NELSON'S

Complete Concordance

of the

Revised Standard Version Bible

NELSON'S

Complete Concordance

of the

Revised Standard Version Bible

Compiled under the supervision of

JOHN W. ELLISON

THOMAS NELSON & SONS

Edinburgh NEW YORK *Toronto*

Library of Congress Catalogue Card Number: 57–7122
MANUFACTURED IN THE UNITED STATES OF AMERICA

Preface to the Concordance of the Revised Standard Version Bible

The wide-spread use of the REVISED STANDARD VERSION of the HOLY BIBLE is itself the justification or *raison d'être* for a Concordance of that translation. A few details about the preparation and form of this Concordance may prove helpful.

An exhaustive concordance of the Bible, such as that of James Strong, takes about a quarter of a century of careful, tedious work to guarantee accuracy. Few students would want to wait a generation for a CONCORDANCE of the REVISED STANDARD VERSION of the HOLY BIBLE. To distribute the work among a group of scholars would be to run the risk of fluctuating standards of accuracy and completeness. The use of mechanical or electronic assistance was feasible and at hand. The Univac I computer at the offices of Remington Rand, Inc., was selected for the task. Every means possible, both human and mechanical, was used to guarantee accuracy in the work.

The use of a computer imposed certain limitations upon the Concordance. Although it could be "exhaustive," it could not be "analytical"; the context and location of each and every word could be listed, but not the Hebrew and Greek words from which they were translated. For students requiring that information, the concordance of the Holy Bible in its original tongues or the analytical concordances of the King James' Version must be consulted.

A study of the frequency and significance of the words of the Bible showed that certain words could well be omitted either because of their frequency, or because they would seldom be the key word under whose heading the passage would be sought. Following this preface is a list of words which were not included in this CONCORDANCE, and only a portion of the occurrences of the following words are listed:

had has have having will

These last five words serve a double purpose in English: they may be auxiliary verbs indicating tense (in which case they need not be in the CONCORDANCE), or they may carry the meaning of possession or determination (in which case they should be listed). If the editor had had a list of their occurrences before he began, a more accurate and more useful listing of them would have been possible. In his Concordance, James Strong includes the number of the Hebrew or Greek word from which the key word is translated, the numbers referring to his lexicon; if no number is given, it merely represents an inflectional form or an idiom. A list of the references of the forms of the verb "have" and the word "will" for which Strong gave a number was arranged for use in the computer. If the translators of the REVISED STANDARD VERSION used *had, has, have,* or *having* in a verse in which Strong indicated that the King James' Version used a form of that verb to translate a Hebrew or Greek word meaning "to possess," the word was retained in this CONCORDANCE. Similarly, the word "will" was retained or eliminated. In some instances the translators used a different English word to render the idea of possession, and used a form of *to have* as an auxiliary for another verb in the same verse; these occurrences were retained by the computer in this CONCORDANCE, even though they do not indicate possession or determination.

The problem of length of context was arbitrarily solved. A computer, at least in the present stage of engineering, can perform only the operations specified for it, but it will precisely and almost unerringly perform them. In previous concordances, each context was made up on the basis of a human judgment which took in untold familiarity with the text and almost unconscious decisions in grouping words into familiar phrases. This kind of human judgment could not be performed by the computer; it required a set of definite, invariable rules for its operation. The details of the program are available for those whose interest prompts them to ask for them.

No footnotes in the Old Testament were included. The marginal readings in the New Testament which included half a verse or more of the text were listed and are indicated by an asterisk (*) before the reference.

Hyphens in the transliteration of Hebrew names were usually omitted. The key word in each context is abbreviated to its initial letter, followed by a period.

The editor takes this opportunity to express his personal gratitude for the unqualified cooperation which he received both from the publisher, Thomas Nelson and Sons, and from the computing staff of Remington Rand, Inc., in the many difficulties, complexities, and delays in this pioneering work. In addition, he owes unstinting thanks to Dr. Henry J. Cadbury, one of the translators of the REVISED STANDARD VERSION of the HOLY BIBLE, and to Dr. William H. P. Hatch, the "Daddy" of so many New Testament students, for their unwavering encouragement during his years of experimenting to find methods of applying electronic computing devices to the problems of Biblical scholarship, without which he never could have produced this CONCORDANCE.

JOHN W. ELLISON.

Winchester, Massachusetts
Whitmonday, 1956

Directions and Explanations

Any passage can be looked up under any one of its words (except those words in the list following which were not included in this concordance) exactly as they are spelled in the Revised Standard Version of the Bible.

It will usually be most helpful to choose the least common word. For instance, the quotation: " 'What has God wrought!' " will be found under both "God" and "wrought." Under "God" are listed 4332 entries, and "wrought" are 41 entries; obviously, the examination of the latter group of entries would be easier than the former group. If a passage is not found in this manner, it is probable that the passage has not been correctly recollected. It would then be helpful to look under words of similar meaning or sound.

The key word in each entry is abbreviated to its initial letter, followed by a period. If the key word is capitalized in the text of the Revised Standard Version Bible, the initial letter is also capitalized. Punctuation following the quotation is usually included.

Headings are by single words only, except for those words which are hyphenated in the Revised Standard Version Bible. Hyphens in most proper names have been omitted. Titles to the various books, chapter headings, marginal notes, the musical directions in the Psalms, and footnotes are not included. When the Revised Standard Version Bible omits half a verse or more of the text as it was rendered by the translators of the King James' Version, the entry is included in this concordance, being marked with an asterisk; such entries will not be located in the body of the Revised Standard Version Bible, but in the footnotes at the bottom of the appropriate page. Shorter omissions of words and phrases included in the King James Version, although listed in the footnotes of the Revised Standard Version Bible are omitted from this Concordance.

The following words of very frequent occurrence are omitted, inasmuch as they account for approximately 59% of the text of the Bible. To have included them would have increased the size of this work to two and a half times its present size; and no text of any significance is made up of these words alone:

a
about
above
after
again
against
all
also
among
an
and
any
are
around
as
ask
asked
asking
at
be
because
been
before
but
by
can
could
did
didst
do
does
doest
doing
done
dost
down
for

from
go
goes
goest
going
gone
he
her
hers
him
his
I
if
in
into
is
it
its
like
may
mayest
me
mine
my
no
not
now
O
of
oh
on
one
or
our
ours
out
over

said
saw
say
sayest
saying
says
see
seeing
seen
shall
shalt
she
should
so
that
the
thee
their
them
then
there
these
they
this
those
thou
through
thy
to
under
unto
up
upon
us
very
was
wast

we
went
wentest
were
what
when
which
who
whom
whose
why
with
within
would
wouldest
wouldst
ye
you
your
yours

Some occurrences of the following words are omitted:

had
has
have
having
will

"art" is not omitted because sometimes it is a noun.

"am" is not omitted because it is often desired to identify the great "I AM" passages.

The following abbreviations of the names of the books of the Bible were regularly used:

Gen	Genesis	Nah	Nahum
Ex	Exodus	Hab	Habakkuk
Lev	Leviticus	Zep	Zephaniah
Num	Numbers	Hag	Haggai
Deu	Deuteronomy	Zec	Zechariah
Jos	Joshua	Mal	Malachi
Ju	Judges	Mt	Matthew
Ru	Ruth	Mk	Mark
1Sa	1 Samuel	Lk	Luke
2Sa	2 Samuel	Jn	John
1Ki	1 Kings	Ac	Acts of the Apostles
2Ki	2 Kings	Rom	Romans
1Ch	1 Chronicles	1Co	1 Corinthians
2Ch	2 Chronicles	2Co	2 Corinthians
Ez	Ezra	Gal	Galatians
Neh	Nehemiah	Eph	Ephesians
Est	Esther	Php	Philippians
Job	Job	Col	Colossians
Ps	Psalms	1Th	1 Thessalonians
Pro	Proverbs	2Th	2 Thessalonians
Ecc	Ecclesiastes	1Ti	1 Timothy
Sol	Song of Solomon	2Ti	2 Timothy
Is	Isaiah	Tit	Titus
Jer	Jeremiah	Phm	Philemon
Lam	Lamentations	Heb	Hebrews
Eze	Ezekiel	Jas	James
Dan	Daniel	1Pe	1 Peter
Hos	Hosea	2Pe	2 Peter
Joe	Joel	1Jn	1 John
Amo	Amos	2Jn	2 John
Ob	Obadiah	3Jn	3 John
Jon	Jonah	Jud	Jude
Mic	Micah	Rev	Revelation

NELSON'S
Complete Concordance
of the
Revised Standard Version Bible

AARON

"Is there not A., your brother the	Ex 4.14
The LORD said to A., "Go into	4.27
And Moses told A. all the words of	4.28
Then Moses and A. went and gathered	4.29
And A. spoke all the words which	4.30
Afterward Moses and A. went to	5.01
"Moses and A., why do you take the	5.04
They met Moses and A., who were	5.20
But the LORD spoke to Moses and A.,	6.13
and she bore him A. and Moses,	6.20
A. took to wife Elisheba, the	6.23
These are the A. and Moses to whom	6.26
from Egypt, this Moses and this A.	6.27
and A. your brother shall be your	7.01
and A. your brother shall tell	7.02
And Moses and A. did so; they did	7.06
and A. eighty-three years old, when	7.07
And the LORD said to Moses and A.,	7.08
miracle,' then you shall say to A.,	7.09
So Moses and A. went to Pharaoh and	7.10
A. cast down his rod before Pharaoh	7.10
"Say to A., 'Take your rod and	7.19
Moses and A. did as the LORD	7.20
"Say to A., 'Stretch out your hand	8.05
So A. stretched out his hand over	8.06
Then Pharaoh called Moses and A.,	8.08
So Moses and A. went out from	8.12
"Say to A., 'Stretch out your rod	8.16
A. stretched out his hand with his	8.17
Then Pharaoh called Moses and A.,	8.25
And the LORD said to Moses and A.,	9.08
sent, and called Moses and A.,	9.27
So Moses and A. went in to Pharaoh,	10.03
So Moses and A. were brought back	10.08
called Moses and A. in haste,	10.16
Moses and A. did all these wonders	11.10
to Moses and A. in the land of	12.01
commanded Moses and A., so they did.	12.28
And he summoned Moses and A. by night,	12.31
And the LORD said to Moses and A.,	12.43
commanded Moses and A., so they did.	12.50
the sister of A., took a timbrel in	15.20
Moses and A. in the wilderness,	16.02
So Moses and A. said to all the	16.06
And Moses said to A., "Say to	16.09
And as A. spoke to the whole	16.10
And Moses said to A., "Take a	16.33
so A. placed it before the Testimony,	16.34
and Moses, A., and Hur went up to	17.10
and A. and Hur held up his hands,	17.12
and A. came with all the elders of	18.12
and come up bringing A. with you;	19.24
you and A., Nadab, and Abihu, and	24.01
Then Moses and A., Nadab, and Abihu	24.09
and behold, A. and Hur are with you;	24.14
A. and his sons shall tend it from	27.21
"Then bring near to you A. your brother,	28.01
A. and Aaron's sons, Nadab and Abihu,	28.01
holy garments for A. your brother,	28.02
garments for A. your brother and	28.04
and A. shall bear their names	28.12
So A. shall bear the names of the	28.29
thus A. shall bear the judgment of	28.30
shall be upon A. when he ministers,	28.35
and A. shall take upon himself any	28.38
put them upon A. your brother,	28.41
and they shall be upon A.,	28.43
You shall bring A. and his sons to	29.04
and put on A. the coat and the robe	29.05
you shall ordain A. and his sons.	29.09
A. and his sons shall lay their	29.10
and A. and his sons shall lay their	29.15
and A. and his sons shall lay their	29.19
right ear of A. and upon the tips	29.20
sprinkle it upon A. and his garments,	29.21

in the hands of A. and in the	29.24
since it is for A. and for his	29.27
It shall be for A. and his sons as	29.28
garments of A. shall be for his	29.29
and A. and his sons shall eat the	29.32
"Thus you shall do to A. and to his	29.35
A. also and his sons I will consecrate,	29.44
And A. shall burn fragrant incense	30.07
and when A. sets up the lamps in	30.08
A. shall make atonement upon its	30.10
with which A. and his sons shall	30.19
And you shall anoint A. and his sons,	30.30
garments for A. the priest and the	31.10
gathered themselves together to A.,	32.01
And A. said to them, "Take off the	32.02
their ears, and brought them to A.	32.03
When A. saw this, he built an altar	32.05
and A. made proclamation and said,	32.05
And Moses said to A., "What did	32.21
And A. said, "Let not the anger of	32.22
loose (for A. had let them break	32.25
they made the calf which A. made.	32.35
And when A. and all the people of	34.30
and A. and all the leaders of the	34.31
holy garments for A. the priest,	35.19
Ithamar the son of A. the priest.	38.21
they made the holy garments for A.;	39.01
fine linen, and A. and his sons,	39.27
holy garments for A. the priest,	39.41
Then you shall bring A. and his	40.12
and put upon A. the holy garments,	40.13
with which Moses and A. and his	40.31
and the sons of A. the priest shall	Lev 1.07
shall be for A. and his sons;	2.03
shall be for A. and his sons;	2.10
and the sons of A. shall throw its	3.13
"Command A. and his sons, saying	6.09
The sons of A. shall offer it	6.14
And the rest of it A. and his sons	6.16
the children of A. may eat of it,	6.18
offering which A. and his sons	6.20
"Say to A. and his sons, This is the	6.25
shall be for all the sons of A.,	7.10
shall be for A. and his sons.	7.31
the sons of A. who offers the	7.33
given them to A. the priest and to	7.34
the portion of A. and of his sons	7.35
"Take A. and his sons with him, and	8.02
And Moses brought A. and his sons,	8.06
and A. and his sons laid their	8.14
and A. and his sons laid their	8.18
and A. and his sons laid their	8.22
in the hands of A. and in the	8.27
sprinkled it upon A. and his	8.30
he consecrated A. and his garments,	8.30
And Moses said to A. and his sons,	8.31
'A. and his sons shall eat it';	8.31
And A. and his sons did all the	8.36
Moses called A. and his sons and	9.01
and he said to A., "Take a bull	9.02
Then Moses said to A., "Draw near	9.07
So A. drew near to the altar, and	9.08
And the sons of A. presented the	9.09
the right thigh A. waved for a	9.21
Then A. lifted up his hands toward	9.22
And Moses and A. went into the tent	9.23
the sons of A., each took his	10.01
Then Moses said to A., "This is	10.03
And A. held his peace.	10.03
the sons of Uzziel the uncle of A.,	10.04
And Moses said to A. and to Eleazar	10.06
And the LORD spoke to A., saying,	10.08
And Moses said to A. and to Eleazar	10.12
the sons of A. who were left, saying,	10.16
And A. said to Moses, "Behold, today	10.19
and the LORD said to Moses and A.,	11.01

AARON (cont.)

the LORD said to Moses and A., Lev 13.01
be brought to A. the priest or to 13.02
The LORD said to Moses and A., 14.33
The LORD said to Moses and A., 15.01
the death of the two sons of A., 16.01
"Tell A. your brother not to come 16.02
But thus shall A. come into the 16.03
"And A. shall offer the bull as a 16.06
and A. shall cast lots upon the two 16.08
And A. shall present the goat on 16.09
"A shall present the bull as a sin 16.11
and A. shall lay both his hands 16.21
"Then A. shall come into the tent 16.23
"Say to A. and his sons, and to all 17.02
the sons of A., and say to them 21.01
"Say to A., None of your descendants 21.17
descendants of A. the priest who 21.21
So Moses spoke to A. and to his 21.24
"Tell A and his sons to keep away 22.02
None of the line of A. who is a 22.04
"Say to A. and his sons and all the 22.18
A. shall keep it in order from 24.03
Every sabbath day A. shall set it 24.08
And it shall be for A. and his sons, 24.09
you and A. shall number them, Num 1.03
Moses and A. took these men who 1.17
whom Moses and A. numbered with 1.44
The LORD said to Moses and A., 2.01
generations of A. and Moses at the 3.01
These are the names of the sons of A.: 3.02
these are the names of the sons of A., 3.03
in the lifetime of A. their father. 3.04
and set them before A. the priest, 3.06
the Levites to A. and his sons; 3.09
And you shall appoint A. and his sons, 3.10
the son of A. the priest was to be 3.32
were Moses and A. and his sons, 3.38
whom Moses and A. numbered at the 3.39
is redeemed to A. and his sons." 3.48
redemption money to A. and his sons, 3.51
The LORD said to Moses and A., 4.01
A. and his sons shall go in and 4.05
And when A. and his sons have 4.15
the son of A. the priest shall 4.16
The LORD said to Moses and A., 4.17
A. and his sons shall go in and 4.19
at the command of A. and his sons, 4.27
Ithamar the son of A. the priest. 4.28
Ithamar the son of A. the priest." 4.33
And Moses and A. and the leaders of 4.34
whom Moses and A. numbered according 4.37
whom Moses and A. numbered according 4.41
whom Moses and A. numbered according 4.45
whom Moses and A. and the leaders 4.46
"Say to A. and his sons, Thus you 6.23
Ithamar the son of A. the priest. 7.08
"Say to A., When you set up the 8.02
And A. did so; he set up 8.03
and A. shall offer the Levites 8.11
Levites to attend A. and his sons, 8.13
as a gift to A. and his sons from 8.19
Thus did Moses and A. and all the 8.20
and A. offered them as a wave 8.21
and A. made atonement for them to 8.21
in attendance upon A. and his sons; 8.22
before Moses and A. on that day; 9.06
And the sons of A., the priests, 10.08
Miriam and A. spoke against Moses 12.01
said to Moses and to A. and Miriam, 12.04
the tent, and called A. and Miriam; 12.05
And A. turned towards Miriam, and 12.10
And A. said to Moses, "Oh, my lord, do 12.11
to Moses and A. and to all the 13.26
murmured against Moses and A.; 14.02
Then Moses and A. fell on their 14.05
And the LORD said to Moses and to A., 14.26
sticks brought him to Moses and A., 15.33
against Moses and against A., 16.03
what is A. that you murmur against 16.11
you and they, and A., tomorrow; 16.16
you also, and A., each his censer." 16.17
tent of meeting with Moses and A. 16.18
And the LORD said to Moses and to A., 16.20
the son of A. the priest to take 16.37
is not of the descendants of A., 16.40
against Moses and against A., 16.41
against Moses and against A., 16.42
And Moses and A. came to the front 16.43
And Moses said to A., "Take your 16.46
So A. took it as Moses said, and ran 16.47
And A. returned to Moses at the 16.50
and the rod of A. was among their 17.06
the rod of A. for the house of Levi 17.08
back the rod of A. before the 17.10
So the LORD said to A., "You and 18.01
Then the LORD said to A., "And 18.08
And the LORD said to A., "You 18.20
LORD's offering to A. the priest. 18.28
Now the LORD said to Moses and to A., 19.01
against Moses and against A. 20.02
Then Moses and A. went from the 20.06
you and A. your brother, and tell 20.08
And Moses and A. gathered the 20.10
And the LORD said to Moses and A., 20.12
said to Moses and A. at Mount Hor, 20.23
"A. shall be gathered to his people 20.24
Take A. and Eleazar his son, and 20.25
and strip A. of his garments and, 20.26
and A. shall be gathered to his 20.26
And Moses stripped A. of his 20.28
and A. died there on the top of the 20.28
congregation saw that A. was dead, 20.29
of Israel wept for A. thirty days. 20.29
son of A. the priest, saw it, he rose 25.07
son of A. the priest, has turned 25.11
Eleazar the son of A., the priest, 26.01
Moses and A. in the company of 26.09
bore to Amram A. and Moses and 26.59
And to A. were born Nadab, Abihu, 26.60
numbered by Moses and A. the priest, 26.64
as your brother A. was gathered, 27.13
the leadership of Moses and A. 33.01
And A. the priest went up Mount Hor 33.38
and A. was a hundred and twenty-three 33.39
so angry with A. that he was ready Deu 9.20
I prayed for A. also at the same 9.20
There A. died, and there he was 10.06
as A. your brother died in Mount 32.50
descendants of A. the priest Jos 21.04
which went to the descendants of A., 21.10
descendants of A. the priest they 21.13
The cities of the descendants of A., 21.19
And I sent Moses and A., and I 24.05
And Eleazar the son of A. died; 24.33
son of A., ministered before it in Ju 20.28
Moses and A. and brought your 1Sa 12.06
and the LORD sent Moses and A., 12.08
A., Moses, and Miriam. The sons 1Ch 6.03
The sons of A.: Nadab, Abihu, Eleazar, 6.03
But A. and his sons made offerings 6.49
These are the sons of A.: Eleazar 6.50
to the sons of A. of the families 6.54
To the sons of A. they gave the 6.57
Jehoiada, of the house of A., 12.27
the sons of A. and the Levites: 15.04
The sons of Amram: A. and Moses 23.13
A. was set apart to consecrate the 23.13
the sons of A. for the service of 23.28
and shall attend the sons of A., 23.32
of the sons of A. were these. 24.01
The sons of A.: Nadab, Abihu, Eleazar, 24.01
for them by A. their father, 24.19
as their brethren the sons of A., 24.31

AARON (cont.)
Kemuel, for A., Zadok; 1Ch 27.17
the sons of A., and the Levites, and 2Ch 13.09
to the LORD who are sons of A., 13.10
but for the priests the sons of A., 26.18
the sons of A. to offer them on 29.21
And for the sons of A., the priests 31.19
the sons of A. were busied in 35.14
and for the priests the sons of A. 35.14
son of A. the chief priest— Ez 7.05
the son of A., shall be with the Neh 10.38
that which was for the sons of A. 12.47
flock by the hand of Moses and A. Ps 77.20
Moses and A. were among his priests, 99.06
and A. whom he had chosen. 105.26
camp were jealous of Moses and A., 106.16
O house of A., put your trust in 115.10
he will bless the house of A.; 115.12
Let the house of A. say, "His 118.03
the beard, upon the beard of A., 133.02
O house of A., bless the LORD! 135.19
before you Moses, A., and Miriam. Mic 6.04
had a wife of the daughters of A., Lk 1.05
saying to A., 'Make for us gods to Ac 7.40
is called by God, just as A. was. Heb 5.04
one named after the order of A.? 7.11

AARON'S
Eleazar, A. son, took to wife one of Ex 6.25
But A. rod swallowed up their rods. 7.12
Aaron and A. sons, Nadab and Abihu, 28.01
that they make A. garments to 28.03
and they shall be upon A. heart, 28.30
It shall be upon A. forehead, 28.38
"And for A. sons you shall make 28.40
of the ram of A. ordination and 29.26
and A. sons the priests shall Lev 1.05
and A. sons the priests shall lay 1.08
and A. sons the priests shall throw 1.11
and bring it to A. sons the priests 2.02
and A. sons the priests shall throw 3.02
Then A. sons shall burn it on the 3.05
and A. sons shall throw its blood 3.08
The priest from among A. sons, 6.22
of the anointing oil on A. head, 8.12
And Moses brought A. sons, and 8.13
on the tip of A. right ear and on 8.23
And A. sons were brought, and Moses 8.24
and A. sons delivered to him the 9.12
and A. sons delivered to him the 9.18
and write A. name upon the rod of Num 17.03
and A. rod that budded, and the Heb 9.04

ABADDON
and A. has no covering. Job 26.06
A. and Death say, 'We have heard a 28.22
be a fire which consumes unto A., 31.12
grave, or thy faithfulness in A.? Ps 88.11
Sheol and A. lie open before the Pro 15.11
Sheol and A. are never satisfied, 27.20
his name in Hebrew is A., and in Rev 9.11

ABAGTHA
Bigtha and A., Zethar and Carkas, Est 1.10

ABANA
Are not A. and Pharpar, the rivers 2Ki 5.12

ABANDON
he will again a. them in the Num 32.15
and thou didst a. them to the hand Neh 9.28
The LORD will not a. him to his Ps 37.33
he will not a. his heritage; 94.14
For thou wilt not a. my soul to Ac 2.27
and a. themselves for the sake of Jud 1.11

ABANDONED
'You a. me, so I have a. you 2Ch 12.05
so I have a. you to the hand of 12.05
For he has crushed and a. the poor, Job 20.19
my house, I have a. my heritage; Jer 12.07
that he was not a. to Hades, Ac 2.31
of our being saved was at last a. 27.20
that you have a. the love you had Rev 2.04

ABARIM
"Go up into this mountain of A., Num 27.12
the mountains of A., before Nebo. 33.47
set out from the mountains of A., 33.48
"Ascend this mountain of the A., Deu 32.49
cry from A., for all your lovers Jer 22.20

ABASE
one that is proud, and a. him. Job 40.11
and a. that which is high. Eze 21.26
who walk in pride he is able to a. Dan 4.37

ABASED
and I will be a. in your eyes; 2Sa 6.22
Yet thou hast cast us off and a. us, Ps 44.09
despised and a. before all the Mal 2.09
I know how to be a., and I Php 4.12

ABASES
For God a. the proud, but he saves Job 22.29

ABASING
commit a sin in a. myself so that 2Co 11.07

ABATE
continued to a. until the tenth Gen 8.05

ABATED
and fifty days the waters had a.; Gen 8.03
to the LORD, and the fire a. Num 11.02
not dim, nor his natural force a. Deu 34.07
their anger against him was a., Ju 8.03
the anger of King Ahasuerus had a., Est 2.01
Then the anger of the king a. 7.10

ABBA
And he said, "A., Father, all things Mk 14.36
When we cry, "A.! Father!" Rom 8.15
Son into our hearts, crying, "A.! Gal 4.06

ABDA
the son of A. was in charge of the 1Ki 4.06
and A. the son of Shammua, son of Neh 11.17

ABDEEL
the son of A. to seize Baruch the Jer 36.26

ABDI
son of A., son of Malluch, 1Ch 6.44
sons of Merari, Kish the son of A., 2Ch 29.12
A., Jeremoth, and Elijah. Ez 10.26

ABDIEL
Ahi the son of A., son of Guni, was 1 Ch 5.15

ABDON
A. with its pasture lands, Jos 21.30
After him A. the son of Hillel the Ju 12.13
Then A. the son of Hillel the 12.15
A. with its pasture lands, 1Ch 6.74
A., Zichri, Hanan, 8.23
A., then Zur, Kish, Baal, Nadab, 8.30
and his first-born son A., 9.36
A. the son of Micah, Shaphan the 2Ch 34.20

ABEDNEGO
Meshach, and Azariah he called A. Dan 1.07
and A. over the affairs of the 2.49
Babylon: Shadrach, Meshach, and A. 3.12
Shadrach, Meshach, and A. be brought. 3.13
and A., that you do not serve my 3.14
and A. answered the king, "O Nebuchadnezzar, 3.16

ABEDNEGO (cont.)
against Shadrach, Meshach, and A. Dan 3.19
and A., and to cast them into the 3.20
took up Shadrach, Meshach, and A. 3.22
and A., fell bound into the burning 3.23
and A., servants of the Most High 3.26
and A. came out from the fire. 3.26
and A., who has sent his angel and 3.28
and A. shall be torn limb from limb, 3.29
and A. in the province of Babylon. 3.30

ABEL
And again, she bore his brother A. Gen 4.02
Now A. was a keeper of sheep, and 4.02
and A. brought of the firstlings of 4.04
had regard for A. and his offering, 4.04
Cain said to A. his brother, "Let us 4.08
rose up against his brother A., 4.08
to Cain, "Where is A. your brother?" 4.09
for me another child instead of A., 4.25
of Israel to A. of Bethmaacah; 2Sa 20.14
besieged him in A. of Bethmaacah; 20.15
'Let them but ask counsel at A.'; 20.18
of innocent A. to the blood of Mt 23.35
from the blood of A. to the blood Lk 11.51
By faith A. offered to God a more Heb 11.04
graciously than the blood of A. 12.24

ABELBETHMAACAH
A., and all Chinneroth, with all the 1Ki 15.20
A., Janoah, Kedesh, Hazor, Gilead, and 2Ki 15.29

ABELKERAMIM
and as far as A., with a very great Ju 11.33

ABELMAIM
A., and all the store-cities of 2Ch 16.04

ABELMEHOLAH
as the border of A., by Tabbath. Ju 7.22
Jezreel, and from Bethshean to A., 1Ki 4.12
of Shaphat of A. you shall anoint 19.16

ABELMIZRAIM
therefore the place was named A.; Gen 50.11

ABELSHITTIM
as far as A. in the plains of Moab. Num 33.49

ABHOR
you, and my soul shall not a. you. Lev 26.11
and my soul will a. you. 26.30
neither will I a. them so as to 26.44
you shall utterly detest and a. it; Deu 7.26
"You shall not a. an Edomite, for he 23.07
you shall not a. an Egyptian, 23.07
pit, and my own clothes will a. me. Job 9.31
All my intimate friends a. me, 19.19
They a. me, they keep aloof from me; 30.10
I hate and a. falsehood, but I love Ps 119.163
and they a. him who speaks the Amo 5.10
"I a. the pride of Jacob, and hate 6.08
who a. justice and pervert all Mic 3.09
You who a. idols, do you rob temples? Rom 2.22

ABHORRED
things, and therefore I a. them. Lev 20.23
and their soul a. my statutes. 26.43
himself utterly a. by his people 1Sa 27.12
and he a. Israel, and reigned over 1Ki 11.25
not despised or a. the affliction Ps 22.24
his people, and he a. his heritage; 106.40
cursed by peoples, a. by nations; Pro 24.24
a. by the nations, the servant of Is 49.07
for you were a., on the day that Eze 16.05

ABHORRENCE
they shall be an a. to all flesh. Is 66.24

ABHORRENT
the king's command was a. to Joab. 1Ch 21.06

ABHORS
and if your soul a. my ordinances, Lev 26.15
the LORD a. bloodthirsty and Ps 5.06

ABI
name was A. the daughter of 2Ki 18.02

ABIALBON
A. the Arbathite, Azmaveth of 2Sa 23.31

ABIASAPH
of Korah: Assir, Elkanah, and A.; Ex 6.24

ABIATHAR
named A., escaped and fled after 1Sa 22.20
And A. told David that Saul had 22.21
And David said to A., 22.22
When A. the son of Ahimelech fled 23.06
and he said to A. the priest, 23.09
And David said to A. the priest, 30.07
So A. brought the Ephod to David. 30.07
Ahimelech the son of A. were priests; 2Sa 8.17
And A. came up, and lo, Zadok came 15.24
you and A., with your two sons, 15.27
son, and Jonathan the son of A. 15.27
So Zadok and A. carried the ark of 15.29
Are not Zadok and A. the priests 15.35
it to Zadok and A. the priests 15.35
said to Zadok and A. the priests, 17.15
to Zadok and A. the priests, 19.11
and Zadok and A. were priests; 20.25
of Zeruiah and with A. the priest; 1Ki 1.07
A. the priest, and Joab the commander 1.19
of the army, and A. the priest; 1.25
the son of A. the priest came; 1.42
on his side are A. the priest and 2.22
And to A. the priest the king said, 2.26
expelled A. from being priest to 2.27
the priest in the place of A. 2.35
Zadok and A. were priests; 4.04
summoned the priests Zadok and A., 1Ch 15.11
Ahimelech the son of A. were priests; 18.16
and Ahimelech the son of A., 24.06
Jehoiada the son of Benaiah, and A. 27.34
when A. was high priest, and ate the Mk 2.26

ABIATHAR'S
Zadok's son, and Jonathan, A. son; 2Sa 15.36

ABIB
to go forth, in the month of A. Ex 13.04
appointed time in the month of A., 23.15
the time appointed in the month A.; 34.18
in the month A. you came out from 34.18
"Observe the month of A., Deu 16.01
in the month of A. the LORD your 16.01

ABIDA
Epher, Hanock, A., and Eldaah. Gen 25.04
Epher, Hanock, A., and Eldaah. 1Ch 1.33

ABIDAN
from Benjamin, A. the son of Gideoni; Num 1.11
Benjamin being A. the son of 2.22
On the ninth day of A. the son of 7.60
the offering of A. the son of 7.65
of Benjamin was A. the son of 10.24

ABIDE
shall not a. in man for ever, for Gen 6.03
Dan, why did he a. with the ships? Ju 5.17
of the LORD, and a. there for ever." 1Sa 1.22
He himself shall a. in prosperity, Ps 25.13
their heritage will a. for ever; 37.18
so shall you a. for ever. 37.27

ABIDE (cont.)

Man cannot a. in his pomp, he is Ps 49.12
Man cannot a. in his pomp, he is 49.20
my hand shall ever a. with him, 89.21
admonition will a. among the wise. Pro 15.31
righteousness a. in the fruitful Is 32.16
My people will a. in a peaceful 32.18
the arrogant man shall not a. Hab 2.05
and it shall a. in his house and Zec 5.04
A. in me, and I in you. Jn 15.04
can you, unless you a. in me. 15.04
If a man does not a. in me, 15.06
If you a. in me, and my words 15.07
and my words a. in you, ask whatever 15.07
have I loved you; a. in my love. 15.09
you will a. in my love, just as I 15.10
commandments and a. in his love. 15.10
and that your fruit should a.; 15.16
So faith, hope, love a., these three; 1Co 13.13
who does not a. by all things Gal 3.10
heard from the beginning a. in you, 1Jn 2.24
then you will a. in the Son and in 2.24
as it has taught you, a. in him. 2.27
a. in him, so that when he appears 2.28
him, how does God's love a. in him? 3.17
keep his commandments a. in him, 3.24
we know that we a. in him and he 4.13
and does not a. in the doctrine of 2Jn 1.09

ABIDES

which a. with them in the midst of Lev 16.16
In his neck a. strength, and terror Job 41.22
who a. in the shadow of the Almighty, Ps 91.01
cannot be moved, but a. for ever. 125.01
Wisdom a. in the mind of a man of Pro 14.33
My Spirit a. among you; Hag 2.05
flesh and drinks my blood a. in me, Jn 6.56
unless it a. in the vine, neither 15.04
He who a. in me, and I in him, he it 15.05
but the word of the Lord a. for ever." 1Pe 1.25
he who says he a. in him ought to 1Jn 2.06
loves his brother a. in the light, 2.10
and the word of God a. in you, 2.14
does the will of God a. for ever. 2.17
heard from the beginning a. in you, 2.24
you received from him a. in you, 2.27
No one who a. in him sins; 3.06
for God's nature a. in him, 3.09
by this we know that he a. in us, 3.24
God a. in us and his love is 4.12
God a. in him, and he in God. 4.15
and he who a. in love a. in God, 4.16
a. in God, and God a. in him. 4.16
the truth which a. in us and will 2Jn 1.02
he who a. in the doctrine of Christ 1.09

ABIDING

a. there, the people of Israel Num 9.22
like a shadow, and there is no a. 1Ch 29.15
you do not have his word a. in you, Jn 5.38
a better possession and an a. one. Heb 10.34
the living and a. word of God; 1Pe 1.23
murderer has eternal life a. in him. 1Jn 3.15

ABIEL

the son of A., son of Zeror, son of 1Sa 9.01
father of Abner was the son of A. 14.51
brooks of Gaash, A. the Arbathite, 1Ch 11.32

ABIEZER

A., Helek. Asriel, Shechem, Hepher, and Jos 17.02
better than the vintage of A.? Ju 8.02
A., of Anathoth, Mebunnai the 2Sa 23.27
bore Ishhod, A., and Mahlah. 1Ch 7.18
Ikkesh of Tekoa, A. of Anathoth, 11.28
was A. of Anathoth, a Benjaminite; 27.12

ABIEZRITE

which belonged to Joash the A., Ju 6.11

ABIEZRITES

at Ophrah, which belongs to the A. Ju 6.24
and the A. were called out to 6.34
his father, at Ophrah of the A. 8.32

ABIGAIL

Nabal, the name of his wife A. 1Sa 25.03
But one of the young men told A., 25.14
Then A. made haste, and took two 25.18
When A. saw David, she made haste, 25.23
And David said to A., "Blessed be 25.32
And A. came to Nabal; and, lo, 25.36
Then David sent and wooed A., 25.39
of David came to A. at Carmel, 25.40
And A. made haste and rose and 25.42
and A. of Carmel, Nabal's widow. 27.03
and A. the widow of Nabal of Carmel 30.05
and A. the widow of Nabal of Carmel 2Sa 2.02
of A. the widow of Nabal of Carmel; 3.03
and their sisters were Zeruiah and A. 1Ch 2.16
A. bore Amasa, and the father of 2.17
second Daniel, by A. the Carmelitess, 3.01

ABIGAL

who had married A. the daughter of 2Sa 17.25

ABIHAIL

of Merari was Zuriel the son of A.; Num 3.35
The name of Abishur's wife was A., 1Ch 2.29
the sons of A. the son of Huri, son 5.14
and of A. the daughter of Eliab the 2Ch 11.18
the daughter of A. the uncle of Est 2.15
Then Queen Esther, the daughter of A., 9.29

ABIHU

A., Eleazar, and Ithamar. Ex 6.23
and A., and seventy of the elders 24.01
and A., and seventy of the elders 24.09
Nadab and A., Eleazar and Ithamar. 28.01
Now Nadab and A., the sons of Aaron, Lev 10.01
and A., Eleazar, and Ithamar; Num 3.02
But Nadab and A. died before the 3.04
A., Eleazar and Ithamar. 26.60
But Nadab and A. died when they 26.61
A., Eleazar, and Ithamar. 1Ch 6.03
A., Eleazar, and Ithamar. 24.01
But Nadab and A. died before their 24.02

ABIHUD

And Bela had sons: Addar, Gera, A., 1Ch 8.03

ABIJAH

and the name of his second, A.; 1Sa 8.02
At that time A. the son of Jeroboam 1Ki 14.01
A. his son, Asa his son, Jehoshaphat 1Ch 3.10
Joel his first-born, the second A. 6.28
A., Anathoth, and Alemeth. 7.08
to Hakkoz, the eighth to A., 24.10
who bore him A., Attai, Ziza, and 2Ch 11.20
appointed A. the son of Maacah as 11.22
and A. his son reigned in his 12.16
King Jeroboam A. began to reign 13.01
was war between A. and Jeroboam. 13.02
A. went out to battle having an 13.03
Then A. stood up on Mount Zemaraim 13.04
and all Israel before A. and Judah. 13.15
A. and his people slew them with a 13.17
And A. pursued Jeroboam, and took 13.19
his power in the days of A.; and the 13.20
But A. grew mighty. And he 13.21
The rest of the acts of A., 13.22
So A. slept with his fathers, and 14.01
name was A. the daughter of 29.01
Meshullam, A., Mijamin, Neh 10.07
Iddo, Ginnethoi, A., 12.04

ABIJAH (cont.)
of A., Zichri; of Miniamin, Neh 12.17
and Rehoboam the father of A., Mt 1.07
and A. the father of Asa, 1.07
Zechariah, of the division of A.; Lk 1.05

ABIJAM
And A. his son reigned in his stead. 1Ki 14.31
A. began to reign over Judah. 15.01
The rest of the acts of A., 15.07
was war between A. and Jeroboam. 15.07
And A. slept with his fathers; 15.08

ABILENE
and Lysanias tetrarch of A., Lk 3.01

ABILITY
you shall speak to all who have a., Ex 28.03
with a. and intelligence, with 31.03
I have given to all able men a., 31.06
women who had a. spun with their 35.25
were moved with a. spun the goats' 35.26
with a., with intelligence, with 35.31
them with a. to do every sort of 35.35
LORD has put a. and intelligence 36.01
in whose mind the LORD had put a., 36.02
according to the a. of him who Lev 27.08
for they were men of great a. 1Ch 26.06
one thousand seven hundred men of a., 26.30
men of great a. among them were 26.31
two thousand seven hundred men of a., 26.32
according to their a. they gave to Ez 2.69
one, to each according to his a. Mt 25.15
every one according to his a., Ac 11.29
to another the a. to distinguish 1Co 12.10

ABIMAEL
Obal, A., Sheba, Gen 10.28
Ebal, A., Sheba, 1Ch 1.22

ABIMELECH
And A. king of Gerar sent and took Gen 20.02
But God came to A. in a dream by 20.03
Now A. had not approached her, 20.04
So A. rose early in the morning, and 20.08
Then A. called Abraham, and said to 20.09
And A. said to Abraham, "What were 20.10
Then A. took sheep and oxen, and 20.14
And A. said, "Behold, my land is 20.15
and God healed A., and also 20.17
of the house of A. because of 20.18
At the time A. and Phicol the 21.22
complained to A. about a well of 21.25
A. said, "I do not know who has done 21.26
sheep and oxen and gave them to A., 21.27
And A. said to Abraham, "What is the 21.29
Then A. and Phicol the commander of 21.32
to A. king of the Philistines. 26.01
A. king of the Philistines looked 26.08
So A. called Isaac, and said, "Behold, 26.09
A. said, "What is this you have done 26.10
So A. warned all the people, saying. 26.11
And A. said to Isaac, "Go away from 26.16
Then A. went to him from Gerar with 26.26
a son, and he called his name A. Ju 8.31
Now A. the son of Jerubbaal went to 9.01
their hearts inclined to follow A., 9.03
with which A. hired worthless and 9.04
and they went and made A. king, 9.06
and honor when you made A. king, 9.16
and have made A., the son of his 9.18
house this day, then rejoice in A., 9.19
but if not, let fire come out from A., 9.20
and from Bethmillo, and devour A. 9.20
there, for fear of A. his brother. 9.21
A. ruled over Israel three years. 9.22
spirit between A. and the men of 9.23
dealt treacherously with A.; 9.23
be laid upon A. their brother, 9.24
along that way; and it was told A. 9.25
and ate and drank and reviled A. 9.27
"Who is A., and who are we of 9.28
then I would remove A. 9.29
I would say to A. 'Increase your 9.29
he sent messengers to A. at Arumah, 9.31
And A. and all the men that were 9.34
and A. and the men that were with 9.35
'Who is A., that we should serve 9.38
men of Shechem, and fought with A. 9.39
And A. chased him, and he fled 9.40
And A. dwelt at Arumah; 9.41
the fields. And A. was told. 9.42
A. and the company that was with 9.44
And A. fought against the city all 9.45
A. was told that all the people of 9.47
And A. went up to Mount Zalmon, he 9.48
and A. took an axe in his hand, and 9.48
and following A. put it against 9.49
Then A. went to Thebez, and encamped 9.50
And A. came to the tower, and fought 9.52
men of Israel saw that A. was dead, 9.55
Thus God requited the crime of A., 9.56
After A. there arose to deliver 10.01
Who killed A. the son of Jerubbesheth 2Sa 11.21

ABIMELECH'S
of water which A. servants had Gen 21.25
an upper millstone upon A. head, Ju 9.53

ABINADAB
it to the house of A. on the hill; 1Sa 7.01
Then Jesse called A., and made 16.08
the first-born, and next to him A., 17.13
Jonathan and A. and Malchishua, 31.02
of the house of A. which was on 2Sa 6.03
the sons of A., were driving the 6.03
A. the second, Shimea the third, 1Ch 2.13
Malchishua, A., and Eshbaal; 8.33
Malchishua, A., and Eshbaal; 9.39
Jonathan and A. and Malchishua, 10.02
a new cart, from the house of A., 13.07

ABINOAM
the son of A. from Kedesh in Ju 4.06
the son of A. had gone up to Mount 4.12
Barak the son of A. on that day: 5.01
away your captives, O son of A. 5.12

ABIRAM
and Dathan and A. the sons of Num 16.01
call Dathan and A. the sons of 16.12
dwelling of Korah, Dathan, and A. 16.24
rose and went to Dathan and A.; 16.25
dwelling of Korah, Dathan, and A.; 16.27
and Dathan and A. came out and 16.27
of Eliab: Nemuel, Dathan, and A. 26.09
These are the Dathan and A., 26.09
to Dathan and A. the sons of Eliab, Deu 11.06
at the cost of A. his first-born, 1Ki 16.34
and covered the company of A. Ps 106.17

ABISHAG
and found A. the Shunammite, and 1Ki 1.03
and A. the Shunammite was ministering 1.15
to give me A. the Shunammite as my 2.17
She said, "Let A. the Shunammite be 2.21
why do you ask A. the Shunammite 2.22

ABISHAI
Joab's brother A. the son of 1Sa 26.06
And A. said, "I will go down with 26.06
So David and A. went to the army by 26.07
Then said A. to David, "God has 26.08
But David said to A., "Do not 26.09
were there, Joab, A., and Asahel. 2Sa 2.18
But Joab and A. pursued Abner; 2.24

ABISHAI (cont.)
So Joab and A. his brother slew 2Sa 3.30
in the charge of A. his brother, 10.10
fled, they likewise fled before A., 10.14
Then A. the son of Zeruiah said to 16.09
And David said to A. and to all his 16.11
the command of A. the son of 18.02
king ordered Joab and A. and Ittai, 18.05
commanded you and A. and Ittai, 18.12
A. the son of Zeruiah answered, 19.21
And David said to A., "Now Sheba 20.06
And there went out after A., 20.07
Then Joab and A. his brother 20.10
But A. the son of Zeruiah came to 21.17
Now A., the brother of Joab, the son 23.18
A., Joab, and Asahel, three. 1Ch 2.16
Now A., the brother of Joab, was 11.20
And A., the son of Zeruiah, slew 18.12
in the charge of A. his brother, 19.11
fled, they likewise fled before A., 19.15

ABISHALOM
name was Maacah the daughter of A. 1Ki 15.02
name was Maacah the daughter of A. 15.10

ABISHUA
of Phinehas, Phinehas of A., 1Ch 6.04
A. of Bukki, Bukki of Uzzi, 6.05
son, Phinehas his son, A. his son, 6.50
A., Naaman, Ahoah, 8.04
son of A., son of Phinehas, son of Ez 7.05

ABISHUR
the sons of Shammai: Nadab and A. 1Ch 2.28

ABISHUR'S
The name of A. wife was Abihail, and 1Ch 2.29

ABITAL
fifth, Shephatiah the son of A.; 2Sa 3.04
the fifth Shephatiah, by A.; 1Ch 3.03

ABITUB
had sons by Hushim: A. and Elpaal. 1Ch 8.11

ABIUD
and Zerubbabel the father of A., Mt 1.13
and A. the father of Eliakim, and 1.13

ABLAZE
of thorns, whether green or a., Ps 58.09
the flame sets the mountains a., 83.14
a forest is set a. by a small fire Jas 3.05

ABLE
if you are a. to number them." Gen 15.05
if you know any a. men among them, 47.06
you are not a. to perform it alone. Ex 18.18
Moreover choose a. men from all the 18.21
you, then you will be a. to endure, 18.23
Moses chose a. men out of all 18.25
I have endowed with an a. mind, 28.03
I have given to all a. men ability, 31.06
"And let every a. man among you 35.10
and every a. man in whom the LORD 36.01
and every a. man in whose mind the 36.02
so that all the a. men who were 36.04
And all the a. men among the 36.08
And Moses was not a. to enter the 40.35
Israel who are a. to go forth to Num 1.03
all who were a. to go forth to war: 1.20
all who were a. to go forth to war: 1.22
all who were a. to go forth to war: 1.24
every man a. to go forth to war: 1.26
every man a. to go forth to war: 1.28
every man a. to go forth to war: 1.30
every man a. to go forth to war: 1.32
every man a. to go forth to war: 1.34
every man a. to go forth to war: 1.36
every man a. to go forth to war: 1.38
every man a. to go forth to war: 1.40
every man a. to go forth to war: 1.42
every man a. to go forth to war in 1.45
I am not a. to carry all this 11.14
or we are well a. to overcome it." 13.30
"We are not a. to go up against the 13.31
LORD was not a. to bring this 14.16
I shall be a. to defeat them and 22.06
I shall be a. to fight against 22.11
Am I not a. to honor you 22.37
I would not be a. to go beyond the 24.13
Israel who are a. to go forth to 26.02
'I am not a. alone to bear you; Deu 1.09
a man shall be a. to stand against 7.24
LORD was not a. to bring them into 9.28
No man shall be a. to stand against 11.25
you are not a. to bring the tithe, 14.24
every man shall give as he is a., 16.17
I am no longer a. to go out and 31.02
No man shall be a. to stand before Jos 1.05
no man has been a. to withstand 23.09
have I been a. to do in comparison Ju 8.03
sent five a. men from the whole 18.02
"Who is a. to stand before the LORD, 1Sa 6.20
If he is a. to fight with me and 17.09
"You are not a. to go against this 17.33
for who is a. to govern this thy 1Ki 3.09
The man Jeroboam was very a., 11.28
all who were a. to put on armor, 2Ki 3.21
if you are a. on your part to set 18.23
he will not be a. to deliver you 18.29
very a. men for the work of the 1Ch 9.13
Elzabad, whose brethren were a. men, 26.07
a. men qualified for the service; 26.08
and brethren, a. men, eighteen. 26.09
of my God, so far as I was a., 29.02
we should be a. thus to offer 29.14
But who is a. to build him a house, 2Ch 2.06
so that none is a. to withstand 20.06
and were not a. to go to Tarshish. 20.37
had no one a. to rule the kingdom. 22.09
a. to handle spear and shield. 25.05
"The LORD is a. to give you much 25.09
lands at all a. to deliver their 32.13
destroyed was a. to deliver his 32.14
God should be a. to deliver you 32.14
has been a. to deliver his people 32.15
we are not a. to work on the wall." Neh 4.10
To them, "We, as far as we are a., 5.08
So that they were not a. to rise; Ps 18.38
that he is not a. to dispute with Ecc 6.10
if you are a. on your part to set Is 36.08
he will not be a. to deliver you. 36.14
you will not be a. to expiate; 47.11
perhaps you may be a. to succeed, 47.12
and he is not a. to conceal himself Jer 49.10
gold are not a. to deliver them in Eze 7.19
shall not be a. to live by his 33.12
lambs shall be as much as he is a., 46.05
with the lambs as much as he is a., 46.07
lambs as much as one is a. to give, 46.11
"Are you a. to make known to me the Dan 2.26
you have been a. to reveal this 2.47
we serve is a. to deliver us from 3.17
god who is a. to deliver in this 3.29
kingdom are not a. to make known 4.18
but you are a., for the spirit of 4.18
walk in pride he is a. to abase. 4.37
been a. to deliver you from the 6.20
But he is not a. to cure you or Hos 5.13
the land is not a. to bear all his Amo 7.10
gold shall be a. to deliver them Zep 1.18
God is a. from these stones to Mt 3.09
believe that I am a. to do this?" 9.28
He who is a. to receive this, let 19.12

ABLE (cont.)
Are you a. to drink the cup that I Mt 20.22
They said to him, "We are a." 20.22
And no one was a. to answer him a 22.46
'I am a. to destroy the temple of 26.61
that house will not be a. to stand. Mk 3.25
them, as they were a. to hear it; 4.33
cast it out, and they were not a." 9.18
my name will be a. soon after to 9.39
Are you a. to drink the cup that I 10.38
And they said to him, "We are a." 10.39
God is a. from these stones to Lk 3.08
you are not a. to do as small a 12.26
seek to enter and will not be a. 13.24
and is not a. to finish, all who see 14.29
to build, and was not a. to finish.' 14.30
whether he is a. with ten thousand 14.31
from here to you may not be a., 16.26
And they were not a. in the presence 20.26
adversaries will be a. to withstand 21.15
and no one is a. to snatch them out Jn 10.29
now they were not a. to haul it in, 21.06
you will not be a. to overthrow Ac 5.39
nor we have been a. to bear? 15.10
which is a. to build you up and to 20.32
you will be a. to learn from him 24.08
that God was a. to do what he had Rom 4.21
will be a. to separate us from the 8.39
the Master is a. to make him stand 14.04
and a. to instruct one another. 15.14
Now to him who is a. to strengthen 16.25
and he is not a. to understand them 1Co 2.14
that you may be a. to endure it. 10.13
that we may be a. to comfort those 2Co 1.04
that you may be a. to answer those 5.12
And God is a. to provide you with 9.08
within us is a. to do far more Eph 3.20
that he may be a. to give to those 4.28
that you may be a. to stand 6.11
that you may be a. to withstand in 6.13
sure that he is a. to guard until 2Ti 1.12
men who will be a. to teach others 2.02
which are a. to instruct you for 3.15
that he may be a. to give instruction Tit 1.09
He is a. to help those who are Heb 2.18
to him who was a. to save him from 5.07
Consequently he is a. for all time 7.25
that God was a. to raise men even 11.19
which is a. to save your souls. Jas 1.21
a. to bridle the whole body also. 3.02
he who is a. to save and to destroy 4.12
you may be a. at any time to 2Pe 1.15
Now to him who is a. to keep you Jud 1.24
door, which no one is a. to shut; Rev 3.08
the earth was a. to open the 5.03

ABLE-BODIED
the Moabites, all strong, a. men; Ju 3.29

ABLUTIONS
with instruction about a., the laying Heb 6.02
with food and drink and various a., 9.10

ABNER
of his army was A. the son of Ner, 1Sa 14.50
the father of A. was the son of 14.51
he said to A., the commander of the 17.55
"A., whose son is this youth?" 17.55
And A. said, "As your soul lives, O 17.55
A. took him, and brought him before 17.57
and A. sat by Saul's side, but David's 20.25
with A. the son of Ner, the commander 26.05
and A. and the army lay around him 26.07
and to A. the son of Ner, saying, 26.14
saying, "Will you not answer, A.?" 26.14
Then A. answered, "Who are you that 26.14
And David said to A., "Are you not 26.15
Now A. the son of Ner, commander of 2Sa 2.08
A. the son of Ner, and the servants 2.12
And A. said to Joab, "Let the young 2.14
and A. and the men of Israel were 2.17
and Asahel pursued A., and as he 2.19
nor to the left from following A. 2.19
Then A. looked behind him and said, 2.20
A. said to him, "Turn aside to your 2.21
And A. said again to Asahel, "Turn 2.22
therefore A. smote him in the belly 2.23
But Joab and Abishai pursued A.; 2.24
themselves together behind A., 2.25
Then A. called to Joab, "Shall the 2.26
And A. and his men went all that 2.29
Joab returned from the pursuit of A.; 2.30
A. was making himself strong in the 3.06
and Ishbosheth said to A., 3.07
Then A. was very angry over the 3.08
God do so to A., and more also, if I 3.09
could not answer A. another word, 3.11
And A. sent messengers to David at 3.12
Then A. said to him, "Go, return"; and 3.16
And A. conferred with the elders of 3.17
A. also spoke to Benjamin; 3.19
and then A. went to tell David at 3.19
When A. came with twenty men to 3.20
a feast for A. and the men who 3.20
And A. said to David, "I will arise 3.21
So David sent A. away; and he went 3.21
But A. was not with David at Hebron, 3.22
"A. the son of Ner came to the king, 3.23
Behold, A. came to you; why is it 3.24
You know that A. the son of Ner 3.25
he sent messengers after A., 3.26
And when A. returned to Hebron, Joab 3.27
for the blood of A. the son of Ner. 3.28
and Abishai his brother slew A., 3.30
on sackcloth, and mourn before A." 3.31
They buried A. at Hebron; and the 3.32
voice and wept at the grave of A.; 3.32
And the king lamented for A., 3.33
"Should A. die as a fool dies? 3.33
will to slay A. the son of Ner. 3.37
heard that A. had died at Hebron, 4.01
it in the tomb of A. at Hebron. 4.12
A. the son of Ner, and Amasa the son 1Ki 2.05
A. the son of Ner, commander of the 2.32
and A. the son of Ner, and Joab the 1Ch 26.28
Benjamin, Jaasiel the son of A.; 27.21

ABNER'S
three hundred and sixty of A. men. 2Sa 2.31

ABOARD
Peter went a. and hauled the net Jn 21.11
intending to take Paul a. there; Ac 20.13
Phoenicia, we went a., and set sail. 21.02

ABODE
by thy strength to thy holy a. Ex 15.13
which thou hast made for thy a., 15.17
because the cloud a. upon it, 40.35
And I will make my a. among you, Lev 26.11
and a. at the rock of Rimmon four Ju 20.47
mount which God desired for his a., Ps 68.16
His a. has been established in 76.02
From thy lofty a. thou waterest the 104.13
he blesses the a. of the righteous Pro 3.33
of jackals, an a. for ostriches. Is 34.13

ABOLISH
and I will a. the bow, the sword, and Hos 2.18
I have come to a. the law and the Mt 5.17
come not to a. them but to fulfil 5.17

ABOLISHED
who a. death and brought life and 2Ti 1.10

ABOLISHES
He a. the first in order to Heb 10.09

ABOLISHING
by a. in his flesh the law of Eph 2.15

ABOMINABLE
God offerings a. to the Egyptians. Ex 8.26
make yourselves a. with any Lev 11.43
any of these a. customs which were 18.30
make yourselves a. by beast or by 20.25
not bring an a. thing into your Deu 7.26
for every a. thing which the LORD 12.31
that such an a. thing has been 13.14
"You shall not eat any a. thing. 14.03
that such an a. thing has been 17.04
to follow the a. practices of 18.09
of these a. practices the LORD 18.12
to all their a. practices which 20.18
with a. practices they provoked him 32.16
she had an a. image made for 1Ki 15.13
according to the a. practices of 2Ki 16.03
according to the a. practices of 21.02
put away the a. idols from all the 2Ch 15.08
she had made an a. image for 15.16
according to the a. practices of 28.03
according to the a. practices of 33.02
less one who is a. and corrupt, Job 15.16
they do a. deeds, there is none that Ps 14.01
are corrupt, doing a. iniquity; 53.01
and broth of a. things is in their Is 65.04
do not do this a. thing that I Jer 44.04
they made their a. images and Eze 7.20
and did a. things before me; 16.50
He has done all these a. things; 18.13
does the same a. things that the 18.24
declare to her all her a. deeds. 22.02
declare to them their a. deeds. 23.36
your iniquities and your a. deeds. 36.31

ABOMINABLY
He did very a. in going after idols, 1Ki 21.26
which you acted more a. than they, Eze 16.52

ABOMINATION
for that is an a. to the Egyptians Gen 43.32
shepherd is an a. to the Egyptians." 46.34
it shall be an a., and he who Lev 7.18
an unclean beast or any unclean a., 7.21
are in the waters, is an a. to you. 11.10
They shall remain an a. to you; 11.11
carcasses you shall have in a. 11.11
fins and scales is an a. to you. 11.12
shall have in a. among the birds, 11.13
they are an a.: the eagle, the 11.13
go upon all fours are an a. to you. 11.20
have four feet are an a. to you. 11.23
swarms upon the earth is an a.; 11.41
shall not eat; for they are an a. 11.42
with a woman; it is an a. 18.22
all on the third day, it is an a.; 19.07
both of them have committed an a.; 20.13
for it is an a. to the LORD your Deu 7.25
for that is an a. to the LORD your 17.01
these things is an a. to the LORD; 18.12
things is an a. to the LORD your 22.05
of these are an a. to the LORD 23.18
for that is an a. before the LORD 24.04
are an a. to the LORD your God. 25.16
an a. to the LORD, a thing made by 27.15
have committed a. and wantonness Ju 20.06
Milcom the a. of the Ammonites. 1Ki 11.05
place for Chemosh the a. of Moab, 11.07
for Molech the a. of the Ammonites, 11.07
Ashtoreth the a. of the Sidonians, 2Ki 23.13
and for Chemosh the a. of Moab, 23.13
for Milcom the a. of the Ammonites 23.13
perverse man is an a. to the LORD, Pro 3.32
seven which are an a. to him: 6.16
wickedness is an a. to my lips. 8.07
false balance is an a. to the LORD, 11.01
perverse mind are an a. to the LORD, 11.20
Lying lips are an a. to the LORD, 12.22
away from evil is an a. to fools. 13.19
of the wicked is an a. to the LORD, 15.08
of the wicked is an a. to the LORD, 15.09
the wicked are an a. to the LORD, 15.26
is arrogant is an a. to the LORD; 16.05
It is an a. to kings to do evil, for 16.12
are both alike an a. to the LORD. 17.15
are both alike an a. to the LORD. 20.10
Diverse weights are an a. to the LORD, 20.23
The sacrifice of the wicked is an a.; 21.27
and the scoffer is an a. to men. 24.09
the law, even his prayer is an a. 28.09
man is an a. to the righteous, but 29.27
is straight is an a. to the wicked. 29.27
incense is an a. to me. New moon Is 1.13
an a. is he who chooses you. 41.24
I make the residue of it an a.? 44.19
swine's flesh and the a. and mice, 66.17
land, and made my heritage an a. Jer 2.07
ashamed when they committed a.? 6.15
ashamed when they committed a.? 8.12
mind, that they should do this a., 32.35
his eyes to the idols, commits a., Eze 18.12
One commits a. with his neighbor's 22.11
set up the a. that makes desolate Dan 11.31
and the a. that makes desolate is 12.11
and a. has been committed in Israel Mal 2.11
among men is an a. in the sight of Lk 16.15
one who practices a. or falsehood, Rev 21.27

ABOMINATIONS
ordinances and do none of these a., Lev 18.26
(for all of these a. the men of the 18.27
For whoever shall do any of these a., 18.29
to all the a. of the nations which 1Ki 14.24
of Judah has committed these a., 2Ki 21.11
and all the a. that were seen in 23.24
away all the a. from all the 2Ch 34.33
and the a. which he did, and what 36.08
following all the a. of the nations; 36.14
peoples of the lands with their a., Ez 9.01
with their a. which have filled it 9.11
the peoples who practice these a.? 9.14
there are seven a. in his heart; Pro 26.25
their soul delights in their a.; Is 66.03
you remove your a. from my presence, Jer 4.01
to go on doing all these a.? 7.10
have set their a. in the house 7.30
I have seen your a., your 13.27
my inheritance with their a." 16.18
They set up their a. in the house 32.34
doings and the a. which you 44.22
of all your a. I will do with you Eze 5.09
things and with all your a., 5.11
have committed, for all their a. 6.09
of all the evil a. of the house of 6.11
I will punish you for all your a. 7.03
while your a. are in your midst. 7.04
I will punish you for all your a. 7.08
while your a. are in your midst. 7.09
the great a. that the house of 8.06
but you will see still greater a." 8.06
see the vile a. that they are 8.09
still greater a. which they commit." 8.13
see still greater a. than these." 8.15
to commit the a. which they commit 8.17
over all the a. that are committed 9.04
detestable things and all its a. 11.18
detestable things and their a., 11.21
all their a. among the nations 12.16

ABOMINATIONS (cont.)
away your faces from all your a. Eze 14.06
make known to Jerusalem her a., 16.02
And in all your a. and your harlotries 16.22
lewdness in addition to all your a.? 16.43
ways, or do according to their a.; 16.47
have committed more a. than they, 16.51
by all the a. which you have 16.51
lewdness and your a., says the LORD. 16.58
them know the a. of their fathers, 20.04
you commit a. and each of you 33.26
of all their a. which they have 33.29
name by their a. which they have 43.08
there be an end to all your a., 44.06
my covenant, with all your a. 44.07
because of the a. which they have 44.13
the wing of a. shall come one who Dan 9.27
and its a. from between its teeth; Zec 9.07
cup full of a. and the impurities Rev 17.04
of harlots and of earth's a. 17.05

ABOUND
will make you a. in prosperity, Deu 28.11
have when their grain and wine a. Ps 4.07
and peace a., till the moon be no 72.07
faithful man will a. with blessings, Pro 28.20
continue in sin that grace may a.? Rom 6.01
the Holy Spirit you may a. in hope. 15.13
your love may a. more and more, Php 1.09
to be abased, and I know how to a.; 4.12
increase and a. in love to one 1Th 3.12
For if these things are yours and a., 2Pe 1.08

ABOUNDED
one man Jesus Christ a. for many. Rom 5.15
increased, grace a. all the more, 5.20

ABOUNDING
and a. in steadfast love and Ex 34.06
and a. in steadfast love, forgiving Num 14.18
to anger and a. in steadfast love, Neh 9.17
a. in steadfast love to all who Ps 86.05
to anger and a. in steadfast love 86.15
to anger and a. in steadfast love. 103.08
to anger and a. in steadfast love. 145.08
were no springs a. with water. Pro 8.24
and a. in steadfast love, and Joe 2.13
and a. in steadfast love, and Jon 4.02
always a. in the work of the Lord, 1Co 15.58
a. in thanksgiving. Col 2.07

ABOUNDS
God's truthfulness a. to his glory, Rom 3.07

ABRAHAM
Abram, but your name shall be A.; Gen 17.05
And God said to A., "As for you 17.09
And God said to A., "As for Sarai 17.15
Then A. fell on his face and 17.17
And A. said to God, "Oh that Ishmael 17.18
with him, God went up from A. 17.22
Then A. took Ishmael his son and 17.23
A. was ninety-nine years old when 17.24
That very day A. and his son 17.26
And A. hastened into the tent to 18.06
And A. ran to the herd, and took a 18.07
Now A. and Sarah were old, advanced 18.11
The LORD said to A., "Why did 18.13
and A. went with them to set them 18.16
I hide from A. what I am about to 18.17
seeing that A. shall become a great 18.18
may bring to A. what he has 18.19
but A. still stood before the LORD. 18.22
Then A. drew near, and said, "Wilt 18.23
A. answered, "Behold, I have taken 18.27
he had finished speaking to A.; 18.33
and A. returned to his place. 18.33
And A. went early in the morning to 19.27
of the valley, God remembered A., 19.29
From there A. journeyed toward the 20.01
And A. said of Sarah his wife, "She 20.02
Then Abimelech called A., and said 20.09
And Abimelech said to A., "What 20.10
A. said, "I did it because I thought, 20.11
female slaves, and gave them to A., 20.14
Then A. prayed to God; and God 20.17
and bore A. a son in his old age at 21.02
A. called the name of his son who 21.03
And A. circumcised his son Isaac 21.04
A. was a hundred years old when his 21.05
have said to A. that Sarah would 21.07
and A. made a great feast on the 21.08
Egyptian, whom she had borne to A., 21.09
So she said to A., "Cast out this 21.10
displeasing to A. on account of 21.11
But God said to A., "Be not 21.12
So A. rose early in the morning, and 21.14
commander of his army said to A., 21.22
And A. said, "I will swear." 21.24
When A. complained to Abimelech 21.25
So A. took sheep and oxen and gave 21.27
A. set seven ewe lambs of the flock 21.28
And Abimelech said to A., "What 21.29
A. planted a tamarisk tree in 21.33
And A. sojourned many days in the 21.34
After these things God tested A., 22.01
A., and said to him, "A.!" And he 22.01
So A. rose early in the morning, 22.03
On the third day A. lifted up his 22.04
Then A. said to his young men, "Stay 22.05
And A. took the wood of the burnt 22.06
said to his father A., "My father!" 22.07
A. said, "God will provide himself 22.08
A. built an altar there, and laid 22.09
Then A. put forth his hand, and took 22.10
from heaven, and said, "A., A.!" 22.11
And A. lifted up his eyes and 22.13
and A. went and took the ram, and 22.13
So A. called the name of that place 22.14
LORD called to A. a second time 22.15
So A. returned to his young men, and 22.19
and A. dwelt at Beersheba. 22.19
Now after these things it was told A., 22.20
and A. went in to mourn for Sarah 23.02
And A. rose up from before his dead, 23.03
The Hittites answered A., 23.05
A. rose and bowed to the Hittites, 23.07
answered A. in the hearing of the 23.10
Then A. bowed down before the 23.12
Ephron answered A., 23.14
A. agreed with Ephron; 23.16
and A. weighed out for Ephron the 23.16
to A. as a possession in the 23.18
After this, A. buried Sarah his wife 23.19
made over to A. as a possession 23.20
Now A. was old, well advanced in 24.01
LORD had blessed A. in all things. 24.01
And A. said to his servant, the 24.02
A. said to him, "See to it that you 24.06
under the thigh of A. his master, 24.09
said, "O LORD, God of my master A., 24.12
steadfast love to my master A. 24.12
the LORD, the God of my master A., 24.27
'O LORD, the God of my master A., 24.42
the LORD, the God of my master A., 24.48
A. took another wife, whose name was 25.01
A. gave all he had to Isaac. 25.05
of his concubines A. gave gifts, 25.06
A. breathed his last and died in a 25.08
the field which A. purchased from 25.10
There A. was buried, with Sarah his 25.10
After the death of A. God blessed 25.11
Egyptian, Sarah's maid, bore to A. 25.12
A. was the father of Isaac, 25.19

ABRAHAM (cont.)

famine that was in the days of A. Gen 26.01
which I swore to A. your father. 26.03
because A. obeyed my voice and kept 26.05
dug in the days of A. his father.) 26.15
dug in the days of A. his father; 26.18
stopped them after the death of A.; 26.18
"I am the God of A. your father; 26.24
the blessing of A. to you and to 28.04
sojournings which God gave to A.!" 28.04
the God of A. your father and the 28.13
the God of A. and the Fear of Isaac, 31.42
The God of A. and the God of Nahor, 31.53
of my father A. and God of my 32.09
which I gave to A. and Isaac I 35.12
where A. and Isaac had sojourned. 35.27
whom my fathers A. and Isaac 48.15
name of my fathers A. and Isaac; 48.16
which A. bought with the field from 49.30
There they buried A. and Sarah his 49.31
which A. bought with the field from 50.13
to the land which he swore to A., 50.24
remembered his covenant with A., Ex 2.24
the God of A., the God of Isaac, and 3.06
God of your fathers, the God of A.; 3.15
the God of A., of Isaac, and of 3.16
the God of A., the God of Isaac, and 4.05
I appeared to A., to Isaac, and to 6.03
land which I swore to give to A., 6.08
Remember A., Isaac, and Israel, thy 32.13
to the land of which I swore to A., 33.01
with Isaac and my covenant with A., Lev 26.42
land which I swore to give to A., Num 32.11
to A., to Isaac, and to Jacob, to Deu 1.08
to A., to Isaac, and to Jacob, to 6.10
to A., to Isaac, and to Jacob. 9.05
A., Isaac, and Jacob; do not 9.27
to A., to Isaac, and to Jacob. 29.13
to A., to Isaac, and to Jacob, to 30.20
is the land of which I swore to A., 34.04
the father of A. and of Nahor; Jos 24.02
your father A. from beyond the 24.03
God of A., Isaac, and Israel, let it 1Ki 18.36
because of his covenant with A., 2Ki 13.23
Abram, that is, A. 1Ch 1.27
The sons of A.: Isaac and Ishmael. 1.28
A. was the father of Isaac. 1.34
O offspring of A. his servant, sons 16.13
the covenant which he made with A., 16.16
the God of A., Isaac, and Israel, our 29.18
the descendants of A. thy friend? 2Ch 20.07
the God of A., Isaac, and Israel, 30.06
Chaldees and give him the name A.; Neh 9.07
as the people of the God of A. Ps 47.09
O offspring of A. his servant, sons 105.06
the covenant which he made with A., 105.09
holy promise, and A. his servant. 105.42
who redeemed A., concerning the Is 29.22
the offspring of A., my friend; 41.08
Look to A. your father and to Sarah 51.02
though A. does not know us and 63.16
to rule over the seed of A., Jer 33.26
'A. was only one man, yet he got Eze 33.24
to Jacob and steadfast love to A., Mic 7.20
the son of David, the son of A. Mt 1.01
A. was the father of Isaac, and 1.02
generations from A. to David were 1.17
yourselves, 'We have A. as our father'; 3.09
stones to raise up children to A. 3.09
and west and sit at table with A., 8.11
'I am the God of A., and the God 22.32
said to him, 'I am the God of A., Mk 12.26
to A. and to his posterity for ever Lk 1.55
which he swore to our father A., 1.73
yourselves, 'We have A. as our father'; 3.08
stones to raise up children to A. 3.08
the son of A., the son of Terah, the 3.34
a daughter of A. whom Satan bound 13.16
when you see A. and Isaac and Jacob 13.28
and saw A. far off and Lazarus in 16.23
'Father A., have mercy upon me, and 16.24
But A. said, 'Son, remember that you 16.25
But A. said, 'They have Moses and 16.29
And he said, 'No, father A.; 16.30
since he also is a son of A. 19.09
Lord the God of A. and the God of 20.37
him, "We are descendants of A., Jn 8.33
that you are descendants of A.; 8.37
They answered him, "A. is our father." 8.39
children, you would do what A. did, 8.39
this is not what A. did. 8.40
A. died, as did the prophets; 8.52
than our father A., who died? 8.53
Your father A. rejoiced that he was 8.56
years old, and have you seen A.?" 8.57
I say to you, before A. was, I am." 8.58
The God of A. and of Isaac and of Ac 3.13
saying to A., 'And in your posterity 3.25
of glory appeared to our father A., 7.02
And so A. became the father of 7.08
the tomb that A. had bought for a 7.16
near, which God had granted to A., 7.17
the God of A. and of Isaac and of 7.32
"Brethren, sons of the family of A., 13.26
What then shall we say about A., Rom 4.01
For if A. was justified by works, he 4.02
"A. believed God, and it was reckoned 4.03
was reckoned to A. as righteousness 4.09
our father A. had before he was 4.12
The promise to A. and his descendants, 4.13
to those who share the faith of A., 4.16
are children of A. because they 9.07
an Israelite, a descendant of A., 11.01
Are they descendants of A.? 2Co 11.22
Thus A. "believed God, and it was Gal 3.06
of faith who are the sons of A. 3.07
the gospel beforehand to A., 3.08
are blessed with A. who had faith. 3.09
the blessing of A. might come upon 3.14
were made to A. and to his offspring. 3.16
but God gave it to A. by a promise. 3.18
it is written that A. had two sons, 4.22
but with the descendants of A. Heb 2.16
For when God made a promise to A., 6.13
And thus A., having patiently 6.15
met A. returning from the slaughter 7.01
and to him A. apportioned a tenth 7.02
A. the patriarch gave him a tithe 7.04
these also are descended from A. 7.05
tithes from A. and blessed him who 7.06
tithes, paid tithes through A., 7.09
By faith A. obeyed when he was 11.08
By faith A., when he was tested, 11.17
Was not A. our father justified by Jas 2.21
"A. believed God, and it was reckoned 2.23
as Sarah obeyed A., calling him 1Pe 3.06

ABRAHAM'S

male among the men of A. house, Gen 17.23
Abimelech because of Sarah, A. wife. 20.18
Milcah bore to Nahor, A. brother. 22.23
A. brother, came out with her water 24.15
So he said, "I am A. servant. 24.34
When A. servant heard their words, 24.52
and A. servant and his men. 24.59
the days of the years of A. life, 25.07
A. son, whom Hagar the Egyptian, 25.12
A. son: Abraham was the father of 25.19
descendants for my servant A. sake." 26.24
the daughter of Ishmael A. son, 28.09
A. concubine: she bore Zimran, 1Ch 1.32
carried by the angels to A. bosom. Lk 16.22
"If you were A. children, you would Jn 8.39
Christ's then you are A. offspring, Gal 3.29

ABRAM

years, he became the father of A., Gen 11.26
Terah was the father of A., 11.27
And A. and Nahor took wives; 11.29
Terah took A. his son and Lot the 11.31
Now the LORD said to A., "Go from 12.01
So A. went, as the LORD had told him; 12.04
A. was seventy-five years old when 12.04
And A. took Sarai his wife, and Lot 12.05
A. passed through the land to the 12.06
Then the LORD appeared to A., 12.07
And A. journeyed on, still going 12.09
So A. went down to Egypt to sojourn 12.10
When A. entered Egypt the Egyptians 12.14
for her sake he dealt well with A.; 12.16
So Pharaoh called A., and said, 12.18
So A. went up from Egypt, he and his 13.01
Now A. was very rich in cattle, in 13.02
and there A. called on the name of 13.04
who went with A., also had flocks 13.05
Then A. said to Lot, "Let there be 13.08
A. dwelt in the land of Canaan, 13.12
The LORD said to A., after Lot 13.14
So A. moved his tent, and came and 13.18
and told A. the Hebrew, who was 14.13
these were allies of A. 14.13
When A. heard that his kinsman had 14.14
"Blessed be A. by God Most High, 14.19
And A. gave him a tenth of everything 14.20
And the king of Sodom said to A., 14.21
But A. said to the king of Sodom, "I 14.22
should say, 'I have made A. rich.' 14.23
of the LORD came to A. in a vision, 15.01
A., I am your shield; your reward 15.01
But A. said, "O LORD GOD, what wilt 15.02
And A. said, "Behold, thou hast given 15.03
A. drove them away. 15.11
down, a deep sleep fell on A.; 15.12
Then the LORD said to A., 15.13
the LORD made a covenant with A., 15.18
and Sarai said to A., "Behold 16.02
And A. hearkened to the voice of 16.02
So, after A. had dwelt ten years in 16.03
and gave her to A. her husband as 16.03
And Sarai said to A., "May the 16.05
But A. said to Sarai, "Behold, your 16.06
And Hagar bore A. a son; and 16.15
and A. called the name of his son, 16.15
A. was eighty-six years old when 16.16
old when Hagar bore Ishmael to A. 16.16
When A. was ninety-nine years old 17.01
years old the LORD appeared to A., 17.01
Then A. fell on his face; 17.03
No longer shall your name be A., 17.05
A., that is, Abraham. 1Ch 1.27
didst choose A. and bring him Neh 9.07

ABRAM'S

the name of A. wife was Sarai, and Gen 11.29
his son A. wife, and they went forth 11.31
plagues because of Sarai, A. wife. 12.17
the herdsmen of A. cattle and the 13.07
the son of A. brother, who dwelt in 14.12
Now Sarai, A. wife, bore him no 16.01
A. wife, took Hagar the Egyptian her 16.03

ABROAD

of the Canaanites spread a. Gen 10.18
nations spread a. on the earth 10.32
we be scattered a. upon the face 11.04
scattered them a. from there over 11.08
scattered them a. over the face of 11.09
shall spread a. to the west and to 28.14
and the more they spread a. Ex 1.12
were scattered a. throughout all 5.12
again and walks a. with his staff, 21.19
whether born at home or born a. Lev 18.09
Then you shall send a. the loud 25.09
you shall send a. the trumpet 25.09
people of the LORD spreading a. 1Sa 2.24
were spread a. over all the land, 30.16
let us send a. to our brethren who 1Ch 13.02
As soon as the command was spread a., 2Ch 31.05
scattered a. and dispersed among Est 3.08
He wanders a. for bread, saying, Job 15.23
when he goes out, he tells it a. Ps 41.06
abundance, O God, thou didst shed a.; 68.09
Should your springs be scattered a., Pro 5.16
let its fragrance be wafted a. Sol 4.16
shoots spread a. and passed over Is 16.08
For you will spread a. to the right 54.03
his sheep have been scattered a., Eze 34.12
till you have scattered them a., 34.21
have spread you a. as the four Zec 2.06
the report went a. concerning him; Lk 5.15
of God who are scattered a. Jn 11.52
The saying spread a. among the 21.23
"He scatters a., he gives to the 2Co 9.09
who go a. to the kings of the whole Rev 16.14

ABRONAH

from Jotbathah, and encamped at A. Num 33.34
And they set out from A., 33.35

ABSALOM

A. the son of Maacah the daughter 2Sa 3.03
Now A., David's son, had a beautiful 13.01
And her brother A. said to her, 13.20
But A. spoke to Amnon neither good 13.22
for A. hated Amnon, because he had 13.22
After two full years A. had sheepshearers 13.23
and A. invited all the king's sons. 13.23
And A. came to the king, and said, 13.24
But the king said to A., "No my 13.25
Then A. said, "If not, pray let my 13.26
But A. pressed him until he let 13.27
Then A. commanded his servants, 13.28
So the servants of A. did to Amnon 13.29
did to Amnon as A. had commanded. 13.29
"A. has slain all the king's sons, 13.30
the command of A. this has been 13.32
But A. fled. And the 13.34
But A. fled, and went to Talmai the 13.37
So A. fled, and went to Geshur, and 13.38
the king longed to go forth to A.; 13.39
the king's heart went out to A. 14.01
go, bring back the young man A." 14.21
and brought A. to Jerusalem. 14.23
So A. dwelt apart in his own house, 14.24
to be praised for his beauty as A.; 14.25
There were born to A. three sons, 14.27
So A. dwelt two full years in 14.28
Then A. sent for Joab, to send him 14.29
arose and went to A. at his house, 14.31
A. answered Joab, "Behold, I sent 14.32
and he summoned A. So he 14.33
and the king kissed A. 14.33
After this A. got himself a chariot 15.01
And A. used to rise early and stand 15.02
A. would call to him, and say, "From 15.02
A. would say to him, "See, your 15.03
A. said moreover, "Oh that I were 15.04
Thus A. did to all of Israel who 15.06
so A. stole the hearts of the men 15.06
of four years A. said to the king, 15.07
But A. sent secret messengers 15.10
'A. is king at Hebron!'" 15.10
With A. went two hundred men from 15.11
And while A. was offering the 15.12
the people with A. kept increasing 15.12
men of Israel have gone after A." 15.13
will be no escape for us from A.; 15.14
is among the conspirators with A." 15.31
and say to A., 'I will be your 15.34

ABSALOM (cont.)
just as A. was entering Jerusalem. 2Sa 15.37
into the hand of your son A. 16.08
Now A. and all the people, the men 16.15
came to A., Hushai said to A., 16.16
And A. said to Hushai, "Is this your 16.17
And Hushai said to A., "No; 16.18
Then A. said to Ahithophel, "Give 16.20
Ahithophel said to A., 16.21
a tent for A. upon the roof; 16.22
and A. went in to his father's 16.22
esteemed, both by David and by A. 16.23
Moreover Ahithophel said to A., 17.01
advice pleased A. and all the 17.04
Then A. said, "Call Hushai the 17.05
And when Hushai came to A., 17.06
A. said to him, "Thus has Ahithophel 17.06
Then Hushai said to A., 17.07
among the people who follow A.' 17.09
And A. and all the men of Israel 17.14
the LORD might bring evil upon A. 17.14
Ahithophel counsel A. and the 17.15
But a lad saw them, and told A.; 17.18
And A. crossed the Jordan with all 17.24
Now A. had set Amasa over the army 17.25
And Israel and A. encamped in the 17.26
for my sake with the young man A." 18.05
to all the commanders about A. 18.05
And A. chanced to meet the servants 18.09
A. was riding upon his mule, and the 18.09
I saw A. hanging in an oak." 18.10
my sake protect the young man A.' 18.12
thrust them into the heart of A., 18.14
surrounded A. and struck him, and 18.15
And they took A., and threw him 18.17
Now A. in his lifetime had taken 18.18
"Is it well with the young man A.?" 18.29
"Is it well with the young man A.?" 18.32
"O my son A., my son, my son A.! 18.33
is weeping and mourning for A." 19.01
"O my son A., O A., my son, my 19.04
perceive that if A. were alive and 19.06
has fled out of the land from A. 19.09
But A., whom we anointed over us, is 19.10
will do us more harm than A.; 20.06
and he was born next after A. 1Ki 1.06
when I fled from A. your brother. 2.07
although he had not supported A.— 2.28
the third A., whose mother was 1Ch 3.02
he took Maacah the daughter of A., 2Ch 11.20
the daughter of A. above all his 11.21

ABSALOM'S
"I love Tamar, my brother A. sister." 2Sa 13.04
woman, in her brother A. house. 13.20
So A. servants set the field on 14.30
When A. servants came to the woman 17.20
it is called A. monument to this 18.18

ABSENCE
to them in the a. of the multitude Lk 22.06
they have made up for your a.; 1Co 16.17
my presence but much more in my a., Php 2.12

ABSENT
when we are a. one from the other. Gen 31.49
For though a. in body I am present 1Co 5.03
that what we say by letter when a., 2Co 10.11
and I warn them now while a., 13.02
I come and see you or am a., Php 1.27
For though I am a. in body, Col 2.05

ABSTAIN
to them to a. from the pollutions Ac 15.20
that you a. from what has been 15.29
they should a. from what has been 21.25
that you a. from immorality; 1Th 4.03
a. from every form of evil. 5.22
and exiles to a. from the passions 1Pe 2.11

ABSTAINS
him who eats despise him who a., Rom 14.03
let not him who a. pass judgment 14.03
while he who a., a. in honor 14.06
a. in honor of the Lord and gives 14.06

ABSTINENCE
and enjoin a. from foods which God 1Ti 4.03

ABUNDANCE
Joseph stored up grain in great a., Gen 41.49
by reason of the a. of all things, Deu 28.47
and the a. of the everlasting hills, 33.15
and sheep in a., and has invited 1Ki 1.19
and sheep in a., and has invited 1.25
came such an a. of spices as these 10.10
You have an a. of workmen: stonecutters, 1Ch 22.15
all this a. that we have provided 29.16
sacrifices in a. for all Israel; 29.21
to prepare timber for me in a., 2Ch 2.09
away sheep in a. and camels. 14.15
Ahab killed an a. of sheep and 18.02
day, and collected money in a. 24.11
Israel gave in a. the first fruits 31.05
made weapons and shields in a. 32.05
himself, and flocks and herds in a.; 32.29
every ten days skins of wine in a.; Neh 5.18
orchards and fruit trees in a.; 9.25
he gives food in a. Job 36.31
But I through the a. of thy steadfast Ps 5.07
They feast on the a. of thy house, 36.08
has than the a. of many wicked. 37.16
in the days of famine they have a. 37.19
boast of the a. of their riches? 49.06
trusted in the a. of his riches, 52.07
Rain in a., O God, thou didst shed 68.09
in the a. of thy steadfast love 69.13
May there be a. of grain in the 72.16
he sent them food in a. 78.25
gave them bread from heaven in a. 105.40
remember the a. of thy steadfast 106.07
according to the a. of his steadfast 106.45
but in an a. of counselors there is Pro 11.14
and a. of costly stones; 20.15
of the diligent lead surely to a., 21.05
and in a. of counselors there is 24.06
and because of the a. of milk which Is 7.22
Therefore the a. they have gained 15.07
and wide, with fire and wood in a.; 30.33
a. of salvation, wisdom, and knowledge 33.06
and spoil in a. will be divided; 33.23
because the a. of the sea shall be 60.05
according to the a. of his steadfast 63.07
delight from the a. of her glory. 66.11
the soul of the priests with a., Jer 31.14
reveal to them a. of prosperity 33.06
wine and summer fruits in great a. 40.12
according to the a. of his steadfast Lam 3.32
nor their a.. nor their wealth; Eze 7.11
In the a. of your trade you were 28.16
silver, and garments in great a. Zec 14.14
For out of the a. of the heart the Mt 12.34
more be given, and he will have a.; 13.12
more be given, and he will have a.; 25.29
all contributed out of their a.; Mk 12.44
for out of the a. of the heart his Lk 6.45
consist in the a. of his possessions 12.15
all contributed out of their a., 21.04
who receive the a. of grace and Rom 5.17
their a. of joy and their extreme 2Co 8.02
equality your a. at the present 814
so that their a. may supply your 8.14
you with every blessing in a., 9.08

ABUNDANCE (cont.)
may provide in a. for every good 2Co 9.08
elated by the a. of revelations, 12.07
plenty and hunger, a. and want. Php 4.12

ABUNDANT
a. provisions of meal, cakes of figs, 1Ch 12.40
and he gave them a. provisions, 2Ch 11.23
and a. righteousness he will not Job 37.23
O how a. is thy goodness, which thou Ps 31.19
themselves in a. prosperity 37.11
according to thy a. mercy blot out 51.01
according to thy a. mercy, 69.16
forth the fame of thy a. goodness, 145.07
Great is our LORD, and a. in power; 147.05
of life and a. welfare will they Pro 3.02
but a. crops come by the strength 14.04
merchandise will supply a. food and Is 23.18
he placed it beside a. waters. Eze 17.05
it to good soil by a. waters, 17.08
of branches by reason of a. water. 19.10
with you because of your a. goods; 27.16
trafficked with you for your a. goods, 27.18
with your a. wealth and merchandise 27.33
from a. water in its shoots. 31.05
its roots went down to a. waters. 31.07
and make it a. and lay no famine 36.29
and the increase of the field a., 36.30
Its leaves were fair and its fruit a., Dan 4.12
whose leaves were fair and its fruit a., 4.21
with a great army and a. supplies. 11.13
he has poured down for you a. rain, Joe 2.23
you know the a. love that I have 2Co 2.04

ABUNDANTLY
they may breed a. on the earth, Gen 8.17
bring forth a. on the earth and 9.07
I came, and it has increased a.; 30.30
years the earth brought forth a., 41.47
and water came forth a., Num 20.11
will make you a. prosperous in all Deu 30.09
they brought in a. the tithe of 2Ch 31.05
pour down, and drop upon man a. Job 36.28
but a. requites him who acts Ps 31.23
Thou waterest its furrows a., 65.10
gave them drink a. as from the 78.15
The trees of the LORD are watered a., 104.16
I will a. bless her provisions; 132.15
it shall blossom a., Is 35.02
to our God, for he will a. pardon. 55.07
they may have life, and have it a. Jn 10.10
For as we share a. in Christ's 2Co 1.05
Christ we share a. in comfort too. 1.05
to do far more a. than all that we Eph 3.20
because your faith is growing a., 2Th 1.03

ABUSE
corrects a scoffer gets himself a., Pro 9.07
and quarreling and a. will cease. 22.10
handed over to them and they a. me." Jer 38.19
you, pray for those who a. you. Lk 6.28
exposed to a. and affliction, Heb 10.33
He considered a. suffered for the 11.26
the camp, bearing a. for him. 13.13
wild profligacy, and they a. you; 1Pe 4.04

ABUSED
and a. her all night until the Ju 19.25
when you are a., those who revile 1Pe 3.16

ABUSIVE
a., disobedient to their parents, 2Ti 3.02

ABYSS
command them to depart into the a. Lk 8.31
or "Who will descend into the a.?" Rom 10.07

ACACIA
tanned rams' skins, goatskins, a. wood, Ex 25.05
"They shall make an ark of a. wood; 25.10
You shall make poles of a. wood, 25.13
"And you shall make a table of a. wood; 25.23
You shall make the poles of a. wood, 25.28
for the tabernacle of a. wood. 26.15
"And you shall make bars of a. wood, 26.26
four pillars of a. overlaid with 26.32
for the screen five pillars of a., 26.37
"You shall make the altar of a. wood, 27.01
poles of a. wood, and overlay them 27.06
of a. wood shall you make it. 30.01
You shall make the poles of a. wood, 30.05
rams' skins, and goatskins, a. wood, 35.07
whom was found a. wood of any use 35.24
for the tabernacle of a. wood. 36.20
And he made bars of a. wood, 36.31
And for it he made four pillars of a., 36.36
Bezalel made the ark of a. wood; 37.01
And he made poles of a. wood, 37.04
He also made the table of a. wood; 37.10
the poles of a. wood to carry the 37.15
the altar of incense of a. wood; 37.25
And he made the poles of a. wood, 37.28
of burnt offering also of a. wood; 38.01
he made the poles of a. wood, 38.06
So I made an ark of a. wood, Deu 10.03
the a., the myrtle, and the olive; Is 41.19

ACCAD
and A., all of them in the land of Gen 10.10

ACCENT
of them, for your a. betrays you." Mt 26.73

ACCEPT
a. it from me, that I may bury my Gen 23.13
perhaps he will a. me." 32.20
then a. my present from my hand; 33.10
A., I pray you, my gift that is 33.11
and the owner shall a. the oath, Ex 22.11
"A. these from them. that they may Num 7.05
Moreover you shall a. no ransom for 35.31
And you shall a. no ransom for him 35.32
and a. the work of his hands; Deu 33.11
for he will not a. boiled meat from 1Sa 2.15
which you shall a. from their hand. 10.04
against me, may be a. an offering; 26.19
the king, "The LORD your God a. you." 2Sa 24.23
so a. now a present from your 2Ki 5.15
said, "Be pleased to a. two talents." 5.23
it a time to a. money and garments, 5.26
sackcloth, but he would not a. them. Est 4.04
and do you not a. their testimony Job 21.29
for I will a. his prayer not to 42.08
I will a. no bull from your house, Ps 50.09
A. my offerings of praise, O LORD, 119.108
and a. my words, that the years of Pro 4.10
He will a. no compensation, nor be 6.35
Listen to advice and a. instruction, 19.20
and to a. his lot and find enjoyment Ecc 5.19
who murmur will a. instruction." Is 29.24
God, and did not a. discipline; Jer 7.28
therefore the LORD does not a. them, 14.10
offering, I will not a. them; 14.12
they refuse to a. the cup from 25.28
there I will a. them, and there I Eze 20.40
As a pleasing odor I will a. you, 20.41
and I will a. you, says the Lord GOD 43.27
a. that which is good and we will Hos 14.02
I will not a. them, and the peace Amo 5.22
fear me, she will a. correction; Zep 3.07
and I will not a. an offering from Mal 1.10
Shall I a. that from your hand? 1.13
and if you are willing to a. it, Mt 11.14
the word and a. it and bear fruit, Mk 4.20

ACCEPT (cont.)
for us Romans to a. or practice." Ac 16.21
they will not a. your testimony 22.18
everywhere we a. this with all 24.03
in God which these themselves a., 24.15
you not to a. the grace of God in 2Co 6.01
or if you a. a different gospel 11.04
a. me as a fool, so that I too may 11.16
refusing to a. release, that they Heb 11.35

ACCEPTABLE
it have been a. in the sight of Lev 10.19
for it will not be a. for you. 22.20
on it shall be a. as an offering 22.27
of my heart be a. in thy sight, Ps 19.14
The sacrifice a. to God is a broken 51.17
At an a. time, O God, in the abundance 69.13
of the righteous know what is a., Pro 10.32
justice is more a. to the LORD 21.03
a fast, and a day a. to the LORD? Is 58.05
Your burnt offerings are not a., Jer 6.20
king, let my counsel be a. to you; Dan 4.27
to proclaim the a. year of the Lord." Lk 4.19
no prophet is a. in his own country 4.24
does what is right is a. to him. Ac 10.35
holy and a. to God, which is your Rom 12.01
what is good and a. and perfect. 12.02
Christ is a. to God and approved 14.18
offering of the Gentiles may be a., 15.16
Jerusalem may be a. to the saints, 15.31
"At the a. time I have listened to 2Co 6.02
Behold, now is the a. time; 6.02
it is a. according to what a man 8.12
a sacrifice a. and pleasing to God. Php 4.18
and it is a. in the sight of God 1Ti 2.03
for this is a. in the sight of God. 5.04
to God a more a. sacrifice than Heb 11.04
let us offer to God a. worship, 12.28
sacrifices a. to God through Jesus 1Pe 2.05

ACCEPTANCE
the LORD, that you may find a.; Lev 23.11
shall come up with a. on my altar, Is 60.07
what will their a. mean but life Rom 11.15
is sure and worthy of full a., 1Ti 1.15
is sure and worthy of full a. 4.09

ACCEPTED
If you do well, will you not be a.? Gen 4.07
they may be a. before the LORD. Ex 28.38
that he may be a. before the LORD; Lev 1.03
and it shall be a. for him to make 1.04
he who offers it shall not be a., 7.18
offer it so that you may be a. 19.05
an abomination; it will not be a., 19.07
to be a. you shall offer a male 22.19
to be a. it must be perfect; 22.21
a votive offering it cannot be a. 22.23
they will not be a. for you." 22.25
sacrifice it so that you may be a. 22.29
would not have a. a burnt offering Ju 13.23
and the LORD a. Job's prayer. Job 42.09
sacrifices will be a. on my altar; Is 56.07
For he not only a. our appeal, 2Co 8.17
who commends himself that is a., 10.18
different gospel from the one you a., 11.04
you a. it not as the word of men 1Th 2.13
you joyfully a. the plundering of Heb 10.34
sake and have a. nothing from the 3Jn 1.07

ACCEPTING
in not a. from his hand what he 2Ki 5.20
churches by a. support from them 2Co 11.08
bearing witness by a. his gifts; Heb 11.04

ACCEPTS
and he a. him, he comes into his Job 33.26
the LORD a. my prayer. Ps 6.09

A wicked man a. a bribe from the Pro 17.23
to no voice, she a. no correction. Zep 3.02
the offering or a. it with favor Mal 2.13

ACCESS
the right of a. among those who Zec 3.07
have obtained a. to this grace in Rom 5.02
we both have a. in one Spirit to Eph 2.18
confidence of a. through our faith 3.12

ACCESSORIES
the bases, and all their a.; Num 3.36
their equipment and all their a.; 4.32

ACCO
drive out the inhabitants of A., Ju 1.31

ACCOMPANIED
a. by the instruments of David king 2Ch 29.27
Now great multitudes a. him; Lk 14.25
men who have a. us during all the Ac 1.21
of the brethren from Joppa a. him. 10.23
These six brethren also a. me, 11.12
Beroea, the son of Pyrrhus, a. him; 20.04
a. by Aristarchus, a Macedonian from 27.02
have the right to be a. by a wife, 1Co 9.05

ACCOMPANY
and a. them without hesitation; Ac 10.20
Paul wanted Timothy to a. him; 16.03
I should go also, they will a. me. 1Co 16.04

ACCOMPLISH
if I do not a. for David what the 2Sa 3.09
sinned, what do you a. against him? Job 35.06
to a. all that he commands them on 37.12
of the LORD of hosts will a. this. Is 37.32
and I will a. all my purpose,' 46.10
but it shall a. that which I 55.11
which he was to a. at Jerusalem. Lk 9.31
who sent me, and to a. his work. Jn 4.34
the Father has granted me to a., 5.36
if only I may a. my course and the Ac 20.24

ACCOMPLISHED
his own house he successfully a. 2Ch 7.11
Thus was a. all the work of Solomon 8.16
the mouth of Jeremiah might be a., 36.22
the mouth of Jeremiah might be a., Ez 1.01
work had been a. with the help of Neh 6.16
executed and a. the intents of his Jer 23.20
executed and a. the intents of his 30.24
they shall be a. before you on 39.16
is a., he will keep you in exile no Lam 4.22
prosper till the indignation is a.; Dan 11.36
end of all these things would be a. 12.07
pass from the law until all is a. Mt 5.18
when these things are all to be a.?" Mk 13.04
which have been a. among us, Lk 1.01
I am constrained until it is a.! 12.50
of man by the prophets will be a. 18.31
having a. the work which thou Jn 17.04
which he a. in Christ when he Eph 1.20

ACCOMPLISHES
of him who a. all things according Eph 1.11

ACCORD
that it has not been of my own a. Num 16.28
with one a. to fight Joshua and Jos 9.02
with one a. are favorable to the 1Ki 22.13
with one a. are favorable to the 2Ch 18.12
Yea, they conspire with one a.; Ps 83.05
my voice, or walked in a. with it, Jer 9.13
the LORD and serve him with one a. Zep 3.09
Son can do nothing of his own a., Jn 5.19
But I have not come of my own a.; 7.28
I came not of my own a., 8.42

ACCORD (cont.)
me, but I lay down of my own a. Jn 10.18
He did not say this of his own a., 11.51
"Do you say this of your own a., 18.34
All these with one a. devoted Ac 1.14
with one a. gave heed to what was 8.06
It opened to them of its own a., 12.10
in a. with Christ Jesus, Rom 15.05
What a. has Christ with Belial? 2Co 6.15
he is going to you of his own a. 8.17
being in full a. and of one mind. Php 2.02
and not in a. with the tradition 2Th 3.06

ACCORDANCE
with you in a. with all these Ex 24.08
in a. with these words I have made 34.27
shall work in a. with all that the 36.01
in a. with the vow which he takes, Num 6.21
in a. with these ordinances; 35.24
in a. with all the curses of the Deu 29.21
In a. with all these words, and in 2Sa 7.17
and in a. with all this vision, 7.17
blindness in a. with the prayer of 2Ki 6.18
in a. with the word of the LORD. 9.26
in a. with all that King Ahaz had 2Ki 16.11
in a. with all the law which I 17.13
in a. with all these words, and in 1Ch 17.15
and in a. with all this vision, 17.15
of God and in a. with the law and 2Ch 31.21
in a. with the word of the LORD, and Jer 32.08
in a. with their conduct and their Eze 36.19
for our sins in a. with the 1Co 15.03
third day in a. with the scriptures, 15.04
in a. with the glorious gospel of 1Ti 1.11
in a. with the prophetic utterances 1.18

ACCORDING
each a. to its kind, upon the earth." Gen 1.11
yielding seed a. to their own 1.12
is their seed, each a. to its kind. 1.12
a. to their kinds, and every winged 1.21
every winged bird a. to its kind. 1.21
living creatures a. to their kinds: 1.24
of the earth a. to their kinds." 1.24
of the earth a. to their kinds and 1.25
and the cattle a. to their kinds, 1.25
upon the ground a. to its kind. 1.25
Of the birds a. to their kinds, and 6.20
of the animals a. to their kinds, 6.20
thing of the ground a. to its kind, 6.20
they and every beast a. to its kind, 7.14
all the cattle a. to their kinds, 7.14
creeps on the earth a. to its kind, 7.14
and every bird a. to its kind, 7.14
a. to their genealogies, in their 10.32
done altogether a. to the outcry 18.21
a. to the weights current among the 23.16
twelve princes a. to their tribes. 25.16
a. to the pace of the cattle which 33.14
before me and a. to the pace of 33.14
and I will give a. as you say to 34.12
a. to their clans in the land of 36.30
a. to their families and their 36.40
a. to their dwelling places in the 36.43
to each man a. to his dream. 41.12
the first-born a. to his birthright 43.33
and the youngest a. to his youth; 43.33
a. to the command of Pharaoh, and 45.21
a. to the number of their dependents 47.12
sons of Levi a. to their generations: Ex 6.16
of the Levites a. to their generations. 6.19
And the LORD did a. to the word of 8.13
man a lamb a. to their fathers' 12.03
shall take a. to the number of 12.04
a. to what each can eat you shall 12.04
for yourselves a. to your families, 12.21
a. to the number of the persons 16.16
each gathered a. to what he could 16.18
a. to the commandment of the LORD, 17.01
a. as the woman's husband shall lay 21.22
be dealt with a. to this same rule. 21.31
nor do a. to their works, but you 23.24
a. to the twelve tribes of Israel. 24.04
A. to all that I show you concerning 25.09
the tabernacle a. to the plan for 26.30
their names a. to the names of the 28.21
a. to all that I have commanded you 29.35
half a shekel a. to the shekel of 30.13
a. to the shekel of the sanctuary, 30.24
you shall make a. to its composition, 30.37
A. to all that I have commanded you 31.11
of Levi did a. to the word of 32.28
a. to the names of the sons of 39.06
their names a. to the names of the 39.14
Israel had done a. to all that the 39.32
A. to all that the LORD had commanded 39.42
a. to all that the LORD commanded 40.16
burnt offering a. to the ordinance Lev 5.10
a. to the shekel of the sanctuary; 5.15
and offered it a. to the ordinance 9.16
And they did a. to the word of 10.07
the kite, the falcon a. to its kind, 11.14
every raven a. to its kind, 11.15
sea gull, the hawk a. to its kind, 11.16
the heron a. to its kind, the hoopoe, 11.19
the locust a. to its kind, the bald 11.22
the bald locust a. to its kind, 11.22
the cricket a. to its kind, and the 11.22
and the grasshopper a. to its kind. 11.22
the great lizard a. to its kind, 11.29
A. to the number of years after the 25.15
and a. to the number of years for 25.15
shall be a. to the number of years 25.50
a. to them he shall refund out of 25.51
a. to the years of service due from 25.52
a. to the shekel of the sanctuary. 27.03
a. to the ability of him who vowed 27.08
shall be a. to the seed for it; 27.16
money-value for it a. to the years 27.18
shall be a. to the shekel of the 27.25
a. to the number of names, every Num 1.02
a. to the number of names, from 1.18
a. to the number of names, head by 1.20
a. to the number of names, head by 1.22
a. to the number of names, from 1.24
a. to the number of names, from 1.26
a. to the number of names, from 1.28
a. to the number of names, from 1.30
a. to the number of names, from 1.32
a. to the number of names, from 1.34
a. to the number of names, from 1.36
a. to the number of names, from 1.38
a. to the number of names, from 1.40
a. to the number of names, from 1.42
they did a. to all that the LORD 1.54
A. to all that the LORD commanded 2.34
a. to his fathers' house. 2.34
numbered them a. to the word of 3.16
Their number a. to the number of 3.22
A. to the number of all the males, 3.28
Their number a. to the number of 3.34
a. to the number of names, from a 3.43
a. to the word of the LORD, as the 3.51
Aaron numbered a. to the commandment 4.37
Aaron numbered a. to the commandment 4.41
Aaron numbered a. to the commandment 4.45
A. to the commandment of the LORD 4.49
LORD shall be a. to his vow as a 6.21
so shall he do a. to the law for 6.21
to each man a. to his service." 7.05
sons of Gershon, a. to their service; 7.07
a. to their service, under the 7.08
a. to the shekel of the sanctuary, 7.13
a. to the shekel of the sanctuary, 7.19

ACCORDING (cont.)
a. to the shekel of the sanctuary, **Num** 7.25
a. to the shekel of the sanctuary, 7.31
a. to the shekel of the sanctuary, 7.37
a. to the shekel of the sanctuary, 7.43
a. to the shekel of the sanctuary, 7.49
a. to the shekel of the sanctuary, 7.55
a. to the shekel of the sanctuary, 7.61
a. to the shekel of the sanctuary, 7.67
a. to the shekel of the sanctuary, 7.73
a. to the shekel of the sanctuary, 7.79
hundred shekels a. to the shekel 7.85
shekels apiece a. to the shekel of 7.86
a. to the pattern which the LORD 8.04
a. to all that the LORD commanded 8.20
a. to all its statutes and all its 9.03
a. to all that the LORD commanded 9.05
a. to all the statute for the 9.12
a. to the statute of the passover 9.14
passover and a. to its ordinance, 9.14
then a. to the command of the LORD 9.20
people of Israel a. to their hosts, 10.28
a. to the command of the LORD, all 13.03
a. to the greatness of thy steadfast 14.19
and a. as thou hast forgiven this 14.19
"I have pardoned, a. to your word; 14.20
A. to the number of the days in 14.34
A. to the number that you prepare, 15.12
with every one a. to their number. 15.12
a. to the ordinance, and one male 15.24
their leaders a. to their fathers' 17.02
a. to their fathers' houses, twelve 17.06
a. to the shekel of the sanctuary, 18.16
The sons of Simeon a. to their 26.12
The sons of Gad a. to their families: 26.15
the sons of Gad a. to their number, 26.18
sons of Judah a. to their families 26.20
of Judah a. to their number, 26.22
of Issachar a. to their families: 26.23
of Issachar a. to their number, 26.25
a. to their families: of Sered, the 26.26
the Zebulunites a. to their number, 26.27
The sons of Joseph a. to their 26.28
sons of Ephraim a. to their 26.35
sons of Ephriam a. to their number, 26.37
sons of Joseph a. to their families 26.37
of Benjamin a. to their families: 26.38
of Benjamin a. to their families; 26.41
the sons of Dan a. to their 26.42
families of Dan a. to their 26.42
a. to their number were sixty-four 26.43
The sons of Asher a. to their 26.44
sons of Asher a. to their number 26.47
of Naphtali a. to their families: 26.48
of Naphtali a. to their families; 26.50
for inheritance a. to the number 26.53
its inheritance a. to its numbers. 26.54
a. to the names of the tribes of 26.55
be divided a. to lot between the 26.56
as numbered a. to their families: 26.57
a. to the ordinance for them, a 29.06
lambs by number a. to the ordinance 29.18
lambs by number a. to the ordinance 29.21
lambs by number a. to the ordinance 29.24
lambs by number a. to the ordinance 29.27
lambs by number a. to the ordinance 29.30
by their number a. to the ordinance 29.33
by their number a. to the ordinance 29.37
he shall do a. to all that proceeds 30.02
their stages a. to their starting 33.02
the land by lot a. to your families 33.54
a. to the tribes of your fathers 33.54
of Israel a. to the word of the 36.05
of Israel a. to all that the LORD **Deu** 1.03
a. to your tribes, and I will 1.13
a. to the common cubit. 3.11
a. to all that the LORD your God 4.34
You shall not do a. to all that we 12.08
a. to the blessing of the LORD your 12.15
a. to the blessing of the LORD your 16.17
God gives you, a. to your tribes; 16.18
Then you shall do a. to what they 17.10
careful to do a. to all that they 17.10
a. to the instructions which they 17.11
and a. to the decision which they 17.11
teach you to do a. to all their 20.18
careful to do a. to all that the 24.08
a. to all thy commandment which 26.13
I have done a. to all that thou 26.14
do to them a. to all the commandment 31.05
of the peoples a. to the number of 32.08
a. to the word of the LORD, 34.05
careful to do a. to all the law **Jos** 1.07
careful to do a. to all that is 1.08
And she said, "A. to your words, so 2.21
a. to the number of the tribes of 4.05
a. to the number of the tribes of 4.08
a. to all that Moses had commanded 4.10
a. to the word of the LORD which he 8.27
a. to all that is written in the 8.34
a. to all that the LORD had spoken 11.23
to Israel a. to their tribal 11.23
as a possession a. to their 12.07
the Reubenites a. to their families 13.15
a. to their families with their 13.23
the Gadites, a. to their families. 13.24
of the Gadites a. to their families, 13.28
the Manassites a. to their families. 13.29
the Machirites a. to their families. 13.31
people of Judah a. to their 15.01
people of Judah a. to their 15.12
A. to the commandment of the LORD 15.13
people of Judah a. to their 15.20
So a. to the commandment of the 17.04
of Benjamin a. to its families 18.11
a. to its families, boundary by 18.20
of Benjamin a. to their families 18.21
of Benjamin a. to its families. 18.28
a. to its families; and its 19.01
tribe of Simeon a. to its families 19.08
a. to its families. And the 19.10
a. to its families—these cities 19.16
of Issachar a. to its families. 19.17
a. to its families—the cities with 19.23
tribe of Asher a. to its families. 19.24
tribe of Asher a. to its families— 19.31
of Naphtali, a. to its families. 19.32
of Naphtali a. to its families— 19.39
of Dan, a. to its families. 19.40
a. to their families—these cities 19.48
The Merarites a. to their families 21.07
do to me a. to what has gone forth **Ju** 11.36
did with her a. to his vow which 11.39
a. to their number, from the dancers 21.23
who shall do a. to what is in my **1Sa** 2.35
a. to the number of the lords of 6.04
a. to the number of all the cities 6.18
A. to all the deeds which they have 8.08
a. to all your heart's desire to 23.20
done to my lord a. to all the good 25.30
the evildoer a. to his wickedness!" **2Sa** 3.39
and a. to thy own heart, thou hast 7.21
a. to all that we have heard with 7.22
"A. to all that my lord the king 9.11
rewarded me a. to my righteousness; 22.21
a. to the cleanness of my hands he 22.21
recompensed me a. to my righteousness, 22.25
a. to my cleanness in his sight. 22.25
Act therefore a. to your wisdom, but **1Ki** 2.06
behold, I now do a. to your word. 3.12
required, each a. to his charge. 4.28
and a. to all its specifications. 6.38
hewn a. to measure, sawed with saws, 7.09
hewn a. to measurement, and cedar. 7.11

ACCORDING (cont.)

a. to the space of each, with 1Ki 7.36
rewarding him a. to his righteousness. 8.32
a. to all his ways (for thou, thou 8.39
and do a. to all for which the 8.43
a. to all that he promised; 8.56
doing a. to all that I have commanded 9.04
he spoke to them a. to the counsel 12.14
a. to the word of the LORD. 12.24
a. to the sign which the man of God 13.05
a. to the word which the LORD spoke 13.26
a. to the word of the LORD, which he 14.18
They did a. to all the abominations 14.24
a. to the word of the LORD which he 15.29
a. to the word of the LORD, which he 16.12
a. to the word of the LORD, which he 16.34
So he went and did a. to the word 17.05
a. to the word of the LORD which he 17.16
a. to the number of the tribes of 18.31
a. to the word of the LORD which he 22.38
So he died a. to the word of the 2Ki 1.17
a. to the word which Elisha spoke. 2.22
a. to the word of the LORD. 4.44
a. to the word of the man of God; 5.14
a. to the word of the LORD. 7.16
and did a. to the word of the man 8.02
a. to the word of the LORD which he 10.17
house of Ahab a. to all that was 10.30
The captains did a. to all that 11.09
a. to the custom, and the captains 11.14
a. to what is written in the book 14.06
a. to the word of the LORD, the GOD 14.25
a. to all that his father Amaziah 15.03
a. to all that his father Uzziah 15.34
a. to the abominable practices of 16.03
day they do a. to the former 17.34
but they did a. to their former 17.40
a. to all that David his father had 18.03
a. to the abominable practices of 21.02
careful to do a. to all that I 21.08
and a. to all the law that my 21.08
to do a. to all that is written 22.13
a. to the word of the LORD which 23.16
he did to them a. to all that he 23.19
a. to all the law of Moses; 23.25
a. to all that his fathers had done 23.32
give the money a. to the command 23.35
from every one a. to his assessment; 23.35
a. to all that his fathers had done. 23.37
a. to the word of the LORD which he 24.02
a. to all that he had done, 24.03
a. to all that his father had done. 24.09
a. to all that Jehoiakim had done. 24.19
the genealogy a. to the birthright; 1Ch 5.01
And their kinsmen a. to their 5.13
of the Levites a. to their fathers 6.19
a. to all that Moses the servant of 6.49
dwelling places a. to their 6.54
To the Gershomites a. to their 6.62
To the Merarites a. to their 6.63
a. to their father's houses were 7.04
a. to their generations, as heads of 7.09
sons of Jediael a. to the heads of 7.11
a. to their generations, chief men. 8.28
and their kinsmen a. to their 9.09
fathers' houses a. to their 9.09
a. to their generations, leaders, who 9.34
a. to the word of the LORD by 11.03
a. to the word of the LORD concerning 11.10
a. to the word of the LORD. 12.23
had commanded a. to the word of 15.15
were to play harps a. to Alamoth; 15.20
lead with lyres a. to the Sheminith. 15.21
a. to all that is written in the 16.40
and a. to thy own heart, thou hast 17.19
a. to all that we have heard with 17.20
were registered a. to the number 23.24
a. to the number required of them 23.31
organized them a. to the appointed 24.03
of the LORD a. to the procedure 24.19
of the Levites a. to their fathers' 24.30
a. to the promise of God to exalt 25.05
a. to the use of each lampstand in 28.15
the work to be done a. to the plan. 28.19
rewarding him a. to his righteousness. 2Ch 6.23
a. to all his ways (for thou, thou 6.30
and do a. to all for which the 6.33
doing a. to all that I have commanded 7.17
offering a. to the commandment of 8.13
A. to the ordinance of David his 8.14
spoke to them a. to the counsel of 10.14
and not a. to the ways of Israel. 17.04
all Judah did a. to all that 23.08
a. to the order of David. 23.18
a. to what is written in the law, in 25.04
a. to all that his father Amaziah 26.04
in divisions a. to the numbers in 26.11
of the LORD a. to all that his 27.02
a. to the abominable practices of 28.03
a. to all that David his father had 29.02
a. to the commandment of David and 29.25
accustomed posts a. to the law of 30.16
even though not a. to the sanctuary's 30.19
each a. to his service, the priests 31.02
their service a. to their offices, 31.16
the priests was a. to their 31.17
and upwards was a. to their 31.17
not make return a. to the benefit 32.25
a. to the abominable practices of 33.02
to do a. to all that is written in 34.21
Jerusalem did a. to the covenant 34.32
Prepare yourselves a. to your 35.04
the holy place a. to the groupings 35.05
to do a. to the word of the LORD by 35.06
their divisions a. to the king's 35.10
distribute them a. to the groupings 35.12
lamb with fire a. to the ordinance 35.13
in their place a. to the command 35.15
a. to the command of King Josiah. 35.16
his good deeds a. to what is 35.26
a. to their ability they gave to Ez 2.69
by number a. to the ordinance as 3.04
a. to the grant which they had from 3.07
a. to the directions of David king 3.10
Then, a. to the word sent by Darius 6.13
a. to the number of the tribes of 6.17
and Jerusalem a. to the law of 7.14
a. to the will of your God. 7.18
a. to the wisdom of your God which 7.25
a. to the counsel of my lord and of 10.03
and let it be done a. to the law. 10.03
a. to their fathers' houses, each of 10.16
the people a. to their families, Neh 4.13
their king, a. to this report. 6.06
to the king a. to these words. 6.07
a. to these things that they did, 6.14
assembly, a. to the ordinance. 8.18
and a. to thy great mercies thou 9.27
deliver them a. to thy mercies. 9.28
a. to our fathers' houses, at times 10.34
a. to the commandment of David the 12.24
for the Levites a. to the fields 12.44
a. to the command of David and his 12.45
and spare me a. to the greatness of 13.22
was lavished a. to the bounty of Est 1.07
And drinking was a. to the law, 1.08
"A. to the law, what is to be done 1.15
house and speak a. to the language 1.22
a. to all that Haman commanded, was 3.12
was written a. to all that Mordecai 8.09
also to do a. to this day's edict. 9.13
these two days a. to what was 9.27
burnt offerings a. to the number Job 1.05
For a. to the work of a man he will 34.11

ACCORDING (cont.)

and a. to his ways he will make it Job 34.11
to deal with you a. to your folly; 42.08
a. to my righteousness and a. to the Ps 7.08
rewarded me a. to my righteousness; 18.20
a. to the cleanness of my hands he 18.20
recompensed me a. to my righteousness, 18.24
a. to the cleanness of my hands in 18.24
a. to thy steadfast love remember 25.07
Requite them a. to their work, and 28.04
and a. to the evil of their deeds; 28.04
requite them a. to the work of 28.04
a. to thy righteousness; and let them 35.24
on me, O God, a. to thy steadfast love; 51.01
a. to thy abundant mercy blot out 51.01
dost requite a man a. to his work. 62.12
a. to thy abundant mercy, turn to me 69.16
but refused to walk a. to his law. 78.10
a. to thy great power preserve 79.11
and do not walk a. to my ordinances, 89.30
and thy wrath a. to the fear of 90.11
not deal with us a. to our sins, 103.10
nor requite us a. to our iniquities 103.10
and relented a. to the abundance of 106.45
Save me a. to thy steadfast love! 109.26
By guarding it a. to thy word. 119.09
revive me a. to thy word! 119.25
strengthen me a. to thy word! 119.28
thy salvation a. to thy promise; 119.41
gracious to me a. to thy promise. 119.58
servant O LORD, a. to thy word. 119.65
to comfort me a. to thy promise to 119.76
me life, O LORD, a. to thy word! 119.107
Uphold me a. to thy promise, that I 119.116
thy servant a. to thy steadfast 119.124
Keep steady my steps a. to thy promise, 119.133
give me life a. to thy promise! 119.154
give me life a. to thy justice. 119.156
Preserve my life a. to thy steadfast 119.159
me understanding a. to thy word! 119.169
deliver me a. to thy word. 119.170
praise him a. to his exceeding 150.02
is commended a. to his good sense, Pro 12.08
he not requite man a. to his work? 24.12
Answer not a fool a. to his folly, 26.04
Answer a fool a. to his folly, lest 26.05
whom it happens a. to the deeds of Ecc 8.14
a. to the years of a hireling, all Is 21.16
A. to their deeds so will he repay 59.18
a. to all that the LORD has granted 63.07
has granted them a. to his mercy, 63.07
a. to the abundance of his steadfast 63.07
a waistcloth a. to the word of the Jer 13.02
give to every man a. to his ways, 17.10
a. to the fruit of his doings. 17.10
every one act a. to the stubbornness 18.12
deal with us a. to all his wonderful 21.02
I will punish you a. to the fruit 21.14
recompense them a. to their deeds 25.14
every man a. to his ways and 32.19
to his ways and a. to the fruit of 32.19
had set free a. to their desire, 34.16
LORD your God a. to your request, 42.04
we do not act a. to all the word 42.05
Requite her a. to her deeds, do to 50.29
do to her a. to all that she has 50.29
a. to all that Jehoiakim had done. 52.02
him by the king a. to his daily 52.34
have compassion a. to the abundance Lam 3.32
a. to the work of their hands. 3.64
but have acted a. to the ordinances Eze 5.07
and will judge you a. to your ways; 7.03
you, and judge you a. to your ways; 7.08
I will punish you a. to your ways, 7.09
A. to their way I will do to them, 7.27
and a. to their own judgments I 7.27
but have acted a. to the ordinances 11.12
or do a. to their abominations; 16.47
every one a. to his ways, says the 18.30
not a. to your evil ways, nor 20.44
nor a. to your corrupt doings, O 20.44
every one a. to his power, have been 22.06
shall judge you a. to their 23.24
a. to your ways and your doings I 24.14
a. to all that he has done you 24.24
do in Edom a. to my anger and 25.14
to my anger and a. to my wrath; 25.14
judge each of you a. to his ways." 33.20
deal with you a. to the anger and 35.11
I dealt with them a. to their 39.24
shall judge it a. to my judgments 44.24
have the land a. to their tribes. 45.08
land among you a. to the tribes of 47.21
and a. to what you see deal with Dan 1.13
and he does a. to his will in the 4.35
a. to the law of the Medes and the 6.08
a. to the law of the Medes and 6.12
a. to the word of the LORD to 9.02
O Lord, a. to all thy righteous acts, 9.16
had spoken to me a. to these words, 10.15
dominion and do a. to his will. 11.03
nor a. to the dominion with which 11.04
him shall do a. to his own will, 11.16
"And the king shall do a. to his will; 11.36
will punish Jacob a. to his ways, Hos 12.02
and requite him a. to his deeds. 12.02
a. to the word of the LORD. Jon 3.03
the prophet, a. to Shigionoth. Hab 3.01
a. to the promise that I made you Hag 2.05
be cut off henceforth a. to it, Zec 5.03
a. to the time which he had ascertained Mt 2.16
"A. to your faith be it done to you." 9.29
one, to each a. to his ability. 25.15
not live a. to the tradition of Mk 7.05
a. to the custom of the priesthood, Lk 1.09
let it be to me a. to your word." 1.38
purification a. to the law of 2.22
a sacrifice a. to what is said in 2.24
to do for him a. to the custom of 2.27
depart in peace, a. to thy word; 2.29
everything a. to the law of the 2.39
old, they went up a. to custom; 2.42
make ready or act a. to his will, 12.47
they rested a. to the commandment. 23.56
You judge a. to the flesh, I judge Jn 8.15
he speaks a. to his own nature, for 8.44
delivered up a. to the definite Ac 2.23
a. to the pattern that he had seen. 7.44
every one a. to his ability, to send 11.29
are circumcised a. to the custom 15.01
educated a. to the strict manner of 22.03
a devout man a. to the law, well 22.12
sitting to judge me a. to the law, 23.03
a. to their instructions, took Paul 23.31
would have judged him a. to our law. * 24.06
that a. to the Way, which they call 24.14
that a. to the strictest party of 26.05
descended from David a. to the flesh Rom 1.03
of God in power a. to the Spirit 1.04
to every man a. to his works: 2.06
a. to my gospel, God judges the 2.16
our forefather a. to the flesh? 4.01
who walk not a. to the flesh but 8.04
to the flesh but a. to the Spirit. 8.04
For those who live a. to the flesh 8.05
those who live a. to the Spirit 8.05
flesh, to live a. to the flesh— 8.12
for if you live a. to the flesh you 8.13
for the saints a. to the will of 8.27
who are called a. to his purpose. 8.28
a. to the flesh, is the Christ 9.05
each a. to the measure of faith 12.03
that differ a. to the grace given 12.06
strengthen you a. to my gospel and 16.25

ACCORDING (cont.)
a. to the revelation of the mystery Rom 16.25
a. to the command of the eternal 16.26
you were wise a. to worldly 1Co 1.26
receive his wages a. to his labor. 3.08
A. to the commission of God given 3.10
by us to live a. to scripture, 4.06
of knowledge a. to the same Spirit 12.08
a. to what he has done in the body. 2Co 5.10
For they gave a. to their means, as 8.03
is acceptable a. to what a man has, 8.12
not a. to what he has not. 8.12
a. to the will of our God and Gal 1.04
offspring, heirs a. to promise. 3.29
the slave was born a. to the flesh, 4.23
he who was born a. to the flesh 4.29
him who was born a. to the Spirit, 4.29
a. to the purpose of his will, Eph 1.05
a. to the riches of his grace 1.07
a. to his purpose which he set 1.09
In him, a. to the purpose of him who 1.11
all things a. to the counsel of 1.11
a. to the working of his great 1.19
made a minister a. to the gift of 3.07
This was a. to the eternal purpose 3.11
that a. to the riches of his glory 3.16
to each of us a. to the measure of 4.07
need of yours a. to his riches in Php 4.19
a. to his glorious might, for all Col 1.11
a minister a. to the divine office 1.25
empty deceit, a. to human tradition, 2.08
a. to the elemental spirits of the 2.08
the universe, and not a. to Christ. 2.08
a. to human precepts and doctrines? 2.22
a. to the grace of our God and the 2Th 1.12
the will of God a. to the promise 2Ti 1.01
unless he competes a. to the rules. 2.05
distributed a. to his own will. Heb 2.04
not a. to a legal requirement 7.16
who offer gifts a. to the law. 8.04
make everything a. to the pattern 8.05
A. to this arrangement, gifts and 9.09
(these are offered a. to the law), 10.08
a. to the scripture, "You shall love Jas 2.08
one impartially a. to his deeds, 1Pe 1.17
who suffer a. to God's will do 4.19
happened to them a. to the true 2Pe 2.22
But a. to his promise we wait for 3.13
wrote to you a. to the wisdom 3.15
and do not live a. to the truth; 1Jn 1.06
we ask anything a. to his will he 5.14

ACCORDINGLY
A., she will be called an adulteress Rom 7.03
A. we have urged Titus that as he 2Co 8.06
A., though I am bold enough in Phm 1.08

ACCORDS
teaching which a. with godliness, 1Ti 6.03
the truth which a. with godliness, Tit 1.01

ACCOUNT
my life may be spared on your a." Gen 12.13
to Abraham on a. of his son. 21.11
but on no a. shall you eat it. Lev 7.24
your flesh on a. of the dead or 19.28
day of the plague on a. of Peor. Num 25.18
was angry with me also on your a., Deu 1.37
LORD was angry with me on your a., 3.26
LORD was angry with me on your a., 4.21
on a. of the evil of your doings, 28.20
in that day on a. of all the evil 31.18
to the LORD on a. of the Midianites, Ju 6.07
On this a. that place is called 18.12
to destroy the city on my a. 1Sa 23.10
And this is the a. of the forced 1Ki 9.15
This is an a. of David's mighty men: 1Ch 11.11
and of little a., and sojourners in 16.19
he rebuked kings on their a., 16.21
of Israel sin on a. of such women? Neh 13.26
and the full a. of the high honor Est 10.02
give him an a. of all my steps; Job 31.37
"Behold, I am of small a.; 40.04
heart, "Thou wilt not call to a."? Ps 10.13
on a. of sins. When our 65.03
of little a., and sojourners in it, 105.12
he rebuked kings on their a., 105.14
it went ill with Moses on their a.; 106.32
is breath, for of what a. is he? Is 2.22
on a. of the violence of all those Eze 12.19
but not on a. of the covenant with 16.61
whom these satraps should give a., Dan 6.02
on a. of my people and my heritage Joe 3.02
Shall not the land tremble on this a., Amo 8.08
know on whose a. this evil has Jon 1.07
on whose a. this evil has come upon 1.08
evil against you falsely on my a. Mt 5.11
men will render a. for every 12.36
persecution arises on a. of the word, 13.21
persecution arises on a. of the word, Mk 4.17
to write an orderly a. for you, Lk 1.03
on a. of the Son of man! 6.22
Turn in the a. of your stewardship, 16.02
on a. of the crowd, because he was 19.03
said this on a. of the people Jn 11.42
not only on a. of Jesus but also to 12.09
because on a. of him many of the 12.11
this they will do to you on my a., 15.21
But I do not a. my life of any Ac 20.24
us shall give a. of himself to God. Rom 14.12
by all, he is called to a. by all, 1Co 14.24
it was not on a. of the one who did 2Co 7.12
nor on a. of the one who suffered 7.12
is weak, and his speech of no a." 10.10
flesh is more necessary on your a. Php 1.24
On a. of these the wrath of God is Col 3.06
on a. of which I am in prison, 4.03
you anything, charge that to my a. Phm 1.18
on their own a. and hold him up to Heb 6.06
as men who will have to give a. 13.17
calls you to a. for the hope that 1Pe 3.15
but they will give a. to him who is 4.05
the earth will wail on a. of him. Rev 1.07
Patmos on a. of the word of God 1.09

ACCOUNTABLE
whole world may be held a. to God. Rom 3.19

ACCOUNTED
and a. as sheep for the slaughter. Ps 44.22
and are a. as the dust on the Is 40.15
they are a. by him as less than 40.17
make many to be a. righteous; 53.11
of the earth are a. as nothing; Dan 4.35
but those who are a. worthy to Lk 20.35

ACCOUNTING
did not ask an a. from the men 2Ki 12.15
But no a. shall be asked from them 22.07

ACCOUNTS
with a. of all his rule and his 1Ch 29.30
A. of his sons, and of the many 2Ch 24.27
to settle a. with his servants. Mt 18.23
came and settled a. with them. 25.19

ACCREDIT
those whom you a. by letter to 1Co 16.03

ACCUMULATE
ears they will a. for themselves 2Ti 4.03

ACCURATE
having a rather a. knowledge of Ac 24.22

ACCURATELY
and taught a. the things concerning Ac 18.25
to him the way of God more a. 18.26

ACCURSED
your house, and become a. like it; Deu 7.26
and abhor it; for it is an a. thing. 7.26
day, for a hanged man is a. by God; 21.23
a. ones, who wander from thy Ps 119.21
a hundred years old shall be a. Is 65.20
and the scant measure that is a.? Mic 6.10
who do not know the law, are a. Jn 7.49
I myself were a. and cut off from Rom 9.03
love for the Lord, let him be a. 1Co 16.22
we preached to you, let him be a. Gal 1.08
which you received, let him be a. 1.09
hearts trained in greed. A. children! 2Pe 2.14
There shall no more be anything a., Rev 22.03

ACCUSATION
they wrote an a. against the Ez 4.06
no one by violence or by false a., Lk 3.14
they might find an a. against him. 6.07
"What a. do you bring against this Jn 18.29
here before you and to make an a., Ac 24.19

ACCUSATIONS
against all the a. of the Jews, Ac 26.02

ACCUSE
any man to a. him of wrongdoing. Deu 19.16
In return for my love they a. me, Ps 109.04
and let none a., for with you is my Hos 4.04
at his right hand to a. him. Zec 3.01
so that they might a. him. Mt 12.10
sabbath, so that they might a. him. Mk 3.02
And they began to a. him, Lk 23.02
that I shall a. you to the Father; Jn 5.45
called, Tertullus began to a. him, Ac 24.02
everything of which we a. him." 24.08
about the man, let them a. him." 25.05
thoughts a. or perhaps excuse them Rom 2.15

ACCUSED
witness and has a. his brother Deu 19.18
and maliciously a. the Jews. Dan 3.08
men who had a. Daniel were brought 6.24
But when he was a. by the chief Mt 27.12
chief priests a. him of many Mk 15.03
real reason why the Jews a. him, Ac 22.30
the charge on which they a. him, 23.28
that he was a. about questions of 23.29
one before the a. met the accusers 25.16
and for this hope I am a. by Jews, 26.07

ACCUSER
I must appeal for mercy to my a. Job 9.15
let an a. bring him to trial. Ps 109.06
Make friends quickly with your a., Mt 5.25
lest your a. hand you over to the 5.25
go with your a. before the magistrate, Lk 12.58
for the a. of our brethren has been Rev 12.10

ACCUSERS
May my a. be put to shame and Ps 71.13
the reward of my a. from the LORD, 109.20
I am an object of scorn to my a.; 109.25
May my a. be clothed with dishonor; 109.29
ordering his a. also to state Ac 23.30
will hear you when your a. arrive. 23.35
commanding his a. to come before * 24.07
accused met the a. face to face, 25.16
When the a. stood up, they brought 25.18

ACCUSES
it is Moses who a. you, on whom you Jn 5.45
who a. them day and night before Rev 12.10

ACCUSING
stood by, vehemently a. him. Lk 23.10

ACCUSTOMED
the ox has been a. to gore in the Ex 21.29
the ox has been a. to gore in the 21.36
Was I ever a. to do so to you?" Num 22.30
They took their a. posts according 2Ch 30.16
can do good who are a. to do evil. Jer 13.23
governor was a. to release for the Mt. 27.15
through being hitherto a. to idols, 1Co 8.07

ACHAIA
But when Gallio was proconsul of A., Ac 18.12
And when he wished to cross to A., 18.27
Macedonia and A. and go to Jerusalem, 19.21
For Macedonia and A. have been Rom 15.26
were the first converts in A., 1Co 16.15
saints who are in the whole of A.: 2Co 1.01
saying that A. has been ready since 9.02
be silenced in the regions of A. 11.10
believers in Macedonia and in A. 1Th 1.07
forth from you in Macedonia and A., 1.08

ACHAICUS
of Stephanas and Fortunatus and A., 1Co 16.17

ACHAN
for A. the son of Carmi, son of Jos 7.01
and A. the son of Carmi, son of 7.18
Then Joshua said to A., "My son, 7.19
And A. answered Joshua, "Of a truth 7.20
with him took A. the son of Zerah, 7.24
Did not A. the son of Zerah break 22.20

ACHAR
A., the troubler of Israel, who 1Ch 2.07

ACHBOR
the son of A. reigned in his stead. Gen 36.38
Baalhanan the son of A. died, 36.39
and A. the son of Micaiah, and 2Ki 22.12
and A., and Shapham, and Asaiah went 22.14
the son of A., reigned in his stead. 1Ch 1.49
the son of A. and others with him, Jer 26.22
Shemaiah, Elnathan the son of A., 36.12

ACHIEVE
so that their hands a. no success. Job 5.12

ACHIM
Zadok, and Zadok the father of A., Mt 1.14
and A. the father of Eliud, 1.14

ACHISH
and went to A. the king of Gath. 1Sa 21.10
And the servants of A. said to him, 21.11
much afraid of A. the king of Gath. 21.12
Then said A. to his servants, "Lo, 21.14
to A. the son of Maoch, king of Gath. 27.02
And David dwelt with A. at Gath, 27.03
Then David said to A., "If I 27.05
So that day A. gave him Ziklag; 27.06
the garments, and came back to A. 27.09
When A. asked, "Against whom have 27.10
And A. trusted David, thinking, "He 27.12
And A. said to David, "Understand 28.01
David said to A., "Very well, you 28.02
And A. said to David, "Very well, I 28.02
passing on in the rear with A., 29.02
And A. said to the commanders of 29.03
Then A. called David and said to 29.06
And David said to A., "But what 29.08
And A. made answer to David, "I know 29.09
of Shimei's slaves ran away to A., 1Ki 2.39
an ass, and went to Gath to A., 2.40

ACHOR
them up to the Valley of A. Jos 7.24
place is called the Valley of A. 7.26
up to Debir from the Valley of A., 15.07
the Valley of A. a place for herds Is 65.10
the Valley of A. a door of hope. Hos 2.15

ACHSAH
him will I give A. my daughter as Jos 15.16
and he gave him A. his daughter as 15.17
I will give him A. my daughter as Ju 1.12
and he gave him A. his daughter as 1.13
and the daughter of Caleb was A. 1Ch 2.49

ACHSHAPH
of Shimron, and to the king of A., Jos 11.01
one; the king of A., one; 12.20
included Helkath, Hali, Beten, A., 19.25

ACHZIB
Keilah, A., and Mareshah: nine cities Jos 15.44
it ends at the sea; Mahalab, A., 19.29
or of A., or of Helbah, or of Aphik, Ju 1.31
the houses of A. shall be a deceitful Mic 1.14

ACKNOWLEDGE
but he shall a. the first-born, the Deu 21.17
and a. thy name, and pray and make 1Ki 8.33
and a. thy name, and turn from their 8.35
they turn again and a. thy name, 2Ch 6.24
and a. thy name, and turn from their 6.26
Then will I also a. to you, Job 40.14
In all your ways a. him, Pro 3.06
over us, but thy name alone we a. Is 26.13
and you who are near, a. my might. 33.13
all who see them shall a. them, 61.09
know us and Israel does not a. us; 63.16
Only a. your guilt, that you rebelled Jer 3.13
We a. our wickedness, O LORD, and the 14.20
those who a. him he shall magnify Dan 11.39
until they a. their guilt and seek Hos. 5.15
I also will a. before my Father who Mt 10.32
man also will a. before the angels Lk 12.08
but the Pharisees a. them all. Ac 23.08
they did not see fit to a. God, Rom 1.28
he should a. that what I am writing 1Co 14.37
the fruit of lips that a. his name. Heb 13.15
who will not a. the coming of 2Jn 1.07
first, does not a. my authority. 3Jn 1.09

ACKNOWLEDGED
Then Judah a. them and said, "She is Gen 38.26
I a. my sin to thee, and I did not Ps 32.05
and having a. that they were Heb 11.13

ACKNOWLEDGES
So every one who a. me before men, Mt 10.32
every one who a. me before men, the Lk 12.08

ACKNOWLEDGING
obedience in a. the gospel of 2Co 9.13

ACQUAINTANCE
the priests take, each from his a.; 2Ki 12.05

ACQUAINTANCES
take no more money from your a., 2Ki 12.07
and my a. are wholly estranged from Job 19.13
an object of dread to my a.; Ps 31.11
him among their kinsfolk and a.; Lk 2.44
And all his a. and the women who 23.49

ACQUAINTED
who are not a. with its ways, and do Job 24.13
and art a. with all my ways. Ps 139.03
man of sorrows, and a. with grief; Is 53.03
you have been a. with the sacred 2Ti 3.15

ACQUIRE
the man of understanding a. skill, Pro 1.05
The simple a. folly, but the prudent 14.18
Do not toil to a. wealth; be wise 23.04
until we a. possession of it, to Eph 1.14

ACQUIRED
which he had a. in Paddan-aram, Gen 31.18
which he had a. in the land of 36.06
work on this wall, and a. no land; Neh 5.16
"I have a. great wisdom, surpassing Ecc 1.16

ACQUIRES
An intelligent mind a. knowledge, Pro 18.15

ACQUIT
for I will not a. the wicked. Ex 23.07
and a. yourselves like men, O 1Sa 4.09
a. yourselves like men and fight." 4.09
and dost not a. me of my iniquity. Job 10.14
who a. the guilty for a bribe, and Is 5.23
Shall I a. the man with wicked Mic 6.11

ACQUITTAL
may they have no a. from thee. Ps 69.27
leads to a. and life for all men. Rom 5.18

ACQUITTED
and I should be a. for ever by my Job 23.07
myself, but I am not thereby a. 1Co 4.04

ACQUITTING
a. the innocent and condemning the Deu 25.01

ACRE
a furrow's length in an a. of land. 1Sa 14.14

ACRES
For ten a. of vineyard shall yield Is 5.10

ACROSS
above the earth a. the firmament Gen 1.20
them and sent them a. the stream, 32.23
do not take us a. the Jordan." Num 32.05
and he drew chains of gold a., 1Ki 6.21
great wind came a. the wilderness, Job 1.19
kings of the coastland a. the sea; Jer 25.22
from the west a. the face of the Dan 8.05
a. the Jordan, Galilee of the Mt 4.15
"Let us go a. to the other side." Mk 4.35
"Let us go a. to the other side of Lk 8.22
and started a. the sea to Capernaum Jn 6.17
He went away again a. the Jordan to 10.40
his disciples a. the Kidron valley, 18.01
we had sailed a. the sea which is Ac 27.05
were drifting a. the sea of Adria, 27.27

ACT
my brothers, do not a. so wickedly. Gen 19.07
since she was not taken in the a.; Num 5.13
to a. treacherously against the 31.16
beware lest you a. corruptly by Deu 4.16
if you a. corruptly by making a 4.25
and not a. presumptuously again. 17.13
all who a. dishonestly, are an 25.16
death you will surely a. corruptly, 31.29
my brethren, do not a. so wickedly; Ju 19.23
A. therefore according to your 1Ki 2.06
and a., and judge thy servants, 8.32
and a., and render to each whose 8.39
and a., and judge thy servants, 2Ch 6.23
be afraid and a. in this way and Neh 6.13
Did not your fathers a. in this way, 13.18
great evil and a. treacherously 13.27
if there are any that a. wisely, Ps 14.02
has ceased to a. wisely and do 36.03
trust in him, and he will a. 37.05
It is time for the LORD to a. 119.126

ACT (cont.)
but those who a. faithfully are his Pro 12.22
and iron, all of them a. corruptly. Jer 6.28
a., O LORD, for thy name's sake: 14.07
will every one a. according to the 18.12
us if we do not a. according to 42.05
of Israel, that I am about to a., Eze 36.22
not for your sake that I will a., 36.32
controversy they shall a. as judges, Eze 44.24
O LORD, give heed and a.: Dan 9.19
with him he shall a. deceitfully; 11.23
possession on the day when I a., Mal 3.17
of your feet, on the day when I a., 4.03
make ready or a. according to his Lk 12.47
been caught in the a. of adultery *Jn 8.04
so one man's a. of righteousness Rom 5.18
because he does not a. from faith; 14.23
Did we not a. in the same spirit? 2Co 12.18
is appointed to a. on behalf of Heb 5.01
desiring to a. honorably in all 13.18
So speak and so a. as those who are Jas 2.12

ACTED
herself and has a. unfaithfully Num 5.27
from Egypt have a. corruptly; Deu 9.12
they on their part a. with cunning, Jos 9.04
if you a. in good faith and honor Ju 9.16
if you then have a. in good faith 9.19
and have a. perversely and wickedly' 1Ki 8.47
and have a. perversely and wickedly' 2Ch 6.37
We have a. very corruptly against Neh 1.07
that they a. insolently against 9.10
and our fathers a. presumptuously 9.16
Yet they a. presumptuously and did 9.29
faithfully and we have a. wickedly; 9.33
but turned away and a. treacherously Ps 78.57
but have a. according to the Eze 5.07
but have a. according to the 11.12
because they have a. faithlessly, 15.08
in which you a. more abominably 16.52
But I a. for the sake of my name, 20.09
But I a. for the sake of my name, 20.14
and a. for the sake of my name, that 20.22
Because Edom a. revengefully 25.12
the Philistines a. revengefully 25.15
and the horn a. and prospered. Dan 8.12
done wrong and a. wickedly and 9.05
conceived them has a. shamefully. Hos 2.05
I know that you a. in ignorance, Ac 3.17
rest of the Jews a. insincerely, Gal 2.13
because I had a. ignorantly in 1Ti 1.13
which likewise a. immorally and Jud 1.07

ACTING
a. as the rear guard of all the Num 10.25
sins against me by a. faithlessly, Eze 14.13
mean for us, that you are a. thus?" 24.19
they are all a. against the Ac 17.07
suspect us of a. in worldly 2Co 10.02

ACTION
and take a. against the holy Dan 11.30
God shall stand firm and take a. 11.32

ACTIONS
knowledge, and by him a. are weighed. 1Sa 2.03
I do not understand my own a. Rom 7.15

ACTIVE
For the word of God is living and a., Heb 4.12
that faith was a. along with his Jas 2.22

ACTIVITY
one by the a. of Satan will be 2Th 2.09

ACTS
arm and with great a. of judgment, Ex 6.06
of Egypt by great a. of judgment. 7.04
goes astray and a. unfaithfully Num 5.12
such works and mighty a. as thine? Deu 3.24
The man who a. presumptuously, by 17.12
Now the rest of the a. of Solomon, 1Ki 11.41
in the book of the a. of Solomon? 11.41
Now the rest of the a. of Jeroboam, 14.19
Now the rest of the a. of Rehoboam, 14.29
The rest of the a. of Abijam, 15.07
Now the rest of all the a. of Asa, 15.23
Now the rest of the a. of Nadab, 15.31
Now the rest of the a. of Baasha, 16.05
Now the rest of the a. of Elah, 16.14
Now the rest of the a. of Zimri, 16.20
Now the rest of the a. of Omri 16.27
Now the rest of the a. of Ahab, 22.39
Now the rest of the a. of Jehoshaphat, 22.45
Now the rest of the a. of Ahaziah 2Ki 1.18
Now the rest of the a. of Joram, 8.23
Now the rest of the a. of Jehu, 10.34
Now the rest of the a. of Joash, 12.19
Now the rest of the a. of Jehoahaz 13.08
Now the rest of the a. of Joash, 13.12
Now the rest of the a. of Jehoash 14.15
Now the rest of the a. of Jeroboam, 14.28
Now the rest of the a. of Azariah, 15.06
Now the rest of the a. of Pekah, 15.31
Now the rest of the a. of Jotham, 15.36
Now the rest of the a. of Ahaz 16.19
Now the rest of the a. of Manasseh, 21.17
Now the rest of the a. of Amon 21.25
Now the rest of the a. of Josiah, 23.28
Now the a. of King David, from first 1Ch 29.29
Now the rest of the a. of Solomon, 2Ch 9.29
Now the a. of Rehoboam, from first 12.15
The rest of the a. of Abijah, 13.22
The a. of Asa, from first to last, 16.11
Now the rest of the a. of Jehoshaphat, 20.34
now the rest of the a. of Uzziah, 26.22
Now the rest of the a. of Jotham, 27.07
Now the rest of his a. and all his 28.26
and these a. of faithfulness 32.01
Now the rest of the a. of Hezekiah, 32.32
Now the rest of the a. of Manasseh, 33.18
Now the rest of the a. of Josiah, 35.26
and his a., first and last, behold, 35.27
Now the rest of the a. of Jehoiakim, 36.08
And all the a. of his power and Est 10.02
requites him who a. haughtily. Ps 31.23
will tell of thy righteous a. 71.15
his a. to the people of Israel. 103.07
Thus they became unclean by their a., 106.39
and shall declare thy mighty a. 145.04
the might of thy terrible a., 145.06
work, the first of his a. of old. Pro 8.22
a wicked man a. shamefully and 13.05
a prudent man a. with knowledge, 13.16
A man of quick temper a. foolishly, 14.17
falls on one who a. shamefully. 14.35
rule over a son who a. shamefully, 17.02
makes himself known by his a., 20.11
haughty man who a. with arrogant 21.24
my four sore a. of judgment, Eze 14.21
will execute a. of judgment upon 30.14
Thus I will execute a. of judgment 30.19
according to all thy righteous a., Dan 9.16
may know the saving a. of the LORD." Mic 6.05
of good works and a. of charity. Ac 9.36
shameless a. with men and receiving Rom 1.27
he who does a. of mercy, with 12.08
that forgets but a doer that a., Jas 1.25

ACTUALLY
he was a. carried by the soldiers Ac 21.35
It is a. reported that there is 1Co 5.01

ADADAH
Kinah, Dimonah, A., Jos 15.22

ADAH
the name of the one was A., Gen 4.19
A. bore Jabal; he was 4.20
"A. and Zillah, hear my voice; 4.23
A. the daughter of Elon the Hittite, 36.02
And A. bore to Esau, Eliphaz; 36.04
the son of A. the wife of Esau, 36.10
are the sons of A., Esau's wife. 36.12
they are the sons of A. 36.16

ADAIAH
the daughter of A. of Bozkath. 2Ki 22.01
of Ethni, son of Zerah, son of A., 1Ch 6.41
A., Beraiah, and Shimrath were the 8.21
and A. the son of Jeroham, son of 9.12
of Obed, Maaseiah the son of A., 2Ch 23.01
A., Jashub, Sheal, and Jeremoth. Ez 10.29
Shelemiah, Nathan, A., 10.39
son of A., son of Joiarib, son of Neh 11.05
and A. the son of Jeroham, son of 11.12

ADALIA
and Poratha and A. and Aridatha Est 9.08

ADAM
And to A. he said, "Because you have Gen 3.17
God made for A. and for his wife 3.21
Now A. knew Eve his wife, and she 4.01
And A. knew his wife again, and she 4.25
the book of the generations of A. 5.01
When A. had lived a hundred and 5.03
The days of A. after he became the 5.04
the days that A. lived were nine 5.05
at A., the city that is beside Jos 3.16
A., Seth, Enosh; 1Ch 1.01
But at A. they transgressed the Hos 6.07
the son of A., the son of God. Lk 3.38
Yet death reigned from A. to Moses, Rom 5.14
not like the transgression of A., 5.14
For as in A. all die, so also in 1Co 15.22
"The first man A. became a living 15.45
the last A. became a life-giving 15.45
For A. was formed first, then Eve; 1Ti 2.13
and A. was not deceived, but the 2.14
generation from A. prophesied, Jud 1.14

ADAMAH
A., Ramah, Hazor, Jos 19.36

ADAMANT
Like a. harder than flint have I Eze 3.09
hearts like a. lest they should Zec 7.12

ADAMINEKEB
and A., and Jabneel, as far as Jos 19.33

ADAR
the third day of the month of A., Ez 6.15
month, which is the month of A. Est 3.07
month, which is the month of A., 3.13
month, which is the month of A., 8.12
month, which is the month of A., 9.01
of the month of A. and they slew 9.15
thirteenth day of the month of A., 9.17
of the month of A. as a day for 9.19
of the month A. and also the 9.21

ADBEEL
and Kedar, A., Mibsam, Gen 25.13
and Kedar, A., Mibsam, 1Ch 1.29

ADD
"May the LORD a. to me another son!" Gen 30.24
and shall a. a fifth to it and give Lev 5.16
and shall a. a fifth to it, and give 6.05
he shall a. the fifth of its value 22.14
he shall a. a fifth to the valuation 27.13
he shall a. a fifth of the valuation 27.15
then he shall a. a fifth of the 27.19
valuation, and a. a fifth to it; 27.27
tithe, he shall a. a fifth to it. 27.31
You shall not a. to the word which Deu 4.02
you shall not a. to it or take from 12.32
then you shall a. three other 19.09
I would a. to give as much more, 2Sa 12.08
LORD your God a. to the people a 24.03
heavy yoke, I will a. to your yoke. 1Ki 12.11
heavy, but I will a. to your yoke; 12.14
And I will a. fifteen years to your 2Ki 20.06
"May the LORD a. to his people a 1Ch 21.03
provided. To these you must a. 22.14
heavy yoke, I will a. to your yoke. 2Ch 10.11
yoke heavy, but I will a. to it; 10.14
A. to them punishment upon punishment Ps 69.27
Do not a. to his words, lest he Pro 30.06
who a. field to field, until there Is 5.08
A. year to year; let the 29.01
that they may a. sin to sin; 30.01
I will a. fifteen years to your 38.05
"A. your burnt offerings to your Jer 7.21
anxious can a. one cubit to his Mt 6.27
anxious can a. a cubit to his span Lk 12.25
God will a. to him the plagues Rev 22.18

ADDAN
A., and Immer, though they could not Ez 2.59

ADDAR
up to A., turns about to Karka, Jos 15.03
And Bela had sons: A., Gera, Abihud, 1Ch 8.03

ADDED
She a., "We have both straw and Gen 24.25
water shall be a. in a vessel; Num 19.17
and a. to the inheritance of the 36.03
inheritance will be a. to the 36.04
loud voice; and he a. no more. Deu 5.22
for we have a. to all our sins this 1Sa 12.19
servant be an a. burden to my lord 2Sa 19.35
And Haman a., "Even Queen Esther Est 5.12
and years will be a. to your life. Pro 9.11
nothing can be a. to it, Ecc 3.14
many similar words were a. to them. Jer 36.32
the LORD has a. sorrow to my pain; 45.03
still more greatness was a. to me. Dan 4.36
a. this to them all, that he shut up Lk 3.20
and there were a. that day about Ac 2.41
And the Lord a. to their number day 2.47
ever believers were a. to the Lord, 5.14
a large company was a. to the Lord. 11.24
were of repute a. nothing to me; Gal 2.06
It was a. because of transgressions, 3.19
then he a., "Lo, I have come to do Heb 10.09

ADDER
like the deaf a. that stops its ear, Ps 58.04
You will tread on the lion and the a., 91.13
a serpent, and stings like an a. Pro 23.32
serpent's root will come forth an a., Is 14.29

ADDER'S
shall put his hand on the a. den. Is 11.08

ADDERS
a. which cannot be charmed, and they Jer 8.17

ADDERS'
They hatch a. eggs, they weave the Is 59.05

ADDI
the son of A., the son of Cosam, the Lk 3.28

ADDICTED
not a. to much wine, not greedy for 1Ti 3.08

ADDING

a. a fifth to it, and giving it to Num 5.07
a. one thing to another to find the Ecc 7.27

ADDITION

on the altar in a. to the burnt Ex 29.25
in a. to the ram of atonement with Num 5.08
in a. to your votive offerings and 29.39
and in a. to them you shall give 35.06
Moreover, in a. to all that I have 1Ch 29.03
the LORD in a. to our present sins 2Ch 28.13
lewdness in a. to all your abominations? Eze 16.43

ADDON

A., and Immer, but they could not Neh 7.61

ADDRESS

I a. my verses to the king; Ps 45.01
could not a. you as spiritual men, 1Co 3.01

ADDRESSED

a. Ezra: "We have broken faith with Ez 10.02
Pilate a. them once more, desiring Lk 23.20
lifted up his voice and a. them, Ac 2.14
when Peter saw it he a. the people, 3.12
heard that he a. them in the 22.02
but this one was a. with an oath, Heb 7.21
Then one of the elders a. me, Rev 7.13

ADDRESSES

exhortation which a. you as sons?— Heb 12.05

ADDRESSING

a. one another in psalms and hymns Eph 5.19

ADDS

For he a. rebellion to his sin; Job 34.37
and he a. no sorrow with it. Pro 10.22
and a. persuasiveness to his lips. 16.23
or a. to it, once it has been Gal 3.15
then he a., "I will remember their Heb 10.17
if any one a. to them, God will add Rev 22.18

ADHERENTS

If it is the a. of the law who are Rom 4.14
not only to the a. of the law but 4.16
which have not benefited their a. Heb 13.09

ADIEL

A., Jesimiel, Benaiah, 1Ch 4.36
Malchijah, and Maasai the son of A., 9.12
treasuries was Azmaveth the son of A.; 27.25

ADIN

The sons of A., four hundred and Ez 2.15
Of the sons of A., Ebed the son of 8.06
The sons of A., six hundred and Neh 7.20
Adonijah, Bigvai, A., 10.16

ADINA

A. the son of Shiza the Reubenite, a 1Ch 11.42

ADITHAIM

Shaaraim, A., Gederah, Gederothaim: Jos 15.36

ADJOINING

A. the twenty cubits which belonged Eze 42.03
A. the territory of Dan, from the 48.02
A. the territory of Asher, from the 48.03
A. the territory of Naphtali, from 48.04
A. the territory of Manasseh, from 48.05
A. the territory of Ephraim, from 48.06
A. the territory of Reuben, from the 48.07
"A. the territory of Judah, from the 48.08
a. the territory of the Levites. 48.12
A. the territory of Benjamin, from 48.24
A. the territory of Simeon, from the 48.25
A. the territory of Issachar, from 48.26
A. the territory of Zebulun, from 48.27
And a. the territory of Gad to the 48.28

ADJURATION

hears a public a. to testify and Lev 5.01

ADJURE

times shall I a. you that you 1Ki 22.16
times shall I a. you that you 2Ch 18.15
I a. you, O daughters of Jerusalem, Sol 2.07
I a. you, O daughters of Jerusalem, 3.05
I a. you, O daughters of Jerusalem, 5.08
beloved, that you thus a. us? 5.09
I a. you, O daughters of Jerusalem, 8.04
"I a. you by the living God, tell us Mt 26.63
I a. you by God, do not torment me." Mk 5.07
"I a. you by the Jesus whom Paul Ac 19.13
I a. you by the Lord that this 1Th 5.27

ADJURED

Then David's men a. him, "You 2Sa 21.17

ADJUSTED

But God has so a. the body, 1Co 12.24

ADLAI

valleys was Shaphat the son of A. 1Ch 27.29

ADMAH

A., and Zeboiim, as far as Lasha. Gen 10.19
of Gomorrah, Shinab king of A., 14.02
the king of A., the king of Zeboiim, 14.08
A. and Zaboiim, which the LORD Deu 29.23
How can I make you like A.! Hos 11.08

ADMATHA

A., Tarshish, Meres, Marsena, and Est 1.14

ADMIN

the son of A., the son of Arni, the Lk 3.33

ADMINISTERED

there also he a. justice to Israel 1Sa 7.17
and David a. justice and equity to 2Sa 8.15
and he a. justice and equity to 1Ch 18.14

ADMINISTERING

this liberal gift which we are a., 2Co 8.20

ADMINISTRATORS

a., speakers in various kinds of 1Co 12.28

ADMISSION

For a. has been secretly gained by Jud 1.04

ADMIT

anointing shall a. them to a Ex 40.15
But this I a. to you, that according Ac 24.14
Never a. any charge against an 1Ti 5.19

ADMITTED

who may be a. to the temple and Eze 44.05

ADMITTING

in a. foreigners, uncircumcised in Eze 44.07

ADMONISH

and solemnly a. you, saying, 'Know 1Ki 2.42
Hear, O my people, while I a. you! Ps 81.08
night or day to a. every one with Ac 20.31
but to a. you as my beloved children 1Co 4.14
you teach and a. one another in Col 3.16
over you in the Lord and a. you, 1Th 5.12
a. the idle, encourage the fainthearted, 5.14

ADMONISHING

after a. him once or twice, have Tit 3.10

ADMONITION
but he who heeds a. is prudent. Pro 15.05
heeds wholesome a. will abide 15.31
he who heeds a. gains understanding 15.32
sayings of a. and knowledge, 22.20

ADNA
A., Chelal, Benaiah, Maaseiah, Mattaniah, Ez 10.30
of Harim, A.; of Meraioth, Neh 12.15

ADNAH
A., Jozabad, Jediael, Michael, Jozabad, 1Ch 12.20
A. the commander, with three hundred 2Ch 17.14

ADONIBEZEK
They came upon A. at Bezek, and Ju 1.05
A. fled; but they pursued 1.06
And A. said, "Seventy kings with 1.07

ADONIJAH
A. the son of Haggith; and the 2Sa 3.04
Now A. the son of Haggith exalted 1Ki 1.05
they followed A. and helped him. 1.07
mighty men were not with A. 1.08
A. sacrificed sheep, oxen, and 1.09
not heard that A. the son of 1.11
Why then is A. king?' 1.13
A. is king, although you, my lord the 1.18
'A. shall reign after me, and he 1.24
and saying, 'Long live King A.!' 1.25
A. and all the guests who were with 1.41
and A. said, "Come in, for you are a 1.42
Johathan answered A., 'No, for our 1.43
Then all the guests of A. trembled, 1.49
And A. feared Solomon; and he 1.50
A. fears King Solomon; for, lo, 1.51
Then A. the son of Haggith came to 2.13
to speak to him on behalf of A. 2.19
be given to A. your brother as his 2.21
ask Abishag the Shunammite for A.? 2.22
word does not cost A. his life! 2.23
A. shall be put to death this day." 2.24
had supported A. although he had 2.28
the fourth A., whose mother was 1Ch 3.02
A., Tobijah, anl Tobadonijah; 2Ch 17.08
A., Bigvai, Adin, Neh 10.16

ADONIKAM
The sons of A., six hundred and Ez 2.13
Of the sons of A., those who came 8.13
The sons of A., six hundred and Neh 7.18

ADONIRAM
and A. the son of Abda was in 1Ki 4.06
A. was in charge of the levy. 5.14

ADONIZEDEK
When A. king of Jerusalem heard how Jos 10.01
So A. king of Jerusalem sent to 10.03

ADOPTED
Mordecai a. her as his own daughter. Est 2.07
who had a. her as his own daughter, 2.15
daughter a. him and brought him up Ac 7.21

ADOPTION
inwardly as we wait for a. as sons, Rom 8.23
that we might receive a. as sons. Gal 4.05

ADORAIM
A., Lachish, Azekah, 2Ch 11.09

ADORAM
and A. was in charge of the forced 2Sa 20.24
Then King Rehoboam sent A., 1Ki 12.18

ADORN
Again you shall a. yourself with Jer 31.04
prophets and a. the monuments of Mt 23.29
women should a. themselves modestly 1Ti 2.09
they may a. the doctrine of God Tit 2.10
in God used to a. themselves and 1Pe 3.05

ADORNED
and a. her head, and looked out of 2Ki 9.30
He a. the house with settings of 2Ch 3.06
how it was a. with noble stones and Lk 21.05
as a bride a. for her husband; Rev 21.02
the city were a. with every jewel; 21.19

ADORNING
be the outward a. with braiding of 1Pe 3.03

ADORNMENT
for your soul and a. for your neck. Pro 3.22

ADORNS
he a. the humble with victory. Ps 149.04
and as a bride a. herself with her Is 61.10

ADRAMMELECH
in the fire to A. and Anammelech, 2Ki 17.31
A. and Sharezer, his sons, slew him 19.37
A. and Sharezer, his sons, slew him Is 37.38

ADRAMYTTIUM
And embarking in a ship of A., Ac 27.02

ADRIA
were drifting across the sea of A., Ac 27.27

ADRIEL
was given to A. the Meholathite 1Sa 18.19
she bore to A. the son of Barzillai 2Sa 21.08

ADRIFT
and a day I have been a. at sea; 2Co 11.25

ADULLAM
of Libnah, one; the king of A., one; Jos 12.15
Jarmuth, A., Soco, Azekah, 15.35
and escaped to the cave of A.; 1Sa 22.01
time to David at the cave of A., 2Sa 23.13
rock to David at the cave of A., 1Ch 11.15
Bethzur, Soco, A., 2Ch 11.07
Zanoah, A., and their villages, Neh 11.30
glory of Israel shall come to A. Mic 1.15

ADULLAMITE
and turned in to a certain A., Gen 38.01
he and his friend Hirah the A. 38.12
sent the kid by his friend the A., 38.20

ADULTERER
both the a. and the adulteress Lev 20.10
The eye of the a. also waits for Job 24.15
offspring of the a. and the harlot. Is 57.03

ADULTERERS
and you keep company with a. Ps 50.18
For they are all a., a company Jer 9.02
For the land is full of a.; 23.10
They are all a.; they are Hos 7.04
against the a., against those who Mal 3.05
a., or even like this tax collector Lk 18.11
nor a., nor homosexuals, 1Co 6.09

ADULTERESS
adulterer and the a. shall be put Lev 20.10
but an a. stalks a man's very life. Pro 6.26
This is the way of an a.: 30.20
beloved of a paramour and is an a.; Hos 3.01
of unchastity, makes her an a.; Mt 5.32
be called an a. if she lives with Rom 7.03
another man she is not an a. 7.03

ADULTERESSES
on them with the sentence of a., Eze 23.45
because they are a., and blood 23.45

ADULTERIES
for all the a. of that faithless Jer 3.08
your a. and neighings, your lewd 13.27

ADULTEROUS
A. wife, who receives strangers Eze 16.32
"An evil and a. generation seeks Mt 12.39
An evil and a. generation seeks for 16.04
words in this a. and sinful Mk 8.38
God will judge the immoral and a. Heb 13.04

ADULTERY
"You shall not commit a." Ex 20.14
"If a man commits a. with the wife Lev 20.10
"'Neither shall you commit a. Deu 5.18
He who commits a. has no sense; Pro 6.32
committing a. with stone and tree. Jer 3.09
they committed a. and trooped to 5.07
commit a., swear falsely, burn 7.09
they commit a. and walk in lies; 23.14
have committed a. with their 29.23
For they have committed a., Eze 23.37
their idols they have committed a.; 23.37
men now commit a. when they 23.43
and her a. from between her breasts; Hos 2.02
stealing, and committing a.; 4.02
harlot, and your brides commit a. 4.13
your brides when they commit a.; 4.14
was said, 'You shall not commit a.' Mt 5.27
committed a. with her in his heart 5.28
a divorced woman commits a. 5.32
a., fornication, theft, false witness, 15.19
and marries another, commits a. 19.09
makes her commit a. * 19.09
marries a divorced woman commits a. * 19.09
You shall not commit a., 19.18
fornication, theft, murder, a., Mk 7.21
another, commits a. against her; 10.11
marries another, she commits a. 10.12
Do not commit a. Do not steal, Do 10.19
and marries another commits a., Lk 16.18
from her husband commits a. 16.18
commandments: 'Do not commit a., 18.20
woman who had been caught in a., *Jn 8.03
has been caught in the act of a. * 8.04
say that one must not commit a., Rom 2.22
do you commit a.? You who abhor 2.22
commandments, "You shall not commit a. 13.09
For he who said "Do not commit a.," Jas 2.11
you do not commit a. but do kill, 2.11
They have eyes full of a., 2Pe 2.14
who commit a. with her I will Rev 2.22

ADUMMIM
is opposite the ascent of A., Jos 15.07
which is opposite the ascent of A.; 18.17

ADVANCE
and shield, and a. for battle! Jer 46.03
A., O horses, and rage, O chariots! 46.09
LORD: "Rise up, a. against Kedar! 49.28
"Rise up, a. against a nation at 49.31
You will a., coming on like a storm, Eze 38.09
and arrange in a. for this gift 2Co 9.05
really served to a. the gospel, Php 1.12

ADVANCED
and Sarah were old, a. in age; Gen 18.11
Now Abraham was old, well a. in years; 24.01
Now Joshua was old and a. in years; Jos 13.01
him, "You are old and a. in years, 13.01
was old and well a. in years, 23.01
"I am now old and well a. in years; 23.02
was already old and a. in years, 1Sa 17.12
King David was old and a. in years; 1Ki 1.01
and a. her and her maids to the Est 2.09
and a. him and set his seat above 3.01
and how he had a. him above the 5.11
Mordecai, to which the king a. him, 10.02
barren, and both were a. in years. Lk 1.07
man, and my wife is a. in years." 1.18
and I a. in Judaism beyond many of Gal 1.14

ADVANTAGE
"The men gained an a. over us, 2Sa 11.23
that you ask, 'What a. have I? Job 35.03
and man has no a. over the beasts; Ecc 3.19
a king is an a. to a land with 5.09
For what a. has the wise man over 6.08
an a. to those who see the sun. 7.11
and the a. of knowledge is that 7.12
there is no a. in a charmer. 10.11
it shall not stand or be to his a. Dan 11.17
it is to your a. that I go away, for Jn 16.07
Then what a. has the Jew? Or what Rom 3.01
I do, not seeking my own a., but that 1Co 10.33
Satan from gaining the a. over us; 2Co 2.11
no one, we have taken a. of no one. 7.02
or takes a. of you, or puts on airs, 11.20
Did I take a. of you through any of 12.17
Did Titus take a. of you? 12.18
Christ will be of no a. to you. Gal 5.02
for that would be of no a. to you. Heb 13.17
flattering people to gain a. Jud 1.16

ADVENTURESS
from the a. with her smooth words, Pro 2.16
and embrace the bosom of an a.? 5.20
from the smooth tongue of the a. 6.24
from the a. with her smooth words. 7.05
a deep pit; an a. is a narrow well. 23.27

ADVERSARIES
majesty thou overthrowest thy a.; Ex 15.07
and an adversary to your a. 23.22
he shall eat up the nations his a., Num 24.08
lest their a. should judge amiss, Deu 32.27
I will take vengeance on my a., 32.41
and takes vengeance on his a., 32.43
him, and be a help against his a. 33.07
crush the loins of his a., 33.11
him, "Are you for us, or for our a.?" Jos 5.13
but they shall become a. to you, Ju 2.03
The a. of the LORD shall be broken 1Sa 2.10
thou didst exalt me above my a., 2Sa 22.49
but if to betray me to my a., 1Ch 12.17
Now when the a. of Judah and Ez 4.01
'Surely our a. are cut off, and what Job 22.20
from their a. at thy right hand. Ps 17.07
thou didst exalt me above my a.; 18.48
my a. and foes, they shall stumble 27.02
Give me not up to the will of my a.; 27.12
I am the scorn of all my a., 31.11
for good are my a. because I 38.20
my a. taunt me, while they say to me 42.10
uproar of thy a. which goes up 74.23
and he put his a. to rout; 78.66
and burns up his a. round about. 97.03
And the waters covered their a.; 106.11
until he sees his desire on his a. 112.08
Many are my persecutors and my a., 119.157
my enemies, and destroy all my a., 143.12
so the LORD raises a. against them, Is 9.11
the fire for thy a. consume them. 26.11
wrath to his a., requital to his 59.18
our a. have trodden it down. 63.18
to make thy name known to thy a., 64.02
them into the hand of their a., Eze 39.23
shall be lifted up over your a., Mic 5.09
vengeance on his a. and keeps wrath Nah 1.02

ADVERSARIES (cont.)
he will make a full end of his a., Nah 1.08
all his a. were put to shame; Lk 13.17
none of your a. will be able to 21.15
to me, and there are many a. 1Co 16.09
of fire which will consume the a. Heb 10.27

ADVERSARY
enemies and an a. to your adversaries Ex 23.22
against the a. who oppresses you, Num 10.09
his stand in the way as his a. 22.22
the battle he become an a. to us. 1Sa 29.04
should this day be as an a. to me? 2Sa 19.22
there is neither a. nor misfortune. 1Ki 5.04
raised up an a. against Solomon, 11.14
God also raised up as an a. to him, 11.23
He was an a. of Israel all the days 11.25
my a. sharpens his eyes against me. Job 16.09
me, and counts me as his a. 19.11
the indictment written by my a.! 31.35
it is not an a. who deals insolently Ps 55.12
Who is my a.? Let him come Is 50.08
"An a. shall surround the land, and Amo 3.11
'Vindicate me against my a.' Lk 18.03
your a. the devil prowls around 1Pe 5.08

ADVERSARY'S
Or, 'Deliver me from the a. hand'? Job 6.23

ADVERSITIES
thou hast taken heed of my a., Ps 31.07

ADVERSITY
know all the a. that has befallen Num 20.14
redeemed my life out of every a., 2Sa 4.09
redeemed my soul out of every a., 1Ki 1.29
affliction, and opens their ear by a. Job 36.15
generations I shall not meet a. Ps 10.06
and a brother is born for a. Pro 17.17
if you faint in the day of a., 24.10
and in the day of a. consider; Ecc 7.14
the bread of a. and the water of Is 30.20

ADVICE
give your a. and counsel here. Ju 20.07
And the a. pleased Absalom and all 2Sa 17.04
This a. pleased the king and the Est 1.21
eyes, but a wise man listens to a. Pro 12.15
with those who take a. is wisdom. 13.10
Listen to a. and accept instruction, 19.20
king, who will no longer take a., Ecc 4.13
so they took his a., and when Ac 5.40
And in this matter I give my a.: 2Co 8.10

ADVISABLE
If it seems a. that I should go 1Co 16.04

ADVISE
"How do you a. me to answer this 1Ki 12.06
"What do you a. that we answer this 12.09
"How do you a. me to answer this 2Ch 10.06
"What do you a. that we answer this 10.09

ADVISED
who had charge of the women, a. Est 2.15
already gone by, Paul a. them, Ac 27.09
the majority a. to put to sea from 27.12

ADVISER
Ahuzzath his a. and Phicol the Gen 26.26

ADVISERS
but with many a. they succeed. Pro 15.22

ADVISES
shall we do as he a.? If not 2Sa 17.06

ADVOCATE
They a. customs which it is not Ac 16.21
we have an a. with the Father, Jesus 1Jn 2.01

AENEAS
There he found a man named A., Ac 9.33
"A., Jesus Christ heals you; Ac 9.34

AENON
was baptizing at A. near Salim, Jn 3.23

AFAR
his eyes and saw the place a. off. Gen 22.04
They saw him a. off, and before he 37.18
and they stood a. off, Ex 20.18
And the people stood a. off, 20.21
of Israel and worship a. off. 24.01
or is a. off on a journey, he shall Num 9.10
like valleys that stretch a., 24.06
bring a nation against you from a., Deu 28.49
have said, "I will scatter them a., 32.26
and stood a. off on the top of the 1Sa 26.13
shout, and the sound was heard a. Ez 3.13
joy of Jerusalem was heard a. off. Neh 12.43
And when they saw him from a., Job 2.12
they hang a. from men, they swing to 28.04
I will fetch my knowledge from a., 36.03
man beholds it from a. 36.25
He smells the battle from a., 39.25
his eyes behold it a. off. 39.29
Why dost thou stand a. off, O Lord? Ps 10.01
and my kinsmen stand a. off. 38.11
yea, I would wander a., 55.07
but the haughty he knows from a. 138.06
discernest my thoughts from a. 139.02
she brings her food from a. Pro 31.14
raise a signal for a nation a. off, Is 5.26
the storm which will come from a.? 10.03
feet carried her to settle a.? 23.07
behold a land that stretches a. 33.17
my sons from a. and my daughters 43.06
and hearken, you peoples from a. 49.01
Lo, these shall come from a., 49.12
and righteousness stands a. off; 59.14
Javan, to the coastlands a. off, 66.19
bringing upon you a nation from a., Jer 5.15
the Lord, and not a God a. off? 23.23
for lo, I will save you from a., 30.10
the Lord appeared to him from a. 31.03
it in the coastlands a. off; 31.10
for lo, I will save you from a., 46.27
Remember the Lord from a., 51.50
decide for strong nations a. off; Mic 4.03
Yea, their horsemen come from a.; Hab 1.08
women there, looking on from a., Mt 27.55
And when he saw Jesus from a., Mk 5.06
were also women looking on from a., 15.40
seen it and greeted it from a., Heb 11.13

AFFAIR
those who died in the a. of Korah. Num 16.49
When the a. was investigated and Est 2.23

AFFAIRS
the course of a. your servant Joab 2Sa 14.20
him, "Why speak any more of your a.? 19.29
land of your a. and of your wisdom, 1Ki 10.06
was a turn of a. brought about by 12.15
to God and for the a. of the king. 1Ch 26.32
land of your a. and of your wisdom, 2Ch 9.05
was a turn of a. brought about by 10.15
who conducts his a. with justice. Ps 112.05
over the a. of the province of Dan 2.49
over the a. of the province of 3.12
anxious about the a. of the Lord, 1Co 7.32
man is anxious about worldly a., 7.33
anxious about the a. of the Lord, 7.34

AFFAIRS (cont.)
woman is anxious about worldly a., 1Co 7.34
Tychicus will tell you all about my a.; Col 4.07
live quietly, to mind your own a., 1Th 4.11

AFFECTION
Let her a. fill you at all times Pro 5.19
love one another with brotherly a.; Rom 12.10
all with the a. of Christ Jesus. Php 1.08
the Spirit, any a. and sympathy, 2.01
the godliness with brotherly a., 2Pe 1.07
and brotherly a. with love. 1.07

AFFECTIONATELY
So, being a. desirous of you, we were 1Th 2.08

AFFECTIONS
you are restricted in your own a. 2Co 6.12

AFFIRM
Now this I a. and testify in the Eph 4.17

AFFIRMING
the charge, a. that all this was so. Ac 24.09

AFFLICT
over them to a. them with heavy Ex 1.11
You shall not a. any widow or 22.22
If you do a. them, and they cry out 22.23
you shall a. yourselves, and shall Lev 16.29
you, and you shall a. yourselves; 16.31
and you shall a. yourselves and 23.27
rest, and you shall a. yourselves; 23.32
and shall a. Asshur and Eber; Num 24.24
convocation, and a. yourselves; 29.07
and any binding oath to a. herself, 30.13
violent men shall a. them no more, 2Sa 7.10
their sin, when thou dost a. them, 1 Ki 8.35
And I will for this a. the descendants 11.39
their sin, when thou dost a. them, 2Ch 6.26
thou didst a. the peoples, but them Ps 44.02
hast wounded, they a. still more. 69.26
O LORD, and a. thy heritage. 94.05
thou keep silent, and a. us sorely? Is 64.12
those who seek their life a. them. Jer 19.09
not willingly a. or grieve the Lam 3.33
you who a. the righteous, who take a Amo 5.12
afflicted you, I will a. you no more. Nah 1.12
but thinking to a. me in my Php 1.17
with affliction those who a. you. 2Th 1.06

AFFLICTED
But the LORD a. Pharaoh and his Gen 12.17
"When a man is a. with leprosy, he Lev 13.09
For whoever is not a. on this same 23.29
and a. us, and laid upon us hard Deu 26.06
of those who a. and oppressed them Ju 2.18
the LORD has a. me and the Almighty Ru 1.21
terrified and a. them with tumors, 1Sa 5.06
and he a. the men of the city, both 5.09
and a. them, and gave them into the 2Ki 17.20
disturbances a. all the inhabitants 2Ch 15.05
and a. him instead of strengthening 28.20
and a. Job with loathsome sores Job 2.07
and he heard the cry of the a. 34.28
but gives the a. their right. 36.06
He delivers the a. by their affliction, 36.15
does not forget the cry of the a. Ps 9.12
up thy hand; forget not the a. 10.12
my a. soul from the horns of the 22.21
abhorred the affliction of the a.; 22.24
The a. shall eat and be satisfied; 22.26
for I am lonely and a. 25.16
let the a. hear and be glad. 34.02
I a. myself with fasting. 35.13
But I am a. and in pain; 69.29
right of the a. and the destitute. 82.03
A. and close to death from my youth 88.15
as many days as thou hast a. us, 90.15
even when I said, "I am greatly a."; 116.10
Before I was a. I went astray; 119.67
It is good for me that I was a., 119.71
in faithfulness thou hast a. me. 119.75
I am sorely a.; give me 119.107
"Sorely have they a. me from my 129.01
"Sorely have they a. me from my 129.02
LORD maintains the cause of the a., 140.12
All the days of the a. are evil, Pro 15.15
poor, or crush the a. at the gate; 22.22
pervert the rights of all the a. 31.05
and in her the a. of his people Is 14.32
and will have compassion on his a. 49.13
you who are a., who are drunk, but 51.21
stricken, smitten by God, and a. 53.04
and he was a., yet he opened not 53.07
"O a. one, storm-tossed, and not 54.11
and satisfy the desire of the a., 58.10
me to bring good tidings to the a.; 61.01
In all their affliction he was a., 63.09
and turn aside the way of the a.; Amo 2.07
away, and those whom I have a.; Mic 4.06
Though I have a. you, I will afflict Nah 1.12
they are a. for want of a shepherd. Zec 10.02
those a. with various diseases and Mt 4.24
sick and those a. with unclean Ac 5.16
If we are a., it is for your 2Co 1.06
We are a. in every way, but not 4.08
rest but we were a. at every turn— 7.05
rest with us to you who are a., 2Th 1.07
relieved the a., and devoted 1Ti 5.10
destitute, a., ill-treated— Heb 11.37

AFFLICTION
the LORD has given heed to your a. Gen 16.11
the LORD has looked upon my a.; 29.32
God saw my a. and the labor of my 31.42
me fruitful in the land of my a. 41.52
"I have seen the a. of my people Ex 3.07
you up out of the a. of Egypt, 3.17
and that he had seen their a., 4.31
the bread of a.—for you came out Deu 16.03
and saw our a., our toil, and our 26.07
and every a. which is not recorded 28.61
look on the a. of thy maidservant, 1Sa 1.11
I have seen the a. of my people, 9.16
that the LORD will look upon my a., 2Sa 16.12
shared in all the a. of my father. 1Ki 2.26
knowing the a. of his own heart 8.38
saw that the a. of Israel was very 2Ki 14.26
Israel, each knowing his own a., 2Ch 6.29
house, and cry to thee in our a., 20.09
didst see the a. of our fathers in Neh 9.09
for our a. is not to be compared Est 7.04
For a. does not come from the dust, Job 5.06
with disgrace and look upon my a. 10.15
days of a. have taken hold of me. 30.16
days of a. come to meet me. 30.27
and caught in the cords of a., 36.08
delivers the afflicted by their a., 36.15
you have chosen rather than a. 36.21
or abhorred the a. of the afflicted Ps 22.24
Consider my a. and my trouble, and 25.18
love, because thou hast seen my a., 31.07
thou forget our a. and oppression? 44.24
thou didst lay a. on our loins; 66.11
prisoners in a. and in irons, 107.10
of their iniquities suffered a.; 107.17
but he raises up the needy out of a., 107.41
comfort in my a. that thy promise 119.50
I should have perished in my a. 119.92
Look on my a. and deliver me, for I 119.153
this is vanity; it is a sore a. Ecc 6.02
of adversity and the water of a., Is 30.20
tried you in the furnace of a. 48.10
In all their a. he was afflicted, 63.09

AFFLICTION (cont.)
I also will choose a. for them, Is 66.04
But I said, "Truly this is an a., Jer 10.19
at hand and his a. hastens apace. 48.16
because of a. and hard servitude; Lam 1.03
the days of her a. and bitterness 1.07
behold my a., for the enemy has 1.09
who has seen a. under the rod of 3.01
Remember my a. and my bitterness, 3.19
I saw the tents of Cushan in a.; Hab 3.07
and great a., and our fathers could Ac 7.11
who comforts us in all our a., 2Co 1.04
to comfort those who are in any a., 1.04
of the a. we experienced in Asia; 1.08
you out of much a. and anguish of 2.04
momentary a. is preparing for us 4.17
With all our a., I am overjoyed. 7.04
for in a severe test of a., 8.02
you received the word in much a., 1Th 1.06
beforehand that we were to suffer a.; 3.04
distress and a. we have been 3.07
to repay with a. those who afflict 2Th 1.06
publicly exposed to abuse and a., Heb 10.33
orphans and widows in their a., Jas 1.27

AFFLICTIONS
your offspring extraordinary a., Deu 28.59
a. severe and lasting, and sicknesses 28.59
they see the a. of that land and 29.22
Many are the a. of the righteous; Ps 34.19
and rescued him out of all his a., Ac 7.10
that imprisonment and a. await me. 20.23
in a., hardships, calamities, 2Co 6.04
in Christ's a. for the sake of his Col 1.24
that no one be moved by these a. 1Th 3.03
and in the a. which you are 2Th 1.04

AFFLICTS
which the LORD a. the nations that Zec 14.18

AFFLUENCE
they suck the a. of the seas and Deu 33.19

AFFORD
"But if he cannot a. a lamb, Lev 5.07
"But if he cannot a. two turtledoves 5.11
And if she cannot a. a lamb, 12.08
he is poor and cannot a. so much, 14.21
young pigeons, such as he can a.; 14.22
young pigeons such as he can a., 14.30
who cannot a. the offerings for his 14.32
apart from what else he can a.; Num 6.21

AFLAME
Scoffers set a city a., but wise Pro 29.08
their faces will be a. Is 13.08
marry than to be a. with passion. 1Co 7.09

AFRAID
and I was a., because I was naked; Gen 3.10
did not laugh"; for she was a. 18.15
for he was a. to dwell in Zoar; 19.30
and the men were very much a. 20.08
And he was a., and said, "How 28.17
Jacob answered Laban, "Because I was a., 31.31
was greatly a. and distressed; 32.07
And the men were a. because they 43.18
replied, "Rest assured, do not be a.; 43.23
do not be a. to go down to Egypt; 46.03
Then Moses was a., and thought, Ex 2.14
face, for he was a. to look at God. 3.06
the people were a. and trembled; 20.18
and they were a. to come near him. 34.30
down, and none shall make you a.; Lev 26.06
were you not a. to speak against Num 12.08
shall not be a. of the face of man, Deu 1.17
'Do not be in dread or a. of them. 1.29
and they will be a. of you. 2.04
for you were a. because of the fire, 5.05
you shall not be a. of them, 7.18
all the peoples of whom you are a. 7.19
For I was a. of the anger and hot 9.19
presumptuously, you need not be a. of him. 18.22
own, you shall not be a. of them; 20.01
and they shall be a. of you. 28.10
of Egypt, which you were a. of; 28.60
to them, "Do not be a. or dismayed; Jos 10.25
"Do not be a. of them, for tomorrow 11.06
he was too a. of his family and Ju 6.27
for he was a., because he was still 8.20
And Samuel was a. to tell the 1Sa 3.15
the Philistines were a.; 4.07
of it they were a. of the Philistines 7.07
they were dismayed and greatly a. 17.11
fled from him, and were much a. 17.24
Saul was a. of David, because the 18.12
Saul was still more a. of David. 18.29
and was much a. of Achish the king 21.12
"Behold, we are a. here in Judah; 23.03
And David was a. because Saul had 23.15
he was a., and his heart trembled 28.05
it you were not a. to put forth 2Sa 1.14
And David was a. of the LORD that 6.09
because the people have made me a.; 14.15
Then he was a., and he arose and 1Ki 19.03
do not be a. of him." So he 2Ki 1.15
But they were exceedingly a., 10.04
Do not be a. because of the words 19.06
"Do not be a. because of the 25.24
for they were a. of the Chaldeans 25.26
And David was a. of God that day; 1Ch 13.12
for he was a. of the sword of the 21.30
Do not be a. or dismayed before the 2Ch 32.07
Judah, and made them a. to build, Ez 4.04
Then I was very much a. Neh 2.02
the people, "Do not be a. of them. 4.14
I should be a. and act in this way 6.13
prophets who wanted to make me a. 6.14
about us were a. and fell greatly 6.16
Tobiah sent letters to make me a. 6.19
you see my calamity, and are a. Job 6.21
I become a. of all my suffering, for 9.28
down, and none will make you a.; 11.19
be a. of the sword, for wrath brings 19.29
I was timid and a. to declare my 32.06
himself up the mighty are a.; 41.25
I am not a. of ten thousands of Ps 3.06
of whom shall I be a.? 27.01
Be not a. when one becomes rich, 49.16
When I am a., I put my trust in 56.03
farthest bounds are a. at thy signs; 65.08
they were a., yea, the deep trembled 77.16
safety, so that they were not a.; 78.53
He is not a. of evil tidings; 112.07
heart is steady, he will not be a., 112.08
and I am a. of thy judgments. 119.120
If you sit down, you will not be a.; Pro 3.24
Do not be a. of sudden panic, or of 3.25
She is not a. of snow for her 31.21
they are a. also of what is high, Ecc 12.05
be not a. of the Assyrians when Is 10.24
I will trust, and will not be a.; 12.02
down, and none will make them a. 17.02
The sinners in Zion are a.; 33.14
Do not be a. because of the words 37.06
The coastlands have seen and are a., 41.05
Fear not, nor be a.; have I not 44.08
that you are a. of man who dies, of 51.12
Be not a. of them, for I am with you Jer 1.08
Be not a. of them, for they cannot 10.05
hand of those of whom you are a., 22.25
he was a. and fled and escaped to 26.21
ease, and none shall make him a. 30.10
was a., nor did they rend their 36.24
"I am a. of the Jews who have 38.19

AFRAID (cont.)

hand of the men of whom you are a. Jer 39.17
"Do not be a. to serve the Chaldeans 40.09
for they were a. of them, because 41.18
of Babylon, of whom you are a.; 42.11
which you are a. shall follow hard 42.16
ease, and none shall make him a. 46.27
be not a. of them, nor be a. of Eze 2.06
nor be a. of their words, though 2.06
be not a. of their words, nor be 2.06
and their kings are horribly a., 27.35
and none shall make them a. 34.28
land with none to make them a., 39.26
I had a dream which made me a.; Dan 4.05
and he shall be a. and withdraw, 11.30
a city, and the people are not a.? Amo 3.06
Then the mariners were a., Jon 1.05
Then the men were exceedingly a., 1.10
tree, and none shall make them a.; Mic 4.04
down, and none shall make them a. Zep 3.13
Ashkelon shall see it, and be a.; Zec 9.05
he was a. to go there, and being Mt 2.22
"Why are you a., O men of little 8.26
they were a., and they glorified 9.08
he was a., and beginning to sink he 14.30
we are a. of the multitude; 21.26
so I was a., and I went and hid 25.25
said to the women, "Do not be a.; 28.05
Then Jesus said to them, "Do not be a.; 28.10
He said to them, "Why are you a.? Mk 4.40
had the legion; and they were a. 5.15
say, for they were exceedingly a. 9.06
and they were a. to ask him. 9.32
and those who followed were a. 10.32
—they were a. of the people, for 11.32
to any one, for they were a. 16.08
"Do not be a., Zechariah, for your Lk 1.13
"Do not be a., Mary, for you have 1.30
And the angel said to them, "Be not a.; 2.10
Jesus said to Simon, "Do not be a.; 5.10
And they were a., and they 8.25
right mind; and they were a. 8.35
and they were a. as they entered 9.34
and they were a. to ask him about 9.45
for I was a. of you, because you are 19.21
do not be a." Then they Jn 6.20
troubled, neither let them be a. 14.27
these words, he was the more a.; 19.08
for they were a. of being stoned by Ac 5.26
and they were all a. of him, 9.26
and they were a. when they heard 16.38
"Do not be a., but speak and do not 18.09
and the tribune also was a., 22.29
a. that Paul would be torn in 23.10
and he said, 'Do not be a., Paul; 27.24
be a., for he does not bear the Rom 13.04
But I am a. that as the serpent 2Co 11.03
I am a. I have labored over you in Gal 4.11
they were not a. of the king's Heb 11.23
not being a. of the anger of the 11.27
is my helper, I will not be a.; 13.06
they are not a. to revile the 2Pe 2.10

AFRESH

skin hardens, then breaks out a. Job 7.05

AFTERBIRTH

her a. that comes out from between Deu 28.57

AFTERNOON

late one a., when David arose from 2Sa 11.02

AFTERWARD

and also a., when the sons of God Gen 6.04
A. the families of the Canaanites 10.18
and a. they shall come out with 15.14
A. his brother came forth, and his 25.26
A. his brother came out with the 38.30
A. Moses and Aaron went to Pharaoh Ex 5.01
And a. all the people of Israel 34.32
And a. he shall kill the burnt Lev 14.19
and a. the priest shall go in to 14.36
and a. he may come into the camp. 16.26
and a. he may come into the camp. 16.28
and a. he may eat of the holy 22.07
and a. shall make the woman drink Num 5.26
a. you shall be gathered to your 31.02
and a. you shall come into the camp 31.24
and a. the hand of all the people. Deu 17.07
vineyard, you shall not glean it a.; 24.21
then a. you may go your way. Jos 2.16
And a. he read all the words of the 8.34
And a. Joshua smote them and put 10.26
A long time a., when the LORD had 23.01
And a. the men of Judah went down Ju 1.09
and a. your hands shall be strengthened 7.11
a. those eat who are invited. 1Sa 9.13
And a. David's heart smote him, 24.05
A. David also arose, and went out of 24.08
A., when David heard of it, he said, 2Sa 3.28
and a. make for yourself and your 1Ki 17.13
A. Benhadad king of Syria mustered 2Ki 6.24
A. Hezron went in to the daughter 1Ch 2.21
A. he built an outer wall to the 2Ch 33.14
And a. they prepared for themselves 35.14
and a. thou wilt receive me to Ps 73.24
but a. his mouth will be full of Pro 20.17
a man will a. find more favor than 28.23
A. you shall be called the city of Is 1.26
A., says the LORD, I will deliver Jer 21.07
But a. they turned around and took 34.11
A. Egypt shall be inhabited as in 46.26
But a. I will restore the fortunes 49.06
in one year and a. a report in 51.46
A. he brought me to the gate, the Eze 43.01
A. he shall turn his face to the Dan 11.18
A. the children of Israel shall Hos 3.05
"And it shall come to pass a., Joe 2.28
forty nights, and a. he was hungry. Mt 4.02
but a. he repented and went. 21.29
you did not a. repent and believe 21.32
A. he sent his son to them, saying, 21.37
A. the other maidens came also, 25.11
Soon a. he went to a city called Lk 7.11
Soon a. he went on through cities 8.01
and a. you shall eat and drink'? 17.08
but a. he said to himself, 'Though I 18.04
A. the woman also died. 20.32
A., Jesus found him in the temple, Jn 5.14
but a. you will understand." 13.07
but you shall follow a." 13.36
four hundred and thirty years a., Gal 3.17
saying through David so long a., Heb 4.07
For you know that a., 12.17
a. destroyed those who did not Jud 1.05

AFTERWARDS

A. she bore a daughter, and called Gen 30.21
and a. I shall see his face; 32.20
a. he will let you go hence; Ex 11.01
and a. he shall come into the camp; Num 19.07
and a. the hand of all the people. Deu 13.09
and a. I brought you out. Jos 24.05
and a. I will send for many hunters, Jer 16.16
from Samuel and those who came a., Ac 3.24

AGABUS

of them named A. stood up and Ac 11.28
a prophet named A. came down from 21.10

AGAG

his king shall be higher than A., Num 24.07
And he took A. the king of the 1Sa 15.08
But Saul and the people spared A., 15.09

AGAG (cont.)

I have brought A. the king of 1Sa 15.20
here to me A. the king of the 15.32
And A. came to him cheerfully. 15.32
A. said, "Surely the bitterness of 15.32
Samuel hewed A. in pieces before 15.33

AGAGITE

Haman the son of Hammedatha the A., Est 3.01
hand and gave it to Haman the A., 3.10
of Haman the A. and the plot which 8.03
letters devised by Haman the A., 8.05
For Haman the A., the son of 9.24

AGATE

a jacinth, an a., and an amethyst; Ex 28.19
a jacinth, an a., and an amethyst; 39.12
I will make your pinnacles of a., Is 54.12
work, fine linen, coral, and a. Eze 27.16
the third a., the fourth emerald, Rev 21.19

AGE

shall be buried in a good old a. Gen 15.15
and Sarah were old, advanced in a.; 18.11
son in his old a. at the time of 21.02
have borne him a son in his old a." 21.07
his last and died in a good old a., 25.08
he was the son of his old a.; 37.03
brother, the child of his old a.; 44.20
eyes of Israel were dim with a., 48.10
and from the a. of fifty years they Num 8.25
died at the a. of one hundred and Ju 2.08
son of Joash died in a good old a., 8.32
and a nourisher of your old a.; Ru 4.15
eyes were dim because of his a. 1Ki 14.04
But in his old a. he was diseased 15.23
those below twenty years of a., 1Ch 27.23
Then he died in a good old a., 29.28
come to your grave in ripe old a., Job 5.26
reach old a., and grow mighty in 21.07
cast me off in the time of old a.; Ps 71.09
So even to old a. and gray hairs, O 71.18
They still bring forth fruit in old a., 92.14
even to your old a. I am He, Is 46.04
for ever, a joy from a. to a. 60.15
you were at the a. for love; Eze 16.08
the youths who are of your own a. Dan 1.10
with staff in hand for very a. Zec 8.04
either in this a. or in the a. to come. Mt 12.32
the harvest is the close of the a., 13.39
will it be at the close of the a. 13.40
So it will be at the close of the a. 13.49
coming and of the close of the a.?" 24.03
you always, to the close of the a." 28.20
and in the a. to come eternal life. Mk 10.30
in her old a. has also conceived a Lk 1.36
she was of a great a., having lived 2.36
was about thirty years of a., 3.23
daughter, about twelve years of a., 8.42
and in the a. to come eternal life. 18.30
sons of this a. marry and are 20.34
attain to that a. and to the 20.35
he is of a., he will speak for Jn 9.21
parents said, "He is of a., ask him." 9.23
Where is the debater of this a.? 1Co 1.20
wisdom of this a. or of the rulers 2.06
the rulers of this a., who are 2.06
rulers of this a. understood this; 2.08
thinks that he is wise in this a., 3.18
us from the present evil a., Gal 1.04
many of my own a. among my people, 1.14
not only in this a. but also in that Eph 1.21
who is under sixty years of a., 1Ti 5.09
and the powers of the a. to come, Heb 6.05
(which is symbolic for the present a.). 9.09
the end of the a. to put away sin 9.26
even when she was past the a., 11.11

AGED

Barzillai was a very a. man, 2Sa 19.32
young man or virgin, old man or a.; 2Ch 36.17
Wisdom is with the a., Job 12.12
grayhaired and the a. are among us, 15.10
withdrew, and the a. rose and stood; 29.08
am young in years, and you are a.; 32.06
nor the a. that understand what is 32.09
I understand more than the a., Ps 119.100
Grandchildren are the crown of the a., Pro 17.06
on the a. you made your yoke Is 47.06
the old folk and the very a. Jer 6.11
Hear this, you a. men, give ear, all Joe 1.02

AGEE

Shammah, the son of A. the Hararite. 2Sa 23.11

AGENT

is Christ then an a. of sin? Gal 2.17

AGES

of bygone a., and consider what the Job 8.08
renown, O LORD, throughout all a. Ps 135.13
A. ago I was set up, at the first, Pro 8.23
been already, in the a. before us. Ecc 1.10
was kept secret for long a. Rom 16.25
before the a. for our glorification 1Co 2.07
whom the end of the a. has come. 10.11
that in the coming a. he might show Eph 2.07
hidden for a. in God who created 3.09
hidden for a. and generations but Col 1.26
To the King of a., immortal, invisible, 1Ti 1.17
he gave us in Christ Jesus a. ago, 2Ti 1.09
who never lies, promised a. ago Tit 1.02
are thy ways, O King of the a.! Rev 15.03

AGHAST

They will look a. at one another; Is 13.08

AGILE

arms were made a. by the hands of Gen 49.24

AGITATOR

an a. among all the Jews throughout Ac 24.05

AGLOW

be a. with the Spirit, serve the Rom 12.11

AGO

asses that were lost three days a., 1Sa 9.20
because I fell sick three days a. 30.13
heard that I determined it long a.? 2Ki 19.25
house that was built many years a., Ez 5.11
old, I remember the years long a. Ps 77.05
Ages a. I was set up, at the first, Pro 8.23
for him who planned it long a. Is 22.11
heard that I determined it long a.? 37.26
Who told this long a.? 45.21
They are created now, not long a.; 48.07
of old, the generations of long a. 51.09
"For long a. you broke your yoke Jer 2.20
as he ordained long a., he has Lam 2.17
darkness like the dead of long a. 3.06
repented long a. in sackcloth and Mt 11.21
they would have repented long a., Lk 10.13
"Four days a., about this hour, I Ac 10.30
what a year a. you began not only 2Co 8.10
fourteen years a. was caught up to 12.02
gave us in Christ Jesus ages a., 2Ti 1.09
who never lies, promised ages a. Tit 1.02
of God heavens existed long a., 2Pe 3.05
some who long a. were designated Jud 1.04

AGONY

disease, and he died in great a. 2Ch 21.19
Pangs and a. will seize them; Is 13.08
Pelusium shall be in great a.; Eze 30.16
And being in an a. he prayed more Lk 22.44

AGREE

will the men a. to dwell with us, Gen 34.22
Only let us a. with them, and they 34.23
"A. with God, and be at peace; Job 22.21
if two of you a. on earth about Mt 18.19
did you not a. with me for a 20.13
him, and their witness did not a. Mk 14.56
not even so did their testimony a. 14.59
this the words of the prophets a., Ac 15.15
I a. that the law is good. Rom 7.16
that all of you a. and that there 1Co 1.10
a. with one another, live in peace, 2Co 13.11
entreat Syntyche to a. in the Lord. Php 4.02
and does not a. with the sound 1Ti 6.03
and the blood; and these three a. 1Jn 5.08

AGREED

Abraham a. with Ephron; Gen 23.16
frogs, as he had a. with Pharaoh. Ex 8.12
So the priests a. that they should 2Ki 12.08
All the assembly a. to do so, 1Ch 13.04
whole assembly a. together to keep 2Ch 30.23
You have a. to speak lying and Dan 2.09
governors are a. that the king 6.07
So he a., and sought an opportunity Lk 22.06
had already a. that if any one Jn 9.22
that you have a. together to tempt Ac 5.09
"The Jews have a. to ask you to 23.20

AGREEING

After a. with the laborers for a Mt 20.02

AGREEMENT

and with Sheol we have an a.; Is 28.15
and your a. with Sheol will not 28.18
satraps came by a. to the king and Dan 6.06
men came by a. and found Daniel 6.11
Then these men came by a. to the king, 6.15
except perhaps by a. for a season, 1Co 7.05
What a. has the temple of God with 2Co 6.16

AGRIPPA

A. the king and Bernice arrived at Ac 25.13
And A. said to Festus, "I should 25.22
So on the morrow A. and Bernice 25.23
"King A. and all who are present 25.24
King A., that, after we have examined 25.26
A. said to Paul, "You have permission 26.01
King A., I am to make my defense 26.02
O King A., I was not disobedient to 26.19
King A., do you believe the prophets? 26.27
And A. said to Paul, "In a short 26.28
And A. said to Festus, "This man 26.32

AGROUND

a shoal they ran the vessel a.; Ac 27.41

AGUR

The words of A. son of Jakeh of Pro 30.01

AH

A., sinful nation, a people laden Is 1.04
"A., I will vent my wrath on my 1.24
A., Assyria, the rod of my anger, the 10.05
A., the thunder of many peoples, 17.12
A., the roar of nations, they roar 17.12
A., land of whirring wings which is 18.01
Then I said, "A., Lord God! Jer 1.06
Then I said, "A., Lord God, surely 4.10
Then I said: "A., Lord God, behold, 14.13
for him, saying, 'A. my brother!' 22.18
or 'A. sister!' They shall not 22.18
lament for him, saying, 'A. lord!' 22.18
or 'A. his majesty!" 22.18
'A. Lord God! It is thou 32.17
A., sword of the Lord! 47.06
A., this is the day we longed for; Lam 2.16
Then I said, "A. Lord God! Eze 4.14
my face, and cried, "A. Lord God! 9.08
loud voice, and said, "A. Lord God! 11.13
Then I said, "A. Lord God! 20.49
A.! it is made like lightning 21.15
"A., but I am rich, I have gained Hos 12.08
"A.! what have you Lk 4.34
"A., now you are speaking plainly, Jn 16.29

AHA

When the trumpet sounds, he says 'A.!' Job 39.25
they say, "A., A.! our eyes Ps 35.21
"A., we have our heart's desire!" 35.25
their shame who say to me. "A., A.!" 40.15
of their shame who say, "A., A.!" 70.03
"A., I am warm, I have seen the fire Is 44.16
Lord God, Because you said, 'A.!' Eze 25.03
'A., the gate of the peoples is 26.02
Because the enemy said of you, 'A.!' 36.02
their heads, and saying, "A.! Mk 15.29

AHAB

and A. his son reigned in his stead. 1Ki 16.28
A. the son of Omri began to reign 16.29
and A. the son of Omri reigned over 16.29
And A. the son of Omri did evil in 16.30
And A. made an Asherah. 16.33
A. did more to provoke the Lord, the 16.33
said to A., "As the Lord the God of 17.01
saying, "Go, show yourself to A.; 18.01
So Elijah went to show himself to A. 18.02
And A. called Obadiah, who was over 18.03
And A. said to Obadiah, "Go through 18.05
A. went in one direction by himself, 18.06
into the hand of A., to kill me? 18.09
I come and tell A. and he cannot 18.12
went to meet A., and told him; 18.16
and A. went to meet Elijah. 18.16
When A. saw Elijah, A. said to him, 18.17
So A. sent to all the people of 18.20
And Elijah said to A., "Go up, 18.41
So A. went up to eat and to drink. 18.42
say to A., 'Prepare your chariot 18.44
And A. rode and went to Jezreel. 18.45
and ran before A. to the entrance 18.46
A. told Jezebel all that Elijah had 19.01
into the city to A. king of Israel, 20.02
came near to A. king of Israel and 20.13
And A. said, "By whom?" 20.14
And A. said, "I will let you go on 20.34
the palace of A. king of Samaria. 21.01
And after this A. said to Naboth, 21.02
But Naboth said to A., "The Lord 21.03
And A. went into his house vexed 21.04
and was dead, Jezebel said to A., 21.15
And as soon as A. heard that Naboth 21.16
A. arose to go down to the vineyard 21.16
"Arise, go down to meet A. king of Israel, 21.18
A. said to Elijah, "Have you found 21.20
will cut off from A. every male, 21.21
belonging to A. who dies in the 21.24
in the sight of the Lord like A., 21.25
And when A. heard those words, he 21.27
"Have you seen how A. has humbled 21.29
the Lord said, 'Who will entice A., 22.20
Now the rest of the acts of A., 22.39
So A. slept with his fathers; 22.40
fourth year of A. king of Israel. 22.41
the son of A. said to Jehoshaphat, 22.49
Ahaziah the son of A. began to 22.51
After the death of A., 2Ki 1.01
the son of A. became king over 3.01
But when A. died, the king of Moab 3.05
fifth year of Joram the son of A., 8.16
as the house of A. had done, 8.18
the daughter of A. was his wife. 8.18
year of Joram the son of A., 8.25
in the way of the house of A., 8.27

AHAB (cont.)
LORD, as the house of A. had done, 2Ki 8.27
was son-in-law to the house of A. 8.27
the son of A. to make war against 8.28
see Joram the son of A. in Jezreel, 8.29
down the house of A. your master, 9.07
the whole house of A. shall perish; 9.08
I will cut off from A. every male, 9.08
the house of A. like the house of 9.09
side by side behind A. his father, 9.25
year of Joram the son of A., 9.29
Now A. had seventy sons in Samaria, 10.01
guardians of the sons of A., saying, 10.01
spoke concerning the house of A.; 10.10
of the house of A. in Jezreel, 10.11
all that remained to A. in Samaria, 10.17
"A. served Baal a little; 10.18
to the house of A. according to 10.30
as A. king of Israel had done, and 21.03
and the plummet of the house of A.; 21.13
made a marriage alliance with A. 2Ch 18.01
he went down to A. in Samaria. 18.02
And A. killed an abundance of sheep 18.02
A. king of Israel said to Jehoshaphat 18.03
"Who will entice A. the king of 18.19
as the house of A. had done; 21.06
the daughter of A. was his wife. 21.06
as the house of A. led Israel into 21.13
in the ways of the house of A., 22.03
LORD, as the house of A. had done; 22.04
the son of A. king of Israel to 22.05
see Joram the son of A. in Jezreel, 22.06
anointed to destroy the house of A., 22.07
judgment upon the house of A., 22.08
concerning A. the son of Kolaiah Jer 29.21
LORD make you like Zedekiah and A., 29.22
all the works of the house of A.; Mic 6.16

AHAB'S
letters in A. name and sealed them 1Ki 21.08

AHARAH
Ashbel the second, A. the third, 1Ch 8.01

AHARHEL
the families of A. the son of 1Ch 4.08

AHASBAI
Eliphelet the son of A. of Maacah, 2Sa 23.34

AHASUERUS
And in the reign of A., Ez 4.06
In the days of A., the A. who Est 1.01
the A. who reigned from India to 1.01
days when King A. sat on his royal 1.02
palace which belonged to King A. 1.09
who served King A. as chamberlains, 1.10
command the King A. conveyed by the 1.15
in all the provinces of King A. 1.16
'King A. commanded Queen Vashti to 1.17
is to come no more before King A.; 1.19
the anger of King A. had abated, 2.01
each maiden to go in to King A., 2.12
taken to King A. into his royal 2.16
and sought to lay hands on King A. 2.21
things King A. promoted Haman the 3.01
throughout the whole kingdom of A. 3.06
in the twelfth year of King A., 3.07
Then Haman said to King A., 3.08
name of King A. and sealed with 3.12
sought to lay hands upon King A. 6.02
Then King A. said to Queen Esther, 7.05
On that day King A. gave to Queen 8.01
Then King A. said to Queen Esther 8.07
name of King A. and sealed with 8.10
all the provinces of King A., 8.12
provinces of King A. to lay hands 9.02
in all the provinces of King A., 9.20
provinces of the kingdom of A., 9.30
King A. laid tribute on the land 10.01
Jew was next in rank to King A., 10.03
first year of Darius the son of A., Dan 9.01

AHAVA
them to the river that runs to A., Ez 8.15
at the river A., that we might 8.21
from the river A. on the twelfth 8.31

AHAZ
and A. his son reigned in his 2Ki 15.38
A. the son of Jotham, king of Judah, 16.01
A. was twenty years old when he 16.02
they besieged A. but could not 16.05
So A. sent messengers to Tiglathpileser 16.07
A. also took the silver and gold 16.08
When King A. went to Damascus to 16.10
And King A. sent to Urijah the 16.10
all that King A. had sent from 16.11
before King A. arrived from Damascus 16.11
And King A. commanded Urijah the 16.15
did all this, as King A. commanded. 16.16
And King A. cut off the frames of 16.17
of the acts of A. which he did, 16.19
And A. slept with his fathers, and 16.20
twelfth year of A. king of Judah 17.01
of Israel, Hezekiah the son of A., 18.01
sun had declined on the dial of A. 20.11
roof of the upper chamber of A., 23.12
A. his son, Hezekiah his son, Manasseh 1Ch 3.13
Pithon, Melech, Tarea, and A. 8.35
A. was the father of Jehoaddah; 8.36
Pithon, Melech, Tahrea, and A.; 9.41
and A. was the father of Jarah, and 9.42
and A. his son reigned in his 2Ch 27.09
A. was twenty years old when he 28.01
At that time King A. sent to the 28.16
low because of A. king of Israel, 28.19
For A. took from the house of the 28.21
to the LORD—this same King A. 28.22
And A. gathered together the 28.24
And A. slept with his fathers, and 28.27
which King A. discarded in his 29.19
A., and Hezekiah, kings of Judah. Is 1.01
In the days of A. the son of Jotham, 7.01
to Isaiah, "Go forth to meet A., 7.03
Again the LORD spoke to A., 7.10
But A. said, "I will not ask, and I 7.12
year that King A. died came this 14.28
on the dial of A. turn back ten 38.08
A., and Hezekiah, kings of Judah, and Hos 1.01
A., and Hezekiah, kings of Judah, Mic 1.01
and Jotham the father of A., Mt 1.09
and A. the father of Hezekiah, 1.09

AHAZIAH
and A. his son reigned in his stead. 1Ki 22.40
Then A. the son of Ahab said to 22.49
A. the son of Ahab began to reign 22.51
Now A. fell through the lattice in 2Ki 1.02
of Judah, because A. had no son. 1.17
of the acts of A. which he did, 1.18
and A. his son reigned in his stead. 8.24
A. the son of Jehoram, king of Judah, 8.25
A. was twenty-two years old when he 8.26
And A. the son of Jehoram king of 8.29
And A. king of Judah had come down 9.16
of Israel and A. king of Judah set 9.21
saying to A., "Treachery, O A.!" 9.23
When A. the king of Judah saw this, 9.27
A. began to reign over Judah. 9.29
the kinsmen of A. king of Judah, 10.13
answered, "We are the kinsmen of A., 10.13
the mother of A. saw that her son 11.01
sister of A., took Joash the son of A., 11.02
Jehosaphat and Jehoram and A., 12.18

AHAZIAH (cont.)
year of Joash the son of A., 2Ki 13.01
son of A., at Bethshemesh, and came 14.13
Joram his son, A. his son, Joash his 1Ch 3.11
joined with A. king of Israel, 2Ch 20.35
"Because you have joined with A., 20.37
Jerusalem made A. his youngest son 22.01
So A. the son of Jehoram king of 22.01
A. was forty-two years old when he 22.02
And A. the son of Jehoram king of 22.06
the downfall of A. should come 22.07
who attended A., and he killed them 22.08
He searched for A., and he was 22.09
the house of A. had no one able to 22.09
the mother of A. saw that her son 22.10
the king, took Joash the son of A., 22.11
because she was a sister of A., 22.11
son of A., at Bethshemesh, and 25.23

AHAZIAH'S
Judah and the sons of A. brothers, 2Ch 22.08

AHBAN
and she bore him A. and Molid. 1Ch 2.29

AHEAD
Then the angel of the LORD went a., Num 22.26
behold, he is just a. of you. 1Sa 9.12
arose, and went to Ziph a. of Saul. 23.24
Gehazi went on a. and laid the 2Ki 4.31
he had sent a man a. of them, Ps 105.17
but each shall go out straight a. Eze 46.09
towns, and got there a. of them. Mk 6.33
and Jesus was walking a. of them; 10.32
and he sent messengers a. of him, Lk 9.51
others, and sent them on a. of him, 10.01
So he ran on a. and climbed up into 19.04
he went on a., going up to Jerusalem 19.28
But going a. to the ship, we set Ac 20.13
each one goes a. with his own meal, 1Co 11.21
straining forward to what lies a., Php 3.13
Any one who goes a. and does not 2Jn 1.09

AHER
sons of Ir, Hushim the sons of A. 1Ch 7.12

AHI
A. the son of Abdiel, son of Guni, 1Ch 5.15

AHIAH
A., Hanan, Anan, Neh 10.16

AHIAM
A. the son of Sharar the Hararite, 2Sa 23.33
A. the son of Sachar the Hararite, 1Ch 11.35

AHIAN
The sons of Shemida were A., 1Ch 7.19

AHIEZER
from Dan, A. the son of Ammishaddai; Num 1.12
of Dan being A. the son of Ammishaddai, 2.25
On the tenth day A. the son of 7.66
the offering of A. the son of 7.71
their host was A. the son of 10.25
The chief was A., then Joash, both 1Ch 12.03

AHIHUD
a leader, A. the son of Shelomi. Num 34.27
who was the father of Uzza and A. 1Ch 8.07

AHIJAH
and A. the son of Ahitub, Ichabod's 1Sa 14.03
And Saul said to A., 14.18
Elihoreph and A. the sons of Shisha 1Ki 4.03
the prophet A. the Shilonite found 11.29
Now A. had clad himself with a new 11.29
Then A. laid hold of the new 11.30
LORD spoke by A. the Shilonite to 12.15
behold, A. the prophet is there, who 14.02
and came to the house of A. 14.04
Now A. could not see, for his eyes 14.04
And the LORD said to A., 14.05
But when A. heard the sound of her 14.06
by his servant A. the prophet. 14.18
Baasha the son of A., 15.27
by his servant A. the Shilonite; 15.29
the son of A. began to reign over 15.33
the house of Baasha the son of A., 21.22
the house of Baasha the son of A. 2Ki 9.09
first-born, Bunah, Oren, Ozem, and A. 1Ch 2.25
Naaman, A., and Gera, that is, Heglam, 8.07
the Mecherathite, A. the Pelonite, 11.36
A. had charge of the treasuries of 26.20
the prophecy of A. the Shilonite, 2Ch 9.29
he spoke by A. the Shilonite to 10.15

AHIKAM
and A. the son of Shaphan, and 2Ki 22.12
and A., and Achbor, and Shaphan, and 22.14
appointed Gedaliah the son of A., 25.22
A. the son of Shaphan, Abdon the son 2Ch 34.20
But the hand of A. the son of Jer 26.24
him to Gedaliah the son of A., 39.14
return to Gedaliah the son of A., 40.05
went to Gedaliah the son of A., 40.06
the son of A. governor in the land, 40.07
Gedaliah the son of A., 40.09
appointed Gedaliah the son of A., 40.11
the son of A. would not believe 40.14
the son of A. said to Johanan the 40.16
Gedaliah the son of A., at Mizpah. 41.01
struck down Gedaliah the son of A., 41.02
"Come in to Gedaliah the son of A." 41.06
committed to Gedaliah the son of A. 41.10
had slain Gedaliah the son of A.— 41.16
had slain Gedaliah the son of A., 41.18
left with Gedaliah the son of A., 43.06

AHILUD
Jehoshaphat the son of A. was recorder; 2Sa 8.16
the son of A. was the recorder; 20.24
Jehoshaphat the son of A. was recorder; 1Ki 4.03
Baana the son of A., 4.12
Jehoshaphat the son of A. was recorder; 1Ch 18.15

AHIMAAZ
was Ahinoam the daughter of A. 1Sa 14.50
A. your son, and Jonathan the son of 2Sa 15.27
A., Zadok's son, and Jonathan, Abiathar's 15.36
Now Johathan and A. were waiting at 17.17
said, "Where are A. and Jonathan?" 17.20
Then said A. the son of Zadok, "Let 18.19
Then A. the son of Zadok said again 18.22
Then A. ran by the way of the plain, 18.23
the running of A. the son of Zadok 18.27
Then A. cried out to the king, "All 18.28
A. answered, "When Joab sent your 18.29
A., in Naphtali (he had taken 1Ki 4.15
Ahitub of Zadok, Zadok of A., 1Ch 6.08
A. of Azariah, Azariah of Johanan, 6.09
Zadok his son, A. his son. 6.53

AHIMAN
and A., Sheshai, and Talmai, the Num 13.22
Sheshai and A. and Talmai, the Jos 15.14
defeated Sheshai and A. and Talmai. Ju 1.10
A., and their kinsmen (Shallum 1Ch 9.17

AHIMELECH
came David to Nob to A. the priest; 1Sa 21.01
and A. came to meet David trembling, 21.01
And David said to A. the priest, 21.02
And David said to A., "And have 21.08
to A. the son of Ahitub, 22.09
king sent to summon A. the priest, 22.11
Then A. answered the king, "And who 22.14

AHIMELECH (cont.)
A., you and all your father's house." 1Sa 22.16
of the sons of A. the son of 22.20
the son of A. fled to David to 23.06
Then David said to A. the Hittite, 26.06
the son of A., "Bring me the ephod." 30.07
of Ahitub and A. the son of 2Sa 8.17
of Ahitub and A. the son of 1Ch 18.16
and A. of the sons of Ithamar, David 24.03
and A. the son of Abiathar, and the 24.06
A., and the heads of fathers' 1Ch 24.31

AHIMOTH
The sons of Elkanah: Amasai and A., 1Ch 6.25

AHINADAB
A. the son of Iddo, in Mahanaim; 1Ki 4.14

AHINOAM
Saul's wife was A. the daughter of 1Sa 14.50
David also took A. of Jezreel; 25.43
A. of Jezreel, and Abigail of Carmel, 27.03
A. of Jezreel, and Abigail the widow 30.05
A. of Jezreel, and Abigail the widow 2Sa 2.02
was Amnon, of A. of Jezreel; 3.02
by A. the Jezreelitess; the 1Ch 3.01

AHIO
and Uzzah and A., the sons of 2Sa 6.03
and A. went before the ark. 6.04
and A., Shashak, and Jeremoth 1Ch 8.14
Gedor, A., Zecher, 8.31
Gedor, A., Zechariah, and Mikloth; 9.37
and Uzzah and A. were driving the 13.07

AHIRA
from Naphtali, A. the son of Enan. Num 1.15
Naphtali being A. the son of Enan, 2.29
On the twelfth day A. the son of 7.78
the offering of A. the son of Enan 7.83
of Naphtali was A. the son of Enan 10.27

AHIRAM
of A., the family of the Ahiramites; Num 26.38

AHIRAMITES
of Ahiram, the family of the A.; Num 26.38

AHISAMACH
the son of A., of the tribe of Dan; Ex 31.06
the son of A. of the tribe of Dan. 35.34
with him was Oholiab the son of A., 38.23

AHISHAHAR
Chenaanah, Zethan, Tarshish, and A. 1Ch 7.10

AHISHAR
A. was in charge of the palace; 1Ki 4.06

AHITHOPHEL
he sent for A. the Gilonite, David's 2Sa 15.12
"A. is among the conspirators with 15.31
the counsel of A. into foolishness 15.31
defeat for me the counsel of A. 15.34
came to Jerusalem, and A. with him. 16.15
Then Absalom said to A., 16.20
A. said to Absalom, "Go in to your 16.21
counsel which A. gave was as if 16.23
was all the counsel of A. esteemed, 16.23
Moreover A. said to Absalom, "Let me 17.01
said to him, "Thus has A. spoken; 17.06
counsel which A. has given is not 17.07
is better than the counsel of A. 17.14
to defeat the good counsel of A., 17.14
"Thus and so did A. counsel Absalom 17.15
thus and so has A. counseled 17.21
When A. saw that his counsel was 17.23
Eliam the son of A. of Gilo, 23.34
A. was the king's counselor, and 1Ch 27.33
A. was succeeded by Jehoiada the 27.34

AHITUB
and Ahijah the son of A., 1Sa 14.03
Nob, to Ahimelech the son of A., 22.09
the son of A., and all his father's 22.11
And Saul said, "Hear now, son of A." 22.12
sons of Ahimelech the son of A., 22.20
the son of A. and Ahimelech the 2Sa 8.17
Meraioth of Amariah, Amariah of A., 1Ch 6.07
A. of Zadok, Zadok of Ahimaaz, 6.08
father of Amariah, Amariah of A., 6.11
A. of Zadok, Zadok of Shallum, 6.12
son, Amariah his son, A. his son, 6.52
son of A., the chief officer of the 9.11
the son of A. and Ahimelech the 18.16
Shallum, son of Zadok, son of A., Ez 7.02
son of A., the ruler of the house of Neh 11.11

AHLAB
or of A., or of Achzib, or of Helbah, Ju 1.31

AHLAI
The sons of Sheshan: A. 1Ch 2.31
Uriah the Hittite, Zabad the son of A., 11.41

AHOAH
Abishua, Naaman, A., 1Ch 8.04

AHOHI
Eleazar the son of Dodo, son of A. 2Sa 23.09

AHOHITE
Zalmon the A., Maharai of Netophah, 2Sa 23.28
Eleazar the son of Dodo, the A. 1Ch 11.12
Sibbecai the Hushathite, Ilai the A., 11.29
Dodai the A. was in charge of the 27.04

AHUMAI
was the father of A. and Lahad. 1Ch 4.02

AHUZZAM
Naarah bore him A., Hepher, Temeni, 1Ch 4.06

AHUZZATH
from Gerar with A. his adviser and Gen 26.26

AHZAI
son of A., son of Meshillemoth, son Neh 11.13

AI
on the west and A. on the east; Gen 12.08
beginning, between Bethel and A., 13.03
Joshua sent men from Jericho to A., Jos 7.02
the men went up and spied out A. 7.02
thousand men go up and attack A.; 7.03
they fled before the men of A., 7.04
and the men of A. killed about 7.05
with you, and arise, go up to A.; 8.01
into your hand the king of A., 8.01
and you shall do to A. and its king 8.02
the fighting men, to go up to A.; 8.03
and lay between Bethel and A., 8.09
to the west of A.; but Joshua 8.09
of Israel, before the people to A. 8.10
encamped on the north side of A., 8.11
with a ravine between them and A. 8.11
in ambush between Bethel and A., 8.12
the king of A. saw this he and all 8.14
was not a man left in A. or Bethel, 8.17
that is in your hand toward A.; 8.18
So when the men of A. looked back, 8.20
back and smote the men of A. 8.21
But the king of A. they took alive, 8.23
inhabitants of A. in the open 8.24
sword, all Israel returned to A., 8.24
thousand, all the people of A. 8.25

AI (cont.)
destroyed all the inhabitants of A. Jos 8.26
So Joshua burned A., and made 8.28
the king of A. on a tree until 8.29
had done to Jericho and to A., 9.03
heard how Joshua had taken A., 10.01
doing to A. and its king as he had 10.01
and because it was greater than A., 10.02
the king of A., which is beside 12.09
The men of Bethel and A., Ez 2.28
The men of Bethel and A., Neh 7.32
"Wail, O Heshbon, for A. is laid waste! Jer 49.03

AIAH
the sons of Zibeon: A. and Anah; Gen 36.24
was Rizpah, the daughter to A.; 2Sa 3.07
sons of Rizpah the daughter of A., 21.08
the daughter of A. took sackcloth, 21.10
what Rizpah the daughter of A., 21.11
The sons of Zibeon: A. and Anah. 1Ch 1.40

AIATH
he has come to A.; he has passed Is 10.28

AID
the son of Zeruiah came to his a., 2Sa 21.17
O thou my help, hasten to my a.! Ps 22.19
but did not a. the poor and needy. Eze 16.49
when they turn to them for a. 29.16
he who gives a., with zeal; Rom 12.08
Jerusalem with a. for the saints. 15.25

AIDE
Jehu said to Bidkar his a., "Take him 2Ki 9.25

AIDED
were about them a. them with Ez 1.06
so that he a. them in the work of 6.22
and they a. the people and the 8.36

AIJA
A., Bethel and its villages, Neh 11.31

AIJALON
and thou Moon in the valley of A. Jos 10.12
Shaalabbin, A., Ithlah, 19.42
A. with its pasture lands, Gathrimmon 21.24
in A., and in Shaalbim, but the hand Ju 1.35
was buried at A. in the land of 12.12
that day from Michmash to A. 1Sa 14.31
A. with its pasture lands, Gathrimmon 1Ch 6.69
houses of the inhabitants of A., 8.13
Zorah, A., and Hebron, fortified 2Ch 11.10
A., Gederoth, Soco with its villages, 28.18

AILMENT
of a bodily a. that I preached the Gal 4.13

AILMENTS
your stomach and your frequent a. 1Ti 5.23

AILS
"What a. you that you come with Ju 18.23
then do you ask me, 'What a. you?'" 18.24
"What a. the people, that they are 1Sa 11.05
What a. you, O sea, that you flee? Ps 114.05

AIM
you will a. at their faces with Ps 21.12
who a. bitter words like arrows, 64.03
Make love your a., and earnestly 1Co 14.01
we make it our a. to please him. 2Co 5.09
for we a. at what is honorable not 8.21
whereas the a. of our charge is 1Ti 1.05
a. at righteousness, godliness, faith, 6.11
since his a. is to satisfy the one 2Ti 2.04
passions and a. at righteousness, 2.22
my a. in life, my faith, my patience, 3.10

AIMLESSLY
I do not run a., I do not box as 1Co 9.26

AIN
to Riblah on the east side of A.; Num 34.11
A., and Rimmon: in all, twenty-nine Jos 15.32
A. with its pasture lands, Juttah 21.16
A., Rimmon, Tochen, and Ashan, five 1Ch 4.32

AIR
sea, and over the birds of the a., Gen 1.26
birds of the a. and over every 1.28
earth, and to every bird of the a., 1.30
the field and every bird of the a., 2.19
cattle, and to the birds of the a., 2.20
creeping things and birds of the a., 6.07
pairs of the birds of the a. also, 7.03
creeping things and birds of the a.; 7.23
and upon every bird of the a., 9.02
winged bird that flies in the a., Deu 4.17
be food for all birds of the a., 28.26
birds of the a. and to the beasts 1Sa 17.44
birds of the a. and to the wild 17.46
birds of the a. to come upon them 2Sa 21.10
the birds of the a. shall eat; 1Ki 14.11
the birds of the a. shall eat. 16.04
the birds of the a. shall eat. 21.24
the birds of the a., and they Job 12.07
concealed from the birds of the a. 28.21
us wiser than the birds of the a.? 35.11
another that no a. can come 41.16
the birds of the a., and the Ps 8.08
I know all the birds of the a., 50.11
to the birds of the a. for food, 79.02
birds of the a. have their habitation 104.12
a bird of the a. will carry your Ecc 10.20
all the birds of the a. had fled. Jer 4.25
be food for the birds of the a., 7.33
birds of the a. and the beasts 9.10
they pant for a. like jackals; 14.06
birds of the a. and the beasts of 15.03
birds of the a. and for the beasts 16.04
birds of the a. and to the beasts 19.07
birds of the a. and the beasts of 34.20
birds of the a. I have given you Eze 29.05
birds of the a. made their nests 31.06
will dwell all the birds of the a., 31.13
birds of the a. to settle on you, 32.04
the sea, and the birds of the a., 38.20
the field, and the birds of the a., Dan 2.38
birds of the a. dwelt in its 4.12
the birds of the a. dwelt— 4.21
of the field, the birds of the a., Hos 2.18
the field, and the birds of the a.; 4.03
them down like birds of the a.; 7.12
birds of the a. and the fish of Zep 1.03
Look at the birds of the a.: Mt 6.26
and birds of the a. have nests; 8.20
birds of the a. come and make 13.32
birds of the a. can make nests in Mk 4.32
the birds of the a. devoured it. Lk 8.05
and birds of the a. have nests; 9.58
birds of the a. made nests in its 13.19
and reptiles and birds of the a. Ac 10.12
and reptiles and birds of the a. 11.06
and threw dust into the a., 22.23
I do not box as one beating the a.; 1Co 9.26
you will be speaking into the a. 14.09
the prince of the power of the a., Eph 2.02
clouds to meet the Lord in the a.; 1Th 4.17
the sun and the a. were darkened Rev 9.02
angel poured his bowl into the a., 16.17

AIRS
or puts on a., or strikes you in 2Co 11.20

AKAN
of Ezer: Bilhan, Zaavan, and A. Gen 36.27

AKELDAMA
was called in their language a., Ac 1.19

AKKUB
A., Johanan, Delaiah, and Anani, seven 1Ch 3.24
A., Talmon, Ahiman, and their kinsmen 9.17
the sons of A., the sons of Hatita, Ez 2.42
sons of Hagabah, the sons of A., 2.45
the sons of A., the sons of Hatita, Neh 7.45
A., Shabbethai, Hodiah, Maaseiah, 8.07
A., Talmon and their brethren, who 11.19
and A. were gatekeepers standing 12.25

AKRABBIM
turn south of the ascent of A., Num 34.04
out southward of the ascent of A., Jos 15.03
Amorites ran from the ascent of A., Ju 1.36

ALABASTER
His legs are a. columns, set upon Sol 5.15
to him with an a. jar of very Mt 26.07
came with an a. jar of ointment of Mk 14.03
brought an a. flask of ointment, Lk 7.37

ALAMOTH
were to play harps according to A.; 1Ch 15.20

ALARM
When you blow an a., Num 10.05
you blow an a. the second time, the 10.06
An a. is to be blown whenever they 10.06
but you shall not sound an a. 10.07
shall sound an a. with the trumpets, 10.09
trumpets for the a. in his hand. 31.06
I had said in my a., Ps 31.22
of the trumpet, and a. of war. Jer 4.19
in the morning and an a. at noon, 20.16
The nations sounded an a. against him; Eze 19.04
dream or the interpretation a. you." Dan 4.19
your thoughts a. you or your color 5.10
east and the north shall a. him, 11.44
Sound the a. at Bethaven; Hos 5.08
sound the a. on my holy mountain! Joe 2.01
what a., what longing, what zeal, 2Co 7.11

ALARMED
and the visions of my head a. me. Dan 4.05
long time, and his thoughts a. him. 4.19
changed, and his thoughts a. him; 5.06
Then King Belshazzar was greatly a., 5.09
and the visions of my head a. me. 7.15
Daniel, my thoughts greatly a. me, 7.28
see that you are not a.; Mt 24.06
and rumors of wars, do not be a.; Mk 13.07
"Do not be a., for his life is in Ac 20.10
Felix was a. and said, "Go away for 24.25

ALARMS
at his thigh, against a. by night. Sol 3.08

ALAS
"A., this people have sinned a Ex 32.31
"A., who shall live when God does Num 24.23
"A., O Lord God, why hast thou Jos 7.07
and Gideon said, "A., O Lord God! Ju 6.22
clothes, and said, "A., my daughter! 11.35
She answered, "A., I am a widow; 2Sa 14.05
over him, saying, "A., my brother!" 1Ki 13.30
Then the king of Israel said, "A.! 2Ki 3.10
and he cried out. "A., my master! 6.05
the servant said, "A., my master! 6.15
A.! that day is so great Jer 30.07
lament for you, saying, "A., lord!"' 34.05
and stamp your foot, and say, A.! Eze 6.11
Lord God: "Wail, 'A. for the day!' 30.02
A. for the day! For the day Joe 1.15
the streets they shall say, 'A.! a.!' Amo 5.16
And a. for those who are with child Mt 24.19
And a. for those who are with child Mk 13.17
A. for those who are with child and Lk 21.23
fear of her torment, and say, "A.! a.! Rev 18.10
"A., a., for the great city that 18.16
"A., a., for the great city where 18.19

ALEMETH
A., with its pasture lands, and 1Ch 6.60
Jeremoth, Abijah, Anathoth, and A. 7.08
and Jehoaddah was the father of A., 8.36
and Jarah of A., Azmaveth, and Zimri 9.42

ALERT
Therefore be a., remembering that Ac 20.31
that end keep a. with all perseverance, Eph 6.18

ALEXANDER
the father of A. and Rufus, to carry Mk 15.21
and Caiaphas and John and A., Ac 4.06
Some of the crowd prompted A., 19.33
And A. motioned with his hand, 19.33
among them Hymenaeus and A., 1Ti 1.20
A. the coppersmith did me great 2Ti 4.14

ALEXANDRIA
a native of A., came to Ephesus. Ac 18.24
found a ship of A. sailing for 27.06
a ship of A., with the Twin Brothers 28.11

ALEXANDRIANS
and of the A., and of those from Ac 6.09

ALGUM
and a. timber from Lebanon, for I 2Ch 2.08
brought a. wood and precious stones 9.10
made of the a. wood steps for the 9.11

ALIAH
were: chiefs Timna, A., Jetheth, 1Ch 1.51

ALIAN
A., Manahath, Ebal, Shephi, and Onam. 1Ch 1.40

ALIEN
and the a., may be refreshed. Ex 23.12
brother or the a. that is with him Deu 1.16
give it to the a. who is within 14.21
I have become an a. in their eyes. Job 19.15
an a. to my mother's sons. Ps 69.08
labors go to the house of an a.; Pro 5.10
and set out slips of an a. god, Is 17.10
and with an a. tongue the Lord 28.11
and to work his work—a. is his work! 28.21
if you do not oppress the a., Jer 7.06
do no wrong or violence to the a., 22.03
In whatever tribe the a. resides, Eze 47.23
for they have borne a. children. Hos 5.07

ALIENATE
they shall not a. this choice Eze 48.14

ALIENATED
O Jerusalem, lest I be a. from you; Jer 6.08
a. from the commonwealth of Israel, Eph 2.12
a. from the life of God because of 4.18

ALIENATES
who repeats a matter a. a friend. Pro 17.09

ALIENS
together the a. who were in the 1Ch 22.02
of all the a. who were in the land 2Ch 2.17
many waters, from the hand of a., Ps 144.07
and deliver me from the hand of a., 144.11
very presence a. devour your land; Is 1.07
is desolate, as overthrown by a. 1.07
and a. will join tnem and will 14.01
the palace of a. is a city no more, 25.02
dost subdue the noise of the a.; 25.05

ALIENS (cont.)
A. shall stand and feed your flocks, Is 61.05
for a. have come into the holy Jer 51.51
over to strangers, our homes to a. Lam 5.02
and for the a. who reside among Eze 47.22
A. devour his strength, and he knows Hos 7.09
a. would devour it. 8.07
would be a. in a land belonging to Ac 7.06
beseech you as a. and exiles to 1Pe 2.11

ALIGHT
curse that is causeless does not a. Pro 26.02
yea, there shall the night hag a., Is 34.14
kindle a fire, who set brands a.! 50.11

ALIGHTED
she a. from the camel, Gen 24.64
and she a. from her ass, and Caleb Jos 15.18
and she a. from her ass, and Caleb Ju 1.14
and Sisera a. from his chariot and 4.15
and a. from the ass, and fell before 1Sa 25.23
he a. from the chariot to meet him, 2Ki 5.21

ALIGHTING
descending like a dove, and a. on him; Mt 3.16

ALIKE
hear the small and the great a.; Deu 1.17
and the clean a. may eat of it. 12.22
and the clean a. may eat it, 15.22
sweeping away of moist and dry a. 29.19
they shall share a." 1Sa 30.24
all of them were cast a., 1Ki 7.37
all a., for there were officers of 1Ch 24.05
house and his younger brother a., 24.31
and great, teacher and pupil a. 25.08
fathers' houses, small and great a., 26.13
old and young a., by divisions, 2Ch 31.15
all a. are to be put to death, Est 4.11
They lie down a. in the dust, and Job 21.26
astray, they are all a. corrupt; Ps 14.03
and the stupid a. must perish and 49.10
they are all a. depraved; 53.03
Singers and dancers a. say, 87.07
are both a. an abomination to the Pro 17.15
are both a. an abomination to the 20.10
day and a contentious woman are a.; 27.15
or whether both a. will be good. Ecc 11.06
and compare me, that we may be a.? Is 46.05
"But they all a. had broken the Jer 5.05
of the inquirer shall be a.— Eze 14.10
But they all a. began to make Lk 14.18
another man esteems all days a. Rom 14.05
For not all flesh is a., 1Co 15.39

ALIVE
the ark, to keep them a. with you; Gen 6.19
come in to you, to keep them a. 6.20
keep their kind a. upon the face 7.03
and remained a. after seeing him 16.13
saying, 'Is your father still a.? 43.07
of whom you spoke? Is he still a.?" 43.27
our father is well, he is still a." 43.28
is my father still a.?" 45.03
and to keep a. for you many survivors 45.07
And they told him, "Joseph is still a., 45.26
Joseph my son is still a.; 45.28
and know that you are still a." 46.30
that many people should be kept a., 50.20
and see whether they are still a." Ex 4.18
beast is found a. in his possession, 22.04
be presented a. before the LORD to Lev 16.10
nakedness while her sister is yet a. 18.18
the son of Jephunneh remained a., Num 14.38
and they go down a. into Sheol, 16.30
to them went down a. into Sheol; 16.33
with him, keep a. for yourselves. 31.18
LORD your God are all a. this day. Deu 4.04
who are all of us here a. this day. 5.03
that he might preserve us a., 6.24
you shall save a. nothing that 20.16
behold, while I am yet a. with you, 31.27
I kill and I make a.; 32.39
and save a. my father and mother, my Jos 2.13
belonged to her, Oshua saved a.; 6.25
But the king of Ai they took a., 8.23
behold, the LORD has kept me a., 14.10
lives, if you had saved them a., Ju 8.19
they had saved a. of the women of 21.14
Agag the king of the Amalekites a., 1Sa 15.08
If I am still a., show me the loyal 20.14
and left neither man nor woman a., 27.09
saved neither man nor woman a., 27.11
"Behold, while the child was yet a., 2Sa 12.18
wept for the child while it was a.; 12.21
said, "While the child was still a., 12.22
while he was still a. in the oak. 18.14
if Absalom were a. and all of us 19.06
says, 'This is my son that is a., 1Ki 3.23
whose son was a. said to the king, 3.26
his father while he was yet a., 12.06
and save the horses and mules a., 18.05
come out for peace, take them a.; 20.18
come out for war, take them a. 20.18
for Naboth is not a., but dead." 21.15
"Am I God, to kill and to make a., 2Ki 5.07
shall take them a. and get into 7.12
He said, "Take them a." 10.14
And they took them a., 10.14
and a hundred thousand men a. 1Ch 5.21
his father while he was yet a., 2Ch 10.06
fell until none remained a.; 14.13
captured another ten thousand a., 25.12
grain, that we may eat and keep a." Neh 5.02
He does not keep the wicked a., Job 36.06
and he who cannot keep himself a. Ps 22.29
death, and keep them a. in famine. 33.19
LORD protects him and keeps him a.; 41.02
let them go down to Sheol a.; 55.15
they would have swallowed us up a., 124.03
let us swallow them a. and whole, Pro 1.12
than the living who are still a.; Ecc 4.02
a man will keep a. a young cow and Is 7.21
children, I will keep them a.; Jer 49.11
they flung me a. into the pit and Lam 3.53
"Yet I will leave some of you a. Eze 6.08
other souls a. for your profit? 13.18
die and keeping a. persons who 13.19
slew, and whom he would he kept a.; Dan 5.19
and one third shall be left a. Zec 13.08
which today is a. and tomorrow is Mt 6.30
said, while he was still a. 27.63
grass which is a. in the field Lk 12.28
my son was dead, and is a. again; 15.24
your brother was dead, and is a.; 15.32
of angels, who said that he was a. 24.23
presented himself a. after his Ac 1.03
that they might not be kept a. 7.19
and widows he presented her a. 9.41
And they took the lad away a., 20.12
but whom Paul asserted to be a. 25.19
dead to sin and a. to God in Rom 6.11
man while her husband is a. 7.03
I was once a. apart from the law, 7.09
spirits are a. because of righteousness 8.10
time, most of whom are still a., 1Co 15.06
in Christ shall all be made a. 15.
had been given which could make a., Gal
And you he made a., Ep
made us a. together with Christ (by
God made a. together with him,
of the Lord, that we who are a.,
then we who are a., who are
long as the one who made it is a.

ALIVE (cont.)
flesh but made a. in the spirit; 1Pe 3.18
and behold I am a. for evermore, Rev 1.18
you have the name of being a., 3.01
two were thrown a. into the lake 19.20

ALLAMMELECH
A., Amad, and Mishal; on the Jos 19.26

ALLEGIANCE
kept their a. to the house of Saul 1Ch 12.29
pledged their a. to King Solomon. 29.24
and swear a. to the LORD of hosts. Is 19.18

ALLEGORICALLY
city which is a. called Sodom and Rev 11.08

ALLEGORIES
of me, 'Is he not a maker of a.?' " Eze 20.49

ALLEGORY
and speak an a. to the house of Eze 17.02
And utter an a. to the rebellious 24.03
Now this is an a.: these women are Gal 4.24

ALLIANCE
Solomon made a marriage a. with 1Ki 3.01
he made a marriage a. with Ahab. 2Ch 18.01
After some years they shall make an a., Dan 11.06
time that an a. is made with him 11.23

ALLIED
Can wicked rulers be a. with thee, Ps 94.20

ALLIES
these were a. of Abram. Gen 14.13
Though they hire a. among the Hos 8.10
All your a. have deceived you, they Ob 1.07

ALLON
son of A., son of Jedaiah, son of 1Ch 4.37

ALLONBACUTH
so the name of it was called A. Gen 35.08

ALLOT
only a. the land of Israel for an Jos 13.06
and didst a. to them every corner; Neh 9.22
"When you a. the land as a possession, Eze 45.01
You shall a. it as an inheritance 47.22
which you shall a. as an inheritance 48.29

ALLOTMENT
The a. of the descendants of Joseph Jos 16.01
Then a. was made to the tribe of 17.01
shall have an a. measuring twenty-five Eze 48.10
shall have an a. twenty-five 48.13

ALLOTMENTS
according to their tribal a. Jos 11.23
possession according to their a., 12.07
And a. were made to the rest of the 17.02
These shall be the a. of the holy Eze 48.10

ALLOTTED
your God has a. to all the peoples Deu 4.19
nd whom he had not a. to them; 29.26
people, Jacob his a. heritage. 32.09
a. to the half-tribe of the Jos 13.29
ere a. to the people of 13.31
led Moses; they a. the land. 14.05
ad and Bashan, because 17.01
a. to the rest of 17.06
o it fell 18.11
n were out of 21.20
e in all twelve 21.40
u as an 23.04
me, Ju 1.03
you." 1.03

families were a. thirteen cities 1Ch 6.62
families were a. twelve cities out 6.63
Merarites were a. out of the tribe 6.77
to his sons was a. the storehouse. 26.15
so I am a. months of emptiness, and Job 7.03
upon the land a. to the righteous. Ps 125.03
and diminished your a. portion, Eze 16.27
they shall be a. an inheritance 47.22
stand in your a. place at the end Dan 12.13
and was a. his share in this Ac 1.17
determined a. periods and the 17.26

ALLOW
"If you will a. me to say so, I have Gen 30.27
and will not a. the destroyer to Ex 12.23
But Sihon would not a. Israel to Num 21.23
they did not a. them to come down Ju 1.34
father would not a. him to go in. 15.01
and she did not a. the birds of the 2Sa 21.10
the eunuchs to a. him not to Dan 1.08
nor a. those who would enter to go Mt 23.13
and he would not a. any one to Mk 11.16
and would not a. them to speak, Lk 4.41
Spirit of Jesus did not a. them; Ac 16.07
as the wind did not a. us to go on, 27.07

ALLOWANCE
had a fixed a. from Pharaoh, Gen 47.22
lived on the a. which Pharaoh gave 47.22
and assigned him an a. of food, 1Ki 11.18
for his a., a regular a. was given him 2Ki 25.30
ate the food a. of the governor Neh 5.14
demand the food a. of the governor, 5.18
gave him an a. of food and a Jer 40.05
as for his a., a regular a. was given 52.34

ALLOWED
your God has not a. you so to do. Deu 18.14
and a. not a man to pass over. Ju 3.28
he a. no one to oppress them; 1Ch 16.21
By these the king a. the Jews who Est 8.11
are in Susa be a. tomorrow also to 9.13
he a. no one to oppress them; Ps 105.14
of heart Moses a. you to divorce Mt 19.08
Am I not a. to do what I choose 20.15
And he a. no one to follow him Mk 5.37
"Moses a. a man to write a certificate 10.04
generations he a. all the nations Ac 14.16
justice has not a. him to live." 28.04
Paul was a. to stay by himself, with 28.16
they were a. to torture them for Rev 9.05
and it was a. to exercise authority 13.05
Also it was a. to make war on the 13.07
which it is a. to work in the 13.14
and it was a. to give breath to the 13.15
and it was a. to scorch men with 16.08

ALLOWS
"The man who a. any of those whom I 2Ki 10.24

ALLOY
as with lye and remove all your a. Is 1.25

ALLURE
I will a. her, and bring her into Hos 2.14

ALLURED
He also a. you out of distree into Job 36.16

ALMIGHTY
and said to him, "I am God A.; Gen 17.01
God A. bless you and make you 28.03
"I am God A.: be fruitful and 35.11
may God A. grant you mercy before 43.14
"God A. appeared to me at Luz in 48.03
by God A. who will bless you with 49.25
as God A., but by my name the LORD Ex 6.03
God, who sees the vision of the A., Num 24.04

ALMIGHTY (cont.)
who sees the vision of the A., Num 24.16
for the A. has dealt very bitterly Ru 1.20
me and the A. has brought calamity 1.21
not the chastening of the A. Job 5.17
For the arrows of the A. are in me; 6.04
friend forsakes the fear of the A. 6.14
Or does the A. pervert the right 8.03
and make supplication to the A., 8.05
you find out the limit of the A.? 11.07
But I would speak to the A., 13.03
God, and bids defiance to the A., 15.25
What is the A., that we should 21.15
them drink of the wrath of the A. 21.20
pleasure to the A. if you are 22.03
us,' and 'What can the A. do to us?' 22.17
return to the A. and humble 22.23
and if the A. is your gold, and your 22.25
will delight yourself in the A., 22.26
the A. has terrified me; 23.16
times of judgment kept by the A., 24.01
and the A., who has made my soul 27.02
Will he take delight in the A.? 27.10
is with the A. I will not conceal. 27.11
oppressors receive from the A.: 27.13
when the A. was yet with me, when my 29.05
my heritage from the A. on high? 31.02
signature! let the A. answer me!) 31.35
in a man, the breath of the A., 32.08
the breath of the A. gives me life. 33.04
and from the A. that he should do 34.10
and the A. will not pervert justice 34.12
cry, nor does the A. regard it. 35.13
The A.—we cannot find him; 37.23
"Shall a faultfinder contend with the A.? 40.02
When the A. scattered kings there, Ps 68.14
abides in the shadow of the A., 91.01
destruction from the A. it will come! Is 13.06
waters, like the thunder of the A., Eze 1.24
the voice of God A. when he speaks. 10.05
destruction from the A. it comes. Joe 1.15
and daughters, says the Lord A. 2Co 6.18
who was and who is to come, the A. Rev 1.08
holy, holy, is the Lord God A., 4.08
Lord God A, who art and who wast, 11.17
are thy deeds, O Lord God the A.! 15.03
Lord God the A., true and just are 16.07
on the great day of God the A. 16.14
For the Lord our God the A. reigns. 19.06
fury of the wrath of God the A. 19.15
the Lord God the A. and the Lamb. 21.22

ALMODAD
Joktan became the father of A., Gen 10.26
Joktan was the father of A., 1Ch 1.20

ALMON
and A. with its pasture lands—four Jos 21.18

ALMOND
rods of poplar and a. and plane, Gen 30.37
the a. tree blossoms, the grasshopper Ecc 12.05
And I said, "I see a rod of a." Jer 1.11

ALMONDIBLATHAIM
from Dibongad, and encamped at A. Num 33.46
And they set out from A., 33.47

ALMONDS
gum, myrrh, pistachio nuts, and a. Gen 43.11
three cups made like a., each Ex 25.33
and three cups made like a., 25.33
itself four cups made like a., 25.34
three cups made like a., each with 37.19
and three cups made like a., 37.19
itself were four cups made like a., 37.20
blossoms, and it bore ripe a. Num 17.08

ALMOST
They are a. ready to stone me. Ex 17.04
my feet had a. stumbled, my steps Ps 73.02
They have a. made an end of me on 119.87
The next sabbath a. the whole city Ac 13.44
at Ephesus but a. throughout all 19.26
When the seven days were a. completed, 21.27
under the law a. everything is Heb 9.22

ALMS
when you give a., sound no trumpet Mt 6.02
But when you give a., 6.03
so that your a. may be in secret; 6.04
But give for a. those things which Lk 11.41
Sell your possessions, and give a.; 12.33
Beautiful to ask a. of those who Ac 3.02
into the temple, he asked for a. 3.03
one who sat for a. at the Beautiful 3.10
gave a. liberally to the people, and 10.02
and your a. have ascended as a 10.04
heard and your a. have been 10.31
to my nation a. and offerings. 24.17

ALMUG
great amount of a. wood and 1Ki 10.11
made of the a. wood supports for 10.12
no such a. wood has come or been 10.12

ALOES
like a. that the LORD has planted, Num 24.06
with myrrh and a. and cassia. Ps 45.08
bed with myrrh, a., and cinnamon. Pro 7.17
myrrh and a., with all chief spices Sol 4.14
bringing a mixture of myrrh and a., Jn 19.39

ALOFT
it towered a. among the thick Eze 19.11
Though you soar a. like the eagle, Ob 1.04
shall remain a. upon its site from Zec 14.10

ALONE
not good that the man should be a.; Gen 2.18
And Jacob was left a.; 32.24
and he a. is left of his mother's 44.20
of the priests a. did not become 47.26
So he let him a. Ex 4.26
'Let us a. and let us serve the 14.12
Why do you sit a., and all 18.14
you are not able to perform it a. 18.18
master's and he shall go out a. 21.04
Moses a. shall come near to the 24.02
now therefore let me a., 32.10
he shall dwell a. in a habitation Lev 13.46
able to carry all this people, a., Num 11.14
you may not bear it yourself a. 11.17
lo, a people dwelling a., 23.09
you, 'I am not able a. to bear you; Deu 1.09
How can I bear a. the weight and 1.12
that man does not live by bread a., 8.03
let me a., that I may destroy them 9.14
the LORD a. did lead him, and there 32.12
safety, the fountain of Jacob a., 33.28
and in Edrei (he a. was left of the Jos 13.12
tribe of Levi a. Moses gave no 13.14
did not perish a. for his iniquity 22.20
he was sitting a. in his cool roof Ju 3.20
if there is dew on the fleece a., 6.37
let me a. two months, that I may go 11.37
"Why are you a., and no one with 1Sa 21.01
"Upon me a., my lord, be the guilt; 25.24
for Amnon a. is dead, for by the 2Sa 13.32
are dead; for Amnon a. is dead." 13.33
Let him a., and let him curse; 16.11
looked, he saw a man running a. 18.24
"If he is a., there are tidings in 18.25
said, "See, another man running a.!" 18.26
give up him a., and I will withdraw 20.21

ALONE (cont.)

and we were a.; there was no one 1Ki 3.18
of them were a. in the open 11.29
"Let her a., for she is in bitter 2Ki 4.27
thou a., of all the kingdoms of the 19.15
know that thou, O LORD, art God a." 19.19
So they let his bones a., 23.18
whom a. God has chosen, is young and 1Ch 29.01
but we a. will build to the LORD, Ez 4.03
let the work on this house of God a.; 6.07
said: "Thou art the LORD, thou a.; Neh 9.06
to lay hands on Mordecai a. Est 3.06
and I a. have escaped to tell you." Job 1.15
and I a. have escaped to tell you." 1.16
and I a. have escaped to tell you." 1.17
and I a. have escaped to tell you." 1.19
Let me a., for my days are a breath 7.16
nor let me a. till I swallow my 7.19
who a. stretched out the heavens, 9.08
Let me a., that I may find a little 10.20
to whom a. the land was given, and 15.19
or have eaten my morsel a., 31.17
for thou a., O LORD, makest me dwell Ps 4.08
For God a. my soul waits in silence; 62.01
For God a. my soul waits in silence, 62.05
praise thy righteousness, thine a. 71.16
who a. does wondrous things. 72.18
Let them know that thou a., 83.18
wondrous things, thou a. art God. 86.10
to him who a. does great wonders, 136.04
LORD, for his name a. is exalted; 148.13
Let them be for yourself a., Pro 5.17
if you scoff, you a. will bear it. 9.12
to him who is a. when he falls and Ecc 4.10
but how can one be warm a.? 4.11
prevail against one who is a., 4.12
Behold, this a. I found, that God 7.29
and the LORD a. will be exalted in Is 2.11
and the LORD a. will be exalted in 2.17
made to dwell a. in the midst of 5.08
us, but thy name a. we acknowledge. 26.13
thou a., of all the kingdoms of the 37.16
may know that thou a. art the LORD." 37.20
who stretched out the heavens a., 44.24
Behold, I was left a.; 49.21
"I have trodden the wine press a., 63.03
I sat a., because thy hand was upon Jer 15.17
no gates or bars, that dwells a. 49.31
Let him sit a. in silence when he Lam 3.28
were smiting, and I was left a., Eze 9.08
they a. would be delivered, but the 14.16
but they a. would be delivered. 14.18
who a. among the sons of Levi may 40.46
And I, Daniel, a. saw the vision, for Dan 10.07
So I was left a. and saw this great 10.08
Ephraim is joined to idols, let him a. Hos 4.17
Assyria, a wild ass wandering a.; 8.09
who dwell a. in a forest in the Mic 7.14
'Man shall not live by bread a.,' Mt 4.04
evening came, he was there a., 14.23
Let them a.; they are blind 15.14
his fault, between you and him a. 18.15
Who can forgive sins but God a.?" Mk 2.07
And when he was a., those who 4.10
the sea, and he was a. on the land. 6.47
No one is good but God a. 10.18
But Jesus said, "Let her a.; 14.06
'Man shall not live by bread a.'" Lk 4.04
he was praying a. the disciples 9.18
had spoken, Jesus was found a. 9.36
my sister has left me to serve a.? 10.40
'Let it a., sir, this year also, till 13.08
No one is good but God a. 18.19
his disciples had gone away a. Jn 6.22
Jesus was left a. with the woman * 8.09
for it is not I a. that judge, 8.16
he has not left me a., 8.29
"Let her a., let her keep it for 12.07
the earth and dies, it remains a.; 12.24
to his home, and will leave me a.; 16.32
yet I am not a., for the Father is 16.32
from these men and let them a.; Ac 5.38
were written not for his sake a., Rom 4.23
and I a. am left, and they seek my 11.03
be in himself a. and not in his Gal 6.04
to be left behind at Athens a., 1Th 3.01
a real widow, and is left all a., 1Ti 5.05
who a. has immortality and dwells 6.16
Luke a. is with me. Get Mark 2Ti 4.11
by works and not by faith a. Jas 2.24
For thou a. art holy. Rev 15.04

ALONG

a. with the child, and sent her away. Gen 21.14
of cloud to lead them a. the way, Ex 13.21
a. with the log of oil, and wave Lev 14.12
a. with a cereal offering; 14.31
a. with the living bird, and dip 14.51
their ancestral tribe a. with them. Num 1.47
by the sea, and a. the Jordan. 13.29
we will go a. the King's Highway, we 20.17
wilderness of Zin a. the side of 34.03
Hazaraddar, and pass a. to Azmon; 34.04
made search all a. the way and Jos 2.22
the lowland all a. the coast of 9.01
passes a. to Zin, and goes up south 15.03
a. by Hezron, up to Addar, turns 15.03
passes a. to Azmon, goes out by the 15.04
and passes a. north of Betharabah; 15.06
boundary passes a. to the waters 15.07
passes a. to the northern shoulder 15.10
Bethshemesh, and passes a. by Timnah; 15.10
and passes a. to Mount Baalah, and 15.11
it passes a. to Ataroth, the territory 16.02
and passes a. beyond it on the east 16.06
an inheritance a. with our brethren 17.04
an inheritance a. with his sons. 17.06
boundary goes a. southward to the 17.07
boundary passes a. southward in 18.13
there it passes a. on the east 19.13
a. with their pasture lands for our 21.02
a. with the pasture lands round 21.11
a. with all the nations that I have 23.04
of the East lay a. the valley like Ju 7.12
all who passed by them a. that way; 9.25
for all a. I have been speaking out 1Sa 1.16
a. with a three-year-old bull, an 1.24
of Bethshemesh a. one highway, 6.12
a. with his men, and killed two 18.27
Shimei went a. on the hillside 2Sa 16.13
a. with all their villages which 1Ch 4.33
and a. with them, by their generations, 7.04
also a. the borders of the Manassites, 7.29
The number of them a. with their 25.07
a. with the sons of Henadad and the Ez 3.09
whatever passes a. the paths of Ps 8.08
they are led a. as they enter the 45.15
all who pass a. the way pluck its 80.12
passing a. the street near her Pro 7.08
with a pestle a. with crushed 27.22
drags itself a. and desire fails; Ecc 12.05
mincing a. as they go, tinkling with Is 3.16
They shall feed a. the ways, 49.09
bound in chains a. with all the Jer 40.01
All who pass a. the way clap their Lam 2.15
and the wheels rose a. with them; Eze 1.20
the wheels rose a. with them; 1.21
I will give it a. with the Ammonites 25.10
pavement ran a. the side of the 40.18
he led me back a. the bank of the 47.06
a. the Jordan between Gilead and 47.18
thence a. the Brook of Egypt to the 47.19
thence a. the Brook of Egypt to the 48.28
sowed, some seeds fell a. the path, Mt 13.04

ALONG (cont.)

this is what was sown a. the path. Mt 13.19
you root up the wheat a. with them. 13.29
and passed a. the Sea of Galilee. 15.29
take one or two others a. with you, 18.16
a. with the Herodians, saying, 22.16
And passing a. by the Sea of Mk 1.16
sowed, some seed fell a. the path, 4.04
And these are the ones a. the path, 4.15
some fell a. the path, and was Lk 8.05
The ones a. the path are those who 8.12
As they were going a. the road, 9.57
he was passing a. between Samaria 17.11
And as he rode a., they spread 19.36
of the high priest a. with Jesus, Jn 18.15
And as they went a. the road they Ac 8.36
For as I passed a., and observed 17.23
purify yourself a. with them and 21.24
You therefore, a. with the council, 23.15
to the ports a. the coast of Asia, 27.02
Coasting a. it with difficulty, we 27.08
weighed anchor and sailed a. Crete, 27.13
not be condemned a. with the world. 1Co 11.32
thinking all a. that we have been 2Co 12.19
Barnabas, taking Titus a. with me. Gal 2.01
a. with those who call upon the 2Ti 2.22
faith was active a. with his works, Jas 2.22
clouds, carried a. by winds; Jud 1.12

ALONGSIDE

"A. the portion set apart as the Eze 45.06
a. the holy district and the 45.07
And a. the territory of the priests, 48.13
of the length a. the holy portion 48.18
and it shall be a. the holy 48.18

ALOOF

you yourself would have stood a." 2Sa 18.13
They abhor me, they keep a. from me; Job 30.10
companions stand a. from my plague, Ps 38.11
for a man to keep a. from strife; Pro 20.03
On the day that you stood a. Ob 1.11

ALOUD

Then Jacob kissed Rachel, and wept a. Gen 29.11
And he wept a., so that the Egyptians 45.02
and cried a. and said to them, Ju 9.07
and all the people wept a. 1Sa 11.04
went away, crying a. as she went. 2Sa 13.19
country wept a. as all the people 15.23
"Cry a., for he is a god; 1Ki 18.27
And they cried a., and cut themselves 18.28
though many shouted a. for joy; Ez 3.12
I call a., but there is no justice. Job 19.07
I cry a. to the LORD, and he answers Ps 3.04
singing a. a song of thanksgiving, 26.07
when I cry a., be gracious to me 27.07
will sing a. of thy deliverance. 51.14
I will sing a. of thy steadfast 59.16
I cried a. to him, and he was 66.17
I cry a. to God, a. to God, that 77.01
a. to God, that he may hear me. 77.01
Sing a. to God our strength; 81.01
and shall sing a. of thy righteousness 145.07
Wisdom cries a. in the street; Pro 1.20
of the portals she cries a.: 8.03
Cry a., O daughter of Gallim! Is 10.30
raise a signal, cry a. to them; 13.02
the armed men of Moab cry a.; 15.04
he shouts a., he shows himself 42.13
forth into singing and cry a., 54.01
"Cry a., spare not, lift up your 58.01
cry a. and say, 'Assemble, and let us Jer 4.05
"Sing a. with gladness for Jacob, 31.07
come and sing a. on the height of 31.12
Cry a. to the Lord! O daughter of Lam 2.18
Sigh, but not a.; make no mourning Eze 24.17
and wail a. over you, and cry 27.30
And the herald proclaimed a., Dan 3.04
He cried a. and said thus, 'Hew down 4.14
The king cried a. to bring in the 5.07
Now why do you cry a.? Mic 4.09
the mighty man cries a. there. Zep 1.14
Sing a., O daughter of Zion; 3.14
Shout a., O daughter of Jerusalem! Zec 9.09
crying a., "Have mercy on us, Son of Mt 9.27
He will not wrangle or cry a., 12.19
Blessed is he who reads a. the Rev 1.03
torment, weeping and mourning a., 18.15

ALPHA

"I am the A. and the Omega," says Rev 1.08
I am the A. and the Omega, the 21.06
I am the A. and the Omega, the first 22.13

ALPHAEUS

James the son of A., and Thaddaeus; Mt 10.03
Levi the son of A. sitting at the Mk 2.14
Thomas, and James the son of A., 3.18
Thomas, and James the son of A., Lk 6.15
the son of A. and Simon the Zealot Ac 1.13

ALREADY

persons; Joseph was a. in Egypt. Ex 1.05
the plague had a. begun among the Num 16.47
purposes which they are a. forming, Deu 31.21
the nations that I have a. cut off, Jos 23.04
Zebah and Zalmunna a. in your hand, Ju 8.06
Zebah and Zalmunna a. in your hand, 8.15
the man was a. old and advanced in 1Sa 17.12
of Israel that have a. perished; 2Ki 7.13
For our guilt is a. great, 2Ch 28.13
daughters have a. been enslaved; Neh 5.05
It has been a., in the ages before Ecc 1.10
Only what he has a. done. 2.12
That which is, a. has been; 3.15
that which is to be, a. has been; 3.15
dead who are a. dead more fortunate 4.02
Whatever has come to be has a. been named, 6.10
and their envy have a. perished, 9.06
for God has a. approved what you do 9.07
to him besides those a. gathered. Is 56.08
a. they are among the nations as a Hos 8.08
indeed I have a. cursed them, Mal 2.02
lustfully has a. committed adultery Mt 5.28
I tell you that Elijah has a. come, 17.12
so that the boat was a. filling. Mk 4.37
as it was a. late, he went out to 11.11
Pilate wondered if he were a. dead; 15.44
asked him whether he was a. dead. 15.44
and would that it were a. kindled! Lk 12.49
know that the summer is a. near. 21.30
does not believe is condemned a., Jn 3.18
the fields are a. white for 4.35
the Jews had a. agreed that if any 9.22
He answered them, "I have told you a., 9.27
Lazarus had a. been in the tomb 11.17
the devil had a. put it into the 13.02
You are a. made clean by the word 15.03
Jesus and saw that he was a. dead, 19.33
the morrow, for it was a. evening. Ac 4.03
the voyage was a. dangerous 27.09
because the fast had a. gone by, 27.09
for I have a. charged that all men, Rom 3.09
not where Christ has a. been named, 15.20
A. you are filled! 1Co 4.08
A. you have become rich! 4.08
I have a. pronounced judgment 5.03
time of his call a. circumcised? 7.18
that as he had a. made a beginning, 2Co 8.06
boasting of work a. done in another's 10.16
Not that I have a. obtained this or Php 3.12
obtained this or am a. perfect; 3.12
but though we had a. suffered and 1Th 2.02

ALREADY (cont.)
of lawlessness is a. at work; 2Th 2.07
For some have a. strayed after 1Ti 5.15
that the resurrection is past a. 2Ti 2.18
For I am a. on the point of being 4.06
in the words a. quoted, "Today, when Heb 4.07
and the true light is a. shining. 1Jn 2.08
and now it is in the world a. 4.03

ALTAR
Then Noah built an a. to the LORD, Gen 8.20
offered burnt offerings on the a. 8.20
he built there an a. to the LORD, 12.07
he built an a. to the LORD and 12.08
he had made an a. at the first; 13.04
there he built an a. to the LORD. 13.18
him, Abraham built an a. there, 22.09
laid him on the a., upon the wood. 22.09
So he built an a. there and called 26.25
There he erected an a. and called 33.20
make there an a. to the God who 35.01
make there an a. to the God who 35.03
and there he built an a., 35.07
And Moses built an a. and called Ex 17.15
An a. of earth you shall make for 20.24
And if you make me an a. of stone, 20.25
shall not go up by steps to my a., 20.26
you shall take him from my a., 21.14
and built an a. at the foot of the 24.04
the blood he threw against the a. 24.06
"You shall make the a. of acacia wood, 27.01
the a. shall be square, and its 27.01
ledge of the a. so that the net 27.05
shall extend half way down the a. 27.05
And you shall make poles for the a., 27.06
be upon the two sides of the a., 27.07
come near the a. to minister in 28.43
horns of the a. with your finger, 29.12
pour out at the base of the a. 29.12
on them, and burn them upon the a. 29.13
it against the a. round about. 29.16
and burn the whole ram upon the a.; 29.18
blood against the a. round about. 29.20
of the blood that is on the a., 29.21
them on the a. in addition to the 29.25
offer a sin offering for the a., 29.36
shall make atonement for the a., 29.37
and the a. shall be most holy; 29.37
touches the a. shall become holy. 29.37
what you shall offer upon the a.: 29.38
the tent of meeting and the a.; 29.44
"You shall make an a. to burn 30.01
the tent of meeting and the a., 30.18
they come near the a. to minister, 30.20
utensils, and the a. of incense, 30.27
and the a. of burnt offering with 30.28
utensils, and the a. of incense, 31.08
and the a. of burnt offering with 31.09
saw this, he built an a. before it; 32.05
and the a. of incense, with its 35.15
the a. of burnt offering, with its 35.16
He made the a. of incense of acacia 37.25
He made the a. of burnt offering 38.01
he made all the utensils of the a., 38.03
And he made for the a. a grating, 38.04
the rings on the sides of the a., 38.07
the bronze a. and the bronze 38.30
it and all the utensils of the a., 38.30
the golden a., the anointing oil 39.38
the bronze a., and its grating of 39.39
put the golden a. for incense 40.05
You shall set the a. of burnt 40.06
the tent of meeting and the a., 40.07
also anoint the a. of burnt 40.10
utensils, and consecrate the a.; 40.10
and the a. shall be most holy. 40.10
put the golden a. in the tent of 40.26
And he set the a. of burnt offering 40.29
the tent of meeting and the a., 40.30
approached the a., they washed; 40.32
round the tabernacle and the a., 40.33
against the a. that is at the door Lev 1.05
priest shall put fire on the a., 1.07
that is on the fire upon the a.; 1.08
shall burn the whole on the a., 1.09
side of the a. before the LORD, and 1.11
blood against the a. round about. 1.11
that is on the fire upon the a.: 1.12
the whole, and burn it on the a.: 1.13
bring it to the a. and wring off 1.15
its head, and burn it on the a.; 1.15
drained out on the side of the a.; 1.15
it beside the a. on the east side. 1.16
the priest shall burn it on the a., 1.17
its memorial portion upon the a., 2.02
he shall bring it to the a. 2.08
portion and burn this on the a., 2.09
offered on the a. for a pleasing 2.12
blood against the a. round about. 3.02
burn it on the a. upon the burnt 3.05
blood against the a. round about. 3.08
burn it on the a. as food offered 3.11
blood against the a. round about. 3.13
them on the a. as food offered by 3.16
horns of the a. of fragrant 4.07
the base of the a. of burnt 4.07
them upon the a. of burnt offering 4.10
horns of the a. which is in the 4.18
the base of the a. of burnt 4.18
take from it and burn upon the a. 4.19
horns of the a. of burnt offering, 4.25
the base of the a. of burnt 4.25
its fat he shall burn on the a., 4.26
horns of the a. of burnt offering, 4.30
of its blood at the base of the a. 4.30
it upon the a. for a pleasing odor 4.31
horns of the a. of burnt offering, 4.34
of its blood at the base of the a. 4.34
the priest shall burn it on the a., 4.35
sin offering on the side of the a., 5.09
drained out at the base of the a.; 5.09
portion and burn this on the a., 5.12
hearth upon the a. all night until 6.09
the fire of the a. shall be kept 6.09
the burnt offering on the a., 6.10
a., and put them beside the a. 6.10
The fire on the a. shall be kept 6.12
burning upon the a. continually; 6.13
the LORD, in front of the a. 6.14
as its memorial portion on the a., 6.15
be thrown on the a. round about. 7.02
them on the a. as an offering by 7.05
shall burn the fat on the a., 7.31
some of it on the a. seven times, 8.11
anointed the a. and all its 8.11
on the horns of the a. round about, 8.15
round about, and purified the a., 8.15
the blood at the base of the a., 8.15
and Moses burned them on the a. 8.16
the blood upon the a. round about. 8.19
burned the whole ram on the a., 8.21
the blood upon the a. round about. 8.24
them on the a. with the burnt 8.28
of the blood which was on the a., 8.30
said to Aaron, "Draw near to the a., 9.07
So Aaron drew near to the a., 9.08
and put it on the horns of the a., 9.09
the blood at the base of the a.; 9.09
sin offering he burned upon the a., 9.10
he threw it on the a. round about. 9.12
and he burned them upon the a. 9.13
with the burnt offering on the a. 9.14
from it, and burned it upon the a., 9.17
he threw upon the a. round about, 9.18

ALTAR (cont.)
and he burned the fat upon the a., Lev 9.20
offering and the fat upon the a.; 9.24
eat it unleavened beside the a., 10.12
and the cereal offering on the a. 14.20
fire from the a. before the LORD, 16.12
go out to the a. which is before 16.18
on the horns of the a. round about. 16.18
and the tent of meeting and the a., 16.20
offering he shall burn upon the a. 16.25
the tent of meeting and for the a., 16.33
blood on the a. of the LORD at the 17.06
you upon the a. to make atonement 17.11
near the veil or approach the a., 21.23
by fire upon the a. to the LORD. 22.22
tabernacle and the a., and its cords; Num 3.26
And over the golden a. they shall 4.11
take away the ashes from the a., 4.13
on it all the utensils of the a., 4.14
basins, all the utensils of the a.; 4.14
around the tabernacle and the a., 4.26
the LORD and bring it to the a.; 5.25
portion, and burn it upon the a., 5.26
consecrated the a. with all its 7.01
dedication of the a. on the day it 7.10
their offering before the a. 7.10
day, for the dedication of the a. 7.11
the dedication offering for the a., 7.84
the dedication offering for the a. 7.88
plates as a covering for the a., 16.38
out as a covering for the a., 16.39
put fire therein from off the a., 16.46
of the sanctuary or to the a., 18.03
sanctuary and the duties of the a., 18.05
concerns the a. and that is within 18.07
sprinkle their blood upon the a., 18.17
offered on each a. a bull and a 23.02
upon each a. a bull and a ram. 23.04
a bull and a ram on each a. 23.14
a bull and a ram on each a. 23.30
on the a. of the LORD your God; Deu 12.27
out on the a. of the LORD your God, 12.27
beside the a. of the LORD your God 16.21
down before the a. of the LORD 26.04
shall build an a. to the LORD your 27.05
the LORD your God, an a. of stones; 27.05
You shall build an a. to the LORD 27.06
whole burnt offering upon thy a. 33.10
Then Joshua built an a. in Mount Jos 8.30
"an a. of unhewn stones, upon which 8.31
congregation and for the a. of the LORD, 9.27
built there an a. by the Jordan, 22.10
by the Jordan, an a. of great size. 22.10
have built an a. at the frontier 22.11
yourselves an a. this day in 22.16
yourselves an a. other than the 22.19
other than the a. of the LORD our 22.19
for building an a. to turn away 22.23
Therefore we said, 'Let us now build an a., 22.26
the copy of the a. of the LORD, 22.28
by building an a. for burnt 22.29
other than the a. of the LORD our 22.29
the Gadites called the a. Witness; 22.34
Then Gideon built an a. there to Ju 6.24
pull down the a. of Baal which 6.25
and build an a. to the LORD your 6.26
the a. of Baal was broken down, and 6.28
upon the a. which had been built. 6.28
pulled down the a. of Baal and cut 6.30
because his a. has been pulled down 6.31
because he pulled down his a. 6.32
went up toward heaven from the a., 13.20
flame of the a. while Manoah and 13.20
rose early, and built there an a., 21.04
to be my priest, to go up to my a., 1Sa 2.28
cut off from my a. shall be spared 2.33
he built there an a. to the LORD. 7.17

And Saul built an a. to the LORD; 14.35
was the first a. that he built to 14.35
rear an a. to the LORD on the 2Sa 24.18
order to build an a. to the LORD, 24.21
built there an a. to the LORD, 24.25
caught hold of the horns of the a. 1Ki 1.50
laid hold of the horns of the a., 1.51
they brought him down from the a. 1.53
caught hold of the horns of the a. 2.28
and behold, he is beside the a., 2.29
burnt offerings upon that a. 3.04
He also made an a. of cedar. 6.20
Also the whole a. that belonged to 6.22
the golden a., the golden table for 7.48
before the a. of the LORD in the 8.22
before thine a. in this house, 8.31
from before the a. of the LORD, 8.54
the bronze a. that was before the 8.64
upon the a. which he built to the 9.25
he offered sacrifices upon the a.; 12.32
He went up to the a. which he had 12.33
went up to the a. to burn incense 12.33
standing by the a. to burn incense 13.01
against the a. by the word of the 13.02
"O a., a., thus says the LORD: 13.02
and a. shall be torn down, and the 13.03
he cried against the a. at Bethel, 13.04
stretched out his hand from the a., 13.04
The a. also was torn down, and the 13.05
the ashes poured out from the a., 13.05
the LORD against the a. in Bethel, 13.32
He erected an a. for Baal in the 16.32
about the a. which they had made. 18.26
he repaired the a. of the LORD 18.30
he built an a. in the name of the 18.32
and he made a trench about the a., 18.32
And the water ran round about the a., 18.35
house, around the a. and the house. 2Ki 11.11
it beside the a. on the right side 12.09
he saw the a. that was at Damascus. 16.10
the priest a model of the a., 16.10
And Urijah the priest built the a.; 16.11
Damascus, the king viewed the a. 16.12
then the king drew near to the a., 16.12
of his peace offerings upon the a. 16.13
And the bronze a. which was before 16.14
between his a. and the house of 16.14
put it on the north side of his a. 16.14
"Upon the great a. burn the morning 16.15
but the bronze a. shall be for me 16.15
before this a. in Jerusalem"? 18.22
come up to the a. of the LORD in 23.09
Moreover the a. at Bethel, the high 23.15
that a. with the high place he 23.15
tombs, and burned them upon the a., 23.16
have done against the a. at Bethel. 23.17
upon the a. of burnt offering and 1Ch 6.49
and upon the a. of incense for all 6.49
LORD upon the a. of burnt offering 16.40
up and rear an a. to the LORD on 21.18
may build on it an a. to the LORD— 21.22
built there an a. to the LORD and 21.26
heaven upon the a. of burnt 21.26
and the a. of burnt offering were 21.29
and here the a. of burnt offering 22.01
for the a. of incense made of 28.18
Moreover the bronze a. that Bezalel 2Ch 1.05
to the bronze a. before the LORD, 1.06
He made an a. of bronze, twenty 4.01
the golden a., the tables for the 4.19
east of the a. with a hundred and 5.12
before the a. of the LORD in the 6.12
oath before thy a. in this house, 6.22
the bronze a. Solomon had made 7.07
dedication of the a. seven days and 7.09
LORD upon the a. of the LORD which 8.12
he repaired the a. of the LORD 15.08

ALTAR (cont.)
house, around the a. and the house. 2Ch 23.10
burn incense on the a. of incense. 26.16
of the LORD, by the a. of incense. 26.19
the a. of burnt offering and all 29.18
they are before the a. of the LORD. 29.19
offer them on the a. of the LORD. 29.21
blood and threw it against the a.; 29.22
blood was thrown against the a.; 29.22
offering with their blood on the a., 29.24
offering be offered on the a. 29.27
"Before one a. you shall worship, 32.12
restored the a. of the LORD and 33.16
offerings on the a. of the LORD, 35.16
they built the a. of the God of Ez 3.02
They set the a. in its place, for 3.03
them upon the a. of the house of 7.17
burn upon the a. of the LORD our Neh 10.34
and go about thy a., O LORD, Ps 26.06
Then I will go to the a. of God, 43.04
bulls will be offered on thy a. 51.19
branches, up to the horns of the a.! 118.27
had taken with tongs from the a. Is 6.06
will be an a. to the LORD in the 19.19
"You shall worship before this a."? 36.07
sacrifices will be accepted on my a.; 56.07
come up with acceptance on my a., 60.07
The Lord has scorned his a., Lam 2.07
north of the a. gate, in the entrance, Eze 8.05
LORD, between the porch and the a., 8.16
in and stood beside the bronze a. 9.02
priests who have charge of the a.; 40.46
and the a. was in front of the 40.47
an a. of wood, three cubits high, two 41.22
dimensions of the a. by cubits (the 43.13
this shall be the height of the a.: 43.14
and the a. hearth, four cubits; 43.15
and from the a. hearth projecting 43.15
The a. hearth shall be square, 43.16
steps of the a. shall face east." 43.17
are the ordinances for the a.: 43.18
put it on the four horns of the a., 43.20
cleanse the a. and make atonement 43.20
and the a. shall be cleansed, as it 43.22
atonement for the a. and purify it, 43.26
offer upon the a. your burnt 43.27
corners of the ledge of the a., 45.19
of the temple, south of the a. 47.01
wail, O ministers of the a. Joe 1.13
vestibule and the a. let the 2.17
beside every a. upon garments Amo 2.08
horns of the a. shall be cut off 3.14
the LORD standing beside the a. 9.01
drenched like the corners of the a., Zec 9.15
be as the bowls before the a.; 14.20
By offering polluted food upon my a. Mal 1.07
not kindle fire upon my a. in vain! 1.10
You cover the LORD's a. with tears, 2.13
are offering your gift at the a., Mt 5.23
gift there before the a. and go; 5.24
swears by the a., it is nothing; 23.18
by the gift that is on the a., 23.18
the gift or the a. that makes the 23.19
So he who swears by the a., 23.20
between the sanctuary and the a. 23.35
right side of the a. of incense Lk 1.11
between the a. and the sanctuary 11.51
I found also an a. with this Ac 17.23
serve at the a. share in the 1Co 9.13
the sacrifices partners in the a.? 10.18
no one has ever served at the a. Heb 7.13
having the golden a. of incense and 9.04
We have an a. from which those who 13.10
offered his son Isaac upon the a.? Jas 2.21
I saw under the a. the souls of Rev 6.09
stood at the a. with a golden 8.03
upon the golden a. before the 8.03
fire from the a. and threw it on 8.05
horns of the golden a. before God, 9.13
of God and the a. and those who 11.01
another angel came out from the a., 14.18
And I heard the a. cry, 16.07

ALTARS
You shall tear down their a., Ex 34.13
and cut down your incense a., Lev 26.30
and a., the vessels of the sanctuary Num 3.31
Balak, "Build for me here seven a., 23.01
him, "I have prepared the seven a., 23.04
top of Pisgah, and built seven a., 23.14
Balak, "Build for me here seven a., 23.29
you shall break down their a., Deu 7.05
you shall tear down their a., 12.03
you shall break down their a.' Ju 2.02
thy covenant, thrown down thy a., 1Ki 19.10
thy covenant, thrown down thy a., 19.14
his a. and his images they broke in 2Ki 11.18
the priest of Baal before the a. 11.18
high places and a. Hezekiah has 18.22
and he erected a. for Baal, 21.03
And he built a. in the house of the 21.04
And he built a. for all the host of 21.05
And the a. on the roof of the upper 23.12
and the a. which Manasseh had made 23.12
upon the a., and burned the bones 23.20
the foreign a. and the high places, 2Ch 14.03
the high places and the incense a. 14.05
his a. and his images they broke 23.17
the priest of Baal before the a. 23.17
he made himself a. in every corner 28.24
and removed the a. that were in 30.14
and all the a. for burning incense 30.14
places and the a. throughout all 31.01
places and his a. and commanded 32.12
and erected a. to the Baals, and 33.03
And he built a. in the house of the 33.04
And he built a. for all the host of 33.05
and all the a. that he had built on 33.15
broke down the a. of the Baals in 34.04
the incense a. which stood above 34.04
bones of the priests on their a., 34.05
he broke down the a., 34.07
all the incense a. throughout all 34.07
at thy a., O LORD of hosts, my king Ps 84.03
they will not have regard for the a., Is 17.08
the Asherim or the a. of incense. 17.08
stones of the a. like chalkstones 27.09
or incense a. will remain standing 27.09
high places and a. Hezekiah has 36.07
Jerusalem are the a. you have set Jer 11.13
a. to burn incense to Baal. 11.13
and on the horns of their a., 17.01
remember their a. and their 17.02
Your a. shall become desolate, and Eze 6.04
your incense a. shall be broken; 6.04
your bones round about your a. 6.05
so that your a. will be waste and 6.06
your incense a. cut down, and your 6.06
their idols round about their a., 6.13
be ashamed because of their a. Hos 4.19
has multiplied a. for sinning, 8.11
have become to him a. for sinning. 8.11
increased the more a. he built; 10.01
the LORD will break down their a., 10.02
thistle shall grow up on their a.; 10.08
their a. also shall be like stone 12.11
I will punish the a. of Bethel, Amo 3.14
they have demolished thy a., Rom 11.03

ALTER
shall put forth a hand to a. this, Ez 6.12
or a. the word that went forth from Ps 89.34

ALTERED
the Medes so that it may not be a., Est 1.19
appearance of his countenance was a., Lk 9.29

ALTERS
that if any one a. this edict, Ez 6.11

ALTHOUGH
A. you have felt through all my Gen 31.37
a. no man is with us, remember, God 31.50
And a. she spoke to Joseph day 39.10
the Philistines, a. that was near; Ex 13.17
a. it is a stiff-necked people; 34.09
a. neither the ark of the covenant Num 14.44
a. I am a numerous people, since Jos 17.14
and, a. he loved Hannah, he would 1Sa 1.05
a. the people of Israel had sworn 2Sa 21.02
and a. they covered him with 1Ki 1.01
a. you, my lord the king, do not know 1.18
Adonijah a. he had not supported 2.28
a. I am but a little child; 3.07
a. I your servant have revered the 18.12
a. there is no wrong in my hands, 1Ch 12.17
left in it (a. up to that time I Neh 6.01
a. you moved me against him, to Job 2.03
a. thou knowest that I am not 10.07
a. there is no violence in my hands, 16.17
a. they had declared Job to be in 32.03
a. man's trouble lies heavy upon him Ecc 8.06
a. he had done no violence, and Is 53.09
in my name a. I did not send them, Jer 14.15
a. the LORD persistently sent to 25.04
LORD,' a. I have not spoken?" Eze 13.07
a. I have not disheartened him, and 13.22
a. the LORD was there— 35.10
A. I trained and strengthened their Hos 7.15
(a. Jesus himself did not baptize, Jn 4.02
and a. there were so many, the net 21.11
a. we gave them no instructions, Ac 15.24
for a. they knew God they did not Rom 1.21
a. the law and the prophets bear 3.21
a. your bodies are dead because of 8.10
a. it is not a wisdom of this age 1Co 2.06
For a. there may be so-called gods 8.05
So a. I wrote to you, it was not on 2Co 7.12
a. his works were finished from Heb 4.03
A. he was a Son, he learned obedience 5.08

ALTOGETHER
they have done a. according to the Gen 18.21
a. his sons and his daughters 46.15
so that you will be a. joyful. Deu 16.15
why then have you become a. vain? Job 27.12
LORD are true, and righteous a. Ps 19.09
and confusion a. who rejoice at my 35.26
transgressors shall be a. destroyed; 37.38
and confusion a. who seek to 40.14
lo, O LORD, thou knowest it a. 139.04
most sweet, and he is a. desirable. Sol 5.16

ALUSH
from Dophkah, and encamped at A. Num 33.13
and they set out from A., Num 33.14

ALVAH
the chiefs Timna, A., Jetheth, Gen 36.40

ALVAN
A., Manahath, Ebal, Shepho, and Onam. Gen 36.23

ALWAYS
Presence on the table before me a. Ex 25.30
it shall a. be upon his forehead, 28.38
they had such a mind as this a., Deu 5.29
for our good a.. that he might 6.24
ordinances, and his commandments a. 11.01
the LORD your God are a. upon it, 11.12
learn to fear the LORD your God a. 14.23
and some of you shall a. be slaves, Jos 9.23
kept from us as a. when I go on an 1Sa 21.05
therefore he shall be my servant a." 27.12
and you shall eat at my table a." 2Sa 9.07
son shall a. eat at my table." 9.10
for he ate a. at the king's table. 9.13
for Hiram a. loved David. 1Ki 5.01
my servant may a. have a lamp 11.36
you shall a. be careful to do. 2Ki 17.37
good concerning me, but a. evil. 2Ch 18.07
needy shall not a. be forgotten, Ps 9.18
I keep the LORD a. before me; 16.08
a. at ease, they increase in riches. 73.12
He will not a. chide, nor will he 103.09
be infatuated a. with her love. Pro 5.19
Bind them upon your heart a.; 6.21
delight, rejoicing before him a., 8.30
Blessed is the man who fears the LORD a.; 28.14
Let your garments be a. white; Ecc 9.08
for ever, nor will I a. be angry; Is 57.16
their angels a. behold the face of Mt 18.10
For you a. have the poor with you, 26.11
you, but you will not a. have me. 26.11
I am with you a., to the close of 28.20
the mountains he was a. crying out, Mk 5.05
For you a. have the poor with you, 14.07
but you will not a. have me. 14.07
you are a. with me, and all that is Lk 15.31
that they ought a. to pray and not 18.01
him, "Lord, give us this bread a." Jn 6.34
yet come, but your time is a. here. 7.06
for I a. do what is pleasing to him." 8.29
I knew that thou hearest me a., 11.42
The poor you a. have with you, but 12.08
you, but you do not a. have me." 12.08
I have a. taught in synagogues and 18.20
him, 'I saw the Lord a. before me, Ac 2.25
you a. resist the Holy Spirit. 7.51
So I a. take pains to have a clear 24.16
I mention you a. in my prayers, Rom 1.09
thanks to God a. for you because 1Co 1.04
a. abounding in the work of the 15.58
but in him it is a. Yes. 2Co 1.19
who in Christ a. leads us in 2.14
a. carrying in the body the death 4.10
we live we are a. being given up 4.11
So we are a. of good courage; 5.06
as sorrowful, yet a. rejoicing; 6.10
so that you may a. have enough of 9.08
purpose it is a. good to be made Gal 4.18
a. and for everything giving thanks Eph 5.20
a. in every prayer of mine for you Php 1.04
courage now as a. Christ will be 1.20
as you have a. obeyed, so now, not 2.12
Rejoice in the Lord a.; 4.04
We a. thank God, the Father of our Col 1.03
Let your speech a. be gracious, 4.06
a. remembering you earnestly in his 4.12
We give thanks to God a. for you all, 1Th 1.02
so as a. to fill up the measure of 2.16
that you a. remember us kindly and 3.06
and so we shall a. be with the Lord. 4.17
but a. seek to do good to one 5.15
Rejoice a., 5.16
to give thanks to God a. for you, 2Th 1.03
To this end we a. pray for you, that 1.11
to give thanks to God a. for you, 2.13
As for you, a. be steady, endure 2Ti 4.05
"Cretans are a. liars, evil beasts, Tit 1.12
I thank my God a. when I remember Phm 1.04
'They a. go astray in their hearts; Heb 3.10
since he a. lives to make intercession 7.25
A. be prepared to make a defense to 1Pe 3.15
Therefore I intend a. to remind you 2Pe 1.12

AM

a. I my brother's keeper?" Gen 4.09
for I a. sorry that I have made 6.07
"Fear not, Abram, I a. your shield; 15.01
"I a. the LORD who brought you from 15.07
how a. I to know that I shall 15.08
She said, "I a. fleeing from my 16.08
and said to him, "I a. God Almighty; 17.01
bear a child, now that I a. old?' 18.13
Abraham what I a. about to do, 18.17
I who a. but dust and ashes. 18.27
And he said, "Here a. I." 22.01
And he said, "Here a. I, my son." 22.07
Abraham!" And he said, "Here a. I." 22.11
"I a. a stranger and a sojourner 23.04
Behold, I a. standing by the spring 24.13
"I a. the daughter of Bethul the 24.24
So he said, "I a. Abraham's servant. 24.34
behold, I a. standing by the spring 24.43
red pottage, for I a. famished!" 25.30
Esau said, "I a. about to die; 25.32
"I a. the God of Abraham your 26.24
for I a. with you and will bless 26.24
and he answered, "Here I a." 27.01
He said, "Behold, I a. old; 27.02
a hairy man, and I a. a smooth man. 27.11
and he said, "Here I a.; 27.18
"I a. Esau your first-born. 27.19
son Esau?" He answered, "I a." 27.24
"I a. your son, your first-born, Esau." 27.32
"I a. weary of my life because of 27.46
"I a. the LORD, the God of Abraham 28.13
Behold, I a. with you and will keep 28.15
the LORD has heard that I a. hated, 29.33
"A. I in the place of God, who has 30.02
And Leah said, "Happy a. I! 30.13
'Jacob,' and I said, 'Here I a.!' 31.11
I a. the God of Bethel, where you 31.13
I a. not worthy of the least of all 32.10
"I a. God Almighty: be fruitful and 35.11
And he said to him, "Here I a." 37.13
"I a. seeking my brothers," he said, 37.16
whom these belong, I a. with child." 38.25
greater in this house than I a.; 39.09
"I a. Pharaoh, and without your 41.44
If I a. bereaved of my children, I a. 43.14
said to his brothers, "I a. Joseph; 45.03
"I a. your brother, Joseph, whom you 45.04
And he said, "Here a. I." 46.02
"I a. God, the God of your father; 46.03
I a. about to die, but God will be 48.21
"I a. to be gathered to my people; 49.29
'I a. about to die: in my tomb which 50.05
for a. I in the place of God? 50.19
to his brothers, "I a. about to die; 50.24
And he said, "Here a. I." Ex 3.04
"I a. the God of your father, the 3.06
"Who a. I that I should go to 3.11
God said to Moses, "I A. WHO I A." 3.14
'I A. has sent me to you.'" 3.14
and thus I a. to be remembered 3.15
I a. not eloquent, either heretofore 4.10
but I a. slow of speech and of 4.10
And God said to Moses, "I a. the LORD. 6.02
'I a. the LORD, and I will bring you 6.06
know that I a. the LORD your God, 6.07
I a. the LORD.'" 6.08
who a. a man of uncircumcised lips?" 6.12
the LORD said to Moses, "I a. the LORD; 6.29
I a. of uncircumcised lips; 6.30
shall know that I a. the LORD, 7.05
you shall know that I a. the LORD: 7.17
to command me when I a. to entreat, 8.09
may know that I a. the LORD in the 8.22
I a. going out from you and I will 8.29
you may know that I a. the LORD." 10.02
execute judgments: I a. the LORD. 12.12
shall know that I a. the LORD." 14.04
shall know that I a. the LORD, 14.18
for I a. the LORD, your healer." 15.26
know that I a. the LORD your God.'" 16.12
I a. coming to you in a thick cloud, 19.09
"I a. the LORD your God, who brought 20.02
the LORD your God a. a jealous God, 20.05
will hear, for I a. compassionate. 22.27
know that I a. the LORD their God, 29.46
among them; I a. the LORD their God. 29.46
lest you die; for so I a. commanded." Lev 8.35
to the LORD; for so I a. commanded. 10.13
For I a. the LORD your God; 11.44
therefore, and be holy, for I am holy. 11.44
For I a. the LORD who brought you 11.45
therefore be holy, for I a. holy." 11.45
I a. the LORD your God. 18.02
Canaan, to which I a. bringing you. 18.03
I a. the LORD your God. 18.04
a man shall live: I a. the LORD. 18.05
nakedness, I a. the LORD. 18.06
name of your God: I a. the LORD. 18.21
the nations I a. casting out 18.24
I a. the LORD your God." 18.30
for I the LORD your God a. holy. 19.02
sabbaths: I a. the LORD your God. 19.03
molten gods: I a. the LORD your God. 19.04
sojourner: I a. the LORD your God. 19.10
name of your God: I a. the LORD. 19.12
shall fear your God: I a. the LORD. 19.14
of your neighbor: I a. the LORD. 19.16
neighbor as yourself: I a. the LORD. 19.18
for you: I a. the LORD your God. 19.25
any marks upon you: I a. the LORD. 19.28
my sanctuary: I a. the LORD. 19.30
by them: I a. the LORD your God. 19.31
shall fear your God: I a. the LORD. 19.32
Egypt: I a. the LORD your God. 19.34
I a. the LORD your God, who brought 19.36
ordinances, and do them: I a. the LORD." 19.37
be holy; for I a. the LORD your God. 20.07
I a. the LORD who sanctify you. 20.08
land where I a. bringing you to 20.22
nation which I a. casting out 20.23
I a. the LORD your God, who have 20.24
for I the LORD a. holy, and have 20.26
LORD, who sanctify you, a. holy. 21.08
his God is upon him: I a. the LORD. 21.12
for I a. the LORD who sanctify him." 21.15
for I a. the LORD who sanctify them." 21.23
holy name; I a. the LORD. 22.02
from my presence: I a. the LORD. 22.03
himself by it: I a. the LORD.' 22.08
I a. the LORD who sanctify them. 22.09
for I a. the LORD who sanctify them." 22.16
of it until morning: I a. the LORD. 22.30
commandments and do them: I a. the LORD. 22.31
I a. the LORD who sanctify you, 22.32
to be your God: I a. the LORD." 22.33
stranger: I a. the LORD your God." 23.22
of Egypt: I a. the LORD your God." 23.43
for I a. the LORD your God." 24.22
for I a. the LORD your God. 25.17
I a. the LORD your God, who brought 25.38
of Egypt: I a. the LORD your God. 25.55
for I a. the LORD your God. 26.01
my sanctuary: I a. the LORD. 26.02
I a. the LORD your God, who brought 26.13
for I a. the LORD their God; 26.44
might be their God: I a. the LORD." 26.45
they shall be mine: I a. the LORD." Num 3.13
I a. the LORD—instead of all the 3.41
shall be mine: I a. the LORD. 3.45
I a. the LORD your God." 10.10
Where a. I to get meat to give to 11.13
I a. not able to carry all this 11.14
among whom I a. number six hundred 11.21

AM (cont.)
I a. the LORD your God, who brought Num 15.41
I a. your portion and your inheritance 18.20
"A. I not your ass, upon which 22.30
A. I not able to honor you 22.37
I a. going to my people; 24.14
'I a. not able alone to bear you; Deu 1.09
for I a. not in the midst of you; 1.42
" 'I a. the LORD your God, who 5.06
the LORD your God a. a jealous God, 5.09
day (since I a. not speaking to 11.02
do all that I a. commanding you. 12.14
may know that I a. the LORD your 29.06
"I a. a hundred and twenty years 31.02
I a. no longer able to go out and 31.02
while I a. yet alive with you, today 31.27
a. he, and there is no god beside me 32.39
the land which I a. giving to them, Jos 1.02
I a. this day eighty-five years old. 14.10
I a. still as strong to this day as 14.11
although I a. a numerous people, 17.14
"I a. now old and well advanced in 23.02
"And now I a. about to go the way 23.14
for I a. thirsty." So she opened Ju 4.19
'I a. the LORD your God; 6.10
and I a. the least in my family." 6.15
behold, I a. laying a fleece of wool 6.37
and I a. pursuing after Zebah and 8.05
also that I a. your bone and your 9.02
this woman?" And he said, "I a." 13.11
"I a. a Levite of Bethlehem in 17.09
and I a. going to sojourn where I 17.09
and I a. going to my home; 19.18
for I a. too old to have a husband. Ru 1.12
of me, when I a. a foreigner?" 2.10
though I a. not one of your maidservants." 2.13
"I a. Ruth, your maidservant; 3.09
is true that I a. a near kinsman, 3.12
A. I not more to you than ten sons?" 1Sa 1.08
I a. a woman sorely troubled; 1.15
I a. the woman who was standing 1.26
and he said, "Here I a.!" 3.04
"Here I a., for you called me." 3.05
"Here I a., for you called me." 3.06
"Here I a., for you called me." 3.08
I a. about to do a thing in Israel, 3.11
tell him that I a. about to punish 3.13
And he said, "Here I a." 3.16
"I a. he who has come from the 4.16
Samuel answered Saul. "I a. the seer; 9.19
"A. I not a Benjaminite, from the 9.21
and behold, I a. coming to you to 10.08
and I a. old and gray, and behold, my 12.02
Here I a.; testify against me 12.03
behold, I a. with you, as is your 14.07
evening and I a. avenged on my 14.24
here I a., I will die." 14.43
A. I not a Philistine, and are you 17.08
for I a. not used to them." 17.39
"A. I a dog, that you come to me 17.43
"I a. the son of your servant Jesse 17.58
"Who a. I, and who are my kinsfolk, 18.18
seeing that I a. a poor man and of 18.23
If I a. still alive, show me the 20.14
he answered, "Here I a., my lord." 22.12
"I a. in great distress; 28.15
He said, "I a. a young man of Egypt, 30.13
And I answered, 'Here I a.' 2Sa 1.07
I answered him, 'I a. an Amalekite.' 1.08
"I a. the son of a sojourner, an 1.13
I a. distressed for you, my brother 1.26
"A. I a dog's head of Judah? 3.08
And I a. this day weak, though 3.39
"Who a. I, O Lord God, and what is my 7.18
and told David, "I a. with child." 11.05
she answered, "Alas, I a. a widow; 14.05
here I a., let him do to me what 15.26
not know that I a. this day king 19.22
I a. this day eighty years old; 19.35
He answered, "I a." Then she said 20.17
And he answered, "I a. listening." 20.17
I a. one of those who are peaceable 20.19
and I a. saved from my enemies. 22.04
"I a. in great distress; 24.14
"I a. about to go the way of all 1Ki 2.02
although I a. but a little child; 3.07
I a. ready to do all you desire in 5.08
I a. about to tear the kingdom from 11.31
came from Judah?" And he said, "I a." 13.14
"I also a. a prophet as you are, and 13.18
For I a. charged with heavy tidings 14.06
I a. sending to you a present of 15.19
and now, I a. gathering a couple of 17.12
a. left a prophet of the LORD; 18.22
and that I a. thy servant and that 18.36
for I a. no better than my fathers. 19.04
and I, even I only, a. left; 19.10
and I, even I only, a. left; 19.14
I a. yours, and all that I have." 20.04
you shall know that I a. the LORD.' " 20.13
you shall know that I a. the LORD.' " 20.28
"I a. as you are, my people as your 22.04
of the battle, for I a. wounded." 22.34
"If I a. a man of God, let fire come 2Ki 1.10
"If I a. a man of God, let fire come 1.12
you, before I a. taken from you." 2.09
you see me as I a. being taken 2.10
I a. as you are, my people as your 3.07
"How a. I to set this before a 4.43
"A. I God, to kill and to make alive, 5.07
"I a. your servant and your son. 16.07
I a. bringing upon Jerusalem and 21.12
"Who a. I, O LORD God, and what is my 1Ch 17.16
"I a. in great distress; let me fall 21.13
"But who a. I, and what is my people, 29.14
Behold, I a. about to build a house 2Ch 2.04
The house which I a. to build will 2.05
Who a. I to build a house for him, 2.06
for the house I a. to build will 2.09
behold I a. sending to you silver 16.03
"I a. as you are, my people as your 18.03
of the battle, for I a. wounded." 18.33
I a. not coming against you this 35.21
the house with which I a. at war; 35.21
me away, for I a. badly wounded." 35.23
I a. ashamed and blush to lift my Ez 9.06
"I a. doing a great work and I Neh 6.03
tomorrow also I a. invited by her Est 5.12
I a. not at ease, nor a. I quiet; Job 3.26
so I a. allotted months of emptiness, 7.03
and I a. full of tossing till the 7.04
A. I the sea, or a sea monster, that 7.12
Though I a. innocent, I cannot 9.15
Though I a. innocent, my own mouth 9.20
though I a. blameless, he would 9.20
I a. blameless; I regard not 9.21
as I a., that I might answer him, 9.32
for I a. not so in myself. 9.35
although thou knowest that I a. not guilty, 10.07
If I a. wicked, woe to me! 10.15
If I a. righteous, I cannot lift up 10.15
for I a. filled with disgrace and 10.15
and I a. clean in God's eyes.' 11.04
I a. not inferior to you. 12.03
I a. a laughingstock to my friends; 12.04
I a. not inferior to you. 13.02
and I a. one before whom men spit. 17.06
but I a. not answered; I call 19.07
and I a. gone. and my hope has he 19.10
I a. repulsive to my wife, loathsome 19.17
When I think of it I a. dismayed, 21.06
Therefore I a. terrified at his 23.15
consider, I a. in dread of him. 23.15
for I a. hemmed in by darkness, and 23.17

AM (cont.)
I a. a byword to them. Job 30.09
I a. a brother of jackals, and a 30.29
"I a. young in years, and you are 32.06
For I a. full of words, the spirit 32.18
Behold, I a. toward God as you are; 33.06
You say, 'I a. clean, without transgression; 33.09
I a. pure, and there is no iniquity 33.09
'I a. innocent, and God has taken 34.05
of my right I a. counted a liar; 34.06
though I a. without transgression.' 34.06
How a. I better off than if I had 35.03
"Behold, I a. of small account; 40.04
I a. not afraid of ten thousands of Ps 3.06
me, O LORD, for I a. languishing; 6.02
I a. weary with my moaning; 6.06
foes rejoice because I a. shaken. 13.04
and I a. saved from my enemies. 18.03
But I a. a worm, and no man; 22.06
I a. poured out like water, and all 22.14
for I a. lonely and afflicted. 25.16
so I a. helped, and my heart exults, 28.07
me, O LORD, for I a. in distress; 31.09
I a. the scorn of all my adversaries, 31.11
"I a. driven far from thy sight." 31.22
"I a. your deliverance!" 35.03
I have been young, and now a. old; 37.25
I a. utterly bowed down and prostrate; 38.06
I a. utterly spent and crushed; 38.08
But I a. like a deaf man, I do not 38.13
Yea, I a. like a man who does not 38.14
For I a. ready to fall, and my pain 38.17
I a. sorry for my sin. 38.18
I a. dumb, I do not open my mouth; 39.09
I a. spent by the blows of thy hand. 39.10
For I a. thy passing guest, a 39.12
As for me, I a. poor and needy; 40.17
"Be still, and know that I a. God. 46.10
I a. exalted among the nations, 46.10
against you. I a. exalted in the earth!" 46.10
I a. God, your God. 50.07
But I a. like a green olive tree in 52.08
I a. overcome by my trouble. 55.02
I a. distraught by the noise of the 55.03
When I a. afraid, I put my trust in 56.03
I a. weary with my crying; 69.03
I a. the talk of those who sit in 69.12
for I a. in distress, make haste to 69.17
my heart, so that I a. in despair. 69.20
But I a. afflicted and in pain; 69.29
But I a. poor and needy; hasten 70.05
Nevertheless I a. continually with 73.23
I a. so troubled that I cannot 77.04
I a. the LORD your God, who brought 81.10
answer me, for I a. poor and needy. 86.01
Preserve my life, for I a. godly; 86.02
I a. reckoned among those who go 88.04
I a. a man who has no strength, 88.04
I a. shut in so that I cannot 88.08
thy terrors; I a. helpless. 88.15
I a. like a vulture of the wilderness, 102.06
I lie awake, I a. like a lonely bird 102.07
For I a. poor and needy, and my 109.22
I a. gone, like a shadow at evening; 109.23
I a. shaken off like a locust. 109.23
I a. an object of scorn to my 109.25
"I a. greatly afflicted"; 116.10
O LORD, I a. thy servant; 116.16
I a. thy servant, the son of thy 116.16
I a. a sojourner on earth; 119.19
I a. a companion of all who fear 119.63
I a. thine, save me; for I have 119.94
I a. sorely afflicted; give me 119.107
and I a. afraid of thy judgments. 119.120
I a. thy servant; give me 119.125
I a. small and despised, yet I do 119.141
I a. for peace; but when 120.07
I a. still with thee." 139.18
for I a. brought very low! 142.06
adversaries, for I a. thy servant. 143.12
I a. pure from my sin"? Pro 20.09
neighbor and says, "I a. only joking!" 26.19
Surely I a. too stupid to be a man. 30.02
"For whom a. I toiling and depriving Ecc 4.08
I a. very dark, but comely, O daughters Sol 1.05
gaze at me because I a. swarthy, 1.06
I a. a rose of Sharon, a lily of the 2.01
for I a. sick with love. 2.05
My beloved is mine and I a. his, 2.16
you tell him I a. sick with love. 5.08
I a. my beloved's and my beloved is 6.03
I a. my beloved's, and his desire is 7.10
I a. weary of bearing them. Is 1.14
For I a. lost; for I a. a man 6.05
for I a. a man of unclean lips, and 6.05
Then I said, "Here I a.! 6.08
Behold, I a. stirring up the Medes 13.17
"I a. a son of the wise, a son of 19.11
I a. bowed down so that I cannot 21.03
I a. dismayed so that I cannot see. 21.03
at my post I a. stationed whole 21.08
I, the LORD, a. its keeper; 27.03
I a. laying in Zion for a foundation 28.16
no inhabitant will say, "I a. sick"; 33.24
I a. consigned to the gates of 38.10
O Lord, I a. oppressed; 38.14
and with the last; I a. He. 41.04
for I a. with you, be not dismayed, 41.10
be not dismayed, for I a. your God; 41.10
"I a. the LORD, I have called you in 42.06
I a. the LORD, that is my name; 42.08
For I a. the LORD your God, the Holy 43.03
Fear not, for I a. with you; 43.05
me and understand that I a. He. 43.10
I, I a. the LORD, and besides me 43.11
"I a. God, and also henceforth I a. He; 43.13
I a. the LORD, your Holy One, the 43.15
Behold, I a. doing a new thing; 43.19
"I, I a. He who blots out your 43.25
'I a. the LORD's,' another will call 44.05
"I a. the first and I a. the last; 44.06
I a. warm, I have seen the fire!" 44.16
"I a. the LORD, who made all things, 44.24
I a. the LORD, and there is no other, 45.05
I a. the LORD, and there is no other. 45.06
I a. the LORD, who do all these 45.07
"I a. the LORD, and there is no 45.18
For I a. God, and there is no other. 45.22
even to your old age I a. He, 46.04
for I a. God, and there is no other; 46.09
I a. God, and there is none like me, 46.09
"I a., and there is no one besides 47.08
"I a., and there is no one besides 47.10
I a. He, I a. the first, and I a. the last; 48.12
"I a. the LORD your God, who teaches 48.17
for I a. honored in the eyes of the 49.05
you will know that I a. the LORD; 49.23
know that I a. the LORD your 49.26
"I, I a. he that comforts you; 51.12
For I a. the LORD your God, who 51.15
it is I who speak; here a. I." 52.06
say, "Behold, I a. a dry tree." 56.03
cry, and he will say, Here I a. 58.09
a. your Savior and your Redeemer, 60.16
I a. the LORD; in its 60.22
I said, "Here a. I, here a. I," to a nation that 65.01
for I a. set apart from you." 65.05
and I a. coming to gather all 66.18
to speak, for I a. only a youth." Jer 1.06
Do not say, 'I a. only a youth'; 1.07
for I a. with you to deliver you, 1.08
for I a. watching over my word to 1.12
For, lo, I a. calling all the tribes 1.15
for I a. with you, says the LORD, to 1.19

AM (cont.)

'I a. not defiled. I have not gone Jer 2.23
you say, 'I a. innocent; 2.35
for I a. merciful, says the LORD; 3.12
for I a. your master; I will 3.14
I a. fainting before murderers." 4.31
I a. making my words in your mouth 5.14
Behold, I a. bringing upon you a 5.15
Therefore I a. full of the wrath of 6.11
I a. weary of holding it in. 6.11
behold, I a. bringing evil upon this 6.19
For behold, I a. sending among you 8.17
that I a. the LORD who practice 9.24
I a. slinging out the inhabitants 10.18
I a. bringing evil upon them which 11.11
I a. weary of relenting. 15.06
for I a. called by thy name, O LORD, 15.16
for I a. with you to save you and 15.20
"Behold, I a. sending for many 16.16
I a. shaping evil against you and 18.11
I a. bringing such evil upon this 19.03
I a. bringing upon this city and 19.15
and I a. weary with holding it in, 20.09
"Behold, I a. against you, O inhabitant 21.13
I a. like a drunken man, like a man 23.09
"A. I a God at hand, says the LORD, 23.23
I a. against the prophets, says the 23.30
Behold, I a. against the prophets, 23.31
Behold, I a. against those who 23.32
a heart to know that I a. the LORD; 24.07
sword which I a. sending among 25.16
sword which I a. sending among you.' 25.27
for I a. summoning a sword against 25.29
for me, behold, I a. in your hands. 26.14
I a. sending on them sword, famine, 29.17
I a. the one who knows, and I a. 29.23
and I a. witness, says the LORD. 29.23
For I a. with you to save you, says 30.11
for I a. a father to Israel, and 31.09
Behold I a. giving this city into 32.03
"Behold, I a. the LORD, the God of 32.27
I a. giving this city into the 32.28
I a. giving this city into the hand 34.02
I a. bringing on Judah and all the 35.17
"I a. debarred from going to the 36.05
I a. not deserting to the Chaldeans 37.14
"I a. afraid of the Jews who have 38.19
for I a. with you, to save you and 42.11
Behold, I a. watching over them for 44.27
I a. weary with my groaning, and I 45.03
I have built I a. breaking down, 45.04
I have planted I a. plucking up— 45.04
I a. bringing evil upon all flesh, 45.05
I a. bringing punishment upon Amon 46.25
says the LORD, for I a. with you. 46.28
For behold, I a. stirring up and 50.09
I a. bringing punishment on the 50.18
"Behold, I a. against you, O proud 50.31
"Behold I a. against you, O destroying 51.25
the evil that I a. bringing upon 51.64
and behold, for I a. despised." Lam 1.11
for I a. in distress, my soul is in 1.20
announced, and let them be as I a. 1.21
I a. the man who has seen affliction 3.01
my head, I said, 'I a. lost.' 3.54
I a. the burden of their songs. 3.63
Behold, I, even I, a. against you; Eze 5.08
you shall know that I a. the LORD. 6.07
they shall know that I a. the LORD; 6.10
And you shall know that I a. the LORD, 6.13
they will know that I a. the LORD." 6.14
you will know that I a. the LORD. 7.04
you will know that I a. the LORD, 7.09
they shall know that I a. the LORD." 7.27
you shall know that I a. the LORD. 11.10
and you shall know that I a. the LORD; 11.12
Say, 'I a. a sign for you: as I have 12.11
they shall know that I a. the LORD, 12.15
and may know that I a. the LORD." 12.16
you shall know that I a. the LORD." 12.20
I a. against you, says the LORD GOD. 13.08
shall know that I a. the Lord GOD. 13.09
you shall know that I a. the LORD. 13.14
I a. against your magic bands with 13.20
you shall know that I a. the LORD. 13.21
you will know that I a. the LORD." 13.23
you shall know that I a. the LORD. 14.08
you will know that I a. the LORD, 15.07
you shall know that I a. the LORD, 16.62
I a. the LORD your God. 20.05
I a. the LORD your God. 20.07
I the LORD a. your God; 20.19
know that I the LORD a. your God. 20.20
they might know that I a. the LORD. 20.26
you will know that I a. the LORD. 20.38
And you shall know that I a. the LORD, 20.42
And you shall know that I a. the LORD, 20.44
I a. against you, and will draw 21.03
you shall know that I a. the LORD." 22.16
so that I a. profaned among them. 22.26
shall know that I a. the Lord GOD." 23.49
I a. about to take the delight of 24.16
will know that I a. the Lord GOD." 24.24
they will know that I a. the LORD." 24.27
therefore I a. handing you over to 25.04
you will know that I a. the LORD. 25.05
you will know I a. the LORD. 25.07
they will know that I a. the LORD. 25.11
they will know that I a. the LORD, 25.17
I a. against you, O Tyre, and will 26.03
they will know that I a. the LORD. 26.06
'I a. perfect in beauty.' 27.03
'I a. a god, I sit in the seat of 28.02
'I a. a god,' in the presence of 28.09
I a. against you, O Sidon, and I will 28.22
know that I a. the LORD when I 28.22
they will know that I a. the LORD. 28.23
will know that I a. the Lord GOD. 28.24
know that I a. the LORD their God." 28.26
I a. against you, Pharaoh king of 29.03
shall know that I a. the LORD. 29.06
they will know that I a. the LORD. 29.09
I a. against you, and against your 29.10
will know that I a. the Lord GOD." 29.16
they will know that I a. the LORD." 29.21
Then they will know that I a. the LORD, 30.08
they will know that I a. the LORD." 30.19
I a. against Pharaoh king of Egypt, 30.22
they shall know that I a. the LORD. 30.25
they will know that I a. the LORD." 30.26
they will know that I a. the LORD. 32.15
Then they will know that I a. the LORD, 33.29
I a. against the shepherds; 34.10
they shall know that I a. the LORD, 34.27
a. with them, and that they, the 34.30
and I a. your God, says the Lord GOD." 34.31
I a. against you, Mount Seir, and I 35.03
you shall know that I a. the LORD. 35.04
you will know that I a. the LORD. 35.09
they will know that I a. the LORD. 35.15
For, behold, I a. for you, and I will 36.09
you will know that I a. the LORD. 36.11
that I a. about to act, but for the 36.22
will know that I a. the LORD, 36.23
they will know that I a. the LORD." 36.38
you shall know that I a. the LORD." 37.06
And you shall know that I a. the LORD, 37.13
I a. about to take the stick of 37.19
I a. against you, O Gog, chief prince 38.03
they will know that I a. the LORD. 38.23
I a. against you, O Gog, chief prince 39.01
they shall know that I a. the LORD. 39.06
shall know that I a. the LORD, 39.07
feast which I a. preparing for you, 39.17

AM (cont.)
feast which I a. preparing for you. Eze 39.19
know that I a. the LORD their God, 39.22
know that I a. the LORD their God 39.28
I a. their inheritance: and you 44.28
in Israel; I a. their possession. 44.28
and when I a. through with him, lo, Dan 10.20
my people and I a. not your God." Hos 1.09
and I a. not her husband—that she 2.02
Therefore I a. like a moth to 5.12
for I a. God and not man, the Holy 11.09
but I a. rich, I have gained wealth 12.08
I a. the LORD your God from the 12.09
I a. the LORD your God from the 13.04
I a. like an evergreen cypress, from 14.08
I a. sending to you grain, wine, and Joe 2.19
know that I a. in the midst of 2.27
a. your God and there is none else 2.27
let the weak say, "I a. a warrior." 3.10
know that I a. the LORD your God, 3.17
I a. setting a plumb line in the Amo 7.08
"I a. no prophet, nor a prophet's son; 7.14
but I a. a herdsman, and a dresser 7.14
And he said to them, "I a. a Hebrew; Jon 1.09
'I a cast out from thy presence; 2.04
this family I a. devising evil, Mic 2.03
I a. filled with power, with the 3.08
Behold I a. against you, says the Nah 2.13
Behold I a. against you, says the 3.05
For I a. doing a work in your days Hab 1.05
For lo, I a. rousing the Chaldeans, 1.06
"I a. and there is none else." Zep 2.15
"I a. with you, says the LORD." Hag 1.13
work, for I a. with you, says the 2.04
I a. about to shake the heavens and 2.21
I a. about to destroy the strength 2.22
I a. exceedingly jealous for Zec 1.14
And I a. very angry with the 1.15
I a. jealous for Zion with great 8.02
and I a. jealous for her with great 8.02
LORD of hosts; I a. going." 8.21
for I a. the LORD their God and I 10.06
For lo, I a. raising up in the land 11.16
"Lo I a. about to make Jerusalem a 12.02
'I a. no prophet, I a. a tiller of 13.05
If then I a. a father, where is my Mal 1.06
And if I a. a master, where is my 1.06
for I a. a great King, says the LORD 1.14
whose sandals I a. not worthy to Mt 3.11
Son, with whom I a. well pleased." 3.17
I a. not worthy to have you come 8.08
For I a. a man under authority, with 8.09
believe that I a. able to do this?" 9.28
for I a. gentle and lowly in heart, 11.29
and I a. unwilling to send them 15.32
them, "But who do you say that I a.?" 16.15
Son, with whom I a. well pleased; 17.05
how long a. I to be with you? 17.17
How long a. I to bear with you? 17.17
there a. I in the midst of them." 18.20
I a. doing you no wrong; 20.13
A. I not allowed to do what I 20.15
drink the cup that I a. to drink?" 20.22
'I a. the God of Abraham, and the 22.32
'I a. the Christ,' and they will 24.05
But after I a. raised up, I will go 26.32
'I a. able to destroy the temple of 26.61
"I a. innocent of this man's blood; 27.24
or he said, 'I a. the Son of God.'" 27.43
and lo, I a. with you always, to the 28.20
whose sandals I a. not worthy to Mk 1.07
with thee I a. well pleased." 1.11
disciples, "Who do men say that I a.?" 8.27
them, "But who do you say that I a.?" 8.29
how long a. I to be with you? 9.19
How long a. I to bear with you? 9.19
baptism with which I a. baptized?" 10.38
baptism with which I a. baptized, 10.39
'I a. the God of Abraham, and the 12.26
come in my name, saying. 'I a. he!' 13.06
where I a. to eat the passover with 14.14
But after I a. raised up, I will go 14.28
And Jesus said, "I a.; and you 14.62
For I a. an old man, and my wife is Lk 1.18
"I a. Gabriel, who stand in the 1.19
"Behold I a. the handmaid of the 1.38
whose sandals I a. not worthy to 3.16
with thee I a. well pleased." 3.22
for I a. a sinful man, O Lord." 5.08
for I a. not worthy to have you 7.06
For I a. a man set under authority, 7.08
"Who do the people say that I a.?" 9.18
them, "But who do you say that I a.?" 9.20
how long a. I to be with you and 9.41
and how I a. constrained until it 12.50
I a. no longer worthy to be called 15.19
I a. no longer worthy to be called 15.21
I a. not strong enough to dig, and I 16.03
to dig, and I a. ashamed to beg. 16.03
houses when I a. put out of the 16.04
for I a. in anguish in this flame.' 16.24
thee that I a. not like other men, 18.11
come in my name, saying, 'I a. he!' 21.08
where I a. to eat the passover with 22.11
But I a. among you as one who 22.27
I a. ready to go with you to prison 22.33
But Peter said, "Man, I a. not." 22.58
he said to them, "You say that I a." 22.70
but confessed. "I a. not the Christ." Jn 1.20
He said, "I a. not." 1.21
He said, "I a. the voice of one 1.23
whose sandal I a. not worthy to 1.27
I a. not the Christ, but I have been 3.28
to her, "I who speak to you a. he." 4.26
and while I a. going another steps 5.07
is working still, and I a. working." 5.17
these very works which I a. doing, 5.36
"I a. the bread of life; 6.35
"I a. the bread which came down 6.41
I a. the bread of life. 6.48
I a. the living bread which came 6.51
I a. not going up to the feast, for 7.08
or whether I a. speaking on my own 7.17
where I a. you cannot come." 7.34
'Where I a. you cannot come'?" 7.36
"I a. the light of the world; 8.12
I have come and whither I a. going, 8.14
I come or whither I a. going. 8.14
where I a. going, you cannot come." 8.21
'Where I a. going, you cannot come'?" 8.22
are from below, I a. from above; 8.23
I a. not of this world. 8.23
unless you believe that I a. he." 8.24
then you will know that I a. he, 8.28
to you, before Abraham was, I a." 8.58
As long as I a. in the world, I a. 9.05
I a. the light of the world." 9.05
He said, "I a. the man." 9.09
I a. the door of the sheep. 10.07
I a. the door; if any one 10.09
I a. the good shepherd. The good shepherd 10.11
I a. the good shepherd; I know my own 10.14
because I said, 'I a. the Son of God'? 10.36
If I a. not doing the works of my 10.37
is in me and I a. in the Father." 10.38
and for your sake I a. glad that I 11.15
"I a. the resurrection and the life 11.25
and where I a., there shall my 12.26
and I, when I a. lifted up from the 12.32
"What I a. doing you do not know 13.07
and you are right, for so I a. 13.13
I a. not speaking of you all; 13.18
place you may believe that I a. he. 13.19
yet a little while I a. with you. 13.33

AM (cont.)

'Where I a. going you cannot come.' Jn 13.33
"Where I a. going you cannot follow 13.36
that where I a. you may be also. 14.03
And you know the way where I a. going." 14.04
"I a. the way, and the truth, and the 14.06
believe that I a. in the Father 14.10
Believe me that I a. in the Father 14.11
will know that I a. in my Father, 14.20
to you, while I a. still with you. 14.25
"I a. the true vine, and my Father 15.01
I a. the vine, you are the branches. 15.05
But now I a. going to him who sent 16.05
again, I a. leaving the world and 16.28
yet I a. not alone, for the Father 16.32
I a. praying for them; I a. 17.09
I a. not praying for the world but 17.09
and I a. glorified in them. 17.10
And now I a. no more in the world, 17.11
the world, and I a. coming to thee. 17.11
But now I a. coming to thee; 17.13
even as I a. not of the world. 17.14
even as I a. not of the world. 17.16
me, may be with me where I a., 17.24
Jesus said to them, "I a. he." 18.05
"I a. he," they drew back and fell 18.06
Jesus answered, "I told you that I a. he; 18.08
man's disciples?" He said, "I a. not." 18.17
He denied it and said, "I a. not." 18.25
Pilate answered,"A. I a Jew? 18.35
answered,"You say that I a. a king. 18.37
I a. bringing him out to you, that 19.04
I a. King of the Jews.'" 19.21
I a. ascending to my Father and 20.17
said to them, "I a. going fishing." 21.03
'I a. the God of your fathers, the Ac 7.32
"I a. Jesus, whom you are persecuting 9.05
And he said, "Here I a., Lord." 9.10
"I a. the one you are looking for; 10.21
I too a. a man." 10.26
"Now I a. sure that the Lord has 12.11
'What do you suppose that I a.? 13.25
I a. not he. No, but 13.25
of whose feet I a. not worthy to 13.25
I a. innocent. From now on 18.06
for I a. with you, and no man shall 18.10
I a. going to Jerusalem, bound in 20.22
this day that I a. innocent of the 20.26
For I a. ready not only to be 21.13
"I a. a Jew, from Tarsus in Cilicia, 21.39
"I a. a Jew, born at Tarsus in 22.03
'I a. Jesus of Nazareth whom you 22.08
I a. a Pharisee, a son of Pharisees; 23.06
resurrection of the dead I a. on trial." 23.06
of the dead I a. on trial before 24.21
"I a. standing before Caesar's 25.10
If then I a. a wrongdoer, and have 25.11
I a. to make my defense today 26.02
for this hope I a. accused by Jews, 26.07
'I a. Jesus whom you are persecuting 26.15
"I a. not mad, most excellent Festus, 26.25
but I a. speaking the sober truth. 26.25
for I a. persuaded that none of 26.26
day might become such as I a.— 26.29
Israel that I a. bound with this 28.20
I a. under obligation both to Rom 1.14
so I a. eager to preach the gospel 1.15
For I a. not ashamed of the gospel: 1.16
why a. I still being condemned as a 3.07
I a. speaking in human terms, 6.19
for I a. speaking to those who know 7.01
but I a. carnal, sold under sin. 7.14
Wretched man that I a.! 7.24
For I a. sure that neither death, 8.38
I a. speaking the truth in Christ, I 9.01
truth in Christ, I a. not lying; 9.01
"Behold I a. laying in Zion a stone 9.33
I myself a. an Israelite, a descendant 11.01
and I alone a. left, and they seek 11.03
Now I a. speaking to you Gentiles. 11.13
then as I a. an apostle to the 11.13
I know and a. persuaded in the Lord 14.14
I myself a. satisfied about you, my 15.14
I a. going to Jerusalem with aid 15.25
I a. thankful that I baptized none 1Co 1.14
I a. not aware of anything against 4.04
but I a. not thereby acquitted. 4.04
in body I a. present in spirit, and 5.03
I wish that all were as I myself a. 7.07
A. I not free? A. I not an apostle? 9.01
If to others I a. not an apostle, at 9.02
an apostle, at least I a. to you; 9.02
nor a. I writing this to secure any 9.15
I a. entrusted with a commission. 9.17
For though I a. free from all men, I 9.19
why a. I denounced because of that 10.30
imitators of me, as I a. of Christ. 11.01
"Because I a. not a hand, I do not 12.15
"Because I a. not an eye, I do not 12.16
I a. a noisy gong or a clanging 13.01
but have not love, I a. nothing. 13.02
What a. I to do? I will 14.15
that what I a. writing to you is a 14.37
For I a. the least of the apostles, 15.09
by the grace of God I a. what I a., 15.10
Why a. I in peril every hour? 15.30
the work of the Lord, as I a. 16.10
for I a. expecting him with the 16.11
I a. filled with comfort. 2Co 7.04
all our affliction, I a. overjoyed. 7.04
But I a. sending the brethren so 9.03
I who a. humble when face to face 10.01
but bold to you when I a. away!— 10.01
you that when I a. present I may 10.02
But I a. afraid that as the serpent 11.03
I think that I a. not in the least 11.05
Even if I a. unskilled in speaking, 11.06
I a. not in knowledge; 11.06
(What I a. saying I say not with 11.17
I a. speaking as a fool—I also 11.21
So a. I. Are they 11.22
of Christ? I a. a better one— 11.23
I a. talking like a madman—with 11.23
Who is weak, and I a. not weak? 11.29
to fall, and I a. not indignant? 11.29
I a. content with weaknesses, 12.10
for when I a. weak, then I a. strong. 12.10
For I a. not at all inferior to 12.11
apostles, even though I a. nothing. 12.11
third time I a. ready to come to 12.14
a. I to be loved the less? 12.15
the third time I a. coming to you. 13.01
this while I a. away from you, 13.10
I a. astonished that you are so Gal 1.06
A. I now seeking the favor of men, 1.10
Or a. I trying to please men? 1.10
(In what I a. writing to you, before 1.20
I a. afraid I have labored over you 4.11
become as I a., for I also have 4.12
not only when I a. present with 4.18
with whom I a. again in travail 4.19
for I a. perplexed about you. 4.20
why a. I still persecuted? 5.11
large letters I a. writing to you 6.11
though I a. the very least of all Eph 3.08
over what I a. suffering for you, 3.13
for which I a. an ambassador in 6.20
may know how I a. and what I a. 6.21
And I a. sure that he who began a Php 1.06
knowing that I a. put here for the 1.16
I a. hard pressed between the two. 1.23
I come and see you or a. absent, 1.27
Even if I a. to be poured as a 2.17
I a. glad and rejoice with you all. 2.17

AM (cont.)
I a. the more eager to send him, Php 2.28
obtained this or a. already perfect 3.12
whatever state I a., to be content. 4.11
I a. filled, having received from 4.18
For though I a. absent in body, yet Col 2.05
yet I a. with you in spirit, rejoicing 2.05
account of which I a. in prison, 4.03
And I a. the foremost of sinners; 1Ti 1.15
and apostle (I a. telling the truth, 2.07
I a. not lying), a teacher of the 2.07
but I a. writing these instructions 3.14
if I a. delayed, you may know how 3.15
I a. reminded of your sincere faith, 2Ti 1.05
I a. sure, dwells in you. 1.05
But I a. not ashamed, for I know 1.12
believed and I a. sure that he is 1.12
for which I a. suffering and 2.09
For I a. already on the point of 4.06
though I a. bold enough in Christ Phm 1.08
I a. sending him back to you, 1.12
for I a. hoping through your 1.22
"Here a. I, and the children God has Heb 2.13
"I a. tempted by God"; for God Jas 1.13
"You shall be holy, for I a. holy." 1Pe 1.16
I a. laying in Zion a stone, a 2.06
as long as I a. in this body, to 2Pe 1.13
Son, with whom I a. well pleased," 1.17
I a. writing this to you so that 1Jn 2.01
Beloved, I a. writing you no new 2.07
Yet I a. writing you a new commandment, 2.08
I a. writing to you, little children, 2.12
I a. writing to you, fathers, because 2.13
I a. writing to you, young men, 2.13
"I a. the Alpha and the Omega," says Rev 1.08
I a. the first and the last, 1.17
and behold I a. alive for evermore, 1.18
know that I a. he who searches 2.23
I a. coming soon; hold fast 3.11
For you say, I a. rich, I have 3.17
("Lo, I a. coming like a thief! 16.15
I a. no widow, mourning I shall 18.07
I a. a fellow servant with you and 19.10
I a. the Alpha and the Omega, the 21.06
And behold, I a. coming soon." 22.07
I John a. he who heard and saw 22.08
I a. a fellow servant with you and 22.09
"Behold, I a. coming soon, bringing 22.12
I a. the Alpha and the Omega, the 22.13
I a. the root and the offspring of 22.16
says, "Surely I a. coming soon." 22.20

AMAD
Allammelech, A., and Mishal; Jos 19.26

AMAL
Zophah, Imna, Shelesh, and A. 1Ch 7.35

AMALEK
she bore A. to Eliphaz.) Gen 36.12
Korah, Gatam, and A.; these are 36.16
Then came A. and fought with Israel Ex 17.08
us men, and go out, fight with A.; 17.09
Moses told him, and fought with A.; 17.10
he lowered his hand, A. prevailed. 17.11
mowed down A. and his people with 17.13
remembrance of A. from under 17.14
have war with A. from generation 17.16
Then he looked on A., Num 24.20
"A. was the first of the nations, 24.20
"Remember what A. did to you on the Deu 25.17
remembrance of A. from under 25.19
punish what A. did to Israel in 1Sa 15.02
Now go and smite A., and utterly 15.03
And Saul came to the city of A., 15.05
I have brought Agag the king of A., 15.20
out his fierce wrath against A., 28.18
A., and from the spoil of Hadadezer 2Sa 8.12
Zephi, Gatam, Kenaz, Timna, and A. 1Ch 1.36
Ammonites, the Philistines, and A. 18.11
Gebal and Ammon and A., Philistia Ps 83.07

AMALEKITE
man of Egypt, servant to an A.; 1Sa 30.13
I answered him, 'I am an A.' 2Sa 1.08
"I am the son of a sojourner, an A." 1.13

AMALEKITES
subdued all the country of the A., Gen 14.07
The A. dwell in the land of the Num 13.29
Now, since the A. and the Canaanites 14.25
For there the A. and the Canaanites 14.43
Then the A. and the Canaanites who 14.45
himself the Ammonites and the A., Ju 3.13
Midianites and the A. and the 6.03
Midianites and the A. and the 6.33
Midianites and the A. and all the 7.12
and the A., and the Maonites, 10.12
in the hill country of the A. 12.15
and smote the A., and delivered 1Sa 14.48
depart, go down from among the A., 15.06
Kenites departed from among the A. 15.06
And Saul defeated the A., 15.07
took Agag the king of the A. alive, 15.08
"They have brought them from the A.; 15.15
the A., and fight against them 15.18
I have utterly destroyed the A. 15.20
here to me Agag the king of the A." 15.32
Geshurites, the Girzites, and the A.; 27.08
the A. had made a raid upon the 30.01
recovered all that the A. had taken; 30.18
from the slaughter of the A., 2Sa 1.01
remnant of the A. that had escaped, 1Ch 4.43

AMAM
A., Shema, Moladah, Jos 15.26

AMANA
Depart from the peak of A., Sol 4.08

AMARIAH
Meraioth of A., A. of Ahitub, 1Ch 6.07
Azariah was the father of A., A. of Ahitub, 6.11
A. his son, Ahitub his son, 6.52
A. the second, Jahaziel the third, 23.19
A. the second, Jahaziel the third, 24.23
And behold, A. the chief priest is 2Ch 19.11
A., and Shecaniah were faithfully 31.15
son of A., son of Azariah, son of Ez 7.03
Shallum, A., and Joseph. 10.42
Pashhur, A., Malchijah, Neh 10.03
son of A., son of Shephatiah, son of 11.04
A., Malluch, Hattush, 12.02
of A., Jehohanan; 12.13
son of A., son of Hezekiah, in the Zep 1.01

AMASA
Now Absalom had set A. over the 2Sa 17.25
A. was the son of a man named Ithra 17.25
And say to A., 'Are you not my bone 19.13
Then the king said to A., "Call 20.04
So A. went to summon Judah; 20.05
A. came to meet them. Now Joab 20.08
And Joab said to A., "Is it 20.09
And Joab took A. by the beard with 20.09
But A. did not observe the sword 20.10
of Joab's men took his stand by A., 20.11
And A. lay wallowing in his blood 20.12
he carried A. out of the highway 20.12
and A. the son of Jether, whom he 1Ki 2.05
and A. the son of Jether, commander 2.32
Abigail bore A., and the father of 1Ch 2.17
the father of A. was Jether the 2.17
and A. the son of Hadlai, stood up 2Ch 28.12

AMASAI

The sons of Elkanah: A. and Ahimoth, 1Ch 6.25
Elkanah, son of Mahath, son of A., 6.35
Then the Spirit came upon A., 12.18
A., Zechariah, Benaiah, and Elezer, 15.24
arose, Mahath the son of A., 2Ch 29.12

AMASHSAI

and A., the son of Azarel, son of Neh 11.13

AMASIAH

and next to him A. the son of 2Ch 17.16

AMAW

in the land of A. to call him, Num 22.05

AMAZED

away, do not be a. at the matter; Ecc 5.08
And all the people were a., Mt 12.23
And they were all a., Mk 1.27
they were all a. and glorified God, 2.12
were greatly a., and ran up to him 9.15
the disciples were a. at his words. 10.24
and they were a., and those who 10.32
And they were a. at him. 12.17
in a white robe; and they were a. 16.05
And he said to them, "Do not be a.; 16.06
heard him were a. at his understanding Lk 2.47
And they were all a. and said to 4.36
And her parents were a.; but he 8.56
Moreover, some women of our company a. us. 24.22
And they were a. and wondered, Ac 2.07
And all were a. and perplexed, 2.12
in the city and a. the nation of 8.09
time he had a. them with his magic 8.11
miracles performed, he was a. 8.13
And all who heard him were a., 9.21
who came with Peter were a., 10.45
opened, they saw him and were a. 12.16

AMAZEMENT

men looked at one another in a. Gen 43.33
immediately they were overcome with a. Mk 5.42
And a. seized them all, and they Lk 5.26
with wonder and a. at what had Ac 3.10

AMAZIAH

and A. his son reigned in his stead. 2Ki 12.21
he fought against A. king of Judah, 13.12
A. the son of Joash, king of Judah, 14.01
Then A. sent messengers to Jehoash 14.08
sent word to A. king of Judah, 14.09
But A. would not listen. So Jehoash 14.11
and he and A. king of Judah faced 14.11
Israel captured A. king of Judah, 14.13
he fought with A. king of Judah, 14.15
A. the son of Joash, king of Judah, 14.17
Now the rest of the deeds of A., 14.18
him king instead of his father A. 14.21
fifteenth year of A. the son of 14.23
of Israel Azariah the son of A., 15.01
to all that his father A. had done. 15.03
A. his son, Azariah his son, Jotham 1Ch 3.12
Meshobab, Jamlech, Joshah the son of A., 4.34
son of A., son of Hilkiah, 6.45
And A. his son reigned in his stead. 2Ch 24.27
A. was twenty-five years old when 25.01
Then A. assembled the men of Judah, 25.05
And A. said to the man of God, "But 25.09
Then A. discharged the army that 25.10
But A. took courage, and led out his 25.11
men of the army whom A. sent back, 25.13
After A. came from the slaughter of 25.14
was angry with A. and sent to him 25.15
then A. king of Judah took counsel 25.17
sent word to A. king of Judah, 25.18
But A. would not listen; for it 25.20
and he and A. king of Judah faced 25.21
Israel captured A. king of Judah, 25.23
A. the son of Joash king of Judah 25.25
Now the rest of the deeds of A., 25.26
him king instead of his father A. 26.01
to all that his father A. had done. 26.04
Then A. the priest of Bethel sent Amo 7.10
And A. said to Amos, "O seer, go, flee 7.12
Then Amos answered A., "I am no 7.14

AMBASSADOR

for which I am an a. in chains; Eph 6.20
an a. and now a prisoner also for Phm 1.09

AMBASSADORS

which sends a. by the Nile, in Is 18.02
against him by sending a. to Egypt, Eze 17.15
So we are a. for Christ, God making 2Co 5.20

AMBITION

thus making it my a. to preach the Rom 15.20
and selfish a. in your hearts Jas 3.14
jealousy and selfish a. exist, 3.16

AMBUSH

lay an a. against the city, behind Jos 8.02
shall lie in a. against the city, 8.04
then you shall rise up from the a., 8.07
and they went to the place of a., 8.09
and set them in a. between Bethel 8.12
there was an a. against him behind 8.14
And the a. rose quickly out of 8.19
saw that the a. had taken the city, 8.21
put men in a. against him on the Ju 9.25
were with him rose from the a. 9.35
set men in a. round about Gibeah. 20.29
who were in a. rushed out of their 20.33
to the men in a. whom they had set 20.36
And the men in a. made haste and 20.37
the men in a. moved out and smote 20.37
and the men in a. was that when 20.38
Jeroboam had sent an a. around to 2Ch 13.13
and the a. was behind them. 13.13
the LORD set an a. against the men 20.22
He sits in a. in the villages; Ps 10.08
as a young lion lurking in a. 17.12
shooting from a. at the blameless, 64.04
let us wantonly a. the innocent; Pro 1.11
they set an a. for their own lives. 1.18
his heart he plans an a. for him. Jer 9.08
of Paul's sister heard of their a.; Ac 23.16
of their men lie in a. for him, 23.21
planning an a. to kill him on the 25.03

AMBUSHES

the enemy and from a. by the way. Ez 8.31
prepare the a.; for the Jer 51.12

AMEN

And the woman shall say, 'A., A.' Num 5.22
people shall answer and say, 'A.' Deu 27.15
And all the people shall say, 'A.' 27.16
And all the people shall say, 'A.' 27.17
And all the people shall say, 'A.' 27.18
And all the people shall say, 'A.' 27.19
And all the people shall say, 'A.' 27.20
And all the people shall say, 'A.' 27.21
And all the people shall say, 'A.' 27.22
And all the people shall say, 'A.' 27.23
And all the people shall say, 'A.' 27.24
And all the people shall say, 'A.' 27.25
And all the people shall say, 'A.' 27.26
of Jehoiada answered the king, "A.! 1Ki 1.36
Then all the people said "A.!" 1Ch 16.36
assembly said "A." and praised the Neh 5.13
"A., A.," lifting up their hands; 8.06
Everlasting! A. and A. Ps 41.13

AMEN (cont.)
the whole earth! A. and A.! 72.19
LORD forever! A. and A. 89.52
And let all the people say, "A.!" 106.48
and the prophet Jeremiah said, "A.! Jer 28.06
power and the glory, for ever. A. *Mt 6.13
who is blessed for ever! A. Rom 1.25
be blessed for ever. A. 9.05
To him be glory for ever. A. 11.36
peace be with you all. A. 15.33
Jesus Christ be with you all. A. *Rom 16.24
through Jesus Christ for ever! A. 16.27
say the "A." to your thanksgiving 1Co 14.16
all in Jesus Christ. A. 16.24
is why we utter the A. through him, 2Co 1.20
glory for ever, and ever. A. Gal 1.05
with your spirit, brethren. A. 6.18
for ever and ever. A. Eph 3.21
glory for ever and ever. A. Php 4.20
glory for ever and ever. A. 1Ti 1.17
eternal dominion. A. 6.16
glory for ever and ever. A. 2Ti 4.18
glory for ever and ever. A. Heb 13.21
all of you. A. 13.25
for ever and ever. A. 1Pe 4.11
for ever and ever. A. 5.11
day of eternity. A. 2Pe 3.18
now and for ever. A. Jud 1.25
for ever and ever. A. Rev 1.06
of him. Even so. A. 1.07
write: 'The words of the A., 3.14
the four living creatures said, "A.!" 5.14
saying, "A.! Blessing and 7.12
for ever and ever! A." 7.12
seated on the throne, saying, "A. 19.04
I am coming soon." A. 22.20
all the saints. A. 22.21

AMEND
A. your ways and your doings, and I Jer 7.03
"For if you truly a. your ways and 7.05
and a. your ways and your doings.' 18.11
Now therefore a. your ways and your 26.13
and a. your doings, and do not go 35.15
that you might a. what was defective, Tit 1.05

AMENDS
and they make a. for their iniquity Lev 26.41
they shall make a. for their 26.43
will make a. for great offences. Ecc 10.04

AMETHYST
row a jacinth. an agate, and an a.; Ex 28.19
a jacinth, an agate, and an a.; 39.12
eleventh jacinth, the twelfth a. Rev 21.20

AMI
Pocherethhazzebaim, and the sons of A. Ez 2.57

AMID
A. thoughts from visions of the Job 4.13
a. the crash they roll on. 30.14
spring up like grass a. waters, Is 44.04
They shall fall a. those who are Eze 32.20
a. the tender grass of the field. Dan 4.15
and Moab shall die a. uproar, Amo 2.02
a. shouting and the sound of the 2.02
the top stone a. shouts of 'Grace, Zec 4.07

AMISS
he has done a. in the holy thing, Lev 5.16
their adversaries should judge a., Deu 32.27

AMITTAI
by his servant Jonah the son of A., 2Ki 14.25
to Jonah the son of A., saying, Jon 1.01

AMMAH
down they came to the hill of A., 2Sa 2.24

AMMIEL
A. the son of Gemalli; Num 13.12
Machir the son of A., at Lodebar. 2Sa 9.04
Machir the son of A., at Lodebar. 9.05
Machir the son of A. from Lodebar, 17.27
by Bathshua, the daughter of A.; 1Ch 3.05
A. the sixth, Issachar the seventh, 26.05

AMMIHUD
Ephraim, Elishama the son of A., Num 1.10
being Elishama the son of A., 2.18
seventh day Elishama the son of A., 7.48
offering of Elishama the son of A. 7.53
host was Elishama the son of A. 10.22
of Simeon, Shemuel the son of A. 34.20
a leader, Pedahel the son of A. 34.28
and went to Talmai the son of A., 2Sa 13.37
Ladan his son, A. his son, Elishama 1Ch 7.26
Uthai the son of A., 9.04

AMMINADAB
the daughter of A. and the sister Ex 6.23
from Judah, Nahshon the son of A.; Num 1.07
Judah being Nahshon the son of A., 2.03
day was Nahshon the son of A., 7.12
offering of Nahshon the son of A. 7.17
host was Nahshon the son of A. 10.14
Hezron of Ram, Ram of A., Ru 4.19
A. of Nahshon, Nahshon of Salmon, 4.20
Ram was the father of A., 1Ch 2.10
and A. was the father of Nahshon, 2.10
A. his son, Korah his son, Assir his 6.22
A. the chief, with a hundred and 15.10
Joel, Shemaiah, Eliel, and A., 15.11
and Ram the father of A., Mt 1.04
and A. the father of Nahshon, and 1.04
the son of A., the son of Admin, the Lk 3.33

AMMISHADDAI
from Dan, Ahiezer the son of A.; Num 1.12
Dan being Ahiezer the son of A., 2.25
tenth day Ahiezer the son of A., 7.66
offering of Ahiezer the son of A. 7.71
host was Ahiezer the son of A. 10.25

AMMIZABAD
A. his son was in charge of his 1Ch 27.06

AMMON
the frontier of the sons of A., Deu 2.19
of the sons of A. as a possession, 2.19
of the sons of A. you did not draw 2.37
of Israel and the people of A. Ju 11.27
the men of A. and Moab and Mount 2Ch 20.10
an ambush against the men of A., 20.22
For the men of A. and Moab rose 20.23
women of Ashdod, A., and Moab; Neh 13.23
Gebal and A. and Amalek, Philistia Ps 83.07
the sons of A., Moab, and all who Jer 9.26
Edom, Moab, and the sons of A.; 25.21
Moab, the king of the sons of A., 27.03

AMMONITE
"No A. or Moabite shall enter the Deu 23.03
Then Nahash the A. went up and 1Sa 11.01
But Nahash the A. said to them, "On 11.02
Zelek the A., Naharai of Beeroth, 2Sa 23.37
A., Edomite, Sidonian, and Hittite 1Ki 11.01
Zelek the A., Naharai of Beeroth, 1Ch 11.39
the A., heard this, it displeased Neh 2.10
the A., and Geshem the Arab heard 2.19
Tobiah the A. was by him, and he 4.03
written that no A. or Moabite 13.01

AMMONITES

the father of the A. to this day. Gen 19.38
to the Jabbok, as far as the A.; Num 21.24
Jazer was the boundary of the A. 21.24
but the A. call them Zamzummim. Deu 2.20
is it not in Rabbah of the A.? 3.11
Jabbok, the boundary of the A.; 3.16
Jabbok, the boundary of the A., Jos 12.02
as far as the boundary of the A.; 13.10
and half the land of the A., 13.25
to himself the A. and the Amalekites, Ju 3.13
gods of Moab, the gods of the A., 10.06
and into the hand of the A., 10.07
And the A. crossed the Jordan to 10.09
from the A. and from the Philistines? 10.11
Then the A. were called to arms, and 10.17
will begin to fight against the A.? 10.18
After a time the A. made war 11.04
And when the A. made war against 11.05
that we may fight with the A." 11.06
go with us and fight with the A., 11.08
me home again to fight with the A., 11.09
to the king of the A. and said, 11.12
And the king of the A. answered the 11.13
again to the king of the A. 11.14
land of the Moab or the land of the A., 11.15
But the king of the A. did not heed 11.28
of Gilead he passed on to the A. 11.29
wilt give the A. into my hand, 11.30
I return victorious from the A., 11.31
over to the A. to fight against 11.32
So the A. were subdued before the 11.33
you on your enemies, on the A." 11.36
cross over to fight against the A., 12.01
had a great feud with the A.; 12.02
and crossed over against the A., 12.03
cut down the A. until the heat of 1Sa 11.11
the king of the A. came against 12.12
against the A., against Edom, 14.47
the A., the Philistines, Amalek, and 2Sa 8.12
After this the king of the A. died, 10.01
came into the land of the A. 10.02
princes of the A. said to Hanun 10.03
When the A. saw that they had 10.06
the A. sent and hired the Syrians 10.06
And the A. came out and drew up in 10.08
and he arrayed them against the A. 10.10
but if the A. are too strong for 10.11
And when the A. saw that the 10.14
from fighting against the A., 10.14
feared to help the A. any more. 10.19
and they ravaged the A., 11.01
slain him with the sword of the A. 12.09
fought against Rabbah of the A., 12.26
he did to all the cities of the A. 12.31
of Nahash from Rabbah of the A., 17.27
Milcom the abomination of the A. 1Ki 11.05
Molech the abomination of the A., 11.07
Moab, and Milcom the god of the A., 11.33
Milcom the abomination of the A. 2Ki 23.13
the Moabites, and bands of the A., 24.02
the A., the Philistines, and Amalek. 1Ch 18.11
Nahash the king of the A. died, 19.01
to Hanun in the land of the A., 19.02
princes of the A. said to Hanun, 19.03
When the A. saw that they had made 19.06
Hanun and the A. sent a thousand 19.06
And the A. were mustered from their 19.07
And the A. came out and drew up in 19.09
they were arrayed against the A. 19.11
but if the A. are too strong for 19.12
And when the A. saw that the 19.15
willing to help the A. any more. 19.19
and ravaged the country of the A., 20.01
did to all the cities of the A. 20.03
After this the Moabites and A., 2Ch 20.01
The A. paid tribute to Uzziah, and 26.08
the king of the A. and prevailed 27.05
and the A. gave him that year a 27.05
The A. paid him the same amount in 27.05
the A., the Moabites, the Egyptians, Ez 9.01
Arabs and the A. and the Ashdodites Neh 4.07
and the A. shall obey them. Is 11.14
and among the A. and in Edom and Jer 40.11
the king of the A. has sent 40.14
set out to cross over to the A. 41.10
with eight men, and went to the A. 41.15
Concerning the A. Thus says 49.01
be heard against Rabbah of the A.; 49.02
fortunes of the A., says the LORD. 49.06
Rabbah of the A. and to Judah and Eze 21.20
the Lord GOD concerning the A., 21.28
man, set your face toward the A., 25.02
Say to the A., Hear the word of the 25.03
cities of the A. a fold for flocks 25.05
along with the A. to the people of 25.10
Moab and the main part of the A. Dan 11.41
"For three transgressions of the A., Amo 1.13
Moab and the revilings of the A., Zep 2.08
and the A. like Gomorrah, a land 2.09

AMMONITESS

mother's name was Naamah the A. 1Ki 14.21
mother's name was Naamah the A. 14.31
mother's name was Naamah the A. 2Ch 12.13
Zabad the son of Shimeath the A., 24.26

AMNON

at Hebron: his first-born was A., 2Sa 3.02
and after a time A., David's son, 13.01
And A. was so tormented that he 13.02
impossible to A. to do anything to 13.02
But A. had a friend, whose name was 13.03
A. said to him, "I love Tamar, my 13.04
So A. lay down, and pretended to be 13.06
A. said to the king, "Pray let my 13.06
And A. said, "Send out every one 13.09
Then A. said to Tamar, "Bring the 13.10
into the chamber to A. her brother. 13.10
Then A. hated her with very great 13.15
And A. said to her, "Arise, be gone." 13.15
"Has A. your brother been with you 13.20
spoke to A. neither good nor bad; 13.22
for Absalom hated A., because he had 13.22
pray let my brother A. go with us." 13.26
until he let A. and all the king's 13.27
'Strike A.,' then kill him. 13.28
Absalom did to A. as Absalom had 13.29
for A. alone is dead, for by the 13.32
are dead; for A. alone is dead." 13.33
for he was comforted about A., 13.39
him in Hebron: the first-born A., 1Ch 3.01
A., Rinnah, Benhanan, and Tilon. 4.20

AMNON'S

"Go to your brother A. house, 2Sa 13.07
Tamar went to her brother A. house, 13.08
"Mark when A. heart is merry with 13.28

AMOK

Sallu, A., Hilkiah, Jedaiah. Neh 12.07
Kallai; of A., Eber; 12.20

AMON

him back to A. the governor of the 1Ki 22.26
and A. his son reigned in his 2Ki 21.18
A. was twenty-two years old when he 21.19
And the servants of A. conspired 21.23
who had conspired against King A., 21.24
of the acts of A. which he did, 21.25
A. his son, Josiah his son. 1Ch 3.14
him back to A. the governor of the 2Ch 18.25
and A. his son reigned in his 33.20
A. was twenty-two years old when he 33.21
A. sacrificed to all the images 33.22

AMON (cont.)
but this A. incurred guilt more and 2Ch 33.23
who had conspired against King A.; 33.25
Pocherethhazzebaim, the sons of A., Neh 7.59
the days of Josiah the son of A., Jer 1.02
year of Josiah the son of A., 25.03
punishment upon A. the Thebes, 46.25
the son of A., king of Judah. Zep 1.01

AMORITE
living by the oaks of Mamre the A., Gen 14.13
captives, to an A. king, Sihon. Num 21.29
given into your hand Sihon the A., Deu 2.24
the A., the Perizzite, the Jebusite, Neh 9.08
your father was an A., and your Eze 16.03
a Hittite and your father an A. 16.45
"Yet I destroyed the A. before them, Amo 2.09
to possess the land of the A. 2.10

AMORITES
the A., the Girgashites, Gen 10.16
and also the A. who dwelt in 14.07
iniquity of the A. is not yet 15.16
the A., the Canaanites, the Girgashites 15.21
the hand of the A. with my sword 48.22
the A., the Perizzites, the Hivites, Ex 3.08
the A., the Perizzites, the Hivites, 3.17
the A., the Hivites, and the Jebusites, 13.05
you, and brings you in to the A., 23.23
the A., the Hittites, the Perizzites, 33.02
I will drive out before you the A., 34.11
and the A. dwell in the hill Num 13.29
from the boundary of the A.; 21.13
of Moab, between Moab and the A. 21.13
to Sihon king of the A., saying, 21.21
in all the cities of the A., 21.25
city of Sihon the king of the A., 21.26
Israel dwelt in the land of the A. 21.31
dispossessed the A. that were there 21.32
as you did to Sihon king of the A., 21.34
all that Israel had done to the A. 22.02
king of the A. and the kingdom of 32.33
dispossessed the A. who were in it. 32.39
defeated Sihon the king of the A., Deu 1.04
go to the hill country of the A., 1.07
way to the hill country of the A., 1.19
come to the hill country of the A., 1.20
the hand of the A., to destroy us. 1.27
Then the A. who lived in that hill 1.44
did to Sihon the king of the A., 3.02
kings of the A. who were beyond 3.08
while the A. call it Senir), 3.09
land of Sihon the king of the A., 4.46
of Bashan, the two kings of the A., 4.47
the A., the Canaanites, the Perizzites, 7.01
them, the Hittites and the A., 20.17
Sihon and Og, the kings of the A., 31.04
kings of the A. that were beyond Jos 2.10
the A., and the Jebusites. 3.10
kings of the A. that were beyond 5.01
the hands of the A., to destroy us? 7.07
the A., the Canaanites, the Perizzites, 9.01
kings of the A. who were beyond 9.10
Then the five kings of the A., 10.05
kings of the A. that dwell in the 10.06
LORD gave the A. over to the men 10.12
the A., the Hittites, the Perizzites, 11.03
Sihon king of the A. who dwelt at 12.02
the A., the Canaanites, the Perizzites, 12.08
Aphek, to the boundary of the A., 13.04
the cities of Sihon king of the A., 13.10
kingdom of Sihon king of the A., 13.21
brought you to the land of the A., 24.08
and also the A., the Perizzites, the 24.11
you, the two kings of the A.; 24.12
the gods of the A. in whose land 24.15
the A. who lived in the land; 24.18
The A. pressed the Danites back Ju 1.34
the A. persisted in dwelling in 1.35
border of the A. ran from the 1.36
the A., the Perizzites, the Hivites, 3.05
reverence to the gods of the A., 6.10
the Jordan in the land of the A., 10.08
from the Egyptians and from the A., 10.11
messengers to Sihon king of the A., 11.19
possession of all the land of the A., 11.21
territory of the A. from the Arnon 11.22
dispossessed the A. from before his 11.23
also between Israel and the A. 1Sa 7.14
but of the remnant of the A.; 2Sa 21.02
king of the A. and of Og king of 1Ki 4.19
the people who were left of the A., 9.20
as the A. had done, whom the LORD 21.26
wicked than all that the A. did, 2Ki 21.11
the A., the Girgashites, 1Ch 1.14
the A., the Perizzites, the Hivites, 2Ch 8.07
Moabites, the Egyptians, and the A. Ez 9.01
king of the A., and Og, king of Ps 135.11
king of the A., for his steadfast 136.19
places of the Hivites and the A., Is 17.09

AMOS
The words of A., who was among the Amo 1.01
"A., what do you see?" And I said 7.08
"A. has conspired against you in 7.10
For thus A. has said, 'Jeroboam 7.11
And Amaziah said to A., "O seer, 7.12
Then A. answered Amaziah, "I am no 7.14
And he said, "A., what do you see?" 8.02
and Manasseh the father of A., Mt 1.10
and A. the father of Josiah, 1.10
the son of A., the son of Nahum, the Lk 3.25

AMOUNT
shall give the a. of the valuation Lev 27.23
spoil of the city, a very great a. 2Sa 12.30
to the a. of four hundred and 1Ki 9.28
a very great a. of almug wood and 10.11
may reckon the a. of the money 2Ki 22.04
spoil of the city, a very great a. 1Ch 20.02
him the same a. in the second and 2Ch 27.05

AMOZ
the prophet Isaiah the son of A. 2Ki 19.02
the son of A. sent to Hezekiah, 19.20
prophet the son of A. came to him, 20.01
the prophet the son of A. wrote. 2Ch 26.22
the son of A., prayed because of 32.20
Isaiah the prophet the son of A., 32.32
The vision of Isaiah the son of A., Is 1.01
the son of A. saw concerning Judah 2.01
which Isaiah the son of A. saw. 13.01
had spoken by Isaiah the son of A., 20.02
the prophet Isaiah the son of A. 37.02
the son of A. sent to Hezekiah, 37.21
prophet the son of A. came to him, 38.01

AMPHIPOLIS
passed through A. and Apollonia, Ac 17.01

AMPLE
you have a. goods laid up for many Lk 12.19
me you may have a. cause to glory Php 1.26

AMPLIATUS
Greet A., my beloved in the Lord. Rom 16.08

AMRAM
A., Izhar, Hebron and Uzziel, the Ex 6.18
A. took to wife Jochebed his 6.20
of the life of A. being one 6.20
A., Izhar, Hebron, and Uzziel. Num 3.19
And Kohath was the father of A. 26.58
and she bore to A. Aaron and Moses 26.59
A., Izhar, Hebron, and Uzziel. 1Ch 6.02

AMRAM (cont.)
The children of A.: 1Ch 6.03
A., Izhar, Hebron, and Uzziel. 6.18
A., Izhar, Hebron, and Uzziel, four. 23.12
The sons of A.: Aaron and Moses. 23.13
Levi: of the sons of A., Shubael; 24.20
the sons of Bani: Maadai, A., Uel, Ez 10.34

AMRAMITES
Of Kohath were the family of the A., Num 3.27
Of the A., the Izharites, the 1Ch 26.23

AMRAM'S
The name of A. wife was Jochebed Num 26.59

AMRAPHEL
In the days of A. king of Shinar, Gen 14.01
A. king of Shinar, and Arioch king 14.09

AMULETS
the perfume boxes, and the a.; Is 3.20

AMZI
son of A., son of Bani, son of 1Ch 6.46
son of A., son of Zechariah, son of Neh 11.12

ANAB
from A., and from all the hill Jos 11.21
A., Eshtemoh, Anim, 15.50

ANAH
the daughter of A. the son of Gen 36.02
the daughter of A. the son of 36.14
the daughter of A., Esau's wife. 36.18
land: Lotan, Shobal, Zibeon, A., 36.20
the sons of Zibeon: Aiah and A.; 36.24
he is the A. who found the hot 36.24
These are the children of A.: 36.25
and Oholibamah the daughter of A. 36.25
chiefs Lotan, Shobal, Zibeon, A., 36.29
A., Dishon, Ezer, and Dishan. 1Ch 1.38
The sons of Zibeon: Aiah and A. 1.40
The sons of A.: Dishon. The sons 1.41

ANAHARATH
Hapharaim, Shion, A., Jos 19.19

ANAIAH
A., Uriah, Hilkiah, and Maaseiah on Neh 8.04
Pelatiah, Hanan, A., 10.22

ANAK
the descendants of A., were there. Num 13.22
we saw the descendants of A. there. 13.28
we saw the Nephilim (the sons of A., 13.33
can stand before the sons of A.?' Deu 9.02
Hebron (Arba was the father of A.). Jos 15.13
from there the three sons of A., 15.14
and Talmai, the descendants of A. 15.14
being the father of A. (that is, 21.11
out from it the three sons of A. Ju 1.20

ANAKIM
have seen the sons of the A. there. Deu 1.28
great and many, and tall as the A.; 2.10
like the A. they are also known as 2.11
great and many, and tall as the A.; 2.21
great and tall, the sons of the A., 9.02
wiped out the A. from the hill Jos 11.21
There was none of the A. left in 11.22
on that day how the A. were there, 14.12
was the greatest man among the A. 14.15
O remnant of the A., how long Jer 47.05

ANAMIM
A., Lehabim, Naphtuhim, Gen 10.13
A., Lehabim, Naphtuhim, 1Ch 1.11

ANAMMELECH
in the fire to Adrammelech and A., 2Ki 17.31

ANAN
Ahiah, Hanan, A., Neh 10.26

ANANI
Johanan, Delaiah, and A., seven. 1Ch 3.24

ANANIAH
son of A. repaired beside his own Neh 3.23
Anathoth, Nob, A., 11.32

ANANIAS
But a man named A. with his wife Ac 5.01
"A., why has Satan filled your 5.03
When A. heard these words, he fell 5.05
a disciple at Damascus named A. 9.10
Lord said to him in a vision, "A." 9.10
a man named A. come in and lay his 9.12
But A. answered, "Lord, I have heard 9.13
So A. departed and entered the 9.17
"And one A., a devout man according 22.12
And the high priest A. commanded 23.02
the high priest A. came down with 24.01

ANATH
After him was Shamgar the son of A., Ju 3.31
son of A., in the days of Jael, 5.06

ANATHOTH
A. with its pasture lands, and Almon Jos 21.18
Abiezer, of A., Mebunnai the Hushathite, 2Sa 23.27
"Go to A., to your estate; 1Ki 2.26
and A. with its pasture lands. 1Ch 6.60
Jeremoth, Abijah, A., and Alemeth. 7.08
of Ikkesh of Tekoa, Abiezer of A., 11.28
Beracah, Jehu of A., 12.03
was Abiezer of A., a Benjaminite; 27.12
The men of A., one hundred and Ez 2.23
The men of A., a hundred and twenty Neh 7.27
Hariph, A., Nebai, 10.19
A., Nob, Ananiah, 11.32
Answer her, O A.! Is 10.30
who were in A. in the land of Jer 1.01
the LORD concerning the men of A., 11.21
will bring evil upon the men of A., 11.23
Jeremiah of A. who is prophesying 29.27
say, 'Buy my field which is at A., 32.07
which is at A. in the land of 32.08
the field at A. from Hanamel my 32.09

ANCESTOR
after the name of Dan their a. Jos 19.47
after the name of Dan their a., Ju 18.29
loins of his a. when Melchizedek Heb 7.10

ANCESTRAL
the leaders of their a. tribes, Num 1.16
by their a. tribe along with them. 1.47

ANCHOR
they weighed a. and sailed along Ac 27.13
sure and steadfast a. of the soul, Heb 6.19

ANCHORS
let out four a. from the stern, Ac 27.29
of laying out a. from the bow, 27.30
cast off the a. and left them in 27.40

ANCIENT
finest produce of the a. mountains, Deu 33.15
to Lehem (now the records are a.) 1Ch 4.22
and be lifted up, O a. doors! Ps 24.07
and be lifted up, O a. doors! 24.09
in the heavens, the a. heavens; 68.33
Remove not the a. landmark which Pro 22.28
Do not remove an a. landmark or 23.10
of the wise, a son of a. kings"? Is 19.11

ANCIENT (cont.)
and from a. times things not yet Is 46.10
And your a. ruins shall be rebuilt; 58.12
They shall build up the a. ruins, 61.04
it is an a. nation, a nation whose Jer 5.15
and look, and ask for the a. paths, 6.16
in the a. roads, and have gone into 18.15
you and me from a. times prophesied 28.08
and, 'The a. heights have become Eze 36.02
one that was a. of days took his Dan 7.09
he came to the A. of Days and was 7.13
until the A. of Days came, and 7.22
is from of old, from a. days. Mic 5.02
if he did not spare the a. world, 2Pe 2.05
that a. serpent, who is called the Rev 12.09
that a. serpent, who is the Devil 20.02

ANCIENTS
As the proverb of the a. says, 1Sa 24.13

ANDREW
is called Peter and A. his brother, Mt 4.18
called Peter, and A. his brother; 10.02
saw Simon and A. the brother of Mk 1.16
entered the house of Simon and A., 1.29
A., and Philip, and Bartholomew, and 3.18
and John and A. asked him privately, 13.03
and A. his brother, and James and Lk 6.14
was A., Simon Peter's brother. Jn 1.40
Bethsaida, the city of A. and Peter. 1.44
A., Simon Peter's brother, said to 6.08
Philip went and told A.; 12.22
A. went with Philip and they told 12.22
Peter and John and James and A., Ac 1.13

ANDRONICUS
Greet A. and Junias, my kinsmen and Rom 16.07

ANEM
and A. with its pasture lands; 1Ch 6.73

ANER
brother of Ashcol and of A.; Gen 14.13
let A., Eshcol, and Mamre take their 14.24
A. with its pasture lands, and 1Ch 6.70

ANEW
say to you, unless one is born a., Jn 3.03
said to you, 'You must be born a.' 3.07
have been born a. to a living hope 1Pe 1.03
You have been born a., 1.23

ANGEL
The a. of the LORD found her by a Gen 16.07
The a. of the LORD said to her, 16.09
The a. of the LORD also said to her, 16.10
And the a. of the LORD said to her, 16.11
and the a. of God called to Hagar 21.17
But the a. of the LORD called to 22.11
And the a. of the LORD called to 22.15
he will send his a. before you, 24.07
will send his a. with you and 24.40
Then the a. of God said to me in 31.11
the a. who has redeemed me from all 48.16
And the a. of the LORD appeared to Ex 3.02
Then the a. of God who went before 14.19
I send an a. before you, to guard 23.20
"When my a. goes before you, and 23.23
behold, my a. shall go before you. 32.34
And I will send an a. before you, 33.02
and sent an a. and brought us forth Num 20.16
and the a. of the LORD took his 22.22
And the ass saw the a. of the LORD 22.23
Then the a. of the LORD stood in a 22.24
the ass saw the a. of the LORD, 22.25
Then the a. of the LORD went ahead, 22.26
When the ass saw the a. of the LORD, 22.27
and he saw the a. of the LORD 22.31
And the a. of the LORD said to him, 22.32
Then Balaam said to the a. of the LORD, 22.34
And the a. of the LORD said to 22.35
Now the a. of the LORD went up from Ju 2.01
When the a. of the LORD spoke these 2.04
says the a. of the LORD, curse 5.23
Now the a. of the LORD came and sat 6.11
And the a. of the LORD appeared to 6.12
And the a. of God said to him, "Take 6.20
Then the a. of the LORD reached out 6.21
and the a. of the LORD vanished 6.21
that he was the a. of the LORD; 6.22
I have seen the a. of the LORD 6.22
And the a. of the LORD appeared to 13.03
the countenance of the a. of God, 13.06
and the a. of God came again to the 13.09
And the a. of the LORD said to 13.13
Manoah said to the a. of the LORD, 13.15
And the a. of the LORD said to 13.16
that he was the a. of the LORD.) 13.16
And Manoah said to the a. of the LORD, 13.17
And the a. of the LORD said to him, 13.18
the a. of the LORD ascended in the 13.20
The a. of the LORD appeared no more 13.21
that he was the a. of the LORD. 13.21
in my sight as an a. of God; 1Sa 29.09
is like the a. of God to discern 2Sa 14.17
wisdom of the a. of God to know 14.20
the king is like the a. of God; 19.27
And when the a. stretched forth his 24.16
and said to the a. who was working 24.16
And the a. of the LORD was by the 24.16
when he saw the a. who was smiting 24.17
and an a. spoke to me by the word 1Ki 13.18
and a. touched him, and said to him, 19.05
And the a. of the LORD came again a 19.07
But the a. of the LORD said to 2Ki 1.03
Then the a. of the LORD said to 1.15
And that night the a. of the LORD 19.35
and the a. of the LORD destroying 1Ch 21.12
And God sent the a. to Jerusalem to 21.15
to the destroying a., "It is enough; 21.15
And the a. of the LORD was 21.15
and saw the a. of the LORD standing 21.16
Then the a. of the LORD commanded 21.18
he turned and saw the a., 21.20
Then the LORD commanded the a.; 21.27
of the sword of the a. of the LORD. 21.30
And the LORD sent an a., 2Ch 32.21
If there be for him an a., Job 33.23
The a. of the LORD encamps around Ps 34.07
with the a. of the LORD driving 35.05
with the a. of the LORD pursuing 35.06
And the a. of the LORD went forth, Is 37.36
and the a. of his presence saved 63.09
has sent his a. and delivered his Dan 3.28
My God sent his a. and shut the 6.22
He strove with the a. and prevailed, Hos 12.04
The a. who talked with me said to Zec 1.09
answered the a. of the LORD who 1.11
Then the a. of the LORD said, 'O 1.12
words to the a. who talked with me 1.13
So the a. who talked with me said 1.14
And I said to the a. who talked 1.19
the a. who talked with me came 2.03
and another a. came forward to meet 2.03
standing before the a. of the LORD, 3.01
Now Joshua was standing before the a., 3.03
And the a. said to those who were 3.04
and the a. of the LORD was standing 3.05
And the a. of the LORD enjoined 3.06
And the a. who talked with me came 4.01
And I said to the a. who talked 4.04
Then the a. who talked with me 4.05
Then the a. who talked with me came 5.05
Then I said to the a. who talked 5.10
Then I said to the a. who talked 6.04

ANGEL (cont.)

And the a. answered me, "These are Zec 6.05
like the a. of the LORD, at their 12.08
an a. of the Lord appeared to him Mt 1.20
he did as the a. of the Lord 1.24
an a. of the Lord appeared to 2.13
an a. of the Lord appeared in a 2.19
for an a. of the Lord descended 28.02
But the a. said to the women, "Do 28.05
to him an a. of the Lord standing Lk 1.11
But the a. said to him, "Do not be 1.13
And Zechariah said to the a., 1.18
And the a. answered him, "I am 1.19
sixth month the a. Gabriel was 1.26
And the a. said to her, "Do not be 1.30
And Mary said to the a., 1.34
And the a. said to her, "The Holy 1.35
And the a. departed from her. 1.38
And an a. of the Lord appeared to 2.09
And the a. said to them, "Be not 2.10
was with the a. a multitude of the 2.13
given by the a. before he was 2.21
appeared to him an a. from heaven, 22.43
for an a. of the Lord went down *Jn 5.04
"An a. has spoken to him." 12.29
But at night an a. of the Lord Ac 5.19
face was like the face of an a. 6.15
an a. appeared to him in the 7.30
the hand of the a. that appeared 7.35
with the a. who spoke to him at 7.38
But an a. of the Lord said to 8.26
in a vision an a. of God coming in 10.03
When the a. who spoke to him had 10.07
by a holy a. to send for you to 10.22
he had seen the a. standing in his 11.13
and behold, an a. of the Lord 12.07
And the a. said to him, "Dress 12.08
what was done by the a. was real, 12.09
and immediately the a. left him. 12.10
has sent his a. and rescued me 12.11
They said, "It is his a.!" 12.15
Immediately an a. of the Lord smote 12.23
resurrection, nor a., nor spirit; 23.08
if a spirit or an a. spoke to him?" 23.09
stood by me an a. of the God to 27.23
disguises himself as an a. of light. 2Co 11.14
or an a. from heaven, should preach Gal 1.08
but received me as an a. of God, 4.14
For to what a. did God ever say, Heb 1.05
But to what a. has he ever said, 1.13
by sending his a. to his servant Rev 1.01
"To the a. of the church in Ephesus 2.01
to the a. of the church in Smyrna 2.08
to the a. of the church in Pergamum 2.12
to the a. of the church in Thyatira 2.18
to the a. of the church in Sardis 3.01
to the a. of the church in Philadelphia 3.07
to the a. of the church in Laodicea 3.14
and I saw a strong a. proclaiming 5.02
Then I saw another a. ascend from 7.02
And another a. came and stood at 8.03
from the hand of the a. before God. 8.04
Then the a. took the censer and 8.05
The first a. blew his trumpet, and 8.07
The second a. blew his trumpet, and 8.08
The third a. blew his trumpet, and a 8.10
The fourth a. blew his trumpet, and 8.12
And the fifth a. blew his trumpet, 9.01
over them the a. of the bottomless 9.11
Then the sixth a. blew his trumpet, 9.13
saying to the sixth a. who had the 9.14
another mighty a. coming down from 10.01
And the a. whom I saw standing on 10.05
to be sounded by the seventh a., 10.07
the hand of the a. who is standing 10.08
So I went to the a. and told him to 10.09
from the hand of the a. and ate it; 10.10
Then the seventh a. blew his 11.15
Then I saw another a. flying in 14.06
Another a., a second, followed, 14.08
And another a., a third, followed, 14.09
And another a. came out of the 14.15
And another a. came out of the 14.17
Then another a. came out from the 14.18
the a. who has power over fire, and 14.18
So the a. swung his sickle on the 14.19
So the first a. went and poured his 16.02
The second a. poured his bowl into 16.03
The third a. poured his bowl into 16.04
And I heard the a. of water say, 16.05
The fourth a. poured his bowl on 16.08
The fifth a. poured his bowl on the 16.10
The sixth a. poured his bowl on the 16.12
The seventh a. poured his bowl into 16.17
But the a. said to me, "Why marvel? 17.07
I saw another a. coming down from 18.01
Then a mighty a. took up a stone 18.21
And the a. said to me, "Write this: 19.09
Then I saw an a. standing in the 19.17
Then I saw an a. coming down from 20.01
has sent his a. to show his servants 22.06
the feet of the a. who showed them 22.08
have sent my a. to you with this 22.16

ANGEL'S

by a man's measure, that is, an a. Rev 21.17

ANGELS

The two a. came to Sodom in the Gen 19.01
the a. urged Lot, saying, "Arise, take 19.15
the a. of God were ascending and 28.12
his way and the a. of God met him; 32.01
and his a. he charges with error; Job 4.18
Man ate of the bread of the a.; Ps 78.25
distress, a company of destroying a. 78.49
will give his a. charge of you to 91.11
O you his a., you mighty ones who 103.20
all his a., praise him, all his host 148.02
'He will give his a. charge of you, Mt 4.06
a. came and ministered to him. 4.11
of the age, and the reapers are a. 13.39
The Son of man will send his a., 13.41
The a. will come out and separate 13.49
come with his a. in the glory of 16.27
in heaven their a. always behold 18.10
marriage, but are like a. in heaven. 22.30
send out his a. with a loud 24.31
not even the a. of heaven, nor the 24.36
and all the a. with him, then he 25.31
prepared for the devil and his a.; 25.41
me more than twelve legions of a. 26.53
and the a. ministered to him. Mk 1.13
of his Father with the holy a. 8.38
marriage, but are like a. in heaven. 12.25
And then he will send out the a., 13.27
not even the a. in heaven, nor the 13.32
When the a. went away from them Lk 2.15
'He will give his a. charge of you, 4.10
of the Father and of the holy a. 9.26
acknowledge before the a. of God; 12.08
be denied before the a. of God. 12.09
joy before the a. of God over one 15.10
carried by the a. to Abraham's 16.22
are equal to a. and are sons of 20.36
they had even seen a vision of a., 24.23
and the a. of God ascending and Jn 1.51
and she saw two a. in white, 20.12
as delivered by a. and did not Ac 7.53
nor a., nor principalities, nor Rom 8.38
to the world, to a. and to men. 1Co 4.09
not know that we are to judge a.? 6.03
on her head, because of the a. 11.10
in the tongues of men and of a., 13.01
was ordained by a. through an Gal 3.19
self-abasement and worship of a., Col 2.18

ANGELS (cont.)

with his mighty a. in flaming fire, 2Th 1.07
seen by a., preached among the 1Ti 3.16
of the elect a. I charge you to 5.21
superior to a. as the name he has Heb 1.04
says, "Let all God's a. worship him." 1.06
Of the a. he says, "Who makes his 1.07
he says, "Who makes his a. winds, 1.07
declared by a. was valid and every 2.02
For it was not to a. that God 2.05
a little while lower than the a., 2.07
while was made lower than the a., 2.09
it is not with a. that he is 2.16
to innumerable a. in festal 12.22
some have entertained a. unawares. 13.02
things into which a. long to look. 1Pe 1.12
with a., authorities, and powers 3.22
not spare the a. when they sinned, 2Pe 2.04
whereas a., though greater in might 2.11
And the a. that did not keep their Jud 1.06
stars are the a. of the seven Rev 1.20
before my Father and before his a. 3.05
the elders the voice of many a., 5.11
After this I saw four a. standing 7.01
to the four a. who had been given 7.02
And all the a. stood round the 7.11
Then I saw the seven a. who stand 8.02
Now the seven a. who had the seven 8.06
which the three a. are about to 8.13
the four a. who are bound at the 9.14
So the four a. were released, who 9.15
Michael and his a. fighting 12.07
and the dragon and his a. fought, 12.07
and his a. were thrown down with 12.09
of the holy a. and in the presence 14.10
seven a. with seven plagues, which 15.01
came the seven a. with the seven 15.06
gave the seven a. seven golden 15.07
plagues of the seven a. were ended. 15.08
the temple telling the seven a., 16.01
of the seven a. who had the seven 17.01
of the seven a. who had the seven 21.09
gates, and at the gates twelve a., 21.12

ANGER

until your brother's a. turns away, Gen 27.45
Jacob's a. was kindled against 30.02
treated me," his a. was kindled. 39.19
let not your a. burn against your 44.18
for in their a. they slay men, and 49.06
Cursed be their a., for it is 49.07
Then the a. of the LORD was kindled Ex 4.14
he went out from Pharaoh in hot a. 11.08
Moses' a. burning hot, and he threw 32.19
"Let not the a. of my lord burn hot 32.22
slow to a., and abounding in 34.06
his a. was kindled, and the fire of Num 11.01
and the a. of the LORD blazed hotly, 11.10
the a. of the LORD was kindled 11.33
And the a. of the LORD was kindled 12.09
'The LORD is slow to a., 14.18
But God's a. was kindled because he 22.22
and Balaam's a. was kindled, and he 22.27
And Balak's a. was kindled against 24.10
And the a. of the LORD was kindled 25.03
that the fierce a. of the LORD may 25.04
And the LORD's a. was kindled on 32.10
And the LORD's a. was kindled 32.13
more the fierce a. of the LORD 32.14
God, so as to provoke him to a., Deu 4.25
lest the a. of the LORD your God be 6.15
then the a. of the LORD would be 7.04
of the LORD, to provoke him to a. 9.18
afraid of the a. and hot displeasure 9.19
and the a. of the LORD be kindled 11.17
turn from the fierceness of his a., 13.17
of blood in hot a. pursue the 19.06
but rather the a. of the LORD and 29.20
overthrew in his a. and wrath— 29.23
means the heat of this great a.?' 29.24
therefore the a. of the LORD was 29.27
their land in a. and fury and 29.28
Then my a. will be kindled against 31.17
provoking him to a. through the 31.29
practices they provoked him to a. 32.16
For a fire is kindled by my a., 32.22
and the a. of the LORD burned Jos 7.01
LORD turned from his burning a. 7.26
Then the a. of the LORD will be 23.16
and they provoked the LORD to a. Ju 2.12
So the a. of the LORD was kindled 2.14
So the a. of the LORD was kindled 2.20
Therefore the a. of the LORD was 3.08
"Let not thy a. burn against me, let 6.39
Then their a. against him was 8.03
son of Ebed, his a. was kindled. 9.30
And the a. of the LORD was kindled 10.07
In hot a. he went back to his 14.19
and his a. was greatly kindled. 1Sa 11.06
and Eliab's a. was kindled against 17.28
Then Saul's a. was kindled against 20.30
table in fierce a. and ate no food 20.34
And the a. of the LORD was kindled 2Sa 6.07
if the king's a. rises, and if he 11.20
Then David's a. was greatly kindled 12.05
Again the a. of the LORD was 24.01
molten images, provoking me to a., 1Ki 14.09
Asherim, provoking the LORD to a. 14.15
because of the a. to which he 15.30
provoking me to a. with their sins, 16.02
provoking him to a. with the work 16.07
of Israel to a. with their idols. 16.13
of Israel, to a. by their idols. 16.26
to a. than all the kings of Israel 16.33
for the a. to which you have 21.22
to a. in every way that his father 22.53
And the a. of the LORD was kindled 2Ki 13.03
things, provoking the LORD to a., 17.11
of the LORD, provoking him to a., 17.17
of the LORD, provoking him to a. 21.06
sight and have provoked me to a., 21.15
provoke me to a. with all the work 22.17
had made, provoking the LORD to a., 23.19
by which his a. was kindled against 23.26
For because of the a. of the LORD 24.20
And the a. of the LORD was kindled 1Ch 13.10
Jehoram the a. of the Philistines 2Ch 21.16
and returned home in fierce a. 25.10
provoking to a. the LORD, the God of 28.25
that his fierce a. may turn away 29.10
that his fierce a. may turn away 30.08
of the LORD, provoking him to a. 33.06
provoke me to a. with all the 34.25
provoked thee to a. before the Neh 4.05
slow to a. and abounding in steadfast 9.17
and his a. burned within him. Est 1.12
when the a. of King Ahasuerus had 2.01
Then the a. of the king abated. 7.10
blast of his a. they are consumed. Job 4.09
when he overturns them in his a.; 9.05
"God will not turn back his a.; 9.13
You who tear yourself in your a., 18.04
will send his fierce a. into him, 20.23
God distributes pains in his a.? 21.17
because his a. does not punish, and 35.15
"The godless in heart cherish a.; 36.13
is jealous with a. against iniquity. 36.33
Pour forth the overflowings of your a., 40.11
O LORD, rebuke me not in thy a., Ps 6.01
in thy a., lift thyself up against 7.06
Turn not thy servant away in a., 27.09
For his a. is but for a moment, and 30.05
Refrain from a., and forsake wrath! 37.08
O LORD, rebuke me not in thy a., 38.01

ANGER (cont.)
and in a. they cherish enmity Ps 55.03
let thy burning a. overtake them. 69.24
Why does thy a. smoke against the 74.01
thee when once thy a. is roused? 76.07
Has he in a. shut up his compassion?" 77.09
his a. mounted against Israel; 78.21
the a. of God rose against them and 78.31
he restrained his a. often, 78.38
He let loose on them his fierce a., 78.49
He made a path for his a.; 78.50
provoked him to a. with their high 78.58
Pour out thy a. on the nations that 79.06
thou didst turn from thy hot a. 85.03
prolong thy a. to all generations? 85.05
slow to a. and abounding in steadfast 86.15
For we are consumed by thy a.; 90.07
Who considers the power of thy a., 90.11
Therefore I swore in my a. that 95.11
because of thy indignation and a.; 102.10
slow to a. and abounding in steadfast 103.08
nor will he keep his a. for ever. 103.09
The LORD to a. with their doings, 106.29
Then the a. of the LORD was kindled 106.40
when their a. was kindled against 124.03
slow to a. and abounding in steadfast 145.08
He who is slow to a. has great Pro 14.29
but a harsh word stirs up a. 15.01
who is slow to a. quiets contention 15.18
He who is slow to a. is better than 16.32
Good sense makes a man slow to a., 19.11
provokes him to a. forfeits his 20.02
A gift in secret averts a.; 21.14
friendship with a man given to a., 22.24
and turn away his a. from him. 24.18
a. is overwhelming; 27.04
A fool gives full vent to his a., 29.11
a man given to a. causes much 29.22
and pressing a. produces strife. 30.33
Be not quick to a., Ecc 7.09
for a. lodges in the bosom of fools 7.09
If the a. of the ruler rises 10.04
Therefore the a. of the LORD was Is 5.25
all this his a. is not turned away 5.25
at the fierce a. of Rezin and Syria 7.04
all this his a. is not turned away 9.12
all this his a. is not turned away 9.17
all this his a. is not turned away 9.21
all this his a. is not turned away 10.04
the rod of my a., the staff of my 10.05
and my a. will be directed to their 10.25
thy a. turned away, and thou didst 12.01
my mighty men to execute my a., 13.03
cruel, with wrath and fierce a., 13.09
hosts in the day of his fierce a. 13.13
the nations in a. with unrelenting 14.06
from far, burning with his a., 30.27
in furious a. and a flame of 30.30
the heat of his a. and the might 42.25
"For my name's sake I defer my a., 48.09
trod them in my a. and trampled 63.03
I trod down the peoples in my a., 63.06
to render his a. in fury, and his 66.15
surely his a. has turned from me.' Jer 2.35
I will not look on you in a., 3.12
for the fierce a. of the LORD has 4.08
the LORD, before his fierce a. 4.26
to other gods, to provoke me to a. 7.18
my a. and my wrath will be poured 7.20
provoked me to a. with their 8.19
not in thy a., lest thou bring me 10.24
provoking me to a. by burning 11.17
of the fierce a. of the LORD." 12.13
for in my a. a fire is kindled 15.14
for in my a. a fire is kindled 17.04
with them in the time of thine a. 18.23
in a., and in fury, and in great 21.05
The a. of the LORD will not turn 23.20
provoke me to a. with the work of 25.06
provoke me to a. with the work of 25.07
of the fierce a. of the LORD. 25.37
LORD, and because of his fierce a." 25.38
The fierce a. of the LORD will not 30.24
to other gods, to provoke me to a. 32.29
provoke me to a. by the work of 32.30
This city has aroused my a. and wrath, 32.31
they did to provoke me to a. 32.32
them in my a. and my wrath and in 32.37
shall smite in my a. and my wrath, 33.05
great is the a. and wrath that the 36.07
As my a. and my wrath were poured 42.18
they committed, provoking me to a., 44.03
Therefore my wrath and my a. were 44.06
provoke me to a. with the works of 44.08
them, my fierce a., says the LORD. 49.37
from the fierce a. of the LORD! 51.45
Surely because of the a. of the 52.03
on the day of his fierce a. Lam 1.12
How the Lord in his a. has set the 2.01
his footstool in the day of his a. 2.01
down in fierce a. all the might of 2.03
the day of thy a. thou hast slain 2.21
the day of the a. of the LORD none 2.22
thyself with a. and pursued us, 3.43
pursue them in a. and destroy them 3.66
wrath, he poured out his hot a.; 4.11
"Thus shall my a. spend itself, and Eze 5.13
judgments on you in a. and fury, 5.15
I will let loose my a. upon you, 7.03
and spend my a. against you, and 7.08
and provoke me further to a.? 8.17
shall be a deluge of rain in my a., 13.13
your harlotry, to provoke me to a. 16.26
and spend my a. against them in 20.08
and spend my a. against them in 20.21
you in my a. and in my wrath, and I 22.20
according to my a. and according 25.14
according to the a. and envy which 35.11
so I have consumed them in my a. 43.08
let thy a. and thy wrath turn away Dan 9.16
moved with a., shall come out and 11.11
neither in a. nor in battle. 11.20
all night their a. smolders; Hos 7.06
My a. burns against them. 8.05
I will not execute my fierce a., 11.09
I have given you kings in my a., 13.11
for my a. has turned from them. 14.04
slow to a., and abounding in Joe 2.13
and his a. tore perpetually, and he Amo 1.11
repent and turn from his fierce a., Jon 3.09
slow to a., and abounding in 4.02
And in a. and wrath I will execute Mic 5.15
not retain his a. for ever because 7.18
The LORD is slow to a. and of great Nah 1.03
who can endure the heat of his a.? 1.06
Was thy a. against the rivers, or Hab 3.08
didst trample the nations in a. 3.12
upon you the fierce a. of the LORD, Zep 2.02
indignation, all the heat of my a.; 3.08
"My a. is hot against the shepherds, Zec 10.03
And in a. his lord delivered him to Mt 18.34
And he looked around at them with a., Mk 3.05
householder in a. said to his Lk 14.21
a., selfishness, slander, gossip, 2Co 12.20
a., selfishness, dissension, party Gal 5.20
let the sun go down on your a., Eph 4.26
and wrath and a. and clamor and 4.31
do not provoke your children to a., 6.04
a., wrath, malice, slander, and foul Col 3.08
hands without a. or quarreling; 1Ti 2.08
being afraid of the a. of the king; Heb 11.27
hear, slow to speak, slow to a., Jas 1 19
for the a. of man does not work the 1.20
unmixed into the cup of his a., Rev 14.10

ANGERED
words, and was a., and he swore, Deu 1.34
our fathers had a. the God of Ez 5.12
They a. him at the waters of Ps 106.32

ANGLE
at the Valley Gate and at the A., 2Ch 26.09
the ascent to the armory at the A. Neh 3.19
from the A. to the door of the 3.20
the house of Azariah to the A. 3.24
opposite the A. and the tower 3.25

ANGRY
So Cain was very a., Gen 4.05
"Why are you a., and why has your 4.06
he said, "Oh let not the LORD be a., 18.30
he said, "Oh let not the LORD be a., 18.32
not my lord be a. that I cannot 31.35
Then Jacob became a., 31.36
the men were indignant and very a., 34.07
And Pharaoh was a. with his two 40.02
When Pharaoh was a. with his 41.10
or a. with yourselves, because you 45.05
and Moses was a. with them. Ex 16.20
And he was a. with Eleazar and Lev 10.16
And Moses was very a., Num 16.15
wilt thou be a. with all the 16.22
And Moses was a. with the officers 31.14
The LORD was a. with me also on Deu 1.37
But the LORD was a. with me on your 3.26
Furthermore the LORD was a. with me 4.21
the LORD was so a. with you that 9.08
And the LORD was so a. with Aaron 9.20
he will be a. with the whole Jos 22.18
lest a. fellows fall upon you, Ju 18.25
And his concubine became a. with him, 19.02
And Samuel was a.; and he 1Sa 15.11
And Saul was very a., and this 18.08
but if he is a., then know that 20.07
the Philistines were a. with him; 29.04
Then Abner was very a. over the 2Sa 3.08
And David was a. because the LORD 6.08
all these things, he was very a. 13.21
then are you a. over this matter 19.42
and quaked, because he was a. 22.08
and thou art a. with them, and dost 1Ki 8.46
And the LORD was a. with Solomon, 11.90
But Naaman was a., and went away, 2Ki 5.11
Then the man of God was a. with him, 13.19
Therefore the LORD was very a. with Israel, 17.18
And David was a. because the LORD 1Ch 13.11
and thou art a. with them, and dost 2Ch 6.36
Then Asa was a. with the seer, and 16.10
And they became very a. with Judah, 25.10
Therefore the LORD was a. with 25.15
Then Uzziah was a. Now he 26.19
when he became a. with the priests 26.19
was a. with Judah, he gave them into 28.09
thou not be a. with us till thou Ez 9.14
he was a. and greatly enraged, and Neh 4.01
to be closed, they were very a.; 4.07
I was very a. when I heard their 5.06
And I was very a., and I threw all 13.08
became a. and sought to lay hands Est 2.21
of the family of Ram, became a. Job 32.02
He was a. at Job because he justified 32.02
he was a. also at Job's three 32.03
of these three men, he became a. 32.05
lest he be a., and you perish in Ps 2.12
Be a., but sin not; commune 4.04
and quaked, because he was a. 18.07
thou hast been a.; oh, restore 60.01
Wilt thou be a. for ever? 79.05
wilt thou be a. with thy people's 80.04
Wilt thou be a. with us for ever? 85.05
The wicked man sees it and is a.; 112.10
the LORD is a. will fall into it. Pro 22.14
and a backbiting tongue, a. looks. 25.23
why should God be a. at your voice, Ecc 5.06
My mother's sons were a. with me, Sol 1.06
for though thou wast a. with me, Is 12.01
I was a. with my people, I profaned 47.06
I will not be a. with you and will 54.09
for ever, nor will I always be a.; 57.16
of his covetousness I was a., 57.17
him, I hid my face and was a.; 57.17
thou wast a., and we sinned; 64.05
Be not exceedingly a., 64.09
will he be a. for ever, will he be Jer 3.05
I will not be a. for ever. 3.12
Art thou exceedingly a. with us? Lam 5.22
be calm, and will no more be a. Eze 16.42
the king was a. and very furious, Dan 2.12
Jonah exceedingly, and he was a. Jon 4.01
LORD said, "Do you do well to be a.?" 4.04
you do well to be a. for the plant?" 4.09
And he said, "I do well to be a., 4.09
do well to be a., a. enough to die." 4.09
"The LORD was very a. with your Zec 1.02
And I am very a. with the nations 1.15
for while I was a. but a little 1.15
with whom the LORD is a. for ever. Mal 1.04
one who is a. with his brother Mt 5.22
The king was a., and he sent his 22.07
But he was a. and refused to go in. Lk 15.28
are you a. with me because on the Jn 7.23
Now Herod was a. with the people of Ac 12.20
foolish nation I will make you a. Rom 10.19
Be a. but do not sin; do not let Eph 4.26
Then the dragon was a. with the woman, Rev 12.17

ANGUISH
and be in a. because of you.' Deu 2.25
for a. has seized me, and yet my 2Sa 1.09
will speak in the a. of my spirit; Job 7.11
distress and a. terrify him; 15.24
a. as of a woman in travail. Ps 48.06
My heart is in a. within me, the 55.04
I suffered distress and a. 116.03
Trouble and a. have come upon me, 119.143
when distress and a. come upon you. Pro 1.27
and darkness, the gloom of a.; Is 8.22
be no gloom for her that was in a. 9.01
they will be in a. like a woman in 13.08
Therefore my loins are filled with a.; 21.03
they will be in a. over the report 23.05
Through a land of trouble and a., 30.06
and shall wail for a. of spirit. 65.14
My a., my a.! I writhe Jer 4.19
a. as of one bringing forth her 4.31
smitten them, but they felt no a.; 5.03
a. has taken hold of us, pain as of 6.24
I have made a. and terror fall upon 15.08
a. and sorrows have taken hold of 49.24
a. seized him, pain as of a woman in 50.43
When a. comes, they will seek peace, Eze 7.25
and a. shall be in Ethiopia, when 30.04
and a. shall come upon them on the 30.09
in a tone of a. and said to Daniel, Dan 6.20
Before them peoples are in a., Joe 2.06
a. is on all loins, all faces grow Nah 2.10
that day, a day of distress and a., Zep 1.15
Gaza too, and shall writhe in a.; Zec 9.05
for I am in a. in this flame. Lk 16.24
comforted here, and you are in a. 16.25
she no longer remembers the a., Jn 16.21
and unceasing a. in my heart. Rom 9.02
affliction and a. of heart and 2Co 2.04
pangs of birth, in a. for delivery. Rev 12.02
gnawed their tongues in a. 16.10

ANIAM
were Ahian, Shechem, Likhi, and A. 1Ch 7.19

ANIM
Anab, Eshtemoh, A., Jos 15.50

ANIMAL
of every clean a. and of every Gen 8.20
and slaughter an a. and make ready, 43.16
if he offers an a. from the herd, Lev 3.01
the LORD is an a. from the flock, 3.06
The fat of an a. that dies of 7.24
the fat of an a. of which an 7.25
whatever, whether of fowl or of a., 7.26
Every a. which parts the hoof but 11.26
"And if any a. of which you may eat 11.39
Any a. which has its testicles 22.24
"If it is an a. such as men offer 27.09
is an unclean a. such as is not 27.11
shall bring the a. before the 27.11
And if it is an unclean a., 27.27
every tenth a. of all that pass 27.32
Every a. that parts the hoof and Deu 14.06

ANIMALS
all cattle, and above all wild a.; Gen 3.14
and of the a. according to their 6.20
you seven pairs of all clean a., 7.02
a pair of the a. that are not 7.02
Of clean a., and of a. that are not 7.08
man and a. and creeping things and 7.23
birds and a. and every creeping 8.17
time for the a. to be gathered 29.07
the cud, among the a., you may eat. Lev 11.03
among the a. that go on all fours, 11.27
A. blind or disabled or mutilated 22.22
God any such a. gotten from a 22.25
"But a firstling of a., which as a 27.26
These are the a. you may eat: the ox, Deu 14.04
the cud, among the a., you may eat. 14.06
alive, and not lose some of the a. 1Ki 18.05
the men and a. that are on the Jer 27.05
When you offer blind a. in sacrifice, Mal 1.08
all kinds of a. and reptiles and Ac 10.12
I observed a. and beasts of prey 11.06
man or birds or a. or reptiles. Rom 1.23
another for a., another for birds, 1Co 15.39
bodies of those a. whose blood is Heb 13.11
But these, like irrational a., 2Pe 2.12
by instinct as irrational a. do, Jud 1.10

ANKLE-DEEP
through the water; and it was a. Eze 47.03

ANKLES
his feet and a. were made strong. Ac 3.07

ANKLETS
take away the finery of the a., Is 3.18

ANNA
A., the daughter ot Phanuel, of the Lk 2.36

ANNAS
high-priesthood of A. and Caiaphas, Lk 3.02
First they led him to A.; for he was Jn 18.13
A. then sent him bound to Caiaphas 18.24
with A. the high priest and Caiaphas Ac 4.06

ANNIHILATE
and to a. all Jews, young and old, Est 3.13
and to a. any armed force of any 8.11

ANNIHILATED
destroyed, to be slain, and to be a. Est 7.04

ANNOUNCE
watchman, let him a. what he sees. Is 21.06
the God of Israel, I a. to you. 21.10
a. to Jerusalem, "Besiegers come Jer 4.16

ANNOUNCED
or now a. to us such things as Ju 13.23
Who has a. from of old the things Is 44.07
they came to pass I a. them to you, 48.05
Bring thou the day thou hast a., Lam 1.21
those who a. beforehand the coming Ac 7.52
have now been a. to you by those 1Pe 1.12
as he a. to his servants the Rev 10.07

ANNOUNCING
"It is I, a. vindication, mighty to Is 63.01

ANNOYED
a. because they were teaching the Ac 4.02
But Paul was a., and turned and 16.18

ANNUAL
and the three a. feasts—the feast 2Ch 8.13

ANNUALLY
had to deliver a. to the king of 2Ki 3.04

ANNUL
has purposed, and who will a. it? Is 14.27
does not a. a covenant previously Gal 3.17

ANNULLED
covenant with death will be a., Is 28.18
So it was a. on that day, and the Zec 11.11

ANNULLING
a. the covenant which I had made Zec 11.10
a. the brotherhood between Judah 11.14

ANNULS
no one a. even a man's will, or adds Gal 3.15

ANOINT
and shall a. them and ordain them Ex 28.41
and pour it on his head and a. him. 29.07
and shall a. it, to consecrate it. 29.36
And you shall a. with it the tent 30.26
And you shall a. Aaron and his sons, 30.30
and a. the tabernacle and all that 40.09
You shall also a. the altar of 40.10
You shall also a. the laver and its 40.11
and you shall a. him and consecrate 40.13
and a. them, as you anointed their 40.15
you shall not a. yourself with the Deu 28.40
went forth to a. a king over them; Ju 9.08
Wash therefore and a. yourself, Ru 3.03
and you shall a. him to be prince 1Sa 9.16
LORD sent me to a. you king over 15.01
and you shall a. for me him whom I 16.03
And the LORD said, "Arise, a. him; 16.12
do not a. yourself with oil, but 2Sa 14.02
prophet there a. him king over 1Ki 1.34
you shall a. Hazael to be king over 19.15
you shall a. to be king over 19.16
you shall a. to be prophet in your 19.16
I a. you king over Israel.' 2Ki 9.03
I a. you king over the people of 9.06
I a. you king over Israel.' " 9.12
oil of the wicked never a. my head; Ps 141.05
and to a. a most holy place. Dan 9.24
nor did I a. myself at all, for the 10.03
and a. themselves with the finest Amo 6.06
but not a. yourselves with oil; Mic 6.15
a. your head and wash your face, Mt 6.17
so that they might go and a. him. Mk 16.01
You did not a. my head with oil, but Lk 7.46
servant Jesus, whom thou didst a., Ac 4.27
and salve to a. your eyes, that you Rev 3.18

ANOINTED
where you a. a pillar and made a Gen 31.13
to be a. in them and ordained in Ex 29.29
as you a. their father, that they 40.15
if it is the a. priest who sins, Lev 4.03

ANOINTED (cont.)
And the priest shall take some Lev 4.05
Then the a. priest shall bring some 4.16
the LORD on the day when he is a.: 6.20
who is a. to succeed him, shall 6.22
on the day that they were a.; 7.36
and a. the tabernacle and all that 8.10
and a. the altar and all its 8.11
and a. him, to consecrate him. 8.12
priest who is a. and consecrated 16.32
the a. priests, whom he ordained to Num 3.03
and had a. and consecrated it with 7.01
of the altar on the day it was a.; 7.10
altar, on the day when it was a., 7.84
for the altar, after it was a. 7.88
priest who was a. with the holy 35.25
and exalt the power of his a. 1Sa 2.10
in and out before my a. for ever. 2.35
the LORD has a. you to be prince 10.01
before the LORD and before his a. 12.03
and his a. is witness this day, that 12.05
The LORD a. you king over Israel. 15.17
"Surely the LORD's a. is before him." 16.06
and a. him in the midst of his 16.13
the LORD's a., to put forth my hand 24.06
him, seeing he is the LORD's a." 24.06
for he is the LORD's a.' 24.10
his hand against the LORD's a., 26.09
my hand against the LORD's a.; 26.11
over your lord, the LORD's a. 26.16
my hand against the LORD's a. 26.23
your hand to destroy the LORD's a.?" 2Sa 1.14
'I have slain the LORD's a.' " 1.16
shield of Saul, not a. with oil. 1.21
and there they a. David king over 2.04
of Judah has a. me king over them." 2.07
I am this day weak, though a. king; 3.39
and they a. David king over Israel. 5.03
David had been a. king over Israel, 5.17
'I a. you king over Israel, and I 12.07
and a. himself, and changed his 12.20
whom we a. over us, is dead in 19.10
because he cursed the LORD's a.?" 19.21
and shows steadfast love to his a., 22.51
the a. of the God of Jacob, the 23.01
oil from the tent, and a. Solomon. 1Ki 1.39
prophet have a. him king at Gihon; 1.45
that they had a. him king in place 5.01
proclaimed him king, and a. him; 2Ki 11.12
and a. him, and made him king in his 23.30
and they a. David king over Israel, 1Ch 11.03
David had been a. king over all 14.08
"Touch not my a. ones, do my prophets 16.22
and they a. him as prince for the 29.22
turn away the face of thy a. one! 2Ch 6.42
the LORD had a. to destroy the 22.07
and Jehoiada and his sons a. him, 23.11
with food and drink, and a. them; 28.15
the LORD and his a., saying, Ps 2.02
and shows steadfast love to his a., 18.50
that the LORD will help his a.; 20.06
he is the saving refuge of his a. 28.08
has a. you with the oil of gladness 45.07
look upon the face of thine a.! 84.09
with my holy oil I have a. him; 89.20
art full of wrath against thy a. 89.38
they mock the footsteps of thy a. 89.51
"Touch not my a. ones, do my prophets 105.15
turn away the face of thy a. one. 132.10
I have prepared a lamp for my a. 132.17
Thus says the LORD to his a., Is 45.01
the LORD has a. me to bring good 61.01
the LORD's a., was taken in their Lam 4.20
from you, and a. you with oil. Eze 16.09
With an a. guardian cherub I placed 28.14
Jerusalem to the coming of an a. one, Dan 9.25
an a. one shall be cut off, and 9.26
for the salvation of thy a. Hab 3.13
are the two a. who stand by the Zec 4.14
and a. with oil many that were sick Mk 6.13
she has a. my body beforehand for 14.08
because he has a. me to preach Lk 4.18
and a. them with the ointment. 7.38
but she has a. my feet with ointment 7.46
the spittle and a. the man's eyes Jn 9.06
made clay and a. my eyes and said 9.11
It was Mary who a. the Lord with 11.02
pure nard and a. the feet of Jesus 12.03
the LORD and against his A.'— Ac 4.26
how God a. Jesus of Nazareth with 10.38
has a. thee with the oil of gladness Heb 1.09
But you have been a. by the Holy 1Jn 2.20

ANOINTEST
thou a. my head with oil, my cup Ps 23.05

ANOINTING
spices for the a. oil and for the Ex 25.06
And you shall take the a. oil, 29.07
and of the a. oil, and sprinkle it 29.21
these a sacred a. oil blended as 30.25
a holy a. oil it shall be. 30.25
be my holy a. oil throughout your 30.31
and the a. oil and the fragrant 31.11
spices for the a. oil and for the 35.08
and the a. oil and the fragrant 35.15
and for the a. oil, and for the 35.28
He made the holy a. oil also, 37.29
the a. oil and the fragrant incense, 39.38
Then you shall take the a. oil, 40.09
and their a. shall admit them to a 40.15
and the a. oil, and the bull of the Lev 8.02
Then Moses took the a. oil, 8.10
some of the a. oil on Aaron's head, 8.12
some of the a. oil and of the 8.30
for the a. oil of the LORD is upon 10.07
whose head the a. oil is poured, 21.10
consecration of the a. oil of his 21.12
and the a. oil, with the oversight Num 4.16
faith you are a. me king over you, Ju 9.15
your a. oils are fragrant, your name Sol 1.03
while from a. king and princes. Hos 8.10
a. him with oil in the name of the Jas 5.14
but the a. which you received from 1Jn 2.27
as his a. teaches you about everything, 2.27

ANOTHER
appointed for me a. child instead Gen 4.25
He waited a. seven days, and again 8.10
Then he waited a. seven days, and 8.12
And they said to one a., 11.03
Abraham took a. wife, whose name was 25.01
Then they dug a. well, and they 26.21
moved from there and dug a. well, 26.22
early and took oath with one a.; 26.31
for serving me a. seven years. 29.27
served Laban for a. seven years. 29.30
"May the LORD add to me a. son!" 30.24
for now you will have a. son." 35.17
Then he dreamed a. dream, 37.09
"Behold, I have dreamed a. dream; 37.09
They said to one a., "Here comes 37.19
sons, "Why do you look at one a.?" 42.01
Then they said to one a., "In truth 42.21
they turned trembling to one a., 42.28
the man that you had a. brother?" 43.06
Have you a. brother?' What we 43.07
men looked at one a. in amazement. 43.33
they did not see one a., nor did Ex 10.23
they said to one a., "What is it?" 16.15
If he takes a. wife to himself, he 21.10
willfully attacks a. to kill him 21.14
and it feeds in a. man's field, 22.05
their wings, their faces one to a.; 25.20

ANOTHER (cont.)
curtains shall be coupled to one a.; Ex 26.03
the loops shall be opposite one a. 26.05
two bases under a. frame for its 26.19
and two bases under a. frame; 26.21
and two bases under a. frame. 26.25
he coupled five curtains to one a., 36.10
the loops were opposite one a. 36.12
two bases under a. frame for its 36.24
frame and two bases under a. frame. 36.26
wings, with their faces one to a.; 37.09
sons of Aaron, one as well as a. Lev 7.10
deal falsely, nor lie to one a. 19.11
betrothed to a. man and not yet 19.20
neighbor, you shall not wrong one a. 25.14
You shall not wrong one a., 25.17
one over a., with harshness. 25.46
They shall stumble over one a., 26.37
if he has sold the field to a. man, 27.20
you shall take a. young bull for a Num 8.08
And they said to one a., 14.04
to him, "Come with me to a. place, 23.13
now, I will take you to a. place; 23.27
transferred from one tribe to a.; 36.07
transferred from one tribe to a.; 36.09
from the midst of a. nation, Deu 4.34
one kind of homicide and a., 17.08
one kind of legal right and a., 17.08
or one kind of assault and a., 17.08
the battle and a. man dedicate it. 20.05
the battle and a. man enjoy its 20.06
in the battle and a. man take her. 20.07
lying with the wife of a. man, 22.22
goes and becomes a. man's wife, 24.02
"When men fight with one a., 25.11
and a. man shall lie with her; 28.30
shall be given to a. people, 28.32
wrath, and cast them into a. land, 29.28
Then the boundary goes in a. direction, Jos 18.14
and there arose a. generation after Ju 2.10
And they said to one a., "Who has 6.29
said one to a., "Who is the man 10.18
for you are the son of a. woman." 11.02
go to glean in a. field or leave Ru 2.08
lest in a. field you be molested." 2.22
before one could recognize a.; 3.14
a. carrying three loaves of bread, 1Sa 10.03
and a. carrying a skin of wine. 10.03
them and be turned into a. man. 10.06
Samuel, God gave him a. heart; 10.09
prophets, the people said to one a., 10.11
a. company turned toward Bethhorn, 13.18
And he turned away from him toward a., 17.30
sang to one a. as they made merry, 18.07
and they kissed one a., 20.41
and wept with one a., until David 20.41
not sing to one a. of him in 21.11
whom they sing to one a. in dances, 29.05
could not answer Abner a. word, 2Sa 3.11
sword devours now one and now a.; 11.25
quarreled with one a. in the field; 14.06
you may carry tidings a. day, 18.20
And the watchman saw a. man running; 18.26
"See, a. man running alone!" 18.26
So he went a. way, and did not 1Ki 13.10
came, she pretended to be a. woman. 14.05
why do you pretend to be a.? 14.06
Obadiah went in a. direction by 18.06
encamped opposite one a. seven days. 20.29
Then he found a. man, and said, 20.37
I will give you a. vineyard for it'; 21.06
there not here a. prophet of the 22.07
one thing, and a. said a. 22.20
sent to him a. captain of fifty 2Ki 1.11
fought together, and slain one a. 3.23
to her son, "Bring me a. vessel." 4.06
he said to her, "There is not a." 4.06
and they said to one a., 7.03
army, so that they said to one a., 7.06
and entered a. tent, and carried off 7.08
Then they said to one a., 7.09
(a. third being at the gate Sur and 11.06
let us look one a. in the face." 14.08
Judah faced one a. in battle at 14.11
Jerusalem from one end to a., 21.16
Jerahmeel also had a. wife, 1Ch 2.26
from one kingdom to a. people, 16.20
there not here a. prophet of the 2Ch 18.06
one thing, and a. said a. 18.19
they all helped to destroy one a. 20.23
Judah captured a. ten thousand 25.12
let us look one a. in the face." 25.17
Judah faced one a. in battle at 25.21
keep the feast for a. seven days; 30.23
kept it for a. seven days with 30.23
and outside it he built a. wall; 32.05
repaired a. section and the Tower Neh 3.11
repaired a. section opposite the 3.19
Zabbai repaired a. section from 3.20
Hakkoz repaired a. section from 3.21
son of Henadad repaired a. section, 3.24
repaired a section opposite the 3.27
son of Zalaph repaired a. section. 3.30
on the wall, far from one a. 4.19
for a. fourth of it they made 9.03
position to a. who is better than Est 1.19
rise for the Jews from a. quarter, 4.14
send choice portions too one a. 9.19
portions to one a. and gifts to 9.22
there came a., and said, "The fire Job 1.16
there came a., and said, "The 1.17
there came a., and said, "Your sons 1.18
my eyes shall behold, and not a. 19.27
A. dies in bitterness of soul, never 21.25
then let me sow, and a. eat; 31.08
then let my wife grind for a., 31.10
One is so near to a. that no air 41.16
They are joined one to a.; 41.17
Those who choose a. god multiply Ps 16.04
putting down one and lifting up a. 75.07
from one kingdom to a. people, 105.13
may a. seize his goods! 109.08
generation shall laud thy works to a., 145.04
a. withholds what he should give, Pro 11.24
a. pretends to be poor, yet has 13.07
I awake? I will seek a. drink." 23.35
Let a. praise you, and not your own 27.02
iron, and one man sharpens a. 27.17
is burdened with the blood of a., 28.17
and has not a. to lift him up. Ecc 4.10
one thing to a. to find the sum, 7.27
your beloved more than a. beloved, Sol 5.09
And the people will oppress one a., Is 3.05
And one called to a. and said: 6.03
They will look aghast at one a.; 13.08
a. will call himself by the name 44.05
and a. will write on his hand, 'The 44.05
My glory I will not give to a. 48.11
They shall not build and a. inhabit; 65.22
they shall not plant and a. eat; 65.22
from him and becomes a. man's wife, Jer 3.01
truly execute justice one with a., 7.05
And I will dash them one against a., 13.14
and he reworked it into a. vessel, 18.04
who bore you into a. country, 22.26
dreams which they tell one a., 23.27
who steal my words from one a. 23.30
one after a., and all the kingdoms 25.26
There was a. man who prophesied in 26.20
they turned one to a. in fear; 36.16
"Take a. scroll and write on it all 36.28
Then Jeremiah took a. scroll and 36.32
and fell, and they said one to a., 46.16
One runner runs to meet a., 51.31

ANOTHER (cont.)
and one messenger to meet a., Jer 51.31
and afterward a report in a. year, 51.46
their wings touched one a.; Eze 1.09
of which touched the wing of a., 1.11
out straight, one toward a.; 1.23
creatures as they touched one a., 3.13
and look at one a. in dismay, 4.17
your place to a. place in their 12.03
"But there was a. great eagle with 17.07
she took a. of her whelps and made 19.05
a. lewdly defiles his daughter-in-law; 22.11
a. in you defiles his sister, his 22.11
iniquities and groan to one a. 24.23
say to one a., each to his brother, 33.30
then take a. stick and write upon 37.16
one over a., thirty in each story. 41.06
and a. door toward the south; 41.11
A. section, twenty-five thousand 45.05
After you shall arise a. kingdom Dan 2.39
will mix with one a. in marriage, 2.43
sovereignty be left to a. people. 2.44
and give your rewards to a.; 5.17
of the sea, different from one a. 7.03
And behold, a. beast, a second one, 7.05
a., like a leopard, with four wings 7.06
there came up among them a. horn, 7.08
and a. shall arise after them; 7.24
and a. holy one said to the one 8.13
the harlot, or belong to a. man; Hos 3.03
and their children a. generation. Joe 1.03
They do not jostle one a., 2.08
and send no rain upon a. city; Amo 4.07
And they said to one a., Jon 1.07
and a. angel came forward to meet Zec 2.03
do: Speak the truth to one a., 8.16
evil in your hearts against one a., 8.17
inhabitants of one city shall go to a., 8.21
left devour the flesh of one a." 11.09
then are we faithless to one a., Mal 2.10
feared the LORD spoke with one a.; 3.16
to their own country by a. way. Mt 2.12
and to a., 'Come,' and he comes, and 8.09
A. of the disciples said to him, 8.21
to come, or shall we look for a.?" 11.03
in a. sixty, and in a. thirty." 13.23
A. parable he put before them, 13.24
A. parable he put before them, 13.31
He told them a. parable. 13.33
and marries a., commits adultery." 19.09
And they argued with one a., 21.25
"Hear a. parable. There was a 21.33
tenants, and went into a. country. 21.33
beat one, killed a., and stoned a. 21.35
one to his farm, a. to his business, 22.05
not be left here one stone upon a., 24.02
will fall away, and betray one a., 24.10
one a., and hate one a. 24.10
he gave five talents, to a. two, 25.15
to a. one, to each according to his 25.15
them one from a. as a shepherd 25.32
began to say to him one after a., 26.22
a. maid saw him, and she said to the 26.71
And a. took a spear and pierced * 27.49
with awe, and said to one a., Mk 4.41
And they discussed it with one a., 8.16
with one a. who was the greatest. 9.34
and be at peace with one a." 9.50
divorces his wife and marries a., 10.11
divorces her husband and marries a., 10.12
And they argued with one a., 11.31
tenants, and went into a. country. 12.01
Again he sent to them a. servant, 12.04
And he sent a., and him they killed; 12.05
But those tenants said to one a., 12.07
heard them disputing with one a., 12.28
not be left here one stone upon a., 13.02
say to him one after a., "Is it I?" 14.19
and in three days I will build a., 14.58
him to one a. with the scribes, 15.31
And they were saying to one a., 16.03
the shepherds said to one a., Lk 2.15
were all amazed and said to one a., 4.36
On a. sabbath, when he entered the 6.06
with one a. what they might do to 6.11
and to a., 'Come,' and he comes; 7.08
to come, or shall we look for a.?" 7.19
to come, or shall we look for a.?' " 7.20
market place and calling to one a., 7.32
saying to one a., "Who then is this, 8.25
And they went on to a. village. 9.56
To a. he said, "Follow me." 9.59
A. said, "I will follow you, Lord; 9.61
together that they trod upon one a., 12.01
And a. said, 'I have bought five 14.19
And a. said, 'I have married a wife, 14.20
going to encounter a. king in war, 14.31
Then he said to a., 'And how much 16.07
and marries a. commits adultery, 16.18
Then a. came, saying, 'Lord, here is 19.20
not leave one stone upon a. in you; 19.44
And they discussed it with one a., 20.05
and went into a. country for a long 20.09
And he sent a. servant; him also 20.11
one stone upon a. that will not be 21.06
And they began to question one a., 22.23
of about an hour still a. insisted, 22.59
So the disciples said to one a., Jn 4.33
holds true, 'One sows and a. reaps." 4.37
I am going a. steps down before me 5.07
there is a. who bears witness to me, 5.32
if a. comes in his own name, him you 5.43
glory from one a. and do not seek 5.44
The Jews said to one a., "Where does 7.35
the door but climbs in by a. way, 10.01
saying to one a. as they stood in 11.56
The Pharisees then said to one a., 12.19
The disciples looked at one a., 13.22
give to you, that you love one a.; 13.34
you, that you also love one a. 13.34
if you have love for one a." 13.35
and he will give you a. Counselor, 14.16
you love one a. as I have loved 15.12
This I command you, to love one a. 15.17
Some of his disciples said to one a., 16.17
Jesus, and so did a. disciple. 18.15
so they said to one a., "Let us not 19.24
And again a. scripture says, "They 19.37
and a. will gird you and carry you 21.18
and 'His office let a. take.' Ac 1.20
saying to one a., "What does this 2.12
they conferred with one a., 4.15
over Egypt a. king who had not 7.18
or to visit any one of a. nation; 10.28
he departed and went to a. place. 12.17
Therefore he says also in a. psalm, 13.35
that there is a. king, Jesus." 17.07
Now some cried one thing, some a.; 19.32
them bring charges against one a. 19.38
we prayed and bade one a. farewell. 21.05
crowd shouted one thing, some a.; 21.34
had withdrawn, they said to one a., 26.31
from his hand, they said to one a., 28.04
consumed with passion for one a., Rom 1.27
whoever you are, when you judge a.; 2.01
she lives with a. man while her 7.03
if she marries a. man she is not 7.03
so that you may belong to a., 7.04
in my members a. law at war with 7.23
for beauty and a. for menial use? 9.21
and individually members one of a. 12.05
love one a. with brotherly affection 12.10
outdo one a. in showing honor. 12.10

ANOTHER (cont.)

Live in harmony with one a.; Rom 12.16
anything, except to love one a.; 13.08
pass judgment on the servant of a.? 14.04
esteems one day as better than a., 14.05
while a. man esteems all days alike 14.05
us no more pass judgment on one a., 14.13
live in such harmony with one a., 15.05
Welcome one a., therefore, as Christ 15.07
knowledge, and able to instruct one a. 15.14
lest I build on a. man's foundation, 15.20
Greet one a. with a holy kiss. 16.16
and a., "I belong to Apollos," are 1Co 3.04
and a. man is building upon it. 3.10
up in favor of one against a. 4.06
at all with one a. is defeat for 6.07
Do not refuse one a. except perhaps 7.05
God, one of one kind and one of a. 7.07
be determined by a. man's scruples? 10.29
and one is hungry and a. is drunk. 11.21
together to eat, wait for one a. 11.33
and to a. the utterance of knowledge 12.08
to a. faith by the same Spirit, to 12.09
to a. gifts of healing by the one 12.09
to a. the working of miracles, to 12.10
to a. prophecy, to a. the ability 12.10
to a. various kinds of tongues, to 12.10
to a. the interpretation of tongues 12.10
may have the same care for one a. 12.25
revelation is made to a. sitting by, 14.30
a. for animals, a. for birds, and a. for fish. 15.39
the glory of the terrestrial is a. 15.40
and a. glory of the moon, and 15.41
and a. glory of the stars; 15.41
Greet one a. with a holy kiss. 16.20
not to make you a. painful visit. 2Co 2.01
from one degree of glory to a.; 3.18
they measure themselves by one a., 10.12
and compare themselves with one a., 10.12
and preaches a. Jesus than the one 11.04
heed my appeal, agree with one a., 13.11
Greet one a. with a holy kiss. 13.12
not that there is a. gospel, Gal 1.07
through love be servants of one a. 5.13
and devour one a. take heed that 5.15
you are not consumed by one a. 5.15
self-conceit, no provoking of one a., 5.26
of one a., no envy of one a. 5.26
patience, forbearing one a. in love, Eph 4.02
for we are members one of a. 4.25
and be kind to one a., tenderhearted, 4.32
forgiving one a., as God in Christ 4.32
addressing one a. in psalms and 5.19
Be subject to one a. out of reverence 5.21
Do not lie to one a., Col 3.09
forbearing one a. and, if one has a 3.13
if one has a complaint against a., 3.13
and admonish one a. in all wisdom, 3.16
in love to one a. and to all men, 1Th 3.12
been taught by God to love one a.; 4.09
Therefore comfort one a. with these 4.18
encourage one a. and build one a. up, 5.11
to do good to one a. and to all. 5.15
of you for one a. is increasing. 2Th 1.03
nor participate in a. man's sins; 1Ti 5.22
hated by men and hating one a.; Tit 3.03
But exhort one a. every day, as long Heb 3.13
would not speak later of a. day. 4.08
as he says also in a. place, 5.06
have been for a. priest to arise 7.11
are spoken belonged to a. tribe, 7.13
evident when a. priest arises in 7.15
to stir up one a. to love and good 10.24
of some, but encouraging one a., 10.25
messengers and sent them out a. way? Jas 2.25
evil against one a., brethren. 4.11
against one a., that you may not be 5.09
Therefore confess your sins to one a., 5.16
and pray for one a., that you may 5.16
love one a. earnestly from the 1Pe 1.22
unfailing your love for one a., 4.08
hospitality ungrudgingly to one a. 4.09
a gift, employ it for one a., 4.10
you, with humility toward one a., 5.05
Greet one a. with the kiss of love. 5.14
we have fellowship with one a., 1Jn 1.07
that we should love one a., 3.11
Son Jesus Christ and love one a., 3.23
Beloved, let us love one a.; 4.07
us, we also ought to love one a. 4.11
if we love one a., 4.12
the beginning, that we love one a. 2Jn 1.05
And out came a. horse, bright red; Rev 6.04
so that men should slay one a.; 6.04
Then I saw a. angel ascend from the 7.02
And a. angel came and stood at the 8.03
Then I saw a. mighty angel coming 10.01
And a. portent appeared in heaven; 12.03
Then I saw a. beast which rose out 13.11
Then I saw a. angel flying in 14.06
A. angel, a second, followed, saying, 14.08
And a. angel, a third, followed, 14.09
And a. angel came out of the temple, 14.15
And a. angel came out of the temple 14.17
Then a. angel came out from the 14.18
Then I saw a. portent in heaven, 15.01
After this I saw a. angel coming 18.01
Then I heard a. voice from heaven 18.04
Also a. book was opened, which is 20.12

ANOTHER'S

may not understand one a. speech." Gen 11.07
"When one man's ox hurts a., Ex 21.35
and do not disclose a. secret; Pro 25.09
been faithful in that which is a., Lk 16.12
you also ought to wash one a. feet. Jn 13.14
of work already done in a. field. 2Co 10.16
Bear one a. burdens, and so fulfil Gal 6.02

ANSWER

So my honesty will a. for me later, Gen 30.33
will give Pharaoh a favorable a." 41.16
told him was in a. to these 43.07
but his brothers could not a. him, 45.03
And if its a. to you is peace and Deu 20.11
and she shall a. and say, 'So shall 25.09
the people shall a. and say, 'Amen.' 27.15
Manasseh said to a. to the heads of Jos 22.21
Her wisest ladies make a., Ju 5.29
nay, she gives a. to herself, 5.29
But there was no a. 19.28
But she did not a. or give heed. 1Sa 4.20
LORD will not a. you in that day." 8.18
But he did not a. him that day. 14.37
saying, "Will you not a., Abner?" 26.14
And David made a., "Here is the 26.22
the LORD, the LORD did not a. him, 28.06
And Achish made a. to David, 29.09
could not a. Abner another word, 2Sa 3.11
the LORD, but he did not a. them. 22.42
and decide what a. I shall return 24.13
do you advise me to a. this people?" 1Ki 12.06
words to them when you a. them, 12.07
advise that we a. this people who 12.09
the people did not a. him a word. 18.21
until noon, saying, "O Baal, a. us!" 18.26
A. me, O LORD, a. me, that this people 18.37
king's command was, "Do not a. him." 2Ki 18.36
Now decide what a. I shall return 1Ch 21.12
do you advise me to a. this people?" 2Ch 10.06
advise that we a. this people who 10.09
The king sent an a.: "To Rehum Ez 4.17
Darius and then a. be returned by 5.05
told them to return a. to Esther, Est 4.13

ANSWER (cont.)
is there any one who will a. you? Job 5.01
one could not a. him once in a 9.03
How then can I a. him, choosing my 9.14
Though I am innocent, I cannot a. him; 9.15
that I might a. him, that we should 9.32
Then call, and I will a.; 13.22
wouldest call, and I would a. thee; 14.15
"Should a wise man a. with windy 15.02
Or what provokes you that you a.? 16.03
my servant, but he gives me no a.; 19.16
"Therefore my thoughts a. me, 20.02
I would learn what he would a. me, 23.05
to thee and thou dost not a. me; 30.20
makes inquiry, what shall I a. him? 31.14
let the Almighty a. me! 31.35
So these three men ceased to a. Job, 32.01
because they had found no a., 32.03
there was no a. in the mouth of 32.05
and I will not a. him with your 32.14
"They are discomfited, they a. no more; 32.15
they stand there, and a. no more? 32.16
I also will give my a.; 32.17
I must open my lips and a. 32.20
A. me, if you can; set your 33.05
I will a. you. God is greater 33.12
'He will a. none of my words'? 33.13
If you have anything to say, a. me; 33.32
I will a. you and your friends with 35.04
There they cry out, but he does not a., 35.12
who argues with God, let him a. it. 40.02
what shall I a. thee? I lay my 40.04
spoken once, and I will not a.; 40.05
A. me when I call, O God of my right Ps 4.01
Consider and a. me, O LORD my God; 13.03
thee, for thou wilt a. me, O God; 17.06
the LORD, but he did not a. them. 18.41
The LORD a. you in the day of 20.01
he will a. him from his holy heaven 20.06
a. us when we call. 20.09
I cry by day, but thou dost not a.; 22.02
aloud, be gracious to me and a. me! 27.07
thou, O LORD my God, who wilt a. 38.15
Attend to me, and a. me; 55.02
by thy right hand and a. us! 60.05
deeds thou dost a. us with deliverance, 65.05
of thy steadfast love a. me. 69.13
A. me, O LORD, for thy steadfast love 69.16
in distress, make haste to a. me. 69.17
and a. me, for I am poor and needy. 86.01
call on thee, for thou dost a. me. 86.07
When he calls to me, I will a. him; 91.15
O LORD our God, thou didst a. them; 99.08
a. me speedily in the day when I 102.02
help by thy right hand, and a. me! 108.06
told of my ways, thou didst a. me; 119.26
then shall I have an a. for those 119.42
a. me, O LORD! 119.145
to the LORD, that he may a. me: 120.01
thou didst a. me, my strength of 138.03
In thy faithfulness a. me, 143.01
Make haste to a. me, O LORD! 143.07
call upon me, but I will not a.; Pro 1.28
A soft a. turns away wrath, but a 15.01
To make an apt a. is a joy to a man, 15.23
of the righteous ponders how to a., 15.28
but the a. of the tongue is from 16.01
If one gives a. before he hears, it 18.13
entreaties, but the rich a. roughly. 18.23
may give a true a. to those who 22.21
gives a right a. kisses the lips. 24.26
A. not a fool according to his 26.04
A. a fool according to his folly, 26.05
seven men who can a. discreetly. 26.16
that I may a. him who reproaches me 27.11
I called him, but he gave no a. Sol 3.01
I called him, but he gave no a. 5.06
A. her, O Anathoth! Is 10.30
What will one a. the messengers of 14.32
when he hears it, he will a. you. 30.19
king's command was, "Do not a. him." 36.21
thirst, I the LORD will a. them, 41.17
who, when I ask, gives an a. 41.28
it does not a. or save him from his 46.07
I called, was there no one to a.? 50.02
shall call, and the LORD will a.; 58.09
you did not a., when I spoke, you 65.12
Before they call I will a., 65.24
when I called you, you did not a., Jer 7.13
to them, but they will not a. you. 7.27
And they will a., "Because they 22.09
Call to me and I will a. you, 33.03
people who had given him this a.: 44.20
I the LORD will a. him myself Eze 14.04
me, I the LORD will a. him myself; 14.07
have no need to a. you in this Dan 3.16
there she shall a. as in the days Hos 2.15
I will a. the heavens and they 2.21
and they shall a. the earth; 2.21
and the earth shall a. the grain, 2.22
the oil, and they shall a. Jezreel; 2.22
It is I who a. and look after you. 14.08
the LORD, but he will not a. them; Mic 3.04
lips, for there is no a. from God. 3.07
I wearied you? A. me! 6.03
and what I will a. concerning my Hab 2.01
LORD their God and I will a. them. Zec 10.06
on my name, and I will a. them. 13.09
does this, any to witness or a., Mal 2.12
But he did not a. her a word. Mt 15.23
and if you tell me the a., 21.24
And no one was able to a. him a word, 22.46
Then the righteous will a. him, 25.37
And the King will a. them, 25.40
Then they also will a., 25.44
Then he will a. them, 'Truly, I say 25.45
and said, "Have you no a. to make? 26.62
priests and elders, he made no a. 27.12
But he gave him no a., 27.14
a. me, and I will tell you by what Mk 11.29
heaven or from men? A. me 11.30
they did not know what to a. him. 14.40
Jesus, "Have you no a. to make? 14.60
But he was silent and made no a. 14.61
asked him, "Have you no a. to make? 15.04
But Jesus made no further a., 15.05
and he will a. from within, 'Do not Lk 11.07
what you are to a. or what you are 12.11
He will a. you, 'I do not know 13.25
marveling at his a. they were 20.26
to meditate beforehand how to a.; 21.14
and if I ask you, you will not a. 22.68
but he made no a. 23.09
Let us have an a. for those who Jn 1.22
"Is that how you a. the high priest?" 18.22
But Jesus gave no a. 19.09
a maid named Rhoda came to a. Ac 12.13
are you, a man, to a. back to God? Rom 9.20
granted us in a. to many prayers. 2Co 1.11
may be able to a. those who pride 5.12
know how you ought to a. every one. Col 4.06

ANSWERED
Abraham a., "Behold, I have taken Gen 18.27
He a., "For the sake of forty I 18.29
He a., "I will not do it, if I find 18.30
He a., "For the sake of twenty I 18.31
He a., "For the sake of ten I 18.32
The Hittites a. Abraham, 23.05
the Hittite a. Abraham in the 23.10
Ephron a. Abraham, 23.14
Then Laban and Bethuel a., 24.50
and he a., "Here I am." 27.01
He a., "Because the LORD your God 27.20

ANSWERED (cont.)
my son Esau?" He a., "I am." Gen 27.24
He a., "I am your son, your first-born 27.32
Isaac a. Esau, "Behold, I have made 27.37
Then Isaac his father a. him: 27.39
Then Rachel and Leah a. him, 31.14
Jacob a. Laban, "Because I was 31.31
Then Laban a. and said to Jacob, 31.43
Jacob a., "To find favor in the 33.08
The sons of Jacob a. Shechem and 34.13
to the God who a. me in the day of 35.03
He a., "I will send you a kid from 38.17
And Joseph a., "This is its interpretation: 40.18
Joseph a. Pharaoh, "It is not in me; 41.16
And Reuben a. them, "Did I not tell 42.22
And Joseph a., "Give your cattle, 47.16
He a., "I will do as you have said." 47.30
And Pharaoh a., "Go up, and bury 50.06
He a., "Who made you a prince and a Ex 2.14
Then Moses a., "But behold, they 4.01
And all the people a. together and 19.08
spoke, and God a. him in thunder. 19.19
all the people a. with one voice, 24.03
But Balaam a. and said to the Num 22.18
And he a., "Must I not take heed to 23.12
But Balaam a. Balak, "Did I not tell 23.26
of Gad and the sons of Reuben a., 32.31
And you a. me, 'The thing that you Deu 1.14
"Then you a. me, 'We have sinned 1.41
And they a. Joshua, "All that you Jos 1.16
And Achan a. Joshua, "Of a truth I 7.20
They a. Joshua, "Because it was told 9.24
Then the people a., 24.16
And his comrade a., Ju 7.14
men of Penuel a. him as the men of 8.08
him as the men of Succoth had a. 8.08
They a., 'As you are, so were they, 8.18
And they a., "We will willingly 8.25
the Ammonites a. the messengers of 11.13
a. and said, "I came to Gibeah that 20.04
and they a., "The LORD bless you." Ru 2.04
was in charge of the reapers a., 2.06
But Boaz a. her, "All that you have 2.11
And she a., "I am Ruth, your maidservant 3.09
But Hannah a., "No, my lord, I am a 1Sa 1.15
Then Eli a., "Go in peace, and the 1.17
brought the tidings a. and said, 4.17
They a., "Let the ark of the God of 5.08
They a., "Five golden tumors and 6.04
for Israel, and the LORD a. him. 7.09
The servant a Saul again, "Here, I 9.08
They a., "He is; behold, he is 9.12
Samuel a. Saul, "I am the seer; 9.19
Saul a., "Am I not a Benjaminite, 9.21
And a man of the place a., 10.12
among all the people that a. him. 14.39
hast thou not a. thy servant this 14.41
One of the young men a., 16.18
And the people a. him in the same 17.27
and the people a. him again as 17.30
And David a., "I am the son of your 17.58
And Michal a. Saul, "He said to me, 19.17
Jonathan a. Saul, "David earnestly 20.28
Then Jonathan a. Saul his father, 20.32
And the priest a. David, "I have no 21.04
And David a. the priest, "Of a truth 21.05
Then a. Doeg the Edomite, who stood 22.09
And he a., "Here I am, my lord." 22.12
Then Ahimelech a. the king, "And who 22.14
And the LORD a. him, "Arise, go down 23.04
And Nabal a. David's servants, "Who 25.10
Then Abner a., "Who are you that 26.14
Saul a., "I am in great distress; 28.15
He a. him, "Pursue; 30.08
And he a., "The people have fled 2Sa 1.04
And I a., 'Here I am.' 1.07
I a. him, 'I am an Amalekite.' 1.08
And he a., "I am the son of a 1.13
And he a., "It is I." 2.20
But David a. Rechab and Baanah his 4.09
And he a., "Behold, your servant." 9.06
She a. him, "No, my brother, do not 13.12
She a., "Alas, I am a widow; 14.05
Then the king a. the woman, "Do not 14.18
The woman a. and said, "As surely as 14.19
Absalom a. Joab, "Behold, I sent word 14.32
But Ittai a. the king, "As the LORD 15.21
Ziba a., "The asses are for the 16.02
Ahimaaz a., "When Joab sent your 18.29
And the Cushite a., "May the 18.32
Abishai the son of Zeruiah a., 19.21
He a., "My lord, O king, my servant 19.26
And the king a., "Chimham shall go 19.38
men of Judah a. the men of Israel, 19.42
men of Israel a. the men of Judah, 19.43
He a., "I am." Then she 20.17
And he a., "I am listening." 20.17
Joab a., "Far be it from me, far be 20.20
Then King David a., "Call 1Ki 1.28
the son of Jehoiada a. the king, 1.36
Jonathan a. Adonijah, "No, for our 1.43
King Solomon a. his mother, "And why 2.22
thus said Joab, and thus he a. me. 2.30
Then the king a. and said, "Give the 3.27
And Solomon a. all her questions; 10.03
And the king a. the people harshly, 12.13
the people a. the king, "What 12.16
And he a. him, "It is I. 18.08
And he a., "I have not troubled 18.18
And all the people a., 18.24
there was no voice, and no one a. 18.26
no one a., no one heeded. 18.29
And the king of Israel a., 20.04
And the king of Israel a., 20.11
He a., "You." 20.14
and he a., 'I will not give you my 21.06
He a., "I have found you, because 21.20
And he a. him, "Go up and triumph; 22.15
They a. him, "He wore a garment of 2Ki 1.08
But Elijah a. the captain of fifty, 1.10
But Elijah a. them, "If I am a man 1.12
And he a., "Yes, I know it; 2.05
Jehoram a., "By the way of the 3.08
the king of Israel's servants a., 3.11
She a., "I dwell among my own 4.13
Gehazi a., "Well, she has no son, 4.14
And she a., "It is well." 4.26
And he a., "Go." 6.02
And he a., "I will go." 6.03
He a., "You shall not slay them. 6.22
She a., "This woman said to me, 6.28
the captain had a. the man of God, 7.19
He a., "Because I know the evil 8.12
Elisha a., "The LORD has shown me 8.13
And he a., "He told me that you 8.14
And Jehu a., "What have you to 9.19
He a., "What peace can there be, 9.22
And they a., "We are the kinsmen 10.13
And Jehonadab a., "It is." 10.15
were silent and a. him not a word, 18.36
And Hezekiah a., "It is an easy 20.10
And Hezekiah a., "They have seen 20.15
and he a. him with fire from heaven 1Ch 21.26
the LORD had a. him at the threshing 21.28
God a. Solomon, "Because this was in 2Ch 1.11
king of Tyre a. in a letter which 2.11
And Solomon a. all her questions; 9.02
And the king a. them harshly, and 10.13
the people a. the king, "What 10.16
He a. him, "I am as you are, my 18.03
And he a., "Go up and triumph; 18.14
The man of God a., "The LORD 25.09
a. him, "Since they began to bring 31.10

ANSWERED (cont.)

and he a. him and gave him a sign	2Ch 32.24
the assembly a. with a loud voice,	Ez 10.12
this way and I a. them in the same	Neh 6.04
and all the people a., "Amen,	8.06
Then Queen Esther a., "If I have	Est 7.03
Satan a. the LORD, "From going to	Job 1.07
Then Satan a. the LORD, "Does Job	1.09
Satan a. the LORD, "From going to	2.02
Then Satan a. the LORD, "Skin for	2.04
Then Eliphaz the Temanite a.:	4.01
Then Job a.:	6.01
Then Bildad the Shuhite a.:	8.01
Then Job a.:	9.01
If I summoned him and he a. me,	9.16
Then Zophar the Naamathite a.:	11.01
Then Job a.:	12.01
who called upon God and he a. me,	12.04
Then Eliphaz the Temanite a.:	15.01
Then Job a.:	16.01
Then Bildad the Shuhite a.:	18.01
Then Job a.:	19.01
but I am not a.;	19.07
Then Zophar the Naamathite a.:	20.01
Then Job a.:	21.01
Then Eliphaz the Temanite a.:	22.01
Then Job a.:	23.01
Then Bildad the Shuhite a.:	25.01
Then Job a.:	26.01
the son of Barachel the Buzite a.:	32.06
or that a. his words, among you.	32.12
Then the LORD a. Job out of the	38.01
Then Job a. the LORD:	40.03
Then the LORD a. Job out of the	40.06
Then Job a. the LORD:	42.01
and he a. me, and delivered me from	Ps 34.04
I a. you in the secret place of	81.07
cried to the LORD, and he a. them.	99.06
the LORD a. me and set me free	118.05
that thou hast a. me and hast	118.21
And he a., "Fallen, fallen is	Is 21.09
were silent and a. him not a word,	36.21
Hezekiah a., "They have seen all	39.04
In a time of favor I have a. you,	49.08
no one a., when I spoke they did	66.04
Then I a., "So be it, LORD."	Jer 11.05
his brother, "What has the LORD a.?'	23.35
prophet, 'What has the LORD a. you?'	23.37
But they a., "We will drink no wine,	35.06
to them and they have not a.	35.17
Baruch a. them, "He dictated all	36.18
and he a. them as the king had	38.27
in the land of Egypt, a. Jeremiah:	44.15
And I a., "O Lord GOD, thou	Eze 37.03
The king a. the Chaldeans, "The word	Dan 2.05
They a. a second time, "Let the king	2.07
The king a., "I know with certainty	2.08
The Chaldeans a. the king, "There is	2.10
Daniel a. the king, "No wise men,	2.27
and Abednego a. the king, "O Nebuchadnezzar,	3.16
They a. the king, "True, O king."	3.24
He a., "But I see four men loose,	3.25
Belteshazzar a., "My lord, may the	4.19
Then Daniel a. before the king, "Let	5.17
The king a., "The thing stands	6.12
Then they a. before the king, "That	6.13
The LORD a. and said to his people,	Joe 2.19
Then Amos a. Amaziah, "I am no	Amo 7.14
out of my distress, and he a. me;	Jon 2.02
what Balaam the son of Beor a. him,	Mic 6.05
And the LORD a. me: "Write the	Hab 2.02
The priests a., "No."	Hag 2.12
The priests a., "It does become	2.13
standing among the myrtle trees a.,	Zec 1.10
And they a. the angel of the LORD	1.11
And the LORD a. gracious and	1.13
And he a. me, "These are the horns	1.19

He a., "These are the horns which	1.21
the angel who talked with me a. me,	4.05
I a., "I see a flying scroll;	5.02
And the angel a. me, "These are	6.05
But Jesus a. him, "Let it be so now;	Mt 3.15
But he a., "It is written, 'Man	4.04
But the centurion a. him,	8.08
And Jesus a. them, "Go and tell John	11.04
But he a. them, "An evil and adulterous	12.39
And he a. them, "To you it has been	13.11
He a., "He who sows the good seed	13.37
And Peter a. him, "Lord, if it is you,	14.28
He a. them, "And why do you transgress	15.03
He a., "Every plant which my	15.13
He a., "I was sent only to the lost	15.24
And he a., "It is not fair to take	15.26
Then Jesus a. her, "O woman, great is	15.28
He a. them, "When it is evening, you	16.02
And Jesus a. him, "Blessed are you,	16.17
And Jesus a., "O faithless and	17.17
He a., "Have you not read that he	19.04
But Jesus a., "You do not know what	20.22
And Jesus a. them, "Truly, I say to	21.21
Jesus a. them, "I also will ask you	21.24
So they a. Jesus, "We do not know."	21.27
And he a., 'I will not'; but afterward	21.29
and he a., 'I go, sir,' but did not	21.30
But Jesus a. them, "You are wrong,	22.29
But he a. them, "You see all these,	24.02
And Jesus a. them, "Take heed that	24.04
But his master a. him, "You wicked	25.26
He a., "He who has dipped his hand	26.23
They a., "He deserves death."	26.66
And all the people a.,	27.25
But he a. them, "You give them	Mk 6.37
But she a. him, "Yes, Lord;	7.28
And his disciples a. him,	8.04
Peter a. him, "You are the Christ."	8.29
And one of the crowd a. him,	9.17
And he a. them, "O faithless generation,	9.19
He a. them, "What did Moses command	10.03
And Jesus a. them, "Have faith in	11.22
So they a. Jesus, "We do not know."	11.33
and seeing that he a. them well,	12.28
Jesus a., "The first is, 'Hear, O	12.29
And when Jesus saw that he a. wisely,	12.34
And he a. him, "You have said so."	15.02
And he a. them, "Do you want me to	15.09
And the angel a. him, "I am Gabriel,	Lk 1.19
And he a. them, "He who has two	3.11
John a. them all, "I baptize you	3.16
And Jesus a. him, "It is written,	4.04
And Jesus a. him, "It is written,	4.08
And Jesus a. him, "It is said, 'You	4.12
And Simon a., "Master, we toiled all	5.05
he a. them, "Why do you question in	5.22
And Jesus a. them, "Those who are	5.31
And Jesus a., "Have you not read	6.03
And he a. them, "Go and tell John	7.22
And he a., "What is it, Teacher?"	7.40
Simon a., "The one, I suppose, to	7.43
But Jesus on hearing this a. him,	8.50
And they a., "John the Baptist;	9.19
And Peter a., "The Christ of God."	9.20
Jesus a., "O faithless and perverse	9.41
John a., "Master, we saw a man	9.49
And he a., "You shall love the Lord	10.27
And he said to him, "You have a. right;	10.28
But the Lord a. her, "Martha, Martha,	10.41
One of the lawyers a. him,	11.45
And he a. them, "Do you think that	13.02
And he a. him, 'Let it alone, sir,	13.08
Then the Lord a. him, "You hypocrites	13.15
but he a. his father, 'Lo, these many	15.29
he a. them, "The kingdom of God is	17.20
He a., "I tell you, if these were	19.40
He a. them, "I also will ask you a	20.03

ANSWERED (cont.)
So they a. that they did not know Lk 20.07
And some of the scribes a., 20.39
And he a. him, "You have said so." 23.03
a. him, "Are you the only visitor to 24.18
And he a., "No." Jn 1.21
John a. them, "I baptize with water; 1.26
Jesus a. him, "Before Philip 1.48
Nathanael a. him, "Rabbi, you are the 1.49
Jesus a. him, "Because I said to you, 1.50
Jesus a. them, "Destroy this temple, 2.19
Jesus a. him, "Truly, truly, I say to 3.03
Jesus a., "Truly, truly, I say to you, 3.05
Jesus a. him, "Are you a teacher of 3.10
John a. "No one can receive 3.27
Jesus a. her, "If you knew the gift 4.10
The woman a. him, "I have no husband 4.17
The sick man a. him, "Sir, I have no 5.07
But he a. them, "The man who healed 5.11
But Jesus a. them, "My Father is 5.17
Philip a. him, "Two hundred denarii 6.07
Jesus a. them, "Truly, truly, I say to 6.26
Jesus a. them, "This is the work of 6.29
Jesus a. them, "Do not murmur among 6.43
Simon Peter a. him, "Lord, to whom 6.68
Jesus a. them, "Did I not choose you, 6.70
So Jesus a. them, "My teaching is 7.16
The people a. "You have a demon! 7.20
Jesus a. them, "I did one deed, and 7.21
The officers a., "No man ever spoke 7.46
The Pharisees a. them, "Are you led 7.47
Jesus a., "Even if I do bear 8.14
Jesus a., "You know neither me 8.19
They a. him, "We are descendants of 8.33
Jesus a. them, "Truly, truly, I say to 8.34
They a. him, "Abraham is our father." 8.39
The Jews a. him, "Are we not right 8.48
Jesus a., "I have not a demon; 8.49
Jesus a., "If I glorify myself, my 8.54
Jesus a., "It was not that this man 9.03
He a., "The man called Jesus made 9.11
His parents a., "We know that this 9.20
He a., "Whether he is a sinner, I do 9.25
He a. them, "I have told you already, 9.27
The man a., "Why, this is a marvel! 9.30
They a. him, "You were born in utter 9.34
He a., "And who is he, sir, that I 9.36
Jesus a. them, "I told you, and you 10.25
Jesus a. them, "I have shown you 10.32
The Jews a. him, "We stone you for 10.33
Jesus a. them, "Is it not written in 10.34
Jesus a., "Are there not twelve 11.09
And Jesus a. them, "The hour has 12.23
Jesus a., "This voice has come for 12.30
The crowd a. him, "We have heard 12.34
Jesus a. him, "What I am doing you 13.07
Jesus a. him, "If I do not wash 13.08
Jesus a., "It is he to whom I shall 13.26
Jesus a., "Where I am going you 13.36
Jesus a., "Will you lay down your 13.38
Jesus a. him, "If a man loves me, he 14.23
Jesus a. them, "Do you now believe? 16.31
They a. him, "Jesus of Nazareth." 18.05
Jesus a., "I told you that I am he; 18.08
Jesus a. him, "I have spoken openly 18.20
Jesus a. him, "If I have spoken 18.23
They a. him, "If this man were not 18.30
Jesus a., "Do you say this of your 18.34
Pilate a., "Am I a Jew? 18.35
Jesus a., "My kingship is not of 18.36
Jesus a., "You say that I am a 18.37
The Jews a. him, "We have a law, and 19.07
Jesus a. him, "You would have no 19.11
The chief priests a., "We have no 19.15
Pilate a., "What I have written I 19.22
Thomas a. him, "My Lord and my God!" 20.28
They a. him, "No." 21.05
But Peter and John a. them, Ac 4.19
But Peter and the apostles a., 5.29
And Simon a., "Pray for me to the 8.24
But Ananias a., "Lord, I have heard 9.13
But the voice a. a second time from 11.09
But the evil spirit a. them, 19.15
Then Paul a., "What are you doing, 21.13
And I a., 'Who are you, Lord?' 22.08
The tribune a., "I bought this 22.28
a., "You have appealed to Caesar; 25.12
I a. them that it was not the 25.16

ANSWERING
And Jesus a. said to him, "Simon, I Lk 7.40

ANSWERS
me if your father a. you roughly?" 1Sa 20.10
away from me and a. me no more, 28.15
and the God who a. by fire, 1Ki 18.24
of my understanding a spirit a. me. Job 20.03
left of your a. but falsehood." 21.34
because he a. like wicked men. 34.36
and he a. me from his holy hill. Ps 3.04
As in water face a. to face, Pro 27.19
life, and money a. everything. Ecc 10.19
the LORD a. you I will tell you; Jer 42.04
at his understanding and his a. Lk 2.47

ANT
Go to the a., O sluggard; Pro 6.06

ANTELOPE
the a., and the mountain-sheep. Deu 14.05
every street like an a. in a net; Is 51.20

ANTHOTHIJAH
Hananiah, Elam, A., 1Ch 8.24

ANTICHRIST
you have heard that a. is coming, 1Jn 2.18
This is the a., he who denies the 2.22
This is the spirit of a., 4.03
one is the deceiver and the a. 2Jn 1.07

ANTICHRISTS
coming, so now many a. have come; 1Jn 2.18

ANTIMONY
a., colored stones, all sorts of 1Ch 29.02
I will set your stones in a., Is 54.11

ANTIOCH
and Nicolaus, a proselyte of A. Ac 6.05
far as Phoenicia and Cyprus and A., 11.19
on coming to A. spoke to the 11.20
and they sent Barnabas to A. 11.22
found him, he brought him to A. 11.26
and in A. the disciples were for 11.26
came down from Jerusalem to A. 11.27
the church at A. there were 13.01
Perga and came to A. of Pisidia. 13.14
came there from A. and Iconium; 14.19
Lystra and to Iconium and to A., 14.21
and from there they sailed to A., 14.26
send them to A. with Paul and 15.22
the Gentiles in A. and Syria and 15.23
sent off, they went down to A.; 15.30
But Paul and Barnabas remained in A., 15.35
church, and then went down to A. 18.22
Cephas came to A. I opposed him to Gal 2.11
sufferings, what befell me at A., 2Ti 3.11

ANTIPAS
even in the days of A. my witness, Rev 2.13

ANTIPATRIS
and brought him by night to A. Ac 23.31

ANTS
the a. are a people not strong, yet Pro 30.25

ANUB
Koz was the father of A., 1Ch 4.08

ANVIL
the hammer him who strikes the a., Is 41.07

ANXIETIES
I want you to be free from a. 1Co 7.32
Cast all your a. on him, for he 1Pe 5.07

ANXIETY
out of my great a. and vexation. 1Sa 1.16
A. in a man's heart weighs him down, Pro 12.25
in this tent, we sigh with a.; 2Co 5.04
upon me of my a. for all the 11.28
Have no a. about anything, but in Php 4.06

ANXIOUS
the asses and become a. about us. 1Sa 9.05
the asses and is a. about you, 10.02
rest, eating the bread of a. toil; Ps 127.02
and is not a. in the year of Jer 17.08
within me was a. and the visions Dan 7.15
do not be a. about your life, what Mt 6.25
of you by being a. can add one 6.27
And why are you a. about clothing? 6.28
Therefore do not be a., 6.31
"Therefore do not be a. about tomorrow, 6.34
for tomorrow will be a. for itself. 6.34
do not be a. how you are to speak 10.19
do not be a. beforehand what you Mk 13.11
you are a. and troubled about many Lk 10.41
do not be a. how or what you are to 12.11
do not be a. about your life, what 12.22
of you by being a. can add a cubit 12.25
why are you a. about the rest? 12.26
are to drink, nor be of a. mind. 12.29
unmarried man is a. about the 1Co 7.32
married man is a. about worldly 7.33
or girl is a. about the affairs of 7.34
woman is a. about worldly affairs, 7.34
be genuinely a. for your welfare. Php 2.20
again, and that I may be less a. 2.28

ANXIOUSLY
inhabitants of Maroth wait a. for good, Mic 1.12
and I have been looking for you a." Lk 2.48

ANYBODY
who will listen to a. and can never 2Ti 3.07

ANYTHING
a sandal-thong or a. that is yours, Gen 14.23
Is a. too hard for the LORD 18.14
hand on the lad or do a. to him; 22.12
said, "You shall not give me a.; 30.31
no concern for a. but the food 39.06
no concern about a. in the house, 39.08
he kept back a. from me except 39.09
paid no heed to a. that was in 39.23
a. that remains until the morning Ex 12.10
any likeness of a. that is in 20.04
or a. that is your neighbor's. 20.17
"If a man borrows a. of his neighbor, 22.14
them to bring a. for the work 35.29
nor woman do a. more for the 36.06
or a. about which he has sworn Lev 6.05
But a. in seas or the rivers 11.10
And a. upon which any of them falls 11.32
in a skin or in a. made of skin, 13.48
or in skin or in a. made of skin, 13.49
or a. of skin, for it is a malignant 13.52
in warp or woof or in a. of skin, 13.53
or in a. of skin, it is spreading; 13.57
or a. of skin from which the 13.58
or in a. of skin, to decide whether 13.59
And whoever sits on a. on which he 15.06
And whoever touches a. that was 15.10
And whoever touches a. upon which 15.22
is the bed or a. upon which she 15.23
and a. left over until the third 19.06
by bird or by a. with which the 20.25
Whoever touches a. that is unclean 22.04
You shall not offer a. that has a 22.20
not substitute a. for it or 27.10
of a. that he has, whether of man or 27.28
for him who does a. unwittingly, Num 15.29
person who does a. with a high 15.30
I now any power at all to speak a.? 22.38
a. by which she has bound herself, 30.09
or hurled a. on him without lying 35.22
the likeness of a. that creeps on Deu 4.18
in the form of a. which the LORD 4.23
a graven image in the form of a., 4.25
any likeness of a. that is in 5.08
or a. that is your neighbor's. 5.21
"You shall not eat a. that dies of 14.21
shall not wear a. that pertains to 22.05
he may not see a. indecent among 23.14
interest on a. that is lent for 23.19
She may not eat of a. that comes Ju 13.14
is no lack of a. that is in the 18.10
there is no lack of a. 19.19
if you hide a. from me of all that 1Sa 3.17
had spoken, he did not tell him a. 10.16
us or taken a. from any man's hand. 12.04
you have not found a. in my hand. 12.05
and if I learn a. I will tell you. 19.03
Yet Saul did not say a. that day; 20.26
'Let no one know a. of the matter 21.02
the king impute a. to his servant 22.15
we did not miss a. when we were in 25.15
spoil or a. that had been taken; 30.19
taste bread or a. else till the 2Sa 3.35
impossible to Amnon to do a. to her. 13.02
"If any one says a. to you bring 14.10
"Do not hide from me a. I ask you." 14.18
the left from a. that my lord the 14.19
considered as a. in the days of 1Ki 10.21
turn aside from a. that he commanded 15.05
considered as a. in the days of 2Ch 9.20
will not save a. in which he Job 20.20
"If I have withheld a. that the 31.16
If you have a. to say, answer me; 33.32
set before my eyes a. that is base. Ps 101.03
added to it, nor a. taken from it; Ecc 3.14
has not seen the sun or known a.; 6.05
not find out a. that will be after 7.14
My son, beware of a. beyond these. 12.12
is a. too hard for me? Jer 32.27
your God in a. that he sent me to 42.21
Is wood taken from it to make a.? Eze 15.03
it is charred, is it useful for a.? 15.04
charred, can it ever be used for a.! 15.05
his army got a. from Tyre to pay 29.18
themselves with a. that causes 44.18
The priests shall not eat of a., 44.31
that speaks a. against the God of Dan 3.28
beast, herd nor flock, taste a.; Jon 3.07
longer good for a. except to be Mt 5.13
a. more than this comes from evil. 5.37
"Never was a. like this seen in 9.33
agree on earth about a. they ask, 18.19
If any one says a. to you, 21.03
saying, "We never saw a. like this!" Mk 2.12
nor is a. secret, except to come to 4.22
him to do a. for his father or 7.12
him, he asked him, "Do you see a.?" 8.23
but if you can do a., 9.22
be driven out by a. but prayer. 9.29
to see if he could find a. on it. 11.13
one to carry a. through the temple 11.16

ANYTHING (cont.)
if you have a. against any one; Mk 11.25
enter his house, to take a. away; 13.15
nor a. secret that shall not be Lk 8.17
in those days a. of what they had 9.36
I cannot get up and give you a.'? 11.07
up and give him a. because he is 11.08
and no one gave him a. 15.16
if I have defrauded any one of a., 19.08
they did not find a. they could do, 19.48
or bag or sandals, did you lack a.? 22.35
to them, "Have you a. here to eat?" 24.41
him was not a. made that was made. Jn 1.03
"Can a. good come out of Nazareth?" 1.46
one can receive a. except what is 3.27
if you ask a. in my name, I will do 14.14
if you ask a. of the Father, he will 16.23
never eaten a. that is common or Ac 10.14
hands, as though he needed a., 17.25
But if you seek a. further, 19.39
declaring to you a. that was 20.20
accusation, if they have a. against me. 24.19
and if there is a. wrong about the 25.05
have committed a. for which I 25.11
nor a. else in all creation, will be Rom 8.39
Owe no one a., except to love one 13.08
One believes he may eat a., 14.02
wine or do a. that makes your 14.21
to speak of a. except what Christ 15.18
who plants nor he who waters is a., 1Co 3.07
I am not aware of a. against myself, 4.04
For who sees a. different in you? 4.07
but I will not be enslaved by a. 6.12
counts for a. nor uncircumcision, 7.19
but we endure a. rather than put an 9.12
That food offered to idols is a., 10.19
is anything, or that an idol is a.? 10.19
If there is a. they desire to know, 14.35
forgiven, if I have forgiven a., 2Co 2.10
to claim a. as coming from us; 3.05
For we cannot do a. against the 13.08
neither circumcision counts for a., Gal 6.15
but when a. is exposed by the light Eph 5.13
for a. that becomes visible is 5.13
frightened in a. by your opponents Php 1.28
and if in a. you are otherwise 3.15
Have no anxiety about a., 4.06
if there is a. worthy of praise, 4.08
everywhere, so that we need not say a. 1Th 1.08
no need to have a. written to you. 5.01
we cannot take a. out of the world 1Ti 6.07
or owes you a., charge that to my Phm 1.18
will receive a. from the Lord. Jas 1.07
that if we ask a. according to his 1Jn 5.14
There shall no more be a. accursed, Rev 22.03

ANYWHERE
look back or stop a. in the valley; Gen 19.17

APACE
And he came a., and drew near. 2Sa 18.25
hand and his affliction hastens a. Jer 48.16

APART
seven ewe lambs of the flock a. Gen 21.28
ewe lambs which you have set a.?" 21.29
and he put his own droves a., 30.40
day I will set a. the land of Ex 8.22
you shall set a. to the LORD all 13.12
I have set a. for you to hold Lev 20.25
a. from what else he can afford; Num 6.21
Then Moses set a. three cities in Deu 4.41
the LORD set a. the tribe of Levi 10.08
you shall set a. three cities for 19.02
you, You shall set a. three cities. 19.07
which were set a. for the Ephraimites Jos 16.09
So they set a. Kedesh in Galilee in 20.07
a. from Benjamin, mustered four Ju 20.17
"Let him dwell a. in his own house; 2Sa 14.24
Absalom dwelt a. in his own house, 14.24
Aaron was set a. to consecrate the 1Ch 23.13
also set a. for the service 25.01
officials had set a. to attend the Ez 8.20
Then I set a. twelve of the leading 8.24
and they set a. that which was for Neh 12.47
the Levites set a. that which was 12.47
LORD has set a. the godly for Ps 4.03
I have no good a. from thee. 16.02
for a. from him who can eat or who Ecc 2.25
near me, for I am set a. from you." Is 65.05
and set them a. for the day of Jer 12.03
They will set a. men to pass Eze 39.14
you shall set a. for the LORD a 45.01
"Alongside the portion set a. as 45.06
the portion which you shall set a., 48.08
you shall set a. for the LORD 48.09
you shall set a. shall be twenty-five 48.20
in a boat to a lonely place a. Mt 14.13
and led them up a high mountain a. 17.01
but the chains he wrenched a., Mk 5.04
a high mountain a. by themselves; 9.02
and withdrew a. to a city called Lk 9.10
for a. from me you can do nothing. Jn 15.05
"Set a. for me Barnabas and Saul Ac 13.02
set a. for the gospel of God Rom 1.01
has been manifested a. from law, 3.21
by faith a. from works of law. 3.28
righteousness a. from works: 4.06
A. from the law sin lies dead. 7.08
I was once alive a. from the law, 7.09
And, a. from other things, there is 2Co 11.28
who had set me a. before I was Gal 1.15
that a. from us they should not be Heb 11.40
me your faith a. from your works, Jas 2.18
that faith a. from works is barren? 2.20
For as the body a. from the spirit 2.26
so faith a. from works is dead. 2.26

APELLES
Greet A., who is approved in Christ. Rom 16.10

APES
silver, ivory, a., and peacocks. 1Ki 10.22
silver, ivory, a., and peacocks. 2Ch 9.21

APHEK
the king of A., one; Jos 12.18
to A., to the boundary of the 13.04
Ummah, A. and Rehob—twenty-two 19.30
and the Philistines encamped at A. 1Sa 4.01
gathered all their forces at A.; 29.01
the Syrians, and went up to A., 1Ki 20.26
And the rest fled into the city of A.; 20.30
the Syrians in A. until you have 2Ki 13.17

APHEKAH
Janim, Bethtappuah, A., Jos 15.53

APHIAH
son of A., a Benjaminite, a man of 1Sa 9.01

APHIK
of Helbah, or of A., or of Rehob; Ju 1.31

APIECE
you shall take an omer a., Ex 16.16
twice as much bread, two omers a.; 16.22
you shall take five shekels a.; Num 3.47
ten shekels a. according to the 7.86
The doors had two leaves a., Eze 41.24

APIS
Why has A. fled? Jer 46.15

APOLLONIA
passed through Amphipolis and A., Ac 17.01

APOLLOS
Now a Jew named A., Ac 18.24
While A. was at Corinth, Paul passed 19.01
belong to Paul," or "I belong to A.," 1Co 1.12
"I belong to A.," are you not 3.04
What then is A.? 3.05
I planted, A. watered, but God gave 3.06
whether Paul or A. or Cephas or the 3.22
to myself and A. for your benefit, 4.06
As for our brother A., 16.12
the lawyer and A. on their way; Tit 3.13

APOLLYON
and in Greek he is called A. Rev 9.11

APOLOGIZED
so they came and a. to them. Ac 16.39

APOSTASIES
are many, their a. are great. Jer 5.06

APOSTASY
and your a. will reprove you. Jer 2.19
if they then commit a., Heb 6.06

APOSTLE
Jesus Christ, called to be an a., Rom 1.01
then as I am an a. to the Gentiles, 11.13
of God to be an a. of Christ Jesus, 1Co 1.01
Am I not an a.? 9.01
If to others I am not an a., 9.02
apostles, unfit to be called an a., 15.09
Paul, an a. of Christ Jesus by the 2Co 1.01
The signs of a true a. were performed 12.12
Paul an a.—not from men nor Gal 1.01
Paul, an a. of Christ Jesus by the Eph 1.01
Paul an a. of Christ Jesus by the Col 1.01
Paul, an a. of Christ Jesus by 1Ti 1.01
a preacher and a. (I am telling 2.07
Paul, an a. of Christ Jesus by the 2Ti 1.01
a preacher and a. and teacher, 1.11
of God and an a. of Jesus Christ, Tit 1.01
the a. and high priest of our Heb 3.01
Peter, and a. of Jesus Christ, To the 1Pe 1.01
a servant and a. of Jesus Christ, To 2Pe 1.01

APOSTLES
The names of the twelve a. are these: Mt 10.02
The a. returned to Jesus, and told Mk 6.30
from them twelve, whom he named a.; Lk 6.13
return the a. told him what they 9.10
'I will send them prophets and a., 11.49
The a. said to the Lord, "Increase 17.05
sat at table, and the a. with him. 22.14
with them who told this to the a.; 24.10
Spirit to the a. whom he had Ac 1.02
he was enrolled with the eleven a. 1.26
to Peter and the rest of the a., 2.37
and signs were done through the a. 2.43
great power the a. gave their 4.33
surnamed by the a. Barnabas (which 4.36
the people by the hands of the a. 5.12
they arrested the a. and put them 5.18
But Peter and the a. answered, 5.29
and when they had called in the a., 5.40
These they set before the a., 6.06
Judea and Samaria, except the a. 8.01
Now when the a. at Jerusalem heard 8.14
him, and brought him to the a., 9.27
Now the a. and the brethren who 11.01
the Jews, and some with the a. 14.04
But when the a. Barnabas and Paul 14.14
Jerusalem to the a. and the elders 15.02
church and the a. and the elders, 15.04
The a. and the elders were gathered 15.06
good to the a. and the elders, 15.22
both the a. and the elders, to the 15.23
reached by the a. and elders who 16.04
they are men of note among the a., Rom 16.07
has exhibited us a. as last of all, 1Co 4.09
as the other a. and the brothers of 9.05
appointed in the church first a., 12.28
Are all a.? Are all prophets? 12.29
to James, then to all the a. 15.07
For I am the least of the a., 15.09
inferior to these superlative a. 2Co 11.05
For such men are false a., 11.13
disguising themselves as a. of Christ. 11.13
inferior to these superlative a., 12.11
to those who were a. before me, Gal 1.17
of the other a. except James the 1.19
foundation of the a. and prophets, Eph 2.20
to his holy a. and prophets by the 3.05
gifts were that some should be a., 4.11
have made demands as a. of Christ. 1Th 2.06
Lord and Savior through your a. 2Pe 3.02
predictions of the a. of our Lord Jud 1.17
who call themselves a. but are not, Rev 2.02
O saints and a. and prophets, for 18.20
names of the twelve a. of the Lamb. 21.14

APOSTLES'
themselves to the a. teaching and Ac 2.42
and laid it at the a. feet; 4.35
money and laid it at the a. feet. 4.37
a part and laid it at the a. feet. 5.02
the laying on of the a. hands, 8.18

APOSTLESHIP
ministry and a. from which Judas Ac 1.25
grace and a. to bring about Rom 1.05
are the seal of my a. in the Lord. 1Co 9.02

APPAIM
The sons of Nadab: Seled and A.; 1Ch 2.30
The sons of A.: Ishi. 2.31

APPALLED
from my head and beard, and sat a. Ez 9.03
me while I sat a. until the 9.04
Upright men are a. at this, Job 17.08
They of the west are a. at his day, 18.20
and be a., and lay your hand upon 21.05
Let them be a. because of their Ps 40.15
Let them be a. because of their 70.03
my heart within me is a. 143.04
My mind reels, horror has a. me; Is 21.04
I was a., but there was no one to 63.05
Be a., O heavens, at this, be shocked, Jer 2.12
shall be a. and the prophets 4.09
fold shall be a. at their fate. 49.20
who passes by Babylon shall be a., 50.13
fold shall be a. at their fate. 50.45
the land was a. and all who were Eze 19.07
every moment, and be a. at you. 26.16
of the coastlands are a. at you; 27.35
among the peoples are a. at you; 28.19
I will make many peoples a. at you, 32.10
but I was a. by the vision and did Dan 8.27

APPALLING
An a. and horrible thing has Jer 5.30

APPAREL
and a suit of a., and your living. Ju 17.10
put ornaments of gold upon your a. 2Sa 1.24
he that is glorious in his a., Is 63.01
Why is thy a. red, and thy garments 63.02
and I will clothe you with rich a. Zec 3.04
then, arraying him in gorgeous a., Lk 23.11
men stood by them in dazzling a.; 24.04
man stood before me in bright a., Ac 10.30
no one's silver or gold or a. 20.33
modestly and sensibly in seemly a., 1Ti 2.09

APPARELED
are gorgeously a. and live in Lk 7.25

APPEAL
went forth to a. to the king for 2Ki 8.03
I must a. for mercy to my accuser. Job 9.15
that I cannot a. to my Father, Mt 26.53
I a. to Caesar." Ac 25.11
I was compelled to a. to Caesar— 28.19
I a. to you therefore, brethren, by Rom 12.01
I a. to you, brethren, by our Lord 15.30
I a. to you, brethren, to take note 16.17
I a. to you, brethren, by the name of 1Co 1.10
God making his a. through us. 2Co 5.20
For he not only accepted our a., 8.17
heed my a., agree with one another, 13.11
For our a. does not spring from 1Th 2.03
love's sake I prefer to a. to you— Phm 1.09
I a. to you for my child, Onesimus, 1.10
I a. to you, brethren, bear with my Heb 13.22
body but as an a. to God for a 1Pe 3.21

APPEALED
restored to life a. to the king for 2Ki 8.05
answered, "You have a. to Caesar; Ac 25.12
But when Paul had a. to be kept in 25.21
as he himself a. to the emperor, 25.25
free if he had not a. to Caesar." 26.32

APPEALING
to write a. to you to contend for Jud 1.03

APPEAR
one place, and let the dry land a." Gen 1.09
to a. before him in Goshen; 46.28
say, 'The LORD did not a. to you.'" Ex 4.01
None shall a. before me empty-handed. 23.15
all your males a. before the Lord 23.17
And none shall a. before me empty. 34.20
all your males a. before the LORD 34.23
you go up to a. before the LORD 34.24
for today the LORD will a. to you.'" Lev 9.04
glory of the LORD will a. to you." 9.06
he shall a. again before the priest; 13.07
for I will a. in the cloud upon the 16.02
males shall a. before the Lord Deu 16.16
They shall not a. before the LORD 16.16
dispute shall a. before the LORD, 19.17
Israel comes to a. before the LORD 31.11
that he may a. in the presence of 1Sa 1.22
them as a blazing oven when you a. Ps 21.09
up Zion, he will a. in his glory; 102.16
The flowers a. on the earth, the Sol 2.12
"When you come to a. before me, Is 1.12
to those who are in darkness, 'A.' 49.09
your sisters a. righteous by all Eze 16.51
made your sisters a. righteous. 16.52
in all your doings your sins a. 21.24
Forces from him shall a. and Dan 11.31
it and that I may a. in my glory, Hag 1.08
Then the LORD will a. over them, Zec 9.14
which outwardly a. beautiful, Mt 23.27
also outwardly a. righteous to men, 23.28
then will a. the sign of the Son of 24.30
of God was to a. immediately. Lk 19.11
those in which I will a. to you, Ac 26.16
For we must all a. before the 2Co 5.10
not that we may a. to have met the 13.07
you also will a. with him in glory Col 3.04
but the sins of others a. later. 1Ti 5.24
now to a. in the presence of God on Heb 9.24
will a. a second time, not to deal 9.28
made out of things which do not a. 11.03
will the impious and sinner a.? 1Pe 4.18
it does not yet a. what we shall be, 1Jn 3.02

APPEARANCE
Now the a. of the glory of the LORD Ex 24.17
like the a. of leprosy in the skin Lev 13.43
like the a. of fire until morning. Num 9.15
and the a. of fire by night. 9.16
and its a. like that of bdellium. 11.07
not look on his a. or on the 1Sa 16.07
man looks on the outward a., 16.07
a youth, ruddy and comely in a. 17.42
He said to her, "What is his a.?" 28.14
but I could not discern its a. Job 4.16
His a. is like Lebanon, choice as Sol 5.15
his a. was so marred, beyond human Is 52.14
And this was their a.: Eze 1.05
As for the a. of the wheels and 1.16
their a. was like the gleaming of a 1.16
of a throne, in a. like sapphire; 1.26
what had the a. of his loins I saw 1.27
like the a. of fire enclosed round 1.27
what had the a. of his loins I saw 1.27
I saw as it were the a. of fire, 1.27
Like the a. of the bow that is in 1.28
so was the a. of the brightness 1.28
Such was the a. of the likeness of 1.28
a form that had the a. of a man; 8.02
it was like the a. of brightness, 8.02
and the a. of the wheels was like 10.09
And as for their a., 10.10
faces whose a. I had seen by the 10.22
whose a. was like bronze, with a 40.03
the temple and its a. and plan, 43.10
Then let our a. and the a. Dan 1.13
the a. of the youths who eat the 1.13
were better in a. and fatter in 1.15
and its a. was frightening. 2.31
and the a. of the fourth is like a 3.25
me one having the a. of a man. 8.15
his face like the a. of lightning, 10.06
my radiant a. was fearfully changed, 10.08
Again one having the a. of a man 10.18
Their a. is like the a. of horses, Joe 2.04
how to interpret the a. of the sky, Mt 16.03
His a. was like lightning, and his 28.03
the a. of his countenance was Lk 9.29
interpret the a. of earth and sky; 12.56
These have indeed an a. of wisdom Col 2.23
In a. the locusts were like horses Rev 9.07

APPEARANCES
Do not judge by a., but judge Jn 7.24

APPEARED
Then the LORD a. to Abram, and said, Gen 12.07
to the LORD, who had a. to him. 12.07
years old the LORD a. to Abram, 17.01
And the LORD a. to him by the oaks 18.01
And the LORD a. to him, and said, "Do 26.02
And the LORD a. to him the same 26.24
to the God who a. to you when you 35.01
God a. to Jacob again, when he came 35.09
"God Almighty a. to me at Luz in 48.03
of the LORD a. to him in a flame Ex 3.02
has a. to me, saying, "I have observed 3.16
the God of Jacob, has a. to you." 4.05
I a. to Abraham, to Isaac, and to 6.03
wonted flow when the morning a.; 14.27
glory of the LORD a. in the cloud. 16.10
of the LORD a. to all the people. Lev 9.23
of the LORD a. at the tent of Num 14.10
of the LORD a. to all the congregation 16.19
it, and the glory of the LORD a. 16.42
the glory of the LORD a. to them, 20.06
And the LORD a. in the tent in a Deu 31.15
of the LORD a. to him and said to Ju 6.12
of the LORD a. to the woman and 13.03
to me the other day has a. to me. 13.10
of the LORD a. no more to Manoah 13.21
And as morning a., the woman came 19.26
And the LORD a. again at Shiloh, for 1Sa 3.21
At Gibeon the LORD a. to Solomon in 1Ki 3.05
the LORD a. to Solomon a second 9.02
as he had a. to him at Gibeon. 9.02
Israel, who had a. to him twice, 11.09

APPEARED (cont.)
In that night God a. to Solomon, 2Ch 1.07
the LORD had a. to David his 3.01
Then the LORD a. to Solomon in the 7.12
the LORD a. to him from afar. Jer 31.03
below what a. to be his loins it Eze 8.02
cherubim there a. above them 10.01
The cherubim a. to have the form of 10.08
of a man's hand a. and wrote on Dan 5.05
King Belshazzar a vision a. to me, 8.01
that which a. to me at the first. 8.01
of the Lord a. to him in a dream, Mt 1.20
from them what time the star a.; 2.07
of the Lord a. to Joseph in a 2.13
of the Lord a. in a dream to 2.19
bore grain, then the weeds a. also. 13.26
there a. to them Moses and Elijah, 17.03
into the holy city and a. to many. 27.53
John the baptizer a. in the wilderness, Mk 1.04
And there a. to them Elijah with 9.04
And there a. to him an angel of the Lk 1.11
And an angel of the Lord a. to them, 2.09
by some that Elijah had a., 9.08
who a. in glory and spoke of his 9.31
And there a. to him an angel from 22.43
He a. to be going further, 24.28
risen indeed, and has a. to Simon! 24.34
And there a. to them tongues as of Ac 2.03
God of glory a. to our father 7.02
following day he a. to them as they 7.26
an angel a. to him in the wilderness 7.30
the angel that a. to him in the 7.35
Lord Jesus who a. to you on the 9.17
and behold, an angel of the Lord a., 12.07
many days he a. to those who came 13.31
And a vision a. to Paul in the 16.09
for I have a. to you for this 26.16
sun nor stars a. for many a day, 27.20
and that he a. to Cephas, then to 1Co 15.05
Then he a. to more than five 15.06
Then he a. to James, then to all the 15.07
untimely born, he a. also to me. 15.08
of God has a. for the salvation of Tit 2.11
kindness of God our Savior a., 3.04
But when Christ a. as a high priest Heb 9.11
he has a. once for all at the end 9.26
You know that he a. to take away 1Jn 3.05
the Son of God a. was to destroy 3.08
who sat there a. like jasper and Rev 4.03
And a great portent a. in heaven, 12.01
And another portent a. in heaven; 12.03
And I saw what a. to be a sea of 15.02

APPEARING
a. to them during forty days, and Ac 1.03
him by his a. and his coming. 2Th 2.08
until the a. of our Lord Jesus 1Ti 6.14
through the a. of our Savior 2Ti 1.10
and by his a. and his kingdom: 4.01
also to all who have loved his a. 4.08
the a. of the glory of our great Tit 2.13

APPEARS
and the disease a. to be deeper Lev 13.03
and a. no deeper than the skin, and 13.04
But when raw flesh a. on him, 13.14
and if it a. deeper than the skin 13.20
white and it a. deeper than the 13.25
and if it a. deeper than the skin, 13.30
and if a. no deeper than the skin 13.31
and the itch a. to be no deeper 13.32
the skin and it a. to be no deeper 13.34
then if it a. again in the garment, 13.57
and if it a. to be deeper than the 14.37
is gone, and the new growth a., Pro 27.25
And if any one again a. as a prophet, Zec 13.03
and who can stand when he a.? Mal 3.02
and when the Christ a., Jn 7.27
they said, "When the Christ a., 7.31
When Christ who is our life a., Col 3.04
are a mist that a. for a little Jas 4.14
so that when he a. we may have 1Jn 2.28
that when he a. we shall be like 3.02

APPEASE
"I may a. him with the present that Gen 32.20
death, and a wise man will a. it. Pro 16.14

APPEASED
nor be a. though you multiply gifts Pro 6.35
Shall I be a. for these things? Is 57.06

APPENDAGE
and the a. of the liver, and the two Ex 29.13
and the a. of the liver, and the two 29.22
and the a. of the liver which he Lev 3.04
and the a. of the liver which he 3.10
and the a. of the liver which he 3.15
and the a. of the liver which he 4.09
and the a. of the liver which he 7.04
and the a. of the liver, and the two 8.16
and the a. of the liver, and the two 8.25
kidneys and the a. of the liver 9.10
kidneys, and the a. of the liver; 9.19

APPETITE
drink, whatever your a. craves; Deu 14.26
My a. refuses to touch them; Job 6.07
bread, and his a. dainty food. 33.20
or satisfy the a. of the young 38.39
to satisfy his a. when he is Pro 6.30
has enough to satisfy his a., 13.25
A worker's a. works for him; 16.26
if you are a man given to a. 23.02
yet his a. is not satisfied. Ecc 6.07
enlarged its a. and opened its Is 5.14
The dogs have a mighty a.; 56.11

APPETITES
but their own a., and by fair and Rom 16.18

APPHIA
and A. our sister and Archippus our Phm 1.02

APPIUS
as the Forum of A. and Three Ac 28.15

APPLE
he kept him as the a. of his eye. Deu 32.10
Keep me as the a. of the eye; Ps 17.08
my teachings as the a. of your eye; Pro 7.02
As an a. tree among the trees of Sol 2.03
Under the a. tree I awakened you. 8.05
and a., all the trees of the field Joe 1.12
you touches the a. of his eye: Zec 2.08

APPLES
spoken is like a. of gold in a Pro 25.11
with raisins, refresh me with a.; Sol 2.05
the scent of your breath like a., 7.08

APPLIED
gold evenly a. upon the carved 1Ki 6.35
And I a. my mind to seek and to Ecc 1.13
And I a. my mind to know wisdom and 1.17
When I a. my mind to know wisdom, 8.16
I have a. all this to myself and 1Co 4.06

APPLY
and a. your mind to my knowledge; Pro 22.17
A. your mind to instruction and 23.12
and a. it to the boil, that he may Is 38.21
be careful to a. themselves to Tit 3.08
people learn to a. themselves to 3.14

APPLYING
observed while a. my mind to all Ecc 8.09

APPOINT

proceed to a. overseers over the Gen 41.34
then I will a. for you a place to Ex 21.13
and shall a. it for the service of 30.16
I will a. over you sudden terror, Lev 26.16
but a. the Levites over the tabernacle Num 1.50
And you shall a. Aaron and his sons, 3.10
shall go in and a. them each to 4.19
a. a man over the congregation, 27.16
and I will a. them as your heads. Deu 1.13
"You shall a. judges and officers 16.18
'A. the cities of refuge, of which I Jos 20.02
now a. for us a king to govern us 1Sa 8.05
your sons and a. them to his 8.11
and he will a. for himself commanders 8.12
to a. me as prince over Israel, the 2Sa 6.21
And I will a. a place for my people 7.10
the Levites to a. their brethren 1Ch 15.16
And I will a. a place for my people 17.09
a. magistrates and judges who may Ez 7.25
A. guards from among the inhabitants Neh 7.03
And let the king a. officers in all Est 2.03
thou wouldest a. me a set time, Job 14.13
time which I a. I will judge with Ps 75.02
place which thou didst a. for them. 104.08
A. a wicked man against him; 109.06
"I will a. over them four kinds of Jer 15.03
and I will a. over her whomever I 49.19
and I will a. over her whomever I 50.44
a. a marshal against her, bring up 51.27
Yet I will a. them to keep charge Eze 44.14
besought the king to a. him a time, Dan 2.16
and they shall a. for themselves Hos 1.11
kingdom for me, so do I a. for you Lk 12.29
whom we may a. to this duty. Ac 6.03
to a. you to serve and bear witness 26.16
and a. elders in every town as I Tit 1.05

APPOINTED

"God has a. for me another child Gen 4.25
At the a. time I will return to you, 18.14
whom thou hast a. for thy servant 24.14
the LORD has a. for my master's son 24.44
ordinance at its a. time from year Ex 13.10
days at the a. time in the month 23.15
I have a. with him Oholiab, the son 31.06
at the time a. in the month Abib; 34.18
The a. feasts of the LORD which you Lev 23.02
my a. feasts, are these. 23.02
"These are the a. feasts of the 23.04
proclaim at the time a. for them. 23.04
"These are the a. feasts of the 23.37
of Israel the a. feasts of the 23.44
And the a. charge of the sons of Num 3.36
LORD through Moses they were a., 4.49
keep the passover at its a. time. 9.02
you shall keep it at its a. time; 9.03
offering at its a. time among the 9.07
the LORD's offering at its a. time; 9.13
and at your a. feasts, and at the 10.10
offering or at your a. feasts, 15.03
to the LORD at your a. feasts, 29.39
shall be a. at the head of the Deu 20.09
whom he had a., a man from each Jos 4.04
they a. Bezer in the wilderness on 20.08
Now the a. signal between the men Ju 20.38
was kept for you until the hour a., 1Sa 9.24
who a. Moses and Aaron and brought 12.06
seven days, the time a. by Samuel; 13.08
did not come within the days a., 13.11
the LORD has a. him to be prince 13.14
and has a. you prince over Israel, 25.30
from the time that I a. judges over 2Sa 7.11
the set time which had been a. him. 20.05
from the morning until the a. time; 24.15
and I have a. him to be ruler over 1Ki 1.35
and a. priests from among all the 12.31
And Jeroboam a. a feast on the 12.32
Now the king had a. the captain on 2Ki 7.17
So the king a. an official for her, 8.06
and a. from among themselves all 17.32
he a. Gedaliah the son of Ahikam, 25.22
of Babylon had a. Gedaliah governor, 25.23
Levites were a. for all the 1Ch 6.48
Others of them were a. over the 9.29
So the Levites a. Heman the son of 15.17
Moreover he a. certain of the 16.04
day David first a. that thanksgiving 16.07
of Juduthun were a. to the gate. 16.42
from the time that I a. judges over 17.10
according to the a. duties in their 24.03
These had as their a. duty in their 24.19
his sons were a. to outside duties 26.29
King David a. him and his brethren, 26.32
moons and the a. feasts of the 2Ch 2.04
at the place that David had a., 3.01
he a. the divisions of the priests 8.14
and he a. his own priests for the 11.15
and Rehoboam a. Abijah the son of 11.22
He a. judges in the land in all the 19.05
Jehoshaphat a. certain Levites and 19.08
he a. those who were to sing to the 20.21
And Hezekiah a. the divisions of 31.02
and the a. feasts, as it is written 31.03
land which I a. for your fathers, 33.08
He a. the priests to their offices 35.02
and at all the a. feasts of the Ez 3.05
They a. the Levites, from twenty 3.08
foreign wives come at a. times, 10.14
time that I was a. to be their Neh 5.14
and the Levites had been a., 7.01
their neck and a. a leader to 9.17
the a. feasts, the holy things, and 10.33
at times a., year by year, to burn 10.34
and a. two great companies which 12.31
day men were a. over the chambers 12.44
who was a. over the chambers of the 13.04
And I a. as treasurers over the 13.13
at a. times, and for the first 13.31
who had been a. to attend her, and Est 4.05
and at the time a. every year, 9.27
be observed at their a. seasons, 9.31
and thou hast a. his bounds that he Job 14.05
and to the house a. for all living. 30.23
For he has not a. a time for any 34.23
thou hast a. a judgment. Ps 7.06
Like sheep they are a. for Sheol; 49.14
and a. a law in Israel, which he 78.05
the a. time has come. 102.13
Thou hast a. thy testimonies in 119.138
for he has a. a time for every Ecc 3.17
moons and your a. feasts my soul Is 1.14
Zion, the city of our a. feasts! 33.20
I a. you a prophet to the nations." Jer 1.05
us the weeks a. for the harvest.' 5.24
will not come at their a. time, 33.20
king of Babylon a. governor of the 40.05
of Babylon had a. Gedaliah the son 40.07
Judah and had a. Gedaliah the son 40.11
of Babylon had a. governor in the 41.02
against the seashore he has a. it." 47.07
for none come to the a. feasts; Lam 1.04
ruins the place of his a. feasts; 2.06
an end in Zion a. feast and 2.06
LORD as on the day of an a. feast. 2.07
the day of an a. feast my terrors 2.22
the a. time of your years has come. Eze 22.04
at Jerusalem during her a. feasts, 36.38
be burnt in the a. place belonging 43.21
my statutes in all my a. feasts, 44.24
all the a. feasts of the house of 45.17
before the LORD at the a. feasts, 46.09
feasts and the a. seasons the 46.11
who a. your food and your drink, Dan 1.10

APPOINTED (cont.)
of the eunuchs had a. over Daniel, Dan 1.11
the king had a. to destroy the 2.24
and he a. Shadrach, Meshach, and 2.49
whom you have a. over the affairs 3.12
pertains to the a. time of the end 8.19
end is yet to be at the time a. 11.27
"At the time a. he shall return and 11.29
end, for it is yet for the time a. 11.35
sabbaths, and all her a. feasts. Hos 2.11
you also, O Judah, a harvest is a. 6.11
you do on the day of a. festival, 9.05
so they are a. to the yoke, and none 11.07
as in the days of the a. feast. 12.09
And the LORD a. a great fish to Jon 1.17
And the LORD God a. a plant, 4.06
God a. a worm which attacked the 4.07
God a. a sultry east wind, and the 4.08
And he a. twelve, to be with him, and Mk 3.14
"Collect no more than is a. you." Lk 3.13
After this the Lord a. seventy others, 10.01
as my Father a. a kingdom for me, so 22.29
I chose you and a. you that you Jn 15.16
he may send the Christ a. for you, Ac 3.20
On an a. day Herod put on his royal 12.21
And when they had a. elders for 14.23
the others were a. to go up to 15.02
righteousness by a man whom he has a., 17.31
told all that is a. for you to do. 22.10
of our fathers a. you to know his 22.14
When they had a. a day for him, they 28.23
authorities resists what God has a., Rom 13.02
the a. time has grown very short; 1Co 7.29
And God has a. in the church first 12.28
but he has been a. by the churches 2Co 8.19
destined and a. to live for the Eph 1.12
For this I was a. a preacher and 1Ti 2.07
gospel I was a. a preacher and 2Ti 1.11
whom he a. the heir of all things, Heb 1.02
He was faithful to him who a. him, 3.02
among men is a. to act on behalf 5.01
but was a. by him who said to him, 5.05
high priest is a. to offer gifts 8.03
And just as it is a. for men to die 9.27

APPOINTING
faithful by a. me to his service, 1Ti 1.12

APPOINTMENT
the field to the a. with David, 1Sa 20.35
I have made an a. with the young 21.02
by the a. of Hezekiah the king and 2Ch 31.13
They made an a. together to come to Job 2.11
By thy a. they stand this day; Ps 119.91
unless they have made an a.? Amo 3.03

APPOINTS
he will complete what he a. for me; Job 23.14
the law a. men in their weakness as Heb 7.28
a. a Son who has been made perfect 7.28

APPORTION
to a. the contribution reserved for 2Ch 31.14
to a. the desolate heritages; Is 49.08

APPORTIONED
inheritance had not yet been a. Jos 18.02
there Joshua a. the land to the 18.10
and nights of misery are a. to me. Job 7.03
he a. them for a possession and Ps 78.55
keep to the limits God has a. us, 2Co 10.13
and to him Abraham a. a tenth part Heb 7.02

APPORTIONS
who a. to each one individually as 1Co 12.11

APPROACH
"None of you shall a. any one near Lev 18.06
that is, you shall not a. his wife; 18.14
"You shall not a. a woman to 18.19
a blemish may a. to offer the 21.17
come near the veil or a. the altar, 21.23
and when you a. the frontier of the Deu 2.19
the days a. when you must die; 31.14
who are with me, will a. the city. Jos 8.05
like a prince I would a. him. Job 31.37
let them a., then let them speak; Is 41.01
and he shall a. me, for who would Jer 30.21
who would dare of himself to a. me? 30.21
Jerusalem at the a. of Pharaoh's 37.11
neighbor's wife or a. a woman in Eze 18.06
the priests who a. the LORD shall 42.13
sanctuary, and they shall a. my table, 44.16
sanctuary and a. the LORD to 45.04

APPROACHED
Now Abimelech had not a. her; Gen 20.04
and when they a. the altar, they Ex 40.32
Then Saul a. Samuel in the gate, and 1Sa 9.18
they a. Zerubbabel and the heads of Ez 4.02
the officials a. me and said, "The 9.01
Then Esther a. and touched the top Est 5.02
I a. one of those who stood there Dan 7.16
Now as he journeyed he a. Damascus, Ac 9.03

APPROACHES
If a woman a. any beast and lies Lev 20.16
generations a. the holy things, 22.03
and whoever a. the ranks is to be 2Ki 11.08
where no thief a. and no moth Lk 12.33

APPROACHING
of mourning for my father are a.; Gen 27.41

APPROVAL
our husbands' a. that we made Jer 44.19
good, and you will receive his a., Rom 13.03
the men of old received divine a. Heb 11.02
which he received a. as righteous, 11.04
it patiently, you have God's a. 1Pe 2.20

APPROVE
Nevertheless the lords do not a. of you. 1Sa 29.06
in his cause, the Lord does not a. Lam 3.36
do them but a. those who practice Rom 1.32
his will and a. what is excellent, 2.18
so that you may a. what is excellent, Php 1.10

APPROVED
a., mighty warriors, chief of the 1Ch 7.40
and when the eye saw, it a.; Job 29.11
for God has already a. what you do. Ecc 9.07
is acceptable to God and a. by men. Rom 14.18
Greet Apelles, who is a. in Christ. 16.10
as we have been a. by God to be 1Th 2.04
present yourself to God as one a., 2Ti 2.15
For one is a. if, mindful of God, he 1Pe 2.19

APPROVES
to judge himself for what he a. Rom 14.22

APPROVING
I also was standing by and a., Ac 22.20

APRONS
together and made themselves a. Gen 3.07
handkerchiefs or a. were carried Ac 19.12

APT
To make an a. answer is a joy to a Pro 15.23
dignified, hospitable, an a. teacher, 1Ti 3.02
an a. teacher, forbearing, 2Ti 2.24

AQUILA
And he found a Jew named A., Ac 18.02
and with him Priscilla and A. 18.18
when Priscilla and A. heard him, 18.26
greet Prisca and A., Rom 16.03
A. and Prisca, together with the 1Co 16.19
Greet Prisca and A., and the 2Ti 4.19

AR
that extends to the seat of A., Num 21.15
It devoured A. of Moab, the lords of 21.28
I have given A. to the sons of Lot Deu 2.09
over the boundary of Moab at A.; 2.18
Moabites who live in A. did for me, 2.29
Because A. is laid waste in a night Is 15.01

ARA
Jether: Jephunneh, Pispa, and A. 1Ch 7.38

ARAB
A., Dumah, Eshan, Jos 15.52
and Geshem the A. heard of it, Neh 2.19
to Geshem the A. and to the rest 6.01
no A. will pitch his tent there, no Is 13.20
lovers like an A. in the wilderness Jer 3.02

ARABAH
in the A. over against Suph, between Deu 1.01
to all their neighbors in the A., 1.07
away from the A. road from Elath 2.08
the A. also, with the Jordan as the 3.17
as far as the sea of the A., 3.17
together with all the A. on the 4.49
Jordan as far as the Sea of the A., 4.49
the Canaanites who live in the A., 11.30
down toward the sea of the A., Jos 3.16
toward the A. to meet Israel in 8.14
and in the A. south of Chinneroth, 11.02
lowland and the A. and the hill 11.16
Hermon, with all the A. eastward: 12.01
and the A. to the Sea of Chinneroth 12.03
Bethjeshimoth, to the sea of the A., 12.03
in the A., in the slopes, in the 12.08
Betharabah it goes down to the A.; 18.18
in the A. to the south of Jeshimon. 1Sa 23.24
went all that night through the A.; 2Sa 2.29
by the way of the A. all night, 4.07
Hamath as far as the Sea of the A., 2Ki 14.25
went in the direction of the A. 25.04
and they went toward the A. Jer 39.04
went in the direction of the A. 52.07
region and goes down into the A.; Eze 47.08
of Hamath to the Brook of the A. Amo 6.14

ARABIA
the kings of A. and from the 1Ki 10.15
the kings of A. and the governors 2Ch 9.14
The oracle concerning A. Is 21.13
the thickets in A. you will lodge, 21.13
all the kings of A. and all the Jer 25.24
A. and all the princes of Kedar Eze 27.21
and all A., and Libya, and the 30.05
before me, but I went away into A.; Gal 1.17
Now Hagar is Mount Sinai in A.; 4.25

ARABIANS
Cretans and A., we hear them Ac 2.11

ARABS
and the A. also brought him seven 2Ch 17.11
and of the A. who are near the 21.16
came with the A. to the camp had 22.01
and against the A. that dwelt in 26.07
Tobiah and the A. and the Ammonites Neh 4.07

ARAD
the king of A., who dwelt in the Num 21.01
the king of A., who dwelt in the 33.40
the king of A., one; Jos 12.14
which lies in the Negeb near A.; Ju 1.16
Zebadiah, A., Eder, 1Ch 8.15

ARAH
A., Hanniel, and Rizia. 1Ch 7.39
The sons of A., seven hundred and Ez 2.05
son-in-law of Shecaniah the son of A.: Neh 6.18
The sons of A., six hundred and 7.10

ARAM
Asshur, Arpachshad, Lud, and A. Gen 10.22
The sons of A.: Uz, Hul, Gether, and 10.23
brother, Kemuel the father of A., 22.21
"From A. Balak has brought me, the Num 23.07
put garrisons in A. of Damascus; 2Sa 8.06
vow while I dwelt at Geshur in A., 15.08
A., Uz, Hul, Gether, and Meshech. 1Ch 1.17
But Geshur and A. took from them 2.23
brother: Rohgah, Jehubbah, and A. 7.34
(Jacob fled to the land of A., Hos 12.12
the LORD belong the cities of A., Zec 9.01

ARAMAIC
your servants in the A. language, 2Ki 18.26
was written in A. and translated. Ez 4.07
"Pray, speak to your servants in A., Is 36.11

ARAMEAN
of Bethuel the A. of Paddan-aram, Gen 25.20
Paddan-aram, the sister of Laban the A. 25.20
Laban, the son of Bethuel the A., 28.05
And Jacob outwitted Laban the A., 31.20
to Laban the A. in a dream by 31.24
God, 'A wandering A. was my father; Deu 26.05
Asriel, whom his A. concubine bore; 1Ch 7.14

ARAMMAACAH
from A., and from Zobah. 1Ch 19.06

ARAN
These are the sons of Dishan: Uz and A. Gen 36.28
The sons of Dishan: Uz and A. 1Ch 1.42

ARARAT
to rest upon the mountains of A. Gen 8.04
and escaped into the land of A. 2Ki 19.37
and escaped into the land of A. Is 37.38
A., Minni, and Ashkenaz; appoint Jer 51.27

ARAUNAH
threshing floor of A. the Jebusite. 2Sa 24.16
threshing floor of A. the Jebusite. 24.18
And when A. looked down, he saw the 24.20
and A. went forth, and did obeisance 24.20
And A. said, "Why has my lord the 24.21
Then A. said to David, "Let my lord 24.22
A. gives to the king." And 24.23
And A. said to the king, "The LORD 24.23
But the king said to A., "No, but 24.24

ARBA
this A. was the greatest man among Jos 14.15
Hebron (A. was the father of Anak). 15.13
A. being the father of Anak (that 21.11

ARBATHITE
Abialbon the A., Azmaveth of 2Sa 23.31
the brooks of Gaash, Abiel the A., 1Ch 11.32

ARBITE
Hezro of Carmel, Paarai the A., 2Sa 23.35

ARCHANGEL
But when the a. Michael, contending Jud 1.09

ARCHANGEL'S
with the a. call, and with the sound 1Th 4.16

ARCHELAUS
he heard that A. reigned over Mt 2.22

ARCHER
Like an a. who wounds everybody is Pro 26.10
of horseman and a. every city Jer 4.29
Let not the a. bend his bow, and let 51.03

ARCHERS
The a. fiercely attacked him, shot Gen 49.23
upon Saul, and the a. found him; 1Sa 31.03
and he was badly wounded by the a. 31.03
Then the a. shot at your servants 2Sa 11.24
upon Saul, and the a. found him; 1Ch 10.03
and he was wounded by the a. 10.03
And the a. shot King Josiah; 2Ch 35.23
his a. surround me. He slashes Job 16.13
remainder of the a. of the mighty Is 21.17
"Summon a. against Babylon, all Jer 50.29

ARCHIPPUS
And say to A., "See that you fulfil Col 4.17
our sister and A. our fellow Phm 1.02

ARCHITE
Hushai the A. came to meet him with 2Sa 15.32
And when Hushai the A., David's 16.16
said, "Call Hushai the A. also, 17.05
of Hushai the A. is better than 17.14
and Hushai the A. was the king's 1Ch 27.33

ARCHITES
Ataroth, the territory of the A.; Jos 16.02

ARCHIVES
in the royal a. there in Babylon, Ez 5.17
house of the a. where the documents 6.01

ARD
Ehi, Rosh, Muppim, Huppim, and A. Gen 46.21
sons of Bela were A. and Naaman: Num 26.40
of A., the family of the Ardites; 26.40

ARDITES
of Ard, the family of the A.; Num 26.40

ARDON
her sons: Jesher, Shobab, and A. 1Ch 2.18

AREA
its whole a., was made over Gen 23.17
three parts the a. of the land Deu 19.03
the outside of the temple a., Eze 40.05
the interior of the temple a., 42.15
measured the temple a. round about. 42.15
the temple, outside the sacred a. 43.21
of the city an a. five thousand 45.06

ARELI
Shuni, Ezbon, Eri, Arodi, and A. Gen 46.16
of A., the family of the Arelites. Num 26.17

ARELITES
of Areli, the family of the A. Num 26.17

AREOPAGITE
Dionysius the A. and a woman named Ac 17.34

AREOPAGUS
of him and brought him to the A., Ac 17.19
standing in the middle of the A., 17.22

ARETAS
under King A. guarded the city of 2Co 11.32

ARGOB
cities, the whole region of A., Deu 3.04
Og, that is, all the region of A., 3.13
Manassite took all the region of A., 3.14
and he had the region of A., 1Ki 4.13

ARGUE
and I desire to a. my case with Job 13.03
Should he a. in unprofitable talk, 15.03
A. your case with your neighbor Pro 25.09
in remembrance, let us a. together; Is 43.26
came and began to a. with him, Mk 8.11

ARGUED
And they a. with one another, "If Mt 21.25
And they a. with one another, "If we Mk 11.31
three weeks he a. with them from Ac 17.02
So he a. in the synagogue with the 17.17
And he a. in the synagogue every 18.04
the synagogue and a. with the Jews. 18.19
and a. daily in the hall of Tyrannus 19.09
And as he a. about justice and self 24.25

ARGUES
He who a. with God, let him answer Job 40.02

ARGUING
them, and scribes a. with them. Mk 9.14
a. and pleading about the kingdom Ac 19.08

ARGUMENT
my humiliation an a. against me, Job 19.05
If a wise man has an a. with a fool, Pro 29.09
And an a. arose among them as to Lk 9.46

ARGUMENTS
him and fill my mouth with a. Job 23.04
We destroy a. and every proud 2Co 10.05

ARIDAI
and Arisai and A. and Vaizatha, Est 9.09

ARIDATHA
and Poratha and Adalia and A. Est 9.08

ARIEL
A., Shemaiah, Elnathan, Jarib, Elnathan, Ez 8.16
Ho A., A., the city where David Is 29.01
Yet I will distress A., and there 29.02
and she shall be to me like an A. 29.02
the nations that fight against A., 29.07

ARIELS
he smote two a. of Moab. He also 2Sa 23.20
he smote two a. of Moab. He also 1Ch 11.22

ARIGHT
"If you set your heart a., Job 11.13
orders his way a. I will show the Ps 50.23
a man of understanding walks a. Pro 15.21
For he is instructed a.; Is 28.26
but they have not spoken a.; Jer 8.06

ARIMATHEA
there came a rich man from A., Mt 27.57
Joseph of A., a respected member of Mk 15.43
Joseph from the Jewish town of A. Lk 23.50
After this Joseph of A., Jn 19.38

ARIOCH
A. king of Ellasar, Chedorlaomer Gen 14.01
and A. king of Ellasar, four kings 14.09
with prudence and discretion to A., Dan 2.14
he said to A., the king's captain, 2.15
Then A. made the matter known to 2.15
Therefore Daniel went in to A., 2.24
Then A. brought in Daniel before 2.25

ARISAI
and Parmashta and A. and Aridai and Est 9.09

ARISE
A., walk through the length and the Gen 13.17
"A., take your wife and your two 19.15
A., lift up the lad, and hold him 21.18

ARISE (cont.)
to his father, "Let my father a., Gen 27.31
a., flee to Laban my brother in 27.43
A., go to Paddan-aram to the house of 28.02
Now a., go forth from this land, and 31.13
"A., go up to Bethel, and dwell 35.01
then let us a. and go up to Bethel, 35.03
them there will a. seven years of 41.30
and we will a. and go, that we may 43.08
and a., go again to the man; 43.13
"A., O LORD, and let thy enemies be Num 10.35
'A., go down quickly from here; Deu 9.12
'A., go on your journey at the head 10.11
then you shall a. and go up to the 17.08
now therefore a., go over this Jos 1.02
"A., why have you thus fallen upon 7.10
men with you, and a., go up to Ai; 8.01
A., Barak, lead away your captives, O Ju 5.12
"A., go down against the camp; 7.09
the camp of Israel, and said, "A.; 7.15
They said, "A., and let us go up 18.09
you shall a. early in the morning 19.09
and a., go and look for the asses. 1Sa 9.03
and the LORD said, "A., anoint him; 16.12
"A., go down to Keilah; for I 23.04
the young men a. and play before 2Sa 2.14
And Joab said, "Let them a." 2.14
"I will a. and go, and will gather 3.21
And Amnon said to her, "A., be gone." 13.15
"A., and let us flee; or else 15.14
"A., and go quickly over the water; 17.21
Now therefore a., go out and speak 19.07
none like you shall a. after you. 1Ki 3.12
"A., and disguise yourself, that it 14.02
A. therefore, go to your house. 14.12
"A., go to Zarephath, which belongs 17.09
him, and said to him, "A. and eat." 19.05
"A. and eat, else the journey will 19.07
A., and eat bread, and let your 21.07
"A., take possession of the vineyard 21.15
"A., go down to meet Ahab king of 21.18
"A., go up to meet the messengers 2Ki 1.03
"A., and depart with your household, 8.01
or did any like him a. after him. 23.25
A. and be doing! The LORD 1Ch 22.16
A. and build the sanctuary of the 22.19
"And now a., O LORD GOD, and go to 2Ch 6.41
A., for it is your task, and we are Ez 10.04
we his servants will a. and build; Neh 2.20
with Urim and Thummim should a. 7.65
I lie down I say, 'When shall I a.?' Job 7.04
Upon whom does his light not a.? 25.03
A., O LORD! Deliver me, Ps 3.07
A., O LORD, in thy anger, lift 7.06
A., O LORD! Let not man 9.19
A., O LORD; O God 10.12
I will now a.," says the LORD; 12.05
A., O Lord! Confront 17.13
though war a. against me, yet I will 27.03
Let God a., let his enemies be 68.01
A., O God, plead thy cause; 74.22
and a. and tell them to their 78.06
A., O God, judge the earth; 82.08
Thou wilt a. and have pity on Zion; 102.13
A., O LORD, and go to thy resting 132.08
When will you a. from your sleep? Pro 6.09
"A., my love, my fair one, and come Sol 2.10
A., my love, my fair one, and come 2.13
A., O princes, oil the shield! Is 21.05
a., pass over to Cyprus, even there 23.12
they are shades, they will not a.; 26.14
but will a. against the house of 31.02
"Now I will a.," says the LORD "Now 33.10
of rulers: "Kings shall see and a.; 49.07
Shake yourself from the dust, a.; 52.02
A., shine; for your 60.01
but the LORD will a. upon you, 60.02
a., and say to them everything that Jer 1.17
trouble they say, 'A. and save us!' 2.27
Let them a., if they can save you, 2.28
and a., go to the Euphrates, and 13.04
"A., go to the Euphrates, and take 13.06
"A., and go down to the potter's 18.02
'A., and let us go up to Zion, to 31.06
'A., and let us go back to our own 46.16
A., cry out in the night, at the Lam 2.19
"A., go forth into the plain and Eze 3.22
After you shall a. another kingdom Dan 2.39
'A., devour much flesh.' 7.05
kings who shall a. out of the 7.17
of this kingdom ten kings shall a., 7.24
and another shall a. after them; 7.24
kingdoms shall a. from his nation, 8.22
who understands riddles, shall a. 8.23
more kings shall a. in Persia; 11.02
Then a mighty king shall a., 11.03
her roots shall a. in his place; 11.07
"Then shall a. in his place one who 11.20
In his place shall a. a contemptible 11.21
"At that time shall a. Michael, 12.01
of war shall a. among your people, Hos 10.14
"A., go to Nineveh, that great city, Jon 1.02
A., call upon your god! Perhaps 1.06
"A., go to Nineveh, that great city, 3.02
A. and go, for this is no place to Mic 2.10
A. and thresh, O daughter of Zion, 4.13
A., plead your case before the 6.01
strife and contention a. Hab 1.03
Will not your debtors suddenly a., 2.07
to a dumb stone, A.! Can this 2.19
"for the day when I a. as a witness. Zep 3.08
of Nineveh will a. at the judgment Mt 12.41
the South will a. at the judgment 12.42
prophets will a. and lead many 24.11
prophets will a. and show great 24.24
"Little girl, I say to you, a." Mk 5.41
prophets will a. and show signs 13.22
said, "Young man, I say to you, a." Lk 7.14
hand he called, saying, "Child, a.," 8.54
the South will a. at the judgment 11.31
of Nineveh will a. at the judgment 11.32
I will a. and go to my father, and I 15.18
own selves will a. men speaking Ac 20.30
and a. from the dead, and Christ Eph 5.14
priest to a. after the order of Heb 7.11

ARISEN
And there has not a. a prophet Deu 34.10
and see how this sin has a. today. 1Sa 14.38
And when he has a., his kingdom Dan 11.04
"A great prophet has a. among us!" Lk 7.16

ARISES
"If a prophet a. among you, or a Deu 13.01
"If any case a. requiring decision 17.08
or persecution a. on account of Mt 13.21
or persecution a. on account of Mk 4.17
another priest a. in the likeness Heb 7.15

ARISTARCHUS
dragging with them Gaius and A., Ac 19.29
the Thessalonians, A. and Secundus; 20.04
we put to sea, accompanied by A., 27.02
A. my fellow prisoner greets you, Col 4.10
A., Demas, and Luke, my fellow Phm 1.24

ARISTOBULUS
who belong to the family of A. Rom 16.10

ARK
Make yourself an a. of gopher wood; Gen 6.14
make rooms in the a., and cover 6.14
length of the A. three hundred 6.15
Make a roof for the a., and finish 6.16
set the door of the a. in its side; 6.16

ARK (cont.)

and you shall come into the a., Gen 6.18
two of every sort into the a., 6.19
"Go into the a., you and all your 7.01
wives with him went into the a., 7.07
went into the a. with Noah, as God 7.09
his sons with them entered the a., 7.13
They went into the a. with Noah, 7.15
increased, and bore up the a., 7.17
and the a. floated on the face of 7.18
those that were with him in the a. 7.23
that were with him in the a. 8.01
the a. came to rest upon the 8.04
window of the a. which he had made, 8.06
and she returned to him to the a., 8.09
brought her into the a. with him. 8.09
sent forth the dove out of the a.; 8.10
removed the covering of the a., 8.13
"Go forth from the A., you and 8.16
forth by families out of the a. 8.19
you, as many as came out of the a. 9.10
went forth from the a. were Shem, 9.18
"They shall make an a. of acacia wood; Ex 25.10
the rings on the sides of the a., 25.14
the a., to carry the a. by them. 25.14
remain in the rings of the a.; 25.15
put into the a. the testimony 25.16
mercy seat on the top of the a.; 25.21
and in the a. you shall put the 25.21
are upon the a. of the testimony, I 25.22
and bring the a. of the testimony 26.33
seat upon the a. of the testimony 26.34
that is by the a. of the testimony, 30.06
meeting and the a. of the testimony, 30.26
and the a. of the testimony, and the 31.07
the a. with its poles, the mercy 35.12
Bezalel made the a. of acacia wood; 37.01
the rings on the sides of the a., 37.05
sides of the a., to carry the a. 37.05
the a. of the testimony with its 39.35
put in it the a. of the testimony, 40.03
shall screen the a. with the veil. 40.03
before the a. of the testimony, and 40.05
testimony and put it into the a., 40.20
and put the poles on the a., and 40.20
set the mercy seat above on the a.; 40.20
and he brought the a. into the 40.21
screened the a. of the testimony; 40.21
which is upon the a.; lest he die; Lev 16.02
And their charge was to be the a., Num 3.31
and cover the a. of the testimony 4.05
was upon the a. of the testimony, 7.89
and the a. of the covenant of the 10.33
And whenever the a. set out, 10.35
neither the a. of the covenant of 14.44
mountain, and make an a. of wood. Deu 10.01
and you shall put them in the a.' 10.02
So I made an a. of acacia wood, and 10.03
tables in the a. which I had made; 10.05
to carry the a. of the covenant of 10.08
who carried the a. of the covenant 31.09
who carried the a. of the covenant 31.25
the side of the a. of the covenant 31.26
you see the a. of the covenant of Jos 3.03
"Take up the a. of the covenant, and 3.06
took up the a. of the covenant, and 3.06
who bear the a. of the covenant, 3.08
Behold, the a. of the covenant of 3.11
who bear the a. of the LORD, 3.13
bearing the a. of the covenant 3.14
who bore the a. had come to the 3.15
bearing the a. were dipped in the 3.15
who bore the a. of the covenant of 3.17
on before the a. of the LORD your 4.05
off before the a. of the covenant 4.07
bearing the a. of the covenant had 4.09
who bore the a. stood in the midst 4.10
the a. of the LORD and the priests 4.11
who bear the a. of the testimony 4.16
bearing the a. of the covenant of 4.18
of rams' horns before the a.; 6.04
"Take up the a. of the covenant, and 6.06
horns before the a. of the LORD. 6.06
pass on before the a. of the LORD. 6.07
with the a. of the covenant of the 6.08
the rear guard came after the a., 6.09
So he caused the a. of the LORD to 6.11
priests took up the a. of the LORD. 6.12
before the a. of the LORD passed 6.13
came after the a. of the LORD, 6.13
face before the a. of the LORD 7.06
sides of the a. before the Levitical 8.33
who carried the a. of the covenant 8.33
LORD (for the a. of the covenant of Ju 20.27
the LORD, where the a. of God was. 1Sa 3.03
us bring the a. of the covenant of 4.03
from there the a. of the covenant 4.04
there with the a. of the covenant 4.04
When the a. of the covenant of the 4.05
that the a. of the LORD had come 4.06
And the a. of God was captured; 4.11
heart trembled for the a. of God. 4.13
and the a. of God has been captured 4.17
When he mentioned the a. of God, 4.18
that the a. of God was captured, 4.19
because the a. of God had been 4.21
for the a. of God has been captured 4.22
Philistines captured the a. of God, 5.01
took the a. of God and brought it 5.02
ground before the a. of the LORD. 5.03
ground before the a. of the LORD, 5.04
"The a. of the God of Israel must 5.07
we do with the a. of the God of 5.08
"Let the a. of the God of Israel be 5.08
brought the a. of the God of 5.08
So they sent the a. of God to Ekron 5.10
But when the a. of God came to 5.10
to us the a. of the God of Israel 5.10
"Send away the a. of the God of 5.11
The a. of the LORD was in the 6.01
we do with the a. of the LORD? 6.02
send away the a. of the God of 6.03
And take the a. of the LORD and 6.08
And they put the a. of the LORD on 6.11
up their eyes and saw the a., 6.13
took down the a. of the LORD and 6.15
they set down the a. of the LORD, 6.18
looked into the a. of the LORD; 6.19
have returned the a. of the LORD. 6.21
and took up the a. of the LORD, 7.01
have charge of the a. of the LORD. 7.01
day that the a. was lodged at 7.02
Ahijah, "Bring hither the a. of God." 14.18
For the a. of God went at that time 14.18
bring up from there the a. of God, 2Sa 6.02
carried the a. of God upon a new 6.03
with the a. of God; and Ahio 6.04
and Ahio went before the a. 6.04
his hand to the a. of God and took 6.06
he put forth his hand to the a.; 6.07
he died there beside the a. of God. 6.07
"How can the a. of the LORD come to 6.09
to take the a. of the LORD into 6.10
And the a. of the LORD remained in 6.11
to him, because of the a. of God. 6.12
brought up the a. of God from the 6.12
who bore the a. of the LORD had 6.13
brought up the a. of the LORD with 6.15
As the a. of the LORD came into the 6.16
they brought in the a. of the LORD, 6.17
but the a. of God dwells in a tent. 7.02
"The a. and Israel and Judah dwell 11.11
bearing the a. of the covenant of 15.24
and they set down the a. of God, 15.24

ARK (cont.)
"Carry the a. of God back into the 2Sa 15.25
carried the a. of God back to 15.29
you bore the a. of the LORD GOD 1Ki 2.26
before the a. of the covenant of 3.15
set there the a. of the covenant 6.19
to bring up the a. of the covenant 8.01
and the priests took up the a. 8.03
they brought up the a. of the LORD, 8.04
him, were with him before the a., 8.05
brought the a. of the covenant of 8.06
wings over the place of the a., 8.07
covering above the a. and its poles. 8.07
nothing in the a. except the two 8.09
I have provided a place for the a., 8.21
LORD, after the a. rested there. 1Ch 6.31
bring again the a. of our God to 13.03
to bring the a. of God from Kiriathjearim. 13.05
bring up from there the a. of God, 13.06
carried the a. of God upon a new 13.07
put out his hand to hold the a., 13.09
he put forth his hand to the a.; 13.10
can I bring the a. of God home to 13.12
not take the a. home into the city 13.13
And the a. of God remained with the 13.14
prepared a place for the a. of God, 15.01
Levites may carry the a. of God, 15.02
to carry the a. of the LORD and to 15.02
to bring up the a. of the LORD to 15.03
may bring up the a. of the LORD, 15.12
to bring up the a. of the LORD, 15.14
carried the a. of God upon their 15.15
were to be gatekeepers for the a. 15.23
the trumpets before the a. of God. 15.24
were to be gatekeepers for the a. 15.24
to bring up the a. of the covenant 15.25
carrying the a. of the covenant of 15.26
Levites who were carrying the a., 15.27
brought up the a. of the covenant 15.28
And as the a. of the covenant of 15.29
And they brought in the a. of God, 16.01
ministers before the a. of the LORD, 16.04
before the a. of the covenant of 16.06
before the a. of the covenant of 16.37
before the a. as each day required, 16.37
but the a. of the covenant of the 17.01
so that the a. of the covenant of 22.19
of rest for the a. of the covenant 28.02
and covered the a. of the covenant 28.18
brought up the a. of God from 2Ch 1.04
to bring up the a. of the covenant 5.02
and the Levites took up the a. 5.04
And they brought up the a., 5.05
before him, were before the a., 5.06
brought the a. of the covenant of 5.07
wings over the place of the a., 5.08
covering above the a. and its poles. 5.08
nothing in the a. except the two 5.10
And there I have set the a., 6.11
thou and the a. of thy might. 6.41
to which the a. of the LORD has 8.11
"Put the holy a. in the house which 35.03
thou and the a. of thy might. Ps 132.08
"The a. of the covenant of the LORD Jer 3.16
the day when Noah entered the a., Mt 24.38
the day when Noah entered the a., Lk 17.27
incense and the a. of the covenant Heb 9.04
constructed an a. for the saving 11.07
during the building of the a., 1Pe 3.20
and the a. of his covenant was seen Rev 11.19

ARKITES
the Hivites, the A., the Sinites, Gen 10.17
the Hivites, the A., the Sinites, 1Ch 1.15

ARM
an outstretched a. and with great Ex 6.06
because of the greatness of thy a., 15.16
"A. men from among you for the war, Num 31.03
mighty hand and an outstretched a., Deu 4.34
mighty hand and an outstretched a.; 5.15
hand, and the outstretched a., 7.19
power and by thy outstretched a., 9.29
hand and his outstretched a., 11.02
mighty hand and an outstretched a., 26.08
he tears the a., and the crown of 33.20
and the armlet which was on his a., 2Sa 1.10
hand, and of thy outstretched a.), 1Ki 8.42
the seat were a. rests and two 10.19
standing beside the a. rests, 10.19
leaning on my a., and I bow myself 2Ki 5.18
power and with an outstretched a.; 17.36
hand, and thy outstretched a., 2Ch 6.32
the seat were a. rests and two 9.18
standing beside the a. rests, 9.18
With him is an a. of flesh; 32.08
have saved the a. that has no Job 26.02
and let my a. be broken from its 31.22
because of the a. of the mighty. 35.09
and their uplifted a. is broken. 38.15
Have you an a. like God, and can you 40.09
Break thou the a. of the wicked and Ps 10.15
did their own a. give them victory 44.03
and thy a., and the light of thy 44.03
Thou didst with thy a. redeem thy 77.15
are the strong a. of the children 83.08
thy enemies with thy mighty a. 89.10
Thou hast a mighty a.; strong 89.13
my a. also shall strengthen him. 89.21
and his holy a. have gotten him 98.01
strong hand and an outstretched a., 136.12
your heart, as a seal upon your a.; Sol 8.06
grain and his a. harvests the ears, Is 17.05
descending blow of his a. to be seen, 30.30
with brandished a. he will fight 30.32
be our a. every morning, our salvation 33.02
might, and his a. rules for him; 40.10
and forges it with his strong a.; 44.12
and his a. shall be against the 48.14
for me, and for my a. they hope. 51.05
put on strength, O a. of the LORD; 51.09
bared his holy a. before the eyes 52.10
to whom has the a. of the LORD 53.01
then his own a. brought him victory, 59.16
right hand and by his mighty a.: 62.08
so my own a. brought me victory, and 63.05
his glorious a. to go at the right 63.12
in man and makes flesh his a., Jer 17.05
outstretched hand and strong a., 21.05
my outstretched a. have made the 27.05
power and by thy outstretched a.! 32.17
a strong hand and outstretched a., 32.21
and his a. is broken, says the LORD. 48.25
of Jerusalem, with your a. bared; Eze 4.07
take a strong a. or many people to 17.09
mighty hand and an outstretched a., 20.33
mighty hand and an outstretched a., 20.34
have broken the a. of Pharaoh king 30.21
both the strong a. and the one 30.22
not retain the strength of her a., Dan 11.06
sword smite his a. and his right Zec 11.17
Let his a. be wholly withered, his 11.17
He had shown strength with his a., Lk 1.51
to whom has the a. of the Lord Jn 12.38
with uplifted a. he led them out Ac 13.17
a. yourselves with the same thought, 1Pe 4.01

ARMAGEDDON
place which is called in Hebrew A. Rev 16.16

ARMED
tribe, twelve thousand a. for war. Num 31.05
and every a. man of you will pass 32.21
over, every man who is a. for war, 32.27
man who is a. to battle before the 32.29

ARMED (cont.)
will not pass over with you a., Num 32.30
We will pass over a. before the 32.32
shall pass over a. before your Deu 3.18
shall pass over a. before your Jos 1.14
passed over a. before the people 4.12
thousand ready a. for war passed 4.13
and let the a. men pass on before 6.07
And the a. men went before the 6.09
and the a. men went before them, and 6.13
outposts of the a. men that were Ju 7.11
a. with weapons of war, set forth 18.11
a. with their weapons of war, stood 18.16
six hundred men a. with weapons of 18.17
and he was a. with a coat of mail, 1Sa 17.05
of the divisions of the a. troops, 1Ch 12.23
thousand eight hundred a. troops. 12.24
thousand men a. with shield and 12.34
thousand men a. with all the 12.37
a. with bucklers and spears, and two 2Ch 14.08
thousand men a. with bow and 17.17
and eighty thousand a. for war. 17.18
So the a. men left the captives and 28.14
annihilate any a. force of any Est 8.11
a. with the bow, turned back on the Ps 78.09
vagabond, and want like an a. man. Pro 6.11
a robber, and want like an a. man. 24.34
therefore the a. men of Moab cry Is 15.04
fully a., guards his own palace, his Lk 11.21

ARMIES
with all their a. and encamped Jos 10.05
gathered their a. for battle; 1Sa 17.01
should defy the a. of the living 17.26
has defied the a. of the living 17.36
hosts, the God of the a. of Israel, 17.45
against the a. of the Philistines?" 23.03
two commanders of the a. of Israel, 1Ki 2.05
commanders of his a. against the 15.20
men of the a. were Asahel the 1Ch 11.26
commanders of his a. against the 2Ch 16.04
Is there any number to his a.? Job 25.03
and hast not gone out with our a. Ps 44.09
not go forth, O God, with our a. 60.10
"The kings of the a., they flee 68.12
not go forth, O God, with our a. 108.11
as upon a dance before two a.? Sol 6.13
A. shall be utterly swept away Dan 11.22
you see Jerusalem surrounded by a., Lk 21.20
in war, put foreign a. to flight. Heb 11.34
And the a. of heaven, arrayed in Rev 19.14
with their a. gathered to make war 19.19

ARMLET
head and the a. which was on his 2Sa 1.10

ARMLETS
earrings and signet rings and a., Ex 35.22
a. and bracelets, signet rings, Num 31.50
the a., the sashes, the perfume Is 3.20

ARMONI
A. and Mephiboseth; and the 2Sa 21.08

ARMOR
to the young man who bore his a., 1Sa 14.01
to the young man who bore his a., 14.06
Then Saul clothed David with his a.; 17.38
David girded his sword over his a., 17.39
but he put his a. in his tent. 17.54
and his a., and even his sword and 18.04
his head, and stripped off his a., 31.09
They put his a. in the temple of 31.10
girds on his a. boast himself as 1Ki 20.11
the scale a. and the breastplate; 22.34
all who were able to put on a., 2Ki 3.21
him and took his head and his a., 1Ch 10.09
And they put his a. in the temple 10.10
the scale a. and the breastplate; 2Ch 18.33
warriors clothed in full a., Eze 23.12
all of them clothed in full a., 38.04
takes away his a. in which he Lk 11.22
darkness and put on the a. of light; Rom 13.12
Put on the whole a. of God, Eph 6.11
Therefore take the whole a. of God, 6.13

ARMOR-BEARER
hastily to the young man his a., Ju 9.54
And his a. said to him, "Do all that 1Sa 14.07
garrison hailed Jonathan and his a., 14.12
And Jonathan said to his a., 14.12
and feet, and his a. after him. 14.13
and his a. killed them after him; 14.13
which Jonathan and his a. made, 14.14
Jonathan and his a. were not there. 14.17
him greatly, and he became his a. 16.21
Then Saul said to his a., "Draw 31.04
But his a. would not; for he 31.04
And when his a. saw that Saul was 31.05
and his a., and all his men, on the 31.06
the a. of Joab the son of Zeruiah, 2Sa 23.37
Then Saul said to his a., "Draw 1Ch 10.04
But his a. would not; for he 10.04
And when his a. saw that Saul was 10.05
the a. of Joab the son of Zeruiah, 11.39

ARMOR-BEARERS
Joab's a., surrounded Absalom and 2Sa 18.15

ARMORY
his a., all that was found in his 2Ki 20.13
the ascent to the a. at the Angle. Neh 3.19
his whole a., all that was found in Is 39.02
The LORD has opened his a., Jer 50.25

ARMPITS
between your a. and the ropes." Jer 38.12

ARMS
bracelets for her a. weighing ten Gen 24.22
the bracelets on his sister's a., 24.30
nose, and the bracelets on her a. 24.47
his a. were made agile by the hands 49.24
but we will take up a., ready Num 32.17
will take up a. to go before the 32.20
underneath are the everlasting a. Deu 33.27
Then the Ammonites were called to a., Ju 10.17
The men of Ephraim were called to a., 12.01
were on his a. became as flax that 15.14
the ropes off his a. like a thread. 16.12
so that my a. can bend a bow of 2Sa 22.35
touches them a. himself with iron 23.07
and the a. of the fatherless were Job 22.09
so that my a. can bend a bow of Ps 18.34
For the a. of the wicked shall be 37.17
strength and makes her a. strong. Pro 31.17
His a. are rounded gold, set with Sol 5.14
he will gather the lambs in his a., Is 40.11
and my a. will rule the peoples; 51.05
daughters shall be carried in the a. 60.04
and I will tear them from your a.; Eze 13.20
and put bracelets on your a., 16.11
of Egypt, and will break his a., 30.22
strengthen the a. of the king of 30.24
but I will break the a. of Pharaoh, 30.24
strengthen the a. of the king of 30.25
but the a. of Pharaoh shall fall; 30.25
gold, its breast and a. of silver, Dan 2.32
his a. and legs like the gleam of 10.06
trained and strengthened their a., Hos 7.15
to walk, I took them up in my a.; 11.03
and taking him in his a., he said Mk 9.36
them in his a. and blessed them, 10.16
him up in his a. and blessed God Lk 2.28

ARMY
commander of his a. said to Abraham, Gen 21.22
commander of his a. rose up and 21.32
and Phicol the commander of his a. 26.26
saw them he said, "This is God's a.!" 32.02
chariot and took his a. with him, Ex 14.06
and his horsemen and his a., 14.09
angry with the officers of the a., Num 31.14
were over the thousands of the a., 31.48
and what he did to the a. of Egypt, Deu 11.04
chariots and an a. larger than 20.01
go out with the a. or be charged 24.05
commander of the a. of the LORD I Jos 5.14
of the LORD's a. said to Joshua, 5.15
the commander of his a. was Sisera, Ju 4.02
Sisera, the general of Jabin's a., 4.07
and all his a. before Barak at the 4.15
chariots and the a. to Haroshethhagoiim, 4.16
and all the a. of Sisera fell by 4.16
about the camp, and all the a. ran; 7.21
his fellow and against all the a.; 7.22
and the a. fled as far as Bethshittah 7.22
we should give bread to your a." 8.06
were in Karkor with their a., 8.10
left of all the a. of the people 8.10
and Jogbehah, and attacked the a.; 8.11
for the a. was off its guard. 8.11
he threw all the a. into a panic. 8.12
"Increase your a., and come out.'" 9.29
the whole a., went up and came to 20.26
commander of the a. of Jabin king 1Sa 12.09
command of his a. was Abner the 14.50
drew up for battle, a. against a. 17.21
to Abner, the commander of the a., 17.55
of Ner, the commander of his a.; 26.05
while the a. was encamped around 26.05
Abishai went to the a. by night; 26.07
Abner and the a. lay around him. 26.07
and David called to the a., 26.14
are to go out with me in the a." 28.01
When Saul saw the a. of the Philistines, 28.05
will give the a. of Israel also 28.19
son of Ner, commander of Saul's a., 2Sa 2.08
and all the a. that was with him 3.23
to smite the a. of the Philistines." 5.24
defeated the whole a. of Hadadezer, 8.09
the son of Zeruiah was over the a.; 8.16
commander of the a. of Hadadezer at 10.16
Shobach the commander of their a., 10.18
Amasa over the a. instead of Joab. 17.25
And David sent forth the a., 18.02
while all the a. marched out by 18.04
So the a. went out into the field 18.06
commander of my a. henceforth in 19.13
in command of all the a. of Israel; 20.23
Joab and the commanders of the a., 24.02
Joab and the commanders of the a. 24.04
commanders of the a. went out from 24.04
and Joab the commander of the a.; 1Ki 1.19
sons, Joab the commander of the a., 1.25
Ner, commander of the a. of Israel, 2.32
commander of the a. of Judah. 2.32
over the a. in place of Joab, and 2.35
Jehoiada was in command of the a.; 4.04
commander of the a. went up to bury 11.15
the commander of the a. was dead, 11.21
made Omri, the commander of the a., 16.16
Syria gathered all his a. together; 20.01
and the a. which followed them. 20.19
and muster an a. like the a., that you 20.25
like the a. that you have lost, 20.25
sunset a cry went through the a., 22.36
water for the a. or for the beasts 2Ki 3.09
king or to the commander of the a.? 4.13
commander of the a. of the king of 5.01
horses and chariots and a great a.; 6.14
an a. with horses and chariots was 6.15
of Syria mustered his entire a., 6.24
has made the a. of the Syrians 7.06
of horses, the sound of a great a., 7.06
them after the a. of the Syrians, 7.14
but his a. fled home. 8.21
commanders of the a. were in 9.05
captains who were set over the a., 11.15
to Jehoahaz an a. of more than 13.07
with a great a. from Lachish to 18.17
with all his a. against Jerusalem, 25.01
But the a. of the Chaldeans pursued 25.05
and all his a. was scattered from 25.05
And all the a. of the Chaldeans, who 25.10
commander of the a. who mustered 25.19
were units of the a. for war, 1Ch 7.04
saw that the a. had fled and that 10.07
when the a. of Philistines was 11.15
These Gadites were officers of the a., 12.14
and were commanders in the a. 12.21
him, until there was a great a., 12.22
a great a., like an a. of God. 12.22
to smite the a. of the Philistines." 14.15
the Philistine a. from Gibeon to 14.16
defeated the whole a. of Hadadezer, 18.09
the son of Zeruiah was over the a.; 18.15
and the king of Maacah with his a., 19.07
and all the a. of the mighty men. 19.08
commander of the a. of Hadadezer at 19.16
Shophach the commander of their a. 19.18
to battle, Joab led out the a., 20.01
and the commanders of the a., 21.02
commanders of the a., had dedicated. 26.26
commanders of the a. for the first 27.03
was commander of the king's a. 27.34
having an a. of valiant men of war, 2Ch 13.03
And Asa had an a. of three hundred 14.08
them with an a. of a million men 14.09
broken before the LORD and his a. 14.13
the a. of the king of Syria has 16.07
Libyans a huge a. with exceedingly 16.08
array, as they went before the a., 20.21
captains who were set over the a., 23.14
of the year the a. of the Syrians 24.23
Though the a. of the Syrians had 24.24
into their hand a very great a., 24.24
do not let the a. of Israel go 25.07
I have given to the a. of Israel?" 25.09
discharged the a. that had come to 25.10
But the men of the a. whom Amaziah 25.13
Moreover Uzziah had an a. of soldiers, 26.11
command was an a. of three hundred 26.13
prepared for all the a. shields, 26.14
out to meet the a. that came to 28.09
commanders of the a. of the king of 33.11
commanders of the a. in all the 33.14
me officers of the a. and horsemen. Neh 2.09
brethren and of the a. of Samaria, 4.02
the a. chiefs of Persia and Media Est 1.03
A king is not saved by his great a.; Ps 33.16
terrible as an a. with banners. Sol 6.04
terrible as an a. with banners?" 6.10
at Jerusalem, with a great a. Is 36.02
chariot and horse, a. and warrior; 43.17
At that time the a. of the king of Jer 32.02
and all his a. and all the kingdoms 34.01
when the a. of the king of Babylon 34.07
the hand of the a. of the king of 34.21
for fear of the a. of the Chaldeans 35.11
Chaldeans and the a. of the Syrians. 35.11
The a. of Pharaoh had come out of 37.05
Pharaoh's a. which came to help you 37.07
the whole a. of Chaldeans who are 37.10
the Chaldean a. had withdrawn from 37.11
at the approach of Pharaoh's a., 37.11
the hand of the a. of the king of 38.03
and all his a. came against 39.01
But the a. of the Chaldeans pursued 39.05

ARMY (cont.)
Concerning the a. of Pharaoh Neco, Jer 46.02
with all his a. against Jerusalem, 52.04
But the a. of the Chaldeans pursued 52.08
and all his a. was scattered from 52.08
And all the a. of the Chaldeans, who 52.14
commander of the a. who mustered 52.25
give him horses and a large a. Eze 17.15
Pharaoh with his mighty a. and 17.17
were in your a. as your men of war 27.10
made his a. labor hard against 29.18
he nor his a. got anything from 29.18
it shall be the wages for his a. 29.19
multitude, Pharaoh and all his a., 32.31
and all your a., horses and horsemen, 38.04
horses, a great host, a mighty a.; 38.15
men of his a. to bind Shadrach, Dan 3.20
against the a. and enter the 11.07
on with a great a. and abundant 11.13
king of the south with a great a.; 11.25
an exceedingly great and mighty a.; 11.25
his a. shall be swept away, and many 11.26
like a powerful a. drawn up for Joe 2.05
utters his voice before his a., 2.11
my great a., which I sent among you 2.25
upon the horse and against his a. Rev 19.19

ARNAN
his son A., his son Obadiah, his son 1Ch 3.21

ARNI
the son of A., the son of Hezron, Lk 3.33

ARNON
on the other side of the A., Num 21.13
for the A. is the boundary of Moab, 21.13
Suphah, and the valleys of the A., 21.14
his land from the A. to the Jabbok, 21.24
out of his hand, as far as the A. 21.26
the lords of the heights of the A. 21.28
on the boundary formed by the A., 22.36
and go over the valley of the A.; Deu 2.24
the edge of the valley of the A., 2.36
valley of the A. to Mount Hermon 3.08
the edge of the valley of the A., 3.12
as far as the valley of the A., 3.16
the edge of the valley of the A., 4.48
valley of the A. to Mount Hermon, Jos 12.01
the edge of the valley of the A., 12.02
the edge of the valley of the A., 13.09
the edge of the valley of the A., 13.16
from the A. to the Jabbok and to Ju 11.13
camped on the other side of the A.; 11.18
for the A. was the boundary of Moab 11.18
from the A. to the Jabbok and from 11.22
that are on the banks of the A., 11.26
which is by the valley of the A., 2Ki 10.33
of Moab at the fords of the A. Is 16.02
Tell it by the A., Jer 48.20

AROD
of A., the family of the Arodites; Num 26.17

ARODI
Shuni, Ezbon, Eri, A., and Areli. Gen 46.16

ARODITES
of Arod, the family of the A.; Num 26.17

AROER
of Gad built Dibon, Ataroth, A., Num 32.34
From A., which is on the edge of Deu 2.36
the territory beginning at A., 3.12
from A., which is on the edge of 4.48
at Heshbon, and ruled from A., Jos 12.02
from A., which is on the edge of 13.09
So their territory was from A., 13.16
to A., which is east of Rabbah, 13.25
and in A. and its villages, and in Ju 11.26
smote them from A. to the neighborhood 11.33
in A., in Siphmoth, in Eshtemoa, 1Sa 30.28
the Jordan, and began from A., 2Sa 24.05
from A., which is by the valley of 2Ki 10.33
who dwelt in A., as far as Nebo and 1Ch 5.08
way and watch, O inhabitant of A.! Jer 48.19

AROERITE
Jeiel the sons of Hotham the A., 1Ch 11.44

AROMA
For we are the a. of Christ to God 2Co 2.15

AROMATIC
and of a. cane two hundred and Ex 30.23

AROSE
when she lay down or when she a. Gen 19.33
and the younger a., and lay 19.35
when she lay down or when she a. 19.35
and a. and went to the place of 22.03
and they a. and went together to 22.19
and he a., and went to Mesopotamia, 24.10
When they a. in the morning, he said, 24.54
Then Rebekah and her maids a., 24.61
So Jacob a., and set his sons and 31.17
and a. and crossed the Euphrates, 31.21
Early in the morning Laban a., 31.55
The same night he a. and took his 32.22
my sheaf a. and stood upright; 37.07
Then she a. and went away, and 38.19
and they a. and went down to Egypt, 43.15
Now there a. a new king over Egypt, Ex 1.08
So Joshua a., and all the fighting Jos 8.03
And Joshua a. early in the morning 8.10
a. and fought against Israel; 24.09
and there a. another generation Ju 2.10
And he a. from his seat. 3.20
Then Deborah a., and went with 4.09
Israel, they ceased until you a., 5.07
a. as a mother in Israel. 5.07
And Gideon a. and slew Zebah and 8.21
After Abimelech there a. to deliver 10.01
After him a. Jair the Gileadite, who 10.03
And Manoah a. and went after his 13.11
at midnight he a. and took hold of 16.03
Then her husband a. and went after 19.03
fourth day they a. early in the 19.05
fifth day he a. early in the 19.08
And all the people a. as one man, 20.08
of Israel a. and went up to Bethel, 20.18
but a. before one could recognize Ru 3.14
and Samuel a. and went to Eli, and 1Sa 3.06
And he a. and went to Eli, and said, 3.08
So Saul a., and both he and Samuel 9.26
And Samuel a., and went up from 13.15
and if he a. against me, I caught 17.35
When the Philistine a. and came and 17.48
David a. and went, along with his 18.27
a. and departed from Keilah, and 23.13
And they a., and went to Ziph ahead 23.24
Then David a. and stealthily cut 24.04
Afterward David also a., 24.08
So Saul a. and went down to the 26.02
So David a. and went over, he and 27.02
So he a. from the earth, and sat 28.23
all the valiant men a., 31.12
Then they a. and passed over by 2Sa 2.15
And David a. and went with all the 6.02
when David a. from his couch and 11.02
then David a. from the earth, and 12.20
child died, you a. and ate food." 12.21
Then all the king's sons a., 13.29
Then the king a., and rent his 13.31
So Joab a. and went to Geshur, and 14.23
Then Joab a. and went to Absalom at 14.31
So he a., and went to Hebron. 15.09

AROSE (cont.)

Then David a., and all the people 2Sa 17.22
Then the king a., and took his seat 19.08
And when David a. in the morning, 24.11
and he a., and went, and caught hold 1Ki 1.50
Shimei a. and saddled an ass, and 2.40
And she a. at midnight, and took my 3.20
he a. from before the altar of the 8.54
but Jeroboam a., and fled into 11.40
she a., and went to Shiloh, and came 14.04
Then Jeroboam's wife a., 14.17
So he a. and went to Zarephath; 17.10
and he a. and went for his life, and 19.03
And he a., and ate and drank, and 19.08
Then he a. and went after Elijah, 19.21
Ahab a. to go down to the vineyard 21.16
So he a. and went down with him to 2Ki 1.15
So he a. and followed her. 4.30
So they a. at twilight to go to the 7.05
So the woman a., and did according 8.02
So he a., and went into the house; 9.06
she a. and destroyed all the royal 11.01
His servants a. and made a conspiracy, 12.20
and when men a. early in the 19.35
and the captains of the forces a., 25.26
all the valiant men a., 1Ch 10.12
this there a. war with the Philistines 20.04
she a. and destroyed all the royal 2Ch 22.10
Then the Levites a., 29.12
and the Levites a. and blessed the 30.27
Then a. Jeshua the son of Jozadak, Ez 3.02
son of Jozadak a. and began to 5.02
Then Ezra a. and made the leading 10.05
Then I a. in the night, I and a few Neh 2.12
and a., and said to the nobles and 4.14
Now there a. a great outcry of the 5.01
Then Job a., and rent his robe, and Job 1.20
when God a. to establish judgment Ps 76.09
I a. to open to my beloved, and my Sol 5.05
and when men a. early in the Is 37.36
of the land a. and spoke to all Jer 26.17
of the LORD a. from its place, Eze 3.12
So I a. and went forth into the 3.23
the king a. and went in haste to Dan 6.19
in place of which four others a., 8.22
So Jonah a. and went to Nineveh, Jon 3.03
and he a. from his throne, removed 3.06
there a. a great storm on the sea, Mt 8.24
her by the hand, and the girl a. 9.25
And a great storm of wind a., Mk 4.37
And from there he a. and went away 7.24
hand and lifted him up, and he a. 9.27
In those days Mary a. and went with Lk 1.39
And he a. and left the synagogue, 4.38
and when a flood a., 6.48
And an argument a. among them as to 9.46
a great famine a. in that country, 15.14
And he a. and came to his father. 15.20
A dispute also a. among them, which 22.24
Then the whole company of them a., 23.01
Now a discussion a. between John's Jn 3.25
For before these days Theudas a., Ac 5.36
the Galilean a. in the days of the 5.37
a. and disputed with Stephen. 6.09
till there a. over Egypt another 7.18
persecution a. against the church 8.01
Saul a. from the ground; 9.08
persecution that a. over Stephen 11.19
And there a. a sharp contention, so 15.39
About that time there a. no little 19.23
a dissension a. between the Pharisees 23.07
Then a great clamor a.; 23.09
prophets also a. among the people, 2Pe 2.01
Now war a. in heaven, Michael and Rev 12.07

AROUSE

to a. you by way of reminder, 2Pe 1.13

AROUSED

I have a. him in righteousness, and Is 45.13
This city has a. my anger and wrath, Jer 32.31
Then all the city was a., Ac 21.30
a. by the law, were at work in our Rom 7.05
of them I have a. your sincere 2Pe 3.01

ARPACHSHAD

Elam, Asshur, A., Lud, and Aram. Gen 10.22
A. became the father of Shelah; 10.24
the father of A. two years after 11.10
the birth of A. five hundred years, 11.11
When A. had lived thirty-five years 11.12
and A. lived after the birth of 11.13
A., Lud, Aram, Uz, Hul, Gether, and 1Ch 1.17
A. was the father of Shelah; 1.18
Shem, A., Shelah; 1.24

ARPAD

Where are the gods of Hamath and A.? 2Ki 18.34
the king of A., the king of the 19.13
Is not Hamath like A.? Is 10.09
Where are the gods of Hamath and A.? 36.19
the king of A., the king of the 37.13
"Hamath and A. are confounded, for Jer 49.23

ARPHAXAD

the son of A., the son of Shem, the Lk 3.36

ARRANGE

and a. in advance for this gift you 2Co 9.05

ARRANGED

for so he had a., intending himself Ac 20.13
God a. the organs in the body, each 1Co 12.18

ARRANGEMENT

its a., its exits and its entrances, Eze 43.11
According to this a., Heb 9.09

ARRANGEMENTS

the table, and set its a. in order; Ex 40.04
the same exits and a. and doors. Eze 42.11

ARRANGING

studying and a. proverbs with Ecc 12.09

ARRAY

themselves in a. against Gibeah, Ju 20.30
set themselves in a. at Baaltamar; 20.33
up in battle a. at the entrance of 2Sa 10.08
Worship the LORD in holy a.; 1Ch 16.29
up in battle a. at the entrance of 19.09
the battle in a. against the 19.17
the LORD and praise him in holy a., 2Ch 20.21
let him a. the man whom the king Est 6.09
worship the LORD in holy a. Ps 29.02
Worship the LORD in holy a.; tremble 96.09
set in a. as a man for battle, Jer 6.23
and they shall a. themselves 50.09
Set yourselves in a. against 50.14
like flame when mustered in a.; Nah 2.03
and all who a. themselves in Zep 1.08
of the earth set themselves in a., Ac 4.26

ARRAYED

and a. him in garments of fine Gen 41.42
to all who were a. against him, Ju 6.31
and a. them against the Syrians; 2Sa 10.09
and he a. them against the Ammonites 10.10
And the Syrians a. themselves 10.17
a. in their robes, at the threshing 1Ki 22.10
a. in battle order, came to Hebron 1Ch 12.38
and a. them against the Syrians; 19.10
and they were a. against the 19.11
a. in fine linen, with cymbals, harps, 2Ch 5.12
their thrones, a. in their robes; 18.09
and he a. Mordecai and made him Est 6.11

ARRAYED (cont.)
terrors of God are a. against me. Job 6.04
I wage, for many are a. against me. Ps 55.18
a. as a man for battle against you, Jer 50.42
glory was not a. like one of these Mt 6.29
glory was not a. like one of these Lk 12.27
and a. him in a purple robe; Jn 19.02
were like horses a. for battle; Rev 9.07
The woman was a. in purple and 17.04
a. in fine linen, white and pure, 19.14

ARRAYING
then, a. him in gorgeous apparel, he Lk 23.11

ARREST
But when they tried to a. him, Mt 21.46
in order to a. Jesus by stealth 26.04
And they tried to a. him, Mk 12.12
seeking how to a. him by stealth, 14.01
So they sought to a. him; Jn 7.30
Pharisees sent officers to a. him. 7.32
Some of them wanted to a. him, 7.44
Again they tried to a. him, 10.39
know, so that they might a. him. 11.57
he proceeded to a. Peter also. Ac 12.03

ARRESTED
he heard that John had been a., Mt 4.12
Now after John was a., Mk 1.14
but no one a. him, because his hour Jn 8.20
was guide to those who a. Jesus. Ac 1.16
And they a. them and put them in 4.03
they a. the apostles and put them 5.18
Then the tribune came up and a. him, 21.33

ARRIVAL
tabernacle was set up before their a. Num 10.21

ARRIVE
I can do nothing till you a. there." Gen 19.22
serve the LORD until we a. there." Ex 10.26
and when you a., you shall anoint 1Ki 19.15
And when you a., look there for 2Ki 9.02
hear you when your accusers a." Ac 23.35
And when I a., I will send those 1Co 16.03
and can never a. at a knowledge of 2Ti 3.07

ARRIVED
When he a., he sounded the trumpet Ju 3.27
and a. on the east side of the land 11.18
and a. opposite Jebus (that is, 19.10
When he a., Eli was sitting upon 1Sa 4.13
of David a. with Joab from a raid, 2Sa 3.22
a. weary at the Jordan; and there 16.14
the messenger a. Elisha said to 2Ki 6.32
before King Ahaz a. from Damascus. 16.11
When they a., they came and stood 18.17
king's eunuchs a. and brought Est 6.14
eighty men a. from Shechem and Jer 41.05
And they a. at Tahpanhes. 43.07
became tall and a. at full maidenhood; Eze 16.07
Jedaiah, who have a. from Babylon; Zec 6.10
Then they a. at the country of the Lk 8.26
friend of mine has a. on a journey, 11.06
three men a. at the house in which Ac 11.11
When they a. at Salamis, they 13.05
And when they a., they gathered the 14.27
and when they a. they went into the 17.10
and Timothy a. from Macedonia, 18.05
When he a., he greatly helped those 18.27
from Tyre, we a. at Ptolemais; 21.07
and Bernice a. at Caesarea to 25.13
and a. with difficulty off Cnidus, 27.07
made a circuit and a. at Rhegium; 28.13
but when he a. in Rome he searched 2Ti 1.17
of the brethren a. and testified 3Jn 1.03

ARROGANCE
let not a. come from your mouth; 1Sa 2.03
me and your a. has come into my 2Ki 19.28
In a. the wicked hotly pursue the Ps 10.02
Let not the foot of a. come upon me, 36.11
Pride and a. and the way of evil Pro 8.13
say in pride and in a. of heart: Is 9.09
of his a., his pride, and his 16.06
me and your a. has come to my ears, 37.29
and his a., and the haughtiness of Jer 48.29
As it is, you boast in your a. Jas 4.16

ARROGANT
For I was envious of the a., Ps 73.03
They pour out their a. words, 94.04
looks and a. heart I will not 101.05
A. men have hidden a trap for me, 140.05
Every one who is a. is an abomination Pro 16.05
haughty man who acts with a. pride. 21.24
will punish the a. boasting of the Is 10.12
put an end to the pride of the a., 13.11
the a. man shall not abide. Hab 2.05
Henceforth we deem the a. blessed; Mal 3.15
when all the a. and all evildoers 4.01
Some are a., as though I were not 1Co 4.18
talk of these a. people but their 4.19
And you are a.! Ought 5.02
it is not a. or rude. 13.05
a., abusive, disobedient to their 2Ti 3.02
he must not be a. or quick-tempered Tit 1.07

ARROGANTLY
when they dealt a. with them." Ex 18.11
transgressions, that they are behaving a. Job 36.09
with their mouths they speak a. Ps 17.10

ARROW
lad ran, he shot an a. beyond him. 1Sa 20.36
place of the a. which Jonathan had 20.37
and said, "Is not the a. beyond you?" 20.37
so that the a. pierced his heart, 2Ki 9.24
"The LORD's a. of victory, the a. of 13.17
to this city or shoot an a. there, 19.32
a bronze a. will strike him through Job 20.24
The a. cannot make him flee; 41.28
have fitted their a. to the string, Ps 11.02
But God will shoot his a. at them; 64.07
nor the a. that flies by day, 91.05
till an a. pierces its entrails; Pro 7.23
club, or a sword, or a sharp a. 25.18
or shoot an a. there, or come before Is 37.33
he made me a polished a., 49.02
Their tongue is a deadly a.; Jer 9.08
and set me as a mark for his a. Lam 3.12
I have made Ephraim its a. Zec 9.13
and his a. go forth like lightning; 9.14

ARROWS
pierce them through with his a. Num 24.08
I will spend my a. upon them; Deu 32.23
I will make my a. drunk with blood, 32.42
shoot three a. to the side of it, 1Sa 20.20
the lad, saying, 'Go, find the a.' 20.21
the a. are on this side of you, take 20.21
the a. are beyond you,' then go; 20.22
"Run and find the a. which I shoot." 20.36
Jonathan's lad gathered up the a., 20.38
And he sent out a., and 2Sa 22.15
said to him, "Take a bow and a."; 2Ki 13.15
so he took a bow and a. 13.15
And he said, "Take the a."; 13.18
and could shoot a. and sling 1Ch 12.02
to shoot a. and great stones. 2Ch 26.15
For the a. of the Almighty are in Job 6.04
weapons, making his a. fiery shafts. Ps 7.13
And he sent out his a., and 18.14
For thy a. have sunk into me, and 38.02
Your a. are sharp in the heart of 45.05

ARROWS (cont.)
their teeth are spears and a., Ps 57.04
who aim bitter words like a., 64.03
There he broke the flashing a., 76.03
thy a. flashed on every side. 77.17
A warrior's sharp a., with 120.04
Like a. in the hand of a warrior 127.04
send out thy a. and rout them! 144.06
throws firebrands, a., and death, Pro 26.18
their a. are sharp, all their bows Is 5.28
With bow and a. men will come there, 7.24
Their a. are like a skilled warrior Jer 50.09
spare no a., for she has sinned 50.14
"Sharpen the a.! Take up 51.11
into my heart the a. of his quiver; Lam 3.13
against you my deadly a. of famine, Eze 5.16
a. for destruction, which I will 5.16
he shakes the a., he consults the 21.21
will make your a. drop out of your 39.03
bows and a., handpikes and spears, 39.09
bow, and put the a. to the string. Hab 3.09
the light of thine a. as they sped, 3.11

ARSENAL
built for an a., whereon hang a Sol 4.04

ART
"Thou a. a God of seeing"; for she Gen 16.13
a. in the midst of this people; Num 14.14
a. seen face to face, and thy cloud 14.14
Therefore thou a. great O LORD God; 2Sa 7.22
thou a. God, and thy words are true, 7.28
Yea, thou a. my lamp, O LORD, and my 22.29
and thou a. angry with them, and 1Ki 8.46
day that thou a. God in Israel, 18.36
a. God, and that thou hast turned 18.37
who a. enthroned above the cherubim, 2Ki 19.15
thou a. the God, thou alone, of all 19.15
that thou, O LORD, a. God alone." 19.19
thou a. God, and thou hast promised 1Ch 17.26
"Blessed a. thou, O LORD, the God of 29.10
and thou a. exalted as head above 29.11
and thou a. angry with them, and 2Ch 6.36
O LORD, thou a. our God; 14.11
prepared by the perfumer's a.; 16.14
a. thou not God in heaven? 20.06
thou a. just, for we are left a Ez 9.15
"Thou a. the LORD, thou alone; Neh 9.06
Thou a. the LORD, the God who didst 9.07
thy promise, for thou a. righteous. 9.08
But thou a. a God ready to forgive, 9.17
for thou a. a gracious and merciful 9.31
a. a shield about me, my glory, and Ps 3.03
For thou a. not a God who delights 5.04
is man that thou a. mindful of him, 8.04
I say to the LORD, "Thou a. my Lord; 16.02
Why a. thou so far from helping me, 22.01
Yet thou a. holy, enthroned on the 22.03
Yet thou a. he who took me from the 22.09
for thou a. with me; thy rod 23.04
for thou a. the God of my salvation; 25.05
Yea, thou a. my rock and my fortress; 31.03
for me, for thou a. my refuge. 31.04
O LORD, I say, "Thou a. my God." 31.14
Thou a. a hiding place for me, thou 32.07
Thou a. my help and my deliverer; 40.17
know that thou a. pleased with me, 41.11
For thou a. the God in whom I take 43.02
Thou a. my King and my God, who 44.04
so that thou a. justified in thy 51.04
God of hosts, a. God of Israel. 59.05
for thou, O God, a. my fortress. 59.09
a. my fortress, the God who shows me 59.17
for thou a. my refuge, a strong 61.03
O God, thou a. my God, I seek thee, my 63.01
who a. the hope of all the ends of 65.05
Thou a. my help and my deliverer; 70.05
for thou a. my rock and my fortress. 71.03
a. my hope, my trust, O LORD, from my 71.05
thou a. he who took me from my 71.06
but thou a. my strong refuge. 71.07
Glorious a. thou, more majestic than 76.04
But thou, terrible a. thou! 76.07
Thou a. the God who workest wonders, 77.14
Thou who a. enthroned upon the 80.01
a. the Most High over all the earth 83.18
Thou a. my God; be gracious 86.03
a. good and forgiving, abounding in 86.05
For thou a. great and doest wondrous 86.10
wondrous things, thou alone a. God. 86.10
a. a God merciful and gracious, slow 86.15
of hosts, who is mighty as thou a., 89.08
For thou a. the glory of their 89.17
'Thou a. my Father, my God, and the 89.26
thou a. full of wrath against thy 89.38
everlasting to everlasting thou a. God. 90.02
O LORD, a. on high for ever. 92.08
thou a. from everlasting. 93.02
a. most high over all the earth; 97.09
thou a. exalted far above all gods. 97.09
a. enthroned for ever; 102.12
but thou a. the same, and thy years 102.27
O LORD my God, thou a. very great! 104.01
Thou a. clothed with honor and 104.01
Thou a. my God, and I will give 118.28
thou a. my God, I will extol thee. 118.28
Thou a. good and doest good; 119.68
Thou a. my hiding-place and my 119.114
Righteous a. thou, O LORD, and right 119.137
But thou a. near, O LORD, and all thy 119.151
O thou who a. enthroned in the 123.01
and a. acquainted with all my ways. 139.03
If I ascend to heaven, thou a. there! 139.08
my bed in Sheol, thou a. there! 139.08
for thou a. fearful and wonderful. 139.14
I say to the LORD, Thou a. my God; 140.06
I say, Thou a. my refuge, my portion 142.05
to do thy will, for thou a. my God! 143.10
O LORD, thou a. my God; I will Is 25.01
thou a. glorified; thou hast 26.15
who a. enthroned above the cherubim, 37.16
thou a. the God, thou alone, of all 37.16
know that thou alone a. the LORD." 37.20
"Deliver me, for thou a. my god!" 44.17
Truly, thou a. a God who hidest 45.15
For thou a. our Father, though 63.16
thou, O LORD, a. our Father, our 63.16
Yet, O LORD, thou a. our Father; 64.08
the clay, and thou a. our potter; 64.08
thou a. the friend of my youth— Jer 3.04
for thou a. the LORD our God. 3.22
thou a. great, and thy name is great 10.06
Righteous a. thou, O LORD, when I 12.01
thou a. near in their mouth and far 12.02
a. in the midst of us, and we are 14.09
A. thou not he, O LORD our God? 14.22
for thou a. my praise. 17.14
thou a. my refuge in the day of 17.17
thou a. stronger than I, and thou 20.07
for thou a. the LORD my God. 31.18
A. thou exceedingly angry with us Lam 5.22
and he shall say, 'Thou a. my God.'" Hos 2.23
knew that thou a. a gracious God Jon 4.02
A. thou not from everlasting, O LORD Hab 1.12
Thou who a. of purer eyes than to 1.13
and a. silent when the wicked 1.13
this: Our Father who a. in heaven, Mt 6.09
heaven, "Thou a. my beloved Son; Mk 1.11
heaven, "Thou a. my beloved Son; Lk 3.22
if thou a. willing, remove this cup 22.42
a. in me, and I in thee, that they Jn 17.21
'Thou a. my Son, today I have Ac 13.33
representation by the a. and 17.29
and prevail when thou a. judged." Rom 3.04

ART (cont.)
shout, thou who a. not in travail; Gal 4.27
"Thou a. my Son, today I have Heb 1.05
But thou a. the same, and thy years 1.12
is man that thou a. mindful of him, 2.06
"Thou a. my Son, today I have 5.05
"Thou a. a priest for ever, after 5.06
"Thou a. a priest for ever, after 7.17
'Thou a. a priest for ever.' 7.21
"Worthy a. thou, our Lord and God, to Rev 4.11
"Worthy a. thou to take the scroll 5.09
who a. and who wast, that thou hast 11.17
For thou alone a. holy. 15.04
"Just a. thou in these thy judgments, 16.05
thou who a. and wast, O Holy One. 16.05

ARTAXERXES
And in the days of A., Bishlam Ez 4.07
associates wrote to A. king of Persia; 4.07
Jerusalem to A. the king as 4.08
"To A. the king: Your servants, the 4.11
and Darius and A. king of Persia; 6.14
in the reign of A. king of Persia, 7.01
in the seventh year of A. the king, 7.07
which King A. gave to Ezra the 7.11
"A., king of Kings, to Ezra the 7.12
"And I, A. the king, make a decree to 7.21
in the reign of A. the king: 8.01
in the twentieth year of King A., Neh 2.01
thirty-second year of A. the king, 5.14
thirty-second year of A. king of 13.06

ARTAXERXES'
copy of King A. letter was read Ez 4.23

ARTEMAS
When I send A. or Tychicus to you, Tit 3.12

ARTEMIS
who made silver shrines of A., Ac 19.24
great goddess A. may count for Ac 19.27
"Great is A. of the Ephesians!" 19.28
"Great is A. of the Ephesians!" 19.34
is temple keeper of the great A., 19.35

ARTICLE
it is an a. of wood or a garment Lev 11.32
every a. of skin, all work of goats' Num 31.20
goats' hair, and every a. of wood. 31.20

ARTICLES
a. of gold, armlets and bracelets, Num 31.50
from them the gold, all wrought a. 31.51
brought with him a. of silver, 2Sa 8.10
a. of silver and gold, garments, 1Ki 10.25
he sent all sorts of a. of gold, 1Ch 18.10
a. of silver and of gold, garments, 2Ch 9.24
all a. of ivory, all articles of Rev 18.12
all a. of costly wood, bronze, iron 18.12

ARTIFICIAL
to the a. pool, and to the house of Neh 3.16

ARTISANS
together with the rest of the a. Jer 52.15

ARTISTIC
to devise a. designs, to work in Ex 31.04
to devise a. designs, to work in 35.32

ARTS
did the same by their secret a. Ex 7.11
did the same by their secret a.; 7.22
did the same by their secret a.; 8.07
by their secret a. to bring forth 8.18
practiced magic a. brought their Ac 19.19

ARUBBOTH
Benhesed, in A. (to him belonged 1Ki 4.10

ARUMAH
sent messengers to Abimelech at A., Ju 9.31
And Abimelech dwelt at A.; 9.41

ARVAD
of Sidon and A. were your rowers; Eze 27.08
The men of A. and Helech were upon 27.11

ARVADITES
the A., the Zemarites, and the Gen 10.18
the A., the Zemarites, and the 1Ch 1.16

ARZA
himself drunk in the house of A., 1Ki 16.09

ASA
And A. his son reigned in his stead. 1Ki 15.08
king of Israel A. began to reign 15.09
And A. did what was right in the 15.11
and A. cut down her image and 15.13
the heart of A. was wholly true to 15.14
was war between A. and Baasha king 15.16
out or come in to A. king of Judah. 15.17
Then A. took all the silver and the 15.18
and King A. sent them to Benhadad 15.18
And Benhadad hearkened to King A., 15.20
Then King A. made a proclamation to 15.22
with them King A. built Geba of 15.22
Now the rest of all the acts of A., 15.23
And A. slept with his fathers, and 15.24
second year of A. king of Judah; 15.25
the third year of A. king of Judah, 15.28
was war between A. and Baasha king 15.32
the third year of A. king of Judah, 15.33
twenty-sixth year of A. king of Judah, 16.08
twenty-seventh year of A. king of Judah, 16.10
twenty-seventh year of A. king of 16.15
thirty-first year of A. king of Judah, 16.23
thirty-eighth year of A. king of Judah, 16.29
Jehoshaphat the son of A. began to 22.41
in all the way of A. his father; 22.43
in the days of his father A., 22.46
A. his son, Jehoshaphat his son, 1Ch 3.10
and Berechiah the son of A., 9.16
and A. his son reigned in his 2Ch 14.01
And A. did what was good and right 14.02
And A. had an army of three hundred 14.08
And A. went out to meet him, and 14.10
And A. cried to the LORD his God, "O 14.11
Ethiopians before A. and before 14.12
A. and the people that were with 14.13
and he went out to meet A., 15.02
A., and all Judah and Benjamin: The 15.02
When A. heard these words, the 15.08
fifteenth year of the reign of A. 15.10
King A. removed from being queen 15.16
A. cut down her image, crushed it, 15.16
the heart of A. was blameless all 15.17
thirty-fifth year of the reign of A. 15.19
thirty-sixth year of the reign of A. 16.01
out or come in to A. king of Judah. 16.01
Then A. took silver and gold from 16.02
And Benhadad hearkened to King A., 16.04
Then King A. took all Judah, and 16.06
the seer came to A. king of Judah, 16.07
Then A. was angry with the seer, and 16.10
And A. inflicted cruelties upon 16.10
The acts of A., from first to last, 16.11
of his reign A. was diseased in 16.12
And A. slept with his fathers, dying 16.13
Ephraim which A. his father had 17.02
in the way of A. his father and 20.32
in the ways of A. king of Judah, 21.12
which king A. had made for defense Jer 41.09
and Abijah the father of A., Mt 1.07
and A. the father of Jehoshaphat, 1.08

ASAHEL
were there, Joab, Abishai, and A. 2Sa 2.18
Now A. was as swift of foot as a 2.18
and A. pursued Abner, and as he went 2.19
behind him and said, "Is it you, A.?" 2.20
But A. would not turn aside from 2.21
And Abner said again to A., 2.22
the place where A. had fallen and 2.23
servants nineteen men besides A. 2.30
And they took up A., 2.32
for the blood of A. his brother. 3.27
their brother A. in the battle at 3.30
A. the brother of Joab was one of 23.24
Abishai, Joab, and A., three. 1Ch 2.16
the armies were A. the brother of 11.26
A. the brother of Joab was fourth, 27.07
A., Shemiramoth, Jehonathan, Adonijah, 2Ch 17.08
A., Jerimoth, Jozabad, Eliel, Ismachiah, 31.13
the son of A. and Jahzeiah the son Ez 10.15

ASAIAH
and A. the king's servant, saying, 2Ki 22.12
and A. went to Huldah the prophetess, 22.14
A., Adiel, Jesimiel, Benaiah, 1Ch 4.36
Haggiah his son, and A. his son. 6.30
A. the first-born, and his sons. 9.05
A. the chief, with two hundred and 15.06
A., Joel, Shemaiah, Eliel, and Amminadab, 15.11
and A. the king's servant, saying, 2Ch 34.20

ASAPH
Joah the son of A., the recorder. 2Ki 18.18
secretary, and Joah the son of A., 18.37
and his brother A., 1Ch 6.39
A. the son of Berechiah, son of 6.39
of Mica, son of Zichri, son of A.; 9.15
of his brethren A. the son of 15.17
A., and Ethan, were to sound bronze 15.19
A. was the chief, and second to him 16.05
A. was to sound the cymbals, 16.05
to the LORD by A. and his brethren 16.07
So David left A. and his brethren 16.37
service certain of the sons of A., 25.01
Of the sons of A.: Zaccur, Joseph, 25.02
sons of A., under the direction of 25.02
Asaph, under the direction of A., 25.02
A., Jeduthun, and Heman were under 25.06
The first lot fell for A. to Joseph; 25.09
the son of Kore, of the sons of A. 26.01
A., Heman, and Jeduthun, their sons 2Ch 5.12
Mattaniah, a Levite of the sons of A., 20.14
and of the sons of A., Zechariah 29.13
words of David and of A. the seer. 29.30
the sons of A., were in their place 35.15
and A., and Heman, and Jeduthun the 35.15
the sons of A., one hundred and Ez 2.41
the sons of A., with cymbals, to 3.10
and a letter to A., the keeper Neh 2.08
the sons of A., a hundred and forty 7.44
son of A., who was the leader to 11.17
son of Mica, of the sons of A., 11.22
Micaiah, son of Zaccur, son of A.; 12.35
of David and A. of old there was a 12.46
Joah the son of A., the recorder. Is 36.03
secretary, and Joah the son of A., 36.22

ASAREL
Ziph, Ziphah, Tiria, and A. 1Ch 4.16

ASCEND
"A. this mountain of the Abarim, Deu 32.49
and die on the mountain which you a., 32.50
Who shall a. the hill of the LORD? Ps 24.03
Thou didst a. the high mount, 68.18
If I a. to heaven, thou art there! 139.08
your heart, 'I will a. to heaven; Is 14.13
I will a. above the heights of the 14.14
For David did not a. into the Ac 2.34
heart, "Who will a. into heaven?" Rom 10.06
another angel a. from the rising Rev 7.02
and is to a. from the bottomless 17.08

ASCENDED
of the LORD a. in the flame of the Ju 13.20
When Jehoram had a. the throne of 2Ch 21.04
Who has a. to heaven and come down? Pro 30.04
No one has a. into heaven but he Jn 3.13
I have not yet a. to the Father; 20.17
your alms have a. as a memorial Ac 10.04
"When he a. on high he led a host Eph 4.08
"He a.," what does it mean but that 4.09
is he who also a. far above all 4.10

ASCENDING
of God were a. and descending on Gen 28.12
angels of God a. and descending Jn 1.51
the Son of man a. where he was 6.62
I am a. to my Father and your 20.17

ASCENDS
the beast that a. from the bottomless Rev 11.07

ASCENT
turn south of the a. of Akrabbim, Num 34.04
by the way of the a. of Bethhoron, Jos 10.10
going down the a. of Bethhoron, 10.11
southward of the a. of Akrabbim, 15.03
is opposite the a. of Adummim, 15.07
is opposite the a. of Adummim; 18.17
ran from the a. of Akrabbim, Ju 1.36
from the battle by the a. of Heres. 8.13
went up the a. of the Mount of 2Sa 15.30
in the chariot at the a. of Gur, 2Ki 9.27
they will come up by the a. of Ziz; 2Ch 20.16
him in the a. of the tombs of the 32.33
opposite the a. to the armory at Neh 3.19
at the a. of the wall, above the 12.37
For at the a. of Luhith they go up Is 15.05
For at the a. of Luhith they go up Jer 48.05

ASCERTAIN
As you may a., it is not more than Ac 24.11

ASCERTAINED
weight of the bronze was not a. 2Ch 4.18
secretly and a. from them what Mt 2.07
which he had a. from the wise men. 2.16

ASCRIBE
A. greatness to our God! Deu 32.03
A. to the LORD, O families of the 1Ch 16.28
a. to the LORD glory and strength! 16.28
A. to the LORD the glory due his 16.29
and a. righteousness to my Maker. Job 36.03
A. to the LORD, O heavenly beings, Ps 29.01
a. to the LORD glory and strength. 29.01
A. to the Lord the glory of his 29.02
A. power to God, whose majesty is 68.34
A. to the LORD, O families of the 96.07
a. to the LORD glory and strength! 96.07
A. to the LORD the glory due his 96.08

ASCRIBED
"They have a. to David ten thousands, 1Sa 18.08
and to me they have a. thousands; 18.08

ASENATH
and he gave him in marriage A., Gen 41.45
whom A., the daughter of Potiphera 41.50
whom A., the daughter of Potiphera 64.20

ASH
lifts the needy from the a. heap, 1Sa 2.08
lifts the needy from the a. heap, Ps 113.07
up in purple lie on a. heaps. Lam 4.05

ASHAMED
were both naked, and were not a. Gen 2.25
them, for the men were greatly a. 2Sa 10.05
in who are a. when they flee in 19.03
when they urged him till he was a., 2Ki 2.17
and stared at him, until he was a. 8.11
them, for the men were greatly a. 1Ch 19.05
For I was a. to ask the king for a Ez 8.22
I am a. and blush to lift my face 9.06
are you not a. to wrong me? Job 19.03
shall be a. and sorely troubled; Ps 6.10
let them be a. who are wantonly 25.03
so your faces shall never be a. 34.05
For you shall be a. of the oaks in Is 1.29
Be a., O Sidon, for the sea has 23.04
will be confounded, and the sun a.; 24.23
thy zeal for thy people, and be a. 26.11
Jacob: "Jacob shall no more be a., 29.22
to him shall come and be a., 45.24
"Fear not, for you will not be a.; 54.04
harlot's brow, you refuse to be a. Jer 3.03
Were they a. when they committed 6.15
No, they were not at all a.; 6.15
Were they a. when they committed 8.12
No, they were not at all a.; 8.12
They shall be a. of their harvests 12.13
they are a. and confounded and 14.03
on the land, the farmers are a., 14.04
you will be a. and confounded 22.22
I was a., and I was confounded, 31.19
Then Moab shall be a. of Chemosh, 48.13
house of Israel was a. of Bethel, 48.13
who were a. of your lewd behavior. Eze 16.27
So be a., you also, and bear your 16.52
disgrace and be a. of all that you 16.54
and be a. when I take your sisters, 16.61
Be a. and confounded for your ways, 36.32
they may be a. of their iniquities. 43.10
And if they are a. of all that they 43.11
they shall be a. because of their Hos 4.19
and Israel shall be a. of his idol. 10.06
see and be a. of all their might; Mic 7.16
prophet will be a. of his vision Zec 13.04
For whoever is a. of me and of my Mk 8.38
him will the Son of man also be a., 8.38
For whoever is a. of me and of my Lk 9.26
Son of man be a. when he comes in 9.26
enough to dig, and I am a. to beg. 16.03
For I am not a. of the gospel: it is Rom 1.16
the things of which you are now a.? 6.21
I do not write this to make you a., 1Co 4.14
hope that I shall not be at all a., Php 1.20
to do with him, that he may be a. 2Th 3.14
Do not be a. then of testifying to 2Ti 1.08
But I am not a., for I know whom I 1.12
he was not a. of my chains, 1.16
a workman who has no need to be a., 2.15
why he is not a. to call them Heb 2.11
God is not a. to be called their 11.16
as a Christian, let him not be a., 1Pe 4.16

ASHAN
Libnah, Ether, A., Jos 15.42
and A.—four cities with their 19.07
Tochen, and A., five cities, 1Ch 4.32
A. with its pasture lands, and 6.59

ASHARELAH
and A., sons of Asaph, under the 1Ch 25.02

ASHBEL
A., Gera, Naaman, Ehi, Rosh, Muppim, Gen 46.21
of A., the family of the Ashbelites; Num 26.38
A. the second, Aharah the third, 1Ch 8.01

ASHBELITES
of Ashbel, the family of the A.; Num 26.38

ASHDOD
and in A., did some remain. Jos 11.22
A., Ashkelon, Gath, and Ekron), and 13.03
all that were by the side of A., 15.46
A., its towns and its villages; 15.47
carried it from Ebenezer to A.; 1Sa 5.01
the people of A. rose early the 5.03
threshold of Dagon in A. to this day. 5.05
was heavy upon the people of A., 5.06
both A. and its territory 5.06
And when the men of A. saw how 5.07
one for A., one for Gaza, one for 6.17
wall of Jabneh and the wall of A.; 2Ch 26.06
territory of A. and elsewhere 26.06
Jews who had married women of A., Neh 13.23
children spoke the language of A., 13.24
came to A. and fought against it Is 20.01
Ekron, and the remnant of A.); Jer 25.20
cut off the inhabitants from A., Amo 1.08
a mongrel people shall dwell in A.; Zec 9.06

ASHDODITES
Ammonites and the A. heard that the Neh 4.07

ASHDOD'S
A. people shall be driven out at Zep 2.04

ASHER
so she called his name A. Gen 30.13
of Zilpah, Leah's maid: Gad and A. 35.26
The sons of A.: Imnah, Ishvah, Ishvi, 46.17
Dan and Naphtali, Gad and A. Ex 1.04
from A., Pagiel the son of Ochran; Num 1.13
Of the people of A., their 1.40
of the tribe of A. was forty-one 1.41
to him shall be the tribe of A., 2.27
the people of A. being Pagiel the 2.27
the leader of the men of A.: 7.72
of the men of A. was Pagiel the 10.26
from the tribe of A., 13.13
The sons of A. according to their 26.44
of the daughter of A. was Serah. 26.46
of the sons of A. according to 26.47
tribe of the sons of A. a leader, 34.27
A., Zebulun, Dan, and Naphtali. Deu 27.13
And of A. he said, "Blessed above 33.24
he said, "Blessed above sons be A.; 33.24
reached from A. to Michmethath, Jos 17.07
on the north A. is reached, and on 17.10
Issachar and in A. Manasseh had 17.11
the tribe of A. according to its 19.24
of the tribe of A. according to 19.31
and A. on the west, and Judah on the 19.34
of Issachar, from the tribe of A., 21.06
and out of the tribe of A., 21.30
A. did not drive out the inhabitants Ju 1.31
A. sat still at the coast of the 5.17
And he sent messengers to A., 6.35
and from A. and from all Manasseh, 7.23
son of Hushai, in A. and Bealoth; 1Ki 4.16
Benjamin, Naphtali, Gad, and A. 1Ch 2.02
A., Naphtali, and Manasseh in Bashan. 6.62
out of the tribe of A.: Mashal 6.74
The sons of A.: Imnah, Ishvah, Ishvi, 7.30
All of these were men of A., 7.40
Of A. forty thousand seasoned 12.36
Only a few men of A., of Manasseh 2Ch 30.11
side to the west, A., one portion. Eze 48.02
Adjoining the territory of A., 48.03
the gate of A., and the gate of 48.34
of Phanuel, of the tribe of A.; Lk 2.36
twelve thousand of the tribe of A., Rev 7.06

ASHERAH
any tree as an A. beside the altar Deu 16.21
cut down the A. that is beside it; Ju 6.25
the wood of the A. which you shall 6.26
and the A. beside it was cut down, 6.28

ASHERAH (cont.)
Baal and cut down the A. beside it. Ju 6.30
an abominable image made for A.; 1Ki 15.13
And Ahab made an A. Ahab did 16.33
the four hundred prophets of A., 18.19
and the A. also remained in 2Ki 13.06
and they made an A., and 17.16
the pillars, and cut down the A. 18.04
and made an A., as Ahab king of 21.03
graven image of A. that he had 21.07
for A., and for all the host of 23.04
brought out the A. from the house 23.06
the women wove hangings for the A. 23.07
also he burned the A. 23.15
made an abominable image for A. 2Ch 15.16

ASHERAHS
destroyed the A. out of the land, 2Ch 19.03
and made A., and worshiped all the 33.03

ASHERIM
pillars, and cut down their A. Ex 34.13
pillars, and hew down their A., Deu 7.05
and burn their A. with fire; 12.03
because they have made their A., 1Ki 14.15
and A. on every high hill and under 14.23
pillars and A. on every high hill 2Ki 17.10
the pillars, and cut down the A., 23.14
the pillars and hewed down the A., 2Ch 14.03
places and the A. out of Judah. 17.06
and served the A. and the idols. 24.18
hewed down the A. and broke down 31.01
and set up the A. and the images, 33.19
the A., and the graven and the 34.03
in pieces the A. and the graven 34.04
and beat the A. and the images into 34.07
either the A. or the altars of Is 17.08
no A. or incense altars will remain 27.09
remember their altars and their A., Jer 17.02
root out your A. from among you Mic 5.14

ASHERITES
but the A. dwelt among the Canaanites, Ju 1.32

ASHEROTH
and serving the Baals and the A. Ju 3.07

ASHER'S
A. food shall be rich, and he shall Gen 49.20

ASHES
the LORD, I who am but dust and a. Gen 18.27
"Take handfuls of a. from the kiln, Ex 9.08
So they took a. from the kiln, and 9.10
make pots for it to receive its a., 27.03
the east side, in the place for a.; Lev 1.16
where the a. are poured out, and 4.12
where the a. are poured out it 4.12
take up the a. to which the fire 6.10
carry forth the a. outside the 6.11
take away the a. from the altar, Num 4.13
gather up the a. of the heifer 19.09
who gathers the a. of the heifer 19.10
shall take some a. of the burnt 19.17
And Tamar put a. on her head, and 2Sa 13.19
and the a. that are upon it shall 1Ki 13.03
and the a. poured out from the 13.05
and carried their a. to Bethel. 2Ki 23.04
and put on sackcloth and a., Est 4.01
of them lay in sackcloth and a. 4.03
himself, and sat among the a. Job 2.08
Your maxims are proverbs of a., 13.12
and I have become like dust and a. 30.19
myself, and repent in dust and a. 42.06
For I eat a. like bread, and mingle Ps 102.09
he scatters hoarfrost like a. 147.16
He feeds on a.; a deluded Is 44.20
spread sackcloth and a. under him? 58.05
give them a garland instead of a., 61.03
gird on sackcloth, and roll in a.; Jer 6.26
and roll in a., you lords of the 25.34
of the dead bodies and the a., 31.40
on gravel, and made me cower in a.; Lam 3.16
on their heads and wallow in a.; Eze 27.30
I turned you to a. upon the earth 28.18
with fasting and sackcloth and a. Dan 9.03
with sackcloth, and sat in a. Jon 3.06
they will be a. under the soles of Mal 4.03
long ago in sackcloth and a. Mt 11.21
ago, sitting in sackcloth and a. Lk 10.13
and with the a. of a heifer Heb 9.13
and Gomorrah to a. he condemned 2Pe 2.06

ASHHUR
his father, and she bore him A., 1Ch 2.24
A., the father of Tekoa, had two 4.05

ASHIMA
Nergal, the men of Hamath made A., 2Ki 17.30

ASHIMAH
Those who swear by A. of Samaria, Amo 8.14

ASHKELON
A., Gath, and Ekron), and those of Jos 13.03
and A. with its territory, and Ekron Ju 1.18
he went down to A. and killed 14.19
one for A., one for Gath, one for 1Sa 6.17
it not in the streets of A.; 2Sa 1.20
of the land of the Philistines (A., Jer 25.20
come upon Gaza, A. has perished. 47.05
Against A. and against the seashore 47.07
him that holds the scepter from A.; Amo 1.08
and A. shall become a desolation; Zep 2.04
the houses of A. they shall lie 2.07
A. shall see it, and be afraid; Zec 9.05
A. shall be uninhabited; 9.05

ASHKENAZ
A., Riphath, and Togarmah. Gen 10.03
A., Diphath, and Togarmah. 1Ch 1.06
kingdoms, Ararat, Minni, and A.; Jer 51.27

ASHNAH
the lowland, Eshtaol, Zorah, A., Jos 15.33
Iphtah, A., Nezib, 15.43

ASHORE
men drew it a. and sat down and Mt 13.48
As he went a. he saw a great throng 14.14
went aboard and hauled the net a., Jn 21.11
if possible to bring the ship a. Ac 27.39

ASHPENAZ
Then the king commanded A., Dan 1.03

ASHTAROTH
who lived in A. and in Edrei. Deu 1.04
Og king of Bashan, who dwelt in A. Jos 9.10
who dwelt at A. and at Edrei 12.04
who reigned in A. and Idrei (the 13.12
and A., and Edrei, the cities of the 13.31
and served the Baals and the A. Ju 2.13
and served the Baals and the A., 10.06
gods and the A. from among you, 1Sa 7.03
put away the Baals and the A., 7.04
have served the Baals and the A.; 12.10
They put his armor in the temple of A.; 31.10
lands and A. with its pasture 1Ch 6.71

ASHTERATHITE
Uzzia the A., Shama and Jeiel the 1Ch 11.44

ASHTEROTHKARNAIM
came and subdued the Rephaim in A., Gen 14.05

ASHTORETH
went after a. the goddess of the 1Ki 11.05
and worshiped A. the goddess of the 11.33
had built for A. the abomination 2Ki 23.13

ASHURITES
Gilead and the A. and Jezreel and 2Sa 2.09

ASHVATH
of Japhlet: Pasach, Bimhal, and A. 1Ch 7.33

ASIA
and Cappadocia, Pontus and A., Ac 2.09
and of those from Cilicia and A., 6.09
Spirit to speak the word in A. 16.06
residents of A. heard the word of 19.10
himself stayed in A. for a while. 19.22
throughout all A. this Paul has 19.26
she whom all A. and the world 19.27
might not have to spend time in A.; 20.16
first day that I set foot in A., 20.18
the Jews from A., who had seen him 21.27
But some Jews from A.— 24.18
to the ports along the coast of A., 27.02
the first convert in A. for Christ. Rom 16.05
The churches of A. send greetings. 1Co 16.19
affliction we experienced in A.; 2Co 1.08
all who are in A. turned away from 2Ti 1.15
Cappadocia, A., and Bithynia, 1Pe 1.01
the seven churches that are in A.: Rev 1.04

ASIANS
and the A., Tychicus and Trophimus. Ac 20.04

ASIARCHS
some of the A. also, who were Ac 19.31

ASIDE
turn a., I pray you, to your servant's Gen 19.02
so they turned a. to him and 19.03
"I will turn a. and see this great Ex 3.03
LORD saw that he turned a. to see, 3.04
turning a. after a multitude, so as 23.02
they have turned a. quickly out of 32.08
have not turned a. to uncleanness, Num 5.19
will not turn a. to the right hand 20.17
will not turn a. into field or 21.22
the ass turned a. out of the road, 22.23
and turned a. before me these three 22.23
If she had not turned a. from me, 22.23
I will turn a. neither to the right Deu 2.27
shall not turn a. to the right 5.32
have turned a. quickly out of the 9.12
you had turned a. quickly from the 9.16
and you turn a. and serve other 11.16
but turn a. from the way which I 11.28
shall not turn a. from the verdict 17.11
he may not turn a. from the 17.20
you do not turn a. from any of the 28.14
and turn a. from the way which I 31.29
turning a. from it neither to the Jos 23.06
soon turned a. from the way in Ju 2.17
"Turn a., my lord, turn a. to me; 4.18
So he turned a. to her into the 4.18
and he turned a. to see the carcass 14.08
and they turned a. and said to him, 18.03
And they turned a. thither, 18.15
let us turn a. to this city of the 19.11
will not turn a. into the city of 19.12
and they turned a. there, 19.15
So Boaz said, "Turn a., friend; Ru 4.01
and he turned a. and sat down. 4.01
his ways, but turned a. after gain; 1Sa 8.03
of which I said to you, 'Put it a.' " 9.23
yet do not turn a. from following 12.20
and do not turn a. after vain 12.21
"Turn a. to your right hand or to 2Sa 2.21
would not turn a. from following 2.21
"Turn a. from following me; 2.22
But he refused to turn a.; 2.23
Joab took him a. into the midst of 3.27
David took it a. to the house of 6.10
"Turn a., and stand here." 18.30
So he turned a., and stood still. 18.30
his statutes I did not turn a. 22.23
But if you turn a. from following 1Ki 9.06
did not turn a. from anything that 15.05
he is musing, or he has gone a., 18.27
he did not turn a. from it, 22.43
and when one is full, set it a." 2Ki 4.04
did not turn a. from the sins of 10.29
he did not turn a. to the right 22.02
but took it a. to the house of 1Ch 13.13
"But if you turn a. and forsake my 2Ch 7.19
did not turn a. from what the king 8.15
father and did not turn a. from it; 20.32
he did not turn a. to the right or 34.02
And they set a. the burnt offerings 35.12
The caravans turn a. from their Job 6.18
his way and have not turned a. 23.11
my step has turned a. from the way, 31.07
that he may turn man a. from his deed, 33.17
because they turned a. from following 34.27
greatness of the ransom turn you a. 36.18
I do not turn a. from thy ordinances, Ps 119.102
But those who turn a. upon their 125.05
not your heart turn a. to her ways, Pro 7.25
of the upright turns a. from evil; 16.17
to turn a. the needy from justice Is 10.02
empty plea turn a. him who is in 29.21
turn a. from the path, let us hear 30.11
they have turned a. and gone away. Jer 5.23
who turns a. to tarry for a night? 14.08
Who will turn a. to ask about your 15.05
to turn a. the right of a man in Lam 3.35
turning a. from thy commandments Dan 9.05
transgressed thy law and turned a., 9.11
men themselves go a. with harlots, Hos 4.14
and turn a. the way of the afflicted Amo 2.07
and turn a. the needy in the gate. 5.12
But you have turned a. from the way; Mal 2.08
those who thrust a. the sojourner, 3.05
you have turned a. from my statutes 3.07
he took the twelve disciples a., Mt 20.17
And taking him a. from the multitude Mk 7.33
laid a. his garments, and girded Jn 13.04
apostleship from which Judas turned a., Ac 1.25
them to go a. out of the council, 4.15
wronging his neighbor thrust him a., 7.27
to obey him, but thrust him a., 7.39
and going a. asked him privately, 23.19
All have turned a., Rom 3.12
put something a. and store it up, 1Co 16.02
this he set a., nailing it to the Col 2.14
commandment is set a. because of Heb 7.18
let us also lay a. every weight, 12.01

ASIEL
Joshibiah, son of Seraiah, son of A., 1Ch 4.35

ASKS
and a. you, 'To whom do you belong Gen 32.17
in time to come your son a. you, Ex 13.14
"When your son a. you in time to Deu 6.20
and if any man comes and a. you, Ju 4.20
with riches, so that he never a., Ecc 4.08
or a priest a. you, 'What is the Jer 23.33
that the king a. is difficult, Dan 2.11
And if one a. him, 'What are these Zec 13.06
For every one who a. receives, Mt 7.08
if his son a. him for a loaf, will 7.09
Or if he a. for a fish, will give 7.10
For every one who a. receives, Lk 11.10
if his son a. for a fish, will 11.11
or if he a. for an egg, will give 11.12

ASKS (cont.)
an embassy and a. terms of peace. Lk 14.32
If any one a. you, 'Why are you 19.31
yet none of you a. me, 'Where Jn 16.05

ASLEEP
And he fell a. and dreamed a second Gen 41.05
was lying fast a. from weariness. Ju 4.21
for they were all a., because 1Sa 26.12
perhaps he is a. and must be 1Ki 18.27
and had lain down, and was fast a. Jon 1.05
Your shepherds are a., O king Nah 3.18
the waves; but he was a. Mt 8.24
who had fallen a. were raised, 27.52
stole him away while we were a. 28.13
in the stern, a. on the cushion; Mk 4.38
lest he come suddenly and find you a. 13.36
said to Peter, "Simon, are you a.? 14.37
and as they sailed he fell a. Lk 8.23
"Our friend Lazarus has fallen a., Jn 11.11
to him, "Lord, if he has fallen a., 11.12
when he had said this, he fell a. Ac 7.60
fell a., and was laid with his 13.36
alive, though some have fallen a. 1Co 15.06
who have fallen a. in Christ have 15.18
fruits of those who have fallen a. 15.20
concerning those who are a., 1Th 4.13
with him those who have fallen a. 4.14
precede those who have fallen a. 4.15
their destruction has not been a. 2Pe 2.03
For ever since the fathers fell a., 3.04

ASNAH
the sons of A., the sons of Meunim, Ez 2.50

ASP
shall play over the hole of the a., Is 11.08

ASPATHA
Parshandatha and Dalphon and A. Est 9.07

ASPIRE
to a. to live quietly, to mind your 1Th 4.11

ASPIRES
If any one a. to the office of 1Ti 3.01

ASPS
serpents, and the cruel venom of a. Deu 32.33
it is the gall of a. within him. Job 20.14
He will suck the poison of a.; 20.16
"The venom of a. is under their Rom 3.13

ASRIEL
and of A., the family of the Num 26.31
A., Shechem, Hepher, and Shemida; Jos 17.02
A., whom his Aramaean concubine 1Ch 7.14

ASRIELITES
and of Asriel, the family of the A.; Num 26.31

ASS
He shall be a wild a. of a man, Gen 16.12
saddled his a., and took two of his 22.03
young men, "Stay here with the a.; 22.05
to give his a. provender at the 42.27
and every man loaded his a., 44.13
Issachar is a strong a., 49.14
and his sons and set them on an a., Ex 4.20
Every firstling of an a. you shall 13.13
or his a., or anything that is your 20.17
and an ox or an a. falls into it, 21.33
it is an ox or an a. or a sheep, 22.04
for a., for sheep, for clothing, or 22.09
his neighbor an a. or an ox or a 22.10
enemy's ox or his a. going astray, 23.04
If you see the a. of one who hates 23.05
your ox and your a. may have rest, 23.12
The firstling of an a. you shall 34.20
I have not taken one a. from them, Num 16.15
in the morning, and saddled his a., 22.21
Now he was riding on the a., 22.22
And the a. saw the angel of the 22.23
and the a. turned aside out of the 22.23
and Balaam struck the a., 22.23
And when the a. saw the angel of 22.25
When the a. saw the angel of the 22.27
he struck the a. with his staff. 22.27
LORD opened the mouth of the a., 22.28
And Balaam said to the a., 22.29
And the a. said to Balaam, "Am I not 22.30
said to Balaam, "Am I not your a., 22.30
you struck your a. these three 22.32
and the a. saw me, and turned aside 22.33
or your a., or any of your cattle, Deu 5.14
or his a., or anything that is your 5.21
And so you shall do with his a.; 22.03
your brother's a. or his ox fallen 22.04
plow with an ox and an a. together. 22.10
your a. shall be violently taken 28.31
and she alighted from her a., Jos 15.18
and she alighted from her a., Ju 1.14
Israel, and no sheep or ox or a. 6.04
And he found a fresh jawbone of an a., 15.15
said, "With the jawbone of an a., 15.16
jawbone of an a. have I slain a 15.16
Then he put her upon the a.; 19.28
Or whose a. have I taken? 1Sa 12.03
suckling, ox and sheep, camel and a. 15.03
And Jesse took an a. laden with 16.20
And as she rode on the a., 25.20
haste, and alighted from the a., 25.23
and rose and mounted on an a., 25.42
not followed, he saddled his a., 2Sa 17.23
'Saddle an a. for me, that I may 19.26
Shimei arose and saddled an a., 1Ki 2.40
to his sons, "Saddle the a. for me." 13.13
saddled the a. for him and he 13.13
he saddled the a. for the prophet 13.23
and the a. stood beside it; 13.24
to his sons, "Saddle the a. for me." 13.13
and the a. and the lion standing 13.28
not eaten the body or torn the a. 13.28
man of God and laid it upon the a., 13.29
Then she saddled the a., 2Ki 4.24
Does the wild a. bray when he has Job 6.05
They drive away the a. of the 24.03
"Who has let the wild a. go free? 39.05
loosed the bonds of the swift a., 39.05
for the horse, a bridle for the a., Pro 26.03
and the a. its master's crib; Is 1.03
of the ox and the a. range free. 32.20
a wild a. used to the wilderness, in Jer 2.24
burial of an a. he shall be buried, 22.19
Be like a wild a. in the desert! 48.06
a wild a. wandering alone; Hos 8.09
is he, humble and riding on an a., Zec 9.09
on a colt the foal of an a. 9.09
immediately you will find an a. tied, Mt 21.02
you, humble, and mounted on an a., 21.05
and on a colt, the foal of an a. 21.05
they brought the a. and the colt, 21.07
his ox or his a. from the manger, Lk 13.15
having an a. or an ox that has 14.05
found a young a. and sat upon it; Jn 12.14
a dumb a. spoke with human voice 2Pe 2.16

ASSAIL
When evildoers a. me, uttering Ps 27.02
to a. the waste places which are Eze 38.12

ASSAILANTS
didst make my a. sink under me. 2Sa 22.40
didst make my a. sink under me. Ps 18.39
thy name we tread down our a. 44.05
have heard the doom of my evil a. 92.11

ASSAILANTS (cont.)
Let my a. be put to shame; Ps 109.28
thoughts of my a. are against me Lam 3.62

ASSAILED
the torrents of perdition a. me; 2Sa 22.05
the torrents of perdition a. me; Ps 18.04

ASSAILS
stronger than he a. him and overcomes Lk 11.22

ASSASSINS
men of the A. out into the wilderness? Ac 21.38

ASSAULT
or one kind of a. and another, Deu 17.08
and every a. shall be settled. 21.05
"Will he even a. the queen in my Est 7.08

ASSAULTED
and laid siege to it, and a. it: Jos 10.31
they laid siege to it, and a. it; 10.34
and they a. it, 10.36
turned back to Debir and a. it, 10.38

ASSAULTS
thy dread a. destroy me. Ps 88.16

ASSAY
you may know and a. their ways. Jer 6.27

ASSAYER
made you an a. and tester among my Jer 6.27

ASSEMBLE
A. and hear, O sons of Jacob, and Gen 49.02
and a. all the congregation at the Lev 8.03
and a. the whole congregation of Num 8.09
and a. the congregation, you and 20.08
A. the people, men, women, and little Deu 31.12
A. to me all the elders of your 31.28
that they should a. at Jerusalem, Ez 10.07
into my mind to a. the nobles and Neh 7.05
and will a. the outcasts of Israel, Is 11.12
together, and let the peoples a. 43.09
let them all a., let them stand 44.11
"A. yourselves and come, draw near 45.20
"A., all of you, and hear! 48.14
'A., and let us go into the fortified Jer 4.05
Go, a. all the wild beasts; 12.09
and a. you out of the countries Eze 11.17
'A. and come, gather from all sides 39.17
Nebuchadnezzar sent to a. the satraps, Dan 3.02
wage war and a. a multitude of 11.10
a. the elders; Joe 2.16
"A. yourselves upon the mountains Amo 3.09
I will a. the lame and gather those Mic 4.06
to a. kingdoms, to pour out upon Zep 3.08
when you a. as a church, I hear that 1Co 11.18
to a. them for battle on the great Rev 16.14

ASSEMBLED
Moses a. all the congregation of Ex 35.01
congregation was a. at the door of Lev 8.04
they a. the whole congregation Num 1.18
and they a. themselves together 16.03
Then Korah a. all the congregation 16.19
congregation had a. against Moses 16.42
and they a. themselves together 20.02
the people of Israel a. at Shiloh, Jos 18.01
congregation a. as one man to the Ju 20.01
and all Israel a. and mourned for 1Sa 25.01
The Philistines a., and came 28.04
and all the Bichrites a., and 2Sa 20.14
Then Solomon a. the elders of 1Ki 8.01
men of Israel a. to King Solomon 8.02
who had a. before him, were with him 8.05
he a. all the house of Judah, and 12.21
Then Jehu a. all the people, and 2Ki 10.18
So David a. all Israel from the 1Ch 13.05
And David a. all Israel at Jerusalem, 15.03
David a. all the leaders of Israel 23.02
David a. at Jerusalem all the 28.01
Then Solomon a. the elders of 2Ch 5.02
men of Israel a. before the king 5.03
who had a. before him, were before 5.06
he a. the house of Judah, and 11.01
And Judah a. to seek help from the 20.04
fourth day they a. in the Valley 20.26
Then Amaziah a. the men of Judah, 25.05
and a. them in the square on the 29.04
had the people a. in Jerusalem— 30.03
and Benjamin a. at Jerusalem Ez 10.09
of Israel were a. with fasting and Neh 9.01
the kings a., they came on together Ps 48.04
utter ruin in the a. congregation. Pro 5.14
and spoke to all the a. people, Jer 26.17
the hosts that are a. about you, Eze 38.07
Have you a. your hosts to carry off 38.13
were a. for the dedication of the Dan 3.03
Now many nations are a. against you, Mic 4.11
And when they had a. with the Mt 28.12
the elders and the scribes were a. Mk 14.53
multitudes who a. to see the sight, Lk 23.48
When you are a., and my spirit is 1Co 5.04
And they a. them at the place which Rev 16.16

ASSEMBLES
whole church a. and all speak in 1Co 14.23

ASSEMBLIES
and sabbath and the calling of a.— Is 1.13
and over her a. a cloud by day, 4.05
take no delight in your solemn a. Amo 5.21

ASSEMBLING
and a. all the chief priests and Mt 2.04
Christ and our a. to meet him, 2Th 2.01

ASSEMBLY
when the whole a. of the congregation Ex 12.06
first day you shall hold a holy a., 12.16
and on the seventh day a holy a.; 12.16
to kill this whole a. with hunger." 16.03
is hidden from the eyes of the a., Lev 4.13
the a. shall offer a young bull for 4.14
it is the sin offering for the a. 4.21
house and for all the a. of Israel. 16.17
and for all the people of the a. 16.33
it is a solemn a.; you shall 23.36
But when the a. is to be gathered Num 10.07
before all the a. of the congregation 14.05
For the a., there shall be one 15.15
congregation, chosen from the a., 16.02
yourselves above the a. of the LORD?" 16.03
perished from the midst of the a. 16.33
and ran into the midst of the a.; 16.47
cut off from the midst of the a., 19.20
you brought the a. of the LORD 20.04
presence of the a. to the door of 20.06
gathered the a. together before 20.10
not bring this a. into the land 20.12
day you shall have a solemn a.: 29.35
to all your a. at the mountain out Deu 5.22
of the fire on the day of the a. 9.10
of the fire on the day of the a.; 10.04
be a solemn a. to the LORD your 16.08
God at Horeb on the day of the a., 18.16
shall not enter the a. of the LORD. 23.01
"No bastard shall enter the a. of the 23.02
descendants shall enter the a. 23.02
or Moabite shall enter the a. 23.03
belonging to them shall enter the a. 23.03
them may enter the a. of the LORD. 23.08
the ears of all the a. of Israel: 31.30
a possession for the a. of Jacob. 33.04

ASSEMBLY (cont.)
read before all the a. of Israel, Jos 8.35
the whole a. of the people of 22.12
themselves in the a. of the people Ju 20.02
not come up in the a. to the LORD?" 21.05
camp from Jabeshgilead, to the a. 21.08
and that all this a. may know that 1Sa 17.47
and blessed all the a. of Israel, 1Ki 8.14
while all the a. of Israel stood. 8.14
presence of all the a. of Israel, 8.22
blessed all the a. of Israel with 8.55
a great a., from the entrance of 8.65
and all the a. of Israel came and 12.03
him to the a. and made him king 12.20
"Sanctify a solemn a. for Baal." 2Ki 10.20
David said to all the a. of Israel, 1Ch 13.02
All the a. agreed to do so, for the 13.04
the a. of the LORD, and in the 28.08
And David the king said to all the a., 29.01
LORD in the presence of all the a.; 29.10
Then David said to all the a., 29.20
And all the a. blessed the LORD, 29.20
and all the a. with him, went to the 2Ch 1.03
Solomon and the a. sought the LORD 1.05
and blessed all the a. of Israel, 6.03
while all the a. of Israel stood. 6.03
presence of all the a. of Israel, 6.12
presence of all the a. of Israel, 6.13
eighth day they held a solemn a.; 7.09
stood in the a. of Judah and 20.05
of Asaph, in the midst of the a. 20.14
And all the a. made a covenant with 23.03
before the princes and all the a. 28.14
brought to the king and the a., 29.23
The whole a. worshiped, and the 29.28
And the a. brought sacrifices and 29.31
which the a. brought was seventy 29.32
and all the a. in Jerusalem had 30.02
right to the king and all the a. 30.04
the second month, a very great a. 30.13
many in the a. who had not sanctified 30.17
Then the whole a. agreed together 30.23
Judah gave the a. a thousand bulls 30.24
gave the a. a thousand bulls and 30.24
The whole a. of Judah, and the 30.25
and the whole a. that came out of 30.25
The whole a. together was forty-two Ez 2.64
a very great a. of men, women, and 10.01
Then all the a. answered with a 10.12
officials stand for the whole a.; 10.14
I held a great a. against them, Neh 5.07
And all the a. said "Amen" and 5.13
The whole a. together was forty-two 7.66
brought the law before the a., 8.02
And all the a. of those who had 8.17
eighth day there was a solemn a., 8.18
should ever enter the a. of God; 13.01
I stand up in the a., and cry Job 30.28
Let the a. of the peoples be Ps 7.07
faithfulness in the a. of the holy 89.05
praise him in the a. of the elders. 107.32
praise in the a. of the faithful! 149.01
will rest in the a. of the dead. Pro 21.16
wickedness will be exposed in the a. 26.26
endure iniquity and solemn a. Is 1.13
on the mount of a. in the far 14.13
a great a., all the people who Jer 44.15
he summoned an a. against me to Lam 1.15
Sanctify a fast, call a solemn a. Joe 1.14
call a solemn a.; 2.15
line by lot in the a. of the LORD. Mic 2.05
"Hear, O tribe and a. of the city! 6.09
Come together and hold a., Zep 2.01
the a. of the elders of the people Lk 22.66
And all the a. kept silence; Ac 15.12
good to us in a. to choose men and 15.25
for the a. was in confusion, and 19.32
shall be settled in the regular a. 19.39
had said this, he dismissed the a. 19.41
and the a. was divided. 23.07
and to the a. of the first-born who Heb 12.23
fine clothing comes into your a., Jas 2.02

ASSERTED
dead, but whom Paul a. to be alive. Ac 25.19

ASSERTIONS
things about which they make a. 1Ti 1.07

ASSES
and maidservants, camels and a. Gen 24.35
and menservants, and camels and a. 30.43
a., flocks, menservants, and maidservants; 32.05
their a., and whatever was in the 34.28
he pastured the a. of Zibeon his 36.24
loaded their a. with their grain, 42.26
make slaves of us and seize our a." 43.18
he had given their a. provender, 43.24
men were sent away with their a. 44.03
ten a. loaded with the good things 45.23
and the a.: and he supplied them 47.17
the a., the camels, the herds, and Ex 9.03
oxen and of the a. and of the Num 31.28
of the a., and of the flocks, of all 31.30
sixty-one thousand a., 31.34
The a. were thirty thousand five 31.39
and thirty thousand five hundred a., 31.45
and a., with the edge of the sword. Jos 6.21
and his oxen and a. and sheep, 7.24
took worn-out sacks upon their a., 9.04
"Tell of it, you who ride on tawny a., Ju 5.10
thirty sons who rode on thirty a.; 10.04
grandsons, who rode on seventy a.; 12.14
him his servant and a couple of a. 19.03
with him a couple of saddled a., 19.10
straw and provender for our a., 19.19
house, and gave the a. provender; 19.21
best of your cattle and your a., 1Sa 8.16
Now the a. of Kish, Saul's father, 9.03
and arise, go and look for the a." 9.03
care about the a. and become 9.05
As for your a. that were lost three 9.20
'The a. which you went to seek are 10.02
care about the a. and is anxious 10.02
And he said, "To seek the a.; 10.14
plainly that the a. had been found. 10.16
a. and sheep, he put to the sword. 22.19
cakes of figs, and laid them on a. 25.18
the a., the camels, and the garments, 27.09
him, with a couple of a. saddled, 2Sa 16.01
"The a. are for the king's household 16.02
of the servants and one of the a., 2Ki 4.22
and their a., leaving the camp as 7.07
and the a. tied, and the tents as 7.10
two thousand a., and a hundred 1Ch 5.21
bringing food on a. and on camels 12.40
all the feeble among them on a., 2Ch 28.15
and their a. were six thousand Ez 2.67
and their a. six thousand seven Neh 7.69
of grain and loading them on a.; 13.15
plowing and the a. feeding beside Job 1.14
like wild a. in the desert they go 24.05
the wild a. quench their thirst. Ps 104.11
riders on a., riders on camels, let Is 21.07
their riches on the backs of a., 30.06
oxen and the a. that till the 30.24
a joy of wild a., a pasture of 32.14
The wild a. stand on the bare Jer 14.06
members were like those of a., Eze 23.20
his dwelling was with the wild a.; Dan 5.21
the a., and whatever beasts may be Zec 14.15

ASSESSED
money for which each man is a.— 2Ki 12.04

ASSESSMENT
—the money from the a. of persons— 2Ki 12.04
from every one according to his a., 23.35

ASSHUR
A., Arpachshad, Lud, and Aram. Gen 10.22
How long shall A. take you away Num 24.22
and shall afflict A. and Eber; 24.24
A., Arpachshad, Lud, Aram, Uz, Hul, 1Ch 1.17
A., and Chilmad traded with you. Eze 27.23

ASSHURIM
The sons of Dedan were A., Gen 25.03

ASSIGN
and you shall a. to their charge Num 4.27
and you shall a. by name the 4.32
For I a. to you a number of days, Eze 4.05
forty days I a. you, a day for each 4.06
you shall a. for the possession of 45.06
there you shall a. him his inheritance, 47.23

ASSIGNED
the place to which you have a. him; 1Sa 29.04
he a. Uriah to the place where he 2Sa 11.16
and a. him an allowance of food, and 1Ki 11.18
And Solomon a. seventy thousand men 2Ch 2.02
any design that may be a. him, 2.14
of them he a. to bear burdens, 2.18
when he a. to the sea its limit, so Pro 8.29
The king a. them a daily portion of Dan 1.05
of faith which God has a. him. Rom 12.03
believed, as the Lord a. to each. 1Co 3.05
life which the Lord has a. to him, 7.17

ASSIGNING
to the Levites in a. their duties. Num 8.26

ASSIGNS
the day when he a. his possessions Deu 21.16

ASSIR
A., Elkanah, and Abiasaph; Ex 6.24
son, Korah his son, A. his son, 1Ch 6.22
son, Ebiasaph his son, A. his son, 6.23
son of A., son of Ebiasaph, son of 6.37

ASSIST
shall be to a. the sons of Aaron 1Ch 23.28
to a. also with the showbread, the 23.29
And they had John to a. them. Ac 13.05
who are widows, let her a. them; 1Ti 5.16
so that it may a. those who are 5.16

ASSISTANT
and as their a. Hanan the son of Neh 13.13

ASSISTED
be a. by the men of his place with Ez 1.04

ASSISTING
were overseers a. Conaniah and 2Ch 31.13
were faithfully a. him in the 31.15

ASSOCIATE
therefore do not a. with one who Pro 20.19
is for a Jew to a. with or to Ac 10.28
be haughty, but a. with the lowly; Rom 12.16
letter not to a. with immoral men; 1Co 5.09
to you not to a. with any one who 5.11
Therefore do not a. with them, Eph 5.07

ASSOCIATED
children of Israel a. with him'; Eze 37.16
the house of Israel a. with him', 37.16
the tribes of Israel a. with him; 37.19

ASSOCIATES
rest of their a. wrote to Artaxerxes Ez 4.07
scribe, and the rest of their a., 4.09
rest of their a. who live in 4.17
Shimshai the scribe and their a., 4.23
and their a. came to them and 5.03
Shetharbozenai and his a. the 5.06
and your a. the governors who are 6.06
and their a. did with all diligence 6.13

ASSOS
to the ship, we set sail for A., Ac 20.13
And when he met us at A., 20.14

ASS'S
vine and his a. colt to the choice Gen 49.11
until an a. head was sold for 2Ki 6.25
when a wild a. colt is born a man. Job 11.12
is coming, sitting on an a. colt!" Jn 12.15

ASSUAGE
of my lips would a. your pain. Job 16.05

ASSUAGED
"If I speak, my pain is not a., Job 16.06

ASSUAGING
There is no a. your hurt, your wound Nah 3.19

ASSUMING
a. that you have heard of the Eph 3.02
a. that you have heard about him 4.21

ASSURANCE
dread, and have no a. of your life. Deu 28.66
he has given a. to all men by Ac 17.31
the full a. of hope until the end, Heb 6.11
a true heart in full a. of faith, 10.22
Now faith is the a. of things hoped 11.01

ASSURED
"Rest a., do not be afraid; Gen 43.23
Be a., an evil man will not go Pro 11.21
be a., he will not go unpunished. 16.05
I will give you a. peace in this Jer 14.13
the riches of a. understanding and Col 2.02
and fully a. in all the will of 4.12

ASSUREDLY
know a. that the LORD your God will Jos 23.13
therefore know a. that God has Ac 2.36

ASSYRIA
Hiddekel, which flows east of A. Gen 2.14
From that land he went into A., 10.11
Egypt in the direction of A.; 25.18
Pul the king of A. came against the 2Ki 15.19
man, to give to the king of A. 15.20
So the king of A. turned back, 15.20
Tiglathpileser king of A. came and 15.29
carried the people captive to A. 15.29
to Tiglathpileser king of A., 16.07
sent a present to the king of A. 16.08
And the king of A. hearkened to him 16.09
the king of A. marched up against 16.09
to meet Tiglathpileser king of A., 16.10
LORD, because of the king of A. 16.18
him came up Shalmaneser king of A.; 17.03
But the king of A. found treachery 17.04
no tribute to the king of A., 17.04
therefore the king of A. shut him up, 17.04
Then the king of A. invaded all the 17.05
the king of A. captured Samaria, 17.06
carried the Israelites away to A., 17.06
own land to A. until this day. 17.23
And the king of A. brought people 17.24
So the king of A. was told, "The 17.26
Then the king of A. commanded, 17.27
He rebelled against the king of A., 18.07
Shalmaneser king of A. came up 18.09

ASSYRIA (cont.)
The king of A. carried the Israelites 2Ki 18.11
carried the Israelites away to A., 18.11
Sennacherib king of A. came up 18.13
sent to the king of A. at Lachish, 18.14
And the king of A. required of 18.14
and gave it to the king of A. 18.16
And the king of A. sent the Tartan, 18.17
the king of A.: On what do you rest 18.19
with my master the king of A.: 18.23
of the great king, the king of A.! 18.28
into the hand of the king of A.' 18.30
for thus says the king of A.: 18.31
out of the hand of the king of A.? 18.33
the king of A. has sent to mock 19.04
of the king of A. have reviled me. 19.06
the king of A. fighting against 19.08
into the hand of the king of A. 19.10
the kings of A. have done to all 19.11
the kings of A. have laid waste the 19.17
Sennacherib king of A. I have heard. 19.20
the LORD concerning the king of A., 19.32
Then Sennacherib king of A. departed, 19.36
out of the hand of the king of A., 20.06
to the king of A. to the river 23.29
Tilgathpilneser king of A. carried 1Ch 5.06
up the spirit of Pul king of A., 5.26
of Tilgathpilneser king of A., 5.26
sent to the king of A. for help. 2Ch 28.16
Tilgathpilneser king of A. came 28.20
and gave tribute to the king of A.; 28.21
from the hand of the kings of A. 30.06
Sennacherib king of A. came and 32.01
the kings of A. come and find much 32.04
the king of A. and all the horde 32.07
After this Sennacherib king of A., 32.09
"Thus says Sennacherib king of A., 32.10
from the hand of the king of A."? 32.11
in the camp of the king of A. 32.21
Sennacherib king of A. and from the 32.22
of the army of the king of A., 33.11
Esarhaddon king of A. who brought Ez 4.02
heart of the king of A. to them, 6.22
of the kings of A. until this day. Neh 9.32
A. also has joined them; they are Ps 83.08
departed from Judah—the king of A. Is 7.17
the bee which is in the land of A. 7.18
the River—with the king of A.— 7.20
carried away before the king of A. 8.04
the king of A. and all his glory; 8.07
Ah, A., the rod of my anger, the 10.05
of the king of A. and his haughty 10.12
from A., from Egypt, from Pathros, 11.11
a highway from A. for the remnant 11.16
will be a highway from Egypt to A., 19.23
Egypt, and the Egyptian into A., 19.23
be the third with Egypt and A., 19.24
and A. the work of my hands, and 19.25
was sent by Sargon the king of A., 20.01
the king of A. lead away the 20.04
be delivered from the king of A.! 20.06
it was not A. They destined 23.13
in the land of A. and those who 27.13
Sennacherib king of A. came up 36.01
And the king of A. sent the Rabshakeh 36.02
the king of A.: On what do you rest 36.04
with my master the king of A.: 36.08
of the great king, the king of A.! 36.13
into the hand of the king of A." 36.15
for thus says the king of A.: 36.16
out of the hand of the king of A.? 36.18
the king of A. has sent to mock 37.04
of the king of A. have reviled me. 37.06
the king of A. fighting against 37.08
into the hand of the king of A. 37.10
the kings of A. have done to all 37.11
the kings of A. have laid waste all 37.18
concerning Sennacherib king of A., 37.21
the LORD concerning the king of A.: 37.33
Then Sennacherib king of A. departed, 37.37
out of the hand of the king of A., 38.06
Or what do you gain by going to A., Jer 2.18
as you were put to shame by A. 2.36
first the king of A. devoured him, 50.17
land, as I punished the king of A. 50.18
and to A., to get bread enough. Lam 5.06
the choicest men of A. all of them; Eze 23.07
"A. is there, and all her company, 32.22
his wound, then Ephraim went to A., Hos 5.13
calling to Egypt, going to A. 7.11
For they have gone up to A., 8.09
they shall eat unclean food in A. 9.03
For behold, they are going to A.; 9.06
itself shall be carried to A., 10.06
and A. shall be their king, because 11.05
and like doves from the land of A.; 11.11
they make a bargain with A., 12.01
A. shall not save us, we will not 14.03
Proclaim to the strongholds in A. Amo 3.09
rule the land of A. with the sword, Mic 5.06
from A. to Egypt, and from Egypt to 7.12
shepherds are asleep, O king of A.; Nah 3.18
against the north, and destroy A.; Zep 2.13
of Egypt, and gather them from A.; Zec 10.10
The pride of A. shall be laid low, 10.11

ASSYRIAN
that I will break the A. in my land, Is 14.25
and the A. will come into Egypt, and 19.23
"And the A. shall fall by a sword, 31.08
and the A. oppressed them for 52.04
when the A. comes into our land and Mic 5.05
us from the A. when he comes into 5.06

ASSYRIANS
thousand in the camp of the A.; 2Ki 19.35
afraid of the A. when they smite Is 10.24
Egyptians will worship with the A. 19.23
The A. will be terror-stricken at 30.31
thousand in the camp of the A.; 37.36
played the harlot also with the A., Eze 16.28
she doted on her lovers the A., 23.05
lovers, into the hands of the A., 23.09
She doted upon the A., governors 23.12
and all the A. with them, desirable 23.23

ASTONISHED
who settle in it shall be a. at it. Lev 26.32
by it will be a., and will hiss; 1Ki 9.08
every one passing by will be a., 2Ch 7.21
As many were a. at him—his appearance Is 52.14
Nebuchadnezzar was a. and rose up Dan 3.24
the crowds were a. at his teaching, Mt 7.28
synagogue, so that they were a., 13.54
heard this they were greatly a., 19.25
they were a. at his teaching. 22.33
And they were a. at his teaching, Mk 1.22
and many who heard him were a., 6.02
And they were a. beyond measure, 7.37
And they were exceedingly a., 10.26
multitude was a. at his teaching. 11.18
And when they saw him they were a.; Lk 2.48
and they were a. at his teaching, 4.32
For he was a., and all that were 5.09
And all were a. at the majesty of 9.43
The Pharisee was a. to see that he 11.38
for he was a. at the teaching of Ac 13.12
I am a. that you are so quickly Gal 1.06

ASTONISHING
and shall speak a. things against Dan 11.36

ASTONISHMENT
of a., and of hissing, as you see 2Ch 29.08
trembling and a. had come upon Mk 16.08

ASTOUNDED
tremble, and are a. at his rebuke. Job 26.11
they were a., they were in panic, Ps 48.05
be appalled and the prophets a. Jer 4.09
wonder and be a. For I am Hab 1.05
And they were utterly a., Mk 6.51
the portico called Solomon's, a. Ac 3.11

ASTRAY
enemy's ox or his ass going a., Ex 23.04
man's wife goes a. and acts Num 5.12
But if you have gone a., though 5.20
goes a. and defiles herself, 5.29
brother's ox or his sheep go a., Deu 22.01
unfaithfulness, and made Judah go a. 2Ch 21.11
They have all gone a., they are Ps 14.03
to those who go a. after false 40.04
The wicked go a. from the womb, they 58.03
Before I was afflicted I went a.; 119.67
all who go a. from thy statutes; 119.118
I have gone a. like a lost sheep; 119.176
but he who rejects reproof goes a. Pro 10.17
way of the wicked leads them a. 12.26
whoever is led a. by it is not 20.01
who lead this people lead them a., Is 9.16
of her tribes have led Egypt a. 19.13
the peoples a bridle that leads a. 30.28
a deluded mind has led him a., 44.20
and your knowledge led you a., 47.10
All we like sheep have gone a.; 53.06
Baal and led my people Israel a. Jer 23.13
lead my people a. by their lies 23.32
that you have gone a. at the cost 42.20
their shepherds have led them a., 50.06
Israel may go no more a. from me, Eze 14.11
fathers and go a. after their 20.30
going a. from me after their idols 44.10
their idols when Israel went a., 44.10
people of Israel went a. from me, 44.15
who did not go a. when the people 48.11
when the people of Israel went a., 48.11
spirit of harlotry has led them a., Hos 4.12
but their lies have led them a., Amo 2.04
the prophets who lead my people a., Mic 3.05
sheep, and one of them has gone a., Mt 18.12
in search of the one that went a.? 18.12
the ninety-nine that never went a. 18.13
"Take heed that no one leads you a. 24.04
Christ,' and they will lead many a. 24.05
will arise and lead many a. 24.11
so as to lead a., if possible, even 24.24
"Take heed that no one leads you a. Mk 13.05
and they will lead many a. 13.06
to lead a., if possible, the elect. 13.22
"Take heed that you are not led a.; Lk 21.08
"No, he is leading the people a." Jn 7.12
them, "Are you led a., you also? 7.47
you were led a. to dumb idols, 1Co 12.02
will be led a. from a sincere and 2Co 11.03
led a., slaves to various passions Tit 3.03
'They always go a. in their hearts; Heb 3.10
Forsaking the right way they have gone a.; 2Pe 2.15

ASTROLOGERS
or a. can show to the king the Dan 2.27
the Chaldeans, and the a. came in; 4.07
enchanters, the Chaldeans, and the a. 5.07
enchanters, Chaldeans, and a., 5.11

ASUNDER
wings, but shall not divide it a. Lev 1.17
the ground under them split a.; Num 16.31
tore the lion a. as one tears a Ju 14.06
I was at ease, and he broke me a.; Job 16.12
"Let us burst their bonds a., Ps 2.03
gloom, and broke their bonds a. 107.14
broken, the earth is rent a., Is 24.19
bronze and cut a. the bars of iron, 45.02
and the rocks are broken a. by him. Nah 1.06
you and will burst your bonds a." 1.13
joined together, let no man put a." Mt 19.06
together, let not man put a." Mk 10.09

ASYNCRITUS
Greet A., Phlegon, Hermes, Patrobas, Rom 16.14

ATAD
came to the threshing floor of A., Gen 50.10
on the threshing floor of A., 50.11

ATARAH
another wife, whose name was A.; 1Ch 2.26

ATAROTH
"A., Dibon, Jazer, Nimrah, Heshbon, Num 32.03
of Gad built Dibon, A., Aroer, 32.24
to Luz, it passes along to A., Jos 16.02
from Janoah to A. and to Naarah, 16.07

ATAROTHADDAR
on the east was A. as far as upper Jos 16.05
then the boundary goes down to A., 18.13

ATE
wise, she took of its fruit and a.; Gen 3.06
some to her husband, and he a. 3.06
me fruit of the tree, and I a." 3.12
"The serpent beguiled me, and I a." 3.13
them under the tree while they a. 18.08
unleavened bread, and they a. 19.03
men who were with him a. and drank, 24.54
Esau, because he a. of his game; 25.28
and he a. and drank, and rose and 25.34
a feast, and they a. and drank. 26.30
So he brought it to him, and he a.; 27.25
and I a. it all before you came, and 27.33
and they a. there by the heap. 31.46
and they a. bread and tarried all 31.54
anything but the food which he a. 39.06
and thin cows a. up the seven 41.04
and gaunt cows a. up the first 41.20
Egyptians who a. with him by 43.32
and they a. all the plants in the Ex 10.15
fleshpots and a. bread to the full 16.03
of Israel a. the manna forty years, 16.35
they a. the manna, till they came to 16.35
they beheld God, and a. and drank. 24.11
he neither a. bread nor drank water. 34.28
the fish we a. in Egypt for Num 11.05
of their gods, and the people a., 25.02
I neither a. bread nor drank water. Deu 9.09
I neither a. bread nor drank water, 9.18
and he a. the produce of the field; 32.13
who a. the fat of their sacrifices, 32.38
they a. of the produce of the land, Jos 5.11
when they a. of the produce of the 5.12
but a. of the fruit of the land of 5.12
and a. and drank and reviled Ju 9.27
and gave some to them, and they a. 14.09
so they a. and drank, and lodged 19.04
two men sat and a. and drank 19.06
So they a., both of them. 19.08
their feet, and a. and drank. 19.21
and she a. until she was satisfied, Ru 2.14
Then the woman went her way and a., 1Sa 1.18
So Saul a. with Samuel that day. 9.24
and the people a. them with the 14.32
anger and a. no food the second 20.34
and they a. Then they arose 28.25
and they gave him bread and he a., 30.11
So Mephibosheth a. at David's table, 2Sa 9.11
for he a. always at the king's table. 9.13
and he a. in his presence and drank, 11.13
set food before him, and he a. 12.20
child died, you arose and a. food." 12.21

ATE (cont.)
they a. and drank and were happy. 1Ki 4.20
and a. bread in his house, and drank 13.19
and her household a. for many days. 17.15
And he a. and drank, and lay down 19.06
and a. and drank, and went in the 19.08
gave it to the people, and they a. 19.21
And they a., and had some left, 2Ki 4.44
So we boiled my son, and a. him. 6.29
and a. and drank, and they carried 7.08
Then he went in and a. and drank; 9.34
but they a. unleavened bread among 23.09
and they a. and drank before the 1Ch 29.22
yet they a. the passover otherwise 2Ch 30.18
So the people a. the food of the 30.22
nor my brethren a. the food Neh 5.14
so they a., and were filled and 9.25
and a. bread with him in his house; Job 42.11
who a. of my bread, has lifted his Ps 41.09
Man a. of the bread of the angels; 78.25
And they a. and were well filled, 78.29
and a. up the fruit of their ground. 105.35
and a. sacrifices offered to the 106.28
All who a. of it became guilty; Jer 2.03
and I a. them, and thy words became 15.16
As they a. bread together there at 41.01
Then I a. it; and it was Eze 3.03
you a. fine flour and honey and oil. 16.13
of the rich food which the king a., Dan 1.05
the youths who a. the king's rich 1.15
and a. grass like an ox, and his 4.33
I a. no delicacies, no meat or wine 10.03
of God and a. the bread of the Mt 12.04
And they all a. and were satisfied. 14.20
And those who a. were about five 14.21
And they all a. and were satisfied; 15.37
Those who a. were four thousand men, 15.38
and a. locusts and wild honey. Mk 1.06
and a. the bread of the Presence, 2.26
And they all a. and were satisfied. 6.42
And those who a. the loaves were 6.44
his disciples a. with hands 7.02
And they a., and were satisfied; 8.08
And he a. nothing in those days; Lk 4.02
plucked and a. some ears of grain, 6.01
and took and a. the bread of the 6.04
And all a. and were satisfied. 9.17
'We a. and drank in your presence, 13.26
fed on the pods that the swine a.; 15.16
They a., they drank, they married, 17.27
They a., they drank, they bought, 17.28
and he took it and a. before them. 24.43
where they a. the bread after the Jn 6.23
but because you a. your fill of 6.26
Our fathers a. the manna in the 6.31
Your fathers a. the manna in the 6.49
such as the fathers a. and died; 6.58
'He who a. my bread has lifted his 13.18
sight and neither a. nor drank. Ac 9.09
who a. and drank with him after he 10.41
encouraged and a. some food 27.36
and all a. the same supernatural 1Co 10.03
he a. with the Gentiles; Gal 2.12
the hand of the angel and a. it; Rev 10.10

ATER
The sons of A., namely of Hezekiah, Ez 2.16
the sons of A., the sons of Talmon, 2.42
The sons of A., namely of Hezekiah, Neh 7.21
the sons of A., the sons of Talmon, 7.45
A., Hezekiah, Azzur, 10.17

ATHACH
in Hormah, in Borashan, in A., 1Sa 30.30

ATHAIAH
A. the son of Uzziah, son of Zechariah, Neh 11.04

ATHALIAH
His mother's name was A.; 2Ki 8.26
Now when A. the mother of Ahaziah 11.01
Thus she hid him from A., 11.02
while A. reigned over the land. 11.03
When A. heard the noise of the 11.13
And A. rent her clothes, and cried, 11.14
was quiet after A. had been slain 11.20
Shamsherai, Shehariah, A., 1Ch 8.26
His mother's name was A., 2Ch 22.02
Now when A. the mother of Ahaziah 22.10
hid him from A., so that she did 22.11
while A. reigned over the land. 22.12
When A. heard the noise of the 23.12
And A. rent her clothes, and cried, 23.13
after A. had been slain with the 23.21
For the sons of A., that wicked woman 24.07
of Elam, Jeshaiah the son of A., Ez 8.07

ATHARIM
Israel was coming by the way of A., Num 21.01

ATHENIANS
Now all the A. and the foreigners Ac 17.21

ATHENS
Paul brought him as far as A.; Ac 17.15
Paul was waiting for them at A., 17.16
"Men of A., I perceive that in 17.22
After this he left A. and went to 18.01
to be left behind at A. alone, 1Th 3.01

ATHLAI
Jehohanan, Hananiah, Zabbai, and A. Ez 10.28

ATHLETE
Every a. exercises self-control in 1Co 9.25
An a. is not crowned unless he 2Ti 2.05

ATONE
upon you, for which you cannot a.; Is 47.11
and to a. for inquity, to bring in Dan 9.24

ATONED
faithfulness iniquity is a. for, Pro 16.06

ATONEMENT
things with which a. was made, Ez 29.33
a bull as a sin offering for a. 29.36
when you make a. for it, and shall 29.36
you shall make a. for the altar, 29.37
Aaron shall make a. upon its horns 30.10
sin offering of a. he shall make 30.10
he shall make a. for it once in 30.10
offering to make a. for yourselves. 30.15
shall take the a. money from the 30.16
so as to make a. for yourselves." 30.16
perhaps I can make a. for your sin." 32.30
accepted for him to make a. for him. Lev 1.04
the priest shall make a. for them, 4.20
shall make a. for him for his sin, 4.26
the priest shall make a. for him, 4.31
shall make a. for him for the sin 4.35
shall make a. for him for his sin. 5.06
shall make a. for him for the sin 5.10
shall make a. for him for the sin 5.13
shall make a. for him with the ram 5.16
shall make a. for him for the 5.18
shall make a. for him before the 6.07
meeting to make a. in the holy 6.30
who makes a. with it shall have it 7.07
consecrated it, to make a. for it. 8.15
to be done to make a. for you. 8.34
and make a. for yourself and for 9.07
the people, and make a. for them; 9.07
to make a. for them before the LORD? 10.17
the LORD, and make a. for her; 12.07
shall make a. for her and she 12.08

ATONEMENT (cont.)
shall make a. for him before the Lev 14.18
to make a. for him who is to be 14.19
the priest shall make a. for him, 14.20
to make a. for him, and a tenth of 14.21
to make a. for him before the LORD. 14.29
shall make a. before the LORD for 14.31
so he shall make a. for the house, 14.53
shall make a. for him before the 15.15
shall make a. for her before the 15.30
and shall make a. for himself and 16.06
before the LORD to make a. over it, 16.10
and shall make a. for himself and 16.11
thus he shall make a. for the holy 16.16
enters to make a. in the holy 16.17
and has made a. for himself and 16.17
before the LORD and make a. for it, 16.18
and make a. for himself and for the 16.24
in to make a. in the holy place, 16.27
this day shall a. be made for you, 16.30
his father's place shall make a., 16.32
he shall make a. for the sanctuary, 16.33
he shall make a. for the tent of 16.33
he shall make a. for the priests 16.33
that a. may be made for the people 16.34
altar to make a. for your souls; 17.11
or it is the blood that makes a., 17.11
shall make a. for him with the ram 19.22
seventh month is the day of a.; 23.27
for it is a day of a., to make 23.28
to make a. for you before the LORD 23.28
on the day of a. you shall send 25.09
to the ram of a. with which Num 5.08
with which a. is made for him. 5.08
and make a. for him, because he 6.11
to make a. for the Levites. 8.12
and to make a. for the people of 8.19
and Aaron made a. for them to 8.21
shall make a. for all the congregation 15.25
shall make a. before the LORD for 15.28
unwittingly, to make a. for him; 15.28
congregation, and make a. for them; 16.46
incense, and made a. for the people. 16.47
and made a. for the people of 25.13
a sin offering, to make a. for you. 28.22
with one male goat, to make a. for you. 28.30
a sin offering, to make a. for you; 29.05
besides the sin offering of a., 29.11
to make a. for ourselves before the 31.50
and to make a. for Israel, according 1Ch 6.49
altar, to make a. for all Israel. 2Ch 29.24
offerings to make a. for Israel, Neh 10.33
the altar and make a. for it. Eze 43.20
shall they make a. for the altar 43.26
to make a. for them, says the Lord 45.15
to make a. for the house of Israel. 45.17
you shall make a. for the temple. 45.20

ATONING
made an end of a. for the holy Lev 16.20

ATROTH-SHOPHAN
A., Jazer, Jogbehah, Num 32.35

ATROTHEBETHJOAB
A., and half of the Manahathites, 1Ch 2.54

ATTACH
and you shall a. the corded chains Ex 28.14
cords you shall a. to the two 28.25
and so a. it in front to the 28.25
and a. them in front to the lower 28.27

ATTACHED
shoulder-pieces a. to its two Ex 28.07
cords they had a. to the two 39.18
thus they a. it in front to the 39.18
and a. them in front to the lower 39.20

valiant man, he a. him to himself. 1Sa 14.52
which were a. to the throne, and on 2Ch 9.18
Then they a. themselves to the Baal Ps 106.28

ATTACK
themselves against me and a. me, Gen 34.30
in an a. of leprosy, to be very Deu 24.08
three thousand men go up and a. Ai; Jos 7.03
the East would come up and a. them; Ju 6.03
Philistines drew near to a. Israel; 1Sa 7.10
"Shall I go and a. these Philistines?" 23.02
"Go and a. the Philistines and save 23.02
and did not permit them to a. Saul. 24.07
water shaft to a. the lame and the 2Sa 5.08
strengthen your a. upon the city, 11.25
of the people fall at the first a., 17.09
or province that might a. them, Est 8.11
me, those who a. me with lies. Ps 69.04
and a. me without cause. 109.03
up, and let us a. at noon!" Jer 6.04
and let us a. by night, and destroy 6.05
the king of the south shall a. him; Dan 11.40
them underfoot and turn to a. you. Mt 7.06
no man shall a. you to harm you; Ac 18.10
made a united a. upon Paul and 18.12

ATTACKED
The archers fiercely a. him, Gen 49.23
how he a. you on the way, when you Deu 25.18
and Jogbehah, and a. the army; Ju 8.11
and a. the Philistine and killed 2Sa 21.17
he a. and slew with the sword two 1Ki 2.32
Israelites rose and a. the Moabites, 2Ki 3.24
and a. and killed Gedaliah and the 25.25
appointed a worm which a. the plant, Jon 4.07
and a. the house of Jason, seeking Ac 17.05

ATTACKING
that of a man a. and murdering his Deu 22.26
the king of Israel, who are a. me." 2Ki 16.07
refrain from a. the king of the Dan 11.08
The crowd joined in a. them; Ac 16.22

ATTACKS
a man willfully a. another to kill Ex 21.14
and a. him, and wounds him mortally Deu 19.11
"He who a. Kiriathsepher and takes Ju 1.12

ATTAI
his slave; and she bore him A. 1Ch 2.35
A. was the father of Nathan and 2.36
A. sixth, Eliel seventh, 12.11
Abijah, A., Ziza, and Shelomith 2Ch 11.20

ATTAIN
but he did not a. to the three. 2Sa 23.19
but he did not a. to the three. And 23.23
but he did not a. to the three. 1Ch 11.21
but he did not a. to the three. And 11.25
it is high, I cannot a. it. Ps 139.6
worthy to a. to that age and to Lk 20.35
which our twelve tribes hope to a., Ac 26.07
until we all a. to the unity of the Eph 4.13
possible I may a. the resurrection Php 3.11

ATTAINABLE
had been a. through the Levitical Heb 7.11

ATTAINED
they have not a. to the days of Gen 47.09
pursue righteousness have a. it, Rom 9.30
us hold true to what we have a. Php 3.16

ATTALIA
in Perga, they went down to A.; Ac 14.25

ATTEMPT
When an a. was made by both Gentiles Ac 14.05

ATTEMPTED
any god ever a. to go and take a Deu 4.34
to Jerusalem he a. to join the Ac 9.26
they a. to go into Bithynia, but the 16.07
when they a. to do the same, were Heb 11.29

ATTEND
names of the men who shall a. you. Num 1.05
and a. to the duties for the people 3.08
and they shall a. to their priesthood 3.10
the Levites to a. Aaron and his 8.13
They shall a. you and a. to all 18.03
and a. to all duties of the tent 18.03
and a. to the tent of meeting, for 18.04
And you shall a. to the duties of 18.05
with you shall a. to your priesthood 18.07
and shall a. the sons of Aaron, 1Ch 23.32
had set apart to a. the Levites. Ez 8.20
who had been appointed to a. her, Est 4.05
a. to my cry! Give ear Ps 17.01
A. to me, and answer me; I am 55.02
will a. and listen for the time to Is 42.23
I will a. to you for your evil Jer 23.02
and they shall a. on the people, Eze 44.11
and they shall a. on me to offer me 44.15
Till I come, a. to the public 1Ti 4.13

ATTENDANCE
of meeting in a. upon Aaron and Num 8.22
and the a. of his servants, their 1Ki 10.05
and the a. of his servants, and 2Ch 9.04
of the eunuchs in a. on the king, Est 7.09

ATTENDANT
it back to the a., and sat down; Lk 4.20

ATTENDANTS
And all his a. went out from his Ju 3.19
and her a., her child, and he who Dan 11.06
Then the king said to the a., Mt 22.13

ATTENDED
favor in his sight and a. him, Gen 39.04
ass, and her five maidens a. her; 1Sa 25.42
son of Hachmoni a. the king's sons. 1Ch 27.32
who a. Ahaziah, and he killed them. 2Ch 22.08
king's servants who a. him said, Est 2.02
king's servants who a. him said, 6.03
away, and you have not a. to them. Jer 23.02
the Spirit be a. with greater 2Co 3.08

ATTENDING
a. to the duties of the sanctuary. Num 3.28
death the women a. her said to her, 1Sa 4.20
a. the temple together and breaking Ac 2.46
be prevented from a. to his needs. 24.23
a. to this very thing. Rom 13.06

ATTENTION
yet God pays no a. to their prayer. Job 24.12
I gave you my a., and, behold, there 32.12
O foolish men, pay a. Pro 8.05
flocks, and give a. to your herds; 27.23
the day when I give a. to them, Jer 27.22
and he fixed his a. upon them, Ac 3.05
But Gallio paid no a. to this. 18.17
paid more a. to the captain and to 27.11
pay the closer a. to what we have Heb 2.01
and you pay a. to the one who wears Jas 2.03
do well to pay a. to this as to a 2Pe 1.19

ATTENTIVE
and thy ears a. to a prayer of 2Ch 6.40
and my ears a. to the prayer that 7.15
let thy ear be a., and thy eyes Neh 1.06
let thy ear be a. to the prayer of 1.11
the people were a. to the book of 8.03
Let thy ears be a. to the voice of Ps 130.02
making your ear a. to wisdom and Pro 2.02
and be a., that you may gain 4.01
My son, be a. to my words; incline 4.20
My son, be a. to my wisdom, incline 5.01
and be a. to the words of my mouth. 7.24

ATTENTIVELY
"But if you harken a. to his voice Ex 23.22

ATTEST
son of Jeberechiah, to a. for me. Is 8.02

ATTESTED
a man a. to you by God with mighty Ac 2.22
must be well a. for her good deeds, 1Ti 5.10
and it was a. to us by those who Heb 2.03
taken he was a. as having pleased 11.05
though well a. by their faith, did 11.39

ATTESTING
was the manner of a. in Israel. Ru 4.07

ATTIRE
her ornaments, or a bride her a.? Jer 2.32
who array themselves in a foreign a. Zep 1.08
or gold or pearls or costly a. 1Ti 2.09

AUDIENCE
entered the a. hall with the Ac 25.23

AUGMENTS
He who a. his wealth by interest Pro 28.08

AUGUR
or an a., or a sorcerer, Deu 18.10

AUGURY
not practice a. or witchcraft. Lev 19.26
and practiced soothsaying and a., 2Ki 21.06
soothsaying and a. and sorcery, 2Ch 33.06

AUGUSTAN
to a centurion of the A. Cohort, Ac 27.01

AUGUSTUS
from Caesar A. that all the world Lk 2.01

AUNT
his wife; she is your a. Lev 18.14

AUTHOR
and killed the A. of life, whom God Ac 3.15

AUTHORITIES
synagogues and the rulers and the a., Lk 12.11
it be that the a. really know that Jn 7.26
Have any of the a. or of the 7.48
even of the a. believed in him, but 12.42
of the brethren before the city a., Ac 17.06
and the city a. were disturbed 17.08
be subject to the governing a. Rom 13.01
who resists the a. resists what 13.02
for the a. are ministers of God, 13.06
dominions or principalities or a.— Col 1.16
to be submissive to rulers and a., Tit 3.01
a., and powers subject to him. 1Pe 3.22

AUTHORITY
grain under the a. of Pharaoh for Gen 41.35
you were under your husband's a., Num 5.19
you are under your husband's a., 5.20
though under her husband's a., 5.29
invest him with some of your a., 27.20
who exercised a. over the people. 2Ch 8.10
Elkanah the next in a. to the king. 28.07
the Jew gave full written a., Est 9.29
When the righteous are in a., Pro 29.02
When the wicked are in a., 29.16
or a. over the day of death; Ecc 8.08

AUTHORITY (cont.)
will commit your a. to his hand; Is 22.21
for he taught them as one who had a., Mt 7.29
For I am a man under a., 8.09
Son of man has a. on earth to 9.06
God, who had given such a. to men. 9.08
and gave them a. over unclean 10.01
great men exercise a. over them. 20.25
"By what a. are you doing these 21.23
things, and who gave you this?" 21.23
you by what a. I do these things. 21.24
you by what a. I do these things. 21.27
"All a. in heaven and on earth has 28.18
he taught them as one who had a.. Mk 1.22
With a. he commands even the 1.27
Son of man has a. on earth to 2.10
and have a. to cast out demons: 3.15
and gave them a. over the unclean 6.07
great men exercise a. over them. 10.42
"By what a. are you doing these 11.28
or who gave you this a. to do them?" 11.28
you by what a. I do these things. 11.29
you by what a. I do these things." 11.33
give all this a. and their glory; Lk 4.06
teaching, for his word was with a. 4.32
For with a. and power he commands 4.36
Son of man has a. on earth to 5.24
For I am a man set under a., 7.08
them power and a. over all demons 9.01
have given you a. to tread upon 10.19
you shall have a. over ten cities.' 19.17
"Tell us by what a. you do these 20.02
or who it is that gave you this a." 20.02
you by what a. I do these things." 20.08
him up to the a. and jurisdiction 20.20
and those in a. over them are 22.25
and has given him a. to execute Jn 5.27
"I can do nothing on my own a.; 5.30
whether I am speaking on my own a. 7.17
on his own a. seeks his own glory; 7.18
on my own a. but speak thus as the 8.28
For I have not spoken on my own a.; 12.49
to you I do not speak on my own a.; 14.10
he will not speak on his own a., 16.13
the Father has fixed by his own a. Ac 1.07
and here he had a. from the chief 9.14
"let the men of a. among you go 25.05
by a. from the chief priests, but 26.10
with the a. and commission of the 26.12
For there is no a. except from God, Rom 13.01
have no fear of him who is in a.? 13.03
Do I say this on human a.? 1 Co 9.08
every rule and every a. and power. 15.24
boast a little too much of our a., 2Co 10.08
with the Lord's a. but as a fool, 11.17
my use of the a. which the Lord 13.10
all rule and a. and power and Eph 1.21
who is the head of all rule and a. Col 2.10
to teach or to have a. over men; 1Ti 2.12
exhort and reprove with all a. Tit 2.15
of defiling passion and despise a. 2Pe 2.10
first, does not acknowledge my a. 3Jn 1.09
reject a., and revile the glorious Jud 1.08
and a., before all time and now and 1.25
our God and the a. of his Christ Rev 12.10
power and his throne and great a. 13.02
he had given his a. to the beast, 13.04
to exercise a. for forty-two 13.05
And a. was given it over every 13.07
exercises all the a. of the first 13.12
are to receive a. as kings for one 17.12
their power and a. to the beast; 17.13
down from heaven, having great a.; 18.01

AUTUMN
as I was in my a. days, when the Job 29.04
The sluggard does not plow in the a.; Pro 20.04
the a. rain and the spring rain, and Jer 5.24
fruitless trees in late a., Jud 1.12

AVAIL
whether Mordecai's words would a.; Est 3.04
Will your cry a. to keep you from Job 36.19
sword reaches him, it does not a.; 41.26
silent, I held my peace to no a.; Ps 39.02
can a. against the LORD. Pro 21.30
trust in deceptive words to no a. Jer 7.08
at the same table, but to no a.; Dan 11.27
gives life, the flesh is of no a.; Jn 6.63
a. yourself of the opportunity. 1Co 7.21
nor uncircumcision is of any a., Gal 5.06

AVEN
The high places of A., the sin of Hos 10.08
inhabitants from the Valley of A., Amo 1.05

AVENGE
"A. the people of Israel on the Num 31.02
you, may the LORD a. me upon you; 1Sa 24.12
that I may a. on Jezebel the blood 2Ki 9.07
he said, "May the LORD see and a.!" 2Ch 24.22
on that day to a. themselves upon Est 8.13
and a. myself on my foes. Is 1.24
and shall I not a. myself on a Jer 5.09
and shall I not a. myself on a 5.29
and shall I not a. myself on a 9.09
to a. himself on his foes. 46.10
I will a. their blood, and I will Joe 3.21
Beloved, never a. yourselves, but Rom 12.19
wilt judge and a. our blood on Rev 6.10

AVENGED
If Cain is a. sevenfold, truly Gen 4.24
the LORD has a. you on your Ju 11.36
do, I swear I will be a. upon you, 15.07
that I may be a. upon the Philistines 16.28
evening and I am a. on my enemies." 1Sa 14.24
that he may be a. of the king's 18.25
LORD who has a. the insult I 25.39
the LORD has a. my lord the king 2Sa 4.08
the LORD has a. upon you all the 16.08
oppressed man and a. him by striking Ac 7.24
and he has a. on her the blood of Rev 19.02

AVENGER
be for you a refuge from the a., Num 35.12
The a. of blood shall himself put 35.19
the a. of blood shall put the 35.21
the manslayer and the a. of blood, 35.24
from the hand of the a. of blood, 35.25
and the a. of blood finds him 35.27
and the a. of blood slays the 35.27
lest the a. of blood in hot anger Deu 19.06
hand him over to the a. of blood, 19.12
you a refuge from the a. of blood. Jos 20.03
And if the a. of blood pursues him, 20.05
die by the hand of the a. of blood, 20.09
that the a. of blood slay no more, 2Sa 14.11
to still the enemy and the a. Ps 8.02
the sight of the enemy and the a. 44.16
but an a. of their wrongdoings. 99.08
the Lord is an a. in all these 1Th 4.06

AVENGES
for he a. the blood of his servants, Deu 32.43
For he who a. blood is mindful of Ps 9.12

AVENGING
and from a. myself with my own 1Sa 25.33
a. in the time of peace blood which had 1Ki 2.05
Let the a. of the outpoured blood Ps 79.10
The LORD is a jealous God and a., Nah 1.02
the LORD is a. and wrathful; 1.02

AVERT
with tears to a. the evil design Est 8.03
and sacrificial flesh a. your doom? Jer 11.15

AVERTED
plague may be a. from the people." 2Sa 24.21
and the plague was a. from Israel. 24.25
plague may be a. from the people." 1Ch 21.22
God over this matter be a. from us." Ez 10.14

AVERTS
A gift in secret a. anger; Pro 21.14

AVITH
the name of his city being A. Gen 36.35
and the name of his city was A. 1Ch 1.46

AVOID
A. it; do not go on it; Pro 4.15
that one may a. the snares of death. 13.14
that one may a. the snares of death. 14.27
life, that he may a. Sheol beneath. 15.24
not only to a. God's wrath but also Rom 13.05
you have been taught; a. them. 16.17
A. the godless chatter and contradictions 1Ti 6.20
the Lord to a. disputing about 2Ti 2.14
A. such godless chatter, for it will 2.16
power of it. A. such people. 3.05
to a. quarreling, to be gentle, and Tit 3.02
But a. stupid controversies, genealogies, 3.09

AVOIDED
and whom they a. and did not 2Ch 20.10
thy lips I have a. the ways of the Ps 17.04

AVOIDS
the fear of the LORD a man a. evil. Pro 16.06

AVVA
A., Hamath and Sepharvaim, and 2Ki 17.24

AVVIM
As for the A., who lived in villages Deu 2.23
and Ekron), and those of the A., Jos 13.03
A., Parah, Ophrah, 18.23

AVVITES
and the A. made Nibhaz and Tartak; 2Ki 17.31

AWAIT
imprisonment and afflictions a. me. Ac 20.23
heaven, and from it we a. a Savior, Php 3.20

AWAITING
you have sat a. lovers like an Jer 3.02
a. our blessed hope, the appearing Tit 2.13

AWAITS
For still the vision a. its time; Hab 2.03

AWAKE
"A., a., Deborah! Ju 5.12
A., a., utter a song! Arise, Barak, 5.12
saw it, or knew it, nor did any a.; 1Sa 26.12
heavens are no more he will not a., Job 14.12
a., O my God; thou hast Ps 7.06
when I a., I shall be satisfied 17.15
and a. for my right, for my cause, my 35.23
A.! Do not cast us off 44.23
A., my soul! A., O harp and lyre! 57.08
I will a. the dawn! 57.08
A. to punish all the nations; 59.05
I lie a., I am like a lonely bird 102.07
I will sing praises! A., my soul! 108.01
A., O harp and lyre! 108.02
I will a. the dawn! 108.02
My eyes are a. before the watches 119.148
the watchman stays a. in vain. 127.01
When I a., I am still with thee. 139.18
and when you a., they will talk Pro 6.22
When shall I a.? I will seek 23.35
A., O north wind, and come, O south Sol 4.16
I slept, but my heart was a. 5.02
a. and sing for joy! For thy dew Is 26.19
A., a., put on strength, O arm of 51.09
a., as in days of old, the generations 51.09
A., a., put on your strength, O 52.01
in the dust of the earth shall a., Dan 12.02
A., you drunkards, and weep; Joe 1.05
and those a. who will make you Hab 2.07
him who says to a wooden thing, A.; 2.19
"A., O sword, against my shepherd, Zec 13.07
were heavy with sleep but kept a., Lk 9.32
the master finds a. when he comes; 12.37
would have been a. and would not 12.39
but I go to a. him out of sleep." Jn 11.11
"A., O sleeper, and arise from the Eph 5.14
but let us keep a. and be sober. 1Th 5.06
A., and strengthen what remains and Rev 3.02
If you will not a., I will come 3.03
Blessed is he who is a., keeping 16.15

AWAKED
and told him, "The child has not a." 2 Ki 4.31

AWAKEN
stir not up nor a. love until it Sol 2.07
stir not up nor a. love until it 3.05
stir not up nor a. love until it 8.04

AWAKENED
he is asleep and must be a." 1Ki 18.27
Under the apple tree I a. you. Sol 8.05
it has a. against you. Eze 7.06

AWAKES
They are like a dream when one a., Ps 73.20
is eating and a. with his hunger Is 29.08
dreams he is drinking and a. a faint, 29.08

AWAKING
on a. you despise their phantoms. Ps 73.20

AWARD
will a. to me on that Day, and not 2Ti 4.08

AWARE
Before I was a., my fancy set me in Sol 6.12
Jesus, a. of this, withdrew from Mt 12.15
But Jesus, a. of this, said, "O men of 16.08
But Jesus, a. of their malice, said, 22.18
But Jesus, a. of this, said to them, 26.10
And being a. of it, Jesus said to Mk 8.17
I am not a. of anything against 1Co 4.04
You are a. that all who are in Asia 2Ti 1.15

AWAY
me this day a. from the ground; Gen 4.14
Then Cain went a. from the presence 4.16
their faces were turned a., 9.23
the carcasses, Abram drove them a. 15.11
with the child, and sent her a. 21.14
So they sent a. Rebekah their 24.59
he sent them a. from his son Isaac, 25.06
said to Isaac, "Go a. from us; 26.16
me and have sent me a. from you?" 26.27
good and have sent you a. in peace. 26.29
and he has taken a. your blessing." 27.35
He took a. my birthright; 27.36
now he has taken a. my blessing." 27.36
a. from the fatness of the earth 27.39
and a. from the dew of heaven on 27.39
until your brother's fury turns a.; 27.44
until your brother's anger turns a., 27.45
Thus Isaac sent Jacob a.; 28.05
and sent him a. to Paddan-aram to 28.06
that you have taken a. my husband? 30.15

AWAY (cont.)

Would you take a. my son's mandrakes **Gen** 30.15
"God has taken a. my reproach"; 30.23
"Send me a., that I may go to my 30.25
Thus God has taken a. the cattle of 31.09
God has taken a. from our father 31.16
and he drove a. all his cattle, all 31.18
and carried a. my daughters like 31.26
have sent you a. with mirth and 31.27
you have gone a. because you 31.30
would have sent me a. empty-handed. 31.42
of Shechem's house, and went a. 34.26
"Put a. the foreign gods that are 35.02
into a land a. from his brother 36.06
And the man said, "They have gone a., 37.17
Then she arose and went a., 38.19
Then he turned a. from them and 42.24
men were sent a. with their asses. 44.03
Then he sent his brothers a., 45.24
said to her, "Take this child a., **Ex** 2.09
The shepherds came and drove them a.; 2.17
take the people a. from their work? 5.04
LORD to take a. the frogs from me 8.08
only you shall not go very far a. 8.28
said to him, "Get a. from me; 10.28
he will drive you a. completely. 11.01
you shall put a. leaven out of 12.15
have taken us a. to die in the 14.11
inhabitants of Canaan have melted a. 15.15
wife, after he had sent her a., 18.02
it dies or is hurt or is driven a., 22.10
take sickness a. from the midst of 23.25
then I will take a. my hand, 33.23
and he shall take a. its crop with **Lev** 1.16
he shall take a. with the kidneys. 3.04
taking it a. close by the backbone, 3.09
he shall take a. with the kidneys. 3.10
he shall take a. with the kidneys. 3.15
he shall take a. with the kidneys 4.09
he shall take a. with the kidneys; 7.04
it may be sent a. into the wilderness 16.10
and send him a. into the wilderness 16.21
sons to keep a. from the holy 22.02
the eyes and cause life to pine a. 26.16
left shall pine a. in your enemies' 26.39
they shall pine a. like them. 26.39
And they shall take a. the ashes **Num** 4.13
your thigh fall a. and your body 5.21
body swell and your thigh fall a. 5.22
swell, and her thigh shall fall a., 5.27
Get a. from about the dwelling of 16.24
you be swept a. with all their 16.26
So they got a. from about the 16.27
"Get a. from the midst of this 16.45
so Israel turned a. from him. 20.21
that he take a. the serpents from 21.07
shall Asshur take you a. captive?" 24.22
the LORD may turn a. from Israel." 25.04
father be taken a. from his family, 27.04
For if you turn a. from following 32.15
will be taken a. from the lot of 36.03
So we went on, a. from our brethren **Deu** 2.08
a. from the Arabah road from Elath 2.08
you be drawn a. and worship them 4.19
and clears a. many nations before 7.01
For they would turn a. your sons 7.04
LORD will take a. from you all 7.15
God will clear a. these nations 7.22
to draw you a. from the LORD your 13.10
and have drawn a. the inhabitants 13.13
himself, lest his heart turn a.; 17.17
he may not put her a. all his days. 22.19
he may not put her a. all his days. 22.29
among you, and turn a. from you. 23.14
who sent her a., may not take her 24.04
shall be none to frighten them a. 28.26
violently taken a. before your 28.31
where the LORD will lead you a. 28.37
heart turns a. this day from the 29.18
to the sweeping a. of moist and 29.19
But if your heart turns a., 30.17
but are drawn a. to worship other 30.17
of the land melt a. before you. **Jos** 2.09
Then she sent them a., 2.21
I have rolled a. the reproach of 5.09
until you take a. the devoted 7.13
have drawn them a. from the city; 8.06
they were drawn a. from the city. 8.16
blessed them, and sent them a.; 22.06
sent them a. to their homes and 22.07
in turning a. this day from 22.16
that you must turn a. this day from 22.18
altar to turn a. from following 22.23
and turn a. this day from following 22.29
put a. the gods which your fathers 24.14
"Then put a. the foreign gods which 24.23
So Joshua sent the people a., 24.28
he sent a. the people that carried **Ju** 3.18
his tent as far a. as the oak in 4.11
his chariot and fled a. on foot. 4.15
But Sisera fled a. on foot to the 4.17
lead a. your captives, O son of 5.12
The torrent Kishon swept them a., 5.21
And Jotham ran a. and fled, and went 9.21
So they put a. the foreign gods 10.16
coming from Egypt took a. my land, 11.13
did not take a. the land of Moab 11.15
And he sent her a. for two months; 11.38
he threw a. the jawbone out of his 15.17
and pulled a. the pin, the loom, and 16.14
and go a., and what have I left? 18.24
and she went a. from him to her 19.02
rose up and went a. to his home. 19.28
and put a. evil from Israel." 20.13
and were drawn a. from the city; 20.31
and draw them a. from the city to 20.32
I went a. full, and the LORD has **Ru** 1.21
Put a. your wine from you." **1Sa** 1.14
"Send a. the ark of the God of 5.11
"If you send a. the ark of the God 6.03
his hand does not turn a. from you." 6.03
their calves home, a. from them. 6.07
to whom shall he go up a. from us?" 6.20
then put a. the foreign gods and 7.03
So Israel put a. the Baals and the 7.04
Then Samuel sent all the people a., 10.25
LORD will not cast a. his people, 12.22
do wickedly, you shall be swept a., 12.25
As Samuel turned to go a., 15.27
and takes a. the reproach from 17.26
And he turned a. from him toward 17.30
and he fled a. and escaped. 19.12
and send you a., that you may go in 20.13
for the LORD has sent you a. 20.22
let me get a., and see my brothers.' 20.29
bread on the day it is taken a. 21.06
and brought a. their cattle, and 23.05
making haste to get a. from Saul, 23.26
enemy, will he let him go a. safe? 24.19
are breaking a. from their masters. 25.10
So David's young men turned a., 25.12
and they went a. No man saw it, 26.12
to the earth a. from the presence 26.20
but took a. the sheep, the oxen, the 27.09
God has turned a. from me and 28.15
they rose and went a. that night. 28.25
man may lead a. his wife and 30.22
So David sent Abner a.; and he went **2Sa** 3.21
at Hebron, for he had sent him a., 3.22
is it that you have sent him a., 3.24
David and his men carried them a. 5.21
whom I put a. from before you. 7.15
at their hips, and sent them a. 10.04
"The LORD also has put a. your sin; 12.13

AWAY (cont.)

in sending me a. is greater than 2Sa 13.16
and went a., crying aloud as she 13.19
will not take a. the life of him 14.14
so both of them went a. quickly, 17.18
the men of Judah stolen you a., 19.41
all like thorns that are thrown a.; 23.06
take a. the iniquity of thy servant 24.10
and thus take a. from me and from 1Ki 2.31
Shimei's slaves ran a. to Achish, 2.39
are carried a. captive to the land 8.46
eighth day he sent the people a.; 8.66
they will turn a. your heart after 11.02
and his wives turned a. his heart. 11.03
wives turned a. his heart after 11.04
heart had turned a. from the LORD, 11.09
However I will not tear a. all the 11.13
So the people went a. 12.05
And as he went a. a lion met him on 13.24
the kingdom a. from the house of 14.08
he took a. the treasures of the 14.26
he took a. everything. He also 14.26
He also took a. all the shields of 14.26
He put a. the male cult prostitutes 15.12
But the high places were not taken a. 15.14
they carried a. the stones of 15.22
utterly sweep a. Baasha and his 16.03
now, O LORD, take a. my life; 19.04
they seek my life, to take it a." 19.10
they seek my life, to take it a." 19.14
pleases them, and take it a.' " 20.06
take the bandage a. from his eyes; 20.41
and turned a. his face, and would 21.04
I will utterly sweep you a., 21.21
the high places were not taken a., 22.43
LORD will take a. your master from 2Ki 2.03
LORD will take a. your master from 2.05
for he put a. the pillar of Baal 3.02
And Gehazi came to thrust her a. 4.27
and went a., saying, "Behold, I 5.11
So he turned and went a. in a rage. 5.12
and he sent the men a., 5.24
he sent them a., and they went to 6.23
So they fled a. in the twilight and 7.07
had thrown a. in their haste. 7.15
and stole him a. from among the 11.02
Nevertheless the high places were not taken a.; 12.03
Then Hazael went a. from Jerusalem. 12.18
Nevertheless the high places were not taken a.; 15.04
he did not turn a. from the sins of 15.24
the Israelites a. to Assyria, 17.06
the LORD carried a. before them. 17.11
have carried a. and placed in the 17.26
priests whom you carried a. thence; 17.27
had carried a. from Samaria came 17.28
whom they had been carried a. 17.33
the Israelites a. to Assyria, 18.11
and take you a. to a land like 18.32
are born to you, shall be taken a.; 20.18
Moreover Josiah put a. the mediums 23.24
But he took Jehoahaz a.; 23.34
He carried a. all Jerusalem, and all 24.14
And he carried a. Jehoiachin to 24.15
And they took a. the pots, and the 25.14
of the guard took a. as gold, 25.15
of Assyria carried a. into exile; 1Ch 5.06
of Assyria, and he carried them a., 5.26
he had sent a. Hushim and Baara 8.08
and took a. the body of Saul and 10.12
took counsel and sent him a., 12.19
at their hips, and sent them a.; 19.04
take a. the inquity of thy servant 21.08
are carried a. captive to a land 2Ch 6.36
do not turn a. the face of thy 6.42
sent the people a. to their homes, 7.10
So the people went a. 10.05
he took a. the treasures of the 12.09
he took a. everything. 12.09
He also took a. the shields of gold 12.09
He took a. the foreign altars and 14.03
Judah carried a. very much booty. 14.13
and carried a. sheep in abundance 14.15
and put a. the abominable idols 15.08
they carried a. the stones of 16.06
God drew them a. from him, 18.31
places, however, were not taken a.; 20.33
and carried a. all the possessions 21.17
and stole him a. from among the 22.11
when he turned a. from the LORD 25.27
Judah, and carried a. captives. 28.17
and have turned a. their faces 29.06
fierce anger may turn a. from us. 29.10
fierce anger may turn a. from you. 30.08
will not turn a. his face from you, 30.09
they took a. and threw into the 30.14
Hezekiah taken a. his high places 32.12
And he took a. the foreign gods and 33.15
And Josiah took a. all the abominations 34.33
did not turn a. from following the 34.33
Nevertheless Josiah would not turn a. from him, 35.22
"Take me a., for I am badly wounded." 35.23
had carried a. from Jerusalem and Ez 1.07
and carried a. the people to 5.12
province Beyond the River, keep a.; 6.06
our God to put a. all these wives 10.03
themselves to put a. their wives, 10.19
they put them a. with their 10.44
been carried a. from Jerusalem Est 2.06
captives carried a. with Jeconiah 2.06
king of Babylon had carried a. 2.06
Mordecai then went a. and did 4.17
God, and turned a. from evil. Job 1.01
fears God and turns a. from evil?" 1.08
gave, and the LORD has taken a.; 1.21
fears God and turns a. from evil? 2.03
torrent-bed, as freshets that pass a., 6.15
long wilt thou not look a. from me, 7.19
transgression and take a. my iniquity? 7.21
Behold, he snatches a.; 9.12
they flee a., they see no good. 9.25
Let him take his rod a. from me, 9.34
put it far a., and let not wickedness 11.14
it as waters that have passed a. 11.16
He leads counselors a. stripped, 12.17
He leads priests a. stripped, 12.19
and takes a. the discernment of the 12.20
enlarges nations, and leads them a. 12.23
He takes a. understanding from the 12.24
Man wastes a. like a rotten thing, 13.28
look a. from him, and desist, that he 14.06
a river wastes a. and dries up, 14.11
the mountain falls and crumbles a., 14.18
the waters wear a. the stones; 14.19
torrents wash a. the soil of the 14.19
countenance, and sendest him a. 14.20
But you are doing a. with the fear 15.04
Why does your heart carry you a., 15.12
will be swept a. by the wind. 15.30
He will fly a. like a dream, and not 20.08
will be chased a. like a vision of 20.08
of his house will be carried a., 20.28
chaff that the storm carries a.? 21.18
You have sent widows a. empty, 22.09
They were snatched a. before their 22.16
their foundation was washed a. 22.16
They drive a. the ass of the 24.03
swiftly carried a. upon the face 24.18
Drought and heat snatch a. the snow 24.19
who has taken a. my right, and the 27.02
I will not put a. my integrity 27.05
off, when God takes a. his life? 27.08
in a valley a. from where men live; 28.04
prosperity has passed a. like a cloud. 30.15
is so wasted a. that it cannot be 33.21

AWAY (cont.)

and God has taken a. my right; Job 34.05
the people are shaken and pass a., 34.20
are taken a. by no human hand. 34.20
chaff which the wind drives a. Ps 1.04
My eye wastes a. because of grief, 6.07
dragging me a., with none to rescue 7.02
statutes I did not put a. from me. 18.22
Sweep me not a. with sinners, nor my 26.09
Turn not thy servant a. in anger, 27.09
my misery, and my bones waste a. 31.10
my body wasted a. through my 32.03
the hand of the wicked drive me a. 36.11
vanish—like smoke they vanish a. 37.20
Look a. from me, that I may know 39.13
who seek to snatch a. my life; 40.14
and their form shall waste a.; 49.14
he dies he will carry nothing a.; 49.17
Cast me not a. from thy presence, 51.11
They have all fallen a.; 53.03
I would fly a. and be at rest; 55.06
let them go a. in terror into their 55.15
vanish like water that runs a.; 58.07
or ablaze, may he sweep them a.! 58.09
As smoke is driven a., so 68.02
so drive them a.; as wax melts 68.02
swept a. utterly by terrors! 73.19
but turned a. and acted treacherously 78.57
and put a. thy indignation toward 85.04
Thou dost sweep men a.; 90.05
our days pass a. under thy wrath, 90.09
they are soon gone, and we fly a. 90.10
hate the work of those who fall a.; 101.03
For my days pass a. like smoke, 102.03
hast taken me up and thrown me a. 102.10
I wither a. like grass. 102.11
like raiment, and they pass a.; 102.26
they get them a. and lie down in 104.22
when thou takest a. their breath, 104.29
to turn a. his wrath from destroying 106.23
courage melted a. in their evil 107.26
he gnashes his teeth and melts a.; 112.10
take a. from me their scorn and 119.22
My soul melts a. for sorrow; 119.28
Turn a. the reproach which I dread; 119.39
but I do not turn a. from thy law. 119.51
then the flood would have swept us a., 124.04
LORD will lead a. with evildoers! 125.05
do not turn a. the face of thy 132.10
it takes a. the life of its possessors Pro 1.19
are killed by their turning a., 1.32
the LORD, and turn a. from evil. 3.07
and do not turn a. from the words 4.05
turn a. from it and pass on. 4.15
Put a. from you crooked speech, and 4.24
turn your foot a. from evil. 4.27
his disgrace will not be wiped a. 6.33
but lawlessness takes a. lives. 11.30
A righteous man turns a. from evil, 12.26
but to turn a. from evil is an 13.19
but it is swept a. through injustice 13.23
is cautious and turns a. from evil, 14.16
A soft answer turns a. wrath, 15.01
and chases a. his mother is a son 19.26
but when he goes a., then he boasts. 20.14
blows that wound cleanse a. evil; 20.30
of the wicked will sweep them a., 21.07
who are being taken a. to death; 24.11
and turn a. his anger from him. 24.18
Take a. the dross from the silver, 25.04
take a. the wicked from the presence 25.05
near than a brother who is far a. 27.10
If one turns a. his ear from 28.09
aflame, but wise men turn a. wrath. 29.08
a time to cast a. stones, and a time Ecc 3.05
to keep, and a time to cast a.; 3.06
God seeks what has been driven a. 3.15
and right violently taken a., 5.08
which he may carry a. in his hand. 5.15
and put a. pain from your body; 11.10
my love, my fair one, and come a.; Sol 2.10
my love, my fair one, and come a. 2.13
they took a. my mantle, those 5.07
Turn a. your eyes from me, for they 6.05
and will smelt a. your dross as Is 1.25
And the idols shall utterly pass a. 2.18
Turn a. from man in whose nostrils 2.22
is taking a. from Jerusalem and 3.01
Lord will take a. the finery of 3.18
take a. our reproach." 4.01
have washed a. the filth of the 4.04
is not turned a. and his hand is 5.25
your guilt is taken a., 6.07
and the LORD removes men far a., 6.12
it will sweep a. the beard also. 7.20
will be carried a. before the king 8.04
is not turned a. and his hand is 9.12
is not turned a. and his hand is 9.17
is not turned a. and his hand is 9.21
is not turned a. and his hand is 10.04
be as when a sick man wastes a. 10.18
angry with me, thy anger turned a., 12.01
a. from your sepulchre, like a 14.19
up they carry a. over the Brook of 15.07
are taken a. from the fruitful 16.10
will flee a. in a day of grief and 17.11
them, and they will flee far a., 17.13
spreading branches he will hew a. 18.05
up, reeds and rushes will rot a. 19.06
be driven a., and be no more. 19.07
of Assyria lead a. the Egyptians 20.04
though they had fled far a. 22.03
"Look a. from me, let me weep bitter 22.04
He has taken a. the covering of 22.08
LORD will hurl you a. violently, 22.17
but I say, "I pine a., I pine a. 24.16
God will wipe a. tears from all 25.08
he will take a. from all the earth 25.08
hail will sweep a. the refuge of 28.17
therefore you shall speed a.; 30.16
one shall cast a. his idols of 31.07
His rock shall pass a. in terror, 31.09
is confounded and withers a.; 33.09
All the host of heaven shall rot a., 34.04
sorrow and sighing shall flee a. 35.10
and take you a. to a land like 36.17
are born to you, shall be taken a.; 39.07
and the wind shall carry them a. 41.16
I have swept a. your transgressions 44.22
arrow, in his quiver he hid me a. 49.02
swallowed you up will be far a. 49.19
and barren, exiled and put a., 49.21
divorce, with which I put her a.? 50.01
transgressions your mother was put a. 50.01
sorrow and sighing shall flee a. 51.11
my people are taken a. for nothing? 52.05
and judgment he was taken a.; 53.08
devout men are taken a., 57.01
man is taken a. from calamity, 57.01
off, a breath will take them a. 57.13
"If you take a. from the midst of 58.09
and turning a. from following our 59.13
iniquities, like the wind, take us a. 64.06
pot, facing a. from the north." Jer 1.13
you will come a. with your hands 2.37
I had sent her a. with a decree of 3.08
strip a. her branches, for they are 5.10
they have turned aside and gone a. 5.23
Your iniquities have turned these a., 5.25
Cut off your hair and cast it a.; 7.29
and none will frighten them a. 7.33
If one turns a., does he not return? 8.04
people turned a. in perpetual 8.05
gave them has passed a. from them." 8.13

AWAY (cont.)

my people and go a. from them! Jer 9.02
beasts and the birds are swept a., 12.04
she has swooned a.; her sun went 15.09
in thy forbearance take me not a.; 15.15
I have taken a. my peace from this 16.05
whose heart turns a. from the LORD. 17.05
those who turn a. from thee shall 17.13
to turn a. thy wrath from them. 18.20
weep bitterly for him who goes a., 22.10
and who went a. from this place: "He 22.11
my flock, and have driven them a., 23.02
up and cast you a. from my presence, 23.39
I have sent a. from this place to 24.05
king of Babylon did not take a., 27.20
of Babylon took a. from this place 28.03
whom I sent a. from Jerusalem to 29.20
For after I had turned a. I repented; 31.19
I will not turn a. from doing good 32.40
will surely stay a. from us," 37.09
us," for they will not stay a. 37.09
in the mire, they turn a. from you.' 38.22
had carried a. captive from Mizpah 41.14
had carried a. captive from Mizpah 41.16
them and carry them a. captive; 43.12
and he shall go a. from there in 43.12
The swift cannot flee a., nor the 46.06
a sound like a serpent gliding a.; 46.22
to Moab, for she would fly a.; 48.09
have been taken a. from the 48.33
suddenly make them run a. from her; 49.19
of the flock shall be dragged a.; 49.20
camels shall be borne a. from them, 49.29
wander far a., dwell in the depths, 49.30
both man and beast shall flee a. 50.03
turning them a. on the mountains; 50.06
a hunted sheep driven a. by lions. 50.17
suddenly make them run a. from her; 50.44
of their flock shall be dragged a.; 50.45
till they swoon a. and sleep a 51.39
guard carried a. captive some of 52.15
And they took a. the pots, and the 52.18
of the guard took a. as gold, 52.19
Nebuchadrezzar carried a. captive: 52.28
he carried a. captive from Jerusalem 52.29
guard carried a. captive of the 52.30
her maidens have been dragged a., Lam 1.04
her children have gone a., 1.05
groans, and turns her face a. 1.08
made my flesh and my skin waste a., 3.04
who pined a., stricken by want of 4.09
"A.! Unclean!" men cried 4.15
"A.! A! Touch not!" 4.15
Spirit lifted me up and took me a., Eze 3.14
and waste a. under their punishment. 4.17
Repent and turn a. from your idols; 14.06
and turn a. your faces from all 14.06
wither a. on the bed where it grew?" 17.10
men of the land he had taken a., 17.13
man turns a. from all his sins 18.21
man turns a. from his righteousness 18.24
man turns a. from his righteousness 18.26
man turns a. from the wickedness 18.27
and turned a. from all the transgressions 18.28
Cast a. from you all the transgressions 18.31
Cast a. the detestable things your 20.07
every man cast a. the detestable 20.08
and take a. your fine jewels. 23.26
and take a. all the fruit of your 23.29
of your eyes a. from you at a 24.16
you shall pine a. in your iniquities 24.23
and her wealth is carried a., 30.04
the sword comes and takes him a., 33.04
man is taken a. in his iniquity, 33.06
and we waste a. because of them; 33.10
to carry a. silver and gold, to take 38.13
to take a. cattle and goods, to 38.13
took more a. from them than from 42.05
Now let them put a. their idolatry 43.09
Put a. violence and oppression, and 45.09
steward took a. their rich food Dan 1.16
and the wind carried them a., 2.35
their dominion was taken a., 7.12
dominion, which shall not pass a., 7.14
and his dominion shall be taken a., 7.26
offering was taken a. from him, 8.11
are near and those that are far a., 9.07
thy wrath turn a. from thy city 9.16
utterly swept a. before him and 11.22
his army shall be swept a., 11.26
and shall take a. the continual 11.31
continual burnt offering is taken a., 12.11
that she put a. her harlotry from Hos 2.02
and I will take a. my wool and my 2.09
the fish of the sea are taken a. 4.03
new wine take a. the understanding. 4.11
I, even I, will rend and go a., 5.14
like the dew that goes early a. 6.04
Ephraim's glory shall fly a. like a bird— 9.11
are bent on turning a. from me; 11.07
or like the dew that goes early a., 13.03
I have taken them a. in my wrath. 13.11
say to him, "Take a. all iniquity; 14.02
shall flee a. naked in that day," Amo 2.16
they shall take you a. with hooks, 4.02
I carried a. your horses; 4.10
Take a. from me the noise of your 5.23
O you who put far a. the evil day, 6.03
stretch themselves shall pass a." 6.07
go into exile a. from his land.'" 7.11
flee a. to the land of Judah, and 7.12
go into exile a. from its land.'" 7.17
not one of them shall flee a., 9.01
a. from the presence of the LORD. Jon 1.03
shall take a. from you its standing Mic 1.11
and houses, and take them a.; 2.02
you take a. my glory for ever. 2.09
those who have been driven a., 4.06
you shall put a., but not save, and 6.14
they will be cut off and pass a. Nah 1.12
is like a pool whose waters run a. 2.08
Yet she was carried a., she went 3.10
spreads its wings and flies a. 3.16
when the sun rises, they fly a.; 3.17
utterly sweep a. everything from Zep 1.02
"I will sweep a. man and beast; 1.03
I will sweep a. the birds of the 1.03
before you are driven a. like the 2.02
The LORD has taken a. the judgments 3.15
you brought it home, I blew it a. Hag 1.09
taken your iniquity a. from you, Zec 3.04
I will take a. its blood from its 9.07
you, till heaven and earth pass a., Mt 5.18
sin, pluck it out and throw it a.; 5.29
to sin, cut it off and throw it a.; 5.30
send us a. into the herd of swine." 8.31
bridegroom is taken a. from them, 9.15
the patch tears a. from the 9.16
But they went a. and spread his 9.31
As they were going a., behold, 9.32
As they went a., Jesus began to 11.07
they had no root they withered a. 13.06
even what he has will be taken a. 13.12
and snatches a. what is sown in 13.19
the word, immediately he falls a. 13.21
weeds among the wheat, and went a. 13.25
into vessels but threw a. the bad. 13.48
parables, he went a. from there, 13.53
send the crowds a. to go into the 14.15
Jesus said, "They need not go a.; 14.16
And Jesus went a. from there and 15.21
"Send her a., for she is crying 15.23
unwilling to send them a. hungry, 15.32

AWAY (cont.)

And sending a. the crowds, he got Mt 15.39
he went a. from Galilee and entered 19.01
of divorce, and to put her a?" 19.07
laid his hands on them and went a. 19.15
heard this he went a. sorrowful; 19.22
will be taken a. from you and 21.43
and they left him and went a. 22.22
Jesus left the temple and was going a., 24.01
And then many will fall a., 24.10
will not pass a. till all these 24.34
Heaven and earth will pass a., 24.35
but my words will not pass a. 24.35
flood came and swept them all a., 24.39
his ability. Then he went a. 25.15
even what he has will be taken a. 25.29
And they will go a. into eternal 25.46
will all fall a. because of me 26.31
they all fall a. because of you, 26.33
of you, I will never fall a." 26.33
he went a. and prayed, "My Father, if 26.42
he went a. and prayed for the third 26.44
him and led him a. and delivered 27.02
him, and led him a. to crucify him. 27.31
his disciples go and steal him a., 27.64
and stole him a. while we were 28.13
him, and sent him a. at once, Mk 1.43
bridegroom is taken a. from them, 2.20
does, the patch tears a. from it, 2.21
it had no root it withered a. 4.06
comes and takes a. the word which 4.15
the word, immediately they fall a. 4.17
even what he has will be taken a." 4.25
And he went a. and began to proclaim 5.20
He went a. from there and came to 6.01
"Come a. by yourselves to a lonely 6.31
And they went a. in the boat to a 6.32
send them a., to go into the 6.36
arose and went a. to the region of 7.24
and if I send them a. hungry to 8.03
And he sent them a.; and immediately 8.10
And he sent him a. to his home, 8.26
of divorce, and to put her a." 10.04
fell, and he went a. sorrowful; 10.22
And they went a., and found a colt 11.04
fig tree withered a. to its roots. 11.20
him, and sent him a. empty-handed. 12.03
so they left him and went a. 12.12
his house, to take anything a.; 13.15
will not pass a. before all these 13.30
Heaven and earth will pass a., 13.31
but my words will not pass a. 13.31
said to them, "You will all fall a.; 14.27
they all fall a., I will not." 14.29
And again he went a. and prayed, 14.39
seize him and lead him a. safely." 14.44
the linen cloth and ran a. naked. 14.52
and led him a. and delivered him 15.01
soldiers led him a. inside the 15.16
"Who will roll a. the stone for us 16.03
to take a. my reproach among men." Lk 1.25
and the rich he has sent empty a. 1.53
When the angels went a. from them 2.15
the midst of them he went a. 4.30
bridegroom is taken a. from them, 5.35
him who takes a. your cloak do not 6.29
and of him who takes a. your goods, 6.30
it withered a., because it had no 8.06
comes and takes a. the word from 8.12
and in time of temptation fall a. 8.13
that he has will be taken a." 8.18
but he sent him a., saying, 8.38
And he went a., proclaiming 8.39
Now the day began to wear a.; 9.12
and said to him, "Send the crowd a., 9.12
shall not be taken a. from her." 10.42
he takes a. his armor in which he 11.22
you have taken a. the key of 11.52
As he went a. from there, the 11.53
manger, and lead it a. to water it? 13.15
"Get a. from here, for Herod wants 13.31
should perish a. from Jerusalem. 13.33
men throw it a. He who has 14.35
taking the stewardship a. from me? 16.03
for heaven and earth to pass a., 16.17
not come down to take them a.; 17.31
which I kept laid a. in a napkin; 19.20
even what he has will be taken a. 19.26
were sent went a. and found it as 19.32
him, and sent him a. empty-handed. 20.10
and sent him a. empty-handed. 20.11
will not pass a. till all has 21.32
Heaven and earth will pass a., 21.33
but my words will not pass a. 21.33
he went a. and conferred with the 22.04
Then they seized him and led him a., 22.54
they led him a. to their council, 22.66
"A. with this man, and release to us 23.18
And as they led him a., they seized 23.26
were led a. to be put to death with 23.32
the stone rolled a. from the tomb, 24.02
who takes a. the sin of the world! Jn 1.29
the pigeons, "Take these things a.; 2.16
had gone a. into the city to buy 4.08
and went a. into the city, and said 4.28
The man went a. and told the Jews 5.15
his disciples had gone a. alone. 6.22
to the twelve, "Will you also go a.?" 6.67
when they heard it, they went a., * 8.09
"I go a., and you will seek me and 8.21
He went a. again across the Jordan 10.40
Jesus said, "Take a. the stone." 11.39
So they took a. the stone. 11.41
Jews were going a. and believing 12.11
'I go a., and I will come to you.' 14.28
he takes a., and every branch that 15.02
to you to keep you from falling a. 16.01
is to your advantage that I go a., 16.07
I go a., for if I do not go a., 16.07
"A. with him, a. with him, crucify 19.15
and that they might be taken a. 19.31
he might take a. the body of Jesus, 19.38
So he came and took a. his body. 19.38
had been taken a. from the tomb. 20.01
"Because they have taken a. my Lord, 20.13
"Sir, if you have carried him a., 20.15
laid him, and I will take him a." 20.15
Jerusalem, a sabbath day's journey a.; Ac 1.12
census and drew a. some of the 5.37
keep a. from these men and let them 5.38
seeking to turn a. the proconsul 13.08
with him and sailed a. to Cyprus, 15.39
Paul and Silas a. by night to 17.10
were carried a. from his body to 19.12
and turned a. a considerable 19.26
but we sailed a. from Philippi 20.06
And they took the lad a. alive, 20.12
to draw a. the disciples after them 20.30
followed, crying, "A. with him!" 21.36
and wash a. your sins, calling on 22.16
send you far a. to the Gentiles.'" 22.21
"A. with such a fellow from the 22.22
"Go a. for the present; 24.25
soldiers cut a. the ropes of the 27.32
lest any should swim a. and escape; 27.42
them when I take a. their sins." Rom 11.27
age, who are doomed to pass a. 1Co 2.06
form of this world is passing a. 7.31
If I give a. all I have, and if I 13.03
as for prophecy, it will pass a.; 13.08
as for knowledge, it will pass a. 13.08
comes, the imperfect will pass a. 13.10
For if what faded a. came with 2Co 3.11
only through Christ is it taken a. 3.14

AWAY (cont.)

our outer nature is wasting a., 2Co 4.16
the body we are a. from the Lord, 5.06
would rather be a. from the body 5.08
So whether we are at home or a., 5.09
the old has passed a., behold, 5.17
but bold to you when I am a.! 10.01
I write this while I am a. from you, 13.10
me, but I went a. into Arabia; Gal 1.17
was carried a. by their insincerity. 2.13
you have fallen a. from grace. 5.04
putting a. falsehood, let every one Eph 4.25
and slander be put a. from you, 4.31
But now put them all a.: anger, Col 3.08
that you keep a. from any brother 2Th 3.06
have wandered a. into vain discussion, 1Ti 1.06
have wandered a. from the faith 6.10
who are in Asia turned a. from me, 2Ti 1.15
and will turn a. from listening to 4.04
heard, lest we drift a. from it. Heb 2.01
you to fall a. from the living God 3.12
growing old is ready to vanish a. 8.13
the age to put a. sin by the 9.26
and goats should take a. sins. 10.04
which can never take a. sins. 10.11
Therefore do not throw a. your 10.35
Do not be led a. by diverse and 13.09
of the grass he will pass a. Jas 1.10
rich man fade a. in the midst of 1.11
Therefore put a. all filthiness and 1.21
and goes a. and at once forgets 1.24
So put a. all malice and all guile 1Pe 2.01
let him turn a. from evil and do 3.11
will pass a. with a loud noise, and 2Pe 3.10
you be carried a. with the error 3.17
is passing a. and the true light 1Jn 2.08
And the world passes a., 2.17
that he appeared to take a. sins, 3.05
God will wipe a. every tear from Rev 7.17
to sweep her a. with the flood. 12.15
And every island fled a., 16.20
And he carried me a. in the Spirit 17.03
his presence earth and sky fled a., 20.11
and the first earth had passed a., 21.01
he will wipe a. every tear from 21.04
the former things have passed a. 21.04
Spirit he carried me a. to a great, 21.10
any one takes a. from the words of 22.19
God will take a. his share in the 22.19

AWE

and they stood in a. of him, Jos 4.14
as they had stood in a. of Moses, 4.14
success, he stood in a. of him. 1Sa 18.15
and they stood in a. of the king, 1Ki 3.28
is to be held in a. above all gods. 1Ch 16.25
and stand in a. of him, all you sons Ps 22.23
of the world stand in a. of him! 33.08
my heart stand in a. of thy words, 119.161
will stand in a. of the God of Is 29.23
me, he stood in a. of my name. Mal 2.05
faces, and were filled with a. Mt 17.06
place, they were filled with a., 27.54
And they were filled with a., Mk 4.41
God and were filled with a., Lk 5.26
not become proud, but stand in a. Rom 11.20
worship, with reverence and a.; Heb 12.28

AWESOME

and said, "How a. is this place! Gen 28.17

AWFUL

may fear this glorious and a. name, Deu 28.58

AWL

bore his ear through with an a.; Ex 21.06
then you shall take an a., Deu 15.17

AWNING

the coasts of Elishah was your a. Eze 27.07

AWOKE

When Noah a. from his wine and knew Gen 9.24
Then Jacob a. from his sleep and 28.16
and fat cows. And Pharaoh a. 41.04
And Pharaoh a., and behold, it was a 41.07
at the beginning. Then I a. 41.21
But he a. from his sleep, and pulled Ju 16.14
And he a. from his sleep, and said, 16.20
And Solomon a., and behold, it was a 1Ki 3.15
Then the Lord a. as from sleep, like Ps 78.65
Thereupon I a. and looked, and my Jer 31.26
And he a. and rebuked the wind, and Mk 4.39
And he a. and rebuked the wind Lk 8.24

AXE

hand swings the a. to cut down a Deu 19.05
by wielding an a. against them; 20.19
Abimelech took an a. in his hand, Ju 9.48
his mattock, his a., or his sickle; 1Sa 13.20
hammer nor a. nor any tool of iron 1Ki 6.07
his a. head fell into the water; 2Ki 6.05
Shall the a. vaunt itself over him Is 10.15
thickets of the forest with an a., 10.34
worked with an a. by the hands of Jer 10.03
Even now the a. is laid to the root Mt 3.10
Even now the a. is laid to the root Lk 3.09

AXES

sharpening the a. and for setting 1Sa 13.21
saws and iron picks and iron a., 2Sa 12.31
with saws and iron picks and a.; 1Ch 20.03
hacked the wooden trellis with a. Ps 74.05
and come against her with a., like those Jer 46.22
and with his a. he will break down Eze 26.09

AXLES

bronze wheels and a. of bronze; 1Ki 7.30
the a. of the wheels were of one 7.32
their a., their rims, their spokes, 7.33

AYYAH

its towns, and A. and its towns; 1Ch 7.28

AZALIAH

king sent Shaphan the son of A., 2Ki 22.03
he sent Shaphan the son of A., 2Ch 34.08

AZANIAH

And the Levites: Jeshua the son of A., Neh 10.09

AZAREL

A., Joezer, and Jashobeam, the 1Ch 12.06
the eleventh to A., 25.18
for Dan, A. the son of Jeroham. 27.22
A., Shelemiah, Shemariah, Ez 10.41
the son of A., son of Ahzai, son of Neh 11.13
A., Milalai, Gilalai, Maai, Nethanel, 12.36

AZARIAH

A. the son of Zadok was the priest; 1Ki 4.02
A. the son of Nathan was over the 4.05
And all the people of Judah took A., 2 Ki 14.21
king of Israel A. the son of 15.01
Now the rest of the acts of A., 15.06
And A. slept with his fathers, and 15.07
thirty-eighth year of A. king of 15.08
thirty-ninth year of A. king of 15.17
fiftieth year of A. king of Judah 15.23
fifty-second year of A. king of 15.27
and Ethan's son was A. 1Ch 2.08
the father of Jehu, and Jehu of A. 2.38
A. was the father of Helez, and 2.39
A. his son, Jotham his son, 3.12
Ahimaaz of A., A. of Johanan, 6.09
and Johanan of A. (it was he who 6.10

AZARIAH (cont.)
A. was the father of Amariah, 1Ch 6.11
Shallum of Hilkiah, Hilkiah of A., 6.13
A. of Seraiah, Seraiah of Jehozadak; 6.14
son of A., son of Zephaniah, 6.36
and A. the son of Hilkiah, son of 9.11
God came upon A. the son of Oded, 2Ch 15.01
the prophecy of A. the son of Oded, 15.08
A., Jehiel, Zechariah, A., Michael, 21.02
A. the son of Jeroham, Ishmael the 23.01
A. the son of Obed, Maaseiah the son 23.01
But A. the priest went in after him, 26.17
And A. the chief priest, and all the 26.20
A. the son of Johanan, Berechiah the 28.12
of Amasai, and Joel the son of A., 29.12
and A. the son of Jehallelel; 29.12
A. the chief priest, who was of the 31.10
the king and A. the chief officer 31.13
son of A., son of Hilkiah, Ez 7.01
son of A., son of Meraioth, 7.03
After them A. the son of Maaseiah, Neh 3.23
from the house of A. to the Angle 3.24
A., Raamiah, Nahamani, Mordecai, 7.07
A., Jozabad, Hanan, Pelaiah, the 8.07
Seraiah, A., Jeremiah, 10.02
and A., Ezra, Meshullam, 12.33
of Kareah and A. the son of Jer 42.01
A. the son of Hoshaiah and Johanan 43.02
and A. of the tribe of Judah. Dan 1.06
and A. he called Abednego. 1.07
Daniel, Hananiah, Mishael, and A.; 1.11
Daniel, Hananiah, Mishael, and A.; 1.19
and A., his companions, 2.17

AZAZ
and Bela the son of A., 1Ch 5.08

AZAZEL
the LORD and the other lot for A. Lev 16.08
lot fell for A. shall be presented 16.10
away into the wilderness to A. 16.10
the goat go to A. shall wash his 16.26

AZAZIAH
and A. were to lead with lyres 1Ch 15.21
Ephraimites, Hoshea the son of A.; 27.20
while Jehiel, A., Nahath, Asahel, 2Ch 31.13

AZBUK
After him Nehemiah the son of A., Neh 3.16

AZEKAH
smote them as far as A. and Makkedah. Jos 10.10
as far as A., and they died; there were 10.11
Jarmuth, Adullam, Soco, A., 15.35
and encamped between Soco and A., 1Sa 17.01
Adoraim, Lachish, A., 2Ch 11.09
and A. and its villages. Neh 11.30
that were left, Lachish and A.; Jer 34.07

AZEL
son, Eleasah his son, A. his son. 1Ch 8.37
A. had six sons, and these are their 8.38
All these were the sons of A. 8.38
son, Eleasah his son, A. his son. 9.43
A. had six sons and these are their 9.44
these were the sons of A. 9.44

AZGAD
The sons of A., one thousand two Ez 2.12
Of the sons of A., Johanan the son 8.12
The sons of A., two thousand three Neh 7.17
Bunni, A., Bebai, 10.15

AZIEL
Zechariah, A., Shemiramoth, Jehiel, 1Ch 15.20

AZIZA
Mattaniah, Jeremoth, Zabad, and A. Ez 10.27

AZMAVETH
Abialbon the Arbathite, A. of Bahurim, 2Sa 23.31
father of Alemeth, A., and Zimri; 1Ch 8.36
Jarah of Alemeth, A., and Zimri; 9.42
A. of Baharum, Eliahba of Shaalbon, 11.33
Jeziel and Pelet the sons of A.; 12.03
treasuries was A. the son of Adiel 27.25
The sons of A., forty-two. Ez 2.24
and from the region of Geba and A.; Neh 12.29

AZMON
Hazaraddar, and pass along to A.; Num 34.04
shall turn from A. to the Brook of 34.05
passes along to A., Jos 15.04

AZNOTHTABOR
then the boundary turns westward to A., Jos 19.34

AZOR
and Eliakim the father of A., Mt 1.13
and A. the father of Zadok, and 1.14

AZOTUS
But Philip was found at A., Ac 8.40

AZRIEL
A., Jeremiah, Hodaviah, and Jahdiel, 1Ch 5.24
Naphtali, Jeremoth the son of A.; 27.19
the son of A. and Shelemiah the Jer 36.26

AZRIKAM
Elioenia, Hizkiah, and A., three. 1Ch 3.23
A., Bocheru, Ishmael, Sheariah, 8.38
son of A., son of Hashabiah, of the 9.14
A., Bocheru, Ishmael, Sheariah, 9.44
king's son and A. the commander of 2Ch 28.07
son of A., son of Hashabiah, son of Neh 11.15

AZUBAH
name was A. the daughter of Shilhi. 1Ki 22.42
Hezron had children by his wife A., 1Ch 2.18
When A. died, Caleb married Ephrath, 2.19
name was A. the daughter of Shilhi. 2Ch 20.31

AZZAN
a leader, Paltiel the son of A. Num 34.26

AZZUR
Ater, Hezekiah, A., Neh 10.17
year, Hananiah the son of A., Jer 28.01
among them Jaazaniah the son of A., Eze 11.01

B

BAAL
Israel yoked himself to B. of Peor. Num 25.03
yoked themselves to B. of Peor. 25.05
men who followed the B. of Peor; Deu 4.03
the altar of B. which your father Ju 6.25
the altar of B. was broken down, and 6.28
the altar of B. and cut down the 6.30
him, "Will you contend for B.? 6.31
"Let B. contend against him," 6.32
Sidonians, and went and served B., 1Ki 16.31
an altar for B. in the house of B., 16.32
prophets of B. and the four 18.19
but if B., then follow him." 18.21
Then Elijah said to the prophets of B., 18.25
on the name of B. from morning 18.26
noon, saying, "O B., answer us!" 18.26

BAAL (cont.)

to them, "Seize the prophets of B.; 1Ki 18.40
knees that have not bowed to B., 19.18
He served B. and worshiped him, and 22.53
the pillar of B. which his father 2Ki 3.02
to them, "Ahab served B. a little; 10.18
call to me all the prophets of B., 10.19
a great sacrifice to offer to B.; 10.19
to destroy the worshipers of B. 10.19
"Sanctify a solemn assembly for B." 10.20
and all the worshipers of B. came, 10.21
And they entered the house of B., 10.21
the house of B. was filled from 10.21
for all the worshipers of B." 10.22
the house of B. with Jehonadab the 10.23
he said to the worshipers of B., 10.23
you, but only the worshipers of B." 10.23
the inner room of the house of B. 10.25
in the house of B., and burned it. 10.26
And they demolished the pillar of B., 10.27
and demolished the house of B., 10.27
Thus Jehu wiped out B. from Israel. 10.28
the land went to the house of B., 11.18
the priest of B. before the altars. 11.18
the host of heaven, and served B. 17.16
and he erected altars for B., 21.03
LORD all the vessels made for B., 23.04
also who burned incense to B., 23.05
about these cities as far as B. 1Ch 4.33
son, Reaiah his son, B. his son, 5.05
Abdon, then Zur, Kish, B., Nadab, 8.30
then Zur, Kish, B., Ner, Nadab, 9.36
the people went to the house of B., 2Ch 23.17
the priest of B. before the altars. 23.17
themselves to the B. of Peor, Ps 106.28
the prophets prophesied by B., Jer 2.08
swear falsely, burn incense to B., 7.09
altars to burn incense to B. 11.13
to anger by burning incense to B." 11.17
taught my people to swear by B., 12.16
high places of B. to burn their 19.05
the fire as burnt offerings to B., 19.05
prophesied by B. and led my people 23.13
fathers forgot my name for B.? 23.27
been offered to B. and drink 32.29
high places of B. in the valley of 32.35
and gold which they used for B. Hos 2.08
no longer will you call me, 'My B.' 2.16
They turn to B.; they are like a 7.16
and consecrated themselves to B., 9.10
incurred guilt through B. and died. 13.01
the remnant of B. and the name of Zep 1.04
who have not bowed the knee to B." Rom 11.04

BAALAH

bends round to B. (that is Kiriathjearim); Jos 15.09
circles west of B. to Mount Seir, 15.10
and passes along to Mount B., 15.11
B., Iim, Ezem, 15.29
David and all Israel went up to B., 1Ch 13.06

BAALATH

Eltekeh, Gibbethon, B., Jos 19.44
and B. and Tamir in the wilderness, 1Ki 9.18
and B., and all the store-cities 2Ch 8.06

BAALATHBEER

about these cities as far as B., Jos 19.08

BAALBERITH

the Baals, and made B. their god. Ju 8.33
of the house of B. with which 9.04

BAALEJUDAH

the people who were with him to B., 2Sa 6.02

BAALGAD

as far as B. in the valley of Jos 11.17
from B. in the valley of Lebanon to 12.07
from B. below Mount Hermon to the 13.05

BAALHAMON

Solomon had a vineyard at B.; Sol 8.11

BAALHANAN

and B. the son of Achbor reigned in Gen 36.38
B. the son of Achbor died, and Hadar 36.39
B., the son of Achbor, reigned in 1Ch 1.49
When B. died, Hadad reigned in his 1.50
the Shephelah was B. the Gederite; 27.28

BAALHAZOR

Abasalom had sheepshearers at B., 2Sa 13.23

BAALHERMON

from Mount B. as far as the entrance Ju 3.03
very numerous from Bashan to B., 1Ch 5.23

BAALIS

you know that B. the king of the Jer 40.14

BAALMEON

Nebo, and B. (their names to be Num 32.38
in Aroer, as far as Nebo and B. 1Ch 5.08
Bethjeshimoth, B., and Kiriathaim. Eze 25.09

BAALPEOR

have seen what the LORD did at B., Deu 4.03
But they came to B., Hos 9.10

BAALPERAZIM

And David came to B., 2Sa 5.20
name of that place is called B. 5.20
And he went up to B., 1Ch 14.11
name of that place is called B. 14.11

BAAL'S

but B. prophets are four hundred 1Ki 18.22

BAALS

of the LORD and served the B.; Ju 2.11
and served the B. and the Ashtaroth. 2.13
and serving the B. and the Asheroth. 3.07
and played the harlot after the B., 8.33
and served the B. and the Ashtaroth, 10.06
our God and have served the B." 10.10
put away the B. and the Ashtaroth, 1Sa 7.04
have served the B. and the Ashtaroth; 12.10
of the LORD and followed the B. 1Ki 18.18
he did not seek the B., 2Ch 17.03
the house of the LORD for the B. 24.07
even made molten images for the B.; 28.02
down, and erected altars to the B., 33.03
altars of the B. in his presence; 34.04
defiled, I have not gone after the B.'? Jer 2.23
hearts and have gone after the B., 9.14
days of the B. when she burned Hos 2.13
the names of the B. from her mouth, 2.17
they kept sacrificing to the B., 11.02

BAALSHALISHAH

A man came from B., bringing the 2Ki 4.42

BAALTAMAR

and set themselves in array at B.; Ju 20.33

BAALZEBUB

inquire of B., the god of Ekron, 2Ki 1.02
you are going to inquire of B., 1.03
you are sending to inquire of B., 1.06
sent messengers to inquire of B., 1.16

BAALZEPHON

Migdol and the sea, in front of B.; Ex 14.02
sea, by Pihahiroth, in front of B. 14.09
to Pihahiroth, which is east of B.; Num 33.07

BAANA
B. the son of Ahilud, in Taanach, 1Ki 4.12
B. the son of Hushai, in Asher and 4.16
them Zadok the son of B. repaired. Neh 3.04

BAANAH
the name of the one was B., 2Sa 4.02
Rechab and B., set out, and about 4.05
so Rechab and B. his brother 4.06
answered Rechab and B. his brother, 4.09
Heleb the son of B. of Netophah, 23.29
Heled the son of B. of Netophah, 1Ch 11.30
Mispar, Bigvai, Rehum, and B. Ez 2.02
Mispereth, Bigvai, Nehum, B. Neh 7.07
Malluch, Harim, B. 10.27

BAARA
sent away Hushim and B. his wives. 1Ch 8.08

BAASEIAH
son of B., son of Malchijah, 1Ch 6.40

BAASHA
between Asa and B. king of Israel 1Ki 15.16
B. king of Israel went up against 15.17
your league with B. king of Israel, 15.19
And when B. heard of it, he stopped 15.21
with which B. had been building; 15.22
B. the son of Ahijah, of the house 15.27
and B. struck him down at Gibbethon, 15.27
So B. killed him in the third year 15.28
between Asa and B. king of Israel 15.32
B. the son of Ahijah began to reign 15.33
son of Hanani against B., saying, 16.01
sweep away B. and his house, 16.03
belonging to B. who dies in the 16.04
Now the rest of the acts of B., 16.05
And B. slept with his fathers, and 16.06
of Hanani against B. and his house, 16.07
Elah the son of B. began to reign 16.08
he killed all the house of B.; 16.11
destroyed all the house of B., 16.12
spoke against B. by Jehu the 16.12
for all the sins of B. and the sins 16.13
the house of B. the son of Ahijah, 21.22
the house of B. the son of Ahijah. 2Ki 9.09
B. king of Israel went up against 2Ch 16.01
your league with B. king of Israel, 16.03
And when B. heard of it, he stopped 16.05
with which B. had been building, and 16.06
defense against B. king of Israel; Jer 41.09

BABBLE
Should your b. silence men, and when Job 11.03

BABBLER
some said, "What would this b. say?" Ac 17.18

BABBLING
but the b. of a fool brings ruin Pro 10.14

BABE
and lo, the b. was crying. Ex 2.06
the b. leaped in her womb; Lk 1.41
the b. in my womb leaped for joy. 1.44
you will find a b. wrapped in 2.12
and the b. lying in a manger. 2.16

BABEL
The beginning of his kingdom was B., Gen 10.10
Therefore its name was called B., 11.09

BABES
by the mouth of b. and infants, Ps 8.02
leave something over to their b. 17.14
and b. shall rule over them. Is 3.04
infants and b. faint in the Lam 2.11
understanding and revealed them to b.; Mt 11.25
of the mouth of b. and sucklings 21.16
understanding and revealed them to b.; Lk 10.21
men of the flesh, as b. in Christ. 1Co 3.01
be b. in evil, but in thinking be 14.20
Like newborn b., long for the pure 1Pe 2.02

BABYLON
of Assyria brought people from B., 2Ki 17.24
the men of B. made Succothbenoth, 17.30
king of B., sent envoys with 20.12
come from a far country, from B. 20.14
this day, shall be carried to B.; 20.17
in the palace of the king of B. 20.18
Nebuchadnezzar king of B. came up, 24.01
for the king of B. had taken all 24.07
Nebuchadnezzar king of B. came up 24.10
Nebuchadnezzar king of B. came to 24.11
gave himself up to the king of B., 24.12
The king of B. took him prisoner in 24.12
And he carried away Jehoiachin to B.; 24.15
captivity from Jerusalem to B. 24.15
And the king of B. brought captive 24.16
captive to B. all the men of valor, 24.16
And the king of B. made Mattaniah, 24.17
rebelled against the king of B. 24.20
Nebuchadnezzar king of B. came with 25.01
him up to the king of B. at Riblah. 25.06
him in fetters, and took him to B. 25.07
king of B.—Nebuzaradan, the captain 25.08
a servant of the king of B., 25.08
who had deserted to the king of B., 25.11
and carried the bronze to B. 25.13
them to the king of B. at Riblah. 25.20
And the king of B. smote them, 25.21
Nebuchadnezzar king of B. had left, 25.22
the king of B. had appointed 25.23
the land, and serve the king of B., 25.24
the month, Evilmerodach king of B., 25.27
the kings who were with him in B. 25.28
into exile in B. because of their 1Ch 9.01
of the envoys of the princes of B., 2Ch 32.31
of bronze and brought him to B. 33.11
came up Nebuchadnezzar king of B., 36.06
him in fetters to take him to B. 36.06
of the LORD to B. and put them in 36.07
and put them in his palace in B. 36.07
Nebuchadnezzar sent and brought him to B. 36.10
princes, all these he brought to B. 36.18
into exile in B. those who had 36.20
the king of B. had carried captive Ez 2.01
hand of Nebuchadnezzar king of B., 5.12
the first year of Cyrus king of B., 5.13
and brought into the temple of B., 5.14
king took out of the temple of B., 5.14
in the royal archives there in B., 5.17
is in Jerusalem and brought to B., 6.05
the king of B. had carried into Neh 7.06
Artaxerxes king of B. I went to the 13.06
Nebuchadnezzar king of B. had Est 2.06
who know me I mention Rahab and B.; Ps 87.04
By the waters of B., 137.01
O daughter of B., you devastator! 137.08
concerning B. which Isaiah the son Is 13.01
And B., the glory of kingdoms, the 13.19
this taunt against the king of B.: 14.04
cut off from B. name and remnant, 14.22
he answered, "Fallen, fallen is B.; 21.09
king of B., sent envoys with 39.01
to me from a far country, from B." 39.03
this day, shall be carried to B.; 39.06
in the palace of the king of B." 39.07
I will send to B. and break down 43.14
the dust, O virgin daughter of B.; 47.01
he shall perform his purpose on B., 48.14
Go forth from B., flee from Chaldea, 48.20
into the hand of the king of B.; Jer 20.04
he shall carry them captive to B., 20.04
seize them, and carry them to B. 20.05
to B. you shall go; and there 20.06

BABYLON (cont.)
Nebuchadrezzar king of B. is making Jer 21.02
the king of B. and against the 21.04
Nebuchadrezzar king of B. and into 21.07
into the hand of the king of B., 21.10
Nebuchadrezzar king of B. and into 22.25
Nebuchadrezzar king of B. had taken 24.01
smiths, and had brought them to B., 24.01
of Nebuchadrezzar king of B.), 25.01
for Nebuchadrezzar the king of B., 25.09
serve the king of B. seventy years. 25.11
the king of B. and that nation, the 25.12
them the king of B. shall drink. 25.26
the king of B., my servant, and I 27.06
this Nebuchadnezzar king of B., 27.08
under the yoke of the king of B., 27.08
You shall not serve the king of B.' 27.09
of the king of B. and serve him, 27.11
under the yoke of the king of B., 27.12
will not serve the king of B.? 27.13
You shall not serve the king of B., 27.14
shortly be brought back from B., 27.16
serve the king of B. and live. 27.17
and in Jerusalem may not go to B. 27.18
Nebuchadnezzar king of B. did not 27.20
Jerusalem to B. Jeconiah the son 27.20
be carried to B. and remain there 27.22
broken the yoke of the king of B. 28.02
Nebuchadnezzar king of B. took away 28.03
from this place and carried to B. 28.03
exiles from Judah who went to B., 28.04
break the yoke of the king of B." 28.04
this place from B. the vessels of 28.06
Nebuchadnezzar king of B. from the 28.11
to Nebuchadnezzar king of B., 28.14
into exile from Jerusalem to B. 29.01
Judah sent to B. to Nebuchadnezzar 29.03
to Nebuchadnezzar king of B. 29.03
into exile from Jerusalem to B.: 29.04
seventy years are completed for B., 29.10
up prophets for us in B.,'— 29.15
I sent away from Jerusalem to B.: 29.20
hand of Nebuchadrezzar king of B., 29.21
by all the exiles from Judah in B.: 29.22
the king of B. roasted in the fire, 29.22
For he has sent to us in B., 29.28
of the king of B. was besieging 32.02
into the hand of the king of B., 32.03
into the hand of the king of B., 32.04
and he shall take Zedekiah to B., 32.05
hand of Nebuchadrezzar king of B., 32.28
hand of the king of B. by sword, 32.36
Nebuchadrezzar king of B. and all 34.01
into the hand of the king of B., 34.02
see the king of B. eye to eye and 34.03
and you shall go to B.' 34.03
of the king of B. was fighting 34.07
of the king of B. which has 34.21
Nebuchadrezzar king of B. came up 35.11
the king of B. will certainly come 36.29
Nebuchadrezzar king of B. made king 37.01
into the hand of the king of B." 37.17
'The king of B. will not come 37.19
of the king of B. and be taken." 38.03
to the princes of the king of B., 38.17
to the princes of the king of B., 38.18
of the king of B. and were saying, 38.22
shall be seized by the king of B.; 38.23
Nebuchadrezzar king of B. and all 39.01
of the king of B. came and sat in 39.03
of the officers of the king of B. 39.03
up to Nebuchadrezzar king of B., 39.05
The king of B. slew the sons of 39.06
and the king of B. slew all the 39.06
him in fetters to take him to B. 39.07
into exile to B. the rest of the 39.09
Nebuchadrezzar king of B. gave 39.11
officers of the king of B. 39.13
Judah who were being exiled to B. 40.01
good to you to come with me to B., 40.04
to come with me to B., do not come. 40.04
the king of B. appointed governor 40.05
the king of B. had appointed 40.07
not been taken into exile to B., 40.07
the land, and serve the king of B., 40.09
the king of B. had left a remnant 40.11
the king of B. had appointed 41.02
the king of B. had made governor 41.18
Do not fear the king of B., 42.11
us or take us into exile in B. 43.03
take Nebuchadrezzar the king of B., 43.10
hand of Nebuchadrezzar king of B., 44.30
Nebuchadrezzar king of B. defeated 46.02
Nebuchadrezzar king of B. to smite 46.13
Nebuchadrezzar king of B. and his 46.26
Nebuchadrezzar king of B. smote. 49.28
Nebuchadrezzar king of B. has made 49.30
which the LORD spoke concerning B., 50.01
'B. is taken; Bel is put to shame, 50.02
"Flee from the midst of B., 50.08
bringing against B. a company of 50.09
who passes by B. shall be appalled, 50.13
in array against B. round about, 50.14
Cut off from B. the sower, and the 50.16
Nebuchadrezzar king of B. has 50.17
on the king of B. and his land, 50.18
How B. has become a horror among 50.23
O B., and you did not know it; 50.24
and escape from the land of B., 50.28
"Summon archers against B., 50.29
unrest to the inhabitants of B. 50.34
and upon the inhabitants of B., 50.35
and jackals shall dwell in B., 50.39
against you, O daughter of B.! 50.42
"The king of B. heard the report of 50.43
which the LORD has made against B., 50.45
the capture of B. the earth shall 50.46
spirit of a destroyer against B., 51.01
and I will send to B. winnowers, 51.02
"Flee from the midst of B., 51.06
B. was a golden cup in the LORD's 51.07
Suddenly B. has fallen and been 51.08
We would have healed B., 51.09
concerning B. is to destroy it, for 51.11
a standard against the walls of B.; 51.12
concerning the inhabitants of B. 51.12
"I will requite B. and all the 51.24
LORD's purposes against B. stand, 51.29
make the land of B. a desolation, 51.29
The warriors of B. have ceased 51.30
the king of B. that his city is 51.31
The daughter of B. is like a 51.33
"Nebuchadrezzar the king of B. has 51.34
to me and to my kinsmen be upon B., 51.35
and B. shall become a heap of ruins, 51.37
"How B. is taken, the praise of the 51.41
How B. has become a horror among 51.41
The sea has come up on B.; 51.42
And I will punish Bel in B., 51.44
the wall of B. has fallen. 51.44
I will punish the images of B.; 51.47
them, shall sing for joy over B.; 51.48
B. must fall for the slain of 51.49
as for B. have fallen the slain of 51.49
Though B. should mount up to heaven, 51.53
a cry from B.! The noise of 51.54
For the LORD is laying B. waste, 51.55
destroyer has come upon her, upon B.; 51.56
broad wall of B. shall be leveled 51.58
with Zedekiah king of Judah to B., 51.59
the evil that should come upon B., 51.60
that are written concerning B. 51.60
to Seraiah: "When you come to B., 51.61
'Thus shall B. sink, to rise no more, 51.64

BABYLON (cont.)
rebelled against the king of B. Jer 52.03
Nebuchadrezzar king of B. came with 52.04
to the king of B. at Riblah in the 52.09
The king of B. slew the sons of 52.10
and the king of B. took him to 52.11
took him to B., and put him in prison 52.11
king of B.—Nebuzaradan the captain 52.12
bodyguard who served the king of B., 52.12
who had deserted to the king of B., 52.15
and carried all the bronze to B. 52.17
them to the king of B. at Riblah. 52.26
And the king of B. smote them, 52.27
the month, Evilmerodach king of B., 52.31
the kings who were with him in B. 52.32
bring him to B. in the land of the Eze 12.13
the king of B. came to Jerusalem, 17.12
and brought them to him to B. 17.12
him he broke, in B. he shall die. 17.16
bring him to B. and enter into 17.20
and brought him to the king of B.; 19.09
sword of the king of B. to come; 21.19
For the king of B. stands at the 21.21
The king of B. has laid siege to 24.02
north Nebuchadrezzar king of B., 26.07
Nebuchadrezzar king of B. made his 29.18
Egypt to Nebuchadrezzar king of B.; 29.19
hand of Nebuchadrezzar king of B. 30.10
strengthen the arms of the king of B., 30.24
strengthen the arms of the king of B., 30.25
into the hand of the king of B., 30.25
of the king of B. shall come upon 32.11
Nebuchadnezzar king of B. came to Dan 1.01
the wise men of B. be destroyed. 2.12
out to slay the wise men of B.; 2.14
the rest of the wise men of B. 2.18
to destroy the wise men of B.; 2.24
"Do not destroy the wise men of B.; 2.24
ruler over the whole province of B., 2.48
over all the wise men of B. 2.48
the affairs of the province of B.; 2.49
of Dura, in the province of B. 3.01
the affairs of the province of B.: 3.12
and Abednego in the province of B. 3.30
the wise men of B. should be 4.06
roof of the royal palace of B., 4.29
king said, "Is not this great B., 4.30
king said to the wise men of B., 5.07
year of Belshazzar king of B., 7.01
you shall go to B. There you shall Mic 4.10
who dwell with the daughter of B. Zec 2.07
Jedaiah, who have arrived from B.; 6.10
the time of the deportation to B. Mt 1.11
And after the deportation to B.: 1.12
deportation to B. fourteen generations, 1.17
deportation to B. to the Christ 1.17
and I will remove you beyond B. Ac 7.43
She who is at B., who is likewise 1Pe 5.13
fallen is B. the great, she who made Rev 14.08
fell, and God remembered great B., 16.19
"B. the great, mother of harlots and 17.05
"Fallen, fallen is B. the great! 18.02
great city, thou mighty city, B.! 18.10
"So shall B. the great city be 18.21

BABYLONIA
brought up from B. to Jerusalem. Ez 1.11
Babylon had carried captive to B.; 2.01
and carried away the people to B. 5.12
decree, and search was made in B., 6.01
this Ezra went up from B. He was 7.06
month he began to go up from B., 7.09
find in the whole province of B., 7.16
those who went up with me from B., 8.01

BABYLONIANS
the B., the men of Susa, that is, the Ez 4.09
a picture of B. whose native land Eze 23.15

And the B. came to her into the bed 23.17
the B. and all the Chaldeans, Pekod 23.23

BACA
the valley of B. they make it a Ps 84.06

BACAME
and Jehoiakim b. his servant three 2Ki 24.01

BACK
and the dove came b. to him in the Gen 8.11
then they turned b. and came to 14.07
Then he brought b. all the goods, 14.16
also brought b. his kinsman Lot 14.16
And they shall come b. here in the 15.16
But they said, "Stand b.!" 19.09
do not look b. or stop anywhere in 19.17
But Lot's wife behind him looked b., 19.26
take your son b. to the land from 24.05
you do not take my son b. there. 24.06
you must not take my son b. there." 24.08
he said, "Send me b. to my master." 24.54
and will bring you b. to this land; 28.15
put the stone b. in its place upon 29.03
But as he drew b. his hand, behold, 38.29
nor has he kept b. anything from me 39.09
brothers, "My money has been put b.; 42.28
if I do not bring him b. to you; 42.37
and I will bring him b. to you." 42.37
not bring him b. to you and set 43.09
carry b. with you the money that 43.12
he may send b. your other brother 43.14
we brought b. to you from the land 44.08
When we went b. to your servant my 44.24
'If I do not bring him b. to you, 44.32
let the lad go b. with his brothers. 44.33
For how can I go b. to my father if 44.34
beasts and go b. to the land of 45.17
us and pay us b. for all the evil 50.15
"Put your hand b. into your bosom." Ex 4.07
he put his hand b. into his bosom; 4.07
Moses went b. to Jethro his father-in-law 4.18
"Let me go b., I pray, to my kinsmen 4.18
to Moses in Midian, "Go b. to Egypt; 4.19
and went b. to the land of Egypt; 4.20
"When you go b. to Egypt, see that 4.21
Aaron were brought b. to Pharaoh; 10.08
Israel to turn b. and encamp in 14.02
drove the sea b. by a strong east 14.21
water may come b. upon the Egyptians, 14.26
LORD brought b. the waters of the 15.19
you shall bring it b. to him. 23.04
hang over the b. of the tabernacle. 26.12
my hand, and you shall see my b.; 33.23
spot is on the b. or on the front. Lev 13.55
sold it and pay b. the overpayment 25.27
means to get it b. for himself, 25.28
and go b. to his own family, and 25.41
he shall buy it b. at your valuation, 27.27
they brought b. word to them and to Num 13.26
be better for us to go b. to Egypt?" 14.03
a captain, and go b. to Egypt." 14.04
you have turned b. from following 14.43
"Put b. the rod of Aaron before the 17.10
and I will bring b. word to you, 22.08
in thy sight, I will go b. again." 22.34
LORD has held you b. from honor." 24.11
rose, and went b. to his place; 24.25
has turned b. my wrath from the 25.11
and turned b. to Pihahiroth, which 33.07
Let him go b. to his house, lest he Deu 20.05
Let him go b. to his house, lest he 20.06
Let him go b. to his house, lest he 20.07
Let him go b. to his house, lest the 20.08
shall take them b. to your brother. 22.01
and turn b. and cover up your 23.13
you shall not go b. to get it; 24.19
will bring you b. in ships to 28.68

BACK (cont.)
So when the men of Ai looked b., Jos 8.20
wilderness turned b. upon the 8.20
they turned b. and smote the men 8.21
For Joshua did not draw b. his hand, 8.26
turned b. to Debir and assaulted it, 10.38
And Joshua turned b. at that time, 11.10
"Go b. to your homes with much 22.08
and brought b. word to them. 22.32
God will push them b. before you, 23.05
For if you turn b., 23.12
the Danites b. into the hill Ju 1.34
they turned b. and behaved worse 2.19
himself turned b. at the sculptured 3.19
of Shechem fall b. upon their 9.57
LORD, and I cannot take b. my vow." 11.35
anger he went b. to his father's 14.19
he turned and went b. to his home. 18.26
kindly to her and bring her b. 19.03
Israel turned b. against the 20.48
"Turn b., my daughters, why will you Ru 1.11
Turn b., my daughters, go your way, 1.12
has gone b. to her people and to 1.15
the LORD has brought me b. empty. 1.21
who came b. with Naomi from the 2.06
'You must not go b. empty-handed to 3.17
who has come b. from the country of 4.03
then they went b. to their house at 1Sa 1.19
Dagon and put him b. in his place. 5.03
Then he would come b. to Ramah, 7.17
let us go b., lest my father cease 9.05
When he turned his b. to leave 10.09
he has turned b. from following me, 15.11
So Samuel turned b. after Saul; 15.31
but David went b. and forth from 17.15
Israelites came b. from chasing 17.53
and come b. to me with sure information. 23.23
and came b. and told him all this. 25.12
and has kept b. his servant from 25.39
garments, and came b. to Achish. 27.09
"Send the man b., that he may 29.04
So go b. now; and go 29.07
David brought b. all. 30.19
the bow of Jonathan turned not b., 2Sa 1.22
that the spear came out at his b.; 2.23
brought him b. from the cistern of 3.26
and then draw b. from him, that he 11.15
we drove them b. to the entrance 11.23
Can I bring him b. again? 12.23
go, bring b. the young man Absalom." 14.21
indeed bring me b. to Jerusalem, 15.08
Go b., and stay with the king; 15.19
Go b., and take your brethren with 15.20
the ark of God b. into the city. 15.25
will bring me b. and let me see 15.25
go b. to the city in peace, you and 15.27
the ark of God b. to Jerusalem; 15.29
will give me b. the kingdom of my 16.03
all the people b. to you as a 17.03
the troops came b. from pursuing 18.16
nothing about bringing the king b.?" 19.10
to bring the king b. to his house, 19.11
be the last to bring b. the king?' 19.12
So the king came b. to the Jordan; 19.15
until the day he came b. in safety. 19.24
to speak of bringing b. our king?" 19.43
did not turn b. until they were 22.38
The LORD will bring b. his bloody 1Ki 2.32
blood come b. upon the head of 2.33
LORD will bring b. your evil upon 2.44
in the other court b. of the hall, 7.08
b. and front, even from the foundation 7.09
turned and went b. to her own land, 10.13
and at the b. of the throne was a 10.19
will turn b. to the house of David; 12.26
he could not draw it b. to himself. 13.04
'Bring him b. with you into your 13.18
So he went b. with him, and ate 13.19
the prophet who had brought him b.; 13.20
but have come b., and have eaten 13.22
the prophet whom he had brought b. 13.23
had brought him b. from the way 13.26
ass, and brought it b. to the city, 13.29
and have cast me behind your b.; 14.09
brought them b. to the guardroom. 14.28
thou hast turned their hearts b." 18.37
And he said to him. "Go b. again; 19.20
and take him b. to Amon the governor 22.26
they turned b. from pursuing him. 22.33
'Go b. to the king who sent you, and 2Ki 1.06
and went b. and stood on the bank 2.13
And they came b. to him, while he 2.18
the man of God, and come b. again." 4.22
then they came b., and entered 7.08
them, but he is not coming b." 9.18
them, but he is not coming b. 9.20
When they came b. and told him, he 9.36
So the king of Assyria turned b., 15.20
I will turn you b. on the way by 19.28
"Turn b., and say to Hezekiah the 20.05
ten steps, or go b. ten steps?" 20.09
let the shadow go b. ten steps." 20.10
he brought the shadow b. ten steps, 20.11
they brought b. word to the king. 22.20
Israel, and came b. to Jerusalem. 1Ch 21.04
put his sword b. into its sheath. 21.27
turned and went b. to her own land, 2Ch 9.12
brought them b. to the guardroom. 12.11
and take him b. to Amon the governor 18.25
they turned b. from pursuing him. 18.32
and brought them b. to the LORD, 19.04
them to bring them b. to the LORD; 24.19
of the army whom Amaziah sent b., 25.13
and send b. the captives from your 28.11
they brought b. word to the king. 34.28
and brought b. to the temple which Ez 6.05
and I turned b. and entered by the Neh 2.15
turn b. their taunt upon their own 4.04
have bought b. our Jewish brethren 5.08
behind their b. and killed thy 9.26
in order to turn them b. to thee, 9.26
order to turn them b. to thy law. 9.29
and I brought b. thither the 13.09
she came b. to the second harem in Est 2.14
"God will not turn b. his anger; Job 9.13
his hands will give b. his wealth. 20.10
He will give b. the fruit of his 20.18
he keeps b. his soul from the Pit, 33.18
to bring b. his soul from the Pit, 33.30
If he should take b. his spirit to 34.14
he does not turn b. from the sword. 39.22
His b. is made of rows of shields, 41.15
they shall turn b., and be put Ps 6.10
When my enemies turned b., 9.03
did not turn b. till they were 18.37
Keep b. thy servant also from 19.13
them be turned b. and confounded 35.04
The wicked borrows, and cannot pay b., 37.21
them be turned b. and brought to 40.14
Thou hast made us turn b. from the foe; 44.10
our heart has not turned b., 44.18
will be turned b. in the day when 56.09
Each evening they come b., 59.06
Each evening they come b., 59.14
"I will bring them b. from Bashan, 68.22
will bring them b. from the depths 68.22
them be turned b. and brought to 70.02
Why dost thou hold b. thy hand, 74.11
turned b. on the day of battle. 78.09
Then we will never turn b. from thee; 80.18
hast turned b. the edge of his 89.43
Thou turnest man b. to the dust, 90.03
"Turn b., O children of men!" 90.03
He will bring b. on them their 94.23

BACK (cont.)
looked and fled, Jordan turned b. Ps 114.03
O Jordan, that you turn b.? 114.05
I hold b. my feet from every evil 119.101
The plowers plowed upon my b.; 129.03
from which he will not turn b.: 132.11
hold b. your foot from their paths; Pro 1.15
go to her come b. nor do they 2.19
rod is for the b. of him who lacks 10.13
curse him who holds b. grain, 11.26
of a man's hand comes b. to him. 12.14
talk of a fool is a rod for his b., 14.03
not even bring it b. to his mouth. 19.24
righteous gives and does not hold b. 21.26
hold b. those who are stumbling to 24.11
pay the man b. for what he has 24.29
ass, and a rod for the b. of fools. 26.03
out to bring it b. to his mouth. 26.15
stone will come b. upon him who 26.27
but a wise man quietly holds it b. 29.11
and does not turn b. before any; 30.30
its b. of gold, its seat of purple; Sol 3.10
out, and who will turn it b.? Is 14.27
come b. again." 21.12
those who turn b. the battle at 28.06
he does not call b. his words, 31.02
I will turn you b. on the way by 37.29
the dial of Ahaz turn b. ten steps." 38.08
the sun turned b. on the dial the 38.08
thou hast held b. my life from the 38.17
cast all my sins behind thy b. 38.17
They shall be turned b. and utterly 42.17
who turns wise men b., 44.25
servant, to bring Jacob b. to him, 49.05
I gave my b. to the smiters, and my 50.06
have made your b. like the ground 51.23
hold not b., lengthen your cords 54.02
"If you turn b. your foot from the 58.13
Justice is turned b., 59.14
they have turned their b. to me, Jer 2.27
the LORD has not turned b. from us." 4.08
not relented nor will I turn b." 4.28
They have turned b. to the iniquities 11.10
will bring them b. to their own 16.15
I will show them my b., not my face, 18.17
I will turn b. the weapons of war 21.04
I will bring them b. to their fold, 23.03
will not turn b. until he has 23.20
I will bring them b. to this land. 24.06
do not hold b. a word. 26.02
shortly be brought b. from Babylon, 27.16
will bring them b. and restore 27.22
I will bring b. to this place all 28.03
I will also bring b. to this place 28.04
and bring b. to this place from 28.06
and bring you b. to this place. 29.10
will bring you b. to the place 29.14
will bring them b. to the land 30.03
will not turn b. until he has 30.24
consolations I will lead them b., 31.09
they shall come b. from the land 31.16
shall come b. to their own country. 31.17
bring me b. that I may be restored, 31.18
to me their b. and not their face; 32.33
I will bring them b. to this place, 32.37
around and took b. the male and 34.11
of you took b. his male and female 34.16
will bring them b. to this city; 34.22
shall come b. and fight against 37.08
do not send me b. to the house of 37.20
not send me b. to the house of 38.26
Mizpah turned about and came b., 41.14
Johanan brought b. from Gibeon. 41.16
I will keep nothing b. from you." 42.04
they look not b.—terror on every 46.05
and let us go b. to our own people 46.16
look not b. to their children, so 47.03
is he who keeps b. his sword from 48.10
Moab has turned his b. in shame! 48.39
Flee, turn b., dwell in the depths, O 49.08
he turned me b.; Lam 1.13
had the face of an eagle at the b. Eze 1.10
writing on the front and on the b., 2.10
it shall not turn b.; 7.13
brought b. word, saying, "I have done 9.11
me and cast me behind your b., 23.35
I will not go b., I will not spare, 24.14
and bring them b. to the land of 29.14
turn b., turn b. from your evil ways; 33.11
gives b. what he had taken by 33.15
strayed you have not brought b., 34.04
and I will bring b. the strayed, 34.16
brought them b. from the peoples 39.27
gate from the b. of the one side 40.13
side room to the b. of the other, 40.13
were set b. from the ground more 42.06
Then he brought me b. to the outer 44.01
Then he brought me b. to the door 47.01
Then he led me b. along the bank 47.06
As I went b., I saw upon the bank 47.07
four wings of a bird on its b.; Dan 7.06
turn his insolence b. upon him. 11.18
turn his face b. toward the 11.19
and shall turn b. and be enraged 11.30
He shall turn b. and give heed to 11.30
Therefore I will take b. my grain Hos 2.09
and will turn b. upon him his 12.14
Are you paying me b. for something? Joe 3.04
If you are paying me b., I will 3.04
hard to bring the ship b. to land, Jon 1.13
but none turns b. Nah 2.08
those who have turned b. from Zep 1.06
he thrust her b. into the ephah, Zec 5.08
will bring them b. because I have 10.06
'What are these wounds on your b.?' 13.06
field not turn b. to take his Mt 24.18
"Put your sword b. into its place; 26.52
and brought b. the thirty pieces 27.03
and came and rolled b. the stone, 28.02
will send it b. here immediately.'" Mk 11.03
field not turn b. to take his 13.16
saw that the stone was rolled b.; 16.04
and gave it b. to the attendant, and Lk 4.20
will be the measure you get b." 6.38
boy, and gave him b. to his father. 9.42
plow and looks b. is fit for the 9.62
I will repay you when I come b.' 10.35
turned b., praising God with a loud 17.15
who is in the field not turn b. 17.31
apparel, he sent him b. to Pilate. 23.11
Herod, for he sent him b. to us. 23.15
and they came b. saying that they 24.23
disciples drew b. and no longer Jn 6.66
then went b. to the chief priests 7.45
went and washed and came b. seeing. 9.07
they drew b. and fell to the 18.06
disciples went b. to their homes. 20.10
knowledge he kept b. some of the Ac 5.02
and to keep b. part of the proceeds 5.03
were carried b. to Shechem and 7.16
of slavery to fall b. into fear, Rom 8.15
you, a man, to answer b. to God? 9.20
be grafted b. into their own olive 11.24
and to come b. to you from Macedonia 2Co 1.16
came he drew b. and separated Gal 2.12
can you turn b. again to the weak 4.09
will be paid b. for the wrong he Col 3.25
I am sending him b. to you, Phm 1.12
you might have him b. for ever, 1.15
by faith, and if he shrinks b., Heb 10.38
who shrink b. and are destroyed, 10.39
speaking, he did receive him b. 11.19
fields, which you kept b. by fraud, Jas 5.04
truth and some one brings him b., 5.19

BACK (cont.)
whoever brings b. a sinner from Jas 5.20
it to turn b. from the holy 2Pe 2.21
The dog turns b. to his own vomit, 2.22
written within and on the b., Rev 5.01
holding b. the four winds of the 7.01

BACKBITING
and a b. tongue, angry looks. Pro 25.23

BACKBONE
taking it away close by the b., Lev 3.09

BACKS
your enemies turn their b. to you. Ex 23.27
turned their b. before their Jos 7.08
they turn their b. before their 7.12
turned their b. before the men of Ju 20.42
my enemies turn their b. to me, 2Sa 22.41
of the LORD, and turned their b. 2Ch 29.06
my enemies turn their b. to me, Ps 18.40
and flogging for the b. of fools. Pro 19.29
their riches on the b. of asses, Is 30.06
with their b. to the temple of the Eze 8.16
see, and bend their b. for ever. Rom 11.10

BACKSLIDING
but he went on b. in the way of his Is 57.17
people turned away in perpetual b.? Jer 8.05

BACKSLIDINGS
for our b. are many, we have sinned Jer 14.07
from all the b. in which they have Eze 37.23

BACKWARD
and walked b. and covered the Gen 9.23
heels so that his rider falls b. 49.17
Eli fell over b. from his seat by 1Sa 4.18
and b., but I cannot perceive him; Job 23.08
Zion be put to shame and turned b.! Ps 129.05
and fall b., and be broken, and Is 28.13
not rebellious, I turned not b. 50.05
and went b. and not forward. Jer 7.24
says the LORD, you keep going b.; 15.06
are dismayed and have turned b. 46.05

BAD
we cannot speak to you b. or good. Gen 24.50
a word to Jacob, either good or b." 31.24
speak to Jacob neither good nor b.' 31.29
a good for a b., or a b. for a good; Lev 27.10
value it as either good or b.; 27.12
value it as either good or b.; 27.14
inquire whether it is good or b., 27.33
that they dwell in is good or b., Num 13.19
either good or b. of my own will; 24.13
spoke to Amnon neither good nor b.; 2Sa 13.22
but the water is b., 2Ki 2.19
A b. messenger plunges men into Pro 13.17
"It is b., it is b.," says the 20.14
is like a b. tooth or a foot that 25.19
riches were lost in a b. venture; Ecc 5.14
the other basket had very b. figs, Jer 24.02
so b. that they could not be eaten. 24.02
and the b. figs very b., so b. that 24.03
Like the b. figs which are so b. 24.08
which are so b. they cannot be 29.17
but the b. tree bears evil fruit. Mt 7.17
nor can a b. tree bear good fruit. 7.18
make the tree b., and its fruit b.; 12.33
into vessels but threw away the b. 13.48
whom they found, both b. and good; 22.10
"For no good tree bears b. fruit, Lk 6.43
nor again does a b. tree bear good 6.43
had done nothing either good or b., Rom 9.11
terror to good conduct, but to b. 13.03
"B. company ruins good morals." 1Co 15.33
will go on from b. to worse, 2Ti 3.13

BADE
The man did as Joseph b. him, Gen 43.17
till the morning, as Moses b. them; Ex 16.24
did to them as the LORD b. him; Jos 11.09
and some b. me kill you, but I 1Sa 24.10
It was your servant Joab who b. me; 2Sa 14.19
we prayed and b. one another Ac 21.05

BADGER
And the rock b., because it chews Lev 11.05
and the rock b., because they chew Deu 14.07

BADGERS
the rocks are a refuge for the b. Ps 104.18
The b. are a people not mighty, yet Pro 30.26

BADLY
and he was b. wounded by the 1Sa 31.03
"Take me away, for I am b. wounded." 2Ch 35.23

BAFFLED
When she saw that she was b., Eze 19.05

BAG
have in your b. two kinds of Deu 25.13
his shepherd's b., in his wallet; 1Sa 17.40
his hand in his b. and took out a 17.49
transgression would be sealed up in a b., Job 14.17
he took a b. of money with him; Pro 7.20
the weights in the b. are his work. 16.11
My beloved is to me a b. of myrrh, Sol 1.13
and with a b. of deceitful weights? Mic 6.11
to put them into a b. with holes. Hag 1.06
no b. for your journey, nor two Mt 10.10
no bread, no b., no money in their Mk 6.08
nor b., nor bread, nor money; Lk 9.03
Carry no purse, no b., no sandals; 10.04
out with no purse or b. or sandals, 22.35
a purse take it, and likewise a b. 22.36

BAGGAGE
he has hidden himself among the b." 1Sa 10.22
in charge of the keeper of the b., 17.22
two hundred remained with the b. 25.13
his share be who stays by the b.; 30.24
at Michmash he stores his b.; Is 10.28
Prepare yourselves b. for exile, Jer 46.19
prepare for yourself an exile's b., Eze 12.03
bring out your b. by day in their 12.04
in their sight, as b. for exile; 12.04
shall lift the b. upon your 12.06
I brought out my b. by day, 12.07
as b. for exile, and in the evening 12.07
shall lift his b. upon his shoulder 12.12

BAGPIPE
b., and every kind of music, you are Dan 3.05
b., and every kind of music, all the 3.07
b., and every kind of music, shall 3.10
b., and every kind of music, to fall 3.15

BAGS
orders to fill their b. with grain, Gen 42.25
fruits of the land in your b., 43.11
up two talents of silver in two b., 2Ki 5.23
and tied up in b. the money that 12.10

BAHARUM
Azmaveth of B., Eliahba of Shaalbon, 1Ch 11.33

BAHURIM
after her all the way to B. 2Sa 3.16
When King David came to B., 16.05
came to the house of a man at B., 17.18
from B., made haste to come down 19.16
Abialbon the Arbathite, Azmaveth of B., 23.31
of Gera, the Benjaminite from B., 1Ki 2.08

BAKBAKKAR
and B., Heresh, Galal, and Mattaniah 1Ch 9.15

BAKBUK
the sons of B., the sons of Hakupha, Ez 2.51
the sons of B., the sons of Hakupha, Neh 7.53

BAKBUKIAH
and B., the second among his Neh 11.17
And B. and Unno their brethren 12.09
Mattaniah, B., Obadiah, Meshullam, 12.25

BAKE
b. what you will b. and boil what Ex 16.23
and b. twelve cakes of it; Lev 24.05
ten women shall b. your bread in 26.26
they shall b. the cereal offering, Eze 46.20

BAKED
and b. unleavened bread, and they Gen 19.03
all sorts of b. food for Pharaoh, 40.17
And they b. unleavened cakes of the Ex 12.39
cereal offering b. in the oven as Lev 2.04
a cereal offering b. on a griddle, 2.05
It shall not be b. with leaven. 6.17
in b. pieces like a cereal offering, 6.21
cereal offering b. in the oven and 7.09
they shall be b. with leaven, as 23.17
the taste of cakes b. with oil. Num 11.08
kneaded it and b. unleavened bread 1Sa 28.24
in his sight, and b. the cakes. 2Sa 13.08
your God lives, I have nothing b., 1Ki 17.12
his head a cake b. on hot stones 19.06
the b. offering, the offering mixed 1Ch 23.29
I also b. bread on its coals, I Is 44.19

BAKER
Egypt and his b. offended their Gen 40.01
the chief butler and the chief b., 40.02
butler and the b. of the king of 40.05
When the chief b. saw that the 40.16
of the chief b. among his servants 40.20
but he hanged the chief b., 40.22
and the chief b. in custody in the 41.10
my office, and the b. was hanged." 41.13
whose b. ceases to stir the fire, Hos 7.04

BAKERS
to be perfumers and cooks and b. 1Sa 8.13

BAKERS'
given him daily from the b. street, Jer 37.21

BAKES
he kindles a fire and b. bread; Is 44.15

BAKING
b. it in their sight on human dung. Eze 4.12

BALAAM
sent messengers to B. the son of Num 22.05
and they came to B., and gave him 22.07
the princes of Moab stayed with B. 22.08
And God came to B. and said, 22.09
And B. said to God, "Balak the son 22.10
God said to B., "You shall not go 22.12
So B. rose in the morning, and said 22.13
"B. refuses to come with us." 22.14
And they came to B. and said to him, 22.16
But B. answered and said to the 22.18
And God came to B. at night and 22.20
So B. rose in the morning, and 22.21
and B. struck the ass, to turn her 22.23
of the LORD, she lay down under B.; 22.27
of the ass, and she said to B., 22.28
And B. said to the ass, "Because you 22.29
And the ass said to B., 22.30
Then the LORD opened the eyes of B., 22.31
Then B. said to the angel of the 22.34
And the angel of the LORD said to B., 22.35
So B. went on with the princes of 22.35
When Balak heard that B. had come, 22.36
And Balak said to B., "Did I not 22.37
B. said to Balak, "Lo, I have come to 22.38
Then B. went with Balak, and they 22.39
and sent to B. and to the princes 22.40
Balak took B. and brought him up 22.41
And B. said to Balak, "Build for me 23.01
Balak did as B. had said; 23.02
and Balak and B. offered on each 23.02
And B. said to Balak, "Stand beside 23.03
And God met B.; and B. said 23.04
And B. took up his discourse, and 23.07
And Balak said to B., "What have 23.11
B. said to Balak, "Stand here beside 23.15
And the LORD met B., and put 23.16
And B. took up his discourse, and 23.18
And Balak said to B., "Neither 23.25
But B. answered Balak, "Did I not 23.26
And Balak said to B., "Come now 23.27
So Balak took B. to the top of Peor, 23.28
And B. said to Balak, "Build for me 23.29
And Balak did as B. had said, 23.30
When B. saw that it pleased the 24.01
And B. lifted up his eyes, and saw 24.02
"The oracle of B. the son of Beor, 24.03
anger was kindled against B., 24.10
and Balak said to B., "I called 24.10
And B. said to Balak, "Did I not 24.12
"The oracle of B. the son of Beor, 24.15
Then B. rose, and went back to his 24.25
they also slew B. the son of Beor 31.08
of Israel, by the counsel of B., 31.16
against you B. the son of Beor Deu 23.04
your God would not hearken to B.; 23.05
B. also, the son of Beor, the soothsayer, Jos 13.22
and invited B. the son of Beor to 24.09
but I would not listen to B.; 24.10
but hired B. against them to curse Neh 13.02
and what B. the son of Beor answered Mic 6.05
they have followed the way of B., 2Pe 2.15
there who hold the teaching of B., Rev 2.14

BALAAM'S
and pressed B. foot against the Num 22.25
and B. anger was kindled, and he 22.27
And the LORD put a word in B. mouth, 23.05
for the sake of gain to B. error, Jud 1.11

BALADAN
time Merodachbaladan the son of B., 2Ki 20.12
time Merodachbaladan the son of B., Is 39.01

BALAH
Hazarshual, B., Ezem, Jos 19.03

BALAK
And B. the son of Zippor saw all Num 22.02
So B. the son of Zippor, who was 22.04
"B. the son of Zippor, king of Moab, 22.10
and said to the princes of B., 22.13
of Moab rose and went to B., 22.14
Once again B. sent princes, more in 22.15
"Thus says B. the son of Zippor: 22.16
and said to the servants of B., 22.18
"Though B. were to give me his 22.18
went on with the princes of B. 22.35
When B. heard that Balaam had come, 22.36
And B. said to Balaam, "Did I not 22.37
Balaam said to B., "Lo, I have come 22.38
Then Balaam went with B., 22.39
And B. sacrificed oxen and sheep, 22.40
And on the morrow B. took Balaam 22.41
And Balaam said to B., 23.01
B. did as Balaam had said; 23.02
and B. and Balaam offered on each 23.02
And Balaam said to B., 23.03
"Return to B., and thus you shall 23.05
"From Aram B. has brought me, the 23.07

BALAK (cont.)
And B. said to Balaam, "What have Num 23.11
And B. said to him, "Come with me to 23.13
Balaam said to B., "Stand here 23.15
"Return to B., and thus shall you 23.16
And B. said to him, "What has the 23.17
and said, "Rise, B., and hear; 23.18
And B. said to Balaam, "Neither 23.25
But Balaam answered B., "Did I 23.26
And B. said to Balaam, "Come now, I 23.27
So B. took Balaam to the top of 23.28
And Balaam said to B., "Build 23.29
And B. did as Balaam had said, and 23.30
and B. said to Balaam, "I called you 24.10
And Balaam said to B., "Did I 24.12
'If B. should give me his house 24.13
and B. also went his way. 24.25
Then B. the son of Zippor, king of Jos 24.09
any better than B. the son of Ju 11.25
remember what B. king of Moab Mic 6.05
who taught B. to put a stumbling Rev 2.14

BALAK'S
to Balaam, and gave him B. message. Num 22.07
And B. anger was kindled against 24.10

BALANCE
(Let me be weighed in a just b., Job 31.06
A false b. is an abomination to the Pro 11.01
A just b. and scales are the LORD's; 16.11
in scales and the hills in a b.? Is 40.12
and its rider had a b. in his hand; Rev 6.05

BALANCES
You shall have just b., Lev 19.36
and all my calamity laid in the b.! Job 6.02
in the b. they go up; Ps 62.09
then take b. for weighing, and Eze 5.01
"You shall have just b., 45.10
weighed in the b. and found Dan 5.27
in whose hands are false b., Hos 12.07
deal deceitfully with false b., Amo 8.05

BALANCINGS
Do you know the b. of the clouds, Job 37.16

BALD
the b. locust according to its kind, Lev 11.22
he is b. but he is clean. 13.40
there is on the b. head or the 13.42
or the b. forehead a reddish-white 13.42
on his b. head or his b. forehead. 13.42
b. head or on his b. forehead, 13.43
or make himself b. for them. Jer 16.06
they make themselves b. for you, Eze 27.31
head was made b. and every shoulder 29.18
Make yourselves b. and cut off your Mic 1.16
make yourselves as b. as the eagle, 1.16

BALDHEAD
"Go up, you b.! Go up, you b.!" 2Ki 2.23

BALDNESS
he has b. of the forehead but he is Lev 13.41
or make any b. on your foreheads Deu 14.01
and instead of well-set hair, b.; Is 3.24
On every head is b., every beard 15.02
to b. and girding with sackcloth; 22.12
B. has come upon Gaza, Ashkelon has Jer 47.05
and b. on all their heads. Eze 7.18
all loins, and b. on every head; Amo 8.10

BALL
you like a b. into a wide land; Is 22.18

BALLAD
Therefore the b. singers say, "Come Num 21.27

BALM
b., and myrrh, on their way to carry Gen 37.25
a little b. and a little honey, gum, 43.11
Is there no b. in Gilead? Jer 8.22
and take b., O virgin daughter of 46.11
Take b. for her pain; perhaps 51.08
and early figs, honey, oil, and b. Eze 27.17

BALSAM
upon them opposite the b. trees. 2Sa 5.23
in the tops of the b. trees, 5.24
upon them opposite the b. trees. 1Ch 14.14
in the tops of the b. trees, 14.15

BAMAH
its name is called B. to this day. Eze 20.29

BAMOTH
Nahaliel, and from Nahaliel to B., Num 21.19
and from B. to the valley lying in 21.20

BAMOTHBAAL
Balaam and brought him up to B.; Num 22.41
Dibon, and B., and Bethbaalmeon, Jos 13.17

BAND
And the skilfully woven b. upon it, Ex 28.08
skilfully woven b. of the ephod. 28.27
skilfully woven b. of the ephod. 28.28
skilfully woven b. of the ephod; 29.05
And the skilfully woven b. upon it, 39.05
skilfully woven b. of the ephod. 39.20
skilfully woven b. of the ephod, 39.21
skilfully woven b. of the ephod, Lev 8.07
you will meet a b. of prophets 1Sa 10.05
a b. of prophets met him; and the 10.10
LORD, "Shall I pursue after this b.? 30.08
"Will you take me down to this b.?" 30.15
I will take you down to this b." 30.15
our hand the b. that came against 30.23
behind Abner, and became one b., 2Sa 2.25
when a b. of Philistines was 23.13
was a round b. half a cubit high; 1Ki 7.35
became leader of a marauding b., 11.24
a marauding b. was seen and the man 2Ki 13.21
of Mount Zion a b. of survivors. 19.31
David against the b. of raiders; 1Ch 12.21
for the b. of men that came with 2Ch 22.01
the king for a b. of soldiers and Ez 8.22
thick darkness its swaddling b., Job 38.09
They b. themselves together, they Ps 56.06
fierce men b. themselves against me. 59.03
a b. of ruthless men seek my life, 86.14
They b. together against the life 94.21
and when a b. of shepherds is Is 31.04
of Mount Zion a b. of survivors. 37.32
bound with a b. of iron and bronze, Dan 4.15
bound with a b. of iron and bronze, 4.23
A b. of drunkards, they give themselves Hos 4.18
procuring a b. of soldiers and some Jn 18.03
So the b. of soldiers and their 18.12

BANDAGE
himself with a b. over his eyes. 1Ki 20.38
to take the b. away from his eyes; 20.41
to heal it by binding it with a b., Eze 30.21

BANDAGES
his hands and feet bound with b., Jn 11.44

BANDED
so the priests are b. together; Hos 6.09

BANDITS
breaks in, and the b. raid without. Hos 7.01

BANDS
who were captains of raiding b.; 2Sa 4.02
Now b. of Moabites used to invade 2Ki 13.20

BANDS (cont.)
against him b. of the Chaldeans, 2Ki 24.02
and b. of the Syrians, and 24.02
and b. of the Moabites, and 24.02
and b. of the Ammonites, and sent 24.02
who sew magic b. upon all wrists, Eze 13.18
your magic b. with which you hunt 13.20
with salt, nor swathed with b. 16.04
with the b. of love, and I became to Hos 11.04

BANI
of Nathan of Zobah, B. the Gadite, 2Sa 23.36
son of B., son of Shemer, 1Ch 6.46
son of B., from the sons of Perez 9.04
The sons of B., six hundred and Ez 2.10
Of the sons of B., Shelomith the 8.10
Of the sons of B. were Meshullam, 10.29
Of the sons of B.: Maadai, Amram, Uel, 10.34
repaired: Rehum the son of B.; Neh 3.17
Also Jeshua, B., Sherebiah, Jamin, 8.07
B., Kadmiel, Shebaniah, Bunni, Sherebiah, 9.04
Bunni, Sherebiah, B., and Chenani; 9.04
B., Hashabneiah, Sherebiah, Hodiah, 9.05
Hodiah, B., Beninu. 10.13
Pahathmoab, Elam, Zattu, B., 10.14
Jerusalem was Uzzi the son of B., 11.22

BANISH
I will b. from them the voice of Jer 25.10
of peace and b. wild beasts from Eze 34.25
he will b. ungodliness from Jacob"; Rom 11.26

BANISHED
not bring his b. one home again. 2Sa 14.13
not to keep his b. one an outcast. 14.14
the gladness of the earth is b. Is 24.11

BANISHMENT
death or for b. or for confiscation Ez 7.26

BANK
other cows on the b. of the Nile. Gen 41.03
and stood on the b. of the Jordan. 2Ki 2.13
me back along the b. of the river. Eze 47.06
I saw upon the b. of the river 47.07
standing on the b. of the river. Dan 8.03
standing on the b. of the river, 8.06
standing on the b. of the great 10.04
one on this b. of the stream and 12.05
and one on that b. of the stream. 12.05
down the steep b. into the sea, Mt 8.32
down the steep b. into the sea, Mk 5.13
down the steep b. into the lake Lk 8.33
you not put my money into the b., 19.23
will cast up a b. about you and 19.43

BANKERS
have invested my money with the b., Mt 25.27

BANKS
was standing on the b. of the Nile; Gen 41.17
to all the b. of the river Jabbok Deu 2.37
overflows all its b. throughout the Jos 3.15
overflowed all its b., as before. 4.18
that are on the b. of the Arnon, Ju 11.26
when it was overflowing all its b., 1Ch 12.15
channels and go over all its b.; Is 8.07
And on the b., on both sides of the Eze 47.12
voice between the b. of the Ulai, Dan 8.16

BANNED
and he himself b. from the congregation Ez 10.08

BANNER
the name of it, The LORD is my b., Ex 17.15
saying, "A hand upon the b. of the LORD! 17.16
Thou hast set up a b. for those who Ps 60.04
and his b. over me was love. Sol 2.04
set up a b. and proclaim, conceal it Jer 50.02

BANNERS
the name of our God set up our b.! Ps 20.05
terrible as an army with b. Sol 6.04
sun, terrible as an army with b.?" 6.10

BANQUET
reign he gave a b. for all his Est 1.03
a b. lasting for seven days, in the 1.05
also gave a b. for the women in 1.09
gave a great b. to all his princes 2.18
it was Esther's b. He also 2.18
the king to the b. she prepared 5.12
in haste to the b. that Esther had 6.14
birthday gave a b. for his courtiers Mk 6.21
"When you give a dinner or a b., Lk 14.12
to him, "A man once gave a great b., 14.16
time for the b. he sent his 14.17
who were invited shall taste my b.' " 14.24

BANQUETING
He brought me to the b. house, Sol 2.04
his lords, came into the b. hall; Dan 5.10

BAPTISM
and Sadducees coming for b., Mt 3.07
The b. of John, whence was it? 21.25
preaching a b. of repentance for Mk 1.04
with the b. with which I am 10.38
and with the b. with which I am 10.39
Was the b. of John from heaven or 11.30
preaching a b. of repentance for Lk 3.03
been baptized with the b. of John; 7.29
I have a b. to be baptized with; 12.50
Was the b. of John from heaven or 20.04
beginning from the b. of John until Ac 1.22
after the b. which John preached: 10.37
had preached a b. of repentance to 13.24
though he knew only the b. of John. Ac 18.25
They said, "Into John's b." 19.03
baptized with the b. of repentance, 19.04
therefore with him by b. into death, Rom 6.04
one Lord, one faith, one b., Eph 4.05
and you were buried with him in b., Col 2.12
B., which corresponds to this, now 1Pe 3.21

BAPTIST
In those days came John the B., Mt 3.01
no one greater than John the B.; 11.11
of John the B. until now the 11.12
his servants, "This is John the B., 14.02
of John the B. here on a platter." 14.08
And they said, "Some say John the B., 16.14
speaking to them of John the B. 17.13
head of John the B. on a platter." Mk 6.25
And they told him, "John the B.; 8.28
"John the B. has sent us to you, Lk 7.20
For John the B. has come eating no 7.33
And they answered, "John the B.; 9.19

BAPTIZE
"I b. you with water for repentance, Mt 3.11
he will b. you with the Holy Spirit 3.11
but he will b. you with the Holy Mk 1.08
them all, "I b. you with water; Lk 3.16
he will b. you with the Holy Spirit 3.16
John answered them, "I b. with water; Jn 1.26
who sent me to b. with water said 1.33
(although Jesus himself did not b., 4.02
(I did b. also the household of 1Co 1.16
not send me to b. but to preach 1.17

BAPTIZED
and they were b. by him in the Mt 3.06
Jordan to John, to be b. by him. 3.13
"I need to be b. by you, and do you 3.14
And when Jesus was b., 3.16
and they were b. by him in the Mk 1.05
I have b. you with water; 1.08

BAPTIZED (cont.)

Galilee and was b. by John in the Mk 1.09
or to be b. with the baptism with 10.38
the baptism with which I am b.?" 10.38
the baptism with which I am b., 10.39
which I am b., you will be b.; 10.39
that came out to be b. by him, Lk 3.07
Tax collectors also came to be b., 3.12
Now when all the people were b., 3.21
also had been b. and was praying, 3.21
having been b. with the baptism of 7.29
themselves, not having been b. by him. 7.30
I have a baptism to be b. with; 12.50
there he remained with them and b. Jn 3.22
and people came and were b. 3.23
the place where John at first b., 10.40
for John b. with water, but before Ac 1.05
you shall be b. with the Holy 1.05
and be b. every one of you in the 2.38
who received his word were b., 2.41
they were b., both men and women. 8.12
and after being b. he continued 8.13
had only been b. in the name of 8.16
What is to prevent my being b.?" 8.36
and the eunuch, and he b. him. 8.38
Then he rose and was b., 9.18
them to be b. in the name of Jesus 10.48
'John b. with water, but you shall 11.16
you shall be b. with the Holy 11.16
And when she was b., with her 16.15
and he was b. at once, with all his 16.33
hearing Paul believed and were b. 18.08
said, "Into what then were you b.?" 19.03
"John b. with the baptism of 19.04
they were b. in the name of the 19.05
Rise and be b., and wash away your 22.16
who have been b. into Christ Jesus Rom 6.03
Jesus were b. into his death? 6.03
Or were you b. in the name of Paul? 1Co 1.13
thankful that I b. none of you 1.14
say that you were b. in my name. 1.15
not know whether I b. any one else. 1.16
and all were b. into Moses in the 10.02
we were all b. into one body— 12.13
mean by being b. on behalf of the 15.29
why are people b. on their behalf? 15.29
of you as were b. into Christ have Gal 3.27

BAPTIZER

John the b. appeared in the wilderness, Mk 1.04
"John the b. has been raised from 6.14
she said, "The head of John the b." 6.24

BAPTIZES

this is he who b. with the Holy Jn 1.33

BAPTIZING

b. them in the name of the Father Mt 28.19
They asked him, "Then why are you b., Jn 1.25
the Jordan, where John was b. 1.28
but for this I came b. with water, 1.31
John also was b. at Aenon near 3.23
b., and all are going to him. 3.26
was making and b. more disciples 4.01
water for b. these people who have Ac 10.47

BAR

The middle b., halfway up the Ex 26.28
made the middle b. to pass through 36.33
and a b. of gold weighing fifty Jos 7.21
and the mantle and the b. of gold, 7.24
b. and all, and put them on his Ju 16.03
let them shut and b. the doors. Neh 7.03
I will break the b. of Damascus, Amo 1.05

BARABBAS

a notorious prisoner, called B. Mt 27.16
B. or Jesus who is called Christ?" 27.17
to ask for B. and destroy Jesus. 27.20
And they said, "B." 27.21
Then he released for them B., 27.26
insurrection, there was a man called B. Mk 15.07
him release for them B. instead. 15.11
the crowd, released for them B.; 15.15
this man, and release to us B."— Lk 23.18
out again, "Not this man, but B.!" Jn 18.40
Now B. was a robber. 18.40

BARACHEL

Then Elihu the son of B. the Buzite, Job 32.02
the son of B. the Buzite answered: 32.06

BARACHIAH

blood of Zechariah the son of B., Mt 23.35

BARAK

and summoned B. the son of Abinoam Ju 4.06
B. said to her, "If you will go with 4.08
arose, and went with B. to Kedesh. 4.09
And B. summoned Zebulun and Naphtali 4.10
was told that B. the son of 4.12
And Deborah said to B., "Up! 4.14
So B. went down from Mount Tabor 4.14
his army before B. at the edge of 4.15
And B. pursued the chariots and the 4.16
And behold, as B. pursued Sisera, 4.22
Deborah and B. the son of Abinoam 5.01
Arise, B., lead away your captives, O 5.12
and Issachar faithful to B.; 5.15
And the LORD sent Jerubbaal and B., 1Sa 12.11
B., Samson, Jephthah, of David and Heb 11.32

BARBARIAN

b., Scythian, slave, free man, but Col 3.11

BARBARIANS

obligation both to Greeks and to b., Rom 1.14

BARBER'S

use it as a b. razor and pass it Eze 5.01

BARE

shall not strip your vineyard b., Lev 19.10
And he went to a b. height. Num 23.03
foundations of the world were laid b., 2Sa 22.16
put it under him on the b. steps, 2Ki 9.13
foundations of the world were laid b., Ps 18.15
whirl, and strips the forests b.; 29.09
LORD will lay b. their secret Is 3.17
On a b. hill raise a signal, cry 13.02
There will be b. places by the Nile, 19.07
strip, and make yourselves b., 32.11
will open rivers on the b. heights, 41.18
on all b. heights shall be their 49.09
Lift up your eyes to the b. heights, Jer 3.02
A voice on the b. heights is heard, 3.21
wind from the b. heights in the 4.11
a lamentation on the b. heights, 7.29
Upon all the b. heights in the 12.12
wild asses stand on the b. heights, 14.06
But I have stripped Esau b., 49.10
become drunk and strip yourself b. Lam 4.21
its foundation will be laid b.; Eze 13.14
yet you were naked and b. 16.07
youth, when you were naked and b., 16.22
shame was laid b. and your nakedness 16.36
jewels, and leave you naked and b. 16.39
labor, and leave you naked and b., 23.29
she put it on the b. rock, 24.07
have set on the b. rock the blood 24.08
from her, and make her a b. rock. 26.04
I will make you a b. rock; 26.14
and every shoulder was rubbed b.; 29.18
laying him b. from thigh to neck. Hab 3.13
for her cedar work will be laid b. Zep 2.14
but a b. kernel, perhaps of wheat or 1Co 15.37
open and laid b. to the eyes of Heb 4.13

BARED

The LORD has b. his holy arm before Is 52.10
of Jerusalem, with your arm b.; Eze 4.07

BAREFOOT

b. and with his head covered; 2Sa 15.30
done so, walking naked and b.— Is 20.02
naked and b. for three years as a 20.03
naked and b., with buttocks uncovered, 20.04

BARELY

men who have b. escaped from those 2Pe 2.18

BARGAIN

and b. over your friend. Job 6.27
Will traders b. over him? Will they 41.06
you have made a b. for yourself Is 57.08
they make a b. with Assyria, and oil Hos 12.01

BARIAH

B., Neariah, and Shaphat, six. 1Ch 3.22

BAR-JESUS

a Jewish false prophet, named B. Ac 13.06

BAR-JONA

him, "Blessed are you, Simon B.! Mt 16.17

BARK

are all dumb dogs, they cannot b.; Is 56.10
off their b. and thrown it down; Joe 1.07

BARKOS

the sons of B., the sons of Sisera, Ez 2.53
the sons of B., the sons of Sisera, Neh 7.55

BARLEY

(the flax and the b. were ruined, Ex 9.31
for the b. was in the ear and the 9.31
of a homer of b. shall be valued Lev 27.16
a tenth of an ephah of b. meal; Num 5.15
a land of wheat and b., of vines Deu 8.08
a cake of b. bread tumbled into the Ju 7.13
at the beginning of b. harvest. Ru 1.22
and it was about an ephah of b. 2.17
the end of the b. and wheat 2.23
he is winnowing b. tonight at the 3.02
he measured out six measures of b., 3.15
six measures of b. he gave to me, 3.17
next to mine, and he has b. there; 2Sa 14.30
b., meal, parched grain, beans and 17.28
at the beginning of b. harvest. 21.09
B. also and straw for the horses 1Ki 4.28
first fruits, twenty loaves of b., 2Ki 4.42
two measures of b. for a shekel, 7.01
two measures of b. for a shekel, 7.16
"Two measures of b. shall be sold 7.18
was a plot of ground full of b., 1Ch 11.13
wheat, twenty thousand cors of b., 2Ch 2.10
Now therefore the wheat and b., 2.15
of wheat and ten thousand of b. 27.05
and foul weeds instead of b. Job 31.40
in rows and b. in its proper place, Is 28.25
b., oil, and honey hidden in the Jer 41.08
"And you, take wheat and b., Eze 4.09
And you shall eat it as a b. cake, 4.12
for handfuls of b. and for pieces 13.19
of an ephah from each homer of b., 45.13
and a homer and a lethech of b. Hos 3.02
vinedressers, for the wheat and the b.; Joe 1.11
who has five b. loaves and two Jn 6.09
fragments from the five b. loaves, 6.13
three quarts of b. for a denarius; Rev 6.06

BARN

Is the seed yet in the b.? Hag 2.19
but gather the wheat into my b.'" Mt 13.30
have neither storehouse nor b., Lk 12.24

BARNABAS

by the apostles B. (which means, Ac 4.36
But B. took him, and brought him to 9.27
and they sent B. to Antioch. 11.22
So B. went to Tarsus to look for 11.25
elders by the hand of B. and Saul. 11.30
And B. and Saul returned from 12.25
B., Symeon who was called Niger, 13.01
apart for me B. and Saul for the 13.02
who summoned B. and Saul and sought 13.07
to Judaism followed Paul and B., 13.43
And Paul and B. spoke out boldly, 13.46
up persecution against Paul and B., 13.50
B. they called Zeus, and Paul, 14.12
the apostles B. and Paul heard of 14.14
day he went on with B. to Derbe. 14.20
And when Paul and B. had no small 15.02
Paul and B. and some of the others 15.02
listened to B. and Paul as they 15.12
them to Antioch with Paul and B. 15.22
you with our beloved B. and Paul, 15.25
But Paul and B. remained in Antioch, 15.35
And after some days Paul said to B., 15.36
And B. wanted to take with them 15.37
B. took Mark with him and sailed 15.39
Or is it only B. and I who have no 1Co 9.06
went up again to Jerusalem with B., Gal 2.01
gave to me and B. the right hand 2.09
so that even B. was carried away by 2.13
the cousin of B. (concerning whom Col 4.10

BARNS

the blessing upon you in your b., Deu 28.08
then your b. will be filled with Pro 3.10
sow nor reap nor gather into b., Mt 6.26
do this: I will pull down my b., Lk 12.18

BARRACKS

him to be brought into the b. Ac 21.34
about to be brought into the b., 21.37
him to be brought into the b., 22.24
them and bring him into the b. 23.10
and entered the b. and told Paul. 23.16
the morrow they returned to the b., 23.32

BARREN

Now Sarai was b.; she had no Gen 11.30
for his wife, because she was b.; 25.21
her womb; but Rachel was b. 29.31
her young or be b. in your land; Ex 23.26
not be male or female b. among you, Deu 7.14
his wife was b. and had no children Ju 13.02
you are b. and have no children; 13.03
The b. has borne seven, but she who 1Sa 2.05
Yea, let that night be b.; Job 3.07
For the company of the godless is b., 15.34
"They feed on the b. childless 24.21
He gives the b. woman a home, making Ps 113.09
Sheol, the b. womb, the earth ever Pro 30.16
I was bereaved and b., exiled and put Is 49.21
"Sing, O b. one, who did not bear; 54.01
no child, because Elizabeth was b., Lk 1.07
month with her who was called b. 1.36
they will say, 'Blessed are the b., 23.29
O b. one that dost not bear; Gal 4.27
that faith apart from works is b.? Jas 2.20

BARRENNESS

considered the b. of Sarah's womb. Rom 4.19

BARRIER

a perpetual b. which it cannot pass; Jer 5.22
There was a b. before the side Eze 40.12

BARS

"And you shall make b. of acacia wood, Ex 26.26
and five b. for the frames of the 26.27
of gold for holders for the b.; 26.29

BARS (cont.)
you shall overlay the b. with gold. Ex 26.29
its b., its pillars, and its bases; 35.11
And he made b. of acacia wood, five 36.31
and five b. for the frames of the other 36.32
five b. for the frames of the tabernacle 36.32
of gold for holders for the b., 36.34
and overlaid the b. with gold. 36.34
its b., its pillars, and its bases; 39.33
have broken the b. of your yoke Lev 26.13
the b., the pillars, the bases, and Num 3.36
with its b., pillars, and bases, 4.31
and b., besides very many unwalled Deu 3.05
Your b. shall be iron and bronze; 33.25
a town that has gates and b. 1Sa 23.07
cities with walls and bronze b.); 1Ki 4.13
cities with walls, gates, and b., 2Ch 8.05
walls and towers, gates and b.; 14.07
its doors, its bolts, and its b. Neh 3.03
its doors, its bolts, and its b. 3.06
and its b., and repaired a thousand 3.13
its doors, its bolts, and its b. Neh 3.14
its doors, its bolts, and its b.; 3.15
Will it go down to the b. of Sheol? Job 17.16
for it, and set b. and doors, 38.10
bronze, his limbs like b. of iron. 40.18
and cuts in two the b. of iron. Ps 107.16
strengthens the b. of your gates; 147.13
quarreling is like the b. of a castle. Pro 18.19
Babylon and break down all the b., Is 43.14
and cut asunder the b. of iron, 45.02
LORD: You have broken wooden b., Jer 28.13
make in their place b. of iron. 28.13
the LORD, that has no gates or b., 49.31
are on fire, her b. are broken. 51.30
he has ruined and broken her b.; Lam 2.09
when I break the b. of their yoke, Eze 34.27
walls, and having no b. or gates'; 38.11
consume the b. of their gates, and Hos 11.06
the land whose b. closed upon me Jon 2.06
fire has devoured your b. Nah 3.13

BARSABBAS
Joseph called B., who was surnamed Ac 1.23
They sent Judas called B., 15.22

BARTER
were in you, to b. for your wares. Eze 27.09

BARTERED
calamus were b. for your merchandise. Eze 27.19

BARTHOLOMEW
Philip and B.; Thomas and Matthew Mt 10.03
and B., and Matthew, and Thomas, and Mk 3.18
and John, and Philip, and B., Lk 6.14
B. and Matthew, James the son of Ac 1.13

BARTIMAEUS
B., a blind beggar, the son of Mk 10.46

BARUCH
After him B. the son of Zabbai Neh 3.20
Daniel, Ginnethon, B., 10.06
and Maaseiah the son of B., 11.05
of purchase to B. the son of Jer 32.12
I charged B. in their presence, 32.13
of purchase to B. the son of 32.16
Then Jeremiah called B. the son of 36.04
and B. wrote upon a scroll at the 36.04
And Jeremiah ordered B., 36.05
And B. the son of Neriah did all 36.08
B. read the words of Jeremiah from 36.10
when B. read the scroll in the 36.13
to say to B., "Take in your hand 36.14
So B. the son of Neriah took the 36.14
So B. read it to them. 36.15
and they said to B., "We must 36.16
Then they asked B., "Tell us 36.17
B. answered them, "He dictated all 36.18
Then the princes said to B., 36.19
Abdeel to seize B. the secretary 36.26
the words which B. wrote at 36.27
and gave it to B. the scribe, 36.32
but B. the son of Neriah has set 43.03
the prophet and B. the son of 43.06
spoke to B. the son of Neriah, when 45.01
the God of Israel, to you, O B.: 45.02

BARZILLAI
and B. the Gileadite from Rogelim, 2Sa 17.27
Now B. the Gileadite had come down 19.31
B. was a very aged man, eighty years 19.32
And the king said to B., "Come over 19.33
But B. said to the king, "How many 19.34
the king kissed B. and blessed him, 19.39
the son of B. the Meholathite; 21.08
with the sons of B. the Gileadite, 1Ki 2.07
and the sons of B. (who had taken Ez 2.61
the daughters of B. the Gileadite, 2.61
the sons of B. (who had taken a Neh 7.63
daughters of B. the Gileadite and 7.63

BASE
The b. and the shaft of the lampstand Ex 25.31
pour out at the b. of the altar. 29.12
with its b. of bronze, for washing. 30.18
utensils and the laver and its b.; 30.28
utensils, and the laver and its b.; 31.09
its utensils, the laver and its b.; 35.16
The b. and the shaft of the lampstand 37.17
of bronze and its b. of bronze, 38.08
hundred talents, a talent for a b. 38.27
its utensils; the laver and its b.; 39.39
also anoint the laver and its b., 40.11
pour out at the b. of the altar of Lev 4.07
pour out at the b. of the altar of 4.18
blood at the b. of the altar of 4.25
its blood at the b. of the altar. 4.30
its blood at the b. of the altar. 4.34
drained out at the b. of the altar; 5.09
utensils, and the laver and its b., 8.11
the blood at the b. of the altar, 8.15
the blood at the b. of the altar; 9.09
from its b. to its flowers, it was Num 8.04
that certain b. fellows have gone Deu 13.13
lest there be a b. thought in your 15.09
b. fellows, beset the house round Ju 19.22
the b. fellows in Gibeah, that we 20.13
your maidservant as a b. woman, 1Sa 1.16
the wicked and b. fellows among 30.22
and set two b. fellows opposite him, 1Ki 21.10
And the two b. fellows came in and 21.13
and the b. fellows brought a charge 21.13
before my eyes anything that is b. Ps 101.03
and the b. fellow to the honorable. Is 3.05
its b., and its walls were of wood. Eze 41.22
its b. shall be one cubit high, and 43.13
from the b. on the ground to the 43.14
and its b. one cubit round about. 43.17
set the ephah down there on its b. Zec 5.11
them up to a b. mind and to Rom 1.28
dissension, slander, b. suspicions, 1Ti 6.04
by teaching for b. gain what they Tit 1.11

BASED
which is b. on law did not succeed Rom 9.31
but as if it were b. on works. 9.32
which is b. on the law shall live 10.05
the righteousness b. on faith says, 10.06
b. on law, but that which is through Php 3.09

BASEMATH
and B. the daughter of Elon the Gen 26.34
and B., Ishmael's daughter, the 36.03
Eliphaz; B. bore Reuel; 36.04

BASEMATH (cont.)
the son of B. the wife of Esau. Gen 36.10
are the sons of B., Esau's wife. 36.13
are the sons of B., Esau's wife. 36.17
(he had taken B. the daughter of 1Ki 4.15

BASES
and forty b. of silver you shall Ex 26.19
two b. under one frame for its two 26.19
and two b. under another frame for 26.19
and their forty b. of silver, 26.21
two b. under one frame, and two 26.21
and two b. under another frame; 26.21
with their b. of silver, sixteen b.; 26.25
two b. under one frame, and two b. 26.25
of gold, upon four b. of silver. 26.32
shall cast five b. of bronze for 26.37
be twenty and their b. twenty, 27.10
pillars twenty and their b. twenty, 27.11
with ten pillars and ten b. 27.12
with three pillars and three b. 27.14
with three pillars and three b. 27.15
four pillars and with them four b. 27.16
of silver, and their b. of bronze. 27.17
fine twined linen and b. of bronze. 27.18
its bars, its pillars, and its b.; 35.11
the court, its pillars and its b., 35.17
and he made forty b. of silver 36.24
two b. under one frame for its two 36.24
and two b. under another frame for 36.24
and their forty b. of silver, 36.26
two b. under one frame and two b. 36.26
frames with their b. of silver: 36.30
sixteen b., under every frame two 36.30
b., under every frame two b. 36.30
he cast for them four b. of silver. 36.36
but their five b. were of bronze. 36.38
were twenty and their b. twenty, 38.10
their b. twenty, of bronze, but the 38.11
with three pillars and three b. 38.14
with three pillars and three b. 38.15
And the b. for the pillars were of 38.17
their four b. were of bronze, their 38.19
for casting the b. of the sanctuary, 38.27
sanctuary, and the b. of the veil; 38.27
a hundred b. for the hundred 38.27
with it he made the b. for the door 38.30
the b. round about the court, and 38.31
and the b. of the gate of the court, 38.31
its bars, its pillars, and its b.; 39.33
and its b., and the screen for the 39.40
he laid its b., and set up its 40.18
the b., and all their accessories; Num 3.36
with their b. and pegs and cords. 3.37
with its bars, pillars, and b., 4.31
court round about with their b., 4.32
On what were its b. sunk, Job 38.06
columns, set upon b. of gold. Sol 5.15

BASHAN
and went up by the way to B.; Num 21.33
Og the king of B. came out against 21.33
and the kingdom of Og king of B., 32.33
in Heshbon, and Og the king of B., Deu 1.04
turned and went up the way to B.; 3.01
Og the king of B. came out against 3.01
the king of B., and all his people; 3.03
of Argob, the kingdom of Og in B. 3.04
tableland and all Gilead and all B., 3.10
cities of the kingdom of Og in B. 3.10
Og the king of B. was left of the 3.11
and all B., the kingdom of Og, that 3.13
whole of that B. is called the 3.13
B., as far as the border of the 3.14
and Golan in B. for the Manassites. 4.43
and the land of Og the king of B., 4.47
Og the king of B. came out against 29.07
herds of B. and goats, with the 32.14
whelp, that leaps forth from B. 33.22
king of Heshbon, and Og king of B., Jos 9.10
and Og king of B., one of the 12.04
Salecah and all B. to the boundary 12.05
Hermon, and all B. to Salecah; 13.11
all the kingdom of Og in B., 13.12
through all B., the whole kingdom 13.30
the whole kingdom of Og king of B., 13.30
which are in B., sixty cities, 13.30
cities of the kingdom of Og in B.; 13.31
were allotted Gilead and B., 17.01
besides the land of Gilead and B., 17.05
and Golan in B., from the tribe of 20.08
the half-tribe of Manasseh in B., 21.06
Golan in B. with its pasture lands, 21.27
Moses had given a possession in B.; 22.07
which is in B., sixty great cites 1Ki 4.13
the Amorites and of Og king of B. 4.19
the Arnon, that is, Gilead and B. 2Ki 10.33
in the land of B. as far as 1Ch 5.11
second, Janai, and Shaphat in B. 5.12
in B. and in its towns, and in all 5.16
numerous from B. to Baalhermon, 5.23
Naphtali, and Manasseh in B. 6.62
Golan in B. with its pasture lands 6.71
and the land of Og king of B. Neh 9.22
me, strong bulls of B. surround me; Ps 22.12
O mighty mountain, mountain of B.; 68.15
many-peaked mountain, mountain of B. 68.15
"I will bring them back from B., 68.22
king of B., and all the kingdoms of 135.11
king of B., for his steadfast love 136.20
and against all the oaks of B.; Is 2.13
and B. and Carmel shake off their 33.09
out, and lift up your voice in B.; Jer 22.20
he shall feed on Carmel and in B., 50.19
Of oaks of B. they made your oars; Eze 27.06
bulls, all of them fatlings of B. 39.18
you cows of B., who are in the Amo 4.01
them feed in B. and Gilead as in Mic 7.14
B. and Carmel wither, the bloom of Nah 1.04
Wail, oaks of B., for the thick Zec 11.02

BASIN
it in the blood which is in the b., Ex 12.22
one silver b. of seventy shekels, Num 7.13
one silver b. of seventy shekels, 7.19
one silver b. of seventy shekels, 7.25
one silver b. of seventy shekels, 7.31
one silver b. of seventy shekels, 7.37
one silver b. of seventy shekels, 7.43
one silver b. of seventy shekels, 7.49
one silver b. of seventy shekels, 7.55
one silver b. of seventy shekels, 7.61
one silver b. of seventy shekels, 7.67
one silver b. of seventy shekels, 7.73
one silver b. of seventy shekels, 7.79
thirty shekels and each b. seventy, 7.85
Then he poured water into a b., Jn 13.05

BASINS
half of the blood and put it in b., Ex 24.06
and shovels and b. and forks and 27.03
the b., the forks, and the fire pans: 38.03
and the b., all the utensils of the Num 4.14
twelve silver b., twelve golden 7.84
brought beds, b., and earthen 2Sa 17.28
the pots, the shovels, and the b. 1Ki 7.40
and the b., all these vessels in 7.45
b., dishes for incense, and firepans, 7.50
the house of the LORD b. of silver, 2Ki 12.13
the forks, the b., and the cups; 1Ch 28.17
And he made a hundred b. of gold. 2Ch 4.08
the pots, the shovels, and the b. 4.11
the snuffers, b., dishes for incense, 4.22
a thousand b. of gold, a thousand Ez 1.09
a thousand b. of silver, twenty-nine 1.09
fifty b., five hundred and thirty Neh 7.70

BASINS (cont.)
and the b., and the dishes for Jer 52.18
and the b., and the pots, and the 52.19

BASIS
it is no longer on the b. of works; Rom 11.06

BASKET
the uppermost b. there were all Gen 40.17
eating it out of the b. on my head." 40.17
took for him a b. made of bulrushes, Ex 2.03
she saw the b. among the reeds and 2.05
put them in one b. and bring them 29.03
b. and bring them in the b., 29.03
out of the b. of unleavened bread 29.23
and the bread that is in the b., 29.32
and the b. of unleavened bread; Lev 8.02
and out of the b. of unleavened 8.26
that is in the b. of ordination 8.31
and a b. of unleavened bread, cakes Num 6.15
with the b. of unleavened bread; 6.17
one unleavened cake out of the b., 6.19
you, and you shall put it in a b., Deu 26.02
shall take the b. from your hand, 26.04
Blessed shall be your b. and your 28.05
Cursed shall be your b. and your 28.17
the meat he put in a b., Ju 6.19
our hands were freed from the b. Ps 81.06
Like a b. full of birds, their Jer 5.27
One b. had very good figs, like 24.02
but the other b. had very bad figs, 24.02
a b. of summer fruit. Amo 8.01
"A b. of summer fruit." 8.02
the wall, lowering him in a b. Ac 9.25
let down in a b. through a window 2Co 11.33

BASKETS
were three cake b. on my head, Gen 40.16
the three b. are three days; 40.18
persons, and put their heads in b., 2Ki 10.07
two b. of figs placed before the Jer 24.01
took up twelve b. full of the Mt 14.20
took up seven b. full of the 15.37
and how many b. you gathered? 16.09
and how many b. you gathered? 16.10
took up twelve b. full of broken Mk 6.43
pieces left over, seven b. full. 8.08
how many b. full of broken pieces 8.19
how many b. full of broken pieces 8.20
twelve b. of broken pieces. Lk 9.17
filled twelve b. with fragments Jn 6.13

BASTARD
"No b. shall enter the assembly of Deu 23.02

BAT
its kind, the hoopoe, and the b. Lev 11.19
the hoopoe and the b. Deu 14.18

BATH
of vineyard shall yield but one b., Is 5.10
a just ephah, and a just b. Eze 45.10
The ephah and the b. shall be of 45.11
the b. containing one tenth of a 45.11
one tenth of a b. from each cor 45.14

BATHE
came down to b. at the river, Ex 2.05
and b. himself in water, and he Lev 14.08
and b. his body in water, and he 14.09
and b. himself in water, and be 15.05
and b. himself in water, and be 15.06
and b. himself in water, and be 15.07
and b. himself in water, and be 15.08
and b. himself in water, and be 15.10
and b. himself in water, and be 15.11
and he shall b. his body in running 15.13
he shall b. his whole body in water, 15.16
of them shall b. themselves in 15.18
and b. himself in water, and be 15.21
and b. himself in water, and be 15.22
and b. himself in water, and be 15.27
He shall b. his body in water, and 16.04
and he shall b. his body in water 16.24
his clothes and b. his body in 16.26
his clothes and b. his body in 16.28
and b. himself in water, and be 17.15
does not wash them or b. his flesh, 17.16
his clothes and b. his body in Num 19.07
in water and b. his body in water, 19.08
his clothes and b. himself in 19.19
he shall b. himself in water, and Deu 23.11
he will b. his feet in the blood of Ps 58.10
that you may b. your feet in blood, 68.23

BATHED
unless he has b. his body in water. Lev 22.06
I had b. my feet, how could I soil Sol 5.03
b. in milk, fitly set. 5.12
Then I b. you with water and washed Eze 16.09
For them you b. yourself, painted 23.40
"He who has b. does not need to Jn 13.10

BATHING
he saw from the roof a woman b.; 2Sa 11.02

BATHRABBIM
in Heshbon, by the gate of B. Sol 7.04

BATHS
it held two thousand b. 1Ki 7.26
each laver held forty b., 7.38
barley, twenty thousand b. of wine, 2Ch 2.10
and twenty thousand b. of oil. 2.10
it held over three thousand b. 4.05
a hundred b. of wine, a hundred Ez 7.22
a hundred b. of oil and salt 7.22
like the homer, contains ten b.); Eze 45.14

BATHSHEBA
"Is not this B., the daughter of 2Sa 11.03
B., and went in to her, and lay with 12.24
Then Nathan said to B. the mother 1Ki 1.11
So B. went to the king into his 1.15
B. bowed and did obeisance to the 1.16
King David answered, "Call B. to me." 1.28
Then B. bowed with her face to the 1.31
Haggith came to B. the mother of 2.13
B. said, "Very well; I will speak 2.18
So B. went to King Solomon, to speak 2.19

BATHSHUA
these three B. the Canaanitess 1Ch 2.03
four by B., the daughter of Ammiel; 3.05

BATS
to the moles and to the b., Is 2.20

BATTALION
gathered the whole b. before him. Mt 27.27
they called together the whole b. Mk 15.16

BATTERED
city, the gates are b. into ruins. Is 24.12

BATTERING
and they were b. the wall, to throw 2Sa 20.15
a b. down of walls and a shouting Is 22.05
and plant b. rams against it round Eze 4.02
to set b. rams against the gates, to 21.22
shock of his b. rams against your 26.09

BATTLE
and they joined b. in the Valley Gen 14.08
the land of Egypt equipped for b. Ex 13.18
and all his people, to b. at Edrei. Num 21.33
the men of war who had gone to b.: 31.21

BATTLE (cont.)

who went out to b. and all the Num 31.27
the men of war who went out to b., 31.28
for war, before the LORD to b., 32.27
who is armed to b. before the LORD, 32.29
Moab or contend with them in b., Deu 2.09
possession, and contend with him in b. 2.24
and all his people, to b. at Jahaz. 2.32
and all his people, to b. at Edrei. 3.01
And when you draw near to the b., 20.02
this day to b. against your 20.03
he die in the b. and another man 20.05
he die in the b. and another man 20.06
he die in the b. and another man 20.07
Bashan came out against us to b., 29.07
passed over before the LORD for b., Jos 4.13
the Arabah to meet Israel in b.; 8.14
they took all in b. 11.19
should come against Israel in b., 11.20
from the b. by the ascent of Heres. Ju 8.13
to go out to b. against the people 20.14
go up first to b. against the 20.18
went out to b. against Benjamin; 20.20
drew up the b. line against them 20.20
formed the b. line in the same 20.22
draw near to b. against our 20.23
again go out to b. against our 20.28
of all Israel, and the b. was hard; 20.34
the men of Israel should turn in b. 20.39
down before us, as in the first b." 20.39
but the b. overtook them, and those 20.42
each man of them his wife in b., 21.22
went out to b. against the Philistines; 1Sa 4.01
and when the b. spread, Israel was 4.02
thousand men on the field of b. 4.02
of Benjamin ran from the b. line, 4.12
"I am he who has come from the b.; 4.16
I fled from the b. today." 4.16
the day of the b. there was 13.22
him rallied and went into the b.; 14.20
followed hard after them in the b. 14.22
and the b. passed beyond Bethaven. 14.23
gathered their armies for b.; 17.01
up in line of b. against the 17.02
you come out to draw up for b.? 17.08
Jesse had followed Saul to the b.; 17.13
who went to the b. were Eliab the 17.13
was going forth to the b. line, 17.20
and the Philistines drew up for b., 17.21
you have come down to see the b." 17.28
for the b. is the LORD's and he will 17.47
toward the b. line to meet the 17.48
of the Philistines came out to b., 18.30
shall go down into b. and perish. 26.10
he shall not go down with us to b., 29.04
lest in the b. he become an adversary 29.04
shall not go up with us to the b.' 29.09
share is who goes down into the b., 30.24
The b. pressed hard upon Saul, and 31.03
"The people have fled from the b., 2Sa 1.04
fallen in the midst of the b.! 1.25
And the b. was very fierce that day 2.17
brother Asahel in the b. at Gibeon. 3.30
and drew up in b. array at the 10.08
saw that the b. was set against 10.09
drew near to b. against the 10.13
the time when kings go forth to b., 11.01
and that you go to b. in person. 17.11
and the b. was fought in the forest 18.06
The b. spread over the face of all 18.08
are ashamed when they flee in b. 19.03
we anointed over us, is dead in b. 19.10
shall no more go out with us to b., 21.17
gird me with strength for the b.; 22.40
who were gathered there for b., 23.09
go out to b. against their enemy, 1Ki 8.44
he said, "Who shall begin the b.?" 20.14
the seventh day the b. was joined; 20.29
went out into the midst of the b.; 20.39
go with me to b. at Ramothgilead?" 22.04
"Shall I go to b. against Ramothgilead, 22.06
shall we go to Ramothgilead to b., 22.15
disguise myself and go into b., 22.30
disguised himself and went into b. 22.30
about, and carry me out of the b., 22.34
And the b. grew hot that day, and 22.35
you go with me to b. against Moab?" 2Ki 3.07
saw that the b. was going against 3.26
one another in b. at Bethshemesh, 14.11
for they cried to God in the b., 1Ch 5.20
The b. pressed hard upon Saul, and 10.03
Philistines were gathered there for b. 11.13
Philistines for the b. against Saul. 12.19
equipped for b. with all the 12.33
six hundred men equipped for b. 12.35
seasoned troops ready for b. 12.36
arrayed in b. order, came to Hebron 12.38
balsam trees, then go out to b.; 14.15
from their cities and came to b. 19.07
and drew up in b. array at the 19.09
saw that the b. was set against 19.10
near before the Syrians for b.; 19.14
David set the b. in array against 19.17
the time when kings go forth to b., 20.01
go out to b. against their enemies, 2Ch 6.34
Abijah went out to b. having an 13.03
up his line of b. against him with 13.03
with their b. trumpets to sound 13.12
sound the call to b. against you. 13.12
the b. was before and behind them; 13.14
men of Judah raised the b. shout. 13.15
their lines of b. in the valley of 14.10
"Shall we go to b. against Ramothgilead, 18.05
shall we go to Ramothgilead to b., 18.14
disguise myself and go into b., 18.29
and they went into b. 18.29
about, and carry me out of the b., 18.33
And the b. grew hot that day, and 18.34
came against Jehoshaphat for b. 20.01
for the b. is not yours but God's. 20.15
You will not need to fight in this b.; 20.17
without letting go with him to b., 25.13
one another in b. at Bethshemesh, 25.21
but joined b. in the plain of 35.22
him, like a king prepared for b. Job 15.24
trouble, for the day of b. and war? 38.23
He smells the b. from afar, 39.25
think of the b.; you will not 41.08
gird me with strength for the b.; Ps 18.39
and mighty, the LORD, mighty in b.! 24.08
in safety from the b. that I wage, 55.18
bow, turned back on the day of b. 78.09
thou hast not made him stand in b. 89.43
covered my head in the day of b. 140.07
for war, and my fingers for b.; 144.01
is made ready for the day of b., Pro 21.31
nor the b. to the strong, nor bread Ecc 9.11
sword and your mighty men in b. Is 3.25
warrior in b. tumult and every 9.05
hosts is mustering a host for b. 13.04
harvest the b. shout has fallen. 16.09
bent bow, and from the press of b. 21.15
slain with the sword or dead in b. 22.02
that I had thorns and briers to b.! 27.04
who turn back the b. at the gate. 28.06
of his anger and the might of b.; 42.25
set in array as a man for b., Jer 6.23
a horse plunging headlong into b. 8.06
youths be slain by the sword in b. 18.21
and shield, and advance for b.! 46.03
will cause the b. cry to be heard 49.02
against her, and rise up for b.! 49.14
The noise of b. is in the land, and 50.22
as a man for b. against you, 50.42

BATTLE (cont.)
but none goes to b., for my wrath Eze 7.14
might stand in b. in the day of 13.05
broken, neither in anger nor in b. Dan 11.20
destroyed Betharbel on the day of b.; Hos 10.14
a powerful army drawn up for b. Joe 2.05
with shouting in the day of b., Amo 1.14
let us rise against her for b.!" Ob 1.01
blast and b. cry against the Zep 1.16
and the b. bow shall be cut off, and Zec 9.10
them like his proud steed in b. 10.03
tent peg, out of them the b. bow, 10.04
shall be like mighty men in b., 10.05
nations against Jerusalem to b., 14.02
as when he fights on a day of b. 14.03
sound, who will get ready for b.? 1Co 14.08
were like horses arrayed for b.; Rev 9.07
with horses rushing into b.; 9.09
them for b. on the great day of 16.14
and Magog, to gather them for b.; 20.08

BATTLEMENT
will build upon her a b. of silver; Sol 8.09

BATTLEMENTS
cities and against the lofty b. Zep 1.16
their b. are in ruins; I have laid 3.06

BATTLES
go out before us and fight our b." 1Sa 8.20
for me and fight the LORD's b." 18.17
is fighting the b. of the LORD; 25.28
From spoil won in b. they dedicated 1Ch 26.27
to help us and to fight our b." 2Ch 32.08

BATTLING
b. with brandished arm he will Is 30.32

BAVVAI
B. the son of Henadad, ruler of half Neh 3.18

BAY
from the b. that faces southward; Jos 15.02
runs from the b. of the sea at the 15.05
at the northern b. of the Salt Sea, 18.19
but they noticed a b. with a beach, Ac 27.39

BAZAARS
may establish b. for yourself in 1Ki 20.34

BAZLITH
the sons of B., the sons of Mehida, Neh 7.54

BAZLUTH
the sons of B., the sons of Mehida, Ez 2.52

BDELLIUM
b. and onyx stone are there. Gen 2.12
and its appearance like that of b. Num 11.07

BEACH
the whole crowd stood on the b. Mt 13.02
breaking, Jesus stood on the b.; Jn 21.04
down on the b. we prayed and bade Ac 21.05
but they noticed a bay with a b., 27.39
to the wind they made for the b. 27.40

BEADS
and b., to make atonement for Num 31.50

BEALIAH
B., Shemariah, Shephatiah the 1Ch 12.05

BEALOTH
Ziph, Telem, B., Jos 15.24
the son of Hushai, in Asher and B.; 1Ki 4.16

BEAM
his spear was like a weaver's b., 1Sa 17.07
whose spear was like a weaver's b. 2Sa 21.19
hand a spear like a weaver's b.; 1Ch 11.23
whose spear was like a weaver's b. 20.05
a b. shall be pulled out of his Ez 6.11
and the b. from the woodwork Hab 2.11

BEAMS
the supporting b. should not be 1Ki 6.06
of the house of b. and planks of 6.09
stone and one course of cedar b. 6.36
with cedar b. upon the pillars. 1Ki 7.02
about, and a course of cedar b. 7.12
its b., its thresholds, its walls, 2Ch 3.07
for binders and b. for the buildings 34.11
timber to make b. for the gates of Neh 2.08
they laid its b. and set its doors, 3.03
they laid its b. and set its doors, 3.06
who hast laid the b. of thy chambers Ps 104.03
the b. of our house are cedar, our Sol 1.17

BEANS
parched grain, b. and lentils, 2Sa 17.28
b. and lentils, millet and spelt, and Eze 4.09

BEAR
punishment is greater than I can b. Gen 4.13
are with child, and shall b. a son; 16.11
is ninety years old, b. a child?" 17.17
Sarah your wife shall b. you a son, 17.19
Sarah shall b. to you at this 17.21
say, 'Shall I indeed b. a child, 18.13
that she may b. upon my knees, and 30.03
then let me b. the blame for ever; 43.09
then I shall b. the blame in the 44.32
so he bowed his shoulder to b., 49.15
and they will b. the burden with Ex 18.22
"You shall not b. false witness 20.16
nor shall you b. witness in a suit, 23.02
and Aaron shall b. their names 28.12
So Aaron shall b. the names of the 28.29
Aaron shall b. the judgment of the 28.30
speak, he shall b. his iniquity. Lev 5.01
guilty and shall b. his iniquity. 5.17
eats of it shall b. his iniquity. 7.18
that you may b. the iniquity of 10.17
The goat shall b. all their iniquities 16.22
flesh, he shall b. his iniquity." 17.16
who eats it shall b. his iniquity, 19.08
lest you b. sin because of him. 19.17
vengeance or b. any grudge against 19.18
nakedness, he shall b. his iniquity. 20.17
they shall b. their iniquity. 20.19
they shall b. their sin, they shall 20.20
lest they b. sin for it and die 22.09
cause them to b. iniquity and 22.16
curses his God shall b. his sin. 24.15
the woman shall b. her iniquity." Num 5.31
that man shall b. his sin. 9.13
and they shall b. the burden of the 11.17
you may not b. it yourself alone. 11.17
you shall b. your iniquity, forty 14.34
with you shall b. iniquity in 18.01
meeting, lest they b. sin and die. 18.22
and they shall b. their iniquity; 18.23
And you shall b. no sin by reason 18.32
then he shall b. her iniquity." 30.15
'I am not able alone to b. you; Deu 1.09
How can I b. alone the weight and 1.12
shall you b. false witness against 5.20
the priests who b. the ark of the Jos 3.08
the priests who b. the ark of the 3.13
"Command the priests who b. the ark 4.16
priests shall b. seven trumpets of 6.04
seven priests b. seven trumpets of 6.06
those who b. the marshal's staff; Ju 5.14
you shall conceive and b. a son. 13.03
you shall conceive and b. a son. 13.05
you shall conceive and b. a son; 13.07
this night and should b. sons, Ru 1.12

BEAR (cont.)
or a b., and took a lamb from the 1Sa 17.34
lion and from the paw of the b., 17.37
like a b. robbed of her cubs in the 2Sa 17.08
let not the king b. it in mind. 19.19
whatever you impose on me I will b." 2Ki 18.14
root downward, and b. fruit upward; 19.30
thousand men to b. burdens and 2Ch 2.02
of them he assigned to b. burdens, 2.18
Many years thou didst b. with them, Neh 9.30
who made the B. and Orion, the Job 9.09
"B with me, and I will speak, and 21.03
"B. with me a little, and I will 36.02
you guide the B. with its children? 38.32
Make them b. their guilt, O God; Ps 5.10
How long must I b. pain in my soul, 13.02
who taunts me—then I could b. it; 55.12
Jerusalem kings b. gifts to thee. 68.29
Let the mountains b. prosperity for 72.03
how I b. in my bosom the insults of 89.50
On their hands they will b. you up, 91.12
if you scoff, you alone will b. it. Pro 9.12
but a broken spirit who can b.? 18.14
or a charging b. is a wicked ruler 28.15
under four it cannot b. up: 30.21
all of which b. twins, and not one Sol 4.02
all of them b. twins, not one among 6.06
woman shall conceive and b. a son, Is 7.14
The cow and the b. shall feed; 11.07
root downward, and b. fruit upward; 37.31
I have made, and I will b.; 46.04
you who b. the vessels of the LORD. 52.11
and he shall b. their iniquities. 53.11
"Sing, O barren one, who did not b.; 54.01
or b. children for calamity; 65.23
is an affliction, and I must b. it." Jer 10.19
that for thy sake I b. reproach. 15.15
for it does not cease to b. fruit." 17.08
and do not b. a burden on the 17.21
and not to b. a burden and enter by 17.27
that they may b. sons and daughters; 29.06
now, and see, can a man b. a child? 30.06
could no longer b. your evil 44.22
He is to me like a b. lying in wait, Lam 3.10
a man that he b. the yoke in his 3.27
and we b. their iniquities. 5.07
you shall b. their punishment. Eze 4.04
long shall you b. the punishment 4.05
and b. the punishment of the house 4.06
And they shall b. their punishment— 14.10
B. your disgrace, you also, for you 16.52
and b. your disgrace, for you have 16.52
that you may b. your disgrace and 16.54
You b. the penalty of your lewdness 16.58
and b. fruit, and become a noble 17.08
bring forth boughs and b. fruit, 17.23
therefore b. the consequences of 23.35
and you shall b. the penalty for 23.49
and they b. their shame with those 32.24
and they b. their shame with those 32.25
and b. their shame with those who 32.30
shall no longer b. the disgrace of 36.15
shall b. their punishment. 44.10
that they shall b. their punishment. 44.12
but they shall b. their shame, 44.13
but they will b. fresh fruit every 47.12
beast, a second one, like a b. Dan 7.05
dried up, they shall b. no fruit. Hos 9.16
now they must b. their guilt. 10.02
them like a b. robbed of her cubs, 13.08
Samaria shall b. her guilt, because 13.16
fled from a lion, and a b. met him; Amo 5.19
is not able to b. all his words. 7.10
so you shall b. the scorn of the Mic 6.16
I will b. the indignation of the 7.09
you will not b. reproach for it. Zep 3.18
and shall b. royal honor, and shall Zec 6.13
in the field shall not fail to b., Mal 3.11
she will b. a son, and you shall Mt 1.21
virgin shall conceive and b. a son, 1.23
B. fruit that befits repentance, 3.08
that does not b. good fruit is cut 3.10
On their hands they will b. you up, 4.06
A sound tree cannot b. evil fruit, 7.18
A sound tree cannot b. evil fruit, 7.18
that does not b. good fruit is cut 7.19
to b. testimony before them and the 10.18
How long am I to b. with you? 17.17
You shall not b. false witness, 19.18
hard to b., and lay them on men's 23.04
word and accept it and b. fruit, Mk 4.20
How long am I to b. with you? 9.19
because you b. the name of Christ, 9.41
Do not b. false witness, Do not 10.19
to b. testimony before them. 13.09
wife Elizabeth will b. you a son, Lk 1.13
conceive in your womb and b. a son, 1.31
B. fruits that befit repentance, and 3.08
that does not b. good fruit is cut 3.09
On their hands they will b. you up, 4.11
does a bad tree b. good fruit; 6.43
I to be with you and b. with you? 9.41
load men with burdens hard to b., 11.46
Whoever does not b. his own cross 14.27
Do not b. false witness, Honor your 18.20
be a time for you to b. testimony. 21.13
to b. witness to the light, that all Jn 1.07
but came to b. witness to the light 1.08
needed no one to b. witness of man; 2.25
and b. witness to what we have seen 3.11
You yourselves b. me witness, that I 3.28
If I b. witness to myself, my 5.31
b. me witness that the Father has 5.36
it is they that b. witness to me; 5.39
"Even if I do b. witness to myself, 8.14
I b. witness to myself, and the 8.18
you cannot b. to hear my word. 8.43
name, they b. witness to me; 10.25
that does b. fruit he prunes, that 15.02
it may b. more fruit 15.02
branch cannot b. fruit by itself, 15.04
that you b. much fruit, and so prove 15.08
should go and b. fruit and that 15.16
Father, he will b. witness to me; 15.26
to you, but you cannot b. them now. 16.12
b. witness to the wrong; but if I have 18.23
to b. witness to the truth. Every one 18.37
the prophets b. witness that every Ac 10.43
nor we have been able to b.? 15.10
should have reason to b. with you, 18.14
council of elders b. me witness. 22.05
so you must b. witness also at Rome." 23.11
to serve and b. witness to the 26.16
and the prophets b. witness to it, Rom 3.21
order that we may b. fruit for God. 7.04
our members to b. fruit for death. 7.05
I b. them witness that they have a 10.02
for he does not b. the sword in 13.04
strong ought to b. with the 15.01
we shall also b. the image of the 1Co 15.49
I wish you would b. with me in a 2Co 11.01
foolishness. Do b. with me! 11.01
For you gladly b. with fools, being 11.19
For you b. it if a man makes slaves 11.20
For I b. you witness that, if Gal 4.15
O barren one that dost not b.; 4.27
troubling you will b. his judgment, 5.10
B. one another's burdens, and so 6.02
man will have to b. his own load. 6.05
for I b. on my body the marks of 6.17
For I b. him witness that he has Col 4.13
Therefore when we could b. it no longer, 1Th 3.01
when I could b. it no longer, I sent 3.05
b. children, rule their households, 1Ti 5.14

BEAR (cont.)

offered once to b. the sins of — Heb 9.28
b. with my word of exhortation, for — 13.22
how you cannot b. evil men but — Rev 2.02
woman who was about to b. a child, — 12.04
of God and b. testimony to Jesus. — 12.17

BEARD

a disease on the head or the b., — Lev 13.29
a leprosy of the head or the b. — 13.30
shave off his b. and his eyebrows, — 14.09
or mar the edges of your b. — 19.27
against me, I caught him by his b., — 1Sa 17.35
let his spittle run down his b. — 21.13
and shaved off half the b. of each, — 2Sa 10.04
his feet, nor trimmed his b., — 19.24
Amasa by the b. with his right — 20.09
pulled hair from my head and b., — Ex 9.03
the head, running down upon the b., — Ps 133.02
upon the b. of Aaron, running down — 133.02
and it will sweep away the b. also. — Is 7.20
is baldness, every b. is shorn; — 15.02
to those who pulled out the b.; — 50.06
is shaved and every b. cut off; — Jer 48.37
pass it over your head and your b.; — Eze 5.01

BEARDS

shave off the edges of their b., — Lev 21.05
Jericho until your b. have grown, — 2Sa 10.05
Jericho until your b. have grown, — 1Ch 19.05
with their b. shaved and their — Jer 41.05

BEARERS

the bier, and the b. stood still. — Lk 7.14

BEARING

and fruit trees b. fruit in which — Gen 1.11
and trees b. fruit in which is — 1.12
has prevented me from b. children; — 16.02
name Judah; then she ceased b. — 29.35
that she had ceased b. children, — 30.09
Gilead, with their camels b. gum, — 37.25
Gershonites, in serving and b. burdens: — Num 4.24
and the work of b. burdens in the — 4.47
you a root b. poisonous and bitter — Deu 29.18
b. them on its pinions, — 32.11
the priests b. the ark of the — Jos 3.14
of the priests b. the ark were — 3.15
of the priests b. the ark of the — 4.09
the priests b. the ark of the — 4.18
seven priests b. the seven trumpets — 6.08
seven priests b. the seven trumpets — 6.13
b. the ark of the covenant of God; — 2Sa 15.24
b. two hundred loaves of bread, a — 16.01
with camels b. spices, and very much — 1Ki 10.02
The men of Judah b. shield and — 1Ch 12.24
and camels b. spices and very much — 2Ch 9.01
b. the seed for sowing, shall come — Ps 126.06
no mischance or failure in b.; — 144.14
to me, I am weary of b. them. — Is 1.14
cakes for her b. her image and — Jer 44.19
"You are b. witness to yourself; — Jn 8.13
b. his own cross, to the place — 19.17
disciple who is b. witness to — 21.24
Spirit himself b. witness with our — Rom 8.16
b. children for slavery; — Gal 4.24
world it is b. fruit and growing— — Col 1.06
b. fruit in every good work and — 1.10
ill be saved through b. children, — 1Ti 2.15
b. this seal: "The Lord knows those — 2Ti 2.19
God b. witness by accepting his — Heb 11.04
outside the camp, b. abuse for him. — 13.13
patiently and b. up for my name's — Rev 2.03

BEAR'S

a leopard, its feet were like a b., — Rev 13.02

BEARS

let loose, that b. comely fawns. — Gen 49.21
a wife and she b. him sons or — Ex 21.04
and b. a male child, then she shall — Lev 12.02
But if she b. a female child, then — 12.05
is the law for her who b. a child, — 12.07
as a man b. his son, in all the way — Deu 1.31
son whom she b. shall succeed to — 25.06
feet and her children whom she b., — 28.57
has killed both lions and b.; — 1Sa 17.36
Blessed be the Lord, who daily b. us up; — Ps 68.19
A man who b. false witness against — Pro 25.18
We all growl like b., we moan — Is 59.11
the tree b. its fruit, the fig tree — Joe 2.22
So, every sound tree b. good fruit, — Mt 7.17
but the bad tree b. evil fruit. — 7.17
he indeed b. fruit, and yields, in — 13.23
"For no good tree b. bad fruit, — Lk 6.43
And if it b. fruit next year, well — 13.09
He b. witness to what he has seen — Jn 3.32
there is another who b. witness to me, — 5.32
testimony which he b. to me is true. — 5.32
who sent me b. witness to me." — 8.18
but if it dies, it b. much fruit. — 12.24
Every branch of mine that b. no fruit, — 15.02
he it is that b. much fruit, for — 15.05
conscience also b. witness and — Rom 2.15
my conscience b. me witness in the — 9.01
any one who b. the name of brother — 1Co 5.11
Love b. all things, believes all — 13.07
of God and b. the very stamp of — Heb 1.03
But if it b. thorns and thistles, it — 6.08
Holy Spirit also b. witness to us; — 10.15

BEAST

And to every b. of the earth, and to — Gen 1.30
formed every b. of the field and — 2.19
air, and to every b. of the field; — 2.20
man and b. and creeping things and — 6.07
they and every b. according to its — 7.14
And every b., every creeping thing, — 8.19
be upon every b. of the earth, — 9.02
of every b. I will require it and — 9.05
and every b. of the earth with you, — 9.10
say that a wild b. has devoured — 37.20
a wild b. has devoured him; — 37.33
and there came gnats on man and b.; — Ex 8.17
so there were gnats on man and b. — 8.18
on man and b. throughout all the — 9.09
breaking out in sores on man and b. — 9.10
every man and b. that is in the — 9.19
upon man and b. and every plant of — 9.22
the land of Egypt, both man and b.; — 12.12
both of man and of b., is mine." — 13.02
whether b. or man, he shall not live — 19.13
and the dead b. shall be his. — 21.34
and the dead b. also they shall — 21.35
ox, and the dead b. shall be his. — 21.36
If the stolen b. is found alive in — 22.04
or lets his b. loose and it feeds — 22.05
an ox or a sheep or any b. to keep, — 22.10
"Whoever lies with a b. shall be — 22.19
of an unclean b. or a carcass of — Lev 5.02
or an unclean b. or any unclean — 7.21
pertaining to b. and bird and — 11.46
in hunting any b. or bird that may — 17.13
lie with any b. and defile yourself — 18.23
herself to a b. to lie with it: — 18.23
If a man lies with a b., he shall be — 20.15
and you shall kill the b. — 20.15
approaches any b. and lies with it. — 20.16
shall kill the woman and the b.; — 20.16
the clean b. and the unclean, and — 20.25
abominable by b. or by bird or by — 20.25
He who kills a b. shall make it — 24.18
He who kills a b. shall make it — 24.21
makes any exchange of b. for b., — 27.10

BEAST (cont.)

that he has, whether of man or b., Lev 27.28
in Israel, both of man and of b.; Num 3.13
are mine, both of man and of b.; 8.17
of all flesh, whether man or b., 18.15
the booty, both of man and of b. 31.11
was taken, both of man and of b., 31.26
the likeness of any b. that is on Deu 4.17
be he who lies with any kind of b.' 27.21
to her servant, "Urge the b. on; 2Ki 4.24
and a wild b. of Lebanon passed 14.09
and a wild b. of Lebanon passed 2Ch 25.18
There was no b. with me but the Neh 2.12
with me but the b. on which I rode. 2.12
place for the b. that was under me 2.14
that the wild b. may trample them. Job 39.15
man and b. thou savest, O LORD. Ps 36.06
For every b. of the forest is mine, 50.10
I was like a b. toward thee. 73.22
drink to every b. of the field; 104.11
of Egypt, both of man and of b.; 135.08
has regard for the life of his b., Pro 12.10
spirit of the b. goes down to the Ecc 3.21
any ravenous b. come up on it; Is 35.09
upon man and b., upon the trees of Jer 7.20
of this city, both man and b.; 21.06
the seed of man and the seed of b. 31.27
is a desolation, without man or b.; 32.43
'It is a waste without man or b., 33.10
without man or inhabitant or b., 33.10
which is waste, without man or b., 33.12
will cut off from it man and b.?" 36.29
both man and b. shall flee away. 50.03
dwell in it, neither men nor b., 51.62
and cut off from it man and b., Eze 14.13
and I cut off from it man and b.; 14.17
to cut off from it man and b.; 14.19
to cut off from it man and b.! 14.21
and cut off from it man and b.; 25.13
will cut off from you man and b.; 29.08
and no foot of b. shall pass 29.11
will multiply upon you man and b.; 36.11
of anything, whether bird or b., 44.31
mind was made like that of a b., Dan 5.21
another b., a second one, like a 7.05
and the b. had four heads; 7.06
a fourth b., terrible and dreadful 7.07
the b. was slain, and its body 7.11
the truth concerning the fourth b., 7.19
"Thus he said: 'As for the fourth b., 7.23
no b. could stand before him, and 8.04
as a wild b. would rend them. Hos 13.08
his nobles: Let neither man nor b., Jon 3.07
but let man and b. be covered with 3.08
"I will sweep away man and b.; Zep 1.03
no wage for man or any wage for b., Zec 8.10
him on his own b. and brought him Lk 10.34
"If even a b. touches the mountain, Heb 12.20
For every kind of b. and bird, Jas 3.07
the b. that ascends from the Rev 11.07
And I saw a b. rising out of the 13.01
And the b. that I saw was like a 13.02
earth followed the b. with wonder. 13.03
had given his authority to the b., 13.04
b., and they worshiped the b., 13.04
b., saying, "Who is like the b., 13.04
And the b. was given a mouth 13.05
Then I saw another b. which rose 13.11
of the first b. in its presence, 13.12
inhabitants worship the first b., 13.12
to work in the presence of the b., 13.14
image for the b. which was wounded 13.14
image of the b. so that the image 13.15
image of the b. should even speak, 13.15
the image of the b. to be slain. 13.15
the name of the b. or the number 13.17
reckon the number of the b., 13.18
one worships the b. and its image, 14.09
worshipers of the b. and its image, 14.11
conquered the b. and its image and 15.02
the mark of the b. and worshiped 16.02
his bowl on the throne of the b., 16.10
mouth of the b. and from the mouth 16.13
on a scarlet b. which was full of 17.03
and of the b. with seven heads and 17.07
The b. that you saw was, and is not, 17.08
will marvel to behold the b., 17.08
As for the b. that was and is not, 17.11
for one hour, together with the b. 17.12
power and authority to the b.; 17.13
they and the b. will hate the 17.16
over their royal power to the b., 17.17
And I saw the b. and the kings of 19.19
And the b. was captured, and with it 19.20
the mark of the b. and those who 19.20
worshiped the b. or its image and 20.04
where the b. and the false prophet 20.10

BEAST'S

and let a b. mind be given to him; Dan 4.16

BEASTS

things and b. of the earth according Gen 1.24
And God made the b. of the earth 1.25
b., all swarming creatures that 7.21
and all the b. and all the cattle 8.01
torn by wild b. I did not bring to 31.39
property and all their b. be ours? 34.23
all his b., and all his property 36.06
load your b. and go back to the 45.17
If it is torn by b., let him bring Ex 22.13
that is torn by b. in the field; 22.31
they leave the wild b. may eat. 23.11
and the wild b. multiply against 23.29
the fat of one that is torn by b., Lev 7.24
among all the b. that are on the 11.02
of itself or what is torn by b., 17.15
or is torn by b. he shall not eat, 22.08
and for the b. that are in your 25.07
will remove evil b. from the land, 26.06
let loose the wild b. among you, 26.22
of unclean b. you shall redeem. Num 18.15
fifty, both of persons and of b., 31.47
livestock and for all their b. 35.03
lest the wild b. grow too numerous Deu 7.22
ground, and the fruit of your b., 28.04
air, and for the b. of the earth; 28.26
send the teeth of b. against them, 32.24
men and b. and all that they found. Ju 20.48
the air and to the b. of the field. Isa 17.44
and to the wild b. of the earth; 17.46
or the b. of the field by night. 2Sa 21.10
he spoke also of b., and of birds, 1Ki 4.33
army or for the b. which followed 2Ki 3.09
you, your cattle, and your b. 3.17
and gold, with goods and with b., Ez 1.04
with b., and with costly wares, 1.06
shall not fear the b. of the earth. Job 5.22
and the b. of the field shall be at 5.23
"But ask the b., and they will 12.07
The proud b. have not trodden it; 28.08
us more than the b. of the earth, 35.11
Then the b. go into their lairs, and 37.08
for him where all the wild b. play. 40.20
and also the b. of the field, Ps 8.07
he is like the b. that perish. 49.12
he is like the b. that perish. 49.20
Rebuke the b. that dwell among the 68.30
soul of thy dove to the wild b.; 74.19
thy saints to the b. of the earth. 79.02
when all the b. of the forest creep 104.20
He gives to the b. their food, 147.09
B. and all cattle, creeping things 148.10
She has slaughtered her b., Pro 9.02
mightiest among b. and does not 30.30

BEASTS (cont.)

to show them that they are but b.	Ecc 3.18
men and the fate of b. is the same;	3.19
man has no advantage over the b.;	3.19
of rams and the fat of fed b.;	Is 1.11
But wild b. will lie down there, and	13.21
mountains and to the b. of the earth.	18.06
and all the b. of the earth will	18.06
They destined Tyre for wild b.	23.13
An oracle on the b. of the Negeb.	30.06
And wild b. shall meet with hyenas,	34.14
nor are its b. enough for a burnt	40.16
The wild b. will honor me, the	43.20
their idols are on b. and cattle;	46.01
are loaded as burdens on weary b.	46.01
All you b. of the field, come to	56.09
to devour—all you b. in the forest.	56.09
air, and for the b. of the earth;	Jer 7.33
the air and the b. have fled and	9.10
dwell in it the b. and the birds	12.04
Go, assemble all the wild b.;	12.09
the air and the b. of the earth to	15.03
air and for the b. of the earth.	16.04
the air and to the b. of the earth.	19.07
him also the b. of the field to	27.06
to him even the b. of the field.'"	28.14
of the air and the b. of the earth.	34.20
"Therefore wild b. and jackals	50.39
died of itself or was torn by b.,	Eze 4.14
famine and wild b. against you,	5.17
and loathsome b., and all the idols	8.10
If I cause wild b. to pass through	14.15
may pass through because of the b.;	14.15
evil b., and pestilence, to cut off	14.21
it will dwell all kinds of b.;	17.23
To the b. of the earth and to the	29.05
branches all the b. of the field	31.06
will be all the b. of the field.	31.13
will gorge the b. of the whole	32.04
destroy all its b. from beside	32.13
shall the hoofs of b. trouble them.	32.13
will give to the b. to be devoured;	33.27
became food for all the wild b.	34.05
become food for all the wild b.,	34.08
and banish wild b. from the land,	34.25
nor shall the b. of the land devour	34.28
and the b. of the field, and all	38.20
and to the wild b. to be devoured.	39.04
sort and to all b. of the field,	39.17
the b. of the field, and the birds	Dan 2.38
The b. of the field found shade	4.12
let the b. flee from under it and	4.14
lot be with the b. in the grass of	4.15
under which b. of the field found	4.21
lot be with the b. of the field,	4.23
shall be with the b. of the field;	4.25
shall be with the b. of the field;	4.32
And four great b. came up out of	7.03
from all the b. that were before	7.07
As for the rest of the b.,	7.12
'These four great b. are four kings	7.17
and the b. of the field shall	Hos 2.12
that day with the b. of the field,	2.18
and also the b. of the field, and	4.03
how the b. groan! The herds	Joe 1.18
Even the wild b. cry to thee	1.20
Fear not, you b. of the field, for	2.22
of your fatted b. I will not look	Amo 5.22
a lion among the b. of the forest,	Mic 5.08
destruction of the b. will terrify	Hab 2.17
of her, all the b. of the field;	Zep 2.14
she has become, a lair for wild b.!	2.15
and whatever b. may be in those	Zec 14.15
and he was with the wild b.;	Mk 1.13
to me slain b. and sacrifices,	Ac 7.42
animals and b. of prey and reptiles	11.06
I fought with b. at Ephesus?	1Co 15.32
liars, evil b., lazy gluttons.	Tit 1.12
and by wild b. of the earth.	Rev 6.08

BEAT

and you shall b. some of it very	Ex 30.36
it in mills or b. it in mortars,	Num 11.08
as bees do and b. you down in Seir	Deu 1.44
When you b. your olive trees, you	24.20
should go on to b. him with more	25.03
"Then loud b. the horses' hoofs	Ju 5.22
then she b. out what she had	Ru 2.17
I b. them fine as the dust of the	2Sa 22.43
and b. it to dust and cast the dust	2Ki 23.06
and b. the Asherim and the images	2Ch 34.07
cursed them and b. some of them	Neh 13.25
I b. them fine as dust before the	Ps 18.42
if you b. him with a rod, he will	Pro 23.13
If you b. him with the rod you will	23.14
they b. me, but I did not feel it.	23.35
they b. me, they wounded me, they	Sol 5.07
and they shall b. their swords into	Is 2.04
B. upon your breasts for the	32.12
Then Pashhur b. Jeremiah the	Jer 20.02
and they b. him and imprisoned him	37.15
B. your plowshares into swords, and	Joe 3.10
and the sun b. upon the head of	Jon 4.08
and they shall b. their swords into	Mic 4.03
you shall b. in pieces many peoples.	4.13
winds blew and b. upon that house,	Mt 7.25
winds blew and b. against that	7.27
took his servants and b. one,	21.35
and begins to b. his fellow servants,	24.49
and the waves b. into the boat, so	Mk 4.37
And they took him and b. him,	12.03
some they b. and some they killed.	12.05
who stripped him and b. him,	Lk 10.30
and begins to b. the menservants	12.45
but b. his breast, saying, 'God, be	18.13
but the tenants b. him,	20.10
him also they b. and treated	20.11
Jesus mocked him and b. him;	22.63
they b. them and charged them not	Ac 5.40
gave orders to b. them with rods.	16.22
and b. him in front of the tribunal	18.17
imprisoned and b. those who	22.19

BEATEN

were b., and were asked, "Why have	Ex 5.14
and behold, your servants are b.;	5.16
to you pure b. olive oil for the	27.20
with a fourth of a hin of b. oil,	29.40
handfuls of sweet incense b. small;	Lev 16.12
pure oil from b. olives for the	24.02
with a fourth of a hin of b. oil.	Num 28.05
the guilty man deserves to be b.,	Deu 25.02
lie down and be b. in his presence	25.02
a pretence of being b. before them,	Jos 8.15
of Israel were b. before the	2Sa 2.17
and twenty thousand cors of b. oil.	1Ki 5.11
hundred large shields of b. gold;	10.16
three hundred shields of b. gold;	10.17
hundred large shields of b. gold;	2Ch 9.15
shekels of b. gold went into each	9.15
three hundred shields of b. gold;	9.16
it, as when an olive tree is b.—	Is 17.06
as when an olive tree is b.,	24.13
through you will be b. down by it.	28.18
but dill is b. out with a stick, and	28.27
B. silver is brought from Tarshish,	Jer 10.09
Their warriors are b. down,	46.05
All her images shall be b. to pieces,	Mic 1.07
from the land, b. by the waves;	Mt 14.24
and you will be b. in synagogues;	Mk 13.09
"They have b. us publicly, uncondemned,	Ac 16.37
Three times I have been b. with rods;	2Co 11.25
wrong and are b. for it you take	1Pe 2.20

BEATING
and he saw an Egyptian b. a Hebrew, Ex 2.11
from the hand of him who is b. him, Deu 25.11
son Gideon was b. out wheat in the Ju 6.11
house round about, b. on the door; 19.22
the poor is a b. rain that leaves Pro 28.03
My heart is b. wildly; Jer 4.19
like doves, and b. their breasts. Nah 2.07
will, shall receive a severe b. Lk 12.47
know, and did what deserved a b., 12.48
shall receive a light b. Every one 12.48
returned home b. their breasts. 23.48
the soldiers, they stopped b. Paul. Ac 21.32
I do not box as one b. the air; 1Co 9.26

BEATINGS
b., imprisonments, tumults, labors, 2Co 6.05
imprisonments, with countless b., 11.23

BEAUTEOUS
a heritage most b. of all nations. Jer 3.19

BEAUTIFUL
that you are a woman b. to behold; Gen 12.11
saw that the woman was very b. 12.14
weak, but Rachel was b. and lovely. 29.17
and see among the captives a b. woman, Deu 21.11
the spoil a b. mantle from Shinar, Jos 7.21
and had b. eyes, and was handsome. 1Sa 16.12
was of good understanding and b., 25.03
and the woman was very b. 2Sa 11.02
had a b. sister. whose name was 13.01
she was a b. woman. 14.27
sought for a b. maiden throughout 1Ki 1.03
The maiden was very b.; 1.04
"Let b. young virgins be sought out Est 2.02
gather all the b. young virgins to 2.03
the maiden was b. and lovely, 2.07
b. in elevation, is the joy of all Ps 48.02
he will bestow on you a b. crown. Pro 4.09
snout is a b. woman without 11.22
has made everything b. in its time; Ecc 3.11
Behold, you are b., my love; Sol 1.15
behold, you are b.; your eyes are 1.15
you are b., my beloved, truly lovely. 1.16
you are b., my love, behold, you are 4.01
behold you are b.! Your eyes are doves 4.01
You are b. as Tirzah, my love, comely 6.04
and against all the b. craft. Is 2.16
the LORD shall be b. and glorious, 4.02
large and b. houses, without inhabitant. 5.09
put on your b. garments, O Jerusalem, 52.01
How b. upon the mountains are the 52.07
Our holy and b. house, where our 64.11
for your b. crown has come down Jer 13.18
that was given you, your b. flock? 13.20
"A b. heifer is Egypt, but a gadfly 46.20
Their b. ornament they used for Eze 7.20
and a b. crown upon your head. 16.12
You grew exceedingly b., 16.13
and b. crowns upon their heads. 23.42
It was b. in its greatness, in the 31.07
I made it b. in the mass of its 31.09
songs with a b. voice and plays 33.32
tombs, which outwardly appear b., Mt 23.27
for she has done a b. thing to me. 26.10
She has done a b. thing to me. Mk 14.06
which is called B. to ask alms of Ac 3.02
for alms at the B. Gate of the 3.10
was born, and was b. before God. 7.20
"How b. are the feet of those who Rom 10.15
they saw that the child was b.; Heb 11.23

BEAUTIFY
to b. the house of the LORD which Ez 7.27
to b. the place of my sanctuary; Is 60.13
In vain you b. yourself. Your lovers Jer 4.30

BEAUTIFYING
was the regular period of their b., Est 2.12

BEAUTY
your brother, for glory and for b. Ex 28.02
shall make them for glory and b. 28.40
be praised for his b. as Absalom; 2Sa 14.25
the peoples and the princes her b.; Est 1.11
to behold the b. of the LORD, and to Ps 27.04
and the king will desire your b. 45.11
Out of Zion, the perfection of b., 50.02
strength and b. are in his sanctuary. 96.06
Do not desire her b. in your heart, Pro 6.25
but the b. of old men is their gray 20.29
and b. is vain, but a woman who 31.30
instead of b., shame. Is 3.24
fading flower of its glorious b., 28.01
fading flower of its glorious b., 28.04
crown of glory, and a diadem of b., 28.05
Your eyes will see the king in his b.; 33.17
and all its b. is like the flower 40.06
with the b. of a man, to dwell in a 44.13
and no b. that we should desire him. 53.02
be a crown of b. in the hand of 62.03
was called the perfection of b., Lam 2.15
the b. of their form was like 4.07
the nations because of your b., Eze 16.14
"But you trusted in your b., 16.15
place and prostituted your b., 16.25
you have said, 'I am perfect in b.' 27.03
your builders made perfect your b. 27.04
they made perfect your b. 27.11
against the b. of your wisdom and 28.07
full of wisdom and perfect in b. 28.12
heart was proud because of your b.; 28.17
garden of God was like it in b. 31.08
'Whom do you surpass in b.? 32.19
his b. shall be like the olive, and Hos 14.06
one vessel for b. and another for Rom 9.21
flower falls, and its b. perishes. Jas 1.11

BEBAI
The sons of B., six hundred and Ez 2.11
Of the sons of B., Zechariah, the 8.11
the son of B., and with him twenty-eight 8.11
Of the sons of B. were Jehohanan, 10.28
The sons of B., six hundred and Neh 7.16
Bunni, Azgad, B., 10.15

BECAME
and man b. a living being. Gen 2.07
it divided and b. four rivers. 2.10
he b. the father of a son in his 5.03
Adam after he b. the father of 5.04
he b. the father of Enosh. 5.06
he b. the father of Kenan. 5.09
he b. the father of Mahalalel. 5.12
he b. the father of Jared. 5.15
years he b. the father of Enoch. 5.18
he b. the father of Methuselah. 5.21
he b. the father of Lamech. 5.25
he b. the father of a son, 5.28
Noah b. the father of Shem, Ham, and 5.32
and b. drunk, and lay uncovered in 9.21
Cush b. the father of Nimrod; 10.08
Egypt b. the father of Ludim, Anamim, 10.13
Canaan b. the father of Sidon his 10.15
Arpachshad b. the father of Shelah; 10.24
and Shelah b. the father of Eber. 10.24
Joktan b. the father of Almodad, 10.26
he b. the father of Arpachshad two 11.10
years he b. the father of Shelah; 11.12
he b. the father of Eber. 11.14
he b. the father of Peleg; 11.16
he b. the father of Reu; 11.18
he b. the father of Serug; 11.20
he b. the father of Nahor; 11.22
he b. the father of Terah; 11.24

BECAME (cont.)

he b. the father of Abraham, Nahor, and Gen 11.26
and she b. a pillar of salt. 19.26
my mother; and she b. my wife. 20.12
wilderness and b. an expert with 21.20
Bethuel b. the father of Rebekah. 22.23
took Rebekah, and she b. his wife; 24.67
and the man b. rich, and gained more 26.13
and more until he b. very wealthy. 26.13
Then Jacob b. angry, and upbraided 31.36
and he b. a successful man; 39.02
For your servant b. surety for the 44.32
upon them. The land b. Pharaoh's; 47.20
and b. a slave at forced labor. 49.15
daughter, and he b. her son; Ex 2.10
on the ground, and it b. a serpent; 4.03
and it b. a rod in his hand— 4.04
his servants, and it b. a serpent. 7.10
down his rod, and they b. serpents. 7.12
and the Nile b. foul, so that the 7.21
of the earth b. gnats throughout 8.17
and it b. boils breaking out in 9.10
land of Egypt since it b. a nation. 9.24
the water, and the water b. sweet. 15.25
and it bred worms and b. foul; 16.20
and the land b. defiled, so that I Lev 18.25
you, so that the land b. defiled); 18.27
and the people b. impatient on the Num 21.04
men; and they b. a warning. 26.10
and there he b. a nation, great, Deu 26.05
fat, you grew thick, you b. sleek; 32.15
Thus the LORD b. king in Jeshurun, 33.05
the people melted, and b. as water. Jos 7.05
So they b. hewers of wood and 9.21
So Hebron b. the inheritance of 14.14
it b. an inheritance of the descendants 24.32
and b. subject to forced labor. Ju 1.30
of Bethanath b. subject to forced 1.33
and they b. subject to forced labor. 1.35
and it b. a snare to Gideon and to 8.27
and he b. indignant over the misery 10.16
And it b. a custom in Israel 11.39
on his arms b. as flax that has 15.14
one of his sons, who b. his priest. 17.05
the young man b. to him like one 17.11
and the young man b. his priest, 17.12
And his concubine b. angry with him, 19.02
Boaz took Ruth and she b. his wife; Ru 4.13
him in her bosom, and b. his nurse. 4.16
When Samuel b. old, he made his sons 1Sa 8.01
Therefore it b. a proverb, "Is Saul 10.12
and it b. a very great panic. 14.15
his mouth; and his eyes b. bright. 14.27
and he b. his armor-bearer. 16.21
and he b. captain over them. 22.02
within him, and he b. as a stone. 25.37
messengers of David, and b. his wife. 25.42
and both of them b. his wives. 25.43
and b. one band, and took their 2Sa 2.25
house of Saul b. weaker and weaker. 3.01
in her haste, he fell, and b. lame. 4.04
And David b. greater and greater, 5.10
the Moabites b. servants to David 8.02
and the Syrians b. servants to 8.06
the Edomites b. David's servants. 8.14
in Ziba's house b. Mephibosheth's 9.12
and b. subject to them. 10.19
and she b. his wife, and bore him a 11.27
wife bore to David, and it b. sick. 12.15
and b. their commander; but he did 23.19
and she b. the king's nurse and 1Ki 1.04
about him and b. leader of a 11.24
And this thing b. a sin, for the 12.30
and b. as it was before. 13.06
And this thing b. sin to the house 13.34
so Tibni died, and Omri b. king. 16.22
the mistress of the house, b. ill; 17.17
b. king in his stead in the second 2Ki 1.17
the son of Ahab b. king over 3.01
the flesh of the child b. warm. 4.34
And Hazael b. king in his stead. 8.15
thirty-two years old when he b. king, 8.17
Benhadad his son b. king in his 13.24
and Hoshea b. his vassal, and paid 17.03
and b. false, and they followed the 17.15
days Hezekiah b. sick and was at 20.01
eighteen years old when he b. king, 24.08
twenty-one years old when he b. king, 24.18
though Judah b. strong among his 1Ch 5.02
went up first, so he b. chief. 11.06
And David b. greater and greater, 11.09
and b. their commander; 11.21
the Moabites b. servants to David 18.02
and the Syrians b. servants to 18.06
the Edomites b. David's servants. 18.13
with David, and b. subject to him. 19.19
therefore they b. a father's house 23.11
Eleazar and Ithamar b. the priests. 24.02
feet, and his disease b. severe; 2Ch 16.12
thirty-two years old when he b. king, 21.05
And they b. very angry with Judah, 25.10
of Egypt, for he b. very strong. 26.08
and when he b. angry with the 26.19
So Jotham b. mighty, because he 27.06
his distress he b. yet more 28.22
days Hezekiah b. sick and was at 32.24
and they b. servants to him and to 36.20
ate, and were filled and b. fat, Neh 9.25
b. angry and sought to lay hands on Est 2.21
of the family of Ram, b. angry. Job 32.02
of these three men, he b. angry. 32.05
my heart b. hot within me. Ps 39.03
with fasting, it b. my reproach. 69.10
I b. a byword to them. 69.11
who b. dung for the ground. 83.10
rebuked the Red Sea, and it b. dry; 106.09
which b. a snare to them. 106.36
Thus they b. unclean by their acts, 106.39
Judah b. his sanctuary, Israel his 114.02
So I b. great and surpassed all who Ecc 2.09
days Hezekiah b. sick and was at Is 38.01
falsely; and he b. their Savior. 63.08
All who ate of it b. guilty; Jer 2.03
worthlessness, and b. worthless? 2.05
and thy words b. to me a joy and 15.16
and they b. a waste and a desolation, 44.06
twenty-one years old when he b. king; 52.01
in the year that he b. king, 52.31
grievously, therefore she b. filthy; Lam 1.08
they b. their food in the destruction 4.10
"So they b. fugitives and wanderers 4.15
you grew up and b. tall and Eze 16.07
says the Lord GOD, and you b. mine. 16.08
and it sprouted and b. a low 17.06
So it b. a vine, and brought forth 17.06
he b. a young lion, and he learned 19.03
he b. a young lion, and he learned 19.06
Its strongest stem b. a ruler's 19.11
They b. mine, and they bore sons and 23.04
and she b. a byword among women, 23.10
and they b. food for all the wild 34.05
so that you b. the possession of 36.03
and you b. the talk and evil gossip 36.03
side chambers b. broader as they 41.07
their idols and b. a stumbling 44.12
and b. like the chaff of the summer Dan 2.35
the image b. a great mountain and 2.35
The tree grew and b. strong, 4.11
you saw, which grew and b. strong, 4.20
Then this Daniel b. distinguished 6.03
who b. king over the realm of the 9.01
the princes b. sick with the heat Hos 7.05
and b. detestable like the thing 9.10
and I b. to them as one who eases 11.04

BECAME (cont.)
Then the LORD b. jealous for his Joe 2.18
So I b. the shepherd of the flock Zec 11.07
But I b. impatient with them, and 11.08
and his garments b. white as light. Mt 17.02
trembled and b. like dead men. 28.04
and his garments b. glistening, Mk 9.03
child grew and b. strong in spirit, Lk 1.80
And the child grew and b. strong, 2.40
Judas Iscariot, who b. a traitor. 6.16
and his raiment b. dazzling white. 9.29
For as Jonah b. a sign to the men 11.30
and it grew and b. a tree, 13.19
But when he heard this he b. sad, 18.23
and his sweat b. like great drops 22.44
and Pilate b. friends with each 23.12
And the Word b. flesh and dwelt Jn 1.14
And it b. known to all the inhabitants Ac 1.19
And so Abraham b. the father of 7.08
and Isaac b. the father of Jacob, 7.08
Joseph's family b. known to 7.13
and b. an exile in the land of 7.29
where he b. the father of two sons. 7.29
but their plot b. known to Saul. 9.24
And it b. known throughout all 9.42
And he b. hungry and desired 10.10
And this b. known to all residents 19.17
And when the dissension b. violent, 23.10
but they b. futile in their thinking Rom 1.21
Claiming to be wise, they b. fools, 1.22
you that Christ b. a servant to 15.08
For I b. your father in Christ 1Co 4.15
To the Jews I b. as a Jew, in order 9.20
the law I b. as one under 9.20
the law I b. as one outside the 9.21
To the weak I b. weak, that I might 9.22
when I b. a man, I gave up childish 13.11
first man Adam b. a living being"; 15.45
the last Adam b. a life-giving 15.45
rich, yet for your sake he b. poor, 2Co 8.09
himself and b. obedient unto death, Php 2.08
of which I, Paul, b. a minister. Col 1.23
of which I b. a minister according 1.25
And you b. imitators of us and of 1Th 1.06
so that you b. an example to all 1.07
b. imitators of the churches of God 2.14
was deceived and b. a transgressor. 1Ti 2.14
made perfect he b. the source of Heb 5.09
Those who formerly b. priests took 7.21
the world and b. an heir of the 11.07
b. mighty in war, put foreign armies 11.34
and the sun b. black as sackcloth, Rev 6.12
the full moon b. like blood, 6.12
and a third of the sea b. blood, 8.09
a third of the waters b. wormwood, 8.11
and it b. like the blood of a dead 16.03
of water, and they b. blood. 16.04

BECHER
B., Ashbel, Gera, Naaman, Ehi, Rosh, Gen 6.21
of B., the family of the Becherites; Num 26.35
Bela, B., and Jediael, three. 1Ch 7.06
The sons of B.: Zemirah, Joash, 7.08
All these were the sons of B.; 7.09

BECHERITES
of Becher, the family of the B.; Num 26.35

BECKONED
they b. to their partners in the Lk 5.07
so Simon Peter b. to him and said, Jn 13.24

BECOME
to his wife, and they b. one flesh. Gen 2.24
the man has b. like one of us, 3.22
never again b. a flood to destroy 9.15
Abraham shall b. a great and 18.18
its people has b. great before the 19.13
my master, and he has b. great; 24.35
that you may b. a company of 28.03
and now I have b. two companies. 32.10
that you will b. as we are and 34.15
dwell with you and b. one people. 34.16
to b. one people: that every male 34.22
see what will b. of his dreams." 37.20
priests alone did not b. Pharaoh's. 47.26
he also shall b. a people, and he 48.19
descendants shall b. a multitude of 48.19
he shall b. a haven for ships, and 49.13
the Nile will b. blood upon the Ex 4.09
Pharaoh, that it may b. a serpent.'" 7.09
die, and the Nile shall b. foul, 7.18
of water, that they may b. blood; 7.19
that it may b. gnats throughout all 8.16
And it shall b. fine dust over all 9.09
and b. boils breaking out in sores 9.09
song, and he has b. my salvation; 15.02
and it did not b. foul, and there 16.24
wives shall b. widows and your 22.24
lest the land b. desolate and the 23.29
touches the altar shall b. holy. 29.37
whatever touches them will b. holy. 30.29
we do not know what has b. of him." 32.01
we do not know what has b. of him.' 32.23
lest it b. a snare in the midst of 34.12
and it shall b. holy. 40.09
and he has b. unclean, he shall be Lev 5.02
when one has sinned and b. guilty, 6.04
one may do and thereby b. guilty." 6.07
whoever touches them shall b. holy." 6.18
"And by these you shall b. unclean; 11.24
with them, lest you b. unclean. 11.43
and the land b. full of wickedness. 19.29
that your ways shall b. desolate. 26.22
the woman shall b. an execration Num 5.27
and our little ones will b. a prey; 14.03
ones, who you said would b. a prey, 14.31
lest he b. as Korah and as his 16.40
seventh day, he will not b. clean. 19.12
ones, who you said would b. a prey, Deu 1.39
and b. accursed like it; 7.26
day you have b. the people of the 27.09
And you shall b. a horror, a proverb, 28.37
they have b. a thing for destruction. Jos 7.12
day but have b. slaves to do 16.10
but they shall b. adversaries to Ju 2.03
and you have b. the cause of great 11.35
then I shall b. weak, and be like 16.07
then I shall b. weak, and be like 16.11
then I shall b. weak, and be like 16.13
and I shall b. weak, and be like any 16.17
hired me, and I have b. his priest." 18.04
that they may b. your husbands? Ru 1.11
lest you b. slaves to the Hebrews 1Sa 4.09
the asses and b. anxious about us." 9.05
that Israel had b. odious to the 13.04
see how my eyes have b. bright, 14.29
now then b. the king's son-in-law.'" 18.22
little thing to b. the king's 18.23
that he might b. the king's son-in-law. 18.27
turned from you and b. your enemy? 28.16
the battle he b. an adversary to 29.04
thou, O LORD, didst b. their God. 2Sa 7.24
that they had b. odious to David, 10.06
of Haggith has b. king and David 1Ki 1.11
turned about and b. my brother's, 2.15
and Israel will b. a proverb and a 9.07
And this house will b. a heap of 9.08
and have b. like plants of the 2Ki 19.26
and they shall b. a prey and a 21.14
they should b. a desolation and a 22.19
thou, O LORD, didst b. their God. 1Ch 17.22
and you wish to b. their king, Neh 6.06
Such you have now b. to me; Job 6.21
Why have I b. a burden to thee? 7.20

BECOME (cont.)

I b. afraid of all my suffering, for Job 9.28
were destined to b. heaps of ruins; 15.28
I have b. an alien in their eyes. 19.15
then have you b. altogether vain? 27.12
"And now I have b. their song, 30.09
and I have b. like dust and ashes. 30.19
let his flesh b. fresh with youth; 33.25
The waters b. hard like stone, and 38.30
Their young ones b. strong, 39.04
I b. like those who go down to the Ps 28.01
I have b. like a broken vessel. 31.12
and his children b. a blessing. 37.26
I have b. a stranger to my brethren, 69.08
own table before them b. a snare; 69.22
We have b. a taunt to our neighbors, 79.04
he has b. the scorn of his neighbors. 89.41
But the LORD has b. my stronghold, 94.22
fasting; my body has b. gaunt. 109.24
he has b. my salvation. 118.14
me and hast b. my salvation. 118.21
rejected has b. the chief cornerstone. 118.22
For I have b. like a wineskin in 119.83
if you have b. surety for your Pro 6.01
who b. surety for debts. 22.26
lest he b. weary of you and hate 25.17
like Sodom, and b. like Gomorrah. Is 1.09
they have b. a burden to me, I am 1.14
crimson, they shall b. like wool. 1.18
How the faithful city has b. a harlot, 1.21
Your silver has b. dross, 1.22
And the strong shall b. tow, 1.31
will b. briers and thorns. 7.23
but they will b. a place where 7.25
And he will b. a sanctuary, and a 8.14
The light of Israel will b. a fire, 10.17
song, and has b. my salvation. 12.02
'You too have b. as weak as we! 14.10
You have b. like us!' 14.10
and will b. a heap of ruins. 17.01
and its canals will b. foul, 19.06
The princes of Zoan have b. fools, 19.13
of Judah will b. a terror to the 19.17
and he will b. a throne of honor to 22.23
of all this has b. to you like the 29.11
watchtower will b. dens for ever, 32.14
her land shall b. burning pitch. 34.09
the burning sand shall b. a pool, 35.07
haunt of jackals shall b. a swamp, 35.07
the grass shall b. reeds and 35.07
and have b. like plants of the 37.27
the uneven ground shall b. level, 40.04
they have b. a prey with none to 42.22
and my God has b. my strength— 49.05
The least one shall b. a clan, 60.22
We have b. like those over whom 63.19
We have all b. like one who is 64.06
Thy holy cities have b. a wilderness, 64.10
Zion has b. a wilderness, Jerusalem 64.10
our pleasant places have b. ruins. 64.11
Sharon shall b. a pasture for 65.10
Why then has he b. a prey? Jer 2.14
degenerate and b. a wild vine? 2.21
The prophets will b. wind; 5.13
they have b. great and rich, 5.27
b. a den of robbers in your eyes? 7.11
for the land shall b. a waste. 7.34
For your gods have b. as many as 11.13
My heritage has b. to me like a 12.08
let their wives b. childless and 18.21
I have b. a laughingstock all the 20.07
of the LORD has b. for me a 20.08
this house shall b. a desolation. 22.05
of them have b. like Sodom to me, 23.14
land shall be a ruin and a waste, 25.11
their land has b. a waste because 25.38
Jerusalem shall b. a heap of ruins, 26.18
should this city b. a desolation? 27.17
who despoil you shall b. a spoil, 30.16
You shall b. an execration, a horror, 42.18
be cut off and b. a curse and a 44.08
and they shall b. an execration, 44.12
your land has b. a desolation and 44.22
For Memphis shall b. a waste, 46.19
and shall b. an overflowing torrent 47.02
her cities shall b. a desolation, 48.09
of Nimrim also have b. desolate. 48.34
So Moab has b. a derision and a 48.39
it shall b. a desolate mound, and 49.02
that Bozrah shall b. a horror, 49.13
"Edom shall b. a horror; 49.17
Damascus has b. feeble, she turned 49.24
Their camels shall b. booty, 49.32
Hazor shall b. a haunt of jackals, 49.33
How Babylon has b. a horror among 50.23
diviners, that they may b. fools! 50.36
her midst, that they may b. women! 50.37
has failed, they have b. women; 51.30
and Babylon shall b. a heap of 51.37
How Babylon has b. a horror among 51.41
Her cities have b. a horror, 51.43
How like a widow has she b., Lam 1.01
among the cities has b. a vassal. 1.01
with her, they have b. her enemies. 1.02
Her foes have b. the head, her 1.05
princes have b. like harts that 1.06
Jerusalem has b. a filthy thing 1.17
The Lord has b. like an enemy, he 2.05
I have b. the laughingstock of all 3.14
daughter of my people has b. cruel, 4.03
bones, it has b. as dry as wood. 4.08
you shall b. drunk and strip 4.21
We have b. orphans, fatherless; 5.03
For this our heart has b. sick, 5.17
Your altars shall b. desolate, Eze 6.04
and the land shall b. a desolation; 12.20
Now you have b. like her an object 16.57
bear fruit, and b. a noble vine. 17.08
bear fruit, and b. a noble cedar; 17.23
lamentation, and has b. a lamentation. 19.14
You have b. guilty by the blood 22.04
house of Israel has b. dross to me; 22.18
lead in the furnace, have b. dross. 22.18
GOD: Because you have all b. dross, 22.19
that it may b. hot, and its copper 24.11
and she shall b. a spoil to the 26.05
your heart has b. proud in your 28.05
so that it may b. strong to wield 30.21
because my sheep have b. a prey, 34.08
my sheep have b. food for all the 34.08
and you shall b. a desolation; 35.04
heights have b. our possession, 36.02
which have b. a prey and derision 36.04
desolate has b. like the garden of 36.35
that they may b. one in your hand. 37.17
the sea, the water will b. fresh. 47.08
the waters of the sea may b. fresh; 47.09
and marshes will not b. fresh; 47.11
king, who have grown and b. strong. Dan 4.22
thy people have b. a byword among 9.16
and when he has b. strong through 11.02
and he shall b. strong with a small 11.23
He shall b. ruler of the treasures 11.43
O Israel, let not Judah b. guilty. Hos 4.15
Ephraim shall b. a desolation in 5.09
of Judah have b. like those who 5.10
they have b. to him altars for 8.11
"Egypt shall b. a desolation and Joe 3.19
temple shall b. wailings in that Amo 8.03
see what would b. of the city. Jon 4.05
Jerusalem shall b. a heap of ruins, Mic 3.12
For I have b. as when the summer 7.01
and Ashkelon shall b. a desolation; Zep 2.04
The seacoast shall b. the possession 2.07

BECOME (cont.)
"Moab shall b. like Sodom, and the Zep 2.09
What a desolation she has b., 2.15
any kind of food, does it b. holy?'" Hag 2.12
any of these, does it b. unclean?" 2.13
answered, "It does b. unclean." 2.13
and they shall b. plunder for Zec 2.09
Zerubbabel you shall b. a plain; 4.07
Then Ephraim shall b. like a mighty 10.07
"B. shepherd of the flock doomed to 11.04
be the LORD, I have b. rich'; 11.05
And the LORD will b. king over all 14.09
these stones to b. loaves of bread." Mt 4.03
you turn and b. like children, 18.03
wife, and the two shall b. one'? 19.05
rejected has b. the head of the 21.42
I will make you b. fishers of men." Mk 1.17
for Jesus' name had b. known. 6.14
and the two shall b. one.' 10.08
rejected has b. the head of the 12.10
command this stone to b. bread." Lk 4.03
for one dot of the law to b. void. 16.17
rejected has b. the head of the 20.17
among you b. as the youngest, and 22.26
gave power to b. children of God; Jn 1.12
feast tasted the water now b. wine, 2.09
give him will b. in him a spring 4.14
you too want to b. his disciples?" 9.27
that those who see may b. blind." 9.39
that you may b. sons of light." 12.36
that they may b. perfectly one, so 17.23
'Let his habitation b. desolate, Ac 1.20
these men must b. with us a 1.22
but which has b. the head of the 4.11
we do not know what has b. of him.' 7.40
soldiers over what had b. of Peter. 12.18
me this day might b. such as I am— 26.29
that he should b. the father of Rom 4.18
of sin have b. obedient from the 6.17
have b. slaves of righteousness. 6.18
from sin and have b. slaves of God, 6.22
commandment might b. sinful beyond 7.13
"Let their feast b. a snare and a 11.09
So do not b. proud, but stand in awe. 11.20
each man's work will b. manifest; 1Co 3.13
let him b. a fool that he may b. wise. 3.18
Already you have b. rich! 4.08
Without us you have b. kings! 4.08
because we have b. a spectacle to 4.09
we have b., and are now, as the 4.13
is written, "The two shall b. one." 6.16
do not b. slaves of men. 7.23
yours somehow b. a stumbling block 8.09
I have b. all things to all men, 9.22
in him we might b. the righteousness 2Co 5.21
by his poverty you might b. rich. 8.09
having b. a curse for us—for it is Gal 3.13
b. as I am, for I also have b. as you 4.12
What has b. of the satisfaction you 4.15
Have I then b. your enemy by 4.16
they have b. callous and have given Eph 4.19
his wife, and the two shall b. one." 5.31
so that it has b. known throughout Php 1.13
children, lest they b. discouraged. Col 3.21
because you had b. very dear to us. 1Th 2.08
his grace and b. heirs in hope of Tit 3.07
father I have b. in my imprisonment Phm 1.10
having b. as much superior to Heb 1.04
that he might b. a merciful and 2.17
since you have b. dull of hearing. 5.11
and have b. partakers of the Holy 6.04
having b. a high priest for ever 6.20
who has b. a priest, not according 7.16
and by it the many b. defiled; 12.15
and b. judges with evil thoughts? Jas 2.04
one point has b. guilty of all of 2.10
you have b. a transgressor of the 2.11
Let not many of you b. teachers, 3.01
rejected has b. the head of the 1Pe 2.07
and b. partakers of the divine 2Pe 1.04
last state has b. worse for them 2.20
the world has b. the kingdom of Rev 11.15
dwellers on earth have b. drunk. 17.02
It has b. a dwelling place of 18.02

BECOMES
which they have committed b. known, Lev 4.14
may be with which one b. unclean, 5.03
raw flesh of the burn b. a spot, 13.24
"If your brother b. poor, and sells 25.25
then himself b. prosperous and 25.26
"And if your brother b. poor, 25.35
"And if your brother b. poor beside 25.39
or sojourner with you b. rich, 25.47
beside him b. poor and sells 25.47
nostrils and b. loathsome to you, Num 11.20
and if she goes and b. another man's Deu 24.02
or seven rams b. a priest of what 2Ch 13.09
Be not afraid when one b. rich, Ps 49.16
He who walks with wise men b. wise, Pro 13.20
and b. surety in the presence of 17.18
is punished, the simple b. wise; 21.11
a slave when he b. king, 30.22
and the flower b. a ripening grape, Is 18.05
the wilderness b. a fruitful field, 32.15
he b. hungry and his strength fails, 44.12
Then it b. fuel for a man; 44.15
from him and b. another man's wife, Jer 3.01
of that man b. worse than the Mt 12.45
greatest of shrubs and b. a tree, 13.32
and when he b. a proselyte, you make 23.15
as its branch b. tender and puts 24.32
it grows up and b. the greatest of Mk 4.32
and grinds his teeth and b. rigid; 9.18
as its branch b. tender and puts 13.28
of that man b. worse than the Lk 11.26
circumcision b. uncircumcision. Rom 2.25
Then what b. of our boasting? 3.27
to a prostitute b. one body with 1Co 6.16
to the Lord b. one spirit with him 6.17
exposed by the light it b. visible, Eph 5.13
anything that b. visible is light. 5.13
This b. even more evident when Heb 7.15

BECOMING
b. unclean thereby; Lev 15.32
Fine speech is not b. to a fool; Pro 17.07
b. a consolation to them. Eze 16.54
b. like him in his death, Php 3.10
And what is b. obsolete and growing Heb 8.13

BECOMINGLY
conduct ourselves b. as in the day, Rom 13.13

BECORATH
son of B., son of Aphiah, a Benjaminite. 1Sa 9.01

BED
himself upon the head of his b. Gen 47.31
his strength, and sat up in b. 48.02
you went up to your father's b.; 49.04
he drew up his feet into the b., 49.33
your bedchamber and on your b., Ex 8.03
man does not die but keeps his b., 21.18
Every b. on which he who has the Lev 15.04
who touches his b. shall wash his 15.05
touches her b. shall wash his 15.21
whether it is the b. or anything 15.23
and every b. on which he lies shall 15.24
Every b. on which she lies, all the 15.26
to her as the b. of her impurity; 15.26
a b. was spread for Saul upon the 1Sa 9.25
laid it on the b. and put a pillow 19.13
"Bring him up to me in the b., 19.15
behold, the image was in the b., 19.16

BED (cont.)
the earth, and sat upon the b. 1Sa 28.23
he lay on his b. in his bedchamber, 2Sa 4.07
man in his own house upon his b., 4.11
Jonadab said to him, "Lie down on your b., 13.05
the king bowed himself upon the b. 1Ki 1.47
and laid him upon his own b. 17.19
And he lay down on his b., 21.04
down from the b. to which you have 2Ki 1.04
down from the b. to which you have 1.06
down from the b. to which you have 1.16
walls, and put there for him a b., 4.10
laid him on the b. of the man of 4.21
saw the child lying dead on his b. 4.32
the priest, and slew him on his b. 2Ch 24.25
'My b. will comfort me, my couch Job 7.13
the stones of the torrent b., 22.24
He goes to b. rich, but will do so 27.19
chastened with pain upon his b., 33.19
night I flood my b. with tears; Ps 6.06
He plots mischief while on his b.; 36.04
when I think of thee upon my b., 63.06
enter my house or get into my b.; 132.03
If I make my b. in Sheol, thou art 139.08
I have perfumed by b. with myrrh, Pro 7.17
why should your b. be taken from 22.27
so does a sluggard on his b. 26.14
Upon my b. by night I sought him Sol 3.01
maggots are the b. beneath you, Is 14.11
For the b. is too short to stretch 28.20
mountain you have set your b., 57.07
me, you have uncovered your b., 57.08
with them, you have loved their b., 57.08
From the b. where it was planted Eze 17.07
away on the b. where it grew?" 17.10
came to her into the b. of love, 23.17
They have made her a b. among the 32.25
head as you lay in b. are these: Dan 2.28
as you lay in b. came thoughts of 2.29
as I lay in b. the fancies and the 4.05
my head as I lay in b. were these: 4.10
visions of my head as I lay in b., 4.13
of his head as he lay in his b. 7.01
corner of a couch and part of a b. Amo 3.12
him a paralytic, lying on his b.; Mt 9.02
—"Rise, take up your b. and go home." 9.06
or under a b., and not on a stand? Mk 4.21
and found the child lying in b., 7.30
bringing on a b. a man who was Lk 5.18
down with his b. through the tiles 5.19
rise, take up your b. and go home." 5.24
a vessel, or puts it under a b., 8.16
and my children are with me in b.; 11.07
there will be two men in one b.; 17.34
rise and make your b." And Ac 9.34
let the marriage b. be undefled; Heb 13.04

BEDAD
Husham died, and Hadad the son of B., Gen 36.35
When Husham died, Hadad the son of B., 1Ch 1.46

BEDAN
The sons of Ulam: B. These were 1Ch 7.17

BEDCHAMBER
and into your b. and on your bed, Ex 8.03
as he lay on his bed in his b., 2Sa 4.07
words that you speak in your b." 2Ki 6.12
she put him and his nurse in a b. 11.02
she put him and his nurse in a b. 2Ch 22.11
nor in your b. curse the rich; Ecc 10.20

BEDECKED
and b. with gold and jewels and Rev 17.04
b. with gold, with jewels, and with 18.16

BEDEIAH
Benaiah, B., Cheluhi, Ez 10.35

BEDRIDDEN
who had been b. for eight years and Ac 9.33

BEDS
brought b., basins, and earthen 2Sa 17.28
while they slumber on their b., Job 33.15
hearts on your b., and be silent. Ps 4.04
His cheeks are like b. of spices, Sol 5.13
to the b. of spices to pasture his 6.02
rest in their b. who walk in their Is 57.02
heart, but they wail upon their b.; Hos 7.14
all the stream b. of Judah shall Joe 3.18
Woe to those who lie upon b. of ivory, Amo 6.04
and work evil upon their b.! Mic 2.01
and laid them on b. and pallets, Ac 5.15

BEDSTEAD
behold, his b. was a b. of iron; Deu 3.11

BEE
and for the b. which is in the land Is 7.18

BEELIADA
Elishama, B., and Eliphelet. 1Ch 14.07

BEELZEBUL
called the master of the house B., Mt 10.25
it they said, "It is only by B., 12.24
And if I cast out demons by B., 12.27
said, "He is possessed by B., Mk 3.22
said, "He casts out demons by B., Lk 11.15
say that I cast out demons by B. 11.18
And if I cast out demons by B., 11.19

BEER
And from there they continued to B.; Num 21.16
and went to B. and dwelt there, for Ju 9.21

BEERA
Shamma, Shilshah, Ithran, and B. 1Ch 7.37

BEERAH
B. his son, whom Tilgathpilneser 1Ch 5.06

BEERELIM
Eglaim, the wailing reaches to B. Is 15.08

BEERI
the daughter of B. the Hittite, Gen 26.34
that came to Hosea the son of B., Hos 1.01

BEERLAHAIROI
Therefore the well was called B.; Gen 16.14
Now Isaac had come from B., 24.62
And Isaac dwelt at B. 25.11

BEEROTH
journeyed from B. Benejaakan to Deu 10.06
B., and Kiriathjearim. Jos 9.17
Gibeon, Ramah, B., 18.25
Benjamin from B. (for B. also is 2Sa 4.02
Naharai of B., the armor-bearer of 23.37
Naharai of B., the armor-bearer of 1Ch 11.39
and B., seven hundred and forty-three Ez 2.25
and B., seven hundred and forty-three Neh 7.29

BEEROTHITE
Now the sons of Rimmon the B., 2Sa 4.05
brother, the sons of Rimmon the B., 4.09

BEEROTHITES
the B. fled to Gittaim, and have 2Sa 4.03

BEERSHEBA
wandered in the wilderness of B. Gen 21.14
Therefore that place was called B.; 21.31
So they made a covenant at B. 21.32
Abraham planted a tamarisk tree in B., 21.33
they arose and went together to B.; 22.19

BEERSHEBA (cont.)
and Abraham dwelt at B. Gen 22.19
From there he went up to B. 26.23
name of the city is B. to this day. 26.33
Jacob left B., and went toward 28.10
and came to B., and offered sacrifices 46.01
Then Jacob set out from B.; 46.05
Hazarshual, B., Biziothiah, Jos 15.28
And it had for its inheritance B., 19.02
from Dan to B., including the land Ju 20.01
from Dan to B. knew that Samuel 1Sa 3.20
they were judges in B. 8.02
and over Judah, from Dan to B. 2Sa 3.10
from Dan to B., as the sand by the 17.11
from Dan to B., and number the 24.02
out to the Negeb of Judah at B. 24.07
from Dan to B. seventy thousand 24.15
in safety, from Dan even to B., 1Ki 4.25
and came to B., which belongs to 19.03
His mother's name was Zibiah of B. 2Ki 12.01
burned incense, from Geba to B.; 23.08
They dwelt in B., Moladah, Hazarshual, 1Ch 4.28
from B. to Dan, and bring me a 21.02
from B. to the hill country of 2Ch 19.04
his mother's name was Zibiah of B. 24.01
from B. to Dan, that the people 30.05
in B. and its villages, Neh 11.27
encamped from B. to the valley of 11.30
into Gilgal or cross over to B.; Amo 5.05
Dan,' and, 'As the way of B. lives, 8.14

BEES
chased you as b. do and beat you Deu 1.44
was a swarm of b. in the body of Ju 14.08
They surrounded me like b., Ps 118.12

BEESHTERAH
and B. with its pasture lands—two Jos 21.27

BEFALL
which are to b. the land of Egypt, Gen 41.36
he feared that harm might b. him. 42.04
If harm should b. him on the 42.38
you what shall b. you in days to 49.01
if war b. us, they join our enemies Ex 1.10
the days to come evil will b. you, Deu 31.29
And this which shall b. your two sons, 1Sa 2.34
Does not calamity b. the unrighteous, Job 31.03
to his ways he will make it b. him. 34.11
no evil shall b. you, no scourge Ps 91.10
befalls the fool will b. me also; Ecc 2.15
moons predict what shall b. you. Is 47.13
what is to b. your people in the Dan 10.14
Does evil b. a city, unless the LORD Amo 3.06
no more, that nothing worse b. you." Jn 5.14
knowing all that was to b. him, 18.04
not knowing what shall b. me there; Ac 20.22

BEFALLEN
him all that had b. them, saying, Gen 42.29
such things as these have b. me! Lev 10.19
all the adversity that has b. us: Num 20.14
they told him all that had b. them. Jos 2.23
us, why then has all this b. us? Ju 6.13
he thought, "Something has b. him; 1Sa 20.26
because evil had b. his house. 1Ch 7.23
friends everything that had b. him. Est 6.13
matter, and of what had b. them, 9.26
These two things have b. you— Is 51.19
testimonies, that this evil has b. you, Jer 44.23
Remember, O LORD, what has b. us; Lam 5.01

BEFALLS
and harm b. him, you will bring down Gen 44.29
upon me, and what I dread b. me. Job 3.25
No ill b. the righteous, but the Pro 12.21
but trouble b. the income of the 15.06
"What b. the fool will befall me Ecc 2.15

BEFELL
trials which b. me through the Ac 20.19
what b. me at Antioch, at Iconium, 2Ti 3.11

BEFIT
Bear fruits that b. repentance, Lk 3.08

BEFITS
Praise b. the upright. Ps 33.01
holiness b. thy house, O LORD, for 93.05
Bear fruit that b. repentance, Mt 3.08
her in the Lord as b. the saints, Rom 16.02
as b. women who profess religion. 1Ti 2.10
you, teach what b. sound doctrine. Tit 2.01
their journey as b. God's service. 3Jn 1.06

BEFOREHAND
Lo, I have told you b. Mt 24.25
not be anxious b. what you are to Mk 13.11
I have told you all things b. 13.23
anointed my body b. for burying. 14.08
not to meditate b. how to answer; Lk 21.14
Spirit spoke b. by the mouth of Ac 1.16
who announced b. the coming of the 7.52
which he promised b. through his Rom 1.02
which he has prepared b. for glory, 9.23
preached the gospel b. to Abraham, Gal 3.08
good works, which God prepared b., Eph 2.10
we told you b. that we were to 1Th 3.04
knowing this b., beware lest you be 2Pe 3.17

BEFORETIME
and b., that we might say, "He is Is 41.26

BEG
and said, "I b. you, my brothers, do Gen 19.07
Haman stayed to b. his life from Est 7.07
May his children wander about and b.; Ps109.10
the children b. for food, but no one Lam 4.04
And they began to b. Jesus to Mk 5.17
I b. you to look upon my son, for he Lk 9.38
to dig, and I am ashamed to b. 16.03
'Then I b. you, father, to send him 16.27
the man who used to sit and b.?" Jn 9.08
I b. you, let me speak to the people." Ac 21.39
I b. you in your kindness to hear 24.04
therefore I b. you to listen to me 26.03
So I b. you to reaffirm your love 2Co 2.08
I b. of you that when I am present 10.02
b. you to lead a life worthy of the Eph 4.01
to meet him, we b. you, brethren, 2Th 2.01
And now I b. you, lady, not as though 2Jn 1.05

BEGAN
that time men b. to call upon the Gen 4.26
When men b. to multiply on the face 6.01
seven years of famine b. to come, 41.54
the people b. to play the harlot Num 25.01
their boundary b. at the Jordan; Jos 18.12
of the LORD b. to stir him in Ju 13.25
Then she b. to torment him, and his 16.19
of his head b. to grow again after 16.22
And as the dawn b. to break, 19.25
times they b. to smite and kill 20.31
But when the signal b. to rise out 20.40
years old when he b. to reign; 1Sa 13.01
old when he b. to reign over 2Sa 2.10
years old when he b. to reign, 5.04
and b. from Aroer, and from the city 24.05
he b. to build the house of the 1Ki 6.01
years old when he b. to reign, 14.21
Abijam b. to reign over Judah. 15.01
of Israel Asa b. to reign over 15.09
son of Jeroboam b. to reign over 15.25
son of Ahijah b. to reign over all 15.33
son of Baasha b. to reign over 16.08
When he b. to reign, as soon as he 16.11
Omri b. to reign over Israel, and 16.23

BEGAN (cont.)
the son of Omri b. to reign over 1 Ki 16.29
Jehoshaphat the son of Asa b. to 22.41
years old when he b. to reign, 22.42
Ahaziah the son of Ahab b. to reign 22.51
Jehoshaphat, king of Judah, b. to reign. 2Ki 8.16
Jehoram, king of Judah, b. to reign. 8.25
years old when he b. to reign, 8.26
Ahaziah b. to reign over Judah. 9.29
days the LORD b. to cut off parts 10.32
years old when he b. to reign. 11.21
year of Jehu Jehoash b. to reign, 12.01
the son of Jehu b. to reign over 13.01
son of Jehoahaz b. to reign over 13.10
Joash, king of Judah, b. to reign. 14.01
years old when he b. to reign, 14.02
b. to reign in Samaria, and he 14.23
Amaziah, king of Judah, b. to reign. 15.01
years old when he b. to reign, 15.02
son of Jabesh b. to reign in the 15.13
the son of Gadi b. to reign over 15.17
son of Menahem b. to reign over 15.23
son of Remaliah b. to reign over 15.27
Uzziah, king of Judah, b. to reign. 15.32
years old when he b. to reign, 15.33
days the LORD b. to send Rezin the 15.37
Jotham, king of Judah, b. to reign. 16.01
years old when he b. to reign, 16.02
the son of Elah b. to reign in 17.01
Ahaz, king of Judah, b. to reign. 18.01
years old when he b. to reign, 18.02
years old when he b. to reign, 21.01
years old when he b. to reign, 21.19
years old when he b. to reign, 22.01
years old when he b. to reign, 23.31
years old when he b. to reign, 23.36
in the year that he b. to reign, 25.27
he b. to be a mighty one in the 1Ch 1.10
Joab the son of Zeruiah b. to number, 27.24
Then Solomon b. to build the house 2Ch 3.01
He b. to build in the second month 3.02
years old when he b. to reign, 12.13
Jeroboam Abijah b. to reign over 13.01
And when they b. to sing and praise, 20.22
years old when he b. to reign, 20.31
years old when he b. to reign, 21.20
years old when he b. to reign, 22.02
years old when he b. to reign, 24.01
years old when he b. to reign, 25.01
years old when he b. to reign, 26.03
years old when he b. to reign, 27.01
years old when he b. to reign, 27.08
years old when he b. to reign, 28.01
Hezekiah b. to reign when he was 29.01
They b. to sanctify on the first 29.17
And when the burnt offering b., 29.27
the song to the LORD b. also, 29.27
month they b. to pile up the heaps, 31.07
"Since they b. to bring the contributions 31.10
years old when he b. to reign, 33.01
years old when he b. to reign, 33.21
years old when he b. to reign, 34.01
he b. to seek the God of David his 34.03
twelfth year he b. to purge Judah 34.03
years old when he b. to reign; 36.02
years old when he b. to reign, 36.05
years old when he b. to reign, 36.09
years old when he b. to reign, 36.11
month they b. to offer burnt Ez 3.06
arose and b. to rebuild the house 5.02
first month he b. to go up from 7.09
When it b. to be dark at the gates Neh 13.19
the morning since your days b., Job 38.12
So they b. with the elders who Eze 9.06
there I b. to hate them. Hos 9.15
Jonah b. to go into the city, going Jon 3.04
From that time Jesus b. to preach, Mt 4.17
Jesus b. to speak to the crowds 11.07
Then he b. to upbraid the cities 11.20
and they b. to pluck ears of grain 12.01
From that time Jesus b. to show his 16.21
took him and b. to rebuke him, 16.22
When he b. the reckoning, one was 18.24
and b. to say to him one after 26.22
he b. to be sorrowful and troubled. 26.37
Then he b. to invoke a curse on 26.74
But he went out and b. to talk Mk 1.45
his disciples b. to pluck ears of 2.23
Again he b. to teach beside the sea. 4.01
And they b. to beg Jesus to depart 5.17
went away and b. to proclaim in 5.20
the sabbath he b. to teach in the 6.02
and b. to send them out two by two, 6.07
and he b. to teach them many things. 6.34
neighborhood and b. to bring sick 6.55
came and b. to argue with him, 8.11
And he b. to teach them that the 8.31
took him, and b. to rebuke him. 8.32
Peter b. to say to him, "Lo, we have 10.28
he b. to tell them what was to 10.32
they b. to be indignant at James 10.41
he b. to cry out and say, "Jesus, Son 10.47
the temple and b. to drive out 11.15
And he b. speak to them in 12.01
And Jesus b. to say to them, "Take 13.05
They b. to be sorrowful, and to say 14.19
and b. to be greatly distressed and 14.33
And some b. to spit on him, and to 14.65
and b. again to say to the bystanders, 14.69
But he b. to invoke a curse on 14.71
came up and b. to ask Pilate to do 15.08
And they b. to salute him, "Hail, 15.18
Jesus, when he b. his ministry, was Lk 3.23
And he b. to say to them, "Today 4.21
the boats, so that they b. to sink. 5.07
and the Pharisees b. to question 5.21
dead man sat up, and b. to speak. 7.15
he b. to speak to the crowds 7.24
she b. to wet his feet with her 7.38
table with him b. to say among 7.49
Now the day b. to wear away; 9.12
he b. to say, "This generation is an 11.29
the Pharisees b. to press him hard, 11.53
he b. to say to his disciples first, 12.01
But they all alike b. to make 14.18
'This man b. to build, and was not 14.30
country, and he b. to be in want. 15.14
And they b. to make merry. 15.24
the disciples b. to rejoice and 19.37
the temple and b. to drive out 19.45
And he b. to tell the people this 20.09
And they b. to question one another, 22.23
And they b. to accuse him, saying, 23.02
them the hour when he b. to mend, Jn 4.52
Never since the world b. has it 9.32
and b. to wash the disciples' feet, 13.05
all that Jesus b. to do and teach, Ac 1.01
Holy Spirit and b. to speak in 2.04
But Peter b. and explained to them 11.04
As I b. to speak, the Holy Spirit 11.15
He b. to speak boldly in the 18.26
Tertullus b. to accuse him, saying: 24.02
they b. next day to throw the cargo 27.18
of all he broke it and b. to eat. 27.35
a year ago you b. not only to do 2Co 8.10
that he who b. a good work in you Php 1.06

BEGET
"When you b. children and children's Deu 4.25
You shall b. sons and daughters, but 28.41

BEGETS
he who b. a wise son will be glad Pro 23.24
If a man b. a hundred children, and Ecc 6.03

BEGETS (cont.)
"If he b. a son who is a robber, a Eze 18.10
"But if this man b. a son who sees 18.14

BEGETTING
says to a father, 'What are you b.?' Is 45.10

BEGGAR
a blind b., the son of Timaeus, was Mk 10.46
who had seen him before as a b., Jn 9.08

BEGGARLY
to the weak and b. elemental Gal 4.09

BEGGED
And the demons b. him, "If you cast Mt 8.31
they b. him to leave their neighborhood. 8.34
and his disciples came and b. him, 15.23
And he b. him eagerly not to send Mk 5.10
and they b. him, "Send us to the 5.12
with demons b. him that he might 5.18
And she b. him to cast the demon 7.26
and b. him to touch him. 8.22
And they b. him not to command them Lk 8.31
and they b. him to let them enter 8.32
demons had gone b. that he might 8.38
And I b. your disciples to cast it 9.40
he went and b. him to come down and Jn 4.47
the people b. that these things Ac 13.42
sent to him and b. him not to 19.31
people there b. him not to go up 21.12

BEGGING
forsaken or his children b. bread. Ps 37.25
man was sitting by the roadside b.; Lk 18.35
b. us earnestly for the favor of 2Co 8.04

BEGIN
b. to take possession, and contend Deu 2.24
This day I will b. to put the dread 2.25
b. to take possession, that you may 2.31
b. to count the seven weeks from 16.09
"This day I will b. to exalt you in Jos 3.07
man that will b. to fight against Ju 10.18
and he shall b. to deliver Israel 13.05
he said, "Who shall b. the battle?" 1Ki 20.14
the leader to b. the thanksgiving Neh 11.17
For behold, I b. to work evil at the Jer 25.29
And b. at my sanctuary." So they Eze 9.06
and do not b. to say to yourselves, Lk 3.08
you will b. to stand outside and to 13.25
Then you will b. to say, 'We ate and 13.26
then you will b. with shame to 14.09
all who see it b. to mock him, 14.29
when these things b. to take place, 21.28
Then they will b. to say to the 23.30
To b. with, the Jews are entrusted Rom 3.02
for judgment to b. with the 1Pe 4.17

BEGINNING
In the b. God created the heavens Gen 1.01
The b. of his kingdom was Babel, 10.10
is only the b. of what they will 11.06
where his tent had been at the b., 13.03
were still as gaunt as at the b. 41.21
b. with the eldest and ending with 44.12
shall be for you the b. of months; Ex 12.02
day of the month b. at evening, Lev 23.32
Gadites the territory b. at Aroer, Deu 3.12
from the b. of the year to the end 11.12
the camp at the b. of the middle Ju 7.19
Bethlehem at the b. of barley Ru 1.22
concerning his house, from b. to end. 1Sa 3.12
at the b. of barley harvest. 2Sa 21.09
from the b. of harvest until rain 21.10
And at the b. of their dwelling 2Ki 17.25
the son of Jozadak made a b., Ez 3.08
in the b. of his reign, they wrote 4.06
the breaches were b. to be closed, Neh 4.07
And though your b. was small, Job 8.07
days of Job more than his b.; 42.12
of the LORD is the b. of wisdom; Ps 111.10
of the LORD is the b. of knowledge; Pro 1.07
The b. of wisdom is this: Get wisdom, 4.07
created me at the b. of his work, 8.22
first, before the b. of the earth. 8.23
of the LORD is the b. of wisdom, 9.10
The b. of strife is like letting 17.24
hastily in the b. will in the end 20.21
has done from the b. to the end. Ecc 3.11
Better is the end of a thing than its b.; 7.08
The b. of the words of his mouth is 10.13
and your counselors as at the b. Is 1.26
it not been told you from the b.? 40.21
the generations from the b.? 41.04
Who declared it from the b., 41.26
end from the b. and from ancient 46.10
from the b. I have not spoken in 48.16
high from the b. is the place of Jer 17.12
In the b. of the reign of Jehoiakim 26.01
In the b. of the reign of Zedekiah 27.01
at the b. of the reign of Zedekiah 28.01
in the b. of the reign of Zedekiah 49.34
night, at the b. of the watches! Lam 2.19
at the b. of the year, on the tenth Eze 40.01
B. at the northern border, from the 48.01
At the b. of your supplications a Dan 9.23
locusts in the b. of the shooting Amo 7.01
you were the b. of sin to the Mic 1.13
and b. to sink he cried out, "Lord, Mt 14.30
them from the b. made them male 19.04
but from the b. it was not so. 19.08
b. with the last, up to the first.' 20.08
all this is but the b. of the 24.08
been from the b. of the world 24.21
but rather that a riot was b., 27.24
The b. of the gospel of Jesus Mk 1.01
But from the b. of creation, 'God 10.06
this is but the b. of the sufferings. 13.08
been from the b. of the creation 13.19
who from the b. were eyewitnesses Lk 1.02
Preparation, and the sabbath was b. 23.54
And b. with Moses and all the 24.27
to all nations, b. from Jerusalem. 24.47
In the b. was the Word, and the Word Jn 1.01
He was in the b. with God; 1.02
they went away, one by one, b. with * 8.09
what I have told you from the b. 8.25
He was a murderer from the b., 8.44
you have been with me from the b. 15.27
these things to you from the b., 16.04
b. from the baptism of John until Ac 1.22
and b. with this scripture he told 8.35
b. from Galilee after the baptism 10.37
on them just as on us at the b. 11.15
spent from the b. among my own 26.04
Are we b. to commend ourselves 2Co 3.01
that as he had already made a b., 8.06
know that in the b. of the gospel, Php 4.15
he is the b., the first-born from Col 1.18
chose you from the b. to be saved, 2Th 2.13
didst found the earth in the b., Heb 1.10
and has neither b. of days nor end 7.03
they were from the b. of creation. 2Pe 3.04
That which was from the b., 1Jn 1.01
commandment which you had from the b.; 2.07
you know him who is from the b. 2.13
you know him who is from the b. 2.14
you heard from the b. abide in you. 2.24
heard from the b. abides in you, 2.24
the devil has sinned from the b. 3.08
which you have heard from the b., 3.11
the one we have had from the b., 2Jn 1.05
as you have heard from the b., 1.06
the b. of God's creation. Rev 3.14

BEGINNING (cont.)
and the Omega, and b. and the end. Rev 21.06
and the last, the b. and the end." 22.13

BEGINNINGS
and at the b. of your months, you Num 10.10
"At the b. of your months you shall 28.11

BEGINS
southern side b. at the outskirts Jos 18.15
where the outside wall b. Eze 42.10
and b. to beat his fellow servants, Mt 24.49
and b. to beat the menservants Lk 12.45
and if it b. with us, what will be 1Pe 4.17

BEGONE
"B., b., you man of blood, you 2Sa 16.07
you will say to them, "B!" Is 30.22
Then Jesus said to him, "B., Satan! Mt 4.10

BEGOT
unmindful of the Rock that b. you, Deu 32.18
and David b. more sons and daughters. 1Ch 14.03
Hearken to your father who b. you, Pro 23.22
the fathers who b. them in this Jer 16.03

BEGOTTEN
b. by your father, since she is your Lev 18.11
or who has b. the drops of dew? Job 38.28
are my son, today I have b. you. Ps 2.07
you and have b. children among you Eze 47.22
art my Son, today I have b. thee.' Ac 13.33
art my Son, today I have b. thee"? Heb 1.05
art my Son, today I have b. thee"; 5.05

BEGRUDGE
Or do you b. my generosity?' Mt 20.15

BEGS
Give to him who b. from you, Mt 5.42
Give to every one who b. from you; Lk 6.30

BEGUILED
said, "The serpent b. me, and I ate." Gen 3.13
with which they b. you in the Num 25.18

BEGUILING
one may delude you with b. speech. Col 2.04
is teaching and b. my servants to Rev 2.20

BEGUN
from the LORD, the plague has b. Num 16.46
had already b. among the people; 16.47
I have b. to give Sihon and his Deu 2.31
thou hast only b. to show thy 3.24
Benjamin had b. to smite and kill Ju 20.39
whose eyesight had b. to grow dim, 1Sa 3.02
before whom you have b. to fall, Est 6.13
undertook to do as they had b. 9.23
Therefore I have b. to smite you, Mic 6.13
because it had b. to rain and was Ac 28.02
Having b. with the Spirit, are you Gal 3.03
thy great power and b. to reign. Rev 11.17

BEHALF
continually on b. of the people of Lev 24.08
words on his b. in the ears of all Ju 9.03
to speak to him on b. of Adonijah. 1Ki 2.19
spoken on your b. to the king or 2Ki 4.13
his might in b. of those whose 2Ch 16.09
the victory of the LORD on your b., 20.17
in Susa, and hold a fast on my b., Est 4.16
yet something to say on God's b. Job 36.02
deal on my b. for thy name's sake; Ps 109.21
the dead on b. of the living? Is 8.19
up a cry or prayer on their b., Jer 11.14
with thee on b. of the enemy in 15.11
and pray to the LORD on its b., 29.07
introduced on b. of this nation, Ac 24.02
in your prayers to God on my b., Rom 15.30
being baptized on b. of the dead? 1Co 15.29
are people baptized on their b.? 15.29
thanks on our b. for the blessing 2Co 1.11
We beseech you on b. of Christ, 5.20
On b. of this man I will boast, but 12.05
but on my own b. I will not boast, 12.05
Christ Jesus on b. of you Gentiles— Eph 3.01
minister of Christ on our b. Col 1.07
me on your b. during my imprisonment Phm 1.13
to act on b. of men in relation to Heb 5.01
has gone as a forerunner on our b., 6.20
in the presence of God on our b. 9.24

BEHAVE
but b. like a woman who has been 2Sa 14.02
one ought to b. in the household 1Ti 3.15

BEHAVED
turned back and b. worse than Ju 2.19
that we have b. in the world, 2Co 1.12

BEHAVING
that they are b. arrogantly. Job 36.09
and b. like ordinary men? 1Co 3.03
that he is not b. properly toward 7.36

BEHAVIOR
So he changed his b. before them, 1Sa 21.13
of the queen's b. will be telling Est 1.18
who were ashamed of your lewd b. Eze 16.27
blameless was our b. to you believers 1Th 2.10
likewise to be reverent in b., Tit 2.03
a word by the b. of their wives, 1Pe 3.01
see your reverent and chaste b. 3.02
your good b. in Christ may be put 3.16

BEHEADED
him, and slew him, and b. him. 2Sa 4.07
and had John b. in the prison, Mt 14.10
whom I b., has been raised." Mk 6.16
He went and b. him in the prison, 6.27
Herod said, "John I b.; Lk 9.09
who had been b. for their testimony Rev 20.04

BEHELD
and b., and lo, the smoke of the Gen 19.28
they b. God, and ate and drank. Ex 24.11
He has not b. misfortune in Jacob; Num 23.21
Thy eyes b. my unformed substance; Ps 139.16
Then I b., and, lo, a form that had Eze 8.02
whenever the unclean spirits b. him, Mk 3.11
we have b. his glory, glory as of Jn 1.14

BEHEMOTH
"Behold, B., which I made as I made Job 40.15

BEHIND
listening at the tent door b. him. Gen 18.10
But Lot's wife b. him looked back, 19.26
b. him was a ram, caught in a 22.13
and moreover he is b. us.'" 32.18
your servant Jacob is b. us.'" 32.20
flocks and your herds remain b." Ex 10.24
not a hoof shall be left b., 10.26
the maidservant who is b. the mill; 11.05
of Israel moved and went b. them; 14.19
before them and stood b. them, 14.19
were to encamp b. the tabernacle Num 3.23
at your rear all who lagged b. you; Deu 25.18
an ambush against the city, b. it." Jos 8.02
in ambush against the city, b. it; 8.04
an ambush against him b. the city. 8.14
the Benjaminites looked b. them; Ju 20.40
coming from the field b. the oxen; 1Sa 11.05
wrapped in a cloth b. the ephod; 21.09
And when Saul looked b. him, 24.08

BEHIND (cont.)
those stayed who were left b. 1Sa 30.09
two hundred stayed b., 30.10
master left me b. because I fell 30.13
And when he looked b. him, 2Sa 1.07
Then Abner looked b. him and said, 2.20
themselves together b. Abner, 2.25
and have cast me b. your back; 1Ki 14.09
sound of his master's feet b. him?" 2Ki 6.32
Turn around and ride b. me." 9.18
Turn round and ride b. me." 9.19
side by side b. Ahab his father, 9.25
a third at the gate b. the guards), 11.06
she wags her head b. you— 19.21
around to come on them from b.; 2Ch 13.13
Judah, and the ambush was b. them. 13.13
the battle was before and b. them; 13.14
parts of the space b. the wall, Neh 4.13
leaders stood b. all the house of 4.16
cast thy law b. their back and 9.26
B. him he leaves a shining wake; Job 41.32
and you cast my words b. you. Ps 50.17
Thou dost beset me b. and before, 139.05
there he stands b. our wall, Sol 2.09
Your eyes are doves b. your veil. 4.01
of a pomegranate b. your veil. 4.03
of a pomegranate b. your veil. 6.07
chambers, and shut your doors b. you; Is 26.20
your ears shall hear a word b. you, 30.21
she wags her head b. you—the daughter 37.22
hast cast all my sins b. thy back. 38.17
B. the door and the doorpost you 57.08
I heard b. me the sound of a great Eze 3.12
me and cast me b. your back, 23.35
whom you left b. shall fall by the 24.21
and b. them a flame burns. Joe 2.03
and leave a blessing b. him, 2.14
and plague followed close b. Hab 3.05
and b. him were red, sorrel, and Zec 1.08
years came up b. him and touched Mt 9.20
said to Peter, "Get b. me, Satan! 16.23
and came up b. him in the crowd and Mk 5.27
Peter, and said, "Get b. me, Satan! 8.33
boy Jesus stayed b. in Jerusalem. Lk 2.43
and standing b. him at his feet, 7.38
came up b. him, and touched the 8.44
the cross, to carry it b. Jesus. 23.26
what lies b. and straining forward Php 3.13
to be left b. at Athens alone, 1Th 3.01
the inner shrine b. the curtain, Heb 6.19
B. the second curtain stood a tent 9.03
and I heard b. me a loud voice like Rev 1.10
full of eyes in front and b.: 4.06

BEHOLD
And God said, "B., I have given you Gen 1.29
and b., it was very good. 1.31
"B., the man has become like one of 3.22
B., thou hast driven me this day 4.14
and b., it was corrupt; 6.12
b., I will destroy them with the 6.13
For b., I will bring a flood of 6.17
and b., the face of the ground was 8.13
"B., I establish my covenant with 9.09
"B., they are one people, and they 11.06
you are a woman beautiful to b.; 12.11
"B., thou hast given me no offspring; 15.03
And b., the word of the LORD came 15.04
b., a smoking fire pot and a 15.17
"B. now, the LORD has prevented me 16.02
"B., your maid is in your power; 16.06
"B., you are with child, and shall 16.11
"B., my covenant is with you, and 17.04
b., I will bless him and make him 17.20
and b., three men stood in front of 18.02
"B., I have taken upon myself to 18.27
He said, "B., I have taken upon 18.31
B., I have two daughters who have 19.08
b., your servant has found favor in 19.19
B., yonder city is near enough to 19.20
"B., I grant you this favor also, 19.21
"B., I lay last night with my 19.34
"B., you are a dead man, because of 20.03
"B., my land is before you; 20.15
"B., I have given your brother a 20.16
He said, "B., the fire and the wood; 22.07
and b., behind him was a ram, caught 22.13
"B., Milcah also has borne children 22.20
B., I am standing by the spring of 24.13
b.. Rebekah, who was born to Bethuel 24.15
and b., he was standing by the 24.30
b., I am standing by the spring of 24.43
b., Rebekah came out with her water 24.45
B., Rebekah is before you, take her 24.51
and b., there were camels coming. 24.63
b., there were twins in her womb. 25.24
"B., she is your wife; how then 26.09
He said, "B., I am old; I do not 27.02
"B., my brother Esau is a hairy man, 27.11
and b., now he has taken away my 27.36
"B., I have made him your lord, and 27.37
"B., away from the fatness of the 27.39
"B., your brother Esau comforts 27.42
and b., the angels of God were 28.12
And b., the LORD stood above it and 28.13
B., I am with you and will keep you 28.15
He said, "B., it is still high day, 29.07
And in the morning, b., it was Leah; 29.25
and b., Esau was coming, and four 33.01
for b., the land is large enough 34.21
b., we were binding sheaves in the 37.07
and b., your sheaves gathered round 37.07
"B., I have dreamed another dream; 37.09
and b., the sun, the moon, and eleven 37.09
b., his brother came out; 38.29
and b., there came up out of the 41.02
And b., seven other cows, gaunt and 41.03
and b., seven ears of grain, plump 41.05
And b., after them sprouted seven 41.06
and b., it was a dream. 41.07
"B., in my dream I was standing on 41.17
"B., I have set you over all the 41.41
And he said, "B., I have heard that 42.02
and b., the youngest is this day 42.13
b., every man's bundle of money was 42.35
B., the money which we found in the 44.08
b., we are my lord's slaves, both we 44.16
"B., I have this day bought you and 47.23
"B., your father is ill"; so he took 48.01
'B.' I will make you fruitful, and 48.04
"B., I am about to die, but God will 48.21
"B., we are your servants." 50.18
"B., the people of Israel are too Ex 1.09
b., two Hebrews were struggling 2.13
And now, b., the cry of the people 3.09
"But b., they will not believe me 4.01
b., his hand was leprous, as white 4.06
b., it was restored like the rest 4.07
and b., he is coming out to meet 4.14
b., I will slay your first-born son 4.23
"B., the people of the land are now 5.05
And b., your servants are beaten; 5.16
"B., the people of Israel have not 6.12
"B., I am of uncircumcised lips; 6.30
and b., you have not yet obeyed." 7.16
b., I will strike the water that is 7.17
b., I will plague all your country 8.02
b., I will send swarms of flies on 8.21
"B., I am going out from you and I 8.29
b., the hand of the LORD will fall 9.03
and b., not one of the cattle of 9.07
B., tomorrow about this time I will 9.18
b., tomorrow I will bring locusts 10.04
and b., the Egyptians were marching 14.10

BEHOLD (cont.)

"B., I will rain bread from heaven Ex 16.04
and b., the glory of the LORD 16.10
B., I will stand before you there 17.06
"B., I send an angel before you, to 23.20
"B. the blood of the covenant which 24.08
and, b., Aaron and Hur are with you; 24.14
And b., I have appointed with him 31.06
and b., it is stiff-necked people; 32.09
b., my angel shall go before you. 32.34
"B., there is a place by me where 33.21
And he said, "B., I make a covenant. 34.10
B., I will drive out before you the 34.11
b., the skin of his face shone, and 34.30
and b., they had done it; 39.43
offering, and b., it was burned! Lev 10.16
B., its blood was not brought into 10.18
"B., today they have offered their 10.19
"B., I have taken the Levites from Num 3.12
b., Miriam was leprous, as white as 12.10
and b., she was leprous. 12.10
and b., the cloud covered it, and 16.42
and b., the plague had already 16.47
and b., the rod of Aaron for the 17.08
"B., we perish, we are undone, we are 17.12
And b., I have taken your brethren 18.06
"And b., I have given you whatever 18.08
"B., a people has come out of Egypt; 22.05
'B., a people has come out of Egypt, 22.11
B., I have come forth to withstand 22.32
I see him, from the hills I b. him; 23.09
and b., you have done nothing but 23.11
B., I received a command to bless: 23.20
B., a people! As a lioness 23.24
and b., you have blessed them these 24.10
And now, b., I am going to my people; 24.14
I b. him, but not nigh: a star shall 24.17
And b., one of the people of Israel 25.06
'B., I give to him my covenant of 25.12
B., these caused the people of 31.16
and b., the place was a place for 32.01
And b., you have risen in your 32.14
b., you have sinned against the 32.23
B., I have set the land before you; Deu 1.08
and b., you are this day as the 1.10
B., the LORD your God has set the 1.21
b., I have given into your hand 2.24
'B., I have begun to give Sihon and 2.31
b., his bedstead was a bedstead of 3.11
and b. it with your eyes; for you 3.27
B., I have taught you statutes and 4.05
and you said, 'B., the LORD our God 5.24
and b., it is a stubborn people; 9.13
and b., you had sinned against the 9.16
B., to the LORD your God belong 10.14
"B., I set before you this day a 11.26
and b., if it be true and certain 13.14
And b., now I bring the first of 26.10
"B., the days approach when you 31.14
"B., you are about to sleep with 31.16
b., while I am yet alive with you, 31.27
"B., certain men of Israel have Jos 2.02
B., when we come into the land, you 2.18
B., the ark of the covenant of the 3.11
and b., a man stood before him with 5.13
and b., they are hidden in the 7.21
and b., it was hidden in his tent 7.22
"B., you shall lie in ambush 8.04
b., the smoke of the city went up 8.20
but now, b., it is dry and moldy; 9.12
and b., they are burst; and these 9.13
And now, b., we are in your hand: do 9.25
And now, b., the LORD has kept me 14.10
"B., the Reubenites and the Gadites 22.11
'B. the copy of the altar of the 22.28
B., I have allotted to you as an 23.04
"B., this stone shall be a witness 24.27
b., I have given the land into his Ju 1.02
And b., as Barak pursued Sisera, 4.22
B., my clan is the weakest in 6.15
b., the altar of Baal was broken 6.28
b., I am laying a fleece of wool on 6.37
b. a man was telling a dream to his 7.13
and he said, "B., I dreamed a dream; 7.13
"B. Zebah and Zalmunna, about whom 8.15
"B., Gaal the son of Ebed and his 9.31
and b., his daughter came out to 11.34
"B., you are barren and have no 13.03
'B., you shall conceive and bear a 13.07
"B., the man who came to me the 13.10
And b., a young lion roared against 14.05
and b., there was a swarm of bees 14.08
"B., I have not told my father nor 14.16
"B., you have mocked me, and told me 16.10
b., the silver is with me; 17.02
and b., it is very fertile. 18.09
b., it is west of Kiriathjearim. 18.12
"B., now the day has waned toward 19.09
B., the day draws to its close; 19.09
And b., an old man was coming from 19.16
b., the men of the city, base 19.22
B., here are my virgin daughter and 19.24
b. there was his concubine lying at 19.27
B., you people of Israel, all of you, 20.07
and b., the whole of the city went 20.40
And b., no one had come to the camp 21.08
b., not one of the inhabitants of 21.09
So they said, "B., there is the 21.19
And b., Boaz came from Bethlehem; Ru 2.04
and b., a woman lay at his feet! 3.08
and b., the next of kin, of whom 4.01
B., the days are coming, when I will 1Sa 2.31
"B., I am about to do a thing in 3.11
b., Dagon had fallen face downward 5.03
b., Dagon had fallen face downward 5.04
"B., you are old and your sons do 8.05
"B., there is a man of God in this 9.06
b., he is just ahead of you. 9.12
and b., I am coming to you to offer 10.08
b., a band of prophets met him; 10.10
"B., he has hidden himself among 10.22
"B., I have hearkened to your voice 12.01
And now, b., the king walks before 12.02
and b., my sons are with you; 12.02
And now b. the king whom you have 12.13
b., the LORD has set a king over 12.13
burnt offering, b., Samuel came; 13.10
b., I am with you, as is your mind 14.07
"B., we will cross over to the men, 14.08
and b., the multitude was surging 14.16
b., Jonathan and his armor-bearer 14.17
and b., every man's sword was 14.20
b., the honey was dropping, but no 14.26
"B., the people are sinning against 14.33
and b., he set up a monument for 15.12
B., to obey is better than sacrifice, 15.22
but b., he is keeping the sheep." 16.11
"B. now, an evil spirit from God is 16.15
"B., I have seen a son of Jesse the 16.18
b., the champion, the Philistine of 17.23
'B., the king has delight in you, 18.22
b., the image was in the bed, with 19.16
"B., David is at Naioth in Ramah." 19.19
"B., they are at Naioth in Ramah." 19.22
B., my father does nothing either 20.02
"B., tomorrow is the new moon, and I 20.05
b., if he is well disposed toward 20.12
And b., I will send the lad, saying, 20.21
b., the LORD is between you and me 20.23
b., it is here wrapped in a cloth 21.09
"B., the Philistines are fighting 23.01
"B., we are afraid here in Judah; 23.03
"B., David is in the wilderness of 24.01
'B., I will give your enemy into 24.04

BEHOLD (cont.)

'B., David seeks your hurt'? 1Sa 24.09
And now, b., I know that you shall 24.20
"B., David sent messengers out of 25.14
b., I come after you." But she did 25.19
b., David and his men came down 25.20
"B., your handmaid is a servant to 25.41
b., I have played the fool, and have 26.21
B., as your life was precious this 26.24
"B., there is a medium at Endor." 28.07
"B., your handmaid has hearkened to 28.21
b., they were spread abroad over 30.16
b., a man came from Saul's camp, with 2Sa 1.02
b., it is written in the Book of 1.18
and b., my hand shall be with you 3.12
B., Abner came to you; 3.24
And b., the doorkeeper of the house 4.06
'B., Saul is dead,' and thought he 4.10
"B., we are your bone and flesh. 5.01
And he answered, "B., your servant." 9.06
'B., I will raise up evil against 12.11
"B., while the child was yet alive, 12.18
"B., your servant has sheepshearers 13.24
and b., many people were coming 13.34
"B., the king's sons have come; 13.35
b., the king's sons came, and lifted 13.36
"B. now, I grant this; 14.21
"B., I sent word to you, 'Come here, 14.32
"B., your servants are ready to do 15.15
b., here I am, let him do to me 15.26
b., Hushai the Archite came to meet 15.32
B., their two sons are with them 15.36
"B., he remains in Jerusalem; 16.03
"B., all that belonged to Mephibosheth 16.04
"B., my own son seeks my life; 16.11
B., even now he has hidden himself 17.09
"B., I saw Absalom hanging in an 18.10
And b., the Cushite came; 18.31
"B., the king is weeping and 19.01
"B., the king is sitting in the 19.08
therefore, b., I have come this day, 19.20
"B., his head shall be thrown to 20.21
And now, b., Adonijah is king, 1Ki 1.18
and b., they are eating and drinking 1.25
b., Jonathan the son of Abiathar 1.42
"B., Adonijah fears King Solomon; 1.51
and b., he is beside the altar," 2.29
"B., your slaves are in Gath," 2.39
b., I now do according to your word. 3.12
B., I give you a wise and discerning 3.12
and b., it was a dream. 3.15
to nurse my child, b., it was dead; 3.21
b., it was not the child that I had 3.21
B., heaven and the highest heaven 8.27
and, b., the half was not told me; 10.07
'B., I am about to tear the kingdom 11.31
B. your gods, O Israel, who brought 12.28
And b., a man of God came out of 13.01
'B., a son shall be born to the 13.02
'B., the altar shall be torn down, 13.03
And b., men passed by, and saw the 13.25
b., Ahijah the prophet is there, who 14.02
"B., the wife of Jeroboam is coming 14.05
therefore b., I will bring evil 14.10
b., they are written in the Book of 14.19
b., I am sending to you a present 15.19
b., I will utterly sweep away 16.03
B., I have commanded a widow there 17.09
b., a widow was there gathering 17.10
b., Elijah met him; and Obadiah 18.07
tell your lord, 'B., Elijah is here.'" 18.08
tell your lord, "B., Elijah is here."' 18.11
lord, "B., Elijah is here"'; and 18.14
"B., a little cloud like a man's 18.44
and b., an angel touched him, and 19.05
and b., there was at his head a 19.06
and b., the word of the LORD came 19.09

And b., the LORD passed by, and a 19.11
And b., there came a voice to him, 19.13
And b., a prophet came near to Ahab 20.13
B., I will give it into your hand 20.13
"B. now, we have heard that the 20.31
b., as soon as you have gone from 20.36
and b., a soldier turned and 20.39
b., he is in the vineyard of Naboth, 21.18
B., I will bring evil upon you; 21.21
"B., the words of the prophets with 22.13
Now therefore b., the LORD has put 22.23
"B., you shall see on that day when 22.25
b., a chariot of fire and horses of 2Ki 2.11
"B. now, there are with your servants 2.16
"B., the situation of this city is 2.19
b., water came from the direction 3.20
"B. now, I perceive that this is a 4.09
"B., I thought that he would surely 5.11
and he said, "B., I know that there 5.15
told him, "B., he is in Dothan." 6.13
b., an army with horses and chariots 6.15
and b., the mountain was full of 6.17
and b., he had sackcloth beneath 6.30
b., there was no one there. 7.05
"B., the king of Israel has hired 7.06
and b., there was no one to be seen 7.10
b., the woman whose son he had 8.05
b., the commanders of the army were 9.05
"B., the two kings could not stand 10.04
b., they are written in the Book of 15.11
b., they are written in the Book of 15.15
b., they are written in the Book of 15.26
b., they are written in the Book of 15.31
and b., they are killing them, 17.26
B., you are relying now on Egypt, 18.21
B., I will put a spirit in him, so 19.07
"B., he has set out to fight 19.09
B., you have heard what the kings 19.11
b., these were all dead bodies. 19.35
b., I will heal you; on the third 20.05
B., the days are coming, when all 20.17
B., I am bringing upon Jerusalem 21.12
B., I will bring evil upon this 22.16
Therefore, b., I will gather you to 22.20
"B., we are your bone and flesh. 1Ch 11.01
"B., I dwell in a house of cedar, 17.01
B., a son shall be born to you; 22.09
And b. the divisions of the priests 28.21
B., I am about to build a house for 2Ch 2.04
B., heaven and the highest heaven 6.18
and b., half the greatness of 9.06
B., God is with us at our head, and 13.12
b., the battle was before and 13.14
b., I am sending to you silver 16.03
"B., the words of the prophets with 18.12
Now therefore b., the LORD has put 18.22
"B., you shall see on that day when 18.24
And b., Amariah the chief priest is 19.11
and, b., they are in Hazazontamar" 20.02
And now b., the men of Ammon and 20.10
b., they reward us by coming to 20.11
b., they will come up by the 20.16
and b., they were dead bodies 20.24
b., the LORD will bring a great 21.14
"B., the king's son! Let 23.03
and b., he was leprous in his 26.20
b., they are written in the Book of 27.07
"B., because the LORD, the God of 28.09
b., they are written in the Book of 28.26
and b., they are before the altar 29.19
b., they are written in the vision 32.32
b., they are in the Chronicles of 33.18
b., they are written in the Chronicles 33.19
B., I will bring evil upon this 34.24
B., I will gather you to your 34.28
b., they are written in the 35.25
b., they are written in the Book of 35.27

BEHOLD (cont.)

b., they are written in the Book of 2Ch 36.08
B., we are before thee in our guilt, Ez 9.15
B., we are slaves this day; Neh 9.36
its good gifts, b., we are slaves. 9.36
for she was fair to b. Est 1.11
"B., I have given Esther the house 8.07
"B., all that he has is in your Job 1.12
and b., a great wind came across 1.19
"B., he is in your power; 2.06
B., you have instructed many, and 4.03
"B., happy is the man whom God 5.17
him who sees me will b. me no more; 7.08
B., this is the joy of his way; 8.19
"B., God will not reject a blameless 8.20
B., he snatches away; who can 9.12
is a contest of strength, b. him! 9.19
B., he will slay me; I have 13.15
B., I have prepared my case; 13.18
B., God puts no trust in his holy 15.15
Even now, b., my witness is in 16.19
B., I cry out, 'Violence!' 19.07
on my side, and my eyes shall b., 19.27
nor will his place any more b. him. 20.09
B., is not their prosperity in 21.16
"B., I know your thoughts, and your 21.27
"B., I go forward, but he is not 23.08
I seek him, but I cannot b. him; 23.09
B., like wild asses in the desert 24.05
B., even the moon is not bright and 25.05
B., all of you have seen it yourselves 27.12
'B., the fear of the Lord, that is 28.28
"B., I waited for your words, I 32.11
b., there was none that confuted 32.12
B., my heart is like wine that has 32.19
B., I open my mouth; the tongue 33.02
B., I am toward God as you are; 33.06
B., no fear of me need terrify you; 33.07
B., he finds occasions against me, 33.10
"B., in this you are not right. 33.12
"B., God does all these things, 33.29
who can b. him, whether it be a 34.29
and b. the clouds, which are higher 35.05
"B., God is mighty, and does not 36.05
B., God is exalted in his power; 36.22
B., God is great, and we know him 36.26
B., he scatters his lightning about 36.30
his eyes b. it afar off. 39.29
"B., I am of small account; 40.04
"B., Behemoth, which I made as I 40.15
B., his strength in his loins, and 40.16
B., if the river is turbulent he is 40.23
B., the hope of a man is disappointed; 41.09
B., the wicked man conceives evil, Ps 7.14
B. what I suffer from those who 9.13
his eyes b., his eyelids test, the 11.04
the upright shall b. his face. 11.07
I shall b. thy face in righteousness; 17.15
to b. the beauty of the LORD, and to 27.04
B., the eye of the LORD is on those 33.18
and b. the upright, for there is 37.37
B., thou hast made my days a few 39.05
I come and b. the face of God? 42.02
Come, b. the works of the LORD, how 46.08
B., I was brought forth in iniquity, 51.05
B., thou desirest truth in the 51.06
B., God is my helper; the Lord 54.04
B., these are the wicked; 73.12
B. our shield, O God; look upon 84.09
b., Philistia and Tyre, with Ethiopia 87.04
and all the peoples b. his glory. 97.06
that I may b. wondrous things out 119.18
B., I long for thy precepts; 119.40
B., he who keeps Israel will 121.04
B., as the eyes of servants look to 123.02
B., how good and pleasant it is 133.01
b., I will pour out my thoughts to Pro 1.23

If you say, "B., we did not know 24.12
and b., all is vanity and a striving Ecc 1.14
But b., this also was vanity. 2.01
and b., all was vanity and a 2.11
And b., the tears of the oppressed, 4.01
B., what I have seen to be good and 5.18
B., this is what I found, says the 7.27
B., this alone I found, that God 7.29
pleasant for the eyes to b. the sun. 11.07
B., you are beautiful, my love; Sol 1.15
b., you are beautiful; your eyes 1.15
B., you are beautiful, my beloved, 1.16
B., he comes, leaping upon the 2.08
B., there he stands behind our wall, 2.09
B., it is the litter of Solomon! 3.07
and b. King Solomon, with the crown 3.11
B., you are beautiful, my love, 4.01
b., you are beautiful! Your eyes 4.01
For, b., the Lord, the LORD of hosts, Is 3.01
for justice, but b., bloodshed; 5.07
for righteousness, but b., a cry! 5.07
b., darkness and distress; 5.30
"B., this has touched your lips; 6.07
B., a young woman shall conceive 7.14
therefore, b., the Lord is bringing 8.07
B., I and the children whom the 8.18
but b., distress and darkness, the 8.22
B., the Lord, the LORD of hosts will 10.33
"B., God is my salvation; 12.02
B., the day of the LORD comes, cruel, 13.09
B., I am stirring up the Medes 13.17
B., Damascus will cease to be a 17.01
At evening time, b., terror! 17.14
B., the LORD is riding on a swift 19.01
'B., this is what has happened to 20.06
And, b., here come riders, horsemen 21.09
and b., joy and gladness, slaying 22.13
B., the LORD will hurl you away 22.17
B. the land of the Chaldeans! 23.13
B., the LORD will lay waste the 24.01
For b., the LORD is coming forth 26.21
B., the Lord has one who is mighty 28.02
"B., I am laying in Zion for a 28.16
therefore, b., I will again do 29.14
B., the name of the LORD comes from 30.27
B., a king will reign in righteousness, 32.01
B. the valiant ones cry without; 33.07
they will b. a land that stretches 33.17
b., it descends for judgment upon 34.05
B., your God will come with vengeance, 35.04
B., you are relying on Egypt, that 36.06
B., I will put a spirit in him, so 37.07
B., you have heard what the kings 37.11
b., these were all dead bodies. 37.36
b., I will add fifteen years to 38.05
B., I will make the shadow cast by 38.08
B., the days are coming, when all 39.06
the cities of Judah, "B. your God!" 40.09
B., the Lord GOD comes with might, 40.10
b., his reward is with him, and his 40.10
B., the nations are like a drop 40.15
b., he takes up the isles like fine 40.15
B., all who are incensed against 41.11
B., I will make of you a threshing 41.15
B., you are nothing, and your work 41.24
B., they are all a delusion; 41.29
B. my servant, whom I uphold, my 42.01
B., the former things have come to 42.09
B., I am doing a new thing; 43.19
B., all his fellows shall be put to 44.11
B., they are like stubble, the fire 47.14
you should say, 'B., I knew them.' 48.07
B., I have refined you, but not like 48.10
B., I have graven you on the palms 49.16
B., I was left alone; 49.21
"B., I will lift up my hand to the 49.22
B., for your iniquities you were 50.01

BEHOLD (cont.)
B., by my rebuke I dry up the sea, I Is 50.02
B., the Lord God helps me; 50.09
B., all of them will wear out like 50.09
B., all you who kindle a fire, who 50.11
"B., I have taken from your hand 51.22
B., my servant shall prosper, he 52.13
b., I will set your stones in 54.11
B., I have created the smith who 54.16
B., I made him a witness to the 55.04
B., you shall call nations that you 55.05
"B., I am a dry tree." 56.03
B., in the day of your fast you 58.03
B., you fast only to quarrel and to 58.04
B., the Lord's hand is not shortened, 59.01
and b., darkness, and for brightness, 59.09
For b., darkness shall cover the 60.02
B., the Lord has proclaimed to the 62.11
"B., your salvation comes; 62.11
b., his reward is with him, and his 62.11
B., thou wast angry, and we sinned; 64.05
B., consider, we are all thy people. 64.09
B., it is written before me: "I will 65.06
"B., my servants shall eat, but you 65.13
b., my servants shall drink, but you 65.13
b., my servants shall rejoice, but 65.13
b., my servants shall sing for 65.14
"For b., I create new heavens and a 65.17
for b., I create Jerusalem a 65.18
"B., I will extend prosperity to 66.12
"For b., the Lord will come in fire, 66.15
B., I do not know how to speak, for Jer 1.06
"B., I have put my words in your 1.09
And I, b., I make you this day a 1.18
B., I will bring you to judgment 2.35
B., you have spoken, but you have 3.05
"B., we come to thee; 3.22
B., he comes up like clouds, his 4.13
b., I am making my words in your 5.14
B., I am bringing upon you a nation 5.15
B., their ears are closed, they 6.10
b., the word of the Lord is to them 6.10
b., I am bringing evil upon this 6.19
'B., I will lay before this people 6.21
"B., a people is coming from the 6.22
"B., you trust in deceptive words 7.08
B., I myself have seen it, says the 7.11
B., my anger and my wrath will be 7.20
Therefore, b., the days are coming, 7.32
But, b., the false pen of the 8.08
a time of healing, but b., terror. 8.15
For b., I am sending among you 8.17
"B., I will refine them and test 9.07
B., I will feed this people with 9.15
"B., the days are coming, says the 9.25
"B., I am slinging out the inhabitants 10.18
B., it comes!—a great 10.22
B., I am bringing evil upon them 11.11
"B., I will punish them; 11.22
"B., I will pluck them up from 12.14
And b., the waistcloth was spoiled; 13.07
B., I will fill with drunkenness 13.13
b., the prophets say to them, 'You 14.13
b., those slain by the sword! 14.18
b., the diseases of famine! 14.18
a time of healing, but b., terror. 14.19
B., I will make to cease from this 16.09
for b., every one of you follows 16.12
"Therefore, b., the days are coming, 16.14
"B., I am sending for many fishers, 16.16
"Therefore, b., I will make them 16.21
B., they say to me, "Where is the 17.15
B., like the clay in the potter's 18.06
B., I am shaping evil against you 18.11
B., I am bringing such evil upon 19.03
therefore, b., days are coming, says 19.06
B., I am bringing upon this city 19.15
B., I will make you a terror to 20.04
B., I will turn back the weapons of 21.04
B., I set before you the way of 21.08
"B., I am against you, O inhabitant 21.13
B., I will attend to you for your 23.02
"B., the days are coming, says the 23.05
"Therefore, b., the days are coming, 23.07
"B., I will feed them with wormwood, 23.15
B., the storm of the Lord! 23.19
Therefore, b., I am against the 23.30
B., I am against the prophets, says 23.31
B., I am against those who prophesy 23.32
therefore, b., I will surely lift 23.39
B., two baskets of figs placed 24.01
b., I will send for all the tribes 25.09
For b., I begin to work evil at the 25.29
B., evil is going forth from nation 25.32
But as for me, b., I am in your 26.14
'B., the vessels of the Lord's house 27.16
'B., I will remove you from the 28.16
'B., I am sending on them sword, 29.17
B., I will deliver them into the 29.21
B., I will punish Shemaiah of 29.32
For b., days are coming, says the 30.03
B., I will restore the fortunes of 30.18
B. the storm of the Lord! 30.23
B., I will bring them from the 31.08
"B., the days are coming, says the 31.27
"B., the days are coming, says the 31.31
"B., the days are coming, says the 31.38
B. I am giving this city into the 32.03
B., Hanamel the son of Shallum your 32.07
B., the siege mounds have come up 32.24
to pass, and b., thou seest it. 32.24
"B., I am the Lord, the God of all 32.27
B., I am giving this city into the 32.28
B., I will gather them from all the 32.37
B., I will bring to it health and 33.06
"B., the days are coming, says the 33.14
B., I am giving this city into the 34.02
b., I proclaim to you liberty to 34.17
B., I will command, says the Lord, 34.22
B., I am bringing on Judah and all 35.17
'B., Pharaoh's army which came to 37.07
"B., he is in your hands; for the 38.05
B., all the women left in the house 38.22
B. I will fulfil my words against 39.16
Now, b., I release you today from 40.04
b., I will pray to the Lord your 42.04
B., I will send and take Nebuchadrezzar 43.10
B., this day they are a desolation, 44.02
B., I will set my face against you 44.11
B., I have sworn by my great name, 44.26
B., I am watching over them for 44.27
B., I will give Pharaoh Hophra king 44.30
B., what I have built I am breaking 45.04
for, b., I am bringing evil upon all 45.05
"B., I am bringing punishment upon 46.25
B., waters are rising out of the 47.02
"Therefore, b., the days are coming, 48.12
"B., one shall fly swiftly like an 48.40
Therefore, b., the days are coming, 49.02
B., I will bring terror upon you, 49.05
For b., I will make you small among 49.15
B., like a lion coming up from the 49.19
B., one shall mount up and fly 49.22
"B., I will break the bow of Elam, 49.35
For b., I am stirring up and 50.09
B., I am bringing punishment on the 50.18
"B., I am against you, O proud one, 50.31
"B., a people comes from the north; 50.41
"B., like a lion coming up from the 50.44
"B., I will stir up the spirit of a 51.01
"B., I am against you, O destroying 51.25
"B., I will plead your cause and 51.36
"Therefore, b., the days are coming 51.47
"Therefore, b., the days are coming, 51.52

BEHOLD (cont.)

"O LORD, b. my affliction, for the	Lam 1.09
and b., for I am despised."	1.11
you peoples, and b. my suffering;	1.18
"B., O LORD, for I am in distress, my	1.20
B. their sitting and their rising;	3.63
b., and see our disgrace!	5.01
As I looked, b., a stormy wind came	Eze 1.04
b., a hand was stretched out to me,	2.09
B., I have made your face hard	3.08
B., cords will be placed upon you,	3.25
And, b., I will put cords upon you,	4.08
B., I have never defiled myself;	4.14
b., I will break the staff of bread	4.16
B., I, even I, am against you;	5.08
B., I, even I, will bring a sword	6.03
disaster! B., it comes.	7.05
against you. B., it comes.	7.06
"B., the day! B., it comes!	7.10
And b., the glory of the God of	8.04
and b., north of the altar gate, in	8.05
b., there was a hole in the wall.	8.07
and b., there sat women weeping for	8.14
and b., at the door of the temple	8.16
and b., on the firmament that was	10.01
and b., there were four wheels	10.09
And b., at the door of the gateway	11.01
"Son of man, b., they of the house	12.27
therefore b., I am against you, says	13.08
B., I am against your magic bands	13.20
B., when it was whole, it was used	15.05
b., you were at the age for love;	16.08
B., therefore, I stretched out my	16.27
therefore, b., I will gather all	16.37
therefore, b., I will requite your	16.43
B., every one who uses proverbs	16.44
B., this was the guilt of your	16.49
and b., this vine bent its roots	17.07
B., when it is transplanted, will it	17.10
Tell them, B., the king of Babylon	17.12
B., all souls are mine; the soul of	18.04
b., he shall die for his iniquity.	18.18
B., I will kindle a fire in you, and	20.47
B., I am against you, and will draw	21.03
B., it comes and it will be fulfilled,	21.07
"B., the princes of Israel in you,	22.06
"B., therefore, I strike my hands	22.13
b., I will gather you into the	22.19
"B., I will rouse against you your	23.22
B., I will deliver you into the	23.28
"Son of man, b., I am about to take	24.16
B., I will profane my sanctuary, the	24.21
therefore, b., I have stretched out	25.07
B., the house of Judah is like all	25.08
B., I will stretch out my hand	25.16
B., I am against you, O Tyre, and	26.03
B., I will bring upon Tyre from the	26.07
therefore, b., I will bring strangers	28.07
"B., I am against you, O Sidon, and I	28.22
"B., I am against you, Pharaoh king	29.03
B., I will bring a sword upon you,	29.08
therefore, b., I am against you, and	29.10
B., I will give the land of Egypt	29.19
B., I am against Pharaoh king of	30.22
B., I will liken you to a cedar in	31.03
B., I am against the shepherds;	34.10
B., I, I myself will search for my	34.11
B., I judge between sheep and sheep,	34.17
B., I, I myself will judge between	34.20
B., I am against you, Mount Seir, and	35.03
B., I speak in my jealous wrath,	36.06
For, b., I am for you, and I will	36.09
and b., there were very many upon	37.02
B., I will cause breath to enter	37.05
was a noise, and b., a rattling;	37.07
B., they say, 'Our bones are dried	37.11
B., I will open your graves, and	37.12
B., I am about to take the stick of	37.19
B., I will take the people of	37.21
B., I am against you, O Gog, chief	38.03
B., I am against you, O Gog, chief	39.01
B., it is coming and it will be	39.08
b., there was a man, whose appearance	40.03
And b., there was a wall all around	40.05
and b., there were chambers and a	40.17
and b., there was a gate which	40.20
and b., there was a gate on the	40.24
and b., there were two chambers in	40.44
And b., the glory of the God of	43.02
and b., the glory of the LORD	43.05
B., this is the law of the temple.	43.12
and b., the glory of the LORD	44.04
and b., water was issuing from	47.01
saw, O king, and b., a great image.	Dan 2.31
and b., a tree in the midst of the	4.10
and b., a watcher, a holy one, came	4.13
and b., the four winds of heaven	7.02
And b., another beast, a second one,	7.05
and b., a fourth beast, terrible and	7.07
and b., there came up among them	7.08
and b., in this horn were eyes like	7.08
and b., with the clouds of heaven	7.13
and b., a ram standing on the bank	8.03
b., a he-goat came from the west	8.05
and b., there stood before me one	8.15
He said, "B., I will make known to	8.19
thy eyes and b. our desolations,	9.18
and b., a man clothed in linen,	10.05
And b., a hand touched me and set	10.10
And b., one in the likeness of the	10.16
B., three more kings shall arise in	11.02
and b., two others stood, one on	12.05
"Therefore, b., I will allure her,	Hos 2.14
For b., they are going to Assyria;	9.06
"B., I am sending to you grain, wine,	Joe 2.19
"For b., in those days and at that	3.01
"B., I will press you down in your	Amo 2.13
b., the days are coming upon you,	4.02
For b., the LORD commands, and the	6.11
"For b., I will raise up against	6.14
b., he was forming locusts in the	7.01
b., the Lord GOD was calling for a	7.04
He showed me: b., the Lord was	7.07
"B., I am setting a plumb line in	7.08
b., a basket of summer fruit.	8.01
"B., the days are coming," says the	8.11
B., the eyes of the Lord GOD are	9.08
"B., the days are coming," says the	9.13
B., I will make you small among the	Ob 1.02
For b., the LORD is coming forth	Mic 1.03
B., against this family I am	2.03
I shall b. his deliverance.	7.09
B., on the mountains the feet of	Nah 1.15
B. I am against you, says the LORD of	2.13
B. I am against you, says the LORD	3.05
B. your troops are women in your	3.13
eyes than to b. evil and canst not	Hab 1.13
B., he whose soul is not upright in	2.04
B., is it not from the LORD of	2.13
B., it is overlaid with gold and	2.19
B., at that time I will deal with	Zep 3.19
and b., a man riding upon a red	Zec 1.08
and b., all the earth remains at	1.11
eyes and saw, and b., four horns!	1.18
and b., a man with a measuring line	2.01
And b., the angel who talked with	2.03
"B., I will shake my hand over them,	2.09
"B., I have taken your iniquity	3.04
b., I will bring my servant the	3.08
For b., upon the stone which I have	3.09
and b., a lampstand all of gold,	4.02
and saw, and b., a flyng scroll!	5.01
And b., the leaden cover was lifted,	5.07
and b., two women coming forward!	5.09

BEHOLD (cont.)

and b., four chariots came out from	Zec 6.01
"B., those who go toward the north	6.08
"B., the man whose name is the	6.12
B., I will save my people from the	8.07
B., a day of the LORD is coming,	14.01
B., I will rebuke your offspring,	Mal 2.03
"B., I send my messenger to prepare	3.01
b., he is coming, says the LORD of	3.01
"For b., the day comes, burning like	4.01
"B., I will send you Elijah the	4.05
b., an angel of the Lord appeared	Mt 1.20
"B., a virgin shall conceive and	1.23
b., wise men from the East came to	2.01
b., an angel of the Lord appeared	2.13
b., an angel of the Lord appeared	2.19
and b., the heavens were opened and	3.16
and b., angels came and ministered	4.11
and b., a leper came to him and	8.02
And b., there arose a great storm	8.24
And b., they cried out, "What have	8.29
and b., the whole herd rushed down	8.32
And b., all the city came out to	8.34
And b., they brought to him a	9.02
And b., some of the scribes said to	9.03
b., many tax collectors and sinners	9.10
b., a ruler came in and knelt	9.18
And b., a woman who had suffered	9.20
b., a dumb demoniac was brought to	9.32
"B., I send you out as sheep in the	10.16
go out into the wilderness to b.?	11.07
B., those who wear soft raiment are	11.08
'B., I send my messenger before thy	11.10
'B., a glutton and a drunkard, a	11.19
and b., there was a man with a	12.10
"B., my servant whom I have chosen,	12.18
and b., something greater than	12.41
and b., something greater than	12.42
b., his mother and his brothers	12.46
And b., a Canaanite woman from that	15.22
And b., there appeared to them	17.03
angels always b. the face of my	18.10
And b., one came up to him, saying,	19.16
"B., we are going up to Jerusalem;	20.18
And b., two blind men sitting by	20.30
B., your king is coming to you,	21.05
B., I have made ready my dinner, my	22.04
B., your house is forsaken and	23.38
'B., the bridegroom! Come out	25.06
B., the hour is at hand, and the Son	26.45
And b., one of those who were with	26.51
And b., the curtain of the temple	27.51
And b., there was a great earthquake;	28.02
and b., he is going before you to	28.07
And b., Jesus met them and said,	28.09
b., some of the guard went into the	28.11
"B., I send my messenger before thy	Mk 1.02
saying, "B., we are going up to	10.33
"B., he is calling Elijah."	15.35
And b., you will be silent and	Lk 1.20
And b., you will conceive in your	1.31
And b., your kinswoman Elizabeth in	1.36
"B. I am the handmaid of the Lord;	1.38
For b., when the voice of your	1.44
For b., henceforth all generations	1.48
for b., I bring you good news of a	2.10
"B., this child is set for the fall	2.34
B., your father and I have been	2.48
And b., men were bringing on a bed	5.18
for b., your reward is great in	6.23
b., a man who had died was being	7.12
go out into the wilderness to b.?	7.24
B., those who are gorgeously	7.25
'B., I send my messenger before thy	7.27
and you say, 'B., a glutton and a	7.34
And b., a woman of the city, who was	7.37
And b., two men talked with him,	9.30

And b., a man from the crowd cried,	9.38
and b., a spirit seizes him, and he	9.39
b., I send you out as lambs in the	10.03
B., I have given you authority to	10.19
And b., a lawyer stood up to put	10.25
and b., something greater than	11.31
and b., something greater than	11.32
and b., everything is clean for you.	11.41
And b., some are last who will be	13.30
'B., I cast out demons and perform	13.32
B., your house is forsaken.	13.35
And b., there was a man before him	14.02
for b., the kingdom of God is in	17.21
"B., we are going up to Jerusalem,	18.31
"B., Lord, the half of my goods I	19.08
"B., when you have entered the city,	22.10
But b. the hand of him who betrays	22.21
"Simon, Simon, b., Satan demanded to	22.31
b., I did not find this man guilty	23.14
B., nothing deserving death has	23.15
For b., the days are coming when	23.29
b., two men stood by them in	24.04
And b., I send the promise of my	24.49
"B., the Lamb of God, who takes away	Jn 1.29
"B., the Lamb of God!"	1.36
"B., an Israelite indeed, in whom is	1.47
b., your king is coming, sitting on	12.15
to b. my glory which thou hast	17.24
"B., I am bringing him out to you,	19.04
to his mother, "Woman, b. your son!"	19.26
to the disciple, "B. your mother!"	19.27
b., two men stood by them in white	Ac 1.10
and he said, "B., I see the heavens	7.56
And b., an Ethiopian, a eunuch, a	8.27
for b., he is praying,	9.11
b., the men that were sent by	10.17
"B., three men are looking for you.	10.19
and b., a man stood before me in	10.30
and b., an angel of the Lord	12.07
And now, b., the hand of the Lord is	13.11
'B., you scoffers, and wonder, and	13.41
b., we turn to the Gentiles.	13.46
And now, b., I am going to Jerusalem,	20.22
And now, b., I know that all you	20.25
"B. I am laying in Zion a stone	Rom 9.33
b., the new has come.	2Co 5.17
"B., now is the acceptable time;	6.02
b., now is the day of salvation.	6.02
as dying, and b. we live;	6.09
B., the wages of the laborers who	Jas 5.04
B., the farmer waits for the	5.07
b., the Judge is standing at the	5.09
B., we call those happy who were	5.11
"B., I am laying in Zion a stone, a	1Pe 2.06
"B., the Lord came with his holy	Jud 1.14
B., he is coming with the clouds,	Rev 1.07
I died, and b. I am alive for	1.18
B., the devil is about to throw	2.10
B., I will throw her on a sickbed,	2.22
B., I have set before you an open	3.08
B., I will make those of the	3.09
b., I will make them come and bow	3.09
B., I stand at the door and knock;	3.20
B., now is the acceptable time;	6.02
and b., a black horse, and its rider	6.05
And I saw, and b., a pale horse, and	6.08
and b., there was a great earthquake;	6.12
and b., a great multitude which no	7.09
b., two woes are still to come.	9.12
b., the third woe is soon to come.	11.14
b. a great red dragon, with seven	12.03
world, will marvel to b. the beast,	17.08
opened, and b., a white horse!	19.11
"B., the dwelling of God is with	21.03
"B., I make all things new."	21.05
And b., I am coming soon."	22.07
"B., I am coming soon, bringing my	22.12

BEHOLDING
be satisfied with b. thy form. Ps 17.15
b. thy power and glory. 63.02
b. the glory of the Lord, are being 2Co 3.18

BEHOLDS
and he b. the form of the LORD. Num 12.08
man b. it from afar. Job 36.25
He b. everything that is high; 41.34

BEING
and man became a living b. Gen 2.07
the LORD b. merciful to him, and 19.16
the name of his city b. Dinhabah. 36.32
the name of his city b. Avith. 36.35
stead, the name of his city b. Pau; 36.39
Joseph, b. seventeen years old, was 37.02
As she was b. brought out, she sent 38.25
b. a hundred and ten years old; 50.26
life of Levi b. a hundred and Ex 6.16
life of Kohath b. a hundred and 6.18
life of Amram b. one hundred and 6.20
kneading bowls b. bound up in 12.34
the waters b. a wall to them on 14.22
the waters b. a wall to them on 14.29
the owner not b. with it, he shall 22.14
which is b. shown you on the 25.40
LORD for him who is b. cleansed. Lev 14.31
each man b. the head of the house Num 1.04
people of Judah b. Nahshon the son 2.03
as numbered b. seventy-four 2.04
of Issachar b. Nethanel the son of 2.05
as numbered b. fifty-four thousand 2.06
of Zebulun b. Eliab the son of 2.07
as numbered b. fifty-seven thousand 2.08
of Reuben b. Elizur the son of 2.10
as numbered b. forty-six thousand 2.11
of Simeon b. Shelumiel the son of 2.12
as numbered b. fifty-nine thousand 2.13
people of Gad b. Eliasaph the son 2.14
as numbered b. forty-five thousand 2.15
of Ephraim b. Elishama the son of 2.18
as numbered b. forty thousand five 2.19
of Manasseh b. Gamaliel the son of 2.20
as numbered b. thirty-two thousand 2.21
of Benjamin b. Abidan the son of 2.22
as numbered b. thirty-five thousand 2.23
people of Dan b. Ahiezer the son 2.25
as numbered b. sixty-two thousand 2.26
people of Asher b. Pagiel the son 2.27
as numbered b. forty-one thousand 2.28
of Naphtali b. Ahira the son of 2.29
as numbered b. fifty-three thousand 2.30
of the dishes b. a hundred and 7.86
cubits, the city b. in the middle; 35.05
without b. at enmity with him in Deu 4.42
b. careful to do all this commandment 15.05
b. careful to do all his commandments 28.01
this day, b. careful to do them, 28.13
our enemies themselves b. judges. 32.31
b. careful to do according to all Jos 1.07
LORD your God b. carried by the 3.03
a pretence of b. beaten before 8.15
to the south b. Ephraim's and that 17.10
that to the north b. Manasseh's, 17.10
Arba b. the father of Anak (that is, 21.11
b. a hundred and ten years old. 24.29
had left over after b. satisfied. Ru 2.18
rejected me from b. king over them. 1Sa 8.07
has also rejected you from b. king." 15.23
you from b. king over Israel. 15.26
him from b. king over Israel? 16.01
and b. stronger than she, he forced 2Sa 13.14
Abiathar from b. priest to the 1Ki 2.27
the temple, while it was b. built. 6.07
Hadad b. yet a little child. 11.17
his mother from b. queen mother 15.13
in b. like the house of Jeroboam, 16.07
see me as I am b. taken from you, 2Ki 2.10
(another third b. at the gate Sur 11.06
And as a man was b. buried, 13.21
in the days of David b. twenty-two 1Ch 7.02
kinsmen (Shallum b. the chief), 9.17
father's house b. chosen for 24.06
b. a man of understanding and a 27.32
removed from b. queen mother 2Ch 15.16
and b. a leper dwelt in a separate 26.21
foundation of this house b. laid, Ez 3.12
It is b. built with huge stones, and 5.08
their names b. Eliphelet, Jeuel, and 8.13
of the provinces b. before him, Est 1.03
the men next to him b. Carshena, 1.14
after b. twelve months under the 2.12
the inner court without b. called, 4.11
b. wholly at ease and secure, Job 21.23
desirest truth in the inward b.; Ps 51.06
b. girded with might; 65.06
Yet he, b. compassionate, forgave 78.38
praise to my God while I have b. 104.33
when I was b. made in secret, 139.15
praises to my God while I have b. 146.02
ones, will you love b. simple? Pro 1.22
will keep your foot from b. caught. 3.26
Rescue those who are b. taken away 24.11
Besides b. wise, the Preacher also Ecc 12.09
cease from b. a nation before me Jer 31.36
of Judah were b. led out to the 38.22
Judah who were b. exiled to 40.01
us cut her off from b. a nation!' 48.02
in a moment, no hand b. laid on it. Lam 4.06
construction b. as it were a wheel Eze 1.16
hand of the LORD b. strong upon me; 3.14
instead of b. the desolation that 36.34
each b. a cubit and a handbreath 40.05
(the cubit b. a cubit and a handbreath): 43.13
of the city b. named after the 48.31
b. about sixty-two years old. Dan 5.31
reject you from b. a priest to me. Hos 4.06
which came into b. in a night, Jon 4.10
b. a just man and unwilling to put Mt 1.19
And b. warned in a dream not to 2.12
and b. warned in a dream he withdrew 2.22
And which of you by b. anxious can 6.27
the boat was b. swamped by the 8.24
and b. called rabbi by men. 23.07
you to escape b. sentenced to hell? 23.33
shortened, no human b. would be saved; 24.22
And b. aware of it, Jesus said to Mk 8.17
And as for the dead b. raised, 12.26
days, no human b. would be saved; 13.20
b. delivered from the hand of our Lk 1.74
Pontius Pilate b. governor of 3.01
and Herod b. tetrarch of Galilee, 3.01
b. the son (as was supposed) of 3.23
synagogues, b. glorified by all. 4.15
who had died was b. carried out, 7.12
And which of you by b. anxious can 12.25
and in Hades, b. in torment, he 16.23
B. asked by the Pharisees when the 17.20
b. sons of the resurrection. 20.36
And b. in an agony he prayed more 22.44
because you, b. a man, make yourself Jn 10.33
but b. high priest that year he 11.51
the doors b. shut where the disciples 20.19
B. therefore a prophet, and knowing Ac 2.30
B. therefore exalted at the right 2.33
day by day those who were b. saved. 2.47
man lame from birth was b. carried, 3.02
if we are b. examined today concerning 4.09
were afraid of b. stoned by the 5.26
And seeing one of them b. wronged, 7.24
and after b. baptized he continued 8.13
what is to prevent my b. baptized?" 8.36
So, b. sent out by the Holy Spirit, 13.04

BEING (cont.)
So, b. sent on their way by the Ac 15.03
b. commended by the brethren to the 15.40
b. Lord of heaven and earth, does 17.24
we live and move and have our b.'; 17.28
B. then God's offspring, we ought not 17.29
and b. fervent in spirit, he spoke 18.25
in danger of b. charged with 19.40
there b. no cause that we can give 19.40
and b. overcome by sleep, he fell 20.09
b. zealous for God as you all are 22.03
that Paul was b. kept at Caesarea, 25.04
B. at a loss how to investigate 25.20
by b. the first to rise from the 26.23
all hope of our b. saved was at 27.20
for every human b. who does evil; Rom 2.09
why am I still b. condemned as a 3.07
For no human b. will be justified 3.20
believe without b. circumcised and 4.11
that Christ b. raised from the 6.09
thy sake we are b. killed all the 8.36
For, b. ignorant of the righteousness 10.03
If your brother is b. injured by 14.15
to us who are b. saved it is the 1Co 1.18
so that no human b. might boast in 1.29
b. under no necessity but having 7.37
through b. hitherto accustomed to 8.07
conscience, b. weak, is defiled. 8.07
though not b. myself under the law— 9.20
not b. without law toward God but 9.21
people mean by b. baptized on 15.29
first man Adam became a living b."; 15.45
those who are b. saved and among 2Co 2.15
are b. changed into his likeness 3.18
we are always b. given up to death 4.11
inner nature is b. renewed every 4.16
but b. himself very earnest he is 8.17
nothing of you—for b. so confident. 9.04
b. ready to punish every disobedience, 10.06
bear with fools, b. wise youselves! 11.19
And to keep me from b. too elated 12.07
harass me, to keep me from b. too elated. 12.07
Jesus himself b. the chief cornerstone, Eph 2.20
that you, b. rooted and grounded in 3.17
complete my joy by b. of the same Php 2.02
b. in full accord and of one mind. 2.02
b. born in the likeness of men. 2.07
And b. found in human form he 2.08
which is b. renewed in knowledge Col 3.10
b. watchful in it with thanksgiving 4.02
So, b. affectionately desirous of 1Th 2.08
after b. captured by him to do his 2Ti 2.26
on the point of b. sacrificed; 4.06
the charge of b. profligate or Tit 1.06
and b. made perfect he became the Heb 5.09
b. designated by God a high priest 5.10
is worthless and near to b. cursed; 6.08
sometimes b. publicly exposed to 10.33
and sometimes b. partners with 10.33
By faith Noah, b. warned by God 11.07
not b. afraid of the anger of the 11.27
b. no hearer that forgets but a Jas 1.25
but no human b. can tame the tongue 3.08
b. patient over it until it receives 5.07
b. put to death in the flesh but 1Pe 3.18
your charge but b. examples to the 5.03
keep you from b. ineffective or 2Pe 1.08
b. kept until the day of judgment 3.07
Beloved, b. very eager to write to Jud 1.03
you have the name of b. alive, Rev 3.01
of your nakedness from b. seen, 3.18
his purpose by b. of one mind and 17.17

BEINGS
O heavenly b., ascribe to the LORD Ps 29.01
the heavenly b. is like the LORD, 89.06
in bondage to b. that by nature Gal 4.08

BEKA
a b. a head (that is, half a shekel, Ex 38.26

BEL
B. bows down, Nebo stoops, their Is 46.01
B. is put to shame, Merodach is Jer 50.02
And I will punish B. in Babylon, 51.44

BELA
Zeboiim, and the king of B. (that is, Gen 14.02
Zeboiim, and the king of B. (that is, 14.08
B. the son of Beor reigned in Edom, 36.32
B. died, and Jobab the son of Zerah 36.33
B., Becher, Ashbel, Gera, Naaman, Ehi, 46.21
of B., the family of the Belaites; Num 26.38
And the sons of B. were Ard and 26.40
B. the son of Beor, the name of 1Ch 1.43
When B. died, Jobab the son of Zerah 1.44
and B. the son of Azaz, son of Shema, 5.08
B., Becher, and Jediael, three. 7.06
The sons of B.: Ezbon, Uzzi, Uzziel, 7.07
the father of B. his first-born, 8.01
And B. had sons: Addar, Gera, Abihud, 8.03

BELAITES
of Bela, the family of the B.; Num 26.38

BELIAL
What accord has Christ with B.? 2Co 6.15

BELIEF
by the Spirit and b. in the truth. 2Th 2.13

BELIEVE
fainted, for he did not b. them. Gen 45.26
they will not b. me or listen to my Ex 4.01
"that they may b. that the LORD, the 4.05
"If they will not b. you, 4.08
they may b. the latter sign. 4.08
If they will not b. even these two 4.09
you, and may also b. you for ever." 19.09
how long will they not b. in me, Num 14.11
"Because you did not b. in me, 20.12
you did not b. the LORD your God, Deu 1.32
and did not b. him or obey his 9.23
but I did not b. the reports until 1Ki 10.07
who did not b. in the LORD their 2Ki 17.14
but I did not b. the reports until 2Ch 9.06
B. in the LORD your God, and you 20.20
b. his prophets, and you will 20.20
and do not b. him, for no god of any 32.15
I would not b. that he was listening Job 9.13
He does not b. that he will return 15.22
I b. that I shall see the goodness Ps 27.13
his wonders they did not b. 78.32
for I b. in thy commandments. 119.66
b. him not, for there are seven Pro 26.25
If you will not b., Is 7.09
may know and b. me and understand 43.10
b. them not, though they speak fair Jer 12.06
son of Ahikam would not b. them. 40.14
The kings of the earth did not b., Lam 4.12
days that you would not b. if told. Hab 1.05
"Do you b. that I am able to do Mt 9.28
little ones who b. in me to sin, 18.06
us, 'Why then did you not b. him?' 21.25
righteousness, and you did not b. him, 21.32
not afterward repent and b. him. 21.32
'There he is!' do not b. it. 24.23
in the inner rooms,' do not b. it. 24.26
the cross, and we will b. in him. 27.42
repent, and b. in the gospel." Mk 1.15
synagogue, "Do not fear, only b." 5.36
the child cried out and said, "I b.; 9.24
little ones who b. in me to sin, 9.42
b. that you receive it, and you will 11.24
say, 'Why then did you not b. him?' 11.31

BELIEVE (cont.)
there he is!' do not b. it. Mk 13.21
the cross, that we may see and b." 15.32
because you did not b. my words, Lk 1.20
that they may not b. and be saved. 8.12
they b. for a while and in time of 8.13
only b., and she shall be well." 8.50
will say, 'Why did you not b. him?' 20.05
"If I tell you, you will not b.; 22.67
tale, and they did not b. them. 24.11
of heart to b. all that the 24.25
that all might b. through him. Jn 1.07
you under the fig tree, do you b.? 1.50
earthly things and you do not b., 3.12
how can you b. if I tell you 3.12
he who does not b. is condemned 3.18
b. me, the hour is coming when 4.21
because of your words that we b., 4.42
signs and wonders you will not b." 4.48
for you do not b. him whom he has 5.38
How can you b., who receive glory 5.44
you would b. me, for he wrote of me. 5.46
But if you do not b. his writings, 5.47
writings, how will you b. my words?" 5.47
that you b. in him whom he has sent." 6.29
do, that we may see, and b. you? 6.30
you have seen me and yet do not b. 6.36
are some of you that do not b." 6.64
who those were that did not b., 6.64
his brothers did not b. in him. 7.05
sins unless you b. that I am he." 8.24
I tell the truth, you do not b. me. 8.45
the truth, why do you not b. me? 8.46
The Jews did not b. that he had 9.18
"Do you b. in the Son of man?" 9.35
is he, sir, that I may b. in him?" 9.36
He said, "Lord, I b."; and he 9.38
"I told you, and you do not b. 10.25
but you do not b., because you do 10.26
of my Father, then do not b. me; 10.37
them, even though you do not b. me, 10.38
b. the works, that you may know and 10.38
was not there, so that you may b. 11.15
shall never die. Do you b. this?" 11.26
I b. that you are the Christ, the 11.27
if you would b. you would see the 11.40
that they may b. that thou didst 11.42
on thus, every one will b. in him, 11.48
b. in the light, that you may become 12.36
them, yet they did not b. in him; 12.37
Therefore they could not b. 12.39
take place you may b. that I am he. 13.19
b. in God, b. also in me. 14.01
Do you not b. that I am in the 14.10
B. me that I am in the Father and 14.11
or else b. me for the sake of the 14.11
it does take place, you may b. 14.29
of sin, because they do not b. in me; 16.09
by this we b. that you came from 16.30
Jesus answered them, "Do you now b.? 16.31
who are to b. in me through their 17.20
the world may b. that thou hast 17.21
the truth—that you also may b. 19.35
my hand in his side, I will not b." 20.25
those who have not seen and yet b." 20.29
that you may b. that Jesus is the 20.31
"If you b. with all your heart, you *Ac 8.37
"I b. that Jesus Christ is the Son * 8.37
they did not b. that he was a 9.26
days, a deed you will never b., 13.41
hear the word of the gospel and b. 15.07
But we b. that we shall be saved 15.11
"B. in the Lord Jesus, and you will 16.31
the people to b. in the one who 19.04
King Agrippa, do you b. the prophets? 26.27
I know that you b." 26.27
in Jesus Christ for all who b. Rom 3.22
of all who b. without being 4.11
to us who b. in him that raised 4.24
we b. that we shall also live with 6.08
is Lord and b. in your heart that 10.09
how are they to b. in him of whom 10.14
we preach to save those who b. 1Co 1.21
among you; and I partly b. it, 11.18
we too b., and so we speak, 2Co 4.13
might be given to those who b. Gal 3.22
greatness of his power in us who b., Eph 1.19
should not only b. in him but also Php 1.29
For since we b. that Jesus died and 1Th 4.14
to make them b. what is false, 2Th 2.11
who did not b. the truth but had 2.12
who were to b. in him for eternal 1Ti 1.16
by those who b. and know the truth. 4.03
men, especially of those who b. 4.10
to God must b. that he exists and Heb 11.06
You b. that God is one; Jas 2.19
Even the demons b.—and shudder. 2.19
now see him you b. in him and 1Pe 1.08
To you therefore who b., he is 2.07
but for those who do not b., 2.07
that we should b. in the name of 1Jn 3.23
do not b. every spirit, but test the 4.01
So we know and b. the love God has 4.16
He who does not b. God, 5.10
this to you who b. in the name of 5.13
destroyed those who did not b. Jud 1.05

BELIEVED
And he b. the LORD; and he Gen 15.06
And the people b.; and when Ex 4.31
and they b. in the LORD and in his 14.31
Then they b. his words; Ps 106.12
Who has b. what we have heard? Is 53.01
And the people of Nineveh b. God; Jon 3.05
be it done for you as you have b." Mt 8.13
collectors and the harlots b. him; 21.32
is she who b. that there would be Lk 1.45
who b. in his name, he gave power to Jn 1.12
and his disciples b. in him. 2.11
and they b. the scripture and the 2.22
many b. in his name when they saw 2.23
he has not b. in the name of the 3.18
from that city b. in him because 4.39
And many more b. because of his 4.41
The man b. the word that Jesus 4.50
and he himself b., and all 4.53
If you b. Moses, you would believe 5.46
and we have b., and have come to 6.69
Yet many of the people b. in him; 7.31
which those who b. in him were to 7.39
or of the Pharisees b. in him? 7.48
As he spoke thus, many b. in him. 8.30
said to the Jews who had b. in him, 8.31
And many b. in him there. 10.42
had seen what he did, b. in him; 11.45
who has b. our report, and to whom 12.38
even of the authorities b. in him, 12.42
me and have b. that I came from 16.27
and they have b. that thou didst 17.08
also went in, and he saw and b.; 20.08
"Have you b. because you have seen 20.29
And all who b. were together and Ac 2.44
of those who heard the word b.; 4.04
of those who b. were of one heart 4.32
But when they b. Philip as he 8.12
Even Simon himself b., and after 8.13
all Joppa, and many b. in the Lord. 9.42
to us when we b. in the Lord Jesus 11.17
number that b. turned to the Lord. 11.21
Then the proconsul b., when he 13.12
were ordained to eternal life b. 13.48
so spoke that a great company b., 14.01
them to the Lord in whom they b. 14.23
household that he had b. in God. 16.34

BELIEVED (cont.)

Many of them therefore b., Ac 17.12
But some men joined him and b., 17.34
b. in the Lord, together with all 18.08
hearing Paul b. and were baptized. 18.08
those who through grace had b., 18.27
the Holy Spirit when you b.?" 19.02
the Jews of those who have b.; 21.20
But as for the Gentiles who have b., 21.25
and beat those who b. in thee. 22.19
"Abraham b. God, and it was reckoned Rom 4.03
presence of the God in whom he b., 4.17
In hope he b. against hope, that he 4.18
upon him in whom they have not b.? 10.14
who has b. what he has heard from 10.16
to us now than when we first b.; 13.11
Servants through whom you b., 1Co 3.05
hold it fast—unless you b. in vain. 15.02
they, so we preach and so you b. 15.11
"I b., and so I spoke," we too 2Co 4.13
even we have b. in Christ Jesus, in Gal 2.16
Thus Abraham "b. God, and it was 3.06
and have b. in him, were sealed with Eph 1.13
be marveled at in all who have b., 2Th 1.10
our testimony to you was b. 1.10
b. on in the world, taken up in 1Ti 3.16
whom I have b. and I am sure that 2Ti 1.12
have learned and have firmly b., 3.14
those who have b. in God may be Tit 3.08
For we who have b. enter that rest, Heb 4.03
"Abraham b. God, and it was reckoned Jas 2.23
he has not b. in the testimony 1Jn 5.10

BELIEVER

son of a Jewish woman who was a b.; Ac 16.01
Or what has a b. in common with an 2Co 6.15

BELIEVERS

And more than ever b. were added to Ac 5.14
And the b. from among the circumcised 10.45
But some b. who belonged to the 15.05
also of those who were now b. came, 19.18
a sign not for b. but for unbelievers, 1Co 14.22
is not for unbelievers but for b. 14.22
to all the b. in Macedonia and in 1Th 1.07
blameless was our behavior to you b.; 2.10
of God, which is at work in you b. 2.13
but set the b. an example in speech 1Ti 4.12
their service are b. and beloved. 6.02
children are b. and not open to Tit 1.06

BELIEVES

The simple b. everything, but the Pro 14.15
'He who b. will not be in haste.' Is 28.16
things are possible to him who b." Mk 9.23
but b. that what he says will come 11.23
that whoever b. in him may have Jn 3.15
that whoever b. in him should not 3.16
He who b. in him is not condemned; 3.18
He who b. in the Son has eternal 3.36
my word and b. him who sent me, has 5.24
and he who b. in me shall never 6.35
the Son and b. in him should have 6.40
he who b. has eternal life. 6.47
He who b. in me, as the scripture 7.38
he who b. in me, though he die, yet 11.25
lives and b. in me shall never die. 11.26
"He who b. in me, b. not in me 12.44
that whoever b. in me may not 12.46
he who b. in me will also do the 14.12
every one who b. in him receives Ac 10.43
every one that b. is freed from 13.39
and he who b. in him will not be Rom 9.33
For man b. with his heart and so is 10.10
"No one who b. in him will be put 10.11
One b. he may eat anything, while 14.02
b. all things, hopes all things, 1Co 13.07
and he who b. in him will not be 1Pe 2.06
Every one who b. that Jesus is the 1Jn 5.01
but he who b. that Jesus is the 5.05
He who b. in the Son of God has the 5.10

BELIEVING

were going away and b. in Jesus. Jn 12.11
do not be faithless, but b." 20.27
and that b. you may have life in 20.31
b. everything laid down by the law Ac 24.14
you with all joy and peace in b., Rom 15.13
If any b. woman has relatives who 1Ti 5.16
Those who have b. masters must not 6.02

BELITTLES

He who b. his neighbor lacks sense, Pro 11.12

BELL

a golden b. and a pomegranate, a Ex 28.34
a b. and a pomegranate, a b. and a 39.26

BELLOWING

b. with their mouths, and snarling Ps 59.07

BELLOWS

The b. blow fiercely, the lead is Jer 6.29

BELLS

with b. of gold between them, Ex 28.33
They also made b. of pure gold, and 39.25
and put the b. between the pomegranates 39.25
inscribed on the b. of the horses, Zec 14.20

BELLY

upon your b. you shall go, and dust Gen 3.14
Whatever goes on its b., Lev 11.42
thigh, and thrust it into his b.; Ju 3.21
not draw the sword out of his b.; 3.22
him in the b. with the butt of his 2Sa 2.23
and there he smote him in the b., 3.27
God casts them out of his b. Job 20.15
To fill his b. to the full God will 20.23
his power in the muscles of his b. 40.16
May their b. be filled with what Ps 17.14
but the b. of the wicked suffers Pro 13.25
Your b. is a heap of wheat, encircled Sol 7.02
has filled his b. with my delicacies, Jer 51.34
its b. and thighs of bronze, Dan 2.32
was in the b. of the fish three Jon 1.17
his God from the b. of the fish, 2.01
out of the b. of Sheol I cried, and 2.02
nights in the b. of the whale, Mt 12.40
destruction, their god is the b., Php 3.19

BELONG

and asks you, 'To whom do you b.? Gen 32.17
'They b. to your servant Jacob; 32.18
"By the man to whom these b., 38.25
"Do not interpretations b. to God? 40.08
a griddle shall b. to the priest Lev 7.09
it shall b. to the priest who 7.14
this shall b. to them as pasture Num 35.05
of the tribe to which they b.; 36.03
of the tribe to which they b.; 36.04
LORD your God b. heaven and the Deu 10.14
"The secret things b. to the LORD 29.29
are revealed b. to us and to our 29.29
and all who b. to them, and deliver Jos 2.13
and all who b. to her, as you swore 6.22
cities of Manasseh, b. to Ephraim. 17.09
who do not b. to the people of Ju 19.12
as one male of all who b. to him." 1Sa 25.22
said to him, "To whom do you b.? 30.13
saying, "To whom does the land b.? 2Sa 3.12
the shields of the earth b. to God; Ps 47.09
for to thee b. all the nations! 82.08
The plans of the mind b. to man, Pro 16.01

BELONG (cont.)
offerings, shall b. to the priests; Eze 44.30
it shall b. to the whole house of 45.06
prince shall b. the land on both 45.07
it shall b. to his sons, it is their 46.16
And it shall b. to them as a 48.12
of the city shall b. to the prince. 48.21
portions, it shall b. to the prince. 48.21
to whom b. wisdom and might. Dan 2.20
Lord our God b. mercy and forgiveness; 9.09
the harlot, or b. to another man; Hos 3.03
For to the LORD b. the cities of Zec 9.01
because you do not b. to my sheep. Jn 10.26
God to whom I b. and whom I Ac 27.23
are called to b. to Jesus Christ; Rom 1.06
so that you may b. to another, 7.04
of Christ does not b. to him. 8.09
and to them b. the sonship, the 9.04
to them b. the patriarchs, and of 9.05
descended from Israel b. to Israel, 9.06
Greet those who b. to the family of 16.10
in the Lord who b. to the family 16.11
"I b. to Paul," or "I b. to Apollos," 1Co 1.12
"I b. to Cephas," or "I b. to Christ." 1.12
"I b. to Paul," and another, "I 3.04
"I b. to Apollos," are you not 3.04
I do not b. to the body," that would 12.15
I do not b. to the body," that would 12.16
his coming those who b. to Christ. 15.23
And those who b. to Christ Jesus Gal 5.24
But, since we b. to the day, let us 1Th 5.08
better things that b. to salvation. Heb 6.09
To him b. glory and dominion for 1Pe 4.11
and glory and power b. to our God, Rev 19.01

BELONGED
the men that b. to Korah and all Num 16.32
and all that b. to them went down 16.33
and brothers and all who b. to her; Jos 6.23
and all who b. to her, Joshua saved 6.25
The land of Tappuah b. to Manasseh, 17.08
of Manasseh b. to the sons of 17.08
Kohathites who b. to the Levites; 21.10
which b. to Joash the Abiezrite, as Ju 6.11
made, and the priest who b. to him, 18.27
of land which b. to our kinsman Ru 4.03
Naomi all that b. to Elimelech and 4.09
and all that b. to Chilion and to 4.09
was missed of all that b. to him; 1Sa 25.21
Ziklag has b. to the kings of 27.06
"All that b. to Saul and to all his 2Sa 9.09
all that b. to Mephibosheth is now 16.04
Arubboth (to him b. Soco and all 1Ki 4.10
altar that b. to the inner sanctuary 6.22
which b. to the Philistines; 15.27
which b. to the Philistines, 16.15
it b. to the priests. 2Ki 12.16
which had b. to Judah, are they not 14.28
taken all that b. to the king of 24.07
former inhabitants there b. to Ham. 1Ch 4.40
yet the birthright b. to Joseph), 5.02
they found that b. to the king's 2Ch 21.17
burial field which b. to the kings, 26.23
territory that b. to the people of 34.33
descent, whether they b. to Israel: Ez 2.59
descent, whether they b. to Israel: Neh 7.61
palace which b. to King Ahasuerus. Est 1.09
cubits which b. to the inner court, Eze 42.03
pavement which b. to the outer 42.03
of a ruler who b. to the Pharisees, Lk 14.01
learned that he b. to Herod's 23.07
sold a field which b. to him, Ac 4.37
of those who b. to the synagogue 6.09
upon some who b. to the church. 12.01
believers who b. to the party of 15.05
he asked to what province he b. 23.34

as if you still b. to the world? Col 2.20
are spoken b. to another tribe, Heb 7.13

BELONGING
All the persons b. to Jacob who Gen 46.26
of common land b. to their cities Lev 25.34
a near kinsman b. to his family 25.49
fathers' house b. to the Simeonites. Num 25.14
generation none b. to them shall Deu 23.03
The cities b. to the tribe of the Jos 15.21
a city b. to the tribe of Judah. 18.14
the Kohathites b. to the Kohathite 21.20
the part of the field b. to Boaz, Ru 2.03
the Philistines b. to the five 1Sa 6.18
Any one b. to Jeroboam who dies in 1Ki 14.11
Any one b. to Baasha who dies in 16.04
Any one b. to Ahab who dies in the 21.24
plot of ground b. to Naboth the 2Ki 9.25
Their kinsmen b. to all the families 1Ch 7.05
of the Gershonites b. to Ladan, 26.21
fathers' houses b. to Ladan the 26.21
of common land b. to their cities, 2Ch 31.19
'B. to Mahershalalhashbaz.'" Is 8.01
hunt down souls b. to my people, Eze 13.18
b. to the outer court. He measured 40.20
appointed place b. to the temple, 43.21
the parts of Libya b. to Cyrene, Ac 2.10
be aliens in a land b. to others, 7.06
that if he found any b. to the Way, 9.02
were lands b. to the chief man of 28.07

BELONGINGS
all its gains, all its prized b., Jer 20.05

BELONGS
from our father b. to us and to Gen 31.16
feet, until he comes to whom it b.; 49.10
die of all that b. to the people Ex 9.04
and give it to him to whom it b., Lev 6.05
the sin offering, b. to the priest; 14.13
whom the land b. as a possession 27.24
as a firstling b. to the LORD, 27.26
furnishings, and over all that b. to it; Num 1.50
with all that b. to them, and they 16.30
Mearah which b. to the Sidonians, Jos 13.04
the side that b. to the people of 22.11
which b. to the Abiezrites. Ju 6.24
the valley which b. to Bethrehob. 18.28
near Gibeah, which b. to Benjamin, 19.14
came to Gibeah that b. to Benjamin, 20.04
which b. to Judah, and encamped 1Sa 17.01
upon that which b. to Judah and 30.14
of Obededom and all that b. to him, 2Sa 6.12
which b. to Sidon, and dwell there. 1Ki 17.09
which b. to Judah, and left his 19.03
know that Ramothgilead b. to us, 22.03
at Bethshemesh, which b. to Judah. 2Ki 14.11
to Kiriathjearim which b. to Judah, 1Ch 13.06
at Bethshemesh, which b. to Judah. 2Ch 25.21
Deliverance b. to the LORD; Ps 3.08
For dominion b. to the LORD, and he 22.28
I heard this: that power b. to God; 62.11
to thee, O Lord, b. steadfast love. 62.12
the Lord, b. escape from death. 68.20
For our shield b. to the LORD, our 89.18
but the victory b. to the LORD. Pro 21.31
of that which b. to the prince. Eze 48.22
b. righteousness, but to us confusion Dan 9.07
To us, O Lord, b. confusion of face, 9.08
Deliverance b. to the LORD! Jon 2.09
for to such b. the kingdom of Mt 19.14
Take what b. to you, and go; 20.14
what I choose with what b. to me? 20.15
for to such b. the kingdom of God. Mk 10.14
for to such b. the kingdom of God. Lk 18.16
is of the earth b. to the earth, Jn 3.31
transcendent power b. to God and 2Co 4.07

BELONGS (cont.)

the one hope that b. to your call, Eph 4.04
nature which b. to your former 4.22
but the substance b. to Christ. Col 2.17
"Salvation b. to our God who sits Rev 7.10
an eighth but it b. to the seven, 17.11

BELOVED

"The b. of the LORD, he dwells in Deu 33.12
"Saul and Jonathan, b. and lovely! 2Sa 1.23
and he was b. by his God, and God Neh 13.26
That thy b. may be delivered, give Ps 60.05
That thy b. may be delivered, give 108.06
for he gives to his b. in sleep. 127.02
My b. is to me a bag of myrrh, that Sol 1.13
My b. is to me a cluster of henna 1.14
are beautiful, my b., truly lovely. 1.16
so is my b. among young men. 2.03
The voice of my b.! Behold, he comes, 2.08
My b. is like a gazelle, or a young 2.09
My b. speaks and says to me: "Arise, 2.10
My b. is mine and I am his, he 2.16
my b., be like a gazelle, or a young 2.17
Let my b. come to his garden, and 4.16
my b. is knocking. "Open to me, 5.02
My b. put his hand to the latch, and 5.04
I arose to open to my b., 5.05
I opened to my b., but my b. 5.06
but my b. had turned and gone. 5.06
of Jerusalem, if you find my b., 5.08
What is your b. more than another b., 5.09
What is your b. more than another b., 5.09
My b. is all radiant and ruddy, 5.10
This is my b. and this is my friend, 5.16
Whither has your b. gone, 6.01
Whither has your b. turned, 6.01
My b. has gone down to his garden, 6.02
I am my beloved's and my b. is mine; 6.03
Come, my b., let us go forth into 7.11
I have laid up for you, O my b. 7.13
wilderness, leaning upon her b.? 8.05
Make haste, my b., and be like a 8.14
Let me sing for my b. a love song Is 5.01
My b. had a vineyard on a very 5.01
What right has my b. in my house, Jer 11.15
have given the b. of my soul into 12.07
it to you, for you are greatly b.; Dan 9.23
man greatly b., give heed to the 10.11
And he said, "O man greatly b., 10.19
fathers, or to the one b. by women; 11.37
a woman who is b. of a paramour Hos 3.01
I will slay their b. children. 9.16
"This is my b. Son, with whom I am Mt 3.17
my b. with whom my soul is well 12.18
"This is my b. Son, with whom I am 17.05
from heaven, "Thou art my b. Son; Mk 1.11
of the cloud, "This is my b. Son; 9.07
He had still one other, a b. son; 12.06
from heaven, "Thou art my b. Son; Lk 3.22
I will send my b. son; it may be 20.13
to you with our b. Barnabas and Ac 15.25
To all God's b. in Rome, who are Rom 1.07
her who was not b. I will call 'my b.'" 9.25
they are b. for the sake of their 11.28
B., never avenge yourselves, but 12.19
Greet my b. Epaenetus, who was the 16.05
Greet Ampliatus, my b. in the Lord. 16.08
in Christ, and my b. Stachys. 16.09
Greet the b. Persis, who has worked 16.12
to admonish you as my b. children. 1Co 4.14
my b. and faithful child in the 4.17
Therefore, my b., shun the worship 10.14
Therefore, my b. brethren, be steadfast, 15.58
b., let us cleanse ourselves from 2Co 7.01
and all for your upbuilding, b. 12.19
he freely bestowed on us in the B. Eph 1.06
imitators of God, as b. children. 5.01
Tychicus the b. brother and faithful 6.21
Therefore, my b., as you have always Php 2.12
stand firm thus in the Lord, my b. 4.01
Epaphras our b. fellow servant. Col 1.07
us to the kingdom of his b. Son, 1.13
holy and b., compassion, kindness, 3.12
he is a b. brother and faithful 4.07
the faithful and b. brother, 4.09
Luke the b. physician and Demas 4.14
brethren b. by God, that he has 1Th 1.04
brethren b. by the Lord, because God 2Th 2.13
their service are believers and b. 1Ti 6.02
To Timothy, my b. child: Grace, mercy, 2Ti 1.02
To Philemon our b. fellow worker Phm 1.01
as a b. brother, especially to me 1.16
b., we feel sure of better things Heb 6.09
Do not be deceived, my b. brethren. Jas 1.16
Know this, my b. brethren. Let every 1.19
Listen, my b. brethren. Has not God 2.05
B., I beseech you as aliens and 1Pe 2.11
B., do not be surprised at the 4.12
"This is my b. Son, with whom I am 2Pe 1.17
b., and in both of them I have 3.01
b., that with the Lord one day is 3.08
Therefore, b., since you wait for 3.14
So also our b. brother Paul wrote 3.15
You therefore, b., knowing this 3.17
B., I am writing you no new commandment, 1Jn 2.07
B., we are God's children now; 3.02
B., if our hearts do not condemn us, 3.21
B., do not believe every spirit, but 4.01
B., let us love one another; 4.07
B., if God so loved us, we also 4.11
The elder to the b. Gaius, 3Jn 1.01
B., I pray that all may go well 1.02
B., it is a loyal thing you do when 1.05
B., do not imitate evil but imitate 1.11
b. in God the Father and kept for Jud 1.01
B., being very eager to write to 1.03
b., the predictions of the apostles 1.17
But you, b., build yourselves up on 1.20
camp of the saints and the b. city; Rev 20.09

BELOVED'S

I am my b. and my beloved is mine; Sol 6.03
I am my b., and his desire is for 7.01

BELOW

was buried under an oak b. Bethel; Gen 35.08
valley of Lebanon b. Mount Hermon. Jos 11.17
from Baalgad b. Mount Hermon to the 13.05
of Midian was b. him in the valley Ju 7.08
smote them, as far as b. Bethcar. 1Sa 7.11
is beside Zarethan b. Jezreel, 1Ki 4.12
both above and b. the lions and 7.29
number those b. twenty years of 1Ch 27.23
The shades b. tremble, the waters Job 26.05
bind their faces in the world b. 40.13
of the earth b. can be explored, Jer 31.37
b. what appeared to be his loins it Eze 8.02
B. these chambers was an entrance 42.09
And b. the south chambers was an 42.12
issuing from b. the threshold of 47.01
down from b. the south end of the 47.01
And as Peter was b. in the courtyard, Mk 14.66
"You are from b., I am from above; Jn 8.23

BELSHAZZAR

King B. made a great feast for a Dan 5.01
B., when he tasted the wine, commanded 5.02
Then King B. was greatly alarmed, 5.09
B., have not humbled your heart, 5.22
Then B. commanded, and Daniel was 5.29
That very night B. the Chaldean 5.30
first year of B. king of Babylon, 7.01
reign of King B. a vision appeared 8.01

BELT
and looses the b. of the strong. Job 12.21
like a b. with which he daily girds Ps 109.19

BELTESHAZZAR
them names: Daniel he called B., Dan 1.07
said to Daniel, whose name was B., 2.26
who was named B. after the name of 4.08
"O B., chief of the magicians, 4.09
And you, O B., declare the interpretation, 4.18
Then Daniel, whose name was B., 4.19
B., let not the dream or the 4.19
B. answered, "My lord, may the 4.19
Daniel, whom the king named B. 5.12
to Daniel, who was named B. 10.01

BELTS
girded with b. on their loins, with Eze 23.15
nor silver, nor copper in your b., Mt 10.09
no bag, no money in their b.; Mk 6.08

BEMOAN
O Jerusalem, or who will b. you? Jer 15.05
or go to lament, or b. them; 16.05
for him who is dead, nor b. him; 22.10
B. him, all you who are round about 48.17
who will b. her? whence shall I Nah 3.07

BEMOANING
I have heard Ephraim b., Jer 31.18

BENABINADAB
B., in all Naphathdor (he had 1Ki 4.11

BENAIAH
and B. the son of Jehoiada was over 2Sa 8.18
and B. the son of Jehoiada was in 20.23
And B. the son of Jehoiada was a 23.20
but B. went down to him with a 23.21
These things did B. the son of 23.22
B. of Pirathon, Hiddai of the brooks 23.30
and B. the son of Jehoiada, and 1Ki 1.08
the prophet or B. or the mighty 1.10
and B. the son of Jehoiada, and your 1.26
and B. the son of Jehoiada. 1.32
And B. the son of Jehoiada answered 1.36
and B. the son of Jehoiada, and the 1.38
and B. the son of Jehoiada, and the 1.44
Solomon sent B. the son of Jehoiada; 2.25
"Solomon sent B. the son of 2.29
So B. came to the tent of the LORD, 2.30
Then B. brought the king word again, 2.30
Then B. the son of Jehoiada went up, 2.34
The king put B. the son of Jehoiada 2.35
king commanded B. the son of 2.46
B. the son of Jehoiada was in 4.04
Asaiah, Adiel, Jesimiel, B., 1Ch 4.36
And B. the son of Jehoiada was a 11.22
but B. went down to him with a 11.23
These things did B. the son of 11.24
the Benjaminites, B. of Pirathon, 11.31
B., Maaseiah, Mattithiah, Eliphelehu, 15.18
and B. were to play harps according 15.20
B., and Eliezer, the priests, should 15.24
B., Obededom, and Jeiel, who were to 16.05
and B. and Jahaziel the priests 16.06
and B. the son of Jehoiada was over 18.17
was B., the son of Jehoiada the 27.05
This is the B. who was a mighty man 27.06
was B. of Pirathon, of the sons of 27.14
the son of B., and Abiathar. 27.34
son of B., son of Jeiel, son of 2Ch 20.14
and B. were overseers assisting 31.13
Mijamin, Eleazar, Hashabiah, and B. Ez 10.25
B., Maaseiah, Mattaniah, Bezalel, 10.30
B., Bedeiah, Cheluhi, 10.35
Zebina, Jaddai, Joel, and B. 10.43
Azzur, and Pelatiah the son of B., Eze 11.01
that Pelatiah the son of B. died. 11.13

BENAMMI
bore a son, and called his name B.; Gen 19.38

BEND
my arms can b. a bow of bronze. 2Sa 22.35
the wicked b. the bow, they have Ps 11.02
my arms can b. a bow of bronze. 18.34
draw the sword and b. their bows, 37.14
They b. their tongue like a bow; Jer 9.03
about, all you that b. the bow; 50.14
Babylon, all those who b. the bow. 50.29
Let not the archer b. his bow, 51.03
and b. their backs for ever." Rom 11.10

BENDEKER
B., in Makaz, Shaalbim, Bethshemesh, 1Ki 4.09

BENDING
you shall come b. low to you; Is 60.14

BENDS
the boundary b. round to Baalah Jos 15.09
the boundary b. round to Shikkeron, 15.11
then it b. in a northerly direction 18.17
on to Rimmon it b. toward Neah; 19.13

BENEATH
of the deep that couches b., Gen 49.25
above, or that is in the earth b., Ex 20.04
they shall be separate b., but joined 26.24
And they were separate b., but joined 36.29
heaven above and on the earth b.; Deu 4.39
above, or that is on the earth b., 5.08
and of the deep that couches b., 33.13
in heaven above and on earth b. Jos 2.11
in heaven above or on earth b., 1Ki 8.23
he had sackcloth b. upon his body— 2Ki 6.30
b. him bowed the helpers of Rahab. Job 9.13
His roots dry up b., and his branches 18.16
life, that he may avoid Sheol b. Pro 15.24
with which he toils b. the sun? Ecc 2.22
Sheol b. is stirred up to meet you Is 14.09
maggots are the bed b. you, 14.11
heavens, and look at the earth b.; 51.06
return and dwell b. my shadow, Hos 14.07
his fruit above, and his roots b. Amo 2.09
my bones, my steps totter b. me. Hab 3.16
above and signs on the earth b., Ac 2.19

BENEBERAK
Jehud, B., Gathrimmon, Jos 19.45

BENEFACTORS
authority over them are called b. Lk 22.25

BENEFIT
according to the b. done to him, 2Ch 32.25
to myself and Apollos for your b., 1Co 4.06
I say this for your own b., 7.35
how shall I b. you unless I bring 14.06
since those who b. by their 1Ti 6.02
I want some b. from you in the Lord. Phm 1.20
which they heard did not b. them, Heb 4.02

BENEFITED
which have not b. their adherents. Heb 13.09

BENEFITS
soul, and forget not all his b., Ps 103.02
A man who is kind b. himself, Pro 11.17
much if we reap your material b.? 1Co 9.11

BENEJAAKAN
from Moseroth, and encamped at B. Num 33.31
And they set out from B., 33.32
journeyed from Beeroth B. to Moserah. Deu 10.06

BENGEBER

B., in Ramothgilead (he had the 1Ki 4.13

BENHADAD

sent them to B. the son of Tabrimmon, 1Ki 15.18
And B. hearkened to King Asa, and 15.20
B. the king of Syria gathered all 20.01
and said to him, "Thus says B.: 20.02
"Thus says B.: 'I sent to you, saying, 20.05
So he said to the messengers of B., 20.09
B. sent to him and said, "The gods 20.10
When B. heard this message as he 20.12
while B. was drinking himself drunk 20.16
And B. sent out scouts, and they 20.17
but B. king of Syria escaped on a 20.20
In the spring B. mustered the 20.26
B. also fled, and entered an inner 20.30
"Your servant B. says, 'Pray, let me 20.32
him and said, "Yes, your brother B." 20.33
Then B. came forth to him; 20.33
And B. said to him, "The cities 20.34
Afterward B. king of Syria mustered 2Ki 6.24
B. the king of Syria was sick; 8.07
"Your son B. king of Syria has sent 8.09
the hand of B. the son of Hazael. 13.03
B. his son became king in his stead. 13.24
took again from B. the son of 13.25
and sent them to B. king of Syria, 2Ch 16.02
And B. hearkened to King Asa, and 16.04
it shall devour the palaces of B." Jer 49.27
shall devour the strongholds of B. Amo 1.04

BENHAIL

B., Obadiah, Zechariah, Nethanel, and 2Ch 17.07

BENHANAN

Amnon, Rinnah, B., and Tilon. 1Ch 4.20

BENHESED

B., in Arubboth (to him belonged 1Ki 4.10

BENHINNOM

the Valley of B. at the entry of Jer 19.02
Topheth, or the Valley of B., 19.06

BENHUR

B., in the hill country of Ephraim; 1Ki 4.08

BENINU

Hodiah, Bani, B. Neh 10.13

BENJAMIN

but his father called his name B. Gen 35.18
The sons of Rachel: Joseph and B. 35.24
But Jacob did not send B., 42.04
no more, and now you would take B.; 42.36
back your other brother and B. 43.14
double the money with them, and B.; 43.15
When Joseph saw B. with them, 43.16
his eyes, and saw his brother B., 43.29
and the eyes of my brother B. see, 45.12
and B. wept upon his neck. 45.14
but to B. he gave three hundred 45.22
Jacob's wife: Joseph and B. 46.19
And the sons of B.: Bela, Becher, 46.21
B. is a ravenous wolf, in the 49.27
Issachar, Zebulun, and B., Ex 1.03
from B., Abidan the son of Gideoni; Num 1.11
Of the people of B., their generations, 1.36
of the tribe of B. was thirty-five 1.37
Then the tribe of B., the leader 2.22
the people of B. being Abidan the 2.22
the leader of the men of B.: 7.60
of the men of B. was Abidan the 10.24
from the tribe of B., Palti the 13.09
The sons of B. according to their 26.38
These are the sons of B. according 26.41
Of the tribe of B., Elidad 34.21
Judah, Issachar, Joseph, and B. Deu 27.12
Of B. he said, "The beloved of the 33.12
of the tribe of B. according to Jos 18.11
the inheritance of the tribe of B., 18.20
of the tribe of B. according to 18.21
of the tribe of B. according to 18.28
Simeon, and B., thirteen cities. 21.04
then out of the tribe of B., 21.17
But the people of B. did not drive Ju 1.21
the people of B. in Jerusalem to 1.21
B., with your kinsmen; from Machir 5.14
and against B. and against the 10.09
near Gibeah, which belongs to B., 19.14
came to Gibeah that belongs to B., 20.04
come they may requite Gibeah of B., 20.10
men through all the tribe of B., 20.12
apart from B., mustered four 20.17
went out to battle against B.; 20.20
And B. went against them out of 20.25
the LORD defeated B. before Israel; 20.35
one hundred men of B. that day; 20.35
men of Israel gave ground to B., 20.36
Now B. had begun to smite and kill 20.39
and the men of B. were dismayed, 20.41
Eighteen thousand men of B. fell, 20.44
that day of B. were twenty-five 20.46
his daughter in marriage to B." 21.01
compassion for B. their brother, 21.06
And B. returned at that time; 21.14
compassion on B. because the LORD 21.15
the women are destroyed out of B.?" 21.16
inheritance for the survivors of B., 21.17
be he who gives a wife to B." 21.18
Shiloh, and go to the land of B. 21.21
A man of B. ran from the battle 1Sa 4.12
There was a man of B. whose name 9.01
they passed through the land of B., 9.04
to you a man from the land of B., 9.16
the families of the tribe of B.? 9.21
in the territory of B. at Zelzah, 10.02
the tribe of B. was taken by lot. 10.20
the tribe of B. near by its 10.21
were with Jonathan in Gibeah of B.; 13.02
up from Gilgal to Gibeah of B. 13.15
with them, stayed in Geba of B.; 13.16
of Saul in Gibeah of B. looked; 14.16
and Ephraim and B. and all Israel. 2Sa 2.09
twelve for B. and Ishbosheth the 2.15
had slain of B. three hundred and 2.31
Abner also spoke to B.; and then 3.19
whole house of B. thought good to 3.19
Rimmon a man of B. from Beeroth 4.02
(for Beeroth also is reckoned to B.; 4.02
him were a thousand men from B. 19.17
Jonathan in the land of B. in Zela, 21.14
Shimei the son of Ela, in B.; 1Ki 4.18
of Judah, and the tribe of B., 12.21
to all the house of Judah and B., 12.23
Asa built Geba of B. and Mizpah. 15.22
Dan, Joseph, B., Naphtali, Gad, and 1Ch 2.02
and from the tribe of B., 6.60
and B. these cities which are 6.65
The sons of B.: Bela, Becher, and 7.06
B., Ehud, Chenaanah, Zethan, Tarshish, 7.10
B. was the father of Bela his first-born, 8.01
B., Ephraim, and Manasseh dwelt in 9.03
of the men of B. and Judah came to 12.16
Levi and B. in the numbering, for 21.06
for B., Jaasiel the son of Abner; 27.21
and B., a hundred and eighty 2Ch 11.01
and to all Israel in Judah and B., 11.03
which are in Judah and in B. 11.10
So he held Judah and B. 11.12
all the districts of Judah and B., 11.23
and eighty thousand men from B., 14.08
"Hear me, Asa, and all Judah and B.: 15.02
of Judah and B. and from the 15.08

BENJAMIN (cont.)
And he gathered all Judah and B., 2Ch 15.09
Of B.: Eliada, a mighty man of valor, 17.17
of hundreds for all Judah and B. 25.05
altars throughout all Judah and B., 31.01
all Judah and B. and from the 34.09
in Jerusalem and in B. stand to it. 34.32
fathers' houses of Judah and B., Ez 1.05
of Judah and B. heard that the 4.01
of Judah and B. assembled at 10.09
B., Malluch, and Shemariah. 10.32
After them B. and Hasshub repaired Neh 3.23
of Judah and of the sons of B. 11.04
And these are the sons of B.: 11.07
The people of B. also lived from 11.31
Levites in Judah were joined to B. 11.36
Judah, B., Shemaiah, and Jeremiah, 12.34
There is B., the least of them, in Ps 68.27
before Ephraim and B. and Manasseh! 80.02
in Anathoth in the land of B., Jer 1.01
O people of B., from the midst of 6.01
to me: "Go and stand in the B. Gate, 17.19
Jerusalem, from the land of B., 17.26
in the upper B. Gate of the house 20.02
is at Anathoth in the land of B., 32.08
and witnessed, in the land of B., 32.44
of the Negeb, in the land of B., 33.13
to the land of B. to receive his 37.12
When he was at the B. Gate, 37.13
king was sitting in the B. Gate— 38.07
of Judah and the territory of B. Eze 48.22
side to the west, B., one portion. 48.23
Adjoining the territory of B., 48.24
the gate of B., and the gate of Dan. 48.32
at Bethaven; tremble, O B.! Hos 5.08
of Samaria and B. shall possess Ob 1.19
the Gate of B. to the place of the Zec 14.10
of Kish, a man of the tribe of B., Ac 13.21
a member of the tribe of B. Rom 11.01
of Israel, of the tribe of B., Php 3.05
sealed out of the tribe of B. Rev 7.08

BENJAMINITE
the B., a left-handed man. Ju 3.15
of Aphiah, a B., a man of wealth; 1Sa 9.01
"Am I not a B., from the least of 9.21
how much more now may this B.! 2Sa 16.11
was Sheba, the son of Bichri, a B.; 20.01
the B. from Bahurim, who cursed me 1Ki 2.08
was Abiezer of Anathoth, a B.; 1Ch 27.12
son of Shimei, son of Kish, a B., Est 2.05

BENJAMINITES
the men of the place were B. Ju 19.16
(Now the B. heard that the people 20.03
But the B. would not listen to the 20.13
And the B. came together out of the 20.14
And the B. mustered out of their 20.15
up first to battle against the B.?" 20.18
The B. came out of Gibeah, and 20.21
battle against our brethren the B.?" 20.23
near against the B. the second day. 20.24
battle against our brethren the B., 20.28
up against the B. on the third day, 20.30
And the B. went out against the 20.31
And the B. said, "They are routed 20.32
but the B. did not know that 20.34
So the B. saw that they were 20.36
the B. looked behind them; 20.40
Cutting down the B., they pursued 20.43
Israel turned back against the B., 20.48
word to the B. who were at the 21.13
And they commanded the B., 21.20
And the B. did so, and took their 21.23
stood about him, "Hear now, you B.; 1Sa 22.07
And the B. gathered themselves 2Sa 2.25
son of Ribai of Gibeah of the B., 23.29
one hundred and fifty. All these were B. 1Ch 8.40
Of the B.: Sallu the son of Meshullam, 9.07
son of Ribai of Gibeah of the B., 11.31
they were B., Saul's kinsmen. 12.02
Of the B., the kinsmen of Saul, 12.29

BENJAMIN'S
but B. portion was five times as Gen 43.34
and the cup was found in B. sack. 44.12
upon his brother B. neck and wept; 45.14

BENO
The sons of Jaaziah: B. 1Ch 24.26
B., Shoham, Zaccur, and Ibri. 24.27

BENONI
she died), she called his name B.; Gen 35.18

BENT
he has b. and strung his bow; Ps 7.12
tremble, and the strong men are b., Ecc 12.03
are sharp, all their bows b., Is 5.28
from the b. bow, and from the press 21.15
He has b. his bow like an enemy, Lam 2.04
he b. his bow and set me as a mark 3.12
this vine b. its roots toward him, Eze 17.07
have been b. on shedding blood. 22.06
minds shall be b. on mischief; Dan 11.27
and I b. down to them and fed them. Hos 11.04
My people are b. on turning away 11.07
For I have b. Judah as my bow; Zec 9.13
she was b. over and could not fully Lk 13.11
Jesus b. down and wrote with his *Jn 8.06
And once more he b. down and wrote * 8.08
But Paul went down and b. over him, Ac 20.10

BENZOHETH
The sons of Ishi: Zoheth and B. 1Ch 4.20

BEON
Elealeh, Sebam, Nebo, and B., Num 32.03

BEOR
Bela the son of B. reigned in Edom, Gen 36.32
to Balaam the son of B. at Pethor, Num 22.05
"The oracle of Balaam the son of B., 24.03
"The oracle of Balaam the son of B., 24.15
the son of B. with the sword. 31.08
the son of B. from Pethor of Deu 23.04
the son of B., the soothsayer, the Jos 13.22
Balaam the son of B. to curse you, 24.09
the Israelites: Bela the son of B., 1Ch 1.43
Balaam the son of B. answered him, Mic 6.05
the son of B., who loved gain from 2Pe 2.15

BEQUEATH
You may b. them to your sons after Lev 25.46

BERA
made war with B. king of Sodom, Gen 14.02

BERACAH
B., Jehu of Anathoth, 1Ch 12.03
they assembled in the Valley of B., 2Ch 20.26
the Valley of B. to this day. 20.26

BERAIAH
Adaiah, B., and Shimrath were the 1Ch 8.21

BEREAVE
In the open the sword shall b., Deu 32.25
shall no longer b. them of children. Eze 36.12
and you b. your nation of children,' 36.13
and no longer b. your nation of 36.14
I will b. them till none is left. Hos 9.12

BEREAVED
"You have b. me of my children: Gen 42.36
If I am b. of my children, I am b." 43.14
and not one among them is b. Sol 4.02

BEREAVED (cont.)
twins, not one among them is b. Sol 6.06
I was b. and barren, exiled and put Is 49.21
I have b. them, I have destroyed my Jer 15.07

BEREAVEMENT
time of your b. will yet say in Is 49.20

BEREAVES
In the street the sword b.; Lam 1.20

BERECHIAH
B., Hasadiah, and Jushabhesed, five. 1Ch 3.20
hand, namely, Asaph the son of B., 6.39
and B. the son of Asa, son of 9.16
his brethren Asaph the son of B.; 15.17
B. and Elkanah were to be gatekeepers 15.23
B. the son of Meshillemoth, Jehizkiah 2Ch 28.12
to them Meshullam the son of B., Neh 3.04
the son of B. repaired opposite 3.30
Meshullam the son of B. as his wife. 6.18
came to Zechariah the son of B., Zec 1.01
came to Zechariah the son of B., 1.07

BERED
it lies between Kadesh and B. Gen 16.14
and B. his son, Tahath his son, 1Ch 7.20

BEREFT
Why should I be b. of you both in Gen 27.45
the woman was b. of her two sons Ru 1.05
my soul is b. of peace, I have Lam 3.17
But since we were b. of you, 1Th 2.17
in mind and b. of the truth, 1Ti 6.05

BERI
Suah, Harnepher, Shual, B., Imrah, 1Ch 7.36

BERIAH
B., with Serah their sister. Gen 46.17
And the sons of B.: Heber and 46.17
of B., the family of the Beriites Num 26.44
Of the sons of B.: of Heber, the 26.45
and he called his name B., 1Ch 7.23
B., and their sister Serah. 7.30
The sons of B.: Heber and Malchiel, 7.31
and B. and Shema (they were heads 8.13
Michael, Ishpah, and Joha were sons of B. 8.16
Jahath, Zina, and Jeush, and B. 23.10
but Jeush and B. had not many 23.11

BERIITES
of Beriah, the family of the B. Num 26.44

BERNICE
the king and B. arrived at Caesarea Ac 25.13
Agrippa and B. came with great 25.23
governor and B. and those who were 26.30

BEROEA
Paul and Silas away by night to B.: Ac 17.10
was proclaimed by Paul at B. also, 17.13
Sopater of B., the son of Pyrrhus, 20.04

BEROTHAH
B., Sibraim (which lies on the Eze 47.16

BEROTHAI
And from Betah and from B., 2Sa 8.08

BERRIES
two or three b. in the top of the Is 17.06

BERYL
and the fourth row a b., an onyx Ex 28.20
a b., an onyx, and a jasper; 39.13
b., and onyx, sapphire, carbuncle, and Eze 28.13
His body was like b., his face Dan 10.06
the eighth b., the ninth topaz, the Rev 21.20

BESAI
sons of Paseah, the sons of B., Ez 2.49
the sons of B., the sons of Meunim, Neh 7.52

BESEECH
LORD, "Heal her, O God, I b. thee." Num 12.13
I b. thee, tell thy servant." 1Sa 23.11
I b. thee, from his hand, that all 2Ki 19.19
I b. thee, how I have walked before 20.03
I must b. him with my mouth. Job 19.16
I b. thee, save my life!" Ps 116.04
Save us, we b. thee, O LORD! 118.25
O LORD, we b. thee, give us success! 118.25
I b. thee, how I have walked before Is 38.03
"O Lord GOD, forgive, I b. thee! Amo 7.02
said, "O Lord GOD, cease, I b. thee! 7.05
"We b. thee, O LORD, let us not Jon 1.14
I b. thee, for it is better for me 4.03
I b. you, do not torment me." Lk 8.28
We b. you on behalf of Christ, be 2Co 5.20
Brethren, I b. you, become as I am, Gal 4.12
we b. and exhort you in the Lord 1Th 4.01
But we b. you, brethren, to respect 5.12
Beloved, I b. you as aliens and 1Pe 2.11

BESEECHING
came forward to him, b. him Mt 8.05
And a leper came to him b. him, Mk 1.40
was standing b. him and saying, Ac 16.09

BESET
b. the house round about, beating on Ju 19.22
and b. the house round about me by 20.05
me when I was b. as in a besieged Ps 31.21
They b. me with words of hate, and 109.03
Thou dost b. me behind and before, 139.05
he himself is b. with weakness. Heb 5.02

BESIDE
three flocks of sheep lying b. it; Gen 29.02
her maidens walked b. the river; Ex 2.05
and cast it b. the altar on the Lev 1.16
altar, and put them b. the altar. 6.10
and eat it unleavened b. the altar, 10.12
that your brother may live b. you. 25.36
your brother becomes poor b. you, 25.39
your brother b. him becomes poor 25.47
any man dies very suddenly b. him, Num 6.09
sea, and let them fall b. the camp, 11.31
"Stand b. your burnt offering, and I 23.03
were standing b. his burnt offering 23.06
"Stand here b. your burnt offering, 23.15
he was standing b. his burnt 23.17
like gardens b. a river, like aloes 24.06
like cedar trees b. the waters. 24.06
against Gilgal, b. the oak of Moreh? Deu 11.30
as an Asherah b. the altar of the 16.21
am he, and there is no god b. me; 32.39
Adam, the city that is b. Zarethan, Jos 3.16
of Ai, which is b. Bethel, one; 12.09
a possession b. their brethren in 22.07
cut down the Asherah that is b. it; Ju 6.25
and the Asherah b. it was cut down, 6.28
and cut down the Asherah b. it." 6.30
and encamped b. the spring of 7.01
b. her he had neither son nor 11.34
So she sat b. the reapers, and he Ru 2.14
on the seat b. the doorpost of the 1Sa 1.09
of Dagon and set it up b. Dagon. 5.02
LORD and the box that was b. it, 6.15
b. which they set down the ark of 6.18
out and stand b. my father in the 19.03
and remain b. yonder stone heap. 20.19
David rose from b. the stone heap 20.41
which is b. the road on the east of 26.03
to me, 'Stand b. me and slay me; 2Sa 1.09
So I stood b. him, and slew him, 1.10
and hanged them b. the pool at 4.12

BESIDE (cont.)

he died there b. the ark of God. 2Sa 6.07
elders of his house stood b. him, 12.17
early and stand b. the way of the 15.02
them, and won a name b. the three. 23.18
and won a name b. the three mighty 23.22
which is b. Enrogel, and he invited 1Ki 1.09
he is b. the altar," Solomon sent 2.29
midnight, and took my son from b. me, 3.20
which is b. Zarethan below Jezreel, 4.12
projection which was b. the network; 7.20
lions standing b. the arm rests, 10.19
the road, and the ass stood b. it; 13.24
the lion also stood b. the body. 13.24
and the lion standing b. the body. 13.28
lay my bones b. his bones. 13.31
b. the palace of Ahab king of 21.01
heaven standing b. him on his 22.19
and the trumpeters b. the king, 2Ki 11.14
and set it b. the altar on the 12.09
them, and won a name b. the three. 1Ch 11.20
and won a name b. the three mighty 11.24
lions standing b. the arm rests, 2Ch 9.18
and the trumpeters b. the king, 23.13
to me (the queen sitting b. him), Neh 2.06
Ananiah repaired b. his own house. 3.23
who sounded the trumpet was b. me. 4.18
and b. him stood Mattithiah, Shema, 8.04
and the asses feeding b. them; Job 1.14
crashing they are b. themselves. 41.25
He leads me b. still waters; Ps 23.02
who dwells trustingly b. you. Pro 3.29
On the heights b. the way, in the 8.02
b. the gates in front of the town, 8.03
then I was b. him, like a master 8.30
at my gates, waiting b. my doors. 8.34
one who wanders b. the flocks of Sol 1.07
your kids b. the shepherds' tents. 1.08
are like doves b. springs of water, 5.12
set me in a chariot b. my prince. 6.12
Happy are you who sow b. all waters, Is 32.20
b. every green tree, and on the high Jer 17.02
the princes who stood b. the king. 36.21
upon the earth b. the living Eze 1.15
went, the wheels went b. them; 1.19
the sound of the wheels b. them, 3.13
in and stood b. the bronze altar. 9.02
he went in and stood b. a wheel. 10.06
were four wheels b. the cherubim, 10.09
the cherubim, one b. each cherub; 10.09
went, the wheels went b. them; 10.16
wheels did not turn from b. them. 10.16
forth, with the wheels b. them; 10.19
wings, with the wheels b. them; 11.22
he placed it b. abundant waters. 17.05
all its beasts from b. many waters; 32.13
were pillars b. the jambs on 40.49
While the man was standing b. me, 43.06
their doorposts b. my doorposts, 43.08
Fishermen will stand b. the sea; 47.10
a leopard I will lurk b. the way. Hos 13.07
themselves down b. every altar Amo 2.08
was standing b. a wall built with 7.07
saw the LORD standing b. the altar, 9.01
which are b. the two golden pipes Zec 4.12
of the house and sat b. the sea. Mt 13.01
He went out again b. the sea; Mk 2.13
for they said, "He is b. himself." 3.21
Again he began to teach b. the sea. 4.01
whole crowd was b. the sea on the 4.01
and he was b. the sea. 5.21
his journey, sat down b. the well. Jn 4.06
had been healed standing b. them, Ac 4.14
out and buried her b. her husband. 5.10
the widows stood b. him weeping, 9.39
For if we are b. ourselves, it is 2Co 5.13
standing b. the sea of glass with Rev 15.02

BESIDES

B. she is indeed my sister, the Gen 20.12
b. the former famine that was in 26.01
b. the wives he had, Mahalath the 28.09
if you take wives b. my daughters, 31.50
b. women and children. Ex 12.37
b. the burnt offering of the Lev 9.17
b. the sabbaths of the LORD, and 23.38
b. your gifts, and b. all your votive 23.38
and b. all your votive offerings, 23.38
and b. all your freewill offerings, 23.38
and b., we saw the descendants of Num 13.28
b. those who died in the affair of 16.49
b. the continual burnt offering and 28.10
be offered b. the continual burnt 28.15
offer these b. the burnt offering 28.23
be offered b. the continual burnt 28.24
B. the continual burnt offering and 28.31
b. the burnt offering of the new 29.06
b. the sin offering of atonement, 29.11
b. the continual burnt offering, its 29.16
b. the continual burnt offering 29.19
b. the continual burnt offering and 29.22
b. the continual burnt offering, its 29.25
b. the continual burnt offerings 29.28
b. the continual burnt offering, its 29.31
b. the continual burnt offering, its 29.34
b. the continual burnt offering and 29.38
b. very many unwalled villages. Deu 3.05
there is no other b. him. 4.35
b. what he receives from the sale 18.08
b. the covenant which he had made 29.01
b. the land of Gilead and Bashan, Jos 17.05
b. the crescents and the pendants Ju 8.26
and b. the collars that were about 8.26
b. the inhabitants of Gibeah, who 20.15
"B., he said to me, 'You shall keep Ru 2.21
there is no one b. you to redeem 4.04
the LORD, there is none b. thee; 1Sa 2.02
servants nineteen men b. Asahel. 2Sa 2.30
thee, and there is no God b. thee, 7.22
B., your father is expert in war; 17.08
b. harts, gazelles, roebucks, and 1Ki 4.23
b. Solomon's three thousand three 5.16
she asked b. what was given her by 10.13
b. that which came from the traders 10.15
b. the sin which he made Judah to 2Ki 21.16
b. the sons of the concubines; 1Ch 3.09
b. their kinsmen, heads of their 9.13
LORD, and there is no God b. thee, 17.20
b. great quantities of onyx and 29.02
she asked b. what she had brought 2Ch 9.12
b. that which the traders and 9.14
b. those whom the king had placed 17.19
B. the great number of burnt 29.35
b. freewill offerings for the house Ez 1.04
b. all that was freely offered. 1.06
b. their menservants and maidservants, 2.65
b. two hundred and twenty of the 8.20
b. forty shekels of silver. Neh 5.15
b. those who came to us from the 5.17
b. their menservants and maidservants, 7.67
upon earth that I desire b. thee. Ps 73.25
B. being wise, the Preacher also Ecc 12.09
other lords b. thee have ruled over Is 26.13
and b. me there is no savior. 43.11
I am the last; b. me there is no god. 44.06
Is there a God b. me? There is no 44.08
b. me there is no God; I gird you, 45.05
the west, that there is none b. me; 45.06
there is no other, no god b. him.'" 45.14
And there is no other god b. me, 45.21
a Savior; there is none b. me. 45.21
"I am, and there is no one b. me; 47.08
"I am, and there is no one b. me." 47.10
others to him b. those already 56.08
ear, no eye has seen a God b. thee, 64.04

BESIDES (cont.)
up and go to others b. these. Dan 11.04
and b. me there is no savior. Hos 13.04
men, b. women and children. Mt 14.21
men, b. women and children. 15.38
B., while he was sitting on the 27.19
And b. all this, between us and you Lk 16.26
Yes, and b. all this, it is now the 24.21
B. this you know what hour it is, Rom 13.11
And b. our own comfort we rejoiced 2Co 7.13
B. that, they learn to be idlers, 1Ti 5.13
B. this, we have had earthly fathers Heb 12.09

BESIEGE
against you, then you shall b. it; Deu 20.12
"When you b. a city for a long time, 20.19
They shall b. you in all your towns, 28.52
and they shall b. you in all your 28.52
to Keilah, to b. David and his men. 1Sa 23.08
their enemies b. them in any of 2Ch 6.28
and will b. you with towers and I Is 29.03

BESIEGED
men that they should be b. by you? Deu 20.19
went up and b. Jabeshgilead; 1Sa 11.01
the Ammonites, and b. Rabbah. 2Sa 11.01
Joab came and b. him in Abel of 20.15
with him, and they b. Tirzah. 1Ki 16.17
and he went up and b. Samaria, 20.01
army, and went up, and b. Samaria. 2Ki 6.24
as they b. it, until an ass's head 6.25
and they b. Ahaz but could not 16.05
and for three years he b. it. 17.05
came up against Samaria and b. it 18.09
to Jerusalem, and the city was b. 24.10
So the city was b. till the eleventh 25.02
Ammonites, and came and b. Rabbah. 1Ch 20.01
when I was beset as in a b. city. Ps 31.21
king came against it and b. it, Ecc 9.14
a cucumber field, like a b. city. Is 1.08
came against Jerusalem and b. it; Jer 39.01
So the city was b. till the eleventh 52.05
he has b. and enveloped me with Lam 3.05
came to Jerusalem and b. it. Dan 1.01

BESIEGERS
"B. come from a distant land; Jer 4.16

BESIEGES
if their enemy b. them in any of 1Ki 8.37

BESIEGING
And as Joab was b. the city, 2Sa 11.16
while his servants were b. it; 2Ki 24.11
who was b. Lachish with all his 2Ch 32.09
Chaldeans who are b. you outside Jer 21.04
Chaldeans who are b. you shall live 21.09
king of Babylon was b. Jerusalem, 32.02
who were b. Jerusalem heard news 37.05

BESMEAR
The godless b. me with lies, but Ps 119.69

BESODEIAH
the son of B. repaired the Old Neh 3.06

BESOR
him, and they came to the brook B., 1Sa 30.09
exhausted to cross the brook B. 30.10
who had been left at the brook B.; 30.21

BESOUGHT
when he b. us and we would not Gen 42.21
But Moses b. the LORD his God, and Ex 32.11
"And I b. the LORD at that time, Deu 3.23
David therefore b. God for the 2Sa 12.16
Then Jehoahaz b. the LORD, and the 2Ki 13.04
So we fasted and b. our God for Ez 8.23
at his feet and b. him with tears Est 8.03
went in and b. the king to appoint Dan 2.16
and b. him that they might only Mt 14.36
servant fell down and b. him, 18.29
all that debt because you b. me; 18.32
and b. him, saying, "My little Mk 5.23
and b. him that they might touch 6.56
and they b. him to lay his hand 7.32
fever, and they b. him for her. Lk 4.38
he fell on his face and b. him, 5.12
they b. him earnestly, saying, "He is 7.04
Jesus' feet he b. him to come to 8.41
Meanwhile the disciples b. him, Jn 4.31
she b. us, saying, "If you have Ac 16.15
Three times I b. the Lord about 2Co 12.08

BEST
took the b. garments of Esau her Gen 27.15
give you the b. of the land of 45.18
for the b. of all the land of Egypt 45.20
brothers in the b. of the land; 47.06
in the b. of the land, in the land 47.11
from the b. in his own field and Ex 22.05
All the b. of the oil, and all the Num 18.12
and all the b. of the wine and of 18.12
from all the b. of them, giving the 18.29
have offered from it the b. of it, 18.30
when you have offered the b. of it. 18.32
'Let them marry whom they think b.; 36.06
towns, where it pleases him b.; Deu 23.16
with the b. gifts of the earth and 33.16
He chose the b. of the land for 33.21
companion, who had been his b. man. Ju 14.20
and put on your b. clothes and go Ru 3.03
to her, "Do what seems b. to you, 1Sa 1.23
He will take the b. of your fields 8.14
and the b. of your cattle and your 8.16
and the b. of the sheep and of the 15.09
spared the b. of the sheep and of 15.15
the b. of the things devoted to 15.21
"Whatever seems b. to you I will do." 2Sa 18.04
select the b. and fittest of your 2Ki 10.03
maids to the b. place in the harem. Est 2.09
kisses like the b. wine that goes Sol 7.09
your wares the b. of all kinds of Eze 27.22
Eden, the choice and b. of Lebanon, 31.16
The b. of them is like a brier, the Mic 7.04
feasts and the b. seats in the Mt 23.06
and the b. seats in the synagogues Mk 12.39
you love the b. seat in the Lk 11.43
servants, 'Bring quickly the b. robe, 15.22
places and the b. seats in the 20.46
But Paul thought b. not to take Ac 15.38
it is b. for you now to complete 2Co 8.10
Do your b. to present yourself to 2Ti 2.15
Do your b. to come to me soon. 4.09
Do your b. to come before winter. 4.21
do your b. to come to me at Nicopolis, Tit 3.12
Do your b. to speed Zenas the 3.13

BESTIR
the balsam trees, then b. yourself; 2Sa 5.24
B. thyself, and awake for my right, Ps 35.23
securely, you will b. yourself Eze 38.14
Let the nations b. themselves, Joe 3.12

BESTIRS
that b. himself to take hold of Is 64.07

BESTOW
that he may b. a blessing upon you Ex 32.29
and majesty thou dost b. upon him. Ps 21.05
she will b. on you a beautiful Pro 4.09

BESTOWED
which shall be b. upon Israel; 1Sa 2.32
and b. upon him such royal majesty 1Ch 29.25
has been b. on Mordecai for this?" Est 6.03

BESTOWED (cont.)
splendor which I had b. upon you, Eze 16.14
She b. her harlotries upon them, the 23.07
many that were blind he b. sight. Lk 7.21
understand the gifts b. on us by God. 1Co 2.12
which he freely b. on us in the Eph 1.06
exalted him and b. on him the name Php 2.09

BESTOWER
the b. of crowns, whose merchants Is 23.08

BESTOWING
b. honor on the woman as the weaker 1Pe 3.07

BESTOWS
he b. favor and honor. No good Ps 84.11
Lord of all and b. his riches upon Rom 10.12

BESTRIDE
Thou didst b. the earth in fury, Hab 3.12

BETAH
And from B. and from Berothai, 2Sa 8.08

BETEN
Helkath, Hali, B., Achshaph, Jos 19.25

BETHANATH
B., and Bethshemesh—nineteen Jos 19.38
Bethshemesh, or the inhabitants of B., Ju 1.33
Bethshemesh and of B. became subject 1.33

BETHANOTH
Maarath, B., and Eltekon: six cities Jos 15.59

BETHANY
of the city to B. and lodged there Mt 21.17
Jesus was at B. in the house of 26.06
to Jerusalem, to Bethphage and B., Mk 11.01
he went out to B. with the twelve. 11.11
they came from B., he was hungry. 11.12
And while he was at B. in the house 14.03
When he drew near to Bethphage and B., Lk 19.29
Then he led them out as far as B., 24.50
This took place in B. beyond the Jn 1.28
Lazarus of B., the village of Mary 11.01
B. was near Jerusalem, about two 11.18
Jesus came to B., where Lazarus was, 12.01

BETHARABAH
and passes along north of B.; Jos 15.06
wilderness, B., Middin, Secacah, 15.61
the shoulder of B. it goes down to 18.18
B., Zemariam, Bethel, 18.22

BETHARBEL
destroyed B. on the day of battle; Hos 10.14

BETHASHBEA
the house of linen workers at B.; 1Ch 4.21

BETHAVEN
which is near B., east of Bethel, Jos 7.02
it ends at the wilderness of B. 18.12
in Michmash, to the east of B. 1Sa 13.05
and the battle passed beyond B. 14.23
nor go up to B., and swear not, "As Hos 4.15
Sound the alarm at B.; tremble 5.08
Samaria tremble for the calf of B. 10.05

BETHAZMAVETH
The men of B., forty-two. Neh 7.28

BETHBAALMEON
Dibon, and Bamothbaal, and B., Jos 13.17

BETHBARAH
as far as B., and also the Jordan. Ju 7.24
seized the waters as far as B., 7.24

BETHBIRI
Bethmarcaboth, Hazarsusim, B., and Shaaraim. 1Ch 4.31

BETHCAR
and smote them, as far as below B. 1Sa 7.11

BETHDAGON
Gederoth, B., Naamah, and Makkedah; Jos 15.41
it goes to B., and touches Zebulun 19.27

BETHDIBLATHAIM
and Dibon, and Nebo, and B., Jer 48.22

BETHEDEN
him that holds the scepter from B.; Amo 1.05

BETHEKED
when he was at B. of the Shepherds, 2Ki 10.12
and slew them at the pit of B., 10.14

BETHEL
to the mountain on the east of B., Gen 12.08
with B. on the west and Ai on the 12.08
on from the Negeb as far as B., 13.03
the beginning, between B. and Ai, 13.03
He called the name of that place B.; 28.19
I am the God of B., where you 31.13
go up to B., and dwell there; 35.01
then let us arise and go up to B., 35.03
B.), which is in the land of Canaan, 35.06
was buried under an oak below B.; 35.08
where God had spoken with him, B. 35.15
Then they journeyed from B.; 35.16
east of B., and said to them, "Go up Jos 7.02
ambush, and lay between B. and Ai, 8.09
them in ambush between B. and Ai, 8.12
There was not a man left in Ai or B., 8.17
of Ai, which is beside B., one; 12.09
one; the king of B., one; 12.16
into the hill country to B.; 16.01
then going from B. to Luz, 16.02
shoulder of Luz (the same is B.), 18.13
Betharabah, Zemaraim, B., 18.22
of Joseph also went up against B.; Ju 1.22
house of Joseph sent to spy out B. 1.23
Ramah and B. in the hill country 4.05
of Israel arose and went up to B., 20.18
went up and came to B. and wept; 20.26
goes up to B. and the other to 20.31
And the people came to B., and sat 21.02
at Shiloh, which is north of B., 21.19
that goes up from B. to Shechem, 21.19
on a circuit year by year to B., 1Sa 7.16
up to God at B. will meet you 10.03
Michmash and the hill country of B., 13.02
it was for those in B., in Ramoth 30.27
And he set one in B., and the 1Ki 12.29
to the one at B. and to the other 12.30
so he did in B., sacrificing to the 12.32
he placed in B. the priests of the 12.32
he had made in B. on the fifteenth 12.33
by the word of the LORD to B. 13.01
he cried against the altar at B., 13.04
by the way that he came to B. 13.10
Now there dwelt an old prophet in B. 13.11
man of God had done that day in B.; 13.11
the LORD against the altar in B., 13.32
In his days Hiel of B. built Jericho; 16.34
the LORD has sent me as far as B." 2Ki 2.02
not leave you." So they went down to B. 2.02
who were in B. came out to Elisha, 2.03
He went up from there to B.; 2.23
calves that were in B., and in Dan. 10.29
from Samaria came and dwelt in B., 17.28
and carried their ashes to B. 23.04
Moreover the altar at B., the high 23.15
have done against the altar at B." 23.17
to all that he had done at B. 23.19

BETHEL (cont.)
settlements were B. and its towns, 1Ch 7.28
B. with its villages and Jeshanah 2Ch 13.19
The men of B. and Ai, two hundred Ez 2.28
The men of B. and Ai, a hundred and Neh 7.32
Aija, B. and its villages, 11.31
house of Israel was ashamed of B., Jer 48.13
He met God at B., and there God Hos 12.04
I will punish the altars of B., Amo 3.14
"Come to B., and transgress; 4.04
but do not seek B., and do not 5.05
and B. shall come to nought." 5.05
with none to quench it for B., 5.06
the priest of B. sent to Jeroboam 7.10
but never again prophesy at B., 7.13
Now the people of B. had sent Zec 7.02

BETHEMEK
Iphtahel northward to B. and Neiel; Jos 19.27

BETHEZEL
the wailing of B. shall take away Mic 1.11

BETHGADER
and Hareph the father of B. 1Ch 2.51

BETHGAMUL
and Kiriathaim, and B., and Bethmeon, Jer 48.23

BETHGILGAL
also from B. and from the region of Neh 12.29

BETHHACCHEREM
ruler of the district of B., Neh 3.14
in Tekoa, and raise a signal on B.; Jer 6.01

BETHHAGGAN
he fled in the direction of B. 2Ki 9.27

BETHHARAM
and in the valley B., Bethnimrah, Jos 13.27

BETHHARAN
Bethnimrah and B., fortified cities, Num 32.36

BETHHOGLAH
and the boundary goes up to B., Jos 15.06
to the north of the shoulder of B.; 18.19
were Jericho, B., Emekkeziz, 18.21

BETHHORON
by the way of the ascent of B., Jos 10.10
were going down the ascent of B., 10.11
far as the territory of lower B., 16.03
Atarothaddar as far as upper B., 16.05
that lies south of Lower B. 18.13
opposite B., and it ends at Kiriathbaal 18.14
B. with its pasture lands—four 21.22
another company turned toward B., 1Sa 13.18
rebuilt Gezer) and B. the lower 1Ki 9.17
B. with its pasture lands, 1Ch 6.68
who built both lower and upper B., 7.24
He also built Upper B. and Lower B., 2Ch 8.05
of Judah, from Samaria to B., 25.13

BETHJESHIMOTH
the Jordan from B. as far as Num 33.49
eastward, and in the direction of B., Jos 12.03
and the slopes of Pisgah, and B., 13.20
B., Baalmeon, and Kiriathaim. Eze 25.09

BETHLEAPHRAH
in B. roll yourselves in the dust. Mic 1.10

BETHLEBAOTH
B., and Sharuhen—thirteen cities Jos 19.06

BETHLEHEM
the way to Ephrath (that is, B.), Gen 35.19
on the way to Ephrath (that is, B.). 48.07
and B.—twelve cities with their Jos 19.15
After him Ibzan of B. judged Israel. Ju 12.08
Then Ibzan died, and was buried at B. 12.10
was a young man of B. in Judah, 17.07
from the town of B. in Judah, 17.08
him, "I am a Levite of B. in Judah, 17.09
a concubine from B. in Judah. 19.01
her father's house at B. in Judah, 19.02
passing from B. in Judah to the 19.18
I went to B. in Judah; 19.18
certain man of B. in Judah went to Ru 1.01
were Ephrathites from B. in Judah. 1.02
them went on until they came to B. 1.19
And when they came to B., 1.19
they came to B. at the beginning 1.22
And behold, Boaz came from B.; 2.04
in Ephrathah and be renowned in B.; 4.11
the LORD commanded, and came to B. 1Sa 16.04
of an Ephrathite of B. in Judah, 17.12
to feed his father's sheep at B. 17.15
leave of me to run to B. his city; 20.06
asked leave of me to go to B.; 20.28
of his father, which was at B. 2Sa 2.32
of the Philistines was then at B. 23.14
the well of B. which is by the 23.15
of the well of B. which was by the 23.16
Elhanan the son of Dodo of B., 23.24
the father of B., and Hareph the 1Ch 2.51
B., the Netophathites, Atrothbethjoab, 2.54
of Ephrathah the father of B. 4.04
of the Philistines was then at B. 11.16
the well of B. which is by the 11.17
of the well of B. which was by the 11.18
Elhanan the son of Dodo of B., 11.26
He built B., Etam, Tekoa, 2Ch 11.06
The sons of B., one hundred and Ez 2.21
The men of B. and Netophah, a Neh 7.26
stayed at Geruth Chimham near B., Jer 41.17
But you, O B. Ephrathah, who are Mic 5.02
was born in B. of Judea in the Mt 2.01
They told him, "In B. of Judea; 2.05
'And you, O B., in the land of Judah, 2.06
and he sent them to B., 2.08
children in B. and in all that 2.16
city of David, which is called B., Lk 2.04
us go over to B. and see this 2.15
from David, and comes from B., Jn 7.42

BETHLEHEMITE
I will send you to Jesse the B., 1Sa 16.01
I have seen a son of Jesse the B., 16.18
son of your servant Jesse the B. 17.58
the B., slew Goliath the Gittite, 2Sa 21.19

BETHMAACAH
the tribes of Israel to Abel of B.; 2Sa 20.14
and besieged him in Abel of B.; 20.15

BETHMARCABOTH
Ziklag, B., Hazarsusah, Jos 19.05
B., Hazarsusim, Bethbiri, and Shaaraim. 1Ch 4.31

BETHMEON
Kiriathaim, and Bethgamul, and B., Jer 48.23

BETHMILLO
and all B., and they went and made Ju 9.06
the citizens of Shechem, and B.; 9.20
and from B., and devour Abimelech. 9.20

BETHNIMRAH
B. and Bethharan, fortified cities, Num 32.36
B., Succoth, and Zaphon, the rest of Jos 13.27

BETHPAZZEZ
Remeth, Engannim, Enhaddah, B.; Jos 19.21

BETHPELET
Hazargaddah, Heshmon, B., Jos 15.27
and in Jeshua and in Moladah and B., Neh 11.26

BETHPEOR
remained in the valley opposite B. Deu 3.29
Jordan in the valley opposite B., 4.46
in the land of Moab opposite B.; 34.06
and B., and the slopes of Pisgah, Jos 13.20

BETHPHAGE
near to Jerusalem and came to B., Mt 21.01
to B. and Bethany, at the Mount of Mk 11.01
When he drew near to B. and Bethany, Lk 19.29

BETHRAPHA
Eshton was the father of B., 1Ch 4.12

BETHREHOB
in the valley which belongs to B. Ju 18.28
sent and hired the Syrians of B., 2Sa 10.06

BETHSAIDA
woe to you, B.! for if Mt 11.21
to B., while he dismissed the crowd Mk 6.45
And they came to B. And some 8.22
withdrew apart to a city called B. Lk 9.10
woe to you, B.! for if 10.13
Now Philip was from B., the city Jn 1.44
who was from B. in Galilee, and said 12.21

BETHSHAN
fastened his body to the wall of B. 1Sa 31.10
of his sons from the wall of B.; 31.12
them from the public square of B., 2Sa 21.12

BETHSHEAN
Manasseh and B. and its villages, Jos 17.11
both those in B. and its villages 17.16
inhabitants of B. and its villages, Ju 1.27
and all B. which is beside Zarethan 1Ki 4.12
and from B. to Abelmeholah, as far 4.12
B. and its town, Taanach and its 1Ch 7.29

BETHSHEMESH
is Chesalon), and goes down to B., Jos 15.10
and B., and its boundary ends at 19.22
and B.—nineteen cities with their 19.38
B. with its pasture lands—nine 21.16
drive out the inhabitants of B., Ju 1.33
inhabitants of B. and of Bethanath 1.33
to B., then it is he who has done 1Sa 6.09
direction of B. along one highway, 6.12
them as far as the border of B. 6.12
Now the people of B. were reaping 6.13
into the field of Joshua of B., 6.14
and the men of B. offered burnt 6.15
day in the field of Joshua of B. 6.18
And he slew some of the men of B., 6.19
Then the men of B. said, "Who is 6.20
Shaalbim, B., and Elonbethhanan; 1Ki 4.09
faced one another in battle at B., 2Ki 14.11
at B., and came to Jerusalem, and 14.13
and B. with its pasture lands; 1Ch 6.59
faced one another in battle at B., 2Ch 25.21
at B., and brought him to Jerusalem, 25.23
and had taken B., Aijalon, Gederoth, 28.18

BETHSHITTAH
fled as far as B. toward Zererah, Ju 7.22

BETHTAPPUAH
Janim, B., Aphekah, Jos 15.53

BETHTOGARMAH
B. exchanged for your wares horses, Eze 27.14
B. from the uttermost parts of the 38.06

BETHUEL
Chesed, Hazo, Pildash, Jidlaph, and B. Gen 22.22
B. became the father of Rebekah. 22.23
who was born to B. the son of 24.15
the daughter of B. the son of 24.24
She said, 'The daughter of B., 24.47
Then Laban and B. answered, "The 24.50
the daughter of B. the Aramean of 25.20
the house of B. your mother's 28.02
the son of B. the Aramean, the 28.05
B., Hormah, Ziklag, 1Ch 4.30

BETHUL
Eltolad, B., Hormah, Jos 19.04

BETHZATHA
gate a pool, in Hebrew called B., Jn 5.02

BETHZUR
Halhul, B., Gedor, Jos 15.58
and Maon was the father of B. 1Ch 2.45
B., Soco, Adullam, 2Ch 11.07
ruler of half the district of B., Neh 3.16

BETONIM
Heshbon to Ramathmizpeh and B., Jos 13.26

BETRAY
but if to b. me to my adversaries, 1Ch 12.17
hide the outcasts, b. not the fugitive; Is 16.03
and b. one another, and hate one Mt 24.10
he sought an opportunity to b. him. 26.16
say to you, one of you will b. me." 26.21
in the dish with me, will b. me. 26.23
priests in order to b. him to them. Mk 14.10
he sought an opportunity to b. him. 14.11
say to you, one of you will b. me, 14.18
how he might b. him to them. Lk 22.04
opportunity to b. him to them in 22.06
would you b. the Son of man with a 22.48
and who it was that should b. him. Jn 6.64
one of the twelve, was to b. him. 6.71
(he who was to b. him), said, 12.04
Iscariot, Simon's son, to b. him, 13.02
For he knew who was to b. him; 13.11
say to you, one of you will b. me." 13.21
who is it that is going to b. you?" 21.20

BETRAYED
and Judas Iscariot, who b. him. Mt 10.04
man by whom the Son of man is b.! 26.24
Judas, who b. him, said, "Is it I, 26.25
Son of man is b. into the hands of 26.45
and Judas Iscariot, who b. him. Mk 3.19
man by whom the Son of man is b.! 14.21
Son of man is b. into the hands of 14.41
woe to that man by whom he is b.!" Lk 22.22
Now Judas, who b. him, also knew the Jn 18.02
Judas, who b. him, was standing 18.05
whom you have now b. and murdered, Ac 7.52
night when he was b. took bread, 1Co 11.23

BETRAYER
but one who utters lies is a b. Pro 14.25
see, my b. is at hand." Mt 26.46
Now the b. had given them a sign, 26.48
his b., saw that he was condemned, 27.03
see, my b. is at hand." Mk 14.42
Now the b. had given them a sign, 14.44

BETRAYING
"I have sinned in b. innocent blood." Mt 27.04

BETRAYS
who b. nations with her harlotries, Nah 3.04
of them, for your accent b. you." Mt 26.73
hand of him who b. me is with me Lk 22.21

BETROTH
You shall b. a wife, and another man Deu 28.30
And I will b. you to me for ever; Hos 2.19
I will b. you to me in righteousness 2.19
I will b. you to me in faithfulness 2.20

BETROTHED
man seduces a virgin who is not b., Ex 22.16
b. to another man and not yet Lev 19.20
there that has b. a wife and has Deu 20.07
"If there is a b. virgin, and a man 22.23
man meets a young woman who is b., 22.25
and though the b. young woman 22.27
a man meets a virgin who is not b., 22.28
whom I b. at the price of a hundred 2Sa 3.14
mother Mary had been b. to Joseph, Mt 1.18
to a virgin b. to a man whose name Lk 1.27
his b., who was with child. 2.05
behaving properly toward his b., 1Co 7.36
his heart, to keep her as his b., 7.37
he who marries his b. does well; 7.38
for I b. you to Christ to present 2Co 11.02

BETTER
"It is b. that I give her to you Gen 29.19
would have been b. for us to serve Ex 14.12
would it not be b. for us to go Num 14.03
of Ephraim b. than the vintage of Ju 8.02
'Which is b. for you, that all 9.02
Now are you any b. than Balak the 11.25
Is it b. for you to be priest to 18.19
How much b. if the people had eaten 1Sa 14.30
to obey is b. than sacrifice, and to 15.22
of yours, who is b. than you. 15.28
is nothing b. for me than that I 27.01
It would be b. for me to be there 2Sa 14.32
the Archite is b. than the counsel 17.14
therefore it is b. that you send us 18.03
more righteous and b. than himself, 1Ki 2.32
for I am no b. than my fathers." 19.04
will give you a b. vineyard for it 21.02
b. than all the waters of Israel? 2Ki 5.12
house, who were b. than yourself; 2Ch 21.13
to another who is b. than she. Est 1.19
How am I b. off than if I had Job 35.03
B. is a little that the righteous Ps 37.16
thy steadfast love is b. than life, 63.03
thy courts is b. than a thousand 84.10
It is b. to take refuge in the LORD 118.08
It is b. to take refuge in the LORD 118.09
of thy mouth is b. to me than 119.72
gain from it is b. than gain from Pro 3.14
silver and its profit b. than gold. 3.14
for wisdom is b. than jewels, and 8.11
My fruit is b. than gold, even fine 8.19
B. is a man of humble standing who 12.09
B. is a little with the fear of the 15.16
B. is a dinner of herbs where love 15.17
B. is a little with righteousness 16.08
To get wisdom is b. than gold; 16.16
It is b. to be of a lowly spirit 16.19
to anger is b. than the mighty, and 16.32
B. is a dry morsel with quiet than 17.01
B. is a poor man who walks in his 19.01
and a poor man is b. than a liar. 19.22
It is b. to live in a corner of the 21.09
It is b. to live in a desert land 21.19
and favor is b. than silver or gold. 22.01
for it is b. to be told, "Come up 25.07
It is b. to live in a corner of the 25.24
B. is open rebuke than hidden love. 27.05
B. is a neighbor who is near than a 27.10
B. is a poor man who walks in his 28.06
There is nothing b. for a man than Ecc 2.24
is nothing b. for them than to be 3.12
is nothing b. than that a man 3.22
but b. than both is he who has not 4.03
B. is a handful of quietness than 4.06
Two are b. than one, because they 4.09
B. is a poor and wise youth than an 4.13
to listen is b. than to offer the 5.01
It is b. that you should not vow 5.05
untimely birth is b. off than he. 6.03
B. is the sight of the eyes than 6.09
vanity, and what is man the b.? 6.11
A good name is b. than precious 7.01
It is b. to go to the house of 7.02
Sorrow is b. than laughter, for by 7.03
It is b. for a man to hear the 7.05
B. is the end of a thing than its 7.08
in spirit is b. than the proud in 7.08
were the former days b. than these? 7.10
a living dog is b. than a dead 9.04
I say that wisdom is b. than might, 9.16
in quiet are b. than the shouting 9.17
Wisdom is b. than weapons of war, 9.18
For your love is b. than wine, Sol 1.02
how much b. is your love than wine, 4.10
and a name b. than sons and Is 56.05
that they were b. in appearance Dan 1.15
them ten times b. than all the 1.20
for it was b. with me then than now Hos 2.07
Are they b. than these Kingdoms? Amo 6.02
for it is b. for me to die than to Jon 4.03
"It is b. for me to die than to 4.08
Are you b. than Thebes that sat by Nah 3.08
it is b. that you lose one of your Mt 5.29
it is b. that you lose one of your 5.30
it would be b. for him to have a 18.06
it is b. for you to enter life 18.08
it is b. for you to enter life with 18.09
would have been b. for that man if 26.24
and was no b. but rather grew worse. Mk 5.26
it would be b. for him if a great 9.42
it is b. for you to enter life 9.43
it is b. for you to enter life lame 9.45
it is b. for you to enter the 9.47
would have been b. for that man if 14.21
It would be b. for him if a millstone Lk 17.02
Are we Jews any b. off? Rom 3.09
esteems one day as b. than another, 14.05
For it is b. to marry than to be 1Co 7.09
refrains from marriage will do b. 7.38
do not eat, and no b. off if we do. 8.08
is not for the b. but for the 11.17
I am a b. one—I am talking like a 2Co 11.23
and got the b. of you by guile. 12.16
is no b. than a slave, though he is Gal 4.01
be with Christ, for that is far b. Php 1.23
count others b. than yourselves. 2.03
serve all the b. since those who 1Ti 6.02
we feel sure of b. things that Heb 6.09
a b. hope is introduced, through 7.19
Jesus the surety of a b. covenant. 7.22
as the covenant he mediates is b., 8.06
since it is enacted on b. promises. 8.06
themselves with b. sacrifices than 9.23
yourselves had a b. possession and 10.34
they desire a b. country, that is, a 11.16
they might rise again to a b. life. 11.35
had foreseen something b. for us, 11.40
For it is b. to suffer for doing 1Pe 3.17
would have been b. for them never 2Pe 2.21

BETWEEN
I will put enmity b. you and the Gen 3.15
and b. your seed and her seed; 3.15
which I make b. me and you and 9.12
of the covenant b. me and the 9.13
which is b. me and you and every 9.15
covenant b. God and every living 9.16
established b. me and all flesh 9.17
Resen b. Nineveh and Calah; 10.12
the beginning, b. Bethel and Ai, 13.03

BETWEEN (cont.)

was strife b. the herdsmen of Gen 13.07
there be no strife b. you and me, 13.08
and b. your herdsmen and my herdsmen; 13.08
torch passed b. these pieces. 15.17
May the LORD judge b. you and me!" 16.05
it lies b. Kadesh and Bered. 16.14
make my covenant b. me and you, 17.02
my covenant b. me and you and your 17.07
b. me and you and your descendants 17.10
sign of the covenant b. me and you. 17.11
and dwelt b. Kadesh and Shur; 20.01
silver, what is that b. you and me? 23.15
let there be an oath b. you and us, 26.28
days' journey b. himself and Jacob; 30.36
that they may decide b. us two. 31.37
let it be a witness b. you and me." 31.44
is a witness b. you and me today." 31.48
said, "The LORD watch b. you and me, 31.49
God is witness b. you and me." 31.50
which I have set b. you and me. 31.51
God of their father, judge b. us." 31.53
and put a space b. drove and drove." 32.16
there was an interpreter b. them. 42.23
the ruler's staff from b. his feet, 49.10
ass, crouching b. the sheepfolds; 49.14
put a division b. my people and Ex 8.23
a distinction b. the cattle of 9.04
a distinction b. the Egyptians and 11.07
and as a memorial b. your eyes, 13.09
hand or frontlets b. your eyes; 13.16
b. Migdol and the sea, in front of 14.02
coming b. the host of Egypt and the 14.20
which is b. Elim and Sinai, on the 16.01
me and I decide b. a man and his 18.16
LORD shall be b. them both to see 22.11
from b. the two cherubim that are 25.22
with bells of gold b. them, 28.33
shall put it b. the tent of 30.18
this is a sign b. me and you 31.13
a sign for ever b. me and the 31.17
put the bells b. the pomegranates 39.25
round about, b. the pomegranates; 39.25
and place the laver b. the tent of 40.07
set the laver b. the tent of 40.30
to distinguish b. the holy and the Lev 10.10
and b. the unclean and the clean; 10.10
a distinction b. the unclean and 11.47
the clean and b. the living 11.47
a distinction b. the clean beast 20.25
and b. the unclean bird and the 20.25
the LORD made b. him and the 26.46
from b. the two cherubim; Num 7.89
While the meat was yet b. their teeth, 11.33
it on a pole b. two of them; 13.23
And he stood b. the dead and the 16.48
b. Moab and the Amorites. 21.13
in a narrow path b. the vineyards, 22.24
according to lot b. the larger and 26.56
as b. a man and his wife, and 30.16
and b. a father and his daughter, 30.16
b. the warriors who went out to 31.27
shall judge b. the manslayer and 35.24
b. Paran and Tophel, Laban, Hazeroth, Deu 1.01
'Hear the cases b. your brethren, 1.16
righteously b. a man and his 1.16
while I stood b. the LORD and you 5.05
shall be as frontlets b. your eyes. 6.08
shall be as frontlets b. your eyes. 11.18
decision b. one kind of homicide 17.08
"If there is a dispute b. men, 25.01
and the judges decide b. them, 25.01
comes out from b. her feet and her 28.57
his dwelling b. his shoulders. 33.12
shall be a space b. you and it, Jos 3.04
and lay b. Bethel and Ai, to the 8.09
Ai, with a ravine b. them and Ai. 8.11
them in ambush b. Bethel and Ai, 8.12
to it fell b. the tribe of Judah 18.11
Jordan a boundary b. us and you, 22.25
but to be a witness b. us and you, 22.27
and b. the generations after us, 22.27
but to be a witness b. us and you.' 22.28
"it is a witness b. us that the 22.34
he put darkness b. you and the 24.07
palm of Deborah b. Ramah and Ju 4.05
there was peace b. Jabin the king 4.17
an evil spirit b. Abimelech and 9.23
"The LORD will be witness b. us; 11.10
decide this day b. the people of 11.27
Mahanehdan, b. Zorah and Eshtaol. 13.25
and put a torch b. each pair of 15.04
They made him stand b. the pillars; 16.25
and buried him b. Zorah and 16.31
appointed signal b. the men of 20.38
and set it up b. Mizpah and 1Sa 7.12
was peace also b. Israel and the 7.14
"Cast the lot b. me and my son 14.42
and encamped b. Soco and Azekah, **in** 17.01
other side, with a valley b. them. 17.03
of bronze slung b. his shoulders. 17.06
is but a step b. me and death." 20.03
the LORD is b. you and me for ever." 20.23
'The LORD shall be b. me and you, 20.42
and b. my descendants and your 20.42
May the LORD judge b. me and you, 24.12
and give sentence b. me and you, 24.15
mountain, with a great space b. them; 26.13
There was a long war b. the house 2Sa 3.01
While there was war b. the house of 3.06
left hanging b. heaven and earth, 18.09
David was sitting b. the two gates; 18.24
silver or gold b. us and Saul or 21.04
oath of the LORD which was b. them, 21.07
b. David and Jonathan the son of 21.07
I may discern b. good and evil; 1Ki 3.09
there was peace b. Hiram and 5.12
the clay ground b. Succoth and 7.46
And there was war b. Rehoboam and 14.30
Now there was war b. Rehoboam and 15.06
there was war b. Abijam and 15.07
And there was war b. Asa and Baasha 15.16
"Let there be a league b. me and you, 15.19
as b. my father and your father: 15.19
And there was war b. Asa and Baasha 15.32
the land b. them to pass through 18.06
and put his face b. his knees. 18.42
king of Israel b. the scale armor 22.34
and shot Joram b. the shoulders, 2Ki 9.24
army, "Bring her out b. the ranks; 11.15
made a covenant b. the LORD and 11.17
and also b. the king and the people. 11.17
from the place b. his altar and 16.14
way of the gate b. the two walls, 25.04
LORD standing b. earth and heaven, 1Ch 21.16
the clay ground b. Succoth and 2Ch 4.17
continual wars b. Rehoboam and 12.15
there was war b. Abijah and 13.02
b. the mighty and the weak. 14.11
"Let there be a league b. me and you, 16.03
as b. my father and your father; 16.03
king of Israel b. the scale armor 18.33
them, "Bring her out b. the ranks; 23.14
made a covenant b. himself and all 23.16
And b. the upper chamber of the Neh 3.32
B. morning and evening they are Job 4.20
There is no umpire b. us, 9.33
at the boundary b. light and 26.10
that no air can come b. them. 41.16
b. them maidens playing timbrels: Ps 68.25
in the valleys; they flow b. the hills, 104.10
and decides b. powerful contenders Pro 18.18
of myrrh, that lies b. my breasts. Sol 1.13
He shall judge b. the nations, and Is 2.04

BETWEEN (cont.)
b. me and my vineyard. Is 5.03
a reservoir b. the two walls for 22.11
a separation b. you and your God, 59.02
in two and passed b. its parts— Jer 34.18
land who passed b. the parts of 34.19
and clothes b. your armpits and 38.12
through the gate b. the two walls; 39.04
the way of a gate b. the two walls, 52.07
as an iron wall b. you and the Eze 4.03
lifted me up b. earth and heaven, 8.03
b. the porch and the altar, were 8.16
burning coals from b. the cherubim, 10.02
"Take fire from b. the whirling 10.06
from b. the cherubim," he went in 10.06
his hand from b. the cherubim to 10.07
the fire that was b. the cherubim, 10.07
true justice b. man and man, 18.08
as a sign b. me and them, that they 20.12
they may be a sign b. me and you, 20.20
no distinction b. the holy and the 22.26
the difference b. the unclean and 22.26
I judge b. sheep and sheep, rams and 34.17
will judge b. the fat sheep and 34.20
I will judge b. sheep and sheep. 34.22
and the space b. the side rooms, 40.07
B. the platform of the temple and 41.09
a palm tree b. cherub and cherub. 41.18
a separation b. the holy and the 42.20
with only a wall b. me and them. 43.08
the difference b. the holy and the 44.23
to distinguish b. the unclean and 44.23
on the border b. Damascus and of 47.16
from Hazarenon b. Hauran and 47.18
the Jordan b. Gilead and the land 47.18
shall lie b. the territory of 48.22
ribs in its mouth b. its teeth; Dan 7.05
had a conspicuous horn b. his eyes. 8.05
a man's voice b. the banks of the 8.16
the great horn b. his eyes is the 8.21
palatial tents b. the sea and the 11.45
her adultery from b. her breasts; Hos 2.02
B. the vestibule and the altar let Joe 2.17
He shall judge b. many peoples, and Mic 4.03
up the ephah b. earth and heaven. Zec 5.09
came out from b. two mountains; 6.01
understanding shall be b. them both."' 6.13
its abominations from b. its teeth; 9.07
the brotherhood b. Judah and 11.14
to the covenant b. you and the Mal 2.14
distinguish b. the righteous and 3.18
b. one who serves God and one who 3.18
b. you and him alone. Mt 18.15
you murdered b. the sanctuary and 23.35
who perished b. the altar and the Lk 11.51
And he divided his living b. them. 15.12
b. us and you a great chasm has 16.26
passing along b. Samaria and 17.11
discussion arose b. John's disciples Jn 3.25
on either side, and Jesus b. them. 19.18
Peter was sleeping b. two soldiers, Ac 12.06
made no distinction b. us and them, 15.09
dissension arose b. the Pharisees 23.07
is no distinction b. Jew and Greek; Rom 10.12
keep b. yourself and God; 14.22
to decide b. members of the 1Co 6.05
ability to distinguish b. spirits, 12.10
I am hard pressed b. the two. Php 1.23
is one mediator b. God and men, 1Ti 2.05
And b. the throne and the four Rev 5.06

BEVELED
there were wreaths of b. work. 1Ki 7.29

BEWAIL
may b. the burning which the LORD Lev 10.06
your house and b. her father and Deu 21.13
and b. my virginity, I and my Ju 11.37

BEWAILED
and b. her virginity upon the Ju 11.38
of women who b. and lamented him. Lk 23.27

BEWAILING
And all were weeping and b. her; Lk 8.52

BEWARE
b. lest you act corruptly by making Deu 4.16
And b. lest you lift up your eyes 4.19
B. lest you say in your heart, 'My 8.17
B. lest there be among you a man or 29.18
Therefore b., and drink no wine or Ju 13.04
I said to the woman let her b. 13.13
"B. that you do not pass this place, 2Ki 6.09
B. lest you say, 'We have found Job 32.13
B. lest wrath entice you into 36.18
My son, b. of anything beyond these. Ecc 12.12
B. lest Hezekiah mislead you by Is 36.18
Let every one b. of his neighbor, Jer 9.04
"B. of practicing your piety before Mt 6.01
"B. of false prophets, who come to 7.15
B. of men; for they will 10.17
"Take heed and b. of the leaven of 16.06
B. of the leaven of the Pharisees 16.11
tell them to b. of the leaven of 16.12
b. of the leaven of the Pharisees Mk 8.15
"B. of the scribes, who like to go 12.38
"B. of the leaven of the Pharisees, Lk 12.01
and b. of all covetousness; 12.15
"B. of the scribes, who like to go 20.46
B., therefore, lest there come upon Ac 13.40
B. of him yourself, for he strongly 2Ti 4.15
b. lest you be carried away with 2Pe 3.17

BEWILDERED
and they were b., because each one Ac 2.06

BEWITCHED
Who has b. you, before whose eyes Gal 3.01

BEYOND
his tent b. the tower of Eder. Gen 35.21
are mighty b. the blessings of the 49.26
which is b. the Jordan, they lamented 50.10
Abelmizraim; it is b. the Jordan. 50.11
has a discharge b. the time of her Lev 15.25
plains of Moab b. the Jordan at Num 22.01
I could not go b. the command of 22.18
be able to go b. the word of the 24.13
other side of the Jordan and b.; 32.19
shall remain with us b. the Jordan." 32.32
inheritance b. the Jordan at 34.15
give three cities b. the Jordan, 35.14
at any time go b. the bounds of 35.26
to all Israel b. the Jordan in the Deu 1.01
B. the Jordan, in the land of Moab, 1.05
Amorites who were b. the Jordan, 3.08
your God gives them b. the Jordan; 3.20
see the good land b. the Jordan, 3.25
cities in the east b. the Jordan, 4.41
b. the Jordan in the valley opposite 4.46
lived to the east b. the Jordan; 4.47
Are they not b. the Jordan, west of 11.30
Neither is it b. the sea, that you 30.13
which Moses gave you b. the Jordan; Jos 1.14
LORD gave you b. the Jordan toward 1.15
Amorites that were b. the Jordan, 2.10
that were b. the Jordan to the 5.01
content to dwell b. the Jordan! 7.07
kings who were b. the Jordan in 9.01
Amorites who were b. the Jordan, 9.10
of their land b. the Jordan toward 12.01
b. the Jordan eastward, as Moses the 13.08
Chinnereth, eastward b. the Jordan. 13.27
b. the Jordan east of Jericho. 13.32
and one-half tribes b. the Jordan; 14.03
passes along b. it on the east to 16.06

BEYOND (cont.)
inheritance b. the Jordan eastward, Jos 18.07
And b. the Jordan east of Jericho, 20.08
lived of old b. the Euphrates, 24.02
Abraham from b. the River and led 24.03
your fathers served b. the River, 24.14
served in the region b. the River, 24.15
and passed b. the sculptured stones, Ju 3.26
Gilead stayed b. the Jordan; 5.17
and Zeeb to Gideon b. the Jordan. 7.25
that were b. the Jordan in the 10.08
and the battle passed b. Bethaven. 1Sa 14.23
the arrows are b. you,' then go; 20.22
lad ran, he shot an arrow b. him. 20.36
and said, "Is not the arrow b. you?" 20.37
and those b. the Jordan saw that 31.07
Syrians who were b. the Euphrates; 2Sa 10.16
had passed a little b. the summit, 16.01
but he delayed b. the set time 20.05
and understanding b. measure, 1Ki 4.29
and scatter them b. the Euphrates, 14.15
of all these vessels was b. weight. 2Ki 25.16
and b. the Jordan at Jericho, on the 1Ch 6.78
of Manasseh from b. the Jordan, 12.37
Syrians who were b. the Euphrates, 19.16
bronze in quantities b. weighing, 22.03
and bronze and iron b. weighing, 22.14
you from Edom, from b. the sea; 2Ch 20.02
rest of the province B. the River, Ez 4.10
men of the province B. the River, 4.11
in the province B. the River. 4.16
rest of the province B. the River, 4.17
the whole province B. the River, 4.20
of the province B. the River and 5.03
of the province B. the River and 5.06
in the province B. the River sent 5.06
of the province B. the River, 6.06
are in the province B. the River, 6.06
of the province from B. the River. 6.08
of the province B. the River, 6.13
in the province B. the River: 7.21
in the province B. the River, 7.25
of the province B. the River; 8.36
of the province B. the River, Neh 2.07
of the province B. the River, 2.09
of the province B. the River. 3.07
does great things b. understanding, Job 9.10
his understanding is b. measure. Ps 147.05
he will be broken b. healing. Pro 6.15
will suddenly be broken b. healing. 29.01
My son, beware of anything b. these. Ecc 12.12
and opened its mouth b. measure, Is 5.14
razor which is hired b. the River— 7.20
the land b. the Jordan, Galilee of 9.01
wings which is b. the rivers of 18.01
b. human semblance, and his form 52.14
and his form b. that of the sons of 52.14
be like this day, great b. measure." 56.12
My grief is b. healing, my heart is Jer 8.18
and cast forth b. the gates of 22.19
of all these things was b. weight. 52.20
breadth, twenty cubits, b. the nave. Eze 41.04
take you into exile b. Damascus, Amo 5.27
From b. the rivers of Ethiopia my Zep 3.10
the LORD, b. the border of Israel!" Mal 1.05
and Judea and from b. the Jordan. Mt 4.25
the region of Judea b. the Jordan; 19.01
Idumea and from b. the Jordan and Mk 3.08
And they were astonished b. measure, 7.37
region of Judea and b. the Jordan, 10.01
place in Bethany b. the Jordan, Jn 1.28
he who was with you b. the Jordan, 3.26
and I will remove you b. Babylon.' Ac 7.43
might become sinful b. measure. Rom 7.13
B. that, I do not know whether I 1Co 1.16
you be tempted b. your strength, 10.13
weight of glory b. all comparison, 2Co 4.17
and b. their means, of their own 8.03
But we will not boast b. limit, 10.13
We do not boast b. limit, 10.15
preach the gospel in lands b. you, 10.16
in Judaism b. many of my own age Gal 1.14
oil of gladness b. thy comrades." Heb 1.09
It is b. dispute that the inferior 7.07

BEZAI
The sons of B., three hundred and Ez 2.17
The sons of B., three hundred and Neh 7.23
Hodiah, Hashum, B., 10.18

BEZALEL
called by name B. the son of Uri, Ex 31.02
called by name B. the son of Uri, 35.30
B. and Oholiab and every able man 36.01
And Moses called B. and Oholiab and 36.02
B. made the ark of acacia wood; 37.01
B. the son of Uri, son of Hur, of the 38.22
Uri, and Uri was the father of B. 1Ch 2.20
altar that B. the son of Uri, 2Ch 1.05
Mattaniah, B., Binnui, and Manasseh. Ez 10.30

BEZEK
defeated ten thousand of them at B. Ju 1.04
They came upon Adonibezek at B., 1.05
When he mustered them at B., 1Sa 11.08

BEZER
B. in the wilderness on the tableland Deu 4.43
they appointed B. in the wilderness Jos 20.08
B. with its pasture lands, Jahaz 21.36
B. in the steppe with its pasture 1Ch 6.78
B., Hod, Shamma, Shilshah, Ithran, and 7.37

BICHRI
the son of B., a Benjaminite; 2Sa 20.01
and followed Sheba the son of B.; 20.02
the son of B. will do us more harm 20.06
to pursue Sheba the son of B. 20.07
pursued Sheba the son of B. 20.10
Joab to pursue Sheba the son of B. 20.13
Ephraim, called Sheba the son of B., 20.21
the head of Sheba the son of B., 20.22

BICHRITES
and all the B. assembled, and 2Sa 20.14

BID
and b. them to make tassels on the Num 15.38
but only what I b. you, that shall 22.20
but only the word which I b. you, 22.35
"What does my lord b. his servant?" Jos 5.14
until the day I b. you shout; 6.10
be before you b. your people turn 2Sa 2.26
and go in and b. him rise from 2Ki 9.02
and we will do all that you b. us. 10.05
b. steadfast love and faithfulness Ps 61.07
b. me come to you on the water." Mt 14.28
you want us to b. fire come down Lk 9.54
b. my brother divide the inheritance 12.13
I now b. you take heart; for there Ac 27.22
given to me I b. every one among Rom 12.03
B. the older men be temperate, Tit 2.02
B. the older women likewise to be 2.03
B. slaves to be submissive to their 2.09

BIDDEN
of Israel, as Moses had b. them; Jos 4.12
on fire, doing as the LORD has b.; 8.08
him curse; for the LORD has b. him. 2Sa 16.11
I say as the Father has b. me." Jn 12.50

BIDDING
b. them make an image for the beast Rev 13.14

BIDKAR
Jehu said to B. his aide, "Take him 2Ki 9.25

BIDS
and b. defiance to the Almighty, Job 15.25

BIER
And King David followed the b. 2Sa 3.31
laid him on a b. which had been 2Ch 16.14
And he came and touched the b., Lk 7.14

BIGTHA
B. and Abagtha, Zethar and Carkas, Est 1.10

BIGTHAN
B. and Teresh, two of the king's Est 2.21

BIGTHANA
had told about B. and Teresh, Est 6.02

BIGVAI
Mispar, B., Rehum, and Baanah. Ez 2.02
The sons of B., two thousand and 2.14
Of the sons of B., Uthai and Zakkur, 8.14
Mispereth, B., Nehum, Baanah. Neh 7.07
The sons of B., two thousand and 7.19
Adonijah, B., Adin, 10.16

BILDAD
B. the Shuhite, and Zophar the Job 2.11
Then B. the Shuhite answered: 8.01
Then B. the Shuhite answered: 18.01
Then B. the Shuhite answered: 25.01
Temanite and B. the Shuhite and 42.09

BILEAM
and B. with its pasture lands, for 1Ch 6.70

BILGAH
the fifteenth to B., the sixteenth 1Ch 24.14
Mijamin, Maadiah, B., Neh 12.05
of B., Shammua; of Shemaiah, 12.18

BILGAI
Maaziah, B., Shemaiah; these are Neh 10.08

BILHAH
(Laban gave his maid B. to his Gen 29.29
Then she said, "Here is my maid B.; 30.03
she gave him her maid B. as a wife; 30.04
And B. conceived and bore Jacob a 30.05
Rachel's maid B. conceived again and 30.07
and lay with B. his father's concubine, 35.22
The sons of B., Rachel's maid: Dan 35.25
lad with the sons of B. and Zilpah, 37.02
(these are the sons of B., whom Laban 46.25
B., Ezem, Tolad, 1Ch 4.29
and Shallum, the offspring of B. 7.13

BILHAN
sons of Ezer: B., Zaavan, and Akan. Gen 36.27
B., Zaavan, and Jaakan. The sons of 1Ch 1.42
The sons of Jediael: B. And the 7.10
And the sons of B.: Jeush, 7.10

BILL
he writes her a b. of divorce and Deu 24.01
writes her a b. of divorce and 24.03
is your mother's b. of divorce, Is 50.01
'Take your b., and sit down quickly Lk 16.06
'Take your b., and write eighty.' 16.07

BILLOWS
waves and thy b. have gone over me. Ps 42.07
waves and thy b. passed over me. Jon 2.03

BILSHAN
B., Mispar, Bigvai, Rehum, and Baanah. Ez 2.02
B., Mispereth, Bigvai, Nehum, Baanah. Neh 7.07

BIMHAL
Japhlet: Pasach, B., and Ashvath. 1Ch 7.33

BIND
And they shall b. the breastpiece Ex 28.28
with girdles and b. caps on them; 29.09
an oath to b. himself by a pledge, Num 30.02
And you shall b. them as a sign Deu 6.08
and you shall b. them as a sign 11.18
and b. up the money in your hand, 14.25
you shall b. this scarlet cord in Jos 2.18
said, "We have come up to b. Samson, Ju 15.10
him, "We have come down to b. you, 15.12
we will only b. you and give you 15.13
that we may b. him to subdue him; 16.05
"If they b. me with seven fresh 16.07
"If they b. me with new ropes that 16.11
I would b. it on me as a crown; Job 31.36
"Can you b. the chains of the 38.31
Can you b. him in the furrow with 39.10
b. their faces in the world below. 40.13
B. the festal procession with Ps 118.27
to b. their kings with chains and 149.08
b. them about your neck, write them Pro 3.03
B. them upon your heart always; 6.21
b. them on your fingers, write them 7.03
B. up the testimony, seal the Is 8.16
and will b. your girdle on him, and 22.21
you shall b. them on as a bride 49.18
has sent me to b. up the brokenhearted, 61.01
b. a stone to it, and cast it into Jer 51.63
and b. them in the skirts of your Eze 5.03
B. on your turban, and put your 24.17
and I will b. up the crippled, and I 34.16
men of his army to b. Shadrach, Dan 3.20
has stricken, and he will b. us up. Hos 6.01
weeds first and b. them in bundles Mt 13.30
whatever you b. on earth shall be 16.19
whatever you b. on earth shall be 18.18
'B. him hand and foot, and cast him 22.13
They b. heavy burdens, hard to bear, 23.04
and no one could b. him any more, Mk 5.03
priests to b. all who call upon Ac 9.14
at Jerusalem b. the man who owns 21.11

BINDER
his hand or the b. of sheaves his Ps 129.07

BINDERS
and timber for b. and beams for 2Ch 34.11

BINDING
we were b. sheaves in the field, and Gen 37.07
B. his foal to the vine and his 49.11
with a woven b. around the opening, Ex 28.32
with a b. around the opening, that 39.23
of the ephod, b. it to him therewith. Lev 8.07
Any vow and any b. oath to afflict Num 30.13
to heal it by b. it with a bandage, Eze 30.21
b. and delivering to prison both Ac 22.04
that the law is b. on a person only during Rom 7.01

BINDS
and b. herself by a pledge, while Num 30.03
For he wounds, but he b. up; Job 5.18
and b. a waistcloth on their loins. 12.18
He b. up the waters in his thick 26.08
He b. up the streams so that they 28.11
it b. me about like the collar of 30.18
not cry for help when he b. them. 36.13
brokenhearted, and b. up their wounds. Ps 147.03
Like one who b. the stone in the Pro 26.08
when the LORD b. up the hurt of Is 30.26
unless he first b. the strong man? Mt 12.29
unless he first b. the strong man; Mk 3.27
which b. everything together in Col 3.14

BINEA
Moza was the father of B.; Raphah was 1Ch 8.37
Moza was the father of B.; and Rephaiah 9.43

BINNUI
Jeshua and Noadiah the son of B. Ez 8.33
Mattaniah, Bezalel, B., and Manasseh. 10.30
Of the sons of B.: Shimei, 10.38
After him B. the son of Henadad Neh 3.24
The sons of B., six hundred and 7.15
B. of the sons of Henadad, Kadmiel; 10.09
B., Kadmiel, Sherebiah, Judah, and 12.08

BIRD
every winged b. according to its Gen 1.21
and to every b. of the air, and to 1.30
the field and every b. of the air, 2.19
and every b. according to its kind, 7.14
its kind, every b. of every sort. 7.14
and every b., everything that moves 8.19
clean animal and of every clean b., 8.20
and upon every b. of the air, 9.02
to beast and b. and every living Lev 11.46
take the living b. with the 14.06
and the living b. in the blood of 14.06
blood of the b. that was killed 14.06
let the living b. go into the open 14.07
stuff, along with the living b., 14.51
blood of the b. that was killed 14.51
the house with the blood of the b., 14.52
water, and with the living b., 14.52
let the living b. go out of the 14.53
any beast or b. that may be eaten 17.13
the unclean b. and the clean; 20.25
by beast or by b. or by anything 20.25
of any winged b. that flies in the Deu 4.17
"That path no b. of prey knows, and Job 28.07
Will you play with him as with a b., 41.05
"Flee like a b. to the mountains; Ps 11.01
like a lonely b. on the housetop. 102.07
escaped as a b. from the snare of 124.07
net spread in the sight of any b.; Pro 1.17
like a b. from the hand of the 6.05
as a b. rushes into a snare; 7.23
Like a b. that strays from its nest, 27.08
for a b. of the air will carry your Ecc 10.20
one rises up at the voice of a b., 12.04
calling a b. of prey from the east, Is 46.11
to me like a speckled b. of prey? Jer 12.09
hunted like a b. by those who were Lam 3.52
whether b. or beast, that has died Eze 44.31
four wings of a b. on its back; Dan 7.06
Ephraim's glory shall fly away like a b.— Hos 9.11
Does a b. fall in a snare on the Amo 3.05
For every kind of beast and b., Jas 3.07
haunt of every foul and hateful b.; Rev 18.02

BIRD'S
"If you chance to come upon a b. nest, Deu 22.06

BIRDS
and let b. fly above the earth Gen 1.20
and let b. multiply on the earth." 1.22
and over the b. of the air, and over 1.26
and over the b. of the air and 1.28
and to the b. of the air, and to 2.20
creeping things and b. of the air, 6.07
Of the b. according to their kinds, 6.20
pairs of the b. of the air also, 7.03
and of b., and of everything that 7.08
b., cattle, beasts, all swarming 7.21
creeping things and b. of the air; 7.23
b. and animals and every creeping 8.17
the b., the cattle, and every beast 9.10
but he did not cut the b. in two. 15.10
And when b. of prey came down upon 15.11
but the b. were eating it out of 40.17
and the b. will eat the flesh from 40.19
the LORD is a burnt offering of b., Lev 1.14
have in abomination among the b., 11.13
living clean b. and cedarwood and 14.04
kill one of the b. in an earthen 14.05
house he shall take two small b., 14.49
kill one of the b. in an earthen 14.50
"You may eat all clean b. Deu 14.11
be food for all b. of the air, 28.26
flesh to the b. of the air and to 1Sa 17.44
this day to the b. of the air and 17.46
not allow the b. of the air to 2Sa 21.10
and of b., and of reptiles, and of 1Ki 4.33
country the b. of the air shall 14.11
the field the b. of the air shall 16.04
country the b. of the air shall 21.24
the b. of the air, and they will Job 12.07
concealed from the b. of the air. 28.21
us wiser than the b. of the air?' 35.11
the b. of the air, and the fish of Ps 8.08
I know all the b. of the air, and 50.11
winged b. like the sand of the seas; 78.27
servants to the b. of the air for 79.02
By them the b. of the air have 104.12
In them the b. build their nests; 104.17
creeping things and flying b.! 148.10
and like b. which are caught in a Ecc 9.12
Like fluttering b., like scattered Is 16.02
be left to the b. of prey of the 18.06
And the b. of prey will summer upon 18.06
Like b. hovering, so the LORD of 31.05
and all the b. of the air had fled. Jer 4.25
Like a basket full of b., their houses 5.27
will be food for the b. of the air, 7.33
both the b. of the air and the 9.10
beasts and the b. are swept away, 12.04
Are the b. of prey against her 12.09
and the b. of the air and the 15.03
be food for the b. of the air and 16.04
for food to the b. of the air and 19.07
be food for the b. of the air and 34.20
that you hunt go free like b. Eze 13.20
of its branches b. of every sort 17.23
and to the b. of the air I have 29.05
All the b. of the air made their 31.06
will dwell all the b. of the air, 31.13
cause all the b. of the air to 32.04
and the b. of the air, and the 38.20
give you to b. of prey of every 39.04
Speak to the b. of every sort and 39.17
and the b. of the air, making you Dan 2.38
and the b. of the air dwelt in its 4.12
it and the b. from its branches. 4.14
branches the b. of the air dwelt— 4.21
the b. of the air, and the creeping Hos 2.18
the field, and the b. of the air; 4.03
bring them down like b. of the air; 7.12
come eagerly like b. from Egypt, 11.11
sweep away the b. of the air and Zep 1.03
Look at the b. of the air: they Mt 6.26
and b. of the air have nests; 8.20
and the b. came and devoured them. 13.04
so that the b. of the air come and 13.32
and the b. came and devoured it. Mk 4.04
so that the b. of the air can make 4.32
and the b. of the air devoured it. Lk 8.05
and b. of the air have nests; 9.58
more value are you than the b.! 12.24
and the b. of the air made nests in 13.19
and reptiles and b. of the air. Ac 10.12
and reptiles and b. of the air. 11.06
mortal man or b. or animals or Rom 1.23
another for b., and another for 1Co 15.39
to all the b. that fly in midheaven, Rev 19.17
and all the b. were gorged with 19.21

BIRDS'
and his nails were like b. claws. Dan 4.33

BIRSHA
B. king of Gomorrah, Shinab king of Gen 14.02

BIRTH

Seth lived after the b. of Enosh Gen 5.07
Enosh lived after the b. of Kenan 5.10
Kenan lived after the b. of Mahalalel 5.13
Mahalalel lived after the b. of 5.16
Jared lived after the b. of Enoch 5.19
God after the b. of Methuselah 5.22
Methuselah lived after the b. of 5.26
Lamech lived after the b. of Noah 5.30
lived after the b. of Arpachshad 11.11
lived after the b. of Shelah four 11.13
lived after the b. of Eber four 11.15
lived after the b. of Peleg four 11.17
lived after the b. of Reu two 11.19
lived after the b. of Serug two 11.21
lived after the b. of Nahor two 11.23
lived after the b. of Terah a 11.25
father Terah in the land of his b., 11.28
house and from the land of my b., 24.07
named in the order of their b.: 25.13
and return to the land of your b.' " 31.13
stone, in the order of their b. Ex 28.10
you forgot the God who gave you b. Deu 32.18
shall be a Nazirite to God from b.; Ju 13.05
to God from b. to the day of his 13.07
was with child, about to give b. 1Sa 4.19
were dead, she bowed and gave b.; 4.19
and I gave b. to a child while she 1Ki 3.17
delivered, this woman also gave b.; 3.18
children have come to the b., 2Ki 19.03
mouth and cursed the day of his b. Job 3.01
"Why did I not die at b., come forth 3.11
was I not as a hidden untimely b., 3.16
who has given b. to the hoarfrost 38.29
Upon thee was I cast from my b., Ps 22.10
err from their b., speaking lies. 58.03
the untimely b. that never sees 58.08
Upon thee I have leaned from by b.; 71.06
an untimely b. is better off than Ecc 6.03
day of death, than the day of b. 7.01
sepulchre, like a loathed untimely b., Is 14.19
neither travailed nor given b., 23.04
children have come to the b., 37.03
have been borne by me from your b., 46.03
and that from b. you were called a 48.08
"Before she was in labor she gave b.; 66.07
Shall I bring to the b. and not 66.09
and to a stone, 'You gave me b.' Jer 2.27
people and to the land of our b., 46.16
origin and your b. are of the land Eze 16.03
And as for your b., on the day 16.04
by b. a Mede, who became king over Dan 9.01
no b., no pregnancy, no conception! Hos 9.11
Now the b. of Jesus Christ took Mt 1.18
eunuchs who have been so from b., 19.12
a Greek, a Syrophoenician by b. Mk 7.26
and many will rejoice at his b.; Lk 1.14
delivered, and she gave b. to a son. 1.57
And she gave b. to her first-born 2.07
by, he saw a man blind from his b. Jn 9.01
And a man lame from b. was being Ac 3.02
he was a cripple from b., who had 14.08
powerful, not many were of noble b.; 1Co 1.26
who are Jews by b. and not Gentile Gal 2.15
it has conceived gives b. to sin; Jas 1.15
she cried out in her pangs of b., Rev 12.02

BIRTHDAY

third day, which was Pharaoh's b., Gen 40.20
But when Herod's b. came, the Mt 14.06
Herod on his b. gave a banquet for Mk 6.21

BIRTHRIGHT

Jacob said, "First sell me your b." Gen 25.31
of what use is a b. to me?" 25.32
to him, and sold his b. to Jacob. 25.33
Thus Esau despised his b. 25.34
He took away my b.; and behold, 27.36
according to his b. and the youngest 43.33
his b. was given to the sons of 1Ch 5.01
the genealogy according to the b.; 5.01
yet the b. belonged to Joseph), 5.02
who sold his b. for a single meal. Heb 12.16

BIRTHSTOOL

women, and see them upon the b., Ex 1.16

BIRZAITH

Malchiel, who was the father of B. 1Ch 7.31

BISHLAM

B. and Mithredath and Tabeel and Ez 4.07

BISHOP

one aspires to the office of b., 1Ti 3.01
Now a b. must be above reproach, 3.02
For a b., as God's steward, must be Tit 1.07

BISHOPS

Philippi, with the b. and deacons: Php 1.01

BIT

and they b. the people, so that many Num 21.06
and if a serpent b. any man, 21.09
your nose and my b. in your mouth, 2Ki 19.28
must be curbed with b. and bridle, Ps 32.09
your nose and my b. in your mouth, Is 37.29
the wall, and a serpent b. him. Amo 5.19

BITE

a serpent will b. him who breaks Ecc 10.08
be charmed, and they shall b. you, Jer 8.17
the serpent, and it shall b. them. Amo 9.03
But if you b. and devour one Gal 5.15

BITES

that b. the horse's heels so that Gen 49.17
At the last it b. like a serpent, Pro 23.32
If the serpent b. before it is Ecc 10.11

BITHIAH

These are the sons of B., the daughter 1Ch 4.17

BITHYNIA

they attempted to go into B., Ac 16.07
Galatia, Cappadocia, Asia, and B., 1Pe 1.01

BITS

and the little house into b. Amo 6.11
If we put b. into the mouths of Jas 3.03

BITTEN

and every one who is b., when he sees Num 21.08

BITTER

and they made life b. for Isaac and Gen 26.35
an exceedingly great and b. cry, 27.34
their lives b. with hard service, Ex 1.14
bread and b. herbs they shall eat 12.08
water of Marah because it was b.; 15.23
enter into her and cause b. pain. Num 5.24
enter into her and cause b. pain, 5.27
with unleavened bread and b. herbs. 9.11
bearing poisonous and b. fruit, Deu 29.18
of poison, their clusters are b.; 32.32
is exceedingly b. to me for your Ru 1.13
all the people were b. in soul, 1Sa 30.06
not know that the end will be b.? 2Sa 2.26
alone, for she is in b. distress; 2Ki 4.27
affliction of Israel was very b., 14.26
wailing with a loud and b. cry; Est 4.01
and life to the b. in soul, Job 3.20
For thou writest b. things against 13.26
"Today also my complaint is b., 23.02
Almighty, who has made my soul b.; 27.02
who aim b. words like arrows, Ps 64.03

BITTER (cont.)
for they made his spirit b., Ps 106.33
but in the end she is b. as wormwood, Pro 5.04
is hungry everything b. is sweet. 27.07
and wine to those in b. distress; 31.06
And I found more b. than death the Ecc 7.26
who put b. for sweet and sweet for b.! Is 5.20
away from me, let me weep b. tears; 22.04
strong drink is b. to those who 24.09
it is evil and b. for you to Jer 2.19
This is your doom, and it is b.; 4.18
an only son, most b. lamentation; 6.26
Ramah, lamentation and b. weeping. 31.15
heart and b. grief before their Eze 21.06
bitterness of soul, with b. mourning. 27.31
Ephraim has given b. provocation; Hos 12.14
and the end of it like a b. day. Amo 8.10
and wail with b. lamentation, and Mic 2.04
that b. and hasty nation, who march Hab 1.06
sound of the day of the LORD is b., Zep 1.14
But if you have b. jealousy and Jas 3.14
the water, because it was made b. Rev 8.11
it will be b. to your stomach, but 10.09
eaten it my stomach was made b. 10.10

BITTERLY
curse b. its inhabitants, because Ju 5.23
lifted up their voices and wept b. 21.02
Almighty has dealt very b. with me. Ru 1.20
prayed to the LORD, and wept b. 1Sa 1.10
and all his servants wept very b. 2Sa 13.36
thy sight." And Hezekiah wept b. 2Ki 20.03
of Israel; for the people wept b. Ez 10.01
the envoys of peace weep b. Is 33.07
thy sight." And Hezekiah wept b. 38.03
eyes will weep b. and run down Jer 13.17
but weep b. for him who goes away, 22.10
She weeps b. in the night, tears on Lam 1.02
away, and she herself suffers b. 1.04
and wail aloud over you, and cry b. Eze 27.30
and weep b. over him, as one weeps Zec 12.10
three times." And he went out and wept b. Mt 26.75
And he went out and wept b. Lk 22.62

BITTERNESS
the water of b. that brings the Num 5.18
this water of b. that brings the 5.19
wash them off into the water of b.; 5.23
the water of b. that brings the 5.24
"Surely the b. of death is past." 1Sa 15.32
will complain in the b. of my soul. Job 7.11
my breath, but fills me with b. 9.18
I will speak in the b. of my soul. 10.01
Another dies in b. of soul, 21.25
The heart knows its own b., Pro 14.10
his father and b. to her who bore 17.25
fled because of the b. of my soul. Is 38.15
for my welfare that I had great b.; 38.17
affliction and b. all the precious Lam 1.07
enveloped me with b. and tribulation; 3.05
He has filled me with b., he has 3.15
Remember my affliction and my b., 3.19
and I went in b. in the heat of my Eze 3.14
they weep over you in b. of soul, 27.31
in the gall of b. and in the bond Ac 8.23
"Their mouth is full of curses and b." Rom 3.14
Let all b. and wrath and anger and Eph 4.31
that no "root of b." spring up and Heb 12.15

BITUMEN
brick for stone, and b. for mortar. Gen 11.03
of Siddim was full of b. pits; 14.10
and daubed it with b. and pitch; Ex 2.03

BIZIOTHIAH
Hazarshual, Beersheba, B., Jos 15.28

BIZTHA
B., Harbona, Bigtha and Abagtha, Est 1.10

BLACK
spotted sheep and every b. lamb, Gen 30.32
the goats and b. among the lambs, 30.33
on it, and every lamb that was b., 30.35
and all the b. in the flock of 30.40
skin and there is no b. hair in it, Lev 13.31
and b. hair has grown in it, the 13.37
heavens grew b. with clouds and 1Ki 18.45
My skin turns b. and falls from me, Job 30.30
his locks are wavy, b. as a raven. Sol 5.11
mourn, and the heavens above be b.; Jer 4.28
and the day shall be b. over them; Mic 3.06
red horses, the second b. horses, Zec 6.02
with the b. horses goes toward the 6.06
cannot make one hair white or b. Mt 5.36
a b. horse, and its rider had a Rev 6.05
and the sun became b. as sackcloth, 6.12

BLACKENED
I go about b., but not by the sun; Job 30.28

BLACKER
Now their visage is b. than soot, Lam 4.08

BLACKNESS
let the b. of the day terrify it. Job 3.05
I clothe the heavens with b., and make Is 50.03
Like b. there is spread upon the Joe 2.02

BLADE
the hilt also went in after the b., Ju 3.22
and the fat closed over the b., 3.22
then let my shoulder b. fall from Job 31.22
first the b., then the ear, then the Mk 4.28

BLAME
then let me bear the b. for ever; Gen 43.09
shall bear the b. in the sight of 44.32
no one should b. us about this 2Co 8.20

BLAMELESS
b. in his generation; Gen 6.09
walk before me, and be b. 17.01
and the rest of you shall be b." 44.10
You shall be b. before the LORD Deu 18.13
time I shall be b. in regard to Ju 15.03
that you are as b. in my sight as 1Sa 29.09
I was b. before him, and I kept 2Sa 22.24
with the b. man thou dost show 22.26
man thou dost show thyself b.; 22.26
heart of Asa was b. all his days. 2Ch 15.17
those whose heart is b. toward him. 16.09
the LORD, yet not with a b. heart. 25.02
and that man was b. and upright, Job 1.01
a b. and upright man, who fears God 1.08
a b. and upright man, who fears God 2.03
"Behold, God will not reject a b. man, 8.20
though I am b., he would prove me 9.20
I am b.; I regard not 9.21
destroys both the b. and the wicked. 9.22
a just and b. man, am a laughingstock 12.04
to him if you make your ways b.? 22.03
I was b. before him, and I kept Ps 18.23
b. man thou dost show thyself b.; 18.25
Then I shall be b., and innocent 19.13
The LORD knows the days of the b., 37.18
Mark the b. man, and behold the 37.37
sentence and b. in thy judgment. 51.04
shooting from ambush at the b., 64.04
give heed to the way that is b. 101.02
the way that is b. shall minister 101.06
Blessed are those whose way is b., 119.01
May my heart be b. in thy statutes, 119.80
righteousness of the b. keeps his Pro 11.05
but those of b. ways are his 11.20

BLAMELESS (cont.)
but the b. will have a goodly Pro 28.10
Bloodthirsty men hate one who is b., 29.10
You were b. in your ways from the Eze 28.15
because I was found b. before him; Dan 6.22
and ordinances of the Lord b. Lk 1.06
should be holy and b. before him. Eph 1.04
may be pure and b. for the day of Php 1.10
that you may be b. and innocent, 2.15
to righteousness under the law b. 3.06
you holy and b. and irreproachable Col 1.22
righteous and b. was our behavior 1Th 2.10
kept sound and b. at the coming of 5.23
themselves b. let them serve as 1Ti 3.10
men who are b., married only once, Tit 1.06
as God's steward, must be b.; 1.07
b., unstained, separated from Heb 7.26

BLAMELESSLY
He who walks b., and does what is Ps 15.02

BLASPHEME
synagogues and tried to make them b.; Ac 26.11
that they may learn not to b. 1Ti 1.20
Is it not they who b. that honorable Jas 2.07

BLASPHEMED
Israelite woman's son b. the Name, Lev 24.11
In this again your fathers b. me, Eze 20.27
name of God is b. among the Rom 2.24
though I formerly b. and persecuted 1Ti 1.13

BLASPHEMERS
sacrilegious nor b. of our goddess. Ac 19.37

BLASPHEMES
He who b. the name of the LORD Lev 24.16
when he b. the Name, shall be put to 24.16
but whoever b. against the Holy Mk 3.29
but he who b. against the Holy Lk 12.10

BLASPHEMIES
of Egypt,' and had committed great b., Neh 9.18
thee, and they committed great b. 9.26
of men, and whatever b. they utter; Mk 3.28
saying, "Who is this that speaks b.? Lk 5.21
its mouth to utter b. against God, Rev 13.06

BLASPHEMING
knew, because his sons were b. God, 1Sa 3.13
said to themselves, "This man is b." Mt 9.03
'You are b.,' because I said, 'I am Jn 10.36
b. his name and his dwelling, that Rev 13.06

BLASPHEMOUS
heard him speak b. words against Ac 6.11
its horns and a b. name upon its Rev 13.01
uttering haughty and b. words, 13.05
beast which was full of b. names, 17.03

BLASPHEMY
every sin and b. will be forgiven Mt 12.31
but the b. against the Spirit will 12.31
robes, and said, "He has uttered b. 26.65
witnesses? You have now heard his b. 26.65
It is b.! Who can Mk 2.07
You have heard his b. What is 14.64
you for no good work but for b.; Jn 10.33

BLAST
At the b. of thy nostrils the Ex 15.08
When the trumpet sounds a long b., 19.13
mountain, and a very loud trumpet b., 19.16
proclaimed with b. of trumpets, Lev 23.24
make a long b. with the ram's horn, Jos 6.05
at the b. of the breath of his 2Sa 22.16
and by the b. of his anger they are Job 4.09
at the b. of the breath of thy Ps 18.15
for the b. of the ruthless is like Is 25.04
with his fierce b. in the day of 27.08
a day of trumpet b. and battle cry Zep 1.16

BLASTING
and with b., and with mildew; Deu 28.22

BLASTS
at the b. of the other trumpets Rev 8.13

BLASTUS
in a body, and having persuaded B., Ac 12.20

BLAZE
take up the censers out of the b.; Num 16.37

BLAZED
and the anger of the LORD b. hotly, Num 11.10
they b. like a fire of thorns; Ps 118.12

BLAZES
the morning it b. like a flaming Hos 7.06

BLAZING
make them as a b. oven when you Ps 21.09
the b. flame shall not be quenched, Eze 20.47
and in my b. wrath I declare, On 38.19
of Judah like a b. pot in the Zec 12.06
a b. fire, and darkness, and gloom, Heb 12.18
b. like a torch, and it fell on a Rev 8.10

BLEACH
no fuller on earth could b. them. Mk 9.03

BLEATING
then is this b. of the sheep in my 1Sa 15.14

BLEEDING
bruises and sores and b. wounds; Is 1.06

BLEMISH
Your lamb shall be without b., Ex 12.05
bull and two rams without b., 29.01
he shall offer a male without b.; Lev 1.03
he shall offer a male without b.; 1.10
it without b. before the LORD. 3.01
he shall offer it without b. 3.06
bull without b. to the LORD for a 4.03
offering a goat, a male without b., 4.23
a goat, a female without b., 4.28
shall bring a female without b., 4.32
a ram without b. out of the flock, 5.15
a ram without b. out of the flock, 5.18
a ram without b. out of the flock, 6.06
both without b., and offer them 9.02
a lamb, both a year old without b., 9.03
take two male lambs without b., 14.10
one ewe lamb a year old without b., 14.10
who has a b. may approach to offer 21.17
one who has a b. shall draw near, a 21.18
who has a b. shall come near to 21.21
since he has a b., he shall 21.21
the altar, because he has a b., 21.23
you shall offer a male without b., 22.19
not offer anything that has a b., 22.20
there shall be no b. in it. 22.21
Since there is a b. in them, 22.25
old without b. as a burnt offering 23.12
seven lambs a year old without b., 23.18
old without b. for a burnt offering, Num 6.14
old without b. as a sin offering, 6.14
one ram without b. as a peace 6.14
defect, in which there is no b., 19.02
male lambs a year old without b., 28.03
male lambs a year old without b., 28.09
male lambs a year old without b.; 28.11
see that they are without b.; 28.19
See that they are without b. 28.31

BLEMISH (cont.)
male lambs a year old without b.; Num 29.02
they shall be to you without b.; 29.08
old; they shall be without b.; 29.13
male lambs a year old without b., 29.17
male lambs a year old without b., 29.20
male lambs a year old without b., 29.23
male lambs a year old without b., 29.26
male lambs a year old without b., 29.29
male lambs a year old without b., 29.32
male lambs a year old without b., 29.36
But if it has any b., if it is Deu 15.21
or has any serious b. whatever, 15.21
an ox or a sheep in which is a b., 17.01
his children because of their b.; 32.05
of his head there was no b. in him. 2Sa 14.25
will lift up your face without b.; Job 11.15
he-goat without b. for a sin Eze 43.22
a bull without b. and a ram from 43.23
a ram from the flock without b. 43.23
without b., shall be provided. 43.25
shall take a young bull without b., 45.18
bulls and seven rams without b., 45.23
lambs without b. and a ram without b.; 46.04
offer a young bull without b., 46.06
a ram, which shall be without b.; 46.06
old without b. for a burnt offering 46.13
youths without b., handsome and Dan 1.04
she might be holy and without b. Eph 5.27
of God without b. in the midst of Php 2.15
offered himself without b. to God, Heb 9.14
that of a lamb without b. or spot. 1Pe 1.19
without spot or b., and at peace. 2Pe 3.14
you without b. before the presence Jud 1.24

BLEMISHED
sacrifices to the Lord what is b.; Mal 1.14

BLEMISHES
They are blots and b., 2Pe 2.13
These are b. on your love feasts, as Jud 1.12

BLENDED
anointing oil b. as by the perfumer Ex 30.25
and make an incense b. as by the 30.35
incense, b. as by the perfumer. 37.29

BLESS
and I will b. you, and make your Gen 12.02
I will b. those who b. you, and 12.03
of the earth will b. themselves. 12.03
I will b. her, and moreover I will 17.16
I will b. her, and she shall be a 17.16
I will b. him and make him fruitful 17.20
the earth shall b. themselves by 18.18
I will indeed b. you, and I will 22.17
nations of the earth b. themselves, 22.18
will be with you, and will b. you; 26.03
of the earth shall b. themselves: 26.04
you and will b. you and multiply 26.24
that I may b. you before I die." 27.04
and b. you before the LORD before I 27.07
so that he may b. you before he 27.10
eat of my game, that you may b. me." 27.19
eat of my son's game and b. you." 27.25
his son's game, that you may b. me." 27.31
"B. me, even me also, O my father!" 27.34
B. me, even me also, O my father." 27.38
God Almighty b. you and make you 28.03
families of the earth b. themselves. 28.14
not let you go, unless you b. me." 32.26
me, I pray you, that I may b. them." 48.09
me from all evil, b. the lads; 48.16
who will b. you with blessings of 49.25
be gone; and b. me also!" Ex 12.32
I will come to you and b. you. 20.24
and I will b. your bread and your 23.25
Thus you shall b. the people of Num 6.23
The LORD b. you and keep you: 6.24
of Israel, and I will b. them." 6.27
that he whom you b. is blessed, 22.06
you have done nothing but b. them." 23.11
Behold, I received a command to b.: 23.20
them at all, nor b. them at all." 23.25
it pleased the LORD to b. Israel, 24.01
and b. you, as he has promised you! Deu 1.11
b. you, and multiply you; 7.13
he will also b. the fruit of your 7.13
and you shall b. the LORD your God 8.10
to him and to b. in his name, 10.08
your God may b. you in all the 14.29
the LORD will b. you in the land 15.04
For the LORD your God will b. you, 15.06
your God will b. you in all your 15.10
your God will b. you in all that 15.18
your God will b. you in all your 16.15
to him and to b. in the name of 21.05
your God may b. you in all that 23.20
may sleep in his cloak and b. you; 24.13
your God may b. you in all the 24.19
and b. thy people Israel and the 26.15
Mount Gerizim to b. the people: 27.12
and he will b. you in the land 28.08
season and to b. all the work of 28.12
your God will b. you in the land 30.16
B., O LORD, his substance, and accept 33.11
they should b. the people of Jos 8.33
themselves willingly, b. the LORD! Ju 5.02
the people. B. the LORD. 5.09
And they answered, "The LORD b. you." Ru 2.04
Then Eli would b. Elkanah and his 1Sa 2.20
since he must b. the sacrifice; 9.13
David returned to b. his household. 2Sa 6.20
please thee to b. the house of thy 7.29
that you may b. the heritage of the 21.03
thou wouldst b. me and enlarge my 1Ch 4.10
went home to b. his household. 16.43
please thee to b. the house of thy 17.27
"B. the LORD your God." And all the 29.20
"Stand up and b. the LORD your God Neh 9.05
For thou dost b. the righteous, O Ps 5.12
I b. the LORD who gives me counsel; 16.07
congregation I will b. the LORD. 26.12
thy people, and b. thy heritage; 28.09
May the LORD b. his people with 29.11
I will b. the LORD at all times; 34.01
They b. with their mouths, but 62.04
So I will b. thee as long as I live 63.04
B. our God, O peoples, let the sound 66.08
to us and b. us and make his face 67.01
"B. God in the great congregation, 68.26
May men b. themselves by him, all 72.17
Sing to the LORD, b. his name; 96.02
Give thanks to him, b. his name! 100.04
B. the LORD, O my soul; and all 103.01
is within me, b. his holy name! 103.01
B. the LORD, O my soul, and forget 103.02
B. the LORD, O you his angels, you 103.20
B. the LORD, all his hosts, his 103.21
B. the LORD, all his works, in all 103.22
B. the LORD, O my soul! 103.22
B. the LORD, O my soul! 104.01
B. the LORD, O my soul! 104.35
Let them curse, but do thou b.! 109.28
mindful of us; he will b. us; 115.12
he will b. the house of Israel; 115.12
he will b. the house of Aaron; 115.12
he will b. those who fear the LORD, 115.13
But we will b. the LORD from this 115.18
We b. you from the house of the 118.26
The LORD b. you from Zion! 128.05
We b. you in the name of the LORD!" 129.08
I will abundantly b. her provisions; 132.15
Come, b. the LORD, all you servants 134.01
to the holy place, and b. the LORD! 134.02

BLESS (cont.)
May the LORD b. you from Zion, he Ps 134.03
O house of Israel, b. the LORD! 135.19
O house of Aaron, b. the LORD! 135.19
O house of Levi, b. the LORD! 135.20
that fear the LORD, b. the LORD! 135.20
and b. thy name for ever and ever. 145.01
Every day I will b. thee, 145.02
and all thy saints shall b. thee! 145.10
let all flesh b. his holy name for 145.21
and do not b. their mothers. Pro 30.11
the land shall b. himself by the Is 65.16
nations shall b. themselves in him, Jer 4.02
'The LORD b. you, O habitation of 31.23
and I will b. them and multiply Eze 37.26
From this day on I will b. you. Hag 2.19
b. those who curse you, pray for Lk 6.28
to b. you in turning every one of Ac 3.26
B. those who persecute you; Rom 12.14
b. and do not curse them. 12.14
When reviled, we b.; when 1Co 4.12
The cup of blessing which we b., 10.16
if you b. with the spirit, how can 14.16
saying, "Surely I will b. you and Heb 6.14
With it we b. the Lord and Father, Jas 3.09
but on the contrary b., for to this 1Pe 3.09

BLESSED
And God b. them, saying, "Be fruitful Gen 1.22
And God b. them, and God said to 1.28
So God b. the seventh day and 2.03
and he b. them and named them Man 5.02
And God b. Noah and his sons, and 9.01
He also said, "B. by the LORD my God 9.26
And he b. him and said, "Blessed be 14.19
"B. be Abram by God Most High, maker 14.19
and b. be God Most High, who has 14.20
the LORD had b. Abraham in all 24.01
and said, "B. be the LORD, the God 24.27
He said, "Come in, O b. of the LORD; 24.31
The LORD has greatly b. my master, 24.35
and b. the LORD, the God of my 24.48
And they b. Rebekah, and said to her, 24.60
of Abraham God b. Isaac his son. 25.11
a hundred-fold. The LORD b. him, 26.12
You are now the b. of the LORD." 26.29
Esau's hands; so he b. him. 27.23
and b. him, and said, "See, the smell 27.27
of a field which the LORD has b.! 27.27
and b. be every one who blesses you 27.29
before you came, and I have b. him? 27.33
him?—yes, and he shall be b." 27.33
with which his father had b. him, 27.41
Then Isaac called Jacob and b. him, 28.01
that Isaac had b. Jacob and sent 28.06
and that as he b. him he charged 28.06
the LORD has b. me because of you; 30.27
the LORD has b. you wherever I 30.30
and his daughters and b. them; 31.55
my name?" And there he b. him. 32.29
came from Paddan-aram, and b. him. 35.09
he had the LORD b. the Egyptian's 39.05
Pharaoh, and Jacob b. Pharaoh. 47.07
And Jacob b. Pharaoh, and went out 47.10
in the land of Canaan and b. me, 48.03
And he b. Joseph, and said, "The God 48.15
So he b. them that day, saying, "By 48.20
father said to them as he b. them, 49.28
"B. be the LORD, who has delivered Ex 18.10
the LORD b. the sabbath day and 20.11
done it. And Moses b. them. 39.43
toward the people and b. them; Lev 9.22
they came out they b. the people, 9.23
know that he whom you bless is b., Num 22.06
curse the people, for they are b." 22.12
he has b., and I cannot revoke it. 23.20
B. be every one who blesses you, and 24.09
you have b. them these three times. 24.10
your God has b. you in all the Deu 2.07
You shall be b. above all peoples; 7.14
which the LORD your God has b. you. 12.07
as the LORD your God has b. you, 15.14
B. shall you be in the city, and 28.03
and b. shall you be in the field. 28.03
B. shall be the fruit of your body, 28.04
B. shall be your basket and your 28.05
B. shall you be when you come in, 28.06
and b. shall you be when you go out. 28.06
the man of God b. the children of 33.01
"B. by the LORD be his land, with 33.13
"B. be he who enlarges Gad! 33.20
"B. above sons be Asher; 33.24
Then Joshua b. him; and he gave Jos 14.13
since hitherto the LORD has b. me?" 17.14
So Joshua b. them, and sent them 22.06
away to their homes and b. them, 22.07
of Israel b. God and spoke no more 22.33
therefore he b. you; so I delivered 24.10
"Most b. of women be Jael, the wife Ju 5.24
of tent-dwelling women most b. 5.24
the boy grew, and the LORD b. him. 13.24
"B. be my son by the LORD." 17.02
B. be the man who took notice of Ru 2.19
"B. be he by the LORD, whose kindness 2.20
"May you be b. by the LORD, my 3.10
"B. be the LORD, who has not left 4.14
"B. be you to the LORD; I have 1Sa 15.13
said, "May you be b. by the LORD; 23.21
"B. be the LORD, the God of Israel, 25.32
B. be your discretion, and b. be you, 25.33
"B. be the LORD who has avenged the 25.39
"B. be you, my son David! 26.25
"May you be b. by the LORD, because 2Sa 2.05
and the LORD b. Obededom and all 6.11
"The LORD has b. the household of 6.12
he b. the people in the name of the 6.18
house of thy servant be b. for ever." 7.29
and did obeisance, and b. the king; 14.22
"B. be the LORD your God, who has 18.28
king kissed Barzillai and b. him, 19.39
and b. be my rock, and exalted be my 22.47
'B. be the LORD, the God of Israel, 1Ki 1.48
But King Solomon shall be b., 2.45
"B. be the LORD this day, who has 5.07
and b. all the assembly of Israel, 8.14
And he said, "B. be the LORD, the God 8.15
and b. all the assembly of Israel 8.55
"B. be the LORD who has given rest 8.56
and they b. the king, and went to 8.66
B. be the LORD your God, who has 10.09
and the LORD b. the household of 1Ch 13.14
he b. the people in the name of the 16.02
B. be the LORD, the God of Israel, 16.36
thou, O LORD, hast b. is b. for ever." 17.27
the eighth; for God b. him. 26.05
Therefore David b. the LORD in the 29.10
"B. art thou, O LORD, the God of 29.10
and all the assembly b. the LORD, 29.20
"B. be the LORD God of Israel, who 2Ch 2.12
and b. all the assembly of Israel, 6.03
And he said, "B. be the LORD, the God 6.04
B. be the LORD your God, who has 9.08
Beracah, for there they b. the LORD; 20.26
Levites arose and b. the people, 30.27
they b. the LORD and his people 31.08
for the LORD has b. his people, 31.10
B. be the LORD, the God of our Ez 7.27
And Ezra b. the LORD, the great God; Neh 8.06
B. be thy glorious name which is 9.05
And the people b. all the men who 11.02
Thou hast b. the work of his hands, Job 1.10
b. be the name of the LORD." 1.21
it called me b., and when the eye 29.11
if his loins have not b. me, 31.20

BLESSED (cont.)

And the LORD b. the latter days of Job 42.12
B. is the man who walks not in the Ps 1.01
B. are all who take refuge in him. 2.12
and b. be my rock, and exalted be 18.46
dost make him most b. for ever; 21.06
B. be the LORD! for he has 28.06
B. be the LORD, for he has wondrously 31.21
B. is he whose transgression is 32.01
B. is the man to whom the LORD 32.02
B. is the nation whose God is the 33.12
for those b. by the LORD shall 37.22
B. is the man who makes the LORD 40.04
B. is he who considers the poor! 41.01
he is called b. in the land; 41.02
B. be the LORD, the God of Israel, 41.13
therefore God has b. you for ever. 45.02
B. is he whom thou dost choose and 65.04
B. be God, because he has not 66.20
God, our God, has b. us. 67.06
God has b. us; let all the 67.07
B. be the Lord, who daily bears us 68.19
B. be God! 68.35
by him, all nations call him b.! 72.17
B. be the LORD, the God of Israel, 72.18
B. be his glorious name for ever; 72.19
B. are those who dwell in thy house, 84.04
B. are the men whose strength is in 84.05
b. is the man who trusts in thee! 84.12
B. are the people who know the 89.15
B. be the LORD for ever! Amen and 89.52
B. is the man whom thou dost 94.12
B. are they who observe justice, who 106.03
B. be the LORD, the God of Israel, 106.48
B. is the man who fears the LORD, 112.01
generation of the upright will be b. 112.02
B. be the name of the LORD from 113.02
May you be b. by the LORD, who made 115.15
B. be he who enters in the name of 118.26
B. are those whose way is blameless, 119.01
B. are those who keep his testimonies, 119.02
B. be thou, O LORD; teach me thy 119.12
B. be the LORD, who has not given us 124.06
B. is every one who fears the LORD, 128.01
the man be b. who fears the LORD. 128.04
B. be the LORD from Zion, he who 135.21
B. be the LORD, my rock, who trains 144.01
Let your fountain be b., and rejoice Pro 5.18
b. are his sons after him! 20.07
beginning will in the end not be b. 20.21
who has a bountiful eye will be b., 22.09
B. is the man who fears the LORD 28.14
but b. is he who keeps the law. 29.18
Her children rise up and call her b.; 31.28
whom the LORD of hosts has b., Is 19.25
"B. be Egypt my people, and Assyria 19.25
b. are all those who wait for him. 30.18
and I b. him and made him many. 51.02
B. is the man who does this, and the 56.02
are a people whom the LORD has b. 61.09
offspring of the b. of the LORD, 65.23
"B. is the man who trusts in the Jer 17.07
mother bore me, let it not be b.! 20.14
Then Daniel b. the God of heaven. Dan 2.19
Daniel said: "B. be the name of God 2.20
"B. be the God of Shadrach, Meshach, 3.28
and I b. the Most High, and praised 4.34
B. is he who waits and comes to the 12.12
'B. be the LORD, I have become rich'; Zec 11.05
Then all nations will call you b., Mal 3.12
Henceforth we deem the arrogant b.; 3.15
"B. are the poor in spirit, for Mt 5.03
"B. are those who mourn, for they 5.04
"B. are the meek, for they shall 5.05
"B. are those who hunger and thirst 5.06
"B. are the merciful, for they shall 5.07
"B. are the pure in heart, for they 5.08
"B. are the peacemakers, for they 5.09
"B. are those who are persecuted 5.10
"B. are you when men revile you and 5.11
And b. is he who takes no offense 11.06
But b. are your eyes, for they see, 13.16
and b., and broke and gave the 14.19
"B. are you, Simon Bar-Jona! 16.17
B. be he who comes in the name of 21.09
'B. be he who comes in the name of 23.39
B. is that servant whom his master 24.46
O b. of my Father, inherit the 25.34
and b., and broke it, and gave it to 26.26
and b., and broke the loaves, and Mk 6.41
and having b. them, he commanded 8.07
took them in his arms and b. them, 10.16
B. be he who comes in the name of 11.09
B. be the kingdom of our father 11.10
and b., and broke it, and gave it to 14.22
you the Christ, the Son of the B.?" 14.61
"B. are you among women, and blessed Lk 1.42
and b. is the fruit of your womb! 1.42
And b. is she who believed that 1.45
all generations will call me b.; 1.48
"B. be the Lord God of Israel, for 1.68
in his arms and b. God and said, 2.28
and Simeon b. them and said to Mary 2.34
"B. are your poor, for yours is the 6.20
"B. are you that hunger now, for you 6.21
"B. are you that weep now, for you 6.21
"B. are you when men hate you, and 6.22
And b. is he who takes no offense 7.23
and b. and broke them, and gave them 9.16
"B. are the eyes which see what you 10.23
"B. is the womb that bore you, and 11.27
But he said, "B. rather are those 11.28
B. are those servants whom the 12.37
finds them so, b. are those servants! 12.38
B. is that servant whom his master 12.43
'B. be he who comes in the name of 13.35
and you will be b., because they 14.14
"B. is he who shall eat bread in 14.15
saying, "B. be the King who comes in 19.38
'B. are the barren, and the wombs 23.29
them, he took the bread and b., 24.30
lifting up his hands he b. them. 24.50
While he b. them, he parted from 24.51
B. be he who comes in the name of Jn 12.13
b. are you if you do them. 13.17
B. are those who have not seen and 20.29
the families of the earth be b.' Ac 3.25
'It is more b. to give than to 20.35
the Creator, who is b. for ever! Rom 1.25
"B. are those whose iniquities are 4.07
b. is the man against whom the Lord 4.08
God who is over all be b. for ever. 9.05
B. be the God and Father of our 2Co 1.03
he who is b. for ever, knows that I 11.31
thee shall all the nations be b. Gal 3.08
of faith are b. with Abraham who 3.09
B. be the God and Father of our Eph 1.03
who has b. us in Christ with every 1.03
gospel of the b. God with which I 1Ti 1.11
time by the b. and only Sovereign, 6.15
awaiting our b. hope, the appearing Tit 2.13
slaughter of the kings and b. him; Heb 7.01
Abraham and b. him who had the 7.06
the inferior is b. by the superior 7.07
b. each of the sons of Joseph, 11.21
B. is the man who endures trial, for Jas 1.12
acts, he shall be b. in his doing. 1.25
B. be the God and Father of our 1Pe 1.03
righteousness' sake, you will be b. 3.14
you are b., because the spirit of 4.14
B. is he who reads aloud the words Rev 1.03
and b. are those who hear, and who 1.03
B. are the dead who die in the Lord 14.13
"B. indeed," says the Spirit, "that 14.13

BLESSED (cont.)
B. is he who is awake keeping his Rev 16.15
B. are those who are invited to the 19.09
B. and holy is he who shares in the 20.06
B. is he who keeps the words of 22.07
B. are those who wash their robes, 22.14

BLESSES
blessed be every one who b. you!" Gen 27.29
Blessed be every one who b. you, Num 24.09
when the LORD your God b. you, Deu 14.24
give as the LORD your God b. you; 16.10
b. himself in his heart, saying, 'I 29.19
he b. your sons within you. Ps 147.13
but he b. the abode of the righteous Pro 3.33
He who b. his neighbor with a loud 27.14
So that he who b. himself in the Is 65.16
frankincense, like him who b. an idol. 66.03

BLESSING
great, so that you will be a b. Gen 12.02
a curse upon myself and not a b." 27.12
as Isaac had finished b. Jacob, 27.30
and he has taken away your b." 27.35
now he has taken away my b." 27.36
"Have you not reserved a b. for me?" 27.36
"Have you but one b., my father? 27.38
because of the b. with which his 27.41
May he give the b. of Abraham to 28.04
the b. of the LORD was upon all 39.05
b. each with the b. suitable to him. 49.28
he may bestow a b. upon you this Ex 32.29
I will command my b. upon you in Lev 25.21
you this day a b. and a curse: Deu 11.26
the b., if you obey the commandments 11.27
shall set the b. on Mount Gerizim 11.29
according to the b. of the LORD 12.15
according to the b. of the LORD 16.17
turned the curse into a b. for you, 23.05
command the b. upon you in your 28.08
the b. and the curse, which I have 30.01
you life and death, b. and curse; 30.19
This is the b. with which Moses the 33.01
and full of the b. of the LORD, 33.23
the b. and the curse, according to Jos 8.34
and with thy b. shall the house of 2Sa 7.29
would not go but gave him his b. 13.25
is exalted above all b. and praise." Neh 9.05
our God turned the curse into a b. 13.02
The b. of him who was about to Job 29.13
the LORD; thy b. be upon thy people! Ps 3.08
He will receive b. from the LORD, 24.05
and his children become a b. 37.26
it with showers, and b. its growth. 65.10
By his b. they multiply greatly; 107.38
He did not like b.; may it be 109.17
This b. has fallen to me, that I 119.56
"The b. of the LORD be upon you! 129.08
the LORD has commanded the b., 133.03
The memory of the righteous is a b., Pro 10.07
The b. of the LORD makes rich, and 10.22
By the b. of the upright a city is 11.11
but a b. is on the head of him who 11.26
and a good b. will be upon them. 24.25
a b. in the midst of the earth, Is 19.24
and my b. on your offspring. 44.03
it, for there is a b. in it, 65.08
places round about my hill a b.; Eze 34.26
they shall be showers of b. 34.26
that a b. may rest on your house. 44.30
and leave a b. behind him, a cereal Joe 2.14
I save you and you shall be a b. Zec 8.13
down for you an overflowing b. Mal 3.10
loosed, and he spoke, b. God. Lk 1.64
continually in the temple b. God. 24.53
pronounces a b. upon the man to Rom 4.06
Is this b. pronounced only upon the 4.09
in the fulness of the b. of Christ. 15.29
The cup of b. which we bless, is it 1Co 10.16
behalf for the b. granted us in 2Co 1.11
you with every b. in abundance, 9.08
Jesus the b. of Abraham might come Gal 3.14
every spiritual b. in the heavenly Eph 1.03
cultivated, receives a b. from God. Heb 6.07
when he desired to inherit the b., 12.17
the same mouth come b. and cursing. Jas 3.10
called, that you may obtain a b. 1Pe 3.09
might and honor and glory and b.!" Rev 5.12
to the Lamb be b. and honor and 5.13
B. and glory and wisdom and thanksgiving 7.12

BLESSINGS
"By you Israel will pronounce b., Gen 48.20
bless you with b. of heaven above, 49.25
b. of the deep that couches beneath, 49.25
b. of the breasts and of the womb. 49.25
The b. of your father are mighty 49.26
beyond the b. of the eternal 49.26
And all these b. shall come upon Deu 28.02
and pronounce b. in his name for 1Ch 23.13
For thou dost meet him with goodly b.; Ps 21.03
and b. invoked for him all the day! 72.15
Happy the people to whom such b. fall! 144.15
B. are on the head of the righteous, Pro 10.06
A faithful man will abound with b., 28.20
upon you and I will curse your b.; Mal 2.02
you the holy and sure b. of David.' Ac 13.34
to share in their spiritual b., Rom 15.27
of service to them in material b. 15.27
gospel, that I may share in its b. 1Co 9.23
invoked future b. on Jacob and Heb 11.20

BLEW
the priests who b. the trumpets, Jos 6.09
while the trumpets b. continually. 6.09
while the trumpets b. continually. 6.13
and they b. the trumpets and Ju 7.19
three companies b. the trumpets 7.20
When they b. the three hundred 7.22
And Saul b. the trumpet throughout 1Sa 13.03
So Joab b. the trumpet; and all the 2Sa 2.28
Then Joab b. the trumpet, and the 18.16
and he b. the trumpet, and said, "We 20.01
So he b. the trumpet, and they 20.22
Then they b. the trumpet; and all the 1Ki 1.39
and they b. the trumpet, and proclaimed, 2Ki 9.13
and the priests b. the trumpets. 2Ch 13.14
you brought it home, I b. it away. Hag 1.09
and the winds b. and beat upon that Mt 7.25
and the winds b. and beat against 7.27
And when the south wind b. gently, Ac 27.13
The first angel b. his trumpet, Rev 8.07
The second angel b. his trumpet, 8.08
The third angel b. his trumpet, 8.10
The fourth angel b. his trumpet, 8.12
And the fifth angel b. his trumpet, 9.01
Then the sixth angel b. his trumpet, 9.13
Then the seventh angel b. his trumpet, 11.15

BLIGHT
pestilence or b. or mildew or locust 1Ki 8.37
pestilence or b. or mildew or locust 2Ch 6.28
"I smote you with b. and mildew; Amo 4.09
your toil with b. and mildew and Hag 2.17

BLIGHTED
seven ears, thin and b. by the east wind. Gen 41.06
and b. by the east wind, sprouted 41.23
empty ears b. by the east wind are 41.27
the housetop; b. before it is grown? 2Ki 19.26
the housetops, b. before it is grown. Is 37.27

BLIND
dumb, or deaf, or seeing, or b.? Ex 4.11
a stumbling block before the b., Lev 19.14

BLIND (cont.)

a man b. or lame, or one who has a Lev 21.18
Animals b. or disabled or mutilated 22.22
any blemish, if it is lame or b., Deu 15.21
who misleads a b. man on the road. 27.18
as the b. grope in darkness, and you 28.29
a bribe to b. my eyes with it? 1Sa 12.03
but the b. and the lame will ward 2Sa 5.06
to attack the lame and the b., 5.08
"The b. and the lame shall not come 5.08
I was eyes to the b., and feet Job 29.15
the LORD opens the eyes of the b. Ps 146.08
in a stupor, b. yourselves and be b.! Is 29.09
the eyes of the b. shall see. 29.18
Then the eyes of the b. shall be 35.05
to open the eyes that are b., 42.07
And I will lead the b. in a way 42.16
and look, you b., that you may see! 42.18
Who is b. but my servant, or deaf as 42.19
Who is b. as my dedicated one, or 42.19
or b. as the servant of the LORD? 42.19
Bring forth the people who are b., 43.08
His watchmen are b., they are all 56.10
We grope for the wall like the b., 59.10
among them the b. and the lame, Jer 31.08
They wandered, b., through the Lam 4.14
that they shall walk like the b., Zep 1.17
When you offer b. animals in Mal 1.08
two b. men followed him, crying Mt 9.27
the b. men came to him; and Jesus 9.28
the b. receive their sight and the 11.05
Then a b. and dumb demoniac was 12.22
Let them alone; they are b. guides. 15.14
And if a b. man leads a b. man, 15.14
the b., the dumb, and many others, 15.30
lame walking, and the b. seeing; 15.31
two b. men sitting by the roadside, 20.30
And the b. and the lame came to him 21.14
"Woe to you, b. guides, who say, 'If 23.16
You b. fools! For which is 23.17
You b. men! For which is 23.19
You b. guides, straining out a gnat 23.24
You b. Pharisee! first cleanse 23.26
people brought to him a b. man, Mk 8.22
And he took the b. man by the hand, 8.23
a b. beggar, the son of Timaeus, was 10.46
And they called the b. man, 10.49
And the b. man said to him, 10.51
and recovering of sight to the b., Lk 4.18
"Can a b. man lead a b. man? Will 6.39
many that were b. he bestowed 7.21
the b. receive their sight, the lame 7.22
the maimed, the lame, the b., 14.13
poor and maimed and b. and lame.' 14.21
a b. man was sitting by the roadside 18.35
of invalids, b., lame, paralyzed. Jn 5.03
by, he saw a man b. from his birth. 9.01
his parents, that he was born b.?" 9.02
the man who had formerly been b. 9.13
So they again said to the b. man, 9.17
he had been b. and had received 9.18
your son, who you say was born b.? 9.19
our son, and that he was born b.; 9.20
called the man who had been b., 9.24
that though I was b., now I see." 9.25
opened the eyes of a man born b. 9.32
that those who see may become b." 9.39
they said to him, "Are we also b.?" 9.40
"If you were b., you would have no 9.41
a demon open the eyes of the b.?" 10.21
the eyes of the b. man have kept 11.37
you shall be b. and unable to see Ac 13.11
that you are a guide to the b., Rom 2.19
these things is b. and shortsighted 2Pe 1.09
pitiable, poor, b., and naked. Rev 3.17

BLINDED

and b. their eyes which turn Eze 6.09
withered, his right eye utterly b.!" Zec 11.17
"He has b. their eyes and hardened Jn 12.40
this world has b. the minds of the 2Co 4.04
the darkness has b. his eyes. 1Jn 2.11

BLINDFOLDED

they also b. him and asked him, Lk 22.64

BLINDNESS

struck with b. the men who were at Gen 19.11
madness and b. and confusion of Deu 28.28
this people, I pray thee, with b." 2Ki 6.18
b. in accordance with the prayer 6.18
every horse of the peoples with b. Zec 12.04

BLINDS

for a bribe b. the officials, and Ex 23.08
for a bribe b. the eyes of the wise Deu 16.19

BLOCK

put a stumbling b. before the Lev 19.14
I fall down before a b. of wood? Is 44.19
I lay a stumbling b. before him, Eze 3.20
the stumbling b. of their iniquity 7.19
the stumbling b. of their iniquity 14.03
the stumbling b. of his iniquity 14.04
the stumbling b. of his iniquity 14.07
it will b. the travelers, for there 39.11
a stumblng b. of iniquity to the 44.12
put a stumbling b. or hindrance in Rom 14.13
a stumbling b. to Jews and folly to 1Co 1.23
become a stumbling b. to the weak. 8.09
the stumbling b. of the cross has Gal 5.11
put a stumbling b. before the sons Rev 2.14

BLOCKED

he has b. my ways with hewn stones, Lam 3.09

BLOCKS

stumbling b. against which they Jer 6.21

BLOOD

your brother's b. is crying to me Gen 4.10
your brother's b. from your hand. 4.11
with its life, that is, its b. 9.04
Whoever sheds the b. of man, 9.06
man, by man shall his b. be shed; 9.06
And Reuben said to them, "Shed no b.; 37.22
our brother and conceal his b.? 37.26
and dipped the robe in the b.; 37.31
there comes a reckoning for his b." 42.22
his vesture in the b. of grapes; 49.11
will become b. upon the dry ground." Ex 4.09
you are a bridegroom of b. to me!" 4.25
said, "You are a bridegroom of b., 4.26
and it shall be turned to b., 7.17
of water, that they may become b.; 7.19
there shall be b. throughout all 7.19
that was in the Nile turned to b. 7.20
and there was b. throughout all the 7.21
Then they shall take some of the b. 12.07
The b. shall be a sign for you, upon 12.13
and when I see the b., I will pass 12.13
dip it in the b. which is in the 12.22
with the b. which is in the basin; 12.22
he sees the b. on the lintel and 12.23
not offer the b. of my sacrifice 23.18
half of the b. and put it in 24.06
and half of the b. he threw 24.06
And Moses took the b. and threw it 24.08
"Behold the b. of the covenant 24.08
part of the b. of the bull and put 29.12
the rest of the b. you shall pour 29.12
shall take its b. and throw it 29.16
part of its b. and put it upon the 29.20
the rest of the b. against the 29.20

BLOOD (cont.)
part of the b. that is on the Ex 29.21
with the b. of the sin offering of 30.10
not offer the b. of my sacrifice 34.25
the priests shall present the b., Lev 1.05
and throw the b. round about 1.05
shall throw its b. against the 1.11
and its b. shall be drained out on 1.15
shall throw the b. against the 3.02
shall throw its b. against the 3.08
shall throw its b. against the 3.13
that you eat neither fat nor b." 3.17
some of the b. of the bull and 4.05
finger in the b. and sprinkle part 4.06
part of the b. seven times before 4.06
put some of the b. on the horns of 4.07
the rest of the b. of the bull he 4.07
some of the b. of the bull to the 4.16
finger in the b. and sprinkle it 4.17
put some of the b. on the horns of 4.18
the rest of the b. he shall pour 4.18
some of the b. of the sin offering 4.25
the rest of its b. at the base of 4.25
some of its b. with his finger and 4.30
the rest of its b. at the base of 4.30
some of the b. of the sin offering 4.34
the rest of its b. at the base of 4.34
some of the b. of the sin offering 5.09
the rest of the b. shall be 5.09
when any of its b. is sprinkled on 6.27
from which any b. is brought into 6.30
and its b. shall be thrown on the 7.02
who throws the b. of the peace 7.14
Moreover you shall eat no b. whatever, 7.26
Whoever eats any b., 7.27
who offers the b. of the peace 7.33
and took the b., and with his 8.15
poured out the b. at the base of 8.15
and threw the b. upon the altar 8.19
some of its b. and put it on the 8.23
put some of the b. on the tips of 8.24
Moses threw the b. upon the altar 8.24
oil and of the b. which was on the 8.30
of Aaron presented the b. to him, 9.09
finger in the b. and put it on the 9.09
poured out the b. at the base of 9.09
sons delivered to him the b., 9.12
sons delivered to him the b., 9.18
Behold, its b. was not brought into 10.18
days in the b. of her purifying; 12.04
continue in the b. of her purifying 12.05
be clean from the flow of her b. 12.07
bird in the b. of the bird that 14.06
some of the b. of the guilt 14.14
upon the b. of the guilt offering; 14.17
some of the b. of the guilt 14.25
place where the b. of the guilt 14.28
dip them in the b. of the bird 14.51
the house with the b. of the bird, 14.52
a discharge of b. which is her 15.19
a discharge of b. for many days, 15.25
take some of the b. of the bull, 16.14
sprinkle the b. with his finger 16.14
and bring its b. within the veil, 16.15
and do with its b. as he did with 16.15
as he did with the b. of the bull, 16.15
some of the b. of the bull and of 16.18
the bull and of the b. of the goat, 16.18
some of the b. upon it with his 16.19
whose b. was brought in to make 16.27
he has shed b.; and that man 17.04
sprinkle the b. on the altar of 17.06
sojourn among them eats any b., 17.10
against that person who eats b., 17.10
the life of the flesh is in the b.; 17.11
for it is the b. that makes atonement, 17.11
No person among you shall eat b., 17.12

who sojourns among you eat b. 17.12
pour out its b. and cover it with 17.13
of every creature is the b. of it; 17.14
not eat the b. of any creature, for 17.14
life of every creature is its b.; 17.14
eat any flesh with the b. in it. 19.26
or his mother, his b. is upon him. 20.09
to death, their b. is upon them. 20.11
incest, their b. is upon them. 20.12
to death, their b. is upon them. 20.13
to death, their b. is upon them. 20.16
uncovered the fountain of her b.; 20.18
their b. shall be upon them." 20.27
sprinkle their b. upon the altar, Num 18.17
some of her b. with his finger, and 19.04
some of her b. toward the front of 19.04
and her b., with her dung, shall be 19.05
and drinks the b. of the slain. 23.24
The avenger of b. shall himself put 35.19
the avenger of b. shall put the 35.21
manslayer and the avenger of b., 35.24
from the hand of the avenger of b., 35.25
and the avenger of b. finds him 35.27
the avenger of b. slays the 35.27
he shall not be guilty of b. 35.27
for b. pollutes the land, and no 35.33
for the b. that is shed in it, 35.33
except by the b. of him who shed it. 35.33
Only you shall not eat the b.; Deu 12.16
be sure that you do not eat the b.; 12.23
for the b. is the life, and you 12.23
offerings, the flesh and the b., 12.27
the b. of your sacrifices shall be 12.27
Only you shall not eat its b.; 15.23
lest the avenger of b. in hot anger 19.06
lest innocent b. be shed in your 19.10
hand him over to the avenger of b., 19.12
guilt of innocent b. from Israel, 19.13
'Our hands did not shed this b., 21.07
of innocent b. in the midst of thy 21.08
the guilt of b. be forgiven them." 21.08
of innocent b. from your midst, 21.09
the guilt of b. upon your house, if 22.08
and of the b. of the grape you 32.14
I will make my arrows drunk with b., 32.42
with the b. of the slain and the 32.42
he avenges the b. of his servants, 32.43
his b. shall be upon his head, and Jos 2.19
house, his b. shall be on our head. 2.19
a refuge from the avenger of b. 20.03
And if the avenger of b. pursues him, 20.05
by the hand of the avenger of b., 20.09
come and their b. be laid upon Ju 9.24
the people ate them with the b. 1Sa 14.32
the LORD, by eating with the b." 14.33
the LORD by eating with the b.'" 14.34
innocent b. by killing David without 19.05
for having shed b. without cause 25.31
let not my b. fall to the earth 26.20
"Your b. be upon your head; 2Sa 1.16
"From the b. of the slain, from the 1.22
for the b. of Asahel his brother. 3.27
LORD for the b. of Abner the son 3.28
now require his b. at your hand, 4.11
the avenger of b. slay no more, 14.11
you man of b., you worthless fellow! 16.07
you all the b. of the house of 16.08
is on you; for you are a man of b." 16.08
wallowing in his b. in the highway. 20.12
"There is b. guilt on Saul and on 21.01
I drink the b. of the men who went 23.17
time of peace b. which had been 1Ki 2.05
innocent b. upon the girdle about 2.05
his head down with b. to the grave." 2.09
guilt for the b. which Joab shed 2.31
So shall their b. come back upon 2.33
your b. shall be upon your own head." 2.37

BLOOD (cont.)
until the b. gushed out upon them. 1Ki 18.28
licked up the b. of Naboth shall 21.19
Naboth shall dogs lick your own b."'" 21.19
and the b. of the wound flowed into 22.35
and the dogs licked up his b., 22.38
water opposite them as red as b. 2Ki 3.22
And they said, "This is b.; the kings 3.23
on Jezebel the b. of my servants 9.07
and the b. of all the servants of 9.07
yesterday the b. of Naboth and the 9.26
of Naboth and the b. of his sons— 9.26
and some of her b. spattered on the 9.33
and threw the b. of his peace offering 16.13
upon it all the b. of the burnt 16.15
and all the b. of the sacrifice; 16.15
Manasseh shed very much innocent b., 21.16
the innocent b. that he had shed; 24.04
filled Jerusalem with innocent b., 24.04
have shed much b. and have waged 1Ch 22.08
shed so much b. before me upon the 22.08
you are a warrior and have shed b.' 28.03
because of the b. of the son of 2Ch 24.25
received the b. and threw it 29.22
rams and their b. was thrown 29.22
lambs and their b. was thrown 29.22
offering with their b. on the altar, 29.24
threw the b. which they received 30.16
sprinkled the b. which they 35.11
cover not my b., and let my cry Job 16.18
His young ones suck up b.; 39.30
For he who avenges b. is mindful of Ps 9.12
libations of b. I will not pour 16.04
of bulls, or drink the b. of goats? 50.13
men of b. and treachery shall not 55.23
his feet in the b. of the wicked. 58.10
that you may bathe your feet in b., 68.23
precious is their b. in his sight. 72.14
He turned their rivers to b., 78.44
out their b. like water round 79.03
the outpoured b. of thy servants 79.10
He turned their waters into b., 105.29
they poured out innocent b., 106.38
the b. of their sons and daughters, 106.38
and the land was polluted with b. 106.38
and that men of b. would depart 139.19
with us, let us lie in wait for b., Pro 1.11
and they make haste to shed b. 1.16
men lie in wait for their own b., 1.18
and hands that shed innocent b., 6.17
of the wicked lie in wait for b., 12.06
is burdened with the b. of another, 28.17
pressing the nose produces b., 30.33
do not delight in the b. of bulls, Is 1.11
listen; your hands are full of b. 1.15
rolled in b. will be burned as 9.05
the waters of Dibon are full of b.; 15.09
will disclose the b. shed upon her, 26.21
mountains shall flow with their b. 34.03
a sword; it is sated with b., 34.06
with the b. of lambs and goats, with 34.06
Their land shall be soaked with b., 34.07
with their own b. as with wine. 49.26
defiled with b. and your fingers 59.03
make haste to shed innocent b.; 59.07
like him who offers swine's b.; 66.03
or shed innocent b. in this place, Jer 7.06
place with the b. of innocents, 19.04
nor shed innocent b. in this place. 22.03
gain, for shedding innocent b., 22.17
bring innocent b. upon yourselves 26.15
and drink its fill of their b. 46.10
"My b. be upon the inhabitants of 51.35
of her the b. of the righteous. Lam 4.13
so defiled with b. that none could 4.14
but his b. I will require at your Eze 3.18
but his b. I will require at your 3.20
pestilence and b. shall pass 5.17
the land is full of b., and the city 9.09
pour out my wrath upon it with b., 14.19
and saw you weltering in your b., 16.06
I said to you in your b., 'Live, 16.06
and washed off your b. from you, 16.09
and bare, weltering in your b. 16.22
because of the b. of your children 16.36
wedlock and shed b. are judged, 16.38
upon you the b. of wrath and 16.38
a shedder of b., who does none of 18.10
his b. shall be upon himself. 18.13
your b. shall be in the midst of 21.32
city that sheds b. in the midst of 22.03
guilty by the b. which you have 22.04
have been bent on shedding b. 22.06
men in you who slander to shed b., 22.09
In you men take bribes to shed b.; 22.12
and at the b. which has been in the 22.13
shedding b., destroying lives to 22.27
and b. is upon their hands; with their 23.37
the sentence of women that shed b.; 23.45
and b. is upon their hands." 23.45
For the b. she has shed is still in 24.07
the bare rock the b. she has shed, 24.08
and b. into her streets; and the 28.23
the mountains with your flowing b.; 32.06
his b. shall be upon his own head. 33.04
his b. shall be upon himself. 33.05
but his b. I will require at the 33.06
but his b. I will require at your 33.08
GOD: You eat flesh with the b., 33.25
eyes to your idols, and shed b., 33.25
GOD, I will prepare you for b., 35.06
and b. shall pursue you; because 35.06
because you are guilty of b., 35.06
therefore b. shall pursue you. 35.06
them for the b. which they had 36.18
you shall eat flesh and drink b. 39.17
and drink the b. of the princes of 39.18
and drink b. till you are drunk, at 39.19
it and for throwing b. against it, 43.18
And you shall take some of its b., 43.20
to me my food, the fat and the b. 44.07
me to offer me the fat and the b., 44.15
some of the b. of the sin offering 45.19
of Jehu for the b. of Jezreel, Hos 1.04
city of evildoers, tracked with b. 6.08
b. and fire and columns of smoke. Joe 2.30
to darkness, and the moon to b., 2.31
shed innocent b. in their land. 3.19
I will avenge their b., and I will 3.21
and lay not on us innocent b.; Jon 1.14
who build Zion with b. and Jerusalem Mic 3.10
they all lie in wait for b., 7.02
for the b. of men and violence to Hab 2.08
Woe to him who builds a town with b., 2.12
for the b. of men and violence to 2.17
their b. shall be poured out like Zep 1.17
take away its b. from its mouth, Zec 9.07
because of the b. of my covenant 9.11
shall drink their b. like wine, 9.15
For flesh and b. has not revealed Mt 16.17
in shedding the b. of the prophets 23.30
all the righteous b. shed on earth, 23.35
from the b. of innocent Abel to the 23.35
Abel to the b. of Zechariah the 23.35
for this is my b. of the covenant, 26.28
sinned in betraying innocent b." 27.04
treasury, since they are b. money." 27.06
called the Field of B. to this day. 27.08
"I am innocent of this man's b.; 27.24
"His b. be on us and on our children!" 27.25
his side, and out came water and b. * 27.49
had a flow of b. for twelve years, Mk 5.25
"This is my b. of the covenant, 14.24
had a flow of b. for twelve years Lk 8.43

BLOOD (cont.)
immediately her flow of b. ceased. Lk 8.44
that the b. of all the prophets, 11.50
the b. of Abel to the b. of Zechariah, 11.51
Galileans whose b. Pilate had 13.01
is the new covenant in my b." * 22.20
great drops of b. falling down 22.44
not of b. nor of the will of the Jn 1.13
of the Son of man and drink his b., 6.53
and drinks my b. has eternal life, 6.54
food indeed, and my b. is drink indeed. 6.55
and drinks my b. abides in me, 6.56
once there came out b. and water. 19.34
Akeldama, that is, Field of B. Ac 1.19
b., and fire, and vapor of smoke; 2.19
into darkness and the moon into b., 2.20
to bring this man's b. upon us." 5.28
from what is strangled and from b. 15.20
idols and from b. and from what is 15.29
"Your b. be upon your heads! 18.06
innocent of the b. of all of you, 20.26
which he obtained with his own b. 20.28
idols and from b. and from what is 21.25
And when the b. of Stephen thy 22.20
"Their feet are swift to shed b., Rom 3.15
forward as an expiation by his b., 3.25
we are now justified by his b., 5.09
participation in the b. of Christ? 1Co 10.16
cup is the new covenant in my b. 11.25
the body and b. of the Lord. 11.27
flesh and b. cannot inherit the 15.50
did not confer with flesh and b., Gal 1.16
we have redemption through his b., Eph 1.07
brought near in the b. of Christ. 2.13
contending against flesh and b., 6.12
peace by the b. of his cross. Col 1.20
the children share in flesh and b., Heb 2.14
without taking b. which he offers 9.07
taking not the b. of goats and 9.12
of goats and calves but his own b., 9.12
with the b. of goats and bulls and 9.13
how much more shall the b. of Christ, 9.14
was not ratified without b. 9.18
he took the b. of calves and goats, 9.19
"This is the b. of the covenant 9.20
with the b. both the tent and all 9.21
everything is purified with b., 9.22
the shedding of b. there is no 9.22
Place yearly with b. not his own; 9.25
that the b. of bulls and goats 10.04
the sanctuary by the b. of Jesus, 10.19
profaned the b. of the covenant by 10.29
the Passover and sprinkled the b., 11.28
to the point of shedding your b. 12.04
the sprinkled b. that speaks more 12.24
graciously than the b. of Abel. 12.24
animals whose b. is brought into 13.11
the people through his own b. 13.12
by the b. of the eternal covenant, 13.20
and for sprinkling with his b.: 1Pe 1.02
but with the precious b. of Christ, 1.19
and the b. of Jesus his Son cleanses 1Jn 1.07
This is he who came by water and b., 5.06
only but with the water and the b. 5.06
the Spirit, the water, and the b.; 5.08
freed us from our sins by his b. Rev 1.05
and by thy b. didst ransom men for 5.09
and avenge our b. on those who 6.10
the full moon became like b., 6.12
them white in the b. of the Lamb. 7.14
mixed with b., which fell on the 8.07
and a third of the sea became b., 8.09
the waters to turn them into b., 11.06
him by the b. of the Lamb and by 12.11
and b. flowed from the wine press, 14.20
became like the b. of a dead man, 16.03
of water, and they became b. 16.04
have shed the b. of saints and 16.06
thou hast given them b. to drink. 16.06
drunk with the b. of the saints 17.06
saints and the b. of the martyrs 17.06
was found the b. of prophets and 18.24
on her the b. of his servants. 19.02
He is clad in a robe dipped in b., 19.13

BLOODGUILT
dies, there shall be no b. for him; Ex 22.02
him, there shall be b. for him. 22.03
b. shall be imputed to that man; Lev 17.04
LORD has restrained you from b., 1Sa 25.26
this day from b. and from avenging 25.33
LORD will leave his b. upon him, Hos 12.14

BLOODGUILTINESS
Deliver me from b., O God, Ps 51.14

BLOODSHED
and so the guilt of b. be upon you. Deu 19.10
concerning b., law or commandment, 2Ch 19.10
looked for justice, but behold, b.; Is 5.07
stops his ears from hearing of b., 33.15
who keeps back his sword from b. Jer 48.10
With pestilence and b. I will enter Eze 38.22

BLOODSTAINS
cleansed the b. of Jerusalem from Is 4.04

BLOODTHIRSTY
the LORD abhors b. and deceitful Ps 5.06
sinners, nor my life with b. men, 26.09
work evil, and save me from b. men. 59.02
B. men hate one who is blameless, Pro 29.10

BLOODY
bring back his b. deeds upon his 1Ki 2.32
land is full of b. crimes and the Eze 7.23
judge, will you judge the b. city? 22.02
Woe to the b. city, to the pot whose 24.06
the Lord GOD: Woe to the b. city! 24.09
Woe to the b. city, all full of lies Nah 3.01

BLOOM
whether the pomegranates were in b. Sol 6.11
and the pomegranates are in b. 7.12
wither, the b. of Lebanon fades. Nah 1.04

BLOSSOM
and his b. will be swept away by Job 15.30
like the vine, and cast off his b., 15.33
and may men b. forth from the Ps 72.16
its figs, and the vines are in b.; Sol 2.13
for our vineyards are in b. 2.15
and their b. go up like dust; Is 5.24
and make them b. in the morning 17.11
when the b. is over, and the flower 18.05
Israel shall b. and put forth 27.06
the desert shall rejoice and b.; 35.01
it shall b. abundantly, and rejoice 35.02
he shall b. as the lily, he shall Hos 14.05
they shall b. as the vine, their 14.07
Though the fig tree do not b., Hab 3.17

BLOSSOMED
injustice has b., pride has budded. Eze 7.10

BLOSSOMS
its b. shot forth, and the clusters Gen 40.10
and produced b., and it bore ripe Num 17.08
the almond tree b., the grasshopper Ecc 12.05
of henna b. in the vineyards of Sol 1.14
to look at the b. of the valley, 6.11
the grape b. have opened and the 7.12

BLOT
"I will b. out man whom I have Gen 6.07
made I will b. out from the face 7.04

BLOT (cont.)
I will utterly b. out the remembrance Ex 17.14
the Jebusites, and I b. them out, 23.23
b. me, I pray thee, out of thy book 32.32
me, him will I b. out of my book. 32.33
them and b. out their name from Deu 9.14
you shall b. out the remembrance of 25.19
the LORD would b. out his name 29.20
that he would b. out the name of 2Ki 14.27
abundant mercy b. out my transgressions. Ps 51.01
and b. out all my iniquities. 51.09
nor b. out their sin from thy sight. Jer 18.23
When I b. you out, I will cover the Eze 32.07
and I will not b. his name out of Rev 3.05

BLOTS
I am He who b. out your transgressions Is 43.25
They are b. and blemishes, reveling 2Pe 2.13

BLOTTED
He b. out every living thing that Gen 7.23
they were b. out from the earth. 7.23
name may not be b. out of Israel. Deu 25.06
a tribe be not b. out from Israel. Ju 21.17
their sin be b. out from thy sight; Neh 4.05
thou hast b. out their name for Ps 9.05
Let them be b. out of the book of 69.28
may his name be b. out in the 109.13
the sin of his mother be b. out! 109.14
that your sins may be b. out, Ac 3.19

BLOW
God made a wind b. over the earth, Gen 8.01
Thou didst b. with thy wind, the sea Ex 15.10
But if they b. only one, then the Num 10.04
When you b. an alarm, the camps that 10.05
And when you b. an alarm the second 10.06
you shall b., but you shall not 10.07
the priests, shall b. the trumpets. 10.08
you shall b. the trumpets over your 10.10
a day for you to b. the trumpets, 29.01
who struck the b. shall be put to 35.21
she struck Sisera a b., she crushed Ju 5.26
When I b. the trumpet, I and all who 7.18
then b. the trumpets also on every 7.18
right hands the trumpets to b.; 7.20
without striking a second b.; 2Sa 20.10
then b. the trumpet, and say, 'Long 1Ki 1.34
should b. the trumpets before the 1Ch 15.24
priests were to b. trumpets 16.06
the east wind to b. in the heavens, Ps 78.26
B. the trumpet at the new moon, at 81.03
he makes his wind b., and the 147.18
B. upon my garden, let its fragrance Sol 4.16
the wounds inflicted by his b. Is 30.26
the descending b. of his arm to be 30.30
"B. the trumpet through the land; Jer 4.05
B. the trumpet in Tekoa, and raise a 6.01
The bellows b. fiercely, the lead is 6.29
wound, with a very grievous b. 14.17
have dealt you the b. of an enemy, 30.14
b. the trumpet among the nations; 51.27
I will b. upon you with the fire of Eze 21.31
to b. the fire upon it in order to 22.20
gather you and b. upon you with 22.21
coming and does not b. the trumpet, 33.06
B. the horn in Gibeah, the trumpet Hos 5.08
B. the trumpet in Zion; sound the Joe 2.01
B. the trumpet in Zion; sanctify a 2.15
no wind might b. on earth or sea Rev 7.01
trumpets made ready to b. them. 8.06
the three angels are about to b.!" 8.13

BLOWING
times, the priests b. the trumpets. Jos 6.04
b. the trumpets, with the ark of the 6.08
b. the trumpets continually; and the 6.13
the land rejoicing and b. trumpets. 2Ki 11.14
the land rejoicing and b. trumpets, 2Ch 23.13
And when you see the south wind b., Lk 12.55
rose because a strong wind was b. Jn 6.18

BLOWN
And when both are b., all the Num 10.03
alarm is to be b. whenever they 10.06
the priests had b. the trumpets, Jos 6.16
shouted, and the trumpets were b. 6.20
a fire not b. upon will devour him; Job 20.26
look! When a trumpet is b., hear! Is 18.03
day a great trumpet will be b., 27.13
"They have b. the trumpet and made Eze 7.14
Is a trumpet b. in a city, and the Amo 3.06

BLOWS
I am spent by the b. of thy hand. Ps 39.10
than a hundred b. into a fool. Pro 17.10
B. that wound cleanse away evil; 20.30
The wind b. to the south, and goes Ecc 1.06
peoples in wrath with unceasing b., Is 14.06
the breath of the LORD b. upon it; 40.07
when he b. upon them, and they 40.24
the smith who b. the fire of coals, 54.16
the land and b. the trumpet and Eze 33.03
the guards received him with b. Mk 14.65
The wind b. where it wills, and you Jn 3.08
had inflicted many b. upon them, Ac 16.23

BLUE
b. and purple and scarlet stuff and Ex 25.04
linen and b. and purple and 26.01
make loops of b. on the edge of 26.04
make a veil of b. and purple and 26.31
of b. and purple and scarlet stuff 26.36
of b. and purple and scarlet stuff 27.16
b. and purple and scarlet stuff, and 28.05
of b. and purple and scarlet stuff, 28.06
b. and purple and scarlet stuff, and 28.08
of gold, b. and purple and scarlet 28.15
of the ephod with a lace of b., 28.28
the robe of the ephod all of b. 28.31
pomegranates of b. and purple and 28.33
it on the turban by a lace of b.; 28.37
b. and purple and scarlet stuff and 35.06
whom was found b. or purple or 35.23
had spun in b. and purple and 35.25
embroiderer in b. and purple and 35.35
linen and b. and purple and 36.08
made loops of b. on the edge of 36.11
the veil of b. and purple and 36.35
of b. and purple and scarlet stuff 36.37
needlework in b. and purple and 38.18
embroiderer in b. and purple and 38.23
And of the b. and purple and 39.01
b. and purple and scarlet stuff, and 39.02
work into the b. and purple and 39.03
b. and purple and scarlet stuff, and 39.05
b. and purple and scarlet stuff, and 39.08
of the ephod with a lace of b., 39.21
robe of the ephod woven all of b.; 39.22
pomegranates of b. and purple and 39.24
linen and of b. and purple and 39.29
And they tied to it a lace of b., 39.31
spread over that a cloth all of b., Num 4.06
they shall spread a cloth of b., 4.07
And they shall take a cloth of b., 4.09
they shall spread a cloth of b., 4.11
and put them in a cloth of b., 4.12
tassel of each corner a cord of b.; 15.38
and b. fabrics, trained also in 2Ch 2.07
b., and crimson fabrics and fine 2.14
the veil of b. and purple and 3.14
curtains and b. hangings caught up Est 1.06
in royal robes of b. and white, 8.15
b. and purple from the coasts of Eze 27.07
in clothes of b. and embroidered 27.24

BLUNT
If the iron is b., and one does not Ecc 10.10

BLUSH
am ashamed and b. to lift my face Ez 9.06
and you shall b. for the gardens Is 1.29
they did not know how to b. Therefore Jer 6.15
they did not know how to b. Therefore 8.12

BOANERGES
of James, whom he surnamed B., Mk 3.17

BOAR
The b. from the forest ravages it, Ps 80.13

BOARD
and went on b., to go with them to Jon 1.03
we took him on b. and came to Ac 20.14
Then we went on b. the ship, and they 21.06
sailing for Italy, and put us on b. 27.06
they put on b. whatever we needed. 28.10

BOARDS
You shall make it hollow, with b.; Ex 27.08
with them; he made it hollow, with b. 38.07
on the inside with b. of cedar; 1Ki 6.15
of the house with b. of cypress. 6.15
the house with b. of cedar from 6.16
will enclose her with b. of cedar. Sol 8.09

BOAST
on his armor b. himself as he that 1Ki 20.11
Some b. of chariots, and some of Ps 20.07
but we b. of the name of the LORD 20.07
My soul makes its b. in the LORD; 34.02
who b. against me when my foot 38.16
wealth and b. of the abundance of 49.06
Why do you b., O mighty man, of 52.01
"Do not b.," and to the wicked, "Do 75.04
words, they b., all the evildoers. 94.04
who make their b. in worthless 97.07
Do not b. about tomorrow, for you do Pro 27.01
their hope and of Egypt their b. Is 20.05
Why do you b. of your valleys, O Jer 49.04
the law and b. of your relation to Rom 2.17
You who b. in the law, do you 2.23
he has something to b. about, 4.02
do not b. over the branches. 11.18
If you do b., remember it is not 11.18
being might b. in the presence of 1Co 1.29
"Let him who boasts, b. of the Lord." 1.31
So let no one b. of men. For all 3.21
why do you b. as if it were not a 4.07
For our b. is this, the testimony of 2Co 1.12
of which I b. about you to the 9.02
For even if I b. a little too much 10.08
But we will not b. beyond limit, 10.13
We do not b. beyond limit, in other 10.15
"Let him who boasts, b. of the Lord." 10.17
this b. of mine shall not be 11.10
so that I too may b. a little. 11.16
since many b. of worldly things, I 11.18
of worldly things, I too will b.) 11.18
whatever any one dares to b. of— 11.21
as a fool—I also dare to b. of that. 11.21
If I must b., I will b. of the 11.30
I must b.; there is nothing 12.01
On behalf of this man I will b., 12.05
but on my own behalf I will not b., 12.05
Though if I wish to b., I shall not 12.06
the more gladly b. of my weaknesses, 12.09
his reason to b. will be in Gal 6.04
of works, lest any man should b. Eph 2.09
Therefore we ourselves b. of you in 2Th 1.04
lowly brother b. in his exaltation, Jas 1.09
do not b. and be false to the truth. 3.14
As it is, you b. in your arrogance. 4.16

BOASTED
In God we have b. continually, and Ps 44.08
should not have b. in the day of Ob 1.12
scoffed and b. against the people Zep 2.10
that in their b. mission they work 2Co 11.12

BOASTERS
loud-mouthed b., flattering people Jud 1.16

BOASTFUL
The b. may not stand before thy Ps 5.05
I say to the b., "Do not boast," and 75.04
b., inventors of evil, disobedient Rom 1.30
and kind; love is not jealous or b.; 1Co 13.04
as a fool, in this b. confidence; 2Co 11.17

BOASTFULNESS
your heart has lifted you up in b. 2Ch 25.19

BOASTING
the arrogant b. of the king of Is 10.12
Then what becomes of our b.? It is Rom 3.27
Your b. is not good. Do you not 1Co 5.06
one deprive me of my ground for b. 9.15
that gives me no ground for b. 9.16
so our b. before Titus has proved 2Co 7.14
love and of our b. about you to 8.24
so that our b. about you may not 9.03
without b. of work already done in 10.16
joy or crown of b. before our Lord 1Th 2.19
your arrogance. All such b. is evil. Jas 4.16

BOASTS
For the wicked b. of the desires of Ps 10.03
the tongue that makes great b., 12.03
but when he goes away, then he b. Pro 20.14
is a man who b. of a gift he does 25.14
and his insolence—his b. are false. Is 16.06
his b. are false, his deeds are Jer 48.30
people and made b. against their Zep 2.08
"Let him who b., boast of the Lord." 1Co 1.31
"Let him who b., boast of the Lord." 2Co 10.17
member and b. of great things. Jas 3.05
uttering loud b. of folly, they 2Pe 2.18

BOAT
in the b. with Zebedee their father, Mt 4.21
Immediately they left the b. and 4.22
And when he got into the b., 8.23
so that the b. was being swamped by 8.24
And getting into a b. he crossed 9.01
he got into a b. and sat there; 13.02
from there in a b. to a lonely 14.13
get into the b. and go before him 14.22
but the b. by this time was many 14.24
got out of the b. and walked on 14.29
And when they got into the b., 14.32
And those in the b. worshiped him, 14.33
he got into the b. and went to the 15.39
were in their b. mending the nets. Mk 1.19
Zebedee in the b. with the hired 1.20
to have a b. ready for him because 3.09
he got into a b. and sat in it on 4.01
them, just as he was, in the b. 4.36
and the waves beat into the b., 4.37
so that the b. was already filling. 4.37
And when he had come out of the b., 5.02
And as he was getting into the b., 5.18
again in the b. to the other side, 5.21
away in the b. to a lonely place 6.32
get into the b. and go before him 6.45
the b. was out on the sea, and he 6.47
And he got into the b. with them 6.51
And when they got out of the b., 6.54
he got into the b. with his disciples, 8.10
into the b. again he departed to 8.13
only one loaf with them in the b. 8.14
and taught the people from the b. Lk 5.03

BOAT (cont.)

in the other b. to come and help Lk 5.07
he got into a b. with his disciples, 8.22
so he got into the b. and returned. 8.37
got into a b., and started across Jn 6.17
the sea and drawing near to the b. 6.19
were glad to take him into the b., 6.21
immediately the b. was at the land 6.21
there had been only one b. there, 6.22
not entered the b. with his 6.22
They went out and got into the b.; 21.03
net on the right side of the b., 21.06
the other disciples came in the b., 21.08
with difficulty to secure the b.; Ac 27.16
had lowered the b. into the sea, 27.30
the ropes of the b., and let it go. 27.32

BOATS

And other b. were with him. Mk 4.36
And he saw two b. by the lake; Lk 5.02
Getting into one of the b., 5.03
they came and filled both the b., 5.07
they had brought their b. to land, 5.11
However, b. from Tiberias came near Jn 6.23
got into the b. and went to 6.24

BOAZ

of Elimelech, whose name was B. Ru 2.01
part of the field belonging to B., 2.03
And behold, B. came from Bethlehem; 2.04
Then B. said to his servant who was 2.05
Then B. said to Ruth, "Now, listen, my 2.08
But B. answered her, "All that you 2.11
And at mealtime B. said to her, 2.14
B. instructed his young men, saying, 2.15
with whom I worked today is B." 2.19
kept close to the maidens of B., 2.23
Now is not B. our kinsman, with 3.02
And when B. had eaten and drunk, and 3.07
And B. went up to the gate and sat 4.01
of whom B. had spoken, came by. 4.01
So B. said, "Turn aside, friend; 4.01
Then B. said, "The day you buy the 4.05
So when the next of kin said to B., 4.08
Then B. said to the elders and all 4.09
So B. took Ruth and she became his 4.13
Salmon of B., B. of Obed, 4.21
the north and called its name B. 1Ki 7.21
the father of Salma, Salma of B., 1Ch 2.11
B. of Obed, Obed of Jesse. 2.12
Jachin, and that on the north B. 2Ch 3.17
and Salmon the father of B. by Rahab, Mt 1.05
and B. the father of Obed by Ruth, 1.05
the son of B., the son of Sala, the Lk 3.32

BOCHERU

Azrikam, B., Ishmael, Sheriah, 1Ch 8.38
B., Ishmael, Sheariah, Obadiah, and 9.44

BOCHIM

the LORD went up from Gilgal to B. Ju 2.01
called the name of that place B.; 2.05

BODIES

my lord but our b. and our lands. Gen 47.18
poured upon the b. of ordinary men, Ex 30.32
cast your dead b. upon the dead Lev 26.30
upon the dead b. of your idols; 26.30
your dead b. shall fall in this Num 14.29
your dead b. shall fall in this 14.32
of your dead b. lies in the 14.33
give the dead b. of the host of 1Sa 17.46
of Saul and the b. of his sons 31.12
behold, these were all dead b. 2Ki 19.35
of Saul and the b. of his sons, 1Ch 10.12
they were dead b. lying on the 2Ch 20.24
also over our b. and over our Neh 9.37
their b. are sound and sleek. Ps 73.04
They have given the b. of thy 79.02
shall live, their b. shall rise. Is 26.19
behold, these were all dead b. 37.36
on the dead b. of the men that 66.24
And the dead b. of this people will Jer 7.33
'The dead b. of men shall fall like 9.22
and their dead b. shall be food 16.04
give their dead b. for food to the 19.07
of the dead b. and the ashes, 31.40
with the dead b. of men whom I 33.05
Their dead b. shall be food for the 34.20
and their b. gashed, bringing cereal 41.05
cast all the b. of the men whom he 41.09
their b. were more ruddy than coral, Lam 4.07
another, while two covered their b. Eze 1.11
lay the dead b. of the people of 6.05
and by the dead b. of their kings, 43.07
and the dead b. of their kings far 43.09
any power over the b. of those men; Dan 3.27
up their b. rather than serve and 3.28
"the dead b. shall be many; Amo 8.03
heaps of corpses, dead b. without end— Nah 3.03
end—they stumble over the b.! 3.03
and many b. of the saints who had Mt 27.52
to prevent the b. from remaining Jn 19.31
of their b. among themselves, Rom 1.24
therefore reign in your mortal b., 6.12
although your b. are dead because 8.10
to your mortal b. also through his 8.11
as sons, the redemption of our b. 8.23
to present your b. as a living 12.01
know that your b. are members of 1Co 6.15
There are celestial b. and there 15.40
and there are terrestrial b.; 15.40
may also be manifested in our b. 2Co 4.10
our b. had no rest but we were 7.05
love their wives as their own b. Eph 5.28
whose b. fell in the wilderness? Heb 3.17
conscience and our b. washed with 10.22
For the b. of those animals whose 13.11
obey us, we guide their whole b. Jas 3.03
and their dead b. will lie in the Rev 11.08
at their dead b. and refuse to let 11.09

BODILY

descended upon him in b. form, Lk 3.22
but his b. presence is weak, and his 2Co 10.10
because of a b. ailment that I Gal 4.13
makes b. growth and upbuilds itself Eph 4.16
whole fulness of deity dwells b., Col 2.09
for while b. training is of some 1Ti 4.08
concerning b. descent but by the Heb 7.16

BODY

all his b. like a hairy mantle; Gen 25.25
it is his mantle for his b.; Ex 22.27
put his linen breeches upon his b., Lev 6.10
the skin of his b. a swelling or 13.02
disease on the skin of his b., 13.02
diseased spot on the skin of his b.; 13.03
be deeper than the skin of his b., 13.03
is white in the skin of his b., 13.04
leprosy in the skin of his b., 13.11
the leprosy has covered all his b., 13.13
skin of one's b. a boil that has 13.18
"Or, when the b. has a burn on its 13.24
the skin of the b., white spots, 13.38
the skin of the b. are of a dull 13.39
of leprosy in the skin of the b., 13.43
and bathe his b. in water, and he 14.09
man has a discharge from his b., 15.02
whether his b. runs with his 15.03
or his b. is stopped from discharge, 15.03
touches the b. of him who has the 15.07
shall bathe his b. in running 15.13
shall bathe his whole b. in water, 15.16
her regular discharge from her b., 15.19

BODY (cont.)

have the linen breeches on his b., Lev 16.04
He shall bathe his b. in water, 16.04
shall bathe his b. in water in a 16.24
clothes and bathe his b. in water, 16.26
clothes and bathe his b. in water, 16.28
he shall not go in to any dead b., 21.11
he has bathed his b. in water. 22.06
thigh fall away and your b. swell; Num 5.21
and make your b. swell and your 5.22
and her b. shall swell, and her 5.27
he shall not go near a dead b. 6.06
he sinned by reason of the dead b. 6.11
go with a razor over all their b., 8.07
touching the dead b. of a man, 9.06
touching the dead b. of a man; 9.07
unclean through touching a dead b., 9.10
clothes and bathe his b. in water, 19.07
in water and bathe his b. in water, 19.08
the dead b. of any person shall be 19.11
the b. of any man who has died, and 19.13
or a dead b., or a bone of a man, 19.16
and the woman, through her b. 25.08
fruit of your b. and the fruit of Deu 7.13
his b. shall not remain all night 21.23
Blessed shall be the fruit of your b., 28.04
prosperity, in the fruit of your b., 28.11
Cursed shall be the fruit of your b., 28.18
And your dead b. shall be food for 28.26
eat the offspring of your own b., 28.53
your hand, in the fruit of your b., 30.09
they took his b. down from the Jos 8.29
of bees in the b. of the lion, Ju 14.08
fastened his b. to the wall of 1Sa 31.10
and took the b. of Saul and the 31.12
who shall come forth from your b., 2Sa 7.12
Joab struck him with it in the b., 20.10
your b. shall not come to the tomb 1Ki 13.22
And his b. was thrown in the road, 13.24
the lion also stood beside the b. 13.24
and saw the b. thrown in the road, 13.25
and the lion standing by the b. 13.25
and found his b. thrown in the 13.28
the lion standing beside the b. 13.28
not eaten the b. or torn the ass. 13.28
took up the b. of the man of God 13.29
And he laid the b. in his own grave; 13.30
sackcloth beneath upon his b.— 2Ki 6.30
took away the b. of Saul and the 1Ch 10.12
He feels only the pain of his own b., Job 14.22
forth and comes out of his b., 20.25
his b. full of fat and the marrow 21.24
my b. also dwells secure. Ps 16.09
from grief, my soul and my b. also. 31.09
my b. wasted away through my 32.03
As with a deadly wound in my b., 42.10
our b. cleaves to the ground. 44.25
may it soak into his b. like water, 109.18
fasting; my b. has become gaunt. 109.24
sons of your b. I will set on your 132.11
your flesh and b. are consumed, Pro 5.11
to the soul and health to the b. 16.24
into the inner parts of the b. 18.08
into the inner parts of the b. 26.22
mind how to cheer my b. with wine— Ecc 2.03
and put away pain from your b.; 11.10
His b. is ivory work, encrusted with Sol 5.14
both soul and b., and it will be as Is 10.18
like a dead b. trodden under foot. 14.19
from the b. of my mother he named 49.01
cast his dead b. into the burial Jer 26.23
and his dead b. shall be cast out 36.30
had two wings covering its b. Eze 1.23
and his b. was wet with the dew of Dan 4.33
and his b. was wet with the dew of 5.21
and its b. destroyed and given over 7.11
His b. was like beryl, his face like 10.06
the fruit of my b. for the sin of Mic 6.07
I hear, and my b. trembles, my lips Hab 3.16
with a dead b. touches any of Hag 2.13
that your whole b. be thrown into Mt 5.29
that your whole b. go into hell. 5.30
"The eye is the lamp of the b. 6.22
your whole b. will be full of light; 6.22
your whole b. will be full of darkness. 6.23
you shall drink, nor about your b., 6.25
and the b. more than clothing? 6.25
who kill the b. but cannot kill 10.28
destroy both soul and b. in hell. 10.28
came and took the b. and buried it; 14.12
Wherever the b. is, there the eagles 24.28
ointment on my b. she has done it 26.12
"Take, eat; this is my b." 26.26
and asked for the b. of Jesus. 27.58
And Joseph took the b., 27.59
she felt in her b. that she was Mk 5.29
of it, they came and took his b., 6.29
has anointed my b. beforehand for 14.08
and said, "Take; this is my b." 14.22
but a linen cloth about his b.; 14.51
and asked for the b. of Jesus. 15.43
dead, he granted the b. to Joseph. 15.45
Your eye is the lamp of your b.; Lk 11.34
your whole b. is full of light; 11.34
your b. is full of darkness. 11.34
If then your whole b. is full of 11.36
do not fear those who kill the b., 12.04
you shall eat, nor about your b., 12.22
and the b. more than clothing. 12.23
"Where the b. is, there the eagles 17.37
it to them, saying, "This is my b. 22.19
and asked for the b. of Jesus. 23.52
the tomb, and how his b. was laid; 23.55
went in they did not find the b. 24.03
and did not find his b.; and they 24.23
But he spoke of the temple of his b. Jn 2.21
I made a man's whole b. well? 7.23
he might take away the b. of Jesus, 19.38
So he came and took away his b. 19.38
They took the b. of Jesus, and bound 19.40
where the b. of Jesus had lain, one 20.12
summoned the b. of the disciples Ac 6.02
then turning to the b. he said, 9.40
and they came to him in a b., 12.20
away from his b. to the sick, 19.12
when he considered his own b., Rom 4.19
that the sinful b. might be 6.06
the law through the b. of Christ, 7.04
deliver me from this b. of death? 7.24
the deeds of the b. you will live. 8.13
For as in one b. we have many 12.04
are one b. in Christ, and individually 12.05
absent in b. I am present in 1Co 5.03
The b. is not meant for immorality, 6.13
the Lord, and the Lord for the b. 6.13
prostitute becomes one b. with her? 6.16
a man commits is outside the b.; 6.18
man sins against his own b. 6.18
know that your b. is a temple of 6.19
So glorify God in your b. 6.20
wife does not rule over her own b., 7.04
does not rule over his own b., 7.04
how to be holy in b. and spirit; 7.34
but I pommel my b. and subdue it, 9.27
participation in the b. of Christ? 10.16
loaf, we who are many are one b., 10.17
"This is my b. which is for you. 11.24
profaning the b. and blood of the 11.27
discerning the b. eats and drinks 11.29
For just as the b. is one and has 12.12
and all the members of the b., 12.12
are one b., so it is with Christ. 12.12
we were all baptized into one b.— 12.13
For the b. does not consist of one 12.14

BODY (cont.)
a hand, I do not belong to the b.," 1Co 12.15
make it any less a part of the b. 12.15
an eye, I do not belong to the b.," 12.16
make it any less a part of the b. 12.16
If the whole b. were an eye, where 12.17
If the whole b. were an ear, where 12.17
God arranged the organs in the b., 12.18
organ, where would the b. be? 12.19
there are many parts, yet one b. 12.20
parts of the b. which seem to be 12.22
parts of the b. which we think 12.23
But God has so adjusted the b., 12.24
that there may be no discord in the b., 12.25
Now you are the b. of Christ and 12.27
if I deliver my b. to be burned, 13.03
with what kind of b. do they come?" 15.35
sow is not the b. which is to be, 15.37
But God gives it a b. as he has 15.38
to each kind of seed its own b. 15.38
It is sown a physical b. 15.44
it is raised a spiritual b. If there 15.44
If there is a physical b., 15.44
there is also a spiritual b. 15.44
always carrying in the b. the death 2Co 4.10
at home in the b. we are away from 5.06
away from the b. and at home with 5.08
to what he has done in the b. 5.10
every defilement of b. and spirit, 7.01
whether in the b. or out of the 12.02
or out of the b. I do not know, 12.02
whether in the b. or out of the 12.03
or out of the b. I do not know, 12.03
I bear on my b. the marks of Jesus Gal 6.17
which is his b., the fulness of him Eph 1.23
following the desires of b. and mind, 2.03
to God in one b. through the cross, 2.16
heirs, members of the same b., 3.06
There is one b. and one Spirit, just 4.04
for building up the b. of Christ, 4.12
from whom the whole b., joined and 4.16
his b., and is himself its Savior. 5.23
because we are members of his b. 5.30
Christ will be honored in my b., Php 1.20
our lowly b. to be like his glorious b., 3.21
He is the head of the b., the church; Col 1.18
reconciled in his b. of flesh by 1.22
afflictions for the sake of his b., 1.24
For though I am absent in b., 2.05
putting off the b. of flesh in the 2.11
the Head, from whom the whole b., 2.19
self-abasement and severity to the b., 2.23
you were called in the one b. 3.15
and soul and b. be kept sound and 1Th 5.23
regulations for the b. imposed Heb 9.10
but a b. hast thou prepared for me; 10.05
offering of the b. of Jesus Christ 10.10
since you also are in the b. 13.03
them the things needed for the b., Jas 2.16
For as the b. apart from the spirit 2.26
able to bridle the whole b. also. 3.02
our members, staining the whole b., 3.06
our sins in his b. on the tree, 1Pe 2.24
dirt from the b. but as an appeal 3.21
right, as long as I am in this b., 2Pe 1.13
putting off of my b. will be soon, 1.14
disputed about the b. of Moses, Jud 1.09

BODYGUARD
son-in-law, and captain over your b., 1Sa 22.14
I will make you my b. for life." 28.02
And David set him over his b. 2Sa 23.23
—Nebuzaradan, the captain of the b., 2Ki 25.08
And David set him over his b. 1Ch 11.25
captain of the b. who served the Jer 52.12

BOG
desolate pit, out of the miry b., Ps 40.02

BOHAN
to the stone of B. the son of Jos 15.06
to the stone of B. the son of 18.17

BOIL
will bake and b. what you will b., Ex 16.23
"You shall not b. a kid in its 23.19
and b. its flesh in a holy place; 29.31
You shall not b. a kid in its 34.26
"B. the flesh at the door of the Lev 8.31
of one's body a b. that has healed, 13.18
place of the b. there comes a 13.19
it has broken out in the b. 13.20
spread, it is the scar of the b.; 13.23
"You shall not b. a kid in its Deu 14.21
And you shall b. it and eat it at 16.07
and b. pottage for the sons of the 2Ki 4.38
let them take and lay it on the b., 20.07
He makes the deep b. like a pot; Job 41.31
of figs, and apply it to the b., Is 38.21
and the fire causes water to b.— 64.02
b. its pieces, seethe also its bones Eze 24.05
b. well the flesh, and empty out the 24.10
priests shall b. the guilt offering 46.20
temple shall b. the sacrifices of 46.24
of them and b. the flesh of the Zec 14.21

BOILED
eat any of it raw or b. with water, Ex 12.09
in which it is b. shall be broken; Lev 6.28
but if it is b. in a bronze vessel, 6.28
when it is b., and one unleavened Num 6.19
and b. it in pots, and made cakes of 11.08
will not accept b. meat from you, 1Sa 2.15
and b. their flesh with the yokes 1Ki 19.21
So we b. my son, and ate him. 2Ki 6.29
and they b. the holy offerings in 2Ch 35.13
women have b. their own children; Lam 4.10

BOILING
Once when Jacob was b. pottage, Gen 25.29
would come, while the meat was b., 1Sa 2.13
as from a b. pot and burning rushes. Job 41.20
"I see a b. pot, facing away from Jer 1.13

BOILS
and become b. breaking out in sores Ex 9.09
and it became b. breaking out in 9.10
before Moses because of the b., 9.11
for the b. were upon the magicians 9.11
smite you with the b. of Egypt, Deu 28.27
with grievous b. of which you 28.35

BOLD
A wicked man puts on a b. face, Pro 21.29
but the righteous are b. as a lion. 28.01
a king of b. countenance, one who Dan 8.23
Then Isaiah is so b. as to say, Rom 10.20
have such a hope, we are very b., 2Co 3.12
but b. to you when I am away!— 10.01
are much more b. to speak the word Php 1.14
though I am b. enough in Christ to Phm 1.08
B. and wilful, they are not afraid 2Pe 2.10

BOLDLY
but he who b. reproves makes peace. Pro 10.10
he had preached b. in the name of Ac 9.27
preaching b. in the name of the 9.29
And Paul and Barnabas spoke out b., 13.46
speaking b. for the Lord, who bore 14.03
He began to speak b. in the synagogue 18.26
and for three months spoke b., 19.08
to you very b. by way of reminder, Rom 15.15
my mouth b. to proclaim the Eph 6.19
that I may declare it b., as I ought 6.20
as they b. carouse together, looking Jud 1.12

BOLDNESS
they saw the b. of Peter and John, Ac 4.13
to speak thy word with all b., 4.29
and spoke the word of God with b. 4.31
have to show b. with such confidence 2Co 10.02
in whom we have b. and confidence Eph 3.12

BOLT
presence, and b. the door after her." 2Sa 13.17
myrrh, upon the handles of the b. Sol 5.05

BOLTED
her out, and b. the door after her. 2Sa 13.18

BOLTS
its doors, its b., and its bars. Neh 3.03
its doors, its b., and its bars. 3.06
its b., and its bars, and repaired a 3.13
its doors, its b., and its bars. 3.14
its doors, its b., and its bars; 3.15

BOND
is none remaining, b. or free. Deu 32.36
both b. and free in Israel, and will 1Ki 14.10
every male, b. or free, in Israel; 21.21
every male, b. or free, in Israel. 2Ki 9.08
b. or free, and there was none to 14.26
from this b. on the sabbath day?" Lk 13.16
bitterness and in the b. of iniquity. Ac 8.23
of the Spirit in the b. of peace. Eph 4.03
having canceled the b. which stood Col 2.14

BONDAGE
of Israel groaned under their b., Ex 2.23
their cry under b. came up to God. 2.23
Egyptians hold in b. and I have 6.05
I will deliver you from their b., 6.06
broken spirit and their cruel b. 6.09
from Egypt, out of the house of b., 13.03
out of Egypt, from the house of b. 13.14
of Egypt, out of the house of b. 20.02
of Egypt, out of the house of b. Deu 5.06
of Egypt, out of the house of b. 6.12
redeemed you from the house of b., 7.08
of Egypt, out of the house of b., 8.14
redeemed you out of the house of b., 13.05
of Egypt, out of the house of b. 13.10
us, and laid upon us hard b. 26.06
of Egypt, out of the house of b., Jos 24.17
brought you out of the house of b.; Ju 6.08
us a little reviving in our b. Ez 9.08
God has not forsaken us in our b., 9.09
to return to their b. in Egypt. Neh 9.17
out of the house of b., saying, Jer 34.13
redeemed you from the house of b.; Mic 6.04
have never been in b. to any one. Jn 8.33
free from its b. to decay and Rom 8.21
that they might bring us into b.— Gal 2.04
you were in b. to beings that by 4.08
death were subject to lifelong b. Heb 2.15

BONDMAID
have rest, and the son of your b., Ex 23.12

BONDMAN
and he shall be your b. for ever. Deu 15.17

BONDMEN
For we are b.; yet our God Ez 9.09

BONDS
and his b. melted off his hands. Ju 15.14
Neco put him in b. at Riblah in 2Ki 23.33
He looses the b. of kings, and binds Job 12.18
has loosed the b. of the swift ass, 39.05
"Let us burst their b. asunder, Ps 2.03
not despise his own that are in b. 69.33
gloom, and broke their b. asunder. 107.14
handmaid. Thou hast loosed my b. 116.16
scoff, lest your b. be made strong; Is 28.22
loose the b. from your neck, O 52.02
to loose the b. of wickedness, to 58.06
broke your yoke and burst your b.; Jer 2.20
the yoke, they had burst the b. 5.05
neck, and I will burst their b., 30.08
you and will burst your b. asunder." Nah 1.13
he broke the b. and was driven by Lk 8.29
bring them in b. to Jerusalem to Ac 22.05

BONDWOMAN
And to your b. you shall do likewise. Deu 15.17

BONE
"This at last is b. of my bones and Gen 2.23
"Surely you are my b. and my flesh!" 29.14
and you shall not break a b. of it. Ex 12.46
the morning, nor break a b. of it; Num 9.12
or a b. of a man, or a grave, shall 19.16
and upon him who touched the b., 19.18
that I am your b. and your flesh." Ju 9.02
"Behold, we are your b. and flesh. 2Sa 5.01
kinsmen, you are my b. and my flesh; 19.12
'Are you not my b. and my flesh? 19.13
"Behold, we are your b. and flesh. 1Ch 11.01
and touch his b. and his flesh, and Job 2.05
and a soft tongue will break a b. Pro 25.15
came together, b. to its b. Eze 37.07
land and any one sees a man's b., 39.15
"Not a b. of him shall be broken." Jn 19.36

BONES
is bone of my b. and flesh of my Gen 2.23
you shall carry up my b. from here." 50.25
And Moses took the b. of Joseph Ex 13.19
must carry my b. with you from 13.19
and shall break their b. in pieces, Num 24.08
The b. of Joseph which the people Jos 24.32
And they took their b. and buried 1Sa 31.13
and took the b. of Saul and the 2Sa 21.12
of Saul and the b. of his son 21.12
from there the b. of Saul and the 21.13
of Saul and the b. of his son 21.13
gathered the b. of those who were 21.13
And they buried the b. of Saul and 21.14
and men's b. shall be burned upon 1Ki 13.02
is buried; lay my b. beside his b. 13.31
the man touched the b. of Elisha, 2Ki 13.21
their places with the b. of men. 23.14
and took the b. out of the tombs, 23.16
"Let him be; let no man move his b." 23.18
So they let his b. alone, with the 23.18
with the b. of the prophet who came 23.18
and burned the b. of men upon them 23.20
buried their b. under the oak in 1Ch 10.12
He also burned the b. of the 2Ch 34.05
trembling, which made all my b. shake. Job 4.14
and death rather than my b. 7.15
me together with b. and sinews. 10.11
My b. cleave to my skin and to my 19.20
His b. are full of youthful vigor, 20.11
fat and the marrow of his b. moist. 21.24
The night racks my b., and the 30.17
from me, and my b. burn with heat. 30.30
with continual strife in his b.; 33.19
and his b. which were not seen 33.21
His b. are tubes of bronze, his 40.18
heal me, for my b. are troubled. Ps 6.02
and all my b. are out of joint; 22.14
I can count all my b.—they stare 22.17
of my misery, and my b. waste away. 31.10
He keeps all his b.; not one 34.20
All my b. shall say, "O LORD, who is 35.10
no health in my b. because of my 38.03
let the b. which thou hast broken 51.08
will scatter the b. of the ungodly; 53.05

BONES (cont.)
and my b. burn like a furnace. Ps 102.03
groaning my b. cleave to my flesh. 102.05
like water, like oil into his b.! 109.18
so shall their b. be strewn at the 141.07
flesh and refreshment to your b. Pro 3.08
shame is like rottenness in his b. 12.04
but passion makes the b. rot. 14.30
and good news refreshes the b. 15.30
a downcast spirit dries up the b. 17.22
comes to the b. in the womb of a Ecc 11.05
like a lion he breaks all my b.; Is 38.13
things, and make your b. strong; 58.11
your b. shall flourish like the 66.14
the b. of the kings of Judah, the Jer 8.01
the b. of its princes, the b. of the priests, 8.01
the b. of the prophets, and the 8.01
and the b. of the inhabitants of 8.01
a burning fire shut up in my b., 20.09
broken within me, all my b. shake; 23.09
king of Babylon has gnawed his b. 50.17
into my b. he made it descend; Lam 1.13
skin waste away, and broken my b.; 3.04
skin has shriveled upon their b., 4.08
scatter your b. round about your Eze 6.05
shoulder; fill it with choice b. 24.04
pieces, seethe also its b. in it. 24.05
broth, and let the b. be burned up. 24.10
whose shields are upon their b.; 32.27
the valley; it was full of b. 37.01
me, "Son of man, can these b. live?" 37.03
said to me, "Prophesy to these b., 37.04
O dry b., hear the word of the LORD. 37.04
Thus says the Lord GOD to these b.: 37.05
and the b. came together, bone to 37.07
these b. are the whole house of 37.11
'Our b. are dried up, and our hope 37.11
and broke all their b. in pieces. Dan 6.24
to lime the b. of the king of Edom. Amo 2.01
up to bring the b. out of the 6.10
and their flesh from off their b.; Mic 3.02
them, and break their b. in pieces, 3.03
rottenness enters into my b., Hab 3.16
of dead men's b. and all uncleanness. Mt 23.27
not flesh and b. as you see that I Lk 24.39

BOOK
This is the b. of the generations Gen 5.01
a memorial in a b. and recite it Ex 17.14
Then he took the b. of the covenant, 24.07
out of thy b. which thou hast 32.32
me, him will I blot out of my b. 32.33
shall write these curses in a b., Num 5.23
is said in the B. of the Wars of 21.14
himself in a b. a copy of this law, Deu 17.18
law which are written in this b., 28.58
not recorded in the b. of this law, 28.61
written in this b. would settle 29.20
written in this b. of the law. 29.21
all the curses written in this b.; 29.27
are written in this b. of the law, 30.10
the words of this law in a b., 31.24
"Take this b. of the law, and put it 31.26
This b. of the law shall not depart Jos 1.08
written in the b. of the law of 8.31
is written in the b. of the law. 8.34
not written in the B. of Jashar? 10.13
set down in a b. a description of 18.09
written in the b. of the law of 23.06
words in the b. of the law of God; 24.26
wrote them in a b. and laid it up 1Sa 10.25
it is written in the B. of Jashar. 2Sa 1.18
written in the b. of the acts of 1Ki 11.41
written in the B. of the Chronicles 14.19
written in the B. of the Chronicles 14.29
written in the B. of the Chronicles 15.07
written in the B. of the Chronicles 15.23
written in the B. of the Chronicles 15.31
written in the B. of the Chronicles 16.05
written in the B. of the Chronicles 16.14
written in the B. of the Chronicles 16.20
written in the B. of the Chronicles 16.27
written in the B. of the Chronicles 22.39
written in the B. of the Chronicles 22.45
written in the B. of the Chronicles 2Ki 1.18
written in the B. of the Chronicles 8.23
written in the B. of the Chronicles 10.34
written in the B. of the Chronicles 12.19
written in the B. of the Chronicles 13.08
written in the B. of the Chronicles 13.12
written in the b. of the law of 14.06
written in the B. of the Chronicles 14.15
written in the B. of the Chronicles 14.18
written in the B. of the Chronicles 14.28
written in the B. of the Chronicles 15.06
written in the B. of the Chronicles 15.11
written in the B. of the Chronicles 15.15
written in the B. of the Chronicles 15.21
written in the B. of the Chronicles 15.26
written in the B. of the Chronicles 15.31
written in the B. of the Chronicles 15.36
written in the B. of the Chronicles 16.19
written in the B. of the Chronicles 20.20
written in the B. of the Chronicles 21.17
written in the B. of the Chronicles 21.25
have found the b. of the law in 22.08
And Hilkiah gave the b. to Shaphan, 22.08
the priest has given me a b." And 22.10
the words of the b. of the law, he rent 22.11
words of this b. that has been found 22.13
not obeyed the words of this b., 22.13
words of the b. which the king of 22.16
words of the b. of the covenant 23.02
that were written in this b.; and all 23.03
written in this b. of the covenant." 23.21
written in the b. that Hilkiah the 23.24
written in the B. of the Chronicles 23.28
written in the B. of the Chronicles 24.05
written in the B. of the Kings of 1Ch 9.01
written in the B. of the Kings of 2Ch 16.11
having the b. of the law of the 17.09
recorded in the B. of the Kings of 20.34
Commentary on the B. of the Kings. 24.27
in the b. of Moses, where the LORD 25.04
written in the B. of the Kings of 25.26
written in the B. of the Kings of 27.07
written in the B. of the Kings of 28.26
in the B. of the Kings of Judah and 32.32
found the b. of the law of the 34.14
have found the b. of the law in 34.15
and Hilkiah gave the b. to Shaphan. 34.15
Shaphan brought the b. to the king, 34.16
the priest has given me a b." 34.18
words of the b. that has been 34.21
to all that is written in this b." 34.21
written in the b. which was read 34.24
words of the b. of the covenant 34.30
that were written in this b. 34.31
it is written in the b. of Moses. 35.12
written in the B. of the Kings of 35.27
written in the B. of the Kings of 36.08
be made in the b. of the records Ez 4.15
find in the b. of the records and 4.15
it is written in the b. of Moses. 6.18
And I found the b. of the genealogy Neh 7.05
to bring the b. of the law of 8.01
attentive to the b. of the law. 8.03
And Ezra opened the b. in the sight 8.05
And they read from the b., from the 8.08
read from the b. of the law of God. 8.18
read from the b. of the law of the 9.03
written in the B. of the Chronicles 12.23
read from the b. of Moses in the 13.01
recorded in the B. of the Chronicles Est 2.23

BOOK (cont.)
to bring the b. of memorable deeds, Est 6.01
written in the B. of the Chronicles 10.02
that they were inscribed in a b.! Job 19.23
the roll of the b. it is written Ps 40.07
thy bottle! Are they not in thy b.? 56.08
out of the b. of the living; 69.28
in thy b. were written, every one of 139.16
the words of a b. that is sealed. Is 29.11
they give the b. to one who cannot 29.12
deaf shall hear the words of a b., 29.18
a tablet, and inscribe it in a b., 30.08
Seek and read from the b. of the LORD: 34.16
it, everything written in this b., Jer 25.13
Write in a b. all the words that I 30.02
words in a b. at the dictation of 45.01
Jeremiah wrote in a b. all the evil 51.60
When you finish reading this b., 51.63
is inscribed in the b. of truth: Dan 10.21
shall be found written in the b. 12.01
and seal the b., until the time of 12.04
The b. of the vision of Nahum of Nah 1.01
and a b. of remembrance was written Mal 3.16
The b. of the genealogy of Jesus Mt 1.01
you not read in the b. of Moses, Mk 12.26
written in the b. of the words of Lk 3.04
to him the b. of the prophet 4.17
He opened the b. and found the 4.17
And he closed the b., and gave 4.20
himself says in the B. of Psalms, 20.42
which are not written in this b.; Jn 20.30
In the first b., O Theophilus, I Ac 1.01
For it is written in the B. of Psalms, 1.20
written in the b. of the prophets: 7.42
written in the b. of the law, Gal 3.10
whose names are in the b. of life. Php 4.03
both the b. itself and all the Heb 9.19
of me in the roll of the b." 10.07
you see in a b. and send it to the Rev 1.11
his name out of the b. of life; 3.05
world in the b. of life of the 13.08
written in the b. of life from the 17.08
Also another b. was opened, which is 20.12
opened, which is the b. of life. 20.12
found written in the b. of life, 20.15
written in the Lamb's b. of life. 21.27
words of the prophecy of this b. 22.07
who keep the words of this b. 22.09
words of the prophecy of this b., 22.10
words of the prophecy of this b.: 22.18
the plagues described in this b., 22.18
words of the b. of this prophecy, 22.19
which are described in this b. 22.19

BOOKS
Of making many b. there is no end, Ecc 12.12
judgment, and the b. were opened. Dan 7.10
perceived in the b. the number of 9.02
not contain the b. that would be Jn 21.25
brought their b. together and Ac 19.19
also the b., and above all the 2Ti 4.13
the throne, and b. were opened. Rev 20.12
by what was written in the b., 20.12

BOOT
For every b. of the tramping Is 9.05

BOOTH
like a b. which a watchman makes. Job 27.18
is left like a b. in a vineyard, Is 1.08
broken down his b. like that of a Lam 2.06
raise up the b. of David that is Amo 9.11
and made a b. for himself there. Jon 4.05

BOOTHS
house, and made b. for his cattle; Gen 33.17
is the feast of b. to the LORD. Lev 23.34
You shall dwell in b. for seven days; 23.42
in Israel shall dwell in b. 23.42
Israel dwell in b. when I brought 23.43
keep the feast of b. seven days, Deu 16.13
of weeks, and at the feast of b. 16.16
of release, at the feast of b., 31.10
and Israel and Judah dwell in b.; 2Sa 11.11
drinking with the kings in the b., 1Ki 20.12
drinking himself drunk in the b., 20.16
And they kept the feast of b., Ez 3.04
should dwell in b. during the Neh 8.14
and other leafy trees to make b., 8.15
them and made b. for themselves, 8.16
captivity made b. and dwelt in the b.; 8.17
hosts, and to keep the feast of b. Zec 14.16
not go up to keep the feast of b. 14.18
not go up to keep the feast of b. 14.19
wish, I will make three b. here, Mt 17.04
let us make three b., one for Mk 9.05
let us make three b., one for Lk 9.33

BOOTY
they took as b. all their cattle, Num 31.09
and took all the spoil and all the b., 31.11
captives and the b. and the spoil 31.12
the count of the b. that was taken, 31.26
and divide the b. into two parts, 31.27
Now the b. remaining of the spoil 31.32
(The men of war had taken b., 31.53
with the b. of the cities which we Deu 2.35
of the cities we took as our b. 3.07
shall take as b. for yourselves; 20.14
shall take as b. for yourselves; Jos 8.02
that city Israel took as their b., 8.27
people of Israel took for their b.; 11.14
of Judah carried away very much b. 2Ch 14.13
Their camels shall become b., Jer 49.32
city, all full of lies and b.— Nah 3.01
Then you will be b. for them. Hab 2.07

BORASHAN
in Hormah, in B., in Athach, 1Sa 30.30

BORDER
Elparan on the b. of the wilderness; Gen 14.06
and his b. shall be at Sidon. 49.13
came to the b. of the land of Ex 16.35
the mountain or touch the b. of it; 19.12
not reap your field to its very b., Lev 19.09
not reap your field to its very b., 23.22
on the b. of the land of Edom, Num 20.23
of Ar, and leans to the b. of Moab." 21.15
as far as the b. of the Geshurites Deu 3.14
the LORD your God enlarges your b., 19.08
Gilgal on the east b. of Jericho. Jos 4.19
And the b. of the people of Reuben 13.23
down to the b. of the mountain 18.16
Jordan: this is the southern b. 18.19
And the b. of the Amorites ran from Ju 1.36
as far as the b. of Abelmeholah, by 7.22
as far as the b. of Bethshemesh. 1Sa 6.12
toward the b. that looks down upon 13.18
Philistines and to the b. of Egypt; 1Ki 4.21
He restored the b. of Israel from 2Ki 14.25
wouldst bless me and enlarge my b., 1Ch 4.10
Philistines, and to the b. of Egypt. 2Ch 9.26
spread even to the b. of Egypt, 26.08
and a pillar to the LORD at its b. Is 19.19
proper place, and spelt as the b.? 28.25
will judge you at the b. of Israel; Eze 11.10
will judge you at the b. of Israel; 11.11
as far as the b. of Ethiopia. 29.10
lies on the b. between Damascus 47.16
which is on the b. of Hauran. 47.16
is on the northern b. of Damascus, 47.17
with the b. of Hamath to the north. 47.17
Beginning at the northern b., from the 48.01
northern b. of Damascus over against Hamath), 48.01
of the holy portion to the east b., 48.21

BORDER (cont.)
thousand cubits to the west b., Eze 48.21
removing them far from their own b. Joe 3.06
that they might enlarge their b. Amo 1.13
they have driven you to the b.; Ob 1.07
our land and treads within our b. Mic 5.06
the LORD, beyond the b. of Israel!" Mal 1.05

BORDERS
before you, and enlarge your b.; Ex 34.24
and possess it to its farthest b.; Jos 17.18
any longer within the b. of Israel, 1Sa 27.01
their settlements within their b.: 1Ch 6.54
also along the b. of the Manassites, 7.29
He makes peace in your b.; he fills Ps 147.14
enlarged all the b. of the land. Is 26.15
or destruction within your b.; 60.18
Your b. are in the heart of the Eze 27.04
which b. thereon, Tyre and Sidon, Zec 9.02

BORE
and she conceived and b. Cain, Gen 4.01
And again, she b. his brother Abel. 4.02
and she conceived and b. Enoch; 4.17
Adah b. Jabal; he was the 4.20
Zillah b. Tubalcain; he was the 4.22
and she b. a son and called his 4.25
and they b. children to them. 6.04
and b. up the ark, and it rose high 7.17
b. him no children. She had an 16.01
And Hagar b. Abram a son; and Abram called 16.15
of his son, whom Hagar b., Ishmael. 16.15
old when Hagar b. Ishmael to Abram. 16.16
The first-born b. a son, and called 19.37
The younger also b. a son, 19.38
slaves so that they b. children. 20.17
and b. Abraham a son in his old age 21.02
to him, whom Sarah b. him, Isaac. 21.03
These eight Milcah b. to Nahor, 22.23
b. Tebah, Gaham, Tahash, and Maacah. 22.24
of Milcah, whom she b. to Nahor." 24.24
master's wife b. a son to my 24.36
Nahor's son, whom Milcah b. to him.' 24.47
She b. him Zimran, Jokshan, Medan, 25.02
Sarah's maid, b. to Abraham. 25.12
sixty years old when she b. them. 25.26
And Leah conceived and b. a son, 29.32
She conceived again and b. a son, 29.33
Again she conceived and b. a son, 29.34
And she conceived again and b. a son, 29.35
saw that she b. Jacob no children, 30.01
conceived and b. Jacob a son. 30.05
again and b. Jacob a second son. 30.07
Then Leah's maid Zilpah b. Jacob a son. 30.10
Leah's maid Zilpah b. Jacob a second 30.12
conceived and b. Jacob a fifth son. 30.17
and she b. Jacob a sixth son. 30.19
Afterwards she b. a daughter, and 30.21
She conceived and b. a son, 30.23
then all the flock b. spotted; 31.08
then all the flock b. striped. 31.08
I b. the loss of it myself; 31.39
And Adah b. to Esau, Eliphaz; 36.04
Eliphaz; Basemath b. Reuel; 36.04
and Oholibamah b. Jeush, Jalam, and 36.05
she b. Amalek to Eliphaz.) 36.12
she b. to Esau Jeush, Jalam, and 36.14
and she conceived and b. a son, 38.03
Again she conceived and b. a son, 38.04
Yet again she b. a son, and she 38.05
she was in Chezib when she b. him. 38.05
Potiphera priest of On, b. to him. 41.50
know that my wife b. me two sons; 44.27
whom she b. to Jacob in Paddan-aram, 46.15
and these she b. to Jacob—sixteen 46.18
the priest of On, b. to him. 46.20
and these she b. to Jacob—seven 46.25

The woman conceived and b. a son; Ex 2.02
She b. a son, and he called his name 2.22
sister and she b. him Aaron and 6.20
and she b. him Nadab, Abihu, Eleazar, 6.23
and she b. him Phinehas. These are 6.25
and how I b. you on eagles' wings 19.04
master shall b. his ear through 21.06
blossoms, and it b. ripe almonds. Num 17.08
and she b. to Amram Aaron and Moses 26.59
seen how the LORD your God b. you, Deu 1.31
which the LORD b. against you, 9.19
and when those who b. the ark had Jos 3.15
the priests who b. the ark of the 3.17
For the priests who b. the ark 4.10
of Israel b. harder and harder on Ju 4.24
was in Shechem also b. him a son, 8.31
And Gilead's wife also b. him sons; 11.02
And the woman b. a son, and called 13.24
whom Tamar b. to Judah, because of Ru 4.12
her conception, and she b. a son. 4.13
time Hannah conceived and b. a son, 1Sa 1.20
conceived and b. three sons and 2.21
to the young man who b. his armor, 14.01
to the young man who b. his armor, 14.06
and when those who b. the ark of 2Sa 6.13
became his wife, and b. him a son. 11.27
that Uriah's wife b. to David, 12.15
and she b. a son, and he called his 12.24
whom she b. to Saul, Armoni and 21.08
whom she b. to Adriel the son of 21.08
because you b. the ark of the LORD 1Ki 2.26
of Tahpenes b. him Genubath his 11.20
the guard b. them and brought them 14.28
and she b. a son about that time 2Ki 4.17
she b. Zimran, Jokshan, Medan, Midian, 1Ch 1.32
Bathshua the Canaanitess b. to him. 2.03
Tamar also b. him Perez and Zerah. 2.04
Abigail b. Amasa, and the father of 2.17
married Ephrath, who b. him Hur. 2.19
years old; and she b. him Segub; 2.21
and she b. him Ashhur, the father of 2.24
and she b. him Ahban and Molid. 2.29
his slave; and she b. him Attai. 2.35
b. Haran, Moza, and Gazez; 2.46
concubine, b. Sheber and Tirhanah. 2.48
She also b. Shaaph the father of 2.49
Naarah b. him Ahuzzam, Hepher, Temeni, 4.06
saying, "Because I b. him in pain." 4.09
and she conceived and b. Miriam, 4.17
And his Jewish wife b. Jered the 4.18
whom his Aramaean concubine b.; 7.14
she b. Machir the father of Gilead. 7.14
Maacah the wife of Machir b. a son, 7.16
And his sister Hammolecheth b. Ishhod, 7.18
and she conceived and b. a son; 7.23
and she b. him sons, Jeush, Shemariah, 2Ch 11.19
who b. him Abijah, Attai, Ziza, and 11.20
LORD, the guard came and b. them, 12.11
since my mother b. me thou hast Ps 22.10
host of those who b. the tidings: 68.11
and bitterness to her who b. him. Pro 17.25
glad, let her who b. you rejoice. 23.25
flawless to her that b. her. Sol 6.09
there she who b. you was in travail. 8.05
and she conceived and b. a son. Is 8.03
And Elam b. the quiver with chariots 22.06
father and to Sarah who b. you; 51.02
yet he b. the sin of many, and made 53.12
She who b. seven has languished; Jer 15.09
that you b. me, a man of strife and 15.10
the mothers who b. them and the 16.03
The day when my mother b. me, 20.14
the mother who b. you into another 22.26
because I b. the disgrace of my 31.19
and she who b. you shall be disgraced. 50.12
and they b. sons and daughters. Eze 23.04
and she conceived and b. him a son. Hos 1.03

BORE (cont.)
She conceived again and b. a daughter. Hos 1.06
pitied, she conceived and b. a son. 1.08
and mother who b. him will say to Zec 13.03
and mother who b. him shall pierce 13.03
infirmities and b. our diseases. Mt 8.17
the plants came up and b. grain, 13.26
For many b. false witness against Mk 14.56
stood up and b. false witness 14.57
"Blessed is the womb that b. you, Lk 11.27
and the wombs that never b., 23.29
(John b. witness to him, and cried, Jn 1.15
And John b. witness, "I saw the 1.32
to whom you b. witness, here he is, 3.26
him from the dead b. witness. 12.17
forty years he b. with them in the Ac 13.18
who b. witness to the word of his 14.03
knows the heart b. witness to them, 15.08
while God also b. witness by signs Heb 2.04
He himself b. our sins in his body 1Pe 2.24
who b. witness to the word of God Rev 1.02
the men who b. the mark of the 16.02

BORED
and b. a hole in the lid of it, and 2Ki 12.09

BORN
To Enoch was b. Irad; and Irad Gen 4.18
To Seth also a son was b., and he 4.26
and daughters were b. to them, 6.01
sons were b. to them after the 10.01
of Japheth, children were b. 10.21
To Eber were b. two sons: the name 10.25
b. in his house, three hundred and 14.14
and a slave b. in my house will be 15.03
whether b. in your house, or bought 17.12
both he that is b. in your house 17.13
a child be b. to a man who is a 17.17
all the slaves b. in his house or 17.23
those b. in the house and those 17.27
name of his son who was b. to him, 21.03
when his son Isaac was b. to him. 21.05
who was b. to Bethuel the son of 24.15
b. of you, shall be divided; 25.23
Jacob who were b. to him in 35.26
Esau who were b. to him in the 36.05
are the chiefs b. of Oholibamah 36.18
of Egypt were b. Manasseh and 46.20
who were b. to Jacob—fourteen 46.22
who were b. to him in Egypt, were 46.27
who were b. to you in the land of 48.05
And the offspring b. to you after 48.06
Manasseh were b. upon Joseph's 50.23
son that is b. to the Hebrews you Ex 1.22
whether b. at home or b. abroad. Lev 18.09
those that are b. in his house may 22.11
"When a bull or sheep or goat is b., 22.27
you, who have been b. in your land; 25.45
who was b. to Levi in Egypt; Num 26.59
And to Aaron were b. Nadab, 26.60
males that are b. of your herd and Deu 15.19
that are b. to them may enter the 23.08
that were b. on the way in the Jos 5.05
to do with the boy that will be b." Ju 13.08
ancestor, who was b. to Israel; 18.29
saying, "A son has been b. to Naomi." Ru 4.17
And sons were b. to David at Hebron: 2Sa 3.02
These were b. to David in Hebron. 3.05
and daughters were b. to David. 5.13
those who were b. to him in 5.14
child that is b. to you shall die." 12.14
There were b. to Absalom three sons, 14.27
and he was b. next after Absalom. 1Ki 1.06
who shall be b. to you shall build 8.19
a son shall be b. to the house of 13.02
who are b. to you, shall be taken 2Ki 20.18
To Eber were b. two sons: the name 1Ch 1.19
that were b. to him: Jerahmeel, Ram, 2.09
David that were b. to him in 3.01
six were b. to him in Hebron, where 3.04
These were b. to him in Jerusalem: 3.05
Gath who were b. in the land slew, 7.21
Behold, a son shall be b. to you; 22.09
Also to his son Shemaiah were sons b., 26.06
who shall be b. to you shall build 2Ch 6.09
There were b. to him seven sons and Job 1.02
"Let the day perish wherein I was b., 3.03
but man is b. to trouble as the 5.07
when a wild ass's colt is b. a man. 11.12
"Man that is b. of a woman is of 14.01
"Are you the first man that was b.? 15.07
Or he that is b. of a woman, that he 15.14
can he who is b. of woman be clean? 25.04
for you were b. then, and the number 38.21
"This one was b. there," they say. Ps 87.04
one and that one were b. in her"; 87.05
the peoples, "This one was b. there." 87.06
and a brother is b. for adversity. Pro 17.17
had slaves who were b. in my house; Ecc 2.07
a time to be b., and a time to die; 3.02
his own kingdom had been b. poor. 4.14
For to us a child is b., to us a Is 9.06
who are b. to you, shall be taken 39.07
The children b. in the time of your 49.20
Shall a land be b. in one day? 66.08
before you were b. I consecrated Jer 1.05
daughters who are b. in this place, 16.03
Cursed be the day on which I was b.! 20.14
"A son is b. to you," making him 20.15
country, where you were not b., 22.26
day you were b. your navel string Eze 16.04
on the day that you were b. 16.05
make her as in the day she was b., Hos 2.03
of Mary, of whom Jesus was b., Mt 1.16
Now when Jesus was b. in Bethlehem 2.01
he who has been b. king of the 2.02
them where the Christ was to be b. 2.04
among those b. of women there has 11.11
for that man if he had not been b." 26.24
for that man if he had not been b." Mk 14.21
the child to be b. will be called Lk 1.35
for to you is b. this day in the 2.11
among those b. of women none is 7.28
who were b., not of blood nor of Jn 1.13
unless one is b. anew, he cannot see 3.03
"How can a man be b. when he is old? 3.04
into his mother's womb and be b.?" 3.04
unless one is b. of water and the 3.05
That which is b. of the flesh is 3.06
that which is b. of the Spirit is 3.06
said to you, 'You must be b. anew.' 3.07
every one who is b. of the Spirit." 3.08
him, "We were not b. of fornication; 8.41
his parents, that he was b. blind?" 9.02
your son, who you say was b. blind? 9.19
our son, and that he was b. blind; 9.20
opened the eyes of a man b. blind. 9.32
"You were b. in utter sin, and would 9.34
that a child is b. into the world. 16.21
For this I was b., and for this 18.37
At this time Moses was b., Ac 7.20
"I am a Jew, b. at Tarsus in Cilicia, 22.03
Paul said, "But I was b. a citizen." 22.28
were not yet b. and had done Rom 9.11
man, so man is now b. of woman. 1Co 11.12
Last of all, as to one untimely b., 15.08
had set me apart before I was b., Gal 1.15
b. of woman, b. under the law, 4.04
the slave was b. according to the 4.23
time he who was b. according to 4.29
b. according to the Spirit, 4.29
being b. in the likeness of men. Php 2.07
Benjamin, a Hebrew b. of Hebrews; 3.05
were b. descendants as many as the Heb 11.12

BORN (cont.)

when he was b., was hid for three Heb 11.23
we have been b. anew to a living 1Pe 1.03
You have been b. anew, not of 1.23
b. to be caught and killed, reviling 2Pe 2.12
one who does right is b. of him. 1Jn 2.29
No one b. of God commits sin; 3.09
cannot sin because he is b. of God. 3.09
he who loves is b. of God and 4.07
For whatever is b. of God overcomes 5.04
that any one b. of God does not 5.18
but He who was b. of God keeps him, 5.18

BORNE

Yet I have b. him a son in his old Gen 21.07
whom she had b. to Abraham, playing 21.09
Milcah also has b. children to 22.20
because I have b. him three sons"; 29.34
because I have b. him six sons"; 30.20
When Rachel had b. Joseph, 30.25
their children whom they have b. 31.43
whom she had b. to Jacob, went out 34.01
and they have b. him children, both Deu 21.15
to you than seven sons, has b. him." Ru 4.15
The barren has b. seven, but she 1Sa 2.05
"Fear not, for you have b. a son." 4.20
it was not the child that I had b." 1Ki 3.21
When he is b. to the grave, watch is Job 21.32
to God, 'I have b. chastisement; 34.31
thy sake that I have b. reproach, Ps 69.07
who have been b. by me from your Is 46.03
your heart: 'Who has b. me these? 49.21
her among all the sons she has b.; 51.18
Surely he has b. our griefs and 53.04
camels shall be b. away from them, Jer 49.29
whom you had b. to me, and these you Eze 16.20
the sons whom they had b. to me. 23.37
for they have b. alien children. Hos 5.07
her not until she had b. a son; Mt 1.25
to us who have b. the burden of 20.12
seen and have b. witness that this Jn 1.34
and he has b. witness to the truth. 5.33
me has himself b. witness to me. 5.37
He who saw it has b. witness— 19.35
Just as we have b. the image of the 1Co 15.49
to which was b. at the proper time. 1Ti 2.06
the voice was b. to him by the 2Pe 1.17
we heard this voice b. from heaven, 1.18
God that he has b. witness to his 1Jn 5.09
testimony that God has b. to his Son. 5.10
and for the witness they had b.; Rev 6.09
woman who had b. the male child. 12.13

BORROW

many nations, but you shall not b.; Deu 15.06
many nations, but you shall not b. 28.12
b. vessels of all your neighbors, 2Ki 4.03
refuse him who would b. from you. Mt 5.42

BORROWED

"Alas, my master! It was b." 2Ki 6.05
"We have b. money for the king's tax Neh 5.04
nor have I b., yet all of them Jer 15.10

BORROWER

and the b. is the slave of the Pro 22.07
as with the lender, so with the b.; Is 24.02

BORROWS

"If a man b. anything of his Ex 22.14
The wicked b., and cannot pay back, Ps 37.21

BOSOM

to him, "Put your hand into your b." Ex 4.06
And he put his hand into his b.; 4.06
"Put your hand back into your b." 4.07
he put his hand back into his b.; 4.07
say to me, 'Carry them in your b., Num 11.12
daughter, or the wife of your b., Deu 13.06
his brother, to the wife of his b., 28.54
grudge to the husband of her b., 28.56
the child and laid him in her b., Ru 4.16
from his cup, and lie in his b., 2Sa 12.03
your master's wives into your b., 12.08
let her lie in your b., that my 1Ki 1.02
slept, and laid it in her b., 3.20
and laid her dead son in my b. 3.20
And he took him from her b., 17.19
treasured in my b. the words of Job 23.12
by hiding my iniquity in my b., 31.33
I prayed with head bowed on my b Ps 35.13
Even my b. friend in whom I trusted, 41.09
thou keep thy right hand in thy b.? 74.11
into the b. of our neighbors the 79.12
I bear in my b. the insults of the 89.50
or the binder of sheaves his b., 129.07
and embrace the b. of an adventuress? Pro 5.20
fire in his b. and his clothes not 6.27
bribe from the b. to pervert the 17.23
a bribe in the b., strong wrath. 21.14
anger lodges in the b. of fools. Ecc 7.09
arms, he will carry them in his b., Is 40.11
shall bring your sons in their b., 49.22
yea, I will repay into their bosom 65.06
into their b. payment for their 65.07
is poured out on their mothers' b. Lam 2.12
her virgin b. and poured out their Eze 23.08
handled your b. and pressed your 23.21
mouth from her who lies in your b.; Mic 7.05
by the angels to Abraham's b. Lk 16.22
far off and Lazarus in his b. 16.23
who is in the b. of the Father, he Jn 1.18

BOSOMS

and their virgin b. handled. Eze 23.03

BOTH

the man and his wife were b. naked, Gen 2.25
Then the eyes of b. were opened, 3.07
laid it upon b. their shoulders, and 9.23
not support b. of them dwelling 13.06
b. he that is born in your house 17.13
b. young and old, all the people to 19.04
b. small and great, so that they 19.11
Thus b. the daughters of Lot were 19.36
because there b. of them swore an 21.31
So they went b. of them together. 22.06
So they went b. of them together. 22.08
"We have b. straw and provender 24.25
I be bereft of you b. in one day?" 27.45
destroyed, b. I and my household." 34.30
And one night they b. dreamed— 40.05
b. we and you and also our little 43.08
b. we and he also in whose hand the 44.16
b. we and our fathers,' in order 46.34
b. we and our land? Buy us 47.19
And Joseph took them b., Ephraim 48.13
up with him b. chariots and 50.09
b. in vessels of wood and in Ex 7.19
land of Egypt, b. man and beast; 9.25
land of Egypt, b. man and beast; 12.12
b. you and the people of Israel; 12.31
cattle, b. flocks and herds. 12.38
b. of man and of beast, is mine." 13.02
b. the first-born of man and the 13.15
the case of b. parties shall 22.09
be between them b. to see whether 22.11
thus shall it be with b. of them; 26.24
that were written on b. sides; 32.15
So they came, b. men and women; 35.22
b. him and Oholiab the son of 35.34
b. without blemish, and offer them Lev 9.02
b. a year old without blemish, for a 9.03
b. of them shall bathe themselves 15.18
and Aaron shall lay b. his hands 16.21

BOTH (cont.)

b. the adulterer and the adulteress Lev 20.10
b. of them shall be put to death, 20.11
b. of them shall be put to death; 20.12
b. of them have committed an 20.13
b. he and they, that there may be no 20.14
b. of them shall be cut off from 20.18
b. of the most holy and of the holy 21.22
shall not kill b. her and her 22.28
then b. it and that for which it is 27.10
then b. it and that for which it is 27.33
b. of man and of beast; they shall Num 3.13
you shall put out b. male and 5.03
b. of them full of fine flour mixed 7.13
b. of them full of fine flour mixed 7.19
b. of them full of fine flour mixed 7.25
b. of them full of fine flour mixed 7.31
b. of them full of fine flour mixed 7.37
b. of them full of fine flour mixed 7.43
b. of them full of fine flour mixed 7.49
b. of them full of fine flour mixed 7.55
b. of them full of fine flour mixed 7.61
b. of them full of fine flour mixed 7.67
b. of them full of fine flour mixed 7.73
b. of them full of fine flour mixed 7.79
b. of man and of beast; on the day 8.17
b. for the sojourner and for the 9.14
And when b. are blown, all the 10.03
and they b. came forward. 12.05
die here, b. we and our cattle? 20.04
and pierced b. of them, the man of 25.08
b. he and all the people of Israel 27.21
the booty, b. of man and of beast. 31.11
b. of man and of beast, you and 31.26
b. of persons and of beasts, and 31.47
then b. parties to the dispute Deu 19.17
b. the loved and the disliked, and 21.15
b. of them shall die, the man who 22.22
bring them b. out to the gate of 22.24
for b. of these are an abomination 23.18
b. he who hews your wood and he who 29.11
destroying b. young man and virgin, 32.25
b. men and women, young and old, oxen, Jos 6.21
b. men and women, were twelve 8.25
b. those in Bethshean and its 17.16
b. they and their camels could not Ju 6.05
day declines." So they ate, b. of them. 19.08
and b. Mahlon and Chilion died, so Ru 1.05
continued to grow b. in stature and 1Sa 2.26
b. of them shall die on the same 2.34
of Dagon and b. his hands were 5.04
b. Ashdod and its territory. 5.06
b. young and old, so that tumors 5.09
b. fortified cities and unwalled 6.18
and b. he and Samuel went out into 9.26
and if b. you and the king who 12.14
swept away, b. you and your king." 12.25
So b. of them showed themselves to 14.11
but kill b. man and woman, infant 15.03
has killed b. lions and bears; 17.36
So they b. went out into the field. 20.11
we have sworn b. of us in the name 20.42
b. men and women, children and 22.19
a wall to us b. by night and by 25.16
and b. of them became his wives. 25.43
b. small and great; they killed 30.02
b. men and women, to each a cake of 2Sa 6.19
Now he was lame in b. his feet. 9.13
set against him b. in front and in 10.09
and let me see b. it and his 15.25
b. by David and by Absalom. 16.23
so b. of them went away quickly, and 17.18
b. you and all your servants." 19.14
b. riches and honor, so that no 1Ki 3.13
b. the nave and the inner sanctuary; 6.05
b. cherubim had the same measure 6.25
b. above and below the lions and 7.29
b. bond and free in Israel, and will 14.10
b. because of all the evil that he 16.07
as they b. were standing by the 2Ki 2.07
b. small and great; and he read 23.02
b. small and great, and the captains 25.26
who built b. lower and upper 1Ch 7.24
b. sons of Shemaah of Gibeah; 12.03
b. men and women, to each a loaf of 16.03
set against him b. in front and in 19.10
of God among b. the sons of 24.05
B. riches and honor come from thee, 29.12
b. for the service and for the 2Ch 24.14
b. in the Shephelah and in the 26.10
b. he and the inhabitants of 32.26
all the people b. great and small; 34.30
b. men and women and all who could Neh 8.02
So b. companies of those who gave 12.40
b. great and small, a banquet Est 1.05
the men were b. hanged on the 2.23
King Ahasuerus, b. near and far, 9.20
he destroys b. the blameless and Job 9.22
who might lay his hand upon us b. 9.33
B. the grayhaired and the aged are 15.10
In peace I will b. lie down and Ps 4.08
b. low and high, rich and poor 49.02
b. rider and horse lay stunned. 76.06
living things b. small and great. 104.25
B. we and our fathers have sinned; 106.06
the LORD, b. small and great. 115.13
of Egypt, b. of man and of beast; 135.08
righteous are b. alike an abomination Pro 17.15
measures are b. alike an abomination 20.10
eye, the LORD has made them b. 20.12
ruin that will come from them b.? 24.22
provocation is heavier than b. 27.03
LORD gives light to the eyes of b. 29.13
b. men and women, and many concubines, Ecc 2.08
but better than b. is he who has 4.03
or whether b. alike will be good. 11.06
and b. of them shall burn together, Is 1.31
of stumbling to b. houses of 8.14
b. soul and body, and it will be as 10.18
b. the young and the old, naked and 20.04
shall fail b. king and princes; Jer 4.09
b. husband and wife shall be taken, 6.11
b. the birds of the air and the 9.10
They are b. stupid and foolish; 10.08
For b. prophet and priest ply their 14.18
B. great and small shall die in 16.06
of this city, b. man and beast; 21.06
"B. prophet and priest are ungodly; 23.11
b. this sealed deed of purchase and 32.14
b. we and our fathers, our kings and 44.17
they have b. fallen together." 46.12
b. man and beast shall flee away. 50.03
the LORD has b. planned and done 51.12
fire has consumed b. ends of it, Eze 15.04
b. the fortunes of Sodom and her 16.53
b. your elder and your younger, and 16.61
off from you b. righteous and 21.03
off from you b. righteous and 21.04
b. of them shall come forth from 21.19
they b. took the same way. 23.13
b. the strong arm and the one that 30.22
the land on b. sides of the holy 45.07
on b. sides of the river, there will 47.12
"What remains on b. sides of the 48.21
b. of the royal family and of the Dan 1.03
and b. horns were high, but one was 8.03
to seal b. vision and prophet, and 9.24
consume it, b. timber and stones." Zec 5.04
understanding shall be between them b."' 6.13
wineskins, and so b. are preserved." Mt 9.17
who can destroy b. soul and body 10.28
Let b. grow together until the 13.30
blind man, b. will fall into a pit." 15.14
whom they found, b. bad and good; 22.10

BOTH (cont.)

And they were b. righteous before Lk 1.06
and b. were advanced in years. 1.07
they came and filled b. the boats, 5.07
Will they not b. fall into a pit? 6.39
could not pay, he forgave them b. 7.42
who invited you b. will come and 14.09
b. chief priests and scribes; 22.66
and destroy b. our holy place and Jn 11.48
seen and hated b. me and my Father. 15.24
They b. ran, but the other disciple 20.04
from Rome, b. Jews and proselytes, Ac 2.10
David that he b. died and was 2.29
has made him b. Lord and Christ, 2.36
b. Herod and Pontius Pilate, with 4.27
multitudes b. of men and women, 5.14
God sent as b. ruler and deliverer 7.35
were baptized, b. men and women. 8.12
and they b. went down into the 8.38
all that he did b. in the country 10.39
believed, b. of Jews and of Greeks. 14.01
was made by b. Gentiles and Jews, 14.05
passed through b. Phoenicia and 15.03
b. the apostles and the elders, to 15.23
the Lord, b. Jews and Greeks. 19.10
b. Jews and Greeks; and fear 19.17
testifying b. to Jews and to Greeks 20.21
to prison b. men and women, 22.04
resurrection of b. the just and 24.15
b. at Jerusalem and here, shouting 25.24
here testifying b. to small and 26.22
proclaim light b. to the people 26.23
about Jesus b. from the law of 28.23
other's faith, b. yours and mine. Rom 1.12
obligation b. to Greeks and to 1.14
b. to the wise and to the foolish: 1.14
b. Jews and Greeks, are under the 3.09
might be Lord b. of the dead and 14.09
Jesus Christ, b. their Lord and ours: 1Co 1.02
b. Jews and Greeks, Christ the power 1.24
will destroy b. one and the other. 6.13
our peace, who has made us b. one, Eph 2.14
reconcile us b. to God in one body 2.16
for through him we b. have access 2.18
that he who is b. their Master and 6.09
b. in my imprisonment and in the Php 1.07
b. to will and to work for his good 2.13
who killed b. the Lord Jesus and 1Th 2.15
you will save b. yourself and your 1Ti 4.16
b. in the flesh and in the Lord. Phm 1.16
and sprinkled b. the book itself Heb 9.19
with the blood b. the tent and all 9.21
and in b. of them I have aroused 2Pe 3.01
be the glory b. now and to the day 3.18
of Christ has b. the Father and 2Jn 1.09
b. small and great, and for destroying Rev 11.18
b. small and great, b. rich and poor, 13.16
b. free and slave, to be marked on 13.16
b. free and slave, b. small and great." 19.18

BOTHER

answer from within, 'Do not b. me; Lk 11.07

BOTHERS

yet because this widow b. me, Lk 18.05

BOTTLE

the waters of the sea as in a b.; Ps 33.07
put thou my tears in thy b.! 56.08

BOTTOM

flowed into the b. of the chariot. 1Ki 22.35
made at the b. of the rows round Eze 46.23
reached the b. of the den the Dan 6.24
from my sight at the b. of the sea, Amo 9.03
was torn in two, from top to b.; Mt 27.51
was torn in two, from top to b. Mk 15.38
without seam, woven from top to b.; Jn 19.23

BOTTOMLESS

the key of the shaft of the b. pit; Rev 9.01
he opened the shaft of the b. pit, 9.02
over them the angel of the b. pit; 9.11
from the b. pit will make war upon 11.07
ascend from the b. pit and go to 17.08
the key of the b. pit and a great 20.01

BOUGH

Joseph is a fruitful b., a fruitful b. Gen 49.22
in the top of the highest b., Is 17.06

BOUGHS

and b. of leafy trees, and willows Lev 23.40
you shall not go over the b. again; Deu 24.20
will lop the b. with terrifying Is 10.33
When its b. are dry, they are broken; 27.11
may bring forth b. and bear fruit, Eze 17.23
towered aloft among the thick b.; 19.11
its b. grew large and its branches 31.05
the air made their nests in its b.; 31.06
it, nor the fir trees equal its b.; 31.08
and its b. will lie broken in all 31.12

BOUGHT

or b. with your money from any Gen 17.12
and he that is b. with your money, 17.13
in his house or b. with his money, 17.23
house and those b. with money from 17.27
he b. for a hundred pieces of money 33.19
b. him from the Ishmaelites who had 39.01
for the grain which they b.; 47.14
So Joseph b. all the land of Egypt 47.20
I have this day b. you and your 47.23
which Abraham b. with the field 49.30
which Abraham b. with the field 50.13
slave that is b. for money may eat Ex 12.44
hand of him who b. it until the Lev 25.28
in perpetuity to him who b. it, 25.30
with him who b. him from the year 25.50
the LORD a field which he has b., 27.22
return to him from whom it was b., 27.24
which Jacob b. from the sons of Jos 24.32
day that I have b. from the hand Ru 4.09
I have b. to be my wife, to perpetuate 4.10
little ewe lamb, which he had b. 2Sa 12.03
So David b. the threshing floor and 24.24
He b. the hill of Samaria from 1Ki 16.24
have b. back our Jewish brethren Neh 5.08
I b. male and female slaves, and had Ecc 2.07
You have not b. me sweet cane with Is 43.24
So I b. a waistcloth according to Jer 13.02
"Take the waistcloth which you have b., 13.04
"And I b. the field at Anathoth 32.09
shall again be b. in this land.' 32.15
Fields shall be b. in this land of 32.43
Fields shall be b. for money, 32.44
drink, the wood we get must be b. Lam 5.04
So I b. her for fifteen shekels of Hos 3.02
and sold all that he had and b. it. Mt 13.46
all who sold and b. in the temple, 21.12
and b. with them the potter's field, 27.07
and those who b. in the temple, Mk 11.15
And he b. a linen shroud, and taking 15.46
b. spices, so that they might go and 16.01
'I have b. a field, and I must go Lk 14.18
'I have b. five yoke of oxen, and I 14.19
they b., they sold, they planted, 17.28
(Now this man b. a field with the Ac 1.18
Abraham had b. for a sum of silver 7.16
"I b. this citizenship for a large 22.28
you were b. with a price. So glorify 1Co 6.20
You were b. with a price; do not 7.23
denying the Master who b. them, 2Pe 2.01

BOUND

and b. Isaac his son, and laid him Gen 22.09
took and b. on his hand a scarlet 38.28

BOUND (cont.)
from them and b. him before their Gen 42.24
as his life is b. up in the lad's 44.30
bowls being b. up in their mantles Ex 12.34
And they b. the breastpiece by its 39.21
and b. caps on them, as the LORD Lev 8.13
pledge by which she has b. herself, Num 30.04
which she has b. herself shall 30.04
pledge by which she has b. herself, 30.05
lips by which she has b. herself, 30.06
which she has b. herself shall 30.07
her lips, by which she b. herself; 30.08
by which she has b. herself, 30.09
or b. herself by a pledge with an 30.10
by which she b. herself shall 30.11
and she b. the scarlet cord in the Jos 2.21
So they b. him with two new ropes, Ju 15.13
lies, and how you might be b., 16.06
dried, and she b. him with them. 16.08
please tell me how you might be b." 16.10
new ropes and b. him with them, 16.12
tell me how you might be b." And he 16.13
and b. him with bronze fetters; 16.21
Lord shall be b. in the bundle of 1Sa 25.29
Your hands were not b., your feet 2Sa 3.34
shut him up, and b. him in prison. 2Ki 17.04
and b. him in fetters, and took him 25.07
with hooks and b. him with fetters 2Ch 33.11
and b. him in fetters to take him 36.06
in Judah were b. by oath to him, Neh 6.18
thou settest a b. to the soles of Job 13.27
to the farthest b. the ore in 28.03
And if they are b. in fetters and 36.08
Thou didst set a b. which they Ps 104.09
a city which is b. firmly together, 122.03
Folly is b. up in the heart of a Pro 22.15
or b. up, or softened with oil. Is 1.06
of the prison to those who are b.; 61.01
the sand as the b. for the sea, Jer 5.22
and b. him in fetters to take him 39.07
he took him b. in chains along 40.01
and b. him in fetters, and the king 52.11
transgressions were b. into a yoke; Lam 1.14
you, and you shall be b. with them, Eze 3.25
b. with cords and made secure; 27.24
and lo, it has not been b. up, 30.21
the crippled you have not b. up, 34.04
Then these men were b. in their Dan 3.21
fell b. into the burning fiery 3.23
cast three men b. into the fire?" 3.24
b. with a band of iron and bronze, 4.15
b. with a band of iron and bronze, 4.23
The iniquity of Ephraim is b. up, Hos 13.12
her great men were b. in chains. Nah 3.10
seized John and b. him and put him Mt 14.03
on earth shall be b. in heaven, 16.19
on earth shall be b. in heaven, 18.18
the temple, he is b. by his oath.' 23.16
on the altar, he is b. by his oath.' 23.18
and they b. him and led him away 27.02
had often been b. with fetters and Mk 5.04
and b. him in prison for the sake 6.17
and they b. Jesus and led him away 15.01
and b. with chains and fetters, but Lk 8.29
and went to him and b. up his wounds, 10.34
whom Satan b. for eighteen years, 13.16
hands and feet b. with bandages, Jn 11.44
the Jews seized Jesus and b. him. 18.12
Annas then sent him b. to Caiaphas 18.24
and b. it in linen cloths with the 19.40
might bring them b. to Jerusalem. Ac 9.02
to bring them b. before the chief 9.21
b. with two chains, and sentries 12.06
b. in the Spirit, not knowing what 20.22
girdle and b. his own feet and 21.11
him to be b. with two chains. 21.33
citizen and that he had b. him. 22.29
made a plot and b. themselves by 23.12
have strictly b. ourselves by an 23.14
having b. themselves by an oath 23.21
that I am b. with this chain." 28.20
woman is b. by law to her husband Rom 7.02
the brother or sister is not b. 1Co 7.15
Are you b. to a wife? Do not 7.27
A wife is b. to her husband as long 7.39
that he is b. to keep the whole Gal 5.03
We are b. to give thanks to God 2Th 1.03
But we are b. to give thanks to God 2.13
Because of this he is b. to offer Heb 5.03
angels who are b. at the great Rev 9.14
and b. him for a thousand years, 20.02

BOUNDARIES
be your land with its b. all round." Num 34.12
but maintains the widow's b. Pro 15.25
I have removed the b. of peoples, Is 10.13
"These are the b. by which you Eze 47.13
periods and the b. of their Ac 17.26

BOUNDARY
from the b. of the Amorites; Num 21.13
for the Arnon is the b. of Moab, 21.13
Jazer was the b. of the Ammonites. 21.24
on the b. formed by the Arnon, at 22.36
Arnon, at the extremity of the b. 22.36
your southern b. shall be from the 34.03
and your b. shall turn south of the 34.04
and the b. shall turn from Azmon to 34.05
"For the western b. you shall have 34.06
this shall be your western b. 34.06
"This shall be your northern b.: 34.07
the end of the b. shall be at 34.08
then the b. shall extend to Ziphron, 34.09
this shall be your northern b. 34.09
your eastern b. from Hazarenan to 34.10
and the b. shall go down from 34.11
and the b. shall go down, and reach 34.11
and the b. shall go down to the 34.12
to pass over the b. of Moab at Ar; Deu 2.18
the middle of the valley as a b., 3.16
Jabbok, the b. of the Ammonites; 3.16
also, with the Jordan as the b., 3.17
the b. of the Ammonites, that is, Jos 12.02
Bashan to the b. of the Geshurites 12.05
Gilead to the b. of Sihon king of 12.05
northward to the b. of Ekron, 13.03
to the b. of the Amorites, 13.04
as far as the b. of the Ammonites; 13.10
of Reuben was the Jordan as a b. 13.23
Heshbon, having the Jordan as a b., 13.27
southward to the b. of Edom, 15.01
And their south b. ran from the end 15.02
This shall be your south b. 15.04
And the east b. is the Salt Sea, to 15.05
And the b. on the north side runs 15.05
and the b. goes up to Bethhoglah, 15.06
and the b. goes up to the stone of 15.06
and the b. goes up to Debir from 15.07
and the b. passes along to the 15.07
then the b. goes up by the valley 15.08
and the b. goes up to the top of 15.08
then the b. extends from the top of 15.09
then the b. bends round to Baalah 15.09
and the b. circles west of Baalah 15.10
the b. goes out to the shoulder of 15.11
then the b. bends round to Shikkeron, 15.11
then the b. comes to an end at the 15.11
And the west b. was the Great Sea 15.12
is the b. round about the people of 15.12
toward the b. of Edom, were Kabzeel, 15.21
the b. of their inheritance on the 16.05
and the b. goes thence to the sea; 16.06
on the east the b. turns round 16.06
From Tappuah the b. goes westward 16.08
then the b. goes along southward to 17.07

BOUNDARY (cont.)
Tappuah on the b. of Manasseh Jos 17.08
Then the b. went down to the brook 17.09
Then the b. of Manasseh goes on the 17.09
with the sea forming its b.; 17.10
side their b. began at the Jordan; 18.12
then the b. goes up to the shoulder 18.12
From there the b. passes along 18.13
then the b. goes down to Atarothaddar, 18.13
Then the b. goes in another direction, 18.14
and the b. goes from there to 18.15
then the b. goes down to the border 18.16
then the b. passes on to the north 18.19
and the b. ends at the northern bay 18.19
forms its b. on the eastern side. 18.20
families, b. by b. round about. 18.20
then its b. goes up westward, and on 19.11
sunrise to the b. of Chislothtabor; 19.12
the north the b. turns about to 19.14
the b. also touches Tabor, Shahazumah, 19.22
and its b. ends at the Jordan— 19.22
then the b. turns to Ramah, reaching 19.29
then the b. turns to Hosah, and it 19.29
And its b. ran from Heleph, from the 19.33
then the b. turns westward to 19.34
the Jordan a b. between us and you, 22.25
for the Arnon was the b. of Moab. Ju 11.18
waters at the b. between light and Job 26.10
to the eastern b. of the land. Eze 45.07
"This shall be the b. of the land: 47.15
So the b. shall run from the sea to 47.17
the b. shall run from Hazarenon 47.18
shall be the b. to a point opposite 47.20
the b. shall run from Tamar to the 48.28
In that day the b. shall be far Mic 7.11

BOUNDING
the mountains, b. over the hills. Sol 2.08
galloping horse and b. chariot! Nah 3.02

BOUNDS
And you shall set b. for the people Ex 19.12
'Set b. about the mountain, and 19.23
And I will set your b. from the Red 23.31
go beyond the b. of his city of Num 35.26
him outside the b. of his city of 35.27
he fixed the b. of the peoples Deu 32.08
him within the b. of his inheritance Ju 2.09
Jezebel within the b. of Jezreel.' 1Ki 21.23
appointed his b. that he cannot Job 14.05
and prescribed b. for it, and set 38.10
farthest b. are afraid at thy Ps 65.08
hast fixed all the b. of the earth; 74.17
he fixed their b. which cannot be 148.06
They know no b. in deeds of wickedness; Jer 5.28
they break all b. and murder follows Hos 4.02

BOUNTIES
the b. of the everlasting hills; Gen 49.26

BOUNTIFUL
He who has a b. eye will be blessed, Pro 22.09

BOUNTIFULLY
because he has dealt b. with me. Ps 13.06
for the LORD has dealt b. with you. 116.07
Deal b. with thy servant, that I may 119.17
for thou wilt deal b. with me. 142.07
and he who sows b. will also reap b. 2Co 9.06

BOUNTY
her by the b. of King Solomon. 1Ki 10.13
according to the b. of the king. Est 1.07
Thou crownest the year with thy b.; Ps 65.11
to the LORD for all his b. to me? 116.12

BOW
I set my b. in the cloud, and it Gen 9.13
earth and the b. is seen in the 9.14
When the b. is in the clouds, I will 9.16
and became an expert with the b. 21.20
weapons, your quiver and your b., 27.03
you, and nations b. down to you. 27.29
your mother's sons b. down to you. 27.29
indeed come to b. ourselves to the 37.10
they cried before him, "B. the knee!" 41.43
with my sword and with my b." 48.22
sons shall b. down before you. 49.08
yet his b. remained unmoved, his 49.24
and b. down to me, saying, 'Get you Ex 11.08
you shall not b. down to them or 20.05
you shall not b. down to their gods, 23.24
made haste to b. his head toward 34.08
in your land, to b. down to them; Lev 26.01
you shall not b. down to them or Deu 5.09
or b. down yourselves to them, Jos 23.07
other gods and b. down to them. 23.16
not by your sword or by your b. 24.12
sword and his b. and his girdle. 1Sa 18.04
the b. of Jonathan turned not back, 2Sa 1.22
my arms can bend a b. of bronze. 22.35
man drew his b. at a venture, 1Ki 22.34
and I b. myself in the house of 2Ki 5.18
b. myself in the house of Rimmon, 5.18
with your sword and with your b.? 6.22
And Jehu drew his b. with his full 9.24
said to him, "Take a b. and arrows"; 13.15
so he took a b. and arrows. 13.15
the king of Israel, "Draw the b."; 13.16
other gods or b. yourselves to 17.35
you shall b. yourselves to him, 17.36
and drew the b., expert in war, 1Ch 5.18
men armed with b. and shield, 2Ch 17.17
man drew his b. at a venture, 18.33
Mordecai did not b. down or do Est 3.02
Mordecai did not b. down or do 3.05
and my b. ever new in my hand.' Job 29.20
and let others b. down upon her. 31.10
he has bent and strung his b.; Ps 7.12
for lo, the wicked bend the b., 11.02
my arms can bend a b. of bronze. 18.34
all the proud of the earth b. down; 22.29
him shall b. all who go down to 22.29
For not in my b. do I trust, nor can 44.06
Since he is your lord, b. to him; 45.11
he breaks the b., and shatters the 46.09
thee, to rally to it from the b. 60.04
May his foes b. down before him, and 72.09
The Ephraimites, armed with the b., 78.09
they twisted like a deceitful b. 78.57
you shall not b. down to a foreign 81.09
shall come and b. down before thee, 86.09
O come, let us worship and b. down, 95.06
all gods b. down before him. 97.07
I b. down toward thy holy temple 138.02
B. thy heavens, O LORD, and come down! 144.05
The evil b. down before the good, Pro 14.19
they b. down to the work of their Is 2.08
With b. and arrows men will come 7.24
from the bent b., and from the 21.15
without the b. they were captured. 22.03
like driven stubble with his b. 41.02
over in chains and b. down to you. 45.14
return: 'To me every knee shall b., 45.23
they b. down together, they cannot 46.02
ground they shall b. down to you, 49.23
'B. down, that we may pass over'; and 51.23
Is it to b. down his head like a 58.05
you shall b. down at your feet; 60.14
of you shall b. down to the 65.12
who draw the b., to Tubal and Javan, 66.19
They lay hold on b. and spear, Jer 6.23
They bend their tongue like a b.; 9.03
of Lud, skilled in handling the b. 46.09
I will break the b. of Elam, 49.35
about, all you that bend the b.; 50.14
Babylon, all those who bend the b. 50.29

BOW (cont.)
They lay hold of b. and spear; Jer 50.42
Let not the archer bend his b., 51.03
He has bent his b. like an enemy, Lam 2.04
he bent his b. and set me as a mark 3.12
appearance of the b. that is in the Eze 1.28
strike your b. from your left hand, 39.03
will break the b. of Israel in the Hos 1.05
I will not deliver them by b., 1.07
and I will abolish the b., 2.18
they are like a treacherous b., 7.16
he who handles the b. shall not Amo 2.15
and you shall b. down no more to Mic 5.13
and b. myself before God on high? 6.06
didst strip the sheath from thy b., Hab 3.09
those who b. down on the roofs to Zep 1.05
those who b. down and swear to the 1.05
earth, and to him shall b. down, 2.11
and the battle b. shall be cut off, Zec 9.10
For I have bent Judah as my b.; 9.13
peg, out of them the battle b., 10.04
of laying out anchors from the b., Ac 27.30
the b. stuck and remained immovable, 27.41
Lord, every knee shall b. to me, Rom 14.11
For this reason I b. my knees Eph 3.14
name of Jesus every knee should b., Php 2.10
them come and b. down before your Rev 3.09
horse, and its rider had a b.; 6.02

BOWED
and b. himself to the earth, Gen 18.02
and b. himself with his face to the 19.01
Abraham rose and b. to the Hittites, 23.07
Then Abraham b. down before the 23.12
The man b. his head and worshiped 24.26
Then I b. my head and worshiped the 24.48
he b. himself to the earth before 24.52
and their children, and b. down; 33.06
her children drew near and b. down; 33.07
Rachel drew near, and they b. down. 33.07
round it, and b. down to my sheaf." 37.07
and b. themselves before him with 42.06
and b. down to him to the ground. 43.26
And they b. their heads and made 43.28
Then Israel b. himself upon the 47.31
and he b. himself with his face to 48.12
so he b. his shoulder to bear, and 49.15
they b. their heads and worshiped. Ex 4.31
And the people b. their heads and 12.27
and he b. his head, and fell on his Num 22.31
and b. down to their gods. 25.02
about them, and b. down to them; Ju 2.12
other gods and b. down to them; 2.17
Then he b. with all his might; 16.30
were dead, she b. and gave birth; 1Sa 4.19
to the ground, and b. three times; 20.41
David b. with his face to the earth, 24.08
on her face, and b. to the ground. 25.23
And she rose and b. with her face 25.41
and he b. with his face to the 28.14
and b. himself on his face to the 2Sa 14.33
The Cushite b. before Joab, and ran. 18.21
And he b. before the king with his 18.28
He b. the heavens, and came down; 22.10
Bathsheba b. and did obeisance to 1Ki 1.16
he b. before the king, with his face 1.23
Then Bathsheba b. with her face to 1.31
And the king b. himself upon the 1.47
to meet her, and b. down to her; 2.19
and he b. himself down upon the 18.42
the knees that have not b. to Baal, 19.18
and b. to the ground before him. 2Ki 2.15
and b. their heads, and worshiped 1Ch 29.20
they b. down with their faces to 2Ch 7.03
Then Jehoshaphat b. his head with 20.18
with him b. themselves and worshiped. 29.29
and they b. down and worshiped. 29.30
and they b. their heads and worshiped Neh 8.06
the king's gate b. down and did Est 3.02
beneath him b. the helpers of Rahab. Job 9.13
He b. the heavens, and came down; Ps 18.09
I prayed with head b. on my bosom, 35.13
mother, b. down and in mourning. 35.14
I am utterly b. down and prostrate; 38.06
For our soul is b. down to the dust; 44.25
my soul was b. down. They dug 57.06
Their hearts were b. down with hard 107.12
and raises up all who are b. down. 145.14
lifts up those who are b. down; 146.08
Man is b. down, and men are brought Is 5.15
I am b. down so that I cannot hear, 21.03
He who is b. down shall speedily be 51.14
green tree you b. down as a harlot. Jer 2.20
Jerusalem have b. their heads to Lam 2.10
of it and is b. down within me. 3.20
frightened and b. their faces to Lk 24.05
and he b. his head and gave up his Jn 19.30
who have not b. the knee to Baal. Rom 11.04

BOWELS
pass into your b. and make your Num 5.22
and shed his b. to the ground, 2Sa 20.10
sickness with a disease of your b., 2Ch 21.15
until your b. come out because of 21.15
him in his b. with an incurable 21.18
his b. came out because of the 21.19
middle and all his b. gushed out. Ac 1.18

BOWING
b. himself to the ground seven Gen 33.03
eleven stars were b. down to me." 37.09
serving them and b. down to them; Ju 2.19
b. to the ground, and said to him, Ru 2.10
fell at his feet, b. to the ground; 2Ki 4.37
b. in worship over the head of his Heb 11.21

BOWL
brought him curds in a lordly b. Ju 5.25
the fleece to fill a b. with water. 6.38
He said, "Bring me a new b., 2Ki 2.20
or the golden b. is broken, or the Ecc 12.06
is a rounded b. that never lacks Sol 7.02
to the dregs the b. of staggering. Is 51.17
the b. of my wrath you shall drink 51.22
with a b. on the top of it, and Zec 4.02
right of the b. and the other on 4.03
like wine, and be full like a b., 9.15
A b. full of vinegar stood there; Jn 19.29
and poured his b. on the earth, Rev 16.02
angel poured his b. into the sea, 16.03
poured his b. into the rivers and 16.04
angel poured his b. on the sun, 16.08
poured his b. on the throne of the 16.10
poured his b. on the great river 16.12
angel poured his b. into the air, 16.17

BOWLS
your ovens and your kneading b.; Ex 8.03
their kneading b. being bound up 12.34
its flagons and b. with which to 25.29
and its b. and flagons with which 37.16
the b., and the flagons for the Num 4.07
the two b. of the capitals that 1Ki 7.41
to cover the two b. of the capitals 7.41
cover the two b. of the capitals 7.42
b., trumpets, or any vessels of gold, 2Ki 12.13
the firepans also, and the b. 25.15
for the golden b. and the weight of 1Ch 28.17
for the silver b. and the weight of 28.17
the b., and the two capitals on the 2Ch 4.12
cover the two b. of the capitals 4.12
cover the two b. of the capitals 4.13
thirty b. of gold, two thousand four Ez 1.10
four hundred and ten b. of silver, 1.10
twenty b. of gold worth a thousand 8.27
also the small b., and the firepans, Jer 52.19

BOWLS (cont.)
incense, and the b. for libation. Jer 52.19
who drink wine in b., and anoint Amo 6.06
shall be as the b. before the Zec 14.20
and with golden b. full of incense, Rev 5.08
seven golden b. full of the wrath 15.07
earth the seven b. of the wrath of 16.01
had the seven b. came and said to 17.01
had the seven b. full of the seven 21.09

BOWMEN
b., having many sons and grandsons, 1Ch 8.40
They were b., and could shoot 12.02

BOWS
The b. of the mighty are broken, but 1Sa 2.04
that carried shields and drew b.; 2Ch 14.08
of mail, b., and stones for slinging. 26.14
swords, their spears, and their b. Neh 4.13
b., and coats of mail; and the 4.16
aim at their faces with your b. Ps 21.12
draw the sword and bend their b., 37.14
and their b. shall be broken. 37.15
all their b. bent, their horses' Is 5.28
Their b. will slaughter the young 13.18
Bel b. down, Nebo stoops, their idols 46.01
their b. are broken in pieces; Jer 51.56
b. and arrows, handpikes and spears, Eze 39.09

BOWSHOT
off, about the distance of a b.; Gen 21.16

BOWSTRINGS
seven fresh b. which have not been Ju 16.07
her seven fresh b. which had not 16.08
But he snapped the b., as a string 16.09

BOX
and put in a b. at its side the 1Sa 6.08
and the b. with the golden mice and 6.11
LORD and the b. that was beside it, 6.15
had the money b. he used to take Jn 12.06
because Judas had the money b., 13.29
I do not b. as one beating the air; 1Co 9.26

BOXES
the perfume b., and the amulets; Is 3.20

BOY
for the b. shall be a Nazirite to Ju 13.05
for the b. shall be a Nazirite to 13.07
to do with the b. that will be 13.08
and the b. grew, and the LORD 13.24
And the b. ministered to the LORD, 1Sa 2.11
a b. girded with a linen ephod. 2.18
And the b. Samuel grew in the 2.21
Now the b. Samuel continued to grow 2.26
Now the b. Samuel was ministering 3.01
that the LORD was calling the b. 3.08
his reign, while he was yet a b., 2Ch 34.03
and have given a b. for a harlot, Joe 3.03
and the b. was cured instantly. Mt 17.18
And they brought the b. to him; Mk 9.20
immediately it convulsed the b., 9.20
and the b. was like a corpse; 9.26
the b. Jesus stayed behind in Lk 2.43
unclean spirit, and healed the b., 9.42

BOY'S
is to be the b. manner of life, Ju 13.12

BOYS
When the b. grew up, Esau was a Gen 25.27
some small b. came out of the city 2Ki 2.23
woods and tore forty-two of the b. 2.24
And I will make b. their princes, Is 3.04
and b. stagger under loads of wood. Lam 5.13
be full of b. and girls playing in Zec 8.05

BOZEZ
the name of the one was B., and the name 1Sa 14.04

BOZKATH
Lachish, B., Eglon, Jos 15.39
the daughter of Adaiah of B. 2Ki 22.01

BOZRAH
son of Zerah of B. reigned in his Gen 36.33
son of Zerah of B. reigned in his 1Ch 1.44
For the LORD has a sacrifice in B., Is 34.06
in crimsoned garments from B., 63.01
and B., and all the cities of the Jer 48.24
that B. shall become a horror, a 49.13
and spread his wings against B., 49.22
shall devour the strongholds of B. Amo 1.12

BRACELETS
and two b. for her arms weighing Gen 24.22
and the b. on his sister's arms, and 24.30
her nose, and the b. on her arms. 24.47
armlets and b., signet rings, Num 31.50
pendants, the b., and the scarfs; Is 3.19
and put b. on your arms, and a chain Eze 16.11
and they put b. upon the hands of 23.42

BRACKISH
same opening fresh water and b.? Jas 3.11

BRAIDED
not with b. hair or gold or pearls 1Ti 2.09

BRAIDING
outward adorning with b. of hair, 1Pe 3.03

BRAMBLE
Then all the trees said to the b., Ju 9.14
And the b. said to the trees, 'If in 9.15
come out of the b. and devour the 9.15
are grapes picked from a b. bush. Lk 6.44

BRAMBLES
As a lily among b., so is my Sol 2.02

BRANCH
on one b., and three cups made like Ex 25.33
on the other b.—so for the six 25.33
on one b., and three cups made like 37.19
on the other b.—so for the six 37.19
from there a b. with a single Num 13.23
and his b. will not be green. Job 15.32
In that day the b. of the LORD Is 4.02
palm b. and reed in one day— 9.14
and a b. shall grow out of his 11.01
or tail, palm b. or reed, may do. 19.15
raise up for David a righteous B., Jer 23.05
a righteous B. to spring forth for 33.15
lo, they put the b. to their nose. Eze 8.17
the vine b. which is among the 15.02
"In those times a b. from her roots Dan 11.07
I will bring my servant the B. Zec 3.08
the man whose name is the B.: 6.12
leave them neither root nor b. Mal 4.01
as soon as its b. becomes tender Mt 24.32
as soon as its b. becomes tender Mk 13.28
Every b. of mine that bears no Jn 15.02
and every b. that does bear fruit 15.02
As the b. cannot bear fruit by 15.04
is cast forth as a b. and withers; 15.06

BRANCHES
and on the vine there were three b.; Gen 40.10
the three b. are three days; 40.12
spring; his b. run over the wall. 49.22
shall be six b. going out of its Ex 25.32
three b. of the lampstand out of 25.32
of it and three b. of the lampstand 25.32
so for the six b. going out of the 25.33
pair of the six b. going out from 25.35
and their b. shall be of one piece 25.36
And there were six b. going out of 37.18
three b. of the lampstand out of 37.18
of it and three b. of the lampstand 37.18

BRANCHES (cont.)
so for the six b. going out of the Ex 37.19
pair of the six b. going out of it. 37.21
and their b. were of one piece 37.22
b. of palm trees, and boughs of Lev 23.40
under the thick b. of a great oak, 2Sa 18.09
to the hills and bring b. of olive, Neh 8.15
and put forth b. like a young Job 14.09
beneath, and his b. wither above. 18.16
with the dew all night on my b., 29.19
the mighty cedars with its b.; Ps 80.10
it sent out its b. to the sea, 80.11
habitation; they sing among the b. 104.12
Bind the festal procession with b., 118.27
palm tree and lay hold of its b. Sol 7.08
nations have struck down its b., Is 16.08
or five on the b. of a fruit tree, 17.06
the spreading b. he will hew away. 18.05
and the b. of Egypt's Nile will 19.06
he lies down, and strips its b. 27.10
strip away her b., for they Jer 5.10
pass your hand again over its b." 6.09
and its b. will be consumed. 11.16
Your b. passed over the sea, reached 48.32
and its b. turned toward him, and Eze 17.06
brought forth b. and put forth 17.06
shot forth its b. toward him that 17.07
that it might bring forth b., 17.08
up its roots and cut off its b., 17.09
shade of its b. birds of every 17.23
and full of b. by reason of 19.10
its height with the mass of its b. 19.11
has consumed its b. and fruit, 19.14
with fair b. and forest shade, and 31.03
boughs grew large and its b. long, 31.05
under its b. all the beasts of the 31.06
greatness, in the length of its b.; 31.07
as nothing compared with its b.; 31.08
it beautiful in the mass of its b., 31.09
all the valleys its b. will fall, 31.12
and upon its b. will be all the 31.13
Israel, shall shoot forth your b., 36.08
birds of the air dwelt in its b., Dan 4.12
down the tree and cut off its b., 4.14
under it and the birds from its b. 4.14
and in whose b. the birds of the 4.21
it down; their b. are made white. Joe 1.07
stripped them and ruined their b.) Nah 2.02
are these two b. of the olive Zec 4.12
air comes and make nests in its b." Mt 13.32
and others cut b. from the trees 21.08
shrubs, and puts forth large b., Mk 4.32
spread leafy b. which they had cut 11.08
of the air made nests in its b." Lk 13.19
So they took b. of palm trees and Jn 12.13
I am the vine, you are the b. 15.05
and the b. are gathered, thrown into 15.06
if the root is holy, so are the b. Rom 11.16
But if some of the b. were broken 11.17
do not boast over the b. If you do 11.18
You will say, "B. were broken off so 11.19
God did not spare the natural b., 11.21
these natural b. be grafted back 11.24
robes, with palm b. in their hands, Rev 7.09

BRAND
you were as a b. plucked out of Amo 4.11
Is not this a b. plucked from the Zec 3.02

BRANDISH
when I b. my sword before them; Eze 32.10
I will b. your sons, O Zion, over Zec 9.13

BRANDISHED
battling with b. arm he will fight Is 30.32

BRANDS
kindle a fire, who set b. alight! Is 50.11
and by the b. which you have kindled! 50.11

BRASS
like iron and your earth like b.; Lev 26.19
heavens over your head shall be b., Deu 28.23
iron sinew and your forehead b., Is 48.04

BRAVEST
twelve thousand of their b. men, Ju 21.10

BRAWLER
Wine is a mocker, strong drink a b.; Pro 20.01

BRAY
Does the wild ass b. when he has Job 6.05
Among the bushes they b.; under the 30.07

BRAZEN
things, the deeds of a b. harlot; Eze 16.30

BRAZIER
fire burning in the b. before him. Jer 36.22
throw them into the fire in the b., 36.23
in the fire that was in the b. 36.23

BREACH
"What a b. you have made for Gen 38.29
"For every b. of trust, whether it Ex 22.09
one commits a b. of faith and sins Lev 5.15
and commits a b. of faith against 6.02
rebellion or in b. of faith toward Jos 22.22
LORD had made a b. in the tribes Ju 21.15
closed up the b. of the city of 1Ki 11.27
Then a b. was made in the city; 2Ki 25.04
there was no b. left in it (although Neh 6.01
He breaks me with b. upon b.; Job 16.14
As through a wide b. they come; 30.14
stood in the b. before him, to turn Ps 106.23
be called the repairer of the b., Is 58.12
month, a b. was made in the city. Jer 39.02
Then a b. was made in the city; 52.07
stand in the b. before me for the Eze 22.30
He who opens the b. will go up Mic 2.13

BREACHED
Thou hast b. all his walls; Ps 89.40
enters a city which has been b. Eze 26.10
Thebes shall be b., and its 30.16

BREACHES
and that the b. were beginning to Neh 4.07
repair its b., for it totters. Ps 60.02
saw that the b. of the city of Is 22.09
You have not gone up into the b., Eze 13.05
And you shall go out through the b., Amo 4.03
that is fallen and repair its b., 9.11

BREAD
you shall eat b. till you return Gen 3.19
of Salem brought out b. and wine; 14.18
while I fetch a morsel of b., 18.05
baked unleavened b., and they ate. 19.03
and took b. and a skin of water, and 21.14
Then Jacob gave Esau b. and pottage 25.34
gave the savory food and the b., 27.17
will give me b. to eat and clothing 28.20
and called his kinsmen to eat b.; 31.54
and they ate b. and tarried all 31.54
all the land of Egypt there was b. 41.54
the people cried to Pharaoh for b.; 41.55
that they should eat b. there. 43.25
might not eat b. with the Hebrews, 43.32
b., and provision for his father on 45.23
Call him, that he may eat b." Ex 2.20
with unleavened b. and bitter herbs 12.08
Seven days you shall eat unleavened b.; 12.15
observe the feast of unleavened b., 12.17
you shall eat unleavened b., 12.18
you shall eat unleavened b." 12.20
no leavened b. shall be eaten. 13.03
Seven days you shall eat unleavened b., 13.06

BREAD (cont.)
Unleavened b. shall be eaten for Ex 13.07
no leavened b. shall be seen with 13.07
fleshpots and ate b. to the full; 16.03
I will rain b. from heaven for you; 16.04
and in the morning b. to the full, 16.08
you shall be filled with b.; 16.12
"It is the b. which the LORD has 16.15
day they gathered twice as much b., 16.22
day he gives you b. for two days; 16.29
may see the b. with which I fed 16.32
Israel to eat b. with Moses' 18.12
keep the feast of unleavened b.; 23.15
eat unleavened b. for seven days 23.15
of my sacrifice with leavened b., 23.18
will bless your b. and your water; 23.25
shall set the b. of the Presence 25.30
and unleavened b., unleavened cakes 29.02
loaf of b., and one cake of b. with oil, 29.23
of unleavened b. that is before 29.23
the ram and the b. that is in the 29.32
or of the b., remain until the 29.34
of unleavened b. you shall keep. 34.18
days you shall eat unleavened b., 34.18
he neither ate b. nor drank water. 34.28
utensils, and the b. of the Presence; 35.13
utensils, and the b. of the Presence; 39.36
and set the b. in order on it 40.23
offering with cakes of leavened b. Lev 7.13
and the basket of unleavened b.; 8.02
of unleavened b. which was before 8.26
cake, and one cake of b. with oil, 8.26
eat it and the b. that is in the 8.31
flesh and the b. you shall burn 8.32
to the LORD, the b. of their God; 21.06
for he offers the b. of your God; 21.08
approach to offer the b. of his God. 21.17
near to offer the b. of his God. 21.21
He may eat the b. of his God, both 21.22
offer as the b. of your God any 22.25
feast of unleavened b. to the LORD; 23.06
days you shall eat unleavened b. 23.06
eat neither b. nor grain parched 23.14
two loaves of b. to be waved, 23.17
with the b. seven lambs a year old 23.18
them with the b. of the first 23.20
may go with the b. as a memorial 24.07
you shall eat your b. to the full, 26.05
When I break your staff of b., 26.26
shall bake your b. in one oven, 26.26
deliver your b. again by weight; 26.26
table of the b. of the Presence Num 4.07
the continual b. also shall be on 4.07
and a basket of unleavened b., 6.15
with the basket of unleavened b.; 6.17
with unleavened b. and bitter 9.11
the land, for they are b. for us; 14.09
days shall unleavened b. be eaten. 28.17
that man does not live by b. alone, Deu 8.03
you will eat b. without scarcity, 8.09
I neither ate b. nor drank water. 9.09
I neither ate b. nor drank water, 9.18
You shall eat no leavened b. with it; 16.03
shall eat it with unleavened b., 16.03
the b. of affliction—for you came 16.03
days you shall eat unleavened b.; 16.08
at the feast of unleavened b., 16.16
meet you with b. and with water on 23.04
you have not eaten b., and you 29.06
Here is our b.; it was still Jos 9.12
cake of barley b. tumbled into the Ju 7.13
give loaves of b. to the people 8.05
we should give b. to your army?" 8.06
we should give b. to your men who 8.15
your heart with a morsel of b., 19.05
with b. and wine for me and your 19.19
and eat some b., and dip your Ru 2.14
have hired themselves out for b., 1Sa 2.05
a piece of silver or a loaf of b., 2.36
that I may eat a morsel of b."'" 2.36
For the b. in our sacks is gone, and 9.07
carrying three loaves of b., 10.03
you and give you two loaves of b., 10.04
And Jesse took an ass laden with b., 16.20
Give me five loaves of b., 21.03
David, "I have no common b. at hand, 21.04
at hand, but there is holy b.; 21.04
So the priest gave him the holy b.; 21.06
there was no b. there but the 21.06
there but the b. of the Presence, 21.06
replaced by hot b. on the day it 21.06
you have given him b. and a sword, 22.13
Shall I take my b. and my water and 25.11
me set a morsel of b. before you; 28.22
it and baked unleavened b. of it, 28.24
and they gave him b. and he ate, 30.11
had not eaten b. or drunk water 30.12
by the sword, or who lacks b.!" 2Sa 3.29
David to eat b. while it was yet 3.35
if I taste b. or anything else till 3.35
and women, to each a cake of b., 6.19
master's son may have b. to eat; 9.10
Tamar come and give me b. to eat, 13.05
bearing two hundred loaves of b., 16.01
the b. and summer fruit for the 16.02
table for the b. of the Presence, 1Ki 7.48
I will not eat b. or drink water 13.08
saying, 'You shall neither eat b., 13.09
him, "Come home with me and eat b." 13.15
will I eat b. nor drink water with 13.16
neither eat b. nor drink water 13.17
that he may eat b. and drink water.'" 13.18
and ate b. in his house, and drank 13.19
and have eaten b. and drunk water 13.22
"Eat no b., and drink no water"; 13.22
And after he had eaten b. and drunk, 13.23
brought him b. and meat in the 17.06
and b. and meat in the evening; 17.06
me a morsel of b. in your hand." 17.11
and fed them with b. and water.) 18.04
and fed them with b. and water? 18.13
and eat b., and let your heart be 21.07
with scant fare of b. and water, 22.27
the man of God b. of the first 2Ki 4.42
Set b. and water before them, that 6.22
a land of b. and vineyards, a land 18.32
ate unleavened b. among their 23.09
and women, to each a loaf of b., 1Ch 16.03
the wafers of unleavened b., 23.29
tables for the b. of the Presence, 2Ch 4.19
feasts—the feast of unleavened b., 8.13
with scant fare of b. and water, 18.26
of unleavened b. in the second 30.13
of unleavened b. seven days with 30.21
feast of unleavened b. seven days. 35.17
of unleavened b. seven days with Ez 6.22
neither eating b. nor drinking 10.06
Thou didst give them b. from heaven Neh 9.15
of Israel with b. and water, 13.02
For my sighing comes as my b., Job 3.24
He wanders abroad for b., saying, 15.23
have withheld b. from the hungry. 22.07
As for the earth, out of it comes b.; 28.05
so that his life loathes b., 33.20
and ate b. with him in his house; 42.11
eat up my people as they eat b., Ps 14.04
forsaken or his children begging b. 37.25
who ate of my b., has lifted his 41.09
eat up my people as they eat b., 53.04
Can he also give b., or provide meat 78.20
Man ate of the b. of the angels; 78.25
hast fed them with the b. of tears, 80.05
withered; I forget to eat my b. 102.04
For I eat ashes like b., and mingle 102.09

BREAD (cont.)
and b. to strengthen man's heart. Ps 104.15
land, and broke every staff of b., 105.16
and gave them b. from heaven in 105.40
eating the b. of anxious toil; 127.02
I will satisfy her poor with b. 132.15
For they eat the b. of wickedness Pro 4.17
may be hired for a loaf of b., 6.26
eat of my b. and drink of the wine 9.05
and b. eaten in secret is pleasant." 9.17
plays the great man but lacks b. 12.09
his land will have plenty of b., 12.11
and you will have plenty of b. 20.13
B. gained by deceit is sweet to a 20.17
for he shares his b. with the poor. 22.09
Do not eat the b. of a man who is 23.06
is hungry, give him b. to eat; 25.21
his land will have plenty of b., 28.19
for a piece of b. a man will do 28.21
does not eat the b. of idleness. 31.27
Go, eat your b. with enjoyment, and Ecc 9.07
nor b. to the wise, nor riches to 9.11
B. is made for laughter, and wine 10.19
Cast your b. upon the waters, for 11.01
and staff, the whole stay of b., Is 3.01
there is neither b. nor mantle; 3.07
eat our own b. and wear our own 4.01
water, meet the fugitive with b., 21.14
Does one crush b. grain? 28.28
give you the b. of adversity and 30.20
his b. will be given him, his water 33.16
wine, a land of b. and vineyards. 36.17
he kindles a fire and bakes b.; 44.15
I also baked b. on its coals, I 44.19
the Pit, neither shall his b. fail. 51.14
money for that which is not b., 55.02
to the sower and b. to the eater, 55.10
to share your b. with the hungry, 58.07
No one shall break b. for the Jer 16.07
and a loaf of b. was given him 37.21
until all the b. of the city was 37.21
for there is no b. left in the 38.09
As they ate b. together there at 41.01
the trumpet, or be hungry for b., 42.14
people groan as they search for b.; Lam 1.11
mothers, "Where is b. and wine?" 2.12
and to Assyria, to get b. enough. 5.06
We get our b. at the peril of our 5.09
single vessel, and make b. of them. Eze 4.09
of Israel eat their b. unclean, 4.13
on which you may prepare your b." 4.15
break the staff of b. in Jerusalem; 4.16
they shall eat b. by weight and 4.16
that they may lack b. and water, 4.17
you, and break your staff of b. 5.16
eat your b. with quaking, and drink 12.18
shall eat their b. with fearfulness, 12.19
of barley and for pieces of b., 13.19
its staff of b. and send famine 14.13
Also my b. which I gave you—I fed 16.19
gives his b. to the hungry and 18.07
but gives his b. to the hungry and 18.16
lips, nor eat the b. of mourners." 24.17
lips, nor eat the b. of mourners. 24.22
in it to eat b. before the LORD; 44.03
days unleavened b. shall be eaten. 45.21
who give me my b. and my water, Hos 2.05
Their b. shall be like mourners' b.; 9.04
for their b. shall be for their 9.04
and lack of b. in all your places, Amo 4.06
and eat b. there, and prophesy there 7.12
not a famine of b., nor a 8.11
and touches with his skirt b., Hag 2.12
stones to become loaves of b." Mt 4.03
'Man shall not live by b. alone, 4.04
Give us this day our daily b.; 6.11
God and ate the b. of the Presence, 12.04
the children's b. and throw it to 15.26
are we to get b. enough in the 15.33
they had forgotten to bring any b. 16.05
themselves, saying, "We brought no b." 16.07
the fact that you have no b.? 16.08
that I did not speak about b.? 16.11
them to beware of the leaven of b., 16.12
of Unleavened B. the disciples 26.17
Jesus took b., and blessed, and 26.26
and ate the b. of the Presence, Mk 2.26
no b.. no bag, no money in their 6.08
two hundred denarii worth of b., 6.37
the children's b. and throw it to 7.27
these men with b. here in the 8.04
Now they had forgotten to bring b.; 8.14
one another, saying, "We have no b." 8.16
the fact that you have no b.? 8.17
and the feast of Unleavened B. 14.01
And on the first day of Unleavened B., 14.12
who is dipping b. in the same dish 14.20
he took b., and blessed, and broke 14.22
command this stone to become b." Lk 4.03
'Man shall not live by b. alone.'" 4.04
and ate the b. of the Presence, 6.04
come eating no b. and drinking no 7.33
staff, nor bag, nor b., nor money; 9.03
Give us each day our daily b.; 11.03
who shall eat b. in the kingdom of 14.15
servants have b. enough and to 15.17
feast of Unleavened B. drew near, 22.01
Then came the day of Unleavened B., 22.07
And he took b., and when he had 22.19
he took the b. and blessed, and 24.30
to them in the breaking of the b. 24.35
to Philip, "How are we to buy b., Jn 6.05
not buy enough b. for each of them 6.07
they ate the b. after the Lord had 6.23
'He gave them b. from heaven to eat.'" 6.31
who gave you the b. from heaven; 6.32
gives you the true b. from heaven. 6.32
For the b. of God is that which 6.33
him, "LORD, give us this b. always." 6.34
Jesus said to them, "I am the b. of life; 6.35
"I am the b. which came down from 6.41
I am the b. of life. 6.48
This is the b. which comes down 6.50
I am the living b. which came down 6.51
if any one eats of this b., 6.51
and the b. which I shall give for 6.51
This is the b. which came down from 6.58
who eats this b. will live for 6.58
'He who ate my b. has lifted his 13.18
with fish lying on it, and b. 21.09
and took the b. and gave it to 21.13
the breaking of b. and the prayers. Ac 2.42
and breaking b. in their homes, 2.46
during the days of Unleavened B. 12.03
after the days of Unleavened B., 20.06
were gathered together to break b., 20.07
up and had broken b. and eaten, 20.11
he took b., and giving thanks to 27.35
the unleavened b. of sincerity and 1Co 5.08
The b. which we break, is it not a 10.16
when he was betrayed took b., 11.23
as you eat this b. and drink the 11.26
eats the b. or drinks the cup of 11.27
so eat of the b. and drink of the 11.28
the sower and b. for food will 2Co 9.10
eat any one's b. without paying, 2Th 3.08
table and the b. of the Presence; Heb 9.02

BREADTH
its b. fifty cubits, and its height Gen 6.15
the length and the b. of the land, 13.17
length, a cubit and a half its b., Ex 25.10
and a cubit and a half its b. 25.17
a cubit its b., and a cubit and a 25.23

BREADTH (cont.)
and the b. of each curtain four Ex 26.02
and the b. of each curtain four 26.08
and a half the b. of each frame. 26.16
And for the b. of the court on the 27.12
The b. of the court on the front to 27.13
the b. fifty, and the height five 27.18
span its length and a span its b. 28.16
be its length, and a cubit its b.; 30.02
and the b. of each curtain four 36.09
and the b. of each curtain four 36.15
and a half the b. of each frame. 36.21
length, a cubit and a half its b., 37.01
and a cubit and a half its b. 37.06
a cubit its b., and a cubit and a 37.10
a cubit, and its b. was a cubit; 37.25
its length, and five cubits its b.; 38.01
and five cubits high in its b., 38.18
and a span its b. when doubled. 39.09
its length, and four cubits its b., Deu 3.11
and its b. fifty cubits, and its 1Ki 7.02
cubits, and its b. thirty cubits; 7.06
cubits, and the b. twenty cubits. 2Ch 3.03
corresponding to the b. of the house, 3.08
and its b. was twenty cubits; 3.08
cubits and its b. sixty cubits, Ez 6.03
will fill the b. of your land, Is 8.08
from the length and b. of the land: Jer 8.19
Then he measured the b. of the Eze 40.11
and the b. of the gateway, thirteen 40.11
a b. of five and twenty cubits, from 40.13
He measured its length and its b. 40.20
and its b. twenty-five cubits. 40.21
and its b. twenty-five cubits. 40.25
and its b. twenty-five cubits. 40.29
and its b. twenty-five cubits. 40.33
and its b. twenty-five cubits. 40.36
and the b. of the gate was fourteen 40.48
cubits, and the b. twelve cubits; 40.49
six cubits was the b. of the jambs. 41.01
And the b. of the entrance was ten 41.02
cubits, and its b., twenty cubits. 41.02
and the b. of the entrance, six 41.03
and its b., twenty cubits, beyond 41.04
and the b. of the side chambers 41.05
the court was a b. of twenty 41.10
and the b. of the part that was 41.11
also the b. of the east front of 41.14
cubits, and the b. fifty cubits. 42.02
north, of the same length and b., 42.11
two cubits, with a b. of one cubit; 43.14
four cubits, with a b. of one cubit; 43.14
twenty-five thousand cubits in b., 48.08
length, and twenty thousand in b. 48.09
cubits in b. on the western side, 48.10
ten thousand in b. on the eastern 48.10
in length and ten thousand in b. 48.13
cubits and the b. twenty thousand. 48.13
cubits in b. and twenty-five 48.15
sixty cubits and its b. six cubits. Dan 3.01
city, three days' journey in b. Jon 3.03
march through the b. of the earth, Hab 1.06
see what is its b. and what is its Zec 2.02
cubits, and its b. ten cubits. 5.02
what is the b. and length and Eph 3.18
its length the same as its b.; Rev 21.16
its length and b. and height are 21.16

BREAK
Lot, and drew near to b. the door. Gen 19.09
b. loose you shall b. his yoke from 27.40
and you shall not b. a bone of it. Ex 12.46
redeem it you shall b. its neck. 13.13
lest they b. through to the LORD to 19.21
lest the LORD b. out upon them." 19.22
and the people b. through to come 19.24
lest he b. out against them." 19.24
them and b. their pillars in 23.24
(for Aaron had let them b. loose, 32.25
and b. their pillars, and cut down 34.13
redeem it you shall b. its neck. 34.20
you shall b. it in pieces, and pour Lev 2.06
be unclean, and you shall b. it. 11.33
And he shall b. down the house, its 14.45
commandments, but b. my covenant, 26.15
and I will b. the pride of your 26.19
When I b. your staff of bread, ten 26.26
utterly and b. my covenant with 26.44
the morning, nor b. a bone of it; Num 9.12
and shall b. their bones in pieces, 24.08
and b. down all the sons of Sheth. 24.17
a pledge, he shall not b. his word; 30.02
you shall b. down their altars, and Deu 7.05
and shall b. the heifer's neck there 21.04
forsake me and b. my covenant 31.16
and despise me and b. my covenant. 31.20
son of Zerah b. faith in the Jos 22.20
'I will never b. my covenant with Ju 2.01
you shall b. down their altars.' 2.02
I will b. down this tower." 8.09
And as the dawn began to b., 19.25
Then at the b. of dawn Samuel 1Sa 9.26
go, b. your league with Baasha king 1Ki 15.19
hundred swordsmen to b. through, 2Ki 3.26
go b. your league with Baasha 2Ch 16.03
shall we b. thy commandments again Ez 9.14
on it he will b. down their stone Neh 4.03
spears from the b. of dawn till 4.21
and b. me in pieces with words? Job 19.02
They b. up my path, they promote my 30.13
You shall b. them with a rod of Ps 2.09
thou dost b. the teeth of the 3.07
B. thou the arm of the wicked and 10.15
he will b. them down and build them 28.05
But God will b. you down for ever; 52.05
O God, b. the teeth in their mouths; 58.06
thou didst b. the heads of the 74.13
b. forth into joyous song and sing 98.04
pretexts to b. out against all Pro 18.01
and a soft tongue will b. a bone. 25.15
a time to b. down, and a time to Ecc 3.03
I will b. down its wall, and it Is 5.05
they b. forth into singing. 14.07
that I will b. the Assyrian in my 14.25
be to you like a b. in a high wall, 30.13
waters shall b. forth in the 35.06
a bruised reed he will not b., 42.03
to Babylon and b. down all the 43.14
b. forth into singing, O mountains, O 44.23
I will b. in pieces the doors of 45.02
b. forth, O mountains, into singing! 49.13
B. forth together into singing, you 52.09
b. forth into singing and cry aloud, 54.01
you shall b. forth into singing, 55.12
go free, and to b. every yoke? 58.06
your light b. forth like the dawn, 58.08
kingdoms, to pluck up and to b. down, Jer 1.10
evil shall b. forth upon all the 1.14
"B. up your fallow ground, and sow 4.03
and do not b. thy covenant with us 14.21
Can one b. iron, iron from the north, 15.12
No one shall b. bread for the 16.07
pluck up and b. down and destroy 18.07
"Then you shall b. the flask in the 19.10
So will I b. this people and this 19.11
for I will b. the yoke of the king 28.04
Even so will I b. the yoke of 28.11
that I will b. the yoke from off 30.08
over them to pluck up and b. down, 31.28
If you can b. my covenant with the 33.20
He shall b. the obelisks of Heliopolis 43.13
and b. his jars in pieces. 48.12
I will b. the bow of Elam, the 49.35
with you I b. nations in pieces; 51.20

BREAK (cont.)

with you I b. in pieces the horse Jer 51.21
with you I b. in pieces the chariot 51.21
with you I b. in pieces man and 51.22
with you I b. in pieces the old man 51.22
with you I b. in pieces the young 51.22
with you I b. in pieces the shepherd 51.23
with you I b. in pieces the farmer 51.23
with you I b. in pieces governors 51.23
I will b. the staff of bread in Eze 4.16
and b. your staff of bread. 5.16
fall, and a stormy wind b. out; 13.11
a stormy wind b. out in my wrath; 13.13
And I will b. down the wall that 13.14
and b. its staff of bread and send 14.13
as women who b. wedlock and shed 16.38
chamber and b. down your lofty 16.39
Can he b. the covenant and yet 17.15
I will b. off from the topmost of 17.22
and b. down her towers; and I will 26.04
axes he will b. down your towers. 26.09
they will b. down your walls and 26.12
when I b. there the dominion of 30.18
and will b. his arms, both the 30.22
but I will b. the arms of Pharaoh, 30.24
when I b. the bars of their yoke, 34.27
it shall b. and crush all these. Dan 2.40
It shall b. it pieces all these 2.44
b. off your sins by practicing 4.27
Then, at b. of day, the king arose 6.19
it down, and b. it to pieces. 7.23
I will b. the bow of Israel in the Hos 1.05
they b. all bounds and murder 4.02
The LORD will b. down their altars, 10.02
b. up your fallow ground, for it is 10.12
I will b. the bar of Damascus, and Amo 1.05
lest he b. out like fire in the 5.06
that the ship threatened to b. up. Jon 1.04
they will b. through and pass the Mic 2.13
and b. their bones in pieces, and 3.03
And now I will b. his yoke from off Nah 1.13
and where thieves b. in and steal, Mt 6.19
thieves do not b. in and steal. 6.20
he will not b. a bruised reed or 12.20
did not want to b. his word to her. Mk 6.26
dead, they did not b. his legs. Jn 19.33
were gathered together to b. bread, Ac 20.07
but if you b. the law, your circumcision Rom 2.25
and circumcision but b. the law. 2.27
The bread which we b., is it not 1Co 10.16
b. forth and shout, thou who art not Gal 4.27
open the scroll and b. its seals?" Rev 5.02

BREAKFAST

Jesus said to them, "Come and have b." Jn 21.12
When they had finished b., Jesus said 21.15

BREAKING

with him until the b. of the day. Gen 32.24
said, "Let me go, for the day is b." 32.26
become boils b. out in sores on Ex 9.09
it became boils b. out in sores on 9.10
If a thief is found b. in, and is 22.02
it is leprosy b. out on his bald Lev 13.42
men commit by b. faith with the Num 5.06
the congregation, and for b. camp. 10.02
nowadays who are b. away from their 1Sa 25.10
and its b. is like that of a Is 30.14
you did not find them b. in. Jer 2.34
what I have built I am b. down, 45.04
the oath in b. the covenant, Eze 16.59
sigh with b. heart and bitter grief 21.06
and as their nets were b., Lk 5.06
to them in the b. of the bread. 24.35
Just as day was b., Jesus stood Jn 21.04
to the b. of bread and the prayers. Ac 2.42
together and b. bread in their 2.46
you doing, weeping and b. my heart? 21.13
do you dishonor God by b. the law? Rom 2.23

BREAKS

"When fire b. out and catches in Ex 22.06
And if the leprosy b. out in the Lev 13.12
"If the disease b. out again in the 14.43
skin hardens, then b. out afresh. Job 7.05
His confidence b. in sunder, and his 8.14
He b. me with breach upon breach; 16.14
He b. me down on every side, and I 19.10
The voice of the LORD b. the cedars, Ps 29.05
the LORD b. the cedars of Lebanon. 29.05
he b. the bow, and shatters the 46.09
perverseness in it b. the spirit. Pro 15.04
to quit before the quarrel b. out. 17.14
bite him who b. through a wall. Ecc 10.08
like a lion he b. all my bones; Is 38.13
lamb, like him who b. a dog's neck; 66.03
as one b. a potter's vessel, so that Jer 19.11
a hammer which b. the rock in 23.29
because iron b. to pieces and Dan 2.40
the thief b. in, and the bandits Hos 7.01

BREAST

shall take the b. of the ram of Ex 29.26
consecrate the b. of the wave 29.27
he shall bring the fat with the b., Lev 7.30
that the b. may be waved as a wave 7.30
but the b. shall be for Aaron and 7.31
For the b. that is waved and the 7.34
And Moses took the b., and waved 8.29
But the b. that is waved and the 10.14
offered and the b. that is waved 10.15
with the b. that is waved and the Num 6.20
as the b. that is waved and as the 18.18
the fatherless child from the b., Job 24.09
wax, it is melted within my b.; Ps 22.14
a child quieted at its mother's b.; 131.02
me, that nursed at my mother's b.! Sol 8.01
the milk, those taken from the b.? Is 28.09
you shall suck the b. of kings; 60.16
give the b. and suckle their young, Lam 4.03
its b. and arms of silver, its belly Dan 2.32
cubs, I will tear open their b., Hos 13.08
but beat his b., saying, 'God, be Lk 18.13
was lying close to the b. of Jesus; Jn 13.23
close to the b. of Jesus, he said to 13.25
close to his b. at the supper and 21.20
with a golden girdle round his b.; Rev 1.13

BREASTPIECE

for the ephod and for the b. Ex 25.07
a b., an ephod, a robe, a coat of 28.04
"And you shall make a b. of judgment, 28.15
make for the b. twisted chains 28.22
make for the b. two rings of gold, 28.23
rings on the two edges of the b. 28.23
two rings at the edges of the b.; 28.24
put them at the two ends of the b., 28.26
shall bind the b. by its rings to 28.28
and that the b. shall not come 28.28
Israel in the b. of judgment upon 28.29
And in the b. of judgment you shall 28.30
and the b., and gird him with the 29.05
for the ephod and for the b. 35.09
set, for the ephod and for the b., 35.27
He made the b., in skilled work, 39.08
the b. was made double, a span its 39.09
made on the b. twisted chains like 39.15
rings on the two edges of the b.; 39.16
two rings at the edges of the b. 39.17
put them at the two ends of the b., 39.19
And they bound the b. by its rings 39.21
and that the b. should not come 39.21
And he placed the b. on him, Lev 8.08
and in the b. he put the Urim and 8.08

BREASTPLATE
between the scale armor and the b.; 1Ki 22.34
between the scale armor and the b.; 2Ch 18.33
He put on righteousness as a b., Is 59.17
put on the b. of righteousness, Eph 6.14
and put on the b. of faith and 1Th 5.08

BREASTPLATES
they had scales like iron b., Rev 9.09
the riders wore b. the color of 9.17

BREASTS
blessings of the b. and of the womb. Gen 49.25
and they put the fat upon the b., Lev 9.20
but the b. and the right thigh 9.21
Or why the b., that I should suck? Job 3.12
keep me safe upon my mother's b. Ps 22.09
of myrrh, that lies between my b. Sol 1.13
Your two b. are like two fawns, 4.05
Your two b. are like two fawns, 7.03
and your b. are like its clusters. 7.07
Oh, may your b. be like clusters of 7.08
a little sister, and she has no b. 8.08
and my b. were like towers; 8.10
Beat upon your b. for the pleasant Is 32.12
be satisfied with her consoling b.; 66.11
your b. were formed, and your hair Eze 16.07
there their b. were pressed and 23.03
bosom and pressed your young b." 23.21
out your hair, and tear your b.; 23.34
her adultery from between her b.; Hos 2.02
them a miscarrying womb and dry b. 9.14
like doves, and beating their b. Nah 2.07
and the b. that you sucked!" Lk 11.27
and the b. that never gave suck!' 23.29
returned home beating their b. 23.48
and their b. girded with golden Rev 15.06

BREATH
everything that has the b. of life, Gen 1.30
into his nostrils the b. of life; 2.07
in which is the b. of life from 6.17
in which there was the b. of life. 7.15
nostrils was the b. of life died. 7.22
blast of the b. of his nostrils. 2Sa 22.16
that there was no b. left in him. 1Ki 17.17
By the b. of God they perish, and by Job 4.09
"Remember that my life is a b.; 7.07
Let me alone, for my days are a b. 7.16
he will not let me get my b., 9.18
thing and the b. of all mankind. 12.10
as long as my b. is in me, and the 27.03
the b. of the Almighty, that makes 32.08
and the b. of the Almighty gives me 33.04
and gather to himself his b., 34.14
By the b. of God ice is given, and 37.10
His b. kindles coals, and a flame 41.21
blast of the b. of thy nostrils. Ps 18.15
their host by the b. of his mouth. 33.06
every man stands as a mere b.! 39.05
surely every man is a mere b.! 39.11
Men of low estate are but a b., 62.09
are together lighter than a b. 62.09
made their days vanish like a b., 78.33
of man, that they are but a b. 94.11
when thou takest away their b., 104.29
is there any b. in their mouths. 135.17
Man is like a b., his days are like 144.04
When his b. departs he returns to 146.04
They all have the same b., Ecc 3.19
the scent of your b. like apples, Sol 7.08
from man in whose nostrils is b., Is 2.22
and with the b. of his lips he 11.04
his b. is like an overflowing 30.28
the b. of the LORD, like a stream of 30.33
your b. is a fire that will consume 33.11
when the b. of the LORD blows upon 40.07
who gives b. to the people upon it 42.05
a b. will take them away. 57.13
and I have made the b. of life. 57.16
daughter of Zion gasping for b., Jer 4.31
false, and there is no b. in them. 10.14
false, and there is no b. in them. 51.17
The b. of our nostrils, the LORD's Lam 4.20
I will cause b. to enter you, and Eze 37.05
and put b. in you, and you shall 37.06
but there was no b. in them. 37.08
Then he said to me, "Prophesy to the b., 37.09
son of man, and say to the b., 37.09
O b., and breathe upon these slain, 37.09
and the b. came into them, and they 37.10
the God in whose hand is your b., Dan 5.23
in me, and no b. is left in me." 10.17
and there is no b. at all in it. Hab 2.19
all men life and b. and everything. Ac 17.25
him with the b. of his mouth and 2Th 2.08
a half days a b. of life from God Rev 11.11
allowed to give b. to the image of 13.15

BREATHE
and their hope is to b. their last." Job 11.20
me, and they b. out violence. Ps 27.12
and b. upon these slain, that they Eze 37.09

BREATHED
and b. into his nostrils the breath Gen 2.07
Abraham b. his last and died in a 25.08
he b. his last and died, and was 25.17
And Isaac b. his last; 35.29
and b. his last, and was gathered to 49.33
but utterly destroyed all that b., Jos 10.40
there was none left that b., 11.11
and they did not leave any that b. 11.14
house of Jeroboam not one that b., 1Ki 15.29
a loud cry, and b. his last. Mk 15.37
him, saw that he thus b. his last, 15.39
having said this he b. his last. Lk 23.46
he b. on them, and said to them, Jn 20.22

BREATHES
shall save alive nothing that b., Deu 20.16
man b. his last, and where is he? Job 14.10
Let everything that b. praise the Ps 150.06
a false witness who b. out lies, Pro 6.19
but a false witness b. out lies. 14.05
Until the day b. and the shadows Sol 2.17
Until the day b. and the shadows 4.06

BREATHING
still b. threats and murder against Ac 9.01

BRED
And since they b. when they came to Gen 30.38
the flocks b. in front of the rods 30.39
and it b. worms and became foul; Ex 16.20
and delicately b. among you will Deu 28.54
and delicately b. woman among you, 28.56
since, b. from the royal stud. Est 8.10
and delicately b. I will destroy, Jer 6.02

BREECHES
for them linen b. to cover their Ex 28.42
and the linen b. of fine twined 39.28
and put his linen b. upon his body, Lev 6.10
have the linen b. on his body, 16.04
and linen b. upon their loins; Eze 44.18

BREED
that they may b. abundantly on the Gen 8.17
that they might b. among the rods, 30.41
let your cattle b. with a different Lev 19.19
you know that they b. quarrels. 2Ti 2.23

BREEDER
Now Mesha king of Moab was a sheep b.; 2Ki 3.04

BREEDING
the flock were b. Jacob laid the Gen 30.41

BREEDS

Their bull b. without fail; Job 21.10

BRETHREN

carry your b. from before the Lev 10.04
but your b., the whole house of 10.06
"The priest who is chief among his b., 21.10
but over your b. the people of 25.46
to their b. in the tent of meeting, Num 8.26
and all your b. the sons of Levi 16.10
And with you bring your b. also, 18.02
have taken your b. the Levites 18.06
died when our b. died before the 20.03
a possession among our father's b." 27.04
their father's b. and cause the 27.07
"Shall your b. go to the war while 32.06
'Hear the cases between your b., Deu 1.16
Our b. have made our hearts melt, 1.28
territory of your b. the sons of 2.04
away from our b. the sons of Esau 2.08
before your b. the people of 3.18
until the LORD gives rest to your b., 3.20
one of your b., in any of your 15.07
from among your b. you shall set 17.15
may not be lifted up above his b., 17.20
have no inheritance among their b.; 18.02
from your b.—him you shall heed— 18.15
like you from among their b.; 18.18
is found stealing one of his b., 24.07
is one of your b. or one of the 24.14
before your b. and shall help them, Jos 1.14
rest to your b. as well as to you, 1.15
But my b. who went up with me made 14.08
an inheritance along with our b." 17.04
among the b. of their father. 17.04
forsaken your b. these many days, 22.03
your God has given rest to your b, 22.04
beside their b. in the land west 22.07
spoil of your enemies with your b." 22.08
came to their b. at Zorah and Ju 18.08
their b. said to them, "What do you 18.08
said to their b., "Do you know that 18.14
my b., do not act so wickedly; 19.23
listen to the voice of their b., 20.13
against our b. the Benjaminites?" 20.23
against our b. the Benjaminites, or 20.28
from among his b. and from the Ru 4.10
turn from the pursuit of their b.?" 2Sa 2.26
pursuit of their b. in the morning." 2.27
Go back, and take your b. with you; 15.20
"Why have our b. the men of Judah 19.41
unleavened bread among their b. 2Ki 23.09
hand were their b. the sons of 1Ch 6.44
and their b. the Levites were 6.48
for their b. had made preparation 12.39
abroad to our b. who remain in all 13.02
a hundred and twenty of his b.; 15.05
two hundred and twenty of his b.; 15.06
a hundred and thirty of his b.; 15.07
chief, with two hundred of his b.; 15.08
the chief, with eighty of his b.; 15.09
a hundred and twelve of his b. 15.10
you and your b., so that you may 15.12
appoint their b. as the singers 15.16
and of his b. Asaph the son of 15.17
their b., Ethan the son of Kushaiah; 15.17
and with them their b. of the 15.18
to the LORD by Asaph and his b. 16.07
Asaph and his b. there before the 16.37
Obededom and his sixty-eight b.; 16.38
priest and his b. the priests 16.39
their b., for the service of the 23.32
just as their b. the sons of Aaron, 24.31
number of them along with their b., 25.07
to him and his b. and his sons, 25.09
his sons and his b., twelve; 25.10
Izri, his sons and his b., twelve; 25.11
his sons and his b., twelve; 25.12
his sons and his b., twelve; 25.13
his sons and his b., twelve; 25.14
his sons and his b., twelve; 25.15
his sons and his b., twelve; 25.16
his sons and his b., twelve; 25.17
his sons and his b., twelve; 25.18
his sons and his b., twelve; 25.19
his sons and his b., twelve; 25.20
his sons and his b., twelve; 25.21
his sons and his b., twelve; 25.22
his sons and his b., twelve; 25.23
his sons and his b., twelve; 25.24
his sons and his b., twelve; 25.25
his sons and his b., twelve; 25.26
his sons and his b., twelve; 25.27
his sons and his b., twelve; 25.28
his sons and his b., twelve; 25.29
his sons and his b., twelve; 25.30
his sons and his b., twelve. 25.31
whose b. were able men, Elihu and 26.07
of Obededom with their sons and b., 26.08
And Meshelemiah had sons and b., 26.09
the sons and b. of Hosah were 26.11
just as their b. did, ministering in 26.12
His b.: from Eliezer were his son 26.25
Shelomoth and his b. were in charge 26.26
the care of Shelomoth and his b. 26.28
Hebronites, Hashabiah and his b., 26.30
King David appointed him and his b., 26.32
said: "Hear me, my b. and my people. 28.02
not go up or fight against your b. 2Ch 11.04
you from your b. who live in their 19.10
may not come upon you and your b. 19.10
They gathered their b., and 29.15
themselves their b. the Levites 29.34
be like your fathers and your b., 30.07
your b. and your children will find 30.09
distribute the portions to their b., 31.15
houses of your b. the lay people, 35.05
yourselves, and prepare for your b., 35.06
for their b. the Levites prepared 35.15
together with the rest of their b., Ez 3.08
to you and your b. to do with the 7.18
to Iddo and his b. the temple 8.17
the son of Jozadak and his b. 10.18
one of my b., came with certain men Neh 1.02
up with his b. the priests and 3.01
After him their b. repaired: 3.18
presence of his b. and of the army 4.02
terrible, and fight for your b., 4.14
I nor my b. nor my servants nor 4.23
wives against their Jewish b. 5.01
flesh is as the flesh of our b., 5.05
back our Jewish b. who have been 5.08
even sell your b. that they may be 5.08
Moreover I and my b. and my servants 5.10
I nor my b. ate the food allowance 5.14
and their b., Shebaniah, Hodiah, 10.10
join with their b., their nobles, 10.29
and their b. who did the work of 11.12
and his b., heads of fathers' 11.13
and their b., mighty men of valor, a 11.14
Bakbukiah, the second among his b.; 11.17
gatekeepers, Akkub, Talmon and their b., 11.19
and of their b. in the days of 12.07
who with his b. was in charge of 12.08
and Unno their b. stood opposite 12.09
with their b. over against them, to 12.24
duty was to distribute to their b. 13.13
with the multitude of his b., Est 10.03
My b. are treacherous as a torrent-bed, Job 6.15
"He has put my b. far from me, and 19.13
I will tell of thy name to my b.; Ps 22.22
I have become a stranger to my b., 69.08
For my b. and companions' sake I 122.08
"Your b. who hate you and cast you Is 66.05

BRETHREN (cont.)
bring all your b. from all the Is 66.20
your b., even your b., your fellow Eze 11.15
the rest of his b. shall return to Mic 5.03
And if you salute only your b., Mt 5.47
one teacher, and you are all b. 23.08
to one of the least of these my b., 25.40
go and tell my b. to go to Galilee, 28.10
turned again, strengthen your b." Lk 22.32
but go to my b. and say to them, I Jn 20.17
among the b. that this disciple 21.23
up among the b. (the company of Ac 1.15
"B., the scripture had to be 1.16
"B., I may say to you confidently 2.29
apostles, "B., what shall we do?" 2.37
"And now, b., I know that you acted 3.17
from your b. as he raised me up. 3.22
Therefore, b., pick out from among 6.03
"B. and fathers, hear me. The God 7.02
into his heart to visit his b., 7.23
that his b. understood that God 7.25
you are b., why do you wrong each 7.26
from your b. as he raised me up.' 7.37
And when the b. knew it, they 9.30
and some of the b. from Joppa 10.23
apostles and the b. who were in 11.01
These six b. also accompanied me, 11.12
relief to the b. who lived in 11.29
"Tell this to James and to the b." 12.17
"B., if you have any word of 13.15
"B., sons of the family of Abraham, 13.26
b., that through this man forgiveness 13.38
poisoned their minds against the b. 14.02
Judea and were teaching the b., 15.01
they gave great joy to all the b. 15.03
"B., you know that in the early 15.07
James replied, "B., listen to me. 15.13
Silas, leading men among the b., 15.22
"The b., both the apostles and the 15.23
to the b. who are of the Gentiles 15.23
exhorted the b. with many words and 15.32
in peace by the b. to those who 15.33
and visit the b. in every city 15.36
commended by the b. to the grace of 15.40
of by the b. at Lystra and Iconium. 16.02
and when they had seen the b., 16.40
and some of the b. before the city 17.06
The b. immediately sent Paul and 17.10
Then the b. immediately sent Paul 17.14
leave of the b. and sailed for 18.18
the b. encouraged him, and wrote to 18.27
we greeted the b. and stayed with 21.07
the b. received us gladly. 21.17
"B. and fathers, hear the defense 22.01
them I received letters to the b., 22.05
"B., I have lived before God in all 23.01
b., that he was the high priest; 23.05
"B., I am a Pharisee, a son of 23.06
There we found b., and were invited 28.14
And the b. there, when they heard of 28.15
"B., though I had done nothing 28.17
and none of the b. coming here has 28.21
b., that I have often intended to Rom 1.13
b.—for I am speaking to those who 7.01
Likewise, my b., you have died to 7.04
so then, b., we are debtors, not to 8.12
be the first-born among many b. 8.29
from Christ for the sake of my b., 9.03
B., my heart's desire and prayer to 10.01
b.: a hardening has come upon part 11.25
b., by the mercies of God, to 12.01
my b., that you yourselves are full 15.14
b., by our Lord Jesus Christ and by 15.30
and the b. who are with them. 16.14
b., to take note of those who 16.17
b., by the name of our Lord Jesus 1Co 1.10
is quarreling among you, my b. 1.11
For consider your call, b.; not many 1.26
b., I did not come proclaiming to 2.01
But I, b., could not address you as 3.01
b., that you may learn by us to 4.06
defraud, and that even your own b. 6.08
So, b., in whatever state each was 7.24
I mean, b., the appointed time has 7.29
against your b. and wounding their 8.12
b., that our fathers were all under 10.01
So then, my b., when you come 11.33
b., I do not want you to be uninformed. 12.01
Now, b., if I come to you speaking 14.06
B., do not be children in your 14.20
What then, b.? When you come 14.26
So, my b., earnestly desire to 14.39
b., in what terms I preached to you 15.01
than five hundred b. at one time, 15.06
I protest, b., by my pride in you 15.31
b.: flesh and blood cannot inherit 15.50
my beloved b., be steadfast, immovable, 15.58
for I am expecting him with the b. 16.11
him to visit you with the other b., 16.12
Now, b., you know that the household 16.15
All the b. send greetings. 16.20
b., of the affliction we experienced 2Co 1.08
b., about the grace of God which 8.01
and as for our b., they are 8.23
am sending the b. so that our 9.03
to urge the b. to go on to you 9.05
supplied by the b. who came from 11.09
at sea, danger from false b.; 11.26
Finally, b., farewell. Mend your 13.11
and all the b. who are with me, To Gal 1.02
b., that the secretly brought in, 2.04
b.: no one annuls even a man's will, 3.15
B., I beseech you, become as I am, 4.12
Now we, b., like Isaac, are children 4.28
So, b., we are not children of the 4.31
But if I, b., still preach circumcision, 5.11
For you were called to freedom, b.; 5.13
B., if a man is overtaken in any 6.01
Christ be with your spirit, b. 6.18
Peace be to the b., and love Eph 6.23
b., that what has happened to me Php 1.12
and most of the b. have been made 1.14
Finally, my b., rejoice in the Lord. 3.01
B., I do not consider that I have 3.13
B., join in imitating me, and mark 3.17
Therefore, my b., whom I love and 4.01
Finally, b., whatever is true, 4.08
The b. who are with me greet you. 4.21
faithful b. in Christ at Col 1.02
my greetings to the b. at Laodicea, 4.15
For we know, b. beloved by God, that 1Th 1.04
b., that our visit to you was not 2.01
remember our labor and toil, b.; 2.09
For you, b., became imitators of the 2.14
b., for a short time, in person not 2.17
b., in all our distress and affliction 3.07
Finally, b., we beseech and exhort 4.01
love of the b. you have no need to 4.09
do love all the b. throughout 4.10
b., to do so more and more, 4.10
b., concerning those who are asleep, 4.13
b., you have no need to have 5.01
b., for that day to surprise you 5.04
b., to respect those who labor 5.12
b., admonish the idle, encourage the 5.14
B., pray for us. 5.25
Greet all the b. with a holy kiss 5.26
this letter be read to all the b. 5.27
b., as is fitting, because your 2Th 1.03
to meet him, we beg you, b., 2.01
b. beloved by the Lord, because God 2.13
So then, b., stand firm and hold to 2.15
Finally, b., pray for us, that the 3.01
b., in the name of our Lord Jesus 3.06

BRETHREN (cont.)
B., do not be weary in well-doing. 2Th 3.13
these instructions before the b., 1Ti 4.06
on the ground that they are b.; 6.02
Linus and Claudia and all the b. 2Ti 4.21
he is not ashamed to call them b., Heb 2.11
saying, "I will proclaim thy name to my b., 2.12
made like his b. in every respect, 2.17
holy b., who share in a heavenly 3.01
Take care, b., lest there be in any 3.12
from their b., though these also 7.05
Therefore, b., since we have confidence 10.19
b., bear with my word of exhortation, 13.22
my b., when you meet various trials, Jas 1.02
Do not be deceived, my beloved b. 1.16
Know this, my beloved b. Let every 1.19
My b., show no partiality as you 2.01
Listen, my beloved b. Has not 2.05
my b., if a man says he has faith 2.14
my b., for you know that we who 3.01
My b., this ought not to be so. 3.10
my b., yield olives, or a grapevine 3.12
speak evil against one another, b. 4.11
b., until the coming of the Lord. 5.07
b., against one another, that you 5.09
b., take the prophets who spoke in 5.10
my b., do not swear, either by 5.12
My b., if any one among you wanders 5.19
truth for a sincere love of the b., 1Pe 1.22
love of the b., a tender heart and 3.08
Therefore, b., be the more zealous 2Pe 1.10
Do not wonder, b., that the world 1Jn 3.13
into life, because we love the b. 3.14
to lay down our lives for the b. 3.16
some of the b. arrived and testified 3Jn 1.03
you render any service to the b., 1.05
refuses himself to welcome the b., 1.10
and their b. should be complete, Rev 6.11
accuser of our b. has been thrown 12.10
you and your b. who hold the 19.10
with you and your b. the prophets, 22.09

BRIBE
are trustworthy and who hate a b.; Ex 18.21
And you shall take no b., 23.08
for a b. blinds the officials, and 23.08
who is not partial and takes no b. Deu 10.17
and you shall not take a b., 16.19
for a b. blinds the eyes of the 16.19
he who takes a b. to slay an 27.25
have I taken a b. to blind my eyes 1Sa 12.03
offer a b. for me'? Job 6.22
does not take a b. against the Ps 15.05
A b. is like a magic stone in the Pro 17.08
man accepts a b. from the bosom to 17.23
and a b. in the bosom, strong wrath. 21.14
foolish, and a b. corrupts the mind. Ecc 7.07
one loves a b. and runs after gifts. Is 1.23
who acquit the guilty for a b., 5.23
his hands, lest they hold a b., 33.15
who take a b., and turn aside the Amo 5.12
Its heads give judgment for a b., Mic 3.11
prince and the judge ask for a b., 7.03

BRIBERY
and fire consumes the tents of b. Job 15.34

BRIBES
they took b. and perverted justice. 1Sa 8.03
God, or partiality, or taking b." 2Ch 19.07
whose right hands are full of b. Ps 26.10
but he who hates b. will live. Pro 15.27
In you men take b. to shed blood; Eze 22.12

BRIBING
b. them to come to you from every Eze 16.33

BRICK
And they had b. for stone, and Ex 1.14
take a b. and lay it before you, and Eze 4.01
mortar, take hold of the b. mold! Nah 3.14

BRICKKILNS
axes, and made them toil at the b.; 2Sa 12.31

BRICKS
let us make b., and burn them Gen 11.03
straw to make b., as heretofore; Ex 5.07
But the number of b. which they 5.08
all your task of making b. today, 5.14
yet they say to us, 'Make b.!' 5.16
deliver the same number of b." 5.18
lessen your daily number of b." 5.19
"The b. have fallen, but we will Is 9.10
and burning incense upon b.; 65.03

BRIDE
to you as a b. comes home to her 2Sa 17.03
Come with me from Lebanon, my b.; Sol 4.08
my b., you have ravished my heart 4.09
is your love, my sister, my b.! 4.10
Your lips distil nectar, my b.; 4.11
my b., a garden locked, a fountain 4.12
my b., I gather my myrrh with my 5.01
shall bind them on as a b. does. Is 49.18
and as a b. adorns herself with her 61.10
bridegroom rejoices over the b., 62.05
of your youth, your love as a b., Jer 2.02
her ornaments, or a b. her attire? 2.32
bridegroom and the voice of the b.; 7.34
bridegroom and the voice of the b., 25.10
bridegroom and the voice of the b., 33.11
his room, and the b. her chamber. Joe 2.16
He who has the b. is the bridegroom; Jn 3.29
you as a pure b. to her one 2Co 11.02
bridegroom and b. shall be heard Rev 18.23
and his B. has made herself ready; 19.07
prepared as a b. adorned for her 21.02
"Come, I will show you the B., 21.09
The Spirit and the B. say, "Come." 22.17

BRIDEGROOM
"Surely you are a b. of blood to me!" Ex 4.25
"You are a b. of blood," because of 4.26
forth like a b. leaving his Ps 19.05
as a b. decks himself with a Is 61.10
and as the b. rejoices over the 62.05
voice of the b. and the voice of Jer 7.34
voice of the b. and the voice of 16.09
voice of the b. and the voice of 25.10
voice of the b. and the voice of 33.11
sackcloth for the b. of her youth. Joe 1.08
Let the b. leave his room, and the 2.16
as long as the b. is with them? Mt 9.15
when the b. is taken away from them, 9.15
lamps and went to meet the b. 25.01
As the b. was delayed, they all 25.05
there was a cry, 'Behold, the b.! 25.06
the b. came, and those who were 25.10
wedding guests fast while the b. is with Mk 2.19
long as they have the b. with them, 2.19
when the b. is taken away from them, 2.20
fast while the b. is with them? Lk 5.34
when the b. is taken away from them, 5.35
of the feast called the b. Jn 2.09
He who has the bride is the b.; 3.29
the friend of the b., who stands 3.29
the voice of b. and bride shall be Rev 18.23

BRIDEGROOM'S
rejoices greatly at the b. voice; Jn 3.29

BRIDES
and your b. commit adultery. Hos 4.13
nor your b. when they commit 4.14

BRIDLE
must be curbed with bit and b., Ps 32.09
I will b. my mouth, so long as the 39.01
peoples a b. that leads astray. Is 30.28
and does not b. his tongue but Jas 1.26
able to b. the whole body also 3.02
press, as high as a horse's b., Rev 14.20

BRIEF
But now for a b. moment favor has Ez 9.08
For a b. moment I forsook you, but Is 54.07

BRIEFLY
you in your kindness to hear us b. Ac 24.04
revelation, as I have written b. Eph 3.03
for I have written to you b. Heb 13.22
him, I have written b. to you, 1Pe 5.12

BRIER
instead of the b. shall come up the Is 55.13
be no more a b. to prick or a Eze 28.24
The best of them is like a b., Mic 7.04

BRIERS
of the wilderness and with b." Ju 8.07
wilderness and b. and with them 8.16
and b. and thorns shall grow up; Is 5.06
silver, will become b. and thorns. 7.23
all the land will be b. and thorns; 7.24
there for fear of b. and thorns; 7.25
a fire, it consumes b. and thorns; 9.18
his thorns and b. in one day. 10.17
that I had thorns and b. to battle! 27.04
people growing up in thorns and b.; 32.13
though b. and thorns are with you Eze 2.06

BRIGHT
and his eyes became b. 1Sa 14.27
see how my eyes have become b., 14.29
vessels of fine b. bronze as Ez 8.27
the moon is not b. and the stars Job 25.05
light when it is b. in the skies, 37.21
thee, the night is b. as the day; Ps 139.12
b. as the sun, terrible as an army Sol 6.10
and the fire was b., Eze 1.13
All the b. lights of heaven will I 32.08
a b. cloud overshadowed them, and a Mt 17.05
no part dark, it will be wholly b., Lk 11.36
man stood before me in b. apparel, Ac 10.30
And out came another horse, b. red; Rev 6.04
robed in pure b. linen, and their 15.06
earth was made b. with his splendor. 18.01
b. and pure"—for the fine linen is 19.08
b. as crystal, flowing from the 22.01
of David, the b. morning star." 22.16

BRIGHTEN
our God may b. our eyes and grant Ez 9.08

BRIGHTER
life will be b. than the noonday; Job 11.17
which shines b. and b. until Pro 4.18
b. than the sun, shining round me Ac 26.13

BRIGHTNESS
Out of the b. before him coals of 2Sa 22.13
Out of the b. before him there Ps 18.12
and for b., but we walk in gloom. Is 59.09
and kings to the b. of your rising. 60.03
nor for b. shall the moon give 60.19
her vindication goes forth as b., 62.01
with b. round about it, and fire Eze 1.04
and there was b. round about him. 1.27
appearance of the b. round about. 1.28
it was like the appearance of b., 8.02
was full of the b. of the glory of 10.04
image, mighty and of exceeding b., Dan 2.31
shine like the b. of the firmament; 12.03
light, and gloom with no b. in it? Amo 5.20
His b. was like the light, rays Hab 3.04
because of the b. of that light, Ac 22.11
at Moses' face because of its b., 2Co 3.07

BRIM
round, ten cubits from b. to b., 1Ki 7.23
Under its b. were gourds, for thirty 7.24
its b. was made like the b. of a cup, 7.26
round, ten cubits from b. to b., 2Ch 4.02
its b. was made like the b. of a cup, 4.05
And they filled them up to the b. Jn 2.07

BRIMSTONE
and Gomorrah b. and fire from the Gen 19.24
the whole land b. and salt, and a Deu 29.23
b. is scattered upon his habitation. Job 18.15
he will rain coals of fire and b.; Ps 11.06
like a stream of b., kindles it. Is 30.33
into pitch, and her soil into b.; 34.09
rains and hailstones, fire and b. Eze 38.22
Sodom fire and b. rained from Lk 17.29
with fire and b. in the presence Rev 14.10
lake of fire that burns with b. 19.20
of fire and b. where the beast and 20.10
lake that burns with fire and b., 21.08

BRING
"Let the waters b. forth swarms of Gen 1.20
"Let the earth b. forth living 1.24
pain you shall b. forth children, 3.16
thistles it shall b. forth to you; 3.18
this one shall b. us relief from 5.29
I will b. a flood of waters upon 6.17
you shall b. two of every sort into 6.19
B. forth with you every living 8.17
b. forth abundantly on the earth 9.07
When I b. clouds over the earth and 9.14
"B. me a heifer three years old, a 15.09
but I will b. judgment on the 15.14
the LORD may b. to Abraham what he 18.19
B. them out to us, that we may know 19.05
let me b. them out to you, and do to 19.08
b. them out of the place; 19.12
and b. it to me that I may eat; 27.04
field to hunt for game and b. it, 27.05
'B. me game, and prepare for me 27.07
and you shall b. it to your father 27.10
and b. a curse upon myself and not 27.12
Then he said, "B. it to me, that I 27.25
and will b. you back to this land; 28.15
by wild beasts I did not b. to you; 31.39
the flock; and b. me word again." 37.14
"B. her out, and let her be burned." 38.24
and God will shortly b. it to pass. 41.32
and let him b. your brother, while 42.16
and b. your youngest brother to me; 42.20
B. your youngest brother to me; 42.34
if I do not b. him back to you; 42.37
and I will b. him back to you." 42.37
you would b. down my gray hairs 42.38
'B. your brother down'?" 43.07
If I do not b. him back to you and 43.09
"B. the men into the house, and 43.16
'B. him down to me, that I may set 44.21
you will b. down my gray hairs in 44.29
servants will b. down the gray 44.31
'If I do not b. him back to you, 44.32
Make haste and b. my father down 45.13
and b. your father, and come. 45.19
and I will also b. you up again; 46.04
"B. them to me, I pray you, that I 48.09
and will b. you again to the land 48.21
to b. it about that many people 50.20
and b. you up out of this land to 50.24
and to b. them up out of that land Ex 3.08
that you may b. forth my people, 3.10
and b. the sons of Israel out of 3.11
that I will b. you up out of the 3.17
and I will b. you out from under 6.06

BRING (cont.)

And I will b. you into the land Ex 6.08
of Egypt to b. the people of 6.13
"B. out the people of Israel from 6.26
upon Egypt and b. forth my hosts, 7.04
upon Egypt and b. out the people 7.05
secret arts to b. forth gnats, 8.18
tomorrow I will b. locusts into 10.04
more I will b. upon Pharaoh and 11.01
to b. them out of the land of Egypt; 12.42
Thou wilt b. them in, and plant them 15.17
when they prepare what they b. in, 16.05
"Why did you b. us up out of Egypt, 17.03
before God, and b. their cases to God; 18.19
great matter they shall b. to you, 18.22
then his master shall b. him to God, 21.06
and he shall b. him to the door or 21.06
beasts, let him b. it as evidence; 22.13
you shall b. it back to him. 23.04
you shall b. into the house of the 23.19
the way and to b. you to the place 23.20
and b. the ark of the testimony in 26.33
that they b. to you pure beaten 27.20
"Then b. near to you Aaron your 28.01
to b. them to continual remembrance 28.29
lest they b. guilt upon themselves 28.43
one basket and b. them in the 29.03
and b. the bull and the two rams. 29.03
You shall b. Aaron and his sons to 29.04
Then you shall b. his sons, and put 29.08
"Then you shall b. the bull before 29.10
that it may b. the people of Israel 30.16
your daughters, and b. them to me." 32.02
evil intent did he b. them forth, 32.12
'B. up this people'; but thou hast 33.12
you shall b. to the house of the 34.26
let him b. the LORD's offering: gold, 35.05
moved them to b. anything for the 35.29
"The people b. much more than 36.05
And you shall b. in the table, and 40.04
and you shall b. in the lampstand, 40.04
Then you shall b. Aaron and his 40.12
You shall b. his sons also and put 40.14
you shall b. your offering of Lev 1.02
then he shall b. his offering of 1.14
priest shall b. it to the altar 1.15
and b. it to Aaron's sons the 2.02
"When you b. a cereal offering 2.04
And you shall b. the cereal offering 2.08
he shall b. it to the altar. 2.08
which you b. to the LORD shall be 2.11
fruits you may b. them to the LORD, 2.12
He shall b. the bull to the door of 4.04
of the bull and b. it to the tent 4.05
offering and b. it before the tent 4.14
priest shall b. some of the blood 4.16
he shall b. as his offering a goat, 4.23
to him he shall b. for his offering 4.28
he shall b. a female without 4.32
and he shall b. his guilt offering 5.06
then he shall b., as his guilt 5.07
He shall b. them to the priest, who 5.08
then he shall b., as his offering 5.11
And he shall b. it to the priest, 5.12
he shall b., as his guilt offering 5.15
He shall b. to the priest a ram 5.18
And he shall b. to the priest his 6.06
you shall b. it well mixed, in baked 6.21
he shall b. his offering with 7.13
the LORD shall b. his offering to 7.29
he shall b. with his own hands the 7.30
he shall b. the fat with the breast, 7.30
of Israel to b. their offerings to 7.38
and b. the offering of the people, 9.07
they shall b. with the offerings 10.15
she shall b. to the priest at the 12.06
day he shall b. them for his cleansing 14.23
and b. them to the priest, to the 15.29
and he shall b. it within the veil 16.12
and b. its blood within the veil, 16.15
and does not b. it to the door of 17.04
of Israel may b. their sacrifices 17.05
that they may b. them to the LORD, 17.05
and does not b. it to the door of 17.09
but he shall b. a guilt offering 19.21
you shall b. the sheaf of the first 23.10
You shall b. from your dwellings 23.17
of Israel to b. you pure oil from 24.02
"B. out of the camp him who cursed; 24.14
so that it will b. forth fruit for 25.21
I will b. more plagues upon you, 26.21
And I will b. a sword upon you, that 26.25
then he shall b. the person before 27.08
the man shall b. the animal before 27.11
"B. the tribe of Levi near, and set Num 3.06
which they b. to the priest, shall 5.09
then the man shall b. his wife to 5.15
and b. the offering required of her, 5.15
"And the priest shall b. her near, 5.16
the LORD and b. it to the altar; 5.25
day he shall b. two turtledoves or 6.10
and b. a male lamb a year old for a 6.12
Did I b. them forth, that thou 11.12
and b. them to the tent of meeting, 11.16
and b. some of the fruit of the 13.20
Why does the LORD b. us into this 14.03
he will b. us into this land and 14.08
for thou didst b. up this people 14.13
was not able to b. this people 14.16
I will b. into the land into which 14.24
I will b. in, and they shall know 14.31
into the land to which I b. you 15.18
to b. you near to himself, to do 16.09
one of you b. before the LORD his 16.17
And with you b. your brethren also, 18.02
which they b. to the LORD, shall be 18.13
of Israel to b. you a red heifer 19.02
to b. us to this evil place? 20.05
so you shall b. water out of the 20.08
shall we b. forth water for you out 20.10
you shall not b. this assemply 20.12
and b. them up to Mount Hor; 20.25
and I will b. back word to you, as 22.08
shall lead them out and b. them in; 27.17
you shall b. to me, and I will hear Deu 1.17
and b. us word again of the way by 1.22
to b. you in, to give you their land 4.38
that he might b. us in and give us 6.23
And you shall not b. an abominable 7.26
from which thou didst b. us say, 9.28
was not able to b. them into the 9.28
whom thou didst b. out by thy 9.29
you shall b. your burnt offerings 12.06
you shall b. all that I command 12.11
you are not able to b. the tithe, 14.24
years you shall b. forth all the 14.28
then you shall b. forth to your 17.05
that city shall b. the heifer down 21.04
then you shall b. her home to your 21.12
hold of him and b. him out to the 21.19
you shall b. it home to your house, 22.02
you may not b. the guilt of blood 22.08
shall take and b. out the tokens 22.15
then they shall b. out the young 22.21
then you shall b. them both out to 22.24
You shall not b. the hire of a 23.18
you shall not b. guilt upon the 24.04
the loan shall b. the pledge out 24.11
now I b. the first of the fruit of 26.10
"The LORD will b. you, and your king 28.36
The LORD will b. a nation against 28.49
then the LORD will b. on you and 28.59
And he will b. upon you again all 28.60
the LORD will b. upon you, until you 28.61

BRING (cont.)
And the LORD will b. you back in Deu 28.68
your God will b. you into the land 30.05
and b. it to us, that we may hear it 30.12
and b. it to us, that we may hear it 30.13
for you shall b. the children of 31.23
and b. him in to his people. 33.07
"B. forth the men that have come to Jos 2.03
destruction, and b. trouble upon it. 6.18
and b. out from it the woman, and 6.22
said, "Why did you b. trouble on us? 7.25
and b. those five kings out to me 10.22
divisions and b. the description 18.06
the LORD will b. upon you all the 23.15
not the LORD b. us up from Egypt?' Ju 6.13
and b. out my present, and set it 6.18
"B. out your son, that he may die, 6.30
Gilead went to b. Jephthah from 11.05
"If you b. me home again to fight 11.09
kindly to her and b. her back. 19.03
"B. out the man who came into your 19.22
let me b. them out now. Ravish 19.24
to b. provisions for the people, 20.10
And he said, "B. the mantle you are Ru 3.15
I will b. him, that he may appear in 1Sa 1.22
Let us b. the ark of the covenant 4.03
if we go, what can we b. the man? 9.07
no present to b. to the man of God. 9.07
"B. the portion I gave you, of which 9.23
B. the men, that we may put them to 11.12
So Saul said, "B. the burnt offering 13.09
"B. hither the ark of God." For the 14.18
'Let every man b. his ox or his 14.34
"B. here to me Agag the king of the 15.32
can play well, and b. him to me." 16.17
and b. some token from them." 17.18
"B. him up to me in the bed, that I 19.15
why should you b. me to your 20.08
the priest, "B. the ephod here." 23.09
to b. tidings to Gath, thinking, 27.11
and b. up for me whomever I shall 28.08
for my life to b. about my death?" 28.09
said, "Whom shall I b. up for you?" 28.11
He said, "B. up Samuel for me." 28.11
son of Ahimelech, "B. me the ephod." 30.07
be with you to b. over all Israel 2Sa 3.12
face, unless you first b. Michal, 3.13
Now then b. it about; for the LORD 3.18
to b. up from there the ark of God, 6.02
and shall b. in the produce, that 9.10
Can I b. him back again? I shall 12.23
"B. the food into the chamber, that 13.10
says anything to you b. him to me, 14.10
king does not b. his banished one 14.13
go, b. back the young man Absalom." 14.21
will indeed b. me back to Jerusalem, 15.08
and b. down evil upon us, and smite 15.14
he will b. me back and let me see 15.25
and I will b. all the people back 17.03
all Israel will b. ropes to that 17.13
the LORD might b. evil upon 17.14
be the last to b. the king back to 19.11
be the last to b. back the king?' 19.12
the king and to b. the king over 19.15
the ford to b. over the king's 19.18
upon the haughty to b. them down. 22.28
and b. him down to Gihon; 1Ki 1.33
are a worthy man and b. good news." 1.42
and you shall b. his head down with 2.09
The LORD will b. back his bloody 2.32
the LORD will b. back your evil 2.44
And the king said, "B. me a sword." 3.24
My servants shall b. it down to the 5.09
to b. up the ark of the covenant of 8.01
and b. them again to the land which 8.34
which thou didst b. out of Egypt, 8.51
when thou didst b. our fathers out 8.53
'B. him back with you into your 13.18
I will b. evil upon the house of 14.10
"B. me a little water in a vessel, 17.10
And as she was going to b. it, 17.11
"B. me a morsel of bread in your 17.11
little cake of it and b. it to me, 17.13
come to me to b. my sin to remembrance, 17.18
Then he said, "Go and b. him." 20.33
and let them b. a charge against 21.10
Behold, I will b. evil upon you; 21.21
I will not b. the evil in his days; 21.29
in his son's days I will b. the evil 21.29
"B. quickly Micaiah the son of 22.09
He said, "B. me a new bowl, and put 2Ki 2.20
But now b. me a minstrel." 3.15
"B. me another vessel." 4.06
He said, "Then b. meal." 4.41
and I will b. you to the man whom 6.19
"B. out the vestments for all the 10.22
"B. her out between the ranks; 11.15
prompts him to b. into the house 12.04
is no strength to b. them forth. 19.03
days of old what now I b. to pass, 19.25
And Isaiah said, "B. a cake of figs. 20.07
I will b. evil upon this place and 22.16
which I will b. upon this place.'" 22.20
to b. out of the temple of the LORD 23.04
Then let us b. again the ark of our 1Ch 13.03
to b. the ark of God from Kiriathjearim. 13.05
to b. up from there the ark of God, 13.06
"How can I b. the ark of God home 13.12
to b. up the ark of the LORD to its 15.03
so that you may b. up the ark of 15.12
themselves to b. up the ark of the 15.14
went to b. up the ark of the 15.25
b. an offering, and come before 16.29
and b. me a report, that I may know 21.02
Why should he b. guilt upon Israel?" 21.03
and b. it to you in rafts by sea to 2Ch 2.16
to b. up the ark of the covenant of 5.02
and b. them again to the land which 6.25
"B. quickly Micaiah the son of 18.08
the LORD will b. a great plague on 21.14
"B. her out between the ranks; 23.14
the Levites to b. in from Judah 24.06
to b. in for the LORD the tax that 24.09
among them to b. them back to the 24.19
and it will b. you no honor from 26.18
"You shall not b. the captives in 28.13
you propose to b. upon us guilt 28.13
they did not b. him into the tombs 28.27
come near, b. sacrifices and thank 29.31
they began to b. the contributions 31.10
I will b. evil upon this place and 34.24
which I will b. upon this place 34.28
All these did Sheshbazzar b. up, Ez 1.11
the Tyrians to b. cedar trees from 3.07
to b. them to Jerusalem, to the 8.30
them thence and b. them to the Neh 1.09
the scribe to b. the book of the 8.01
the hills and b. branches of olive, 8.15
Abram and b. him forth out of Ur 9.07
hunger and b. forth water for them 9.15
and thou didst b. them into the 9.23
of the land b. in wares or any 10.31
to b. it into the house of our God, 10.34
ourselves to b. the first fruits 10.35
also to b. to the house of our God, 10.36
and to b. the first of our coarse 10.37
and to b. to the Levites the tithes 10.37
Levites shall b. up the tithe of 10.38
of Levi shall b. the contribution 10.39
cast lots to b. one out of ten to 11.01
to b. them to Jerusalem to celebrate 12.27
did not our God b. all this evil 13.18
Yet you b. more wrath upon Israel 13.18
to b. Queen Vashti before the king Est 1.11

BRING (cont.)

“B. Haman quickly, that we may do as Est 5.05
gave orders to b. the book of 6.01
thou dost b. fresh hosts against me. Job 10.17
“Why didst thou b. me forth from 10.18
who b. their god in their hand. 12.06
such a one and b. him into judgment 14.03
Who can b. a clean thing out of an 14.04
mischief and b. forth evil and 15.35
know that thou wilt b. me to death, 30.23
and his life to those who b. death. 33.22
to b. back his soul from the Pit, 33.30
to b. rain on a land where no man 38.26
when the mountain goats b. forth? 39.01
know the time when they b. forth, 39.02
b. forth their offspring, and are 39.03
and b. your grain to your threshing 39.12
one that is proud, and b. him low; 40.12
him who made him b. near his sword! 40.19
the haughty eyes thou dost b. down. Ps 18.27
and b. me out of my distresses. 25.17
He will b. forth your vindication 37.06
to b. down the poor and needy, to 37.14
let them b. me to thy holy hill and 43.03
For they b. trouble upon me, and in 55.03
and b. them down, O Lord, our shield! 59.11
Who will b. me to the fortified 60.09
tongue he will b. them to ruin; 64.08
whom thou dost choose and b. near, 65.04
Thou didst b. us into the net; 66.11
“I will b. them back from Bashan, I 68.22
I will b. them back from the depths 68.22
the earth thou wilt b. me up again. 71.20
kings of Sheba and Seba b. gifts! 72.10
all around him b. gifts to him who 76.11
Thou didst b. a vine out of Egypt; 80.08
They still b. forth fruit in old 92.14
He will b. back on them their 94.23
b. an offering, and come into his 96.08
that he may b. forth food from the 104.14
Who will b. me to the fortified 108.10
let an accuser b. him to trial. 109.06
B. me out of prison, that I may give 142.07
righteousness b. me out of trouble! 143.11
may our sheep b. forth thousands 144.13
the clouds that b. the spring rain. Pro 16.15
A fool’s lips b. strife, and his 18.06
will not even b. it back to his 19.24
do not hastily b. into court; 25.08
he who hears you b. shame upon you, 25.10
him out to b. it back to his mouth. 26.15
not know what a day may b. forth. 27.01
A man’s pride will b. him low, 29.23
who can b. him to see what will be Ecc 3.22
things God will b. you into 11.09
For God will b. every deed into 12.14
lead you and b. you into the house Sol 8.02
each one was to b. for its fruit a 8.11
B. no more vain offerings; Is 1.13
The LORD will b. upon you and upon 7.17
take them and b. them to their 14.02
yet I will b. upon Dibon even more, 15.09
she has caused I b. to an end. 21.02
To the thirsty b. water, meet the 21.14
of his walls he will b. down, 25.12
chaff, you b. forth stubble; 33.11
is no strength to b. them forth. 37.03
days of old what now I b. to pass, 37.26
to night thou dost b. me to an end; 38.12
to night thou dost b. me to an end. 38.13
b. your proofs, says the King of 41.21
Let them b. them, and tell us what 41.22
he will b. forth justice to the 42.01
will faithfully b. forth justice. 42.03
to b. out the prisoners from the 42.07
I will b. your offspring from the 43.05
b. my sons from afar and my daughters 43.06
B. forth the people who are blind, 43.08
Let them b. their witnesses to 43.09
spoken, and I will b. it to pass; 46.11
I b. near my deliverance, it is not 46.13
to b. Jacob back to him, and that 49.05
and they shall b. your sons in 49.22
making it b. forth and sprout, 55.10
these I will b. to my holy mountain, 56.07
and b. the homeless poor into your 58.07
mischief and b. forth iniquity. 59.04
They shall b. gold and frankincense, 60.06
to b. your sons from far, their 60.09
that men may b. to you the wealth 60.11
Instead of bronze I will b. gold, 60.17
instead of iron I will b. silver; 60.17
anointed me to b. good tidings to 61.01
I will b. forth descendants from 65.09
and b. their fears upon them; 66.04
Shall I b. to the birth and not 66.09
birth and not cause to b. forth? 66.09
who cause to b. forth, shut the womb? 66.09
And they shall b. all your brethren 66.20
the Israelites b. their cereal 66.20
I will b. you to judgment for Jer 2.35
family, and I will b. you to Zion. 3.14
for I b. evil from the north, and 4.06
and I will b. distress on them, that 10.18
anger, lest thou b. me to nothing. 10.24
For I will b. evil upon the men of 11.23
they grow and b. forth fruit; 12.02
wild beasts; b. them to devour. 12.09
and I will b. them again each to 12.15
of the nations that can b. rain? 14.22
For I will b. them back to their 16.15
b. upon them the day of evil; 17.18
sabbath day or b. it in by the 17.21
and b. in no burden by the gates of 17.24
and I will b. them together into 21.04
and I will b. them back to their 23.03
for I will b. evil upon them in the 23.12
And I will b. upon you everlasting 23.40
and I will b. them back to this 24.06
and I will b. them against this 25.09
I will b. upon that land all the 25.13
you will b. innocent blood upon 26.15
we are about to b. great evil upon 26.19
which will b. its neck under the 27.11
“B. your necks under the yoke of 27.12
Then I will b. them back and 27.22
years I will b. back to this place 28.03
I will also b. back to this place 28.04
and b. back to this place from 28.06
my promise and b. you back to this 29.10
and I will b. you back to the place 29.14
and I will b. them back to the land 30.03
Behold, I will b. them from the 31.08
b. me back that I may be restored, 31.18
and b. evil, so I will watch over 31.28
by the hand to b. them out of the 31.32
Thou didst b. thy people Israel out 32.21
I will b. them back to this place, 32.37
so I will b. upon them all the good 32.42
Behold, I will b. to it health and 33.06
as they b. thank offerings to the 33.11
and will b. them back to this city; 34.22
and b. them to the house of the 35.02
I will b. upon them, and upon the 36.31
the evil which I will b. upon them. 42.17
And I will b. to an end in Moab, 48.35
For I will b. these things upon 48.44
Behold, I will b. terror upon you, 49.05
For I will b. the calamity of Esau 49.08
I will b. you down from there, says 49.16
and I will b. their calamity from 49.32
and I will b. upon Elam the four 49.36
I will b. evil upon them, my fierce 49.37
b. up horses like bristling locusts. 51.27

BRING (cont.)
I will b. them down like lambs to Jer 51.40
B. thou the day thou hast announced, Lam 1.21
and when I b. more and more famine Eze 5.16
and I will b. the sword upon you. 5.17
will b. a sword upon you, and I will 6.03
I will b. the worst of the nations 7.24
and I will b. the sword upon you, 11.08
And I will b. you forth out of the 11.09
You shall b. out your baggage by 12.04
and I will b. him to Babylon in the 12.13
and b. it down to the ground, so 13.14
Or if I b. a sword upon that land, 14.17
and b. upon you the blood of wrath 16.38
They shall b. up a host against you, 16.40
that it might b. forth branches, and 17.08
and I will b. him to Babylon and 17.20
that it may b. forth boughs and 17.23
that I the LORD b. low the high 17.24
that I would b. them out of the 20.06
I would not b. them into the land 20.15
I will b. you out from the peoples 20.34
and I will b. you into the wilderness 20.35
I will b. them out of the land 20.38
when I b. you out from the peoples, 20.41
when I b. you into the land of 20.42
and I will b. them against you from 23.22
"B. up a host against them, and make 23.46
and will b. up many nations against 26.03
I will b. upon Tyre from the north 26.07
when I b. up the deep over you, and 26.19
I will b. you to a dreadful end, and 26.21
I will b. strangers upon you, the 28.07
I will b. a sword upon you, and will 29.08
and b. them back to the land of 29.14
I will b. desolation upon the land 30.12
"They shall b. to nought the pride 32.12
If I b. the sword upon a land, and 33.02
I will b. them out from the peoples, 34.13
will b. them into their own land; 34.13
and I will b. back the strayed, and 34.16
and b. you into your own land. 36.24
and I will b. you home into the 37.12
and b. them to their own land; 37.21
and I will b. you forth, and all 38.04
days I will b. you against my land, 38.16
that I would b. you against them? 38.17
and b. you up from the uttermost 39.02
in order not to b. them out into 46.20
to b. some of the people of Israel, Dan 1.03
b. me in before the king, and I will 2.24
kingdoms and b. them to an end, 2.44
cried aloud to b. in the enchanters, 5.07
who didst b. thy people out of the 9.15
to b. in everlasting righteousness, 9.24
and he shall b. terms of peace and 11.17
and b. her into the wilderness, and Hos 2.14
I will b. them down like birds of 7.12
Even if they b. up children, I will 9.12
Even though they b. forth, 9.16
the nations and b. them down to Joe 3.02
B. down thy warriors, O LORD. 3.11
and b. down your defenses from you, Amo 3.11
husbands, 'B., that we may drink!' 4.01
b. your sacrifices every morning, 4.04
"Did you b. to me sacrifices and 5.25
and b. near the seat of violence? 6.03
take him up to b. the bones out of 6.10
and b. the poor of the land to an 8.04
I will b. sackcloth upon all loins, 8.10
from there I will b. them down. 9.02
"Did I not b. up Israel from the 9.07
"Who will b. me down to the ground?" Ob 1.03
thence I will b. you down, says the 1.04
rowed hard to b. the ship back to Jon 1.13
yet thou didst b. up my life from 2.06
I will again b. a conqueror upon Mic 1.15
He will b. me forth to the light; 7.09
I will b. distress on men, so that Zep 1.17
dispersed ones, shall b. my offering. 3.10
At that time I will b. you home, 3.20
the hills and b. wood and build Hag 1.08
I will b. my servant the Branch. Zec 3.08
and he shall b. forward the top 4.07
and I will b. them to dwell in the 8.08
I will b. them back because I have 10.06
I will b. them home from the land 10.10
will b. them to the land of Gilead 10.10
You b. what has been taken by Mal 1.13
and this you b. as your offering! 1.13
or to b. an offering to the LORD of 2.12
B. the full tithes into the storehouse, 3.10
when you have found him b. me word, Mt 2.08
I have come to b. peace on earth; 10.34
I have not come to b. peace, but 10.34
And he said, "B. them here to me." 14.18
they had forgotten to b. any bread. 16.05
bear with you? B. him here to me." 17.17
untie them and b. them to me. 21.02
and gave orders to b. his head. Mk 6.27
and began to b. sick people on 6.55
Now they had forgotten to b. bread; 8.14
to bear with you? B. him to me." 9.19
has ever sat; untie it and b. it. 11.02
B. me a coin, and let me look at it." 12.15
And when they b. you to trial and 13.11
many charges they b. against you." 15.04
and to b. you this good news. Lk 1.19
for behold, I b. you good news of a 2.10
they sought to b. him in and lay 5.18
but finding no way to b. him in, 5.19
and b. forth fruit with patience. 8.15
bear with you? B. your son here." 9.41
And when they b. you before the 12.11
and b. in the poor and maimed and 14.21
'B. quickly the best robe, and put 15.22
and b. the fatted calf and kill it, 15.23
b. them here and slay them before 19.27
has ever sat; untie it and b. it here. 19.30
to them, "Why did you not b. him?" Jn 7.45
might have some charge to b. against *8.06
I must b. them also, and they will 10.16
and b. to your remembrance all that 14.26
accusation do you b. against this 18.29
"B. some of the fish that you have 21.10
you intend to b. this man's blood Ac 5.28
he might b. them bound to Jerusalem. 9.02
to b. them bound before the chief 9.21
and b. one Simon who is called 10.05
to Joppa and b. Simon called Peter; 11.13
the Passover to b. him out to the 12.04
when Herod was about to b. him out, 12.06
And we b. you the good news that 13.32
that you may b. salvation to the 13.47
and b. you good news, that you 14.15
seeking to b. them out to the 17.05
For you b. some strange things to 17.20
let them b. charges against one 19.38
were there and b. them in bonds to 22.05
among them and b. him into the 23.10
the tribune to b. him down to you, 23.15
"B. this young man to the tribune; 23.17
and asked me to b. this young man 23.18
to ask you to b. Paul down to the 23.20
and b. him safely to Felix the 23.24
you what they now b. up against me. 24.13
years I came to b. to my nation 24.17
if possible to b. the ship ashore. 27.39
no charge to b. against my nation. 28.19
apostleship to b. about obedience Rom 1.05
is good, then, b. death to me? 7.13
Who shall b. any charge against 8.33
(that is, to b. Christ down) 10.06
(that is, to b. Christ up from the 10.07

BRING (cont.)
to b. about obedience to the faith— Rom 16.26
to b. to nothing things that are, 1Co 1.28
who will b. to light the things now 4.05
you unless I b. you some revelation 14.06
with Jesus and b. us with you into 2Co 4.14
that they might b. us into bondage— Gal 2.04
but b. them up in the discipline Eph 6.04
in you will b. it to completion at Php 1.06
God will b. with him those who have 1Th 4.14
Get Mark and b. him with you; 2Ti 4.11
When you come, b. the cloak that I 4.13
that he might b. us to God, being 1Pe 3.18
will secretly b. in destructive 2Pe 2.01
you and does not b. this doctrine, 2Jn 1.10
I will b. up what he is doing, 3Jn 1.10
the earth shall b. their glory Rev 21.24
they shall b. into it the glory and 21.26

BRINGEST
when thou b. the marauder suddenly Jer 18.22

BRINGING
of Egypt about b. out the people Ex 6.27
done to us, in b. us out of Egypt? 14.11
and come up b. Aaron with you; 19.24
They still kept b. him freewill 36.03
the people were restrained from b.; 36.06
thus b. guilt on the people, then Lev 4.03
of Canaan, to which I am b. you. 18.03
land where I am b. you to dwell 20.22
b. iniquity to remembrance. Num 5.15
against him by b. up an evil 14.36
your God is b. you into a good Deu 8.07
take delight in b. ruin upon you 28.63
b. upon it all the curses written 29.27
have you disturbed me by b. me up?" 1Sa 28.15
b. much spoil with them. But Abner 2Sa 3.22
and thought he was b. good news, 4.10
say nothing about b. the king back?" 19.10
first to speak of b. back our king?" 19.43
the guilty by b. his conduct upon 1Ki 8.32
of Tarshish used to come b. gold, 10.22
b. the man of God bread of the 2Ki 4.42
of the city, who were b. them up. 10.06
I am b. upon Jerusalem and Judah 21.12
came b. food on asses and on camels 1Ch 12.40
the guilty by b. his conduct upon 2Ch 6.23
of Tarshish used to come b. gold, 9.21
While they were b. out the money 34.14
and b. in heaps of grain and Neh 13.15
shouts of joy, b. his sheaves with him. Ps 126.06
the Lord is b. up against them the Is 8.07
as of one b. forth her first child, Jer 4.31
Behold, I am b. upon you a nation 5.15
behold, I am b. evil upon this 6.19
I am b. evil upon them which they 11.11
b. burnt offerings and sacrifices, 17.26
and b. thank offerings to the house 17.26
I am b. such evil upon this place 19.03
I am b. upon this city and upon all 19.15
I am b. on Judah and all the 35.17
b. cereal offerings and incense to 41.05
I am b. evil upon all flesh, says 45.05
I am b. punishment upon Amon of 46.25
stirring up and b. against Babylon 50.09
I am b. punishment on the king of 50.18
of the evil that I am b. upon her.'" 51.64
to them in b. them out of the land Eze 20.09
by b. upon us a great calamity; Dan 9.12
b. with them the lame, the maimed, Mt 15.30
b. five talents more, saying, 'Master, 25.20
And they came, b. to him a paralytic Mk 2.03
And they were b. children to him, 10.13
men were b. on a bed a man who was Lk 5.18
preaching and b. the good news of 8.01
Now they were b. even infants to 18.15
b. him into the high priest's house. 22.54
I am b. him out to you, that you may Jn 19.04
came b. a mixture of myrrh and 19.39
b. the sick and those afflicted Ac 5.16
b. with them John whose other name 12.25
b. us to the house of Mnason of 21.16
b. against him many serious charges 25.07
thereby b. the hostility to an end. Eph 2.16
in b. many sons to glory, should Heb 2.10
b. upon themselves swift destruction. 2Pe 2.01
b. my recompense, to repay every one Rev 22.12

BRINGS
And when the LORD b. you into the Ex 13.05
"And when the LORD b. you into the 13.11
and b. you in to the Amorites, and 23.23
any man of you b. an offering to Lev 1.02
"When any one b. a cereal offering 2.01
"If he b. a lamb as his offering 4.32
of bitterness that b. the curse. Num 5.18
of bitterness that b. the curse. 5.19
may this water that b. the curse 5.22
of bitterness that b. the curse, 5.24
the water that b. the curse shall 5.24
the water that b. the curse shall 5.27
then he who b. his offering shall 15.04
God b. them out of Egypt; they have 23.22
God b. him out of Egypt; he has as it 24.08
LORD your God b. you into the land Deu 6.10
LORD your God b. you into the land 7.01
LORD your God b. you into the land 11.29
and b. an evil name upon her, saying, 22.14
The LORD b. trouble on you today." Jos 7.25
The LORD kills and b. to life; 1Sa 2.06
he b. down to Sheol and raises up. 2.06
he b. low, he also exalts. 2.07
The king said, "He also b. tidings." 2Sa 18.26
When disaster b. sudden death, he Job 9.23
and b. deep darkness to light. 12.22
for wrath b. the punishment of the 19.29
that is hid he b. forth to light. 28.11
with mischief, and b. forth lies. Ps 7.14
The LORD b. the counsel of the 33.10
He who b. thanksgiving as his 50.23
the rain and b. forth the wind 135.07
way of the wicked he b. to ruin. 146.09
son who sleeps in harvest b. shame. Pro 10.05
babbling of a fool b. ruin near. 10.14
of the righteous b. forth wisdom, 10.31
but she who b. shame is like 12.04
the tongue of the wise b. healing. 12.18
the word b. destruction on himself, 13.13
but a faithful envoy b. healing. 13.17
compresses his lips b. evil to pass. 16.30
for him and b. him before great 18.16
When a man's folly b. his way to 19.03
Wealth b. many new friends, but a 19.04
who causes shame and b. reproach. 19.26
the mighty and b. down the stronghold 21.22
more when he b. it with evil 21.27
The north wind b. forth rain; 25.23
left to himself b. shame to his 29.15
she b. her food from afar. 31.14
in his eyes as one who b. peace. Sol 8.10
that b. neither help nor profit, but Is 30.05
And yet he is wise and b. disaster, 31.02
who b. princes to nought, and makes 40.23
He who b. out their host by number, 40.26
who b. forth chariot and horse, army 43.17
feet of him who b. good tidings, 52.07
who b. good tidings of good, who 52.07
For as the earth b. forth its 61.11
and he b. forth the wind from his Jer 10.13
your God before he b. darkness, 13.16
and he b. forth the wind from his 51.16
but he b. their guilt to remembrance, Eze 21.23
you, as the sea b. up its waves. 26.03
feet of him who b. good tidings, Nah 1.15
He b. all of them up with a hook, he Hab 1.15

BRINGS (cont.)
oil, upon what the ground b. forth, Hag 1.11
till he b. justice to victory; Mt 12.20
of his good treasure b. forth good, 12.35
of his evil treasure b. forth evil. 12.35
Then he goes and b. with him seven 12.45
householder who b. out of his 13.52
Then he goes and b. seven other Lk 11.26
For the law b. wrath, but where Rom 4.15
many trespasses b. justification. 5.16
to salvation and b. no regret, 2Co 7.10
when he b. the first-born into the Heb 1.06
and b. forth vegetation useful to 6.07
it is full-grown b. forth death. Jas 1.15
truth and some one b. him back, 5.19
that whoever b. back a sinner from 5.20

BRINK
among the reeds at the river's b. Ex 2.03
wait for him by the river's b., 7.15
you come to the b. of the waters Jos 3.08
dipped in the b. of the water (the 3.15
on the b. of the Nile, and all that Is 19.07

BRISTLING
bring up horses like b. locusts. Jer 51.27

BRITTLE
be partly strong and partly b. Dan 2.42

BROAD
of that land to a good and b. land, Ex 3.08
cubits long and five cubits b.; 27.01
The land is b.; yea, God has Ju 18.10
He brought me forth into a b. place; 2Sa 22.20
The lowest story was five cubits b., 1Ki 6.06
the middle one was six cubits b., 6.06
and the third was seven cubits b.; 6.06
pasture, and the land was very b., 1Ch 4.40
Jerusalem as far as the B. Wall. Neh 3.08
of the Furnaces, to the B. Wall, 12.38
distress into a b. place where Job 36.16
and the b. waters are frozen fast. 37.10
He brought me forth into a b. place; Ps 18.19
hast set my feet in a b. place. 31.08
thy commandment is exceedingly b. 119.96
us a place of b. rivers and Is 33.21
The b. wall of Babylon shall be Jer 51.58
one reed long, and one reed b.; Eze 40.07
cubits long and five cubits b. 40.30
long, and a cubit and a half b., 40.42
a hundred cubits b., foursquare; 40.47
west side was seventy cubits b.; 41.12
two cubits long, and two cubits b.; 41.22
long and five hundred cubits b., 42.20
and one cubit b., with a rim of one 43.13
twelve cubits long by twelve b. 43.16
fourteen cubits long by fourteen b., 43.17
a rim around it half a cubit b., 43.17
long and twenty thousand cubits b.; 45.01
cubits long and ten thousand b., 45.03
long and ten thousand cubits b., 45.05
an area five thousand cubits b., 45.06
forty cubits long and thirty b.; 46.22
them like a lamb in a b. pasture? Hos 4.16
darken the earth in b. daylight. Amo 8.09
phylacteries b. and their fringes Mt 23.05
up over the b. earth and surrounded Rev 20.09

BROADER
the earth, and b. than the sea. Job 11.09
chambers became b. as they rose Eze 41.07

BROILED
They gave him a piece of b. fish, Lk 24.42

BROKE
his hands and b. them at the foot Ex 32.19
on the first tables, which you b. 34.01
and b. them before your eyes Deu 9.17
on the first tables which you b., 10.02
because you b. faith with me in the 32.51
of Israel b. faith in regard to Jos 7.01
blew the trumpets and b. the jars, Ju 7.20
And he b. down the tower of Penuel, 8.17
so that tumors b. out upon them. 1Sa 5.09
and the day b. upon them at Hebron. 2Sa 2.32
mighty men b. through the camp of 23.16
and b. in pieces the rocks before 1Ki 19.11
and his images they b. in pieces, 2Ki 11.18
and b. down the wall of Jerusalem 14.13
and b. the pillars, and cut down the 18.04
And he b. in pieces the bronze 18.04
And he b. down the houses of the 23.07
and he b. down the high places of 23.08
he pulled down and b. in pieces, 23.12
And he b. in pieces the pillars, and 23.14
down and he b. in pieces its 23.15
b. down the walls around Jerusalem. 25.10
the Chaldeans b. in pieces, and 25.13
mighty men b. through the camp of 1Ch 11.18
the LORD our God b. forth upon us, 15.13
and b. down the pillars and hewed 2Ch 14.03
and his images they b. in pieces, 23.17
and b. down the wall of Jerusalem 25.23
and b. down the wall of Gath and 26.06
priests leprosy b. out on his 26.19
of Judah and b. in pieces the 31.01
the Asherim and b. down the high 31.01
And they b. down the altars of the 34.04
and he b. in pieces the Asherim 34.04
he b. down the altars, and beat the 34.07
and b. down the wall of Jerusalem, 36.19
I was at ease, and he b. me asunder; Job 16.12
I b. the fangs of the unrighteous, 29.17
him there b. through his clouds Ps 18.12
wood they b. down with hatchets 74.06
There he b. the flashing arrows, the 76.03
and b. every staff of bread, 105.16
Fire also b. out in their company; 106.18
and a plague b. out among them. 106.29
and b. their bonds asunder. 107.14
by his knowledge the deeps b. forth, Pro 3.20
and you b. down the houses to Is 22.10
"For long ago you b. your yoke and Jer 2.20
Jeremiah the prophet, and b. them. 28.10
Egypt, my covenant which they b., 31.32
and b. down the walls of Jerusalem. 39.08
b. down all the walls round about 52.14
the Chaldeans b. in pieces, and 52.17
he b. off the topmost of its young Eze 17.04
and whose covenant with him he b., 17.16
the oath and b. the covenant, 17.18
and my covenant which he b., 17.19
you b., and tore all their shoulders; 29.07
you b., and made all their loins to 29.07
and clay, and b. them in pieces; Dan 2.34
and that it b. in pieces the iron, 2.45
them and b. all their bones in 6.24
it devoured and b. in pieces, 7.07
which devoured and b. in pieces, 7.19
the ram and b. his two horns; 8.07
and I b. it, annulling the covenant Zec 11.10
Then I b. my second staff Union, 11.14
and b. and gave the loaves to the Mt 14.19
given thanks he b. them and gave 15.36
and b. it, and gave it to the 26.26
and the fetters he b. in pieces; Mk 5.04
and b. the loaves, and gave them to 6.41
given thanks he b. them and gave 8.06
When I b. the five loaves for the 8.19
and she b. the jar and poured it 14.03
and b. it, and gave it to them, and 14.22
And he b. down and wept. 14.72
the stream b. against that house, Lk 6.48
against which the stream b., 6.49
but he b. the bonds and was driven 8.29

BROKE (cont.)
to heaven, and blessed and b. them, Lk 9.16
given thanks he b. it and gave it 22.19
and b. it, and gave it to them. 24.30
he not only b. the sabbath but Jn 5.18
came and b. the legs of the first, 19.32
the meeting of the synagogue b. up, Ac 13.43
of all he b. it and began to eat. 27.35
he b. it, and said, "This is my body 1Co 11.24

BROKEN
his people; he has b. my covenant." Gen 17.24
of their b. spirit and their cruel Ex 6.09
the people had b. loose (for Aaron 32.25
in which it is boiled shall be b.; Lev 6.28
or stove, it shall be b. in pieces; 11.35
it has b. out in the boil. 13.20
it has b. out in the burn, and the 13.25
tetter that has b. out in the skin; 13.39
the discharge touches shall be b.; 15.12
and I have b. the bars of your yoke 26.13
and has b. his commandment, that Num 15.31
whose neck was b. in the valley; Deu 21.06
the altar of Baal was b. down, Ju 6.28
The bows of the mighty are b., 1Sa 2.04
of the LORD shall be b. to pieces; 2.10
and his neck was b. and he died, 4.18
"The LORD has b. through my enemies 2Sa 5.20
the LORD had b. forth upon Uzzah; 6.08
and I will have them b. up there, 1Ki 5.09
that b. reed of a staff, which will 2Ki 18.21
the LORD had b. forth upon Uzzah; 1Ch 13.11
"God has b. through my enemies by 14.11
for they were b. before the LORD 2Ch 14.13
They were b. in pieces, nation 15.06
had b. into the house of God; 24.07
up all the wall that was b. down, 32.05
his father Hezekiah had b. down, 33.03
"We have b. faith with our God and Ez 10.02
the wall of Jerusalem is b. down, Neh 1.03
which were b. down and its gates 2.13
teeth of the young lions, are b. Job 4.10
My spirit is b., my days are 17.01
my plans are b. off, the desires of 17.11
so wickedness is b. like a tree.' 24.20
let my arm be b. from its socket. 31.22
and their uplifted arm is b. 38.15
I have become like a b. vessel. Ps 31.12
all his bones; not one of them is b. 34.20
heart, and their bows shall be b. 37.15
the arms of the wicked shall be b.; 37.17
shouldst have b. us in the place 44.19
bones which thou hast b. rejoice. 51.08
acceptable to God is a b. spirit; 51.17
a b. and contrite heart, O God, thou 51.17
hast rejected us, b. our defenses; 60.01
Insults have b. my heart, so that I 69.20
Why then hast thou b. down its walls, 80.12
He has b. my strength in mid-course; 102.23
to act, for thy law has been b. 119.126
the snare is b., and we have 124.07
he will be b. beyond healing. Pro 6.15
sorrow of heart the spirit is b. 15.13
but a b. spirit who can bear? 18.14
and its stone wall was b. down. 24.31
is like a city b. into and left 25.28
will suddenly be b. beyond healing. 29.01
A threefold cord is not quickly b. Ecc 4.12
snapped, or the golden bowl is b., 12.06
the pitcher is b. at the fountain, 12.06
or the wheel b. at the cistern, 12.06
is loose, not a sandal-thong b.; Is 5.27
Ephraim will be b. to pieces so 7.08
Be b., you peoples, and be dismayed; 8.09
they shall fall and be b.; 8.15
thou hast b. as on the day of 9.04
The LORD has b. the staff of the 14.05
that the rod which smote you is b., 14.29
b. the everlasting covenant. 24.05
The city of chaos is b. down, 24.10
The earth is utterly b., 24.19
When its boughs are dry, they are b.; 27.11
and be b., and snared, and taken. 28.13
Covenants are b., witnesses are 33.08
nor will any of its cords be b. 33.20
that b. reed of a staff, which will 36.06
b. cisterns, that can hold no water. Jer 2.13
Tahpanhes have b. the crown of 2.16
But they all alike had b. the yoke, 5.05
destroyed, and all my cords are b.; 10.20
of Judah have b. my covenant which 11.10
b. pot, a vessel no one cares for? 22.28
My heart is b. within me, all my 23.09
I have b. the yoke of the king of 28.02
Hananiah had b. the yoke-bars from 28.12
You have b. wooden bars, but I will 28.13
with David my servant may be b., 33.21
is put to shame and b. down; 48.01
say, 'How the mighty scepter is b., 48.17
Moab is put to shame, for it is b.; 48.20
and his arm is b., says the LORD. 48.25
for I have b. Moab like a vessel 48.38
How it is b.! How they wail! 48.39
the whole earth is cut down and b.! 50.23
Suddenly Babylon has fallen and been b.; 51.08
are on fire, her bars are b. 51.30
taken, their bows are b. in pieces; 51.56
wrath he has b. down the strongholds Lam 2.02
He has b. down his booth like that 2.06
he has ruined and b. her bars; 2.09
skin waste away, and b. my bones; 3.04
your incense altars shall be b.; Eze 6.04
your idols b. and destroyed, your 6.06
when I have b. their wanton heart 6.09
Aha, the gate of the peoples is b., 26.02
Egypt, and all her helpers are b. 30.08
be breached, and its walls b. down. 30.16
I have b. the arm of Pharaoh king 30.21
strong arm and the one that was b.; 30.22
boughs will lie b. in all the 31.12
So you shall be b. and lie among 32.28
You have b. my covenant, with all 44.07
all together were b. in pieces, Dan 2.35
was strong, the great horn was b., 8.08
As for the horn that was b., 8.22
by no human hand, he shall be b. 8.25
shall be b. and divided toward the 11.04
within a few days he shall be b., 11.20
swept away before him and b., 11.22
because they have b. my covenant, Hos 8.01
of Samaria shall be b. to pieces. 8.06
the rocks are b. asunder by him. Nah 1.06
full of the b. pieces left over. Mt 14.20
full of the b. pieces left over. 15.37
on this stone will be b. to pieces; * 21.44
not have let his house be b. into. 24.43
baskets full of b. pieces and of Mk 6.43
took up the b. pieces left over, 8.08
baskets full of b. pieces did you 8.19
baskets full of b. pieces did you 8.20
over, twelve baskets of b. pieces. Lk 9.17
have left his house to be b. into. 12.39
on that stone will be b. to pieces; 20.18
the law of Moses may not be b., Jn 7.23
came (and scripture cannot be b.), 10.35
Pilate that their legs might be b., 19.31
"Not a bone of him shall be b." 19.36
gone up and had b. bread and eaten, Ac 20.11
the stern was b. up by the surf. 27.41
some of the branches were b. off, Rom 11.17
"Branches were b. off so that I 11.19
They were b. off because of their 11.20
and has b. down the dividing wall Eph 2.14
when earthen pots are b. in pieces, Rev 2.27

BROKENHEARTED
The LORD is near to the b., Ps 34.18
needy and the b. to their death. 109.16
He heals the b., and binds up their 147.03
he has sent me to bind up the b., Is 61.01

BRONZE
of all instruments of b. and iron. Gen 4.22
from them: gold, silver, and b., Ex 25.03
"And you shall make fifty clasps of b., 26.11
cast five bases of b. for them. 26.37
and you shall overlay it with b. 27.02
its utensils you shall make of b. 27.03
for it a grating, a network of b.; 27.04
shall make four b. rings at its 27.04
wood, and overlay them with b.; 27.06
of b., but the hooks of the pillars 27.10
of b., but the hooks of the pillars 27.11
of silver, and their bases of b. 27.17
fine twined linen and bases of b. 27.18
pegs of the court, shall be of b. 27.19
"You shall also make a laver of b., 30.18
with its base of b., for washing. 30.18
to work in gold, silver, and b., 31.04
offering: gold, silver, and b.; 35.05
offering, with its grating of b., 35.16
of silver or b. brought it as the 35.24
to work in gold and silver and b., 35.32
fifty clasps of b. to couple the 36.18
but their five bases were of b. 36.38
it, and he overlaid it with b. 38.02
all its utensils he made of b. 38.03
a network of b., under its ledge, 38.04
corners of the b. grating as 38.05
wood, and overlaid them with b. 38.06
the laver of b. and its base of b., 38.08
of b., but the hooks of the pillars 38.10
of b., but the hooks of the pillars 38.11
bases for the pillars were of b., 38.17
their four bases were of b., 38.19
the court round about were of b. 38.20
And the b. that was contributed was 38.29
the b. altar and the b. grating for it 38.30
the b. altar, and its grating of b., 39.39
but if it is boiled in a b. vessel, Lev 6.28
the priest took the b. censers, Num 16.39
So Moses made a b. serpent, 21.09
look at the b. serpent and live. 21.09
the b., the iron, the tin, and the 31.22
Your bars shall be iron and b.; Deu 33.25
gold, and vessels of b. and iron, Jos 6.19
and the vessels of b. and of iron, 6.24
b., and iron, and with much clothing; 22.08
and bound him with b. fetters; Ju 16.21
He had a helmet of b. on his head, 1Sa 17.05
was five thousand shekels of b. 17.05
he had greaves of b. upon his legs, 17.06
a javelin of b. slung between his 17.06
he put a helmet of b. on his head, 17.38
King David took very much b. 2Sa 8.08
of silver, of gold, and of b.; 8.10
three hundred shekels of b., 21.16
that my arms can bend a bow of b. 22.35
cities with walls and b. bars); 1Ki 4.13
was a man of Tyre, a worker in b.; 7.14
skill, for making any work in b. 7.14
He cast two pillars of b. 7.15
made two capitals of molten b., 7.16
He also made the ten stands of b.; 7.27
stand had four b. wheels and axles of b., 7.30
And he made ten lavers of b.; 7.38
King Solomon, were of burnished b. 7.45
weight of the b. was not found out. 7.47
because the b. altar that was 8.64
made in their stead shields of b., 14.27
And the b. altar which was before 2Ki 16.14
but the b. altar shall be for me 16.15
from off the b. oxen that were 16.17
in pieces the b. serpent that 18.04
And the pillars of b. that were in 25.13
stands and the b. sea that were in 25.13
and carried the b. to Babylon. 25.13
the vessels of b. used in the 25.14
the b. of all these vessels was 25.16
and upon it was a capital of b.; 25.17
all of b., were upon the capital 25.17
Ethan, were to sound b. cymbals; 1Ch 15.19
Hadadezer, David took very much b.; 18.08
made the b. sea and the pillars 18.08
the pillars and the vessels of b. 18.08
of gold, of silver, and of b.; 18.10
as well as b. in quantities beyond 22.03
and b. and iron beyond weighing, for 22.14
gold, silver, b., and iron. 22.16
and the b. for the things of b., 29.02
eighteen thousand talents of b., 29.07
Moreover the b. altar that Bezalel 2Ch 1.05
up there to the b. altar before 1.06
b., and iron, and in purple, crimson, 2.07
b., iron, stone, and wood, and in 2.14
He made an altar of b., 4.01
and overlaid their doors with b., 4.09
of burnished b. for King Solomon 4.16
weight of the b. was not ascertained. 4.18
Solomon had made a b. platform five 6.13
because the b. altar Solomon had 7.07
made in their stead shields of b., 12.10
in iron and b. to repair the house 24.12
with fetters of b. and brought him 33.11
of fine bright b. as precious as Ez 8.27
of stones, or is my flesh b.? Job 6.12
a b. arrow will strike him through. 20.24
His bones are tubes of b., 40.18
as straw, and b. as rotten wood. 41.27
that my arms can bend a bow of b. Ps 18.34
Let b. be brought from Egypt; 68.31
For he shatters the doors of b., 107.16
the doors of b. and cut asunder Is 45.02
Instead of b. I will bring gold, and 60.17
b., instead of stones, iron. 60.17
and b. walls, against the whole land, Jer 1.18
they are b. and iron, all of them 6.28
iron, iron from the north, and b.? 15.12
this people a fortified wall of b.; 15.20
And the pillars of b. that were in 52.17
stands and the b. sea that were in 52.17
and carried all the b. to Babylon. 52.17
the vessels of b. used in the 52.18
the twelve b. bulls which were 52.20
the b. of all these things was 52.20
Upon it was a capital of b.; 52.22
all of b., were upon the capital 52.22
the fire, as it were gleaming b. Eze 1.04
they sparkled like burnished b. 1.07
loins I saw as it were gleaming b., 1.27
of brightness, like gleaming b. 8.02
in and stood beside the b. altar. 9.02
silver and b. and tin and iron and 22.18
silver and b. and iron and lead 22.20
and vessels of b. for your merchandise. 27.13
man, whose appearance was like b., 40.03
its belly and thighs of b., Dan 2.32
the b., the silver, and the gold, all 2.35
you, and yet a third kingdom of b., 2.39
the b., the clay, the silver, and the 2.45
bound with a band of iron and b., 4.15
bound with a band of iron and b., 4.23
b., iron, wood, and stone. 5.04
of b., iron, wood, and stone, which do 5.23
its teeth of iron and claws of b.; 7.19
like the gleam of burnished b., 10.06
your horn iron and your hoofs b.; Mic 4.13
the mountains were mountains of b. Zec 6.01
of cups and pots and vessels of b.) Mk 7.04

BRONZE (cont.)
his feet were like burnished b., Rev 1.15
whose feet are like burnished b. 2.18
and silver and b. and stone and 9.20
costly wood, b., iron and marble, 18.12

BROOCHES
heart brought b. and earrings and Ex 35.22

BROOD
a b. of sinful men, to increase Num 32.14
A senseless, a disreputable b., Job 30.08
that gathers a b. which she did Jer 17.11
he said to them, "You b. of vipers! Mt 3.07
You b. of vipers! how can you 12.34
you b. of vipers, how are you to 23.33
hen gathers her b. under her wings, 23.37
baptized by him, "You b. of vipers! Lk 3.07
hen gathers her b. under her wings, 13.34

BROOK
leafy trees, and willows of the b.; Lev 23.40
turn from Azmon to the B. of Egypt, Num 34.05
'Now rise up, and go over the b. Zered.' Deu 2.13
So we went over the b. Zered. 2.13
we crossed the b. Zered was thirty-eight 2.14
of it into the b. that descended 9.21
Azmon, goes out by the b. of Egypt, Jos 15.04
to the b. of Egypt, and the great 15.47
goes westward to the b. Kanah, 16.08
went down to the b. Kanah. 17.09
here, to the south of the b., 17.09
side of the b. and ends at the sea; 17.09
then the b. which is east of 19.11
five smooth stones from the b., 1Sa 17.40
him, and they came to the b. Besor, 30.09
exhausted to cross the b. Besor. 30.10
who had been left at the b. Besor; 30.21
and the king crossed the b. Kidron, 2Sa 15.23
have gone over the b. of water." 17.20
and cross the b. Kidron, know for 1Ki 2.37
of Hamath to the B. of Egypt, 8.65
and burned it at the b. Kidron. 15.13
hide yourself by the b. Cherith, 17.03
You shall drink from the b., 17.04
dwelt by the b. Cherith that is 17.05
the evening; and he drank from the b. 17.06
And after a while the b. dried up, 17.07
brought them down to the b. Kishon, 18.40
to the b. Kidron, and burned it at 2Ki 23.06
and burned it at the b. Kidron, 23.06
dust of them into the b. Kidron. 23.12
Egypt from the B. of Egypt to the 24.07
of Hamath to the B. of Egypt. 2Ch 7.08
it, and burned it at the b. Kidron. 15.16
carried it out to the b. Kidron. 29.16
springs and the b. that flowed 32.04
the willows of the b. surround him. Job 40.22
He will drink from the b. by the way; Ps 110.07
away over the B. of the Willows. Is 15.07
Euphrates to the B. of Egypt the 27.12
thou be to me like a deceitful b., Jer 15.18
the fields as far as the b. Kidron, 31.40
along the B. of Egypt to the Great Eze 47.19
along the B. of Egypt to the Great 48.28
of Hamath to the B. of the Arabah. Amo 6.14

BROOKS
a land of b. of water, of fountains Deu 8.07
Jotbathah, a land with b. of water. 10.07
Pirathon, Hiddai of the b. of Gaash, 2Sa 23.30
Hurai of the b. of Gaash, Abiel the 1Ch 11.32
Thou didst cleave open springs and b.; Ps 74.15
there will be b. running with Is 30.25
will make them walk by b. of water, Jer 31.09
because the water b. are dried up, Joe 1.20

BROOM
came and sat down under a b. tree; 1Ki 19.04
lay down and slept under a b. tree; 19.05
themselves the roots of the b. Job 30.04
with glowing coals of the b. tree! Ps 120.04
it with the b. of destruction, Is 14.23

BROTH
and the b. he put in a pot, and Ju 6.19
rock, and pour the b. over them." 6.20
and b. of abominable things is in Is 65.04
the flesh, and empty out the b., Eze 24.10

BROTHER
And again, she bore his b. Abel. Gen 4.02
Cain said to Abel his b., 4.08
Cain rose up against his b. Abel, 4.08
to Cain, "Where is Abel your b.?" 4.09
of every man's b. I will require the 9.05
the elder b. of Japheth, children 10.21
took Lot, the son of Abram's b., 14.12
b. of Eshcol and of Aner; these were 14.13
And she herself said, 'He is my b.' 20.05
we come, say of me, He is my b.'" 20.13
have given your b. a thousand 20.16
borne children to your b. Nahor: 22.20
Buz his b., Kemuel the father of 22.21
Milcah bore to Nahor, Abraham's b. 22.23
Abraham's b., came out with her 24.15
Rebekah had a b. whose name was 24.29
gave to her b. and to her mother 24.53
Her b. and her mother said, "Let the 24.55
Afterward his b. came forth, and his 25.26
your father speak to your b. Esau, 27.06
my b. Esau is a hairy man, and I am 27.11
hairy like his b. Esau's hands; 27.23
Esau his b. came in from his 27.30
"Your b. came with guile, and he has 27.35
live, and you shall serve your b.; 27.40
then I will kill my b. Jacob." 27.41
your b. Esau comforts himself by 27.42
flee to Laban my b. in Haran, 27.43
daughters of Laban your mother's b. 28.02
the b. of Rebekah, Jacob's and Esau's 28.05
daughter of Laban his mother's b., 29.10
the sheep of Laban his mother's b., 29.10
the flock of Laban his mother's b. 29.10
him to Esau his b. in the land of 32.03
saying, "We came to your b. Esau, 32.06
pray thee, from the hand of my b., 32.11
him a present for his b. Esau, 32.13
"When Esau my b. meets you, and asks 32.17
until he came near to his b. 33.03
But Esau said, "I have enough, my b.; 33.09
when you fled from your b. Esau." 35.01
to him when he fled from his b. 35.07
into a land away from his b. Jacob. 36.06
if we slay our b. and conceal his 37.26
for he is our b., our own flesh." 37.27
and raise up offspring for your b." 38.08
he should give offspring to his b. 38.09
his hand, behold, his b. came out; 38.29
Afterward his b. came out with the 38.30
Joseph's b., with his brothers, for 42.04
unless your youngest b. comes here. 42.15
of you, and let him bring your b., 42.16
and bring your youngest b. to me; 42.20
we are guilty concerning our b., 42.21
Bring your youngest b. to me; 42.34
and I will deliver to you your b., 42.34
for his b. is dead, and he only is 42.38
face, unless your b. is with you.' 43.03
If you will send our b. with us, 43.04
face, unless your b. is with you.'" 43.05
the man that you had another b.?" 43.06
Have you another b.?' What we told 43.07
he would say, 'Bring your b. down'?" 43.07
Take also your b., and arise, go 43.13

BROTHER (cont.)
back your other b. and Benjamin. Gen 43.14
and saw his b. Benjamin, his mother's 43.29
and said, "Is this your youngest b., 43.29
for his heart yearned for his b., 43.30
'Have you a father, or a b.?' 44.19
and a young b., the child of his 44.20
and his b. is dead, and he alone is 44.20
your youngest b. comes down with 44.23
If our youngest b. goes with us, 44.26
unless our youngest b. is with us.' 44.26
"I am your b., Joseph, whom you sold 45.04
and the eyes of my b. Benjamin see, 45.12
fell upon his b. Benjamin's neck 45.14
his younger b. shall be greater 48.19
not Aaron, your b., the Levite? Ex 4.14
and Aaron your b. shall be your 7.01
and Aaron your b. shall tell 7.02
"Then bring near to you Aaron your b., 28.01
holy garments for Aaron your b., 28.02
for Aaron your b. and his sons to 28.04
shall put them upon Aaron your b., 28.41
camp, and slay every man his b., 32.27
the cost of his son and of his b., 32.29
"Tell Aaron your b. not to come at Lev 16.02
the nakedness of your father's b., 18.14
not hate your b. in your heart, 19.17
his son, his daughter, his b., 21.02
"If your b. becomes poor, and sells 25.25
and redeem what his b. has sold. 25.25
"And if your b. becomes poor, and 25.35
that your b. may live beside you. 25.36
"And if your b. becomes poor beside 25.39
and your b. beside him becomes poor 25.47
nor for b. or sister, if they die, Num 6.07
congregation, you and Aaron your b., 20.08
of Edom, "Thus says your b. Israel: 20.14
as your b. Aaron was gathered, because 27.13
Zelophehad our b. to his daughters. 36.02
a man and his b. or the alien that Deu 1.16
"If your b., the son of your mother, 13.06
his b., because the LORD's release 15.02
is with your b. your hand shall 15.03
your hand against your poor b., 15.07
eye be hostile to your poor b., 15.09
open wide your hand to your b., 15.11
"If your b., a Hebrew man, or a 15.12
over you, who is not your b. 17.15
and has accused his b. falsely, 19.18
as he had meant to do to his b.; 19.19
shall take them back to your b. 22.01
be with you until your b. seeks it; 22.02
an Edomite, for he is your b.; 23.07
not lend upon interest to your b., 23.19
but to your b. you shall not lend 23.20
your b. be degraded in your sight. 25.03
her husband's b. shall go in to her, 25.05
the duty of a husband's b. to her. 25.05
to the name of his b. who is dead, 25.06
'My husband's b. refuses to perpetuate 25.07
the duty of a husband's b. to me.' 25.07
you will grudge food to his b., 28.54
as Aaron your b. died in Mount Hor 32.50
the b. of Caleb, took it; Jos 15.17
And Judah said to Simeon his b., Ju 1.03
Kenaz, Caleb's younger b., took it; 1.13
And Judah went with Simeon his b., 1.17
son of Kenaz, Caleb's younger b. 3.09
for they said, "He is our b." 9.03
there, for fear of Abimelech his b. 9.21
be laid upon Abimelech their b., 9.24
compassion for Benjamin their b., 21.06
Ichabod's b., son of Phinehas, son of 1Sa 14.03
his eldest b. heard when he spoke 17.28
and my b. has commanded me to be 20.29
and to Joab's b. Abishai the son of 26.06
distressed for you, my b. Jonathan; 2Sa 1.26
I lift up my face to your b. Joab?" 2.22
for the blood of Asahel his b. 3.27
Joab and Abishai his b. slew Abner, 3.30
killed their b. Asahel in the 3.30
and Baanah his b. slipped in. 4.06
answered Rechab and Baanah his b., 4.09
in the charge of Abishai his b., 10.10
the son of Shimeah, David's b.; 13.03
"I love Tamar, my b. Absalom's sister." 13.04
"Go to your b. Amnon's house, and 13.07
Tamar went to her b. Amnon's house, 13.08
into the chamber to Amnon her b. 13.10
my b., do not force me; for such a 13.12
But she said to him, "No, my b.; 13.16
And her b. Absalom said to her, "Has 13.20
"Has Amnon your b. been with you? 13.20
he is your b.; do not take 13.20
in her b. Absalom's house. 13.20
pray let my b. Amnon go with us." 13.26
David's b., said, "Let not my lord 13.32
'Give up the man who struck his b., 14.07
the life of his b. whom he slew'; 14.07
Joab's b., and one third under the 18.02
Amasa, "Is it well with you, my b.?" 20.09
and Abishai his b. pursued Sheba 20.10
of Shimei, David's b., slew him. 21.21
the b. of Joab, the son of Zeruiah, 23.18
Asahel the b. of Joab was one of 23.24
the mighty men or Solomon his b. 1Ki 1.10
when I fled from Absalom your b. 2.07
to Adonijah your b. as his wife." 2.21
for he is my elder b., and on his 2.22
which you have given me, my b.?" 9.13
over him, saying, "Alas, my b.!" 13.30
"Does he still live? He is my b." 20.32
and said, "Yes, your b. Benhadad." 20.33
Jehoram, his b., became king in his 2Ki 1.17
and the name of his b. Joktan. 1Ch 1.19
Shammai's b.: Jether and Jonathan; 2.32
The sons of Caleb the b. of Jerahmeel: 2.42
Chelub, the b. of Shuhah, was the 4.11
and his b. Asaph, who stood on his 6.39
and the name of his b. was Sheresh; 7.16
The sons of Shemer his b.: Rohgah, 7.34
The sons of Heler his b.: Zophah, 7.35
The sons of Eshek his b.: Ulam his 8.39
the b. of Joab, was chief of the 11.20
armies were Asahel the b. of Joab, 11.26
Joel the b. of Nathan, Mibhar the 11.38
and Joha his b., the Tizite, 11.45
in the charge of Abishai his b., 19.11
Joab's b., and entered the city. 19.15
slew Lahmi the b. of Goliath the 20.05
of Shimea, David's b., slew him. 20.07
The b. of Micah, Isshiah; 24.25
house and his younger b. alike, 24.31
of Jehieli, Zetham and Joel his b., 26.22
Asahel the b. of Joab was fourth, 27.07
with Shimei his b. as second; 2Ch 31.12
assisting Conaniah and Shimei his b., 31.13
Eliakim his b. king over Judah and 36.04
Jehoahaz his b. and carried him to 36.04
and made his b. Zedekiah king over 36.10
exacting interest, each from his b." Neh 5.07
I gave my b. Hanani and Hananiah 7.02
I am a b. of jackals, and a companion Job 30.29
I grieved for my friend or my b.; Ps 35.14
You sit and speak against your b.; 50.20
and a b. is born for adversity. Pro 17.17
his work is a b. to him who 18.09
A b. helped is like a strong city, 18.19
friend who sticks closer than a b. 18.24
is near than a b. who is far away. 27.10
either son or b., yet there is no Ecc 4.08
O that you were like a b. to me, Sol 8.01
hold of his b. in the house of his Is 3.06
for the fire; no man spares his b. 9.19

BROTHER (cont.)
man against his b. and every man Is 19.02
and says to his b., "Take courage!" 41.06
neighbor, and put no trust in any b.; Jer 9.04
for every b. is a supplanter, and 9.04
lament for him, saying, 'Ah my b.!' 22.18
neighbor and every one to his b., 23.35
teach his neighbor and each his b., 31.34
one should enslave a Jew, his b. 34.09
one to his b. and to his neighbor; 34.17
robbed his b., and did what is not Eze 18.18
each to his b., 'Come, and hear what 33.30
man's sword will be against his b. 38.21
for b. or unmarried sister they may 44.25
Say to your b., "My people," and to Hos 2.01
womb he took his b. by the heel, 12.03
he pursued his b. with the sword, Amo 1.11
the violence done to your b. Jacob, Ob 1.10
the day of your b. in the day of 1.12
and each hunts his b. with a net. Mic 7.02
kindness and mercy each to his b., Zec 7.09
evil against his b. in your heart." 7.10
"Is not Esau Jacob's b.?" Mal 1.02
is called Peter and Andrew his b., Mt 4.18
the son of Zebedee and John his b., 4.21
angry with his b. shall be liable 5.22
insults his b. shall be liable to 5.22
that your b. has something against 5.23
first be reconciled to your b., 5.24
Or how can you say to your b., 7.04
is called Peter, and Andrew his b.; 10.02
son of Zebedee, and John his b.; 10.02
B. will deliver up b. to death, and 10.21
of my Father in heaven is my b., 12.50
of Herodias, his b. Philip's wife; 14.03
Peter and James and John his b., 17.01
"If your b. sins against you, go and 18.15
to you, you have gained your b. 18.15
often shall my b. sin against me, 18.21
forgive your b. from your heart." 18.35
his b. must marry the widow, and 22.24
and raise up children for his b.' 22.24
children left his wife to his b. 22.25
and Andrew the b. of Simon casting Mk 1.16
the son of Zebedee and John his b., 1.19
Zebedee and John the b. of James, 3.17
Whoever does the will of God is my b., 3.35
and James and John the b. of James. 5.37
son of Mary and b. of James and 6.03
of Herodias, his b. Philip's wife; 6.17
that if a man's b. dies and leaves 12.19
and raise up children for his b. 12.19
And b. will deliver up b. to death, 13.12
and his b. Philip tetrarch of the Lk 3.01
he named Peter, and Andrew his b., 6.14
Or how can you say to your b., 6.42
'B., let me take out the speck that 6.42
bid my b. divide the inheritance 12.13
'Your b. has come, and your father 15.27
for this your b. was dead, and is 15.32
if your b. sins, rebuke him, and if 17.03
for us that if a man's b. dies, 20.28
and raise up children for his b. 20.28
him, was Andrew, Simon Peter's b. Jn 1.40
He first found his b. Simon, 1.41
Simon Peter's b., said to him, 6.08
whose b. Lazarus was ill. 11.02
console them concerning their b. 11.19
been here, my b. would not have died. 11.21
to her, "Your b. will rise again." 11.23
been here, my b. would not have died." 11.32
"B. Saul, the Lord Jesus who appeared Ac 9.17
James the b. of John with the 12.02
b., how many thousands there are 21.20
'B. Saul, receive your sight.' 22.13
Why do you pass judgment on your b.? Rom 14.10
Or you, why do you despise your b.? 14.10
or hindrance in the way of a b. 14.13
If your b. is being injured by what 14.15
anything that makes your b. stumble. 14.21
and our b. Quartus, greet you. 16.23
Jesus, and our b. Sosthenes, 1Co 1.01
the name of b. if he is guilty of 5.11
you has a grievance against a b., 6.01
but b. goes to law against b., and 6.06
that if any b. has a wife who is an 7.12
such a case the b. or sister is 7.15
the b. for whom Christ died. 8.11
meat, lest I cause my b. to fall. 8.13
As for our b. Apollos, I strongly 16.12
will of God, and Timothy our b. 2Co 1.01
I did not find my b. Titus there. 2.13
are sending the b. who is famous 8.18
are sending our b. whom we have 8.22
to go, and sent the b. with him. 12.18
apostles except James the Lord's b. Gal 1.19
the beloved b. and faithful Eph 6.21
Epaphroditus my b. and fellow Php 2.25
will of God, and Timothy our b., Col 1.01
he is a beloved b. and faithful 4.07
the faithful and beloved b., 4.09
our b. and God's servant in the 1Th 3.02
and wrong his b. in this matter, 4.06
away from any b. who is living in 2Th 3.06
as an enemy, but warn him as a b. 3.15
Christ Jesus, and Timothy our b., Phm 1.01
my b., because the hearts of the 1.07
as a beloved b., especially to me 1.16
Yes, b., I want some benefit from 1.20
one his fellow or every one his b., Heb 8.11
that our b. Timothy has been 13.23
Let the lowly b. boast in his Jas 1.09
If a b. or sister is ill-clad and 2.15
evil against a b. or judges his b., 4.11
a faithful b. as I regard him, I 1Pe 5.12
our beloved b. Paul wrote to you 2Pe 3.15
and hates his b. is in the darkness 1Jn 2.09
He who loves his b. abides in the 2.10
who hates his b. is in the darkness 2.11
nor he who does not love his b. 3.10
the evil one and murdered his b. 3.12
one who hates his b. is a murderer, 3.15
goods and sees his b. in need, 3.17
and hates his b., he is a liar; 4.20
not love his b. whom he has seen, 4.20
loves God should love his b. also. 4.21
one sees his b. committing what is 5.16
of Jesus Christ and b. of James, Jud 1.01
I John, your b., who share with you Rev 1.09

BROTHERHOOD
not remember the covenant of b. Amo 1.09
annulling the b. between Judah and Zec 11.14
decide between members of the b., 1Co 6.05
Love the b. Fear God. Honor 1Pe 2.17
required of your b. throughout the 5.09

BROTHER-IN-LAW
perform the duty of a b. to her, Gen 38.08

BROTHERLY
love one another with b. affection; Rom 12.10
Let b. love continue. Heb 13.01
and godliness with b. affection, 2Pe 1.07
and b. affection with love. 1.07

BROTHER'S
"I do not know; am I my b. keeper?" Gen 4.09
voice of your b. blood is crying 4.10
to receive your b. blood from your 4.11
His b. name was Jubal; 4.21
and his b. name was Joktan. 10.25
and Lot his b. son, and all their 12.05
until your b. fury turns away; 27.44
until your b. anger turns away, and 27.45
to Onan, "Go in to your b. wife, 38.08

BROTHER'S (cont.)

went in to his b. wife he spilled Gen 38.09
the nakedness of your b. wife; Lev 18.16
she is your b. nakedness. 18.16
If a man takes his b. wife, 20.21
he has uncovered his b. nakedness, 20.21
not see your b. ox or his sheep go Deu 22.01
do with any lost thing of your b., 22.03
not see your b. ass or his ox 22.04
does not wish to take his b. wife, 25.07
then his b. wife shall go up to the 25.07
perpetuate his b. name in Israel; 25.07
then his b. wife shall go up to him 25.09
who does not build up his b. house.' 25.09
has turned about and become my b., 1Ki 2.15
wine in their eldest b. house; Job 1.13
wine in their eldest b. house; 1.18
not go to your b. house in the day Pro 27.10
the speck that is in your b. eye, Mt 7.03
take the speck out of your b. eye. 7.05
for you to have your b. wife." Mk 6.18
his b. wife, and for all the evil Lk 3.19
the speck that is in your b. eye, 6.41
the speck that is in your b. eye. 6.42
food is a cause of my b. falling, 1Co 8.13
were evil and his b. righteous. 1Jn 3.12

BROTHERS

and told his two b. outside. Gen 9.22
of slaves shall he be to his b." 9.25
my b., do not act so wickedly. 19.07
Be lord over your b., and may your 27.29
and all his b. I have given to him 27.37
"My b., where do you come from?" 29.04
said to her father and to her b., 34.11
Dinah's b., took their swords and 34.25
shepherding the flock with his b.; 37.02
But when his b. saw that their 37.04
loved him more than all his b., 37.04
told it to his b. they only hated 37.05
His b. said to him, "Are you indeed 37.08
dream, and told it to his b., 37.09
it to his father and to his b., 37.10
mother and your b. indeed come to 37.10
And his b. were jealous of him, but 37.11
Now his b. went to pasture their 37.12
"Are not your b. pasturing the 37.13
see if it is well with your b., 37.14
"I am seeking my b.," he said, 37.16
So Joseph went after his b., 37.17
So when Joseph came to his b., 37.23
Then Judah said to his b., 37.26
And his b. heeded him. 37.27
and returned to his b., 37.30
that Judah went down from his b., 38.01
that he would die, like his b. 38.11
So ten of Joseph's b. went down to 42.03
with his b., for he feared that 42.04
And Joseph's b. came, and bowed 42.06
Joseph saw his b., and knew them, 42.07
Thus Joseph knew his b., 42.08
are twelve b., the sons of one man 42.13
let one of your b. remain confined 42.19
and he said to his b., 42.28
we are twelve b., sons of our 42.32
men: leave one of your b. with me, 42.33
When Judah and his b. came to 44.14
let the lad go back with his b. 44.33
made himself known to his b. 45.01
Joseph said to his b., "I am Joseph; 45.03
But his b. could not answer him, for 45.03
So Joseph said to his b., 45.04
kissed all his b. and wept upon 45.15
after that his b. talked with him. 45.15
"Joseph's b. have come," it pleased 45.16
"Say to your b., 'Do this: load your 45.17
Then he sent his b. away, 45.24
Joseph said to his b. and to his 46.31
'My b. and my father's household, who 46.31
told Pharaoh, "My father and my b., 47.01
And from among his b. he took five 47.02
Pharaoh said to his b., "What is your 47.03
father and your b. have come to 47.05
father and your b. in the best of 47.06
settled his father and his b., 47.11
his b., and all his father's household 47.12
name of their b. in their inheritance. 48.06
than to your b. one mountain slope 48.22
Simeon and Levi are b.; weapons of 49.05
Judah, your b. shall praise you; 49.08
him who was separate from his b. 49.26
his b., and his father's household; 50.08
Egypt with his b. and all who had 50.14
When Joseph's b. saw that their 50.15
transgression of your b. and their sin, 50.17
His b. also came and fell down 50.18
And Joseph said to his b., "I am about 50.24
and all his b., and all that Ex 1.06
one of his b. may redeem him, Lev 25.48
give his inheritance to his b. Num 27.09
And if he has no b., then you shall 27.10
his inheritance to his father's b. 27.10
And if his father has no b., 27.11
to sons of their father's b. 36.11
portion or inheritance with his b.; Deu 10.09
"If b. dwell together, and one of 25.05
he disowned his b., and ignored 33.09
of him that is prince among his b. 33.16
let him be the favorite of his b., 33.24
my b. and sisters, and all who Jos 2.13
your b., and all your father's 2.18
and mother and b. and all who 6.23
"They were my b., the sons of my Ju 8.19
and slew his b. the sons of Jerubbaal, 9.05
strengthened his hands to slay his b. 9.24
father in killing his seventy b.; 9.56
Then Jephthah fled from his b., 11.03
Then his b. and all his family came 16.31
or their b. come to complain to us, 21.22
anointed him in the midst of his b.; 1Sa 16.13
"Take for your b. an ephah of this 17.17
quickly to the camp to your b.; 17.17
See how your b. fare, and bring some 17.18
ranks, and went and greeted his b. 17.22
let me get away, and see my b.' 20.29
and when his b. and all his father's 22.01
my b., with what the LORD has given 30.23
to his b., and to his friends, and 2Sa 3.08
Enrogel, and he invited all his b., 1Ki 1.09
Jabez was more honorable than his b.; 1Ch 4.09
but his b. had not many children, 4.27
among his b. and a prince was from 5.02
and his b. came to comfort him. 7.22
for Judah, Elihu, one of David's b.; 27.18
as chief prince among his b., 2Ch 11.22
He had b., the sons of Jehoshaphat: 21.02
he slew all his b. with the sword, 21.04
and also you have killed your b., 21.13
Judah and the sons of Ahaziah's b., 22.08
and Shemaiah and Nethanel his b., 35.09
pledges of your b. for nothing, Job 22.06
to him all his b. and sisters and 42.11
them inheritance among their b. 42.15
it is when b. dwell in unity! Ps 133.01
a man who sows discord among b. Pro 6.19
the inheritance as one of the b. 17.02
All a poor man's b. hate him; 19.07
For even your b. and the house of Jer 12.06
and his b., and all his sons, and 35.03
and his b., and his neighbors; 49.10
the father of Judah and his b., Mt 1.02
the father of Jechoniah and his b., 1.11
he saw two b., Simon who is called 4.18
on from there he saw two other b., 4.21

BROTHERS (cont.)
mother and his b. stood outside, Mt 12.46
mother and your b. are standing * 12.47
is my mother, and who are my b.?" 12.48
said, "Here are my mother and my b.! 12.49
And are not his b. James and Joseph 13.55
left houses or b. or sisters or 19.29
they were indignant at the two b. 20.24
Now there were seven b. among us; 22.25
And his mother and his b. came; Mk 3.31
mother and your b. are outside, 3.32
"Who are my mother and my b.?" 3.33
said, "Here are my mother and my b.! 3.34
left house or b. or sisters or 10.29
houses and b. and sisters and 10.30
There were seven b.; the first took 12.20
Then his mother and his b. came to him, Lk 8.19
mother and your b. are standing 8.20
mother and my b. are those who 8.21
friends or your b. or your kinsmen 14.12
and children and b. and sisters, 14.26
for I have five b., so that he 16.28
or wife or b. or parents or 18.29
Now there were seven b.; 20.29
by parents and b. and kinsmen and 21.16
mother and his b. and his disciples; Jn 2.12
So his b. said to him, "Leave here 7.03
For even his b. did not believe in 7.05
But after his b. had gone up to the 7.10
mother of Jesus, and with his b. Ac 1.14
made himself known to his b., 7.13
with the Twin B. as figurehead. 28.11
apostles and the b. of the Lord and 1Co 9.05
a father; treat younger men like b., 1Ti 5.01

BROUGHT
The earth b. forth vegetation, Gen 1.12
and b. them to the man to see what 2.19
into a woman and b. her to the man. 2.22
of time Cain b. to the LORD an 4.03
and Abel b. of the firstlings of 4.04
took her and b. her into the ark 8.09
Then he b. back all the goods, and 14.16
and also b. back his kinsman Lot 14.16
king of Salem b. out bread and 14.18
And he b. him outside and said, 15.05
am the LORD who b. you from Ur of 15.07
And he b. him all these, cut them in 15.10
Let a little water be b., 18.04
their hands and b. Lot into the 19.10
and they b. him forth and set him 19.16
And when they had b. them forth, 19.17
that you have b. on me and my 20.09
And the servant b. forth jewelry of 24.53
Then Isaac b. her into the tent, and 24.67
you would have b. guilt upon us." 26.10
took them and b. them to his 27.14
So he b. it to him, and he ate; 27.25
and he b. him wine, and he drank. 27.25
and b. it to his father. 27.31
that hunted game and b. it to me, 27.33
and b. him to his house. Jacob told 29.13
daughter Leah and b. her to Jacob; 29.23
and b. them to his mother Leah. 30.14
and so the flocks b. forth striped, 30.39
you, my gift that is b. to you, 33.11
"You have b. trouble on me by 34.30
and Joseph b. an ill report of them 37.02
sleeves and b. it to their father, 37.32
As she was being b. out, she sent 38.25
Ishmaelites who had b. him down there. 39.01
he has b. among us a Hebrew to 39.14
whom you have b. among us, came in 39.17
and they b. him hastily out of the 41.14
years the earth b. forth abundantly, 41.47
grain which they had b. from Egypt, 43.02
and b. the men to Joseph's house. 43.17
they were b. to Joseph's house, and 43.18
that we are b. in, so that he may 43.18
so we have b. it again with us, 43.21
and we have b. other money down in 43.22
Then he b. Simeon out to them. 43.23
the man had b. the men into 43.24
they b. into the house to him the 43.26
we b. back to you from the land of 44.08
offspring he b. with him into 46.07
and they have b. their flocks, and 46.32
Then Joseph b. in Jacob his father, 47.07
and Joseph b. the money into Pharaoh's 47.14
So they b. their cattle to Joseph; 47.17
So Joseph b. them near him; 48.10
right hand, and b. them near him. 48.13
and she b. him to Pharaoh's daughter, Ex 2.10
when you have b. forth the people 3.12
who has b. you out from under the 6.07
and b. frogs upon the land of Egypt. 8.07
is in the field and is not b. home, 9.19
and Aaron were b. back to Pharaoh; 10.08
and the LORD b. an east wind upon 10.13
the east wind had b. the locusts. 10.13
this very day I b. your hosts out 12.17
which they had b. out of Egypt, 12.39
day the LORD b. the people of 12.51
hand the LORD b. you out from this 13.03
the LORD has b. you out of Egypt. 13.09
hand the LORD b. us out of Egypt, 13.14
hand the LORD b. us out of Egypt." 13.16
the LORD b. back the waters of the 15.19
for you have b. us out into this 16.03
the LORD who b. you out of the 16.06
when I b. you out of the land of 16.32
the LORD had b. Israel out of 18.01
hard cases they b. to Moses, 18.26
eagles' wings and b. you to myself. 19.04
Then Moses b. the people out of the 19.17
who b. you out of the land of Egypt, 20.02
who b. them forth out of the land 29.46
the man who b. us up out of the 32.01
their ears, and b. them to Aaron. 32.03
who b. you up out of the land of 32.04
offerings and b. peace offerings; 32.06
whom you b. up out of the land of 32.07
who b. you up out of the land of 32.08
whom thou hast b. forth out of the 32.11
that you have b. a great sin upon 32.21
the man who b. us up out of the 32.23
whom you have b. up out of the 33.01
and b. the LORD's offering to be 35.21
a willing heart b. brooches and 35.22
rams' skins or goatskins, b. them. 35.23
or bronze b. it as the LORD's 35.24
wood of any use in the work, b. it. 35.24
and b. what they had spun in blue 35.25
And the leaders b. onyx stones and 35.27
b. it as their freewill offering to 35.29
of Israel had b. for doing the 36.03
And they b. the tabernacle to Moses, 39.33
and he b. the ark into the tabernacle, 40.21
any blood is b. into the tent of Lev 6.30
And Moses b. Aaron and his sons, and 8.06
And Moses b. Aaron's sons, and 8.13
Then he b. the bull of the sin 8.14
And Aaron's sons were b., 8.24
And they b. what Moses commanded 9.05
blood was not b. into the inner 10.18
am the LORD who b. you up out of 11.45
he shall be b. to Aaron the priest 13.02
he shall be b. to the priest; 13.09
He shall be b. to the priest; 14.02
whose blood was b. in to make 16.27
who b. you out of the land of Egypt. 19.36
who b. you out of the land of Egypt 22.33
until you have b. the offering of 23.14
day that you b. the sheaf of the 23.15

BROUGHT (cont.)
booths when I b. them out of the Lev 23.43
And they b. him to Moses. His mother's 24.11
and they b. him who had cursed out 24.23
who b. you forth out of the land of 25.38
whom I b. forth out of the land of 25.42
servants whom I b. forth out of 25.55
who b. you forth out of the land of 26.13
to them and b. them into the land 26.41
whom I b. forth out of the land of 26.45
he shall be b. to the door of the Num 6.13
offered and b. their offerings 7.03
and it b. quails from the sea, and 11.31
after that she may be b. in again." 12.14
march till Miriam was b. in again. 12.15
they b. also some pomegranates and 13.23
they b. back word to them and to 13.26
So they b. to the people of Israel 13.32
the men who b. up an evil report of 14.37
and they have b. their offering, an 15.25
gathering sticks b. him to Moses 15.33
congregation b. him outside the 15.36
who b. you out of the land of Egypt, 15.41
and that he has b. you near him, 16.10
that you have b. us up out of a 16.13
Moreover you have not b. us into a 16.14
Then Moses b. out all the rods from 17.09
Why have you b. the assembly of the 20.04
an angel and b. us forth out of 20.16
"Why have you b. us up out of Egypt 21.05
took Balaam and b. him up to 22.41
said, "From Aram Balak has b. me, 23.07
Israel came and b. a Midianite 25.06
Moses b. their case before the LORD. 27.05
Then they b. the captives and the 31.12
And we have b. the LORD's offering, 31.50
and b. it into the tent of meeting, 31.54
until we have b. them to their 32.17
of the land and b. it down to us, Deu 1.25
and b. us word again, and said, 'It 1.25
hated us he has b. us forth out of 1.27
and b. you forth out of the iron 4.20
and b. you out of Egypt with his 4.37
who b. you out of the land of Egypt, 5.06
LORD your God b. you out thence 5.15
who b. you out of the land of Egypt, 6.12
and the LORD b. us out of Egypt 6.21
and he b. us out from there, that he 6.23
the LORD has b. you out with a 7.08
which the LORD your God b. you out; 7.19
who b. you out of the land of Egypt, 8.14
who b. you water out of the flinty 8.15
the LORD has b. me in to possess 9.04
whom you have b. from Egypt have 9.12
whom thou hast b. out of Egypt 9.26
he has b. them out to slay them in 9.28
who b. you out of the land of Egypt 13.05
who b. you out of the land of Egypt, 13.10
LORD your God b. you out of Egypt 16.01
who b. you up out of the land of 20.01
because he has b. an evil name 22.19
and the LORD b. us out of Egypt 26.08
and he b. us into this place and 26.09
them when he b. them out of the 29.25
For when I have b. them into the 31.20
before I have b. them into the land 31.21
But she had b. them up to the roof, Jos 2.06
and b. out Rahab, and her father and 6.23
and they b. all her kindred, and set 6.23
why hast thou b. this people over 7.07
you shall be b. near by your 7.14
and b. Israel near tribe by tribe, 7.16
and he b. near the families of 7.17
and he b. near the family of the 7.17
and he b. near his household man by 7.18
of the tent and b. them to Joshua 7.23
and they b. them up to the Valley 7.24
took alive, and b. him to Joshua. 8.23
and b. those five kings out to him 10.23
And when they b. those kings out to 10.24
and I b. him word again as it was 14.07
of Israel, and b. back word to them. 22.32
and afterwards I b. you out. 24.05
Then I b. your fathers out of Egypt, 24.06
Then I b. you to the land of the 24.08
our God who b. us and our fathers 24.17
of Israel b. up from Egypt were 24.32
And they b. him to Jerusalem, and he Ju 1.07
"I b. you up from Egypt, and b. you 2.01
who had b. them out of the land of 2.12
she b. him curds in a lordly bowl. 5.25
And Israel was b. very low because 6.06
and b. you out of the house of 6.08
and b. them to him under the oak 6.19
So he b. the people down to the 7.05
and they b. the heads of Oreb and 7.25
you have b. me very low, and you 11.35
daughters he b. in from outside 12.09
they b. thirty companions to be 14.11
and b. him up from the rock. 15.13
the Philistines b. her seven fresh 16.08
and b. the money in their hands. 16.18
and b. him down to Gaza, and bound 16.21
took him and b. him up and buried 16.31
and said to him, "Who b. you here? 18.03
So he b. him into his house, and 19.21
how was this wickedness b. to pass?" 20.03
and they b. them to the camp at 21.12
and the LORD has b. me back empty. Ru 1.21
Almighty has b. calamity upon me?" 1.21
and she also b. out and gave her 2.18
and she b. him to the house of the 1Sa 1.24
and they b. the child to Eli. 1.25
that the fork b. up the priest would 2.14
and b. from there the ark of the 4.04
He who b. the tidings answered and 4.17
ark of God and b. it into the 5.02
God of Israel be b. around to Gath." 5.08
So they b. the ark of the God of 5.08
But after they had b. it around, 5.09
"They have b. around to us the ark 5.10
and b. it to the house of Abinadab 7.01
from the day I b. them up out of 8.08
his servant and b. them into the 9.22
'I b. up Israel out of Egypt, and I 10.18
Then Samuel b. all the tribes of 10.20
He b. the tribe of Benjamin near by 10.21
finally he b. the family of the 10.21
despised him, and b. him no present. 10.27
and Aaron and b. your fathers up 12.06
who b. forth your fathers out of 12.08
of the people b. his ox with him 14.34
"They have b. them from the Amalekites; 15.15
I have b. Agag the king of Amalek, 15.20
And he sent, and b. him in. 16.12
Philistine and b. it to Jerusalem; 17.54
and b. him before Saul with the 17.57
and David b. their foreskins, which 18.27
And Jonathan b. David to Saul, and 19.07
for you have b. your servant into a 20.08
For I have b. neither my sword nor 21.08
why then have you b. him to me? 21.14
that you have b. this fellow to 21.15
and b. away their cattle, and made a 23.05
servant has b. to my lord be given 25.27
from her hand what she had b. him; 25.35
So Abiathar b. the ephod to David. 30.07
open country, and b. him to David; 30.11
had been taken; David b. back all. 30.19
and I have b. them here to my lord." 2Sa 1.10
And David b. up his men who were 2.03
and b. him over to Mahanaim; 2.08
and they b. him back from the 3.26
and b. the head of Ishbosheth to 4.08

BROUGHT (cont.)
you that led out and b. in Israel; 2Sa 5.02
and b. it out of the house of 6.03
David went and b. up the ark of 6.12
house of Israel b. up the ark of 6.15
And they b. in the ark of the LORD, 6.17
since the day I b. up the people 7.06
that thou hast b. me thus far? 7.18
servants to David and b. tribute. 8.02
servants to David and b. tribute. 8.06
and b. them to Jerusalem. 8.07
And Joram b. with him articles of 8.10
David sent and b. him from the 9.05
and b. out the Syrians who were 10.16
David sent and b. her to his house, 11.27
And he b. it up, and it grew up with 12.03
And he b. forth the spoil of the 12.30
And he b. forth the people who were 12.31
and b. them into the chamber to 13.10
But when she b. them near him to 13.11
and b. Absalom to Jerusalem. 14.23
to Ziba, "Why have you b. these?" 16.02
b. beds, basins, and earthen vessels, 17.28
b. the king on his way. 19.40
and b. the king and his household 19.41
and he b. up from there the bones 21.13
He b. me forth into a broad place; 22.20
vengeance and b. down peoples 22.48
who b. me out from my enemies; 22.49
gate, and took and b. it to David. 23.16
Shunammite, and b. her to the king. 1Ki 1.03
Has this thing been b. about by my 1.27
David's mule, and b. him to Gihon. 1.38
and they b. him down from the altar. 1.53
and had a seat b. for the king's 2.19
Then Benaiah b. the king word again, 2.30
Shimei went and b. his slaves from 2.40
and b. her into the city of David, 3.01
So a sword was b. before the king. 3.24
they b. tribute and served Solomon 4.21
steeds they b. to the place where 4.28
sent and b. Hiram from Tyre. 7.13
And Solomon b. in the things which 7.51
And they b. up the ark of the LORD, 8.04
priests and the Levites b. them up. 8.04
Then the priests b. the ark of the 8.06
'Since the day that I b. my people 8.16
when he b. them out of the land of 8.21
their God who b. their fathers out 9.09
the LORD has b. all this evil upon 9.09
and b. from there gold, to the 9.28
and they b. it to King Solomon. 9.28
which b. gold from Ophir, b. from 10.11
Every one of them b. his present, 10.25
turn of affairs b. about by the 12.15
who b. you up out of the land of 12.28
to the prophet who had b. him back; 13.20
the prophet whom he had b. back. 13.23
prophet who had b. him back from 13.26
and b. it back to the city, to mourn 13.29
bore them and b. them back to the 14.28
And he b. into the house of the 15.15
And the ravens b. him bread and 17.06
hast thou b. calamity even upon the 17.20
and b. him down from the upper 17.23
and Elijah b. them down to the 18.40
departed and b. him word again. 20.09
soldier turned and b. a man to me, 20.39
base fellows b. a charge against 21.13
king died, and was b. to Samaria; 22.37
salt in it." So they b. it to him. 2Ki 2.20
she poured they b. the vessels to 4.05
and b. him to his mother, the child 4.20
And he b. the letter to the king of 5.06
accepting from his hand what he b. 5.20
"They have b. the heads of the 10.08
So he b. out the vestments for 10.22
and they b. out the pillar that was 10.26
sent and b. the captains of the 11.04
and each b. his men who were to go 11.09
Then he b. out the king's son, and 11.12
and they b. the king down from the 11.19
things which is b. into the house 12.04
money that was b. into the house 12.09
money that was b. into the house 12.13
offerings was not b. into the house 12.16
And they b. him upon horses; 14.20
who had b. them up out of the land 17.07
king of Assyria b. people from 17.24
who b. you out of the land of Egypt 17.36
and he b. the shadow back ten 20.11
the conduit and b. water into the 20.20
which has been b. into the house 22.04
And they b. back word to the king. 22.20
And he b. out the Asherah from the 23.06
And he b. all the priests out of 23.08
and b. him to Jerusalem, and buried 23.30
king of Babylon b. captive to 24.16
and b. him up to the king of 25.06
and b. them to the king of Babylon 25.20
and b. them to Halah, Habor, Hara, and 1Ch 5.26
when they were b. in and taken out 9.28
of his sons, and b. them to Jabesh. 10.12
you that led out and b. in Israel; 11.02
gate, and took and b. it to David. 11.18
the risk of their lives they b. it." 11.19
and the LORD b. the fear of him 14.17
So all Israel b. up the ark of the 15.28
And they b. in the ark of God, and 16.01
that thou hast b. me thus far? 17.16
servants to David and b. tribute. 18.02
servants to David, and b. tribute. 18.06
and b. them to Jerusalem. 18.07
messengers and b. out the Syrians 19.16
And he b. forth the spoil of the 20.02
And he b. forth the people who were 20.03
and Tyrians b. great quantities of 22.04
of God may be b. into a house 22.19
(But David had b. up the ark of God 2Ch 1.04
And Solomon b. in the things which 5.01
And they b. up the ark, the tent of 5.05
priests and the Levites b. them up. 5.05
So the priests b. the ark of the 5.07
'Since the day that I b. my people 6.05
fathers who b. them out of the 7.22
therefore he has b. all this evil 7.22
Solomon b. Pharaoh's daughter up 8.11
of gold and b. it to King Solomon. 8.18
of Solomon, who b. gold from Ophir, 9.10
b. algum wood and precious stones. 9.10
what she had b. to the king. 9.12
which the traders and merchants b.; 9.14
of the land b. gold and silver to 9.14
Every one of them b. his present, 9.24
turn of affairs b. about by God 10.15
and b. them back to the guardroom. 12.11
from the spoil which they had b., 15.11
And he b. into the house of God the 15.18
and all Judah b. tribute to 17.05
the Philistines b. Jehoshaphat 17.11
the Arabs also b. him seven 17.11
and b. them back to the LORD, the 19.04
and he was b. to Jehu and put to 22.09
They each b. his men, who were to go 23.08
Then he b. out the king's son, and 23.11
the priest b. out the captains who 23.14
and they b. the king down from 23.20
rejoiced and b. their tax and 24.10
the chest was b. to the king's 24.11
they b. the rest of the money 24.14
he b. the gods of the men of Seir, 25.14
and b. him to Jerusalem, and broke 25.23
And they b. him upon horses; 25.28
his people and b. them to Damascus. 28.05

BROUGHT (cont.)
from them and b. the spoil to 2Ch 28.08
they b. them to their kinsfolk at 28.15
For the LORD b. Judah low because 28.19
He b. in the priests and the 29.04
and they b. out all the uncleanness 29.16
And they b. seven bulls, seven rams, 29.21
offering were b. to the king and 29.23
the assembly b. sacrifices and 29.31
a willing heart b. burnt offerings. 29.31
the assembly b. was seventy bulls, 29.32
and b. burnt offerings into the 30.15
and they b. in abundantly the 31.05
of Judah also b. in the tithe of 31.06
And they faithfully b. in the 31.12
And many b. gifts to the LORD to 32.23
Therefore the LORD b. upon them the 33.11
of bronze and b. him to Babylon. 33.11
supplication and b. him again to 33.13
that had been b. into the house 34.09
that had been b. into the house of 34.14
Shaphan b. the book to the king, and 34.16
And they b. back word to the king. 34.28
chariot and b. him to Jerusalem. 35.24
Nebuchadnezzar sent and b. him to Babylon, 36.10
Therefore he b. up against them the 36.17
princes, all these he b. to Babylon. 36.18
Cyrus the king also b. out the Ez 1.07
Cyrus king of Persia b. these out 1.08
the exiles were b. up from Babylonia 1.11
king of Assyria who b. us here." 4.02
Jerusalem and b. into the temple 5.14
offered and burnt offerings are b.; 6.03
is in Jerusalem and b. to Babylon, 6.05
be restored and b. back to the 6.05
they b. us a man of discretion, of 8.18
and I b. charges against the nobles Neh 5.07
And Ezra the priest b. the law 8.02
went out and b. them and made 8.16
is your God who b. you up out of 9.18
Then I b. up the princes of Judah 12.31
and I b. back thither the vessels 13.09
Then all Judah b. the tithe of the 13.12
which they b. into Jerusalem on the 13.15
b. in fish and all kinds of wares 13.16
burden might be b. in on the 13.19
Queen Vashti to be b. before him, Est 1.17
He had b. up Hadassah, that is 2.07
just as when she was b. up by him. 2.20
let royal robes be b., which the king 6.08
arrived and b. Haman in haste to 6.14
"Now a word was b. to me stealthily, Job 4.12
of the wily are b. to a quick end. 5.13
they are b. low, and he perceives it 14.21
Or were you b. forth before the 15.07
and is b. to the king of terrors. 18.14
when they b. a complaint against me; 31.13
evil that the LORD had b. upon him; 42.11
He b. me forth into a broad place; Ps 18.19
thou hast b. up my soul from Sheol, 30.03
condemned when he is b. to trial. 37.33
turned back and b. to dishonor who 40.14
Behold, I was b. forth in iniquity, 51.05
yet thou hast b. us forth to a 66.12
Let bronze be b. from Egypt; let 68.31
seek thee be b. to dishonor 69.06
turned back and b. to dishonor who 70.02
And he b. them to his holy land, to 78.54
had young he b. him to be the 78.71
to meet us, for we are b. very low. 79.08
who b. you up out of the land of 81.10
Before the mountains were b. forth, 90.02
and he b. quails, and gave them 105.40
and they were b. into subjection 106.42
and were b. low through their 106.43
he b. them out of darkness and 107.14
and he b. them to their desired 107.30
diminished and b. low through 107.39
when I was b. low, he saved me. 116.06
and b. Israel out from among them, 136.11
my cry; for I am b. very low! 142.06
were no depths I was b. forth, Pro 8.24
before the hills, I was b. forth; 8.25
the daughters of song are b. low; Ecc 12.04
The king has b. me into his chambers. Sol 1.04
He b. me to the banqueting house, 2.04
go until I had b. him into my 3.04
"Sons have I reared and b. up, Is 1.02
and men are b. low—forgive them 2.09
looks of man shall be b. low, 2.11
the pride of men shall be b. low; 2.17
For they have b. evil upon themselves. 3.09
and men are b. low, and the eyes of 5.15
former time he b. into contempt 9.01
a bull I have b. down those who 10.13
down, and the lofty will be b. low. 10.33
Your pomp is b. down to Sheol, the 14.11
But you are b. down to Sheol, to the 14.15
of Moab will be b. into contempt, 16.14
the glory of Jacob will be b. low, 17.04
gifts will be b. to the LORD of 18.07
reared young men nor b. up virgins." 23.04
For he has b. low the inhabitants 26.05
we have as it were b. forth wind. 26.18
You have not b. me your sheep for 43.23
I have b. him, and he will prosper 48.15
put away, but who has b. up these? 49.21
among all the sons she has b. up. 51.18
you have b. a cereal offering. 57.06
then his own arm b. him victory, 59.16
so my own arm b. me victory, and my 63.05
Where is he who b. up out of the 63.11
a nation be b. forth in one moment? 66.08
was in labor she b. forth her sons. 66.08
is the LORD who b. us up from the Jer 2.06
And I b. you into a plentiful land 2.07
Have you not b. this upon yourself 2.17
your doings have b. this upon you. 4.18
the day that I b. them out of the 7.22
shall be b. out of their tombs; 8.01
Beaten silver is b. from Tarshish, 10.09
fathers when I b. them out of the 11.04
fathers when I b. them up out of 11.07
Therefore I b. upon them all the 11.08
I have b. against the mothers of 15.08
LORD lives who b. up the people of 16.14
LORD lives who b. up the people of 16.15
Cursed be the man who b. the news 20.15
LORD lives who b. up the people of 23.07
LORD lives who b. up and led the 23.08
and had b. them to Babylon, the LORD 24.01
from Egypt and b. him to King 26.23
now shortly be b. back from 27.16
Just as I have b. all this great 32.42
and b. them into subjection as 34.11
fathers when I b. them out of the 34.13
and you b. them into subjection to 34.16
I b. them to the house of the LORD 35.04
Jeremiah and b. him to the princes. 37.14
they b. him up to Nebuchadrezzar 39.05
the LORD has b. it about, and has 40.03
whom Johanan b. back from Gibeon. 41.16
the evil that I b. upon Jerusalem 44.02
O Madmen, shall be b. to silence; 48.02
and b. out the weapons of his wrath, 50.25
The LORD has b. forth our vindication; 51.10
and b. him up to the king of 52.09
and b. them to the king of Babylon 52.26
of Judah and b. him out of prison; 52.31
my sorrow which was b. upon me, Lam 1.12
he has b. down to the ground in 2.02
the LORD has b. to an end in Zion 2.06
he has driven and b. me into 3.02
those who were b. up in purple lie 4.05

BROUGHT (cont.)
and b. me in visions of God to Eze 8.03
And he b. me to the door of the 8.07
Then he b. me to the entrance of 8.14
And he b. me into the inner court 8.16
b. back word, saying, "I have done as 9.11
and b. me to the east gate of the 11.01
you shall be b. forth out of the 11.07
me up and b. me in the vision by 11.24
I b. out my baggage by day, as 12.07
evil that I have b. upon Jerusalem, 14.22
for all that I have b. upon it. 14.22
and b. forth branches and put forth 17.06
her princes and b. them to him to 17.12
And she b. up one of her whelps; 19.03
and they b. him with hooks to the 19.04
and b. him to the king of Babylon; 19.09
they b. him into custody, that his 19.09
of Egypt and b. them into the 20.10
in whose sight I had b. them out. 20.14
in whose sight I had b. them out. 20.22
For when I had b. them into the 20.28
and you have b. your day near, the 22.04
your harlotry b. from the land of 23.27
have b. this upon you, because you 23.30
drunkards were b. from the wilderness; 23.42
they b. you in payment ivory tusks 27.15
Your rowers have b. you out into 27.26
so I b. forth fire from the midst 28.18
shall be b. in to destroy the land; 30.11
of the field b. forth their young; 31.06
You shall be b. down with the trees 31.18
the strayed you have not b. back, 34.04
and he b. me out by the Spirit of 37.01
its people were b. out from the 38.08
is coming and it will be b. about, 39.08
when I have b. them back from the 39.27
and b. me in the visions of God 40.02
When he b. me there, behold, there 40.03
for you were b. here in order that 40.04
Then he b. me into the outer court; 40.17
Then he b. me to the inner court by 40.28
Then he b. me to the inner court on 40.32
Then he b. me to the north gate, and 40.35
Then he b. me from without into the 40.44
Then he b. me to the vestibule of 40.48
Then he b. me to the nave, and 41.01
and he b. me to the chambers which 42.01
Afterward he b. me to the gate, the 43.01
and b. me into the inner court; 43.05
Then he b. me back to the outer 44.01
Then he b. me by way of the north 44.04
Then he b. me through the entrance, 46.19
Then he b. me forth to the outer 46.21
Then he b. me back to the door of 47.01
Then he b. me out by way of the 47.02
and he b. them to the land of Dan 1.02
commanded that they should be b. in, 1.18
of the eunuchs b. them in before 1.18
Then Arioch b. in Daniel before the 2.25
Meshach, and Abednego be b. 3.13
Then they b. these men before the 3.13
of Babylon should be b. before me, 4.06
of the temple in Jerusalem be b., 5.02
Then they b. in the golden and 5.03
Then Daniel was b. in before the 5.13
the king my father b. from Judah. 5.13
have been b. in before me to read 5.15
house have been b. in before you, 5.23
your kingdom and b. it to an end; 5.26
and Daniel was b. and cast into 6.16
And a stone was b. and laid upon 6.17
no diversions were b. to him, 6.18
Daniel were b. and cast into the 6.24
the calamity and has b. it upon us; 9.14
the LORD b. Israel up from Egypt, Hos 12.13
Also I b. you up out of the land of Amo 2.10
family which I b. up out of the 3.01
she who is in travail has b. forth; Mic 5.03
For I b. you up from the land of 6.04
lions, where the lion b. his prey, Nah 2.11
and when you b. it home, I blew it Hag 1.09
and they b. him all the sick, those Mt 4.24
That evening they b. to him many 8.16
they b. to him a paralytic, lying on 9.02
a dumb demoniac was b. to him. 9.32
You shall be b. down to Hades. 11.23
and dumb demoniac was b. to him, 12.22
on good soil and b. forth grain, 13.08
and his head was b. on a platter 14.11
and she b. it to her mother. 14.11
that region and b. to him all that 14.35
themselves, saying, "We b. no bread." 16.07
And I b. him to your disciples, and 17.16
one was b. to him who owed him ten 18.24
Then children were b. to him that 19.13
they b. the ass and the colt, and 21.07
thou hast b. perfect praise'?" 21.16
And they b. him a coin. 22.19
he repented and b. back the thirty 27.03
they b. to him all who were sick or Mk 1.32
into good soil and b. forth grain, 4.08
"Is a lamp b. in to be put under a 4.21
and b. his head on a platter, and 6.28
And they b. to him a man who was 7.32
And some people b. to him a blind 8.22
I b. my son to you, for he has a 9.17
And they b. the boy to him; 9.20
And they b. the colt to Jesus, and 11.07
And they b. one. And he said 12.16
And they b. him to the place called 15.22
they b. him up to Jerusalem to Lk 2.22
the parents b. in the child Jesus, 2.27
mountain and hill shall be b. low, 3.05
Nazareth, where he had been b. up; 4.16
various diseases b. them to him; 4.40
And when they had b. their boats to 5.11
b. an alabaster flask of ointment, 7.37
You shall be b. down to Hades. 10.15
his own beast and b. him to an inn, 10.34
of a rich man b. forth plentifully; 12.16
charges were b. to him that this 16.01
and commanded him to be b. to him; 18.40
And they b. it to Jesus, and throwing 19.35
and you will be b. before kings 21.12
and b. him before Pilate. 23.01
"You b. me this man as one who was 23.14
He b. him to Jesus. Jesus looked Jn 1.42
another, "Has any one b. him food?" 4.33
scribes and the Pharisees b. a woman * 8.03
They b. to the Pharisees the man 9.13
When he has b. out all his own, he 10.04
who kept the door, and b. Peter in. 18.16
he b. Jesus out and sat down on the 19.13
and b. the proceeds of what was Ac 4.34
and b. the money and laid it at the 4.37
and b. only a part and laid it at 5.02
doors and b. them out and said, 5.19
sent to the prison to have them b. 5.21
with the officers went and b. them, 5.26
And when they had b. them, 5.27
seized him and b. him before the 6.12
And he was b. up for three months 7.20
adopted him and b. him up as her 7.21
Our fathers in turn b. it in with 7.45
by the hand and b. him into 9.08
and b. him to the apostles, and 9.27
they b. him down to Caesarea, and 9.30
found him, he b. him to Antioch. 11.26
the Lord had b. him out of the 12.17
posterity God has b. to Israel a 13.23
b. oxen and garlands to the gates 14.13
divination and b. her owners much 16.16
and when they had b. them to the 16.20

BROUGHT (cont.)
and b. them out and said, "Men, what Ac 16.30
Then he b. them up into his house, 16.34
conducted Paul b. him as far as 17.15
hold of him and b. him to the 17.19
upon Paul and b. him before the 18.12
magic arts b. their books together 19.19
b. no little business to the 19.24
For you have b. these men here who 19.37
And they b. him to the ship. 20.38
b. us on our way till we were 21.05
moreover he also b. Greeks into the 21.28
that Paul had b. him into the 21.29
him to be b. into the barracks. 21.34
was about to be b. into the 21.37
but b. up in this city at the feet 22.03
him to be b. into the barracks, and 22.24
and he b. Paul down and set him 22.30
So he took him and b. him to the 23.18
I b. him down to their council. 23.28
took Paul and b. him by night to 23.31
tribunal and ordered Paul to be b. 25.06
and ordered the man to be b. in. 25.17
they b. no charge in his case of 25.18
command of Festus Paul was b. in. 25.23
Therefore I have b. him before you, 25.26
one trespass b. condemnation, Rom 5.16
who have been b. from death to 6.13
of false brethren secretly b. in, Gal 2.04
off have been b. near in the blood Eph 2.13
and has b. us the good news of your 1Th 3.06
as one who has b. up children, 1Ti 5.10
for we b. nothing into the world, 6.07
death and b. life and immortality 2Ti 1.10
whose blood is b. into the sanctuary Heb 13.11
of peace who b. again from the 13.20
Of his own will be b. us forth by Jas 1.18
and the earth b. forth its fruit. 5.18
when he b. a flood upon the world 2Pe 2.05
her child when she b. it forth; Rev 12.04
she b. forth a male child, one who 12.05

BROW
and on the b. of him who was Gen 49.26
yet you have a harlot's b., Jer 3.03
led him to the b. of the hill on Lk 4.29

BRUISE
he shall b. your head, and you shall Gen 3.15
head, and you shall b. his heel." 3.15
was the will of the LORD to b. him; Is 53.10

BRUISED
its testicles b. or crushed or Lev 22.24
a b. reed he will not break, and a Is 42.03
he was b. for our iniquities; 53.05
not break a b. reed or quench a Mt 12.20

BRUISES
but b. and sores and bleeding Is 1.06

BRUISING
and b. himself with stones. Mk 5.05

BRUSHWOOD
hand, and cut down a bundle of b., Ju 9.48
fire kindles b. and the fire Is 64.02

BRUTAL
you into the hands of b. men, Eze 21.31

BUCKET
nations are like a drop from a b., Is 40.15

BUCKETS
Water shall flow from his b., Num 24.07

BUCKLER
Take hold of shield and b., Ps 35.02
faithfulness is a shield and b. 91.04
"Prepare b. and shield, and advance Jer 46.03
against you on every side with b., Eze 23.24
all of them with b. and shield, 38.04

BUCKLERS
armed with b. and spears, and two 2Ch 14.08
arsenal, whereon hang a thousand b., Sol 4.04
shields and b., bows and arrows, Eze 39.09

BUD
in the ear and the flax was in b. Ex 9.31
water it will b. and put forth Job 14.09

BUDDED
as soon as it b., its blossoms shot Gen 40.10
to see whether the vines had b., Sol 6.11
and see whether the vines have b., 7.12
has blossomed, pride has b. Eze 7.10
the manna, and Aaron's rod that b., Heb 9.04

BUDS
Levi had sprouted and put forth b., Num 17.08

BUFFETED
are ill-clad and b. and homeless, 1Co 4.11

BUGLE
And if the b. gives an indistinct 1Co 14.08

BUILD
let us b. ourselves a city, and a Gen 11.04
you shall not b. it of hewn stones; Ex 20.25
"B. for me here seven altars, and Num 23.01
"B. for me here seven altars, and 23.29
"We will b. sheepfolds here for our 32.16
B. cities for your little ones, and 32.24
cities, which you did not b., Deu 6.10
that you may b. siegeworks against 20.20
"When you b. a new house, you shall 22.08
who does not b. up his brother's 25.09
And there you shall b. an altar to 27.05
You shall b. an altar to the LORD 27.06
you shall b. a house, and you shall 28.30
'Let us now b. an altar, not for Jos 22.26
and b. an altar to the LORD your Ju 6.26
and I will b. him a sure house, and 1Sa 2.35
Would you b. me a house to dwell in? 2Sa 7.05
He shall b. a house for my name, and 7.13
saying, 'I will b. you a house'; 7.27
in order to b. an altar to the LORD, 24.21
"B. yourself a house in Jerusalem, 1Ki 2.36
could not b. a house for the name 5.03
And so I purpose to b. a house for 5.05
shall b. the house for my name.' 5.05
and the stone to b. the house. 5.18
he began to b. the house of the 6.01
of Israel in which to b. a house, 8.16
my father to b. a house for the 8.17
your heart to b. a house for my 8.18
nevertheless you shall not b. the house, 8.19
to you shall b. the house for my 8.19
all that Solomon desired to b., 9.01
levied to b. the house of the LORD 9.15
Solomon desired to b. in Jerusalem, 9.19
and will b. you a sure house, as I 11.38
carpenters to b. a house for him. 1Ch 14.01
You shall not b. me a house to 17.04
that the LORD will b. you a house. 17.10
He shall b. a house for me, and I 17.12
that thou wilt b. a house for him; 17.25
that I may b. on it an altar to 21.22
charged him to b. a house for the 22.06
in my heart to b. a house to the 22.07
you shall not b. a house to my 22.08
He shall b. a house for my name. 22.10
Arise and b. the sanctuary of the 22.19
in my heart to b. a house of rest 28.02
'You may not b. a house for my name, 28.03
son who shall b. my house and my 28.06
chosen you to b. a house for the 28.10

BUILD (cont.)
and that he may b. the palace for 1Ch 29.19
purposed to b. a temple for the 2Ch 2.01
him cedar to b. himself a house to 2.03
I am about to b. a house for the 2.04
which I am to b. will be great, 2.05
But who is able to b. him a house, 2.06
Who am I to b. a house for him, 2.06
house I am to b. will be great and 2.09
who will b. a temple for the LORD, 2.12
began to b. the house of the LORD 3.01
He began to b. in the second month 3.02
of Israel in which to b. a house, 6 05
my father to b. a house for the 6.07
your heart to b. a house for my 6.08
nevertheless you shall not b. the house, 6.09
to you shall b. the house for my 6.09
Solomon desired to b. in Jerusalem, 8.06
"Let us b. these cities, and surround 14.07
charged me to b. him a house at 36.23
charged me to b. him a house at Ez 1.02
said to them, "Let us b. with you; 4.02
but we alone will b. to the LORD, 4.03
Judah, and made them afraid to b., 4.04
you a decree to b. this house and 5.03
you a decree to b. this house and 5.09
Come, let us b. the wall of Jerusalem, Neh 2.17
they said, "Let us rise up and b." 2.18
we his servants will arise and b.; 2.20
seized a house which he did not b. Job 20.19
them down and b. them up no more. Ps 28.05
and b. your throne for all generations.'" 89.04
For the LORD will b. up Zion, 102.16
In them the birds b. their nests; 104.17
those who b. it labor in vain. 127.01
and after that b. your house. Pro 24.27
to break down, and a time to b. up; Ecc 3.03
we will b. upon her a battlement of Sol 8.09
but we will b. with dressed stones; Is 9.10
he shall b. my city and set my 45.13
"B. up, b. up, prepare the way, 57.14
Foreigners shall b. up your walls, 60.10
They shall b. up the ancient ruins, 61.04
b. up, b. up the highway, clear it 62.10
They shall b. houses and inhabit 65.21
They shall not b. and another 65.22
house which you would b. for me, 66.01
to overthrow, to b. and to plant." Jer 1.10
that I will b. and plant it, 18.09
'I will b. myself a great house 22.14
I will b. them up, and not tear them 24.06
B. houses and live in them; 29.05
b. houses and live in them, and 29.28
Again I will b. you, and you shall 31.04
watch over them to b. and to plant, 31.28
you shall not b. a house; you shall not 35.07
and not to b. houses to dwell in. 35.09
then I will b. you up and not pull 42.10
and b. a siege wall against it, and Eze 4.02
'The time is not near to b. houses; 11.03
because, when the people b. a wall, 13.10
cast up mounds, to b. siege towers. 21.22
them who should b. up the wall and 22.30
and they shall b. houses and plant 28.26
to restore and b. Jerusalem to the Dan 9.25
and I will b. a wall against her, so Hos 2.06
who b. Zion with blood and Jerusalem Mic 3.10
Though they b. houses, they shall Zep 1.13
and bring wood and b. the house, Hag 1.08
of Shinar, to b. a house for it; Zec 5.11
and he shall b. the temple of the 6.12
It is he who shall b. the temple of 6.13
and help to b. the temple of the 6.15
"They may b., but I will tear down, Mal 1.04
on this rock I will b. my church, Mt 16.18
for you b. the tombs of the prophets 23.29
and to b. it in three days.'" 26.61
the temple and b. it in three days, 27.40
in three days I will b. another, Mk 14.58
the temple and b. it in three days, 15.29
for you b. the tombs of the prophets Lk 11.47
them, and you b. their tombs. 11.48
down my barns, and b. larger ones; 12.18
desiring to b. a tower, does not 14.28
saying, 'This man began to b., 14.30
forty-six years to b. this temple, Jn 2.20
What house will you b. for me, Ac 7.49
is able to b. you up and to give 20.32
lest I b. on another man's foundation, Rom 15.20
lawful," but not all things b. up. 1Co 10.23
But if I b. up again those things Gal 2.18
one another and b. one another up, 1Th 5.11
b. yourselves up on your most holy Jud 1.20

BUILDER
skilled master b. I laid a foundation, 1Co 3.10
Moses as the b. of a house has Heb 3.03
but the b. of all things is God.) 3.04
whose b. and maker is God. 11.10

BUILDERS
So Solomon's b. and Hiram's b. and 1Ki 5.18
carpenters and the b. who worked 2Ki 12.11
and to the b., and to the masons, as 22.06
carpenters and the b. to buy 2Ch 34.11
And when the b. laid the foundation Ez 3.10
thee to anger before the b. Neh 4.05
And each of the b. had his sword 4.18
The stone which the b. rejected has Ps 118.22
Your b. outstrip your destroyers, Is 49.17
your b. made perfect your beauty. Eze 27.04
stone which the b. rejected has Mt 21.42
stone which the b. rejected has Mk 12.10
stone which the b. rejected has Lk 20.17
stone which was rejected by you b., Ac 4.11
stone which the b. rejected has 1Pe 2.07

BUILDING
and they left off b. the city. Gen 11.08
by b. yourselves an altar this day Jos 22.16
us as rebels by b. yourselves an 22.19
for b. an altar to turn away from 22.23
the LORD by b. an altar for burnt 22.29
he had finished b. his own house 1Ki 3.01
"Concerning this house which you are b., 6.12
He was seven years in b. it. 6.38
Solomon was b. his own house 7.01
had finished b. the house of the 9.01
he stopped b. Ramah, and he dwelt in 15.21
with which Baasha had been b.; 15.22
stones for b. the house of God. 1Ch 22.02
may succeed in b. the house of the 22.11
and I made preparations for b. 28.02
provided for b. thee a house for 29.16
measurements for b. the house of 2Ch 3.03
he stopped b. Ramah, and let his 16.05
with which Baasha had been b., 16.06
He joined him in b. ships to go to 20.36
and did much b. on the wall of 27.03
exiles were b. a temple to the Ez 4.01
do with us in b. a house to our 4.03
the men who are b. this b.?" 5.04
time until now it has been in b., 5.16
finished their b. by command of 6.14
heard that we were b. the wall, Neh 4.01
what they are b.—if a fox goes up 4.03
who were b. on the wall. 4.17
that is why you are b. the wall; 6.06
b. great siegeworks against it. Ecc 9.14
b. your vaulted chamber at the head Eze 16.31
The b. that was facing the temple 41.12
the wall of the b. was five cubits 41.12
the yard and the b. with its walls, 41.13
length of the b. facing the yard 41.15
and opposite the b. on the north. 42.01

BUILDING (cont.)
The length of the b. which was on Eze 42.02
and middle chambers in the b. 42.05
the yard and opposite the b., 42.10
A day for the b. of your walls! Mic 7.11
he is like a man b. a house, Lk 6.48
you are God's field, God's b. 1Co 3.09
and another man is b. upon it. 3.10
to excel in b. up the church. 14.12
we have a b. from God, a house not 2Co 5.01
Lord gave for b. you up and not 10.08
given me for b. up and not for 13.10
for b. up the body of Christ, Eph 4.12
during the b. of the ark, in which a 1Pe 3.20

BUILDINGS
beams for the b. which the kings 2Ch 34.11
out to him the b. of the temple. Mt 24.01
stones and what wonderful b.!" Mk 13.01
to him, "Do you see these great b.? 13.02

BUILDS
The house which he b. is like a Job 27.18
Unless the LORD b. the house, Ps 127.01
The LORD b. up Jerusalem; 147.02
Wisdom b. her house, but folly with Pro 14.01
"Woe to him who b. his house by Jer 22.13
who b. his upper chambers in the Amo 9.06
Woe to him who b. a town with blood, Hab 2.12
man take care how he b. upon it. 1Co 3.10
Now if any one b. on the foundation 3.12
"Knowledge" puffs up, but love b. up. 8.01

BUILT
and he b. a city, and called the Gen 4.17
Then Noah b. an altar to the LORD, 8.20
and b. Nineveh, Rehoboth-Ir, Calah, 10.11
which the sons of men had b. 11.05
So he b. there an altar to the LORD, 12.07
and there he b. an altar to the 12.08
and there he b. an altar to the 13.18
Abraham b. an altar there, and laid 22.09
So he b. an altar there and called 26.25
and b. himself a house, and made 33.17
and there he b. an altar, and called 35.07
and they b. for Pharaoh store-cities Ex 1.11
And Moses b. an altar and called 17.15
and b. an altar at the foot of the 24.04
he b. an altar before it; and harm 32.05
(Hebron was b. seven years before Num 13.22
let it be b., let the city of Sihon 21.27
and b. seven altars, and offered a 23.14
And the sons of Gad b. Dibon, 32.34
And the sons of Reuben b. Heshbon, 32.37
names to the cities which they b. 32.38
and have b. goodly houses and live Deu 8.12
for ever, it shall not be b. again. 13.16
there that has b. a new house and 20.05
her house was b. into the city Jos 2.15
Then Joshua b. an altar in Mount 8.30
of Manasseh b. there an altar by 22.10
Manasseh have b. an altar at the 22.11
and cities which you had not b., 24.13
land of the Hittites and b. a city, Ju 1.26
Then Gideon b. an altar there to 6.24
upon the altar which had been b. 6.28
and b. there an altar, and offered 21.04
who together b. up the house of Ru 4.11
And he b. there an altar to the 1Sa 7.17
And Saul b. an altar to the LORD; 14.35
first altar that he b. to the LORD. 14.35
And David b. the city round about 2Sa 5.09
and masons who b. David a house. 5.11
have you not b. me a house of 7.07
And David b. there an altar to the 24.25
had yet been b. for the name of 1Ki 3.02
King Solomon b. for the LORD was 6.02
He also b. a structure against the 6.05
When the house was b., it was 6.07
the temple, while it was being b. 6.07
So he b. the house, and finished it; 6.09
He b. the structure against the 6.10
So Solomon b. the house, and finished 6.14
He b. twenty cubits of the rear of 6.16
and he b. this within as an inner 6.16
He b. the inner court with three 6.36
He b. the House of the Forest of 7.02
and it was b. upon three rows of 7.02
I have b. thee an exalted house, a 8.13
and I have b. the house for the 8.20
less this house which I have b.! 8.27
which I have b. is called by thy 8.43
which I have b. for thy name, 8.44
house which I have b. for thy name; 8.48
this house which you have b., 9.03
Solomon had b. the two houses, 9.10
house which Solomon had b. for her; 9.24
then he b. the Millo. 9.24
the altar which he b. to the LORD, 9.25
King Solomon b. a fleet of ships at 9.26
Solomon, the house that he had b., 10.04
Then Solomon b. a high place for 11.07
Solomon b. the Millo, and closed up 11.27
as I b. for David, and I will give 11.38
Then Jeroboam b. Shechem in the 12.25
went out from there and b. Penuel. 12.25
For they also b. for themselves 14.23
and b. Ramah, that he might permit 15.17
them King Asa b. Geba of Benjamin 15.22
he did, and the cities which he b., 15.23
the name of the city which he b., 16.24
of Baal, which he b. in Samaria. 16.32
his days Hiel of Bethel b. Jericho; 16.34
the stones he b. an altar in the 18.32
and the ivory house which he b., 22.39
and all the cities that he b., 22.39
He b. Elath and restored it to 2Ki 14.22
He b. the upper gate of the house 15.35
And Urijah the priest b. the altar; 16.11
which had been b. inside the 16.18
They b. for themselves high places 17.09
And he b. altars in the house of 21.04
And he b. altars for all the host 21.05
of Israel had b. for Ashtoreth the 23.13
and they b. siegeworks against it 25.01
that Solomon b. in Jerusalem). 1Ch 6.10
Solomon had b. the house of the 6.32
who b. both lower and upper Bethhoron, 7.24
who b. Ono and Lod with its towns, 8.12
And he b. the city round about from 11.08
David b. houses for himself in the 15.01
have you not b. me a house of 17.06
And David b. there an altar to the 21.26
that is to be b. for the LORD must 22.05
into a house b. for the name of 22.19
I have b. thee an exalted house, a 2Ch 6.02
and I have b. the house for the 6.10
less this house which I have b.! 6.18
which I have b. is called by thy 6.33
which I have b. for thy name, 6.34
which I have b. for thy name, 6.38
Solomon had b. the house of the 8.01
He b. Tadmor in the wilderness and 8.04
store-cities which he b. in Hamath. 8.04
He also b. Upper Bethhoron and 8.05
the house which he had b. for her, 8.11
which he had b. before the vestibule, 8.12
Solomon, the house that he had b., 9.03
and he b. cities for defense in 11.05
He b. Bethlehem, Etam, Tekoa, 11.06
He b. fortified cities in Judah, for 14.06
So they b. and prospered. 14.07
and b. Ramah, that he might permit 16.01
with them he b. Geba and Mizpah. 16.06
He b. in Judah fortresses and store-cities, 17.12

BUILT (cont.)
and have b. thee in it a sanctuary 2Ch 20.08
and they b. the ships in Eziongeber. 20.36
He b. Eloth and restored it to 26.02
and he b. cities in the territory 26.06
Moreover Uzziah b. towers in 26.09
And he b. towers in the wilderness, 26.10
He b. the upper gate of the house 27.03
Moreover he b. cities in the hill 27.04
resolutely and b. up all the wall 32.05
and outside it he b. another wall; 32.05
And he b. altars in the house of 33.04
And he b. altars for all the host 33.05
Afterward he b. an outer wall to 33.14
that he had b. on the mountain of 33.15
on which he b. high places and set 33.19
son of David, king of Israel, b.; 35.03
and they b. the altar of the God of Ez 3.02
It is being b. with huge stones, and 5.08
house that was b. many years ago, 5.11
king of Israel b. and finished. 5.11
of the Jews b. and prospered, 6.14
priests and they b. the Sheep Gate. Neh 3.01
And next to him the men of Jericho b. 3.02
to them Zaccur the son of Imri b. 3.02
sons of Hassenaah b. the Fish Gate; 3.03
and he b. the wall of the Pool of 3.15
So we b. the wall; and all the 4.06
girded at his side while he b. 4.18
that I had b. the wall and that 6.01
wall had been b. and I had set up 7.01
were few and no houses had been b. 7.04
the singers had b. for themselves 12.29
He b. his sanctuary like the high Ps 78.69
Jerusalem, b. as a city which is 122.03
Wisdom has b. her house, she has set Pro 9.01
By wisdom a house is b., and by 24.03
I b. houses and planted vineyards Ecc 2.04
b. for an arsenal, whereon hang a Sol 4.04
he b. a watchtower in the midst of Is 5.02
cities of Judah, 'They shall be b., 44.26
'She shall be b.,' and of the 44.28
And they have b. the high place of Jer 7.31
they shall be b. up in the midst 12.16
and have b. the high places of Baal 19.05
build you, and you shall be b., 31.04
from the day it was b. to this day, 32.31
They b. the high places of Baal in 32.35
what I have b. I am breaking down, 45.04
siege to it and b. siegeworks 52.04
or b. up a wall for the house of Eze 13.05
you b. yourself a vaulted chamber, 16.24
street you b. your lofty place and 16.25
and siege walls b. to cut off many 17.17
which I have b. by my mighty power Dan 4.30
it shall be b. again with squares 9.25
forgotten his Maker, and b. palaces; Hos 8.14
increased the more altars he b.; 10.01
you have b. houses of hewn stone, Amo 5.11
beside a wall b. with a plumb line, 7.07
my house shall be b. in it, Zec 1.16
laid, that the temple might be b. 8.09
Tyre has b. herself a rampart, and 9.03
a wise man who b. his house upon Mt 7.24
foolish man who b. his house upon 7.26
and b. a tower, and let it out to 21.33
and b. a tower, and let it out to Mk 12.01
hill on which their city was b., Lk 4.29
it, because it had been well b. 6.48
like a man who b. a house on the 6.49
and he b. us our synagogue." 7.05
they sold, they planted, they b., 17.28
was Solomon who b. a house for him. Ac 7.47
Samaria had peace and was b. up; 9.31
any man has b. on the foundation 1Co 3.14
b. upon the foundation of the Eph 2.20
you also are b. into it for a 2.22
rooted and b. up in him and established Col 2.07
(For every house is b. by some one, Heb 3.04
be yourselves b. into a spiritual 1Pe 2.05
The wall was b. of jasper, while the Rev 21.18

BUKKI
a leader, B. the son of Jogli. Num 34.22
Abishua of B., B. of Uzzi, 1Ch 6.05
B. his son, Uzzi his son, Zerahiah 6.51
Zerahiah, son of Uzzi, son of B., Ez 7.04

BUKKIAH
B., Mattaniah, Uzziel, Shebuel, and 1Ch 25.04
the sixth to B., his sons and his 25.13

BUL
eleventh year, in the month of B., 1Ki 6.38

BULGING
b. out, and about to collapse, whose Is 30.13

BULL
Take one young b. and two rams Ex 29.01
and bring the b. and the two rams. 29.03
shall bring the b. before the tent 29.10
hands upon the head of the b., 29.10
shall kill the b. before the LORD, 29.11
blood of the b. and put it upon 29.12
But the flesh of the b., and its 29.14
shall offer a b. as a sin offering 29.36
shall kill the b. before the LORD; Lev 1.05
committed a young b. without 4.03
He shall bring the b. to the door 4.04
lay his hand on the head of the b., 4.04
and kill the b. before the LORD. 4.04
blood of the b. and bring it to 4.05
blood of the b. he shall pour out 4.07
the fat of the b. of the sin 4.08
But the skin of the b. and all its 4.11
the whole b. he shall carry forth 4.12
offer a young b. for a sin offering 4.14
the head of the b. before the LORD, 4.15
and the b. shall be killed before 4.15
blood of the b. to the tent of 4.16
Thus shall he do with the b.; 4.20
he did with the b. of the sin 4.20
carry forth the b. outside the 4.21
burn it as he burned the first b.; 4.21
and the b. of the sin offering, and 8.02
Then he brought the b. of the sin 8.14
the head of the b. of the sin 8.14
But the b., and its skin, and its 8.17
"Take a b. calf for a sin offering, 9.02
with a young b. for a sin offering 16.03
shall offer the b. as a sin 16.06
present the b. as a sin offering 16.11
shall kill the b. as a sin offering 16.11
take some of the blood of the b., 16.14
as he did with the blood of the b., 16.15
blood of the b. and of the blood 16.18
And the b. for the sin offering and 16.27
A b. or a lamb which has a part too 22.23
"When a b. or sheep or goat is born, 22.27
and one young b., and two rams; 23.18
one young b., one ram, one male lamb Num 7.15
one young b., one ram, one male lamb 7.21
one young b., one ram, one male lamb 7.27
one young b., one ram, one male lamb 7.33
one young b., one ram, one male lamb 7.39
one young b., one ram, one male lamb 7.45
one young b., one ram, one male lamb 7.51
one young b., one ram, one male lamb 7.57
one young b., one ram, one male lamb 7.63
one young b., one ram, one male lamb 7.69
one young b., one ram, one male lamb 7.75
one young b., one ram, one male lamb 7.81
take a young b. and its cereal 8.08
another young b. for a sin offering. 8.08

BULL (cont.)

you prepare a b. for a burnt Num 15.08
offer with the b. a cereal offering 15.09
shall be done for each b. or ram, 15.11
offer one young b. for a burnt 15.24
on each altar a b. and a ram. 23.02
upon each altar a b. and a ram." 23.04
and offered a b. and a ram on each 23.14
and offered a b. and a ram on each 23.30
mixed with oil, for each b.; 28.12
be a half a hin of wine for a b., 28.14
an ephah shall you offer for a b., 28.20
tenths of an ephah for each b., 28.28
one young b., one ram, seven male 29.02
tenths of an ephah for the b., 29.03
one young b., one ram, seven male 29.08
tenths of an ephah for the b., 29.09
one b., one ram, seven male lambs a 29.36
and the drink offerings for the b., 29.37
His firstling b. has majesty, and Deu 33.17
said to him, "Take your father's b., Ju 6.25
the second b. seven years old, and 6.25
then take the second b., and offer it 6.26
and the second b. was offered upon 6.28
along with a three-year-old b., 1Sa 1.24
Then they slew the b., and they 1.25
them choose one b. for themselves, 1Ki 18.23
the other b. and lay it on the 18.23
yourselves one b. and prepare it 18.25
And they took the b. which was 18.26
and cut the b. in pieces and laid 18.33
with a young b. or seven rams 2Ch 13.09
Their b. breeds without fail; Job 21.10
I will accept no b. from your house, Ps 50.09
than an ox or a b. with horns and 69.31
like a b. I have brought down those Is 10.13
Why did not your b. stand? Jer 46.15
the Lord GOD, a b. for a sin offering. Eze 43.19
also take the b. of the sin 43.21
as it was cleansed with the b. 43.22
shall offer a b. without blemish 43.23
also a b. and a ram from the flock, 43.25
take a young b. without blemish, 45.18
land a young b. for a sin offering. 45.22
offering an ephah for each b., 45.24
offer a young b. without blemish, 46.06
ephah with the b. and an ephah 46.07
with a young b. shall be an ephah, 46.11

BULLS

their colts, forty cows and ten b., Gen 32.15
of the b. or the sheep or the goats. Lev 22.19
for the burnt offering twelve b., Num 7.87
of peace offerings twenty-four b., 7.88
hands upon the heads of the b.; 8.12
me here seven b. and seven rams." 23.01
me here seven b. and seven rams." 23.29
two young b., one ram, seven male 28.11
two young b., one ram, and seven 28.19
two young b., one ram, seven male 28.27
to the LORD, thirteen young b., 29.13
ephah for each of the thirteen b., 29.14
"On the second day twelve young b., 29.17
and the drink offerings for the b., 29.18
"On the third day eleven b., two rams, 29.20
and the drink offerings for the b., 29.21
"On the fourth day ten b., two rams, 29.23
and the drink offerings for the b., 29.24
"On the fifth day nine b., two rams, 29.26
and the drink offerings for the b., 29.27
"On the sixth day eight b., two rams, 29.29
and the drink offerings for the b., 29.30
"On the seventh day seven b., two rams, 29.32
and the drink offerings for the b., 29.33
Let two b. be given to us; and let 1Ki 18.23
sacrificed seven b. and seven rams. 1Ch 15.26
a thousand b., a thousand rams, and 29.21
And they brought seven b., seven rams, 2Ch 29.21
So they killed the b., and the 29.22
assembly brought was seventy b., 29.32
six hundred b. and three thousand 29.33
a thousand b. and seven thousand 30.24
a thousand b. and ten thousand 30.24
thousand, and three thousand b. 35.07
and kids and three hundred b. 35.08
lambs and kids and five hundred b. 35.09
And so they did with the b. 35.12
young b., rams, or sheep for burnt Ez 6.09
this house of God one hundred b., 6.17
shall with all diligence buy b., 7.17
twelve b. for all Israel, ninety-six 8.35
take seven b. and seven rams, Job 42.08
Many b. encompass me, strong Ps 22.12
strong b. of Bashan surround me; 22.12
Do I eat the flesh of b., or drink 50.13
then b. will be offered on thy 51.19
make an offering of b. and goats. 66.15
the herd of b. with the calves of 68.30
do not delight in the blood of b., Is 1.11
young steers with the mighty b. 34.07
Slay all her b., let them go down Jer 50.27
twelve bronze b. which were under 52.20
of b., all of them fatlings of Eze 39.18
seven young b. and seven rams 45.23
if in Gilgal they sacrifice b., Hos 12.11
of goats and b. and with the ashes Heb 9.13
the blood of b. and goats should 10.04

BULRUSHES

took for him a basket made of b., Ex 2.03

BULWARK

hast founded a b. because of thy Ps 8.02
the pillar and b. of the truth. 1Ti 3.15

BULWARKS

sets up salvation as walls and b. Is 26.01
her b. have fallen, her walls are Jer 50.15
the b. are burned with fire, and the 51.32

BUNAH

B., Oren, Ozem, and Ahijah. 1Ch 2.25

BUNCH

Take a b. of hyssop and dip it in Ex 12.22

BUNCHES

a hundred b. of raisins, a hundred 2Sa 16.01

BUNDLE

every man's b. of money was in his Gen 42.35
and cut down a b. of brushwood, Ju 9.48
cut down his b. and following 9.49
be bound in the b. of the living 1Sa 25.29
Gather up your b. from the ground, O Jer 10.17
Paul had gathered a b. of sticks Ac 28.03

BUNDLES

their father saw their b. of money, Gen 42.35
pull out some from the b. for her, Ru 2.16
and bind them in b. to be burned, Mt 13.30

BUNNI

B., Sherebiah, Bani, and Chenani; Neh 9.04
B., Azgad, Bebai, 10.15
son of Hashabiah, son of B.; 11.15

BURDEN

and they will bear the b. with you. Ex 18.22
who hates you lying under its b., 23.05
each to his task and to his b., Num 4.19
dost lay the b. of all this people 11.11
the b. is too heavy for me. 11.14
shall bear the b. of the people 11.17
the weight and b. of you and your Deu 1.12
on with me, you will be a b. to me. 2Sa 15.33

BURDEN (cont.)
be an added b. to my lord the king 2Sa 19.35
servant two mules' b. of earth; 2Ki 5.17
that no b. might be brought in on Neh 13.19
Why have I become a b. to thee? Job 7.20
weigh like a b. too heavy for me. Ps 38.04
Cast your b. on the LORD, and he 55.22
"I relieved your shoulder of the b.; 81.06
they have become a b. to me, Is 1.14
For the yoke of his b., and the 9.04
And in that day his b. will depart 10.27
and his b. from their shoulder." 14.25
and the b. that was upon it will be 22.25
together, they cannot save the b., 46.02
do not bear a b. on the sabbath Jer 17.21
And do not carry a b. out of your 17.22
and bring in no b. by the gates of 17.24
not to bear a b. and enter by the 17.27
you, 'What is the b. of the LORD?' 23.33
'You are the b., and I will cast 23.33
'The b. of the LORD,' I will punish 23.34
But 'the b. of the LORD' you shall 23.36
for the b. is every man's own word, 23.36
'The b. of the LORD,' thus says the 23.38
"The b. of the LORD," when I sent to 23.38
"You shall not say, 'The b. of the LORD,'" 23.38
the b. of their songs all day long. Lam 3.14
rising; I am the b. of their songs. 3.63
yoke is easy, and my b. is light." Mt 11.30
have borne the b. of the day and 20.12
you no greater b. than these Ac 15.28
I did not b. any one, for my needs 2Co 11.09
that I myself did not b. you? Forgive 12.13
And I will not be a b., for I seek 12.14
that I myself did not b. you, 12.16
that we might not b. any of you, 1Th 2.09
that we might not b. any of you. 2Th 3.08
I do not lay upon you any other b.; Rev 2.24

BURDEN-BEARERS
thousand b. and eighty thousand 1Ki 5.15
were over the b. and directed all 2Ch 34.13
"The strength of the b. is failing, Neh 4.10

BURDENED
If a man is b. with the blood of Pro 28.17
I have not b. you with offerings, or Is 43.23
But you have b. me with your sins, 43.24
others should be eased and you b., 2Co 8.13
let the church not be b., so that 1Ti 5.16
b. with sins and swayed by various 2Ti 3.06

BURDENING
refrain from b. you in any way. 2Co 11.09

BURDENS
them to afflict them with heavy b.; Ex 1.11
his people and looked on their b.; 2.11
from their work! Get to your b." 5.04
you make them rest from their b.!" 5.05
from under the b. of the Egyptians, 6.06
from under the b. of the Egyptians. 6.07
Gershonites, in serving and bearing b.: Num 4.24
work of bearing b. in the tent of 4.47
men to bear b. and eighty thousand 2Ch 2.02
of them he assigned to bear b., 2.18
who carried b. were laden in such Neh 4.17
me laid heavy b. upon the people, 5.15
grapes, figs, and all kinds of b., 13.15
are loaded as b. on weary beasts. Is 46.01
They bind heavy b., hard to Mt 23.04
you load men with b. hard to bear, Lk 11.46
not touch the b. with one of your 11.46
Bear one another's b., and so Gal 6.02

BURDENSOME
not all go, lest we be b. to you." 2Sa 13.25
And his commandments are not b. 1Jn 5.03

BURIAL
the place of his b. to this day. Deu 34.06
fathers in the b. field which 2Ch 26.23
good things, and also has no b., Ecc 6.03
will not be joined with them in b., Is 14.20
With the b. of an ass he shall be Jer 22.19
body into the b. place of the 26.23
to Gog a place for b. in Israel, Eze 39.11
has done it to prepare me for b. Mt 26.12
her keep it for the day of my b. Jn 12.07
as is the b. custom of the Jews. 19.40
gave directions concerning his b. Heb 11.22

BURIED
you shall be b. in a good old age. Gen 15.15
Abraham b. Sarah his wife in the 23.19
his sons b. him in the cave of 25.09
There Abraham was b., with Sarah 25.10
and she was b. under an oak below 35.08
and she was b. on the way to 35.19
and his sons Esau and Jacob b. him. 35.29
and I b. her there on the way to 48.07
There they b. Abraham and Sarah his 49.31
there they b. Isaac and Rebekah his 49.31
and there I b. Leah— 49.31
and b. him in the cave of the field 50.13
After he had b. his father, Joseph 50.14
there they b. the people who had Num 11.34
died there, and was b. there. 20.01
Aaron died, and there he was b.; Deu 10.06
and he b. him in the valley in the 34.06
And they b. him in his own inheritance Jos 24.30
up from Egypt were b. at Shechem, 24.32
and they b. him at Gibeah, the town 24.33
And they b. him within the bounds Ju 2.09
and was b. in the tomb of Joash his 8.32
Then he died, and was b. at Shamir. 10.02
And Jair died, and was b. in Kamon. 10.05
and was b. in his city in Gilead. 12.07
died, and was b. at Bethlehem. 12.10
and was b. at Aijalon in the land 12.12
and was b. at Pirathon in the land 12.15
him up and b. him between Zorah 16.31
I will die, and there will I be b. Ru 1.17
and they b. him in his house at 1Sa 25.01
for him and b. him in Ramah, 28.03
their bones and b. them under the 31.13
men of Jabeshgilead who b. Saul," 2Sa 2.04
to Saul your lord, and b. him! 2.05
and b. him in the tomb of his father, 2.32
They b. Abner at Hebron; and the 3.32
and b. it in the tomb of Abner at 4.12
and was b. in the tomb of his 17.23
And they b. the bones of Saul and 21.14
and was b. in the city of David. 1Ki 2.10
and he was b. in his own house in 2.34
and was b. in the city of David his 11.43
And after he had b. him, he said 13.31
in which the man of God is b.; 13.31
And all Israel b. him and mourned 14.18
fathers and was b. with his 14.31
and they b. him in the city of 15.08
and was b. with his fathers in the 15.24
his fathers, and was b. at Tirzah; 16.06
his fathers, and was b. in Samaria; 16.28
and they b. the king in Samaria. 22.37
and was b. with his fathers in the 22.50
and was b. with his fathers in the 2Ki 8.24
and b. him in his tomb with his 9.28
fathers, and they b. him in Samaria. 10.35
And they b. him with his fathers in 12.21
fathers, and they b. him in Samaria; 13.09
and Joash was b. in Samaria with 13.13
So Elisha died, and they b. him. 13.20
And as a man was being b., lo, 13.21
and was b. in Samaria with the 14.16
and he was b. in Jerusalem with 14.20

BURIED (cont.)
and they b. him with his fathers in 2Ki 15.07
and was b. with his fathers in the 15.38
and was b. with his fathers in the 16.20
and was b. in the garden of his 21.18
And he was b. in his tomb in the 21.26
and b. him in his own tomb. 23.30
And they b. their bones under the 1Ch 10.12
and was b. in the city of David his 2Ch 9.31
and was b. in the city of David; 12.16
and they b. him in the city of 14.01
They b. him in the tomb which he 16.14
and was b. with his fathers in the 21.01
They b. him in the city of David, 21.20
They b. him, for they said, "He is 22.09
And they b. him in the city of 24.16
and they b. him in the city of 24.25
and he was b. with his fathers in 25.28
and they b. him with his fathers in 26.23
and they b. him in the city of 27.09
and they b. him in the city, in 28.27
and they b. him in the ascent of 32.33
and they b. him in his house; 33.20
and was b. in the tombs of his 35.24
Then I saw the wicked b.; they used Ecc 8.10
they shall not be gathered or b.; Jer 8.02
be lamented, nor shall they be b.; 16.04
they shall not be b., and no one 16.06
die, and there you shall be b., 20.06
burial of an ass he shall be b., 22.19
be lamented, or gathered, or b.; 25.33
field, and not be gathered and b. Eze 29.05
and all his multitude will be b.; 39.11
buriers have b. it in the Valley 39.15
came and took the body and b. it; Mt 14.12
the rich man also died and was b.; Lk 16.22
David that he both died and was b., Ac 2.29
up and carried him out and b. him. 5.06
those that have b. your husband 5.09
her out and b. her beside her 5.10
Devout men b. Stephen, and made 8.02
We were b. therefore with him by Rom 6.04
that he was b., that he was raised 1Co 15.04
and you were b. with him in baptism, Col 2.12

BURIERS
till the b. have buried it in the Eze 39.15

BURIES
Those who survive him the pestilence b., Job 27.15
The sluggard b. his hand in the Pro 19.24
The sluggard b. his hand in the 26.15

BURN
bricks, and b. them thoroughly." Gen 11.03
not your anger b. against your 44.18
until the morning you shall b. Ex 12.10
b. for b., wound for wound, stripe 21.25
and my wrath will b., and I will 22.24
may be set up to b. continually. 27.20
and b. them upon the altar. 29.13
you shall b. with fire outside the 29.14
and b. the whole ram upon the altar; 29.18
and b. them on the altar in addition 29.25
then you shall b. the remainder 29.34
make an altar to b. incense upon; 30.01
And Aaron shall b. fragrant incense 30.07
dresses the lamps he shall b. it, 30.07
he shall b. it, a perpetual incense 30.08
to b. an offering by fire to the 30.20
my wrath may b. hot against them 32.10
does thy wrath b. hot against thy 32.11
not the anger of my lord b. hot; 32.22
priest shall b. the whole on the Lev 1.09
and b. it on the altar; it is a 1.13
and b. it on the altar; and its 1.15
priest shall b. it on the altar, 1.17
priest shall b. this as its 2.02
portion and b. this on the altar, 2.09
for you shall b. no leaven nor any 2.11
priest shall b. as its memorial 2.16
sons shall b. it on the altar upon 3.05
priest shall b. it on the altar as 3.11
priest shall b. them on the altar 3.16
priest shall b. them upon the 4.10
and shall b. it on a fire of wood; 4.12
take from it and b. upon the altar. 4.19
and b. it as he burned the first 4.21
its fat he shall b. on the altar, 4.26
priest shall b. it upon the altar 4.31
priest shall b. it on the altar, 4.35
portion and b. this on the altar, 5.12
priest shall b. wood on it every 6.12
and shall b. on it the fat of the 6.12
and b. this as its memorial portion 6.15
the priest shall b. them on the 7.05
The priest shall b. the fat on the 7.31
the bread you shall b. with fire. 8.32
the body has a b. on its skin and 13.24
raw flesh of the b. becomes a spot, 13.24
it has broken out in the b., 13.25
dim, it is a swelling from the b., 13.28
for it is the scar of the b. 13.28
And he shall b. the garment, whether 13.52
you shall b. it in the fire, whether 13.55
you shall b. with fire that in 13.57
offering he shall b. upon the altar. 16.25
and b. the fat for a pleasing odor 17.06
and b. it upon the altar, and Num 5.26
draw near to b. incense before the 16.40
and shall b. their fat as an 18.17
and b. their graven images with Deu 7.05
their gods you shall b. with fire; 7.25
and b. their Asherim with fire; 12.03
for they even b. their sons and 12.31
and b. the city and all its spoil 13.16
and b. their chariots with fire." Jos 11.06
that stood on mounds did Israel b., 11.13
"Let not thy anger b. against me, Ju 6.39
of the tower to b. it with fire. 9.52
We will b. your house over you with 12.01
lest we b. you and your father's 14.15
"Let them b. the fat first, and then 1Sa 2.16
to b. incense, to wear an ephod 2.28
went up to the altar to b. incense. 1Ki 12.33
standing by the altar to b. incense. 13.01
high places who b. incense upon 13.02
sacrifice and b. incense on the 2Ki 12.03
the great altar b. the morning 16.15
had ordained to b. incense in the 23.05
no one might b. his son or his 23.10
for ever should b. incense before 1Ch 23.13
as a place to b. incense before 2Ch 2.06
of pure gold to b. before the 4.20
its lamps may b. every evening; 13.11
of the LORD to b. incense on the 26.16
to b. incense to the LORD, but for 26.18
who are consecrated to b. incense. 26.18
a censer in his hand to b. incense, 26.19
high places to b. incense to other 28.25
ministers and b. incense to him." 29.11
it you shall b. your sacrifices"? 32.12
to b. upon the altar of the LORD Neh 10.34
from me, and my bones b. with heat. Job 30.30
and it would b. to the root all my 31.12
thy jealous wrath b. like fire? Ps 79.05
long will thy wrath b. like fire? 89.46
and my bones b. like a furnace. 102.03
and both of them shall b. together, Is 1.31
and it will b. and devour his 10.17
I would b. them up together. 27.04
you who b. with lust among the oaks, 57.05
and b. with none to quench it, Jer 4.04
b. incense to Baal, and go after 7.09
it will b. and not be quenched." 7.20

BURN (cont.)
to b. their sons and their daughters Jer 7.31
the gods to whom they b. incense, 11.12
altars to b. incense to Baal. 11.13
is kindled which shall b. for ever." 15.14
is kindled which shall b. for ever." 17.04
they b. incense to false gods; 18.15
of Baal to b. their sons in the 19.05
and he shall b. it with fire.' 21.10
and b. with none to quench it, 21.12
and b. it, with the houses on whose 32.29
to b. cereal offerings, and to make 33.18
and he shall b. it with fire. 34.02
so men shall b. spices for you and 34.05
and take it, and b. it with fire. 34.22
the king not to b. the scroll, 36.25
shall take it and b. it with fire. 37.08
rise up and b. this city with fire.'" 37.10
and they shall b. it with fire, 38.18
and he shall b. them and carry them 43.12
of Egypt he shall b. with fire.'" 43.13
they went to b. incense and serve 44.03
wickedness and b. no incense to 44.05
b. incense to the queen of heaven 44.17
to b. incense to the queen of 44.25
part you shall b. in the fire in Eze 5.02
and b. them in the fire; from there 5.04
And they shall b. your houses and 16.41
daughters, and b. up their houses. 23.47
become hot, and its copper may b., 24.11
fires of the weapons and b. them, 39.09
oven their hearts b. with intrigue; Hos 7.06
they shall b. them and consume them, Ob 1.18
and I will b. your chariots in Nah 2.13
day that comes shall b. them up, Mal 4.01
chaff he will b. with unquenchable Mt 3.12
temple of the Lord and b. incense. Lk 1.09
chaff he will b. with unquenchable 3.17
not our hearts b. within us while 24.32
the throne b. seven torches of Rev 4.05
her flesh and b. her up with fire, 17.16

BURNED
"Bring her out, and let her be b." Gen 38.24
Moses' anger b. hot, and he threw Ex 32.19
are poured out it shall be b. Lev 4.12
burn it as he b. the first bull; 4.21
the whole of it shall be b. 6.22
of a priest shall be wholly b.; 6.23
it shall be b. with fire. 6.30
third day shall be b. with fire. 7.17
it shall be b. with fire. 7.19
and Moses b. them on the altar. 8.16
he b. with fire outside the camp, as 8.17
Moses b. the head and the pieces 8.20
Moses b. the whole ram on the altar, 8.21
and b. them on the altar with the 8.28
sin offering he b. upon the altar, 9.10
and the skin he b. with fire 9.11
and he b. them upon the altar. 9.13
and b. them with the burnt offering 9.14
and b. it upon the altar, besides 9.17
and he b. the fat upon the altar, 9.20
offering, and behold, it was b.! 10.16
it shall be b. in the fire. 13.52
their dung shall be b. with fire. 16.27
third day shall be b. with fire. 19.06
they shall be b. with fire, both he 20.14
she shall be b. with fire. 21.09
the fire of the LORD b. among them, Num 11.01
the fire of the LORD b. among them. 11.03
those who were b. had offered; 16.39
hiefer shall be b. in his sight; 19.05
blood, with her dung, shall be b.; 19.05
encampments, they b. with fire, 31.10
the mountain b. with fire to the Deu 4.11
and b. it with fire and crushed it, 9.21
And they b. the city with fire, and Jos 6.24
of the LORD b. against the people 7.01
things shall be b. with fire, 7.15
they b. them with fire, and stoned 7.25
So Joshua b. Ai, and made it for 8.28
and b. their chariots with fire. 11.09
and he b. Hazor with fire. 11.11
Hazor only; that Joshua b. 11.13
and b. up the shocks and the Ju 15.05
and b. her and her father with fire. 15.06
and b. the city with fire. 18.27
Moreover, before the fat was b., 1Sa 2.15
Ziklag, and b. it with fire, 30.01
they found it b. with fire, and 30.03
and we b. Ziklag with fire." 30.14
who b. incense and sacrificed to 1Ki 11.08
men's bones shall be b. upon you.'" 13.02
her image and b. it at the brook 15.13
and b. the king's house over him 16.18
sacrificed and b. incense on the 22.43
in the house of Baal, and b. it. 2Ki 10.26
sacrificed and b. incense on the 14.04
sacrificed and b. incense on the 15.04
sacrificed and b. incense on the 15.35
He even b. his son as an offering, 16.03
sacrificed and b. incense on the 16.04
and b. his burnt offering and his 16.13
and there they b. incense on all 17.11
And they b. their sons and their 17.17
the Sepharvites b. their children 17.31
of Israel had b. incense to it; 18.04
And he b. his son as an offering, 21.06
me and have b. incense to other 22.17
he b. them outside Jerusalem in 23.04
those also who b. incense to Baal, 23.05
and b. it at the brook Kidron, and 23.06
where the priests had b. incense, 23.08
and he b. the chariots of the sun 23.11
also he b. the Asherah. 23.15
and b. them upon the altar, and 23.16
and b. the bones of men upon them. 23.20
And he b. the house of the LORD, and 25.09
every great house he b. down. 25.09
gave command, and they were b. 1Ch 14.12
and b. it at the brook Kidron. 2Ch 15.16
and he b. incense in the valley of 28.03
and b. his sons as an offering, 28.03
sacrificed and b. incense on the 28.04
and have not b. incense or offered 29.07
And he b. his sons as an offering 33.06
He also b. the bones of the priests 34.05
me and have b. incense to other 34.25
And they b. the house of God, and 36.19
and b. all its palaces with fire, 36.19
lies in ruins with its gates b. Neh 2.17
of rubbish, and b. ones at that?" 4.02
and his anger b. within him. Est 1.12
from heaven and b. up the sheep Job 1.16
As I mused, the fire b.; then I Ps 39.03
they b. all the meeting places of 74.08
They have b. it with fire, they have 80.16
company; the flame b. up the wicked. 106.18
bosom and his clothes not be b.? Pro 6.27
your cities are b. with fire; Is 1.07
it will be b. again, like a terebinth 6.13
blood will be b. as fuel for the 9.05
the LORD of hosts the land is b., 9.19
peoples will be as if b. to lime, 33.12
cut down, that are b. in the fire." 33.12
it b. him, but he did not take it to 42.25
through fire you shall not be b., 43.02
Half of it I b. in the fire, I also 44.19
has been b. by fire, and all our 64.11
because they b. incense upon the 65.07
they have b. incense to other gods, Jer 1.16
has been b. to all the host of 19.13
as spices were b. for your fathers, 34.05

BURNED (cont.)
the king had b. the scroll with Jer 36.27
Jehoiakim the king of Judah has b. 36.28
You have b. this scroll, saying, "Why 36.29
king of Judah had b. in the fire; 36.32
city shall not be b. with fire, 38.17
this city shall be b. with fire." 38.23
The Chaldeans b. the king's house 39.08
"When we b. incense to the queen of 44.19
that you b. in the cities of Judah 44.21
It is because you b. incense, 44.23
its villages shall be b. with fire; 49.02
the bulwarks are b. with fire, 51.32
high gates shall be b. with fire. 51.58
And he b. the house of the LORD, and 52.13
every great house he b. down. 52.13
he has b. like a flaming fire in Lam 2.03
broth, and let the bones be b. up. Eze 24.10
and given over to be b. with fire. Dan 7.11
Baals when she b. incense to them Hos 2.13
and flame has b. all the trees of Joe 1.19
because he b. to lime the bones of Amo 2.01
her hires shall be b. with fire, Mic 1.07
and bind them in bundles to be b., Mt 13.30
are gathered and b. with fire, 13.40
those murderers and b. their city. 22.07
thrown into the fire and b. Jn 15.06
together and b. them in the sight Ac 19.19
If any man's work is b. up, 1Co 3.15
and if I deliver my body to be b., 13.03
cursed; its end is to be b. Heb 6.08
for sin are b. outside the camp. 13.11
that are upon it will be b. up. 2Pe 3.10
and she shall be b. wtih fire; Rev 18.08

BURNING
the bush was b., yet it was not Ex 3.02
the altar shall be kept b. on it. Lev 6.09
the altar shall be kept b. on it, 6.12
Fire shall be kept b. upon the 6.13
may bewail the b. which the LORD 10.06
a light may be kept b. continually. 24.02
the midst of the b. of the heifer. Num 19.06
the mountain was b. with fire, Deu 5.23
and the mountain was b. with fire; 9.15
devoured with b. heat and poisonous 32.24
the LORD turned from his b. anger. Jos 7.26
b. incense before the LORD. 1Ki 9.25
to him for the b. of incense of 2Ch 2.04
the altars for b. incense they 30.14
from a boiling pot and b. rushes. Job 41.20
For my loins are filled with b., Ps 38.07
and let thy b. anger overtake them. 69.24
Let b. coals fall upon them! 140.10
of judgment and by a spirit of b. Is 4.04
in his hand a b. coal which he had 6.06
his glory a b. will be kindled, 10.16
be kindled, like the b. of fire. 10.16
b. with his anger, and in thick 30.27
For a b. place has long been 30.33
her land shall become b. pitch. 34.09
the b. sand shall become a pool, and 35.07
and a dimly b. wick he will not 42.03
and her salvation as a b. torch. 62.01
in gardens and b. incense upon 65.03
me to anger by b. incense to Baal." Jer 11.17
this place by b. incense in it to 19.04
as it were a b. fire shut up in my 20.09
was a fire b. in the brazier 36.22
b. incense to other gods in the 44.08
we left off b. incense to the 44.18
an oven with the b. heat of famine. Lam 5.10
that looked like b. coals of fire, Eze 1.13
your hands with b. coals from 10.02
be cast into a b. fiery furnace." Dan 3.06
be cast into a b. fiery furnace. 3.11
be cast into a b. fiery furnace; 3.15
us from the b. fiery furnace; 3.17
them into the b. fiery furnace. 3.20
cast into the b. fiery furnace. 3.21
bound into the b. fiery furnace. 3.23
the door of the b. fiery furnace 3.26
flames, its wheels were b. fire. 7.09
and b. incense to idols. Hos 11.02
as a brand plucked out of the b.; Amo 4.11
b. like an oven, when all the Mal 4.01
loins be girded and your lamps b., Lk 12.35
He was a b. and shining lamp, and Jn 5.35
you will heap b. coals upon his Rom 12.20
b. with fire, was thrown into the Rev 8.08
when they see the smoke of her b.; 18.09
as they saw the smoke of her b., 18.18

BURNINGS
us can dwell with everlasting b.?" Is 33.14

BURNISHED
King Solomon, were of b. bronze. 1Ki 7.45
Huramabi made of b. bronze for King 2Ch 4.16
and they sparkled like b. bronze. Eze 1.07
legs like the gleam of b. bronze, Dan 10.06
his feet were like b. bronze, Rev 1.15
and whose feet are like b. bronze. 2.18

BURNS
And he who b. them shall wash his Lev 16.28
He who b. the heifer shall wash his Num 19.08
you any one who b. his son or his Deu 18.10
and it b. to the depths of Sheol, 32.22
as a man b. up dung until it is all 1Ki 14.10
he b. the chariots with fire! Ps 46.09
and b. up his adversaries round 97.03
For wickedness b. like a fire, it Is 9.18
Half of it he b. in the fire; 44.16
nostrils, a fire that b. all the day. 65.05
high place and b. incense to his Jer 48.35
My anger b. against them. How long Hos 8.05
them, and behind them a flame b. Joe 2.03
he who b. him, shall take him up to Amo 6.10
to his net and b. incense to his Hab 1.16
of fire that b. with brimstone. Rev 19.20
the lake that b. with fire and 21.08

BURNT
and offered b. offerings on the Gen 8.20
him there as a b. offering upon 22.02
cut the wood for the b. offering, 22.03
took the wood of the b. offering, 22.06
is the lamb for a b. offering?" 22.07
himself the lamb for a b. offering, 22.08
it up as a b. offering instead of 22.13
sight, why the bush is not b." Ex 3.03
have sacrifices and b. offerings, 10.25
offered a b. offering and sacrifices 18.12
on it your b. offerings and your 20.24
who offered b. offerings and 24.05
it is a b. offering to the LORD; 29.18
in addition to the b. offering, 29.25
be a continual b. offering throughout 29.42
nor b. offering, nor cereal offering; 30.09
and the altar of b. offering with 30.28
and the altar of b. offering with 31.09
and offered b. offerings and 32.06
and b. it with fire, and ground it 32.20
the altar of b. offering, with its 35.16
the altar of b. offering also of 38.01
the altar of b. offering before 40.06
the altar of b. offering and all 40.10
and b. fragrant incense upon it; 40.27
the altar of b. offering at the 40.29
upon it the b. offering and the 40.29
offering is a b. offering from the Lev 1.03
upon the head of the b. offering, 1.04
shall flay the b. offering and cut 1.06
as a b. offering, an offering by 1.09

BURNT (cont.)
"If his gift for a b. offering is Lev 1.10
it is a b. offering, an offering by 1.13
the LORD is a b. offering of birds, 1.14
it is a b. offering, an offering by 1.17
on the altar upon the b. offering, 3.05
of the altar of b. offering which 4.07
them upon the altar of b. offering. 4.10
of the altar of b. offering which 4.18
they kill the b. offering before 4.24
horns of the altar of b. offering, 4.25
base of the altar of b. offering. 4.25
in the place of b. offering. 4.29
horns of the altar of b. offering, 4.30
where they kill the b. offering. 4.33
horns of the altar of b. offering, 4.34
and the other for a b. offering. 5.07
second for a b. offering according 5.10
This is the law of the b. offering. 6.09
The b. offering shall be on the 6.09
consumed the b. offering on the 6.10
shall lay the b. offering in order 6.12
place where the b. offering is 6.25
they kill the b. offering they 7.02
any man's b. offering shall have 7.08
the skin of the b. offering which 7.08
This is the law of the b. offering, 7.37
presented the ram of the b. offering; 8.18
as a b. offering, a pleasing odor, an 8.21
on the altar with the b. offering, 8.28
and a ram for a b. offering, 9.02
blemish, for a b. offering, 9.03
sin offering and your b. offering, 9.07
And he killed the b. offering; 9.12
delivered the b. offering to him, 9.13
them with the b. offering on the 9.14
And he presented the b. offering, 9.16
besides the b. offering of the 9.17
offering and the b. offering and 9.22
consumed the b. offering and the 9.24
and their b. offering before the 10.19
lamb a year old for a b. offering, 12.06
one for a b. offering and the other 12.08
sin offering and the b. offering, 14.13
he shall kill the b. offering; 14.19
shall offer the b. offering and 14.20
and the other a b. offering. 14.22
and the other for a b. offering, 14.31
and the other for a b. offering; 15.15
and the other for a b. offering; 15.30
and a ram for a b. offering. 16.03
and one ram for a b. offering. 16.05
and offer his b. offering and the 16.24
and the b. offering of the people, 16.24
who offers a b. offering or sacrifice, 17.08
to the LORD as a b. offering, 22.18
blemish as a b. offering to the 23.12
they shall be a b. offering to the 23.18
b. offerings and cereal offerings, 23.37
and the other for a b. offering, Num 6.11
without blemish for a b. offering, 6.14
sin offering and his b. offering, 6.16
lamb a year old, for a b. offering; 7.15
lamb a year old, for a b. offering; 7.21
lamb a year old, for a b. offering; 7.27
lamb a year old, for a b. offering; 7.33
lamb a year old, for a b. offering; 7.39
lamb a year old, for a b. offering; 7.45
lamb a year old, for a b. offering; 7.51
lamb a year old, for a b. offering; 7.57
lamb a year old, for a b. offering; 7.63
lamb a year old, for a b. offering; 7.69
lamb a year old, for a b. offering; 7.75
lamb a year old, for a b. offering; 7.81
cattle for the b. offering twelve 7.87
the other for a b. offering to the 8.12
over your b. offerings and over 10.10
by fire or a b. offering or a 15.03
shall prepare with the b. offering, 15.05
prepare a bull for a b. offering, 15.08
one young bull for a b. offering, 15.24
some ashes of the b. sin offering, 19.17
"Stand beside your b. offering, 23.03
standing beside his b. offering. 23.06
"Stand here beside your b. offering, 23.15
standing beside his b. offering, 23.17
It is a continual b. offering, 28.06
this is the b. offering of every 28.10
the continual b. offering and its 28.10
shall offer a b. offering to the 28.11
for a b. offering of pleasing odor, 28.13
this is the b. offering of each 28.14
the continual b. offering and its 28.15
a b. offering to the LORD: two young 28.19
besides the b. offering of the 28.23
is for a continual b. offering. 28.23
the continual b. offering and its 28.24
but offer a b. offering, a pleasing 28.27
Besides the continual b. offering 28.31
and you shall offer a b. offering, 29.02
besides the b. offering of the new 29.06
the continual b. offering and its 29.06
shall offer a b. offering to the 29.08
the continual b. offering and its 29.11
and you shall offer a b. offering, 29.13
besides the continual b. offering, 29.16
the continual b. offering and its 29.19
the continual b. offering and its 29.22
besides the continual b. offering, 29.25
the continual b. offerings and its 29.28
besides the continual b. offering, 29.31
besides the continual b. offering, 29.34
but you shall offer a b. offering, 29.36
the continual b. offering and its 29.38
for your b. offerings, and for your 29.39
bring your b. offerings and your Deu 12.06
your b. offerings and your sacrifices, 12.11
not offer your b. offerings at 12.13
you shall offer your b. offerings, 12.14
and offer your b. offerings, the 12.27
as a whole b. offering to the LORD 13.16
you shall offer b. offerings on it 27.06
and whole b. offering upon thy 33.10
offered on it b. offerings to the Jos 8.31
did so to offer b. offerings or 22.23
not for b. offering, nor for sacrifice, 22.26
with our b. offerings and sacrifices 22.27
not for b. offerings, nor for 22.28
building an altar for b. offering, 22.29
offer it as a b. offering with the Ju 6.26
offer him up for a b. offering." 11.31
if you make ready a b. offering, 13.16
have accepted a b. offering and a 13.23
and offered b. offerings and peace 20.26
and offered b. offerings and peace 21.04
the cows as a b. offering to the 1Sa 6.14
Bethshemesh offered b. offerings 6.15
it as a whole b. offering to the 7.09
was offering up the b. offering, 7.10
to you to offer b. offerings and 10.08
"Bring the b. offering here to me, 13.09
And he offered the b. offering. 13.09
finished offering the b. offering, 13.10
and offered the b. offering." 13.12
delight in b. offerings and 15.22
came to Jabesh and b. them there. 31.12
David offered b. offerings and 2Sa 6.17
offering the b. offerings and the 6.18
are the oxen for the b. offering, 24.22
will not offer b. offerings to the 24.24
and offered b. offerings and peace 24.25
sacrificed and b. incense at the 1Ki 3.03
a thousand b. offerings upon that 3.04
and offered up b. offerings and 3.15

BURNT (cont.)
he offered the b. offering and the 1Ki 8.64
was too small to receive the b. offering 8.64
captured Gezer and b. it with fire, 9.16
to offer up b. offerings and peace 9.25
and his b. offerings which he 10.05
and pour it on the b. offering, 18.33
fell, and consumed the b. offering, 18.38
him for a b. offering upon the 2Ki 3.27
will not offer b. offering or 5.17
offer sacrifices and b. offerings. 10.24
an end of offering the b. offering, 10.25
and burned his b. offering and his 16.13
altar burn the morning b. offering, 16.15
offering, and the king's b. offering, 16.15
with the b. offering of all the 16.15
all the blood of the b. offering, 16.15
the altar of b. offering and upon 1Ch 6.49
they offered b. offerings and 16.01
offering the b. offerings and the 16.02
to offer b. offerings to the LORD 16.40
the altar of b. offering continually 16.40
I give the oxen for b. offerings, 21.23
nor offer b. offerings which cost 21.24
and presented b. offerings and 21.26
upon the altar of b. offering. 21.26
the altar of b. offering were at 21.29
the altar of b. offering for 22.01
and whenever b. offerings are 23.31
day offered b. offerings to the 29.21
a thousand b. offerings upon it. 2Ch 1.06
and for b. offerings morning and 2.04
what was used for the b. offering, 4.06
consumed the b. offering and the 7.01
he offered the b. offering and the 7.07
could not hold the b. offering and 7.07
offered up b. offerings to the 8.12
and his b. offerings which he 9.04
every evening b. offerings and 13.11
to offer b. offerings to the LORD, 23.18
service and for the b. offerings, 24.14
they offered b. offerings in the 24.14
or offered b. offerings in the 29.07
the altar of b. offering and all 29.18
that the b. offering and the sin 29.24
that the b. offering be offered on 29.27
And when the b. offering began, the 29.27
until the b. offering was finished. 29.28
willing heart brought b. offerings. 29.31
The number of the b. offerings 29.32
were for a b. offering to the LORD. 29.32
not flay all the b. offerings, 29.34
great number of b. offerings there 29.35
the libations for the b. offerings. 29.35
and brought b. offerings into the 30.15
for b. offerings and peace offerings, 31.02
possessions was for the b. offerings: 31.03
the b. offerings of morning and 31.03
the b. offerings for the sabbaths, the 31.03
set aside the b. offerings that 35.12
in offering the b. offerings and 35.14
and to offer b. offerings on the 35.16
to offer b. offerings upon it, as it Ez 3.02
they offered b. offerings upon it 3.03
b. offerings morning and evening. 3.03
the daily b. offerings by number 3.04
that the continual b. offerings, 3.05
began to offer b. offerings to the 3.06
are offered and b. offerings are 6.03
or sheep for b. offerings to the 6.09
offered b. offerings to the God of 8.35
all this was a b. offering to the 8.35
the continual b. offering, the Neh 10.33
and offer b. offerings according Job 1.05
up for yourselves a b. offering; 42.08
with favor your b. sacrifices! Ps 20.03
B. offering and sin offering thou 40.06
your b. offerings are continually 50.08
were I to give a b. offering, 51.16
in b. offerings and whole b. offerings; 51.19
into thy house with b. offerings; 66.13
offer to thee b. offerings of 66.15
had enough of b. offerings of rams Is 1.11
with sacrifice and b. offering, 19.21
beasts enough for a b. offering. 40.16
me your sheep for b. offerings, 43.23
their b. offerings and their 56.07
Your b. offerings are not acceptable, Jer 6.20
"Add your b. offerings to your 7.21
them concerning b. offerings and 7.22
they offer b. offering and cereal 14.12
bringing b. offerings and sacrifices, 17.26
in the fire as b. offerings to 19.05
my presence to offer b. offerings, 33.18
crags, and make you a b. mountain. 51.25
where the b. offering was to be Eze 40.38
on which the b. offering and the 40.39
of hewn stone for the b. offering, 40.42
with which the b. offerings and the 40.42
for offering b. offerings upon it 43.18
and it shall be b. in the appointed 43.21
them up as a b. offering to the 43.24
the altar your b. offerings and 43.27
shall slay the b. offering and the 44.11
b. offerings, and peace offerings, to 45.15
duty to furnish the b. offerings, 45.17
b. offerings, and peace offerings, to make 45.17
provide as a b. offering to the 45.23
b. offerings, and cereal offerings, 45.25
shall offer his b. offering and 46.02
The b. offering that the prince 46.04
either a b. offering or peace 46.12
he shall offer his b. offering or his 46.12
blemish for a b. offering to the 46.13
for the continual b. offering. 46.14
for a continual b. offering. 46.15
the continual b. offering was Dan 8.11
the continual b. offering through 8.12
concerning the continual b. offering, 8.13
away the continual b. offering. 11.31
the continual b. offering is taken 12.11
of God, rather than b. offerings. Hos 6.06
offer me your b. offerings and Amo 5.22
come before him with b. offerings, Mic 6.06
than all whole b. offerings and Mk 12.33
in b. offerings and sin offerings Heb 10.06
offerings and b. offerings and sin 10.08
and a third of the earth was b. up, Rev 8.07
a third of the trees were b. up, 8.07
and all green grass was b. up. 8.07

BURNT-OUT
and a b. waste, unsown, and growing Deu 29.23

BURST
fountains of the great deep b. forth, Gen 7.11
them, and behold, they are b.; Jos 9.13
new wineskins, it is ready to b. Job 32.19
when it b. forth from the womb; 38.08
"Let us b. their bonds asunder, and Ps 2.03
broke your yoke and b. your bonds; Jer 2.20
the yoke, they had b. the bonds. 5.05
it will b. upon the head of the 23.19
and I will b. their bonds, and 30.08
it will b. upon the head of the 30.23
you b. forth in your rivers, trouble Eze 32.02
they b. through the weapons and are Joe 2.08
you and will b. your bonds asunder." Nah 1.13
the skins b., and the wine is Mt 9.17
the wine will b. the skins, and the Mk 2.22
new wine will b. the skins and it Lk 5.37
headlong he b. open in the middle Ac 1.18

BURSTING
enemies before me, like a b. flood." 2Sa 5.20
by my hand, like a b. flood." 1Ch 14.11
and your vats will be b. with wine. Pro 3.10

BURY
that I may b. my dead out of my Gen 23.04
B. your dead in the choicest of our 23.06
that I should b. my dead out of my 23.08
I give it to you; b. your dead." 23.11
me, that I may b. my dead there." 23.13
between you and me? B. your dead." 23.15
with me. Do not b. me in Egypt, 47.29
of Egypt and b. me in their 47.30
b. me with my fathers in the cave 49.29
of Canaan, there shall you b. me.' 50.05
I pray you, and b. my father; 50.05
and b. your father, as he made you 50.06
So Joseph went up to b. his father; 50.07
gone up with him to b. his father. 50.14
but you shall b. him the same day, Deu 21.23
said, strike him down and b. him; 1Ki 2.31
the army went up to b. the slain, 11.15
the city, to mourn and to b. him. 13.29
b. me in the grave in which the man 13.31
shall mourn for him, and b. him; 14.13
of Jezreel, and none shall b. her." 2Ki 9.10
to this cursed woman, and b. her; 9.34
But when they went to b. her, 9.35
they did not b. him in the tombs 2Ch 24.25
and there was none to b. them. Ps 79.03
for they will b. in Topheth, because Jer 7.32
with none to b. them—them, their 14.16
Men shall b. in Topheth because 19.11
there will be no place else to b. 19.11
people of the land will b. them; Eze 39.13
continually and b. those remaining 39.14
gather them, Memphis shall b. them. Hos 9.06
let me first go and b. my father." Mt 8.21
the dead to b. their own dead." 8.22
potter's field, to b. strangers in. 27.07
let me first go and b. my father." Lk 9.59
the dead to b. their own dead; 9.60

BURYING
property among you a b. place, Gen 23.04
or hinder you from b. your dead." 23.06
as a possession for a b. place." 23.09
possession for a b. place by the 23.20
and bury me in their b. place." 47.30
Hittite to possess as a b. place. 49.30
Hittite, to possess as a b. place. 50.13
Egyptians were b. all their first-born, Num 33.04
house of Israel will be b. them, Eze 39.12
anointed my body beforehand for b. Mk 14.08

BUSH
of fire out of the midst of a b.; Ex 3.02
the b. was burning, yet it was not 3.02
sight, why the b. is not burnt." 3.03
to him out of the b., "Moses, Moses!" 3.04
favor of him that dwelt in the b. Deu 33.16
Moses, in the passage about the b., Mk 12.26
grapes picked from a bramble b. Lk 6.44
in the passage about the b., 20.37
Sinai, in a flame of fire in a b. Ac 7.30
that appeared to him in the b. 7.35

BUSHEL
light a lamp and put it under a b., Mt 5.15
brought in to be put under a b., Mk 4.21
puts it in a cellar or under a b., Lk 11.33

BUSHES
cast the child under one of the b. Gen 21.15
they pick mallow and the leaves of b., Job 30.04
Among the b. they bray; under the 30.07

BUSIED
of Aaron were b. in offering the 2Ch 35.14

BUSINESS
the army or be charged with any b.; Deu 24.05
If you do not tell this b. of ours, Jos 2.14
But if you tell this b. of ours, 2.20
place? What is your b. here?" Ju 18.03
the king's b. is required haste." 1Sa 21.08
in Maon, whose b. was in Carmel. 25.02
who have charge of the king's b., Est 3.09
doing b. on the great waters; Ps 107.23
is an unhappy b. that God has Ecc 1.13
I have seen the b. that God has 3.10
also is vanity and an unhappy b. 4.08
For a dream comes with much b., 5.03
and to see the b. that is done on 8.16
rose and went about the king's b.; Dan 8.27
to his farm, another to his b., Mt 22.05
and the money-changers at their b. Jn 2.14
no little b. to the craftsmen. Ac 19.24
that from this b. we have our 19.25

BUSY
your servant was b. here and there, 1Ki 20.40
to b. myself with wicked deeds in Ps 141.04
to the sons of men to be b. with. Ecc 1.13
to the sons of men to be b. with. 3.10
while you b. yourselves each with Hag 1.09

BUSYBODIES
mere b., not doing any work. 2Th 3.11
not only idlers but gossips and b., 1Ti 5.13

BUTLER
the b. of the king of Egypt and his Gen 40.01
the chief b. and the chief baker, 40.02
the b. and the baker of the king of 40.05
So the chief b. told his dream to 40.09
as formerly, when you were his b. 40.13
of the chief b. and the head of 40.20
the chief b. to his butlership, and 40.21
Yet the chief b. did not remember 40.23
Then the chief b. said to Pharaoh, 41.09

BUTLERSHIP
restored the chief butler to his b., Gen 40.21

BUTT
the belly with the b. of his spear, 2Sa 2.23

BUTTER
His speech was smoother than b., Ps 55.21

BUTTOCKS
with b. uncovered, to the shame of Is 20.04

BUY
to Egypt to Joseph to b. grain, Gen 41.57
go down and b. grain for us there, 42.02
went down to b. grain in Egypt. 42.03
Israel came to b. among the others 42.05
the land of Canaan, to b. food." 42.07
but to b. food have your servants 42.10
"Go again, b. us a little food." 43.02
we will go down and b. you food; 43.04
down the first time to b. food; 43.20
money down in our hand to b. food. 43.22
'Go again, b. us a little food,' 44.25
B. us and our land for food, and we 47.19
land of the priests he did not b.; 47.22
When you b. a Hebrew slave, he shall Ex 21.02
neighbor or b. from your neighbor, Lev 25.14
you shall b. from your neighbor, and 25.15
you may b. male and female slaves 25.44
You may also b. from among the 25.45
then he shall b. it back at your 27.27
you shall also b. water of them Deu 2.06
slaves, but no man will b. you." 28.68

BUY (cont.)
B. it in the presence of those Ru 4.04
"The day you b. the field from the 4.05
"B. it for yourself," he drew off 4.08
"To b. the threshing floor of you, 2Sa 24.21
but I will b. it of you for a price; 24.24
as well as to b. timber and quarried 2Ki 12.12
but I will b. it for the full price; 1Ch 21.24
the builders to b. quarried stone, 2Ch 34.11
shall with all diligence b. bulls, Ez 7.17
we will not b. from them on the Neh 10.31
a price in his hand to b. wisdom, Pro 17.16
B. truth, and do not sell it; 23.23
b. wisdom, instruction, and understanding. 23.23
who has no money, come, b. and eat! Is 55.01
Come, b. wine and milk without money 55.01
"Go and b. a linen waistcloth, and Jer 13.01
b. a potter's earthen flask, and take 19.01
'B. my field which is at Anathoth, 32.07
'B. my field which is at Anathoth 32.08
redemption is yours; b. it for yourself. 32.08
"B. the field for money and get 32.25
that we may b. the poor for silver Amo 8.06
Those who b. them slay them and go Zec 11.05
villages and b. food for themselves." Mt 14.15
the dealers and b. for yourselves.' 25.09
And while they went to b., 25.10
round about and b. themselves Mk 6.36
"Shall we go and b. two hundred 6.37
are to go and b. food for all Lk 9.13
sword sell his mantle and b. one. 22.36
gone away into the city to b. food. Jn 4.08
to Philip, "How are we to b. bread, 6.05
would not b. enough bread for each 6.07
"B. what we need for the feast"; or, 13.29
and those who b. as though they had 1Co 7.30
counsel you to b. from me gold Rev 3.18
so that no one can b. or sell 13.17

BUYER
"It is bad, it is bad," says the b.; Pro 20.14
as with the b., so with the seller; Is 24.02
Let not the b. rejoice, nor the Eze 7.12

BUYING
you are also b. Ruth the Moabitess, Ru 4.05
as well as for b. timber and 2Ki 22.06

BUYS
but if a priest b. a slave as his Lev 22.11
She considers a field and b. it; Pro 31.16

all that he has and b. that field. Mt 13.44
since no one b. their cargo any Rev 18.11

BUZ
B. his brother, Kemuel the father of Gen 22.21
Jeshishai, son of Jahdo, son of B.; 1Ch 5.14
Dedan, Tema, B., and all who cut the Jer 25.23

BUZI
the son of B., in the land of the Eze 1.03

BUZITE
Then Elihu the son of Barachel the B., Job 32.02
son of Barachel the B. answered: 32.06

BUZZARD
the b., the kite, after their kinds; Deu 14.13

BYGONE
of b. ages, and consider what the Job 8.08

BYPATHS
roads, and have gone into b., Jer 18.15

BYSTANDERS
saw him, and she said to the b., Mt 26.71
while the b. came up and said to 26.73
And some of the b. hearing it said, 27.47
and began again to say to the b., Mk 14.69
while again the b. said to Peter, 14.70
And some of the b. hearing it said, 15.35

BYWAYS
and travelers kept to the b. Ju 5.06

BYWORD
and a b., among all the peoples Deu 28.37
a proverb and a b. among all 1Ki 9.07
a proverb and a b. among all 2Ch 7.20
"He has made me a b. of the peoples, Job 17.06
their song, I am a b. to them. 30.09
Thou hast made us a b. among the Ps 44.14
my clothing, I became a b. to them. 69.11
a b., a taunt, and a curse in all Jer 24.09
a sign and a b. and cut him off Eze 14.08
sister Sodom a b. in your mouth in 16.56
and she became a b. among women, 23.10
have become a b. among all who are Dan 9.16
a b. among the nations. Why should Joe 2.17
you have been a b. of cursing Zec 8.13

C

CABBON
C. Lahmam, Chitlish, Jos 15.40

CABUL
it continues in the north to C., Jos 19.27
called the land of C. to this day. 1Ki 9.13

CAESAR
lawful to pay taxes to C., or not?" Mt 22.17
therefore to C. the things that 22.21
lawful to pay taxes to C., or not? Mk 12.14
"Render to C. the things that are 12.17
went out from C. Augustus that all Lk 2.01
year of the reign of Tiberius C., 3.01
us to give tribute to C., or not?" 20.22
"Then render to C. the things that 20.25
forbidding us to give tribute to C., 23.02
a king sets himself against C." Jn 19.12
answered, "We have no king but C." 19.15
acting against the decrees of C., Ac 17.07
nor against C. have I offended at 25.08
up to them. I appeal to C." 25.11
answered, "You have appealed to C.; 25.12
to C. you shall go." 25.12
held until I could send him to C." 25.21
free if he had not appealed to C." 26.32
you must stand before C.; 27.24
I was compelled to appeal to C.— 28.19

CAESAREA
into the district of C. Philippi, Mt 16.13
to the villages of C. Philippi; Mk 8.27
all the towns till he came to C. Ac 8.40
it, they brought him down to C., 9.30
At C. there was a man named Cornelius, 10.01
the following day they entered C. 10.24
which we were, sent to me from C. 11.11
Then he went down from Judea to C., 12.19
When he had landed at C., he went 18.22
morrow we departed and came to C.; 21.08
the disciples from C. went with us, 21.16
spearmen to go as far as C. 23.23
When they came to C. and delivered 23.33
he went up to Jerusalem from C. 25.01

CAESAREA (cont.)
that Paul was being kept at C., Ac 25.04
or ten days, he went down to C.; 25.06
arrived at C. to welcome Festus. 25.13

CAESAR'S
They said, "C." Then he said to Mt 22.21
to Caesar the things that are C., 22.21
They said to him, "C." Mk 12.16
to Caesar the things that are C., 12.17
has it?" They said, "C." Lk 20.24
to Caesar the things that are C., 20.25
this man, you are not C. friend; Jn 19.12
"I am standing before C. tribunal, Ac 25.10
especially those of C. household. Php 4.22

CAGE
With hooks they put in a c., Eze 19.09

CAIAPHAS
high priest, who was called C., Mt 26.03
led him to C. the high priest, 26.57
high-priesthood of Annas and C., Lk 3.02
C., who was high priest that year, Jn 11.49
for he was the father-in-law of C., 18.13
It was C. who had given counsel to 18.14
him bound to C. the high priest. 18.24
the house of C. to the praetorium. 18.28
high priest and C. and John and Ac 4.06

CAIN
and she conceived and bore C., Gen 4.01
and C. a tiller of the ground. 4.02
course of time C. brought to the 4.03
but for C. and his offering he had 4.05
So C. was very angry, and his 4.05
The LORD said to C., "Why are you 4.06
C. said to Abel his brother, "Let us 4.08
C. rose up against his brother Abel, 4.08
Then the LORD said to C., "Where 4.09
C. said to the LORD, "My punishment 4.13
If any one slays C., 4.15
And the LORD put a mark on C., 4.15
Then C. went away from the presence 4.16
C. knew his wife, and she conceived 4.17
If C. is avenged sevenfold, truly 4.24
instead of Abel, for C. slew him." 4.25
more acceptable sacrifice than C., Heb 11.04
and not be like C. who was of the 1Jn 3.12
For they walk in the way of C., Jud 1.11

CAINAN
the son of C., the son of Arphaxad, Lk 3.36
son of Mahalaleel, the son of C., 3.37

CAKE
were three c. baskets on my head, Gen 40.16
and one c. of bread with oil, and Ex 29.23
shall offer one c. from each Lev 7.14
the LORD he took one unleavened c., 8.26
and one c. of bread with oil, and 8.26
of an ephah shall be in each c. 24.05
one unleavened c. out of the Num 6.19
shall present a c. as an offering; 15.20
and lo, a c. of barley bread tumbled Ju 7.13
a piece of a c. of figs and two 1Sa 30.12
to each a c. of bread, a portion of 2Sa 6.19
of meat, and a c. of raisins. 6.19
me a little c. of it and bring it 1Ki 17.13
at his head a c. baked on hot 19.06
And Isaiah said, "Bring a c. of figs. 2Ki 20.07
of meat, and a c. of raisins. 1Ch 16.03
said, "Let them take a c. of figs, Is 38.21
And you shall eat it as a barley c., Eze 4.12
Ephraim is a c. not turned. Hos 7.08

CAKES
fine meal, knead it, and make c." Gen 18.06
unleavened c. of the dough which Ex 12.39
unleavened c. mixed with oil, and 29.02
be unleavened c. of fine flour Lev 2.04
unleavened c. mixed with oil, 7.12
and c. of fine flour well mixed 7.12
offering with c. of leavened bread 7.13
flour, and bake twelve c. of it; 24.05
c. of fine flour mixed with oil, and Num 6.15
it in pots, and made c. of it; 11.08
the taste of c. baked with oil. 11.08
unleavened c. and parched grain. Jos 5.11
and unleavened c. from an ephah of Ju 6.19
the meat and the unleavened c., 6.20
the meat and the unleavened c.; 6.21
the flesh and the unleavened c.; 6.21
raisins, and two hundred c. of figs, 1Sa 25.18
make a couple of c. in my sight, 2Sa 13.06
and made c. in his sight, and baked 13.08
in his sight, and baked the c. 13.08
And Tamar took the c. she had made, 13.10
some c., and a jar of honey, and go 1Ki 14.03
in charge of making the flat c. 1Ch 9.31
c. of figs, clusters of raisins, and 12.40
to make c. for the queen of heaven; Jer 7.18
that we made c. for her bearing 44.19
other gods and love c. of raisins." Hos 3.01

CALAH
Nineveh, Rehoboth-Ir, C., and Gen 10.11
Resen between Nineveh and C.; 10.12

CALAMITIES
from all your c. and your distresses; 1Sa 10.19
in afflictions, hardships, c., 2Co 6.04
hardships, persecutions, and c.; 12.10

CALAMITY
all the tribes of Israel for c., Deu 29.21
for the day of their c. is at hand, 32.35
Almighty has brought c. upon me?" Ru 1.21
They came upon me in the day of my c.; 2Sa 22.19
thou brought c. even upon the 1Ki 17.20
to see the c. that is coming to my Est 8.06
and all my c. laid in the balances! Job 6.02
you see my c., and are afraid. 6.21
Cannot my taste discern c.? 6.30
he mocks at the c. of the innocent. 9.23
and c. is ready for his stumbling. 18.12
That their c. comes upon them? 21.17
man is spared in the day of c., 21.30
up my path, they promote my c.; 30.13
Does not c. befall the unrighteous, 31.03
For I was in terror of c. from God, 31.23
They came upon me in the day of my c.; Ps 18.18
altogether who rejoice at my c.! 35.26
I also will laugh at your c.; Pro 1.26
and your c. comes like a whirlwind, 1.27
therefore c. will come upon him 6.15
who is glad at c. will not go 17.05
a perverse tongue falls into c. 17.20
He who sows injustice will reap c., 22.08
the wicked are overthrown by c. 24.16
house in the day of your c. 27.10
his heart will fall into c. 28.14
righteous man is taken away from c., Is 57.01
in vain, or bear children for c.; 65.23
my face, in the day of their c." Jer 18.17
day of their c. has come upon them, 46.21
The c. of Moab is near at hand and 48.16
will bring the c. of Esau upon him, 49.08
bring their c. from every side of 49.32
the sword at the time of their c., Eze 35.05
us, by bringing upon us a great c.; Dan 9.12
all this c. has come upon us, yet we 9.13
kept ready the c. and has brought 9.14
of my people in the day of his c.; Ob 1.13
his disaster in the day of his c.; 1.13
looted his goods in the day of his c. 1.13

CALAMUS
c. and cinnamon, with all trees of Sol 4.14
and c. were bartered for your Eze 27.19

CALCOL
C., and Darda, the sons of Mahol; 1Ki 4.31
C., and Dara, five in all. 1Ch 2.06

CALDRON
the pan, or kettle, or c., or pot; 1Sa 2.14
this city is the c., Eze 11.03
the flesh, and this city is the c.; 11.07
This city shall not be your c., 11.11
in a kettle, like flesh in a c. Mic 3.03

CALDRONS
in c., and in pans, and carried them 2Ch 35.13

CALEB
C. the son of Jephunneh; Num 13.06
But C. quieted the people before 13.30
son of Nun and C. the son of 14.06
But my servant C., because he has a 14.24
except C. the son of Jephunneh and 14.30
son of Nun and C. the son of 14.38
except C. the son of Jephunneh and 26.65
none except C. the son of Jephunneh 32.12
C. the son of Jephunneh. 34.19
except C. the son of Jephunneh; Deu 1.36
and C. the son of Jephunneh the Jos 14.06
gave Hebron to C. the son of 14.13
inheritance of C. the son of 14.14
he gave to C. the son of Jephunneh 15.13
And C. drove out from there the 15.14
And C. said, "Whoever smites Kiriathsepher, 15.16
Kenaz, the brother of C., took it; 15.17
and C. said to her, "What do you 15.18
And C. gave her the upper springs 15.19
been given to C. the son of 21.12
And C. said, "He who attacks Kiriathsepher Ju 1.12
and C. said to her, "What do you 1.14
And C. gave her the upper springs 1.15
And Hebron was given to C., as Moses 1.20
to Judah and upon the Negeb of C.; 1Sa 30.14
C. the son of Hezron had children 1Ch 2.18
C. married Ephrath, who bore him Hur. 2.19
C. went in to Ephrathah, the wife of 2.24
The sons of C. the brother of 2.42
and the daughter of C. was Achsah. 2.49
These were the descendants of C. 2.50
The sons of C. the son of Jephunneh: 4.15
they gave to C. the son of Jephunneh. 6.56

CALEB'S
C. younger brother, took it; Ju 1.13
son of Kenaz, C. younger brother. 3.09
Ephah also, C. concubine, bore Haran, 1Ch 2.46
Maacah, C. concubine, bore Sheber and 2.48

CALEBITE
and ill-behaved; he was a C. 1Sa 25.03

CALF
and took a c., tender and good, and Gen 18.07
and the c. which he had prepared, 18.08
graving tool, and made a molten c.; Ex 32.04
made for themselves a molten c., 32.08
and saw the c. and the dancing, 32.19
And he took the c. which they had 32.20
fire, and there came out this c." 32.24
they made the c. which Aaron made. 32.35
"Take a bull c. for a sin offering, Lev 9.02
and a c. and a lamb, both a year old 9.03
and killed the c. of the sin 9.08
had made yourselves a molten c.; Deu 9.16
the c. which you had made, and 9.21
woman had a fatted c. in the house, 1Sa 28.24
themselves a molten c. and said, Neh 9.18
calves, and does not cast her c. Job 21.10
He makes Lebanon to skip like a c., Ps 29.06
They made a c. in Horeb and worshiped 106.19
and the c. and the lion and the Is 11.06
there the c. grazes, there he lies 27.10
her newborn c. because there is no Jer 14.05
chastened, like an untrained c.; 31.18
make like the c. which they cut in 34.18
passed between the parts of the c.; 34.19
I have spurned your c., O Samaria. Hos 8.05
The c. of Samaria shall be broken 8.06
tremble for the c. of Bethaven. 10.05
and bring the fatted c. and kill it, Lk 15.23
father has killed the fatted c.,' 15.27
you killed for him the fatted c.!' 15.30
And they made a c. in those days, Ac 7.41

CALF'S
back of the throne was a c. head, 1Ki 10.19
were like the sole of a c. foot; Eze 1.07

CALL
man to see what he would c. them; Gen 2.19
men began to c. upon the name of 4.26
you shall c. his name Ishmael; 16.11
you shall not c. her name Sarai, but 17.15
and you shall c. his name Isaac. 17.19
"We will c. the maiden, and ask her." 24.57
For the women will c. me happy"; 30.13
"Shall I go and c. you a nurse from Ex 2.07
C. him, that he may eat bread." 2.20
And Moses sent to c. Dathan and Num 16.12
in the land of Amaw to c. him, 22.05
"If the men have come to c. you, 22.20
"Did I not send to you to c. you? 22.37
but the Moabites c. them Emim. Deu 2.11
the Ammonites c. them Zamzummim, 2.20
(the Sidonians c. Hermon Sirion, 3.09
while the Amorites c. it Senir), 3.09
is to us, whenever we c. upon him? 4.07
I c. heaven and earth to witness 4.26
elders of his city shall c. him, 25.08
and you c. them to mind among all 30.01
I c. heaven and earth to witness 30.19
c. Joshua, and present yourselves in 31.14
their ears and c. heaven and earth 31.28
They shall c. peoples to their 33.19
not to c. us when you went to fight Ju 8.01
and did not c. us to go with you? 12.01
"C. Samson, that he may make sport 16.25
"Do not c. me Naomi, c. me Mara, Ru 1.20
Why c. me Naomi, when the LORD has 1.21
But he said, "I did not c.; 1Sa 3.05
But he said, "I did not c., my son; 3.06
I will c. upon the LORD, that he may 12.17
Absalom would c. to him, and say, 2Sa 15.02
"C. Hushai the Archite also, and let 17.05
"C. the men of Judah together to me 20.04
I c. upon the LORD, who is worthy to 22.04
"C. Bathsheba to me." So she came 1Ki 1.28
"C. to me Zadok the priest, Nathan 1.32
to them whenever they c. to thee. 8.52
And you c. on the name of your god 18.24
I will c. on the name of the Lord; 18.24
and c. on the name of your god, but 18.25
"C. this Shunammite." When he 2Ki 4.12
He said, "C. her." And when 4.15
"C. this Shunammite." So he called 4.36
and c. on the name of the LORD his 5.11
Now therefore c. to me all the 10.19
c. on his name, make known his deeds 1Ch 16.08
to sound the c. to battle against 2Ch 13.12
"C. now; is there any one Job 5.01
Then c., and I will answer; 13.22
Thou wouldest c., and I would 14.15
I c. aloud, but there is no justice. 19.07
I c. to my servant, but he gives me 19.16
Will he c. upon God at all times? 27.10

CALL (cont.)

they c. for help because of the arm Job 35.09
Answer me when I c., O God of Ps 4.01
the LORD hears when I c. to him. 4.03
"Thou wilt not c. to account"? 10.13
bread, and do not c. upon the LORD? 14.04
I c. upon thee, for thou wilt answer 17.06
I c. upon the LORD, who is worthy to 18.03
O LORD; answer us when we c. 20.09
To thee, O LORD, I c.; my rock 28.01
to shame, O LORD, for I c. on thee; 31.17
and c. upon me in the day of 50.15
eat bread, and do not c. upon God? 53.04
But I c. upon God; and the LORD 55.16
turned back in the day when I c. 56.09
from the end of the earth I c. to thee, 61.02
up my hands and c. on thy name. 63.04
by him, all nations c. him blessed! 72.17
we c. on thy name and recount thy 75.01
I will c. to mind the deeds of the 77.11
kingdoms that do not c. on thy name! 79.06
life, and we will c. on thy name! 80.18
steadfast love to all who c. on thee. 86.05
the day of my trouble I c. on thee, 86.07
I c. for help by day; I cry out 88.01
Every day I c. upon thee, O LORD; 88.09
me speedily in the day when I c.! 102.02
c. on his name, make known his deeds 105.01
therefore I will c. on him as long 116.02
salvation and c. on the name of 116.13
thanksgiving and c. on the name of 116.17
I c. upon thee, O LORD; make haste 141.01
ear to my voice, when I c. to thee! 141.01
is near to all who c. upon him, 145.18
to all who c. upon him in truth. 145.18
Then they will c. upon me, but I Pro 1.28
and c. insight your intimate 7.04
Does not wisdom c., does not 8.01
I c., and my cry is to the sons of 8.04
her maids to c. from the highest 9.03
children rise up and c. her blessed; 31.28
Woe to those who c. evil good and Is 5.20
and shall c. his name Immanuel. 7.14
"C. his name Mahershalalhashbaz; 8.03
"Do not c. conspiracy all that this 8.12
all that this people c. conspiracy, 8.12
to the LORD, c. upon his name; 12.04
In that day I will c. my servant 22.20
he does not c. back his words, but 31.02
sun, and he shall c. on my name; 41.25
"Yet you did not c. upon me, 43.22
another will c. himself by the 44.05
of Israel, who c. you by your name, 45.03
I c. you by your name, I surname you, 45.04
For they c. themselves after the 48.02
when I c. to them, they stand forth 48.13
you shall c. nations that you know 55.05
c. upon him while he is near; 55.06
will you c. this a fast, and a day 58.05
Then you shall c., and the LORD 58.09
and c. the sabbath a delight and 58.13
they shall c. you the City of the 60.14
you shall c. your walls Salvation, 60.18
nation that did not c. on my name. 65.01
servants he will c. by a different 65.15
Before they c. I will answer, while 65.24
And I thought you would c. me, Jer 3.19
You shall c. to them, but they will 7.27
and c. for the mourning women to 9.17
peoples that c. not on thy name; 10.25
when they c. to me in the time of 11.14
LORD does not c. your name Pashhur, 20.03
Then you will c. upon me and come 29.12
watchmen will c. in the hill 31.06
C. to me and I will answer you, and 33.03
C. the name of Pharaoh, king of 46.17
though I c. and cry for help, he Lam 3.08
But this I c. to mind, and therefore 3.21
"C. his name Jezreel; for yet a Hos 1.04
"C. her name Not pitied, for I will 1.06
"C. his name Not my people, for you 1.09
you will c. me, 'My husband,' and no 2.16
no longer will you c. me, 'My Baal.' 2.16
c. a solemn assembly. Gather the Joe 1.14
a fast; c. a solemn assembly; 2.15
that all who c. upon the name of 2.32
They shall c. the farmers to Amo 5.16
Arise, c. upon your god! Jon 1.06
all of them may c. on the name of Zep 3.09
They will c. on my name, and I will Zec 13.09
Then all nations will c. you blessed, Mal 3.12
and you shall c. his name Jesus, for Mt 1.21
For I came not to c. the righteous, 9.13
'C. the laborers and pay them their 20.08
his servants to c. those who were 22.03
And c. no man your father on earth, 23.09
his angels with a loud trumpet c., 24.31
I came not to c. the righteous, but Mk 2.17
said to him, "Why do you c. me good? 10.18
And Jesus stopped and said, "C. him." 10.49
man whom you c. the King of the 15.12
and you shall c. his name John. Lk 1.13
and you shall c. his name Jesus. 1.31
all generations will c. me blessed; 1.48
I have not come to c. the righteous, 5.32
"Why do you c. me 'Lord, Lord,' and 6.46
said to him, "Why do you c. me good? 18.19
c. your husband, and come here." Jn 4.16
You c. me Teacher and Lord; 13.13
No longer do I c. you servants, for 15.15
to bind all who c. upon thy name." Ac 9.14
cleansed, you must not c. common." 10.15
I should not c. any man common or 10.28
cleansed you must not c. common.' 11.09
which they c. a sect, I worship the 24.14
But if you c. yourself a Jew and Rom 2.17
of works but because of his c., 9.11
not my people I will c. 'my people,' 9.25
not beloved I will c. 'my beloved.'" 9.25
riches upon all who c. upon him. 10.12
But how are men to c. upon him in 10.14
gifts and the c. of God are 11.29
in every place c. on the name of 1Co 1.02
For consider your c., brethren; 1.26
the time of his c. already circumcised? 7.18
the time of his c. uncircumcised? 7.18
But I c. God to witness against me— 2Co 1.23
one hope that belongs to your c., Eph 4.04
of the upward c. of God in Christ Php 3.14
command, with the archangel's c., 1Th 4.16
God may make you worthy of his c., 2Th 1.11
with those who c. upon the Lord 2Ti 2.22
not ashamed to c. them brethren, Heb 2.11
brethren, who share in a heavenly c., 3.01
Behold, we c. those happy who were Jas 5.11
Let him c. for the elders of the 5.14
to confirm your c. and election, 2Pe 1.10
those who c. themselves apostles Rev 2.02
what some c. the deep things of 2.24
of the trumpet c. to be sounded by 10.07
Here is a c. for the endurance and 13.10
Here is a c. for the endurance of 14.12

CALLED

God c. the light Day, and the Gen 1.05
Day, and the darkness he c. Night. 1.05
And God c. the firmament Heaven. 1.08
God c. the dry land Earth, and the 1.10
were gathered together he c. Seas. 1.10
whatever the man c. every living 2.19
she shall be c. Woman, because she 2.23
But the LORD God c. to the man, 3.09
The man c. his wife's name Eve, 3.20
and c. the name of the city after 4.17

CALLED (cont.)

bore a son and c. his name Seth, Gen 4.25
was born, and he c. his name Enosh. 4.26
and c. his name Noah, saying, "Out of 5.29
Therefore its name was c. Babel, 11.09
to the LORD and c. on the name of 12.08
So Pharaoh c. Abram, and said, "What 12.18
and there Abram c. on the name of 13.04
So she c. the name of the LORD who 16.13
Therefore the well was c. Beerlahairoi; 16.14
and Abram c. the name of his son, 16.15
and they c. to Lot, "Where are the 19.05
the name of the city was c. Zoar. 19.22
bore a son, and c. his name Moab; 19.37
and c. his name Benammi; 19.38
and c. all his servants, and told 20.08
Then Abimelech c. Abraham, and said 20.09
Abraham c. the name of his son who 21.03
angel of God c. to Hagar from 21.17
Therefore that place was c. Beersheba; 21.31
and c. there on the name of the 21.33
of the LORD c. to him from heaven, 22.11
So Abraham c. the name of that 22.14
of the LORD c. to Abraham a second 22.15
And they c. Rebekah, and said to her, 24.58
so they c. his name Esau. 25.25
so his name was c. Jacob. 25.26
(Therefore his name was c. Edom.) 25.30
So Abimelech c. Isaac, and said, 26.09
So he c. the name of the well Esek, 26.20
so he c. its name Sitnah. 26.21
so he c. its name Rehoboth, saying, 26.22
altar there and c. upon the name 26.25
He c. it Shibah; therefore the 26.33
he c. Esau his older son, and said 27.01
so she sent and c. Jacob her 27.42
Then Isaac c. Jacob and blessed him, 28.01
He c. the name of that place Bethel; 28.19
and she c. his name Reuben; for she said, 29.32
son also"; and she c. his name Simeon. 29.33
therefore his name was c. Levi. 29.34
therefore she c. his name Judah; 29.35
therefore she c. his name Dan. 30.06
so she c. his name Naphtali. 30.08
so she c. his name Gad. 30.11
so she c. his name Asher. 30.13
so she c. his name Issachar. 30.18
so she c. his name Zebulun. 30.20
a daughter, and c. her name Dinah. 30.21
and she c. his name Joseph, saying, 30.24
So Jacob sent and c. Rachel and 31.04
Laban c. it Jegarsahadutha: but 31.47
Jegarsahadutha: but Jacob c. it Galeed. 31.47
mountain and c. his kinsmen to eat 31.54
So he c. the name of that place 32.02
name shall no more be c. Jacob, 32.28
So Jacob c. the name of the place 32.30
name of the place is c. Succoth. 33.17
an altar and c. it El-Elohe-Israel. 33.20
and c. the place Elbethel, because 35.07
the name of it was c. Allonbacuth. 35.08
longer shall your name be c. Jacob, 35.10
your name." So his name was c. Israel. 35.10
So Jacob c. the name of the place 35.15
she c. his name Benoni; but his 35.18
but his father c. his name Benjamin. 35.18
bore a son, and he c. his name Er. 38.03
a son, and she c. his name Onan. 38.04
and she c. his name Shelah. 38.05
Therefore his name was c. Perez. 38.29
she c. his name was c. Zerah. 38.30
she c. to the men of her household 39.14
and he sent and c. for all the 41.08
Then Pharaoh sent and c. Joseph, 41.14
Pharaoh c. Joseph's name Zaphenathpaneah; 41.45
Joseph c. the name of the first-born 41.51
The name of the second he c. Ephraim, 41.52
he c. his son Joseph and said to 47.29
they shall be c. by the name of 48.06
Then Jacob c. his sons, and said, 49.01
So the king of Egypt c. the midwives, Ex 1.18
girl went and c. the child's mother. 2.08
and he c. his name Gershom; 2.22
God c. to him out of the bush, 3.04
Then Pharaoh c. Moses and Aaron, and 8.08
Then Pharaoh c. Moses and Aaron, and 8.25
and c. Moses and Aaron, and said to 9.27
Then Pharaoh c. Moses and Aaron in 10.16
Then Pharaoh c. Moses, and said, "Go, 10.24
Then Moses c. all the elders of 12.21
house of Israel c. its name manna; 16.31
And he c. the name of the place 17.07
an altar and c. the name of it, 17.15
and the LORD c. him out of the 19.03
So Moses came and c. the elders of 19.07
and the LORD c. Moses to the top of 19.20
seventh day he c. to Moses out of 24.16
"See, I have c. by name Bezalel the 31.02
and he c. it the tent of meeting. 33.07
But Moses c. to them; 34.31
the LORD has c. by name Bezalel the 35.30
And Moses c. Bezalel and Oholiab 36.02
The LORD c. Moses, and spoke to him Lev 1.01
day Moses c. Aaron and his sons 9.01
And Moses c. Mishael and Elzaphan, 10.04
name of that place was c. Taberah, Num 11.03
that place was c. Kibrothhattaavah, 11.34
and c. Aaron and Miriam; 12.05
And Moses c. Hoshea the son of Nun 13.16
That place was c. the Valley of 13.24
name of the place was c. Hormah. 21.03
"I c. you to curse my enemies, and 24.10
and c. them Havvothjair. 32.41
and c. it Nobah, after his own name. 32.42
that Bashan is c. the land of Deu 3.13
and c. the villages after his own 3.14
of his house shall be c. in Israel, 25.10
that you are c. by the name of the 28.10
Then Joshua c. the twelve men from Jos 4.04
that place is c. Gilgal to this 5.09
the son of Nun c. the priests and 6.06
that place is c. the Valley of 7.26
the city were c. together to 8.16
and the Gadites c. the altar 22.34
the name of the city was c. Hormah. Ju 1.17
built a city, and c. its name Luz; 1.26
And they c. the name of that place 2.05
Sisera c. out all his chariots, nine 4.13
and c. it, The LORD is peace. 6.24
Therefore on that day he was c. Jerubbaal, 6.32
Abiezrites were c. out to follow 6.34
they too were c. out to follow him 6.35
of Israel were c. out from Naphtali 7.23
all the men of Ephraim were c. out, 7.24
and he c. his name Abimelech. 8.31
Then he c. hastily to the young man 9.54
c. Havvothjair to this day, which 10.04
Then the Ammonites were c. to arms, 10.17
The men of Ephraim were c. to arms, 12.01
and when I c. you, you did not 12.02
and c. his name Samson; 13.24
and that place was c. Ramathlehi. 15.17
and he c. on the LORD and said, 15.18
the name of it was c. Enhakkore; 15.19
she sent and c. the lords of the 16.18
and she c. a man, and had him shave 16.19
So they c. Samson out of the prison, 16.25
Then Samson c. to the LORD and said, 16.28
that place is c. Mahanehdan to 18.12
near Micah's house were c. out, 18.22
and she c. his name Samuel, for she 1Sa 1.20
Then the LORD c., "Samuel!" 3.04
and said, "Here I am, for you c. me." 3.05
And the LORD c. again, "Samuel!" 3.06

CALLED (cont.)
and said, "Here I am, for you c. me." 1Sa 3.06
And the LORD c. Samuel again the 3.08
and said, "Here I am, for you c. me." 3.08
But Eli c. Samuel and said, "Samuel, 3.16
And the Philistines c. for the 6.02
and c. its name Ebenezer; 7.12
he who is now c. a prophet was 9.09
a prophet was formerly c. a seer. 9.09
of dawn Samuel c. to Saul upon the 9.26
Now Samuel c. the people together 10.17
So Samuel c. upon the LORD, and the 12.18
the people were c. out to join 13.04
Then Jesse c. Abinadab, and made him 16.08
And Jonathan c. David, and Jonathan 19.07
Jonathan c. after the lad and said, 20.37
And Jonathan c. after the lad, 20.38
that place was c. the Rock of 23.28
and c. after Saul, "My lord the king!" 24.08
and David c. to the army, and to 26.14
Then Achish c. David and said to 29.06
him, he saw me, and c. to me. 2Sa 1.07
Then David c. one of the young men 1.15
that place was c. Helkathhazzurim, 2.16
Then Abner c. to Joab, "Shall the 2.26
and c. it the city of David. 5.09
of that place is c. Baalperazim. 5.20
which is c. by the name of the LORD 6.02
and that place is c. Perezuzzah, 6.08
was Ziba, and they c. him to David; 9.02
Then the king c. Ziba, Saul's servant, 9.09
and he c. his name Solomon. 12.24
so he c. his name Jedidiah, because 12.25
the city, and it be c. by my name." 12.28
He c. the young man who served him 13.17
he c. the pillar after his own name, 18.18
and it is c. Absalom's monument to 18.18
And the watchman c. out and told 18.25
the watchman c. to the gate and 18.26
Then a wise woman c. from the city, 20.16
c. Sheba the son of Bichri, has 20.21
So the king c. the Gibeonites. 21.02
"In my distress I c. upon the LORD; 22.07
to my God I c. From his temple 22.07
the south and c. its name Jachin; 1Ki 7.21
on the north and c. its name Boaz. 7.21
I have built is c. by thy name. 8.43
So they are c. the land of Cabul to 9.13
And they sent and c. him; 12.03
they sent and c. him to the assembly 12.20
and c. the name of the city which 16.24
and he c. to her and said, "Bring me 17.10
he c. to her and said, "Bring me a 17.11
And Ahab c. Obadiah, who was over 18.03
and c. on the name of Baal from 18.26
king of Israel c. all the elders 20.07
The LORD has c. these three kings 2Ki 3.10
LORD who has c. these three kings 3.13
were c. out, and were drawn up at 3.21
When he had c. her, she stood 4.12
And when he had c. her, she stood 4.15
Then she c. to her husband, and said, 4.22
So he c. her. And when she 4.36
and he c. his servants and said to 6.11
So they came and c. to the gatekeepers 7.10
Then the gatekeepers c. out, 7.11
for the LORD has c. for a famine, 8.01
the prophet c. one of the sons of 9.01
and c. it Joktheel, which is its 14.07
incense to it; it was c. Nehushtan. 18.04
And when they c. for the king, there 18.18
stood and c. out in a loud voice 18.28
and his mother c. his name Jabez, 1Ch 4.09
Jabez c. on the God of Israel, 4.10
and she c. his name Peresh; 7.16
and he c. his name Beriah, because 7.23
therefore it was c. the city of 11.07
which is c. by the name of the LORD 13.06
that place is c. Perezuzza to this 13.11
of that place is c. Baalperazim. 14.11
and c. upon the LORD, and he answered 21.26
Then he c. for Solomon his son, and 22.06
that on the south he c. Jachin, 2Ch 3.17
I have built is c. by thy name. 6.33
people who are c. by my name 7.14
And they sent and c. him; 10.03
place has been c. the Valley of 20.26
Gileadite, was c. by their name). Ez 2.61
And I c. the priests, and took an Neh 5.12
Gileadite and was c. by their name). 7.63
Then Esther c. for Hathach, one of Est 4.05
the inner court without being c., 4.11
I have not been c. to come in to 4.11
Therefore they c. these days Purim, 9.26
I, who c. upon God and he answered Job 12.04
it c. me blessed, and when the eye 29.11
or c. fine gold my confidence; 31.24
And he c. the name of the first 42.14
In my distress I c. upon the LORD; Ps 18.06
he is c. blessed in the land; 41.02
In distress you c., and I delivered 81.07
was among those who c. on his name. 99.06
Then I c. on the name of the LORD: 116.04
Out of my distress I c. on the LORD; 118.05
On the day I c., thou didst answer 138.03
Because I have c. and you refused Pro 1.24
who hold her fast are c. happy. 3.18
of heart is c. a man of discernment, 16.21
do evil will be c. a mischief-maker. 24.08
I c. him, but he gave no answer. Sol 3.01
I c. him, but he gave no answer. 5.06
maidens saw her and c. her happy; 6.09
you shall be c. the city of Is 1.26
only let us be c. by your name; 4.01
in Jerusalem will be c. holy, 4.03
And one c. to another and said: 6.03
shook at the voice of him who c., 6.04
name will be c. "Wonderful Counselor, 9.06
these will be c. the City of the 19.18
c. to weeping and mourning, to 22.12
therefore I have c. her "Rahab who 30.07
of shepherds is c. forth against 31.04
The fool will no more be c. noble, 32.05
and it shall be c. the Holy Way; 35.08
stood and c. out in a loud voice 36.13
and c. from its farthest corners, 41.09
I have c. you in righteousness, I 42.06
I have c. you by name, you are mine. 43.01
every one who is c. by my name, 43.07
no more be c. tender and delicate. 47.01
no more be c. the mistress of 47.05
who are c. by the name of Israel, 48.01
from birth you were c. a rebel. 48.08
me, O Jacob, and Israel, whom I c.! 48.12
I, even I, have spoken and c. him, 48.15
The LORD c. me from the womb, from 49.01
When I c., was there no one to 50.02
for when he was but one I c. him, 51.02
God of the whole earth he is c. 54.05
For the LORD has c. you like a wife 54.06
house shall be c. a house of 56.07
you shall be c. the repairer of the 58.12
they may be c. oaks of righteousness, 61.03
but you shall be c. the priests of 61.06
you shall be c. by a new name 62.02
you shall be c. My delight is in 62.04
And they shall be c. The holy 62.12
and you shall be c. Sought out, 62.12
those who are not c. by thy name. 63.19
when I c., you did not answer, when 65.12
when I c., no one answered, when I 66.04
Have you not just now c. to me, Jer 3.04
shall be c. the throne of the LORD, 3.17
Refuse silver they are c., 6.30

CALLED (cont.)

which is c. by my name, and say, 'We Jer 7.10
which is c. by my name, become a den 7.11
and when I c. you, you did not 7.13
the house which is c. by my name, 7.14
the house which is c. by my name, 7.30
when it will no more be c. Topheth, 7.32
The LORD once c. you, 'A green olive 11.16
of us, and we are c. by thy name; 14.09
for I am c. by thy name, O LORD, God 15.16
place shall no more be c. Topheth, 19.06
is the name by which he will be c.: 23.06
at the city which is c. by my name, 25.29
they have c. you an outcast: 30.17
the house which is c. by my name, 32.34
is the name by which it will be c.: 33.16
The house which is c. by my name; 34.15
I have c. to them and they have not 35.17
Then Jeremiah c. Baruch the son of 36.04
"I c. to my lovers but they deceived Lam 1.19
city which was c. the perfection 2.15
"I c. on thy name, O LORD, from the 3.55
Thou didst come near when I c. on thee; 3.57
and he c. to the man clothed in Eze 9.03
they were c. in my hearing the 10.13
So its name is c. Bamah to this day.) 20.29
it will be c. the Valley of Hamongog. 39.11
Daniel he c. Belteshazzar, Hananiah Dan 1.07
Hananiah he c. Shadrach, Mishael he 1.07
Mishael he c. Meshach, and Azariah 1.07
Meshach, and Azariah he c. Abednego. 1.07
Now let Daniel be c., and he will 5.12
and it c., "Gabriel, make this man 8.16
the city which is c. by thy name; 9.18
and thy people are c. by thy name." 9.19
him, and out of Egypt I c. my son. Hos 11.01
The more I c. them, the more they 11.02
the nations who are c. by my name, Amo 9.12
saying, "I c. to the LORD, out of my Jon 2.02
And I have c. for a drought upon Hag 1.11
"As I c., and they would not hear, Zec 7.13
so they c., and I would not hear," 7.13
shall be c. the faithful city, and 8.03
till they are c. the wicked country, Mal 1.04
Jesus was born, who is c. Christ. Mt 1.16
name shall be c. Emmanuel" (which 1.23
and he c. his name Jesus. 1.25
"Out of Egypt have I c. my son." 2.15
and dwelt in a city c. Nazareth, 2.23
fulfilled, "He shall be c. a Nazarene." 2.23
Simon who is c. Peter and Andrew 4.18
mending their nets, and he c. them. 4.21
for they shall be c. sons of God. 5.09
shall be c. least in the kingdom of 5.19
them shall be c. great in the 5.19
he saw a man c. Matthew sitting at 9.09
And he c. to him his twelve disciples 10.01
who is c. Peter, and Andrew his 10.02
If they have c. the master of the 10.25
Is not his mother c. Mary? 13.55
And he c. the people to him and 15.10
Then Jesus c. his disciples to him 15.32
But Jesus c. them to him and said, 20.25
And Jesus stopped and c. them, 20.32
house shall be c. a house of 21.13
For many are c., but few are chosen." 22.14
places, and being c. rabbi by men. 23.07
But you are not to be c. rabbi, 23.08
Neither be c. masters, for you have 23.10
on a journey c. his servants and 25.14
high priest, who was c. Caiaphas, 26.03
who was c. Judas Iscariot, went to 26.14
with them to a place c. Gethsemane, 26.36
field has been c. the Field of 27.08
a notorious prisoner, c. Barabbas. 27.16
Barabbas or Jesus who is c. Christ?" 27.17
I do with Jesus who is c. Christ?" 27.22
came to a place c. Golgotha (which 27.33
And immediately he c. them; Mk 1.20
and c. to him those whom he desired; 3.13
And he c. them to him, and said to 3.23
they sent to him and c. him. 3.31
And he c. to him the twelve, and 6.07
and he c. the people to him again, 7.14
he c. his disciples to him, and said 8.01
And he c. to him the multitude with 8.34
And he sat down and c. the twelve; 9.35
And Jesus c. them to him and said 10.42
And they c. the blind man, saying 10.49
house shall be c. a house of 11.17
And he c. his disciples to him, and 12.43
to a place which was c. Gethsemane; 14.32
there was a man c. Barabbas. 15.07
and they c. together the whole 15.16
to the place c. Golgotha (which 15.22
and will be c. the Son of the Most Lk 1.32
child to be born will be c. holy, 1.35
month with her who was c. barren. 1.36
"Not so; he shall be c. John." 1.60
of your kindred is c. by this name." 1.61
inquiring what he would have him c. 1.62
will be c. the prophet of the Most 1.76
which is c. Bethlehem, because he 2.04
he was c. Jesus, the name given by 2.21
womb shall be c. holy to the Lord") 2.23
he c. his disciples, and chose from 6.13
and Simon who was c. the Zealot, 6.15
afterward he went to a city c. Nain, 7.11
c. Magdalene, from whom seven demons 8.02
he c. out, "He who has ears to hear, 8.08
But taking her by the hand he c., 8.54
And he c. the twelve together and 9.01
apart to a city c. Bethsaida. 9.10
And she had a sister c. Mary, 10.39
he c. her and said to her, "Woman, 13.12
no longer worthy to be c. your son; 15.19
no longer worthy to be c. your son.' 15.21
And he c. one of the servants and 15.26
And he c. him and said to him, 'What 16.02
And he c. out, 'Father Abraham, have 16.24
But Jesus c. them to him, saying, 18.16
to be c. to him, that he might know 19.15
at the mount that is c. Olivet, 19.29
and lodged on the mount c. Olivet. 21.37
near, which is c. the Passover. 22.01
entered into Judas c. Iscariot, 22.03
over them are c. benefactors. 22.25
and the man c. Judas, one of the 22.47
Pilate then c. together the chief 23.13
to the place which is c. The Skull, 23.33
You shall be c. Cephas" (which means Jn 1.42
answered him, "Before Philip c. you, 1.48
of the feast c. the bridegroom 2.09
c. Sychar, near the field that Jacob 4.05
is coming (he who is c. Christ); 4.25
in Hebrew c. Bethzatha, which has 5.02
sabbath but also c. God his Father, 5.18
"The man c. Jesus made clay and 9.11
until they c. the parents of the 9.18
time they c. the man who had been 9.24
If he c. them gods to whom the word 10.35
Thomas, c. the Twin, said to his 11.16
she went and c. her sister Mary, 11.28
wilderness, to a town c. Ephraim; 11.54
him when he c. Lazarus out of the 12.17
but I have c. you friends, for all 15.15
the praetorium again and c. Jesus, 18.33
seat at a place c. The Pavement, 19.13
to the place c. the place of a 19.17
which is c. in Hebrew Golgotha. 19.17
c. the Twin, was not with them when 20.24
Thomas c. the Twin, Nathanael of 21.02
Jerusalem from the mount c. Olivet, Ac 1.12
the field was c. in their language 1.19

CALLED (cont.)

Joseph c. Barsabbas, who was surnamed Ac 1.23
temple which is c. Beautiful to 3.02
them in the portico c. Solomon's, 3.11
So they c. them and charged them 4.18
with him and c. together the 5.21
when they had c. in the apostles, 5.40
of the Freedmen (as it was c.), 6.09
And Joseph sent and c. to him Jacob 7.14
power of God which is c. Great. 8.10
and go to the street c. Straight, 9.11
of those who c. on this name? 9.21
bring one Simon who is c. Peter; 10.05
he c. two of his servants and a 10.07
and c. out to ask whether Simon who 10.18
Simon who was c. Peter was lodging 10.18
So he c. them in to be his guests. 10.23
them and had c. together his 10.24
and ask for Simon who is c. Peter; 10.32
to Joppa and bring Simon c. Peter; 11.13
for the first time c. Christians. 11.26
Barnabas, Symeon who was c. Niger, 13.01
the work to which I have c. them." 13.02
who is also c. Paul, filled with the 13.09
Barnabas they c. Zeus, and Paul, 14.12
the chief speaker, they c. Hermes. 14.12
Gentiles who are c. by my name, 15.17
They sent Judas c. Barsabbas, 15.22
to take with them John c. Mark. 15.37
that God had c. us to preach the 16.10
And he c. for lights and rushed in, 16.29
to Ephesus and c. to him the 20.17
And Paul c. one of the centurions 23.17
the prisoner c. me and asked me to 23.18
Then he c. two of the centurions 23.23
and when he was c., Tertullus 24.02
we came to a place c. Fair Havens, 27.08
c. the northeaster, struck down from 27.14
the lee of a small island c. Cauda, 27.16
then learned that the island was c. Malta. 28.01
After three days he c. together the 28.17
c. to be an apostle, set apart for Rom 1.01
yourselves who are c. to belong to 1.06
who are c. to be saints: Grace to 1.07
she will be c. an adulteress if she 7.03
who are c. according to his purpose 8.28
whom he predestined he also c.; 8.30
those whom he c. he also justified; 8.30
even us whom he has c., not from 9.24
they will be c. 'sons of the 9.26
Paul, c. by the will of God to be an 1Co 1.01
c. to be saints together with all 1.02
whom you were c. into the fellowship 1.09
but to those who are c., both Jews 1.24
For God has c. us to peace. 7.15
him, and in which God has c. him. 7.17
in the state in which he was c. 7.20
Were you a slave when c.? 7.21
For he who was c. in the Lord as a 7.22
was free when c. is a slave of 7.22
in whatever state each was c., 7.24
he is c. to account by all, 14.24
unfit to be c. an apostle, because I 15.09
deserting him who c. you in the Gal 1.06
and had c. me through his grace, 1.15
persuasion is not from him who c. you. 5.08
For you were c. to freedom, brethren; 5.13
is the hope to which he has c. you, Eph 1.18
c. the uncircumcision by what is 2.11
by what is c. the circumcision, 2.11
calling to which you have been c., 4.01
as you were c. to the one hope 4.04
indeed you were c. in the one body. Col 3.15
and Jesus who is c. Justus. 4.11
For God has not c. us for uncleanness, 1Th 4.07
To this he c. you through our 2Th 2.14
which you were c. when you made 1Ti 6.12
of what is falsely c. knowledge, 6.20
who saved us and c. us with a holy 2Ti 1.09
day, as long as it is c. "today," Heb 3.13
but he is c. by God, just as Aaron 5.04
Presence; it is c. the Holy Place. 9.02
stood a tent c. the Holy of Holies, 9.03
those who are c. may receive the 9.15
when he was c. to go out to a 11.08
is not ashamed to be c. their God, 11.16
refused to be c. the son of Pharaoh's 11.24
honorable name by which you are c.? Jas 2.07
and he was c. the friend of God. 2.23
but as he who c. you is holy, be 1Pe 1.15
of him who c. you out of darkness 2.09
For to this you have been c., 2.21
for to this you have been c., 3.09
who has c. you to his eternal glory 5.10
of him who c. us to his own glory 2Pe 1.03
we should be c. children of God; 1Jn 3.01
of James, To those who are c., Jud 1.01
on the island c. Patmos on account Rev 1.09
and he c. with a loud voice to the 7.02
and in Greek he is c. Appollyon. 9.11
and c. out with a loud voice, like a 10.03
when he c. out, the seven thunders 10.03
allegorically c. Sodom and Egypt, 11.08
who is c. the Devil and Satan, the 12.09
and he c. with a loud voice to him 14.18
at the place which is c. in Hebrew 16.16
with him are c. and chosen and 17.14
And he c. out with a mighty voice, 18.02
sat upon it is c. Faithful and 19.11
by which he is c. is The Word of 19.13
a loud voice he c. to all the 19.17

CALLING

c. Leshem, Dan, after the name of Dan Jos 19.47
that the LORD was c. the boy. 1Sa 3.08
c. as at other times, "Samuel! 3.10
c. to those who pass by, who are Pro 9.15
sabbath and the c. of assemblies— Is 1.13
One is c. to me from Seir, "Watchman, 21.11
c. them all by name; by the greatness 40.26
c. the generations from the beginning? 41.04
c. a bird of prey from the east, the 46.11
For, lo, I am c. all the tribes of Jer 1.15
c. to Egypt, going to Assyria. Hos 7.11
Lord GOD was c. for a judgment by Amo 7.04
places and c. to their playmates, Mt 11.16
And c. to him a child, he put him in 18.02
it said, "This man is c. Elijah." 27.47
"Take heart; rise, he is c. you." Mk 10.49
it said, "Behold, he is c. Elijah." 15.35
And John, c. to him two of his Lk 7.19
market place and c. to one another, 7.32
C. ten of his servants, he gave them 19.13
Teacher is here and is c. for you." Jn 11.28
Then c. the saints and widows he Ac 9.41
away your sins, c. on his name.' 22.16
worthy of the c. to which you have Eph 4.01
us and called us with a holy c., 2Ti 1.09
as Sarah obeyed Abraham, c. him lord. 1Pe 3.06
c. to the mountains and rocks, "Fall Rev 6.16
c. with a loud voice to him who sat 14.15

CALLOUS

they have become c. and have given Eph 4.19

CALLS

When Pharaoh c. you, and says, 'What Gen 46.33
and if he c. you, you shall say, 1Sa 3.09
"Who are you that c. to the king?" 26.14
for which the foreigner c. to thee; 1Ki 8.43
for which the foreigner c. to thee; 2Ch 6.33
and c. to judgment, who can hinder Job 11.10
Deep c. to deep at the thunder of Ps 42.07
He c. to the heavens above and to 50.04
For he delivers the needy when he c., 72.12

CALLS (cont.)
When he c. to me, I will answer him; Ps 91.15
There is no one that c. upon thy name, Is 64.07
fallen; and none of them c. upon me. Hos 7.07
shall be those whom the LORD c. Joe 2.32
who c. for the waters of the sea, Amo 5.08
who c. for the waters of the sea, 9.06
the Spirit, c. him Lord, saying, Mt 22.43
If David thus c. him Lord, how is he 22.45
David himself c. him Lord; Mk 12.37
he c. together his friends and his Lk 15.06
she c. together her friends and 15.09
where he c. the Lord the God of 20.37
David thus c. him Lord; so how 20.44
and he c. his own sheep by name and Jn 10.03
be that whoever c. on the name of Ac 2.21
whom the Lord our God c. to him." 2.39
to the dead and c. into existence Rom 4.17
For, "every one who c. upon the name 10.13
who c. you into his own kingdom and 1Th 2.12
He who c. you is faithful, and he 5.24
to any one who c. you to account 1Pe 3.15
who c. herself a prophetess and is Rev 2.20
This c. for wisdom: let him who has 13.18
This c. for a mind with wisdom: the 17.09

CALM
I will be c., and will no more be Eze 16.42
and there was a great c. Mt 8.26
ceased, and there was a great c. Mk 4.39
they ceased, and there was a c. Lk 8.24

CALMED
But I have c. and quieted my soul, Ps 131.02

CALNEH
Pass over to C., and see; Amo 6.02

CALNO
Is not C. like Carchemish? Is 10.09

CALVES
the cart, but take their c. home, 1Sa 6.07
cart, and shut up their c. at home. 6.10
and took sheep and oxen and c., 14.32
counsel, and made two c. of gold. 1Ki 12.28
sacrificing to the c. that he had 12.32
the golden c. that were in Bethel, 2Ki 10.29
themselves molten images of two c.; 17.16
and for the c. which he had made. 2Ch 11.15
you the golden c. which Jeroboam 13.08
their cow c., and does not cast her Job 21.10
bulls with the c. of the peoples. Ps 68.30
in her midst are like fatted c.; Jer 46.21
they say. Men kiss c.! Hos 13.02
and c. from the midst of the stall; Amo 6.04
offerings, with c. a year old? Mic 6.06
leaping like c. from the stall. Mal 4.02
my oxen and my fat c. are killed, Mt 22.04
of goats and c. but his own blood, Heb 9.12
he took the blood of c. and goats, 9.19

CALVING
Do you observe the c. of the hinds? Job 39.01

CAME
when the sons of God c. in to the daughters Gen 6.04
waters of the flood c. upon the earth. 7.10
and the dove c. back to him in the evening, 8.11
Casluhim (whence c. the Philistines), 10.14
And the LORD c. down to see the city 11.05
when they c. to Haran, they settled 11.31
tent, and c. and dwelt by the oaks of 13.18
kings who were with him c. and subdued 14.05
turned back and c. to Enmishpat (that 14.07
one who had escaped c., and told 14.13
the word of the LORD c. to Abram in 15.01
the word of the LORD c. to him, "This 15.04
when birds of prey c. down upon the 15.11
two angels c. to Sodom in the evening; 19.01
"Where are the men who c. to you tonight? 19.05
"This fellow c. to sojourn, and he would 19.09
But God c. to Abimelech in a dream by 20.03
When they c. to the place of which God 22.09
son back to the land from which you c.?" 24.05
c. out with her water jar upon her shoulder. 24.15
spring, and filled her jar, and c. up. 24.16
So the man c. into the house; and Laban 24.32
"I c. today to the spring, and said, 24.42
Rebekah c. out with her water jar on her 24.45
The first c. forth red, all his body like a 25.25
his brother c. forth, and his hand had taken 25.26
Esau c. in from the field, and he was 25.29
Isaac's servants c. and told him about the well 26.32
So he c. near and kissed him; and he 27.27
Esau his brother c. in from his hunting. 27.30
and I ate it all before you c., and I have 27.23
"Your brother c. with guile, and he has taken 27.35
and c. to the land of the people of the east. 29.01
them, Rachel c. with her father's sheep; 29.09
When Jacob c. from the field in the evening, 30.16
you had little before I c., and it has 30.30
troughs, where the flocks c. to drink. 30.38
since they bred when they c. to drink, 30.38
God c. to Laban the Aramean in a dream 31.24
"We c. to your brother Esau, and he is 32.06
seven times, until he c. near to his brother. 33.03
Jacob c. safely to the city of Shechem, 33.18
so Jacob held his peace until they c. 34.05
The sons of Jacob c. in from the field when 34.07
Hamor and his son Shechem c. to the gate 34.20
took their swords and c. upon the city 34.25
the sons of Jacob c. upon the slain, and 34.27
Jacob c. to Luz (that is, Bethel), which 35.06
Jacob again, when he c. from Paddan-aram, 35.09
Jacob c. to his father Isaac at Mamre, or 35.27
valley of Hebron, and he c. to Shechem. 37.14
before he c. near to them they conspired 37.18
Joseph c. to his brothers, they stripped him of 37.23
the time of her delivery c., there were twins 38.27
scarlet thread, saying, "This c. out first." 38.28
behold, his brother c. out; and she said, 38.29
his brother c. out with the scarlet thread 38.30
he c. in to me to lie with me, and I cried out 39.14
garment by her until his master c. home, 39.16
brought among us, c. in to me to insult me; 39.17
Joseph c. to them in the morning and saw them, 40.06
there c. up out of the Nile seven cows sleek 41.02
seven other cows, gaunt and thin, c. up out 41.03
as he interpreted to us, so it c. to pass; 41.13
his clothes, he c. in before Pharaoh. 41.14
cows, fat and sleek, c. up out of the Nile and 41.18
seven other cows c. up after them, poor 41.19
lean and gaunt cows that c. up after them 41.27
Before the year of famine c., Joseph had 41.50
all the earth c. to Egypt to Joseph to buy 41.57
Israel c. to buy among the others who c., 42.05
Joseph's brothers c., and bowed themselves 42.06
they c. to Jacob their father in the land 42.29
we c. down the first time to buy food; 43.20
when we c. to the lodging place we opened 43.21
Joseph c. home, they brought into the house 43.26
Judah and his brothers c. to Joseph's house, 44.14
And they c. near. And he said, "I am 45.04
out of Egypt, and c. to the land of Canaan 45.25
all that he had, and c. to Beersheba, 46.01
the land of Canaan, and c. into Egypt, 46.06
descendents of Israel, who c. into Egypt, 46.08
belonging to Jacob who c. into Egypt, who 46.26
Jacob, that c. into Egypt, were seventy. 46.27
and they c. into the land of Goshen. 46.28
all the Egyptians c. to Joseph, and said, 47.15
they c. to him the following year, and said 47.18
before I c. to you in Egypt, are mine; 48.05
when I c. from Paddan, Rachel to my sorrow 48.07

CAME (cont.)
they c. to the threshing floor of Atad, Gen 50.10
sons of Israel who c. to Egypt with Jacob, Ex 1.01
the daughter of Pharaoh c. down to bathe at 2.05
and they c. and drew water, and filled the 2.16
The shepherds c. and drove them away; 2.17
When they c. to their father Reuel, he said, 2.18
and their cry under bondage c. up to God. 2.23
and c. to Horeb, the mountain of God 3.01
of the people of Israel c. and cried to 5.15
who were waiting for them, as they c. forth 5.20
For since I c. to Pharaoh to speak in thy 5.23
and the frogs c. up and covered the land of 8.06
there c. great swarms of flies into the 8.24
day, in which you c. out from Egypt, 13.03
LORD did for me when I c. out of Egypt,' 13.08
When they c. to Marah, they could not 15.23
Then they c. to Elim, where there were 15.27
the people of Israel c. to the wilderness of 16.01
quails c. up and covered the camp; and in 16.13
leaders of the congregation c. and told Moses, 16.22
years, till they c. to a habitable land; 16.35
they c. to the border of the land of Canaan. 16.35
Then c. Amalek and fought with Israel 17.08
c. with his sons and his wife to Moses in 18.05
and Aaron c. with all the elders of Israel 18.12
on that day they c. into the wilderness of 19.01
from Rephidim and c. into the wilderness 19.02
So Moses c. and called the elders of 19.07
the LORD c. down from Mount Sinai, 19.20
If it was hired, it c. for its hire. 22.15
of Abib, for in it you c. out of Egypt. 23.15
Moses c. and told the people all the 24.03
as soon as he c. near the camp and saw 32.19
the fire, and there c. out this calf." 32.24
in the month Abib you c. out from Egypt. 34.18
When Moses c. down from Mount Sinai, 34.29
in his hand as he c. down from the 34.29
all the people of Israel c. near, and he 34.32
him, he took the veil off, until he c. out; 34.34
when he c. out, and told the people of 34.34
And they c., every one whose heart stirred 35.21
So they c., both men and women; all 35.22
every sort of task on the sanctuary c., each 36.04
he c. down from offering the sin offering Lev 9.22
they c. out they blessed the people, 9.23
fire c. forth from before the LORD 9.24
they c. before Moses and Aaron on that day; Num 9.06
the LORD c. down in the cloud and 11.25
And the three of them c. out. 12.04
the LORD c. down in a pillar of cloud, 12.05
and Miriam; and they both c. forward. 12.05
into the Negeb, and c. to Hebron; 13.22
they c. to the Valley of Eshcol, and cut 13.23
they c. to Moses and Aaron and to 13.26
"We c. to the land to which you sent 13.27
who dwelt in that hill country c. down, 14.45
and Dathan and Abiram c. out and 16.27
And fire c. forth from the LORD, 16.35
Moses and Aaron c. to the front of 16.43
c. into the wilderness of Zin in the 20.01
and water c. forth abundantly, and the 20.11
Edom c. out against them with many 20.20
whole congregation, c. to Mount Hor. 20.22
Moses and Eleazar c. down from the 20.28
And the people to c. to Moses, and said, 21.07
c. to Jahaz, and fought against Israel. 21.23
they c. to Balaam, and gave him Balak's 22.07
God c. to Balaam and said, "Who 22.09
they c. to Balaam and said to him, 22.16
God c. to Balaam at night and said 22.20
went with Balak, and they c. to 22.39
he c. to him, and, lo, he was standing 23.17
And the Spirit of God c. upon him, 24.02
one of the people of Israel c. and brought 25.06
the captains of hundreds, c. near to Moses, 31.48
and the sons of Reuben c. and said to 32.02
of the men who c. up out of Egypt, 32.11
they c. near to him, and said, 32.16
set out from Marah, and c. to Elim; 33.09
c. near and spoke before Moses and 36.01
us; and we c. to Kadeshbarnea. Deu 1.19
Then all of you c. near me, and said, 1.22
and c. to the Valley of Eshcol and 1.24
that you went until you c. to this place.' 1.31
c. out against you and chased you as 1.44
the Caphtorim, who c. from Caphtor, 2.23
Sihon c. out against us, he and all 2.32
Og the king of Bashan c. out against 3.01
And you c. near and stood at the 4.11
of Israel when they c. out of Egypt, 4.45
defeated when they c. out of Egypt. 4.46
you c. near to me, all the heads of 5.23
day you c. out of the land of Egypt, 9.07
turned and c. down from the mountain, 9.15
c. down from the mountain, and put 10.05
wilderness, until you c. to this place; 11.05
for you c. out of the land of Egypt in 16.03
remember the day when you c. out of 16.03
sun, at the time you c. out of Egypt. 16.06
when I c. near her, I did not find in 22.14
way, when you c. forth out of Egypt, 23.04
on the way as you c. forth out of Egypt. 24.09
on the way as you c. out of Egypt, 25.17
you c. to this place, Sihon the king of 29.07
Og the king of Bashan c. out against 29.07
we c. through the midst of the nations 29.16
Moses c. and recited all the words 32.44
"The LORD c. from Sinai, and dawned 33.02
he c. from the ten thousands of holy 33.02
and he c. to the heads of the people, 33.21
c. into the house of a harlot whose Jos 2.01
men c. to me, but I did not know 2.04
down, she c. up to them on the roof, 2.08
before you when you c. out of Egypt, 2.10
two men c. down again from the hills, 2.23
and they c. to the Jordan, and lodged 3.01
c. up from the midst of the Jordan, 4.18
The people c. up out of the Jordan 4.19
males of the people who c. out of Egypt, 5.04
all the people who c. out had been 5.05
the men of war that c. forth out of 5.06
none went out, and none c. in. 6.01
the rear guard c. after the ark, 6.09
and they c. into the camp, and spent 6.11
rear guard c. after the ark of the LORD, 6.13
So Joshua c. upon them suddenly, 10.09
Then they c. near, and put their feet 10.24
king of Gezer c. up to help Lachish; 10.33
c. and encamped together at the 11.05
So Joshua c. suddenly upon them 11.07
Joshua c. at that time, and wiped 11.21
people of Judah c. to Joshua at 14.06
When she c. to him, she urged him 15.18
They c. before Eleazar the priest and 17.04
they c. to Joshua in the camp at Shiloh, 18.09
Benjamin according to its families c. up, 18.11
The second lot c. out for Simeon, 19.01
lot c. up for the tribe of Zebulun, 19.10
fourth lot c. out for Issachar, 19.17
lot c. out for the tribe of Asher 19.24
lot c. out for the tribe of Naphtali, 19.32
seventh lot c. out for the tribe of Dan, 19.40
c. to Eleazar the priest and to Joshua 21.01
c. out for the families of the Kohathites. 21.04
of Israel had failed; all c. to pass. 21.45
when they c. to the region about the 22.10
And they c. to the Reubenites, the 22.15
out of Egypt, and you c. to the sea; 24.06
went over the Jordan and c. to Jericho, 24.11
When she c. to him, she urged him Ju 1.14
The Spirit of the Lord c. upon him, 3.10
And Ehud c. to him, as he was sitting 3.20
out of his belly; and the dirt c. out. 3.22

CAME (cont.)
the servants c.; and when they saw Ju 3.24
and the people of Israel c. up to her for 4.05
"The kings c., they fought; then 5.19
because they c. not to the help of the 5.23
the angel of the LORD c. and sat 6.11
When Gideon c., behold a man was 7.13
and c. to the tent, and struck it so 7.13
men who were with him c. to the 7.19
Gideon c. to the Jordan and passed 8.04
he c. to the men of Succoth, and 8.15
Abimelech c. to the tower, and fought 9.52
upon them c. the curse of Jotham the 9.57
but when they c. up from Egypt, Israel 11.16
wilderness to the Red Sea and c. to Kadesh. 11.16
Spirit of the LORD c. upon Jephthah, 11.29
Jephthah c. to his home at Mizpah; 11.34
his daughter c. out to meet him with 11.34
the woman c. and told her husband, 13.06
"A man of God c. to me, and his 13.06
angel of God c. again to the woman 13.09
the man who c. to me the other day 13.10
and c. to the man and said to him, 13.11
he c. up, and told his father and 14.02
and he c. to the vineyards at Timnah. 14.05
Spirit of the LORD c. mightily upon 14.06
and he c. to his father and mother, 14.09
"out of the eater c. something to eat. 14.14
Out of the strong c. something sweet." 14.14
Spirit of the LORD c. mightily upon him, 14.19
And the Philistines c. up, and burned 15.06
he c. to Lehi, the Philistines c. shouting 15.14
Spirit of the LORD c. mightily upon him, 15.14
is at Lehi, and there c. water from it; 15.19
Philistines c. to her and said to her, 16.05
lords of the Philistines c. up to her, 16.18
all his family c. down and took him 16.31
he c. to the hill country of Ephraim 17.08
they c. to the hill country of Ephraim, 18.02
five men departed, and c. to Laish, 18.07
when they c. to their brethren at Zorah 18.08
Ephraim, and c. to the house of Micah. 18.13
and c. to the house of the young Levite, 18.15
Danites c. to Laish, to a people quiet 18.27
out the man who c. into your house, 19.22
the woman c. and fell down at the 19.26
people of Israel c. up out of the land 19.30
"I c. to Gibeah that belongs to 20.04
Benjaminites c. out of Gibeah, and 20.21
people of Israel c. near against the 20.24
went up and c. to Bethel and wept; 20.26
c. against Gibeah ten thousand picked 20.34
who c. out of the cities destroyed them 20.42
the people c. to Bethel, and sat there 21.02
went on until they c. to Bethlehem. Ru 1.19
when they c. to Bethlehem, the whole 1.19
c. to Bethlehem at the beginning of 1.22
And behold, Boaz c. from Bethlehem; 2.04
who c. back with Naomi from the country 2.06
So she c., and she has continued 2.07
c. to a people that you did not know before. 2.11
she c. softly, and uncovered his feet, 3.07
that the woman c. to the threshing floor." 3.14
she c. to her mother-in-law, she said, 3.16
of whom Boaz had spoken, c. by. 4.01
to all the Israelites who c. there. 1Sa 2.14
And there c. a man of God to Eli, 2.27
And the LORD c. and stood forth, 3.10
the word of Samuel c. to all Israel. 4.01
And when the troops c. to the camp, 4.03
ark of the covenant of the LORD c. into 4.05
line, and c. to Shiloh the same day, 4.12
man c. into the city and told the news, 4.13
the man hastened and c. and told Eli. 4.14
birth; for her pains c. upon her. 4.19
But when the ark of God c. to Ekron, 5.10
The cart c. into the field of Joshua of 6.14
the men of Kiriathjearim c. and took 7.01
gathered together and c. to Samuel at 8.04
When they c. to the land of Zuph, Saul 9.05
Now the day before Saul c., the LORD 9.15
c. down from the high place into the city, 9.25
and all these signs c. to pass that day. 10.09
When they c. to Gibeah, behold, a band 10.10
Spirit of God c. mightily upon him, and 10.10
prophesying, he c. to the high place. 10.13
the messengers c. to Gibeah of Saul, 11.04
the Spirit of God c. mightily upon Saul 11.06
people, and they c. out as one man. 11.07
messengers c. and told the men of Jabesh, 11.09
they c. into the midst of the camp in the 11.11
Nahash the king of the Ammonites c. against 12.12
they c. up and encamped at Michmash, to 13.05
Samuel c.; and Saul went out to meet 13.10
raiders c. out of the camp of the Philistines 13.17
And all the people c. into the forest; 14.25
the way, when they c. up out of Egypt. 15.02
Saul c. to the city of Amalek, and lay 15.05
Israel when they c. up out of Egypt." 15.06
The word of the LORD c. to Samuel: 15.10
"Saul c. to Carmel, and behold, he set up 15.12
Samuel c. to Saul, and Saul said to 15.13
And Agag c. to him cheerfully. Agag said, 15.32
LORD commanded, and c. to Bethlehem. 16.04
elders of the city c. to meet him trembling, 16.04
When they c., he looked on Eliab and 16.06
Spirit of the Lord c. mightily upon David 16.13
David c. to Saul, and entered his service. 16.21
he c. to the encampment as the host 17.20
c. up out of the ranks of the Philistines, 17.23
c. a lion, or a bear, and took a lamb from 17.34
Philistine c. on and drew near to David, 17.41
and c. and drew near to meet David, 17.48
women c. out of all the cities of Israel, 18.06
he went out and c. in before the people. 18.13
for he went out and c. in before them. 18.16
princes of the Philistines c. out to battle, 18.30
as often as they c. out David had more 18.30
when the messengers c. in, behold, the image 19.16
escaped, and he c. to Samuel at Ramah, 19.18
and c. to the great well that is in Secu; 19.22
and the Spirit of God c. upon him also, 19.23
Ramah, and c. and said before Jonathan, 20.01
when the new moon c., the king sat down 20.24
the lad c. to the place of the arrow which 20.37
gathered up the arrows, and c. to his master. 20.38
Then c. David to Nob to Ahimelech 21.01
at Nob; and all of them c. to the king. 22.11
he c. down with an ephod in his hand. 23.06
when a messenger c. to Saul, saying, 23.27
And he c. to the sheepfolds by the way, 24.03
When David's young men c., they said 25.09
away, and c. back and told him all this. 25.12
c. down under cover of the mountain, 25.20
David and his men c. down toward her; 25.20
And Abigail c. to Nabal; and, lo, 25.36
servants of David c. to Abigail at Carmel, 25.40
Then the Ziphites c. to Saul at Gibeah, 26.01
when he saw that Saul c. after him 26.03
David rose and c. to the place where 26.05
one of the people c. in to destroy the king 26.15
and the garments, and c. back to Achish. 27.09
and c. and encamped at Shunem; and 28.04
him; and they c. to the woman by night. 28.08
And the woman c. to Saul, and when she 28.21
the servants of your lord who c. with you; 29.10
David and his men c. to Ziklag on the 30.01
when David and his men c. to the city, 30.03
and they c. to the brook Besor, where those 30.09
Then David c. to the two hundred men, 30.21
our hand the band that c. against us. 30.23
David c. to Ziklag, he sent part of the 30.26
the Philistines c. and dwelt in them. 31.07
when the Philistines c. to strip the slain, 31.08

CAME (cont.)

they c. to Jabesh and burnt them there. 1Sa 31.12
a man c. from Saul's camp, with his clothes 2Sa 1.02
when he c. to David, he fell to the ground 1.02
the men of Judah c., and there they 2.04
so that the spear c. out at his back; 2.23
And all who c. to the place where 2.23
they c. to the hill of Ammah, which lies 2.24
the whole forenoon they c. to Mahanaim. 2.29
Abner c. with twenty men to David at 3.20
Joab and all the army that was with him c., 3.23
"Abner the son of Ner c. to the king, and he 3.23
Behold, Abner c. to you; why is it that 3.24
that Abner the son of Ner c. to deceive you, 3.25
Joab c. out from David's presence, he sent 3.26
the people c. to persuade David to eat 3.35
news about Saul and Jonathan c. from Jezreel; 4.04
they c. to the house of Ishbosheth, as he 4.05
When they c. into the house, as he lay 4.07
all the tribes of Israel c. to David at 5.01
elders of Israel c. to the king at Hebron; 5.03
from Jerusalem, after he c. from Hebron; 5.13
David c. to Baalperazim, and David 5.20
Philistines c. up yet again, and spread 5.22
they c. to the threshing floor of Nacon, 6.06
ark of the LORD c. into the city of David, 6.16
Michal the daughter of Saul c. out to meet 6.20
the word of the LORD c. to Nathan, 7.04
when the Syrians of Damascus c. to help 8.05
son of Saul, c. to David, and fell on his 9.06
David's servants c. into the land of the 10.02
Ammonites c. out and drew up in battle array 10.08
the Ammonites, and c. to Jerusalem. 10.14
and they c. to Helam, with Shobach the 10.16
and crossed the Jordan, and c. to Helam. 10.17
and she c. to him, and he lay with her. 11.04
When Uriah c. to him, David asked how 11.07
men of the city c. out and fought with Joab; 11.17
and c. and told David all that Joab had 11.22
us, and c. out against us in the field; 11.23
David. He c. to him, and said to him, 12.01
there c. a traveler to the rich man, and he 12.04
and when the king c. to see him, Ammon 13.06
Absalom c. to the king, and said, "Behold, 13.24
were on the way, tidings c. to David, 13.30
king's sons c., and lifted up their voice 13.36
So he c. to the king, and bowed himself 14.33
man c. near to do obeisance to him, 15.05
Israel who c. to the king for judgment; 15.06
a messenger c. to David, saying, "The 15.13
You c. only yesterday, and shall I today 15.20
When David c. to the summit, where God 15.32
Hushai the Archite c. to meet him with his 15.32
Hushai, David's friend, c. into the city, 15.37
When King David c. to Bahurim, there 16.05
there c. out a man of the family of the 16.05
Gera; and as he c. he cursed continually. 16.05
the men of Israel, c. to Jerusalem, and 16.15
Archite, David's friend, c. to Absalom, 16.16
when Hushai c. to Absalom, Absalom said to 17.06
c. to the house of a man at Bahurim, 17.18
Absalom's servants c. to the woman at the 17.20
had gone, the men c. up out of the well, 17.21
David c. to Mahanaim. And Absalom 17.24
When David c. to Mahanaim, Shobi the 17.27
mouth." And he c. apace, and drew near. 18.25
the Cushite c.; and the Cushite said, 18.31
Joab c. into the house to the king, and 19.05
and all the people c. before the king. 19.08
So the king c. back to the Jordan; and 19.15
and Judah c. to Gilgal to meet the king 19.15
Mephibosheth the son of Saul c. down to meet 19.24
departed until the day he c. back in safety. 19.24
when he c. from Jerusalem to meet the 19.25
all the men of Israel c. to the king, and 19.41
David c. to his house at Jerusalem; 20.03
who c. by, seeing him, stopped; and when 20.12
all the men who were with Joab c. and 20.15
he c. near her; and the woman said, 20.17
He bowed the heavens, and c. down; 22.10
and c. about harvest time to David at 23.13
they c. to Gilead, and to Kadesh in the 24.06
and they c. to Dan, and from Dan they 24.06
and c. to the fortress of Tyre and to all 24.07
they c. to Jerusalem at the end of nine 24.08
word of the LORD c. to the prophet Gad, 24.11
Gad c. to David and told him, and said 24.13
Gad c. that day to David, and said to 24.18
with the king, Nathan the prophet c. in. 1Ki 1.22
when he c. in before the king, he bowed 1.23
So she c. into the king's presence, and stood 1.28
Jehoiada." So they c. before the king. 1.32
Jonathan the son of Abiathar the priest c.; 1.42
the king's servants c. to congratulate our 1.47
he c. and did obeisance to King Solomon; 1.53
when he c. down to meet me at the Jordan, 2.08
the son of Haggith c. to Bathsheba the 2.13
When the news c. to Joab—for Joab 2.28
Benaiah c. to the tent of the LORD, and 2.30
he c. to Jerusalem, and stood before the 3.15
two harlots c. to the king, and stood 3.16
and for all who c. to King Solomon's table, 4.27
men c. from all peoples to hear the 4.34
year after the people of Israel c. out of 6.01
Now the word of the LORD c. to Solomon, 6.11
He c. to King Solomon, and did all his 7.14
all the elders of Israel c., and the priests 8.03
when they c. out of the land of Egypt. 8.09
when the priests c. out of the holy place, 8.10
Hiram c. from Tyre to see the cities 9.12
she c. to test him with hard questions. 10.01
She c. to Jerusalem with a very great retinue, 10.02
she c. to Solomon, she told him all that 10.02
until I c. and my own eyes had seen it; 10.07
never again c. such an abundance of spices 10.10
the weight of the gold that c. to Solomon 10.14
set out from Midian and c. to Paran, 11.18
with them from Paran and c. to Egypt, 11.18
all the assembly of Israel c. and said to 12.03
Jeroboam and all the people c. to Rehoboam 12.12
Rehoboam c. to Jerusalem, he assembled 12.21
the word of God c. to Shemaiah the man 12.22
a man of God c. out of Judah by the 13.01
nor return by the way that you c.'" 13.09
not return by the way that he c. to Bethel. 13.10
his sons c. and told him all that the 13.11
man of God who c. from Judah had gone. 13.12
the man of God who c. from Judah?" 13.14
there, nor return by the way that you c.'" 13.17
the word of the LORD c. back to the prophet 13.20
cried to the man of God who c. from Judah, 13.21
they c. and told it in the city where the 13.25
to Shiloh, and c. to the house of Ahijah. 14.04
she c., she pretended to be another woman. 14.05
sound of her feet, as she c. in at the door, 14.06
arose, and departed, and c. to Tirzah. 14.17
as she c. to the threshold of the house, 14.17
Shishak king of Egypt c. up against Jerusalem; 14.25
the word of the LORD c. to Jehu the son 16.01
c. by the prophet Jehu the son of 16.07
And the word of the LORD c. to him, 17.02
Then the word of the LORD c. to him, 17.08
and when he c. to the gate of the city, 17.10
soul of the child c. into him again, and 17.22
word of the LORD c. to Elijah, in the third 18.01
Elijah c. near to all the people, and said, 18.21
and all the people c. near to him. 18.30
Jacob, to whom the word of the LORD c., 18.31
Elijah the prophet c. near and said, 18.36
and went for his life, and c. to Beersheba, 19.03
and c. and sat down under a broom tree; 19.04
angel of the LORD c. again a second time, 19.07
there he c. to a cave, and lodged there; 19.09
word of the LORD c. to him, and he said 19.09

CAME (cont.)
there c. a voice to him, and said, 1Ki 19.13
messengers c. again, and said, "Thus says 20.05
a prophet c. near to Ahab king of Israel 20.13
prophet c. near to the king of Israel, 20.22
a man of God c. near and said to the king 20.28
Benhadad c. forth to him; and he caused 20.33
resentful and sullen, and c. to Samaria. 20.43
Jezebel his wife c. to him, and said to 21.05
the two base fellows c. in and sat 21.13
the word of the LORD c to Elijah the 21.17
word of the LORD c. to Elijah the Tishbite, 21.28
Jehoshaphat the king of Judah c. down to 22.02
a spirit c. forward and stood before the 22.21
"There c. a man to meet us, and said to 2Ki 1.06
who c. to meet you and told you these 1.07
fire c. down from heaven, and consumed 1.10
the fire of God c. down from heaven and 1.12
and c. and fell on his knees before Elijah, 1.13
fire c. down from heaven, and consumed 1.14
prophets who were in Bethel c. out to Elisha, 2.03
will not leave you." So they c. to Jericho. 2.04
they c. to meet him, and bowed to the 2.15
they c. back to him, while he tarried at 2.18
some small boys c. out of the city and 2.23
two she-bears c. out of the woods and tore 2.24
the power of the LORD c. upon him. 3.15
water c. from the direction of Edom, 3.20
when they c. to the camp of Israel, the 3.24
She c. and told the man of God, and he 4.07
One day he c. there, and he turned into 4.11
and c. to the man of God at Mount Carmel. 4.25
she c. to the mountain to the man of God, 4.27
Gehazi c. to thrust her away. But the 4.27
Elisha c. into the house, he saw the 4.32
when she c. to him, he said, "Take up 4.36
Elisha c. again to Gilgal when there was 4.38
c. and cut them up into the pot of pottage, 4.39
A man c. from Baalshalishah, bringing 4.42
So Naaman c. with his horses and chariots, 5.09
But his servants c. near and said to him, 5.13
company, and he c. and stood before him; 5.15
he c. to the hill, he took them from their 5.24
c. to the Jordan, they cut down trees. 6.04
they c. by night, and surrounded the city. 6.14
the Syrians c. down against him, Elisha 6.18
the Syrians c. no more on raids into the 6.23
them, the king c. down to him and said, 6.33
they c. to the edge of the camp of the Syrians, 7.05
these lepers c. to the edge of the camp, they 7.08
then they c. back, and entered another tent, 7.08
c. and called to the gatekeepers of the city, 7.10
"We c. to the camp of the Syrians, and 7.10
had said when the king c. down to him. 7.17
Elisha c. to Damascus. Benhadad the 8.07
When he c. and stood before him, he said, 8.09
departed from Elisha, and c. to his master, 8.14
when he c., behold, the commanders of 9.05
Jehu c. out to the servants of his master, 9.11
he spied the company of Jehu as he c., 9.17
a second horseman, who c. to them, 9.19
Jehu c. to Jezreel, Jezebel heard of 9.30
When they c. back and told him, he said, 9.36
the letter c. to them, they took the king's 10.07
messenger c. and told him, "They have 10.08
he c. to Samaria, he slew all that remained 10.17
all the worshipers of Baal c., so that 10.21
sabbath, and c. to Jehoiada the priest. 11.09
king's secretary and the high priest c. up 12.10
at Bethshemesh, and c. to Jerusalem, and 14.13
fourth generation." And so it c. to pass.) 15.12
c. up from Tirzah and c. to Samaria, 15.14
Pul the king of Assyria c. against the land; 15.19
king of Assyria c. and captured Ijon, 15.29
Of Israel, c. up to wage war on Jerusalem, 16.05
the Edomites c. to Elath, where they 16.06
the king c. from Damascus, the king 16.12
c. up Shalmaneser king of Assyria; 17.03
invaded all the land and c. to Samaria, 17.05
from Samaria c. and dwelt in Bethel, 17.28
c. up against Samaria and besieged it 18.09
Sennacherib king of Assyria c. up against 18.13
And they went up and c. to Jerusalem. 18.17
they c. and stood by the conduit of the 18.17
c. out to them Eliakim the son of Hilkiah, 18.18
c. to Hezekiah with their clothes rent, and 18.37
servants of King Hezekiah c. to Isaiah, 19.05
you back on the way by which you c. 19.28
way that he c., by the same he shall return, 19.33
Isaiah the prophet the son of Amoz c. to 20.01
court, the word of the LORD c. to him: 20.04
Isaiah the prophet c. to King Hezekiah, 20.14
since the day their fathers c. out of Egypt, 21.15
Shaphan the secretary c. to the king, 22.09
tomb of the man of God who c. from Judah 23.17
bones of the prophet who c. out of Samaria. 23.18
away; and he c. to Egypt, and died there. 23.34
Nebuchadnezzar king of Babylon c. up, 24.01
this c. upon Judah at the command of 24.03
king of Babylon c. up to Jerusalem, and 24.10
king of Babylon c. to the city, while his 24.11
it c. to the point in Jerusalem and Judah 24.20
king of Babylon c. with all his army 25.01
a servant of the king of Babylon, c. to 25.08
they c. with their men to Gedaliah at 25.23
c. with ten men, and attacked and killed 25.25
Casluhim (whence c. the Philistines), 1Ch 1.12
these c. the Zorathites and the Estaolites. 2.53
Kenites who c. from Hamath, the father 2.55
c. in the days of Hezekiah, king of Judah, 4.41
because they c. down to raid their cattle. 7.21
and his brothers c. in to comfort him. 7.22
and the Philistines c. and dwelt in them. 10.07
when the Philistines c. to strip the slain, 10.08
elders of Israel c. to the king at Hebron; 11.03
these are the men who c. to David at 12.01
of Benjamin and Judah c. to the stronghold 12.16
the Spirit c. upon Amasai, chief of the 12.18
deserted to David when he c. with the 12.19
armed troops, who c. to David in Hebron, 12.23
c. to Hebron with full intent to make 12.38
when they c. to the threshing floor of Chidon, 13.09
the covenant of the LORD c. to the city 15.29
night the word of the LORD c. to Nathan, 17.03
the Syrians of Damascus c. to help 18.05
David's servants c. to Hanun in the land 19.02
who c. and encamped before Medeba. 19.07
mustered from their cities and c. to battle. 19.07
Ammonites c. out and drew up in battle 19.09
the city. Then Joab c. to Jerusalem. 19.15
and crossed the Jordan, and c. to them, 19.17
Ammonites, and c. and besieged Rabbah. 20.01
all Israel, and c. back to Jerusalem. 21.04
So Gad c. to David and said to him, 21.11
As David c. to Ornan, Ornan looked and 21.21
the word of the LORD c. to me, saying, 22.08
counselor, and his lot c. out for the north. 26.14
Shuppim and Hosah it c. out for the west, 26.16
concerning the divisions that c. and went, 27.01
So Solomon c. from the high place at 2Ch 1.13
all the elders of Israel c., and the Levites 5.04
people of Israel, when they c. out of Egypt. 5.10
when the priests c. out of the holy place 5.11
fire c. down from heaven and consumed 7.01
she c. to Jerusalem to test him with hard 9.01
When she c. to Solomon, she told him 9.01
until I c. and my own eyes had seen it; 9.06
weight of gold that c. to Solomon in 9.13
Jeroboam and all Israel c. and said to 10.03
c. to Rehoboam the third day, as the king 10.12
Rehoboam c. to Jerusalem, he assembled 11.01
word of the LORD c. to Shemaiah the 11.02
their holdings and c. to Judah and 11.14
LORD God of Israel c. after them from 11.16

CAME (cont.)
Shishak king of Egypt c. up against 2Ch 12.02
number who c. with him from Egypt— 12.03
of Judah and c. as far as Jerusalem. 12.04
Shemaiah the prophet c. to Rehoboam 12.05
the word of the LORD c. to Shemaiah: 12.07
Shishak king of Egypt c. up against 12.09
the guard c. and bore them, and brought 12.11
Zerah the Ethiopian c. out against them 14.09
chariots, and c. as far as Mareshah. 14.09
The Spirit of God c. upon Azariah the 15.01
him who went out or to him who c. in, 15.05
Hanani the seer c. to Asa King of Judah, 16.07
a spirit c. forward and stood before the 18.20
son of Chenaanah c. near and struck 18.23
of the Meunites, c. against Jehoshaphat for 20.01
Some men c. and told Jehoshaphat, 20.02
cities of Judah they c. to seek the LORD. 20.04
not let Israel invade when they c. from the 20.10
the Spirit of the LORD c. upon Jahaziel the 20.14
Judah c. to the watchtower of the 20.24
his people c. to take the spoil from them, 20.25
They c. to Jerusalem, with harps and lyres 20.28
And a letter c. to him from Elijah the 21.12
they c. up against Judah, and invaded it, 21.17
his bowels c. out because of the disease, 21.19
the band of men that c. with the Arabs 22.01
he c. there he went out with Jehoram to 22.07
of Israel, and they c. to Jerusalem. 23.02
princes of Judah c. and did obeisance 24.17
wrath c. upon Judah and Jerusalem for 24.18
army of the Syrians c. up against Joash. 24.23
They c. to Judah and Jerusalem, and 24.23
But a man of God c. to him and said, 25.07
After Amaziah c. from the slaughter of the 25.14
out to meet the army that c. to Samaria, 28.09
king of Assyria c. against him, and 28.20
month they c. to the vestibule of the LORD; 29.17
humbled themselves and c. to Jerusalem. 30.11
the whole assembly that c. out of Israel, 30.25
sojourners who c. out of the land of 30.25
their prayer c. to his holy habitation in 30.27
Hezekiah and the princes c. and saw 31.08
Sennacherib king of Assyria c. and invaded 32.01
when he c. into the house of his god, 32.21
They c. to Hilkiah the high priest and 34.09
Against him c. up Nebuchadnezzar king 36.06
who c. up out of the captivity of those Ez 2.01
They c. with Zerubbabel, Jeshua, Nehemiah, 2.02
when they c. to the house of the LORD 2.68
the seventh month c., and the sons of 3.01
the Jews who c. up from you to us have 4.12
their associates c. to them and spoke to 5.03
Sheshbazzar c. and laid the foundations of 5.16
he c. to Jerusalem in the fifth month, 7.08
on the first day of the fifth month he c. to 7.09
We c. to Jerusalem, and there we remained 8.32
one of my brethren, c. with certain men Neh 1.02
I c. to the governors of the province 2.09
I c. to Jerusalem and was there three 2.11
who lived by them c. they said to us ten 4.12
besides those who c. to us from the nations 5.17
and Tobiah's letters c. to them. 6.17
genealogy of those who c. up at the first, 7.05
who c. up out of the captivity of those 7.06
They c. with Zerubbabel, Jeshua, Nehemiah, 7.07
and c. to Jerusalem, and I then discovered 13.07
when the turn c. for each maiden to go in Est 2.12
in the morning she c. back to the second 2.14
the turn c. for Esther the daughter of 2.15
wherever the king's command and his decree c., 4.03
Esther's maids and her eunuchs c. and told 4.04
the king and Haman c. to the dinner that 5.05
So Haman c. in, and the king said to 6.06
Mordecai c. before the king, for Esther 8.01
wherever the king's command and his edict c., 8.17
when Esther c. before the king, he gave orders 9.25
a day when the sons of God c. to present Job 1.06
the LORD, and Satan also c. among them. 1.06
there c. a messenger to Job, and said, 1.14
he was yet speaking, there c. another, 1.16
speaking, there c. another, and said, 1.17
While he was yet speaking, there c. another, 1.18
a great wind c. across the wilderness, and 1.19
"Naked I c. from my mother's womb, and 1.21
c. to present themselves before the LORD, 2.01
Satan also c. among them to present 2.01
him, they c. each from his own place, 2.11
dread c. upon me, and trembling, 4.14
him who was about to perish c. upon me, 29.13
But when I looked for good, evil c.; 30.26
and when I waited for light, darkness c. 30.26
Then c. to him all his brothers and sisters 42.11
He bowed the heavens, and c. down; Ps 18.09
until what he has said c. to pass 105.19
Then Israel c. to Egypt; Jacob sojourned 105.23
He spoke, and there c. swarms of flies, 105.31
He spoke, and the locusts c., and 105.34
As he c. from his mother's womb he shall Ecc 5.15
naked as he c., and shall take nothing 5.15
just as he c., so shall he go; and what 5.16
a great king c. against it and beseiged it, 9.14
the king of Israel c. up to Jerusalem to wage Is 7.01
when they c. up from the land of Egypt. 11.16
c. to Ashdod and fought against it and 20.01
king of Assyria c. up against all the 36.01
And there c. out to him Eliakim the son 36.03
recorder, c. to Hezekiah with their clothes rent, 36.22
the servants of King Hezekiah c. to Isaiah, 37.05
I c. to its remotest height, its densest forest. 37.24
you back on the way by which you c.' 37.29
the way that he c., by the same he shall return, 37.34
Isaiah the prophet the son of Amoz c. to him, 38.01
Then the word of the LORD c. to Isaiah: 38.04
Isaiah the prophet c. to King Hezekiah, 39.03
who c. forth from the loins of Judah; 48.01
suddenly I did them and they c. to pass. 48.03
before they c. to pass I announced them to 48.05
from the time it c. to be I have been there." 48.16
Why, when I c., was there no man? 50.02
before her pain c. upon her she was 66.07
to whom the word of the LORD c. in the days Jer 1.02
It c. also in the days of Jehoiakim the 1.03
the word of the LORD c. to me saying, 1.04
c. to me, saying, "Jeremiah, what do 1.11
c. to me a second time, saying, "What 1.13
The word of the LORD c. to me, saying, 2.01
evil c. upon them, says the LORD." 2.03
But when you c. in you defiled my land, 2.07
word that c. to Jeremiah from the LORD: 7.01
that your fathers c. out of the land of 7.25
We looked for peace, but no good c., 8.15
word that c. to Jeremiah from the LORD: 11.01
word of the LORD c. to me a second time, 13.03
Then the word of the LORD c. to me: 13.08
which c. to Jeremiah concerning the drought: 14.01
The word of the LORD c. to me: 16.01
that which c. out of my lips was before 17.16
The word that c. to Jeremiah from the 18.01
Then the word of the LORD c. to me: 18.05
Jeremiah c. from Topheth, where the 19.14
word which c. to Jeremiah from the LORD, 21.01
Then the word of the LORD c. to me: 24.04
that c. to Jeremiah concerning all the 25.01
king of Judah, this word c. from the LORD, 26.01
they c. up from the king's house to the 26.10
this word c. to Jeremiah from the LORD 27.01
prophet, the word of the LORD c. to Jeremiah: 28.12
the word of the LORD c. to Jeremiah: 29.30
The word that c. to Jeremiah from the 30.01
c. to Jeremiah from the LORD in the tenth 32.01
said, "The word of the LORD c. to me: 32.06
Hanamel my cousin c. to me in the court 32.08
The word of the LORD c. to Jeremiah: 32.26

CAME (cont.)
c. to Jeremiah a second time, while Jer 33.01
The word of the LORD c. to Jeremiah: 33.19
The word of the LORD c. to Jeremiah: 33.23
which c. to Jeremiah from the LORD, when 34.01
The word which c. to Jeremiah from 34.08
the LORD c. to Jeremiah from the LORD: 34.12
c. to Jeremiah from the LORD in the days 35.01
king of Babylon c. up against the land, 35.11
Then the word of the LORD c. to Jeremiah: 35.12
this word c. to Jeremiah from the LORD: 36.01
all the people who c. from the cities of 36.09
took the scroll in his hand and c. to them. 36.14
the word of the LORD c. to Jeremiah: 36.27
of the LORD c. to Jeremiah the prophet: 37.06
Pharaoh's army which c. to help you is 37.07
all the princes c. to Jeremiah and asked him, 38.27
his army c. against Jerusalem and besieged it; 39.01
princes of the king of Babylon c. and sat 39.03
c. to Jeremiah while he was shut up in 39.15
c. to Jeremiah from the LORD after 40.01
which they had been driven and c. to the land of 40.12
the open country c. to Gedaliah at Mizpah 40.13
c. with ten men to Gedaliah the son of 41.01
c. out from Mizpah to meet them, weeping 41.06
When they c. into the city, Ishmael the son 41.07
people from the least to the greatest, c. near 42.01
end of the ten days the word of the LORD c. 42.07
And they c. into the land of Egypt, for 43.07
word of the LORD c. to Jeremiah in Tahpanhes: 43.08
c. to Jeremiah concerning all the Jews 44.01
c. to Jeremiah the prophet concerning the 46.01
c. to Jeremiah the prophet concerning the 47.01
If grape-gatherers c. to you, would they 49.09
c. to Jeremiah the prophet concerning Elam, 49.34
c. to such a pass in Jerusalem and Judah 52.03
c. with all his army against Jerusalem, 52.04
Who has commanded and it c. to pass, Lam 3.37
word of the LORD c. to Ezekiel the priests, Eze 1.03
a stormy wind c. out of the north, and 1.04
c. the likeness of four living creatures. 1.05
and I c. to the exiles at Telabib, who 3.15
days, the word of the LORD c. to me: 3.16
The word of the LORD c. to me: 6.01
The word of the LORD c. to me: 7.01
six men c. from the direction of the 9.02
And it c. to pass, while I was prophesying, 11.13
And the word of the LORD c. to me: 11.14
The word of the LORD c. to me: 12.01
In the morning the word of the LORD c. 12.08
Moreover the word of the LORD c. to me: 12.17
And the word of the LORD c. to me: 12.21
Again the word of the LORD c. to me: 12.26
The word of the LORD c. to me: 13.01
c. certain of the elders of Israel to me, 14.01
And the word of the LORD c. to me: 14.02
And the word of the LORD c. to me: 14.12
And the word of the LORD c. to me: 15.01
Again the word of the LORD c. to me: 16.01
The word of the LORD c. to me: 17.01
c. to Lebanon and took the top of the 17.03
Then the word of the LORD c. to me: 17.11
the king of Babylon c. to Jerusalem, and 17.12
word of the LORD c. to me again: 18.01
certain of the elders of Israel c. to inquire 20.01
And the word of the LORD c. to me: 20.02
And the word of the LORD c. to me: 20.45
The word of the LORD c. to me: 21.01
And the word of the LORD c. to me; 21.08
The word of the LORD c. to me again: 21.18
Moreover the word of the LORD c. to me, 22.01
And the word of the LORD c. to me: 22.17
the word of the LORD c. to me: 22.23
The word of the LORD c. to me: 23.01
the Babylonians c. to her into the bed 23.17
they c. into the sanctuary to profane it. 23.39
to whom a messenger was sent, and lo, they c. 23.40
month, the word of the LORD c. to me: 24.01
Also the word of the LORD c. to me: 24.15
them, "The word of the LORD c. to me: 24.20
The word of the LORD c. to me: 25.01
month, the word of the LORD c. to me: 26.01
The word of the LORD c. to me: 27.01
When your wares c. from the seas, 27.33
The word of the LORD c. to me: 28.01
Moreover the word of the LORD c. to me: 28.11
The word of the LORD c. to me: 28.20
month, the word of the LORD c. to me: 29.01
the word of the LORD c. to me: 29.17
The word of the LORD c. to me: 30.01
the word of the LORD c. to me: 30.20
month, the word of the LORD c. to me: 31.01
the word of the LORD c. to me: 32.01
month, the word of the LORD c. to me: 32.17
The word of the LORD c. to me: 33.01
a man who had escaped from Jerusalem c. 33.21
upon me the eveining before the fugitive c.; 33.22
by the time the man c. to me in the morning; 33.22
The word of the LORD to me: 33.23
The word of the LORD c. to me: 34.01
The word of the LORD c. to me: 35.01
word of the LORD c. to me: 36.16
and the bones c. together, bone to its bone. 37.07
and the breath c. into them, and they 37.10
The word of the LORD c. to me: 37.15
The word of the LORD c. to me: 38.01
glory of the God of Israel c. from the east; 43.02
had seen when he c. to destroy the city, 43.03
Nebuchadnezzar king of Babylon c. to Dan 1.01
So they c. in and stood before the king. 2.02
c. thoughts of what would be hereafter, 2.29
certain Chaldeans c. forward and maliciously 3.08
Nebuchadnezzar c. near to the door of 3.26
Meshach, and Abednego c. out from the fire. 3.26
the Chaldeans, and the astrologers c. in; 4.07
At last Daniel c. in before me—he who 4.08
a watcher, a holy one, c. down from heaven. 4.13
All this c. upon King Nebuchadnezzar. 4.28
all the king's wise men c. in, but they 5.08
and his lords, c. into the banqueting hall; 5.10
they c. near and said before the king, 6.12
he c. near to the den where Daniel was, 6.20
four great beasts c. up out of the sea, 7.03
there c. up among them another horn, 7.08
A stream of fire issued and c. forth from 7.10
of heaven there c. one like a son of man, 7.13
and he c. to the Ancient of Days and was 7.13
the other horn which c. up and before which 7.20
until the Ancient of Days c., and judgment was 7.22
time c. when the saints received the kingdom. 7.22
the other, and the higher one c. up last. 8.03
a he-goat c. from the west across the face 8.05
He c. to the ram with the two horns, 8.06
there c. up four conspicuous horns 8.08
Out of one of them c. forth a little horn, 8.09
he c. near where I stood; and when he c., 8.17
c. to me in swift flight at the time 9.21
He c. and he said to me, "O Daniel, 9.22
one of the chief princes, c. to help me, 10.13
and c. to make you understand what is to 10.14
that c. to Hosea the son of Beeri, Hos 1.01
time when she c. out of the land of Egypt. 2.15
LORD that c. to Joel, the son of Pethuel: Joe 1.01
If thieves c. to you, if plunderers by Ob 1.05
If grape-gatherers c. to you, would they 1.05
the LORD c. to Jonah the son of Amittai, Jon 1.01
the captain c. and said to him, "What 1.06
and my prayer c. to thee, into thy 2.07
word of the LORD c. to Jonah a second time, 3.01
when dawn c. up the next day, God appointed 4.07
which c. into being in a night, and 4.10
that c. to Micah of Moresheth in the days Mic 1.01
days when you c. out of the land of Egypt 7.15
God c. from Teman, and the Holy One Hab 3.03

CAME (cont.)
warriors, who c. like a whirlwind to scatter Hab 3.14
the LORD which c. to Zephaniah the son of Zep 1.01
c. by Haggai the prophet to Zerubbabel Hag 1.01
word of the LORD c. by Haggai the prophet, 1.03
looked for much, and, lo, it c. to little; 1.09
they c. and worked on the house of the LORD 1.14
word of the LORD c. by Haggai the prophet, 2.01
promise that I made you when you c. out 2.05
of the LORD c. by Haggai the prophet, 2.10
When one c. to a heap of twenty measures, 2.16
one c. to the winevat to draw fifty 2.16
The word of the LORD c. a second time to 2.20
c. to Zechariah the son of Berechiah, Zec 1.01
the word of the LORD c. to Zechariah 1.07
angel who talked with me c. forward, 2.03
and another angel c. forward to meet him, 2.03
the angel who talked with me c. again, 4.01
the word of the LORD c. to me, saying, 4.08
four chariots c. out from between two 6.01
And the word of the LORD c. to me: 6.09
c. to Zechariah in the fourth day of the 7.01
the word of the LORD of hosts c. to me; 7.04
word of the LORD c. to Zechariah, saying, 7.08
great wrath c. from the LORD of hosts. 7.12
word of the LORD of hosts c. to me, 8.01
from the foe for him who went out or c. in; 8.10
the word of the LORD of hosts c. to me, 8.18
before they c. together she was found to be Mt 1.18
wise men from the East c. to Jerusalem, 2.01
c. to rest over the place where the child was. 2.09
c. John the Baptist, preaching in the 3.01
Jesus c. from Galilee to the Jordan to John, 3.13
And the tempter c. and said to him, "If 4.03
behold, angels c. and ministered to him. 4.11
when he sat down his disciples c. to him. 5.01
and the rain fell, and the floods c., 7.25
the floods c., and the winds blew and 7.27
When he c. down from the mountain, great 8.01
a leper c. to him and knelt before him, 8.02
centurion c. forward to him, beseeching him 8.05
And a scribe c. up and said to him, 8.19
when he c. to the other side, to the country 8.28
they c. out and went into the swine; 8.32
behold, all the city c. out to meet Jesus; 8.34
he crossed over and c. to his own city. 9.01
tax collectors and sinners c. and sat down 9.10
I c. not to call the righteous, but sinners." 9.13
the disciples of John c. to him, saying, 9.14
a ruler c. in and knelt before him, saying, 9.18
c. up behind him and touched the fringe 9.20
Jesus c. to the ruler's house, and saw the 9.23
the house, the blind men c. to him; 9.28
For John c. neither eating nor drinking, 11.18
the Son of man c. eating and drinking, 11.19
she c. from the ends of the earth to hear 12.42
'I will return to my house from which I c.' 12.44
and the birds c. and devoured them. 13.04
Then the disciples c. and said to him, 13.10
his enemy c. and sowed weeds among the 13.25
when the plants c. up and bore grain, 13.26
servants of the householder c. and said to 13.27
disciples c. to him, saying, "Explain to us 13.36
disciples c. and took the body and buried it, 14.12
evening, the disciples c. to him and said, 14.15
When evening c., he was there alone, 14.23
walked on the water and c. to Jesus; 14.29
over, they c. to land at Gennesaret. 14.34
Pharisees and scribes c. to Jesus from 15.01
Then the disciples c. and said to him, 15.12
Canaanite woman from that region c. out 15.22
And his disciples c. and begged him, 15.23
But she c. and knelt before him, saying, 15.25
great crowds c. to him, bringing with 15.30
the Pharisees and Sadducees c., and to test 16.01
Jesus c. into the district of Caesarea Philippi 16.13
Jesus c. and touched them, saying, 17.07
they c. to the crowd, a man c. up to him 17.14
the demon c. out of him, and the boy 17.18
disciples c. to Jesus privately and said, 17.19
they c. to Capernaum, the collectors of 17.24
he c. home. Jesus spoke to him first, 17.25
that time the disciples c. to Jesus, 18.01
For the Son of man c. to save the lost * 18.11
Then Peter c. up and said to him, 18.21
Pharisees c. up to him and tested him 19.03
one c. up to him, saying, "Teacher, what 19.16
when evening c., the owner of the vineyard 20.08
those hired about the eleventh hour c. 20.09
the first c., they thought they would 20.10
mother of the sons of Zebedee c. up to him, 20.20
Son of man c. not to be served but to serve, 20.28
near to Jerusalem and c. to Bethphage, 21.01
the blind and the lame c. to him in the 21.14
priests and the elders of the people c. up to 21.23
John c. to you in the way of righteousness, 21.32
when the king c. in to look at the guests, 22.11
The same day Sadducees c. to him, 22.23
his disciples c. to point out to him the 24.01
the disciples c. to him privately, saying, 24.03
until the flood c. and swept them all away, 24.39
while they went to buy, the bridegroom c., 25.10
Afterward the other maidens c. also, 25.11
the master of those servants c. and settled 25.19
who had received the five talents c. forward, 25.20
he also who had the two talents c. forward, 25.22
who had received the one talent c. forward, 25.24
me, I was in prison and you c. to me.' 25.36
woman c. up to him with an alabaster jar 26.07
Unleavened Bread the disciples c. to Jesus, 26.17
he c. to the disciples and found them 26.40
again he c. and found them sleeping, 26.43
he c. to the disciples and said to them, 26.45
Judas c., one of the twelve, and with 26.47
And he c. up to Jesus at once and said, 26.49
they c. up and laid hands on Jesus and 26.50
false witnesses c. forward. At last two c. 26.60
a maid c. up to him, and said, "You 26.69
the bystanders c. up and said to Peter, 26.73
When morning c., all the chief priests and 27.01
they c. upon a man of Cyrene, Simon by 27.32
when they c. to a place called Golgotha 27.33
there c. a rich man from Arimathea, 27.57
heaven and c. and rolled back the stone, 28.02
they c. and took hold of his feet and 28.09
'His disciples c. by night and stole him 28.13
Jesus c. and said to them, "All authority 28.18
Jesus c. from Nazareth of Galilee and Mk 1.09
when he c. up out of the water, immediately 1.10
a voice c. from heaven, "Thou art my 1.11
Jesus c. into Galilee, preaching the gospel 1.14
and crying with a loud voice, c. out of him. 1.26
he c. and took her by the hand and 1.31
preach there also; for that is why I c. out." 1.38
a leper c. to him beseeching him, 1.40
and people c. to him from every quarter. 1.45
and they c., bringing to him a paralytic 2.03
I c. not to call the righteous, but sinners." 2.17
people c. and said to him, "Why do 2.18
multitude, hearing all that he did, c. to him. 3.08
whom he desired; and they c. to him. 3.13
crowd c. together again, so that they could 3.20
scribes who c. down from Jerusalem said, 3.22
his mother and his brothers c.; and 3.31
and the birds c. and devoured it. 4.04
They c. to the other side of the sea, to 5.01
people c. to see what it was that had 5.14
they c. to Jesus, and saw the demoniac 5.15
c. one of the rulers of the synagogue, 5.22
c. up behind him in the crowd and 5.27
c. in fear and trembling and fell down 5.33
there c. from the ruler's house some who 5.35
c. to the house of the ruler of the 5.38
from there and c. to his own country; 6.01

CAME (cont.)

an opportunity c. when Herod on his Mk 6.21
Herodias' daughter c. in and danced, 6.22
she c. in immediately with haste to the 6.25
they c. and took his body, and laid it in 6.29
late, his disciples c. to him and said, 6.35
when evening c., the boat was out on the sea, 6.47
fourth watch of the night he c. to them, 6.48
they c. to land at Gennesaret, and moored 6.53
wherever he c., in villages, cities, or 6.56
of him, and c. and fell down at his feet. 7.25
Pharisees c. and began to argue with him, 8.11
And they c. to Bethsaida. And some 8.22
them, and a voice c. out of the cloud, 9.07
when they c. to the disciples, they saw 9.14
it c. out, and the boy was like a corpse; 9.26
they c. to Capernaum; and when he was 9.33
Pharisees c. up and in order to test him 10.02
the sons of Zebedee, c. forward to him, 10.35
Son of man also c. not to be served but 10.45
they c. to Jericho; and as he was leaving 10.46
mantle he sprang up and c. to Jesus. 10.50
when they c. from Bethany, he was hungry. 11.12
c. to it, he found nothing but leaves, 11.13
c. to Jerusalem. And he entered the 11.15
when evening c. they went out of the city. 11.19
And they c. again to Jerusalem. 11.27
and the scribes and the elders c. to him, 11.27
c. and said to him, "Teacher, we know 12.14
Sadducees c. to him, who say that there 12.18
one of the scribes c. up and heard them 12.28
a poor widow c., and put in two copper 12.42
woman c. with an alabaster jar of ointment 14.03
when it was evening he c. with the twelve. 14.17
he c. and found them sleeping, and he 14.37
again he c. and found them sleeping, 14.40
he c. the third time, and said to them, 14.41
Judas c., one of the twelve, and with him 14.43
when he c., he went up to him at once, 14.45
one of the maids of the high priest c.; 14.66
women who c. up with him to Jerusalem. 15.41
when he c. out, he could not speak Lk 1.22
he c. to her and said, "Hail, O favored 1.28
when the voice of your greeting c. to my ears, 1.44
time c. for Elizabeth to be delivered, 1.57
day they c. to circumcise the child; 1.59
And fear c. on all their neighbors. 1.65
when the time c. for their purification 2.22
inspired by the Spirit he c. into the temple; 2.27
went down with them and c. to Nazareth, 2.51
word of God c. to John the son of 3.02
multitudes that c. out to be baptized 3.07
Tax collectors also c. to be baptized, 3.12
as a dove, and a voice c. from heaven, 3.22
he c. to Nazareth, where he had been 4.16
he c. out of him, having done him no 4.35
demons also c. out of many, crying, 4.41
the people sought him and c. to him, 4.42
c. and filled both the boats, so that 5.07
cities, there c. a man full of leprosy; 5.12
c. down with them and stood on a level 6.17
who c. to hear him and to be healed 6.17
when they c. to Jesus, they besought him 7.04
he c. and touched the bier, and the 7.14
from the time I c. in she has not ceased 7.45
a great crowd c. together and people from 8.04
people from town after town c. to him, 8.04
his mother and his brothers c. to him, 8.19
a storm of wind c. down on the lake, 8.23
demons c. out of the man and entered 8.33
had happened, and they c. to Jesus, 8.35
c. a man named Jairus, who was a ruler 8.41
c. up behind him, and touched the 8.44
she was not hidden, she c. trembling, 8.47
a man from the ruler's house c. and said, 8.49
c. to the house, he permitted no one 8.51
and the twelve c. and said to him, 9.12

this, a cloud c. and overshadowed them; 9.34
And a voice c. out of the cloud, saying, 9.35
the Son of man c. not to destroy men's lives * 9.56
a Levite, when he c. to the place and 10.32
as he journeyed, c. to where he was; 10.33
'I will return to my house from which I c.' 11.24
she c. from the ends of the earth to hear 11.31
"I c. to cast fire upon the earth; and 12.49
he c. seeking fruit on it and found none. 13.06
At that very hour some Pharisees c., and 13.31
the servant c. and reported this to his 14.21
when he c. to himself he said, 'How many 15.17
And he arose, and c. to his father. 15.20
as he c. and drew near to the house, 15.25
His father c. out and entreated him, 15.28
this son of yours c., who has devoured your 15.30
moreover the dogs c. and licked his sores. 16.21
and the flood c. and destroyed them all. 17.27
when he c. near, he asked him, 18.40
Jesus c. to the place, he looked up and 19.05
So he made haste and c. down, and 19.06
Son of man c. to seek and to save the lost." 19.10
first c. before him, saying, 'Lord, your 19.16
the second c., saying, 'Lord, your pound 19.18
another c., saying, 'Lord, here is your pound, 19.20
and the scribes with the elders c. up 20.01
the time c., he sent a servant to the tenants, 20.10
There c. to him some Sadducees, those who 20.27
all the people c. to him in the temple to 21.38
Then c. the day of Unleavened Bread, on 22.07
when the hour c., he sat at table, and 22.14
he c. out, and went, as was his custom, 22.39
when he c. to the place he said to them, 22.40
he c. to the disciples and found them sleeping 22.45
there c. a crowd, and the man called Judas, 22.47
day c., the assembly of the elders of the 22.66
c. to the place which is called The Skull, 23.33
they c. back saying that they had even 24.23
He c. for testimony, to bear witness Jn 1.07
not the light, but c. to bear witness to 1.08
He c. to his own home, and his own people 1.11
grace and truth c. through Jesus Christ. 1.17
but for this I c. baptizing with water, 1.31
c. and saw where he was staying; and 1.39
man c. to Jesus by night and said to 3.02
there; and people c. and were baptized. 3.23
And they c. to John, and said to him, 3.26
he c. to a city of Samaria, called Sychar, 4.05
c. a woman of Samaria to draw water. 4.07
Just then his disciples c. They 4.27
when the Samaritans c. to him, they 4.40
when he c. to Galilee, the Galileans 4.45
So he c. again to Cana in Galilee, 4.46
evening c., his disciples went down to 6.16
boats from Tiberias c. near the place 6.23
"I am the bread which c. down from heaven." 6.41
I am the living bread which c. down 6.51
is the bread which c. down from heaven, 6.58
morning he c. again to the temple; * 8.02
all the people c. to him, and he sat * 8.02
for I proceeded and c. forth from God; 8.42
I c. not of my own accord, but he sent 8.42
he went and washed and c. back seeing. 9.07
"For judgment I c. into this world, that 9.39
All who c. before me are thieves and 10.08
them gods to whom the word of God c. 10.35
And many c. to him, and they said, 10.41
Jesus c., he found that Lazarus had 11.17
when she c. where Jesus was and saw 11.32
the Jews who c. with her also weeping, 11.33
deeply moved again, c. to the tomb; 11.38
The dead man c. out, his hands and 11.44
Jesus c. to Bethany, where Lazarus was, 12.01
they c., not only on account of Jesus 12.09
these c. to Philip, who was from Bethsaida 12.21
a voice c. from heaven, "I have glorified 12.28
He c. to Simon Peter; and Peter said 13.06

CAME (cont.)
have believed that I c. from the Father. Ju 16.27
I c. from the Father and have come into 16.28
By this we believe that you c. from God." 16.30
and know in truth that I c. from thee; 17.08
befall him, c. forward and said to them, 18.04
c. up to him, saying, "Hail, King of the 19.03
Jesus c. out, wearing the crown of thorns 19.05
soldiers c. and broke the legs of the 19.32
c. to Jesus and saw that he was already 19.33
and at once there c. out blood and water. 19.34
So he c. and took away his body. 19.38
c. bringing a mixture of myrrh and aloes, 19.39
Mary Magdalene c. to the tomb early, 20.01
Peter then c. out with the other disciple, 20.03
Simon Peter c., following him, and 20.06
Jesus c. and stood among them and said 20.19
Twin, was not with them when Jesus c. 20.24
but Jesus c. and stood among them, and 20.26
the other disciples c. in the boat, dragging 21.08
Jesus c. and took the bread and gave 21.13
a sound c. from heaven like the rush Ac 2.02
at this sound the multitude c. together, 2.06
fear c. upon every soul; and many 2.43
temple and the Sadducees c. upon them, 4.01
great fear c. upon all who heard of it. 5.05
interval of about three hours his wife c. in, 5.07
young men c. in they found her dead, 5.10
great fear c. upon the whole church, 5.11
high priest c. and those who were with him 5.21
when the officers c., they did not find 5.22
some one c. and told them, "The men 5.25
they c. upon him and seized him 6.12
c. a famine throughout all Egypt and 7.11
it c. into his heart to visit his brethren, 7.23
near to look, the voice of the Lord c., 7.31
unclean spirits c. out of many who 8.07
who c. down and prayed for them 8.15
along the road they c. to some water, 8.36
c. up out of the water, the Spirit of 8.39
all the towns till he c. to Caesarea. 8.40
to you on the road by which you c., 9.17
he c. down also to the saints that lived 9.32
c. a voice to him, "Rise, Peter; kill 10.13
the voice c. to him again a second time, 10.15
I was sent for, I c. without objection. 10.29
circumcised who c. with Peter were 10.45
four corners; and it c. down to me. 11.05
News of this c. to the ears of the 11.22
he c. and saw the grace of God, he was 11.23
prophets c. down from Jerusalem to 11.27
c. to the iron gate leading into the city. 12.10
Peter c. to himself, and said, "Now I am 12.11
a maid named Rhoda c. to answer. 12.13
when day c., there was no small stir 12.18
they c. to him in a body, and having 12.20
Paphos, and c. to Perga in Pamphylia. 13.13
from Perga and c. to Antioch of Pisidia. 13.14
those who c. up with him from Galilee 13.31
But Jews c. there from Antioch and 14.19
Pisidia, and c. to Pamphylia. 14.24
some men c. down from Judea and 15.01
they c. to Jersalem, they were welcomed 15.04
he c. also to Derbe and to Lystra. 16.01
of her." And it c. out that very hour. 16.18
so they c. and apologized to them. 16.39
they c. to Thessalonica, where there 17.01
they c. there too, stirring up and inciting 17.13
c. to Ephesus, and he left them there; 18.19
Apollos, a native of Alexandria, c. to 18.24
the upper country and c. to Ephesus. 19.01
upon them, the Holy Spirit c. on them; 19.06
also of those who were now believers c., 19.18
much encouragement, he c. to Greece. 20.02
and in five days we c. to them at Troas, 20.06
took him on board and c. to Mitylene. 20.14
we c. the following day opposite Chios; 20.15
the day after that we c. to Miletus. 20.15
when they c. to him, he said to them: 20.18
we c. by a straight course to Cos, and 21.01
morrow we departed and c. to Caesarea; 21.08
named Agabus c. down from Judea. 21.10
word c. to the tribune of the cohort 21.31
the tribune c. up and arrested him, 21.33
he c. to the steps, he was actually carried 21.35
were with me, and c. into Damascus. 22.11
c. to me, and standing by me said 22.13
So the tribune c. and said to him, 22.27
when I c. upon them with the soldiers 23.27
c. to Caesarea and delivered the letter 23.33
high priest Ananias c. down with 24.01
Lysias c. and with great violence took * 24.07
I c. to bring to my nation alms and 24.17
Felix c. with his wife Drussila, who was 24.24
they c. together here, I made no delay, 25.17
Agrippa and Bernice c. with great pomp, 25.23
Pamphylia, we c. to Myra in Lycia. 27.05
we c. to a place called Fair Havens, 27.08
a viper c. out because of the heat and 28.03
who had diseases also c. and were cured. 28.09
on the second day we c. to Puteoli. 28.13
seven days. And so we c. to Rome. 28.14
c. as far as the Forum of Appius and 28.15
we c. into Rome, Paul was allowed to 28.16
they c. to him at his lodging in great 28.23
and welcomed all who c. to him, 28.30
Law c. in, to increase the trespass; but Rom 5.20
commandment c., sin revived and I died; 7.09
When I c. to you, brethren, I did not 1Co 2.01
For as by a man c. death, by a man has 15.21
when I c. I might not be pained by those 2Co 2.03
I c. to Troas to preach the gospel of 2.12
we c. into Macedonia, our bodies had 7.05
by the brethren who c. from Macedonia. 11.09
it c. through a revelation of Jesus Christ. Gal 1.12
Cephas c. to Antioch I opposed him 2.11
before certain men c. from James, he ate 2.12
they c. he drew back and separated himself, 2.12
the law, which c. four hundred and thirty 3.17
before faith c., we were confined under 3.23
the law was our custodian until Christ c., 3.24
he c. and preached peace to you who Eph 2.17
our gospel c. to you not only in word, 1Th 1.05
Christ Jesus c. into the world to save sinners. 1Ti 1.15
when Christ c. into the world, he said, Heb 10.05
no prophecy ever c. by the impulse of man, 2Pe 1.21
This is he who c. by water and blood, 1Jn 5.06
the Lord c. with his holy myriads, Jud 1.14
and the last, who died and c. to life. Rev 2.08
another angel c. and stood at the altar 8.03
from the smoke c. locusts on the earth, 9.03
the nations raged, but thy wrath c., 11.18
angel c. out of the temple, calling with 14.15
angel c. out of the temple in heaven, 14.17
c. out from the altar, the angel who 14.18
out of the temple c. the seven angels 15.06
and a great voice c. out of the temple, 16.17
angels who had the seven bowls c. and 17.01
And from the throne c. a voice crying, 19.05
but fire c. down from heaven and 20.09
c. one of the seven angels who had 21.09

CAMEL
Isaac, she alighted from the c., Gen 24.64
The c., because it chews the cud Lev 11.04
the c., the hare, and the rock Deu 14.07
suckling, ox and sheep, c. and ass.'" 1Sa 15.03
goods of Damascus, forty c. loads. 2Ki 8.09
a restive young c. interlacing her Jer 2.23
is easier for a c. to go through Mt 19.24
out a gnat and swallowing a c.! 23.24
It is easier for a c. to go through Mk 10.25
is easier for a c. to go through Lk 18.25

CAMEL'S

gods and put them in the c. saddle, Gen 31.34
Now John wore a garment of c. hair, Mt 3.04
Now John was clothed with c. hair, Mk 1.06

CAMELS

Maidservants, she-asses, and c. Gen 12.16
of his master's c. and departed, 24.10
And he made the c. kneel down 24.11
'Drink, and I will water your c.'— 24.14
said, "I will draw for your c. also, 24.19
draw, and she drew for all his c. 24.20
When the c. had done drinking, the 24.22
standing by the c. at the spring. 24.30
the house and a place for the c." 24.31
and Laban ungirded the c., 24.32
him straw and provender for the c., 24.32
and maidservants, c. and asses. 24.35
and I will draw for your c. also," 24.44
and I will give your c. drink also." 24.46
and she gave the c. drink also. 24.46
rode upon the c. and followed the 24.61
and behold, there were c. coming. 24.63
and menservants, and c. and asses. 30.43
set his sons and his wives on c.; 31.17
and the flocks and herds and c., 32.07
thirty milch c. and their colts, 32.15
with their c. bearing gum, balm, and 37.25
the c., the herds, and the flocks. Ex 9.03
they and their c. could not be Ju 6.05
and their c. were without number, as 7.12
that were on the necks of their c. 8.21
were about the necks of their c. 8.26
the c., and the garments, and came 1Sa 27.09
young men, who mounted c. and fled. 30.17
with c. bearing spices, and very 1Ki 10.02
livestock: fifty thousand of their c., 1Ch 5.21
on asses and on c. and on mules 12.40
Over the c. was Obil the Ishmaelite; 27.30
retinue and c. bearing spices and 2Ch 9.01
away sheep in abundance and c. 14.15
their c. were four hundred and Ez 2.67
their c. four hundred and thirty-five, Neh 7.69
thousand sheep, three thousand c., Job 1.03
a raid upon the c. and took them, 1.17
six thousand c., a thousand yoke of 42.12
riders on c., let him listen Is 21.07
their treasures on the humps of c., 30.06
A multitude of c. shall cover you, 60.06
the young c. of Midian and Ephah; 60.06
their c. shall be borne away from Jer 49.29
Their c. shall become booty, their 49.32
a pasture for c. and the cities of Eze 25.05
the c., the asses, and whatever Zec 14.15

CAMEST

thou c. down, the mountains quaked Is 64.03

CAMP

lodged that night in the c. Gen 32.21
quails came up and covered the c.; Ex 16.13
morning dew lay round about the c. 16.13
people who were in the c. trembled. 19.16
people out of the c. to meet God; 19.17
burn with fire outside the c.; 29.14
"There is a noise of war in the c." 32.17
came near the c. and saw the calf 32.19
then Moses stood in the gate of the c., 32.26
gate to gate throughout the c., 32.27
tent and pitch it outside the c., 33.07
far off from the c.; and he called 33.07
meeting, which was outside the c. 33.07
Moses turned again into the c., 33.11
was proclaimed throughout the c., 36.06
outside the c. to a clean place, Lev 4.12
forth the bull outside the c., 4.21
outside the c. to a clean place. 6.11
he burned with fire outside the c., 8.17
he burned with fire outside the c. 9.11
before the sanctuary out of the c." 10.04
them in their coats out of the c., 10.05
in a habitation outside the c. 13.46
and the priest shall go out of the c., 14.03
that he shall come into the c., 14.08
afterward he may come into the c. 16.26
be carried forth outside the c.; 16.27
afterward he may come into the c. 16.28
ox or a lamb or a goat in the c., 17.03
camp, or kills it outside the c., 17.03
man of Israel quarreled in the c., 24.10
"Bring out of the c. him who cursed; 24.14
him who had cursed out of the c., 24.23
man by his own c. and every man by Num 1.52
standard of the c. of Judah by 2.03
The whole number of the c. of Judah, 2.09
standard of the c. of Reuben by 2.10
The whole number of the c. of Reuben, 2.16
with the c. of the Levites in the 2.17
standard of the c. of Ephraim by 2.18
The whole number of the c. of Ephraim, 2.24
standard of the c. of Dan by their 2.25
number of the c. of Dan is a 2.31
When the c. is to set out, Aaron and 4.05
as the c. sets out, after that the 4.15
they put out of the c. every leper, 5.02
putting them outside the c., 5.03
that they may not defile their c., 5.03
so, and drove them outside the c.; 5.04
tabernacle, they remained in c. 9.18
of the LORD they remained in c.; 9.20
remained in c. and did not set out; 9.22
congregation, and for breaking c. 10.02
The standard of the c. of the men 10.14
standard of the c. of Reuben set 10.18
standard of the c. of the men of 10.22
standard of the c. of the men of 10.25
whenever they set out from the c. 10.34
some outlying parts of the c. 11.01
dew fell upon the c. in the night, 11.09
Now two men remained in the c., 11.26
and so they prophesied in the c. 11.26
Medad are prophesying in the c." 11.27
of Israel returned to the c. 11.30
and let them fall beside the c., 11.31
the other side, round about the c., 11.31
for themselves all around the c. 11.32
shut up outside the c. seven days, 12.14
shut up outside the c. seven days; 12.15
nor Moses, departed out of the c. 14.44
him with stones outside the c." 15.35
congregation brought him outside the c., 15.36
outside the c. and slaughtered 19.03
afterwards he shall come into the c.; 19.07
outside the c. in a clean place; 19.09
at the c. on the plains of Moab by 31.12
forth to meet them outside the c. 31.13
Encamp outside the c. seven days; 31.19
afterward you shall come into the c." 31.24
of war, had perished from the c., Deu 2.14
them, to destroy them from the c., 2.15
against your enemies and are in c., 23.09
then he shall go outside the c., 23.10
he shall not come within the c.; 23.10
is down, he may come within the c. 23.11
outside the c. and you shall go 23.12
God walks in the midst of your c., 23.14
therefore your c. must be holy, 23.14
the sojourner who is in your c., 29.11
"Pass through the c., and command Jos 1.11
the officers went through the c. 3.02
places in the c. till they were 5.08
and they came into the c., 6.11
and spent the night in the c. 6.11
once, and returned into the c. 6.14

CAMP (cont.)
and make the c. of Israel a thing Jos 6.18
set them outside the c. of Israel. 6.23
went to Joshua in the c. at Gilgal, 9.06
sent to Joshua at the c. in Gilgal, 10.06
with him, to the c. at Gilgal. 10.15
to Joshua in the c. at Makkedah; 10.21
with him, to the c. at Gilgal. 10.43
to Joshua in the c. at Shiloh, 18.09
and the c. of Midian was north of Ju 7.01
and the c. of Midian was below him 7.08
him, "Arise, go down against the c.; 7.09
go down to the c. with Purah your 7.10
strengthened to go down against the c." 7.11
the armed men that were in the c. 7.11
tumbled into the c. of Midian, 7.13
he returned to the c. of Israel, 7.15
outskirts of the c., do as I do. 7.17
also on every side of all the c., 7.18
outskirts of the c. at the beginning 7.19
in his place round about the c., 7.21
had come to the c. from Jabeshgilead, 21.08
brought them to the c. at Shiloh, 21.12
And when the troops came to the c., 1Sa 4.03
of the LORD came into the c., 4.05
shouting in the c. of the Hebrews 4.06
of the LORD had come to the c., 4.06
"The gods have come into the c." 4.07
midst of the c. in the morning 11.11
came out of the c. of the Philistines 13.17
And there was a panic in the c., 14.15
tumult in the c. of the Philistines 14.19
had gone up with them into the c., 14.21
out from the c. of the Philistines 17.04
quickly to the c. to your brothers; 17.17
and they plundered their c. 17.53
down with me into the c. to Saul?" 26.06
behold, a man came from Saul's c., 2Sa 1.02
have escaped from the c. of Israel." 1.03
through the c. of the Philistines, 23.16
over Israel that day in the c. 1Ki 16.16
when they came to the c. of Israel, 2Ki 3.24
and such a place shall be my c." 6.08
go over to the c. of the Syrians; 7.04
to go to the c. of the Syrians; 7.05
the edge of the c. of the Syrians, 7.05
leaving the c. as it was, and fled 7.07
lepers came to the edge of the c., 7.08
"We came to the c. of the Syrians, 7.10
gone out of the c. to hide themselves 7.12
plundered the c. of the Syrians. 7.16
thousand in the c. of the Assyrians; 19.35
gatekeepers of the c. of the Levites. 1Ch 9.18
in charge of the c. of the LORD, 9.19
through the c. of the Philistines, 11.18
Arabs to the c. had slain all the 2Ch 22.01
gates of the c. of the LORD and to 31.02
officers in the c. of the king of 32.21
May their c. be a desolation, let no Ps 69.25
them fall in the midst of their c., 78.28
When men in the c. were jealous of 106.16
thousand in the c. of the Assyrians; Is 37.36
stench of your c. go up into your Amo 4.10
for sin are burned outside the c. Heb 13.11
us go forth to him outside the c., 13.13
surrounded the c. of the saints Rev 20.09

CAMPAIGN
march out and in with me in the c.; 1Sa 29.06

CAMPED
and he c. before the city. Gen 33.18
of the LORD, and c. at Rephidim; Ex 17.01
and c. on the other side of the Ju 11.18

CAMPING
of my lord are c. in the open 2Sa 11.11

CAMPS
the Levites in the midst of the c.; Num 2.17
all in the c. who were numbered by 2.32
the c. that are on the east side Num 10.05
the c. that are on the south side 10.06
as the rear guard of all the c., 10.25
dwell in are c. or strongholds, 13.19
set c. also against it, and plant Eze 4.02
whatever beasts may be in those c. Zec 14.15

CANA
was a marriage at C. in Galilee, Jn 2.01
Jesus did at C. in Galilee, and 2.11
So he came again to C. in Galilee, 4.46
Nathanael of C. in Galilee, the sons 21.02

CANAAN
Ham was the father of C. Gen 9.18
the father of C., saw the nakedness 9.22
he said, "Cursed be C.; a slave of 9.25
be Shem; and let C. be his slave. 9.26
of Shem; and let C. be his slave." 9.27
of Ham: Cush, Egypt, Put, and C. 10.06
C. became the father of Sidon his 10.15
Chaldeans to go into the land of C.; 11.31
set forth to go to the land of C. 12.05
they had come to the land of C., 12.05
Abram dwelt in the land of C., 13.12
dwelt ten years in the land of C., 16.03
sojournings, all the land of C., 17.08
(that is, Hebron) in the land of C.; 23.02
(that is, Hebron) in the land of C. 23.19
to the land of C. to his father 31.18
Shechem, which is in the land of C., 33.18
Bethel), which is in the land of C., 35.06
were born to him in the land of C. 36.05
he had acquired in the land of C.; 36.06
sojournings, in the land of C. 37.01
the famine was in the land of C. 42.05
"From the land of C., to buy food." 42.07
sons of one man in the land of C.; 42.13
their father in the land of C., 42.29
with our father in the land of C.' 42.32
back to you from the land of C.; 44.08
and go back to the land of C.; 45.17
to the land of C. to their father 45.25
they had gained in the land of C., 46.06
and Onan died in the land of C.); 46.12
household, who were in the land of C., 46.31
have come from the land of C.; 47.01
famine is severe in the land of C." 47.04
and the land of C. languished by 47.13
of Egypt and in the land of C., 47.14
of Egypt and in the land of C., 47.15
in the land of C. and blessed me, 48.03
died in the land of C. on the way, 48.07
east of Mamre, in the land of C., 49.30
out for myself in the land of C., 50.05
sons carried him to the land of C., 50.13
them, to give them the land of C., Ex 6.04
inhabitants of C. have melted away. 15.15
to the border of the land of C. 16.35
"When you come into the land of C., Lev 14.34
do as they do in the land of C., 18.03
Egypt to give you the land of C., 25.38
"Send men to spy out the land of C., Num 13.02
them to spy out the land of C., 13.17
Er and Onan died in the land of C. 26.19
among you in the land of C." 32.30
the LORD into the land of C., 32.32
in the Negeb in the land of C., 33.40
the Jordan into the land of C., 33.51
the land of C. (this is the land 34.02
the land of C. in its full extent), 34.02
people of Israel in the land of C." 34.29
the Jordan into the land of C., 35.10
and three cities in the land of C., 35.14

CANAAN (cont.)
and view the land of C., Deu 32.49
fruit of the land of C. that year. Jos 5.12
Israel received in the land of C., 14.01
them at Shiloh in the land of C., 21.02
Shiloh, which is in the land of C., 22.09
that lies in the land of C., 22.10
at the frontier of the land of C., 22.11
land of Gilead to the land of C., 22.32
led him through all the land of C., 24.03
had no experience of any war in C.; Ju 3.01
into the hand of Jabin king of C., 4.02
the king of C. before the people 4.23
and harder on Jabin the king of C., 4.24
they destroyed Jabin king of C. 4.24
then fought the kings of C., 5.19
Shiloh, which is in the land of C. 21.12
of Ham: Cush, Egypt, Put, and C. 1Ch 1.08
C. was the father of Sidon his 1.13
saying, "To you I will give the land of C., 16.18
the land of C. as your portion for Ps 105.11
they sacrificed to the idols of C.; 106.38
and all the kingdoms of C., 135.11
the language of C. and swear Is 19.18
concerning C. to destroy its 23.11
O C., land of the Philistines; Zep 2.05
famine throughout all Egypt and C., Ac 7.11
seven nations in the land of C., 13.19

CANAANITE
not marry one of the C. women. Gen 28.01
not marry one of the C. women," 28.06
saw that the C. women did not 28.08
of a certain C. whose name was 38.02
and Shaul, the son of a C. woman; Ex 6.15
C., and Hittite from before you. 23.28
When the C., the king of Arad, who Num 21.01
And the C., the king of Arad, who 33.40
of Ekron, it is reckoned as C.; Jos 13.03
his descendants the land of the C., Neh 9.08
And behold, a C. woman from that Mt 15.22

CANAANITES
families of the C. spread abroad. Gen 10.18
territory of the C. extended from 10.19
that time the C. were in the land. 12.06
that time the C. and the Perizzites 13.07
the C., the Girgashites and the 15.21
son from the daughters of the C., 24.03
son from the daughters of the C., 24.37
the C. and the Perizzites; my numbers 34.30
Esau took his wives from the C.: 36.02
the C., saw the mourning on the 50.11
and honey, to the place of the C., Ex 3.08
of Egypt, to the land of the C., 3.17
brings you into the land of the C., 13.05
brings you into the land of the C., 13.11
and the C., the Hivites, and the 23.23
you, and I will drive out the C., 33.02
the C., the Hittites, the Perizzites, 34.11
and the C. dwell by the sea, and Num 13.29
Amalekites and the C. dwell in the 14.25
Amalekites and the C. are before you, 14.43
Amalekites and the C. who dwelt in 14.45
of Israel, and gave over the C.; 21.03
the seacoast, the land of the C., Deu 1.07
the C., the Perizzites, the Hivites, 7.01
the land of the C. who live in the 11.30
the C. and the Perizzites, the 20.17
drive out from before you the C., Jos 3.10
kings of the C. that were by the 5.01
For the C. and all the inhabitants 7.09
the C., the Perizzites, the Hivites, 9.01
to the C. in the east and the west, 11.03
the C., the Perizzites, the Hivites, 12.08
in the south, all the land of the C., 13.04
drive out the C. that dwelt in 16.10
so the C. have dwelt in the midst 16.10
but the C. persisted in dwelling in 17.12
they put the C. to forced labor, and 17.13
yet all the C. who dwell in the 17.16
for you shall drive out the C., 17.18
the C., the Hittites, the Girgashites, 24.11
go up first for us against the C., Ju 1.01
that we may fight against the C.; 1.03
LORD gave the C. and the Perizzites 1.04
defeated the C. and the Perizzites 1.05
against the C. who dwelt in the 1.09
against the C. who dwelt in Hebron 1.10
defeaded the C. who inhabited 1.17
but the C. persisted in dwelling in 1.27
they put the C. to forced labor, but 1.28
drive out the C. who dwelt in 1.29
but the C. dwelt in Gezer among 1.29
but the C. dwelt among them, and 1.30
but the Asherites dwelt among the C., 1.32
Bethanath, but dwelt among the C., 1.33
and all the C., and the Sidonians, 3.03
of Israel dwelt among the C., 3.05
the cities of the Hivites and C.; 2Sa 24.07
had slain the C. who dwelt in the 1Ki 9.16
from the C., the Hittites, the Ez 9.01
the C., and didst give them into Neh 9.24
birth are of the land of the C.; Eze 16.03

CANAANITESS
three Bathshua the C. bore to him. 1Ch 2.03

CANAANITISH
and Shaul, the son of a C. woman. Gen 46.10

CANALS
their c., and their ponds, and all Ex 7.19
over the c., and over the pools, and 8.05
and its c. will become foul, and the Is 19.06

CANANEAN
Simon the C., and Judas Iscariot, Mt 10.04
and Thaddaeus, and Simon the C., Mk 3.18

CANCELED
having c. the bond which stood Col 2.14

CANDACE
a minister of C. the queen of the Ac 8.27

CANE
and of aromatic c. two hundred and Ex 30.23
not bought me sweet c. with money, Is 43.24
or sweet c. from a distant land? Jer 6.20

CANNEH
Haran, C., Eden, Asshur, and Chilmad Eze 27.23

CANNOT
that they c. be numbered for multitude." Gen 16.10
but I c. flee to the hills, lest the 19.19
we c. speak to you bad or good. 24.50
"We c. until all the flocks are 29.08
be angry that I c. rise before you, 31.25
which c. be numbered for multitude.'" 32.12
"We c. do this thing, to give our 34.14
'The lad c. leave his father, for if 44.22
we said, 'We c. go down. If our 44.26
for we c. see the man's face unless 44.26
"The people c. come up to Mount Ex 19.23
But," he said, "you c. see my face; 33.20
"But if he c. afford a lamb, then he Lev 5.07
"But if he c. afford two turtledoves 5.11
And if she c. afford a lamb, then 12.08
he is poor and c. afford so much, 14.21
who c. afford the offerings for his 14.32
votive offering it c. be accepted. 22.23
and c. maintain himself with you, 25.35
he has blessed, and I c. revoke it. Num 23.20

CANNOT (cont.)
and whatever c. stand the fire, you Num 31.23
itch, of which you c. be healed. Deu 28.27
boils of which you c. be healed, 28.35
of Israel c. stand before their Jos 7.12
you c. stand before your enemies, 7.13
the people, "You c. serve the LORD; 24.19
LORD, and I c. take back my vow." Ju 11.35
but if you c. tell me what it is, 14.13
Yet we c. give them wives of our 21.18
"I c. redeem it for myself, lest I Ru 4.06
yourself, for I c. redeem it." 4.06
things which c. profit or save, 1Sa 12.21
said to Saul, "I c. go with these; 17.39
your soul lives, O king, I c. tell." 17.55
ill-natured that one c. speak to him." 25.17
thinking, "David c. come in here." 2Sa 5.06
which c. be gathered up again; 14.14
one c. turn to the right hand or to 14.19
for they c. be taken with the hand; 23.06
that c. be numbered or counted for 1Ki 3.08
the highest heaven c. contain thee; 8.27
and tell Ahab and he c. find you, 18.12
will do; but this thing I c. do.'" 20.09
highest heaven, c. contain him? 2Ch 2.06
the highest heaven c. contain thee; 6.18
fathers; for you c. succeed." 13.12
the LORD, so that you c. prosper? 24.20
we c. stand in the open. Ez 10.13
a great work and I c. come down. Neh 6.03
with the king's ring c. be revoked." Est 8.08
C. my taste discern calamity? Job 6.30
Though I am innocent, I c. answer him; 9.15
I c. lift up my head, for I am 10.15
appointed his bounds that he c. pass, 14.05
so that I c. pass, and he has set 19.08
so that you c. see, and a flood of 22.11
backward, but I c. perceive him; 23.08
I seek him, but I c. behold him; 23.09
the right hand, but I c. see him. 23.09
It c. be gotten for gold, and silver 28.15
and silver c. be weighed as its 28.15
It c. be valued in the gold of 28.16
Gold and glass c. equal it, nor can 28.17
of Ethiopia c. compare with it, nor 28.19
so wasted away that it c. be seen; 33.21
things which we c. comprehend. 37.05
we c. draw up our case because of 37.19
"And now men c. look on the light 37.21
The Almighty—we c. find him; 37.23
he c. stand still at the sound of 39.24
each other and c. be separated. 41.17
The arrow c. make him flee; 41.28
and he who c. keep himself alive. Ps 22.29
and by its great might it c. save. 33.17
his iniquity c. be found out and 36.02
and c. pay back, but the righteous 37.21
have overtaken me, till I c. see; 40.12
Man c. abide in his pomp, he is like 49.12
Man c. abide in his pomp, he is like 49.20
be darkened, so that they c. see; 69.23
I am so troubled that I c. speak. 77.04
I am shut in so that I c. escape; 88.08
The dull man c. know, the stupid 92.06
the stupid c. understand this: 92.06
which c. be moved, but abides for 125.01
it is high, I c. attain it. 139.06
their bounds which c. be passed. 148.06
For they c. sleep unless they have Pro 4.16
you may desire c. compare with her 8.11
trembles; under four it c. bear up: 30.21
a man c. utter it; the eye Ecc 1.08
What is crooked c. be made straight, 1.15
and what is lacking c. be numbered. 1.15
yet so that he c. find out what 3.11
that man c. find out the work that 8.17
claims to know, he c. find it out. 8.17

Many waters c. quench love, neither Sol 8.07
I c. endure iniquity and solemn Is 1.13
I am bowed down so that I c. hear, 21.03
I am dismayed so that I c. see. 21.03
"I c., for it is sealed." 29.11
give the book to one who c. read, 29.12
"Read this," he says, "I c. read." 29.12
a people that c. profit them, 30.05
to a people that c. profit them. 30.06
speech which you c. comprehend, 33.19
a tongue which you c. understand. 33.19
it c. hold the mast firm in its 33.23
For Sheol c. thank thee, death 38.18
thank thee, death c. praise thee; 38.18
down to the pit c. hope for thy 38.18
with nails so that it c. be moved. 41.07
they c. rise, they are extinguished, 43.17
shut their eyes, so that they c. see, 44.18
minds, so that they c. understand. 44.18
and he c. deliver himself or say, 44.20
on praying to a god that c. save. 45.20
they c. save the burden, but themselves 46.02
it c. move from its place. If one 46.07
upon you, for which you c. atone; 47.11
they c. deliver themselves from the 47.14
hand shortened, that it c. redeem? 50.02
are all dumb dogs, they c. bark; 56.10
for it c. rest, and its waters toss 57.20
is not shortened, that it c. save, 59.01
or his ear dull, that it c. hear; 59.01
squares, and uprightness c. enter. 59.14
I c. keep silent; for I hear Jer 4.19
perpetual barrier which it c. pass; 5.22
though the waves toss, they c. prevail, 5.22
they roar, they c. pass over it. 5.22
ears are closed, they c. listen; 6.10
adders which c. be charmed, and they 8.17
and nails so that it c. move 10.04
cucumber field, and they c. speak; 10.05
to be carried, for they c. walk. 10.05
for they c. do evil, neither is it 10.05
and the nations c. endure his 10.10
upon them which they c. escape; 11.11
but they c. save them in the time 11.12
like a mighty man who c. save? 14.09
weary with holding it in, and I c. 20.09
secret places so that I c. see him? 23.24
bad, so bad that they c. be eaten." 24.03
which are so bad they c. be eaten, 24.08
which are so bad they c. be eaten. 29.17
host of heaven c. be numbered and 33.22
sands of the sea c. be measured, 33.22
The swift c. flee away, nor the 46.06
like the sea which c. be quiet. 49.23
hands of those whom I c. withstand. Lam 1.14
me about so that I c. escape; 3.07
whose words you c. understand. Eze 3.06
so that you c. go out among the 3.25
so that you c. turn from one side 4.08
they c. satisfy their hunger or 7.19
so that it c. be changed, according Dan 6.08
the Persians, which c. be revoked." 6.08
and Persians, which c. be revoked." 6.12
her, so that she c. find her paths. Hos 2.06
from which you c. remove your Mic 2.03
A city set on a hill c. be hid. Mt 5.14
for you c. make one hair white or 5.36
You c. serve God and mammon. 6.24
A sound tree c. bear evil fruit, nor 7.18
kill the body but c. kill the soul; 10.28
but you c. interpret the signs of 16.03
if this c. pass unless I drink it, 26.42
think that I c. appeal to my 26.53
he c. save himself. He is the 27.42
bridegroom with them, they c. fast. Mk 2.19
itself, that kingdom c. stand." 3.24
he c. stand, but is coming to an end. 3.26

CANNOT (cont.)
a man from outside c. defile him, Mk 7.18
"This kind c. be driven out by 9.29
others; he c. save himself. 15.31
I c. get up and give you anything'? Lk 11.07
for it c. be that a prophet should 13.33
blessed, because they c. repay you. 14.14
a wife, and therefore I c. come.' 14.20
his own life, he c. be my disciple. 14.26
come after me, c. be my disciple. 14.27
all that he has c. be my disciple. 14.33
You c. serve God and mammon." 16.13
for they c. die any more, because 20.36
he c. see the kingdom of God." Jn 3.03
he c. enter the kingdom of God. 3.05
The world c. hate you, but it hates 7.07
find me; where I am you c. come." 7.34
me,' and, 'Where I am you c. come'?" 7.36
where I am going, you c. come." 8.21
'Where I am going, you c. come'?" 8.22
is because you c. bear to hear my 8.43
came (and scripture c. be broken), 10.35
you, 'Where I am going you c. come.' 13.33
I am going you c. follow me now; 13.36
why c. I follow you now? I will 13.37
truth, whom the world c. receive, 14.17
As the branch c. bear fruit by 15.04
to you, but you c. bear them now. 16.12
of Jerusalem, and we c. deny it. Ac 4.16
for we c. but speak of what we have 4.20
custom of Moses, you c. be saved." 15.01
these things c. be contradicted, 19.36
stay in the ship, you c. be saved." 27.31
will what is right, but I c. do it. Rom 7.18
submit to God's law, indeed it c.; 8.07
who are in the flesh c. please God. 8.08
be darkened so that they c. see, 11.10
But if they c. exercise self-control, 1Co 7.09
You c. drink the cup of the Lord 10.21
You c. partake of the table of the 10.21
The eye c. say to the hand, "I have 12.21
flesh and blood c. inherit the 15.50
and he heard things that c. be told, 2Co 12.04
For we c. do anything against the 13.08
Yet which I shall choose I c. tell. Php 1.22
Here there c. be Greek and Jew, Col 3.11
are not, they c. remain hidden. 1Ti 5.25
and we c. take anything out of the 6.07
faithful—for he c. deny himself. 2Ti 2.13
and sound speech that c. be censured, Tit 2.08
these things we c. now speak in Heb 9.05
offered which c. perfect the 9.09
order that what c. be shaken may 12.27
a kingdom that c. be shaken, 12.28
for God c. be tempted with evil and Jas 1.13
And you covet and c. obtain; 4.02
and he c. sin because he is born of 1Jn 3.09
c. love God whom he has not seen. 4.20
and how you c. bear evil men but Rev 2.02
which c. either see or hear or walk; 9.20

CANOPY
He made darkness around his his c., 2Sa 22.12
with pillars, and a c. before them. 1Ki 7.06
his c. thick clouds dark with water Ps 18.11
there will be a c. and a pavilion. Is 4.05
will spread his royal c. over them. Jer 43.10
and there was a c. of wood in front Eze 41.25

CAPERNAUM
he went and dwelt in C. by the sea, Mt 4.13
As he entered C., a centurion came 8.05
And you, C., will you be exalted to 11.23
When they came to C., the collectors 17.24
And they went into C.; and immediately Mk 1.21
he returned to C. after some days, 2.01
And they came to C.; and when 9.33
what we have heard you did at C., Lk 4.23
And he went down to C., 4.31
of the people he entered C. 7.01
And you, C., will you be exalted to 10.15
After this he went down to C., Jn 2.12
And at C. there was an official 4.46
and started across the sea to C. 6.17
and went to C., seeking Jesus. 6.24
the synagogue, as he taught at C. 6.59

CAPHTOR
who came from C., destroyed them Deu 2.23
the remnant of the coastland of C. Jer 47.04
Philistines from C. and the Syrians Amo 9.07

CAPHTORIM
came the Philistines), and C. Gen 10.14
the C., who came from Caphtor, Deu 2.23
came the Philistines), and C. 1Ch 1.12

CAPITAL
each with c. and flower, on one Ex 25.33
made like almonds, each with c. and 25.33
and a c. of one piece with it under 25.35
each with c. and flower, on one 37.19
made like almonds, each with c. and 37.19
and a c. of one piece with it under 37.21
of the one c. was five cubits, and 1Ki 7.16
of the other c. was five cubits. 7.16
a net for the one c., and a net 7.17
and a net for the other c. 7.17
to cover the c. that was upon the 7.18
he did the same with the other c. 7.18
about; and so with the other c. 7.20
and upon it was a c. of bronze; 2Ki 25.17
height of the c. was three cubits; 25.17
were upon the c. round about. 25.17
with a c. of five cubits on the top 2Ch 3.15
the c. which is in the province of Ez 6.02
year, as I was in Susa the c., Neh 1.01
his royal throne in Susa the c., Est 1.02
the people present in Susa the c., 1.05
to the harem in Susa the c., 2.03
Jew in Susa the c. whose name was 2.05
in Susa the c. in custody of Hegai, 2.08
decree was issued in Susa the c. 3.15
decree was issued in Susa the c. 8.14
In Susa the c. itself the Jews slew 9.06
in Susa the c. was reported to the 9.11
"In Susa the c. the Jews have slain 9.12
Upon it as a c. of bronze; Jer 52.22
of the one c. was five cubits; 52.22
were upon the c. round about. 52.22
when I saw, I was in Susa the c., Dan 8.02

CAPITALS
its cups, its c., and its flowers Ex 25.31
almonds, with their c. and flowers, 25.34
Their c. and their branches shall 25.36
He overlaid their c, and their 36.38
its cups, its c., and its flowers 37.17
almonds, with their c. and flowers, 37.20
Their c. and their branches were of 37.22
of their c. was also of silver, and 38.17
of their c. and their fillets of 38.19
overlaid their c. and made fillets 38.28
He also made two c. of molten 1Ki 7.16
work for the c. upon the tops of 7.17
Now the c. that were upon the tops 7.19
The c. were upon the two pillars 7.20
bowls of the c. that were on the 7.41
to cover the two bowls of the c. 7.41
bowls of the c. that were upon the 7.42
and the two c. on the top of the 2Ch 4.12
bowls of the c. that were on the 4.12
bowls of the c. that were upon the 4.13
"Smite the c. until the thresholds Amo 9.01
the hedgehog shall lodge in her c.; Zep 2.14

CAPPADOCIA
Judea and C., Pontus and Asia, Ac 2.09
Galatia, C., Asia, and Bithynia, 1Pe 1.01

CAPS
make coats and girdles and c.; Ex 28.40
with girdles and bind c. on them; 29.09
and the c. of fine linen, and the 39.28
and bound c. on them, as the LORD Lev 8.13

CAPTAIN
of Pharaoh, the c. of the guard. Gen 37.36
the c. of the guard, an Egyptian, 39.01
the house of the c. of the guard, 40.03
The c. of the guard charged Joseph 40.04
the house of the c. of the guard, 41.10
a servant of the c. of the guard; 41.12
to one another, "Let us choose a c., Num 14.04
and he became c. over them. 1Sa 22.02
and c. over your bodyguard, and 22.14
sent to him a c. of fifty men with 2Ki 1.09
But Elijah answered the c. of fifty, 1.10
to him another c. of fifty men 1.11
king sent the c. of a third fifty 1.13
And the third c. of fifty went up, 1.13
Then the c. on whose hand the king 7.02
appointed the c. on whose hand he 7.17
the c. had answered the man of God, 7.19
his c., conspired against him with 15.25
a single c. among the least of my 18.24
the c. of the bodyguard, a servant 25.08
who were with the c. of the guard, 25.10
Nebuzaradan the c. of the guard 25.11
But the c. of the guard left some 25.12
was of gold the c. of the guard 25.15
And the c. of the guard took 25.18
And Nebuzaradan the c. of the guard 25.20
the c. of fifty and the man of rank, Is 3.03
a single c. among the least of my 36.09
the c. of the guard, carried into Jer 39.09
the c. of the guard, left in the 39.10
the c. of the guard, saying, 39.11
So Nebuzaradan the c. of the guard, 39.13
Nebuzaradan the c. of the guard 40.01
The c. of the guard took Jeremiah 40.02
So the c. of the guard gave him 40.05
the c. of the guard, had committed 41.10
Nebuzaradan the c. of the guard 43.06
Nebuzaradan the c. of the bodyguard 52.12
who were with the c. of the guard, 52.14
And Nebuzaradan the c. of the guard 52.15
But Nebuzaradan the c. of the guard 52.16
was of gold the c. of the guard 52.19
And the c. of the guard took 52.24
And Nebuzaradan the c. of the guard 52.26
Nebuzaradan the c. of the guard 52.30
the c. of the King's guard, who had Dan 2.14
the king's c., "Why is the decree of 2.15
So the c. came and said to him, Jon 1.06
and their c. and the officers of Jn 18.12
priests and the c. of the temple Ac 4.01
Now when the c. of the temple and 5.24
Then the c. with the officers went 5.26
But the chief c. Lysias came and * 24.07
attention to the c. and to the 27.11

CAPTAINS
the c. of thousands and the Num 31.48
the c. of hundreds, came near to 31.48
men who were c. of raiding bands; 2Sa 4.02
his c., his chariot commanders and 1Ki 9.22
the thirty-two c. of his chariots, 22.31
And when the c. of the chariots saw 22.32
And when the c. of the chariots saw 22.33
the two former c. of fifty men 2Ki 1.14
and brought the c. of the Carites 11.04
The c. did according to all that 11.09
delivered to the c. the spears and 11.10
and the c. and the trumpeters 11.14
commanded the c. who were set over 11.15
And he took the c., 11.19
Now when all the c. of the forces 25.23
and the c. of the forces arose, and 25.26
commanded the c. of his chariots, 2Ch 18.30
And when the c. of the chariots saw 18.31
for when the c. of the chariots saw 18.32
delivered to the c. the spears and 23.09
and the c. and the trumpeters 23.13
brought out the c. who were set 23.14
And he took the c., the nobles, 23.20
from afar, the thunder of the c., Job 39.25
When all the c. of the forces in Jer 40.07
priests and c. how he might betray Lk 22.04
priests and c. of the temple and 22.52
the flesh of c., the flesh of Rev 19.18

CAPTIVE
that his kinsman had been taken c., Gen 14.14
first-born of the c. who was in the Ex 12.29
Israel, and took some of them c. Num 21.01
long shall Asshur take you away c.?" 24.22
of Israel took c. the women of 31.09
your hands, and you take them c., Deu 21.10
and taken c. the women and all who 1Sa 30.02
and sons and daughters taken c. 30.03
David's two wives also had been taken c., 30.05
carried away c. to the land of the 1Ki 8.46
to which they have been carried c., 8.47
their enemies, who carried them c., 8.48
sight of those who carried them c., 8.50
you have taken c. with your sword 2Ki 6.22
carried the people c. to Assyria. 15.29
it, carrying its people c. to Kir, 16.09
Babylon brought c. to Babylon all 24.16
the c.: Shealtiel his son, 1Ch 3.17
carried away c. to a land far or 2Ch 6.36
to which they have been carried c., 6.37
to which they were carried c., 6.38
him and took c. a great number of 28.05
of Israel took c. two hundred 28.08
had carried c. to Babylonia; Ez 2.01
by all those who held them c. Ps 106.46
treacherous are taken c. by their lust. Pro 11.06
a king is held c. in the tresses. Sol 7.05
they will take c. those who were Is 14.02
O c. Jerusalem; loose the 52.02
your neck, O c. daughter of Zion. 52.02
the LORD's flock has been taken c. Jer 13.17
he shall carry them c. to Babylon, 20.04
where they have carried him c., 22.12
Then Ishmael took c. all the rest 41.10
took them c. and set out to cross 41.10
carried away c. from Mizpah turned 41.14
carried away c. from Mizpah after 41.16
burn them and carry them away c.; 43.12
for your sons have been taken c., 48.46
who took them c. have held them 50.33
carried away c. some of the 52.15
was carried c. out of its land. 52.57
Nebuchadrezzar carried away c.: 52.28
he carried away c. from Jerusalem 52.29
carried away c. of the Jews seven 52.30
nations where they are carried c., Eze 6.09
I carry you c. among the nations, 32.09
and be led c. among all nations; Lk 21.24
law, dead to that which held us c., Rom 7.06
and making me c. to the law of sin 7.23
every thought c. to obey Christ, 2Co 10.05
If any one is to be taken c., Rev 13.10

CAPTIVE'S
And she shall put off her c. garb, Deu 21.13

CAPTIVES

my daughters like c. of the sword? Gen 31.26
fugitives, and his daughters c., Num 21.29
brought the c. and the booty and 31.12
and your c. on the third day and 31.19
and see among the c. a beautiful Deu 21.11
the blood of the slain and the c., 32.42
Arise, Barak, lead away your c., Ju 5.12
ten thousand c., and all the 2Ki 24.14
send back the c. from your kinsfolk 2Ch 28.11
"You shall not bring the c. in here, 28.13
men left the c. and the spoil 28.14
by name rose and took the c., 28.15
defeated Judah, and carried away c. 28.17
in a land where they are c. Neh 4.04
among the c. carried away with Est 2.06
leading c. in thy train, and receiving Ps 68.18
the Egyptians c. and the Ethiopians Is 20.04
or the c. of a tyrant be rescued? 49.24
"Even the c. of the mighty shall be 49.25
to proclaim liberty to the c., 61.01
with all the c. of Jerusalem and Jer 40.01
have gone away, c. before the foe. Lam 1.05
them. They gather c. like sand. Hab 1.09
I will set your c. free from the Zec 9.11
release to the c. and recovering Lk 4.18
on high he led a host of c., Eph 4.08

CAPTIVITY

for they shall go into c. Deu 28.41
the day of the c. of the land. Ju 18.30
he took into c. from Jerusalem to 2Ki 24.15
to thee in the land of their c., 2Ch 6.37
heart in the land of their c., 6.38
and our wives are in c. for this. 29.09
up out of the c. of those exiles Ez 2.01
had come to Jerusalem from the c. 3.08
time those who had come from c., 8.35
to c., to plundering, and to utter 9.07
up out of the c. of those exiles Neh 7.06
from the c. made booths and dwelt 8.17
and delivered his power to c., Ps 78.61
burden, but themselves go into c. Is 46.02
until the c. of Jerusalem in the Jer 1.03
famine, and those who are for c., to c."' 15.02
in your house, shall go into c.; 20.06
and your lovers shall go into c.; 22.22
offspring from the land of their c. 30.10
one of them, shall go into c.; 30.16
to c. those who are doomed to c., and 43.11
offspring from the land of their c. 46.27
captive, and your daughters into c. 48.46
year of the c. of Jehoiachin king 52.31
and my young men have gone into c. Lam 1.18
they shall go into exile, into c.' Eze 12.11
and the women shall go into c. 30.17
and her daughters shall go into c. 30.18
went into c. for their iniquity, 39.23
by c. and plunder, for some days. Dan 11.33
they go into c. before their Amo 9.04
was carried away, she went into c.; Nah 3.10
to be taken captive, to c. he goes; Rev 13.10

CAPTORS

to thee in the land of their c., 1Ki 8.47
will find compassion with their c., 2Ch 30.09
For there our c. required of us Ps 137.03
captive those who were their c., Is 14.02
Among our c. he divides our fields." Mic 2.04

CAPTURE

upon David and his men to c. them, 1Sa 23.26
do not let her c. you with her Pro 6.25
sound of the c. of Babylon the Jer 50.46
with swords and clubs to c. me? Mt 26.55
with swords and clubs to c. me? Mk 14.48
into households and c. weak women, 2Ti 3.06

CAPTURED

they c. and made their prey. Gen 34.29
And we c. all his cities at that Deu 2.34
booty of the cities which we c. 2.35
And the ark of God was c.; 1Sa 4.11
and the ark of God has been c." 4.17
tidings that the ark of God was c., 4.19
of God had been c. and because of 4.21
for the ark of God has been c." 4.22
When the Philistines c. the ark of God, 5.01
David also c. all the flocks and 30.20
had gone up and c. Gezer and burnt 1Ki 9.16
and c. the horses and chariots, and 20.21
king of Israel c. Amaziah king of 2Ki 14.13
king of Assyria came and c. Ijon, 15.29
the king of Assyria c. Samaria, 17.06
Then they c. the king, and brought 25.06
and he was c. while hiding in 2Ch 22.09
The men of Judah c. another ten 25.12
king of Israel c. Amaziah king of 25.23
And they c. fortified cities and a Neh 9.25
without the bow they were c. Is 22.03
all of you who were found were c., 22.03
shall surely be c. and delivered Jer 34.03
Then they c. the king, and brought 52.09
remembrance, that they may be c. Eze 21.32
after being c. by him to do his 2Ti 2.26
And the beast was c., and with Rev 19.20

CAPTURING

and after c. it and putting it to Jos 19.47

CARAVAN

up they saw a c. of Ishmaelites Gen 37.25
went up by the c. route east of Ju 8.11

CARAVANS

c. ceased and travelers kept to the Ju 5.06
The c. turn aside from their course Job 6.18
The c. of Tema look, the travelers 6.19
you will lodge, O c. of Dedanites. Is 21.13

CARBUNCLE

and c. shall be the first row; Ex 28.17
topaz, and c. was the first row; 39.10
onyx, sapphire, c., and emerald; Eze 28.13

CARBUNCLES

your gates of c., and all your wall Is 54.12

CARCASS

whether the c. of an unclean beast Lev 5.02
beast or a c. of unclean cattle or 5.02
cattle or a c. of unclean swarming 5.02
touches their c. shall be unclean 11.24
part of their c. shall wash his 11.25
touches their c. shall be unclean 11.27
carries their c. shall wash his 11.28
part of their c. falls shall be 11.35
touches their c. shall be unclean. 11.36
part of their c. falls upon any 11.37
any part of their c. falls on it, 11.38
who touches its c. shall be 11.39
who eats of its c. shall wash his 11.40
who carries the c. shall wash his 11.40
aside to see the c. of the lion, Ju 14.08
the honey from the c. of the lion. 14.09
Thou didst crush Rahab like a c., Ps 89.10
and fill the valleys with your c. Eze 32.05

CARCASSES

of prey came down upon the c., Gen 15.11
and their c. you shall not touch; Lev 11.08
and their c. you shall have in 11.11
and their c. you shall not touch. Deu 14.08
land with the c. of their detestable Jer 16.18

CARCHEMISH

up to fight at C. on the Euphrates 2Ch 35.20
Is not Calno like C.? Is not Is 10.09
Euphrates at C. and which Nebuchadrezzar Jer 46.02

CARE

herds giving suck are a c. to me; Gen 33.13
to Joseph's c. all the prisoners 39.22
anything that was in Joseph's c., 39.32
with the c. of the holy things Num 7.09
Take good c. to observe the commandment Jos 22.05
they will take c. to walk in the Ju 2.22
I will c. for all your wants; 19.20
father cease to c. about the asses 1Sa 9.05
has ceased to c. about the asses 10.02
living in the c. of the LORD your 25.29
we flee, they will not c. about us. 2Sa 18.03
us die, they will not c. about us. 18.03
he had left to c. for the house, 20.03
we did not c. for it in the way 1Ch 15.13
having the c. of the courts and the 23.28
were in the c. of Shelomoth and 26.28
in the c. of Jehiel the Gershonite. 29.08
and c. for the golden lampstand 2Ch 13.11
And take c. not to be slack in this Ez 4.22
and thy c. has preserved my spirit. Job 10.12
For what do they c. for their 21 21
of man that thou dost c. for him? Ps 8.04
arranging proverbs with great c. Ecc 12.09
send to Kedar and examine with c.; Jer 2.10
the shepherds who c. for my people: 23.02
over them who will c. for them, 23.04
they c. nothing for you; for I 30.14
the children of their tender c.? Lam 2.20
who does not c. for the perishing, Zec 11.16
God truthfully, and c. for no man; Mt 22.16
"Teacher, do you not c. if we perish?" Mk 4.38
you are true, and c. for no man; 12.14
him to an inn, and took c. of him. Lk 10.34
innkeeper, saying, 'Take c. of him; 10.35
do you not c. that my sister has 10.40
take c. what you do with these men. Ac 5.35
each man take c. how he builds 1Co 3.10
Only take c. lest this liberty of 8.09
have the same c. for one another. 12.25
same earnest c. for you into the 2Co 8.16
a nurse taking c. of her children. 1Th 2.07
how can he c. for God's church? 1Ti 3.05
Take c., brethren, lest there be in Heb 3.12

CARED

he c. for him, he kept him as the Deu 32.10
not that he c. for the poor but Jn 12.06
to go to his friends and be c. for. Ac 27.03

CAREFREE

The sound of a c. multitude was Eze 23.42

CAREFUL

learn them and be c. to do them. Deu 5.01
You shall be c. to do therefore as 5.32
O Israel, and be c. to do them; 6.03
if we are c. to do all this commandment 6.25
therefore be c. to do the commandment, 7.11
you this day you shall be c. to do, 8.01
For if you will be c. to do all 11.22
you shall be c. to do all the 11.32
you shall be c. to do in the land 12.01
Be c. to heed all these words which 12.28
command you you shall be c. to do; 12.32
being c. to do all this commandment 15.05
you shall be c. to observe these 16.12
you shall be c. to do according to 17.10
provided you are c. to keep all 19.09
You shall be c. to perform what has 23.23
to be very c. to do according to 24.08
them, so you shall be c. to do. 24.08
therefore be c. to do them with 26.16
being c. to do all his commandments 28.01
you this day, being c. to do them, 28.13
your God or be c. to do all his 28.15
"If you are not c. to do all the 28.58
Therefore be c. to do the words of 29.09
and be c. to do all the words of 31.12
they may be c. to do all the words 32.46
being c. to do according to all the Jos 1.07
that you may be c. to do according 1.08
but have been c. to keep the charge 22.03
But Jehu was not c. to walk in the 2Ki 10.31
you, you shall always be c. to do. 17.37
they will be c. to do according to 21.08
if you are c. to observe the 1Ch 22.13
they will be c. to do all that I 2Ch 33.08
and is c. to observe my ordinances— Exe 18.09
and has been c. to observe all my 18.19
and be c. to observe my ordinances, 20.19
and were not c. to observe my 20.21
statutes and be c. to observe my 36.27
ordinances and be c. to observe my 37.24
Therefore be c. lest the light in Lk 11.35
in God may be c. to apply themselves Tit 3.08

CAREFULLY

questioned us c. about ourselves Gen 43.07
Listen c. to my words, and let my Job 13.17
"Listen c. to my words, and let this 21.02
observe c. what is before you; Pro 23.01
Look c. then how you walk, not as Eph 5.15

CARELESS

throws off restraint and is c. Pro 14.16
for every c. word they utter; Mt 12.36

CARES

which the LORD your God c. for; Deu 11.12
When the c. of my heart are many, Ps 94.19
remains to me, no man c. for me. 142.04
broken pot, a vessel no one c. for? Jer 22.28
'It is Zion, for whom no one c.!' 30.17
for which no one c., says the LORD 48.38
the LORD of hosts c. for his flock, Zec 10.03
but the c. of the world and the Mt 13.22
but the c. of the world, and the Mk 4.19
choked by the c. and riches and Lk 8.14
drunkenness and c. of this life, 21.34
a hireling and c. nothing for the Jn 10.13
on him, for he c. about you. 1Pe 5.07

CAREST

son of man, that thou c. for him? Heb 2.06

CARGO

the ship was to unload its c. Ac 21.03
not only of the c. and the ship, 27.10
next day to throw the c. overboard; 27.18
no one buys their c. any more, Rev 18.11
c. of gold, silver, jewels and pearls, 18.12

CARITES

captains of the C. and of the 2Ki 11.04
the C., the guards, and all the 11.19

CARKAS

Zethar and C., the seven eunuchs Est 1.10

CARMEL

the king of Jokneam in C., one; Jos 12.22
Maon, C., Ziph, Juttah, 15.55
west it touches C. and Shihorlibnath, 19.26
"Saul came to C., and behold, he set 1Sa 15.12
in Maon, whose business was in C. 25.02
He was shearing his sheep in C. 25.02
"Go up to C., and go to Nabal, and 25.05
all the time they were in C. 25.07
of David came to Abigail at C., 25.40

CARMEL (cont.)
and Abigail of C., Nabal's widow. 1Sa 27.03
Abigail the widow of Nabal of C. 30.05
Abigail the widow of Nabal of C. 2Sa 2.02
Abigail the widow of Nabal of C.; 3.03
Hezro of C., Paarai the Arbite, 23.35
all Israel to me at Mount C., 1Ki 18.19
the prophets together at Mount C. 18.20
Elijah went up to the top of C.; 18.42
From there he went on to Mount C., 2Ki 2.25
came to the man of God at Mount C. 4.25
Hezro of C., Naarai the son of 1Ch 11.37
Your head crowns you like C., Sol 7.05
and Bashan and C. shake off their Is 33.09
it, the majesty of C. and Sharon. 35.02
and like C. by the sea, shall one Jer 46.18
he shall feed on C. and in Bashan, 50.19
mourn, and the top of C. withers. Amo 1.02
hide themselves on the top of C., 9.03
Bashan and C. wither, the bloom of Nah 1.04

CARMELITESS
second Daniel, by Abigail the C., 1Ch 3.01

CARMI
Hanoch, Pallu, Hezron, and C. Gen 46.09
Hanoch, Pallu, Hezron and C., Ex 6.14
of C., the family of the Carmites. Num 26.06
for Achan the son of C., son of Jos 7.01
by man, and Achan the son of C., 7.18
The sons of C.: Achar, the troubler 1Ch 2.07
Hezron, C., Hur, and Shobal. 4.01
Hanoch, Pallu, Hezron, and C. 5.03

CARMITES
of Carmi, the family of the C. Num 26.06

CARNAL
spiritual; but I am c., sold under sin. Rom 7.14

CARNALLY
shall not lie c. with your neighbor's Lev 18.20
"If a man lies c. with a woman who 19.20
if a man lies with her c., and it Num 5.13

CARNELIAN
c., topaz, and jasper, chrysolite, Eze 28.13
sat there appeared like jasper and c., Rev 4.03
the sixth c., the seventh chrysolite, 21.20

CAROUSE
feasts, as they boldly c. together, Jud 1.12

CAROUSING
envy, drunkenness, c., and the like. Gal 5.21
revels, c., and lawless idolatry. 1Pe 4.03
in their dissipation, c. with you. 2Pe 2.13

CARPENTER
The c. stretches a line, he marks it Is 44.13
Is not this the c., the son of Mk 6.03

CARPENTER'S
Is not this the c. son? Is not his Mt 13.55

CARPENTERS
also c. and masons who built David 2Sa 5.11
it out to the c. and the builders 2Ki 12.11
to the c., and to the builders, and 22.06
also masons and c. to build a 1Ch 14.01
c., and all kinds of craftsmen 22.15
masons and c. to restore the house 2Ch 24.12
They gave it to the c. and the 34.11
money to the masons and the c., Ez 3.07

CARPETS
who sit on rich c. and you who Ju 5.10
and in c. of colored stuff, bound Eze 27.24

CARPUS
cloak that I left with C. at Troas, 2Ti 4.13

CARRIED
and c. away my daughters like Gen 31.26
sons of Israel c. Jacob their 46.05
for his sons c. him to the land of 50.13
the table shall be c. with these. Ex 25.28
sides of the altar, when it is c. 27.07
and c. them in their coats out of Lev 10.05
shall be c. forth outside the camp; 16.27
which had to be c. on the shoulder Num 7.09
who c. the tabernacle, set out. 10.17
and they c. it on a pole between 13.23
who c. the ark of the covenant of Deu 31.09
the Levites who c. the ark of the 31.25
your God being c. by the Levitical Jos 3.03
and they c. them over with them to 4.08
priests who c. the ark of the 8.33
the people that c. the tribute. Ju 3.18
shoulders and c. them to the top 16.03
from the dancers whom they c. off; 21.23
they c. it from Ebenezer to Ashdod; 1Sa 5.01
but c. them off, and went their way. 30.02
and David and his men c. them away. 2Sa 5.21
And they c. the ark of God upon a 6.03
gold which were c. by the servants 8.07
and Abiathar c. the ark of God 15.29
he c. Amasa out of the highway into 20.12
of the people who c. on the work. 1Ki 5.16
that they are c. away captive to 8.46
to which they have been c. captive, 8.47
who c. them captive, and pray to 8.48
sight of those who c. them captive, 8.50
of the people who c. on the work. 9.23
and they c. away the stones of 15.22
and c. him up into the upper chamber, 17.19
their raids had c. off a little 2Ki 5.02
and they c. them before Gehazi. 5.23
and they c. off silver and gold and 7.08
and c. off things from it, and went 7.08
His servants c. him in a chariot to 9.28
and he c. the people captive to 15.29
and he c. the Israelites away to 17.06
whom the LORD c. away before them. 17.11
which you have c. away and placed 17.26
priests whom you c. away thence; 17.27
whom they had c. away from Samaria 17.28
among whom they had been c. away. 17.33
The king of Assyria c. the Israelites 18.11
this day, shall be c. to Babylon; 20.17
and c. their ashes to Bethel. 23.04
And his servants c. him dead in a 23.30
and c. off all the treasures of the 24.13
He c. away all Jerusalem, and all 24.14
And he c. away Jehoiachin to 24.15
captain of the guard c. into exile. 25.11
and c. the bronze to Babylon. 25.13
king of Assyria c. away into exile; 1Ch 5.06
who c. shield and sword, and drew 5.18
They c. off their livestock: fifty 5.21
and he c. them away, namely, the 5.26
and they were c. into exile to 8.06
And they c. the ark of God upon a 13.07
And the Levites c. the ark of God 15.15
gold which were c. by the servants 18.07
which he had c. off from all the 18.11
that they are c. away captive to a 2Ch 6.36
to which they have been c. captive, 6.37
to which they were c. captive, 6.38
that c. shields and drew bows; 14.08
men of Judah c. away very much 14.13
and c. away sheep in abundance and 14.15
and they c. away the stones of 16.06
and c. away all the possessions 21.17
Judah, and c. away captives. 28.17
took it and c. it out to the brook 29.16

CARRIED (cont.)

and c. it round Ophel, and raised it 2Ch 33.14
and c. them quickly to all the lay 35.13
the chariot and c. him in his 35.24
his brother and c. him to Egypt. 36.04
Nebuchadnezzar also c. part of the 36.07
Nebuchadnezzar had c. away from Ez 1.07
of Babylon had c. captive to 2.01
this house and c. away the people 5.12
Those who c. burdens were laden in Neh 4.17
king of Babylon had c. into exile; 7.06
who had been c. away from Jerusalem Est 2.06
the captives c. away with Jeconiah 2.06
king of Babylon had c. away. 2.06
c. from the womb to the grave. Job 10.19
of his house will be c. away, 20.28
are swiftly c. away upon the face 24.18
Samaria will be c. away before the Is 8.04
whose feet c. her to settle afar? 23.07
this day, shall be c. to Babylon; 39.06
from your birth, c. from the womb; 46.03
shall be c. on their shoulders. 49.22
our griefs and c. our sorrows; 53.04
daughters shall be c. in the arms. 60.04
them up and c. them all the days 63.09
you shall be c. upon her hip, and 66.12
they have to be c., for they Jer 10.05
where they have c. him captive, 22.12
They shall be c. to Babylon and 27.22
from this place and c. to Babylon. 28.03
c. into exile to Babylon the rest 39.09
Ishmael had c. away captive from 41.14
Nethaniah had c. away captive from 41.16
of the guard c. away captive some 52.15
and c. all the bronze to Babylon. 52.17
So Judah was c. captive out of its 52.27
Nebuchadrezzar c. away captive: 52.28
Nebuchadrezzar he c. away captive 52.29
of the guard c. away captive of 52.30
he purposed, has c. out his threat; Lam 2.17
nations where they are c. captive, Eze 6.09
young twigs and c. it to a land of 17.04
But she c. her harlotry further; 23.14
When she c. on her harlotry so 23.18
Egypt, and her wealth is c. away, 30.04
and the wind c. them away, so that Dan 2.35
itself shall be c. to Assyria, Hos 10.06
Assyria, and oil is c. to Egypt. 12.01
and have c. my rich treasures into Joe 3.05
because they c. into exile a whole Amo 1.06
I c. away your horses; and I made 4.10
that strangers c. off his wealth, Ob 1.11
she is c. off, her maidens lamenting, Nah 2.07
Yet she was c. away, she went into 3.10
to him a paralytic c. by four men. Mk 2.03
man who had died was being c. out, Lk 7.12
died and was c. by the angels to 16.22
if you have c. him away, tell me Jn 20.15
a man lame from birth was being c., Ac 3.02
him up and c. him out and buried 5.06
and they c. her out and buried her 5.10
so that they even c. out the sick 5.15
and they were c. back to Shechem 7.16
or aprons were c. away from his 19.12
he was actually c. by the soldiers 21.35
Barnabas was c. away by their Gal 2.13
to and fro and c. about with every Eph 4.14
lest you be c. away with the error 2Pe 3.17
waterless clouds, c. along by winds; Jud 1.12
And he c. me away in the Spirit Rev 17.03
the Spirit he c. me away to a 21.10

CARRIES

and whoever c. any part of their Lev 11.25
and he who c. their carcass shall 11.28
he also who c. the carcass shall 11.40
and he who c. such a thing shall 15.10
as a nurse c. the sucking child, to Num 11.12
like chaff that the storm c. away? Job 21.18
the night a whirlwind c. him off. 27.20
the man who c. out evil devices! Ps 37.07
and the tempest c. them off like Is 40.24
'If one c. holy flesh in the skirt Hag 2.12
heads and ten horns that c. her. Rev 17.07

CARRION

the c. vulture and the cormorant, Deu 14.17

CARRY

on their way to c. it down to Gen 37.25
the rest go and c. grain for the 42.19
and c. down to the man a present, a 43.11
c. back with you the money that was 43.12
with food, as much as they can c., 44.01
which Joseph had sent to c. him, 45.27
which Pharaoh had sent to c. him. 46.05
c. me out of Egypt and bury me in 47.30
and you shall c. up my bones from 50.25
you shall not c. forth any of the Ex 12.46
then you must c. my bones with you 13.19
of the ark, to c. the ark by them. 25.14
for the poles to c. the table. 25.27
for poles with which to c. it. 30.04
with me, do not c. us up from here. 33.15
sides of the ark, to c. the ark. 37.05
for the poles to c. the table. 37.14
of acacia wood to c. the table, 37.15
for the poles with which to c. it. 37.27
of the altar, to c. it with them; 38.07
bull he shall c. forth outside the Lev 4.12
And he shall c. forth the bull 4.21
and c. forth the ashes outside the 6.11
c. your brethren from before the 10.04
and he shall c. them forth out of 14.45
they are to c. the tabernacle and Num 1.50
of Kohath shall come to c. these, 4.15
which the sons of Kohath are to c. 4.15
they shall c. the curtains of the 4.25
sons, in all that they are to c., 4.27
charge all that they are to c. 4.27
is what they are charged to c., 4.31
which they are required to c. 4.32
'C. them in your bosom, as a nurse 11.12
I am not able to c. all this people 11.14
and c. it quickly to the congregation, 16.46
of Levi to c. the ark of the Deu 10.08
You shall c. much seed into the 28.38
and c. them over with you, and lay Jos 4.03
and c. them quickly to the camp to 1Sa 17.17
"Go and c. them to the city." 20.40
and did not c. out his fierce wrath 28.18
to c. the good news to their idols 31.09
As for me, where could I c. my shame? 2Sa 13.13
"C. the ark of God back into the 15.25
and c. tidings to the king that the 18.19
"You are not to c. tidings today; 18.20
you may c. tidings another day, but 18.20
but today you shall c. no tidings, 18.20
the LORD will c. you whither I 1Ki 18.12
and c. me out of the battle, for I 22.34
servant, "C. him to his mother." 2Ki 4.19
to c. the good news to their idols 1Ch 10.09
the Levites may c. the ark of God, 15.02
chose them to c. the ark of the 15.02
Because you did not c. it the first 15.13
longer need to c. the tabernacle 23.26
and c. me out of the battle, for I 2Ch 18.33
until they could c. no more. 20.25
and c. out the filth from the holy 29.05
need no longer c. it upon your 35.03
Why does your heart c. you away, Job 15.12
hungry, they c. the sheaves; 24.10
Surely I would c. it on my shoulder; 31.36
shepherd, and c. them for ever. Ps 28.09

CARRY (cont.)
he dies he will c. nothing away; Ps 49.17
Can a man c. fire in his bosom and Pro 6.27
which he may c. away in his hand. Ecc 5.15
bird of the air will c. your voice, 10.20
they c. it off, and none can rescue. Is 5.29
laid up they c. away over the 15.07
"who c. out a plan, but not mine; 30.01
they c. their riches on the backs 30.06
he will c. them in his bosom, and 40.11
and the wind shall c. them away, 41.16
knowledge who c. about their 45.20
things you c. are loaded as 46.01
and to gray hairs I will c. you. 46.04
will bear; I will c. and will save. 46.04
they c. it, they set it in its place, 46.07
The wind will c. them off, a breath 57.13
And do not c. a burden out of your Jer 17.22
he shall c. them captive to Babylon, 20.04
seize them, and c. them to Babylon. 20.05
burn them and c. them away captive 43.12
and c. it out in the dark; you shall Eze 12.06
and he shall c. off its wealth and 29.19
when I c. you captive among the 32.09
to seize spoil and c. off plunder; 38.12
your hosts to c. off plunder, 38.13
to c. away silver and gold, to take 38.13
He shall also c. off to Egypt their Dan 11.08
and again shall c. the war as far 11.10
I will c. off, and none shall rescue Hos 5.14
sandals I am not worthy to c.; Mt 3.11
man they compelled to c. his cross. 27.32
any one to c. anything through the Mk 11.16
Alexander and Rufus, to c. his cross. 15.21
C. no purse, no bag, no sandals; Lk 10.04
the cross, to c. it behind Jesus. 23.26
lawful for you to c. your pallet." Jn 5.10
gird you and c. you where you do 21.18
the door, and they will c. you out." Ac 5.09
of mine to c. my name before the 9.15
by letter to c. your gift to 1Co 16.03
their hearts to c. out his purpose Rev 17.17

CARRYING
and put it upon the c. frame. Num 4.10
and put them on the c. frame. 4.12
each to his task of serving or c.; 4.49
c. the holy things, and the tabernacle 10.21
meet you there, one c. three kids, 1Sa 10.03
another c. three loaves of bread, 10.03
and another c. a skin of wine. 10.03
done well in c. out what is right 2Ki 10.30
c. its people captive to Kir, and he 16.09
who were c. the ark of the covenant 1Ch 15.26
the Levites who were c. the ark, 15.27
and c. all the feeble among them 2Ch 28.15
c. my outfit upon my shoulder in Eze 12.07
and a man c. a jar of water will Mk 14.13
a man c. a jar of water will meet Lk 22.10
kept them from c. out their Ac 27.43
always c. in the body the death of 2Co 4.10
gracious work which we are c. on, 8.19
we are not c. on a worldly war, 10.03

CARSHENA
the men next to him being C., Est 1.14

CART
prepare a new c. and two milch 1Sa 6.07
yoke, and yoke the cows to the c., 6.07
of the LORD and place it on the c., 6.08
cows and yoked them to the c., 6.10
put the ark of the LORD on the c., 6.11
The c. came into the field of 6.14
the wood of the c. and offered the 6.14
the ark of God upon a new c., 2Sa 6.03
Abinadab, were driving the new c. 6.03
the ark of God upon a new c., 1Ch 13.07
Uzzah and Ahio were driving the c. 13.07
who draw sin as with c. ropes, Is 5.18
nor is a c. wheel rolled over 28.27
he drives his c. wheel over it 28.28
as a c. full of sheaves presses Amo 2.13

CARVE
and c. a habitation for yourself in Is 22.16

CARVED
the house was c. in the form of 1Ki 6.18
He c. all the walls of the house 6.29
about with c. figures of cherubim 6.29
On them he c. cherubim and palm 6.35
evenly applied upon the c. work. 6.35
he c. cherubim, lions, and palm trees, 7.36
and he c. cherubim on the walls. 2Ch 3.07
And then all its c. wood they broke Ps 74.06
and the nave were c. likenesses Eze 41.17
They were c. on the whole temple 41.19
and palm trees were c. on the wall. 41.20
the nave were c. cherubim and palm 41.25
such as were c. on the walls; 41.25
c. in letters on stone, came with 2Co 3.07

CARVING
and in c. wood, for work in every Ex 31.05
and in c. wood, for work in every 35.33

CARVINGS
of olivewood with c. of cherubim, 1Ki 6.32
At its opening there were c.; and its 7.31

CASE
the c. of both parties shall Ex 22.09
of Israel in c. the people of Num 8.19
Moses brought their c. before the 27.05
and the c. that is too hard for you, Deu 1.17
"If any c. arises requiring decision 17.08
any c. within your towns which is 17.08
for this c. is like that of a man 22.26
and explain his c. to the elders Jos 20.04
whenever a c. comes to you from 2Ch 19.10
I desire to argue my c. with God. Job 13.03
him, will you plead the c. for God? 13.08
Behold, I have prepared my c.; 13.18
I would lay my c. before him and 23.04
that the c. is before him, and you 35.14
draw up our c. because of darkness. 37.19
He who states his c. first seems Pro 18.17
Argue your c. with your neighbor 25.09
Set forth your c., says the LORD; Is 41.21
set forth your c., that you may 43.26
Declare and present your c.; 45.21
I would plead my c. before thee. Jer 12.01
with a writing c. at his side. Eze 9.02
who had the writing c. at his side. 9.03
with the writing c. at his side, 9.11
plead your c. before the mountains, Mic 6.01
in one c. a hundredfold, in another Mt 13.23
"If such is the c. of a man with 19.10
So in the present c. I tell you, Ac 5.38
to determine his c. more exactly. 23.15
the governor their c. against Paul; 24.01
comes down, I will decide your c." 24.22
laid Paul's c. before the king, 25.14
charge in his c. of such evils as 25.18
for the death penalty in my c. 28.18
in such a c. the brother or sister 1Co 7.15
in this c., what once had splendor 2Co 3.10
In their c. the god of this world 4.04
you may not prove vain in this c., 9.03
In that c. the stumbling block of Gal 5.11
yet in your c., beloved, we feel Heb 6.09
so that in c. they speak against 1Pe 2.12

CASES
God, and bring their c. to God; Ex 18.19
hard c. they brought to Moses, but 18.26
"This is the law in c. of jealousy, Num 5.29
'Hear the c. between your brethren, Deu 1.16
the LORD and to decide disputed c. 2Ch 19.08
you incompetent to try trivial c.? 1Co 6.02
If then you have such c., why do 6.04
so as to help c. of urgent need, and Tit 3.14

CASIPHIA
the leading man at the place C., Ez 8.17
temple servants at the place C. 8.17

CASLUHIM
Pathrusim, C. (whence came the Gen 10.14
Pathrusim, C. (whence came the 1Ch 1.12

CASSIA
and of c. five hundred, according to Ex 30.24
with myrrh and aloes and c. Ps 45.08
wrought iron, c., and calamus were Eze 27.19

CAST
"C. out this slave woman with her Gen 21.10
she c. the child under one of the 21.15
c. him into this pit here in the 37.22
took him and c. him into a pit. 37.24
master's wife c. her eyes upon 39.07
Hebrews you shall c. into the Nile, Ex 1.22
And he said, "C. it on the ground." 4.03
So he c. it on the ground, and it 4.03
your rod and c. it down before 7.09
Aaron c. down his rod before 7.10
For every man c. down his rod, and 7.12
and his host he c. into the sea; 15.04
you shall c. it to the dogs. 22.31
None shall c. her young or be 23.26
And you shall c. four rings of gold 25.12
and you shall c. five bases of 26.37
For I will c. out nations before 34.24
and he c. for them four bases of 36.36
And he c. for it four rings of gold 37.03
He c. for it four rings of gold, and 37.13
He c. four rings on the four 38.05
and c. it beside the altar on the Lev 1.16
and Aaron shall c. lots upon the 16.08
and c. your dead bodies upon the 26.30
and c. them into the midst of the Num 19.06
without seeing him c. it upon him, 35.23
and c. them out of my two hands, and Deu 9.17
and c. them into another land, as at 29.28
and c. it at the entrance of the Jos 8.29
and I will c. lots for you here 18.06
and I will c. lots for you here 18.08
and Joshua c. lots for them in 18.10
But now the LORD has c. us off, Ju 6.13
and every man c. in it the earrings 8.25
LORD will not c. away his people, 1Sa 12.22
"C. the lot between me and my son 14.42
and Saul c. the spear, for he 18.11
But Saul c. his spear at him to 20.33
Did not a woman c. an upper millstone 2Sa 11.21
they c. up a mound against the city, 20.15
He c. two pillars of bronze. 1Ki 7.15
two rows, c. with it when it was c. 7.24
The supports were c., with wreaths 7.30
and their hubs, were all c. 7.33
all of them were c. alike, 7.37
of the Jordan the king c. them, 7.46
my name I will c. out of my sight; 9.07
and have c. me behind your back; 14.09
by him and c. his mantle upon him. 19.19
whom the LORD c. out before the 21.26
him up and c. him upon some 2Ki 2.16
and c. him on the plot of ground 9.25
take him up and c. him on the plot 9.26
the officers c. them out and went 10.25
and the man was c. into the grave 13.21
nor has he c. them from his 13.23
until he had c. them out of his 17.20
and have c. their gods into the 19.18
a shield or c. up a mound against 19.32
And I will c. off the remnant of my 21.14
it to dust and c. the dust of it 23.06
and c. the dust of them into the 23.12
and I will c. off this city which I 23.27
Judah that he c. them out from his 24.20
c. lots, just as their brethren the 1Ch 24.31
And they c. lots for their duties, 25.08
and they c. lots by fathers' houses, 26.13
They c. lots also for his son 26.14
he will c. you off for ever. 28.09
two rows, c. with it when it was c. 2Ch 4.03
of the Jordan the king c. them, 4.17
I will c. out of my sight, and will 7.20
and his sons c. them out from 11.14
God will c. you down before the 25.08
has power to help or to c. down. 25.08
letters to c. contempt on the LORD 32.17
and thou didst c. their pursuers Neh 9.11
thee and c. thy law behind their 9.26
We have likewise c. lots, 10.34
of the people c. lots to bring one 11.01
they c. Pur, that is the lot, before Est 3.07
and they c. it month after month 3.07
and had c. Pur, that is the lot, to 9.24
You would even c. lots over the Job 6.27
and c. off his blossom, like the 15.33
For he is c. into a net by his own 18.08
times you have c. reproach upon me; 19.03
they have c. up siegeworks against 19.12
calves, and does not c. her calf. 21.10
countenance they did not c. down. 29.24
they have c. off restraint in my 30.11
they c. up against me their ways of 30.12
God has c. me into the mire, and I 30.19
firmly c. upon him and immovable. 41.23
and c. their cords from us." Ps 2.03
many transgressions c. them out, 5.10
their eyes to c. me to the ground. 17.11
I c. them out like the mire of the 18.42
Upon thee was I c. from my birth, 22.10
and for my raiment they c. lots. 22.18
C. me not off, forsake me not, O God 27.09
fall, he shall not be c. headlong, 37.24
Why are you c. down, O my soul, and 42.05
My soul is c. down within me, 42.06
Why are you c. down, O my soul, and 42.11
why hast thou c. me off? 43.02
Why are you c. down, O my soul, and 43.05
Yet thou hast c. us off and abased 44.09
Do not c. us off for ever! 44.23
and you c. my words behind you. 50.17
C. me not away from thy presence, 51.11
C. your burden on the LORD, and he 55.22
wilt c. them down into the lowest 55.23
in wrath c. down the peoples, O God! 56.07
upon Edom I c. my shoe; over Philistia 60.08
Do not c. me off in the time of old 71.09
why dost thou c. us off for ever? 74.01
O LORD, why dost thou c. me off? 88.14
But now thou hast c. off and 89.38
and c. his throne to the ground. 89.44
upon Edom I c. my shoe; over Philistia 108.09
Let them be c. into pits, no more to 140.10
The lot is c. into the lap, but the Pro 16.33
the wicked are c. down to ruin. 21.12
the people c. off restraint, 29.18
a time to c. away stones, and a time Ecc 3.05
to keep, and a time to c. away; 3.06
C. your bread upon the waters, for 11.01
day men will c. forth their idols Is 2.20
but you are c. out, away from your 14.19

CAST (cont.)
all who c. hook in the Nile; Is 19.08
and you will be c. down from your 22.19
covering that is c. over all 25.07
and c. to the ground, even to the 25.12
he will c. down to the earth with 28.02
every one shall c. away his idols 31.07
Their slain shall be c. out, 34.03
He has c. the lot for them, his hand 34.17
and have c. their gods into the 37.19
or c. up a siege mound against it. 37.33
make the shadow c. by the declining 38.08
for thou hast c. all my sins behind 38.17
chosen you and not c. you off"; 41.09
a wife of youth when she is c. off, 54.06
hate you and c. you out for my 66.05
c. up a siege mound against Jerusalem. Jer 6.06
And I will c. you out of my sight, 7.15
as I c. out all your kinsmen, all 7.15
Cut off your hair and c. it away; 7.29
they have c. down our dwellings.'" 9.19
shall be c. out in the streets of 14.16
and c. them into the fire. 22.07
dragged and c. forth beyond the 22.19
hurled and c. into a land which 22.28
and I will c. you off, says the LORD.' 23.33
lift you up and c. you away from 23.39
the sword and c. his dead body 26.23
then I will c. off all the descendants 31.37
body shall be c. out to the heat 36.30
Jeremiah and c. him into the 38.06
and c. them into a cistern. 41.07
which Ishmael c. all the bodies of 41.09
and c. it into the midst of the 51.63
Judah that he c. them out from his 52.03
He has c. down from heaven to earth Lam 2.01
they have c. dust on their heads 2.10
the Lord will not c. off for ever, 3.31
into the pit and c. stones on me; 3.53
and c. up a mound against it; Eze 4.02
and c. them into the fire, and burn 5.04
and I will c. down your slain 6.04
They c. their silver into the 7.19
but you were c. out on the open 16.05
when mounds are c. up and siege 17.17
C. away from you all the transgressions 18.31
c. down to the ground; the east wind 19.12
C. away the detestable things your 20.07
not every man c. away the detestable 20.08
to c. up mounds, to build siege 21.22
forgotten me and c. me behind your 23.35
soil they will c. into the midst 26.12
They c. dust on their heads and 27.30
so I c. you as profane thing from 28.16
I c. you to the ground; 28.17
And I will c. you forth into the 29.05
deserves. I have c. it out. 31.11
when I c. it down to Sheol with 31.16
And I will c. you on the ground, on 32.04
immediately be c. into a burning Dan 3.06
shall be c. into a burning fiery 3.11
immediately be c. into a burning 3.15
and to c. them into the burning 3.20
and they were c. into the burning 3.21
"Did we not c. three men bound into 3.24
shall be c. into the den of lions. 6.07
shall be c. into the den of lions?" 6.12
was brought and c. into the den of 6.16
brought and c. into the den of 6.24
but he c. him down to the ground 8.07
of the stars it c. down to the 8.10
and truth was c. down to the ground, 8.12
and he shall c. down tens of 11.12
My God will c. them off, because Hos 9.17
and have c. lots for my people, and Joe 3.03
and c. off all pity, and his anger Amo 1.11
you shall be c. forth into Harmon," 4.03
and c. down righteousness to the 5.07
they shall be c. out in silence." 8.03
his gates and c. lots for Jerusalem, Ob 1.11
let us c. lots, that we may know on Jon 1.07
So they c. lots, and the lot fell 1.07
For thou didst c. me into the deep, 2.03
'I am c. out from thy presence; 2.04
have none to c. the line by lot in Mic 2.05
and those who were c. off, a strong 4.07
Thou wilt c. all our sins into the 7.19
for her honored men lots were c., Nah 3.10
he has c. out your enemies. Zep 3.15
to c. down the horns of the nations Zec 1.21
"C. it into the treasury"—the 11.13
of silver and c. them into the 11.13
and c. out demons in your name, Mt 7.22
and he c. out the spirits with a 8.16
"If you c. us out, send us away into 8.31
And when the demon had been c. out, 9.33
to c. them out, and to heal every 10.01
cleanse lepers, c. out demons. 10.08
And if I c. out demons by Beelzebul, 12.27
by whom do your sons c. them out? 12.27
Spirit of God that I c. out demons, 12.28
said, "Why could we not c. it out?" 17.19
them, go to the sea and c. a hook, 17.27
'Be taken up and c. into the sea, 21.21
took him and c. him out of the 21.39
and c. him into the outer darkness; 22.13
And c. the worthless servant into 25.30
and c. out many demons; and he Mk 1.34
and have authority to c. out demons: 3.15
parables, "How can Satan c. out Satan? 3.23
And they c. out many demons, and 6.13
begged him to c. the demon out of 7.26
asked your disciples to c. it out, 9.18
And it has often c. him into the 9.22
privately, "Why could we not c. it out?" 9.28
'Be taken up and c. into the sea, 11.23
and c. him out of the vineyard. 12.08
and c. out your name as evil, on Lk 6.22
begged your disciples to c. it out, 9.40
you say that I c. out demons by 11.18
And if I c. out demons by Beelzebul, 11.19
by whom do your sons c. them out? 11.19
finger of God that I c. out demons, 11.20
killed, has power to c. into hell; 12.05
"I came to c. fire upon the earth; 12.49
I c. out demons and perform cures 13.32
neck and he were c. into the sea, 17.02
enemies will c. up a bank about 19.43
this one they wounded and c. out. 20.12
And they c. him out of the vineyard 20.15
And they c. lots to divide his 23.34
who comes to me I will not c. out. Jn 6.37
teach us?" And they c. him out. 9.34
Jesus heard that they had c. him out, 9.35
the ruler of this world be c. out; 12.31
he is c. forth as a branch and 15.06
but c. lots for it to see whose it 19.24
and for my clothing they c. lots." 19.24
"C. the net on the right side of 21.06
So they c. it, and now they were 21.06
And they c. lots for them, and the Ac 1.26
Then they c. him out of the city 7.58
and do they now c. us out secretly? 16.37
put to death I c. my vote against 26.10
third day they c. out with their 27.19
So they c. off the anchors and left 27.40
Let us then c. off the works of Rom 13.12
"C. out the slave and her son; Gal 4.30
C. all your anxieties on him, for he 1Pe 5.07
but c. them into hell and committed 2Pe 2.04
they c. their crowns before the Rev 4.10
and c. them to the earth. And the 12.04

CASTANETS
and tambourines and c. and cymbals. 2Sa 6.05

CASTING
silver were for c. the bases of — Ex 38.27
nations I am c. out before you — Lev 18.24
which I am c. out before you; — 20.23
weeping and c. himself down before — Ez 10.01
the prophet by c. him into the — Jer 38.09
c. a net into the sea; for they — Mt 4.18
his garments among them by c. lots; — 27.35
of Simon c. a net in the sea; — Mk 1.16
their synagogues and c. out demons. — 1.39
we saw a man c. out demons in your — 9.38
c. lots for them, to decide what — 15.24
we saw a man c. out demons in your — Lk 9.49
Now he was c. out a demon that was — 11.14
c. up the foam of their own shame; — Jud 1.13

CASTLE
governor of the c. charge over — Neh 7.02
quarreling is like the bars of a c. — Pro 18.19

CASTS
and c. me into the hands of the — Job 16.11
God c. them out of his belly. — 20.15
he c. the wicked to the ground. — Ps 147.06
He c. forth his ice like morsels; — 147.17
Slothfulness c. into a deep sleep, — Pro 19.15
to the ground, c. it to the dust. — Is 26.05
a workman c. it, and a goldsmith — 40.19
and c. for it silver chains. — 40.19
Who fashions a god or c. an image, — 44.10
"He c. out demons by the prince of — Mt 9.34
demons, that this man c. out demons." — 12.24
and if Satan c. out Satan, he is — 12.26
of demons he c. out the demons." — Mk 3.22
"He c. out demons by Beelzebul, the — Lk 11.15
love, but perfect love c. out fear. — 1Jn 4.18

CATARACTS
to deep at the thunder of thy c.; — Ps 42.07

CATCH
A slothful man will not c. his prey, — Pro 12.27
C. us the foxes, the little foxes, — Sol 2.15
They set a trap; they c. men. — Jer 5.26
the LORD, and they shall c. them; — 16.16
lion, and he learned to c. prey; — Eze 19.03
lion, and he learned to c. prey; — 19.06
and let down your nets for a c." — Lk 5.04
at the c. of fish which they had — 5.09
to c. at something he might say. — 11.54
the people to c. him by what he — 20.26

CATCHES
breaks out and c. in thorns so — Ex 22.06
"He c. the wise in their craftiness, — 1Co 3.19

CATCHING
c. them, bearing them on its pinions, — Deu 32.11
henceforth you will be c. men." — Lk 5.10

CATERPILLAR
blight or mildew or locust or c.; — 1Ki 8.37
blight or mildew or locust or c.; — 2Ch 6.28
He gave their crops to the c., — Ps 78.46
is gathered as the c. gathers; — Is 33.04

CATTLE
c. and creeping things and beasts — Gen 1.24
kinds and the c. according to — 1.25
and over the c., and over all the — 1.26
The man gave names to all c., — 2.20
this, cursed are you above all c., — 3.14
who dwell in tents and have c. — 4.20
and all the c. according to their — 7.14
c., beasts, all swarming creatures — 7.21
and all the c. that were with him — 8.01
the c., and every beast of the — 9.10
Now Abram was very rich in c., — 13.02
of Abram's c. and the herdsmen of — 13.07
and the herdsmen of Lot's c. — 13.07
and how your c. have fared with me. — 30.29
taken away the c. of your father, — 31.09
and he drove away all his c., — 31.18
the c. in his possession which he — 31.18
the pace of the c. which are — 33.14
house, and made booths for his c.; — 33.17
sons were with his c. in the field, — 34.05
Will not their c., their property — 34.23
his c., all his beasts, and all his — 36.06
support them because of their c. — 36.07
They also took their c. and their — 46.06
for they have been keepers of c.; — 46.32
been keepers of c. from our youth — 46.34
them, put them in charge of my c." — 47.06
"Give your c., and I will give you — 47.16
you food in exchange for your c., — 47.16
So they brought their c. to Joseph; — 47.17
exchange for all their c. that year. — 47.17
and the herds of c. are my lord's; — 47.18
upon your c. which are in the — Ex 9.03
between the c. of Israel and the — 9.04
of Israel and the c. of Egypt, — 9.04
all the c. of the Egyptians died, — 9.06
but of the c. of the people of — 9.06
not one of the c. of the Israelites — 9.07
get your c. and all that you have — 9.19
slaves and his c. flee into the — 9.20
his slaves and his c. in the field. — 9.21
Our c. also must go with us; — 10.26
and all the first-born of the c. — 11.05
and all the first-born of the c. — 12.29
and very many c., both flocks and — 12.38
firstlings of your c. that are — 13.12
of man and the first-born of c. — 13.15
children and our c. with thirst?" — 17.03
or your c., or the sojourner who is — 20.10
all your male c., the firstlings of — 34.19
offering of c. from the herd or — Lev 1.02
of unclean c. or a carcass of — 5.02
not let your c. breed with a — 19.19
for your c. also and for the beasts — 25.07
your children, and destroy your c., — 26.22
and the c. of the Levites instead — Num 3.41
among the c. of the people of — 3.41
and the c. of the Levites instead — 3.45
of the Levites instead of their c.; — 3.45
all the c. for the burnt offering — 7.87
and all the c. for the sacrifice of — 7.88
die here, both we and our c.? — 20.04
to the congregation and their c." — 20.08
congregation drank, and their c. — 20.11
I and my c., then I will pay for it — 20.19
they took as booty all their c., — 31.09
of all the c., and give them to the — 31.30
seventy-two thousand c., — 31.33
The c. were thirty-six thousand, of — 31.38
thirty-six thousand c., — 31.44
had a very great multitude of c.; — 32.01
the place was a place for c. — 32.01
of Israel, is a land for c.; — 32.04
and your servants have c." — 32.04
and all our c., shall remain there — 32.26
be for their c. and for their — 35.03
only the c. we took as spoil for — Deu 2.35
But all the c. and the spoil of the — 3.07
and your c. (I know that you have — 3.19
you have many c.) shall remain in — 3.19
ox, or your ass, or any of your c., — 5.14
increase of your c. and the young — 7.13
barren among you, or among your c. — 7.14
grass in your fields for your c., — 11.15
all who are in it and its c., — 13.15
the c., and everything else in the — 20.14
beasts, the increase of your c., — 28.04
body, and in the fruit of your c., — 28.11

CATTLE (cont.)
ground, the increase of your c., Den 28.18
offspring of your c. and the fruit 28.51
increase of your c. or the young of 28.51
body, and in the fruit of your c., 30.09
and your c. shall remain in the Jos 1.14
spoil and its c. you shall take as 8.02
Only the c. and the spoil of that 8.27
spoil of these cities and the c., 11.14
lands for their c. and their 14.04
their pasture lands for our c. 21.02
much wealth, and with very many c., 22.08
up with their c. and their tents, Ju 6.05
ones and the c. and the goods in 18.21
the best of your c. and your asses, 1Sa 8.16
Philistines, and brought away their c., 23.05
people drove those c. before him, 30.20
oxen, and twenty pasture-fed c., 1Ki 4.23
drink, you, your c., and your beasts.' 2Ki 3.17
because their c. had multiplied in 1Ch 5.09
they came down to raid their c. 7.21
property and c. of the king and 28.01
the tents of those who had c., 2Ch 14.15
they found c. in great numbers, 20.25
in the tithe of c. and sheep, 31.06
and stalls for all kinds of c., 32.28
and over our c. at their pleasure, Neh 9.37
first-born of our sons and of our c., 10.36
Why are we counted as c.? Why are we Job 18.03
the c. on a thousand hills. Ps 50.10
He gave over their c. to the hail, 78.48
cause the grass to grow for the c., 104.14
he does not let their c. decrease. 107.38
may our c. be heavy with young, 144.14
Beasts and all c., creeping things 148.10
a place where c. are let loose and Is 7.25
that day your c. will graze in 30.23
their idols are on beasts and c.; 46.01
Like c. that go down into the valley, 63.14
and the lowing of c. is not heard; Jer 9.10
booty, their herds of c. a spoil. 49.32
who have gotten c. and goods, who Eze 38.12
to take away c. and goods, to seize 38.13
The herds of c. are perplexed because Joe 1.18
from their left, and also much c.?" Jon 4.11
upon men and c., and upon all their Hag 1.11
the multitude of men and c. in it. Zec 2.04
himself, and his sons, and his c.?" Jn 4.12
c. and sheep, horses and chariots, Rev 18.13

CAUDA
lee of a small island called C., Ac 27.16

CAUGHT
c. in a thicket by his horns; Gen 22.13
she c. him by his garment, saying, 39.12
so he put out his hand and c. it, Ex 4.04
and c. him, and cut off his thumbs Ju 1.06
And he c. a young man of Succoth, 8.14
So Samson went and c. three hundred 15.04
became as flax that has c. fire, 15.14
I c. him by his beard, and smote him 1Sa 17.35
And each c. his opponent by the 2Sa 2.16
and his head c. fast in the oak, and 18.09
and c. hold of the horns of the 1Ki 1.50
of the LORD and c. hold of the 2.28
of the LORD has c. him up and cast 2Ki 2.16
man of God, she c. hold of his feet. 4.27
blue hangings c. up with cords of Est 1.06
in fetters and c. in the cords of Job 36.08
hid has their own foot been c. Ps 9.15
let them be c. in the schemes which 10.02
will keep your foot from being c. Pro 3.26
and he is c. in the toils of his 5.22
c. in the words of your mouth; 6.02
And if he is c., he will pay 6.31
slaughter, or as a stag is c. fast 7.22
like birds which are c. in a snare, Ecc 9.12
and whoever is c. will fall by the Is 13.15
the pit shall be c. in the snare. 24.18
"As a thief is shamed when c., Jer 2.26
the pit shall be c. in the snare. 48.44
you were found and c., because you 50.24
reached out his hand and c. him, Mt 14.31
woman who had been c. in adultery, *Jn 8.03
this woman has been c. in the act * 8.04
but that night they c. nothing. 21.03
of the fish that you have just c." 21.10
Spirit of the Lord c. up Philip; Ac 8.39
the ship was c. and could not face 27.15
years ago was c. up to the third 2Co 12.02
this man was c. up into Paradise— 12.03
shall be c. up together with them 1Th 4.17
born to be c. and killed, reviling 2Pe 2.12
her child was c. up to God and to Rev 12.05

CAULKERS
your c., your dealers in merchandise, Eze 27.27

CAULKING
men were in you, c. your seams; Eze 27.09

CAUSE
and c. frogs to come upon the land Ex 8.05
time I will c. very heavy hail to 9.18
place where I c. my name to be 20.24
subverts the c. of those who are 23.08
whoever has a c., let him go to 24.14
and he shall c. the inside of the Lev 14.41
and so c. them to bear iniquity and 22.16
the eyes and c. life to pine away. 26.16
enter into her and c. bitter pain. Num 5.24
enter into her and c. bitter pain, 5.27
And you shall c. the Levites to 8.13
and will c. him to come near to him; 16.05
he will choose he will c. to come near 16.05
brethren and c. the inheritance of 27.07
then you shall c. his inheritance 27.08
c. him to stand before Eleazar the 27.19
for he shall c. Israel to inherit Deu 1.38
subverts the c. of the righteous. 16.19
or c. the people to return to Egypt 17.16
the judge shall c. him to lie down 25.02
"The LORD will c. your enemies who 28.07
"The LORD will c. you to be defeated 28.25
for you shall c. this people to Jos 1.06
Or will you defend his c.? Whoever Ju 6.31
have become the c. of great trouble 11.35
blood by killing David without c.?" 1Sa 19.05
and plead my c., and deliver me 24.15
my lord shall have no c. of grief, 25.31
blood without c. or for my lord 25.31
with a suit or c. might come to me, 2Sa 15.04
fortified cities, and c. us trouble." 20.06
For will he not c. to prosper all 23.05
and c. Solomon my son to ride on my 1Ki 1.33
blood which Joab shed without c. 2.31
supplication, and maintain their c. 8.45
supplication, and maintain their c. 8.49
he maintain the c. of his servant, 8.59
and the c. of his people Israel, as 8.59
and to c. the death of my son!" 17.18
and I will c. him to fall by the 2Ki 19.07
and I will not c. the feet of 21.08
supplication, and maintain their c. 2Ch 6.35
maintain their c. and forgive thy 6.39
Jerusalem and to c. confusion in it. Neh 4.08
him, to destroy him without c." Job 2.03
and to God would I commit my c.; 5.08
multiplies my wounds without c.; 9.17
searched out the c. of him whom I 29.16
rejected the c. of my manservant 31.13
or plundered my enemy without c., Ps 7.04
For thou hast maintained my just c.; 9.04

CAUSE (cont.)

Hear a just c., O LORD; attend to Ps 17.01
"He committed his c. to the LORD; 22.08
For without c. they hid their net 35.07
without c. they dug a pit for my 35.07
the eye who hate me without c. 35.19
for my c., my God and my Lord! 35.23
are my foes without c. are mighty, 38.19
and defend my c. against an ungodly 43.01
victoriously for the c. of truth 45.04
I will c. your name to be celebrated 45.17
day long they seek to injure my c.; 56.05
are those who hate me without c.; 69.04
May he defend the c. of the poor of 72.04
Arise, O God, plead thy c.; remember 74.22
Thou dost c. the grass to grow for 104.14
of hate, and attack me without c. 109.03
Plead my c. and redeem me; give me 119.154
Princes persecute me without c., 119.161
maintains the c. of the afflicted, 140.12
plead their c. and despoil of life Pro 22.23
he will plead their c. against you. 23.11
Who has wounds without c.? Who has 23.29
against your neighbor without c., 24.28
and the widow's c. does not come Is 1.23
and the LORD will c. his majestic 30.30
of recompense for the c. of Zion. 34.08
and let it c. righteousness to 45.08
who pleads the c. of his people: 51.22
Lord GOD will c. righteousness and 61.11
birth and not c. to bring forth? 66.09
shall I, who c. to bring forth, shut 66.09
justice the c. of the fatherless, Jer 5.28
for to thee have I committed my c. 11.20
and will c. their people to fall by 19.07
for to thee have I committed my c. 20.12
He judged the c. of the poor and 22.16
There is none to uphold your c., 30.13
abomination, to c. Judah to sin. 32.35
time I will c. a righteous Branch 33.15
when I will c. the battle cry to be 49.02
He will surely plead their c., 50.34
will plead your c. and take 51.36
but, though he c. grief, he will have Lam 3.32
to subvert a man in his c., 3.36
my eyes c. me grief at the fate of 3.51
who were my enemies without c.; 3.52
"Thou hast taken up my c., O Lord, 3.58
O LORD; judge thou my c. 3.59
If I c. wild beasts to pass through Eze 14.15
done without c. all that I have 14.23
"On that day I will c. a horn to 29.21
and will c. all the birds of the 32.04
I will c. your multitude to fall by 32.12
and c. their rivers to run like oil, 32.14
and I will c. you to be inhabited 36.11
and no longer c. your nation to 36.15
and c. you to walk in my statutes 36.27
I will c. the cities to be inhabited, 36.33
I will c. breath to enter you, and 37.05
and will c. flesh to come upon you, 37.06
and he shall c. fearful destruction, Dan 8.24
c. thy face to shine upon thy 9.17
week he shall c. sacrifice and 9.27
he pleads my c. and executes Mic 7.09
and I will c. the remnant of this Zec 8.12
Lo, I will c. men to fall each into 11.06
to divorce one's wife for any c.?" Mt 19.03
that he should c. one of these Lk 17.02
law, 'They hated me without a c.' Jn 15.25
there being no c. that we can give Ac 19.40
what you eat c. the ruin of one Rom 14.15
if food is a c. of my brother's 1Co 8.13
lest I c. my brother to fall. 8.13
For if I c. you pain, who is there 2Co 2.02
not to c. you pain but to let you 2.04
but giving you c. to be proud of 5.12
may have ample c. to glory in Php 1.26
bitterness" spring up and c. trouble, Heb 12.15
in it there is no c. for stumbling. 1Jn 2.10
and to c. those who will not Rev 13.15

CAUSED

God had not c. it to rain upon the Gen 2.05
So the LORD God c. a deep sleep to 2.21
And when God c. me to wander from 20.13
that the LORD c. all that he did 39.03
took Joshua and c. him to stand Num 27.22
Behold, these c. the people of 31.16
until they have c. you to perish. Deu 28.51
So he c. the ark of the LORD to Jos 6.11
went down and c. Solomon to ride on 1Ki 1.38
and they have c. him to ride on the 1.44
and he c. him to come up into the 20.33
May the God who has c. his name to Ex 6.12
and I c. the widow's heart to sing Job 29.13
or have c. the eyes of the widow to 31.16
and c. the death of its owners; 31.39
so that they c. the cry of the poor 34.28
and c. the dawn to know its place, 38.12
and c. waters to flow down like Ps 78.16
He c. the east wind to blow in the 78.26
Thou hast c. my companions to shun 88.08
Thou hast c. lover and friend to 88.18
blood, and c. their fish to die. 105.29
He c. them to be pitied by all 106.46
He has c. his wonderful works to be 111.04
sighing she has c. I bring to an Is 21.02
who c. his glorious arm to go at 63.12
he c. my strength to fail; the Lord Lam 1.14
he c. rampart and wall to lament, 2.08
which they c. by their might; Eze 32.30
house of Israel c. to be profaned 36.21
you have c. many to stumble by your Mal 2.08
But if any one has c. pain, 2Co 2.05
he has c. it not to be, but in some 2.05

CAUSELESS

a curse that is c. does not alight Pro 26.02

CAUSES

"When a man c. a field or vineyard Ex 22.05
When a man c. a disfigurement in Lev 24.19
or for love, he c. it to happen. Job 37.13
and c. the lightning of his cloud 37.15
A slack hand c. poverty, but the Pro 10.04
He who winks the eye c. trouble, 10.10
is a son who c. shame and brings 19.26
given to anger c. much transgression. 29.22
and as a garden c. what is sown in Is 61.11
and the fire c. water to boil— 64.02
with anything that c. sweat. Eze 44.18
If your right eye c. you to sin, Mt 5.29
And if your right hand c. you to sin, 5.30
his kingdom all c. of sin and all 13.41
but whoever c. one of these little 18.06
hand or your foot c. you to sin, 18.08
And if your eye c. you to sin, 18.09
"Whoever c. one of these little Mk 9.42
And if your hand c. you to sin, 9.43
And if your foot c. you to sin, 9.45
And if your eye c. you to sin, 9.47
What c. wars, and what c. fightings Jas 4.01
Also it c. all, both small and great, Rev 13.16

CAUSING

c. a very great panic, and he 1Sa 5.09
c. them to look with contempt upon Est 1.17

CAUTIONED

And he c. them, saying, "Take heed, Mk 8.15

CAUTIOUS

A wise man is c. and turns away Pro 14.16

CAVALRY
the troops of c. was twice ten Rev 9.16

CAVE
he dwelt in a c. with his two Gen 19.30
he may give me the c. of Machpelah, 23.09
I give you the c. that is in it; 23.11
field with the c. which was in it 23.17
his wife in the c. of the field of 23.19
The field and the c. that is in it 23.20
buried him in the c. of Machpelah, 25.09
fathers in the c. that is in the 49.29
in the c. that is in the field at 49.30
the field and the c. that is in it 49.32
him in the c. of the field at 50.13
themselves in the c. at Makkedah. Jos 10.16
hidden in the c. at Makkedah." 10.17
stones against the mouth of the c., 10.18
said, "Open the mouth of the c., 10.22
five kings out to me from the c." 10.22
five kings out to him from the c., 10.23
them into the c. where they had 10.27
stones against the mouth of the c., 10.27
and escaped to the c. of Adullam; 1Sa 22.01
by the way, where there was a c.; 24.03
in the innermost parts of the c. 24.03
And Saul rose up and left the c., 24.07
also arose, and went out of the c., 24.08
you today into my hand in the c.; 24.10
time to David at the c. of Adullam, 2Sa 23.13
and hid them by fifties in a c., 1Ki 18.04
LORD's prophets by fifties in a c., 18.13
And there he came to a c., and 19.09
stood at the entrance of the c. 19.13
rock to David at the c. of Adullam, 1Ch 11.15
the c. of the young lions, where the Nah 2.11
it was a c., and a stone lay upon Jn 11.38

CAVERNS
to enter the c. of the rocks and Is 2.21

CAVES
and the c. and the strongholds. Ju 6.02
themselves in c. and in holes and 1Sa 13.06
shall enter the c. of the rocks Is 2.19
strongholds and in c. shall die by Eze 33.27
he filled his c. with prey and his Nah 2.12
and in dens and c. of the earth. Heb 11.38
hid in the c. and among the rocks Rev 6.15

CEASE
day and night, shall not c." Gen 8.22
the thunder will c., and there will Ex 9.29
I will make to c. from me the Num 17.05
poor will never c. out of the land; Deu 15.11
remembrance of them c. from among men, 32.26
our children c. to worship the Jos 22.25
the Benjaminites, or shall we c.?" Ju 20.28
"Do not c. to cry to the LORD our 1Sa 7.08
lest my father c. to care about 9.05
building Ramah, and let his work c. 2Ch 16.05
C. opposing God, who is with me, lest 35.21
that these men be made to c., Ez 4.21
by force and power made them c. 4.23
of these days c. among their Est 9.28
There the wicked c. from troubling, Job 3.17
and that its shoots will not c. 14.07
He makes wars c. to the end of the Ps 46.09
C., my son, to hear instruction only Pro 19.27
and quarreling and abuse will c. 22.10
the grinders c. because they are Ecc 12.03
before my eyes; c. to do evil, Is 1.16
Damascus will c. to be a city, and 17.01
come to nought and the scoffer c., 29.20
And I will make to c. from the Jer 7.34
night and day, and let them not c., 14.17
I will make to c. from this place, 16.09
for it does not c. to bear fruit." 17.08
of Israel c. from being a nation 31.36
made the wine c. from the wine 48.33
c. your evictions of my people, says Eze 45.09
cause sacrifice and offering to c.; Dan 9.27
And they shall c. for a little Hos 8.10
c., I beseech thee! How can Amo 7.05
they did not c. teaching and Ac 5.42
years I did not c. night or day to 20.31
as for tongues, they will c.; 1Ch 13.08
I do not c. to give thanks for you, Eph 1.16
and night they never c. to sing, Rev 4.08

CEASED
it had c. to be with Sarah after Gen 18.11
name Judah; then she c. bearing. 29.35
that she had c. bearing children, 30.09
until he c. to measure it, for it 41.49
and the thunder and the hail c., Ex 9.33
the hail and the thunder had c., 9.34
And the manna c. on the morrow, when Jos 5.12
caravans c. and travelers kept to Ju 5.06
The peasantry c. in Israel, they 5.07
they c. until you arose, Deborah, 5.07
who were hungry have c. to hunger. 1Sa 2.05
your father has c. to care about 10.02
and it c. until the second year Ez 4.24
So these three men c. to answer Job, Job 32.01
he has c. to act wisely and do good Ps 36.03
Has his steadfast love for ever c.? 77.08
Babylon: "How the oppressor has c., Is 14.04
has c., the insolent fury c.! 14.04
is no more, and destruction has c., 16.04
the noise of the jubilant has c., 24.08
When you have c. to destroy, you 33.01
of Babylon have c. fighting, Jer 51.30
The joy of our hearts has c.; Lam 5.15
and the sea c. from its raging. Jon 1.15
got into the boat, the wind c. Mt 14.32
And the wind c., and there was a Mk 4.39
And immediately the hemorrhage c.; 5.29
the boat with them and the wind c. 6.51
And when he had c. speaking, Lk 5.04
in she has not c. to kiss my feet. 7.45
and they c., and there was a calm. 8.24
immediately her flow of blood c. 8.44
and when he c., one of his disciples 11.01
After the uproar c., Paul sent Ac 20.01
we c. and said, "The will of the 21.14
we have not c. to pray for you, Col 1.09
they not have c. to be offered? Heb 10.02
in the flesh has c. from sin, 1Pe 4.01

CEASES
is no whisperer, quarreling c. Pro 26.20
lie waste, the wayfaring man c. Is 33.08
steadfast love of the LORD never c., Lam 3.22
whose baker c. to stir the fire, Hos 7.04
"This man never c. to speak words Ac 6.13
God's rest also c. from his labors Heb 4.10

CEASING
the LORD by c. to pray for you; 1Sa 12.23
I knew not slandered me without c.; Ps 35.15
"My eyes will flow without c., Lam 3.49
that without c. I mention you Rom 1.09

CEDAR
like c. trees beside the waters. Num 24.06
and c. trees, also carpenters and 2Sa 5.11
"See now, I dwell in a house of c., 7.02
you not built me a house of c.?"' 7.07
from the c. that is in Lebanon to 1Ki 4.33
the matter of c. and cypress 5.08
the timber of c. and cypress that 5.10
house of beams and planks of c. 6.09
to the house with timbers of c. 6.10
on the inside with boards of c.; 6.15

CEDAR (cont.)
with boards of c. from the floor 1Ki 6.16
The c. within the house was carved 6.18
all was c., no stone was seen. 6.18
He also made an altar of c. 6.20
stone and one course of c. beams. 6.36
upon three rows of c. pillars, 7.02
with c. beams upon the pillars. 7.02
covered with c. above the chambers 7.03
finished with c. from floor to 7.07
according to measurement, and c. 7.11
about, and a course of c. beams; 7.12
Solomon with c. and cypress timber 9.11
and he made c. as plentiful as the 10.27
on Lebanon sent to a c. on Lebanon, 2Ki 14.09
and c. trees, also masons and 1Ch 14.01
"Behold, I dwell in a house of c., 17.01
you not built me a house of c.?"' 17.06
and c. timbers without number; 22.04
great quantities of c. to David. 22.04
and he made c. as plentiful as the 2Ch 1.15
and sent him c. to build himself a 2.03
Send me also c., cypress, and algum 2.08
and c. as plentiful as the sycamore 9.27
on Lebanon sent to a c. on Lebanon, 25.18
to bring c. trees from Lebanon to Ez 3.07
He makes his tail stiff like a c.; Job 40.17
and towering like a c. of Lebanon. Ps 37.35
and grow like a c. in Lebanon 92.12
the beams of our house are c., Sol 1.17
will enclose her with boards of c. 8.09
I will put in the wilderness the c., Is 41.19
he plants a c. and the rain nourishes 44.14
for it, paneling it with c., Jer 22.14
a king because you compete in c.? 22.15
Lebanon and took the top of the c.; Eze 17.03
sprig from the lofty top of the c., 17.22
bear fruit, and become a noble c.; 17.23
they took a c. from Lebanon to make 27.05
will liken you to a c. in Lebanon, 31.03
for her c. work will be laid bare. Zep 2.14
for the c. has fallen, for the Zec 11.02

CEDARS
and devour the c. of Lebanon.' Ju 9.15
command that c. of Lebanon be cut 1Ki 5.06
I felled its tallest c., its choicest 2Ki 19.23
The voice of the LORD breaks the c., Ps 29.05
the LORD breaks the c. of Lebanon. 29.05
the mighty c. with its branches; 80.10
the c. of Lebanon which he planted. 104.16
all hills, fruit trees and all c.! 148.09
is like Lebanon, choice as the c. Sol 5.15
against all the c. of Lebanon, Is 2.13
but we will put c. in their place." 9.10
the c. of Lebanon, saying, 'Since you 14.08
I felled its tallest c., its choicest 37.24
He cuts down c.; or he chooses 44.14
shall cut down your choices c., Jer 22.07
of Lebanon, nested among the c., 22.23
The c. in the garden of God could Eze 31.08
was like the height of the c., Amo 2.09
that the fire may devour your c.! Zec 11.01

CEDARWOOD
clean birds and c. and scarlet Lev 14.04
bird with the c. and the scarlet 14.06
with c. and scarlet stuff and 14.49
and shall take the c. and the 14.51
and with the c. and hyssop and 14.52
shall take c. and hyssop and Num 19.06

CEILING
and he made the c. of the house of 1Ki 6.09
the house to the rafters of the c., 6.15

CELEBRATE
to Jerusalem to c. the dedication Neh 12.27
you shall c. the feast of the Eze 45.21
c. the festival, not with the old 1Co 5.08

CELEBRATED
c. the dedication of this house of Ez 6.16
your name to be c. in all generations; Ps 45.17

CELEBRATION
instruments leading in the c. 2Ch 23.13

CELESTIAL
There are c. bodies and there are 1Co 15.40
but the glory of the c. is one, 15.40

CELL
and a light shone in the c.; and he Ac 12.07

CELLAR
puts it in a c. or under a bushel, Lk 11.33

CELLARS
for the wine c. was Zabdi the 1Ch 27.27

CELLS
Jeremiah had come to the dungeon c., Jer 37.16

CENCHREAE
At C. he cut his hair, for he had a Ac 18.18
a deaconess of the church at C., Rom 16.01

CENSER
each took his c., and put fire in Lev 10.01
And he shall take a c. full of 16.12
and let every one of you take his c., Num 16.17
you bring before the LORD his c., 16.17
you also, and Aaron, each his c." 16.17
So every man took his c., and they 16.18
"Take your c., and put fire therein 16.46
Now he had a c. in his hand to burn 2Ch 26.19
Each had his c. in his hand, and the Eze 8.11
at the altar with a golden c.; Rev 8.03
angel took the c. and filled it 8.05

CENSERS
Do this: take c., Korah and all his Num 16.06
censer, two hundred and fifty c.; 16.17
to take up the c. out of the blaze; 16.37
the c. of these men who have sinned 16.38
the priest took the bronze c., 16.39
basins of silver, twenty-nine c., Ez 1.09

CENSURE
I hear c. which insults me, and out Job 20.03

CENSURED
and sound speech that cannot be c., Tit 2.08

CENSUS
"When you take the c. of the people Ex 30.12
numbered in the c. shall give this: 30.13
Every one who is numbered in the c., 30.14
one who was numbered in the c., 38.26
"Take a c. of all the congregation Num 1.02
not take a c. of them among the 1.49
"Take a c. of the sons of Kohath 4.02
"Take a c. of the sons of Gershon 4.22
"Take a c. of all the congregation 26.02
"Take a c. of the people, from 26.04
Then Solomon took a c. of all the 2Ch 2.17
after the c. of them which David 2.17
the days of the c. and drew away Ac 5.37

CENTER
down from the c. of the land, Ju 9.37
set her in the c. of the nations, Eze 5.05
who dwell at the c. of the earth. 38.12

CENTURION
a c. came forward to him, beseeching Mt 8.05
But the c. answered him, "Lord, I am 8.08

CENTURION (cont.)
And to the c. Jesus said, "Go; Mt 8.13
When the c. and those who were with 27.54
And when the c., who stood facing Mk 15.39
and summoning the c., he asked him 15.44
from the c. that he was dead, he 15.45
Now a c. had a slave who was dear Lk 7.02
the c. sent friends to him, saying 7.06
Now when the c. saw what had taken 23.47
a c. of what was known as the Italian Ac 10.01
a c., an upright and God-fearing 10.22
said to the c. who was standing by, 22.25
When the c. heard that, he went to 22.26
orders to the c. that he should be 24.23
prisoners to a c. of the Augustan 27.01
There the c. found a ship of 27.06
But the c. paid more attention to 27.11
Paul said to the c. and the soldiers, 27.31
but the c., wishing to save Paul, 27.43

CENTURIONS
He at once took soldiers and c., Ac 21.32
Paul called one of the c. and said, 23.17
Then he called two of the c. and said, 23.23

CEPHAS
shall be called C." (which means Jn 1.42
to Apollos," or "I belong to C.," 1Co 1.12
or Apollos or C. or the world or 3.22
the brothers of the Lord and C.? 9.05
and that he appeared to C., then to 15.05
I went up to Jerusalem to visit C., Gal 1.18
James and C. and John, who were 2.09
But when C. came to Antioch I 2.11
I said to C. before them all, "If 2.14

CEREAL
offer with it a c. offering and Ex 29.41
burnt offering, nor c. offering; 30.09
burnt offering and the c. offering; 40.29
one brings a c. offering as an Lev 2.01
is left of the c. offering shall 2.03
"When you bring a c. offering baked 2.04
offering is a c. offering baked on 2.05
oil on it; it is a c. offering. 2.06
offering is a c. offering cooked 2.07
shall bring the c. offering that 2.08
take from the c. offering its 2.09
is left of the c. offering shall 2.10
"No c. offering which you bring to 2.11
season all your c. offerings with 2.13
be lacking from your c. offering; 2.13
"If you offer a c. offering of 2.14
the c. offering of your first fruits 2.14
on it; it is a c. offering. 2.15
the priest, as in the c. offering." 5.13
this is the law of the c. offering. 6.14
flour of the c. offering with its 6.15
which is on the c. offering, 6.15
flour as a regular c. offering, 6.20
in baked pieces like a c. offering, 6.21
Every c. offering of a priest shall 6.23
And every c. offering baked in the 7.09
And every c. offering, mixed with 7.10
of the c. offering, of the sin 7.37
and a c. offering mixed with oil; 9.04
And he presented the c. offering, 9.17
"Take the c. offering that remains 10.12
and a c. offering of three tenths 14.10
offering and the c. offering on the 14.20
mixed with oil for a c. offering, 14.21
offering, along with a c. offering; 14.31
And the c. offering with it shall 23.13
shall present a c. offering of new 23.16
with their c. offering and their 23.18
burnt offerings and c. offerings, 23.37
the continual c. offering, and the Num 4.16
for it is a c. offering of jealousy, 5.15
a c. offering of remembrance, bringing 5.15
her hands the c. offering of remembrance, 5.18
which is the c. offering of jealousy 5.18
shall take the c. offering of 5.25
shall wave the c. offering before 5.25
take a handful of the c. offering, 5.26
and their c. offering and their 6.15
offer also its c. offering and its 6.17
mixed with oil for a c. offering; 7.13
mixed with oil for a c. offering; 7.19
mixed with oil for a c. offering; 7.25
mixed with oil for a c. offering; 7.31
mixed with oil for a c. offering; 7.37
mixed with oil for a c. offering; 7.43
mixed with oil for a c. offering; 7.49
mixed with oil for a c. offering; 7.55
mixed with oil for a c. offering; 7.61
mixed with oil for a c. offering; 7.67
mixed with oil for a c. offering; 7.73
mixed with oil for a c. offering; 7.79
a year old, with their c. offering; 7.87
bull and its c. offering of fine 8.08
to the LORD a c. offering of a tenth 15.04
prepare for a c. offering two tenths 15.06
with the bull a c. offering of 15.09
with its c. offering and its drink 15.24
every c. offering of theirs and 18.09
of fine flour for a c. offering, 28.05
like the c. offering of the morning, 28.08
of fine flour for a c. offering, 28.09
ephah of fine flour for a c. offering, 28.12
of fine flour for a c. offering, mixed 28.12
with oil as a c. offering for 28.13
also their c. offering of fine 28.20
you offer a c. offering of new 28.26
also their c. offering of fine 28.28
burnt offering and its c. offering, 28.31
also their c. offering of fine 29.03
and its c. offering, and the continual 29.06
burnt offering and its c. offering, 29.06
and their c. offering of fine flour 29.09
burnt offering and its c. offering, 29.11
and their c. offering of fine flour 29.14
its c. offering and its drink 29.16
with the c. offering and the drink 29.18
offering and its c. offering, 29.19
with the c. offering and the drink 29.21
offering and its c. offering and 29.22
with the c. offering and the drink 29.24
its c. offering and its drink 29.25
with the c. offering and the drink 29.27
offerings and its c. offering and 29.28
with the c. offering and the drink 29.30
its c. offering, and its drink 29.31
with the c. offering and the drink 29.33
its c. offering, and its drink 29.34
and the c. offering, and the drink 29.37
offering and its c. offering and 29.38
and for your c. offerings, and for 29.39
offerings or c. offerings or peace Jos 22.23
c. offering, or sacrifice, other than 22.29
took the kid with the c. offering, Ju 13.19
offering and a c. offering at our 13.23
offering and the c. offering and 1Ki 8.64
offering and the c. offering and 8.64
burnt offering and his c. offering, 2Ki 16.13
and the evening c. offering, 16.15
and his c. offering, with the burnt 16.15
of the land, and their c. offering, 16.15
and the wheat for a c. offering. 1Ch 21.23
the flour for the c. offering, 23.29
offering and the c. offering and 2Ch 7.07
with their c. offerings and their Ez 7.17
the continual c. offering, the Neh 10.33
had previously put the c. offering, 13.05
with the c. offering and the 13.09

CEREAL (cont.)
you have brought a c. offering. Is 57.06
he who presents a c. offering, 66.03
bring their c. offering in a clean 66.20
burnt offering and c. offering, Jer 14.12
c. offerings and frank incense, and 17.26
to burn c. offerings, and to make 33.18
bringing c. offerings and incense 41.05
the c. offering, the sin offering, Eze 42.13
They shall eat the c. offering, 44.29
is the offering for c. offerings, 45.15
c. offerings, and drink offerings, at 45.17
c. offerings, burnt offerings, and 45.17
provide as a c. offering an ephah 45.24
and c. offerings, and for the oil. 45.25
and the c. offering with the ram 46.05
and the c. offering with the lambs 46.05
as a c. offering he shall provide 46.07
seasons the c. offering with a 46.11
shall provide a c. offering with 46.14
as a c. offering to the LORD; 46.14
they shall bake the c. offering, 46.20
The c. offering and the drink Joe 1.09
Because c. offering and drink 1.13
a c. offering and a drink offering 2.14
burnt offerings and c. offerings, Amo 5.22

CERTAIN
And he came to a c. place, and stayed Gen 28.11
and turned in to a c. Adullamite, 38.01
daughter of a c. Canaanite whose 38.02
And there were c. men who were Num 9.06
that c. base fellows have gone out Deu 13.13
it be true and c. that such an 13.14
it is true and c. that such an 17.04
c. men of Israel have come here Jos 2.02
And a c. woman threw an upper Ju 9.53
And there was a c. man of Zorah, 13.02
a c. Levite was sojourning in the 19.01
and a c. man of Bethlehem in Judah Ru 1.01
There was a c. man of Ramathaimzophim 1Sa 1.01
Now a c. man of the servants of 21.07
"There were two men in a c. city, 2Sa 12.01
And a c. man saw it, and told Joab, 18.10
know for c. that you shall die; 1Ki 2.37
'Know for c. that on the day you go 2.42
together with c. Edomites of his 11.17
And a c. man of the sons of the 20.35
But a c. man drew his bow at a 22.34
Moreover he appointed c. of the 1Ch 16.04
for the service c. of the sons of 25.01
and c. worthless scoundrels gathered 2Ch 13.07
But a c. man drew his bow at a 18.33
appointed c. Levites and priests 19.08
C. chiefs also of the men of 28.12
came with c. men out of Judah; Neh 1.02
Jerusalem lived c. of the sons of 11.04
And c. divisions of the Levites in 11.36
and c. of the priests' sons with 12.35
"There is a c. people scattered Est 3.08
Only know for c. that if you put me Jer 26.15
And c. of the elders of the land 26.17
Jehoiakim sent to Egypt c. men, 26.22
Then came c. of the elders of Eze 14.01
c. of the elders of Israel came to 20.01
The dream is c., and its interpretation Dan 2.45
Therefore at that time c. Chaldeans 3.08
There are c. Jews whom you have 3.12
And he ordered c. mighty men of his 3.20
"A c. creditor had two debtors; Lk 7.14
He was praying in a c. place, 11.01
He said, "In a c. city there was a 18.02
down at c. seasons into the pool *Jn 5.04
Now a c. man was ill, Lazarus of 11.01
they came upon a c. magician, Ac 13.06
but they had c. points of dispute 25.19
For before c. men came from James, Gal 2.12
you may charge c. persons not to 1Ti 1.03
C. persons by swerving from these 1.06
c. persons have made shipwreck of 1.19
again he sets a c. day, "Today," Heb 4.07

CERTAINLY
You c. ought to have eaten it in Lev 10.18
'I will c. honor you,' but the LORD Num 24.11
the LORD will c. make my lord a 1Sa 25.28
for I will c. give the Philistines 2Sa 5.19
say to him, 'You shall c. recover'; 2Ki 8.10
has shown me that he shall c. die." 8.10
told me that you would c. recover." 8.14
of Babylon will c. come and Jer 36.29
"C. you are also one of them, for Mt 26.73
"C. you are one of them; Mk 14.70
"C. this man also was with him; Lk 22.59
and said, "C. this man was innocent!" 23.47
They will c. hear that you have Ac 21.22
we shall c. be united with him in a Rom 6.05
an agent of sin? C. not! Gal 2.17
C. not; for if a law 3.21

CERTAINTY
servants for a c. that the LORD Jos 9.24
learned of a c. that Saul had come. 1Sa 26.04
Know for a c. that I have warned Jer 42.19
know for a c. that you shall die 42.22
"I know with c. that you are trying Dan 2.08

CERTIFICATE
let him give her a c. of divorce.' Mt 5.31
one to give a c. of divorce, 19.07
a man to write a c. of divorce, Mk 10.04

CHAFF
a driven leaf and pursue dry c.? Job 13.25
and like c. that the storm carries 21.18
but are like c. which the wind Ps 1.04
Let them be like c. before the wind, 35.05
dust, like c. before the wind. 83.13
chased like c. on the mountains Is 17.13
of the ruthless like passing c. 29.05
You conceive c., you bring forth 33.11
you shall make the hills like c.; 41.15
you like c. driven by the wind Jer 13.24
became like the c. of the summer Dan 2.35
like the c. that swirls from the Hos 13.03
driven away like the drifting c., Zep 2.02
but the c. he will burn with Mt 3.12
but the c. he will burn with Lk 3.17

CHAIN
and put a gold c. about his neck; Gen 41.42
with wreaths of c. work for the 1Ki 7.17
your arms, and a c. on your neck. Eze 16.11
and have a c. of gold about his Dan 5.07
and have a c. of gold about your 5.16
a c. of gold was put about his neck, 5.29
bind him any more, even with a c.; Mk 5.03
that I am bound with this c." Ac 28.20
the bottomless pit and a great c. Rev 20.01

CHAINS
and two c. of pure gold, twisted Ex 28.14
the corded c. to the settings. 28.14
breastpiece twisted c. like cords, 28.22
breastpiece twisted c. like cords, 39.15
and he drew c. of gold across, in 1Ki 6.21
gold, and made palms and c. on it. 2Ch 3.05
He made c. like a necklace and put 3.16
pomegranates, and put them on the c. 3.16
"Can you bind the c. of the Pleiades, Job 38.31
kings with c. and their nobles Ps 149.08
gold, and casts for it silver c. Is 40.19
come over in c. and bow down to 45.14
him bound in c. along with all the Jer 40.01
today from the c. on your hands. 40.04

CHAINS (cont.)
he has put heavy c. on me; Lam 3.07
all her great men were bound in c. Nah 3.10
been bound with fetters and c., Mk 5.04
but the c. he wrenched apart, and 5.04
and bound with c. and fetters, Lk 8.29
two soldiers, bound with two c., Ac 12.06
And the c. fell off his hands. 12.07
him to be bound with two c. 21.33
such as I am—except for these c." 26.29
for which I am an ambassador in c.; Eph 6.20
he was not ashamed of my c., 2Ti 1.16
and even c. and imprisonment. Heb 11.36
him in eternal c. in the nether Jud 1.06

CHAIR
a c., and a lamp, so that whenever 2Ki 4.10

CHALDEA
flee from C., declare this with a Is 48.20
C. shall be plundered; all who Jer 50.10
against the inhabitants of C.; 51.01
inhabitants of C. before your very 51.24
be upon the inhabitants of C., 51.35
of God into C., to the exiles. Eze 11.24
also with the trading land of C.; 16.29
Babylonians whose native land was C. 23.15
and sent messengers to them in C. 23.16

CHALDEAN
afraid because of the C. officials; 2Ki 25.24
the C., who destroyed this house Ez 5.12
Now when the C. army had withdrawn Jer 37.11
and the C. soldiers who happened to 41.03
of any magician or enchanter or C. Dan 2.10
Belshazzar the C. king was slain. 5.30

CHALDEANS
land of his birth, in Ur of the C. Gen 11.28
from Ur of the C. to go into the 11.31
who brought you from Ur of the C., 15.07
sent against him bands of the C., 2Ki 24.02
though the C. were around the city. 25.04
But the army of the C. pursued the 25.05
And all the army of the C., 25.10
the C. broke in pieces, and carried 25.13
Jews and the C. who were with him 25.25
for they were afraid of the C. 25.26
up against them the king of the C., 2Ch 36.17
"The C. formed three companies, and Job 1.17
the splendor and pride of the C., Is 13.19
Behold the land of the C.! 23.13
shouting of the C. will be turned 43.14
a throne, O daughter of the C.! 47.01
darkness, O daughter of the C.; 47.05
his arm shall be against the C. 48.14
and against the C. who are besieging Jer 21.04
surrenders to the C. who are 21.09
and into the hand of the C. 22.25
this place to the land of the C. 24.05
that nation, the land of the C., 25.12
escape out of the hand of the C., 32.04
though you fight against the C., 32.05
hands of the C. who are fighting 32.24
is given into the hands of the C.' " 32.25
hands of the C. and into the hand 32.28
The C. who are fighting against 32.29
is given into the hands of the C. 32.43
The C. are coming in to fight and 33.05
the army of the C. and the army of 35.11
and when the C. who were besieging 37.05
And the C. shall come back and 37.08
"The C. will surely stay away from 37.09
whole army of C. who are fighting 37.10
"You are deserting to the C." 37.13
I am not deserting to the C." 37.14
who goes out to the C. shall live; 38.02
be given into the hand of the C., 38.18
Jews who have deserted to the C., 38.19
sons shall be led out to the C., 38.23
But the army of the C. pursued them, 39.05
The C. burned the king's house and 39.08
"Do not be afraid to serve the C. 40.09
you before the C. who will come to 40.10
because of the C.; for they were 41.18
deliver us into the hand of the C., 43.03
concerning the land of the C., 50.01
and go out of the land of the C., 50.08
a work to do in the land of the C. 50.25
"A sword upon the C., says the LORD, 50.35
formed against the land of the C.: 50.45
down slain in the land of the C., 51.04
the land of the C. is full of 51.05
destruction from the land of the C.! 51.54
while the C. were round about the 52.07
But the army of the C. pursued the 52.08
And all the army of the C., 52.14
the C. broke in pieces, and carried 52.17
the land of the C. by the river Eze 1.03
to Babylon in the land of the C., 12.13
images of the C. portrayed in 23.14
the Babylonians and all the C., 23.23
the letters and language of the C. Dan 1.04
and the C. be summoned, to tell the 2.02
Then the C. said to the king, "O 2.04
The king answered the C., 2.05
The C. answered the king, "There is 2.10
time certain C. came forward and 3.08
the C., and the astrologers came in 4.07
the C., and the astrologers. 5.07
enchanters, C., and astrologers, 5.11
king over the realm of the C.— 9.01
For lo, I am rousing the C., Hab 1.06
departed from the land of the C., Ac 7.04

CHALDEES
of Ur of the C. and give him the Neh 9.07

CHALKSTONES
the altars like c. crushed to Is 27.09

CHAMBER
he entered his c. and wept there. Gen 43.30
sitting alone in his cool roof c. Ju 3.20
the doors of the roof c. upon him, 3.23
doors of the roof c. were locked, 3.24
in the closet of the cool c." 3.24
not open the doors of the roof c., 3.25
"I will go in to my wife in the c." 15.01
men lying in wait in an inner c. 16.09
lying in wait were in an inner c. 16.12
Tamar, "Bring the food into the c., 2Sa 13.10
them into the c. to Amnon her 13.10
went up to the c. over the gate, 18.33
king into his c. (now the king was 1Ki 1.15
carried him up into the upper c., 17.19
from the upper c. into the house, 17.23
entered an inner c. in the city. 20.30
into an inner c. to hide yourself." 22.25
lattice in his upper c. in Samaria, 2Ki 1.02
us make a small roof c. with walls, 4.10
there, and he turned into the c. 4.11
and lead him to an inner c. 9.02
by the c. of Nathanmelech the 23.11
the roof of the upper c. of Ahaz, 23.12
into an inner c. to hide yourself." 2Ch 18.24
and went to the c. of Jehohanan Ez 10.06
Berechiah repaired opposite his c. Neh 3.30
and to the upper c. of the corner. 3.31
the upper c. of the corner and the 3.32
Tobiah a large c. where they had 13.05
for him a c. in the courts of the 13.07
furniture of Tobiah out of the c. 13.08
From its c. comes the whirlwind, and Job 37.09
like a bridegroom leaving his c., Ps 19.05
decked in her c. with gold-woven 45.13

CHAMBER (cont.)

and into the c. of her that conceived Sol 3.04
and into the c. of her that conceived 8.02
LORD into the c. of the sons of Jer 35.04
was near the c. of the princes, 35.04
above the c. of Maaseiah the son of 35.04
in the c. of Gemariah the son of 36.10
house, into the secretary's c.; 36.12
scroll in the c. of Elishama the 36.20
it from the c. of Elishama the 36.21
you built yourself a vaulted c., Eze 16.24
building your vaulted c. at the 16.31
your vaulted c. and break down 16.39
There was a c. with its door in the 40.38
This c. which faces south is for 40.45
and the c. which faces north is for 40.46
in his upper c. open toward Dan 6.10
his room, and the bride her c. Joe 2.16
in the upper c. where we were Ac 20.08

CHAMBERLAIN

the chamber of Nathanmelech the c., 2Ki 23.11
the king's c., they asked for peace, Ac 12.20

CHAMBERLAINS

who served King Ahasuerus as c., Est 1.10

CHAMBERS

and in the c. shall be terror, Deu 32.25
and he made side c. all around. 1Ki 6.05
cedar above the c. that were upon 7.03
charge of the c. and the treasures 1Ch 9.26
dwelling in the c. of the temple 9.33
the care of the courts and the c., 23.28
and its inner c., and of the room 28.11
the LORD, all the surrounding c., 28.12
he overlaid the upper c. with gold. 2Ch 3.09
them to prepare c. in the house of 31.11
within the c. of the house of the Ez 8.29
to the c. of the house of our God; Neh 10.37
to the c., to the storehouse. 10.38
of grain, wine, and oil to the c., 10.39
appointed over the c. for the stores, 12.44
over the c. of the house of our 13.04
orders and they cleansed the c.; 13.09
Pleiades and the c. of the south; Job 9.09
the beams of thy c. on the waters, Ps 104.03
even in the c. of their kings. 105.30
going down to the c. of death. Pro 7.27
king has brought me into his c. Sol 1.04
enter your c., and shut your doors Is 26.20
of the LORD, into one of the c.; Jer 35.02
there were c. and a pavement, round Eze 40.17
thirty c. fronted on the pavement. 40.17
there were two c. in the inner 40.44
and the breadth of the side c., 41.05
And the side c. were in three 41.06
serve as supports for the side c., 41.06
And the side c. became broader as 41.07
of the side c. measured a full 41.08
of the side c. was five cubits; 41.09
c. of the court was a breadth of 41.10
of the side c. opened on the part 41.11
me to the c. which were opposite 42.01
And before the c. was a passage 42.04
Now the upper c. were narrower, for 42.05
and middle c. in the building. 42.05
hence the upper c. were set back 42.06
a wall outside parallel to the c., 42.07
opposite the c., fifty cubits long. 42.07
For the c. on the outer court were 42.08
Below these c. was an entrance on 42.09
opposite the building, there were c. 42.10
similar to the c. on the north, 42.11
And below the south c. was an 42.12
"The north c. and the south c. opposite 42.13
opposite the yard are the holy c., 42.13
and lay them in the holy c.; and they 44.19
row of the holy c. for the priests 46.19
builds his upper c. in the heavens, Amo 9.06

CHAMELEON

the sand lizard, and the c. Lev 11.30

CHAMPION

the Philistines a c. named Goliath, 1Sa 17.04
the c., the Philistine of Gath, 17.23
Philistines saw that their c. was dead, 17.51

CHANCE

"If you c. to come upon a bird's Deu 22.06
struck us, it happened to us by c." 1Sa 6.09
"By c. I happened to be on Mount 2Sa 1.06
but time and c. happen to them all. Ecc 9.11
Now by c. a priest was going down Lk 10.31
on the c. that somehow they could Ac 27.12
for he found no c. to repent, Heb 12.17

CHANCED

And Absalom c. to meet the servants 2Sa 18.09
day with those who c. to be there. Ac 17.17

CHANCES

reason of what c. to him by night, Deu 23.10

CHANGE

yourselves, and c. your garments; Gen 35.02
In order to c. the course of 2Sa 14.20
to his own hurt and does not c.; Ps 15.04
fear though the earth should c., 46.02
has sworn and will not c. his mind, 110.04
Can the Ethiopian c. his skin or Jer 13.23
words before me till the times c. Dan 2.09
thoughts alarm you or your color c. 5.10
shall think to c. the times and 7.25
I will c. their glory into shame. Hos 4.07
time I will c. the speech of the Zep 3.09
and I will c. their shame into 3.19
"For I the LORD do not c.; therefore Mal 3.06
and will c. the customs which Moses Ac 6.14
with you now and to c. my tone, Gal 4.20
who will c. our lowly body to be Php 3.21
For when there is a c. in the Heb 7.12
necessarily a c. in the law as 7.12
has sworn and will not c. his mind, 7.21
no variation or shadow due to c. Jas 1.17

CHANGED

cheated me and c. my wages ten Gen 31.07
and you have c. my wages ten times. 31.41
shaved himself and c. his clothes, 41.14
servants was c. toward the people, Ex 14.05
turns again and is c. to white, Lev 13.16
the diseased spot has not c. color, 13.55
(their names to be c.), and Sibmah; Num 32.38
So he c. his behavior before them, 1Sa 21.13
himself, and c. his clothes; 2Sa 12.20
and c. his name to Jehoiakim. 2Ki 23.34
and c. his name to Zedekiah. 24.17
and c. his name to Jehoiakim; 2Ch 36.04
which had been c. to a day when Est 9.01
It is c. like clay under the seal, Job 38.14
right hand of the Most High has c." Ps 77.10
hardness of his countenance is c. Ecc 8.01
Has a nation c. its gods, even Jer 2.11
my people have c. their glory for 2.11
in him, and his scent is not c. 48.11
grown dim, how the pure gold is c.! Lam 4.01
of his face was c. against Shadrach, Dan 3.19
let his mind be c. from a man's, 4.16
Then the king's color c., and his 5.06
greatly alarmed, and his color c.; 5.09
document, so that it cannot be c., 6.08
the king establishes can be c. 6.15
might be c. concerning Daniel. 6.17

CHANGED (cont.)
alarmed me, and my color c.; but I kept Dan 7.28
appearance was fearfully c., and I 10.08
they c. their minds and said that Ac 28.06
all sleep, but we shall all be c., 1Co 15.51
imperishable, and we shall be c. 15.52
are being c. into his likeness from 2Co 3.18
roll them up, and they will be c. Heb 1.12

CHANGES
He c. times and seasons; Dan 2.21
he c. the portion of my people; Mic 2.04

CHANGEST
thou c. his countenance, and sendest Job 14.20
Thou c. them like raiment, and they Ps 102.26

CHANGING
lightly you gad about, c. your way! Jer 2.36

CHANNEL
"Who has cleft a c. for the torrents Job 38.25

CHANNELS
Then the c. of the sea were seen, 2Sa 22.16
He cuts out c. in the rocks, and his Job 28.10
Then the c. of the sea were seen, Ps 18.15
over all its c. and go over all Is 8.07
it into seven c. that men may cross 11.15

CHANT
daughters of the nations shall c. it; Eze 32.16
shall they c. it, says the LORD GOD." 32.16

CHANTED
whose glory above the heavens is c. Ps 8.01
is a lamentation which shall be c.; Eze 32.16

CHAOS
the land of gloom and c., where Job 10.22
The city of c. is broken down, every Is 24.10
the plummet of c. over its nobles. 34.11
he did not create it a c., he formed 45.18
offspring of Jacob, 'Seek me in c.' 45.19

CHARACTER
and endurance produces c., Rom 5.04
and c. produces hope, 5.04
the unchangeable c. of his purpose, Heb 6.17

CHARACTERS
and write upon it in common c., Is 8.01

CHARCOAL
As c. to hot embers and wood to Pro 26.21
and officers had made a c. fire, Jn 18.18
they saw a c. fire there, with fish 21.09

CHARGE
that he may c. his children and his Gen 18.19
who had c. of all that he had, "Put 24.02
obeyed my voice and kept my c., 26.05
and put them in c. of his sons; 30.35
and put him in c. of all that he 39.04
all that he had in Joseph's c.; 39.06
them, put them in c. of my cattle." 47.06
and gave them a c. to the people Ex 6.13
for thou thyself didst c. us, saying, 19.23
Keep far from a false c., and do 23.07
So keep my c. never to practice any Lev 18.30
They shall therefore keep my c., 22.09
shall keep c. of the tabernacle of Num 1.53
they shall have c. of all the 3.08
And the c. of the sons of Gershon 3.25
And their c. was to be the ark, the 3.31
those who had c. of the sanctuary. 3.32
And the appointed c. of the sons of 3.36
having c. of the rites within the 3.38
shall have c. of the oil for the 4.16
assign to their c. all that they 4.27
to keep the c., and they shall do 8.26
of Israel kept the c. of the LORD, 9.19
they kept the c. of the LORD, at the 9.23
who have c. of the tabernacle of 31.30
Levites who had c. of the tabernacle 31.47
But c. Joshua, and encourage and Deu 3.28
and keep his c., his statutes, his 11.01
which is in c. of the Levitical 17.18
witnesses, shall a c. be sustained. 19.15
to keep the c. of the LORD your Jos 22.03
who was in c. of the reapers, Ru 2.05
who was in c. of the reapers 2.06
to have c. of the ark of the LORD. 1Sa 7.01
and the c. was a pim for the 13.21
his father c. the people with the 14.27
the things in c. of the keeper of 17.22
and yet you c. me today with a 2Sa 3.08
he put in the c. of Abishai his 10.10
and Adoram was in c. of the forced 20.24
and keep the c. of the LORD your 1Ki 2.03
Ahishar was in c. of the palace; 4.06
of Abda was in c. of the forced 4.06
required, each according to his c. 4.28
Adoniram was in c. of the levy. 5.14
who had c. of the people who 5.16
who had c. of the people who 9.23
he gave him c. over all the forced 11.28
let them bring a c. against him, 21.10
brought a c. against Naboth, 21.13
under your c. is too small for us. 2Ki 6.01
he leaned to have c. of the gate; 7.17
him who was in c. of the wardrobe, 10.22
David put in c. of the service of 1Ch 6.31
were in c. of the work of the 9.19
had been in c. of the camp of the 9.19
sons were in c. of the gates of 9.23
were in c. of the chambers and the 9.26
and they had c. of opening it every 9.27
Some of them had c. of the utensils 9.28
was in c. of making the flat cakes. 9.31
Kohathites had c. of the showbread, 9.32
he put in the c. of Abishai his 19.11
he gives you c. over Israel you 22.12
"shall have c. of the work in the 23.04
Thus they shall keep c. of the tent 23.32
Ahijah had c. of the treasuries of 26.20
were in c. of the treasuries of the 26.22
officer in c. of the treasuries. 26.24
brethren were in c. of all the 26.26
Zabdiel was in c. of the first 27.02
Ahohite was in c. of the division 27.04
his son was in c. of his division. 27.06
for we keep the c. of the LORD our 2Ch 13.11
shall keep c. of the LORD. 23.06
to be in c. of the house of the 23.18
those who had c. of the work of 24.12
officer in c. of them was Conaniah 31.12
these out in c. of Mithredath the Ez 1.08
of the castle c. over Jerusalem, Neh 7.02
obligation to c. ourselves yearly 10.32
brethren was in c. of the songs of 12.08
eunuch who is in c. of the women; Est 2.03
of Hegai who had c. of the women. 2.08
who was in c. of the concubines; 2.14
who had c. of the women, advised. 2.15
those who have c. of the king's 3.09
it to her and c. her to go to the 4.08
did not sin or c. God with wrong. Job 1.22
Who gave him c. over the earth and 34.13
you, and lay the c. before you. Ps 50.21
give his angels c. of you to guard 91.11
I did not send them or c. them; Jer 23.32
Give them this c. for their masters: 27.04
to have c. in the house of the LORD 29.26
when the LORD has given it a c.? 47.07
priests who have c. of the temple, Eze 40.45

CHARGE (cont.)
priests who have c. of the altar; Eze 40.46
have not kept c. of my holy things; 44.08
to keep my c. in my sanctuary. 44.08
them to keep c. of the temple, 44.14
who kept the c. of my sanctuary 44.15
to me, and they shall keep my c. 44.16
who kept my c., who did not go 48.11
prince who has c. of your people. Dan 12.01
Like warriors they c., like soldiers Joe 2.07
walk in my ways and keep my c., Zec 3.07
my house and have c. of my courts, 3.07
our keeping his c. or of walking Mal 3.14
'He will give his angels c. of you, Mt 4.06
no answer, not even to a single c.; 27.14
head they put the c. against him, 27.37
home and puts his servants in c., Mk 13.34
inscription of the c. against him 15.26
'He will give his angels c. of you, Lk 4.10
might have some c. to bring against *Jn 8.06
this c. I have received from my 10.18
in c. of all her treasure, had come Ac 8.27
though they could c. him with 13.28
and to c. them to keep the law of 15.05
"I c. you in the name of Jesus 16.18
Having received this c., he put 16.24
to know the c. on which they 23.28
The Jews also joined in the c., 24.09
concerning the c. laid against him. 25.16
they brought no c. in his case of 25.18
though I have no c. to bring 28.19
slanderously c. us with saying. Rom 3.08
Who shall bring any c. against God's 8.33
To the married I give c., not I but 1Co 7.10
I may make the gospel free of c., 9.18
Any c. must be sustained by the 2Co 13.01
that you may c. certain persons 1Ti 1.03
whereas the aim of our c. is love 1.05
This c. I commit to you, Timothy, my 1.18
Never admit any c. against an elder 5.19
elect angels I c. you to keep 5.21
I c. you to keep the commandment 6.14
c. them not to be haughty, nor to 6.17
and c. them before the Lord to 2Ti 2.14
I c. you in the presence of God and 4.01
not open to the c. of being Tit 1.06
anything, c. that to my account. Phm 1.18
tend the flock of God that is your c., 1Pe 5.02
those in your c. but being examples 5.03

CHARGED
and c. him, "You shall not marry one Gen 28.01
that as he blessed him he c. him, 28.06
of the guard c. Joseph with them, 40.04
Then he c. them, and said to them, "I 49.29
signs which he had c. him to do. Ex 4.28
what the LORD has c., lest you die; Lev 8.35
And this is what they are c. to carry, Num 4.31
they were c. with the care of the 7.09
And I c. your judges at that time, Deu 1.16
the army or be c. with any business 24.05
And Moses c. the people the same 27.11
and Joshua c. those who went to Jos 18.08
Have I not c. the young men not to Ru 2.09
father strictly c. the people with 1Sa 14.28
"The king has c. me with a matter, 21.02
you, and with which I have c. you.' 21.02
he c. Solomon his son, saying, 1Ki 2.01
commandment with which I c. you?" 2.43
For I am c. with heavy tidings for 14.06
and c. him to build a house for the 1Ch 22.06
And he c. them: "Thus you shall do 2Ch 19.09
and he has c. me to build him a 36.23
and he has c. me to build him a Ez 1.02
Mordecai had c. her not to make it Est 2 10
her people, as Mordecai had c. her; 2.20
I c. Baruch in their presence, Jer 32.13
And Jesus sternly c. them, "See that Mt 9.30
Then he strictly c. the disciples 16.20
And he sternly c. him, and sent him Mk 1.43
And he strictly c. them that no one 5.43
He c. them to take nothing for 6.08
And he c. them to tell no one; 7.36
but the more he c. them, the more 7.36
And he c. them to tell no one about 8.30
he c. them to tell no one what they 9.09
And he c. him to tell no one; Lk 5.14
but he c. them to tell no one what 8.56
But he c. and commanded them to 9.21
with them he c. them not to depart Ac 1.04
called them and c. them not to 4.18
"We strictly c. you not to teach in 5.28
beat them and c. them not to speak 5.40
danger of being c. with rioting 19.40
but c. with nothing deserving death 23.29
for I have already c. that all men, Rom 3.09
you and encouraged you and c. you 1Th 2.11
work with your hands, as we c. you; 4.11
May it not be c. against them! 2Ti 4.16

CHARGERS
mustered in array; the c. prance. Nah 2.03

CHARGES
and c. her with shameful conduct, Deu 22.14
has made shameful c. against her, 22.17
and I brought c. against the nobles Neh 5.07
and his angels he c. with error; Job 4.18
See how many c. they bring against Mk 15.04
and c. were brought to him that Lk 16.01
of any of your c. against him; 23.14
let them bring c. against one Ac 19.38
many serious c. which they could 25.07
be tried on these c. before me?" 25.09
is nothing in their c. against me, 25.11
not to indicate the c. against him." 25.27

CHARGING
When Jacob finished c. his sons, Gen 49.33
lion or a c. bear is a wicked Pro 28.15
I saw the ram c. westward and Dan 8.04
Horsemen c., flashing sword and Nah 3.03
c. them, "Go nowhere among the Mt 10.05
c. the jailer to keep them safely. Ac 16.23
c. him, "Tell no one that you have 23.22

CHARIOT
made him to ride in his second c.; Gen 41.43
made ready his c. and went up to 46.29
made ready his c. and took his Ex 14.06
clogging their c. wheels so that 14.25
from his c. and fled away on foot. Ju 4.15
'Why is his c. so long in coming? 5.28
David hamstrung all the c. horses, 2Sa 8.04
got himself a c. and horses, 15.01
The wheels were made like a c. wheel; 1Ki 7.33
his c. commanders and his horsemen. 9.22
stationed in the c. cities and with 10.26
A c. could be imported from Egypt 10.29
Rehoboam made haste to mount his c., 12.18
'Prepare your c. and go down, lest 18.44
lost, horse for horse, and c. for c.; 20.25
caused him to come up into the c. 20.33
he said to the driver of his c., 22.34
up in his c. facing the Syrians, 22.35
flowed into the bottom of the c. 22.35
And they washed the c. by the pool 22.38
a c. of fire and horses of fire 2Ki 2.11
alighted from the c. to meet him, 5.21
man turned from his c. to meet you? 5.26
and he and his c. commanders smote 8.21
Then Jehu mounted his c., and went 9.16
And they made ready his c. Then 9.21
each in his c., and went to meet 9.21
his heart and he sank in his c. 9.24

CHARIOT (cont.)
shot him in the c. at the ascent 2Ki 9.27
carried him in a c. to Jerusalem, 9.28
took him up with him into the c. 10.15
So he had him ride in his c. 10.16
him dead in a c. from Megiddo, 23.30
David hamstrung all the c. horses, 1Ch 18.04
for the golden c. of the cherubim 28.18
stationed in the c. cities and with 2Ch 1.14
They imported a c. from Egypt for 1.17
stationed in the c. cities and with 9.25
Rehoboam made haste to mount his c., 10.18
he said to the driver of his c., 18.33
up in his c. facing the Syrians 18.34
surrounded him and his c. commanders. 21.09
him out of the c. and carried him 35.24
in his second c. and brought him 35.24
track of thy c. drip with fatness Ps 65.11
who makest the clouds thy c., 104.03
set me in a c. beside my prince. Sol 6.12
who brings forth c. and horse, Is 43.17
in pieces the c. and the charioteer; Jer 51.21
galloping horse and bounding c.! Nah 3.02
thy horses, upon thy c. of victory? Hab 3.08
the first c. had red horses, the Zec 6.02
and the fourth c. dappled gray 6.03
The c. with the black horses goes 6.06
cut off the c. from Ephraim and 9.10
seated in his c., he was reading Ac 8.28
to Philip, "Go up and join this c." 8.29
And he commanded the c. to stop, 8.38

CHARIOTEER
in pieces the chariot and the c.; Jer 51.21

CHARIOTRY
With mighty c., twice ten thousand, Ps 68.17

CHARIOTS
up with him both c. and horsemen; Gen 50.09
hundred picked c. and all the Ex 14.07
all the other c. of Egypt with 14.07
horses and c. with his horsemen and 14.09
his host, his c., and his horsemen. 14.17
Pharaoh, his c., and his horsemen." 14.18
horses, his c., and his horsemen. 14.23
upon this c., and upon their 14.26
and covered the c. and the horsemen 14.28
"Pharaoh's c. and his host he cast 15.04
with his c. and his horsemen went 15.19
to their horses and to their c.; Deu 11.04
see horses and c. and an army 20.01
with very many horses and c. Jos 11.04
and burn their c. with fire." 11.06
and burned their c. with fire. 11.09
dwell in the plain have c. of iron, 17.16
though they have c. of iron, 17.18
fathers with c. and horsemen to 24.06
plain, because they had c. of iron. Ju 1.19
for he had nine hundred c. of iron, 4.03
Kishon with his c. and his troops; 4.07
Sisera called out all his c., 4.13
nine hundred c. of iron, and all the 4.13
and all his c. and all his army 4.15
pursued the c. and the army to 4.16
why tarry the hoofbeats of his c.?' 5.28
them to his c. and to be his 1Sa 8.11
horsemen, and to run before his c.; 8.11
of war and the equipment of his c. 8.12
with Israel, thirty thousand c., 13.05
and lo, the c. and the horsemen were 2Sa 1.06
but left enough for a hundred c. 8.04
the men of seven hundred c., and forty 10.18
for himself c. and horsemen, and fifty 1Ki 1.05
stalls of horses for his c., and twelve 4.26
had, and the cities for his c., 9.19
gathered together c. and horsemen; 10.26
fourteen hundred c. and twelve 10.26
Zimri, commander of half his c., 16.09
were with him, and horses and c.; 20.01
and captured the horses and c., 20.21
the thirty-two captains of his c., 22.31
captains of the c. saw Jehosphaphat, 22.32
captains of the c. saw that it was 22.33
the c. of Israel and its horsemen!" 2Ki 2.12
Naaman came with his horses and c., 5.09
horses and c. and a great army; 6.14
with horses and c. was round about 6.15
of horses and c. of fire round 6.17
the Syrians hear the sound of c., 7.06
over to Zair with all his c., 8.21
there are with you c. and horses, 10.02
horsemen and ten c. and ten thousand 13.07
The c. of Israel and its horsemen!" 13.14
on Egypt for c. and for horsemen? 18.24
'With my many c. I have gone up the 19.23
he burned the c. of the sun with 23.11
And David took from him a thousand c., 1Ch 18.04
but left enough for a hundred c. 18.04
silver to hire c. and horsemen 19.06
thousand c. and the king of Maacah 19.07
the men of seven thousand c., 19.18
Solomon gathered together c. and horsemen; 2Ch 1.14
fourteen hundred c. and twelve 1.14
had, and all the cities for his c., 8.06
officers, the commanders of his c., 8.09
thousand stalls for horses and c., 9.25
with twelve hundred c. and sixty 12.03
a million men and three hundred c., 14.09
exceedingly many c. and horsemen? 16.08
commanded the captains of his c., 18.30
captains of the c. saw Jehoshaphat, 18.31
captains of the c. saw that it was 18.32
with his commanders and all his c., 21.09
Some boast of c., and some of Ps 20.07
spear, he burns the c. with fire! 46.09
my love, to a mare of Pharaoh's c. Sol 1.09
and there is no end to their c. Is 2.07
the quiver with c. and horsemen, 22.06
Your choicest valleys were full of c., 22.07
there shall be your splendid c., 22.18
who trust in c. because they are 31.01
on Egypt for c. and for horsemen? 36.09
With my many c. I have gone up the 37.24
and his c. like the stormwind, to 66.15
and in c., and in litters, and upon 66.20
his c. like the whirlwind; Jer 4.13
riding in c. and on horses, they and 17.25
riding in c. and on horses, they, and 22.04
Advance, O horses, and rage, O c.! 46.09
stallions, at the rushing of his c., 47.03
upon her horses and upon her c., 50.37
the north with c. and wagons and a Eze 23.24
king of kings, with horses and c., 26.07
of the horsemen and wagons and c., 26.10
with c. and horsemen, and with many Dan 11.40
trusted in your c. and in the Hos 10.13
As with the rumbling of c., they leap Joe 2.05
Harness the steeds to the c., Mic 1.13
among you and will destroy your c.; 5.10
The c. flash like flame when Nah 2.03
The c. rage in the streets, they 2.04
and I will burn your c. in smoke, 2.13
overthrow the c. and their riders; Hag 2.22
four c. came out from between two Zec 6.01
noise of many c. with horses Rev 9.09
horses and c., and slaves, that is, 18.13

CHARITY
full of good works and acts of c. Ac 9.36

CHARM
C. is deceitful, and beauty is vain, Pro 31.30

CHARMED
If the serpent bites before it is c., Ecc 10.11
serpents, adders which cannot be c., Jer 8.17

CHARMER
or a c., or a medium, or a wizard, or Deu 18.11
there is no advantage in a c. Ecc 10.11

CHARMERS
the voice of c. or of the cunning Ps 58.05

CHARMS
magician and the expert in c. Is 3.03
harlot, graceful and of deadly c., Nah 3.04
harlotries, and people with her c. 3.04

CHARRED
of it, and the middle of it is c., Eze 15.04
fire has consumed it and it is c., 15.05

CHASE
And you shall c. your enemies, and Lev 26.07
Five of you shall c. a hundred, 26.08
of you shall c. ten thousand; 26.08
How should one c. a thousand, and Deu 32.30
every side, and c. him at his heels. Job 18.11

CHASED
against you and c. you as bees do Deu 1.44
and c. them before the gate as far Jos 7.05
and c. them by the way of the ascent 10.10
smote them and c. them as far as 11.08
And Abimelech c. him, and he fled Ju 9.40
therefore I c. him from me. Neh 13.28
he will be c. away like a vision of Job 20.08
c. like chaff on the mountains Is 17.13
they c. us on the mountains, they Lam 4.19

CHASES
his father and c. away his mother Pro 19.26

CHASING
came back from c. the Philistines, 1Sa 17.53

CHASM
and you a great c. has been fixed, Lk 16.26

CHASTE
c., domestic, kind, and submissive to Tit 2.05
see your reverent and c. behavior. 1Pe 3.02
themselves with women, for they are c.; Rev 14.04

CHASTEN
I will c. him with the rod of men, 2Sa 7.14
anger, nor c. me in thy wrath. Ps 6.01
anger, nor c. me in thy wrath! 38.01
When thou dost c. man with rebukes 39.11
Blessed is the man whom thou dost c., 94.12
Your wickedness will c. you, and your Jer 2.19
I will c. you in just measure, and I 30.11
I will c. you in just measure, and I 46.28
Those whom I love, I reprove and c.; Rev 3.19

CHASTENED
"Man is also c. with pain upon his Job 33.19
stricken and c. every morning. Ps 73.14
The LORD has c. me sorely, but he 118.18
'Thou hast c. me, and I was c., like Jer 31.18
we are c. so that we may not be 1Co 11.32

CHASTENING
despise not the c. of the Almighty. Job 5.17
a prayer when thy c. was upon them. Is 26.16

CHASTENS
He who c. the nations, does he not Ps 94.10

CHASTISE
then I will c. you again sevenfold Lev 26.18
and c. you myself sevenfold for your 26.28
though they c. him, will not give Deu 21.18
but I will c. you with scorpions.'" 1Ki 12.11
but I will c. you with scorpions." 12.14
but I will c. you with scorpions.'" 2Ch 10.11
but I will c. you with scorpions." 10.14
the nations, does he not c.? He who Ps 94.10
Shittim; but I will c. all of them. Hos 5.02
I will c. them for their wicked 7.12
the wayward people to c. them; 10.10
I will therefore c. him and release Lk 23.16
will therefore c. him and release 23.22

CHASTISED
My father c. you with whips, but I 1Ki 12.11
my father c. you with whips, but I 12.14
My father c. you with whips, but I 2Ch 10.11
my father c. you with whips, but I 10.14
when they are c. for their double Hos 10.10

CHASTISEMENT
one said to God, 'I have borne c.; Job 34.31
the nations and c. on the peoples, Ps 149.07
it, but folly is the c. of fools. Pro 16.22
him was the c. that made us whole, Is 53.05
For the c. of the daughter of my Lam 4.06
Rock, hast established them for c. Hab 1.12

CHASTISEMENTS
and fury, and with furious c.— Eze 5.15
vengeance upon them with wrathful c. 25.17

CHASTISES
and c. every son whom he receives." Heb 12.06

CHATTER
the godless c. and contradictions 1Ti 6.20
Avoid such godless c., for it will 2Ti 2.16

CHEAT
and c. me, and did not tell me, so Gen 31.27
Cursed be the c. who has a male in Mal 1.14

CHEATED
yet your father has c. me and Gen 31.07
that you have c. me, and carried 31.26

CHEBAR
among the exiles by the river C., Eze 1.01
of the Chaldeans by the river C.; 1.03
Telabib, who dwelt by the river C. 3.15
which I had seen by the river C.; 3.23
creatures that I saw by the river C. 10.15
the God of Israel by the river C.; 10.20
appearance I had seen by the river C. 10.22
which I had seen by the river C.; 43.03

CHECKED
the disease is c. and the disease Lev 13.05
But if in his eyes the itch is c., 13.37

CHECKER
a coat of c. work, a turban, and a Ex 28.04
the coat in c. work of fine linen, 28.39
two nets of c. work with wreaths 1Ki 7.17

CHECKING
of no value in c. the indulgence Col 2.23

CHEDORLAOMER
C. king of Elam, and Tidal king of Gen 14.01
Twelve years they had served C., 14.04
fourteenth year C. and the kings 14.05
with C. king of Elam, Tidal king of 14.09
the defeat of C. and the kings who 14.17

CHEEK
near and struck Micaiah on the c., 1Ki 22.24
near and struck Micaiah on the c., 2Ch 18.23
struck me insolently upon the c., Job 16.10

CHEEK (cont.)
smite all my enemies on the c., Ps 3.07
let him give his c. to the smiter, Lam 3.30
strike upon the c. the ruler of Mic 5.01
one strikes you on the right c., Mt 5.39
To him who strikes you on the c., Lk 6.29

CHEEKS
and the two c. and the stomach. Deu 18.03
Your c. are comely with ornaments, Sol 1.10
Your c. are like halves of a 4.03
His c. are like beds of spices, 5.13
Your c. are like halves of a 6.07
and my c. to those who pulled out Is 50.06
in the night, tears on her c.; Lam 1.02

CHEER
countenance, and be of good c.,' Job 9.27
many, thy consolations c. my soul. Ps 94.19
my mind how to c. my body with Ecc 2.03
let your heart c. you in the days 11.09
but be of good c., I have Jn 16.33

CHEERED
so that I may be c. by news of you. Php 2.19

CHEERFUL
bread, and let your heart be c.; 1Ki 21.07
A glad heart makes a c. countenance, Pro 15.13
but a c. heart has a continual feast. 15.15
A c. heart is a good medicine, but a 17.22
of joy and gladness, and c. feasts; Zec 8.19
compulsion, for God loves a c. giver. 2Co 9.07
Is any c.? Let him sing praise. Jas 5.13

CHEERFULLY
And Agag came to him c. Agag said, 1Sa 15.32
this nation, I c. make my defense. Ac 24.10

CHEERFULNESS
he who does acts of mercy, with c. Rom 12.08

CHEERS
my wine which c. gods and men, Ju 9.13

CHEESE
and sheep and c. from the herd, 2Sa 17.29
like milk and curdle me like c.? Job 10.10

CHEESES
also take these ten c. to the 1Sa 17.18

CHELAL
C., Benaiah, Maaseiah, Mattaniah, Ez 10.30

CHELUB
C., the brother of Shuhah, was the 1Ch 4.11
the soil was Ezri the son of C.; 27.26

CHELUBAI
to him: Jerahmeel, Ram, and C. 1Ch 2.09

CHELUHI
Benaiah, Bedeiah, C., Ez 10.35

CHEMOSH
You are undone, O people of C.! Num 21.29
possess what C. your god gives you Ju 11.24
high place for C. the abomination 1Ki 11.07
C. the god of Moab, and Milcom the 11.33
and for C. the abomination of Moab, 2Ki 23.13
and C. shall go forth into exile, Jer 48.07
Then Moab shall be ashamed of C., 48.13
The people of C. is undone; for your 48.46

CHENAANAH
the son of C. made for himself horns of 1Ki 22.11
the son of C. came near and struck 22.24
C., Zethan, Tarshish, and Ahishahar. 1Ch 7.10
the son of C. made for himself horns of 2Ch 18.10
the son of C. came near and struck 18.23

CHENANI
Bunni, Sherebiah, Bani, and C.; and they Neh 9.04

CHENANIAH
C., leader of the Levites in music, 1Ch 15.22
and C. the leader of the music of 15.27
C. and his sons were appointed to 26.29

CHEPHARAMMONI
C., Ophni, Geba—twelve cities with Jos 18.24

CHEPHIRAH
C., Beeroth, and Kiriathjearim. Jos 9.17
Mizpeh, C., Mozah 18.26
C., and Beeroth, seven hundred and Ez 2.25
C., and Beeroth, seven hundred and Neh 7.29

CHERAN
Hemdan, Eshban, Ithran, and C. Gen 36.26
Hamran, Eshban, Ithran, and C. 1Ch 1.41

CHERETHITES
Negeb of the C. and upon that 1Sa 30.14
was over the C. and the Pelethites 2Sa 8.18
and all the C., and all the Pelethites, 15.18
Joab and the C. and the Pelethites, 20.07
command of the C. and the Pelethites 20.23
and the C. and the Pelethites, went 1Ki 1.38
and the C. and the Pelethites; 1.44
was over the C. and the Pelethites 1Ch 18.17
Philistines, and I will cut off the C., Eze 25.16
the seacoast, you nation of the C.! Zep 2.05

CHERISH
"The godless in heart c. anger; Job 36.13
in anger they c. enmity against me. Ps 55.03
forsaken the LORD to c. harlotry. Hos 4.10

CHERISHED
If I had c. iniquity in my heart, Ps 66.18
Because you c. perpetual enmity, and Eze 35.05

CHERISHES
own flesh, but nourishes and c. it, Eph 5.29

CHERITH
and hide yourself by the brook C., 1Ki 17.03
by the brook C. that is east of 17.05

CHERUB
Make one c. on the one end, and one Ex 25.19
and one c. on the other end; 25.19
one c. on the one end, and one 37.08
and one c. on the other end; 37.08
He rode on a c., and flew; he was 2Sa 22.11
the length of one wing of the c., 1Ki 6.24
length of the other wing of the c.; 6.24
The other c. also measured ten 6.25
The height of one c. was ten cubits, 6.26
and so was that of the other c. 6.26
of the other c. touched the other 6.27
touched the wing of the other c.; 2Ch 3.11
and of this c., one wing, of five 3.12
joined to the wing of the first c. 3.12
C., Addan, and Immer, though they Ez 2.59
C., Addon, and Immer, but they could Neh 7.61
He rode on a c., and flew; he came Ps 18.10
And a c. stretched forth his hand Eze 10.07
the cherubim, one beside each c.; 10.09
first face was the face of the c., 10.14
anointed guardian c. I placed you; 28.14
the guardian c. drove you out from 28.16
a palm tree between c. and c. 41.18
Every c. had two faces: 41.18

CHERUBIM
garden of Eden he placed the c., Gen 3.24
And you shall make two c. of gold; Ex 25.18
you make the c. on its two ends. 25.19
The c. shall spread out their wings 25.20
seat shall the faces of the c. be. 25.20
between the two c. that are upon 25.22
with c. skilfully worked shall you 26.01
work shall it be made, with c.; 26.31
stuff, with c. skilfully worked. 36.08
with c. skilfully worked he made it 36.35
And he made two c. of hammered gold; 37.07
he made the c. on its two ends. 37.08
The c. spread out their wings above, 37.09
mercy seat were the faces of the c. 37.09
testimony, from between the two c.; Num 7.89
hosts, who is enthroned on the c.; 1Sa 4.04
hosts who sits enthroned on the c. 2Sa 6.02
he made two c. of olivewood, each ten 1Ki 6.23
both c. had the same measure and 6.25
He put the c. in the innermost part 6.27
wings of the c. were spread out so 6.27
And he overlaid the c. with gold. 6.28
figures of c. and palm trees and 6.29
of olivewood with carvings of c., 6.32
gold upon the c. and upon the palm 6.32
On them he carved c. and palm trees 6.35
frames were lions, oxen, and c. 7.29
he carved c., lions, and palm trees, 7.36
underneath the wings of the c. 8.06
For the c. spread out their wings 8.07
so that the c. made a covering above 8.07
who art enthroned above the c., 2Ki 19.15
who sits enthroned above the c. 1Ch 13.06
chariot of the c. that spread 28.18
and he carved c. on the walls. 2Ch 3.07
he made two c. of wood and overlaid 3.10
The wings of the c. together 3.11
The wings of these c. extended 3.13
the c. stood on their feet, facing 3.13
fine linen, and worked c. on it. 3.14
underneath the wings of the c. 5.07
For the c. spread out their wings 5.08
so that the c. made a covering 5.08
enthroned upon the c., shine forth Ps 80.01
He sits enthroned upon the c.; 99.01
who art enthroned above the c., Is 37.16
up from the c. on which it rested Eze 9.03
heads of the c. there appeared 10.01
whirling wheels underneath the c.; 10.02
burning coals from between the c., 10.02
Now the c. were standing on the 10.03
up from the c. to the threshold of 10.04
wings of the c. was heard as far 10.05
wheels, from between the c., 10.06
between the c. to the fire that 10.07
the fire that was between the c., 10.07
The c. appeared to have the form of 10.08
were four wheels beside the c., 10.09
And the c. mounted up. These were 10.15
And when the c. went, the wheels 10.16
and when the c. lifted up their 10.16
the house, and stood over the c. 10.18
And the c. lifted up their wings 10.19
and I knew that they were c. 10.20
Then the c. lifted up their wings, 11.22
of c. and palm trees, a palm tree 41.18
above the door c. and palm trees 41.20
nave were carved c. and palm trees, 41.25
above it were the c. of glory Heb 9.05

CHESALON
of Mount Jearim (that is C.), Jos 15.10

CHESED
C., Hazo, Pildash, Jidlaph, and Gen 22.22

CHESIL
Eltolad, C., Hormah, Jos 15.30

CHEST
Then Jehoiada the priest took a c., 2Ki 12.09
there was much money in the c., 12.10
king commanded, and they made a c., 2Ch 24.08
it into the c. until they had 24.10
And whenever the c. was brought to 24.11
and empty the c. and take it and 24.11

CHESULLOTH
included Jezreel, C., Shunem, Jos 19.18

CHEW
those that c. the cud or part the Lev 11.04
cloven-footed but does not c. the cud, 11.07
or does not c. the cud is unclean 11.26
Yet of those that c. the cud or Deu 14.07
because they c. the cud but do not 14.07
the hoof but does not c. the cud, 14.08

CHEWS
is cloven-footed and c. the cud, Lev 11.03
because it c. the cud but does not 11.04
because it c. the cud but does not 11.05
because it c. the cud but does not 11.06
and c. the cud, among the animals, Deu 14.06

CHEZIB
She was in C. when she bore him. Gen 38.05

CHIDE
He will not always c., nor will he Ps 103.09

CHIDON
came to the threshing floor of C., 1Ch 13.09

CHIEF
the c. butler and the c. baker, Gen 40.02
So the c. butler told his dream to 40.09
When the c. baker saw that the 40.16
the head of the c. butler and the 40.20
the head of the c. baker among his 40.20
He restored the c. butler to his 40.21
but he hanged the c. baker, as Joseph 40.22
Yet the c. butler did not remember 40.23
Then the c. butler said to Pharaoh, 41.09
put me and the c. baker in custody 41.10
his hand on the c. men of the Ex 24.11
"The priest who is c. among his Lev 21.10
was to be c. over the leaders of Num 3.32
Edomite, the c. of Saul's herdsmen. 1Sa 21.07
he was c. of the three; he wielded 2Sa 23.08
of the thirty c. men went down, 23.13
of Zeruiah, was c. of the thirty. 23.18
three hundred c. officers who were 1Ki 5.16
These were the c. officers who were 9.23
and the c. men of the land, he took 2Ki 24.15
guard took Seraiah the c. priest, 25.18
the c., Jeiel and Zechariah, 1Ch 5.07
Joel the c., Shapham the second, 5.12
was c. in their fathers' houses; 5.15
Isshiah, five, all of them c. men; 7.03
mighty warriors, c. of the princes. 7.40
to their generations, c. men. 8.28
the c. officer of the house of God; 9.11
kinsmen (Shallum being the c.), 9.17
for the four c. gatekeepers, who 9.26
first shall be c. and commander." 11.06
went up first, so he became c. 11.06
a Hachmonite, was c. of the three; 11.11
Three of the thirty c. men went 11.15
of Joab, was c. of the thirty. 11.20
The c. was Ahiezer, then Joash, both 12.03
Ezer the c., Obadiah second, Eliab 12.09
c. of the thirty, and he said, "We 12.18
Uriel the c., with a hundred and 15.05

CHIEF (cont.)

Asaiah the c., with two hundred and 1Ch 15.06
Joel the c., with a hundred and 15.07
Shemaiah the c., with two hundred 15.08
Eliel the c., with eighty of his 15.09
Amminadab the c., with a hundred 15.10
Asaph was the c., and second to him 16.05
sons were the c. officials in the 18.17
Jehiel the c., and Zetham, and Joel, 23.08
Jahath was the c., and Zizah the 23.11
The sons of Gershom: Shebuel the c. 23.16
The sons of Eliezer: Rehabiah the c.; 23.17
The sons of Izhar: Shelomith the c. 23.18
Jemah the c., Amariah the second, 23.19
Micah the c. and Isshiah the second. 23.20
Since more c. men were found among 24.04
sons of Rehabiah, Isshiah the c. 24.21
Jeriah the c., Amariah the second, 24.23
Shimri the c. (for though he was 26.10
first-born, his father made him c.), 26.10
corresponding to their c. men, 26.12
was c. officer in charge of the 26.24
Jerijah was c. of the Hebronites of 26.31
and was c. of all the commanders of 27.03
son of Jehoiada the priest, as c.; 27.05
the son of Zichri was c. officer; 27.16
And these were the c. officers of 2Ch 8.10
of Maacah as c. prince among his 11.22
Amariah the c. priest is over you 19.11
So the king summoned Jehoiada the c., 24.06
officer of the c. priest would 24.11
And Azariah the c. priest, and all 26.20
Azariah the c. priest, who was of 31.10
The c. officer in charge of them 31.12
and Azariah the c. officer of the 31.13
the c. officers of the house of God, 35.08
Eleazar, son of Aaron the c. priest— Ez 7.05
them before the c. priests and the 8.29
officials and c. men hast been 9.02
old there was a c. of the singers, Neh 12.46
and sat as c., and I dwelt like a Job 29.25
has become the c. cornerstone. Ps 118.22
Without having any c., officer or Pro 6.07
and aloes, with all c. spices— Sol 4.14
In the year that the commander in c., Is 20.01
who was c. officer in the house of Jer 20.01
shouts for the c. of the nations; 31.07
and all the c. officers of the king 39.13
one of the c. officers of the king, 41.01
guard took Seraiah the c. priest, 52.24
(The c. men of the land he had Eze 17.13
the c. prince of Meshech and Tubal, 38.02
c. prince of Meshech and Tubal; 38.03
c. prince of Meshech and Tubal; 39.01
his c. eunuch, to bring some of the Dan 1.03
And the c. of the eunuchs gave them 1.07
he asked the c. of the eunuchs to 1.08
the sight of the c. of the eunuchs; 1.09
and the c. of the eunuchs said to 1.10
whom the c. of the eunuchs had 1.11
the c. of the eunuchs brought them 1.18
and c. prefect over all the wise 2.48
c. of the magicians, because I know 4.09
made him c. of the magicians, 5.11
one of the c. princes, came to help 10.13
assembling all the c. priests and Mt 2.04
the elders and c. priests and 16.21
delivered to the c. priests and 20.18
But when the c. priests and the 21.15
the c. priests and the elders of 21.23
When the c. priests and the Pharisees 21.45
Then the c. priests and the elders 26.03
Iscariot, went to the c. priests 26.14
from the c. priests and the elders 26.47
Now the c. priests and the whole 26.59
all the c. priests and the elders 27.01
silver to the c. priests and the 27.03
But the c. priests, taking the 27.06
accused by the c. priests and 27.12
Now the c. priests and the elders 27.20
So also the c. priests, with the 27.41
the c. priests and the Pharisees 27.62
and told the c. priests all that 28.11
elders and the c. priests and the Mk 8.31
delivered to the c. priests and the 10.33
And the c. priests and the scribes 11.18
the c. priests and the scribes and 11.27
And the c. priests and the scribes 14.01
went to the c. priests in order to 14.10
from the c. priests and the scribes 14.43
and all the c. priests and the 14.53
Now the c. priests and the whole 14.55
as it was morning the c. priests, 15.01
And the c. priests accused him of 15.03
envy that the c. priests had 15.10
But the c. priests stirred up the 15.11
So also the c. priests mocked him 15.31
the elders and c. priests and Lk 9.22
he was a c. tax collector, and rich. 19.02
The c. priests and the scribes and 19.47
the c. priests and the scribes with 20.01
The scribes and the c. priests 20.19
And the c. priests and the scribes 22.02
with the c. priests and captains 22.04
said to the c. priests and captains 22.52
both c. priests and scribes; 22.66
said to the c. priests and the 23.04
The c. priests and the scribes 23.10
together the c. priests and the 23.13
and how our c. priests and rulers 24.20
and the c. priests and Pharisees Jn 7.32
back to the c. priests and Pharisees, 7.45
So the c. priests and the Pharisees 11.47
Now the c. priests and the Pharisees 11.57
So the c. priests planned to put 12.10
from the c. priests and the 18.03
nation and the c. priests have 18.35
When the c. priests and the officers 19.06
The c. priests answered, "We have 19.15
The c. priests of the Jews then 19.21
what the c. priests and the elders Ac 4.23
temple and the c. priests heard 5.24
from the c. priests to bind all 9.14
them bound before the c. priests." 9.21
because he was the c. speaker, 14.12
commanded the c. priests and all 22.30
went to the c. priests and elders, 23.14
But the c. captain Lysias came and *24.07
And the c. priests and the principal 25.02
the c. priests and the elders of 25.15
by authority from the c. priests, 26.10
and commission of the c. priests. 26.12
belonging to the c. man of the 28.07
himself being the c. cornerstone, Eph 2.20
And when the c. Shepherd is manifested 1Pe 5.04

CHIEFS

These are the c. of the sons of Gen 36.15
the c. Teman, Omar, Zepho, Kenaz, 36.15
these are the c. of Eliphaz in the 36.16
the c. Nahath, Zerah, Shammah, and 36.17
these are the c. of Reuel in the 36.17
the c. Jeush, Jalam, and Korah; 36.18
these are the c. born of Oholibamah 36.18
is, Edom), and these are their c. 36.19
These are the c. of the Horites, the 36.21
These are the c. of the Horites: the 36.29
the c. Lotan, Shobal, Zibeon, Anah, 36.29
these are the c. of the Horites, 36.30
These are the names of the c. of Esau, 36.40
the c. Timna, Alvah, Jetheth, 36.40
these are the c. of Edom (that is, 36.43
Now are the c. of Edom dismayed; Ex 15.15
"Take all the c. of the people, and Num 25.04

CHIEFS (cont.)

and said to the c. of the men of Jos 10.24
and with him ten c., one from 22.14
priest and the c. of the congregation, 22.30
and the c., returned from the 22.32
And the c. of all the people, of all Ju 20.02
The c. of Edom were: c. Timna, 1Ch 1.51
and Iram; these are the c. of Edom. 1.54
Now these are the c. of David's 11.10
c. of thousands in Manasseh. 12.20
two hundred c., and all their 12.32
commanded the c. of the Levites to 15.16
David and the c. of the service 25.01
Certain c. also of the men of 2Ch 28.12
the c. of the Levites, gave to the 35.09
The c. of the people: Parosh, Pahathmoab, Neh 10.14
These are the c. of the province 11.03
of the c. of the Levites, who were 11.16
These were the c. of the priests 12.07
And the c. of the Levites: Hashabiah, 12.24
the army c. of Persia and Media and Est 1.03
from the c. of the people of the Job 12.24
he will shatter c. over the wide Ps 110.06
The mighty c. shall speak of them, Eze 32.21

CHIEFTAIN

he was a c. of the Reubenites. 1Ch 5.06

CHILD

for me another c. instead of Abel, Gen 4.25
was barren; she had no c. 11.30
you are with c., and shall bear a 16.11
"Shall a c. be born to a man who is 17.17
who is ninety years old, bear a c.?" 17.17
and say. "Shall I indeed bear a c., 18.13
Lot were with c. by their father. 19.36
And the c. grew, and was weaned; 21.08
on her shoulder, along with the c., 21.14
she cast the c. under one of the 21.15
not look upon the death of the c." 21.16
the c. lifted up his voice and wept. 21.16
moreover she is with c. by harlotry." 38.24
to whom these belong, I am with c." 38.25
brother, the c. of his old age; 44.20
she saw that he was a goodly c., Ex 2.02
and she put the c. in it and placed 2.03
When she opened it she saw the c.; 2.06
women to nurse the c. for you?" 2.07
"Take this c. away, and nurse him 2.09
woman took the c. and nursed him. 2.09
And the c. grew, and she brought him 2.10
together, and hurt a woman with c., 21.22
conceives, and bears a male c., Lev 12.02
But if she bears a female c., 12.05
is the law for her who bears a c., 12.07
and has no c., and returns to her 22.13
as a nurse carries the sucking c., Num 11.12
the sucking c. with the man of gray Deu 32.25
she was his only c.; beside her Ju 11.34
Then Naomi took the c. and laid him Ru 4.16
"As soon as the c. is weaned, 1Sa 1.22
at Shiloh; and the c. was young. 1.24
and they brought the c. to Eli. 1.25
For this c. I prayed; and the 1.27
was with c., about to give birth. 4.19
And she named the c. Ichabod, 4.21
of Saul had no c. to the day of 2Sa 6.23
sent and told David, "I am with c." 11.05
the c. that is born to you shall 12.14
LORD struck the c. that Uriah's 12.15
David therefore besought God for the c.; 12.16
On the seventh day the c. died. 12.18
to tell him that the c. was dead; 12.18
while the c. was yet alive, we spoke 12.18
can we say to him the c. is dead? 12.18
perceived that the c. was dead; 12.19
to his servants, "Is the c. dead?" 12.19
wept for the c. while it was alive; 12.21
but when the c. died, you arose and 12.21
"While the c. was still alive, I 12.22
to me, that the c. may live?' 12.22
although I am but a little c.; 1Ki 3.07
gave birth to a c. while she was 3.17
rose in the morning to nurse my c., 3.21
it was not the c. that I had borne." 3.21
the living c. is mine, and the dead 3.22
is mine, and the dead c. is yours." 3.22
"No, the dead c. is yours, and 3.22
and the living c. is mine." Thus 3.22
said, "Divide the living c. in two, 3.25
my lord, give her the living c., 3.26
"Give the living c. to the first 3.27
Hadad being yet a little c. 11.17
you what shall happen to the c." 14.03
enter the city, the c. shall die. 14.12
threshold of the house, the c. died. 14.17
himself upon the c. three times, 17.21
the soul of the c. came into him 17.22
And Elijah took the c., 17.23
When the c. had grown, he went out 2Ki 4.18
the c. sat on her lap till noon, and 4.20
Is it well with the c.?" And she 4.26
my staff upon the face of the c." 4.29
Then the mother of the c. said, 4.30
the staff upon the face of the c., 4.31
told him, "The c. has not awaked." 4.31
he saw the c. lying dead on his bed. 4.32
Then he went up and lay upon the c., 4.34
the flesh of the c. became warm. 4.34
the c. sneezed seven times, and the 4.35
and the c. opened his eyes. 4.35
like the flesh of a little c., 5.14
and rip up their women with c." 8.12
the women in it who were with c. 15.16
the fatherless c. from the breast, Job 24.09
like a c. quieted at its mother's Ps 131.02
like a c. that is quieted is my 131.02
Even a c. makes himself known by Pro 20.11
train up a c. in the way he should 22.06
Folly is bound up in the heart of a c., 22.15
Do not withhold discipline from a c.; 23.13
but a c. left to himself brings 29.15
O land, when your king is a c., Ecc 10.16
in the womb of a woman with c., 11.05
For before the c. knows how to Is 7.16
for before the c. knows how to cry 8.04
For to us a c. is born, to us a son 9.06
so few that a c. can write them 10.19
and a little c. shall lead them. 11.06
The sucking c. shall play over the 11.08
and the weaned c. shall put his 11.08
Like a woman with c., who writhes 26.17
we were with c., we writhed, we have 26.18
"Can a woman forget her sucking c., 49.15
for the c. shall die a hundred 65.20
of one bringing forth her first c., Jer 4.31
Ask now, and see, can a man bear a c.? 30.06
the woman with c. and her who is 31.08
Is he my darling c.? For as 31.20
infant and c., from the midst of 44.07
her c., and he who got possession Dan 11.06
When Israel was a c., I loved Hos 11.01
ripped up women with c. in Gilead, Amo 1.13
him, as one mourns for an only c., Zec 12.10
to be with c. of the Holy Spirit; Mt 1.18
and search diligently for the c., 2.08
over the place where the c. was. 2.09
they saw the c. with Mary his 2.11
take the c. and his mother, and flee 2.13
is about to search for the c., 2.13
and took the c. and his mother by 2.14
take the c. and his mother, and go 2.20
and took the c. and his mother, 2.21
to death, and the father his c., 10.21

CHILD (cont.)
And calling to him a c., he put Mt 18.02
Whoever humbles himself like this c., 18.04
one such c. in my name receives me 18.05
twice as much a c. of hell as 23.15
who are with c. and for those who 24.19
The c. is not dead but sleeping." Mk 5.39
him, and went in where the c. was. 5.40
and found the c. lying in bed, and 7.30
father of the c. cried out and 9.24
And he took a c., and put him in 9.36
one such c. in my name perceives me 9.37
of God like a c. shall not enter 10.15
but leaves no c., the man must take 12.19
to death, and the father his c., 13.12
who are with c. and for those who 13.17
But they had no c., because Lk 1.07
therefore the c. to be born will be 1.35
day they came to circumcise the c.; 1.59
saying, "What then will this c. be?" 1.66
And you, c., will be called the 1.76
And the c. grew and became strong 1.80
his betrothed, who was with c. 2.05
been told them concerning this c.; 2.17
parents brought in the c. Jesus, 2.27
this c. is set for the fall and 2.34
And the c. grew and became strong, 2.40
the father and mother of the c. 8.51
hand he called, saying, "C., arise." 8.54
upon my son, for he is my only c.; 9.38
he took a c. and put him by his 9.47
receives this c. in my name 9.48
of God like a c. shall not enter 18.17
who are with c. and for those who 21.23
"Sir, come down before my c. dies." Jn 4.49
when she is delivered of the c., 16.21
for joy that a c. is born into the 16.21
after him, though he had no c. Ac 7.05
and faithful c. in the Lord, 1Co 4.17
When I was a c., I spoke like a c., 13.11
I thought like a c., I reasoned like a c.; 13.11
the heir, as long as he is a c., Gal 4.01
travail comes upon a woman with c., 1Th 5.03
my true c. in the faith: Grace, mercy, 1Ti 1.02
my beloved c.: Grace, mercy, and peace 2Ti 1.02
my true c. in a common faith: Grace Tit 1.04
I appeal to you for my c., Onesimus, Phm 1.10
of righteousness, for he is a c. Heb 5.13
they saw that the c. was beautiful; 11.23
Jesus is the Christ is a c. of God, 1Jn 5.01
who loves the parent loves the c. 5.01
she was with c. and she cried out Rev 12.02
woman who was about to bear a c., 12.04
devour her c. when she brought it 12.04
she brought forth a male c., 12.05
but her c. was caught up to God and 12.05
woman who had borne the male c. 12.13

CHILDBEARING
greatly multiply your pain in c.; Gen 3.16

CHILDBIRTH
The pangs of c. come for him, but he Hos 13.13

CHILDHOOD
He who pampers his servant from c., Pro 29.21
had this?" And he said, "From c. Mk 9.21
and how from c. you have been 2Ti 3.15

CHILDISH
I became a man, I gave up c. ways. 1Co 13.11

CHILDLESS
thou give me, for I continue c., Gen 15.02
bear their sin, they shall die c. Lev 20.20
nakedness, they shall be c. 20.21
"As your sword has made women c., 1Sa 15.33
your mother be c. among women." 15.33
and Appaim; and Seled died c. 1Ch 2.30
Jonathan; and Jether died c. 2.32
"They feed on the barren c. woman, Job 24.21
their wives become c. and widowed. Jer 18.21
LORD: "Write this man down as c., 22.30

CHILDREN
in pain you shall bring forth c., Gen 3.16
of men, and they bore c. to them. 6.04
the father of all the c. of Eber, 10.21
brother of Japheth, c. were born. 10.21
Abram's wife, bore him no c. 16.01
has prevented me from bearing c.; 16.02
be that I shall obtain c. by her." 16.02
may charge his c. and his household 18.19
female slaves so that they bore c. 20.17
Abraham that Sarah would suckle c.? 21.07
also has borne c. to your brother 22.20
All these were the c. of Keturah. 25.04
The c. struggled together within 25.22
saw that she bore Jacob no c., 30.01
"Give me c., or I shall die!" 30.01
and even I may have c. through her." 30.03
saw that she had ceased bearing c., 30.09
my wives and my c. for whom I have 30.26
father belongs to us and to our c.; 31.16
are my daughters, the c. are my c., 31.43
or to their c. whom they have borne? 31.43
us all, the mothers with the c. 32.11
his two maids, and his eleven c., 32.22
he divided the c. among Leah and 33.01
the maids with their c. in front, 33.02
in front, then Leah with her c., 33.02
his eyes and saw the women and c., 33.05
"The c. whom God has graciously 33.05
maids drew near, they and their c., 33.06
likewise and her c. drew near and 33.07
lord knows that the c. are frail, 33.13
according to the pace of the c., 33.14
These are the c. of Anah: Dishon and 36.25
more than any other of his c., 37.03
"You have bereaved me of my c.: 42.36
bereaved of my c., I am bereaved. 43.14
alone is left of his mother's c.; 44.20
you and your c. and your children's c., 45.10
God has let me see your c. also." 48.11
only their c., their flocks, and 50.08
saw Ephraim's c. of the third 50.23
the c. also of Machir the son of 50.23
them, but let the male c. live. Ex 1.17
this, and let the male c. live?" 1.18
"This is one of the Hebrews' c." 2.06
he did not let the c. of Israel go. 10.20
your c. also may go with you; 10.24
And when your c. say to you, 'What 12.26
men on foot, besides women and c. 12.37
kill us and our c. and our cattle 17.03
faultfinding of the c. of Israel, 17.07
shall speak to the c. of Israel." 19.06
upon the c. to the third and the 20.05
wife and her c. shall be her 21.04
love my master, my wife, and my c.; 21.05
widows and your c. fatherless. 22.24
upon the c. and the children's c., 34.07
Every male among the c. of Aaron Lev 6.18
any of your c. to devote them by 18.21
any of his c. to Molech shall be 20.02
has given one of his c. to Molech, 20.03
he gives one of his c. to Molech, 20.04
sight of the c. of their people; 20.17
not profane his c. among his 21.15
he and his c. with him, and go back 25.41
of jubilee, he and his c. with him. 25.54
which shall rob you of your c., 26.22
and they had no c. So Eleazer Num 3.04
be free and shall conceive c. 5.28

CHILDREN (cont.)

the iniquity of fathers upon c., Num 14.18
And your c. shall be shepherds in 14.33
him and to his c. I will give the Deu 1.36
and your c., who this day have no 1.39
every city, men, women, and c.; 2.34
every city, men, women, and c. 3.06
known to your c. and your children's c.— 4.09
that they may teach their c. so.' 4.10
"When you beget c. and children's c., 4.25
and with your c. after you, and that 4.40
Moses set before the c. of Israel; 4.44
spoke to the c. of Israel when 4.45
Moses and the c. of Israel defeated 4.46
upon the c. to the third and 5.09
them and with their c. for ever! 5.29
teach them dilgently to your c., 6.07
speaking to your c. who have not 11.02
And you shall teach them to your c., 11.19
days of your c. may be multiplied 11.21
you and with your c. after you, 12.25
and with your c. after you for 12.28
kingdom, he and his c., in Israel. 17.20
disliked, and they have borne him c., 21.15
The c. of the third generation that 23.08
not be put to death for the c., 24.16
nor shall the c. be put to death 24.16
the last of the c. who remain to 28.54
flesh of his c. whom he is eating, 28.55
her feet and her c. whom she bears, 28.57
your c. who rise up after you, and 29.22
to us and to our c. for ever, 29.29
you and your c., and obey his voice 30.02
and that their c., who have not 31.13
shall bring the c. of Israel into 31.23
no longer his c. because of their 32.05
c. in whom is no faithfulness. 32.20
you may command them to your c., 32.46
God blessed the c. of Israel 33.01
his brothers, and ignored his c. 33.09
when your c. ask in time to come, Jos 4.06
"When your c. ask their fathers in 4.21
then you shall let your c. know, 4.22
So it was their c., whom he 5.07
for you and your c. for ever, 14.09
to come your c. might say to our c., 22.24
So your c. might make our c. cease 22.25
lest your c. say to our c. in 22.27
Jacob and his c. went down to 24.04
oppressed the c. of Israel that Ju 10.08
his wife was barren and had no c. 13.02
you are barren and have no c.; 13.03
because of the c. that the LORD Ru 4.12
And Peninnah had c., but Hannah 1Sa 1.02
had c., but Hannah had no c. 1.02
but she who has many c. is forlorn. 2.05
LORD give you c. by this woman for 2.20
c. and sucklings, oxen, asses and 22.19
away his wife and c., and depart." 30.22
grew up with him and with his c.; 2Sa 12.03
will dwell among the c. of Israel, 1Ki 6.13
the hearts of all the c. of men); 8.39
you or your c., and do not keep my 9.06
fairest wives and c. also are mine.'" 20.03
your gold, your wives and your c."; 20.05
sent to me for my wives and my c., 20.07
to take my two c. to be his slaves." 2Ki 4.01
to death the c. of the murderers; 14.06
not be put to death for the c., 14.06
or the c. be put to death for the 14.06
burned their c. in the fire to 17.31
the LORD commanded the c. of Jacob, 17.34
their c. likewise, and their children's c.— 17.41
c. have come to birth, and 19.03
of Hezron had c. by his wife 1Ch 2.18
but his brothers had not many c., 4.27
The c. of Amram: Aaron, Moses, and 6.03
names of the c. whom he had in 14.04
and had no c., so Eleazar and 24.02
inheritance to your c. after you 28.08
the hearts of the c. of men); 2Ch 6.30
When all the c. of Israel saw the 7.03
ones, their wives, and their c. 20.13
your c., your wives, and all your 21.14
But he did not put their c. to death, 25.04
shall not be put to death for the c., 25.04
or the c. be put to death for the 25.04
and your c. will find compassion 30.09
enrolled with all their little c., 31.18
our c., and all our goods. Ez 8.21
an inheritance to your c. for ever.' 9.12
and c., gathered to him out of 10.01
away all these wives and their c., 10.03
they put them away with their c. 10.44
the welfare of the c. of Israel. Neh 2.10
our c. are as their c.; yet we 5.05
the c. of Israel were in their 7.73
the women and c. also rejoiced. 12.43
not meet the c. of Israel with 13.02
and half of their c. spoke the 13.24
women and c., in one day, the Est 3.13
with their c. and women, and to 8.11
If your c. have sinned against him, Job 8.04
the eyes of his c. will fail. 17.05
Even young c. despise me; when I 19.18
His c. will seek the favor of the 20.10
Their c. are established in their 21.08
like a flock, and their c. dance. 21.11
wilderness as food for their c. 24.05
If his c. are multiplied, it is for 27.14
with me, when my c. were about me; 29.05
can you guide the Bear with its c.? 38.32
his eyelids test, the c. of men. Ps 11.04
from heaven upon the c. of men, 14.02
may their c. have more than enough; 17.14
and their c. from among the sons of 21.10
and his c. shall possess the land. 25.13
The c. of men take refuge in the 36.07
forsaken or his c. begging bread. 37.25
and his c. become a blessing. 37.26
but the c. of the wicked shall be 37.28
the c. of his servants shall 69.36
untrue to the generation of thy c. 73.15
We will not hide them from their c., 78.04
our fathers to teach to their c.; 78.05
the c. yet unborn, and arise and 78.06
arise and tell them to their c., 78.06
the strong arm of the c. of Lot. 83.08
If his c. forsake my law and do not 89.30
and sayest, "Turn back, O c. of men!" 90.03
and thy glorious power to their c. 90.16
The c. of thy servants shall dwell 102.28
As a father pities his c., so the 103.13
righteousness to children's c., 103.17
May his c. be fatherless, and his 109.09
May his c. wander about and beg; 109.10
nor any to pity his fatherless c.! 109.12
making her the joyous mother of c. 113.09
give you increase, you and your c.! 115.14
your c. will be like olive shoots 128.03
May you see your children's c.! 128.06
maidens together, old men and c.! 148.12
inheritance to his children's c., Pro 13.22
and his c. will have a refuge. 14.26
Her c. rise up and call her blessed 31.28
If a man begets a hundred c., Ecc 6.03
My people—c. are their oppressors, Is 3.12
I and the c. whom the LORD has 8.18
their eyes will not pity c. 13.18
like the glory of the c. of Israel, 17.03
because of the c. of Israel, 17.09
For when he sees his c., the work 29.23
"Woe to the rebellious c.," says the 30.01
c. have come to the birth, and there 37.03

CHILDREN (cont.)

known to the c. thy faithfulness.	Is 38.19
"Will you question me about my c.,	45.11
a widow or know the loss of c.":	47.08
the loss of c. and widowhood shall	47.09
The c. born in the time of your	49.20
with you, and I will save your c.	49.25
For the c. of the desolate one will	54.01
more than the c. of her that is	54.01
Are you not c. of transgression, the	57.04
who slay your c. in the valleys,	57.05
or out of the mouth of your c.,	59.21
of the mouth of your children's c.,	59.21
in vain, or bear c. for calamity;	65.23
the LORD, and their c. with them.	65.23
your children's c. I will contend.	Jer 2.09
In vain have I smitten your c.,	2.30
Return, O faithless c., says the LORD;	3.14
they are stupid c., they have no	4.22
Your c. have forsaken me, and have	5.07
it out upon the c. in the street,	6.11
The c. gather wood, the fathers	7.18
cutting off the c. from the	9.21
my c. have gone from me, and they	10.20
while their c. remember their	17.02
Therefore deliver up their c. to famine;	18.21
are he and his c. hurled and cast	22.28
Their c. shall be as they were of	30.20
Rachel is weeping for her c.;	31.15
refuses to be comforted for her c.,	31.15
and your c. shall come back to	31.17
of fathers to their c. after them,	32.18
the good of their c. after them.	32.39
and c., those of the poorest of the	40.07
c., and eunuchs, whom Johanan	41.16
the c., the princesses, and every	43.06
fathers look not back to their c.,	47.03
His c. are destroyed, and his	49.10
Leave your fatherless c., I will	49.11
her c. have gone away, captives	Lam 1.05
my c. are desolate, for the enemy	1.16
to him for the lives of your c.,	2.19
the c. of their tender care?	2.20
the c. beg for food, but no one	4.04
women have boiled their own c.;	4.10
and they will rob you of your c.;	Eze 5.17
little c. and women, but touch no	9.06
slaughtered my c. and delivered	16.21
blood of your c. that you gave to	16.36
who loathed her husband and her c.;	16.45
their husbands and their c.	16.45
"And I said to their c. in the	20.18
But the c. rebelled against me;	20.21
slaughtered their c. in sacrifice	23.39
shall no longer bereave them of c.	36.12
you bereave your nation of c.,	36.13
longer bereave your nation of c.,	36.14
and the c. of Israel associated	37.16
they and their c. and their children's c.	37.25
you and have begotten c. among you.	47.22
their c., and their wives; and before	Dan 6.24
harlotry and have c. of harlotry,	Hos 1.02
Upon her c. also I will have no	2.04
because they are c. of harlotry.	2.04
For the c. of Israel shall dwell	3.04
Afterward the c. of Israel shall	3.05
God, I also will forget your c.	4.06
for they have borne alien c.	5.07
Even if they bring up c.,	9.12
I will slay their beloved c.	9.16
dashed in pieces with their c.	10.14
Tell your c. of it, and let your	Joe 1.03
and let your c. tell their c.,	1.03
and their c. another generation.	1.03
gather the c., even nursing infants.	2.16
for the c. of your delight;	Mic 1.16
their young c. you take away my	2.09
Their c. shall see it and rejoice,	Zec 10.07
and with their c. they shall live	10.09
to their c. and the hearts of	Mal 4.06
the hearts of c. to their fathers,	4.06
all the male c. in Bethlehem and	Mt 2.16
lamentation, Rachel weeping for her c.;	2.18
stones to raise up c. to Abraham.	3.09
how to give good gifts to your c.,	7.11
and c. will rise against parents	10.21
It is like c. sitting in the market	11.16
thousand men, besides women and c.	14.21
thousand men, besides women and c.	15.38
unless you turn and become like c.,	18.03
his wife and c. and all that he	18.25
Then c. were brought to him that he	19.13
"Let the c. come to me, and do not	19.14
or father or mother or c. or lands,	19.29
and the c. crying out in the temple,	21.15
having no c., his brother must	22.24
and raise up c. for his brother.'	22.24
and having no c. left his wife to	22.25
gathered your c. together as a hen	23.37
"His blood be on us and on our c.!"	27.25
"Let the c. first be fed, for it is	Mk 7.27
And they were bringing c. to him,	10.13
"Let the c. come to me, do not	10.14
"C., how hard it is to enter the	10.24
or mother or father or c. or lands,	10.29
and mothers and c. and lands,	10.30
and raise up c. for his brother.	12.19
wife, and when he died left no c.;	12.20
took her, and died, leaving no c.;	12.21
and the seven left no c. Last of	12.22
and c. will rise against parents	13.12
hearts of the fathers to the c.,	Lk 1.17
stones to raise up c. to Abraham.	3.08
They are like c. sitting in the	7.32
Yet wisdom is justified by all her c."	7.35
and my c. are with me in bed;	11.07
how to give good gifts to your c.,	11.13
gathered your c. together as a hen	13.34
and wife and c. and brothers and	14.26
"Let the c. come to me, and do not	18.16
wife or brothers or parents or c.,	18.29
you and your c. within you, and they	19.44
dies, having a wife but no c.,	20.28
and raise up c. for his brother.	20.28
took a wife, and died without c.;	20.29
all seven left no c. and died.	20.31
for yourselves and for your c.	23.28
he gave power to become c. of God;	Jn 1.12
to them, "If you were Abraham's c.,	8.39
into one the c. of God who are	11.52
Little c., yet a little while I am	13.33
"C., have you any fish?"	21.05
you and to your c. and to all that	Ac 2.39
to us their c. by raising Jesus;	13.33
and they all, with wives and c.,	21.05
circumcise their c. or observe the	21.21
a teacher of c., having in the law	Rom 2.20
our spirit that we are c. of God,	8.16
and if c., then heirs, heirs of God	8.17
glorious liberty of the c. of God.	8.21
and not all are c. of Abraham	9.07
it is not the c. of the flesh who	9.08
of the flesh who are the c. of God,	9.08
but the c. of the promise are	9.08
had conceived c. by one man, our	9.10
Lord of hosts had not left us c.,	9.29
to admonish you as my beloved c.	1Co 4.14
your c. would be unclean, but as it	7.14
do not be c. in your thinking;	14.20
I speak as to c.—widen your hearts	2Co 6.13
for c. ought not to lay up for	12.14
parents, but parents for their c.	12.14
when we were c., we were slaves to	Gal 4.03
My little c., with whom I am again	4.19

CHILDREN (cont.)
Sinai, bearing c. for slavery; Gal 4.24
for she is in slavery with her c. 4.25
hath more c. than she who hath a 4.27
like Isaac, are c. of promise. 4.28
we are not c. of the slave but of 4.31
so we were by nature c. of wrath, Eph 2.03
so that we may no longer be c., 4.14
be imitators of God, as beloved c. 5.01
the Lord; walk as c. of light 5.08
C., obey your parents in the Lord, 6.01
Fathers, do not provoke your c. to anger, 6.04
c. of God without blemish in the Php 2.15
C., obey your parents in everything, Col 3.20
Fathers, do not provoke your c., 3.21
like a nurse taking care of her c. 1Th 2.07
how, like a father with his c., 2.11
will be saved through bearing c., 1Ti 2.15
keeping his c. submissive and 3.04
manage their c. and their households 3.12
If a widow has c. or grandchildren, 5.04
as one who has brought up c., 5.10
bear c., rule their households, and 5.14
whose c. are believers and not open Tit 1.06
to love their husbands and c., 2.04
and the c. God has given me." Heb 2.13
Since therefore the c. share in 2.14
are illegitimate c. and not sons. 12.08
As obedient c., do not be conformed 1Pe 1.14
you are now her c. if you do right 3.06
trained in greed. Accursed c.! 2Pe 2.14
My little c., I am writing this to 1Jn 2.01
little c., because your sins are 2.12
c., because you know the Father. 2.13
C., it is the last hour; and as 2.18
little c., abide in him, so that 2.28
that we should be called c. of God; 3.01
Beloved, we are God's c. now; 3.02
Little c., let no one deceive you. 3.07
may be seen who are the c. of God, 3.10
and who are the c. of the devil: 3.10
Little c., let us not love in word 3.18
Little c., you are of God, and have 4.04
we know that we love the c. of God, 5.02
Little c., keep yourselves from 5.21
elder to the elect lady and her c., 2Jn 1.01
some of your c. following the 1.04
The c. of your elect sister greet 1.13
to hear that my c. follow the 3Jn 1.04
and I will strike her c. dead. Rev 2.23

CHILDREN'S
your children and your c. children, Gen 45.10
the children and the c. children, Ex 34.07
children and your c. children— Deu 4.09
you beget children and c. children, 4.25
and their c. children—as their 2Ki 17.41
his righteousness to c. children, Ps 103.17
May you see your c. children! 128.06
an inheritance to his c. children, Pro 13.22
of the mouth of your c. children, Is 59.21
and with your c. children I will Jer 2.09
and the c. teeth are set on edge.' 31.29
and the c. teeth are set on edge'? Eze 18.02
and their c. children shall dwell 37.25
to take the c. bread and throw it Mt 15.26
to take the c. bread and throw it Mk 7.27
under the table eat the c. crumbs." 7.27

CHILD'S
girl went and called the c. mother. Ex 2.08
let this c. soul come into him 1Ki 17.21
who sought the c. life are dead." Mt 2.20
and took the c. father and mother Mk 5.40

CHILEAB
C., of Abigail the widow of Nabal 2Sa 3.03

CHILION
of his two sons were Mahlon and C.; Ru 1.02
and both Mahlon and C. died, 1.05
that belonged to C. and to Mahlon. 4.09

CHILMAD
Asshur, and C. traded with you. Eze 27.23

CHIMHAM
But here is your servant C.; 2Sa 19.37
"C. shall go over with me, and I 19.38
and C. went on with him; all the 19.40
stayed at Geruth C. near Bethlehem, Jer 41.17

CHINNERETH
of the sea of C. on the east; Num 34.11
from C. as far as the sea of the Deu 3.17
to the lower end of the Sea of C., Jos 13.27
Ziddim, Zer, Hammath, Rakkath, C., 19.35

CHINNEROTH
and in the Arabah south of C., Jos 11.02
Arabah to the Sea of C. eastward, 12.03
and all C., with all the land of 1Ki 15.20

CHIOS
came the following day opposite C.; Ac 20.15

CHIP
like a c. on the face of the waters. Hos 10.07

CHIRP
and the wizards who c. and mutter, Is 8.19

CHIRPED
a wing, or opened the mouth, or c." Is 10.14

CHISLEV
Now it happened in the month of C., Neh 1.01
of the ninth month, which is C. Zec 7.01

CHISLON
of Benjamin, Elidad the son of C. Num 34.21

CHISLOTHTABOR
the sunrise to the boundary of C.; Jos 19.12

CHITLISH
Cabbon, Lahmam, C., Jos 15.40

CHLOE'S
to me by C. people that there is 1Co 1.11

CHOICE
all sorts of c. gifts from his Gen 24.10
some of the c. fruits of the land 43.11
and his ass's colt to the c. vine, 49.11
and every c. city, and shall fell 2Ki 3.19
day was one ox and six c. sheep; Neh 5.18
which they send c. portions to one Est 9.19
for sending c. portions to one 9.22
and knowledge rather than c. gold; Pro 8.10
gold, and my yield than c. silver. 8.19
of the righteous is c. silver; 10.20
is like Lebanon, c. as the cedars. Sol 5.15
over our doors are all c. fruits, 7.13
Yet I planted it with c. vines; Is 5.02
Yet I planted you a c. vine, Jer 2.21
and you shall fall like c. rams. 25.34
the shoulder; fill it with c. bones. Eze 24.04
after piece, without making any c. 24.06
These traded with you in c. garments, 27.24
the c. and best of Lebanon, all that 31.16
alienate this c. portion of the 48.14
early days God made c. among you, Ac 15.07

CHOICEST
dead in the c. of our sepulchres; Gen 23.06
with the c. gifts of heaven above. Deu 33.13

CHOICEST (cont.)
with the c. fruits of the sun, and Deu 33.14
upon the c. parts of every offering 1Sa 2.29
tallest cedars, its c. cypresses; 2Ki 19.23
of pomegranates with all c. fruits, Sol 4.13
his garden, and eat its c. fruits. 4.16
Your c. valleys were full of Is 22.07
tallest cedars, its c. cypresses; 37.24
they shall cut down your c. cedars, Jer 22.07
and the c. of his young men have 48.15
contributions and the c. of your gifts, Eze 20.40
the c. men of Assyria all of them; 23.07
Take the c. one of the flock, pile 24.05

CHOKE
the delight in richest c. the word, Mt 13.22
enter in and c. the word, and it Mk 4.19

CHOKED
and the thorns grew up and c. them. Mt 13.07
and the thorns grew up and c. it, Mk 4.07
the thorns grew with it and c. it. Lk 8.07
way they are c. by the cares and 8.14

CHOOSE
"C. for us men, and go out, fight Ex 17.09
Moreover c. able men from all the 18.21
"Let us c. a captain, and go back to Num 14.04
whom he will c. he will cause to 16.05
of the man whom I c. shall sprout; 17.05
C. wise, understanding, and experienced Deu 1.13
your God will c. out of all your 12.05
which the LORD your God will c., 12.11
the LORD will c. in one of your 12.14
which the LORD your God will c., 12.18
your God will c. to put his name 12.21
the place which the LORD will c., 12.26
God, in the place which he will c., 14.23
the place which the LORD will c. 15.20
the place which the LORD will c., 16.02
which the LORD your God will c., 16.06
which the LORD your God will c.; 16.07
which the LORD your God will c., 16.11
the place which the LORD will c.; 16.15
God at the place which he will c.: 16.16
which the LORD your God will c., 17.08
that place which the LORD will c.; 17.10
him whom the LORD your God will c. 17.15
the place which the LORD will c., 18.06
which he shall c. within one of 23.16
which the LORD your God will c., 26.02
therefore c. life, that you and your 30.19
God at the place which he will c., 31.11
in the place which he should c. Jos 9.27
c. this day whom you will serve, 24.15
C. a man for yourselves, and let him 1Sa 17.08
"Let me c. twelve thousand men, and 2Sa 17.01
c. one of them, that I may do it to 24.12
and let them c. one bull for 1Ki 18.23
"C. for yourselves one bull and 18.25
c. one of them, that I may do it 1Ch 21.10
God who didst c. Abram and bring Neh 9.07
so that I would c. strangling and Job 7.15
and you c. the tongue of the crafty 15.05
Let us c. what is right; let us 34.04
For you must c., and not I; 34.33
Those who c. another god multiply Ps 16.04
in the way that he should c. 25.12
whom thou dost c. and bring near, 65.04
he did not c. the tribe of Ephraim; 78.67
and did not c. the fear of the Pro 1.29
and do not c. any of his ways; 3.31
to refuse the evil and c. the good. Is 7.15
to refuse the evil and c. the good, 7.16
on Jacob and will again c. Israel, 14.01
who c. the things that please me 56.04
Is such the fast that I c., a day 58.05
"Is not this the fast that I c.: 58.06
I also will c. affliction for them, 66.04
and will not c. one of his descendants Jer 33.26
I will appoint over her whomever I c. 49.19
appoint over her whomever I c. For who 50.44
Zion and again c. Jerusalem.'" Zec 1.17
land, and will again c. Jerusalem." 2.12
I c. to give to this last as I give Mt 20.14
to do what I c. with what belongs 20.15
"Did I not c. you, the twelve, and Jn 6.70
You did not c. me, but I chose you 15.16
to c. men from among them and send Ac 15.22
in assembly to c. men and send 15.25
Yet which I shall c. I cannot tell. Php 1.22

CHOOSES
whom the LORD c. shall be the holy Num 16.07
you, which the LORD your God c., Deu 14.24
place which the LORD your God c., 14.25
is impoverished c. for an offering Is 40.20
an abomination is he who c. you. 41.24
or he c. a holm tree or an oak and 44.14
to whom the Son c. to reveal him. Mt 11.27
to whom the Son c. to reveal him." Lk 10.22

CHOOSING
answer him, c. my words with him? Job 9.14
c. rather to share ill-treatment Heb 11.25

CHOP
and c. them up like meat in a Mic 3.03

CHORAZIN
"Woe to you, C.! woe to you, Mt 11.21
"Woe to you, C.! woe to you, Lk 10.13

CHOSE
to wife such of them as they c. Gen 6.02
So Lot c. for himself all the 13.11
Moses c. able men out of all Israel, Ex 18.25
fathers and c. their descendants Deu 4.37
set his love upon you and c. you, 7.07
fathers and c. their descendants 10.15
He c. the best of the land for 33.21
and Joshua c. thirty thousand Jos 8.03
And I c. him out of all the tribes 1Sa 2.28
Saul c. three thousand men of 13.02
and c. five smooth stones from the 17.40
who c. me above your father, and 2Sa 6.21
he c. some of the picked men of 10.09
I c. no city in all the tribes of 1Ki 8.16
but I c. David to be over my people 8.16
sake of David my servant whom I c., 11.34
for the LORD c. them to carry the 1Ch 15.02
he c. some of the picked men of 19.10
God of Israel c. me from all my 28.04
for he c. Judah as leader, and in 28.04
I c. no city in all the tribes of 2Ch 6.05
and I c. no man as prince over my 6.05
I c. their way, and sat as chief, and Job 29.25
He c. our heritage for us, the pride Ps 47.04
but he c. the tribe of Judah, Mount 78.68
He c. David his servant, and took 78.70
and c. what I did not delight in." Is 65.12
and c. that in which I did not 66.04
the two families which he c.'? Jer 33.24
GOD: On the day when I c. Israel, Eze 20.05
whom he c., he shortened the days. Mk 13.20
and c. from them twelve, whom he Lk 6.13
marked how they c. the places of 14.07
but I c. you and appointed you that Jn 15.16
but I c. you out of the world, 15.19
and they c. Stephen, a man full of Ac 6.05
people Israel c. our fathers and 13.17
but Paul c. Silas and departed, 15.40
but God c. what is foolish in the 1Co 1.27
God c. what is weak in the world to 1.27
God c. what is low and despised in 1.28

CHOSE (cont.)

body, each one of them, as he c. 1Co 12.18
even as he c. us in him before the Eph 1.04
To them God c. to make known how Col 1.27
because God c. you from the beginning 2Th 2.13

CHOSEN

No, for I have c. him, that he may Gen 18.19
These were the ones c. from the Num 1.16
one of his c. men, said, "My lord 11.28
c. from the assembly, well-known men 16.02
c. from the congregation, who 26.09
your God has c. you to be a people Deu 7.06
the LORD has c. you to be a people 14.02
your God has c. him out of all 18.05
your God has c. them to minister 21.05
yourselves that you have c. the LORD, Jos 24.22
When new gods were c., when war Ju 5.08
cry to the gods whom you have c.; 10.14
whom you have c. for yourselves; 1Sa 8.18
you see him whom the LORD has c.? 10.24
behold the king whom you have c., 12.13
"Neither has the LORD c. this one." 16.08
"Neither has the LORD c. this one." 16.09
Jesse, "The LORD has not c. these." 16.10
that you have c. the son of Jesse 20.30
three thousand c. men out of all 24.02
three thousand c. men of Israel, 26.02
gathered all the c. men of Israel, 2Sa 6.01
and all the men of Israel have c., 16.18
of thy people whom thou hast c., 1Ki 3.08
which thou hast c. and the house 8.44
the city which thou hast c., 8.48
sake of Jerusalem which I have c." 11.13
which I have c. out of all the 11.32
where I have c. to put my name. 11.36
and eighty thousand c. warriors, 12.21
the LORD had c. out of all the 14.21
which I have c. out of all the 2Ki 21.07
cast off this city which I have c., 23.27
who were c. as gatekeepers at the 1Ch 9.22
servant, sons of Jacob, his c. ones! 16.13
rest of those c. and expressly 16.41
house being c. for Eleazar and one 24.06
for Eleazar and one c. for Ithamar. 24.06
sons) he has c. Solomon my son to 28.05
for I have c. him to be my son, and 28.06
the LORD has c. you to build a 28.10
my son, whom alone God has c., 29.01
But I have c. Jerusalem that my 2Ch 6.06
and I have c. David to be over my 6.06
which thou has c. and the house 6.34
the city which thou hast c., 6.38
and have c. this place for myself 7.12
For now I have c. and consecrated 7.16
and eighty thousand c. warriors, 11.01
the LORD had c. out of all the 12.13
the LORD has c. you to stand in 29.11
which I have c. out of all the 33.07
them to the place which I have c., Neh 1.09
and with seven c. maids from the Est 2.09
this you have c. rather than Job 36.21
The LORD is my c. portion and my Ps 16.05
whom he has c. as his heritage! 33.12
made covenant with my c. one, 89.03
exalted one c. from the people. 89.19
servant, sons of Jacob, his c. ones! 105.06
servant, and Aaron whom he had c. 105.26
with joy, his c. ones with singing. 105.43
see the prosperity of thy c. ones, 106.05
his c. one, stood in the breach 106.23
I have c. the way of faithfulness, I 119.30
me, for I have c. thy precepts. 119.173
For the LORD has c. Zion; he has 132.13
For the LORD has c. Jacob for himself, 135.04
is to be c. rather than silver. Pro 16.16
name is to be c. rather than great 22.01
for the gardens which you have c. Is 1.29
whom I have c., the offspring of 41.08
I have c. you and not cast you off"; 41.09
my c., in whom my soul delights; 42.01
"and my servant whom I have c., 43.10
to give drink to my c. people, 43.20
my servant, Israel whom I have c.! 44.01
servant, Jeshurun whom I have c. 44.02
and Israel my c., I call you by 45.04
Holy One of Israel, who has c. you." 49.07
my c. shall inherit it, and my 65.09
your name to my c. for a curse, 65.15
and my c. shall long enjoy the work 65.22
These have c. their own ways, and 66.03
for I have c. you, says the LORD of Hag 2.23
LORD who has c. Jerusalem rebuke Zec 3.02
"Behold, my servant whom I have c., Mt 12.18
For many are called, but few are c." 22.14
saying, "This is my Son, my C.; Lk 9.35
Mary has c. the good portion, which 10.42
is the Christ of God, his C. One!" 23.35
I know whom I have c.; it is that Jn 13.18
to the apostles whom he had c. Ac 1.02
one of these two thou hast c. 1.24
for he is a c. instrument of mine 9.15
to us who were c. by God as 10.41
there is a remnant, c. by grace. Rom 11.05
But God gives it a body as he has c., 1Co 15.38
as God's c. ones, holy and beloved, Col 3.12
beloved by God, that he has c. you; 1Th 1.04
high priest c. from among men is Heb 5.01
Has not God c. those who are poor Jas 2.05
c. and destined by God the Father 1Pe 1.02
but in God's sight c. and precious; 2.04
a cornerstone c. and precious, and 2.06
But you are a c. race, a royal 2.09
is at Babylon, who is likewise c., 5.13
him are called and c. and faithful." Rev 17.14

CHRIST

The book of the genealogy of Jesus C., Mt 1.01
Jesus was born, who is called C. 1.16
Babylon to the C. fourteen generations. 1.17
birth of Jesus C. took place in 1.18
them where the C. was to be born. 2.04
prison about the deeds of the C., 11.02
"You are the C., the Son of the 16.16
to tell no one that he was the C. 16.20
saying, "What do you think of the C.? 22.42
for you have one master, the C. 23.10
'I am the C.,' and they will lead 24.05
says to you, 'Lo, here is the C.!' 24.23
God, tell us if you are the C., 26.63
saying, "Prophesy to us, you C.! 26.68
Barabbas or Jesus who is called C.?" 27.17
I do with Jesus who is called C.?" 27.22
beginning of the Gospel of Jesus C., Mk 1.01
Peter answered him, "You are the C." 8.29
because you bear the name of C., 9.41
say that the C. is the son of 12.35
says to you, 'Look, here is the C.!' 13.21
"Are you the C., the Son of the 14.61
Let the C., the King of Israel, come 15.32
David a Savior, who is C. the Lord. Lk 2.11
before he had seen the Lord's C. 2.26
whether perhaps he were the C., 3.15
they knew that he was the C. 4.41
And Peter answered, "The C. of God." 9.20
say that the C. is David's son? 20.41
"If you are the C., tell us." 22.67
that he himself is C. a king." 23.02
if he is the C. of God, his Chosen 23.35
at him, saying, "Are you not the C.? 23.39
that the C. should suffer these 24.26
that the C. should suffer and on 24.46
and truth came through Jesus C. Jn 1.17
but confessed, "I am not the C." 1.20

CHRIST (cont.)
baptizing, if you are neither the C., Jn 1.25
found the Messiah" (which means C.). 1.41
I am not the C., but I have been 3.28
is coming (he who is called C.); 4.25
ever did. Can this be the C.?" 4.29
really know that this is the C.? 7.26
and when the C. appears, no one will 7.27
"When the C. appears, will he do 7.31
Others said, "This is the C." 7.41
"Is the C. to come from Galilee? 7.41
said that the C. is descended from 7.42
one should confess him to be C., 9.22
If you are the C., tell us 10.24
I believe that you are the C., 11.27
law that the C. remains for ever. 12.34
and Jesus C. whom thou hast sent. 17.03
may believe that Jesus is the C., 20.31
of the resurrection of the C., Ac 2.31
God has made him both Lord and C., 2.36
name of Jesus C. for the forgiveness 2.38
the name of Jesus C. of Nazareth, 3.06
that his C. should suffer, he thus 3.18
he may send the C. appointed for 3.20
the name of Jesus C. of Nazareth, 4.10
and preaching Jesus as the C. 5.42
and proclaimed to them the C. 8.05
of God and the name of Jesus C., 8.12
"I believe that Jesus C. is the Son * 8.37
by proving that Jesus was the C. 9.22
to him, "Aeneas, Jesus C. heals you; 9.34
peace by Jesus C. (he is Lord of 10.36
baptized in the name of Jesus C. 10.48
we believed in the Lord Jesus C., 11.17
for the sake of our Lord Jesus C. 15.26
name of Jesus C. to come out of 16.18
necessary for the C. to suffer and 17.03
whom I proclaim to you, is the C." 17.03
to the Jews that the C. was Jesus. 18.05
scriptures that the C. was Jesus. 18.28
and of faith in our Lord Jesus C. 20.21
him speak upon faith in C. Jesus. 24.24
that the C. must suffer, and that, by 26.23
the Lord Jesus C. quite openly and 28.31
Paul, a servant of Jesus C., Rom 1.01
from the dead, Jesus C. our Lord, 1.04
are called to belong to Jesus C.; 1.06
our Father and the Lord Jesus C. 1.07
through Jesus C. for all of you. 1.08
the secrets of men by C. Jesus. 2.16
faith in Jesus C. for all who 3.22
redemption which is in C. Jesus, 3.24
with God through our Lord Jesus C. 5.01
the right time C. died for the 5.06
we were yet sinners C. died for us. 5.08
in God through our Lord Jesus C., 5.11
one man Jesus C. abounded for many 5.15
life through the one man Jesus C. 5.17
life through Jesus C. our Lord. 5.21
baptized into C. Jesus were 6.03
so that as C. was raised from the 6.04
But if we have died with C., 6.08
For we know that C. being raised 6.09
sin and alive to God in C. Jesus. 6.11
eternal life in C. Jesus our Lord. 6.23
to the law through the body of C., 7.04
to God through Jesus C. our Lord! 7.25
for those who are in C. Jesus. 8.01
of life in C. Jesus has set me 8.02
the Spirit of C. does not belong 8.09
But if C. is in you, although your 8.10
he who raised C. Jesus from the 8.11
of God and fellow heirs with C., 8.17
Is it C. Jesus, who died, yes, who was 8.34
separate us from the love of C.? 8.35
love of God in C. Jesus our Lord. 8.39
I am speaking the truth in C., 9.01
cut off from C. for the sake of my 9.03
according to the flesh, is the C. 9.05
For C. is the end of the law, that 10.04
(that is, to bring C. down) 10.06
to bring C. up from the dead). 10.07
heard comes by the preaching of C. 10.17
though many, are one body in C., 12.05
But put on the Lord Jesus C., 13.14
For to this end C. died and lived 14.09
the ruin of one for whom C. died. 14.15
he who thus serves C. is acceptable 14.18
For C. did not please himself; 15.03
another, in accord with C. Jesus, 15.05
and Father of our Lord Jesus C. 15.06
as C. has welcomed you, for the 15.07
For I tell you that C. became a 15.08
a minister of C. Jesus to the 15.16
In C. Jesus, then, I have reason to 15.17
except what C. has wrought through 15.18
fully preached the gospel of C., 15.19
not where C. has already been named, 15.20
the fulness of the blessing of C. 15.29
our Lord Jesus C. and by the love 15.30
my fellow workers in C. Jesus, 16.03
the first convert in Asia for C. 16.05
and they were in C. before me. 16.07
Greet Urbanus, our fellow worker in C., 16.09
Greet Apelles, who is approved in C. 16.10
All the churches of C. greet you. 16.16
persons do not serve our Lord C., 16.18
of our Lord Jesus C. be with you. 16.20
The grace of our Lord Jesus C. * 16.24
and the preaching of Jesus C., 16.25
for evermore through Jesus C.! 16.27
God to be an apostle of C. Jesus, 1Co 1.01
to those sanctified in C. Jesus, 1.02
on the name of our Lord Jesus C., 1.02
our Father and the Lord Jesus C. 1.03
which was given you in C. Jesus, 1.04
testimony to C. was confirmed 1.06
the revealing of our Lord Jesus C.; 1.07
in the day of our Lord Jesus C. 1.08
of his Son, Jesus C. our Lord. 1.09
by the name of our Lord Jesus C., 1.10
to Cephas," or "I belong to C." 1.12
Is C. divided? Was Paul 1.13
For C. did not send me to baptize 1.17
the cross of C. be emptied of its 1.17
but we preach C. crucified, a 1.23
C. the power of God and the wisdom 1.24
source of your life in C. Jesus, 1.30
except Jesus C. and him crucified. 2.02
But we have the mind of C. 2.16
men of the flesh, as babes in C. 3.01
which is laid, which is Jesus C. 3.11
you are Christ's: and C. is God's. 3.23
as servants of C. and stewards of 4.01
sake, but you are wise in C. 4.10
you have countless guides in C., 4.15
your father in C. Jesus through 4.15
to remind you of my ways in C., 4.17
For C., our paschal lamb, has been 5.07
the Lord Jesus C. and in the 6.11
that your bodies are members of C.? 6.15
the members of C. and make them 6.15
free when called is a slave of C. 7.22
Jesus C., through whom are all 8.06
the brother for whom C. died. 8.11
it is weak, you sin against C. 8.12
in the way of the gospel of C. 9.12
God but under the law of C.— 9.21
followed them, and the Rock was C. 10.04
a participation in the blood of C.? 10.16
a participation in the body of C.? 10.16
Be imitators of me, as I am of C. 11.01
that the head of every man is C., 11.03
husband, and the head of C. is God. 11.03

CHRIST (cont.)
are one body, so it is with C. 1Co 12.12
are the body of C. and individually 12.27
that C. died for our sins in 15.03
Now if C. is preached as raised 15.12
then C. has not been raised; 15.13
if C. has not been raised, then our 15.14
testified of God that he raised C., 15.15
then C. has not been raised. 15.16
If C. has not been raised, your 15.17
fallen asleep in C. have perished. 15.18
we who are in C. have only hope, 15.19
But in fact C. has been raised from 15.20
so also in C. shall all be made 15.22
C. the first fruits, then at his 15.23
his coming those who belong to C. 15.23
which I have in C. Jesus our Lord, 15.31
victory through our Lord Jesus C. 15.57
My love be with you all in C. Jesus. 16.24
an apostle of C. Jesus by the will 2Co 1.01
our Father and the Lord Jesus C. 1.02
and Father of our Lord Jesus C., 1.03
so through C. we share abundantly 1.05
Jesus C., whom we preached among 1.19
who establishes us with you in C., 1.21
your sake in the presence of C., 2.10
Troas to preach the gospel of C., 2.12
who in C. always leads us in 2.14
the aroma of C. to God among those 2.15
in the sight of God we speak in C. 2.17
a letter from C. delivered by us, 3.03
that we have through C. toward God. 3.04
only through C. is it taken away. 3.14
of the gospel of the glory of C., 4.04
but Jesus C. as Lord, with ourselves 4.05
the glory of God in the face of C. 4.06
before the judgment seat of C., 5.10
For the love of C. controls us, 5.14
once regarded C. from a human 5.16
Therefore, if any one is in C., 5.17
who through C. reconciled us to 5.18
God was in C. reconciling the world 5.19
So we are ambassadors for C., 5.20
We beseech you on behalf of C., 5.20
What accord has C. with Belial? 6.15
the grace of our Lord Jesus C., 8.09
of the churches, the glory of C. 8.23
in acknowledging the gospel of C., 9.13
the meekness and gentleness of C.— 10.01
every thought captive to obey C., 10.05
way to you with the gospel of C. 10.14
betrothed you to C. to present you 11.02
a sincere and pure devotion to C. 11.03
As the truth of C. is in me, 11.10
themselves as apostles of C. 11.13
Are they servants of C.? I am 11.23
I know a man in C. who fourteen 12.02
the power of C. may rest upon me. 12.09
For the sake of C., then, I am 12.10
that we have been speaking in C., 12.19
proof that C. is speaking in me. 13.03
realize that Jesus C. is in you? 13.05
the Lord Jesus C. and the love of 13.14
through Jesus C. and God the Gal 1.01
the Father and our Lord Jesus C., 1.03
in the grace of C. and turning to 1.06
want to pervert the gospel of C. 1.07
I should not be a servant of C. 1.10
through a revelation of Jesus C. 1.12
to the churches of C. in Judea; 1.22
freedom which we have in C. Jesus, 2.04
law but through faith in Jesus C., 2.16
even we have believed in C. Jesus, 2.16
to be justified by faith in C., 2.16
our endeavor to be justified in C., 2.17
is C. then an agent of sin? 2.17
I have been crucified with C.; 2.20
but C. who lives in me; and the 2.20
then C. died to no purpose. 2.21
eyes Jesus C. was publicly portrayed 3.01
C. redeemed us from the curse of 3.13
that in C. Jesus the blessing of 3.14
to your offspring," which is C. 3.16
faith in Jesus C. might be given 3.22
was our custodian until C. came, 3.24
for in C. Jesus you are all sons of 3.26
baptized into C. have put on C. 3.27
for you are all one in C. Jesus. 3.28
me as an angel of God, as C. Jesus. 4.14
travail until C. be formed in you! 4.19
For freedom C. has set us free; 5.01
C. will be of no advantage to you. 5.02
You are severed from C., you who 5.04
For in C. Jesus neither circumcision 5.06
who belong to C. Jesus have 5.24
and so fulfil the law of C. 6.02
be persecuted for the cross of C. 6.12
in the cross of our Lord Jesus C., 6.14
our Lord Jesus C. be with your 6.18
an apostle of C. Jesus by the will Eph 1.01
who are also faithful in C. Jesus: 1.01
our Father and the Lord Jesus C. 1.02
and Father of our Lord Jesus C., 1.03
blessed us in C. with every 1.03
to be his sons through Jesus C., 1.05
purpose which he set forth in C. 1.09
first hoped in C. have been 1.12
that the God of our Lord Jesus C., 1.17
accomplished in C. when he raised 1.20
together with C. (by grace you 2.05
the heavenly places in C. Jesus, 2.06
in kindness toward us in C. Jesus. 2.07
created in C. Jesus for good works, 2.10
at that time separated from C., 2.12
But now in C. Jesus you who once 2.13
brought near in the blood of C. 2.13
C. Jesus himself being the chief 2.20
a prisoner for C. Jesus on behalf 3.01
my insight into the mystery of C., 3.04
the promise in C. Jesus through 3.06
the unsearchable riches of C., 3.08
has realized in C. Jesus our Lord, 3.11
and that C. may dwell in your 3.17
the love of C. which surpasses 3.19
church and in C. Jesus to all 3.21
for building up the body of C., 4.12
the stature of the fulness of C.; 4.13
into him who is the head, into C., 4.15
You did not so learn C.! 4.20
another, as God in C. forgave you. 4.32
as C. loved us and gave himself up 5.02
in the kingdom of C. and of God. 5.05
and C. shall give you light." 5.14
our Lord Jesus C. to God the 5.20
another out of reverence for C. 5.21
of the wife as C. is the head of 5.23
As the church is subject to C., 5.24
as C. loved the church and gave 5.25
cherishes it, as C. does the church, 5.29
take it to mean C. and the church; 5.32
in singleness of heart, as to C.; 6.05
men-pleasers, but as servants of C., 6.06
the Father and the Lord Jesus C. 6.23
our Lord Jesus C. with love undying. 6.24
servants of C. Jesus, to all the Php 1.01
the saints in C. Jesus who are at 1.01
our Father and the Lord Jesus C. 1.02
completion at the day of Jesus C. 1.06
all with the affection of C. Jesus. 1.08
and blameless for the day of C., 1.10
which come through Jesus C., 1.11
that my imprisonment is for C.; 1.13
Some indeed preach C. from envy and 1.15
the former proclaim C. out of 1.17

CHRIST (cont.)
or in truth, C. is proclaimed; Php 1.18
Spirit of Jesus C. this will turn 1.19
now as always C. will be honored 1.20
For to me to live is C., and to 1.21
desire is to depart and be with C., 1.23
ample cause to glory in C. Jesus, 1.26
life be worthy of the gospel of C., 1.27
for the sake of C. you should not 1.29
there is any encouragement in C., 2.01
yourselves, which you have in C. Jesus, 2.05
confess that Jesus C. is Lord, 2.11
in the day of C. I may be proud 2.16
interests, not those of Jesus C. 2.21
for he nearly died for the work of C., 2.30
and glory in C. Jesus, and put no 3.03
counted as loss for the sake of C. 3.07
worth of knowing C. Jesus my Lord. 3.08
in order that I may gain C. 3.08
that which is through faith in C., 3.09
because C. Jesus has made me his 3.12
the upward call of God in C. Jesus. 3.14
live as enemies of the cross of C. 3.18
await a Savior, the Lord Jesus C., 3.20
hearts and your minds in C. Jesus. 4.07
to his riches in glory in C. Jesus. 4.19
Greet every saint in C. Jesus. 4.21
the Lord Jesus C. be with your 4.23
an apostle of C. Jesus by the will Col 1.01
faithful brethren in C. at Colossae: 1.02
the Father of our Lord Jesus C., 1.03
your faith in C. Jesus and of the 1.04
minister of C. on our behalf 1.07
which is C. in you, the hope of 1.27
may present every man mature in C. 1.28
knowledge of God's mystery, of C., 2.02
the firmness of your faith in C. 2.05
you received C. Jesus the Lord, 2.06
universe, and not according to C. 2.08
of flesh in the circumcision of C.; 2.11
but the substance belongs to C. 2.17
If with C. you died to the elemental 2.20
If then you have been raised with C., 3.01
where C. is, seated at the right 3.01
your life is hid with C. in God. 3.03
When C. who is our life appears, 3.04
but C. is all, and in all. 3.11
the peace of C. rule in your 3.15
Let the word of C. dwell in you 3.16
you are serving the Lord C. 3.24
word, to declare the mystery of C., 4.03
a servant of C. Jesus, greets you, 4.12
the Father and the Lord Jesus C.: 1Th 1.01
of hope in our Lord Jesus C. 1.03
made demands as apostles of C. 2.06
of God in C. Jesus which are in 2.14
God's servant in the gospel of C., 3.02
And th edead in C. will rise first; 4.16
salvation through our Lord Jesus C., 5.09
will of God in C. Jesus for you. 5.18
at the coming of our Lord Jesus C. 5.23
of our Lord Jesus C. be with you. 5.28
our Father and the Lord Jesus C.: 2Th 1.01
the Father and the Lord Jesus C. 1.02
of our God and the Lord Jesus C. 1.12
our Lord Jesus C. and our assembling 2.01
the glory of our Lord Jesus C. 2.14
Now may our Lord Jesus C. himself, 2.16
God and to the steadfastness of C. 3.05
in the name of our Lord Jesus C., 3.06
the Lord Jesus C. to do their work 3.12
our Lord Jesus C. be with you all. 3.18
an apostle of C. Jesus by command 1Ti 1.01
Savior and of C. Jesus our hope, 1.01
the Father and C. Jesus our Lord. 1.02
C. Jesus our Lord, because he judged 1.12
and love that are in C. Jesus. 1.14
that C. Jesus came into the world 1.15
Jesus C. might display his perfect 1.16
God and men, the man C. Jesus, 2.05
in the faith which is in C. Jesus. 3.13
be a good minister of C. Jesus, 4.06
wanton against C. they desire to 5.11
of God and of C. Jesus and of the 5.21
our Lord Jesus C. and the teaching 6.03
and of C. Jesus who in his testimony 6.13
the appearing of our Lord Jesus C.; 6.14
an apostle of C. Jesus by the will 2Ti 1.01
of the life which is in C. Jesus, 1.01
the Father and C. Jesus our Lord. 1.02
he gave us in C. Jesus ages ago, 1.09
appearing of our Savior C. Jesus, 1.10
and love which are in C. Jesus; 1.13
in the grace that is in C. Jesus, 2.01
as a good soldier of C. Jesus. 2.03
Remember Jesus C., risen from the 2.08
which in C. Jesus goes with 2.10
a godly life in C. Jesus will be 3.12
salvation through faith in C. Jesus. 3.15
of God and of C. Jesus who is to 4.01
of God and an apostle of Jesus C., Tit 1.01
the Father and C. Jesus our Savior. 1.04
our great God and Savior Jesus C., 2.13
through Jesus C. our Savior, 3.06
Paul, a prisoner for C. Jesus, Phm 1.01
our Father and the Lord Jesus C. 1.03
of all the good that is ours in C. 1.06
bold enough in C. to command you 1.08
now a prisoner also for C. Jesus— 1.09
the Lord. Refresh my heart in C. 1.20
Epaphras, my fellow prisoner in C. Jesus, 1.23
the Lord Jesus C. be with your 1.25
but C. was faithful over God's house Heb 3.06
For we share in C., if only 3.14
So also C. did not exalt himself to 5.05
doctrines of C. and go on to 6.01
But as it is, C. has obtained a 8.06
But when C. appeared as a high 9.11
how much more shall the blood of C., 9.14
For C. has entered, not into a 9.24
so C., having been offered once to 9.28
when C. came into the world, he said, 10.05
the body of Jesus C. once for all. 10.10
But when C. had offered for all 10.12
suffered for the C. greater wealth 11.26
Jesus C. is the same yesterday and 13.08
in his sight through Jesus C.; 13.21
of God and of the Lord Jesus C., Jas 1.01
the faith of our Lord Jesus C., 2.01
Peter, an apostle of Jesus C., 1Pe 1.01
to Jesus C. and for sprinkling 1.02
and Father of our Lord Jesus C.! 1.03
resurrection of Jesus C. from the dead, 1.03
at the revelation of Jesus C. 1.07
the Spirit of C. within them when 1.11
sufferings of C. and the subsequent 1.11
you at the revelation of Jesus C. 1.13
but with the precious blood of C., 1.19
acceptable to God through Jesus C. 2.05
because C. also suffered for you, 2.21
your hearts reverence C. as Lord. 3.15
behavior in C. may be put to shame. 3.16
For C. also died for sins once for 3.18
the resurrection of Jesus C., 3.21
Since therefore C. suffered in the 4.01
may be glorified through Jesus C. 4.11
are reproached for the name of C., 4.14
sufferings of C. as well as a 5.01
you to his eternal glory in C., 5.10
Peace to all of you that are in C. 5.14
a servant and apostle of Jesus C., 2Pe 1.01
of our God and Savior Jesus C.: 1.01
the knowledge of our Lord Jesus C. 1.08
of our Lord and Savior Jesus C. 1.11

CHRIST (cont.)
as our Lord Jesus C. showed me. 2Pe 1.14
and coming of our Lord Jesus C., 1.16
of our Lord and Savior Jesus C., 2.20
of our Lord and Savior Jesus C. 3.18
Father and with his Son Jesus C. 1Jn 1.03
the Father, Jesus C. the righteous; 2.01
he who denies that Jesus is the C.? 2.22
his Son Jesus C. and love one 3.23
that Jesus C. has come in the 4.02
Jesus is the C. is a child of God, 5.01
Jesus C., not with the water only 5.06
who is true, in his Son Jesus C. 5.20
and from Jesus C. the Father's Son, 2Jn 1.03
coming of Jesus C. in the flesh; 1.07
the doctrine of C. does not have 1.09
the Doctrine of C. has both the 1.09
of Jesus C. and brother of James, Jud 1.01
the Father and kept for Jesus C.: 1.01
our only Master and Lord, Jesus C. 1.04
the apostles of our Lord Jesus C.; 1.17
our Lord Jesus C. unto eternal 1.21
Savior through Jesus C. our Lord, 1.25
The revelation of Jesus C., Rev 1.01
and to the testimony of Jesus C., 1.02
and from Jesus C. the faithful 1.05
kingdom of our Lord and of his C., 11.15
the authority of his C. have come, 12.10
reigned with C. a thousand years. 20.04
shall be priests of God and of C., 20.06

CHRIST'S
and you are C.; and Christ 1Co 3.23
We are fools for C. sake, but you 4.10
share abundantly in C. sufferings, 2Co 1.05
any one is confident that he is C., 10.07
that as he is C., so are we. 10.07
And if you are C. then you are Gal 3.29
according to the measure of C. gift. Eph 4.07
is lacking in C. afflictions for Col 1.24
so far as you share C. sufferings, 1Pe 4.13

CHRISTIAN
time you think to make me a C.!" Ac 26.28
yet if one suffers as a C., 1Pe 4.16

CHRISTIANS
were for the first time called C. Ac 11.26

CHRISTS
For false C. and false prophets Mt 24.24
False C. and false prophets will Mk 13.22

CHRONIC
it is a c. leprosy in the skin of Lev 13.11

CHRONICLES
the Book of the C. of the Kings of 1Ki 14.19
the Book of the C. of the Kings of 14.29
the Book of the C. of the Kings of 15.07
the Book of the C. of the Kings of 15.23
the Book of the C. of the Kings of 15.31
the Book of the C. of the Kings of 16.05
the Book of the C. of the Kings of 16.14
the Book of the C. of the Kings of 16.20
the Book of the C. of the Kings of 16.27
the Book of the C. of the Kings of 22.39
the Book of the C. of the Kings of 22.45
the Book of the C. of the Kings of 2Ki 1.18
the Book of the C. of the Kings of 8.23
the Book of the C. of the Kings of 10.34
the Book of the C. of the Kings of 12.19
the Book of the C. of the Kings of 13.08
the Book of the C. of the Kings of 13.12
the Book of the C. of the Kings of 14.15
the Book of the C. of the Kings of 14.18
the Book of the C. of the Kings of 14.28
the Book of the C. of the Kings of 15.06
the Book of the C. of the Kings of 15.11
the Book of the C. of the Kings of 15.15
the Book of the C. of the Kings of 15.21
the Book of the C. of the Kings of 15.26
the Book of the C. of the Kings of 15.31
the Book of the C. of the Kings of 15.36
the Book of the C. of the Kings of 16.19
the book of the C. of the Kings of 20.20
the Book of the C. of the Kings of 21.17
the Book of the C. of the Kings of 21.25
the Book of the C. of the Kings of 23.28
the book of the C. of the Kings of 24.05
entered in the c. of King David. 1Ch 27.24
written in the C. of Samuel the 29.29
and in the C. of Nathan the prophet, 29.29
and in the C. of Gad the seer, 29.29
written in the c. of Shemaiah the 2Ch 12.15
written in the c. of Jehu the son 20.34
they are in the C. of the Kings of 33.18
are written in the C. of the Seers. 33.19
the Book of the C. until the Days Neh 12.23
the Book of the C. in the presence Est 2.23
the c., and they were read before 6.01
the Book of the C. of the Kings of 10.02

CHRYSOLITE
was like the gleaming of a c.; Eze 1.16
the wheels was like sparkling c.. 10.09
c., beryl, and onyx, sapphire, carbuncle, 28.13
the seventh c., the eighth beryl, Rev 21.20

CHRYSOPRASE
the tenth c., the eleventh jacinth, Rev 21.20

CHURCH
on this rock I will build my c., Mt 16.18
listen to them, tell it to the c.; 18.17
refuses to listen even to the c., 18.17
And great fear came upon the whole c., Ac 5.11
arose against the c. in Jerusalem; 8.01
But Saul laid waste the c., 8.03
So the c. throughout all Judea and 9.31
to the ears of the c. in Jerusalem, 11.22
a whole year they met with the c., 11.26
upon some who belonged to the c. 12.01
for him was made to God by the c. 12.05
Now in the c. at Antioch there were 13.01
elders for them in every c., 14.23
gathered the c. together and 14.27
So, being sent on their way by the c., 15.03
welcomed by the c. and the apostles 15.04
and the elders, with the whole c., 15.22
he went up and greeted the c., 18.22
called to him the elders of the c. 20.17
to feed the c. of the Lord which he 20.28
deaconess of the c. at Cenchreae, Rom 16.01
greet also the c. in their house. 16.05
me and to the whole c., greets you. 16.23
To the c. of God which is at 1Co 1.02
teach them everywhere in every c. 4.17
inside the c. whom you are to 5.12
who are least esteemed by the c.? 6.04
or to Greeks or to the c. of God, 10.32
place, when you assemble as a c., 11.18
you despise the c. of God and 11.22
appointed in the c. first apostles, 12.28
he who prophesies edifies the c. 14.04
so that the c. may be edified. 14.05
to excel in building up the c. 14.12
in c. I would rather speak five 14.19
the whole c. assembles and all 14.23
keep silence in c. and speak to 14.28
shameful for a woman to speak in c. 14.35
because I persecuted the c. of God. 15.09
together with the c. in their house, 16.19
To the c. of God which is at 2Co 1.01
persecuted the c. of God violently Gal 1.13

CHURCH (cont.)
head over all things for the c., Eph 1.22
that through the c. the manifold 3.10
be glory in the c. and in Christ 3.21
as Christ is the head of the c., 5.23
As the c. is subject to Christ, so 5.24
loved the c. and gave himself up 5.25
that the c. might be presented 5.27
cherishes it, as Christ does the c., 5.29
take it to mean Christ and the c.; 5.32
as to zeal a persecutor of the c., Php 3.06
no c. entered into partnership with 4.15
He is the head of the body, in the c.; Col 1.18
sake of his body, that is, the c., 1.24
to Nympha and the c. in her house. 4.15
also in the c. of the Laodiceans; 4.16
To the c. of the Thessalonians in 1Th 1.01
To the c. of the Thessalonians in 2Th 1.01
How can he care for God's c.? 1Ti 3.05
which is the c. of the living God, 3.15
let the c. not be burdened, so that 5.16
soldier, and the c. in your house: Phm 1.02
him call for the elders of the c., Jas 5.14
testified to your love before the c. 3Jn 1.06
I have written something to the c.; 1.09
them and puts them out of the c. 1.10
angel of the c. in Ephesus write: Rev 2.01
angel of the c. in Smyrna write: 2.08
angel of the c. in Pergamum write: 2.12
angel of the c. in Thyatira write: 2.18
angel of the c. in Sardis write: 3.01
angel of the c. in Philadelphia 3.07
angel of the c. in Laodicea write: 3.14

CHURCHES
and Cilicia, strengthening the c. Ac 15.41
So the c. were strengthened in the 16.05
also all the c. of the Gentiles Rom 16.04
All the c. of Christ greet you. 16.16
This is my rule in all the c. 1Co 7.17
practice, nor do the c. of God. 11.16
As in all the c. of the saints, 14.33
should keep silence in the c. 14.34
as I directed the c. of Galatia, 16.01
The c. of Asia send greetings. 16.19
been shown in the c. of Macedonia, 2Co 8.01
among all the c. for his preaching 8.18
appointed by the c. to travel with 8.19
they are messengers of the c., 8.23
before the c., of your love and of 8.24
I robbed other c. by accepting 11.08
me of my anxiety for all the c. 11.28
favored than the rest of the c., 12.13
are with me, to the c. of Galatia: Gal 1.02
by sight to the c. of Christ in 1.22
imitators of the c. of God in 1Th 2.14
of you in the c. of God for your 2Th 1.04
John to the seven c. that are in Rev 1.04
a book and send it to the seven c., 1.11
of the seven c. and the seven 1.20
seven lampstands are the seven c. 1.20
what the Spirit says to the c. 2.07
what the Spirit says to the c. 2.11
what the Spirit says to the c. 2.17
And all the c. shall know that I am 2.23
what the Spirit says to the c.' 2.29
what the Spirit says to the c.' 3.06
what the Spirit says to the c.' 3.13
what the Spirit says to the c.'" 3.22
you with this testimony for the c. 22.16

CHURLISH
but the man was c. and ill-behaved; 1Sa 25.03

CHUZA
the wife of C., Herod's steward, and Lk 8.03

CILICIA
and of those from C. and Asia, Ac 6.09
Antioch and Syria and C., greeting. 15.23
And he went through Syria and C., 15.41
"I am a Jew, from Tarsus in C., 21.39
"I am a Jew, born at Tarsus in C., 22.03
learned that he was from C. 23.34
sea which is off C. and Pamphylia, 27.05
into the regions of Syria and C. Gal 1.21

CINNAMON
of sweet-smelling c. half as much, Ex 30.23
my bed with myrrh, aloes, and c. Pro 7.17
calamus and c., with all trees of Sol 4.14
c., spice, incense, myrrh, frankincense, Rev 18.13

CIRCLE
He has described a c. upon the face Job 26.10
when he drew a c. on the face of Pro 8.27
who sits above the c. of the earth, Is 40.22

CIRCLES
and the boundary c. west of Baalah Jos 15.10

CIRCUIT
And he went on a c. year by year to 1Sa 7.16
from the Millo in complete c.; 1Ch 11.08
from the c. round Jerusalem and Neh 12.28
and its c. to the end of them; Ps 19.06
there we made a c. and arrived at Ac 28.13

CIRCUITOUS
they had made a c. march of seven 2Ki 3.09

CIRCUITS
and on its c. the wind returns. Ecc 1.06

CIRCUMCISE
C. therefore the foreskin of your Deu 10.16
your God will c. your heart and 30.06
knives and c. the people of Israel Jos 5.02
C. yourselves to the LORD, remove Jer 4.04
day they came to c. the child; Lk 1.59
and you c. a man upon the sabbath. Jn 7.22
said, "It is necessary to c. them, Ac 15.05
them not to c. their children or 21.21

CIRCUMCISED
Every male among you shall be c. Gen 17.10
You shall be c. in the flesh of 17.11
days old among you shall be c.; 17.12
with your money, shall be c. 17.13
male who is not c. in the flesh of 17.14
and he c. the flesh of their 17.23
old when he was c. in the flesh of 17.24
old when he was c. in the flesh of 17.25
and his son Ishmael were c.; 17.26
from a foreigner, were c. with him. 17.27
And Abraham c. his son Isaac when 21.04
we are and every male of you be c. 34.15
will not listen to us and be c., 34.17
among us be c. as they are c. 34.22
and every male was c., all who 34.24
eat of it after you have c. him. Ex 12.44
the LORD, let all his males be c., 12.48
flesh of his foreskin shall be c. Lev 12.03
and c. the people of Israel at Jos 5.03
is the reason why Joshua c. them: 5.04
people who came out had been c., 5.05
come out of Egypt had not been c. 5.05
up in their stead, that Joshua c.; 5.07
they had not been c. on the way. 5.07
those who are c. but yet uncircumcised— Jer 9.25
when he was c., he was called Jesus, Lk 2.21
and c. him on the eighth day; Ac 7.08
from among the c. who came with 10.45
"Unless you are c. according to the 15.01
he took him and c. him because of 16.03

CIRCUMCISED (cont.)

justify the c. on the ground of Rom 3.30
pronounced only upon the c., 4.09
it before or after he had been c.? 4.10
not after, but before he was c. 4.10
without being c. and who thus have 4.11
father of the c. who are not 4.12
are not merely c. but also follow 4.12
Abraham had before he was c. 4.12
servant to the c. to show God's 15.08
at the time of his call already c.? 1Co 7.18
me, was not compelled to be c., Gal 2.03
with the gospel to the c. 2.07
mission to the c. worked through 2.08
to the Gentiles and they to the c.; 2.09
that would compel you to be c., 6.12
to have you c. that they may glory 6.13
c. on the eighth day, of the people Php 3.05
also you were c. with a circumcision Col 2.11
c. and uncircumcised, barbarian, 3.11

CIRCUMCISING

When the c. of all the nation was Jos 5.08

CIRCUMCISION

of blood," because of the c. Ex 4.26
Moses gave you c. (not that it is Jn 7.22
If on the sabbath a man receives c., 7.23
And he gave him the covenant of c. Ac 7.08
the c. party criticized him, 11.02
C. indeed is of value if you obey Rom 2.25
your c. becomes uncircumcision. 2.25
uncircumcision be regarded as c.? 2.26
code and c. but break the law. 2.27
nor is true c. something external 2.28
and real c. is a matter of the 2.29
Or what is the value of c.? 3.01
He received c. as a sign or seal of 4.11
not seek to remove the marks of c. 1Co 7.18
Let him not seek c. 7.18
For neither c. counts for anything 7.19
himself, fearing the c. party. Gal 2.12
say to you that if you receive c., 5.02
who receives c. that he is bound 5.03
Jesus neither c. nor uncircumcision 5.06
still preach c., why am I still 5.11
who receive c. do not themselves 6.13
For neither c. counts for anything, 6.15
uncircumcision by what is called the c., Eph 2.11
For we are the true c., who worship Php 3.03
circumcised with a c. made without Col 2.11
body of flesh in the c. of Christ; 2.11
only men of the c. among my fellow 4.11
deceivers, especially the c. party; Tit 1.10

CIRCUMFERENCE

of twelve cubits measured its c.; 1Ki 7.15
of thirty cubits measured its c. 7.23
of thirty cubits measured its c. 2Ch 4.02
its c. was twelve cubits, and its Jer 52.21
The c. of the city shall be eighteen Eze 48.35

CIRCUMSTANCES

and of the c. that came upon him 1Ch 29.30
in any and all c. I have learned Php 4.12
give thanks in all c.; for this 1Th 5.18

CISTERN

Nevertheless a spring or a c. Lev 11.36
him back from the c. of Sirah; 2Sa 3.26
will drink the water of his own c.; 2Ki 18.31
Drink water from your own c., Pro 5.15
or the wheel broken at the c., Ecc 12.06
or to dip up water out of the c." Is 30.14
will drink the water of his own c.; 36.16
cast him into the c. of Malchiah, Jer 38.06
And there was no water in the c., 38.06
had put Jeremiah into the c.— 38.07
prophet by casting him into the c.; 38.09
out of the c. before he dies." 38.10
to Jeremiah in the c. by ropes. 38.11
ropes and lifted him out of the c. 38.13
slew them, and cast them into a c. 41.07
Now the c. into which Ishmael cast 41.09
was the large c. which King Asa 41.09

CISTERNS

and c. hewn out, which you did not Deu 6.11
in rocks and in tombs and in c., 1Sa 13.06
wilderness, and hewed out many c., 2Ch 26.10
c. hewn out, vineyards, olive orchards Neh 9.25
and hewed out c. for themselves, Jer 2.13
broken c., that can hold no water. 2.13
they come to the c., they find 14.03

CITADEL

went into the c. of the king's 1Ki 16.18
in the c. of the king's house; 2Ki 15.25

CITADELS

Within her c. God has shown himself Ps 48.03
her ramparts, go through her c.; 48.13

CITIES

dwelt among the c. of the valley Gen 13.12
and he overthrew those c., and all 19.25
and all the inhabitants of the c., 19.25
God destroyed the c. of the valley, 19.29
overthrew the c. in which Lot 19.29
fell upon the c. that were round 35.05
of Pharaoh for food in the c., 41.35
and stored up food in the c.; 41.48
Nevertheless the c. of the Levites, Lev 25.32
houses in the c. of their possession, 25.32
houses in the c. of the Levites 25.33
to their c. may not be sold; 25.34
within your c. I will send pestilence 26.25
And I will lay your c. waste, 26.31
and your c. shall be a waste. 26.33
and whether the c. that they dwell Num 13.19
and the c. are fortified and very 13.28
I will utterly destroy their c." 21.02
destroyed them and their c.; 21.03
And Israel took all these c., 21.25
in all the c. of the Amorites, in 21.25
the survivors of c. be destroyed!" 24.19
All their c. in the places where 31.10
and c. for our little ones, 32.16
the fortified c. because of the 32.17
Build c. for your little ones, and 32.24
remain there in the c. of Gilead; 32.26
land and its c. with their territories, 32.33
the c. of the land throughout the 32.33
fortified c., and folds for sheep. 32.36
names to the c. which they built. 32.38
their possession, c. to dwell in; 35.02
pasture lands round about the c. 35.02
The c. shall be theirs to dwell in, 35.03
The pasture lands of the c., 35.04
them as pasture land for their c. 35.05
The c. which you give to the 35.06
shall be the six c. of refuge, 35.06
them you shall give forty-two c. 35.06
All the c. which you give to the 35.07
And as for the c. which you shall 35.08
give of its c. to the Levites." 35.08
c. to be c. of refuge for you, 35.11
The c. shall be for you a refuge 35.12
And the c. which you give shall be 35.13
shall be your six c. of refuge. 35.13
give three c. beyond the Jordan, 35.14
and three c. in the land of Canaan, 35.14
land of Canaan, to be c. of refuge. 35.14
These six c. shall be for refuge 35.15
go up and the c. into which we Deu 1.22
the c. are great and fortified up 1.28

CITIES (cont.)
captured all his c. at that time Deu 2.34
booty of the c. which we captured. 2.35
Jabbok and the c. of the hill 2.37
And we took all his c. at that time— 3.04
sixty c., the whole region of Argob, 3.04
All these were c. fortified with 3.05
spoil of the c. we took as our 3.07
all the c. of the tableland and all 3.10
c. of the kingdom of Og in Bashan. 3.10
hill country of Gilead with its c.; 3.12
remain in the c. which I have 3.19
set apart three c. in the east 4.41
to one of these c. he might save 4.42
give you, with great and goodly c., 6.10
c. great and fortified up to heaven, 9.01
"If you hear in one of your c., 13.12
dwell in their c. and in their 19.01
set apart three c. for you in the 19.02
to one of these c. and save his 19.05
you, You shall set apart three c. 19.07
add three other c. to these three, 19.09
man flees into one of these c., 19.11
do to all the c. which are very 20.15
which are not c. of the nations 20.15
But in the c. of these peoples that 20.16
distance to the c. which are 21.02
reached their c. on the third day. Jos 9.17
Now their c. were Gibeon, Chephirah, 9.17
city, like one of the royal c., 10.02
do not let them enter their c.; 10.19
had entered into the fortified c., 10.20
And all the c. of those kings, and 11.12
But none of the c. that stood on 11.13
spoil of these c. and the cattle, 11.14
destroyed them with their c. 11.21
and all the c. of Sihon king of the 13.10
and all its c. that are in the 13.17
all the c. of the tableland, and all 13.21
families with their c. and villages. 13.23
and all the c. of Gilead, and half 13.25
families, with their c. and villages. 13.28
which are in Bashan, sixty c., 13.30
the c. of the kingdom of Og in 13.31
but only c. to dwell in, with their 14.04
there, with great fortified c.: 14.12
there to the c. of Mount Ephron; 15.09
The c. belonging to the tribe of 15.21
twenty-nine c., with their villages. 15.32
fourteen c. with their villages. 15.36
sixteen c. with their villages. 15.41
nine c. with their villages. 15.44
eleven c. with their villages. 15.51
nine c. with their villages. 15.54
ten c. with their villages. 15.57
six c. with their villages. 15.59
two c. with their villages. 15.60
six c. with their villages. 15.62
The c. here, to the south of the 17.09
among the c. of Manasseh, belong to 17.09
not take possession of those c.; 17.12
Now the c. of the tribe of Benjamin 18.21
twelve c. with their villages: 18.24
fourteen c. with their villages. 18.28
thirteen c. with their villages; 19.06
four c. with their villages; 19.07
about these c. as far as Baalathbeer, 19.08
twelve c. with their villages. 19.15
these c. with their villages. 19.16
sixteen c. with their villages. 19.22
the c. with their villages. 19.23
twenty-two c. with their villages. 19.30
these c. with their villages. 19.31
The fortified c. are Ziddim, Zer, 19.35
nineteen c. with their villages. 19.38
the c. with their villages. 19.39
these c. with their villages. 19.48
'Appoint the c. of refuge, of which 20.02
to one of these c. and shall stand 20.04
These were the c. designated for 20.09
that we be given c. to dwell in, 21.02
the following c. and pasture lands 21.03
Simeon, and Benjamin, thirteen c. 21.04
the half-tribe of Manasseh, ten c. 21.05
of Manasseh in Bashan, thirteen c. 21.06
the tribe of Zebulun, twelve c. 21.07
These c. and their pasture lands 21.08
the following c. mentioned by name, 21.09
nine c. out of these two tribes; 21.16
with its pasture lands—four c. 21.18
The c. of the descendants of Aaron, 21.19
in all thirteen c. with their 21.19
the c. allotted to them were out of 21.20
with its pasture lands—four c.; 21.22
with its pasture lands—four c.; 21.24
with its pasture lands—two c. 21.25
The c. of the families of the rest 21.26
with its pasture lands—two c.; 21.27
with its pasture lands—four c.; 21.29
with its pasture lands—four c.; 21.31
with its pasture lands—three c. 21.32
The c. of the several families of 21.33
in all thirteen c. with their 21.33
with its pasture lands—four c.; 21.35
with its pasture lands—four c.; 21.37
its pasture lands—four c. in all. 21.39
As for the c. of the several 21.40
to them were in all but twelve c. 21.40
The c. if the Levites in the midst 21.41
all forty-eight c. with their 21.41
These c. had each its pasture lands 21.42
so it was with all these c. 21.42
and c. which you had not built, and 24.13
and they had thirty c., Ju 10.04
and in all the c. that are on the 11.26
twenty c., and as far as Abelkeramim, 11.33
together out of the c. of Gibeah, 20.14
out of their c. on that day 20.15
came out of the c. destroyed them 20.42
of all the c. of the Philistines 1Sa 6.18
both fortified c. and unwalled 6.18
The c. which the Philistines had 7.14
came out of all the c. of Israel, 18.06
in the c. of the Jerahmeelites, in 30.29
in the c. of the Kenites, 30.29
they forsook their c. and fled; 31.07
go up into any of the c. of Judah?" 2Sa 2.01
c. of Hadadezer, King David took 8.08
people, and for the c. of our God; 10.12
did to all the c. of the Ammonites. 12.31
lest he get himself fortified c., 20.06
and to all the c. of the Hivites 24.07
sixty great c. with walls and 1Ki 4.13
besieges them in any of their c.; 8.37
to Hiram twenty c. in the land of 9.11
Tyre to see the c. which Solomon 9.12
"What kind of c. are these which 9.13
and the c. for his chariots, and the 9.19
and the c. for his horsemen, and 9.19
in the chariot c. and with the 10.26
who dwelt in the c. of Judah. 12.17
which are in the c. of Samaria, 13.32
armies against the c. of Israel, 15.20
and the c. which he built, are they 15.23
"The c. which my father took from 20.34
and all the c. that he built, are 22.39
And they overthrew the c., 2Ki 3.25
fortified c. also, and weapons, 10.02
of Hazael the c. which he had 13.25
him and recovered the c. of Israel. 13.25
Gozan, and in the c. of the Medes. 17.06
them in the c. of Samaria instead 17.24
of Samaria, and dwelt in its c. 17.24
placed in the c. of Samaria do not 17.26

CITIES (cont.)
nation in the c. in which they 2Ki 17.29
Gozan, and in the c. of the Medes, 18.11
the fortified c. of Judah and took 18.13
turn fortified c. into heaps of 19.25
places at the c. of Judah and 23.05
the priests out of the c. of Judah, 23.08
that were in the c. of Samaria, 23.19
twenty-three c. in the land of 1Ch 2.22
were their c. until David reigned. 4.31
Tochen, and Ashan, five c., 4.32
about these c. as far as Baal. 4.33
Aaron they gave the c. of refuge: 6.57
All their c. throughout their 6.60
the half of Manasseh, ten c. 6.61
thirteen c. out of the tribes of 6.62
allotted twelve c. out of the 6.63
the Levites the c. with their 6.64
Benjamin these c. which are 6.65
of Kohath had c. of their territory 6.66
They were given the c. of refuge: 6.67
possessions in their c. were Israel, 9.02
they forsook their c. and fled; 10.07
Levites in the c. that have 13.02
c. of Hadadezer, David took very 18.08
from their c. and came to battle. 19.07
people, and for the c. of our God; 19.13
did to all the c. of the Ammonites. 20.03
in the c., in the villages and in 27.25
in the chariot c. and with the 2Ch 1.14
besiege them in any of their c.; 6.28
Solomon rebuilt the c. which Huram 8.02
fortified c. with walls, gates, and 8.05
and all the c. for his chariots, and 8.06
and the c. for his horsemen, and 8.06
in the chariot c. and with the 9.25
who dwelt in the c. of Judah. 10.17
and he built c. for defense in 11.05
fortified c. which are in Judah and 11.10
shields and spears in all the c., 11.12
Benjamin, in all the fortified c.; 11.23
the fortified c. of Judah and came 12.04
and took c. from him, Bethel with 13.19
out of all the c. of Judah the 14.05
He built fortified c. in Judah, 14.06
to Judah, "Let us build these c., 14.07
smote all the c. round about Gerar, 14.14
They plundered all the c., 14.14
and from the c. which he had taken 15.08
armies against the c. of Israel, 16.04
in all the fortified c. of Judah, 17.02
and in the c. of Ephraim which Asa 17.02
to teach in the c. of Judah; 17.07
through all the c. of Judah and 17.09
great stores in the c. of Judah. 17.13
the fortified c. throughout all 17.19
in all the fortified c. of Judah, 19.05
your brethren who live in their c., 19.10
from all the c. of Judah they 20.04
together with fortified c. in Judah; 21.03
Levites from all the c. of Judah, 23.02
to them, "Go out to the c. of Judah, 24.05
fell upon the c. of Judah, from 25.13
and he built c. in the territory 26.06
Moreover he built c. in the hill 27.04
raids on the c. in the Shephelah 28.18
went out to the c. of Judah and 31.01
of Israel returned to their c., 31.01
lived in the c. of Judah also 31.06
him in the c. of the priests, 31.15
common land belonging to their c., 31.19
in the several c. who were designated 31.19
encamped against the fortified c., 32.01
He likewise provided c. for himself, 32.29
in all the fortified c. in Judah. 33.14
And in the c. of Manasseh, Ephraim, 34.06
settled in the c. of Samaria and Ez 4.10
let all in our c. who have taken 10.14
fortified c. and a rich land, and Neh 9.25
in their c. throughout all the Est 9.02
and has lived in desolate c., Job 15.28
their c. thou hast rooted out; Ps 9.06
Zion and rebuild the c. of Judah; 69.35
forth from the c. like the grass 72.16
your c. are burned with fire; Is 1.07
"Until c. lie waste without inhabitant, 6.11
like a desert and overthrew its c., 14.17
fill the face of the world with c." 14.21
Her c. will be deserted for ever; 17.02
their strong c. will be like the 17.09
will be five c. in the land of 19.18
c. of ruthless nations will fear 25.03
the fortified c. of Judah and took 36.01
make fortified c. crash into heaps 37.26
say to the c. of Judah, "Behold your 40.09
desert and its c. lift up their 42.11
and of the c. of Judah, 'They 44.26
and will people the desolate c. 54.03
they shall repair the ruined c., 61.04
Thy holy c. have become a wilderness, 64.10
and against all the c. of Judah. Jer 1.15
his c. are in ruins, without inhabitant. 2.15
as many as your c. are your gods, 2.28
let us go into the fortified c.!' 4.05
your c. will be ruins without 4.07
they shout against the c. of Judah. 4.16
and all its c. were laid in ruins 4.26
all the c. are forsaken, and no man 4.29
is watching against their c., 5.06
your fortified c. in which you 5.17
doing in the c. of Judah and in 7.17
cease from the c. of Judah and 7.34
the fortified c. and perish there; 8.14
I will make the c. of Judah a 9.11
to make the c. of Judah a desolation, 10.22
all these words in the c. of Judah, 11.06
Then the c. of Judah and the 11.12
become as many as your c., O Judah; 11.13
The c. of the Negeb are shut up, 13.19
come from the c. of Judah and the 17.26
man be like the c. which the LORD 20.16
Jerusalem and the c. of Judah, 25.18
to all the c. of Judah which come 26.02
Israel, return to these your c. 31.21
in the land of Judah and in its c., 31.23
and all its c. shall dwell there 31.24
and in the c. of Judah, in the 32.44
in the c. of the hill country, in 32.44
in the c. of the Shephelah, and in 32.44
Shephelah, and in the c. of the Negeb; 32.44
in the c. of Judah and the 33.10
man or beast, and in all of its c., 33.12
In the c. of the hill country, in 33.13
in the c. of the Shephelah, and in 33.13
and in the c. of the Negeb, in the 33.13
and in the c. of Judah, flocks shall 33.13
Jerusalem and all of its c.: 34.01
against all the c. of Judah that 34.07
only fortified c. of Judah that 34.07
I will make the c. of Judah a 34.22
of Judah who come out of their c. 36.06
came from the c. of Judah to 36.09
governor of the c. of Judah, 40.05
dwell in your c. that you have 40.10
and upon all the c. of Judah. 44.02
kindled in the c. of Judah and in 44.06
in the c. of Judah and in the 44.17
burned in the c. of Judah and in 44.21
I will destroy c. and their 46.08
her c. shall become a desolation, 48.09
of Moab and his c. has come up, 48.15
and all the c. of the land of Moab, 48.24
"Leave the c., and dwell in the 48.28
the c. shall be taken and the 48.41

CITIES (cont.)

and his people settled in its c.? Jer 49.01
and all her c. shall be perpetual 49.13
their neighbor c. were overthrown, 49.18
and I will kindle a fire in his c., 50.32
and Gomorrah and their neighbor c., 50.40
Her c. have become a horror, a land 51.43
among the c. has become a vassal. Lam 1.01
Wherever you dwell your c. shall be Eze 6.06
And the inhabited c. shall be laid 12.20
strongholds, and laid waste their c.; 19.07
camels and the c. of the Ammonites 25.05
Moab from the c. on its frontier, 25.09
like the c. that are not inhabited, 26.19
and her c. shall be a desolation 29.12
years among c. that are laid waste. 29.12
countries and her c. shall be in 30.07
in the midst of c. that are laid 30.07
I will lay your c. waste, 35.04
and your c. shall not be inhabited. 35.09
desolate wastes and the deserted c., 36.04
the c. shall be inhabited and the 36.10
will cause the c. to be inhabited, 36.33
and ruined c. are now inhabited 36.35
shall the waste c. be filled with 36.38
dwell in the c. of Israel will go 39.09
their possession for c. to live in. 45.05
Judah has multiplied fortified c.; Hos 8.14
but I will send a fire upon his c., 8.14
The sword shall rage against their c., 11.06
cleanness of teeth in all your c., Amo 4.06
so two or three c. wandered to one 4.08
the ruined c. and inhabit them; 9.14
shall possess the c. of the Negeb. Ob 1.20
cut off the c. of your land and Mic 5.11
from among you and destroy your c. 5.14
to c. and all who dwell therein. Hab 2.08
to c. and all who dwell therein. 2.17
the fortified c. and against the Zep 1.16
their c. have been made desolate, 3.06
on Jerusalem and the c. of Judah, Zec 1.12
My c. shall again overflow with 1.17
with her c. round about her, and the 7.07
even the inhabitants of many c.; 8.20
to the Lord belong the c. of Aram, 9.01
went about all the c. and villages, Mt 9.35
to teach and preach in their c. 11.01
to upbraid the c. where most of 11.20
c., or country, they laid the sick Mk 6.56
of God to the other c. also; Lk 4.43
While he was in one of the c., 5.12
he went on through c. and villages, 8.01
shall have authority over ten c.' 19.17
'And you are to be over five c.' 19.19
c. of Lycaonia. and to the surrounding Ac 14.06
went on their way through the c., 16.04
persecuted them even to foreign c. 26.11
if by turning the c. of Sodom and 2Pe 2.06
Gomorrah and the surrounding c., Jud 1.07
and the c. of the nations fell, and Rev 16.19

CITIZEN

in Cilicia, a c. of no mean city; Ac 21.39
to scourge a man who is a Roman c., 22.25
For this man is a Roman c." 22.26
him, "Tell me, are you a Roman c.?" 22.27
Paul said, "But I was born a c." 22.28
was a Roman c. and that he had 22.29
learned that he was a Roman c. 23.27

CITIZENS

the ears of all the c. of Shechem, Ju 9.02
And all the c. of Shechem came 9.06
king over the c. of Shechem, because 9.18
and devour the c. of Shechem, 9.20
come out from the c. of Shechem, 9.20
to one of the c. of that country, Lk 15.15
But his c. hated him and sent an 19.14
uncondemned, men who are Roman c., Ac 16.37
they heard that they were Roman c.; 16.38
you are fellow c. with the saints Eph 2.19

CITIZENSHIP

"I bought this c. for a large sum." Ac 22.28

CITY

and he built a c., and called Gen 4.17
the name of the c. after the name 4.17
that is the great c. 10.12
"Come, let us build ourselves a c., 11.04
down to see the c. and the tower, 11.05
and they left off building the c. 11.08
are fifty righteous within the c.; 18.24
at Sodom fifty righteous in the c., 18.26
the whole c. for lack of five 18.28
they lay down, the men of the c., 19.04
or any one you have in the c., 19.12
Lord is about to destroy the c." 19.14
in the punishment of the c." 19.15
forth and set him outside the c. 19.16
Behold, yonder c. is near enough to 19.20
overthrow the c. of which you have 19.21
the name of the c. was called Zoar. 19.22
who went in at the gate of his c., 23.10
who went in at the gate of his c. 23.18
to Mesopotamia, to the c. of Nahor. 24.10
outside the c. by the well of 24.11
the men of the c. are coming out 24.13
the name of the c. is Beersheba to 26.33
the name of the c. was Luz at the 28.19
came safely to the c. of Shechem, 33.18
and he camped before the c. 33.18
gate of their c. and spoke to the 34.20
to the men of their c., saying, 34.20
the gate of his c. hearkened to 34.24
who went out of the gate of his c. 34.24
and came upon the c. unawares, 34.25
the slain, and plundered the c., 34.27
was in the c. and in the field; 34.28
the name of his c. being Dinhabah. 36.32
the name of his c. being Avith. 36.35
the name of his c. being Pau; 36.39
up in every c. the food from the 41.48
but a short distance from the c., 44.04
ass, and they returned to the c. 44.13
soon as I have gone out of the c., Ex 9.29
went out of the c. from Pharaoh, 9.33
an unclean place outside the c.; Lev 14.40
an unclean place outside the c.; 14.41
out of the c. to an unclean place. 14.45
go out of the c. into the open 14.53
a dwelling house in a walled c., 25.29
in the walled c. shall be made 25.30
was sold in a c. of their possession 25.33
a c. on the edge of your territory. Num 20.16
For Heshbon was the c. of Sihon the 21.26
let the c. of Sihon be established. 21.27
Heshbon, flame from the c. of Sihon. 21.28
out to meet him at the c. of Moab, 22.36
the wall of the c. outward a 35.04
outside the c., for the east side 35.05
the c. being in the middle; 35.05
restore him to his c. of refuge, 35.25
bounds of his c. of refuge to 35.26
the bounds of his c. of refuge, 35.27
remain in his c. of refuge until 35.28
who has fled to his c. of refuge, 35.32
and utterly destroyed every c., Deu 2.34
and from the c. that is in the 2.36
there was not a c. too high for us 2.36
there was not a c. which we did 3.04
of Heshbon, destroying every c., 3.06
away the inhabitants of the c., 13.13
inhabitants of that c. to the sword, 13.15

CITY (cont.)

and burn the c. and all its spoil	Deu 13.16
elders of his c. shall send and	19.12
draw near to a c. to fight against	20.10
and everything else in the c.,	20.14
"When you besiege a c. for a long	20.19
against the c. that makes war with	20.20
elders of the c. which is nearest	21.03
elders of that c. shall bring the	21.04
elders of that c. nearest to the	21.06
elders of his c. at the gate of	21.19
shall say to the elders of his c.,	21.20
the men of the c. shall stone him	21.21
the elders of the c. in the gate;	22.15
before the elders of the c.	22.17
elders of that c. shall take the	22.18
the men of her c. shall stone her	22.21
her in the c. and lies with her,	22.23
both out to the gate of that c.,	22.24
for help though she was in the c.,	22.24
elders of his c. shall call him,	25.08
Blessed shall you be in the c.,	28.03
Cursed shall you be in the c.,	28.16
of Jericho the c. of palm trees,	34.03
house was built into the c. wall,	Jos 2.15
the c. that is beside Zarethan, and	3.16
You shall march around the c.,	6.03
of war going around the c. once.	6.03
march around the c. seven times,	6.04
the wall of the c. will fall down	6.05
march around the c., and let	6.07
ark of the LORD to compass the c.,	6.11
they march around the c. once,	6.14
around the c. in the same manner	6.15
marched around the c. seven times.	6.15
or the LORD has given you the c.	6.16
And the c. and all that is within	6.17
the people went up into the c.,	6.20
before him, and they took the c.	6.20
utterly destroyed all in the c.,	6.21
And they burned the c. with fire,	6.24
up and rebuilds this c., Jericho.	6.26
his people, his c., and his land;	8.01
ambush against the c., behind it."	8.02
ambush against the c., behind it;	8.04
do not go very far from the c.,	8.04
are with me, will approach the c.	8.05
have drawn them away from the c.;	8.06
from the ambush, and seize the c.;	8.07
And when you have taken the c.,	8.08
you shall set the c. on fire, doing	8.08
up, and drew near before the c.,	8.11
and Ai, to the west of the c.	8.12
north of the c. and its rear guard	8.13
and its rear guard west of the c.	8.13
all his people, the men of the c.,	8.14
ambush against him behind the c.	8.14
who were in the c. were called	8.16
they were drawn away from the c.	8.16
they left the c. open, and pursued	8.17
that was in his hand toward the c.	8.18
ran and entered the c. and took it;	8.19
made haste to set the c. on fire.	8.19
smoke of the c. went up to heaven;	8.20
that the ambush had taken the c.,	8.21
that the smoke of the c. went up,	8.21
forth from the c. against them;	8.22
spoil of that c. Israel took as	8.27
the entrance of the gate of the c.,	8.29
because Gibeon was a great c.,	10.02
There was not a c. that made peace	11.19
and the c. that is in the middle of	13.09
and the c. that is in the middle of	13.16
Nibshan, the C. of Salt, and Engedi:	15.62
a c. belong to the tribe of	18.14
to the fortified c. of Tyre;	19.29
gave him the c. which he asked,	19.50
and he rebuilt the c.,	19.50
the entrance of the gate of the c.,	20.04
his case to the elders of that c.;	20.04
they shall take him into the c.,	20.04
remain in that c. until he has	20.06
fields of the c. and its villages	21.12
the c. of refuge for the slayer,	21.13
the c. of refuge for the slayer,	21.21
the c. of refuge for the slayer, and	21.27
the c. of refuge for the slayer,	21.32
the c. of refuge for the slayer,	21.38
the sword, and set the c. on fire.	Ju 1.08
Judah from the c. of palms into	1.16
the name of the c. was called	1.17
the name of the c. was formerly	1.23
saw a man coming out of the c.,	1.24
"Pray, show us the way into the c.,	1.24
he showed them the way into the c.;	1.25
they smote the c. with the edge of	1.25
of the Hittites and built a c.,	1.26
took possession of the c. of palms.	3.13
elders of the c. and he took	8.16
Penuel, and slew the men of the c.	8.17
it and put it in his c., in Ophrah;	8.27
ruler of the c. heard the words of	9.30
are stirring up the c. against you.	9.31
rise early and rush upon the c.;	9.33
the entrance of the gate of the c.;	9.35
saw the men coming out of the c.,	9.43
the entrance of the gate of the c.,	9.44
fought against the c. all that day;	9.45
he took the c., and killed the	9.45
he razed the c. and sowed it with	9.45
was a strong tower within the c.,	9.51
the people of the c. fled to it,	9.51
and was buried in his c. in Gilead.	12.07
And the men of the c. said to him	14.18
all night at the gate of the c.	16.02
the gate of the c. and the two	16.03
sword, and burned the c. with fire.	18.27
And they rebuilt the c.,	18.28
And they named the c. Dan,	18.29
the name of the c. was Laish at	18.29
aside to this c. of the Jebusites,	19.11
aside into the c. of foreigners,	19.12
down in the open square of the c.;	19.15
in the open square of the c.;	19.17
merry, behold, the men of the c.,	19.22
of Israel gathered against the c.,	20.11
and were drawn away from the c.;	20.31
away from the c. to the highways."	20.32
smote all the c. with the edge of	20.37
of smoke rise up out of the c.	20.38
rise out of the c. in a column of	20.40
whole of the c. went up in smoke	20.40
took it up and went into the c.;	Ru 2.18
upon her; then she went into the c.	3.15
ten men of the elders of the c.,	4.02
year from his c. to worship and to	1Sa 1.03
came into the c. and told the news,	4.13
the news, all the c. cried out.	4.13
of the LORD was against the c.,	5.09
and he afflicted the men of the c..	5.09
panic throughout the whole c.	5.11
the cry of the c. went up to	5.12
of Israel, "Go every man to his c."	8.22
there is a man of God in this c.,	9.06
went to the c. where the man of	9.10
As they went up to the hill to the c.,	9.11
he has come just now to the c.,	9.12
As soon as you enter the c.,	9.13
So they went up to the c.	9.14
As they were entering the c.,	9.14
from the high place into the c.,	9.25
down to the outskirts of the c.,	9.27
and there, as you come to the c.,	10.05
And Saul came to the c. of Amalek,	15.05

CITY (cont.)
elders of the c. came to meet him 1Sa 16.04
of me to run to Bethlehem his c.; 20.06
family holds a sacrifice in the c., 20.29
him, "Go and carry them to the c." 20.40
and Jonathan went into the c. 20.42
And Nob, the c. of the priests, he 22.19
to destroy the c. on my account. 23.10
dwell in the royal c. with you?" 27.05
buried him in Ramah, his own c. 28.03
David and his men came to the c., 30.03
of Zion, that is, the c. of David. 2Sa 5.07
and called it the c. of David. 5.09
David built the c. round about 5.09
of the LORD into the c. of David; 6.10
Obededom to the c. of David with 6.12
the LORD came into the c. of David, 6.16
servants to you to search the c., 10.03
before Abishai, and entered the c. 10.14
And as Joab was besieging the c., 11.16
And the men of the c. came out and 11.17
did you go so near the c. to fight? 11.20
strengthen your attack upon the c., 11.25
"There were two men in a certain c., 12.01
Ammonites, and took the royal c. 12.26
I have taken the c. of waters. 12.27
encamp against the c., and take it; 12.28
lest I take the c., and it be called 12.28
brought forth the spoil of the c., 12.30
him, and say, "From what c. are you?" 15.02
counselor, from his c. Giloh. 15.12
and smite the c. with the edge of 15.14
had all passed out of the c. 15.24
the ark of God back into the c. 15.25
"Look, go back to the c. in peace, 15.27
But if you return to the c., 15.34
came into the c., just as Absalom 15.37
If he withdraws into a c., then all 17.13
Israel will bring ropes to that c., 17.13
must not be seen entering the c. 17.17
and went off home to his own c. 17.23
that you send us help from the c." 18.03
stole into the c. that day as 19.03
that I may die in my own c., 19.37
cast up a mound against the c., 20.15
woman called from the c., "Hear! 20.16
to destroy a c. which is a mother 20.19
and I will withdraw from the c." 20.21
and they dispersed from the c., 20.22
and from the c. that is in the 24.05
does this uproar in the c. mean?" 1Ki 1.41
so that the c. is in an uproar. 1.45
and was buried in the c. of David. 2.10
brought her into the c. of David, 3.01
of the LORD out of the c. of David, 8.01
I chose no c. in all the tribes of 8.16
LORD toward the c. which thou hast 8.44
the c. which thou hast chosen, and 8.48
the Canaanites who dwelt in the c., 9.16
up from the c. of David to her own 9.24
breach of the c. of David his 11.27
the c. which I have chosen out of 11.32
the c. where I have chosen to put 11.36
buried in the c. of David his 11.43
told it in the c. where the old 13.25
ass, and brought it back to the c., 13.29
who dies in the c. the dogs shall 14.11
When your feet enter the c., 14.12
the c. which the LORD had chosen 14.21
his fathers in the c. of David. 14.31
they buried him in the c. of David. 15.08
fathers in the c. of David his 15.24
who dies in the c. the dogs shall 16.04
Zimri saw that the c. was taken, 16.18
the name of the c. which he built, 16.24
when he came to the gate of the c., 17.10
into the c. to Ahab king of Israel, 20.02
their positions against the c. 20.12
So these went out of the c., 20.19
the rest fled into the c. of Aphek; 20.30
entered an inner chamber in the c. 20.30
who dwelt with Naboth in his c. 21.08
And the men of his c., the elders 21.11
and the nobles who dwelt in his c., 21.11
So they took him outside the c., 21.13
who dies in the c. the dogs shall 21.24
governor of the c. and to Joash 22.26
the army, "Every man to his c., 22.36
fathers in the c. of David his 22.50
Now the men of the c. said to Elisha, 2Ki 2.19
situation of this c. is pleasant, 2.19
came out of the c. and jeered at 2.23
shall conquer every fortified c., 3.19
and every choice c., and shall fell 3.19
by night, and surrounded the c. 6.14
chariots was round about the c. 6.15
the way, and this is not the c.; 6.19
If we say, 'Let us enter the c.,' 7.04
the famine is in the c., and we 7.04
to the gatekeepers of the c., 7.10
'When they come out of the c., 7.12
them alive and get into the c.'" 7.12
his fathers in the c. of David; 8.24
slip out of the c. to go and tell 9.15
his fathers in the c. of David. 9.28
Samaria, to the rulers of the c., 10.01
palace, and he who was over the c., 10.05
were with the great men of the c., 10.06
and the c. was quiet after Athaliah 11.20
his fathers in the c. of David, 12.21
his fathers in the c. of David. 14.20
his fathers in the c. of David, 15.07
fathers in the c. of David his 15.38
his fathers in the c. of David; 16.20
from watch tower to fortified c.; 17.09
from watchtower to fortified c. 18.08
and this c. will not be given into 18.30
the king of the c. of Sepharvaim, 19.13
come to this c. or shoot an arrow 19.32
come into this c., says the LORD. 19.33
For I will defend this c. to save it, 19.34
you and this c. out of the hand of 20.06
defend this c. for my own sake and 20.06
and brought water into the c., 20.20
of Joshua the governor of the c., 23.08
one's left at the gate of the c. 23.08
And the men of the c. told him, 23.17
cast off this c. which I have 23.27
Jerusalem, and the c. was besieged. 24.10
king of Babylon came to the c., 24.11
So the c. was besieged till the 25.02
severe in the c. that there was no 25.03
Then a breach was made in the c.; 25.04
the Chaldeans were around the c. 25.04
left in the c. and the deserters 25.11
and from the c. he took an officer 25.19
council who were found in the c.; 25.19
the land who were found in the c. 25.19
the name of whose c. was Dinhabah. 1Ch 1.43
and the name of his c. was Avith. 1.46
and the name of his c. was Pai, 1.50
fields of the c. and its villages 6.56
of Zion, that is, the c. of David. 11.05
it was called the c. of David. 11.07
And he built the c. round about 11.08
Joab repaired the rest of the c. 11.08
the ark home into the c. of David, 13.13
for himself in the c. of David; 15.01
the LORD came to the c. of David, 15.29
array at the entrance of the c., 19.09
Joab's brother, and entered the c. 19.15
brought forth the spoil of the c., 20.02
of the LORD out of the c. of David, 2Ch 5.02
I chose no c. in all the tribes of 6.05

CITY (cont.)
toward this c. which thou hast 2Ch 6.34
the c. which thou hast chosen, and 6.38
up from the c. of David to the 8.11
buried in the c. of David his 9.31
the c. which the LORD had chosen 12.13
and was buried in the c. of David; 12.16
they buried him in the c. of David; 14.01
against nation and c. against c., 15.06
out for himself in the c. of David. 16.14
governor of the c. and to Joash 18.25
cities of Judah, c. by c., 19.05
his fathers in the c. of David; 21.01
they buried him in the c. of David, 21.20
and the c. was quiet, after 23.21
him in the c. of David among the 24.16
they buried him in the c. of David, 24.25
his fathers in the c. of David. 25.28
they buried him in the c. of David; 27.09
at Jericho, the c. of palm trees. 28.15
In every c. of Judah he made high 28.25
and they buried him in the c., 28.27
gathered the officials of the c., 29.20
went from c. to c. through the 30.10
springs that were outside the c.; 32.03
the Millo in the c. of David. 32.05
the gate of the c. and spoke 32.06
order that they might take the c. 32.18
the west side of the c. of David. 32.30
wall to the c. of David west of 33.14
he threw them outside of the c. 33.15
Maaseiah the governor of the c., 34.08
that rebellious and wicked c.; Ez 4.12
if this c. is rebuilt and the walls 4.13
learn that this c. is a rebellious c., 4.15
was why this c. was laid waste. 4.15
if this c. is rebuilt and its walls 4.16
found that this c. from of old has 4.19
and that this c. be not rebuilt, 4.21
the elders and judges of every c., 10.14
when the c., the place of my Neh 2.03
to the c. of my fathers' sepulchres, 2.05
temple, and for the wall of the c., 2.08
that go down from the C. of David. 3.15
The c. was wide and large, but the 7.04
to live in Jerusalem the holy c., 11.01
Hassenuah was second over the c. 11.09
in the holy c. were two hundred 11.18
by the stairs of the c. of David, 12.37
Men of Tyre also, who lived in the c., 13.16
all this evil on us and on this c.? 13.18
but the c. of Susa was perplexed. Est 3.15
went out into the midst of the c., 4.01
square of the c. in front of the 4.06
through the open square of the c., 6.09
through the open square of the c., 6.11
were in every c. to gather and 8.11
while the c. of Susa shouted and 8.15
And in every province and in every c., 8.17
and c., and that these days of 9.28
From out of the c. the dying groan, Job 24.12
When I went out to the gate of the c., 29.07
He scorns the tumult of the c.; 39.07
I was beset as in a besieged c. Ps 31.21
streams make glad the c. of God, 46.04
to be praised in the c. of our God! 48.01
the c. of the great King. 48.02
we seen in the c. of the LORD of 48.08
in the c. of our God, which God 48.08
see violence and strife in the c. 55.09
dogs and prowling about the c. 59.06
dogs and prowling about the c. 59.14
Who will bring me to the fortified c.? 60.09
mount stands the c. he founded; 87.01
are spoken of you, O c. of God. 87.03
evildoers from the c. of the LORD. 101.08
finding no way to a c. to dwell in; 107.04
till they reached a c. to dwell in. 107.07
and they establish a c. to live in; 107.36
Who will bring me to the fortified c.? 108.10
built as a c. which is bound firmly 122.03
the LORD watches over the c., 127.01
entrance of the c. gates she Pro 1.21
rich man's wealth is his strong c.; 10.15
the righteous, the c. rejoices; 11.10
of the upright a c. is exalted, 11.11
his spirit than he who takes a c. 16.32
rich man's wealth is his strong c., 18.11
brother helped is like a strong c., 18.19
man scales the c. of the mighty 21.22
is like a c. broken into and left 25.28
Scoffers set a c. aflame, but wise 29.08
than ten rulers that are in a c. Ecc 7.19
praised in the c. where they had 8.10
There was a little c. with few men 9.14
he by his wisdom delivered the c. 9.15
he does not know the way to the c. 10.15
"I will rise now and go about the c., Sol 3.02
me, as they went about in the c. 3.03
me, as they went about in the c.; 5.07
cucumber field, like a besieged c. Is 1.08
How the faithful c. has become a 1.21
be called the c. of righteousness, 1.26
of righteousness, the faithful c." 1.26
cry, O c.; melt in fear, 14.31
Damascus will cease to be a c., 17.01
c. against c., kingdom against 19.02
will be called the C. of the Sun. 19.18
tumultuous c., exultant town? 22.02
breaches of the c. of David were 22.09
your exultant c. whose origin is 23.07
go about the c., O forgotten harlot 23.16
The c. of Chaos is broken down, 24.10
Desolation is left in the c., 24.12
For thou hast made the c. a heap, 25.02
a heap, the fortified c. a ruin; 25.02
palace of aliens is a c. no more, 25.02
land of Judah: "We have a strong c.; 26.01
of the height, the lofty c. 26.05
For the fortified c. is solitary, 27.10
the c. where David encamped! 29.01
the joyous houses in the joyful c. 32.13
forsaken, the populous c. deserted; 32.14
and the c. will be utterly laid low 32.19
the c. of our appointed feasts! 33.20
this c. will not be given into the 36.15
the king of the c. of Sepharvaim, 37.13
He shall not come into this c., 37.33
come into this c., says the LORD. 37.34
For I will defend this c. to save it, 37.35
you and this c. out of the hand of 38.06
of Assyria, and defend this c. 38.06
shall build my c. and set my 45.13
call themselves after the holy c., 48.02
garments, O Jerusalem, the holy c.; 52.01
shall call you the C. of the LORD, 60.14
Sought out, a c. not forsaken. 62.12
"Hark, an uproar from the c.! 66.06
I make you this day a fortified c., Jer 1.18
one from a c. and two from a family, 3.14
archer every c. takes to flight; 4.29
This is the c. which must be 6.06
the c. and those who dwell in it. 8.16
And if I enter the c., 14.18
gates of this c. on the sabbath 17.24
gates of this c. kings who sit on 17.25
and this c. shall be inhabited for 17.25
And I will make this c. a horror, 19.08
I break this people and this c., 19.11
making this c. like Topheth. 19.12
upon this c. and upon all its 19.15
will give all the wealth of the c., 20.05
together into the midst of this c. 21.04
smite the inhabitants of this c., 21.06

CITY (cont.)
people in this c. who survive the Jer 21.07
stays in this c. shall die by the 21.09
against this c. for evil and not 21.10
you a desert, an uninhabited c. 22.06
many nations will pass by this c., 22.08
LORD dealt thus with this great c.?" 22.08
you and the c. which I gave to you 23.39
evil at the c. which is called by 25.29
will make this c. a curse for all 26.06
and this c. shall be desolate, 26.09
he has prophesied against this c., 26.11
house and this c. all the words 26.12
and upon this c. and its inhabitants, 26.15
against this c. and against this 26.20
Why should this c. become a desolation? 27.17
vessels which are left in this c., 27.19
welfare of the c. where I have 29.07
the people who dwell in this c., 29.16
the c. shall be rebuilt upon its 30.18
when the c. shall be rebuilt for 31.38
am giving this c. into the hand of 32.03
have come up to the c. to take it, 32.24
pestilence the c. is given into 32.24
though the c. is given into the 32.25
am giving this c. into the hands 32.28
against this c. shall come and set 32.29
and set this c. on fire, and burn it, 32.29
This c. has aroused my anger and 32.31
concerning this c. of which you 32.36
houses of this c. and the houses 33.04
face from this c. because of all 33.05
And this c. shall be to me a name 33.09
am giving this c. into the hand of 34.02
will bring them back to this c.; 34.22
back and fight against this c.; 37.08
rise up and burn this c. with fire.' " 37.10
all the bread of the c. was gone. 37.21
stays in this c. shall die by the 38.02
This c. shall surely be given into 38.03
soldiers who are left in this c., 38.04
there is no bread left in the c." 38.09
and this c. shall not be burned 38.17
then this c. shall be given into 38.18
and this c. shall be burned with 38.23
month, a breach was made in the c. 39.02
out of the c. at night by way of 39.04
the people who were left in the c., 39.09
against this c. for evil and not 39.16
When they came into the c., 41.07
the c. and those who dwell in it. 47.02
destroyer shall come upon every c., 48.08
and no c. shall escape; the valley 48.08
famous c. is forsaken, the joyful c.! 49.25
that his c. is taken on every side; 51.31
So the c. was besieged till the 52.05
the famine was so severe in the c., 52.06
Then a breach was made in the c.; 52.07
out from the c. by night by the 52.07
Chaldeans were round about the c. 52.07
left in the c. and the deserters 52.15
and from the c. he took an officer 52.25
council, who were found in the c.; 52.25
who were found in the midst of the c. 52.25
How lonely sits the c. that was Lam 1.01
and elders perished in the c., 1.19
faint in the streets of the c. 2.11
men in the streets of the c., 2.12
"Is this the c. which was called 2.15
fate of all the maidens of my c. 3.51
The old men have quit the c. gate, 5.14
you, and portray upon it a c., Eze 4.01
iron wall between you and the c.; 4.03
you shall prophesy against the c. 4.07
in the fire in the midst of the c., 5.02
with the sword round about the c.; 5.02
that is in the c. famine and 7.15
crimes and the c. is full of 7.23
near, you executioners of the c.. 9.01
said to him, "Go through the c., 9.04
"Pass through the c. after him, 9.05
went forth, and smote in the c. 9.07
and the c. full of injustice; 9.09
and scatter them over the c." 10.02
who give wicked counsel in this c.; 11.02
this c. is the caldron, and we are 11.03
multiplied your slain in this c., 11.06
flesh, and this c. is the caldron; 11.07
This c. shall not be your caldron, 11.11
went up from the midst of the c., 11.23
is on the east side of the c. 11.23
and set it in a c. of merchants. 17.04
it at the head of the way to a c.; 21.19
will you judge the bloody c.? 22.02
A c. that sheds blood in the midst 22.03
the Lord GOD: Woe to the bloody c., 24.06
the Lord GOD: Woe to the bloody c.! 24.09
as one enters a c. which has been 26.10
O c. renowned, that was mighty on 26.17
When I make you a c. laid waste, 26.19
to me and said, "The c. has fallen." 33.21
(A c. Hamonah is there also.) 39.16
year after the c. was conquered, 40.01
a structure like a c. opposite me. 40.02
when he came to destroy the c., 43.03
possession of the c. an area five 45.06
district and the property of the c., 45.07
property of the c., on the west and 45.07
be for ordinary use for the c., 48.15
In the midst of it shall be the c.; 48.15
And the c. shall have open land: on 48.17
be food for the workers of the c. 48.18
And the workers of the c., 48.19
with the property of the c. 48.20
property of the c. shall belong to 48.21
and the property of the c., 48.22
"These shall be the exits of the c.: 48.30
gates of the c. being named after 48.31
circumference of the c. shall be 48.35
the name of the c. henceforth 48.35
turn away from thy c. Jerusalem, Dan 9.16
and the c. which is called by thy 9.18
because thy c. and thy people are 9.19
your people and your holy c., 9.24
destroy the c. and the sanctuary. 9.26
and take a well-fortified c. 11.15
Gilead is a c. of evildoers, tracked Hos 6.08
They leap upon the c., they run Joe 2.09
Is a trumpet blown in a c., Amo 3.06
Does evil befall a c., unless 3.06
I would send rain upon one c., 4.07
and send no rain upon another c.; 4.07
wandered to one c. to drink water, 4.08
"The c. that went forth a thousand 5.03
deliver up the c. and all that is 6.08
wife shall be a harlot in the c., 7.17
that great c., and cry against it; Jon 1.02
that great c., and proclaim to it 3.02
was an exceedingly great c., 3.03
Jonah began to go into the c., 3.04
went out of the c. and sat to the 4.05
city and sat to the east of the c., 4.05
see what would become of the c. 4.05
that great c., in which there are 4.11
forth from the c. and dwell in the Mic 4.10
voice of the LORD cries to the c.— 6.09
O tribe and assembly of the c.! 6.09
Woe to the bloody c., all full Nah 3.01
blood, and founds a c. on iniquity! Hab 2.12
This is the exultant c. that dwelt Zep 2.15
and defiled, the oppressing c.! 3.01
shall be called the faithful c., Zec 8.03
streets of the c. shall be full of 8.05
inhabitants of one c. shall go to 8.21

CITY (cont.)

and the c. shall be taken and the Zec 14.02
half of the c. shall go into exile, 14.02
shall not be cut off from the c. 14.02
and dwelt in a c. called Nazareth, Mt 2.23
Then the devil took him to the holy c., 4.05
A c. set on a hill cannot be hid. 5.14
for it is the c. of the great King. 5.35
going into the c. they told 8.33
all the c. came out to meet Jesus; 8.34
over and came to his own c. 9.01
and no c. or house divided against 12.25
all the c. was stirred, saying, "Who 21.10
went out of the c. to Bethany and 21.17
returning to the c., he was hungry. 21.18
murderers and burned their c. 22.07
"Go into the c. to such a one, and 26.18
into the holy c. and appeared to 27.53
went into the c. and told the 28.11
And the whole c. was gathered Mk 1.33
told it in the c. and in the 5.14
came they went out of the c. 11.19
"Go into the c., and a man carrying 14.13
disciples set out and went to the c., 14.16
from God to a c. of Galilee named Lk 1.26
hill country, to a c. of Judah, 1.39
to be enrolled, each to his own c. 2.03
from the c. of Nazareth, to Judea, to 2.04
to the c. of David, which is called 2.04
this day in the c. of David a 2.11
Galilee, to their own c., Nazareth. 2.39
rose up and put him out of the c., 4.29
hill on which their c. was built, 4.29
down to Capernaum, a c. of Galilee. 4.31
he went to a c. called Nain, 7.11
he drew near to the gate of the c., 7.12
crowd from the c. was with her. 7.12
And behold, a woman of the c., 7.37
a man from the c. who had demons; 8.27
told it in the c. and in the 8.34
the whole c. how much Jesus had 8.39
apart to a c. called Bethsaida. 9.10
to the streets and lanes of the c., 14.21
"In a certain c. there was a judge 18.02
a widow in that c. who kept coming 18.03
and saw the c. he wept over it, 19.41
those who are inside the c. depart, 21.21
when you have entered the c., 22.10
an insurrection started in the c., 23.19
but stay in the c., until you are 24.49
the c. of Andrew and Peter. Jn 1.44
So he came to a c. of Samaria, 4.05
gone away into the c. to buy food. 4.08
jar, and went away into the c., 4.28
They went out of the c. and were 4.30
from that c. believed in him 4.39
was crucified was near the c.; 19.20
for truly in this c. there were Ac 4.27
him out of the c. and stoned him; 7.58
Philip went down to a c. of Samaria, 8.05
So there was much joy in that c. 8.08
magic in the c. and amazed the 8.09
but rise and enter the c., 9.06
journey and coming near the c., 10.09
"I was in the c. of Joppa praying; 11.05
the iron gate leading into the c. 12.10
the whole c. gathered together to 13.44
and the leading men of the c., 13.50
But the people of the c. were divided; 14.04
temple was in front of the c., 14.13
Paul and dragged him out of the c., 14.19
him, he rose up and entered the c.; 14.20
gospel to that c. and had made 14.21
had in every c. those who preach 15.21
in every c. where we proclaimed 15.36
is the leading c. of the district 16.12
We remained in this c. some days; 16.12
from the c. of Thyatira, a seller of 16.14
and they are disturbing our c. 16.20
out and asked them to leave the c. 16.39
set the c. in an uproar, and attacked 17.05
brethren before the c. authorities, 17.06
people and the c. authorities were 17.08
he saw that the c. was full of 17.16
or I have many people in this c." 18.10
So the c. was filled with the 19.29
know that the c. of the Ephesians 19.35
to me in every c. that imprisonment 20.23
way till we were outside the c.; 21.05
the Ephesian with him in the c., 21.29
Then all the c. was aroused, and the 21.30
Cilicia, a citizen of no mean c.; 21.39
up in this c. at the feet of 22.03
or in the synagogues, or in the c. 24.12
and the prominent men of the c. 25.23
near which was the c. of Lasea. 27.08
Erastus, the c. treasurer, and our Rom 16.23
danger in the c., danger in the 2Co 11.26
guarded the c. of Damascus in 11.32
forward to the c. which has Heb 11.10
for he has prepared for them a c. 11.16
Zion and to the c. of the living 12.22
For here we have no lasting c., 13.14
but we seek the c. which is to 13.14
and the name of the c. of my God, Rev 3.12
over the holy c. for forty-two 11.02
of the great c. which is allegorically 11.08
earthquake, and a tenth of the c. fell; 11.13
press was trodden outside the c., 14.20
The great c. was split into three 16.19
is the great c. which has dominion 17.18
thou great c., thou mighty c., 18.10
for the great c. that was clothed 18.16
"What c. was like the great c.?" 18.18
for the great c. where all who had 18.19
the great c. be thrown down with 18.21
of the saints and the beloved c.; 20.09
And I saw the holy c., a new 21.02
me the holy c. Jerusalem coming 21.10
And the wall of the c. had twelve 21.14
to measure the c. and its gates 21.15
The c. lies foursquare, its length 21.16
he measured the c. with his rod, 21.16
while the c. was pure gold, clear as 21.18
the wall of the c. were adorned 21.19
the street of the c. was pure gold, 21.21
And I saw no temple in the c., 21.22
And the c. had no need of sun or 21.23
the middle of the street of the c.; 22.02
they may enter the c. by the gates. 22.14
tree of life and in the holy c., 22.19

CIVILIAN

gets entangled in c. pursuits, 2Ti 2.04

CLAD

daughters of the king c. of old. 2Sa 13.18
Now Ahijah had c. himself with a 1Ki 11.29
shall be c. thus in white garments, Rev 3.05
c. in white garments, with golden 4.04
He is c. in a robe dipped in blood, 19.13

CLAIM

let gloom and deep darkness c. it. Job 3.05
died! Who do you c. to be?" Jn 8.53
share this rightful c. upon you, 1Co 9.12
of ourselves to c. anything as 2Co 3.05
undermine the c. of those who 11.12
would like to c. that in their 11.12

CLAIMING

C. to be wise, they became fools, Rom 1.22

CLAIMS

your c. are good and right; 2Sa 15.03
even though a wise man c. to know, Ecc 8.17

CLAMOR
Do not forget the c. of thy foes, Ps 74.23
Like a swallow or a crane I c., Is 38.14
The c. will resound to the ends of Jer 25.31
a c. was raised in the house of the Lam 2.07
Then a great c. arose; and some Ac 23.09
and anger and c. and slander be Eph 4.31

CLAMPS
the doors of the gates and for c., 1Ch 22.03

CLAN
Behold, my c. is the weakest in Ju 6.15
to the whole c. of his mother's 9.01
he gave in marriage outside his c., 12.09
The least one shall become a c., Is 60.22
it shall be like a c. in Judah, Zec 9.07

CLANGING
I am a noisy gong or a c. cymbal. 1Co 13.01

CLANS
to their c. in the land of Seir. Gen 36.30
the heads of the c. of Israel. Num 1.16
of a family among the c. of Israel. Jos 22.14
Among the c. of Reuben there were Ju 5.15
Among the c. of Reuben there were 5.16
little to be among the c. of Judah, Mic 5.02
Then the c. of Judah shall say to Zec 12.05
I will make the c. of Judah like a 12.06

CLAP
C. your hands, all peoples! Ps 47.01
Let the floods c. their hands; 98.08
of the field shall c. their hands. Is 55.12
along the way c. their hands at Lam 2.15
"C. your hands, and stamp your foot, Eze 6.11
c. your hands and let the sword 21.14
I also will c. my hands, and I will 21.17
the news of you c. their hands Nah 3.19

CLAPPED
and they c. their hands, and said, 2Ki 11.12
you have c. your hands and stamped Eze 25.06

CLAPS
It c. its hands at him, and hisses Job 27.23
he c. his hands among us, and 34.37

CLASHING
praise him with loud c. cymbals! Ps 150.05

CLASP
they c. each other and cannot be Job 41.17

CLASPS
And you shall make fifty c. of gold, Ex 26.06
one to the other with the c., 26.06
"And you shall make fifty c. of bronze, 26.11
and put the c. into the loops, and 26.11
shall hang the veil from the c., 26.33
And he made fifty c. of gold, 36.13
curtains one to the other with c.; 36.13
And he made fifty c. of bronze to 36.18

CLASS
we venture to c. or compare 2Co 10.12

CLAUDIA
and Linus and C. and all the 2Ti 4.21

CLAUDIUS
this took place in the days of C. Ac 11.28
because C. had commanded all the 18.02
"C. Lysias to his Excellency the 23.26

CLAWS
and his nails were like birds' c. Dan 4.33
its teeth of iron and c. of bronze; 7.19

CLAY
in the c. ground between Succoth 1Ki 7.46
in the c. ground between Succoth 2Ch 4.17
those who dwell in houses of c., Job 4.19
Remember that thou hast made me of c.; 10.09
your defenses are defenses of c. 13.12
dust, and pile up clothing like c.; 27.16
too was formed from a piece of c. 33.06
It is changed like c. under the seal, 38.14
the potter be regarded as the c.; Is 29.16
on mortar, as the potter treads c. 41.25
Does the c. say to him who fashions 45.09
we are the c., and thou art our 64.08
was making of c. was spoiled in Jer 18.04
like the c. in the potter's hand, so 18.06
partly of iron and partly of c. Dan 2.33
image on its feet of iron and c., 2.34
the c., the bronze, the silver, and 2.35
of potter's c. and partly of iron, 2.41
saw iron mixed with the miry c. 2.41
were partly iron and partly c., 2.42
saw the iron mixed with miry c., 2.43
just as iron does not mix with c. 2.43
the c., the silver, and the gold. 2.45
go into the c., tread the mortar, Nah 3.14
ground and made c. of the spittle Jn 9.06
anointed the man's eyes with the c., 9.06
Jesus made c. and anointed my eyes 9.11
Jesus made the c. and opened his 9.14
"He put c. on my eyes, and I washed, 9.15
Has the potter no right over the c., Rom 9.21

CLEAN
you seven pairs of all c. animals, Gen 7.02
of the animals that are not c., 7.02
Of c. animals, and of animals that 7.08
and of animals that are not c., 7.08
every c. animal and of every c. bird, 8.20
outside the camp to a c. place, Lev 4.12
outside the camp to a c. place. 6.11
All who are c. may eat flesh, 7.19
and between the unclean and the c.; 10.10
you shall eat in any c. place, 10.14
then it shall be c. 11.32
cistern holding water shall be c.; 11.36
that is to be sown, it is c.; 11.37
unclean and the c. and between the 11.47
she shall be c. from the flow of 12.07
for her and she shall be c." 12.08
the priest shall pronounce him c.; 13.06
shall wash his clothes, and be c. 13.06
pronounce him c. of the disease; 13.13
has all turned white, and he is c. 13.13
the diseased person c.; he is c. 13.17
the priest shall pronounce him c. 13.23
the priest shall pronounce him c.; 13.28
the priest shall pronounce him c.; 13.34
shall wash his clothes, and be c. 13.34
it, the itch is healed, he is c.; 13.37
the priest shall pronounce him c. 13.37
in the skin; he is c. 13.39
his head, he is bald but he is c. 13.40
of the forehead but he is c. 13.41
be washed a second time, and be c." 13.58
decide whether it is c. or unclean. 13.59
two living c. birds and cedarwood 14.04
then he shall pronounce him c., 14.06
in water, and he shall be c.; 14.08
body in water, and he shall be c. 14.09
for him, and he shall be c. 14.20
shall pronounce the house c., 14.48
for the house, and it shall be c." 14.53
it is unclean and when it is c. 14.57
discharge spits on one who is c., 15.08
in running water, and shall be c. 15.13
and after that she shall be c. 15.28
you shall be c. before the LORD. 16.30

CLEAN (cont.)

evening; then he shall be c. Lev 17.15
between the c. beast and the 20.25
the unclean bird and the c.; 20.25
of the holy things until he is c. 22.04
When the sun is down he shall be c.; 22.07
has not defiled herself and is c., Num 5.28
But the man who is c. and is not on 9.13
one who is c. in your house may 18.11
one who is c. in your house may 18.13
And a man who is c. shall gather up 19.09
outside the camp in a c. place; 19.09
on the seventh day, and so be c.; 19.12
seventh day, he will not become c. 19.12
then a c. person shall take hyssop, 19.18
and the c. person shall sprinkle 19.19
and at evening he shall be c. 19.19
the fire, and it shall be c. 31.23
seventh day, and you shall be c.; 31.24
unclean and the c. may eat of it, Deu 12.15
unclean and the c. alike may eat 12.22
"You may eat all c. birds. 14.11
All c. winged things you may eat. 14.20
unclean and the c. alike may eat 15.22
man who is not c. by reason of 23.10
he is not c., surely he is not c." 1Sa 20.26
be restored, and you shall be c." 2Ki 5.10
I not wash in them, and be c." 5.12
he says to you, 'Wash, and be c.?'" 5.13
of a little child, and he was c. 5.14
lamb for every one who was not c., 2Ch 30.17
all of them were c. So they Ez 6.20
is pure, and I am in c. in God's eyes.' Job 11.04
Who can bring a c. thing out of an 14.04
What is man, that he can be c.? 15.14
heavens are not c. in his sight; 15.15
and he that has c. hands grows 17.09
can he who is born of woman be c.? 25.04
the stars are not c. in his sight; 25.05
You say, 'I am c., without transgression; 33.09
the fear of the LORD is c., Ps 19.09
He who has c. hands and a pure 24.04
Purge me with hyssop, and I shall be c.; 51.07
Create in me a c. heart, O God, and 51.10
I kept my heart c. and washed my 73.13
Who can say, "I have made my heart c.; Pro 20.09
strokes make c. the innermost parts. 20.30
to the c. and the unclean, to him Ecc 9.02
make yourselves c.; remove the Is 1.16
offering in a c. vessel to the 66.20
will it be before you are made c.?" Jer 13.27
and he shall c. the land of Egypt, 43.12
between the unclean and the c., Eze 22.26
I will sprinkle c. water upon you, 36.25
you shall be c. from all your 36.25
is lost; we are c. cut off.' 37.11
between the unclean and the c. 44.23
days, and then he shall be c. 44.26
"Let them put a c. turban on his Zec 3.05
put a c. turban on his head and 3.05
if you will, you can make me c." Mt 8.02
be c." And immediately 8.03
that the outside also may be c. 23.26
wrapped it in a c. linen shroud, 27.59
"If you will, you can make me c." Mk 1.40
"I will; be c." 1.41
left him, and he was made c. 1.42
(Thus he declared all foods c.) 7.19
if you will, you can make me c." Lk 5.12
"I will; be c." 5.13
behold, everything is c. for you. 11.41
his feet, but he is c. all over; Jn 13.10
and you are c., but not all of you." 13.10
why he said, "You are not all c." 13.11
already made c. by the word which 15.03
Everything is indeed c., but it is Rom 14.20
sprinkled c. from an evil conscience Heb 10.22

CLEANING

of the house had been c. wheat, 2Sa 4.06

CLEANNESS

according to the c. of my hands he 2Sa 22.21
according to my c. in his sight. 22.25
to the sanctuary's rules of c." 2Ch 30.19
through the c. of your hands." Job 22.30
according to the c. of my hands he Ps 18.20
according to the c. of my hands in 18.24
"I gave you c. of teeth in all your Amo 4.06

CLEANS

as a shepherd c. his cloak of Jer 43.12

CLEANSE

Thus he shall c. the house with the Lev 14.52
and c. it and hallow it from the 16.19
atonement be made for you, to c. you; 16.30
the people of Israel, and c. them. Num 8.06
to c. them: sprinkle the water of 8.07
their clothes and c. themselves. 8.07
made atonement for them to c. them. 8.21
he shall c. himself with the water 19.12
if he does not c. himself on the 19.12
and does not c. himself, defiles the 19.13
on the seventh day he shall c. him, 19.19
is unclean and does not c. himself, 19.20
to c. the house of the LORD. 2Ch 29.15
of the house of the LORD to c. it, 29.16
snow, and c. my hands with lye, Job 9.30
my iniquity, and c. me from my sin! Ps 51.02
Blows that wound c. away evil; Pro 20.30
of my people, not to winnow or c., Jer 4.11
I will c. them from all the guilt 33.08
you washed with water to c. you, Eze 16.04
from all your idols I will c. you. 36.25
the day that I c. you from all 36.33
they have sinned, and will c. them; 37.23
them, in order to c. the land. 39.12
face of the land, so as to c. it; 39.14
Thus shall they c. the land. 39.16
thus you shall c. the altar and 43.20
blemish, and c. the sanctuary. 45.18
refine and to c. them and to make Dan 11.35
of Jerusalem to c. them from sin Zec 13.01
c. lepers, cast out demons. Mt 10.08
for you c. the outside of the cup 23.25
first c. the inside of the cup and 23.26
you Pharisees c. the outside of Lk 11.39
C. out the old leaven that you may 1Co 5.07
let us c. ourselves from every 2Co 7.01
C. your hands, you sinners, and Jas 4.08
our sins and c. us from all 1Jn 1.09

CLEANSED

who is to be c. two living clean Lev 14.04
him who is to be c. of leprosy; 14.07
And he who is to be c. shall wash 14.08
who is to be c. and these things 14.11
right ear of him who is to be c., 14.14
right ear of him who is to be c., 14.17
on the head of him who is to be c. 14.18
who is to be c. from his uncleanness. 14.19
right ear of him who is to be c., 14.25
right ear of him who is to be c., 14.28
on the head of him who is to be c., 14.29
the LORD for him who is being c. 14.31
a discharge is c. of his discharge, 15.13
But if she is c. of her discharge, 15.28
when you have c. them and offered Num 8.15
even yet we have not c. ourselves, Jos 22.17
"We have c. all the house of the 2Ch 29.18
had not c. themselves, yet they ate 30.18
orders and they c. the chambers; Neh 13.09
Thus I c. them from everything 13.30
eyes but are not c. of their filth. Pro 30.12

CLEANSED (cont.)
of Zion and c. the bloodstains of Is 4.04
her, You are a land that is not c., Eze 22.24
I would have c. you and you were 24.13
you were not c. from your filthiness, 24.13
shall not be c. any more till I 24.13
offering; and the altar shall be c., 43.22
c., as it was c. with the bull. 43.22
And immediately his leprosy was c. Mt 8.03
lepers are c. and the deaf hear, and 11.05
and none of them was c., but only Lk 4.27
lepers are c., and the deaf hear, 7.22
And as they went they were c. 17.14
Then said Jesus, "Were not ten c.? 17.17
"What God has c., you must not call Ac 10.15
'What God has c. you must not call 11.09
but c. their hearts by faith. 15.09
having c. her by the washing of Eph 5.26
If the worshippers had once been c., Heb 10.02
that he was c. from his old sins. 2Pe 1.09

CLEANSES
And the priest who c. him shall set Lev 14.11
Jesus his Son c. us from all sin. 1Jn 1.07

CLEANSING
himself to the priest for his c., Lev 13.07
spreads in the skin after his c., 13.35
of the leper for the day of his c. 14.02
them for his c. to the priest, 14.23
afford the offerings for his c." 14.32
And for the c. of the house he 14.49
for himself seven days for his c., 15.13
his head on the day of his c.; Num 6.09
the c. of all that is holy, and any 1Ch 23.28
When you have finished c. it, Eze 43.23
offer for your c. what Moses Mk 1.44
and make an offering for your c., Lk 5.14

CLEAR
Or how can we c. ourselves? Gen 44.16
he that struck him shall be c.; Ex 21.19
the owner of the ox shall be c. 21.28
who will by no means c. the guilty, 34.07
and you shall c. out the old to Lev 26.10
he will by no means c. the guilty, Num 14.18
your God will c. away these Deu 7.22
and there c. ground for yourselves Jos 17.15
you shall c. it and possess it to 17.18
have made it c. today that commanders 2Sa 19.06
All this he made c. by the writing 1Ch 28.19
understand that is not c. to us? Job 15.09
C. thou me from hidden faults. Ps 19.12
Thou didst c. the ground for it; 80.09
dwelling like c. heat in sunshine, Is 18.04
c. it of stones, lift up an ensign 62.10
Then I will make their waters c., Eze 32.14
and to drink of c. water, that you 34.18
and I will not c. the guilty, Joe 3.21
will by no means c. the guilty. Nah 1.03
and he will c. his threshing floor Mt 3.12
to c. his threshing floor, and to Lk 3.17
pains to have a c. conscience Ac 24.16
what eagerness to c. yourselves, 2Co 7.11
This is a c. omen to them of their Php 1.28
that I may make it c., as I ought Col 4.04
of the faith with a c. conscience. 1Ti 3.09
whom I serve with a c. conscience, 2Ti 1.03
thus make it c. that they are Heb 11.14
sure that we have a c. conscience, 13.18
and keep your conscience c., 1Pe 3.16
appeal to God for a c. conscience, 3.21
like a jasper, c. as crystal. Rev 21.11
city was pure gold, c. as glass. 21.18

CLEARED
the wind has passed and c. them. Job 37.21
He digged it and c. it of stones, Is 5.02

CLEARLY
c., and not in dark speech; Num 12.08
the book, from the law of God, c.; Neh 8.08
days you will understand it c. Jer 23.20
you will see c. to take the speck Mt 7.05
restored, and saw everything c. Mk 8.25
you will see c. to take out the Lk 6.42
that it may be c. seen that his Jn 3.21
the day he saw c. in a vision an Ac 10.03
has been c. perceived in the things Rom 1.20

CLEARNESS
stone, like the very heaven for c. Ex 24.10

CLEARS
and c. away many nations before you, Deu 7.01

CLEAVE
of Israel shall c. to the inheritance Num 36.07
of Israel shall c. to its own 36.09
you shall serve him and c. to him, Deu 10.20
you shall serve him and c. to him. 13.04
things shall c. to your hand; 13.17
the pestilence c. to you until he 28.21
afraid of; and they shall c. to you. 28.60
and to c. to him, and to serve him Jos 22.05
but c. to the LORD your God as you 23.08
leprosy of Naaman shall c. to you, 2Ki 5.27
My bones c. to my skin and to my Job 19.20
and the clods c. fast together? 38.38
The folds of his flesh c. together, 41.23
Thou didst c. open springs and Ps 74.15
fall away; it shall not c. to me. 101.03
groaning my bones c. to my flesh. 102.05
I c. to thy testimonies, O LORD; 119.31
Let my tongue c. to the roof of my 137.06
them and will c. to the house of Is 14.01
your tongue c. to the roof of your Eze 3.26
Thou didst c. the earth with rivers Hab 3.09

CLEAVED
their tongue c. to the roof of Job 29.10
and if any spot has c. to my hands; 31.07

CLEAVES
and his mother and c. to his wife, Gen 2.24
and my tongue c. to my jaws; Ps 22.15
our body c. to the ground. 44.25
Because he c. to me in love, I will 91.14
My soul c. to the dust; 119.25
rock which one c. and shatters on 141.07
of the nursling c. to the roof of Lam 4.04

CLEAVING
in all his ways, and c. to him, Deu 11.22
obeying his voice, and c. to him; 30.20

CLEFT
I will put you in a c. of the rock, Ex 33.22
stayed in the c. of the rock of Ju 15.08
down to the c. of the rock of Etam, 15.11
"Who has c. a channel for the Job 38.25
He c. rocks in the wilderness, and Ps 78.15
he c. the rock and the water gushed Is 48.21
hide it there in a c. of the rock." Jer 13.04
him and the valleys will be c., Mic 1.04

CLEFTS
in the c. of the rock, in the covert Sol 2.14
the rocks and the c. of the cliffs, Is 2.21
and in the c. of the rocks, and on 7.19
valleys, under the c. of the rocks? 57.05
and out of the c. of the rocks. Jer 16.16
you who live in the c. of the rock, 49.16
you who live in the c. of the rock, Ob 1.03

CLEMENT
together with C. and the rest of Php 4.03

CLEOPAS
named C., answered him, "Are you the Lk 24.18

CLERK
And when the town c. had quieted Ac 19.35

CLEVER
cleverness of the c. I will thwart." 1Co 1.19

CLEVERLY
did not follow c. devised myths 2Pe 1.16

CLEVERNESS
and the c. of the clever I will thwart." 1Co 1.19

CLIFF
the rock, in the covert of the c., Sol 2.14

CLIFFS
the rocks and the clefts of the c., Is 2.21
and the c. shall fall, and every Eze 38.20

CLIMB
I say I will c. the palm tree and Sol 7.08
they c. among rocks; all the cities Jer 4.29
they c. up into the houses, they Joe 2.09
though they c. up to heaven, from Amo 9.02

CLIMBED
Then Jonathan c. up on his hands 1Sa 14.13
on ahead and c. up into a sycamore Lk 19.04

CLIMBS
and he who c. out of the pit shall Is 24.18
and he who c. out of the pit shall Jer 48.44
by the door but c. in by another Jn 10.01

CLING
and c. to the rock for want of Job 24.08
the whole house of Judah c. to me, Jer 13.11

CLINGS
My soul c. to thee; Ps 63.08
the waistcloth c. to the loins of Jer 13.11
of your town that c. to our feet, Lk 10.11
and sin which c. so closely, and let Heb 12.01

CLOAK
corners of your c. with which you Deu 22.12
may sleep in his c. and bless you; 24.13
a shepherd cleans his c. of vermin; Jer 43.12
coat, let him have your c. as well; Mt 5.40
And they clothed him in a purple c., Mk 15.17
they stripped him of the purple c., 15.20
takes away your c. do not withhold Lk 6.29
or a c. for greed, as God is witness 1Th 2.05
bring the c. that I left with 2Ti 4.13

CLOAKS
the mantles, the c., and the handbags; Is 3.22

CLODS
The c. of the valley are sweet to Job 21.33
a mass and the c. cleave fast 38.38
The seed shrivels under the c., Joe 1.17

CLOGGING
c. their chariot wheels so that Ex 14.25

CLOPAS
sister, Mary the wife of C., Jn 19.25

CLOSE
and followed c. after him into the Gen 31.23
Joseph's hand shall c. your eyes." 46.04
C. to the frame the rings shall lie, Ex 25.27
C. to the frame were the rings, as 37.14
taking it away c. by the backbone, Lev 3.09
Behold, the day draws to its c.; Ju 19.09
that disaster was c. upon them. 20.34
saw that disaster was c. upon them. 20.41
one, but keep c. to my maidens. Ru 2.08
'You shall keep c. by my servants, 2.21
So she kept c. to the maidens of 2.23
and the horsemen were c. upon him. 2Sa 1.06
and let us c. the doors of the Neh 6.10
My kinsfolk and my c. friends have Job 19.14
They c. their hearts to pity; Ps 17.10
or the pit c. its mouth over me. Ps 69.15
Afflicted and c. to death from my 88.15
they c. in upon me together. 88.17
a whisperer separates c. friends. Pro 16.28
its time is c. at hand and its days Is 13.22
'Do not c. thine ear to my cry for Lam 3.56
I saw him come c. to the ram, and he Dan 8.07
and plague followed c. behind. Hab 3.05
the harvest is the c. of the age, Mt 13.39
so will it be at the c. of the age. 13.40
So it will be at the c. of the age. 13.49
coming and of the c. of the age?" 24.03
you always, to the c. of the age." 28.20
was lying c. to the breast of Jesus; Jn 13.23
So lying thus, c. to the breast of 13.25
Preparation, as the tomb was c. at hand, 19.42
who had lain c. to his breast at 21.20
together his kinsmen and c. friends. Ac 10.24
and sailed along Crete, c. inshore. 27.13
to do right, evil lies c. at hand. Rom 7.21

CLOSED
of his ribs and c. up its place Gen 2.21
the windows of the heavens were c., 8.02
For the LORD had c. all the wombs 20.18
and the earth c. over them, and they Num 16.33
and when the gate was to be c., Jos 2.05
and the fat c. over the blade, for Ju 3.22
and c. the doors of the roof 3.23
because the LORD had c. her womb. 1Sa 1.05
because the LORD had c. her womb. 1.06
and c. up the breach of the city of 1Ki 11.27
This same Hezekiah c. the upper 2Ch 32.30
breaches were beginning to be c., Neh 4.07
Since thou hast c. their minds to Job 17.04
and c. his net about me. 19.06
and has c. your eyes, the prophets, Is 29.10
of those who see will not be c., 32.03
him that gates may not be c.: 45.01
Behold their ears are c., they cannot Jer 6.10
water c. over my head; I said, Lam 3.54
The waters c. in over me, the deep Jon 2.05
land whose bars c. upon me for 2.06
and their eyes they have c., Mt 13.15
And he c. the book, and gave it back Lk 4.20
and their eyes they have c.; Ac 28.27

CLOSELY
I looked at it c. in the morning, 1Ki 3.21
shields, shut up c. as with a seal. Job 41.15
all things c. for some time past, Lk 1.03
Looking at it c. I observed animals Ac 11.06
inquire somewhat more c. about him. 23.20
weight, and sin which clings so c., Heb 12.01

CLOSER
who sticks c. than a brother. Pro 18.24
Therefore we must pay the c. Heb 2.01

CLOSES
when he c. his lips, he is deemed Pro 17.28
He who c. his ear to the cry of the 21.13
yet c. his heart against him, how 1Jn 3.17

CLOSET
himself in the c. of the cool Ju 3.24

CLOSING
his men were c. in upon David and 1Sa 23.26
Thou dost hold my eyelids from c.; Ps 77.04

CLOTH

a garment of c. made of two kinds Lev 19.19
spread over that a c. all of blue, Num 4.06
they shall spread a c. of blue, 4.07
spread over them a c. of scarlet, 4.08
And they shall take a c. of blue, 4.09
they shall spread a c. of blue, 4.11
and put them in a c. of blue, 4.12
and spread a purple c. over it; 4.13
wrapped in a c. behind the ephod; 1Sa 21.09
embroidered c. and shod you with Eze 6.10
and silk, and embroidered c.; 16.13
of unshrunk c. on an old garment, Mt 9.16
of unshrunk c. on an old garment; Mk 2.21
but a linen c. about his body; 14.51
left the linen c. and ran away 14.52
and his face wrapped with a c. Jn 11.44

CLOTHE

she sent garments to c. Mordecai, Est 4.04
Thou didst c. me with skin and Job 10.11
Do you c. his neck with strength? 39.19
c. yourself with glory and splendor. 40.10
the meadows c. themselves with Ps 65.13
Her priests I will c. with salvation, 132.16
His enemies I will c. with shame, 132.18
drowsiness will c. a man with rags. Pro 23.21
and I will c. him with your robe, Is 22.21
I c. the heavens with blackness, and 50.03
they will c. themselves with Eze 26.16
I will c. Lebanon in gloom for it, 31.15
you c. yourselves with the wool, you 34.03
you c. yourselves, but no one is Hag 1.06
and I will c. you with rich apparel." Zec 3.04
oven, will he not much more c. you, Mt 6.30
welcome thee, or naked and c. thee? 25.38
me, naked and you did not c. me, 25.43
oven, how much more will he c. you, Lk 12.28
C. yourselves, all of you, with 1Pe 5.05
garments to c. you and to keep the Rev 3.18

CLOTHED

garments of skins, and c. them. Gen 3.21
and c. him with the robe, and put Lev 8.07
and c. them with coats, and girded 8.13
Then Saul c. David with his armor; 1Sa 17.38
and c. him with a coat of mail. 17.38
who c. you daintily in scarlet, who 2Sa 1.24
David was c. with a robe of fine 1Ch 15.27
c. in sackcloth, fell upon their 21.16
be c. with salvation, and let thy 2Ch 6.41
the spoil they c. all that were 28.15
they c. them, gave them sandals, 28.15
the king's gate c. with sackcloth. Est 4.02
My flesh is c. with worms and dirt; Job 7.05
who hate you will be c. with shame, 8.22
put on righteousness, and it c. me; 29.14
God is c. with terrible majesty. 37.22
Let them be c. with shame and Ps 35.26
Thou art c. with honor and majesty, 104.01
He c. himself with cursing as his 109.18
May my accusers be c. with dishonor; 109.29
Let thy priests be c. with righteousness, 132.09
her household are c. in scarlet. Pro 31.21
c. with the slain, those pierced by Is 14.19
c. with sackcloth, to the prophet 37.02
for he has c. me with the garments 61.10
with them was a man c. in linen, Eze 9.02
he called to the man c. in linen, 9.03
the man c. in linen, with the 9.11
And he said to the man c. in linen, 10.02
he commanded the man c. in linen, 10.06
the hands of the man c. in linen, 10.07
I c. you also with embroidered 16.10
warriors c. in purple, governors and 23.06
warriors c. in full armor, horsemen 23.12
all of them c. in full armor, a 38.04
shall be c. with purple, and have a Dan 5.07
you shall be c. with purple, and 5.16
and Daniel was c. with purple, 5.29
a man c. in linen, whose loins were 10.05
And I said to the man c. in linen, 12.06
The man c. in linen, who was above 12.07
his soldiers are c. in scarlet, Nah 2.03
angel, c. with filthy garments. Zec 3.03
on his head and c. him with 3.05
To see a man c. in soft rainment? Mt 11.08
I was naked and you c. me, I was sick 25.36
Now John was c. with camel's hair, Mk 1.06
c. and in his right mind, the man 5.15
And they c. him in a purple cloak, 15.17
A man c. in soft raiment? Behold, Lk 7.25
c. and in his right mind; and they 8.35
who was c. in purple and fine linen 16.19
until you are c. with power from on 24.49
but that we would be further c., 2Co 5.04
c. with a long robe and with a Rev 1.13
c. in white robes, with palm branches 7.09
c. in white robes, and whence have 7.13
and sixty days, c. in sackcloth. 11.03
a woman c. with the sun, with the 12.01
city that was c. in fine linen, 18.16
her to be c. with fine linen, 19.08

CLOTHES

in the pit, he rent his c. Gen 37.29
shaved himself and changed his c., 41.14
Then they rent their c., 44.13
loose, and do not rend your c., Lev 10.06
shall wash his c. and be unclean 11.25
shall wash his c. and be unclean 11.28
shall wash his c. and be unclean 11.40
carries the carcass shall wash his c. 11.40
he shall wash his c., and be clean. 13.06
he shall wash his c., and be clean. 13.34
shall wear torn c. and let the 13.45
to be cleansed shall wash his c., 14.08
Then he shall wash his c., 14.09
in the house shall wash his c.; 14.47
in the house shall wash his c.; 14.47
touches his bed shall wash his c., 15.05
discharge has sat shall wash his c., 15.06
the discharge shall wash his c., 15.07
clean, then he shall wash his c.. 15.08
such a thing shall wash his c., 15.10
hands in water shall wash his c., 15.11
for his cleansing, and wash his c.; 15.13
touches her bed shall wash his c., 15.21
which she sits shall wash his c., 15.22
be unclean, and shall wash his c., 15.27
shall wash his c. and bathe his 16.26
shall wash his c. and bathe his 16.28
or a sojourner, shall wash his c., 17.15
head hang loose, nor rend his c.; 21.10
and wash their c. and cleanse Num 8.07
from sin, and washed their c.; 8.21
spied out the land, rent their c., 14.06
shall wash his c. and bathe his 19.07
shall wash his c. in water and 19.08
of the heifer shall wash his c., 19.10
shall wash his c. and bathe 19.19
for impurity shall wash his c.; 19.21
You must wash your c. on the 31.24
your c. have not worn out upon you, Deu 29.05
Then Joshua rent his c., Jos 7.06
on their feet, and worn-out c.; 9.05
it on his right thigh under his c. Ju 3.16
he rent his c., and said, "Alas, my 11.35
on your best c. and go down to the Ru 3.03
with his c. rent and with earth 1Sa 4.12
head, and covered it with the c. 19.13
And he too stripped off his c., 19.24
with his c. rent and earth upon his 2Sa 1.02
took hold of his c., and rent them; 1.11

CLOTHES (cont.)
"Rend your c., and gird on sackcloth, 2Sa 3.31
himself, and changed his c.; 12.20
his beard, nor washed his c.. 19.24
although they covered him with c., 1Ki 1.01
he rent his c., and put sackcloth 21.27
hold of his own c. and rent them 2Ki 2.12
he rent his c. and said, "Am I God, 5.07
the king of Israel had rent his c., 5.08
saying, "Why have you rent your c.? 5.08
words of the woman he rent his c.— 6.30
And Athaliah rent her c., 11.14
to Hezekiah with their c. rent, 18.37
he rent his c., and covered himself 19.01
book of the law, he rent his c. 22.11
have rent your c. and wept before 22.19
And Athaliah rent her c., 2Ch 23.13
words of the law he rent his c. 34.19
have rent your c. and wept before 34.27
me, none of us took off our c.; Neh 4.23
their c. did not wear out and their 9.21
rent his c. and put on sackcloth Est 4.01
a pit, and my own c. will abhor me. Job 9.31
his bosom and his c. not be burned? Pro 6.27
our own bread and wear our own c., Is 4.01
to Hezekiah with their c. rent, 36.22
he rent his c., and covered himself 37.01
there old rags and worn-out c., Jer 38.11
the rags and c. between your 38.12
beards shaved and their c. torn, 41.05
you of your c. and take your fair Eze 16.39
you of your c. and take away your 23.26
in c. of blue and embroidered work, 27.24
But if God so c. the grass of the Mt 6.30
robe, and put his own c. on him, 27.31
cloak, and put his own c. on him. Mk 15.20
or a long time he had worn no c., Lk 8.27
But if God so c. the grass which is 12.28
he put on his c., for he was Jn 21.07

CLOTHING
me bread to eat and c. to wear, Gen 28.20
and c., and you shall put them on Ex 3.22
of silver and of gold, and c.; 12.35
her c., or her marital rights. 21.10
for c., or for any kind of lost 22.09
Your c. did not wear out upon you, Deu 8.04
sojourner, giving him food and c. 10.18
bronze, and iron, and with much c.; Jos 22.08
their c., his cupbearers, and his 1Ki 10.05
carried off silver and gold and c., 2Ki 7.08
and their c., his cupbearers, and 2Ch 9.04
and their c., and his burnt offerings 9.04
c., and precious things, which they 20.25
and stripped the naked of their c. Job 22.06
without c., and have no covering in 24.07
They go about naked, without c.; 24.10
dust, and pile up c. like clay; 27.16
seen any one perish for lack of c., 31.19
When I made sackcloth my c., Ps 69.11
the lambs will provide your c., Pro 27.26
her c. is fine linen and purple. 31.22
Strength and dignity are her c., 31.25
food and fine c. for those who Is 23.18
Their webs will not serve as c.; 59.06
on garments of vengeance for c., 59.17
their c. is violet and purple; Jer 10.09
food, and the body more than c.? Mt 6.25
And why are you anxious about c.? 6.28
you in sheep's c. but inwardly are 7.15
food, and the body more than c. Lk 12.23
them, and for my c. they cast lots." Jn 19.24
but if we have food and c., with these 1Ti 6.08
and in fine c. comes into your Jas 2.02
man in shabby c. also comes in, 2.02
one who wears the fine c. and say, 2.03

CLOTHS
and wrapped him in swaddling c., Lk 2.07
in swaddling c. and lying in a 2.12
he saw the linen c. by themselves; * 24.12
it in linen c. with the spices, as Jn 19.40
he saw the linen c. lying there, 20.05
he saw the linen c. lying, 20.06
with the linen c. but rolled up in 20.07

CLOUD
I set my bow in the c., Gen 9.13
in a pillar of c. to lead them Ex 13.21
the pillar of c. by day and the 13.22
the pillar of c. moved from before 14.19
there was the c. and the darkness; 14.20
of fire and of c. looked down upon 14.24
of the LORD appeared in the c. 16.10
I am coming to you in a thick c., 19.09
and a thick c. upon the mountain, 19.16
near to the thick c. where God was. 20.21
and the c. covered the mountain. 24.15
and the c. covered it six days; 24.16
Moses out of the midst of the c. 24.16
And Moses entered the c., 24.18
the pillar of c. would descend and 33.09
the pillar of c. standing at the 33.10
descended in the c. and stood with 34.05
Then the c. covered the tent of 40.34
because the c. abode upon it, and 40.35
whenever the c. was taken up from 40.36
but if the c. was not taken up, then 40.37
journeys the c. of the LORD was 40.38
appear in the c. upon the mercy Lev 16.02
that the c. of the incense may 16.13
the c. covered the tabernacle, the Num 9.15
the c. covered it by day, and the 9.16
And whenever the c. was taken up 9.17
place where the c. settled down, 9.17
as long as the c. rested over the 9.18
Even when the c. continued over the 9.19
Sometimes the c. was a few days 9.20
And sometimes the c. remained from 9.21
and when the c. was taken up in the 9.21
when the c. was taken up they set 9.21
that the c. continued over the 9.22
the c. was taken up from over the 10.11
and the c. settled down in the 10.12
And the c. of the LORD was over 10.34
down in the c. and spoke to him, 11.25
LORD came down in a pillar of c., 12.05
and when the c. removed from over 12.10
and they c. stands over them and 14.14
in a pillar of c. by day and in a 14.14
the c. covered it, and the glory of 16.42
should go, and in the c. by day. Deu 1.33
wrapped in darkness, c., and gloom. 4.11
the c., and the deep gloom, with a 5.22
in the tent in a pillar of c.; 31.15
the pillar of c. stood by the door 31.15
made a great c. of smoke rise up Ju 20.38
a c. filled the house of the LORD, 1Ki 8.10
to minister because of the c.; 8.11
a little c. like a man's hand is 18.44
of the LORD, was filled with a c., 2Ch 5.13
to minister because of the c.; 5.14
By a pillar of c. thou didst lead Neh 9.12
the pillar of c. which led them in 9.19
As the c. fades and vanishes. so he Job 7.09
and the c. is not rent under them. 26.08
moon, and spreads over it his c. 26.09
prosperity has passed away like a c. 30.15
He loads the thick c. with moisture; 37.11
the lightning of his c. to shine? 37.15
In the daytime he led them with a c., Ps 78.14
He spoke to them in the pillar of c.; 99.07
He spread a c. for a covering, and 105.39
over her assemblies a c. by day. Is 4.05

CLOUD (cont.)
like a c. of dew in the heat of Ps 18.04
on a swift c. and comes to Egypt; 19.01
as heat by the shade of a c., 25.05
away your transgressions like a c., 44.22
Who are these that fly like a c., 60.08
the daughter of Zion under a c.! Lam 2.01
thyself with a c. so that no 3.44
and a great c., with brightness Eze 1.04
that is in the c. on the day of 1.28
smoke of the c. of incense went up 8.11
and a c. filled the inner court. 10.03
the house was filled with the c., 10.04
she shall be covered by a c., 30.18
I will cover the sun with a c., 32.07
will be like a c. covering the 38.09
like a c. covering the land. 38.16
Your love is like a morning c., Hos 6.04
a bright c. overshadowed them, and a Mt 17.05
them, and a voice from the c. said, 17.05
And a c. overshadowed them, and a Mk 9.07
and a voice came out of the c., 9.07
a c. came and overshadowed them; Lk 9.34
were afraid as they entered the c. 9.34
And a voice came out of the c., 9.35
"When you see a c. rising in the 12.54
man coming in a c. with power and 21.27
and a c. took him out of their Ac 1.09
our fathers were all under the c., 1Co 10.01
Moses in the c. and in the sea, 10.02
by so great a c. of witnesses. Heb 12.01
wrapped in a c., with a rainbow Rev 10.01
they went up to heaven in a c.; 11.12
a white c., and seated on the c. one 14.14
voice to him who sat upon the c., 14.15
sat upon the c. swung his sickle 14.16

CLOUDBURST
with a c. and tempest and hailstones. Is 30.30

CLOUDLESS
shining forth upon a c. morning, 2Sa 23.04

CLOUDS
When I bring c. over the earth and Gen 9.14
and the bow is seen in the c., 9.14
When the bow is in the c., 9.16
dropped, yea, the c. dropped water. Ju 5.04
thick c., a gathering of water. 2Sa 22.12
grew black with c. and wind, 1Ki 18.45
Let c. dwell upon it; Job 3.05
and his head reach to the c., 20.06
Thick c. enwrap him, so that he does 22.14
up the waters in his thick c., 26.08
and behold the c., 35.05
understand the spreading of the c., 36.29
the c. scatter his lightning. 37.11
Do you know the balancings of the c., 37.16
when I made c. its garment, and 38.09
"Can you lift up your voice to the c., 38.34
Who has put wisdom in the c., 38.36
Who can number the c. by wisdom? 38.37
canopy thick c. dark with water. Ps 18.11
through his c. hailstones and 18.12
heavens, thy faithfulness to the c. 36.05
heavens, thy faithfulness to the c. 57.10
song to him who rides upon the c.; 68.04
The c. poured out water; the skies 77.17
C. and thick darkness are round 97.02
who makest the c. thy chariot, 104.03
thy faithfulness reaches to the c. 108.04
who makes the c. rise at the end 135.07
He covers the heavens with c., 147.08
and the c. drop down the dew. Pro 3.20
is like the c. that bring the 16.15
Like c. and wind without rain is a 25.14
If the c. are full of rain, they Ecc 11.03
who regards the c. will not reap. 11.04
darkened and the c. return after 12.02
command the c. that they rain no Is 5.06
the light is darkened by its c. 5.30
ascend above the heights of the c., 14.14
Behold, he comes up like c., Jer 4.13
it will be a day of c., a time Eze 30.03
great height, its top among the c. 31.03
high and set its top among the c., 31.10
or set their tops among the c., and 31.14
on a day of c. and thick darkness. 34.12
with the c. of heaven there came Dan 7.13
a day of c. and thick darkness! Joe 2.02
and the c. are the dust of his feet. Nah 1.03
scribes like c. of locusts settling 3.17
a day of c. and thick darkness, Zep 1.15
the LORD who makes the storm c., Zec 10.01
coming on the c. of heaven with Mt 24.30
and coming on the c. of heaven." 26.64
man coming in c. with great power Mk 13.26
and coming with the c. of heaven." 14.62
them in the c. to meet the Lord in 1Th 4.17
waterless c., carried along by Jud 1.12
Behold, he is coming with the c., Rev 1.07

CLOVE
and his hand c. to the sword; 2Sa 23.10

CLOVEN
hoof and has the hoof c. in two, Deu 14.06
have the hoof c. you shall not eat 14.07

CLOVEN-FOOTED
the hoof and is c. and chews the Lev 11.03
the hoof and is c. but does not 11.07
hoof but is not c. or does not 11.26

CLUB
his neighbor is like a war c., Pro 25.18

CLUBS
C. are counted as stubble; Job 41.29
a great crowd with swords and c.. Mt 26.47
with swords and c. to capture me? 26.55
him a crowd with swords and c., Mk 14.43
with swords and c. to capture me? 14.48
a robber, with swords and c.? Lk 22.52

CLUNG
mother-in-law, but Ruth c. to her. Ru 1.14
Solomon c. to these in love. 1Ki 11.02
Nevertheless he c. to the sin of 2Ki 3.03
While he c. to Peter and John, all Ac 3.11

CLUSTER
branch with a single c. of grapes, Num 13.23
because of the c. which the men of 13.24
is to me a c. of henna blossoms in Sol 1.14
"As the wine is found in the c., Is 65.08
there is no c. to eat, no first-ripe Mic 7.01

CLUSTERS
and the c. ripened into grapes. Gen 40.10
of poison, their c. are bitter; Deu 32.32
and a hundred c. of raisins, and two 1Sa 25.18
cake of figs and two c. of raisins. 30.12
c. of raisins, and wine and oil, oxen 1Ch 12.40
and your breasts are like its c. Sol 7.07
breasts be like c. of the vine, 7.08
and gather the c. of the vine of Rev 14.18

CNIDUS
and arrived with difficulty off C., Ac 27.07

COAL
would quench my c. which is left, 2Sa 14.07
hand a burning c. which he had Is 6.06
No c. for warming oneself is this, 47.14

COALS
censer full of c. of fire from the Lev 16.12
glowing c. flamed forth from him. 2Sa 22.09
before him c. of fire flamed forth. 22.13
His breath kindles c., and a Job 41.21
he will rain c. of fire and Ps 11.06
glowing c. flamed forth from him. 18.08
clouds hailstones and c. of fire. 18.12
voice, hailstones and c. of fire. 18.13
with glowing c. of the broom tree! 120.04
Let burning c. fall upon them! 140.10
walk upon hot c. and his feet not Pro 6.28
for you will heap c. of fire on his 25.22
it and works it over the c.; Is 44.12
fire, I also baked bread on its c., 44.19
the smith who blows the fire of c., 54.16
looked like burning c. of fire, Eze 1.13
with burning c. from between the 10.02
Then set it empty upon the c., 24.11
will heap burning c. upon his head." Rom 12.20

COARSE
first of your c. meal you shall Num 15.20
first of your c. meal you shall 15.21
and to bring the first of our c. meal, Neh 10.37
priests the first of your c. meal, Eze 44.30

COAST
have the Great Sea and its c.; Num 34.06
all along the c. of the Great Sea Jos 9.01
sat still at the c. of the sea, Ju 5.17
Be still, O inhabitants of the c., Is 23.02
wail, O inhabitants of the c.! 23.06
to the ports along the c. of Asia, Ac 27.02

COASTING
C. along it with difficulty, we came Ac 27.08

COASTLAND
From these the c. peoples spread. Gen 10.05
inhabitants of this c. will say in Is 20.06
the kings of the c. across the sea; Jer 25.22
the remnant of the c. of Caphtor. 47.04

COASTLANDS
the land and on the c. of the sea. Est 10.01
let the many c. be glad! Ps 97.01
Hamath, and from the c. of the sea. Is 11.11
in the c. of the sea, to the name of 24.15
Listen to me in silence, O c.; 41.01
The c. have seen and are afraid, the 41.05
and the c. wait for his law. 42.04
the c. and their inhabitants. 42.10
and declare his praise in the c. 42.12
O c., and hearken, you peoples from 49.01
the c. wait for me, and for my arm 51.05
to the c. he will render requital. 59.18
For the c. shall wait for me, the 60.09
to the c. afar off, that have not 66.19
and declare it in the c. afar off; Jer 31.10
Will not the c. shake at the sound Eze 26.15
merchant of the peoples on many c., 27.03
many c. were your own special 27.15
inhabitants of the c. are appalled 27.35
those who dwell securely in the c.; 39.06
Afterward he shall turn his face to the c., Dan 11.18

COAST-LINE
was the Great Sea with its c. Jos 15.12
and the great sea with its c. 15.47

COASTS
For cross to the c. of Cyprus and Jer 2.10
of pines from the c. of Cyprus, Eze 27.06
purple from the c. of Elishah was 27.07

COAT
a c. of checker work, a turban, and a Ex 28.04
shall weave the c. in checker work 28.39
on Aaron the c. and the robe of 29.05
And he put on him the c., Lev 8.07
He shall put on the holy linen c., 16.04
and he was armed with a c. of mail, 1Sa 17.05
weight of the c. was five thousand 17.05
and clothed him with a c. of mail. 17.38
him with his c. rent and earth 2Sa 15.32
penetrate his double c. of mail? Job 41.13
himself with cursing as his c., Ps 109.18
him not stand up in his c. of mail. Jer 51.03
one would sue you and take your c., Mt 5.40
do not withhold your c. as well. Lk 6.29

COATS
you shall make c. and girdles and Ex 28.40
his sons, and put c. on them, 29.08
They also made the c., woven 39.27
his sons also and put c. on them, 40.14
sons, and clothed them with c., Lev 8.13
them in their c. out of the camp, 10.05
c. of mail, bows, and stones for 2Ch 26.14
shields, bows, and c. of mail; Neh 4.16
spears, put on your c. of mail! Jer 46.04
answered them, "He who has two c., Lk 3.11
and showing c. and garments which Ac 9.39

COCK
the strutting c., the he-goat, and a Pro 30.31
before the c. crows, you will deny Mt 26.34
And immediately the c. crowed. 26.74
"Before the c. crows, you will deny 26.75
before the c. crows twice, you will Mk 14.30
And immediately the c. crowed a 14.72
"Before the c. crows twice, you will 14.72
the c. will not crow this day, until Lk 22.34
was still speaking, the c. crowed. 22.60
"Before the c. crows today, you will 22.61
the c. will not crow, till you have Jn 13.38
and at once the c. crowed. 18.27

COCKCROW
or at c., or in the morning— Mk 13.35

CODE
the written c. and circumcision Rom 2.27
the old written c. but in the new 7.06
in a written c. but in the Spirit; 2Co 3.06
for the written c. kills, 3.06

COFFIN
and he was put in a c. in Egypt. Gen 50.26

COHORT
what was known as the Italian C., Ac 10.01
tribune of the c. that all Jerusalem 21.31
of the Augustan C., named Julius. 27.01

COIN
And they brought him a c. Mt 22.19
Bring me a c., and let me look at Mk 12.15
silver coins, if she loses one c., Lk 15.08
have found the c. which I had lost.' 15.09
"Show me a c. Whose likeness 20.24

COINS
came, and put in two copper c., Mk 12.42
"Or what woman, having ten silver c., Lk 15.08
a poor widow put in two copper c. 21.02
poured out the c. of the money-changers Jn 2.15

COLD
c. and heat, summer and winter, day Gen 8.22
and the c. by night, and my sleep 31.40
and have no covering in the c. Job 24.07
and c. from the scattering winds. 37.09
who can stand before his c.? Ps 147.17
Like the c. of snow in the time of Pro 25.13
takes off a garment on a c. day, 25.20

COLD (cont.)
Like c. water to a thirsty soul, so Pro 25.25
run dry, the c. flowing streams? Jer 18.14
on the fences in a day of c.— Nah 3.17
shall be neither c. nor frost. Zec 14.06
even a cup of c. water because he Mt 10.42
most men's love will grow c. 24.12
a charcoal fire, because it was c., Jn 18.18
it had begun to rain and was c. Ac 28.02
without food, in c. and exposure. 2Co 11.27
works: you are neither c. nor hot. Rev 3.15
Would that you were c. or hot! 3.15
and neither c. nor hot, I will spew 3.16

COLHOZEH
And Shallum the son of C., ruler Neh 3.15
son of C. son of Hazaiah, son of 11.05

COLLAPSE
They will c. and fall; but we Ps 20.08
and about to c., whose crash comes Is 30.13

COLLAR
me about like the c. of my tunic. Job 30.18
his neck was put in a c. of iron; Ps 105.18
down on the c. of his robes! 133.02
to put him in the stocks and c. Jer 29.26

COLLARS
and besides the c. that were about Ju 8.26

COLLECT
the Levites who c. the tithes in Neh 10.37
c. all your strength. Nah 2.01
"C. no more than is appointed you." Lk 3.13

COLLECTED
worthless fellows c. round Jephthah, Ju 11.03
threshold have c. from the people; 2Ki 22.04
and c. money in abundance. 2Ch 24.11
had c. from Manasseh and Ephraim 34.09
fixed are the c. sayings which are Ecc 12.11
and you c. the waters of the lower Is 22.09
nations round about shall be c., Zec 14.14
I should have c. it with interest?' Lk 19.23

COLLECTION
let your c. of idols deliver you! Is 57.13

COLLECTOR
Thomas and Matthew the tax c.; Mt 10.03
to you as a Gentile and a tax c. 18.17
and saw a tax c., named Levi, Lk 5.27
a Pharisee and the other a tax c. 18.10
adulterers, or even like this tax c. 18.11
But the tax c., standing far off, 18.13
he was a chief tax c., and rich. 19.02

COLLECTORS
Do not even the tax c. do the same? Mt 5.46
many tax c. and sinners came and 9.10
eat with tax c. and sinners?" 9.11
a friend of tax c. and sinners!' 11.19
the c. of the half-shekel tax went 17.24
the tax c. and the harlots go into 21.31
but the tax c. and the harlots 21.32
many tax c. and sinners were Mk 2.15
was eating with sinners and tax c., 2.16
he eat with tax c. and sinners?" 2.16
Tax c. also came to be baptized, and Lk 3.12
company of tax c. and others 5.29
and drink with tax c. and sinners?" 5.30
and the tax c. justified God, 7.29
a friend of tax c. and sinners!' 7.34
Now the tax c. and sinners were all 15.01

COLLECTS
and c. as his own all peoples. Hab 2.05

COLONY
of Macedonia, and a Roman c. Ac 16.12

COLOR
diseased spot has not changed c., Lev 13.55
Then the king's c. changed, and his Dan 5.06
alarmed, and his c. changed; and his 5.09
thoughts alarm you or your c. change. 5.10
alarmed me, and my c. changed; 7.28
breastplates the c. of fire and of Rev 9.17

COLORED
c. stones, all sorts of precious 1Ch 29.02
c. spreads of Egyptian linen; Pro 7.16
work, and in carpets of c. stuff, Eze 27.24

COLORS
pinions, rich in plumage of many c., Eze 17.03

COLOSSAE
faithful brethren in Christ at C.: Col 1.02

COLT
and his ass's c. to the choice Gen 49.11
when a wild ass's c. is born a man. Job 11.12
an ass, on a c. the foal of an ass. Zec 9.09
an ass tied, and a c. with her; Mt 21.02
and on a c., the foal of an ass." 21.05
they brought the ass and the c., 21.07
enter it you will find a c. tied, Mk 11.02
and found a c. tied at the door out 11.04
"What are you doing, untying the c.?" 11.05
And they brought the c. to Jesus, 11.07
entering you will find a c. tied, Lk 19.30
And as they were untying the c., 19.33
them, "Why are you untying the c.?" 19.33
garments on the c. they set Jesus 19.35
is coming, sitting on an ass's c.!" Jn 12.15

COLTS
thirty milch camels and their c., Gen 32.15

COLUMN
out of the city in a c. of smoke, Ju 20.40
like a c. of smoke, perfumed with Sol 3.06
they roll upward in a c. of smoke. Is 9.18

COLUMNS
His legs are alabaster c., Sol 5.15
As Jehudi read three or four c., Jer 36.23
blood and fire and c. of smoke. Joe 2.30

COMBAT
And he set c. commanders over the 2Ch 32.06

COMBED
The workers in c. flax will be in Is 19.09

COME
and you shall c. into the ark, you, Gen 6.18
two of every sort shall c. in to you, 6.20
When they had c. to the land of Canaan, 12.05
they shall c. out with great possessions. 15.14
And they shall c. back here in the 15.16
where have you c. from and where are 16.08
and kings shall c. forth from you. 17.06
since you have c. to your servant." 18.05
to the outcry which has c. to me, 18.21
they have c. under the shelter of my roof." 19.08
a man on earth to c. in to us after 19.31
C., let us make our father drink 19.32
at every place to which we c., say of 20.13
worship, and c. again to you." 22.05
He said, "C. in, O blessed of the LORD; 24.31
my oath, when you c. to my kindred; 24.41
Isaac had c. from Beerlahairoi, and was 24.62
"Why have you c. to me, seeing that you 26.27
"C. near, that I may feel you, my 27.21

COME (cont.)

him, "C. near and kiss me, my son." Gen 27.26
so that I c. again to my father's house 28.21
"You must c. in to me; for I have hired 30.16
when you c. to look into my wages 30.33
C. now, let us make a covenant, 31.44
fear him, lest he come and slay us 32.11
children, until I c. to my lord in Seir." 33.14
a company of nations shall c. from you, 35.11
c. to bow ourselves to the ground before 37.10
C., I will send you to them." And he 37.13
C. now, let us kill him and throw him 37.20
C., let us sell him to the Ishmaelites, 37.27
"C., let me c. in to you," for he did 38.16
you give me, that you may c. in to me?" 38.16
There will c. seven years of great plenty 41.29
seven years of famine began to c., as 41.54
"Where do you c. from?" he said. 42.07
have c. to see the weakness of the land." 42.09
but to buy food have your servants c. 42.10
of the land that you have c. to see." 42.12
therefore is this distress c. upon us." 42.21
Now therefore, when I c. to your servant 44.30
the evil that would c. upon my father." 44.34
"C. near to me, I pray you." And they 45.04
of all Egypt; c. down to me, do not tarry; 45.09
there are yet five years of famine to c.; 45.11
and all that you have, c. to poverty.' 45.11
"Joseph's brothers have c.," it pleased 45.16
father and your households, and c. to me, 45.18
your wives, and bring your father, and c. 45.19
who were in the land of Canaan, have c. to me; 46.31
possess, have c. from the land of Canaan; 47.01
"We have c. to sojourn in the land; for 47.04
"Your father and your brothers have c. to you. 47.05
to Jacob, "Your son Joseph has c. to you"; 48.02
O my soul, c. not into their council; 49.06
C., let us deal shrewdly with them, lest Ex 1.10
is it that you have c. so soon today?" 2.18
and I have c. down to deliver them out 3.08
of the people of Israel has c. to me, 3.09
C., I will send you to Pharaoh that 3.10
"If I c. to the people of Israel and say 3.13
frogs which shall c. up into your house, 8.03
the frogs shall c. up on you and on your 8.04
cause frogs to c. upon the land of Egypt!'" 8.05
hail shall c. down upon every man and 9.19
that they may c. upon the land of Egypt, 10.12
these your servants shall c. down to me, 11.08
when you c. to the land which the LORD 12.25
then he may c. near and keep it; he 12.48
when in time to c. your son asks you, 13.14
water may c. back upon the Egyptians, 14.26
'C. near before the LORD, for he has 16.09
the rock, and water shall c. out of it, 17.06
all the hardship that had c. upon them 18.08
"Because the people c. to me to inquire 18.15
when they have a dispute, they c. to me 18.16
the LORD will c. down upon Mount Sinai 19.11
blast, they shall c. up to the mountain." 19.13
priests who c. near to the LORD consecrate 19.22
"The people cannot c. up to Mount Sinai; 19.23
and c. up bringing Aaron with you; 19.24
people break through to c. up to the 19.24
for God has c. to prove you, and that 20.20
remembered I will c. to you and bless 20.24
case of both parties shall c. before God; 22.09
the people against whom you shall c., 23.27
"C. up to the LORD, you and Aaron, 24.01
Moses alone shall c. near to the LORD; 24.02
the others shall not c. near, and 24.02
the people shall not c. up with him." 24.02
"C. up to me on the mountain, and 24.12
for us, until we c. to you again; 24.14
when they c. near the altar to minister 28.43
they c. near the altar to minister, to 30.20
Moses delayed to c. down from the 32.01
"Who is on the LORD's side? C. to me." 32.26
and c. up in the morning to Mount Sinai, 34.02
No man shall c. up with you, and let 34.03
and they were afraid to c. near him. 34.30
man among you c. and make all that 35.10
heart stirred him up to c. to do the work; 36.02
lest wrath c. upon all the congregation; Lev 10.06
upon which water may c., shall be 11.34
nor c. into the sanctuary, until the days 12.04
to white, then he shall c. to the priest, 13.16
after that he shall c. into the camp, 14.08
"When you c. into the land of Canaan, 14.34
he who owns the house shall c. and tell 14.35
priest shall c. again on the seventh day, 14.39
and c. before the LORD to the door of 15.14
"Tell Aaron your brother not to c. at all 16.02
thus shall Aaron c. into the holy place: 16.03
until he c. out and has made atonement 16.17
"Then Aaron shall c. into the tent of 16.23
and put on his garments, and c. forth, 16.24
afterward he may c. into the camp. 16.26
and afterward he may c. into the camp. 16.28
nor shall there c. upon you a garment 19.19
"When you c. into the land and 19.23
who has a blemish shall c. near to 21.21
not c. near to offer the bread of his 21.21
he shall not c. near the veil or approach 21.23
When you c. into the land which I give 23.10
you c. into the land which I give you, 25.02
his next of kin shall c. and redeem 25.25
they had c. out of the land of Egypt, Num 1.01
sons of Kohath shall c. to carry these, 4.15
no razor shall c. upon his head; 6.05
Israel should c. near the sanctuary." 8.19
they had c. out of the land of Egypt, 9.01
c. with us, and we will do you good; 10.29
I will c. down and talk with you 11.17
my word will c. true for you or not." 11.23
"C. out, you three, to the tent of 12.04
(the sons of Anak, who c. from the 13.33
not one shall c. into the land where 14.30
When you c. into the land you are to 15.02
you c. into the land to which I bring 15.18
and will cause him to c. near to him; 16.05
he will choose he will cause to c. near 16.05
and they said, "We will not c. up. 16.12
of these men? We will not c. up." 16.14
but shall not c. near to the vessels 18.03
and no one else shall c. near you. 18.04
people of Israel shall not c. near the 18.22
and upon which a yoke has never c. 19.02
and afterwards he shall c. into the camp; 19.07
have you made us c. up out of Egypt, 20.05
lest I c. out with the sword against 20.18
"C. to Heshbon, let it be built, let 21.27
"Behold, a people has c. out of Egypt; 22.05
C. now, curse this people for me, 22.06
a people has c. out of Egypt, and it 22.11
now c., curse them for me; perhaps I 22.11
said, "Balaam refuses to c. with us." 22.14
will do; c., curse this people for me.'" 22.17
"If the men have c. to call you, 22.20
When Balak heard that Balaam had c., 22.36
Why did you not c. to me? Am I 22.37
I have c. to you! Have I now any 22.38
perhaps the LORD will c. to meet me; 23.03
'C., curse Jacob for me, and c., denounce 23.07
"C. with me to another place, from 23.13
"C. now, I will take you to another 23.27
c., I will let you know what this people 24.14
a star shall c. forth out of Jacob, 24.17
But ships shall c. from Kittim and 24.24
and at his word they shall c. in, 27.21
who had c. from service in the war. 31.14
afterward you shall c. into the camp." 31.24
of Israel had c. out of the land of Egypt, 33.38
'You have c. to the hill country of Deu 1.20

COME (cont.)
and the cities into which we shall c.' Deu 1.22
all these things c. upon you in the 4.30
"When your son asks you in time to c., 6.20
and c. up to me on the mountain, and 10.01
of Egypt, from which you have c., 11.10
for you have not as yet c. to the rest 12.09
towns, shall c. and eat and be filled; 14.29
"When you c. to the land which the 17.14
and he may c. when he desires—to the 18.06
c. into the land which the LORD your 18.09
word does not c. to pass or c. true, 18.22
the priest shall c. forward and speak to 20.02
elders and your judges shall c. forth, 21.02
priests the sons of Levi shall c. forward 21.05
he shall not c. within the camp; 23.10
is down, he may c. within the camp. 23.11
between men, and they c. into court, 25.01
you c. into the land which the LORD 26.01
God that I have c. into the land 26.03
all these blessings shall c. upon you 28.02
Blessed shall you be when you c. in, 28.06
they shall c. out against you one way, 28.07
curses shall c. upon you and overtake 28.15
Cursed shall you be when you c. in, 28.19
c. down upon you until you are destroyed. 28.24
you shall c. down lower and lower. 28.43
All these curses shall c. upon you 28.45
c. down throughout all your land; 28.52
the generation to c., your children who 29.22
when all these things c. upon you, 30.01
no longer able to go out and c. in. 31.02
evils and troubles will c. upon them, 31.17
when many evils and troubles have c. 31.21
to new gods that had c. in of late, 32.17
Let these c. upon the head of Joseph, 33.16
have c. here tonight to search out the Jos 2.02
"Bring forth the men that have c. to you, 2.03
have c. to search out all the land." 2.03
when we c. into the land, you shall 2.18
thousand cubits; do not c. near it." 3.04
'When you c. to the brink of the 3.08
"C. hither, and hear the words of the 3.09
who bore the ark had c. to the Jordan, 3.15
when your children ask in time to c., 4.06
the ark of the testimony to c. up out 4.16
the priests, "C. up out of the Jordan." 4.17
children ask their fathers in time to c., 4.21
wilderness after they had c. out of 5.04
after they had c. out of Egypt had not 5.05
the army of the LORD I have now c." 5.14
LORD takes shall c. near by families; 7.14
LORD takes shall c. near by households; 7.14
And when they c. out against us, 8.05
and they will c. out after us, till 8.06
"We have c. from a far country; 9.06
are you? And where do you c. from?" 9.08
very far country your servants have c., 9.09
on the day we set forth to c. to you, 9.12
"C. up to me, and help me, and 10.04
c. up to us quickly, and save us, 10.06
"C. near, put your feet upon the necks 10.24
they should c. against Israel in battle, 11.20
their inheritances, and then c. to me. 18.04
description of the land, and c. again to 18.08
that in time to c. your children might 22.24
say to our children in time to c., 22.27
to our descendants in time to c., we 22.28
all have c. to pass for you, not one of 23.14
"C. up with me into the territory Ju 1.03
allow them to c. down to the plain; 1.34
"C., and I will show you the man 4.22
East would c. up and attack them; 6.03
they would c. up with their cattle and 6.05
until I c. to thee, and bring out my 6.18
when I c. to the outskirts of the camp, 7.17
"C. down against the Midianites and 7.24
"When I c. again in peace, I will 8.09
fig tree, 'C. you, and reign over us.' 9.10
vine, 'C. you, and reign over us.' 9.12
bramble, 'C. you, and reign over us.' 9.14
then c. and take refuge in my shade; 9.15
let fire c. out of the bramble and 9.15
let fire c. out from Abimelech, and 9.20
c. out from the citizens of Shechem, 9.20
might c. and their blood be laid upon 9.24
'Increase your army, and c. out.'" 9.29
and his kinsmen have c. to Shechem, 9.31
that are with him c. out against you, 9.33
"C. and be our leader, that we may 11.06
have you c. to me now when you are 11.07
have c. to me to fight against my land?" 11.12
why then have you c. up to me this day, 12.03
No razor shall c. upon his head, for 13.05
whom thou didst send c. again to us, 13.08
when your words c. true, what is to 13.12
words c. true, we may honor you?" 13.17
said, "Why have you c. up against us?" 15.10
"We have c. up to bind Samson, to 15.10
'We have c. down to bind you, that we 15.12
Gazites were told, "Samson has c. here," 16.02
"A razor has never c. upon my head; 16.17
"C. up this once, for he has told me 16.18
to him, "From where do you c.?" 17.09
you will c. to an unsuspecting people. 18.10
you that you c. with such a company?" 18.23
"C. now, let us turn aside to this city 19.11
"C. and let us draw near to one of 19.13
you going? and whence do you c.?" 19.17
seeing that this man has c. into my 19.23
when they c. they may requite Gibeah 20.10
why has this c. to pass in Israel, that 21.03
did not c. up in the assembly to the 21.05
concerning him who did not c. up to 21.05
not c. up to the LORD to Mizpah?" 21.08
no one had c. to the camp from 21.08
daughters of Shiloh c. out to dance 21.21
then c. out of the vineyards and seize 21.21
or their brothers c. to complain to us, 21.22
she happened to c. to the part of the field Ru 2.03
under whose wings you have c. to take 2.12
"C. here, and eat some bread, and dip 2.14
"Naomi, who has c. back from the country 4.03
let not arrogance c. from your mouth; 1Sa 2.03
sacrifice, the priest's servant would c., 2.13
the priest's servant would c. and say 2.15
shall c. to implore him for a piece of 2.36
that he may c. among us and save us from 4.03
that the ark of the LORD had c. to the camp, 4.06
"The gods have c. into the camp." And 4.07
"I am he who has c. from the battle; 4.16
upon which there has never c. a yoke, and 6.07
C. down and take it up to you." 6.21
"C., let us go back, lest my father cease 9.05
"C., let us go to the seer"; for he who 9.09
his servant, "Well said; c., let us go." 9.10
he has c. just now to the city, because 9.12
people, because their cry has c. to me." 9.16
there further and c. to the oak of Tabor; 10.03
you shall c. to Gibeathelohim, where there 10.05
as you c. to the city, you will meet a 10.05
of the LORD will c. mightily upon you, 10.06
until I c. to you and show you what you 10.08
"What has c. over the son of Kish. Is 10.11
the LORD, "Did the man c. hither?" and 10.22
does not c. out after Saul and Samuel, 11.07
they said to the messengers who had c., 11.09
"C., let us go to Gilgal and there renew 11.14
but Samuel did not c. to Gilgal, and 13.08
that you did not c. within the days 13.11
Philistines will c. down upon me at Gilgal, 13.12
"C., let us go over to the Philistine garrison 14.01
"C., let us go over to the garrison of these 14.06
say to us, 'Wait until we c. to you,' 14.09

COME (cont.)
'C. up to us,' then we will go up; for 1Sa 14.10
"C. up to us, and we will show you a 14.12
"C. up after me; for the LORD has given 14.12
say, 'I have c. to sacrifice to the LORD.' 16.02
and said, "Do you c. peaceably?" 16.04
"Peaceably; I have c. to sacrifice to the LORD; 16.05
yourselves, and c. with me to the sacrifice." 16.05
have you c. out to draw up for battle? 17.08
yourselves, and let him c. down to me. 17.08
"Have you seen this man who has c. up? 17.25
Surely he has c. up to defy Israel; and 17.25
"Why have you c. down? And with whom 17.28
"Am I a dog, that you c. to me with sticks?" 17.43
"C. to me, and I will give your flesh to 17.44
"You c. to me with a sword and with a 17.45
by my father that evil should c. upon you, 20.09
David, "C., let us go out into the field." 20.11
you are to c., for, as the LORD lives, it 20.21
has not the son of Jesse c. to the meal, 20.27
reason he has not c. to the king's table." 20.29
Shall this fellow c. into my house?" 21.15
was told Saul that David had c. to Keilah, 23.07
heard that Saul seeks to c. to Keilah, 23.10
Saul c. down, as thy servant has heard? 23.11
And the LORD said, "He will c. down." 23.11
because Saul had c. out to seek his life. 23.15
Now c. down, O king, according to all 23.20
your heart's desire to c. down; and our 23.20
and c. back to me with sure information. 23.23
"Make haste and c.; for the Philistines 23.27
After whom has the king of Israel c. out? 24.14
in your eyes; for we c. on a feast day. 25.08
"Go on before me; behold, I c. after you." 25.19
unless you had made haste and c. to meet me, 25.34
learned of a certainty that Saul had c. 26.04
or his day shall c. to die; or he shall go 26.10
the king of Israel has c. out to seek my life, 26.20
one of the young men c. over and fetch it. 26.22
lest these uncircumcised c. and thrust me 31.04
said to him, "Where do you c. from?" 2Sa 1.03
daughter, when you c. to see my face." 3.13
"You will not c. in here, but the blind 5.06
thinking, "David cannot c. in here." 5.06
blind and the lame shall not c. into the 5.08
the Philistines had c. and spread out in 5.18
and c. upon them opposite the balsam trees. 5.23
"How can the ark of the LORD c. to me?" 6.09
thy servant's house for a great while to c., 7.19
for you, then I will c. and help you. 10.11
"Have you not c. from a journey? Why did 11.10
to prepare for the wayfarer who had c. to him, 12.04
it for the man who had c. to him." 12.04
'Let my sister Tamar c. and give me 13.05
"Pray let my sister Tamar c. and make a 13.06
said to her, "C., lie with me, my sister." 13.11
king, "Behold, the king's sons have c.; 13.35
as your servant said, so it has c. about." 13.35
Now I have c. to say this to my lord the 14.15
the king; but Joab would not c. to him. 14.29
a second time, but Joab would not c. 14.29
'C. here, that I may send you to the king, 14.32
"Why have I c. from Geshur? It would 14.32
any man had a suit to c. before the king 15.02
suit or cause might c. to me, and I 15.04
I will c. upon him while he is weary 17.02
we shall c. upon him in some place where 17.12
word of all Israel has c. to the king? 19.11
made haste to c. down with the men of 19.16
I have c. this day, the first of all the 19.20
since my lord the king has c. safely home." 19.30
Barzillai the Gileadite had c. down from 19.31
"C. over with me, and I will provide for 19.33
Joab, 'C. here, that I may speak to you.'" 20.16
"Shall three years of famine c. to you in 24.13
has my lord the king c. to his servant?" 24.21
Now therefore c., let me give you counsel, 1Ki 1.12
I also will c. in after you and confirm 1.14
You shall then c. up after him, and 1.35
he shall c. and sit upon my throne; 1.35
"C. in, for you are a worthy man and bring 1.42
And she said, "Do you c. peaceably?" 2.13
him, "The king commands, 'C. forth.'" 2.30
child; I do not know how to go out or c. in. 3.07
no such almug wood has c. or been seen, 10.12
ships of Tarshish used to c. bringing gold, 10.22
for all Israel had c. to Shechem to make 12.01
"Depart for three days, then c. again to me." 12.05
king said, "C. to me again the third day." 12.12
"C. home with me, and refresh yourself, 13.07
him, "C. home with me and eat bread." 13.15
but have c. back, and have eaten bread 13.22
your body shall not c. to the tomb of your 13.22
cities of Samaria, shall surely c. to pass." 13.32
"C. in, wife of Jeroboam; why do you pretend 14.06
he only of Jeroboam shall c. to the grave, 14.13
permit no one to go out or c. in to Asa 15.17
You have c. to me to bring my sin to 17.18
let this child's soul c. into him again." 17.21
when I c. and tell Ahab and he cannot 18.12
said to all the people, "C. near to me"; 18.30
"If they have c. out for peace, take them 20.18
they have c. out for war, take them alive." 20.18
"C., strengthen yourself, and consider well 20.22
he caused him to c. up into the chariot. 20.33
he had c. to the king, the king said to 22.15
of bread and water, until I c. in peace."'" 22.27
'You shall not c. down from the bed to 2Ki 1.04
Therefore you shall not c. down from 1.06
"O man of God, the king says, 'C. down.'" 1.09
let fire c. down from heaven and consume 1.10
this is the king's order, 'C. down quickly!'" 1.11
"If I am a man of God, let fire c. down from 1.12
not c. down from the bed to which you 1.16
the kings had c. up to fight against them, 3.21
the creditor has c. to take my two children 4.01
whenever he c. to us, he can go in there." 4.10
to the man of God, and c. back again." 4.22
Let him c. now to me, that he may know 5.08
I thought that he would surely c. out to me, 5.11
just now c. to me from the hill country 5.22
c., let us go over to the camp of the Syrians; 7.04
and the kings of Egypt to c. upon us." 7.06
c., let us go and tell the king's household." 7.09
'When they c. out of the city, we shall 7.12
it will c. upon the land for seven years." 8.01
told him, "The man of God has c. here," 8.07
Why did this mad fellow c. to you?" 9.11
king of Judah had c. down to visit Joram. 9.16
and c. to me at Jezreel tomorrow at this 10.06
"C. with me, and see my zeal for the LORD." 10.16
there was not a man left who did not c. 10.21
with those who were to c. on duty on 11.09
"C., let us look one another in the face." 14.08
C. up, and rescue me from the hand of 16.07
have c. up against this place to destroy it? 18.25
your peace with me and c. out to me; 18.31
until I c. and take you away to a land 18.32
children have c. to the birth, and there 19.03
your arrogance has c. into my ears, 19.28
He shall not c. to this city or shoot 19.32
or c. before it with a shield or cast up a 19.32
he shall not c. into this city, says the 19.33
say? And whence did they c. to you?" 20.14
"They have c. from a far country, from 20.14
priests of the high places did not c. up to 23.09
the king of Egypt did not c. again out 24.07
were obliged to c. in every seven days, 1Ch 9.25
lest these uncircumcised c. and make 10.04
said to David, "You will not c. in here." 11.05
"If you have c. to me in friendship to 12.17
named to c. and make David king. 12.31
the Philistines had c. and made a raid 14.09
go around and c. upon them opposite the 14.14

COME (cont.)

bring an offering, and c. before him! 1Ch 16.29
servant's house for a great while to c., 17.17
Have not his servants c. to you to search 19.03
kings who had c. were by themselves 19.09
service to c. into the house of the LORD 24.19
riches and honor c. from thee, and thou 29.12
all things c. from thee, and of thy own 29.14
knowledge to go out and c. in before 2Ch 1.10
saw the fire c. down and the glory of 7.03
which the ark of the LORD has c. are holy." 8.11
ships of Tarshish used to c. bringing gold, 9.21
for all Israel had c. to Shechem to make 10.01
them, "C. to me again in three days." 10.05
king said, "C. to me again the third day." 10.12
around to c. on them from behind; 13.13
permit no one to go out or c. in to 16.01
he had c. to the king, the king said to 18.14
wrath may not c. upon you and your 19.10
they will c. up by the ascent of Ziz; 20.16
who had c. against Judah, so that they 20.22
the downfall of Ahaziah should c. about 22.07
with those who were to c. on duty on 23.08
of the chief priest would c. and empty 24.11
army of the Syrians had c. with few men, 24.24
army that had c. to him from Ephraim, 25.10
"C., let us look one another in the face." 25.17
c. near, bring sacrifices and thank offerings 29.31
they should c. to the house of the LORD at 30.01
people should c. and keep the passover 30.05
Sennacherib had c. and intended to 32.02
of Assyria c. and find much water?" 32.04
wrath of the LORD did not c. upon them 32.26
who had c. to Jerusalem from the captivity. Ez 3.08
those who had c. from captivity, the 8.35
all that had c. upon us for our evil deeds 9.13
if any one did not c. within three days, 10.08
taken foreign wives c. at appointed times, 10.14
let me pass through until I c. to Judah; Neh 2.07
some one had c. to seek the welfare of 2.10
C., let us build the wall of Jerusalem, 2.17
they all plotted together to c. and fight 4.08
till w. c. into the midst of them and 4.11
they live they will c. up against us." 4.12
"C. and let us meet together in one of 6.02
doing a great work and I cannot c. down. 6.03
while I leave it and c. down to you?" 6.03
now c., and let us take counsel together." 6.07
month had c., the children of Israel were 7.73
Thou didst c. down upon Mount Sinai, 9.13
seem little to thee that has c. upon us, 9.32
that time on they did not c. on the sabbath. 13.21
purify themselves and c. and guard the gates, 13.22
Queen Vashti refused to c. at the king's Est 1.12
brought before him, and she did not c.' 1.17
that Vashti is to c. no more before 1.19
I have not been called to c. in to the king 4.11
king and Haman c. this day to a dinner 5.04
let the king and Haman c. tomorrow to 5.08
"Even Queen Esther let no one c. with the 5.12
you have not c. to the kingdom for such 5.14
And the king said, "Let him c. in." 6.05
LORD said to Satan, "Whence have you c.?" Job 1.07
said to Satan, "Whence have you c.?" Satan 2.02
of all this evil that had c. upon him, 2.11
to c. to condole with him and comfort 2.11
let it not c. into the number of the 3.06
c. forth from the womb and expire? 3.11
But now it has c. to you, and you are 4.05
For affliction does not c. from the dust, 5.06
You shall c. to your grave in ripe old age, 5.26
they c. thither and are confounded. 6.20
he who goes down to Sheol does not c. up; 7.09
him, that we should c. to trial together. 9.32
will speak, and let c. on me what may. 13.13
a godless man shall not c. before him. 13.16
would wait, till my release should c. 14.14
His sons c. to honor, and he does not 14.21
in prosperity the destroyer will c. upon him. 15.21
when a few years have c. I shall go the 16.22
But you, c. on again, all of you, 17.10
His troops c. on together; they have 19.12
all the force of misery will c. upon him. 20.22
of his gall; terrors c. upon him. 20.25
at peace; thereby good will c. to you. 22.21
him, that I might c. even to his seat! 23.03
has tried me, I shall c. forth as gold. 23.10
and whose spirit has c. forth from you? 26.04
As through a wide breach they c.; 30.14
the cry of the poor to c. to him, 34.28
'Thus far you shall c., and no farther, 38.11
From whose womb did the ice c. forth, 38.29
another that no air can c. between them. 41.16
let the evil of the wicked c. to an end, Ps 7.09
deliverance for Israel would c. out of Zion! 14.07
From thee let my vindication c.! 17.02
that the King of glory may c. in. 24.07
that the King of glory may c. in! 24.09
C., O sons, listen to me, I will teach 34.11
Let ruin c. upon them unawares! And let 35.08
Let not the foot of arrogance c. upon me, 36.11
"Lo, I c.; in the roll of the book it is 40.07
When shall I c. and behold the face 42.02
All this has c. upon us, though we 44.17
C., behold the works of the LORD, how 46.08
deliverance for Israel would c. from Zion! 53.06
Fear and trembling c. upon me, and 55.05
prayer! To thee shall all flesh c. 65.02
C. and see what God has done: he 66.05
C. and hear, all you who fear God, 66.16
For the waters have c. up to my neck. 69.01
I have c. into deep waters, and the flood 69.02
thy might to all the generations to c. 71.18
the heathen have c. into thy inheritance; 79.01
the groans of the prisoners c. before thee; 79.11
Stir up thy might, and c. to save us! 80.02
"C., let us wipe them out as a nation; 83.04
nations thou hast made shall c. and bow 86.09
Let my prayer c. before thee, incline 88.02
right hand; but it will not c. near you. 91.07
befall you, no scourge c. near your tent. 91.10
O c., let us sing to the LORD; let us 95.01
Let us c. into his presence with thanksgiving; 95.02
O c., let us worship and bow down, let 95.06
bring an offering, and c. into his courts! 96.08
gladness! C. into his presence with singing! 100.02
blameless. Oh when wilt thou c. to me? 101.02
O LORD; let my cry c. to thee! 102.01
favor her; the appointed time has c. 102.13
Let this be recorded for a generation to c., 102.18
He loved to curse; let curses c. on him! 109.17
Let thy steadfast love c. to me, O LORD, 119.41
Let thy mercy c. to me, that I may live; 119.77
Let my cry c. before thee, O LORD; 119.169
Let my supplication c. before thee; 119.170
sowing, shall c. home with shouts of joy, 126.06
Bow thy heavens, O LORD, and c. down! 144.05
hills. From whence does my help c.? 121.01
"C. with us, let us lie in wait for blood, Pro 1.11
when distress and anguish c. upon you. 1.27
from his mouth c. knowledge and understanding; 2.06
"Go, and c. again, tomorrow I will give 3.28
for you have c. into your neighbor's power: 6.03
and poverty will c. upon you like a 6.11
therefore calamity will c. upon him 6.15
so now I have c. out to meet you, 7.15
C., let us take our fill of love till 7.18
him; at full moon he will c. home." 7.20
"C., eat of my bread and drink of the 9.05
but a prating fool will c. to ruin. 10.08
What the wicked dreads will c. upon him, 10.24
Poverty and disgrace c. to him who ignores 13.18
abundant crops c. by the strength of the ox. 14.04
Love not sleep, lest you c. to poverty; 20.13

COME (cont.)
or gives to the rich, will only c. to want, Pro 22.16
drunkard and the glutton will c. to poverty, 23.21
poverty will c. upon you like a robber, 24.34
for it is better to be told, "C. up here," 25.07
does not know that want will c. upon him. 28.22
and she laughs at the time to c. 31.25
to happen among those who c. after. Ecc 1.11
in the days to c. all will have been long 2.16
those who c. later will not rejoice in 4.16
who fears God shall c. forth from them 7.18
before the evil days c., and the years 12.01
"Arise, my love, my fair one, and c. away; Sol 2.10
earth, the time of singing has c., 2.12
Arise, my love, my fair one, and c. away. 2.13
that have c. up from the washing, 4.02
C. with me from Lebanon, my bride; c. with 4.08
O north wind, and c., O south wind! 4.16
Let my beloved c. to his garden, and 4.16
I c. to my garden, my sister, my bride, 5.01
C., my beloved, let us go forth into 7.11
"When you c. to appear before me, who Is 1.12
"C. now, let us reason together, says the 1.18
and the widow's cause does not c. to them. 1.23
It shall c. to pass in the latter days that 2.02
peoples shall c., and say, "C., let us go 2.03
c., let us walk in the light of the LORD. 2.05
and let it c., that we may know it!" 5.19
stand, and it shall not c. to pass. 7.07
such days as have not c. since the day 7.17
they will all c. and settle in the steep 7.19
With bows and arrows men will c. there, 7.24
you will not c. there for fear of briers and 7.25
counsel together, but it will c. to nought; 8.10
in the storm which will c. from afar? 10.03
he has c. to Aiath; he has passed through 10.28
shall c. forth a shoot from the stump of 11.01
They c. from a distant land, from the 13.05
as destruction from the Almighty it will c.! 13.06
stirred up to meet you when you c., 14.09
from the serpent's root will c. forth an adder, 14.29
and the Assyrian will c. into Egypt, 19.23
behold, here c. riders, horsemen in pairs!" 21.09
If you will inquire, inquire; c. back again." 21.12
C., my people, enter your chambers, and shut 26.20
In the days to c. Jacob shall take root, 27.06
broken; women c. and make a fire of them. 27.11
will c. and worship the LORD on the 27.13
scourge passes through it will not c. to us; 28.15
from low in the dust your words shall c.; 29.04
your voice shall c. from the ground like 29.04
the ruthless shall c. to nought and the scoffer 29.20
who err in spirit will c. to understanding, 29.24
from where c. the lioness and the lion, 30.06
it may be for the time to c. as a witness 30.08
so the LORD of hosts will c. down to 31.04
will fail, the fruit harvest will not c. 32.10
Behold, your God will c. with vengeance, 35.04
of God. He will c. and save you." 35.04
nor shall any ravenous beast c. up on it; 35.09
return, and c. to Zion with singing, 35.10
that I have c. up against this land to destroy 36.10
Make your peace with me and c. out to me; 36.16
until I c. and take you away to a land 36.17
children have c. to birth, and there is no 37.03
and your arrogance has c. to my ears, 37.29
He shall not c. into this city, or shoot an 37.33
not c. into this city, says the LORD. 37.34
say? And whence did they c. to you?" 39.03
"They have c. to me from a far country, 39.03
tremble; they have drawn near and c. 41.05
or declare to us the things to c. 41.22
Tell us what is to c. hereafter, that 41.23
one from the north, and he has c., 41.25
Behold, the former things have c. to pass, 42.09
will attend and listen for the time to c.? 42.23
announced from of old the things to c.? 44.07
stature, shall c. over to you and be yours, 45.14
they shall c. over in chains and bow down 45.14
"Assemble yourselves and c., draw near 45.20
to him shall c. and be ashamed, all who 45.24
C. down and sit in the dust, O virgin 47.01
two things shall c. to you in a moment, 47.09
widowhood shall c. upon you in full 47.09
But evil shall c. upon you, for which 47.11
ruin shall c. on you suddenly, of which 47.11
saying to the prisoners, 'C. forth,' to those 49.09
Lo, these shall c. from afar, and lo, these 49.12
see; they all gather, they c. to you. 49.18
alone; whence then have these c.?'" 49.21
adversary? Let him c. near to me. 50.08
shall return, and c. with singing to Zion; 51.11
for there shall no more c. into you the 52.01
and from terror, for it shall not c. near you. 54.14
every one who thirsts, c. to the waters; 55.01
he who has no money, c., buy and eat! 55.01
C., buy wine and milk without money and 55.01
Incline your ear, and c. to me; hear, 55.03
rain and the snow c. down from heaven, 55.10
Instead of the thorn shall c. up the cypress; 55.13
instead of the brier shall c. up the myrtle; 55.13
for soon my salvation will c., and my 56.01
All you beasts of the field, c. to devour— 56.09
"C.," they say, "let us get wine, let us 56.12
for he will c. like a rushing stream, 59.19
"And he will c. to Zion as Redeemer, to 59.20
Arise, shine; for your light has c., and 60.01
nations shall c. to your light, and kings 60.03
they all gather together, they c. to you; 60.04
your sons shall c. from far, and your 60.04
the wealth of the nations shall c. to you. 60.05
Ephah; all those from Sheba shall c. 60.06
they shall c. up with acceptance on my 60.07
The glory of Lebanon shall c. to you, the 60.13
who oppressed you shall c. bending low 60.14
heart, and my year of redemption has c. 63.04
thou wouldst rend the heavens and c. down, 64.01
do not c. near me, for I am set apart from 65.05
not be remembered or c. into mind. 65.17
behold, the LORD will c. in fire, 66.15
shall c. to an end together, says the LORD. 66.17
they shall c. and shall see my glory, 66.18
all flesh shall c. to worship before me, 66.23
they shall c. and every one shall set his Jer 1.15
are free, we will c. no more to thee'? 2.31
you will c. away with your hands upon 2.37
withheld, and the spring rain has not c.; 3.03
It shall not c. to mind, or be remembered, 3.16
they shall c. from the land of the north 3.18
"Behold, we c. to thee; for thou art 3.22
"Beseigers c. from a distant land; they 4.16
no evil will c. upon us, nor shall 5.12
Shepherds with their flocks shall c. against 6.03
does frankincense c. to me from Sheba, 6.20
suddenly the destroyer will c. upon us. 6.26
then c. and stand before me in this house, 7.10
command, nor did it c. into my mind. 7.31
They c. and devour the land and all that 8.16
and call for the mourning women to c.; 9.17
send for the skilled women to c.; 9.17
death has c. up into our windows, it 9.21
heights in the desert destroyers have c.; 12.12
c. to pass, if they will diligently 12.16
crown has c. down from your head." 13.18
and see those who c. from the north. 13.20
'Why have these things c. upon me?' 13.22
they c. to the cisterns, they find no 14.03
to thee shall the nations c. from the ends 16.19
and shall not see any good c. 17.06
is the word of the LORD? Let it c.!" 17.15
people shall c. from the cities of Judah 17.26
"C., let us make plots against Jeremiah, 18.18
C., let us smite him with the tongue, and 18.18
or decree, nor did it c. into my mind; 19.05

COME (cont.)
Why did I c. forth from the womb to Jer 20.18
'Who shall c. down against us, or who 21.13
will groan when pangs c. upon you, 22.23
they say, 'No evil shall c. upon you.'" 23.17
the word of the LORD has c. to me, 25.03
c. to worship in the house of LORD 26.02
c. to Jerusalem to Zedekiah king of Judah. 27.03
"And it shall c. to pass in that day, 30.08
With weeping they shall c., and with 31.09
shall c. and sing aloud on the height of 31.12
c. back from the land of the enemy. 31.16
children shall c. back to their own country. 31.17
c. to pass that as I have watched over 31.28
Shallum your uncle will c. to you and say, 32.07
thou hast made all this evil c. upon them. 32.23
have c. up to the city to take it, 32.24
What thou didst speak has c. to pass, 32.24
this city shall c. and set this city on fire, 32.29
'C., and let us go to Jerusalem for fear 35.11
men of Judah who c. out of their cities. 36.06
read in the hearing of the people, and c." 36.14
will certainly c. and destroy this land, 36.29
army of Pharaoh had c. out of Egypt; 37.05
Chaldeans shall c. back and fight against 37.08
will not c. against you and against this land'? 37.19
with you and c. to you and say to you, 38.25
obey his voice, this thing has c. upon you. 40.03
to c. with me to Babylon, c., and I will 40.04
to you to c. with me to Babylon, do not c. 40.04
before the Chaldeans who will c. to us; 40.10
"C. in to Gedaliah the son of Ahikam." 41.06
He shall c. and smite the land of Egypt, 43.11
it? Did it not c. into his mind? 44.21
and like Carmel by the sea, shall one c. 46.18
a gadfly from the north has c. upon her. 46.20
of their calamity has c. upon them, 46.21
c. against her with axes, like those 46.22
Baldness has c. upon Gaza, Ashkelon 47.05
'C., let us cut her off from being a 48.02
destroyer shall c. upon every city, and 48.08
"C. down from your glory, and sit on 48.18
the destroyer of Moab has c. up against you; 48.18
"Judgment has c. upon the tableland, 48.21
saying, 'Who will c. against me?' 49.04
"Gather yourselves together and c. against 49.14
which those driven out of Elam shall not c. 49.36
the north a nation has c. up against her, 50.03
Judah shall c. together, weeping as they c.; 50.04
'C., let us join ourselves to the LORD 50.05
C. against her from every quarter; open 50.26
for their day has c., the time of their 50.27
your day has c., the time when I will 50.31
c., let us declare in Zion the work of 51.10
your end has c., the thread of your 51.13
and the time of her harvest will c." 51.33
The sea has c. up on Babylon; she is 51.42
destroyers shall c. against them out of 51.48
and let Jerusalem c. into your mind: 51.50
aliens have c. into the holy places of 51.51
destroyers would c. from me upon her, 51.53
destroyer has c. upon her, upon Babylon; 51.56
all the evil that should c. upon Babylon, 51.60
"When you c. to Babylon, see that you read 51.61
for none c. to the appointed feasts; Lam 1.04
"Let all their evil doing c. before thee; 1.22
panic and pitfall have c. upon us, 3.47
were numbered; for our end had c. 4.18
nor has foul flesh c. into my mouth." Eze 4.14
a fire will c. forth into all the house of 5.04
The end has c. upon the four corners of 7.02
An end has c., the end has c.; it has 7.06
Your doom has c. to you, O inhabitant of the 7.07
the time has c., the day is near, a day of 7.07
Your doom has c., injustice has blossomed, 7.10
The time has c., the day draws near. Let 7.12
I know the things that c. into your mind. 11.05
when they c. there, they will remove from 11.18
when they c. forth to you, and you see 14.22
bribing them to c. to you from every side 16.33
GOD, Is it to inquire of me that you c.? 20.03
for the sword of the king of Babylon to c.; 21.19
both of them shall c. forth from the same land. 21.19
mark a way for the sword to c. to Rabbah 21.20
because you have c. to remembrance, you 21.24
wicked one, prince of Israel, whose day has c., 21.25
unhallowed wicked, whose day has c., 21.29
in the midst of her, that her time may c., 22.03
the appointed time of your years has c. 22.04
they shall c. against you from the north 23.24
They even sent for men to c. from far, 23.40
I the LORD have spoken; it shall c. to pass, 24.14
a fugitive will c. to you to report to you 24.26
their ships c. all that handle the oar. 27.29
you have c. to a dreadful end and shall 27.36
you have c. to a dreadful end and shall be 28.19
A sword shall c. upon Egypt, and anguish 30.04
fall, and her proud might shall c. down; 30.06
anguish shall c. upon them on the day of 30.09
and her proud might shall c. to an end; 30.18
sword of the king of Babylon shall c. upon you. 32.11
'C., and hear what the word is that 33.30
And they c. to you as people c., and they 33.31
and c. it will!—then they will know 33.33
people Israel; for they will soon c. home. 36.08
and flesh had c. upon them, and skin 37.08
C. from the four winds, O breath, and 37.09
On that day thoughts will c. into your mind, 38.10
'Have you c. to seize spoil? Have you 38.13
c. from your place out of the uttermost 38.15
you will c. up against my people Israel, 38.16
when Gog shall c. against the land of Israel, 38.18
'Assemble and c., gather from all sides to 39.17
the sons of Levi may c. near to the LORD to 40.46
They shall not c. near to me, to serve. 44.13
nor c. near any of my sacred things and 44.13
me, shall c. near to me to minister to me; 44.15
people of the land c. before the LORD at 46.09
provinces to c. to the dedication of the image Dan 3.02
of the Most High God c. forth, and c. here!" 3.26
which has c. upon my lord, the king, 4.24
I saw him c. close to the ram, and he 8.07
Moses, all this calamity has c. upon us, 9.13
I have now c. out to give you wisdom and 9.22
went forth, and I have c. to tell it to you, 9.23
prince who is to c. shall destroy the city 9.26
Its end shall c. with a flood, and to the 9.26
abominations shall c. one who makes desolate, 9.27
and I have c. because of your words. 10.12
For the vision is for days yet to c." 10.14
"Do you know why I have c. to you? 10.20
with him, lo, the prince of Greece will c. 10.20
shall c. to the king of the north to 11.06
he shall c. against the army and enter 11.07
the latter shall c. into the realm of the 11.09
which shall c. on and overflow and pass 11.10
shall c. out and fight with the king of 11.11
he shall c. on with a great army and 11.13
the king of the north shall c. and throw 11.15
he shall c. in without warning and obtain 11.21
he shall c. into the richest parts of 11.24
he shall return and c. into the south; 11.29
ships of Kittim shall c. against him, 11.30
he shall c. into countries and shall 11.40
He shall c. into the glorious land. And 11.41
he shall c. to his end, with none to help 11.45
"C., let us return to the LORD; for he Hos 6.01
he will c. to us as the showers, as the 6.03
it shall not c. to the house of the LORD. 9.04
The days of puishment have c., 9.07
the days of recompense have c.; Israel 9.07
that he may c. and rain salvation upon you. 10.12
The pangs of childbirth c. for him, 13.13
east wind, the wind of the LORD, shall c., 13.15

COME (cont.)

For a nation has c. up against my land, Joe 1.06
"And it shall c. to pass afterward, that I 2.28
shall c. to pass that all who call upon 2.32
men of war draw near, let them c. up. 3.09
Hasten and c., all you nations round about, 3.11
and c. up to the valley of Jehoshaphat; 3.12
a fountain shall c. forth from the house 3.18
"C. to Bethel, and transgress; to Gilgal, Amo 4.04
exile, and Bethel shall c. to nought." 5.05
nations, to whom the house of Israel c.! 6.01
"The end has c. upon my people Israel; 8.02
their wickedness has c. up before me." Jon 1.02
"C., let us cast lots, that we may know 1.07
on whose account this evil has c. upon us? 1.08
And whence do you c.? What is your 1.08
that this great tempest has c. upon you." 1.12
plant, and made it c. up over Jonah, 4.06
will c. down and tread upon the high Mic 1.03
and it has c. to Judah, it has reached 1.09
the inhabitants of Zaanan do not c. forth; 1.11
because evil has c. down from the LORD 1.12
glory of Israel shall c. to Adullam. 1.15
midst of us? No evil shall c. upon us." 3.11
It shall c. to pass in the latter days 4.01
and many nations shall c., and say, 4.02
"C., let us go up to the mountain of the LORD, 4.02
shall it c., the former dominion shall c., 4.08
from you shall c. forth for me one who 5.02
"With what shall I c. before the LORD, 6.06
Shall I c. before him with burnt offerings, 6.06
watchmen, of their punishment, has c.; 7.04
they will c. to you, from Assyria to Egypt, 7.12
Did one not c. out from you, who plotted Nah 1.11
for never again shall the wicked c. against you, 1.15
the shatterer has c. up against you. 2.01
upon whom has not c. your unceasing evil? 3.19
Yea, their horsemen c. from afar; they Hab 1.08
They all c. for violence; terror of them 1.09
it will surely c., it will not delay. 2.03
cup in the LORD's right hand will c. around 2.16
and shame will c. upon your glory! 2.16
the day of trouble to c. upon people who invade 3.16
C. together and hold assembly, O shameless Zep 2.01
time has not yet c. to rebuild the house Hag 1.02
the treasures of all nations shall c. in, 2.07
consider what will c. to pass from this day 2.15
and these have c. to terrify them, Zec 1.21
I c. and I will dwell in the midst of you, 2.10
those who are far off shall c. and help 6.15
shall c. to pass, if you will diligently 6.15
Peoples shall yet c., even the inhabitants 8.20
shall c. to seek the LORD of hosts in 8.22
Out of them shall c. the cornerstone, out 10.04
all the nations that c. against Jerusalem. 12.09
Then the LORD your God will c., and 14.05
nations that have c. against Jerusalem 14.16
c. the plague with which the Lord afflicts 14.18
all who sacrifice may c. and take of them 14.21
Lord whom you seek will suddenly c. to his Mal 3.01
lest I c. and smite the land with a curse." 4.06
in the East, and have c. to worship him." Mt 2.02
from you shall c. a ruler who will govern 2.06
that I too may c. and worship him." 2.08
Who warned you to flee from the wrath to c.? 3.07
baptized by you, and do you c. to me?" 3.14
not that I have c. to abolish the law 5.17
c. not to abolish them but to fulfil them. 5.17
brother, and then c. and offer your gift. 5.24
Thy kingdom c., Thy will be done, 6.10
who c. to you in sheeps clothing but 7.15
said to him, "I will c. and heal him." 8.07
I am not worthy to have you c. under my 8.08
and to another, 'C.,' and he comes, 8.09
many will c. from east and west and 8.11
Have you c. here to torment us before 8.29
The days will c., when the bridegroom is 9.15
c. and lay your hand on her, and she will 9.18
house is worthy, let your peace c. upon it; 10.13
not think that I have c. to bring peace on 10.34
have not c. to bring peace, but a sword. 10.34
I have c. to set a man against his father, 10.35
"Are you he who is to c., or shall we 11.03
to accept it, he is Elijah who is to c. 11.14
C. to me, all who labor and are heavy-laden, 11.28
then the kingdom of God has c. upon you. 12.28
either in this age or in the age to c. 12.32
the birds of the air c. and make nests 13.32
angels will c. out and separate the evil 13.49
is you, bid me c. to you on the water." 14.28
He said, "C." So Peter got out of the 14.29
out of the heart c. evil thoughts, murder, 15.19
any man would c. after me, let him deny 16.24
Son of man is to c. with his angels in 16.27
the scribes say that first Elijah must c.?" 17.10
"Elijah does c., and he is to restore all 17.11
but I tell you that Elijah has already c., 17.12
For it is necessary that temptations c., 18.07
"Let the children c. to me, and do not hinder 19.14
treasure in heaven; and c., follow me." 19.21
"May no fruit ever c. from you again!" 21.19
c., let us kill him and have his inheritance.' 21.38
marriage feast; but they would not c. 22.03
is ready; c. to the marriage feast.' 22.04
may c. all the righteous blood shed on 23.35
all this will c. upon this generation. 23.36
For many will c. in my name, saying, 24.05
to all nations; and then the end will c. 24.14
master of that servant will c. on a day 24.50
the bridegroom! C. out to meet him.' 25.06
'C., O blessed of my Father, inherit the 25.34
"Have you c. out as against a robber, with 26.55
the Son of God, c. down from the cross." 27.40
let him c. down now from the cross, 27.42
let us see whether Elijah will c. to save him." 27.49
C., see the place where he lay. 28.06
Have you c. to destroy us? I know who Mk 1.24
saying, "Be silent, and c. out of him!" 1.25
days will c., when the bridegroom is 2.20
is anything secret, except to c. to light. 4.22
in the sickle, because the harvest has c." 4.29
when evening had c., he said to them, 4.35
he had c. out of the boat, there met him 5.02
"C. out of the man, you unclean spirit!" 5.08
C. and lay your hands on her, so that 5.23
"C. away by yourselves to a lonely place, 6.31
of the scribes, who had c. from Jerusalem, 7.01
when they c. from the market place, 7.04
things which c. out of a man are what defile 7.15
evil things c. from within, and they defile 7.23
and some of them have c. a long way." 8.03
"If any man would c. after me, let him deny 8.34
see the kingdom of God c. with power." 9.01
scribes say that first Elijah must c.?" 9.11
"Elijah does c. first to restore all 9.12
But I tell you that Elijah has c., and 9.13
c. out of him, and never enter him again." 9.25
"Let the children c. to me, do not hinder 10.14
treasure in heaven; and c., follow me." 10.21
and in the age to c. eternal life. 10.30
believes that what he says will c. to pass, 11.23
c., let us kill him, and the inheritance 12.07
He will c. and destroy the tenants, and 12.09
Many will c. in my name, saying, 'I am 13.06
for you do not know when the time will c. 13.33
when the master of the house will c., 13.35
lest he c. suddenly and find you asleep. 13.36
It is enough; the hour has c.; the Son 14.41
"Have you c. out as against a robber, 14.48
save yourself, and c. down from the cross!" 15.30
King of Israel, c. down now from the cross, 15.32
when the sixth hour had c., there was 15.33
whether Elijah will c. to take him down." 15.36
evening had c., since it was the day of 15.42

COME (cont.)

trembling and astonishment had c. upon Mk 16.08
until the day that these things c. to pass, Lk 1.20
"The Holy Spirit will c. upon you, and 1.35
mother of my Lord should c. to me? 1.43
Who warned you to flee from the wrath to c.? 3.07
Have you c. to destroy us? I know who 4.34
saying, "Be silent, and c. out of him!" 4.35
the unclean spirits, and they c. out." 4.36
in the other boat to c. and help them. 5.07
who had c. from every village of Galilee 5.17
I have not c. to call the righteous, but 5.32
days will c., when the bridegroom is 5.35
asking him to c. and heal his slave. 7.03
not worthy to have you c. under my roof; 7.06
therefore I did not presume to c. to you. 7.07
and to another, 'C.,' and he comes; 7.08
"Are you he who is to c., or shall we 7.19
when the men had c. to him, they said, 7.20
saying, 'Are you he who is to c., or 7.20
John the Baptist has c. eating no bread 7.33
Son of man has c. eating and drinking; 7.34
that shall not be known and c. to light. 8.17
he had commanded the unclean spirit to c. 8.29
he besought him to c. to his house, 8.41
"If any man would c. after me, let him 9.23
they had c. down from the mountain, 9.37
"Lord, do you want us to bid fire c. down 9.54
place where he himself was about to c. 10.01
'The kingdom of God has c. near to you.' 10.09
this, that the kingdom of God has c. near.' 10.11
spend, I will repay you when I c. back.' 10.35
hallowed by thy name. Thy kingdom c. 11.02
the kingdom of God has c. upon you. 11.20
master to c. home from the marriage 12.36
at table, and he will c. and serve them. 12.37
master of that servant will c. on a day 12.46
that I have c. to give peace on earth? 12.51
I have c. seeking fruit on this fig tree, 13.07
c. on those days and be healed, and not 13.14
men will c. from east and west, and from 13.29
he who invited you both will c. and say 14.09
been invited, 'C.; for all is now ready.' 14.17
married a wife, and therefore I cannot c.' 14.20
compel people to c. in, that my house 14.23
not bear his own cross and c. after me, 14.27
'Your brother has c., and your father 15.27
they also c. into this place of torment.' 16.28
"Temptations to sin are sure to c.; but 17.01
but woe to him by whom they c.! 17.01
say to him when he has c. in from the field, 17.07
'C. at once and sit down at table'? 17.07
the house, not c. down to take them away; 17.31
"Let the children c. to me, and do not hinder 18.16
treasure in heaven; and c., follow me." 18.22
time, and in the age to c. eternal life." 18.30
"Zacchaeus, make haste and c. down; for 19.05
"Today salvation has c. to this house, 19.09
to them, 'Trade with these till I c.' 19.13
days shall c. upon you, when your enemies 19.43
He will c. and destroy those tenants, and 20.16
will c. when there shall not be left 21.06
many will c. in my name, saying, 'I am 21.08
then know that its desolation has c. near. 21.20
as soon as they c. out in leaf, you see 21.30
that day c. upon you suddenly like a snare; 21.34
it will c. upon all who dwell upon the 21.35
elders, who had c. out against him, 22.52
"Have you c. out as against a robber, 22.52
remember me when you c. in your kingly power." 23.42
who had c. with him from Galilee 23.55
He said to them, "C. and see." They Jn 1.39
"Can anything good c. out of Nazareth?" 1.46
Philip said to him, "C. and see." 1.46
do with me? My hour has not yet c." 2.04
know that you are a teacher c. from God; 3.02
that the light has c. into the world, 3.19
the light, and does not c. to the light, 3.20
I may not thirst, nor c. here to draw." 4.15
"Go, call your husband, and c. here." 4.16
"C., see a man who told me all that I 4.29
that Jesus had c. from Judea to Galilee, 4.47
begged him to c. down and heal his son, 4.47
him, "Sir, c. down before my child dies." 4.49
when he had c. from Judea to Galilee. 4.54
he does not c. into judgment, but has 5.24
and c. forth, those who have done good, 5.29
you refuse to c. to me that you may have 5.40
I have c. in my Father's name, and 5.43
the prophet who is to c. into the world!" 6.14
were about to c. and take him by force. 6.15
and Jesus had not yet c. to them. 6.17
to him, "Rabbi, when did you c. here?" 6.25
that the Father gives me will c. to me; 6.37
I have c. down from heaven, not to do my 6.38
now say, 'I have c. down from heaven'?" 6.42
No one can c. to me unless the Father 6.44
can c. to me unless it is granted him by 6.65
we have believed, and have c. to know, 6.69
"My time has not yet c., but your time 7.06
feast, for my time has not yet fully c." 7.08
me, and you know where I c. from? 7.28
But I have not c. of my own accord; 7.28
I know him, for I c. from him, and 7.29
because his hour had not yet c. 7.30
find me; where I am you cannot c." 7.34
and, 'Where I am you cannot c.'?" 7.36
one thirst, let him c. to me and drink. 7.37
said, "Is the Christ to c. from Galilee? 7.41
whence I have c. and whither I am going, 8.14
but you do not know whence I c. or 8.14
him, because his hour had not yet c. 8.20
sin; where I am going, you cannot c." ' 8.21
says, 'Where I am going, you cannot c.'?" 8.22
many of the Jews had c. to Martha and 11.19
Jesus had not yet c. to the village, 11.30
They said to him, "Lord, c. and see." 11.34
cried with a loud voice, "Lazarus, c. out." 11.43
who had c. with Mary and had seen 11.45
the Romans will c. and destroy both 11.48
think? That he will not c. to the feast?" 11.56
a great crowd who had c. to the feast 12.12
"The hour has c. for the Son of man to 12.23
for this purpose I have c. to this hour. 12.27
voice has c. for your sake, not for mine. 12.30
I have c. as light into the world, that 12.46
I did not c. to judge the world but 12.47
Jesus knew that his hour had c. to 13.01
he had c. from God and was going to God, 13.03
you, 'Where I am going you cannot c.' 13.33
I will c. again and will take you 14.03
not leave you desolate; I will c. to you. 14.18
we will c. to him and make our home 14.23
you, 'I go away, and I will c. to you.' 14.28
If I had not c. and spoken to them, 15.22
away, the Counselor will not c. to you; 16.07
declare to you the things that are to c. 16.13
has sorrow, because her hour has c.; 16.21
the Father and have c. into the world; 16.28
it has c., when you will be scattered, 16.32
"Father, the hour has c.; glorify thy 17.01
for this I have c. into the world, to 18.37
who had first c. to him by night, 19.39
said to them, "C. and have breakfast." 21.12
"If it is my will that he remain until I c., 21.22
remain until I c., what is that to you?" 21.23
they had c. together, they asked him, Ac 1.06
when the Holy Spirit has c. upon you; 1.08
will c. in the same way as you saw him 1.11
When the day of Pentecost had c., they 2.01
may c. from the presence of the Lord, 3.19
they shall c. out and worship me in 7.07
and I have c. down to deliver them. 7.34
And now c., I will send you to Egypt.' 7.34

COME (cont.)

what you have said may c. upon me." Ac 8.24
had c. to Jerusalem to worship 8.27
invited Philip to c. up and sit with him. 8.31
Ananias c. in and lay his hands on 9.12
he has c. here for this purpose, to 9.21
he had c. to Jerusalem he attempted 9.26
him, "Please c. to us without delay." 9.38
he had c., they took him to the upper room. 9.39
and you have been kind enough to c. 10.33
c. upon you what is said in the prophets: 13.40
c. down to us in the likeness of men!" 14.11
c. opposite Mysia, they attempted to 16.07
"C. over to Macedonia and help us." 16.09
and spoke to the women who had c. 16.13
the Lord, c. to my house and stay." 16.15
name of Jesus Christ to c. out of her." 16.18
them c. themselves and take us out." 16.37
world upside down have c. here also; 17.06
Silas and Timothy to c. to him as 17.15
lately c. from Italy with his wife Priscilla, 18.02
who was to c. after him, that is, Jesus." 19.04
did not know why they had c. together. 19.32
c. to Jerusalem, the brethren received us 21.17
will certainly hear that you have c. 21.22
commanding his accusers to c. before you * 24.08
when Festus had c. into is province, 25.01
when he had c., the Jews who had 25.07
night had c., as we were drifting 27.27
time and saw no misfortune c. to him, 28.06
that I have often intended to c. to you Rom 1.13
And why not do evil that good may c.? 3.08
who was a type of the one who was to c. 5.14
nor things present, nor things to c., nor 8.38
through their trespass salvation has c. 11.11
a hardening has c. upon part of Israel, 11.25
"The Deliverer will c. from Zion, he will 11.26
longed for many years to c. to you, 15.23
if the Gentiles have c. to share in 15.27
when I c. to you I shall c. in the fulness 15.29
by God's will I may c. to you with joy 15.32
I did not c. proclaiming to you the 1Co 2.01
I will c. to you soon, if the Lord wills, 4.19
Shall I c. to you with a rod, or with 4.21
c. together again, lest Satan tempt you 7.05
upon whom the end of the ages has c. 10.11
you c. together it is not for the better 11.17
you c. together to eat, wait for one another— 11.33
lest you c. together to be condemned. 11.34
things I will give directions when I c. 11.34
if I c. to you speaking in tongues, how 14.06
you c. together, each one has a hymn, a 14.26
c. also the resurrection of the dead. 15.21
With what kind of body do they c.?" 15.35
contributions need not be made when I c. 16.02
He will c. when he has opportunity. 16.12
let him be accursed. Our Lord, c.! 16.22
I wanted to c. to you first, so that 2Co 1.15
to c. back to you from Macedonia and 1.16
c. out from them, and be separate 6.17
if some Macedonians c. with me and find 9.04
to c. all the way to you with the gospel 10.14
third time I am ready to c. to you. 12.14
I may c. and find you not what I wish, 12.20
I c. again my God may humble me before 12.21
that if I c. again I will not spare them— 13.02
the blessing of Abraham might c. upon the Gal 3.14
till the offspring should c. to whom 3.19
now that faith has c., we are no longer 3.25
the time had fully c., God sent forth 4.04
but now that you have c. to know God, 4.09
age but also in that which is to c.; Eph 1.21
the fruits of righteousness which c. Php 1.11
whether I c. and see you or am absent, 1.27
Lord that shortly I myself shall c. also. 2.24
c. to you, as indeed in the whole world Col 1.06
you have c. to fulness of life in him, 2.10

These are only a shadow of what is to c.; 2.17
Jesus who delivers us from the wrath to c. 1Th 1.10
God's wrath has c. upon them at last! 2.16
because we wanted to c. to you— 2.18
just as it has c. to pass, and as you know. 3.04
that Timothy has c. to us from you, 3.06
day of the Lord will c. like a thief in 5.02
then sudden destruction will c. upon them 5.03
to the effect that the day of the Lord has c. 2Th 2.02
that day will not c., unless the rebellion 2.03
and to c. to the knowledge of the truth. 1Ti 2.04
I hope to c. to you soon, but I am 3.14
present life and also for the life to c. 4.08
Till I c., attend to the public reading of 4.13
that they will repent and c. to know 2Ti 2.25
in the last days there will c. times of stress. 3.01
sacrificed; the time of my departure has c. 4.06
Do your best to c. to me soon. 4.09
When you c., bring the cloak that I left 4.13
Do your best to c. before winter. 4.21
do your best to c. to me at Nicopolis, Tit 3.12
angels that God subjected the world to c., Heb 2.05
of God and the powers of the age to c., 6.05
"The days will c., says the Lord, when I 8.08
priest of the good things that have c., 9.11
but a shadow of the good things to c. 10.01
'Lo, I have c. to do they will, O God,' 10.07
he added, "Lo, I have c. to do thy will." 10.09
the coming one shall c. and shall not tarry; 10.37
you have not c. to what may be touched, 12.18
you have c. to Mount Zion and to the 12.22
but we seek the city which is to c. 13.14
Those who c. from Italy send you greetings. 13.24
C. now, you who say, "Today or Jas 4.13
C. now, you rich, weep and howl for 5.01
C. to him, to that living stone, rejected 1Pe 2.04
time has c. for judgment to begin with 1Pe 4.17
scoffers will c. in the last days with 2Pe 3.03
the day of the Lord will c. like a thief, 3.10
coming, so now many antichrists have c.; 1Jn 2.18
Jesus Christ has c. in the flesh is of 4.02
we know that the Son of God has c. 5.20
I hope to c. to see you and talk with 2Jn 1.12
if I c., I will bring up what he is doing, 3Jn 1.10
who is and who was and who is to c., Rev 1.04
was and who is to c., the Almighty. 1.08
I will c. to you and remove your 2.05
I will c. to you soon and war against 2.16
hold fast what you have, until I c. 2.25
will not awake, I will c. like a thief, 3.03
you will not know at what hour I will c. 3.03
I will make them c. and bow down 3.09
I will c. in to him and eat with him, 3.20
"C. up hither, and I will show you 4.01
Almighty, who was and is and is to c.!" 4.08
say, as with a voice of thunder, "C.!" 6.01
I heard the second living creature say, "C.!" 6.03
heard the third living creature say, "C.!" 6.05
voice of the fourth living creature say, "C.!" 6.07
the great day of their wrath has c., 6.17
in white robes, and whence have they c.?" 7.13
who have c. out of the great tribulation; 7.14
behold, two woes are still to c. 9.12
heaven saying to them, "C. up hither!" 11.12
behold, the third woe is soon to c. 11.14
and the authority of his Christ have c., 12.10
devil has c. down to you in great wrath, 12.12
fire c. down from heaven to earth in 13.13
glory, for the hour of his judgment has c.; 14.07
All nations shall c. and worship thee, 15.04
"C., I will show you the judgment of 17.01
one is, the other has not yet c., and 17.10
"C. out of her, my people, lest you 18.04
so shall her plagues c. in a single day, 18.08
Babylon! In one hour has thy judgment c." 18.10
for the marriage of the Lamb has c., 19.07
"C., gather for the great supper of God, 19.17

COME (cont.)
"C., I will show you the Bride, the Rev 21.09
The Spirit and the Bride say, "C." 22.17
let him who hears say, "C." And let 22.17
who is thirsty c., let him who desires 22.17
coming soon." Amen. C., Lord Jesus! 22.20

COMELINESS
had no form or c. that we should Is 53.02

COMELY
let loose, that bears c. fawns. Gen 49.21
youth, ruddy and c. in appearance. 1Sa 17.42
but c., O daughters of Jerusalem, Sol 1.05
Your cheeks are c. with ornaments, 1.10
is sweet, and your face is c. 2.14
c. as Jerusalem, terrible as an army 6.04
The c. and delicately bred I will Jer 6.02

COMES
let the young woman who c. out to draw, Gen 24.43
"If Esau c. to the one company and 32.08
one another, "Here c. this dreamer. 37.19
unless your youngest brother c. here. 42.15
'Unless your youngest brother c. down with 44.23
until he c. to whom it belongs; and 49.10
delivered before the midwife c. to them." Ex 1.19
If he c. in single, he shall go out 21.03
if he c. in married, then his wife shall 21.03
LORD, and when he c. out, lest he die. 28.35
when he c. into the tent of meeting to 29.30
priest c. and makes an examination, Lev 14.48
when its produce c. in, you shall eat 25.22
if any one else c. near, he shall be Num 1.51
c. near, he shall be put to death." 3.10
if the spirit of jealousy c. upon him, 5.14
c. upon him, and he is jealous of his 5.14
the spirit of jealousy c. upon a man 5.30
until it c. out at your nostrils and 11.20
when he c. out of his mother's womb." 12.12
Every one who c. near, who c. near to 17.13
else who c. near shall be put to death." 18.07
every one who c. into the tent, and 19.14
wonder which he tells you c. to pass, Deu 13.02
"And if a Levite c. from any of your 18.06
but when evening c. on, he shall 23.11
her afterbirth that c. out from between 28.57
and the foreigner who c. from a far 29.22
when all Israel c. to appear before 31.11
at hand, and their doom c. swiftly. 32.35
any man c. and asks you, "Is any one Ju 4.20
whoever c. forth from the doors of 11.31
of anything that c. from the vine, 13.14
held in honor; all that he says c. true. 1Sa 9.06
for the people will not eat until he c., 9.13
we will not sit down till he c. here." 16.11
and when your father c. to see you, 2Sa 13.05
until word c. from you to inform me." 15.28
is a good man, and c. with good tidings." 18.27
c. and swears his oath before thine altar 1Ki 8.31
c. from a far country for thy name's sake 8.41
when he c. and prays toward this house, 8.42
when the messenger c., shut the door, 2Ki 6.32
as soon as this letter c. to you, seeing 10.02
king when he goes out and when he c. in." 11.08
the LORD, for he c. to judge the earth. 1Ch 16.33
c. from thy hand and is all thy own. 29.16
c. and swears his oath before thy altar 2Ch 6.22
c. from a far country for the sake of 6.32
when he c. and prays toward this house, 6.32
Whoever c. to consecrate himself with a 13.09
whenever a case c. to you from your 19.10
'If evil c. upon us, the sword, judgment, 20.09
with the king when he c. in, and when 23.07
who long for death, but it c. not, Job 3.21
For my sighing c. as my bread, and 3.24
For the thing that I fear c. upon me, 3.25
quiet; I have no rest; but trouble c." 3.26
shall not fear destruction when it c. 5.21
a shock of grain c. up to the threshing 5.26
He c. forth like a flower, and withers; 14.02
drawn forth and c. out of his body, 20.25
the glittering point c. out of his gall; 20.25
out? That their calamity c. upon them? 21.17
his cry, when trouble c. upon him? 27.09
As for the earth, out of it c. bread; 28.05
"Whence then c. wisdom? And where 28.20
From its chamber c. the whirlwind, and 37.09
Out of the north c. golden splendor; God 37.22
which c. forth like a bridegroom leaving Ps 19.05
night, but joy c. with the morning. 30.05
when one c. to see me, he utters empty 41.06
Our God c., he does not keep silence, 50.03
in silence; from him c. my salvation. 62.01
and not from the wilderness c. lifting up; 75.06
flesh, a wind that passes and c. not again. 78.39
for he c., for he c. to judge the earth. 96.13
the LORD, for he c. to rule the earth. 98.09
My help c. from the LORD, who made 121.02
and your calamity c. like a whirlwind, Pro 1.27
or of the ruin of the wicked, when it c.; 3.25
the expectation of the wicked c. to nought. 10.28
When pride c., then c. disgrace; but 11.02
evil c. to him who searches for it. 11.27
strong tower of the wicked c. to ruin, 12.12
the work of a man's hand c. back to him. 12.14
he who opens wide his lips c. to ruin. 13.03
When wickedness c., contempt c. also; 18.03
and with dishonor c. disgrace. 18.03
until the other c. and examines him. 18.17
A generation goes, and a generation c., Ecc 1.04
what can the man do who c. after the king? 2.12
a dream c. with much business, and a 5.03
it c. into vanity and goes into darkness, 6.04
one fate c. to all, to the righteous and 9.02
will be many. All that c. is vanity. 11.08
Behold, he c., leaping upon the mountains, Sol 2.08
earth; and lo, swiftly, speedily it c.! Is 5.26
Behold, the day of the LORD c., cruel, 13.09
laid low, no hewer c. up against us.' 14.08
smoke c. out of the north, and there is 14.31
when he c. to his sanctuary to pray, 16.12
is riding on a swift cloud and c. to Egypt; 19.01
it c. from the desert, from a terrible land. 21.01
says: "Morning c., and also the night. 21.12
this also c. from the LORD of hosts; 28.29
every one c. to shame through a people 30.05
whose crash c. suddenly, in an instant; 30.13
Behold, the name of the LORD c. from far, 30.27
fills it; the world, and all that c. from it. 34.01
Behold, the Lord GOD c. with might, 40.10
spread forth the earth and what c. from it, 42.05
"Behold, your salvation c.; behold, his 62.11
Who is this that c. from Edom, in 63.01
a wind too full for this c. for me. Jer 4.12
he c. up like clouds, his chariots like 4.13
what will you do when the end c.? 5.31
Hark, a rumor! Behold, it c.! 10.22
and does not fear when heat c., 17.08
grandson, until the time of his own land c.; 27.07
when the word of that prophet c. to pass, 28.09
"Behold, a people c. from the north; 50.41
report c. in one year and afterward a 51.46
Disaster after disaster! Behold, it c. Eze 7.05
it has awakened against you. Behold, it c. 7.06
"Behold, the day! Behold, it c.! Your 7.10
When anguish c., they will seek peace, but 7.25
Disaster c. upon disaster, rumor follows 7.26
before his face, and yet c. to the prophet, 14.04
yet c. to a prophet to inquire for himself of 14.07
When it c., every heart will melt and all 21.07
Behold, it c. and it will be fulfilled,' " 21.07
even a trace of it until he c. whose right it is; 21.27
When this c., then you will know that I am 24.24

COMES (cont.)

on the day of Egypt's doom; for, lo, it c.! Eze 30.09
the sword c. and takes him away, his blood 33.04
and the sword c., and takes any one of them; 33.06
what the word is that c. forth from the LORD.' 33.30
When this c.—and come it will!—then 33.33
he who c. against him shall do according Dan 11.16
power of the holy people c. to an end 12.07
Blessed is he who waits and c. to the 12.12
and as destruction from the Almighty it c. Joe 1.15
before the great and terrible day of the LORD c. 2.31
so that destruction c. upon the fortress. Amo 5.09
when the Assyrian c. into our land and Mic 5.05
when he c. into our land and treads within 5.06
before there c. upon you the fierce anger Zep 2.02
c. upon you the day of the wrath of the LORD. 2.02
Lo, your king c. to you; triumphant and Zec 9.09
the day c., burning like an oven, when Mal 4.01
the day that c. shall burn them up, says 4.01
the great and terrible day of th LORD c. 4.05
anything more than this c. from evil. Mt 5.37
and he c., and to my slave, 'Do this.' 8.09
towns of Israel, before the Son of man c. 10.23
when he c. he finds it empty, swept, and 12.44
the evil one c. and snatches away what is 13.19
what c. out of the mouth, this defiles a man." 15.11
what c. out of the mouth proceeds from 15.18
kind never c. out except by prayer and * 17.21
and take the first fish that c. up, 17.27
to the man by whom the temptation c.! 18.07
be he who c. in the name of the Lord! 21.09
therefore the owner of the vineyard c., 21.40
be he who c. in the name of the Lord.' " 23.39
as the lightening c. from the east and 24.27
his master when he c. will find so doing. 24.46
"When the Son of man c. in his glory, 25.31
And if this c. to the governor's ears, 28.14
"After me c. he who is mightier than I, Mk 1.07
Satan immediately c. and takes away the 4.15
"What c. out of a man is what defiles 7.20
when he c. in the glory of his Father 8.38
be he who c. in the name of the Lord! 11.09
who c. to me and hears my words and Lk 6.47
and to another, 'Come,' and he c.; and 7.08
the devil c. and takes away the word 8.12
be ashamed when he c. in his glory and 9.26
when he c. he finds it swept and put 11.25
may open to him at once when he c. 12.36
whom the master finds awake when he c.; 12.37
If he c. in the second watch, or in 12.38
whom his master when he c. will find 12.43
he who c. in the name of the Lord!' " 13.55
when your host c. he may say to you, 14.10
"If any one c. to me and does not hate 14.26
to meet him who c. against him with 14.31
when he c. home, he calls together his 15.06
Son of man c., will he find faith on earth?" 18.08
the King who c. in the name of the Lord! 19.38
the vine until the kingdom of God c." 22.18
'He who c. after me ranks before me, Jn 1.15
who c. after me, the thong of whose 1.27
'After me c. a man who ranks before 1.30
but you do not know whence it c. or 3.08
who does what is true c. to the light, 3.21
He who c. from above is above all; 3.31
he who c. from heaven is above all. 3.31
when he c., he will show us all things." 4.25
are yet four months, then c. the harvest'? 4.35
c. in his own name, him you will receive. 5.43
seek the glory that c. from the only God? 5.44
God is that which c. down from heaven, 6.33
he who c. to me shall not hunger, and 6.35
him who c. to me I will not cast out. 6.37
and learned from the Father c. to me. 6.45
is the bread which c. down from heaven, 6.50
Yet we know where this man c. from; 7.27
appears, no one will know where he c. from." 7.27
descended from David, and c. from Bethlehem, 7.42
day; night c., when no one can work. 9.04
thief c. only to steal and kill and destroy; 10.10
be he who c. in the name of the Lord, 12.13
no one c. to the Father, but by me. 14.06
But when the Counselor c., whom I 15.26
when their hour c. you may remember 16.04
when he c., he will convince the world 16.08
the Spirit of truth c., he will guide you 16.13
before the day of the Lord c., the great Ac 2.20
are ready to kill him before he c. near." 23.15
"When Lysias the tribune c. down, I 24.22
I have had the help that c. from God, 26.22
faith c. from what is heard, and Rom 10.17
what is heard c. by the preaching of Christ. 10.17
before the time, before the Lord c., 1Co 4.05
you proclaim the Lord's death until he c. 11.26
the perfect c., the imperfect will pass 13.10
c. the end, when he delivers the kingdom 15.24
Timothy c., see that you put him at ease 16.10
some one c. and preaches another Jesus 2Co 11.04
wrath of God c. upon the sons of disobedience. Eph 5.06
instructions—if he c. to you, receive him), Col 4.10
as travail c. upon a woman with child, 1Th 5.03
when he c. on that day to be glorified 2Th 1.10
unless the rebellion c. first, and the 2.03
with whom I shall see you if he c. soon. Heb 13.23
in fine clothing c. into your assembly, Jas 2.02
a poor man in shabby clothing also c. in, 2.02
wisdom is not such as c. down from above, 3.15
the fiery ordeal which c. upon you to 1Pe 4.12
If any one c. to you and does not bring 2Jn 1.10
New Jerusalem which c. down from my Rev 3.12
he c. he must remain only a little while. 17.10

COMFORT

his daughters rose up to c. him; Gen 37.35
and his brothers came to c. him. 1Ch 7.22
to condole with him and c. him. Job 2.11
'My bed will c. me, my couch will 7.13
alone, that I may find a little c. 10.20
How then will you c. me with empty 21.34
thy rod and thy staff, they c. me. Ps 23.04
increase my honor, and c. me again. 71.21
This is my c. in my affliction that 119.50
from of old, I take c., O LORD. 119.52
be ready to c. me according to thy 119.76
I ask, "When will thou c. me?" 119.82
and they had no one to c. them! Ecc 4.01
and there was no one to c. them. 4.01
turned away, and thou didst c. me. Is 12.01
do not labor to c. me for the 22.04
C., c. my people, says your God. 40.01
For the LORD will c. Zion; he will 51.03
he will c. all her waste places, and 51.03
and sword, who will c. you? 51.19
lead him and requite him with c., 57.18
of our God, to c. all who mourn; 61.02
mother comforts, so I will c. you; 66.13
to c. him for the dead; nor shall Jer 16.07
I will c. them, and give them 31.13
her lovers she has none to c. her; Lam 1.02
hands, but there is none to c. her; 1.17
there is none to c. me. All my 1.21
that I may c. you, O virgin daughter 2.13
he will c. himself for all his Eze 22.31
LORD will again c. Zion and again Zec 1.17
Lord and in the c. of the Holy Ac 9.31
of mercies and God of all c., 2Co 1.03
may be able to c. those who are in 1.04
with the c. with which we ourselves 1.04
we share abundantly in c. too. 1.05
it is for your c. and salvation; 1.06
are comforted, it is for your c., 1.06
you will also share in our c. 1.07
rather turn to forgive and c. him, 2.07
I am filled with c. With all 7.04

COMFORT (cont.)
but also by the c. with which he 2Co 7.07
besides our own c. we rejoiced 7.13
God, and they have been a c. to me. Col 4.11
Therefore c. one another with these 1Th 4.18
gave us eternal c. and good hope 2Th 2.16
c. your hearts and establish them 2.17
much joy and c. from your love, Phm 1.07

COMFORTED
So Isaac was c. after his mother's Gen 24.67
but he refused to be c., and said, 37.35
and when Judah was c., he went 38.12
Thus he reassured them and c. them. 50.21
for you have c. me and spoken Ru 2.13
Then David c. his wife, Bathsheba, 2Sa 12.24
for he was c. about Amnon, seeing he 13.39
sympathy and c. him for all the Job 42.11
wearying; my soul refuses to be c. Ps 77.02
LORD, hast helped me and c. me. 86.17
For the LORD has c. his people. Is 49.13
for the LORD has c. his people, 52.09
and not c., behold, I will set your 54.11
you shall be c. in Jerusalem. 66.13
refuses to be c. for her children, Jer 31.15
will be c. in the nether world. Eze 31.16
who mourn, for they shall be c. Mt 5.04
but now he is c. here, and you are Lk 16.25
alive, and were not a little c. Ac 20.12
which we ourselves are c. by God. 2Co 1.04
and if we are c., it is for your 1.06
c. us by the coming of Titus, 7.06
with which he was c. in you, 7.07
Therefore we are c. And besides 7.13
we have been c. about you through 1Th 3.07

COMFORTER
fall is terrible, she has no c. Lam 1.09
for a c. is far from me, one to 1.16

COMFORTERS
because David has sent c. to you, 2Sa 10.03
because David has sent c. to you. 1Ch 19.03
miserable c. are you all. Job 16.02
and for c., but I found none. Ps 69.20
whence shall I seek c. for her? Nah 3.07

COMFORTING
gracious and c. words to the angel Zec 1.13

COMFORTS
brother Esau c. himself by planning Gen 27.42
troops, like one who c. mourners. Job 29.25
"I, I am he that c. you; Is 51.12
As one whom his mother c.. so I will 66.13
who c. us in all our affliction, so 2Co 1.04
But God, who c. the downcast, comforted 7.06

COMING
men of the city are c. out to draw water. Gen 24.13
looked, and behold, there were camels c. 24.63
Rachel his daughter is c. with the sheep!" 29.06
Esau, and he is c. to meet you, and 32.06
Esau was c., and four hundred men with 33.01
a caravan of Ishmaelites c. from Gilead, 37.25
all the food of these good years that are c., 41.35
ready the present for Joseph's c. at noon, 43.25
he is c. out to meet you, and when Ex 4.14
c. between the host of Egypt and the host 14.20
without one c. near the other all night. 14.20
your father-in-law Jethro is c. to you with 18.06
I am c. to you in a thick cloud, that the 19.09
heard that Israel was c. by the way Num 21.01
nothing hinder you from c. to me; 22.16
heard of the c. of the people of Israel. 33.40
and c. to the Levitical priests, and Deu 17.09
the waters c. down from above shall Jos 3.13
the waters c. down from above 4.16
then, for war, and for going and c. 14.11
spies saw a man c. out of the city, Ju 1.24
'Why is his chariot so long in c.? 5.28
tents; c. like locusts for number; 6.05
men are c. down from the mountain tops!" 9.36
men are c. down from the center of the 9.37
one company is c. from the direction 9.37
saw the men c. out of the city, and 9.43
"Because Israel on c. from Egypt took 11.13
an old man was c. from his work 19.16
woman, who is c. into your house, Ru 4.11
Behold, the days are c., when I will 1Sa 2.31
they saw Samuel c. out toward them 9.14
a band of prophets c. down from the high 10.05
I am c. to you to offer burnt offerings 10.08
Saul was c. from the field behind the 11.05
Hebrews are c. out of the holes where they 14.11
As they were c. home, when David 18.06
"I saw the son of Jesse c. to Nob, to 22.09
"An old man is c. up; and he is wrapped 28.14
from the day of your c. to me to this day. 29.06
to know your going out and your c. in, 2Sa 3.25
people were c. from the Horonaim road 13.34
king and his servants c. on toward him; 24.20
wife of Jeroboam is c. to inquire of you 1Ki 14.05
him, "Men are c. out from Samaria." 20.17
man of God saw her c., he said to 2Ki 4.25
reached them, but he is not c. back." 9.18
"He reached them, but he is not c. back. 9.20
Jehonadab the son of Rechab c. to meet him; 10.15
down and your going out and c. in, 19.27
the days are c., when all that is in your 20.17
men kept c. to David to help him, 1Ch 12.22
"A great multitude is c. against you 2Ch 20.02
they reward us by c. to drive us out 20.11
against this great multitude that is c. 20.12
against those who were c. from the war, 28.12
I am not c. against you this day, 35.21
second year of their c. to the house of Ez 3.08
the temple; for they are c. to kill you, Neh 6.10
at night they are c. to kill you." 6.10
the calamity that is c. to my people? Est 8.06
wicked, for he sees that his day is c. Ps 37.13
but tell to the c. generation the glorious 78.04
LORD will keep your going out and your c. in 121.08
What is that c. up from the wilderness, Sol 3.06
Who is that c. up from the wilderness, 8.05
the LORD is c. forth out of his place Is 26.21
down and your going out and your c. in., 37.28
the days are c., when all that is in your 39.06
I am c. to gather all nations and tongues; 66.18
Warn the nations that he is c.; Jer 4.16
a people is c. from the north country, 6.22
behold, the days are c., says the LORD, 7.32
and crane keep the time of their c.; 8.07
the days are c., says the LORD, when I will 9.25
the days are c., says the LORD, when it 16.14
days are c., says the LORD, when this place 19.06
c., says the LORD, when I shall raise up for 23.05
c., says the LORD, when men shall no 23.07
c., says the LORD, when I will restore the 30.03
"Behold, the days are c., says the LORD, 31.27
c., says the LORD, when I will make a 31.31
are c., says the LORD, when the city 31.38
Chaldeans are c. in to fight and to 33.05
are c., says the LORD, when I will fulfil 33.14
that is c. to destroy all the Philistines, 47.04
"Therefore, behold, the days are c., says the 48.12
days are c., says the LORD, when I will 49.02
like a lion c. up from the jungle of 49.19
"Behold, like a lion c. up from the 50.44
days are c. when I will punish the 51.47
behold, the days are c., says the LORD, 51.52
if he sees the sword c. upon the land and Eze 33.03
watchman sees the sword c. and does not 33.06
You will advance, c. on like a storm, 38.09
it is c. and it will be brought about, 39.08

COMING (cont.)
sound of his c. was like the sound of Eze 43.02
a holy one, c. down from heaven and Dan 4.23
for the day of the LORD is c., it is near, Joe 2.01
the days are c. upon you, when they shall Amo 4.02
the days are c.," says the LORD GOD, "when 8.11
"Behold, the days are c.," says the LORD 9.13
the LORD is c. forth out of his place, Mic 1.03
And I said, "What are these c. to do?" Zec 1.21
and behold, two women c. forward! 5.09
a day of the LORD is c., when the spoil 14.01
behold, he is c., says the LORD of hosts. Mal 3.01
But who can endure the day of his c., 3.02
Pharisees and Sadducees c. for baptism, Mt 3.07
he who is c. after me is mightier than I, 3.11
demoniacs met him, c. out of the tombs, 8.28
c. to his own country he taught them 13.54
they see the Son of man c. in his kingdom." 16.28
as they were c. down the mountain, 17.09
your king is c. to you, humble, and 21.05
sign of your c. and of the close of the age?" 24.03
so will be the c. of the Son of man. 24.27
Son of man c. on the clouds of heaven 24.30
days of Noah, so will be the c. of the Son 24.37
do not know on what day your Lord is c. 24.42
in what part of the night the thief was c., 24.43
the Son of man is c. at an hour you do not 24.44
at my c. I should have received what 25.27
Power, and c. on the clouds of heaven." 26.64
c. out of the tombs after his resurrection 27.53
he cannot stand, but is c. to an end. Mk 3.26
many were c. and going, and they had 6.31
as they were c. down the mountain, 9.09
kingdom of our father David that is c.! 11.10
will see the Son of man c. in clouds with 13.26
Power, and c. with the clouds of heaven." 14.62
who was c. in from the country, the 15.21
c. up at that very hour she gave Lk 2.38
but he who is mightier than I is c., the 3.16
he was c., the demons tore him and 9.42
known at what hour the thief was c., 12.39
Son of man is c. at an hour you do not 12.40
himself, 'My master is delayed in c.,' 12.45
you say at once, 'A shower is c.'; and 12.54
when the kingdom of God was c., he 17.20
kingdom of God is not c. with signs to 17.20
"The days are c. when you will desire to 17.22
widow in that city who kept c. to him 18.03
will wear me out by her continual c.'" 18.05
at my c. I should have collected it with 19.23
with foreboding of what is c. on the world; 21.26
will see the Son of man c. in a cloud 21.27
Simon of Cyrene, who was c. in from the 23.26
the days are c. when they will say, 23.29
mocked him, c. up and offering him vinegar, 23.36
true light that enlightens every man was c. Jn 1.09
Jesus saw Nathanael c. to him, and said 1.47
the hour is c. when neither on this mountain 4.21
But the hour is c., and now is, when the 4.23
said to him, "I know that Messiah is c. 4.25
went out of the city and were c. to him. 4.30
hour is c., and now is, when the dead 5.25
hour is c. when all who are in the tombs 5.28
seeing that a multitude was c. to him, 6.05
sees the wolf c. and leaves the sheep 10.12
When Martha heard that Jesus was c., 11.20
Christ, the Son of God, he who is c. into 11.27
heard that Jesus was c. to Jerusalem. 12.12
behold, your king is c., sitting on 12.15
you, for the ruler of the world is c. 14.30
hour is c. when whoever kills you will 16.02
hour is c. when I shall no longer speak 16.25
The hour is c., indeed it has come, 16.32
are in the world, and I am c. to thee. 17.11
now I am c. to thee; and these things 17.13
beforehand the c. of the Righteous One, Ac 7.52
angel of God c. in and saying to him, 10.03
for; what is the reason for your c.?" 10.21
who on c. to Antioch spoke to the 11.20
Before his c. John had preached a 13.24
after me one is c., the sandals of 13.25
c. to us he took Paul's girdle and 21.11
brethren c. here has reported or spoken 28.21
may now at last succeed in c. to you. Rom 1.10
often been hindered from c. to you. 15.22
arrogant, as though I were not c. to you. 1Co 4.18
at his c. those who belong to Christ. 15.23
I rejoice at the c. of Stephanas and 16.17
that I refrained from c. to Corinth. 2Co 1.23
comforted us by the c. of Titus, 7.06
only by his c. but also by the comfort 7.07
This is the third time I am c. to you. 13.01
in the c. ages he might show the Eph 2.07
Jesus, because of my c. to you again. Php 1.26
account of these the wrath of God is c. Col 3.06
boasting before our Lord Jesus at his c.? 1Th 2.19
at the c. of our Lord Jesus with all his 3.13
who are left until the c. of the Lord 4.15
blameless at the c. of our Lord Jesus Christ. 5.23
concerning the c. of our Lord Jesus Christ 2Th 2.01
destroy him by his appearing and his c. 2.08
the c. of the lawless one by the activity 2.09
time is c. when people will not endure 2Ti 4.03
the c. one shall come and shall not tarry; Heb 10.37
c. down from the Father of lights Jas 1.17
therefore, brethren, until the c. of the Lord. 5.07
for the c. of the Lord is at hand. 5.08
power and c. of our Lord Jesus Christ, 2Pe 1.16
"Where is the promise of his c.? For 3.04
hastening the c. of the day of God, 3.12
as you have heard that antichrist is c., 1Jn 2.18
not shrink from him in shame at his c. 2.28
of which you heard that it was c., 4.03
not acknowledge the c. of Jesus Christ 2Jn 1.07
he is c. with the clouds, and every Rev 1.07
trial which is c. on the whole world, 3.10
I am c. soon; hold fast what you have, 3.11
I saw another mighty angel c. down from 10.01
("Lo, I am c. like a thief! Blessed is he 16.15
I saw another angel c. down from heaven, 18.01
I saw an angel c. down from heaven, 20.01
Jerusalem, c. down out of heaven from God, 21.02
And behold, I am c. soon." Blessed is 22.07
I am c. soon, bringing my recompense, to 22.12
things says, "Surely I am c. soon." 22.20

COMMAND
my son, obey my word as I c. you. Gen 27.08
shall order themselves as you c.; 41.40
C. them also, "Do this: take wagons 45.19
according to the c. of Pharaoh, 45.21
father gave this c. before he died, 50.16
You shall speak all that I c. you; Ex 7.02
"Be pleased to c. me when I am to 8.09
the LORD our God as he will c. us." 8.27
"And you shall c. the people of 27.20
"Observe what I c. you this day. 34.11
So Moses gave c., and word was 36.06
"C. Aaron and his sons, saying, This Lev 6.09
priest shall c. that they wash the 13.54
the priest shall c. them to take 14.04
priest shall c. them to kill one 14.05
priest shall c. that they empty 14.36
priest shall c. that they take out 14.40
"C. the people of Israel to bring 24.02
I will c. my blessing upon you in 25.21
shall be at the c. of Aaron and Num 4.27
"C. the people of Israel that they 5.02
the LORD will c. concerning you." 9.08
At the c. of the LORD the people of 9.18
and at the c. of the LORD they 9.18
to the c. of the LORD they remained 9.20
the c. of the LORD they set out. 9.20
At the c. of the LORD they encamped, 9.23

COMMAND (cont.)

at the c. of the LORD they set out; Num 9.23
at the c. of the LORD by Moses. 9.23
time at the c. of the LORD by 10.13
according to the c. of the LORD, 13.03
transgressing the c. of the LORD, 14.41
against my c. at the waters of 20.24
go beyond the c. of the LORD my 22.18
I received a c. to bless: he has 23.20
"C. the people of Israel, and say to 28.02
men of war who are under our c., 31.49
So Moses gave c. concerning them to 32.28
stage by stage, by c. of the LORD; 33.02
up Mount Hor at the c. of the LORD, 33.38
"C. the people of Israel, and say to 34.02
"C. the people of Israel, that they 35.02
against the c. of the LORD your Deu 1.26
rebelled against the c. of the LORD, 1.43
And c. the people, You are about to 2.04
not add to the word which I c. you, 4.02
the LORD your God which I c. you. 4.02
which I c. you this day, that it may 4.40
which I c. you, all the days of your 6.02
words which I c. you this day 6.06
ordinances, which I c. you this day. 7.11
commandent which I c. you this day 8.01
statutes. which I c. you this day: 8.11
which I c. you this day for your 10.13
commandment which I c. you this day, 11.08
commandments which I c. you this day, 11.13
commandment which I c. you to do, 11.22
your God, which I c. you this day, 11.27
the way which I c. you this day, 11.28
you shall bring all that I c. you: 12.11
all these words which I c. you, 12.28
"Everything that I c. you you shall 12.32
commandments which I c. you this day, 13.18
commandment which I c. you this day. 15.05
therefore I c. you, You shall open 15.11
you; therefore I c. you this today. 15.15
speak to them all that I c. him. 18.18
Therefore I c. you, You shall set 19.07
which I c. you this day, by loving 19.09
therefore I c. you to do this. 24.18
therefore I c. you to do this. 24.22
commandment which I c. you this day. 27.01
concerning which I c. you this day, 27.04
statutes, which I c. you this day." 27.10
commandments which I c. you this day, 28.01
The LORD will c. the blessing upon 28.08
which I c. you this day, being 28.13
the words which I c. you this day, 28.14
statutes which I c. you this day, 28.15
in all that I c. you this day, 30.02
commandments which I c. you this day. 30.08
commandment which I c. you this day 30.11
your God which I c. you this day, 30.16
that you may c. them to your 32.46
and c. the people, 'Prepare your Jos 1.11
whatever you c. him, shall be put to 1.18
And you shall c. the priests who 3.08
and c. them, 'Take twelve stones 4.03
"C. the priests who bear the ark of 4.16
By c. of the LORD they gave him the 19.50
So by c. of the LORD the people of 21.03
themselves by c. of the LORD 22.09
But you have not obeyed my c. Ju 2.02
c. you, "Go, gather your men at Mount 4.06
Let our lord now c. your servants, 1Sa 16.16
for by the c. of Absalom this has 2Sa 13.32
one third under the c. of Joab, 18.02
third under the c. of Abishai the 18.02
third under the c. of Ittai the 18.02
Now Joab was in c. of all the army 20.23
Jehoiada was in c. of the Cherethites 20.23
of Jehoiada was in c. of the army; 1Ki 4.04
Now therefore c. that cedars of 5.06

At the king's c., they quarried out 5.17
will hearken to all that I c. you, 11.38
his fellow at the c. of the LORD, 20.35
not a word, for the king's c. was, 2Ki 18.36
according to the c. of Pharaoh. 23.35
upon Judah at the c. of the LORD, 24.03
who had been in c. of the men of 25.19
he did not keep the c. of the LORD, 1Ch 10.13
all their kinsmen under their c. 12.32
gods there, and David gave c., 14.12
for the king's c. was abhorrent to 21.06
not I who gave c. to number the 21.17
the thirty and in c. of the thirty; 27.06
people will be wholly at your c." 28.21
or c. the locust to devour the land, 2Ch 7.13
and by c. of the king they stoned 24.21
Under their c. was an army of three 26.13
As soon as the c. was spread abroad, 31.05
divisions according to the king's c. 35.10
place according to the c. of David, 35.15
according to the c. of King Josiah. 35.16
building by c. of the God of Ez 6.14
which thou didst c. by thy servants 9.11
thou didst c. thy servant Moses. Neh 1.07
thou didst c. thy servant Moses, 1.08
sabbath and c. them commandments 9.14
For there was a c. from the king 11.23
according to the c. of David and 12.45
at the king's c. conveyed by the Est 1.12
performed the c. of King Ahasuerus 1.15
do you transgress the king's c.?" 3.03
the king's c. and his decree came, 4.03
in haste, urged by the king's c.; 8.14
the king's c. and his edict came, 8.17
when the king's c. and edict were 9.01
The c. of Queen Esther fixed these 9.32
know how God lays his c. upon them, Job 37.15
Is it at your c. that the eagle 39.27
The Lord gives the c.; great is Ps 68.11
He sends forth his c. to the earth; 147.15
stormy wind fulfilling his c.! 148.08
waters might not transgress his c., Pro 8.29
Keep the king's c., and because Ecc 8.02
He who obeys a c. will meet no harm, 8.05
I will also a. the clouds that they Is 5.06
the people of my wrath I c. him, 10.06
LORD has given c. concerning 23.11
not a word, for the king's c. was, 36.21
or c. me concerning the work of my 45.11
and whatever I c. you you shall Jer 1.07
to them everything that I c. you. 1.17
your fathers or c. them concerning 7.22
But this c. I gave them, 'Obey my 7.23
walk in all the way that I c. you, 7.23
which I did not c., nor did it 7.31
my voice, and do all that I c. you. 11.04
nor did I c. them or speak to them. 14.14
Baal, which I did not c. or decree, 19.05
words that I c. you to speak to 26.02
words which I did not c. them. 29.23
of all thou didst c. them to do. 32.23
Molech, though I did not c. them, 32.35
Behold, I will c., says the LORD, and 34.22
The c. which Jonadab the son of 35.14
they have obeyed their father's c. 35.14
have kept the c. which their 35.16
have obeyed the c. of Jonadab your 35.18
of Babylon gave c. concerning 39.11
who had been in c. of the men of 52.25
"I have done as thou didst c. me." Eze 9.11
and set at nought the king's c., Dan 3.28
there I will c. the serpent, and it Amo 9.03
there I will c. the sword, and it 9.04
I will c., and shake the house of 9.09
and he shall c. peace to the Zec 9.10
now, O priests, this c. is for you. Mal 2.01
that I have sent this c. to you, 2.04

COMMAND (cont.)
c. these stones to become loaves of Mt 4.03
then did Moses c. one to give a 19.07
"C. that these two sons of mine may 20.21
I c. you, come out of him, and never Mk 9.25
them, "What did Moses c. you?" 10.03
c. this stone to become bread." Lk 4.03
him not to c. them to depart into 8.31
you, and I never disobeyed your c.; 15.29
my friends if you do what I c. you. Jn 15.14
This I c. you, to love one another. 15.17
and receiving a c. for Silas and Ac 17.15
Then by c. of Festus Paul was 25.23
according to the c. of the eternal Rom 16.26
by the way of concession, not of c. 1Co 7.06
I have no c. of the Lord, but I give 7.25
writing to you is a c. of the Lord. 14.37
I say this not as a c., but to prove 2Co 8.08
so that you may c. the respect of 1Th 4.12
from heaven with a cry of c., 4.16
and will do the things which we c. 2Th 3.04
Now we c. you, brethren, in the name 3.06
were with you, we gave you this c.: 3.10
Now such persons we c. and exhort 3.12
Christ Jesus by c. of God our 1Ti 1.01
C. and teach these things. 4.11
C. this, so that they may be without 5.07
entrusted by c. of God our Savior; Tit 1.03
in Christ to c. you to do what is Phm 1.08

COMMANDED
And the LORD God c. the man, Gen 2.16
tree of which I c. you not to eat?" 3.11
of the tree of which I c. you, 3.17
he did all that God c. him. 6.22
did all that the LORD had c. him. 7.05
ark with Noah, as God had c. Noah. 7.09
flesh, went in as God had c. him; 7.16
eight days old, as God had c. him. 21.04
Then he c. the steward of his house, 44.01
land of Rameses, as Pharaoh had c. 47.11
And Joseph c. his servants the 50.02
sons did for him as he had c. them; 50.12
do as the king of Egypt c. them, Ex 1.17
Then Pharaoh c. all his people, 1.22
day Pharaoh c. the taskmasters of 5.06
they did as the LORD c. them. 7.06
to Pharaoh and did as the LORD c.; 7.10
Moses and Aaron did as the LORD c.; 7.20
as the LORD had c. Moses and Aaron, 12.28
as the LORD c. Moses and Aaron, so 12.50
This is what the LORD has c.: 16.16
them, "This is what the LORD has c.: 16.23
said, "This is what the LORD has c.: 16.32
As the LORD c. Moses, so Aaron 16.34
words which the LORD had c. him. 19.07
as I c. you, you shall eat unleavened 23.15
according to all that I have c. you; 29.35
may make all that I have c. you: 31.06
to all that I have c. you shall do." 31.11
out of the way which I c. them; 32.08
Sinai, as the LORD had c. him, 34.04
as I c. you, at the time appointed 34.18
people of Israel what he was c., 34.34
which the LORD has c. you to do. 35.01
is the thing which the LORD has c. 35.04
and make all that the LORD has c.: 35.10
the LORD had c. by Moses to be 35.29
with all that the LORD has c." 36.01
which the LORD has c. us to do." 36.05
made all that the LORD c. Moses; 38.22
for Aaron; as the LORD had c. Moses. 39.01
linen; as the LORD had c. Moses. 39.05
of Israel; as the LORD had c. Moses. 39.07
ephod; as the LORD had c. Moses. 39.21
ministering; as the LORD had c. Moses. 39.26
needlework; as the LORD had c. Moses. 39.29
above; as the LORD had c. Moses. 39.31
to all that the LORD had c. Moses; 39.32
According to all that the LORD had c. Moses, 39.42
as the LORD had c., 39.43
that the LORD c. him, so he did. 40.16
over it, as the LORD had c. Moses. 40.19
testimony; as the LORD had c. Moses. 40.21
the LORD; as the LORD had c. Moses. 40.23
the LORD; as the LORD had c. Moses. 40.25
upon it; as the LORD had c. Moses. 40.27
offering; as the LORD had c. Moses. 40.29
washed; as the LORD c. Moses. 40.32
the LORD has c. not to be done, Lev 4.02
the LORD has c. not to be done and 4.13
LORD his God has c. not to be done, 4.22
the LORD has c. not to be done, 4.27
the LORD has c. not to be done, 5.17
the LORD c. this to be given them 7.36
which the LORD c. Moses on Mount 7.38
the day that he c. the people of 7.38
And Moses did as the LORD c. him; 8.04
which the LORD has c. to be done." 8.05
holy crown, as the LORD c. Moses. 8.09
caps on them, as the LORD c. Moses. 8.13
the camp, as the LORD c. Moses. 8.17
to the LORD, as the LORD c. Moses. 8.21
ordination, as the LORD c. Moses. 8.29
as I c., saying, 'Aaron and his sons 8.31
the LORD has c. to be done to make 8.34
lest you die; for so I am c." 8.35
things which the LORD c. by Moses. 8.36
what Moses c. before the tent of 9.05
thing which the LORD c. you to do; 9.06
for them; as the LORD has c." 9.07
the altar, as the LORD c. Moses. 9.10
the LORD; as Moses c. 9.21
LORD, such as he had not c. them. 10.01
the LORD; for so I am c. 10.13
as the LORD has c." 10.15
eaten it in the sanctuary, as I c." 10.18
and Moses did as the LORD c. him. 16.34
is the thing which the LORD has c. 17.02
of Israel did as the LORD c. Moses. 24.23
which the LORD c. Moses for the 27.34
as the LORD c. Moses. So he Num 1.19
to all that the LORD c. Moses. 1.54
of Israel, as the LORD c. Moses. 2.33
to all that the LORD c. Moses, 2.34
the word of the LORD, as he was c. 3.16
of Israel, as the LORD c. him. 3.42
of the LORD, as the LORD c. Moses. 3.51
by him, as the LORD c. Moses. 4.49
lampstand, as the LORD c. Moses. 8.03
that the LORD c. Moses concerning 8.20
as the LORD had c. Moses concerning 8.22
to all that the LORD c. Moses, 9.05
all that the LORD has c. you by Moses, 15.23
with stones, as the LORD c. Moses. 15.36
as the LORD c. him, so he did. 17.11
of the law which the LORD has c.: 19.02
from before the LORD, as he c. him. 20.09
Moses did as the LORD c.; 20.27
and upward," as the LORD c. Moses. 26.04
ordinance, as the LORD c. Moses.'" 27.11
And Moses did as the LORD c. him; 27.22
just as the LORD had c. Moses. 29.40
"This is what the LORD has c. 30.01
statutes which the LORD c. Moses, 30.16
as the LORD c. Moses, and slew every 31.07
law which the LORD has c. Moses: 31.21
priest did as the LORD c. Moses. 31.31
the priest, as the LORD c. Moses. 31.41
the LORD; as the LORD c. Moses. 31.47
Moses c. the people of Israel, 34.13
the LORD has c. to give to the 34.13
whom the LORD c. to divide the 34.29
"The LORD c. my lord to give the 36.02

COMMANDED (cont.)

and my lord was c. by the LORD to	Num 36.02
And Moses c. the people of Israel	36.05
Zelophehad did as the LORD c. Moses;	36.10
which the LORD c. by Moses to the	36.13
And I c. you at that time all the	Deu 1.18
Amorites, as the LORD our God c. us;	1.19
just as the LORD our God c. us.'	1.41
"And I c. you at that time, saying,	3.18
And I c. Joshua at that time, 'Your	3.21
ordinances, as the LORD my God c. me,	4.05
which he c. you to perform, that is,	4.13
And the LORD c. me at that time to	4.14
holy, as the LORD your God c. you.	5.12
LORD your God c. you to keep the	5.15
as the LORD your God c. you;	5.16
as the LORD your God has c. you;	5.32
which the LORD your God has c. you,	5.33
LORD your God c. me to teach you,	6.01
his statutes, which he has c. you.	6.17
which the LORD our God has c. you?'	6.20
And the LORD c. us to do all these	6.24
the LORD our God, as he has c. us.'	6.25
out of the way which I c. them;	9.12
the way which the LORD had c. you.	9.16
there they are, as the LORD c. me.	10.05
has given you, as I have c. you;	12.21
the LORD your God c. you to walk.	13.05
which I have not c. him to speak,	18.20
as the LORD your God has c.;	20.17
as I c. them, so you shall be	24.08
commandment which thou hast c. me;	26.13
to all that thou hast c. me.	26.14
the elders of Israel c. the people,	27.01
and his statutes which he c. you.	28.45
which the LORD c. Moses to make	29.01
commandment which I have c. you.	30.05
And Moses c. them, "At the end of	31.10
Moses c. the Levites who carried	31.25
from the way which I have c. you;	31.29
when Moses c. us a law, as a possession	33.04
and did as the LORD had c. Moses.	34.09
law which Moses my servant c. you;	Jos 1.07
Have I not c. you? Be strong and	1.09
Then Joshua c. the officers of the	1.10
the servant of the LORD c. you,	1.13
"All that you have c. us we will do,	1.16
and c. the people, "When you see the	3.03
the men of Israel did as Joshua c.,	4.08
that the LORD c. Joshua to tell	4.10
to all that Moses had c. Joshua.	4.10
Joshua therefore c. the priests,	4.17
And as Joshua had c. the people,	6.08
But Joshua c. the people, "You shall	6.10
my covenant which I c. them;	7.11
And he c. them, "Behold, you shall	8.04
has bidden; see, I have c. you."	8.08
of the LORD which he c. Joshua.	8.27
going down of the sun Joshua c.,	8.29
of the LORD had c. the people of	8.31
of the LORD had c. at the first,	8.33
all that Moses c. which Joshua did	8.35
your God had c. his servant Moses	9.24
Joshua c., and they took them down	10.27
as the LORD God of Israel c.	10.40
the servant of the LORD had c.	11.12
As the LORD had c. Moses his	11.15
so Moses c. Joshua, and so Joshua	11.15
of all that the LORD had c. Moses.	11.15
exterminated, as the LORD c. Moses.	11.20
an inheritance, as I have c. you.	13.06
as the LORD had c. Moses for the	14.02
of Israel did as the LORD c. Moses;	14.05
"The LORD c. Moses to give us an	17.04
"The LORD c. through Moses that we	21.02
as the LORD had c. through Moses.	21.08
the servant of the LORD c. you,	22.02
my voice in all that I have c. you;	22.02
the servant of the LORD c. you,	22.05
which he c. you, and go and serve	23.16
covenant which I c. their fathers,	Ju 2.20
which he c. their fathers by Moses.	3.04
And he c., "Silence." And all	3.19
all that I c. her let her observe."	13.14
and c. them, "Go and smite the	21.10
And they c. the Benjaminites, saying,	21.20
and my offerings which I c.,	1Sa 2.29
the LORD your God, which he c. you;	13.13
have not kept what the LORD c. you."	13.14
Samuel did what the LORD c.,	16.04
and went, as Jesse had c. him;	17.20
And Saul c. his servants, "Speak to	18.22
my brother has c. me to be there.	20.29
And David c. his young men, and they	2Sa 4.12
And David did as the LORD c. him,	5.25
whom I c. to shepherd my people	7.07
Then Absalom c. his servants, "Mark	13.28
have I not c. you? Be courageous	13.28
did to Amnon as Absalom had c.	13.29
the king c. you and Abishai and	18.12
and they did all that the king c.	21.14
up at Gad's word, as the LORD c.	24.19
Then the king c. Benaiah the son of	1Ki 2.46
ordinances, which he c. our fathers.	8.58
according to all that I have c. you,	9.04
and had c. him concerning this	11.10
he did not keep what the LORD c.	11.10
my statutes which I have c. you,	11.11
for so was it c. me by the word of	13.09
which the LORD your God c. you,	13.21
anything that he c. him all the	15.05
and I have c. the ravens to feed	17.04
I have c. a widow there to feed you."	17.09
of Syria had c. the thirty-two	22.31
the prophet had c. you to do some	2Ki 5.13
And he c. them, "This is the thing	11.05
to all that Jehoiada the priest c.,	11.09
the priest c. the captains who	11.15
law of Moses, where the LORD c.,	14.06
And King Ahaz c. Urijah the priest,	16.15
did all this, as King Ahaz c.	16.16
the law which I c. your fathers,	17.13
the LORD had c. them that they	17.15
Then the king of Assyria c.,	17.27
which the LORD c. the children of	17.34
and c. them, "You shall not fear	17.35
commandments which the LORD c. Moses.	18.06
Moses the servant of the LORD c.;	18.12
according to all that I have c. them,	21.08
law that my servant Moses c. them."	21.08
And the king c. Hilkiah the priest,	22.12
and the king c. Hilkiah, the high	23.04
And the king c. all the people,	23.21
Moses the servant of God had c.	1Ch 6.49
And David did as God c. him,	14.16
as Moses had c. according to the	15.15
David also c. the chiefs of the	15.16
for ever, of the word that he c.,	16.15
law of the LORD which he c. Israel.	16.40
whom I c. to shepherd my people,	17.06
of the LORD c. Gad to say to David	21.18
Then the LORD c. the angel;	21.27
David c. to gather together the	22.02
which the LORD c. Moses for Israel.	22.13
David also c. all the leaders of	22.17
the LORD God of Israel had c. him.	24.19
all that I have c. you and keeping	2Ch 7.17
for so David the man of God had c.	8.14
the king had c. the priests and	8.15
and c. Judah to seek the LORD, the	14.04
of Syria had c. the captains of	18.30
to all that Jehoiada the priest c.	23.08
So the king c., and they made a	24.08
book of Moses, where the LORD c.,	25.04

COMMANDED (cont.)
and went in as the king had c., 2Ch 29.15
And he c. the priests the sons of 29.21
For the king c. that the burnt 29.24
Then Hezekiah c. that the burnt 29.27
and the princes c. the Levites to 29.30
his princes, as the king had c., 30.06
and the princes c. by the word of 30.12
And he c. the people who lived in 31.04
Then Hezekiah c. them to prepare 31.11
his altars and c. Judah and 32.12
to do all that I have c. them, 33.08
and he c. Judah to serve the LORD 33.16
And the king c. Hilkiah, Ahikam the 34.20
and God has c. me to make haste. 35.21
Cyrus the king of Persia has c. us." Ez 4.03
Whatever is c. by the God of heaven, 7.23
the LORD had c. by Moses that the Neh 8.14
I c. that the doors should be shut 13.19
And I c. the Levites that they 13.22
he c. Mehuman, Biztha, Harbona, Bigtha Est 1.10
'King Ahasuerus c. Queen Vashti to 1.17
the king had so c. concerning him. 3.02
according to all that Haman c., 3.12
that Mordecai c. concerning the 8.09
So the king c. this to be done; 9.14
"Have you c. the morning since your Job 38.12
he c., and it stood forth. Ps 33.09
which he c. our fathers to teach to 78.05
Yet he c. the skies above, and 78.23
for ever, of the word that he c., 105.08
the peoples, as the LORD c. them, 106.34
For he c., and raised the stormy 107.25
he has c. his covenant for ever. 111.09
Thou hast c. thy precepts to be 119.04
there the LORD has c. the blessing, 133.03
For he c. and they were created. 148.05
I myself have c. my consecrated Is 13.03
For the mouth of the LORD has c., 34.16
heavens, and I c. all their host. 45.12
image and my molten image c. them.' 48.05
which I c. your fathers when I Jer 11.04
which I c. them to do, but they did 11.08
the Euphrates, as the LORD c. me. 13.05
waistcloth which I c. you to hide 13.06
day holy, as I c. your fathers. 17.22
the LORD had c. him to speak to 26.08
c. us, 'You shall not drink wine, 35.06
our father, in all that he c. us, 35.08
all that Jonadab our father c. us. 35.10
and done all that he c. you, 35.18
And the king c. Jerahmeel the king's 36.26
Then the king c. Ebedmelech, the 38.10
and do all that I have c. you. 50.21
the prophet c. Seraiah the son of 51.59
the LORD has c. against Jacob that Lam 1.17
Who has c. and it came to pass, 3.37
And when he c. the man clothed in Eze 10.06
And I did as I was c. I brought 12.07
the next morning I did as I was c. 24.18
So I prophesied as I was c.; 37.07
So I prophesied as he c. me, 37.10
Then the king c. Ashpenaz, his chief Dan 1.03
the king had c. that they should 1.18
Then the king c. that the magicians, 2.02
and c. that all the wise men of 2.12
and c. that an offering and incense 2.46
"You are c., O peoples, nations, and 3.04
in furious rage c. that Shadrach, 3.13
And as it was c. to leave the stump 4.26
c. that the vessels of gold and of 5.02
Then Belshazzar c., and Daniel 5.29
Then the king c., and Daniel was 6.16
and c. that Daniel be taken up out 6.23
And the king c., and those men who 6.24
and c. the prophets, saying, 'You Amo 2.12
which I c. my servants the prophets, Zec 1.06
ordinances that I c. him at Horeb Mal 4.04
as the angel of the Lord c. him; Mt 1.24
and offer the gift that Moses c., 8.04
his guests he c. it to be given; 14.09
For God c., 'Honor your father and 15.04
Jesus c. them, "Tell no one the 17.09
to observe all that I have c. you; 28.20
For your cleansing what Moses c., Mk 1.44
Then he c. them all to sit down by 6.39
And he c. the crowd to sit down on 8.06
he c. that these also should be set 8.07
as Moses c., for a proof to the Lk 5.14
For he had c. the unclean spirit to 8.29
But he charged and c. them to tell 9.21
what you c. has been done, and still 14.22
servant because he did what was c.? 17.09
you have done all that is c. you, 17.10
and c. him to be brought to him; 18.40
he c. these servants, to whom he had 19.15
Now in the law Moses c. us to stone *Jn 8.05
but I do as the Father has c. me, 14.31
But when they had c. them to go Ac 4.15
And he c. the chariot to stop, and 8.38
that you have been c. by the LORD." 10.33
And he c. us to preach to the 10.42
And he c. them to be baptized in 10.48
For so the Lord has c. us, 13.47
Claudius had c. all the Jews to 18.02
the tribune c. him to be brought 22.24
and c. the chief priests and all 22.30
priest Ananias c. those who stood 23.02
c. the soldiers to go down and take 23.10
And he c. him to be guarded in 23.35
I c. him to be held until I could 25.21
the Lord c. that those who proclaim 1Co 9.14
of the covenant which God c. you." Heb 9.20
one another, just as he has c. us. 1Jn 3.23
as we have been c. by the Father. 2Jn 1.04

COMMANDER
and Phicol the c. of his army said Gen 21.22
and Phicol the c. of his army rose 21.32
and Phicol the c. of his army. 26.26
but as c. of the army of the LORD I Jos 5.14
And the c. of the LORD's army said 5.15
the c. of his army was Sisera, who Ju 4.02
c. of the army of Jabin king of 1Sa 12.09
the name of the c. of his army was 14.50
cheeses to the c. of their thousand 17.18
the c. of the army, "Abner, whose son 17.55
and made him a c. of a thousand; 18.13
the son of Ner, the c. of his army; 26.05
c. of Saul's army, had taken Ishbosheth 2Sa 2.08
Shobach the c. of the army of 10.16
Shobach the c. of their army, 10.18
if you are not c. of my army 19.12
of the thirty, and became their c.; 23.19
and Joab the c. of the army; 1Ki 1.19
Joab the c. of the army, and Abiathar 1.25
c. of the army of Israel, and Amasa 2.32
c. of the army of Judah. 2.32
and Joab the c. of the army went up 11.15
that Joab the c. of the army was 11.21
c. of half his chariots, conspired 16.09
the c. of the army, king over Israel 16.16
the king or to the c. of the army?" 2Ki 4.13
Naaman, c. of the army of the king 5.01
"I have an errand to you, O c." 9.05
And he said, "To you, O c." 9.05
secretary of the c. of the army who 25.19
first shall be chief and c." 1Ch 11.06
of the thirty, and became their c.; 11.21
Shophach the c. of the army of 19.16
also Shophach the c. of their army. 19.18
The third c., for the third month, 27.05
The fifth c., for the fifth month, 27.08
Joab was c. of the king's army. 27.34

COMMANDER (cont.)
Adnah the c., with three hundred 2Ch 17.14
and next to him Jehohanan the c., 17.15
and Azrikam the c. of the palace 28.07
Rehum the c. and Shimshai the Ez 4.08
then wrote Rehum the c., 4.09
"To Rehum the c. and Shimshai the 4.17
In the year that the c. in chief, Is 20.01
a leader and c. for the peoples. 55.04
secretary of the c. of the army who Jer 52.25
but a c. shall put an end to his Dan 11.18

COMMANDER'S
for there a c. portion was reserved; Deu 33.21

COMMANDERS
army, the c. of thousands and the Num 31.14
the c. of hundreds, who had come 31.14
from the c. of thousands and the 31.52
the c. of hundreds, was sixteen 31.52
gold from the c. of thousands and 31.54
c. of thousands, c. of hundreds, Deu 1.15
c. of fifties, c. of tens, and 1.15
then c. shall be appointed at the 20.09
goes out to the c. of Israel who Ju 5.09
from Machir marched down the c., 5.14
c. of thousands and c. of fifties, 1Sa 8.12
c. of thousands and c. of hundreds, 22.07
the c. of the Philistines said, 29.03
Achish said to the c. of the Philistines, 29.03
But the c. of the Philistines were 29.04
and the c. of the Philistines said 29.04
nevertheless the c. of the Philistines 29.09
c. of thousands and c. of hundreds. 2Sa 18.01
orders to all the c. about Absalom. 18.05
today that c. and servants are 19.06
to Joab and the c. of the army, 24.02
Joab and the c. of the army. 24.04
So Joab and the c. of the army went 24.04
with the two c. of the armies of 1Ki 2.05
his c., his captains, his chariot c. and 9.22
and sent the c. of his armies 15.20
and put c. in their places; 20.24
and his chariot c. smote the 2Ki 8.21
the c. of the army were in council; 9.05
of valor, and were c. in the army. 1Ch 12.21
and twenty-two c. from his own 12.28
a thousand c. with whom were 12.34
with the c. of the thousands and of 13.01
and the c. of thousands, went to 15.25
said to Joab and the c. of the army, 21.02
and the c. of the army, had dedicated 26.26
the c. of thousands and hundreds, 27.01
of all the c. of the army for the 27.03
the c. of thousands, the c. of hundreds, 28.01
the c. of thousands and of hundreds, 29.06
to the c. of thousands and of 2Ch 1.02
the c. of his chariots, and his 8.09
and put c. in them, and stores of 11.11
and sent the c. of his armies 16.04
the c. of thousands: Adnah the 17.14
over with his c. and all his chariots, 21.09
surrounded him and his chariot c. 21.09
a compact with the c. of hundreds, 23.01
houses under c. of thousands and 25.05
of Hananiah, one of the king's c. 26.11
And he set combat c. over the 32.06
warriors and c. and officers in 32.21
upon them the c. of the army of 33.11
he also put c. of the army in all 33.14
for he says: "Are not my c. all kings? Is 10.08
Then all the c. of the forces, and Jer 42.01
and all the c. of the forces who 42.08
and all the c. of the forces and 43.04
and all the c. of the forces took 43.05
I break in pieces governors and c. 51.23
her c., and her warriors; they shall 51.57
governors and c., all of them Eze 23.06
governors and c., warriors clothed 23.12
governors and c. all of them, 23.23

COMMANDING
you shall do all that I am c. you. Deu 12.14
And c. the crowd to sit down on the Mt 15.35
c. his accusers to come before you. *Ac 24.08

COMMANDMENT
according to the c. of the LORD, Ex 17.01
of stone, with the law and the c., 24.12
give you in c. for the people of 25.22
he gave them in c. all that the 34.32
were counted at the c. of Moses, 38.21
numbered at the c. of the LORD, Num 3.39
according to the c. of the LORD by 4.37
according to the c. of the LORD. 4.41
according to the c. of the LORD by 4.45
According to the c. of the LORD 4.49
from the day that the LORD gave c., 15.23
of the LORD, and has broken his c., 15.31
LORD had given him in c. to them, Deu 1.03
you all the c. and the statutes 5.31
"Now this is the c., 6.01
to do all this c. before the LORD 6.25
therefore be careful to do the c., 7.11
"All the c. which I command you 8.01
against the c. of the LORD your 9.23
keep all the c. which I command 11.08
to do all this c. which I command 11.22
to do all this c. which I command 15.05
he may not turn aside from the c., 17.20
are careful to keep all this c., 19.09
to all thy c. which thou hast 26.13
"Keep all the c. which I command 27.01
"For this c. which I command you 30.11
to all the c. which I have commanded 31.05
against your c. and disobeys your Jos 1.18
According to the c. of the LORD to 15.13
according to the c. of the LORD he 17.04
to observe the c. and the law 22.05
rebel against the c. of the LORD, 1Sa 12.14
rebel against the c. of the LORD, 12.15
not kept the c. of the LORD your 13.13
have performed the c. of the LORD. 15.13
transgressed the c. of the LORD and 15.24
LORD and the c. with which I 1Ki 2.43
not kept the c. which the LORD 13.21
the law or the c. which the LORD 2Ki 17.34
the law and the c. which he wrote 17.37
according to the c. of Moses for 2Ch 8.13
and to keep the law and the c. 14.04
law or c., statutes or ordinances, 19.10
according to the c. of David and of 29.25
for the c. was from the LORD 29.25
who tremble at the c. of our God; Ez 10.03
according to the c. of David the Neh 12.24
were given by c. to the Levites, 13.05
departed from the c. of his lips; Job 23.12
the c. of the LORD is pure, enlightening Ps 19.08
but thy c. is exceedingly broad. 119.96
Thy c. makes me wiser than my 119.98
My son, keep your father's c., Pro 6.20
For the c. is a lamp and the 6.23
respects the c. will be rewarded. 13.13
He who keeps the c. keeps his life; 19.16
fear of me is a c. of men learned Is 29.13
the LORD has given c. about you: Nah 1.14
transgress the c. of God for the Mt 15.03
"Teacher, which is the great c. in the law?" 22.36
This is the great and first c. 22.38
You leave the c. of God, and hold Mk 7.08
way of rejecting the c. of God, 7.09
of heart he wrote you this c. 10.05
"Which c. is the first of all?" 12.28
is no other c. greater than these." 12.31

COMMANDMENT (cont.)

they rested according to the c.	Lk 23.56
given me c. what to say and what	Jn 12.49
And I know that his c. is eternal	12.50
A new c. I give to you, that you	13.34
"This is my c., that you love one	15.12
he had given c. through the Holy	Ac 1.02
sin, finding opportunity in the c.,	Rom 7.08
but when the c. came, sin revived	7.09
the very c. which promised life	7.10
sin, finding opportunity in the c.,	7.11
and the c. is holy and just and	7.12
and through the c. might become	7.13
shall not covet," and any other c.,	13.09
is the first c. with a promise,	Eph 6.02
you to keep the c. unstained and	1Ti 6.14
office have a c. in the law to	Heb 7.05
a former c. is set aside because of	7.18
For when every c. of the law had	9.19
from the holy c. delivered to them	2Pe 2.21
prophets and the c. of the Lord and	3.02
Beloved, I am writing you no new c.,	1Jn 2.07
but an old c. which you had from	2.07
the old c. is the word which you	2.07
Yet I am writing you a new c.,	2.08
And this is his c., that we should	3.23
And this c. we have from him, that	4.21
though I were writing you a new c.,	2Jn 1.05
this is the c., as you have heard	1.06

COMMANDMENTS

my c., my statutes, and my laws."	Gen 26.05
heed to his c. and keep all his	Ex 15.26
refuse to keep my c. and my laws?	16.28
those who love me and keep my c.	20.06
words of the covenant, the ten c.	34.28
"So you shall keep my c. and do them:	Lev 22.31
and observe my c. and do them,	26.03
me, and will not do all these c.,	26.14
so that you will not do all my c.,	26.15
These are the c. which the Lord	27.34
all these c. which the Lord has	Num 15.22
remember all the c. of the Lord,	15.39
shall remember and do all my c.,	15.40
These are the c. and the ordinances	36.13
may keep the c. of the Lord your	Deu 4.02
to perform, that is, the ten c.;	4.13
shall keep his statutes and his c.,	4.40
those who love me and keep my c.	5.10
to fear me and to keep all my c.,	5.29
all his statutes and his c.,	6.02
keep the c. of the Lord your God,	6.17
those who love him and keep his c.,	7.09
you would keep his c., or not.	8.02
shall keep the c. of the Lord your	8.06
not keeping his c. and his ordinances	8.11
the ten c. which the Lord had	10.04
and to keep the c. and statutes of	10.13
his ordinances, and his c. always.	11.01
will obey my c. which I command	11.13
if you obey the c. of the Lord	11.27
do not obey the c. of the Lord	11.28
and keep his c. and obey his voice,	13.04
keeping all his c. which I command	13.18
not transgressed any of thy c.,	26.13
statutes and his c. and his ordinances,	26.17
that you are to keep all his c.,	26.18
keeping his c. and his statutes,	27.10
to do all his c. which I command	28.01
if you keep the c. of the Lord	28.09
if you obey the c. of the Lord your	28.13
to do all his c. and his statutes	28.15
to keep his c. and his statutes	28.45
keep all his c. which I command	30.08
to keep his c. and his statutes	30.10
If you obey the c. of the Lord your	30.16
by keeping his c. and his statutes	30.16
all his ways, and to keep his c.,	Jos 22.05
who had obeyed the c. of the Lord,	Ju 2.17
would obey the c. of the Lord,	3.04
me, and has not performed my c."	1Sa 15.11
his c., his ordinances, and his	1Ki 2.03
keeping my statues and my c.,	3.14
and keep all my c. and walk in	6.12
all his ways, and to keep his c.,	8.58
in his statutes and keeping his c.,	8.61
do not keep my c. and my statutes	9.06
who kept my c. and my statutes;	11.34
by keeping my statutes and my c.,	11.38
who kept my c., and followed me	14.08
forsaken the c. of the Lord and	18.18
and keep my c. and my statutes, in	2Ki 17.13
forsook all the c. of the Lord	17.16
not keep the c. of the Lord their	17.19
but kept the c. which the Lord	18.06
and to keep his c. and his testimonies	23.03
in keeping my c. and my ordinances,	1Ch 28.07
out all the c. of the Lord your	28.08
a whole heart he may keep thy c.,	29.19
statutes and my c. which I have	2Ch 7.19
of his father and walked in his c.,	17.04
you transgress the c. of the Lord,	24.20
accordance with the law and the c.,	31.21
and to keep his c. and his testimonies	34.31
matters of the c. of the Lord and	Ez 7.11
For we have forsaken thy c.,	9.10
shall we break thy c. again and	9.14
those who love him and keep his c.;	Neh 1.05
thee, and have not kept the c.,	1.07
to me and keep my c. and do them,	1.09
true laws, good statutes and c.,	9.13
command them c. and statutes and a	9.14
their neck and did not obey thy c.;	9.16
presumptuously and did not obey thy c.,	9.29
or heeded thy c. and thy warnings	9.34
and do all the c. of the Lord our	10.29
the works of God, but keep his c.;	Ps 78.07
my statutes and do not keep my c.,	89.31
covenant and remember to do his c.	103.18
who greatly delights in his c.!	112.01
having my eyes fixed on all thy c.	119.06
let me not wander from thy c.!	119.10
on earth; hide not thy c. from me!	119.19
ones, who wander from thy c.;	119.21
the way of thy c. when thou	119.32
Lead me in the path of thy c.,	119.35
my delight in thy c., which I love.	119.47
I revere thy c., which I love, and I	119.48
and do not delay to keep thy c.	119.60
knowledge, for I believe in thy c.	119.66
understanding that I may learn thy c.	119.73
All thy c. are sure; they persecute	119.86
that I may keep the c. of my God.	119.115
Therefore I love thy c. above gold,	119.127
I pant, because I long for thy c.	119.131
upon me, but thy c. are my delight.	119.143
O Lord, and all thy c. are true.	119.151
salvation, O Lord, and I do thy c.	119.166
thy word, for all they c. are right.	119.172
servant, for I do not forget thy c.	119.176
and treasure up my c. with you,	Pro 2.01
but let your heart keep my c.;	3.01
my words; keep my c., and live;	4.04
and treasure up my c. with you;	7.01
keep my c. and live, keep my teachings	7.02
The wise of heart will heed c.,	10.08
Fear God, and keep his c.; for this	Ecc 12.13
O that you had hearkened to my c.!	Is 48.18
who love him and keep his c.,	Dan 9.04
aside from thy c. and ordinances;	9.05
least of these c. and teaches men	Mt 5.19
you would enter life, keep the c."	19.17
On these two c. depend all the law	22.40
You know the c.: 'Do not kill, Do not	Mk 10.19

COMMANDMENTS (cont.)
in all the c. and ordinances of Lk 1.06
You know the c.: 'Do not commit 18.20
"If you love me, you will keep my c. Jn 14.15
He who has my c. and keeps them, he 14.21
If you keep my c., you will abide 15.10
my Father's c. and abide in his 15.10
The c., "You shall not commit adultery, Rom 13.09
uncircumcision, but keeping the c. of God. 1Co 7.19
flesh the law of c. and ordinances, Eph 2.15
we know him, if we keep his c. 1Jn 2.03
him" but disobeys his c. is a liar, 2.04
we keep his c. and do what pleases 3.22
All who keep his c. abide in him, 3.24
when we love God and obey his c. 5.02
love of God, that we keep his c. 5.03
And his c. are not burdensome. 5.03
is love, that we follow his c.; 2Jn 1.06
who keep the c. of God and bear Rev 12.17
who keep the c. of God and the 14.12

COMMANDS
and God so c. you, then you will be Ex 18.23
servants will do as my lord c. Num 32.25
what the LORD c. concerning the 36.06
LORD your God c. you do these Deu 26.16
he executed the c. and just 33.21
my lord the king c. his servant, 2Sa 9.11
to him, "The king c., 'Come forth.'" 1Ki 2.30
who c. the sun, and it does not rise; Job 9.07
and c. that they return from iniquity. 36.10
and c. it to strike the mark. 36.32
all that he c. them on the face of 37.12
By day the LORD c. his steadfast Ps 42.08
because they do not keep thy c. 119.158
the LORD c., and the great house Amo 6.11
humble of the land, who do his c.; Zep 2.03
authority he c. even the unclean Mk 1.27
and c. the doorkeeper to be on the 13.34
and power he c. the unclean spirits, Lk 4.36
that he c. even wind and water, and 8.25
but now he c. all men everywhere to Ac 17.30
myths or to c. of men who reject Tit 1.14

COMMEMORATION
nor should the c. of these days Est 9.28

COMMEND
And I c. enjoyment, for man has no Ecc 8.15
And now I c. you to God and to the Ac 20.32
I c. to you our sister Phoebe, a Rom 16.01
Food will not c. us to God. 1Co 8.08
I c. you because you remember me in 11.02
instructions I do not c. you, because 11.17
Shall I c. you in this? No, I 11.22
Are we beginning to c. ourselves 2Co 3.01
truth we would c. ourselves to 4.02
of God we c. ourselves in every 6.04
some of those who c. themselves. 10.12

COMMENDATION
man will receive his c. from God. 1Co 4.05

COMMENDED
A man is c. according to his good Pro 12.08
The master c. the dishonest steward Lk 16.08
they had been c. to the grace of Ac 14.26
being c. by the brethren to the 15.40
for I ought to have been c. by you. 2Co 12.11

COMMENDING
We are not c. ourselves to you 2Co 5.12

COMMENDS
not the man who c. himself that is 2Co 10.18
but the man whom the LORD c. 10.18

COMMENTARY
written in the C. on the Book of 2Ch 24.27

COMMISSION
and you shall c. him in their sight. Num 27.19
tent of meeting, that I may c. him." Deu 31.14
authority and c. of the chief Ac 26.12
According to the c. of God given to 1Co 3.10
own will, I am entrusted with a c. 9.17

COMMISSIONED
and c. him as the LORD directed Num 27.23
And the LORD c. Joshua the son of Deu 31.23
with you in Christ, and has c. us; 2Co 1.21
as c. by God, in the sight of God we 2.17

COMMISSIONS
the king's c. to the king's satraps Ez 8.36

COMMIT
"You shall not c. adultery. Ex 20.14
sins that men c. by breaking faith Num 5.06
" 'Neither shall you c. adultery. Deu 5.18
never again c. any such evil among 19.20
LORD and made them c. great sin. 2Ki 17.21
and to God would I c. my cause; Job 5.08
Into thy hand I c. my spirit; Ps 31.05
C. your way to the LORD; trust 37.05
C. your work to the LORD, and your Pro 16.03
and will c. your authority to his Is 22.21
c. adultery, swear falsely, burn Jer 7.09
they c. iniquity and are too weary 9.05
they c. adultery and walk in lies; 23.14
Why do you c. this great evil 44.07
greater abominations which they c." Eze 8.13
of Judah to c. the abominations 8.17
abominations which they c. here, 8.17
men c. lewdness in your midst. 22.09
and I will c. the judgment to them, 23.24
Do not men now c. adultery when 23.43
and to Oholibah to c. lewdness. 23.44
warning and not c. lewdness as you 23.48
you c. abominations and each of you 33.26
and your brides c. adultery. Hos 4.13
your brides when they c. adultery; 4.14
to Shechem, yea, they c. villainy. 6.09
said, 'You shall not c. adultery.' Mt 5.27
makes her c. adultery * 19.09
You shall not c. adultery, You shall 19.18
Do not c. adultery, Do not steal, Do Mk 10.19
him to whom men c. much they will Lk 12.48
'Do not c. adultery, Do not kill, Do 18.20
into thy hands I c. my spirit!" 23.46
say that one must not c. adultery, Rom 2.22
adultery, do you c. adultery? 2.22
commandments, "You shall not c. adultery, 13.09
Did I c. a sin in abasing myself so 2Co 11.07
This charge I c. to you, Timothy, my 1Ti 1.18
if they then c. apostasy, since they Heb 6.06
you c. sin, and are convicted by the Jas 2.09
"Do not c. adultery," said also, "Do 2.11
If you do not c. adultery but do kill, 2.11
and those who c. adultery with her Rev 2.22

COMMITS
of Israel c. a sin unwittingly and Lev 4.13
"If any one c. a breach of faith 5.15
one sins and c. a breach of faith 6.02
"If a man c. adultery with the wife 20.10
a man or woman c. any of the sins Num 5.06
for the person who c. an error, 15.28
When he c. iniquity, I will chasten 2Sa 7.14
the hapless c. himself to thee; Ps 10.14
He who c. adultery has no sense; Pro 6.32
his righteousness and c. iniquity, Eze 3.20
c. no robbery, gives his bread to 18.07
c. robbery, does not restore the 18.12
eyes to the idols, c. abomination, 18.12
c. no robbery, but gives his bread 18.16
righteousness and c. iniquity and 18.24

COMMITS (cont.)
his righteousness and c. iniquity, Eze 18.26
One c. abomination with his neighbor's 22.11
his righteousness and c. iniquity, 33.13
and c. iniquity, he shall die for it. 33.18
for the land c. great harlotry by Hos 1.02
a divorced woman c. adultery. Mt 5.32
and marries another, c. adultery." 19.09
a divorced woman c. adultery. * 19.09
c. adultery against her; Mk 10.11
marries another, she c. adultery." 10.12
and marries another c. adultery, Lk 16.18
from her husband c. adultery. 16.18
every one who c. sin is a slave to Jn 8.34
sin which a man c. is outside the 1Co 6.18
Every one who c. sin is guilty of 1Jn 3.04
He who c. sin is of the devil; 3.08
No one born of God c. sin; 3.09

COMMITTED
of the prison c. to Joseph's care Gen 39.22
which he has c. a young bull Lev 4.03
which they have c. becomes known, 4.14
which he has c. is made known to 4.23
which he has c. is made known to 4.28
for his sin which he has c. 4.28
him for the sin which he has c., 4.35
shall confess the sin he has c., 5.05
LORD for the sin which he has c., 5.06
LORD for the sin which he has c., 5.07
him for the sin which he has c., 5.10
for the sin which he has c., 5.11
which he has c. in any one of 5.13
the error which he c. unwittingly, 5.18
or the deposit which was c. to him, 6.04
LORD for his sin which he has c.; 19.22
which he has c. shall be forgiven 19.22
they have c. incest, their blood is 20.12
of them have c. an abomination; 20.13
treachery which they c. against me, 26.40
confess his sin which he has c.; Num 5.07
of all the sin which you had c., Deu 9.18
with any offence that he has c.; 19.15
"And if a man has c. a crime 21.22
which you have c. against the God Jos 22.16
you have not c. this treachery 22.31
which he c. against his father in Ju 9.56
for they have c. abomination and 20.06
crime which they have c. in Israel." 20.10
which they have c. against thee; 1Ki 8.50
with their sins which they c., 14.22
and c. them to the hands of the 14.27
because of his sins which he c., 16.19
and for his sin which he c., 16.19
of Judah has c. these abominations, 2Ki 21.11
he did, and the sin that he c., 21.17
and c. them to the hands of the 2Ch 12.10
"All that was c. to your servants 34.16
and had c. great blasphemies, Neh 9.18
and they c. great blasphemies. 9.26
"He c. his cause to the LORD; Ps 22.08
we have c. iniquity, we have done 106.06
for my people have c. two evils: Jer 2.13
they c. adultery and trooped to the 5.07
ashamed when they c. abomination? 6.15
ashamed when they c. abomination? 8.12
for to thee have I c. my cause. 11.20
that we have c. against the LORD 16.10
for to thee have I c. my cause. 20.12
because they have c. folly in 29.23
they have c. adultery with their 29.23
and they c. Jeremiah to the court 37.21
and had c. to him men, women, and 40.07
had c. to Gedaliah the son of 41.10
because of the wickedness which they c., 44.03
which they c. in the land of Judah 44.09
and the abominations which you c.; 44.22
for the evils which they have c., Eze 6.09
the abominations that are c. in it." 9.04
"Have you not c. lewdness in 16.43
Samaria has not c. half your sins; 16.51
you have c. more abominations than 16.51
the abominations which you have c. 16.51
the treason he has c. against me. 17.20
which he has c. and keeps all my 18.21
which he has c. shall be remembered 18.22
the sin he has c., he shall die. 18.24
which he has c. he shall die. 18.26
wickedness he has c. and does what 18.27
the transgressions which he had c., 18.28
which you have c. against me, 18.31
for all the evils that you have c. 20.43
practiced extortion and c. robbery; 22.29
For they have c. adultery, and blood 23.37
their idols they have c. adultery; 23.37
that he has c. he shall die. 33.13
that he has c. shall be remembered 33.16
abominations which they have c. 33.29
abominations which they have c., 43.08
abominations which they have c. 44.13
which they have c. against thee. Dan 9.07
has been c. in Israel and in Mal 2.11
has already c. adultery with her Mt 5.28
who had c. murder in the insurrection, Mk 15.07
and women and c. them to prison. Ac 8.03
they c. them to the LORD in whom 14.23
and have c. anything for which I 25.11
of teaching to which you were c., Rom 6.17
and if he has c. sins, he will be Jas 5.15
He c. no sin; no guile 1Pe 2.22
into hell and c. them to pits of 2Pe 2.04
which they have c. in such an Jud 1.15
of the earth have c. fornication, Rev 17.02
the earth have c. fornication with 18.03
who c. fornication and were wanton 18.09
were those to whom judgment was c. 20.04

COMMITTING
c. adultery with stone and tree. Jer 3.09
the house of Israel are c. here, Eze 8.06
abominations that they are c. here." 8.09
statutes of life, c. no iniquity; 33.15
killing, stealing, and c. adultery; Hos 4.02
men c. shameless acts with me and Rom 1.27
his brother c. what is not a mortal 1Jn 5.16

COMMON
"If any one of the c. people sins Lev 4.27
between the holy and the c., and 10.10
But the fields of c. land belonging 25.34
men die the c. death of all men, or Num 16.29
breadth, according to the c. cubit. Deu 3.11
"I have no c. bread at hand, but 1Sa 21.04
holy, even when it is a c. journey; 21.05
made silver as c. in Jerusalem as 1Ki 10.27
upon the graves of the c. people. 2Ki 23.06
and gold as c. in Jerusalem as 2Ch 1.15
made silver as c. in Jerusalem as 9.27
left their c. lands and their 11.14
the fields of c. land belonging to 31.19
and write upon it in c. characters, Is 8.01
What has straw in c. with wheat? Jer 23.28
the burial place of the c. people. 26.23
between the holy and the c., Eze 22.26
with men of the c. sort drunkards 23.42
separation between the holy and the c. 42.20
between the holy and the c., and show 44.23
together and had all things in c.; Ac 2.44
c. men, they wondered; and they 4.13
own, but they had everything in c. 4.32
and put them in the c. prison. 5.18
anything that is c. or unclean." 10.14
has cleansed, you must not call c." 10.15
not call any man c. or unclean. 10.28

COMMON (cont.)
for nothing c. or unclean has ever Ac 11.08
has cleansed you must not call c.' 11.09
overtaken you that is not c. to man. 1Co 10.13
of the Spirit for the c. good. 12.07
a believer in c. with an unbeliever? 2Co 6.15
Titus, my true child in a c. faith: Tit 1.04
write to you of our c. salvation, Jud 1.03

COMMONWEALTH
alienated from the c. of Israel, Eph 2.12
But our c. is in heaven, and from it Php 3.20

COMMOTION
—a great c. out of the north Jer 10.22
we can give to justify this c." Ac 19.40

COMMUNE
c. with your own hearts on your Ps 4.04
I c. with my heart in the night; 77.06

COMMUNICATE
lest they c. holiness to the people Eze 44.19
court and so c. holiness to the 46.20

COMPACT
entered into a c. with the commanders 2Ch 23.01

COMPANIES
and herds and camels, into two c., Gen 32.07
and now I have become two c. 32.10
pitch their tents by their c., Num 1.52
of the camp of Judah by their c., 2.03
by their c., is a hundred and 2.09
of the camp of Reuben by their c., 2.10
by their c., is a hundred and fifty 2.16
of the camp of Ephraim by their c., 2.18
by their c., is a hundred and eight 2.24
of the camp of Dan by their c., 2.25
by their c. were six hundred and 2.32
of Judah set out first by their c.; 10.14
camp of Reuben set out by their c.; 10.18
men of Ephraim set out by their c.; 10.22
all the camps, set out by their c.; 10.25
three hundred men into three c., Ju 7.16
And the three c. blew the trumpets 7.20
wait against Shechem in four c. 9.34
men and divided them into three c., 9.43
while the two c. rushed upon all 9.44
Saul put the people in three c.; 1Sa 11.11
of the Philistines in three c.; 13.17
two great c. which gave thanks and Neh 12.31
So both c. of those who gave thanks 12.40
"The Chaldeans formed three c., Job 1.17
to sit down by c. upon the green Mk 6.39
disciples, "Make them sit down in c., Lk 9.14

COMPANION
his brother, and every man his c., Ex 32.27
And Samson's wife was given to his c., Ju 14.20
so I gave her to your c. 15.02
his wife and given her to his c." 15.06
of jackals, and a c. of ostriches. Job 30.29
equal, my c., my familiar friend. Ps 55.13
My c. stretched out his hand against 55.20
I am a c. of all who fear thee, of 119.63
who forsakes the c. of her youth Pro 2.17
but the c. of fools will suffer 13.20
but a c. of gluttons shames his 28.07
is the c. of a man who destroys. 28.24
she is your c. and your wife by Mal 2.14

COMPANIONS
bewail my virginity, I and my c." Ju 11.37
she and her c., and bewailed her 11.38
brought thirty c. to be with him. 14.11
My friends and c. stand aloof from Ps 38.11
to the king, with her virgin c., 45.14
Thou hast caused my c. to shun me; 88.08
shun me; my c. are in darkness. 88.18
beside the flocks of your c.? Sol 1.07
my c. are listening for your voice; 8.13
are rebels and c. of thieves. Is 1.23
did not kill them with their c. Jer 41.08
Daniel and his c., to slay them. Dan 2.13
Mishael, and Azariah, his c., 2.17
Daniel and his c. might not perish 2.18
who were Paul's c. in travel. Ac 19.29

COMPANIONS'
For my brethren and c. sake I will Ps 122.08

COMPANY
you may become a c. of peoples. Gen 28.03
to the one c. and destroys it, then 32.08
then the c. which is left will 32.08
mean by all this c. which I met?" 33.08
a nation and a c. of nations shall 35.11
I will make of you a c. of peoples, 48.04
spirit, be not joined to their c.; 49.06
it was a very great c. 50.09
shall number them c. by c. Num 1.03
and he said to Korah and all his c., 16.05
take censers, Korah and all his c.; 16.06
and all your c. have gathered 16.11
"Be present, you and all your c., 16.16
he become as Korah and as his c.— 16.40
Moses and Aaron in the c. of Korah, 26.09
when that c. died, when the fire 26.10
not among the c. of those who 27.03
the LORD in the c. of Korah, 27.03
and one c. is coming from the Ju 9.37
Abimelech and the c. that was with 9.44
you that you come with such a c.?" 18.23
one c. turned toward Ophrah, to the 1Sa 13.17
another c. turned toward Bethhoron, 13.18
another c. turned toward the border 13.18
they saw the c. of the prophets 19.20
the man of God, he and all his c., 2Ki 5.15
he spied the c. of Jehu as he came, 9.17
as he came, and said, "I see a c." 9.17
The other c. of those who gave Neh 12.38
For the c. of the godless is barren, Job 15.34
he has made desolate all my c. 16.07
who goes in c. with evildoers and 34.08
a c. of evildoers encircle me; Ps 22.16
I hate the c. of evildoers, and I 26.05
and you keep c. with adulterers. 50.18
distress, a c. of destroying angels. 78.49
and covered the c. of Abiram. 106.17
Fire also broke out in their c.; 106.18
in the c. of the upright, in the 111.01
wicked deeds in c. with men who 141.04
one who keeps c. with harlots Pro 29.03
a c. of teacherous men. Jer 9.02
not sit in the c. of merrymakers, 15.17
a great c., they shall return here. 31.08
Babylon a c. of great nations, from 50.09
army and great c. will not help Eze 17.17
with all your c. that is in your 27.27
and all her c., their graves round 32.22
and her c. is round about her grave 32.23
a great c., all of them with 38.04
of Herodias danced before the c., Mt 14.06
to be in the c. they went a day's Lk 2.44
was a large c. of tax collectors 5.29
Then the whole c. of them arose, and 23.01
Moreover, some women of our c. amazed us. 24.22
brethren (the c. of persons was in Ac 1.
Now the c. of those who believed
And a large c. was added to the
and taught a large c. of people;
Now Paul and his c. set sail from
so spoke that a great c. believed,
away a considerable c. of people,

COMPANY (cont.)

have enjoyed your c. for a little. Rom 15.24
joy and be refreshed in your c. 15.32
deceived: "Bad c. ruins good morals." 1Co 15.33

COMPARE

no other king shall c. with you, 1Ki 3.13
of Ethiopia cannot c. with it, Job 28.19
toward us; none can c. with thee! Ps 40.05
nothing you desire can c. with her. Pro 3.15
you may desire cannot c. with her. 8.11
I c. you, my love, to a mare of Sol 1.09
God, or what likeness c. with him? Is 40.18
To whom then will you c. me, 40.25
and c. me, that we may be alike? 46.05
to what c. you, O daughter of Lam 2.13
"But to what shall I c. this Mt 11.16
what can we c. the kingdom of God, Mk 4.30
then shall I c. the men of this Lk 7.31
like? And to what shall I c. it? 13.18
"To what shall I c. the kingdom of 13.20
to class or c. ourselves with some 2Co 10.12
and c. themselves with one another, 10.12

COMPARED

is not to be c. with the loss to Est 7.04
in the skies can be c. to the LORD? Ps 89.06
were as nothing c. with its Eze 31.08
heaven may be c. to a man who Mt 13.24
heaven may be c. to a king who 18.23
heaven may be c. to a king who 22.02
heaven shall be c. to ten maidens 25.01

COMPARING

are not worth c. with the glory Rom 8.18

COMPARISON

have I done now in c. with you? Ju 8.02
I been able to do in c. with you?" 8.03
weight of glory beyond all c., 2Co 4.17

COMPASS

the ark of the LORD to c. the city, Jos 6.11
planes, and marks it with a c.; Is 44.13

COMPASSING

c. the sea round about; the gourds 1Ki 7.24
c. the sea round about; the gourds 2Ch 4.03

COMPASSION

and have c. on you, and multiply you, Deu 13.17
and have c. upon you, and he will 30.03
people and have c. on his servants, 32.36
of Israel had c. for Benjamin Ju 21.06
And the people had c. on Benjamin 21.15
for you have had c. on me. 1Sa 23.21
and grant them c. in the sight of 1Ki 8.50
that they may have c. on them 8.50
gracious to them and had c. on them, 2Ki 13.23
will find c. with their captors, 2Ch 30.09
because he had c. on his people 36.15
[illegible]d had no c. on young man or 36.17
[illegible] he in anger shut up his c.?" Ps 77.09
[illegible] c. come speedily to meet us, 79.08
[illegible] c. on his servants. 135.14
[illegible] is over all that he has 145.09
[illegible] on their fatherless Is 9.17
[illegible] have c. on Jacob and 14.01
[illegible] not have c. on them, 27.11
[illegible] his afflicted. 49.13
[illegible] the son of 49.15
[illegible] will gather 54.07
[illegible] have c. on you, 54.08
[illegible] c. on you, 54.10
[illegible] held from 63.15
[illegible] them, Jer 12.15
[illegible] c., 13.14
[illegible] 21.07

and have c. on his dwellings; 30.18
he will have c. according to the Lam 3.32
things to you out of c. for you; Eze 16.05
favor and c. in the sight of the Dan 1.09
I led them with cords of c., Hos 11.04
my c. grows warm and tender. 11.08
destruction? C. is hid from my eyes. 13.14
He will again have c. upon us, Mic 7.19
have returned to Jerusalem with c.; Zec 1.16
back because I have c. on them, 10.06
a spirit of c. and supplication, so 12.10
he had c. for them, because they Mt 9.36
and he had c. on them, and healed 14.14
"I have c. on the crowd, because 15.32
and he had c. on them, because they Mk 6.34
"I have c. on the crowd, because 8.02
he had c. on her and said to her, Lk 7.13
and when he saw him, he had c., 10.33
his father saw him and had c., 15.20
and I will have c. on whom I have c." Rom 9.15
c., kindness, lowliness, meekness, and Col 3.12
For you had c. on the prisoners, and Heb 10.34

COMPASSIONATE

to me, I will hear, for I am c. Ex 22.27
Yet he, being c., forgave their Ps 78.38
The hands of c. women have boiled Lam 4.10
how the Lord is c. and merciful. Jas 5.11

COMPEL

and c. people to come in, that my Lk 14.23
how can you c. the Gentiles to live Gal 2.14
that would c. you to be circumcised, 6.12

COMPELLED

you go unless c. by a mighty hand. Ex 3.19
according to the law, no one was c.; Est 1.08
Young men are c. to grind at the Lam 5.13
this man they c. to carry his cross. Mt 27.32
And they c. a passer-by, Simon of Mk 15.21
I was c. to appeal to Caesar—though Ac 28.19
was not c. to be circumcised, though Gal 2.03

COMPELS

with her smooth talk she c. him. Pro 7.21

COMPENSATION

He will accept no c., nor be Pro 6.35

COMPETE

you, how will you c. with horses? Jer 12.05
are a king because you c. in cedar? 22.15
that in a race all the runners c., 1Co 9.24

COMPETENT

and c. to serve in the king's palace, Dan 1.04

COMPETES

unless he c. according to the 2Ti 2.05

COMPILE

undertaken to c. a narrative of Lk 1.01

COMPLACENCE

and the c. of fools destroys them; Pro 1.32

COMPLACENT

you c. daughters, give ear to my Is 32.09
you will shudder, you c. women; 32.10
are at ease, shudder, you c. ones; 32.11

COMPLAIN

or their brothers come to c. to us, Ju 21.22
I will c. in the bitterness of my Job 7.11
"Why do you c. against me? Jer 2.29
thou, O LORD, when I c. to thee; 12.01
Why should a living man c., Lam 3.39
Not that I c. of want; for I have Php 4.11

COMPLAINED
When Abraham c. to Abimelech about Gen 21.25
And the people c. in the hearing of Num 11.01

COMPLAINING
Who has c.? Who has wounds Pro 23.29

COMPLAINT
me, my couch will ease my c.,' Job 7.13
If I say, 'I will forget my c., 9.27
will give free utterance to my c.; 10.01
As for me, is my c. against man? 21.04
"Today also my c. is bitter, his 23.02
when they brought a c. against me; 31.13
and at noon I utter my c. and moan, Ps 55.17
Hear my voice, O God, in my c.; 64.01
I pour out my c. before him, I tell 142.02
a ground for c. against Daniel Dan 6.04
they could find no ground for c. or 6.04
any ground for c. against this 6.05
I will answer concerning my c. Hab 2.01
with him have a c. against any one, Ac 19.38
if one has a c. against another, Col 3.13

COMPLETE
of the Amorites is not yet c." Gen 15.16
C. the week of this one, and we will 29.27
"C. your work, your daily task, as Ex 5.13
about from the Millo in c. circuit; 1Ch 11.08
so as not to make a c. destruction; 2Ch 12.12
For he will c. what he appoints for Job 23.14
they c. their days in prosperity, 36.11
his hands shall also c. it. Zec 4.09
whether he has enough to c. it? Lk 14.28
he should also c. among you this 2Co 8.06
for you now to c. what a year ago 8.10
disobedience, when your obedience is c. 10.06
c. my joy by being of the same mind, Php 2.02
his life to c. your service to me. 2.30
in my flesh I c. what is lacking Col 1.24
that the man of God may be c., 2Ti 3.17
that you may be perfect and c., Jas 1.04
this that our joy may be c. 1Jn 1.04
to face, so that our joy may be c. 2Jn 1.12
and their brethren should be c., Rev 6.11

COMPLETED
go in to her, for my time is c." Gen 29.21
Jacob did so, and c. her week; 29.28
the days of your ordination are c., Lev 8.33
the days of her purifying are c. 12.04
the days of her purifying are c., 12.06
the time is c. for which he Num 6.05
time of his separation has been c.: 6.13
So the house of the LORD was c. 2Ch 8.16
And when these days were c., Est 1.05
Then after seventy years are c., Jer 25.12
seventy years are c. for Babylon, 29.10
And when you have c. these, Eze 4.06
till you have c. the days of your 4.08
when the days of the siege are c.; 5.02
And when they have c. these days, 43.27
When the seven days were almost c., Ac 21.27
When therefore I have c. this, Rom 15.28
works, and faith was c. by works, Jas 2.22

COMPLETELY
you go, he will drive you away c. Ex 11.01
who seek the LORD understand it c. Pro 28.05

COMPLETING
matched by your c. it out of what 2Co 8.11

COMPLETION
bring it to c. at the day of Jesus Php 1.06

COMPLIMENTARY
honey, so be sparing of c. words. Pro 25.27

COMPOSITION
shall make no other like it in c.; Ex 30.32
you shall make according to its c., 30.37

COMPOUNDS
Whoever c. any like it or whoever Ex 30.33

COMPREHEND
great things which we cannot c. Job 37.05
obscure speech which you cannot c., Is 33.19
may have power to c. with all the Eph 3.18

COMPREHENDED
Have you c. the expanse of the Job 38.18

COMPREHENDS
So also no one c. the thoughts of 1Co 2.11

COMPRESSES
he who c. his lips brings evil to Pro 16.30

COMPULSION
mind, not reluctantly or under c., 2Co 9.07
might not be by c. but of your own Phm 1.14

COMPUTE
priest shall c. the money-value Lev 27.18
priest shall c. the valuation for 27.23

COMRADE
man was telling a dream to his c.; Ju 7.13
And his c. answered, "This is no 7.14

COMRADES
the oil of gladness beyond thy c." Heb 1.09

CONANIAH
charge of them was C. the Levite, 2Ch 31.12
assisting C. and Shimei his 31.13
C. also, and Shemaiah and Nethanel 35.09

CONCEAL
slay our brother and c. his blood? Gen 37.26
spare him, nor shall you c. him; Deu 13.08
thou wouldest c. me until thy Job 14.13
is with the Almighty I will not c. 27.11
he will c. me under the cover of Ps 27.05
It is the glory of God to c. things, Pro 25.02
and he is not able to c. himself. Jer 49.10
c. it not, and say: 'Babylon is taken, 50.02

CONCEALED
and c. from the birds of the air. Job 28.21
if I have c. my transgressions from 31.33
I have not c. thy steadfast love Ps 40.10
is their iniquity c. from my eyes. Jer 16.17
and it was c. from them, that they Lk 9.45

CONCEALS
mouth of the wicked c. violence. Pro 10.06
mouth of the wicked c. violence. 10.11
He who c. hatred has lying lips, and 10.18
A prudent man c. his knowledge, but 12.23
He who c. his transgressions will 28.13

CONCEIT
any who are wise in their own c. Job 37.24
slander, gossip, c., and disorder. 2Co 12.20
Do nothing from selfishness or c., Php 2.03
puffed up with c., and fall into 1Ti 3.06
he is puffed up with c., he knows 6.04
swollen with c., lovers of pleasure 2Ti 3.04

CONCEITED
with the lowly; never be c. Rom 12.16

CONCEITS
Lest you be wise in your own c., Rom 11.25

CONCEIVE

be free and shall c. children. Num 5.28
Did I c. all this people? Did I 11.12
but you shall c. and bear a son. Ju 13.03
for lo, you shall c. and bear a son. 13.05
you shall c. and bear a son; 13.07
They c. mischief and bring forth Job 15.35
the land they c. words of deceit. Ps 35.20
and in sin did my mother c. me. 51.05
woman shall c. and bear a son, Is 7.14
You c. chaff, you bring forth 33.11
they c. mischief and bring forth 59.04
"Behold, a virgin shall c. and bear a son, Mt 1.23
you will c. in your womb and bear a Lk 1.31
Sarah herself received power to c., Heb 11.11

CONCEIVED

and she c. and bore Cain, saying, "I Gen 4.01
wife, and she c. and bore Enoch; 4.17
And he went in to Hagar, and she c.; 16.04
and when she saw that she had c., 16.04
and when she saw that she had c., 16.05
And Sarah c., and bore Abraham a 21.02
prayer, and Rebekah his wife c. 25.21
And Leah c. and bore a son, and she 29.32
She c. again and bore a son, and 29.33
Again she c. and bore a son, and 29.34
And she c. again and bore a son, and 29.35
And Bilhah c. and bore Jacob a son. 30.05
Rachel's maid Bilhah c. again and 30.07
and she c. and bore Jacob a fifth 30.17
And Leah c. again, and she bore 30.19
She c. and bore a son, and said, "God 30.23
and she c. and bore a son, and he 38.03
Again she c. and bore a son, and she 38.04
went in to her, and she c. by him. 38.18
The woman c. and bore a son; Ex 2.02
due time Hannah c. and bore a son, 1Sa 1.20
and she c. and bore three sons and 2.21
And the woman c.; and she 2Sa 11.05
But the woman c., and she bore a 2Ki 4.17
and she c. and bore Miriam, 1Ch 4.17
wife, and she c. and bore a son; 7.23
which said, 'A man-child is c.' Job 3.03
thought out a cunningly c. plot. Ps 64.06
into the chamber of her that c. me. Sol 3.04
into the chamber of her that c. me. 8.02
prophetess, and she c. and bore a son. Is 8.03
and she c. and bore him a son. Hos 1.03
She c. again and bore a daughter. 1.06
Not pitied, she c. and bore a son. 1.08
she that c. them has acted shamefully 2.05
that which is c. in her is of the Mt 1.20
After these days his wife Elizabeth c., Lk 1.24
in her old age has also c. a son; 1.36
angel before he was c. in the womb. 2.21
Rebecca had c. children by one man, Rom 9.10
ear heard, nor the heart of man c., 1Co 2.09
when it has c. gives birth to sin; Jas 1.15

CONCEIVES

If a woman c., and bears a male Lev 12.02
Behold, the wicked man c. evil, Ps 7.14

CONCEIVING

c. and uttering from the heart Is 59.13

CONCEPTION

to her, and the LORD gave her c., Ru 4.13
—no birth, no pregnancy, no c.! Hos 9.11

CONCERN

him he had no c. for anything but Gen 39.06
master has no c. about anything in 39.08
But I had c. for my holy name, which Eze 36.21
you have revived your c. for me; Php 4.10

CONCERNED

Is it for oxen that God is c.? 1Co 9.09
you were indeed c. for me, but you Php 4.10
that he is c. but with the descendants Heb 2.16

CONCERNING

And Pharaoh gave men orders c. him; Gen 12.20
and swore to him c. this matter. 24.09
truth we are guilty c. our brother, 42.21
it a statute c. the land of Egypt, 47.26
cried to the LORD c. the frogs, Ex 8.12
that I show you c. the pattern of 25.09
commanded Moses c. the Levites, Num 8.20
had commanded Moses c. the Levites, 8.22
what the LORD will command c. you." 9.08
out of her lips c. her vows, 30.12
or c. her pledge of herself, shall 30.12
gave command c. them to Eleazar 32.28
LORD commands c. the daughters of 36.06
this day c. the LORD that he is Deu 26.17
this day c. you that you are a 26.18
c. which I command you this day, on 27.04
God in Kadeshbarnea c. you and me. Jos 14.06
the LORD your God promised c. you; 23.14
God promised c. you have been 23.15
a great oath c. him who did not Ju 21.05
times in Israel c. redeeming and Ru 4.07
that I have spoken c. his house, 1Sa 3.12
before the LORD c. all the saving 12.07
the good that he has spoken c. you, 25.30
me today with a fault c. a woman. 2Sa 3.08
c. thy servant and c. his house, 7.25
to console him c. his father. 10.02
and I will give orders c. you." 14.08
his word which he spoke c. me, 1Ki 2.04
he had spoken c. the house of Eli 2.27
"C. this house which you are 6.12
fame of Solomon c. the name of the 10.01
from the nations c. which the LORD 11.02
and had commanded him c. this thing, 11.10
to inquire of you c. her son; 14.05
prophesies good c. me, but evil." 22.08
not prophesy good c. me, but evil?" 22.18
the LORD has spoken evil c. you." 22.23
the LORD spoke c. the house of 2Ki 10.10
c. whom the LORD had commanded them 17.15
the king heard c. Tirhakah king of 19.09
that the LORD has spoken c. him: 19.21
says the LORD c. the king of 19.32
c. the words of this book that has 22.13
to all that is written c. us." 22.13
to the word of the LORD c. Israel. 1Ch 11.10
hast spoken c. thy servant and 17.23
c. his house be established for ever, 17.23
to console him c. his father. 19.02
When David was told c. the men, 19.05
your God, as he has spoken c. you. 22.11
in all matters c. the divisions 27.01
from the hand of the LORD c. it, 28.19
c. any matter and c. the treasuries. 2Ch 8.15
Iddo the seer c. Jeroboam the son 9.29
for he never prophesies good c. me, 18.07
not prophesy good c. me, but evil?" 18.17
the LORD has spoken evil c. you." 18.22
c. bloodshed, law or commandment, 19.10
the LORD spoke c. the sons of 23.03
c. the words of the book that has 34.21
answer be returned by letter c. it. Ez 5.05
C. the house of God at Jerusalem, 6.03
I asked them c. the Jews that Neh 1.02
escaped exile, and c. Jerusalem. 1.02
to proclaim c. you in Jerusalem, 6.07
a command from the king c. them, 11.23
hand in all matters c. the people. 11.24
c. this, and wipe not out my good 13.14
the king had so commanded c. him. Est 3.02
commanded c. the Jews to the 8.09

CONCERNING (cont.)
I will teach you c. the hand of God; Job 27.11
Its crashing declares c. him, 36.33
will not keep silence c. his limbs, 41.12
For my enemies speak c. me, Ps 71.10
which he saw c. Judah and Jerusalem Is 1.01
son of Amoz saw c. Judah and 2.01
a love song c. his vineyard: 5.01
The oracle c. Babylon which Isaiah 13.01
is purposed c. the whole earth; 14.26
An oracle c. Moab. Because Ar 15.01
the LORD spoke c. Moab in the past 16.13
An oracle c. Damascus. Behold, 17.01
An oracle c. Egypt. Behold, the 19.01
The oracle c. the wilderness of the 21.01
The oracle c. Dumah. One is 21.11
The oracle c. Arabia. In the 21.13
The oracle c. the valley of vision. 22.01
The oracle c. Tyre. Wail, O ships 23.01
given command c. Canaan to destroy 23.11
c. the house of Jacob: "Jacob shall 29.22
ungodliness, to utter error c. the LORD 32.06
Now the king heard c. Tirhakah king 37.09
prayed to me c. Sennacherib king 37.21
that the LORD has spoken c. him: 37.22
says the LORD c. the king of 37.33
or command me c. the work of my 45.11
or command them c. burnt offerings Jer 7.22
says the LORD c. the men of 11.21
Thus says the LORD c. all my evil 12.14
came to Jeremiah c. the drought: 14.01
Thus says the LORD c. this people: 14.10
says the LORD c. the prophets who 14.15
says the LORD c. the sons and 16.03
and c. the mothers who bore them 16.03
time I declare c. a nation or a 18.07
c. which I have spoken, turns from 18.08
time I declare c. a nation or a 18.09
says the LORD c. the house of the 22.06
says the LORD c. Shallum the son 22.11
says the LORD c. Jehoiakim the son 22.18
c. the shepherds who care for my 23.02
C. the prophets: My heart is broken 23.09
the LORD of hosts c. the prophets: 23.15
to Jeremiah c. all the people of 25.01
LORD has spoken c. any nation 27.13
the LORD of hosts c. the pillars, 27.19
c. the vessels which are left in 27.21
Thus says the LORD c. the king who 29.16
and c. all the people who dwell in 29.16
c. Ahab the son of Kolaiah and 29.21
says the LORD c. Shemaiah of 29.31
the LORD spoke c. Israel and Judah: 30.04
c. this city of which you say, 'It 32.36
c. the houses of this city and the 33.04
Thus says the LORD c. you: 34.04
And c. Jehoiakim king of Judah you 36.29
says the LORD c. Jehoiakim king of 36.30
gave command c. Jeremiah through 39.11
to Jeremiah c. all the Jews that 44.01
Jeremiah the prophet c. the nations. 46.01
C. the army of Pharaoh Neco, king of 46.02
the prophet c. the Philistines, 47.01
C. Moab. Thus says the LORD 48.01
C. the Ammonites. Thus says the LORD: 49.01
C. Edom. Thus says the LORD 49.07
C. Damascus. "Hamath and 49.23
C. Kedar and the kingdoms of Hazor 49.28
to Jeremiah the prophet c. Elam, 49.34
which the LORD spoke c. Babylon, 50.01
c. the land of the Chaldeans, by 50.01
his purpose c. Babylon is to 51.11
what he spoke c. the inhabitants 51.12
words that are written c. Babylon. 51.60
thou hast said c. this place that 51.62
the Lord GOD c. the inhabitants of Eze 12.19
who prophesied c. Jerusalem and 13.16
this proverb c. the land of Israel, 18.02
says the Lord GOD c. the Ammonites. 21.28
Ammonites, and c. their reproach; 21.28
because Tyre said c. Jerusalem, 26.02
Therefore prophesy c. the land of 36.06
shall tell you c. all the ordinances 44.05
therefore I have sworn c. them, 44.12
understanding c. which the king Dan 1.20
the God of heaven c. this mystery, 2.18
and proclamation was made c. him, 5.29
c. the interdict, "O king! Did you 6.12
nothing might be changed c. Daniel. 6.17
asked him the truth c. all this. 7.16
know the truth c. the fourth beast, 7.19
and c. the ten horns that were on 7.20
is the vision c. the continual 8.13
are decreed c. your people and 9.24
which he saw c. Israel in the days Amo 1.01
The LORD repented c. this; 7.03
The LORD repented c. this; 7.06
Thus says the Lord GOD c. Edom: Ob 1.01
which he saw c. Samaria and Jerusalem. Mic 1.01
Thus says the LORD c. the prophets 3.05
An oracle c. Nineveh. The book Nah 1.01
what I will answer c. my complaint. Hab 2.01
The word of the LORD c. Israel: Zec 12.01
to speak to the crowds c. John: Mt 11.07
twelve asked him c. the parables. Mk 4.10
know the truth c. the things of Lk 1.04
had been told them c. this child; 2.17
questioned in their hearts c. John, 3.15
and a report c. him went out 4.14
more the report went abroad c. him; 5.15
And this report c. him spread 7.17
to speak to the crowds c. John: 7.24
"C. Jesus of Nazareth, who was a 24.19
scriptures the things c. himself. 24.27
to console them c. their brother. Jn 11.19
c. Judas who was guide to those who Ac 1.16
For David says c. him, 'I saw the 2.25
examined today c. a good deed done 4.09
accurately the things c. Jesus, 18.25
arose no little stir c. the Way. 19.23
his defense c. the charge laid 25.16
the gospel c. his Son, who was Rom 1.03
made him waver c. the promise of 4.20
from the law c. the husband. 7.02
And Isaiah cries out c. Israel: 9.27
Now c. the matters about which you 1Co 7.01
Now c. the unmarried, I have no 7.25
Now c. food offered to idols: we 8.01
Now c. spiritual gifts, brethren, I 12.01
Now c. the contribution for the 16.01
of Barnabas (c. whom you have Col 4.10
themselves report c. us what a 1Th 1.09
But c. love of the brethren you 4.09
c. those who are asleep, that you 4.13
Now c. the coming of our Lord Jesus 2Th 2.01
requirement c. bodily descent but Heb 7.16
warned by God c. events as yet 11.07
and gave directions c. his burial. 11.22
our hands, c. the word of life— 1Jn 1.01

CONCERNS
for all that c. the altar and that Num 18.07
Your wickedness c. a man like Job 35.08
This oracle c. the prince in Eze 12.10

CONCESSION
I say this by the way of c., not of 1Co 7.06

CONCILIATE
when slandered, we try to c.; 1Co 4.13

CONCLUDING
c. that God had called us to preach Ac 16.10

CONCUBINE

Moreover, his c., whose name was Gen 22.24
lay with Bilhah his father's c.; 35.22
(Timna was a c. of Eliphaz, Esau's 36.12
And his c. who was in Shechem also Ju 8.31
to himself a c. from Bethlehem in 19.01
And his c. became angry with him, 19.02
the man and his c. and his servant 19.09
asses, and his c. was with him. 19.10
are my virgin daughter and his c.; 19.24
So the man seized his c., 19.25
there was his c. lying at the door 19.27
hold of his c. he divided her, 19.29
I and my c., to spend the night. 20.04
kill me, and they ravished my c., 20.05
And I took my c. and cut her in 20.06
Now Saul had a c., whose name was 2Sa 3.07
have you gone in to my father's c.?" 3.07
of Aiah, the c. of Saul, had done, 21.11
Abraham's c.: she bore Zimran, Jokshan, 1Ch 1.32
Caleb's c.. bore Haran, Moza, and 2.46
Caleb's c., bore Sheber and Tirhanah. 2.48
Asriel, whom his Aramean c. bore; 7.14

CONCUBINES

the sons of his c. Abraham gave Gen 25.06
and David took more c. and wives 2Sa 5.13
king left ten c. to keep the house. 15.16
Absalom, "Go in to your father's c., 16.21
to his father's c. in the sight of 16.22
lives of your wives and your c., 19.05
took the ten c. whom he had left 20.03
princesses, and three hundred c.; 1Ki 11.03
sons, besides the sons of the c.; 1Ch 3.09
his wives and c. (he took eighteen 2Ch 11.21
took eighteen wives and sixty c., 11.21
eunuch who was in charge of the c.; Est 2.14
women, and many c., man's delight. Ecc 2.08
There are sixty queens and eighty c., Sol 6.08
the queens and c. also, and they 6.09
and his c. might drink from them. Dan 5.02
and his c. drank from them. 5.03
and your c. have drunk wine from 5.23

CONDEMN

whom God shall c. shall pay double Ex 22.09
innocent, my own mouth would c. me; Job 9.20
I will say to God, Do not c. me; 10.02
Will you c. him who is righteous 34.17
When he is quiet, who can c.? 34.29
Will you c. me that you may be 40.08
and c. the innocent to death. Ps 94.21
him from those who c. him to death. 109.31
over to those who shall c. them, 141.06
with this generation and c. it; Mt 12.41
with this generation and c. it; 12.42
and they will c. him to death, 20.18
and they will c. him to death, and Mk 10.33
c. not, and you will not be condemned; Lk 6.37
men of this generation and c. them; 11.31
with this generation and c. it; 11.32
'I will c. you out of your own 19.22
not to c. the world, but that the Jn 3.17
Neither do I c. you; go, and do * 8.11
judgment upon him you c. yourself, Rom 2.01
the law will c. you who have the 2.27
who is to c.? Is it Christ 8.34
I do not say this to c. you, 2Co 7.03
whenever our hearts c. us; 1Jn 3.20
Beloved, if our hearts do not c. us, 3.21

CONDEMNATION

C. is ready for scoffers, and Pro 19.29
you will receive greater c. *Mt 23.14
They will receive the greater c." Mk 12.40
They will receive the greater c." Lk 20.47
are under the same sentence of c.? 23.40
with saying. Their c. is just. Rom 3.08
following one trespass brought c., 5.16
trespass led to c. for all men, 5.18
therefore now no c. for those who 8.01
splendor in the dispensation of c., 2Co 3.09
and fall into the c. of the devil; 1Ti 3.06
and so they incur c. for having 5.12
no, that you may not fall under c. Jas 5.12
of old their c. has not been idle, 2Pe 2.03
ago were designated for this c., Jud 1.04

CONDEMNED

I shall be c.; why then do I Job 9.29
who hate the righteous will be c. Ps 34.21
who take refuge in him will be c. 34.22
or let him be c. when he is brought 37.33
would not have c. the guiltless. Mt 12.07
and by your words you will be c." 12.37
his betrayer, saw that he was c., 27.03
And they all c. him as deserving Mk 14.64
not, and you will not be c.; Lk 6.37
delivered him up to be c. to death, 24.20
He who believes in him is not c.; Jn 3.18
who does not believe is c. already, 3.18
where are they? Has no one c. you?" * 8.10
am I still being c. as a sinner? Rom 3.07
and for sin, he c. sin in the flesh, 8.03
But he who has doubts is c., 14.23
we may not be c. along with the 1Co 11.32
—lest you come together to be c. 11.34
to his face, because he stood c. Gal 2.11
so that all may be c. who did not 2Th 2.12
by this he c. the world and became Heb 11.07
You have c., you have killed the Jas 5.06
to ashes he c. them to extinction 2Pe 2.06

CONDEMNING

the innocent and c. the guilty, Deu 25.01
c. the guilty by bringing his 1Ki 8.32
sabbath, fulfilled these by c. him. Ac 13.27

CONDEMNS

Your own mouth c. you, and not I; Job 15.06
but a man of evil devices he c. Pro 12.02
and he who c. the righteous are 17.15

CONDITION

Only on this c. will we consent to Gen 34.15
Only on this c. will the men agree 34.22
of Israel, and God knew their c. Ex 2.25
"On this c. I will make a treaty 1Sa 11.02
to its proper c. and strengthened 2Ch 24.13
Know well the c. of your flocks, and Pro 27.23
were in poorer c. than the youths Dan 1.10
and though my c. was a trial to you, Gal 4.14

CONDITIONS

moreover, c. were good in Judah 2Ch 12.12
containing the terms and c., Jer 32.11

CONDOLE

to come to c. with him and comfort Job 2.11
befallen you—who will c. with you? Is 51.19

CONDUCT

and charges her with shameful c., Deu 22.14
by bringing his c. upon his own 1Ki 8.32
by bringing his c. upon his own 2Ch 6.23
and let him c. the man on horseback Est 6.09
but wise c. is pleasure to a man of Pro 10.23
but the c. of the pure is right. 21.08
knows how to c. himself before the Ecc 6.08
their c. before me was like the Eze 36.17
with their c. and their deeds I 36.19
to a base mind and to improper c. Rom 1.28
a terror to good c., but to bad. 13.03
let us c. ourselves becomingly as 13.13
C. yourselves wisely toward outsiders, Col 4.05

CONDUCT (cont.)
give you in our c. an example to 2Th 3.09
an example in speech and c., 1Ti 4.12
my c., my aim in life, my faith, my 2Ti 3.10
be holy yourselves in all your c.; 1Pe 1.15
c. yourselves with fear throughout 1.17
Maintain good c. among the Gentiles, 2.12

CONDUCTED
Those who c. Paul brought him as Ac 17.15

CONDUCTS
who c. his affairs with justice. Ps 112.05

CONDUIT
stood by the c. of the upper pool, 2Ki 18.17
pool and the c. and brought water 20.20
the end of the c. of the upper Is 7.03
he stood by the c. of the upper 36.02

CONFEDERATES
your c. have prevailed against you; Ob 1.07

CONFER
I did not c. with flesh and blood, Gal 1.16

CONFERRED
And Abner c. with the elders of 2Sa 3.17
He c. with Joab the son of Zeruiah 1Ki 1.07
he went away and c. with the chief Lk 22.04
the council, they c. with one another, Ac 4.15
when he had c. with his council, 25.12

CONFESS
he shall c. the sin he has committed, Lev 5.05
and c. over him all the iniquities 16.21
"But if they c. their iniquity and 26.40
he shall c. his sin which he has Num 5.07
"I will c. my transgressions to the Ps 32.05
I c. my iniquity, I am sorry for my 38.18
and c. the God of Israel, but not in Is 48.01
that they may c. all their abominations Eze 12.16
any one should c. him to be Christ, Jn 9.22
the Pharisees they did not c. it, 12.42
if you c. with your lips that Jesus Rom 10.09
and every tongue c. that Jesus Php 2.11
we c., is the mystery of our 1Ti 3.16
Therefore c. your sins to one Jas 5.16
If we c. our sins, he is faithful 1Jn 1.09
which does not c. Jesus is not of 4.03
I will c. his name before my Father Rev 3.05

CONFESSED
and stood and c. their sins and the Neh 9.02
He c., he did not deny, but Jn 1.20
but c., "I am not the Christ." 1.20

CONFESSES
but he who c. and forsakes them Pro 28.13
and he c. with his lips and so is Rom 10.10
He who c. the Son has the Father 1Jn 2.23
spirit which c. that Jesus Christ 4.02
Whoever c. that Jesus is the Son of 4.15

CONFESSING
c. the sins of the people of Israel, Neh 1.06
c. my sin and the sin of my people Dan 9.20
in the river Jordan, c. their sins. Mt 3.06
in the river Jordan, c. their sins. Mk 1.05
c. and divulging their practices. Ac 19.18

CONFESSION
While Ezra prayed and made c., Ez 10.01
Now then make c. to the LORD the 10.11
of it they made c. and worshiped Neh 9.03
to the LORD my God and made c., Dan 9.04
made the good c. in the presence 1Ti 6.12
Pontius Pilate made the good c., 6.13
apostle and high priest of our c. Heb 3.01
of God, let us hold fast our c. 4.14
hold fast the c. of our hope 10.23

CONFIDENCE
the men of Shechem put c. in him. Ju 9.26
what do you rest this c. of yours? 2Ki 18.19
the people took c. from the words 2Ch 32.08
Is not your fear of God your c., Job 4.06
His c. breaks in sunder, and his 8.14
And you will have c., because 11.18
smiled on them when they had no c.; 29.24
trust, or called fine gold my c.; 31.24
fate of those who have foolish c., Ps 49.13
Put no c. in extortion, set no vain 62.10
in the LORD than to put c. in man. 118.08
the LORD than to put c. in princes. 118.09
will be your c. and will keep your Pro 3.26
but the upright are in his c. 3.32
fear of the LORD one has strong c., 14.26
what do you rest this c. of yours? Is 36.04
was ashamed of Bethel, their c. Jer 48.13
a neighbor, have no c. in a friend; Mic 7.05
Such is the c. that we have through 2Co 3.04
I have great c. in you; I have 7.04
because I have perfect c. in you. 7.16
because of his great c. in you. 8.22
with such c. as I count on showing 10.02
but as a fool, in this boastful c.; 11.17
I have c. in the Lord that you will Gal 5.10
boldness and c. of access through Eph 3.12
Jesus, and put no c. in the flesh. Php 3.03
have reason for c. in the flesh 3.04
man thinks he has reason for c. in 3.04
And we have c. in the Lord about 2Th 3.04
and also great c. in the faith 1Ti 3.13
hold fast our c. and pride in our Heb 3.06
hold our first c. firm to the end, 3.14
Let us then with c. draw near to 4.16
since we have c. to enter the 10.19
Therefore do not throw away your c., 10.35
Through him you have c. in God, 1Pe 1.21
we may have c. and not shrink from 1Jn 2.28
condemn us, we have c. before God; 3.21
we may have c. for the day of 4.17
And this is the c. which we have in 5.14

CONFIDENT
disappointed because they were c.; Job 6.20
he is c. though Jordan rushes 40.23
arise against me, yet I will be c. Ps 27.03
say nothing of you—for being so c. 2Co 9.04
If any one is c. that he is Christ's, 10.07
have been made c. in the Lord Php 1.14
C. of your obedience, I write to you, Phm 1.21

CONFIDENTLY
may say to you c. of the patriarch Ac 2.29
Hence we can c. say, "The Lord is my Heb 13.06

CONFINED
where the king's prisoners were c., Gen 39.20
in the prison where Joseph was c. 40.03
who were c. in the prison—each his 40.05
brothers remain c. in your prison, 42.19
we were c. under the law, kept under Gal 3.23

CONFIRM
and will c. my covenant with you. Lev 26.09
that he may c. his covenant which Deu 8.18
and that he may c. the words which 9.05
he who does not c. the words of 27.26
to c. a transaction, the one drew Ru 4.07
c. for ever the word which thou 2Sa 7.25
in after you and c. your words." 1Ki 1.14
help him to c. his hold of the 2Ki 15.19
but I will c. him in my house and 1Ch 17.14
C. to thy servant thy promise, which Ps 119.38

CONFIRM (cont.)
Then c. your vows and perform Jer 44.25
I stood up to c. and strengthen him. Dan 11.01
in order to c. the promises given Rom 15.08
more zealous to c. you call and 2Pe 1.10

CONFIRMATION
the defense and c. of the gospel. Php 1.07
disputes an oath is final for c. Heb 6.16

CONFIRMED
God of Israel, let thy word be c., 1Ki 8.26
which he c. as a statute to Jacob, 1Ch 16.17
God of Israel, let thy word be c., 2Ch 6.17
which he c. to Jacob as a statute, Ps 105.10
I have sworn an oath and c. it, 119.106
He has c. his words, which he spoke Dan 9.12
word may be c. by the evidence of Mt 18.16
to Christ was c. among you— 1Co 1.06

CONFIRMING
c. this second letter about Purim. Est 9.29

CONFIRMS
who c. the word of his servant, and Is 44.26

CONFISCATION
banishment or for c. of his goods Ez 7.26

CONFLICT
was true, and it was a great c. Dan 10.01
engaged in the same c. which you Php 1.30

CONFLICTING
and their c. thoughts accuse or Rom 2.15

CONFORM
me, men who do not c. to thy law. Ps 119.85

CONFORMED
predestined to be c. to the image Rom 8.29
Do not be c. to this world but be 12.02
do not be c. to the passions of 1Pe 1.14

CONFOUND
You would c. the plans of the poor, Ps 14.06
out, and I will c. their plans; Is 19.03
and they shall c. the riders on Zec 10.05

CONFOUNDED
of strength, are dismayed and c., 2Ki 19.26
they come thither and are c. Job 6.20
turned back and c. who devise evil Ps 35.04
be dismayed and c. because of Is 20.05
Then the moon will be c.. 24.33
Lebanon is c. and withers away; 33.09
of strength, are dismayed and c., 37.27
you shall be put to shame and c.; 41.11
All of them are put to shame and c., 45.16
put to shame or c. to all eternity 45.17
therefore I have not been c.; 50.07
be not c., for you will not be put 54.04
are ashamed and c. and cover their Jer 14.03
be ashamed and c. because of all 22.22
and I was c., because I bore the 31.19
"Hamath and Arpad are c., for they 49.23
that you may remember and be c., Eze 16.63
Be ashamed and c .for your ways, 36.32
Be c., O tillers of the soil, wail, O Joe 1.11
also, because its hopes are c. Zec 9.05
and c. the Jews who lived in Ac 9.22

CONFRONT
this song shall c. them as a Deu 31.21
c. them, overthrow them! Deliver Ps 17.13

CONFRONTED
me, the snares of death c. me. 2Sa 22.06
me, the snares of death c. me. Ps 18.05

CONFUSE
and there c. their language, that Gen 11.07
plans, O Lord, c. their tongues; Ps 55.09
and c. the course of your paths. Is 3.12

CONFUSED
there the LORD c. the language of Gen 11.09
they are c. with wine, they stagger Is 28.07
Why shouldst thou be like a man c., Jer 14.09

CONFUSION
will throw into c. all the people Ex 23.27
you, and throw them into great c., Deu 7.23
c., and frustration, in all that you 28.20
and blindness and c. of mind; 28.28
Philistines and threw them into c.; 1Sa 7.10
and there was very great c. 14.20
Jerusalem and to cause c. in it. Neh 4.08
to shame and c. altogether who Ps 35.26
to shame and c. altogether who 40.14
and hast put to c. those who hate 44.07
to shame and c. who seek my life! 70.02
mingled within her a spirit of c.; Is 19.14
trampling and c. in the valley of 22.05
stretch the line of c. over it, 34.11
makers of idols go in c. together. 45.16
it not themselves, to their own c.? Jer 7.19
but to us c. of face, as at this day, Dan 9.07
belongs c. of face, to our kings, to 9.08
has come; now their c. is at hand. Mic 7.04
So the city was filled with the c.; Ac 19.29
for the assembly was in c., and most 19.32
that all Jerusalem was in c. 21.31
is not a God of c. but of peace. 1Co 14.33

CONFUTE
and you shall c. every tongue that Is 54.17
and also to c. those who contradict Tit 1.09

CONFUTED
behold, there was none that c. Job, Job 32.12
for he powerfully c. the Jews in Ac 18.28

CONCEALED
the deeps c. in the heart of the Ex 15.08

CONGRATULATE
and to c. him because he had fought 2Sa 8.10
servants come to c. our lord King 1Ki 1.47
and to c. him because he had fought 1Ch 18.10

CONGREGATION
Tell all the c. of Israel that on Ex 12.03
assembly of the c. of Israel shall 12.06
be cut off from the c. of Israel, 12.19
All the c. of Israel shall keep it. 12.47
and all the c. of the people of 16.01
And the whole c. of the people of 16.02
to the whole c. of the people of 16.09
to the whole c. of the people of 16.10
leaders of the c. came and told 16.22
All the c. of the people of Israel 17.01
leaders of the c. returned to him, 34.31
assembled all the c. of the people 35.01
Moses said to all the c. of the 35.04
Then all the c. of the people of 35.20
those of the c. who were numbered 38.25
"If the whole c. of Israel commits Lev 4.13
elders of the c. shall lay their 4.15
assemble all the c. at the door of 8.03
and the c. was assembled at the 8.04
And Moses said to the c., "This is 8.05
and all the c. drew near and stood 9.05
lest wrath come upon all the c.; 10.06
may bear the iniquity of the c., 10.17
take from the c. of the people of 16.05
"Say to all the c. of the people of 19.02
head, and let all the c. stone him. 24.14

CONGREGATION (cont.)
death; all the c. shall stone him; Lev 24.16
of all the c. of the people of Num 1.02
These were the ones chosen from the c., 1.16
assembled the whole c. together, 1.18
wrath upon the c. of the people of 1.53
for the whole c. before the tent 3.07
leaders of the c. numbered the 4.34
the whole c. of the people of 8.09
and all the c. of the people of 8.20
use them for summoning the c., 10.02
all the c. shall gather themselves 10.03
and to all the c. of the people of 13.26
word to them and to all the c., 13.26
Then all the c. raised a loud cry; 14.01
the whole c. said to them, "Would 14.02
assembly of the c. of the people 14.05
and said to all the c. of the 14.07
But all the c. said to stone them 14.10
this wicked c. murmur against me 14.27
all this wicked c. that are 14.35
made all the c. to murmur against 14.36
without the knowledge of the c., 15.24
all the c. shall offer one young 15.24
for all the c. of the people of 15.25
And all the c. of the people of 15.26
Moses and Aaron, and to all the c. 15.33
all the c. shall stone him with 15.35
And all the c. brought him outside 15.36
and fifty leaders of the c., 16.02
For all the c. are holy, every one 16.03
separated you from the c. of Israel, 16.09
before the c. to minister to them; 16.09
assembled all the c. against them 16.19
of the LORD appeared to all the c. 16.19
"Separate yourselves from among this c., 16.21
wilt thou be angry with all the c.?" 16.22
"Say to the c., Get away from about 16.24
And he said to the c., "Depart, 16.26
morrow all the c. of the people of 16.41
And when the c. had assembled 16.42
"Get away from the midst of this c., 16.45
it, and carry it quickly to the c., 16.46
be kept for the c. of the people 19.09
the whole c., came into the wilderness 20.01
Now there was no water for the c.; 20.02
"Take the rod, and assemble the c., 20.08
drink to the c. and their cattle." 20.08
and the c. drank, and their cattle. 20.11
the whole c., came to Mount Hor. 20.22
Hor in the sight of all the c. 20.27
And when all the c. saw that Aaron 20.29
of the whole c. of the people of 25.06
saw it, he rose and left the c., 25.07
of all the c. of the people of 26.02
and Abiram, chosen from the c., 26.09
before the leaders and all the c., 27.02
of Zin during the strife of the c., 27.14
flesh, appoint a man over the c., 27.16
that the c. of the LORD may not be 27.17
Eleazar the priest and all the c., 27.19
that all the c. of the people of 27.20
of Israel with him, the whole c." 27.21
the priest and the whole c., 27.22
and to the c. of the people of 31.12
and all the leaders of the c., 31.13
came among the c. of the LORD. 31.16
of the fathers' houses of the c.; 31.26
went out to battle and all the c. 31.27
and to the leaders of the c., 32.02
LORD smote before the c. of Israel, 32.04
stands before the c. for judgment. 35.12
then the c. shall judge between the 35.24
and the c. shall rescue the manslayer 35.25
and the c. shall restore him to his 35.25
leaders of the c. swore to them. Jos 9.15
leaders of the c. had sworn to 9.18
Then all the c. murmured against 9.18
all the leaders said to all the c., 9.19
drawers of water for all the c., 9.21
water for the c. and for the altar 9.27
Then the whole c. of the people of 18.01
stood before the c. for judgment, 20.06
blood, till he stood before the c. 20.09
"Thus says the whole c. of the LORD, 22.16
a plague upon the c. of the LORD, 22.17
with the whole c. of Israel 22.18
fell upon all the c. of Israel? 22.20
priest and the chiefs of the c., 22.30
and the c. assembled as one man to Ju 20.01
So the c. sent thither twelve 21.10
Then the whole c. sent word to the 21.13
Then the elders of the c. said, 21.16
Solomon and all the c. of Israel, 1Ki 8.05
Solomon and all the c. of Israel, 2Ch 5.06
a very great c., from the entrance 7.08
on the c. of Israel for the tent of 24.06
banned from the c. of the exiles. Ez 10.08
sinners in the c. of the righteous Ps 1.05
midst of the c. I will praise thee: 22.22
comes my praise in the great c.; 22.25
in the great c. I will bless the 26.12
Then I will thank thee in the great c.; 35.18
of deliverance in the great c.; 40.09
thy faithfulness from the great c. 40.10
"Bless God in the great c., 68.26
Remember thy c., which thou hast 74.02
extol him in the c. of the people, 107.32
company of the upright, in the c. 111.01
of utter ruin in the assembled c. Pro 5.14
O c., what will happen to them. Jer 6.18
and their c. shall be established 30.20
thou didst forbid to enter thy c. Lam 1.10
Sanctify the c.; assemble the Joe 2.16
who was in the c. in the wilderness Ac 7.38
having gathered the c. together, 15.30
evil of the Way before the c., 19.09
midst of the c. I will praise thee Heb 2.12

CONGREGATION'S
now the c. half was three hundred Num 31.43

CONIAH
though C. the son of Jehoiakim, king Jer 22.24
Is this man C. a despised, broken 22.28
instead of C. the son of Jehoiakim 37.01

CONJUGAL
give to his wife her c. rights, 1Co 7.03

CONNECTED
God, and who was c. with Tobiah, Neh 13.04

CONNECTING
the edge of the other c. curtain. Ex 36.17

CONNECTION
iniquity in c. with the sanctuary; Num 18.01
iniquity in c. with your priesthood. 18.01
any wrong in c. with any offense Deu 19.15
we find it in c. with the law of Dan 6.05
and in c. with that tribe Moses Heb 7.14

CONQUER
and you shall c. every fortified 2Ki 3.19
besieged Ahaz but could not c. him. 16.05
it, but they could not c. it. Is 7.01
and let us c. it for ourselves, and 7.06
he went out conquering and to c. Rev 6.02
upon them and c. them and kill 11.07
war on the saints and to c. them. 13.07
Lamb, and the Lamb will c. them, 17.14

CONQUERED
and c. Ijon, Dan, Abelbethmaacah, and 1Ki 15.20
the slingers surrounded and c. it. 2Ki 3.25

CONQUERED (cont.)
and they c. Ijon, Dan, Abelmaim, and 2Ch 16.04
fourteenth year after the city was c., Eze 40.01
who through faith c. kingdoms, Heb 11.33
as I myself c. and sat down with my Rev 3.21
has c., so that he can open the 5.05
And they have c. him by the blood 12.11
those who had the beast and its 15.02

CONQUERING
and far, a nation mighty and c., Is 18.02
and far, a nation mighty and c., 18.07
and he went out c. and to conquer. Rev 6.02

CONQUEROR
I will again bring a c. upon you, Mic 1.15

CONQUERORS
to others and their fields to c., Jer 8.10
are more than c. through him who Rom 8.37

CONQUERS
To him who c. I will grant to eat Rev 2.07
He who c. shall not be hurt by the 2.11
To him who c. I will give some of 2.17
He who c. and who keeps my works 2.26
He who c. shall be glad thus in 3.05
He who c., I will make him a pillar 3.12
He who c., I will grant him to sit 3.21
He who c. shall have this heritage, 21.07

CONSCIENCE
or pangs of c., for having shed 1Sa 25.31
God in all good c. up to this day." Ac 23.01
to have a clear c. toward God and 24.16
while their c. also bears witness Rom 2.15
my c. bears me witness in the Holy 9.01
wrath but also for the sake of c. 13.05
and their c., being weak, is defiled. 1Co 8.07
if his c. is weak, to eat food 8.10
wounding their c. when it is weak, 8.12
any question on the ground of c. 10.25
any question on the ground of c. 10.27
I mean his c., not yours—do not 10.29
testimony of our c. that we have 2Co 1.12
to every man's c. in the sight of 4.02
I hope it is known also to your c. 5.11
and a good c. and sincere faith. 1Ti 1.05
holding faith and a good c. 1.19
By rejecting c., certain persons 1.19
of the faith with a clear c. 3.09
God whom I serve with a clear c., 2Ti 1.03
perfect the c. of the worshiper, Heb 9.09
purify your c. from dead works to 9.14
from an evil c. and our bodies 10.22
are sure that we have a clear c., 13.18
and keep your c. clear, so that, when 1Pe 3.16
as an appeal to God for a clear c., 3.21

CONSCIENCE'
informed you, and for c. sake— 1Co 10.28

CONSCIENCES
of liars whose c. are seared, 1Ti 4.02
very minds and c. are corrupted. Tit 1.15

CONSCIOUSNESS
would no longer have any c. of sin. Heb 10.02

CONSECRATE
"C. to me all the first-born; Ex 13.02
the people and c. them today and 19.10
near to the LORD c. themselves, 19.22
about the mountain, and c. it.'" 19.23
garments to c. him for my priesthood. 28.03
them and ordain them and c. them, 28.41
you shall do to them to c. them, 29.01
And you shall c. the breast of the 29.27
to ordain and c. them, but an 29.33
it, and shall anoint it, to c. it. 29.36
and c. it, and the altar shall be 29.37
I will c. the tent of meeting and 29.44
Aaron also and his sons I will c., 29.44
you shall c. them, that they may be 30.29
and c. them that they may serve me 30.30
and c. it and all its furniture; 40.09
all its utensils, and c. the altar; 40.10
the laver and its base, and c. it. 40.11
you shall anoint him and c. him, 40.13
the laver and its base, to c. them. Lev 8.11
head, and anointed him, to c. him. 8.12
c. yourselves therefore, and be holy, 11.44
C. yourselves therefore, and be holy; 20.07
You shall c. him, for he offers the 21.08
And he shall c. his head that same Num 6.11
'C. yourselves for tomorrow, and you 11.18
flock you shall c. to the LORD Deu 15.19
"I c. the silver to the LORD from Ju 17.03
c. yourselves, and come with me to 1Sa 16.05
set apart to c. the most holy 1Ch 23.13
comes to c. himself with a young 2Ch 13.09
altar and purify it, and so c. it. Eze 43.26
And for their sake I c. myself, Jn 17.19

CONSECRATED
to the people, and c. the people; Ex 19.14
"You shall be men c. to me; 22.31
c. to them on the day they were Lev 7.35
all that was in it, and c. them. 8.10
and c. it, to make atonement for it. 8.15
so he c. Aaron and his garments, and 8.30
is anointed and c. as priest in 16.32
who has been c. to wear the garments, 21.10
I c. for my own all the first-born Num 3.13
him, and he defiles his c. head, 6.09
shall shave his c. head at the 6.18
hair from his c. head and put it 6.18
anointed and c. it with all its 7.01
and c. the altar with all its utensils, 7.01
land of Egypt I c. them for myself, 8.17
all the c. things of the people of 18.08
all those c. to him were in his Deu 33.03
and they c. his son, Eleazar, to have 1Sa 7.01
And he c. Jesse and his sons, and 16.05
day the king c. the middle of the 1Ki 8.64
I have c. this house which you have 9.03
which I have c. for my name I will 9.07
he c. to be priests of the high 13.33
And Solomon c. the middle of the 2Ch 7.07
have chosen and c. this house that 7.16
which I have c. for my name, I will 7.20
who are c. to burn incense. 26.18
"You have now c. yourselves to the 29.31
And the c. offerings were six 29.33
which had been c. to the LORD 31.06
They c. it and set its doors; Neh 3.01
they c. it as far as the Tower of 3.01
I myself have commanded my c. ones, Is 13.03
and before you were born I c. you; Jer 1.05
This shall be for the c. priests, Eze 48.11
and c. themselves to Baal, and Hos 9.10
a sacrifice and c. his guests. Zep 1.07
whom the Father c. and sent into Jn 10.36
that they also may be c. in truth. 17.19
husband is c. through his wife, and 1Co 7.14
unbelieving wife is c. through her 7.14
for then it is c. by the word of 1Ti 4.05
c. and useful to the master of the 2Ti 2.21

CONSECRATING
c. himself today to the LORD?" 1Ch 29.05

CONSECRATION
of the c., and of the peace offerings, Lev 7.37
for the c. of the anointing oil of 21.12
he has shaven the hair of his c., Num 6.19

CONSENT
this condition will we c. to you: Gen 34.15
without your c. no man shall lift 41.44
king of Moab, but he would not c. Ju 11.17
said to him, "Do not heed or c." 1Ki 20.08
if sinners entice you, do not c. Pro 1.10
witnesses and c. to the deeds of Lk 11.48
without your c. in order that your Phm 1.14

CONSENTED
righteousness." Then he c. Mt 3.15
who had not c. to their purpose and Lk 23.51

CONSENTING
And Saul was c. to his death. Ac 8.01

CONSENTS
and she c. to live with him, he 1Co 7.12
and he c. to live with her, she 7.13

CONSEQUENCES
bear the c. of your lewdness and Eze 23.35

CONSEQUENTLY
C. he is able for all time to save Heb 7.25
C., when Christ came into the world, 10.05

CONSIDER
C. too that this nation is thy Ex 33.13
And c. this day (since I am not Deu 11.02
c. the discipline of the LORD your 11.02
c. the years of many generations; 32.07
Now therefore c. what you will do." Ju 18.14
c. it, take counsel, and speak." 19.30
for c. what great things he has 1Sa 12.24
know this and c. what you should 25.17
Now c., and decide what answer I 2Sa 24.13
and c. well what you have to do; 1Ki 20.22
Only c., and see how he is seeking 2Ki 5.07
"C. what you do, for you judge not 2Ch 19.06
and c. what the fathers have found; Job 8.08
sees iniquity, will he not c. it? 11.11
words? C., and then we will speak. 18.02
when I c., I am in dread of him. 23.15
stop and c. the wondrous works of 37.14
C. and answer me, O LORD my God; Ps 13.03
C. my affliction and my trouble, and 25.18
C. how many are my foes, and with 25.19
c., and incline your ear; forget 45.10
c. well her ramparts, go through her 48.13
I c. the days of old, I remember the 77.05
did not c. thy wonderful works; 106.07
let men c. the steadfast love of 107.43
destroy me; but I c. thy testimonies. 119.95
C. how I love thy precepts! 119.159
c. her ways, and be wise. Pro 6.06
So I turned to c. wisdom and Ecc 2.12
C. the work of God; who can 7.13
and in the day of adversity c.; 7.14
may c. and understand together, that Is 41.20
that we may c. them, that we may 41.22
nor c. the things of old. 43.18
"Remember this and c., recall 46.08
Behold, c., we are all thy people. 64.09
"C., and call for the mourning Jer 9.17
c. well the highway, the road by 31.21
though you c. yourself as wise as a Eze 28.02
"Because you c. yourself as wise as 28.06
"You c. yourself a lion among the 32.02
therefore c. the word and understand Dan 9.23
But they do not c. that I remember Hos 7.02
of hosts: C. how you have fared. Hag 1.05
of hosts: C. how you have fared. 1.07
Pray now, c. what will come to pass 2.15
C. from this day onward, from the 2.18
of the LORD's temple was laid, c.: 2.18
C. the lilies of the field, how they Mt 6.28
C. the ravens: they neither sow nor Lk 12.24
C. the lilies, how they grow; 12.27
gathered together to c. this matter. Ac 15.06
So you also must c. yourselves dead Rom 6.11
I c. that the sufferings of this 8.18
For c. your call, brethren; not many 1Co 1.26
C. the practice of Israel; are not 10.18
I do not c. that I have made it my Php 3.13
So if you c. me your partner, Phm 1.17
c. Jesus, the apostle and high Heb 3.01
and let us c. how to stir up one 10.24
C. him who endured from sinners 12.03
c. the outcome of their life, and 13.07

CONSIDERABLE
turned away a c. company of people, Ac 19.26

CONSIDERATELY
live c. with your wives, bestowing 1Pe 3.07

CONSIDERATION
then out of c. for the man who 1Co 10.28

CONSIDERED
it was not c. as anything in the 1Ki 10.21
silver was not c. as anything in 2Ch 9.20
"Have you c. my servant Job, that Job 1.08
"Have you c. my servant Job, that 2.03
a fool who keeps silent is c. wise; Pro 17.28
Then I saw and c. it; I looked 24.32
Then I c. all that my hands had Ecc 2.11
who c. that he was cut off out of Is 53.08
Because he c. and turned away from Eze 18.28
I c. the horns, and behold, there Dan 7.08
But as he c. this, behold, an angel Mt 1.20
and c. in her mind what sort of Lk 1.29
in faith when he c. his own body, Rom 4.19
or when he c. the barrenness of 4.19
rule well be c. worthy of double 1Ti 5.17
since she c. him faithful who had Heb 11.11
He c. that God was able to raise 11.19
He c. abuse suffered for the Christ 11.26

CONSIDERING
As I was c., behold, a he-goat came Dan 8.05

CONSIDERS
Blessed is he who c. the poor! Ps 41.01
Who c. the power of thy anger, and 90.11
but an upright man c. his ways. Pro 21.29
She c. a field and buys it; with the 31.16
No one c., nor is there knowledge Is 44.19

CONSIGNED
I am c. to the gates of Sheol for Is 38.10
For God has c. all men to disobedience, Rom 11.32
But the scripture c. all things to Gal 3.22

CONSIST
life does not c. in the abundance Lk 12.15
of God does not c. in talk but in 1Co 4.20
body does not c. of one member but 12.14

CONSOLATION
This would be my c.; I would Job 6.10
my words, and let this be your c. 21.02
him the cup of c. to drink for his Jer 16.07
have done, becoming a c. to them. Eze 16.54
false dreams, and give empty c. Zec 10.02
looking for the c. of Israel, Lk 2.25
for you have received your c. 6.24
upbuilding and encouragement and c. 1Co 14.03

CONSOLATIONS
Are the c. of God too small for you, Job 15.11
are many, thy c. cheer my soul. Ps 94.19
and with c. I will lead them back, I Jer 31.09

CONSOLE
his servants to c. him concerning 2Sa 10.02
messengers to c. him concerning 1Ch 19.02

CONSOLE (cont.)
land of the Ammonites, to c. him. 1Ch 19.02
They will c. you, when you see their Eze 14.23
and Mary to c. them concerning Jn 11.19

CONSOLED
you will be c. for the evil that I Eze 14.22
she refused to be c., because Mt 2.18

CONSOLING
be satisfied with her c. breasts; Is 66.11
c. her, saw Mary rise quickly and go Jn 11.31

CONSORT
nor do I c. with dissemblers; Ps 26.04

CONSPICUOUS
the goat had a c. horn between his Dan 8.05
came up four c. horns toward the 8.08
The sins of some men are c., pointing 1Ti 5.24
So also good deeds are c.; and even 5.25

CONSPIRACY
And the c. grew strong, and the 2Sa 15.12
and the c. which he made, are they 1Ki 16.20
His servants arose and made a c., 2Ki 12.20
And they made a c. against him in 14.19
and the c. which he made, behold, 15.15
of Elah made a c. against Pekah 15.30
they made a c. against him in 2Ch 25.27
"Do not call c. all that this Is 8.12
people call c., and do not fear 8.12
more than forty who made this c. Ac 23.13

CONSPIRATORS
is among the c. with Absalom." 2Sa 15.31

CONSPIRE
Why do the nations c., and the Ps 2.01
Yea, they c. with one accord; 83.05

CONSPIRED
to them they c. against him to Gen 37.18
that all of you have c. against me? 1Sa 22.08
"Why have you c. against me, you and 22.13
house of Issachar, c. against him; 1Ki 15.27
half his chariots, c. against him. 16.09
"Zimri has c., and he has killed 16.16
the son of Nimshi c. against Joram. 2Ki 9.14
It was I who c. against my master, 10.09
Shallum the son of Jabesh c. against him, 15.10
c. against him with fifty men of 15.25
servants of Amon c. against him, 21.23
those who had c. against King Amon, 21.24
But they c. against him, and by 2Ch 24.21
his servants c. against him because 24.25
Those who c. against him were Zabad 24.26
And his servants c. against him and 33.24
those who had c. against King Amon 33.25
"Amos has c. against you in the Amo 7.10

CONSTANT
in tribulation, be c. in prayer. Rom 12.12

CONSTANTLY
the people, and prayed c. to God. Ac 10.02
c. mentioning you in our prayers, 1Th 1.02
And we also thank God c. for this, 2.13
pray c., 5.17
I remember you c. in my prayers. 2Ti 1.03

CONSTELLATIONS
and the c., and all the host of the 2Ki 23.05
and their c. will not give their Is 13.10

CONSTERNATION
I said in my c., "Men are all a Ps 116.11

CONSTRAINED
and how I am c. until it is accomplished! Lk 12.50
but they c. him, saying, "Stay with 24.29

CONSTRAINS
words, the spirit within me c. me. Job 32.18

CONSTRAINT
not by c. but willingly, not for 1Pe 5.02

CONSTRUCTED
took heed and c. an ark for the Heb 11.07

CONSTRUCTION
any work in the c. of the sanctuary Ex 36.01
in all the c. of the sanctuary, the 38.24
This was the c. of the stands: they 1Ki 7.28
half of my servants worked on c., Neh 4.16
appearance of the wheels and their c.: Eze 1.16
their c. being as it were a wheel 1.16

CONSULT
you shall c. them, and they shall Deu 17.09
be a priest to c. Urim and Thummim. Ez 2.63
who watch for my life c. together, Ps 71.10
they c. together against thy 83.03
"C. the mediums and the wizards who Is 8.19
should not a people c. their God? 8.19
Should they c. the dead on behalf 8.19
and they will c. the idols and the 19.03
Holy One of Israel or c. the LORD! 31.01
Whom did he c. for his enlightenment, 40.14

CONSULTATION
and the whole council held a c.; Mk 15.01

CONSULTED
was as if one c. the oracle of God 2Sa 16.23
and also c. a medium, seeking 1Ch 10.13
David c. with the commanders of 13.01

CONSULTS
he c. the teraphim, he looks at the Eze 21.21

CONSUME
Egypt; the famine will c. the land, Gen 41.30
hot against them and I may c. them; Ex 32.10
and to c. them from the face of the 32.12
lest I c. you in the way, for you 33.03
go up among you, I would c. you. 33.05
that I may c. them in a moment." Num 16.21
that I may c. them in a moment." 16.45
that I did not c. the people of 25.11
For this great fire will c. us; Deu 5.25
for the locust shall c. it. 28.38
and c. you, after having done you Jos 24.20
will utterly c. the house of 1Ki 14.10
from heaven and c. you and your 2Ki 1.10
from heaven and c. you and your 1.12
with us till you wouldst c. us, Ez 9.14
and fire will c. them. Ps 21.09
thou dost c. like a moth what is 39.11
c. them in wrath, c. them till 59.13
but the lips of a fool c. him. Ecc 10.12
fire for thy adversaries c. them. Is 26.11
breath is a fire that will c. you. 33.11
and the flame shall not c. you. 43.02
but I will c. them by the sword, by Jer 14.12
fire, the fire shall yet c. them; Eze 15.07
and I will c. your filthiness out 22.15
c. the bars of their gates, and Hos 11.06
they shall burn them and c. them, Ob 1.18
shall abide in his house and c. it, Zec 5.04
moth and rust c. and where thieves Mt 6.19
come down from heaven and c. them?" Lk 9.54
"Zeal for thy house will c. me." Jn 2.17
fire which will c. the adversaries Heb 10.27

CONSUMED

lest you be c. in the punishment of Gen 19.15
flee to the hills, lest you be c." 19.17
by day the heat c. me, and the 31.40
was burning, yet it was not c. Ex 3.02
standing grain or the field is c., 22.06
the fire has c. the burnt offering Lev 6.10
the LORD and c. the burnt offering 9.24
and c. some outlying parts of the Num 11.01
before it was c., the anger of the 11.33
flesh is half c. when he comes out 12.12
and c. the two hundred and fifty 16.35
in the sight of the LORD was c. 32.13
until he has c. you off the land Deu 28.21
the rock and c. the flesh and the Ju 6.21
against them until they are c.' 1Sa 15.18
"The man who c. us and planned to 2Sa 21.05
not turn back until they were c. 22.38
I c. them; I thrust them 22.39
and they are utterly c. with fire." 23.07
and c. the burnt offering, and the 1Ki 18.38
and c. him and his fifty. 2Ki 1.10
from heaven and c. him and his 1.12
and c. the two former captains of 1.14
from heaven and c. the burnt 2Ch 7.01
and the servants, and c. them; Job 1.16
the blast of his anger they are c. 4.09
By disease his skin is c., the 18.13
is left in his tent will be c. 20.26
and what they left the fire has c. 22.20
not turn back till they were c. Ps 18.37
For zeal for thy house has c. me, 69.09
my accusers be put to shame and c.; 71.13
For we are c. by thy anger; by thy 90.07
Let sinners be c. from the earth, 104.35
My soul is c. with longing for thy 119.20
when your flesh and body are c., Pro 5.11
who forsake the LORD shall be c. Is 1.28
thou hast c. them, but they refused Jer 5.03
fiercely, the lead is c. by the fire; 6.29
after them, until I have c. them." 9.16
they have devoured him and c. him, 10.25
to it, and its branches will be c. 11.16
famine those prophets shall be c. 14.15
until I have c. it by his hand. 27.08
scroll was c. in the fire that was 36.23
to live, and they shall all be c.; 44.12
and by famine they shall be c.; 44.12
and have been c. by the sword and 44.18
Egypt shall be c. by the sword and 44.27
after them, until I have c. them; 49.37
which c. its foundations. Lam 4.11
pestilence and be c. with famine in Eze 5.12
the fire has c. both ends of it, 15.04
the fire has c. it and it is 15.05
withered; the fire c. it. 19.12
has c. its branches and fruit, so 19.14
I have c. them with the fire of my 22.31
may be melted in it, its rust c. 24.11
it c. you, and I turned you to ashes 28.18
no more be c. with hunger in the 34.29
so I have c. them in my anger. 43.08
to be c. and destroyed to the end. Dan 7.26
Like entangled thorns they are c., Nah 1.10
wrath, all the earth shall be c.; Zep 1.18
wrath all the earth shall be c. 3.08
you, O sons of Jacob, are not c. Mal 3.06
women and were c. with passion for Rom 1.27
that you are not c. by one another. Gal 5.15
came down from heaven and c. them, Rev 20.09

CONSUMES

thy fury, it c. them like stubble. Ex 15.07
and fire c. the tents of bribery. Job 15.34
first-born of death c. his limbs. 18.13
be a fire which c. unto Abaddon, 31.12
As fire c. the forest, as the flame Ps 83.14
My zeal c. me, because my foes 119.139
it c. briers and thorns; it kindles Is 9.18
are like stubble, the fire c. them; 47.14
moth nor rust c. and where thieves Mt 6.20
from their mouth and c. their foes; Rev 11.05

CONSUMING

fire in Jacob, c. all around. Lam 2.03
for our God is a c. fire. Heb 12.29

CONSUMPTION

c., and fever that waste the eyes Lev 26.16
The LORD will smite you with c., Deu 28.22

CONTACT

unclean through c. with the dead Lev 22.04
unclean through c. with the dead; Num 5.02
is unclean by c. with a dead body Hag 2.13

CONTAIN

the highest heaven cannot c. thee; 1Ki 8.27
great as would c. two measures of 18.32
even highest heaven, cannot c. him? 2Ch 2.06
the highest heaven cannot c. thee; 6.18
could not c. the books that would Jn 21.25

CONTAINED

which c. a golden urn holding the Heb 9.04

CONTAINING

c. the terms and conditions, and the Jer 32.11
the bath c. one tenth of a homer, Eze 45.11

CONTAINS

land will be stripped of all it c., Eze 12.19
held in derision, for it c. much; 23.32
cor, like the homer, c. ten baths); 45.14

CONTEMPT

she looked with c. on her mistress. Gen 16.04
conceived, she looked on me with c. 16.05
the offering of the LORD with c. 1Sa 2.17
letters to cast c. on the LORD the 2Ch 32.17
to look with c. upon their husbands, Est 1.17
there will be c. and wrath in 1.18
at ease there is c. for misfortune; Job 12.05
He pours c. on princes, and looses 12.21
and the c. of families terrified me, 31.34
the righteous in pride and c. Ps 31.18
he pours c. upon princes and makes 107.40
take away from me their scorn and c., 119.22
we have had more than enough of c. 123.03
are at ease, the c. of the proud. 123.04
When wickedness comes, c. comes also; Pro 18.02
he brought into c. the land of Is 9.01
of Moab will be brought into c., 16.14
mother are treated with c. in you; Eze 22.07
who have treated them with c. 28.24
who have treated them with c. 28.26
with wholehearted joy and utter c., 36.05
some to shame and everlasting c. Dan 12.02
for the son treats the father with c., Mic 7.06
filth at you and treat you with c., Nah 3.06
be sated with c. instead of glory. Hab 2.16
many things and be treated with c.? Mk 9.12
treated him with c. and mocked him; Lk 23.11
own account and hold him up to c. Heb 6.06

CONTEMPTIBLE

make myself yet more c. than this, 2Sa 6.22
shall arise a c. person to whom Dan 11.21

CONTEND

do not c. with them; for I will Deu 2.05
harass Moab or c. with them in 2.09
do not harass them or c. with them, 2.19
and c. with him in battle. 2.24
With thy hands c. for him, 33.07

CONTEND (cont.)

against him, "Will you c. for Baal? Ju 6.31
let him c. for himself, because his 6.31
"Let Baal c. against him," because 6.32
If one wished to c. with him, Job 9.03
know why thou dost c. against me. 10.02
Who is there that will c. with me? 13.19
Would he c. with me in the greatness 23.06
Why do you c. against him, saying, 33.13
"Shall a faultfinder c. with the 40.02
C., O LORD, with those who c. Ps 35.01
Do not c. with a man for no reason, Pro 3.30
The LORD has taken his place to c., Is 3.13
by exile thou didst c. with them; 27.08
You shall seek those who c. with you, 41.12
for I will c. with those who c. with you, 49.25
Who will c. with me? Let us 50.08
For I will not c. for ever, nor will 57.16
"Therefore I still c. with you, Jer 2.09
your children's children I will c. 2.09
Yet let no one c., and let none Hos 4.04
people, and he will c. with Israel. Mic 6.02
to you to c. for the faith which Jud 1.03

CONTENDED

Esek, because they c. with him. Gen 26.20
And the people c. with Moses, and Num 20.03
people of Israel c. with the LORD, 20.13
who c. against Moses and Aaron in 26.09
when they c. against the LORD, 26.09
And I c. with them and cursed them Neh 13.25
Pharisees' party stood up and c., Ac 23.09

CONTENDERS

and decides between powerful c. Pro 18.18

CONTENDING

For we are not c. against flesh and Eph 6.12
c. with the devil disputed about Jud 1.09

CONTENDS

Whoever c. for him shall be put to Ju 6.31
is none who c. by my side against Dan 10.21

CONTENT

And Moses was c. to dwell with the Ex 2.21
And when Moses heard that he was c. Lev 10.20
we had been c. to dwell beyond the Jos 7.07
and the Levite was c. to dwell with Ju 17.11
Be c. with your glory, and stay at 2Ki 14.10
Yet you were not c. to walk in Eze 16.47
accusation, and be c. with your wages." Lk 3.14
I am c. with weaknesses, insults, 2Co 12.10
in whatever state I am, to be c. Php 4.11
clothing, with these we shall be c. 1Ti 6.08
and be c. with what you have; Heb 13.05
And not c. with that, he refuses 3Jn 1.10

CONTENTION

he who is slow to anger quiets c. Pro 15.18
of strife and c. to the whole land! Jer 15.10
for with you is my c., O priest. Hos 4.04
before me; strife and c. arise. Hab 1.03
And there arose a sharp c., Ac 15.39

CONTENTIOUS

in a house shared with a c. woman. Pro 21.09
than with a c. and fretful woman. 21.19
in a house shared with a c. woman. 25.24
rainy day and a c. woman are alike; 27.15
If any one is disposed to be c., 1Co 11.16

CONTENTMENT

is great gain in godliness with c.; 1Ti 6.06

CONTEST

If it is a c. of strength, behold Job 9.19

CONTINUAL

bring them to c. remembrance Ex 28.29
It shall be a c. burnt offering 29.42
the c. bread also shall be on it; Num 4.07
the c. cereal offering, and the 4.16
day by day, as a c. offering. 28.03
It is a c. burnt offering, which was 28.06
besides the c. burnt offering and 28.10
besides the c. burnt offering and 28.15
which is for a c. burnt offering. 28.23
besides the c. burnt offering and 28.24
Besides the c. burnt offering and 28.31
and the c. burnt offering and its 29.06
and the c. burnt offering and its 29.11
besides the c. burnt offering, its 29.16
besides the c. burnt offering and 29.19
besides the c. burnt offering and 29.22
besides the c. burnt offering, its 29.25
besides the c. burnt offerings and 29.28
besides the c. burnt offering, its 29.31
besides the c. burnt offering, its 29.34
besides the c. burnt offering and 29.38
and for the c. offering of the 2Ch 2.04
There were c. wars between Rehoboam 12.15
and after that the c. burnt offerings, Ez 3.05
the c. cereal offering, the c. burnt Neh 10.33
and with c. strife in his bones; Job 33.19
a cheerful heart has a c. feast. Pro 15.15
quarreling is a c. dripping of 19.13
A c. dripping on a rainy day and a 27.15
Israel, which had been a c. waste; Eze 38.08
ordinance for the c. burnt offering. 46.14
morning, for a c. burnt offering. 46.15
and the c. burnt offering was taken Dan 8.11
with the c. burnt offering through 8.12
concerning the c. burnt offering, 8.13
take away the c. burnt offering. 11.31
time that the c. burnt offering is 12.11
will wear me out by her c. coming.'" Lk 18.05

CONTINUALLY

of his heart was only evil c. Gen 6.05
waters receded from the earth c. 8.03
fire flashing c. in the midst of Ex 9.24
a lamp may be set up to burn c. 27.20
upon his heart before the LORD c. 28.30
two lambs a year old day by day c. 29.38
be kept burning upon the altar c.; Lev 6.13
a light may be kept burning c. 24.02
to morning before the LORD c.; 24.03
of pure gold before the LORD c. 24.04
before the LORD c. on behalf of 24.08
So it was c.; the cloud Num 9.16
be only oppressed and robbed c., Deu 28.29
be only oppressed and crushed c.; 28.33
ark, while the trumpets blew c. Jos 6.09
passed on, blowing the trumpets c.; 6.13
LORD, while the trumpets blew c. 6.13
So Saul was David's enemy c. 1Sa 18.29
and as he came he cursed c. 2Sa 16.05
who c. stand before you and hear 1Ki 10.08
between Rehoboam and Jeroboam c. 14.30
who is c. passing our way. 2Ki 4.09
he gave them c. into the hand of 13.03
priests were to blow trumpets c., 1Ch 16.06
his strength, seek his presence c.! 16.11
to minister c. before the ark as 16.37
burnt offering c. morning and 16.40
of them, c. before the LORD. 23.31
who c. stand before you and hear 2Ch 9.07
of the LORD c. all the days of 24.14
hearts." Thus Job did c. Job 1.05
his praise shall c. be in my mouth. Ps 34.01
who love thy salvation say c., 40.16
and night, while men say to me c., 42.03
taunt me, while they say to me c., 42.10
In God we have boasted c., and we 44.08

CONTINUALLY (cont.)
burnt offerings are c. before me. Ps 50.08
and make their loins tremble c. 69.23
womb. My praise is c. of thee. 71.06
But I will hope c., and will 71.14
May prayer be made for him c., 72.15
Nevertheless I am c. with thee; 73.23
thy adversaries which goes up c.! 74.23
his strength, seek his presence c.! 105.04
Let them be before the LORD c.; 109.15
I will keep thy law c., for ever 119.44
I hold my life in my hand c., 119.109
have regard for thy statutes c.! 119.117
their heart, and stir up wars c. 140.02
my prayer is c. against their 141.05
devises evil, c. sowing discord; Pro 6.14
c. by day, and at my post I am Is 21.08
Does he who plows for sowing plow c.? 28.24
does he c. open and harrow his 28.24
your walls are c. before me. 49.16
and fear c. all the day because of 51.13
and c. all the day my name is 52.05
And the LORD will guide you c., 58.11
Your gates shall be open c.; 60.11
who provoke me to my face c., 65.03
They say c. to those who despise Jer 23.17
My soul c. thinks of it and is Lam 3.20
it, and fire flashing forth c., Eze 1.04
the land c. and bury those remaining 39.14
whom you serve c., deliver you!" Dan 6.16
has your God, whom you serve c., 6.20
justice, and wait c. for your God." Hos 12.06
and were c. in the temple blessing Lk 24.53
the priests go c. into the outer Heb 9.06
which are c. offered year after 10.01
Through him then let us c. offer up 13.15

CONTINUE
for I c. childless, and the heir of Gen 15.02
Then she shall c. for thirty-three Lev 12.04
and she shall c. in the blood of 12.05
she shall c. in uncleanness; 15.25
so that he may c. long in his Deu 17.20
to c. to this day, in the place Jos 9.27
God will not c. to drive out these 23.13
But now your kingdom shall not c.; 1Sa 13.14
that it may c. for ever before thee; 2Sa 7.29
that it may c. for ever before thee; 1Ch 17.27
O c. thy steadfast love to those Ps 36.10
that he should c. to live on for 49.09
his fame c. as long as the sun! 72.17
lies shall c. in my presence. 101.07
but c. in the fear of the LORD all Pro 23.17
knowledge its stability will long c. 28.02
be smitten, that you c. to rebel? Is 1.05
it shall c. in summer as in winter. Zec 14.08
"If you c. in my word, you are truly Jn 8.31
The slave does not c. in the house 8.35
urged them to c. in the grace of Ac 13.43
exhorting them to c. in the faith, 14.22
Are we to c. in sin that grace may Rom 6.01
God's purpose of election might c., 9.11
provided you c. in his kindness; 11.22
And what I do I will c. to do, 2Co 11.12
I shall remain and c. with you all, Php 1.25
provided that you c. in the faith, Col 1.23
C. steadfastly in prayer, being 4.02
c. in what you have learned and 2Ti 3.14
for they did not c. in my covenant, Heb 8.09
Let brotherly love c. 13.01

CONTINUED
The flood c. forty days upon the Gen 7.17
And the waters c. to abate until 8.05
and they c. for some time in 40.04
Even when the cloud c. over the Num 9.19
or if it c. for a day and a night, 9.21
that the cloud c. over the tabernacle, 9.22
And from there they c. to Beer; 21.16
So Moses c. to speak these words to Deu 31.01
and she has c. from early morning Ru 2.07
As she c. praying before the LORD, 1Sa 1.12
Now the boy Samuel c. to grow both 2.26
Syria and Israel c. without war. 1Ki 22.01
the people c. to sacrifice and burn 2Ki 12.03
all this c. until the burnt 2Ch 29.28
and I c. fasting and praying before Neh 1.04
And Elihu c., and said: Job 36.01
therefore I have c. my faithfulness Jer 31.03
And Daniel c. until the first year Dan 1.21
there they have c. Shall not Hos 10.09
all night he c. in prayer to God. Lk 6.12
those who have c. with me in my 22.28
And as they c. to ask him, *Jn 8.07
being baptized he c. with Philip. Ac 8.13
But Peter c. knocking; and when 12.16
This c. for two years, so that all 19.10
that you have c. in suspense and 27.33
all things have c. as they were 2Pe 3.04
of us, they would have c. with us; 1Jn 2.19

CONTINUES
then it c. in the north to Cabul, Jos 19.27
for ever if he c. resolute in 1Ch 28.07
he flees like a shadow, and c. not. Job 14.02
for ever; the son c. for ever. Jn 8.35
if she c. in faith and love and 1Ti 2.15
hope on God and c. in supplications 5.05
Son of God he c. a priest for ever. Heb 7.03
permanently, because he c. for ever. 7.24

CONTINUING
Judah c. in his territory on the Jos 18.05
prevented by death from c. in office; Heb 7.23

CONTINUOUS
And there shall be c. day (it is Zec 14.07

CONTRADICT
will be able to withstand or c. Lk 21.15
also to confute those who c. it. Tit 1.09

CONTRADICTED
and c. what was spoken by Paul, and Ac 13.45
that these things cannot be c., 19.36

CONTRADICTIONS
chatter and c. of what is falsely 1Ti 6.20

CONTRARY
"Then if you walk c. to me, and will Lev 26.21
turned to me, but walk c. to me, 26.23
then I also will walk c. to you, 26.24
hearken to me, but walk c. to me, 26.27
then I will walk c. to you in fury, 26.28
me, and also in walking c. to me, 26.40
so that I walked c. to them and 26.41
men to worship God c. to the law." Ac 18.13
and yet c. to the law you order me 23.03
On the c., we uphold the law. Rom 3.31
to a disobedient and c. people." 10.21
c. to nature, into a cultivated 11.24
On the c., the parts of the body 1Co 12.22
On the c., I worked harder than any 15.10
to you a gospel c. to that which Gal 1.08
to you a gospel c. to that which 1.09
but on the c., when they saw that I 2.07
whatever else is c. to sound 1Ti 1.10
but on the c. bless, for to this you 1Pe 3.09

CONTRIBUTE
C. to the needs of the saints, Rom 12.13

CONTRIBUTED
bronze that was c. was seventy Ex 38.29
Then Josiah c. to the lay people, as 2Ch 35.07

CONTRIBUTED (cont.)
And his princes c. willingly to the 2Ch 35.08
For they all c. out of their Mk 12.44
for they all c. out of their Lk 21.04

CONTRIBUTES
he who c., in liberality; he who gives Rom 12.08

CONTRIBUTING
those who are c. to the treasury. Mk 12.43

CONTRIBUTION
The c. of the king from his own 2Ch 31.03
apportion the c. reserved for the 31.14
Levi shall bring the c. of grain, Neh 10.39
to make some c. for the poor among Rom 15.26
Now concerning the c. for the saints: 1Co 16.01
generosity of your c. for them and 2Co 9.13

CONTRIBUTIONS
to bring the c. into the house of 2Ch 31.10
And they faithfully brought in the c., 31.12
and our c., the fruit of every tree, Neh 10.37
the c., the first fruits, and the 12.44
and the c. for the priests. 13.05
require your c. and the choicest Eze 20.40
so that c. need not be made when I 1Co 16.02

CONTRITE
a broken and c. heart, O God, thou Ps 51.17
him who is of a c. and humble Is 57.15
and to revive the heart of the c. 57.15
he that is humble and c. in spirit, 66.02

CONTRIVED
that you have c. this deed in your Ac 5.04

CONTROL
could not c. himself before all Gen 45.01
but having his desire under c., 1Co 7.37
the younger men to c. themselves. Tit 2.06
he left nothing outside his c. Heb 2.08

CONTROLLING
and c. himself he said, "Let food be Gen 43.31

CONTROLS
For the love of Christ c. us, 2Co 5.14

CONTROVERSIES
all customs and c. of the Jews; Ac 26.03
to do with stupid, senseless c.; 2Ti 2.23
But avoid stupid c., genealogies, Tit 3.09

CONTROVERSY
In a c. they shall act as judges, Eze 44.24
the LORD has a c. with the inhabitants Hos 4.01
the c. of the LORD, and you enduring Mic 6.02
the LORD has a c. with his people, 6.02
craving for c. and for disputes 1Ti 6.04

CONVERSATION
for the c. had not been overheard. Jer 38.27
"What is this c. which you are Lk 24.17

CONVERSE
We used to hold sweet c. together; Ps 55.14

CONVERSED
he c. with them a long while, until Ac 20.11
sent for him often and c. with him. 24.26

CONVERSION
reporting the c. of the Gentiles, Ac 15.03

CONVERT
was the first c. in Asia for Rom 16.05
He must not be a recent c., or he 1Ti 3.06

CONVERTS
Jews and devout c. to Judaism Ac 13.43
were the first c. in Achaia, 1Co 16.15

CONVEY
and also to c. the silver and gold Ez 7.15

CONVEYED
king's command c. by the eunuchs. Est 1.12
King Ahasuerus c. by the eunuchs?" 1.15

CONVICT
and to c. all the ungodly of all Jud 1.15

CONVICTED
he is c. by all, he is called to 1Co 14.24
and are c. by the law as transgressors. Jas 2.09

CONVICTION
the Holy Spirit and with full c. 1Th 1.05
hoped for, the c. of things not seen. Heb 11.01

CONVICTS
this decision the king c. himself, 2Sa 14.13
Which of you c. me of sin? If I tell Jn 8.46

CONVINCE
he will c. the world of sin and of Jn 16.08
and trying to c. them about Jesus Ac 28.23
c., rebuke, and exhort, be unfailing 2Ti 4.02
And c. some, who doubt; Jud 1.22

CONVINCED
will they be c. if some one should Lk 16.31
for they are c. that John was a 20.06
"I myself was c. that I ought to do Ac 26.09
And some were c. by what he said, 28.24
fully c. that God was able to do Rom 4.21
one be fully c. in his own mind. 14.05
because we are c. that one has 2Co 5.14
C. of this, I know that I shall Php 1.25

CONVINCINGLY
to show more c. to the heirs of Heb 6.17

CONVOCATION
sabbath of solemn rest, a holy c.; Lev 23.03
first day you shall have a holy c.; 23.07
on the seventh day is a holy c.; 23.08
you shall hold a holy c.; you shall 23.21
with blast of trumpets, a holy c. 23.24
shall be for you a time of holy c., 23.27
On the first day shall be a holy c.; 23.35
hold a holy c. and present an offering 23.36
shall proclaim as times of holy c., 23.37
first day there shall be a holy c.: Num 28.18
day you shall have a holy c.; 28.25
of weeks, you shall have a holy c.; 28.26
month you shall have a holy c.; 29.01
month you shall have a holy c., 29.07
month you shall have a holy c.; 29.12

CONVOCATIONS
you shall proclaim as holy c., Lev 23.02
the holy c., which you shall 23.04

CONVULSED
horribly afraid, their faces are c. Eze 27.35
saw him, immediately it c. the boy, Mk 9.20
the demon tore him and c. him. Lk 9.39

CONVULSES
it c. him till he foams, and shatters Lk 9.39

CONVULSING
c. him and crying with a loud voice, Mk 1.26
crying out and c. him terribly, 9.26

COOK
And Samuel said to the c., "Bring 1Sa 9.23
So the c. took up the leg and the 9.24

COOKED
is a cereal offering c. in a pan, Lev 2.07

COOKS
to be perfumers and c. and bakers. 1Sa 8.13

COOL
in the garden in the c. of the day, Gen 3.08
alone in his c. roof chamber. Ju 3.20
in the closet of the c. chamber." 3.24
he who has a c. spirit is a man of Pro 17.27
finger in water and c. my tongue; Lk 16.24

COPIED
men of Hezekiah king of Judah c. Pro 25.01

COPIES
necessary for the c. of the heavenly Heb 9.23

COPING
even from the foundation to the c., 1Ki 7.09

COPPER
out of whose hills you can dig c. Deu 8.09
and c. is smelted from the ore. Job 28.02
and its c. may burn, that its Eze 24.11
nor silver, nor c. in your belts, Mt 10.09
came, and put in two c. coins, Mk 12.42
you have paid the very last c." Lk 12.59
a poor widow put in two c. coins. 21.02

COPPERSMITH
Alexander the c. did me great harm; 2Ti 4.14

COPY
himself in a book a c. of this law, Deu 17.18
the stones a c. of the law of Jos 8.32
'Behold the c. of the altar of the 22.28
and now this is a c. of the letter Ez 4.11
Then, when the c. of King Artaxerxes' 4.23
The c. of the letter which Tattenai 5.06
This is a c. of the letter which 7.11
A c. of the document was to be Est 3.14
Mordecai also gave him a c. of the 4.08
A c. of what was written was to be 8.13
and conditions, and the open c.; Jer 32.11
They serve a c. and shadow of the Heb 8.05
a c. of the true one, but into 9.24

COR
of a bath from each c. (the c., Eze 45.14

CORAL
shall be made of c. or of crystal; Job 28.18
bodies were more ruddy than c., Lam 4.07
work, fine linen, c., and agate. Eze 27.16

CORBAN
have gained from me is C.' (that is, Mk 7.11

CORD
replied, "Your signet and your c., Gen 38.18
signet and the c. and the staff." 38.25
tassel of each corner a c. of blue; Num 15.38
this scarlet c. in the window Jos 2.18
bound the scarlet c. in the window. 2.21
has loosed my c. and humbled me, Job 30.11
or press down his tongue with a c.? 41.01
A threefold c. is not quickly Ecc 4.12
before the silver c. is snapped, 12.06

CORDED
attach the c. chains to the Ex 28.14

CORDS
of pure gold, twisted like c.; Ex 28.14
chains like c., of pure gold; 28.22
put the two c. of gold in the two 28.24
ends of the two c. you shall 28.25
pegs of the court, and their c.; 35.18
chains like c., of pure gold; 39.15
put the two c. of gold in the two 39.17
Two ends of the two c. they had 39.18
of the court, its c., and its pegs; 39.40
tabernacle and the altar, and its c.; Num 3.26
with their bases and pegs and c. 3.37
and their c., and all the equipment 4.26
and c., with all their equipment 4.32
the c. of Sheol entangled me, the 2Sa 22.06
caught up with c. of fine linen Est 1.06
caught in the c. of affliction, Job 36.08
Pleiades, or loose the c. of Orion? 38.31
asunder, and cast their c. from us. Ps 2.03
The c. of death encompassed me, the 18.04
the c. of Shoel entangled me, the 18.05
Though the c. of the wicked ensnare 119.61
he has cut the c. of the wicked. 129.04
and with c. they have spread a net, 140.05
draw iniquity with c. of falsehood, Is 5.18
nor will any of its c. be broken. 33.20
lengthen your c. and strengthen 54.02
destroyed, and all my c. are broken; Jer 10.20
c. will be placed upon you, and you Eze 3.25
I will put c. upon you, so that you 4.08
bound with c. and made secure; 27.24
I led them with c. of compassion, Hos 11.04
And making a whip of c., he drove Jn 2.15

CORIANDER
it was like c. seed, white, and the Ex 16.31
Now the manna was like c. seed, Num 11.07

CORINTH
this he left Athens and went to C. Ac 18.01
While Apollos was at C., Paul passed 19.01
To the church of God which is at C., 1Co 1.02
the church of God which is at C., 2Co 1.01
that I refrained from coming to C. 1.23
Erastus remained at C.; Trophimus 2Ti 4.20

CORINTHIANS
and many of the C. hearing Paul Ac 18.08
Our mouth is open to you, C.; 2Co 6.11

CORMORANT
the owl, the c., the ibis, Lev 11.17
the carrion vulture and the c., Deu 14.17

CORNELIUS
At Caesarea there was a man named C., Ac 10.01
coming in and saying to him, "C." 10.03
the men that were sent by C., having 10.17
"C., a centurion, an upright and 10.22
C. was expecting them and had 10.24
C. met him and fell down at his 10.25
And C. said, "Four days ago, about 10.30
saying, 'C., your prayer has been 10.31

CORNER
tassel of each c. a cord of blue; Num 15.38
on the southeast c. of the house. 1Ki 7.39
the Ephraim Gate too the C. Gate. 2Ki 14.13
at the southeast c. of the house. 2Ch 4.10
the Ephraim Gate to the C. Gate. 25.23
Jerusalem at the C. Gate and at the 26.09
altars in every c. of Jerusalem. 28.24
and to the c. Palal the Neh 3.25
and to the upper chamber of the c. 3.31
chamber of the c. and the Sheep 3.32
and didst allot to them every c.; 9.22
daughters like c. pillars cut for Ps 144.12
passing along the street near her c., Pro 7.08
and at every c. she lies in wait. 7.12
to live in a c. of the housetop 21.09
to live in a c. of the housetop 25.24
tower of Hananel to the C. Gate. Jer 31.38
to the c. of the Horse Gate toward 31.40

CORNER (cont.)
from you for a c. and no stone for Jer 51.26
and in each c. of the court there Eze 46.21
with the c. of a couch and part of Amo 3.12
to the C. Gate, and from the Tower Zec 14.10
has become the head of the c.; Mt 21.42
has become the head of the c.; Mk 12.10
has become the head of the c.'? Lk 20.17
has become the head of the c. Ac 4.11
for this was not done in a c. 26.26
has become the head of the c.," 1Pe 2.07

CORNERS
to the four c. at its four legs. Ex 25.26
two frames for c. of the tabernacle 26.23
they shall form the two c. 26.24
make horns for it on its four c.; 27.02
four bronze rings at its four c. 27.04
two frames for c. of the tabernacle 36.28
two of them thus, for the two c. 36.29
four rings of gold for its four c., 37.03
to the four c. at its four legs. 37.13
He made horns for it on its four c.; 38.02
on the four c. of the bronze 38.05
tassels on the c. of their garments Num 15.38
on the four c. of your cloak with Deu 22.12
and at the four c. were supports 1Ki 7.30
at the four c. of each stand; 7.34
to be on the towers and the c., 2Ch 26.15
struck the four c. of the house, Job 1.19
lightning to the c. of the earth. 37.03
from the four c. of the earth. Is 11.12
and called from its farthest c., 41.09
that cut the c. of their hair; Jer 9.26
all who cut the c. of their hair; 25.23
those who cut the c. of their hair, 49.32
come upon the four c. of the land. Eze 7.02
its c., its base, and its walls were 41.22
and on the four c. of the ledge, 43.20
the four c. of the ledge of the 45.19
led me to the four c. of the court; 46.21
in the four c. of the court were 46.22
drenched like the c. of the altar. Zec 9.15
synagogues and at the street c., Mt 6.05
let down by four c. upon the earth. Ac 10.11
let down from heaven by four c.; 11.05
at the four c. of the earth, holding Rev 7.01
are at the four c. of the earth, 20.08

CORNERSTONE
bases sunk, or who laid its c., Job 38.06
rejected has become the chief c. Ps 118.22
a precious c., of a sure foundation: Is 28.16
Out of them shall come the c., Zec 10.04
Jesus himself being the chief c., Eph 2.20
a c. chosen and precious, and he who 1Pe 2.06

CORNERSTONES
who are the c. of her tribes have Is 19.13

CORPSE
and the c. of Jezebel shall be as 2Ki 9.37
out, and the boy was like a c.; Mk 9.26

CORPSES
the nations, filling them with c.; Ps 110.06
and their c. were as refuse in the Is 5.25
the stench of their c. shall rise; 34.03
heaps of c., dead bodies without Nah 3.03

CORRECT
seek justice, c. oppression; Is 1.17
C. me, O LORD, but in just measure; Jer 10.24

CORRECTING
c. his opponents with gentleness. 2Ti 2.25

CORRECTION
Whether for c., or for his land, or Job 37.13
your children, they took no c.; Jer 2.30
them, but they refused to take c. 5.03
to no voice, she accepts no c. Zep 3.02
will fear me, she will accept c.; 3.07
for c., and for training in righteousness, 2Ti 3.16

CORRECTOR
a c. of the foolish, a teacher of Rom 2.20

CORRECTS
He who c. a scoffer gets himself Pro 9.07

CORRESPOND
Their end will c. to their deeds. 2Co 11.15

CORRESPONDED
goes up. Watch c. to watch. 1Ch 26.16

CORRESPONDING
c. to the hangings of the court. Ex 38.18
in divisions c. to the sons of 1Ch 23.06
c. to their chief men, had duties, 26.12
its length, c. to the breadth of 2Ch 3.08
the man of God, watch c. to watch. Neh 12.24
c. to the length of the gates; Eze 40.18
c. to the enlargement of the offset 41.07
c. in length to one of the tribal 45.07

CORRESPONDS
she c. to the present Jerusalem, for Gal 4.25
Baptism, which c. to this, now saves 1Pe 3.21

CORRUPT
Now the earth was c. in God's sight, Gen 6.11
the earth, and behold, it was c.; 6.12
people still followed c. practices. 2Ch 27.02
less one who is abominable and c., Job 15.16
They are c., they do abominable Ps 14.01
gone astray, they are all alike c.; 14.03
They are c., doing abominable 53.01
all things, and desperately c.; Jer 17.09
you were more c. than they in all Eze 16.47
nor according to your c. doings, 20.44
she was more c. than she in her 23.11
speak lying and c. words before me Dan 2.09
eager to make all their deeds c." Zep 3.07
of life and is c. through deceitful Eph 4.22
men of c. mind and counterfeit 2Ti 3.08
but to the c. and unbelieving Tit 1.15

CORRUPTED
all flesh had c. their way upon Gen 6.12
land of Egypt, have c. themselves; Ex 32.07
you c. your wisdom for the sake of Eze 28.17
They have deeply c. themselves as Hos 9.09
you have c. the covenant of Levi, Mal 2.08
we have c. no one, we have taken 2Co 7.02
very minds and consciences are c. Tit 1.15
harlot who c. the earth with her Rev 19.02

CORRUPTION
to the south of the mount of c., 2Ki 23.13
the c. of Ephraim is revealed, and Hos 7.01
Hades, nor let thy Holy One see c. Ac 2.27
to Hades, nor did his flesh see c. 2.31
the dead, no more to return to c., 13.34
wilt not let thy Holy One see c.' 13.35
laid with his fathers, and saw c.; 13.36
but he whom God raised up saw no c. 13.37
flesh will from the flesh reap c.; Gal 6.08
escape from the c. that is in the 2Pe 1.04
they themselves are slaves of c.; 2.19

CORRUPTLY
beware lest you act c. by making a Deu 4.16
if you act c. by making a graven 4.25

CORRUPTLY (cont.)
brought from Egypt have acted c.; Deu 9.12
my death you will surely act c., 31.29
They have dealth c. with him, 32.05
We have acted very c. against thee, Neh 1.07
of evildoers, sons who deal c.! sI 1.04
and iron, all of them act c. Jer 6.28

CORRUPTS
foolish, and a bribe c. the mind. Ecc 7.07

CORS
twenty thousand c. of wheat as 1Ki 5.11
twenty thousand c. of beaten oil. 5.11
twenty thousand c. of crushed 2Ch 2.10
twenty thousand c. of barley, 2.10
ten thousand c. of wheat and ten 27.05

COS
we came by a straight course to C., Ac 21.01

COSAM
the son of C., the son of Elmadam, Lk 3.28

COST
each one at the c. of his son and Ex 32.29
sinned at the c. of their lives; Num 16.38
for at half the c. of a hired Deu 15.18
At the c. of his first-born shall Jos 6.26
And at the c. of his youngest son 6.26
Lord my God which c. me nothing. 2Sa 24.24
word does not c. Adonijah his life! 1Ki 2.23
foundation at the c. of Abiram his 16.34
gates at the c. of his youngest 16.34
offerings which c. me nothing." 1Ch 21.24
let the c. be paid from the royal Ez 6.04
the c. is to be paid to these men 6.08
know that it will c. him his life. Pro 7.23
astray at the c. of your lives. Jer 42.20
first sit down and count the c., Lk 14.28
God's gospel without c. to you? 2Co 11.07

COSTLY
and to her mother c. oranaments. Gen 24.53
c. stones in order to lay the 1Ki 5.17
All these were made of c. stones, 7.09
The foundation was of c. stones, 7.10
And above were c. stones, hewn 7.11
and for all kinds of c. vessels; 2Ch 32.27
and with c. wares, besides all that Ez 1.06
for the ransom of his life is c., Ps 49.08
gold, and abundance of c. stones; Pro 20.15
with precious stones and c. gifts. Dan 11.38
very c., and she broke the jar and Mk 14.03
Mary took a pound of c. ointment of Jn 12.03
or gold or pearls or c. attire 1Ti 2.09
of ivory, all articles of c. wood, Rev 18.12

COTTON
There were white c. curtain and Est 1.06
and the weavers of white c. Is 19.09

COUCH
you defiled it—you went up to my c.! Gen 49.04
arose from his c. and was walking 2Sa 11.02
to lie on his c. with the servants 11.13
he polluted his father's c., 1Ch 5.01
falling on the c. where Esther was Est 7.08
my c. will ease my complaint,' Job 7.13
if I spread my c. in darkness, 17.13
I drench my c. with my weeping. Ps 6.06
I have decked my c. with coverings, Pro 7.16
While the king was on his c., Sol 1.12
truly lovely. Our c. is green; 1.16
you sat upon a stately c., Eze 23.41
the corner of a c. and part of a Amo 3.12

COUCHED
he c. as a lion, and as a lioness; Gen 49.09
He c., he lay down like a lion, and Num 24.09
She c. in the midst of young lions, Eze 19.02

COUCHES
of the deep that c. beneath, Gen 49.25
and of the deep that c. beneath, Deu 33.13
Gad c. like a lion, he tears the arm, 33.20
and also c. of gold and silver on a Est 1.06
let them sing for joy on their c. Ps 149.05
stretch themselves upon their c., Amo 6.04

COUCHING
not do well, sin is c. at the door; Gen 4.07

COUNCIL
O my soul, come not into their c.; Gen 49.06
commanders of the army were in c.; 2Ki 9.05
of the king's c. who were found in 25.19
Have you listened in the c. of God? Job 15.08
taken his place in the divine c.; Ps 82.01
feared in the c. of the holy ones, 89.07
stood in the c. of the Lord to Jer 23.18
But if they had stood in my c., 23.22
and seven men of the king's c., 52.25
not be in the c. of my people, Eze 13.09
brother shall be liable to the c., Mt 5.22
and the whole c. sought false 26.59
and the whole c. sought testimony Mk 14.55
and the whole c. held a consultation 15.01
a respected member of the c., 15.43
and they led him away to their c., Lk 22.66
He was a member of the c., 23.50
and the Pharisees gathered the c., Jn 11.47
them to go aside out of the c., Ac 4.15
together the c. and all the senate 5.21
them, they set them before the c. 5.27
Pharisee in the c. named Gamaliel, 5.34
Then they left the presence of the c., 5.41
him and brought him before the c., 6.12
who sat in the c. saw that his 6.15
and the whole c. of elders bear me 22.05
priests and all the c. to meet, 22.30
And Paul, looking intently at the c., 23.01
Pharisees, he cried out in the c., 23.06
You therefore, along with the c., 23.15
bring Paul down to the c. tomorrow, 23.20
I brought him down to their c. 23.28
found when I stood before the c., 24.20
when he had conferred with his c., 25.12

COUNCILS
for they will deliver you up to c., Mt 10.17
for they will deliver you up to c.; Mk 13.09

COUNSEL
I will give you c., and God Ex 18.19
by the c. of Balaam, to act treacherously Num 31.16
"For they are a nation void of c., Deu 32.28
consider it, take c., and speak." Ju 19.30
you, give your advice and c. here." 20.07
turn the c. of Ahithophel into 2Sa 15.31
defeat for me the c. of Ahithophel. 15.34
said to Ahithophel, "Give your c.; 16.20
those days the c. which Ahithophel 16.23
so was all the c. of Ahithophel 16.23
"This time the c. which Ahithophel 17.07
But my c. is that all Israel be 17.11
"The c. of Hushai the Archite is 17.14
better than the c. of Ahithophel." 17.14
defeat the good c. of Ahithophel, 17.14
did Ahithophel c. Absalom and the 17.15
saw that his c. was not followed, 17.23
'Let them but ask c. at Abel'; 20.18
therefore come, let me give you c., 1Ki 1.12
Rehoboam took c. with the old men, 12.06
But he forsook the c. which the old 12.08

COUNSEL (cont.)
and took c. with the young men who 1Ki 12.08
forsaking the c. which the old men 12.13
according to the c. of the young 12.14
So the king took c., and made 12.28
he took c. with his servants, saying, 2Ki 6.08
mere words are c. and strength for 18.20
Philistines took c. and sent him 1Ch 12.19
Rehoboam took c. with the old men, 2Ch 10.06
But he forsook the c. which the old 10.08
and took c. with the young men who 10.08
forsaking the c. of the old men, 10.13
according to the c. of the young 10.14
he had taken c. with the people, he 20.21
He even followed their c., and went 22.05
and have not listened to my c." 25.16
of Judah took c. and sent to Joash 25.17
had taken c. to keep the passover 30.02
according to the c. of my lord and Ez 10.03
I took c. with myself, and I brought Neh 5.07
come, and let us take c. together." 6.07
This c. pleased Haman, and he had Est 5.14
he has c. and understanding. Job 12.13
The c. of the wicked is far from me. 21.16
but the c. of the wicked is far 22.18
waited, and kept silence for my c. 29.21
that darkens c. by words without 38.02
this that hides c. without knowledge?' 42.03
walks not in the c. of the wicked, Ps 1.01
and the rulers take c. together, 2.02
I bless the LORD who gives me c.; 16.07
I will c. you with my eye upon you. 32.08
The LORD brings the c. of the 33.10
The c. of the LORD stands for ever, 33.11
Thou dost guide me with thy c., 73.24
they did not wait for his c. 106.13
and spurned the c. of the Most 107.11
ignored all my c. and would have Pro 1.25
would have none of my c., and 1.30
I have c. and sound wisdom, I have 8.14
Without c. plans go wrong, but with 15.22
Plans are established by c.; 20.18
no c., can avail against the LORD. 21.30
Take c. together, but it will come Is 8.10
the spirit of c. and might, the 11.02
"Give c., grant justice; make your 16.03
counselors of Pharaoh give stupid c. 19.11
he is wonderful in c., 28.29
hide deep from the LORD their c., 29.15
to Egypt, without asking for my c., 30.02
performs the c. of his messengers; 44.26
let them take c. together! Who told 45.21
'My c. shall stand, and I will 46.10
the man of my c. from a far country. 46.11
nor c. from the wise, nor the word Jer 18.18
great in c. and mighty in deed; 32.19
And if I give you c., you will 38.15
Has c. perished from the prudent? 49.07
and c. from the elders. Eze 7.26
who give wicked c. in this city; 11.02
let my c. be acceptable to you; Dan 4.27
went out and took c. against him Mt 12.14
went and took c. how to entangle 22.15
and took c. together in order to 26.04
the people took c. against Jesus 27.01
So they took c., and brought with 27.07
with the elders and taken c., 28.12
immediately held c. with the Mk 3.06
first and take c. whether he is Lk 14.31
on they took c. how to put him to Jn 11.53
who had given c. to the Jews that 18.14
had served the c. of God in his Ac 13.36
declaring to you the whole c. of God. 20.27
according to the c. of his will, Eph 1.11
Therefore I c. you to buy from me Rev 3.18

COUNSELED
and thus and so have I c. 2Sa 17.15
so has Ahithophel c. against you." 17.21
How you have c. him who has no Job 26.03
against the LORD, and c. villainy? Nah 1.11

COUNSELOR
David's c., from his city Giloh. 2Sa 15.12
a shrewd c., and his lot came out 1Ch 26.14
was a c., being a man of understanding 27.32
Ahithophel was the king's c., 27.33
mother was his c. in doing wickedly. 2Ch 22.03
him, "Have we made you a royal c.? 25.16
the c. and the skilful magician and Is 3.03
name will be called "Wonderful C., 9.06
or as his c. has instructed him? 40.13
among these there is no c. who, 41.28
Has your c. perished, that pangs Mic 4.09
and he will give you another C., Jn 14.16
But the C., the holy Spirit, whom 14.26
But when the C. comes, whom I shall 15.26
the C. will not come to you; 16.07
the Lord, or who has been his c.?" Rom 11.34

COUNSELORS
of his father they were his c., 2Ch 22.04
and hired c. against them to Ez 4.05
and his seven c. to make inquiries 7.14
king and his c. have freely 7.15
love before the king and his c., 7.28
king and his c. and his lords and 8.25
with kings and c. of the earth who Job 3.14
He leads c. away stripped, and 12.17
are my delight, they are my c. Ps 119.24
an abundance of c. there is safety. Pro 11.14
in abundance of c. there is 24.06
and your c. as at the beginning. Is 1.26
the wise c. of Pharaoh give stupid 19.11
the c., the treasurers, the justices, Dan 3.02
the c., the treasurers, the justices, 3.03
He said to his c., "Did we not 3.24
and the king's c. gathered together 3.27
My c. and my lords sought me, and I 4.36
the c. and the governors are agreed 6.07

COUNSELS
let them fall by their own c.; Ps 5.10
hearts, to follow their own c. 81.12
the c. of the wicked are treacherous. Pro 12.05
You are wearied with your many c.; Is 47.13
in their own c. and the stubbornness Jer 7.24
and you have walked in their c.; Mic 6.16

COUNT
that if one can c. the dust of the Gen 13.16
shall make your c. for the lamb. Ex 12.04
then he shall c. for himself seven Lev 15.13
she shall c. for herself seven days, 15.28
then you shall c. their fruit as 19.23
"And you shall c. from the morrow 23.15
"And you shall c. seven weeks of 25.08
Who can c. the dust of Jacob, or Num 23.10
"Take the c. of the booty that was 31.26
"You shall c. seven weeks; Deu 16.09
begin to c. the seven weeks from 16.09
required to c. them when they were 1Ch 9.28
thy face, and c. me as thy enemy? Job 13.24
my maidservants c. me as a stranger; 19.15
I can c. all my bones—they stare Ps 22.17
Thou hast kept c. of my tossings; 56.08
of the earth thou dost c. as dross; 119.119
If I would c. them, they are more 139.18
hatred; I c. them my enemies. 139.22
he shall c. for himself seven days, Eze 44.26
not first sit down and c. the cost, Lk 14.28
goddess Artemis may c. for nothing, Ac 19.27
confidence as I c. on showing 2Co 10.02
but in humility c. others better Php 2.03
did not c. equality with God a 2.06
Indeed I c. everything as loss 3.08

COUNT (cont.)
and c. them as refuse, in order that Php 3.08
C. it all joy, my brethren, when you Jas 1.02
They c. it pleasure to revel in the 2Pe 2.13
his promise as some c. slowness, 3.09
And c. the forbearance of our Lord 3.15

COUNTED
your descendants also can be c. Gen 13.16
found with me, shall be c. stolen." 30.33
as they were c. at the commandment Ex 38.21
servants have c. the men of war Num 31.49
and their camels could not be c.; Ju 6.05
son Solomon will be c. offenders." 1Ki 1.21
be numbered or c. for multitude. 3.08
they could not be c. or numbered. 8.05
up and they c. and tied up in bags 2Ki 12.10
they could not be c. or numbered. 2Ch 5.06
who c. them out to Sheshbazzar the Ez 1.08
The whole was c. and weighed, and 8.34
Mattaniah, for they were c. faithful; Neh 13.13
Why are we c. as cattle? Why are Job 18.03
in spite of my right I am c. a liar; 34.06
Clubs are c. as stubble; he laughs 41.29
let his prayer be c. as sin! Ps 109.07
Let my prayer be c. as incense 141.02
the morning, will be c. as cursing. Pro 27.14
and you c. the houses of Jerusalem, Is 22.10
on the terror: "Where is he who c., 33.18
Where is he who c. the towers?" 33.18
that they were c. worthy to suffer Ac 5.41
and they c. the value of them and 19.19
but sin is not c. where there is Rom 5.13
I c. as loss for the sake of Christ Php 3.07
Yet Jesus has been c. worthy of as Heb 3.03

COUNTENANCE
was very angry, and his c. fell. Gen 4.05
angry, and why has your c. fallen? 4.06
The LORD lift up his c. upon you, Num 6.26
a nation of stern c., who shall Deu 28.50
his c. was like the c. of the angel Ju 13.06
and her c. was no longer sad. 1Sa 1.18
complaint, I will put off my sad c., Job 9.27
thou changest his c., and sendest 14.20
the light of my c. they did not 29.24
up the light of thy c. upon us, Ps 4.06
pride of his c. the wicked does 10.04
thy arm, and the light of thy c.; 44.03
perish at the rebuke of thy c.! 80.16
O LORD, in the light of thy c., 89.15
secret sins in the light of thy c. 90.08
A glad heart makes a cheerful c., Pro 15.13
by sadness of c. the heart is made Ecc 7.03
the hardness of his c. is changed. 8.01
full measure, a king of bold c., Dan 8.23
At that saying his c. fell, and he Mk 10.22
appearance of his c. was altered, Lk 9.29

COUNTERFEIT
men of corrupt mind and c. faith; 2Ti 3.08

COUNTING
c. fifty days to the morrow after Lev 23.16
not c. their trespasses against 2Co 5.19

COUNTLESS
And all for the c. harlotries of Nah 3.04
For though you have c. guides in 1Co 4.15
with c. beatings, and often near 2Co 11.23

COUNTRIES
the gods of the c. have delivered 2Ki 18.35
delivered their c. out of my hand, 18.35
upon all the kingdoms of the c. 1Ch 29.30
service of the kingdoms of the c." 2Ch 12.08
kingdoms of the c. when they heard 20.29
give ear, all you far c.; gird Is 8.09
gods of these c. have delivered 36.20
delivered their c. out of my hand, 36.20
out of all the c. where he had Jer 16.15
out of all the c. where I have 23.03
out of all the c. where he had 23.08
against many c. and great kingdoms. 28.08
from all the c. to which I drove 32.37
nations, with c. round about her. Eze 5.05
more than the c. round about her, 5.06
you are scattered through the c., 6.08
I scattered them among the c., 11.16
a while in the c. where they have 11.16
you out of the c. where you have 11.17
and scatter them through the c. 12.15
and disperse them through the c., 20.23
nations, like the tribes of the c., 20.32
you out of the c. where you are 20.34
you out of the c. where you have 20.41
and a mocking to all the c. 22.04
and disperse you through the c., 22.15
will make you perish out of the c.; 25.07
in the midst of desolated c.; 29.12
and disperse them among the c. 29.12
of desolated c. and her cities 30.07
disperse them throughout the c. 30.26
into the c. which you have not 32.09
and gather them from the c., 34.13
and these two c. shall be mine, 35.10
they were dispersed through the c.; 36.19
and gather you from all the c., 36.24
shall come into c. and shall overflow Dan 11.40
out his hand against the c., and the 11.42
yet in far c. they shall remember Zec 10.09

COUNTRY
Sephar to the hill c. of the east. Gen 10.30
"Go from your c. and your kindred 12.01
subdued all the c. of the Amalekites, 14.07
but will go to my c. and to my 24.04
son Isaac, eastward to the east c. 25.06
Laban said, "It is not so done in our c., 29.26
I may go to my own home and c. 30.25
face toward the hill c. of Gilead. 31.21
him into the hill c. of Gilead. 31.23
pitched his tent in the hill c., 31.25
encamped in the hill c. of Gilead. 31.25
the land of Seir, the c. of Edom, 32.03
'Return to your c. and to your 32.09
So Esau dwelt in the hill c. of Seir; 36.08
Edomites in the hill c. of Seir. 36.09
defeated Midian in the c. of Moab, 36.35
will plague all your c. with frogs; Ex 8.02
I will bring locusts into your c., 10.04
settled on the whole c. of Egypt, 10.14
was left in all the c. of Egypt. 10.19
and he went his way to his own c. 18.27
And in all the c. you possess, you Lev 25.24
reckoned with the fields of the c.; 25.31
yonder, and go up into the hill c., Num 13.17
the Amorites dwell in the hill c.; 13.29
up to the heights of the hill c., 14.40
up to the heights of the hill c., 14.44
dwelt in that hill c. came down, 14.45
of the land throughout the c. 32.33
go to the hill c. of the Amorites, Deu 1.07
in the hill c. and in the lowland, 1.07
way to the hill c. of the Amorites, 1.19
to the hill c. of the Amorites, 1.20
and went up into the hill c., and came 1.24
it easy to go up into the hill c. 1.41
presumptuous and went up into the hill c. 1.43
in that hill c. came out against 1.44
about this mountain c. long enough; 2.03
and the cities of the hill c., and 2.57
half the hill c. of Gilead with 3.12
that goodly hill c., and Lebanon.' 3.25
found slain, lying in the open c., 21.01

COUNTRY (cont.)

"But if in the open c. a man meets Deu 22.25
because he came upon her in the open c., 22.27
in the hill c. and in the lowland Jos 9.01
Israel, "We have come from a far c.; 9.06
"From a very far c. your servants 9.09
inhabitants of our c. said to us, 9.11
dwell in the hill c. are gathered 10.06
the hill c. and the Negeb and the 10.40
and all the c. of Goshen, as far as 10.41
who were in the northern hill c., 11.02
and the Jebusites in the hill c., 11.03
the hill c. and all the Negeb and 11.16
and the hill c. of Israel and its 11.16
out the Anakim from the hill c., 11.21
and from all the hill c. of Judah, 11.21
and from all the hill c. of Israel; 11.21
in the hill c., in the lowland, in 12.08
of the hill c. from Lebanon to 13.06
me this hill c. of which the LORD 14.12
And in the hill c., Shamir, 15.48
Jericho into the hill c. to Bethel; 16.01
since the hill c. of Ephraim is 17.15
"The hill c. is not enough for us; 17.16
but the hill c. shall be yours, for 17.18
up through the hill c. westward; 18.12
Timnathserah in the hill c. of Ephraim; 19.50
Galilee in the hill c. of Naphtali, 20.07
Shechem in the hill c. of Ephraim, 20.07
Hebron) in the hill c. of Judah. 20.07
in the hill c. of Judah, along with 21.11
lands in the hill c. of Ephraim, 21.21
Esau the hill c. of Seir to possess 24.04
which is in the hill c. of Ephraim, 24.30
given him in the hill c. of Ephraim. 24.33
Canaanites who dwelt in the hill c., Ju 1.09
he took possession of the hill c., 1.19
the Danites back into the hill c., 1.34
in the hill c. of Ephraim, north of 2.09
trumpet in the hill c. of Ephraim; 3.27
down with him from the hill c., 3.27
Bethel in the hill c. of Ephraim; 4.05
throughout all the hill c. of Ephraim, 7.24
Shamir in the hill c. of Ephraim. 10.01
pray, through your land to our c.' 11.19
Amorites, who inhabited that c. 11.21
in the hill c. of the Amalekites. 12.15
our hand, the ravager of our c., 16.24
a man of the hill c. of Ephraim, 17.01
to the hill c. of Ephraim to the 17.08
came to the hill c. of Ephraim, 18.02
there to the hill c. of Ephraim, 18.13
gone to spy out the c. of Laish, 18.14
parts of the hill c. of Ephraim, 19.01
was from the hill c. of Ephraim, 19.16
parts of the hill c. of Ephraim, 19.18
throughout all the c. of the 20.06
to Gibeah, and in the open c., 20.31
went to sojourn in the c. of Moab, Ru 1.01
went into the c. of Moab and remained 1.02
to return from the c. of Moab, 1.06
heard in the c. of Moab that the 1.06
who returned from the c. of Moab. 1.22
with Naomi from the c. of Moab. 2.06
has come back from the c. of Moab, 4.03
Ramathaimzophim of the hill c. of Ephraim, 1Sa 1.01
LORD was in the c. of the Philistines 6.01
the hill c. of Ephraim and passed 9.04
Michmash and the hill c. of Bethel, 13.02
in the hill c. of Ephraim heard 14.22
in the hill c. of the Wilderness of 23.14
be given me in one of the c. towns, 27.05
dwelt in the c. of the Philistines 27.07
he dwelt in the c. of the Philistines 27.11
They found an Egyptian in the open c., 30.11
were by themselves in the open c. 2Sa 10.08
And all the c. wept aloud as all 15.23
spread over the face of all the c.; 18.08
a man of the hill c. of Ephraim, 20.21
Benhur, in the hill c. of Ephraim; 1Ki 4.08
the c. of Sihon king of the Amorites 4.19
hewers of stone in the hill c., 5.15
from a far c. for thy name's sake 8.41
depart, that I may go to my own c." 11.21
now seeking to go to your own c.?" 11.22
of them were alone in the open c. 11.29
Shechem in the hill c. of Ephraim, 12.25
in the open c. the birds of the 14.11
but the Syrians filled the c. 20.27
in the open c. the birds of the 21.24
his city, and every man to his c.!" 22.36
till the c. was filled with water. 2Ki 3.20
from the hill c. of Ephraim two 5.22
to hide themselves in the open c., 7.12
come from a far c., from Babylon." 20.14
in the open c. and their men heard 25.23
defeated Midian in the c. of Moab, 1Ch 1.46
lands in the hill c. of Ephraim, 6.67
had sons in the c. of Moab after 8.08
were by themselves in the open c. 19.09
and ravaged the c. of the Ammonites, 20.01
and over the treasuries in the c., 27.25
thousand to quarry in the hill c., 2Ch 2.02
thousand to quarry in the hill c., 2.18
from a far c. for the sake of thy 6.32
which is in the hill c. of Ephraim, 13.04
taken in the hill c. of Ephraim, 15.08
Beersheba to the hill c. of Ephraim, 19.04
places in the hill c. of Judah, 21.11
cities in the hill c. of Judah, 27.04
through the c. of Ephraim and 30.10
peoples of the c. declared themselves Est 8.17
and gnats throughout their c. Ps 105.31
shattered the trees of their c. 105.33
so is good news from a far c. Pro 25.25
Your c. lies desolate, your cities Is 1.07
to me from a far c., from Babylon." 39.03
man of my counsel from a far c. 46.11
people is coming from the north c., Jer 6.22
of the north c. to make the cities 10.22
of the north c. and out of all the 16.15
on the mountains in the open c. 17.03
from the hill c., and from the 17.26
who bore you into another c., 22.26
of the north c. and out of all the 23.08
call in the hill c. of Ephraim: 31.06
will bring them from the north c., 31.08
shall come back to their own c. 31.17
in the cities of the hill c., 32.44
in the cities of the hill c., 33.13
in the open c. and their men heard 40.07
in the open c. came to Gedaliah at 40.13
in the north c. by the river 46.10
great nations, from the north c.; 50.09
and let us go each to his own c.; 51.09
the c. which I swore to give to Eze 20.42
its frontier, the glory of the c., 25.09
all the inhabited places of the c. 34.13
for dwellings and for open c. 48.15
as his c. improved he improved his Hos 10.01
What is your c.? And of what Jon 1.08
I said when I was yet in my c.? 4.02
make Samaria a heap in the open c., Mic 1.06
the city and dwell in the open c.; 4.10
horses goes toward the north c., Zec 6.06
white ones go toward the west c., 6.06
dappled ones go toward the south c." 6.06
the north c. have set my Spirit at 6.08
my Spirit at rest in the north c." 6.08
from the east c. and from the west c.; 8.07
waste his hill c. and left his Mal 1.03
till they are called the wicked c., 1.04
to their own c. by another way. Mt 2.12
to the c. of the Gadarenes, two 8.28

COUNTRY (cont.)
to his own c. he taught them in Mt 13.54
in his own c. and in his own house 13.57
tenants, and went into another c. 21.33
out to him all the c. of Judea, Mk 1.05
a town, but was out in the c.; 1.45
of the sea, to the c. of the Gerasenes. 5.01
not to send them out of the c. 5.10
told it in the city and in the c. 5.14
from there and came to his own c.; 6.01
honor, except in his own c., and 6.04
to go into the c. and villages 6.36
or c., they laid the sick in the 6.56
tenants, and went into another c. 12.01
who was coming in from the c., 15.21
went with haste into the hill c., Lk 1.39
through all the hill c. of Judea; 1.65
out through all the surrounding c. 4.14
Capernaum, do here also in your own c.'" 4.23
prophet is acceptable in his own c. 4.24
Judea and all the surrounding c. 7.17
arrived at the c. of the Gerasenes, 8.26
told it in the city and in the c. 8.34
the surrounding c. of the Gerasenes 8.37
the villages and c. round about, 9.12
and took his journey into a far c., 15.13
a great famine arose in that c., 15.14
to one of the citizens of that c., 15.15
went into a far c. to receive 19.12
into another c. for a long while. 20.09
who are out in the c. enter it; 21.21
who was coming in from the c., 23.26
prophet has no honor in his own c. Jn 4.44
there to the c. near the wilderness, 11.54
up from the c. to Jerusalem before 11.55
did both in the c. of the Jews and Ac 10.39
because their c. depended on the 12.20
depended on the king's c. for food. 12.20
Lycaonia, and to the surrounding c.; 14.06
the upper c. and came to Ephesus. 19.01
and throughout all the c. of Judea, 26.20
But as it is, they desire a better c., Heb 11.16

COUNTRYMEN
you have put a riddle to my c., Ju 14.16
Then she told the riddle to her c. 14.17
from your own c. as they did from 1Th 2.14

COUNTRYSIDE
cry of your pilots the c. shakes, Eze 27.28

COUNTS
and c. me as his adversary. Job 19.11
against me, he c. me as his enemy; 33.10
He c. iron as straw, and bronze as 41.27
he c. himself happy, and though a Ps 49.18
the hands of the one who c. them, Jer 33.13
circumcision c. for anything nor 1Co 7.19
circumcision c. for anything, Gal 6.15

COUPLE
and c. the curtains one to the Ex 26.06
And you shall c. five curtains by 26.09
and c. the tent together that it 26.11
of bronze to c. the tent together 36.18
him his servant and a c. of asses. Ju 19.03
had with him a c. of saddled asses, 19.10
come and make a c. of cakes in my 2Sa 13.06
with a c. of asses saddled, bearing 16.01
now, I am gathering a c. of sticks, 1Ki 17.12

COUPLED
curtains shall be c. to one another; Ex 26.03
the other five curtains shall be c. to 26.03
And he c. five curtains to one 36.10
five curtains he c. to one another. 36.10
and c. the curtains one to the 36.13
He c. five curtains by themselves, 36.16

COURAGE
Be of good c., and bring some of Num 13.20
Be strong and of good c., do not Deu 31.06
Israel, "Be strong and of good c.; 31.07
and said, "Be strong and of good c.; 31.23
Be strong and of good c.; for you Jos 1.06
Be strong and of good c.; be not 1.09
Only be strong and of good c." 1.18
there was no c. left in any man, 2.11
be strong and of good c.; for thus 10.25
took c., and again formed the Ju 20.22
Take c., and acquit yourselves like 1Sa 4.09
his c. failed, and all Israel was 2Sa 4.01
has found c. to pray this prayer 7.27
Be of good c., and let us play the 10.12
has found c. to pray before thee. 1Ch 17.25
Be of good c., and let us play the 19.13
Be strong, and of good c. Fear not 22.13
strong and of good c., and do it. 28.20
But you, take c.! Do not let 2Ch 15.07
he took c., and put away the 15.08
the seventh year Jehoiada took c., 23.01
But Amaziah took c., and led out 25.11
"Be strong and of good c. Do not 32.07
I took c., for the hand of the LORD Ez 7.28
strong, and let your heart take c.; Ps 27.14
Be strong, and let your heart take c., 31.24
their c. melted away in their evil 107.26
and says to his brother, "Take c.!" Is 41.06
c. shall fail both king and princes; Jer 4.09
far from me, one to revive my c.; Lam 1.16
Can your c. endure, or can your Eze 22.14
be strong and of good c." And when Dan 10.19
power and his c. against the king 11.25
Yet now take c., O Zerubbabel, says Hag 2.04
take c., O Joshua, son of Jehozadak, 2.04
take c., all you people of the land, 2.04
took c. and went to Pilate, and Mk 15.43
"Take c., for as you have testified Ac 23.11
them Paul thanked God and took c. 28.15
So we are always of good c.; we know 2Co 5.06
We are of good c., and we would 5.08
that with full c. now as always Php 1.20
we had c. in our God to declare to 1Th 2.02
nor lose c. when you are punished Heb 12.05

COURAGEOUS
Only be strong and very c., Jos 1.07
you? Be c. and be valiant." 2Sa 13.28
His heart was c. in the ways of the 2Ch 17.06
in your faith, be c., be strong. 1Co 16.13

COURAGEOUSLY
Deal c., and may the LORD be with 2Ch 19.11

COURIERS
So c. went throughout all Israel 2Ch 30.06
So the c. went from city to city 30.10
Letters were sent by c. to all the Est 3.13
The c. went in haste by order of 3.15
sent by mounted c. riding on swift 8.10
So the c., mounted on their swift 8.14

COURSE
In the c. of time Cain brought to Gen 4.03
In c. of time the wife of Judah, 38.12
In the c. of those many days the Ex 2.23
to change the c. of affairs your 2Sa 14.20
stone and one c. of cedar beams. 1Ki 6.36
about, and a c. of cedar beams; 7.12
In c. of time, at the end of two 2Ch 21.19
great stones and one c. of timber; Ez 6.04
days of the feast had run their c., Job 1.05
The caravans turn aside from their c.; 6.18
a strong man runs its c. with joy. Ps 19.05
and confuse the c. of your paths. Is 3.12
you direct your c. to seek lovers! Jer 2.33
Every one turns to his own c., 8.06

COURSE (cont.)
Their c. is evil, and their might is Jer 23.10
and the third day I finish my c. Lk 13.32
And as John was finishing his c., Ac 13.25
accomplish my c. and the ministry 20.24
we came by a straight c. to Cos, 21.01
following the c. of this world, Eph 2.02

COURSES
from their c. they fought against Ju 5.20
with three c. of hewn stone and 1Ki 6.36
court had three c. of hewn stone 7.12
with three c. of great stones and Ez 6.04
and the Levites in then c., 6.18

COURT
"You shall make the c. of the Ex 27.09
south side the c. shall have 27.09
breadth of the c. on the west side 27.12
The breadth of the c. on the front 27.13
For the gate of the c. there shall 27.16
around the c. shall be filleted 27.17
The length of the c. shall be a 27.18
pegs and all the pegs of the c., 27.19
the hangings of the c., its pillars 35.17
the screen for the gate of the c.; 35.17
tabernacle and the pegs of the c., 35.18
And he made the c.; for the 38.09
hangings of the c. were of fine 38.09
the gate of the c. were hangings 38.15
round about the c. were of fine 38.16
pillars of the c. were filleted 38.17
the gate of the c. was embroidered 38.18
corresponding to the hangings of the c. 38.18
and for the c. round about were of 38.20
the bases round about the c., and the 38.31
the bases of the gate of the c., 38.31
and all the pegs round about the c. 38.31
the hangings of the c., its pillars, 39.40
the screen for the gate of the c., 39.40
shall set up the c. round about, 40.08
the screen for the gate of the c. 40.08
And he erected the c. round the 40.33
the screen of the gate of the c. 40.33
in the c. of the tent of meeting Lev 6.16
in the c. of the tent of meeting. 6.26
the hangings of the c., the screen Num 3.26
the door of the c. which is around 3.26
Also the pillars of the c. round about, 3.37
and the hangings of the c., 4.26
the gate of the c. which is around 4.26
pillars of the c. round about with 4.32
between men, and they come into c., Deu 25.01
He built the inner c. with three 1Ki 6.36
in the other c. back of the hall, 7.08
and from the c. of the house of the 7.09
house of the LORD to the great c. 7.09
The great c. had three courses of 7.12
had the inner c. of the house of 7.12
middle of the c. that was before 8.64
had gone out of the middle c., 2Ki 20.04
He made the c. of the priests, and 2Ch 4.09
and the great c., and doors for the 4.09
and doors for the c., and overlaid 4.09
high, and had set it in the c.; 6.13
middle of the c. that was before 7.07
of the LORD, before the new c., 20.05
stones in the c. of the house of 24.21
LORD into the c. of the house of 29.16
of the king at the c. of the guard. Neh 3.25
in the c. of the garden of the Est 1.05
in front of the c. of the harem, 2.11
the inner c. without being called, 4.11
in the inner c. of the king's 5.01
Queen Esther standing in the c., 5.02
And the king said, "Who is in the c.?" 6.04
the outer c. of the king's palace 6.04
"Haman is there, standing in the c." 6.05
do not hastily bring into c.; Pro 25.08
he stood in the c. of the LORD's Jer 19.14
Stand in the c. of the LORD's house, 26.02
shut up in the c. of the guard 32.02
came to me in the c. of the guard, 32.08
sitting in the c. of the guard. 32.12
shut up in the c. of the guard: 33.01
secretary, which was in the upper c., 36.10
So they went into the c. to the king, 36.20
Jeremiah to the c. of the guard; 37.21
remained in the c. of the guard. 37.21
which was in the c. of the guard, 38.06
remained in the c. of the guard. 38.13
remained in the c. of the guard 38.28
Jeremiah from the c. of the guard. 39.14
shut up in the c. of the guard: 39.15
of the inner c. that faces north, Eze 8.03
brought me to the door of the c.; 8.07
into the inner c. of the house of 8.16
and a cloud filled the inner c. 10.03
and the c. was full of the brightness 10.04
was heard as far as the outer c., 10.05
vestibule of the gateway was the c. 40.14
Then he brought me into the outer c.; 40.17
and a pavement, round about the c.; 40.17
to the outer front of the inner c., 40.19
north, belonging to the outer c. 40.20
east, was a gate to the inner c.; 40.23
gate on the south of the inner c.; 40.27
me to the inner c. by the south 40.28
Its vestibule faced the outer c., 40.31
me to the inner c. on the east 40.32
Its vestibule faced the outer c., 40.34
Its vestibule faced the outer c., 40.37
me from without into the inner c., 40.44
were two chambers in the inner c., 40.44
And he measured the c., a hundred 40.47
chambers of the c. was a breadth of 41.10
Then he led me out into the inner c., 42.01
which belonged to the inner c., 42.03
which belonged to the outer c., 42.03
like the pillars of the outer c.; 42.06
the chambers, toward the outer c., 42.07
on the outer c. were fifty cubits 42.08
one enters them from the outer c., 42.09
into the outer c. without laying 42.14
and brought me into the inner c.; 43.05
enter the gates of the inner c., 44.17
gates of the inner c., and within. 44.17
into the outer c. to the people, 44.19
wine, when he enters the inner c. 44.21
the holy place, into the inner c., 44.27
posts of the gate of the inner c. 45.19
of the inner c. that faces east 46.01
into the outer c. and so communicate 46.20
brought me forth to the outer c., 46.21
me to the four corners of the c.; 46.21
corner of the c. there was a c.— 46.21
corners of the c. were small 46.22
Daniel remained at the king's c. Dan 2.49
the c. sat in judgment, and the 7.10
But the c. shall sit in judgment, 7.26
while you are going with him to c., Mt 5.25
he entered the c. of the high Jn 18.15
a member of the c. of Herod the Ac 13.01
judged by you or by any human c. 1Co 4.03
it not they who drag you into c.? Jas 2.06
not measure the c. outside the Rev 11.02

COURTESY
to show perfect c. toward all men. Tit 3.02

COURTIERS
banquet for his c. and officers Mk 6.21

COURTS
in the two c. of the house of the 2Ki 21.05
made in the two c. of the house of 23.12

COURTS (cont.)

the care of the c. and the chambers, 1Ch 23.28
who shall build my house and my c., 28.06
in mind for the c. of the house of 28.12
shall be in the c. of the house of 2Ch 23.05
in the two c. of the house of the 33.05
and in their c. and in the c. of the Neh 8.16
chamber in the c. of the house of 13.07
and bring near, to dwell in thy c.! Ps 65.04
yea, faints for the c. of the LORD; 84.02
For a day in thy c. is better than 84.10
they flourish in the c. of our God. 92.13
an offering, and come into his c.! 96.08
thanksgiving, and his c. with praise! 100.04
in the c. of the house of the LORD, 116.19
in the c. of the house of our God! 135.02
of you this trampling of my c.? Is 1.12
drink it in the c. of my sanctuary." 62.09
and fill the c. with the slain. Eze 9.07
corners of the court were small c., 46.22
of the four c. was a row of 46.23
my house and have charge of my c., Zec 3.07
live in luxury are in king's c. Lk 7.25
the c. are open, and there are Ac 19.38

COURTYARD

Bahurim, who had a well in his c.; 2Sa 17.18
as far as the c. of the high priest, Mt 26.58
was sitting outside in the c. 26.69
right into the c. of the high Mk 14.54
And as Peter was below in the c., 14.66
middle of the c. and sat down Lk 22.55

COURTYARDS

the houses and c. and out of the Ex 8.13

COUSIN

or his c. may redeem him, or a near Lev 25.49
Then Hanamel my c. came to me in Jer 32.08
at Anathoth from Hanamel my c., 32.09
in the presence of Hanamel my c., 32.12
and Mark the c. of Barnabas (concerning Col 4.10

COVENANT

But I will establish my c. with you; Gen 6.18
"Behold, I establish my c. with you 9.09
I establish my c. with you, that 9.11
the sign of the c. which I make 9.12
a sign of the c. between me and 9.13
remember my c. which is between me 9.15
the everlasting c. between God and 9.16
the sign of the c. which I have 9.17
day the LORD made a c. with Abram, 15.18
And I will make my c. between me 17.02
"Behold, my c. is with you, and you 17.04
establish my c. between me and you 17.07
generations for an everlasting c., 17.07
"As for you, you shall keep my c., 17.09
This is my c., which you shall keep, 17.10
a sign of the c. between me and 17.11
my c. be in your flesh an everlasting c. 17.13
his people; he has broken my c." 17.14
establish my c. with him as an everlasting c. 17.19
But I will establish my c. with Isaac, 17.21
Abimelech, and the two men made a c. 21.27
So they made a c. at Beersheba. 21.32
us, and let us make a c. with you, 26.28
Come now, let us make a c., you and I; 31.44
God remembered his c. with Abraham, Ex 2.24
I also established my c. with them, 6.04
in bondage and I have remembered my c. 6.05
will obey my voice and keep my c., 19.05
You shall make no c. with them or 23.32
Then he took the book of the c., 24.07
blood of the c. which the LORD has 24.08
generations, as a perpetual c. 31.16
And he said, "Behold, I make a c. 34.10
lest you make a c. with the inhabitants 34.12
lest you make a c. with the inhabitants 34.15
I have made a c. with you and with 34.27
the tables the words of the c., 34.28
the salt of the c. with your God Lev 2.13
people of Israel as a c. for ever. 24.08
and will confirm my c. with you. 26.09
my commandments, but break my c., 26.15
shall execute vengeance for the c.; 26.25
then I will remember my c. with Jacob, 26.42
remember my c. with Isaac and my 26.42
with Isaac and my c. with Abraham, 26.42
utterly and break my c. with them; 26.44
remember the c. with their forefathers, 26.45
the ark of the c. of the LORD went Num 10.33
the ark of the c. of the LORD, 14.44
it is a c. of salt for ever before 18.19
I give to him my c. of peace; 25.12
the c. of a perpetual priesthood, 25.13
And he declared to you his c., Deu 4.13
you forget the c. of the LORD your 4.23
or forget the c. with your fathers 4.31
our God made a c. with us in Horeb. 5.02
fathers did the LORD make this c., 5.03
you shall make no c. with them, 7.02
God who keeps c. and steadfast 7.09
with you the c. and the steadfast 7.12
may confirm his c. which he swore 8.18
tables of the c. which the LORD 9.09
of stone, the tables of the c. 9.11
tables of the c. were in my two 9.15
the ark of the c. of the LORD, 10.08
your God, in transgressing his c., 17.02
words of the c. which the LORD 29.01
besides the c. which he had made 29.01
careful to do the words of this c., 29.09
into the sworn c. of the LORD your 29.12
only that I make this sworn c., 29.14
hears the words of this sworn c., 29.19
curses of the c. written in this 29.21
they forsook the c. of the LORD, 29.25
the ark of the c. of the LORD, 31.09
me and break my c. which I have 31.16
and despise me and break my c. 31.20
the ark of the c. of the LORD, 31.25
the ark of the c. of the LORD your 31.26
observed thy word, and kept thy c. 33.09
the ark of the c. of the LORD your Jos 3.03
priests, "Take up the ark of the c., 3.06
And they took up the ark of the c., 3.06
priests who bear the ark of the c., 3.08
Behold, the ark of the c. of the 3.11
the ark of the c. before the 3.14
the ark of the c. of the LORD 3.17
the ark of the c. of the LORD 4.07
the ark of the c. had stood; 4.09
the ark of the c. of the LORD came 4.18
to them, "Take up the ark of the c., 6.06
the ark of the c. of the LORD 6.08
transgressed my c. which I commanded 7.11
transgressed the c. of the LORD, 7.15
the ark of the c. of the LORD, 8.33
so now make a c. with us." 9.06
then how can we make a c. with you?" 9.07
come now, make a c. with us."' 9.11
and made a c. with them, to let them 9.15
after they had made a c. with them, 9.16
transgress the c. of the LORD your 23.16
So Joshua made a c. with the people 24.25
I will never break my c. with you, Ju 2.01
shall make no c. with the inhabitants 2.02
transgressed my c. which I commanded 2.20
the ark of the c. of God was there 20.27
the ark of the c. of the LORD here 1Sa 4.03
the ark of the c. of the LORD of 4.04
with the ark of the c. of God. 4.04
When the ark of the c. of the LORD 4.05
Then Jonathan made a c. with David, 18.03

COVENANT (cont.)
servant into a sacred c. with you. 1Sa 20.08
of them made a c. before the LORD; 23.18
Make your c. with me, and behold, my 2Sa 3.12
I will make a c. with you; but one 3.13
that they may make a c. with you, 3.21
David made a c. with them at Hebron 5.03
bearing the ark of the c. of God; 15.24
has made with me an everlasting c., 23.05
the ark of the c. of the LORD, 1Ki 3.15
the ark of the c. of the LORD. 6.19
the ark of the c. of the LORD out 8.01
the ark of the c. of the LORD to 8.06
the LORD made a c. with the people 8.09
in which is the c. of the LORD 8.21
keeping c. and showing steadfast 8.23
not kept my c. and my statutes 11.11
of Israel have forsaken thy c., 19.10
of Israel have forsaken thy c., 19.14
So he made a c. with him and let 20.34
and he made a c. with them and put 2Ki 11.04
And Jehoiada made a c. between the 11.17
because of his c. with Abraham, 13.23
and his c. that he made with their 17.15
The LORD made a c. with them, 17.35
not forget the c. that I have made 17.38
their God but transgressed his c., 18.12
the book of the c. which had been 23.02
and made a c. before the LORD, to 23.03
words of this c. that were written 23.03
all the people joined in the c. 23.03
is written in this book of the c. 23.21
David made a c. with them at 1Ch 11.03
the ark of the c. of the LORD from 15.25
the ark of the c. of the LORD, 15.26
the ark of the c. of the LORD with 15.28
the ark of the c. of the LORD came 15.29
before the ark of the c. of God. 16.06
He is mindful of his c. for ever, 16.15
the c. which he made with Abraham, 16.16
as an everlasting c. to Israel, 16.17
the ark of the c. of the LORD to 16.37
the ark of the c. of the LORD is 17.01
the ark of the c. of the LORD and 22.19
for the ark of the c. of the LORD, 28.02
the ark of the c. of the LORD. 28.18
the ark of the c. of the LORD out 2Ch 5.02
the ark of the c. of the LORD to 5.07
the LORD made a c. with the people 5.10
in which is the c. of the LORD 6.11
keeping c. and showing steadfast 6.14
David and his sons by a c. of salt? 13.05
entered into a c. to seek the LORD, 15.12
because of the c. which he had 21.07
assembly made a c. with the king 23.03
And Jehoiada made a c. between 23.16
heart to make a c. with the LORD, 29.10
the book of the c. which had been 34.30
and made a c. before the LORD, to 34.31
words of the c. that were written 34.31
did according to the c. of God, 34.32
Therefore let us make a c. with our Ez 10.03
God who keeps c. and steadfast Neh 1.05
with him the c. to give to his 9.08
who keepest c. and steadfast love, 9.32
we make a firm c. and write it, 9.38
priesthood and the c. of the 13.29
"I have made a c. with my eyes; Job 31.01
Will he make a c. with you to take 41.04
who keep his c. and his testimonies. Ps 25.10
and he makes known to them his c. 25.14
thee, or been false to thy c. 44.17
who made a c. with me by sacrifice!" 50.05
statutes, or take my c. on your lips? 50.16
his friends, he violated his c. 55.20
Have regard for thy c.; for the 74.20
They did not keep God's c., 78.10
they were not true to his c. 78.37
against thee they make a c.— 83.05
"I have made a c. with my chosen 89.03
and my c. will stand firm for him. 89.28
I will not violate my c., or alter 89.34
renounced the c. with thy servant; 89.39
who keep his c. and remember to do 103.18
He is mindful of his c. for ever, 105.08
the c. which he made with Abraham, 105.09
to Israel as an everlasting c., 105.10
He remembered for their sake his c., 106.45
he is ever mindful of his c. 111.05
he has commanded his c. for ever. 111.09
sons keep my c. and my testimonies 132.12
and forgets the c. of her God; Pro 2.17
statutes, broken the everlasting c. Is 24.05
said, "We have made a c. with death, 28.15
Then your c. with death will be 28.18
given you as a c. to the people, 42.06
given you as a c. to the people, 49.08
and my c. of peace shall not be 54.10
make with you an everlasting c., 55.03
please me and hold fast my c., 56.04
profane it, and holds fast my c.— 56.06
this is my c. with them, says the 59.21
make an everlasting c. with them. 61.08
say, "The ark of the c. of the LORD." Jer 3.16
"Hear the words of this c., and speak 11.02
does not heed the words of this c. 11.03
the words of this c. and do them. 11.06
upon them all the words of this c., 11.08
have broken my c. which I made 11.10
and do not break thy c. with us. 14.21
forsook the c. of the LORD their 22.09
will make a new c. with the house 31.31
not like the c. which I made with 31.32
my c. which they broke, though I was 31.32
But this is the c. which I will 31.33
make with them an everlasting c., 32.40
can break my c. with the day and 33.20
and my c. with the night, so that 33.20
then also my c. with David my 33.21
and my c. with the Levitical 33.21
established my c. with day and 33.25
had made a c. with all the people 34.08
into the c. that every one would 34.10
I made a c. with your fathers when 34.13
and you made a c. before me in the 34.15
transgressed my c. and did not 34.18
terms of the c. which they made 34.18
an everlasting c. which will never 50.05
you and entered into a c. with you, Eze 16.08
despised the oath in breaking the c., 16.59
remember my c. with you in the 16.60
establish with you an everlasting c. 16.60
not on account of the c. with you. 16.61
I will establish my c. with you, 16.62
seed royal and made a c. with him, 17.13
by keeping his c. it might stand.) 17.14
Can he break the c. and yet escape? 17.15
and whose c. with him he broke, in 17.16
despised the oath and broke the c., 17.18
and my c. which he broke, I will 17.19
with them a c. of peace and banish 34.25
I will make a c. of peace with them 37.26
be an everlasting c. with them; 37.26
You have broken my c., with all 44.07
who keepest c. and steadfast love Dan 9.04
make a strong c. with many for one 9.27
and the prince of the c. also. 11.22
shall be set against the holy c. 11.28
take action against the holy c. 11.30
to those who forsake the holy c. 11.30
flattery those who violate the c.; 11.32
make for you a c. on that day with Hos 2.18
But at Adam they transgressed the c.; 6.07
because they have broken my c., 8.01

COVENANT (cont.)
not remember the c. of brotherhood. Amo 1.09
of the blood of my c. with you, Zec 9.11
annulling the c. which I had made 11.10
that my c. with Levi may hold, says Mal 2.04
My c. with him was a c. of life and 2.05
you have corrupted the c. of Levi, 2.08
profaning the c. of our fathers? 2.10
witness to the c. between you and 2.14
your companion and your wife by c. 2.14
messenger of the c. in whom you 3.01
for this is my blood of the c., Mt 26.28
them, "This is my blood of the c., Mk 14.24
and to remember his holy c., Lk 1.72
for you is the new c. in my blood." * 22.20
and of the c. which God gave to Ac 3.25
And he gave him the c. of circumcision. 7.08
"and this will be my c. with them Rom 11.27
"This cup is the new c. in my blood. 1Co 11.25
us to be ministers of a new c., 2Co 3.06
day, when they read the old c., 3.14
not annul a c. previously ratified Gal 3.17
Jesus the surety of a better c. Heb 7.22
the old as the c. he mediates is 8.06
For if that first c. had been faultless, 8.07
establish a new c. with the house 8.08
not like the c. that I made with 8.09
for they did not continue in my c., 8.09
This is the c. that I will make 8.10
of a new c. he treats the first as 8.13
Now even the first c. had regulations 9.01
the ark of the c. covered on all 9.04
budded, and the tables of the c.; 9.04
Therefore he is the mediator of a new c., 9.15
transgressions under the first c. 9.15
Hence even the first c. was not 9.18
blood of the c. which God commanded 9.20
"This is the c. that I will make 10.16
blood of the c. by which he was 10.29
to Jesus, the mediator of a new c., 12.24
by the blood of the eternal c., 13.20
the ark of his c. was seen within Rev 11.19

COVENANTED
as I c. with David your father, 2Ch 7.18

COVENANTS
C. are broken, witnesses are despised, Is 33.08
with empty oaths they make c.; Hos 10.04
the c., the giving of the law, the Rom 9.04
allegory: these women are two c. Gal 4.24
and strangers to the c. of promise, Eph 2.12

COVER
and c. it inside and out with pitch. Gen 6.14
and they shall c. the face of the Ex 10.05
The floods c. them; they went 15.05
man digs a pit and does not c. it, 21.33
this side and that side, to c. it. 26.13
breeches to c. their naked flesh; 28.42
and I will c. you with my hand 33.22
and he shall c. his upper lip and Lev 13.45
the incense may c. the mercy seat 16.13
out its blood and c. it with dust. 17.13
and c. the ark of the testimony Num 4.05
and c. the same with a covering of 4.08
and c. the lampstand for the light, 4.09
and c. it with a covering of goatskin, 4.11
and c. them with a covering of goatskin, 4.12
which has no c. fastened upon it, is 19.15
they c. the face of the earth, and 22.05
cloak with which you c. yourself. Deu 22.12
turn back and c. up your excrement. 23.13
the sea come upon them and c. them; Jos 24.07
came down under c. of the mountain, 1Sa 25.20
to c. the capital that was upon the 1Ki 7.18
two networks to c. the two bowls 7.41
to c. the two bowls of the capitals 7.42
two networks to c. the two bowls 2Ch 4.12
to c. the two bowls of the capitals 4.13
Do not c. their guilt, and let not Neh 4.05
thou wouldest c. over my iniquity. Job 14.17
"O earth, c. not my blood, and let my 16.18
in the dust, and the worms c. them. 21.26
that a flood of waters may c. you? 38.34
For his shade the lotus trees c. him; 40.22
thou dost c. him with favor as with Ps 5.12
me under the c. of his tent, he will 27.05
he will c. you with his pinions, and 91.04
Thou didst c. it with the deep as 104.06
they might not again c. the earth. 104.09
If I say, "Let only darkness c. me, 139.11
the LORD as the waters c. the sea. Is 11.09
her, and will no more c. her slain. 26.21
to c. him, and not to hide yourself 58.07
men will not c. themselves with 59.06
darkness shall c. the earth, and thick 60.02
A multitude of camels shall c. you, 60.06
shame, and let our dishonor c. us; Jer 3.25
and confounded and c. their heads. 14.03
are ashamed, they c. their heads. 14.04
I will c. the earth, I will destroy 46.08
you shall c. your face, that you may Eze 12.06
he shall c. his face, that he may 12.12
embroidered garments to c. them, 16.18
upon the ground to c. it with dust. 24.07
do not c. your lips, nor eat the 24.17
you shall not c. your lips, nor eat 24.22
many that their dust will c. you; 26.10
you, and the great waters c. you, 26.19
I will c. the heavens, and make 32.07
I will c. the sun with a cloud, and 32.07
and c. you with skin, and put breath 37.06
which were to c. her nakedness. Hos 2.09
C. us, and to the hills, Fall upon us 10.08
shame shall c. you, and you shall be Ob 1.10
they shall all c. their lips, Mic 3.07
and shame will c. her who said to 7.10
the LORD, as the waters c. the sea. Hab 2.14
the leaden c. was lifted, and there Zec 5.07
You c. the LORD's altar with tears, Mal 2.13
and to c. his face, and to strike Mk 14.65
on us'; and to the hills, 'C. us.' Lk 23.30
For a man ought not to c. his head, 1Co 11.07
death and will c. a multitude of Jas 5.20

COVERED
under the whole heaven were c.; Gen 7.19
backward and c. the nakedness of 9.23
she took her veil and c. herself. 24.65
a harlot, for she had c. her face. 38.15
came up and c. the land of Egypt. Ex 8.06
For they c. the face of the whole 10.15
returned and c. the chariots and 14.28
with thy wind, the sea c. them; 15.10
quails came up and c. the camp; 16.13
and the cloud c. the mountain. 24.15
and the cloud c. it six days; 24.16
Then the cloud c. the tent of 40.34
if the leprosy has c. all his body, Lev 13.13
six c. wagons and twelve oxen, a Num 7.03
the cloud c. the tabernacle, the 9.15
the cloud c. it by day, and the 9.16
the cloud c. it, and the glory of 16.42
tent, and she c. him with a rug. Ju 4.18
and gave him a drink and c. him. 4.19
its head, and c. it with the clothes. 1Sa 19.13
barefoot and with his head c.; 2Sa 15.30
who were with him c. their heads, 15.30
The king c. his face, and the king 19.04
"You have today c. with shame the 19.05
although they c. him with clothes, 1Ki 1.01
he c. them on the inside with wood; 6.15
and he c. the floor of the house 6.15
He c. the two doors of olivewood 6.32

COVERED (cont.)
And it was c. with cedar above the 1Ki 7.03
man threw a stone, until it was c.; 2Ki 3.25
And the c. way for the sabbath 16.18
and c. himself with sackcloth, and 19.01
c. with sackcloth, to the prophet 19.02
their wings and c. the ark of the 1Ch 28.18
and c. it with fine gold, and made 2Ch 3.05
rebuilt it and c. it and set its Neh 3.15
mourning and with his head c. Est 6.12
of the king, they c. Haman's face. 7.08
because he has c. his face with his Job 15.27
is forgiven, whose sin is c. Ps 32.01
me, and shame has c. my face, 44.15
and c. us with deep darkness. 44.19
—the wings of a dove c. with silver, 68.13
reproach, that shame has c. my face. 69.07
may they be c. who seek my hurt. 71.13
The mountains were c. with its shade, 80.10
youth; thou hast c. him with shame. 89.45
And the waters c. their adversaries; 106.11
Dathan, and c. the company of Abiram. 106.17
thou hast c. my head in the day of 140.07
the ground was c. with nettles, Pro 24.31
though his hatred be c. with guile, 26.26
and in darkness its name is c.; Ecc 6.04
with two he c. his face, and with Is 6.02
face, and with two he c. his feet, 6.02
and c. your heads, the seers. 29.10
and c. himself with sackcloth, and 37.01
he has c. me with the robe of 61.10
she is c. with its tumultuous waves. Jer 51.42
dishonor has c. our face, for aliens 51.51
another, while two c. their bodies. Eze 1.11
and c. your nakedness: yea, I plighted 16.08
in fine linen and c. you with silk. 16.10
has shed, that it may not be c. 24.08
she shall be c. by a cloud, and her 30.18
upon them, and skin had c. them; 37.08
windows (now the windows were c.), 41.16
and c. himself with sackcloth, and Jon 3.06
man and beast be c. with sackcloth, 3.08
His glory c. the heavens, and the Hab 3.03
for nothing is c. that will not be Mt 10.26
field, which a man found and c. up; 13.44
Nothing is c. up that will not be Lk 12.02
forgiven, and whose sins are c.; Rom 4.07
with his head c. dishonors his 1Co 11.04
of the covenant c. on all sides Heb 9.04

COVEREST
who c. thyself with light as with a Ps 104.02

COVERING
mountains, c. them fifteen cubits deep. Gen 7.20
and Noah removed the c. of the ark, 8.13
for that is his only c., it is Ex 22.27
for the tent a c. of tanned rams' 26.14
its tent and its c., its hooks 35.11
for the tent a c. of tanned rams' 36.19
the c. of tanned rams' skins and 39.34
and put the c. of the tent over it, 40.19
offer the fat c. the entrails and Lev 3.03
the fat c. the entails, and all the 3.14
tabernacle, the tent with its c., Num 3.25
shall put on it a c. of goatskin, 4.06
the same with a c. of goatskin, 4.08
utensils in a c. of goatskin and 4.10
and cover it with a c. of goatskin, 4.11
cover them with a c. of goatskin, 4.12
spread upon it a c. of goatskin, 4.14
have finished c. the sanctuary and 4.15
the tent of meeting with its c., 4.25
and the c. of sheepskin that is on 4.25
plates as a c. for the altar, for they 16.38
hammered out as a c. for the altar, 16.39
and spread a c. over the well's 2Sa 17.19
cherubim made a c. above the ark 1Ki 8.07
cherubim made a c. above the ark 2Ch 5.08
clothing, and have no c. in the cold. Job 24.07
before God, and Abaddon has no c. 26.06
clothing, or a poor man without c.; 31.19
He made darkness his c. around him, Ps 18.11
He spread a cloud for a c., and fire 105.39
Like the glaze c. an earthen vessel Pro 26.23
beneath you, and worms are your c. Is 14.11
He has taken away the c. of Judah. 22.08
mountain the c. that is cast over 25.07
and the c. too narrow to wrap 28.20
blackness, and make sackcloth their c." 50.03
creature had two wings c. its body. Eze 1.23
every precious stone was your c., 28.13
will be like a cloud c. the land, 38.09
Israel, like a cloud c. the land. 38.16
and c. one's garment with violence, Mal 2.16
her hair is given to her for a c. 1Co 11.15

COVERINGS
I have decked my couch with c., Pro 7.16
She makes herself c.; her clothing 31.22

COVERLET
he took the c. and dipped it in 2Ki 8.15

COVERS
all the fat that c. the entrails, Ex 29.13
and the fat that c. the entrails, 29.22
and the fat that c. the entrails, Lev 3.09
the fat that c. the entrails and 4.08
the fat that c. the entrails, 7.03
and that which c. the entrails, 9.19
the leprosy c. all the skin of the 13.12
and it c. the face of the earth; Num 22.11
he c. the faces of its judges—if Job 9.24
see, and a flood of water c. you. 22.11
and thick darkness c. my face. 23.17
He c. the face of the moon, and 26.09
and c. the roots of the sea. 36.30
He c. his hands with the lightning, 36.32
violence c. them as a garment. Ps 73.06
early rain also c. it with pools. 84.06
He c. the heavens with clouds, he 147.08
strife, but love c. all offenses. Pro 10.12
with sackcloth, and horror c. them; Eze 7.18
the hungry and c. the naked with a 18.07
the hungry and c. the naked with a 18.16
lighting a lamp c. it with a vessel, Lk 8.16
since love c. a multitude of sins. 1Pe 4.08

COVERT
dens, or lie in wait in their c.? Job 38.40
in the c. of the reeds and in the 40.21
in secret like a lion in his c.; Ps 10.09
In the c. of thy presence thou 31.20
in the c. of the cliff, let me see Sol 2.14
a c. from the tempest, like streams Is 32.02
Like a lion he has left his c., Jer 25.38

COVET
"You shall not c. your neighbor's Ex 20.17
shall not c. your neighbor's wife, 20.17
shall you c. your neighbor's wife; Deu 5.21
you shall not c. the silver or the 7.25
They c. fields, and seize them; Mic 2.02
not have known what it is to c. if Rom 7.07
law had not said, "You shall not c." 7.07
You shall not c.," and any other 13.09
And you c. and cannot obtain; Jas 4.02

COVETED
then I c. them, and took them; Jos 7.21
I c. no one's silver or gold or Ac 20.33

COVETING
c., wickedness, deceit, licentiousness, Mk 7.22

COVETOUS
or one who is c. (that is, an idolater), Eph 5.05

COVETOUSNESS
the iniquity of his c. I was angry, Is 57.17
"Take heed, and beware of all c.; Lk 12.15
of wickedness, evil, c., malice. Rom 1.29
wrought in me all kinds of c. 7.08
all impurity or c. must not even Eph 5.03
desire, and c., which is idolatry. Col 3.05

COVETS
and c. many days, that he may enjoy Ps 34.12
All day long the wicked c., Pro 21.26

COW
the firstlings of c. and sheep. Ex 34.19
the mother is a c. or a ewe, you Lev 22.28
But the firstling of a c., or the Num 18.17
their c. calves, and does not cast Job 21.10
alive a young c. and two sheep; Is 7.21
The c. and the bear shall feed; 11.07

COWARDLY
But as for the c., the faithless, Rev 21.08

COWER
on gravel, and made me c. in ashes; Lam 3.16

COW'S
let you have c. dung instead of Eze 4.15

COWS
forty c. and ten bulls, twenty Gen 32.15
of the Nile seven c. sleek and fat, 41.02
seven other c., gaunt and thin, came 41.03
by the other c. on the bank of the 41.03
gaunt and thin c. ate up the seven 41.04
ate up the seven sleek and fat c. 41.04
and seven c., fat and sleek, came up 41.18
and seven other c. came up after 41.19
thin and gaunt c. ate up the first 41.20
ate up the first seven fat c., 41.20
The seven good c. are seven years, 41.26
lean and gaunt c. that came up 41.27
and two milch c. upon which there 1Sa 6.07
and yoke the c. to the cart, but 6.07
took two milch c. and yoked them 6.10
And the c. went straight in the 6.12
and offered the c. as a burnt 6.14
you c. of Bashan, who are in the Amo 4.01

COZBI
was slain was C. the daughter of Num 25.15
of Peor, and in the matter of C., 25.18

COZEBA
and Jokim, and the men of C., 1Ch 4.22

CRACK
The c. of whip, and rumble of wheel, Nah 3.02

CRACKLING
For as the c. of thorns under a pot, Ecc 7.06
like the c. of a flame of fire Joe 2.05

CRAFT
carving wood, for work in every c. Ex 31.05
wood, for work in every skilled c. 35.33
and against all the beautiful c. Is 2.16
craftsman of any c. shall be found Rev 18.22

CRAFTILY
to deal c. with his servants. Ps 105.25
He dealt c. with our race and Ac 7.19

CRAFTINESS
He takes the wise in their own c.; Job 5.13
But he perceived their c., and said Lk 20.23
"He catches the wise in their c.," 1Co 3.19
by their c. in deceitful wiles. Eph 4.14

CRAFTSMAN
work done by a c. or by a designer Ex 35.35
a c. and designer and embroiderer 38.23
a thing made by the hands of a c., Deu 27.15
out a skilful c. to set up an Is 40.20
The c. encourages the goldsmith, and 41.07
with an axe by the hands of a c. Jer 10.03
the work of the c. and of the 10.09
and a c. of any craft shall be Rev 18.22

CRAFTSMANSHIP
intelligence, with knowledge and all c., Ex 31.03
with knowledge, and with all c., 35.31

CRAFTSMEN
and all the c. and the smiths; 2Ki 24.14
and the c. and the smiths, one 24.16
so-called because they were c. 1Ch 4.14
and all kinds of c. without number, 22.15
and for all the work to be done by c., 29.05
with your c., the c. of my lord, 2Ch 2.14
Lod, and Ono, the valley of c. Neh 11.35
to shame, and the c. are but men; Is 44.11
the c., and the smiths, and had Jer 24.01
the c., and the smiths had departed 29.02
silver, all of them the work of c. Hos 13.02
no little business to the c. Ac 19.24
Demetrius and the c. with him have 19.38

CRAFTY
and Jonadab was a very c. man. 2Sa 13.03
He frustrates the devices of the c., Job 5.12
you choose the tongue of the c. 15.05
They lay c. plans against thy Ps 83.03
I was c., you say, and got the 2Co 12.16

CRAG
was a rocky c. on the one side and 1Sa 14.04
and a rocky c. on the other side; 14.04
The one c. rose on the north in 14.05
in the fastness of the rocky c. Job 39.28

CRAGS
of Lebanon leave the c. of Sirion? Jer 18.14
you, and roll you down from the c., 51.25

CRAMPING
broad place where there was no c., Job 36.16

CRANE
Like a swallow or a c. I clamor, Is 38.14
and c. keep the time of their Jer 8.07

CRASH
come; amid the c. they roll on. Job 30.14
The c. of thy thunder was in the Ps 77.18
whose c. comes suddenly, in an Is 30.13
fortified cities c. into heaps of 37.26
Quarter, a loud c. from the hills. Zep 1.10

CRASHING
Its c. declares concerning him, who Job 36.33
at the c. they are beside themselves 41.25

CRAVE
because you c. flesh, you may eat Deu 12.20

CRAVED
by demanding the food they c. Ps 78.18
for he gave them what they c. 78.29

CRAVES
drink, whatever your appetite c.; Deu 14.26
The soul of the sluggard c., Pro 13.04

CRAVING
was among them had a strong c.; Num 11.04
buried the people who had the c. 11.34
But before they had sated their c., Ps 78.30
had a wanton c. in the wilderness, 106.14
he thwarts the c. of the wicked. Pro 10.03
to leave the c. of the hungry Is 32.06
he has a morbid c. for controversy 1Ti 6.04
is through this c. that some have 6.10

CRAWLING
with venom of c. things of the dust. Deu 32.24
like the c. things of the earth; Mic 7.17
like c. thinks that have no ruler. Hab 1.14

CRAWLS
thing that c. upon the earth. Lev 11.44

CRAZED
stagger and be c. because of the Jer 25.16

CREATE
C. in me a clean heart, O God, and Ps 51.10
Then the LORD will c. over the Is 4.05
I form light and c. darkness, 45.07
darkness, I make weal and c. woe, 45.07
he did not c. it a chaos, he formed 45.18
"For behold, I c. new heavens and a 65.17
rejoice for ever in that which I c.; 65.18
for behold, I c. Jerusalem a rejoicing, 65.18
of those who c. dissensions and Rom 16.17
that he might c. in himself one new Eph 2.15
for thou didst c. all things, Rev 4.11

CREATED
beginning God c. the heavens and Gen 1.01
So God c. the great sea monsters 1.21
So God c. man in his own image, in 1.27
in the image of God he c. him; 1.27
him; male and female he c. them. 1.27
and the earth when they were c. 2.04
When God c. man, he made him in the 5.01
Male and female he c. them, and he 5.02
named them Man when they were c. 5.02
man whom I have c. from the face 6.07
day that God c. man upon the earth, Deu 4.32
who c. you, who made you and established 32.06
and the south, thou hast c. them; Ps 89.12
thou hast c. all the sons of men! 89.47
forth thy Spirit, they are c.; 104.30
for he commanded and they were c. 148.05
The LORD c. me at the beginning of Pro 8.22
eyes on high and see: who c. these? Is 40.26
the Holy One of Israel has c. it. 41.20
who c. the heavens and stretched 42.05
he who c. you, O Jacob, he who formed 43.01
whom I c. for my glory, whom I 43.07
up also; I the LORD have c. it. 45.08
made the earth, and c. man upon it; 45.12
who c. the heavens (he is God!), 45.18
They are c. now, not long ago; 48.07
Behold, I have c. the smith who 54.16
I have also c. the ravager to destroy; 54.16
the LORD has c. a new thing on the Jer 31.22
In the place where you were c., Eze 21.30
that you were c. they were prepared 28.13
your ways from the day you were c., 28.15
Has not one God c. us? Why then Mal 2.10
creation which God c. until now, Mk 13.19
Neither was man c. for woman, 1Co 11.09
c. in Christ Jesus for good works, Eph 2.10
for ages in God who c. all things; 3.09
c. after the likeness of God in 4.24
for in him all things were c., Col 1.16
—all things were c. through him and 1.16
foods which God c. to be received 1Ti 4.03
For everything c. by God is good, 4.04
through whom also he c. the world. Heb 1.02
the world was c. by the word of 11.03
thy will they existed and were c." Rev 4.11
who c. heaven and what is in it, the 10.06

CREATES
But if the LORD c. something new, Num 16.30
and c. the wind, and declares to man Amo 4.13

CREATING
c. for his mourners the fruit of Is 57.18

CREATION
his work which he had done in c. Gen 2.03
in his own c. when he makes dumb Hab 2.18
But from the beginning of c., Mk 10.06
beginning of the c. which God 13.19
Ever since the c. of the world his Rom 1.20
For the c. waits with eager longing 8.19
for the c. was subjected to futility, 8.20
because the c. itself will be set 8.21
that the whole c. has been groaning 8.22
and not only the c., 8.23
depth, nor anything else in all c., 8.39
one is in Christ, he is a new c.; 2Co 5.17
nor uncircumcision, but a new c. Gal 6.15
God, the first-born of all c.; Col 1.15
hands, that is, not of this c.) Heb 9.11
they were from the beginning of c." 2Pe 3.04
witness, the beginning of God's c. Rev 3.14

CREATOR
Remember also your C. in the days Ecc 12.01
the C. of the ends of the earth. Is 40.28
the C. of Israel, your King. 43.15
the creature rather than the C., Rom 1.25
knowledge after the image of its c. Col 3.10
their souls to a faithful c. 1Pe 4.19

CREATURE
the man called every living c., Gen 2.19
any other wild c. that the LORD 3.01
every living c. as I have done. 8.21
every living c. that is with you, 9.10
every living c. that is with you, 9.12
and every living c. of all flesh; 9.15
every living c. of all flesh that 9.16
every living c. that moves through Lev 11.46
and every c. that swarms upon the 11.46
the living c. that may be eaten 11.47
and the living c. that may not be 11.47
life of every c. is the blood of 17.14
shall not eat the blood of any c., 17.14
the life of every c. is its blood; 17.14
is not his like, a c. without fear. Job 41.33
or some winged c. tell the matter. Ecc 10.20
each c. had two wings, each of which Eze 1.11
and each c. had two wings covering 1.23
every living c. which swarms will 47.09
natives saw the c. hanging from Ac 28.04
shook off the c. into the fire and 28.05
and served the c. rather than the Rom 1.25
preached to every c. under heaven, Col 1.23
And before him no c. is hidden, Heb 4.13
and bird, of reptile and sea c., Jas 3.07
the first living c. like a lion, Rev 4.07
the second living c. like an ox, 4.07
third living c. with the face of a 4.07
fourth living c. like a flying 4.07
And I heard every c. in heaven and 5.13
the second living c. say, "Come!" 6.03
the third living c. say, "Come!" 6.05
of the fourth living c. say, "Come!" 6.07

CREATURES
bring forth swarms of living c., Gen 1.20
forth living c. according to their 1.24
all swarming c. that swarm upon the 7.21
of the swarming c. in the waters Lev 11.10

CREATURES (cont.)
of the living c. that are in the Lev 11.10
as food for the c. of the wilderness. Ps 74.14
the earth is full of thy c. 104.24
houses will be full of howling c.; Is 13.21
the likeness of four living c. Eze 1.05
of the living c. there was something 1.13
to and fro among the living c.; 1.13
And the living c. darted to and fro, 1.14
Now as I looked at the living c., 1.15
upon the earth beside the living c., 1.15
And when the living c. went, 1.19
when the living c. rose from the 1.19
of the living c. was in the wheels. 1.20
of the living c. was in the wheels. 1.21
of the living c. there was the 1.22
of the living c. as they touched 3.13
were the living c. that I saw by 10.15
of the living c. was in them. 10.17
These were the living c. that I saw 10.20
a kind of first fruits of his c. Jas 1.18
Unfaithful c.! Do you not 4.04
c. of instinct, born to be caught 2Pe 2.12
of the throne, are four living c., Rev 4.06
And the four living c., each of them 4.08
the living c. give glory and honor 4.09
the four living c. and among the 5.06
the four living c. and the twenty-four 5.08
and the living c. and the elders 5.11
And the four living c. said, "Amen!" 5.14
one of the four living c. say, 6.01
midst of the four living c. saying, 6.06
the elders and the four living c., 7.11
of the living c. in the sea died, 8.09
the four living c. and before the 14.03
the four living c. gave the seven 15.07
the four living c. fell down and 19.04

CREDIT
love you, what c. is that to you? Lk 6.32
to you, what c. is that to you? 6.33
to receive, what c. is that to you? 6.34
fruit which increases to your c. Php 4.17
For what c. is it, if when you do 1Pe 2.20

CREDITED
neither shall it be c. to him; Lev 7.18

CREDITOR
you shall not be to him as a c., Ex 22.25
every c. shall release what he has Deu 15.02
but the c. has come to take my two 2Ki 4.01
May the c. seize all that he has; Ps 109.11
as with the c., so with the debtor. Is 24.02
"A certain c. had two debtors; Lk 7.41

CREDITORS
Or which of my c. is it to whom I Is 50.01

CREEP
the beasts of the forest c. forth. Ps 104.20
things that c. on the ground, Eze 38.20

CREEPING
cattle and c. things and beasts of Gen 1.24
and over every c. thing that creeps 1.26
and beast and c. things and birds 6.07
of every c. thing of the ground 6.20
and every c. thing that creeps on 7.14
and animals and c. things and 7.23
and every c. thing that creeps on 8.17
every c. thing, and every bird, 8.19
touches a c. thing by which he may Lev 22.05
cattle, c. things and flying birds! Ps 148.10
about, were all kinds of c. things, Eze 8.10
and all c. things that creep on the 38.20
and the c. things of the ground; Hos 2.18

CREEPS
everything that c. upon the ground Gen 1.25
thing that c. upon the earth." 1.26
to everything that c. on the earth, 1.30
everything that c. on the ground, 7.08
thing that c. on the earth according 7.14
thing that c. on the earth—that they 8.17
everything that c. on the ground 9.02
of anything that c. on the ground, Deu 4.18

CRESCENS
C. has gone to Galatia, Titus to 2Ti 4.10

CRESCENTS
and he took the c. that were on the Ju 8.21
besides the c. and the pendants and 8.26
anklets, the headbands, and the c.; Is 3.18

CRETANS
C. and Arabians, we hear them Ac 2.11
"C. are always liars, evil beasts, Tit 1.12

CRETE
under the lee of C. off Salmone. Ac 27.07
a harbor of C., looking northeast 27.12
and sailed along C., close inshore. 27.13
set sail from C. and incurred this 27.21
This is why I left you in C., that you Tit 1.05

CREW
and all your c. have sunk with you. Eze 27.34

CRIB
Will he spend the night at your c.? Job 39.09
owner, and the ass its master's c.; Is 1.03

CRICKET
the c. according to its kind, and Lev 11.22

CRIED
he c. out with an exceedingly great Gen 27.34
and I c. out with a loud voice; 39.14
that I lifted up my voice and c., 39.15
as I lifted up my voice and c., 39.18
and they c. before him, "Bow the 41.43
the people c. to Pharaoh for bread; 41.55
and he c., "Make every one go out 45.01
and c. out for help, and their cry Ex 2.23
of Israel came and c. to Pharaoh, 5.15
and Moses c. to the LORD concerning 8.12
of Israel c. out to the LORD; 14.10
And he c. to the LORD; and the 15.25
So Moses c. to the LORD, "What shall 17.04
Then the people c. to Moses; and Num 11.02
And Moses c. to the LORD, "Heal her, 12.13
and when we c. to the LORD, he heard 20.16
young woman c. for help there was Deu 22.27
Then we c. to the LORD the God of 26.07
And when they c. to the LORD, he put Jos 24.07
people of Israel c. to the LORD, Ju 3.09
people of Israel c. to the LORD, 3.15
of Israel c. to the LORD for help; 4.03
of Israel c. for help to the LORD. 6.06
of Israel c. to the LORD on account 6.07
and they c., "A sword for the LORD 7.20
army ran; they c. out and fled. 7.21
and c. aloud and said to them, 9.07
people of Israel c. to the LORD, 10.10
and you c. to me, and I delivered 10.12
told the news, all the city c. out. 1Sa 4.13
Ekron, the people of Ekron c. out, 5.10
and Samuel c. to the LORD for 7.09
your fathers c. to the LORD and 12.08
And they c. to the LORD, and said, 12.10
and he c. to the LORD all night. 15.11
she c. out with a loud voice; 28.12
The Ahimaaz c. out to the king, 2Sa 18.28
and the king c. with a loud voice, 19.04

CRIED (cont.)
they c. to the LORD, but he did not 2Sa 22.42
And the man c. against the altar by 1Ki 13.02
which he c. against the altar at 13.04
and he c. to the man of God who 13.21
saying which he c. by the word of 13.32
And he c. to the LORD, "O LORD my 17.20
and c. to the LORD, "O LORD my God, 17.21
And they c. aloud, and cut themselves 18.28
he c. to the king and said, "Your 20.39
against him; and Jehoshaphat c. out. 22.32
And Elisha saw it and he c., 2Ki 2.12
sons of the prophets c. to Elisha, 4.01
they c. out, "O man of God, there is 4.40
and he c. out, "Alas, my master! 6.05
a woman c. out to him, saying, "Help, 6.26
rent her clothes, and c., "Treason! 11.14
And Isaiah the prophet c. to the LORD; 20.11
for they c. to God in the battle, 1Ch 5.20
and they c. to the LORD, and the 2Ch 13.14
And Asa c. to the LORD his God, "O 14.11
and Jehoshaphat c. out, and the 18.31
rent her clothes, and c., "Treason! 23.13
because of this and c. to heaven. 32.20
and they c. with a loud voice to Neh 9.04
suffering they c. to thee and thou 9.27
they turned and c. to thee thou 9.28
because I delivered the poor who c., Job 29.12
"If my land has c. out against me, 31.38
to my God I c. for help. From his Ps 18.06
They c. for help, but there was none 18.41
they c. to the LORD, but he did not 18.41
To thee they c., and were saved; 22.05
but has heard, when he c. to him. 22.24
I c. to thee for help, and thou hast 30.02
To thee, O LORD, I c.; and to the 30.08
hear my supplications, when I c. to 31.22
This poor man c., and the LORD 34.06
I c. aloud to him, and he was 66.17
They c. to the LORD, and he answered 99.06
Then they c. to the LORD in their 107.06
Then they c. to the LORD in their 107.13
Then they c. to the LORD in their 107.19
Then they c. to the LORD in their 107.28
Then he who saw c.: "Upon a Is 21.08
men c. at them; "Away! Away! Lam 4.15
Then he c. in my ears with a loud Eze 9.01
upon my face, and c., "Ah Lord God! 9.08
and c. with a loud voice, and said, 11.13
He c. aloud and said thus, 'Hew down Dan 4.14
The king c. aloud to bring in the 5.07
he c. out in a tone of anguish and 6.20
afraid, and each c. to his god; Jon 1.05
Therefore they c. to the LORD, "We 1.14
out of the belly of Sheol I c., 2.02
And he c., "Yet forty days, and 3.04
to whom the former prophets c. out, Zec 1.04
Then he c. to me, "Behold, those who 6.08
they c. out, "What have you to do Mt 8.29
And they c. out for fear. 14.26
and beginning to sink he c. out, 14.30
from that region came out and c., 15.22
c. out, "Have mercy on us, Son of 20.30
but they c. out the more, "Lord, have 20.31
hour Jesus c. with a loud voice, 27.46
And Jesus c. again with a loud 27.50
and he c. out, "What have you to do Mk 1.24
fell down before him and c. out, 3.11
thought it was a ghost, and c. out; 6.49
of the child c. out and said, 9.24
but he c. out all the more, "Son of 10.48
those who followed c. out, "Hosanna! 11.09
And they c. out again, "Crucify him." 15.13
hour Jesus c. with a loud voice, 15.34
and he c. out with a loud voice, Lk 4.33
he c. out and fell down before him, 8.28
And behold, a man from the crowd c., 9.38
And he c., "Jesus, Son of David, have 18.38
but he c. out all the more, "Son of 18.39
But they all c. out together, "Away 23.18
and c., "This was he of whom I said, Jn 1.15
he c. with a loud voice, "Lazarus, 11.43
And Jesus c. out and said, "He who 12.44
They c. out again, "Not this man, but 18.40
they c. out, "Crucify him, crucify 19.06
but the Jews c. out, "If you release 19.12
They c. out, "Away with him, away 19.15
But they c. out with a loud voice Ac 7.57
knelt down and c. with a loud 7.60
But Paul c. with a loud voice, "Do 16.28
and c. out, "Great is Artemis of the 19.28
Now some c. one thing, some another; 19.32
they all with one voice c. out, 19.34
And as they c. out and waved their 22.23
he c. out in the council, "Brethren, 23.06
thing which I c. out while standing 24.21
they c. out with a loud voice, "O Rev 6.10
child and she c. out in her pangs 12.02
and c. out as they saw the smoke of 18.18
Once more they c., "Hallelujah! 19.03

CRIES
And if he c. to me, I will hear, for Ex 22.27
soul of the wounded c. for help; Job 24.12
Wisdom c. aloud in the street; Pro 1.20
on the top of the walls she c. out; 1.21
entrance of the portals she c. aloud: 8.03
My heart c. out for Moab; his Is 15.05
who writhes and c. out in her 26.17
A voice c.: "In the wilderness 40.03
he c. out, he shouts aloud, he shows 42.13
If one c. to it, it does not answer 46.07
The voice of the LORD c. to the city— Mic 6.09
the mighty man c. aloud there. Zep 1.14
seizes him, and he suddenly c. out; Lk 9.39
with loud c. that he should be 23.23
And Isaiah c. out concerning Israel: Rom 9.27
with loud c. and tears, to him who Heb 5.07
and the c. of the harvesters have Jas 5.04

CRIME
a man for any c. or for any wrong Deu 19.15
has committed a c. punishable by 21.22
Thus God requited the c. of Abimelech, Ju 9.56
all the wanton c. which they have 20.10
For that would be a heinous c.; Job 31.11
so recompense them for their c.; Ps 56.07
multitudes, "I find no c. in this man." Lk 23.04
found in him no c. deserving death 23.22
and told them, "I find no c. in him. Jn 18.38
may know that I find no c. in him." 19.04
him, for I find no c. in him." 19.06
matter of wrongdoing or vicious c., Ac 18.14

CRIMES
Who can search out our c.? We have Ps 64.06
full of bloody c. and the city is Eze 7.23

CRIMINAL
and wearing fetters, like a c. 2Ti 2.09

CRIMINALS
who were c., were led away to be Lk 23.32
and the c., one on the right and 23.33
One of the c. who were hanged 23.39

CRIMSON
c., and blue fabrics, trained also 2Ch 2.07
and c. fabrics and fine linen, and 2.14
and purple and c. fabfrics and fine 3.14
though they are red like c., Is 1.18

CRIMSONED
in c. garments from Bozrah, he that Is 63.01

CRINGE
that thy enemies c. before thee. Ps 66.03
hate the LORD would c. toward him, 81.15

CRINGING
Foreigners came c. to me; as soon as 2Sa 22.45
obeyed me; foreigners came c. to me. Ps 18.44

CRIPPLE
concerning a good deed done to a c., Ac 4.09
he was a c. from birth, who had 14.08

CRIPPLED
had a son who was c. in his feet. 2Sa 4.04
of Jonathan; he is c. in his feet." 9.03
the c. you have not bound up, the Eze 34.04
strayed, and I will bind up the c., 34.16

CRIPPLES
c. whom I knew not slandered me Ps 35.15

CRISPUS
C., the ruler of the synagogue, Ac 18.08
none of you except C. and Gaius; 1Co 1.14

CRITICIZED
the circumcision party c. him, Ac 11.02

CROAK
the raven c. on the threshold; Zep 2.14

CROCODILE
the land c., the lizard, the sand Lev 11.30

CROCUS
shall rejoice and blossom; like the c. Is 35.01

CROOKED
are a perverse and c. generation. Deu 32.05
and with the c. thou dost show 2Sa 22.27
and with the c. thou dost show Ps 18.26
upon their c. ways the LORD will 125.05
men whose paths are c., and who are Pro 2.15
Put away from you c. speech, 4.24
man, goes about with c. speech, 6.12
is nothing twisted or c. in them. 8.08
A man of c. mind does not prosper, 17.20
The way of the guilty is c., 21.08
What is c. cannot be made straight, Ecc 1.15
make straight what he has made c.? 7.13
they have made their roads c., no one Is 59.08
stones, he has made my paths c. Lam 3.09
and the c. shall be made straight, Lk 3.05
yourselves from this c. generation." Ac 2.40
not stop making c. the straight 13.10
the midst of a c. and perverse Php 2.15

CROOKEDNESS
but the c. of the treacherous Pro 11.03

CROP
take away its c. with the feathers, Lev 1.16
we may not sow or gather in our c.?' 25.20
the c. which you have sown and the Deu 22.09
thresh in hope of a share in the c. 1Co 9.10

CROPS
of years for c. he shall sell to Lev 25.15
number of the c. that he is selling 25.16
will forego the c. of the seventh Neh 10.31
He gave their c. to the caterpillar, Ps 78.46
but abundant c. come by the strength Pro 14.04
for I have nowhere to store my c.?' Lk 12.17
to have the first share of the c. 2Ti 2.06

CROSS
and c. to Zin, and its end shall be Num 34.04
When you c. the Jordan into the 35.10
that I should not c. the Jordan, Deu 4.21
"Why did you c. over to fight Ju 12.01
we will c. over to the men, and we 1Sa 14.08
exhausted to c. the brook Besor. 30.10
as he was about to c. the Jordan, 2Sa 19.18
and c. the brook Kidron, know for 1Ki 2.37
channels that men may c. dryshod. Is 11.15
For c. to the coasts of Cyprus and Jer 2.10
and set out to c. over to the 41.10
into Gilgal or c. over to Beersheba; Amo 5.05
not take his c. and follow me is Mt 10.38
and take up his c. and follow me. 16.24
man they compelled to carry his c. 27.32
Son of God, come down from the c." 27.40
let him come down now from the c., 27.42
and take up his c. and follow me. Mk 8.34
Alexander and Rufus, to carry his c. 15.21
yourself, and come down from the c.!" 15.30
Israel, come down now from the c., 15.32
and take up his c. daily and Lk 9.23
bear his own c. and come after me, 14.27
and none may c. from there to us.' 16.26
country, and laid on him the c., 23.26
he went out, bearing his own c., Jn 19.17
wrote a title and put it on the c.; 19.19
standing by the c. of Jesus were 19.25
remaining on the c. on the sabbath 19.31
And when he wished to c. to Achaia, Ac 18.27
lest the c. of Christ be emptied of 1Co 1.17
For the word of the c. is folly to 1.18
block of the c. has been removed. Gal 5.11
be persecuted for the c. of Christ. 6.12
except in the c. of our Lord Jesus 6.14
to God in one body through the c., Eph 2.16
unto death, even death on a c. Php 2.08
as enemies of the c. of Christ. 3.18
peace by the blood of his c. Col 1.20
he set aside, nailing it to the c. 2.14
was set before him endured the c., Heb 12.02

CROSSED
and arose and c. the Euphrates, and Gen 31.21
only my staff I c. this Jordan; 32.10
and c. the ford of the Jabbok. 32.22
until we c. the brook Zered was Deu 2.14
of Israel until they had c. over, Jos 5.01
And the Ammonites c. the Jordan to Ju 10.09
So Jephthah c. over to the Ammonites 11.32
and they c. to Zaphon and said to 12.01
and c. over against the Ammonites, 12.03
or c. the fords of the Jordan to 1Sa 13.07
they c. the Jordan, and marching the 2Sa 2.29
and c. the Jordan, and came to Helam. 10.17
and the king c. the brook Kidron, 15.23
with him, and they c. the Jordan; 17.22
was left who had not c. the Jordan. 17.22
And Absalom c. the Jordan with all 17.24
and they c. the ford to bring over 19.18
They c. the Jordan, and began from 24.05
When they had c., Elijah said to 2Ki 2.09
These are the men who c. the Jordan 1Ch 12.15
and c. the Jordan, and came to them, 19.17
they have c. over the pass, at Geba Is 10.29
into a boat he c. over and came to Mt 9.01
And when they had c. over, they came 14.34
And when Jesus had c. again in the Mk 5.21
And when they had c. over, they came 6.53
the people c. the Red Sea as if on Heb 11.29

CROSSING
c. his hands, for Manasseh was the Gen 48.14
and c. the Jordan they encamped in Ju 6.33
found a ship c. to Phoenicia, Ac 21.02

CROUCH
when thy c. in their dens, or lie Job 38.40
when they c., bring forth their 39.03
Nothing remains but to c. among the Is 10.04

CROUCHING
c. between the sheepfolds; Gen 49.14

CROW
the cock will not c. this day, Lk 22.34
I say to you, the cock will not c., Jn 13.38

CROWD
and the c. making a tumult, Mt 9.23
But when the c. had been put 9.25
and the whole c. stood on the beach. 13.02
said, "I have compassion on the c., 15.32
the desert to feed so great a c.?" 15.33
And commanding the c. to sit down 15.35
And when they came to the c., 17.14
Jericho, a great c. followed him. 20.29
The c. rebuked them, telling them to 20.31
Most of the c. spread their garments 21.08
And when the c. heard it, they were 22.33
him a great c. with swords and 26.47
release for the c. any one prisoner 27.15
and washed his hands before the c., 27.24
not get near him because of the c., Mk 2.04
and all the c. gathered about him, 2.13
ready for him because of the c., 3.09
and the c. came together again, so 3.20
And a c. was sitting about him; 3.32
a very large c. gathered about him, 4.01
and the whole c. was beside the sea 4.01
And leaving the c., they took 4.36
a great c. gathered about him; 5.21
And a great c. followed him and 5.24
him in the c. and touched his 5.27
immediately turned about in the c., 5.30
"You see the c. pressing around you, 5.31
Bethsaida, while he dismissed the c. 6.45
when again a great c. had gathered, 8.01
"I have compassion on the c., 8.02
commanded the c. to sit down on 8.06
and they set them before the c. 8.06
they saw a great c. about them, 9.14
And immediately all the c., 9.15
And one of the c. answered him, 9.17
saw that a c. came running together, 9.25
and with him a c. with swords and 14.43
And the c. came up and began to ask 15.08
stirred up the c. to have him 15.11
So Pilate, wishing to satisfy the c., 15.15
to bring him in, because of the c., Lk 5.19
with a great c. of his disciples 6.17
And all the c. sought to touch him, 6.19
and a great c. went with him. 7.11
and a large c. from the city was 7.12
And when a great c. came together 8.04
could not reach him for the c. 8.19
the c. welcomed him, for they were 8.40
"Send the c. away, to go into the 9.12
the disciples to set before the c. 9.16
the mountain, a great c. met him. 9.37
And behold, a man from the c. cried, 9.38
a woman in the c. raised her voice 11.27
could not, on account of the c., 19.03
there came a c., and the man called 22.47
as there was a c. in the place. Jn 5.13
heard the c. thus muttering about 7.32
But this c., who do not know the 7.49
When the great c. of the Jews 12.09
day a great c. who had come to the 12.12
The c. that had been with him when 12.17
The reason why the c. went to meet 12.18
The c. standing by heard it and 12.29
The c. answered him, "We have heard 12.34
The c. joined in attacking them; Ac 16.22
of the rabble, they gathered a c., 17.05
Paul wished to go in among the c., 19.30
Some of the c. prompted Alexander, 19.33
the town clerk had quieted the c., 19.35
the temple, stirred up all the c., 21.27
Some in the c. shouted one thing, 21.34
because of the violence of the c.; 21.35
with any one or stirring up a c., 24.12
temple, without any c. or tumult. 24.18

CROWDS
And great c. followed him from Mt 4.25
Seeing the c., he went up on the 5.01
the c. were astonished at his 7.28
mountain, great c. followed him; 8.01
when Jesus saw great c. around him, 8.18
When the c. saw it, they were afraid, 9.08
and the c. marveled, saying, "Never 9.33
When he saw the c., he had 9.36
to speak to the c. concerning John: 11.07
And great c. gathered about him, so 13.02
Jesus said to the c. in parables; 13.34
Then he left the c. and went into 13.36
But when the c. heard it, they 14.13
send the c. away to go into the 14.15
Then he ordered the c. to sit down 14.19
the disciples gave them to the c. 14.19
side, while he dismissed the c. 14.22
And after he had dismissed the c., 14.23
And great c. came to him, bringing 15.30
the disciples gave them to the c. 15.36
And sending away the c., he got into 15.39
and large c. followed him, and he 19.02
And the c. that went before him and 21.09
And the c. said, "This is the 21.11
Jesus to the c. and to his disciples, 23.01
At that hour Jesus said to the c., 26.55
and c. gathered to him again; Mk 10.01
to speak to the c. concerning John: Lk 7.24
When the c. learned it, they followed 9.11
When the c. were increasing, he 11.29
And when the c. saw what Paul had Ac 14.11
stirring up and inciting the c. 17.13

CROWED
And immediately the cock c. Mt 26.74
immediately the cock c. a second time. Mk 14.72
he was still speaking, the cock c. Lk 22.60
denied it; and at once the cock c. Jn 18.27

CROWN
put the holy c. upon the turban. Ex 29.06
plate of the holy c. of pure gold, 39.30
the holy c., as the LORD commanded Lev 8.09
your foot to the c. of your head. Deu 28.35
and upon the c. of the head of him 33.16
the arm, and the c. of the head. 33.20
and I took the c. which was on his 2Sa 1.10
And he took the c. of their king 12.30
his foot to the c. of his head 14.25
was within a c. which projected 1Ki 7.31
and put the c. upon him, and gave 2Ki 11.12
And David took the c. of their king 1Ch 20.02
and put the c. upon him, and gave 2Ch 23.11
before the king with her royal c., Est 1.11
set the royal c. on her head and 2.17
on whose head a royal c. is set; 6.08
a great golden c. and a mantle of 8.15
of his foot to the c. of his head. Job 2.07
and taken the c. from my head. 19.09
I would bind it on me as a c.; 31.36
and dost c. him with glory and Ps 8.05
thou dost set a c. of fine gold 21.03
the hairy c. of him who walks in 68.21
"I have set the c. upon one who is 89.19
hast defiled his c. in the dust. 89.39
himself his c. will shed its 132.18
will bestow on you a beautiful c. Pro 4.09
good wife is the c. of her husband, 12.04
The c. of the wise is their wisdom, 14.24
A hoary head is a c. of glory; 16.31

CROWN (cont.)
Grandchildren are the c. of the aged. Pro 17.06
and does a c. endure to all generations? 27.24
with the c. with which his mother Sol 3.11
Woe to the proud c. of the drunkards Is 28.01
The proud c. of the drunkards of 28.03
of hosts will be a c. of glory, 28.05
You shall be a c. of beauty in the 62.03
have broken the c. of your head. Jer 2.16
your beautiful c. has come down 13.18
the c. of the sons of tumult. 48.45
The c. has fallen from our head; Lam 5.16
and a beautiful c. upon your head. Eze 16.12
the turban, and take off the c.; 21.26
and make a c., and set it upon the Zec 6.11
And the c. shall be in the temple 6.14
the jewels of a c. they shall 9.16
and plaiting a c. of thorns they Mt 27.29
and plaiting a c. of thorns they Mk 15.17
soldiers plaited a c. of thorns, Jn 19.02
wearing the c. of thorns and the 19.05
my joy and c., stand firm thus in Php 4.01
hope or joy or c. of boasting 1Th 2.19
up for me the c. of righteousness, 2Ti 4.08
receive the c. of life which God Jas 1.12
obtain the unfading c. of glory. 1Pe 5.04
and I will give you the c. of life. Rev 2.10
so that no one may seize your c. 3.11
and a c. was given to him, and he 6.02
on her head a c. of twelve stars; 12.01
with a golden c. on his head, and a 14.14

CROWNED
the prudent are c. with knowledge. Pro 14.18
his mother c. him on the day of Sol 3.11
And athlete is not c. unless he 2Ti 2.05
thou hast c. him with glory and Heb 2.07
c. with glory and honor because of 2.09

CROWNEST
Thou c. the year with thy bounty; Ps 65.11

CROWNS
who c. you with steadfast love and Ps 103.04
Your head c. you like Carmel, and Sol 7.05
against Tyre, the bestower of c., Is 23.08
and beautiful c. upon their heads. Eze 23.42
with golden c. upon their heads. Rev 4.04
they cast their c. before the 4.10
were what looked like c. of gold; 9.07

CROWS
very night, before the cock c., Mt 26.34
of Jesus, "Before the cock c., 26.75
night, before the cock c. twice, Mk 14.30
to him, "Before the cock c. twice, 14.72
to him, "Before the cock c. today, Lk 22.61

CRUCIBLE
The c. is for silver, and the Pro 17.03
The c. is for silver, and the 27.21

CRUCIFIED
to be mocked and scourged and c., Mt 20.19
man will be delivered up to be c." 26.02
They all said, "Let him be c." 27.22
all the more, "Let him be c." 27.23
Jesus, delivered him to be c. 27.26
And when they had c. him, they divided 27.35
Then two robbers were c. with him, 27.38
who were c. with him also reviled 27.44
that you seek Jesus who was c. 28.05
Jesus, he delivered him to be c. Mk 15.15
And they c. him, and divided his 15.24
the third hour, when they c. him. 15.25
And with him they c. two robbers, 15.27
Those who were c. with him also 15.32
seek Jesus of Nazareth, who was c. 16.06
loud cries that he should be c. Lk 23.23
there they c. him, and the criminals, 23.33
and be c., and on the third day 24.07
be condemned to death, and c. him 24.20
handed him over to them to be c. Jn 19.16
There they c. him, and with him two 19.18
where Jesus was c. was near the 19.20
soldiers had c. Jesus they took 19.23
the other who had been c. with him; 19.32
where he was c. there was a garden, 19.41
you c. and killed by the hands of Ac 2.23
and Christ, this Jesus whom you c." 2.36
whom you c., whom God raised from 4.10
old self was c. with him so that Rom 6.06
Was Paul c. for you? Or were 1Co 1.13
but we preach Christ c., a stumbling 1.23
you except Jesus Christ and him c. 2.02
would not have c. the Lord of 2.08
For he was c. in weakness, but lives 2Co 13.04
I have been c. with Christ; Gal 2.20
was publicly portrayed as c.? 3.01
Jesus have c. the flesh with its 5.24
which the world has been c. to me, 6.14
and Egypt, where their Lord was c. Rev 11.08

CRUCIFY
some of whom you will kill and c., Mt 23.34
on him, and led him away to c. him. 27.31
And they cried out again, "C. him." Mk 15.13
they shouted all the more, "C. him." 15.14
And they led him out to c. him. 15.20
But they shouted out, "C., c. him!" Lk 23.21
"C. him, c. him!" Pilate said Jn 19.06
"Take him yourselves and c. him, 19.06
release you, and power to c. you?" 19.10
with him, away with him, c. him!" 19.15
said to them, "Shall I c. your King?" 19.15
since they c. the Son of God on Heb 6.06

CRUEL
and their wrath, for it is c.! Gen 49.07
broken spirit and their c. bondage. Ex 6.09
serpents, and the c. venom of asps. Deu 32.33
Thou hast turned c. to me; with the Job 30.21
the grasp of the unjust and c. man. Ps 71.04
Rescue me from the c. sword, and deliver 144.11
himself, but a c. man hurts himself. Pro 11.17
but the mercy of the wicked is c. 12.10
and a c. messenger will be sent 17.11
Wrath is c., anger is overwhelming; 27.04
understanding is a c. oppressor; 28.16
death, jealousy is c. as the grave. Sol 8.06
c., with wrath and fierce anger, to Is 13.09
they are c. and have no mercy, the Jer 6.23
they are c., and have no mercy. 50.42
daughter of my people has become c., Lam 4.03

CRUELLY
of Israel c. for twenty years. Ju 4.03
She deals c. with her young, as if Job 39.16

CRUELTIES
Asa inflicted c. upon some of the 2Ch 16.10

CRUMBLES
"But the mountain falls and c. away, Job 14.18

CRUMBS
dogs eat the c. that fall from Mt 15.27
the table eat the children's c." Mk 7.28

CRUSE
in a jar, and a little oil in a c.; 1Ki 17.12
and the c. of oil shall not fail, 17.14
neither did the c. of oil fail, 17.16

CRUSH
it shall c. the forehead of Moab, Num 24.17
c. the loins of his adversaries, of Deu 33.11

CRUSH (cont.)

by thee I can c. a troop, and by my 2Sa 22.30
is the lot, to c. and destroy them; Est 9.24
that it would please God to c. me, Job 6.09
forgetting that a foot may c. them, 39.15
Yea, by thee I can c. a troop; Ps 18.29
to the needy, and c. the oppressor! 72.04
Thou didst c. the heads of Leviathan, 74.14
Thou didst c. Rahab like a carcass, 89.10
I will c. his foes before him and 89.23
They c. thy people, O LORD, and 94.05
or c. the afflicted at the gate; Pro 22.22
C. a fool in a mortar with a pestle 27.22
Does one c. bread grain? No, he does Is 28.28
with his horses, he does not c. it. 28.28
thresh the mountains and c. them, 41.15
against me to c. my young men; Lam 1.15
To c. under foot all the prisoners 3.34
it shall break and c. all these. Dan 2.40
who c. the needy, who say to their Amo 4.01
Thou didst c. the head of the Hab 3.13
and they shall c. the earth, and I Zec 11.06
falls on any one, it will c. him. *Mt 21.44
the crowd, lest they should c. him; Mk 3.09
it falls on any one it will c. him." Lk 20.18
peace will soon c. Satan under Rom 16.20

CRUSHED

first fruits c. new grain from Lev 2.14
part of the c. grain and of the 2.16
disease or scabs or c. testicles; 21.20
bruised or c. or torn or cut, 22.24
and burned it with fire and c. it, Deu 9.21
testicles are c. or whose male 23.01
only oppressed and c. continually; 28.33
she c. his head, she shattered and Ju 5.26
Abimelech's head, and c. his skull. 9.53
and they c. and oppressed the 10.08
I c. them and stamped them down 2Sa 22.43
twenty thousand cors of c. wheat, 2Ch 2.10
c. it, and burned it at the brook 15.16
who are c. before the moth. Job 4.19
they are c. in the gate, and there 5.04
For he has c. and abandoned the 20.19
the arms of the fatherless were c. 22.09
them in the night, and they are c. 34.25
The hapless is c., sinks down, and Ps 10.10
brokenhearted, and saves the c. in spirit. 34.18
I am utterly spent and c.; I groan 38.08
he has c. my life to the ground; 143.03
with a pestle along with c. grain, Pro 27.22
the pillars of the land will be c., Is 19.10
like chalkstones c. to pieces, 27.09
one which is c. a viper is hatched 59.05
has devoured me, he has c. me; Jer 51.34
and c. you from all sides, so that Eze 36.03
c. in judgment, because he was Hos 5.11
unbearably c. that we despaired of 2Co 1.08
afflicted in every way, but not c.; 4.08

CRUSHES

For he c. me with a tempest, and Job 9.17
and like iron which c., it shall Dan 2.40

CRUSHING

pieces its stones, c. them to dust; 2Ki 23.15
What do you mean by c. my people, Is 3.15

CRY

an exceedingly great and bitter c., Gen 27.34
and their c. under bondage came up Ex 2.23
heard their c. because of their 3.07
the c. of the people of Israel has 3.09
therefore they c., 'Let us go 5.08
be a great c. throughout all the 11.06
and there was a great c. in Egypt, 12.30
said to Moses, "Why do you c. to me? 14.15
and they c. out to me, I will surely 22.23
to me, I will surely hear their c.; 22.23
or the sound of the c. of defeat, 32.18
shall cover his upper lip and c., Lev 13.45
the congregation raised a loud c.; Num 14.01
round about them fled at their c.; 16.34
and he c. to the LORD against you, Deu 15.09
she did not c. for help though she 22.24
lest he c. against you to the LORD, 24.15
Go and c. to the gods whom you have Ju 10.14
and the c. of the city went up to 1Sa 5.12
"Do not cease to c. to the Lord our 7.08
day you will c. out because of 8.18
because their c. has come to me." 9.16
battle line, shouting the war c. 17.20
have I, then, to c. to the king?" 2Sa 19.28
my voice, and my c. came to his ears. 22.07
hearkening to the c. and to the 1Ki 8.28
"C. aloud, for he is a god; 18.27
And about sunset a c. went through 22.36
hearkening to the c. and to the 2Ch 6.19
and c. to thee in our affliction, 20.09
and hear their c. at the Red Sea, Neh 9.09
wailing with a loud and bitter c.; Est 4.01
let no joyful c. be heard in it. Job 3.07
and let my c. find no resting place. 16.18
Behold, I c. out, 'Violence!' 19.07
Will God hear his c., when trouble 27.09
I c. to thee and thou dost not 30.20
and in his disaster c. for help? 30.24
in the assembly, and c. for help. 30.28
they caused the c. of the poor to 34.28
he heard the c. of the afflicted— 34.28
of oppressions people c. out; 35.09
There they c. out, but he does not 35.12
Surely God does not hear an empty c., 35.13
they do not c. for help when he 36.13
Will your c. avail to keep you from 36.19
when its young ones c. to God, 38.41
I c. aloud to the LORD, and he Ps 3.04
Hearken to the sound of my c., 5.02
not forget the c. of the afflicted. 9.12
attend to my c.! Give ear 17.01
and my c. to him reached his ears. 18.06
O my God, I c. by day, but thou dost 22.02
when I c. aloud, be gracious to me 27.07
as I c. to thee for help, as I lift 28.02
and in his temple all c., "Glory!" 29.09
and his ears toward their c. 34.15
When the righteous c. for help, 34.17
O LORD, and give ear to my c.; 39.12
he inclined to me and heard my c. 40.01
I c. to God Most High, to God who 57.02
Hear my c., O God, listen to my 61.01
I c. aloud to God, aloud to God, that 77.01
for to thee do I c. all the day. 86.03
hearken to my c. of supplication. 86.06
I c. out in the night before thee. 88.01
thee, incline thye ar to my c.! 88.02
But I, O LORD, c. to thee; 88.13
He shall c. to me, 'Thou art my 89.26
let my c. come to thee! 102.01
distress, when he heard their c. 106.44
With my whole heart I c.; answer 119.145
I c. to thee; save me, that 119.146
I rise before dawn and c. for help; 119.147
Let my c. come before thee, O LORD; 119.169
In my distress I c. to the LORD, 120.01
Out of the depths I c. to thee, 130.01
I c. with my voice to the LORD, with 142.01
I c. to thee, O LORD; I say, Thou 142.05
Give heed to my c.; for I am 142.06
may there be no c. of distress in 144.14
fear him, he also hears their c., 145.19
and to the young ravens which c. 147.09
yes, if you c. out for insight and Pro 2.03
and my c. is to the sons of men. 8.04
his ear to the c. of the poor will 21.13

CRY (cont.)
will himself c. out and not be Pro 21.13
"Give, give," they c. Three things 30.15
righteousness, but behold, a c.! Is 5.07
knows how to c. 'My father' or 'My 8.04
C. aloud, O daughter of Gallim! 10.30
raise a signal, c. aloud to them; 13.02
Hyenas will c. in its towers, and 13.22
c., O city; melt in fear, 14.31
Heshbon and Elealeh c. out, 15.04
the armed men of Moab c. aloud; 15.04
they raise a c. of destruction; 15.05
For a c. has gone round the land of 15.08
when they c. to the LORD because of 19.20
to you at the sound of your c.; 30.19
Behold the valiant ones c. without; 33.07
the satyr shall c. to his fellow; 34.14
I c. for help until morning; 38.13
and c. to her that her warfare is 40.02
A voice says, "C.!" And I said, 40.06
And I said, "What shall I c.?" 40.06
He will not c. or lift up his voice, 42.02
now I will c. out like a woman in 42.14
forth into singing and c. aloud, 54.01
When you c. out, let your collection 57.13
"C. aloud, spare not, lift up your 58.01
you shall c., and he will say, Here 58.09
but you shall c. out for pain of 65.14
of weeping and the c. of distress. 65.19
c. aloud and say, 'Assemble, and let Jer 4.05
For I heard a c. as of a woman in 4.31
the c. of the daughter of Zion 4.31
or lift up a c. or prayer for them, 7.16
Hark, the c. of the daughter of my 8.19
though they c. to me, I will not 11.11
will go and c. to the gods to whom 11.12
or lift up a c. or prayer on their 11.14
they are in full c. after you; 12.06
and the c. of Jerusalem goes up. 14.02
fast, I will not hear their c., 14.12
May a c. be heard from their houses, 18.22
I c. out, I shout, "Violence and 20.08
let him near a c. in the morning 20.16
and c. out, and lift up your voice 22.20
c. from Abarim, for all your lovers 22.20
and c., and roll in ashes, you lords 25.34
Hark, the c. of the shepherds, and 25.36
LORD: We have heard a c. of panic, 30.05
Why do you c. out over your hurt? 30.15
and the earth is full of your c.; 46.12
Men shall c. out, and every inhabitant 47.02
a c. from Horonaim, 'Desolation and 48.03
a c. is heard as far as Zoar. 48.04
have heard the c. of destruction. 48.05
wail and c.! Tell it by 48.20
I c. out for all Moab; 48.31
"Heshbon and Elealeh c. out; 48.34
the battle c. to be heard against 49.02
C., O daughters of Rabbah! Gird 49.03
sound of their c. shall be heard 49.21
and men shall c. to them: 'Terror on 49.29
and her c. shall be heard among the 50.46
a c. from Babylon! The noise 51.54
They c. to their mothers, "Where is Lam 2.12
they c.: "We have destroyed her! 2.16
C. aloud to the Lord! O daughter 2.18
Arise, c. out in the night, at the 2.19
though I call and c. for help, 3.08
close thine ear to my c. for help! 3.56
and though they c. in my ears with Eze 8.18
C. and wail, son of man, for it is 21.12
to open the mouth with a c., 21.22
sound of the c. of your pilots the 27.28
aloud over you, and c. bitterly. 27.30
They do not c. to me from the heart, Hos 7.14
To me they c., My God, we Israel 8.02
your God; and c. to the LORD. Joe 1.14
Unto thee, O LORD, I c. For fire 1.19
Even the wild beasts c. to thee 1.20
a young lion c. out from his den, Amo 3.04
that great city, and c. against it; Jon 1.02
and let them c. mightily to God; 3.08
Then they will c. to the LORD, but Mic 3.04
who c. "Peace" when they have 3.05
Now why do you c. aloud? 4.09
they c.; but none turns Nah 2.08
LORD, how long shall I c. for help, Hab 1.02
Or c. to thee "Violence!" 1.02
For the stone will c. out from the 2.11
"a c. will be heard from the Fish Zep 1.10
and battle c. against the fortified 1.16
'C. out, Thus says the LORD of hosts: Zec 1.14
C. again, Thus says the LORD of 1.17
He will not wrangle or c. aloud, Mt 12.19
But at midnight there was a c., 25.06
he began to c. out and say, "Jesus, Mk 10.47
And Jesus uttered a loud c., 15.37
and she exclaimed with a loud c., Lk 1.42
who c. to him day and night? 18.07
the very stones would c. out." 19.40
When we c., "Abba! Father!" Rom 8.15
from heaven with a c. of command, 1Th 4.16
you kept back by fraud, c. out; Jas 5.04
And I heard the altar c., Rev 16.07

CRYING
blood is c. to me from the ground. Gen 4.10
and lo, the babe was c. She took Ex 2.06
went away, c. aloud as she went. 2Sa 13.19
c., "My father, my father! The chariots 2Ki 13.14
I am weary with my c.; my throat Ps 69.03
voice of one c. in the wilderness: Mt 3.03
c. aloud, "Have mercy on us, Son of 9.27
her away, for she is c. after us." 15.23
the children c. out in the temple, 21.15
the voice of one c. in the wilderness: Mk 1.03
convulsing him and c. with a loud 1.26
the mountains he was always c. out, 5.05
and c. out with a loud voice, he 5.07
And after c. out and convulsing him 9.26
voice of one c. in the wilderness: Lk 3.04
c., "You are the Son of God!" 4.41
Then Jesus, c. with a loud voice, 23.46
voice of one c. in the wilderness, Jn 1.23
went out to meet him, c., "Hosana! 12.13
c. with a loud voice; and many Ac 8.07
out among the multitude, c., 14.14
c., "These men are servants of the 16.17
c., "These men who have turned the 17.06
c. out, "Men of Israel, help! 21.28
followed, c., "Away with him!" 21.36
his Son into our hearts, c., "Abba! Gal 4.06
and c. out with a loud voice, Rev 7.10
heard an eagle c. with a loud 8.13
c. out, "Alas, alas, for the great 18.19
multitude in heaven, c., "Hallelujah! 19.01
And from the throne came a voice c., 19.05
thunderpeals, c., "Hallelujah! 19.06
be mourning nor c. nor pain any 21.04

CRYSTAL
shall be made of coral or of c.; Job 28.18
shining like c., spread out above Eze 1.22
as it were a sea of glass, like c. Rev 4.06
jewel, like a jasper, clear as c. 21.11
bright as c., flowing from the 22.01

CUBIT
ark, and finish it to a c. above; Gen 6.16
a c. and a half its breadth, and a Ex 25.10
and a c. and a half its height. 25.10
and a c. and a half its breadth. 25.17
its length, a c. its breadth, and 25.23
and a c. and a half its height. 25.23
And the c. on the one side, and the 26.13

CUBIT (cont.)
and the c. on the other side, of Ex 26.13
and a c. and a half the breadth of 26.16
A c. shall be its length, and a 30.02
its length, and a c. its breadth; 30.02
and a c. and a half the breadth of 36.21
a c. and a half its breadth, and a 37.01
and a c. and a half its height. 37.01
and a c. and a half its breadth. 37.06
its length, a c. its breadth, 37.10
and a c. and a half its height, 37.10
acacia wood; its length was a c., 37.25
and its breadth was a c.; it was 37.25
breadth, according to the common c. Deu 3.11
with two edges, a c. in length; Ju 3.16
which projected upward one c.; 1Ki 7.31
a c. and a half deep. At its opening 7.31
of a wheel was a c. and a half. 7.32
was a round band half a c. high; 7.35
each being a c. and a handbreadth Eze 40.05
side rooms, one c. on either side; 40.12
a c. and a half long, and a 40.42
and a c. and a half broad, and one 40.42
and one c. high, on which the 40.42
by cubits (the c. being a c. and 43.13
its base shall be one c. high, 43.13
and one c. broad, with a rim of one 43.13
cubits, with a breadth of one c.; 43.14
cubits, with a breadth of one c.; 43.14
upward, four horns, one c. high. 43.15
a rim around it half a c. broad, 43.17
and its base one c. round about. 43.17
can add one c. to his span of life? Mt 6.27
can add a c. to his span of life? Lk 12.25

CUBITS
length of the ark three hundred c., Gen 6.15
its breadth fifty c., and its 6.15
and its height thirty c. 6.15
covering them fifteen c. deep. 7.20
two c. and a half shall be its Ex 25.10
two c. and a half shall be its 25.17
two c. shall be its length, a cubit 25.23
curtain shall be twenty-eight c., 26.02
breadth of each curtain four c.; 26.02
of each curtain shall be thirty c., 26.08
breadth of each curtain four c.; 26.08
Ten c. shall be the length of a 26.16
five c. long and five c. broad; 27.01
and its height shall be three c. 27.01
linen a hundred c. long for one 27.09
be hangings a hundred c. long, 27.11
shall be hangings for fifty c., 27.12
to the east shall be fifty c. 27.13
of the gate shall be fifteen c., 27.14
the hangings shall be fifteen c., 27.15
shall be a screen twenty c. long, 27.16
of the court shall be a hundred c., 27.18
fifty, and the height five c., 27.18
and two c. shall be its height; 30.02
each curtain was twenty-eight c., 36.09
breadth of each curtain four c.; 36.09
of each curtain was thirty c., 36.15
breadth of each curtain four c.; 36.15
Ten c. was the length of a frame, 36.21
two c. and a half was its length, a 37.01
two c. and a half was its length, 37.06
two c. was its length, a cubit its 37.10
square, and two c. was its height; 37.25
five c. was its length, and five 38.01
length, and five c. its breadth; 38.01
and three c. was its height. 38.01
of fine twined linen, a hundred c.; 38.09
And for the north side a hundred c., 38.11
side were hangings of fifty c., 38.12
the front to the east, fifty c. 38.13
side of the gate were fifteen c., 38.14
court were hangings of fifteen c., 38.15
it was twenty c. long and five c. high 38.18
and about two c. deep on the face Num 11.31
outward a thousand c. all round. 35.04
for the east side two thousand c., 35.05
for the south side two thousand c., 35.05
for the west side two thousand c., 35.05
for the north side two thousand c., 35.05
Nine c. was its length, and four c. Deu 3.11
distance of about two thousand c.; Jos 3.04
whose height was six c. and a span. 1Sa 17.04
for the LORD was sixty c. long, 1Ki 6.02
twenty c. wide, and thirty c. high. 6.02
of the house was twenty c. long, 6.03
and ten c. deep in front of the 6.03
The lowest story was five c. broad, 6.06
the middle one was six c. broad, 6.06
and the third was seven c. broad; 6.06
house, each story five c. high, 6.10
He built twenty c. of the rear of 6.16
inner sanctuary, was forty c. long. 6.17
inner sanctuary was twenty c. long, 6.20
twenty c. wide, and twenty c. high; 6.20
of olivewood, each ten c. high. 6.23
Five c. was the length of one wing 6.24
and five c. the length of the other 6.24
it was ten c. from the tip of one 6.24
The other cherub also measured ten c.; 6.25
The height of one cherub was ten c., 6.26
its length was a hundred c., and its 7.02
its breadth fifty c., and its height thirty c., 7.02
its length was fifty c., and its breadth thirty c.; 7.06
stones, stones of eight and ten c. 7.10
Eighteen c. was the height of one 7.15
line of twelve c. measured its 7.15
of the one capital was five c., 7.16
of the other capital was five c. 7.16
vestibule were of lily-work, four c. 7.19
ten c. from brim to brim, and five 7.23
and five c. high, and a line of 7.23
line of thirty c. measured its 7.23
for thirty c., compassing the sea 7.24
each stand was four c. long, 7.27
four c. wide. and three c. high. 7.27
baths, each laver measured four c., 7.38
of Jerusalem for four hundred c., 2Ki 14.13
of the one pillar was eighteen c., 25.17
height of the capital was three c.; 25.17
man of great stature, five c. tall. 1Ch 11.23
in c. of the old standard, was sixty c., 2Ch 3.03
c., and the breadth twenty c. 3.03
of the house was twenty c. long, 3.04
height was a hundred and twenty c. 3.04
of the house, was twenty c., and its 3.08
and its breadth was twenty c., 3.08
together extended twenty c.: 3.11
of five c., touched the wall of the 3.11
and its other wing, of five c., 3.11
of five c., touched the wall of the 3.12
also of five c., was joined to the 3.12
these cherubim extended twenty c.; 3.13
two pillars thirty-five c. high, 3.15
capital of five c. on the top of 3.15
altar of bronze, twenty c. long, 4.01
and twenty c. wide, and ten c. high. 4.01
ten c. from brim to brim, and five 4.02
and five c. high, and a line of 4.02
a line of thirty c. measured its 4.02
for thirty c., compassing the sea 4.03
a bronze platform five c. long, 6.13
five c. wide, and three c. high, 6.13
of Jerusalem for four hundred c., 25.23
shall be sixty c. and its breadth Ez 6.03
and its breadth sixty c., 6.03
repaired a thousand c. of the wall, Neh 3.13
a gallows fifty c. high be made, Est 5.14
in Haman's house, fifty c. high. 7.09
of the one pillar was eighteen c., Jer 52.21

CUBITS (cont.)

its circumference was twelve c., Jer 52.21
of the one capital was five c.; 52.22
in the man's hand was six long c., Eze 40.05
between the side rooms, five c.; 40.07
vestibule of the gateway, eight c.; 40.08
and its jambs, two c.; and the 40.09
the opening of the gateway, ten c.; 40.11
of the gateway, thirteen c. 40.11
rooms were six c. on either side. 40.12
a breadth of five and twenty c.; 40.13
also the vestibule, twenty c.; 40.14
vestibule of the gate was fifty c. 40.15
of the inner court, a hundred c. 40.19
first gate; its length was fifty c., 40.21
and its breadth twenty-five c. 40.21
from gate to gate, a hundred c. 40.23
the others; its length was fifty c., 40.25
and its breadth twenty-five c. 40.25
toward the south, a hundred c. 40.27
vestibule; its length was fifty c., 40.29
and its breadth twenty-five c. 40.29
twenty-five c. long and five c. broad. 40.30
vestibule; its length was fifty c., 40.33
and its breadth twenty-five c. 40.33
round about; its length was fifty c., 40.36
and its breadth twenty-five c. 40.36
a hundred c. long, and a hundred 40.47
and a hundred c. broad, foursquare; 40.47
vestibule, five c. on either side; 40.48
of the gate was fourteen c.; 40.48
gate were three c. on either side. 40.48
of the vestibule was twenty c., 40.49
and the breadth twelve c.; 40.49
each side six c. was the breadth 41.01
breadth of the entrance was ten c.; 41.02
were five c. on either side; 41.02
the length of the nave forty c., 41.02
and its breadth, twenty c. 41.02
the jambs of the entrance, two c.; 41.03
breadth of the entrance, six c.; 41.03
sidewalls of the entrance, seven c. 41.03
twenty c., and its breadth, twenty 41.04
twenty c., beyond the nave. 41.04
wall of the temple, six c. thick; 41.05
four c., round about the temple. 41.05
measured a full reed of six long c. 41.08
of the side chambers was five c.; 41.09
which was left free was five c. 41.09
of twenty c. round about the 41.10
left free was five c. round about. 41.11
the west side was seventy c. broad; 41.12
was five c. thick round about, and 41.12
and its length ninety c. 41.12
the temple, a hundred c. long; 41.13
with its walls, a hundred c. long; 41.13
temple and the yard, a hundred c. 41.14
walls on either side, a hundred c. 41.15
three c. high, two c. long, and 41.22
two c. long, and two c. broad; 41.22
on the north side was a hundred c., 42.02
c., and the breadth fifty c. 42.02
Adjoining the twenty c. which 42.03
ten c. wide and a hundred c. long, 42.04
the chambers, fifty c. long. 42.07
the outer court were fifty c. long, 42.08
the temple were a hundred c. long. 42.08
five hundred c. by the measuring 42.16
five hundred c. by the measuring 42.17
five hundred c. by the measuring 42.18
five hundred c. by the measuring 42.19
five hundred c. long and five 42.20
long and five hundred c. broad, 42.20
of the altar by c. (the cubit 43.13
two c., with a breadth of one cubit; 43.14
ledge to the larger ledge, four c., 43.14
and the altar hearth, four c.; 43.15
twelve c. long by twelve broad. 43.16
fourteen c. long by fourteen broad, 43.17
twenty-five thousand c. long and 45.01
long and twenty thousand c. broad; 45.01
by five hundred c. shall be for 45.02
with fifty c. for an open space 45.02
thousand c. long and ten thousand 45.03
thousand c. long and ten thousand 45.05
long and ten thousand c. broad, 45.05
an area five thousand c. broad, 45.06
and twenty-five thousand c. long; 45.06
forty c. long and thirty broad; 46.22
the man measured a thousand c., 47.03
twenty-five thousand c. in breadth, 48.08
twenty-five thousand c. in length, 48.09
thousand c. on the northern side, 48.10
ten thousand c. in breadth on the 48.10
thousand c. in length and ten 48.13
thousand c. and the breadth twenty 48.13
five thousand c. in breadth and 48.15
side four thousand five hundred c., 48.16
the north two hundred and fifty c., 48.17
be ten thousand c. to the east, 48.18
be twenty-five thousand c. square, 48.20
thousand c. of the holy portion to 48.21
thousand c. to the west border, 48.21
five hundred c. by measure, 48.30
be four thousand five hundred c., 48.32
thousand five hundred c. by measure, 48.33
be four thousand five hundred c., 48.34
was sixty c. and its breadth six c. Dan 3.01
cubits and its breadth six c. 3.01
its length is twenty c., Zec 5.02
and its breadth ten c. 5.02
and forty-four c. by a man's Rev 21.17

CUBS

bear robbed of her c. in the field. 2Sa 17.08
meet a she-bear robbed of her c., Pro 17.12
them like a bear robbed of her c., Hos 13 08
where his c. were, with none to Nah 2.11

CUCUMBER

vineyard, like a lodge in a c. field, Is 1.08
are like scarecrows in a c. field, Jer 10.05

CUCUMBERS

the c., the melons, the leeks, the Num 11.05

CUD

is cloven-footed and chews the c., Lev 11.03
that chew the c. or part the hoof, 11.04
it chews the c. but does not part 11.04
it chews the c. but does not part 11.05
it chews the c. but does not part 11.06
cloven-footed but does not chew the c., 11.07
not chew the c. is unclean to you; 11.26
and chews the c., among the animals, Deu 14.06
that chew the c. or have the hoof 14.07
they chew the c. but do not part 14.07
the hoof but does not chew the c., 14.08

CULT

"There shall be no c. prostitute of Deu 23.17
there be a c. prostitute of the 23.17
were also male c. prostitutes in 1Ki 14.24
away the male c. prostitutes out 15.12
of the male c. prostitutes who 22.46
houses of the c. prostitutes which 2Ki 23.07
and sacrifice with c. prostitutes, Hos 4.14

CULTIVATE

cattle, and plants for man to c., Ps 104.14

CULTIVATED

advantage to a land with a c. fields. Ecc 5.09
into a c. olive tree, how much more Rom 11.24
to those for whose sake it is c., Heb 6.07

CUMI
hand he said to her, "Talitha c."; Mk 5.41

CUMMIN
sow c., and put in wheat in rows Is 28.25
nor is a cartwheel rolled over c.; 28.27
with a stick, and c. with a rod. 28.27
for you tithe mint and dill and c., Mt 23.23

CUN
And from Tibhath and from C., 1Ch 18.08

CUNNING
they on their part acted with c., Jos 9.04
it is told me that he is very c. 1Sa 23.22
did it with c. in order to destroy 2Ki 10.19
of charmers or of the c. enchanter. Ps 58.05
thy statutes; yea, their c. is in vain. 119.118
By his c. he shall make deceit Dan 8.25
to practice c. or to tamper with 2Co 4.02
the serpent deceived Eve by his c., 11.03
by the c. of men, by their craftiness Eph 4.14

CUNNINGLY
thought out a c. conceived plot. Ps 64.06

CUP
Pharaoh's c. was in my hand; Gen 40.11
and pressed them into Pharaoh's c., 40.11
and placed the c. in Pharaoh's hand." 40.11
place Pharaoh's c. in his hand as 40.13
he placed the c. in Pharaoh's hand; 40.21
and put my c., the silver c., in 44.02
Why have you stolen my silver c.? 44.04
and the c. was found in Benjamin's 44.12
whose hand the c. has been found." 44.16
whose hand the c. was found shall 44.17
his morsel, and drink from his c., 2Sa 12.03
was made like the brim of a c., 1Ki 7.26
was made like the brim of a c., 2Ch 4.05
shall be the portion of their c. Ps 11.06
is my chosen portion and my c.; 16.05
my head with oil, my c. overflows. 23.05
the hand of the LORD there is a c., 75.08
lift up the c. of salvation and 116.13
sparkles in the c. and goes down Pro 23.31
of the LORD the c. of his wrath, Is 51.17
your hand the c. of staggering; 51.22
give him the c. of consolation to Jer 16.07
my hand this c. of the wine of 25.15
So I took the c. from the LORD's 25.17
to accept the c. from your hand to 25.28
to drink the c. must drink it, 49.12
Babylon was a golden c. in the 51.07
but to you also the c. shall pass; Lam 4.21
I will give her c. into your hand. Eze 23.31
your sister's c. which is deep and 23.32
A c. of horror and desolation, is 23.33
is the c. of your sister Samaria; 23.33
drink of the c. of his wrath, Hab 2.15
The c. in the LORD's right hand will 2.16
Jerusalem a c. of reeling to all Zec 12.02
ones even a c. of cold water Mt 10.42
to drink the c. that I am to drink?" 20.22
said to them, "You will drink my c., 20.23
outside of the c. and of the plate, 23.25
inside of the c. and of the plate, 23.26
And he took a c., and when he had 26.27
possible, let this c. pass from me; 26.39
gives you a c. of water to drink Mk 9.41
able to drink the c. that I drink, 10.38
"The c. that I drink you will drink; 10.39
And he took a c., and when he had 14.23
remove this c. from me; yet not what 14.36
outside of the c. and of the dish, Lk 11.39
And he took a c., and when he had 22.17
likewise the c. after supper, * 22.20
"This c. which is poured out for * 22.20
willing, remove this c. from me; 22.42
I not drink the c. which the Jn 18.11
The c. of blessing which we bless, 1Co 10.16
drink the c. of the Lord and the 10.21
of the Lord and the c. of demons. 10.21
In the same way also the c., 11.25
"This c. is the new covenant in my 11.25
eat this bread and drink the c., 11.26
or drinks the c. of the Lord in an 11.27
of the bread and drink of the c. 11.28
unmixed into the c. of his anger, Rev 14.10
her drain the c. of the fury of 16.19
hand a golden c. full of abominations 17.04
for her in the c. she mixed. 18.06

CUPBEARER
Now I was c. to the king. Neh 1.11

CUPBEARERS
his c., and his burnt offerings 1Ki 10.05
his c., and their clothing, and his 2Ch 9.04

CUPS
its c., its capitals, and its Ex 25.31
three c. made like almonds, each 25.33
itself four c. made like almonds, 25.34
its c., its capitals, and its 37.17
three c. made like almonds, each 37.19
were four c. made like almonds, 37.20
the c., snuffers, basins, dishes for 1Ki 7.50
the forks, the basins, and the c.; 1Ch 28.17
from the c. to all the flagons. Is 22.24
and fill c. of mixed wine for 65.11
pitchers full of wine, and c.; Jer 35.05
the washing of c. and pots and Mk 7.04

CURBED
which must be c. with bit and Ps 32.09

CURDLE
like milk and c. me like cheese? Job 10.10

CURDS
Then he took c., and milk, and the Gen 18.08
C. from the herd, and milk from the Deu 32.14
she brought him c. in a lordly Ju 5.25
honey and c. and sheep and cheese 2Sa 17.29
streams flowing with honey and c. Job 20.17
For pressing milk produces c., Pro 30.33
He shall eat c. and honey when he Is 7.15
which they give, he will eat c.; 7.22
in the land will eat c. and honey. 7.22

CURE
He would c. him of his leprosy." 2Ki 5.03
that you may c. him of his leprosy." 5.06
word to me to c. a man of his 5.07
over the place, and c. the leper. 5.11
is not able to c. you or heal your Hos 5.13
all demons and to c. diseases, Lk 9.01

CURED
him, and the boy was c. instantly. Mt 17.18
with unclean spirits were c. Lk 6.18
In that hour he c. many of diseases 7.21
and c. those who had need of 9.11
Jews said to the man who was c., Jn 5.10
had diseases also came and were c. Ac 28.09

CURES
and perform c. today and tomorrow, Lk 13.32

CURRENT
to the weights c. among the Gen 23.16

CURSE
never again c. the ground because Gen 8.21
and him who curses you I will c.; 12.03
and bring a c. upon myself and not 27.12

CURSE (cont.)

to him, "Upon me be your c., my son; Gen 27.13
nor c. a ruler of your people. Ex 22.28
You shall not c. the deaf or put a Lev 19.14
of bitterness that brings the c. Num 5.18
of bitterness that brings the c. 5.19
the woman take the oath of the c., 5.21
that brings the c. pass into your 5.22
of bitterness that brings the c. 5.24
the water that brings the c. shall 5.24
that brings the c. shall enter 5.27
Come now, c. this people for me, 22.06
and he whom you c. is cursed." 22.06
now come, c. them for me; 22.11
you shall not c. the people, for 22.12
come, c. this people for me.'" 22.17
c. Jacob for me, and come, denounce 23.07
How can I c. whom God has not 23.08
I took you to c. my enemies, and 23.11
then c. them for me from there." 23.13
"Neither c. them at all, nor bless 23.25
that you may c. them for me from 23.27
"I called you to c. my enemies, 24.10
you this day a blessing and a c.: Deu 11.26
and the c., if you do not obey the 11.28
Gerizim and the c. on Mount Ebal. 11.29
Pethor of Mesopotamia, to c. you. 23.04
God turned the c. into a blessing 23.05
stand upon Mount Ebal for the c.: 27.13
upon you, the blessing and the c., 30.01
life and death, blessing and c.; 30.19
the law, the blessing and the c., Jos 8.34
Balaam the son of Beor to c. you, 24.09
"C. Meroz, says the angel of the Ju 5.23
c. bitterly its inhabitants, because 5.23
them came the c. of Jotham the son 9.57
you, about which you uttered a c., 17.02
this dead dog c. my lord the king 2Sa 16.09
'C. David,' who then shall say, 'Why 16.10
Let him alone, and let him c.; 16.11
with a grievous c. on the day when 1Ki 2.08
become a desolation and a c., 2Ki 22.19
enter into a c. and an oath to Neh 10.29
Balaam against them to c. them— 13.02
God turned the c. into a blessing. 13.02
and he will c. thee to thy face. Job 1.11
and he will c. thee to thy face. 2.05
your integrity? C. God, and die." 2.09
Let those c. it who c. the day, 3.08
by asking for his life with a c.: 31.30
their mouths, but inwardly they c. Ps 63.04
who deride me use my name for a c. 102.08
He loved to c.; let curses come 109.17
Let them c., but do thou bless! 109.28
The LORD's c. is on the house of the Pro 3.33
The people c. him who holds back 11.26
a c. that is causeless does not 26.02
hides his eyes will get many a c. 28.27
he hears the c., but discloses 29.24
lest he c. you, and you be held 30.10
There are those who c. their 30.11
do not c. the king, nor in your Ecc 10.20
nor in your bedchamber c. the rich; 10.20
and will c. their king and their Is 8.21
Therefore a c. devours the earth, 24.06
your name to my chosen for a c., 65.15
I borrowed, yet all of them c. me. Jer 15.10
because of the c. the land mourns, 23.10
and a c. in all the places where I 24.09
and a waste, a hissing and a c., 25.18
this city a c. for all the nations 26.06
to be a c., a terror, a hissing, and 29.18
Because of them this c. shall be 29.22
a horror, a c., and a taunt. You shall 42.18
and become a c. and a taunt among 44.08
a horror, a c., and a taunt. 44.12
a desolation and a waste and a c., 44.22
horror, a taunt, a waste, and a c.; 49.13
of heart; thy c. will be on them. Lam 3.65
And the c. and oath which are Dan 9.11
"This is the c. that goes out over Zec 5.03
for there shall be no more c.; 14.11
I will send the c. upon you and I Mal 2.02
you and I will c. your blessings; 2.02
You are cursed with a c., for you are 3.09
come and smite the land with a c." 4.06
to invoke a c. on himself and to Mt 26.74
to invoke a c. on himself and to Mk 14.71
bless those who c. you, Lk 6.28
bless and do not c. them. Rom 12.14
on works of the law are under a c.; Gal 3.10
redeemed us from the c. of the law, 3.13
having become a c. for us—for it 3.13
and Father, and with it we c. men, Jas 3.09

CURSED

c. are you above all cattle, and Gen 3.14
c. is the ground because of you; 3.17
And now you are c. from the ground, 4.11
the LORD has c. this one shall 5.29
he said, "C. be Canaan; a slave 9.25
C. be every one who curses you, and 27.29
C. be their anger, for it is fierce; 49.07
he has c. his father or his mother, Lev 20.09
son blasphemed the Name, and c. 24.11
"Bring out of the camp him who c.; 24.14
him who had c. out of the camp, and 24.23
and he whom you curse is c." Num 22.06
How can I curse whom God has not c.? 23.08
and c. be every one who curses you." 24.09
" 'C. be the man who makes a graven Deu 27.15
" 'C. be he who dishonors his father 27.16
" 'C. be he who removes his neighbor's 27.17
" 'C. be who misleads a blind man 27.18
" 'C. be he who perverts the justice 27.19
" 'C. be he who lies with his father's 27.20
" 'C. be he who lies with any kind 27.21
" 'C. be he who lies with his sister, 27.22
" 'C. be he who lies with his mother-in-law.' 27.33
" 'C. be he who slays his neighbor 27.24
" 'C. be he who takes a bribe to 27.25
" 'C. be he who does not confirm the 27.26
C. shall you be in the city, and 28.16
and c. shall you be in the field. 28.16
C. shall be your basket and your 28.17
C. shall be the fruit of your body, 28.18
C. shall you be when you come in, 28.19
and c. shall you be when you go out. 28.19
"C. before the LORD be the man that Jos 6.26
Now therefore you are c., and some 9.23
"C. be he who gives a wife to Ju 21.18
"C. be the man who eats food until 1Sa 14.24
'C. be the man who eats food this 14.28
the Philistine c. David by his 17.43
may they be c. before the LORD, for 26.19
and as he came he c. continually. 2Sa 16.05
And Shimei said as he c., "Begone, 16.07
opposite him and c. as he went, 16.13
because he c. the LORD's anointed 19.21
who c. me with a grievous curse on 1Ki 2.08
'You have c. God and the king. 21.10
"Naboth c. God and the king.' 21.13
he c. them in the name of the LORD. 2Ki 2.24
he said, "See now to this c. woman, 9.34
with them and c. them and beat Neh 13.25
and c. God in their hearts." Thus Job Job 1.05
his mouth and c. the day of his 3.01
but suddenly I c. his dwelling. 5.03
their portion is c. in the land; 24.18
but those c. by him shall be cut Ps 37.22
will be c. by peoples, abhorred by Pro 24.24
times you have yourself c. others. Ecc 7.22
C. be the man who does not heed the Jer 11.03
"C. is the man who trusts in man 17.05

CURSED (cont.)
C. be the day on which I was born! Jer 20.14
C. be the man who brought the news 20.15
"C. is he who does the work of the 48.10
and c. is he who keeps back his 48.10
C. be the cheat who has a male in Mal 1.14
indeed I have already c. them, 2.02
You are c. with a curse, for you are 3.09
you c., into the eternal fire Mt 25.41
fig tree which you c. has withered." Mk 11.21
of God ever says "Jesus be c.!" 1Co 12.03
"C. be every one who does not abide Gal 3.10
"C. be every one who hangs on a 3.13
is worthless and near to being c.; Heb 6.08
and they c. the name of God who had Rev 16.09
and c. the God of heaven for their 16.11
till men c. God for the plague of 16.21

CURSES
and him who c. you I will curse; Gen 12.03
Cursed be every one who c. you, 27.29
"Whoever c. his father or his Ex 21.17
For every one who c. his father or Lev 20.09
Whoever c. his God shall bear his 24.15
shall write these c. in a book, Num 5.23
and cursed be every one who c. you." 24.09
then all these c. shall come upon Deu 28.15
"The LORD will send upon you c., 28.20
All these c. shall come upon you 28.45
and the c. written in this book 29.20
with all the c. of the covenant 29.21
upon it all the c. written in this 29.27
put all these c. upon your foes 30.07
all the c. that are written in the 2Ch 34.24
greedy for gain c. and renounces Ps 10.03
let c. come on him! He did not 109.17
If one c. his father or his mother, Pro 20.20
mouth is full of c. and bitterness." Rom 3.14

CURSING
If he is c. because the LORD has 2Sa 16.10
with good for this c. of me today." 16.12
is filled with c. and deceit and Ps 10.07
For the c. and lies which they 59.12
himself with c. as his coat, 109.18
the morning, will be counted as c. Pro 27.14
lest you hear your servant c. you; Ecc 7.21
a byword of c. among the nations, O Zec 8.13
same mouth come blessing and c. Jas 3.10

CURTAIN
The length of each c. shall be Ex 26.02
the breadth of each c. four cubits; 26.02
of the outmost c. in the first set; 26.04
loops on the edge of the outmost c. in 26.04
loops you shall make on the one c., 26.05
edge of the c. that is in the second 26.05
The length of each c. shall be 26.08
the breadth of each c. four cubits; 26.08
and the sixth c. you shall double 26.09
the edge of the c. that is outmost 26.10
the c. which is outmost in the second 26.10
the half c. that remains, shall hang 26.12
The length of each c. was twenty-eight 36.09
the breadth of each c. four cubits; 36.09
of the outmost c. of the first set; 36.11
of the outmost c. of the second 36.11
he made fifty loops on the one c., 36.12
the edge of the c. that was in the 36.12
The length of each c. was thirty 36.15
the breadth of each c. four cubits; 36.15
of the outmost c. of the one set, 36.17
edge of the other connecting c. 36.17
stretches out the heavens like a c., Is 40.22
the c. of the temple was torn in Mt 27.51
And the c. of the temple was torn Mk 15.38
and the c. of the temple was torn Lk 23.45
the inner shrine behind the c., Heb 6.19
Behind the second c. stood a tent 9.03
he opened for us through the c., 10.20

CURTAINS
with ten c. of fine twined linen Ex 26.01
all the c. shall have one measure. 26.02
Five c. shall be coupled to one 26.03
the other five c. shall be coupled 26.03
and couple the c. one to the other 26.06
"You shall also make c. of goats' 26.07
eleven c. shall you make. 26.07
the eleven c. shall have the same 26.08
shall couple five c. by themselves, 26.09
and six c. by themselves, and the 26.09
that remains of the c. of the tent, 26.12
length of the c. of the tent shall 26.13
made the tabernacle with ten c.; 36.08
all the c. had the same measure. 36.09
And he coupled five c. to one another, 36.10
the other five c. he coupled to one 36.10
and coupled the c. one to the 36.13
He also made c. of goats' hair for 36.14
over the tabernacle; he made eleven c. 36.14
the eleven c. had the same measure. 36.15
He coupled five c. by themselves, 36.16
themselves, and six c. by themselves. 36.16
they shall carry the c. of the Num 4.25
white cotton c. and blue hangings Est 1.06
of Kedar, like the c. of Solomon. Sol 1.05
and let the c. of your habitations Is 54.02
are destroyed, my c. in a moment. Jer 4.20
my tent again, and to set up my c. 10.20
their c. and all their goods; 49.29
the c. of the land of Midian did Hab 3.07

CUSH
flows around the whole land of C. Gen 2.13
C., Egypt, Put, and Canaan. 10.06
The sons of C.: Seba, Havilah, Sabtah, 10.07
C. became the father of Nimrod; 10.08
C., Egypt, Put, and Canaan. 1Ch 1.08
The sons of C.: Seba, Havilah, Sabta, 1.09
C. was the father of Nimrod; 1.10
Persia, C., and Put are with them, Eze 38.05

CUSHAN
I saw the tents of C. in affliction; Hab 3.07

CUSHANRISHATHAIM
the hand of C. king of Mesopotamia Ju 3.08
of Israel served C. eight years. 3.08
the LORD gave C. king of Mesopotamia 3.10
and his hand prevailed over C. 3.10

CUSHI
son of C., to say to Baruch, "Take Jer 36.14
came to Zephaniah the son of C., Zep 1.01

CUSHION
was in the stern, asleep on the c.; Mk 4.38

CUSHITE
because of the C. woman whom he Num 12.01
for he had married a C. woman; 12.01
Then Joab said to the C., "Go, tell 2Sa 18.21
The C. bowed before Joab, and ran. 18.21
may, let me also run after the C." 18.22
of the plain, and outran the C. 18.23
And behold, the C. came; and the C. 18.31
The king said to the C., "Is it 18.32
And the C. answered, "May the 18.32

CUSTODIAN
the law was our c. until Christ Gal 3.24
come, we are no longer under a c.; 3.25

CUSTODY
and he put them in c. in the house Gen 40.03
they continued for some time in c. 40.04

CUSTODY (cont.)

with him in c. in his master's Gen 40.07
chief baker in c. in the house of 41.10
And they put him in c., till the Lev 24.12
They put him in c., because it Num 15.34
under c. of Hegai the king's eunuch Est 2.03
in Susa the capital in c. of Hegai, 2.08
and put in c. of Hegai who had 2.08
second harem in c. of Shaashgaz 2.14
they brought him into c., that his Eze 19.09
and put them in c. until the Ac 4.03
be kept in c. but should have some 24.23
to be kept in c. for the decision 25.21

CUSTOM

And it became a c. in Israel Ju 11.39
Now this was the c. in former times Ru 4.07
The c. of the priests with the 1Sa 2.13
Such was his c. all the while he 27.11
after their c. with swords and 1Ki 18.28
by the pillar, according to the c., 2Ki 11.14
c., or toll, and the royal revenue Ez 4.13
tribute, c., and toll were paid. 4.20
c., or toll upon any one of the 7.24
as his c. was, he taught them. Mk 10.01
according to the c. of the priesthood, Lk 1.09
according to the c. of the law, 2.27
old, they went up according to c.; 2.42
as his c. was, on the sabbath day. 4.16
as was his c., to the Mount of 22.39
But you have a c. that I should Jn 18.39
as is the burial c. of the Jews. 19.40
according to the c. of Moses, Ac 15.01
as was his c., and for three weeks 17.02
it was not the c. of the Romans to 25.16

CUSTOMS

abominable c. which were practiced Lev 18.30
not walk in the c. of the nation 20.23
and walked in the c. of the nations 2Ki 17.08
and in the c. which the kings of Israel 17.08
walked in the c. which Israel had 17.19
for the c. of the peoples are false. Jer 10.03
will change the c. which Moses Ac 6.14
They advocate c. which it is not 16.21
their children or observe the c. 21.21
with all c. and controversies of 26.03
people or the c. of our fathers, 28.17

CUT

all flesh be c. off by the waters Gen 9.11
c. them in two, and laid each half 15.10
but he did not c. the birds in two. 15.10
shall be c. off from his people; 17.14
and he c. the wood for the burnt 22.03
a flint and c. off her son's Ex 4.25
would have been c. off from the 9.15
person shall be c. off from Israel. 12.15
person shall be c. off from the 12.19
Then you shall c. the ram into 29.17
shall be c. off from his people.' " 30.33
shall be c. off from his people." 30.38
soul shall be c. off from among 31.14
"C. two tables of stone like the 34.01
So Moses c. two tables of stone 34.04
pillars, and c. down their Asherim 34.13
hammered out and c. into threads to 39.03
offering and c. it into pieces; Lev 1.06
And he shall c. it into pieces, with 1.12
person shall be c. off from his 7.20
person shall be c. off from his 7.21
LORD shall be c. off from his 7.25
person shall be c. off from his 7.27
And when the ram was c. into pieces, 8.20
man shall be c. off from among his 17.04
man shall be c. off from his 17.09
and will c. him off from among his 17.10
whoever eats it shall be c. off. 17.14
them shall be c. off from among 18.29
person shall be c. off from his 19.08
and will c. him off from among his 20.03
and will c. them off from among 20.05
and will c. him off from among his 20.06
they shall be c. off in the sight 20.17
them shall be c. off from among 20.18
person shall be c. off from my 22.03
bruised or crushed or torn or c., 22.24
day shall be c. off from his 23.29
and c. down your incense altars, and 26.30
person shall be c. off from his Num 9.13
and c. down from there a branch 13.23
men of Israel c. down from there. 13.24
person shall be c. off from among 15.30
person shall be utterly c. off; 15.31
person shall be c. off from Israel; 19.13
person shall be c. off from the 19.20
you shall not c. yourselves or make Deu 14.01
forest with his neighbor to c. wood, 19.05
swings the axe to c. down a tree, 19.05
but you shall not c. them down. 20.19
may destroy and c. down that you 20.20
male member is c. off shall not 23.01
then you shall c. off her hand; 25.12
and c. off at your rear all who 25.18
the Salt Sea, were wholly c. off; Jos 3.16
the Jordan were c. off before the 4.07
waters of the Jordan were c. off. 4.07
and c. off our name from the earth; 7.09
nations that I have already c. off, 23.04
and c. off his thumbs and his great Ju 1.06
great toes c. off used to pick up 1.07
and c. down the Asherah that is 6.25
Asherah which you shall c. down." 6.26
the Asherah beside it was c. down, 6.28
of Baal and c. down the Asherah 6.30
and c. down a bundle of brushwood, 9.48
of the people c. down his bundle 9.49
my concubine and c. her in pieces, 20.06
of them were c. down in the 20.45
"One tribe is c. off from Israel 21.06
dead may not be c. off from among Ru 4.10
wicked shall be c. off in darkness; 1Sa 2.09
when I will c. off your strength 2.31
I shall not c. off from my altar 2.33
were lying c. off upon the threshold; 5.04
and c. them in pieces and sent them 11.07
and c. down the Ammonites until the 11.11
you down, and c. off your head; 17.46
and c. off his head with it. 17.51
and do not c. off your loyalty from 20.15
of Jonathan be c. off from the 20.16
and stealthily c. off the skirt of 24.04
because he had c. off Saul's skirt. 24.05
the fact that I c. off the skirt 24.11
you will not c. off my descendants 24.21
how he has c. off the mediums and 28.09
And they c. off his head, and 31.09
and c. off their hands and feet, and 2Sa 4.12
and have c. off all your enemies 7.09
and c. off their garments in the 10.04
And when he c. the hair of his head 14.26
end of every year he used to c. it; 14.26
he c. it, he weighed the hair of 14.26
And they c. off the head of Sheba 20.22
cedars of Lebanon be c. for me; 1Ki 5.06
knows how to c. timber like the 5.06
then I will c. off Israel from the 9.07
until he had c. off every male in 11.16
so as to c. it off and to destroy 13.34
and will c. off from Jeroboam every 14.10
who shall c. off the house of 14.14
and Asa c. down her image and 15.13
and when Jezebel c. off the prophets 18.04
and c. it in pieces and lay it on 18.23
and c. themselves after their 18.28

CUT (cont.)

and c. the bull in pieces and laid	1Ki 18.33
and will c. off from Ahab every	21.21
and came and c. them up into the	2Ki 4.39
to the Jordan, they c. down trees.	6.04
he c. off a stick, and threw it in	6.06
and I will c. off from Ahab every	9.08
LORD began to c. off parts of	10.32
And King Ahaz c. off the frames of	16.17
and c. down the Asherah. And he	18.04
and c. down the Asherim, and filled	23.14
and c. in pieces all the vessels of	24.13
and have c. off all your enemies	1Ch 17.08
and c. off their garments in the	19.04
know how to c. timber in Lebanon.	2Ch 2.08
servants, the hewers who c. timber,	2.10
and we will c. whatever timber you	2.16
Asa c. down her image, crushed it,	15.16
of God and c. in pieces the	28.24
who c. off all the mighty warriors	32.21
Or where were the upright c. off?	Job 4.07
let loose his hand and c. me off!	6.09
While yet in flower and not c. down,	8.12
if it be c. down, that it will	14.07
number of their months is c. off?	21.21
'Surely our adversaries are c. off,	22.20
they are c. off like the heads of	24.24
and c. off pride from man;	33.17
peoples are c. off in their place.	36.20
May the LORD c. off all flattering	Ps 12.03
to c. off the remembrance of them	34.16
For the wicked shall be c. off;	37.09
cursed by him shall be c. off.	37.22
of the wicked shall be c. off.	37.28
of the wicked shall be c. off.	37.38
horns of the wicked he will c. off,	75.10
it with fire, they have c. it down;	80.16
for they are c. off from thy hand.	88.05
Thou hast c. short the days of his	89.45
May his posterity be c. off;	109.13
his memory be c. off from the	109.15
the name of the LORD I c. them off!	118.10
the name of the LORD I c. them off!	118.11
the name of the LORD I c. them off!	118.12
he has c. the cords of the wicked.	129.04
steadfast love c. off my enemies,	143.12
corner pillars c. for the structure	144.12
wicked will be c. off from the	Pro 2.22
the perverse tongue will be c. off.	10.31
and your hope will not be c. off.	23.18
and your hope will not be c. off.	24.14
the sycamores have been c. down,	Is 9.10
So the LORD c. off from Israel head	9.14
and to c. off nations not a few;	10.07
He will c. down the thickets of the	10.34
who harass Judah shall be c. off;	11.13
How you are c. down to the ground,	14.12
"and will c. off from Babylon name	14.22
he will c. off the shoots with	18.05
and it will be c. down and fall,	22.25
burden that was upon it will be c. off,	22.25
watch to do evil shall be c. off,	29.20
like thorns c. down, that are burned	33.12
of bronze and c. asunder the bars	45.02
for you, that I may not c. you off.	48.09
would never be c. off or destroyed	48.19
thou that didst c. Rahab in pieces,	51.09
that he was c. off out of the land	53.08
sign which shall not be c. off."	55.13
name which shall not be c. off.	56.05
it is c. off from their lips.	Jer 7.28
C. off your hair and cast it away;	7.29
the desert that c. the corners of	9.26
a tree from the forest is c. down,	10.03
let us c. him off from the land of	11.19
for them or c. himself or make	16.06
and they shall c. down your choicest	22.07
and all who c. the corners of their	25.23
calf which they c. in two and	34.18
the king would c. them off with a	36.23
and will c. off from it man and	36.29
to c. off from you man and woman,	44.07
that you may be c. off and become	44.08
you for evil, to c. off all Judah.	44.11
They shall c. down her forest, says	46.23
to c. off from Tyre and Sidone every	47.04
let us c. her off from being a	48.02
The horn of Moab is c. off, and his	48.25
is shaved and every beard c. off;	48.37
wind those who c. the corners of	49.32
C. off from Babylon the sower, and	50.16
whole earth is c. down and broken!	50.23
Be not c. off in her punishment, for	51.06
the thread of your life is c.	51.13
place that thou wilt c. it off,	51.62
He has c. down in fierce anger all	Lam 2.03
therefore I will c. you down;	Eze 5.11
your incense altars c. down,	6.06
a byword and c. him off from the	14.08
and c. off from it man and beast,	14.13
and I c. off from it man and beast;	14.17
to c. off from it man and beast;	14.19
to c. off from it man and beast!	14.21
born your navel string was not c.,	16.04
stone you and c. you to pieces	16.40
its roots and c. off its branches,	17.09
walls built to c. off many lives.	17.17
and will c. off from you both	21.03
Because I will c. off from you both	21.04
C. sharply to right and left where	21.16
They shall c. off your nose and	23.25
and I will c. you off from the	25.07
and c. off from it man and beast;	25.13
and I will c. off the Cherethites,	25.16
and will c. off from you man and	29.08
and c. off the multitude of Thebes.	30.15
will c. it down and leave it.	31.12
and I will c. off from it all who	35.07
is lost; we are clean c. off.'	37.11
of the field or c. down any out of	39.10
a stone was c. out by no human hand,	Dan 2.34
a stone was c. from a mountain by	2.45
the tree and c. off its branches,	4.14
an anointed one shall be c. off,	9.26
of Israel shall be utterly c. off.	Hos 10.15
for it is c. off from your mouth.	Joe 1.05
offering are c. off from the house	1.09
Is not the food c. off before our	1.16
and c. off the inhabitants from the	Amo 1.05
I will c. off the inhabitants from	1.08
I will c. off the ruler from its	2.03
altar shall be c. off and fall to	3.14
Esau will be c. off by slaughter.	Ob 1.09
and you shall be c. off for ever.	1.10
of the ways to c. off his fugitives;	1.14
yourselves bald and c. off your hair,	Mic 1.16
all your enemies shall be c. off.	5.09
I will c. off your horses from	5.10
and I will c. off the cities of	5.11
and I will c. off sorceries from	5.12
and I will c. off your images and	5.13
they will be c. off and pass away.	Nah 1.12
gods I will c. off the graven	1.14
against you, he is utterly c. off.	1.15
I will c. off your prey from the	2.13
you, the sword will c. you off.	3.15
the flock be c. off from the fold	Hab 3.17
I will c. off mankind from the face	Zep 1.03
and I will c. off from this place	1.04
who weigh out silver are c. off.	1.11
"I have c. off nations; their	3.06
steals shall be c. off henceforth	Zec 5.03
shall be c. off henceforth according	5.03
I will c. off the chariot from	9.10

CUT (cont.)
and the battle bow shall be c. off, Zec 9.10
I will c. off the names of the 13.02
thirds shall be c. off and perish, 13.08
shall not be c. off from the city. 14.02
May the LORD c. off from the tents Mal 2.12
good fruit is c. down and thrown Mt 3.10
c. it off and throw it away; 5.30
good fruit is c. down and thrown 7.19
c. it off and throw it from you; 18.08
and others c. branches from the 21.08
high priest, and c. off his ear. 26.51
hand causes you to sin, c. it off; Mk 9.43
foot causes you to sin, c. it off; 9.45
which they had c. from the fields. 11.08
the high priest and c. off his ear. 14.47
good fruit is c. down and thrown Lk 3.09
C. it down; why should it 13.07
but if not, you can c. it down.' " 13.09
high priest and c. off his right 22.50
slave and c. off his right ear. Jn 18.10
the man whose ear Peter had c. off, 18.26
this they were c. to the heart, Ac 2.37
At Cenchreae he c. his hair, for he 18.18
Then the soldiers c. away the ropes 27.32
accursed and c. off from Christ Rom 9.03
otherwise you too will be c. off. 11.22
you have been c. from what is by 11.24
then she should c. off her hair; 1Co 11.06

CUTH
the men of C. made Nergal, the men 2Ki 17.30

CUTHAH
C., Avva, Hamath, and Sepharvaim, and 2Ki 17.24

CUTS
LORD your God c. off before you Deu 12.29
LORD your God c. off the nations 19.01
When the LORD c. off every one of 1Sa 20.15
of the godless when God c. him off, Job 27.08
He c. out channels in the rocks, and 28.10
who c. off the spirit of princes, Ps 76.12
and c. in two the bars of iron. 107.16
hand of a fool c. off his own feet Pro 26.06
he c. me off from the loom; from Is 38.12
He c. down cedars; or he 44.14
and c. out windows for it, paneling Jer 22.14

CUTTER
and the c., my great army, which I Joe 2.25

CUTTING
in c. stones for setting, and in Ex 31.05
in c. stones for setting, and in 35.33
C. down the Benjaminites, they Ju 20.43
c. off all the evildoers from the Ps 101.08
c. off the children from the Jer 9.21
What the c. locust left, the swarming Joe 1.04
your house by c. off many peoples; Hab 2.10

CUTTINGS
not make any c. in your flesh on Lev 19.28
nor make any c. in their flesh. 21.05

CYCLE
setting on fire the c. of nature, Jas 3.06

CYMBAL
I am a noisy gong or a clanging c. 1Co 13.01

CYMBALS
tambourines and castanets and c. 2Sa 6.05
tambourines and c. and trumpets. 1Ch 13.08
instruments, on harps and lyres and c., 15.16
and Ethan, were to sound bronze c.; 15.19
and c., and made loud music on 15.28
and lyres; Asaph was to sound the c., 16.05
trumpets and c. for the music and 16.42
lyres, with harps, and with c. 25.01
in the house of the LORD with c., 25.06
with c., harps, and lyres, stood east 2Ch 5.12
trumpets and c. and other musical 5.13
in the house of the LORD with c., 29.25
with c., to praise the LORD, according Ez 3.10
with singing, with c., harps, and lyres. Neh 12.27
Praise him with sounding c.; Ps 150.05
praise him with loud clashing c.! 150.05

CYPRESS
the matter of cedar and c. timber. 1Ki 5.08
of cedar and c. that he desired, 5.10
of the house with boards of c. 6.15
and two doors of c. wood; the two 6.34
with cedar and c. timber and gold, 9.11
c., and algum timber from Lebanon, 2Ch 2.08
The nave he lined with c., and covered 3.05
I will set in the desert the c., Is 41.19
Instead of the thorn shall come up the c.; 55.13
the c., the plane, and the pine, to 60.13
I am like an evergreen c., from me Hos 14.08
Wail, O c., for the cedar has fallen, Zec 11.02

CYPRESSES
tallest cedars, its choicest c.; 2Ki 19.23
The c. rejoice at you, the cedars of Is 14.08
tallest cedars, its choicest c.; 37.24

CYPRUS
the land of C. it is revealed to Is 23.01
pass over to C., even there you 23.12
For cross to the coasts of C. and see, Jer 2.10
of pines from the coasts of C., Eze 27.06
encouragement), a Levite, a native of C., Ac 4.36
as Phoenicia and C. and Antioch, 11.19
men of C. and Cyrene, who on coming 11.20
and from there they sailed to C. 13.04
with him and sailed away to C., 15.39
When we had come in sight of C., 21.03
us to the house of Mnason of C., 21.16
we sailed under the lee of C., 27.04

CYRENE
upon a man of C., Simon by name; Mt 27.32
Simon of C., who was coming in from Mk 15.21
away, they seized one Simon of C., Lk 23.26
the parts of Libya belonging to C., Ac 2.10
some of them, men of Cyprus and C., 11.20
Lucius of C., Manaen a member of 13.01

CYRENIANS
and of the C., and of the Alexandrians, Ac 6.09

CYRUS
first year of C. king of Persia, 2Ch 36.22
the spirit of C. king of Persia so 36.22
"Thus says C. king of Persia, 'The 36.23
first year of C. king of Persia, Ez 1.01
the spirit of C. king of Persia so 1.01
"Thus says C. king of Persia: The 1.02
C. the king also brought out the 1.07
C. king of Persia brought these out 1.08
they had from C. king of Persia. 3.07
as King C. the king of Persia has 4.03
all the days of C. king of Persia, 4.05
first year of C. king of Babylon, 5.13
C. the king made a decree that this 5.13
these C. the king took out of the 5.14
was issued by C. the king for the 5.17
In the first year of C. the king, 6.03
C. the king issued a decree: Concerning 6.03
by decree of C. and Darius and 6.14
who says of C., 'He is my shepherd, Is 44.28
to C., whose right hand I have 45.01
until the first year of King C. Dan 1.21
and the reign of C. the Persian. 6.28
third year of C. king of Persia a 10.01

DABBESHETH
and touches D., then the brook Jos 19.11

DABERATH
thence it goes to D., then up to Jos 19.13
lands, D. with its pasture lands, 21.28
lands, D. with its pasture lands, 1Ch 6.72

DAGON
a great sacrifice to D. their god, Ju 16.23
the house of D. and set it up beside D. 1Sa 5.02
D. had fallen face downward on the 5.03
So they took D. and put him back in 5.03
D. had fallen face downward on the 5.04
and the head of D. and both his 5.04
the trunk of D. was left to him. 5.04
the priests of D. and all who 5.05
the house of D. do not tread on 5.05
threshold of D. in Ashdod to this 5.05
heavy upon us and upon D. our god." 5.07
his head in the temple of D. 1Ch 10.10

DAILY
your d. task, as when there was Ex 5.13
lesson your d. number of bricks." 5.19
be twice as much as they gather d. 16.05
In the same way you shall offer d., Num 28.24
and offered the d. burnt offerings Ez 3.04
gave the d. portions for the Neh 12.47
Blessed be the Lord, who d. bears us up; Ps 68.19
with which he d. girds himself! 109.19
and I was d. his delight, rejoicing Pro 8.30
watching d. at my gates, waiting 8.34
Yet they seek me d., and delight Is 58.02
was given him d. from the bakers' Jer 37.21
the king according to his d. need, 52.34
shall provide d. a goat for a sin Eze 43.25
and a he-goat d. for a sin offering 45.23
a burnt offering to the LORD d.; 46.13
assigned them a d. portion of the Dan 1.05
Give us this day our d. bread; Mt 6.11
take up his cross d. and follow me. Lk 9.23
Give us each day our d. bread; 11.03
And he was teaching d. in the temple. 19.47
whom they laid d. at that gate of Ac 3.02
neglected in the d. distribution. 6.01
and they increased in numbers d. 16.05
the scriptures d. to see if these 17.11
and argued d. in the hall of 19.09
there is the d. pressure upon me of 2Co 11.28
priests, to offer sacrifices d., Heb 7.27
priest stands d. at his service, 10.11
ill-clad and in lack of d. food, Jas 2.15

DAINTIES
rich, and he shall yield royal d. Gen 49.20
and let me not eat of their d.! Ps 141.04
Those who feasted on d. perish in Lam 4.05
and all thy d. and thy splendor are Rev 18.14

DAINTILY
who clothed you d. in scarlet, 2Sa 1.24

DAINTY
bread, and his appetite d. food. Job 33.20

DALMANUTHA
and went to the district of D. Mk 8.10

DALMATIA
has gone to Galatia, Titus to D. 2Ti 4.10

DALPHON
Parshandatha and D. and Aspatha Est 9.07

DAM
seven days it shall be with its d.; Ex 22.30

DAMAGE
why should d. grow to the hurt of Ez 4.22

DAMARIS
a woman named D. and others with Ac 17.34

DAMASCUS
pursued them to Hobah, north of D. Gen 14.15
heir of my house is Eliezer of D.?" 15.02
the Syrians of D. came to help 2Sa 8.05
Then David put garrisons in Aram of D.; 8.06
and they went to D., and dwelt 1Ki 11.24
there, and made him king in D. 11.24
of Syria, who dwelt in D., saying, 15.18
your way to the wilderness of D.; 19.15
establish bazaars for yourself in D., 20.34
the rivers of D., better than all 2Ki 5.12
Now Elisha came to D. Benhadad 8.07
with him, all kinds of goods of D., 8.09
recovered for Israel D. and Hamath, 14.28
of Assyria marched up against D., 16.09
Ahaz went to D. to meet Tiglathpileser 16.10
he saw the altar that was at D. 16.10
that King Ahaz had sent from D., 16.11
before King Ahaz arrived from D. 16.11
And when the king came from D., 16.12
the Syrians of D. came to help 1Ch 18.05
David put garrisons in Syria of D.; 18.06
of Syria, who dwelt in D., saying, 2Ch 16.02
all their spoil to the king of D. 24.23
his people and brought them to D. 28.05
to the gods of D. which had defeated 28.23
a tower of Lebanon, overlooking D. Sol 7.04
For the head of Syria is D., and the Is 7.08
and the head of D. is Rezin. (Within 7.08
the wealth of D. and the spoil of 8.04
like Arpad? Is not Samaria like D.? 10.09
An oracle concerning D. Behold, D. 17.01
Ephraim, and the kingdom from D.; 17.03
Concerning D. "Hamath and Arpad Jer 49.23
D. has become feeble, she turned to 49.24
kindle a fire in the wall of D., 49.27
D. trafficked with you for your Eze 27.18
border between D. and of Hamath), 47.16
is on the northern border of D. 47.17
Hazarenon between Hauran and D.; 47.18
border of D. over against Hamath), 48.01
"For three transgressions of D., Amo 1.03
I will break the bar of D., and cut 1.05
will take you into exile beyond D.," 5.27
of Hadrach and will rest upon D. Zec 9.01
letters to the synagogues at D., Ac 9.02
Now as he journeyed he approached D., 9.03
the hand and brought him into D. 9.08
was a disciple at D. named Ananias. 9.10
he was with the disciples at D. 9.19
who lived in D. by proving that 9.22
and how at D. he had preached 9.27
I journeyed to D. to take those 22.05
my journey and drew near to D., 22.06
and go into D., and there you will 22.10
who were with me, and came into D. 22.11
"Thus I journeyed to D. with the 26.12
but declared first to those at D., 26.20
At D., the governor under King 2Co 11.32
the city of D. in order to seize 11.32
Arabia; and again I returned to D. Gal 1.17

DAN
and went in pursuit as far as D. Gen 14.14
therefore she called his name D. 30.06
Rachel's maid: D. and Naphtali. 35.25
The sons of D.: Hushim. 46.23
D. shall judge his people as one of 49.16
D. shall be a serpent in the way, 49.17
D. and Naphtali, Gad and Asher. Ex 1.04

DAN (cont.)

of Ahisamach, of the tribe of D.; Ex 31.06
of Ahisamach of the tribe of D, 35.34
of Ahisamach, of the tribe of D., 38.23
of Dibri, of the tribe of D. Lev 24.11
from D., Ahiezer the son of Ammishaddai; Num 1.12
Of the people of D., their 1.38
of the tribe of D. was sixty-two 1.39
of the camp of D. by their companies, 2.25
the people of D. being Ahiezer the 2.25
of the camp of D. is a hundred and 2.31
the leader of the men of D.: 7.66
of the camp of the men of D., acting 10.25
from the tribe of D., Ammiel 13.12
These are the sons of D. according 26.42
the families of D. according to 26.42
tribe of the sons of D. a leader. 34.22
Asher, Zebulun, D., and Naphtali. Deu 27.13
And of D. he said, "D. is a lion's whelp, 33.22
all the land, Gilead as far as D., 34.01
lot came out for the tribe of D., Jos 19.40
D., after the name of D. their ancestor. 19.47
the inheritance of the tribe of D., 19.48
the tribe of D. and the half-tribe 21.05
and out of the tribe of D., Elteke 21.23
and D., why did he abide with the Ju 5.17
six hundred men of the tribe of D., 18.11
And they named the city D., after 18.29
the name of D. their ancestor, 18.29
from D. to Beersheba, including the 20.01
And all Israel from D. to Beersheba 1Sa 3.20
over Judah, from D. to Beersheba. 2Sa 3.10
from D. to Beersheba, as the sand by 17.11
from D. to Beersheba, and number the 24.02
and they came to D., and from D. 24.06
the people from D. to Beersheba 24.15
from D. even to Beersheba, every man 1Ki 4.25
Bethel, and the other he put in D. 12.29
and to the other as far as D. 12.30
D., Abelbethmaacah, and all Chinneroth, 15.20
that were in Bethel, and in D. 2Ki 10.29
D., Joseph, Benjamin, Naphtali, Gad, 1Ch 2.02
Israel, from Beersheba to D., 21.02
for D., Azarel the son of Jeroham. 27.22
of a woman of the daughters of D., 2Ch 2.14
D., Abelmaim, and all the store-cities 16.04
all Israel, from Beersheba to D., 30.05
declares from D. and proclaims Jer 4.15
of their horses is heard from D.; 8.16
side of the west, D., one portion. Eze 48.01
adjoining the territory of D., 48.02
of Benjamin, and the gate of D, 48.32
O D.,' and, 'As the way of Beersheba Amo 8.14

DANCE

come out to d. in the dances, Ju 21.21
a flock, and their children d. Job 21.11
Praise him with timbrel and d.; Ps 150.04
time to mourn, and a time to d.; Ecc 3.04
as upon a d. before two armies? Sol 6.13
dwell, and there satyrs will d. Is 13.21
go forth in the d. of the merrymakers Jer 31.04
the maidens rejoice in the d., 31.13
'We piped to you, and you did not d.; Mt 11.17
piped to you, and you did not d.; Lk 7.32
to eat and drink and rose up to d." 1Co 10.07

DANCED

And David d. before the LORD with 2Sa 6.14
and Herodias d. before the company, Mt 14.06
Herodias' daughter came in and d., Mk 6.22

DANCERS

from the d. whom they carried off; Ju 21.23
Singers and d. alike say, "All my Ps 87.07

DANCES

meet him with timbrels and with d.; Ju 11.34
Shiloh come out to dance in the d., 21.21
sing to one another of him in d., 1Sa 21.11
they sing to one another in d., 29.05
strength, and terror d. before him. Job 41.22

DANCING

out after her with timbrels and d. Ex 15.20
camp and saw the calf and d., 32.19
singing and d., to meet King Saul, 1Sa 18.06
land, eating and drinking and d., 30.16
leaping and d. before the LORD; 2Sa 6.16
saw King David d. and making merry 1Ch 15.29
turned for me my mourning into d.; Ps 30.11
Let them praise his name with d., 149.03
our d. has been turned to mourning. Lam 5.15
the house, he heard music and d. Lk 15.25

DANDLED

her lip, and d. upon her knees. Is 66.12
those whom I d. and reared my enemy Lam 2.22

DANGER

is safe for you and there is no d. 1Sa 20.21
man sees d. and hides himself; Pro 22.03
man sees d. and hides himself; 27.12
filling with water, and were in d. Lk 8.23
And there is d. not only that this Ac 19.27
For we are in d. of being charged 19.40
in d. from rivers, d. from robbers, 2Co 11.26
d. from my own people, d. from Gentiles, 11.26
d. in the city, d. in the wilderness, 11.26
d. at sea, d. from false brethren; 11.26

DANGEROUS

was already d. because the fast Ac 27.09

DANIEL

the second D., by Abigail the 1Ch 3.01
Of the sons of Ithamar, D. Of the Ez 8.02
D., Ginnethon, Baruch, Neh 10.06
D., and Job, were in it, they would Eze 14.14
even if Noah, D., and Job were in it, 14.20
you are indeed wiser than D.; 28.03
Among these were D., Hananiah, Dan 1.06
D. he called Belteshazzar, Hananiah 1.07
But D. resolved that he would not 1.08
And God gave D. favor and compassion 1.09
chief of the Eunuchs said to D., 1.10
Then D. said to the steward whom 1.11
the eunuchs had appointed over D., 1.11
and D. had understanding in all 1.17
them all none was found like D., 1.19
And D. continued until the first 1.21
and they sought D. and his companions, 2.13
Then D. replied with prudence and 2.14
Arioch made the matter known to D. 2.15
And D. went in and besought the 2.16
Then D. went to his house and made 2.17
so that D. and his companions might 2.18
was revealed to D. in a vision of 2.19
Then D. blessed the God of heaven. 2.19
D. said: "Blessed be the name of God 2.20
Therefore D. went in to Arioch, whom 2.24
brought in D. before the king in 2.25
The king said to D., whose 2.26
D. answered the king, "No wise men, 2.27
his face, and did homage to D., 2.46
The king said to D., "Truly, 2.47
Then the king gave D. high honors 2.48
D. made request of the king, and he 2.49
At last D. came in before me—he 4.08
Then D., whose name was Belteshazzar, 4.19
problems were found in this D., 5.12
Now let D. be called, and he will 5.12
Then D. was brought in before the 5.13

DANIEL (cont.)

The king said to D., "You are that D., Dan 5.13
Then D. answered before the king, 5.17
and D. was clothed with purple, a 5.29
of whom D. was one, to whom these 6.02
Then this D. became distinguished 6.03
complaint against D. with regard to 6.04
against this D. unless we find it 6.05
When D. knew that the document had 6.10
and found D. making petition and 6.11
"That D., who is one of the exiles 6.13
and set his mind to deliver D.; 6.14
and D. was brought and cast into 6.16
The king said to D., "May your 6.16
might be changed concerning D. 6.17
came near to the den where D. was, 6.20
a tone of anguish and said to D., 6.20
"O D., servant of the living God, 6.20
Then D. said to the king, "O king, 6.21
commanded that D. be taken up out 6.23
So D. was taken up out of the den, 6.23
who had accused D. were brought 6.24
and fear before the God of D., 6.26
who has saved D. from the power of 6.27
So this D. prospered during the 6.28
D. had a dream and visions of his 7.01
D. said, "I saw in my vision by 7.02
"As for me, D., my spirit within me 7.15
As for me, D., my thoughts greatly 7.28
D., after that which appeared to me 8.01
When I, D., had seen the vision, I 8.15
And I, D., was overcome and lay sick 8.27
D., perceived in the books the 9.02
"O D., I have now come out to give 9.22
Persia a word was revealed to D., 10.01
D., was mourning for three weeks. 10.02
And I, D., alone saw the vision, for 10.07
"O D., man greatly beloved, give 10.11
D., for from the first day that you 10.12
But you, D., shut up the words, and 12.04
Then I D. looked, and behold, two 12.05
D., for the words are shut up and 12.09
spoken of by the prophet D., Mt 24.15

DANITES

territory of the D. was lost to Jos 19.47
the D. went up and fought against 19.47
pressed the D. back into the hill Ju 1.34
of Zorah, of the tribe of the D., 13.02
tribe of the D. was seeking for 18.01
So the D. sent five able men from 18.02
Now the six hundred men of the D., 18.16
out, and they overtook the D. 18.22
And they shouted to the D., 18.23
And the D. said to him, "Do not let 18.25
Then the D. went their way; 18.26
the D. came to Laish, to a people 18.27
And the D. set up the graven image 18.30
tribe of the D. until the day of 18.30
Of the D. twenty-eight thousand six 1Ch 12.35

DANNAH

D., Kiriathsannah (that is, Debir), Jos 15.49

DAPPLED

the fourth chariot d. gray horses. Zec 6.03
and the d. ones go toward the south 6.06

DARA

Heman, Calcol, and D., five in all. 1Ch 2.06

DARDA

and D., the sons of Mahol; and his 1Ki 4.31

DARE

for who would d. of himself to Jer 30.21
day did any one d. to ask him any Mt 22.46
trembled and did not d. to look. Ac 7.32
a good man one will d. even to die. Rom 5.07
does he d. go to law before the 1Co 6.01
I also d. to boast of that. 2Co 11.21

DARED

that no one d. to ask him any Mk 12.34
For they no longer d. to ask him Lk 20.40
none of the disciples d. ask him, Jn 21.12
None of the rest d. join them, Ac 5.13

DARES

a lioness; who d. rouse him up? Gen 49.09
fierce that he d. to stir him up. Job 41.10
whatever any one d. to boast of— 2Co 11.21

DARICS

and ten thousand d. of gold, 1Ch 29.07
work sixty-one thousand d. of gold, Ez 2.69
twenty bowls of gold worth a thousand d., 8.27
the treasury a thousand d. of gold, Neh 7.70
twenty thousand d. of gold and two 7.71
was twenty thousand d. of gold, 7.72

DARIUS

the reign of D. king of Persia. Ez 4.05
of the reign of D. king of Persia. 4.24
should reach D. and then answer be 5.05
the River sent to D. the king; 5.06
follows: "To D. the king, all peace. 5.07
Then D. the king made a decree, and 6.01
I D. make a decree; let it be 6.12
to the word sent by D. the king, 6.13
diligence what D. the king had 6.13
of Cyrus and D. and Artaxerxes 6.14
year of the reign of D. the king. 6.15
until the reign of D. the Persian. Neh 12.22
And D. the Mede received the Dan 5.31
It pleased D. to set over the 6.01
to him, "O King D., live for ever! 6.06
Therefore King D. signed the 6.09
Then King D. wrote to all the 6.25
the reign of D. and the reign of 6.28
first year of D. the son of 9.01
in the first year of D. the Mede, 11.01
In the second year of D. the king, Hag 1.01
In the second year of D. the king, 2.01
month, in the second year of D. 2.10
month, in the second year of D., Zec 1.01
Shebat, in the second year of D., 1.07
In the fourth year of King D., 7.01

DARK

sun had gone down and it was d., Gen 15.17
clearly, and not in d. speech; Num 12.08
at d., the men went out; Jos 2.05
When it began to be d. at the gates Neh 13.19
Let the stars of its dawn be d.; Job 3.09
which are d. with ice, and where the 6.16
They grope in the d. without light; 12.25
The light is d. in his tent, and his 18.06
The murderer rises in the d., 24.14
In the d. they dig through houses; 24.16
to shoot in the d. at the upright Ps 11.02
canopy thick clouds d. with water. 18.11
Let their way be d. and slippery, 35.06
for the d. places of the land are 74.20
I will utter d. sayings from of old, 78.02
Pit, in the regions d. and deep. 88.06
darkness, and made the land d.; 105.28
even the darkness is not d. to thee, 139.12
I am very d., but comely, O daughters Sol 1.05
the sun will be at its rising Is 13.10
counsel, whose deeds are in the d., 29.15
of Israel are doing in the d., Eze 8.12
shoulder, and carry it out in the d.; 12.06
I went forth in the d., carrying 12.07
upon his shoulder in the d., and shall 12.12
At Tehaphnehes the day shall be d., 30.18

DARK (cont.)
heavens, and make their stars d.; Eze 32.07
of heaven will I make d. over you, 32.08
What I tell you in the d., utter Mk 10.27
full of light, having no part d., Lk 11.36
said in the d. shall be heard in 12.03
It was now d., and Jesus had not Jn 6.17
tomb early, while it was still d., 20.01
as to a lamp shining in a d. place, 2Pe 1.19

DARKEN
and d. the earth in broad daylight. Amo 8.09

DARKENED
land, so that the land was d., Ex 10.15
your light is d., so that you Job 22.11
Let their eyes be d., so that Ps 69.23
the stars are d. and the clouds Ecc 12.02
and the light is d. by its clouds. Is 5.30
The sun and the moon are d., Joe 2.10
The sun and the moon are d., 3.15
of those days the sun will be d., Mt 24.29
tribulation, the sun will be d., Mk 13.24
and their senseless minds were d. Rom 1.21
let their eyes be d. so that they 11.10
they are d. in their understanding, Eph 4.18
that a third of their light was d.; Rev 8.12
the air were d. with the smoke 9.02

DARKENS
"Who is this that d. counsel by Job 38.02
and d. the day into night, who calls Amo 5.08

DARKNESS
and d. was upon the face of the Gen 1.02
separated the light from the d. 1.04
and the d. he called Night. And there 1.05
to separate the light from the d. 1.18
a dread and great d. fell upon him. 15.12
there may be d. over the land of Ex 10.21
land of Egypt, a d. to be felt." 10.21
there was thick d. in all the land 10.22
And there was the cloud and the d.; 14.20
wrapped in d., cloud, and gloom. Deu 4.11
voice out of the midst of the d., 5.23
noonday, as the blind grope in d., 28.29
he put d. between you and the Jos 24.07
the wicked shall be cut off in d.; 1Sa 2.09
thick d. was under his feet. 2Sa 22.10
He made d. around him his canopy, 22.12
O Lord, and my God lightens my d. 22.29
that he would dwell in thick d. 1Ki 8.12
that he would dwell in thick d. 2Ch 6.01
Let that day be d.! May God Job 3.04
Let gloom and deep d. claim it. 3.05
That night—let thick d. seize it! 3.06
They meet with d. in the daytime, 5.14
to the land of gloom and deep d., 10.21
and chaos, where light is as d. 10.22
its d. will be like the morning. 11.17
He uncovers the deeps out of d., 12.22
and brings deep d. to light. 12.22
that he will return out of d., 15.22
that a day of d. is ready at his 15.23
he will not escape from d.; 15.30
and on my eyelids is deep d.; 16.16
they say, 'is near to the d.' 17.12
house, if I spread my couch in d., 17.13
He is thrust from light into d., 18.18
and he has set d. upon my paths. 19.08
Utter d. is laid up for his treasures 20.26
Can he judge through the deep d.? 22.13
for I am hemmed in by d., and thick d. 23.17
For deep d. is morning to all of 24.17
with the terrors of deep d. 24.17
the boundary between light and d. 26.10
Men put an end to d., and search 28.03
bound the ore in gloom and deep d. 28.03
by his light I walked through d.; 29.03
when I waited for light, d. came. 30.26
gloom or deep d. where evildoers 34.22
draw up our case because of d. 37.19
and thick d. its swaddling band, 38.09
have you seen the gates of deep d.? 38.17
and where is the place of d., 38.19
thick d. was under his feet. Ps 18.09
He made d. his covering around him, 18.11
the Lord my God lightens my d. 18.28
and covered us with deep d. 44.19
understanding, they walk about in d.; 82.05
Are thy wonders known in the d., 88.12
my companions are in d. 88.18
nor the pestilence that stalks in d., 91.06
Clouds and thick d. are round about 97.02
Thou makest d., and it is night, 104.20
He sent d., and made the land dark; 105.28
Some sat in d. and in gloom, prisoners 107.10
he brought them out of d. and gloom, 107.14
Light rises in the d. for the 112.04
"Let only d. cover me, and the light 139.11
even the d. is not d. to thee, the 139.12
for d. is as light with thee. 139.12
made me sit in d. like those long 143.03
uprightness to walk in the ways of d., Pro 2.13
The way of the wicked is like deep d.; 4.19
evening, at the time of night and d. 7.09
lamp will be put out in utter d. 20.20
excels folly as light excels d. Ecc 2.13
his head, but the fool walks in d.; 2.14
spent all his days in d. and grief, 5.17
comes into vanity and goes into d., 6.04
and in d. its name is covered; 6.04
that the days of d. will be many. 11.08
who put d. for light and light for d., Is 5.20
the land, behold, d. and distress; 5.30
distress and d., the gloom of 8.22
they will be thrust into thick d. 8.22
who walked in d. have seen a great 9.02
who dwelt in a land of deep d., 9.02
their gloom and d. the eyes of the 29.18
the prison those who sit in d. 42.07
I will turn the d. before them into 42.16
treasures of d. and the hoards in 45.03
I form light and create d., 45.07
speak in secret, in a land of d.; 45.19
and go into d., O daughter of the 47.05
to those who are in d., 'Appear.' 49.09
who walks in d. and has no light, 50.10
rise in the d. and your gloom be 58.10
d., and for brightness, but we walk 59.09
For behold, d. shall cover the earth, 60.02
earth, and thick d. the peoples; 60.02
in a land of drought and deep d., Jer 2.06
to Israel, or a land of thick d.? 2.31
Lord your God before he brings d., 13.16
it into gloom and makes it deep d. 13.16
them like slippery paths in the d., 23.12
brought me into d. without any Lam 3.02
me dwell in d. like the dead of 3.06
and put d. upon your land, says the Eze 32.08
on a day of clouds and thick d. 34.12
he knows what is in the d., Dan 2.22
a day of d. and gloom, a day of Joe 2.02
a day of clouds and thick d.! 2.02
The sun shall be turned to d., 2.31
who makes the morning d., Amo 4.13
and turns deep d. into the morning, 5.08
the Lord? It is d., and not light; 5.18
Is not the day of the Lord d., 5.20
and d. to you, without divination. Mic 3.06
when I sit in d., the Lord will be 7.08
will pursue his enemies into d. Nah 1.08
a day of d. and gloom, a day of Zep 1.15
a day of clouds and thick d., 1.15
who sat in d. have seen a great Mt 4.16

DARKNESS (cont.)
your whole body will be full of d. Mt 6.23
If then the light in you is d., 6.23
is d., how great is the d.! 6.23
will be thrown into the outer d.; 8.12
and cast him into the outer d.; 22.13
worthless servant into the outer d.; 25.30
hour there was d. over all the 27.45
there was d. over the whole land Mk 15.33
who sit in d. and in the shadow of Lk 1.79
not sound, your body is full of d. 11.34
lest the light in you be d. 11.35
is your hour, and the power of d." 22.53
and there was d. over the whole 23.44
The light shines in the d., Jn 1.05
and the d. has not overcome it. 1.05
and men loved d. rather than light, 3.19
who follows me will not walk in d., 8.12
light, lest the d. overtake you; 12.35
walks in the d. does not know 12.35
believes in me may not remain in d. 12.46
be turned into d. and the moon Ac 2.20
mist and d. fell upon him and he 13.11
may turn from d. to light and from 26.18
a light to those who are in d., Rom 2.19
the works of d. and put on the 13.12
now hidden in d. and will disclose 1Co 4.05
said, "Let light shine out of d.," 2Co 4.06
what fellowship has light with d.? 6.14
for once you were d., Eph 5.08
part in the unfruitful works of d., 5.11
world rulers of this present d., 6.12
the dominion of d. and transferred Col 1.13
But you are not in d., brethren, 1Th 5.04
we are not of the night or of d. 5.05
and d., and gloom, and a tempest, Heb 12.18
you out of d. into his marvelous 1Pe 2.09
nether gloom of d. has been 2Pe 2.17
light and in him is no d. at all. 1Jn 1.05
with him while we walk in d., 1.06
because the d. is passing away and 2.08
his brother is in the d. still. 2.09
is in the d. and walks in the d., 2.11
because the d. has blinded his eyes. 2.11
nether gloom of d. has been Jud 1.13
beast, and its kingdom was in d.; Rev 16.10

DARKON
the sons of D., the sons of Giddel, Ez 2.56
the sons of D., the sons of Giddel, Neh 7.58

DARLING
the d. of her mother, flawless to Sol 6.09
Is he my d. child? For as often Jer 31.20

DART
nor the spear, the d., or the javelin. Job 41.26
torches, they d. like lightning. Nah 2.04

DARTED
the living creatures d. to and fro, Eze 1.14

DARTS
and he took three d. in his hand, 2Sa 18.14
all the flaming d. of the evil one Eph 6.16

DASH
and d. in pieces their pillars, and Deu 7.05
and d. in pieces their pillars, and 12.03
and d. in pieces their little ones, 2Ki 8.12
and d. them in pieces like a Ps 2.09
lest you d. your foot against a 91.12
And I will d. them one against Jer 13.14
and d. you to the ground, you and Lk 19.44

DASHED
and they were all d. to pieces. 2Ch 25.12
me by the neck and d. me to pieces; Job 16.12
Their infants will be d. in pieces Is 13.16
mothers were d. in pieces with Hos 10.14
little ones shall be d. in pieces, 13.16
ones were d. in pieces at the head Nah 3.10

DASHES
little ones and d. them against Ps 137.09
it seizes him, it d. him down; Mk 9.18

DATE
until the d. set by the father. Gal 4.02

DATHAN
and D. and Abiram the sons of Eliab, Num 16.01
sent to call D. and Abiram the 16.12
dwelling of Korah, D., and Abiram. 16.24
rose and went to D. and Abiram; 16.25
dwelling of Korah, D., and Abiram; 16.27
and D. and Abiram came out and 16.27
of Eliab: Nemuel, D., and Abiram. 26.09
These are the D. and Abiram, chosen 26.09
and what he did to D. and Abiram Deu 11.06
the earth opened and swallowed up D., Ps 106.17

DAUB
these prophets d. it with whitewash; Eze 13.10
say to those who d. it with whitewash 13.11

DAUBED
and d. it with bitumen and pitch; Ex 2.03
the daubing with which you d. it?' Eze 13.12
that you have d. with whitewash, 13.14
those who have d. it with whitewash 13.15
is no more, nor those who d. it, 13.15
prophets have d. for them with 22.28

DAUBING
'Where is the d. with which you Eze 13.12

DAUGHTER
the d. of Haran the father of Gen 11.29
the d. of my father but not the d. of 20.12
and said, "Tell me whose d. you are. 24.23
"I am the d. of Bethuel the son of 24.24
Then I asked her, 'Whose d. are you?' 24.47
'The d. of Bethuel, Nahor's son, whom 24.47
way to take the d. of my master's 24.48
the d. of Bethuel the Aramean of 25.20
wife Judith the d. of Beeri the 26.34
Basemath the d. of Elon the 26.34
Mahalath the d. of Ishmael Abraham's 28.09
Rachel his d. is coming with the 29.06
saw Rachel the d. of Laban his 29.10
years for your younger d. Rachel." 29.18
he took his d. Leah and brought 29.23
Zilpah to his d. Leah to be her 29.24
gave him his d. Rachel to wife. 29.28
Bilhah to his d. Rachel to be her 29.29
Afterwards she bore a d., 30.21
Now Dinah the d. of Leah, whom she 34.01
was drawn to Dinah the d. of Jacob; 34.03
that he had defiled his d. Dinah; 34.05
in Israel by lying with Jacob's d., 34.07
my son Shechem longs for your d.; 34.08
circumcised, then we will take our d., 34.17
he had delight in Jacob's d. Now 34.19
Adah the d. of Elon the Hittite, 36.02
Oholibamah the d. of Anah the son 36.02
Ishmael's d., the sister of Nebaioth 36.03
Oholibamah the d. of Anah the son 36.14
born of Oholibamah the d. of Anah, 36.18
and Oholibamah the d. of Anah. 36.25
the d. of Matred, d. of Mezahab. 36.39
There Judah saw the d. of a certain 38.02
the wife of Judah, Shua's d., died; 38.12
the d. of Potiphera priest of On. 41.45
the d. of Potiphera priest of On, 41.50
Paddan-aram, together with his d. Dinah; 46.15

DAUGHTER (cont.)

whom Laban gave to Leah his d.;	Gen 46.18
the d. of Potiphera the priest of	46.20
whom Laban gave to Rachel his d.,	46.25
but if it is a d., she shall	Ex 1.16
but you shall let every d. live."	1.22
went and took to wife a d. of Levi.	2.01
Now the d. of Pharaoh came down to	2.05
Then his sister said to Pharaoh's d.,	2.07
And Pharaoh's d. said to her, "Go."	2.08
And Pharaoh's d. said to her, "Take	2.09
she brought him to Pharaoh's d.,	2.10
and he gave Moses his d. Zipporah.	2.21
the d. of Amminadab and the sister	6.23
or your d., your manservant, or your	20.10
"When a man sells his d. as a slave,	21.07
shall deal with her as with a d.	21.09
If it gores a man's son or d.,	21.31
whether for a son or for a d., she	Lev 12.06
the d. of your father or the d. of your	18.09
of your son's d. or of your daughter's d.,	18.10
nakedness of your father's wife's d.,	18.11
nakedness of a woman and of her d.,	18.17
take her son's d. or her daughter's d.	18.17
profane your d. by making her a	19.29
a d. of his father or a d. of his mother,	20.17
his son, his d., his brother,	21.02
And the d. of any priest, if she	21.09
If a priest's d. is married to an	22.12
But if a priest's d. is a widow or	22.13
the d. of Dibri, of the tribe of Dan	24.11
was slain was Cozbi the d. of Zur,	Num 25.15
the d. of the prince of Midian,	25.18
And the name of the d. of Asher was	26.46
wife was Jochebed the d. of Levi,	26.59
his inheritance to pass to his d.	27.08
And if he has no d., then you	27.09
and between a father and his d.,	30.16
And every d. who possesses an	36.08
or your d., or your manservant, or	Deu 5.14
you and your son and your d.,	12.18
or your d., or the wife of your	13.06
God, you and your son and your d.,	16.11
you and your son and your d.,	16.14
his son or his d. as an offering,	18.10
'I gave my d. to this man to wife,	22.16
find in your d. the tokens of	22.17
whether the d. of his father or the d.	27.22
bosom, to her son and to her d.,	28.56
will I give Achsah my d. as wife."	Jos 15.16
he gave him Achsah his d. as wife.	15.17
will give him Achsah my d. as wife."	Ju 1.12
he gave him Achsah his d. as wife.	1.13
his d. came out to meet him with	11.34
her he had neither son nor d.	11.34
his clothes, and said, "Alas, my d.!	11.35
to lament the d. of Jephthah the	11.40
are my virgin d. and his concubine	19.24
shall give his d. in marriage to	21.01
And she said to her, "Go, my d."	Ru 2.02
my d., do not go to glean in	2.08
my d., that you go out with his	2.22
"My d., should I not seek a home	3.01
you be blessed by the LORD, my d.;	3.10
And now, my d., do not fear, I will	3.11
she said, "How did you fare, my d.?"	3.16
my d., until you learn how the	3.18
wife was Ahinoam the d. of Ahimaaz.	1Sa 14.50
riches, and will give him his d..	17.25
David, "Here is my elder d. Merab;	18.17
Saul's d., should have been given to	18.19
Now Saul's d. Michal loved David;	18.20
gave him his d. Michal for a wife.	18.27
Saul had given Michal his d.,	25.44
of Maacah the d. of Talmai king of	2Sa 3.03
name was Rizpah, the d. of Aiah;	3.07
Saul's d., when you come to see my	3.13
Michal the d. of Saul looked out of	6.16
But Michal the d. of Saul came out	6.20
And Michal the d. of Saul had no	6.23
the d. of Eliam, the wife of Uriah	11.03
bosom, and it was like a d. to him.	12.03
and one d. whose name was Tamar;	14.27
married Abigal the d. of Nahash,	17.25
two sons of Rizpah the d. of Aiah,	21.08
five sons of Merob the d. of Saul,	21.08
Then Rizpah the d. of Aiah took	21.10
told what Rizpah the d. of Aiah,	21.11
he took Pharaoh's d., and brought	1Ki 3.01
had Taphath the d. of Solomon as	4.11
Basemath the d. of Solomon as his	4.15
for Pharaoh's d. whom he had taken	7.08
had given it as dowry to his d.,	9.16
But Pharaoh's d. went up from the	9.24
the d. of Pharaoh, and Moabite,	11.01
was Maacah the d. of Abishalom.	15.02
was Maacah the d. of Abishalom.	15.10
Jezebel the d. of Ethbaal king of	16.31
name was Azubah the d. of Shilhi.	22.42
for the d. of Ahab was his wife.	2Ki 8.18
bury her; for she is a king's d."	9.34
the d. of King Joram, sister of	11.02
'Give your d. to my son for a wife';	14.09
name was Jerusha the d. of Zadok.	15.33
name was Abi the d. of Zechariah.	18.02
scorns you—the virgin d. of Zion;	19.21
head behind you—the d. of Jerusalem.	19.21
Meshullemeth the d. of Haruz of	21.19
was Jedidah the d. of Adaiah of	22.01
his son or his d. as an offering	23.10
was Hamutal the d. of Jeremiah of	23.31
was Zebidah the d. of Pedaiah of	23.36
Nehushta the d. of Elnathan of	24.08
was Hamutal the d. of Jeremiah of	24.18
Mehetabel the d. of Matred, the d. of	1Ch 1.50
went in to the d. of Machir the	2.21
gave his d. in marriage to Jarha	2.35
and the d. of Caleb was Achsah.	2.49
the d. of Pharaoh, whom heard	4.17
four by Bathshua, the d. of Ammiel;	3.05
the d. of Pharaoh, whom Mered	4.17
His d. was Sheerah, who built both	7.24
Michal the d. of Saul looked out of	15.29
Pharaoh's d. up from the city of	2Ch 8.11
Mahalath the d. of Jerimoth the	11.18
of Abihail the d. of Eliab the son	11.18
he took Maacah the d. of Absalom,	11.20
Maacah the d. of Absalom above all	11.21
was Micaiah the d. of Uriel of	13.02
name was Azubah the d. of Shilhi.	20.31
for the d. of Ahab was his wife.	21.06
the d. of the king, took Joash the	22.11
the d. of King Jehoram and wife of	22.11
'Give your d. to my son for a wife';	25.18
name was Jerushah the d. of Zadok.	27.01
was Abijah the d. of Zechariah.	29.01
had taken the d. of Meshullam the	Neh 6.18
the d. of his uncle, for she had	Est 2.07
Mordecai adopted her as his own d.	2.07
for Esther the d. of Abihail the	2.15
who had adopted her as his own d.,	2.15
the d. of Abihail, and Mordecai the	9.29
gates of the d. of Zion I may	Ps 9.14
Hear, O d., consider, and incline	45.10
O d. of Babylon, you devastator!	137.08
And the d. of Zion is left like a	Is 1.08
Cry aloud, O d. of Gallim!	10.30
at the mount of the d. of Zion,	10.32
The d. of Dibon has gone up to the	15.02
to the mount of the d. of Zion.	16.01
destruction of the d. of my people."	22.04
like the Nile. O d. of Tarshish;	23.10
O oppressed virgin d. of Sidon;	23.12
scorns you—the virgin d. of Zion;	37.22

DAUGHTER (cont.)

behind you—the d. of Jerusalem. Is 37.22
the dust, O virgin d. of Babylon; 47.01
O d. of the Chaldeans! For you shall 47.01
O d. of the Chaldeans; for you shall 47.05
your neck, O captive d. of Zion 52.02
Say to the d. of Zion, "Behold your 62.11
desert toward the d. of my people, Jer 4.11
the cry of the d. of Zion gasping 4.31
I will destroy, the d. of Zion. 6.02
battle, against you, O d. of Zion!" 6.23
O d. of my people, gird on sackcloth, 6.26
Hark, the cry of the d. of my people 8.19
wound of the d. of my people is my 8.21
health of the d. of my people not 8.22
the slain of the d. of my people! 9.01
for the virgin d. of my people is 14.17
will you waver, O faithless d.? 31.22
take balm, O virgin d. of Egypt! 46.11
The d. of Egypt shall be put to 46.24
O faithless d., who trusted in her 49.04
against you, O d. of Babylon! 50.42
The d. of Babylon is like a threshing 51.33
was Hamutal the d. of Jeremiah of 52.01
From the d. of Zion has departed Lam 1.06
wine press the virgin d. of Judah. 1.15
has set the d. of Zion under a 2.01
the strongholds of the d. of Judah; 2.02
eyes in the tent of the d. of Zion; 2.04
multiplied in the d. of Judah 2.05
ruins the wall of the d. of Zion; 2.08
The elders of the d. of Zion sit on 2.10
destruction of the d. of my people, 2.11
compare you, O d. of Jerusalem? 2.13
comfort you, O virgin d. of Zion? 2.13
their heads at the d. of Jerusalem; 2.15
O d. of Zion! Let tears 2.18
destruction of the d. of my people. 3.48
but the d. of my people has become 4.03
chastisement of the d. of my people 4.06
destruction of the d. of my people. 4.10
O d. of Edom, dweller in the land of 4.21
O d. of Zion, is accomplished, he 4.22
O d. of Edom, he will punish, he will 4.22
would deliver neither son nor d.; Eze 14.20
about you, 'Like mother, like d.' 16.44
You are the d. of your mother, who 16.45
his sister, his father's d. 22.11
for son or d., for brother or 44.25
and the d. of the king of the south Dan 11.06
give him the d. of women to 11.17
and took Gomer the d. of Diblaim, Hos 1.03
She conceived again and bore a d. 1.06
beginning of sin to the d. of Zion, Mic 1.13
hill of the d. of Zion, to you shall 4.08
the kingdom of the d. of Jerusalem. 4.08
O d. of Zion, like a woman in 4.10
O d. of Zion, for I will make your 4.13
the d. rises up against her mother, 7.06
the d. of my dispersed ones, shall Zep 3.10
Sing aloud, O d. of Zion; shout, 3.14
all your heart, O d. of Jerusalem! 3.14
who dwell with the d. of Babylon. Zec 2.07
Sing and rejoice, O d. of Zion; 2.10
Rejoice greatly, O d. of Zion! Shout 9.09
Shout aloud, O d. of Jerusalem! 9.09
has married the d. of a foreign Mal 2.11
him, saying, "My d. has just died; Mt 9.18
seeing her he said, "Take heart, d.; 9.22
and a d. against her mother, and a 10.35
loves son or d. more than me is 10.37
the d. of Herodias danced before 14.06
my d. is severely possessed by a 15.22
And her d. was healed instantly. 15.28
"Tell the d. of Zion, Behold, your 21.05
"My little d. is at the point of Mk 5.23
"D., your faith has made you well; 5.34
some who said, "Your d. is dead. 5.35
For when Herodias' d. came in and 6.22
whose little d. was possessed by an 7.25
to cast the demon out of her d. 7.26
the demon has left your d." 7.29
the d. of Phanuel, of the tribe of Lk 2.36
for he had an only d., 8.42
"D., your faith has made you well; 8.48
came and said, "Your d. is dead; 8.49
mother against d. and d. against 12.53
a d. of Abraham whom Satan bound 13.16
"Fear not, d. of Zion; Jn 12.15
Pharaoh's d. adopted him and brought Ac 7.21
be called the son of Pharaoh's d., Heb 11.24

DAUGHTER-IN-LAW

and Sarai his d., his son Abram's Gen 11.31
Then Judah said to Tamar his d., 38.11
did not know that she was his d. 38.16
"Tamar your d. has played the 38.24
uncover the nakedness of your d.; Lev 18.15
If a man lies with his d., 20.12
Ruth the Moabitess her d. with her, Ru 1.22
And Naomi said to her d., 2.20
her d., "It is well, my daughter, 2.22
for your d. who loves you, who is 4.15
Now his d., the wife of Phinehas, 1Sa 4.19
His d. Tamar also bore him Perez 1Ch 2.04
another lewdly defiles his d.; Eze 22.11
the d. against her mother-in-law; Mic 7.06
and a d. against her mother-in-law; Mt 10.35
mother-in-law against her d. and d. Lk 12.53

DAUGHTER'S

daughter or of your d. daughter, Lev 18.10
daughter or her d. daughter to 18.17
are the tokens of my d. virginity." Deu 22.17

DAUGHTERS

and he had other sons and d. Gen 5.04
years, and had other sons and d. 5.07
years, and had other sons and d. 5.10
years, and had other sons and d. 5.13
years, and had other sons and d. 5.16
years, and had other sons and d. 5.19
years, and had other sons and d. 5.22
years, and had other sons and d. 5.26
years, and had other sons and d. 5.30
ground, and d. were born to them, 6.01
saw that the d. of men were fair; 6.02
of God came in to the d. of men, 6.04
years, and had other sons and d. 11.11
years, and had other sons and d. 11.13
years, and had other sons and d. 11.15
years, and had other sons and d. 11.17
years, and had other sons and d. 11.19
years, and had other sons and d. 11.21
years, and had other sons and d. 11.23
years, and had other sons and d. 11.25
I have two d. who have not known 19.08
d., or any one you have in the city, 19.12
sons-in-law, who were to marry his d., 19.14
wife and your two d. who are here, 19.15
wife and his two d. by the hand, 19.16
dwelt in the hills with his two d., 19.30
he dwelt in a cave with his two d. 19.30
Thus both the d. of Lot were with 19.36
my son from the d. of the Canaanites, 24.03
and the d. of the men of the city 24.13
my son from the d. of the Canaanites, 24.37
one of the d. of Laban your 28.02
Now Laban had two d.; the name 29.16
carried away my d. like captives 31.26
to kiss my sons and my d. farewell? 31.28
would take your d. from me by 31.31
you fourteen years for your two d., 31.41
"The d. are my d., the children 31.43

DAUGHTERS (cont.)
can I do this day to these my d., Gen 31.43
If you ill-treat my d., or if you 31.50
or if you take wives besides my d., 31.50
grandchildren and his d. and 31.55
give your d. to us, and take our d. 34.09
Then we will give our d. to you, 34.16
we will take your d. to ourselves, 34.16
let us take their d. in marriage, 34.21
and let us give them our d. 34.21
his d., and all the members of his 36.06
and all his d. rose up to comfort 37.35
his d., and his sons' d.; all his 46.07
sons and his d. numbered thirty-three). 46.15
Now the priest of Midian had seven d.; Ex 2.16
He said to his d., "And where is he? 2.20
them on your sons and on your d.; 3.22
to wife one of the d. of Putiel; 6.25
our sons and d. and with our 10.09
wife and she bears him sons or d., 21.04
and your d. and bring them to me." 32.02
you take of their d. for your sons, 34.16
and their d. play the harlot after 34.16
and your sons and your d. with you; Lev 10.14
you shall eat the flesh of your d. 26.29
and to your sons and d. with you, Num 18.11
and to your sons and d. with you, 18.19
and his d. captives, to an Amorite 21.29
the harlot with the d. of Moab. 25.01
but d.: and the names of the d. of 26.33
Then drew near the d. of Zelophehad 27.01
The names of his d. were: 27.01
"The d. of Zelophehad are right; 27.07
Zelophehad our brother to his d. 36.02
concerning the d. of Zelophehad, 36.06
the d. of Zelophehad did as the 36.10
the d. of Zelophehad, were married 36.11
giving your d. to their sons or Deu 7.03
or taking their d. for your sons. 7.03
God, you and your sons and your d., 12.12
sons and their d. in the fire to 12.31
prostitute of the d. of Israel, 23.17
Your sons and your d. shall be 28.32
You shall beget sons and d., 28.41
the flesh of your sons and d., 28.53
provocation of his sons and his d. 32.19
bar of gold, and his sons and d., Jos 7.24
Manasseh, had no sons. but only d.; 17.03
and these are the names of his d.: 17.03
because the d. of Manasseh received 17.06
and they took their d. to themselves Ju 3.06
and their own d. they gave to their 3.06
that the d. of Israel went year by 11.40
and thirty d. he gave in marriage 12.09
and thirty d. he brought in from 12.09
saw one of the d. of the Philistines. 14.01
saw one of the d. of the Philistines 14.02
woman among the d. of your kinsmen, 14.03
give them any of our d. for wives?" 21.07
cannot give them wives of our d." 21.18
if the d. of Shiloh come out to 21.21
man his wife from the d. of Shiloh, 21.21
my d., why will you go with me? Ru 1.11
Turn back, my d., go your way, for I 1.12
No, my d., for it is exceedingly 1.13
wife and to all her sons and d.; 1Sa 1.04
and bore three sons and two d. 2.21
He will take your d. to be perfumers 8.13
the names of his two d. were these: 14.49
and sons and d. taken captive. 30.03
in soul, each for his sons and d. 30.06
sons or d., spoil or anything that 30.19
lest the d. of the Philistines 2Sa 1.20
lest the d. of the uncircumcised 1.20
"Ye d. of Israel, weep over Saul, who 1.24
more sons and d. were born to 5.13
were the virgin d. of the king 13.18
the lives of your sons and your d., 19.05
sons and their d. as offerings, 2Ki 17.17
Now Sheshan had no sons, only d.; 1Ch 2.34
Shimei had sixteen sons and six d.; 4.27
and Zelophehad had d. 7.15
and David begot more sons and d. 14.03
Eleazar died having no sons, but only d.; 23.22
Heman fourteen sons and three d. 25.05
the son of a woman of the d. of Dan, 2Ch 2.14
twenty-eight sons and sixty d.); 11.21
had twenty-two sons and sixteen d. 13.21
two wives, and he had sons and d. 24.03
kinsfolk, women, sons, and d.; 28.08
sons and our d. and our wives are 29.09
and their d., the whole multitude; 31.18
a wife from the d. of Barzillai Ez 2.61
some of their d. to be wives for 9.02
Therefore give not your d. to their sons, 9.12
take their d. for your sons, 9.12
Jerusalem, repaired, he and his d. Neh 3.12
your d., your wives, and your homes." 4.14
our sons and our d., we are many; 5.02
our sons and our d. to be slaves, 5.05
and some of our d. have already 5.05
a wife of the d. of Barzillai the 7.63
their d., all who have knowledge 10.28
not give our d. to the peoples of 10.30
land or take their d. for our sons; 10.30
not give your d. to their sons, or 13.25
or take their d. for your sons or 13.25
to him seven sons and three d. Job 1.02
his sons and d. were eating and 1.13
"Your sons and d. were eating and 1.18
He had also seven sons and three d. 42.13
were no women so fair as Job's d.; 42.15
d. of kings are among your ladies Ps 45.09
Let the d. of Judah rejoice because 48.11
and the d. of Judah rejoice, because 97.08
sons and their d. to the demons; 106.37
the blood of their sons and d., 106.38
our d. like corner pillars cut for 144.12
The leech has two d.; "Give, give," Pro 30.15
and all the d. of song are brought Ecc 12.04
O d. of Jerusalem, like the tents of Sol 1.05
O d. of Jerusalem, by the gazelles 2.07
O d. of Jerusalem, by the gazelles 3.05
within by the d. of Jerusalem. 3.10
Go forth, O d. of Zion, and behold 3.11
O d. of Jerusalem, if you find my 5.08
is my friend, O d. of Jerusalem. 5.16
O d. of Jerusalem, that you stir not 8.04
Because the d. of Zion are haughty Is 3.16
a scab the heads of the d. of Zion, 3.17
filth of the d. of Zion and 4.04
so are the d. of Moab at the fords 16.02
you complacent d., give ear 32.09
afar and my d. from the end of the 43.06
and your d. shall be carried on 49.22
and a name better than sons and d.; 56.05
and your d. shall be carried in the 60.04
herds, their sons and their d. Jer 3.24
shall eat up your sons and your d.; 5.17
sons and their d. in the fire; 7.31
teach to your d. a lament, and each 9.20
sons and their d. shall die by 11.22
wives, their sons, and their d. 14.16
you have sons or d. in this place. 16.02
the sons and d. who are born in 16.03
flesh of their sons and their d., 19.09
Take wives and have sons and d.; 29.06
and give your d. in marriage, that 29.06
that they may bear sons and d.; 29.06
up their sons and d. to Molech, 32.35
our wives, our sons, or our d., 35.08
the king's d. and all the people who 41.10
captive, and your d. into captivity. 48.46
Cry, O d. of Rabbah! Gird 49.03

DAUGHTERS (cont.)
face against the d. of your people, Eze 13.17
would deliver neither sons nor d.; 14.16
would deliver neither sons nor d., 14.18
survivors to lead out sons and d., 14.22
And you took your sons and your d., 16.20
the d. of the Philistines, who were 16.27
lived with her d. to the north of 16.46
south of you, is Sodom with her d. 16.46
Sodom and her d. have not done as 16.48
you and your d. have done. 16.48
she and her d. had pride, surfeit of 16.49
the fortunes of Sodom and her d., 16.53
the fortunes of Samaria and her d., 16.53
Sodom and her d. shall return to 16.55
Samaria and her d. shall return to 16.55
you and your d. shall return to 16.55
reproach for the d. of Edom and all 16.57
and for the d. of the Philistines. 16.57
younger, and give them to you as d., 16.61
two women, the d. of one mother; 23.02
mine, and they bore sons and d. 23.04
they seized her sons and her d.; 23.10
shall seize your sons and your d., 23.25
shall slay their sons and their d., 23.47
sons and your d. whom you left 24.21
and also their sons and d., 24.25
and her d. on the mainland shall be 26.06
the sword your d. on the mainland; 26.08
and her d. shall go into captivity. 30.18
the d. of the nations shall chant 32.16
her and the d. of majestic nations, 32.18
Therefore your d. play the harlot, Hos 4.13
not punish your d. when they play 4.14
sons and your d. shall prophesy, Joe 2.28
sons and you d. into the hand of 3.08
sons and your d. shall fall by the Amo 7.17
he had a wife of the d. of Aaron, Lk 1.05
"D. of Jerusalem, do not weep for me, 23.28
sons and your d. shall prophesy, Ac 2.17
And he had four unmarried d., 21.09
and you shall be my sons and d., 2Co 6.18

DAUGHTERS-IN-LAW
with her d. to return from the Ru 1.06
with her two d., and they went on 1.07
But Naomi said to her two d., 1.08

DAUNTED
shouting or d. at their noise, Is 31.04

DAVID
father of Jesse. the father of D. Ru 4.17
Obed of Jesse, and Jesse of D. 4.22
mightily upon D. from that day 1Sa 16.13
"Send me D. your son, who is with 16.19
sent them by D. his son to Saul. 16.20
And D. came to Saul, and entered his 16.21
"Let D. remain in my service, for he 16.22
D. took the lyre and played it with 16.23
Now D. was the son of an Ephrathite 17.12
D. was the youngest; the three 17.14
but D. went back and forth from 17.15
And Jesse said to D. his son, 17.17
And D. rose early in the morning, 17.20
And D. left the things in charge of 17.22
as before. And D. heard him. 17.23
And D. said to the men who stood by 17.26
anger was kindled against D., 17.28
And D. said, "What have I done now? 17.29
When the words which D. spoke were 17.31
And D. said to Saul, "Let no man's 17.32
And Saul said to D., 17.33
But D. said to Saul, "Your servant 17.34
And D. said, "The LORD who delivered 17.37
And Saul said to D., "Go, and 17.37
Then Saul clothed D. with his armor; 17.38
And D. girded his sword over his 17.39
Then D. said to Saul, "I cannot go 17.39
And D. put them off. 17.39
came on and drew near to D., 17.41
and saw D., he disdained him; 17.42
And the Philistine said to D., "Am I a 17.43
Philistine cursed D. by his gods. 17.43
The Philistine said to D., 17.44
Then D. said to the Philistine, "You 17.45
and came and drew near to meet D., 17.48
D. ran quickly toward the battle 17.48
And D. put his hand in his bag and 17.49
So D. prevailed over the Philistine 17.50
was no sword in the hand of D. 17.50
Then D. ran and stood over the 17.51
And D. took the head of the Philistine 17.54
When Saul saw D. go forth against 17.55
And as D. returned from the slaughter 17.57
And D. answered, "I am the son of 17.58
Jonathan was knit to the soul of D., 18.01
Then Jonathan made a covenant with D., 18.03
was upon him, and gave it to D., 18.04
And D. went out and was successful 18.05
when D. returned from slaying the 18.06
thousands, and D. his ten thousands." 18.07
have ascribed to D. ten thousands, 18.08
And Saul eyed D. from that day on. 18.09
while D. was playing the lyre, as he 18.10
thought, "I will pin D. to the wall." 18.11
But D. evaded him twice. 18.11
Saul was afraid of D., because the 18.12
And D. had success in all his 18.14
But all Israel and Judah loved D.; 18.16
Then Saul said to D., "Here is 18.17
And D. said to Saul, "Who am I, and 18.18
should have been given to D., 18.19
Now Saul's daughter Michal loved D.; 18.20
Saul said to D. a second time, 18.21
"Speak to D. in private and say, 18.22
those words in the ears of D. 18.23
and D. said, "Does it seem to you a 18.23
told him, "Thus and so did D. speak." 18.24
said, "Thus shall you say to D., 18.25
thought to make D. fall by the 18.25
his servants told D. these words, 18.26
it pleased D. well to be the king's 18.26
D. arose and went, along with his 18.27
and D. brought their foreskins, 18.27
and knew that the LORD was with D., 18.28
Saul was still more afraid of D. 18.29
they came out D. had more success 18.30
servants, that they should kill D. 19.01
Saul's son, delighted much in D. 19.01
And Jonathan told D., "Saul my 19.02
spoke well of D. to Saul his 19.04
king sin against his servant D.; 19.04
blood of killing D. without cause? 19.05
And Jonathan called D., 19.07
and Jonathan brought D. to Saul, 19.07
and D. went out and fought with the 19.08
and D. was playing the lyre. 19.09
sought to pin D. to the wall with 19.10
And D. fled, and escaped. 19.10
So Michal let D. down through the 19.12
Saul sent messengers to take D., 19.14
Saul sent the messengers to see D., 19.15
Now D. fled and escaped, and he came 19.18
"Behold, D. is at Naioth in Ramah." 19.19
Then Saul sent messengers to take D.; 19.20
he asked, "Where are Samuel and D.?" 19.22
Then D. fled from Naioth in Ramah, 20.01
But D. replied, "Your father knows 20.03
Then said Jonathan to D., "Whatever 20.04
D. said to Jonathan, "Behold, tomorrow 20.05
'D. earnestly asked leave of me to 20.06
Then said D. to Jonathan, "Who will 20.10

DAVID (cont.)

And Jonathan said to D., "Come, let 1Sa 20.11
And Jonathan said to D., "The LORD, 20.12
if he is well disposed toward D., 20.12
the enemies of D. from the face of 20.15
be cut off from the house of D. 20.16
And Jonathan made D. swear again by 20.17
So D. hid himself in the field; 20.24
"D. earnestly asked leave of me to 20.28
was determined to put D. to death. 20.33
month, for he was grieved for D., 20.34
field to the appointment with D., 20.35
Jonathan and D. knew the matter. 20.39
D. rose from beside the stone heap 20.41
until D. recovered himself. 20.41
Then Jonathan said to D., "Go in 20.42
Then came D. to Nob to Ahimelech 21.01
Ahimelech came to meet D. trembling, 21.01
And D. said to Ahimelech the priest, 21.02
And the priest answered D., "I have 21.04
And D. answered the priest, "Of a 21.05
And D. said to Ahimelech, "And have 21.08
And D. said, "There is none like 21.09
And D. rose and fled that day from 21.10
"Is not this D. the king of the 21.11
And D. his ten thousands'?" 21.11
And D. took these words to heart, 21.12
D. departed from there and escaped 22.01
And D. went from there to Mizpeh of 22.03
the time that D. was in the 22.04
Then the prophet Gad said to D., 22.05
So D. departed, and went into the 22.05
Now Saul heard that D. was discovered, 22.06
your servants is so faithful as D., 22.14
because their hand also is with D., 22.17
Abiathar, escaped and fled after D. 22.20
And Abiathar told D. that Saul had 22.21
And D. said to Abiathar, "I knew on 22.22
Now they told D., "Behold, the 23.01
Therefore D. inquired of the LORD, 23.02
And the LORD said to D., "Go and 23.02
Then D. inquired of the LORD again. 23.04
And D. and his men went to Keilah, 23.05
So D. delivered the inhabitants of 23.05
of Ahimelech fled to D. to Keilah, 23.06
told Saul that D. had come to 23.07
Keilah, to besiege D. and his men. 23.08
D. knew that Saul was plotting evil 23.09
Then said D., "O LORD, the God of 23.10
Then said D., "Will the men of 23.12
Then D. and his men, who were about 23.13
was told that D. had escaped from 23.13
And D. remained in the strongholds 23.14
And D. was afraid because Saul had 23.15
D. was in the Wilderness of Ziph at 23.15
and went to D. at Horesh, and 23.16
D. remained at Horesh, and Jonathan 23.18
"Does not D. hide among us in the 23.19
Now D. and his men were in the 23.24
And D was told; therefore he went 23.25
pursued after D. in the wilderness 23.25
and D. and his men on the other 23.26
and D. was making haste to get away 23.26
closing in upon D. and his men to 23.26
returned from pursuing after D., 23.28
And D. went up from there, and dwelt 23.29
D. is in the wilderness of Engedi." 24.01
went to seek D. and his men in 24.02
Now D. and his men were sitting in 24.03
And the men of D. said to him, "Here 24.04
Then D. arose and stealthily cut 24.04
So D. persuaded his men with these 24.07
Afterward D. also arose, and went 24.08
D. bowed with his face to the earth, 24.08
And D. said to Saul, "Why do you 24.09
'Behold, D. seeks your hurt'? 24.09
When D. had finished speaking these 24.16
"Is this your voice, my son D.?" 24.16
He said to D., "You are more 24.17
And D. swore this to Saul. 24.22
but D. and his men went up to the 24.22
Then D. rose and went down to the 25.01
D. heard in the wilderness that 25.04
So D. sent ten young men; 25.05
and D. said to the young men, "Go up 25.05
your servants and to your son D. 25.08
this to Nabal in the name of D.; 25.09
David's servants, "Who is D.? 25.10
And D. said to his men, "Every man 25.13
D. also girded on his sword; 25.13
four hundred men went up after D., 25.13
D. sent messengers out of the 25.14
D. and his men came down toward her 25.20
Now D. had said, "Surely in vain 25.21
God do so to D. and more also, if by 25.22
When Abigail saw D., she made 25.23
and fell before D. on her face, 25.23
And D. said to Abigail, "Blessed be 25.32
Then D. received from her hand what 25.35
When D. heard that Nabal was dead, 25.39
Then D. sent and wooed Abigail, to 25.39
the servants of D. came to Abigail 25.40
"D. has sent us to you to take you 25.40
went after the messengers of D., 25.42
D. also took Ahinoam of Jezreel; 25.43
"Is not D. hiding himself on the 26.01
to seek D. in the wilderness of 26.02
But D. remained in the wilderness; 26.03
D. sent out spies, and learned of a 26.04
Then D. rose and came to the place 26.05
and D. saw the place where Saul lay, 26.05
Then D. said to Ahimelech the 26.06
So D. and Abishai went to the army 26.07
Then said Abishai to D., "God has 26.08
But D. said to Abishai, "Do not 26.09
And D. said, "As the LORD lives, the 26.10
So D. took the spear and the jar of 26.12
Then D. went over to the other side, 26.13
and D. called to the army, and to 26.14
And D. said to Abner, "Are you not a 26.15
"Is this your voice, my son D.?" 26.17
And D. said, "It is my voice, my lord, 26.17
my son D., for I will no more do 26.21
And D. made answer, "Here is the 26.22
said to D., "Blessed be you, my son D.! 26.25
So D. went his way, and Saul returned 26.25
And D. said in his heart, "I shall 27.01
So D. arose and went over, he and 27.02
And D. dwelt with Achish at Gath, he 27.03
and D. with his two wives, Ahinoam 27.03
told Saul that D. had fled to Gath, 27.04
Then D. said to Achish, "If I have 27.05
the days that D. dwelt in the 27.07
Now D. and his men went up, and made 27.08
And D. smote the land, and left 27.09
D. would say, "Against the Negeb of 27.10
And D. saved neither man nor woman 27.11
about us, and say, 'So D. has done.'" 27.11
And Achish trusted D., thinking, "He 27.12
And Achish said to D., "Understand 28.01
D. said to Achish, "Very well, you 28.02
And Achish said to D., "Very well, 28.02
and given it to your neighbor, D. 28.17
and D. and his men were passing on 29.02
"Is not this D., the servant of 29.03
Is not this D., of whom they sing 29.05
And D. his ten thousands'?" 29.05
Then Achish called D. and said to 29.06
And D. said to Achish, "But what 29.08
And Achish made answer to D., 29.09
So D. set out with his men early in 29.11
Now when D. and his men came to 30.01
And when D. and his men came to the 30.03
Then D. and the people who were 30.04

DAVID (cont.)
And D. was greatly distressed; 1Sa 30.06
But D. strengthened himself in the 30.06
And D. said to Abiathar the priest, 30.07
Abiathar brought the ephod to D. 30.07
And D. inquired of the LORD, "Shall 30.08
So D. set out, and the six hundred 30.09
But D. went on with the pursuit, he 30.10
country, and brought him to D.; 30.11
And D. said to him, "To whom do you 30.13
And D. said to him. "Will you take 30.15
And D. smote them from twilight 30.17
D. recovered all that the Amalekites 30.18
and D. rescued his two wives. 30.18
had been taken; D. brought back all. 30.19
D. also captured all the flocks and 30.20
Then D. came to the two hundred men, 30.21
been too exhausted to follow D., 30.21
out to meet D. and to meet the 30.21
and when D. drew near to the people 30.21
the men who had gone with D. said, 30.22
But D. said, "You shall not do so, my 30.23
When D. came to Ziklag, he sent part 30.26
places where D. and his men had 30.31
when D. had returned from the 2Sa 1.01
D. remained two days in Ziklag; 1.01
And when he came to D., he fell 1.02
D. said to him, "Where do you come 1.03
And D. said to him, "How did it go 1.04
Then D. said to the young man who 1.05
Then D. took hold of his clothes, 1.11
And D. said to the young man who 1.13
D. said to him, "How is it you were 1.14
Then D. called one of the young men 1.15
And D. said to him, "Your blood be 1.16
And D. lamented with this lamentation 1.17
After this D. inquired of the LORD, 2.01
D. said, "To which shall I go up?" 2.01
So D. went up there, and his two 2.02
And D. brought up his men who were 2.03
they anointed D. king over the 2.04
When they told D., "It was the 2.04
D. sent messengers to the men of 2.05
But the house of Judah followed D. 2.10
And the time that D. was king in 2.11
of Zeruiah, and the servants of D., 2.13
and twelve of the servants of D. 2.15
beaten before the servants of D. 2.17
But the servants of D. had slain of 2.31
house of Saul and the house of D.; 3.01
and D. grew stronger and stronger, 3.01
And sons were born to D. at Hebron: 3.02
These were born to D. in Hebron. 3.05
house of Saul and the house of D., 3.06
not given you into the hand of D.; 3.08
accomplish for D. what the LORD 3.09
the throne of D. over Israel and 3.10
sent messengers to D. at Hebron, 3.12
Then D. sent messengers to Ishbosheth 3.14
been seeking D. as king over you. 3.17
for the LORD has promised D., 3.18
of my servant D. I will save my 3.18
went to tell D. at Hebron all that 3.19
with twenty men to D. at Hebron, 3.20
D. made a feast for Abner and the 3.20
And Abner said to D., "I will arise 3.21
So D. sent Abner away; and he went 3.21
the servants of D. arrived with 3.22
Abner was not with D. at Hebron, 3.22
but D. did not know about it. 3.26
when D. heard of it, he said, "I and 3.28
Then D. said to Joab and to all the 3.31
And King D. followed the bier. 3.31
to persuade D. to eat bread while 3.35
but D. swore, saying, "God do so to 3.35
head of Ishbosheth to D. at Hebron. 4.08
But D. answered Rechab and Baanah 4.09

And D. commanded his young men, and 4.12
of Israel came to D. at Hebron, 5.01
and King D. made a covenant with 5.03
they anointed D. king over Israel. 5.03
D. was thirty years old when he 5.04
who said to D., "You will not come 5.06
thinking, "D. cannot come in here." 5.06
Nevertheless D. took the stronghold 5.07
of Zion, that is, the city of D. 5.07
And D. said on that day, "Whoever 5.08
and D. dwelt in the stronghold, and 5.09
and called it the city of D. 5.09
And D. built the city round about 5.09
And D. became greater and greater, 5.10
king of Tyre sent messengers to D., 5.11
and masons who built D. a house. 5.11
And D. perceived that the LORD had 5.12
And D. took more concubines and 5.13
sons and daughters were born to D. 5.13
heard that D. had been anointed 5.17
Philistines went up in search of D.; 5.17
but D. heard of it and went down to 5.17
and D. inquired of the LORD, "Shall 5.19
And the LORD said to D., "Go up; 5.19
And D. came to Baalperazim, and 5.20
and D. defeated them there; and he said, 5.20
and D. and his men carried them 5.21
And when D. inquired of the LORD, he 5.23
And D. did as the LORD commanded 5.25
D. again gathered all the chosen 6.01
And D. arose and went with all the 6.02
And D. and all the house of Israel 6.05
And D. was angry because the LORD 6.08
And D. was afraid of the LORD that 6.09
So D. was not willing to take the 6.10
of the LORD into the city of D.; 6.10
but D. took it aside to the house 6.10
And it was told King D., "The LORD 6.12
So D. went and brought up the ark 6.12
to the city of D. with rejoicing; 6.12
And D. danced before the LORD with 6.14
and D. was girded with a linen 6.14
So D. and all the house of Israel 6.15
the LORD came into the city of D., 6.16
and saw King D. leaping and dancing 6.16
the tent which D. had pitched for 6.17
and D. offered burnt offerings and 6.17
And when D. had finished offering 6.18
And D. returned to bless his household. 6.20
of Saul came out to meet D., and said, 6.20
And D. said to Michal, "It was 6.21
"Go and tell my servant D., 7.05
you shall say to my servant D., 7.08
this vision, Nathan spoke to D. 7.17
Then King D. went in and sat before 7.18
And what more can D. say to thee? 7.20
of thy servant D. will be established 7.26
After this D. defeated the Philistines 8.01
and D. took Metheghammah out of the 8.01
servants to D. and brought tribute 8.02
D. also defeated Hadadezer the son 8.03
And D. took from him a thousand and 8.04
and D. hamstrung all the chariot 8.04
D. slew twenty-two thousand men of 8.05
Then D. put garrisons in Aram of 8.06
servants to D. and brought tribute 8.06
gave victory to D. wherever he 8.06
And D. took the shields of gold 8.07
King D. took very much bronze. 8.08
heard that D. had defeated the 8.09
Tou sent his son Joram to King D., 8.10
these also King D. dedicated to the 8.11
And D. won a name for himself. 8.13
gave victory to D. wherever he 8.14
So D. reigned over all Israel; 8.15
and D. administered justice and 8.15
And D. said, "Is there still any one 9.01

DAVID (cont.)

Ziba, and they called him to D.; 2Sa 9.02
Then King D. sent and brought him 9.05
came to D., and fell on his face 9.06
and D. said, "Mephibosheth!" 9.06
And D. said to him, "Do not fear; 9.07
And D. said, "I will deal loyally 10.02
So D. sent by his servants to 10.02
because D. has sent comforters to 10.03
Has not D. sent his servants to you 10.03
When it was told D., he sent 10.05
that they had become odious to D., 10.06
And when D. heard of it, he sent 10.07
And when it was told D., he gathered 10.17
arrayed themselves against D., 10.17
and D. slew of the Syrians the men 10.18
D. sent Joab, and his servants with 11.01
But D. remained at Jerusalem. 11.01
when D. arose from his couch and 11.02
And D. sent and inquired about the 11.03
So D. sent messengers, and took her; 11.04
and she sent and told D., 11.05
So D. sent word to Joab, "Send me 11.06
And Joab sent Uriah to D. 11.06
D. asked how Joab was doing, and how 11.07
Then D. said to Uriah, "Go down to 11.08
When they told D., "Uriah did not 11.10
D. said to Uriah, "Have you not 11.10
Uriah said to D., "The ark and 11.11
Then D. said to Uriah, "Remain here 11.12
And D. invited him, and he ate in 11.13
In the morning D. wrote a letter to 11.14
the servants of D. among the 11.17
sent and told D. all the news 11.18
came and told D. all that Joab had 11.22
The messenger said to D., 11.23
D. said to the messenger, "Thus 11.25
D. sent and brought her to his house, 11.27
the thing that D. had done displeased 11.27
And the LORD sent Nathan to D. 12.01
Nathan said to D., "You are the man. 12.07
D. said to Nathan, "I have sinned 12.13
And Nathan said to D., "The LORD 12.13
child that Uriah's wife bore to D., 12.15
D. therefore besought God for the 12.16
and D. fasted, and went in and lay 12.16
the servants of D. feared to tell 12.18
But when D. saw that his servants 12.19
D. perceived that the child was 12.19
and D. said to his servants, "Is the 12.19
Then D. arose from the earth, and 12.20
Then D. comforted his wife, Bathsheba, 12.24
And Joab sent messengers to D., 12.27
So D. gathered all the people 12.29
Then D. and all the people returned 12.31
Then D. sent home to Tamar, saying, 13.07
When King D. heard of all these 13.21
on the way, tidings came to D., 13.30
And D. mourned for his son day 13.37
And a messenger came to D., saying, 15.13
Then D. said to all his servants 15.14
And D. said to Ittai, "Go then, pass 15.22
But D. went up the ascent of the 15.30
And it was told D., "Ahithophel 15.31
And D. said, "O LORD, I pray thee, 15.31
When D. came to the summit, where 15.32
D. said to him, "If you go on with 15.33
When D. had passed a little beyond 16.01
When King D. came to Bahurim, there 16.05
And he threw stones at D., and at all 16.06
and at all the servants of King D.; 16.06
'Curse D.,' who then shall say, 'Why 16.10
And D. said to Abishai and to all 16.11
So D. and his men went on the road, 16.13
esteemed, both by D. and by Absalom. 16.23
will set out and pursue D. tonight. 17.01
therefore send quickly and tell D., 17.16
and they would go and tell King D.; 17.17
well, and went and told King D. 17.21
They said to D., "Arise, and go 17.21
Then D. arose, and all the people 17.22
Then D. came to Mahanaim. And Absalom 17.24
When D. came to Mahanaim, Shobi the 17.27
for D. and the people with him to 17.29
Then D. mustered the men who were 18.01
And D. sent forth the army, one 18.02
there by the servants of D., and the 18.07
chanced to meet the servants of D. 18.09
Now D. was sitting between the two 18.24
And King D. sent this message to 19.11
the men of Judah to meet King D.; 19.16
But D. said, "What have I to do with 19.22
and in D. also we have more than 19.43
and said, "We have no portion in D., 20.01
the men of Israel withdrew from D., 20.02
And D. came to his house at Jerusalem; 20.03
And D. said to Abishai, "Now Sheba 20.06
favors Joab, and whoever is for D., 20.11
lifted up his hand against King D.; 20.21
in the days of D. for three years, 21.01
and D. sought the face of the LORD. 21.01
And D. said to the Gibeonites, "What 21.03
between D. and Jonathan the son of 21.07
When D. was told what Rizpah the 21.11
D. went and took the bones of Saul 21.12
and D. went down together with his 21.15
the Philistines; and D. grew weary. 21.15
a new sword, thought to kill D. 21.16
by the hand of D. and by the hand 21.22
And D. spoke to the LORD the words 22.01
to D., and his descendants for ever." 22.51
Now these are the last words of D.: 23.01
The oracle of D., the son of Jesse, 23.01
of the mighty men whom D. had: 23.08
He was with D. when they defied the 23.09
harvest time to D. at the cave of 23.13
D. was then in the stronghold; 23.14
And D. said longingly, "O that some 23.15
and took and brought it to D. 23.16
And D. set him over his bodyguard. 23.23
and he incited D. against them, 24.01
And D. said to the LORD, "I have 24.10
And when D. arose in the morning, 24.11
"Go and say to D., 'Thus says the 24.12
So Gad came to D. and told him, and 24.13
Then D. said to Gad, "I am in great 24.14
Then D. spoke to the LORD when he 24.17
And Gad came that day to D., 24.18
So D. went up at Gad's word, as the 24.19
D. said, "To buy the threshing floor 24.21
Then Araunah said to D., 24.22
So D. bought the threshing floor 24.24
And D. built there an altar to the 24.25
Now King D. was old and advanced in 1Ki 1.01
become king and D. our lord does 1.11
Go in at once to King D., 1.13
Then King D. answered, "Call Bathsheba 1.28
"May my lord King D. live for ever!" 1.31
King D. said, "Call to me Zadok the 1.32
than the throne of my lord King D." 1.37
our lord King D. has made Solomon 1.43
to congratulate our lord King D., 1.47
Then D. slept with his fathers, and 2.10
and was buried in the city of D. 2.10
And the time that D. reigned over 2.11
upon the throne of D. his father; 2.12
me on the throne of D. my father, 2.24
the LORD GOD before D. my father, 2.26
the knowledge of my father D., 2.32
but to D., and to his descendants, 2.33
evil that you did to D. my father; 2.44
the throne of D. shall be established 2.45
brought her into the city of D., 3.01
in the statutes of D. his father; 3.03

DAVID (cont.)
love to thy servant D. my father, 1Ki 3.06
king in place of D. my father, 3.07
commandments, as your father D. walked, 3.14
his father; for Hiram always loved D. 5.01
"You know that D. my father could 5.03
as the LORD said to D. my father, 5.05
has given to D. a wise son to be 5.07
which I spoke to D. your father. 6.12
things which D. his father had 7.51
of the city of D., which is Zion. 8.01
with his mouth to D. my father, 8.15
but I chose D. to be over my people 8.16
in the heart of D. my father to 8.17
But the LORD said to D. my father, 8.18
risen in the place of D. my father, 8.20
thy servant D. my father what thou 8.24
thy servant D. my father what thou 8.25
spoken to thy servant D. my father. 8.26
had shown to D. his servant and to 8.66
as D. your father walked, with 9.04
as I promised D. your father, saying, 9.05
the city of D. to her own house 9.24
as was the heart of D. his father. 11.04
as D. his father had done. 11.06
Yet for the sake of D. your father 11.12
for the sake of D. my servant and 11.13
For when D. was in Edom, and Joab 11.15
in Egypt that D. slept with his 11.21
band, after the slaughter by D.; 11.24
of the city of D. his father. 11.27
of my servant D. and for the sake 11.32
ordinances, as D. his father did. 11.33
for the sake of D. my servant whom 11.34
that D. my servant may always have 11.36
as D. my servant did, I will be with 11.38
a sure house, as I built for D., 11.38
this afflict the descendants of D., 11.39
in the city of D. his father; 11.43
king, "What portion have we in D.? 12.16
Look now to your own house, D." 12.16
the house of D. to this day. 12.19
none that followed the house of D., 12.20
will turn back to the house of D.; 12.26
shall be born of the house of D., 13.02
the house of D. and gave it to you 14.08
have not been like my servant D., 14.08
with his fathers in the city of D. 14.31
God, as the heart of D. his father. 15.03
because D. did what was right in 15.05
they buried him in the city of D. 15.08
as D. his father had done. 15.11
in the city of D. his father; 15.24
in the city of D. his father; 22.50
for the sake of D. his servant, 2Ki 8.19
with his fathers in the city of D.; 8.24
with his fathers in the city of D. 9.28
with his fathers in the city of D., 12.21
LORD, yet not like D. his father; 14.03
with his fathers in the city of D. 14.20
with his fathers in the city of D., 15.07
in the city of D. his father; 15.38
God, as his father D. had done, 16.02
with his fathers in the city of D.; 16.20
the house of D. they made Jeroboam 17.21
to all that D. his father had done 18.03
and for the sake of my servant D." 19.34
the God of D. your father: I have 20.05
LORD said to D. and to Solomon his 21.07
in all the way of D. his father, 22.02
Ozem the sixth, D. the seventh; 1Ch 2.15
These are the sons of D. that were 3.01
were their cities until D. reigned. 4.31
the men whom D. put in charge of 6.31
in the days of D. being twenty-two 7.02
D. and Samuel the seer established 9.22
kingdom over to D. the son of 10.14
gathered together to D. at Hebron, 11.01
and D. made a covenant with them 11.03
they anointed D. king over Israel, 11.03
And D. and all Israel went to 11.04
The inhabitants of Jebus said to D., 11.05
Nevertheless D. took the stronghold 11.05
of Zion, that is, the city of D. 11.05
D. said, "Whoever shall smite the 11.06
And D. dwelt in the stronghold; 11.07
it was called the city of D. 11.07
And D. became greater and greater, 11.09
He was with D. at Pasdammim when 11.13
to the rock to D. at the cave of 11.15
D. was then in the stronghold; 11.16
And D. said longingly, "O that some 11.17
and took and brought it to D. 11.18
But D. would not drink of it; 11.18
And D. set him over his bodyguard. 11.25
the men who came to D. at Ziklag, 12.01
went over to D. at the stronghold 12.08
Judah came to the stronghold to D. 12.16
D. went out to meet them and said 12.17
and he said, "We are yours, O D.; 12.18
Then D. received them, and made 12.18
deserted to D. when he came with 12.19
They helped D. against the band of 12.21
men kept coming to D. to help him, 12.22
who came to D. in Hebron, to turn 12.23
named to come and make D. king. 12.31
to help D. with singleness of 12.33
intent to make D. king over all 12.38
of a single mind to make D. king. 12.38
were there with D. for three days, 12.39
D. consulted with the commanders of 13.01
And D. said to all the assembly of 13.02
So D. assembled all Israel from the 13.05
And D. and all Israel went up to 13.06
And D. and all Israel were making 13.08
And D. was angry because the LORD 13.11
And D. was afraid of God that day; 13.12
So D. did not take the ark home 13.13
the ark home into the city of D., 13.13
king of Tyre sent messengers to D., 14.01
And D. perceived that the LORD had 14.02
And D. took more wives in Jerusalem, 14.03
and D. begot more sons and daughters 14.03
heard that D. had been anointed 14.08
Philistines went up in search of D.; 14.08
and D. heard of it and went out 14.08
And D. inquired of God, "Shall I go 14.10
and D. defeated them there; and D. 14.11
and D. gave command, and they were 14.12
And when D. again inquired of God, 14.14
And D. did as God commanded him, and 14.16
And the fame of D. went out into 14.17
D. built houses for himself in the 15.01
for himself in the city of D.; 15.01
Then D. said, "No one but the 15.02
And D. assembled all Israel at 15.03
And D. gathered together the sons 15.04
Then D. summoned the priests Zadok 15.11
D. also commanded the chiefs of the 15.16
So D. and the elders of Israel, and 15.25
D. was clothed with a robe of fine 15.27
singers; and D. wore a linen ephod. 15.27
of the LORD came to the city of D., 15.29
and saw King D. dancing and making 15.29
the tent which D. had pitched for 16.01
And when D. had finished offering 16.02
Then on that day D. first appointed 16.07
So D. left Asaph and his brethren 16.37
and D. went home to bless his 16.43
Now when D. dwelt in his house, 17.01
D. said to Nathan the prophet, 17.01
And Nathan said to D., "Do all 17.02
"Go and tell my servant D., 17.04
shall you say to my servant D., 17.07

DAVID (cont.)

this vision, Nathan spoke to D.	1Ch 17.15
Then King D. went in and sat before	17.16
And what more can D. say to thee	17.18
of thy servant D. will be established	17.24
After this D. defeated the Philistines	18.01
servants to D. and brought tribute	18.02
D. also defeated Hadadezer king of	18.03
And D. took from him a thousand	18.04
and D. hamstrung all the chariot	18.04
D. slew twenty-two thousand men of	18.05
Then D. put garrisons in Syria of	18.06
the Syrians became servants to D.,	18.06
gave victory to D. wherever he	18.06
And D. took the shields of gold	18.07
D. took very much bronze; with it	18.08
heard that D. had defeated the	18.09
he sent his son Hadoram to King D.,	18.10
these also King D. dedicated to the	18.11
gave victory to D. wherever he	18.13
So D. reigned over all Israel;	18.14
And D. said, "I will deal loyally	19.02
So D. sent messengers to console	19.02
because D. has sent comforters to	19.03
When D. was told concerning the men,	19.05
had made themselves odious to D.,	19.06
When D. heard of it, he sent Joab	19.08
And when it was told D., he gathered	19.17
And when D. set the battle in array	19.17
and D. slew of the Syrians the	19.18
by Israel, they made peace with D.,	19.19
But D. remained at Jerusalem.	20.01
And D. took the crown of their king	20.02
and thus D. did to all the cities	20.03
Then D. and all the people returned	20.03
by the hand of D. and by the hand	20.08
and incited D. to number Israel.	21.01
So D. said to Joab and the commanders	21.02
the numbering of the people to D.	21.05
And D. said to God, "I have sinned	21.08
"Go and say to D., 'Thus says the	21.10
So Gad came to D. and said to him,	21.11
Then D. said to Gad, "I am in great	21.13
And D. lifted his eyes and saw the	21.16
Then D. and the elders, clothed in	21.16
And D. said to God, "Was it not I	21.17
Gad to say to D. that D. should go up	21.18
So D. went up at Gad's word, which he	21.19
As D. came to Ornan, Ornan looked	21.21
looked and saw D. and went forth	21.21
obeisance to D. with his face to	21.21
And D. said to Ornan, "Give me the	21.22
Then Ornan said to D., "Take it;	21.23
But King D. said to Ornan, "No, but I	21.24
So D. paid Ornan six hundred	21.25
And D. built there an altar to the	21.26
when D. saw that the LORD had	21.28
but D. could not go before it to	21.30
Then D. said, "Here shall be the	22.01
D. commanded to gather together the	22.02
D. also provided great stores of	22.03
great quantities of cedar to D.	22.04
For D. said, "Solomon my son is	22.05
So D. provided materials in great	22.05
D. said to Solomon, "My son, I had it	22.07
D. also commanded all the leaders	22.17
When D. was old and full of days, he	23.01
D. assembled all the leaders of	23.02
D. said, "shall have charge of the	23.04
And D. organized them in divisions	23.06
For D. said, "The LORD, the God of	23.25
last words of D. these were the	23.27
D. organized them according to the	24.03
Aaron, in the presence of King D.,	24.31
D. and the chiefs of the service	25.01
dedicated gifts which D. the king,	26.26
King D. appointed him and his	26.32
D. did not number those below	27.23
in the chronicles of King D.	27.24
D. assembled at Jerusalem all the	28.01
Then King D. rose to his feet and	28.02
Then D. gave Solomon his son the	28.11
Then D. said to Solomon his son, "Be	28.20
And D. the king said to all the	29.01
D. the king also rejoiced greatly	29.09
Therefore D. blessed the LORD in	29.10
and D. said: "Blessed art thou, O	29.10
Then D. said to all the assembly,	29.20
the son of D. king the second time,	29.22
as king instead of D. his father;	29.23
and also all the sons of King D.,	29.24
Thus D. the son of Jesse reigned	29.26
Now the acts of King D., from first	29.29
Solomon the son of D. established	2Ch 1.01
(But D. had brought up the ark of	1.04
the place that D. had prepared for	1.04
and steadfast love to D. my father,	1.08
thy promise to D. my father be now	1.09
you dealt with D. my father and	2.03
Jerusalem, whom D. my father provided.	2.07
who has given King D. a wise son,	2.12
craftsmen of my lord, D. your father.	2.14
of them which D. his father had	2.17
LORD had appeared to D. his father,	3.01
at the place that D. had appointed,	3.01
things which D. his father had	5.01
of the city of D., which is Zion.	5.02
with his mouth to D. my father,	6.04
I have chosen D. to be over my	6.06
in the heart of D. my father to	6.07
But the LORD said to D. my father,	6.08
risen in the place of D. my father,	6.10
thy servant D. my father what thou	6.15
thy servant D. my father what thou	6.16
thou hast spoken to thy servant D.	6.17
steadfast love for D. thy servant."	6.42
LORD which King D. had made for	7.06
whenever D. offered praises by	7.06
had shown to D. and to Solomon and	7.10
as D. your father walked, doing	7.17
I covenanted with D. your father,	7.18
the city of D. to the house which	8.11
in the house of D. king of Israel,	8.11
According to the ordinance of D. his father,	8.14
for so D. the man of God had commanded.	8.14
in the city of D. his father;	9.31
king, "What portion have we in D.?	10.16
Look now to your own house, D."	10.16
the house of D. to this day.	10.19
years in the way of D. and Solomon.	11.17
daughter of Jerimoth the son of D.,	11.18
and was buried in the city of D.;	12.16
for ever to D. and his sons by a	13.05
a servant of Solomon the son of D.,	13.06
LORD in the hand of the sons of D.,	13.08
they buried him in the city of D.;	14.01
out for himself in the city of D.	16.14
with his fathers in the city of D.;	21.01
would not destroy the house of D.,	21.07
covenant which he had made with D.,	21.07
the God of D. your father, 'Because	21.12
they buried him in the city of D.,	21.20
spoke concerning the sons of D.	23.03
Levites whom D. had organized to	23.18
singing, according to the order of D.	23.18
in the city of D. among the kings,	24.16
they buried him in the city of D.,	24.25
with his fathers in the city of D.	25.28
they buried him in the city of D.;	27.09
of the LORD, like his father D.,	28.01
to all that D. his father had done.	29.02
commandment of D. and of Gad the	29.25
stood with the instruments of D.,	29.26
instruments of D. king of Israel.	29.27

DAVID (cont.)
the words of D. and of Asaph the 2Ch 29.30
the son of D. king of Israel there 30.26
the Millo in the city of D. 32.05
to the west side of the city of D. 32.30
of the tombs of the sons of D.; 32.33
God said to D. and to Solomon his 33.07
to the city of D. west of Gihon, 33.14
in the ways of D. his father; 34.02
to seek the God of D. his father; 34.03
house which Solomon the son of D., 35.03
directions of D. king of Israel 35.04
according to the command of D., 35.15
directions of D. king of Israel; Ez 3.10
Of the sons of D., Hattush, 8.02
whom D. and his officials had set 8.20
that go down from the City of D. Neh 3.15
opposite the sepulchres of D., 3.16
commandment of D. the man of God, 12.24
instruments of D. the man of God; 12.36
by the stairs of the city of D., 12.37
of the wall, above the house of D., 12.37
the command of D. and his son 12.45
For in the days of D. and Asaph of 12.46
to D. and his descendants for ever. Ps 18.50
The prayers of D., the son of Jesse, 72.20
He chose D. his servant, and took 78.70
I have sworn to D. my servant: 89.03
I have found D., my servant; 89.20
holiness; I will not lie to D. 89.35
faithfulness thou didst swear to D.? 89.49
the thrones of the house of D. 122.05
The LORD swore to D. a sure oath 132.11
will make a horn to sprout for D.; 132.17
kings, who rescuest D. thy servant. 144.10
Solomon, son of D., king of Israel: Pro 1.01
the son of D. king in Jerusalem. Ecc 1.01
Your neck is like the tower of D., Sol 4.04
When the house of D. was told, Is 7.02
And he said, "Hear then, O house of D.! 7.13
be no end, upon the throne of D., 9.07
in the tent of D. one who judges 16.05
of the city of D. were many, and you 22.09
shoulder the key of the house of D.; 22.22
Ariel, the city where D. encamped! 29.01
and for the sake of my servant D. 37.35
the God of D. your father: I have 38.05
my steadfast, sure love for D. 55.03
kings who sit on the throne of D., Jer 17.25
O house of D.! Thus says 21.12
Judah, who sit on the throne of D., 22.02
kings who sit on the throne of D., 22.04
in sitting on the throne of D., 22.30
raise up for D. a righteous Branch, 23.05
king who sits on the throne of D., 29.16
LORD their God and D. their king, 30.09
Branch to spring forth for D.; 33.15
D. shall never lack a man to sit on 33.17
covenant with D. my servant may be 33.21
the descendants of D. my servant, 33.22
of Jacob and D. my servant and 33.26
none to sit upon the throne of D., 36.30
my servant D., and he shall feed Eze 34.23
and my servant D. shall be prince 34.24
"My servant D. shall be king over 37.24
and D. my servant shall be their 37.25
LORD their God, and D. their king; Hos 3.05
and like D. invent for themselves Amo 6.05
up the booth of D. that is fallen 9.11
of the house of D. and the glory Zec 12.07
them on that day shall be like D., 12.08
the house of D. shall be like God, 12.08
on the house of D. and the inhabitants 12.10
of the house of D. by itself, 12.12
the house of D. and the inhabitants 13.01
the son of D., the son of Abraham. Mt 1.01
and Jesse the father of D. the king. 1.06
And D. was the father of Solomon by 1.06
from Abraham to D. were fourteen 1.17
and from D. to the deportation to 1.17
son of D., do not fear to take Mary 1.20
aloud, "Have mercy on us, Son of D." 9.27
"Have you not read what D. did, 12.03
said, "Can this be the Son of D.?" 12.23
mercy on me, O Lord, Son of D.; 15.22
out, "Have mercy on us, Son of D.!" 20.30
"Lord, have mercy on us, Son of D.!" 20.31
shouted, "Hosanna to the son of D.! 21.09
temple, "Hosanna to the Son of D.!" 21.15
They said to him, "The son of D." 22.42
to them, "How is it then that D., 22.43
If D. thus calls him Lord, how is he 22.45
"Have you never read what D. did, Mk 2.25
"Jesus, Son of D., have mercy on me!" 10.47
"Son of D., have mercy on me!" 10.48
of our father D. that is coming! 11.10
that the Christ is the son of D.? 12.35
D. himself, inspired by the Holy 12.36
D. himself calls him Lord; so how 12.37
was Joseph, of the house of D.; Lk 1.27
him on the throne of his father D., 1.32
us in the house of his servant D., 1.69
to Judea, to the city of D., 2.04
of the house and lineage of D., 2.04
day in the city of D. a Savior, 2.11
the son of Nathan, the son of D., 3.31
not read what D. did when he was 6.03
Son of D., have mercy on me!" 18.38
"Son of D., have mercy on me!" 18.39
For D. himself says in the Book of 20.42
D. thus calls him Lord; so how 20.44
the Christ is descended from D., Jn 7.42
Bethlehem, the village where D. was?" 7.42
beforehand by the mouth of D., Ac 1.16
For D. says concerning him, 'I saw 2.25
the patriarch D. that he both died 2.29
For D. did not ascend into the 2.34
who by the mouth of our father D., 4.25
So it was until the days of D., 7.45
he raised up D. to be their king; 13.22
'I have found in D. the son of 13.22
the holy and sure blessings of D.' 13.34
For D., after he had served the 13.36
I will rebuild the dwelling of D., 15.16
descended from D. according to the Rom 1.03
So also D. pronounces a blessing 4.06
And D. says, "Let their feast become 11.09
from the dead, descended from D., 2Ti 2.08
saying through D. so long afterward, Heb 4.07
of D. and Samuel and the prophets— 11.32
true one, who has the key of D., Rev 3.07
the Root of D., has conquered, so 5.05
the root and the offspring of D., 22.16

DAVID'S
So Saul was D. enemy continually. 1Sa 18.29
messengers to D. house to watch 19.11
But Michal, D. wife, told him, "If you 19.11
LORD take vengeance on D. enemies." 20.16
Saul's side, but D. place was empty. 20.25
D. place was empty. And Saul said to 20.27
But D. men said to him, "Behold, we 23.03
And afterward D. heart smote him, 24.05
When D. young men came, they said 25.09
And Nabal answered D. servants, 25.10
So D. young men turned away, and 25.12
D. wife, to Palti the son of Laish, 25.44
Saul recognized D. voice, and said, 26.17
D. two wives also had been taken 30.05
him, and said, "This is D. spoil." 30.20
were missing of D. servants nineteen 2Sa 2.30
sixth, Ithream of Eglah, D. wife. 3.05
When Joab came out from D. presence, 3.26
blind, who are hated by D. soul." 5.08

DAVID'S (cont.)
the Edomites became D. servants. 2Sa 8.14
Pelethites; and D. sons were priests. 8.18
So Mephibosheth ate at D. table, 9.11
And D. servants came into the land 10.02
So Hanun took D. servants, and 10.04
Then D. anger was greatly kindled 12.05
and it was placed on D. head. 12.30
Now Absalom, D. son, had a beautiful 13.01
a time Amnon, D. son, loved her. 13.01
the son of Shimeah, D. brother; 13.03
D. brother, said, "Let not my lord 13.32
D. counselor, from his city Giloh. 15.12
So Hushai, D. friend, came into the 15.37
D. friend, came to Absalom, Hushai 16.16
Jordan, and all D. men with him?" 19.41
Ira the Jairite was also D. priest. 20.26
Then D. men adjured him, "You shall 21.17
Shimei, D. brother, slew him. 21.21
But D. heart smote him after he had 24.10
the prophet Gad, D. seer, saying, 24.11
and D. mighty men were not with 1Ki 1.08
Solomon to ride on King D. mule, 1.38
When D. time to die drew near, he 2.01
Nevertheless for D. sake the LORD 15.04
and shields that had been King D., 2Ki 11.10
sake and for my servant D. sake." 20.06
All these were D. sons, besides the 1Ch 3.09
are the chiefs of D. mighty men, 11.10
This is an account of D. mighty men: 11.11
the Edomites became D. servants. 18.13
and D. sons were the chief 18.17
And D. servants came to Hanun in 19.02
So Hanun took D. servants, and 19.04
and it was placed on D. head. 20.02
Shimea, D. brother, slew him. 20.07
spoke to Gad, D. seer, saying, 21.09
fortieth year of D. reign search 26.31
for Judah, Elihu, one of D. brothers; 27.18
were stewards of King D. property. 27.31
Jonathan, D. uncle, was a counselor, 27.32
shields that had been King D., 2Ch 23.09
in D. favor, all the hardships he Ps 132.01
For thy servant D. sake do not turn 132.10
the kings who sit on D. throne, Jer 13.13
they say that the Christ is D. son? Lk 20.41

DAWN
they rose early at the d. of day, Jos 6.15
And as the d. began to break, they Ju 19.25
Then at the break of d. Samuel 1Sa 9.26
the break of d. till the stars Neh 4.21
Let the stars of its d. be dark; Job 3.09
I am full of tossing till the d. 7.04
and caused the d. to know its 38.12
are like the eyelids of the d. 41.18
and lyre! I will awake the d.! Ps 57.08
and lyre! I will awake the d.! 108.02
I rise before d. and cry for help; 119.147
righteous is like the light of d., Pro 4.18
youth and the d. of life are vanity. Ecc 11.10
this that looks forth like the d., Sol 6.10
which they speak there is no d. Is 8.20
from heaven, O Day Star, son of D.! 14.12
your light break forth like the d., 58.08
is going forth is sure as the d.; Hos 6.03
But when d. came up the next day, Jon 4.07
each d. he does not fail; but the Zep 3.05
toward the d. of the first day of Mt 28.01
the day shall d. upon us from on Lk 1.78
at early d., they went to the tomb, 24.01
As day was about to d., Paul urged Ac 27.33

DAWNED
When morning d., the angels urged Gen 19.15
and d. from Seir upon us; he shone Deu 33.02
and shadow of death light has d." Mt 4.16

DAWNS
he d. on them like the morning 2Sa 23.04
Light d. for the righteous, and joy Ps 97.11
When the morning d., they perform Mic 2.01
until the day d. and the morning 2Pe 1.19

DAY
God called the light D., and the Gen 1.05
and there was morning, one d. 1.05
and there was morning, a second d. 1.08
and there was morning, a third d. 1.13
to separate the d. from the night; 1.14
the greater light to rule the d., 1.16
to rule over the d. and over the 1.18
and there was morning, a fourth d. 1.19
and there was morning, a fifth d. 1.23
and there was morning, a sixth d. 1.31
And on the seventh d. God finished 2.02
he rested on the seventh d. 2.02
the seventh d. and hallowed it, 2.03
In the d. that the LORD God made 2.04
for in the d. that you eat of it 2.17
the garden in the cool of the d., 3.08
driven me this d. away from the 4.14
on the seventeenth d. of the month, 7.11
on that d. all the fountains of the 7.11
on the very same d. Noah and his sons, 7.13
on the seventeenth d. of the month, 8.04
on the first d. of the month, the 8.05
the first d. of the month, the 8.13
the twenty-seventh d. of the month, 8.14
d. and night, shall not cease." 8.22
On that d. the LORD made a covenant 15.18
on their foreskins that very d., 17.23
That very d. Abraham and his son 17.26
of his tent in the heat of the d. 18.01
And on the next d., 19.34
father of the Moabites to this d. 19.37
father of the Ammonites to this d. 19.38
feast on the d. that Isaac was 21.08
On the third d. Abraham lifted up 22.04
as it is said to this d., 22.14
That same d. Isaac's servants came 26.32
the city is Beersheba to this d. 26.33
I do not know the d. of my death. 27.02
I be bereft of you both in one d.?" 27.45
He said, "Behold, it is still high d., 29.07
But that d. Laban removed the 30.35
on the third d. that Jacob had 31.22
stolen by d. or stolen by night. 31.39
by d. the heat consumed me, and the 31.40
can I do this d. to these my 31.43
him until the breaking of the d. 32.24
"Let me go, for the d. is breaking." 32.26
Therefore to this d. the Israelites 32.32
if they are overdriven for one d., 33.13
returned that d. on his way to 33.16
On the third d., when they were 34.25
me in the d. of my distress and 35.03
tomb, which is there to this d. 35.20
she spoke to Joseph d. after d., 39.10
But one d., when he went into the 39.11
On the third d., which was Pharaoh's 40.20
youngest is this d. with our father, 42.13
On the third d. Joseph said to them, 42.18
youngest is this day with our father 42.32
I have this d. bought you and your 47.23
of Egypt, and it stands to this d., 47.26
me all my life long to this d., 48.15
So he blessed them that d., saying, 48.20
One d., when Moses had grown up, he Ex 2.11
When he went out the next d., behold, 2.13
The same d. Pharaoh commanded the 5.06
On the d. when the LORD spoke to 6.28
But on that d. I will set apart the 8.22
Egypt from the d. it was founded 9.18
from the d. they came on earth to this d. 10.06

DAY (cont.)

land all that d. and all that night; Ex 10.13
for in the d. you see my face you 10.28
on the tenth d. of this month they 12.03
the fourteenth d. of this month, 12.06
"This d. shall be for you a memorial d., 12.14
on the first d. you shall put away 12.15
from the first d. until the seventh d.? 12.15
On the first d. you shall hold a 12.16
on the seventh d. a holy assembly; 12.16
on this very d. I brought your 12.17
therefore you shall observe this d., 12.17
the fourteenth d. of the month at 12.18
twenty-first d. of the month at 12.18
on that very d., all the hosts of 12.41
And on that very d. the LORD 12.51
to the people, "Remember this d., 13.03
This d. you are to go forth, in the 13.04
on the seventh d. there shall be a 13.06
you shall tell your son on that d., 13.08
before them by d. in a pillar of 13.21
might travel by d. and by night; 13.21
of cloud by d. and the pillar of 13.22
Israel that d. from the hand of 14.30
the fifteenth d. of the second 16.01
gather a day's portion every d., 16.04
On the sixth d., when they prepare 16.05
On the sixth d. they gathered twice 16.22
'Tomorrow is a d. of solemn rest, 16.23
but on the seventh d., which is 16.26
On the seventh d. some of the 16.27
on the sixth d. he gives you bread 16.29
out of his place on the seventh d." 16.29
people rested on the seventh d. 16.30
on that d. they came into the 19.01
and be ready by the third d.; 19.11
on the third d. the LORD will come 19.11
people, "Be ready by the third d.; 19.15
of the third d. there were thunders 19.16
"Remember the sabbath d., to keep 20.08
but the seventh d. is a sabbath to 20.10
in them, and rested the seventh d.; 20.11
the sabbath d. and hallowed it. 20.11
But if the slave survives a d. or two, 21.21
on the eighth d. you shall give it 22.30
on the seventh d. you shall rest; 23.12
on the seventh d. he called to 24.16
and every d. you shall offer a bull 29.36
a year old d. by d. continually. 29.38
but the seventh d. is a sabbath of 31.15
work on the sabbath d. shall be 31.15
and on the seventh d. he rested, 31.17
the people that d. about three 32.28
bestow a blessing upon you this d." 32.29
in the d. when I visit, I will visit 32.34
"Observe what I command you this d. 34.11
on the seventh d. you shall rest; 34.21
on the seventh d. you shall have a 35.02
your habitations on the sabbath d." 35.03
"On the first d. of the first month 40.02
on the first d. of the month, the 40.17
onward till the d. that it was 40.37
LORD was upon the tabernacle by d., 40.38
on the d. of his guilt offering. Lev 6.05
the LORD on the d. when he is 6.20
be eaten on the d. of his offering 7.15
be eaten on the d. that he offers 7.16
on the third d. shall be burned 7.17
offering is eaten on the third d., 7.18
to them on the d. they were 7.35
on the d. that they were anointed; 7.36
on the d. that he commanded the 7.38
shall remain d. and night for 8.35
On the eighth d. Moses called Aaron 9.01
And on the eighth d. the flesh of 12.03
examine him on the seventh d., 13.05
him again on the seventh d., 13.06
shall examine him the seventh d.; 13.27
and on the seventh d. the priest 13.32
and on the seventh d. the priest 13.34
the disease on the seventh d. 13.51
leper for the d. of his cleansing. 14.02
And on the seventh d. he shall 14.09
"And on the eighth d. he shall take 14.10
And on the eighth d. he shall bring 14.23
again on the seventh d., and look; 14.39
And on the eighth d. he shall take 15.14
And on the eighth d. she shall take 15.29
on the tenth d. of the month, you 16.29
for on this d. shall atonement be 16.30
be eaten the same d. you offer it, 19.06
until the third d. shall be burned 19.06
it is eaten at all on the third d., 19.07
from the eighth d. on it shall be 22.27
both her and her young in one d. 22.28
It shall be eaten on the same d., 22.30
on the seventh d. is a sabbath of 23.03
the fourteenth d. of the month in 23.05
the fifteenth d. of the same month 23.06
On the first d. you shall have a 23.07
on the seventh d. is a holy convocation 23.08
And on the d. when you wave the 23.12
or fresh until this same d., until you 23.14
from the d. that you brought the 23.15
make proclamation on the same d.; 23.21
on the first d. of the month, you 23.24
shall observe a d. of solemn rest, 23.24
"On the tenth d. of this seventh 23.27
month is the d. of atonement; 23.27
shall do no work on this same d.; 23.28
for it is a d. of atonement, to make 23.28
on this same d. shall be cut off 23.29
does any work on this same d., 23.30
on the ninth d. of the month 23.32
the fifteenth d. of this seventh 23.34
On the first d. shall be a holy 23.35
on the eighth d. you shall hold a 23.36
offerings, each on its proper d.; 23.37
"On the fifteenth d. of the seventh 23.39
on the first d. shall be a solemn 23.39
on the eight d. shall be a solemn 23.39
on the first d. the fruit of 23.40
Every sabbath d. Aaron shall set it 24.08
on the tenth d. of the seventh 25.09
on the d. of atonement you shall 25.09
valuation on that d. as a holy 27.23
on the first d. of the second month, Num 1.01
and on the first d. of the second 1.18
on the d. that I slew all the first 3.13
his head on the d. of his cleansing 6.09
on the seventh d. he shall shave it 6.09
On the eighth d. he shall bring two 6.10
consecrate his head that same d., 6.11
On the d. when Moses had finished 7.01
altar on the d. it was anointed; 7.10
offerings, one leader each d., 7.11
the first d. was Nahshon the son 7.12
On the second d. Nethanel the son 7.18
On the third d. Eliab the son of 7.24
On the fourth d. Elizur the son of 7.30
On the fifth d. Shelumiel the son 7.36
On the sixth d. Eliasaph the son of 7.42
On the seventh d. Elishama the son 7.48
On the eighth d. Gamaliel the son 7.54
On the ninth d. Abidan the son of 7.60
On the tenth d. Ahiezer the son of 7.66
On the eleventh d. Pagiel the son 7.72
On the twelfth d. Ahira the son of 7.78
on the d. when it was anointed, from 7.84
on the d. that I slew all the first 8.17
On the fourteenth d. of this month, 9.03
on the fourteenth d. of the month, 9.05
not keep the passover on that d.; 9.06
before Moses and Aaron on that d.; 9.06

DAY (cont.)
the fourteenth d. in the evening Num 9.11
On the d. that the tabernacle was 9.15
the cloud covered it by d., and the 9.16
it continued for a d. and a night, 9.21
On the d. of your gladness also, and 10.10
on the twentieth d. of the month, 10.11
of the LORD was over them by d., 10.34
You shall not eat one d., or two 11.19
And the people rose all that d., 11.32
and all night, and all the next d., 11.32
of cloud by d. and in a pillar of 14.14
for every d. a year, you shall bear 14.34
from the d. that the LORD gave 15.23
gathering sticks on the sabbath d. 15.32
on the third d. and on the seventh d. 19.12
on the third d. and on the seventh d. 19.19
on the seventh d. he shall cleanse 19.19
all your life long to this d.? 22.30
slain on the d. of the plague on 25.18
d. by d., as a continual offering. 28.03
"On the sabbath d. two male lambs a 28.09
"On the fourteenth d. of the first 28.16
the fifteenth d. of this month is 28.17
On the first d. there shall be a 28.18
And on the seventh d. you shall 28.25
"On the d. of the first fruits, when 28.26
"On the first d. of the seventh 29.01
It is a d. for you to blow the 29.01
"On the tenth d. of this seventh 29.07
"On the fifteenth d. of the seventh 29.12
"On the second d. twelve young 29.17
"On the third d. eleven bulls, two 29.20
"On the fourth d. ten bulls, two 29.23
"On the fifth d. nine bulls, two 29.26
"On the sixth d. eight bulls, two 29.29
"On the seventh d. seven bulls, 29.32
"On the eighth d. you shall have a 29.35
to her on the d. that he hears of 30.05
to her on the d. that he hears; 30.07
But if on the d. that her husband 30.08
and void on the d. that he hears 30.12
says nothing to her from d. to d., 30.14
to her on the d. that he heard of 30.14
on the third d. and on the seventh d. 31.19
your clothes on the seventh d., 31.24
anger was kindled on that d., 32.10
the fifteenth d. of the first 33.03
on the d. after the passover the 33.03
on the first d. of the fifth month. 33.38
on the first d. of the eleventh Deu 1.03
you are this d. as the stars of 1.10
should go, and in the cloud by d., 1.33
who this d. have no knowledge of 1.39
'This d. you are to pass over the 2.18
in their stead even to this d. 2.22
This d. I will begin to put the 2.25
him into your hand, as at this d. 2.30
Havvothjair, as it is to this d. 3.14
your God are all alive this d. 4.04
law which I set before you this d.? 4.08
how on the d. that you stood before 4.10
no form on the d. that the LORD 4.15
his own possession, as at this d. 4.20
to witness against you this d., 4.26
since the d. that God created man 4.32
for an inheritance, as at this d.; 4.38
know therefore this d., and lay 4.39
which I command you this d., 4.40
I speak in your hearing this d., 5.01
are all of us here alive this d. 5.03
"'Observe the sabbath d., to keep 5.12
but the seventh d. is a sabbath to 5.14
commanded you to keep the sabbath d. 5.15
we have this d. seen God speak with 5.24
you this d. shall be upon your 6.06
preserve us alive, as at this d. 6.24
which I command you this d. 7.11
you this d. you shall be careful 8.01
which I command you this d.: 8.11
to your fathers, as at this d. 8.18
warn you this d. that you shall 8.19
to pass over the Jordan this d., 9.01
Know therefore this d. that he who 9.03
From the d. you came out of the 9.07
The fire on the d. of the assembly 9.10
LORD from the d. that I knew you. 9.24
the fire on the d. of the assembly 10.04
to bless in his name, to this d. 10.08
command you this d. for your good? 10.13
above all peoples, as at this d. 10.15
And consider this d. (since I am 11.02
LORD has destroyed them to this d.; 11.04
which I command you this d., 11.08
which I command you this d., 11.13
before you this d. a blessing and 11.26
God, which I command you this d., 11.27
way which I command you this d., 11.28
which I set before you this d. 11.32
all that we are doing here this d., 12.08
which I command you this d., and doing 13.18
commandment which I command you this d. 15.05
remember the d. when you came out 16.03
of the first d. remain all night 16.04
on the seventh d. there shall be a 16.08
at Horeb on the d. of the assembly, 18.16
which I command you this d., by loving 19.09
draw near this d. to battle against 20.03
then on the d. when he assigns his 21.16
but you shall bury him the same d., 21.23
him his hire on the d. he earns it, 24.15
'I declare this d. to the LORD 26.03
"This d. the LORD your God commands 26.16
declared this d. concerning the 26.17
declared this d. concerning you 26.18
which I command you this d. 27.01
And on the d. you pass over the 27.02
which I command you this d., 27.04
this d. you have become the people 27.09
which I command you this d." 27.10
the people the same d., saying, 27.11
which I command you this d., 28.01
God, which I command you this d., 28.13
words which I command you this d., 28.14
which I command you this d., 28.15
with longing for them all the d.; 28.32
night and d. you shall be in dread, 28.66
but to this d. the LORD has not 29.04
"You stand this d. all of you 29.10
your God makes with you this d.; 29.12
establish you this d. as his people, 29.13
with us this d. as well as with 29.15
with us this d. before the LORD 29.15
turns away this d. from the LORD 29.18
into another land, as at this d.' 29.28
in all that I command you this d., 30.02
which I command you this d. 30.08
you this d. is not too hard for 30.11
before you this d. life and good, 30.15
God which I command you this d., 30.16
I declare to you this d., that you 30.18
to witness against you this d., 30.19
and twenty years old this d.; 31.02
be kindled against them in that d., 31.17
so that they will say in that d., 31.17
my face in that d. on account of 31.18
So Moses wrote this song the same d., 31.22
for the d. of their calamity is at 32.35
which I enjoin upon you this d., 32.46
LORD said to Moses that very d., 32.48
he encompasses him all the d. long, 33.12
the place of his burial to this d. 34.06
shall meditate on it d. and night, Jos 1.08
"This d. I will begin to exalt you 3.07

DAY (cont.)
stood; and they are there to this d. Jos 4.09
On that d. the LORD exalted Joshua 4.14
on the tenth d. of the first month, 4.19
"This d. I have rolled away the 5.09
place is called Gilgal to this d. 5.09
the fourteenth d. of the month at 5.10
that very d., they ate of the 5.11
on the seventh d. you shall march 6.04
until the d. I bid you shout; 6.10
And the second d. they marched 6.14
On the seventh d. they rose early 6.15
they rose early at the dawn of d., 6.15
only on that d. that they marched 6.15
and she dwelt in Israel to this d., 6.25
of stones that remains to this d.; 7.26
Therefore to this d. the name of 7.26
And all who fell that d., both men 8.25
heap of ruins, as it is to this d. 8.28
which stands there to this d. 8.29
on the d. we set forth to come to 9.12
their cities on the third d. 9.17
made them that d. hewers of wood 9.27
the LORD, to continue to this d., 9.27
the LORD in the d. when the LORD 10.12
to go down for about a whole d. 10.13
There has been no d. like it before 10.14
cave, which remain to this very d. 10.27
And Joshua took Makkedah on that d., 10.28
and he took it on the second d., 10.32
and they took it on that d., and smote 10.35
in it he utterly destroyed that d., 10.35
in the midst of Israel to this d. 13.13
And Moses swore on that d., saying, 14.09
I am this d. eighty-five years old. 14.10
strong to this d. as I was in the d. 14.11
of which the LORD spoke on that d.; 14.12
heard on that d. how the Anakim 14.12
Jephunneh the Kenizzite to this d., 14.14
of Judah at Jerusalem to this d. 15.63
Ephraim to this d. but have become 16.10
down to this d., but have been 22.03
away this d. from following the 22.16
an altar this d. in rebellion 22.16
turn away this d. from following 22.18
turn away this d. from following 22.29
God as you have done to this d. 23.08
able to withstand you to this d. 23.09
choose this d. whom you will serve, 24.15
a covenant with the people that d., 24.25
Benjamin in Jerusalem to this d. Ju 1.21
that is its name to this d. 1.26
subdued that d. under the hand of 3.30
For this is the d. in which the 4.14
So on that d. God subdued Jabin the 4.23
the son of Abinoam on that d.: 5.01
To this d. it still stands at 6.24
the men of the town to do it by d., 6.27
Therefore on that d. he was called 6.32
against my father's house this d., 9.18
Jerubbaal and with his house this d., 9.19
On the following d. the men went 9.42
against the city all that d.; 9.45
called Havvothjair to this d., 10.04
deliver us, we pray thee, this d." 10.15
decide this d. between the people 11.27
have you come up to me this d., 12.03
from birth to the d. of his death.'" 13.07
to me the other d. has appeared to 13.10
On the fourth d. they said to 14.15
and on the seventh d. he told her, 14.17
on the seventh d. before the sun 14.18
it is at Lehi to this d. 15.19
hard with her words d. after d., 16.16
is called Mahanedan to this d.; 18.12
until the d. of the captivity of 18.30
And on the fourth d. they arose 19.05
And on the fifth d. he arose early 19.08
and tarry until the d. declines." 19.08
now the d. has waned toward evening 19.09
Behold, the d. draws to its close; 19.09
the d. was far spent, and the 19.11
seen from the d. that the people 19.30
of the land of Egypt until this d.; 19.30
cities on that d. twenty-six thousand 20.15
ground on that d. twenty-two thousand 20.21
they had formed it on the first d. 20.22
the Benjaminites the second d. 20.24
them out of Gibeah the second d., 20.25
and fasted that d. until evening, 20.26
the Benjaminites on the third d., 20.30
hundred men of Benjamin that d.; 20.35
who fell that d. of Benjamin were 20.46
is cut off from Israel this d. 21.06
"The d. you buy the field from the Ru 4.05
witnesses this d. that I have 4.09
place; you are witnesses this d." 4.10
left you this d. without next of 4.14
On the d. when Elkanah sacrificed, 1Sa 1.04
of them shall die on the same d. 2.34
On that d. I will fulfil against 3.12
and came to Shiloh the same d., 4.12
of Ashdod rose early the next d., 5.03
of Dagon in Ashdod to this d. 5.05
sacrifices on that d. to the LORD. 6.15
it, they returned that d. to Ekron. 6.16
witness to this d. in the field of 6.18
From the d. that the ark was lodged 7.02
the LORD, and fasted on that d., 7.06
voice that d. against the Philistines 7.10
from the d. I brought them up out 8.08
up out of Egypt even to this d., 8.08
And in that d. you will cry out 8.18
will not answer you in that d." 8.18
Now the d. before Saul came, the 9.15
So Saul ate with Samuel that d. 9.24
these signs came to pass that d. 10.09
But you have this d. rejected your 10.19
Ammonites until the heat of the d.; 11.11
man shall be put to death this d., 11.13
you from my youth until this d. 12.02
his anointed is witness this d., 12.05
LORD sent thunder and rain that d.; 12.18
So on the d. of the battle there 13.22
One d. Jonathan the son of Saul 14.01
So the LORD delivered Israel that d.; 14.23
of Israel were distressed that d.; 14.24
be the man who eats food this d.'" 14.28
Philistines that d. from Michmash 14.31
But he did not answer him that d. 14.37
not answered thy servant this d.? 14.41
he has wrought with God this d." 14.45
kingdom of Israel from you this d., 15.28
again until the d. of his death, 15.35
upon David from that d. forward. 16.13
"I defy the ranks of Israel this d.; 17.10
This d. the LORD will deliver you 17.46
Philistines this d. to the birds of 17.46
And Saul took him that d., and would 18.02
And Saul eyed David from that d. on. 18.09
the lyre, as he did d. by d. 18.10
naked all that d. and all that 19.24
field till the third d. at evening. 20.05
or the third d., behold, if he is 20.12
And on the third d. you will be 20.19
Yet Saul did not say anything that d.; 20.26
But on the second d., the morrow 20.27
no food the second d. of the month, 20.34
bread on the d. it is taken away. 21.06
servants of Saul was there that d., 21.07
rose and fled that d. from Saul, 21.10
me, to lie in wait, as at this d." 22.08
me, to lie in wait, as at this d.?" 22.13
killed on that d. eighty-five 22.18

DAY (cont.)
to Abiathar, "I knew on that d., 1Sa 22.22
And Saul sought him every d., 23.14
"Here is the d. of which the LORD 24.04
Lo, this d. your eyes have seen how 24.10
declared this d. how you have 24.18
what you have done to me this d. 24.19
for we come on a feast d. Pray, 25.08
wall to us both by night and by d., 25.16
who sent you this d. to meet me! 25.32
kept me this d. from bloodguilt 25.33
your enemy into your hand this d.; 26.08
or his d. shall come to die; or he 26.10
me out this d. that I should have 26.19
was precious in your eyes this d.; 26.21
was precious this d. in my sight, 26.24
now perish one d. by hand of 27.01
So that d. Achish gave him Ziklag; 27.06
to the kings of Judah to this d. 27.06
has done this thing to you this d. 28.18
eaten nothing all d. and all night. 28.20
found no fault in him to this d." 29.03
in you from the d. of your coming 29.06
to me to this d. Nevertheless 29.06
from the d. I entered your service 29.08
men came to Ziklag on the third d., 30.01
until the evening of the next d.; 30.17
And from that d. forward he made it 30.25
an ordinance for Israel to this d. 30.25
his men, on the same d. together. 31.06
and on the third d., behold, 2Sa 1.02
the battle was very fierce that d.; 2.17
and the d. broke upon them at 2.32
This d. I keep showing loyalty to 3.08
to eat bread while it was yet d.; 3.35
understood that d. that it had not 3.37
man has fallen this d. in Israel? 3.38
And I am this d. weak, though 3.39
been sojourners there to this d.). 4.03
the heat of the d. they came to 4.05
the king this d. on Saul and on 4.08
And David said on that d., "Whoever 5.08
is called Perezuzzah, to this d. 6.08
was afraid of the LORD that d.; 6.09
no child to the d. of her death. 6.23
house since the d. I brought up 7.06
of Israel from Egypt to this d., 7.06
in Jerusalem that d., and the next. 11.12
On the seventh d. the child died. 12.18
from the d. he forced his sister 13.32
mourned for his son d. after d. 13.37
slaughter there was great on that d., 18.07
more people that d. than the sword. 18.08
Absalom's monument to this d. 18.18
you may carry tidings another d., 18.20
you this d. from the power of all 18.31
victory that d. was turned into 19.02
for the people heard that d., 19.02
the city that d. as people steal 19.03
who have this d. saved your life, 19.05
wrong on the d. my lord the king 19.19
behold, I have come this d., the first 19.20
you should this d. be as an adversary 19.22
be put to death in Israel this d.? 19.22
that I am this d. king over Israel 19.22
from the d. the king departed until 19.24
until the d. he came back in 19.24
I am this d. eighty years old; 19.35
up until the d. of their death, 20.03
of the air to come upon them by d., 21.10
on the d. the Philistines killed 21.12
song on the d. when the LORD 22.01
upon me in the d. of my calamity; 22.19
wrought a great victory that d.; 23.10
in a pit on a d. when snow had 23.20
And Gad came that d. to David, 24.18
For he has gone down this d., 1Ki 1.25
stead'; even so will I do this d." 1.30
to sit on my throne this d., my own 1.48
curse on the d. when I went to 2.08
shall be put to death this d." 2.24
For on the d. you go forth, and 2.37
that on the d. you go forth and go 2.42
a son to sit on his throne this d. 3.06
Then on the third d. after I was 3.18
provision for one d. was thirty 4.22
said, "Blessed be the LORD this d., 5.07
and they are there to this d. 8.08
'Since the d. that I brought my 8.16
thy hand hast fulfilled it this d. 8.24
servant prays before thee this d.; 8.28
open night and d. toward this 8.29
to the LORD our God d. and night, 8.59
people Israel, as each d. requires; 8.59
his commandments, as at this d. 8.61
The same d. the king consecrated 8.64
On the eighth d. he sent the people 8.66
the land of Cabul to this d. 9.13
slaves, and so they are to this d. 9.21
has come or been seen, to this d. 10.12
came to Rehoboam the third d., 12.12
"Come to me again the third d." 12.12
the house of David to this d. 12.19
the fifteenth d. of the eighth month 12.32
the fifteenth d. in the eighth month, 12.33
And he gave a sign the same d., 13.03
of God had done that d. in Bethel; 13.11
over Israel that d. in the camp. 16.16
until the d. that the LORD sends 17.14
be known this d. that thou art God 18.36
give it into your hand this d.; 20.13
on the seventh d. the battle was 20.29
thousand foot soldiers in one d. 20.29
see on that d. when you do into an 22.25
And the battle grew hot that d., 22.35
has been wholesome to this d., 2Ki 2.22
One d. Elisha went on to Shunem, 4.08
One d. he came there, and he turned 4.11
he went out one d. to his father 4.18
And on the next d. I said to her, 6.29
This d. is a d. of good news; 7.09
fields from the d. that she left 8.06
from the rule of Judah to this d. 8.22
and made it a latrine to this d. 10.27
which is its name to this d. 14.07
was a leper to the d. of his death 15.05
Elath, where they dwell to this d. 16.06
own land to Assyria until this d. 17.23
To this d. they do according to the 17.34
fathers did, so they do to this d. 17.41
This d. is a d. of distress, of 19.03
on the third d. you shall go up 20.05
house of the LORD on the third d.?" 20.08
have stored up till this d., 20.17
since the d. their fathers came out 21.15
came out of Egypt, even to this d." 21.15
on the tenth d. of the month, 25.01
On the ninth d. of the fourth month 25.03
on the seventh d. of the month— 25.08
the twenty-seventh d. of the month, 25.27
And every d. of his life he dined 25.29
every d. a portion, as long as he 25.30
and exterminated them to this d., 1Ch 4.41
they have dwelt there to this d. 4.43
and the river Gozan, to this d. 5.26
for they were on duty d. and night. 9.33
in a pit on a d. when snow had 11.22
For from d. to d. men kept coming 12.22
is called Perezuzza to this d. 13.11
And David was afraid of God that d.; 13.12
Then on that d. David first appointed 16.07
of his salvation from d. to d. 16.23
the ark as each d. required, 16.37
the d. I led up Israel to this d., 17.05

DAY (cont.)
On the east there were six each d., 1Ch 26.17
d., on the north four each d., 26.17
d., on the south four each d., 26.17
and on the next d. offered burnt 29.21
LORD on that d. with great gladness 29.22
and they are there to this d. 2Ch 5.09
'Since the d. that I brought my 6.05
thy hand hast fulfilled it this d. 6.15
may be open d. and night toward 6.20
And on the eighth d. they held a 7.09
twenty-third d. of the seventh 7.10
levy and so they are to this d. 8.08
as the duty of each d. required, 8.13
as the duty of each d. required, 8.14
from the d. the foundation of the 8.16
came to Rehoboam the third d., 10.12
"Come to me again the third d." 10.12
the house of David to this d. 10.19
They sacrificed to the LORD on that d., 15.11
see on that d. when you go into an 18.24
And the battle grew hot that d., 18.34
On the fourth d. they assembled in 20.26
the Valley of Beracah to this d. 20.26
from the rule of Judah to this d. 21.10
because of the disease, d. by d. 21.15
Thus they did d. after d., and 24.11
was a leper to the d. of his death, 26.21
twenty thousand in Judah in one d., 28.06
on the first d. of the first month, 29.17
on the eighth d. of the month they 29.17
the sixteenth d. of the first 29.17
the fourteenth d. of the second 30.15
priests praised the LORD d. by d.. 30.21
as the duty of each d. required, 31.16
the fourteenth d. of the first 35.01
of the LORD was prepared that d., 35.16
am not coming against you this d., 35.21
Josiah in their laments to this d. 35.25
ordinance, as each d. required, Ez 3.04
From the first d. of the seventh 3.06
given to them d. by d. without 6.09
on the third d. of the month of 6.15
On the fourteenth d. of the first 6.19
for on the first d. of the first 7.09
on the first d. of the fifth month 7.09
on the twelfth d. of the first 8.31
On the fourth d., within the house 8.33
fathers to this d. we have been in 9.07
and to utter shame, as at this d. 9.07
that has escaped, as at this d. 9.15
on the twentieth d. of the month. 10.09
this a work for one d. or for two; 10.13
On the first d. of the tenth month 10.16
and by the first d. of the first 10.17
before thee d. and night for the Neh 1.06
Will they finish up in a d.? 4.02
protection against them d. and night. 4.09
From that d. on, half of my servants 4.16
us by night and may labor by d." 4.22
Return to them this very d. their fields, 5.11
prepared for one d. was one ox and 5.18
twenty-fifth d. of the month Elul, 6.15
on the first d. of the seventh 8.02
"This d. is holy to the LORD your 8.09
for this d. is holy to our Lord; 8.10
"Be quiet, for this d. is holy; 8.11
On the second d. the heads of 8.13
of Nun to that d. the people of 8.17
d. by d., from the first d. to the last d., 8.18
on the eighth d. there was a 8.18
twenty-fourth d. of this month the 9.01
their God for a fourth of the d.; 9.03
thee a name, as it is to this d. 9.10
thou didst lead them in the d., 9.12
way did not depart from them by d., 9.19
the kings of Assyria until this d. 9.32
Behold, we are slaves this d.; 9.36
grain on the sabbath d. to sell, 10.31
on the sabbath or on a holy d.; 10.31
the singers, as every d. required. 11.23
sacrifices that d. and rejoiced, 12.43
On that d. men were appointed over 12.44
On that d. they read from the book 13.01
into Jerusalem on the sabbath d.; 13.15
them on the d. when they sold food 13.15
doing, profaning the sabbath d.? 13.17
be brought in on the sabbath d. 13.19
gates, to keep the sabbath d. holy. 13.22
On the seventh d., when the heart Est 1.10
This very d. the ladies of Persia 1.18
And every d. Mordecai walked in 2.11
spoke to him d. after d. and he 3.04
the lot, before Haman d. after d.; 3.07
the thirteenth d. of the first 3.12
in one d., the thirteenth d. of the 3.13
peoples to be ready for that d. 3.14
drink for three days, night or d. 4.16
On the third d. Esther put on her 5.01
Haman come this d. to a dinner 5.04
went out that d. joyful and glad 5.09
And on the second d., as they 7.02
On that d. King Ahasuerus gave to 8.01
of Sivan, on the twenty-third d.; 8.09
upon one d. throughout all the 8.12
the thirteenth d. of the twelfth 8.12
ready on that d. to avenge themselves 8.13
on the thirteenth d. of the same, 9.01
on the very d. when the enemies of 9.01
changed to a d. when the Jews 9.01
That very d. the number of those 9.11
the fourteenth d. of the month of 9.15
the thirteenth d. of the month of 9.17
the fourteenth d. they rested and 9.17
and made that a d. of feasting and 9.17
the thirteenth d. and on the 9.18
and rested on the fifteenth d., 9.18
making that a d. of feasting and 9.18
the fourteenth d. of the month of 9.19
of Adar as a d. for gladness and 9.19
and a d. on which they send choice 9.19
the fourteenth d. of the month 9.21
also the fifteenth d. of the same, 9.21
in the house of each on his d.; Job 1.04
Now there was a d. when the sons of 1.06
Now there was a d. when his sons 1.13
Again there was a d. when the sons 2.01
and cursed the d. of his birth. 3.01
"Let the d. perish wherein I was 3.03
Let that d. be darkness! 3.04
the blackness of the d. terrify it. 3.05
Let those curse it who curse the d., 3.08
may enjoy, like a hireling, his d. 14.06
He knows that a d. of darkness is 15.23
They make night into d.; 17.12
of the west are appalled at his d., 18.20
off in the d. of God's wrath. 20.28
is spared in the d. of calamity, 21.30
he is rescued in the d. of wrath? 21.30
by d. they shut themselves up; 24.16
I weep for him whose d. was hard? 30.25
for the d. of battle and war? 38.23
his law he meditates d. and night. Ps 1.02
a God who has indignation every d. 7.11
have sorrow in my heart all the d.? 13.02
upon me in the d. of my calamity; 18.18
D. to d. pours forth speech, and 19.02
answer you in the d. of trouble! 20.01
I cry by d., but thou dost not 22.02
for thee I wait all the d. long. 25.05
his shelter in the d. of trouble; 27.05
through my groaning all d. long. 32.03
For d. and night thy hand was heavy 32.04
and of thy praise all the d. long. 35.28

DAY (cont.)

for he sees that his d. is coming. Ps 37.13
all the d. I go about mourning. 38.06
meditate treachery all the d. long. 38.12
delivers him in the d. of trouble; 41.01
have been my food d. and night, 42.03
By d. the LORD commands his steadfast 42.08
All d. long my disgrace is before 44.15
sake we are slain all the d. long, 44.22
and call upon me in the d. of trouble; 50.15
All the d. you are plotting destruction. 52.01
D. and night they go around it on 55.10
all d. long foemen oppress me; 56.01
trample upon me all d. long, 56.02
All d. long they seek to injure my 56.05
turned back in the d. when I call. 56.09
a refuge in the d. of my distress. 59.16
thy name, as I pay my vows d. after d. 61.08
and with thy glory all the d. 71.08
thy deeds of salvation all the d., 71.15
thy righteous help all the d. long, 71.24
blessings invoked for him all the d.! 72.15
For all the d. long I have been 73.14
Thine is the d., thine also the 74.16
impious scoff at thee all the d.! 74.22
In the d. of my trouble I seek the 77.02
turned back on the d. of battle. 78.09
or the d. when he redeemed them 78.42
at the full moon, on our feast d. 81.03
For a d. in thy courts is better 84.10
for to thee do I cry all the d. 86.03
In the d. of my trouble I call on 86.07
my God, I call for help by d.; 88.01
Every d. I call upon thee, O LORD; 88.09
me like a flood all d. long; 88.17
who exult in thy name all the d., 89.16
nor the arrow that flies by d., 91.05
as on the d. at Massah in the 95.08
tell of his salvation from d. to d. 96.02
from me in the d. of my distress! 102.02
me speedily in the d. when I call! 102.02
All the d. my enemies taunt me, 102.08
freely on the d. you lead your 110.03
kings on the d. of his wrath. 110.05
This is the d. which the LORD has 118.24
thy appointment they stand this d.; 119.91
It is my meditation all the d. 119.97
Seven times a d. I praise thee for 119.164
The sun shall not smite you by d., 121.06
the sun to rule over the d., 136.08
the Edomites the d. of Jerusalem, 137.07
On the d. I called, thou didst 138.03
the night is bright as the d.; 139.12
my head in the d. of battle. 140.07
Every d. I will bless thee, and 145.02
on that very d. his plans perish. 146.04
brighter and brighter until full d. Pro 4.18
Riches do not profit in the d. of wrath, 11.04
the wicked for the d. of trouble. 16.04
All d. long the wicked covets, but 21.26
is made ready for the d. of battle, 21.31
in the fear of the LORD all the d. 23.17
If you faint in the d. of adversity, 24.10
takes off a garment on a cold d., 25.20
not know what a d. may bring forth. 27.01
house in the d. of your calamity. 27.10
on a rainy d. and a contentious 27.15
the d. of death, than the d. of birth. Ecc 7.01
In the d. of prosperity by joyful, 7.14
and in the d. of adversity consider 7.14
or authority over the d. of death; 8.08
how neither d. nor night one's eyes 8.16
in the d. when the keepers of the 12.03
Until the d. breathes and the Sol 2.17
him on the d. of his wedding, 3.11
on the d. of the gladness of his 3.11
Until the d. breathes and the 4.06

on the d. when she is spoken for? 8.08
alone will be exalted in that d. Is 2.11
of hosts has a d. against all that 2.12
alone will be exalted in that d. 2.17
In that d. men will cast forth 2.20
in that d. he will speak out, saying: 3.07
In that d. the Lord will take away 3.18
take hold of one man in that d., 4.01
In that d. the branch of the LORD 4.02
over her assemblies a cloud by d., 4.05
be for a shade by d. from the heat, 4.06
They will growl over it on that d., 5.30
come since the d. that Ephraim 7.17
In that d. the LORD will whistle 7.18
In that d. the Lord will shave with 7.20
In that d. a man will keep alive a 7.21
In that d. every place where there 7.23
hast broken as on the d. of Midian. 9.04
palm branch and reed in one d.— 9.14
you do on the d. of punishment, 10.03
his thorns and briers in one d. 10.17
In that d. the remnant of Israel 10.20
And in that d. his burden will 10.27
This very d. he will halt at Nob, he 10.32
In that d. the root of Jesse shall 11.10
In that d. the Lord will extend his 11.11
You will say in that d.: "I will 12.01
And you will say in that d.: 12.04
Wail, for the d. of the LORD is near; 13.06
Behold, the d. of the LORD comes, 13.09
of hosts in the d. of his fierce 13.13
O D. Star, son of Dawn! How you 14.12
And in that d. the glory of Jacob 17.04
In that d. men will regard their 17.07
In that d. their strong cities will 17.09
grow on the d. that you plant them, 17.11
flee away in a d. of grief and 17.11
In that d. the Egyptians will be 19.16
In that d. there will be five 19.18
In that d. there will be an altar 19.19
LORD in that d. and worship with 19.21
In that d. there will be a highway 19.23
In that d. Israel will be the third 19.24
this coastland will say in that d., 20.06
I stand, O Lord, continually by d., 21.08
of hosts has a d. of tumult and 22.05
In that d. you looked to the 22.08
In that d. the Lord GOD of hosts, 22.12
In that d. I will call my servant 22.20
In that d., says the LORD of hosts, 22.25
In that d. Tyre will be forgotten 23.15
On that d. the LORD will punish the 24.21
It will be said on that d., 25.09
In that d. this song will be sung 26.01
In that d. the LORD with his hard 27.01
In that d.: "A pleasant vineyard, 27.02
harm it, I guard it night and d.; 27.03
blast in the d. of the east wind. 27.08
In that d. from the river Euphrates 27.12
And in that d. a great trumpet will 27.13
In that d. the LORD of hosts will 28.05
pass through, by d. and by night; 28.19
In that d. the deaf shall hear the 29.18
In that d. your cattle will graze 30.23
in the d. of the great slaughter, 30.25
in the d. when the LORD binds up 30.26
For in that d. every one shall cast 31.07
For the LORD has a d. of vengeance, 34.08
Night and d. it shall not be 34.10
'This d. is a d. of distress, of 37.03
from d. to night thou dost bring me 38.12
from d. to night thou dost bring me 38.13
he thanks thee, as I do this d.; 38.19
have stored up till this d., 39.06
come to you in a moment, in one d.; 47.09
in a d. of salvation I have helped 49.08
continually all the d. because of 51.13

DAY (cont.)
continually all the d. my name is Is 52.05
therefore in that d. they shall 52.06
and tomorrow will be like this d., 56.12
in the d. of your fast you seek 58.03
like yours this d. will not make 58.04
a d. for a man to humble himself? 58.05
and a d. acceptable to the LORD? 58.05
doing your pleasure on my holy d., 58.13
and the holy d. of the LORD 58.13
d. and night they shall not be shut; 60.11
shall be no more your light by d., 60.19
and the d. of vengeance of our God, 61.02
and the d. and all the night they 62.06
For the d. of vengeance was in my 63.04
hands all the d. to a rebellious 65.02
a fire that burns all the d. 65.05
Shall a land be born in one d.? 66.08
set you this d. over nations and Jer 1.10
I make you this d. a fortified 1.18
from our youth even to this d.; 3.25
"In that d., says the LORD, courage 4.09
for the d. declines, for the shadows 6.04
For in the d. that I brought them 7.22
From the d. that your fathers came 7.25
of the land of Egypt to this d., 7.25
the prophets to them, d. after d.; 7.25
I might weep d. and night for the 9.01
with milk and honey, as at this d. 11.05
even to this d., saying, Obey my 11.07
them apart for the d. of slaughter. 12.03
run down with tears night and d., 14.17
sun went down while it was yet d.; 15.09
serve other gods d. and night, 16.13
my refuge in the d. of trouble, 16.19
have I desired the d. of disaster, 17.16
art my refuge in the d. of evil. 17.17
bring upon them the d. of evil; 17.18
on the sabbath d. or bring it in 17.21
work, but keep the sabbath d. holy, 17.22
of this city on the sabbath d., 17.24
the sabbath d. holy and do no work 17.24
to me, to keep the sabbath d. holy, 17.27
of Jerusalem on the sabbath d., 17.27
in the d. of their calamity." 18.17
become a laughingstock all the d.; 20.07
reproach and derision all d. long. 20.08
Cursed be the d. on which I was 20.14
The d. when my mother bore me, let 20.14
to this d., the word of the LORD 25.03
hissing and a curse, as at this d.; 25.18
LORD on that d. shall extend from 25.33
there until the d. when I give 27.22
that d. is so great there is none 30.07
"And it shall come to pass in that d., 30.08
shall be a d. when watchmen will 31.06
for light by d. and the fixed 31.35
and to this d. in Israel and among 32.20
made thee a name, as at this d. 32.20
from the d. it was built to this d., 32.31
with the d. and my covenant with 33.20
so that d. and night will not come 33.20
covenant with d. and night and the 33.25
and they drink none of this d., 35.14
from the d. I spoke to you, from the 36.02
and on a fast d. in the hearing of 36.06
to the heat by d. and the frost by 36.30
guard until the d. that Jerusalem 38.28
on the ninth d. of the month, a 39.02
accomplished before you on that d. 39.16
But I will deliver you on that d., 39.17
On the d. after the murder of 41.04
that I have warned you this d. 42.19
And I have this d. declared it to 42.21
Behold, this d. they are a desolation, 44.02
and a desolation, as at this d. 44.06
humbled themselves even to this d., 44.10
inhabitant, as it is this d. 44.22
has befallen you, as at this d." 44.23
That d. is the d. of the Lord GOD 46.10
a d. of vengeance, to avenge himself 46.10
for the d. of their calamity has 46.21
because of the d. that is coming to 47.04
be in that d. like the heart of a 48.41
be in that d. like the heart of a 49.22
shall be destroyed in that d., 49.26
for their d. has come, the time of 50.27
destroyed on that d., says the LORD. 50.30
for your d. has come, the time when 50.31
every side on the d. of trouble. 51.02
on the tenth d. of the month, 52.04
On the ninth d. of the fourth month 52.06
in prison till the d. of his death. 52.11
on the tenth d. of the month—which 52.12
the twenty-fifth d. of the month, 52.31
And every d. of his life he dined 52.33
until the d. of his death as long 52.34
inflicted on the d. of his fierce Lam 1.12
me stunned, faint all the d. long. 1.13
Bring thou the d. thou hast announced, 1.21
footstool in the d. of his anger. 2.01
LORD as on the d. of an appointed 2.07
Ah, this is the d. we longed for; 2.16
down like a torrent d. and night! 2.18
in the d. of thy anger thou hast 2.21
as to the d. of an appointed feast 2.22
and on the d. of the anger of the 2.22
again and again the whole d. long. 3.03
burden of their songs all d. long. 3.14
are against me all the d. long. 3.62
on the fifth d. of the month, as I Eze 1.01
On the fifth d. of the month (it 1.02
is in the cloud on the d. of rain, 1.28
transgressed against me to this very d. 2.03
I assign you, a d. for each year. 4.06
be by weight, twenty shekels a d.; 4.10
once a d. you shall eat it. 4.10
of a hin; once a d. you shall drink. 4.11
the d. is near, a d. of tumult, and 7.07
"Behold, the d.! Behold, it 7.10
The time has come, the d. draws near. 7.12
them in the d. of the wrath of the 7.19
on the fifth d. of the month, as I 8.01
go into exile by d. in their sight; 12.03
your baggage by d. in their sight, 12.04
I brought out my baggage by d., 12.07
in battle in the d. of the LORD. 13.05
on the d. you were born your navel 16.04
on the d. that you were born. 16.05
mouth in the d. of your pride, 16.56
on the tenth d. of the month, 20.01
On the d. when I chose Israel, I 20.05
On that d. I swore to them that I 20.06
name is called Bamah to this d. 20.29
with all your idols to this d. 20.31
whose d. has come, the time of your 21.25
whose d. has come, the time of their 21.29
and you have brought your d. near, 22.04
upon in the d. of indignation. 22.24
on the same d. and profaned my 23.38
on the same d. they came into my 23.39
on the tenth d. of the month, the 24.01
the name of this d., this very d. 24.02
siege of Jerusalem this very d. 24.02
on the d. when I take from them 24.25
on that d. a fugitive will come to 24.26
On that d. your mouth will be 24.27
on the first d. of the month, the 26.01
tremble on the d. of your fall; 26.18
of the seas on the d. of your ruin. 27.27
On the d. that you were created 28.13
ways from the d. you were created, 28.15
on the twelfth d. of the month, 29.01
on the first d. of the month, the 29.17

DAY (cont.)
"On that d. I will cause a horn to Eze 29.21
LORD GOD: "Wail. 'Alas for the d.!' 30.02
For the d. is near, the d. of the LORD 30.03
it will be a d. of clouds, a time of 30.03
"On that d. swift messengers shall 30.09
them on the d. of Egypt's doom; 30.09
At Tehaphnehes the d. shall be dark, 30.18
on the seventh d. of the month, 30.20
on the first d. of the month, the 31.01
on the first d. of the month, the 32.01
own life, on the d. of your downfall. 32.10
on the fifteenth d. of the month, 32.17
on the fifth d. of the month, a man 33.21
scattered on a d. of clouds and 34.12
On the d. that I cleanse you from 36.33
On that d. thoughts will come into 38.10
On that d. when my people Israel 38.14
But on that d., when Gog shall come 38.18
On that d. there shall be a great 38.19
That is the d. of which I have 39.08
"On that d. I will give to Gog a 39.11
honor on the d. that I show my 39.13
their God, from that d. forward. 39.22
on the tenth d. of the month, in the 40.01
on that very d., the hand of the 40.01
On the d. when it is erected for 43.18
And on the second d. you shall 43.22
from the eighth d. onward the 43.27
And on the d. that he goes into the 44.27
on the first d. of the month, you 45.18
on the seventh d. of the month for 45.20
on the fourteenth d. of the month, 45.21
On that d. the prince shall provide 45.22
the fifteenth d. of the month and 45.25
on the sabbath d. it shall be 46.01
and on the d. of the new moon it 46.01
on the sabbath d. shall be six 46.04
On the d. of the new moon he shall 46.06
as he does on the sabbath d. 46.12
three times a d. and prayed and Dan 6.10
his petition three times a d." 6.13
at break of d., the king arose and 6.19
as at this d., to the men of Judah, 9.07
as at this d., we have sinned, we 9.15
twenty-fourth d. of the first 10.04
from the first d. that you set 10.12
And on that d., I will break the Hos 1.05
great shall be the d. of Jezreel. 1.11
make her as in the d. she was born, 2.03
"And in that d., says the LORD, you 2.16
covenant on that d. with the beasts 2.18
"And in that d., says the LORD, I 2.21
You shall stumble by d., the prophet 4.05
desolation in the d. of punishment; 5.09
on the third d. he will raise us up, 6.02
On the d. of our king the princes 7.05
you do on the d. of appointed 9.05
and on the d. of the feast of the 9.05
Betharbel on the d. of battle; 10.14
pursues the east wind all d. long; 12.01
the d.! For the d. of the LORD is near, Joe 1.15
for the d. of the LORD is coming, it 2.01
a d. of darkness and gloom, a d. of clouds 2.02
For the d. of the LORD is great and 2.11
and terrible d. of the LORD comes. 2.31
For the d. of the LORD is near in 3.14
"And in that d. the mountains shall 3.18
with shouting in the d. of battle, Amo 1.14
tempest in the d. of the whirlwind 1.14
shall flee away naked in that d., 2.16
"that on the d. I punish Israel for 3.14
and darkens the d. into night, 5.08
you who desire the d. of the LORD! 5.18
would you have the d. of the LORD? 5.18
Is not the d. of the LORD darkness, 5.20
O you who put far away the evil d., 6.03
shall become wailings in that d., 8.03
"And on that d.," says the Lord GOD, 8.09
and the end of it like a bitter d. 8.10
"In that d. the fair virgins and 8.13
"In that d. I will raise up the 9.11
Will I not on that d., Ob 1.08
On the d. that you stood aloof, on 1.11
on the d. that strangers carried 1.11
over the d. of your brother in the d. of 1.12
of Judah in the d. of their ruin; 1.12
have boasted in the d. of distress. 1.12
people in the d. of his calamity; 1.13
disaster in the d. of his calamity; 1.13
goods in the d. of his calamity. 1.13
survivors in the d. of distress. 1.14
For the d. of the LORD is near upon 1.15
But when dawn came up the next d., Jon 4.07
In that d. they shall take up a Mic 2.04
and the d. shall be black over them 3.06
In that d., says the LORD, I will 4.06
And in that d., says the LORD, I 5.10
The d. of their watchmen, of their 7.04
A d. for the building of your walls! 7.11
In that d. the boundary shall be 7.11
in that d. they will come to you, 7.12
a stronghold in the d. of trouble; Nah 1.07
on the fences in a d. of cold— 3.17
wait for the d. of trouble to come Hab 3.16
For the d. of the LORD is at hand; Zep 1.07
And on the d. of the LORD's sacrifice 1.08
On that d. I will punish every one 1.09
"On that d.," says the LORD, "a cry 1.10
The great d. of the LORD is near, 1.14
sound of the d. of the LORD is 1.14
A d. of wrath is that d., a d. of 1.15
a d. of distress and anguish, a d. 1.15
a d. of ruin and devastation, a d. 1.15
a d. of darkness and gloom, a d. of 1.15
a d. of clouds and thick darkness, 1.15
a d. of trumpet blast and battle 1.16
them on the d. of the wrath of the 1.18
upon you the d. of the wrath of 2.02
hidden on the d. of the wrath of 2.03
"for the d. when I arise as a 3.08
"On that d. you shall not be put to 3.11
On that d. it shall be said to 3.16
as on a d. of festival. "I will 3.18
on the first d. of the month, the Hag 1.01
on the twenty-fourth d. of the month, 1.15
the twenty-first d. of the month, 2.01
twenty-fourth d. of the ninth 2.10
come to pass from this d. onward. 2.15
Consider from this d. onward, 2.18
twenty-fourth d. of the ninth 2.18
Since the d. that the foundation of 2.18
From this d. on I will bless you." 2.19
the twenty-fourth d. of the month, 2.20
On that d., says the LORD of hosts, 2.23
twenty-fourth d. of the eleventh Zec. 1.07
themselves to the LORD in that d., 2.11
guilt of this land in a single d. 3.09
In that d., says the LORD of hosts, 3.10
despised the d. of small things 4.10
and go the same d. to the house of 6.10
in the fourth d. of the ninth 7.01
since the d. that the foundation of 8.09
On that d. the LORD their God will 9.16
So it was annulled on that d., 11.11
On that d. I will make Jerusalem a 12.03
On that d., says the LORD, I will 12.04
"On that d. I will make the clans 12.06
On that d. the LORD will put a 12.08
them on that d. shall be like 12.08
And on that d. I will seek to 12.09
On that d. the mourning in Jerusalem 12.11
"On that d. there shall be a 13.01
"And on that d., says the LORD of 13.02

DAY (cont.)

On that d. every prophet will be Zec 13.04
Behold, a d. of the LORD is coming, 14.01
when he fights on a d. of battle. 14.03
On that d. his feet shall stand on 14.04
On that d. there shall be neither 14.06
be continuous d. (it is known to 14.07
not d. and not night, for at evening 14.07
On that d. living waters shall flow 14.08
on that d. the LORD will be one and 14.09
And on that d. a great panic from 14.13
And on that d. there shall be 14.20
of the LORD of hosts on that d. 14.21
can endure the d. of his coming, Mal 3.02
possession on the d. when I act, 3.17
the d. comes, burning like an oven, 4.01
the d. that comes shall burn them 4.01
on the d. when I act, says the LORD 4.03
and terrible d. of the LORD comes. 4.05
Give us this d. our daily bread; Mt 6.11
trouble be sufficient for the d. 6.34
On that d. many will say to me, 7.22
tolerable on the d. of judgment for 10.15
tolerable on the d. of judgment for 11.22
would have remained until this d. 11.23
tolerable on the d. of judgment for 11.24
on the d. of judgment men will 12.36
That same d. Jesus went out of the 13.01
place, and the d. is now over; 14.15
and on the third d. be raised. 16.21
he will be raised on the third d." 17.23
the laborers for a denarius a d., 20.02
'Why do you stand here idle all d.?' 20.06
burden of the d. and the scorching 20.12
he will be raised on the third d." 20.19
The same d. Sadducees came to him, 22.23
nor from that d. did any one dare 22.46
"But of that d. and hour no one 24.36
until the d. when Noah entered the 24.38
know on what d. your Lord is 24.42
will come on a d. when he does not 24.50
know neither the d. nor the hour. 25.13
Now on the first d. of Unleavened 26.17
vine until that d. when I drink it 26.29
D. after d. I sat in the temple 26.55
the Field of Blood to this d. 27.08
Next d., that is, after the d. of 27.62
be made secure until the third d., 27.64
dawn of the first d. of the week, 28.01
spread among the Jews to this d. 28.15
morning, a great while before d., Mk 1.35
and then they will fast in that d. 2.20
should sleep and rise night and d., 4.27
On that d., when evening had come, 4.35
Night and d. among the tombs and on 5.05
On the following d., when they 11.12
"But of that d. or that hour no one 13.32
And on the first d. of Unleavened 14.12
vine until that d. when I drink it 14.25
D. after d. I was with you in the 14.49
since it was the d. of Preparation, 15.42
that is, the d. before the sabbath, 15.42
on the first d. of the week they 16.02
speak until the d. that these Lk 1.20
And on the eighth d. they came to 1.59
when the d. shall dawn upon us from 1.78
till the d. of his manifestation 1.80
is born this d. in the city of 2.11
fasting and prayer night and d. 2.37
his custom was, on the sabbath d. 4.16
And when it was d. he departed and 4.42
And when it was d., he called 6.13
Rejoice in that d., and leap 6.23
One d. he got into a boat with his 8.22
Now the d. began to wear away; 9.12
and on the third d. be raised." 9.22
On the next d., when they had come 9.37
tolerable on that d. for Sodom than 10.12
And the next d. he took out two 10.35
Give us each d. our daily bread; 11.03
will come on a d. when he does not 12.46
healed, and not on the sabbath d." 13.14
from this bond on the sabbath d.?" 13.16
and the third d. I finish my course 13.32
and tomorrow and the d. following; 13.33
pull him out on a sabbath d.?" 14.05
who feasted sumptuously every d. 16.19
against you seven times in the d., 17.04
will the Son of man be in his d. 17.24
until the d. when Noah entered the 17.27
but on the d. when Lot went out 17.29
it be on the d. when the Son of 17.30
On that d., let him who is on the 17.31
elect, who cry to him d. and night? 18.07
and on the third d. he will rise." 18.33
One d., as he was teaching the 20.01
and that d. come upon you suddenly 21.34
And every d. he was teaching in the 21.37
Then came the d. of Unleavened 22.07
the cock will not crow this d., 22.34
When I was with you d. after d. in 22.53
When d. came, the assembly of the 22.66
with each other that very d., 23.12
It was the d. of Preparation, and 23.54
But on the first d. of the week, 24.01
crucified, and on the third d. rise." 24.07
That very d. two of them were going 24.13
now the third d. since this 24.21
evening and the d. is now far 24.29
on the third d. rise from the dead, 24.46
The next d. he saw Jesus coming Jn 1.29
The next d. again John was standing 1.35
and they stayed with him that d., 1.39
The next d. Jesus decided to go to 1.43
On the third d. there was a marriage 2.01
Now that d. was the sabbath. 5.09
On the next d. the people who 6.22
me, but raise it up at the last d. 6.39
I will raise him up at the last d." 6.40
I will raise him up at the last d. 6.44
I will raise him up at the last d. 6.54
On the last d. of the feast, the 7.37
the great d., Jesus stood up and 7.37
rejoiced that he was to see my d.; 8.56
of him who sent me, while it is d.; 9.04
was a sabbath d. when Jesus made 9.14
there not twelve hours in the d.? 11.09
If any one walks in the d., he does 11.09
in the resurrection at the last d." 11.24
So from that d. on they took counsel 11.53
keep it for the d. of my burial. 12.07
The next d. a great crowd who had 12.12
will be his judge on the last d. 12.48
In that d. you will know that I am 14.20
In that d. you will ask me no 16.23
In that d. you will ask in my name; 16.26
Now it was the d. of Preparation 19.14
Since it was the d. of Preparation, 19.31
(for that sabbath was a high d.), 19.31
of the Jewish d. of Preparation, 19.42
Now on the first d. of the week 20.01
On the evening of that d., 20.19
the first d. of the week, the doors 20.19
Just as d. was breaking, Jesus stood 21.04
until the d. when he was taken up, Ac 1.02
John until the d. when he was 1.22
When the d. of Pentecost had come, 2.01
is only the third hour of the d.; 2.15
before the d. of the Lord comes, the 2.20
comes, the great and manifest d. 2.20
and his tomb is with us to this d. 2.29
were added that d. about three 2.41
And d. by d., attending the temple 2.46
to their number d. by d. those 2.47

DAY (cont.)
And every d. in the temple and at Ac 5.42
circumcised him on the eighth d.; 7.08
the following d. he appeared to 7.26
And on that d. a great persecution 8.01
watching the gates d. and night, 9.24
hour of the d. he saw clearly in a 10.03
The next d., as they were on their 10.09
The next d. he rose and went off 10.23
the following d. they entered 10.24
on the third d. and made him 10.40
Now when d. came, there was no small 12.18
On an appointed d. Herod put on his 12.21
on the sabbath d. they went into 13.14
and on the next d. he went on with 14.20
and the following d. to Neapolis, 16.11
and on the sabbath d. we went 16.13
But when it was d., the magistrates 16.35
place every d. with those who 17.17
because he has fixed a d. on which 17.31
On the first d. of the week, when we 20.07
the following d. opposite Chios; 20.15
the next d. we touched at Samos; 20.15
and the d. after that we came to 20.15
possible, on the d. of Pentecost. 20.16
from the first d. that I set foot 20.18
to you this d. that I am innocent 20.26
cease night or d. to admonish 20.31
and the next d. to Rhodes, and from 21.01
and stayed with them for one d. 21.07
On the following d. Paul went in 21.18
and the next d. he purified himself 21.26
for God as you all are this d. 22.03
all good conscience up to this d." 23.01
When it was d., the Jews made a 23.12
I am on trial before you this d.' " 24.21
and the next d. he took his seat on 25.06
but on the next d. took my seat on 25.17
earnestly worship night and d. 26.07
To this d. I have had the help that 26.22
hear me this d. might become such 26.29
The next d. we put in at Sidon; 27.03
they began next d. to throw the 27.18
and the third d. they cast out with 27.19
nor stars appeared for many a d., 27.20
stern, and prayed for d. to come. 27.29
As d. was about to dawn, Paul urged 27.33
the fourteenth d. that you have 27.33
Now when it was d., they did 27.39
and after one d. a south wind 28.13
on the second d. we came to 28.13
When they had appointed a d. for him, 28.23
yourself on the d. of wrath when Rom 2.05
on that d. when, according to my 2.16
are being killed all the d. long; 8.36
"All d. long I have held out my 10.21
not hear, down to this very d." 11.08
is far gone, the d. is at hand. 13.12
ourselves becomingly as in the d., 13.13
One man esteems one d. as better 14.05
He who observes the d., 14.06
guiltless in the d. of our Lord 1Co 1.08
for the D. will disclose it, because 3.13
be saved in the d. of the Lord 5.05
thousand fell in a single d. 10.08
on the third d. in accordance with 15.04
Jesus our Lord, I die every d.! 15.31
On the first d. of every week, each 16.02
on the d. of the Lord Jesus. 2Co 1.14
for to this d., when they read the 3.14
Yes, to this d. whenever Moses is 3.15
nature is being renewed every d. 4.16
helped you on the d. of salvation." 6.02
behold, now is the d. of salvation. 6.02
a night and a d. I have been adrift 11.25
sealed for the d. of redemption. Eph 4.30
able to withstand in the evil d., 6.13
gospel from the first d. until now. Php 1.05
completion at the d. of Jesus 1.06
blameless for the d. of Christ, 1.10
so that in the d. of Christ I may 2.16
circumcised on the eighth d., 3.05
from the d. you heard and understood Col 1.06
from the d. we heard of it, we have 1.09
we worked night and d., 1Th 2.09
night and d. that we may see you 3.10
well that the d. of the Lord will 5.02
for that d. to surprise you like a 5.04
sons of light and sons of the d.; 5.05
But, since we belong to the d., 5.08
comes on that d. to be glorified 2Th 1.10
effect that the d. of the Lord has 2.02
for that d. will not come, unless 2.03
and labor we worked night and d., 3.08
supplications and prayers night and d.; 1Ti 5.05
I long night and d. to see you, 2Ti 1.04
until that D. what has been 1.12
mercy from the Lord on that D.— 1.18
judge, will award to me on that D., 4.08
on the d. of testing in the wilderness, Heb 3.08
But exhort one another every d., 3.13
of the seventh d. in this way, 4.04
on the seventh d. from all his 4.04
again he sets a certain d., 4.07
not speak later of another d. 4.08
fathers on the d. when I took them 8.09
as you see the D. drawing near. 10.25
your hearts in a d. of slaughter. Jas 5.05
God on the d. of visitation. 1Pe 2.12
until the d. dawns and the morning 2Pe 1.19
righteous soul d. after d. with 2.08
punishment until the d. of judgment, 2.09
kept until the d. of judgment and 3.07
the Lord one d. is as a thousand 3.08
and a thousand years as one d. 3.08
But the d. of the Lord will come 3.10
the coming of the d. of God, 3.12
both now and to the d. of eternity. 3.18
confidence for the d. of judgment, 1Jn 4.17
until the judgment of the great d.; Jud 1.06
was in the Spirit on the Lord's d., Rev 1.10
and d. and night they never cease 4.08
for the great d. of their wrath has 6.17
and serve him d. and night within 7.15
a third of the d. was kept from 8.12
the d., the month, and the year, to 9.15
accuses them d. and night before 12.10
d. or night, these worshipers of the 14.11
on the great d. of God the Almighty 16.14
her plagues come in a single d., 18.08
be tormented d. and night for ever 20.10
gates shall never be shut by d.— 21.25

DAYBREAK
by d. not one was left who had not 2Sa 17.22
the temple at d. and taught. Ac 5.21
until d., and so departed. 20.11

DAYLIGHT
and darken the earth in broad d. Amo 8.09

DAY'S
and gather a d. portion every day, Ex 16.04
a d. journey on this side and a d. Num 11.31
himself went a d. journey into the 1Ki 19.04
to do according to this d. edict. Est 9.13
into the city, going a d. journey. Jon 3.04
Let the d. own trouble be sufficient Mt 6.34
the company they went a d. journey, Lk 2.44
Jerusalem, a sabbath d. journey away; Ac 1.12

DAYS
for seasons and for d. and years, Gen 1.14
shall eat all the d. of your life. 3.14
eat of it all the d. of your life; 3.17

DAYS (cont.)

The d. of Adam after he became the Gen 5.04
Thus all the d. that Adam lived 5.05
Thus all the d. of Seth were nine 5.08
Thus all the d. of Enosh were nine 5.11
Thus all the d. of Kenan were nine 5.14
Thus all the d. of Mahalalel were 5.17
Thus all the d. of Jared were nine 5.20
Thus all the d. of Enoch were three 5.23
Thus all the d. of Methuselah were 5.27
Thus all the d. of Lamech were 5.31
but his d. shall be a hundred and 6.03
were on the earth in those d., 6.04
For in seven d. I will send rain 7.04
the earth forty d. and forty 7.04
And after seven d. the waters of 7.10
the earth forty d. and forty 7.12
continued forty d. upon the earth; 7.17
the earth a hundred and fifty d. 7.24
and fifty d. the waters had abated; 8.03
end of forty d. Noah opened the 8.06
He waited another seven d., 8.10
Then he waited another seven d., 8.12
All the d. of Noah were nine 9.29
for in his d. the earth was divided, 10.25
The d. of Terah were two hundred 11.32
In the d. of Amraphel king of 14.01
He that is eight d. old among you 17.12
son Isaac when he was eight d. old, 21.04
sojourned many d. in the land of 21.34
with us a while, at least ten d.; 24.55
These are the d. of the years of 25.07
When her d. to be delivered were 25.24
that was in the d. of Abraham. 26.01
had dug in the d. of Abraham his 26.15
been dug in the d. of Abraham his 26.18
"The d. of mourning for my father 27.41
him but a few d. because of the 29.20
In the d. of wheat harvest Reuben 30.14
him for seven d. and followed 31.23
Now the d. of Isaac were a hundred 35.28
to his people, old and full of d.; 35.29
and mourned for his son many d. 37.34
the three branches are three d.; 40.12
within three d. Pharaoh will lift 40.13
the three baskets are three d.; 40.18
within three d. Pharaoh will lift 40.19
together in prison for three d. 42.17
many are the d. of the years of 47.08
"The d. of the years of my sojourning 47.09
have been the d. of the years of 47.09
attained to the d. of the years of 47.09
fathers in the d. of their sojourning." 47.09
so the d. of Jacob, the years of his 47.28
shall befall you in d. to come. 49.01
forty d. were required for it, for 50.03
Egyptians wept for him seventy d. 50.03
And when the d. of weeping for him 50.04
a mourning for his father seven d. 50.10
of those many d. the king of Egypt Ex 2.23
Seven d. passed after the LORD had 7.25
in all the land of Egypt three d.; 10.22
rise from his place for three d.; 10.23
Seven d. you shall eat unleavened 12.15
no work shall be done on those d.; 12.16
For seven d. no leaven shall be 12.19
Seven d. you shall eat unleavened 13.06
Unleavened bread shall be eaten for seven d.; 13.07
they went three d. in the wilderness 15.22
Six d. you shall gather it; but on 16.26
day he gives you bread for two d.; 16.29
Six d. you shall labor, and do all 20.09
for in six d. the LORD made heaven 20.11
that your d. may be long in the 20.12
seven d. it shall be with its dam; 22.30
"Six d. you shall do your work, but 23.12
bread for seven d. at the appointed 23.15
will fulfil the number of your d. 23.26
and the cloud covered it six d.; 24.16
mountain forty d. and forty nights 24.18
his place shall wear them seven d., 29.30
through seven d. shall you ordain 29.35
Seven d. you shall make atonement 29.37
Six d. shall work be done, but the 31.15
that in six d. the LORD made 31.17
Seven d. you shall eat unleavened 34.18
"Six d. you shall work, but on the 34.21
the LORD forty d. and forty nights 34.28
Six d. shall work be done, but on 35.02
the tent of meeting for seven d., Lev 8.33
until the d. of your ordination are 8.33
will take seven d. to ordain you. 8.33
remain day and night for seven d., 8.35
then she shall be unclean seven d.; 12.02
thirty-three d. in the blood of 12.04
until the d. of her purifying are 12.04
of her purifying for sixty-six d. 12.05
"And when the d. of her purifying 12.06
the diseased person for seven d.; 13.04
shall shut him up seven d. more; 13.05
priest shall shut him up seven d.; 13.21
priest shall shut him up seven d., 13.26
the itching disease for seven d., 13.31
itching disease for seven d. more; 13.33
which has the disease for seven d.; 13.50
he shall shut it up seven d. more; 13.54
dwell outside his tent seven d. 14.08
and shut up the house seven d. 14.38
himself seven d. for his cleansing, 15.13
be in her impurity for seven d., 15.19
him, he shall be unclean seven d.; 15.24
a discharge of blood for many d., 15.25
all the d. of the discharge she 15.25
as in the d. of her impurity, she 15.25
all the d. of her discharge, shall 15.26
shall count for herself seven d., 15.28
remain seven d. with its mother; 22.27
Six d. shall work be done; 23.03
seven d. you shall eat unleavened 23.06
by fire to the LORD seven d.; 23.08
counting fifty d. to the morrow 23.16
and for seven d. is the feast of 23.34
Seven d. you shall present offerings 23.36
the feast of the LORD seven d.; 23.39
before the LORD your God seven d. 23.40
to the LORD seven d. in the year; 23.41
shall dwell in booths for seven d.; 23.42
All the d. of his separation he Num 6.04
"All the d. of his vow of separation 6.05
"All the d. that he separates 6.06
All the d. of his separation he is 6.08
LORD for the d. of his separation, 6.12
over the tabernacle many d., 9.19
cloud was a few d. over the 9.20
Whether it was two d., 9.22
two d., or five d., or ten d., or twenty d., 11.19
should she not be shamed seven d.? 12.14
shut up outside the camp seven d., 12.14
shut up outside the camp seven d., 12.15
end of forty d. they returned from 13.25
number of the d. in which you 14.34
forty d., for every day a year, you 14.34
person shall be unclean seven d.; 19.11
tent, shall be unclean seven d. 19.14
a grave, shall be unclean seven d. 19.16
of Israel wept for Aaron thirty d. 20.29
do to your people in the latter d." 24.14
seven d. shall unleavened bread be 28.17
for seven d., the food of an 28.24
keep a feast to the LORD seven d.; 29.12
Encamp outside the camp seven d.; 31.19
So you remained at Kadesh many d., Deu 1.46
the d. that you remained there. 1.46
and for many d. we went about Mount 2.01

DAYS (cont.)
your heart all the d. of your life; Deu 4.09
fear me all the d. that they live 4.10
come upon you in the latter d., 4.30
"For ask now of the d. that are past, 4.32
prolong your d. in the land which 4.40
Six d. you shall labor, and do all 5.13
that your d. may be prolonged, and 5.16
you, all the d. of your life; 6.02
and that your d. may be prolonged. 6.02
mountain forty d. and forty nights 9.09
end of forty d. and forty nights 9.09
end of forty d. and forty nights 9.11
forty d. and forty nights; 9.18
for these forty d. and forty 9.25
forty d. and forty nights, and the 10.10
your d. and the d. of your children 11.21
all the d. that you live upon the 12.01
seven d. you shall eat it with 16.03
that all the d. of your life you 16.03
in all your territory for seven d.; 16.04
For six d. you shall eat unleavened 16.08
keep the feast of booths seven d., 16.13
For seven d. you shall keep the 16.15
judge who is in office in those d., 17.09
read in it all the d. of his life, 17.19
who are in office in those d.; 19.17
he may not put her away all his d. 22.19
he may not put her away all his d. 22.29
prosperity all your d. for ever. 23.06
that your d. may be prolonged in 25.15
means life to you and length of d., 30.20
the d. approach when you must die; 31.14
and in the d. to come evil will 31.29
Remember the d. of old, consider the 32.07
and as your d., so shall your 33.25
in the plains of Moab thirty d.; 34.08
then the d. of weeping and mourning 34.08
before you all the d. of your life; Jos 1.05
within three d. you are to pass 1.11
and hide yourselves there three d.. 2.16
hills, and remained there three d., 2.22
end of three d. the officers went 3.02
of Moses, all the d. of his life. 4.14
Thus shall you do for six d. 6.03
So they did for six d. 6.14
end of three d. after they had 9.16
your brethren these many d., 22.03
the LORD all the d. of Joshua, 24.31
and all the d. of the elders who 24.31
the LORD all the d. of Joshua, Ju 2.07
and all the d. of the elders who 2.07
"In the d. of Shamgar, son of Anath, 5.06
in the d. of Jael, caravans ceased 5.06
forty years in the d. of Gideon. 8.28
the Gileadite four d. in the year. 11.40
within the seven d. of the feast, 14.12
not in three d. tell what the 14.14
him the seven d. that their feast 14.17
Israel in the d. of the Philistines 15.20
In those d. there was no king in 17.06
In those d. there was no king in 18.01
And in those d. the tribe of the 18.01
In those d., when there was no king 19.01
and he remained with him three d.; 19.04
of God was there in those d., 20.27
ministered before it in those d.), 20.28
In those d. there was no king in 21.25
In the d. when the judges ruled Ru 1.01
to the LORD all the d. of his life, 1Sa 1.11
Behold, the d. are coming, when I 2.31
of the LORD was rare in those d.; 3.01
Philistines all the d. of Samuel. 7.13
Israel all the d. of his life. 7.15
asses that were lost three d. ago, 9.20
Seven d. you shall wait, until I 10.08
"Give us seven d. respite that we 11.03
He waited seven d., the time 13.08
not come within the d. appointed, 13.11
the Philistines all the d. of Saul; 14.52
In the d. of Saul the man was 17.12
For forty d. the Philistine came 17.16
And about ten d. later the LORD 25.38
number of the d. that David dwelt 27.07
In those d. the Philistines gathered 28.01
been with me now for d. and years, 29.03
water for three d. and three 30.12
because I fell sick three d. ago. 30.13
in Jabesh, and fasted seven d. 31.13
David remained two d. in Ziklag; 2Sa 1.01
When your d. are fulfilled and you 7.12
been mourning many d. for the dead; 14.02
Now in those d. the counsel which 16.23
together to me within three d., 20.04
a famine in the d. of David for 21.01
death in the first d. of harvest, 21.09
end of nine months and twenty d. 24.08
Shimei dwelt in Jerusalem many d. 1Ki 2.38
compare with you, all your d. 3.13
then I will lengthen your d." 3.14
Solomon all the d. of his life. 4.21
fig tree, all the d. of Solomon. 4.25
thee all the d. that they live in 8.40
before the LORD our God, seven d. 8.65
as anything in the d. of Solomon. 10.21
father I will not do it in your d., 11.12
of Israel all the d. of Solomon, 11.25
him ruler all the d. of his life, 11.34
He said to them, "Depart for three d., 12.05
commanded him all the d. of his life, 15.05
Jeroboam all the d. of his life. 15.06
wholly true to the LORD all his d. 15.14
Baasha king of Israel all their d. 15.16
Baasha king of Israel all their d. 15.32
Zimri reigned seven d. in Tirzah. 16.15
In his d. Hiel of Bethel built 16.34
and her household ate for many d. 17.15
After many d. the word of the LORD 18.01
that food forty d. and forty 19.08
opposite one another seven d. 20.29
will not bring the evil in his d.; 21.29
in his son's d. I will bring the 21.29
remained in the d. of his father 22.46
and for three d. they sought him 2Ki 2.17
a circuitous march of seven d., 3.09
In his d. Edom revolted from the 8.20
In those d. the LORD began to cut 10.32
in the eyes of the LORD all his d., 12.02
Israel all the d. of Jehoahaz. 13.22
depart all his d. from all the 15.18
In the d. of Pekah king of Israel 15.29
In those d. the LORD began to send 15.37
for until those d. the people of 18.04
I planned from d. of old what now I 19.25
In those d. Hezekiah became sick 20.01
Behold, the d. are coming, when all 20.17
be peace and security in my d.?" 20.19
kept since the d. of the judges 23.22
during all the d. of the kings of 23.22
In his d. Pharaoh Neco king of 23.29
In his d. Nebuchadnezzar king of 24.01
(for in his d. the earth was 1Ch 1.19
came in the d. of Hezekiah, king of 4.41
And in the d. of Saul they made war 5.10
genealogies in the d. of Jotham 5.17
and in the d. of Jeroboam king of 5.17
number in the d. of David being 7.02
their father mourned many d., 7.22
obliged to come in every seven d., 9.25
oak in Jabesh, and fasted seven d. 10.12
were there with David for three d., 12.39
we neglected it in the d. of Saul." 13.03
When your d. are fulfilled to go to 17.11
or else three d. of the sword of 21.12

DAYS (cont.)

and quiet to Israel in his d.	1Ch 22.09
When David was old and full of d.,	23.01
and feast d., according to the	23.31
our d. on the earth are like a	29.15
full of d., riches, and honor;	29.28
ways all the d. that they live in	2Ch 6.31
held the feast for seven d.,	7.08
the altar seven d. and the feast seven d.	7.09
as anything in the d. of Solomon.	9.20
them, "Come to me again in three d."	10.05
his power in the d. of Abijah;	13.20
In his d. the land had rest for ten	14.01
of Asa was blameless all his d.	15.17
They were three d. in taking the	20.25
In his d. Edom revolted from the	21.08
LORD all the d. of Jehoiada the	24.02
continually all the d. of Jehoiada	24.14
grew old and full of d., and died;	24.15
to seek God in the d. of Zechariah,	26.05
then for eight d. they sanctified	29.17
bread seven d. with great gladness	30.21
food of the festival for seven d.,	30.22
the feast for another seven d.;	30.23
for another seven d. with gladness.	30.23
In those d. Hezekiah became sick	32.24
upon them in the d. of Hezekiah.	32.26
All his d. they did not turn away	34.33
feast of unleavened bread seven d.	35.17
since the d. of Samuel the prophet	35.18
months and ten d. in Jerusalem.	36.09
All the d. that it lay desolate it	36.21
ever since the d. of Esarhaddon	Ez 4.02
all the d. of Cyrus king of Persia,	4.05
And in the d. of Artaxerxes, Bishlam	4.07
unleavened bread seven d. with joy;	6.22
and there we encamped three d.	8.15
and there we remained three d.	8.32
From the d. of our fathers to this	9.07
one did not come within three d.,	10.08
at Jerusalem within the three d.;	10.09
down and wept, and mourned for d.;	Neh 1.04
Jerusalem and was there three d.	2.11
and every ten d. skins of wine in	5.18
of the month Elul, in fifty-two d.	6.15
Moreover in those d. the nobles of	6.17
for from the d. of Jeshua the son	8.17
They kept the feast seven d.;	8.18
their brethren in the d. of Jeshua.	12.07
And in the d. of Joiakim were	12.12
in the d. of Eliashib, Joiada,	12.22
until the d. of Johanan the son of	12.23
These were in the d. of Joiakim the	12.26
and in the d. of Nehemiah the	12.26
For in the d. of David and Asaph of	12.46
Israel in the d. of Zerubbabel and	12.47
and in the d. of Nehmiah gave the	12.47
In those d. I saw in Judah men	13.15
In those d. also I saw the Jews who	13.23
In the d. of Ahasuerus, the Ahasuerus	Est 1.01
in those d. when King Ahasuerus sat	1.02
pomp of his majesty for many d.,	1.04
many d., a hundred and eighty d.	1.04
And when these d. were completed,	1.05
a banquet lasting for seven d.,	1.05
And in those d., as Mordecai was	2.21
in to the king these thirty d."	4.11
drink for three d., night or day.	4.16
as the d. on which the Jews got	9.22
make them d. of feasting and	9.22
d. for sending choice portions to	9.22
Therefore they called these d. Purim,	9.26
keep these two d. according to	9.27
that these d. should be remembered	9.28
and that these d. of Purim should	9.28
of these d. cease among their	9.28
that these d. of Purim should be	9.31
And when the d. of the feast had	Job 1.05
ground seven d. and seven nights.	2.13
rejoice among the d. of the year,	3.06
and are not his d. like the d. of a	7.01
My d. are swifter than a weaver's	7.06
me alone, for my d. are a breath.	7.16
your latter d. will be very great.	8.07
for our d. on earth are a shadow.	8.09
"My d. are swifter than a runner;	9.25
Are thy d. as the d. of man, or	10.05
Are not the d. of my life few?	10.20
and understanding in length of d.	12.12
is born of a woman is of few d.,	14.01
Since his d. are determined, and the	14.05
All the d. of my service I would	14.14
man writhes in pain all his d.,	15.20
my d. are extinct, the grave is	17.01
My d. are past, my plans are broken	17.11
They spend their d. in prosperity,	21.13
who know him never see his d.?	24.01
not reproach me for any of my d.	27.06
as in the d. when God watched over	29.02
as I was in my autumn d., when the	29.04
shall multiply my d. as the sand,	29.18
d. of affliction have taken hold of	30.16
d. of affliction come to meet me.	30.27
I said, 'Let d. speak, and many years	32.07
return to the d. of his youthful	33.25
complete their d. in prosperity,	36.11
the morning since your d. began,	38.12
and the number of your d. is great!	38.21
the latter d. of Job more than his	42.12
died, an old man, and full of d.	42.17
length of d. for ever and ever.	Ps 21.04
follow me all the d. of my life;	23.06
of the LORD all the d. of my life,	27.04
desires life, and covets many d.,	34.12
The LORD knows the d. of the	37.18
in the d. of famine they have	37.19
and what is the measure of my d.;	39.04
hast made my d. a few handbreaths,	39.05
thou didst perform in their d., in the d.	44.01
shall not live out half their d.	55.23
In his d. may righteousness flourish,	72.07
I consider the d. of old, I remember	77.05
So he made their d. vanish like a	78.33
throne as the d. of the heavens.	89.29
hast cut short the d. of his youth;	89.45
For all our d. pass away under thy	90.09
to number our d. that we may get a	90.12
may rejoice and be glad all our d.	90.14
Make us glad as many d. as thou	90.15
him respite from d. of trouble,	94.13
For my d. pass away like smoke, and	102.03
My d. are like an evening shadow;	102.11
mid-course; he has shortened my d.	102.23
me not hence in the midst of my d.,	102.24
As for man, his d. are like grass;	103.15
May his d. be few; may another	109.08
Jerusalem all the d. of your life!	128.05
the d. that were formed for me, when	139.16
I remember the d. of old, I meditate	143.05
his d. are like a passing shadow.	144.04
for length of d. and years of life	Pro 3.02
For by me your d. will be multiplied,	9.11
All the d. of the afflicted are	15.15
unjust gain will prolong his d.	28.16
not harm, all the d. of her life.	31.12
during the few d. of their life.	Ecc 2.03
that in the d. to come all will	2.16
For all his d. are full of pain, and	2.23
and spent all his d. in darkness	5.17
the sun the few d. of his life	5.18
remember the d. of his life	5.20
so that the d. of his years are	6.03
lives the few d. of his vain life,	6.12
were the former d. better than	7.10

DAYS (cont.)
he prolong his d. like a shadow, Ecc 8.13
through the d. of life which God 8.15
all the d. of your vain life which 9.09
for you will find it after many d. 11.01
that the d. of darkness will be 11.08
cheer you in the d. of your youth; 11.09
Creator in the d. of your youth, 12.01
youth, before the evil d. come, 12.01
and Jerusalem in the d. of Uzziah, Is 1.01
in the latter d. that the mountain 2.02
In the d. of Ahaz the son of Jotham, 7.01
house such d. as have not come 7.17
at hand and its d. will not be 13.22
whose origin is from d. of old, 23.07
years, like the d. of one king. 23.15
and after many d. they will be 24.22
In d. to come Jacob shall take root, 27.06
sevenfold, as the light of seven d., 30.26
I planned from d. of old what now I 37.26
In those d. Hezekiah became sick 38.01
noontide of my d. I must depart; 38.10
instruments all the d. of our life, 38.20
Behold, the d. are coming, when all 39.06
be peace and security in my d." 39.08
awake, as in d. of old, the generations 51.09
offspring, he shall prolong his d.; 53.10
"For this is like the d. of Noah to me: 54.09
and your d. of mourning shall be 60.20
and carried them all the d. of old. 63.09
Then he remembered the d. of old, 63.11
an infant that lives but a few d., 65.20
man who does not fill out his d., 65.20
for like the d. of a tree shall the d. of 65.22
came in the d. of Josiah the son Jer 1.02
also in the d. of Jehoiakim the 1.03
forgotten me d. without number. 2.32
to me in the d. of King Josiah: 3.06
in those d., says the LORD, they 3.16
In those d. the house of Judah 3.18
"But even in those d., says the LORD, 5.18
the d. are coming, says the LORD, 7.32
"Behold, the d. are coming, says 9.25
And after many d. the LORD, 16.14
midst of his d. they will leave 17.11
d. are coming, says the LORD, when 19.06
sorrow, and spend my d. in shame? 20.18
who shall not succeed in his d.; 22.30
"Behold, the d. are coming, says the 23.05
In his d. Judah will be saved, and 23.06
the d. are coming, says the LORD, 23.07
In the latter d. you will understand 23.20
for the d. of your slaughter and 25.34
prophesied in the d. of Hezekiah 26.18
For behold, d. are coming, says the 30.03
In the latter d. you will understand 30.24
"Behold, the d. are coming, says the 31.27
In those d. they shall no longer 31.29
"Behold, the d. are coming, says the 31.31
the house of Israel after those d., 31.33
"Behold, the d. are coming, says the 31.38
"Behold, the d. are coming, says the 33.14
In those d. and at that time I will 33.15
In those d. Judah will be saved and 33.16
the LORD in the d. of Jehoiakim 35.01
shall live in tents all your d., 35.07
may live many d. in the land where 35.07
us, to drink no wine all our d., 35.08
from the d. of Josiah until today. 36.02
cells, and remained there many d., 37.16
At the end of ten d. the word of 42.07
be inhabited as in the d. of old, 46.26
the d. are coming, says the LORD, 48.12
in the latter d., says the LORD. 48.47
the d. are coming, says the LORD, 49.02
"But in the latter d. I will 49.39
"In those d. and in that time, says 50.04
In those d. and in that time, says 50.20
the d. are coming when I will 51.47
the d. are coming, says the LORD, 51.52
remembers in the d. of her affliction Lam 1.07
that were hers from d. of old. 1.07
our d. were numbered; for our end 4.18
restored! Renew our d. as of old! 5.21
overwhelmed among them seven d. Eze 3.15
And at the end of seven d., 3.16
number of the d. that you lie upon 4.04
For I assign to you a number of d., 4.05
three hundred and ninety d., equal 4.05
forty d. I assign you, a day for 4.06
completed the d. of your siege. 4.08
the number of d. that you lie upon 4.09
side, three hundred and ninety d., you shall 4.09
when the d. of the siege are completed; 5.02
'The d. grow long, and every vision 12.22
The d. are at hand, and the fulfilment 12.23
but in your d., O rebellious house, 12.25
that he sees is for many d. hence, 12.27
not remember the d. of your youth, 16.22
remembered the d. of your youth, 16.43
with you in the d. of your youth, 16.60
in the d. that I shall deal with 22.14
practiced since her d. in Egypt; 23.08
remembering the d. of her youth, 23.19
After many d. you will be mustered; 38.08
In the latter d. I will bring you 38.16
spoke in former d. by my servants 38.17
who in those d. prophesied for 38.17
For seven d. you shall provide 43.25
Seven d. shall they make atonement 43.26
And when they have completed these d., 43.27
shall count for himself seven d., 44.26
and for seven d. unleavened bread 45.21
And on the seven d. of the festival 45.23
blemish, on each of the seven d.; 45.23
and for the seven d. of the feast, 45.25
be shut on the six working d.; 46.01
"Test your servants for ten d.; Dan 1.12
matter, and tested them for ten d. 1.14
At the end of ten d. it was seen 1.15
what will be in the latter d. 2.28
And in the d. of those kings the 2.44
At the end of the d. I, Nebuchadnezzar, 4.34
In the d. of your father light and 5.11
numbered the d. of your kingdom 5.26
to any god or man for thirty d., 6.07
man within thirty d. except to you, 6.12
was ancient of d. took his seat; 7.09
the Ancient of D. and was presented 7.13
until the Ancient of D. came, 7.22
for it pertains to many d. hence." 8.26
overcome and lay sick for some d.; 8.27
In those d. I, Daniel, was mourning 10.02
Persia withstood me twenty-one d.; 10.13
your people in the latter d. 10.14
the vision is for d. yet to come." 10.14
within a few d. he shall be broken, 11.20
captivity and plunder, for some d. 11.33
thousand two hundred and ninety d. 12.11
three hundred and thirty-five d. 12.12
alloted place at the end of the d." 12.13
in the d. of Uzziah, Jotham, Ahaz, and Hos 1.01
and in the d. of Jeroboam the son 1.01
for the feast d. of the Baals when 2.13
answer as in the d. of her youth, 2.15
"You must dwell as mine for many d.; 3.03
dwell many d. without king or 3.04
to his goodness in the latter d. 3.05
After two d. he will revive us; 6.02
The d. of punishment have come, the 9.07
the d. of recompense have come; 9.07
themselves as in the d. of Gibeah: 9.09
From the d. of Gibeah, you have 10.09
as in the d. of the appointed feast 12.09

DAYS (cont.)
such a thing happened in your d., Joe 1.02
or in the d. of your fathers? 1.02
and maidservants in those d., I will 2.29
in those d. and at that time, when I 3.01
Israel in the d. of Uzziah king of Amo 1.01
and in the d. of Jeroboam the son 1.01
the d. are coming upon you, when 4.02
morning, your tithes every three d.; 4.04
"Behold, the d. are coming," says the 8.11
and rebuild it as in the d. of old; 9.11
"Behold, the d. are coming," says the 9.13
the fish three d. and three nights. Jon 1.17
"Yet forty d., and Nineveh shall be 3.04
of Moresheth in the d. of Jotham, Mic 1.01
in the latter d. that the mountain 4.01
is from of old, from ancient d. 5.02
and Gilead as in the d. of old. 7.14
As in the d. when you came out of 7.15
to our fathers from the d. of old. 7.20
a work in your d. that you would Hab 1.05
in the d. of Josiah the son of Amon, Zep 1.01
remnant of this people in these d., Zec 8.06
who in these d. have been hearing 8.09
For before those d. there was no 8.10
of this people as in the former d., 8.11
in these d. to do good to Jerusalem 8.15
In those d. ten men from the 8.23
earthquake in the d. of Uzziah king 14.05
LORD as in the d. of old and as in Mal 3.04
From the d. of your fathers you 3.07
of Judea in the d. of Herod the Mt 2.01
In those d. came John the Baptist, 3.01
And he fasted forty d. and forty 4.02
The d. will come, when the bridegroom 9.15
From the d. of John the Baptist 11.12
Jonah was three d. and three 12.40
of man be three d. and three 12.40
have been with me now three d., 15.32
And after six d. Jesus took with 17.01
had lived in the d. of our fathers, 23.30
those who give suck in those d.! 24.19
And if those d. had not been 24.22
the elect those d. will be shortened 24.22
of those d. the sun will be 24.29
As were the d. of Noah, so will be 24.37
For as in those d. before the flood 24.38
that after two d. the Passover is 26.02
God, and to build it in three d.'" 26.61
it in three d., save yourself! 27.40
'After three d. I will rise again.' 27.63
In those d. Jesus came from Nazareth Mk 1.09
And he was in the wilderness forty d., 1.13
returned to Capernaum after some d., 2.01
The d. will come, when the bridegroom 2.20
In those d., when again a great 8.01
have been with me now three d., 8.02
and after three d. rise again. 8.31
And after six d. Jesus took with 9.02
after three d. he will rise." 9.31
and after three d. he will rise." 10.34
those who give suck in those d.! 13.17
For in those d. there will be such 13.19
the Lord had not shortened the d., 13.20
whom he chose, he shortened the d. 13.20
"But in those d., after that 13.24
It was now two d. before the 14.01
and in three d. I will build 14.58
temple and build it in three d., 15.29
In the d. of Herod, king of Judea, Lk 1.05
After these d. his wife Elizabeth 1.24
to me in the d. when he looked on 1.25
In those d. Mary arose and went 1.39
before him all the d. of our life. 1.75
In those d. a decree went out from 2.01
And at the end of eight d., 2.21
After three d. they found him in 2.46
for forty d. in the wilderness, 4.02
And he ate nothing in those d.; 4.02
in Israel in the d. of Elijah, 4.25
On one of those d., as he was 5.17
The d. will come, when the bridegroom 5.35
then they will fast in those d." 5.35
In these d. he went out into the 6.12
Now about eight d. after these 9.28
no one in those d. anything of 9.36
When the d. drew near for him to be 9.51
"There are six d. on which work 13.14
come on those d. and be healed, and 13.14
Not many d. later, the younger son 15.13
"The d. are coming when you will 17.22
see one of the d. of the Son of 17.22
As it was in the d. of Noah, 17.26
it be in the d. of the Son of man. 17.26
Likewise as it was in the d. of Lot— 17.28
For the d. shall come upon you, when 19.43
the d. will come when there shall 21.06
for these are d. of vengeance, to 21.22
those who give suck in those d.! 21.23
the d. are coming when they will 23.29
have happened there in these d.?" 24.18
and there they stayed for a few d. Jn 2.12
and in three d. I will raise it up." 2.19
will you raise it up in three d.?" 2.20
and he stayed there two d. 4.40
After the two d. he departed to 4.43
he stayed two d. longer in the 11.06
already been in the tomb four d. 11.17
odor, for he has been dead four d. 11.39
Six d. before the Passover, Jesus 12.01
Eight d. later, his disciples were 20.26
appearing to them during forty d., Ac 1.03
but before many d. you shall be 1.05
In those d. Peter stood up among 1.15
'And in the last d. it shall be, 2.17
in those d. I will pour out my 2.18
afterwards, also proclaimed these d. 3.24
For before these d. Theudas arose, 5.36
arose in the d. of the census and 5.37
Now in these d. when the disciples 6.01
And they made a calf in those d., 7.41
So it was until the d. of David, 7.45
And for three d. he was without 9.09
For several d. he was with the 9.19
When many d. had passed, the Jews 9.23
In those d. she fell sick and died; 9.37
Joppa for many d. with one Simon, 9.43
"Four d. ago, about this hour, I was 10.30
asked him to remain for some d. 10.48
Now in these d. prophets came down 11.27
took place in the d. of Claudius. 11.28
was during the d. of Unleavened 12.03
and for many d. he appeared to 13.31
for I do a deed in your d., a deed 13.41
in the early d. God made choice 15.07
And after some d. Paul said to 15.36
We remained in this city some d.; 16.12
And this she did for many d. 16.18
After this Paul stayed many d. longer, 18.18
after the d. of Unleavened Bread, 20.06
and in five d. we came to them at 20.06
where we stayed for seven d. 20.06
we stayed there for seven d. 21.04
And when our d. there were ended, we 21.05
While we were staying for some d., 21.10
After these d. we made ready and 21.15
notice when the d. of purification 21.26
When the seven d. were almost 21.27
And after five d. the high priest 24.01
than twelve d. since I went up to 24.11
After some d. Felix came with his 24.24
after three d. he went up to 25.01
them not more than eight or ten d., 25.06
Now when some d. had passed, Agrippa 25.13

DAYS (cont.)

And as they stayed there many d., Ac 25.14
We sailed slowly for a number of d., 27.07
entertained us hospitably for three d. 28.07
we stayed there for three d. 28.12
to stay with them for seven d. 28.14
After three d. he called together 28.17
another man esteems all d. alike. Rom 14.05
in former d. was written for our 15.04
and remained with him fifteen d. Gal 1.18
You observe d., and months, and 4.10
the time, because the d. are evil. Eph 5.16
in the last d. there will come 2Ti 3.01
passing our d. in malice and envy, Tit 3.03
but in these last d. he has spoken Heb 1.02
In the d. of his flesh, Jesus 5.07
beginning of d. nor end of life, 7.03
"The d. will come, says the Lord, 8.08
the house of Israel after those d., 8.10
will make with them after those d., 10.16
But recall the former d. when, 10.32
had been encircled for seven d. 11.30
laid up treasure for the last d. Jas 5.03
would love life and see good d., 1Pe 3.10
patience waited in the d. of Noah, 3.20
come in the last d. with scoffing, 2Pe 3.03
and for ten d. you will have Rev 2.10
even in the d. of Antipas my 2.13
And in those d. men will seek death 9.06
but that in the d. of the trumpet 10.07
thousand two hundred and sixty d., 11.03
rain may fall during the d. of their 11.06
For three d. and a half men from 11.09
three and a half d. a breath of life 11.11
thousand two hundred and sixty d. 12.06

DAYS'

of three d. journey between Gen 30.36
us go a three d. journey into the Ex 3.18
a three d. journey into the wilderness, 5.03
We must go three d. journey into 8.27
mount of the LORD three d. journey; Num 10.33
went before them three d. journey, 10.33
went a three d. journey in the 33.08
It is eleven d. journey from Horeb Deu 1.02
there be three d. pestilence in 2Sa 24.13
three d. journey in breadth. Jon 3.03

DAYTIME

They meet with darkness in the d., Job 5.14
In the d. he led them with a cloud, Ps 78.14
it pleasure to revel in the d. 2Pe 2.13

DAZED

will be drunken, you will be d.; Nah 3.11

DAZZLING

and his raiment became d. white. Lk 9.29
men stood by them in d. apparel; 24.04

DEACONESS

a d. of the church at Cenchreae, Rom 16.01

DEACONS

Philippi, with the bishops and d.: Php 1.01
D. likewise must be serious, not 1Ti 3.08
blameless let them serve as d. 3.10
Let d. be married only once, and let 3.12
serve well as d. gain a good 3.13

DEAD

you are a d. man, because of the Gen 20.03
Abraham rose up from before his d., 23.03
I may bury my d. out of sight." 23.04
Bury your d. in the choicest of our 23.06
or hinder you from burying your d." 23.06
should bury my d. out of my sight, 23.08
give it to you; bury your d." 23.11
me, that I may bury my d. there." 23.13
you and me? Bury your d." 23.15
with you, for his brother is d., 42.38
and his brother is d., and he alone 44.20
saw that their father was d., 50.15
who were seeking your life are d. Ex 4.19
cattle of the Israelites was d. 9.07
not a house where one was not d. 12.30
for they said, "We are all d. men." 12.33
the Egyptians d. upon the seashore 14.30
and the d. beast shall be his. 21.34
and the d. beast also they shall 21.35
and the d. beast shall be his. 21.36
when they are d. shall be unclean Lev 11.31
when they are d. shall be unclean, 11.32
account of the d. or tattoo any 19.28
himself for the d. among his people, 21.01
he shall not go in to any d. body, 21.11
with the d. or a man who has had 22.04
your d. bodies upon the d. bodies 26.30
through contact with the d.; Num 5.02
he shall not go near a d. body. 6.06
he sinned by reason of the d. body. 6.11
touching the d. body of a man, 9.06
touching the d. body of a man; 9.07
unclean through touching a d. body, 9.10
Let her not be as one d., 12.12
your d. bodies shall fall in this 14.29
your d. bodies shall fall in this 14.32
last of your d. bodies lies in the 14.33
between the d. and the living; 16.48
"He who touches the d. body of any 19.11
Whoever touches a d. person, the body 19.13
or a d. body, or a bone of a man, or 19.16
the slain, or the d., or the grave; 19.18
congregation saw that Aaron was d., 20.29
and were d. from among the people, Deu 2.16
on your foreheads for the d. 14.01
the wife of the d. shall not be 25.05
the name of his brother who is d., 25.06
or offered any of it to the d.; 26.14
And your d. body shall be food for 28.26
"Moses my servant is d.; now Jos 1.02
lay their lord d. on the floor. Ju 3.25
and there lay Sisera d., with the 4.22
where he sank, there he fell d. 5.27
Israel saw that Abimelech was d., 9.55
So the d. whom he slew at his death 16.30
my concubine, and she is d. 20.05
have dealt with the d. and with me. Ru 1.08
not forsaken the living or the d.!" 2.20
the Moabitess, the widow of the d., 4.05
the name of the d. to his inheritance 4.05
the name of the d. in his inheritance, 4.10
the name of the d. may not be cut 4.10
are d., and the ark of God has been 1Sa 4.17
father-in-law and her husband were d., 4.19
I will give the d. bodies of the 17.46
their champion was d.. they fled. 17.51
After a d. dog! After a flea! 24.14
When David heard that Nabal was d., 25.39
armor-bearer saw that Saul was d., 31.05
and that Saul and his sons were d., 31.07
people also have fallen and are d.; 2Sa 1.04
and his son Jonathan are also d." 1.04
Saul and his son Jonathan are d.?" 1.05
for Saul your lord is d., and the 2.07
Saul is d.,' and thought he was 4.10
look upon a d. dog such as I?" 9.08
Uriah the Hittite is d. also.'" 11.21
some of the king's servants are d.; 11.24
Uriah the Hittite is d. also." 11.24
that Uriah her husband was d., 11.26
to tell him that the child was d.; 12.18
can we say to him the child is d.? 12.18
perceived that the child was d.; 12.19
to his servants, "Is the child d.?" 12.19

DEAD (cont.)

They said, "He is d." 2Sa 12.19
But now he is d.; why should 12.23
king's sons, for Amnon alone is d., 13.32
that all the king's sons are d.; 13.33
for Amnon alone is d." 13.33
about Amnon, seeing he was d. 13.39
been mourning many days for the d.; 14.02
a widow; my husband is d. 14.05
"Why should this d. dog curse my 16.09
because the king's son is d." 18.20
alive and all of us were d. today, 19.06
anointed over us, is d. in battle. 19.10
and laid her d. son in my bosom. 1Ki 3.20
nurse my child, behold, it was d.; 3.21
is mine, and the d. child is yours." 3.22
d. child is yours, and the living child 3.22
that is alive, and your son is d.'; 3.23
'No, but your son is d., and my son 3.23
the commander of the army was d., 11.21
been stoned; he is d." 21.14
Naboth had been stoned and was d., 21.15
For Naboth is not alive but d." 21.15
as Ahab heard that Naboth was d., 21.16
"Your servant my husband is d.; 2Ki 4.01
saw the child lying d. on his bed. 4.32
Elisha had restored the d. to life, 8.05
of Ahaziah saw that her son was d., 11.01
behold, these were all d. bodies. 19.35
carried him d. in a chariot from 23.30
armor-bearer saw that Saul was d., 1Ch 10.05
and that Saul and his sons were d., 10.07
they were d. bodies lying on the 2Ch 20.24
of Ahaziah saw that her son was d., 22.10
the young people, and they are d.; Job 1.19
out of mind like one who is d.; Ps 31.12
like one forsaken among the d., 88.05
Dost thou work wonders for the d.? 88.10
ate sacrifices offered to the d.; 106.28
The d. do not praise the LORD, nor 115.17
sit in darkness like those long d. 143.03
not know that the d. are there, Pro 9.18
rest in the assembly of the d. 21.16
I thought the d. who are already d. Ecc 4.02
and after that they go to the d. 9.03
dog is better than a d. lion. 9.04
but the d. know nothing, and they 9.05
D. flies make the perfumer's ointment 10.01
consult the d. on behalf of the Is 8.19
like a d. body trodden under foot. 14.19
with the sword or d. in battle. 22.02
They are d., they will not live; 26.14
Thy d. shall live, their bodies 26.19
behold, these were all d. bodies. 37.36
in full vigor we are like d. men. 59.10
and look on the d. bodies of the 66.24
And the d. bodies of this people Jer 7.33
'The d. bodies of men shall fall 9.22
and their d. bodies shall be food 16.04
mourner, to comfort him for the d.; 16.07
will give their d. bodies for food 19.07
Weep not for him who is d., 22.10
and cast his d. body into the 26.23
valley of the d. bodies and the 31.40
them with the d. bodies of men 33.05
Their d. bodies shall be food for 34.20
and his d. body shall be cast out 36.30
darkness like the d. of long ago. Lam 3.06
And I will lay the d. bodies of the Eze 6.05
make no mourning for the d. 24.17
and by the d. bodies of their kings, 43.07
idolatry and the d. bodies of their 43.09
by going near to a d. person; 44.25
"the d. bodies shall be many; Amo 8.03
d. bodies without end— they Nah 3.03
contact with a d. body touches any Hag 2.13
who sought the child's life are d." Mt 2.20
and leave the d. to bury their own d." 8.22
the girl is not d. but sleeping." 9.24
raise the d., cleanse lepers, cast 10.08
and the d. are raised up, and the 11.05
he has been raised from the d.; 14.02
Son of man is raised from the d." 17.09
And as for the resurrection of the d., 22.31
He is not God of the d., but of 22.32
are full of d. men's bones and all 23.27
people, 'He has risen from the d.,' 27.64
trembled and became like d. men. 28.04
that he has risen from the d., 28.07
some who said, "Your daughter is d. Mk 5.35
The child is not d. but sleeping." 5.39
has been raised from the d.; 6.14
man should have risen from the d. 9.09
what the rising from the d. meant. 9.10
that most of them said, "He is d." 9.26
For when they rise from the d., 12.25
And as for the d. being raised, have 12.26
He is not God of the d., 12.27
wondered if he were already d.; 15.44
him whether he was already d. 15.44
from the centurion that he was d., 15.45
And the d. man sat up, and began to Lk 7.15
the d. are raised up, the poor have 7.22
came and said, "Your daughter is d.; 8.49
for she is not d. but sleeping." 8.52
at him, knowing that she was d. 8.53
John had been raised from the d., 9.07
"Leave the d. to bury their own d.; 9.60
him, and departed, leaving him half d. 10.30
for this my son was d., and is 15.24
your brother was d., and is alive; 15.32
some one goes to them from the d., 16.30
some one should rise from the d.'" 16.31
from the d. neither marry nor are 20.35
But that the d. are raised, even 20.37
Now he is not God of the d., 20.38
you seek the living among the d.? 24.05
the third day rise from the d., 24.46
therefore he was raised from the d., Jn 2.22
raises the d. and gives them life, 5.21
when the d. will hear the voice of 5.25
told them plainly, "Lazarus is d.; 11.14
Martha, the sister of the d. man, 11.39
odor, for he has been d. four days." 11.39
The d. man came out, his hands and 11.44
whom Jesus had raised from the d. 12.01
whom he had raised from the d. 12.09
him from the d. bore witness. 12.17
and saw that he was already d., 19.33
that he must rise from the d. 20.09
after he was raised from the d. 21.14
life, whom God raised from the d. Ac 3.15
Jesus the resurrection from the d. 4.02
whom God raised from the d., by him 4.10
men came in they found her d., 5.10
with him after he rose from the d. 10.41
be judge of the living and the d. 10.42
But God raised him from the d.; 13.30
that he raised him from the d., 13.34
the city, supposing that he was d. 14.19
to suffer and to rise from the d., 17.03
all men by raising him from the d." 17.31
resurrection of the d., some mocked; 17.32
third story and was taken up d. 20.09
resurrection of the d. I am on trial." 23.06
resurrection of the d. I am on 24.21
who was d., but whom Paul asserted 25.19
any of you that God raises the d.? 26.08
the first to rise from the d., 26.23
swell up or suddenly fall down d.; 28.06
by his resurrection from the d., Rom 1.04
life to the d. and calls into 4.17
was as good as d. because he was 4.19
raised from the d. Jesus our Lord, 4.24

DEAD (cont.)

raised from the d. by the glory of Rom 6.04
raised from the d. will never die 6.09
yourselves d. to sin and alive to 6.11
raised from the d. in order that 7.04
d. to that which held us captive, so 7.06
Apart from the law sin lies d. 7.08
your bodies are d. because of sin, 8.10
Jesus from the d. dwells in you, 8.11
Jesus from the d. will give life 8.11
yes, who was raised from the d., 8.34
to bring Christ up from the d.). 10.07
that God raised him from the d.,— 10.09
acceptance mean but life from the d.? 11.15
both of the d. and of the living. 14.09
is preached as raised from the d., 1Co 15.12
there is no resurrection of the d.? 15.12
there is no resurrection of the d., 15.13
is true that the d. are not raised. 15.15
For if the d. are not raised, then 15.16
Christ has been raised from the d., 15.20
also the resurrection of the d. 15.21
being baptized on behalf of the d.? 15.29
If the d. are not raised at all, why 15.29
If the d. are not raised, "Let us 15.32
will ask, "How are the d. raised? 15.35
it with the resurrection of the d. 15.42
and the d. will be raised imperishable, 15.52
but on God who raises the d.; 2Co 1.09
who raised him from the d.— Gal 1.01
him from the d. and made him sit Eph 1.20
when you were d. through the 2.01
even when we were d. through our 2.05
O sleeper, and arise from the d., 5.14
the resurrection from the d. Php 3.11
beginning, the first-born from the d., Col 1.18
of God, who raised him from the d. 2.12
who were d. in trespasses and the 2.13
heaven, whom he raised from the d., 1Th 1.10
And the d. in Christ will rise 4.16
self-indulgent is d. even while she 1Ti 5.06
Remember Jesus Christ, risen from the d., 2Ti 2.08
is to judge the living and the d., 4.01
repentance from d. works and of Heb 6.01
hands, the resurrection of the d., 6.02
conscience from d. works to serve 9.14
one man, and him as good as d., 11.12
able to raise men even from the d.; 11.19
Women received their d. by resurrection 11.35
again from the d. our Lord Jesus, 13.20
itself, if it has no works, is d. Jas 2.17
body apart from the spirit is d., 2.26
so faith apart from works is d. 2.26
of Jesus Christ from the d., 1Pe 1.03
him from the d. and gave him glory, 1.21
to judge the living and the d. 4.05
gospel was preached even to the d., 4.06
in late autumn, twice d., uprooted; Jud 1.12
witness, the first-born of the d., Rev 1.05
I fell at his feet as though d. 1.17
and I will strike her children d. 2.23
of being alive, and you are d. 3.01
and their d. bodies will lie in the 11.08
gaze at their d. bodies and refuse 11.09
the time for the d. to be judged, 11.18
Blessed are the d. who die in the 14.13
became like the blood of a d. man, 16.03
The rest of the d. did not come to 20.05
And I saw the d., great and small, 20.12
And the d. were judged by what was 20.12
And the sea gave up the d. in it, 20.13
and Hades gave up the d. in them, 20.13

DEADLY

he has prepared his d. weapons, Ps 7.13
my d. enemies who surround me. 17.09
They say, "A d. thing has fastened 41.08
As with a d. wound in my body, my 42.10
fowler and from the d. pestilence; 91.03
Their tongue is a d. arrow; Jer 9.08
They shall die of d. diseases. 16.04
against you my d. arrows of famine, Eze 5.16
harlot, graceful and of d. charms, Nah 3.04
he delivered us from so d. a peril, 2Co 1.10
a restless evil, full of d. poison. Jas 3.08

DEAF

or d., or seeing, or blind? Ex 4.11
not curse the d. or put a stumbling Lev 19.14
be not d. to me, lest, if thou be Ps 28.01
But I am like a d. man, 38.13
like the d. adder that stops its 58.04
In that day the d. shall hear the Is 29.18
and the ears of the d. unstopped; 35.05
Hear, you d.; and look, 42.18
or d. as my messenger whom I send? 42.19
eyes, who are d., yet have ears! 43.08
mouths, their ears shall be d.; Mic 7.16
are cleansed and the d. hear, Mt 11.05
a man who was d. and had an Mk 7.32
even makes the d. hear and the 7.37
"You dumb and d. spirit, I command 9.25
and the d. hear, the dead are raised Lk 7.22

DEAL

Now we will d. worse with you than Gen 19.09
you will not d. falsely with me or 21.23
you will d. with me and with the 21.23
if you will d. loyally and truly 24.49
and promise to d. loyally and 47.29
Come, let us d. shrewdly with them, Ex 1.10
"Why do you d. thus with your 5.15
let not Pharaoh d. falsely again 8.29
he shall d. with her as with a 21.09
nor d. falsely, nor lie to one Lev 19.11
but d. thus with them, that they may Num 4.19
If thou wilt d. thus with me, kill 11.15
But thus shall you d. with them: Deu 7.05
you also will d. kindly with my Jos 2.12
then we will d. kindly and faithfully 2.14
lest you d. falsely with your God." 24.27
and we will d. kindly with you." Ju 1.24
May the Lord d. kindly with you, as Ru 1.08
Therefore d. kindly with your 1Sa 20.08
"I will d. loyally with Hanun the 2Sa 10.02
"D. gently for my sake with the 18.05
But d. loyally with the sons of 1Ki 2.07
their hand, for they d. honestly." 2Ki 22.07
"I will d. loyally with Hanun the 1Ch 19.02
a house to dwell in, so d. with me. 2Ch 2.03
D. courageously, and may the Lord be 19.11
prayer not to d. with you according Job 42.08
your hands d. out violence on earth. Ps 58.02
He does not d. with us according to 103.10
to d. craftily with his servants. 105.25
d. on my behalf for thy name's sake; 109.21
D. bountifully with thy servant, 119.17
D. with thy servant according to 119.124
for thou wilt d. bountifully with 142.07
evildoers. sons who d. corruptly! Is 1.04
the treacherous d. treacherously, 24.16
the treacherous d. very treacherously." 24.16
that you would d. very treacherously, 48.08
sons who will not d. falsely; 63.08
d. with them in the time of thine Jer 18.23
the Lord will d. with us according 21.02
shall reign as king and d. wisely, 23.05
but d. with him as he tells you." 39.12
and d. with them as thou hast dealt Lam 1.22
Therefore I will d. in wrath; Eze 8.18
I will d. with you as you have done, 16.59
when I d. with you for my name's 20.44
the days that I shall d. with you? 22.14
that they may d. with you in fury. 23.25

DEAL (cont.)
and they shall d. with you in Eze 23.29
he shall surely d. with it as its 31.11
I will d. with you according to the 35.11
desolate, so I will d. with you; 35.15
to what you see d. with your Dan 1.13
and he shall d. with them and shall 11.07
He shall d. with the strongest 11.39
for they d. falsely, the thief Hos 7.01
and d. deceitfully with false Amo 8.05
time I will d. with all your Zep 3.19
purposed to d. with us for our Zec 1.06
But now I will not d. with the 8.11
and those who d. with the world as 1Co 7.31
He can d. gently with the ignorant Heb 5.02
but d. only with food and drink and 9.10
not to d. with sin but to save 9.28

DEALERS
were your favored d. in lambs, Eze 27.21
your d. in merchandise, and all your 27.27
rather to the d. and buy for Mt 25.09

DEALING
receive instruction in wise d., Pro 1.03
made an end of d. treacherously, Is 33.01
by d. treacherously with me. Eze 20.27
He is not weak in d. with you, 2Co 13.03
but in d. with you we shall live 13.04

DEALINGS
Sidonians and had no d. with any one. Ju 18.07
and they had no d. with any one. 18.28
of your evil d. from all the people. 1Sa 2.23
Jews have no d. with Samaritans. Jn 4.09
as though they had no d. with it. 1Co 7.31

DEALS
the word that d. gently with you? Job 15.11
She d. cruelly with her young, as if 39.16
adversary who d. insolently with Ps 55.12
the man who d. generously and 112.05
A servant who d. wisely has the Pro 14.35
A slave who d. wisely will rule 17.02
uprightness he d. perversely and Is 26.10
to priest, every one d. falsely. Jer 6.13
to priest every one d. falsely. 8.10

DEALT
And for her sake he d. well with Gen 12.16
Then Sarai d. harshly with her, and 16.06
but as I have d. loyally with you, 21.23
because God has d. graciously with 33.11
So God d. well with the midwives; Ex 1.20
when they d. arrogantly with them. 18.11
since he has d. faithlessly with 21.08
he shall be d. with according to 21.31
"Why hast thou d. ill with thy Num 11.11
the Egyptians d. harshly with us 20.15
They have d. corruptly with him, Deu 32.05
that as I have d. kindly with you, Jos 2.12
and if you have d. well with Ju 9.16
men of Shechem d. treacherously 9.23
"Thus and thus has Micah d. with me: 18.04
as you have d. with the dead and Ru 1.08
Almighty has d. very bitterly with 1.20
he said, "You have d. treacherously; 1Sa 14.33
day how you have d. well with me, 24.18
the LORD has d. well with my lord, 25.31
as his father d. loyally with me." 2Sa 10.02
if I had d. treacherously against 18.13
how he d. with the two commanders 1Ki 2.05
the workmen, for they d. honestly. 2Ki 12.15
and d. with mediums and with 21.06
for his father d. loyally with me. 1Ch 19.02
"As you d. with David my father and 2Ch 2.03
And he d. wisely, and distributed 11.23
for he had d. wantonly in Judah and 28.19
and d. with mediums and with 33.06
for thou hast d. faithfully and we Neh 9.33
because he has d. bountifully with Ps 13.06
the LORD has d. bountifully with 116.07
Thou hast d. well with thy servant, 119.65
He has not d. thus with any other 147.20
whom none has d. treacherously! Is 33.01
you will be d. with treacherously. 33.01
even they have d. treacherously Jer 12.06
has the LORD d. thus with this 22.08
for I have d. you the blow of an 30.14
friends have d. treacherously with Lam 1.02
as thou hast d. with me because of 1.22
With whom hast thou d. thus? 2.20
because they d. so treacherously Eze 39.23
I d. with them according to their 39.24
was hardened so that he d. proudly, Dan 5.20
They have d. faithlessly with the Hos 5.07
there they d. faithlessly with me. Hos 6.07
who has d. wondrously with you. Joe 2.26
and deeds, so has he d. with us. Zec 1.06
I have d. with all that Jesus began Ac 1.01
He d. craftily with our race and 7.19

DEAR
like a moth what is d. to him; Ps 39.11
For thy servants hold her stones d., 102.14
Is Ephraim my d. son? Is he my Jer 31.20
had a slave who was d. to him, Lk 7.02
you had become very d. to us. 1Th 2.08

DEATH
not look upon the d. of the child." Gen 21.16
comforted after his mother's d. 24.67
After the d. of Abraham God blessed 25.11
man or his wife shall be put to d." 26.11
them after the d. of Abraham; 26.18
I do not know the day of my d. 27.02
God only to remove this d. from me." Ex 10.17
the mountain shall be put to d.; 19.12
so that he dies shall be put to d. 21.12
or his mother shall be put to d. 21.15
possession of him, shall be put to d. 21.16
or his mother shall be put to d. 21.17
an ox gores a man or a woman to d., 21.28
its owner also shall be put to d. 21.29
with a beast shall be put to d. 22.19
who profanes it shall be put to d.; 31.14
the sabbath day shall be put to d. 31.15
any work on it shall be put to d.; 35.02
after the d. of the two sons of Lev 16.01
They shall not be put to d., because 19.20
to Molech shall be put to d.; 20.02
Molech, and do not put him to d., 20.04
or his mother shall be put to d.; 20.09
the adulteress shall be put to d. 20.10
both of them shall be put to d.; 20.11
both of them shall be put to d.; 20.12
they shall be put to d., their 20.13
a beast, he shall be put to d.; 20.15
they shall be put to d., their 20.16
or a wizard shall be put to d.; 20.27
of the LORD shall be put to d.; 24.16
the Name, shall be put to d. 24.16
who kills a man shall be put to d. 24.17
who kills a man shall be put to d. 24.21
ransomed; he shall be put to d. 27.29
comes near, he shall be put to d. Num 1.51
comes near, he shall be put to d." 3.10
who came near was to be put to d. 3.38
Moses, "The man shall be put to d.; 15.35
and stoned him to d. with stones, 15.36
men die the common d. of all men, 16.29
who comes near shall be put to d." 18.07
Let me die the d. of the righteous, 23.10
the murderer shall be put to d. 35.16

DEATH (cont.)
the murderer shall be put to d. Num 35.17
the murderer shall be put to d. 35.18
himself put the murderer to d.; 35.19
meets him, he shall put him to d. 35.19
struck the blow shall be put to d.; 35.21
blood shall put the murderer to d., 35.21
in it until the d. of the high 35.25
until the d. of the high priest; 35.28
but after the d. of the high priest 35.28
shall be put to d. on the evidence 35.30
shall be put to d. on the testimony 35.30
of a murderer who is guilty of d.; 35.31
but he shall be put to d. 35.31
land before the d. of the high 35.32
of dreams shall be put to d., Deu 13.05
first against him to put him to d., 13.09
You shall stone him to d. with stones, 13.10
man or woman to d. with stones. 17.05
that is to die shall be put to d.; 17.06
not to be put to d. on the evidence 17.06
first against him to put him to d., 17.07
shall stone him to d. with stones; 21.21
punishable by d. and he is put to d., 21.22
shall stone her to d. with stones, 22.21
shall stone them to d. with stones, 22.24
is no offence punishable by d., 22.26
not be put to d. for the children, 24.16
be put to d. for the fathers; 24.16
shall be put to d. for his own sin 24.16
day life and good, d. and evil. 30.15
I have set before you life and d., 30.19
how much more after my d.! 31.27
that after my d. you will surely 31.29
children of Israel before his d. 33.01
After the d. of Moses the servant Jos 1.01
command him, shall be put to d. 1.18
and deliver our lives from d." 2.13
smote them and put them to d., 10.26
and smote them, and put them to d. 11.17
until the d. of him who is high 20.06
After the d. of Joshua the people Ju 1.01
jeoparded their lives to the d.; 5.18
him shall be put to d. by morning. 6.31
from birth to the day of his d.' " 13.07
him, his soul was vexed to d. 16.16
he slew at his d. were more than 16.30
Gibeah, that we may put them to d., 20.13
saying, "He shall be put to d." 21.05
also if even d. parts me from you." Ru 1.17
since the d. of your husband has 2.11
the time of her d. the women 1Sa 4.20
men, that we may put them to d." 11.12
a man shall be put to d. this day, 11.13
the bitterness of d. is past." 15.32
Saul again until the day of his d., 15.35
lives, he shall not be put to d." 19.06
is but a step between me and d." 20.03
father, "Why should he be put to d.? 20.32
was determined to put David to d. 20.33
occasioned the d. of all the 22.22
for my life to bring about my d.?" 28.09
After the d. of Saul, when David had 2Sa 1.01
In life and in d. they were not 1.23
had no child to the day of her d. 6.23
lines he measured to be put to d., 8.02
whether for d. or for life, there 15.21
not Shimei be put to d. for this, 19.21
one be put to d. in Israel this 19.22
men doomed to d. before my lord 19.28
shut up until the day of their d., 20.03
he put the Gibeonites to d." 21.01
us to put any man to d. in Israel." 21.04
were put to d. in the first days 21.09
"For the waves of d. encompassed me, 22.05
me, the snares of d. confronted me. 22.06
not put you to d. with the sword." 1Ki 2.08
shall be put to d. this day." 2.24
to your estate; for you deserve d. 2.26
not at this time put you to d., 2.26
in Egypt until the d. of Solomon. 11.40
stoned him to d. with stones. 12.18
and to cause the d. of my son!" 17.18
take him out, and stone him to d. 21.10
and stoned him to d. with stones. 21.13
After the d. of Ahab, Moab rebelled 2Ki 1.01
henceforth neither d. nor miscarriage 2.21
man of God, there is d. in the pot!" 4.40
did not put to d. the children of 14.06
not be put to d. for the children, 14.06
be put to d. for the fathers; 14.06
years after the d. of Jehoash son 14.17
was a leper to the day of his d., 15.05
sick and was at the point of d. 20.01
and put them to d. at Riblah in 25.21
After the d. of Hezron, Caleb went 1Ch 2.24
in great quantity before his d. 22.05
stoned him to d. with stones. 2Ch 10.18
God of Israel, should be put to d., 15.13
for after the d. of his father 22.04
was brought to Jehu and put to d. 22.09
and thirty years old at his d. 24.15
Now after the d. of Jehoiada the 24.17
did not put their children to d., 25.04
not to be put to d. for the children, 25.04
be put to d. for the fathers; 25.04
Why should you be put to d.?" 25.16
years after the d. of Joash the 25.25
was a leper to the day of his d., 26.21
sick and was at the point of d., 32.24
Jerusalem did him honor at his d. 32.33
whether for d. or for banishment or Ez 7.26
all alike are to be put to d., Est 4.11
who long for d., but it comes not, Job 3.21
In famine he will redeem you from d., 5.20
strangling and d. rather than my 7.15
When disaster brings sudden d., 9.23
first-born of d. consumes his 18.13
Abaddon and D. say, 'We have heard a 28.22
know that thou wilt bring me to d., 30.23
and caused the d. of its owners; 31.39
and his life to those who bring d. 33.22
Have the gates of d. been revealed 38.17
For in d. there is no remembrance Ps 6.05
liftest me up from the gates of d., 9.13
eyes, lest I sleep the sleep of d.; 13.03
The cords of d. encompassed me, the 18.04
me, the snares of d. confronted me. 18.05
thou dost lay me in the dust of d. 22.15
the valley of the shadow of d., 23.04
"What profit is there in my d., 30.09
that he may deliver their soul from d., 33.19
D. shall be their shepherd; 49.14
the terrors of d. have fallen upon 55.04
Let d. come upon them; 55.15
hast delivered my soul from d., 56.13
the Lord, belongs escape from d. 68.20
he did not spare them from d., 78.50
Afflicted and close to d. from my 88.15
What man can live and never see d.? 89.48
and condemn the innocent to d. 94.21
they drew near to the gates of d. 107.18
and the brokenhearted to their d. 109.16
from those who condemn him to d. 109.31
The snares of d. encompassed me; 116.03
hast delivered my soul from d., 116.08
the LORD is the d. of his saints. 116.15
but he has not given me over to d. 118.18
for her house sinks down to d., Pro 2.18
Her feet go down to d.; her steps 5.05
going down to the chambers of d. 7.27
himself; all who hate me love d." 8.36
but righteousness delivers from d. 10.02
but righteousness delivers from d. 11.04

DEATH (cont.)
but the way of error leads to d. Pro 12.28
one may avoid the snares of d. 13.14
man, but its end is the way to d. 14.12
one may avoid the snares of d. 14.27
A king's wrath is a messenger of d., 16.14
man, but its end is the way to d. 16.25
D. and life are in the power of the 18.21
a fleeting vapor and a snare of d. 21.06
who are being taken away to d.; 24.11
throws firebrands, arrows, and d., 26.18
let him be a fugitive until d.; 28.17
and the day of d., than the Ecc 7.01
bitter than d. the woman whose 7.26
or authority over the day of d.; 8.08
for love is strong as d., Sol 8.06
He will swallow up d. for ever, Is 25.08
"We have made a covenant with d., 28.15
covenant with d. will be annulled, 28.18
sick and was at the point of d. 38.01
d. cannot praise thee; 38.18
and with a rich man in his d., 53.09
he poured out his soul to d.. 53.12
D. shall be preferred to life by Jer 8.03
For d. has come up into our windows, 9.21
their men meet d. by pestilence, 18.21
the way of life and the way of d. 21.08
man deserves the sentence of d., 26.11
certain that if you put me to d., 26.15
not deserve the sentence of d., 26.16
Judah and all Judah put him to d.? 26.19
the king sought to put him to d.; 26.21
over to the people to be put to d. 26.24
king, "Let this man be put to d., 38.04
you not be sure to put me to d.? 38.15
not put you to d. or deliver you 38.16
us and we will not put you to d.,' 38.25
in prison till the day of his d. 52.11
and put them to d. at Riblah in 52.27
the day of his d. as long as he 52.34
in the house it is like d. Lam 1.20
putting to d. persons who should Eze 13.19
pleasure in the d. of the wicked, 18.23
no pleasure in the d. of any one, 18.32
shall die the d. of the slain in 28.08
You shall die the d. of the uncircumcised 28.10
or they are all given over to d., 31.14
pleasure in the d. of the wicked, 33.11
Shall I redeem them from D.? Hos 13.14
O D., where are your plagues? 13.14
like d. he has never enough. He gathers Hab 2.05
there until the d. of Herod. This was Mt 2.15
and shadow of d. light has dawned." 4.16
Brother will deliver up brother to d., 10.21
parents and have them put to d.; 10.21
And though he wanted to put him to d., 14.05
the powers of d. shall not prevail 16.18
will not taste d. before they see 16.28
and they will condemn him to d., 20.18
those wretches to a miserable d., 21.41
to tribulation, and put you to d.; 24.09
soul is very sorrowful, even to d.; 26.38
that they might put him to d., 26.59
They answered, "He deserves d." 26.66
against Jesus to put him to d.; 27.01
daughter is at the point of d. Mk 5.23
will not taste d. before they see 9.01
and they will condemn him to d., 10.33
will deliver up brother to d., 13.12
parents and have them put to d.; 13.12
soul is very sorrowful, even to d.; 14.34
against Jesus to put him to d.; 14.55
all condemned him as deserving d. 14.64
darkness and in the shadow of d., Lk 1.79
should not see d. before he had 2.26
was sick and at the point of d. 7.02
not taste of d. before they see 9.27
some of you they will put to d.; 21.16
were seeking how to put him to d.; 22.02
to go with you to prison and to d." 22.33
deserving d. has been done by him; 23.15
found in him no crime deserving d.; 23.22
led away to be put to d. with him. 23.32
him up to be condemned to d., 24.20
son, for he was at the point of d. Jn 4.47
but has passed from d. to life. 5.24
my word, he will never see d." 8.51
my word, he will never taste d." 8.52
said, "This illness is not unto d.; 11.04
Now Jesus had spoken of his d., 11.13
took counsel how to put him to d. 11.53
planned to put Lazarus also to d., 12.10
to show by what d. he was to die. 12.33
lawful for us to put any man to d." 18.31
to show by what d. he was to die. 18.32
to show by what d. he was to 21.19
up, having loosed the pangs of d., Ac 2.24
And Saul was consenting to his d. 8.01
They put him to d. by hanging him 10.39
that they should be put to d. 12.19
him with nothing deserving d., 13.28
I persecuted this Way to the d., 22.04
deserving d. or imprisonment. 23.29
to die, I do not seek to escape d.; 25.11
he had done nothing deserving d.; 25.25
were put to d. I cast my vote 26.10
to deserve d. or imprisonment." 26.31
reason for the d. penalty in my 28.18
who was put to d. for our trespasses Rom 4.25
to God by the d. of his Son, 5.10
through one man and d. through sin, 5.12
and so d. spread to all men because 5.12
Yet d. reigned from Adam to Moses, 5.14
d. reigned through that one man, 5.17
so that. as sin reigned in d., 5.21
Jesus were baptized into his d.? 6.03
with him by baptism into d., 6.04
united with him in a d. like his, 6.05
d. no longer has dominion over him. 6.09
The d. he died he died to sin, once 6.10
have been brought from d. to life, 6.13
either of sin, which leads to d., 6.16
The end of those things is d. 6.21
For the wages of sin is d., 6.23
our members to bear fruit for d. 7.05
promised life proved to be d. to me. 7.10
is good, then, bring d. to me? 7.13
working d. in me through what is 7.13
deliver me from this body of d.? 7.24
me free from the law of sin and d. 8.02
To set the mind on the flesh is d., 8.06
you put to d. the deeds of the 8.13
For I am sure that neither d., 8.38
or life or d. or the present or 1Co 3.22
of all, like men sentenced to d.; 4.09
the Lord's d. until he comes. 11.26
For as by a man came d., 15.21
The last enemy to be destroyed is d. 15.26
"D. is swallowed up in victory." 15.54
"O d., where is thy victory? 15.55
O d., where is thy sting?" 15.55
The sting of d. is sin, and the 15.56
we had received the sentence of d.; 2Co 1.09
to one a fragrance from d. to d., 2.16
Now if the dispensation of d., 3.07
in the body of d. of Jesus, 4.10
given up to d. for Jesus' sake, so 4.11
So d. is at work in us, but life in 4.12
but worldly grief produces d. 7.10
beatings, and often near d. 11.23
my body, whether by life or by d. Php 1.20
obedient unto d., even d. on a cross. 2.08
Indeed he was ill, near to d. 2.27
becoming like him in his d., 3.10

DEATH (cont.)
in his body of flesh by his d., Col 1.22
Put to d. therefore what is earthly 3.05
who abolished d. and brought life 2Ti 1.10
because of the suffering of d., Heb 2.09
he might taste d. for every one. 2.09
that through d. he might destroy 2.14
him who has the power of d., 2.14
through fear of d. were subject to 2.15
who was able to save him from d., 5.07
prevented by d. from continuing in 7.23
since a d. has occurred which 9.15
the d. of the one who made it must 9.16
For a will takes effect only at d., 9.17
up so that he should not see d.; 11.05
it is full-grown brings forth d. Jas 1.15
his soul from d. and will cover a 5.20
being put to d. in the flesh but 1Pe 3.18
we have passed out of d. into life, 1Jn 3.14
He who does not love remains in d. 3.14
I have the keys of D. and Hades. Rev 1.18
Be faithful unto d., and I will 2.10
shall not be hurt by the second d." 2.11
remains and is on the point of d., 3.02
horse, and its rider's name was D., 6.08
men will seek d. and will not find 9.06
long to die, and d. flies from them. 9.06
loved not their lives even unto d. 12.11
such the second d. has no power, 20.06
D. and Hades gave up the dead in 20.13
Then D. and Hades were thrown into 20.14
This is the second d., the lake of 20.14
and d. shall be no more, neither 21.04
brimstone, which is the second d." 21.08

DEATHLY
For there was a d. panic throughout 1Sa 5.11

DEBARRED
"I am d. from going to the house of Jer 36.05

DEBATE
small dissension and d. with them, Ac 15.02
And after there had been much d., 15.07

DEBATER
Where is the d. of this age? 1Co 1.20

DEBAUCHERY
not in d. and licentiousness, not in Rom 13.13
drunk with wine, for that is d.; Eph 5.18

DEBIR
and to D. king of Eglon, saying, Jos 10.03
turned back to D. and assaulted it, 10.38
so he did to D. and to its king. 10.39
from D., from Anab, and from all 11.21
the king of D., one; the king of 12.13
Mahanaim to the territory of D., 13.26
goes up to D. from the Valley of 15.07
against the inhabitants of D.; 15.15
now the name of D. formerly was 15.15
Dannah, Kiriathsannah (that is, D.), 15.49
D. with its pasture lands, 21.15
went against the inhabitants of D. Ju 1.11
The name of D. was formerly Kiriathsepher. 1.11
D. with its pasture lands, 1Ch 6.58

DEBORAH
And D., Rebekah's nurse, died, and she Gen 35.08
Now D., a prophetess, the wife of Ju 4.04
the palm of D. between Ramah and 4.05
Then D. arose, and went with Barak 4.09
his heels; and D. went up with him. 4.10
And D. said to Barak, "Up! For this 4.14
Then sang D. and Barak the son of 5.01
D., arose as a mother in Israel. 5.07
"Awake, awake, D.! Awake, awake, 5.12
the princes of Issachar came with D., 5.15

DEBT
and every one who was in d., 1Sa 22.02
year and the exaction of every d. Neh 10.31
released him and forgave him the d. Mt 18.27
prison till he should pay the d. 18.30
you all that d. because you 18.32
till he should pay all his d. 18.34
and indeed they are in d. to them, Rom 15.27

DEBTOR
with the creditor, so with the d. Is 24.02
but restores to the d. his pledge, Eze 18.07

DEBTORS
Will not your d. suddenly arise, and Hab 2.07
As we also have forgiven our d.; Mt 6.12
"A certain creditor had two d.; Lk 7.41
summoning his master's d. one by one, 16.05
we are d., not to the flesh, to live Rom 8.12

DEBTS
"Go, sell the oil and pay your d., 2Ki 4.07
pledges, who become surety for d. Pro 22.26
And forgive us our d., Mt 6.12

DECAPOLIS
Galilee and the D. and Jerusalem Mt 4.25
proclaim in the D. how much Jesus Mk 5.20
Galilee, through the region of the D. 7.31

DECAY
its bondage to d. and obtain the Rom 8.21

DECEIT
evil and their heart prepares d." Job 15.35
and my tongue will not utter d. 27.04
and my foot has hastened to d.; 31.05
with cursing and d. and oppression; Ps 10.07
to my prayer from lips free of d.! 17.01
and in whose spirit there is no d. 32.02
and your lips from speaking d. 34.13
the land they conceive words of d. 35.20
of his mouth are mischief and d.; 36.03
evil, and your tongue frames d. 50.19
who practices d. shall dwell in my 101.07
but a false witness utters d. Pro 12.17
D. is in the heart of those who 12.20
Bread gained by d. is sweet to a 20.17
lips and harbors d. in his heart; 26.24
and there was no d. in his mouth. Is 53.09
transgression, the offspring of d., 57.04
They hold fast to d., they refuse Jer 8.05
and d. upon d., they refuse to 9.06
and the d. of their own minds. 14.14
prophesy the d. of their own heart, 23.26
he shall make d. prosper under his Dan 8.25
and the house of Israel with d.; Hos 11.12
d., licentiousness, envy, slander, Mk 7.22
full of all d. and villainy, will Ac 13.10
d., malignity, they are gossips, Rom 1.29
of you by philosophy and empty d., Col 2.08

DECEITFUL
abhors bloodthirsty and d. men. Ps 5.06
from d. and unjust men deliver me! 43.01
all words that devour, O d. tongue. 52.04
fathers; they twisted like a d. bow. 78.57
For wicked and d. mouths are opened 109.02
from lying lips, from a d. tongue. 120.02
be done to you, you d. tongue? 120.03
Charm is d., and beauty is vain, but Pro 31.30
Wilt thou be to me like a d. brook, Jer 15.18
The heart is d. above all things, 17.09
shall be a d. thing to the kings Mic 1.14
and with a bag of d. weights? 6.11
their tongue is d. in their mouth. 6.12
found in their mouth a. d. tongue. Zep 3.13
d. workmen, disguising themselves as 2Co 11.13

DECEITFUL (cont.)
by their craftiness in d. wiles. Eph 4.14
and is corrupt through d. lusts, 4.22
giving heed to d. spirits and 1Ti 4.01

DECEITFULLY
Shechem and his father Hamor d., Gen 34.13
for God, and speak d. for him? Job 13.07
is false, and does not swear d. Ps 24.04
it speaks d.; with his Jer 9.08
is made with him he shall act d.; Dan 11.23
and deal d. with false balances, Amo 8.05

DECEITFULNESS
may be hardened by the d. of sin. Heb 3.13

DECEIVE
"Why did you d. us, saying, 'We are Jos 9.22
the son of Ner came to d. you, 2Sa 3.25
Did I not say, Do not d. me?" 2Ki 4.28
king: 'Do not let Hezekiah d. you, 18.29
whom you rely d. you by promising 19.10
let Hezekiah d. you or mislead you 2Ch 32.15
Or can you d. him, as one deceives a Job 13.09
and do not d. with your lips. Pro 24.28
king: 'Do not let Hezekiah d. you, Is 36.14
whom you rely d. you by promising 37.10
diviners who are among you d. you, Jer 29.08
Do not d. yourselves, saying, "The 37.09
on a hairy mantle in order to d., Zec 13.04
they use their tongues to d. Rom 3.13
words they d. the hearts of the 16.18
Let no one d. himself. If any one 1Co 3.18
Let no one d. you with empty words, Eph 5.06
Let no one d. you in any way; 2Th 2.03
we d. ourselves, and the truth is 1Jn 1.08
you about those who would d. you; 2.26
Little children, let no one d. you. 3.07
that he should d. the nations no Rev 20.03
come out to d. the nations which 20.08

DECEIVED
Why then have you d. me?" Gen 29.25
Take heed lest your heart be d., Deu 11.16
"Why have you d. me thus, and let my 1Sa 19.17
said to Saul, "Why have you d. me? 28.12
"My lord, O king, my servant d. me; 2Sa 19.26
the d. and the deceiver are his. Job 12.16
hast utterly d. this people and Jer 4.10
thou hast d. me, and I was d.; 20.07
"Perhaps he will be d., then we 20.10
friends have d. you and prevailed 38.22
The horror you inspire has d. you, 49.16
called to my lovers but they d. me; Lam 1.19
the prophet be d. and speak a word, Eze 14.09
have d. that prophet, and I will 14.09
The pride of your heart has d. you, Ob 1.03
All your allies have d. you, they have 1.07
d. me and by it killed me. Rom 7.11
Do not be d.; neither the 1Co 6.09
Do not be d.: "Bad company ruins 15.33
as the serpent d. Eve by his 2Co 11.03
Do not be d.; God is not Gal 6.07
Adam was not d., but the woman was d. 1Ti 2.14
bad to worse, deceivers and d. 2Ti 3.13
Do not be d., my beloved brethren. Jas 1.16
all nations were d. by thy sorcery. Rev 18.23
by which he d. those who had 19.20
devil who had d. them was thrown 20.10

DECEIVER
the deceived and the d. are his. Job 12.16
a one is the d. and the antichrist. 2Jn 1.07
the d. of the whole world—he was Rev 12.09

DECEIVERS
from bad to worse, d. and deceived. 2Ti 3.13
insubordinate men, empty talkers and d., Tit 1.10
For many d. have gone out into the 2Jn 1.07

DECEIVES
you deceive him, as one d. a man? Job 13.09
is the man who d. his neighbor and Pro 26.19
Every one d. his neighbor, and no Jer 9.05
when he is nothing, he d. himself. Gal 6.03
bridle his tongue but d. his heart, Jas 1.26
it d. those who dwell on earth, Rev 13.14

DECEIVING
the LORD by d. his neighbor in a Lev 6.02
not trust in emptiness, d. himself; Job 15.31
way, but the folly of fools is d. Pro 14.08
not hearers only, d. yourselves. Jas 1.22

DECENTLY
should be done d. and in order. 1Co 14.40

DECEPTION
and with all wicked d. for those 2Th 2.10

DECEPTIVE
A wicked man earns d. wages, Pro 11.18
delicacies, for they are d. food. 23.03
Do not trust in these d. words: Jer 7.04
you trust in d. words to no avail. 7.08
seen for you false and d. visions; Lam 2.14

DECIDE
that they may d. between us two. Gen 31.37
to me and I d. between a man and Ex 18.16
matter they shall d. themselves; 18.22
to d. whether it is clean or Lev 13.59
and the judges d. between them, Deu 25.01
d. this day between the people of Ju 11.27
and d. what answer I shall return 2Sa 24.13
Now d. what answer I shall return 1Ch 21.12
the LORD and to d. disputed cases. 2Ch 19.08
You will d. on a matter, and it will Job 22.28
and shall d. for many peoples; Is 2.04
eyes see, or d. by what his ears hear; 11.03
and d. with equity for the meek of 11.04
and shall d. for strong nations Mic 4.03
the priests to d. this question, Hag 2.11
to d. what each should take. Mk 15.24
comes down, I will d. your case." Ac 24.22
but rather d. never to put a Rom 14.13
wise enough to d. between members 1Co 6.05

DECIDED
small matter they d. themselves. Ex 18.26
I have d.: you and Ziba shall divide 2Sa 19.29
judgment be; you yourself have d. it." 1Ki 20.40
After this Joash d. to restore the 2Ch 24.04
I have d. what to do, so that people Lk 16.04
The next day Jesus d. to go to Jn 1.43
when he had d. to release him. Ac 3.13
For Paul had d. to sail past 20.16
to the emperor, I d. to send him. 25.25
And when it was d. that we should 27.01
For I d. to know nothing among you 1Co 2.02
for I have d. to spend the winter Tit 3.12

DECIDES
to do whatever my lord the king d." 2Sa 15.15
to disputes and d. between powerful Pro 18.18

DECISION
requiring d. between one kind of Deu 17.08
they shall declare to you the d. 17.09
according to the d. which they 17.11
in giving this d. the king convicts 2Sa 14.13
but the d. is wholly from the LORD. Pro 16.33
the d. by the word of the holy ones, Dan 4.17
Multitudes, multitudes, in the valley of d.! Joe 3.14
LORD is near in the valley of d. 3.14
For my d. is to gather nations, to Zep 3.08
What is your d.?" And they all Mk 14.64
custody for the d. of the emperor, Ac 25.21

DECISIONS
the statutes of God and his d. Ex 18.16
teach them the statutes and the d., 18.20
Inspired d. are on the lips of a Pro 16.10
observance the d. which had been Ac 16.04

DECK
"D. yourself with majesty and Job 40.10
the valleys d. themselves with Ps 65.13
that you d. yourself with ornaments Jer 4.30
Men d. it with silver and gold; 10.04
they made your d. of pines from the Eze 27.06

DECKED
The princess is d. in her chamber Ps 45.13
I have d. my couch with coverings, Pro 7.16
And I d. you with ornaments, and put Eze 16.11
Thus you were d. with gold and 16.13
made for yourself gaily d. shrines, 16.16
and d. yourself with ornaments; 23.40
to them and d. herself with her Hos 2.13

DECKS
with lower, second, and third d. Gen 6.16
as a bridegroom d. himself with a Is 61.10

DECLARATION
and let my d. be in your ears. Job 13.17

DECLARE
to d. to you the word of the LORD; Deu 5.05
and they shall d. to you the 17.09
to what they d. to you from that 17.10
the verdict which they d. to you, 17.11
'I d. this day to the LORD your God 26.03
Levites shall d. to all the men of 27.14
I d. to you this day, that you shall 30.18
father what thou didst d. to him; 1Ki 8.24
as thou didst d. through Moses, thy 8.53
D. his glory among the nations, his 1Ch 16.24
Moreover I d. to you that the LORD 17.10
father what thou didst d. to him; 2Ch 6.15
the fish of the sea will d. to you. Job 12.08
and what I have seen I will d. 15.17
and afraid to d. my opinion to you. 32.06
to me; let me also d. my opinion.' 32.10
answer; I also will d. my opinion. 32.17
My words d. the uprightness of my 33.03
to d. to man what is right for him; 33.23
therefore d. what you know. 34.33
you, and you shall d. to me. 38.03
earth? D., if you know all this. 38.18
question you, and you d. to me. 40.07
question you, and you d. to me.' 42.04
The heavens d. his righteousness, Ps 50.06
to d. thy steadfast love in the 92.02
D. his glory among the nations, his 96.03
that men may d. in Zion the name of 102.21
With my lips I d. all the ordinances 119.13
and shall d. thy mighty acts. 145.04
acts, and I will d. thy greatness. 145.06
or d. to us the things to come. Is 41.22
to pass, and new things I now d.; 42.09
and d. his praise in the coastlands 42.12
Who among them can d. this, 43.09
that they might d. my praise. 43.21
let him d. and set it forth before 44.07
the truth, I d. what is right. 45.19
D. and present your case; 45.21
and will you not d. it? From this 48.06
d. this with a shout of joy, proclaim 48.20
who will d. me guilty? 50.09
d. to my people their transgression, 58.01
and they shall d. my glory among 66.19
D. in Judah, and proclaim in Jerusalem, Jer 4.05
D. this in the house of Jacob, 5.20
the LORD spoken, that he may d. it? 9.12
If at any time I d. concerning a 18.07
at any time I d. concerning a 18.09
and d. it in the coastlands afar 31.10
our God says d. to us and we will 42.20
"D. in Egypt, and proclaim in Migdol 46.14
"D. among the nations and proclaim, 50.02
to d. in Zion the vengeance of the 50.28
come, let us d. in Zion the work of 51.10
Then d. to her all her abominable Eze 22.02
Then d. to them their abominable 23.36
and in my blazing wrath I d., 38.19
d. all that you see to the house of 40.04
d. the interpretation, because all Dan 4.18
tribes of Israel I d. what is sure. Hos 5.09
but d. war against him who puts Mic 3.05
to d. to Jacob his transgression 3.08
today I d. that I will restore to Zec 9.12
And then will I d. to them, Mt 7.23
and d. how much God has done for Lk 8.39
and I d. to the world what I have Jn 8.26
and he will d. to you the things 16.13
take what is mine and d. it to you. 16.14
take what is mine and d. it to you. 16.15
he will d. to you a message by Ac 11.14
worship God and d. that God is 1Co 14.25
that I may d. it boldly, as I ought Eph 6.20
to d. the mystery of Christ, on Col 4.03
in our God to d. to you the gospel 1Th 2.02
For this we d. to you by the word 4.15
D. these things; exhort and Tit 2.15
that you may d. the wonderful deeds 1Pe 2.09

DECLARED
my name may be d. throughout all Ex 9.16
that is in the house be d. unclean; Lev 14.36
Thus Moses d. to the people of 23.44
of the LORD should be d. to them. 24.12
And he d. to you his covenant, which Deu 4.13
You have d. this day concerning the 26.17
and the LORD has d. this day 26.18
And you have d. this day how you 1Sa 24.18
the words that were d. to them. Neh 8.12
of the country d. themselves Jews, Est 8.17
and plentifully d. sound knowledge! Job 26.03
then he saw it and d. it; 28.27
they had d. Job to be in the wrong. 32.03
When I d. not my sin, my body wasted Ps 32.03
thy steadfast love d. in the grave, 88.11
Who d. it from the beginning, that Is 41.26
There was none who d. it, 41.26
I first have d. it to Zion, and I 41.27
I d. and saved and proclaimed, when 43.12
not told you from of old and d. it? 44.08
Who d. it of old? Was it not 45.21
"The former things I d. of old, 48.03
I d. them to your from of old, before 48.05
Who among them has d. these things? 48.14
And I have this day d. it to you, Jer 42.21
your wives have d. with your 44.25
At that time Jesus d., "I thank Mt 11.25
Peter d. to him, "Though they all 26.33
(Thus he d. all foods clean.) Mk 7.19
d., 'The Lord said to my Lord, Sit 12.36
down before him d. in the presence Lk 8.47
and d. to them how on the road he Ac 9.27
extolling God. Then Peter d., 10.46
together and d. all that God had 14.27
and they d. all that God had done 15.04
but d. first to those at Damascus, 26.20
For if the message d. by angels was Heb 2.02
It was d. at first by the Lord, and 2.03
law had been d. by Moses to all 9.19

DECLARES
Therefore the LORD the God of Israel d.: 1Sa 2.30
but now the LORD d.: 'Far be it 2.30
the LORD d. to you that the LORD 2Sa 7.11
Who d. his way to his face, and who Job 21.31

DECLARES (cont.)
then he d. to them their work and Job 36.09
Its crashing d. concerning him, who 36.33
and night to night d. knowledge. Ps 19.02
He d. his word to Jacob, his statutes 147.19
For a voice d. from Dan and proclaims Jer 4.15
and d. to man what is his thought; Amo 4.13
God d., that I will pour out my Ac 2.17
never believe, if one d. it to you.' " 13.41

DECLARING
d. the end from the beginning and Is 46.10
not shrink from d. to you anything Ac 20.20
not shrink from d. to you the 20.27
exhorting and d. that this is the 1Pe 5.12

DECLINED
the sun had d. on the dial of Ahaz 2Ki 20.11
the ten steps by which it had d. Is 38.08
to stay for a longer period, he d.; Ac 18.20

DECLINES
heart, and tarry until the day d.' Ju 19.08
for the day d., for the shadows of Jer 6.04

DECLINING
cast by the d. sun on the dial of Is 38.08

DECORATION
d. of gold, and wearing of robes, 1Pe 3.03

DECREASE
he does not let their cattle d. Ps 107.38
multiply there, and do not d. Jer 29.06
He must increase, but I must d." Jn 3.30

DECREE
And I made a d., and search has Ez 4.19
Therefore make a d. that these men 4.21
rebuilt, until a d. is made by me. 4.21
He must increase, but I must d." Jn 3.30
"Who gave you a d. to build this 5.03
'Who gave you a d. to build this 5.09
the king made a d. that this house 5.13
see whether a d. was issued by 5.17
Then Darius the king made a d., 6.01
king, Cyrus the king issued a d.: 6.03
Moreover I make a d. regarding what 6.08
Also I make a d. that if any one 6.11
I Darius make a d.; let it be 6.12
Israel and by d. of Cyrus and 6.14
I make a d. that any one of the 7.13
make a d. to all the treasurers in 7.21
So when the d. made by the king is Est 1.20
be issued as a d. in every province 3.14
and the d. was issued in Susa the 3.15
the king's command and his d. came, 4.03
of the written d. issued in Susa 4.08
be issued as a d. in every province, 8.13
and the d. was issued in Susa the 8.14
a d. was issued in Susa, and the ten 9.14
when he made a d. for the rain, and Job 28.26
I will tell of the d. of the LORD: Ps 2.07
Do you indeed d. what is right, you 58.01
He made it a d. in Joseph, when he 81.05
reign, and rulers d. what is just; Pro 8.15
Woe to those who d. iniquitous Is 10.01
I have heard a d. of destruction 28.22
sent her away with a d. of divorce; Jer 3.08
which I did not command or d., 19.05
So the d. went forth that the wise Dan 2.13
"Why is the d. of the king so 2.15
have made a d., that every man who 3.10
Therefore I make a d.: Any people, 3.29
Therefore I made a d. that all the 4.06
is by the d. of the watchers, the 4.17
It is a d. of the Most High, which 4.24
I make a d., that in all my royal 6.26
"By the d. of the king and his Jon 3.07
In those days a d. went out from Lk 2.01
Though they know God's d. that those Rom 1.32

DECREED
as d. for ever throughout your Lev 6.18
it to the LORD as d. for ever; 6.22
So they d. to make a proclamation 2Ch 30.05
and what had been d. against her. Est 2.01
let it be d. that they be destroyed, 3.09
the heritage d. for him by God." Job 20.29
as was d. for Israel, to give thanks Ps 122.04
drink and forget what has been d., Pro 31.05
Destruction is d., overflowing Is 10.22
as d., in the midst of all the 10.23
of years are d. concerning your Dan 9.24
shall be war; desolations are d. 9.26
until the d. end is poured out on 9.27
which God d. before the ages for 1Co 2.07

DECREES
commands and just d. of the LORD." Deu 33.21
Thy d. are very sure; holiness Ps 93.05
Woe to those who decree iniquitous d., Is 10.01
acting against the d. of Caesar, Ac 17.07

DEDAN
The sons of Raamah: Sheba and D. Gen 10.07
Jokshan was the father of Sheba and D. 25.03
The sons of D. were Asshurim, 25.03
The sons of Raamah: Sheba and D. 1Ch 1.09
the sons of Jokshan: Sheba and D. 1.32
D., Tema, Buz, and all who cut the Jer 25.23
in the depths, O inhabitants of D.! 49.08
Teman even to D. they shall fall Eze 25.13
D. traded with you in saddlecloths 27.20
Sheba and D. and the merchants of 38.13

DEDANITES
you will lodge, O caravans of D. Is 21.13

DEDICATE
which they d. to me, so that they Lev 22.02
people of Israel d. to the LORD, 22.03
belongs to the LORD, no man may d.; 27.26
the battle and another man d. it. Deu 20.05
LORD my God and d. it to him for 2Ch 2.04

DEDICATED
a new house and has not d. it? Deu 20.05
these also King David d. to the LORD, 2Sa 8.11
gold which he d. from all the 8.11
which David his father had d., 1Ki 7.51
of Israel d. the house of the LORD 8.63
had d., and his own votive gifts, 2Ki 12.18
kings of Judah had d. to the sun, 23.11
these also King David d. to the LORD, 1Ch 18.11
and the treasuries of the d. gifts. 26.20
treasuries of the d. gifts which 26.26
the commanders of the army, had d. 26.26
in battles they d. gifts for the 26.27
Joab the son of Zeruiah had d.— 26.28
all d. gifts were in the care of 26.28
and the treasuries for d. gifts; 28.12
which David his father had d., 2Ch 5.01
all the people d. the house of God. 7.05
used all the d. things of the 24.07
and the d. things which had been 31.06
the tithes and the d. things. 31.12
her hire will be d. to the LORD; Is 23.18
Who is blind as my d. one, 42.19

DEDICATES
"When a man d. his house to be holy Lev 27.14
And if he who d. it wishes to 27.15
"If a man d. to the LORD part of 27.16
If he d. his field from the year of 27.17
but if he d. his field after the 27.18

DEDICATES (cont.)
And if he who d. the field wishes Lev 27.19
If he d. to the LORD a field which 27.22

DEDICATING
every man d. an offering of gold to Ex 35.22

DEDICATION
offerings for the d. of the altar. Num 7.10
each day, for the d. of the altar." 7.11
This was the d. offering for the 7.84
This was the d. offering for the 7.88
had kept the d. of the altar seven 2Ch 7.09
celebrated the d. of this house of Ez 6.16
They offered at the d. of this 6.17
And at the d. of the wall of Neh 12.27
to celebrate the d. with gladness, 12.27
to come to the d. of the image Dan 3.02
assembled for the d. of the image 3.03
the feast of the D. at Jerusalem; Jn 10.22

DEDUCTION
and a d. shall be made from your Lev 27.18

DEED
"What d. is this that you have done? Gen 44.15
Nevertheless, because by this d. you 2Sa 12.14
For this d. of the queen will be Est 1.17
that he may turn man aside from his d., Job 33.17
and he will repay him for his d. Pro 19.17
against an evil d. is not executed Ecc 8.11
will bring every d. into judgment, 12.14
to do his d.—strange is his d.! Is 28.21
I signed the d., sealed it, got Jer 32.10
Then I took the sealed d. of purchase, 32.11
and I gave the d. of purchase to 32.12
who signed the d. of purchase, 32.12
sealed d. of purchase and this open d., 32.14
"After I had given the d. of 32.16
great in counsel and mighty in d.; 32.19
requite your d. upon your own head Joe 3.04
requite your d. upon your own head 3.07
what good d. must I do, to have Mt 19.16
consented to their purpose and d., Lk 23.51
mighty in d. and word before God 24.19
"I did one d., and you all marvel Jn 7.21
concerning a good d. done to a Ac 4.09
contrived this d. in your heart? 5.04
for I do a d. in your days, a d. 13.41
from the Gentiles, by word and d., Rom 15.18
in word or d., do everything in the Col 3.17
disobedient, unfit for any good d. Tit 1.16
or speech but in d. and in truth. 1Jn 3.18

DEEDS
in glorious d., doing wonders? Ex 15.11
his signs and his d. which he did Deu 11.03
and terrible d. which Moses 34.12
his wonderful d. which our fathers Ju 6.13
done to him as his d. deserved— 9.16
According to all the d. which they 1Sa 8.08
all the saving d. of the LORD 12.07
and because his d. have been of 19.04
man of Kabzeel, a doer of great d.; 2Sa 23.20
back his bloody d. upon his own 1Ki 2.32
Now the rest of the d. of Amaziah, 2Ki 14.18
Now the rest of the d. of Zechariah, 15.11
Now the rest of the d. of Shallum, 15.15
Now the rest of the d. of Menahem, 15.21
Now the rest of the d. of Pekahiah, 15.26
The rest of the d. of Hezekiah, 20.20
Now the rest of the d. of Jehoiakim, 24.05
man of Kabzeel, a doer of great d., 1Ch 11.22
make known his d. among the 16.08
Now the rest of the d. of Amaziah, 2Ch 25.26
and his good d., behold, they are 32.32
and his good d. according to what 35.26
us for our evil d. and for our Ez 9.13
of his good d. in my presence, Neh 6.19
not out my good d. that I have 13.14
to bring the book of memorable d., Est 6.01
will tell of all thy wonderful d. Ps 9.01
Tell among the peoples his d.! 9.11
righteous, he loves righteous d.; 11.07
are corrupt, they do abominable d., 14.01
and telling all thy wondrous d. 26.07
according to the evil of their d.; 28.04
all, and observes all their d. 33.15
thy wondrous d. and thy thoughts 40.05
what d. thou didst perform in their 44.01
your right hand teach you dread d.! 45.04
By dread d. thou dost answer us 65.05
Say to God, "How terrible are thy d.! 66.03
he is terrible in his d. among men. 66.05
of thy d. of salvation all the day, 71.15
With the mighty d. of the Lord GOD 71.16
I still proclaim thy wondrous d. 71.17
name and recount thy wondrous d. 75.01
call to mind the d. of the LORD; 77.11
work, and muse on thy mighty d. 77.12
the glorious d. of the LORD, 78.04
make known his d. among the 105.01
and tell of his d. in songs of joy 107.22
they saw the d. of the LORD, his 107.24
and recount the d. of the LORD. 118.17
with wicked d. in company with men 141.04
continually against their wicked d. 141.05
to the sons of men thy mighty d., 145.12
words, and gracious in all his d. 145.13
Praise him for his mighty d.; 150.02
good man with the fruit of his d. Pro 14.14
seen the evil d. that are done Ecc 4.03
according to the d. of the wicked, 8.14
according to the d. of the righteous. 8.14
wise and their d. are in the hand 9.01
and their d. are against the LORD, Is 3.08
shall eat the fruit of their d. 3.10
do not regard the d. of the LORD, 5.12
make known his d. among the nations, 12.04
whose d. are in the dark, and who 29.15
and d. of violence are in their 59.06
According to their d., so will he 59.18
our righteous d. are like a 64.06
know no bounds in d. of wickedness; Jer 5.28
house, when she has done vile d.? 11.15
thou didst show me their evil d. 11.18
according to all his wonderful d., 21.02
to their d. and the work of their 25.14
Take these d., both this sealed 32.14
and d. shall be signed and sealed 32.44
boasts are false, his d. are false. 48.30
Requite her according to her d., 50.29
his righteous d. which he has done Eze 3.20
requite their d. upon their heads." 9.10
requite their d. upon their own 11.21
the d. of a brazen harlot; 16.30
requite your d. upon your head, 16.43
the righteous d. which he has done 18.24
to her all her abominable d. 22.02
to them their abominable d. 23.36
his righteous d. shall be remembered; 33.13
conduct and their d. I judged them. 36.19
and your d. that were not good; 36.31
iniquities and your abominable d. 36.31
and requite them for their d. Hos 4.09
Their d. do not permit them to 5.04
and the wicked d. of Samaria; 7.01
Now their d. encompass them, they 7.02
chastise them for their wicked d. 7.12
of their d. I will drive them out 9.15
requite him according to his d. 12.02
will never forget any of their d. Amo 8.07
your d. shall return on your own Ob 1.15
they have made their d. evil. Mic 3.04
eager to make all their d. corrupt." Zep 3.07

DEEDS (cont.)

because of the d. by which you Zep 3.11
evil ways and from your evil d.' Zec 1.04
deal with us for our ways and d., 1.06
prison about the d. of the Christ, Mt 11.02
Yet wisdom is justified by her d." 11.19
They do all their d. to be seen by 23.05
consent to the d. of your fathers; Lk 11.48
receiving the due reward of our d.; 23.41
light, because their d. were evil. Jn 3.19
lest his d. should be exposed. 3.20
seen that his d. have been wrought 3.21
he was mighty in his words and d. Ac 7.22
God and perform d. worthy of their 26.20
to death the d. of the body you Rom 8.13
end will correspond to their d. 2Co 11.15
hostile in mind, doing evil d., Col 1.21
but by good d., as befits women who 1Ti 2.10
be well attested for her good d., 5.10
So also good d. are conspicuous; 5.25
to do good, to be rich in good d., 6.18
Lord will requite him for his d. 2Ti 4.14
God, but they deny him by their d.; Tit 1.16
in all respects a model of good d., 2.07
own who are zealous for good d. 2.14
not because of d. done by us in 3.05
to apply themselves to good d.; 3.08
to apply themselves to good d., 3.14
impartially according to his d., 1Pe 1.17
the wonderful d. of him who called 2.09
see your good d. and glorify God 2.12
after day with their lawless d.), 2Pe 2.08
Because his own d. were evil and 1Jn 3.12
of all their d. of ungodliness Jud 1.15
labors, for their d. follow them!" Rev 14.13
"Great and wonderful are thy d., 15.03
and did not repent of their d. 16.11
and repay her double for her d.; 18.06
is the righteous d. of the saints. 19.08

DEEM

Henceforth we d. the arrogant Mal 3.15

DEEMED

his lips, he is d. intelligent. Pro 17.28
the fruitful field is d. a forest. Is 32.15

DEEMS

since indeed God d. it just to 2Th 1.06

DEEP

was upon the face of the d.; Gen 1.02
God caused a d. sleep to fall upon 2.21
of the great d. burst forth, 7.11
covering them fifteen cubits d. 7.20
fountains of the d. and the windows 8.02
a d. sleep fell on Abram; 15.12
blessings of the d. that couches 49.25
two cubits d. on the face of the Num 11.31
and the d. gloom, with a loud voice; Deu 5.22
and of the d. that couches beneath, 33.13
because a d. sleep from the LORD 1Sa 26.12
upon you, nor upsurging of the d.! 2Sa 1.21
and ten cubits d. in front of the 1Ki 6.03
is made, a cubit and a half d. 7.31
Let gloom and d. darkness claim it. Job 3.05
when d. sleep falls on men, 4.13
the land of gloom and d. darkness, 10.21
"Can you find out the d. things of God? 11.07
and brings d. darkness to light. 12.22
and on my eyelids is d. darkness? 16.16
he judge through the d. darkness? 22.13
For d. darkness is morning to all 24.17
with the terrors of d. darkness. 24.17
the ore in gloom and d. darkness. 28.03
The d. says, 'It is not in me,' and 28.14
when d. sleep falls upon men, while 33.15
There is no gloom or d. darkness 34.22
walked in the recesses of the d.? 38.16
you seen the gates of d. darkness? 38.17
and the face of the d. is frozen. 38.30
He makes the d. boil like a pot; 41.31
one would think the d. to be hoary. 41.32
to the wicked d. in his heart; Ps 36.01
judgments are like the great d.; 36.06
D. calls to d. at the thunder of 42.07
and covered us with d. darkness. 44.19
mind and heart of a man are d.! 64.06
I sink in d. mire, where there is no 69.02
I have come into d. waters, 69.02
my enemies and from the d. waters 69.14
or the d. swallow me up, or the pit 69.15
were afraid, yea, the d. trembled. 77.16
drink abundantly as from the d. 78.15
it took d. root and filled the land 80.09
Pit, in the regions dark and d. 88.06
O LORD! Thy thoughts are very d.! 92.05
it with the d. as with a garment; 104.06
through the d. as through a desert 106.09
LORD, his wondrous works in the d. 107.24
of the wicked is like d. darkness; Pro 4.19
a circle on the face of the d., 8.27
established the fountains of the d., 8.28
of a man's mouth are d. waters; 18.04
Slothfulness casts into a d. sleep, • 19.15
in a man's mind is like d. water, 20.05
mouth on a loose woman is a d. pit; 22.14
For a harlot is a d. pit; an 23.27
is, is far off, and d., very d.; Ecc 7.24
let it be d. as Sheol or high as Is 7.11
who dwelt in a land of d. darkness, 9.02
Then d. from the earth you shall 29.04
out upon you a spirit of d. sleep, 29.10
those who hide d. from the LORD 29.15
its pyre made d. and wide, with fire 30.33
who says to the d., 44.27
sea, the waters of the great d.; 51.10
a land of drought and d. darkness, Jer 2.06
gloom and makes it d. darkness, 13.16
sister's cup which is d. and large; Eze 23.32
when I bring up the d. over you, 26.19
the d. made it grow tall, making its 31.04
I will make the d. mourn for it, 31.15
threshold of the gate, one reed d.; 40.06
it was d. enough to swim in, a river 47.05
he reveals d. and mysterious things Dan 2.22
I fell into a d. sleep with my face 8.18
on my face in a d. sleep with my 10.09
And they have made d. the pit of Hos 5.02
and turns d. darkness into the Amo 5.08
the great d. and was eating up the 7.04
For thou didst cast me into the d., Jon 2.03
the d. was round about me; weeds were 2.05
the d. gave forth its voice, it Hab 3.10
out into the d. and let down your Lk 5.04
who dug d., and laid the foundation 6.48
to draw with, and the well is d.; Jn 4.11
He sank into a d. sleep as Paul Ac 20.09
for us with sighs too d. for words. Rom 8.26
some call the d. things of Satan, Rev 2.24

DEEPER

appears to be d. than the skin of Lev 13.03
and appears no d. than the skin, 13.04
if it appears d. than the skin and 13.20
and it is not d. than the skin, 13.21
and it appears d. than the skin, 13.25
and it is no d. than the skin, 13.26
and if it appears d. than the skin, 13.30
it appears no d. than the skin and 13.31
appears to be no d. than the skin. 13.32
appears to be no d. than the skin, 13.34
appears to be d. than the surface, 14.37
D. than Sheol—what can you know? Job 11.08
A rebuke goes d. into a man of Pro 17.10

DEEPLY
She was d. distressed and prayed to 1Sa 1.10
And the king was d. moved, and went 2Sa 18.33
her, the queen was d. distressed; Est 4.04
and drink: drink d., O lovers! Sol 5.01
him from whom you have d. revolted, Is 31.06
to one d. despised, abhorred by the 49.07
you may drink d. with delight from 66.11
They have d. corrupted themselves Hos 9.09
And he sighed d. in his spirit, and Mk 8.12
he was d. moved in spirit and Jn 11.33
Then Jesus, d. moved again, came to 11.38

DEEPS
the d. congealed in the heart of Ex 15.08
He uncovers the d. out of darkness, Job 12.22
he put the d. in storehouses. Ps 33.07
on earth, in the seas and all d. 135.06
you sea monsters and all d., 148.07
by his knowledge the d. broke forth, Pro 3.20

DEFAMED
God and the teaching may not be d. 1Ti 6.01

DEFEAT
return from the d. of Chedorlaomer Gen 14.17
or the sound of the cry of d., Ex 32.18
be able to d. them and drive them Num 22.06
them over to you, and you d. them; Deu 7.02
then you will d. for me the 2Sa 15.34
had ordained to d. the good 17.14
if you should d. the whole army of Jer 37.10
all with one another is d. for you. 1Co 6.07

DEFEATED
who d. Midian in the country of Gen 36.35
and d. them and pursued them, even Num 14.45
after he had d. Sihon they king of Deu 1.04
lest you be d. before your enemies.' 1.42
and we d. him and his sons and all 2.33
of Israel d. when they came out of 4.46
against you to be d. before you; 28.07
cause you to be d. before your 28.25
us to battle, but we d. them; 29.07
So Joshua d. the whole land, the Jos 10.40
And Joshua d. them from Kadeshbarnea 10.41
land, whom the people of Israel d., 12.01
and the people of Israel d. them; 12.06
of Israel d. on the west side of 12.07
these Moses had d. and driven out. 13.12
whom Moses d. with the leaders of 13.21
and they d. ten thousand of them at Ju 1.04
and d. the Canaanites and the 1.05
and they d. Sheshai and Ahiman and 1.10
and they d. the Canaanites who 1.17
Amalekites, and went and d. Israel; 3.13
hand of Israel, and they d. them; 11.21
And the LORD d. Benjamin before 20.35
Benjaminites saw that they were d. 20.36
Israel was d. by the Philistines, 1Sa 4.02
Philistines fought, and Israel was d., 4.10
Jonathan d. the garrison of the 13.03
that Saul had d. the garrison of 13.04
And Saul d. the Amalekites, from 15.07
Baalperazim, and David d. them there; 2Sa 5.20
After this David d. the Philistines 8.01
And he d. Moab, and measured them 8.02
David also d. Hadadezer the son of 8.03
that David had d. the whole army 8.09
against Hadadezer and d. him; 8.10
that they had been d. by Israel, 10.15
that they had been d. by Israel, 10.19
of Israel were d. there by the 18.07
Israel are d. before the enemy 1Ki 8.33
Hazael d. them throughout the 2Ki 10.32
times Joash d. him and recovered 13.25
And Judah was d. by Israel, and 14.12
who d. Midian in the country of 1Ch 1.46
Baalperazim, and David d. them there; 14.11
After this David d. the Philistines 18.01
And he d. Moab, and the Moabites 18.02
David also d. Hadadezer king of 18.03
that David had d. the whole army 18.09
against Hadadezer and d. him; 18.10
that they had been d. by Israel, 19.16
that they had been d. by Israel, 19.19
Israel are d. before the enemy 2Ch 6.24
God d. Jeroboam and all Israel 13.15
So the LORD d. the Ethiopians 14.12
And Judah was d. by Israel, and 25.22
who d. him and took captive a great 28.05
who d. him with great slaughter. 28.05
had again invaded and d. Judah, 28.17
gods of Damascus which had d. him, 28.23
king of Babylon d. the fourth Jer 46.02
but they were d. and there was no Rev 12.08

DEFECT
or a man with a d. in his sight or Lev 21.20
bring you a red heifer without d., Num 19.02
is a blemish, any d. whatever; Deu 17.01

DEFECTIVE
that you might amend what was d., Tit 1.05

DEFEND
Or will you d. his cause? Ju 6.31
For I will d. this city to save it, 2Ki 19.34
and I will d. this city for my own 20.06
city to gather and d. their lives, Est 8.11
also gathered to d. their lives, 9.16
yet I will d. my ways to his face. Job 13.15
and do thou d. them, that those who Ps 5.11
and d. my cause against an ungodly 43.01
cause of truth and to d. the right; 45.04
May he d. the cause of the poor of 72.04
d. the fatherless, plead for the Is 1.17
They do not d. the fatherless, and 1.23
and will d. and deliver them. 19.20
For I will d. this city to save it, 37.35
king of Assyria, and d. this city. 38.06
and they do not d. the rights of Jer 5.28
to d. you—those of whom you said, Hos 3.10

DEFENDED
and d. it, and slew the Philistines; 2Sa 23.12
and d. it, and slew the Philistines 1Ch 11.14
he d. the oppressed man and avenged Ac 7.24

DEFENDING
we have been d. ourselves before 2Co 12.19

DEFENSE
he built cities for d. in Judah. 2Ch 11.05
God has shown himself a sure d. Ps 48.03
his place of d. will be the fortresses Is 33.16
down to make a d. against the Jer 33.04
had made for d. against Baasha 41.09
wishing to make a d. to the people Ac 19.33
hear the d. which I now make before 22.01
nation, I cheerfully make my d. 24.10
Paul said in his d., "Neither 25.08
to make his d. concerning the 25.16
out his hand and made his d.: 26.01
I am to make my d. today against 26.02
And as he thus made his d., Festus 26.24
This is my d. to those who would 1Co 9.03
and in the d. and confirmation of Php 1.07
put here for the d. of the gospel; 1.16
At my first d. no one took my part; 2Ti 4.16
to make a d. to any one who calls 1Pe 3.15

DEFENSELESS
I seek refuge; leave me not d.! Ps 141.08

DEFENSES
of ashes, your d. are d. of clay. Job 13.12
hast rejected us, broken our d.; Ps 60.01
and bring down your d. from you, Amo 3.11

DEFER
to the poor or d. to the great, Lev 19.15
"For my name's sake I d. my anger, Is 48.09

DEFERENCE
for d. will make amends for great Ecc 10.04

DEFERRED
Hope d. makes the heart sick, but a Pro 13.12

DEFIANCE
and bids d. to the Almighty, Job 15.25

DEFIANTLY
of Israel as they went forth d. Ex 14.08

DEFIED
seeing he has d. the armies of the 1Sa 17.36
armies of Israel, whom you have d. 177.44
David when they d. the Philistines 2Sa 23.09
about him and d. Rehoboam the son 2Ch 13.07

DEFILE
you shall not d. yourselves with Lev 11.43
You shall not d. yourselves with 11.44
and d. yourself with her. 18.20
any beast and d. yourself with it, 18.23
"Do not d. yourselves by any of 18.24
when you d. it, as it vomited out 18.28
and never to d. yourselves by them: 18.30
of them shall d. himself for the 21.01
for her he may d. himself). 21.03
He shall not d. himself as a 21.04
nor d. himself, even for his father 21.11
that they may not d. their camp, Num 5.03
You shall not d. the land in which 35.34
you shall not d. your land which Deu 21.23
to d. the pride of all glory, to Is 23.09
Then you will d. your silver-covered 30.22
is called by name, to d. it. Jer 7.30
is called by my name, to d. it. 32.34
"D. the house, and fill the courts Eze 9.07
nor d. themselves any more with all 14.11
does not d. his neighbor's wife or 18.06
does not d. his neighbor's wife, 18.15
and do not d. yourselves with the 20.07
nor d. yourselves with their idols. 20.18
will you d. yourselves after the 20.30
you d. yourselves with all your 20.31
and that makes idols to d. herself! 22.03
your wisdom and d. your splendor. 28.07
They shall not d. themselves any 37.23
shall no more d. my holy name, 43.07
They shall not d. themselves by 44.25
sister they may d. themselves. 44.25
he would not d. himself with the Dan 1.08
to allow him not to d. himself. 1.08
These are what d. a man; Mt 15.20
unwashed hands does not d. a man." 15.20
which by going into him can d. him; Mk 7.15
come out of a man are what d. him." 7.15
a man from outside cannot d. him, 7.18
from within, and they d. a man." 7.23
in their dreamings d. the flesh, Jud 1.08

DEFILED
that he had d. his daughter Dinah; Gen 34.05
because he had d. their sister 34.13
because their sister had been d.; 34.27
then you d. it—you went up to my 49.04
out before you d. themselves; Lev 18.24
and the land became d., 18.25
you, so that the land became d.); 18.27
to be d. by them: I am the LORD your 19.31
harlot or a woman who has been d.; 21.07
divorced, or a woman who has been d., 21.14
undetected though she has d. herself, Num 5.13
of his wife who has d. herself; 5.14
though she has not d. herself; 5.14
and if you have d. yourself, 5.20
if she has d. herself and has acted 5.27
woman has not d. herself and is 5.28
because his separation was d. 6.12
since he has d. the sanctuary of 19.20
be his wife, after she has been d.; Deu 2.04
the shield of the mighty was d., 2Sa 1.21
and d. the high places where the 2Ki 23.08
And he d. Topheth, which is in the 23.10
And the king d. the high places 23.13
and d. it, according to the word of 23.16
they have d. the priesthood and Neh 13.29
they have d. thy holy temple; Ps 79.01
thou hast d. his crown the dust. 89.39
For your hands are d. with blood Is 59.03
when you came in you d. my land, Jer 2.07
'I am not d., I have not gone after 2.23
shall be d. like the place of 19.13
for she has proudly d. the LORD, 50.29
so d. with blood that none could Lam 4.14
behold, I have never d. myself; Eze 4.14
you have d. my sanctuary with all 5.11
and I d. them through their very 20.26
and d. by the idols which you have 22.04
and she d. herself with all the 23.07
And I saw that she was d.; 23.13
and they d. her with their lust; 23.17
they have d. my sanctuary on the 23.38
they d. it by their ways and their 36.17
idols with which they had d. it. 36.18
They have d. my holy name by their 43.08
After he is d., he shall count for 44.26
played the harlot, Israel is d. Hos 5.03
harlotry is there, Israel is d. 6.10
all who eat of it shall be d.; 9.04
Woe to her that is rebellious and d., Zep 3.01
of his disciples with hands d., Mk 7.02
the elders, but eat with hands d.?" 7.05
so that they might not be d., Jn 18.28
and he has d. this holy place." Ac 21.28
conscience, being weak, is d. 1Co 8.07
sprinkling of d. persons with the Heb 9.13
and by it the many become d.; 12.15
who have not d. themselves with Rev 14.04

DEFILEMENT
from every d. of body and spirit, 2Co 7.01

DEFILEMENTS
escaped the d. of the world 2Pe 2.20

DEFILES
goes astray and d. herself, Num 5.29
and he d. his consecrated head, then 6.09
d. the tabernacle of the LORD, and 19.13
d. his neighbor's wife, Eze 18.11
another lewdly d. his daughter-in-law; 22.11
another in you d. his sister, 22.11
and each of you d. his neighbor's 33.26
not what goes into the mouth d. a man, Mt 15.11
out of the mouth, this d. a man." 15.11
from the heart, and this d. a man. 15.18
out of a man is what d. a man. Mk 7.20

DEFILING
uncleanness by d. my tabernacle Lev 15.31
d. my sanctuary and profaning my 20.03
d. himself by it: I am the LORD.' 22.08
in the lust of d. passion and 2Pe 2.10

DEFINITE
according to the d. plan and Ac 2.23
But I have nothing d. to write to 25.26

DEFRAUD
Do not d., Honor your father and Mk 10.19
But you yourselves wrong and d., 1Co 6.08

DEFRAUDED
Or whom have I d.? Whom have I 1Sa 12.03
"You have not d. us or oppressed us 12.04
and if I have d. any one of anything Lk 19.08
suffer wrong? Why not rather be d.? 1Co 6.07

DEFY
"I d. the ranks of Israel this day; 1Sa 17.10
surely he has come up to d. Israel; 17.25
that he should d. the armies of 17.26
men who maliciously d. thee, who lift Ps 139.20

DEFYING
the LORD, d. his glorious presence. Is 3.08

DEGENERATE
have you turned d. and become a Jer 2.21

DEGRADED
your brother be d. in your sight. Deu 25.03

DEGRADING
to wear long hair is d. to him, 1Co 11.14

DEGREE
thrones, and exalted those of low d.; Lk 1.52
from one d. of glory to another; 2Co 3.18

DEITY
to think that the D. is like gold, Ac 17.29
namely, his eternal power and d., Rom 1.20
whole fulness of d. dwells bodily, Col 2.09

DEJECTEDLY
in sackcloth, and went about d. 1Ki 21.27

DEJECTION
to mourning and your joy to d. Jas 4.09

DELAIAH
Johanan, D., and Anani, seven. 1Ch 3.24
the twenty-third to D., the 24.18
the sons of D., the sons of Tobiah, Ez 2.60
house of Shemaiah the son of D., Neh 6.10
the sons of D., the sons of Tobiah, 7.62
D. the son of Shemaiah, Elnathan the Jer 36.12
Elnathan and D. and Gemariah urged 36.25

DELAY
"Do not d. me, since the LORD has Gen 24.56
man did not d. to do the thing, 34.19
"You shall not d. to offer from the Ex 22.29
and without d. from the royal Ez 6.08
and do not d. to keep thy commandments. Ps 119.60
a vow to God, do not d. paying it; Ecc 5.04
presence, do not d. when the matter is 8.03
d. not, for thy own sake, O my God, Dan 9.19
will surely come, it will not d. Hab 2.03
wondered at his d. in the temple. Lk 1.21
night? Will he d. long over them? 18.07
him, "Please come to us without d." Ac 9.38
I made no d., but on the next day 25.17
that there should be no more d., Rev 10.06

DELAYED
for if we had not d., we would Gen 43.10
saw that Moses d. to come down Ex 32.01
Ehud escaped while they d., and Ju 3.26
but he d. beyond the set time which 2Sa 20.05
It will no longer be d., but in Eze 12.25
of my words will be d. any longer 12.28
to himself, 'My master is d.,' 24.48
As the bridegroom was d., they all 25.05
'My master is d. in coming,' and Lk 12.45
if I am d., you may know how one 1Ti 3.15

DELECTABLE
you are, O loved one, d. maiden! Sol 7.06

DELIBERATELY
For if we sin d. after receiving Heb 10.26
They d. ignore this fact, that by 2Pe 3.05

DELICACIES
Do not desire his d., for they Pro 23.03
stingy; do not desire his d.; 23.06
he has filled his belly with my d., Jer 51.34
I ate no d., no meat or wine Dan 10.03

DELICATE
because she is so d. and tender, Deu 28.56
no more be called tender and d. Is 47.01

DELICATELY
most tender and d. bred among you Deu 28.54
The most tender and d. bred woman 28.56
The comely and d. bred I will Jer 6.02

DELICIOUS
of a whisperer are like d. morsels; Pro 18.08
of a whisperer are like d. morsels; 26.22

DELIGHT
and that it was a d. to the eyes, Gen 3.06
because he had d. in Jacob's 34.19
Then, if you have no d. in her, Deu 21.14
the LORD took d. in doing you good 28.63
LORD will take d. in bringing ruin 28.63
will again take d. in prospering 30.09
as he took d. in your fathers, 30.09
LORD as great d. in burnt offerings 1Sa 15.22
the king has d. in you, and all his 18.22
my lord the king d. in this thing?" 2Sa 24.03
servants who d. to fear thy name; Neh 1.11
would the king d. to honor more Est 6.06
then you will d. yourself in the Job 22.26
Will he take d. in the Almighty? 27.10
that he should take d. in God.' 34.09
but his d. is in the law of the Ps 1.02
the noble, in whom is all my d. 16.03
Take d. in the LORD, and he will 37.04
and d. themselves in abundant 37.11
I d. to do thy will, O my God; 40.08
countenance; for thou didst d. in them. 44.03
For thou hast no d. sacrifice; 51.16
then wilt thou d. in right sacrifices, 51.19
scatter the peoples who d. in war. 68.30
testimonies I d. as much as in all 119.14
I will d. in thy statutes; I will not 119.16
Thy testimonies are my d., they are 119.24
thy commandments, for I d. in it. 119.35
for I find my d. in thy commandments, 119.47
like fat, but I d. in thy law. 119.70
may live; for thy law is my d. 119.77
If thy law had not been my d., 119.92
me, but thy commandments are my d. 119.143
O LORD, and thy law is my d. 119.174
His d. is not in the strength of 147.10
will scoffers d. in their scoffing Pro 1.22
doing evil and d. in the perverseness 2.14
fill you at all times with d., 5.19
let us d. ourselves with love. 7.18
and I was daily his d., rejoicing 8.30
LORD, but a just weight in his d. 11.01
those of blameless ways are his d. 11.20
who act faithfully are his d. 12.22
prayer of the upright is his d. 15.08
Righteous lips are the d. of a king. 16.13
who rebuke the wicked will have d., 24.25
he will give d. to your heart. 29.17
and many concubines, man's d. Ecc 2.08
With great d. I sat in his shadow, Sol 2.03
I do not d. in the blood of bulls, Is 1.11
And his d. shall be in the fear of 11.03

DELIGHT (cont.)
for silver and do not d. in gold. Is 13.17
the things they d. in do not 44.09
and d. yourselves in fatness. 55.02
and d. to know my ways, as if they 58.02
they d. to draw near to God. 58.02
the sabbath a d. and the holy day 58.13
then you shall take d. in the LORD, 58.14
shall be called My d. is in her, 62.04
and chose what I did not d. in." 65.12
chose that in which I did not d." 66.04
deeply with d. from the abundance 66.11
these things I d., says the LORD. Jer 9.24
to me a joy and the d. of my heart; 15.16
to take the d. of your eyes away Exe 24.16
the d. of your eyes, and the desire 24.21
the d. of their eyes and their 24.25
but the LORD has no d. in them. Hos 8.13
and I take no d. in your solemn Amo 5.21
hair, for the children of your d.; Mic 1.16
of the covenant in whom you d., Mal 3.01
for you will be a land of d., 3.12
world and the d. in riches choke Mt 13.22
and the d. in riches. and the desire Mk 4.19
For I d. in the law of God, in my Rom 7.22

DELIGHTED
Saul's son, d. much in David. 1Sa 19.01
delivered me, because he d. in me. 2Sa 22.20
who has d. in you and set you on 1Ki 10.09
who has d. in you and set you on 2Ch 9.08
and d. themselves in thy great Neh 9.25
unless the king d. in her and she Est 2.14
delivered me, because he d. in me. Ps 18.19
of the oaks in which you d.; Is 1.29

DELIGHTING
world and d. in the sons of men. Pro 8.31

DELIGHTS
If the LORD d. in us, he will bring Num 14.08
the man whom the king d. to honor?" Est 6.06
the man whom the king d. to honor, 6.07
the man whom the king d. to honor, 6.09
the man whom the king d. to honor.'" 6.09
the man whom the king d. to honor." 6.11
not save anything in which he d. Job 20.20
art not a God who d. in wickedness; Ps 5.04
him rescue him, for he d. in him!" 22.08
who d. in the welfare of his 35.27
drink from the river of thy d. 36.08
establishes him in whose way he d.; 37.23
who greatly d. in his commandments! 112.01
as a father the son in whom he d. Pro 3.12
my chosen, in whom my soul d.; Is 42.01
for the LORD d. in you, and your 62.04
and their soul d. in their abominations 66.03
ever because he d. in steadfast Mic 7.18
of the LORD, and he d. in them." Mal 2.17

DELILAH
valley of Sorek, whose name was D. Ju 16.04
And D. said to Samson, "Please tell 16.06
And D. said to Samson, "Behold, you 16.10
So D. took new ropes and bound him 16.12
And D. said to Samson, "Until now 16.13
D. took the seven locks of his head 16.14
When D. saw that he had told her 16.18

DELIVER
D. me, I pray thee, from the hand of Gen 32.11
and I will d. to you your brother, 42.34
come down to d. them out of the Ex 3.08
yet you shall d. the same number of 5.18
and I will d. you from their 6.06
for I will d. the inhabitants of 23.31
and shall d. your bread again by Lev 26.26
is none that can d. out of my hand. Deu 32.39
and d. our lives from death." Jos 2.13
of yours and d. Israel from the Ju 6.14
"Pray, Lord, how can I d. Israel? 6.15
"If thou wilt d. Israel by my hand, 6.36
that thou wilt d. Israel by my 6.37
men that lapped I will d. you, 7.07
there arose to d. Israel Tola the 10.01
"Did I not d. you from the Egyptians 10.11
therefore I will d. you no more. 10.13
let them d. you in the time of your 10.14
only d. us, we pray thee, this day." 10.15
you did not d. me from their hand. 12.02
I saw that you would not d. me, 12.03
shall begin to d. Israel from the 13.05
Who can d. us from the power of 1Sa 4.08
and he will d. you out of the hand 7.03
but now d. us out of the hand of 12.10
will d. me from the hand of this 17.37
the LORD will d. you into my hand, 17.46
cause, and d. me from your hand." 24.15
and may he d. me out of all tribulation." 26.24
or d. me into the hands of my 30.15
and d. his servant from the hand of 2Sa 14.16
Thou dost d. a humble people, but 22.28
"Thou didst d. me from strife with 22.44
Thou didst d. me from men of 22.49
"D. to me your silver and your gold, 1Ki 20.05
and he had to d. annually to the 2Ki 3.04
and he will d. you out of the hand 17.39
not be able to d. you out of my 18.29
saying, The LORD will surely d. us, 18.30
you by saying, The LORD will d. us. 18.32
the LORD should d. Jerusalem out 18.35
I will d. you and this city out of 20.06
Say also: "D. us, O God of our 1Ch 16.35
which did not d. their own people 2Ch 25.15
our God will d. us from the hand 32.11
at all able to d. their lands out 32.13
was able to d. his people from my 32.14
be able to d. you from my hand?'" 32.14
been able to d. his people from my 32.15
will your God d. you out of my 32.15
will not d. his people from my 32.17
you shall d. before the God of Ez 7.19
thou didst d. them according to Neh 9.28
and there is no one to d. them. Job 5.04
He will d. you from six troubles; 5.19
Or, 'D. me from the adversary's hand'? 6.23
is none to d. out of thy hand? 10.07
'D. him from going down into the 33.24
D. me, O my God! Ps 3.07
d. me for the sake of thy steadfast 6.04
from all my pursuers, and d. me, 7.01
D. my life from the wicked by thy 17.13
For thou dost d. a humble people; 18.27
Thou didst d. me from strife with 18.43
thou didst d. me from men of 18.48
trusted, and thou didst d. them. 22.04
let him d. him, let him rescue him, 22.08
D. my soul from the sword, my life 22.20
Oh guard my life, and d. me; 25.20
shame; in thy righteousness d. me! 31.01
d. me from the hand of my enemies 31.15
that he may d. their soul from 33.19
D. me from all my transgressions. 39.08
Be pleased, O LORD, to d. me! 40.13
deceitful and unjust men d. me! 43.01
D. us for the sake of thy steadfast 44.26
I will d. you, and you shall glorify 50.15
I rend, and there be none to d.! 50.22
D. me from bloodguiltiness, O God, 51.14
He will d. my soul in safety from 55.18
D. me from my enemies, O my God, 59.01
d. me from those who work evil, and 59.02
Be pleased, O God, to d. me! 70.01
righteousness d. me and rescue me; 71.02

DELIVER (cont.)

him, for there is none to d. him. Ps 71.11
Do not d. the soul of thy dove to 74.91
d. us, and forgive our sins, for thy 79.09
d. them from the hand of the wicked 82.04
Who can d. his soul from the power 89.48
For he will d. you from the snare 91.03
to me in love, I will d. him; 91.14
thy steadfast love is good, d. me! 109.21
Look on my affliction and d. me, 119.153
d. me according to thy word. 119.170
"D. me, O LORD, from lying lips, from 120.02
d. me, O LORD, from evil men; 140.01
D. me from my persecutors; for they 142.06
D. me, O LORD, from my enemies! 143.09
rescue me and d. me from the many 144.07
and d. me from the hand of aliens, 144.11
for if you d. him, you will only Pro 19.19
will wickedness d. those who are Ecc 8.08
and will defend and d. them. Is 19.20
he will protect and d. it, he will 31.05
for he will not be able to d. you. 36.14
saying, "The LORD will surely d. us; 36.15
you by saying, "The LORD will d. us." 36.18
the LORD should d. Jerusalem out 36.20
I will d. you and this city out of 38.06
is none who can d. from my hand; 43.13
"D. me, for thou art my god!" 44.17
and he cannot d. himself or say, "Is 44.20
they cannot d. themselves from the 47.14
Or have I no power to d.? Behold, 50.02
your collection of idols d. you! 57.13
them, for I am with you to d. you, Jer 1.08
with you, says the LORD, to d. you." 1.19
am with you to save you and d. you, 15.20
I will d. you out of the hand of 15.21
Therefore d. up their children to 18.21
I will d. Zedekiah king of Judah, 21.07
and d. from the hand of the oppressor 21.12
and d. from the hand of the oppressor 22.03
I will d. them into the hand of 29.21
you to death or d. you into the 38.16
But I will d. you on that day, says 39.17
save you and to d. you from his 42.11
to d. us into the hand of the 43.03
I will d. them into the hand of 46.26
is none to d. us from their hand. Lam 5.08
are not able to d. them in the day Eze 7.19
and d. my people out of your hand, 13.21
I will d. my people out of your 13.23
they would d. but their own lives 14.14
they would d. neither sons nor 14.16
they would d. neither sons nor 14.18
they would d. neither son nor 14.20
they would d. but their own lives 14.20
and I will d. you into the hands of 21.31
I will d. you into the hands of 23.28
shall not d. him when he transgresses 33.12
and d. them from the hand of those 34.27
And I will d. you from all your 36.29
god that will d. you out of my Dan 3.15
is able to d. us from the burning 3.17
and he will d. us out of your hand, 3.17
god who is able to d. in this way." 3.29
and set his mind to d. Daniel; 6.14
whom you serve continually, d. you!" 6.16
been able to d. you from the lions?" 6.20
and I will d. them by the LORD Hos 1.07
I will not d. them by bow, nor by 1.07
whole people to d. them up to Edom. Amo 1.06
and I will d. up the city and all 6.08
and they shall d. us from the Mic 5.06
in pieces, and there is none to d. 5.08
be able to d. them on the day of Zep 1.18
and I will d. none from their hand." Zec 11.06
temptation, But d. us from evil. Mt 6.13
for they will d. you up to councils, 10.17
When they d. you up, do not be 10.19
Brother will d. up brother to death, 10.21
and d. him to the Gentiles to be 20.19
"Then they will d. you up to 24.09
you give me if I d. him to you?" 26.15
let God d. him now, if he desires 27.43
death, and d. him to the Gentiles; Mk 10.33
for they will d. you up to councils; 13.09
bring up to trial and d. you up, 13.11
And brother will d. up brother to 13.12
so as to d. him up to the authority Lk 20.20
and I have come down to d. them. Ac 7.34
this girdle and d. him into the 21.11
Who will d. me from this body of Rom 7.24
you are to d. this man to Satan for 1Co 5.05
and if I d. my body to be burned, 13.03
deadly a peril, and he will d. us; 2Co 1.10
our hope that he will d. us again. 1.10
for our sins to d. us from the Gal 1.04
and d. all those who through fear Heb 2.15

DELIVERANCE

this great d. by the hand of thy Ju 15.18
the sun is hot, you shall have d.'" 1Sa 11.09
the LORD has wrought d. in Israel." 11.13
but I will grant them some d., 2Ch 12.07
relief and d. will rise for the Est 4.14
D. belongs to the LORD; thy Ps 3.08
of Zion I may rejoice in thy d. 9.14
O that d. for Israel would come out 14.07
and proclaim his d. to a people yet 22.31
thou dost encompass me with d. 32.07
Say to my soul, "I am your d.!" 35.03
in the LORD, exulting in his d. 35.09
glad news of d. in the great 40.09
tongue will sing aloud of thy d. 51.14
O that d. for Israel would come 53.06
On God rests my d. and my honor; 62.07
deeds thou dost answer us with d., 65.05
give d. to the needy, and crush the 72.04
We have wrought no d. in the earth, Is 26.18
of heart, you who are far from d.: 46.12
I bring near my d., it is not 46.13
"Hearken to me, you who pursue d., 51.01
My d. draws near speedily, my 51.05
and my d. will never be ended. 51.06
but my d. will be for ever, and my 51.08
will come, and my d. be revealed. 56.01
D. belongs to the LORD!" Jon 2.09
light; I shall behold his d. Mic 7.09
God was giving them d. by his hand, Ac 7.25
this will turn out for my d., Php 1.19

DELIVERED

sea; into your hand they are d. Gen 9.02
who has d. your enemies into your 14.20
When her days to be d. were fulfilled, 25.24
These he d. into the hand of his 32.16
he d. him out of their hands, saying, 37.21
vigorous and are d. before the Ex 1.19
"An Egyptian d. us out of the hand 2.19
thou hast not d. thy people at all." 5.23
and d. me from the sword of Pharaoh"). 18.04
way, and how the LORD had d. them. 18.08
in that he had d. them out of the 18.09
who has d. you out of the hand of 18.10
because he d. the people from under 18.11
Aaron's sons d. to him the blood, Lev 9.12
And they d. the burnt offering to 9.13
Aaron's sons d. to him the blood, 9.18
you shall be d. into the hand of 26.25
and d. them out of the hand of the Jos 9.26
so I d. you out of his hand. 24.10
who d. them, Othniel the son of Ju 3.09
oxgoad; and he too d. Israel. 3.31
and I d. you from the hand of the 6.09
me, saying, 'My own hand has d. me.' 7.02

DELIVERED (cont.)

for you have d. us out of the hand Ju 8.22
and I d. you out of their hand. 10.12
and I d. you from the hand of the 1Sa 10.18
and d. you out of the hand of your 12.11
So the LORD d. Israel that day; 14.23
and d. Israel out of the hands of 14.48
smote him and d. it out of his 17.35
"The LORD who d. me from the paw of 17.37
So David d. the inhabitants of 23.05
and I d. you out of the hand of 2Sa 12.07
the LORD had d. him from the power 18.19
who has d. up the men who raised 18.28
the LORD has d. you this day from 18.31
"The king d. us from the hand of 19.09
when the LORD d. him from the hand 22.01
He d. me from my strong enemy, from 22.18
he d. me, because he delighted in me 22.20
Then on the third day after I was d., 1Ki 3.18
and d. him to his mother; and 17.23
And the priest d. to the captains 2Ki 11.10
whose hand they d. the money to 12.15
nations ever d. his land out of 18.33
Have they d. Samaria out of my hand? 18.34
countries have d. their countries 18.35
utterly. And shall you be d.? 19.11
Have the gods of the nations d. them, 19.12
money which is d. into their hand, 22.07
and have d. it into the hand of the 22.09
For he has d. the inhabitants of 1Ch 22.18
the priest d. to the captains the 2Ch 23.09
the LORD d. into their hand a very 24.24
who have not d. their people from 32.17
high priest and d. the money that 34.09
They d. it to the workmen who had 34.10
LORD and have d. it into the hand 34.17
and they were d. to one whose name Ez 5.14
and he d. us from the hand of the 8.31
They also d. the king's commissions 8.36
he has d. them into the power of Job 8.04
you will be d. through the cleanness 22.30
because I d. the poor who cried, and 29.12
offspring, and are d. of their young? 39.03
He d. me from my strong enemy, and Ps 18.17
he d. me, because he delighted in me 18.19
who d. me from my enemies; yea, thou 18.48
and hast not d. me into the hand of 31.08
warrior is not d. by his great 33.16
and d. me from all my fears. 34.04
For thou hast d. me from every 54.07
For thou hast d. my soul from death, 56.13
That thy beloved may be d., give 60.05
let me be d. from my enemies and 69.14
and d. his power to captivity, his 78.61
In distress you called, and I d. you; 81.07
thou hast d. my soul from the 86.13
and d. them from the power of the 106.10
Many times he d. them, but they were 106.43
and he d. them from their distress; 107.06
and he d. them from their distress; 107.13
and he d. them from their distress; 107.19
and d. them from destruction. 107.20
and he d. them from their distress; 107.28
That thy beloved may be d., give 108.06
For thou hast d. my soul from death, 116.08
The righteous is d. from trouble, Pro 11.08
by knowledge the righteous are d. 11.09
those who are righteous will be d. 11.21
He who walks in integrity will be d., 28.18
he who walks in wisdom will be d. 28.26
and he by his wisdom d. the city. Ecc 9.15
for help to be d. from the king of Is 20.06
of the nations d. his land out of 36.18
Have they d. Samaria out of my hand? 36.19
countries have d. their countries 36.20
utterly. And shall you be d.? 37.11
Have the gods of the nations d. them, 37.12
I d. Jacob to utter destruction and 43.28
and hast d. us into the hand of our 64.07
came upon her she was d. of a son. 66.07
by my name, and say, 'We are d.!' Jer 7.10
For he has d. the life of the needy 20.13
be captured and d. into his hand; 34.03
"You shall be d. into the hand of 37.17
she shall be d. into the hand of a 46.24
he has d. into the hand of the Lam 2.07
they alone would be d., but the Eze 14.16
daughters, but they alone would be d. 14.18
my children and d. them up as an 16.21
and d. you to the greed of your 16.27
they are d. over to the sword with 21.12
Therefore I d. her into the hands 23.09
sent his angel and d. his servants, Dan 3.28
these shall be d. out of his hand: 11.41
that time your people shall be d., 12.01
the name of the LORD shall be d.; Joe 2.32
because they d. up a whole people Amo 1.09
should not have d. up his survivors Ob 1.14
have been d. to me by my Father; Mt 11.27
of man is to be d. into the hands 17.22
anger his lord d. him to the jailers, 18.34
of man will be d. to the chief 20.18
you d. to me five talents; here I 25.20
you d. to me two talents; here I 25.22
of man will be d. up to be crucified 26.02
him away and d. him to Pilate the 27.02
of envy that they had d. him up. 27.18
Jesus, d. him to be crucified. 27.26
of man will be d. into the hands Mk 9.31
of man will be d. to the chief 10.33
led him away and d. him to Pilate. 15.01
the chief priests had d. him up. 15.10
Jesus, he d. him to be crucified. 15.15
just as they were d. to us by those Lk 1.02
time came for Elizabeth to be d., 1.57
being d. from the hand of our 1.74
the time came for her to be d. 2.06
for it has been d. to me, and I 4.06
of man is to be d. into the hands 9.44
have been d. to me by my Father; 10.22
For he will be d. to the Gentiles, 18.32
You will be d. up even by parents 21.16
but Jesus he d. up to their will. 23.25
of man must be d. into the hands 24.07
and rulers d. him up to be condemned 24.20
but when she is d. of the child, Jn 16.21
therefore he who d. me to you has 19.11
this Jesus, d. up according to the Ac 2.23
whom you d. up and denied in the 3.13
the customs which Moses d. to us." 6.14
the law as d. by angels and did 7.53
and d. him to four squads of 12.04
together, they d. the letter. 15.30
they d. to them for observance the 16.04
to Caesarea and d. the letter to 23.33
they d. Paul and some other prisoners 27.01
yet I was d. prisoner from Jerusalem 28.17
and have d. to them what has been Rom 15.28
that I may be d. from the unbelievers 15.31
even as I have d. them to you. 1Co 11.02
the Lord what I also d. to you, 11.23
For I d. to you as of first importance 15.03
he d. us from so deadly a peril, and 2Co 1.10
are a letter from Christ d. by us, 3.03
He has d. us from the dominion of Col 1.13
and that we may be d. from wicked 2Th 3.02
whom I have d. to Satan that they 1Ti 1.20
the holy commandment d. to them. 2Pe 2.21
was once for all d. to the saints. Jud 1.03

DELIVERER

raised up a d. for the people of Ju 3.09
the LORD raised up for them a d., 3.15
And there was no d. because it was 18.28
rock, and my fortress, and my d., 2Sa 22.02

DELIVERER (cont.)
and my d., my God, my rock, in whom I Ps 18.02
Thou art my help and my d.; do not 40.17
Thou art my help and my d.; O LORD, 70.05
my strong d., thou hast covered my 140.07
fortress, my stronghold and my d., 144.02
both ruler and d. by the hand of Ac 7.35
"The D. will come from Zion, he will Rom 11.26

DELIVEREST
thou who d. the weak from him who Ps 35.10
people; help me when thou d. them; 106.04

DELIVERING
d. you from the way of evil, from Pro 2.12
d. you up to the synagogues and Lk 21.12
binding and d. to prison both men Ac 22.04
d. you from the people and from the 26.17

DELIVERS
"If a man d. to his neighbor money Ex 22.07
"If a man d. to his neighbor an ass 22.10
He d. the innocent man; you will Job 22.30
He d. the afflicted by their 36.15
those who fear him, and d. them. Ps 34.07
and d. them out of all their 34.17
but the LORD d. him out of them all 34.19
The LORD helps them and d. them; 37.40
he d. them from the wicked, and 37.40
The LORD d. him in the day of 41.01
For he d. the needy when he calls, 72.12
he d. them from the hand of the 97.10
enemies, and thy right hand d. me. 138.07
but righteousness d. from death. Pro 10.02
but righteousness d. from death. 11.04
righteousness of the upright d. them, 11.06
the mouth of the upright d. men. 12.06
she d. girdles to the merchant. 31.24
He d. and rescues, he works signs Dan 6.27
when he d. the kingdom to God the 1Co 15.24
Jesus who d. us from the wrath to 1Th 1.10

DELIVERY
When the time of her d. came, there Gen 38.27
pangs of birth, in anguish for d. Rev 12.02

DELUDE
that no one may d. you with Col 2.04

DELUDED
and the princes of Memphis are d.; Is 19.13
a d. mind has led him astray, and he 44.20

DELUGE
There will be a d. of rain, Eze 13.11
shall be a d. of rain in my anger, 13.13

DELUGED
existed was d. with water and 2Pe 3.06

DELUSION
men of high estate are a d.; in the Ps 62.09
Behold, they are all a d.; their Is 41.29
Truly the hills are a d., the orgies Jer 3.23
They are worthless, a work of d.; 10.15
They are worthless, a work of d.; 51.18
Therefore God sends upon them a strong d., 2Th 2.11

DELUSIONS
you have uttered d. and seen lies, Eze 13.08

DELUSIVE
Have you not seen a d. vision, and Eze 13.07
prophets who see d. visions and who 13.09
no more see d. visions nor practice 13.23

DELVED
which the nobles of the people d., Num 21.18

DEMAND
this I did not d. the food allowance Neh 5.18
earth who can meet the king's d.; Dan 2.10
commit much they will d. the more. Lk 12.48
that their d. should be granted. 23.24
For Jews d. signs and Greeks seek 1Co 1.22

DEMANDED
that you first d. of your servant 1Ki 20.09
Satan d. to have you, that he might Lk 22.31

DEMANDING
trifle, d. no high price for them. Ps 44.12
their heart by d. the food they 78.18
d. with loud cries that he should Lk 23.23

DEMANDS
stood against us with its legal d.; Col 2.14
might have made d. as apostles of 1Th 2.06

DEMAS
beloved physician and D. greet you. Col 4.14
For D., in love with this present 2Ti 4.10
D., and Luke, my fellow workers. Phm 1.24

DEMETRIUS
For a man named D., a silversmith, Ac 19.24
If therefore D. and the craftsmen 19.38
D. has testimony from every one, and 3Jn 1.12

DEMOLISH
and d. all their high places, Num 33.52

DEMOLISHED
And they d. the pillar of Baal, and 2Ki 10.27
and d. the house of Baal, and made 10.27
long ago, he was d. without pity; Lam 2.17
they have d. thy altars, and I alone Rom 11.03

DEMON
And when the d. had been cast out, Mt 9.33
and they say, 'He has a d.'; 11.18
is severely possessed by a d. 15.22
and the d. came out of him, and the 17.18
him to cast the d. out of her Mk 7.26
the d. has left your daughter.' 7.29
lying in bed, and the d. gone. 7.30
had the spirit of an unclean d.; Lk 4.33
And when the d. had thrown him 4.35
wine; and you say, 'He has a d.' 7.33
driven by the d. into the desert.) 8.29
the d. tore him and convulsed him. 9.42
was casting out a d. that was dumb; 11.14
when the d. had gone out, the dumb 11.14
The people answered, "You have a d.! Jn 7.20
you are a Samaritan and have a d.?" 8.48
Jesus answered, "I have not a d.; 8.49
"Now we know that you have a d. 8.52
said, "He has a d., and he is mad; 10.20
the sayings of one who has a d. 10.21
Can a d. open the eyes of the blind?" 10.21

DEMONIAC
a dumb d. was brought to him. Mt 9.32
blind and dumb d. was brought to 12.22
and saw the d. sitting there, Mk 5.15
happened to the d. and to the 5.16

DEMONIACS
d., epileptics, and paralytics, and Mt 4.24
two d. met him, coming out of the 8.28
and what had happened to the d. 8.33

DEMONIC
for they are d. spirits, performing Rev 16.14

DEMONS
They sacrificed to d. which were no Deu 32.17
sons and their daughters to the d.; Ps 106.37

DEMONS (cont.)
and cast out d. in your name, and do Mt 7.22
many who were possessed with d.; 8.16
And the d. begged him, "If you cast 8.31
"He casts out d. by the prince of d." 9.34
dead, cleanse lepers, cast out d. 10.08
prince of d., that this man casts out d." 12.24
And if I cast out d. by Beelzebul, 12.27
Spirit of God that I cast out d., 12.28
who were sick or possessed with d. Mk 1.32
diseases, and cast out many d.; 1.34
would not permit the d. to speak, 1.34
synagogues and casting out d. 1.39
and have authority to cast out d.: 3.15
the prince of d. he casts out the d." 3.22
possessed with d. begged him that 5.18
And they cast out many d., 6.13
a man casting out d. in your name, 9.38
And d. also came out of many, crying, Lk 4.41
from whom seven d. had gone out, 8.02
him a man from the city who had d.; 8.27
"Legion"; for many d. had entered him. 8.30
Then the d. came out of the man and 8.33
the man from whom the d. had gone, 8.35
been possessed with d. was healed. 8.36
from whom the d. had gone begged 8.38
over all d. and to cure diseases, 9.01
a man casting out d. in your name, 9.49
even the d. are subject to us in 10.17
out d. by Beelzebul, the prince of d."; 11.15
that I cast out d. by Beelzebul. 11.18
And if I cast out d. by Beelzebul, 11.19
finger of God that I cast out d., 11.20
I cast out d. and perform cures 13.32
they offer to d. and not to God. 1Co 10.20
want you to be partners with d. 10.20
cup of the Lord and the cup of d. 10.21
of the LORD and the table of d. 10.21
spirits and doctrines of d., 1Ti 4.01
Even the d. believe—and shudder. Jas 2.19
up worshiping d. and idols of gold Rev 9.20
has become a dwelling place of d., 18.02

DEMONSTRATION
but in d. of the Spirit and power, 1Co 2.04

DEN
put his hand on the adder's d. Is 11.08
become a d. of robbers in your eyes? Jer 7.11
shall be cast into the d. of lions. Dan 6.07
shall be cast into the d. of lions?" 6.12
and cast into the d. of lions. 6.16
and laid upon the mouth of the d., 6.17
went in haste to the d. of lions. 6.19
near to the d. where Daniel was, he 6.20
Daniel be taken up out of the d. 6.23
Daniel was taken up out of the d., 6.23
and cast into the d. of lions— 6.24
bottom of the d. the lions overpowered 6.24
a young lion cry out from his d., Amo 3.04
Where is the lions' d., the cave Nah 2.11
but you make it a d. of robbers." Mt 21.13
you have made it a d. of robbers." Mk 11.17
you have made it a d. of robbers." Lk 19.46

DENARII
servants who owed him a hundred d.; Mt 18.28
buy two hundred d. worth of bread, Mk 6.37
for more than three hundred d., 14.05
one owed five hundred d., and the Lk 7.41
he took out two d. and gave them 10.35
"Two hundred d. would not buy Jn 6.07
three hundred d. and given to the 12.05

DENARIUS
with the laborers for a d. a day, Mt 20.02
came, each of them received a d. 20.09
each of them also received a d. 20.10
did you not agree with me for a d.? 20.13
saying, "A quart of wheat for a d., Rev 6.06
three quarts of barley for a d.; 6.06

DENIED
But Sarah d., saying, "I did not Gen 18.15
for I have not d. the words of the Job 6.10
But he d. it before them all, saying, Mt 26.70
And again he d. it with an oath, "I 26.72
But he d. it, saying, "I neither know Mk 14.68
But again he d. it. And after 14.70
When all d. it, Peter said, "Master, Lk 8.25
men will be d. before the angels 12.09
But he d. it, saying, "Woman, I do not 22.57
till you have d. me three times. Jn 13.38
He d. it and said, "I am not." 18.25
Peter again d. it; and at once 18.27
delivered up and d. in the presence Ac 3.13
But you d. the Holy and Righteous 3.14
his humiliation justice was d. him. 8.33
my word and have not d. my name. Rev 3.08

DENIES
but whoever d. me before men, I also Mt 10.33
but he who d. me before men will be Lk 12.09
liar but he who d. that Jesus is 1Jn 2.22
he who d. the Father and the Son. 2.22
No one who d. the Son has the 2.23

DENOUNCE
Jacob for me, and come, d. Israel!' Num 23.07
How can I d. whom the LORD has not 23.08
"D. him! Let us d. him!" Jer 20.10

DENOUNCED
denounce whom the LORD has not d.? Num 23.08
why am I d. because of that for 1Co 10.30

DENS
themselves the d. which are in the Ju 6.02
lairs, and remain in their d. Job 37.08
when they crouch in their d., 38.40
them away and lie down in their d. Ps 104.22
from the d. of lions, from the Sol 4.08
watchtower will become d. for ever, Is 32.14
prey and his d. with torn flesh. Nah 2.12
and in d. and caves of the earth. Heb 11.38

DENSE
such a d. swarm of locusts as had Ex 10.14

DENSEST
farthest retreat, its d. forest. 2Ki 19.23
its remotest height, its d. forest. Is 37.24

DENY
then it will d. him, saying, 'I have Job 8.18
d. them not to me before I die: Pro 30.07
and d. thee, and say, "Who is the 30.09
I also will d. before my Father who Mt 10.33
let him d. himself and take up his 16.24
crows, you will d. me three times." 26.34
die with you, I will not d. you." 26.35
crows, you will d. me three times." 26.75
let him d. himself and take up his Mk 8.34
twice, you will d. me three times." 14.30
die with you, I will not d. you." 14.31
twice, you will d. me three times." 14.72
let him d. himself and take up his Lk 9.23
you three times d. that you know 22.34
today, you will d. me three times." 22.61
he did not d., but confessed, "I am Jn 1.20
of Jerusalem, and we cannot d. it. Ac 4.16
if we d. him, he also will d. us; 2Ti 2.12
faithful—for he cannot d. himself. 2.13
but they d. him by their deeds; Tit 1.16
licentiousness and d. our only Jud 1.04
and you did not d. my faith even Rev 2.13

DENYING

and d. the LORD, and turning away Is 59.13
of religion but d. the power of it 2Ti 3.05
even d. the Master who bought them, 2Pe 2.01

DEPART

The scepter shall not d. from Judah, Gen 49.10
The frogs shall d. from you and Ex 8.11
of flies may d. from Pharaoh, 8.29
night did not d. from before the 13.22
Then Moses let his father-in-law d., 18.27
"D., go up hence, you and the people 33.01
man, did not d. from the tent. 33.11
I will d. to my own land and to my Num 10.30
"D. I pray you, from the tents of 16.26
and lest they d. from your heart Deu 4.09
law shall not d. out of your mouth, Jos 1.08
Do not d. from here, I pray thee, Ju 6.18
arose early in the morning to d.; 19.08
and his servant rose up to d., 19.09
When you d. from me today you will 1Sa 10.02
d., go down from among the Amalekites, 15.06
d., and go into the land of Judah." 22.05
and d. as soon as you have light." 29.10
away his wife and children, and d." 30.22
and tomorrow I will let you d." 2Sa 11.12
shall never d. from your house, 12.10
"Let me d., that I may go to my own 1Ki 11.21
"D. for three days, then come again 12.05
"D. from here and turn eastward, and 17.03
to sin; he did not d. from it. 2Ki 3.03
and d. with your household, and 8.01
he did not d. from them. 13.02
Nevertheless they did not d. from 13.06
he did not d. from all the sins 13.11
he did not d. from all the sins 14.24
He did not d. from the sins of 15.09
he did not d. all his days from 15.18
he did not d. from the sins of 15.28
they did not d. from them, 17.22
he did not d. from following him, 18.06
did not need to d. from their 2Ch 35.15
the way did not d. from them by Neh 9.19
They say to God, 'D. from us! Job 21.14
'D. from us,' and 'What can the 22.17
and to d. from evil is understanding 28.28
D. from me, all you workers of evil; Ps 6.08
The wicked shall d. to Sheol, 9.17
D. from evil and do good; seek 34.14
D. from evil, and do good; so shall 37.27
gladness, before I d. and be no more! 39.13
fraud do not d. from its market 55.11
D. from me, you evildoers, that I may 119.115
men of blood would d. from me, 139.19
and do not d. from the words of my Pro 5.07
evil will not d. from his house. 17.13
he is old he will not d. from it. 22.06
yet his folly will not d. from him. 27.22
D. from the peak of Amana, from the Sol 4.08
his burden will d. from your Is 10.27
The jealousy of Ephraim shall d., 11.13
and his yoke shall d. from them, 14.25
the noontide of my days I must d.; 38.10
D., d., go out thence, touch no 52.11
mountains may d. and the hills be 54.10
steadfast love shall not d. from you, 54.10
shall not d. out of your mouth, or 59.21
and my jealousy shall d. from you; Eze 16.42
Woe to them when I d. from them! Hos 9.12
and the scepter of Egypt shall d. Zec 10.11
d. from me, you evildoers." Mt 7.23
he said, "D.; for the girl 9.24
it, and stay with him until you d. 10.11
'D. from me, you cursed, into the 25.41
to beg Jesus to d. from their Mk 5.17
thou thy servant d. in peace, Lk 2.29
She did not d. from the temple, 2.37
"D. from me, for I am a sinful man, O 5.08
command them to d. into the abyss. 8.31
Gerasenes asked him to d. from them; 8.37
stay there. and from there d. 9.04
d. from me, all you workers of 13.27
those who are inside the city d., 21.21
had come to d. out of this world Jn 13.01
them not to d. from Jerusalem, Ac 1.04
'D. from your land and from your 7.03
intending to d. on the morrow; 20.07
And he said to me, 'D.; for I will 22.21
My desire is to d. and be with Php 1.23
times some will d. from the faith 1Ti 4.01
name of the Lord d. from iniquity. 2Ti 2.19

DEPARTED

years old when he d. from Haran. Gen 12.04
in Sodom, and his goods, and d. 14.12
And she d., and wandered in the 21.14
ten of his master's camels and d., 24.10
So Isaac d. from there, and encamped 26.17
and they d. from him in peace. 26.31
then he d. and returned home. 31.55
asses with their grain, and d. 42.26
and as they d., he said to them, "Do 45.24
after they had d. from the land of Ex 16.01
of Israel d. from the presence of 35.20
kindled against them, and he d.; Num 12.09
nor Moses, d. out of the camp. 14.44
of Midian d. with the fees for 22.07
she sent them away, and they d.; Jos 2.21
They d., and went into the hills, 2.22
they d. every man to his home. Ju 9.55
and she d., she and her companions, 11.38
And the man d. from the town of 17.08
Then the five men d., and came 18.07
So they turned and d., putting 18.21
he rose up and d., and arrived 19.10
of Israel d. from there at that 21.24
"The glory has d. from Israel!" 1Sa 4.21
said, "The glory has d. from Israel, 4.22
let the people go, and they d.? 6.06
So the Kenites d. from among the 15.06
Spirit of the LORD d. from Saul, 16.14
and the evil spirit d. from him. 16.23
was with him but had d. from Saul. 18.12
And he rose and d.; and Jonathan 20.42
David d. from there and escaped to 22.01
So David d., and went into the 22.05
arose and d. from Keilah, and they 23.13
Then all the people d., each to 2Sa 6.19
day the king d. until the day he 19.24
have not wickedly d. from my God. 22.22
So Israel d. to their tents. 1Ki 12.16
and d., and came to Tirzah. 14.17
So he d. from there, and found 19.19
the messengers d. and brought him 20.09
And as soon as he had d. from him, 20.36
So the prophet d., and waited for 20.38
he sent the men away, and they d. 2Ki 5.24
Then he d. from Elisha, and came to 8.14
And when he d. from there, he met 10.15
Then Sennacherib king of Assyria d., 19.36
Then all the people d. each to his 1Ch 16.43
them away; and they d. 19.04
So Joab d. and went throughout all 21.04
So all Israel d. to their tents. 2Ch 10.16
and he d. with no one's regret. 21.20
When they had d. from him, leaving 24.25
Then we d. from the river Ahava on Ez 8.31
I have not d. from the commandment Job 23.12
have not wickedly d. from my God. Ps 18.21
have our steps d. from thy way, 44.18
Egypt was glad when they d., for dread 105.38
the day that Ephraim d. from Judah— Is 7.17
Then Sennacherib king of Assyria d., 37.37
the smiths had d. from Jerusalem. Jer 29.02

DEPARTED (cont.)
of Zion has d. all her majesty. Lam 1.06
wanton heart which has d. from me, Eze 6.09
The kingdom has d. from you, Dan 4.31
its glory which has d. from it. Hos 10.05
they d. to their own country by Mt 2.12
Now when they had d., behold, 2.13
mother by night, and d. to Egypt, 2.14
Jonah." So he left them and d. 16.04
of silver in the temple, he d.; 27.05
to the door of the tomb, and d. 27.60
So they d. quickly from the tomb 28.08
boat again he d. to the other side Mk 8.13
And the angel d. from her. Lk 1.38
he d. from him until an opportune 4.13
it was day he d. and went into a 4.42
And they d. and went through the 9.06
and d., leaving him half dead. 10.30
he left Judea and d. again to Jn 4.03
After the two days he d. to Galilee. 4.43
he d. and hid himself from them. 12.36
Then he d. from the land of the Ac 7.04
So Ananias d. and entered the house 9.17
When the angel who spoke to him had d., 10.07
Then he d. and went to another 12.17
but Paul chose Silas and d., 15.40
brethren, they exhorted them and d. 16.40
him as soon as possible, they d. 17.15
time there he d. and went from 18.23
leave of them and d. for Macedonia. 20.01
while, until daybreak, and so d. 20.11
we d. and went on our journey; 21.05
On the morrow we d. and came to 21.08
they d., after Paul had made one 28.25
Jews d., holding much dispute among * 28.29

DEPARTING
And as her soul was d. (for she died), Gen 35.18

DEPARTS
the disease d. when you have Lev 13.58
and she d. out of his house, Deu 24.01
When his breath d. he returns to Ps 146.04
and he who d. from evil makes Is 59.15
this fixed order d. from before me, Jer 31.36

DEPARTURE
in glory and spoke of his d., Lk 9.31
that after my d. fierce wolves Ac 20.29
the time of my d. has come. 2Ti 4.06
that after my d. you may be able 2Pe 1.15

DEPEND
Will you d. on him because his Job 39.11
commandments d. all the law and Mt 22.40

DEPENDED
their country d. on the king's Ac 12.20

DEPENDENT
of outsiders, and be d. on nobody. 1Th 4.12

DEPENDENTS
according to the number of their d. Gen 47.12

DEPENDS
That is why it d. on faith, in order Rom 4.16
So it d. not upon man's will or 9.16
so far as it d. upon you, live 12.18
righteousness from God that d. on faith; Php 3.09

DEPORTATION
at the time of the d. to Babylon. Mt 1.11
And after the d. to Babylon: Jechoniah 1.12
David to the d. to Babylon fourteen 1.17
and from the d. to Babylon to the 1.17

DEPORTED
noble Osnappar d. and settled in Ez 4.10

DEPOSED
And he d. the idolatrous priests 2Ki 23.05
king of Egypt d. him in Jerusalem 2Ch 36.03
he was d. from his kingly throne, Dan 5.20
she may even be d. from her Ac 19.27

DEPOSIT
in a matter of d. or security, Lev 6.02
or the d. which was committed to 6.04
Then you shall d. them in the tent Num 17.04
and d. them outside the camp in a 19.09

DEPOSITED
And Moses d. the rods before the Num 17.07

DEPRAVED
they are all alike d.; there is Ps 53.03
men who are d. in mind and bereft 1Ti 6.05

DEPRIVE
or to d. a righteous man of justice. Pro 18.05
and d. the innocent of his right! Is 5.23
and to d. the thirsty of drink. 32.06
have any one d. me of my ground 1Co 9.15

DEPRIVES
He d. of speech those who are Job 12.20

DEPRIVING
I toiling and d. myself of pleasure?" Ecc 4.08

DEPTH
for height, and the earth for d., Pro 25.03
up, since they had no d. of soil, Mt 13.05
to be drowned in the d. of the sea. 18.06
up, since it had no d. of soil; Mk 4.05
nor d., nor anything else in all Rom 8.39
O the d. of the riches and wisdom 11.33
and length and height and d., Eph 3.18

DEPTHS
went down into the d. like a stone. Ex 15.05
and it burns to the d. of Sheol, Deu 32.22
cast their pursuers into the d., Neh 9.11
go down into the d. of the earth; Ps 63.09
them back from the d. of the sea, 68.22
from the d. of the earth thou wilt 71.20
my soul from the d. of Sheol. 86.13
Thou has put me in the d. of the Pit, 88.06
In his hand are the d. of the earth; 95.04
heaven, they went down to the d.; 107.26
Out of the d. I cry to thee, O LORD! 130.01
wrought in the d. of the earth. 139.15
When there were no d. I was brought Pro 8.24
her guests are in the d. of Sheol. 9.18
to Sheol, to the d. of the Pit. Is 14.15
shout, O d. of the earth; break 44.23
didst make the d. of the sea a way 51.10
who led them through the d.? 63.13
dwell in the d., O inhabitants of Jer 49.08
dwell in the d., O inhabitants of 49.30
O LORD, from the d. of the pit; Lam 3.55
the seas, in the d. of the waters; Eze 27.34
our sins into the d. of the sea. Mic 7.19
and all the d. of the Nile dried up. Zec 10.11
everything, even the d. of God. 1Co 2.10

DEPUTED
there is no man d. by the king to 2Sa 15.03

DEPUTIES
Medes, with their governors and d., Jer 51.28

DEPUTY
in Edom; a d. was king. 1Ki 22.47

DERBE
of it and fled to Lystra and D., Ac 14.06
day he went on with Barnabas to D. 14.20

DERBE (cont.)
And he came also to D. and Lystra. Ac 16.01
and Gaius of D., and Timothy; 20.04

DERIDE
those who d. me use my name for a Ps 102.08
Godless men utterly d. me., 119.51

DERIDED
they d. us and despised us and said, Neh 2.19
mocked and d. by those round about Ps 79.04
And those who passed by d. him, Mt 27.39
And those who passed by d. him, Mk 15.29

DERIDES
My mouth d. my enemies, because I 1Sa 2.01

DERISION
the LORD has them in d. Ps 2.04
the d. and scorn of those about us. 44.13
dost hold all the nations in d. 59.08
me a reproach and d. all day long. Jer 20.08
and he too shall be held in d. 48.26
Was not Israel a d. to you? Was he 48.27
has become a d. and a horror to 48.39
shall be laughed at and held in d., Eze 23.32
a prey and d. to the rest of the 36.04
shall be their d. in the land of Hos 7.16
in scoffing d. of him, and say, "Woe Hab 2.06

DERIVED
For I have d. much joy and comfort Phm 1.07

DESCEND
of cloud would d. and stand at the Ex 33.09
Shall we d. together into the dust?" Job 17.16
straight to the grave they d., Ps 49.14
into my bones he made it d.; Lam 1.13
with those who d. into the Pit, Eze 26.20
saw the Spirit d. as a dove from Jn 1.32
you see the Spirit d. and remain, 1.33
or "Who will d. into the abyss?" Rom 10.07
himself will d. from heaven with a 1Th 4.16

DESCENDANT
He was a d. of Perez, and was chief 1Ch 27.03
no offspring or d. among his Job 18.19
a d. of Abraham, a member of the Rom 11.01

DESCENDANTS
with you and your d. after you, Gen 9.09
These are the d. of Shem. 11.10
Now these are the d. of Terah. 11.27
"To your d. I will give this land." 12.07
to you and to your d. for ever. 13.15
I will make your d. as the dust of 13.16
your d. also can be counted. 13.16
said to him, "So shall your d. be." 15.05
that your d. will be sojourners in 15.13
"To your d. I give this land, from 15.18
multiply your d. that they cannot 16.10
you and your d. after you throughout 17.07
to you and to your d. after you. 17.07
and to your d. after you, the land 17.08
you and your d. after you throughout 17.09
me and you and your d. after you: 17.10
covenant for his d. after him. 17.19
Isaac shall your d. be named. 21.12
multiply your d. as the stars of 22.17
And your d. shall possess the gate 22.17
and by your d. shall all the 22.18
'To your d. I will give this land,' 24.07
and may your d. possess the gate of 24.60
These are the d. of Ishmael, Abraham's 25.12
These are the d. of Isaac, Abraham's 25.19
you and to your d. I will give all 26.03
multiply your d. as the stars of 26.04
give to your d. all these lands; 26.04
and by your d. all the nations of 26.04
multiply your d. for my servant 26.24
to you and to your d. with you, 28.04
I will give to you and to your d.; 28.13
and your d. shall be like the dust 28.14
by you and your d. shall all the 28.14
and make your d. as the sand of the 32.12
give the land to your d. after you." 35.12
These are the d. of Esau (that is, 36.01
These are the d. of Esau the father 36.09
are the names of the d. of Israel, 46.08
land to your d. after you for an 48.04
and his d. shall become a multitude 48.19
But the d. of Israel were fruitful Ex 1.07
for him and to his d. after him. 28.43
him and to his d. throughout their 30.12
multiply your d. as the stars of 32.13
promised I will give to your d., 32.13
saying, 'To your d. I will give it.' 33.01
None of your d. throughout their Lev 21.17
no man of the d. of Aaron the 21.21
one of all your d. throughout your 22.03
you or of your d. is unclean Num 9.10
the d. of Anak, were there. 13.22
we saw the d. of Anak there. 13.28
and his d. shall possess it. 14.24
who is not of the d. of Aaron, 16.40
and to his d. after him, the covenant 25.13
to them and to their d. after them.' Deu 1.08
and chose their d. after them, 4.37
and chose their d. after them, 10.15
to give to them and to their d., 11.09
none of his d. shall enter the 23.02
wonder, and upon your d. for ever. 28.46
that you and your d. may live, 30.19
unforgotten in the mouths of their d.); 31.21
Jacob, 'I will give it to your d.' 34.04
Ahiman and Talmai, the d. of Anak. Jos 15.14
allotment of the d. of Joseph went 16.01
were the male d. of Manasseh the 17.02
who were d. of Aaron the priest 21.04
which went to the d. of Aaron, 21.10
And to the d. of Aaron the priest 21.13
The cities of the d. of Aaron, 21.19
to us or to our d. in time to come, 22.28
an inheritance of the d. of Joseph. 24.32
And the d. of the Kenite, Moses' Ju 1.16
the d. of Hobab the father-in-law 4.11
Now these are the d. of Perez: Ru 4.18
and between my d. and your d., 1Sa 20.42
will not cut off my d. after me, 24.21
one of the d. of the giants, whose 2Sa 21.16
was one of the d. of the giants. 21.18
to David, and his d. for ever. 22.51
upon the head of his d. for ever; 1Ki 2.33
and to his d., and to his house, and 2.33
their d. who were left after them 9.21
for this afflict the d. of David, 11.39
to you, and to your d. for ever." 2Ki 5.27
LORD rejected all the d. of Israel, 17.20
All these were the d. of Keturah. 1Ch 1.33
All these were d. of Machir, 2.23
These were the d. of Jerahmeel. 2.33
These were the d. of Caleb. 2.50
the d. of Solomon: Rehoboam, Abijah 3.10
The d. of Jehoiakim: Jeconiah his 3.16
was one of the d. of the giants; 20.04
from their d. who were left after 2Ch 8.08
for ever to the d. of Abraham thy 20.07
to give to his d. the land of the Neh 9.08
multiply their d. as the stars of 9.23
So the d. went in and possessed the 9.24
and the d. of Solomon's servants. 11.03
and their d. and all who joined Est 9.27
of these days cease among their d. 9.28
for themselves and for their d., 9.31
also that your d. shall be many, Job 5.25

DESCENDANTS (cont.)

to David and his d. for ever.	Ps 18.50
'I will establish your d. for ever,	89.04
disperse their d. among the	106.27
His d. will be mighty in the land;	112.02
"May the d. of evildoers nevermore	Is 14.20
I will pour my Spirit upon your d.,	44.03
and your d. like its grains;	48.19
and your d. will possess the	54.03
Their d. shall be known among the	61.09
I will bring forth d. from Jacob,	65.09
so shall your d. and your name	66.22
up and led the d. of the house of	Jer 23.08
Shemaiah of Nehelam and his d.;	29.32
then shall the d. of Israel cease	31.36
off all the d. of Israel for all	31.37
multiply the d. of David my	33.22
will reject the d. of Jacob and	33.26
one of his d. to rule over the	33.26
"We are d. of Abraham, and have	Jn 8.33
I know that you are d. of Abraham;	8.37
set one of his d. upon his throne,	Ac 2.30
The promise to Abraham and his d.,	Rom 4.13
and be guaranteed to all his d.—	4.16
had been told, "So shall your d. be."	4.18
of Abraham because they are his d.;	9.07
Isaac shall your d. be named."	9.07
of the promise are reckoned as d.	9.08
Are they d. of Abraham? So am I.	2Co 11.22
concerned but with the d. of Abraham.	Heb 2.16
And those d. of Levi who receive	7.05
were born d. as many as the stars	11.12
Isaac shall your d. be named."	11.18

DESCENDED

the LORD d. upon it in fire;	Ex 19.18
And the LORD d. in the cloud and	34.05
the brook that d. out of the	Deu 9.21
and he also was d. from the giants.	2Sa 21.20
These four were d. from the giants	21.22
and he also was d. from the giants.	1Ch 20.06
These were d. from the giants in	20.08
of the Lord d. from heaven and	Mt 28.02
and the Holy Spirit d. upon him in	Lk 3.22
heaven but he who d. from heaven,	Jn 3.13
that the Christ is d. from David,	7.42
who was d. from David according to	Rom 1.03
not all who are d. from Israel	9.06
he had also d. into the lower	Eph 4.09
He who d. is he who also ascended	4.10
d. from David, as preached in my	2Ti 2.08
these also are d. from Abraham.	Heb 7.05
that our Lord was d. from Judah,	7.14

DESCENDING

of God were ascending and d. on it!	Gen 28.12
heard and the d. blow of his arm	Is 30.30
the Spirit of God d. like a dove,	Mt 3.16
and the Spirit d. upon him like a	Mk 1.10
ascending and d. upon the Son of	Jn 1.51
and something d., like a great	Ac 10.11
something d., like a great sheet,	11.05

DESCENDS

on his own pate his violence d.	Ps 7.16
behold, it d. for judgment upon Edom,	Is 34.05

DESCENT

Shebarim, and slew them at the d.	Jos 7.05
early to the d. toward the Arabah	8.14
their fathers' houses or their d.,	Ez 2.59
their fathers' houses nor their d.,	Neh 7.61
Israel all those of foreign d.	13.03
for at the d. of Horonaim they have	Jer 48.05
at the d. of the Mount of Olives,	Lk 19.37
concerning bodily d. but by the	Heb 7.16

DESCRIBE

And you shall d. the land in seven	Jos 18.06
d. to the house of Israel the	Eze 43.10
Who can d. his generation? For his	Ac 8.33

DESCRIBED

He had d. a circle upon the face of	Job 26.10
he d. to them how the Lord had	Ac 12.17
him the plagues d. in this book,	Rev 22.18
city, which are d. in this book.	22.19

DESCRIPTION

writing a d. of it with a view to	Jos 18.04
and bring the d. here to me;	18.06
went to write the d. of the land,	18.08
"Go up and down and write a d. of	18.08
in a book a d. of it by towns in	18.09

DESECRATED

the ground they d. the dwelling	Ps 74.07

DESERT

which looks down upon the d.	Num 21.20
top of Peor, that overlooks the d.	23.28
"He found him in a d. land,	Deu 32.10
entrance of the d. this side of	1Ch 5.09
heads he will d. to his master	12.19
asses in the d. they go forth to	Job 24.05
on the d. in which there is no man;	38.26
against the Most High in the d.	Ps 78.17
wilderness and grieved him in the d.!	78.40
flowed through the d. like a river.	105.41
through the deep as through a d.	106.09
and put God to the test in the d.;	106.14
Some wandered in d. wastes, finding	107.04
He turns rivers into a d., springs	107.33
He turns a d. into pools of water, a	107.35
to live in a d. land than with a	Pro 21.19
world like a d. and overthrew its	Is 14.17
by way of the d., to the mount of	16.01
to Jazer and strayed to the d.;	16.08
sweep on, it comes from the d.,	21.01
his officers d. the standard in	31.09
Sharon is like a d.; and Bashan	33.09
the d. shall rejoice and blossom;	35.01
wilderness, and streams in the d.;	35.06
straight in the d. a highway for	40.03
I will set in the d. the cypress,	41.19
Let the d. and its cities lift up	42.11
wilderness and rivers in the d.	43.19
rivers in the d., to give drink to	43.20
up the sea, I make the rivers a d.;	50.02
her d. like the garden of the LORD;	51.03
Like a horse in the d., they did	63.13
heights in the d. toward the	Jer 4.11
and lo, the fruitful land was a d.,	4.26
a wolf from the d. shall destroy	5.06
I had in the d. a wayfarers'	9.02
dwell in the d. that cut the	9.26
heights in the d. destroyers have	12.12
driven by the wind from the d.	13.24
He is like a shrub in the d.,	17.06
yet surely I will make you a d.,	22.06
mixed tribes that dwell in the d.;	25.24
Be like a wild ass in the d.!	48.06
nations, a wilderness dry and d.	50.12
horror, a land of drought and a d.,	51.43
desolation, a dry waste like the d.	Zep 2.13
his heritage to jackals of the d."	Mal 1.03
enough in the d. to feed so great	Mt 15.33
men with bread here in the d.?"	Mk 8.04
driven by the demon into the d.'	Lk 8.29
This is a d. road.	Ac 8.26

DESERTED
and since he d. to me I have found 1Sa 29.03
deserters who had d. to the king of 2Ki 25.11
men of Manasseh d. to David when 1Ch 12.19
these men of Manasseh d. to him: 12.20
numbers had d. to him from Israel 2Ch 15.09
but a poor man is d. by his friend. Pro 19.04
kings you are in dread will be d. Is 7.16
Her cities will be d. for ever; 17.02
be like the d. places of the Hivites 17.09
which they d. because of the children 17.09
a habitation d. and forsaken, like 27.10
be forsaken, the populous city d.; 32.14
Jews who have d. to the Chaldeans, Jer 38.19
those who had d. to him, and the 39.09
deserters who had d. to the king of 52.15
desolate wastes and the d. cities, Eze 36.04
For Gaza shall be d., and Ashkelon Zep 2.04
has d. me and gone to Thessalonica; 2Ti 4.10
all d. me. May it not 4.16

DESERTERS
city and the d. who had deserted 2Ki 25.11
city and the d. who had deserted Jer 52.15

DESERTING
for, d. me, you have uncovered your Is 57.08
"You are d. to the Chaldeans." Jer 37.13
I am not d. to the Chaldeans." 37.14
are so quickly d. him who called Gal 1.06

DESERTS
render to the proud their d.! Ps 94.02
when he led them through the d.; Is 48.21
in a land of d. and pits, in a land Jer 2.06
worthless shepherd, who d. the flock! Zec 11.17
wandering over d. and mountains, and Heb 11.38

DESERVE
though the man did not d. to die, Deu 19.06
you d. to die, because you have not 1 Sa 26.16
for you d. death. But I will 1Ki 2.26
man does not d. the sentence of Jer 26.16
who did not d. to drink the cup 49.12
anything for which I d. to die, Ac 25.11
nothing to d. death or imprisonment." 26.31
those who do such things d. to die, Rom 1.32
to each of you as your works d. Rev 2.23

DESERVED
have done to him as his deeds d.— Ju 9.16
our iniquities d. and hast given Ez 9.13
and did what d. a beating, shall Lk 12.48
think will be d. by the man who Heb 10.29

DESERVES
then if the guilty man d. to be beaten, Deu 25.02
man who has done this d. to die; 2Sa 12.05
of you less than your guilt d. Job 11.06
"This man d. the sentence of death, Jer 26.11
deal with it as its wickedness d. Eze 31.11
staff; for the laborer d. his food. Mt 10.10
judgment?" They answered, "He d. death." 26.66
for the laborer d. his wages; Lk 10.07
and, "The laborer d. his wages." 1Ti 5.18

DESERVING
they all condemned him as d. death. Mk 14.64
nothing d. death has been done by Lk 23.15
found in him no crime d. death; 23.22
charge him with nothing d. death, Ac 13.28
with nothing d. death or imprisonment. 23.29
that he had done nothing d. death; 25.25

DESIGN
fine twined lined, in skilled d. Ex 39.03
and execute any d. that may be 2Ch 2.14
avert the evil d. of Haman the Est 8.03

DESIGNATED
who has d. her for himself, then he Ex 21.08
These were the cities d. for all Jos 20.09
cities who were d. by name to 2Ch 31.19
houses, each of them d. by name. Ez 10.16
and d. Son of God in power according Rom 1.04
being d. by God a high priest after Heb 5.10
long ago were d. for this condemnation, Jud 1.04

DESIGNATES
If he d. her for his son, he shall Ex 21.09

DESIGNER
craftsman or by a d. or by an Ex 35.35
by any sort of workman or skilled d. 35.35
a craftsman and d. and embroiderer 38.23

DESIGNS
to devise artistic d., to work Ex 31.04
to devise artistic d., to work 35.32
and favor the d. of the wicked? Job 10.03
or we are not ignorant of his d. 2Co 2.11

DESIRABLE
whom is all that is d. in Israel? 1Sa 9.20
sweet, and he is altogether d. Sol 5.16
all of them d. young men, horsemen Eze 23.06
horses, all of them d. young men. 23.12
d. young men, governors and commanders 23.23

DESIRE
yet your d. shall be for your Gen 3.16
its d. is for you, but you must 4.07
the LORD, for that is what you d." Ex 10.11
my d. shall have its fill of them. 15.09
neither shall any man d. your land, 34.24
you shall not d. your neighbor's Deu 5.21
of your towns, as much as you d., 12.15
may eat as much flesh as you d. 12.20
your towns as much as you d. 12.21
the money for whatever you d., 14.26
and you have d. for her and would 21.11
all your heart's d. to come down; 1Sa 23.20
all that you d. of me I will do 2Sa 19.38
to prosper all my help and my d.? 23.05
and the king said, "What do you d.?" 1Ki 1.16
to do all you d. in the matter of 5.08
had sought him with their whole d., 2Ch 15.15
and that God would grant my d.; Job 6.08
and I d. to argue my case with God. 13.03
We do not d. the knowledge of thy 21.14
speak, for I d. to justify you. 33.32
thou wilt hear the d. of the meek; Ps 10.17
May he grant you your heart's d., 20.04
Thou hast given him his heart's d., 21.02
"Aha, we have our heart's d.!" 35.25
Let those who d. my vindication 35.27
Sacrifice and offering thou dost not d.; 40.06
brought to dishonor who d. my hurt! 40.14
and the king will d. your beauty. 45.11
brought to dishonor who d. my hurt! 70.02
upon earth that I d. besides thee. 73.25
he sees his d. on his adversaries. 112.08
the d. of the wicked man comes to 112.10
satisfiest the d. of every living 145.16
He fulfils the d. of all who fear 145.19
and nothing you d. can compare Pro 3.15
Do not d. her beauty in your heart, 6.25
that you may d. cannot compare 8.11
but the d. of the righteous will be 10.24
The d. of the righteous ends only 11.23
but the d. of the treacherous is 13.02
but a d. fulfilled is a tree of 13.12
A d. fulfilled is sweet to the soul; 13.19
The d. of the sluggard kills him 21.25
Do not d. his delicacies, for they 23.03
stingy; do not d. his delicacies; 23.06
evil men, nor d. to be with them; 24.01

DESIRE (cont.)

or for rulers to d. strong drink; Pro 31.04
the eyes than the wandering of d.; Ecc 6.09
drags itself along and d. fails; 12.05
my beloved's, and his d. is for me. Sol 7.10
memorial name is the d. of our soul. Is 26.08
no beauty that we should d. him. 53.02
and satisfy the d. of the afflicted, 58.10
satisfy your d. with good things, 58.11
had set free according to their d., Jer 34.16
place where you d. to go to live." 42.22
to which they d. to return to dwell 44.14
and his d. shall be satisfied on 50.19
your eyes, and the d. of your soul; Eze 24.21
of their eyes and their heart's d., 24.25
For I d. steadfast love and not Hos 6.06
Woe to you who d. the day of the Amo 5.18
man utters the evil d. of his soul; Mic 7.03
And what does he d.? Godly Mal 2.15
'I d. mercy, and not sacrifice.' Mt 9.13
'I d. mercy, and not sacrifice,' you 12.07
Be it done for you as you d." 15.28
and the d. for other things, enter Mk 4.19
when you will d. to see one of the Lk 17.22
Father, I d. that they also, whom Jn 17.24
But we d. to hear from you what Ac 28.22
my heart's d. and prayer to God for Rom 10.01
but having his d. under control, 1Co 7.37
not to d. evil as they did. 10.06
But earnestly d. the higher gifts. 12.31
and earnestly d. the spiritual 14.01
If there is anything they d. to know, 14.35
earnestly d. to prophesy, and do not 14.39
began not only to do but to d., 2Co 8.10
since you d. proof that Christ is 13.03
you who d. to be under law, do you Gal 4.21
but they d. to have you circumcised 6.13
My d. is to depart and be with Php 1.23
evil d., and covetousness, which is Col 3.05
and with great d. to see you face 1Th 2.17
I d. then that in every place the 1Ti 2.08
against Christ they d. to marry, 5.11
But those who d. to be rich fall 6.09
Indeed all who d. to live a godly 2Ti 3.12
I d. you to insist on these things, Tit 3.08
And we d. each one of you to show Heb 6.11
they d. a better country, that is, a 11.16
is lured and enticed by his own d. Jas 1.14
Then d. when it has conceived gives 1.15
You d. and do not have; so you 4.02
Now I do remind you, though you Jud 1.05
every plague, as often as they d. Rev 11.06

DESIRED

tree was to be d. to make one wise, Gen 3.06
just as you d. of the LORD your God Deu 18.16
of cedar and cypress that he d., 1Ki 5.10
and all that Solomon d. to build, 9.01
as much as he d., King Solomon gave 9.11
whatever Solomon d. to build in 9.19
the queen of Sheba all that she d., 10.13
whatever Solomon d. to build in 2Ch 8.06
the queen of Sheba all that she d., 9.12
his palace to do as every man d. Est 1.08
whatever she d. to take with her 2.13
withheld anything that the poor d., Job 31.16
More to be d. are they than gold, Ps 19.10
mount which God d. for his abode, 68.16
he brought them to their d. haven. 107.30
he has d. it for his habitation: 132.13
I will dwell, for I have d. it. 132.14
What is d. in a man is loyalty, and Pro 19.22
whatever my eyes d. I did not keep Ecc 2.10
nor have I d. the day of disaster, Jer 17.16
"Then I d. to know the truth Dan 7.19
and called to him those whom he d.; Mk 3.13
and kings d. to see what you see, Lk 10.24
who d. to be fed with what fell 16.21
have earnestly d. to eat this 22.15
for he had long d. to see him, 23.08
hungry and d. something to eat; Ac 10.10
So when God d. to show more convincingly Heb 6.17
and offerings thou hast not d., 10.05
hast neither d. nor taken pleasure 10.08
when he d. to inherit the blessing, 12.17

DESIRES

lives—and he may come when he d.— Deu 18.06
'The king d. no marriage present 1Sa 18.25
reign over all that your heart d." 2Sa 3.21
reign over all that your soul d., 1Ki 11.37
that we may do as Esther d." Est 5.05
are broken off, the d. of my heart. Job 17.11
turn him? What he d., that he does. 23.13
boasts of the d. of his heart, Ps 10.03
What man is there who d. life, 34.12
will give you the d. of your heart. 37.04
Grant not, O LORD, the d. of the wicked; 140.08
The soul of the wicked d. evil; Pro 21.10
he lacks nothing of all that he d., Ecc 6.02
no first-ripe fig which my soul d. Mic 7.01
God deliver him now, if he d. him; Mt 27.43
one after drinking old wine d. new; Lk 5.39
will is to do your father's d. Jn 8.44
for the flesh, to gratify its d. Rom 13.14
unbelieving partner d. to separate, 1Co 7.15
do not gratify the d. of the flesh. Gal 5.16
For the d. of the flesh are against 5.17
and the d. of the Spirit are against 5.17
the flesh with its passions and d. 5.24
following the d. of body and mind, Eph 2.03
who d. all men to be saved and to 1Ti 2.04
of bishop, he d. a noble task. 3.01
and hurtful d. that plunge men 6.09
let him who d. take the water of Rev 22.17

DESIREST

Behold, thou d. truth in the inward Ps 51.06

DESIRING

standing outside, d. to see you." Lk 8.20
But he, d. to justify himself, said 10.29
d. to build a tower, does not first 14.28
once more, d. to release Jesus; 23.20
d. to know the real reason why the Ac 22.30
And d. to know the charge on which 23.28
and d. to do the Jews a favor, Felix 24.27
What if God, d. to show his wrath Rom 9.22
readiness in d. it may be matched 2Co 8.11
d. to be teachers of the law, 1Ti 1.07
d. to act honorably in all things. Heb 13.18

DESIROUS

So, being affectionately d. of you, 1Th 2.08

DESIST

and d., that he may enjoy, like a Job 14.06
wealth; be wise enough to d. Pro 23.04

DESOLATE

and that the land may not be d." Gen 47.19
the land become d. and the wild Ex 23.29
so that your ways shall become d. Lev 26.22
and will make your sanctuaries d., 26.31
its sabbaths as long as it lies d., 26.34
As long as it lies d. it shall have 26.35
while it lies d. without them; 26.43
a d. woman, in her brother Absalom's 2Sa 13.20
that it lay d. it kept sabbath, to 2Ch 36.21
and has lived in d. cities, Job 15.28
he has made d. all my company. 16.07
they gnaw the dry and d. ground; 30.03
to satisfy the waste and d. land, 38.27
He drew me up from the d. pit, Ps 40.02
God gives the d. a home to dwell in; 68.06

DESOLATE (cont.)
the rights of all who are left d. Pro 31.08
Your country lies d., your cities are Is 1.07
it is d., as overthrown by aliens. 1.07
"Surely many houses shall be d., 5.09
men, and the land is utterly d., 6.11
lay waste the earth and make it d., 24.01
to apportion the d. heritages; 49.08
waste and your d. places and your 49.19
children of the d. one will be 54.01
and will people the d. cities. 54.03
land shall no more be termed D.; 62.04
be utterly d., says the LORD, Jer 2.12
And you, O d. one, what do you mean 4.30
pleasant portion a d. wilderness. 12.10
a desolation; d., it mourns to me. 12.11
The whole land is made d., 12.11
Shiloh, and this city shall be d., 26.09
streets of Jerusalem that are d., 33.10
of Nimrim also have become d. 48.34
it shall become a d. mound, 49.02
beast, and it shall be d. for ever.' 51.62
all her gates are d., her priests Lam 1.04
my children are d., for the 1.16
to pieces; he has made me d.; 3.11
for Mount Zion which lies d.; 5.18
Your altars shall become d., Eze 6.04
and make the land d. and waste, 6.14
they ravage it, and it be made d., 14.15
delivered, but the land would be d. 14.16
And I will make the land d., because 15.08
land of Israel when it was made d., 25.03
and I will make it d.; from Teman 25.13
land of Egypt d. and when the land 32.15
shall be so d. that none will pass 33.28
Israel, saying, 'They are laid d., 35.12
the whole earth I will make you d. 35.14
house of Israel, because it was d., 35.15
you shall be d., Mount Seir, and all 35.15
yea, because they made you d., 36.03
the d. wastes and the deserted 36.04
land that was d. shall be tilled, 36.34
land that was d. has become like 36.35
the waste and d. and ruined cities 36.35
and replanted that which was d.; 36.36
the transgression that makes d., Dan 8.13
upon thy sanctuary, which is d. 9.17
shall come one who makes d., 9.27
up the abomination that makes d. 11.31
abomination that makes d. is set up, 12.11
the clods, the storehouses are d.; Joe 1.17
but after them a d. wilderness, 2.03
him into a parched and d. land, 2.20
desolation and Edom a d. wilderness, 3.19
places of Isaac shall be made d., Amo 7.09
making you d. because of your sins. Mic 6.13
earth will be d. because of its 7.13
D.! Desolation and ruin! Nah 2.10
their cities have been made d., Zep 3.06
Thus the land they left was d., Zec 7.14
and the pleasant land was made d." 7.14
Behold, your house is forsaken and d. Mt 23.38
"I will not leave you d.; I will Jn 14.18
'Let his habitation become d., Ac 1.20
for the d. hath more children than Gal 4.27
they will make her d. and naked, Rev 17.16

DESOLATED
in the midst of d. countries; Eze 29.12
shall be d. in the midst of d. countries 30.07

DESOLATING
you see the d. sacrilege spoken of Mt 24.15
you see the d. sacrilege set up Mk 13.14

DESOLATION
and your land shall be a d., Lev 26.33
should become a d. and a curse, 2Ki 22.19
that he made them a d., as you see. 2Ch 30.07
May their camp be a d., let no one Ps 69.25
the earth a d. and to destroy its Is 13.09
the waters of Nimrim are a d.; 15.06
of Israel, and there will be d. 17.09
D. is left in the city, the gates 24.12
d. and destruction are in their 59.07
a wilderness, Jerusalem a d. 64.10
LORD, "The whole land shall be a d.; Jer 4.27
lest I make you a d., 6.08
will make the cities of Judah a d., 9.11
to make the cities of Judah a d., 10.22
They have made it a d.; desolate, 12.11
that this house shall become a d. 22.05
to make them a d. and a waste, 25.18
Why should this city become a d.? 27.17
It is a d., without man or beast; 32.43
of Judah a d. without inhabitant." 34.22
Behold, this day they are a d., 44.02
and they became a waste and a d., 44.06
has become a d. and a waste and a 44.22
'D. and great destruction!' 48.03
her cities shall become a d., 48.09
which shall make her land a d., 50.03
inhabited, but shall be an utter d.; 50.13
to make the land of Babylon a d., 51.29
will make you a d. and an object Eze 5.14
and make a d. "Because 7.23
and the land shall become a d.; 12.20
A cup of horror and d., is the 23.33
of Egypt shall be a d. and a waste. 29.09
of Egypt an utter waste and d., 29.10
land of Egypt a d. in the midst of 29.12
shall be a d. forty years among 29.12
I will bring d. upon the land and 30.12
I will make Pathros a d., and will 30.14
make the land a d. and a waste; 33.28
made the land a d. and a waste 33.29
I will make you a d. and a waste. 35.03
waste, and you shall become a d.; 35.04
make Mount Seir a waste and a d.; 35.07
I will make you a perpetual d., 35.09
of being the d. that it was in the 36.34
Ephraim shall become a d. in the Hos 5.09
"Egypt shall become a d. and Edom a Joe 3.19
that I may make you a d., and your Mic 6.16
D. and ruin! Hearts faint Nah 2.10
and Ashkelon shall become a d.; Zep 2.04
and he will make Nineveh a d., 2.13
What a d. she has become, a lair 2.15
know that its d. has come near. Lk 21.20

DESOLATIONS
how he has wrought d. in the earth. Ps 46.08
the end of the d. of Jerusalem, Dan 9.02
open thy eyes and behold our d., 9.18
shall be war; d. are decreed. 9.26

DESOLATOR
end is poured out on the d." Dan 9.27

DESPAIR
then Saul will d. of seeking me any 1Sa 27.01
they rise up when they d. of life. Job 24.22
my heart, so that I am in d. Ps 69.20
my heart up to d. over all the Ecc 2.20
in combed flax will be in d., Is 19.09
the prince is wrapped in d., Eze 7.27
perplexed, but not driven to d.; 2Co 4.08

DESPAIRED
crushed that we d. of life itself. 2Co 1.08

DESPAIRING
the speech of a d. man is wind? Job 6.26

DESPERATELY
above all things, and d. corrupt; Jer 17.09

DESPISE
"How long will this people d. me? Num 14.11
and d. me and break my covenant. Deu 31.20
and those who d. me shall be 1Sa 2.30
Why then did you d. us? Were we 2Sa 19.43
therefore d. not the chastening of Job 5.17
to d. the work of thy hands and 10.03
Even young children d. me; when I 19.18
God is mighty, and does not d. any; 36.05
therefore I d. myself, and repent in 42.06
heart, O God, thou wilt not d. Ps 51.17
and does not d. his own that are in 69.33
on awaking you d. their phantoms. 73.20
and will not d. their supplication. 102.17
fools d. wisdom and instruction. Pro 1.07
My son, do not d. the LORD's discipline 3.11
Do not men d. a thief if he steals 6.30
for he will d. the wisdom of your 23.09
and do not d. your mother when she 23.22
kiss you, and none would d. me. Sol 8.01
"Because you d. this word, and trust Is 30.12
Your lovers d. you; they seek Jer 4.30
to those who d. the word of the 23.17
all who honored her d. her, Lam 1.08
those round about who d. you. Eze 16.57
what could it do if you d. the rod?" 21.13
"I hate, I d. your feasts, and I take Amo 5.21
to you, O priests, who d. my name. Mal 1.06
to the one and d. the other. Mt 6.24
"See that you do not d. one of 18.10
to the one and d. the other. Lk 16.13
him who eats d. him who abstains, Rom 14.03
Or you, why do you d. your brother? 14.10
Or do you d. the church of God and 1Co 11.22
So let no one d. him. Speed 16.11
to you, you did not scorn or d. me, Gal 4.14
do not d. prophesying, 1Th 5.20
Let no one d. your youth, but set 1Ti 4.12
defiling passion and d. authority. 2Pe 2.10

DESPISED
Thus Esau d. his birthright. Gen 25.34
of those who d. me shall see it. Num 14.23
know the land which you have d. 14.31
Because he has d. the word of the 15.31
that these men have d. the LORD." 16.30
Are not these the men whom you d.? Ju 9.38
And they d. him, and brought him no 1Sa 10.27
all that was d. and worthless they 15.09
and she d. him in her heart. 2Sa 6.16
Why have you d. the word of the 12.09
your house, because you have d. me, 12.10
They d. his statutes, and his 2Ki 17.15
and she d. him in her heart. 1Ch 15.29
they derided us and d. us and said, Neh 2.19
Hear, O our God, for we are d.; 4.04
in whose eyes a reprobate is d., Ps 15.04
by men, and d. by the people. 22.06
For he has not d. or abhorred the 22.24
Then they d. the pleasant land, 106.24
I am small and d., yet I do not 119.141
counsel, and d. all my reproof, Pro 1.30
discipline, and my heart d. reproof! 5.12
but one of perverse mind is d. 12.08
though the poor man's wisdom is d., Ecc 9.16
they have d. the Holy One of Israel, Is 1.04
and have d. the word of the Holy 5.24
witnesses are d., there is no 33.08
to one deeply d., abhorred by the 49.07
continually all the day my name is d. 52.05
He was d. and rejected by men; 53.03
he was d., and we esteemed him not. 53.03
and all who d. you shall bow down 60.14
Is this man Coniah a d., Jer 22.28
Thus they have d. my people so that 33.24
among the nations d. among men. 49.15
O LORD, and behold, for I am d." Lam 1.11
who have d. the oath in breaking Eze 16.59
whose oath he d., and whose covenant 17.16
Because he d. the oath and broke 17.18
I live, surely my oath which he d., 17.19
You have d. the rod, my son, with 21.10
You have d. my holy things, and 22.08
nations, you shall be utterly d. Ob 1.02
For whoever has d. the day of small Zec 4.10
you say, 'How have we d. thy name?" Mal 1.06
that the LORD's table may be d. 1.07
and the food for it may be d. 1.12
and so make you d. and abased 2.09
they were righteous and d. others: Lk 18.09
what is low and d. in the world, 1Co 1.28

DESPISES
"She d. you, she scorns you—the 2Ki 19.21
He who d. the word brings destruction Pro 13.13
who is devious in his ways d. him. 14.02
He who d. his neighbor is a sinner, 14.21
A fool d. his father's instruction, 15.05
but a foolish man d. his mother. 15.20
who ignores instruction d. himself, 15.32
he who d. the word will die. 19.16
he who d. the gain of oppressions, Is 33.15
'She d. you, she scorns you—the 37.22

DESPISING
d. his words, and scoffing at his 2Ch 36.16
d. the shame, and is seated at the Heb 12.02

DESPITE
d. his wonders they did not believe. Ps 78.32

DESPOIL
thus you shall d. the Egyptians." Ex 3.22
by night and d. them until the 1Sa 14.36
from the wicked who d. me, my deadly Ps 17.09
All that pass by d. him; he has 89.41
and d. of life those who d. them. Pro 22.23
is the portion of those who d. us, Is 17.14
those who d. you shall become a Jer 30.16
its wealth and d. it and plunder Eze 29.19
they will d. those who despoiled 39.10

DESPOILED
Thus they d. the Egyptians. Ex 12.36
"Because the poor are d., because Ps 12.05
utterly laid waste and utterly d.; Is 24.03
will despoil those who d. them, Eze 39.10
shepherds, for their glory is d.! Zec 11.03

DESPOILING
for the LORD is d. their pasture, Jer 25.36

DESPOILS
weak and needy from him who d. him?" Ps 35.10

DESTINE
I will d. you to the sword, and all Is 65.12

DESTINED
darkness, and he is d. for the sword. Job 15.22
which were d. to become heaps of 15.28
They d. Tyre for wild beasts. They Is 23.13
as I have seen, are d. for a prey; Hos 9.13
He d. us in love to be his sons Eph 1.05
have been d. and appointed to live 1.12
For God has not d. us for wrath, 1Th 5.09
chosen and d. by God the Father and 1Pe 1.02
He was d. before the foundation of 1.20
the word, as they were d. to do. 2.08

DESTINY
and fill cups of mixed wine for D.; Is 65.11

DESTITUTE
right of the afflicted and the d. Ps 82.03
he will regard the prayer of the d., 102.17
goats, d., afflicted, ill-treated— Heb 11.37

DESTROY

I will d. them with the earth. Gen 6.13
to d. all flesh in which is the 6.17
I ever again d. every living 8.21
there be a flood to d. the earth." 9.11
become a flood to d. all flesh. 9.15
thou indeed d. the righteous with 18.23
wilt thou then d. the place and not 18.24
Wilt thou d. the whole city for 18.28
"I will not d. it if I find forty-five 18.28
sake of twenty I will not d. it." 18.31
the sake of ten I will not d. it." 18.32
for we are about to d. this place, 19.13
and the LORD has sent us to d. it." 19.13
the LORD is about to d. the city." 19.14
shall fall upon you to d. you, Ex 12.13
my sword, my hand shall d. them.' 15.09
person I will d. from among his Lev 23.30
and d. your cattle, and make you few 26.22
And I will d. your high places, and 26.30
them so as to d. them utterly and 26.44
I will utterly d. their cities." Num 21.02
and you will d. all this people." 32.15
and d. all their figured stones, and 33.52
and d. all their molten images, and 33.52
the hand of the Amorites, to d. us. Deu 1.27
to d. them from the camp, until they 2.15
not fail you or d. you or forget 4.31
and he d. you from off the face of 6.15
then you must utterly d. them; 7.02
you, and he would d. you quickly. 7.04
And you shall d. all the peoples 7.16
he will d. them and subdue them 9.03
you that he was ready to d. you. 9.08
that I may d. them and blot out 9.14
so that he was ready to d. you. 9.19
Aaron that he was ready to d. him; 9.20
the LORD had said he would d. you. 9.25
d. not thy people and thy heritage, 9.26
the LORD was unwilling to d. you. 10.10
You shall surely d. all the places 12.02
and d. their name out of that place 12.03
but you shall utterly d. them, 20.17
you shall not d. its trees by 20.19
food you may d. and cut down that 20.20
he will d. these nations before you, 31.03
the enemy before you, and said, D. 33.27
hands of the Amorites, to d. us? Jos 7.07
unless you d. the devoted things 7.12
and to d. all the inhabitants of 9.24
to d. the land where the Reubenites 22.33
them and d. the produce of the Ju 6.04
with a male you shall utterly d." 21.11
and utterly d. all that they have; 1Sa 15.03
Amalekites, lest I d. you with them; 15.06
and would not utterly d. them; 15.09
utterly d. the sinners, the Amalekites, 15.18
to d. the city on my account. 23.10
you will not d. my name out of my 24.21
said to Abishai, "Do not d. him; 26.09
came in to d. the king your lord. 26.15
your hand to d. the LORD's anointed 2Sa 1.14
and d. you from the earth?" 4.11
and so they would d. the heir also. 14.07
man who would d. me and my son 14.16
you seek to d. a city which is a 20.19
it, that I shall swallow up or d.! 20.20
consumed us and planned to d. us, 21.05
his hand toward Jerusalem to d. it, 24.16
Israel were unable to d. utterly— 1Ki 9.21
it off and to d. it from the face 13.34
Yet the LORD would not d. Judah, 2Ki 8.19
in order to d. the worshipers of 10.19
and Jacob, and would not d. them; 13.23
up against this place to d. it? 18.25
Go up against this land and d. it.'" 18.25
sent them against Judah to d. it, 24.02
the angel to Jerusalem to d. it; 1Ch 21.15
but when he was about to d. it, 1Ch 21.15
I will not d. them, but I will 2Ch 12.07
whom they avoided and did not d.— 20.10
they all helped to d. one another. 20.23
the LORD will d. what you have made." 20.37
LORD would not d. the house of 21.07
had anointed to d. the house of 22.07
that God has determined to d. you, 25.16
who is with me, lest he d. you." 35.21
or to d. this house of God which is Ez 6.12
Haman sought to d. all the Jews, Est 3.06
to d., to slay, and to annihilate 3.13
he wrote to d. the Jews who are in 8.05
to d., to slay, and to annihilate 8.11
against the Jews to d. them, 9.24
is the lot, to crush and d. them; 9.24
against him, to d. him without cause." Job 2.03
now thou dost turn about and d. me. 10.08
You will d. their offspring from Ps 21.10
D. their plans, O Lord, confuse their 55.09
who seek to d. my life shall go 63.09
mighty are those who would d. me, 69.04
iniquity, and did not d. them; 78.38
thy dread assaults d. me. 88.16
his neighbor secretly I will d. 101.05
morning I will d. all the wicked 101.08
Therefore he said he would d. them— 106.23
They did not d. the peoples, as the 106.34
The wicked lie in wait to d. me; 119.95
and d. all my adversaries, for I am 143.12
but all the wicked he will d. 145.20
godless man would d. his neighbor, Pro 11.09
your ways to those who d. kings. 31.03
and d. the work of your hands? Ecc 5.06
why should you d. yourself? 7.16
but it is in his mind to d., Is 10.07
his fruitful land the LORD will d., 10.18
not hurt or d. in all my holy 11.09
will utterly d. the tongue of the 11.15
to d. the whole earth. 13.05
desolation and to d. its sinners 13.09
Canaan to d. its strongholds. 23.11
And he will d. on this mountain the 25.07
When you have ceased to d., 33.01
come up against this land to d. it? 36.10
Go up against this land, and d. it.'" 36.10
oppressor, when he sets himself to d.? 51.13
also created the ravager to d.; 54.16
'Do not d. it, for there is a 65.08
servants' sake, and not d. them all. 65.08
not hurt or d. in all my holy 65.25
to d. and to overthrow, to build and Jer 1.10
wolf from the desert shall d. them. 5.06
"Go up through her vine-rows and d., 5.10
trust they shall d. with the sword." 5.17
and delicately bred I will d., 6.02
by night, and d. her palaces!" 6.05
"Let us d. the tree with its fruit, 11.19
will utterly pluck it up and d. it, 12.17
compassion, that I should not d. them.'" 13.14
of the earth to devour and d. 15.03
d. them with double destruction! 17.18
pluck up and break down and d. it, 18.07
shepherds who d. and scatter the 23.01
I will utterly d. them, and make 25.09
d., and bring evil, so I will watch 31.28
certainly come and d. this land, 36.29
I will d. cities and their inhabitants. 46.08
is coming to d. all the Philistines, 47.04
would they not d. only enough for 49.09
Kedar! D. the people of the east! 49.28
and d. their king and princes, says 49.38
and utterly d. after them, says the 50.21
heaps of grain, and d. her utterly; 50.26
young men; utterly d. all her host. 51.03
concerning Babylon is to d. it, 51.11

DESTROY (cont.)

with you I d. kingdoms; Jer 51.20
in anger and d. them from under Lam 3.66
which I will loose to d. you, Eze 5.16
and I will d. your high places. 6.03
wilt thou d. all that remains of 9.08
great hailstones in wrath to d. it. 13.13
and will d. him from the midst of 14.09
and I did not d. them or make a 20.17
hands of brutal men, skilful to d. 21.31
the land, that I should not d. it; 22.30
I will d. you. Then you 25.07
of heart to d. in never-ending 25.15
and d. the rest of the seacoast. 25.16
They shall d. the walls of Tyre, and 26.04
your walls and d. your pleasant 26.12
shall be brought in to d. the land; 30.11
I will d. the idols, and put an end 30.13
I will d. all its beasts from 32.13
seen when he came to d. the city, 43.03
appointed to d. the wise men of Dan 2.24
"Do not d. the wise men of Babylon; 2.24
'Hew down the tree and d. it, but 4.23
and d. mighty men and the people of 8.24
Without warning he shall d. many; 8.25
to come shall d. the city and the 9.26
daughter of women to d. the kingdom; 11.17
to exterminate and utterly d. many. 11.44
night; and I will d. your mother. Hos 4.05
their altars, and d. their pillars. 10.02
anger, I will not again d. Ephraim; 11.09
midst, and I will not come to d. 11.09
I will d. you, O Israel; 13.09
and I will d. it from the surface Amo 9.08
not utterly d. the house of Jacob," 9.08
d. the wise men out of Edom, and Ob 1.08
you and will d. your chariots; Mic 5.10
from among you and d. your cities. 5.14
and I will d. you till no inhabitant Zep 2.05
against the north, and d. Assyria; 2.13
I am about to d. the strength of Hag 2.22
I will seek to d. all the nations Zec 12.09
it will not d. the fruits of your Mal 3.11
to search for the child, to d. him." Mt 2.13
him who can d. both soul and body 10.28
counsel against him, how to d. him. 12.14
'I am able to d. the temple of God, 26.61
to ask for Barabbas and d. Jesus. 27.20
"You who would d. the temple and 27.40
Have you come to d. us? I know Mk 1.24
Herodians against him, how to d. him. 3.06
fire and into the water, to d. him; 9.22
it and sought a way to d. him; 11.18
He will come and d. the tenants, 12.09
'I will d. this temple that is made 14.58
You who would d. the temple and 15.29
Have you come to d. us? I know Lk 4.34
do harm, to save life or to d. it?" 6.09
Son of man came not to d. men's * 9.55
men of the people sought to d. him; 19.47
He will come and d. those tenants, 20.16
"D. this temple, and in three days I Jn 2.19
only to steal and kill and d.; 10.10
will come and d. both our holy 11.48
of Nazareth will d. this place, Ac 6.14
d. the work of God. Everything Rom 14.20
"I will d. the wisdom of the wise, 1Co 1.19
God's temple, God will d. him. 3.17
and God will d. both one and the 6.13
divine power to d. strongholds. 2Co 10.04
We d. arguments and every proud 10.05
God violently and tried to d. it; Gal 1.13
the faith he once tried to d." 1.23
his mouth and d. him by his 2Th 2.08
death he might d. him who has the Heb 2.14
he who is able to save and to d. Jas 4.12
appeared was to d. the works of 1Jn 3.08

DESTROYED

before the LORD d. Sodom and Gen 13.10
when God d. the cities of the 19.29
I shall be d., both I and my 34.30
the frogs be d. from you and your Ex 8.09
the LORD only, shall be utterly d. 22.20
is to be utterly d. from among men, Lev 27.29
Kohathites be d. from among the Num 4.18
they utterly d. them and their 21.03
and the survivors of cities be d.!" 24.19
and d. them from before them, and Deu 2.12
but the LORD d. them before them; 2.21
when he d. the Horites before them, 2.22
d. them and settled in their stead.) 2.23
time and utterly d. every city, 2.34
And we utterly d. them, as we did to 3.06
LORD your God d. from among you 4.03
upon it, but will be utterly d. 4.26
hide themselves from you are d. 7.20
great confusion, until they are d. 7.23
you, until you have d. them. 7.24
the LORD has d. them to this day; 11.04
after they have been d. before you, 12.30
until you are d. and perish quickly, 28.20
down upon you until you are d. 28.24
till you are d., because you did 28.45
your neck, until he has d. you. 28.48
of your ground, until you are d.; 28.51
bring upon you, until you are d. 28.61
and to their land, when he d. them. 31.04
Sihon and Og, whom you utterly d. Jos 2.10
Then they utterly d. all in the 6.21
he had utterly d. all the inhabitants 8.26
taken Ai, and had utterly d. it, 10.01
he utterly d. every person in it, he 10.28
in it he utterly d. that day, as he 10.35
and utterly d. it with every person 10.37
and utterly d. every person in it; 10.39
but utterly d. all that breathed, as 10.40
the sword, until they had d. them, 11.14
that they should be utterly d., 11.20
Joshua utterly d. them with their 11.21
until he have d. you from off this 23.15
land, and I d. them before you. 24.08
inhabited Zephath, and utterly d. it. Ju 1.17
until they d. Jabin king of Canaan. 4.24
men of Israel d. twenty-five 20.35
of the cities d. them in the midst 20.42
the women are d. out of Benjamin?" 21.16
and utterly d. all the people with 1Sa 15.08
and worthless they utterly d. 15.09
and the rest we have utterly d." 15.15
I have utterly d. the Amalekites. 15.20
slay no more, and my son be not d." 2Sa 14.11
I pursued my enemies and d. them, 22.38
those who hated me, and I d. them. 22.41
until he had d. it, according to the 1Ki 15.29
Jeroboam, and also because he d. it. 16.07
Thus Zimri d. all the house of 16.12
push the Syrians until they are d.'" 22.11
she arose and d. all the royal 2Ki 11.01
of Syria had d. them and made them 13.07
the nations which my fathers d., 19.12
and stone; therefore they were d. 19.18
which Hezekiah his father had d.; 21.03
whom the LORD d. before the people 21.09
and d. their tents and the Meunim 1Ch 4.41
and they d. the remnant of the 4.43
land, whom God had d. before them. 5.25
the people of Israel had not d.— 2Ch 8.08
push the Syrians until they are d.'" 18.10
for you d. the Asherahs out of the 19.03
she arose and d. all the royal 22.10
and d. all the princes of the 24.23
Manasseh, until they had d. them all. 31.01
fathers utterly d. was able to 32.14
whom the LORD d. before the people 33.09

DESTROYED (cont.)
and d. all its precious vessels. 2Ch 36.19
who d. this house and carried away Ez 5.12
down, and its gates are d. by fire." Neh 1.03
and its gates have been d. by fire?" 2.03
gates which had been d. by fire. 2.13
let it be decreed that they be d., Est 3.09
to be d., to be slain, and to be 7.04
Jews slew and d. five hundred men, 9.06
Between morning and evening they are d.; Job 4.20
If he is d. from his place, then it 8.18
and after my skin has been thus d., 19.26
nations, thou hast d. the wicked; Ps 9.05
if the foundations are d., 11.03
to me, and those who hated me I d. 18.40
transgressors shall be altogether d.; 37.38
How they are d. in a moment, swept 73.19
the enemy has d. everything in the 74.03
them, and frogs, which d. them. 78.45
He d. their vines with hail, and 78.47
who were d. at Endor, who became 83.10
The house of the wicked will be d., Pro 14.11
and sinners shall be d. together, Is 1.28
his yoke will be d. from your neck." 10.27
because you have d. your land, 14.20
who yourself have not been d.; 33.01
ceased to destroy, you will be d.; 33.01
the nations which my fathers d., 37.12
and stone; therefore they were d. 37.19
be cut off or d. from before me." 48.19
Suddenly my tents are d., my curtains Jer 4.20
My tent is d., and all my cords are 10.20
Many shepherds have d. my vineyard, 12.10
out my hand against you and d. you; 15.06
bereaved them, I have d. my people; 15.07
Abarim, for all your lovers are d. 22.20
be utterly d. from the land which 24.10
Moab is d.; a cry is 48.04
perish, and the plain shall be d., 48.08
he has d. your strongholds. 48.18
Moab shall be d. and be no longer a 48.42
it has d. the forehead of Moab, the 48.45
His children are d., and his 49.10
soldiers shall be d. in that day, 49.26
soldiers shall be d. on that day, 50.30
her warriors, that they may be d.! 50.36
The Lord has d. without mercy all Lam 2.02
like an enemy, he has d. Israel; 2.05
he has d. all its palaces, laid in 2.05
teeth, they cry: "We have d. her! 2.16
I dandled and reared my enemy d. 2.22
ruined, your idols broken and d., Eze 6.06
'Who was ever d. like Tyre in the 27.32
all the wise men of Babylon be d. Dan 2.12
a kingdom which shall never be d., 2.44
his kingdom shall never be d., 6.26
and its body d. and given over to 7.11
kingdom one that shall not be d. 7.14
to be consumed and d. to the end. 7.26
My people are d. for lack of Hos 4.06
the sin of Israel, shall be d. 10.08
all your fortresses shall be d., 10.14
as Shalman d. Betharbel on the day 10.14
because the grain is d., the wine Joe 1.10
"Yet I d. the Amorite before them, Amo 2.09
I d. his fruit above, and his roots 2.09
by night—how you have been d.!— Ob 1.05
In one month I d. the three shepherds. Zec 11.08
what is to be d., let it be d.; 11.09
is spilled, and the skins are d.; Mt 9.17
his troops and d. those murderers 22.07
spilled, and the skins will be d. Lk 5.37
and the flood came and d. them all. 17.27
rained from heaven and d. them all— 17.29
shall be d. from the people.' Ac 3.23
And when he had d. seven nations in 13.19
that the sinful body might be d., Rom 6.06
your knowledge this weak man is d., 1Co 8.11
them did and were d. by serpents; 10.09
did and were d. by the Destroyer. 10.10
The last enemy to be d. is death. 15.26
forsaken; struck down, but not d.; 2Co 4.09
the earthly tent we live in is d., 5.01
those who shrink back and are d., Heb 10.39
will be d. in the same destruction 2Pe 2.12
afterward d. those who did not Jud 1.05
irrational animals do, they are d. 1.10
and a third of the ships were d. Rev 8.09

DESTROYER
not allow the d. to enter your Ex 12.23
prosperity the d. will come upon Job 15.21
be a refuge to them from the d. Is 16.04
plunders, and the d. destroys. 21.02
Woe to you, d., who yourself have 33.01
a d. of nations has set out; Jer 4.07
suddenly the d. will come upon us. 6.26
of young men a d. at noonday; 15.08
The d. shall come upon every city, 48.08
The d. of Moab and his cities has 48.15
For the d. of Moab has come up 48.18
and your vintage the d. has fallen. 48.32
the spirit of a d. against Babylon, 51.01
for a d. has come upon her, upon 51.56
the d., and the cutter, my great Joe 2.25
did and were destroyed by the D. 1Co 10.10
so that the D. of the first-born Heb 11.28

DESTROYERS
Your builders outstrip your d., Is 49.17
heights in the desert d. have come; Jer 12.12
appoint over them four kinds of d., 15.03
I will prepare d. against you, each 22.07
for the d. shall come against them 51.48
yet d. would come from me upon her, 51.53
for destroying the d. of the earth." Rev 11.18

DESTROYEST
so thou d. the hope of man. Job 14.19
Thou d. those who speak lies; Ps 5.06

DESTROYING
d. every city, men, women, and children. Deu 3.06
those who hate him, by d. them; 7.10
d. it utterly, all who are in it and 13.15
bringing ruin upon you and d. you; 28.63
d. both young man and virgin, the 32.25
who were in it, utterly d. them; Jos 11.11
utterly d. them, as Moses the 11.12
done to all lands, d. them utterly. 2Ki 19.11
of the LORD d. throughout all the 1Ch 21.12
and he said to the d. angel, 21.15
d. them utterly, and when they had 2Ch 20.23
and d. them, and did as they pleased Est 9.05
distress, a company of d. angels. Ps 78.49
turn away his wrath from d. them. 106.23
a d. tempest, like a storm of mighty, Is 28.02
done to all lands, d. them utterly. 37.11
For the LORD is d. the Philistines, Jer 47.04
O d. mountain, says the LORD, which 51.25
he restrained not his hand from d.; Lam 2.08
each with his d. weapon in his hand." Eze 9.01
d. lives to get dishonest gain. 22.27
left, the d. locust has eaten. Joe 1.04
Father after d. every rule and 1Co 15.24
building you up and not for d. you, 2Co 10.08
and for d. the destroyers of the Rev 11.18

DESTROYS
comes to the one company and d. it, Gen 32.08
and d. it, he shall let the slave go Ex 21.26
he d. both the blameless and the Job 9.22
and he d. them: he enlarges nations, 12.23
the complacence of fools d. them; Pro 1.32
sense; he who does it d. himself. 6.32

DESTROYS (cont.)

crookedness of the treacherous d. them.	Pro 11.03
work is a brother to him who d.	18.09
is the companion of a man who d.	28.24
war, but one sinner d. much good.	Ecc 9.18
plunders, and the destroyer d.	Is 21.02
which d. the whole earth; I will	Jer 51.25
uncleanness that d. with a grievous	Mic 2.10
no thief approaches and no moth d.	Lk 12.33
If any one d. God's temple, God will	1Co 3.17

DESTRUCTION

but in the end he shall come to d."	Num 24.20
and he also shall come to d."	24.24
be devoted to the LORD for d.;	Jos 6.17
from the things devoted to d.,	6.18
the camp of Israel a thing for d.,	6.18
they have become a thing for d.	7.12
best of the things devoted to d.,	1Sa 15.21
who was working d. among the	2Sa 24.16
the man whom I had devoted to d.,	1Ki 20.42
so as not to make a complete d.;	2Ch 12.12
strong he grew proud, to his d.	26.16
treasuries for the d. of the Jews.	Est 4.07
decree issued in Susa for their d.,	4.08
endure to see the d. of my kindred?"	8.06
shall not fear d. when it comes.	Job 5.21
At d. and famine you shall laugh,	5.22
Let their own eyes see their d.,	21.20
up against me their ways of d.	30.12
their heart is d., their throat	Ps 5.09
will look on the d. of the wicked.	37.34
All the day you are plotting d.	52.01
till the storms of d. pass by.	57.01
nor the d. that wastes at noonday.	91.06
they are doomed to d. for ever,	92.07
them, and delivered them from d.	107.20
is upright, but d. to evildoers.	Pro 10.29
the word brings d. on himself,	13.13
Pride goes before d., and a	16.18
who makes his door high seeks d.	17.19
Before d. a man's heart is haughty,	18.12
do not set your heart on his d.	19.18
D. is decreed, overflowing with	Is 10.22
anger will be directed to their d.	10.25
as d. from the Almighty it will	13.06
will sweep it with the broom of d.,	14.23
to Horonaim they raise a cry of d.;	15.05
and d. has ceased, and he who	16.04
me for the d. of the daughter of	22.04
them with d. and wiped out all	26.14
a decree of d. from the Lord GOD	28.22
the nations with the sieve of d.,	30.28
back my life from the pit of d.,	38.17
Jacob to utter d. and Israel to	43.28
with you?—devastation and d.,	51.19
desolation and d. are in their	59.07
devastation or d. within your	60.18
evil from the north, and great d.	Jer 4.06
out of the north, and great d.	6.01
violence and d. are heard within	6.07
destroy them with double d.!	17.18
cry out, I shout, "Violence and d.!"	20.08
Horonaim, 'Desolation and great d.!'	48.03
they have heard the cry of d.	48.05
is in the land, and great d.!	50.22
noise of great d. from the land of	51.54
because of the d. of the daughter	Lam 2.11
come upon us, devastation and d.;	3.47
because of the d. of the daughter	3.48
food in the d. of the daughter of	4.10
arrows for d., which I will loose	Eze 5.16
and he shall cause fearful d.,	Dan 8.24
D. to them, for they have rebelled	Hos 7.13
they made idols for their own d.	8.04
O Sheol, where is your d.?	13.14
and as d. from the Almighty it	Joe 1.15
who makes d. flash forth against	Amo 5.09
so that d. comes upon the fortress.	5.09
that destroys with a grievous d.	Mic 2.10
D. and violence are before me;	Hab 1.03
the d. of the beasts will terrify	2.17
that leads to d., and those who	Mt 7.13
the vessels of wrath made for d.,	Rom 9.22
to Satan for the d. of the flesh,	1Co 5.05
a clear omen to them of their d.,	Php 1.28
Their end is d., their god is the	3.19
then sudden d. will come upon	1Th 5.03
of eternal d. and exclusion from	2Th 1.09
that plunge men into ruin and d.	1Ti 6.09
bringing upon themselves swift d.	2Pe 2.01
and their d. has not been asleep.	2.03
destroyed in the same d. with them,	2.12
of judgment and d. of ungodly men.	3.07
and unstable twist to their own d.,	3.16

DESTRUCTIVE

will secretly bring in d. heresies,	2Pe 2.01

DETAIL

things we cannot now speak in d.	Heb 9.05

DETAILS

its pattern, exact in all its d.	2Ki 16.10

DETAIN

let us d. you, and prepare a kid for	Ju 13.15
"If you d. me, I will not eat of	13.16
But, to d. you no further, I beg you	Ac 24.04

DETAINED

d. before the LORD; his name	1Sa 21.07

DETERMINE

and he shall pay as the judges d.	Ex 21.22
let us d. among ourselves what is	Job 34.04
were going to d. his case more	Ac 23.15

DETERMINED

"I have d. to make an end of all	Gen 6.13
saw that she was d. to go with her,	Ru 1.18
then know that evil is d. by him.	1Sa 20.07
that it was d. by my father that	20.09
his father was d. to put David to	20.33
for evil is d. against our master	25.17
this has been d. from the day he	2Sa 13.32
not heard that I d. it long ago?	2Ki 19.25
that God has d. to destroy you,	2Ch 25.16
that evil was d. against him by	Est 7.07
Since his days are d., and the	Job 14.05
Who d. its measurements—surely you	38.05
not heard that I d. it long ago?	Is 37.26
The LORD d. to lay in ruins the	Lam 2.08
for what is d. shall be done.	Dan 11.36
because he was d. to go after	Hos 5.11
Son of man goes as it has been d.;	Lk 22.22
And the disciples d., every one	Ac 11.29
having d. allotted periods and the	17.26
he d. to return through Macedonia.	20.03
and has d. this in his heart, to	1Co 7.37
my liberty be d. by another man's	10.29

DETERMINES

He d. the number of the stars, he	Ps 147.04

DETEST

you shall utterly d. and abhor it;	Deu 7.26

DETESTABLE

and you have seen their d. things,	Deu 29.17
the carcasses of their d. idols,	Jer 16.18
with all your d. things and with	Eze 5.11
images and their d. things of it;	7.20
from it all its d. things and all	11.18
after their d. things and their	11.21

DETESTABLE (cont.)
Cast away the d. things your eyes Eze 20.07
cast away the d. things their eyes 20.08
go astray after their d. things? 20.30
their idols and their d. things, 37.23
and became d. like the thing they Hos 9.10
they are d., disobedient, unfit for Tit 1.16

DETESTED
with them, and they also d. me. Zec 11.08

DEUEL
from Gad, Eliasaph the son of D.; Num 1.14
sixth day Eliasaph the son of D., 7.42
offering of Eliasaph the son of D. 7.47
of Gad was Eliasaph the son of D. 10.20

DEVASTATE
And I will d. the land, so that your Lev 26.32

DEVASTATED
desolate places and your d. land— Is 49.19
and the peaceful folds are d., Jer 25.37

DEVASTATION
or three months of d. by your foes, 1Ch 21.12
—d. and destruction, famine and Is 51.19
d. or destruction within your 60.18
upon us, d. and destruction; Lam 3.47
and anguish, a day of ruin and d., Zep 1.15

DEVASTATIONS
they shall raise up the former d.; Is 61.04
the d. of many generations. 61.04

DEVASTATOR
O daughter of Babylon, you d.! Ps 137.08

DEVICES
He frustrates the d. of the crafty, Job 5.12
men in whose hands are evil d., Ps 26.10
the man who carries out evil d.! 37.07
way and be sated with their own d. Pro 1.31
but a man of evil d. he condemns. 12.02
but they have sought out many d. Ecc 7.29
devises wicked d. to ruin the poor Is 32.07
not good, following their own d.; 65.02
this people, the fruit of their d., Jer 6.19
vengeance, all their d. against me. Lam 3.60
O Lord, all their d. against me. 3.61

DEVIL
wilderness to be tempted by the d. Mt 4.01
Then the d. took him to the holy 4.05
Again, the d. took him to a very 4.08
Then the d. left him, and behold, 4.11
the enemy who sowed them is the d.; 13.39
prepared for the d. and his angels; 25.41
the wilderness, tempted by the d. Lk 4.02
The d. said to him, "If you are the 4.03
And the d. took him up, and showed 4.05
And when the d. had ended every 4.13
then the d. comes and takes away 8.12
the twelve, and one of you is a d.?" Ju 6.70
You are of your father the d., 8.44
when the d. had already put it into 13.02
all that were oppressed by the d., Ac 10.38
and said, "You son of the d., 13.10
and give no opportunity to the d. Eph 4.27
stand against the wiles of the d. 6.11
into the condemnation of the d.; 1Ti 3.06
reproach and the snare of the d. 3.07
escape from the snare of the d., 2Ti 2.26
power of death, that is, the d., Heb 2.14
Resist the d. and he will flee from Jas 4.07
adversary the d. prowls around 1Pe 5.08
He who commits sin is of the d.; 1Jn 3.08
for the d. has sinned from the 3.08
was to destroy the works of the d. 3.08
and who are the children of the d.: 3.10
Michael, contending with the d., Jud 1.09
Behold, the d. is about to throw Rev 2.10
who is called the D. and Satan, 12.09
for the d. has come down to you in 12.12
who is the D. and Satan, and bound 20.02
and the d. who had deceived them 20.10

DEVILISH
but is earthly, unspiritual, d. Jas 3.15

DEVIOUS
and who are d. in their ways. Pro 2.15
and put d. talk far from you. 4.24
but he who is d. in his ways 14.02

DEVISE
to d. artistic designs, to work in Ex 31.04
to d. artistic designs, to work in 35.32
if they d. mischief, they will not Ps 21.11
confounded who d. evil against me! 35.04
Nay, in your hearts you d. wrongs; 58.02
in the heart of those who d. evil, Pro 12.20
Do they not err that d. evil? 14.22
Those who d. good meet loyalty and 14.22
for their minds d. violence, 24.02
are the men who d. iniquity and Eze 11.02
and you will d. an evil scheme 38.10
He shall d. plans against strongholds, Dan 11.24
yet they d. evil against me. Hos 7.15
Woe to those who d. wickedness and Mic 2.01
let none of you d. evil against Zec 7.10
do not d. evil in your hearts 8.17

DEVISED
which he had d. of his own heart; 1Ki 12.33
which he had d. against the Jews. Est 8.03
the letters d. by Haman the 8.05
which he had d. against the Jews 9.25
in the schemes which they have d. Ps 10.02
has d. evil against you, saying, Is 7.05
it was against me they d. schemes, Jer 11.19
for plots shall be d. against him. Dan 11.25
remember what Balak king of Moab d., Mic 6.05
You have d. shame to your house by Hab 2.10
follow cleverly d. myths when we 2Pe 1.16

DEVISES
life of him who d. means not to 2Sa 14.14
with perverted heart d. evil, Pro 6.14
a heart that d. wicked plans, feet 6.18
he d. wicked devices to ruin the Is 32.07
But he who is noble d. noble things, 32.08

DEVISING
The d. of folly is sin, and the Pro 24.09
or if you have been d. evil, 30.32
against you and d. a plan against Jer 18.11
against this family I am d. evil, Mic 2.03

DEVOID
worldly people, d. of the Spirit. Jud 1.19

DEVOTE
children to d. them by fire to Lev 18.21
and shall d. their gain to the Lord, Mic 4.13
But we will d. ourselves to prayer Ac 6.04
that you may d. yourselves to 1Co 7.05
d. yourself to them, so that all may 1Ti 4.15

DEVOTED
Lord, as a field that has been d.; Lev 27.21
"But no d. thing that a man devotes 27.28
every d. thing is most holy to the 27.28
No one d., who is to be utterly 27.29
Every d. thing in Israel shall be Num 18.14
None of the d. things shall cleave Deu 13.17

DEVOTED (cont.)

it shall be d. to the LORD for Jos 6.17
from the things d. to destruction, 6.18
when you have d. them you take any 6.18
of the d. things and make the camp 6.18
faith in regard to the d. things; 7.01
took some of the d. things; and the 7.01
have taken some of the d. things; 7.11
you destroy the d. things from 7.12
"There are d. things in the midst 7.13
take away the d. things from among 7.13
taken with the d. things shall be 7.15
in the matter of the d. things, 22.20
of the things d. to destruction, 1Sa 15.21
man whom I had d. to destruction, 1Ki 20.42
in the matter of the d. thing; 1Ch 2.07
and every d. thing in Israel shall Eze 44.29
or he will be d. to the one and Mt 6.24
or he will be d. to the one and Lk 16.13
with one accord d. themselves to Ac 1.14
And they d. themselves to the 2.42
and they have d. themselves to the 1Co 16.15
and d. herself to doing good in 1Ti 5.10

DEVOTES

thing that a man d. to the LORD, Lev 27.28

DEVOTION

because of my d. to the house of 1Ch 29.03
I remember the d. of your youth, Jer 2.02
your undivided d. to the Lord. 1Co 7.35
a sincere and pure d. to Christ. 2Co 11.03
rigor of d. and self-abasement and Col 2.23

DEVOUR

and my sword shall d. flesh— Deu 32.42
the bramble and d. the cedars of Ju 9.15
and d. the citizens of Shechem, and 9.20
from Bethmillo, and d. Abimelech." 9.20
Joab, "Shall the sword d. for ever? 2Sa 2.26
command the locust to d. the land, 2Ch 7.13
fire not blown upon will d. him; Job 20.26
You love all words that d., Ps 52.04
that greedily d. the sons of men; 57.04
to d. the poor from off the earth, Pro 30.14
very presence aliens d. your land; Is 1.07
on the west d. Israel with open 9.12
and they d. on the left, but are not 9.20
will burn and d. his thorns and 10.17
a sword, not of man, shall d. him; 31.08
come to d.—all you beasts in the 56.09
wood, and the fire shall d. them. Jer 5.14
They come and d. the land and all 8.16
beasts; bring them to d. 12.09
of the earth to d. and destroy. 15.03
and it shall d. the palaces of 17.27
and it shall d. all that is round 21.14
Therefore all who d. you shall be 30.16
The sword shall d. and be sated, 46.10
the sword shall d. round about you.' 46.14
and it shall d. the palaces of 49.27
and it will d. all that is round 50.32
the city famine and pestilence d. Eze 7.15
and it shall d. every green tree in 20.47
the beasts of the land d. them; 34.28
desolate, they are given us to d.' 35.12
'You d. men, and you bereave your 36.13
shall no longer d. men and no 36.14
it was told, 'Arise, d. much flesh.' Dan 7.05
and it shall d. the whole earth, and 7.23
beasts of the field shall d. them. Hos 2.12
new moon shall d. them with their 5.07
an oven, and they d. their rulers. 7.07
Aliens d. his strength, and he knows 7.09
were to yield, aliens would d. it. 8.07
and it shall d. his strongholds. 8.14
and d. them in their fortresses. 11.06
there I will d. them like a lion, 13.08
and it shall d. the strongholds of Amo 1.04
and it shall d. her strongholds. 1.07
and it shall d. her strongholds." 1.10
and it shall d. the strongholds of 1.12
and it shall d. her strongholds, 1.14
and it shall d. the strongholds of 2.02
and it shall d. the strongholds of 2.05
and it d., with none to quench it 5.06
the sword shall d. your young Nah 2.13
There will the fire d. you, 3.15
It will d. you like the locust. 3.15
they fly like an eagle swift to d. Hab 1.08
as if to d. the poor in secret. 3.14
and they shall d. and tread down Zec 9.15
that the fire may d. your cedars! 11.01
that are left d. the flesh of one 11.09
and they shall d. to the right and 12.06
for you d. widows' houses and for *Mt 23.14
who d. widows' houses and for a Mk 12.40
who d. widows' houses and for a Lk 20.47
But if you bite and d. one another Gal 5.15
lion, seeking some one to d. 1Pe 5.08
that he might d. her child when she Rev 12.04
and d. her flesh and burn her up 17.16

DEVOURED

say that a wild beast has d. him, Gen 37.20
a wild beast has d. him; Joseph is 37.33
presence of the LORD and d. them, Lev 10.02
It d. Ar of Moab, the lords of the Num 21.28
when the fire d. two hundred and 26.10
from them, and they will be d.; Deu 31.17
and d. with burning heat and 32.24
and the forest d. more people that 2Sa 18.08
which d. them, and frogs, which Ps 78.45
Fire d. their young men, and their 78.63
For they have d. Jacob, and laid 79.07
which d. all the vegetation in 105.35
you shall be d. by the sword; Is 1.20
"It is you who have d. the vineyard, 3.14
its hedge, and it shall be d.; 5.05
your own sword d. your prophets Jer 2.30
thing has d. all for which our 3.24
for they have d. Jacob; they have d. him 10.25
Therefore all who devour you shall be d., 30.16
All who found them have d. them, 50.07
First the king of Assyria d. him, 50.17
"Nebuchadnezzar the king of Babylon d. me, 51.34
you sacrificed to them to be d. Eze 16.20
catch prey; he d. men. 19.03
catch prey; he d. men. 19.06
they have d. human lives; 22.25
your survivors shall be d. by fire. 23.25
I will give to the beasts to be d.; 33.27
and to the wild beasts to be d. 39.04
it d. and broke in pieces, and Dan 7.07
and which d. and broke in pieces, 7.19
For fire has d. the pastures of the Joe 1.19
and fire has d. the pastures of the 1.20
and your olive trees the locust d.; Amo 4.09
and it d. the great deep and was 7.04
your foes; fire has d. your bars. Nah 3.13
sea, and she shall be d. by fire. Zec 9.04
and the birds came and d. them. Mt 13.04
path, and the birds came and d. it. Mk 4.04
and the birds of the air d. it. Lk 8.05
who has d. your living with harlots, 15.30

DEVOURER

I will rebuke the d. for you, Mal 3.11

DEVOURING

wolf, in the morning d. the prey, Gen 49.27
LORD was like a d. fire on the top Ex 24.17
For the LORD your God is a d. fire, Deu 4.24
before you as a d. fire is the 9.03
and d. fire from his mouth; 2Sa 22.09

DEVOURING (cont.)
and d. fire from his mouth; Ps 18.08
silence, before him as a d. fire, 50.03
tempest, and the flame of a d. fire. Is 29.06
and his tongue is like a d. fire; 30.27
anger and a flame of d. fire, 30.30
us can dwell with the d. fire? 33.14
of a flame of fire d. the stubble, Joe 2.05

DEVOURS
is a land that d. its inhabitants; Num 13.32
not lie down till it d. the prey, 23.24
d. the earth and its increase, and Deu 32.22
for the sword d. now one and now 2Sa 11.25
mouth of the wicked d. iniquity. Pro 19.28
dwelling, but a foolish man d. it. 21.20
the tongue of fire d. the stubble, Is 5.24
each d. his neighbor's flesh, 9.20
Therefore a curse d. the earth, 24.06
of the LORD d. from one end of the Jer 12.12
Fire d. before them, and behind them Joe 2.03
but d. the flesh of the fat ones, Zec 11.16

DEVOUT
d. men are taken away, while no one Is 57.01
and this man was righteous and d., Lk 2.25
d. men from every nation under Ac 2.05
D. men buried Stephen, and made 8.02
a d. man who feared God with all 10.02
servants and a d. soldier from 10.07
many Jews and d. converts to 13.43
incited the d. women of high 13.50
many of the d. Greeks and not a 17.04
with the Jews and the d. persons, 17.17
a d. man according to the law, well 22.12

DEW
May God give you of the d. of heaven, Gen 27.28
away from the d. of heaven on high. 27.39
in the morning d. lay round about Ex 16.13
And when the d. had gone up, there 16.14
When the d. fell upon the camp in Num 11.09
rain, my speech distil as the d., Deu 32.02
yea, his heavens drop down d. 33.28
if there is d. on the fleece alone, Ju 6.37
he wrung enough d. from the fleece 6.38
on all the ground let there be d." 6.39
and on all the ground there was d. 6.40
let there be no d. or rain upon 2Sa 1.21
upon him as the d. falls on the 17.12
be neither d. nor rain these years, 1Ki 17.01
with the d. all night on my branches, Job 29.19
who has begotten the drops of d.? 38.28
morning like d. your youth will Ps 110.03
It is like the d. of Hermon, which 133.03
and the clouds drop down the d. Pro 3.20
favor is like d. upon the grass. 19.12
for my head is wet with d., Sol 5.02
like a cloud of d. in the heat of Is 18.04
For thy d. is a d. of light, and on 26.19
him be wet with the d. of heaven; Dan 4.15
him be wet with the d. of heaven; 4.23
shall be wet with the d. of heaven, 4.25
wet with the d. of heaven till his 4.33
body was wet with the d. of heaven, 5.21
like the d. that goes early away. Hos 6.04
or like the d. that goes early 13.03
I will be as the d. to Israel; 14.05
many peoples like d. from the LORD, Mic 5.07
above you have withheld the d., Hag 1.10
the heavens shall give their d.; Zec 8.12

DIADEM
and a d. of beauty, to the remnant Is 28.05
and a royal d. in the hand of your 62.03

DIADEMS
horns, and seven d. upon his heads. Rev 12.03
with ten d. upon its horns and a 13.01
fire, and on his head are many d.; 19.12

DIAL
sun had declined on the d. of Ahaz. 2Ki 20.11
sun on the d. of Ahaz turn back on the d. Is 38.08

DIAMOND
an emerald, a sapphire, and a d.; Ex 28.18
an emerald, a sapphire, and a d.; 39.11
with a point of d. it is engraved Jer 17.01

DIBLAIM
and took Gomer the daughter of D., Hos 1.03

DIBON
as far as D., and we laid waste Num 21.30
"Ataroth, D., Jazer, Nimrah, Heshbon, 32.03
And the sons of Gad built D., 32.34
tableland of Medeba as far as D.: Jos 13.09
D., and Bamothbaal, and Bethbaalmeon, 13.17
and in D. and its villages, and in Neh 11.25
The daughter of D. has gone up to Is 15.02
For the waters of D. are full of 15.09
yet I will bring upon D. even more, 15.09
parched ground, O inhabitant of D.! Jer 48.18
and D., and Nebo, and Bethdiblathaim, 48.22

DIBONGAD
out from Iyim, and encampted at D. Num 33.45
And they set out from D., 33.46

DIBRI
was Shelomith, the daughter of D., Lev 24.11

DISCIPLINED
By mere words a servant is not d., Pro 29.19

DICTATED
"He d. all these words to me, while Jer 36.18

DICTATION
a scroll at the d. of Jeremiah all Jer 36.04
which you have written at my d. 36.06
these words? Was it at his d.?" 36.17
Baruch wrote at Jeremiah's d., 36.27
on it at the d. of Jeremiah all 36.32
in a book at the d. of Jeremiah, 45.01

DIE
that you eat of it you shall d." Gen 2.17
shall you touch it, lest you d.'" 3.03
said to the woman, "You will not d. 3.04
that is on the earth shall d. 6.17
the disaster overtake me, and I d. 19.19
her, know that you shall surely d., 20.07
Esau said, "I am about to d.; 25.32
thought, 'Lest I d. because of her.'" 26.09
that I may bless you before I d." 27.04
you before the LORD before I d.' 27.07
"Give me children, or I shall d.!" 30.01
one day, all the flocks will d. 33.13
up"—for he feared that he would d." 38.11
that we may live, and not d." 42.02
be verified, and you shall not d." 42.20
go, that we may live and not d., 43.08
let him d., and we also will be my 44.09
his father, his father would d.' 44.22
the lad is not with us, he will d.; 44.31
I will go and see him before I d." 45.28
"Now let me d., since I have seen 46.30
why should we d. before your eyes? 47.15
Why should we d. before your eyes, 47.19
that we may live, and not d., and that 47.19
time drew near that Israel must d., 47.29
I am about to d., but God will be 48.21

DIE (cont.)
swear, saying, 'I am about to d.: Gen 50.05
to his brothers, "I am about to d.; 50.24
and the fish in the Nile shall d., Ex 7.18
nothing shall d. of all that 9.04
brought home, and they shall d."'" 9.19
day you see my face you shall d." 10.28
in the land of Egypt shall d., 11.05
us away to d. in the wilderness? 14.11
Egyptians than to d. in the wilderness." 14.12
not God speak to us, lest we d." 20.19
him from my altar, that he may d. 21.14
man does not d. but keeps his bed, 21.18
and when he comes out, lest he d. 28.35
bring guilt upon themselves and d. 28.43
wash with water, lest they d. 30.20
lest they d.: it shall be a statute 30.21
the LORD has charged, lest you d.; Lev 8.35
lest you d., and lest wrath come 10.06
the tent of meeting, lest you d.; 10.07
the tent of meeting, lest you d.; 10.09
lest they d. in their uncleanness 15.31
which is upon the ark, lest he d.; 16.02
is upon the testimony, lest he d.; 16.13
their sin, they shall d. childless. 20.20
sin for it and d. thereby when 22.09
the holy things, lest they d. Num 4.15
live and not d. when they come 4.19
even for a moment, lest they d." 4.20
if they d., shall he make himself 6.07
full end, and there they shall d." 14.35
If these men d. the common death of 16.29
murmurings against me, lest they d." 17.10
tabernacle of the LORD, shall d. 17.13
the altar, lest they, and you, d. 18.03
meeting, lest they bear sin and d. 18.22
the people of Israel, lest you d.'" 18.32
wilderness, that we should d. here, 20.04
to his people, and shall d. there." 20.26
out of Egypt to d. in the wilderness? 21.05
Let me d. the death of the righteous, 23.10
Notwithstanding, the sons of Korah did not d. 26.11
"They shall d. in the wilderness." 26.65
manslayer may not d. until he 35.12
in the hand, by which a man may d., 35.17
in the hand, by which a man may d., 35.18
a stone, by which a man may d., 35.23
For I must d. in this land, I must Deu 4.22
Now therefore why should we d.? 5.25
LORD our God any more, we shall d. 5.25
he that is to d. shall be put to 17.06
or the judge, that man shall d.; 17.12
great fire any more, lest I d.' 18.16
gods, that same prophet shall d.' 18.20
the man did not deserve to d., 19.06
of blood, so that he may d. 19.12
lest he d. in the battle and 20.05
lest he d. in the battle and 20.06
lest he d. in the battle and 20.07
another man, both of them shall d., 22.22
the man who lay with her shall d. 22.25
him, then that thief shall d.; 24.07
the days approach when you must d.; 31.14
and d. on the mountain which you 32.50
"Let Reuben live, and not d.; 33.06
he might not d. by the hand of the Jos 20.09
do not fear, you shall not d." Ju 6.23
that he may d., for he has pulled 6.30
to his wife, "We shall surely d., 13.22
and shall I now d. of thirst, 15.18
"Let me d. with the Philistines." 16.30
where you d. I will d., and there Ru 1.17
house shall d. by the sword of men. 1Sa 2.33
of them shall d. on the same day. 2.34
the men who did not d. were stricken 5.12
LORD your God, that we may not d.; 12.19
Jonathan my son, he shall surely d." 14.39
here I am, I will d." 14.43
you shall surely d., Jonathan." 14.44
said to Saul, "Shall Jonathan d., 14.45
ransomed Jonathan, that he did not d. 14.45
You shall not d. Behold, my 1Sa 20.02
of the LORD, that I may not d.; 20.14
him to me, for he shall surely d." 20.31
the king said, "You shall surely d., 22.16
or his day shall come to d.; 26.10
the LORD lives, you deserve to d., 26.16
"Should Abner d. as a fool dies? 2Sa 3.33
that he may be struck down, and d." 11.15
who has done this deserves to d.; 12.05
your sin; you shall not d. 12.13
child that is born to you shall d." 12.14
We must all d., we are like water 14.14
If half of us d., they will not 18.03
said to Shimei, "You shall not d." 19.23
that I may d. in my own city, near 19.37
is found in him, he shall d." 1Ki 1.52
When David's time to d. drew near, 2.01
but he said, "No, I will d. here." 2.30
know for certain that you shall d.; 2.37
any place whatever, you shall d.'? 2.42
"When I d., bury me in the grave in 13.31
enter the city, the child shall d. 14.12
my son, that we may eat it, and d." 17.12
and he asked that he might d., 19.04
have gone, but you shall surely d.'" 2Ki 1.04
you have gone, but shall surely d.'" 1.06
have gone, but you shall surely d.'" 1.16
"Why do we sit here till we d.? 7.03
in the city, and we shall d. there; 7.04
and if we sit here, we d. also. So 7.04
and if they kill us we shall but d." 7.04
me that he shall certainly d." 8.10
the illness of which he was to d., 13.14
every man shall d. for his own sin." 14.06
that you may live, and not d. 18.32
for you shall d., you shall not 20.01
every man shall d. for his own sin." 2Ch 25.04
you over to d. by famine and by 32.11
integrity? Curse God, and d." Job 2.09
"Why did I not d. at birth, come 3.11
do they not d., and that without 4.21
and wisdom will d. with you. 12.02
for then I would be silent and d. 13.19
and its stump d. in the ground, 14.08
If a man d., shall he live again? 14.14
till I d. I will not put away my 27.05
'I shall d. in my nest, and I shall 29.18
In a moment they d.; at midnight 34.20
sword, and d. without knowledge. 36.12
They d. in youth, and their life 36.14
"When will he d., and his name Ps 41.05
he shall see that even the wise d., 49.10
power preserve those doomed to d.! 79.11
you shall d. like men, and fall like 82.07
free those who were doomed to d.; 102.20
they d. and return to their dust. 104.29
blood, and caused their fish to d. 105.29
I shall not d., but I shall live, 118.17
but fools d. for lack of sense. Pro 10.21
but he who pursues evil will d. 11.19
he who hates reproof will d. 15.10
he who despises the word will d. 19.16
him with a rod, he will not d. 23.13
deny them not to me before I d.: 30.07
a time to be born, and a time to d.; Ecc 3.02
why should you d. before your time? 7.17
For the living know that they will d., 9.05
eat and drink, for tomorrow we d." Is 22.13
not be forgiven you till you d., 22.14
there you shall d., and there 22.18
for you shall d., you shall not 38.01
lack of water, and d. of thirst. 50.02
who dwell in it will d. like gnats; 51.06

DIE (cont.)
he shall not d. and go down to the Is 51.14
the child shall d. a hundred years 65.20
for their worm shall not d., 66.24
or you will d. by our hand"— Jer 11.21
young men shall d. by the sword; 11.22
their daughters shall d. by famine; 11.22
They shall d. of deadly diseases. 16.04
and small shall d. in this land; 16.06
and there you shall d., and there 20.06
they shall d. of a great pestilence. 21.06
in this city shall d. by the sword, 21.09
him captive, there shall he d., 22.12
not born, and there you shall d. 22.26
hold of him, saying, "You shall d.! 26.08
and your people d. by the sword, 27.13
This very year you shall d., 28.16
But every one shall d. for his own 31.30
'You shall not d. by the sword. 34.04
You shall d. in peace. And as 34.05
the secretary, lest I d. there." 37.20
in this city shall d. by the sword, 38.02
and he will d. there of hunger, for 38.09
these words and you shall not d. 38.24
the house of Jonathan to d. there.'" 38.26
to Egypt; and there you shall d. 42.16
live there shall d. by the sword, 42.17
that you shall d. by the sword, 42.22
they shall d. by the sword and by 44.12
the wicked, 'You shall surely d.,' Eze 3.18
wicked man shall d. in his iniquity; 3.18
he shall d. in his iniquity; 3.19
block before him, he shall d.; 3.20
he shall d. for his sin, and his 3.20
of you shall d. of pestilence and 5.12
is far off shall d. of pestilence; 6.12
is preserved shall d. of famine. 6.12
see it; and he shall d. there. 12.13
who should not d. and keeping 13.19
he broke, in Babylon he shall d. 17.16
mine: the soul that sins shall d. 18.04
he shall surely d.; his blood 18.13
he shall not d. for his father's 18.17
he shall d. for his iniquity. 18.18
The soul that sins shall d. 18.20
surely live; he shall not d. 18.21
sin he has committed, he shall d. 18.24
iniquity, he shall d. for it; 18.26
which he has committed he shall d. 18.26
shall surely live, he shall not d. 18.28
Why will you d., O house of Israel? 18.31
and you shall d. the death of the 28.08
You shall d. the death of the 28.10
O wicked man, you shall surely d., 33.08
man shall d. is his iniquity, but 33.08
he shall d. in his iniquity, but you 33.09
for why will you d., O house 33.11
that he has committed he shall d. 33.13
the wicked, "You shall surely d.," 33.14
shall surely live, he shall not d. 33.15
iniquity, he shall d. for it. 33.18
in caves shall d. by pestilence. 33.27
and Moab shall d. amid uproar, Amo 2.02
remain in one house, they shall d. 6.09
'Jeroboam shall d. by the sword, 7.11
yourself shall d. in an unclean 7.17
of my people shall d. by the sword, 9.10
better for me to d. than to live." Jon 4.03
and he asked that he might d., 4.08
better for me to d. than to live." 4.08
to be angry, angry enough to d." 4.09
We shall not d. O LORD, Hab 1.12
What is to d., let it d.; Zec 11.09
or mother, let him surely d.' Mt 15.04
to him, "Even if I must d. with you, 26.35
or mother, let him surely d.'; Mk 7.10
where their worm does not d. and * 9.44
where their worm does not d. and * 9.46
where their worm does not d., 9.48
"If I must d. with you, I will not 14.31
for they cannot d. any more, Lk 20.36
a man may eat of it and not d. Jn 6.50
will seek me and d. in your sin; 8.21
you that you would d. in your sins, 8.24
for you will d. in your sins unless 8.24
also go, that we may d. with him." 11.16
though he d., yet shall he live, 11.25
and believes in me shall never d. 11.26
one man should d. for the people, 11.50
Jesus should d. for the nation, 11.51
to show by what death he was to d. 12.33
one man should d. for the people. 18.14
to show by what death he was to d. 18.32
and by that law he ought to d., 19.07
that this disciple was not to d.; 21.23
say to him that he was not to d., 21.23
but even to d. at Jerusalem for Ac 21.13
anything for which I deserve to d., 25.11
who do such things deserve to d., Rom 1.32
Why, one will hardly d. for a 5.07
good man one will dare even to d. 5.07
from the dead will never d. again; 6.09
according to the flesh you will d., 8.13
and if we d., we d. to the Lord; 14.08
whether we live or whether we d., 14.08
I would rather d. than have any 1Co 9.15
For as in Adam all d., so also 15.22
Jesus our Lord, I d. every day! 15.31
eat and drink, for tomorrow we d." 15.32
to d. together and to live together. 2Co 7.03
live is Christ, and to d. is gain. Php 1.21
it is appointed for men to d. once, Heb 9.27
that we might d. to sin and live to 1Pe 2.24
they will long to d., and death Rev 9.06
the dead who d. in the Lord 14.13

DIED
thirty years; and he d. Gen 5.05
twelve years; and he d. 5.08
five years; and he d. 5.11
ten years; and he d. 5.14
ninety-five years; and he d. 5.17
sixty-two years; and he d. 5.20
sixty-nine years; and he d. 5.27
seventy-seven years; and he d. 5.31
And all flesh d. that moved upon 7.21
nostrils was the breath of life d. 7.22
fifty years; and he d. 9.29
Haran d. before his father Terah in 11.28
five years: and Terah d. in Haran. 11.32
And Sarah d. at Kiriatharba (that 23.02
his last and d. in a good old age, 25.08
he breathed his last and d., 25.17
d., and she was buried under an oak 35.08
her soul was departing (for she d.), 35.18
So Rachel d., and she was buried on 35.19
and he d. and was gathered to his 35.29
Bela d., and Jobab the son of Zerah 36.33
Jobab d., and Husham of the land of 36.34
Husham d., and Hadad the son of 36.35
Hadad d., and Samlah of Masrekah 36.36
Samlah d., and Shaul of Rehoboth on 36.37
Shaul d., and Baalhanan the son of 36.38
Baalhanan the son of Achbor d., 36.39
wife of Judah, Shua's daughter, d.; 38.12
(but Er and Onan d. in the land of 46.12
to my sorrow d. in the land of 48.07
gave this command before he d., 50.16
So Joseph d., being a hundred and 50.26
Then Joseph d., and all his brothers, Ex 1.06
many days the king of Egypt d. 2.23
And the fish in the Nile d.; 7.21
the frogs d. out of the houses and 8.13
all the cattle of the Egyptians d., 9.06

DIED (cont.)

of the people of Israel not one d. Ex 9.06
that we had d. by the hand of the 16.03
and they d. before the LORD. Lev 10.02
drew near before the LORD and d.; 16.01
But Nadab and Abihu d. before the Num 3.04
that we had d. in the land of 14.02
that we had d. in this wilderness! 14.02
d. by plague before the LORD. 14.37
Now those who d. by the plague were 16.49
those who d. in the affair of Korah. 16.49
the body of any man who has d., 19.13
and Miriam d. there, and was buried 20.01
that we had d. when our brethren d. 20.03
and Aaron d. there on the top of 20.28
so that many people of Israel d. 21.06
Nevertheless those that d. by the 25.09
with Korah, when that company d., 26.10
and Er and Onan d. in the land of 26.19
But Nadab and Abihu d. when they 26.61
"Our father d. in the wilderness; 27.03
but d. for his own sin; and he had 27.03
and d. there, in the fortieth year 33.38
years old when he d. on Mount Hor. 33.39
so that he d., he is a murderer; 35.16
and he d., he is a murderer; 35.17
and he d., he is a murderer; 35.18
him, lying in wait, so that he d., 35.20
so that he d., then he who struck 35.21
so that he d., though he was not 35.23
There Aaron d., and there he was Deu 10.06
your brother d. in Mount Hor and 32.50
of the LORD d. there in the land 34.05
and twenty years old when he d.; 34.07
had d. on the way in the wilderness Jos 5.04
them as far as Azekah, and they d.; 10.11
there were more who d. because of 10.11
d., being a hundred and ten years 24.29
And Eleazar the son of Aaron d.; 24.33
him to Jerusalem, and he d. there. Ju 1.07
d. at the age of one hundred and 2.08
But whenever the judge d., they turned 2.19
that Joshua left when he d., 2.21
Then Othniel the son of Kenaz d. 3.11
sight of the LORD, after Ehud d. 4.01
weariness. So he d. 4.21
son of Joash d. in a good old age, 8.32
As soon as Gideon d., the people 8.33
of the Tower of Shechem also d., 9.49
man thrust him through, and he d. 9.54
Then he d., and was buried at 10.02
And Jair d., and was buried in 10.05
Then Jephthah the Gileadite d., 12.07
Then Ibzan d., and was buried at 12.10
Then Elon the Zebulunite d., 12.12
son of Hillel the Pirathonite d., 12.15
d., and she was left with her two Ru 1.03
and both Mahlon and Chilion d., 1.05
and his neck was broken and he d., 1Sa 4.18
Now Samuel d.; and all 25.01
and his heart d. within him, and he 25.37
smote Nabal; and he d. 25.38
Now Samuel had d., and all Israel 28.03
upon his sword, and d. with him. 31.05
Thus Saul d., and his three sons, 31.06
And he smote him so that he d. 2Sa 1.15
he fell there, and d. where he was. 2.23
had fallen and d., stood still. 2.23
so that he d., for the blood of 3.27
heard that Abner had d. at Hebron, 4.01
and he d. there beside the ark of 6.07
After this the king of the Ammonites d., 10.01
of their army, so that he d. there. 10.18
the wall, so that he d. at Thebez? 11.21
On the seventh day the child d. 12.18
but when the child d., 12.21
and he d., and was buried in the 17.23
Would I had d. instead of you, O 18.33
and he d. Then Joab and 20.10
and there d. of the people from Dan 24.15
and he struck him down, and he d. 1Ki 2.25
out and struck him down, and he d. 2.46
And this woman's son d. in the night, 3.19
threshold of the house, the child d. 14.17
house over him with fire, and d., 16.18
so Tibni d., and Omri became king. 16.22
Syrians, until at evening he d.; 22.35
So the king d., and was brought to 22.37
So he d. according to the word of 2Ki 1.17
But when Ahab d., the king of Moab 3.05
her lap till noon, and then he d. 4.20
so that he d., as the man of God 7.17
upon him in the gate and he d. 7.20
it over his face, till he d. 8.15
he fled to Megiddo, and d. there. 9.27
who struck him down, so that he d. 12.21
So Elisha d., and they buried him. 13.20
When Hazael king of Syria d., 13.24
and he came to Egypt, and d. there. 23.34
When Bela d., Jobab the son of 1Ch 1.44
When Jobab d., Husham of the land 1.45
When Husham d., Hadad the son of 1.46
When Hadad d., Samlah of Masrekah 1.47
When Samlah d., Shaul of Rehoboth 1.48
When Shaul d., Baalhanan, the son of 1.49
When Baalhanan d., Hadad reigned in 1.50
And Hadad d. The chiefs of 1.51
When Azubah d., Caleb married 2.19
Appaim; and Seled d. childless. 2.30
Jonathan; and Jether d. childless. 2.32
also fell upon his sword, and d. 10.05
Thus Saul d.; he and his 10.06
sons and all his house d. together. 10.06
So Saul d. for his unfaithfulness; 10.13
and he d. there before God. 13.10
the king of the Ammonites d., 19.01
Eleazar d. having no sons, but only 23.22
But Nadab and Abihu d. before their 24.02
Then he d. in a good old age, full 29.28
and the LORD smote him, and he d. 2Ch 13.20
evening; then at sunset he d. 18.34
disease, and he d. in great agony. 21.19
grew old and full of days, and d.; 24.15
So he d.; and they buried 24.25
And he d., and was buried in the 35.24
when her father and her mother d., Est 2.07
that I had d. before any eye had Job 10.18
And Job d., an old man, and full of 42.17
King Uzziah d. I saw the Lord Is 6.01
that king Ahaz d. came this oracle: 14.28
month, the prophet Hananiah d. Jer 28.17
eaten what d. of itself or was Eze 4.14
Pelatiah the son of Benaiah d. 11.13
morning, and at evening my wife d. 24.18
that has d. of itself or is torn. 44.31
incurred guilt through Baal and d. Hos 13.01
But when Herod d., behold, an angel Mt 2.19
saying, "My daughter has just d.; 9.18
and d., and having no children left 22.25
After them all, the woman d. 22.27
and when he d. left no children; Mk 12.20
and d., leaving no children; 12.21
Last of all the woman also d. 12.22
a man who had d. was being carried Lk 7.12
The poor man d. and was carried by 16.22
rich man also d. and was buried; 16.22
a wife, and d. without children; 20.29
all seven left no children and d. 20.31
Afterward the woman also d. 20.32
in the wilderness, and they d. Jn 6.49
not such as the fathers ate and d.; 6.58
Abraham d., as did the prophets; 8.52
than our father Abraham, who d.? 8.53
And the prophets d.! Who do you 8.53

DIED (cont.)
here, my brother would not have d. Jn 11.21
here, my brother would not have d." 11.32
that he both d. and was buried, Ac 2.29
these words, he fell down and d. 5.05
Immediately she fell down at his feet and d. 5.10
And after his father d., God 7.04
And he d., himself and our fathers, 7.15
In those days she fell sick and d.; 9.37
and he was eaten by worms and d. 12.23
time Christ d. for the ungodly. Rom 5.06
were yet sinners Christ d. for us. 5.08
For if many d. through one man's 5.15
How can we who d. to sin still live 6.02
For he who has d. is freed from sin. 6.07
But if we have d. with Christ, we 6.08
The death he d. he d. to sin, once 6.10
you have d. to the law through the 7.04
commandment came, sin revived and I d.; 7.09
who d., yes, who was raised from the 8.34
this end Christ d. and lived again, 14.09
the ruin of one for whom Christ d. 14.15
the brother for whom Christ d. 1Co 8.11
are weak and ill, and some have d. 11.30
that Christ d. for our sins in 15.03
convinced that one has d. for all; 2Co 5.14
all; therefore all have d. 5.14
And he d. for all, that those who 5.15
for their sake d. and was raised. 5.15
For I through the law d. to the law, Gal 2.19
law, then Christ d. to no purpose. 2.21
for he nearly d. for the work of Php 2.30
If with Christ you d. to the Col 2.20
For you have d., and your life is 3.03
that Jesus d. and rose again, 1Th 4.14
who d. for us so that whether we 5.10
If we have d. with him, we shall 2Ti 2.11
he d., but through his faith he is Heb 11.04
These all d. in faith, not having 11.13
For Christ also d. for sins once 1Pe 3.18
I d., and behold I am alive for Rev 1.18
who d. and came to life. 2.08
the living creatures in the sea d., 8.09
and many men d. of the water, 8.11
living thing d. that was in the 16.03

DIES
that he may bless you before he d." Gen 27.10
man so that he d. shall be put to Ex 21.12
and the slave d. under his hand, 21.20
so that it d., then they shall sell 21.35
in, and is struck so that he d., 22.02
and it d. or is hurt or is driven 22.10
his neighbor, and it is hurt or d., 22.14
fat of an animal that d. of itself, Lev 7.24
any animal of which you may eat d., 11.39
that eats what d. of itself or 17.15
That which d. of itself or is torn 22.08
"And if any man d. very suddenly Num 6.09
is the law when a man d. in a tent: 19.14
'If a man d., and has no son, then 27.08
not eat anything that d. of itself; Deu 14.21
his neighbor so that he d.— 19.05
wounds him mortally so that he d., 19.11
house, or if the latter husband d., 24.03
and one of them d. and has no son, 25.05
"Should Abner die as a fool d.? 2Sa 3.33
to Jeroboam who d. in the city the 1Ki 14.11
and any one who d. in the open 14.11
to Baasha who d. in the city the 16.04
who d. in the field the birds of the 16.04
to Ahab who d. in the city the 21.24
who d. in the open country the birds 21.24
But man d., and is laid low; Job 14.10
One d. in full prosperity, being 21.23
Another d. in bitterness of soul, 21.25
For when he d. he will carry Ps 49.17
He d. for lack of discipline, and Pro 5.23
When the wicked d., his hope 11.07
the wise man d. just like the fool! Ecc 2.16
as one d., so d. the other. 3.19
that you are afraid of man who d., Is 51.12
he who eats their eggs d., 59.05
out of the cistern before he d." Jer 38.10
is in the field d. by the sword; Eze 7.15
'If a man d., having no children, Mt 22.24
a man's brother d. and leaves a Mk 12.19
for us that if a man's brother d., Lk 20.28
"Sir, come down before my child d." Jn 4.49
wheat falls into the earth and d., 12.24
but if it d., it bears much fruit. 12.24
if her husband d. she is discharged Rom 7.02
if her husband d. she is free from 7.03
and none of us d. to himself. 14.07
If the husband d., she is free 1Co 7.39
does not come to life unless it d. 15.36
law of Moses d. without mercy at Heb 10.28

DIFFER
Having gifts that d. according to Rom 12.06

DIFFERENCE
they taught the d. between the Eze 22.26
my people the d. between the holy 44.23
(what they were makes no d. to me; Gal 2.06

DIFFERENT
your cattle breed with a d. kind; Lev 19.19
he has a d. spirit and has followed Num 14.24
go limping with two d. opinions? 1Ki 18.21
goblets of d. kinds, and the royal Est 1.07
their laws are d. from those of 3.08
servants he will call by a d. name. Is 65.15
So you were d. from other women in Eze 16.34
given to you; therefore you were d. 16.34
out of the sea, d. from one another. Dan 7.03
It was d. from all the beasts that 7.07
which was d. from all the rest, 7.19
which shall be d. from all the 7.23
he shall be d. from the former ones, 7.24
For who sees anything d. in you? 1Co 4.07
doubtless many d. languages in the 14.10
you receive a d. spirit from the 2Co 11.04
if you accept a d. gospel from the 11.04
of Christ and turning to a d. gospel— Gal 1.06
not to teach any d. doctrine, 1Ti 1.03

DIFFERS
for star d. from star in glory. 1Co 15.41

DIFFICULT
your towns which is too d. for you, Deu 17.08
The thing that the king asks is d., Dan 2.11
and that no mystery is d. for you, 4.09

DIFFICULTIES
who create dissensions and d., Rom 16.17

DIFFICULTY
and arrived with d. off Cnidus, Ac 27.07
Coasting along it with d., 27.08
we managed with d. to secure the 27.16

DIG
of whose hills you can d. copper. Deu 8.09
you shall d. a hole with it, and 23.13
and d. for it more than for hid Job 3.21
In the dark they d. through houses; 24.16
to me, "Son of man, d. in the wall"; Eze 8.08
D. through the wall in their sight, 12.05
he shall d. through the wall and go 12.12
"Though they d. into Sheol, from Amo 9.02
till I d. about it and put on Lk 13.08
I am not strong enough to d., and I am 16.03

DIGGED
He d. it and cleared it of stones, Is 5.02
the quarry from which you were d. 51.01

DIGGING
d. it out, and falls into the hole Ps 7.15

DIGNIFIED
d., hospitable, an apt teacher, 1Ti 3.02

DIGNITY
"What honor or d. has been bestowed Est 6.03
"Deck yourself with majesty and d.; Job 40.10
Strength and d. are her clothing, Pro 31.25
justice and d. proceed from Hab 1.07

DIGS
or when a man d. a pit and does not Ex 21.33
He who d. a pit will fall into it, Pro 26.27
He who d. a pit will fall into it; Ecc 10.08

DIKLAH
Hadoram, Uzal, D., Gen 10.27
Hadoram, Uzal, D., 1Ch 1.21

DILEAN
D., Mizpeh, Joktheel, Jos 15.38

DILIGENCE
let it be done with all d." Ez 6.12
did with all d. what Darius the 6.13
you shall with all d. buy bulls, 7.17
of you, be it done with all d., 7.21

DILIGENT
but the hand of the d. makes rich. Pro 10.04
The hand of the d. will rule, 12.24
but the d. man will get precious 12.27
the soul of the d. is richly 13.04
loves him is d. to discipline him. 13.24
The plans of the d. lead surely to 21.05

DILIGENTLY
"If you will d. hearken to the Ex 15.26
Now Moses d. inquired about the Lev 10.16
"Only take heed, and keep your soul d., Deu 4.09
teach them d. to your children, and 6.07
You shall d. keep the commandments 6.17
inquire and make search and ask d.; 13.14
then you shall inquire d., and if it 17.04
the judges shall inquire d., and if the 19.18
work goes on d. and prospers in Ez 5.08
commanded thy precepts to be kept d. Ps 119.04
will seek me d. but will not find Pro 1.28
and those who seek me d. find me. 8.17
He who d. seeks good seeks favor, 11.27
let him listen d., very d." Is 21.07
Hearken d. to me, and eat what is 55.02
if they will d. learn the ways of Jer 12.16
are upon what is evil, to do it d.; Mic 7.03
if you will d. obey the voice of Zec 6.15
"Go and search d. for the child, Mt 2.08
house and seek d. until she finds Lk 15.08

DILL
surface, does he not scatter d., Is 28.25
D. is not threshed with a threshing 28.27
but d. is beaten out with a stick, 28.27
you tithe mint and d. and cummin, Mt 23.23

DIM
his eyes were d. so that he could Gen 27.01
eyes of Israel were d. with age, 48.10
diseased spot is d. and the disease Lev 13.06
but is d., then the priest shall 13.21
but is d., the priest shall shut 13.26
but is d., it is a swelling from 13.28
the disease is d. after it is 13.56
his eye was not d., nor his Deu 34.07
eyesight had begun to grow d., 1Sa 3.02
his eyes were d. because of his 1Ki 14.04
My eye has grown d. from grief, Job 17.07
My eyes grow d. with waiting for my Ps 69.03
my eye grows d. through sorrow. 88.09
How the gold has grown d., Lam 4.01
things our eyes have grown d., 5.17

DIMENSIONS
"These are the d. of the altar by Eze 43.13
and these shall be its d.: 48.16

DIMINISH
he shall not d. her food, her Ex 21.10
are few you shall d. the price, Lev 25.16
of Egypt's Nile will d. and dry up, Is 19.06

DIMINISHED
When they are d. and brought low Ps 107.39
and d. your allotted portion, and Eze 16.27

DIMLY
and a d. burning wick he will not Is 42.03
For now we see in a mirror d., 1Co 13.12

DIMMED
look through the windows are d., Ecc 12.03

DIMNAH
D. with its pasture lands, Nahalal Jos 21.35

DIMONAH
Kinah, D., Adadah, Jos 15.22

DINAH
a daughter, and called her name D. Gen 30.21
Now D. the daughter of Leah, whom 34.01
was drawn to D. the daughter of 34.03
he had defiled his daughter D.; 34.05
he had defiled their sister D. 34.13
and took D. out of Shechem's house, 34.26
together with his daughter D.; 46.15

DINAH'S
D. brothers, took their swords and Gen 34.25

DINE
the men are to d. with me at noon." Gen 43.16
Pharisee asked him to d. with him; Lk 11.37
when he went to d. at the house of 14.01

DINED
of his life he d. regularly at the 2Ki 25.29
of his life he d. regularly at the Jer 52.33

DINHABAH
the name of his city being D. Gen 36.32
the name of whose city was D. 1Ch 1.43

DINNER
this day to a d. that I have Est 5.04
came to the d. that Esther had 5.05
tomorrow to the d. which I will 5.08
go merrily with the king to the d." 5.14
Better is a d. of herbs where love Pro 15.17
Behold, I have made ready my d., Mt 22.04
he did not first wash before d. Lk 11.38
"When you give a d. or a banquet, 14.12
invites you to d. and you are 1Co 10.27

DIONYSIUS
among them D. the Areopagite and a Ac 17.34

DIOTREPHES
but D., who likes to put himself 3Jn 1.09

DIP
of hyssop and d. it in the blood Ex 12.22
priest shall d. his finger in the Lev 4.06

DIP (cont.)
priest shall d. his finger in the Lev 4.17
and d. them and the living bird in 14.06
and d. his right finger in the oil 14.16
and d. them in the blood of the 14.51
and d. it in the water. and sprinkle Num 19.18
and let him d. his foot in oil. Deu 33.24
and d. your morsel in the wine." Ru 2.14
or to d. up water out of the Is 30.14
lions, and do not d. it in water." Jer 13.01
send Lazarus to d. the end of his Lk 16.24

DIPHATH
Gomer: Ashkenaz, D., and Togarmah. 1Ch 1.06

DIPPED
and d. the robe in the blood; Gen 37.31
and he d. his finger in the blood Lev 9.09
the ark were d. in the brink of Jos 3.15
and d. it in the honeycomb, and put 1Sa 14.27
went down and d. himself seven 2Ki 5.14
coverlet and d. it in water and 8.15
"He who has d. his hand in the dish Mt 26.23
give this morsel when I have d. it." Ju 13.26
So when he had d. the morsel, he gave 13.26
He is clad in a robe d. in blood, Rev 19.13

DIPPING
one who is d. bread in the same Mk 14.20

DIRECT
according to all that they d. you; Deu 17.10
the Levitical priests shall d. you; 24.08
and d. your heart to the LORD, and 1Sa 7.03
to go by sea to the place you d., 1Ki 5.09
should d. the music, for he understood 1Ch 15.22
and d. their hearts toward thee. 29.18
D. thy steps to the perpetual ruins Ps 74.03
Therefore I d. my steps by all thy 119.128
and d. your mind in the way. Pro 23.19
"How well you d. your course to Jer 2.33
in man who walks to d. his steps. 10.23
And I will d. my indignation Eze 23.25
He will d. the shock of his battering 26.09
we made a d. voyage to Samothrace, Ac 16.11
our Lord Jesus, d. our way to you; 1Th 3.11
May the Lord d. your hearts to the 2Th 3.05

DIRECTED
him as the LORD d. through Moses. Num 27.23
of Gihon and d. them down to the 2Ch 32.30
and d. all who did work in every 34.13
He has not d. his words against me, Job 32.14
anger will be d. to their destruction. Is 10.25
Who has d. the Spirit of the LORD, 40.13
and left where your edge is d. Eze 21.16
went and did as Jesus had d. them; Mt 21.06
disciples did as Jesus had d. them, 26.19
potter's field, as the LORD d. me." 27.10
the money and did as they were d.; 28.15
mountain to which Jesus had d. them. 28.16
and he d. that something should be Lk 8.55
And Peter d. his gaze at him, with Ac 3.04
spoke to Moses d. him to make it, 7.44
was d. by a holy angel to send for 10.22
as I d. the churches of Galatia, so 1Co 16.01
elders in every town as I d. you, Tit 1.05

DIRECTION
in the d. of Gerar, as far as Gaza, Gen 10.19
and in the d. of Sodom, Gomorrah, 10.19
Mesha in the d. of Sephar to the 10.30
land of Egypt in the d. of Zoar; 13.10
opposite Egypt in the d. of Assyria; 25.18
under the d. of Ithamar the son of Ex 38.21
under the d. of Ithamar the son of Num 7.08
wilderness in the d. of the Red Sea.' Deu 1.40
wilderness in the d. of the Red Sea, 2.01
and went in the d. of the wilderness 2.08
thy steps, receiving d. from thee, 33.03
and fled in the d. of the wilderness. Jos 8.15
and did not ask d. from the LORD. 9.14
and in the d. of Bethjeshimoth, to 12.03
along southward in the d. of Luz, 18.13
Then the boundary goes in another d., 18.14
in a northerly d. going on to 18.17
in the other d. eastward toward 19.12
coming from the d. of the Diviners' Ju 9.37
Israel in the d. of the wilderness; 20.42
straight in the d. of Bethshemesh 1Sa 6.12
Ahab went in one d. by himself, 1Ki 18.06
Obadiah went in another d. by himself. 18.06
water came from the d. of Edom, 2Ki 3.20
he fled in the d. of Bethhaggan. 9.27
they went in the d. of the Arabah. 25.04
under the d. of Asaph, who prophesied 1Ch 25.02
prophesied under the d. of the king. 25.02
under the d. of their father 25.03
all under the d. of their father 25.06
LORD under the d. of the Levitical 2Ch 23.18
under the d. of Hananiah, one of the 26.11
wander about each in his own d.; Is 47.15
and the priests rule at their d.; Jer 5.31
they went in the d. of the Arabah. 52.07
eyes now in the d. of the north." Eze 8.05
came from the d. of the upper gate, 9.02
but in whatever d. the front wheel 10.11

DIRECTIONS
following the d. of David king of 2Ch 35.04
Israel and the d. of Solomon his 35.04
according to the d. of David king Ez 3.10
of their four d. without turning Eze 1.17
of their four d. without turning 10.11
things I will give d. when I come. 1Co 11.34
and gave d. concerning his burial. Heb 11.22

DIRECTLY
Let your eyes look d. forward, Pro 4.25

DIRECTS
his way, but the LORD d. his steps. Pro 16.09
wherever the will of the pilot d. Jas 3.04

DIRGE
and each to her neighbor a d. Jer 9.20

DIRT
his belly; and the d. came out. Ju 3.22
flesh is clothed with worms and d.; Job 7.05
and its waters toss up mire and d. Is 57.20
gold like the d. of the streets. Zec 9.03
as a removal of d. from the body 1Pe 3.21

DISABLED
Animals blind or d. or mutilated or Lev 22.22

DISAGREED
So, as they d. among themselves, they Ac 28.25

DISAPPEAR
In time of heat they d.; when it is Job 6.17
The fortress will d. from Ephraim, Is 17.03

DISAPPOINT
and hope does not d. us, Rom 5.05

DISAPPOINTED
They are d. because they were Job 6.20
Behold, the hope of a man is d.; 41.09
thee they trusted, and were not d. Ps 22.05

DISAPPROVAL
expresses d. to her on the day Num 30.05
he expresses d., then he shall make 30.08

DISARMED
He d. the principalities and powers Col 2.15

DISASTER
lest the d. overtake me, and I die. Gen 19.19
not know that d. was close upon Ju 20.34
they saw that d. was close upon 20.41
When d. brings sudden death, he Job 9.23
hand, and in his d. cry for help? 30.24
and d. the workers of iniquity? 31.03
for d. from them will rise suddenly, Pro 24.22
And yet he is wise and brings d., Is 31.02
d. shall fall upon you, which you 47.11
D. follows hard on d., the Jer 4.20
the day of d., thou knowest; 17.16
the LORD GOD: D. after d.! Eze 7.05
D. comes upon d., rumor 7.26
his d. in the day of his calamity; Ob 1.13
"I will remove d. from you, Zep 3.18
but a little they furthered the d. Zec 1.15

DISASTERS
will hiss because of all its d. Jer 19.08
will hiss because of all its d. 49.17

DISBELIEVED
And while they still d. for joy, Lk 24.41
but when some were stubborn and d., Ac 19.09
by what he said, while others d. 28.24

DISCARDED
which King Ahaz d. in his reign 2Ch 29.19

DISCERN
they would d. their latter end! Deu 32.29
angel of God to d. good and evil. 2Sa 14.17
can I d. what is pleasant and what 19.35
that I may d. between good and evil; 1Ki 3.09
understanding to d. what is right, 3.11
but I could not d. its appearance. Job 4.16
Cannot my taste d. calamity? 6.30
that you may d. the paths to its 38.20
But who can d. his errors? Ps 19.12
of a prudent man is to d. his way, Pro 14.08
They know not, nor do they d.; Is 44.18

DISCERNED
because they are spiritually d. 1Co 2.14

DISCERNEST
thou d. my thoughts from afar. Ps 139.02

DISCERNING
I give you a wise and d. mind, 1Ki 3.12
of their d. men shall be hid." Is 29.14
whoever is d., let him know them; Hos 14.09
drinks without d. the body eats 1Co 11.29
and d. the thoughts and intentions Heb 4.12

DISCERNMENT
takes away the d. of the elders. Job 12.20
The wise of heart is called a man of d., Pro 16.21
For this is a people without d.; Is 27.11
and the d. of their discerning men 29.14
is there knowledge or d. to say, 44.19
more, with knowledge and all d., Php 1.09

DISCHARGE
man has a d. from his body, his d. Lev 15.02
law of his uncleanness for a d.: 15.03
whether his body runs with his d., 15.03
or his body is stopped from d., 15.03
he who has the d. lies shall be 15.04
he who has the d. has sat shall 15.06
him who has the d. shall wash his 15.07
he who has the d. spits on one who 15.08
he who has the d. rides shall be 15.09
he that has the d. touches without 15.11
he who has the d. touches shall be 15.12
he who has a d. is cleansed of his d., 15.13
for him before the LORD for his d. 15.15
"When a woman has a d. of blood 15.19
which is her regular d. from her body, 15.19
"If a woman has a d. of blood for 15.25
or if she has a d. beyond the time 15.25
the days of the d. she shall continue 15.25
she lies, all the days of her d., 15.26
But if she is cleansed of her d., 15.28
before the LORD for her unclean d. 15.30
him who has a d. and for him who 15.32
who has a d.. and for the man who 15.33
or suffers a d. may eat of the 22.04
or having a d. or an itch or scabs, 22.22
leper, and every one having a d., Num 5.02
never be without one who has a d., 2Sa 3.29
there is no d. from war, nor will Ecc 8.08

DISCHARGED
Then Amaziah d. the army that had 2Ch 25.10
dies she is d. from the law Rom 7.02
But now we are d. from the law, dead 7.06

DISCIPLE
"A d. is not above his teacher, nor Mt 10.24
enough for the d. to be like his 10.25
of cold water because he is a d., 10.42
Joseph, who also was a d. of Jesus. 27.57
A d. is not above his teacher, but Lk 6.40
his own life, he cannot be my d. 14.26
and come after me, cannot be my d. 14.27
all that he has cannot be my d. 14.33
"You are his d., but we are disciples Jn 9.28
Jesus, and so did another d. 18.15
As this d. was known to the high 18.15
So the other d., who was known to 18.16
and the d. whom he loved standing 19.26
Then he said to the d., "Behold 19.27
that hour the d. took her to his 19.27
who was a d. of Jesus, but secretly, 19.38
to Simon Peter and the other d., 20.02
Peter then came out with the other d., 20.03
but the other d. outran Peter and 20.04
Then the other d., who reached the 20.08
That d. whom Jesus loved said to 21.07
them the d. whom Jesus loved, who 21.20
that this d. was not to die; 21.23
This is the d. who is bearing 21.24
Now there was a d. at Damascus Ac 9.10
did not believe that he was a d. 9.26
was at Joppa a d. named Tabitha, 9.36
A d. was there, named Timothy, the 16.01
an early d., with whom we should 21.16

DISCIPLES
seal the teaching among my d. Is 8.16
he sat down his d. came to him. Mt 5.01
Another of the d. said to him, "Lord, 8.21
into the boat, his d. followed him. 8.23
and sat down with Jesus and his d. 9.10
saw this, they said to his d., 9.11
Then the d. of John came to him, 9.14
fast, but your d. do not fast?" 9.14
rose and followed him, with his d. 9.19
Then he said to his d., "The harvest 9.37
him his twelve d. and gave them 10.01
finished instructing his twelve d., 11.01
of the Christ, he sent word by his d. 11.02
his d. were hungry, and they began 12.01
your d. are doing what is not 12.02
stretching out his hand toward his d., 12.49
Then the d. came and said to him, 13.10
And his d. came to him, saying, 13.36
And his d. came and took the body 14.12
the d. came to him and said, "This 14.15
and gave the loaves to the d., and the d. 14.19
Then he made the d. get into the 14.22
But when the d. saw him walking on 14.26

DISCIPLES (cont.)
"Why do your d. transgress the Mt 15.02
Then the d. came and said to him, 15.12
And his d. came and begged him, 15.23
called his d. to him and said, "I 15.32
And the d. said to him, "Where are 15.33
broke them and gave them to the d., 15.36
and the d. gave them to the crowds. 15.36
When the d. reached the other side, 16.05
he asked his d., "Who do men say 16.13
charged the d. to tell no one that 16.20
to show his d. that he must go to 16.21
Then Jesus told his d., 16.24
When the d. heard this, they fell on 17.06
And the d. asked him, "Then why do 17.10
Then the d. understood that he was 17.13
And I brought him to your d., 17.16
Then the d. came to Jesus privately 17.19
At that time the d. came to Jesus, 18.01
The d. said to him, "If such is the 19.10
The d. rebuked the people; 19.13
And Jesus said to his d., "Truly, 19.23
When the d. heard this they were 19.25
he took the twelve d. aside, 20.17
of Olives, then Jesus sent two d., 21.01
The d. went and did as Jesus had 21.06
When the d. saw it they marveled, 21.20
And they sent their d. to him, 22.16
Jesus to the crowds and to his d., 23.01
when his d. came to point out to 24.01
the d. came to him privately, saying, 24.03
these sayings, he said to his d., 26.01
But when the d. saw it, they were 26.08
Unleavened Bread the d. came to Jesus, 26.17
passover at your house with my d.'" 26.18
And the d. did as Jesus had directed 26.19
he sat at table with the twelve d.; 26.20
it, and gave it to the d. and said, 26.26
deny you." And so said all the d. 26.35
Gethsemane, and he said to his d., 26.36
And he came to the d. and found 26.40
Then he came to the d. and said to 26.45
Then all the d. forsook him and 26.56
lest his d. go and steal him away, 27.64
and tell his d. that he has risen 28.07
great joy, and ran to tell his d. 28.08
'His d. came by night and stole him 28.13
Now the eleven d. went to Galilee, 28.16
therefore and make d. of all nations, 28.19
were sitting with Jesus and his d.; Mk 2.15
said to his d., "Why does he eat 2.16
Now John's d. and the Pharisees were 2.18
"Why do John's d. and the d. of the 2.18
Pharisees fast, but your d. do not fast?" 2.18
their way his d. began to pluck 2.23
Jesus withdrew with his d. to the sea, 3.07
And he told his d. to have a boat 3.09
to his own d. he explained everything. 4.34
And his d. said to him, "You see the 5.31
country; and his d. followed him. 6.01
When his d. heard of it, they came 6.29
his d. came to him and said, "This 6.35
them to the d. to set before the 6.41
Immediately he made his d. get into 6.45
some of his d. ate with hands 7.02
"Why do your d. not live according 7.05
his d. asked him about the parable. 7.17
he called his d. to him, and said to 8.01
And his d. answered him, "How can 8.04
them to his d. to set before the 8.06
he got into the boat with his d., 8.10
And Jesus went on with his d., 8.27
he asked his d., "Who do men say 8.27
But turning and seeing his d., 8.33
to him the multitude with his d., 8.34
And when they came to the d., 9.14
and I asked your d. to cast it out, 9.18
his d. asked him privately, "Why 9.28
for he was teaching his d., 9.31
the house the d. asked him again 10.10
touch them; and the d. rebuked them. 10.13
looked around and said to his d., 10.23
And the d. were amazed at his words. 10.24
with his d. and a great multitude, 10.46
of Olives, he sent two of his d., 11.01
you again." And his d. heard it. 11.14
And he called his d. to him, 12.43
one of his d. said to him, "Look, 13.01
his d. said to him, "Where will you 14.12
And he sent two of his d., 14.13
am to eat the passover with my d.?' 14.14
And the d. set out and went to the 14.16
and he said to his d., 14.32
tell his d. and Peter that he is 16.07
scribes murmured against his d., Lk 5.30
"The d. of John fast often and 5.33
and so do the d. of the Pharisees, 5.33
his d. plucked and ate some ears of 6.01
he called his d., and chose from 6.13
crowd of his d. and a great 6.17
And he lifted up his eyes on his d., 6.20
and his d. and a great crowd went 7.11
The d. of John told him of all 7.18
John, calling to him two of his d., 7.19
And when his d. asked him what this 8.09
day he got into a boat with his d., 8.22
And he said to his d., "Make them 9.14
them to the d. to set before the 9.16
praying alone the d. were with him; 9.18
And I begged your d. to cast it out, 9.40
everything he did, he said to his d., 9.43
And when his d. James and John saw 9.54
Then turning to the d. he said 10.23
one of his d. said to him, "Lord, 11.01
us to pray, as John taught his d." 11.01
he began to say to his d. first, 12.01
And he said to his d., "Therefore I 12.22
He also said to the d., "There was 16.01
And he said to his d., "Temptations 17.01
And he said to the d., "The days are 17.22
and when the d. saw it, they rebuked 18.15
Olivet, he sent two of the d., 19.29
multitude of the d. began to 19.37
to him, "Teacher, rebuke your d." 19.39
all the people he said to his d., 20.45
am to eat the passover with my d.?' 22.11
of Olives; and the d. followed him. 22.39
he came to the d. and found them 22.45
was standing with two of his d.; Jn 1.35
The two d. heard him say this, and 1.37
to the marriage, with his d. 2.02
and his d. believed in him. 2.11
mother and his brothers and his d.; 2.12
His d. remembered that it was 2.17
his d. remembered that he had said 2.22
Jesus and his d. went into the 3.22
between John's d. and a Jew over 3.25
and baptizing more d. than John 4.01
did not baptize, but only his d.), 4.02
For his d. had gone away into the 4.08
Just then his d. came. They marveled 4.27
Meanwhile the d. besought him, 4.31
So the d. said to one another, "Has 4.33
and there sat down with his d. 6.03
One of his d., Andrew, Simon Peter's 6.08
he told his d., "Gather up the 6.12
his d. went down to the sea, 6.16
not entered the boat with his d., 6.22
but that his d. had gone away alone. 6.22
nor his d., they themselves got 6.24
Many of his d., when they heard it, 6.60
himself that his d. murmured at it, 6.61
many of his d. drew back and no 6.66
that your d. may see the works you 7.03

DISCIPLES (cont.)
in my word, you are truly my d., Jn 8.31
And his d. asked him, "Rabbi, who 9.02
Do you too want to become his d.?" 9.27
disciple, but we are d. of Moses. 9.28
Then after this he said to the d., 11.07
The d. said to him, "Rabbi, the Jews 11.08
The d. said to him, "Lord, if he has 11.12
the Twin, said to his fellow d., 11.16
and there he stayed with the d. 11.54
one of his d. (he who was to betray 12.04
His d. did not understand this at 12.16
The d. looked at one another, 13.22
One of his d., whom Jesus loved, was 13.23
men will know that you are my d., 13.35
fruit, and so prove to be my d. 15.08
Some of his d. said to one another, 16.17
His d. said, "Ah, now you are speaking 16.29
forth with his d. across the Kidron 18.01
garden, which he and his d. entered. 18.01
Jesus often met there with his d. 18.02
not you also one of this man's d.?" 18.17
Jesus about his d. and his teaching. 18.19
"Are not you also one of his d.?" 18.25
Then the d. went back to their 20.10
Mary Magdalene went and said to the d., 20.18
doors being shut where the d. were, 20.19
Then the d. were glad when they saw 20.20
So the other d. told him, "We have 20.25
his d. were again in the house, and 20.26
signs in the presence of the d., 20.30
again to the d. by the Sea of 21.01
two others of his d. were together. 21.02
yet the d. did not know that it was 21.04
But the other d. came in the boat, 21.08
now none of the d. dared ask him, 21.12
revealed to the d. after he was 21.14
days when the d. were increasing Ac 6.01
the body of the d. and said, 6.02
number of the d. multiplied 6.07
murder against the d. of the Lord, 9.01
he was with the d. at Damascus. 9.19
but his d. took him by night and 9.25
he attempted to join the d.; 9.26
the d., hearing that Peter was 9.38
in Antioch the d. were for the 11.26
And the d. determined, every one 11.29
And the d. were filled with joy and 13.52
But when the d. gathered about him, 14.20
to that city and had made many d., 14.21
strengthening the souls of the d., 14.22
remained no little time with the d. 14.28
the neck of the d. which neither 15.10
Phrygia, strengthening all the d. 18.23
and wrote to the d. to receive him. 18.27
Ephesus. There he found some d. 19.01
taking the d. with him, and argued 19.09
but the d. would not let him; 19.30
sent for the d. and having exhorted 20.01
to draw away the d. after them. 20.30
And having sought out the d., 21.04
And some of the d. from Caesarea 21.16

DISCIPLES'
and began to wash the d. feet, Jn 13.05

DISCIPLINE
"And if by this d. you are not Lev 26.23
his voice, that he might d. you; Deu 4.36
consider the d. of the LORD your 11.02
For you hate d., and you cast my Ps 50.17
the LORD's d. or be weary of his Pro 3.11
"How I hated d., and my heart 5.12
He dies for lack of d., and because 5.23
the reproofs of d. are the way of 6.23
Whoever loves d. loves knowledge, 12.01
loves him is diligent to d. him. 13.24
There is severe d. for him who 15.10
D. your son while there is hope; 19.18
but the rod of d. drives it far 22.15
Do not withhold d. from a child; 23.13
D. your son, and he will give you 29.17
their God, and did not accept d.; Jer 7.28
them up in the d. and instruction Eph 6.04
regard lightly the d. of the Lord, Heb 12.05
It is for d. that you have to 12.07
there whom his father does not d.? 12.07
If you are left without d., in which 12.08
fathers to d. us and we respected 12.09
For the moment all d. seems painful 12.11

DISCIPLINED
For they d. us for a short time at Heb 12.10

DISCIPLINES
as a man d. his son, the LORD your Deu 8.05
his son, the LORD your God d. you. 8.05
For the Lord d. him whom he loves, Heb 12.06
but he d. us for our good, that we 12.10

DISCLOSE
I not then send and d. it to you? 1Sa 20.12
if I do not d. it to you, and send 20.13
he fled, and did not d. it to me." 22.17
and do not d. another's secret; Pro 25.09
the earth will d. the blood shed Is 26.21
for the Day will d. it, because it 1Co 3.13
and will d. the purposes of the 4.05

DISCLOSED
And when it was d. to me that there Ac 23.30
but is now d. and through the Rom 16.26
the secrets of his heart are d.; 1Co 14.25

DISCLOSES
No one d. to me when my son makes a 1Sa 22.08
or d. to me that my son has stirred 22.08
he hears the curse, but d. nothing. Pro 29.24

DISCLOSING
great or small without d. it to me; 1Sa 20.02

DISCOMFITED
and d. the host of the Egyptians, Ex 14.24
"They are d., they answer no more; Job 32.15

DISCOMFORT
his head, to save him from his d. Jon 4.06

DISCONTENTED
in debt, and every one who was d., 1Sa 22.02

DISCORD
evil, continually sowing d.; Pro 6.14
a man who sows d. among brothers. 6.19
that there may be no d. in the body, 1Co 12.25

DISCOURAGE
Why will you d. the heart of the Num 32.07

DISCOURAGED
they d. the heart of the people of Num 32.09
upon him while he is weary and d., 2Sa 17.02
of the land d. the people of Judah, Ez 4.04
not fail or be d. till he has Is 42.04
your children, lest they become d. Col 3.21

DISCOURSE
And Balaam took up his d., Num 23.07
And Balaam took up his d., 23.18
and he took up his d., 24.03
And he took up his d., 24.15
on Amalek, and took up his d., 24.20
on the Kenite, and took up his d., 24.21
And he took up his d., 24.23

DISCOURSE (cont.)
again took up his d., and said: Job 27.01
again took up his d., and said: 29.01

DISCOVER
would not God d. this? For he knows Ps 44.21

DISCOVERED
Now Saul heard that David was d., 1Sa 22.06
wherever any need of repairs is d." 2Ki 12.05
and I then d. the evil that Eliashib Neh 13.07

DISCREDITED
that the word of God may not be d. Tit 2.05

DISCREET
Pharaoh select a man d. and wise, Gen 41.33
is none so d. and wise as you are; 41.39

DISCREETLY
than seven men who can answer d. Pro 26.16

DISCRETION
Blessed be your d., and blessed 1Sa 25.33
LORD grant you d. and understanding, 1Ch 22.12
endued with d. and understanding, 2Ch 2.12
us, they brought us a man of d., Ez 8.18
knowledge and d. to the youth— Pro 1.04
d. will watch over you; understanding 2.11
My son, keep sound wisdom and d.; 3.21
that you may keep d., and your 5.02
and I find knowledge and d. 8.12
is a beautiful woman without d. 11.22
foolishly, but a man of d. is patient. 14.17
with prudence and d. to Arioch, Dan 2.14

DISCUSS
why do you d. among yourselves the Mt 16.08
"Why do you d. the fact that you Mk 8.17

DISCUSSED
And they d. it among themselves, Mt 16.07
And they d. it with one another, Mk 8.16
way they had d. with one another 9.34
with fury and d. with one another Lk 6.11
And they d. it with one another, 20.05

DISCUSSING
them, "What are you d. with them?" Mk 9.16
them, "What were you d. on the way?" 9.33
While they were talking and d. together, Lk 24.15

DISCUSSION
Now a d. arose between John's Jn 3.25
have wandered away into vain d., 1Ti 1.06

DISDAINED
looked, and saw David, he d. him; 1Sa 17.42
But he d. to lay hands on Mordecai Est 3.06
I would have d. to set with the Job 30.01

DISEASE
into a leprous d. on the skin of Lev 13.02
white and the d. appears to be 13.03
skin of his body, it is a leprous d.; 13.03
in his eyes the d. is checked and 13.05
the d. has not spread in the skin, 13.05
is dim and the d. has not spread 13.06
pronounce him clean of the d.; 13.13
and if the d. has turned white, then 13.17
it is the d. of leprosy, it has 13.20
him unclean; it is a leprous d. 13.25
him unclean; it is a leprous d. 13.27
or woman has a d. on the head or 13.29
the priest shall examine the d.; 13.30
the priest examines the itching d., 13.31
person with the itching d. for seven 13.31
the priest shall examine the d.; 13.32
the itching d. for seven days more; 13.33
unclean; his d. is on his head. 13.44
who has the d. shall wear torn 13.45
unclean as long as he has the d.; 13.46
there is a leprous d. in a garment, 13.47
if the d. shows greenish or reddish 13.49
it is a leprous d. and shall be shown 13.49
And the priest shall examine the d., 13.50
that which has the d. for seven days; 13.50
examine the d. on the seventh day. 13.51
If the d. has spread in the garment, 13.51
the d. is a malignant leprosy; 13.51
and the d. has not spread in the 13.53
wash the thing in which is the d., 13.54
though the d. has not spread, it is 13.55
and the d. is dim after it is 13.56
with fire that in which is the d. 13.57
from which the d. departs when you 13.58
for a leprous d. in a garment of 13.59
if the leprous d. is healed in the 14.03
for him in whom is a leprous d., 14.32
I put a leprous d. in a house in 14.34
to be some sort of d. in my house.' 14.35
the priest goes to examine the d., 14.36
And he shall examine the d.; 14.37
and if the d. is in the walls of 14.37
and if the d. has spread in the 14.39
in which is the d. and throw them 14.40
"If the d. breaks out again in the 14.43
and if the d. has spread in the 14.44
and the d. has not spread in the 14.48
house clean, for the d. is healed. 14.48
for any leprous d.: for an itch, 14.54
or an itching d. or scabs or 21.20
his feet, and his d. became severe; 2Ch 16.12
yet even in his d. he did not seek 16.12
sickness with a d. of your bowels, 21.15
out because of the d., day by day.'" 21.15
in his bowels with an incurable d. 21.18
bowels came out because of the d., 21.19
By d. his skin is consumed, the Job 18.13
but sent a wasting d. among them. Ps 106.15
healing every d. and every infirmity Mt 4.23
healing every d. and every infirmity 9.35
to heal every d. and every infirmity 10.01
body that she was healed of her d. Mk 5.29
in peace, and be healed of your d." 5.34
was healed of whatever d. he had. *Jn 5.04

DISEASED
examine the d. spot on the skin of Lev 13.03
the hair in the d. spot has turned 13.03
shut up the d. person for seven 13.04
and if the d. spot is dim and the 13.06
the skin of the d. person from 13.12
pronounce the d. person clean; 13.17
him unclean; it is d. 13.22
forehead a reddish-white d. spot, 13.42
and if the d. swelling is reddish-white 13.43
whether d. in warp or woof, woolen 13.52
examine the d. thing after it has 13.55
And if the d. spot has not changed 13.55
his old age he was d. in his feet. 1Ki 15.23
his reign Asa was d. in his feet, 2Ch 16.12
which he did on those who were d. Jn 6.02

DISEASES
put none of the d. upon you which Ex 15.26
and none of the evil d. of Egypt, Deu 7.15
upon you again all the d. of Egypt, 28.60
iniquity, who heals all your d., Ps 103.03
the city, behold, the d. of famine! Jer 14.18
They shall die of deadly d. They shall 16.04
afflicted with various d. and pains, Mt 4.24
our infirmities and bore our d." 8.17
many who were sick with various d., Mk 1.34
all who had d. pressed upon him to 3.10

DISEASES (cont.)
with various d. brought them to Lk 4.40
him and to be healed of their d.; 6.17
cured many of d. and plagues and 7.21
over all demons and to cure d., 9.01
and d. left them and the evil Ac 19.12
island who had d. also came and 28.09

DISFIGURE
for they d. their faces that their Mt 6.16

DISFIGURED
as he has d. a man, he shall be d. Lev 24.20

DISFIGUREMENT
When a man causes a d. in his Lev 24.19

DISGRACE
for that would be a d. to us. Gen 34.14
and thus put d. upon all Israel." 1Sa 11.02
of distress, of rebuke, and of d.; 2Ki 19.03
that we may no longer suffer d." Neh 2.17
am filled with d. and look upon my Job 10.15
All day long my d. is before me, Ps 44.15
with scorn and d. may they be 71.13
for ever; let them perish in d. 83.17
inherit honor. but fools get d. Pro 3.35
and his d. will not be wiped away. 6.33
When pride comes, then comes d.; 11.02
Poverty and d. come to him who 13.18
and with dishonor comes d. 18.03
help nor profit, but shame and d." Is 30.05
of distress, of rebuke, and of d.; 37.03
because I bore the d. of my youth.' Jer 31.19
befallen us: behold, and see our d.! Lam 5.01
Bear your d., you also, for you have Eze 16.52
may bear your d. and be ashamed of 16.54
longer bear the d. of the peoples 36.15
suffer the d. of famine among the 36.30
things; d. will not overtake us." Mic 2.06

DISGRACED
because his father had d. him. 1Sa 20.34
to shame and d. who sought to do Ps 71.24
she has been shamed and d. And the Jer 15.09
and she who bore you shall be d. 50.12
the seers shall be d., and the Mic 3.07

DISGRACEFUL
but if it is d. for a woman to be 1Co 11.06
We have renounced d., underhanded 2Co 4.02

DISGRACEFULLY
wicked man acts shamefully and d. Pro 13.05

DISGUISE
and d. yourself, that it be not 1Ki 14.02
"I will d. myself and go into 22.30
"I will d. myself and go into 2Ch 18.29
servants also d. themselves as 2Co 11.15

DISGUISED
So Saul d. himself and put on other 1Sa 28.08
king of Israel d. himself and went 1Ki 22.30
And the king of Israel d. himself; 2Ch 18.29
but d. himself in order to fight 35.22

DISGUISES
will see me'; and he d. his face. Job 24.15
for even Satan d. himself as an 2Co 11.14

DISGUISING
d. himself with a bandage over his 1Ki 20.38
d. themselves as apostles of Christ. 2Co 11.13

DISGUST
I look at the faithless with d., Ps 119.158
them, she turned from them in d. Eze 23.17
I turned in d. from her, as I had 23.18
lovers from whom you turned in d. 23.22
those from whom you turned in d.; 23.28

DISH
one golden d. of ten shekels, full Num 7.14
one golden d. of ten shekels, full 7.20
one golden d. of ten shekels, full 7.26
one golden d. of ten shekels, full 7.32
one golden d. of ten shekels, full 7.38
one golden d. of ten shekels, full 7.44
one golden d. of ten shekels, full 7.50
one golden d. of ten shekels, full 7.56
one golden d. of ten shekels, full 7.62
one golden d. of ten shekels, full 7.68
one golden d. of ten shekels, full 7.74
one golden d. of ten shekels, full 7.80
wipe Jerusalem as one wipes a d., 2Ki 21.13
sluggard buries his hand in the d., Pro 19.24
sluggard buries his hand in the d.; 26.15
dipped his hand in the d. with me, Mt 26.23
dipping bread in the same d. with me. Mk 14.20
outside of the cup and of the d., Lk 11.39

DISHAN
Dishon, Ezer, and D.; these are Gen 36.21
These are the sons of D.: Uz and Aran. 36.28
Dishon, Ezer, and D.; these are 36.30
Zibeon, Anah, Dishon, Ezer, and D. 1Ch 1.38
The sons of D.: Uz and Aran. 1.42

DISHEARTENED
Because you have d. the righteous Eze 13.22
although I have not d. him, and you 13.22

DISHES
make its plates and d. for incense, Ex 25.29
its plates and d. for incense, and its 37.16
the d. for incense, the bowls, and Num 4.07
silver basins, twelve golden d., 7.84
the twelve golden d., full of incense, 7.86
the gold of the d. being a hundred 7.86
d. for incense, and firepans, of pure 1Ki 7.50
and the d. for incense and all the 2Ki 25.14
d. for incense, and firepans, of pure 2Ch 4.22
and d. for incense, and vessels of 24.14
and the d. for incense, and all the Jer 52.18
and the d. for incense, and the 52.19

DISHON
D., Ezer, and Dishan; these are Gen 36.21
D. and Oholibamah the daughter of Anah. 36.25
These are the sons of D.: Hemdan, 36.26
D., Ezer, and Dishan; these are 36.30
Anah, D., Ezer, and Dishan. 1Ch 1.38
The sons of Anah: D. The sons of 1.41
The sons of D.: Hamran, Eshban, Ithran, 1.41

DISHONEST
and heart only for your d. gain, Jer 22.17
together at the d. gain which you Eze 22.13
destroying lives to get d. gain. 22.27
commended the d. steward for his Lk 16.08
and he who is d. in a very little 16.10
a very little is d. also in much. 16.10

DISHONESTLY
all who act d., are an abomination Deu 25.16

DISHONOR
for us to witness the king's d., Ez 4.14
to shame and d. who seek after my Ps 35.04
with shame and d. who magnify 35.26
and brought to d. who desire my 40.14
thee be brought to d. through me, 69.06
reproach, and my shame and my d.; 69.19
and brought to d. who desire my 70.02
May my accusers be clothed with d.; 109.29
Wounds and d. will he get, and his Pro 6.33

DISHONOR (cont.)
and with d. comes disgrace. Pro 18.03
to d. all the honored of the earth. Is 23.09
instead of d. you shall rejoice in 61.07
our shame, and let our d. cover us; Jer 3.25
do not d. thy glorious throne; 14.21
Their eternal d. will never be 20.11
d. has covered our face, for aliens 51.51
the ground in d. the kingdom and Lam 2.02
I honor my Father, and you d. me. Jn 8.49
worthy to suffer d. for the name. Ac 5.41
do you d. God by breaking the law? Rom 2.23
It is sown in d., it is raised in 1Co 15.43
in honor and d., in ill repute and 2Co 6.08

DISHONORABLE
God gave them up to d. passions. Rom 1.26

DISHONORED
But you have d. the poor man. Jas 2.06

DISHONORING
to the d. of their bodies among Rom 1.24

DISHONORS
be he who d. his father or his Deu 27.16
with his head covered d. his head, 1Co 11.04
her head unveiled d. her head— 11.05

DISINHERIT
with the pestilence and d. them, Num 14.12

DISLIKED
the one loved and the other d., Deu 21.15
children, both the loved and the d., 21.15
first-born son is hers that is d., 21.15
in preference to the son of the d., 21.16
the first-born, the son of the d., 21.17
The poor is d. even by his neighbor, Pro 14.20

DISLIKES
latter husband d. her and writes Deu 24.03

DISMAL
do not look d., like the hypocrites, Mt 6.16

DISMAY
the righteous, but d. to evildoers. Pro 21.15
by them, lest I d. you before them. Jer 1.17
I mourn, and d. has taken hold on me. 8.21
drink water by measure and in d. Eze 4.16
and look at one another in d., 4.17
fearfulness, and drink water in d., 12.19
are opened, the palace is in d.; Nah 2.06

DISMAYED
bundles of money, they were d. Gen 42.35
for they were d. at his presence. 45.03
Now are the chiefs of Edom d.; the leaders Ex 15.15
has told you; do not fear or be d.' Deu 1.21
forsake you; do not fear or be d." 31.08
be not frightened, neither be d.; Jos 1.09
to Joshua, "Do not fear or be d.; 8.01
to them, "Do not be afraid or d.; 10.25
and the men of Benjamin were d., Ju 20.41
they were d. and greatly afraid. 1Sa 17.11
failed, and all Israel was d. 2Sa 4.01
are d. and confounded, and have 2Ki 19.26
courage. Fear not; be not d. 1Ch 22.13
Fear not, be not d.; for the LORD 28.20
and be not d. at this great multitude; 2Ch 20.15
Fear not, and be not d.; tomorrow go out 20.17
be afraid or d. before the king of 32.07
it touches you, and you are d. Job 4.05
When I think of it I am d., and 21.06
He laughs at fear, and is not d.; 39.22
thou didst hide thy face, I was d. Ps 30.07
be put to shame and d. for ever; 83.17
When thou hidest thy face, they are d.; 104.29
of your sacred oath be not d.; Ecc 8.02
Be broken, you peoples, and be d.; Is 8.09
be d., gird yourselves and be d. 8.09
and they will be d. Pangs and 13.08
Then they shall be d. and confounded 20.05
I am d. so that I cannot see. 21.03
are d. and confounded, and have 37.27
be not d., for I am your God; 41.10
that we may be d. and terrified. 41.23
and be not d. at their revilings. 51.07
Do not be d. by them, lest I dismay Jer 1.17
shame, they shall be d. and taken; 8.09
nor be d. at the signs of the 10.02
because the nations are d. at them, 10.02
Because of the ground which is d., 14.04
let them be d., but let me not be d.; 17.18
nor be d., neither shall any be 23.04
says the LORD, nor be d., O Israel; 30.10
They are d. and have turned backward. 46.05
my servant, nor be d., O Israel; 46.27
is put to shame, Merodach is d. 50.02
are put to shame, her idols are d.' 50.02
nor be d. at their looks, for they Eze 2.06
nor be d. at their looks, for they 3.09
in the sea are d. at your passing.' 26.18
was d. for a long time, and his Dan 4.19
even the flocks of sheep are d. Joe 1.18
And your mighty men shall be d., Ob 1.09

DISMISS
priest did not d. the divisions. 2Ch 23.08

DISMISSED
When Joshua d. the people, the Ju 2.06
other side, while he d. the crowds. Mt 14.22
And after he had d. the crowds, 14.23
Bethsaida, while he d. the crowd. Mk 6.45
had said this, he d. the assembly. Ac 19.41
So the tribune d. the young man, 23.22

DISOBEDIENCE
For as by one man's d. many were Rom 5.19
received mercy because of their d., 11.30
For God has consigned all men to d., 11.32
being ready to punish every d., 2Co 10.06
is now at work in the sons of d. Eph 2.02
of God comes upon the sons of d. 5.06
transgression or d. received a just Heb 2.02
failed to enter because of d., 4.06
no one fall by the same sort of d. 4.11

DISOBEDIENT
"Nevertheless they were d. and Neh 9.26
and the d. to the wisdom of the Lk 1.17
I was not d. to the heavenly vision, Ac 26.19
inventors of evil, d. to parents, Rom 1.30
my hands to a d. and contrary 10.21
you were once d. to God but now 11.30
have now been d. in order that by 11.31
just but for the lawless and d., 1Ti 1.09
d. to their parents, ungrateful, 2Ti 3.02
d., unfit for any good deed. Tit 1.16
d., led astray, slaves to various 3.03
his rest, but to those who were d.? Heb 3.18
not perish with those who were d., 11.31

DISOBEY
king, and do not d. either of them; Pro 24.21
stumble because they d. the word, 1Pe 2.08

DISOBEYED
you have d. the word of the LORD, 1Ki 13.21
who d. the word of the LORD; 13.26
you, and I never d. your command; Lk 15.29

DISOBEYING
d. the voice of the LORD your God Jer 42.13

DISOBEYS
your commandment and d. your words, Jos 1.18
"I know him" but d. his commandments 1Jn 2.04

DISORDER
slander, gossip, conceit, and d. 2Co 12.20
there will be d. and every vile Jas 3.16

DISOWNED
he d. his brothers, and ignored his Deu 33.09
his altar, d. his sanctuary; he has Lam 2.07
he has d. the faith and is worse 1Ti 5.08

DISPATCH
stone them and d. them with their Eze 23.47
upon the earth with vigor and d." Rom 9.28

DISPATCHED
the king had d. a man from his 2Ki 6.32

DISPENSATION
Now if the d. of death, carved in 2Co 3.07
why should not the d. of the Spirit 3.08
splendor in the d. of condemnation, 3.09
the d. of righteousness must far 3.09

DISPENSES
The tongue of the wise d. knowledge, Pro 15.02

DISPERSE
"D. yourselves among the people, and 1Da 14.34
and would d. their descendants Ps 106.27
when I d. them among the nations Eze 12.15
the nations and d. them through 20.23
the nations and d. you through the 22.15
and d. them among the countries. 29.12
and d. them throughout the lands. 30.23
the nations and d. them throughout 30.26

DISPERSED
and they d. from the city, every man 2Sa 20.22
though your d. be under the farthest Neh 1.09
abroad and d. among the peoples in Est 3.08
and gather the d. of Judah from Is 11.12
and they were d. through the countries; Eze 36.19
suppliants, the daughter of my d. ones, Zep 3.10
him were d. and came to nothing. Ac 5.36

DISPERSION
of your slaughter and d. have come, Jer 25.34
to go to the D. among the Greeks Jn 7.35
twelve tribes in the d.: Greeting. Jas 1.01
To the exiles of the d. in Pontus, 1Pe 1.01

DISPLAY
Christ might d. his perfect 1Ti 1.16

DISPLEASE
you may not d. the lords of the 1Sa 29.07
and d. God and oppose all men 1Th 2.15

DISPLEASED
"Be not d. because of the lad and Gen 21.12
the head of Ephraim, it d. him; 48.17
blazed hotly, and Moses was d. Num 11.10
But the thing d. Samuel when they 1Sa 8.06
very angry, and this saying d. him; 18.08
that David had done d. the LORD. 2Sa 11.27
never at any time d. him by asking, 1Ki 1.06
But God was d. with this thing, and 1Ch 21.07
it d. them greatly that some one Neh 2.10
and be d., and turn away his anger Pro 24.18
and it d. him that there was no Is 59.15
But it d. Jonah exceedingly, and he Jon 4.01

DISPLEASING
thing was very d. to Abraham on Gen 21.11
And what he did was d. in the sight 38.10

DISPLEASURE
years, and you shall know my d.' Num 14.34
anger and hot d. which the LORD Deu 9.19

DISPOSAL
it was sold, was it not at your d.? Ac 5.04

DISPOSED
if he is well d. toward David, shall 1Sa 20.12
you to dinner and you are d. to go, 1Co 10.27
If any one is d. to be contentious, 11.16

DISPOSSESS
greater than I; how can I d. them?' Deu 7.17
to go in to d. nations greater and 9.01
and you will d. nations greater and 11.23
whom you shall d. served their 12.02
the nations whom you go in to d., 12.29
and you d. them and dwell in their 12.29
nations, which you are about to d., 18.14
and you d. them and dwell in their 19.01
you, so that you shall d. them; 31.03
Israel shall d. those who dispossessed Jer 49.02

DISPOSSESSED
and d. the Amorites that were there. Num 21.32
Edom shall be d., Seir also, his 24.18
enemies, shall be d., while Israel does 24.18
and d. the Amorites who were in it. 32.39
but the sons of Esau d. them, Deu 2.12
and they d. them, and settled in 2.21
and they d. them, and settled in 2.22
d. the Amorites from before his Ju 11.23
the LORD our God has d. before us, 11.24
Why then has Milcom d. Gad, and his Jer 49.01
shall dispossess those who d. him, 49.02
people shall be d. of his property." Eze 46.18
when they d. the nations which God Ac 7.45

DISPUTE
when they have a d., they come Ex 18.16
parties to the d. shall appear Deu 19.17
word every d. and every assault 21.05
"If there is a d. between men, and 25.01
is not able to d. with one stronger Ecc 6.10
A d. also arose among them, which of Lk 22.24
points of d. with him about their Ac 25.19
holding much d. among themselves. * 28.29
It is beyond d. that the inferior Heb 7.07

DISPUTED
the LORD and to decide d. cases. 2Ch 19.08
The Jews then d. among themselves, Jn 6.52
Asia, arose and d. with Stephen. Ac 6.09
he spoke and d. against the Hellenists; 9.29
d. about the body of Moses, he did Jud 1.09

DISPUTES
puts an end to d. and decides Pro 18.18
him, but not for d. over opinions. Rom 14.01
controversy and for d. about words, 1Ti 6.04
in all their d. an oath is final Heb 6.16

DISPUTING
and heard them d. with one another, Mk 12.28
did not find me d. with any one or Ac 24.12
the Lord to avoid d. about words, 2Ti 2.14

DISQUALIFIED
to others I myself should be d. 1Co 9.27

DISQUALIFY
Let no one d. you, insisting on self Col 2.18

DISQUIETED
soul, and why are you d. within me? Ps 42.05
soul, and why are you d. within me? 42.11
soul, and why are you d. within me? 43.05

DISREGARD
authority. Let no one d. you. Tit 2.15

DISREGARDED
and my right is d. by my God"? Is 40.27
and they have d. my sabbaths, so Eze 22.26

DISREGARDS
whoever d. this, d. not man but God, 1Th 4.08

DISREPUTABLE
A senseless, a d. brood, they have Job 30.08

DISREPUTE
may come into d. but also that the Ac 19.27
are held in honor, but we in d. 1Co 4.10

DISRESPECTFUL
must not be d. on the ground that 1Ti 6.02

DISSEMBLERS
men, nor do I consort with d.; Ps 26.04

DISSEMBLES
He who hates, d. with his lips and Pro 26.24

DISSENSION
had no small d. and debate with Ac 15.02
a d. arose between the Pharisees 23.07
And when the d. became violent, the 23.10
selfishness, d., party spirit, Gal 5.20
d., slander, base suspicions, 1Ti 6.04

DISSENSIONS
who create d. and difficulties, in Rom 16.17
and that there be no d. among you, 1Co 1.10
d., and quarrels over the law, for Tit 3.09

DISSIPATION
down with d. and drunkenness and Lk 21.34
blemishes, reveling in their d., 2Pe 2.13

DISSOLVED
the elements will be d. with fire, 2Pe 3.10
all these things are thus to be d., 3.11
the heavens will be kindled and d., 3.12

DISSOLVES
like the snail which d. into slime, Ps 58.08

DISTAFF
She puts her hands to the d., Pro 31.19

DISTANCE
way off, about the d. of a bowshot; Gen 21.16
and he set a d. of three days' 30.36
were still some d. from Ephrath, 35.16
gone but a short d. from the city, 44.04
was still some d. to go to Ephrath; 48.07
And his sister stood at a d., Ex 2.04
measure the d. to the cities which Deu 21.02
a d. of about two thousand cubits; Jos 3.04
and stood at some d. from them, 2Ki 2.07
had gone from him a short d., 5.19
Then he measured the d. from the Eze 40.19
was feeding at some d. from them. Mt 8.30
But Peter followed him at a d., 26.58
And seeing in the d. a fig tree in Mk 11.13
And Peter had followed him at a d., 14.54
But while he was yet at a d., Lk 15.20
by ten lepers, who stood at a d. 17.12
house. Peter followed at a d.; 22.54
stood at a d. and saw these things 23.49

DISTANT
They come from a d. land, Is 13.05
"Besiegers come from a d. land; Jer 4.16
or sweet cane from a d. land? 6.20
was many furlongs d. from the land, Mt 14.24

DISTIL
my speech d. as the dew, as the Deu 32.02
Your lips d. nectar, my bride; Sol 4.11

DISTILLING
are lilies, d. liquid myrrh. Sol 5.13

DISTILS
of water, he d. his mist in rain Job 36.27

DISTINCT
going with us, so that we are d., Ex 33.16
do not give d. notes, how will any 1Co 14.07

DISTINCTION
will make a d. between the cattle Ex 9.04
LORD makes a d. between the 11.07
to make a d. between the unclean Lev 11.47
therefore make a d. between the 20.25
have made no d. between the holy Eze 22.26
and he made no d. between us and Ac 15.09
who believe. For there is no d.; Rom 3.22
For there is no d. between Jew and 10.12

DISTINCTIONS
have you not made d. among yourselves, Jas 2.04

DISTINCTLY
stammerers will speak readily and d. Is 32.04

DISTINGUISH
You are to d. between the holy and Lev 10.10
could not d. the sound of the Ez 3.13
them how to d. between the unclean Eze 44.23
more you shall d. between the Mal 3.18
the ability to d. between spirits, 1Co 12.10
by practice to d. good from evil. Heb 5.14

DISTINGUISHED
and ruddy, d. among ten thousand. Sol 5.10
Daniel became d. above all the Dan 6.03

DISTRACTED
But Martha was d. with much serving Lk 10.40

DISTRAUGHT
I am d. by the noise of the enemy, Ps 55.03

DISTRESS
the day of my d. and has been with Gen 35.03
in that we saw the d. of his soul, 42.21
therefore is this d. come upon us." 42.21
and in the d. with which your Deu 28.53
which your enemies shall d. you. 28.53
and in the d. with which your 28.55
enemy shall d. you in all your 28.55
and in the d. with which your 28.57
enemy shall d. you in your towns. 28.57
deliver you in the time of your d." Ju 10.14
Then in d. you will look with 1Sa 2.32
And every one who was in d., 22.02
Saul answered, "I am in great d.; 28.15
"In my d. I called upon the LORD; 2Sa 22.07
said to Gad, "I am in gread d.; 24.14
her alone, for she is in bitter d.; 2Ki 4.27
Hezekiah, This day is a day of d., 19.03
said to Gad, "I am in great d.; 1Ch 21.13
but when in their d. they turned to 2Ch 15.04
troubled them with every sort of d. 15.06
In the time of his d. he became yet 28.22
And when he was in d. he entreated 33.12
pleasure, and we are in great d." Neh 9.37
d. and anguish terrify him; Job 15.24
you out of d. into a broad place 36.16
your cry avail to keep you from d., 36.19
given me room when I was in d. Ps 4.01

DISTRESS (cont.)
In my d. I called upon the LORD; Ps 18.06
to me, O LORD, for I am in d.; 31.09
at a time of d., in the rush of 32.06
my d. grew worse, 39.02
and a refuge in the day of my d. 59.16
for I am in d., make haste to 69.17
and d., a company of destroying 78.49
In d. you called, and I delivered 81.07
face from me in the day of my d.! 102.02
Nevetheless he regarded their d., 106.44
he delivered them from their d.; 107.06
he delivered them from their d.; 107.13
he delivered them from their d.; 107.19
he delivered them from their d.; 107.28
I suffered d. and anguish. 116.03
Out of my d. I called on the LORD; 118.05
In my d. I cry to the LORD, that he 120.01
be no cry of d. in our streets! 144.14
when d. and anguish come upon you. Pro 1.27
and wine to those in bitter d.; 31.06
the land, behold, darkness and d.; Is 5.30
d. and darkness, the gloom of 8.22
stronghold to the needy in his d., 25.04
O LORD, in d. they sought thee, they 26.16
Yet I will d. Ariel, and there shall 29.02
her and her stronghold and d. her, 29.07
Hezekiah, 'This day is a day of d., 37.03
sound of weeping and the cry of d. 65.19
time, and I will bring d. on them, Jer 10.18
of trouble and in the time of d.! 15.11
neighbor in the seige and in the d., 19.09
it is a time of d. for Jacob; 30.07
overtaken her in the midst of her d. Lam 1.03
for I am in d., my soul is in 1.20
and in their d. they seek me, saying, Hos 5.15
not have boasted in the day of d. Ob 1.12
up his survivors in the day of d. 1.14
out of my d., and he answered me; Jon 2.02
a day of d. and anguish, a day of Zep 1.15
I will bring d. on men, so that they 1.17
paralyzed at home, in terrible d. Mt 8.06
For great d. shall be upon the Lk 21.23
upon the earth d. of nations in 21.25
tribulation and d. for every human Rom 2.09
or d., or persecution, or famine, or 8.35
the impending d. it is well for a 1Co 7.26
in all our d. and affliction we 1Th 3.07

DISTRESSED
Then Jacob was greatly afraid and d.; Gen 32.07
And now do not be d., or angry 45.05
so that Israel was sorely d. Ju 10.09
She was deeply d. and prayed to the 1Sa 1.10
the men of Israel were d. that day; 14.24
And David was greatly d.; for the 30.06
I am d. for you, my brother Jonathan; 2Sa 1.26
told her, the queen was deeply d.; Est 4.04
the land, greatly d. and hungry; Is 8.21
was much d., and set his mind to Dan 6.14
third day." And they were greatly d. Mt 17.23
taken place, they were greatly d., 18.31
he saw that they were d. in rowing, Mk 6.48
to be greatly d. and troubled. 14.33
and has been d. because you heard Php 2.26
greatly d. by the licentiousness of 2Pe 2.07

DISTRESSES
all your calamities and your d.; 1Sa 10.19
heart, and bring me out of my d. Ps 25.17

DISTRIBUTE
to d. the portions to their brethren, 2Ch 31.15
by name to d. portions to every 31.19
that they might d. them according 35.12
duty was to d. to their brethren. Neh 13.13
that you have and d. to the poor, Lk 18.22

DISTRIBUTED
which Moses d. in the plains of Jos 13.32
of the people of Israel d. to them. 14.01
of Israel d. by lot at Shiloh 19.51
and d. among all the people, the 2Sa 6.19
and d. to all Israel, both men and 1Ch 16.03
and d. some of his sons through all 2Ch 11.23
to the place where the light is d., Job 38.24
He has d. freely, he has given to Ps 112.09
he d. them to those who were seated; Jn 6.11
d. and resting on each one of them. Ac 2.03
and goods and d. them to all, as any 2.45
the Holy Spirit d. according to Heb 2.04

DISTRIBUTES
That God d. pains in his anger? Job 21.17

DISTRIBUTING
had finished d. the several territories Jos 19.49

DISTRIBUTION
and d. was made to each as any had Ac 4.35
were neglected in the daily d. 6.01

DISTRICT
ruler of half the d. of Jerusalem, Neh 3.09
ruler of half the d. of Jerusalem, 3.12
ruler of the d. of Bethhaccherem, 3.14
ruler of the d. of Mizpah, repaired 3.15
ruler of half the d. of Bethzur, 3.16
ruler of half the d. of Keilah, 3.17
of Keilah, repaired for his d. 3.17
ruler of half the d. of Keilah; 3.18
a portion of the land as a holy d., Eze 45.01
And in the holy d. you shall 45.03
as the holy d. you shall assign 45.06
of the holy d. and the property of 45.07
the city, alongside the holy d. and 45.07
he withdrew to the d. of Galilee. Mt 2.22
of this went through all that d. 9.26
his fame through all that d. 9.31
withdrew to the d. of Tyre and 15.21
came into the d. of Caesarea 16.13
and went to the d. of Dalmanutha. Mk 8.10
and drove them out of their d. Ac 13.50
city of the d. of Macedonia, 16.12

DISTRICTS
servants of the governors of the d. 1Ki 20.14
servants of the governors of the d., 20.15
governors of the d. went out first. 20.17
servants of the governors of the d., 20.19
through all the d. of Judah and 2Ch 11.23

DISTRUST
No d. made him waver concerning the Rom 4.20

DISTURB
for they d. me—Your hair is like a Sol 6.05
his cubs were, with none to d.? Nah 2.11

DISTURBANCES
for great d. afflicted all the 2Ch 15.05

DISTURBED
"Why have you d. me by bringing me 1Sa 28.15
their own place, and be d. no more; 2Sa 7.10
their own place, and be d. no more; 1Ch 17.09
authorities were d. when they heard Ac 17.08

DISTURBING
are Jews and they are d. our city. Ac 16.20

DISUSE
never fall into d. among the Jews, Est 9.28

DIVERSE
D. weights and d. measures are Pro 20.10

DIVERSE (cont.)
D. weights are an abomination to Pro 20.23
be led away by d. and strange Heb 13.09

DIVERSIONS
no d. were brought to him, and sleep Dan 6.18

DIVIDE
I will d. them in Jacob and scatter Gen 49.07
your hand over the sea and d. it, Ex 14.16
I will d. the spoil, my desire shall 15.09
the live ox and d. the price of it 21.35
the dead beast also they shall d. 21.35
wings, but shall not d. it asunder. Lev 1.17
and d. the booty into two parts, Num 31.27
men who shall d. the land to you 34.17
to d. the land for inheritance. 34.18
commanded to d. the inheritance 34.29
and d. into three parts the area of Deu 19.03
Now therefore d. this land for an Jos 13.07
They shall d. it into seven portions, 18.05
d. the spoil of your enemies with 22.08
you and Ziba shall d. the land." 2Sa 19.29
"D. the living child in two, and 1Ki 3.25
mine nor yours; d. it." 3.26
And thou didst d. the sea before Neh 9.11
the innocent will d. the silver. Job 27.17
Will they d. him up among the 41.06
they d. my garments among them, and Ps 22.18
exultation I will d. up Shechem and 60.06
The women at home d. the spoil, 68.12
Thou didst d. the sea by thy might; 74.13
exultation I will d. up Shechem, 108.07
poor than to d. the spoil with the Pro 16.19
men rejoice when they d. the spoil. Is 9.03
conquering, whose land the rivers d. 18.02
conquering, whose land the rivers d., 18.07
those who d. the heavens, who gaze 47.13
Therefore I will d. him a portion 53.12
and he shall d. the spoil with the 53.12
for weighing, and d. the hair. Eze 5.01
which you shall d. the land for 47.13
And you shall d. it equally; 47.14
"So you shall d. this land among 47.21
many and shall d. the land for a Dan 11.39
bid my brother d. the inheritance Lk 12.13
"Take this, and d. it among yourselves; 22.17
they cast lots to d. his garments. 23.34

DIVIDED
and there it d. and became four Gen 2.10
for in his days the earth was d., 10.25
And he d. his forces against them 14.15
peoples, born of you, shall be d.; 25.23
and he d. the people that were with 32.07
So he d. the children among Leah 33.01
dry land, and the waters were d. Ex 14.21
land shall be d. for inheritance Num 26.53
But the land shall be d. by lot; 26.55
shall be d. according to lot 26.56
And he d. the three hundred men Ju 7.16
his men and d. them into three 9.43
hold of his concubine he d. her, 19.29
life and in death they were not d.; 2Sa 1.23
of Israel were d. into two parts; 1Ki 16.21
So they d. the land between them to 18.06
(for in his days the earth was d.), 1Ch 1.19
He d. the sea and let them pass Ps 78.13
to him who d. the Red Sea in sunder, 136.13
and spoil in abundance will be d.; Is 33.23
who d. the waters before them to 63.12
and no longer d. into two kingdoms. Eze 37.22
of iron, it shall be a d. kingdom; Dan 2.41
PERES, your kingdom is d. and given 5.28
be broken and d. toward the four 11.04
nations, and have d. up my land, Joe 3.02
you will be d. in the midst of you. Zec 14.01
"Every kingdom d. against itself is Mt 12.25
no city or house d. against itself will 12.25
he is d. against himself; how then 12.26
they d. his garments among them by 27.35
If a kingdom is d. against itself, Mk 3.24
And if a house is d. against itself, 3.25
risen up against himself and is d., 3.26
and he d. the two fish among them 6.41
and d. his garments among them, 15.24
"Every kingdom d. against itself is Lk 11.17
Satan also is d. against himself, 11.18
in one house there will be five d., 12.52
they will be d., father against son 12.53
And he d. his living between them. 15.12
But the people of the city were d.; Ac 14.04
Sadducees; and the assembly was d. 23.07
Is Christ d.? Was Paul 1Co 1.13
and his interests are d. And the 7.34

DIVIDER
who made me a judge or d. over you?" Lk 12.14

DIVIDES
Among our captors he d. our fields. Mic 2.04
which he trusted, and d. his spoil. Lk 11.22

DIVIDING
the prey, and at even d. the spoil." Gen 49.27
So they finished d. the land. Jos 19.51
'Are they not finding and d. the spoil?— Ju 5.30
and opposite there was a d. wall. Eze 42.12
broken down the d. wall of hostility, Eph 2.14

DIVINATION
have learned by d. that the LORD Gen 30.27
with the fees for d. in their hand; Num 22.07
Jacob, no d. against Israel; 23.23
offering, any one who practices d., Deu 18.10
For rebellion is as the sin of d., 1Sa 15.23
and used d. and sorcery, and sold 2Ki 17.17
worthless d., and the deceit of Jer 14.14
or flattering d. within the house Eze 12.24
vision, and uttered a lying d., 13.07
delusive visions nor practice d.; 13.23
head of the two ways, to use d.; 21.21
them it will seem like a false d.; 21.23
and darkness to you, without d. Mic 3.06
had a spirit of d. and brought her Ac 16.16

DIVINATIONS
visions and who give lying d.; Eze 13.09

DIVINE
that such a man as I can indeed d.?" Gen 44.15
And he said, "D. for me by a spirit, 1Sa 28.08
Your d. throne endures for ever and Ps 45.06
taken his place in the d. council; 82.01
while they d. lies for you—to be Eze 21.39
hire, its prophets d. for money; Mic 3.11
because in his d. forbearance he Rom 3.25
but have d. power to destroy 2Co 10.04
I feel a d. jealousy for you, for I 11.02
according to the d. office which Col 1.25
rather than the d. training that 1Ti 1.04
men of old received d. approval. Heb 11.02
His d. power has granted to us all 2Pe 1.03
become partakers of the d. nature. 1.04

DIVINED
have spoken falsehood and d. a lie; Eze 13.06

DIVINER
the prophet, the d. and the elder, Is 3.02

DIVINERS
give heed to soothsayers and to d.; Deu 18.14
the priests and the d. and said, 1Sa 6.02
are full of d. from the east and Is 2.06

DIVINERS (cont.)
of liars, and makes fools of d.; Is 44.25
your d., your dreamers, your soothsayers, Jer 27.09
and your d. who are among you 29.08
A sword upon the d., that they 50.36
disgraced, and the d. put to shame; Mic 3.07
nonsense, and the d. see lies; Zec 10.02

DIVINERS'
for the direction of the D. Oak." Ju 9.37

DIVINES
drinks, and by this that he d.? Gen 44.05

DIVINING
false visions and d. lies for them, Eze 22.28

DIVINITIES
to be a preacher of foreign d."— Ac 17.18

DIVISION
Thus I will put a d. between my Ex 8.23
each d. numbering twenty-four 1Ch 27.01
of the first d. in the first month; 27.02
in his d. were twenty-four thousand. 27.02
charge of the d. of the second 27.04
in his d. were twenty-four thousand. 27.04
in his d. were twenty-four thousand. 27.05
his son was in charge of his d. 27.06
in his d. were twenty-four thousand. 27.07
in his d. were twenty-four thousand. 27.08
in his d. were twenty-four thousand. 27.09
in his d. were twenty-four thousand. 27.10
in his d. were twenty-four thousand. 27.11
in his d. were twenty-four thousand. 27.12
in his d. were twenty-four thousand. 27.13
in his d. were twenty-four thousand. 27.14
in his d. were twenty-four thousand. 27.15
d. by d., each according to 2Ch 31.02
Zechariah, of the d. of Abijah; Lk 1.05
God when his d. was on duty, 1.08
No, I tell you, but rather d.; 12.51
So there was a d. among the people Jn 7.43
There was a d. among them. 9.16
There was again a d. among the Jews 10.19
piercing to the d. of soul and Heb 4.12

DIVISIONS
land in seven d. and bring the Jos 18.06
description of it by towns in seven d.; 18.09
and the two d. of you, which come on 2Ki 11.07
numbers of the d. of the armed 1Ch 12.23
organized them in d. corresponding 23.06
The d. of the sons of Aaron were 24.01
As for the d. of the gatekeepers: of 26.01
These d. of the gatekeepers, corresponding 26.12
These were the d. of the gatekeepers 26.19
concerning the d. that came and 27.01
officers of the d. that served the 28.01
for the d. of the priests and of 28.13
And behold the d. of the priests 28.21
themselves, without regard to their d.; 2Ch 5.11
appointed the d. of the priests 8.14
in their d. for the several gates; 8.14
the priest did not dismiss the d. 23.08
in d. according to the numbers in 26.11
appointed the d. of the priests 31.02
brethren, old and young alike, by d., 31.15
to their officers, by their d. 31.16
to their officers, by their d. 31.17
to your fathers' houses by your d., 35.04
in their d. according to the king's 35.10
in their d. and the Levites in Ez 6.18
And certain d. of the Levites in Neh 11.36
I hear that there are d. among you; 1Co 11.18
It is these who set up d., Jud 1.19

DIVORCE
her a bill of d. and puts it in Deu 24.01
her a bill of d. and puts it in 24.03
"Where is your mother's bill of d., Is 50.01
sent her away with a decree of d.; Jer 3.08
"For I hate d., says the LORD the Mal 2.16
shame, resolved to d. her quietly. Mt 1.19
him give her a certificate of d.' 5.31
"Is it lawful to d. one's wife for 19.03
one to give a certificate of d., 19.07
Moses allowed you to d. your wives, 19.08
it lawful for a man to d. his wife?" Mk 10.02
a man to write a certificate of d., 10.04
the husband should not d. his wife. 1Co 7.11
with him, he should not d. her. 7.12
with her, she should not d. him. 7.13

DIVORCED
marry a woman d. from her husband; Lev 21.07
or one d., or a woman who has been 21.14
priest's daughter is a widow or d., 22.13
vow of a widow or of a d. woman, Num 30.09
or a d. woman, but only a virgin of Eze 44.22
marries a d. woman commits adultery. Mt 5.32
marries a d. woman commits adultery * 19.09
marries a woman d. from her husband Lk 16.18

DIVORCES
"If a man d. his wife and she goes Jer 3.01
'Whoever d. his wife, let him give Mt 5.31
you that every one who d. his wife, 5.32
whoever d. his wife, except for 19.09
"Whoever d. his wife and marries Mk 10.11
and if she d. her husband and 10.12
"Every one who d. his wife and Lk 16.18

DIVULGING
confessing and d. their practices. Ac 19.18

DIZAHAB
Tophel, Laban, Hazeroth, and D. Deu 1.01

DOCTRINE
'My d. is pure, and I am clean in Job 11.04
opposition to the d. which you have Rom 16.17
about with every wind of d., Eph 4.14
not to teach any different d., 1Ti 1.03
else is contrary to sound d., 1.10
and of the good d. which you have 4.06
in sound d. and also to confute Tit 1.09
you, teach what befits sound d. 2.01
may adorn the d. of God our Savior. 2.10
not abide in the d. of Christ does not 2Jn 1.09
who abides in the d. of Christ has both 1.09
to you and does not bring this d., 1.10

DOCTRINES
teaching as d. the precepts of men.'" Mt 15.09
teaching as d. the precepts of men.' Mk 7.07
according to human precepts and d.? Col 2.22
deceitful spirits and d. of demons, 1Ti 4.01
the elementary d. of Christ and go Heb 6.01

DOCUMENT
A copy of the d. was to be issued Est 3.14
the interdict and sign the d., Dan 6.08
Darius signed the d. and interdict. 6.09
knew that the d. had been signed, 6.10

DOCUMENTS
archives where the d. were stored. Ez 6.01

DODAI
D. the Ahohite was in charge of the 1Ch 27.04

DODANIM
Elishah, Tarshish, Kittim, and D. Gen 10.04

DODAVAHU
the son of D. of Mareshah prophesied 2Ch 20.37

DODO
son of D., a man of Issachar; and he Ju 10.01
Eleazar the son of D., son of Ahohi. 2Sa 23.09
Elhanan the son of D. of Bethlehem, 23.24
Eleazar the son of D.. the Ahohite. 1Ch 11.12
Elhanan the son of D. of Bethlehem, 11.26

DOE
a lovely hind, a graceful d. Let her Pro 5.19

DOEG
his name was D. the Edomite, the 1Sa 21.07
Then answered D. the Edomite, who 22.09
Then the king said to D., "You turn 22.18
And D. the Edomite turned and fell 22.18
when D. the Edomite was there, that 22.22

DOER
done there, he was the d. of it; Gen 39.22
of Kabzeel, a d. of great deeds; 2Sa 23.20
of Kabzeel, a d. of great deeds; 1Ch 11.22
a hearer of the word and not a d., Jas 1.23
that forgets but a d. that acts, 1.25
you are not a d. of the law but a 4.11

DOERS
but the d. of the law who will be Rom 2.13
But be d. of the word, and not Jas 1.22

DOG
man or beast, not a d. shall growl; Ex 11.07
of a harlot, or the wages of a d., Deu 23.18
as a d. laps, you shall set by Ju 7.05
"Am I a d., that you come to me 1Sa 17.43
After a dead d.! After a flea! 24.14
look upon a dead d. such as I?" 2Sa 9.08
this dead d. curse my lord the 16.09
who is but a d., that he should do 2Ki 8.13
my life from the power of the d.! Ps 22.20
Like a d. that returns to his vomit Pro 26.11
who takes a passing d. by the ears. 26.17
for a living d. is better than a Ecc 9.04
The d. turns back to his own vomit, 2Pe 2.22

DOGGED
Men d. our steps so that we could Lam 4.18

DOG'S
and said, "Am I a d. head of Judah? 2Sa 3.08
like him who breaks a d. neck; Is 66.03

DOGS
you shall cast it to the d. Ex 22.31
dies in the city the d. shall eat; 1Ki 14.11
dies in the city the d. shall eat; 16.04
the place where d. licked up the 21.19
Naboth shall d. lick your own blood."'" 21.19
'The d. shall eat Jezebel within 21.23
dies in the city the d. shall eat; 21.24
and the d. licked up his blood, and 22.38
And the d. shall eat Jezebel in the 2Ki 9.10
of Jezreel the d. shall eat the 9.36
to set with the d. of my flock. Job 30.01
Yea, d. are round about me; a company Ps 22.16
howling like d. and prowling about 59.06
howling like d. and prowling about 59.14
tongues of your d. may have their 68.23
they are all dumb d., they cannot Is 56.10
The d. have a mighty appetite; 56.11
the d. to tear, and the birds of the Jer 15.03
"Do not give d. what is holy; Mt 7.06
bread and throw it to the d." 15.26
yet even the d. eat the crumbs that 15.27
bread and throw it to the d." Mk 7.27
yet even the d. under the table eat 7.28
moreover the d. came and licked his Lk 16.21
Look out for the d., look out Php 3.02
Outside are the d. and sorcerers Rev 22.15

DOINGS
on account of the evil of your d., Deu 28.20
utter the mighty d. of the LORD, Ps 106.02
the LORD to anger with their d., 106.29
and played the harlot in their d. 106.39
his ways, and kind in all his d. 145.17
evil of your d. from before my Is 1.16
in all her d. as a drunken man 19.14
of your righteousness and your d., 57.12
bosom payment for their former d." 65.07
it, because of the evil of your d." Jer 4.04
Your ways and your d. have brought 4.18
Amend your ways and your d., 7.03
truly amend your ways and your d., 7.05
according to the fruit of his d." 17.10
and amend your ways and your d.' 18.11
quench it, because of your evil d.'" 21.12
fruit of your d., says the LORD; 21.14
for your evil d., says the LORD. 23.02
way, and from the evil of their d. 23.22
from his evil way and wrong d., 25.05
to them because of their evil d. 26.03
amend your ways and your d., 26.13
according to the fruit of his d.; 32.19
his evil way, and amend your d., 35.15
bear your evil d. and the abominations 44.22
you see their ways and their d., Eze 14.22
you see their ways and their d.; 14.23
and all the d. with which you have 20.43
nor according to your corrupt d., 20.44
in all your d. your sins appear— 21.24
ways and your d. I will judge you, 24.14
it by their ways and their d.; 36.17
Are these his d.? Do not Mic 2.07
inhabitants, for the fruit of their d. 7.13
unless they repent of her d.; Rev 2.22

DOMESTIC
d., kind, and submissive to their Tit 2.05

DOMINEERING
not as d. over those in your charge 1Pe 5.03

DOMINION
let them have d. over the fish of Gen 1.26
and have d. over the fish of the 1.28
are you indeed to have d. over us?" 37.08
By Jacob shall d. be exercised, and Num 24.19
the Philistines had d. over Israel. Ju 14.04
For he had d. over all the region 1Ki 4.24
and in all the land of his d. 9.19
and in all the land of his d. 2Ch 8.06
so that they had d. over them; Neh 9.28
"D. and fear are with God; Job 25.02
Thou hast given him d. over the Ps 8.06
let them not have d. over me! 19.13
For d. belongs to the LORD, and he 22.28
May he have d. from sea to sea, and 72.08
his works, in all places of his d. 103.22
his sanctuary, Israel his d. 114.02
and let no iniquity get d. over me. 119.133
and thy d. endures throughout all 145.13
earth under his d. and all the Jer 34.01
and every land under their d. Jer 51.28
when I break there the d. of Egypt, Eze 30.18
and his d. is from generation to Dan 4.03
and your d. to the ends of the 4.22
for his d. is an everlasting d., 4.34
in all my royal d. men tremble and 6.26
and his d. shall be to the end. 6.26
herds; and d. was given to it. 7.06
their d. was taken away, but their 7.12
him was given d. and glory and 7.14
his d. is an everlasting d., which 7.14

DOMINION (cont.)

and his d. shall be taken away, to Dan 7.26
kingdom and the d. and the greatness 7.27
rule with great d. and do according 11.03
according to the d. with which he 11.04
than he and his d. shall be a great d. 11.05
the former d. shall come, the kingdom Mic 4.08
his d. shall be from sea to sea, and Zec 9.10
death no longer has d. over him. Rom 6.09
For sin will have no d. over you, 6.14
and authority and power and d., Eph 1.21
us from the d. of darkness and Col 1.13
To him be honor and eternal d. 1Ti 6.16
glory and d. for ever and ever. 1Pe 4.11
to him be the d. for ever and ever. 5.11
d., and authority, before all time Jud 1.25
be glory and d. for ever and ever. Rev 1.06
city which has d. over the kings 17.18

DOMINIONS

and all d. shall serve and obey Dan 7.27
thrones or d. or principalities or Col 1.16

DOOM

hand, and their d. comes swiftly. Deu 32.35
have heard the d. of my evil Ps 92.11
This is your d., and it is bitter; Jer 4.18
sacrificial flesh avert your d.? 11.15
she took no thought of her d.; Lam 1.09
Your d. has come to you, O inhabitant Eze 7.07
Your d. has come, injustice has 7.10
a time of d. for the nations. 30.03
upon them on the day of Egypt's d.; 30.09

DOOMED

were but men d. to death before my 2Sa 19.28
who are d. with you to eat their 2Ki 18.27
power preserve those d. to die! Ps 79.11
they are d. to destruction for ever, 92.07
set free those who were d. to die; 102.20
he has d. them, has given them over Is 34.02
Edom, upon the people I have d. 34.05
who are d. with you to eat their 36.12
LORD our God has d. us to perish, Jer 8.14
those who are d. to the pestilence, 43.11
those who are d. to captivity, 43.11
those who are d. to the sword. 43.11
of the flock d. to slaughter. Zec 11.04
of the flock d. to be slain for 11.07
this age, who are d. to pass away. 1Co 2.06
them, thus he is d. to be killed. Rev 11.05

DOOR

do well, sin is couching at the d.; Gen 4.07
and set the d. of the ark in its 6.16
he sat at the d. of his tent in 18.01
ran from the tent d. to meet them, 18.02
listening at the tent d. behind him. 18.10
Lot went out of the d. to the men, 19.06
to the men, shut the d. after him, 19.06
Lot, and drew near to break the d. 19.09
the house to them, and shut the d. 19.10
who were at the d. of the house, 19.11
wearied themselves groping for the d. 19.11
with him at the d. of the house, 43.19
go out of the d. of his house Ex 12.22
the LORD will pass over the d., 12.23
him to the d. or the doorpost; 21.06
a screen for the d. of the tent, 26.36
his sons to the d. of the tent of 29.04
at the d. of the tent of meeting, 29.11
at the d. of the tent of meeting. 29.32
generations at the d. of the tent 29.42
and every man stood at his tent d., 33.08
and stand at the d. of the tent, 33.09
cloud standing at the d. of the tent, 33.10
worship, every man at his tent d. 33.10
incense. and the screen for the d., 35.15
at the d. of the tabernacle; 35.15
a screen for the d. of the tent, 36.37
ministered at the d. of the tent of 38.08
bases for the d. of the tent of 38.30
the screen for the d. of the tent; 39.38
screen for the d. of the tabernacle. 40.05
before the d. of the tabernacle of 40.06
his sons to the d. of the tent of 40.12
screen for the d. of the tabernacle. 40.28
offering at the d. of the tabernacle 40.29
offer it at the d. of the tent of Lev 1.03
that is at the d. of the tent of 1.05
kill it at the d. of the tent of 3.02
the bull to the d. of the tent of 4.04
which is at the d. of the tent of 4.07
which is at the d. of the tent of 4.18
congregation at the d. of the tent 8.03
assembled at the d. of the tent of 8.04
flesh at the d. of the tent of 8.31
go out from the d. of the tent of 8.33
At the d. of the tent of meeting 8.35
go out from the d. of the tent of 10.07
priest at the d. of the tent of 12.06
at the d. of the tent of meeting. 14.11
to the d. of the tent of meeting, 14.23
the house to the d. of the house, 14.38
the LORD to the d. of the tent of 15.14
to the d. of the tent of meeting. 15.29
the LORD at the d. of the tent of 16.07
bring it to the d. of the tent of 17.04
priest at the d. of the tent of 17.05
the LORD at the d. of the tent of 17.06
bring it to the d. of the tent of 17.09
to the d. of the tent of meeting, a 19.21
screen for the d. of the tent of Num 3.25
screen for the d. of the court 3.26
screen for the d. of the tent of 4.25
priest to the d. of the tent of 6.10
brought to the d. of the tent of 6.13
head at the d. of the tent of 6.18
every man at the d. of his tent; 11.10
and stood at the d. of the tent, 12.05
and stood at the d. of their tents, 16.27
assembly to the d. of the tent of 20.06
weeping at the d. of the tent of 25.06
at the d. of the tent of meeting, 27.02
it through his ear into the d., Deu 15.17
woman to the d. of her father's 22.21
cloud stood by the d. of the tent. 31.15
at the d. of the tent of meeting. Jos 19.51
"Stand at the d. of the tent, and if Ju 4.20
near to the d. of the tower to 9.52
round about, beating on the d.; 19.22
down at the d. of the man's house 19.26
lying at the d. of the house, 19.27
slept at the d. of the king's house 2Sa 11.09
presence, and bolt the d. after her." 13.17
out, and bolted the d. after her. 13.18
leaves of the one d. were folding, 1Ki 6.34
of the other d. were folding. 6.34
her feet, as she came in at the d., 14.06
who kept the d. of the king's house. 14.27
and shut the d. upon yourself and 2Ki 4.04
and shut the d. upon herself and 4.05
and shut the d. upon him, and went 4.21
in and shut the d. upon the two of 4.33
halted at the d. of Elisha's house. 5.09
shut the d., and hold the d. fast 6.32
Then open the d. and flee; 9.03
Then he opened the d., and fled. 9.10
who kept the d. of the king's house. 2Ch 12.10
Angle to the d. of the house of Neh 3.20
from the d. of the house of 3.21
lain in wait at my neighbor's d.; Job 31.09
keep watch over the d. of my lips! Ps 141.03
do not go near the d. of her house; Pro 5.08

DOOR (cont.)

She sits at the d. of her house,	Pro 9.14
who makes his d. high seeks	17.19
As a d. turns on its hinges, so does	26.14
but if she is a d., we will	Sol 8.09
Behind the d. and the doorpost you	Is 57.08
brought me to the d. of the court;	Eze 8.07
in the wall, lo, there was a d.	8.08
at the d. of the temple of the LORD,	8.16
stood at the d. of the east gate	10.19
at the d. of the gateway there were	11.01
and twenty cubits, from d. to d.	40.13
with its d. in the vestibule of	40.38
one d. toward the north, and another	41.11
and another d. toward the south;	41.11
to the space above the d., even to	41.17
to above the d. cherubim and palm	41.20
holy place had each a double d.	41.23
two swinging leaves for each d.	41.24
me back to the d. of the temple;	47.01
near to the d. of the burning	Dan 3.26
the Valley of Achor a d. of hope.	Hos 2.15
and shut the d. and pray to your	Mt 6.06
feast; and the d. was shut.	25.10
great stone to the d. of the tomb,	27.60
was gathered together about the d.	Mk 1.33
for them, not even about the d.;	2.02
tied at the d. out in the open	11.04
a stone against the d. of the tomb.	15.46
for us from the d. of the tomb?"	16.03
the d. is now shut, and my children	Lk 11.07
"Strive to enter by the narrow d.;	13.24
has risen up and shut the d.,	13.25
outside and to knock at the d.,	13.25
sheepfold by the d. but climbs in	Jn 10.01
enters by the d. is the shepherd	10.02
to you, I am the d. of the sheep.	10.07
I am the d.; if any one	10.09
while Peter stood outside at the d.	18.16
spoke to the maid who kept the d.,	18.16
maid who kept the d. said to Peter,	18.17
buried your husband are at the d.,	Ac 5.09
before the d. were guarding the	12.06
knocked at the d. of the gateway,	12.13
he had opened a d. of faith to the	14.27
house was next d. to the synagogue.	18.07
for a wide d. for effective work	1Co 16.09
a d. was opened for me in the Lord;	2Co 2.12
may open to us a d. for the word,	Col 4.03
I have set before you an open d.,	Rev 3.08
Behold, I stand at the d. and knock,	3.20
hears my voice and opens the d.,	3.20
and lo, in heaven an open d.!	4.01

DOORKEEPER

the d. of the house had been	2Sa 4.06
rather be a d. in the house of my	Ps 84.10
commands the d. to be on the watch.	Mk 13.34

DOORKEEPERS

the d., the temple servants, or	Ez 7.24

DOORPOST

bring him to the door or the d.;	Ex 21.06
seat beside the d. of the temple	1Sa 1.09
door and the d. you have set up	Is 57.08

DOORPOSTS

it on the two d. and the lintel of	Ex 12.07
and the two d. with the blood	12.22
on the lintel and on the two d.,	12.23
them on the d. of your house and	Deu 6.09
them upon the d. of your house and	11.20
lintel and the d. formed a pentagon.	1Ki 6.31
to the nave d. of olivewood,	6.33
and from the d. which Hezekiah king	2Ki 18.16
The d. of the nave were squared;	Eze 41.21
and their d. beside my d.,	43.08
and put it on the d. of the temple,	45.19

DOORS

goes out of the d. of your house	Jos 2.19
and closed the d. of the roof	Ju 3.23
saw that the d. of the roof	3.24
not open the d. of the roof	3.25
forth from the d. of my house to	11.31
hold of the d. of the gate of the	16.03
he opened the d. of the house and	19.27
he opened the d. of the house of	1Sa 3.15
made marks on the d. of the gate,	21.13
sanctuary he made d. of olivewood;	1Ki 6.31
He covered the two d. of olivewood	6.32
and two d. of cypress wood;	6.34
for the d. of the innermost part of	7.50
the d. of the nave of the temple.	7.50
gold from the d. of the temple of	2Ki 18.16
nails for the d. of the gates and	1Ch 22.03
thresholds, its walls, and its d.;	2Ch 3.07
and d. for the court, and overlaid	4.09
and overlaid their d. with bronze;	4.09
for the inner d. to the most holy	4.22
for the d. of the nave of the temple	4.22
he shut up the d. of the house of	28.24
he opened the d. of the house of	29.03
They also shut the d. of the	29.07
They consecrated it and set its d.;	Neh 3.01
they laid its beams and set its d.,	3.03
they laid its beams and set its d.,	3.06
they rebuilt it and set its d.,	3.13
he rebuilt it and set its d.,	3.14
it and covered it and set its d.,	3.15
not set up the d. in the gates),	6.01
let us close the d. of the temple;	6.10
been built and I had set up the d.,	7.01
guard let them shut and bar the d.	7.03
that the d. should be shut and	13.19
not shut the d. of my mother's womb,	Job 3.10
have opened my d. to the wayfarer);	31.32
silence, and did not go out of d.—	31.34
"Or who shut in the sea with d.,	38.08
bounds for it, and set bars and d.,	38.10
Who can open the d. of his face?	41.14
and be lifted up, O ancient d.!	Ps 24.07
and be lifted up, O ancient d.!	24.09
above, and opened the d. of heaven;	78.23
For he shatters the d. of bronze,	107.16
at my gates, waiting beside my d.	Pro 8.34
and the d. on the street are shut;	Ecc 12.04
and over our d. are all choice	Sol 7.13
and shut your d. behind you; hide	Is 26.20
to open d. before him that gates	45.01
in pieces the d. of bronze and cut	45.02
walls and at the d. of the houses,	Eze 33.30
And the d. of the side chambers	41.11
The d. had two leaves apiece, two	41.24
And on the d. of the nave were	41.25
and their d. were on the north.	42.04
same exits and arrangements and d.	42.11
guard the d. of your mouth from her	Mic 7.05
Open your d., O Lebanon, that the	Zec 11.01
among you who would shut the d.,	Mal 1.10
the d. being shut where the disciples	Jn 20.19
The d. were shut, but Jesus came and	20.26
the prison d. and brought them out	Ac 5.19
the sentries standing at the d.,	5.23
immediately all the d. were opened	16.26
saw that the prison d. were open,	16.27
the Judge is standing at the d.	Jas 5.09

DOORWAY

called her, she stood in the d.	2Ki 4.15

DOORWAYS

All the d. and windows had square	1Ki 7.05

DOPHKAH
wilderness of Sin, and encamped at D. Num 33.12
And they set out from D., and encamped 33.13

DOR
the king of D. in Naphathdor, one; Jos 12.23
inhabitants of D. and its villages, 17.11
inhabitants of D. and its villages, Ju 1.27
and its towns, D. and its towns. 1Ch 7.29

DORCAS
Tabitha, which means D. or Gazelle. Ac 9.36
garments which D. made while she 9.39

DOT
not a d., will pass from the law Mt 5.18
than for one d. of the law to Lk 16.17

DOTED
and she d. on her lovers the Eze 23.05
idols of every one on whom she d. 23.07
of the Assyrians, upon whom she d. 23.09
She d. upon the Assyrians, governors 23.12
When she saw them she d. upon them, 23.16
and d. upon her paramours there, 23.20

DOTHAN
I heard them say, 'Let us go to D.'" Gen 37.17
his brothers, and found them at D. 37.17
was told him, "Behold, he is in D." 2Ki 6.13

DOTING
than she in her d. and in her Eze 23.11

DOUBLE
Take d. the money with you; Gen 43.12
and they took d. the money with 43.15
an ass or a sheep, he shall pay d. Ex 22.04
thief is found, he shall pay d. 22.07
shall pay d. to his neighbor. 22.09
you shall d. over at the front of 26.09
It shall be square and d., 28.16
the breastpiece was made d.. 39.09
by giving him a d. portion of all Deu 21.17
me inherit a d. share of your 2Ki 2.09
can penetrate his d. coat of mail? Job 41.13
lips and a d. heart they speak. Ps 12.02
the LORD's hand d. for all her Is 40.02
shame you shall have a d. portion, 61.07
you shall possess a d. portion; 61.07
destroy them with d. destruction! Jer 17.18
the holy place had each a d. door. Eze 41.23
chastised for their d. iniquity. Hos 10.10
that I will restore to you d. Zec 9.12
that you might have a d. pleasure; 2Co 1.15
be considered worthy of d. honor, 1Ti 5.17
not suppose that a d. minded man, Jas 1.07
your hearts, you men of d. mind. 4.08
and repay her d. for her deeds; Rev 18.06
mix a d. draught for her in the cup 18.06

DOUBLED
and a span its breadth when d. Ex 39.09

DOUBLE-MINDED
I hate d. men, but I love thy law. Ps 119.113

DOUBLE-TONGUED
not d., not addicted to much wine, 1Ti 3.08

DOUBLING
And the d. of Pharaoh's dream means Gen 41.32

DOUBLY
And I will d. recompense their Jer 16.18

DOUBT
is without d. torn to pieces." Gen 37.33
your life shall hang in d. before you; Deu 28.66
"No d. you are the people, and Job 12.02
of little faith, why did you d.?" Mt 14.31
if you have faith and never d., 21.21
and does not d. in his heart, but Mk 11.23
"No d. this man is a murderer. Ac 28.04
And convince some, who d.; Jud 1.22

DOUBTED
worshiped him; but some d. Mt 28.17

DOUBTING
with no d., for he who doubts is Jas 1.06

DOUBTLESS
"D. you will quote to me this Lk 4.23
There are d. many different languages 1Co 14.10

DOUBTS
But he who has d. is condemned, if Rom 14.23
for he who d. is like a wave of the Jas 1.06

DOUGH
took their d. before it was Ex 12.34
cakes of the d. which they had 12.39
And she took d., and kneaded it, and 2Sa 13.08
fire, and the women knead d., Jer 7.18
kneading of the d. until it is Hos 7.04
If the d. offered as first fruits Rom 11.16
ferments the whole lump of d.? 1Co 5.06
leaven that you may be fresh d., 5.07

DOVE
Then he sent forth a d. from him, Gen 8.08
but the d. found no place to set 8.09
sent forth the d. out of the ark; 8.10
and the d. came back to him in the 8.11
seven days, and sent forth the d.; 8.12
say, "O that I had wings like a d.! Ps 55.06
the wings of a d. covered with 68.13
the soul of thy d. to the wild 74.19
O my d., in the clefts of the rock, Sol 2.14
my d., my perfect one; for my head 5.02
My d., my perfect one, is only one, 6.09
a crane I clamor, I moan like a d. Is 38.14
Be like the d. that nests in the Jer 48.28
Ephraim is like a d., silly and Hos 7.11
Spirit of God descending like a d., Mt 3.16
descending upon him like a d.; Mk 1.10
as a d., and a voice came from Lk 3.22
Spirit descend as a d. from heaven, Jn 1.32

DOVE'S
of a kab of d. dung for five 2Ki 6.25

DOVES
are beautiful; your eyes are d. Sol 1.15
Your eyes are d. behind your veil. 4.01
His eyes are like d. beside springs 5.12
bears, we moan and moan like d.; Is 59.11
and like d. to their windows? 60.08
like d. of the valleys, all of them Eze 7.16
and like d. from the land of Assyria; Hos 11.11
moaning like d., and beating their Nah 2.07
as serpents and innocent as d. Mt 10.16

DOWNCAST
house, "Why are your faces d. today?" Gen 40.07
but a d. spirit dries up the bones. Pro 17.22
But God, who comforts the d., 2Co 7.06

DOWNFALL
by God that the d. of Ahaziah 2Ch 22.07
have seen the d. of my enemies, Ps 92.11
righteous will look upon their d. Pro 29.16
gloated over her, mocking at her d. Lam 1.07
own life, on the day of your d. Eze 32.10

DOWNTRODDEN
Let not the d. be put to shame; Ps 74.21
The LORD lifts up the d., 147.06

DOWNWARD
shall tend upward only, and not d.; Deu 28.13
the Jebusites, and d. to Enrogel; Jos 18.16
had fallen face d. on the ground 1Sa 5.03
had fallen face d. on the ground 5.04
of Judah shall again take root d., 2Ki 19.30
of Judah shall again take root d., Is 37.31
and d. from what had the appearance Eze 1.27

DOWRY
"God has endowed me with a good d.; Gen 30.20
had given it as d. to his daughter, 1Ki 9.16

DRAG
and we shall d. it into the valley, 2Sa 17.13
lest he d. you to the judge, and the Lk 12.58
it not they who d. you into court? Jas 2.06

DRAGGED
d. off in the day of God's wrath. Job 20.28
d. and cast forth beyond the gates Jer 22.19
ones of the flock shall be d. away; 49.20
of their flock shall be d. away; 50.45
her maidens have been d. away, Lam 1.04
and you will be d. before governors Mt 10.18
he d. off men and women and committed Ac 8.03
stoned Paul and d. him out of the 14.19
and Silas and d. them into the 16.19
they d. Jason and some of the 17.06
seized Paul and d. him out of the 21.30

DRAGGING
d. me away, with none to rescue. Ps 7.02
d. the net full of fish, for they Jn 21.08
d. with them Gaius and Aristarchus, Ac 19.29

DRAGNET
and I will haul you up in my d. Eze 32.03

DRAGON
will slay the d. that is in the Is 27.01
pieces, that didst pierce the d.? 51.09
the great d. that lies in the midst Eze 29.03
but you are like a d. in the seas; 32.02
behold a great red d., with seven Rev 12.03
And the d. stood before the woman 12.04
his angels fighting against the d.; 12.07
and the d. and his angels fought, 12.07
And the great d. was thrown down, 12.09
And when the d. saw that he had 12.13
river which the d. had poured from 12.16
Then the d. was angry with the 12.17
And to it the d. gave his power and 13.02
Men worshiped the d., for he had 13.04
like a lamb and it spoke like a d. 13.11
mouth of the d. and from the mouth 16.13
And he seized the d., that ancient 20.02

DRAGONS
the heads of the d. on the waters. Ps 74.13

DRAGS
the grasshopper d. itself along Ecc 12.05
he d. them out with his net, he Hab 1.15

DRAIN
the earth shall d. it down to the Ps 75.08
you shall drink it and d. it out, Eze 23.34
to make her d. the cup of the fury Rev 16.19

DRAINED
blood shall be d. out on the side Lev 1.15
blood shall be d. out at the base 5.09

DRANK
and he d. of the wine, and became Gen 9.21
So I d., and she gave the camels 24.46
men who were with him ate and d., 24.54
of lentils, and he ate and d., 25.34
them a feast, and they ate and d. 26.30
and he brought him wine, and he d. 27.25
So they d. and were merry with him. 43.34
they beheld God, and ate and d. Ex 24.11
he neither ate bread nor d. water. 34.28
abundantly, and the congregation d., Num 20.11
I neither ate bread nor d. water. Deu 9.09
I neither ate bread nor d. water, 9.18
the blood of the grape you d. wine. 32.14
and d. the wine of their drink 32.38
and ate and d. and reviled Abimelech. Ju 9.27
and when he d., his spirit returned, 15.19
so they ate and d., and lodged 19.04
men sat and ate and d. together; 19.06
washed their feet, and ate and d. 19.21
and he ate in his presence and d., 2Sa 11.13
they ate and d. and were happy. 1Ki 4.20
bread in his house, and d. water. 13.19
and he d. from the brook. 17.06
And he ate and d., and lay 19.06
and ate and d., and went in the 19.08
and ate and d., and they carried 2Ki 7.08
Then he went in and ate and d.; 9.34
I dug wells and d. foreign waters, 19.24
and they ate and d. before the LORD 1Ch 29.22
I dug wells and d. waters, and I Is 37.25
the nations d. of her wine, therefore Jer 51.07
ate, and of the wine which he d. Dan 1.05
food, or with the wine which he d.; 1.08
and d. wine in front of the thousand 5.01
and his concubines d. from them. 5.03
They d. wine, and praised the gods 5.04
it to them. and they all d. of it. Mk 14.23
'We ate and d. in your presence, and Lk 13.26
They ate, they d., they married, they 17.27
they d., they bought, they sold, they 17.28
and d. from it himself, and his sons, Jn 4.12
without sight, and neither ate nor d. Ac 9.09
who ate and d. with him after he 10.41
and all d. the same supernatural 1Co 10.04
they d. from the supernatural Rock 10.04

DRAUGHT
and he will pour a d. from it, Ps 75.08
mix a double d. for her in the cup Rev 18.06

DRAW
time when women go out to d. water. Gen 24.11
city are coming out to d. water. 24.13
"I will d. for your camels also, 24.19
and ran again to the well to d., 24.20
young woman who comes out to d., 24.43
and I will d. for your camels also, 24.44
I will d. my sword, my hand shall Ex 15.09
"D. near to the altar, and offer Lev 9.07
"D. near, carry your brethren from 10.04
who has a blemish shall d. near, 21.18
should d. near to burn incense Num 16.40
sons of Ammon you did not d. near, Deu 2.37
he sought to d. you away from the 13.10
And when you d. near to the battle, 20.02
you d. near this day to battle, 20.03
"When you d. near to a city to 20.10
For Joshua did not d. back his hand, Jos 8.26
for he did not d. the sword out of Ju 3.22
And I will d. out Sisera, the 4.07
But the youth did not d. his sword; 8.20
"D. your sword and kill me, lest men 9.54
"Come and let us d. near to one of 19.13
"Shall we again d. near to battle 20.23
and d. them away from the city to 20.32
maidens coming out to d. water, 1Sa 9.11
"Let us d. near hither to God." 14.36
you come out to d. up for battle? 17.08
"D. your sword, and thrust me 31.04
and then d. back from him, that he 2Sa 11.15

DRAW (cont.)
he could not d. it back to himself. 1Ki 13.04
to the king of Israel, "D. the bow"; 2Ki 13.16
"D. your sword, and thrust me 1Ch 10.04
we cannot d. up our case because of Job 37.19
"Can you d. out Leviathan with a 41.01
D. the spear and javelin against my Ps 35.03
The wicked d. the sword and bend 37.14
D. near to me, redeem me, set me free 69.18
They d. near who persecute me with 119.150
of understanding will d. it out. Pro 20.05
to d. near to listen is better than Ecc 5.01
and the years d. nigh, when you will 12.01
D. me after you, let us make haste. Sol 1.04
Woe to those who d. iniquity with Is 5.18
who d. sin as with cart ropes, 5.18
of the Holy One of Israel d. near, 5.19
With joy you will d. water from the 12.03
this people d. near with their 29.13
D. near, O nations, to hear, and 34.01
let us together d. near for judgment. 41.01
d. near together, you survivors of 45.20
D. near to me, hear this: from the 48.16
But you, d. near hither, sons of the 57.03
they delight to d. near to God. 58.02
who d. the bow, to Tubal and Javan, 66.19
I will make him d. near, and he shall Jer 30.21
"D. near, you executioners of the Eze 9.01
and will d. forth my sword out of 21.03
and they shall d. their swords 28.07
and I will d. you up out of the 29.04
and they shall d. their swords 30.11
who d. near to me to minister to me, 43.19
Let all the men of war d. near, Joe 3.09
D. water for the siege, strengthen Nah 3.14
she does not d. near to her God. Zep 3.02
the winevat to d. fifty measures, Hag 2.16
"Then I will d. near to you for Mal 3.05
"Now d. some out, and take it to the Jn 2.08
a woman of Samaria to d. water. 4.07
"Sir, you have nothing to d. with, 4.11
not thirst, nor come here to d." 4.15
the earth, will d. all men to myself." 12.32
to d. away the disciples after them. Ac 20.30
with confidence d. near to the Heb 4.16
through which we d. near to God. 7.19
save those who d. near to God 7.25
make perfect those who d. near. 10.01
let us d. near with a true heart in 10.22
whoever would d. near to God must 11.06
D. near to God and he will draw Jas 4.08
to God and he will d. near to you. 4.08

DRAWERS
of wood and d. of water for all Jos 9.21
of wood and d. of water for the 9.23
of wood and d. of water for the 9.27

DRAWING
were all d. near to hear him. Lk 15.01
As he was now d. near, at the 19.37
because your redemption is d. near." 21.28
on the sea and d. near to the boat. Jn 6.19
more as you see the Day d. near. Heb 10.25

DRAWN
And his soul was d. to Dinah the Gen 34.03
with a d. sword in his hand; Num 22.23
with his d. sword in his hand; 22.31
shall take one d. out of every 31.30
you be d. away and worship them and Deu 4.19
you and have d. away the inhabitants 13.13
but are d. away to worship other 30.17
him with his d. sword in his hand; Jos 5.13
till we have d. them away from the 8.06
they were d. away from the city. 8.16
and were d. away from the city; Ju 20.31
drink what the young men have d." Ru 2.09
and were d. up at the frontier. 2Ki 3.21
in his hand a d. sword stretched 1Ch 21.16
It is d. forth and comes out of his Job 20.25
for thou hast d. me up, and hast not Ps 30.01
than oil, yet they were d. swords. 55.21
from the d. sword, from the bent bow, Is 21.15
tremble; they have d. near and come. 41.05
I the LORD have d. my sword out of Eze 21.05
a sword is d. for the slaughter, it 21.28
a powerful army d. up for battle. Joe 2.05
land of Nimrod with the d. sword; Mic 5.06
servants who had d. the water knew), Jn 2.09
and all was d. up again into heaven. Ac 11.10

DRAWS
wife of the one d. near to rescue Deu 25.11
wood and he who d. your water, 29.11
Behold, the day d. to its close; Ju 19.09
His soul d. near the Pit, and his Job 33.22
For he d. up the drops of water, he 36.27
poor when he d. him into his net. Ps 10.09
troubles, and my life d. near to Sheol. 88.03
My deliverance d. near speedily, my Is 51.05
The time has come, the day d. near. Eze 7.12
the Father who sent me d. him; Jn 6.44

DREAD
of you and the d. of you shall be Gen 9.02
and lo, a d. and great darkness fell 15.12
Egyptians were in d. of the people Ex 1.12
Terror and d. fall upon them; because of 15.16
Moab was in great d. of the people, Num 22.03
'Do not be in d. or afraid of them. Deu 1.29
to put the d. and fear of you upon 2.25
You shall not be in d. of them; 7.21
of you and the d. of you upon all 11.25
or tremble, or be in d. of them; 20.03
night and day you shall be in d., 28.66
because of the d. which your 28.67
do not fear or be in d. of them: 31.06
Then the d. of the LORD fell upon 1Sa 11.07
upon me, and what I d. befalls me. Job 3.25
d. came upon me, and trembling, which 4.14
and let not d. of him terrify me. 9.34
and the d. of him fall upon you? 13.11
and let not d. of thee terrify me. 13.21
when I consider, I am in d. of him. 23.15
an object of d. to my acquaintances; Ps 31.11
your right hand teach you d. deeds! 45.04
my life from d. of the enemy, 64.01
By d. deeds thou dost answer us 65.05
over me; thy d. assaults destroy me. 88.16
for d. of them had fallen upon it. 105.38
Turn away the reproach which I d.; 119.39
be at ease, without d. of evil. Pro 1.33
The d. wrath of a king is like the 20.02
you are in d. will be deserted. Is 7.16
fear what they fear, nor be in d. 8.12
your fear, and let him be your d. 8.13
Whom did you d. and fear, so that 57.11
LORD is with me as a d. warrior; Jer 20.11
shall turn in d. to the LORD our Mic 7.17
D. and terrible are they; their justice Hab 1.07

DREADED
whom your fathers had never d. Deu 32.17

DREADFUL
I will bring you to a d. end, Eze 26.21
have come to a d. end and shall be 27.36
have come to a d. end and shall be 28.19
terrible and d. and exceedingly Dan 7.07

DREADS
What the wicked d. will come upon Pro 10.24

DREAM

came to Abimelech in a d. by night, Gen 20.03
Then God said to him in the d., 20.06
and saw in a d. that the he-goats 31.10
angel of God said to me in the d., 31.11
Laban the Aramean in a d. by night, 31.24
Now Joseph had a d., and when 37.05
"Hear this d. which I have dreamed: 37.06
Then he dreamed another d., and told 37.09
"Behold, I have dreamed another d.; 37.09
"What is this d. that you have 37.10
each his own d., and each d. 40.05
chief butler told his d. to Joseph, 40.09
"In my d. there was a vine before 40.09
"I also had a d.: there were three 40.16
awoke, and behold, it was a d. 41.07
and Pharaoh told them his d., 41.08
each having a d. with its own 41.11
to each man according to his d. 41.12
"I have had a d., and there is no 41.15
when you hear a d. you can interpret 41.15
in my d. I was standing on the 41.17
I also saw in my d. seven ears 41.22
"The d. of Pharaoh is one; 41.25
are seven years; the d. is one. 41.26
of Pharaoh's d. means that the 41.32
a vision, I speak with him in a d. Num 12.06
was telling a d. to his comrade; Ju 7.13
he said, "Behold, I dreamed a d.; 7.13
telling of the d. and its interpretation, 7.15
to Solomon in a d. by night; and God 1Ki 3.05
awoke, and behold, it was a d. 3.15
He will fly away like a d., Job 20.08
In a d., in a vision of the night, 33.15
They are like a d. when one awakes, Ps 73.20
they are like a d., like grass 90.05
of Zion, we were like those who d. 126.01
For a d. comes with much business, Ecc 5.03
distress her, shall be like a d., Is 29.07
who has a d. tell the d., Jer 23.28
to the dreams which they d., 29.08
"I had a d., and my spirit is Dan 2.03
spirit is troubled to know the d." 2.03
Tell your servants the d., 2.04
known to me the d. and its interpretation, 2.05
But if you show the d. and its 2.06
show me the d. and its interpretation." 2.06
the king tell his servants the d., 2.07
you do not make the d. known to me, 2.09
Therefore tell me the d., and I shall 2.09
known to me the d. that I have 2.26
Your d. and the visions of your 2.28
"This was the d.; now we will 2.36
The d. is certain, and its interpretation 2.45
I had a d. which made me afraid; 4.05
to me the interpretation of the d. 4.06
and I told them the d., but they could 4.07
gods—and I told him the d., saying, 4.08
you, here is the d. which I saw; 4.09
This d. I, King Nebuchadnezzar, saw. 4.18
let not the d. or the interpretation 4.19
may the d. be for those who hate you 4.19
Daniel had a d. and visions of his 7.01
Then he wrote down the d., and told 7.01
your old men shall d. dreams, Joe 2.28
the Lord appeared to him in a d., Mt 1.20
warned in a d. not to return to 2.12
appeared to Joseph in a d. and said, 2.13
appeared in a d. to Joseph in 2.19
warned in a d. he withdrew to the 2.22
much over him today in a d." 27.19
and your old men shall d. dreams; Ac 2.17

DREAMED

And he d. that there was a ladder Gen 28.12
"Hear this dream which I have d.: 37.06
Then he d. another dream, and told 37.09
"Behold, I have d. another dream; 37.09
is this dream that you have d.? 37.10
And one night they both d.— 40.05
Pharaoh d. that he was standing by 41.01
fell asleep and d. a second time; 41.05
we d. on the same night, he and I, 41.11
the dreams which he had d. of them; 42.09
and he said, "Behold, I d. a dream; Ju 7.13
saying, 'I have d., I have d.!' Jer 23.25

DREAMER

to one another, "Here comes this d. Gen 37.19
or a d. of dreams, and gives you a Deu 13.01
prophet or to that d. of dreams; 13.03
prophet or that d. of dreams shall 13.05

DREAMERS

your d., your soothsayers, or your Jer 27.09
the d. tell false dreams, and give Zec 10.02

DREAMING

d., lying down, loving to slumber. Is 56.10

DREAMINGS

men in their d. defile the flesh, Jud 1.08

DREAMS

more for his d. and for his words. Gen 37.08
see what will become of his d." 37.20
"We have had d., and there is no 40.08
him, he interpreted our d. to us, 41.12
remembered the d. which he had 42.09
among you, or a dreamer of d., Deu 13.01
prophet or to that dreamer of d.; 13.03
that dreamer of d. shall be put to 13.05
either by d., or by Urim, or by 1Sa 28.06
more, either by prophets or by d.; 28.15
scare me with d. and terrify me Job 7.14
For when d. increase, empty words Ecc 5.07
a hungry man d. he is eating and Is 29.08
a thirsty man d. he is drinking 29.08
name by their d. which they tell Jer 23.27
those who prophesy lying d., 23.32
listen to the d. which they dream, 29.08
understanding in all visions and d. Dan 1.17
Nebuchadnezzar, Nebuchadnezzar had d.; 2.01
summoned, to tell the king his d. 2.02
and understanding to interpret d., 5.12
your old men shall dream d., Joe 2.28
the dreamers tell false d., Zec 10.02
and your old men shall dream d.; Ac 2.17

DREGS

shall drain it down to the d. Ps 75.08
drunk to the d. the bowl of Is 51.17

DRENCH

I d. my couch with my weeping. Ps 6.06
I d. you with my tears, O Heshbon Is 16.09
I will d. the land even to the Eze 32.06

DRENCHED

d. like the corners of the altar. Zec 9.15

DRESS

You shall plant vineyards and d. them, Deu 28.39
do you mean that you d. in scarlet, Jer 4.30
"D. yourself and put on your Ac 12.08

DRESSED

of wine, and five sheep ready d., 1Sa 25.18
he had neither d. his feet, 2Sa 19.24
of the house with d. stones. 1Ki 5.17
to prepare d. stones for building 1Ch 22.02
d. as a harlot, wily of heart. Pro 7.10
but we will build with d. stones; Is 9.10
d. in a white robe; Mk 16.05

DRESSER
and a d. of sycamore trees, Amo 7.14

DRESSES
morning when he d. the lamps he Ex 30.07

DREW
Then Abraham d. near, and said, "Wilt Gen 18.23
and d. near to break the door. 19.09
and she d. for all his camels. 24.20
went down to the spring, and d. 24.45
Then the maids d. near, they and 33.06
her children d. near and bowed 33.07
and last Joseph and Rachel d. near, 33.07
and they d. Joseph up and lifted 37.28
But as he d. back his hand, behold, 38.29
And when the time d. near that 47.29
he d. up his feet into the bed, and 49.33
"Because I d. him out of the water." Ex 2.10
and they came and d. water, 2.16
and even d. water for us and 2.19
When Pharaoh d. near, the people of 14.10
while Moses d. near to the thick 20.21
congregation d. near and stood Lev 9.05
So Aaron d. near to the altar, and 9.08
So they d. near, and carried them in 10.05
when they d. near before the LORD 16.01
Then d. near the daughters of Num 27.01
and d. near before the city, and Jos 8.11
thousand men who d. the sword. Ju 8.10
and d. near to the door of the 9.52
men on foot that d. the sword. 20.02
thousand men that d. the sword, 20.15
hundred thousand men that d. sword; 20.17
men of Israel d. up the battle 20.20
these were men who d. the sword. 20.25
these were men who d. the sword. 20.35
thousand men that d. the sword, 20.46
the one d. off his sandal and gave Ru 4.07
yourself," he d. off his sandal. 4.08
The Philistines d. up in line 1Sa 4.02
and d. water and poured it out 7.06
the Philistines d. near to attack 7.10
and d. up in line of battle against 17.02
the Philistines d. up for battle, 17.21
and he d. near to the Philistine. 17.40
came on and d. near to David, 17.41
and came and d. near to meet David, 17.48
his sword and d. it out of its 17.51
and when David d. near to the 30.21
came out and d. up in battle array 2Sa 10.08
were with him d. near to battle 10.13
And he came apace, and d. near. 18.25
he d. me out of many waters. 22.17
and d. water out of the well of 23.16
valiant men who d. the sword, 24.09
When David's time to die d. near, 1Ki 2.01
and he d. chains of gold across, in 6.21
But a certain man d. his bow at a 22.34
were at Jericho d. near to Elisha, 2Ki 2.05
And Jehu d. his bow with his full 9.24
and he d. it. And Elisha 13.16
Then the king d. near to the altar, 16.12
and d. the bow, expert in war, 1Ch 5.18
and d. water out of the well of 11.18
came out and d. up in battle array 19.09
were with him d. near before the 19.14
and d. up his forces against them. 19.17
thousand men who d. the sword, 21.05
and seventy thousand who d. the sword. 21.05
and Jeroboam d. up his line of 2Ch 13.03
that carried shields and d. bows; 14.08
and they d. up their lines of 14.10
helped him. God d. them away from him, 18.31
But a certain man d. his bow at a 18.33
he d. me out of many waters. Ps 18.16
He d. me up from the desolate pit, 40.02
and they d. near to the gates of 107.18
when he d. a circle on the face of Pro 8.27
Then they d. Jeremiah up with ropes Jer 38.13
our end d. near; our days were Lam 4.18
men d. it ashore and sat down and Mt 13.48
And when they d. near to Jerusalem 21.01
When the season of fruit d. near, 21.34
out his hand and d. his sword, 26.51
And when they d. near to Jerusalem, Mk 11.01
of those who stood by d. his sword, 14.47
As he d. near to the gate of the Lk 7.12
When the days d. near for him to be 9.51
as he came and d. near to the 15.25
As he d. near to Jericho, a blind 18.35
When he d. near to Bethphage and 19.29
And when he d. near and saw the 19.41
feast of Unleavened Bread d. near, 22.01
He d. near to Jesus to kiss him; 22.47
Jesus himself d. near and went with 24.15
So they d. near to the village to 24.28
his disciples d. back and no Jn 6.66
they d. back and fell to the 18.06
d. it and struck the high priest's 18.10
the census and d. away some of the Ac 5.37
as the time of the promise d. near, 7.17
and as he d. near to look, the voice 7.31
he d. his sword and was about to 16.27
my journey and d. near to Damascus, 22.06
they came he d. back and separated Gal 2.12

DRIED
the waters were d. up from the Gen 8.07
the waters were d. from off the 8.13
grapes or eat grapes, fresh or d. Num 6.03
but now our strength is d. up, 11.06
how the LORD d. up the water of Jos 2.10
LORD your God d. up the waters of 4.23
he d. up for us until we passed over, 4.23
the LORD had d. up the waters of 5.01
bowstrings which have not been d., Ju 16.07
bowstrings which had not been d., 16.08
d. up, so that he could not draw it 1Ki 13.04
And after a while the brook d. up, 17.07
and I d. up with the sole of my 2Ki 19.24
my strength is d. up like a potsherd, Ps 22.15
my strength was d. up as by the 32.04
waters of the Nile will be d. up, Is 19.05
and I d. up with the sole of my 37.25
of the wilderness are d. up. Jer 23.10
her waters, that they may be d. up! 50.38
the east wind d. it up; its fruit Eze 19.12
they say, 'Our bones are d. up, 37.11
their root is d. up, they shall bear Hos 9.16
because the water brooks are d. up, Joe 1.20
all the depths of the Nile d. up. Zec 10.11
Euphrates, and its water was d. up, Rev 16.12

DRIES
and a river wastes away and d. up, Job 14.11
a downcast spirit d. up the bones. Pro 17.22
it dry, he d. up all the rivers; Nah 1.04

DRIFT
heard, lest we d. away from it. Heb 2.01

DRIFTING
are driven away like the d. chaff, Zep 2.02
as we were d. across the sea of Ac 27.27

DRINK
Come, let us make our father d. wine, Gen 19.32
their father d. wine that night; 19.33
let us make him d. wine tonight 19.34
their father d. wine that night 19.35
with water, and gave the lad a d. 21.19
let down your jar that I may d.,' 24.14
'D., and I will water your camels'— 24.14
a little water to d. from your jar." 24.17

DRINK (cont.)
She said, "D., my lord"; and she Gen 24.18
jar upon her hand, and gave him a d. 24.18
When she had finished giving him a d., 24.19
little water from your jar to d.," 24.43
"D., and I will draw for your 24.44
I said to her, 'Pray let me d.' 24.45
'D., and I will give your camels d. 24.46
and she gave the camels d. also. 24.46
where the flocks came to d. 30.38
since they bred when they came to d., 30.38
he poured out a d. offering on it, 35.14
will loathe to d. water from the Ex 7.18
could not d. water from the Nile; 7.21
about the Nile for water to d., 7.24
could not d. the water of the Nile. 7.24
they could not d. the water of 15.23
Moses, saying, "What shall we d.?" 15.24
was no water for the people to d. 17.01
and said, "Give us water to d." 17.02
out of it, that the people may d." 17.06
the people sat down to eat and d., 32.06
made the people of Israel d. it. 32.20
"D. no wine nor strong d., you nor Lev 10.09
and all d. which may be drunk from 11.34
and the d. offering with it shall 23.13
offering and their d. offerings, 23.18
sacrifices and d. offerings, 23.37
the flagons for the d. offering; Num 4.07
make the woman d. the water of 5.24
shall make the woman d. the water. 5.26
And when he has made her d. the water, 5.27
himself from wine and strong d.; 6.03
he shall d. no vinegar made from 6.03
wine or strong d., and shall not d. any 6.03
offering and their d. offerings. 6.15
offering and its d. offering. 6.17
that the Nazirite may d. wine. 6.20
and wine for the d. offering, 15.05
and for the d. offering you shall 15.07
offer for the d. offering half a 15.10
offering and its d. offering, 15.24
and there is no water to d." 20.05
you shall give d. to the congregation 20.08
neither will we d. water from a 20.17
and if we d. of your water, I and my 20.19
we will not d. the water of a well; 21.22
Its d. offering shall be a fourth 28.07
pour out a d. offering of strong d. 28.07
and like its d. offering, you shall 28.08
with oil, and its d. offering: 28.09
burnt offering and its d. offering. 28.10
Their d. offerings shall be half a 28.14
burnt offering and its d. offering. 28.15
burnt offering and its d. offering. 28.24
offer them and their d. offering. 28.31
and their d. offering, according to 29.06
offering, and their d. offerings. 29.11
offering and its d. offering. 29.16
offering and the d. offerings for 29.18
offering, and their d. offerings. 29.19
offering and the d. offerings for 29.21
offering and its d. offering. 29.22
offering and the d. offerings for 29.24
offering and its d. offering. 29.25
offering and the d. offerings for 29.27
offering and its d. offering. 29.28
offering and the d. offerings for 29.30
offering, and its d. offerings. 29.31
offering and the d. offerings for 29.33
offering, and its d. offering. 29.34
offering and the d. offerings for 29.37
offering and its d. offering. 29.38
and for your d. offerings, and for 29.39
was no water for the people to d. 33.14
of them for money, that you may d. Deu 2.06
me water for money, that I may d.; 2.28
or sheep, or wine or strong d., 14.26
shall neither d. of the wine nor 28.39
have not drunk wine or strong d.; 29.06
the wine of their d. offering? 32.38
"Pray, give me a little water to d.; Ju 4.19
and gave him a d. and covered him. 4.19
every one that kneels down to d." 7.05
the people knelt down to d. water. 7.06
and d. no wine or strong d., and 13.04
so then d. no wine or strong d., 13.07
neither let her d. wine or strong d., 13.14
the vessels and d. what the young Ru 2.09
drunk neither wine nor strong d., 1Sa 1.15
he ate, they gave him water to d., 30.11
to eat and to d., and to lie with 2Sa 11.11
and d. from his cup, and lie in his 12.03
who faint in the wilderness to d." 16.02
me water to d. from the well of 23.15
But he would not d. of it; 23.16
Shall I d. the blood of the men who 23.17
Therefore he would not d. it. 23.17
eat bread or d. water in this 1Ki 13.08
nor d. water, nor return by the way 13.09
I eat bread nor d. water with you 13.16
eat bread nor d. water there, 13.17
that he may eat bread and d. water.'" 13.18
"Eat no bread, and d. no water"; 13.22
You shall d. from the brook, and I 17.04
water in a vessel, that I may d." 17.10
said to Ahab, "Go up, eat and d.; 18.41
So Ahab went up to eat and to d. 18.42
with water, so that you shall d., 2Ki 3.17
may eat and d. and go to their 6.22
offering, and poured his d. offering, 16.13
offering, and their d. offering; 16.15
own dung and to d. their own urine?" 18.27
one of you will d. the water of 18.31
me water to d. from the well of 1Ch 11.17
But David would not d. of it; 11.18
Therefore he would not d. it. 11.19
with their d. offerings, and sacrifices 29.21
provided them with food and d., 2Ch 28.15
d., and oil to the Sidonians and Ez 3.07
offerings and their d. offerings, 7.17
eat the fat and d. sweet wine and Neh 8.10
way to eat and d. and to send 8.12
the king and Haman sat down to d.; Est 3.15
neither eat nor d. for three days, 4.16
sisters to eat and d. with them. Job 1.04
and let them d. of the wrath of the 21.20
given no water to the weary to d., 22.07
givest them d. from the river of Ps 36.08
or d. the blood of goats? 50.13
us wine to d. that made us reel. 60.03
thirst they gave me vinegar to d. 69.21
and gave them d. abundantly as from 78.15
they could not d. of their streams. 78.44
them tears to d. in full measure. 80.05
and mingle tears with my d., 102.09
they give d. to every beast of the 104.11
He will d. from the brook by the 110.07
wickedness and d. the wine of Pro 4.17
D. water from your own cistern, 5.15
of my bread and d. of the wine I 9.05
Wine is a mocker, strong d. a brawler; 20.01
"Eat and d.!" he says 23.07
awake? I will seek another d." 23.35
is thirsty, give him water to d.; 25.21
it is not for kings to d. wine, 31.04
or for rulers to desire strong d.; 31.04
lest they d. and forget what has 31.05
Give strong d. to him who is 31.06
let them d. and forget their 31.07
man than that he should eat and d., Ecc 2.24
should eat and d. and take pleasure 3.13
is to eat and d. and find enjoyment 5.18
and d., and enjoy himself, for this 8.15

DRINK (cont.)
and d. your wine with a merry heart; Ecc 9.07
I d. my wine with my milk. Sol 5.01
friends, and d.: d. deeply, O lovers! 5.01
I would give you spiced wine to d., 8.02
that they may run after strong d., Is 5.11
valiant men in mixing strong d., 5.22
spread the rugs, they eat, they d. 21.05
"Let us eat and d., for tomorrow 22.13
strong d. is bitter to those who d. it. 24.09
wine and stagger with strong d.; 28.07
priest and prophet reel with strong d., 28.07
with wine, they stagger with strong d.; 28.07
stagger, but not with strong d.! 29.09
and to deprive the thirsty of d. 32.06
own dung and d. their own urine?" 36.12
one of you will d. the water of 36.16
to give d. to my chosen people, 43.20
of my wrath you shall d. no more; 51.22
us fill ourselves with strong d.; 56.12
you have poured out a d. offering, 57.06
shall not d. your wine for which 62.08
gather it shall d. it in the 62.09
behold, my servants shall d., 65.13
that you may d. deeply with delight 66.11
to d. the waters of the Nile? Jer 2.18
to d. the waters of the Euphrates? 2.18
they pour out d. offerings to 7.18
has given us poisoned water to d., 8.14
give them poisonous water to d. 9.15
consolation to d. for his father 16.07
to sit with them, to eat and d. 16.08
and d. offerings have been poured 19.13
father eat and d. and do justice 22.15
and give them poisoned water to d.; 23.15
nations to whom I send you d. it. 25.15
They shall d. and stagger and be 25.16
to whom the Lord sent me d. it: 25.17
them the king of Babylon shall d. 25.26
D., be drunk and vomit, fall and 25.27
the cup from your hand to d., 25.28
says the LORD of hosts: You must d.! 25.28
to Baal and d. offerings have been 32.29
then offer them wine to d." 35.02
and I said to them, "D. wine." 35.05
"We will d. no wine, for Jonadab the 35.06
commanded us, 'You shall not d. wine, 35.06
to d. no wine all our days, ourselves, 35.08
to d. no wine, has been kept; 35.14
and they d. none to this day, for 35.14
and d. its fill of their blood. 46.10
not deserve to d. the cup must d. it, 49.12
not go unpunished, but you must d. 49.12
We must pay for the water we d., Lam 5.04
And water you shall d. by measure, Eze 4.11
a hin; once a day you shall d. 4.11
and they shall d. water by measure 4.16
and d. water with trembling and 12.18
and d. water in dismay, because 12.19
they poured out their d. offerings. 20.28
"You shall d. your sister's cup 23.32
you shall d. it and drain it out, 23.34
fruit, and they shall d. your milk. 25.04
no trees that d. water may reach 31.14
all that d. water, will be comforted 31.16
and to d. of clear water, that you 34.18
and d. what you have fouled with 34.19
you shall eat flesh and d. blood. 39.17
and d. the blood of the princes of 39.18
and d. blood till you are drunk, at 39.19
No priest shall d. wine, and when 44.21
and d. offerings, at the feasts, the 45.17
appointed your food and your d., Dan 1.10
vegetables to eat and water to d. 1.12
food and the wine they were to d., 1.16
his concubines might d. from them. 5.02
wool and my flax, my oil and my d.' Hos 2.05
offering and the d. offering are Joe 1.09
offering and d. offering are 1.13
offering and a d. offering for the 2.14
their God they d. the wine of Amo 2.08
"But you made the Nazirites d. wine, 2.12
husbands, 'Bring, that we may d.!' 4.01
wandered to one city to d. water, 4.08
but you shall not d. their wine. 5.11
who d. wine in bowls, and anoint 6.06
plant vineyards and d. their wine, 9.14
the nations round about shall d.; Ob 1.16
they shall d., and stagger, and 1.16
let them not feed, or d. water, Jon 3.07
to you of wine and strong d.,' Mic 2.11
tread grapes, but not d. wine. 6.15
his neighbors d. of the cup of his Hab 2.15
D., yourself, and stagger! 2.16
they shall not d. wine from them." Zep 1.13
you d., but you never have your fill; Hag 1.06
And when you eat and when you d., Zec 7.06
for yourselves and d. for yourselves? 7.06
and they shall d. their blood like 9.15
you shall eat or what you shall d., Mt 6.25
or 'What shall we d.?' 6.31
able to d. the cup that I am to d.?" 20.22
"You will d. my cup, but to sit at 20.23
I was thirsty and you gave me d., 25.35
thee, or thirsty and give thee d.? 25.37
was thirsty and you gave me no d., 25.42
"D. of it, all of you; 26.27
you I shall not d. again of this 26.29
that day when I d. it new with you 26.29
if this cannot pass unless I d. it, 26.42
they offered him wine to d., 27.34
he tasted it, he would not d. it. 27.34
a reed, and gave it to him to d. 27.48
cup of water to d. because you Mk 9.41
Are you able to d. the cup that I d., 10.38
"The cup that I d. you will d.; 10.39
I shall not d. again of the fruit 14.25
that day when I d. it new in the 14.25
on a reed and gave it to him to d., 15.36
and he shall d. no wine nor strong d., Lk 1.15
do you eat and d. with tax collectors 5.30
Pharisees, but yours eat and d." 5.33
take your ease, eat, d., be merry.' 12.19
are to eat and what you are to d., 12.29
and to eat and d. and get drunk, 12.45
and serve me, till I eat and d.; 17.08
and afterward you shall eat and d.'? 17.08
on I shall not d. of the fruit of 22.18
that you may eat and d. at my table 22.30
Jesus said to her, "Give me a d." Jn 4.07
ask a d. of me, a woman of Samaria?" 4.09
'Give me a d.,' you would have 4.10
of the Son of man and d. his blood, 6.53
indeed, and my blood is d. indeed. 6.55
thirst, let him come to me and d. 7.37
shall I not d. the cup which the 18.11
to eat nor d. till they had killed Ac 23.12
to eat nor d. till they have 23.21
if he is thirsty, give him d.; Rom 12.20
mean food and d. but righteousness 14.17
to eat meat or d. wine or do 14.21
have the right to our food and d.? 1Co 9.04
all drank the same supernatural d. 10.04
down to eat and d. and rose up to 10.07
You cannot d. the cup of the Lord 10.21
So, whether you eat or d., 10.31
not have houses to eat and d. in? 11.22
Do this, as often as you d. it, 11.25
you eat this bread and d. the cup, 11.26
eat of the bread and d. of the cup. 11.28
all were made to d. of one Spirit. 12.13
are not raised, "Let us eat and d., 15.32
of food and d. or with regard to a Col 2.16
No longer d. only water, but use a 1Ti 5.23

DRINK (cont.)
to be slanderers or slaves to d.; Tit 2.03
with food and d. and various Heb 9.10
all nations d. the wine of her Rev 14.08
he also shall d. the wine of God's 14.10
thou hast given them blood to d. 16.06

DRINKERS
all you d. of wine, because of the Joe 1.05

DRINKING
also, until they have done d." Gen 24.19
When the camels had done d., 24.22
he has finished eating and d. Ru 3.03
eating and d. and dancing, because 1Sa 30.16
they are eating and d. before him, 1Ki 1.25
All King Solomon's d. vessels were 10.21
d. himself drunk in the house of 16.09
as he was d. with the kings in the 20.12
Benhadad was d. himself drunk in 20.16
eating and d., for their brethren 1Ch 12.39
All King Solomon's d. vessels were 2Ch 9.20
neither eating bread nor d. water; Ez 10.06
And d. was according to the law, no Est 1.08
And as they were d. wine, the king 5.06
as they were d. wine, the king again 7.02
the place where they were d. wine, 7.08
were eating and d. wine in their Job 1.13
were eating and d. wine in their 1.18
to those who are heroes at d. wine, Is 5.22
sheep, eating flesh and d. wine. 22.13
dreams he is d. and awakes faint, 29.08
For John came neither eating nor d., Mt 11.18
the Son of man came eating and d., 11.19
the flood they were eating and d., 24.38
And no one after d. old wine Lk 5.39
eating no bread and d. no wine; 7.33
The Son of man has come eating and d.; 7.34
eating and d. what they provide, for 10.07

DRINKS
Is it not from this that my lord d., Gen 44.05
and d. the blood of the slain." Num 23.24
which d. water by the rain from Deu 11.11
taste what he eats or what he d.? 2Sa 19.35
D. were served in golden goblets, Est 1.07
my spirit d. their poison; Job 6.04
a man who d. iniquity like water! 15.16
who d. up scoffing like water, 34.07
off his own feet and d. violence. Pro 26.06
he d. no water and is faint. Is 44.12
and eats and d. with the drunken, Mt 24.49
"Every one who d. of this water Jn 4.13
but whoever d. of the water that I 4.14
my flesh and d. my blood has 6.54
my flesh and d. my blood abides in 6.56
the bread or d. the cup of the 1Co 11.27
who eats and d. without discerning 11.29
eats and d. judgment upon himself. 11.29

DRIP
of thy chariot d. with fatness. Ps 65.11
The pastures of the wilderness d., 65.12
the lips of a loose woman d. honey, Pro 5.03
the mountains shall d. sweet wine, Joe 3.18
the mountains shall d. sweet wine, Amo 9.13

DRIPPED
and my hands d. with myrrh, my Sol 5.05

DRIPPING
quarreling is a continual d. of rain. Pro 19.13
A continual d. on a rainy day and a 27.15

DRIPPINGS
than honey and d. of the honeycomb. Ps 19.10
and the d. of the honeycomb are Pro 24.13

DRIVE
hand he will d. them out of his Ex 6.01
he will d. you away completely. 11.01
which shall d. out Hivite, Canaanite, 23.28
I will not d. them out from before 23.29
little I will d. them out from 23.30
and you shall d. them out before 23.31
and I will d. out the Canaanites, 33.02
I will d. out before you the Amorites, 34.11
defeat them and d. them from the Num 22.06
fight against them and d. them out.'" 22.11
then you shall d. out all the 33.52
But if you do not d. out the 33.55
nations where the LORD will d. you. Deu 4.27
so you shall d. them out, and make 9.03
then the LORD will d. out all these 11.23
without fail d. out from before Jos 3.10
I will myself d. them out from 13.06
Israel did not d. out the Geshurites 13.13
and I shall d. them out as the LORD 14.12
people of Judah could not d. out; 15.63
However they did not d. out the 16.10
and did not utterly d. them out. 17.13
for you shall d. out the Canaanites, 17.18
and d. them out of your sight; 23.05
not continue to d. out these 23.13
he could not d. out the inhabitants Ju 1.19
Benjamin did not d. out the Jebusites 1.21
Manasseh did not d. out the inhabitants 1.27
but did not utterly d. them out. 1.28
And Ephraim did not d. out the 1.29
Zebulun did not d. out the inhabitants 1.30
Asher did not d. out the inhabitants 1.31
for they did not d. them out. 1.32
Naphtali did not d. out the inhabitants 1.33
I will not d. them out before you; 2.03
not henceforth d. out before them 2.21
and d. me out of my father's house? 11.07
d. out the inhabitants of this land 2Ch 20.07
us by coming to d. us out of thy 20.11
They d. away the ass of the fatherless; Job 24.03
they d. me forth, they cast up 30.12
the hand of the wicked d. me away. Ps 36.11
own hand didst d. out the nations, 44.02
is driven away, so d. them away; 68.02
thou didst d. out the nations and 80.08
D. out a scoffer, and strife will go Pro 22.10
the places where I shall d. them. Jer 24.09
and I will d. you out, and you will 27.10
that I will d. you out and you 27.15
the nations whither I will d. them." Eze 4.13
to d. me far from my sanctuary? 8.06
turn you about and d. you forward, 39.02
deeds I will d. them out of my Hos 9.15
and d. him into a parched and Joe 2.20
my people you d. out from their Mic 2.09
and began to d. out those who sold Mk 11.15
and began to d. out those who sold, Lk 19.45
D. out the wicked person from among 1Co 5.13

DRIVEN
thou hast d. me this day away from Gen 4.14
And they were d. out from Pharaoh's Ex 10.11
it dies or is hurt or is d. away, 22.10
the sound of a d. leaf shall put Lev 26.36
until he has d. out his enemies Num 32.21
you shall be d. mad by the sight Deu 28.34
the LORD your God has d. you, 30.01
Moses had defeated and d. out. Jos 13.12
For the LORD has d. out before you 23.09
for they have d. me out this day 1Sa 26.19
Have you not d. out the priests of 2Ch 13.09
me, and any resource is d. from me. Job 6.13
Wilt thou frighten a d. leaf and 13.25
darkness, and d. out of the world. 18.18
They are d. out from among men; 30.05
"I am d. far from thy sight." Ps 31.22

DRIVEN (cont.)
As smoke is d. away, so drive them Ps 68.02
may they be d. out of the ruins 109.10
God seeks what has been d. away. Ecc 3.15
be d. away, and be no more. Is 19.07
those who were d. out to the land 27.13
like d. stubble with his bow. 41.02
the places where I have d. them, Jer 8.03
you like chaff d. by the wind from 13.24
the countries where he had d. them.' 16.15
and have d. them away, and you have 23.02
the countries where I have d. them, 23.03
the countries where he had d. them.' 23.08
which they shall be d. and fall; 23.12
all the places where I have d. you, 29.14
the nations where I have d. them, 29.18
they had been d. and came to the 40.12
to which they had been d.— 43.05
the nations to which I have d. you, 46.28
about you, and you shall be d. out, 49.05
to which those d. out of Elam 49.36
is a hunted sheep d. away by lions. 50.17
he has d. and brought me into Lam 3.02
a yoke on our necks we are hard d.; 5.05
that you shall be d. from among men, Dan 4.25
and you shall be d. from among men, 4.32
He was d. from among men, and ate 4.33
he was d. from among men, and his 5.21
lands to which thou hast d. them, 9.07
they have d. you to the border; Ob 1.07
gather those who have been d. away, Mic 4.06
before you are d. away like the Zep 2.02
people shall be d. out at noon, 2.04
kind cannot be d. out by anything Mk 9.29
bonds and was d. by the demon into Lk 8.29
we gave way to it and were d. Ac 27.15
lowered the gear, and so were d. 27.17
perplexed, but not d. to despair; 2Co 4.08
the sea that is d. and tossed by Jas 1.06
great and are d. by strong winds, 3.04
springs and mists d. by a storm; 2Pe 2.17

DRIVER
he said to the d. of his chariot, 1Ki 22.34
he said to the d. of his chariot, 2Ch 18.33
he hears not the shouts of the d. Job 39.07

DRIVES
Nimshi; for he d. furiously." 2Ki 9.20
like chaff which the wind d. away. Ps 1.04
wicked, and d. the wheel over them. Pro 20.26
of discipline d. it far from him. 22.15
when he d. his cart wheel over it Is 28.28
which the wind of the LORD d. 59.19

DRIVING
d. out before you nations greater Deu 4.38
the LORD is d. them out before you. 9.04
your God is d. them out from 9.05
your God is d. them out before you. 18.12
not d. them out at once, and he did Ju 2.23
of Abinadab, were d. the new cart 2Sa 6.03
by d. out before his people a 7.23
And the d. is like the d. of Jehu 2Ki 9.20
Uzzah and Ahio were d. the cart. 1Ch 13.07
in d. out nations before thy people 17.21
the angel of the LORD d. them on! Ps 35.05

DROMEDARIES
and upon d., to my holy mountain Is 66.20

DROOPING
Therefore lift your d. hands and Heb 12.12

DROP
for your olives shall d. off. Deu 28.40
May my teaching d. as the rain, 32.02
yea, his heavens d. down dew. 33.28
they did not d. any of their Ju 2.19
"Their hands will d. from the work, Neh 6.09
and made him d. his prey from his Job 29.17
and d. upon man abundantly. 36.28
and the clouds d. down the dew. Pro 3.20
are like a d. from a bucket, Is 40.15
your arrows d. out of your right Eze 39.03

DROPPED
earth trembled, and the heavens d., Ju 5.04
dropped, yea, the clouds d. water. 5.04
their tax and d. it into the chest 2Ch 24.10
again, and my word d. upon them. Job 29.22
d. on men from heaven, till men Rev 16.21

DROPPING
the honey was d., but no man put 1Sa 14.26

DROPS
For he draws up the d. of water, Job 36.27
or who has begotten the d. of dew? 38.28
my locks with the d. of the night. Sol 5.02
like great d. of blood falling Lk 22.44

DROPSY
was a man before him who had d. Lk 14.02

DROSS
of the earth thou dost count as d.; Ps 119.119
Take away the d. from the silver, Pro 25.04
Your silver has become d., your Is 1.22
smelt away your d. as with lye and 1.25
of Israel has become d. to me; Eze 22.18
in the furnace, have become d. 22.18
Because you have all become d., 22.19

DROUGHT
and with d., and with blasting, and Deu 28.22
D. and heat snatch away the snow Job 24.19
in a land of d. and deep darkness, Jer 2.06
to Jeremiah concerning the d.: 14.01
is not anxious in the year of d., 17.08
A d. upon her waters, that they may 50.38
a land of d. and a desert, a land in 51.43
the wilderness, in the land of d.; Hos 13.05
called for a d. upon the land and Hag 1.11

DROVE
He d. out the man; and at the Gen 3.24
the carcasses, Abram d. them away. 15.11
and he d. away all his cattle, all 31.18
every d. by itself, and said to his 32.16
put a space between d. and d." 32.16
The shepherds came and d. them away; Ex 2.17
the locusts and d. them into the 10.19
and the LORD d. the sea back by a 14.21
wheels so that they d. heavily; 14.25
and d. them outside the camp; Num 5.04
And Caleb d. out from there the Jos 15.14
which d. them out before you, the 24.12
and the LORD d. out before us all 24.18
and he d. out from it the three Ju 1.20
to him and d. the peg into his 4.21
and d. them out before you, and gave 6.09
and Zebul d. out Gaal and his 9.41
and the people d. those cattle 1Sa 30.20
but we d. them back to the entrance 2Sa 11.23
which the LORD d. out before the 1Ki 14.24
whom the LORD d. out before the 2Ki 16.03
and d. the men of Judah from Elath; 16.06
whom the LORD d. out before the 17.08
And Jeroboam d. Israel from following 17.21
whom the LORD d. out before the 21.02
whom the LORD d. out before the 2Ch 28.03
whom the LORD d. out before the 33.02
He d. out nations before them; Ps 78.55
to which I d. them in my anger and Jer 32.37
He d. into my heart the arrows of Lam 3.13

DROVE (cont.)
guardian cherub d. you out from Eze 28.16
of God and d. out all who sold and Mt 21.12
immediately d. him out into the Mk 1.12
he d. them all, with the sheep and Jn 2.15
and d. them out of their district. Ac 13.50
And he d. them from the tribunal. 18.16
and d. us out, and displease God and 1Th 2.15

DROVES
and he put his own d. apart, Gen 30.40
third and all who followed the d., 32.19

DROWN
love, neither can floods d. it. Sol 8.07

DROWNED
neck and to be d. in the depth of Mt 18.06
the sea, and were d. in the sea. Mk 5.13
bank into the lake and were d. Lk 8.33
attempted to do the same, were d. Heb 11.29

DROWSINESS
and d. will clothe a man with rags. Pro 23.21

DROWSY
wheat, but she grew d. and slept; 2Sa 4.06

DRUNK
and became d., and lay uncovered in Gen 9.21
which may be d. from every such Lev 11.34
you have not d. wine or strong Deu 29.06
I will make my arrows d. with blood, 32.42
And when Boaz had eaten and d., Ru 3.07
After they had eaten and d. in Shiloh, 1Sa 1.09
I have d. neither wine nor strong 1.15
within him, for he was very d.; 25.36
eaten bread or d. water for three 30.12
and drank, so that he made him d.; 2Sa 11.13
eaten bread and d. water in the 1Ki 13.22
And after he had eaten bread and d., 13.23
drinking himself d. in the house of 16.09
drinking himself d. in the booths, 20.16
and when they had eaten and d., 2Ki 6.23
Be d., but not with wine; Is 29.09
For my sword has d. its fill in the 34.05
they shall be d. with their own 49.26
you who have d. at the hand of the 51.17
who have d. to the dregs the bowl 51.17
who are d., but not with wine: 51.21
I made them d. in my wrath, and I 63.06
be d. and vomit, fall and rise no Jer 25.27
"Make him d., because he magnified 48.26
them a feast and make them d., 51.39
I will make d. her princes and her 51.57
shall become d. and strip yourself Lam 4.21
and drink blood till you are d., Eze 39.19
concubines have d. wine from them; Dan 5.23
a girl for wine, and have d. it. Joe 3.03
For as you have d. upon my holy Ob 1.16
of his wrath, and makes them d., Hab 2.15
and to eat and drink and get d., Lk 12.45
and when men have d. freely, Jn 2.10
For these men are not d., as you Ac 2.15
one is hungry and another is d. 1Co 11.21
And do not get d. with wine, for Eph 5.18
those who get d. are d. at night. 1Th 5.07
For land which has d. the rain that Heb 6.07
dwellers on earth have become d." Rev 17.02
d. with the blood of the saints and 17.06
nations have d. the wine of her 18.03

DRUNKARD
he is a glutton and a d.' Deu 21.20
for the d. and the glutton will Pro 23.21
the hand of a d. is a proverb in 26.09
he who hires a passing fool or d. 26.10
say, 'Behold, a glutton and a d., Mt 11.19
say, 'Behold, a glutton and a d., Lk 7.34
d., or robber—not even to eat with 1Co 5.11
no d., not violent but gentle, not 1Ti 3.03
quick-tempered or a d. or violent or Tit 1.07

DRUNKARDS
and the d. make songs about me. Ps 69.12
proud crown of the d. of Ephraim, Is 28.01
crown of the d. of Ephraim will be 28.03
the common sort d. were brought Eze 23.42
A band of d., they give themselves Hos 4.18
Awake, you d., and weep; Joe 1.05
nor d., nor revilers, nor robbers 1Co 6.10

DRUNKEN
Eli took her to be a d. woman. 1Sa 1.13
to her, "How long will you be d.? 1.14
makes them stagger like a d. man. Job 12.25
they reeled and staggered like d. men, Ps 107.27
her doings as a d. man staggers in Is 19.14
The earth staggers like a d. man, 24.20
I am like a d. man, like a man Jer 23.09
hand, making all the earth d.; 51.07
You also will be d., you will be Nah 3.11
and eats and drinks with the d., Mt 24.49

DRUNKENNESS
time, for strength, and not for d.! Ecc 10.17
will fill with d. all the inhabitants Jer 13.13
you will be filled with d. and sorrow. Eze 23.33
dissipation and d. and cares of Lk 21.34
in the day, not in reveling and d., Rom 13.13
envy, d., carousing, and the like. Gal 5.21
d., revels, carousing, and lawless 1Pe 4.03

DRUSILLA
days Felix came with his wife D., Ac 24.24

DRY
place, and let the d. land appear." Gen 1.09
God called the d. land Earth, and 1.10
everything on the d. land in whose 7.22
the face of the ground was d. 8.13
day of the month, the earth was d. 8.14
and pour it upon the d. ground; Ex 4.09
become blood upon the d. ground." 4.09
may go on d. ground through the 14.16
night, and made the sea d. land, 14.21
the midst of the sea on d. ground, 14.22
walked on d. ground through the 14.29
walked on d. ground in the midst 15.19
offering, mixed with oil or d., Lev 7.10
sweeping away of moist and d. alike. Deu 29.19
were passing over on d. ground, Jos 3.17
LORD stood on d. ground in the 3.17
feet were lifted up on d. ground, 4.18
over this Jordan on d. ground.' 4.22
their provisions were d. and moldy. 9.05
now, behold, it is d. and moldy; 9.12
and it is d. on all the ground, then Ju 6.37
let it be d. only on the fleece, and 6.39
for it was d. on the fleece only, 6.40
of them could go over on d. ground. 2Ki 2.08
will make this d. stream-bed full 3.16
the midst of the sea on d. land; Neh 9.11
withholds the waters, they d. up; Job 12.15
a driven leaf and pursue d. chaff? 13.25
the flame will d. up his shoots, 15.30
His roots d. up beneath, and his 18.16
they gnaw the d. and desolate 30.03
as in a d. and weary land where no Ps 63.01
He turned the sea into d. land; 66.06
thou didst d. up ever-flowing 74.15
for his hands formed the d. land. 95.05
the Red Sea, and it became d.; 106.09
Better is a d. morsel with quiet Pro 17.01
and as d. grass sinks down in the Is 5.24
the river will be parched and d.; 19.05

DRY (cont.)

Nile will diminish and d. up, Is 19.06
is sown by the Nile will d. up, 19.07
like heat in a d. place. Thou dost 25.05
When its boughs are d., they are 27.11
streams of water in a d. place, 32.02
wilderness and the d. land shall be 35.01
and the d. land springs of water. 41.18
and d. up all their herbage; 42.15
into islands, and d. up the pools. 42.15
land, and streams on the d. ground; 44.03
'Be d., I will d. up your rivers'; 44.27
by my rebuke I d. up the sea, 50.02
not thou that didst d. up the sea, 51.10
and like a root out of d. ground; 53.02
eunuch say, "Behold, I am a d. tree." 56.03
Do the mountain waters run d., Jer 18.14
nations, a wilderness d. and desert. 50.12
I will d. up her sea and make her 51.36
her sea and make her fountain d.; 51.36
bones, it has become as d. as wood. Lam 4.08
d. up the green tree, and make the Eze 17.24
and make the d. tree flourish. 17.24
in a d. and thirsty land. 19.13
tree in you and every d. tree; 20.47
And I will d. up the Nile, and will 30.12
and lo, they were very d. 37.02
O d. bones, hear the word of the 37.04
and like d. rot to the house of Hos 5.12
a miscarrying womb and d. breasts. 9.14
and his fountain shall d. up, 13.15
who made the sea and the d. land." Jon 1.09
vomited out Jonah upon the d. land. 2.10
He rebukes the sea and makes it d., Nah 1.04
they are consumed, like d. stubble. 1.10
a d. waste like the desert. Zep 2.13
earth and the sea and the d. land; Hag 2.06
what will happen when it is d.?" Lk 23.31
the Red Sea as if on d. land; Heb 11.29

DRYSHOD

channels that men may cross d. Is 11.15

DUE

the justice d. to your poor in his Ex 23.06
as a perpetual d. from the people 29.28
as a perpetual d. from the people Lev 7.34
is a perpetual d. throughout their 7.36
it is your d. and your sons' d., 10.13
given as your d. and your sons' d., 10.14
sons' with you, as a d. for ever; 10.15
fire to the LORD, a perpetual d." 24.09
of service d. from him he shall 25.52
and to your sons as a perpetual d. Num 18.08
with you, as a perpetual d.; 18.11
with you, as a perpetual d.; 18.19
every offering d. to the LORD, 18.29
to offer to me in its d. season.' 28.02
holy things which are d. from you, Deu 12.26
be the priests' d. from the people, 18.03
the justice d. to the sojourner or 24.17
the justice d. to the sojourner, 27.19
here, with stones laid in d. order; Ju 6.26
and in d. time Hannah conceived and 1Sa 1.20
performed their service in d. order. 1Ch 6.32
Ascribe to the LORD the glory d. his name; 16.29
the portion d. to the priests and 2Ch 31.04
LORD the thanks d. to his righteousness, Ps 7.17
render them their d. reward. 28.04
Praise is d. to thee, O God, in Zion; 65.01
Ascribe to the LORD the glory d. his name; 96.08
give them their food in d. season. 104.27
them their food in d. season. 145.15
good from those to whom it is d., Pro 3.27
For this is thy d.; for among Jer 10.07
receiving the d. reward of our Lk 23.41
own persons the d. penalty for Rom 1.27
reckoned as a gift but as his d. 4.04
dues, taxes to whom taxes are d., 13.07
d., revenue to whom revenue is d., 13.07
d., respect to whom respect is d., 13.07
is d., honor to whom honor is d., 13.07
for in d. season we shall reap, if Gal 6.09
d. to their hardness of heart; Eph 4.18
variation or shadow d. to change. Jas 1.17
that in d. time he may exalt you. 1Pe 5.06
to drink. It is their d.!" Rev 16.06

DUES

to the LORD, and his rightful d. Deu 18.01
Pay all of them their d., taxes to Rom 13.07

DUG

witness for me that I d. this well." Gen 21.30
servants had d. in the days of 26.15
And Isaac d. again the wells of 26.18
which had been d. in the days of 26.18
servants d. in the valley and 26.19
Then they d. another well, and they 26.21
from there and d. another well, 26.22
there Isaac's servants d. a well. 26.25
about the well which they had d., 26.32
the Egyptians d. round about the Ex 7.24
the well which the princes d., Num 21.18
I d. wells and drank foreign waters, 2Ki 19.24
cause they d. a pit for my life. Ps 35.07
They d. a pit in my way, but they 57.06
until a pit is d. for the wicked. 94.13
Godless men have d. pitfalls for me, 119.85
I d. wells and drank waters, and I Is 37.25
and d., and I took the waistcloth Jer 13.07
Yet they have d. a pit for my life. 18.20
For they have d. a pit to take me, 18.22
and when I d. in the wall, lo, there Eze 8.08
the evening I d. through the wall 12.07
and d. a wine press in it, and built Mt 21.33
went and d. in the ground and hid 25.18
and d. a pit for the wine press, and Mk 12.01
who d. deep, and laid the foundation Lk 6.48

DULL

skin of the body are of a d. white, Lev 13.39
The d. man cannot know, the stupid Ps 92.06
or his ear d., that it cannot hear; Is 59.01
For this people's heart has grown d., Mt 13.15
For this people's heart has grown d., Ac 28.27
you have become d. of hearing. Heb 5.11

DULLEST

Understand, O d. of the people! Ps 94.08

DULLNESS

Thou wilt give them d. of heart; Lam 3.65

DUMAH

Mishma. D., Massa, Gen 25.14
Arab, D., Eshan, Jos 15.52
Mishma, D., Massa, Hadad, Tema, 1Ch 1.30
The oracle concerning D. One is Is 21.11

DUMB

Who makes him d., or deaf, or seeing, Ex 4.11
Let the lying lips be d., which speak Ps 31.18
like a d. man who does not open his 38.13
I was d. and silent, I held my peace 39.02
I am d., I do not open my mouth; 39.09
Open your mouth for the d., for the Pro 31.08
the tongue of the d. sing for joy. Is 35.06
that before its shearers is d., 53.07
they are all d. dogs, they cannot 56.10
you shall be d. and unable to Eze 3.26
shall speak and be no longer d. 24.27
was opened, and I was no longer d. 33.22
face toward the ground and was d. Dan 10.15
creation when he makes d. idols! Hab 2.18

DUMB (cont.)
to a d. stone, Arise! Can this Hab 2.19
a d. demoniac was brought to him. Mt 9.32
been cast out, the d. man spoke; 9.33
Then a blind and d. demoniac was 12.22
so that the d. man spoke and saw. 12.22
the d., and many others, and they 15.30
when they saw the d. speaking, 15.31
the deaf hear and the d. speak. Mk 7.37
son to you, for he has a d. spirit; 9.17
"You d. and deaf spirit, I command 9.25
made signs to them and remained d. Lk 1.22
casting out a demon that was d.; 11.14
the d. man spoke, and the people 11.14
or a lamb before its shearer is d., Ac 8.32
you were led astray to d. idols, 1Co 12.02
a d. ass spoke with human voice and 2Pe 2.16

DUMBFOUNDED
to shame, let them go d. to Sheol. Ps 31.17

DUNG
and its d., you shall burn with Ex 29.14
legs, its entrails, and its d., Lev 4.11
and its d., he burned with fire 8.17
flesh and their d. shall be burned 16.27
with her d., shall be burned; Num 19.05
a man burns up d. until it is all 1Ki 14.10
a kab of dove's d. for five 2Ki 6.25
shall be as d. upon the face of 9.37
eat their own d. and to drink 18.27
Jackal's Well and to the D. Gate, Neh 2.13
of the wall, as far as the D. Gate. 3.13
Bethhaccherem, repaired the D. Gate; 3.14
right upon the wall to the D. Gate; 12.31
perish for ever like his own d.; Job 20.07
who became d. for the ground. Ps 83.10
eat their own d. and drink their Is 36.12
shall be as d. on the surface of Jer 8.02
shall fall like d. upon the open 9.22
shall be as d. on the surface of 16.04
they shall be d. on the surface of 25.33
it in their sight on human d." Eze 4.12
you have cow's d. instead of human d., 4.15
like dust, and their flesh like d. Zep 1.17
and spread d. upon your faces, the Mal 2.03
the d. of your offerings, and I will 2.03

DUNGEON
they should put me into the d." Gen 40.15
brought him hastily out of the d.; 41.14
of the captive who was in the d., Ex 12.29
out the prisoners from the d., Is 42.07
When Jeremiah had come to the d. cells, Jer 37.16

DUNGHILL
and his house shall be made a d. Ez 6.11
for the land nor for the d.; Lk 14.35

DUNG-PIT
as straw is trodden down in a d. Is 25.10

DURA
He set it up on the plain of D., Dan 3.01

DURING
land of Egypt d. the seven plenteous Gen 41.34
D. the seven plenteous years the 41.47
which she lies d. her impurity Lev 15.20
wilderness of Zin d. the strife of Num 27.14
whom he had slain d. his life. Ju 16.30
or d. all the days of the kings of 2Ki 23.22
dwell in booths d. the feast of Neh 8.14
do under heaven d. the few days of Ecc 2.03
D. the number of days that you lie Eze 4.09
at Jerusalem d. her appointed 36.38
prospered d. the reign of Darius Dan 6.28
"Not d. the feast, lest there be a Mt 26.05
"Not d. the feast, lest there be a Mk 14.02
And d. supper, when the devil had Jn 13.02
appearing to them d. forty days, Ac 1.03
accompanied us d. all the time 1.21
This was d. the days of Unleavened 12.03
people great d. their stay in the 13.17
on a person only d. his life? Rom 7.01
on your behalf d. my imprisonment Phm 1.13
d. the building of the ark, in which 1Pe 3.20
rain may fall d. the days of their Rev 11.06

DUST
formed man of d. from the ground, Gen 2.07
and d. you shall eat all the days 3.14
you are d., and to d. you shall return." 3.19
descendants as the d. of the earth; 13.16
one can count the d. of the earth, 13.16
LORD, I who am but d. and ashes. 18.27
shall be like the d. of the earth, 28.14
rod and strike the d. of the earth, Ex 8.16
and struck the d. of the earth, 8.17
all the d. of the earth became 8.17
become fine d. over all the land 9.09
out its blood and cover it with d. Lev 17.13
some of the d. that is on the Num 5.17
Who can count the d. of Jacob, 23.10
small, until it was as fine as d.; Deu 9.21
and I threw the d. of it into the 9.21
rain of your land powder and d.; 28.24
venom of crawling things of the d. 32.24
and they put d. upon their heads. Jos 7.06
He raises up the poor from the d.; 1Sa 2.08
threw stones at him and flung d. 2Sa 16.13
them fine as the d. of the earth, 22.43
you out of the d. and made you 1Ki 16.02
and the d., and licked up the water 18.38
if the d. of Samaria shall suffice 20.10
made them like the d. at threshing. 2Ki 13.07
and beat it to d. and cast the 23.06
and cast the d. of it upon the 23.06
and cast the d. of them into the 23.12
its stones, crushing them to d.; 23.15
as many as the d. of the earth. 2Ch 1.09
and he made d. of them and strewed 34.04
and sprinkled d. upon their heads Job 2.12
whose foundation is in the d., 4.19
affliction does not come from the d., 5.06
and wilt thou turn me to d. again? 10.09
have laid my strength in the d. 16.15
we descend together into the d." 17.16
will lie down with him in the d. 20.11
They lie down alike in the d., and the 21.26
if you lay gold in the d., and gold 22.24
Though he heap up silver like d., 27.16
sapphires, and it has d. of gold. 28.06
I have become like d. and ashes. 30.19
together, and man would return to d. 34.15
when the d. runs into a mass and 38.38
Hide them all in the d. together; 40.13
myself, and repent in d. and ashes." 42.06
ground, and lay my soul in the d. Ps 7.05
them fine as d. before the wind; 18.42
dost lay me in the d. of death. 22.15
bow all who go down to the d., 22.29
Will the d. praise thee? Will it 30.09
For our soul is bowed down to the d.; 44.25
him, and his enemies lick the d.! 72.09
he rained flesh upon them like d., 78.27
my God, make them like whirling d., 83.13
hast defiled his crown in the d. 89.39
Thou turnest man back to the d., 90.03
dear, and have pity on her d. 102.14
he remembers that we are d. 103.14
they die and return to their d. 104.29
He raises the poor from the d., 113.07
My soul cleaves to the d.; 119.25
the first of the d. of the world. Pro 8.26

DUST (cont.)
all are from the d., and all turn to d. Ecc 3.20
and the d. returns to the earth as 12.07
and hide in the d. from before the Is 2.10
and their blossom go up like d.; 5.24
and whirling d. before the storm. 17.13
cast to the ground, even to the d. 25.12
to the ground, casts it to the d. 26.05
O dwellers in the d., awake and sing 26.19
from low in the d. your words 29.04
speech shall whisper out of the d. 29.04
your foes shall be like small d., 29.05
enclosed the d. of the earth in a 40.12
accounted as the d. on the scales; 40.15
he takes up the isles like fine d. 40.15
makes them like d. with his sword, 41.02
Come down and sit in the d., 47.01
you, and lick the d. of your feet. 49.23
Shake yourself from the d., arise; 52.02
and d. shall be the serpent's food. 65.25
they have cast d. on their heads Lam 2.10
In the d. of the streets lie the 2.21
let him put his mouth in the d.— 3.29
the ground to cover it with d. Eze 24.07
many that their d. will cover you; 26.10
They cast d. on their heads and 27.30
sleep in the d. of the earth shall Dan 12.02
the poor into the d. of the earth, Amo 2.07
Bethleaphrah roll yourselves in the d. Mic 1.10
they shall lick the d. like a serpent, 7.17
the clouds are the d. of his feet. Nah 1.03
blood shall be poured out like d., Zep 1.17
and heaped up silver like d., Zec 9.03
shake off the d. from your feet as Mt 10.14
shake off the d. that is on your Mk 6.11
shake off the d. from your feet as Lk 9.05
'Even the d. of your town that 10.11
shook off the d. from their feet Ac 13.51
garments and threw d. into the air, 22.23
was from the earth, a man of d.; 1Co 15.47
man of d., so are those who are of the d.; 15.48
borne the image of the man of d., 15.49
And they threw d. on their heads, as Rev 18.19

DUTIES
They shall perform d. for him and Num 3.07
attend to the d. for the people of 3.08
attending to the d. of the sanctuary 3.28
the Levites in assigning their d. 8.26
and attend to all d. of the tent; 18.03
attend to the d. of the sanctuary 18.05
sanctuary and the d. of the altar, 18.05
the rights and d. of the kingship; 1Sa 10.25
the appointed d in their service. 1Ch 24.03
did the work and of their d. was: 25.01
And they cast lots for their d., 25.08
had d., just as their brethren did, 26.12
appointed to outside d. for Israel, 26.29
established the d. of the priests Neh 13.30
blood, who does none of these d., Eze 18.10
Practice these d., devote yourself 1Ti 4.15
beloved. Teach and urge these d. 6.02
tent, performing their ritual d.; Heb 9.06

DUTY
and perform the d. of a brother-in-law Gen 38.08
and perform the d. of a husband's Deu 25.05
not perform the d. of a husband's 25.07
who come off d. on the sabbath and 2Ki 11.05
which come on d. in force on the 11.07
were to go off d. on the sabbath, 11.09
were to come on d. on the sabbath, 11.09
upon them lay the d. of watching, 1Ch 9.27
for they were on d. day and night. 9.33
"but their d. shall be to assist 23.28
their appointed d. in their 24.19
and it was the d. of the trumpeters 2Ch 5.13
as the d. of each day required, 8.13
priests as the d. of each day 8.14
who come off d. on the sabbath, 23.04
were to go off d. on the sabbath, 23.08
were to come on d. on the sabbath; 23.08
the LORD as the d. of each day 31.16
and their d. was to distribute to Neh 13.13
for this is the whole d. of man. Ecc 12.13
be the prince's d. to furnish the Eze 45.17
God when his division was on d., Lk 1.08
we have only done what was our d.'" 17.10
whom we may appoint to this d. Ac 6.03
their religious d. to their own 1Ti 5.04

DWARF
or a d., or a man with a defect in Lev 21.20

DWELL
of those who d. in tents and have Gen 4.20
and let him d. in the tents of Shem; 9.27
that they could not d. together, 13.06
and he shall d. over against all 16.12
for he was afraid to d. in Zoar; 19.30
before you; d. where it pleases you." 20.15
the Canaanites, among whom I d., 24.03
the Canaanites, in whose land I d.; 24.37
d. in the land of which I shall 26.02
You shall d. with us; and the land 34.10
d. and trade in it, and get property 34.10
and we will d. with you and become 34.16
let them d. in the land and trade 34.21
will the men agree to d. with us, 34.22
them, and they will d. with us." 34.23
go up to Bethel, and d. there; 35.01
too great for them to d. together; 36.07
you shall d. in the land of Goshen, 45.10
that you may d. in the land of 46.34
your servants d. in the land of 47.04
let them d. in the land of Goshen; 47.06
Zebulun shall d. at the shore of 49.13
was content to d. with the man, Ex 2.21
land of Goshen, where my people d., 8.22
They shall not d. in your land, lest 23.33
that I may d. in their midst. 25.08
And I will d. among the people of 29.45
Egypt that I might d. among them; 29.46
he shall d. alone in a habitation Lev 13.46
but shall d. outside his tent seven 14.08
bringing you to d. may not vomit 20.22
You shall d. in booths for seven 23.42
in Israel shall d. in booths, 23.42
of Israel d. in booths when I 23.43
so you will d. in the land securely. 25.18
your fill, and d. in it securely. 25.19
and d. in your land securely. 26.05
camp, in the midst of which I d." Num 5.03
the people who d. in it are strong 13.18
land that they d. in is good or 13.19
that they d. in are camps or 13.19
Yet the people who d. in the land 13.28
The Amalekites d. in the land of 13.29
the Amorites d. in the hill 13.29
and the Canaanites d. by the sea, 13.29
the Canaanites d. in the valleys, 14.25
I swore that I would make you d., 14.30
you in the land where you d. 33.55
their possession, cities to d. in; 35.02
The cities shall be theirs to d. in, 35.03
may return to d. in the land 35.32
live, in the midst of which I d.; 35.34
for I the LORD d. in the midst of 35.34
choose, to make his name d. there, Deu 12.11
dispossess them and d. in their land, 12.29
your God gives you to d. there, 13.12
choose, to make his name d. there, 14.23
choose, to make his name d. there, 16.02

DWELL (cont.)

choose, to make his name d. in it,	Deu 16.06
choose, to make his name d. there.	16.11
and you possess it and d. in it,	17.14
them and d. in their cities and in	19.01
he shall d. with you, in your midst,	23.16
"If brothers d. together, and one of	25.05
to make his name to d. there.	26.02
house, and you shall not d. in it;	28.30
that you may d. in the land which	30.20
been content to d. beyond the	Jos 7.07
from you,' when you d. among us?	9.22
Amorites that d. in the hill	10.06
and Maacath d. in the midst of	13.13
the land, but only cities to d. in,	14.04
the Jebusites d. with the people	15.63
Canaanites who d. in the plain	17.16
that we be given cities to d. in,	21.02
had not built, and you d. therein;	24.13
the Amorites in whose land you d.;	24.15
the Amorites, in whose land you d.'	Ju 6.10
was content to d. with the man;	17.11
for itself an inheritance to d. in;	18.01
and made them d. in this place.	1Sa 12.08
country towns, that I may d. there;	27.05
your servant d. in the royal city	27.05
I d. in a house of cedar, but the	2Sa 7.02
you build me a house to d. in?	7.05
that they may d. in their own place,	7.10
and Israel and Judah d. in booths;	11.11
"Let him d. apart in his own house;	14.24
and d. there, and do not go forth	1Ki 2.36
woman and I d. in the same house;	3.17
And I will d. among the children of	6.13
His own house where he was to d.,	7.08
that he would d. in thick darkness	8.12
a place for thee to d. in for ever."	8.13
"But will God indeed d. on the earth?	8.27
belongs to Sidon, and d. there.	17.09
She answered, "I d. among my own people."	2Ki 4.13
place where we d. under your	6.01
us make a place for us to d. there."	6.02
Elath, where they d. to this day.	16.06
and let him go and d. there,	17.27
d. in the land, and serve the king	25.24
Now the first to d. again in their	1Ch 9.02
I d. in a house of cedar, but the	17.01
not build me a house to d. in.	17.04
that they may d. in their own place,	17.09
to build himself a house to d. in,	2Ch 2.03
that he would d. in thick darkness.	6.01
a place for thee to d. in for ever."	6.02
"But will God d. indeed with man on	6.18
his name to d. there overthrow any	Ez 6.12
chosen, to make my name d. there.'	Neh 1.09
Israel should d. in booths during	8.14
Let clouds d. upon it; let the	Job 3.05
more those who d. in houses of	4.19
not wickedness d. in your tents.	11.14
of the torrents they must d.,	30.06
O LORD, makest me d. in safety.	Ps 4.08
Who shall d. on thy holy hill?	15.01
and I shall d. in the house of the	23.06
the world and those who d. therein;	24.01
that I may d. in the house of the	27.04
so you will d. in the land, and	37.03
the land, and d. upon it for ever.	37.29
Let me d. in thy tent for ever!	61.04
bring near, to d. in thy courts!	65.04
so that those who d. at earth's	65.08
gives the desolate a home to d. in;	68.06
the rebellious d. in a parched	68.06
where the LORD will d. for ever?	68.16
that the LORD God may d. there.	68.18
Rebuke the beasts that d. among the	68.30
let no one d. in their tents.	69.25
servants shall d. there and possess it;	69.35

who love his name shall d. in it.	69.36
Blessed are those who d. in thy house,	84.04
of my God than d. in the tents of	84.10
him, that glory may d. in our land.	85.09
the world and those who d. in it!	98.07
the land, that they may d. with me;	101.06
deceit shall d. in my house;	101.07
of thy servants shall d. secure;	102.28
finding no way to a city to d. in;	107.04
till they reached a city to d. in.	107.07
And there he lets the hungry d.,	107.36
that I d. among the tents of Kedar!	120.05
here I will d., for I have desired	132.14
it is when brothers d. in unity!	133.01
the morning and d. in the uttermost	139.09
upright shall d. in thy presence.	140.13
to me will d. secure and will be	Pro 1.33
I, wisdom, d. in prudence, and I find	8.12
the wicked will not d. in the land.	10.30
O you who d. in the gardens, my	Sol 8.13
you are made to d. alone in the	Is 5.08
and I d. in the midst of a people	6.05
who d. in Zion, be not afraid of the	10.24
The wolf shall d. with the lamb, and	11.06
there ostriches will d., and there	13.21
you who d. on the earth, when a	18.03
for those who d. before the LORD.	23.18
people in Zion who d. at Jerusalem;	30.19
Then justice will d. in the wilderness,	32.16
among us can d. with the devouring	33.14
among us can d. with everlasting	33.14
He will d. on the heights;	33.16
the people who d. there will be	33.24
owl and the raven shall d. in it.	34.11
to generation they shall d. in it.	34.17
spreads them like a tent to d. in;	40.22
beauty of a man, to d. in a house.	44.13
for me; make room for me to d. in.'	49.20
and they who d. in it will die like	51.06
"I d. in the high and holy place,	57.15
the restorer of streets to d. in.	58.12
it, and my servants shall d. there.	65.09
I will let you d. in this place.	Jer 7.03
then I will let you d. in this place,	7.07
where I made my name d. at first,	7.12
the city and those who d. in it.	8.16
and all who d. in the desert that	9.26
ground, O you who d. under siege!	10.17
of those who d. in it the beasts	12.04
He shall d. in the parched places	17.06
and all who d. in your house, shall	20.06
saved, and Israel will d. securely.	23.06
Then they shall d. in their own land."	23.08
and those who d. in the land of	24.08
and d. upon the land which the LORD	25.05
mixed tribes that d. in the desert;	25.24
own land, to till it and d. there,	27.11
all the people who d. in this city,	29.16
its cities shall d. there together,	31.24
and I will make them d. in safety.	32.37
and Jerusalem will d. securely.	33.16
and not to build houses to d. in.	35.09
then you shall d. in the land	35.15
and d. with him among the people;	40.05
D. in the land, and serve the king	40.09
I will d. at Mizpah, to stand for	40.10
and d. in your cities that you have	40.10
for bread, and we will d. there,'	42.14
those who d. in the land of Egypt,	44.13
they desire to return to d. there;	44.14
of Judah who d. in the land of	44.26
the city and those who d. in it.	47.02
and d. in the rock, O inhabitants of	48.28
d. in the depths, O inhabitants of	49.08
no man shall d. there, no man shall	49.18
d. in the depths, O inhabitants of	49.30
no man shall d. there, no man shall	49.33

DWELL (cont.)
desolation, and none shall d. in it; Jer 50.03
and jackals shall d. in Babylon, 50.39
and ostriches shall d. in her; 50.39
the LORD, so no man shall d. there, 50.40
O you who d. by many waters, rich in 51.13
so that nothing shall d. in it, 51.62
he has made me d. in darkness like Lam 3.06
Wherever you d. your cities shall Eze 6.06
you d. in the midst of a rebellious 12.02
violence of all those who d. in it. 12.19
under it will d. all kinds of 17.23
make you to d. in the nether world, 26.20
then they shall d. in their own 28.25
And they shall d. securely in it, 28.26
They shall d. securely, when I 28.26
Upon its ruin will d. all the birds 31.13
it, when I smite all who d. in it, 32.15
that they may d. securely in the 34.25
they shall d. securely, and none 34.28
You shall d. in the land which I 36.28
They shall d. in the land where 37.25
children shall d. there for ever; 37.25
the nations and now d. securely, 38.08
the quiet people who d. securely, 38.11
who d. at the center of the earth. 38.12
on those who d. securely in the 39.06
"Then those who d. in the cities of 39.09
when they d. securely in their land 39.26
where I will d. in the midst of the 43.07
and I will d. in their midst for 43.09
wherever they d., the sons of men, Dan 2.38
that d. in all the earth: Peace be 4.01
languages that d. in all the earth: 6.25
"You must d. as mine for many days; Hos 3.03
of Israel shall d. many days 3.04
and all who d. in it languish, and 4.03
I will again make you d. in tents, 12.09
return and d. beneath my shadow, 14.07
who d. in Zion, my holy mountain. Joe 3.17
of Israel who d. in Samaria be Amo 3.12
but you shall not d. in them; 5.11
and all who d. in it mourn, and all 9.05
the city and d. in the open Mic 4.10
And they shall d. secure, 5.04
who d. alone in a forest in the 7.14
the world and all that d. therein. Nah 1.05
to cities and all who d. therein. Hab 2.08
to cities and all who d. therein. 2.17
yourselves to d. in your paneled Hag 1.04
you who d. with the daughter of Zec 2.07
come and I will d. in the midst of 2.10
and I will d. in the midst of you, 2.11
and will d. in the midst of Jerusalem, 8.03
bring them to d. in the midst of 8.08
a mongrel people shall d. in Ashdod; 9.06
Jerusalem shall d. in security. 14.11
and they enter and d. there; Mt 12.45
and they enter and d. there; Lk 11.26
upon all who d. upon the face of 21.35
Judea and all who d. in Jerusalem, Ac 2.14
moreover my flesh will d. in hope. 2.26
High does not d. in houses made 7.48
and that Christ may d. in your Eph 3.17
fulness of God was pleased to d., Col 1.19
word of Christ d. in you richly, 3.16
which he has made to d. in us"? Jas 4.05
" 'I know where you d., Rev 2.13
to try those who d. upon the earth. 3.10
on those who d. upon the earth?" 6.10
woe to those who d. on the earth, 8.13
and those who d. on the earth will 11.10
to those who d. on the earth. 11.10
O heaven and you that d. therein! 12.12
that is, those who d. in heaven. 13.06
and all who d. on earth will 13.08
it deceives those who d. on earth, 13.14
proclaim to those who d. on earth, 14.06
He will d. with them, and they shall 21.03

DWELLER
d. in the land of Uz; Lam 4.21

DWELLERS
O d. in the dust, awake and sing for Is 26.19
fornication the d. on earth have Rev 17.02
and the d. on earth whose names 17.08

DWELLING
support both of them d. together; Gen 13.06
Beerlahairoi, and was d. in the Negeb. 24.62
Jacob was a quiet man, d. in tents. 25.27
of the earth shall your d. be, 27.39
their families and their d. places, 36.40
to their d. places in the land of 36.43
in all your d. places, that you eat Lev 3.17
"If a man sells a d. house in a 25.29
away from about the d. of Korah, Num 16.24
away from about the d. of Korah, 16.27
earth, and they are d. opposite me. 22.05
lo, a people d. alone, and not 23.09
said, "Enduring is your d. place, 24.21
and makes his d. between his Deu 33.12
The eternal God is your d. place, 33.27
Canaanites persisted in d. in that land. Jos 17.12
Canaanites persisted in d. in that land. Ju 1.27
persisted in d. in Harheres, in Aijalon, 1.35
moving about in a tent for my d. 2Sa 7.06
hear thou in heaven thy d. place; 1Ki 8.30
then hear thou in heaven thy d. place, 8.39
hear thou in heaven thy d. place, 8.43
in heaven thy d. place their prayer 8.49
at the beginning of their d. there, 2Ki 17.25
These are their d. places according 1Ch 6.54
d. in the chambers of the temple 9.33
to tent and from d. to d. 17.05
hear thou from heaven thy d. place; 2Ch 6.21
hear thou from heaven thy d. place, 6.30
hear thou from heaven thy d. place, 6.33
from heaven thy d. place their 6.39
on his people and on his d. place; 36.15
of Israel, whose d. is in Jerusalem, Ez 7.15
root, but suddenly I cursed his d. Job 5.03
"Where is the way to the d. of light, 38.19
and the salt land for his d. place? 39.06
me to thy holy hill and to thy d.! Ps 43.03
their d. places to all generations, 49.11
thy flock found a d. in it; 68.10
desecrated the d. place of thy 74.07
in Salem, his d. place in Zion. 76.02
He forsook his d. at Shiloh, the 78.60
How lovely is thy d. place, 84.01
than all the d. places of Jacob. 87.02
hast been our d. place in all 90.01
have I had my d. among those who 120.06
a d. place for the Mighty One of 132.05
"Let us go to his d. place; 132.07
treasure remains in a wise man's d., Pro 21.20
man against the d. of the righteous 24.15
look from my d. like clear heat in Is 18.04
My d. is plucked up and removed 38.12
My d. place shall be with them; Eze 37.27
all of them d. without walls, and 38.11
my people Israel are d. securely, 38.14
whose d. is not with flesh.' Dan 2.11
and your d. shall be with the 4.25
and your d. shall be with the 4.32
and his d. was with the wild asses; 5.21
whose d. is high, who say in your Ob 1.03
roused himself from his holy d. Zec 2.13
Now there were d. in Jerusalem Jews, Ac 2.05
and I will rebuild the d. of David, 15.16
long to put on our heavenly d., 2Co 5.02
into it for a d. place of God in Eph 2.22

DWELLING (cont.)
their proper d. have been kept by Jud 1.06
blaspheming his name and his d., Rev 13.06
It has become a d. place of demons, 18.02
the d. of God is with men. He will 21.03

DWELLINGS
in all your d. you shall eat Ex 12.20
or of animal, in any of your d. Lev 7.26
sabbath to the LORD in all your d. 23.03
your generations in all your d. 23.14
bring from your d. two loaves of 23.17
in all your d. throughout your 23.21
your generations in all your d. 23.31
your generations in all your d. Num 35.29
Surely such are the d. of the ungodly, Job 18.21
and his d. shall be glorious. Is 11.10
in secure d., and in quiet resting 32.18
because they have cast down our d.'" Jer 9.19
and have compassion on his d.; 30.18
her d. are on fire, her bars are 51.30
and make their d. in your midst; Eze 25.04
for d. and for open country. In the 48.15

DWELLS
he d. in safety by him; he encompasses Deu 33.12
but the ark of God d. in a tent." 2Sa 7.02
and he d. in Jerusalem for ever. 1Ch 23.25
and my eye d. on their provocation. Job 17.02
In his tent d. that which is none 18.15
On the rock he d. and makes his 39.28
to the LORD, who d. in Zion! Ps 9.11
rejoices; my body also d. secure. 16.09
and the place where thy glory d. 26.08
He who d. in the shelter of the 91.01
from Zion, he who d. in Jerusalem! 135.21
neighbor who d. trustingly beside Pro 3.29
of hosts, who d. on Mount Zion. Is 8.18
LORD is exalted, for he d. on high; 33.05
passes through, where no man d.?' Jer 2.06
forsaken, and no man d. in them. 4.29
desolation, and no one d. in them, 44.02
that d. securely, says the LORD, that 49.31
no gates or bars, that d. alone. 49.31
desert, a land in which no one d., 51.43
she d. now among the nations, but Lam 1.03
where the king d. who made him Eze 17.16
who d. at the entrance to the sea, 27.03
darkness, and the light d. with him. Dan 2.22
guilty, for the LORD d. in Zion." Joe 3.21
and every one mourn who d. in it, Amo 8.08
by it and by him who d. in it; Mt 23.21
the Father who d. in me does his Jn 14.10
for he d. with you, and will be in 14.17
do it, but sin which d. within me. Rom 7.17
that nothing good d. within me, 7.18
do it, but sin which d. within me. 7.20
law of sin which d. in my members. 7.23
the Spirit of God really d. in you. 8.09
Jesus from the dead d. in you, 8.11
through his Spirit which d. in you. 8.11
and that God's Spirit d. in you? 1Co 3.16
whole fulness of deity d. bodily, Col 2.09
immortality and d. in unapproachable 1Ti 6.16
and now, I am sure, d. in you. 2Ti 1.05
the Holy Spirit who d. within us. 1.14
earth in which righteousness d. 2Pe 3.13
killed among you, where Satan d. Rev 2.13

DWELT
and d. in the land of Nod, east of Gen 4.16
and the Perizzites d. in the land. 13.07
Abram d. in the land of Canaan, 13.12
while Lot d. among the cities of 13.12
and came and d. by the oaks of 13.18
Amorites who d. in Hazazontamar. 14.07
who d. in Sodom, and his goods, and 14.12
So, after Abram had d. ten years in 16.03
overthrew the cities in which Lot d. 19.29
and d. in the hills with his two 19.30
so he d. in a cave with his two 19.30
and d. between Kadesh and Shur; 20.01
and Abraham d. at Beersheba. 22.19
And Isaac d. at Beerlahairoi. 25.11
They d. from Havilah to Shur, which 25.18
So Isaac d. in Gerar. 26.06
the valley of Gerar and d. there. 26.17
While Israel d. in that land Reuben 35.22
So Esau d. in the hill country of 36.08
Jacob d. in the land of his father's 37.01
Tamar went and d. in her father's 38.11
Thus Israel d. in the land of Egypt, 47.27
So Joseph d. in Egypt, he and his 50.22
in which they d. as sojourners. Ex 6.04
of Israel had light where they d. 10.23
of Israel d. in Egypt was four 12.40
where you d., and you shall not do Lev 18.03
your sabbaths when you d. upon it. 26.35
Canaanites who d. in that hill Num 14.45
and we d. in Egypt a long time; 20.15
who d. in the Negeb, heard that 21.01
Thus Israel d. in the land of the 21.31
of the Amorites, who d. at Heshbon. 21.34
While Israel d. in Shittim the 25.01
cities in the places where they d., 31.10
who d. in the Negeb in the land of 33.40
of the Amorites, who d. at Heshbon. Deu 3.02
"You know how we d. in the land of 29.16
favor of him that d. in the bush. 33.16
So Israel d. in safety, the fountain 33.28
wall, so that she d. in the wall. Jos 2.15
and she d. in Israel to this day, 6.25
of Bashan, who d. in Ashtaroth. 9.10
and that they d. among them. 9.16
of the Amorites who d. at Heshbon, 12.02
who d. at Ashtaroth and at Edrei 12.04
of Sihon, who d. in the land. 13.21
the Canaanites that d. in Gezer: 16.10
Canaanites have d. in the midst of 16.10
Canaanites who d. in the hill Ju 1.09
Canaanites who d. in Hebron (now 1.10
the Jebusites who d. in Jerusalem; 1.21
Jebusites have d. with the people 1.21
out the Canaanites who d. in Gezer; 1.29
the Canaanites d. in Gezer among 1.29
but the Canaanites d. among them, 1.30
but the Asherites d. among the 1.32
but d. among the Canaanites, the 1.33
the Hivites who d. on Mount 3.03
of Israel d. among the Canaanites, 3.05
who d. in Haroshethhagoiim. 4.02
Joash went and d. in his own house 8.29
and went to Beer and d. there, 9.21
And Abimelech d. at Arumah; 9.41
and d. in the land of Tob; and worthless 11.03
While Israel d. in Heshbon and its 11.26
how they d. in security, after the 18.07
rebuilt the city, and d. in it. 18.28
rebuilt the towns, and d. in them. 21.23
every side; and you d. in safety. 1Sa 12.11
and Samuel went and d. at Naioth. 19.18
and d. in the strongholds of Engedi 23.29
And David d. with Achish at Gath, he 27.03
days that David d. in the country 27.07
the while he d. in the country of 27.11
Philistines came and d. in them. 31.07
and they d. in the towns of Hebron. 2Sa 2.03
And David d. in the stronghold, and 5.09
Now when the king d. in his house, 7.01
I have not d. in a house since the 7.06
And all who d. in Ziba's house 9.12
So Mephibosheth d. in Jerusalem; 9.13
So Tamar d., a desolate woman, in 13.20
So Absalom d. apart in his own 14.24

DWELT (cont.)

So Absalom d. two full years in 2Sa 14.28
a vow while I d. at Geshur in Aram, 15.08
So Shimei d. in Jerusalem many days 1Ki 2.38
And Judah and Israel d. in safety, 4.25
the Canaanites who d. in the city, 9.16
and d. there, and made him king in 11.24
of Israel who d. in the cities of 12.17
country of Ephraim, and d. there; 12.25
Now there d. an old prophet in 13.11
the city where the old prophet d. 13.25
who d. in Damascus, saying, 15.18
building Ramah, and he d. in Tirzah. 15.21
he went and d. by the brook Cherith 17.05
the nobles who d. with Naboth in 21.08
and the nobles who d. in his city, 21.11
of Israel d. in their homes as 2Ki 13.05
and he d. in a separate house. 15.05
of Samaria, and d. in its cities. 17.24
from Samaria came and d. in Bethel, 17.28
in the cities in which they d.; 17.29
and went home, and d. at Nineveh. 19.36
wardrobe (now she d. in Jerusalem in 22.14
of the scribes that d. at Jabez: 1Ch 2.55
they d. there with the king for 4.23
They d. in Beersheba, Moladah, 4.28
and they have d. there to this day. 4.43
who d. in Aroer, as far as Nebo and 5.08
He also d. to the east as far as 5.09
and they d. in their tents throughout 5.10
The sons of Gad d. over against 5.11
and they d. in Gilead, in Bashan and 5.16
And they d. in their place until 5.22
half-tribe of Manasseh d. in the land; 5.23
In these d. the sons of Joseph the 7.29
chief men. These d. in Jerusalem. 8.28
Jeiel the father of Gibeon d. in Gibeon, 8.29
Now these also d. opposite their 8.32
and Manasseh d. in Jerusalem: 9.03
who d. in the villages of the 9.16
In Gibeon d. the father of Gibeon, 9.35
and these also d. opposite their 9.38
Philistines came and d. in them. 10.07
And David d. in the stronghold; 11.07
Now when David d. in his house, 17.01
For I have not d. in a house since 17.05
of Israel who d. in the cities of 2Ch 10.17
Rehoboam d. in Jerusalem, and he 11.05
who d. in Damascus, saying, 16.02
Jehoshaphat d. at Jerusalem; 19.04
And they have d. in it, and have 20.08
the Arabs that d. in Gurbaal, 26.07
being a leper d. in a separate 26.21
and the sojourners who d. in Judah, 30.25
wardrobe (now she d. in Jerusalem in 34.22
made booths and d. in the booths; Neh 8.17
is the tent in which the wicked d.?' Job 21.28
land, and the favored man d. in it. 22.08
and I d. like a king among his 29.25
Mount Zion, where thou hast d. Ps 74.02
the tent where he d. among men, 78.60
would soon have d. in the land of 94.17
those who d. in a land of deep Is 9.02
be inhabited or d. in for all 13.20
and went home and d. at Nineveh. 37.37
So he d. among the people. Jer 39.14
and d. with him among the people 40.06
the Jews that d. in the land of 44.01
the people who d. in Pathros in 44.15
who d. by the river Chebar. And I sat Eze 3.15
of the nations among whom they d., 20.09
its shadow d. all great nations. 31.06
those who d. under its shadow among 31.17
house of Israel d. in their own 36.17
your fathers d. that I gave to my 37.25
of the air d. in its branches, and Dan 4.12
branches the birds of the air d.— 4.21
the exultant city that d. secure, Zep 2.15
And he went and d. in a city called Mt 2.23
he went and d. in Capernaum by the 4.13
all the others who d. in Jerusalem? Lk 13.04
Word became flesh and d. among us, Jn 1.14
a faith that d. first in your 2Ti 1.05

DWINDLE

Wealth hastily gotten will d., Pro 13.11

DYED

spoil of d. stuffs for Sisera, spoil Ju 5.30
spoil of d. stuffs embroidered, two 5.30
two pieces of d. work embroidered 5.30
seal, and it is d. like a garment. Job 38.14

DYING

d. in the forty-first year of his 2Ch 16.13
And when he was d., he said, 24.22
From out of the city the d. groan, Job 24.12
their honored men are d. of hunger, Is 5.13
years of age, and she was d. Lk 8.42
man have kept this man from d.?" Jn 11.37
as d., and behold we live; 2Co 6.09
when d., blessed each of the sons Heb 11.21

DYSENTERY

Publius lay sick with fever and d.; Ac 28.08

E

EACH

e. according to its kind, upon the Gen 1.11
e. according to its kind. And God 1.12
e. with his own language, by their 10.05
thus they separated from e. other. 13.11
and laid e. half over against the 15.10
e. his own dream, and e. dream 40.05
and e. dream with its own meaning. 40.05
e. having a dream with its own 41.11
interpretation to e. man according 41.12
and put e. man's money in the mouth 44.01
To e. and all of them he gave 45.22
blessing e. with the blessing 49.28
with Jacob, e. with his household: Ex 1.01
but e. woman shall ask of her 3.22
according to what e. can eat you 12.04
persons whom e. of you has in his 16.16
e. gathered according to what he 16.18
e. as much as he could eat; 16.21
and they asked e. other of their 18.07
e. with capital and flower, on one 25.33
with it under e. pair of the six 25.35
The length of e. curtain shall be 26.02
the breadth of e. curtain four 26.02
The length of e. curtain shall be 26.08
the breadth of e. curtain four 26.08
and a half the breadth of e. frame. 26.16
There shall be two tenons in e. frame, 26.17
e. engraved with its name, for the 28.21
then e. shall give a ransom for 30.12
E. who is numbered in the census 30.13
frankincense (of e. shall there be 30.34
e. one at the cost of his son and 32.29
e. from the task that he was doing, 36.04
The length of e. curtain was twenty 36.09
the breadth of e. curtain four 36.09
The length of e. curtain was thirty 36.15
the breadth of e. curtain four 36.15
and a half the breadth of e. frame. 36.21
E. frame had two tenons, for fitting 36.22
e. with capital and flower, on one 37.19
with it under e. pair of the six 37.21

EACH (cont.)
e. engraved with its name, for the Ex 39.14
offer one cake from e. offering, Lev 7.14
e. took his censer, and put fire in 10.01
drink offerings, e. on its proper day; 23.37
of an ephah shall be in e. cake. 24.05
put pure frankincense with e. row, 24.07
when e. of you shall return to his 25.10
property and e. of you shall 25.10
year of jubilee e. of you shall 25.13
be with you a man from e. tribe, Num 1.04
e. man being the head of the house 1.04
e. representing his fathers' house. 1.44
shall encamp e. by his own standard, 2.02
e. in position, standard by standard. 2.17
appoint them e. to his task and to 4.19
e. to his task of serving or 4.49
the leaders, and for e. one an ox; 7.03
to e. man according to his service." 7.05
one leader e. day, for the dedication 7.11
e. silver plate weighing a hundred 7.85
shekels and e. basin seventy. 7.85
from e. tribe of their fathers 13.02
or for the sacrifice, for e. lamb. 15.05
shall be done for e. bull or ram, 15.11
or for e. of the male lambs or the 15.11
the tassel of e. corner a cord of 15.38
you also, and Aaron, e. his censer." 16.17
one for e. fathers' house, from all 17.02
Write e. man's name upon his rod, 17.02
for the head of e. fathers' house. 17.03
one for e. leader, according to 17.06
looked, and e. man took his rod. 17.09
offered on e. altar a bull and a 23.02
offered upon e. altar a bull and a 23.04
a bull and a ram on e. altar. 23.14
a bull and a ram on e. altar. 23.30
be a fourth of a hin for e. lamb; 28.07
mixed with oil, for e. bull; 28.12
offering of e. month throughout 28.14
you offer for e. of the seven 28.21
tenths of an ephah for e. bull, 28.28
a tenth for e. of the seven lambs; 28.29
and one tenth for e. of the seven 29.04
a tenth for e. of the seven lambs: 29.10
of an ephah for e. of the thirteen 29.14
two tenths for e. of the two rams, 29.14
and a tenth for e. of the fourteen 29.15
a thousand from e. of the tribes 31.04
Israel, a thousand from e. tribe, 31.05
the war, a thousand from e. tribe, 31.06
what e. man found, articles of gold, 31.50
have inherited e. his inheritance. 32.18
e., in proportion to the inheritance 35.08
for e. of the tribes of the people 36.09
men of you, one man for e. tribe; Deu 1.23
of Israel, from e. tribe a man. Jos 3.12
the people, from e. tribe a man, 4.02
had appointed, a man from e. tribe; 4.04
and take up e. of you a stone upon 4.05
Provide three men from e. tribe, 18.04
of Israel, to e. his portion. 18.10
These cities had e. its pasture 21.42
one from e. of the tribal families 22.14
of Israel went e. to his inheritance Ju 2.06
a torch between e. pair of tails. 15.04
and we will e. give you eleven 16.05
and seize e. man his wife from the 21.21
not take for e. man of them his 21.22
return e. of you to her mother's Ru 1.08
e. of you in the house of her 1.09
robe and take it to him e. year, 1Sa 2.19
people away, e. one to his home. 10.25
e. for his sons and daughters. 30.06
except that e. man may lead away 30.22
And e. caught his opponent by the 2Sa 2.16
to e. a cake of bread, a portion of 6.19
people departed, e. to his house. 6.19
shaved off half the beard of e., 10.04
and e. mounted his mule and fled. 13.29
who had six fingers on e. hand, 21.20
and six toes on e. foot, twenty-four 21.20
and rose, and e. went his own way. 1Ki 1.49
e. man had to make provision for 4.07
e. one in his month; they let 4.27
e. according to his charge. 4.28
e. story five cubits high, and it 6.10
olivewood, e. ten cubits high. 6.23
wings touched e. other in the 6.27
forty-five pillars, fifteen in e. row. 7.03
e. stand was four cubits long, four 7.27
Moreover e. stand had four bronze 7.30
with wreaths at the side of e. 7.30
at the four corners of e. stand; 7.34
according to the space of e., 7.36
of bronze; e. laver held forty baths, 7.38
e. laver measured four cubits, and 7.38
was a laver for e. of the ten 7.38
of pomegranates for e. network, 7.42
e. knowing the affliction of his 8.38
and render to e. whose heart thou 8.39
people Israel, as e. day requires; 8.59
of gold went into e. shield. 10.16
minas of gold went into e. shield; 10.17
and on e. side of the seat were arm 10.19
one on e. end of a step on the six 10.20
And e. killed his man; the Syrians 20.20
e. from his post, and put commanders 20.24
let e. return to his home in peace.'" 22.17
the Jordan and e. of us get there 2Ki 6.02
e. in his chariot, and went to meet 9.21
e. with his weapons in his hand; 11.08
and e. brought his men who were to 11.09
money for which e. man is assessed— 12.04
e. from his acquaintance; and let them 12.05
to e. a loaf of bread, a portion of 1Ch 16.03
before the ark as e. day required, 16.37
people departed e. to his house, 16.43
who had six fingers on e. hand, 20.06
e. hand, and six toes on e. foot, 20.06
the head of e. father's house and 24.31
On the east there were six e. day, 26.17
e. day, on the north four e. day, 26.17
e. day, on the south four e. day, 26.17
e. division numbering twenty-four 27.01
all golden vessels for e. service, 28.14
of silver vessels for e. service, 28.14
of gold for e. lampstand and its 28.15
to the use of e. lampstand in the 28.15
of gold for e. table for the 28.16
golden bowls and the weight of e.; 28.17
silver bowls and the weight of e.; 28.17
of five cubits on the top of e. 2Ch 3.15
of pomegranates for e. network, 4.13
e. knowing his own affliction, and 6.29
and render to e. whose heart thou 6.30
as the duty of e. day required, 8.13
as the duty of e. day required, 8.14
of beaten gold went into e. shield. 9.15
of gold went into e. shield; 9.16
and on e. side of the seat were arm 9.18
one on e. end of a step on the six 9.19
E. of you to your tents, O Israel! 10.16
let e. return to his home in 18.16
e. with his weapons in his hand; 23.07
They e. brought his men, who were to 23.08
e. according to his service, the 31.02
as the duty of e. day required, 31.16
there be for e. a part of a 35.05
the gatekeepers were at e. gate; 35.15
"What have we to do with e. other, 35.21
and let e. survivor, in whatever Ez 1.04
and Judah, e. to his own town. 2.01
the ordinance, as e. day required, 3.04

EACH (cont.)

is in Jerusalem, e. to its place; Ez 6.05
e. of them designated by name. 10.16
e. one opposite his own house. Neh 3.28
to the wall, e. to his work. 4.15
such a way that e. with one hand 4.17
And e. of the builders had his 4.18
e. kept his weapon in his hand. 4.23
e. from his brother." And I held 5.07
e. to his station and e. opposite 7.03
Jerusalem and Judah, e. to his town. 7.06
e. on his roof, and in their courts 8.16
the work, had fled e. to his field. 13.10
but the language of e. people. 13.24
and Levites, e. in his work; 13.30
turn came for e. maiden to go in Est 2.12
in the house of e. on his day; Job 1.04
they came e. from his own place, 2.11
they clasp e. other and cannot be 41.17
and e. of them gave him a piece of 42.11
E. evening they come back, howling Ps 59.06
E. evening they come back, howling 59.14
and peace will kiss e. other. 85.10
e. with his sword at his thigh, Sol 3.08
e. one was to bring for its fruit a 8.11
e. had six wings: with two he Is 6.02
e. devours his neighbor's flesh, 9.20
in glory, e. in his own tomb; 14.18
E. will be like a hiding-place from 32.02
gathered, e. one with her mate. 34.15
wander about e. in his own direction; 47.15
e. to his own gain, one and all. 56.11
e. neighing for his neighbor's wife. Jer 5.08
shall pasture, e. in his place. 6.03
with his mouth e. speaks peaceably 9.08
and e. to her neighbor a dirge. 9.20
them again e. to his heritage and 12.15
to his heritage and e. to his land. 12.15
e. with his weapons; and they 22.07
e. man who eats sour grapes, his 31.30
And no longer shall e. man teach 31.34
his neighbor and e. his brother, 31.34
of six years e. of you must set 34.14
e. to his neighbor, and you made a 34.15
my name when e. of you took back 34.16
and let us go e. to his own country; 51.09
but e. had four faces, and e. of Eze 1.06
and e. of them had four wings. 1.06
e. had the face of a man in front; 1.10
e. creature had two wings, 1.11
e. of which touched the wing of 1.11
And e. went straight forward; 1.12
one for e. of the four of them. 1.15
and e. creature had two wings 1.23
I assign you, a day for e. year. 4.06
E. had his censer in his hand, and 8.11
e. with his destroying weapon in 9.01
the cherubim, one beside e. cherub; 10.09
E. had four faces, and e. four wings, 10.21
I will judge e. of you according to 33.20
abominations and e. of you defiles 33.26
e. to his brother, 'Come, and hear 33.30
e. being a cubit and a handbreadth 40.05
on e. side six cubits was the 41.01
over another, thirty in e. story. 41.06
holy place had e. a double door. 41.23
two swinging leaves for e. door. 41.24
of an ephah from e. homer of wheat, 45.13
an ephah from e. homer of barley, 45.13
of a bath from e. cor (the cor, 45.14
on e. of the seven days; and a he-goat 45.23
offering an ephah for e. bull, 45.24
an ephah for e. ram, and a hin of 45.24
ram, and a hin of oil to e. ephah. 45.24
with a hin of oil to e. ephah. 46.05
with a hin of oil to e. ephah. 46.07
but e. shall go out straight ahead. 46.09
and in e. corner of the court there 46.21
around e. of the four courts was a 46.23
They march e. on his way, they do Joe 2.07
e. marches in his path; they burst 2.08
and e. cried to his god; and they Jon 1.05
peoples walk e. in the name of its Mic 4.05
and e. hunts his brother with a net. 7.02
e. in its place, all the lands of Zep 2.11
e. dawn he does not fail; but the 3.05
busy yourselves e. with his own Hag 1.09
seven lips on e. of the lamps Zec 4.02
and mercy e. to his brother, 7.09
e. with staff in hand for very age. 8.04
men to fall e. into the hand of 11.06
and e. into the hand of his king; 11.06
e. family by itself; the family of 12.12
e. by itself, and their wives by 12.14
so that e. will lay hold on the 14.13
e. of them received a denarius. Mt 20.09
but e. of them also received a 20.10
to e. according to his ability. 25.15
e. with his work, and commands the Mk 13.34
to decide what e. should take. 15.24
to be enrolled, e. to his own city. Lk 2.03
for e. tree is known by its own 6.44
down in companies, about fifty e." 9.14
Give us e. day our daily bread; 11.03
Does not e. of you on the sabbath 13.15
friends with e. other that very 23.12
had been at enmity with e. other. 23.12
and talking with e. other about all 24.14
holding with e. other as you walk?" 24.17
They said to e. other, "Did not our 24.32
e. holding twenty or thirty gallons. Jn 2.06
bread for e. of them to get a 6.07
They went e. to his own house, * 7.53
four parts, one for e. soldier. 19.23
and resting on e. one of them. Ac 2.03
because e. one heard them speaking 2.06
e. of us in his own native language? 2.08
was made to e. as any had need. 4.35
brethren, why do you wrong e. other?' 7.26
that they separated from e. other; 15.39
he is not far from e. one of us, 17.27
encouraged by e. other's faith, Rom 1.12
e. according to the measure of 12.03
So e. of us shall give account of 14.12
let e. of us please his neighbor 15.02
What I mean is that e. one of you 1Co 1.12
believed, as the Lord assigned to e. 3.05
and e. shall receive his wages 3.08
Let e. man take care how he builds 3.10
e. man's work will become manifest; 3.13
what sort of work e. one has done. 3.13
e. man should have his own wife and 7.02
own wife and e. woman her own 7.02
But e. has his own special gift 7.07
in whatever state e. was called, 7.24
For in eating, e. one goes ahead 11.21
To e. is given the manifestation of 12.07
apportions to e. one individually 12.11
e. one of them, as he chose. 12.18
e. one has a hymn, a lesson, a 14.26
or at most three, and e. in turn; 14.27
let e. of them keep silence in 14.28
But e. in his own order: Christ the 15.23
and to e. kind of seed its own body. 15.38
e. of you is to put something aside 16.02
so that e. one may receive good or 2Co 5.10
E. one must do as he has made up 9.07
or these are opposed to e. other, Gal 5.17
But let e. one test his own work, 6.04
For e. man will have to bear his 6.05
was given to e. of us according to Eph 4.07
when e. part is working properly, 4.16
however, let e. one of you love his 5.33
Let e. of you look not only to his Php 2.04

EACH (cont.)
another, forgiving e. other; Col 3.13
we exhorted e. one of you and 1Th 2.11
that e. one of you know how to take 4.04
And we desire e. one of you to show Heb 6.11
blessed e. of the sons of Joseph, 11.21
but e. person is tempted when he is Jas 1.14
him who judges e. one impartially 1Pe 1.17
As e. has received a gift, employ it 4.10
I will give to e. of you as your Rev 2.23
on e. side of the throne, are four 4.06
e. of them with six wings, are full 4.08
e. holding a harp, and with golden 5.08
Then they were e. given a white 6.11
e. of the gates made of a single 21.21
fruit, yielding its fruit e. month; 22.02

EAGER
They are like a lion e. to tear, Ps 17.12
more they were e. to make all Zep 3.07
so I am e. to preach the gospel to Rom 1.15
waits with e. longing for the 8.19
since you are e. for manifestations 1Co 14.12
which very thing I was e. to do. Gal 2.10
e. to maintain the unity of the Eph 4.03
as it is my e. expectation and hope Php 1.20
I am the more e. to send him, 2.28
being very e. to write to you of Jud 1.03

EAGERLY
to seek you e., and I have found Pro 7.15
they shall come e. like birds from Hos 11.11
And he begged him e. not to send Mk 5.10
the more e. and with great desire 1Th 2.17
searched for me e. and found me— 2Ti 1.17
those who are e. waiting for him. Heb 9.28
not for shameful gain but e., 1Pe 5.02

EAGERNESS
they received the word with all e., Ac 17.11
what e. to clear yourselves, what 2Co 7.11

EAGLE
the e., the ossifrage, the osprey, Lev 11.13
the e., the vulture, the osprey, Deu 14.12
earth, as swift as the e. flies, 28.49
Like an e. that stirs up its nest, 32.11
like an e. swooping on the prey. Job 9.26
that the e. mounts up and makes 39.27
flying like an e. toward heaven. Pro 23.05
the way of an e. in the sky, the way 30.19
one shall fly swiftly like an e., Jer 48.40
up and fly swiftly like an e., 49.22
had the face of an e. at the back. Eze 1.10
and the fourth the face of an e. 10.14
A great e. with great wings and 17.03
another great e. with great wings 17.07
Though you soar aloft like the e., Ob 1.04
make yourselves as bald as the e., Mic 1.16
fly like an e. swift to devour. Hab 1.08
living creature like a flying e. Rev 4.07
and I heard an e. crying with a 8.13
of the great e. that she might fly 12.14

EAGLE'S
your youth is renewed like the e. Ps 103.05
make your nest as high as the e., Jer 49.16

EAGLES
they were swifter than e., 2Sa 1.23
shall mount up with wings like e., Is 40.31
his horses are swifter than e.— Jer 4.13
there the e. will be gathered Mt 24.28
there the e. will be gathered Lk 17.37

EAGLES'
I bore you on e. wings and brought Ex 19.04
hair grew as long as e. feathers, Dan 4.33
was like a lion and had e. wings. 7.04

EAR
was in the e. and the flax was in Ex 9.31
shall bore his e. through with an 21.06
of the right e. of Aaron and upon 29.20
Aaron's right e. and on the thumb Lev 8.23
of the right e. of him who is to 14.14
of the right e. of him who is to 14.17
of the right e. of him who is to 14.25
of the right e. of him who is to 14.28
to your voice or give e. to you. Deu 1.45
it through his e. into the door, 15.17
"Give e., O heavens, and I will 32.01
give e., O princes; to the LORD Ju 5.03
giving e. to them whenever they 1Ki 8.52
Incline thy e., O LORD, and hear; 2Ki 19.16
let thy e. be attentive, and thy Neh 1.06
let thy e. be attentive to the 1.11
yet they would not give e. Therefore 9.30
my e. received the whisper of it. Job 4.12
Does not the e. try words as the 12.11
my e. has heard and understood it. 13.01
When the e. heard, it called me 29.11
and give e. to me, you who know; 34.02
for the e. tests words as the 34.03
and opens their e. by adversity. 36.15
of thee by the hearing of the e., 42.05
Give e. to my words, O LORD; give Ps 5.01
heart, thou wilt incline thy e. 10.17
Give e. to my prayer from lips free 17.01
incline thy e. to me, hear my words. 17.06
Incline thy e. to me, rescue me 31.02
O LORD, and give e. to my cry; 39.12
but thou hast given me an open e. 40.06
consider, and incline your e.; 45.10
Give e., all inhabitants of the 49.01
I will incline my e. to a proverb; 49.04
give e. to the words of my mouth. 54.02
Give e. to my prayer, O God; and hide 55.01
God will give e., and humble them, 55.19
the deaf adder that stops its e., 58.04
incline thy e. to me, and save me! 71.02
Give e., O my people, to my teaching 78.01
Give e., O Shepherd of Israel, thou 80.01
my prayer; give e., O God of Jacob! 84.08
Incline thy e., O LORD, and answer 86.01
Give e., O LORD, to my prayer; 86.06
thee, incline thy e. to my cry! 88.02
He who planted the e., does he not 94.09
Incline thy e. to me; answer me 102.02
Because he inclined his e. to me, 116.02
give e. to the voice of my supplications, 140.06
Give e. to my voice, when I call to 141.01
give e. to my supplications! 143.01
making your e. attentive to wisdom Pro 2.02
incline your e. to my sayings. 4.20
incline your e. to my understanding; 5.01
or incline my e. to my instructors. 5.13
He whose e. heeds wholesome admonition 15.31
and the e. of the wise seeks 18.15
The hearing e. and the seeing eye, 20.12
He who closes his e. to the cry of 21.13
Incline your e., and hear the words 22.17
and your e. to words of knowledge. 23.12
a wise reprover to a listening e. 25.12
turns away his e. from hearing the 28.09
nor the e. filled with hearing. Ecc 1.08
Hear, O heavens, and give e., O earth; Is 1.02
Give e. to the teaching of our God, 1.10
give e., all you far countries; 8.09
Give e., and hear my voice; hearken, 28.23
daughters, give e. to my speech. 32.09
Incline thy e., O LORD, and hear; 37.17
Who among you will give e. to this, 42.23
of old your e. has not been opened. 48.08
he wakens my e. to hear as those 50.04
The Lord GOD has opened my e., 50.05
and give e. to me, my nation; 51.04

EAR (cont.)

Incline your e., and come to me; Is 55.03
or his e. dull, that it cannot hear; 59.01
has heard or perceived by the e., 64.04
did not obey or incline their e., Jer 7.24
listen to me, or incline their e., 7.26
and let your e. receive the word of 9.20
did not obey or incline their e., 11.08
Hear and give e.; be not proud, 13.15
did not listen or incline their e., 17.23
incline your e. or listen to me. 35.15
did not listen or incline their e., 44.05
not close thine e. to my cry for Lam 3.56
O my God, incline thy e. and hear; Dan 9.18
give e., all inhabitants of the Joe 1.02
lion two legs, or a piece of an e., Amo 3.12
high priest, and cut off his e. Mt 26.51
the e., then the full grain in the e. Mk 4.28
the high priest and cut off his e. 14.47
priest and cut off his right e. Lk 22.50
he touched his e. and healed him. 22.51
slave and cut off his right e. Jn 18.10
the man whose e. Peter had cut off, 18.26
to you, and give e. to my words. Ac 2.14
nor e. heard, nor the heart of man 1Co 2.09
And if the e. should say, "Because I 12.16
If the whole body were an e., where 12.17
He who has an e., let him hear what Rev 2.07
He who has an e., let him hear what 2.11
He who has an e., let him hear what 2.17
He who has an e., let him hear what 2.29
He who has an e., let him hear what 3.06
He who has an e., let him hear what 3.13
He who has an e., let him hear what 3.22
If any one has an e., let him hear: 13.09

EARLIER

walked in the e. ways of his 2Ch 17.03

EARLY

you may rise up e. and go on your Gen 19.02
And Abraham went e. in the morning 19.27
So Abimelech rose e. in the morning, 20.08
So Abraham rose e. in the morning, 21.14
So Abraham rose e. in the morning, 22.03
they rose e. and took oath with 26.31
So Jacob rose e. in the morning, and 28.18
E. in the morning Laban arose, and 31.55
"Rise up e. in the morning and wait Ex 8.20
"Rise up e. in the morning and 9.13
And he rose e. in the morning, and 24.04
And they rose up e. on the morrow, 32.06
and he rose e. in the morning and 34.04
And they rose e. in the morning, and Num 14.40
the e. rain and the latter rain, that Deu 11.14
E. in the morning Joshua rose and Jos 3.01
Then Joshua rose e. in the morning, 6.12
day they rose e. at the dawn of 6.15
So Joshua rose e. in the morning, 7.16
And Joshua arose e. in the morning 8.10
and went out e. to the descent 8.14
of the town rose e. in the morning, Ju 6.28
When he rose e. next morning and 6.38
with him rose e. and encamped 7.01
rise e. and rush upon the city; 9.33
day they arose e. in the morning, 19.05
day he arose e. in the morning to 19.08
you shall arise e. in the morning 19.09
And on the morrow the people rose e., 21.04
continued from e. morning until Ru 2.07
They rose e. in the morning and 1Sa 1.19
of Ashdod rose e. the next day, 5.03
But when they rose e. on the next 5.04
And Samuel rose e. to meet Saul in 15.12
And David rose e. in the morning, 17.20
Now then rise e. in the morning 29.10
and start e. in the morning, and 29.10
out with his men e. in the morning, 29.11
used to rise e. and stand beside 2Sa 15.02
And when they rose e. in the morning, 2Ki 3.22
man of God rose e. in the morning 6.15
when men arose e. in the morning, 19.35
And they rose e. in the morning and 2Ch 20.20
the king rose e. and gathered the 29.20
Water Gate from e. morning until Neh 8.03
he would rise e. in the morning Job 1.05
God will help her right e. Ps 46.05
the e. rain also covers it with 84.06
It is in vain that you rise up e., 127.02
rising e. in the morning, will be Pro 27.14
let us go out e. to the vineyards, Sol 7.12
those who rise e. in the morning, Is 5.11
when men arose e. in the morning, 37.36
olives and e. figs, honey, oil, and Eze 27.17
like the dew that goes e. away. Hos 6.04
or like the dew that goes e. away, 13.03
has given the e. rain for your Joe 2.23
the e. and the latter rain, as 2.23
who went out e. in the morning to Mt 20.01
And very e. on the first day of the Mk 16.02
And e. in the morning all the Lk 21.38
at e. dawn, they went to the tomb, 24.01
were at the tomb e. in the morning 24.22
E. in the morning he came again * Jn 8.02
It was e. They themselves 18.28
Mary Magdalene came to the tomb e., 20.01
that in the e. days God made Ac 15.07
For from e. generations Moses has 15.21
an e. disciple, with whom we should 21.16
it receives the e. and the late Jas 5.07

EARN

quietness and to e. their own 2Th 3.12

EARNEST

but e. prayer for him was made to Ac 12.05
puts the same e. care for you into 2Co 8.16
himself very e. he is going to you 8.17
and found e. in many matters, but 8.22
who is now more e. than ever 8.22

EARNESTLY

'David e. asked leave of me to run 1Sa 20.06
"David e. asked leave of me to go 20.28
they repented and sought God e. Ps 78.34
my spirit within me e. seeks thee. Is 26.09
to Jesus, they besought him e., Lk 7.04
"I have e. desired to eat this 22.15
in an agony he prayed more e.; 22.44
as they e. worship night and day. Ac 26.07
But e. desire the higher gifts. 1Co 12.31
and e. desire the spiritual gifts, 14.01
e. desire to prophesy, and do not 14.39
begging us e. for the favor of 2Co 8.04
remembering you e. in his prayers, Col 4.12
praying e. night and day that we 1Th 3.10
you the more e. to do this in Heb 13.19
love one another e. from the heart. 1Pe 1.22

EARNESTNESS

For see what e. this godly grief 2Co 7.11
in all e., and in your love for us— 8.07
to prove by the e. of others that 8.08
show the same e. in realizing the Heb 6.11

EARNS

him his hire on the day he e. it, Deu 24.15
A wicked man e. deceptive wages, but Pro 11.18
and he who e. wages e. wages to put Hag 1.06

EARRINGS

brooches and e. and signet rings Ex 35.22
e., and beads, to make atonement for Num 31.50
man of you the e. of his spoil." Ju 8.24
(For they had golden e., 8.24

EARRINGS (cont.)
man cast in it the e. of his spoil. Ju 8.25
of the golden e. that he requested 8.26
and e. in your ears, and a beautiful Eze 16.12

EARS
the rings that were in their e.; Gen 35.04
seven e. of grain, plump and good, 41.05
after them sprouted seven e., 41.06
And the thin e. swallowed up the 41.07
up the seven plump and full e. 41.07
my dream seven e. growing on one 41.22
and seven e., withered, thin, and 41.23
and the thin e. swallowed up the 41.24
swallowed up the seven good e. 41.24
the seven good e. are seven years; 41.26
the seven empty e. blighted by the 41.27
you, speak a word in my lord's e., 44.18
in the e. of Pharaoh, saying, 50.04
and recite it in the e. of Joshua, Ex 17.14
tips of the right e. of his sons, 29.20
which are in the e. of your wives, 32.02
of gold which were in their e., 32.03
crushed new grain from fresh e., Lev 2.14
of their right e. and on the 8.24
may pluck the e. with your hand, Deu 23.25
or eyes to see, or e. to hear. 29.04
words in their e. and call heaven 31.28
in the e. of all the assembly of 31.30
proclaim in the e. of the people, Ju 7.03
"Say in the e. of all the citizens 9.02
behalf in the e. of all the men of 9.03
curse, and also spoke it in my e., 17.02
glean among the e. of grain after Ru 2.02
which the two e. of every one that 1Sa 3.11
repeated them in the e. of the LORD. 8.21
the matter in the e. of the people; 11.04
bleating of the sheep in my e., 15.14
those words in the e. of David. 18.23
let your handmaid speak in your e., 25.24
all that we have heard with our e. 2Sa 7.22
voice, and my cry came to his e. 22.07
and fresh e. of grain in his sack. 2Ki 4.42
your arrogance has come into my e., 19.28
evil that the e. of every one who 21.12
all that we have heard with our e. 1Ch 17.20
be open and thy e. attentive to a 2Ch 6.40
be open and my e. attentive to the 7.15
and the e. of all the people were Neh 8.03
let my declaration be in your e. Job 13.17
Terrifying sounds are in his e.; 15.21
heard a rumor of it with our e. 28.22
then he opens the e. of men, 33.16
He opens their e. to instruction, 36.10
and my cry to him reached his e. Ps 18.06
and his e. toward their cry. 34.15
We have heard with our e., 44.01
incline your e. to the words of my 78.01
my e. have heard the doom of my 92.11
They have e., but do not hear; 115.06
Let thy e. be attentive to the 130.02
they have e., but they hear not, nor 135.17
who takes a passing dog by the e. Pro 26.17
and their e. heavy, and shut their Is 6.10
their eyes, and hear with their e., 6.10
see, or decide by what his e. hear; 11.03
grain and his arm harvests the e., 17.05
one gleans the e. of grain in the 17.05
has revealed himself in my e.: 22.14
And your e. shall hear a word 30.21
and the e. of those who hear will 32.03
who stops his e. from hearing of 33.15
and the e. of the deaf unstopped; 35.05
your arrogance has come to my e., 37.29
his e. are open, but he does not 42.20
eyes, who are deaf, yet have e.! 43.08
bereavement will yet say in your e.: 49.20
see not, who have e., but hear not. Jer 5.21
Behold, their e. are closed, they 6.10
place that the e. of every one who 19.03
nor inclined your e. to hear, 25.04
as you have heard with your own e." 26.11
speak all these words in your e." 26.15
to me or incline their e. to me. 34.14
your heart, and hear with your e. Eze 3.10
they cry in my e. with a loud 8.18
Then he cried in my e. with a loud 9.01
who have e. to hear, but hear not; 12.02
your nose, and earrings in your e., 16.12
cut off your nose and your e., 23.25
your eyes, and hear with your e., 40.04
hear with your e. all that I shall 44.05
their mouths; their e. shall be deaf; Mic 7.16
stopped their e. that they might Zec 7.11
He who has e. to hear, let him hear. Mt 11.15
began to pluck e. of grain and to 12.01
He who has e., let him hear." 13.09
and their e. are heavy of hearing, 13.15
their eyes, and hear with their e., 13.15
see, and your e., for they hear. 13.16
He who has e., let him hear. 13.43
if this comes to the governor's e., 28.14
disciples began to pluck e. of grain. Mk 2.23
"He who has e. to hear, let him hear." 4.09
If any man has e. to hear, let him 4.23
"If any man has e. to hear." * 7.16
he put his fingers into his e., 7.33
And his e. were opened, his tongue 7.35
and having e. do you not hear? 8.18
of your greeting came to my e., Lk 1.44
plucked and ate some e. of grain, 6.01
"He who has e. to hear, let him hear." 8.08
"Let these words sink into your e.; 9.44
He who has e. to hear, let him hear." 14.35
uncircumcised in heart and e., Ac 7.51
stopped their e. and rushed 7.57
came to the e. of the church in 11.22
some strange things to our e.; 17.20
and their e. are heavy of hearing, 28.27
their eyes, and hear with their e., 28.27
not see and e. that should not Rom 11.08
having itching e. they will 2Ti 4.03
reached the e. of the Lord of Jas 5.04
and his e. are open to their prayer. 1Pe 3.12

EARTH
God created the heavens and the e. Gen 1.01
The e. was without form and void, 1.02
God called the dry land E., and the 1.10
"Let the e. put forth vegetation, 1.11
according to its kind, upon the e." 1.11
The e. brought forth vegetation, 1.12
heavens to give light upon the e." 1.15
heavens to give light upon the e., 1.17
fly above the e. across the firmament 1.20
and let birds multiply on the e." 1.22
"Let the e. bring forth living 1.24
beasts of the e. according to 1.24
beasts of the e. according to 1.25
the cattle, and over all the e., 1.26
thing that creeps upon the e." 1.26
and fill the e. and subdue it; 1.28
thing that moves upon the e." 1.28
is upon the face of all the e., 1.29
And to every beast of the e., 1.30
everything that creeps on the e., 1.30
heavens and the e. were finished, 2.01
heavens and the e. when they were 2.04
God made the e. and the heavens, 2.04
was yet in the e. and no herb of 2.05
not caused it to rain upon the e., 2.05
up from the e. and watered the 2.06
fugitive and a wanderer on the e." 4.12
fugitive and a wanderer on the e., 4.14

EARTH (cont.)

were on the e. in those days, Gen 6.04
wickedness of man was great in the e., 6.05
that he had made man on the e., 6.06
Now the e. was corrupt in God's 6.11
and the e. was filled with violence. 6.11
And God saw the e., 6.12
corrupted their way upon the e. 6.12
for the e. is filled with violence 6.13
I will destroy them with the e. 6.13
a flood of waters upon the e., 6.17
that is on the e. shall die. 6.17
alive upon the face of all the e. 7.03
rain upon the e. forty days and 7.04
flood of waters came upon the e. 7.06
of the flood came upon the e. 7.10
fell upon the e. forty days and 7.12
creeps on the e. according to its 7.14
continued forty days upon the e.; 7.17
ark, and it rose high above the e. 7.17
and increased greatly upon the e.; 7.18
upon the e. that all the high 7.19
flesh died that moved upon the e., 7.21
swarm upon the e., and every man; 7.21
they were blotted out from the e. 7.23
upon the e. a hundred and fifty 7.24
God made a wind blow over the e., 8.01
receded from the e. continually. 8.03
waters were dried up from the e. 8.07
still on the face of the whole e. 8.09
waters had subsided from the e. 8.11
waters were dried from off the e.; 8.13
day of the month, the e. was dry. 8.14
thing that creeps on the e.—that they 8.17
may breed abundantly on the e., 8.17
fruitful and multiply upon the e." 8.17
everything that moves upon the e., 8.19
While the e. remains, seedtime and 8.22
and multiply, and fill the e. 9.01
be upon every beast of the e., 9.02
abundantly on the e. and multiply 9.07
and every beast of the e. with you, 9.10
there be a flood to destroy the e." 9.11
the covenant between me and the e. 9.13
clouds over the e. and the bow is 9.14
of all flesh that is upon the e." 9.16
and all flesh that is upon the e." 9.17
these the whole e. was peopled. 9.19
the first on e. to be a mighty man. 10.08
for in his days the e. was divided, 10.25
abroad on the e. after the flood. 10.32
Now the whole e. had one language 11.01
upon the face of the whole e." 11.04
there over the face of all the e., 11.08
confused the language of all the e.; 11.09
abroad over the face of all the e. 11.09
families of the e. will bless 12.03
descendants as the dust of the e.; 13.16
one can count the dust of the e., 13.16
Most High, maker of heaven and e.; 14.19
Most High, maker of heaven and e., 14.22
them, and bowed himself to the e., 18.02
nations of the e. shall bless 18.18
the Judge of all the e. do right?" 18.25
himself with his face to the e., 19.01
risen on the e. when Lot came to 19.23
is not a man on e. to come in to 19.31
us after the manner of all the e. 19.31
nations of the e. bless themselves, 22.18
the God of heaven and of the e., 24.03
himself to the e. before the LORD. 24.52
nations of the e. shall bless 26.04
and filled with e. all the wells 26.15
and of the fatness of the e., 27.28
fatness of the e. shall your 27.39
was a ladder set up on the e., 28.12
shall be like the dust of the e., 28.14
families of the e. bless themselves. 28.14
years the e. brought forth abundantly, 41.47
all the e. came to Egypt to Joseph 41.57
famine was severe over all the e. 41.57
preserve for you a remnant on e., 45.07
himself with his face to the e. 48.12
a multitude in the midst of the e." 48.16
rod and strike the dust of the e., Ex 8.16
rod, and struck the dust of the e., 8.17
the dust of the e. became gnats 8.17
am the LORD in the midst of the e. 8.22
is none like me in all the e. 9.14
have been cut off from the e.; 9.15
be declared throughout all the e. 9.16
hail, and fire ran down to the e. 9.23
may know that the e. is the LORD's. 9.29
rain no longer poured upon the e. 9.33
day they came on e. to this day.' " 10.06
right hand, the e. swallowed them. 15.12
peoples; for all the e. is mine, 19.05
or that is in the e. beneath, 20.04
that is in the water under the e.; 20.04
days the LORD made heaven and e., 29.11
An altar of e. you shall make for 20.24
days the LORD made heaven and e., 31.17
them from the face of the e.'? 32.12
that are upon the face of the e.?" 33.16
head toward the e., and worshiped. 34.08
in all the e. or in any nation; 34.10
all the beasts that are on the e. Lev 11.02
feet, with which to leap on the e. 11.21
things that swarm upon the e.: 11.29
swarms upon the e. is an abomination; 11.41
things that swarm upon the e., 11.42
thing that crawls upon the e. 11.44
creature that swarms upon the e., 11.46
like iron and your e. like brass; 26.19
cubits deep on the face of the e. Num 11.31
that were on the face of the e. 12.03
and as all the e. shall be filled 14.21
and the e. opened its mouth and 16.32
and the e. closed over them, and 16.33
said, "Lest the e. swallow us up!" 16.34
they cover the face of the e., 22.05
and it covers the face of the e.; 22.11
and the e. opened its mouth and 26.10
in heaven or on e. who can do such Deu 3.24
days that they live upon the e., 4.10
of any beast that is on the e., 4.17
that is in the water under the e. 4.18
I call heaven and e. to witness 4.26
that God created man upon the e., 4.32
and on e. he let you see his great 4.36
heaven above and on the e. beneath; 4.39
or that is on the e. beneath, 5.08
that is in the water under the e.; 5.08
you from off the face of the e. 6.15
that are on the face of the e. 7.06
the e. with all that is in it; 10.14
how the e. opened its mouth and 11.06
as the heavens are above the e. 11.21
the days that you live upon the e. 12.01
pour it out upon the e. like water. 12.16
pour it out upon the e. like water. 12.24
one end of the e. to the other, 13.07
that are on the face of the e. 14.02
above all the nations of the e. 28.01
peoples of the e. shall see that 28.10
and the e. under you shall be iron. 28.23
to all the kingdoms of the e. 28.25
air, and for the beasts of the e.; 28.26
from afar, from the end of the e., 28.49
one end of the e. to the other; 28.64
I call heaven and e. to witness 30.19
call heaven and e. to witness 31.28

EARTH (cont.)

and let the e. hear the words of my Deu 32.01
ride on the high places of the e., 32.13
devours the e. and its increase, and 32.22
gifts of the e. and its fulness, 33.16
all of them, to the ends of the e.; 33.17
in heaven above and on e. beneath. Jos 2.11
Lord of all the e. is to pass over 3.11
the LORD, the Lord of all the e., 3.13
peoples of the e. may know that 4.24
Joshua fell on his face to the e., 5.14
and fell to the e. upon his face 7.06
and cut off our name from the e.; 7.09
hidden in the e. inside my tent, 7.21
about to go the way of all the e., 23.14
the e. trembled, and the heavens Ju 5.04
lacking nothing that is in the e., 18.07
lack of anything that is in the e." 18.10
pillars of the e. are the LORD's, 1Sa 2.08
LORD will judge the ends of the e.; 2.10
shout, so that the e. resounded. 4.05
rent and with e. upon his head. 4.12
the e. quaked; and it became 14.15
and to the wild beasts of the e.; 17.46
that all the e. may know that there 17.46
of David from the face of the e., 20.15
the son of Jesse lives upon the e., 20.31
bowed with his face to the e., 24.08
pin him to the e. with one stroke 26.08
fall to the e. away from the 26.20
see a god coming up out of the e." 28.13
So he arose from the e., and sat 28.23
clothes rent and e. upon his head. 2Sa 1.02
hand, and destroy you from the e.?" 4.11
name of the great ones of the e. 7.09
What other nation on e. is like thy 7.23
Then David arose from the e., 12.20
his garments, and lay on the e.; 13.31
remnant upon the face of the e." 14.07
know all things that are on the e." 14.20
his coat rent and e. upon his head. 15.32
left hanging between heaven and e., 18.09
the king with his face to the e., 18.28
"Then the e. reeled and rocked; 22.08
of his hairs shall fall to the e.; 1Ki 1.52
about to go the way of all the e. 2.02
and from all the kings of the e., 4.34
in heaven above or on e. beneath, 8.23
"But will God indeed dwell on the e.? 8.27
peoples of the e. may know thy 8.43
among all the peoples of the e., 8.53
peoples of the e. may know that 8.60
kings of the e. in riches and in 10.23
And the whole e. sought the presence 10.24
destroy it from the face of the e. 13.34
the LORD sends rain upon the e.' " 17.14
and I will send rain upon the e." 18.01
he bowed himself down upon the e., 18.42
no God in all the e. but in Israel; 2Ki 5.15
servant two mules' burden of e.; 5.17
fall to the e. nothing of the word 10.10
of all the kingdoms of the e.; 19.15
thou hast made heaven and e. 19.15
kingdoms of the e. may know that 19.19
began to be a mighty one in the e. 1Ch 1.10
in his days the e. was divided), 1.19
his judgments are in all the e. 16.14
Sing to the LORD, all the e.! 16.23
tremble before him, all the e.; 16.30
and let the e. rejoice, and let them 16.31
LORD, for he comes to judge the e. 16.33
name of the great ones of the e. 17.08
What other nation on e. is like thy 17.21
standing between e. and heaven, 21.16
much blood before me upon the e. 22.08
the heavens and in the e. is thine; 29.11
our days on the e. are like a 29.15
as many as the dust of the e. 2Ch 1.09
of Israel, who made heaven and e., 2.12
God like thee, in heaven or on e., 6.14
dwell indeed with man on the e.? 6.18
peoples of the e. may know thy 6.33
faces to the e. on the pavement, 7.03
kings of the e. in riches and in 9.22
kings of the e. sought the presence 9.23
to and fro throughout the whole e., 16.09
the gods of the peoples of the e., 32.19
me all the kingdoms of the e., 36.23
me all the kingdoms of the e., Ez 1.02
of the God of heaven and e., 5.11
and with e. upon their heads. Neh 9.01
the e. and all that is on it, the 9.06
"From going to and fro on the e., Job 1.07
there is none like him on the e., 1.08
"From going to and fro on the e., 2.02
there is none like him on the e., 2.03
counselors of the e. who rebuilt 3.14
rain upon the e. and sends waters 5.10
not fear the beasts of the e. 5.22
offspring as the grass of the e. 5.25
"Has not man a hard service upon e., 7.01
For now I shall lie in the e.; 7.21
for our days on e. are a shadow. 8.09
and out of the e. others will 8.19
who shakes the e. out of its place, 9.06
The e. is given into the hand of 9.24
Its measure is longer than the e., 11.09
or the plants of the e., and they 12.08
the chiefs of the people of the e., 12.24
Though its root grow old in the e., 14.08
wash away the soil of the e.; 14.19
nor will he strike root in the e.; 15.29
"O e., cover not my blood, and let 16.18
shall the e. be forsaken for you, or 18.04
His memory perishes from the e., 18.17
at last he will stand upon the e.; 19.25
old, since man was placed upon e., 20.04
and the e. will rise up against him. 20.27
the poor of the e. all hide themselves 24.04
and hangs the e. upon nothing. 26.07
Iron is taken out of the e., 28.02
As for the e., out of it comes 28.05
For he looks to the ends of the e., 28.24
in holes of the e. and of the 30.06
charge over the e. and who laid on 34.13
us more than the beasts of the e., 35.11
lightning to the corners of the e. 37.03
the snow he says, 'Fall on the e.'; 37.06
hot when the e. is still because 37.17
I laid the foundation of the e.? 38.04
take hold of the skirts of the e., 38.13
comprehended the expanse of the e.? 38.18
east wind is scattered upon the e.? 38.24
you establish their rule on the e.? 38.33
For she leaves her eggs to the e., 39.14
Upon e. there is not his like, a 41.33
The kings of the e. set themselves, Ps 2.02
the ends of the e. your possession 2.08
be warned, O rulers of the e. 2.10
majestic is thy name in all the e.! 8.01
majestic is thy name in all the e.! 8.09
who is of the e. may strike terror 10.18
Then the e. reeled and rocked; 18.07
voice goes out through all the e., 19.04
their offspring from the e., 21.10
All the ends of the e. shall 22.27
all the proud of the e. bow down; 22.29
The e. is the LORD's and the fulness 24.01
the e. is full of the steadfast 33.05
Let all the e. fear the LORD, let 33.08
on all the inhabitants of the e., 33.14
remembrance of them from the e. 34.16
make them princes in all the e. 45.16

EARTH (cont.)
fear though the e. should change, Ps 46.02
he utters his voice, the e. melts. 46.06
has wrought desolations in the e. 46.08
wars cease to the end of the e.; 46.09
nations, I am exalted in the e.! 46.10
a great king over all the e. 47.02
For God is the king of all the e.; 47.07
shields of the e. belong to God; 47.09
elevation, is the joy of all the e., 48.02
reaches to the ends of the e. 48.10
and summons the e. from the rising 50.01
to the heavens above and to the e., 50.04
Let thy glory be over all the e.! 57.05
Let thy glory be over all the e.! 57.11
your hands deal out violence on e. 58.02
there is a God who judges on e. 58.11
over Jacob to the ends of the e. 59.13
from the end of the e. I call to thee, 61.02
go down into the depths of the e.; 63.09
the hope of all the ends of the e., 65.05
Thou visitest the e. and waterest 65.09
Make a joyful noise to God, all the e.; 66.01
All the e. worships thee; they sing 66.04
that thy way may be known upon e., 67.02
and guide the nations upon e. 67.04
The e. has yielded its increase; 67.06
all the ends of the e. fear him! 67.07
the e. quaked, the heavens poured 68.08
Sing to God, O kingdoms of the e.; 68.32
Let heaven and e. praise him, the 69.34
depths of the e. thou wilt bring 71.20
like showers that water the e.! 72.06
the River to the ends of the e.! 72.08
may his glory fill the whole e.! 72.19
their tongue struts through the e. 73.09
is nothing upon e. that I desire 73.25
salvation in the midst of the e. 74.12
fixed all the bounds of the e.; 74.17
When the e. totters, and all its 75.03
wicked of the e. shall drain it 75.08
the e. feared and was still, 76.08
save all the oppressed of the e. 76.09
is terrible to the kings of the e. 76.12
world; the e. trembled and shook. 77.18
like the e., which he has founded 78.69
thy saints to the beasts of the e. 79.02
foundations of the e. are shaken. 82.05
Arise, O God, judge the e.; for to 82.08
art the Most High over all the e. 83.18
are thine, the e. also is thine; 89.11
the highest of the kings of the e. 89.27
hadst formed the e. and the world, 90.02
Rise up, O judge of the e.; render 94.02
In his hand are the depths of the e.; 95.04
sing to the LORD, all the e.! 96.01
tremble before him, all the e.! 96.09
be glad, and let the e. rejoice; 96.11
for he comes to judge the e. 96.13
let the e. rejoice; let the many 97.01
the e. sees and trembles. 97.04
before the LORD of all the e. 97.05
art most high over all the e.; 97.09
the ends of the e. have seen the 98.03
noise to the LORD, all the e.; 98.04
LORD, for he comes to rule the e. 98.09
cherubim; let the e. quake! 99.01
all the kings of the e. thy glory. 102.15
heaven the LORD looked at the e., 102.19
didst lay the foundation of the e., 102.25
the heavens are high above the e., 103.11
Thou didst set the e. on its 104.05
they might not again cover the e. 104.09
the e. is satisfied with the fruit 104.13
may bring forth food from the e., 104.14
the e. is full of thy creatures. 104.24
who looks on the e. and it trembles, 104.32
Let sinners be consumed from the e., 104.35
his judgments are in all the e. 105.07
the e. opened and swallowed up 106.17
Let thy glory be over all the e.! 108.05
his memory be cut off from the e.! 109.15
shatter chiefs over the wide e. 110.06
down upon the heavens and the e.? 113.06
Tremble, O e., at the presence of 114.07
the LORD, who made heaven and e.! 115.15
but the e. he has given to the sons 115.16
I am a sojourner on e.; hide not 119.19
The e., O LORD, is full of thy 119.64
almost made an end of me on e.; 119.87
thou hast established the e., and it 119.90
wicked of the e. thou dost count 119.119
the LORD, who made heaven and e. 121.02
the LORD, who made heaven and e. 124.08
Zion, he who made heaven and e.! 134.03
he does, in heaven and on e., 135.06
clouds rise at the end of the e., 135.07
spread out the e. upon the waters, 136.06
kings of the e. shall praise thee, 138.04
wrought in the depths of the e. 139.15
departs he returns to his e.; 146.04
who made heaven and e., the sea, 146.06
he prepares rain for the e., 147.08
He sends forth his command to the e.; 147.15
Praise the LORD from the e., 148.07
Kings of the e. and all peoples, 148.11
princes and all rulers of the e.! 148.11
his glory is above e. and heaven. 148.13
The LORD by wisdom founded the e.; Pro 3.19
rule, and nobles govern the e. 8.16
before the beginning of the e. 8.23
before he had made the e. with its 8.26
out the foundations of the e., 8.29
If the righteous is requited on e., 11.31
a fool are on the ends of the e. 17.24
and the e. for depth, so the mind of 25.03
established all the ends of the e.? 30.04
to devour the poor from off the e., 30.14
the e. ever thirsty for water, and 30.16
Under three things the e. trembles; 30.21
Four things on e. are small, but 30.24
comes, but the e. remains for ever. Ecc 1.04
of the beast goes down to the e.? 3.21
God is in heaven, and you upon e.; 5.02
righteous man on e. who does good 7.20
a vanity which takes place on e., 8.14
the business that is done on e., 8.16
not what evil may happen on e. 11.02
they empty themselves on the e.; 11.03
dust returns to the e. as it was, 12.07
The flowers appear on the e., Sol 2.12
Hear, O heavens, and give ear, O e.; Is 1.02
when he rises to terrify the e. 2.19
when he rises to terrify the e. 2.21
for it from the ends of the e.; 5.26
the whole e. is full of his glory." 6.03
and they will look to the e., 8.22
so I have gathered all the e.; 10.14
decreed, in the midst of all the e. 10.23
with equity for the meek of the e.; 11.04
shall smite the e. with the rod of 11.04
for the e. shall be full of the 11.09
from the four corners of the e. 11.12
let this be known in all the e. 12.05
indignation, to destroy the whole e. 13.05
to make the e. a desolation and to 13.09
and the e. will be shaken out of 13.13
The whole e. is at rest and quiet; 14.07
all who were leaders of the e.; 14.09
the man who made the e. tremble, 14.16
lest they rise and possess the e., 14.21
purposed concerning the whole e.; 14.26
the world, you who dwell on the e., 18.03

EARTH (cont.)
and to the beasts of the e. Is 18.06
beasts of the e. will winter upon 18.06
a blessing in the midst of the e., 19.24
traders were the honored of the e.? 23.08
dishonor all the honored of the e. 23.09
the world upon the face of the e. 23.17
lay waste the e. and make it 24.01
The e. shall be utterly laid waste 24.03
The e. mourns and withers, the world 24.04
languish together with the e. 24.04
The e. lies polluted under its 24.05
Therefore a curse devours the e., 24.06
inhabitants of the e. are scorched, 24.06
the gladness of the e. is banished. 24.11
midst of the e. among the nations, 24.13
From the ends of the e. we hear 24.16
upon you, O inhabitant of the e.! 24.17
the foundations of the e. tremble. 24.18
The e. is utterly broken, the e. 24.19
the e. is rent asunder, the e. is 24.19
the e. is violently shaken. 24.19
The e. staggers like a drunken man, 24.20
the kings of the e., on the e. 24.21
he will take away from all the e.; 25.08
when thy judgments are in the e., 26.09
wrought no deliverance in the e., 26.18
inhabitants of the e. for their 26.21
and the e. will disclose the blood 26.21
cast down to the e. with violence. 28.02
Then deep from the e. you shall 29.04
Let the e. listen, and all that 34.01
of all the kingdoms of the e.; 37.16
thou hast made heaven and e. 37.16
kingdoms of the e. may know that 37.20
the dust of the e. in a measure 40.12
from the foundations of the e.? 40.21
sits above the circle of the e., 40.22
the rulers of the e. as nothing. 40.23
their stem taken root in the e., 40.24
the Creator of the ends of the e. 40.28
afraid, the ends of the e. tremble; 41.05
I took from the ends of the e., 41.09
has established justice in the e.; 42.04
forth the e. and what comes from 42.05
his praise from the end of the e.! 42.10
daughters from the end of the e., 43.06
shout, O depths of the e.; break forth 44.23
alone, who spread out the e.—Who was 44.24
let the e. open, that salvation may 45.08
I made the e., and created man upon 45.12
who formed the e. and made it 45.18
be saved, all the ends of the e.! 45.22
hand laid the foundation of the e., 48.13
send it forth to the end of the e.; 48.20
may reach to the end of the e. 49.06
joy, O heavens, and exult, O e.; 49.13
heavens, and look at the e. beneath; 51.06
the e. will wear out like a garment, 51.06
and laid the foundations of the e., 51.13
laying the foundations of the e., 51.16
the ends of the e. shall see the 52.10
God of the whole e. he is called. 54.05
Noah should no more go over the e., 54.09
the heavens are higher than the e., 55.09
not thither but water the e., 55.10
ride upon the heights of the e.; 58.14
darkness shall cover the e., 60.02
For as the e. brings forth its 61.11
and makes it a praise in the e. 62.07
proclaimed to the end of the e.: 62.11
out their lifeblood on the e. 63.06
I create new heavens and a new e.; 65.17
throne and the e. is my footstool; 66.01
and the new e. which I will make 66.22
I looked on the e., and lo, it Jer 4.23
For this the e. shall mourn, and the 4.28
Hear, O e.; behold, I am 6.19
from the farthest parts of the e. 6.22
air, and for the beasts of the e.; 7.33
and righteousness in the e.; 9.24
At his wrath the e. quakes, 10.10
heavens and the e. shall perish 10.11
perish from the e. and from under 10.11
is he who made the e. by his power, 10.12
mist rise from the ends of the e. 10.13
beasts of the e. to devour and 15.03
kingdoms of the e. because of what 15.04
air and for the beasts of the e. 16.04
from the ends of the e. and say: 16.19
thee shall be written in the e., 17.13
air and to the beasts of the e. 19.07
Do I not fill heaven and e.? 23.24
to all the kingdoms of the e., 24.09
which are on the face of the e. 25.26
all the inhabitants of the e., 25.29
all the inhabitants of the e. 25.30
will resound to the ends of the e., 25.31
from the farthest parts of the e.! 25.32
one end of the e. to the other. 25.33
for all the nations of the e.' " 26.06
outstretched arm have made the e., 27.05
men and animals that are on the e., 27.05
remove you from the face of the e. 28.16
to all the kingdoms of the e., 29.18
from the farthest parts of the e., 31.08
has created a new thing on the e.: 31.22
foundations of the e. below can be 31.37
heavens and the e. by thy great 32.17
"Thus says the LORD who made the e., 33.02
nations of the e. who shall hear 33.09
the ordinances of heaven and e., 33.25
kingdoms of the e. under his 34.01
to all the kingdoms of the e. 34.17
the air and the beasts of the e. 34.20
among all the nations of the e.? 44.08
I will rise, I will cover the e., 46.08
and the e. is full of your cry; 46.12
of their fall the e. shall tremble; 49.21
of the whole e. is cut down and 50.23
that he may give rest to the e., 50.34
from the farthest parts of the e. 50.41
of Babylon the e. shall tremble, 50.46
hand, making all the e. drunken; 51.07
is he who made the e. by his power, 51.15
mist rise from the ends of the e. 51.16
LORD, which destroys the whole e.; 51.25
"Set up a standard on the e., 51.27
the praise of the whole e. seized! 51.41
Then the heavens and the e., 51.48
fallen the slain of all the e. 51.49
from heaven to e. the splendor of Lam 2.01
of beauty, the joy of all the e.?" 2.15
foot all the prisoners of the e., 3.34
The kings of the e. did not believe, 4.12
wheel upon the e. beside the Eze 1.15
living creatures rose from the e., 1.19
and when those rose from the e., 1.21
the wicked of the e. for a spoil; 7.21
lifted me up between e. and heaven, 8.03
wings to mount up from the e., 10.16
up from the e. in my sight as they 10.19
you enriched the kings of the e. 27.33
ashes upon the e. in the sight of 28.18
beasts of the e. and to the birds 29.05
peoples of the e. will go from its 31.12
beasts of the whole e. with you. 32.04
over all the face of the e., 34.06
and the e. shall yield its increase, 34.27
of the whole e. I will make you 35.14
who dwell at the center of the e. 38.12
that are upon the face of the e., 38.20
blood of the princes of the e.— 39.18

EARTH (cont.)

and the e. shone with his glory.	Eze 43.02
is not a man on e. who can meet	Dan 2.10
mountain and filled the whole e.	2.35
which shall rule over all the e.	2.39
languages, that dwell in all the e.:	4.01
a tree in the midst of the e.;	4.10
visible to the end of the whole e.	4.11
the stump of its roots in the e.,	4.15
the beasts in the grass of the e.;	4.15
visible to the end of the whole e.;	4.20
dominion to the ends of the e.	4.22
the stump of its roots in the e.,	4.23
inhabitants of the e. are accounted	4.35
among the inhabitants of the e.;	4.35
languages that dwell in all the e.:	6.25
and wonders in heaven and on e.,	6.27
who shall arise out of the e.	7.17
shall be a fourth kingdom on e.,	7.23
and it shall devour the whole e.,	7.23
across the face of the whole e.,	8.05
in the dust of the e. shall awake,	12.02
and they shall answer the e.;	Hos 2.21
and the e. shall answer the grain,	2.22
the spring rains that water the e.	6.03
The e. quakes before them, the	Joe 2.10
in the heavens and on the e.,	2.30
and the heavens and the e. shake.	3.16
the poor into the dust of the e.,	Amo 2.07
of all the families of the e.;	3.02
Does a bird fall in a snare on the e.,	3.05
treads on the heights of the e.—	4.13
cast down righteousness to the e.!	5.07
out upon the surface of the e.,	5.08
and darken the e. in broad daylight.	8.09
he who touches the e. and it melts,	9.05
and founds his vault upon the e.;	9.06
out upon the surface of the e.—	9.06
no pebble shall fall upon the e.	9.09
hearken, O e., and all that is in it	Mic 1.02
upon the high places of the e.	1.03
wealth to the Lord of the whole e.	4.13
be great to the ends of the e.	5.04
you enduring foundations of the e.;	6.02
godly man has perished from the e.,	7.02
But the e. will be desolate because	7.13
like the crawling things of the e.;	7.17
the e. is laid waste before him, the	Nah 1.05
will cut off your prey from the e.,	2.13
through the breadth of the e.,	Hab 1.06
for they heap up e. and take it.	1.10
of men and violence to the e.,	2.08
For the e. will be filled with the	2.14
of men and violence to the e.,	2.17
let all the e. keep silence before	2.20
and the e. was full of his praise.	3.03
He stood and measured the e.;	3.06
didst cleave the e. with rivers.	3.09
Thou didst bestride the e. in fury,	3.12
everything from the face of the e.,	Zep 1.02
mankind from the face of the e.,	1.03
all the e. shall be consumed;	1.18
of all the inhabitants of the e.	1.18
will famish all the gods of the e.,	2.11
wrath all the e. shall be consumed.	3.08
praise and renown in all the e.	3.19
among all the peoples of the e.,	3.20
and the e. has withheld its produce.	Hag 1.10
heavens and the e. and the sea and	2.06
to shake the heavens and the e.,	2.21
the LORD has sent to patrol the e.'	Zec 1.10
trees, 'We have patrolled the e.,	1.11
all the e. remains at rest.'	1.11
which range through the whole e."	4.10
stand by the LORD of the whole e."	4.14
up the ephah between e. and heaven.	5.09
before the LORD of all the e.	6.05
to get off and patrol the e.	6.07
And he said, "Go, patrol the e."	6.07
So they patrolled the e.	6.07
the River to the ends of the e.	9.10
and they shall crush the e.,	11.06
and founded the e. and formed the	12.01
nations of the e. will come	12.03
will become king over all the e.;	14.09
families of the e. do not go up to	14.17
for they shall inherit the e.	Mt 5.05
"You are the salt of the e.;	5.13
you, till heaven and e. pass away,	5.18
or by the e., for it is his footstool,	5.35
On e. as it is in heaven.	6.10
up for yourselves treasures on e.,	6.19
authority on e. to forgive sins"—	9.06
I have come to bring peace on e.;	10.34
Father, Lord of heaven and e.,	11.25
nights in the heart of the e.	12.40
the ends of the e. to hear the	12.42
you bind on e. shall be bound in	16.19
you loose on e. shall be loosed in	16.19
do kings of the e. take toll or	17.25
you bind on e. shall be bound in	18.18
you loose on e. shall be loosed in	18.18
of you agree on e. about anything	18.19
And call no man your father on e.,	23.09
all the righteous blood shed on e.,	23.35
the tribes of the e. will mourn,	24.30
Heaven and e. will pass away, but my	24.35
and the e. shook, and the rocks were	27.51
heaven and on e. has been given to	28.18
authority on e. to forgive sins"—	Mk 2.10
The e. produces of itself, first the	4.28
smallest of all the seeds on e.;	4.31
as no fuller on e. could bleach	9.03
the ends of the e. to the ends of	13.27
Heaven and e. will pass away, but my	13.31
and on e. peace among men with whom	Lk 2.14
authority on e. to forgive sins"—	5.24
Father, Lord of heaven and e.,	10.21
the ends of the e. to hear the	11.31
"I came to cast fire upon the e.;	12.49
I have come to give peace on e.?	12.51
the appearance of e. and sky;	12.56
for heaven and e. to pass away,	16.17
comes, will he find faith on e.?"	18.08
be upon the e. and wrath upon this	21.23
and upon the e. distress of nations	21.25
Heaven and e. will pass away, but my	21.33
upon the face of the whole e.	21.35
who is of the e. belongs to the e.,	Jn 3.31
the e., and of the e. he speaks;	3.31
wheat falls into the e. and dies,	12.24
I, when I am lifted up from the e.,	12.32
I glorified thee on e., having	17.04
Samaria and to the end of the e."	Ac 1.08
above and signs on the e. beneath,	2.19
the families of the e. be blessed.'	3.25
heaven and the e. and the sea and	4.24
The kings of the e. set themselves	4.26
'Heaven is my throne, and e. my footstool.	7.49
his life is taken up from the e."	8.33
down by four corners upon the e.	10.11
to the uttermost parts of the e.' "	13.47
heaven and the e. and the sea and	14.15
in it, being Lord of heaven and e.,	17.24
to live on all the face of the e.,	17.26
with such a fellow from the e.!	22.22
may be proclaimed in all the e."	Rom 9.17
upon the e. with vigor and dispatch."	9.28
voice has gone out to all the e.,	10.18
so-called gods in heaven or on e.—	1Co 8.05
For "the e. is the Lord's, and	10.26
man was from the e., a man of dust;	15.47

EARTH (cont.)
things in heaven and things on e. Eph 1.10
in heaven and on e. is named, 3.15
into the lower parts of the e.? 4.09
that you may live long on the e." 6.03
heaven and on e. and under the e., Php 2.10
were created, in heaven and on e., Col 1.16
whether on e. or in heaven, making 1.20
not on things that are on e. 3.02
didst found the e. in the beginning, Heb 1.10
Now if he were on e., he would 8.04
strangers and exiles on the e. 11.13
and in dens and caves of the e. 11.38
refused him who warned them on e., 12.25
His voice then shook the e.; 12.26
not only the e. but also the 12.26
lived on the e. in luxury and in Jas 5.05
for the precious fruit of the e., 5.07
by heaven or by e. or with any 5.12
months it did not rain on the e. 5.17
and the e. brought forth its fruit. 5.18
and an e. formed out of water and 2Pe 3.05
the heavens and e. that now exist 3.07
and the e. and the works that are 3.10
and a new e. in which righteousness 3.13
dead, and the ruler of kings on e. Rev 1.05
tribes of the e. will wail on 1.07
to try those who dwell upon the e. 3.10
in heaven or on e. or under the 5.03
or under the e. was able to open 5.03
of God sent out into all the e.; 5.06
God, and they shall reign on e." 5.10
heaven and on e. and under the 5.13
and under the e. and in the sea, 5.13
permitted to take peace from the e., 6.04
power over a fourth of the e., 6.08
and by wild beasts of the e. 6.08
on those who dwell upon the e.?" 6.10
sky fell to the e. as the fig tree 6.13
kings of the e. and the great men 6.15
at the four corners of the e., 7.01
back the four winds of the e., 7.01
might blow on e. or sea or against 7.01
given power to harm e. and sea, 7.02
saying, "Do not harm the e. or the 7.03
the altar and threw it on the e.; 8.05
with blood, which fell on the e.; 8.07
and a third of the e. was burnt up, 8.07
woe to those who dwell on the e., 8.13
a star fallen from heaven to e., 9.01
the smoke came locusts on the e., 9.03
the power of scorpions of the e.; 9.03
grass of the e. or any green 9.04
the e. and what is in it, and the 10.06
stand before the Lord of the e. 11.04
to smite the e. with every plague, 11.06
dwell on the e. will rejoice over 11.10
to those who dwell on the e. 11.10
destroying the destroyers of the e." 11.18
of heaven, and cast them to the e. 12.04
world—he was thrown down to the e., 12.09
O e. and sea, for the devil has come 12.12
he had been thrown down to the e., 12.13
But the e. came to the help of the 12.16
and the e. opened its mouth and 12.16
and the whole e. followed the beast 13.03
who dwell on e. will worship it, 13.08
beast which rose out of the e.; 13.11
and makes the e. and its inhabitants 13.12
from heaven to e. in the sight of 13.13
it deceives those who dwell on e., 13.14
who had been redeemed from the e. 14.03
proclaim to those who dwell on e., 14.06
worship him who made heaven and e., 14.07
harvest of the e. is fully ripe." 14.15
cloud swung his sickle on the e., 14.16
the e., and the e. was reaped. 14.16
the clusters of the vine of the e., 14.18
sickle on the e. and gathered the 14.19
and gathered the vintage of the e., 14.19
pour out on the e. the seven bowls 16.01
went and poured his bowl on the e., 16.02
been since men were on the e., 16.18
kings of the e. have committed 17.02
the dwellers on e. have become 17.02
the dwellers on e. whose names 17.08
dominion over the kings of the e." 17.18
and the e. was made bright with his 18.01
kings of the e. have committed 18.03
merchants of the e. have grown rich 18.03
And the kings of the e., who 18.09
merchants of the e. weep and mourn 18.11
were the great men of the e., 18.23
of all who have been slain on e." 18.24
corrupted the e. with her fornication, 19.02
kings of the e. with their armies 19.19
are at the four corners of the e., 20.08
over the broad e. and surrounded 20.09
his presence e. and sky fled away, 20.11
Then I saw a new heaven and a new e.; 21.01
and the first e. had passed away, 21.01
kings of the e. shall bring their 21.24

EARTHEN
And the e. vessel in which it is Lev 6.28
of them falls into any e. vessel, 11.33
the birds in an e. vessel over 14.05
the birds in an e. vessel over 14.50
And the e. vessel which he who has 15.12
take holy water in an e. vessel, Num 5.17
and e. vessels, wheat, barley, meal, 2Sa 17.28
covering an e. vessel are smooth Pro 26.23
an e. vessel with the potter! Is 45.09
LORD, "Go, buy a potter's e. flask, Jer 19.01
how they are reckoned as e. pots, Lam 4.02
have this treasure in e. vessels, 2Co 4.07
as when e. pots are broken in Rev 2.27

EARTHENWARE
deed, and put them in an e. vessel, Jer 32.14
and silver but also of wood and e., 2Ti 2.20

EARTHLY
If I have told you e. things and Jn 3.12
not by e. wisdom but by the grace 2Co 1.12
that if the e. tent we live in is 5.01
to those who are your e. masters, Eph 6.05
shame, with minds set on e. things. Php 3.19
death therefore what is e. in you: Col 3.05
those who are your e. masters, 3.22
for worship and an e. sanctuary. Heb 9.01
we have had e. fathers to discipline 12.09
but is e., unspiritual, devilish. Jas 3.15

EARTHQUAKE
and after the wind an e., but the 1Ki 19.11
but the LORD was not in the e.; 19.11
and after the e. a fire, but the 19.12
and with e. and great noise, with Is 29.06
behind me the sound of a great e.; Eze 3.12
them, that sounded like a great e. 3.13
of Israel, two years before the e. Amo 1.01
fled from the e. in the days of Zec 14.05
saw the e. and what took place, they Mt 27.54
And behold, there was a great e.; 28.02
and suddenly there was a great e., Ac 16.26
and behold, there was a great e.; Rev 6.12
flashes of lightning, and an e. 8.05
And at that hour there was a great e., 11.13
people were killed in the e., 11.13
of thunder, an e., and heavy hail. 11.19
and a great e. such as had never 16.18
on the earth, so great was that e. 16.18

EARTHQUAKES
be famines and e. in various places: Mt 24.07
there will be e. in various places, Mk 13.08
there will be great e., and in Lk 21.11

EARTH'S
who dwell at e. farthest bounds Ps 65.08
of harlots and of e. abominations." Rev 17.05

EASE
these nations you shall find no e., Deu 28.65
There the prisoners are at e. together; Job 3.18
I am not at e., nor am I quiet; 3.26
my couch will e. my complaint,' 7.13
one who is at e. there is contempt 12.05
I was at e., and he broke me 16.12
being wholly at e. and secure, 21.23
always at e., they increase in Ps 73.12
the scorn of those who are at e., 123.04
dwell secure and will be at e., Pro 1.33
women who are at e., hear my voice; Is 32.09
Tremble, you women who are at e., 32.11
shall return and have quiet and e., Jer 30.10
shall return and have quiet and e., 46.27
"Moab has been at e. from his youth 48.11
up, advance against a nation at e., 49.31
surfeit of food, and prosperous e., Eze 16.49
was at e. in my house and prospering Dan 4.04
"Woe to those who are at e. in Zion, Amo 6.01
with the nations that are at e.; Zec 1.15
take your e., eat, drink, be merry.' Lk 12.19
that you put him at e. among you, 1Co 16.10

EASED
should be e. and you burdened, 2Co 8.13

EASES
them as one who e. the yoke on Hos 11.04

EASIER
so it will be e. for you, and they Ex 18.22
For which is e., to say, 'Your sins Mt 9.05
it is e. for a camel to go through 19.24
Which is e., to say to the paralytic, Mk 2.09
It is e. for a camel to go through 10.25
Which is e., to say, 'Your sins are Lk 5.23
But it is e. for heaven and earth 16.17
For it is e. for a camel to go 18.25

EASILY
people might e. have lain with Gen 26.10

EAST
a garden in Eden, in the e.; Gen 2.08
Hiddekel, which flows e. of Assyria. 2.14
and at the e. of the garden of Eden 3.24
in the land of Nod, e. of Eden. 4.16
to the hill country of the e. 10.30
And as men migrated in the e., 11.02
the mountain on the e. of Bethel, 12.08
on the west and Ai on the e.; 12.08
valley, and Lot journeyed e.; 13.11
which was to the e. of Mamre, 23.17
of Machpelah e. of Mamre (that is, 23.19
Isaac, eastward to the e. country. 25.06
of Zohar the Hittite, e. of Mamre, 25.09
west and to the e. and to the 28.14
the land of the people of the e. 29.01
thin and blighted by the e. wind, 41.06
thin, and blighted by the e. wind, 41.23
blighted by the e. wind are also 41.27
to the e. of Mamre, in the land of 49.30
to the e. of Mamre, which Abraham 50.13
LORD brought an e. wind upon the Ex 10.13
was morning the e. wind had 10.13
back by a strong e. wind all night, 14.21
front to the e. shall be fifty 27.13
the front to the e., fifty cubits. 38.13
it beside the altar on the e. side, Lev 1.16
encamp on the e. side toward the Num 2.03
before the tabernacle on the e., 3.38
that are on the e. side shall set 10.05
this side of the Jordan to the e." 32.19
Pihahiroth, which is e. of Baalzephon; 33.07
the end of the Salt Sea on the e.; 34.03
to Riblah on the e. side of Ain; 34.11
of the sea of Chinnereth on the e.; 34.11
for the e. side two thousand cubits, 35.05
the slopes of Pisgah on the e. Deu 3.17
cities in the e. beyond the Jordan, 4.41
lived to the e. beyond the Jordan; 4.47
Arabah on the e. side of the Jordan 4.49
Gilgal on the e. border of Jericho Jos 4.19
e. of Bethel, and said to them, "Go 7.02
Canaanites in the e. and the west, 11.03
which is e. of Egypt, northward to 13.03
to Aroer, which is e. of Rabbah, 13.25
beyond the Jordan e. of Jericho. 13.32
And the e. boundary is the Salt Sea, 15.05
e. of the waters of Jericho, into 16.01
inheritance on the e. was Atarothaddar 16.05
then on the e. the boundary turns 16.06
beyond it on the e. to Janoah, 16.06
Michmethath, which is e. of Shechem; 17.07
is reached, and on the e. Issachar. 17.10
the brook which is e. of Jokneam; 19.11
along on the e. toward the sunrise 19.13
and Judah on the e. at the Jordan. 19.34
And beyond the Jordan e. of Jericho, 20.08
people of the E. would come up and Ju 6.03
the people of the E. came together, 6.33
people of the E. lay along the 7.12
the army of the people of the E.; 8.10
caravan route e. of Nobah and 8.11
arrived on the e. side of the land 11.18
far as opposite Gibeah on the e. 20.43
on the e. of the highway that goes 21.19
in Michmash, to the e. of Bethaven. 1Sa 13.05
far as Shur, which is e. of Egypt. 15.07
which is on the e. of Jeshimon? 26.01
the road on the e. of Jeshimon. 26.03
wisdom of all the people of the e., 1Ki 4.30
facing south, and three facing e.; 7.25
on the mountain e. of Jerusalem. 11.07
Cherith, that is e. of the Jordan. 17.03
Cherith that is e. of the Jordan. 17.05
places that were e. of Jerusalem, 2Ki 23.13
to the e. side of the valley, to 1Ch 4.39
dwelt to the e. as far as the 5.09
all the region e. of Gilead. 5.10
on the e. side of the Jordan, out of 6.78
in the king's gate on the e. side. 9.18
e., west, north, and south; 9.24
valleys, to the e. and to the west. 12.15
The lot for the e. fell to Shelemiah 26.14
On the e. there were six each day, 26.17
facing south, and three facing e.; 2Ch 4.04
stood e. of the altar with a 5.12
e. of the wilderness of Jeruel. 20.16
them in the square on the e., 29.04
keeper of the e. gate, was over the 31.14
Gate, on the e. and the projecting Neh 3.26
keeper of the E. Gate, repaired. 3.29
David, to the Water Gate on the e. 12.37
of all the people of the e. Job 1.03
and fill himself with the e. wind? 15.02
and horror seizes them of the e. 18.20
The e. wind lifts him up and he is 27.21
or where the e. wind is scattered 38.24
By the e. wind thou didst shatter Ps 48.07
For not from the e. or from the 75.06
He caused the e. wind to blow in 78.26
as far as the e. is from the west, 103.12
from the e. and from the west, from 107.03
from the e. and of soothsayers Is 2.06

EAST (cont.)

The Syrians on the e. and the Ps 9.12
shall plunder the people of the e. 11.14
Therefore in the e. give glory to 24.15
blast in the day of the e. wind. 27.08
up one from the e. whom victory 41.02
bring your offspring from the e., 43.05
calling a bird of prey from the e., 46.11
Like the e. wind I will scatter Jer 18.17
of the Horse Gate toward the e., 31.40
Destroy the people of the e.! 49.28
and their faces toward the e., Eze 8.16
worshiping the sun toward the e. 8.16
the door of the e. gate of the 10.19
me to the e. gate of the house of 11.01
house of the LORD, which faces e. 11.01
which is on the e. side of the 11.23
wither when the e. wind strikes it 17.10
the e. wind dried it up; its fruit 19.12
people of the E. for a possession, 25.04
people of the E. as a possession, 25.10
The e. wind has wrecked you in the 27.26
of the Travelers e. of the sea; 39.11
he went into the gateway facing e., 40.06
on either side of the e. gate; 40.10
the gate which faced toward the e.; 40.22
as on the e., was a gate to the 40.23
to the inner court on the e. side, 40.32
breadth of the e. front of the 41.14
was an entrance on the e. side, 42.09
was an entrance on the e. side, 42.12
me out by the gate which faced e., 42.15
He measured the e. side with the 42.16
me to the gate, the gate facing e. 43.01
the God of Israel came from the e.; 43.02
the temple by the gate facing e., 43.04
steps of the altar shall face e. 43.17
of the sanctuary, which faces e.; 44.01
city, on the west and on the e., 45.07
that faces e. shall be shut on the 46.01
the gate facing e. shall be opened 46.12
toward the e. (for the temple faced e.); 47.01
gate, that faces toward the e.; 47.02
"On the e. side, the boundary shall 47.18
This shall be the e. side. 47.18
from the e. side to the west, Dan, 48.01
from the e. side to the west, Asher, 48.02
from the e. side to the west, 48.03
from the e. side to the west, 48.04
from the e. side to the west, 48.05
from the e. side to the west, Reuben, 48.06
from the e. side to the west, Judah, 48.07
from the e. side to the west, shall 48.08
from the e. side to the west, with 48.08
the e. side four thousand five 48.16
on the e. two hundred and fifty, and 48.17
be ten thousand cubits to the e., 48.18
the holy portion to the e. border, 48.21
from the e. side to the west, 48.23
from the e. side to the west, Simeon, 48.24
from the e. side to the west, 48.25
from the e. side to the west, 48.26
from the e. side to the west, Gad, 48.27
On the e. side, which is to be four 48.32
toward the e., and toward the Dan 8.09
from the e. and the north shall 11.44
and pursues the e. wind all day Hos 12.01
the e. wind, the wind of the LORD, 13.15
sea to sea, and from north to e.; Amo 8.12
city and sat to the e. of the city, Jon 4.05
God appointed a sultry e. wind, 4.08
people from the e. country and Zec 8.07
in two from e. to west by a very 14.04
men from the E. came to Jerusalem, Mt 2.01
we have seen his star in the E., 2.02
had seen in the E. went before 2.09
will come from e. and west and sit 8.11
comes from the e. and shines as 24.27
And men will come from e. and west, Lk 13.29
the way for the kings from the e. Rev 16.12
on the e. three gates, on the north 21.13

EASTERN

king of Moab from the e. mountains: Num 23.07
mark out your e. boundary from 34.10
forms its boundary on the e. side. Jos 18.20
western to the e. boundary of the Eze 45.07
toward the e. region and goes down 47.08
to the e. sea and as far as Tamar. 47.18
thousand in breadth on the e. side, 48.10
land, his front into the e. sea, Joe 2.20
of them to the e. sea and half of Zec 14.08

EASTWARD

and southward and e. and westward; Gen 13.14
son Isaac, e. to the east country. 25.06
beyond the Jordan at Jericho e. Num 34.15
and northward and southward and e., Deu 3.27
and e. as far as the valley of Jos 11.08
Hermon, with all the Arabah e.: 12.01
Arabah to the Sea of Chinneroth e., 12.03
gave them, beyond the Jordan e., 13.08
Chinnereth, e. beyond the Jordan. 13.27
inheritance beyond the Jordan e., 18.07
other direction e. toward the 19.12
then it turns e., it goes to 19.27
"Depart from here and turn e., 1Ki 17.03
from the Jordan e., all the land 2Ki 10.33
And he said, "Open the window e."; 13.17
and e. Naaran, and westward Gezer 1Ch 7.28
Going on e. with a line in his hand, Eze 47.03

EASY

and thought it e. to go up into Deu 1.41
"It is an e. thing for the shadow 2Ki 20.10
knowledge is e. for a man of Pro 14.06
the gate is wide and the way is e., Mt 7.13
For my yoke is e., and my burden is 11.30

EAT

"You may freely e. of every tree of Gen 2.16
of good and evil you shall not e., 2.17
day that you e. of it you shall 2.17
'You shall not e. of any tree of 3.01
"We may e. of the fruit of the 3.02
'You shall not e. of the fruit of 3.03
that when you e. of it your eyes 3.05
of which I commanded you not to e.?" 3.11
dust you shall e. all the days of 3.14
you, 'You shall not e. of it,' 3.17
toil you shall e. of it all the 3.17
and you shall e. the plants of the 3.18
face you shall e. bread till you 3.19
and e., and live for ever"— 3.22
Only you shall not e. flesh with 9.04
Then food was set before him to e.; 24.33
"I will not e. until I have told my 24.33
"Let me e. some of that red pottage, 25.30
and bring it to me that I may e.; 27.04
that I may e. it, and bless you 27.07
bring it to your father to e., 27.10
now sit up and e. of my game, 27.19
that I may e. of my son's game and 27.25
and e. of his son's game, that you 27.31
me bread to e. and clothing to 28.20
and called his kinsmen to e. bread; 31.54
Israelites do not e. the sinew of 32.32
Then they sat down to e.; and looking 37.25
the birds will e. the flesh from 40.19
that they should e. bread there. 43.25
might not e. bread with the 43.32
and you shall e. the fat of the 45.18
Call him, that he may e. bread." Ex 2.20
and they shall e. what is left to 10.05
and they shall e. every tree of 10.05

EAT (cont.)

and e. every plant in the land, all Ex 10.12
what each can e. you shall make 12.04
the houses in which they e. them. 12.07
They shall e. the flesh that night, 12.08
and bitter herbs they shall e. it. 12.08
Do not e. any of it raw or boiled 12.09
In this manner you shall e. it: 12.11
and you shall e. it in haste. 12.11
Seven days you shall e. unleavened 12.15
but what every one must e., that only 12.16
you shall e. unleavened bread, and 12.18
You shall e. nothing leavened; 12.20
you shall e. unleavened bread." 12.20
no foreigner shall e. of it; 12.43
for money may e. of it after you 12.44
or hired servant may e. of it. 12.45
uncircumcised person shall e. of it. 12.48
Seven days you shall e. unleavened 13.06
flesh to e. and in the morning 16.08
'At twilight you shall e. flesh, 16.12
which the LORD has given you to e. 16.15
man of you, as much as he can e.; 16.16
according to what he could e. 16.18
it, each as much as he could e.; 16.21
Moses said, "E. it today, for today 16.25
of Israel to e. bread with Moses' 18.12
you shall not e. any flesh that is 22.31
the poor of your people may e.; 23.11
they leave the wild beasts may e. 23.11
you shall e. unleavened bread for 23.15
his sons shall e. the flesh of the 29.32
They shall e. those things with 29.33
an outsider shall not e. of them, 29.33
people sat down to e. and drink, 32.06
invites you, you e. of his sacrifice, 34.15
days you shall e. unleavened bread, 34.18
that you e. neither fat nor blood." Lev 3.17
of it Aaron and his sons shall e.; 6.16
tent of meeting they shall e. it. 6.16
the children of Aaron may e. of it, 6.18
who offers it for sin shall e. it; 6.26
among the priests may e. of it; 6.29
among the priests may e. of it; 7.06
All who are clean may e. flesh, 7.19
You shall e. no fat, of ox, or sheep, 7.23
but on no account shall you e. it. 7.24
Moreover you shall e. no blood 7.26
and there e. it and the bread that 8.31
'Aaron and his sons shall e. it'; 8.31
and e. it unleavened beside the 10.12
you shall e. it in a holy place, 10.13
you shall e. in any clean place, 10.14
which you may e. among all the 11.02
cud, among the animals, you may e. 11.03
you shall not e. these: The camel, 11.04
Of their flesh you shall not e., 11.08
"These you may e., of all that are 11.09
seas or in the rivers, you may e. 11.09
of their flesh you shall not e., 11.11
fours you may e. those which have 11.21
Of them you may e.: the locust 11.22
animal of which you may e. dies, 11.39
upon the earth, you shall not e.; 11.42
No person among you shall e. blood, 17.12
who sojourns among you e. blood. 17.12
You shall not e. the blood of any 17.14
year you may e. of their fruit, 19.25
"You shall not e. any flesh with 19.26
He may e. the bread of his God, both 21.22
a discharge may e. of the holy 22.04
and shall not e. of the holy 22.06
afterward he may e. of the holy 22.07
is torn by beasts he shall not e., 22.08
shall not e. of a holy thing. 22.10
for money, the slave may e. of it; 22.11
in his house may e. of his food. 22.11
she shall not e. of the offering 22.12
she may e. of her father's food; 22.13
yet no outsider shall e. of it. 22.13
days you shall e. unleavened bread 23.06
And you shall e. neither bread nor 23.14
and they shall e. it in a holy 24.09
you shall e. what it yields out of 25.12
and you will e. your fill, and dwell 25.19
'What shall we e. in the seventh 25.20
comes in, you shall e. the old. 25.22
and you shall e. your bread to the 26.05
And you shall e. old store long 26.10
vain, for your enemies shall e. it; 26.16
and you shall e., and not be 26.26
You shall e. the flesh of your sons, 26.29
and you shall e. the flesh of your 26.29
of your enemies shall e. you up. 26.38
any juice of grapes or e. grapes, Num 6.03
he shall e. nothing that is 6.04
they shall e. it with unleavened 9.11
and said, "O that we had meat to e.! 11.04
say, 'Give us meat, that we may e.' 11.13
tomorrow, and you shall e. meat; 11.18
"Who will give us meat to e.? 11.18
give you meat, and you shall e. 11.18
You shall not e. one day, or two 11.19
that they may e. a whole month!' 11.21
and when you e. of the food of the 15.19
most holy place shall you e. of it; 18.10
every male may e. of it; 18.10
clean in your house may e. of it. 18.11
clean in your house may e. of it. 18.13
and you may e. it in any place, you 18.31
he shall e. up the nations his 24.08
them for money, that you may e.; Deu 2.06
that I may e., and give me water 2.28
see, nor hear, nor e., nor smell. 4.28
and when you e. and are full, 6.11
which you will e. bread without 8.09
And you shall e. and be full, and 8.10
and you shall e. and be full. 11.15
and there you shall e. before the 12.07
slaughter and e. flesh within any 12.15
unclean and the clean may e. of it, 12.15
Only you shall not e. the blood; 12.16
You may not e. within your towns 12.17
but you shall e. them before the 12.18
'I will e. flesh,' because you crave 12.20
you may e. as much flesh as you 12.20
and you may e. within your towns as 12.21
hart is eaten, so you may e. of it; 12.22
and the clean alike may e. of it. 12.22
sure that you do not e. the blood; 12.23
you shall not e. the life with the 12.23
You shall not e. it; you shall 12.24
You shall not e. it; that all may 12.25
your God, but the flesh you may e. 12.27
"You shall not e. any abominable 14.03
These are the animals you may e.: 14.04
cud, among the animals, you may e. 14.06
hoof cloven you shall not e. these: 14.07
Their flesh you shall not e., 14.08
are in the waters you may e. these: 14.09
has fins and scales you may e. 14.09
fins and scales you shall not e.; 14.10
"You may e. all clean birds. 14.11
the ones which you shall not e.: 14.12
All clean winged things you may e. 14.20
"You shall not e. anything that 14.21
that he may e. it, or you may sell 14.21
you shall e. the tithe of your 14.23
and you shall e. there before the 14.26
shall come and e. and be filled; 14.29
You shall e. it, you and your 15.20
You shall e. it within your towns; 15.22
and the clean alike may e. it, 15.22
Only you shall not e. its blood; 15.23

EAT (cont.)
You shall e. no leavened bread with Deu 16.03
days you shall e. it with unleavened 16.03
boil it and e. it at the place 16.07
days you shall e. unleavened bread 16.08
they shall e. the offerings by fire 18.01
They shall have equal portions to e., 18.08
for you may e. of them, but you 20.19
you may e. your fill of grapes, as 23.24
that they may e. within your towns 26.12
offerings, and shall e. there; 27.07
eyes, and you shall not e. of it; 28.31
not known shall e. up the fruit of 28.33
for the worm shall e. them. 28.39
and shall e. the offspring of your 28.51
And you shall e. the offspring of 28.53
because she will e. them secretly, 28.57
you e. the fruit of vineyards and Jos 24.13
strong drink, and e. nothing unclean, Ju 13.04
and e. nothing unclean, for the boy 13.07
She may not e. of anything that 13.14
or e. any unclean thing; 13.14
me, I will not e. of your food; 13.16
of the eater came something to e. 14.14
and e. some bread, and dip your Ru 2.14
Hannah wept and would not e. 1Sa 1.07
And why do you not e.? And why 1.08
that I may e. a morsel of bread" ' " 2.36
he goes up to the high place to e.; 9.13
people will not e. till he comes, 9.13
afterward those e. who are invited. 9.13
for today you shall e. with me, 9.19
E.; because it was kept for you 9.24
that you might e. with the guests." 9.24
sheep, and slay them here, and e.; 14.34
came, the king sat down to e. food. 20.24
and e., that you may have strength 28.22
He refused, and said, "I will not e." 28.23
David to e. bread while it was yet 2Sa 3.35
and you shall e. at my table always 9.07
master's son may have bread to e.; 9.10
son shall always e. at my table." 9.10
to e. and to drink, and to lie with 11.11
it used to e. of his morsel, and 12.03
not, nor did he e. food with them. 12.17
Tamar come and give me bread to e., 13.05
and e. it from her hand.' " 13.05
sight, that I may e. from her hand." 13.06
before him, but he refused to e. 13.09
that I may e. from your hand." 13.10
she brought them near him to e., 13.11
fruit for the young men to e., 16.02
and the people with him to e.; 17.29
among those who e. at your table. 19.28
among those who e. at your table; 1Ki 2.07
And I will not e. bread or drink 13.08
'You shall neither e. bread, 13.09
"Come home with me and e. bread." 13.15
neither will I e. bread nor drink 13.16
shall neither e. bread nor drink 13.17
that he may e. bread and drink 13.18
"E. no bread, and drink no water"; 13.22
dies in the city the dogs shall e.; 14.11
the birds of the air shall e.; 14.11
dies in the city the dogs shall e.; 16.04
the birds of the air shall e." 16.04
my son, that we may e. it, and die." 17.12
Asherah, who e. at Jezebel's table." 18.19
said to Ahab, "Go up, e. and drink; 18.41
So Ahab went up to e. and to drink. 18.42
him, and said to him, "Arise and e." 19.05
"Arise and e., else the journey 19.07
his face, and would e. no food. 21.04
so vexed that you e. no food? 21.05
Arise, and e. bread, and let your 21.07
'The dogs shall e. Jezebel within 21.23
dies in the city the dogs shall e.; 21.24
the birds of the air shall e." 21.24
who urged him to e. some food. 2Ki 4.08
he would turn in there to e. food. 4.08
And they poured out for the men to e. 4.40
And they could not e. it. 4.40
out for the men, that they may e." 4.41
"Give to the men, that they may e." 4.42
that they may e., for thus says the 4.43
'They shall e. and have some left.' " 4.43
that they may e. and drink and go 6.22
that we may e. him today, and we 6.28
and we will e. my son tomorrow.' 6.28
'Give your son, that we may e. him'; 6.29
eyes, but you shall not e. of it." 7.02
eyes, but you shall not e. of it." 7.19
And the dogs shall e. Jezebel in 9.10
the dogs shall e. the flesh of 9.36
with you to e. their own dung and 18.27
one of you will e. of his own vine, 18.31
year you shall e. what grows of 19.29
vineyards, and e. their fruit. 19.29
Now because we e. the salt of the Ez 4.14
and e. the good of the land, and 9.12
that we may e. and keep alive." Neh 5.02
e. the fat and drink sweet wine and 8.10
their way to e. and drink and to 8.12
and neither e. nor drink for three Est 4.16
sisters to e. and drink with them. Job 1.04
His harvest the hungry e., and he 5.05
offspring have not enough to e. 27.14
then let me sow, and another e.; 31.08
who e. up my people as they e. bread, Ps 14.04
The afflicted shall e. and be 22.26
Do I e. the flesh of bulls, or drink 50.13
who e. up my people as they e. bread, 53.04
rained down upon them manna to e., 78.24
withered; I forget to e. my bread. 102.04
For I e. ashes like bread, and 102.09
You shall e. the fruit of the labor 128.02
and let me not e. of their dainties 141.04
therefore they shall e. the fruit Pro 1.31
For they e. the bread of wickedness 4.17
"Come, e. of my bread and drink of 9.05
who love it will e. its fruits. 18.21
When you sit down to e. with a ruler, 23.01
Do not e. the bread of a man who is 23.06
"E. and drink!" he says 23.07
My son, e. honey, for it is good, and 24.13
e. only enough for you, lest you be 25.16
is hungry, give him bread to e.; 25.21
It is not good to e. much honey, 25.27
tends a fig tree will e. its fruit, 27.18
and does not e. the bread of 31.27
than that he should e. and drink, Ecc 2.24
him who can e. or who can have 2.25
one should e. and drink and take 3.13
increase, they increase who e. them; 5.11
fitting is to e. and drink and 5.18
good thing under the sun but to e., 8.15
Go, e. your bread with enjoyment, and 9.07
and e. its choicest fruits. Sol 4.16
I e. my honeycomb with my honey, I 5.01
E., O friends, and drink: drink 5.01
you shall e. the good of the land; Is 1.19
for they shall e. the fruit of 3.10
"We will e. our own bread and wear 4.01
He shall e. curds and honey when he 7.15
which they give, he will e. curds; 7.22
the land will e. curds and honey. 7.22
the lion shall e. straw like the 11.07
the rugs, they e., they drink. 21.05
"Let us e. and drink, for tomorrow 22.13
the ground will e. salted provender, 30.24
with you to e. their own dung and 36.12
one of you will e. of his own vine, 36.16

EAT (cont.)

this year e. what grows of itself, Is 37.30
vineyards, and e. their fruit. 37.30
your oppressors e. their own flesh, 49.26
the moth will e. them up. 50.09
For the moth will e. them up like a 51.08
the worm will e. them like wool; 51.08
who has no money, come, buy and e.! 55.01
and e. what is good, and delight 55.02
you shall e. the wealth of the 61.06
garner it shall e. it and praise 62.09
who e. swine's flesh, and broth of 65.04
GOD: "Behold, my servants shall e., 65.13
plant vineyards and e. their fruit. 65.21
shall not plant and another e.; 65.22
the lion shall e. straw like the 65.25
They shall e. up your harvest and Jer 5.17
they shall e. up your sons and your 5.17
they shall e. up your flocks and 5.17
they shall e. up your vines and 5.17
your sacrifices, and e. the flesh. 7.21
to sit with them, to e. and drink. 16.08
will make them e. the flesh of 19.09
every one shall e. the flesh of 19.09
not your father e. and drink and 22.15
plant gardens and e. their produce. 29.05
plant gardens and e. their produce."'" 29.28
Should women e. their offspring, the Lam 2.20
and e. what I give you." Eze 2.08
e. what is offered to you; 3.01
e. this scroll, and go, speak to the 3.01
and he gave me the scroll to e. 3.02
e. this scroll that I give you and 3.03
and ninety days, you shall e. it. 4.09
food which you e. shall be by 4.10
once a day you shall e. it. 4.10
And you shall e. it as a barley 4.12
of Israel e. their bread unclean, 4.13
they shall e. bread by weight and 4.16
Therefore fathers shall e. their 5.10
and sons shall e. their fathers; 5.10
"Son of man, e. your bread with 12.18
They shall e. their bread with 12.19
if he does not e. upon the mountains 18.06
who does not e. upon the mountains 18.15
men in you who e. upon the mountains 22.09
nor e. the bread of mourners." 24.17
nor e. the bread of mourners. 24.22
they shall e. your fruit, and they 25.04
You e. flesh with the blood, and 33.25
You e. the fat, you clothe yourselves 34.03
And must my sheep e. what you have 34.19
and you shall e. flesh and drink 39.17
You shall e. the flesh of the 39.18
And you shall e. fat till you are 39.19
the LORD shall e. the most holy 42.13
sit in it to e. bread before the 44.03
They shall e. the cereal offering, 44.29
The priests shall not e. of anything, 44.31
vegetables to e. and water to Dan 1.12
the youths who e. the king's rich 1.13
be made to e. grass like an ox, and 4.25
be made to e. grass like an ox; 4.32
Even those who e. his rich food 11.26
They shall e., but not be satisfied; Hos 4.10
they sacrifice flesh and e. it; 8.13
and they shall e. unclean food in 9.03
all who e. of it shall be defiled; 9.04
"You shall e. in plenty and be Joe 2.26
and e. lambs from the flock, and Amo 6.04
and e. bread there, and prophesy 7.12
make gardens and e. their fruit. 9.14
who e. the flesh of my people, and Mic 3.03
when they have something to e., 3.05
You shall e., but not be satisfied, 6.14
gleaned: there is no cluster to e., 7.01
you e., but you never have enough; Hag 1.06
And when you e. and when you drink, Zec 7.06
do you not e. for yourselves and 7.06
what you shall e. or what you Mt 6.25
anxious, saying, 'What shall we e.?' 6.31
your teacher e. with tax collectors 9.11
to pluck ears of grain and to e. 12.01
for him to e. nor for those who 12.04
you give them something to e." 14.16
not wash their hands when they e." 15.02
but to e. with unwashed hands does 15.20
even the dogs e. the crumbs that 15.27
three days, and have nothing to e.; 15.32
prepare for you to e. the passover?" 26.17
the disciples and said, "Take, e.; 26.26
"Why does he e. with tax collectors Mk 2.16
for any but the priests to e., 2.26
so that they could not even e. 3.20
them to give her something to e. 5.43
and they had no leisure even to e. 6.31
and buy themselves something to e." 6.36
"You give them something to e." 6.37
bread, and give it to them to e.?" 6.37
do not e. unless they wash their 7.03
they do not e. unless they purify 7.04
elders, but e. with hands defiled?" 7.05
under the table e. the children's 7.28
gathered, and they had nothing to e., 8.01
three days, and have nothing to e.; 8.02
"May no one ever e. fruit from you 11.14
prepare for you to e. the passover?" 14.12
where I am to e. the passover with 14.14
"Why do you e. and drink with tax Lk 5.30
Pharisees, but yours e. and drink." 5.33
for any but the priests to e., 6.04
Pharisees asked him to e. with him, 7.36
something should be given her to e. 8.55
"You give them something to e." 9.13
receive you, e. what is set before you; 10.08
take your ease, e., drink, be merry.' 12.19
about your life, what you shall e., 12.22
what you are to e. and what you 12.29
is he who shall e. bread in the 14.15
it, and let us e. and make merry; 15.23
and serve me, till I e. and drink; 17.08
afterward you shall e. and drink'? 17.08
passover for us, that we may e. it." 22.08
where I am to e. the passover with 22.11
desired to e. this passover with 22.15
you I shall not e. it until it is 22.16
that you may e. and drink at my 22.30
them, "Have you anything here to e.?" 24.41
besought him, saying, "Rabbi, e." Jn 4.31
"I have food to e. of which you do 4.32
bread, so that these people may e.?" 6.05
gave them bread from heaven to e.'" 6.31
that a man may e. of it and not 6.50
this man give us his flesh to e.?" 6.52
unless you e. the flesh of the Son 6.53
defiled, but might e. the passover. 18.28
hungry and desired something to e.; Ac 10.10
"Rise, Peter; kill and e." 10.13
uncircumcised men and e. with them?" 11.03
'Rise, Peter; kill and e.' 11.07
oath neither to e. nor drink till 23.12
oath neither to e. nor drink till 23.21
of all he broke it and began to e. 27.35
One believes he may e. anything, Rom 14.02
is being injured by what you e., 14.15
let what you e. cause the ruin of 14.15
it is right not to e. meat or drink 14.21
not even to e. with such a one. 1Co 5.11
e. food as really offered to an 8.07
are no worse off if we do not e., 8.08
to e. food offered to idols? 8.10
I will never e. meat, lest I cause 8.13

EAT (cont.)

sat down to e. and drink and rose 1Co 10.07
not those who e. the sacrifices 10.18
E. whatever is sold in the meat 10.25
e. whatever is set before you 10.27
conscience, not yours—do not e. it.) 10.29
whether you e. or drink, or whatever 10.31
not the Lord's supper that you e. 11.20
not have houses to e. and drink in? 11.22
For as often as you e. this bread 11.26
and so e. of the bread and drink of 11.28
when you come together to e., 11.33
let him e. at home—lest you come 11.34
"Let us e. and drink, for tomorrow 15.32
we did not e. any one's bread 2Th 3.08
one will not work, let him not e. 3.10
and their talk will e. its way like 2Ti 2.17
serve the tent have no right to e. Heb 13.10
you and will e. your flesh like Jas 5.03
I will grant to e. of the tree of Rev 2.07
that they might e. food sacrificed 2.14
immorality and to e. food sacrificed 2.20
come in to him and e. with him, 3.20
and he said to me, "Take it and e.; 10.09
to e. the flesh of kings, the flesh 19.18

EATEN

Have you e. of the tree of which I Gen 3.11
and have e. of the tree of which I 3.17
you every sort of food that is e., 6.21
but what the young men have e., 14.24
and I have not e. the rams of your 31.38
but when they had e. them no one 41.21
have known that they had e. them, 41.21
And when they had e. the grain 43.02
In one house shall it be e.; Ex 12.46
no leavened bread shall be e. 13.03
Unleavened bread shall be e. for seven days; 13.07
and its flesh shall not be e.; 21.28
it shall not be e., because it is 29.34
it shall be e. unleavened in a holy Lev 6.16
wholly burned; it shall not be e." 6.23
in a holy place it shall be e., 6.26
shall be e. from which any blood 6.30
it shall be e. in a holy place; 7.06
shall be e. on the day of his 7.15
it shall be e. on the day that he 7.16
what remains of it shall be e., 7.16
offering is e. on the third day, he 7.18
any unclean thing shall not be e.; 7.19
"Why have you not e. the sin 10.17
ought to have e. it in the sanctuary, 10.18
If I had e. the sin offering today, 10.19
the birds, they shall not be e., 11.13
Any food in it which may be e., 11.34
abomination; it shall not be e. 11.41
that may be e. and the living 11.47
living creature that may not be e. 11.47
that may be e. shall pour out its 17.13
It shall be e. the same day you 19.06
If it is e. at all on the third day, 19.07
forbidden to you, it must not be e. 19.23
It shall be e. on the same day, you 22.30
days shall unleavened bread be e. Num 28.17
when you have e. and are full, and Deu 8.12
Just as the gazelle or the hart is e., 12.22
unclean for you; they shall not be e. 14.19
I have not e. of the tithe while I 26.14
you have not e. bread, and you have 29.06
and they have e. and are full and 31.20
And when Boaz had e. and drunk, Ru 3.07
After they had e. and drunk in 1Sa 1.09
the people had e. freely today of 14.30
for he had e. nothing all day and 28.20
And when he had e., his spirit 30.12
for he had not e. bread or drunk 30.12
Have we e. at all at the king's 2Sa 19.42
and have e. bread and drunk water 1Ki 13.22
And after he had e. bread and drunk, 13.23
lion had not e. the body or torn 13.28
and when they had e. and drunk, 2Ki 6.23
LORD we have e. and had enough and 2Ch 31.10
it was e. by the people of Israel Ez 6.21
is tasteless be e. without salt, Job 6.06
There was nothing left after he had e.; 20.21
or have e. my morsel alone, and the 31.17
the fatherless has not e. of it 31.17
if I have e. its yield without 31.39
and bread e. in secret is pleasant. Pro 9.17
up the morsels which you have e., 23.08
the valley and e. by the vultures. 30.17
coals, I roasted flesh and have e.; Is 44.19
so bad that they could not be e. Jer 24.02
bad, so bad that they cannot be e." 24.03
which are so bad they cannot be e., 24.08
which are so bad they cannot be e. 29.17
'The fathers have e. sour grapes, 31.29
I have never e. what died of Eze 4.14
'The fathers have e. sour grapes, 18.02
days unleavened bread shall be e. 45.21
you have e. the fruit of lies. Hos 10.13
left, the swarming locust has e. Joe 1.04
left, the hopping locust has e., 1.04
left, the destroying locust has e. 1.04
which the swarming locust has e., 2.25
And when they had e. their fill, Jn 6.12
loaves, left by those who had e. 6.13
I have never e. anything that is Ac 10.14
and he was e. by worms and died. 12.23
up and had broken bread and e., 20.11
And when they had e. enough, they 27.38
but when I had e. it my stomach Rev 10.10

EATER

"Out of the e. came something to Ju 14.14
to the sower and bread to the e., Is 55.10
they fall into the mouth of the e. Nah 3.12

EATERS

or among gluttonous e. of meat; Pro 23.20

EATING

the birds were e. it out of the Gen 40.17
by e. their holy things: for I am Lev 22.16
year, you will be e. old produce; 25.22
of his children whom he is e., Deu 28.55
hands, and went on, e. as he went; Ju 14.09
he has finished e. and drinking. Ru 3.03
the LORD, by e. with the blood." 1Sa 14.33
the LORD by e. with the blood. 14.34
e. and drinking and dancing, because 30.16
they are e. and drinking before him, 1Ki 1.25
while they were e. of the pottage, 2Ki 4.40
e. and drinking, for their brethren 1Ch 12.39
neither e. bread nor drinking water Ez 10.06
daughters were e. and drinking Job 1.13
daughters were e. and drinking 1.18
e. the bread of anxious toil; Ps 127.02
e. flesh and drinking wine. "Let us Is 22.13
dreams he is e. and awakes with 29.08
e. swine's flesh and the abomination 66.17
had finished e. the grass of the Amo 7.02
great deep and was e. up the land. 7.04
For John came neither e. nor drinking, Mt 11.18
the Son of man came e. and drinking, 11.19
flood they were e. and drinking, 24.38
and as they were e., he said, "Truly, 26.21
Now as they were e., Jesus took 26.26
saw that he was e. with sinners Mk 2.16
And as they were at table e., 14.18
betray me, one who is e. with me." 14.18
And as they were e., he took 14.22
has come e. no bread and drinking Lk 7.33

EATING (cont.)

of man has come e. and drinking; Lk 7.34
e. and drinking what they provide, 10.07
as to the e. of food offered to 1Co 8.04
vineyard without e. and of its 9.07
For in e., each one goes ahead with 11.21

EATS

for if any one e. what is leavened, Ex 12.15
for if any one e. what is leavened, 12.19
and he who e. of it shall bear his Lev 7.18
but the person who e. of the flesh 7.20
and then e. of the flesh of the 7.21
person who e. of the fat of an 7.25
Whoever e. any blood, that person 7.27
and he who e. of its carcass shall 11.40
and he who e. in the house shall 14.47
sojourn among them e. any blood, 17.10
against that person who e. blood, 17.10
whoever e. it shall be cut off. 17.14
person that e. what dies of itself 17.15
and every one who e. it shall bear 19.08
And if a man e. of a holy thing 22.14
be the man who e. food until it is 1Sa 14.24
be the man who e. food this day.'" 14.28
taste what he e. or what he drinks 2Sa 19.35
I made you; he e. grass like an ox. Job 40.15
the image of an ox that e. grass. Ps 106.20
of his mouth a good man e. good, Pro 13.02
she e., and wipes her mouth, and 30.20
his hands, and e. his own flesh. Ecc 4.05
whether he e. little or much; 5.12
he e. it up as soon as it is in his Is 28.04
over the half he e. flesh, he roasts 44.16
he who e. their eggs dies, and from 59.05
each man who e. sour grapes, his Jer 31.30
but e. upon the mountains, defiles Eze 18.11
and e. and drinks with the drunken, Mt 24.49
receives sinners and e. with them. Lk 15.02
if any one e. of htis bread, he will Jn 6.51
he who e. my flesh and drinks my 6.54
He who e. my flesh and drinks my 6.56
so he who e. me will live because 6.57
he who e. this bread will live for 6.58
the weak man e. only vegetables. Rom 14.02
Let not him who e. despise him who 14.03
pass judgment on him who e.; 14.03
He also who e., e. in honor of the Lord, 14.06
to make others fall by what he e.; 14.20
if he e., because he does not act 14.23
e. the bread or drinks the cup of 1Co 11.27
For any one who e. and drinks 11.29
the body e. and drinks judgment 11.29

EBAL

Manahath, E., Shepho, and Onam. Gen 36.23
Gerizim and the curse on Mount E. Deu 11.29
on Mount E., and you shall plaster 27.04
stand upon Mount E. for the curse: 27.13
an altar in Mount E. to the LORD, Jos 8.30
half of them in front of Mount E., 8.33
E., Abimael, Sheba, 1Ch 1.22
E., Shephi, and Onam. The sons of 1.40

EBED

And Gaal the son of E. moved into Ju 9.26
And Gaal the son of E. said, 9.28
the words of Gaal the son of E., 9.30
Gaal the son of E. and his kinsmen 9.31
And Gaal the son of E. went out and 9.35
E. the son of Jonathan, and with him Ez 8.06

EBEDMELECH

When E. the Ethiopian, a eunuch, who Jer 38.07
E. went from the king's house and 38.08
Then the king commanded E., 38.10
So E. took the men with him and 38.11
Then E. the Ethiopian said to 38.12
and say to E. the Ethiopian, 'Thus 39.16

EBENEZER

they encamped at E., and the 1Sa 4.01
they carried it from E. to Ashdod; 5.01
Jeshanah, and called its name E.; 7.12

EBER

father of all the children of E., Gen 10.21
and Shelah became the father of E. 10.24
To E. were born two sons: the name 10.25
years, he became the father of E.; 11.14
the birth of E. four hundred and 11.15
When E. had lived thirty-four years, 11.16
and E. lived after the birth of 11.17
and shall afflict Asshur and E.; Num 24.24
and Shelah was the father of E. 1Ch 1.18
To E. were born two sons: the name 1.19
E., Peleg, Reu; 1.25
Jorai, Jacan, Zia, and E., seven. 5.13
E., Misham, and Shemed, who built Ono 8.12
Ishpan, E., Eliel, 8.22
of Sallai, Kallai, of Amok, E.; Neh 12.20
the son of E., the son of Shelah, Lk 3.35

EBEZ

Rabbith, Kishion, E., Jos 19.20

EBIASAPH

E. his son, Assir his son, 1Ch 6.23
of Assir, son of E., son of Korah, 6.37
son of E., son of Korah, and his 9.19

EBONY

you in payment ivory tusks and e. Eze 27.15

EBRON

E., Rehob, Hammon, Kanah, as far as Jos 19.28

ECBATANA

And in E., the capital which is in Ez 6.02

EDEN

a garden in E., in the east; Gen 2.08
flowed out of E. to water the 2.10
the garden of E. to till it and 2.15
him forth from the garden of E., 3.23
the garden of E. he placed the 3.24
in the land of Nod, east of E. 4.16
the people of E. who were in 2Ki 19.12
of Zimmah, and E. the son of Joah; 2Ch 29.12
E., Miniamin, Jeshua, Shemaiah, 31.15
the people of E. who were in Is 37.12
will make her wilderness like E., 51.03
Haran, Canneh, E., Asshur, and Chilmad Eze 27.23
You were in E., the garden of God; 28.13
and all the trees of E. envied it, 31.09
and all the trees of E., the choice 31.16
in greatness among the trees of E. 31.18
the trees of E. to the nether 31.18
has become like the garden of E.; 36.35
like the garden of E. before them, Joe 2.03

EDER

his tent beyond the tower of E. Gen 35.21
of Edom, were Kabzeel, E., Jagur, Jos 15.21
Zebadiah, Arad, E., 1Ch 8.15
Mahli, E., and Jeremoth, three. 23.23
of Mushi: Mahli, E., and Jerimoth. 24.30

EDGE

Etham, on the e. of the wilderness. Ex 13.20
people with the e. of the sword. 17.13
of blue on the e. of the outmost 26.04
loops on the e. of the outmost 26.04
make on the e. of the curtain that 26.05
loops on the e. of the curtain 26.10

EDGE (cont.)
on its inside e. next to the ephod. Ex 28.26
of blue on the e. of the outmost 36.11
loops on the e. of the curtain 36.12
loops on the e. of the outmost 36.17
loops on the e. of the other 36.17
on its inside e. next to the ephod. 39.19
a city on the e. of your territory. Num 20.16
slew him with the e. of the sword, 21.24
which is on the e. of the wilderness 33.06
on the e. of the land of Edom. 33.37
which is on the e. of the valley Deu 2.36
which is on the e. of the valley 3.12
which is on the e. of the valley 4.48
cattle, with the e. of the sword. 13.15
asses, with the e. of the sword. Jos 6.21
had fallen by the e. of the sword, 8.24
smote it with the e. of the sword. 8.24
its king with the e. of the sword; 10.28
smote it with the e. of the sword, 10.30
smote it with the e. of the sword, 10.32
smote it with the e. of the sword; 10.35
smote it with the e. of the sword, 10.37
them with the e. of the sword, 10.39
them with the e. of the sword, 11.12
smote with the e. of the sword, 11.14
which is on the e. of the valley 12.02
which is on the e. of the valley 13.09
which is on the e. of the valley 13.16
smote it with the e. of the sword, Ju 1.08
the city with the e. of the sword, 1.25
Barak at the e. of the sword; 4.15
Sisera fell by the e. of the sword; 4.16
them with the e. of the sword, 18.27
the city with the e. of the sword. 20.37
them with the e. of the sword, 20.48
Jabeshgilead with the e. of the sword; 21.10
people with the e. of the sword. 1Sa 15.08
the city with the e. of the sword." 2Sa 15.14
came to the e. of the camp of the 2Ki 7.05
lepers came to the e. of the camp, 7.08
servants with the e. of the sword; Job 1.15
servants with the e. of the sword; 1.17
turned back the e. of his sword, Ps 89.43
and one does not whet the e., Ecc 10.10
them with the e. of the sword; Jer 21.07
the children's teeth are set on e.' 31.29
his teeth shall be set on e. 31.30
children's teeth are set on e.'? Eze 18.02
and left where your e. is directed. 21.16
a rim of one span around its e. 43.13
they will fall by the e. of the sword, Lk 21.24
escaped the e. of the sword, won Heb 11.34

EDGES
shoulder-pieces attached to its two e., Ex 28.07
on the two e. of the breastpiece. 28.23
rings at the e. of the breastpiece 28.24
shoulder-pieces, joined to it at its two e. 39.04
on the two e. of the breastpiece; 39.16
rings at the e. of the breastpiece 39.17
temples or mar the e. of your beard. Lev 19.27
shave off the e. of their beards, 21.05
for himself a sword with two e., Ju 3.16

EDICT
that if any one alters this e., Ez 6.11
order and his e. were proclaimed, Est 2.08
and an e., according to all that 3.12
for an e. written in the name of 8.08
and an e. was written according to 8.09
the king's command and his e. came, 8.17
command and e. were about to be 9.01
to do according to this day's e. 9.13
were not afraid of the king's e. Heb 11.23

EDIFICATION
Let all things be done for e. 1Co 14.26

EDIFIED
so that the church may be e. 1Co 14.05
but the other man is not e. 14.17

EDIFIES
He who speaks in a tongue e. himself, 1Co 14.04
he who prophesies e. the church. 14.04

EDIFY
neighbor for his good, to e. him. Rom 15.02

EDIFYING
but only such as is good for e., Eph 4.29

EDOM
Therefore his name was called E.) Gen 25.30
land of Seir, the country of E., 32.03
descendants of Esau (that is, E.). 36.01
country of Seir; Esau is E. 36.08
of Eliphaz in the land of E.; 36.16
chiefs of Reuel in the land of E.; 36.17
E., and these are their chiefs. 36.19
the sons of Seir in the land of E. 36.21
who reigned in the land of E., 36.31
Bela the son of Beor reigned in E., 36.32
these are the chiefs of E. (that is, 36.43
the father of E.), according to 36.43
Now are the chiefs of E. dismayed; Ex 15.15
from Kadesh to the king of E., Num 20.14
But E. said to him, "You shall not 20.18
And E. came out against them with 20.20
Thus E. refused to give Israel 20.21
on the border of the land of E., 20.23
Sea, to go around the land of E.; 21.04
E. shall be dispossessed, Seir also, 24.18
Hor, on the edge of the land of E. 33.37
of Zin along the side of E., 34.03
southward to the boundary of E., Jos 15.01
South, toward the boundary of E., 15.21
didst march from the region of E., Ju 5.04
sent messengers to the king of E., 11.17
but the king of E. would not listen 11.17
the land of E. and the land of 11.18
against E., against the kings of 1Sa 14.47
from E., Moab, the Ammonites, the 2Sa 8.12
And he put garrisons in E.; 8.14
throughout all E. he put garrisons, 8.14
of the Red Sea, in the land of E. 1Ki 9.26
he was of the royal house in E. 11.14
For when David was in E., and Joab 11.15
slain, he slew every male in E. 11.15
he had cut off every male in E.); 11.16
There was no king in E.; a deputy 22.47
"By the way of the wilderness of E." 2Ki 3.08
king of Judah and the king of E. 3.09
and the king of E. went down to 3.12
came from the direction of E., 3.20
through, opposite the king of E.; 3.26
In his days E. revolted from the 8.20
So E. revolted from the rule of 8.22
You have indeed smitten E., 14.10
the king of E. recovered Elath for E., 16.06
in the land of E. before any king 1Ch 1.43
The chiefs of E. were: chiefs Timna, 1.51
these are the chiefs of E. 1.54
from E., Moab, the Ammonites, the 18.11
And he put garrisons in E.; 18.13
of the sea, in the land of E. 2Ch 8.17
is coming against you from E., 20.02
In his days E. revolted from the 21.08
So E. revolted from the rule of 21.10
You say, 'S, I have smitten E.,' 25.19
they had sought the gods of E. 25.20
upon E. I cast my shoe; over Philistia Ps 60.08

EDOM (cont.)

fortified city? Who will lead me to E.? Ps 60.09
the tents of E. and the Ishmaelites, 83.06
upon E. I cast my shoe; over Philistia 108.09
fortified city? Who will lead me to E.? 108.10
their hand against E. and Moab, Is 11.14
it descends for judgment upon E., 34.05
great slaughter in the land of E. 34.06
And the streams of E. shall be 34.09
Who is this that comes from E., 63.01
Egypt, Judah, E., the sons of Ammon, Jer 9.26
E., Moab, and the sons of Ammon; 25.21
Send word to the king of E., 27.03
Ammonites and in E. and in other 40.11
Concerning E. Thus says the 49.07
"E. shall become a horror; 49.17
made against E. and the purposes 49.20
the warriors of E. shall be in 49.22
O daughter of E., dweller in the Lam 4.21
O daughter of E., he will punish, he 4.22
daughters of E. and all her Eze 16.57
Because E. acted revengefully 25.12
stretch out my hand against E., 25.13
vengeance upon E. by the hand of 25.14
shall do in E. according to my 25.14
E. trafficked with you because of 27.16
"E. is there, her kings and all her 32.29
Mount Seir, and all E., all of it. 35.15
of the nations, and against all E., 36.05
E. and Moab and the main part of Dan 11.41
desolation and E. a desolate Joe 3.19
people to deliver them up to E. Amo 1.06
delivered up a whole people to E., 1.09
"For three transgressions of E., 1.11
lime the bones of the king of E. 2.01
the remnant of E. and all the 9.12
says the Lord GOD concerning E.: Ob 1.01
destroy the wise men out of E., 1.08
If E. says, "We are shattered but we Mal 1.04

EDOMITE

"You shall not abhor an E., Deu 23.07
his name was Doeg the E., 1Sa 21.07
Then answered Doeg the E., 22.09
And Doeg the E. turned and fell 22.18
when Doeg the E. was there, that he 22.22
E., Sidonian, and Hittite women, 1Ki 11.01
against Solomon, Hadad the E.; 11.14

EDOMITES

father of the E. in the hill Gen 36.09
thousand E. in the Valley of Salt. 2Sa 8.13
and all the E. became David's 8.14
with certain E. of his father's 1Ki 11.17
smote the E. who had surrounded 2Ki 8.21
ten thousand E. in the Valley of 14.07
and the E. came to Elath, where 16.06
thousand E. in the Valley of Salt. 1Ch 18.12
and all the E. became David's 18.13
and smote the E. who had surrounded 2Ch 21.09
came from the slaughter of the E., 25.14
For the E. had again invaded and 28.17
against the E. the day of Jerusalem, Ps 137.07

EDREI

all his people, to battle at E. Num 21.33
who lived in Ashtaroth and in E. Deu 1.04
all his people, to battle at E. 3.01
Bashan, as far as Salecah and E., 3.10
dwelt at Ashtaroth and at E. Jos 12.04
Ashtaroth and in E. (he alone was 13.12
and E., the cities of the kingdom 13.31
Kedesh, E., Enhazor, 19.37

EDUCATED

They were to be e. for three years, Dan 1.05
e. according to the strict manner Ac 22.03

EFFECT

and spoke to her to that e. 2Ch 34.22
And the e. of righteousness will be Is 32.17
to the e. that they ought always to Lk 18.01
And God spoke to this e., Ac 7.06
And he wrote a letter to this e.: 23.25
is not like the e. of that one Rom 5.16
to the e. that the day of the Lord 2Th 2.02
For a will takes e. only at death, Heb 9.17
let steadfastness have its full e., Jas 1.04

EFFECTIVE

for a wide door for e. work has 1Co 16.09

EFFECTS

man has great power in its e. Jas 5.16

EFFORT

make an e. to settle with him on Lk 12.58
make every e. to supplement your 2P 1.05

EGG

or if he asks for an e., will give Lk 11.12

EGGS

young ones or e. and the mother Deu 22.06
upon the young or upon the e., 22.06
For she leaves her e. to the earth, Job 39.14
as men gather e. that have been Is 10.14
They hatch adders' e., they weave the 59.05
he who eats their e. dies, 59.05

EGLAH

sixth, Ithream of E., David's wife. 2Sa 3.05
the sixth Ithream, by his wife E.; 1Ch 3.03

EGLAIM

the wailing reaches to E., the wailing Is 15.08

EGLATHSHELISHIYAH

his fugitives flee to Zoar, to E. Is 15.05
from Zoar to Horonaim and E. Jer 48.34

EGLON

and to Debir king of E., saying, Jos 10.03
of Lachish, and the king of E., 10.05
of Lachish, and the king of E. 10.23
with all Israel from Lachish to E.; 10.34
with all Israel from E. to Hebron; 10.36
remaining, as he had done to E., 10.37
the king of E., one; the king of 12.12
Lachish, Bozkath, E., 15.39
strengthened E. the king of Moab Ju 3.12
Israel served E. the king of Moab 3.14
by him to E. the king of Moab. 3.15
the tribute to E. king of Moab. 3.17
Now E. was a very fat man. 3.17

EGYPT

Ham: Cush, E., Put, and Canaan. Gen 10.06
E. became the father of Ludim, 10.13
went down to E. to sojourn there, 12.10
When he was about to enter E., 12.11
When Abram entered E. the Egyptians 12.14
So Abram went up from E., he and his 13.01
the land of E. in the direction of 13.10
the river of E. to the great river, 15.18
a wife for him from the land of E. 21.21
is opposite E. in the direction of 25.18
and said, "Do not go down to E.; 26.02
their way to carry it down to E. 37.25
of silver; and they took Joseph to E. 37.28
had sold him in E. to Potiphar, 37.36
Now Joseph was taken down to E., 39.01
of the king of E. and his baker 40.01
offended their lord the king of E. 40.01
and the baker of the king of E., 40.05
magicians of E. and all its wise 41.08

EGYPT (cont.)
never seen in all the land of E. Gen 41.19
throughout all the land of E., 41.29
be forgotten in the land of E.; 41.30
and set him over the land of E. 41.33
of the land of E. during the seven 41.34
which are to befall the land of E., 41.36
set you over all the land of E." 41.41
he set him over all the land of E. 41.43
hand or foot in all the land of E." 41.44
went out over the land of E. 41.45
the service of Pharaoh king of E. 41.46
went through all the land of E. 41.46
there was plenty in the land of E., 41.48
in the land of E. came to an end; 41.53
all the land of E. there was bread 41.54
When all the land of E. was famished, 41.55
was severe in the land of E. 41.56
earth came to E. to Joseph to buy 41.57
learned that there was grain in E., 42.01
heard that there is grain in E.; 42.02
went down to buy grain in E. 42.03
which they had brought from E., 43.02
and they arose and went down to E., 43.15
Joseph, whom you sold into E. 45.04
and ruler over all the land of E. 45.08
God has made me lord of all E.; 45.09
my father of all my splendor in E., 45.13
you the best of the land of E., 45.18
the land of E. for your little 45.19
of all the land of E. is yours.'" 45.20
loaded with the good things of E., 45.23
So they went up out of E., 45.25
is ruler over all the land of E." 45.26
do not be afraid to go down to E.; 46.03
I will go down with you to E., 46.04
and came into E., Jacob and all his 46.06
he brought with him into E. 46.07
who came into E., Jacob and his 46.08
in the land of E. were born 46.20
belonging to Jacob who came into E., 46.26
were born to him in E., were two; 46.27
that came into E., were seventy. 46.27
The land of E. is before you; 47.06
a possession in the land of E., 47.11
the land of E. and the land of 47.13
in the land of E. and in the land 47.14
in the land of E. and in the land 47.15
all the land of E. for Pharaoh; 47.20
from one end of E. to the other. 47.21
statute concerning the land of E., 47.26
Thus Israel dwelt in the land of E., 47.27
in the land of E. seventeen years; 47.28
truly with me. Do not bury me in E., 47.29
carry me out of E. and bury me in 47.30
in the land of E. before I came to 48.05
I came to you in E., are mine; 48.05
all the elders of the land of E., 50.07
returned to E. with his brothers 50.14
So Joseph dwelt in E., he and his 50.22
and he was put in a coffin in E. 50.26
Israel who came to E. with Jacob, Ex 1.01
persons; Joseph was already in E. 1.05
Now there arose a new king over E., 1.08
Then the king of E. said to the 1.15
as the king of E. commanded them, 1.17
So the king of E. called the 1.18
many days the king of E. died. 2.23
affliction of my people who are in E., 3.07
the sons of Israel, out of E." 3.10
bring the sons of Israel out of E.?" 3.11
brought forth the people out of E., 3.12
what has been done to you in E.; 3.16
you up out of the affliction of E., 3.17
to the king of E. and say to him, 3.18
the king of E. will not let you go 3.19
hand and smite E. with all the 3.20
my kinsmen in E. and see whether 4.18
to Moses in Midian, "Go back to E.; 4.19
and went back to the land of E.; 4.20
to Moses, "When you go back to E., 4.21
But the king of E. said to them, 5.04
throughout all the land of E., 5.12
Pharaoh king of E. to let the 6.11
Pharaoh king of E. to bring the 6.13
of Israel out of the land of E. 6.13
from the land of E. by their hosts." 6.26
Pharaoh king of E. about bringing 6.27
out the people of Israel from E., 6.27
spoke to Moses in the land of E., 6.28
Pharaoh king of E. all that I say 6.29
and wonders in the land of E., 7.03
my hand upon E. and bring forth my 7.04
of the land of E. by great acts of 7.04
my hand upon E. and bring out the 7.05
and they also, the magicians of E., 7.11
your hand over the waters of E., 7.19
throughout all the land of E., 7.19
throughout all the land of E. 7.21
magicians of E. did the same by 7.22
frogs to come upon the land of E.!'" 8.05
out his hand over the waters of E.; 8.06
came up and covered the land of E. 8.06
brought frogs upon the land of E. 8.07
throughout all the land of E.'" 8.16
throughout all the land of E. 8.17
all the land of E. the land was 8.24
of Israel and the cattle of E., 9.04
fine dust over all the land of E., 9.09
throughout all the land of E." 9.09
has been in E. from the day it was 9.18
may be hail in all the land of E., 9.22
field, throughout the land of E." 9.22
rained hail upon the land of E.; 9.23
all the land of E. since it became 9.24
throughout all the land of E.," 9.25
yet understand that E. is ruined?" 10.07
the land of E. for the locusts, 10.12
they may come upon the land of E., 10.12
forth his rod over the land of E., 10.13
came up over all the land of E., 10.14
settled on the whole country of E., 10.14
field, through all the land of E. 10.15
was left in all the country of E. 10.19
be darkness over the land of E., 10.21
in all the land of E. three days; 10.22
bring upon Pharaoh and upon E.; 11.01
was very great in the land of E. 11.03
I will go forth in the midst of E.; 11.04
in the land of E. shall die, 11.05
cry throughout all the land of E., 11.06
be multiplied in the land of E." 11.09
Moses and Aaron in the land of E., 12.01
through the land of E. that night, 12.12
the first-born in the land of E., 12.12
all the gods of E. I will execute 12.12
you, when I smite the land of E. 12.13
your hosts out of the land of E.: 12.17
of the people of Israel in E., 12.27
the first-born in the land of E., 12.29
and there was a great cry in E., 12.30
which they had brought out of E., 12.39
thrust out of E. and could not 12.39
Israel dwelt in E. was four 12.40
LORD went out from the land of E. 12.41
bring them out of the land of E.; 12.42
of the land of E. by their hosts. 12.51
day, in which you came out from E., 13.03
did for me when I came out of E.' 13.08
the LORD has brought you out of E. 13.09
hand the LORD brought us out of E., 13.14
the first-born in the land of E., 13.15

EGYPT (cont.)

hand the LORD brought us out of E." Ex 13.16
they see war, and return to E." 13.17
of the land of E. equipped for 13.18
When the king of E. was told that 14.05
chariots of E. with officers over 14.07
Pharaoh king of E. and he pursued 14.08
no graves in E. that you have 14.11
to us, in bringing us out of E.? 14.11
not this what we said to you in E., 14.12
the host of E. and the host of 14.20
had departed from the land of E. 16.01
hand of the LORD in the land of E., 16.03
brought you out of the land of E., 16.06
brought you out of the land of E.' " 16.32
"Why did you bring us up out of E., 17.03
LORD had brought Israel out of E. 18.01
gone forth out of the land of E., 19.01
brought you out of the land of E., 20.02
were strangers in the land of E. 22.21
were strangers in the land of E. 23.09
Abib, for in it you came out of E. 23.15
of the land of E. that I might 29.46
us up out of the land of E., 32.01
you up out of the land of E.!" 32.04
brought up out of the land of E., 32.07
you up out of the land of E.!' " 32.08
of the land of E. with great power 32.11
us up out of the land of E., 32.23
brought up out of the land of E., 33.01
month Abib you came out from E. 34.18
you up out of the land of E., Lev 11.45
do as they do in the land of E., 18.03
were strangers in the land of E.: 19.34
brought you out of the land of E. 19.36
of the land of E. to be your God: 22.33
brought them out of the land of E.: 23.43
of the land of E. to give you the 25.38
forth out of the land of E.; 25.42
forth out of the land of E.: 25.55
you forth out of the land of E., 26.13
of the land of E. in the sight of 26.45
out of the land of E, saying, Num 1.01
the first-born in the land of E., 3.13
in the land of E. I consecrated 8.17
out of the land of E., saying, 9.01
the fish we ate in E. for nothing, 11.05
For it was well with us in E." 11.18
"Why did we come forth out of E.?" ' " 11.20
seven years before Zoan in E.) 13.22
that we had died in the land of E.! 14.02
be better for us to go back to E.?" 14.03
a captain and go back to E." 14.04
people, from E. even until now." 14.19
I wrought in E. and in the wilderness, 14.22
brought you out of the land of E., 15.41
have you made us come up out of E., 20.05
how our fathers went down to E., 20.15
and we dwelt in E. a long time; 20.15
and brought us forth out of E.; 20.16
us up out of E. to die in the 21.05
a people has come out of E.; 22.05
'Behold, a people has come out of E., 22.11
God brings them out of E.; they have 23.22
God brings him out of E.; he has 24.08
forth out of the land of E., were: 26.04
Levi, who was born to Levi in E.; 26.59
of the men who came up out of E., 32.11
of the land of E. by their hosts 33.01
had come out of the land of E., 33.38
turn from Azmon to the Brook of E., 34.05
us forth out of the land of E., Deu 1.27
did for you in E. before your eyes, 1.30
out of E., to be a people of his 4.20
did for you in E. before your eyes? 4.34
you out of E. with his own presence, 4.37

Israel when they came out of E., 4.45
defeated when they came out of E. 4.46
brought you out of the land of E., 5.06
were a servant in the land of E., 5.15
brought you out of the land of E., 6.12
'We were Pharaoh's slaves in E.; 6.21
us out of E. with a mighty hand; 6.21
against E. and against Pharaoh and 6.22
the hand of Pharaoh king of E. 7.08
none of the evil diseases of E., 7.15
God did to Pharaoh and to all E., 7.18
brought you out of the land of E., 8.14
day you came out of the land of E., 9.07
brought from E. have acted corruptly 9.12
brought out of E. with a mighty 9.26
were sojourners in the land of E. 10.19
went down to E. seventy persons; 10.22
which he did in E. to Pharaoh the 11.03
the king of E. and to all his land 11.03
and what he did to the army of E., 11.04
of it is not like the land of E., 11.10
of the land of E. and redeemed you 13.05
brought you out of the land of E., 13.10
you were a slave in the land of E., 15.15
God brought you out of E. by night. 16.01
of the land of E. in hurried 16.03
you came out of the land of E. 16.03
at the time you came out of E. 16.06
that you were a slave in E.; 16.12
to return to E. in order to 17.16
you up out of the land of E. 20.01
way, when you came forth out of E., 23.04
way as you came forth out of E. 24.09
were a slave in E. and the LORD 24.18
you were a slave in the land of E.; 24.22
on the way as you came out of E., 25.17
went down into E. and sojourned 26.05
us out of E. with a mighty hand 26.08
smite you with the boils of E., 28.27
you again all the diseases of E., 28.60
will bring you back in ships to E., 28.68
before your eyes in the land of E., 29.02
how we dwelt in the land of E., 29.16
them out of the land of E., 29.25
sent him to do in the land of E., 34.11
before you when you came out of E., Jos 2.10
of the people who came out of E., 5.04
after they had come out of E. 5.04
after they had come out of E., 5.05
of war that came forth out of E., 5.06
away the reproach of E. from you" 5.09
of him, and all that he did in E., 9.09
(from the Shihor, which is east of E., 13.03
Azmon, goes out by the brook of E., 15.04
to the brook of E., 15.47
and his children went down to E. 24.04
and I plagued E. with what I did in 24.05
Then I brought your fathers out of E., 24.06
and your eyes saw what I did to E.; 24.07
and in E., and serve the LORD. 24.14
our fathers up from the land of E., 24.17
brought up from E. were buried at 24.32
he said, "I brought you up from E., Ju 2.01
brought them out of the land of E.; 2.12
of Israel: I led you up from E., 6.08
not the LORD bring us up from E.?' 6.13
on coming from E. took away my 11.13
but when they came up from E., 11.16
of the land of E. until this day; 19.30
they were in E. subject to the 1Sa 2.27
them up out of E. even to this day, 8.08
'I brought up Israel out of E., 10.18
fathers up out of the land of E. 12.06
When Jacob went into E. and the 12.08
forth your fathers out of E., 12.08
way, when they came up out of E. 15.02

EGYPT (cont.)
Israel when they came up out of E." 1Sa 15.06
far as Shur, which is east of E. 15.07
as far as Shur, to the land of E. 27.08
He said, "I am a young man of E., 30.13
of Israel from E. to this day, 2Sa 7.06
alliance with Pharaoh king of E.; 1Ki 3.01
Philistines and to the border of E.; 4.21
the east, and all the wisdom of E. 4.30
Israel came out of the land of E., 6.01
they came out of the land of E. 8.09
brought my people Israel out of E., 8.16
brought them out of the land of E." 8.21
which thou didst bring out of E., 8.51
our fathers out of E., O Lord God." 8.53
of Hamath to the Brook of E., 8.65
fathers out of the land of E., 9.09
(Pharaoh king of E. had gone up and 9.16
of horses was from E. and Kue, 10.28
imported from E. for six hundred 10.29
but Hadad fled to E., together with 11.17
them from Paran and came to E., 11.18
to E., to Pharaoh king of E., 11.18
Hadad heard in E. that David slept 11.21
and fled into E., to Shishak king of E., 11.40
and was in E. until the death of 11.40
heard of it (for he was still in E., 12.02
then Jeroboam returned from E. 12.02
you up out of the land of E." 12.28
Shishak king of E. came up against 14.25
the kings of E. to come upon us." 2Ki 7.06
king of E., and offered no tribute 17.04
of the land of E. from under the 17.07
the hand of Pharaoh king of E., 17.07
of the land of E. with great power 17.36
Behold, you are relying now on E., 18.21
Pharaoh king of E. to all who rely 18.21
you rely on E. for chariots and 18.24
of my foot all the streams of E.' 19.24
day their fathers came out of E., 21.15
Neco king of E. went up to the 23.29
and he came to E., and died there. 23.34
And the king of E. did not come 24.07
to the king of E. from the Brook of E. 24.07
the forces arose, and went to E.; 25.26
Ham: Cush, E., Put, and Canaan. 1Ch 1.08
E. was the father of Ludim, Anamim, 1.11
the Shihor of E. to the entrance 13.05
whom thou didst redeem from E.? 17.21
of horses was from E. and Kue, 2Ch 1.16
a chariot from E. for six hundred 1.17
Israel, when they came out of E. 5.10
my people out of the land of E., 6.05
of Hamath to the Brook of E. 7.08
brought them out of the land of E., 7.22
Philistines, and to the border of E. 9.26
Solomon from E. and from all lands 9.28
Nebat heard of it (for he was in E., 10.02
then Jeroboam returned from E. 10.02
Shishak king of E. came up against 12.02
number who came with him from E.— 12.03
So Shishak king of E. came up 12.09
when they came from the land of E., 20.10
spread even to the border of E., 26.08
Neco king of E. went up to fight at 35.20
Then the king of E. deposed him in 36.03
And the king of E. made Eliakim his 36.04
his brother and carried him to E. 36.04
our fathers in E. and hear their Neh 9.09
to return to their bondage in E. 9.17
God who brought you up out of E., 9.18
Let bronze be brought from E.; Ps 68.31
wrought marvels in the land of E., 78.12
when he wrought his signs in E., 78.43
He smote all the first-born in E., 78.51
Thou didst bring a vine out of E.: 80.08
he went out over the land of E. 81.05
you up out of the land of E. 81.10
Then Israel came to E.; Jacob 105.23
E. was glad when they departed, for 105.38
Our fathers, when they were in E., 106.07
who had done great things in E., 106.21
When Israel went forth from E., 114.01
was who smote the first-born of E., 135.08
O E., sent signs and wonders 135.09
him who smote the first-born of E., 136.10
the sources of the streams of E., Is 7.18
he will lift it as he did in E. 10.26
from E., from Pathros, from Ethiopia, 11.11
the tongue of the sea of E.; 11.15
they came up from the land of E. 11.16
An oracle concerning E. Behold, the 19.01
on a swift cloud and comes to E.; 19.01
the idols of E. will tremble at 19.01
of hosts has purposed against E. 19.12
of her tribes have led E. astray. 19.13
they have made E. stagger in all 19.14
be nothing for E. which head or 19.15
in the land of E. which speak the 19.18
in the midst of the land of E., 19.19
Lord of hosts in the land of E.; 19.20
And the Lord will smite E., smiting 19.22
be a highway from E. to Assyria, 19.23
and the Assyrian will come into E., 19.23
be the third with E. and Assyria, 19.24
"Blessed be E. my people, and 19.25
a portent against E. and Ethiopia, 20.03
uncovered, to the shame of E. 20.04
their hope and of E. their boast. 20.05
When the report comes to E., 23.05
to the Brook of E. the Lord will 27.12
to the land of E. will come and 27.13
who set out to go down to E., 30.02
seek shelter in the shadow of E.! 30.02
the shadow of E. to your humiliation 30.03
who go down to E. for help and 31.01
Behold, you are relying on E., 36.06
Pharaoh king of E. to all who rely 36.06
you rely on E. for chariots and 36.09
of my foot all the streams of E. 37.25
I give E. as your ransom, Ethiopia 43.03
"The wealth of E. and the merchandise 45.14
the first into E. to sojourn there, 52.04
brought us up from the land of E., Jer 2.06
what do you gain by going to E., 2.18
put to shame by E. as you were put 2.36
brought them out of the land of E., 7.22
out of the land of E. to this day, 7.25
E., Judah, Edom, the sons of Ammon, 9.26
brought them out of the land of E., 11.04
them up out of the land of E., 11.07
of Israel out of the land of E.,' 16.14
of Israel out of the land of E.,' 23.07
those who dwell in the land of E. 24.08
Pharaoh king of E., his servants, 25.19
afraid and fled and escaped to E. 26.21
Jehoiakim sent to E. certain men, 26.22
Uriah from E. and brought him to 26.23
bring them out of the land of E., 31.32
and wonders in the land of E., 32.20
of the land of E. with signs and 32.21
brought them out of the land of E., 34.13
army of Pharaoh had come out of E.; 37.05
help you is about to return to E., 37.07
Bethlehem, intending to go to E. 41.17
'No, we will go to the land of E., 42.14
faces to enter E. and go to live 42.15
you there in the land of E.; 42.16
shall follow hard after you to E.; 42.16
faces to go to E. to live there 42.17
out on you when you go to E. 42.18
remnant of Judah, 'Do not go to E.' 42.19
'Do not go to E. to live there'; 43.02

EGYPT (cont.)
And they came into the land of E., Jer 43.07
come and smite the land of E., 43.11
in the temples of the gods of E.; 43.12
and he shall clean the land of E., 43.12
Heliopolis which is in the land of E.; 43.13
of the gods of E. he shall burn 43.13
Jews that dwelt in the land of E., 44.01
in the land of E. where you have 44.08
to come to the land of E. to live, 44.12
in the land of E. they shall fall; 44.12
those who dwell in the land of E., 44.13
in the land of E. shall escape or 44.14
dwelt in Pathros in the land of E., 44.15
Judah who are in the land of E., 44.24
Judah who dwell in the land of E.: 44.26
man of Judah in all the land of E., 44.26
in the land of E. shall be consumed 44.27
the land of E. to the land of 44.28
who came to the land of E. to live, 44.28
Hophra king of E. into the hand of 44.30
About E. Concerning the army 46.02
king of E., which was by the river 46.02
E. rises like the Nile, like rivers 46.08
take balm, O virgin daughter of E.! 46.11
Babylon to smite the land of E.: 46.13
"Declare in E., and proclaim in 46.14
king of E., 'Noisy one who lets the 46.17
for exile, O inhabitants of E.! 46.19
"A beautiful heifer is E., but a 46.20
The daughter of E. shall be put to 46.24
and E. and her gods and her kings, 46.25
Afterward E. shall be inhabited as 46.26
We have given the hand to E., Lam 5.06
him by sending ambassadors to E., Eze 17.15
him with hooks to the land of E. 19.04
known to them in the land of E., 20.05
of the land of E. into a land that 20.06
yourselves with the idols of E.; 20.07
did they forsake the idols of E. 20.08
in the midst of the land of E. 20.08
bringing them out of the land of E. 20.09
of the land of E. and brought them 20.10
the wilderness of the land of E., 20.36
they played the harlot in E.; 23.03
had practiced since her days in E; 23.08
the harlot in the land of Egypt 23.19
brought from the land of E.; 23.27
linen from E. was your sail, 27.07
face against Pharaoh king of E., 29.02
against him and against all E.; 29.02
am against you, Pharaoh king of E., 29.03
inhabitants of E. shall know that 29.06
and the land of E. shall be a 29.09
the land of E. an utter waste and 29.10
the land of E. a desolation in the 29.12
and I will restore the fortunes of E., 29.14
the land of E. to Nebuchadrezzar 29.19
him the land of E. as his recompense 29.20
A sword shall come upon E., 30.04
Ethiopia, when the slain fall in E., 30.04
Those who support E. shall fall, 30.06
LORD, when I have set fire to E., 30.08
put an end to the wealth of E., 30.10
shall draw their swords against E., 30.11
be a prince in the land of E.; 30.13
I will put fear in the land of E. 30.13
Pelusium, the stronghold of E., 30.15
And I will set fire to E.; 30.16
I break there the dominion of E., 30.18
execute acts of judgment upon E. 30.19
the arm of Pharaoh king of E.; 30.21
I am against Pharaoh king of E., 30.22
it out against the land of E.; 30.25
Pharaoh king of E. and to his 31.02
lamentation over Pharaoh king of E., 32.02
bring to nought the pride of E., 32.12
the land of E. desolate and when 32.15
over E., and over all her multitude, 32.16
man, wail over the multitude of E., 32.18
the Brook of E. to the Great Sea. 47.19
the Brook of E. to the Great Sea. 48.28
of the land of E. with a mighty Dan 9.15
carry off to E. their gods with 11.08
and the land of E. shall not 11.42
and all the precious things of E.; 11.43
she came out of the land of E. Hos 2.15
calling to E., going to Assyria 7.11
their derision in the land of E. 7.16
their sins; they shall return to E. 8.13
but Ephraim shall return to E., 9.03
E. shall gather them, Menphis shall 9.06
and out of E. I called my son. 11.01
They shall return to the land of E., 11.05
come eagerly like birds from E., 11.11
Assyria, and oil is carried to E. 12.01
LORD your God from the land of E.; 12.09
the LORD brought Israel up from E., 12.13
LORD Your God from the land of E.; 13.04
"E. shall become a desolation and Joe 3.19
you up out of the land of E., Amo 2.10
brought up out of the land of E.: 3.01
the strongholds in the land of E., 3.09
pestilence after the manner of E.; 4.10
sink again, like the Nile of E.?" 8.08
sinks again, like the Nile of E.; 9.05
up Israel from the land of E., 9.07
brought you up from the land of E., Mic 6.04
come to you, from Assyria to E., 7.12
and from E. to the River, from sea 7.12
of the land of E. I will show them 7.15
E. too, and that without limit; Nah 3.09
I made you when you came out of E. Hag 2.05
them home from the land of E., Zec 10.10
They shall pass through the sea of E., 10.11
and the scepter of E. shall depart. 10.11
the family of E. do not go up and 14.18
punishment to E. and the punishment 14.19
and flee to E., and remain there Mt 2.13
by night, and departed to E., 2.14
"Out of E. have I called my son." 2.15
a dream to Joseph in E., saying, 2.19
E. and the parts of Libya belonging Ac 2.10
of Joseph, sold him into E.; 7.09
king of E., who made him governor over E. 7.10
throughout all E. and Canaan, 7.11
heard that there was grain in E., 7.12
and Jacob went down into E. 7.15
grew and multiplied in E. 7.17
arose over E. another king who had 7.18
that are in E. and heard their 7.34
now come, I will send you to E.' 7.34
and signs in E. and at the Red Sea, 7.36
in their hearts they turned to E., 7.39
who led us out from the land of E., 7.40
their stay in the land of E., 13.17
those who left E. under the Heb 3.16
to lead them out of the land of E.; 8.09
wealth than the treasures of E., 11.26
By faith he left E., not being 11.27
a people out of the land of E., Jud 1.05
allegorically called Sodom and E., Rev 11.08

EGYPTIAN
She had an E. maid whose name was Gen 16.01
wife, took Hagar the E. her maid, 16.03
But Sarah saw the son of Hagar the E., 21.09
Abraham's son, whom Hagar the E., 25.12
an E., bought him from the Ishmaelites 39.01
in the house of his master the E., 39.02
women are not like the E. women; Ex 1.19
and he saw an E. beating a Hebrew, 2.11

EGYPTIAN (cont.)
he killed the E. and hid him in Ex 2.12
to kill me as you killed the E.?" 2.14
They said, "An E. delivered us out 2.19
son, whose father was an E., Lev 24.10
you shall not abhor an E., because Deu 23.07
They found an E. in the open 1Sa 30.11
And he slew an E., a handsome man. 2Sa 23.21
The E. had a spear in his hand; 23.21
but Sheshan had an E. slave, 1Ch 2.34
And he slew an E., a man of great 11.23
The E. had in his hand a spear like 11.23
coverings, colored spreads of E. linen; Pro 7.16
and the E. into Assyria, and the Is 19.23
and avenged him by striking the E. Ac 7.24
me as you killed the E. yesterday?' 7.28
Are you not the E., then, who 21.38

EGYPTIAN'S
blessed the E. house for Joseph's Gen 39.05
the spear out of the E. hand, 2Sa 23.21
the spear out of the E. hand, 1Ch 11.23

EGYPTIANS
and when the E. see you, they will Gen 12.12
Egypt the E. saw that the woman 12.14
said to all the E., "Go to Joseph; 41.55
storehouses, and sold to the E., 41.56
and the E. who ate with him by 43.32
because the E. might not eat bread 43.32
that is an abomination to the E. 43.32
so that the E. heard it, and the 45.02
is an abomination to the E." 46.34
all the E. came to Joseph, and said, 47.15
for all the E. sold their fields, 47.20
And the E. wept for him seventy 50.03
is a grievous mourning to the E." 50.11
And the E. were in dread of the Ex 1.12
them out of the hand of the E., 3.08
with which the E. oppress them. 3.09
favor in the sight of the E.; 3.21
thus you shall despoil the E." 3.22
Israel whom the E. hold in bondage 6.05
from under the burdens of the E., 6.06
from under the burdens of the E. 6.07
And the E. shall know that I am the 7.05
and the E. will loathe to drink 7.18
so that the E. could not drink 7.21
And all the E. dug round about the 7.24
houses of the E. shall be filled 8.21
God offerings abominable to the E. 8.26
abominable to the E. before their 8.26
all the cattle of the E. died, 9.06
the magicians and upon all the E. 9.11
sport of the E. and what signs I 10.02
your servants and of all the E.; 10.06
favor in the sight of the E. 11.03
distinction between the E. and Israel. 11.07
will pass through to slay the E.; 12.23
he slew the E. but spared our 12.27
all his servants, and all the E.; 12.30
And the E. were urgent with the 12.33
asked of the E. jewelry of silver 12.35
favor in the sight of the E., 12.36
Thus they despoiled the E. 12.36
and the E. shall know that I am the 14.04
The E. pursued them, all Pharaoh's 14.09
the E. were marching after them; 14.10
us alone and let us serve the E.'? 14.12
us to serve the E. than to die in 14.12
for the E. whom you see today, you 14.13
I will harden the hearts of the E., 14.17
And the E. shall know that I am the 14.18
The E. pursued, and went in after 14.23
down upon the host of the E., 14.24
discomfited the host of the E., 14.24
and the E. said, "Let us flee from 14.25
fights for them against the E." 14.25
water may come back upon the E., 14.26
and the E. fled into it, and the 14.27
LORD routed the E. in the midst of 14.27
that day from the hand of the E.; 14.30
Israel saw the E. dead upon the 14.30
which the LORD did against the E., 14.31
upon you which I put upon the E.; 15.26
and to the E. for Israel's sake, all 18.08
them out of the hand of the E. 18.09
the hand of the E. and out of the 18.10
from under the hand of the E., 18.11
You have seen what I did to the E., 19.04
Why should the E. say, 'With evil 32.12
"Then the E. will hear of it, for Num 14.13
and the E. dealt harshly with us 20.15
in the sight of all the E., 33.03
while the E. were burying all their 33.04
And the E. treated us harshly, and Deu 26.06
and the E. pursued your fathers Jos 24.06
darkness between you and the E., 24.07
you from the hand of the E., Ju 6.09
you from the E. and from the 10.11
who smote the E. with every sort 1Sa 4.08
hearts as the E. and Pharaoh 6.06
the hand of the E. and from the 10.18
Egypt and the E. oppressed them, 12.08
the E., and the Amorites. Ez 9.01
staff against you as the E. did. Is 10.24
heart of the E. will melt within 19.01
And I will stir up E. against E., 19.02
spirit of the E. within them will 19.03
give over the E. into the hand of 19.04
In that day the E. will be like 19.16
will become a terror to the E.; 19.17
will make himself known to the E.; 19.21
and the E. will know the LORD in 19.21
and the E. will worship with the 19.23
lead away the E. captives and the 20.04
The E. are men, and not God; 31.03
also played the harlot with the E., Eze 16.26
when the E. handled your bosom and 23.21
eyes to the E. or remember them 23.27
scatter the E. among the nations, 29.12
will gather the E. from the 29.13
scatter the E. among the nations, 30.23
scatter the E. among the nations 30.26
in all the wisdom of the E., Ac 7.22
but the E., when they attempted to Heb 11.29

EGYPT'S
the branches of E. Nile will Is 19.06
For E. help is worthless and empty, 30.07
upon them on the day of E. doom; Eze 30.09

EHI
E., Rosh, Muppim, Huppim, and Ard Gen 46.21

EHUD
E., the son of Gera, the Benjaminite, Ju 3.15
And E. made for himself a sword 3.16
And when E. had finished presenting 3.18
And E. came to him, as he was 3.20
And E. said, "I have a message from 3.20
And E. reached with his left hand, 3.21
Then E. went out into the vestibule, 3.23
E. escaped while they delayed, and 3.26
sight of the LORD, after E. died. 4.01
E., Chenaanah, Zethan, Tarshish, and 1Ch 7.10
These are the sons of E.(they were 8.06

EIGHT
of Seth were e. hundred years; Gen 5.04
birth of Enosh e. hundred and 5.07
birth of Kenan e. hundred and 5.10
of Mahalalel e. hundred and forty 5.13
birth of Jared e. hundred and 5.16

EIGHT (cont.)

Mahalalel were e. hundred and Gen 5.17
birth of Enoch e. hundred years, 5.19
He that is e. days old among you 17.12
son Isaac when he was e. days old, 21.04
These e. Milcah bore to Nahor, 22.23
And there shall be e. frames, Ex 26.25
There were e. frames with their 36.30
a hundred and e. thousand one Num 2.24
there were e. thousand six hundred, 3.28
of them were e. thousand five 4.48
and four wagons and e. oxen he gave 7.08
"On the sixth day e. bulls, 29.29
served Cushanrishathaim e. years. Ju 3.08
and he judged Israel e. years. 12.14
named Jesse, who had e. sons. 1Sa 17.12
spear against e. hundred whom he 2Sa 23.08
there were e. hundred thousand 24.09
stones of e. and ten cubits. 1Ki 7.10
and he reigned e. years in Jerusalem 2Ki 8.17
Josiah was e. years old when he 22.01
six thousand e. hundred armed 1Ch 12.24
Ephraimites twenty thousand e. hundred, 12.30
and e. of the sons of Ithamar. 24.04
him with e. hundred thousand 2Ch 13.03
and he reigned e. years in Jerusalem 21.05
and he reigned e. years in Jerusalem 21.20
then for e. days they sanctified 29.17
Josiah was e. years old when he 34.01
Jehoiachin was e. years old when he 36.09
two thousand e. hundred and twelve. Ez 2.06
two thousand e. hundred and eighteen Neh 7.11
e. hundred and forty-five. 7.13
e. hundred and twenty-two; 11.12
or even to e., for you know not Ecc 11.02
escaped from Johanan with e. men, Jer 41.15
from Jerusalem e. hundred and 52.29
vestibule of the gateway, e. cubits; Eze 40.08
and its stairway had e. steps. 40.31
and its stairway had e. steps. 40.34
and its stairway had e. steps. 40.37
e. tables, on which the sacrifices 40.41
shepherds and e. princes of men; Mic 5.05
And at the end of e. days, Lk 2.21
Now about e. days after these 9.28
E. days later, his disciples were Jn 20.26
bedridden for e. years and was Ac 9.33
them not more than e. or ten days, 25.06
e. persons, were saved through water 1Pe 3.20

EIGHTEEN

three hundred and e. of them, Gen 14.14
Eglon the king of Moab e. years. Ju 3.14
For e. years they oppressed all the 10.08
to the ground e. thousand men of 20.25
E. thousand men of Benjamin fell, 20.44
he slew e. thousand Edomites in the 2Sa 8.13
E. cubits was the height of one 1Ki 7.15
Jehoiachin was e. years old when he 2Ki 24.08
of the one pillar was e. cubits, 25.17
half-tribe of Manasseh e. thousand, 1Ch 12.31
slew e. thousand Edomites in the 18.12
sons and brethren, able men, e. 26.09
e. thousand talents of bronze, and a 29.07
concubines (he took e. wives and 2Ch 11.21
with him two hundred and e. men. Ez 8.09
with his sons and kinsmen, e.; 8.18
two thousand eight hundred and e. Neh 7.11
of the one pillar was e. cubits, Jer 52.21
city shall be e. thousand cubits. Eze 48.35
Or those e. upon whom the tower in Lk 13.04
a spirit of infirmity for e. years; 13.11
whom Satan bound for e. years, 13.16

EIGHTEENTH

Now in the e. year of King Jeroboam 1Ki 15.01
In the e. year of Jehoshaphat king 2Ki 3.01
In the e. year of King Josiah, the 22.03
but in the e. year of King Josiah 23.23
to Hezir, the e. to Happizzez, 1Ch 24.15
to the e., to Hanani, his sons and 25.25
In the e. year of King Jeroboam 2Ch 13.01
Now in the e. year of his reign, 34.08
In the e. year of the reign of 35.19
which was the e. year of Nebuchadrezzar Jer 32.01
in the e. year of Nebuchadrezzar he 52.29

EIGHTH

on the e. day you shall give it to Ex 22.30
On the e. day Moses called Aaron Lev 9.01
And on the e. day the flesh of his 12.03
"And on the e. day he shall take 14.10
And on the e. day he shall bring 14.23
And on the e. day he shall take two 15.14
And on the e. day she shall take 15.29
and from the e. day on it shall be 22.27
on the e. day you shall hold a holy 23.36
and on the e. day shall be a solemn 23.39
When you sow in the e. year, 25.22
On the e. day he shall bring two Num 6.10
On the e. day Gamaliel the son of 7.54
"On the e. day you shall have a 29.35
which is the e. month, the house was 1Ki 6.38
On the e. day he sent the people 8.66
day of the e. month like the feast 12.32
the fifteenth day in the e. month, 12.33
prisoner in the e. year of his 2Ki 24.12
Johanan e., Elzabad ninth, 1Ch 12.12
to Hakkoz, the e. to Abijah, 24.10
the e. to Jeshaiah, his sons and his 25.15
the seventh, Peullethai the e.; 26.05
E., for the e. month, was Sibbecai 27.11
And on the e. day they held a 2Ch 7.09
and on the e. day of the month they 29.17
For in the e. year of his reign, 34.03
and on the e. day there was a Neh 8.18
then from the e. day onward the Eze 43.27
In the e. month, in the second year Zec 1.01
And on the e. day they came to Lk 1.59
and circumcised him on the e. day; Ac 7.08
circumcised on the e. day, Php 3.05
it is an e. but it belongs to the Rev 17.11
the e. beryl, the ninth topaz, the 21.20

EIGHTIETH

hundred and e. year after the 1Ki 6.01

EIGHTY

Isaac were a hundred and e. years. Gen 35.28
Now Moses was e. years old, and Ex 7.07
eight thousand five hundred and e. Num 4.48
And the land had rest for e. years. Ju 3.30
Barzillai was a very aged man, e. years old; 2Sa 19.32
I am this day e. years old; can I 19.35
burden-bearers and e. thousand 1Ki 5.15
a hundred and e. thousand chosen 12.21
was sold for e. shekels of silver, 2Ki 6.25
Jehu had stationed e. men outside, 10.24
the chief, with e. of his brethren; 1Ch 15.09
burdens and e. thousand to quarry 2Ch 2.02
e. thousand to quarry in the hill 2.18
a hundred and e. thousand chosen 11.01
two hundred and e. thousand men 14.08
with two hundred and e. thousand, 17.15
a hundred and e. thousand armed 17.18
with e. priests of the LORD who 26.17
of Michael, and with him e. men. Ez 8.08
many days, a hundred and e. days. Est 1.04
are sixty queens and e. concubines, Sol 6.08
e. men arrived from Shechem and Jer 41.05
him, 'Take your bill, and write e.' Lk 16.07

EIGHTY-EIGHT

skilful, was two hundred and e. 1Ch 25.07
and Netophah, a hundred and e. Neh 7.26

EIGHTY-FIVE
lo, I am this day e. years old. Jos 14.10
on that day e. persons who wore 1Sa 22.18
a hundred and e. thousand in the 2Ki 19.35
a hundred and e. thousand in the Is 37.36

EIGHTY-FOUR
holy city were two hundred and e. Neh 11.18
and as a widow till she was e. Lk 2.37

EIGHTY-SEVEN
had lived a hundred and e. years, Gen 5.25
were in all e. thousand mighty 1Ch 7.05

EIGHTY-SIX
Abram was e. years old when Hagar Gen 16.16
a hundred and e. thousand four Num 2.09

EIGHTY-THREE
and Aaron e. years old, when they Ex 7.07

EIGHTY-TWO
Lamech seven hundred and e. years, Gen 5.26
had lived a hundred and e. years, 5.28

EITHER
a word to Jacob, e. good or bad." Gen 31.24
e. heretofore or since thou hast Ex 4.10
e. man or beast, not a dog shall 11.07
bears a child, e. male or female. Lev 12.07
e. in warp or woof, or in anything 13.59
e. the native or the stranger who 16.29
e. the native or the stranger who 18.26
shall value it as e. good or bad; 27.12
shall value it as e. good or bad; 27.14
When e. a man or a woman makes a Num 6.02
vineyards, with a wall on e. side. 22.24
no way to turn e. to the right or 22.26
to do e. good or bad of my own will 24.13
e. to the right hand or to the left Deu 17.11
e. to the right hand or to the left 17.20
does nothing e. great or small 1Sa 20.02
to the meal, e. yesterday or today?" 20.27
e. by dreams, or by Urim, or by 28.06
e. by prophets or by dreams; 28.15
e. he is musing, or he has gone 1Ki 18.27
stones with e. the right or the 1Ch 12.02
e. three years of famine; or three 21.12
and do not disobey e. of them; Pro 24.21
e. son or brother, yet there is no Ecc 4.08
e. the Asherim or the altars of Is 17.08
side rooms on e. side of the east Eze 40.10
the jambs on e. side were of the 40.10
side rooms, one cubit on e. side; 40.12
rooms were six cubits on e. side. 40.12
three on e. side, and its jambs and 40.21
trees on its jambs, one on e. side. 40.26
trees on its jambs, one on e. side; 40.34
trees on its jambs, one on e. side; 40.37
gate were two tables on e. side, 40.39
vestibule, five cubits on e. side; 40.48
gate were three cubits on e. side. 40.48
beside the jambs on e. side. 40.49
were five cubits on e. side; 41.02
the west and its walls on e. side, 41.15
windows and palm trees on e. side, 41.26
e. a burnt offering or peace 46.12
e. by heaven, for it is the throne Mt 5.34
for e. he will hate the one and 6.24
e. in this age or in the age to 12.32
"E. make the tree good, and its 12.33
for e. he will hate the one and Lk 16.13
one on e. side, and Jesus between Jn 19.18
e. in the temple or in the synagogues, Ac 24.12
e. of sin, which leads to death, or Rom 6.16
had done nothing e. good or bad, 9.11
For we never used e. words of 1Th 2.05
e. by spirit or by word, or by 2Th 2.02
e. by word of mouth or by letter. 2.15
understanding e. what they are 1Ti 1.07
e. by heaven or by earth or with Jas 5.12
who sins has e. seen him or known 1Jn 3.06
which cannot e. see or hear or walk Rev 9.20
also, on e. side of the river, the 22.02

EKER
of Jerahmeel: Maaz, Jamin, and E. 1Ch 2.27

EKRON
northward to the boundary of E., Jos 13.03
and E.), and those of the Avvim, 13.03
shoulder of the hill north of E., 15.11
E., with its towns and its villages 15.45
from E. to the sea, all that were by 15.46
Elon, Timnah, E., 19.43
and E. with its territory. Ju 1.18
So they sent the ark of God to E. 1Sa 5.10
But when the ark of God came to E., 5.10
the people of E. cried out, "They 5.10
it, they returned that day to E. 6.16
Ashkelon, one for Gath, one for E.; 6.17
restored to Israel, from E. to Gath; 7.14
as far as Gath and the gates of E., 17.52
Shaaraim as far as Gath and E. 17.52
the god of E., whether I shall 2Ki 1.02
of Baalzebub, the god of E.?" 1.03
of Baalzebub, the god of E.? 1.06
the god of E.,—is it because there 1.16
E., and the remnant of Ashdod: Jer 25.20
I will turn my hand against E.; Amo 1.08
and E. shall be uprooted. Zep 2.04
E. also, because its hopes are Zec 9.05
and E. shall be like the Jebusites. 9.07

ELA
Shimei the son of E., in Benjamin; 1Ki 4.18

ELAH
Oholibamah, E., Pinon, Gen 36.41
and encamped in the valley of E., 1Sa 17.02
Israel, were in the valley of E., 17.19
you killed in the valley of E., 21.09
and E. his son reigned in his stead 1Ki 16.06
E. the son of Baasha began to reign 16.08
and the sins of E. his son which 16.13
Now the rest of the acts of E., 16.14
the son of E. made a conspiracy 2Ki 15.30
the son of E. began to reign in 17.01
the third year of Hoshea son of E., 18.01
seventh year of Hoshea son of E., 18.09
Oholibamah, E., Pinon, 1Ch 1.52
of Jephunneh: Iru, E., and Naam; 4.15
and the sons of E.: Kenaz. 4.15
E. the son of Uzzi, son of Michri, 9.08

ELAM
E., Asshur, Arpachshad, Lud, and Aram. Gen 10.22
Ellasar, Chedorlaomer king of E., 14.01
with Chedorlaomer king of E., 14.09
E., Asshur, Arpachshad, Lud, Aram, Uz, 1Ch 1.17
Hananiah, E., Anthothijah, 8.24
E. the fifth, Jehohanan the sixth, 26.03
The sons of E., one thousand two Ez 2.07
The sons of the other E., one thousand, 2.31
Of the sons of E., Jeshaiah the son 8.07
son of Jehiel, of the sons of E., 10.02
Of the sons of E.: Mattaniah, Zechariah, 10.26
The sons of E., a thousand two Neh 7.12
The sons of the other E., 7.34
Pahathmoab, E., Zattu, Bani, 10.14
Jehohanan, Malchijah, E., and Ezer. 12.42
from E., from Shinar, from Hamath, Is 11.11
Go up, O E., lay siege, O Media; 21.02
And E. bore the quiver with chariots 22.06

ELAM (cont.)
of Zimri, all the kings of E., Jer 25.25
Jeremiah the prophet concerning E., 49.34
"Behold, I will break the bow of E., 49.35
will bring upon E. the four winds 49.36
driven out of E. shall not come. 49.36
I will terrify E. before their 49.37
and I will set my throne in E., 49.38
the fortunes of E., says the LORD." 49.39
the e. shall serve the younger." 25.23
"E. is there, and all her multitude Eze 32.24
which is in the province of E.; Dan 8.02

ELAMITES
the men of Susa, that is, the E., Ez 4.09
Parthians and Medes and E. and Ac 2.09

ELAPSED
But when two years had e., Ac 24.27

ELASAH
Ishmael, Nethanel, Jozabad, and E. Ez 10.22
by the hand of E. the son of Jer 29.03

ELATED
from being too e. by the abundance 2Co 12.07
me, to keep me from being too e. 12.07

ELATH
Arabah road from E. and Eziongeber. Deu 2.08
He built E. and restored it to 2Ki 14.22
king of Edom recovered E. for Edom, 16.06
and drove the men of Judah from E.; 16.06
and the Edomites came to E., 16.06

ELBERITH
the stronghold of the house of E. Ju 9.46

ELBETHEL
an altar, and called the place E., Gen 35.07

ELDAAH
Epher, Hanoch, Abida, and E. Gen 25.04
Epher, Hanoch, Abida, and E. 1Ch 1.33

ELDAD
one named E., and the other named Num 11.26
"E. and Medad are prophesying in 11.27

ELDER
the e. brother of Japheth, children Gen 10.21
the e. shall serve the younger." 25.23
"Here is my e. daughter Merab; 1Sa 18.17
for he is my e. brother, and on his 1Ki 2.22
prophet, the diviner and the e., Is 3.02
youth will be insolent to the e., 3.05
the e. and honored man is the head, 9.15
And your e. sister is Samaria, who Eze 16.46
both your e. and your younger, and 16.61
the name of the e. and Oholibah 23.04
"Now his e. son was in the field; Lk 15.25
"The e. will serve the younger." Rom 9.12
against an e. except on the 1Ti 5.19
as a fellow e. and a witness of the 1Pe 5.01
The e. to the elect lady and her 2Jn 1.01
The e. to the beloved Gaius, whom I 3Jn 1.01

ELDERS
the e. of his household, and all the Gen 50.07
and all the e. of the land of Egypt, 50.07
Go and gather the e. of Israel Ex 3.16
and you and the e. of Israel shall 3.18
together all the e. of the people 4.29
Then Moses called all the e. of Israel, 12.21
with you some of the e. of Israel; 17.05
in the sight of the e. of Israel. 17.06
with all the e. of Israel to eat 18.12
and called the e. of the people, 19.07
and seventy of the e. of Israel, 24.01
seventy of the e. of Israel went 24.09
And he said to the e., "Tarry here 24.14
and the e. of the congregation Lev 4.15
and his sons and the e. of Israel; 9.01
me seventy men of the e. of Israel, Num 11.16
know to be the e. of the people 11.16
men of the e. of the people, 11.24
him and put it upon the seventy e.; 11.25
And Moses and the e. of Israel 11.30
and the e. of Israel followed him. 16.25
And Moab said to the e. of Midian, 22.04
So the e. of Moab and the e. of Midian 22.07
heads of your tribes, and your e.; Deu 5.23
then the e. of his city shall send 19.12
then your e. and your judges shall 21.02
and the e. of the city which is 21.03
And the e. of that city shall bring 21.04
And all the e. of that city nearest 21.06
him out to the e. of his city at 21.19
shall say to the e. of his city, 21.20
virginity to the e. of the city in 22.15
young woman shall say to the e., 22.16
garment before the e. of the city. 22.17
Then the e. of that city shall take 22.18
shall go up to the gate to the e., 25.07
Then the e. of his city shall call 25.08
to him in the presence of the e., 25.09
Now Moses and the e. of Israel 27.01
your e., and your officers, all the 29.10
LORD, and to all the e. of Israel. 31.09
Assemble to me all the e. of your tribes, 31.28
your e., and they will tell you. 32.07
evening, he and the e. of Israel; Jos 7.06
with the e. of Israel, before the 8.10
with their e. and officers and 8.33
And our e. and all the inhabitants 9.11
his case to the e. of that city; 20.04
their e. and heads, their judges and 23.02
to Shechem, and summoned the e., 24.01
the days of the e. who outlived 24.31
the days of the e. who outlived Ju 2.07
the officials and e. of Succoth, 8.14
And he took the e. of the city and 8.16
the e. of Gilead went to bring 11.05
But Jephthah said to the e. of Gilead, 11.07
And the e. of Gilead said to 11.08
Jephthah said to the e. of Gilead, 11.09
And the e. of Gilead said to 11.10
Jephthah went with the e. of Gilead, 11.11
Then the e. of the congregation 21.16
took ten men of the e. of the city, Ru 4.02
presence of the e. of my people. 4.04
said to the e. and all the people, 4.09
and the e., said, "We are witnesses. 4.11
the e. of Israel said, "Why has the 1Sa 4.03
Then all the e. of Israel gathered 8.04
The e. of Jabesh said to him, "Give 11.03
now before the e. of my people and 15.30
The e. of the city came to meet him 16.04
the e. of Judah, saying, "Here is a 30.26
conferred with the e. of Israel, 2Sa 3.17
So all the e. of Israel came to the 5.03
And the e. of his house stood 12.17
Absalom and all the e. of Israel. 17.04
Absalom and the e. of Israel; 17.15
"Say to the e. of Judah, 'Why should 19.11
assembled the e. of Israel and all 1Ki 8.01
And all the e. of Israel came, and 8.03
called all the e. of the land, 20.07
And all the e. and all the people 20.08
letters to the e. and the nobles 21.08
the e. and the nobles who dwelt in 21.11
and the e. were sitting with him. 2Ki 6.32
arrived Elisha said to the e., 6.32
to the e., and to the guardians of 10.01
with the e. and the guardians, sent 10.05

ELDERS (cont.)

and all the e. of Judah and Jerusalem 2Ki 23.01
So all the e. of Israel came to the 1Ch 11.03
So David and the e. of Israel, 15.25
Then David and the e., clothed 21.16
assembled the e. of Israel and all 2Ch 5.02
And all the e. of Israel came, and 5.04
together all the e. of Judah and 34.29
God was upon the e. of the Jews, Ez 5.05
Then we asked those e. and spoke to 5.09
Jews and the e. of the Jews 6.07
do for the e. of the Jews for the 6.08
And the e. of the Jews built and 6.14
officials and the e. all his 10.08
with them the e. and judges of 10.14
away the discernment of the e. Job 12.20
pleasure, and to teach his e. wisdom. Ps 105.22
him in the assembly of the e. 107.32
he sits among the e. of the land. Pro 31.23
with the e. and princes of his Is 3.14
and before his e. he will manifest 24.23
some of the e. of the people and Jer 19.01
And certain of the e. of the land 26.17
Jerusalem to the e. of the exiles, 29.01
my priests and e. perished in the Lam 1.19
The e. of the daughter of Zion sit 2.10
to the priests, no favor to the e. 4.16
no respect is shown to the e. 5.12
priest, and counsel from the e. Eze 7.26
with the e. of Judah sitting before 8.01
men of the e. of the house of 8.11
seen what the e. of the house of 8.12
began with the e. who were before 9.06
certain of the e. of Israel to me, 14.01
certain of the e. of Israel came 20.01
speak to the e. of Israel, and say 20.03
The e. of Gebal and her skilled men 27.09
Gather the e. and all the inhabitants Joe 1.14
assemble the e.; gather the 2.16
transgress the tradition of the e.? Mt 15.02
things from the e. and chief 16.21
priests and the e. of the people 21.23
priests and the e. of the people 26.03
priests and the e. of the people. 26.47
scribes and the e. had gathered. 26.57
priests and the e. of the people 27.01
to the chief priests and the e., 27.03
by the chief priests and e., 27.12
priests and the e. persuaded the 27.20
priests, with the scribes and e., 27.41
with the e. and taken counsel, they 28.12
observing the tradition of the e.; Mk 7.03
according to the tradition of the e., 7.05
rejected by the e. and the chief 8.31
scribes and the e. came to him, 11.27
priests and the scribes and the e. 14.43
priests and the e. and the scribes 14.53
with the e. and scribes, and the 15.01
he sent to him e. of the Jews, Lk 7.03
rejected by the e. and chief 9.22
the scribes with the e. came up 20.01
and captains of the temple and e., 22.52
assembly of the e. of the people 22.66
rulers and e. and scribes were Ac 4.05
them, "Rulers of the people and e., 4.08
priests and the e. had said to 4.23
people and the e. and the scribes, 6.12
it to the e. by the hand of 11.30
had appointed e. for them in every 14.23
apostles and the e. about this 15.02
church and the apostles and the e., 15.04
apostles and the e. were gathered 15.06
good to the apostles and the e., 15.22
both the apostles and the e., 15.23
apostles and e. who were at 16.04
called to him the e. of the church. 20.17
and all the e. were present. 21.18
council of e. bear me witness. 22.05
went to the chief priests and e., 23.14
down with some e. and a spokesman, 24.01
priests and the e. of the Jews 25.15
when the e. laid their hands upon 1Ti 4.14
Let the e. who rule well be considered 5.17
and appoint e. in every town as I Tit 1.05
him call for the e. of the church, Jas 5.14
So I exhort the e. among you, 1Pe 5.01
are younger be subject to the e. 5.05
on the thrones were twenty-four e., Rev 4.04
the twenty-four e. fall down before 4.10
Then one of the e. said to me, 5.05
living creatures and among the e., 5.06
the twenty-four e. fell down 5.08
creatures and the e. the voice of 5.11
and the e. fell down and worshiped. 5.14
and round the e. and the four 7.11
Then one of the e. addressed me, 7.13
And the twenty-four e. who sit on 11.16
living creatures and before the e. 14.03
And the twenty-four e. and the four 19.04

ELDEST

with the e. and ending with the Gen 44.12
The three e. sons of Jesse had 1Sa 17.13
the three e. followed Saul, 17.14
Now Eliab his e. brother heard when 17.28
Then he took his e. son who was to 2Ki 3.27
wine in their e. brother's house; Job 1.13
wine in their e. brother's house; 1.18
one by one, beginning with the e., *Jn 8.09

ELEAD

and Ezer and E., whom the men of 1Ch 7.21

ELEADAH

E. his son, Tahath his son, 1Ch 7.20

ELEALEH

E., Sebam, Nebo, and Beon, Num 32.03
built Heshbon, E., Kiriathaim, 32.37
Heshbon and E. cry out, their voice Is 15.04
with my tears, O Heshbon and E.; 16.09
"Heshbon and E. cry out; Jer 48.34

ELEASAH

father of Helez, and Helez of E. 1Ch 2.39
E. was the father of Sismai, and 2.40
was his son, E. his son, Azel his son. 8.37
was his son, E. his son, Azel his son. 9.43

ELEAZAR

him Nadab, Abihu, E., and Ithamar. Ex 6.23
E., Aaron's son, took to wife one of 6.25
Nadab and Abihu, E. and Ithamar. 28.01
to Aaron and to E. and Ithamar, Lev 10.06
to Aaron and to E. and Ithamar, 10.12
he was angry with E. and Ithamar, 10.16
first-born, and Abihu, E., and Ithamar; Num 3.02
So E. and Ithamar served as priests 3.04
And E. the son of Aaron the priest 3.32
"And E. the son of Aaron the priest 4.16
"Tell E. the son of Aaron the 16.37
So E. the priest took the bronze 16.39
the LORD said to E. through Moses. 16.40
shall give her to E. the priest, 19.03
and E. the priest shall take some 19.04
Take Aaron and E. his son, and bring 20.25
and put them upon E. his son; 20.26
upon E. his son; and Aaron died 20.28
Then Moses and E. came down from 20.28
When Phinehas the son of E., 25.07
"Phinehas the son of E., son of 25.11
to Moses and to E. the son of 26.01
And Moses and E. the priest spoke 26.03

ELEAZAR (cont.)
born Nadab, Abihu, E. and Ithamar. Num 26.60
numbered by Moses and E. the priest, 26.63
and before E. the priest, and before 27.02
to stand before E. the priest and 27.19
shall stand before E. the priest, 27.21
to stand before E. the priest and 27.22
Phinehas the son of E. the priest, 31.06
and to E. the priest, and to the 31.12
Moses, and E. the priest, and all the 31.13
And E. the priest said to the men 31.21
you and E. the priest and the heads 31.26
and give it to E. the priest as an 31.29
And Moses and E. the priest did as 31.31
to E. the priest, as the LORD 31.41
And Moses and E. the priest received 31.51
And Moses and E. the priest received 31.54
to Moses and to E. the priest and 32.02
concerning them to E. the priest, 32.28
E. the priest and Joshua the son of 34.17
and his son E. ministered as priest Deu 10.06
which E. the priest, and Joshua the Jos 14.01
They came before E. the priest and 17.04
inheritances which E. the priest 19.51
Levites came to E. the priest and 21.01
Phinehas the son of E. the priest, 22.13
the son of E. the priest said to 22.31
Then Phinehas the son of E. the priest, 22.32
And E. the son of Aaron died; 24.33
and Phinehas the son of E., Ju 20.28
E., to have charge of the ark of 1Sa 7.01
mighty men was E. the son of Dodo, 2Sa 23.09
Nadab, Abihu, E., and Ithamar. 1Ch 6.03
E. was the father of Phinehas, 6.04
E. his son, Phinehas his son, Abishua 6.50
the son of E. was the ruler over 9.20
mighty men was E. the son of Dodo, 11.12
The sons of Mahli: E. and Kish. 23.21
E. died having no sons, but only 23.22
Nadab, Abihu, E., and Ithamar. 24.01
so E. and Ithamar became the 24.02
help of Zadok of the sons of E., 24.03
the sons of E. than among the sons 24.04
fathers' houses of the sons of E., 24.04
the sons of E. and the sons of 24.05
chosen for E. and one chosen for 24.06
Of Mahli: E., who had no sons. 24.28
son of E., son of Aaron the chief Ez 7.05
with him was E. the son of Phinehas, 8.33
E., Hashabiah, and Benaiah. 10.25
E., Uzzi, Jehohanan, Malchijah, Elam, Neh 12.42
and Eliud the father of E., Mt 1.15
and E. the father of Matthan, and 1.15

ELECT
the sake of the e. those days will Mt 24.22
astray, if possible, even the e. 24.24
will gather his e. from the four 24.31
but for the sake of the e., Mk 13.20
lead astray, if possible, the e. 13.22
and gather his e. from the four 13.27
And will not God vindicate his e., Lk 18.07
bring any charge against God's e.? Rom 8.33
The e. obtained it, but the rest 11.07
and of the e. angels I charge you 1Ti 5.21
everything for the sake of the e., 2Ti 2.10
faith of God's e. and their Tit 1.01
The elder to the e. lady and her 2Jn 1.01
children of your e. sister greet 1.13

ELECTION
God's purpose of e. might continue, Rom 9.11
but as regards e. they are beloved 11.28
to confirm your call and e., 2Pe 1.10

EL-ELOHE-ISRAEL
erected an altar and called it E. Gen 33.20

ELEMENTAL
slaves to the e. spirits of the Gal 4.03
the weak and beggarly e. spirits, 4.09
according to the e. spirits of the Col 2.08
you died to the e. spirits of the 2.20

ELEMENTARY
us leave the e. doctrines of Heb 6.01

ELEMENTS
and the e. will be dissolved with 2Pe 3.10
and the e. will melt with fire! 3.12

ELEVATION
beautiful in e., is the joy of all Ps 48.02

ELEVEN
and his e. children, and crossed the Gen 32.22
and e. stars were bowing down to me 37.09
tabernacle; e. curtains shall you make. Ex 26.07
the e. curtains shall have the same 26.08
tabernacle; he made e. curtains. 36.14
the e. curtains had the same 36.15
"On the third day e. bulls, Num 29.20
It is e. days' journey from Horeb Deu 1.02
e. cities with their villages. Jos 15.51
each give you e. hundred pieces of Ju 16.05
"The e. hundred pieces of silver 17.02
And he restored the e. hundred 17.03
and he reigned e. years in Jerusalem 2Ki 23.36
and he reigned e. years in Jerusalem 24.18
and he reigned e. years in Jerusalem 2Ch 36.05
and he reigned e. years in Jerusalem 36.11
and he reigned e. years in Jerusalem Jer 52.01
Now the e. disciples went to Mt 28.16
all this to the e. and to all the Lk 24.09
they found the e. gathered together 24.33
was enrolled with the e. apostles. Ac 1.26
But Peter, standing with the e., 2.14

ELEVENTH
On the e. day Pagiel the son of Num 7.72
on the first day of the e. month, Deu 1.03
And in the e. year, in the month of 1Ki 6.38
In the e. year of Joram the son of 2Ki 9.29
till the e. year of King Zedekiah. 25.02
Jeremiah tenth, Machbannai e. 1Ch 12.13
the e. to Eliashib, the twelfth to 24.12
the e. to Azarel, his sons and his 25.18
E., for the e. month, was Benaiah 27.14
the end of the e. year of Zedekiah, Jer 1.03
in the e. year of Zedekiah, in the 39.02
till the e. year of King Zedekiah. 52.05
In the e. year, on the first day of Eze 26.01
In the e. year, in the first month, 30.20
In the e. year, in the third month, 31.01
day of the e. month which is the Zec 1.07
And about the e. hour he went out Mt 20.06
those hired about the e. hour came, 20.09
the e. jacinth, the twelfth amethyst. Rev 21.20

ELHANAN
and E. the son of Jaareoregim, the 2Sa 21.19
E. the son of Dodo of Bethlehem, 23.24
E. the son of Dodo of Bethlehem, 1Ch 11.26
and E. the son of Jair slew Lahmi 20.05

ELI
Shiloh, where the two sons of E., 1Sa 1.03
Now E. the priest was sitting on 1.09
E. observed her mouth. 1.12
therefore E. took her to be a 1.13
And E. said to her, "How long will 1.14
Then E. answered, "Go in peace, and 1.17
and they brought the child to E. 1.25
in the presence of E. the priest. 2.11
Now the sons of E. were worthless 2.12

ELI (cont.)
Then E. would bless Elkanah and his 1Sa 2.20
Now E. was very old, and he heard 2.22
And there came a man of God to E., 2.27
ministering to the LORD under E. 3.01
At that time E., whose eyesight had 3.02
and ran to E., and said, "Here I am, 3.05
And Samuel arose and went to E., 3.06
And he arose and went to E., 3.08
Then E. perceived that the LORD was 3.08
Therefore E. said to Samuel, "Go, lie 3.09
fulfil against E. all that I have 3.12
to the house of E. that the 3.14
afraid to tell the vision to E. 3.15
But E. called Samuel and said, 3.16
And E. said, "What was it that he 3.17
and the two sons of E., Hophni and 4.04
and the two sons of E., Hophni and 4.11
E. was sitting upon his seat by the 4.13
When E. heard the sound of the 4.14
man hastened and came and told E. 4.14
Now E. was ninety-eight years old 4.15
And the man said to E., "I am he 4.16
E. fell over backward from his seat 4.18
son of E., the priest of the LORD 14.03
concerning the house of E. in Shiloh. 1Ki 2.27
"E., E., lama sabachthani?" Mt 27.46

ELI'S
the iniquity of E. house shall not 1Sa 3.14

ELIAB
from Zebulun, E. the son of Helon; Num 1.09
Zebulun being E. the son of Helon, 2.07
On the third day E. the son of 7.24
the offering of E. the son of 7.29
of Zebulun was E. the son of Helon 10.16
Dathan and Abiram the sons of E., 16.01
Dathan and Abiram the sons of E.; 16.12
And the sons of Pallu: E. 26.08
The sons of E.: Nemuel, Dathan, and 26.09
the sons of E., son of Reuben; Deu 11.06
he looked on E. and thought, "Surely 1Sa 16.06
the battle were E. the first-born, 17.13
Now E. his eldest brother heard 17.28
the father of E. his first-born, 1Ch 2.13
E. his son, Jeroham his son, Elkanah 6.27
chief, Obadiah second, E. their, 12.09
E., Benaiah, Maaseiah, Mattithiah, 15.18
E., Maaseiah, and Benaiah were to 15.20
E., Benaiah, Obededom, and Jeiel, who 16.05
the daughter of E. the son of 2Ch 11.18

ELIAB'S
and E. anger was kindled against 1Sa 17.28

ELIADA
Elishama, E., and Eliphelet. 2Sa 5.16
to him, Rezon the son of E., 1Ki 11.23
Elishama, E., and Eliphelet, nine. 1Ch 3.08
Of Benjamin: E., a mighty man of 2Ch 17.17

ELIAHBA
E. of Shaalbon, the sons of Jashen, 2Sa 23.32
Azmaveth of Baharum, E. of Shaalbon, 1Ch 11.33

ELIAKIM
out to them E. the son of Hilkiah, 2Ki 18.18
Then E. the son of Hilkiah, and 18.26
Then E. the son of Hilkiah, who was 18.37
And he sent E., who was over the 19.02
Neco made E. the son of Josiah 23.34
of Egypt made E. his brother king 2Ch 36.04
and the priests E., Maaseiah, Neh 12.41
call my servant E. the son of Is 22.20
came out to him E. the son of 36.03
Then E., Shebna, and Joah said to 36.11
Then E. the son of Hilkiah, who was 36.22
And he sent E., who was over the 37.02
Abiud, and Abiud the father of E., Mt 1.13
and E. the father of Azor, 1.13
the son of Jonam, the son of E., Lk 3.30

ELIAM
this Bathsheba, the daugher of E., 2Sa 11.03
E. the son of Ahithophel of Gilo, 23.34

ELIASAPH
from Gad, E. the son of Deuel; Num 1.14
of Gad being E. the son of Reuel, 2.14
with E., the son of Lael as head of 3.24
On the sixth day E. the son of 7.42
the offering of E. the son of 7.47
men of Gad was E. the son of Deuel 10.20

ELIASHIB
E., Pelaiah, Akkub, Johanan, Delaiah, 1Ch 3.24
the eleventh to E., 24.12
chamber of Jehohanan the son of E., Ez 10.06
Of the singers: E. 10.24
E., Mattaniah, Jeremoth, Zabad, and 10.27
Vaniah, Meremoth, E., 10.36
Then E. the high priest rose up Neh 3.01
of the house of E. the high priest 3.20
of the house of E. to the end of 3.21
to the end of the house of E. 3.21
Joiakim, Joiakim the father of E., 12.10
E. the father of Joiada, 12.10
for the Levites, in the days of E., 12.22
the days of Johanan the son of E. 12.23
E. the priest, who was appointed 13.04
the evil that E. had done for 13.07
the son of E. the high priest, was 13.28

ELIATHAH
E., Giddalti, and Romamtiezer, 1Ch 25.04
to E., his sons and his brethren, 25.27

ELIDAD
Benjamin, E. the son of Chislon. Num 34.21

ELIEHOENAI
Jehohanan the sixth, E. the seventh. 1Ch 26.03
E. the son of Zerahiah, and with him Ez 8.04

ELIEL
E., Azriel, Jeremiah, Hodaviah, and 1Ch 5.24
Jeroham, son of E., son of Toah, 6.34
Elienai, Zillethai, E., 8.20
Ishpan, Eber, E., 8.22
E. the Mahavite, and Jeribai, and 11.46
E., and Obed, and Jaasiel the 11.47
Attai sixth, E. seventh, 12.11
E. the chief, with eighty of his 15.09
E., and Amminadab, 15.11
E., Ismachiah, Mahath, and Benaiah 2Ch 31.13

ELIENAI
E., Zillethai, Eliel, 1Ch 8.20

ELIEZER
heir of my house is E. of Damascus?" Gen 15.02
E. (for he said, "The God of my Ex 18.04
E., Elioenai, Omri, Jeremoth, Abijah, 1Ch 7.08
and E., the priests, should blow the 15.24
The sons of Moses: Gershom and E. 23.15
The sons of E.: Rehabiah the chief; 23.17
E. had no other sons, but the sons 23.17
from E. were his son Rehabiah, and 26.25
the Reubenites E. the son of 27.16
Then E. the son of Dodavahu of 2Ch 20.37
Then I sent for E., Ariel, Ez 8.16
E., Jarib, and Gedaliah, of the sons 10.18
Kelita), Pethahiah, Judah, and E. 10.23

ELIEZER (cont.)
E., Isshijah, Malchijah, Shemaiah, Ez 10.31
the son of E., the son of Jorim, the Lk 3.29

ELIHOREPH
E. and Ahijah the sons of Shisha 1Ki 4.03

ELIHU
son of E., son of Tohu, son of Zuph, 1Sa 1.01
E., and Zillethai, chiefs of thousands 1Ch 12.20
were able men, E. and Semachiah. 26.07
for Judah, E., one of David's brothers 27.18
Then E. the son of Barachel the Job 32.02
Now E. had waited to speak to Job 32.04
And when E. saw that there was no 32.05
And E. the son of Barachel the 32.06
Then E. said: 34.01
And E. said: 35.01
And E. continued, and said: 36.01

ELIJAH
Now E. the Tishbite, of Tishbe in 1Ki 17.01
And E. said to her, "Fear not; 17.13
And she went and did as E. said; 17.15
of the LORD which he spoke by E. 17.16
And she said to E., "What have you 17.18
LORD hearkened to the voice of E.; 17.22
And E. took the child, and brought 17.23
and E. said, "See, your son lives." 17.23
And the woman said to E., "Now I know 17.24
the word of the LORD came to E., 18.01
So E. went to show himself to Ahab. 18.02
was on the way, behold, E. met him; 18.07
and said, "Is it you, my lord E.?" 18.07
your lord, 'Behold, E. is here.'" 18.08
tell your lord, "Behold, E. is here."' 18.11
your lord, "Behold, E. is here"'; 18.14
And E. said, "As the LORD of hosts 18.15
and Ahab went to meet E. 18.16
When Ahab saw E., Ahab said to him, 18.17
And E. came near to all the people, 18.21
Then E. said to the people, "I, even 18.22
Then E. said to the prophets of 18.25
And at noon E. mocked them saying, 18.27
Then E. said to all the people, 18.30
E. took twelve stones, according to 18.31
E. the prophet came near and said, 18.36
And E. said to them, "Seize the 18.40
and E. brought them down to the 18.40
And E. said to Ahab, "Go up, eat and 18.41
And E. went up to the top of Carmel 18.42
And the hand of the LORD was on E.; 18.46
Ahab told Jezebel all that E. had done, 19.01
Then Jezebel sent a messenger to E., 19.02
him, "What are you doing here, E.?" 19.09
And when E. heard it, he wrapped his 19.13
said, "What are you doing here, E.?" 19.13
E. passed by him and cast his 19.19
and ran after E., and said, "Let me 19.20
Then he arose and went after E., 19.21
the LORD came to E. the Tishbite, 21.17
Ahab said to E., "Have you found me, 21.20
the LORD came to E. the Tishbite, 21.28
the LORD said to E. the Tishbite, 2Ki 1.03
surely die.'" So E. went. 1.04
And he said, "It is E. the Tishbite." 1.08
He went up to E., who was sitting 1.09
But E. answered the captain of 1.10
But E. answered them, "If I am a man 1.12
and fell on his knees before E., 1.13
Then the angel of the LORD said to E., 1.15
of the LORD which E. had spoken. 1.17
about to take E. up to heaven by a 2.01
E. and Elisha were on their way 2.01
And E. said to Elisha, "Tarry here, I 2.02
E. said to him, "Elisha, tarry here, I 2.04
Then E. said to him, "Tarry here, I 2.06
Then E. took his mantle, and rolled 2.08
E. said to Elisha, "Ask what I shall 2.09
And E. went up by a whirlwind into 2.11
the mantle of E. that had fallen 2.13
the mantle of E. that had fallen 2.14
"Where is the LORD, the God of E.?" 2.14
"The spirit of E. rests on Elisha." 2.15
poured water on the hands of E." 3.11
by his servant E. the Tishbite, 9.36
what he said by his servant E." 10.10
of the LORD which he spoke to E. 10.17
Jaareshiah, E., and Zichri were the 1Ch 8.27
came to him from E. the prophet, 2Ch 21.12
E., Shemaiah, Jehiel, and Uzziah. Ez 10.21
Jehiel, Abdi, Jeremoth, and E. 10.26
"Behold, I will send you E. the Mal 4.05
accept it, he is E. who is to come. Mt 11.14
others say E., and others Jeremiah 16.14
appeared to them Moses and E., 17.03
and one for Moses and one for E.," 17.04
say that first E. must come?" 17.10
He replied, "E. does come, and he is 17.11
but I tell you that E. has already 17.12
it said, "This man is calling E." 27.47
us see whether E. will come to 27.49
But others said, "It is E." Mk 6.15
and others say, E.; and others 8.28
appeared to them E. with Moses; 9.04
and one for Moses and one for E." 9.05
say that first E. must come?" 9.11
"E. does come first to restore all 9.12
But I tell you that E. has come, 9.13
it said, "Behold, he is calling E." 15.35
us see whether E. will come to 15.36
him in the spirit and power of E., Lk 1.17
widows in Israel in the days of E., 4.25
and E. was sent to none of them but 4.26
by some that E. had appeared, and by 9.08
but others say, E.; and others, 9.19
men talked with him, Moses and E., 9.30
and one for Moses and one for E."— 9.33
Are you E.?" He said, "I am not." Jn 1.21
nor E., nor the prophet?" 1.25
know what the scripture says of E., Rom 11.02
E. was a man of like nature with Jas 5.17

ELIKA
Shammah of Harod, E. of Harod. 2Sa 23.25

ELIM
Then they came to E., where there Ex 15.27
They set out from E., and all 16.01
Sin, which is between E. and Sinai, 16.01
set out from Marah, and came to E.; Num 33.09
at E. there were twelve springs of 33.09
And they set out from E., and encamped 33.10

ELIMELECH
of the man was E. and the name of Ru 1.02
But E., the husband of Naomi, died, 1.03
man of wealth, of the family of E., 2.01
Boaz, who was of the family of E. 2.03
which belonged to our kinsman E. 4.03
belonged to E. and all that 4.09

ELIOENAI
E., Hizkiah, and Azrikam, three. 1Ch 3.23
The sons of E.: Hodaviah, Eliashib, 3.24
E., Jaakobah, Jeshohaiah, Asaiah, 4.36
E., Omri, Jeremoth, Abijah, Anathoth, 7.08
E., Maaseiah, Ishmael, Nethanel, Ez 10.22
E., Eliashib, Mattaniah, Jeremoth, 10.27
E., Zechariah, and Hananiah, with Neh 12.41

ELIPHAL
the Hararite, E. the son of Ur, 1Ch 11.35

ELIPHAZ
And Adah bore to Esau, E.; Gen 36.04
E. the son of Adah the wife of Esau, 36.10
The sons of E. were Teman, Omar, 36.11
(Timna was a concubine of E., Esau's son; 36.12
she bore Amalek to E.) 36.12
The sons of E. the first-born of 36.15
the chiefs of E. in the land of 36.16
E., Reuel, Jeush, Jalam, and Korah. 1Ch 1.35
The sons of E.: Teman, Omar, Zephi, 1.36
E. the Temanite, Bildad the Shuhite, Job 2.11
Then E. the Temanite answered: 4.01
Then E. the Temanite answered: 15.01
Then E. the Temanite answered: 22.01
the LORD said to E. the Temanite: 42.07
So E. the Temanite and Bildad the 42.09

ELIPHELEHU
E., and Mikneiah, and the gatekeepers 1Ch 15.18
E., Mikneiah, Obededom, Jeiel, and 15.21

ELIPHELET
Elishama, Eliada, and E. 2Sa 5.16
E. the son of Ahasbai of Maacah, 23.34
then Ibhar, Elishama, E., 1Ch 3.06
Elishama, Eliada, and E., nine. 3.08
Jeush the second, and E. the third. 8.39
Elishama, Beeliada, and E. 14.07
came later, their names being E., Ez 8.13
E., Jeremai, Manasseh, and Shimei. 10.33

ELISHA
and E. the son of Shaphat of 1Ki 19.16
the sword of Jehu shall E. slay. 19.17
and found E. the son of Shaphat, who 19.19
Elijah and E. were on their way 2Ki 2.01
And Elijah said to E., "Tarry here, 2.02
But E. said, "As the LORD lives, 2.02
who were in Bethel came out to E., 2.03
"E., tarry here, I pray you; 2.04
were at Jericho drew near to E., 2.05
had crossed, Elijah said to E., 2.09
And E. said, "I pray you, let me 2.09
And E. saw it and he cried, "My 2.12
to the other; and E. went over. 2.14
"The spirit of Elijah rests on E." 2.15
Now the men of the city said to E., 2.19
according to the word which E. spoke. 2.22
"E. the son of Shaphat is here, who 3.11
And E. said to the king of Israel, 3.13
And E. said, "As the LORD of hosts 3.14
sons of the prophets cried to E., 4.01
And E. said to her, "What shall I do 4.02
One day E. went on to Shunem, where 4.08
as E. had said to her. 4.17
When E. came into the house, he saw 4.32
And E. came again to Gilgal when 4.38
And E. said, "Give to the men, that 4.42
But when E. the man of God heard 5.08
And E. sent a messenger to him, 5.10
Gehazi, the servant of E. the man of God, 5.20
and E. said to him, "Where have you 5.25
sons of the prophets said to E., 6.01
but E., the prophet who is in 6.12
Then E. prayed, and said, "O LORD, I 6.17
chariots of fire round about E. 6.17
E. prayed to the LORD, and said, 6.18
accordance with the prayer of E. 6.18
And E. said to them, "This is not 6.19
E. said, "O LORD, open the eyes of 6.20
of Israel saw them he said to E., 6.21
if the head of E. the son of 6.31
E. was sitting in his house, and the 6.32
messenger arrived E. said to the 6.32
But E. said, "Hear the word of the 7.01
Now E. had said to the woman whose 8.01
the great things that E. has done." 8.04
the king how E. had restored the 8.05
is her son whom E. restored to 8.05
Now E. came to Damascus. 8.07
And E. said to him, "Go, say to him, 8.10
E. answered, "The LORD has shown 8.13
Then he departed from E., 8.14
to him, "What did E. say to you?" 8.14
Then E. the prophet called one of 9.01
Now when E. had fallen sick with 13.14
And E. said to him, "Take a bow and 13.15
And E. laid his hands upon the 13.16
Then E. said, "Shoot"; and he shot. 13.17
So E. died, and they buried him. 13.20
man was cast into the grave of E.; 13.21
as the man touched the bones of E., 13.21
in the time of the prophet E.; Lk 4.27

ELISHAH
E., Tarshish, Kittim, and Dodanim. Gen 10.04
E., Tarshish, Kittim, and Rodanim. 1Ch 1.07
the coasts of E. was your awning. Eze 27.07

ELISHAMA
E. the son of Ammihud, and from Num 1.10
Ephraim being E. the son of 2.18
On the seventh day E. the son of 7.48
the offering of E. the son of 7.53
their host was E. the son of 10.22
E., Eliada, and Eliphelet. 2Sa 5.16
son of E., of the royal family, came 2Ki 25.25
of Jekamiah, and Jekamiah of E. 1Ch 2.41
then Ibhar, E., Eliphelet, 3.06
E., Eliada, and Eliphelet, nine. 3.08
son, Ammihud his son, E. his son, 7.26
E., Beeliada, and Eliphelet. 14.07
Levites, the priests E. and Jehoram. 2Ch 17.08
E. the secretary, Delaiah the son of Jer 36.12
in the chamber of E. the secretary; 36.20
the chamber of E. the secretary; 36.21
son of E., of the royal family, one 41.01

ELISHAPHAT
and E. the son of Zichri. 2Ch 23.01

ELISHA'S
and halted at the door of E. house. 2Ki 5.09

ELISHEBA
Aaron took to wife E., the daughter Ex 6.23

ELISHUA
Ibhar, E., Nepheg, Japhia, 2Sa 5.15
Ibhar, E., Elpelet, 1Ch 14.05

ELIUD
Achim, and Achim the father of E., Mt 1.14
and E. the father of Eleazar, and 1.15

ELIZABETH
of Aaron, and her name was E. Lk 1.05
because E. was barren, and both were 1.07
and your wife E. will bear you a 1.13
After these days his wife E. conceived, 1.24
your kinswoman E. in her old age 1.36
house of Zechariah and greeted E. 1.40
And when E. heard the greeting of 1.41
and E. was filled with the Holy 1.41
time came for E. to be delivered, 1.57

ELIZAPHAN
with E. the son of Uzziel as head Num 3.30
a leader, E. the son of Parnach. 34.25
of the sons of E., Shemaiah the 1Ch 15.08
and of the sons of E., Shimri 2Ch 29.13

ELIZUR
From Reuben, E. the son of Shedeur; Num 1.05
of Reuben being E. the son of 2.10

ELIZUR (cont.)
On the fourth day E. the son of — Num 7.30
the offering of E. the son of — 7.35
their host was E. the son of — 10.18

ELKANAH
of Korah: Assir, E., and Abiasaph; — Ex 6.24
whose name was E. the son of — 1Sa 1.01
On the day when E. sacrificed, — 1.04
And E., her husband, said to her, — 1.08
And E. knew Hannah his wife, and the — 1.19
And the man E. and all his house — 1.21
E. her husband said to her, "Do what — 1.23
Then E. went home to Ramah. — 2.11
Then Eli would bless E. and his wife, — 2.20
E. his son, Ebiasaph his son, Assir — 1Ch 6.23
The sons of E.: Amasai and Ahimoth, — 6.25
E. his son, Zophai his son, Nahath — 6.26
son, Jeroham his son, E. his son. — 6.27
son of E., son of Jeroham, son of — 6.34
son of E., son of Mahath, son of — 6.35
son of E., son of Joel, son of — 6.36
son of E., who dwelt in the villages — 9.16
E., Isshiah, Azarel, Joezer, and — 12.06
Berechiah and E. were to be gatekeepers — 15.23
the palace and E. the next in — 2Ch 28.07

ELKOSH
book of the vision of Nahum of E. — Nah 1.01

ELLASAR
king of Shinar, Arioch king of E., — Gen 14.01
of Shinar, and Arioch king of E., — 14.09

ELMADAM
the son of E., the son of Er, — Lk 3.28

ELNAAM
the sons of E., and Ithmah the — 1Ch 11.46

ELNATHAN
the daughter of E. of Jerusalem. — 2Ki 24.08
E., Jarib, Elnathan, Nathan, Zechariah, — Ez 8.16
E., Nathan, Zechariah, and Meshullam, — 8.16
men, and for Joiarib and E., — 8.16
E. the son of Achbor and others — Jer 26.22
E. the son of Achbor, Gemariah the — 36.12
Even when E. and Delaiah and — 36.25

ELOI
"E., E., lama sabachthani?" — Mk 15.34

ELON
the daughter of E. the Hittite; — Gen 26.34
the daughter of E. the Hittite, — 36.02
of Zebulun: Sered, E., and Jahleel — 46.14
of E., the family of the Elonites; — Num 26.26
E., Timnah, Ekron, — Jos 19.43
After him E. the Zebulunite judged — Ju 12.11
Then E. the Zebulunite died, and was — 12.12

ELONBETHHANAN
Shaalbim, Bethshemesh, and E.; — 1Ki 4.09

ELONITES
of Elon, the family of the E.; — Num 26.26

ELOQUENT
I am not e., either heretofore or — Ex 4.10
He was an e. man, well versed in the — Ac 18.24
and not with e. wisdom, lest the — 1Co 1.17

ELOTH
which is near E. on the shore of — 1Ki 9.26
Eziongeber and E. on the shore of — 2Ch 8.17
He built E. and restored it to — 26.02

ELPAAL
had sons by Hushim: Abitub and E. — 1Ch 8.11
The sons of E.: Eber, Misham, and — 8.12
and Jobab were the sons of E. — 8.18

ELPARAN
Seir as far as E. on the border of — Gen 14.06

ELPELET
Ibhar, Elishua, E., — 1Ch 14.05

ELSE
to Lot, "Have you any one e. here? — Gen 19.12
or e., by the life of Pharaoh, — 42.16
E., if you will not let my people — Ex 8.21
in what e. shall he sleep? — 22.27
And if any one e. comes near, — Num 1.51
but if any one e. comes near, — 3.10
and any one e. who came near was to — 3.38
apart from what e. he can afford; — 6.21
and no one e. shall come near you. — 18.04
and any one e. who comes near shall — 18.07
and everything e. in the city, — Deu 20.14
e. you would now be guilty.'" — Ju 21.22
or anything e. till the sun goes — 2Sa 3.35
or e. there will be no escape for — 15.14
was no one e. with us in the house, — 1Ki 3.18
e. the journey will be too great — 19.07
or e. you shall pay a talent of — 20.39
or e., if it please you, I will give — 21.06
or e. three days of the sword of — 1Ch 21.12
And whatever e. is required for the — Ez 7.20
This is nothing e. but sadness of — Neh 2.02
e. would my Maker soon put an end — Job 32.22
e. it will not keep with you. — Ps 32.09
for what e. can I do, because of my — Jer 9.07
there will be no place e. to bury. — 19.11
am your God and there is none e. — Joe 2.27
herself, "I am and there is none e." — Zep 2.15
later some one e. saw him and said, — Lk 22.58
or e. believe me for the sake of — Jn 14.11
them the works which no one e. did, — 15.24
And there is salvation in no one e., — Ac 4.12
about himself or about some one e.?" — 8.34
Or e. let these men themselves say — 24.20
nor anything e. in all creation, — Rom 8.39
know whether I baptized any one e.) — 1Co 1.16
single or e. be reconciled to her — 7.11
and whatever e. is contrary to — 1Ti 1.10

ELSEWHERE
of Ashdod and e. among the Philistines — 2Ch 26.06
is better than a thousand e. — Ps 84.10
because there is no room e. — Jer 7.32

ELTEKE
E. with its pasture lands, Gibbethon — Jos 21.23

ELTEKEH
E., Gibbethon, Baalath, — Jos 19.44

ELTEKON
and E.: six cities with their — Jos 15.59

ELTOLAD
E., Chesil, Hormah, — Jos 15.30
E., Bethul, Hormah, — 19.04

ELUDED
but he e. Saul, so that he struck — 1Sa 19.10

ELUL
twenty-fifth day of the month E., — Neh 6.15

ELUZAI
E., Jerimoth, Bealiah, Shemariah, — 1Ch 12.05

ELYMAS
But E. the magician (for that is — Ac 13.08

ELZABAD
Johanan eighth, E. ninth, 1Ch 12.12
and E., whose brethren were able 26.07

ELZAPHAN
of Uzziel: Mishael, E., and Sithri. Ex 6.22
And Moses called Mishael and E., Lev 10.04

EMBALM
the physicians to e. his father. Gen 50.02

EMBALMED
So the physicians e. Israel; Gen 50.02
and they e. him, and he was put in a 50.26

EMBALMING
for so many are required for e. Gen 50.03

EMBARKING
And e. in a ship of Adramyttium, Ac 27.02

EMBASSY
he sends an e. and asks terms of Lk 14.32
hated him and sent an e. after him, 19.14

EMBERS
As charcoal to hot e. and wood to Pro 26.21

EMBITTERED
When my soul was e., when I was Ps 73.21

EMBODIMENT
in the law the e. of knowledge and Rom 2.20

EMBRACE
I gave my maid to your e., Gen 16.05
comes round, you shall e. a son." 2Ki 4.16
she will honor you if you e. her. Pro 4.08
loose woman and e. the bosom of an 5.20
a time to e., and a time to refrain Ecc 3.05

EMBRACED
and e. him and kissed him, and Gen 29.13
and e. him, and fell on his neck and 33.04
and he kissed them and e. them. 48.10
and that his right hand e. me! Sol 2.06
and that his right hand e. me! 8.03
and ran and e. him and kissed him. Lk 15.20
all wept and e. Paul and kissed Ac 20.37

EMBRACING
and a time to refrain from e.; Ecc 3.05
and e. him said, "Do not be alarmed, Ac 20.10

EMBROIDERED
twined linen, e. with needlework. Ex 26.36
twined linen, e. with needlework; 27.16
make a girdle e. with needlework. 28.39
e. with needlework; 36.37
the court was e. with needlework 38.18
e. with needlework; 39.29
Sisera, spoil of dyed stuffs e., Ju 5.30
of dyed work e. for my neck as 5.30
you also with e. cloth and shod Eze 16.10
fine linen, and silk, and e. cloth; 16.13
and you took your e. garments to 16.18
and strip off their e. garments; 26.16
Of fine e. linen from Egypt was 27.07
e. work, fine linen, coral, and agate. 27.16
in clothes of blue and e. work, 27.24

EMBROIDERER
or by an e. in blue and purple and Ex 35.35
designer and e. in blue and purple 38.23

EMEKKEZIZ
were Jericho, Bethhoglah, E., Jos 18.21

EMERALD
and the second row an e., a sapphire, Ex 28.18
an e., a sapphire, and a diamond; 39.11
onyx, sapphire, carbuncle, and e.; Eze 28.13
a rainbow that looked like an e. Rev 4.03
the third agate, the fourth e., 21.19

EMERALDS
they exchanged for your wares e., Eze 27.16

EMIM
the E. in Shavehkiriathaim, Gen 14.05
(The E. formerly lived there, a Deu 2.10
but the Moabites call them E. 2.11

EMINENCE
to thrust him down from his e. Ps 62.04

EMINENT
lest a more e. man than you be Lk 14.08
Greet Rufus, e. in the Lord, also his Rom 16.13

EMISSION
"And if a man has an e. of semen, Lev 15.16
a woman and has an e. of semen, 15.18
and for him who has an e. of semen, 15.32
a man who has had an e. of semen, 22.04

EMMANUEL
shall be called E." (which means, Mt 1.23

EMMAUS
were going to a village named E., Lk 24.13

EMPEROR
custody for the decision of the e., Ac 25.21
as he himself appealed to the e., 25.25
it be to the e. as supreme, 1Pe 2.13
Fear God. Honor the e. 2.17

EMPLOY
e. it for one another, as good 1Pe 4.10

EMPLOYED
those who are e. in the temple 1Co 9.13

EMPTIED
So she quickly e. her jar into the Gen 24.20
As they e. their sacks, behold, every 42.35
the pan and e. it out before him, 2Sa 13.09
servants have e. out the money 2Ki 22.09
They have e. out the money that was 2Ch 34.17
So may he be shaken out and e." Neh 5.13
Egyptians within them will be e. out, Is 19.03
he has not been e. from vessel to Jer 48.11
cross of Christ be e. of its power. 1Co 1.17
but e. himself, taking the form of a Php 2.07

EMPTINESS
so I am allotted months of e., Job 7.03
Let him not trust in e., deceiving 15.31
for e. will be his recompense. 15.31
by him as less than nothing and e. Is 40.17

EMPTY
The pit was e., there was no water Gen 37.24
and the seven e. ears blighted by 41.27
when you go, you shall not go e., Ex 3.21
And none shall appear before me e. 34.20
that they e. the house before the Lev 14.36
hands of all of them and e. jars, Ju 7.16
the LORD has brought me back e. Ru 1.21
God of Israel, do not send it e., 1Sa 6.03
because your seat will be e. 20.18
side, but David's place was e. 20.25
the new moon, David's place was e. 20.27
the sword of Saul returned not e. 2Sa 1.22
e. vessels and not too few. 2Ki 4.03

EMPTY (cont.)
would come and e. the chest and 2Ch 24.11
you comfort me with e. nothings? Job 21.34
You have sent widows away e., 22.09
Surely God does not hear an e. cry, 35.13
Job opens his mouth in e. talk, 35.16
he utters e. words, while his heart Ps 41.06
e. words grow many: but do you fear Ecc 5.07
they e. themselves on the earth; 11.03
and with an e. plea turn aside him Is 29.21
For Egypt's help is worthless and e., 30.07
their molten images are e. wind. 41.29
it shall not return to me e., 55.11
they rely on e. pleas, they speak 59.04
they return with their vessels e.; Jer 14.03
and e. his vessels, and break his 48.12
her, and they shall e. her land, 51.02
he has made me an e. vessel, 51.34
and e. out the broth, and let the Eze 24.10
Then set it e. upon the coals, that 24.11
with e. oaths they make covenants; Hos 10.04
dreams, and give e. consolation. Zec 10.02
do not heap up e. phrases as the Mt 6.07
and when he comes he finds it e., 12.44
and the rich he has sent e. away. Lk 1.53
Let no one deceive you with e. words, Eph 5.06
of you by philosophy and e. deceit, Col 2.08
e. talkers and deceivers, especially Tit 1.10

EMPTY-HANDED
now you would have sent me away e. Gen 31.42
None shall appear before me e. Ex 23.15
you, you shall not let him go e.; Deu 15.13
not appear before the LORD e.; 16.16
not go back e. to your mother-in-law.'" Ru 3.17
warrior who does not return e. Jer 50.09
and beat him, and sent him away e. Mk 12.03
beat him, and sent him away e. Lk 20.10
shamefully, and sent him away e. 20.11

EMPTYING
Is he then to keep on e. his net, Hab 1.17

ENABLES
the power which e. him even to Php 3.21

ENACTED
since it is e. on better promises. Heb 8.06

ENAIM
up, and sat at the entrance to E., Gen 38.14
who was at E. by the wayside?" 38.21

ENAM
Zanoah, Engannim, Tappuah, E., Jos 15.34

ENAN
from Naphtali, Ahira the son of E. Num 1.15
Naphtali being Ahira the son of E., 2.29
twelfth day Ahira the son of E., 7.78
offering of Ahira the son of E. 7.83
Naphtali was Ahira the son of E. 10.27

ENCAMP
turn back and e. in front of Ex 14.02
you shall e. over against it, by the 14.02
and shall e. around the tabernacle. Num 1.50
Levites shall e. around the 1.53
of Israel shall e. each by his own 2.02
they shall e. facing the tent of 2.02
Those to e. on the east side toward 2.03
Those to e. next to him shall be 2.05
And those to e. next to him shall 2.12
as they e., so shall they set out, 2.17
And those to e. next to him shall 2.27
Gershonites were to e. behind the 3.23
Kohath were to e. on the south 3.29
they were to e. on the north side 3.35
And those to e. before the tabernacle 3.38
how we are to e. in the wilderness, 10.31
E. outside the camp seven days; 31.19
they would e. against them and Ju 6.04
and e. against the city, and take it 2Sa 12.28
and e. round about my tent. Job 19.12
Though a host e. against me, my Ps 27.03
And I will e. against you round Is 29.03
E. round about her; let no one Jer 50.29
Then I will e. at my house as a Zec 9.08

ENCAMPED
and e. in the valley of Gerar and Gen 26.17
his kinsmen e. in the hill country 31.25
and e. at Etham, on the edge of the Ex 13.20
and overtook them e. at the sea, 14.09
and they e. there by the water. 15.27
where he was e. at the mountain of 18.05
they e. in the wilderness; 19.02
there Israel e. before the mountain. 19 02
so they e. by their standards, and Num 2.34
there the people of Israel e. 9.17
at the command of the LORD they e.; 9.18
At the command of the LORD they e., 9.23
and e. in the wilderness of Paran. 12.16
of Israel set out, and e. in Oboth. 21.10
and e. at Iyeabarim, in the wilderness 21.11
and e. in the Valley of Zered. 21.12
and e. on the other side of the 21.13
and e. in the plains of Moab beyond 22.01
from Rameses, and e. at Succoth. 33.05
and e. at Etham, which is on the 33.06
and they e. before Migdol. 33.07
wilderness of Etham, and e. at Marah. 33.08
palm trees, and they e. there. 33.09
from Elim, and e. by the Red Sea. 33.10
and e. in the wilderness of Sin. 33.11
wilderness of Sin, and e. at Dophkah. 33.12
out from Dophkah, and e. at Alush. 33.13
and e. at Rephidim, where there was 33.14
and e. in the wilderness of Sinai. 33.15
and e. at Kibrothhattaavah. 33.16
Kibrothhattaavah, and e. at Hazeroth. 33.17
from Hazeroth, and e. at Rithmah. 33.18
Rithmah, and e. at Rimmonperez. 33.19
from Rimmonperez, and e. at Libnah. 33.20
out from Libnah, and e. at Rissah. 33.21
from Rissah, and e. at Kehelathah. 33.22
and e. at Mount Shepher. 33.23
Mount Shepher, and e. at Haradah. 33.24
from Haradah, and e. at Makheloth. 33.25
from Makheloth, and e. at Tahath. 33.26
out from Tahath, and e. at Terah. 33.27
out from Terah, and e. at Mithkah. 33.28
from Mithkah, and e. at Hashmonah. 33.29
from Hashmonah, and e. at Moseroth. 33.30
Moseroth, and e. at Benejaakan. 33.31
and e. at Horhaggidgad. 33.32
Horhaggidgad, and e. at Jotbathah. 33.33
from Jotbathah, and e. at Abronah. 33.34
from Abronah, and e. at Eziongeber. 33.35
and e. in the wilderness of Zin 33.36
and e. at Mount Hor, on the edge of 33.37
from Mount Hor, and e. at Zalmonah. 33.41
out from Zalmonah, and e. at Punon. 33.42
out from Punon, and e. at Oboth. 33.43
and e. at Iyeabarim, in the territory 33.44
out from Iyim, and e. at Dibongad. 33.45
and e. at Almondiblathaim. 33.46
and e. in the mountains of Abarim, 33.47
and e. in the plains of Moab by the 33.48
they e. by the Jordan from Bethjeshimoth 33.49
and they e. in Gilgal on the east Jos 4.19
of Israel were e. in Gilgal they 5.10
and e. on the north side of Ai, with 8.11
their armies and e. against Gibeon, 10.05
and came and e. together at the 11.05

ENCAMPED (cont.)
the Jordan they e. in the Valley Ju 6.33
rose early and e. beside the 7.01
and e. against Thebez, and took it. 9.50
to arms, and they e. in Gilead; 10.17
together, and they e. at Mizpah. 10.17
and e. at Jahaz, and fought with 11.20
Philistines came up and e. in Judah, 15.09
and went up and e. at Kiriathjearim 18.12
the morning, and e. against Gibeah. 20.19
they e. at Ebenezer, and the Philistines 1Sa 4.01
and the Philistines e. at Aphek. 4.01
they came up and e. in Michmash, 13.05
but the Philistines e. in Michmash. 13.16
and e. between Soco and Azekah, in 17.01
and e. in the valley of Elah, and 17.02
And Saul e. on the hill of Hachilah, 26.03
to the place where Saul had e.; 26.05
while the army was e. around him. 26.05
assembled, and came and e. at Shunem; 28.04
all Israel, and they e. at Gilboa. 28.04
Israelites were e. by the fountain 29.01
and Absalom e. in the land of 2Sa 17.26
Philistines was e. in the valley 23.13
the troops were e. against Gibbethon, 1Ki 16.15
troops who were e. heard it said, 16.16
of Israel e. before them like two 20.27
And they e. opposite one another 20.29
Philistines was e. in the valley 1Ch 11.15
who came and e. before Medeba. 19.07
Judah and e. against the fortified 2Ch 32.01
Ahava, and there we e. three days. Ez 8.15
So they e. from Beersheba to the Neh 11.30
Ariel, the city where David e.! Is 29.01

ENCAMPING
and saw Israel e. tribe by tribe. Num 24.02

ENCAMPMENT
the main e. which was north of the Jos 8.13
he came to the e. as the host was 1Sa 17.20
Saul was lying within the e., 26.05
lay Saul sleeping within the e., 26.07

ENCAMPMENTS
by their villages and by their e., Gen 25.16
tents, O Jacob, your e., O Israel! Num 24.05
and all their e., they burned with 31.10
shall set their e. among you and Eze 25.04

ENCAMPS
of the LORD e. around those who Ps 34.07

ENCHANTER
of charmers or of the cunning e. Ps 58.05
of any magician or e. or Chaldean. Dan 2.10

ENCHANTERS
magicians and e. that were in all Dan 1.20
the e., the sorcerers, and the 2.02
e., magicians, or astrologers can 2.27
the e., the Chaldeans, and the 4.07
cried aloud to bring in the e., 5.07
e., Chaldeans, and astrologers, 5.11
the e., have been brought in before 5.15

ENCHANTMENT
For there is no e. against Jacob, Num 23.23

ENCHANTMENTS
and the great power of your e. Is 47.09
Stand fast in your e. and your many 47.12

ENCIRCLE
a company of evildoers e. me; Ps 22.16

ENCIRCLED
he e. him, he cared for him, he kept Deu 32.10
is a heap of wheat, e. with lilies. Sol 7.02
they had been e. for seven days. Heb 11.30

ENCLOSE
you shall e. them in settings of Ex 28.11
we will e. her with boards of cedar. Sol 8.09

ENCLOSED
e. in settings of gold filigree and Ex 39.06
they were e. in settings of gold 39.13
e. the dust of the earth in a Is 40.12
appearance of fire e. round about; Eze 1.27
they e. a great shoal of fish; Lk 5.06

ENCOMPASS
Many bulls e. me, strong bulls of Ps 22.12
thou dost e. me with dliverance. 32.07
Now their deeds e. them, Hos 7.02

ENCOMPASSED
"For the waves of death e. me, 2Sa 22.05
The cords of death e. me, Ps 18.04
For evils have e. me without number 40.12
The snares of death e. me; 116.03
Ephraim has e. me with lies, and the Hos 11.12

ENCOMPASSES
he e. him all the day long, and Deu 33.12
great slaughter, which e. them, Eze 21.14

ENCOUNTER
going to e. another king in war, Lk 14.31

ENCOURAGE
e. him, for he shall cause Israel to Deu 1.38
and e. and strengthen him; 3.28
overthrow it.' And e. him." 2Sa 11.25
and that he may e. your hearts. Eph 6.22
and that he may e. your hearts, Col 4.08
Therefore e. one another and build 1Th 5.11
e. the fainthearted, help the weak, 5.14

ENCOURAGED
offices and e. them in the service 2Ch 35.02
and you have e. the wicked, that he Eze 13.22
the brethren e. him, and wrote to Ac 18.27
Then they all were e. and ate some 27.36
may be mutually e. by each other's Rom 1.12
idol's temple, might he not be e., 1Co 8.10
that all may learn and all be e.; 14.31
hearts may be e. as they are knit Col 2.02
one of you and e. you and charged 1Th 2.11

ENCOURAGEMENT
Son of e.), a Levite, a native of Ac 4.36
parts and had given them much e., 20.02
and by the e. of the scriptures we Rom 15.04
steadfastness and e. grant you to 15.05
upbuilding and e. and consolation. 1Co 14.03
So if there is any e. in Christ, Php 2.01
have strong e. to seize the hope Heb 6.18

ENCOURAGES
The craftsman e. the goldsmith, and Is 41.07

ENCOURAGING
but e. one another, and all the more Heb 10.25

ENCOURAGINGLY
And Hezekiah spoke e. to all the 2Ch 30.22
of the city and spoke e. to them, 32.06

ENCRUSTED
is ivory work, e. with sapphires. Sol 5.14

END
determined to make an e. of all flesh; Gen 6.13
At the e. of a hundred and fifty 8.03

END (cont.)

At the e. of forty days Noah opened Gen 8.06
it is at the e. of his field. 23.09
in the land of Egypt came to an e.; 41.53
them from one e. of Egypt to the 47.21
And at the e. of four hundred and Ex 12.41
ingathering at the e. of the year, 23.16
Make one cherub on the one e., 25.19
and one cherub on the other e.; 25.19
shall pass through from e. to e. 26.28
he had made an e. of speaking with 31.18
of ingathering at the year's e. 34.22
through from e. to e. halfway up 36.33
one cherub on the one e., 37.08
and one cherub on the other e.; 37.08
he has made an e. of atoning for Lev 16.20
This is to the e. that the people 17.05
At the e. of forty days they Num 13.25
they shall come to a full e., 14.35
you may make an e. of their 17.10
righteous, and let my e. be like his 23.10
but in the e. he shall come to 24.20
be from the e. of the Salt Sea on 34.03
and its e. shall be south of 34.04
and the e. of the boundary shall be 34.08
and its e. shall be at Hazarenan; 34.09
and its e. shall be at the Salt Sea 34.12
ask from one e. of heaven to the Deu 4.32
may not make an e. of them at once, 7.22
test you, to do you good in the e. 8.16
And at the e. of forty days and 9.11
of the year to the e. of the year. 11.12
from the one e. of the earth to the 13.07
"At the e. of every three years you 14.28
"At the e. of every seven years you 15.01
have made an e. of speaking to the 20.09
from the e. of the earth, as swift 28.49
from one e. of the earth to the 28.64
"At the e. of every seven years, at 31.10
law in a book, to the very e., 31.24
I will see what their e. will be, 32.20
they would discern their latter e. 32.29
At the e. of three days the officers Jos 3.02
At the e. of three days after they 9.16
to the lower e. of the Sea of 13.27
ran from the e. of the Salt Sea, 15.02
and comes to its e. at the sea. 15.04
at the northern e. of the valley 15.08
boundary comes to an e. at the sea. 15.11
is at the north e. of the valley 18.16
at the south e. of the Jordan: this 18.19
And at the e. of two months, she Ju 11.39
until the e. of the barley and Ru 2.23
lie down at the e. of the heap of 3.07
his house, from beginning to e. 1Sa 3.12
know that the e. will be bitter? 2Sa 2.26
head (for at the e. of every year 14.26
And at the e. of four years Absalom 15.07
Jerusalem at the e. of nine months 24.08
happened at the e. of three years 1Ki 2.39
At the e. of twenty years, in which 9.10
one on each e. of a step on the six 10.20
And at the e. of the seven years, 2Ki 8.03
filled from one e. to the other. 10.21
he had made an e. of offering the 10.25
until you have made an e. of them." 13.17
until you had made an e. of it, 13.19
and at the e. of three years he 18.10
Jerusalem from one e. to another, 21.16
At the e. of twenty years, in which 2Ch 8.01
one on each e. of a step on the six 9.19
find them at the e. of the valley, 20.16
had made an e. of the inhabitants 20.23
at the e. of two years, his bowels 21.19
At the e. of the year the army of 24.23
filled it from e. to e. with their Ez 9.11
had come to the e. of all the men 10.17
Eliashib to the e. of the house of Neh 3.21
not make an e. of them or forsake 9.31
the wily are brought to a quick e. Job 5.13
And what is my e., 6.11
and come to their e. without hope. 7.06
Shall windy words have an e.? 16.03
There is no e. to your iniquities. 22.05
Men put an e. to darkness, and 28.03
my Maker soon put an e. to me. 32.22
Would that Job were tried to the e., 34.36
evil of the wicked come to an e., Ps 7.09
their words to the e. of the world. 19.04
is from the e. of the heavens, 19.06
and its circuit to the e. of them; 19.06
"LORD, let me know my e., 39.04
wars cease to the e. of the earth; 46.09
the e. of those who are pleased 49.13
thy faithfulness put an e. to them. 54.05
from the e. of the earth I call to 61.02
then I perceived their e. 73.17
dost put an e. to those who are 73.27
his promises at an e. for all time? 77.08
years come to an e. like a sigh. 90.09
the same, and thy years have no e. 102.27
to the e. that they should keep his 105.45
men, and were at their wits' e. 107.27
and I will keep it to the e. 119.33
almost made an e. of me on earth; 119.87
thy statutes for ever, to the e. 119.112
clouds rise at the e. of the earth, 135.07
but in the e. she is bitter as Pro 5.04
and at the e. of your life you 5.11
but its e. is the way to death. 14.12
and the e. of joy is grief. 14.13
but its e. is the way to death. 16.25
The lot puts an e. to disputes and 18.18
will in the e. not be blessed. 20.21
for what will you do in the e., 25.08
and your ill repute have no e. 25.10
will in the e. find him his heir. 29.21
done from the beginning to the e. Ecc 3.11
yet there is no e. to all his toil, 4.08
there was no e. of all the people; 4.16
for this is the e. of all men, 7.02
Better is the e. of a thing than 7.08
and the e. of his talk is wicked 10.13
making many books there is no e., 12.12
The e. of the matter; all has been 12.13
and there is no e. to their treasures; Is 2.07
and there is no e. to their chariots. 2.07
at the e. of the conduit of the 7.03
and of peace there will be no e., 9.07
LORD of hosts, will make a full e., 10.23
my indignation will come to an e., 10.25
from the e. of the heavens, the LORD 13.05
I will put an e. to the pride of 13.11
she has caused I bring to an e. 21.02
glory of Kedar will come to an e.; 21.16
At the e. of seventy years, it will 23.15
At the e. of seventy years, the LORD 23.17
to that e. thou hast visited them 26.14
have made an e. of dealing treacherously, 33.01
night thou dost bring me to an e.; 38.12
night thou dost bring me to an e. 38.13
praise from the e. of the earth! 42.10
daughters from the e. of the earth, 43.06
declaring the e. from the beginning 46.10
to heart or remember their e. 47.07
send it forth to the e. of the earth; 48.20
may reach to the e. of the earth." 49.06
proclaimed to the e. of the earth: 62.11
mice, shall come to an e. together, 66.17
and until the e. of the eleventh Jer 1.03
will he be indignant to the e.?' 3.05
yet I will not make a full e. 4.27
destroy, but make not a full e.; 5.10
I will not make a full e. of you. 5.18

END (cont.)
what will you do when the e. comes? Jer 5.31
"He will not see our latter e." 12.04
from one e. of the land to the 12.12
and at his e. he will be a fool. 17.11
extend from one e. of the earth to 25.33
make a full e. of all the nations 30.11
of you I will not make a full e. 30.11
'At the e. of six years each of you 34.14
At the e. of ten days the word of 42.07
until there is an e. of them. 44.27
make a full e. of all the nations 46.28
of you I will not make a full e. 46.28
And I will bring to an e. in Moab, 48.35
your e. has come, the thread of your 51.13
brought to an e. in Zion appointed Lam 2.06
his mercies never come to an e.; 3.22
our e. drew near; our days were 4.18
for our e. had come. 4.18
And at the e. of seven days, the Eze 3.16
GOD to the land of Israel: An e. 7.02
The e. has come upon the four 7.02
Now the e. is upon you, and I will 7.03
An e. has come, the e. has come; 7.06
I will put an e. to their proud 7.24
make a full e. of the remnant of 11.13
I will put an e. to this proverb, 12.23
wilderness, to make a full e. of them. 20.13
or make a full e. of them in the 20.17
Thus I will put an e. to your 23.27
Thus will I put an e. to lewdness 23.48
I will bring you to a dreadful e., 26.21
to a dreadful e. and shall be no 27.36
to a dreadful e. and shall be no 28.19
At the e. of forty years I will 29.13
I will put an e. to the wealth of 30.10
and put an e. to the images, in 30.13
proud might shall come to an e.; 30.18
proud might shall come to an e.; 33.28
at the e. of seven months they will 39.14
the gate at the inner e., one reed. 40.07
of the gate was at the inner e. 40.09
entrance to the e. of the inner 40.15
let there be an e. to all your 44.06
at the extreme western e. of them. 46.19
below the south e. of the threshold 47.01
and at the e. of that time they Dan 1.05
At the e. of ten days it was seen 1.15
At the e. of the time, when the king 1.18
kingdoms and bring them to an e., 2.44
visible to the e. of the whole 4.11
to the e. that the living may know 4.17
visible to the e. of the whole 4.20
At the e. of twelve months he was 4.29
At the e. of the days I, Nebuchadnezzar, 4.34
kingdom and brought it to an e.; 5.26
his dominion shall be to the e. 6.26
consumed and destroyed to the e. 7.26
"Here is the e. of the matter. 7.28
vision is for the time of the e." 8.17
at the latter e. of the indignation 8.19
to the appointed time of the e. 8.19
And at the latter e. of their rule, 8.23
pass before the e. of the desolations 9.02
to put an e. to sin, and to atone 9.24
Its e. shall come with a flood, and 9.26
and to the e. there shall be war; 9.26
the decreed e. is poured out on 9.27
shall put an e. to his insolence; 11.18
for the e. is yet to be at the time 11.27
white, until the time of the e., 11.35
"At the time of the e. the king of 11.40
yet he shall come to his e., 11.45
the book, until the time of the e. 12.04
it be till the e. of these wonders?" 12.06
comes to an e. all these things 12.07
sealed until the time of the e. 12.09
But go your way till the e.; 12.13
place at the e. of the days." 12.13
I will put an e. to the kingdom of Hos 1.04
And I will put an e. to all her 2.11
great houses shall come to an e.. Amo 3.15
"The e. has come upon my people 8.02
the poor of the land to an e., 8.04
and the e. of it like a bitter day. 8.10
make a full e. of his adversaries, Nah 1.08
He will make a full e.; he will 1.09
There is no e. of treasure, or 2.09
and booty—no e. to the plunder! 3.01
corpses, dead bodies without e.— 3.03
it hastens to the e.—it will not Hab 2.03
sudden e. he will make of all the Zep 1.18
I will make an e. of the pride of Zec 9.06
endures to the e. will be saved. Mt 10.22
take place, but the e. is not yet. 24.06
endures to the e. will be saved. 24.13
nations; and then the e. will come. 24.14
from one e. of heaven to the other. 24.31
sat with the guards to see the e. 26.58
stand, but is coming to an e. Mk 3.26
take place, but the e. is not yet. 13.07
endures to the e. will be saved. 13.13
of his kingdom there will be no e." Lk 1.33
And at the e. of eight days, when he 2.21
to dip the e. of his finger in 16.24
but the e. will not be at once. 21.09
the world, he loved them to the e. Jn 13.01
Samaria and to the e. of the earth." Ac 1.08
The e. of those things is death. Rom 6.21
sanctification and its e., eternal life. 6.22
For Christ is the e. of the law, 10.04
For to this e. Christ died and 14.09
who will sustain you to the e., 1Co 1.08
upon whom the e. of the ages has 10.11
Then comes the e., when he delivers 15.24
not see the e. of the fading 2Co 3.13
Their e. will correspond to their 11.15
bringing the hostility to an e. Eph 2.16
To that e. keep alert with all 6.18
Their e. is destruction, their god Php 3.19
To this e. we always pray for you, 2Th 1.11
For to this e. we toil and strive, 1Ti 4.10
same, and thy years will never e." Heb 1.12
first confidence firm to the e., 3.14
cursed; its e. is to be burned. 6.08
assurance of hope until the e., 6.11
beginning of days nor e. of life, 7.03
for all at the e. of the age to 9.26
at the e. of his life, made mention 11.22
manifest at the e. of the times 1Pe 1.20
The e. of all things is at hand; 4.07
will be the e. of those who do not 4.17
who keeps my works until the e., Rev 2.26
Omega, the beginning and the e. 21.06
the last, the beginning and the e." 22.13

ENDANGER
So you would e. my head with the Dan 1.10

ENDANGERED
he who splits logs is e. by them. Ecc 10.09

ENDEAVOR
But if, in our e. to be justified in Gal 2.17

ENDEAVORED
we e. the more eagerly and with 1Th 2.17

ENDED
And when that year was e., they came Gen 47.18
and mourning for Moses were e. Deu 34.08
Lakkum; and it e. at the Jordan; Jos 19.33
When Solomon had e. his prayer, 2Ch 7.01
The words of Job are e. Job 31.40
of David, the son of Jesse, are e. Ps 72.20

ENDED (cont.)
cry to her that her warfare is e., Is 40.02
my deliverance will never be e. 51.06
your days of mourning shall be e. 60.20
the summer is e., and we are not Jer 8.20
And when his time of service was e., Lk 1.23
and when the feast was e., as they 2.43
when they were e., he was hungry. 4.02
the devil had e. every temptation, 4.13
After he had e. all his sayings in 7.01
And when our days there were e., Ac 21.05
with them the wrath of God is e. Rev 15.01
seven plagues of the seven angels were e. 15.08
till the thousand years were e. 20.03
until the thousand years were e. 20.05
And when the thousand years are e., 20.07

ENDING
the eldest and e. with the youngest Gen 44.12
touchs Jericho, e. at the Jordan. Jos 16.07
Spirit, are you now e. with the flesh? Gal 3.03

ENDLESS
with myths and e. genealogies 1Ti 1.04

ENDOR
inhabitants of E. and its villages, Jos 17.11
"Behold, there is a medium at E." 1Sa 28.07
who were destroyed at E., who became Ps 83.10

ENDOWED
"God has e. me with a good dowry; Gen 30.20
whom I have e. with an able mind, Ex 28.03
e. with knowledge, understanding Dan 1.04

ENDOWING
e. with wealth those who love me, Pro 8.21

ENDOWMENT
Every good e. and every perfect Jas 1.17

ENDS
on the two e. of the mercy seat. Ex 25.18
make the cherubim on its two e. 25.19
the two e. of the two cords you 28.25
them at the two e. of the breastpiece, 28.26
on the two e. of the mercy seat he 37.07
he made the cherubim on its two e. 37.08
Two e. of the two cords they had 39.18
them at the two e. of the breastpiece, 39.19
of them, to the e. of the earth; Deu 33.17
of Enshemesh, and e. at Enrogel; Jos 15.07
to Gezer, and it e. at the sea. 16.03
the brook Kanah, and e. at the sea. 16.08
of the brook and e. at the sea; 17.09
and it e. at the wilderness of 18.12
and it e. at Kiriathbaal (that is, 18.14
the boundary e. at the northern 18.19
and it e. at the valley of Iphtahel; 19.14
and its boundary e. at the Jordan— 19.22
to Hosah, and it e. at the sea; 19.29
will judge the e. of the earth; 1Sa 2.10
long that the e. of the poles were 1Ki 8.08
long that the e. of the poles were 2Ch 5.09
For he looks to the e. of the earth, Job 28.24
youth, and their life e. in shame. 36.14
and the e. of the earth your possession. Ps 2.08
All the e. of the earth shall remember 22.27
reaches to the e. of the earth. 48.10
over Jacob to the e. of the earth. 59.13
hope of all the e. of the earth, 65.05
let all the e. of the earth fear 67.07
the River to the e. of the earth 72.08
All the e. of the earth have seen 98.03
of the righteous e. in gladness, Pro 10.28
of the righteous e. only in good; 11.23
a fool are on the e. of the earth. 17.24
established all the e. of the earth? 30.04
for it from the e. of the earth; Is 5.26
From the e. of the earth we hear 24.16
the Creator of the e. of the earth. 40.28
the e. of the earth tremble; they have 41.05
I took from the e. of the earth, 41.09
be saved, all the e. of the earth! 45.22
and all the e. of the earth shall 52.10
mist rise from the e. of the earth. Jer 10.13
come from the e. of the earth and 16.19
resound to the e. of the earth, 25.31
mist rise from the e. of the earth. 51.16
fire has consumed both e. of it, Eze 15.04
dominion to the e. of the earth. Dan 4.22
be great to the e. of the earth. Mic 5.04
the River to the e. of the earth. Zec 9.10
came from the e. of the earth to Mt 12.42
the e. of the earth to the e. of heaven. Mk 13.27
came from the e. of the earth to Lk 11.31
their words to the e. of the world. Rom 10.18
Love never e.; as for prophecy, 1Co 13.08

ENDUED
e. with discretion and understanding, 2Ch 2.12
e. with understanding, Huramabi, 2.13

ENDURANCE
By your e. you will gain your lives Lk 21.19
knowing that suffering produces e., Rom 5.03
and e. produces character, and 5.04
through great e., in afflictions, 2Co 6.04
for all e. and patience with joy, Col 1.11
For you have need of e., so that you Heb 10.36
and the kingdom and the patient e., Rev 1.09
your toil and your patient e., and how 2.02
faith and service and patient e., 2.19
have kept my word of patient e., 3.10
a call for the e. and faith of the 13.10
is a call for the e. of the saints, 14.12

ENDURE
you, then you will be able to e., Ex 18.23
For how can I e. to see the calamity Est 8.06
Or how can I e. to see the destruction 8.06
hold of it, but it does not e. Job 8.15
rich, and his wealth will not e., 15.29
therefore his prosperity will not e. 20.21
may his years e. to all generations! Ps 61.06
May his name e. for ever, his fame 72.17
His line shall e. for ever, his 89.36
and arrogant heart I will not e. 101.05
whose years e. throughout all 102.24
They will perish, but thou dost e.; 102.26
May the glory of the LORD e. for ever, 104.31
How long must thy servant e.? 119.84
Truthful lips e. for ever, but a Pro 12.19
A man's spirit will e. sickness; 18.14
word of a man who hears will e. 21.28
does a crown e. to all generations? 27.24
I cannot e. iniquity and solemn Is 1.13
nations cannot e. his indignation. Jer 10.10
Can your courage e., or can your Eze 22.14
he and his offspring shall not e.; Dan 11.06
very terrible; who can e. it? Joe 2.11
Who can e. the heat of his anger? Nah 1.06
But who can e. the day of his Mal 3.02
in themselves, but e. for a while; Mk 4.17
we bless; when persecuted, we e.; 1Co 4.12
but we e. anything rather than put 9.12
that you may be able to e. it. 10.13
you patiently e. the same sufferings 2Co 1.06
Therefore I e. everything for the 2Ti 2.10
if we e., we shall also reign with 2.12
people will not e. sound teaching, 4.03
e. suffering, do the work of an 4.05
for discipline that you have to e. Heb 12.07
For they could not e. the order 12.20

ENDURED
favor, all the hardships he e.; Ps 132.01
has e. with much patience the Rom 9.22
at Lystra, what persecutions I e.; 2Ti 3.11
And thus Abraham, having patiently e., Heb 6.15
you e. a hard struggle with sufferings, 10.32
for he e. as seeing him who is 11.27
was set before him e. the cross, 12.02
Consider him who e. from sinners 12.03

ENDURES
for his steadfast love e. for ever. 1Ch 16.34
for his steadfast love e. for ever. 16.41
for his steadfast love e. for ever, 2Ch 5.13
for his steadfast love e. for ever," 7.03
his steadfast love e. for ever— 7.06
for his steadfast love e. for ever." 20.21
steadfast love e. for ever toward Ez 3.11
Your divine throne e. for ever and Ps 45.06
May he live while the sun e., and as 72.05
his steadfast love e. for ever, 100.05
thy name e. to all generations. 102.12
for his steadfast love e. for ever! 106.01
for his steadfast love e. for ever! 107.01
and his righteousness e. for ever. 111.03
practice it. His praise e. for ever! 111.10
and his righteousness e. for ever. 112.03
his righteousness e. for ever; 112.09
faithfulness of the LORD e. for ever. 117.02
his steadfast love e. for ever! 118.01
"His steadfast love e. for ever." 118.02
"His steadfast love e. for ever." 118.03
"His steadfast love e. for ever." 118.04
for his steadfast love e. for ever! 118.29
Thy faithfulness e. to all generations; 119.90
righteous ordinances e. for ever. 119.160
e. for ever, thy renown, O LORD, 135.13
for his steadfast love e. for ever. 136.01
for his steadfast love e. for ever. 136.02
for his steadfast love e. for ever; 136.03
for his steadfast love e. for ever; 136.04
for his steadfast love e. for ever; 136.05
for his steadfast love e. for ever; 136.06
for his steadfast love e. for ever; 136.07
for his steadfast love e. for ever; 136.08
for his steadfast love e. for ever; 136.09
for his steadfast love e. for ever; 136.10
for his steadfast love e. for ever; 136.11
for his steadfast love e. for ever; 136.12
for his steadfast love e. for ever; 136.13
for his steadfast love e. for ever; 136.14
for his steadfast love e. for ever; 136.15
for his steadfast love e. for ever; 136.16
for his steadfast love e. for ever; 136.17
for his steadfast love e. for ever; 136.18
for his steadfast love e. for ever; 136.19
for his steadfast love e. for ever; 136.20
for his steadfast love e. for ever; 136.21
for his steadfast love e. for ever. 136.22
for his steadfast love e. for ever; 136.23
for his steadfast love e. for ever; 136.24
for his steadfast love e. for ever. 136.25
for his steadfast love e. for ever. 136.26
steadfast love, O LORD, e. for ever. 138.08
and thy dominion e. throughout all 145.13
that whatever God does e. for ever; Ecc 3.14
for his steadfast love e. for ever! Jer 33.11
thy throne e. to all generations. Lam 5.19
and his kingdom e. from generation Dan 4.34
But he who e. to the end will be Mt 10.22
but e. for a while, and when tribulation 13.21
But he who e. to the end will be 24.13
the food which e. to eternal life, Jn 6.27
hopes all things, e. all things. 1Co 13.07
But he who e. to the end will be Mk 13.13
his righteousness e. for ever. 2Co 9.09
Blessed is the man who e. trial, Jas 1.12
he e. pain while suffering unjustly. 1Pe 2.19

ENDURING
"E. is your dwelling place, and your Num 24.21
of the LORD is clean, e. for ever; Ps 19.09
with me, e. wealth and prosperity. Pro 8.18
fool there is no e. remembrance, Ecc 2.16
It is an e. nation, it is an ancient Jer 5.15
he is the living God, e. for ever; Dan 6.26
and you e. foundations of the earth; Mic 6.02
the afflictions which you are e. 2Th 1.04
I know you are e. patiently and Rev 2.03

ENEGLAIM
from Engedi to E. it will be a Eze 47.10

ENEMIES
delivered your e. into your hand!" Gen 14.20
possess the gate of their e., 22.17
shall be on the neck of your e.; 49.08
they join our e. and fight against Ex 1.10
enemy to your e. and an adversary 23.22
make all your e. turn their backs 23.27
to their shame among their e.), 32.25
And you shall chase your e., and they Lev 26.07
and your e. shall fall before you 26.08
in vain, for your e. shall eat it; 26.16
shall be smitten before your e.; 26.17
so that your e. who settle in it 26.32
hearts in the lands of their e.; 26.36
no power to stand before your e. 26.37
land of your e. shall eat you up. 26.38
them into the land of their e.; 26.41
they are in the land of their e., 26.44
you shall be saved from your e. Num 10.09
LORD, and let thy e. be scattered; 10.35
you be struck down before your e., 14.42
I took you to curse my e., and behold, 23.11
"I called you to curse my e., and 24.10
his e., shall be dispossessed, while 24.18
driven out his e. from before him 32.21
you be defeated before your e.' Deu 1.42
out all your e. from before you, as 6.19
rest from all your e. round about, 12.10
go forth to war against your e., 20.01
this day to battle against your e.: 20.03
to fight for you against your e., 20.04
shall enjoy the spoil of your e., 20.14
go forth to war against your e., 21.10
against your e. and are in camp, 23.09
and to give up your e. before you, 23.14
rest from all your e. round about, 25.19
will cause your e. who rise against 28.07
you to be defeated before your e.; 28.25
sheep shall be given to your e., 28.31
serve your e. whom the LORD will 28.48
with which your e. shall distress 28.53
sale to your e. as male and female 28.68
your foes and e. who persecuted 30.07
even our e. themselves being judges. 32.31
Your e. shall come fawning to you; 33.29
turned their backs before their e.! Jos 7.08
cannot stand before their e.; they turn 7.12
turn their backs before their e., 7.12
you cannot stand before your e., 7.13
nation took vengeance on their e. 10.13
pursue your e., fall upon their 10.19
do to all your e. against whom you 10.25
of all their e. had withstood them, 21.44
given all their e. into their 21.44
spoil of your e. with your brethren." 22.08
from all their e. round about, and 23.01
the power of their e. round about, Ju 2.14
could no longer withstand their e. 2.14
hand of their e. all the days of 2.18
has given your e. the Moabites 3.28

ENEMIES (cont.)

"So perish all thine e., O LORD! Ju 5.31
hand of all their e. on every side; 8.34
LORD has avenged you on your e., 11.36
My mouth derides my e., because I 1Sa 2.01
save us from the power of our e." 4.03
the hand of their e. round about. 10.01
us out of the hand of our e., 12.10
the hand of your e. on every side; 12.11
evening and I am avenged on my e." 14.24
spoil of their e. which they found 14.30
against all his e. on every side, 14.47
he may be avenged of the king's e.'" 18.25
one of the e. of David from the 20.15
LORD take vengeance on David's e." 20.16
then let your e. and those who 25.26
lives of your e. he shall sling 25.29
against the e. of my lord the king?" 29.08
the spoil of the e. of the LORD"; 30.26
and from the hand of all their e.'" 2Sa 3.18
has broken through my e. before me, 5.20
rest from all his e. round about. 7.01
off all your e. from before you; 7.09
give you rest from all your e. 7.11
him from the power of his e." 18.19
"May the e. of my lord the king, and 18.32
delivered us from the hand of our e., 19.09
him from the hand of all his e., 22.01
praised, and I am saved from my e. 22.04
I pursued my e. and destroyed them, 22.38
Thou didst make my e. turn their 22.41
who brought me out from my e.; 22.49
or riches or the life of your e., 1Ki 3.11
with which his e. surrounded him, 5.03
heart in the land of their e., 8.48
you out of the hand of all your e." 2Ki 17.39
them into the hand of their e., 21.14
prey and a spoil to all their e., 21.14
broken through my e. by my hand, 1Ch 14.11
off all your e. from before you; 17.08
and I will subdue all your e. 17.10
the sword of your e. overtakes you; 21.12
peace from all his e. round about; 22.09
if their e. besiege them in any 2Ch 6.28
go out to battle against their e., 6.34
made them rejoice over their e. 20.27
fought against the e. of Israel. 20.29
them into the hand of their e., 25.20
and from the hand of all his e.; 32.22
And our e. said, "They will not know Neh 4.11
When our e. heard that it was known 4.15
the taunts of the nations our e.? 5.09
the rest of our e. that I had 6.01
And when all our e. heard of it, 6.16
them into the hand of their e., 9.27
them from the hand of their e. 9.27
them to the hand of their e., 9.28
to avenge themselves upon their e. Est 8.13
day when the e. of the Jews hoped 9.01
smote all their e. with the sword. 9.05
and got relief from their e., 9.16
the Jews got relief from their e., 9.22
dost smite all my e. on the cheek, Ps 3.07
thy righteousness because of my e.; 5.08
All my e. shall be ashamed and 6.10
up against the fury of my e.; awake, 7.06
When my e. turned back, they stumbled 9.03
my deadly e. who surround me. 17.09
praised, and I am saved from my e. 18.03
I pursued my e. and overtook them; 18.37
Thou didst make my e. turn their 18.40
who delivered me from my e.; yea, thou 18.48
Your hand will find out all your e.; 21.08
before me in the presence of my e.; 23.05
shame; let not my e. exult over me. 25.02
up above my e. round about me; 27.06
on a level path because of my e. 27.11
the hand of my e. and persecutors! 31.15
the e. of the LORD are like the 37.20
give him up to the will of his e. 41.02
My e. say of me in malice: "When 41.05
and our e. have gotten spoil. 44.10
in the heart of the king's e.; 45.05
He will requite my e. with evil; 54.05
eye has looked in triumph on my e. 54.07
my e. trample upon me all day long, 56.02
Then my e. will be turned back in 56.09
Deliver me from my e., O my God, 59.01
let me look in triumph on my e. 59.10
power that thy e. cringe before 66.03
God arise, let his e. be scattered; 68.01
will shatter the heads of his e., 68.21
delivered from my e. and from the 69.14
me, set me free because of my e. 69.18
For my e. speak concerning me, those 71.10
him, and his e. lick the dust 72.09
but the sea overwhelmed their e. 78.53
and our e. laugh among themselves. 80.06
I would soon subdue their e., and turn 81.14
For lo, thy e. are in tumult; those 83.02
scatter thy e. with thy mighty arm. 89.10
thou hast made all his e. rejoice. 89.42
with which thy e. taunt, O LORD, with 89.51
For, lo, thy e., O LORD, for, lo, thy e. shall 92.09
have seen the downfall of my e., 92.11
All the day my e. taunt me, those 102.08
Their e. oppressed them, and they 106.42
till I make your e. your footstool." 110.01
commandment makes me wiser than my e., 119.98
he speaks with his e. in the gate. 127.05
His e. I will clothe with shame, but 132.18
hand against the wrath of my e., 138.07
perfect hatred; I count them my e. 139.22
Deliver me, O LORD, from my e.! 143.09
thy steadfast love cut off my e., 143.12
makes even his e. to be at peace Pro 16.07
"Ah, I will vent my wrath on my e., Is 1.24
them, and stirs up their e. 9.11
adversaries, requital to his e.; 59.18
your grain to be food for your e., 62.08
rendering recompense to his e.! 66.06
his indignation is against his e. 66.14
my soul into the hands of her e. Jer 12.07
before their e., says the LORD." 15.09
you serve your e. in a land which 15.14
you serve your e. in a land which 17.04
fall by the sword before their e., 19.07
which their e. and those who seek 19.09
sword of their e. while you look 20.04
of Judah into the hand of their e., 20.05
and into the hand of their e., into 21.07
hand of their e. and into the hand 34.20
hand of their e. and into the hand 34.21
the hand of his e. and into the 44.30
for her e. march in force, and come 46.22
I will terrify Elam before their e., 49.37
and their e. have said. 'We are not 50.07
with her, they have become her e. Lam 1.02
her e. prosper, because the LORD has 1.05
All my e. have heard of my trouble; 1.21
All your e. rail against you; they hiss, 2.16
"All our e. rail against us; 3.46
those who were my e. without cause; 3.52
you to the greed of your e., the Eze 16.27
and its interpretation for your e.! Dan 4.19
go into captivity before their e., Amo 9.04
redeem you from the hand of your e. Mic 4.10
and all your e. shall be cut off. 5.09
a man's e. are the men of his own 7.06
adversaries and keeps wrath for his e. Nah 1.02
will pursue his e. into darkness. 1.08
against you, he has cast out your e. Zep 3.15

ENEMIES (cont.)
Love your e. and pray for those who Mt 5.44
till I put thy e. under thy feet'? 22.44
till I put thy e. under thy feet.' Mk 12.36
that we should be saved from our e., Lk 1.71
delivered from the hand of our e., 1.74
Love your e., do good to those who 6.27
But love your e., and do good, and 6.35
But as for these e. of mine, who did 19.27
when your e. will cast up a bank 19.43
till I make thy e. a stool for thy 20.43
till I make thy e. a stool for thy Ac 2.35
while we were e. we were reconciled Rom 5.10
the gospel they are e. of God, 11.28
has put all his e. under his feet. 1Co 15.25
live as e. of the cross of Christ. Php 3.18
till I make thy e. a stool for thy Heb 1.13
wait until his e. should be made a 10.13

ENEMIES'
while you are in your e. land; Lev 26.34
away in your e. lands because of 26.39
gathered them from their e. lands, Eze 39.27

ENEMY
So the e. took all the goods of Gen 14.11
hand, O LORD, shatters the e. Ex 15.06
The e. said, 'I will pursue, I will 15.09
I will be an e. to your enemies 23.22
delivered into the hand of the e. Lev 26.25
he died, though he was not his e., Num 35.23
with which your e. shall distress Deu 28.55
with which your e. shall distress 28.57
I not feared provocation by the e., 32.27
the long-haired heads of the e.' 32.42
he thrust out the e. before you, 33.27
given Samson our e. into our hand." Ju 16.23
god has given our e. into our hand, 16.24
So Saul was David's e. continually. 1Sa 18.29
and let my e. go, so that he has 19.17
I will give your e. into your hand, 24.04
For if a man finds his e., will he 24.19
has given your e. into your hand 26.08
turned from you and become your e.? 28.16
your e., who sought your life; 2Sa 4.08
He delivered me from my strong e., 22.18
before the e. because they have 1Ki 8.33
if their e. besieges them in any of 8.37
go out to battle against their e., 8.44
them, and dost give them to an e., 8.46
away captive to the land of the e., 8.46
Elijah, "Have you found me O my e.?" 21.20
before the e. because they have 2Ch 6.24
them, and dost give them to an e., 6.36
will cast you down before the e.; 25.08
to help the king against the e. 26.13
us against the e. on our way; since we Ez 8.22
the hand of the e. and from ambushes 8.31
of Hammedatha, the e. of the Jews. Est 3.10
And Esther said, "A foe and e.! 7.06
house of Haman, the e. of the Jews. 8.01
of Hammedatha, the e. of the Jews; 9.10
the e. of all the Jews, had plotted 9.24
thy face, and count me as thy e.? Job 13.24
"Let my e. be as the wicked, and let 27.07
against me, he counts me as his e.; 33.10
or plundered my e. without cause, Ps 7.04
let the e. pursue me and overtake 7.05
to still the e. and the avenger. 8.02
The e. have vanished in everlasting 9.06
long shall my e. be exalted over 13.02
lest my e. say, "I have prevailed 13.04
He delivered me from my strong e., 18.17
delivered me into the hand of the e.; 31.08
in that my e. has not triumphed 41.11
because of the oppression of the e.?" 42.09
because of the oppression of the e.? 43.02
sight of the e. and the avenger. 44.16
distraught by the noise of the e., 55.03
It is not an e. who taunts me—then 55.12
refuge, a strong tower against the e. 61.03
preserve my life from dread of the e., 64.01
the e. has destroyed everything in 74.03
Is the e. to revile thy name for 74.10
how the e. scoffs, and an impious 74.18
The e. shall not outwit him, the 89.22
them from the power of the e. 106.10
For the e. has pursued me; he has 143.03
Do not rejoice when your e. falls, Pro 24.17
If your e. is hungry, give him bread 25.21
friend; profuse are the kisses of an e. 27.06
therefore he turned to be their e., Is 63.10
for the e. has a sword, terror is on Jer 6.25
behalf of the e. in the time of 15.11
I will scatter them before the e. 18.17
I have dealt you the blow of an e., 30.14
come back from the land of the e. 31.16
who was his e. and sought his life. 44.30
affliction, for the e. has triumphed!" Lam 1.09
The e. has stretched out his hands 1.10
desolate for the e. has prevailed." 1.16
right hand in the face of the e.; 2.03
He has bent his bow like an e., with his 2.04
The Lord has become like an e., he has 2.05
the hand of the e. the walls of 2.07
he has made the e. rejoice over you, 2.17
dandled and reared my e. destroyed. 2.22
that foe or e. could enter the 4.12
Because the e. said of you, 'Aha!' Eze 36.02
the good; the e. shall pursue him. Hos 8.03
rise against my people as an e.; Mic 2.08
Rejoice not over me, O my e.; 7.08
Then my e. will see, and shame will 7.10
you will seek a refuge from the e. Nah 3.11
your neighbor and hate your e.' Mt 5.43
his e. came and sowed weeds among 13.25
said to them, 'An e. has done this.' 13.28
and the e. who sowed them in the 13.39
and over all the power of the e.; Lk 10.19
you e. of all righteousness, full of Ac 13.10
No, "if your e. is hungry, feed him; Rom 12.20
The last e. to be destroyed is 1Co 15.26
become your e. by telling you the Gal 4.16
Do not look on him as an e., but 2Th 3.15
and give the e. no occasion to 1Ti 5.14
world makes himself an e. of God. Jas 4.04

ENEMY'S
"If you meet your e. ox or his ass Ex 23.04

ENERGY
with all the e. which he mightily Col 1.29

ENFORCE
an ordinance and e. an interdict, Dan 6.07

ENFORCED
e. justice, received promises, Heb 11.33

ENGAGED
So those who were e. in the work 2Ch 24.13
were glad, and e. to give him money. Lk 22.05
e. in the same conflict which you Php 1.30

ENGANNIM
Zanoah, E., Tappuah, Enam, Jos 15.34
Remeth, E., Enhaddah, Bethpazzez; 19.21
E. with its pasture lands—four 21.29

ENGEDI
Salt, and E.: six cities with their Jos 15.62
and dwelt in the strongholds of E. 1Sa 23.29
David is in the wilderness of E." 24.01
are in Hazazontamar" (that is, E.). 2Ch 20.02

ENGEDI (cont.)
blossoms in the vineyards of E. Sol 1.14
from E. to Eneglaim it will be a Eze 47.10

ENGINES
In Jerusalem he made e., invented 2Ch 26.15

ENGRAVE
and e. on them the names of the Ex 28.09
so shall you e. the two stones with 28.11
and e. on it, like the engraving of 28.36
I will e. its inscription, says the Zec 3.09

ENGRAVED
each e. with its name, for the Ex 28.21
filigree and e. like the engravings 39.06
each e. with its name, for the 39.14
diamond it is e. on the tablet of Jer 17.01

ENGRAVES
As a jeweler e. signets, so shall Ex 28.11

ENGRAVING
like the e. of a signet, 'Holy to Ex 28.36
like the e. of a signet, "Holy to 39.30
blue fabrics, trained also in e., 2Ch 2.07
do all sorts of e. and execute any 2.14

ENGRAVINGS
engraved like the e. of a signet, Ex 39.06
were your settings and your e. Eze 28.13

ENHADDAH
Remeth, Engannim, E., Bethpazzez; Jos 19.21

ENHAKKORE
the name of it was called E.; Ju 15.19

ENHAZOR
Kedesh, Edrei. E., Jos 19.37

ENJOIN
words which I e. upon you this day, Deu 32.46
marriage and e. abstinence from 1Ti 4.03

ENJOINED
and Queen Esther e. upon the Jews, Est 9.31
of all that I have e. upon her.' Zep 3.07
And the angel of the LORD e. Joshua, Zec 3.06

ENJOINING
e. them that they should keep the Est 9.21

ENJOY
"Then the land shall e. its sabbaths Lev 26.34
shall rest, and e. its sabbaths. 26.34
and e. its sabbaths while it lies 26.43
and another man e. its fruit. Deu 20.06
and you shall e. the spoil of your 20.14
our fathers to e. its fruit and Neh 9.36
that he may e., like a hireling, his Job 14.06
many days, that he may e. good? Ps 34.12
dwell in the land, and e. security. 37.03
but the upright e. his favor. Pro 14.09
test of pleasure; e. yourself." Ecc 2.01
to be happy and e. themselves as 3.12
than that a man should e. his work, 3.22
possessions and power to e. them, 5.19
does not give him power to e. them, 6.02
but he does not e. life's good 6.03
yet e. no good—do not all go to 6.06
and e. himself, for this will go 8.15
E. life with the wife whom you love, 9.09
shall long e. the work of their Is 65.22
plentiful land to e. its fruits and Jer 2.07
plant, and shall e. the fruit. 31.05
"Since through you we e. much peace, Ac 24.02
furnishes us with everything to e. 1Ti 6.17
of God than to e. the fleeting Heb 11.25

ENJOYED
vineyard and has not e. its fruit? Deu 20.06
until the land had e. its sabbaths. 2Ch 36.21
leave all to be e. by a man who Ecc 2.21
once I have e. your company for a Rom 15.24

ENJOYMENT
of his trading he will get no e. Job 20.18
and drink, and find e. in his toil. Ecc 2.24
him who can eat or who can have e.? 2.25
drink and find e. in all the toil 5.18
his lot and find e. in his toil— 5.19
And I commend e., for man has no 8.15
Go, eat your bread with e., and drink 9.07

ENJOYS
enjoy them, but a stranger e. them; Ecc 6.02

ENLARGE
God e. Japheth, and let him dwell in Gen 9.27
before you. and e. your borders; Ex 34.24
wouldst bless me and e. my border, 1Ch 4.10
E. the place of your tent, and let Is 54.02
that you e. your eyes with paint? Jer 4.30
that they might e. their border. Amo 1.13

ENLARGED
Therefore Sheol has e. its appetite Is 5.14
thou hast e. all the borders of the 26.15
field among you may be greatly e., 2Co 10.15

ENLARGEMENT
corresponding to the e. of the Eze 41.07

ENLARGES
LORD your God e. your territory, Deu 12.20
the LORD your God e. your border, 19.08
he said, "Blessed be he who e. Gad! 33.20
he e. nations, and leads them away. Job 12.23

ENLARGEST
when thou e. my understanding Ps 119.32

ENLIGHTENED
a zeal for God, but it is not e. Rom 10.02
having the eyes of your hearts e., Eph 1.18
those who have once been e., who have Heb 6.04
days when, after you were e., you 10.32

ENLIGHTENING
of the LORD is pure, e. the eyes; Ps 19.08

ENLIGHTENMENT
Whom did he consult for his e., Is 40.14

ENLIGHTENS
The true light that e. every man Jn 1.09

ENLISTED
is to satisfy the one who e. him. 2Ti 2.04

ENMISHPAT
turned back and came to E.(that is, Gen 14.07

ENMITY
I will put e. between you and the Gen 3.15
or in e. struck him down with his Num 35.21
he stabbed him suddenly without e., 35.22
being at e. with him in time past, Deu 4.42
having been at e. with him in time 19.04
he was not at e. with his neighbor 19.06
having had no e. against him in Jos 20.05
anger they cherish e. against me. Ps 55.03
to destroy in never-ending e.; Eze 25.15
Because you cherished perpetual e., 35.05
had been at e. with each other. Lk 23.12
e., strife, jealousy, anger, selfishness, Gal 5.20
with the world is e. with God? Jas 4.04

ENOCH
and she conceived and bore E.; Gen 4.17
city after the name of his son, E. 4.17
To E. was born Irad; and Irad was 4.18
years he became the father of E. 5.18
the birth of E. eight hundred 5.19
When E. had lived sixty-five years, 5.21
E. walked with God after the birth 5.22
Thus all the days of E. were three 5.23
E. walked with God; and he was 5.24
E., Methuselah, Lamech; 1Ch 1.03
the son of E., the son of Jared, the Lk 3.37
By faith E. was taken up so that he Heb 11.05
these also that E. in the seventh Jud 1.14

ENOS
the son of E.. the son of Seth, the Lk 3.38

ENOSH
born, and he called his name E. Gen 4.26
years, he became the father of E. 5.06
the birth of E. eight hundred and 5.07
When E. had lived ninety years, he 5.09
E. lived after the birth of Kenan 5.10
Thus all the days of E. were nine 5.11
Adam, Seth, E.; 1Ch 1.01

ENOUGH
Behold, yonder city is near e. to flee to, Gen 19.20
have both straw and provender e., 24.25
But Esau said, "I have e., my brother; 33.09
with me, and because I have e." 33.11
the land is large e. for them; 34.21
and Israel said, "It is e.; Joseph 45.28
there has been e. of this thunder Ex 9.28
much more than e. for doing the 36.05
stayed long e. at this mountain; Deu 1.06
this mountain country long e.; 2.03
"The hill country is not e. for us; Jos 17.16
Have we not had e. of the sin at 22.17
he wrung e. dew from the fleece to Ju 6.38
but left e. for a hundred chariots. 2Sa 8.04
destruction among the people, "It is e.; 24.16
have gone up to Jerusalem long e. 1Ki 12.28
he might die, saying, "It is e.; 19.04
but left e. for a hundred chariots. 1Ch 18.04
to the destroying angel, "It is e.; 21.15
eaten and had e. and have plenty 2Ch 31.10
his offspring have not e. to eat. Job 27.14
their children have more than e.; Ps 17.14
have had more than e. of contempt. 123.03
The righteous has e. to satisfy his Pro 13.25
wealth; be wise e. to desist. 23.04
eat only e. for you, lest you be 25.16
there will be e. goats' milk for 27.27
satisfied; four never say, "E.": 30.15
and the fire which never says, "E." 30.16
I have had e. of burnt offerings of Is 1.11
are its beasts e. for a burnt 40.16
they never have e. The shepherds 56.11
not destroy only e. for themselves? Jer 49.09
and to Assyria, to get bread e. Lam 5.06
Is it not e. for you to feed on the Eze 34.18
E., O princes of Israel! Put away 45.09
it was deep e. to swim in, a river 47.05
not steal only e. for themselves? Ob 1.05
well to be angry, angry e. to die." Jon 4.09
The lion tore e. for his whelps and Nah 2.12
like death he has never e. He gathers Hab 2.05
you eat, but you never have e.; Hag 1.06
it is e. for the disciple to be Mt 10.25
we to get bread e. in the desert 15.33
will not be e. for us and for you; 25.09
It is e.; the hour has come; Mk 14.41
whether he has e. to complete it? Lk 14.28
servants have bread e. and to spare, 15.17
I am not strong e. to dig, and I am 16.03
And he said to them, "It is e." 22.38
would not buy e. bread for each Jn 6.07
and you have been kind e. to come. Ac 10.33
And when they had eaten e., they 27.38
among you wise e. to decide 1Co 6.05
For you may give thanks well e., 14.17
punishment by the majority is e.; 2Co 2.06
may always have e. of everything 9.08
accepted, you submit to it readily e. 11.04
I am bold e. in Christ to command Phm 1.08

ENRAGED
mighty men, and that they are e., 2Sa 17.08
wall, he was angry and greatly e., Neh 4.01
At this the king was e., and his Est 1.12
they will be e. and will curse Is 8.21
For the LORD is e. against all the 34.02
And the princes were e. at Jeremiah, Jer 37.15
but have e. me with all these Eze 16.43
and he was e. against him and struck Dan 8.07
back and be e. and take action 11.30
this they were e. and wanted to Ac 5.33
heard these things they were e., 7.54
When they heard this they were e., 19.28

ENRICH
the king will e. with great riches, 1Sa 17.25

ENRICHED
A liberal man will be e., and one Pro 11.25
who trusts in the LORD will be e. 28.25
merchandise you e. the kings of Eze 27.33
way you were e. in him with all 1Co 1.05
You will be e. in every way for 2Co 9.11

ENRICHEST
waterest it, thou greatly e. it; Ps 65.09

ENRIMMON
E., Ether, and Ashan—four cities Jos 19.07
in E., in Zorah, in Jarmuth, Neh 11.29

ENROGEL
waters of Enshemesh, and ends at E.; Jos 15.07
the Jebusites, and downward to E.; 18.16
and Ahimaaz were waiting at E.; 2Sa 17.17
Serpent's Stone, which is beside E., 1Ki 1.09

ENROL
But refuse to e. younger widows; 1Ti 5.11

ENROLLED
that he is not e. in the genealogy 1Ch 5.01
All of these were e. by genealogies 5.17
mighty warriors, e. by genealogy. 7.05
Their number e. by genealogies, for 7.40
So all Israel was e. by genealogies; 9.01
They were e. by genealogies in 9.22
except those e. by genealogy, males 2Ch 31.16
The priests were e. with all their 31.18
one among the Levites who was e. 31.19
among those e. in the genealogies, Ez 2.62
the people to be e. by genealogy. Neh 7.05
among those e. in the genealogies, 7.64
let them not be e. among the Ps 69.28
nor be e. in the register of the Eze 13.09
that all the world should be e. Lk 2.01
And all went to be e., each to 2.03
to be e. with Mary, his betrothed, 2.05
and he was e. with the eleven Ac 1.26
Let no one be e. as a widow who is 1Ti 5.09
first-born who are e. in heaven, Heb 12.23

ENROLLMENT
and their e. by genealogies was 1Ch 7.07
and their e. by genealogies, 7.09
The e. of the priests was according 2Ch 31.17
This was the first e., when Lk 2.02

ENSHEMESH
passes along to the waters of E., Jos 15.07
northerly direction going on to E., 18.17

ENSIGN
stand as an e. to the peoples; Is 11.10
He will raise an e. for the nations, 11.12
lift up an e. over the peoples. 62.10
was your sail, serving as your e.; Eze 27.07

ENSIGNS
with the e. of their fathers' houses; Num 2.02

ENSLAVE
so that no one should e. a Jew, Jer 34.09
who would e. them and ill-treat Ac 7.06

ENSLAVED
our daughters have already been e.; Neh 5.05
so that they would not be e. again; Jer 34.10
from the hand of those who e. them. Eze 34.27
we might no longer be e. to sin. Rom 6.06
but I will not be e. by anything. 1Co 6.12
overcomes a man, to that he is e. 2Pe 2.19

ENSNARE
that he should not e. the people. Job 34.30
let the net which they hid e. them; Ps 35.08
Though the cords of the wicked e. me, 119.61
The iniquities of the wicked e. him, Pro 5.22

ENSNARED
yourselves, lest you be e. by it; Deu 7.25
that you be not e. to follow them, 12.30
An evil man is e. by the transgression Pro 12.13
An evil man is e. in his transgression, 29.06

ENTANGLE
his ways and e. yourself in a Pro 22.25
counsel how to e. him in his talk. Mt 22.15

ENTANGLED
Israel, 'They are e. in the land; Ex 14.03
the cords of Sheol e. me, the snares 2Sa 22.06
the cords of Sheol e. me, the snares Ps 18.05
Like e. thorns they are consumed, Nah 1.10
on service gets e. in civilian 2Ti 2.04
they are again e. in them and 2Pe 2.20

ENTAPPUAH
southward to the inhabitants of E. Jos 17.07

ENTER
When he was about to e. Egypt, Gen 12.11
destroyer to e. your houses to Ex 12.23
was not able to e. the tent of 40.35
all who can e. the service, to do Num 4.03
all who can e. for service, to do 4.23
every one that can e. the service, 4.30
one that could e. the service, 4.35
one that could e. the service for 4.39
one that could e. the service, 4.43
one that could e. to do the work 4.47
the curse shall e. into her and 5.24
the curse shall e. into her and 5.27
he shall not e. the land which I 20.24
When you e. the land of Canaan 34.02
who stands before you, he shall e.; Deu 1.38
I should not e. the good land 4.21
off shall not e. the assembly of 23.01
"No bastard shall e. the assembly 23.02
descendants shall e. the assembly of 23.02
Moabite shall e. the assembly of 23.03
to them shall e. the assembly of 23.03
to them may e. the assembly of the 23.08
pass over to e. the land which the 27.03
that you may e. into the sworn 29.12
over the Jordan to e. and possess. 30.18
do not let them e. their cities; Jos 10.19
they did not e. the territory of Ju 11.18
and e. in and possess the land. 18.09
and all who e. the house of Dagon 1Sa 5.05
did not again e. the territory of 7.13
As soon as you e. the city, you will 9.13
"You shall not e. into marriage 1Ki 11.02
When your feet e. the city, 14.12
'Let us e. the city,' the famine is 2Ki 7.04
could not e. the house of the LORD, 2Ch 7.02
Let no one e. the house of the LORD 23.06
they may e., for they are holy, 23.06
no one should e. who was in any 23.19
their fathers to e. and possess. Neh 9.23
and e. into a curse and an oath to 10.29
should ever e. the assembly of God 13.01
no one might e. the king's gate Est 4.02
steadfast love will e. thy house, Ps 5.07
their sword shall e. their own 37.15
along as they e. the palace of the 45.15
that they should not e. my rest. 95.11
E. his gates with thanksgiving, and 100.04
that I may e. through them and give 118.19
the righteous shall e. through it. 118.20
"I will not e. my house or get into 132.03
E. not into judgment with thy 143.02
Do not e. the path of the wicked, Pro 4.14
landmark or e. the fields of the 23.10
E. into the rock, and hide in the Is 2.10
And men shall e. the caves of the 2.19
to e. the caverns of the rocks and 2.21
for them to e. the gates of the 13.02
is shut up so that none can e. 24.10
nation which keeps faith may e. in. 26.02
e. your chambers, and shut your 26.20
squares, and uprightness cannot e. 59.14
they e. thickets; they climb Jer 4.29
of Judah who e. these gates to 7.02
And if I e. the city, behold, the 14.18
Do not e. the house of mourning, or 16.05
kings of Judah e. and by which 17.19
Jerusalem, who e. by these gates. 17.20
then there shall e. by the gates of 17.25
a burden and e. by the gates of 17.27
or who shall e. our habitations?' 21.13
and your people who e. these gates. 22.02
there shall e. the gates of this 22.04
nor did it e. into my mind, that 32.35
your faces to e. Egypt and go to 42.15
didst forbid to e. thy congregation. Lam 1.10
or enemy could e. the gates of 4.12
robbers shall e. and profane it, Eze 7.22
nor shall they e. the land of 13.09
to Babylon and e. into judgment 17.20
there I will e. into judgment with 20.35
so I will e. into judgment with you, 20.36
they shall not e. the land of 20.38
I will cause breath to e. you, 37.05
bloodshed I will e. into judgment 38.22
When the priests e. the holy place, 42.14
opened, and no one shall e. by it; 44.02
he shall e. by way of the vestibule 44.03
of Israel, shall e. my sanctuary. 44.09
they shall e. my sanctuary, and they 44.16
When they e. the gates of the inner 44.17
The prince shall e. by the vestibule 46.02
the army and e. the fortress of Dan 11.07
E. not into Gilgal, nor go up to Hos 4.15
they e. through the windows like a Joe 2.09
and I will e. into judgment with 3.02
and do not e. into Gilgal or cross Amo 5.05
and it shall e. the house of the Zec 5.04
you will never e. the kingdom of Mt 5.20
"E. by the narrow gate; for the gate 7.13
and those who e. by it are many. 7.13

ENTER (cont.)

shall e. the kingdom of heaven, Mt 7.21
and e. no town of the Samaritans, 10.05
And whatever town or village you e., 10.11
As you e. the house, salute it. 10.12
Or how can one e. a strong man's 12.29
and they e. and dwell there; 12.45
you will never e. the kingdom of 18.03
for you to e. life maimed or lame 18.08
for you to e. life with one eye 18.09
If you would e. life, keep the 19.17
a rich man to e. the kingdom of 19.23
a rich man to e. the kingdom of 19.24
for you neither e. yourselves, 23.13
allow those who would e. to go in. 23.13
e. into the joy of your master.' 25.21
e. into the joy of your master.' 25.23
you may not e. into temptation; 26.41
could no longer openly e. a town, Mk 1.45
But no one can e. a strong man's 3.27
e. in and choke the word, and it 4.19
us to the swine, let us e. them." 5.12
"Where you e. a house, stay there 6.10
saying, "Do not even e. the village." 8.26
out of him, and never e. him again." 9.25
for you to e. life maimed than 9.43
for you to e. life lame than with 9.45
for you to e. the kingdom of God 9.47
God like a child shall not e. it." 10.15
have riches to e. the kingdom of 10.23
hard it is to e. the kingdom of 10.24
a rich man to e. the kingdom of 10.25
immediately as you e. it you will 11.02
nor e. his house, to take anything 13.15
you may not e. into temptation. 14.38
him by lot to e. the temple of the Lk 1.09
that those who e. may see the 8.16
begged him to let them e. these. 8.32
he permitted no one to e. with him, 8.51
And whatever house you e., stay there, 9.04
Whatever house you e., first say, 10.05
Whenever you e. a town and they 10.08
But whenever you e. a town and they 10.10
and they e. and dwell there; 11.26
that those who e. may see the 11.33
you did not e. yourselves, and you 11.52
"Strive to e. by the narrow door; 13.24
will seek to e. and will not be 13.24
God like a child shall not e. it." 18.17
have riches to e. the kingdom of 18.24
a rich man to e. the kingdom of 18.25
who are out in the country e. it; 21.21
you may not e. into temptation." 22.40
you may not e. into temptation." 22.46
these things and e. into his glory?" 24.26
Can he e. a second time into his Jn 3.04
he cannot e. the kingdom of God. 3.05
he who does not e. the sheepfold 10.01
themselves did not e. the praetorium, 18.28
but rise and e. the city, and you Ac 9.06
tribulations we must e. the kingdom 14.22
and outsiders or unbelievers e., 1Co 14.23
'They shall never e. my rest.'" Heb 3.11
that they should never e. his rest, 3.18
were unable to e. because of 3.19
For we who have believed e. that rest, 4.03
'They shall never e. my rest,'" 4.03
said, "They shall never e. my rest." 4.05
it remains for some to e. it, 4.06
news failed to e. because of 4.06
therefore strive to e. that rest, 4.11
confidence to e. the sanctuary by 10.19
no one could e. the temple until Rev 15.08
But nothing unclean shall e. it, 21.27
that they may e. the city by the 22.14

ENTERED

of his sons with them e. the ark, Gen 7.13
And they that e., male and female 7.16
When Abram e. Egypt the Egyptians 12.14
aside to him and e. his house; 19.03
of Leah's tent, and e. Rachel's. 31.33
old when he e. the service of Pharaoh, 41.46
And he e. his chamber and wept 43.30
And Moses e. the cloud, and went up Ex 24.18
When Moses e. the tent, the pillar 33.09
come to you, who e. your house; Jos 2.03
they ran and e. the city and took 8.19
of them had e. into the fortified 10.20
they e. the stronghold of the house Ju 9.46
and e. and took the graven image, 18.17
And when he e. his house, he took a 19.29
And when the people e. the forest, 1Sa 14.26
came to Saul, and e. his service. 16.21
from the day I e. your service 29.08
before Abishai, and e. the city. 2Sa 10.14
and e. an inner chamber in the city. 1Ki 20.30
As soon as they e. Samaria, Elisha 2Ki 6.20
and e. another tent, and carried off 7.08
And as Jehu e. the gate, she said, 9.31
And they e. the house of Baal, and 10.21
side as one e. the house of the 12.09
I e. its farthest retreat, its 19.23
Joab's brother, and e. the city. 1Ch 19.15
number was not e. in the chronicles 27.24
And they e. into a covenant to seek 2Ch 15.12
and e. into a compact with the 23.01
and e. the temple of the LORD to 26.16
all who e. the house of the LORD as 31.16
turned back and e. by the Valley Neh 2.15
Haman had just e. the outer court Est 6.04
"Have you e. into the springs of the Job 38.16
"Have you e. the storehouses of the 38.22
it has e. our palaces, cutting off Jer 9.21
and they e. and took possession of 32.23
people who had e. into the covenant 34.10
the king of Babylon, e. Jerusalem. 52.12
the Spirit e. into me and set me Eze 2.02
But the Spirit e. into me, and set 3.24
to you and e. into a covenant with 16.08
As I e. into judgment with your 20.36
of the LORD e. the temple by the 43.04
the God of Israel, has e. by it; 44.02
by way of the gate by which he e., 46.09
no meat or wine e. my mouth, nor did Dan 10.03
and foreigners e. his gates and Ob 1.11
You should not have e. the gate of 1.13
As he e. Capernaum, a centurion came Mt 8.05
And when Jesus e. Peter's house, he 8.14
When he e. the house, the blind men 9.28
how he e. the house of God and ate 12.04
from there, and e. their synagogue. 12.09
Galilee and e. the region of Judea 19.01
And when he e. Jerusalem, all the 21.10
And Jesus e. the temple of God and 21.12
And when he e. the temple, the chief 21.23
the day when Noah e. the ark, 24.38
the sabbath he e. the synagogue Mk 1.21
and e. the house of Simon and 1.29
how he e. the house of God, when 2.26
Again he e. the synagogue, and a man 3.01
spirits came out, and e. the swine; 5.13
And when he had e., he said to 5.39
And when he had e. the house, 7.17
And he e. a house, and would not 7.24
And when he had e. the house, 9.28
And he e. Jerusalem, and went into 11.11
And he e. the temple and began to 11.15
and she e. the house of Zechariah Lk 1.40
synagogue, and e. Simon's house. 4.38
how he e. the house of God, and took 6.04
when he e. the synagogue and taught, 6.06

ENTERED (cont.)
of the people he e. Capernaum. Lk 7.01
I e. your house, you gave me no 7.44
for many demons had e. him. 8.30
out of the man and e. the swine, 8.33
were afraid as they e. the cloud. 9.34
who went and e. a village of the 9.52
went on their way, he e. a village; 10.38
And as he e. a village, he was met 17.12
until the day when Noah e. the ark, 17.27
He e. Jericho and was passing 19.01
And he e. the temple and began to 19.45
Then Satan e. into Judas called 22.03
when you have e. the city, a man 22.10
and you have e. into their labor." Jn 4.38
Jesus has not e. the boat with his 6.22
the morsel, Satan e. into him. 13.27
which he and his disciples e. 18.01
he e. the court of the high priest 18.15
Pilate e. the praetorium again and 18.33
he e. the praetorium again and said 19.09
and when they had e., they went Ac 1.13
alms of those who e. the temple. 3.02
and walked and e. the temple with 3.08
they e. the temple at daybreak and 5.21
So Ananias departed and e. the house. 9.17
the following day they e. Caesarea. 10.24
When Peter e., Cornelius met him 10.25
or unclean has ever e. my mouth.' 11.08
me, and we e. the man's house. 11.12
Now at Iconium they e. together 14.01
him, he rose up and e. the city; 14.20
And he e. the synagogue and for 19.08
and we e. the house of Philip the 21.08
so he went and e. the barracks and 23.16
and they e. the audience hall with 25.23
no church e. into partnership with Php 4.15
he e. once for all into the Holy Heb 9.12
For Christ has e., not into a sanctuary 9.24
a breath of life from God e. them, Rev 11.11

ENTERING
which you are e. to take possession Deu 4.05
which you are e. to take possession 7.01
which you are e. to take possession 11.10
which you are e. to take possession 11.29
which you are e. to take possession 23.20
which you are e. to take possession 28.21
which you are e. to take possession 28.63
which you are e. to take possession 30.16
As they were e. the city, they saw 1Sa 9.14
himself in by e. a town that has 23.07
just as Absalom was e. Jerusalem. 2Sa 15.37
they must not be seen e. the city. 17.17
saying, 'The land which you are e., Ez 9.11
he is e. into judgment with all Jer 25.31
And e. the tomb, they saw a young Mk 16.05
and you hindered those who were e." Lk 11.52
where on e. you will find a colt 19.30
and e. house after house, he dragged Ac 8.03
the promise of e. his rest remains, Heb 4.01

ENTERS
Moreover he who e. the house while Lev 14.46
meeting when he e. to make atonement 16.17
and whoever e. the house shall be 2Ch 23.07
and e. into judgment with you? Job 22.04
Blessed be he who e. in the name of Ps 118.26
The LORD e. into judgment with the Is 3.14
he e. into peace; they rest in 57.02
No one e. suit justly, no one goes 59.04
when he e. your gates as one e. a city Eze 26.10
as one e. them from the outer court, 42.09
where one e. the passage, and 42.12
when he e. the inner court. 44.21
When the prince e., he shall go 46.08
he who e. by the north gate to 46.09
and he who e. by the south gate 46.09
and when it e. the stagnant waters 47.08
rottenness e. into my bones, my Hab 3.16
since it e., not his heart but his Mk 7.19
and wherever he e., say to the 14.14
and every one e. it violently. Lk 16.16
him into the house which he e., 22.10
but he who e. by the door is the Jn 10.02
if any one e. by me, he will be 10.09
and an unbeliever or outsider e., 1Co 14.24
for whoever e. God's rest also Heb 4.10
a hope that e. into the inner 6.19
the high priest e. the Holy Place 9.25

ENTERTAINED
received us and e. us hospitably Ac 28.07
some have e. angels unawares. Heb 13.02

ENTHRONED
who is e. on the cherubim; and the 1Sa 4.04
hosts who sits e. on the cherubim. 2Sa 6.02
who art e. above the cherubim, thou 2Ki 19.15
LORD who sits e. above the cherubim. 1Ch 13.06
But the LORD sits e. for ever, he has Ps 9.07
art holy, e. on the praises of Israel. 22.03
The LORD sits e. over the flood; 29.10
The LORD sits e. as king for ever. 29.10
from where he sits e. he looks 33.14
them, he who is e. from of old; 55.19
May he be e. for ever before God; 61.07
Thou who art e. upon the cherubim, 80.01
He sits e. upon the cherubim; 99.01
But thou, O LORD, art e. for ever; 102.12
O thou who art e. in the heavens! 123.01
who art e. above the cherubim, thou Is 37.16

ENTICE
"E. your husband to tell us what Ju 14.15
"E. him, and see wherein his great 16.05
'Who will e. Ahab, that he may go up 1Ki 22.20
the LORD, saying, 'I will e. him.' 22.21
'You are to e. him, and you shall 22.22
'Who will e. Ahab the king of 2Ch 18.19
the LORD, saying, 'I will e. him.' 18.20
'You are to e. him, and you shall 18.21
Beware lest wrath e. you into Job 36.18
if sinners e. you, do not consent. Pro 1.10
They e. unsteady souls. They have 2Pe 2.14
they e. with licentious passions of 2.18

ENTICED
"If my heart has been e. to a woman, Job 31.09
and my heart has been secretly e., 31.27
he is lured and e. by his own Jas 1.14

ENTICES
e. you secretly, saying, 'Let us go Deu 13.06
A man of violence e. his neighbor Pro 16.29

ENTIRE
the fat tail e., taking it away Lev 3.09
until the e. generation, that is, the Deu 2.14
years, and he finished his e. house. 1Ki 7.01
king of Syria mustered his e. army, 2Ki 6.24
until the e. scroll was consumed in Jer 36.23
but to show e. and true fidelity, so Tit 2.10

ENTIRELY
Does he not speak e. for our sake? 1Co 9.10

ENTRAILS
all the fat that covers the e., Ex 29.13
and wash its e. and its legs, and 29.17
and the fat that covers the e., 29.22
but its e. and its legs he shall Lev 1.09
but the e. and the legs he shall 1.13
covering the e. and all the fat 3.03
and all the fat that is on the e., 3.03

ENTRAILS (cont.)
and the fat that covers the e., Lev 3.09
and all the fat that is on the e., 3.09
the LORD, the fat covering the e., 3.14
and all the fat that is on the e., 3.14
that covers the e. and all the fat 4.08
and all the fat that is on the e., 4.08
its legs, its e., and its dung, 4.11
tail, the fat that covers the e., 7.03
all the fat that was on the e., 8.16
And when the e. and the legs were 8.21
and all the fat that was on the e., 8.25
And he washed the e. and the legs, 9.14
tail, and that which covers the e., 9.19
till an arrow pierces its e.; Pro 7.23

ENTRANCE
up, and sat at the e. to Enaim, Gen 38.14
screen for the e. of the gate of Num 4.26
to you at the e. of the tent of 10.03
to Rehob, near the e. of Hamath. 13.21
stood at the e. of the tent of 16.18
them at the e. of the tent of 16.19
to Moses at the e. of the tent of 16.50
mark it out to the e. of Hamath, 34.08
cast it at the e. of the gate of Jos 8.29
Mount Hermon to the e. of Hamath, 13.05
stand at the e. of the gate of the 20.04
Baalhermon as far as the e. of Hamath. Ju 3.03
stood in the e. of the gate of the 9.35
wounded, up to the e. of the gate. 9.40
stood at the e. of the gate of the 9.44
war, stood by the e. of the gate; 18.16
stood by the e. of the gate with 18.17
served at the e. to the tent of 1Sa 2.22
battle array at the e. of the gate; 2Sa 10.08
them back to the e. of the gate. 11.23
The e. for the lowest story was on 1Ki 6.08
For the e. to the inner sanctuary 6.31
he made for the e. to the nave 6.33
from the e. of Hamath to the Brook 8.65
before Ahab to the e. of Jezreel. 18.46
and stood at the e. of the cave. 19.13
floor at the e. of the gate of 22.10
were lepers at the e. to the gate; 2Ki 7.03
heaps at the e. of the gate until 10.08
the horses' e. to the king's house, 11.16
Israel from the e. of Hamath as 14.25
and the outer e. for the king he 16.18
were at the e. of the gate of 23.08
at the e. to the house of the LORD, 23.11
They journeyed to the e. of Gedor, 1Ch 4.39
as far as the e. of the desert 5.09
of the LORD, keepers of the e. 9.19
gatekeeper at the e. of the tent of 9.21
of Egypt to the e. of Hamath, 13.05
battle array at the e. of the city, 19.09
from the e. of Hamath to the Brook 2Ch 7.08
floor at the e. of the gate of 18.09
standing by his pillar at the e., 23.13
went into the e. of the horse gate 23.15
to the e. by the Fish Gate, and 33.14
he went up to the e. of the king's Est 4.02
opposite the e. to the palace; 5.01
At the upper e. they hacked the Ps 74.05
at the e. of the city gates she Pro 1.21
at the e. of the portals she cries 8.03
throne at the e. of the gates of Jer 1.15
at the third e. of the temple of 38.14
which is at the e. to Pharaoh's 43.09
to the e. of the gateway of the Eze 8.03
in the e., was this image of 8.05
me to the e. of the north gate of 8.14
who dwells at the e. to the sea, 27.03
the gate at the e. to the end of 40.15
vestibule at the e. of the north 40.40
breadth of the e. was ten cubits; 41.02
sidewalls of the e. were five 41.02
the jambs of the e., two cubits; 41.03
the breadth of the e., six cubits; 41.03
sidewalls of the e., seven cubits. 41.03
chambers was an e. on the east 42.09
chambers was an e. on the east 42.12
worship at the e. of that gate 46.03
Then he brought me through the e., 46.19
way of Hethlon to the e. of Hamath, 47.15
a point opposite the e. of Hamath. 47.20
way of Hethlon to the e. of Hamath, 48.01
you from the e. of Hamath to the Amo 6.14
for you an e. into the eternal 2Pe 1.11

ENTRANCES
arrangement, its exits and its e., Eze 43.11

ENTRAP
Herodians, to e. him in his talk. Mk 12.13

ENTREAT
and e. for me Ephron the son of Gen 23.08
"E. the LORD to take away the frogs Ex 8.08
to command me when I am to e., 8.09
E. the LORD; for there has been 9.28
and e. the LORD your God only to 10.17
"E. me not to leave you or to Ru 1.16
"E. now the favor of the LORD your 1Ki 13.06
to him and e. him for her people. Est 4.08
you afraid; many will e. your favor. Job 11.19
I e. thy favor with all my heart; Ps 119.58
the LORD and e. the favor of the Jer 26.19
their men, to e. the favor of the LORD, Zec 7.02
go at once to e. the favor of the 8.21
and to e. the favor of the LORD. 8.22
And now e. the favor of God, that he Mal 1.09
we e. you not to accept the grace 2Co 6.01
myself e. you, by the meekness and 10.01
I e. Euodia and I e. Syntyche Php 4.02
the hearers e. that no further Heb 12.19

ENTREATED
out from Pharaoh, and e. the LORD. Ex 10.18
Then Manoah e. the LORD, and said, "O, Ju 13.08
and I have not e. the favor of the 1Sa 13.12
And the man of God e. the LORD; 1Ki 13.06
and e. him, "O man of God, I pray you, 2Ki 1.13
in distress he e. the favor of the 2Ch 33.12
if I have not e. thee for their Jer 15.11
yet we have not e. the favor of Dan 9.13
His father came out and e. him, Lk 15.28

ENTREATIES
The poor use e., but the rich Pro 18.23

ENTREATING
there, sent two men to him e. him, Ac 9.38

ENTREATY
very far away. Make e. for me." Ex 8.28
granted their e. because they 1Ch 5.20
received his e. and heard his 2Ch 33.13
and how God received his e., 33.19
this, and he listened to our e. Ez 8.23

ENTRUST
who will e. to you the true riches? Lk 16.11
many witnesses e. to faithful men 2Ti 2.02
do right and e. their souls to a 1Pe 4.19

ENTRUSTED
Moses; he is e. with all my house. Num 12.07
They e. him to Gedaliah the son of Jer 39.14
servants and e. to them his property; Mt 25.14
the Jews are e. with the oracles of Rom 3.02
own will, I am e. with a commission. 1Co 9.17
that I had been e. with the gospel Gal 2.07
Peter had been e. with the gospel 2.07

ENTRUSTED (cont.)
by God to be e. with the gospel, so 1Th 2.04
blessed God with which I have been e. 1Ti 1.11
guard what has been e. to you. Avoid 6.20
that Day what has been e. to me. 2Ti 1.12
that has been e. to you by the 1.14
I have been e. by command of God Tit 1.03

ENTRUSTING
and e. to us the message of reconciliation. 2Co 5.19

ENTRY
Benhinnom at the e. of the Potsherd Jer 19.02
seat in the e. of the New Gate of 26.10
at the e. of the New Gate of the 36.10

ENVELOPED
besieged and e. me with bitterness Lam 3.05

ENVIED
so that the Philistines e. him. Gen 26.14
no children, she e. her sister; and she 30.01
and all the trees of Eden e. it, Eze 31.09

ENVIOUS
will look with e. eye on all the 1Sa 2.32
wicked, be not e. of wrongdoers! Ps 37.01
For I was e. of the arrogant, when I 73.03
Be not e. of evil men, nor desire to Pro 24.01
evildoers, and be not e. of the wicked; 24.19

ENVOY
but a faithful e. brings healing. Pro 13.17

ENVOYS
sent e. with letters and a present 2Ki 20.12
matter of the e. of the princes of 2Ch 32.31
But he sent e. to him, saying, "What 35.21
at Zoan and his e. reach Hanes, Is 30.04
the e. of peace weep bitterly. 33.07
sent e. with letters and a present 39.01
you sent your e. far off, and sent 57.09
the hand of the e. who have come Jer 27.03

ENVY
Why look you with e., O many-peaked Ps 68.16
Do not e. a man of violence and do Pro 3.31
Let not your heart e. sinners, 23.17
from a man's e. of his neighbor. Ecc 4.04
hate and their e. have already 9.06
the anger and e. which you showed Eze 35.11
it was out of e. that they had Mt 27.18
e., slander, pride, foolishness. Mk 7.22
it was out of e. that the chief 15.10
Full of e., murder, strife, deceit, Rom 1.29
e., drunkenness, carousing, and the Gal 5.21
one another, no e. of one another. 5.26
preach Christ from e. and rivalry, Php 1.15
which produce e., dissension, 1Ti 6.04
passing our days in malice and e., Tit 3.03
insincerity and e. and all slander. 1Pe 2.01

ENWRAP
Thick clouds e. him, so that he does Job 22.14

EPAENETUS
Greet my beloved E., who was Rom 16.05

EPAPHRAS
learned it from E. our beloved Col 1.07
E., who is one of yourselves, a 4.12
E., my fellow prisoner in Christ Phm 1.23

EPAPHRODITUS
to send to you E. my brother and Php 2.25
received from E. the gifts you 4.18

EPHAH
The sons of Midian were E., Gen 25.04
(An omer is the tenth part of an e.) Ex 16.36
a tenth of an e. of fine flour for Lev 5.11
a tenth of an e. of fine flour as a 6.20
tenths of an e. of fine flour 14.10
a tenth of an e. of fine flour 14.21
a just e., and a just hin: I am the 19.36
tenths of an e. of fine flour 23.13
waved, made of two tenths of an e.; 23.17
tenths of an e. shall be in each 24.05
a tenth of an e. of barley meal; Num 5.15
of a tenth of an e. of fine flour, 15.04
tenths of an e. of fine flour 15.06
tenths of an e. of fine flour, 15.09
also a tenth of an e. of fine flour 28.05
tenths of an e. of fine flour for 28.09
tenths of an e. of fine flour for 28.12
tenths of an e. shall you offer 28.20
tenths of an e. for each bull, 28.28
three tenths of an e. for the bull, 29.03
three tenths of an e. for the bull, 29.09
tenths of an e. for each of the 29.14
unleavened cakes from an e. of flour; Ju 6.19
and it was about an e. of barley. Ru 2.17
an e. of flour, and a skin of wine; 1Sa 1.24
brothers an e. of this parched 17.17
E., Epher, Hanoch, Abida, and Eldaah. 1Ch 1.33
E. also, Caleb's concubine, bore Haran, 2.46
Geshan, Pelet, E., and Shaaph. 2.47
of seed shall yield but an e." Is 5.10
the young camels of Midian and E.; 60.06
a just e., and a just bath. Eze 45.10
The e. and the bath shall be of the 45.11
and the e. one tenth of a homer; 45.11
sixth of an e. from each homer of wheat, 45.13
sixth of an e. from each homer of barley, 45.13
offering an e. for each bull, 45.24
an e. for each ram, and a hin of oil 45.24
ram, and a hin of oil to each e. 45.24
with the ram shall be an e., 46.05
with a hin of oil to each e. 46.05
provide an e. with the bull and an 46.07
the bull and an e. with the ram, 46.07
with a hin of oil to each e. 46.07
with a young bull shall be an e., 46.11
be an ephah, and with a ram an e., 46.11
together with a hin of oil to an e. 46.11
by morning, one sixth of an e., 46.14
we may make the e. small and the Amo 8.05
"This is the e. that goes forth." Zec 5.06
was a woman sitting in the e.! 5.07
And he thrust her back into the e., 5.08
lifted up the e. between earth and 5.09
me, "Where are they taking the e.?" 5.10
will set the e. down there on its 5.11

EPHAI
the sons of E. the Netophathite, Jer 40.08

EPHER
E., Hanoch, Abida, and Eldaah. All these Gen 25.04
E., Hanoch, Abida, and Eldaah. All these 1Ch 1.33
Jether, Mered, E., and Jalon. These are 4.17
E., Ishi, Eliel, Azriel, Jeremiah, 5.24

EPHESDAMMIM
between Soco and Azekah, in E. 1Sa 17.01

EPHESIAN
Trophimus the E. with him in the Ac 21.29

EPHESIANS
out, "Great is Artemis of the E.!" Ac 19.28
out, "Great is Artemis of the E.!" 19.34
the city of the E. is temple keeper 19.35

EPHESUS
And they came to E., and he left Ac 18.19
wills," and he set sail from E. 18.21
a native of Alexandria, came to E. 18.24

EPHESUS (cont.)
the upper country and came to E. Ac 19.01
known to all residents of E., 19.17
not only at E. but almost throughout 19.26
"Men of E., what man is there who 19.35
For Paul had decided to sail past E., 20.16
he sent to E. and called to him 20.17
speaking, I fought with beasts at E.? 1Co 15.32
But I will stay in E. until Pentecost, 16.08
remain at E. that you may charge 1Ti 1.03
all the service he rendered at E. 2Ti 1.18
Tychicus I have sent to E. 4.12
to E. and to Smyrna and to Pergamum Rev 1.11
angel of the church in E. write: 2.01

EPHLAL
Zabad was the father of E., and E. of Obed. 1Ch 2.37

EPHOD
for the e. and for the breastpiece. Ex 25.07
an e., a robe, a coat of checker 28.04
And they shall make the e. of gold, 28.06
upon the shoulder-pieces of the e., 28.12
the work of the e. you shall make 28.15
to the shoulder-pieces of the e. 28.25
on its inside edge next to the e. 28.26
the two shoulder-pieces of the e., 28.27
the skilfully woven band of the e. 28.27
rings of the e. with a lace of 28.28
the skilfully woven band of the e., 28.28
shall not come loose from the e. 28.28
the robe of the e. all of blue. 28.31
the coat and the robe of the e., 29.05
and the e., and the breastpiece, and 29.05
the skilfully woven band of the e.; 29.05
for the e. and for the breastpiece. 35.09
for the e. and for the breastpiece, 35.27
And he made the e. of gold, blue 39.02
They made for the e. shoulder-pieces, 39.04
on the shoulder-pieces of the e., 39.07
work, like the work of the e., of gold, 39.08
to the shoulder-pieces of the e. 39.18
on its inside edge next to the e. 39.19
the two shoulder-pieces of the e., 39.20
the skilfully woven band of the e. 39.20
rings of the e. with a lace of blue, 39.21
the skilfully woven band of the e., 39.21
should not come loose from the e.; 39.21
the robe of the e. woven all of 39.22
and put the e. upon him, and girded Lev 8.07
the skilfully woven band of the e., 8.07
a leader, Hanniel the son of E. Num 34.23
And Gideon made an e. of it and put Ju 8.27
and he made an e. and teraphim, 17.05
in these houses there are an e., 18.14
the e., the teraphim, and the molten 18.17
the e., the teraphim, and the molten 18.18
he took the e., and the teraphim, 18.20
LORD, a boy girded with a linen e. 1Sa 2.18
incense, to wear an e. before me; 2.28
the LORD in Shiloh, wearing an e. 14.03
wrapped in a cloth behind the e.; 21.09
persons who wore the linen e. 22.18
came down with an e. in his hand. 23.06
the priest, "Bring the e. here." 23.09
son of Ahimelech, "Bring me the e." 30.07
Abiathar brought the e. to David. 30.07
David was girded with a linen e. 2Sa 6.14
and David wore a linen e. 1Ch 15.27
or pillar, without e. or teraphim. Hos 3.04

EPHPHATHA
"E.," that is, "Be opened." Mk 7.34

EPHRAIM
The name of the second he called E., Gen 41.52
of Egypt were born Manasseh and E., 46.20
him his two sons, Manasseh and E. 48.01
E. and Manasseh shall be mine, as 48.05
E. in his right hand toward Israel's 48.13
and laid it upon the head of E., 48.14
his right hand upon the head of E., 48.17
'God make you as E. and as Manasseh'"; 48.20
and thus he put E. before Manasseh. 48.20
from E., Elishama the son of Num 1.10
namely, of the people of E., 1.32
of the tribe of E. was forty 1.33
of the camp of E. by their companies, 2.18
the people of E. being Elishama 2.18
The whole number of the camp of E., 2.24
the leader of the men of E.: 7.48
of the men of E. set out by their 10.22
from the tribe of E., Hoshea 13.08
to their families: Manasseh and E. 26.28
These are the sons of E. according 26.35
of the sons of E. according to 26.37
tribe of the sons of E. a leader, 34.24
such are the ten thousands of E., Deu 33.17
the land of E. and Manasseh, all the 34.02
were two tribes, Manasseh and E.; Jos 14.04
Manasseh and E., received their 16.04
in the midst of E. to this day but 16.10
Manasseh belonged to the sons of E. 17.08
cities of Manasseh, belong to E. 17.09
hill country of E. is too narrow 17.15
to E. and Manasseh, "You are a 17.17
Timnathserah in the hill country of E.; 19.50
Shechem in the hill country of E., 20.07
the families of the tribe of E., 21.05
them were out of the tribe of E. 21.20
lands in the hill country of E., 21.21
which is in the hill country of E., 24.30
him in the hill country of E. 24.33
And E. did not drive out the Ju 1.29
Timnathheres, in the hill country of E., 2.09
trumpet in the hill country of E.; 3.27
Bethel in the hill country of E.; 4.05
From E. they set out thither into 5.14
throughout all the hill country of E., 7.24
all the men of E. were called out, 7.24
And the men of E. said to him, "What 8.01
the grapes of E. better than the 8.02
Shamir in the hill country of E. 10.01
and against the house of E.; 10.09
The men of E. were called to arms, 12.01
men of Gilead and fought with E.; 12.04
and the men of Gilead smote E., 12.04
they said, "You are fugitives of E., 12.04
in the midst of E. and Manasseh." 12.04
any of the fugitives of E. said, 12.05
at Pirathon in the land of E., 12.15
a man of the hill country of E., 17.01
hill country of E. to the house of 17.08
came to the hill country of E., 18.02
there to the hill country of E., 18.13
parts of the hill country of E., 19.01
was from the hill country of E., 19.16
parts of the hill country of E., 19.18
Ramathaimzophim of the hill country of E., 1Sa 1.01
hill country of E. and passed 9.04
hill country of E. heard that the 14.22
and Jezreel and E. and Benjamin 2Sa 2.09
which is near E., and Absalom 13.23
was fought in the forest of E. 18.06
a man of the hill country of E., 20.21
Benhur, in the hill country of E.; 1Ki 4.08
Shechem in the hill country of E., 12.25
hill country of E. two young men 2Ki 5.22
from the E. Gate to the Corner 14.13
territory out of the tribe of E. 1Ch 6.66
lands in the hill country of E., 6.67
The sons of E.: Shuthelah, and Bered 7.20
And E. their father mourned many 7.22
And E. went in to his wife, and she 7.23

EPHRAIM (cont.)

E., and Manasseh dwelt in Jerusalem: 1Ch 9.03
the Pelonite, of the sons of E.; 27.10
of Pirathon, of the sons of E.; 27.14
which is in the hill country of E., 2Ch 13.04
taken in the hill country of E., 15.08
and Benjamin, and those from E., 15.09
the cities of E. which Asa his 17.02
Beersheba to the hill country of E., 19.04
army that had come to him from E., 25.10
from the E. Gate to the Corner Gate. 25.23
And Zichri, a mighty man of E., 28.07
Certain chiefs also of the men of E., 28.12
letters also to E. and Manasseh, 30.01
the country of E. and Manasseh, 30.10
the people, many of them from E., 30.18
and in E. and Manasseh, until they 31.01
E., and Simeon, and as far as 34.06
Manasseh and E. and from all the 34.09
in the square at the Gate of E. Neh 8.16
and above the Gate of E., and by 12.39
E. is my helmet; Judah is my Ps 60.07
he did not choose the tribe of E.; 78.67
before E. and Benjamin and Manasseh 80.02
E. is my helmet; Judah my 108.08
told, 'Syria is in league with E.," Is 7.02
with E. and the son of Remaliah, has 7.05
sixty-five years E. will be broken 7.08
And the head of E. is Samaria, 7.09
the day that E. departed from Judah— 7.17
E. and the inhabitants of Samaria, 9.09
Manasseh E., and E. Manasseh, 9.21
and E. Manasseh, and together they 9.21
The jealousy of E. shall depart, 11.13
E. shall not be jealous of Judah, 11.13
and Judah shall not harass E. 11.13
and Judah shall not harass E. 11.13
The fortress will disappear from E., 17.03
proud crown of the drunkards of E., 28.01
drunkards of E. will be trodden 28.03
and proclaims evil from Mount E. Jer 4.15
kinsmen, all the offspring of E. 7.15
call in the hill country of E.: 31.06
to Israel, and E. is my first-born. 31.09
I have heard E. bemoaning, 'Thou 31.18
Is E. my dear son? Is he my 31.20
on the hills of E. and in Gilead. 50.19
(the stick of E.) and all the house Eze 37.16
in the hand of E.) and the tribes 37.19
side to the west, E., one portion. 48.05
Adjoining the territory of E., 48.06
E. is joined to idols, let him alone. Hos 4.17
I know E., and Israel is not hid 5.03
for now, O E., you have played the 5.03
E. shall stumble in his guilt; 5.05
E. shall become a desolation in the 5.09
E. is oppressed, crushed in judgment, 5.11
Therefore I am like a moth to E., 5.12
When E. saw his sickness, and Judah 5.13
then E. went to Assyria, and sent to 5.13
For I will be like a lion to E., 5.14
What shall I do with you, O E.? 6.04
the corruption of E. is revealed, 7.01
E. mixes himself with the peoples; 7.08
E. is a cake not turned. 7.08
E. is like a dove, silly and without 7.11
alone; E. has hired lovers. 8.09
Because E. has multiplied altars 8.11
but E. shall return to Egypt, and 9.03
The prophet is the watchman of E., 9.08
E. must lead forth his sons to 9.13
E. is stricken, their root is dried 9.16
E. shall be put to shame, and Israel 10.06
E. was a trained heifer that loved 10.11
but I will put E. to the yoke, 10.11
Yet it was I who taught E. to walk, 11.03
How can I give you up, O E.! How can 11.08
anger, I will not again destroy E.; 11.09
E. has encompassed me with lies, and 11.12
E. herds the wind, and pursues the 12.01
E. has said, "Ah, but I am rich, I 12.08
E. has given bitter provocation; 12.14
When E. spoke, men trembled; he was 13.01
The iniquity of E. is bound up, 13.12
O E., what have I to do with idols? 14.08
the land of E. and the land of Ob 1.19
chariot from E. and the war horse Zec 9.10
I have made E. its arrow. I will 9.13
Then E. shall become like a mighty 10.07
wilderness, to a town called E.; Jn 11.54

EPHRAIMITE

Gilead said to him, "Are you an E.?" Ju 12.05
son of Tohu, son of Zuph, an E. 1Sa 1.01
an E. of Zeredah, a servant of 1Ki 11.26

EPHRAIMITES

territory of the E. by their Jos 16.05
tribe of the E. by their families, 16.08
apart for the E. within the 16.09
fords of the Jordan against the E. Ju 12.05
time forty-two thousand of the E. 12.06
Of the E. twenty thousand eight 1Ch 12.30
for the E., Hoshea the son of 27.20
not with Israel, with all these E. 2Ch 25.07
The E., armed with the bow, turned Ps 78.09

EPHRAIM'S

remove it from E. head to Manasseh's Gen 48.17
And Joseph saw E. children of the 50.23
the south being E. and that to the Jos 17.10
E. harlotry is there, Israel is Hos 6.10
E. glory shall fly away like a bird 9.11
E. sons, as I have seen, are destined 9.13

EPHRATH

were still some distance from E., Gen 35.16
buried on the way to E. (that is, 35.19
still some distance to go to E.; 48.07
her there on the way to E. (that is, 48.07
Caleb married E., who bore him Hur. 1Ch 2.19

EPHRATHAH

you prosper in E. and be renowned Ru 4.11
of Hezron, Caleb went in to E., 1Ch 2.24
sons of Hur the first-born of E.: 2.50
first-born of E. the father of 4.04
Lo, we heard of it in E., we found Ps 132.06
O Bethlehem E., who are little to Mic 5.02

EPHRATHITE

the son of an E. of Bethlehem in 1Sa 17.12

EPHRATHITES

they were E. from Bethlehem in Ru 1.02

EPHRON

entreat for me E. the son of Zohar, Gen 23.08
Now E. was sitting among the 23.10
and E. the Hittite answered Abraham 23.10
And he said to E. in the hearing of 23.13
E. answered Abraham, 23.14
Abraham agreed with E.; and Abraham 23.16
weighed out for E. the silver 23.16
So the field of E. in Machpelah, 23.17
in the field of E. the son of 25.09
is in the field of E. the Hittite, 49.29
the field from E. the Hittite to 49.30
with the field from E. the Hittite, 50.13
there to the cities of Mount E.; Jos 15.09
the boundary goes from there to E., 18.15
villages and E. with its villages. 2Ch 13.19

EPICUREAN

Some also of the E. and Stoic Ac 17.18

EPILEPTIC
for he is an e. and he suffers Mt 17.15

EPILEPTICS
e., and paralytics, and he healed Mt 4.24

EQUAL
each shall there be an e. part), Ex 30.34
They shall have e. portions to eat, Deu 18.08
e. to the width of the house, and 1Ki 6.03
e. to the width of the house; 2Ch 3.04
Gold and glass cannot e. it, Job 28.17
my e., my companion, my familiar Ps 55.13
will you liken me and make me e., Is 46.05
e. to the number of the years of Eze 4.05
nor the fir trees e. its boughs; 31.08
and in length e. to one of the 48.08
have made them e. to us who have Mt 20.12
they are e. to angels and are sons Lk 20.36
Father, making himself e. with God. Jn 5.18
plants and he who waters are e., 1Co 3.08
a faith of e. standing with ours 2Pe 1.01
and breadth and height are e. Rev 21.16

EQUALITY
as a matter of e. your abundance 2Co 8.14
your want, that there may be e. 8.14
did not count e. with God a thing Php 2.06

EQUALLY
And you shall divide it e.; I swore Eze 47.14

EQUIP
e. you with everything good that Heb 13.21

EQUIPMENT
and all the e. for their service; Num 4.26
with all their e. and all their 4.32
of war and the e. of his chariots. 1Sa 8.12
garments and e. which the Syrians 2Ki 7.15
and all the e. for these Huramabi 2Ch 4.16
for the e. of the saints, for the Eph 4.12
feet with the e. of the gospel of 6.15

EQUIPPED
of the land of Egypt e. for battle. Ex 13.18
e. for battle with all the weapons 1Ch 12.33
six hundred men e. for battle. 12.35
complete, e. for every good work. 2Ti 3.17

EQUITY
justice and e. to all his people. 2Sa 8.15
justice and e. to all his people. 1Ch 18.14
he judges the peoples with e. Ps 9.08
royal scepter is a scepter of e.; 45.06
peoples with e. and guide the 67.04
I appoint I will judge with e. 75.02
he will judge the peoples with e." 96.10
righteousness, and the peoples with e. 98.09
justice, thou hast established e.; 99.04
righteousness, justice, and e.; Pro 1.03
righteousness and justice and e., 2.09
the poor with e. his throne will 29.14
and decide with e. for the meek of Is 11.04
abhor justice and pervert all e., Mic 3.09

EQUIVALENT
shall pay money e. to the marriage Ex 22.17

ER
a son, and he called his name E. Gen 38.03
took a wife for E. his first-born, 38.06
But E., Judah's first-born, was 38.07
E., Onan, Shelah, Perez, and Zerah 46.12
and Zerah (but E. and Onan died in 46.12
The sons of Judah were E. and Onan; Num 26.19
and E. and Onan died in the land of 26.19
E., Onan, and Shelah; these three 1Ch 2.03
Now E., Judah's first-born, was 2.03
E. the father of Lecah, Laadah the 4.21
the son of Elmadam, the son of E., Lk 3.28

ERAN
of E., the family of the Eranites. Num 26.36

ERANITES
of Eran, the family of the E. Num 26.36

ERASTUS
Timothy and E., he himself stayed Ac 19.22
E., the city treasurer, and our Rom 16.23
E. remained at Corinth; 2Ti 4.20

ERECH
E., and Accad, all of them in the Gen 10.10
the men of E., the Babylonians, the Ez 4.09

ERECT
And you shall e. the tabernacle Ex 26.30
month you shall e. the tabernacle 40.02
no idols and e. no graven image or Lev 26.01
of your yoke and made you walk e. 26.13
house of God, to e. it on its site; Ez 2.68
Moses was about to e. the tent, Heb 8.05

ERECTED
There he e. an altar and called it Gen 33.20
the month, the tabernacle was e. Ex 40.17
Moses e. the tabernacle; he laid 40.18
And he e. the court round the 40.33
He e. an altar for Baal in the 1Ki 16.32
and he e. altars for Baal, and 2Ki 21.03
the high place e. by Jeroboam the 23.15
and e. altars to the Baals, and made 2Ch 33.03
They e. their siege towers, they Is 23.13
day when it is e. for offering Eze 43.18

ERI
Shuni, Ezbon, E., Arodi, and Areli. Gen 46.16
of E., the family of the Erites; Num 26.16

ERITES
of Eri, the family of the E.; Num 26.16

ERR
"But if you e., and do not observe Num 15.22
they e. from their birth, speaking Ps 58.03
"They are a people who e. in heart, 95.10
Do they not e. that devise evil? Pro 14.22
they e. in vision, they stumble in Is 28.07
And those who e. in spirit will 29.24
it, and fools shall not e. therein. 35.08
thou make us e. from thy ways and 63.17

ERRAND
not eat until I have told my e." Gen 24.33
"I have an e. to you, O commander." 2Ki 9.05

ERRED
the fool, and have e. exceedingly." 1Sa 26.21
make me understand how I have e. Job 6.24
And even if it be true that I have e., 19.04

ERROR
for him for the e. which he Lev 5.18
because it was an e., and they have Num 15.25
before the LORD, for their e. 15.25
population was involved in the e. 15.26
for the person who commits an e., 15.28
and his angels he charges with e.; Job 4.18
my e. remains with myself. 19.04
but the way of e. leads to death. Pro 12.28
as it were an e. proceeding from Ecc 10.05
to utter e. concerning the LORD, to Is 32.06
has sinned through e. or ignorance; Eze 45.20
and no e. or fault was found in him Dan 6.04

ERROR (cont.)

the due penalty for their e. Rom 1.27
not spring from e. or uncleanness, 1Th 2.03
sinner from the e. of his way will Jas 5.20
escaped from those who live in e. 2Pe 2.18
away with the e. of lawless men 3.17
of truth and the spirit of e. 1Jn 4.06
the sake of gain to Balaam's e., Jud 1.11

ERRORS

But who can discern his e.? Ps 19.12
and for the e. of the people. Heb 9.07

ERUPTION

body a swelling or an e. or a spot, Lev 13.02
it is only an e.; and he shall 13.06
But if the e. spreads in the skin, 13.07
and if the e. has spread in the 13.08
for a swelling or an e. or a spot, 14.56

ESARHADDON

And E. his son reigned in his stead 2Ki 19.37
the days of E. king of Assyria who Ez 4.02
And E. his son reigned in his stead Is 37.38

ESAU

so they called his name E. Gen 25.25
E. was a skilful hunter, a man of 25.27
Isaac loved E., because he ate of 25.28
E. came in from the field, and he 25.29
And E. said to Jacob, "Let me eat 25.30
E. said, "I am about to die; of what 25.32
Then Jacob gave E. bread and pottage 25.34
Thus E. despised his birthright. 25.34
When E. was forty years old, he took 26.34
he called E. his older son, and said 27.01
when Isaac spoke to his son E. 27.05
So when E. went to the field to 27.05
father speak to your brother E., 27.06
my brother E. is a hairy man, and I 27.11
best garments of E. her older son, 27.15
"I am E. your first-born. I have done 27.19
you are really my son E. or not." 27.21
but the hands are the hands of E." 27.22
He said, "Are you really my son E.?" 27.24
E. his brother came in from his 27.30
"I am your son, your first-born, E." 27.32
When E. heard the words of his 27.34
E. said, "Is he not rightly named 27.36
Isaac answered E., "Behold, I have 27.37
E. said to his father, "Have you but 27.38
And E. lifted up his voice and wept. 27.38
Now E. hated Jacob because of the 27.41
and E. said to himself, "The days of 27.41
But the words of E. her older son 27.42
your brother E. comforts himself by 27.42
Now E. saw that Isaac had blessed 28.06
So when E. saw that the Canaanite 28.08
E. went to Ishmael and took to wife, 28.09
before him to E. his brother in 32.03
"Thus you shall say to my lord E.: 32.04
saying, "We came to your brother E., 32.06
thinking, "If E. comes to the one 32.08
of my brother, from the hand of E., 32.11
him a present for his brother E., 32.13
"When E. my brother meets you, and 32.17
are a present sent to my lord E.; 32.18
same thing to E. when you meet him, 32.19
E. was coming, and four hundred men 33.01
But E. ran to meet him, and embraced 33.04
And when E. raised his eyes and saw 33.05
E. said, "What do you mean by all 33.08
But E. said, "I have enough, my 33.09
Then E. said, "Let us journey on our 33.12
So E. said, "Let me leave with you 33.15
So E. returned that day on his way 33.16
when you fled from your brother E." 35.01
and his sons E. and Jacob buried 35.29
These are the descendants of E. (that is, 36.01
E. took his wives from the Canaanites: 36.02
And Adah bore to E., Eliphaz; 36.04
are the sons of E. who were born 36.05
Then E. took his wives, his sons, his 36.06
So E. dwelt in the hill country of 36.08
country of Seir; E. is Edom. 36.08
descendants of E. the father of 36.09
the son of Adah the wife of E., 36.10
the son of Basemath the wife of E. 36.10
she bore to E. Jeush, Jalam, and 36.14
These are the chiefs of the sons of E. 36.15
of Eliphaz the first-born of E.: 36.15
These are the sons of E.(that is, 36.19
These are the names of the chiefs of E., 36.40
E., the father of Edom), according 36.43
of your brethren the sons of E., Deu 2.04
Mount Seir to E. as a possession. 2.05
the sons of E. who live in Seir, 2.08
but the sons of E. dispossessed 2.12
as he did for the sons of E., 2.22
as the sons of E. who live in Seir 2.29
and to Isaac I gave Jacob and E. Jos 24.04
And I gave E. the hill country of 24.04
The sons of Isaac: E. and Israel. 1Ch 1.34
The sons of E.: Eliphaz, Reuel, Jeush, 1.35
bring the calamity of E. upon him, Jer 49.08
But I have stripped E. bare, 49.10
How E. has been pillaged, his Ob 1.06
and understanding out of Mount E.? 1.08
man from Mount E. will be cut off 1.09
flame, and the house of E. stubble; 1.18
be no survivor to the house of E.; 1.18
the Negeb shall possess Mount E., 1.19
up to Mount Zion to rule Mount E.; 1.21
"Is not E. Jacob's brother?" Mal 1.02
but I have hated E.; I have laid 1.03
"Jacob I loved, but E. I hated." Rom 9.13
future blessings on Jacob and E. Heb 11.20
be immoral or irreligious like E., 12.16

ESAU'S

his hand had taken hold of E. heel; Gen 25.26
hairy like his brother E. hands; 27.23
of Rebekah, Jacob's and E. mother. 28.05
These are the names of E. sons: 36.10
was a concubine of Eliphaz, E. son; 36.12
are the sons of Adah, E. wife. 36.12
are the sons of Basemath, E. wife. 36.13
E. wife: she bore to Esau Jeush, 36.14
E. son: the chiefs Nahath, Zerah, 36.17
are the sons of Basemath, E. wife. 36.17
E. wife: the chiefs Jeush, Jalam, and 36.18
the daughter of Anah, E. wife. 36.18

ESCAPE

to e. the waters of the flood. Gen 7.07
Let me e. there—is it not a little 19.20
Make haste, e. there; for I can do 19.22
the company which is left will e." 32.08
against us and e. from the land." Ex 1.10
as if to e. a sword, though none Lev 26.37
place was called the Rock of E. 1Sa 23.28
that I should e. to the land of 27.01
and I shall e. out of his hand." 27.01
will be no e. for us from Absalom; 2Sa 15.14
let not one of them e." And they 1Ki 18.40
your hands to e. shall forfeit his 2Ki 10.24
let not a man e." So when 10.25
be no remnant, nor any to e.? Ez 9.14
palace you will e. any more than Est 4.13
all way of e. will be lost to them, Job 11.20
he will not e. from darkness; 15.30
the Lord, belongs e. from death. Ps 68.20
I am shut in so that I cannot e.; 88.08
into their own nets, while I e. 141.10

ESCAPE (cont.)
let them not e. from your sight, Pro 3.21
Let them not e. from your sight; 4.21
and he who utters lies will not e. 19.05
a lion for those of Moab who e., Is 15.09
And we, how shall we e.?'" 20.06
upon them which they cannot e.; Jer 11.11
nor e. for the lords of the flock. 23.35
Judah shall not e. out of the hand 32.04
You shall not e. from his hand, but 34.03
you shall not e. from their hand." 38.18
shall not e. from their hand, but 38.23
of Egypt shall e. or survive or 44.14
And those who e. the sword shall 44.28
flee away, nor the warrior e.; 46.06
every city, and no city shall e.; 48.08
they flee and e. from the land of 50.28
let no one e. Requite her 50.29
me about so that I cannot e.; Lam 3.07
the nations some who e. the sword, Eze 6.08
of you who e. will remember me 6.09
And if any survivors e., they will 7.16
a few of them e. from the sword, 12.16
though they e. from the fire, the 15.07
Can a man e. who does such things 17.15
he break the covenant and yet e.? 17.15
all these things, he shall not e. 17.18
and the land of Egypt shall not e. Dan 11.42
there shall be those who e., Joe 2.32
away, not one of them shall e. Amo 9.01
Zion there shall be those that e., Ob 1.17
E. to Zion, you who dwell with the Zec 2.07
they put God to the test they e.'" Mal 3.15
how are you to e. being sentenced Mt 23.33
strength to e. all these things Lk 21.36
to die, I do not seek to e. death; Ac 25.11
were seeking to e. from the ship, 27.30
lest any should swim away and e.; 27.42
you will e. the judgment of God? Rom 2.03
will also provide the way of e., 1Co 10.13
child, and there will be no e. 1Th 5.03
and they may e. from the snare of 2Ti 2.26
how shall we e. if we neglect such Heb 2.03
if they did not e. when they 12.25
less shall we e. if we reject him 12.25
these you may e. from the corruption 2Pe 1.04

ESCAPED
Then one who had e. came, and told Gen 14.13
a slave who has e. from his master Deu 23.15
was left none that survived or e. Jos 8.22
Ehud e. while they delayed, and Ju 3.26
sculptured stones, and e. to Seirah. 3.26
able-bodied men; not a man e. 3.29
Saul were taken, but the people e. 1Sa 14.41
into the wall. And David fled, and e. 19.10
window; and he fled away and e. 19.12
let my enemy go, so that he has e.?" 19.17
Now David fled and e., and he came 19.18
from there and e. to the cave of 22.01
Abiathar, e. and fled after David. 22.20
told that David had e. from Keilah, 23.13
and not a man of them e., except 30.17
"I have e. from the camp of Israel." 2Sa 1.03
king of Syria e. on a horse with 1Ki 20.20
so that they e. from the hand of 2Ki 13.05
and e. into the land of Ararat. 19.37
of the Amalekites that had e., 1Ch 4.43
of the king of Syria has e. you. 2Ch 16.07
on the ground; none had e. 20.24
of you who have e. from the hand 30.06
those who had e. from the sword, 36.20
we are left a remnant that has e., Ez 9.15
who had e. exile, and concerning Neh 1.02
province who e. exile are in great 1.03
and I alone have e. to tell you." Job 1.15
and I alone have e. to tell you." 1.16
and I alone have e. to tell you." 1.17
and I alone have e. to tell you." 1.19
and I have e. by the skin of my 19.20
We have e. as a bird from the snare Ps 124.07
snare is broken, and we have e.! 124.07
and e. into the land of Ararat. Is 37.38
afraid and fled and e. to Egypt. Jer 26.21
of Nethaniah e. from Johanan with 41.15
"You that have e. from the sword, go, 51.50
of the LORD none e. or survived; Lam 2.22
a man who had e. from Jerusalem Eze 33.21
but he e. from their hands. Jn 10.39
supposing that the prisoners had e. Ac 16.27
of these things has e. his notice, 26.26
and so it was that all e. to land. 27.44
After we had e., we then learned 28.01
Though he has e. from the sea, 28.04
in the wall, and e. his hands. 2Co 11.33
e. the edge of the sword, won Heb 11.34
who have barely e. from those who 2Pe 2.18
after they have e. the defilements 2.20

ESCAPES
who e. from the sword of Hazael 1Ki 19.17
him who e. from the sword of Jehu 19.17
but the righteous e. from trouble. Pro 12.13
he who pleases God e. her, but the Ecc 7.26
Ask him who flees and her who e.; Jer 48.19
wilderness, and nothing e. them. Joe 2.03

ESCORT
to e. him over the Jordan. 2Sa 19.31
companions, her e., in her train. Ps 45.14

ESEK
he called the name of the well E., Gen 26.20

ESHAN
Arab, Dumah, E., Jos 15.52

ESHBAAL
Malchishua, Abinadab, and E.; 1Ch 8.33
Malchishua, Abinadab, and E.; 9.39

ESHBAN
Hemdan, E., Ithran, and Cheran. Gen 36.26
Hamran, E., Ithran, and Cheran. 1Ch 1.41

ESHCOL
Amorite, brother of E. and of Aner; Gen 14.13
let Aner, E., and Mamre take their 14.24
And they came to the Valley of E. Num 13.23
That place was called the Valley of E. 13.24
they went up to the Valley of E., 32.09
the Valley of E. and spied it out. Deu 1.24

ESHEK
The sons of E. his brother: Ulam his 1Ch 8.39

ESHTAOL
lowland, E., Zorah, Ashnah, Jos 15.33
included Zorah, E., Irshemesh, 19.41
Mahanehdan, between Zorah and E. Ju 13.25
Zorah and E. in the tomb of Manoah 16.31
tribe, from Zorah and from E., 18.02
to their brethren at Zorah and E., 18.08
war, set forth from Zorah and E., 18.11

ESHTAOLITES
came the Zorathites and the E. 1Ch 2.53

ESHTEMOA
E. with its pasture lands, Jos 21.14
in Aroer, in Siphmoth, in E., 1Sa 30.28
and Ishbah, the father of E. 1Ch 4.17
the Garmite and E. the Maacathite. 4.19
E. with its pasture lands, 6.57

ESHTEMOH
Anab, E., Anim, Jos 15.50

ESHTON
of Mehir, who was the father of E. 1Ch 4.11
E. was the father of Bethrapha, 4.12

ESLI
the son of E., the son of Naggai, Lk 3.25

ESPECIALLY
"Go, view the land, e. Jericho." Jos 2.01
e. before you, King Agrippa, that, Ac 25.26
because you are e. familiar with 26.03
gifts, e. that you may prophesy. 1Co 14.01
and e. to those who are of the Gal 6.10
e. those of Caesar's household. Php 4.22
of all men, e. of those who believe. 1Ti 4.10
and e. for his own family, he has 5.08
e. those who labor in preaching and 5.17
e. the circumcision party; Tit 1.10
e. to me but how much more to you, Phm 1.16
and e. those who indulge in the 2Pe 2.10
to the brethren, e. to strangers, 3Jn 1.05

ESTABLISH
But I will e. my covenant with you; Gen 6.18
"Behold, I e. my covenant with you 9.09
I e. my covenant with you, that 9.11
And I will e. my covenant between 17.07
I will e. my covenant with him as 17.19
But I will e. my covenant with 17.21
herself, her husband may e., Num 30.13
The LORD will e. you as a people Deu 28.09
that he may e. you this day as his 29.13
only, may the LORD e. his word." 1Sa 1.23
body, and I will e. his kingdom. 2Sa 7.12
and I will e. the throne of his 7.13
And thou didst e. for thyself thy 7.24
that the LORD may e. his word which 1Ki 2.04
then I will e. my word with you, 6.12
then I will e. your royal throne 9.05
and you may e. bazaars for yourself 20.34
that he might e. the words of the 2Ki 23.24
sons, and I will e. his kingdom. 1Ch 17.11
and I will e. his throne for ever. 17.12
and I will e. his royal throne in 22.10
I will e. his kingdom for ever if 28.07
then I will e. your royal throne, as 2Ch 7.18
Israel and would e. them for ever, 9.08
Can you e. their rule on the earth? Job 38.33
but e. thou the righteous, thou who Ps 7.09
when God arose to e. judgment to 76.09
the Most High himself will e. her. 87.05
'I will e. your descendants for 89.04
I will e. his line for ever and his 89.29
and e. thou the work of our hands 90.17
the work of our hands e. thou it. 90.17
and they e. a city to live in; 107.36
to e. it, and to uphold it with Is 9.07
to e. the land, to apportion the 49.08
the LORD who formed it to e. it— Jer 33.02
and I will e. with you an everlasting Eze 16.60
I will e. my covenant with you, and 16.62
the king should e. an ordinance Dan 6.07
Now, O king, e. the interdict and 6.08
and e. justice in the gate; Amo 5.15
God, and seeking to e. their own, Rom 10.03
to e. you in your faith and to 1Th 3.02
so that he may e. your hearts 3.13
comfort your hearts and e. them in 2Th 2.17
when I will e. a new covenant with Heb 8.08
first in order to e. the second. 10.09
E. your hearts, for the coming of Jas 5.08
e., and strengthen you. 1Pe 5.10

ESTABLISHED
which I have e. between me and all Gen 9.17
I also e. my covenant with them, to Ex 6.04
O LORD, which thy hands have e. 15.17
built, let the city of Sihon be e. Num 21.27
he has e. them, because he said 30.14
you, who made you and e. you? Deu 32.06
that Samuel was e. as a prophet of 1Sa 3.20
LORD would have e. your kingdom 13.13
you nor your kingdom shall be e. 1Sa 20.31
of Israel shall be e. in your hand. 24.20
the LORD had e. him king over 2Sa 5.12
your throne shall be e. for ever.'" 7.16
David will be e. before thee. 7.26
and his kingdom was firmly e. 1Ki 2.12
who has e. me, and placed me on the 2.24
David shall be e. before the LORD 2.45
the kingdom was e. in the hand of 2.46
Samuel the seer e. them in their 1Ch 9.22
the LORD had e. him king over 14.02
his throne shall be e. for ever.'" 17.14
concerning his house be e. for ever, 17.23
name will be e. and magnified for 17.24
David will be e. before thee. 17.24
the procedure e. for them by Aaron 24.19
son of David e. himself in his 2Ch 1.01
of Rehoboam was e. and was strong, 12.01
So King Rehoboam e. himself in 12.13
Therefore the LORD e. the kingdom 17.05
LORD your God, and you will be e.; 20.20
throne of his father and was e., 21.04
and I e. the duties of the priests Neh 13.30
Their children are e. in their Job 21.08
matter, and it will be e. for you, 22.28
he e. it, and searched it out. 28.27
and the stars which thou hast e.; Ps 8.03
he has e. his throne for judgment; 9.07
and e. it upon the rivers. 24.02
thou hadst e. me as a strong 30.07
thy strength hast e. the mountains, 65.06
thou hast e. the luminaries and the 74.16
His abode has been e. in Salem, 76.02
He e. a testimony in Jacob, and 78.05
thy steadfast love was e. for ever, 89.02
Like the moon it shall be e. for ever; 89.37
Yea, the world is e.; it shall never 93.01
thy throne is e. from of old; 93.02
the world is e., it shall never be 96.10
of justice, thou hast e. equity; 99.04
posterity shall be e. before thee. 102.28
The LORD has e. his throne in the 103.19
they are e. for ever and ever, to be 111.08
thou hast e. the earth, and it 119.90
the slanderer be e. in the land; 140.11
And he e. them for ever and ever; 148.06
by understanding he e. the heavens; Pro 3.19
When he e. the heavens, I was there, 8.27
when he e. the fountains of the 8.28
but the righteous is e. for ever. 10.25
A man is not e. by wickedness, but 12.03
LORD, and your plans will be e. 16.03
the throne is e. by righteousness. 16.12
of the LORD that will be e. 19.21
Plans are e. by counsel; by wise 20.18
and by understanding it is e.; 24.03
throne will be e. in righteousness. 25.05
his throne will be e. for ever. 29.14
Who has e. all the ends of the 30.04
LORD shall be e. as the highest of Is 2.02
believe, surely you shall not be e.'" 7.09
throne will be e. in steadfast 16.05
till he has e. justice in the 42.04
the earth and made it (he e. it; 45.18
In righteousness you shall be e.; 54.14
who e. the world by his wisdom, and Jer 10.12
congregation shall be e. before me; 30.20
If I have not e. my covenant with 33.25

ESTABLISHED (cont.)
who e. the world by his wisdom, and Jer 51.15
and I was e. in my kingdom, and Dan 4.36
LORD shall be e. as the highest of Mic 4.01
hast e. them for chastisement. Hab 1.12
But whoever is firmly e. in his heart, 1Co 7.37
up in him and e. in the faith, Col 2.07
of the one who made it must be e. Heb 9.16
them and are e. in the truth that 2Pe 1.12

ESTABLISHES
then he e. all her vows, or all her Num 30.14
and he e. him in whose way he Ps 37.23
of our God, which God e. for ever. 48.08
rest until he e. Jerusalem and Is 62.07
which the king e. can be changed." Dan 6.15
But it is God who e. us with you in 2Co 1.21

ESTABLISHING
son after him, and e. Jerusalem; 1Ki 15.04
the time for e. all that God spoke Ac 3.21

ESTABLISHMENT
sons until the e. of the kingdom 2Ch 36.20

ESTATE
said, "Go to Anathoth, to your e.; 1Ki 2.26
Men of low e. are but a breath, men Ps 62.09
men of high e. are a delusion; 62.09
he who remembered us in our low e., 136.23
beautiful, and came to regal e. Eze 16.13
shall return to their former e., 16.55
shall return to your former e. 16.55
regarded the low e. of his handmaiden. Lk 1.48
he is the owner of all the e.; Gal 4.01

ESTEEM
and fell greatly in their own e.; Neh 6.16
and to e. them very highly in love 1Th 5.13

ESTEEMED
who despise me shall be lightly e. 1Sa 2.30
so that his name was highly e. 18.30
all the counsel of Ahithophel e., 2Sa 16.23
he was despised, and we e. him not. Is 53.03
yet we e. him stricken, smitten by 53.04
who are least e. by the church? 1Co 6.04

ESTEEMS
One man e. one day as better than Rom 14.05
another man e. all days alike. 14.05

ESTHER
that is E., the daughter of his Est 2.07
E. also was taken into the king's 2.08
E. had not made known her people or 2.10
to learn how E. was and how she 2.11
turn came for E. the daughter of 2.15
Now E. found favor in the eyes of 2.15
And when E. was taken to King 2.16
the king loved E. more than all the 2.17
Now E. had not made known her 2.20
for E. obeyed Mordecai just as when 2.20
Mordecai, and he told it to Queen E., 2.22
and E. told the king in the name of 2.22
Then E. called for Hathach, one of 4.05
show it to E. and explain it to 4.08
went and told E. what Mordecai had 4.09
Then E. spoke to Hathach and gave 4.10
told Mordecai what E. had said. 4.12
told them to return answer to E., 4.13
Then E. told them to reply to 4.15
everything as E. had ordered him. 4.17
On the third day E. put on her 5.01
king saw Queen E. standing in the 5.02
he held out to E. the golden 5.02
Then E. approached and touched the 5.02
said to her, "What is it, Queen E.? 5.03
And E. said, "If it please the king, 5.04
that we may do as E. desires." 5.05
to the dinner that E. had prepared. 5.05
drinking wine, the king said to E., 5.06
But E. said, "My petition and my 5.07
"Even Queen E. let no one come with 5.12
the banquet that E. had prepared. 6.14
went in to feast with Queen E. 7.01
wine, the king again said to E., 7.02
"What is your petition, Queen E.? 7.02
Then Queen E. answered, "If I have 7.03
Then King Ahasuerus said to Queen E., 7.05
And E. said, "A foe and enemy! 7.06
to beg his life from Queen E., 7.07
falling on the couch where E. was; 7.08
gave to Queen E. the house of 8.01
for E. had told what he was to her; 8.01
And E. set Mordecai over the house 8.02
Then E. spoke again to the king; 8.03
held out the golden scepter to E., 8.04
and E. rose and stood before the 8.05
said to Queen E. and to Mordecai 8.07
I have given E. the house of Haman, 8.07
And the king said to Queen E., 9.12
And E. said, "If it please the king, 9.13
but when E. came before the king, he 9.25
Then Queen E., the daughter of 9.29
Jew and Queen E. enjoined upon the 9.31
of Queen E. fixed these practices 9.32

ESTHER'S
it was E. banquet. He also granted Est 2.18
When E. maids and her eunuchs came 4.04

ESTRANGED
acquaintances are wholly e. from me. Job 19.13
He who is e. seeks pretexts to Pro 18.01
One of Israel, they are utterly e. Is 1.04
who are all e. from me through Eze 14.05
who once were e. and hostile in Col 1.21

ETAM
in the cleft of the rock of E. Ju 15.08
to the cleft of the rock of E., 15.11
These were the sons of E.: Jezreel 1Ch 4.03
And their villages were E., Ain, Rimmon, 4.32
He built Bethlehem, E., Tekoa, 2Ch 11.06

ETERNAL
the blessings of the e. mountains, Gen 49.26
The e. God is your dwelling place, Deu 33.27
because man goes to his e. home, Ecc 12.05
Their e. dishonor will never be Jer 20.11
then the e. mountains were scattered, Hab 3.06
feet to be thrown into the e. fire. Mt 18.08
deed must I do, to have e. life?" 19.16
a hundredfold, and inherit e. life. 19.29
into the e. fire prepared for the 25.41
will go away into e. punishment, 25.46
but the righteous into e. life." 25.46
but is guilty of an e. sin"— Mk 3.29
what must I do to inherit e. life?" 10.17
and in the age to come e. life. 10.30
what shall I do to inherit e. life?" Lk 10.25
you into the e. habitations. 16.09
what shall I do to inherit e. life? 18.18
and in the age to come e. life." 18.30
believes in him may have e. life." Jn 3.15
should not perish but have e. life. 3.16
believes in the Son has e. life; 3.36
of water welling up to e. life." 4.14
and gathers fruit for e. life, 4.36
him who sent me, has e. life; 5.24
that in them you have e. life; 5.39
the food which endures to e. life, 6.27
believes in him should have e. life; 6.40
you, he who believes has e. life. 6.47

ETERNAL (cont.)
and drinks my blood has e. life, Jn 6.54
You have the words of e. life; 6.68
and I give them e. life, and they 10.28
world will keep it for e. life. 12.25
that his commandment is e. life. 12.50
to give e. life to all whom thou 17.02
And this is e. life, that they know 17.03
yourselves unworthy of e. life, Ac 13.46
were ordained to e. life believed. 13.48
his e. power and deity, has been Rom 1.20
immortality, he will give e. life; 2.07
righteousness to e. life through 5.21
sanctification and its end, e. life. 6.22
gift of God is e. life in Christ 6.23
to the command of the e. God, to bring 16.26
for us an e. weight of glory beyond all 2Co 4.17
the things that are unseen are e. 4.18
made with hands, e. in the heavens. 5.01
will from the Spirit reap e. life. Gal 6.08
according to the e. purpose which Eph 3.11
punishment of e. destruction and 2Th 1.09
us and gave us e. comfort and good 2.16
were to believe in him for e. life. 1Ti 1.16
hold of the e. life to which you 6.12
To him be honor and e. dominion. 6.16
in Christ Jesus goes with e. glory. 2Ti 2.10
in hope of e. life which God, who Tit 1.02
become heirs in hope of e. life. 3.07
the source of e. salvation to all Heb 5.09
of the dead, and e. judgment. 6.02
thus securing an e. redemption. 9.12
who through the e. Spirit offered 9.14
the promised e. inheritance, 9.15
by the blood of the e. covenant, 13.20
you to his e. glory in Christ, will 1Pe 5.10
into the e. kingdom of our Lord 2Pe 1.11
to you the e. life which was with 1Jn 1.02
what he has promised us, e. life. 2.25
no murderer has e. life abiding in 3.15
testimony, that God gave us e. life, 5.11
you may know that you have e. life. 5.13
This is the true God and e. life. 5.20
kept by him in e. chains in the Jud 1.06
undergoing a punishment of e. fire. 1.07
our Lord Jesus Christ unto e. life. 1.21
with an e. gospel to proclaim to Rev 14.06

ETERNITY
also he has put e. into man's mind, Ecc 3.11
to shame or confounded to all e. Is 45.17
high and lofty One who inhabits e., 57.15
both now and to the day of e. 2Pe 3.18

ETHAM
from Succoth, and encamped at E., Ex 13.20
from Succoth, and encamped at E., Num 33.06
And they set out from E., and turned 33.07
journey in the wilderness of E., 33.08

ETHAN
wiser than E. the Ezrahite, and 1Ki 4.31
E., Heman, Calcol, and Dara, five in 1Ch 2.06
son of E., son of Zimmah, son of 6.42
E. the son of Kishi, son of Abdi, son 6.44
brethren, E. the son of Kushaiah; 15.17
and E., were to sound bronze 15.19

ETHANIM
at the feast in the month E., 1Ki 8.02

ETHAN'S
and E. son was Azariah. 1Ch 2.08

ETHBAAL
the daughter of E. king of the 1Ki 16.31

ETHER
Libnah, E., Ashan, Jos 15.42
Enrimmon, E., and Ashan—four cities 19.07

ETHIOPIA
concerning Tirhakah king of E., 2Ki 19.09
from India to E. over one hundred Est 1.01
of the provinces from India to E., 8.09
The topaz of E. cannot compare with Job 28.19
let E. hasten to stretch out her Ps 68.31
with E.—"This one was born there," 87.04
from E., from Elam, from Shinar, from Is 11.11
which is beyond the rivers of E.; 18.01
a portent against Egypt and E., 20.03
because of E. their hope and of 20.05
concerning Tirhakah king of E., 37.09
E. and Seba in exchange for you. 43.03
of Egypt and the merchandise of E., 45.14
men of E. and Put who handle the Jer 46.09
Syene, as far as the border of E. Eze 29.10
Egypt, and anguish shall be in E., 30.04
E., and Put, and Lud, and all Arabia, 30.05
E. was her strength, Egypt too, and Nah 3.09
the rivers of E. my suppliants, Zep 3.10

ETHIOPIAN
Zerah the E. came out against them 2Ch 14.09
Can the E. change his skin or the Jer 13.23
When Ebedmelech the E., a eunuch, 38.07
the E., "Take three men with you 38.10
Then Ebedmelech the E. said to 38.12
"Go, and say to Ebedmelech the E., 39.16
an E., a eunuch, a minister of Ac 8.27

ETHIOPIANS
from Egypt—Libyans, Sukkiim, and E. 2Ch 12.03
defeated the E. before Asa and 14.12
and before Judah, and the E. fled. 14.12
and the E. fell until none remained 14.13
Were not the E. and the Libyans a 16.08
of the Arabs who are near the E.; 21.16
Egyptians captives and the E. exiles, Is 20.04
me to terrify the unsuspecting E.; Eze 30.09
Libyans and the E. shall follow in Dan 11.43
"Are you not like the E. to me, Amo 9.07
You also, O E., shall be slain by my Zep 2.12
of Candace the queen of the E., Ac 8.27

ETHKAZIN
to E., and going on to Rimmon it Jos 19.13

ETHNAN
of Helah: Zereth, Izhar, and E. 1Ch 4.07

ETHNI
son of E., son of Zerah, son of 1Ch 6.41

EUBULUS
E. sends greetings to you, as do 2Ti 4.21

EUNICE
Lois and your mother E. and now, 2Ti 1.05

EUNUCH
the king's e. who is in charge of Est 2.03
the king's e. who was in charge of 2.14
except what Hegai the king's e., 2.15
and let not the e. say, "Behold, Is 56.03
a e., who was in the king's house, Jer 38.07
his chief e., to bring some of the Dan 1.03
a e., a minister of Candace the Ac 8.27
And the e. said to Philip, "About 8.34
and the e. said, "See, here is water! 8.36
into the water, Philip and the e.. 8.38
and the e. saw him no more, and went 8.39

EUNUCHS
Two or three e. looked out at him. 2Ki 9.32
they shall be e. in the palace of 20.18

EUNUCHS (cont.)
the seven e. who served King Est 1.10
king's command conveyed by the e. 1.12
King Ahasuerus conveyed by the e.?" 1.15
and Teresh, two of the king's e., 2.21
maids and her e. came and told her, 4.04
for Hathach, one of the king's e., 4.05
and Teresh, two of the king's e., 6.02
the king's e. arrived and brought 6.14
one of the e. in attendance on the 7.09
they shall be e. in the palace of Is 39.07
"To the e. who keep my sabbaths, who 56.04
the e., the princes of Judah and Jer 29.02
the e., the priests, and all the 34.19
and e., whom Johanan brought back 41.16
chief of the e. gave them names: Dan 1.07
chief of the e. to allow him not 1.08
the sight of the chief of the e.; 1.09
the chief of the e. said to Daniel, 1.10
chief of the e. had appointed over 1.11
chief of the e. brought them in 1.18
For there are e. who have been so Mt 19.12
there are e. who have been made e. 19.12
there are e. who have made themselves e. 19.12

EUODIA
I entreat E. and I entreat Syntyche Php 4.02

EUPHRATES
And the fourth river is the E. Gen 2.14
to the great river, the river E., 15.18
had, and arose and crossed the E., 31.21
Rehoboth on the E. reigned in his 36.37
and from the wilderness to the E.; Ex 23.31
as the great river, the river E. Deu 1.07
the river E., to the western sea. 11.24
the river E., all the land of the Jos 1.04
fathers lived of old beyond the E. 24.02
restore his power at the river E. 2Sa 8.03
the Syrians who were beyond the E.; 10.16
from the E. to the land of the 1Ki 4.21
west of the E. from Tiphsah to 4.24
over all the kings west of the E.; 4.24
and scatter them beyond the E., 14.15
king of Assyria to the river E. 2Ki 23.29
the Brook of Egypt to the river E. 24.07
Rehoboth on the E. reigned in his 1Ch 1.48
of the desert this side of the E., 5.09
up his monument at the river E. 18.03
the Syrians who were beyond the E., 19.16
kings from the E. to the land of 2Ch 9.26
Carchemish on the E. and Josiah 35.20
from the river E. to the Brook of Is 27.12
to drink the waters of the E.? Jer 2.18
go to the E., and hide it there in 13.04
So I went, and hid it by the E., 13.05
go to the E., and take from there 13.06
Then I went to the E., and dug, 13.07
by the river E. at Carchemish and 46.02
by the river E. they have stumbled 46.06
the north country by the river E. 46.10
cast it into the midst of the E., 51.63
are bound at the great river E. Rev 9.14
his bowl on the great river E., 16.12

EUTYCHUS
young man named E. was sitting in Ac 20.09

EVADED
to the wall." But David e. him twice. 1Sa 18.11

EVANGELIST
entered the house of Philip the e., Ac 21.08
suffering, do the work of an e., 2Ti 4.05

EVANGELISTS
some e., some pastors and teachers, Eph 4.11

EVE
The man called his wife's name E., Gen 3.20
Now Adam knew E. his wife, and she 4.01
serpent deceived E. by his cunning, 2Co 11.03
For Adam was formed first, then E.; 1Ti 2.13

EVEN
"Bless me, e. me also, O my father!" Gen 27.34
Bless me, e. me also, O my father." 27.38
and e. I may have children through 30.03
cattle from our youth e. until now, 46.34
and at e. dividing the spoil. 49.27
and e. drew water for us and Ex 2.19
not believe e. these two signs or 4.09
he did not lay e. this to heart. 7.23
e. to the first-born of the maidservant 11.05
e. to him and to his descendants 30.21
e. for his father or for his mother; Lev 21.11
the holy things e. for a moment, Num 4.20
not e. the seeds or the skins. 6.04
E. when the cloud continued over 9.19
people, from Egypt e. until now. 14.19
and pursued them, e. to Hormah. 14.45
in their stead e. to this day. Deu 2.22
E. at Horeb you provoked the LORD 9.08
for they e. burn their sons and 12.31
e. to the tenth generation none of 23.02
e. to the tenth generation none 23.03
e. our enemies themselves being 32.31
e. I, am he, and there is no god 32.39
e. all the Sidonians. I will myself Jos 13.06
Peor from which e. yet we have not 22.17
e. if I should have a husband this Ru 1.12
more also if e. death parts me 1.17
without resting e. for a moment." 2.07
"Let her glean e. among the sheaves, 2.15
up out of Egypt e. to this day, 1Sa 8.08
garrison and e. the raiders 14.15
e. they also turned to be with the 14.21
and e. his sword and his bow and 18.04
e. when it is a common journey; 21.05
Behold, e. now he has hidden himself 2Sa 17.09
Then e. the valiant man, whose heart 17.10
until not e. a pebble is to be 17.13
"E. if I felt in my hand the weight 18.12
my stead'; e. so will I do this day." 1Ki 1.30
e. so may he be with Solomon, and 1.37
from Dan e. to Beersheba, every man 4.25
e. the Hall of Judgment; it was 7.07
e. from the foundation to the 7.09
calamity e. upon the widow with 17.20
e. I only, am left a prophet of the 18.22
and I, e. I only, am left; and they seek 19.10
and I, e. I only, am left; and they seek 19.14
He e. burned his son as an offering, 2Ki 16.03
e. all that Moses the servant of 18.12
came out of Egypt, e. to this day. 21.15
In times past, e. when Saul was king, 1Ch 11.02
e. my God, is with you. He will not 28.20
and have not e. asked long life, but 2Ch 1.11
e. highest heaven, cannot contain 2.06
E. Maacah, his mother, King Asa 15.16
yet e. in his disease he did not 16.12
He e. followed their counsel, and 22.05
his fame spread e. to the border 26.08
He e. made molten images for the 28.02
e. though not according to the 30.19
e. until the reign of Darius king Ez 4.05
but e. now there is hope for Israel 10.02
but you e. sell your brethren that Neh 5.08
E. their servants lorded it over 5.15
E. when they had made for themselves 9.18
foreign women made e. him to sin. 13.26
e. to the half of my kingdom." Est 5.03
E. to the half of my kingdom, it 5.06
"E. Queen Esther let no one come 5.12
E. to the half of my kingdom, it 7.02

EVEN (cont.)

"Will he e. assault the queen in my Est 7.08
E. in his servants he puts no trust, Job 4.18
and he takes it e. out of thorns; 5.05
I would e. exult in pain unsparing; 6.10
You would e. cast lots over the 6.27
E. now, behold, my witness is in 16.19
And e. if it be true that I have 19.04
E. young children despise me; 19.18
that I might come e. to his seat! 23.03
Behold, e. the moon is not bright 25.05
Will you e. put me in the wrong? 40.08
he is laid low e. at the sight of 41.09
they than gold, e. much fine gold; Ps 19.10
E. though I walk through the valley 23.04
be upon us, e. as we hope in thee. 33.22
E. my bosom friend in whom I trusted, 41.09
Yea, he shall see that e. the wise die, 49.10
e. among the rebellious, that the 68.18
So e. to old age and gray hairs, O 71.18
E. the sparrow finds a home, and the 84.03
or e. by reason of strength fourscore 90.10
e. in the chambers of their kings. 105.30
accuse me, e. as I make prayer for them. 109.04
e. when I said, "I am greatly afflicted"; 116.10
E. though princes sit plotting against 119.23
E. before a word is on my tongue, lo, 139.04
e. there thy hand shall lead me, and 139.10
e. the darkness is not dark to thee, 139.12
e. fine gold, and my yield than Pro 8.19
E. in laughter the heart is sad, and 14.13
is disliked e. by his neighbor, but 14.20
e. the wicked for the day of trouble. 16.04
he makes e. his enemies to be at peace 16.07
E. a fool who keeps silent is considered 17.28
and will not e. bring it back to 19.24
E. a child makes himself known by 20.11
them known to you today, e. to you. 22.19
e. his prayer is an abomination. 28.09
e. in the night his mind does not Ecc 2.23
e. there was wickedness, and in the 3.16
e. though he had gone from prison 4.14
E. though he should live a thousand 6.06
e. though a wise man claims to know, 8.17
E. when the fool walks on the road, 10.03
E. in your thought, do not curse the 10.20
or e. to eight, for you know not 11.02
sole of the foot e. to the head, Is 1.06
e. though you make many prayers, I 1.15
pass on, reaching e. to the neck; 8.08
I will bring upon Dibon e. more, 15.09
e. there you will have no rest." 23.12
cast to the ground, e. to the dust. 25.12
e. when the plea of the needy is 32.07
e. the lame will take the prey. 33.23
E. youths shall faint and be weary, 40.30
e. to your old age I am He, and to 46.04
I, e. I, have spoken and called him, I 48.15
E. these may forget, yet I will 49.15
'E. the captives of the mighty 49.25
far off, and sent down e. to Sheol. 57.09
e. for a long time, and so you do 57.11
e. though they are no gods? But my Jer 2.11
So that e. to wicked women you have 2.33
from our youth e. to this day; 3.25
"But e. in those days, says the LORD, 5.18
E. the stork in the heavens knows 8.07
e. the leaves are withered, and what 8.13
e. to this day, saying, Obey my voice. 11.07
For e. your brothers and the house 12.06
e. they have dealt treacherously 12.06
e. as they taught my people to 12.16
E. so will I spoil the pride of 13.09
E. the hind in the field forsakes 14.05
e. into the hand of Nebuchadrezzar 22.25
e. in my house I have found their 23.11
e. as their fathers forgot my name 23.27
kings shall make slaves e. of them; 25.14
E. so will I break the yoke of 28.11
given to him e. the beasts of the 28.14
E. when Elnathan and Delaiah and 36.25
For e. if you should defeat the 37.10
humbled themselves e. to this day, 44.10
E. her hired soldiers in her midst 46.21
E. the little ones of the flock 49.20
has been lifted up e. to the skies. 51.09
E. the jackals give the breast and Lam 4.03
upon it a city, e. Jerusalem; Eze 4.01
e I, am against you; and I will 5.08
e. I, will bring a sword upon you, 6.03
e. your brethren, your fellow exiles, 11.15
e. if these three men, Noah, Daniel, 14.14
e. if these three men were in it, as 14.16
e. if Noah, Daniel, and Job were in 14.20
and e. with this you were not satisfied. 16.29
shall not be e. a trace of it until he 21.27
and they have e. offered up to them 23.37
They e. sent for men to come from 23.40
from Teman e. to Dedan they shall 25.13
drench the land e. to the mountains 32.06
e. to the shepherds, Thus says the 34.02
e. my people Israel; and they shall 36.12
e. to the inner room, and on the 41.17
It grew great, e. to the host of Dan 8.10
e. up to the Prince of the host; 8.11
and he shall e. rise up against the 8.25
or e. his picked troops, for there 11.15
E. those who eat his rich food 11.26
e. as the LORD loves the people of Hos 3.01
and e. the fish of the sea are 4.03
I, e. I, will rend and go away, I will 5.14
E. if they bring up children, I will 9.12
E. though they bring forth, I will 9.16
e. the flocks of sheep are dismayed Joe 1.18
E. the wild beasts cry to thee 1.20
"Yet e. now," says the LORD, "return 2.12
e. nursing infants. Let the bridegroom 2.16
E. upon the menservants and maidservants 2.29
e. the last of you with fishhooks. Amo 4.02
E. though you offer me your burnt 5.22
e. the inhabitants of many cities; Zec 8.20
e. as all the tribes of Israel; 9.01
ones, tearing off e. their hoofs. 11.16
e. Judah will fight against Jerusalem 14.14
E. now the axe is laid to the root Mt 3.10
Do not e. the tax collectors do the 5.46
Do not e. the Gentiles do the same? 5.47
e. Solomon in all his glory was not 6.29
not e. in Israel have I found such 8.10
that e. winds and sea obey him?" 8.27
But e. the hairs of your head are 10.30
little ones e. a cup of cold water 10.42
e. what he has will be taken away. 13.12
yet e. the dogs eat the crumbs that 15.27
refuses to listen e. to the church, 18.17
e. as the Son of man came not to be 20.28
but e. if you say to this mountain, 21.21
and e. when you saw it, you did not 21.32
astray, if possible, e. the elect. 24.24
not e. the angels of heaven, nor the 24.36
e. what he has will be taken away. 25.29
"E. if I must die with you, I will 26.35
is very sorrowful, e. to death; 26.38
not e. to a single charge; so that the 27.14
he commands e. the unclean spirits, Mk 1.27
for them, not e. about the door; 2.02
of man is lord e. of the sabbath." 2.28
so that they could not e. eat. 3.20
e. what he has will be taken away." 4.25
that e. wind and sea obey him?" 4.41
bind him any more, e. with a chain; 5.03
"If I touch e. his garments, I shall 5.28
I will give you, e. half of my kingdom." 6.23
and they had no leisure e. to eat. 6.31

EVEN (cont.)

might touch e. the fringe of his Mk 6.56
yet e. the dogs under the table eat 7.28
he e. makes the deaf hear and the 7.37
saying, "Do not e. enter the village." 8.26
not e. the angels in heaven, nor the 13.32
"E. though they all fall away, I 14.29
is very sorrowful, e. to death; 14.34
Yet not e. so did their testimony 14.59
Holy Spirit, e. from his mother's womb. Lk 1.15
E. now the axe is laid to the root 3.09
For e. sinners love those who love 6.32
For e. sinners do the same. 6.33
E. sinners lend to sinners, to 6.34
Be merciful, e. as your Father is 6.36
not e. in Israel have I found such 7.09
"Who is this, who e. forgives sins?" 7.49
e. what he thinks that he has will 8.18
that he commands e. wind and water, 8.25
'E. the dust of your town that 10.11
e. the demons are subject to us in 10.17
Why, e. the hairs of your head are 12.07
e. Solomon in all his glory was not 12.27
and e. his own life, he cannot be my 14.26
E. so, I tell you. there will be more 15.07
E. so, I tell you, there is joy 15.10
or e. like this tax collector. 18.11
would not e. lift up his eyes to 18.13
were bringing e. infants to him 18.15
e. what he has will be taken away. 19.26
"Would that e. today you knew the 19.42
e. Moses showed, in the passage 20.37
be delivered up e. by parents and 21.16
from Galilee e. to this place." 23.05
that they had e. seen a vision of 24.23
e. he who comes after me, the thong Jn 1.27
e. as they honor the Father. He who does 5.23
For e. his brothers did not believe 7.05
"E. if I do bear witness to myself, 8.14
Yet e. if I do judge, my judgment is 8.16
"E. what I have told you from the 8.25
fornication; we have one Father, e. God." 8.41
e. though you do not believe me, 10.38
And e. now I know that whatever you 11.22
of the Lord, e. the King of Israel!" 12.13
Nevertheless many e. of the authorities 12.42
e. as I have loved you, that you 13.34
e. the Spirit of truth, whom the 14.17
e. the Spirit of truth, who proceeds 15.26
they may be one, e. as we are one. 17.11
e. as I am not of the world. 17.14
e. as I am not of the world. 17.16
e. as thou, Father, art in me, and I 17.21
they may be one e. as we are one, 17.22
hast loved them e. as thou hast 17.23
has sent me, e. so I send you." 20.21
so that they e. carried out the Ac 5.15
You might e. be found opposing God!" 5.39
not e. a foot's length, but promised 7.05
e. as he who spoke to Moses directed 7.44
E. Simon himself believed, and after 8.13
been poured out e. on the Gentiles 10.45
as e. some of your poets have said, 17.28
we have never e. heard that there 19.02
that she may e. be deposed from 19.27
imprisoned but e. to die at Jerusalem 21.13
He e. tried to profane the temple, 24.06
persecuted them e. to foreign 26.11
e. though they do not have the law. Rom 2.14
no one does good, not e. one." 3.12
a good man one will dare e. to die. 5.07
e. over those whose sins were not 5.14
e. us whom he has called, not from 9.24
And e. the others, if they do not 11.23
e. as the testimony to Christ was 1Co 1.06
e. things that are not, to bring to 1.28
everything, e. the depths of God. 2.10
and e. yet you are not ready, 3.02
court. I do not e. judge myself. 4.03
that is not found e. among pagans; 5.01
not e. to eat with such a one. 5.11
and that e. your own brethren. 6.08
the traditions e. as I have 11.02
e. as I have been fully understood. 13.12
but e. more to prophesy. He who 14.05
If e. lifeless instruments, such as 14.07
and e. then they will not listen to 14.21
be subordinate, as e. the law says. 14.34
We are e. found to be misrepresenting 15.15
with you or e. spend the winter, so 16.06
And e. if our gospel is veiled, it 2Co 4.03
e. though we once regarded Christ 5.16
For e. when we came into Macedonia, 7.05
For e. if I made you sorry with my 7.08
For e. if I boast a little too much 10.08
apportioned us, to reach e. to you. 10.13
E. if I am unskilled in speaking, I 11.06
for e. Satan disguises himself as 11.14
but e. if you do, accept me as a 11.16
apostles, e. though I am nothing. 12.11
But e. if we, or an angel from Gal 1.08
But e. Titus, who was with me, was 2.03
yield submission e. for a moment, 2.05
so that e. Barnabas was carried 2.13
e. we have believed in Christ Jesus, 2.16
no one annuls e. a man's will, or 3.15
For e. those who receive circumcision 6.13
e. as he chose us in him before the Eph 1.04
e. when we were dead through our 2.05
must not e. be named among you, as 5.03
For it is a shame e. to speak of 5.12
E. so husbands should love their 5.28
unto death, e. death on a cross. Php 2.08
E. if I am to be poured as a 2.17
you and now tell you e. with tears, 3.18
enables him e. to subject all 3.21
for e. in Thessalonica you sent me 4.16
e. so, through Jesus, God will bring 1Th 4.14
For e. when we were with you, we 2Th 3.10
self-indulgent is dead e. while she 1Ti 5.06
and e. when they are not, they 5.25
of your owing me e. your own self. Phm 1.19
you will do e. more than I say. 1.21
One might e. say that Levi himself, Heb 7.09
This becomes e. more evident when 7.15
Now e. the first covenant had 9.01
Hence e. the first covenant was not 9.18
e. when she was past the age, since 11.11
able to raise men e. from the dead; 11.19
and e. chains and imprisonment. 11.36
"If e. a beast touches the mountain, 12.20
E. the demons believe—and shudder. Jas 2.19
But e. if you do suffer for righteousness' 1Pe 3.14
gospel was preached e. to the dead, 4.06
e. denying the Master who bought 2Pe 2.01
hating e. the garment spotted by Jud 1.23
Jesus Christ e. to all that he saw. Rev 1.02
on account of him. E. so. 1.07
deny my faith e. in the days of 2.13
e. as I myself have received power 2.27
not their lives e. unto death. 12.11
e. making fire come down from 13.13
image of the beast should e. speak, 13.15

EVENING

And there was e. and there was Gen 1.05
And there was e. and there was 1.08
And there was e. and there was 1.13
And there was e. and there was 1.19
And there was e. and there was 1.23
And there was e. and there was 1.31
dove came back to him in the e., 8.11
two angels came to Sodom in the e.; 19.01
well of water at the time of e., 24.11

EVENING (cont.)
to meditate in the field in the e.; Gen 24.63
But in the e. he took his daughter 29.23
came from the field in the e., 30.16
shall kill their lambs in the e. Ex 12.06
fourteenth day of the month at e., 12.18
twenty-first day of the month at e. 12.18
"At e. you shall know that it was 16.06
you in the e. flesh to eat and in 16.08
In the e. quails came up and 16.13
about Moses from morning till e. 18.13
about you from morning till e.?" 18.14
tend it from e. to morning before 27.21
lamb you shall offer in the e.; 29.39
lamb you shall offer in the e., 29.41
Aaron sets up the lamps in the e., 30.08
in the morning and half in the e. Lev 6.20
shall be unclean until the e., 11.24
and be unclean until the e. 11.25
shall be unclean until the e., 11.27
and be unclean until the e.; 11.28
dead shall be unclean until the e. 11.31
it shall be unclean until the e.; 11.32
shall be unclean until the e., 11.39
and be unclean until the e.; 11.40
up shall be unclean until the e.; 14.46
water, and be unclean until the e. 15.05
water, and be unclean until the e. 15.06
water, and be unclean until the e. 15.07
water, and be unclean until the e. 15.08
him shall be unclean until the e.; 15.10
water, and be unclean until the e. 15.10
water, and be unclean until the e. 15.11
water, and be unclean until the e. 15.16
water, and be unclean until the e. 15.17
water, and be unclean until the e. 15.18
her shall be unclean until the e. 15.19
water, and be unclean until the e. 15.21
water, and be unclean until the e.; 15.22
he shall be unclean until the e. 15.23
water, and be unclean until the e. 15.27
water, and be unclean until the e.; 17.15
until the e. and shall not eat of 22.06
fourteenth day of the month in the e., 23.05
day of the month beginning at e., 23.32
from e. to e. shall you keep your 23.32
in order from e. to morning before 24.03
in the e., you shall keep it at its Num 9.03
in the e., in the wilderness of 9.05
day in the e. they shall keep it; 9.11
and at e. it was over the tabernacle 9.15
remained from e. until morning; 9.21
priest shall be unclean until e. 19.07
and shall be unclean until e. 19.08
clothes, and be unclean until e. 19.10
and at e. he shall be clean. 19.19
impurity shall be unclean until e. 19.21
it shall be unclean until e. 19.22
lamb you shall offer in the e.; 28.04
lamb you shall offer in the e.; 28.08
sacrifice on the e. of the first Deu 16.04
in the e. at the going down of the 16.06
but when e. comes on, he shall bathe 23.11
you shall say, 'Would it were e.!' 28.67
and at e. you shall say, 'Would it 28.67
of the month at e. in the plains Jos 5.10
the ark of the LORD until the e., 7.06
the king of Ai on a tree until e.; 8.29
they hung upon the trees until e.; 10.26
now the day has waned toward e.; Ju 19.09
from his work in the field at e.; 19.16
wept before the LORD until the e.; 20.23
LORD, and fasted that day until e., 20.26
and sat there till e. before God, 21.02
So she gleaned in the field until e.; Ru 2.17
until it is e. and I am avenged on 1Sa 14.24
and took his stand, morning and e. 17.16
the field till the third day at e. 20.05
until the e. of the next day; 30.17
fasted until e. for Saul and for 2Sa 1.12
and in the e. he went out to lie on 11.13
and bread and meat in the e.; 1Ki 17.06
the Syrians, until at e. he died; 22.35
and the e. cereal offering, and the 2Ki 16.15
offering continually morning and e., 1Ch 16.40
the LORD, and likewise at e., 23.30
for burnt offerings morning and e., 2Ch 2.04
and every e. burnt offerings and 13.11
that its lamps may burn every e.; 13.11
facing the Syrians until e.; 18.34
burnt offerings of morning and e., 31.03
burnt offerings morning and e. Ez 3.03
appalled until the e. sacrifice. 9.04
And at the e. sacrifice I rose from 9.05
In the e. she went, and in the Est 2.14
Between morning and e. they are Job 4.20
E. and morning and at noon I utter Ps 55.17
Each e. they come back, howling like 59.06
Each e. they come back, howling like 59.14
morning and the e. to shout for 65.08
in the e. it fades and withers. 90.06
My days are like an e. shadow; 102.11
work and to his labor until the e. 104.23
I am gone, like a shadow at e.; 109.23
up of my hands as an e. sacrifice! 141.02
in the e., at the time of night and Pro 7.09
and at e. withhold not your hand; Ecc 11.06
late into the e. till wine inflames Is 5.11
At e. time, behold, terror! Before 17.14
for the shadows of e. lengthen!" Jer 6.04
yourself at e. in their sight, Eze 12.04
and in the e. I dug through the 12.07
morning, and at e. my wife died. 24.18
upon me the e. before the fugitive 33.22
gate shall not be shut until e. 46.02
at the time of the e. sacrifice. Dan 9.21
more fierce than the e. wolves; Hab 1.08
Ashkelon they shall lie down at e. Zep 2.07
her judges are e. wolves that leave 3.03
for at e. time there shall be light Zec 14.07
That e. they brought to him many Mt 8.16
When it was e., the disciples came 14.15
When e. came, he was there alone, 14.23
"When it is e., you say, 'It will be 16.02
And when e. came, the owner of the 20.08
When it was e., he sat at table 26.20
When it was e., there came a rich 27.57
That e., at sundown, they brought to Mk 1.32
when e. had come, he said to them, 4.35
And when e. came, the boat was out 6.47
And when e. came they went out of 11.19
in the e., or at midnight, or at 13.35
And when it was e. he came with the 14.17
And when e. had come, since it was 15.42
it is toward e. and the day is now Lk 24.29
When e. came, his disciples went Jn 6.16
On the e. of that day, the first day 20.19
the morrow, for it was already e. Ac 4.03
to them from morning till e., testifying 28.23

EVENINGS
and three hundred e. and mornings; Dan 8.14
The vision of the e. and the 8.26

EVENLY
them with gold e. applied upon the 1Ki 6.35

EVENTIDE
all joy has reached its e.; Is 24.11

EVENTS
Now after these e. Paul resolved in Ac 19.21
by God concerning e. as yet unseen, Heb 11.07

EVER

life, and eat, and live for e."— Gen 3.22
shall not abide in man for e., 6.03
neither will I e. again destroy 8.21
you and to your descendants for e. 13.15
Ask of me e. so much as marriage 34.12
then let me bear the blame for e.; 43.09
me to you': this is my name for e., Ex 3.15
Why didst thou e. send me? For since 5.22
if e. I let you and your little 10.10
been before, nor e. shall be again. 10.14
never been, nor e. shall be again. 11.06
observe it as an ordinance for e. 12.14
generations, as an ordinance for e. 12.17
for you and for your sons for e. 12.24
The LORD will reign for e. and e." 15.18
and may also believe you for e." 19.09
If e. you take your neighbor's 22.26
a statute for e. to be observed 27.21
shall be a statute for e. to them, 30.21
It is a sign for e. between me and 31.17
and they shall inherit it for e.' " 32.13
as decreed for e. throughout your Lev 6.18
it to the LORD as decreed for e.; 6.22
a statute for e. throughout your 10.09
sons' with you, as a due for e.; 10.15
to you for e. that in the seventh 16.29
it is a statute for e. 16.31
a statute for e. to them throughout 17.07
a statute for e. throughout your 23.14
a statute for e. in all your 23.21
a statute for e. throughout your 23.31
a statute for e. throughout your 23.41
a statute for e. throughout your 24.03
of Israel as a covenant for e. 24.08
to inherit as a possession for e.; 25.46
of salt for e. before the LORD for Num 18.19
Was I e. accustomed to do so to you 22.30
as this has e. happened or was e. heard Deu 4.32
Did any people e. hear the voice of 4.33
Or has any god e. attempted to go 4.34
the LORD your God gives you for e." 4.40
and with their children for e.! 5.29
your children after you for e., 12.28
it shall be a heap for e., 13.16
he shall be your bondman for e. 15.17
the LORD, him and his sons for e. 18.05
God and by walking e. in his ways— 19.09
the assembly of the LORD for e.; 23.03
prosperity all your days for e. 23.06
and upon your descendants for e. 28.46
to us and to our children for e., 29.29
and swear, As I live for e., 32.40
people of Israel a memorial for e." Jos 4.07
may fear the LORD your God for e." 4.24
and made it for e. a heap of ruins. 8.28
for you and your children for e., 14.09
Did he e. strive against Israel, or Ju 11.25
or did he e. go to war with them? 11.25
the LORD, and abide there for e." 1Sa 1.22
go in and out before me for e.'; 2.30
be an old man in your house for e. 2.32
and out before my anointed for e. 2.35
about to punish his house for e., 3.13
by sacrifice or offering for e." 3.14
your kingdom over Israel for e. 13.13
your loyalty from my house for e. 20.15
LORD is between you and me for e." 20.23
and your descendants, for e.' " 20.42
"Shall the sword devour for e.? 2Sa 2.26
kingdom are for e. guiltless 3.28
the throne of his kingdom for e. 7.13
be made sure for e. before me; 7.16
throne shall be established for e.' " 7.16
Israel to be thy people for e.; 7.24
confirm for e. the word which thou 7.25
and thy name will be magnified for e., 7.26
it may continue for e. before thee; 7.29
of thy servant be blessed for e." 7.29
let me e. find favor in your sight, 16.04
David, and his descendants for e." 22.51
"May my lord King David live for e.!" 1Ki 1.31
the head of his descendants for e.; 2.33
established before the LORD for e." 2.45
place for thee to dwell in for e." 8.13
and put my name there for e.; 9.03
royal throne over Israel for e., 9.05
the LORD loved Israel for e., 10.09
descendants of David, but not for e.' " 11.39
they will be your servants for e." 12.07
and to your descendants for e." 2Ki 5.27
lamp to him and to his sons for e. 8.19
of the nations e. delivered his 18.33
Israel, I will put my name for e.; 21.07
LORD and to minister to him for e." 1Ch 15.02
He is mindful of his covenant for e., 16.15
his steadfast love endures for e.! 16.34
his steadfast love endures for e. 16.41
I will establish his throne for e.' " 17.12
my kingdom for e. and his throne 17.14
throne shall be established for e.' " 17.14
Israel to be thy people for e.; 17.22
his house be established for e., 17.23
established and magnified for e., 17.24
it may continue for e. before thee; 17.27
hast blessed is blessed for e." 17.27
his royal throne in Israel for e.' 22.10
his sons for e. should burn 23.13
blessings in his name for e. 23.13
and he dwells in Jerusalem for e. 23.25
to be king over Israel for e.; 28.04
his kingdom for e. if he continues 28.07
to your children after you for e. 28.08
him, he will cast you off for e. 28.09
Israel our father, for e. and e. 29.10
keep for e. such purposes and thoughts 29.18
God, as ordained for e. for Israel. 2Ch 2.04
his steadfast love endures for e.," 5.13
place for thee to dwell in for e." 6.02
his steadfast love endures for e." 7.03
his steadfast love endures for e.— 7.06
that my name may be there for e.; 7.16
and would establish them for e., 9.08
they will be your servants for e." 10.07
over Israel for e. to David and 13.05
and give it for e. to the descendants 20.07
his steadfast love endures for e." 20.21
lamp to him and to his sons for e. 21.07
which he has sanctified for e., 30.08
Jerusalem shall my name be for e." 33.04
Israel, I will put my name for e.; 33.07
love endures for e. toward Israel." Ez 3.11
sacrificing to him e. since the 4.02
inheritance to your children for e.' 9.12
the king, "Let the king live for e.! Neh 2.03
Moabite should e. enter the 13.01
who that was innocent e. perished? Job 4.07
they perish for e. without any 4.20
I would not live for e. Let me alone, 7.16
Thou prevailest for e. against him, 14.20
were graven in the rock for e.! 19.24
he will perish for e. like his own 20.07
be acquitted for e. by my judge. 23.07
me, and my bow e. new in my hand.' 29.20
the throne he sets them for e., 36.07
Did a man e. wish that he would be 37.20
take him for your servant for e.? 41.04
rejoice, let them e. sing for joy; Ps 5.11
out their name for e. and e. 9.05
But the LORD sits enthroned for e., 9.07
the poor shall not perish for e. 9.18
The LORD is king for e. and e.; 10.16
guard us e. from this generation. 12.07
Wilt thou forget me for e.? How long 13.01

EVER (cont.)

David and his descendants for e.	Ps 18.50
the LORD is clean, enduring for e.;	19.09
length of days for e. and e.	21.04
dost make him most blessed for e.;	21.06
the LORD! May your hearts live for e.!	22.26
in the house of the LORD for e.	23.06
My eyes are e. toward the LORD, for	25.15
shepherd, and carry them for e.	28.09
LORD sits enthroned as king for e.	29.10
I will give thanks to thee for e.	30.12
The counsel of the LORD stands for e.,	33.11
their heritage will abide for e.;	37.18
He is e. giving liberally and	37.26
do good; so shall you abide for e.	37.27
righteous shall be preserved for e.,	37.28
the land, and dwell upon it for e.	37.29
to fall, and my pain is e. with me.	38.17
thy faithfulness e. preserve me!	40.11
and set me in thy presence for e.	41.12
give thanks to thy name for e.	44.08
Awake! Do not cast us off for e.!	44.23
therefore God has blessed you for e.	45.02
throne endures for e. and e.	45.06
will praise you for e. and e.	45.17
God, which God establishes for e.	48.08
is God, our God for e. and e.	48.14
He will be our guide for e.	48.14
should continue to live on for e.,	49.09
Their graves are their homes for e.,	49.11
transgressions, and my sin is e. before me.	51.03
But God will break you down for e.;	52.05
love of God for e. and e.	52.08
I will thank thee for e., because	52.09
Let me dwell in thy tent for e.!	61.04
May he be enthroned for e. before God;	61.07
So will I e. sing praises to thy	61.08
who rules by his might for e.,	66.07
where the LORD will dwell for e.?	68.16
May his name endure for e., his fame	72.17
Blessed be his glorious name for e.;	72.19
of my heart and my portion for e.	73.26
why dost thou cast us off for e.?	74.01
enemy to revile thy name for e.?	74.10
forget the life of thy poor for e.	74.19
But I will rejoice for e., I will sing	75.09
"Will the Lord spurn for e.,	77.07
Has his steadfast love for e. ceased?	77.08
earth, which he has founded for e.	78.69
Wilt thou be angry for e.? Wilt thy	79.05
will give thanks to thee for e.;	79.13
and their fate would last for e.	81.15
put to shame and dismayed for e.;	83.17
thy house, e. singing thy praise!	84.04
Wilt thou be angry with us for e.?	85.05
and I will glorify thy name for e.	86.12
thy steadfast love, O LORD, for e.;	89.01
love was established for e., thy	89.02
establish your descendants for e.,	89.04
my hand shall e. abide with him,	89.21
love I will keep for him for e.,	89.28
his line for e. and his throne as	89.29
His line shall endure for e.,	89.36
it shall be established for e.;	89.37
Wilt thou hide thyself for e.?	89.46
Blessed be the LORD for e.!	89.52
or e. thou hadst formed the earth	90.02
are doomed to destruction for e.,	92.07
but thou, O LORD, art on high for e.	92.08
they are e. full of sap and green,	92.14
his steadfast love endures for e.,	100.05
thou, O LORD, art enthroned for e.;	102.12
nor will he keep his anger for e.	103.09
glory of the LORD endure for e.,	104.31
He is mindful of his covenant for e.,	105.08
his steadfast love endures for e.!	106.01
generation to generation for e.	106.31
his steadfast love endures for e.!	107.01
a priest for e. after the order of	110.04
his righteousness endures for e.	111.03
he is e. mindful of his covenant.	111.05
they are established for e. and e.,	111.08
has commanded his covenant for e.	111.09
practice it. His praise endures for e.!	111.10
his righteousness endures for e.	112.03
he will be remembered for e.	112.06
his righteousness endures for e.;	112.09
faithfulness of the LORD endures for e.	117.02
his steadfast love endures for e.!	118.01
"His steadfast love endures for e."	118.02
"His steadfast love endures for e."	118.03
"His steadfast love endures for e."	118.04
his steadfast love endures for e.!	118.29
law continually, for e. and e.;	119.44
For e., O LORD, thy word is firmly	119.89
my enemies, for it is e. with me.	119.98
testimonies are my heritage for e.;	119.111
thy statutes for e., to the end.	119.112
Thy righteousness is righteous for e.,	119.142
Thy testimonies are righteous for e.;	119.144
that thou hast founded them for e.	119.152
righteous ordinances endures for e.	119.160
cannot be moved, but abides for e.	125.01
sons also for e. shall sit upon your	132.12
"This is my resting place for e.;	132.14
endures for e., thy renown, O LORD,	135.13
his steadfast love endures for e.	136.01
his steadfast love endures for e.	136.02
his steadfast love endures for e.;	136.03
his steadfast love endures for e.;	136.04
his steadfast love endures for e.;	136.05
his steadfast love endures for e.;	136.06
his steadfast love endures for e.;	136.07
his steadfast love endures for e.;	136.08
his steadfast love endures for e.;	136.09
his steadfast love endures for e.;	136.10
his steadfast love endures for e.;	136.11
his steadfast love endures for e.;	136.12
his steadfast love endures for e.;	136.13
his steadfast love endures for e.;	136.14
his steadfast love endures for e.;	136.15
his steadfast love endures for e.;	136.16
his steadfast love endures for e.;	136.17
his steadfast love endures for e.;	136.18
his steadfast love endures for e.;	136.19
his steadfast love endures for e.;	136.20
his steadfast love endures for e.;	136.21
his steadfast love endures for e.	136.22
his steadfast love endures for e.;	136.23
his steadfast love endures for e.;	136.24
his steadfast love endures for e.	136.25
his steadfast love endures for e.	136.26
love, O LORD, endures for e.	138.08
and bless thy name for e. and e.	145.01
praise thy name for e. and e.	145.02
his holy name for e. and e.	145.21
is in them; who keeps faith for e.;	146.06
The LORD will reign for e.,	146.10
established them for e. and e.;	148.06
righteous is established for e.	Pro 10.25
Truthful lips endure for e., but a	12.19
for riches do not last for e.;	27.24
throne will be established for e.	29.14
the earth e. thirsty for water, and	30.16
but the earth remains for e.	Ecc 1.04
whatever God does endures for e.;	3.14
no more for e. any share in all	9.06
Her cities will be deserted for e.;	Is 17.02
He will swallow up death for e.,	25.08
Trust in the LORD for e., for the LORD	26.04
No, he does not thresh it for e.;	28.28
time to come as a witness for e.	30.08
watchtower will become dens for e.,	32.14
righteousness, quietness and trust for e.	32.17

EVER (cont.)
quenched; its smoke shall go up for e. Is 34.10
shall pass through it for e. and e. 34.10
they shall possess it for e., from 34.17
word of our God will stand for e. 40.08
You said. "I shall be mistress for e.," 47.07
but my salvation will be for e., 51.06
but my deliverance will be for e., 51.08
For I will not contend for e., 57.16
I will make you majestic for e., 60.15
they shall possess the land for e., 60.21
and remember not iniquity for e. 64.09
and rejoice for e. in that which I 65.18
will he be angry for e., will he be Jer 3.05
I will not be angry for e. 3.12
and wounds are e. before me. 6.07
gave of old to your fathers for e. 7.07
is kindled which shall burn for e." 15.14
is kindled which shall burn for e." 17.04
city shall be inhabited for e. 17.25
a thing to be hissed at for e. 18.16
grave, and her womb for e. great. 20.17
fathers from of old and for e.; 25.05
being a nation before me for e." 31.36
or overthrown any more for e." 31.40
way, that they may fear me for e., 32.39
his steadfast love endures for e.!' 33.11
and to make sacrifices for e." 33.18
neither you nor your sons for e.; 35.06
shall be peopled no more for e., 50.39
and it shall be desolate for e.' 51.62
the Lord will not cast off for e., Lam 3.31
e. watching vainly for help; 4.17
But thou, O LORD, dost reign for e.; 5.19
Why dost thou forget us for e., 5.20
can it e. be used for anything! Eze 15.05
has never been, nor e. shall be. 16.16
'Who was e. destroyed like Tyre in 27.32
end and shall be no more for e.' " 27.36
end and shall be no more for e." 28.19
do more good to you than e. before. 36.11
children shall dwell there for e.; 37.25
shall be their prince for e. 37.25
of the people of Israel for e. 43.07
I will dwell in their midst for e. 43.09
to the king, "O king, live for e.! Dan 2.04
be the name of God for e. and e., 2.20
an end, and it shall stand for e.; 2.44
Nebuchadnezzar, "O king, live for e.! 3.09
and honored him who lives for e.; 4.34
queen said, "O king, live for e.! 5.10
to him, "O King Darius, live for e.! 6.06
to the king, "O king, live for e.! 6.21
is the living God, enduring for e.; 6.26
and possess the kingdom for e., for e. and e.' 7.18
like the stars for e. and e. 12.03
who lives for e. that it would be 12.07
And I will betroth you to me for e.; Hos 2.19
But Judah shall be inhabited for e., Joe 3.20
and he kept his wrath for e. Amo 1.11
and you shall be cut off for e. Ob 1.10
whose bars closed upon me for e.; Jon 2.06
you take away my glory for e. Mic 2.09
the LORD our God for e. and e. 4.05
his anger for e. because he 7.18
mercilessly slaying nations for e.? Hab 1.17
and salt pits, and a waste for e. Zep 2.09
the prophets, do they live for e.? Zec 1.05
with whom the LORD is angry for e." Mal 1.04
and the power and the glory for e. *Mt 6.13
"May no fruit e. come from you 21.19
tied, on which no one has e. sat; Mk 11.02
"May no one e. eat fruit from you 11.14
over the house of Jacob for e.; Lk 1.33
and to his posterity for e." 1.55
on which no one has e. yet sat; 19.30
where no one had e. yet been laid. 23.53
No one has e. seen God; the only Jn 1.18
man who told me all that I e. did. 4.29
"He told me all that I e. did." 4.39
of this bread, he will live for e.; 6.51
eats this bread will live for e." 6.58
"No man e. spoke like this man!" 7.46
not continue in the house for e.; 8.35
the son continues for e. 8.35
law that the Christ remains for e. 12.34
Counselor, to be with you for e., 14.16
tomb where no one had e. been laid. 19.41
And more than e. believers were Ac 5.14
or unclean has e. entered my mouth." 11.08
E. since the creation of the world Rom 1.20
the Creator, who is blessed for e.! 1.25
who is over all be blessed for e. 9.05
see, and bend their backs for e." 11.10
all things. To him be glory for e. 11.36
Spirit of God e. says "Jesus be 1Co 12.03
earnest than e. because of his 2Co 8.22
his righteousness endures for e." 9.09
Jesus, he who is blessed for e., 11.31
to whom be the glory for e. and e. Gal 1.05
all generations, for e. and e. Eph 3.21
For no man e. hates his own flesh, 5.29
Father be glory for e. and e. Php 4.20
be honor and glory for e. and e. 1Ti 1.17
whom no man has e. seen or can see. 6.16
him be the glory for e. and e. 2Ti 4.18
you might have him back for e., Phm 1.15
For to what angel did God e. say, Heb 1.05
throne, O God, is for e. and e., 1.08
But to what angel has he e. said, 1.13
place, "Thou art a priest for e., 5.06
high priest for e. after the order 6.20
God he continues a priest for e. 7.03
no one has e. served at the altar. 7.13
of him, "Thou art a priest for e., 7.17
mind, 'Thou art a priest for e.' " 7.21
permanently, because he continues for e. 7.24
who has been made perfect for e. 7.28
yesterday and today and for e. 13.08
to whom be glory for e. and e. 13.21
the word of the Lord abides for e." 1Pe 1.25
glory and dominion for e. and e. 4.11
be the dominion for e. and e. 5.11
because no prophecy e. came by the 2Pe 1.21
For e. since the fathers fell 3.04
does the will of God abides for e. 1Jn 2.17
No man has e. seen God; if we love 4.12
in us and will be with us for e.: 2Jn 1.02
darkness has been reserved for e. Jud 1.13
before all time and now and for e. 1.25
glory and dominion for e. and e. Rev 1.06
throne, who lives for e. and e., 4.09
him who lives for e. and e.; 4.10
glory and might for e. and e.!" 5.13
be to our God for e. and e.! 7.12
by him who lives for e. and e., 10.06
and he shall reign for e. and e." 11.15
torment goes up for e. and e.; 14.11
of God who lives for e. and e.; 15.07
from her goes up for e. and e." 19.03
day and night for e. and e. 20.10
they shall reign for e. and e. 22.05

EVER-FLOWING
thou didst dry up e. streams. Ps 74.15
righteousness like an e. stream. Amo 5.24

EVERGREEN
I am like an e. cypress, from me Hos 14.08

EVERLASTING
remember the e. covenant between Gen 9.16
generations for an e. covenant, 17.07

EVERLASTING (cont.)
of Canaan, for an e. possession; Gen 17.08
be in your flesh an e. covenant. 17.13
with him as an e. covenant for his 17.19
the name of the LORD, the E. God. 21.33
after you for an e. possession.' 48.04
the bounties of the e. hills; 49.26
shall be an e. statute for you, Lev 16.34
and the abundance of the e. hills, Deu 33.15
and underneath are the e. arms. 33.27
he has made with me an e. covenant, 2Sa 23.05
as an e. covenant to Israel, 1Ch 16.17
of Israel, from e. to e.!" 16.36
your God from e. to e. Neh 9.05
The enemy have vanished in e. ruins; Ps 9.06
of Israel, from e. to e.! 41.13
majestic than the e. mountains. 76.04
he put them to e. shame. 78.66
from e. to e. thou art God. 90.02
from of old; thou art from e. 93.02
LORD is from e. to e. upon those who 103.17
to Israel as an e. covenant, 105.10
of Israel, from e. to e.! 106.48
in me, and lead me in the way e.! 139.24
Thy kingdom is an e. kingdom, 145.13
Mighty God, E. Father, Prince of Peace." Is 9.06
statutes, broken the e. covenant. 24.05
for the LORD GOD is an e. rock. 26.04
us can dwell with e. burnings?" 33.14
with e. joy upon their heads; 35.10
The LORD is the e. God, the Creator 40.28
by the LORD with e. salvation; 45.17
e. joy shall be upon their heads; 51.11
but with e. love I will have 54.08
will make with you an e. covenant, 55.03
for an e. sign which shall not be 55.13
give them an e. name which shall 56.05
but the LORD will be your e. light, 60.19
for the LORD will be your e. light, 60.20
double portion; yours shall be e. joy. 61.07
I will make an e. covenant with 61.08
to make for himself an e. name, 63.12
is the living God and the e. King. Jer 10.10
bring upon you e. reproach and 23.40
a hissing, and an e. reproach. 25.09
LORD, making the land an e. waste. 25.12
I have loved you with an e. love; 31.03
will make with them an e. covenant, 32.40
a haunt of jackals, an e. waste; 49.33
the LORD in an e. covenant which 50.05
establish with you an e. covenant. Eze 16.60
it shall be an e. covenant with 37.26
His kingdom is an e. kingdom, Dan 4.03
for his dominion is an e. dominion, 4.34
his dominion is an e. dominion, 7.14
kingdom shall be an e. kingdom, 7.27
to bring in e. righteousness, to 9.24
some to e. life, and some to shame 12.02
and some to shame and e. contempt. 12.02
Art thou not from e., O LORD my Hab 1.12
scattered, the e. hills sank low. 3.06

EVERMORE
be peace from the LORD for e." 1Ki 2.33
right hand are pleasures for e. Ps 16.11
and say e., "Great is the LORD, who 35.27
thy salvation say e., "God is great!" 70.04
befits thy house, O LORD, for e. 93.05
from this time forth and for e.! 113.02
from this time forth and for e. 115.18
in from this time forth and for e. 121.08
from this time forth and for e. 125.02
from this time forth and for e. 131.03
commanded the blessing, life for e. 133.03
from this time forth and for e. Is 9.07
from this time forth and for e." 59.21
in the midst of them for e. Eze 37.26
is in the midst of them for e." 37.28
from this time forth and for e. Mic 4.07
be glory for e. through Jesus Christ! Rom 16.27
died, and behold I am alive for e., Rev 1.18

EVERY
and e. winged bird according to its Gen 1.21
and over e. creeping thing that 1.26
air and over e. living thing that 1.28
have given you e. plant yielding 1.29
and e. tree with seed in its fruit; 1.29
And to e. beast of the earth, and to 1.30
and to e. bird of the air, and to 1.30
I have given e. green plant for 1.30
made to grow e. tree that is pleasant 2.09
"You may freely eat of e. tree of the 2.16
LORD God formed e. beast of the 2.19
the field and e. bird of the air, 2.19
the man called e. living creature, 2.19
and to e. beast of the field; 2.20
flaming sword which turned e. way, 3.24
and that e. imagination of the 6.05
And of e. living thing of all flesh, 6.19
bring two of e. sort into the ark, 6.19
of e. creeping thing of the ground 6.20
two of e. sort shall come in to you, 6.20
Also take with you e. sort of food 6.21
and e. living thing that I have 7.04
they and e. beast according to its 7.14
and e. creeping thing that creeps 7.14
e. bird according to its kind, e. bird of e. 7.14
swarm upon the earth, and e. man; 7.21
He blotted out e. living thing that 7.23
Bring forth with you e. living 8.17
and animals and e. creeping thing 8.17
And e. beast, e. creeping thing, and e. bird, 8.19
e. clean animal and of e. clean bird, 8.20
again destroy e. living creature 8.21
shall be upon e. beast of the 9.02
and upon e. bird of the air, upon 9.02
E. moving thing that lives shall be 9.03
of e. beast I will require it and 9.05
of e. man's brother I will require 9.05
and with e. living creature that is 9.10
and e. beast of the earth with you, 9.10
me and you and e. living creature 9.12
me and you and e. living creature 9.15
between God and e. living creature 9.16
hand against e. man and e. man's hand against 16.12
E. male among you shall be circumcised 17.10
e. male throughout your generations, 17.12
e. male among the men of Abraham's 17.23
at e. place to which we come, say of 20.13
and before e. one you are righted." 20.16
e. one who hears will laugh over me 21.06
Cursed be e. one who curses you, and 27.29
and blessed be e. one who blesses 27.29
removing from it e. speckled and 30.32
spotted sheep and e. black lamb, 30.32
E. one that is not speckled and 30.33
e. one that had white on it, and 30.35
and e. lamb that was black, and put 30.35
e. drove by itself, and said to his 32.16
as we are and e. male of you be 34.15
that e. male among us be circumcised 34.22
and e. male was circumcised, all who 34.24
he stored up in e. city the food 41.48
and to replace e. man's money in 42.25
e. man's bundle of money was in his 42.35
and there was e. man's money in the 43.21
Then e. man quickly lowered his 44.11
ground, and e. man opened his sack. 44.11
and e. man loaded his ass, and they 44.13
"Make e. one go out from me." 45.01
for e. shepherd is an abomination 46.34
"E. son that is born to the Hebrews Ex 1.22
but you shall let e. daughter live." 1.22

EVERY (cont.)

For e. man cast down his rod, and Ex 7.12
come down upon e. man and beast 9.19
and beast and e. plant of the 9.22
struck down e. plant of the field, 9.25
and shattered e. tree of the field. 9.25
they shall eat e. tree of yours 10.05
and eat e. plant in the land, all 10.12
e. man of his neighbor and e. woman 11.02
they shall take e. man a lamb 12.03
but what e. one must eat, that only 12.16
but e. slave that is bought for 12.44
E. firstling of an ass you shall 13.13
E. first-born of man among your 13.13
and gather a day's portion e. day, 16.04
e. man of you, as much as he can eat 16.16
remain e. man of you in his place, 16.29
e. great matter they shall bring to 18.22
in e. place where I cause my name 20.24
"For e. breach of trust, whether it 22.09
from e. man whose heart makes him 25.02
of the tabernacle for e. use, 27.19
and e. day you shall offer a bull 29.36
e. morning when he dresses the 30.07
E. one who is numbered in the 30.14
carving wood, for work in e. craft. 31.05
e. one who profanes it shall be put 31.14
'Put e. man his sword on his side, 32.27
and slay e. man his brother, and 32.27
and e. man his companion, and e. man 32.27
And e. one who sought the LORD 33.07
and e. man stood at his tent door, 33.08
and worship, e. man at his tent door. 33.10
"And let e. able man among you come 35.10
And they came, e. one whose heart 35.21
and e. one whose spirit moved him, 35.21
e. man dedicating an offering of 35.22
And e. man with whom was found blue 35.23
E. one who could make an offering 35.24
and e. man with whom was found 35.24
wood, for work in e. skilled craft. 35.33
ability to do e. sort of work done 35.35
Bezalel and Oholiab and e. able man 36.01
and Oboliab and e. able man in 36.02
e. one whose heart stirred him up 36.02
him freewill offerings e. morning, 36.03
who were doing e. sort of task on 36.04
sixteen bases, under e. frame two bases. 36.30
for e. one who was numbered in the 38.26
shall burn wood on it e. morning, Lev 6.12
E. male among the children of Aaron 6.18
E. cereal offering of a priest 6.23
e. male among the priests may 6.29
E. male among the priests may eat 7.06
And e. cereal offering baked in the 7.09
And e. cereal offering, mixed with 7.10
For e. person who eats of the fat 7.25
e. raven according to its kind, 11.15
E. animal which parts the hoof but 11.26
e. one who touches them shall be 11.26
be drunk from e. such vessel shall 11.34
"E. swarming thing that swarms upon 11.41
and bird and e. living creature 11.46
the waters and e. creature that 11.46
E. bed on which he who has the 15.04
And e. garment and e. skin on 15.17
and e. bed on which he lies shall 15.24
E. bed on which she lies, all the 15.26
"For the life of e. creature is the 17.14
for the life of e. creature is its 17.14
And e. person that eats what dies 17.15
E. one of you shall revere his 19.03
and e. one who eats it shall bear 19.08
For e. one who curses his father or 20.09
E. sabbath day Aaron shall set it 24.08
E. valuation shall be according to 27.25
e. devoted thing is most holy to 27.28
e. tenth animal of all that pass 27.32
of names, e. male, head by head; Num 1.02
e. male from twenty years old and 1.20
e. male from twenty years old and 1.22
e. man able to go forth to war: 1.26
e. man able to go forth to war: 1.28
e. man able to go forth to war: 1.30
e. man able to go forth to war: 1.32
e. man able to go forth to war: 1.34
e. man able to go forth to war: 1.36
e. man able to go forth to war: 1.38
e. man able to go forth to war: 1.40
e. man able to go forth to war: 1.42
e. man able to go forth to war in 1.45
e. man by his own camp and e. 1.52
e. man by his own standard; 1.52
the tent of meeting on e. side. 2.02
e. one in his family, according to 2.34
instead of e. first-born that opens 3.12
e. male from a month old and upward 3.15
e. one that can enter the service, 4.30
e. one that could enter the service, 4.35
e. one that could enter the service 4.39
e. one that could enter the service, 4.43
e. one that could enter to do the 4.47
they put out of the camp e. leper, 5.02
and e. one having a discharge, and 5.02
and e. one that is unclean through 5.02
And e. offering, all the holy things 5.09
and e. man's holy things shall be 5.10
a wagon for e. two of the leaders, 7.03
e. man at the door of his tent; 11.10
a man, e. one a leader among them." 13.02
for e. day a year, you shall bear 14.34
you do with e. one according to 15.12
e. one of them, and the LORD is 16.03
and let e. one of you take his 16.17
and e. one of you bring before the 16.17
So e. man took his censer, and they 16.18
E. one who comes near, who comes 17.13
e. cereal offering of theirs and 18.09
of theirs and e. sin offering of 18.09
of theirs and e. guilt offering of 18.09
e. male may eat of it; it is holy 18.10
e. one who is clean in your house 18.11
e. one who is clean in your house 18.13
E. devoted thing in Israel shall be 18.14
I have given e. tithe in Israel 18.21
shall present e. offering due to 18.29
e. one who comes into the tent, and 19.14
and e. one who is in the tent, shall 19.14
And e. open vessel, which has no 19.15
and e. one who is bitten, when he 21.08
Blessed be e. one who blesses you, 24.09
and cursed be e. one who curses you." 24.09
"E. one of you slay his men who 25.05
e. tribe shall be given its inheritance 26.54
e. male from a month old and upward 26.62
the burnt offering of e. sabbath, 28.10
as a cereal offering for e. lamb; 28.13
and e. pledge by which she has 30.04
and e. pledge by which she bound 30.11
commanded Moses, and slew e. male. 31.07
kill e. male among the little ones, 31.17
and kill e. woman who has known man 31.17
You shall purify e. garment, 31.20
e. article of skin, all work of 31.20
and e. article of wood." 31.20
take one drawn out of e. fifty, 31.30
half Moses took one of e. fifty, 31.47
taken booty, e. man for himself.) 31.53
and e. armed man of you will pass 32.21
e. man who is armed for war, before 32.27
e. man who is armed to battle 32.29
You shall take one leader of e. tribe, 34.18
for e. one of the people of Israel 36.07

EVERY (cont.)

And e. daughter who possesses an Num 36.08
so that e. one of the people of 36.08
And e. man of you girded on his Deu 1.41
time and utterly destroyed e. city, 2.34
destroying e. city, men, women, and 3.06
shall return e. man to his possession 3.20
and e. living thing that followed 11.06
E. place on which the sole of your 11.24
the hills and under e. green tree; 12.02
e. man doing whatever is right in 12.08
offerings at e. place that you see 12.13
for e. abominable thing which the 12.31
E. animal that parts the hoof and 14.06
e. raven after its kind; 14.14
"At the end of e. three years you 14.28
"At the end of e. seven years you 15.01
e. creditor shall release what he 15.02
e. man shall give as he is able, 16.17
by their word e. dispute and e. assault 21.05
keep yourself from e. evil thing. 23.09
e. man shall be put to death for 24.16
E. sickness also, and e. affliction 28.61
them, "At the end of e. seven years, 31.10
E. place that the sole of your foot Jos 1.03
shall go up e. man straight before 6.05
e. man straight before him, and they 6.20
utterly destroyed e. person in it, 10.28
of the sword, and e. person in it; 10.30
and e. person in it, as he had done 10.32
and e. person in it he utterly 10.35
and its towns, and e. person in it; 10.37
destroyed it with e. person in it. 10.37
utterly destroyed e. person in it; 10.39
but e. man they smote with the edge 11.14
them rest on e. side just as he 21.44
e. one of them the head of a family 22.14
people away, e. man to his inheritance. 24.28
A maiden or two for e. man; spoil of Ju 5.30
"E. one that laps the water with 7.05
likewise e. one that kneels down to 7.05
the others go e. man to his home." 7.07
rest of Israel e. man to his tent, 7.08
trumpets also on e. side of all the 7.18
They stood e. man in his place 7.21
the LORD set e. man's sword against 7.22
are, so were they, e. one of them; 8.18
give me e. man of you the earrings 8.24
and e. man cast in it the earrings 8.25
of all their enemies on e. side; 8.34
So e. one of the people cut down 9.49
they departed e. man to his home. 9.55
e. man did what was right in his 17.06
e. one could sling a stone at a 20.16
e. male and e. woman that has 21.11
e. man to his tribe and family, and 21.24
out from there e. man to his 21.24
e. man did what was right in his 21.25
parts of e. offering of my people 1Sa 2.29
And e. one who is left in your 2.36
the two ears of e. one that hears 3.11
Egyptians with e. sort of plague 4.08
e. man to his home; and there was 4.10
of Israel, "Go e. man to his city." 8.22
hand of your enemies on e. side; 12.11
sent home, e. man to his tent. 13.02
but e. one of the Israelites went 13.20
and behold, e. man's sword was 14.20
'Let e. man bring his ox or his 14.34
So e. one of the people brought his 14.34
against all his enemies on e. side, 14.47
LORD cuts off e. one of the 20.15
And e. one who was in distress, and 22.02
and e. one who was in debt, and 22.02
and e. one who was discontented, 22.02
of Jesse give e. one of you fields 22.07
And Saul sought him e. day, 23.14
"E. man gird on his sword!" 25.13
And e. man of them girded on his 25.13
The LORD rewards e. man for his 26.23
e. man with his household, and David 27.03
e. one with his household; and they 2Sa 2.03
my life out of e. adversity, 4.09
said, "Send out e. one from me." 13.09
So e. one went out from him. 13.09
at the end of e. year he used to 14.26
Then e. man with a suit or cause 15.04
all Israel fled e. one to his own 18.17
Israel had fled e. man to his own 19.08
e. man to his tents, O Israel!" 20.01
e. man to his home. And Joab 20.22
my soul out of e. adversity, 1Ki 1.29
e. man under his vine and under his 4.25
God has given me rest on e. side; 5.04
e. one passing by it will be 9.08
Once e. three years the fleet of 10.22
E. one of them brought his present, 10.25
the slain, he slew e. male in Edom 11.15
he had cut off e. male in Edom); 11.16
Return e. man to his home, for this 12.24
will cut off from Jeroboam e. male, 14.10
and Asherim on e. high hill and 14.23
high hill and under e. green tree; 14.23
and e. mouth that has not kissed 19.18
and will cut off from Ahab e. male, 21.21
"E. man to his city, and e. man 22.36
and e. man to his country!" 22.36
to anger in e. way that his father 22.53
shall conquer e. fortified city, 2Ki 3.19
and e. choice city, and shall fell e. good tree, 3.19
and ruin e. good piece of land with 3.19
and on e. good piece of land e. man threw 3.25
they stopped e. spring of water, and 3.25
I will cut off from Ahab e. male, 9.08
Then in haste e. man of them took 9.13
e. man with his weapons in his hand, 11.11
but e. man shall die for his own 14.06
by Israel, and e. man fled to his home. 14.12
shekels of silver from e. man, 15.20
the hills, and under e. green tree. 16.04
and Asherim on e. high hill and 17.10
high hill and under e. green tree; 17.10
and Judah by e. prophet and e. seer, 17.13
But e. nation still made gods of 17.29
e. nation in the cities in which 17.29
then e. one of you will eat of 18.31
and e. one of his own fig tree, and 18.31
and e. one of you will drink the 18.31
the ears of e. one who hears of it 21.12
from e. one according to his assessment, 23.35
e. great house he burned down. 25.09
And e. day of his life he dined 25.29
e. day a portion, as long as he 25.30
obliged to come in e. seven days, 1Ch 9.25
charge of opening it e. morning. 9.27
showbread, to prepare it e. Sabbath. 9.32
and of hundreds, with e. leader. 13.01
he not given you peace on e. side? 22.18
And they shall stand e. morning, 23.30
and understands e. plan and thought. 28.09
work will be e. willing man who 28.21
e. one passing by will be astonished, 2Ch 7.21
once e. three years the ships of 9.21
E. one of them brought his present, 9.24
Return e. man to his home, for this 11.04
to the LORD e. morning and e. evening 13.11
that its lamps may burn e. evening; 13.11
he has given us peace on e. side." 14.07
troubled them with e. sort of distress. 15.06
e. man of Judah and Jerusalem, and 20.27
e. man with his weapon in his hand, 23.10
but e. man shall die for his own 25.04
and e. man fled to his home. 25.22
the hills, and under e. green tree. 28.04

EVERY (cont.)
altars in e. corner of Jerusalem. 2Ch 28.24
In e. city of Judah he made high 28.25
lamb for e. one who was not clean, 30.17
saying, "The good LORD pardon e. one 30.18
their cities, e. man to his possession. 31.01
portions to e. male among the 31.19
priests and to e. one among the 31.19
And e. work that he undertook in 31.21
and he gave them rest on e. side. 32.22
who did work in e. kind of service 34.13
e. one whose spirit God had stirred Ez 1.05
offerings of e. one who made a 3.05
and also by e. one who had joined 6.21
the elders and judges of e. city, 10.14
"Let e. man and his servant pass Neh 4.22
God shake out e. man from his 5.13
and e. ten days skins of wine in 5.18
and didst allot to them e. corner; 9.22
year and the exaction of e. debt. 10.31
fruits of all fruit of e. tree, 10.35
the fruit of e. tree, the wine and 10.37
towns of Judah e. one lived on his 11.03
of Judah. e. one in his inheritance. 11.20
the singers, as e. day required. 11.23
his palace to do as e. man desired. Est 1.08
to e. province in its own script 1.22
script and to e. people in its own 1.22
that e. man be lord in his own 1.22
And e. day Mordecai walked in front 2.11
from those of e. other people, 3.08
to e. province in its own script 3.12
own script and e. people in its 3.12
as a decree in e. province by 3.14
And in e. province, wherever the 4.03
to e. province in its own script 8.09
script and to e. people in its own 8.09
who were in e. city to gather and 8.11
issued as a decree in e. province, 8.13
And in e. province and in e. city, 8.17
and at the time appointed e. year, 9.27
and kept throughout e. generation, 9.28
in e. family, province, and city, and 9.28
and all that he has, on e. side? Job 1.10
e. morning, and test him e. moment? 7.18
is the life of e. living thing and 12.10
Terrors frighten him on e. side, 18.11
He breaks me down on e. side, 19.10
and his eye sees e. precious thing. 28.10
He seals up the hand of e. man, 37.07
he searches after e. green thing. 39.08
and look on e. one that is proud, 40.11
Look on e. one that is proud, and 40.12
e. night I flood my bed with tears; Ps 6.06
a God who has indignation e. day. 7.11
E. one utters lies to his neighbor; 12.02
On e. side the wicked prowl, as 12.08
of many—terror on e. side!— as they 31.13
Therefore let e. one who is godly 32.06
Surely e. man stands as a mere 39.05
surely e. man is a mere breath! 39.11
For e. beast of the forest is mine, 50.10
hast delivered me from e. trouble, 54.07
stricken, and chastened e. morning. 73.14
thy arrows flashed on e. side. 77.17
E. day I call upon thee, O LORD; 88.09
they give drink to e. beast of the 104.11
and broke e. staff of bread, 105.16
me, surrounded me on e. side; 118.11
hold back my feet from e. evil way, 119.101
therefore I hate e. false way. 119.104
thy precepts; I hate e. false way. 119.128
and e. one of thy righteous ordinances 119.160
Blessed is e. one who fears the 128.01
yea, e. one who trusts in them! 135.18
e. one of them, the days that were 139.16
E. day I will bless thee, and praise 145.02
the desire of e. living thing. 145.16
justice and equity, e. good path; Pro 2.09
and at e. corner she lies in wait. 7.12
The eyes of the LORD are in e. place, 15.03
E. one who is arrogant is an abomination 16.05
and e. one is a friend to a man who 19.06
but e. fool will be quarreling. 20.03
E. way of a man is right in his own 21.02
but e. one who is hasty comes only 21.05
E. word of God proves true; he is 30.05
and a time for e. matter under Ecc 3.01
to man that e. one should eat and 3.13
has appointed a time for e. matter, 3.17
for every matter, and for e. work. 3.17
E. man also to whom God has given 5.19
For e. matter has its time and way, 8.06
and he says to e. one that he is a 10.03
For God will bring e. deed into 12.14
with e. secret thing, whether good 12.14
E. one loves a bribe and runs after Is 1.23
against e. high tower, and against e. 2.15
e. man his fellow and e. man his neighbor; 3.05
e. one who has been recorded for 4.03
for e. one that is left in the land 7.22
In that day e. place where there 7.23
For e. boot of the tramping warrior 9.05
tumult and e. garment rolled in 9.05
for e. one is godless and an evildoer, 9.17
and e. mouth speaks folly. 9.17
and e. man's heart will melt, 13.07
e. man will turn to his own people, 13.14
and e. man will flee to his own 13.14
On e. head is baldness, e. beard is shorn 15.02
in the squares e. one wails and 15.03
let e. one wail for Moab. Mourn, 16.07
e. man against his brother and e. man against 19.02
e. one to whom it is mentioned will 19.17
e. small vessel, from the cups to 22.24
e. house is shut up so that none 24.10
e. moment I water it. Lest any one 27.03
e. one comes to shame through a 30.05
e. lofty mountain and e. high hill 30.25
And e. stroke of the staff of 30.32
For in that day e. one shall cast 31.07
Be our arm e. morning, our salvation 33.02
then e. one of you will eat of his 36.16
and e. one of his own fig tree, and 36.16
and e. one of you will drink the 36.16
E. valley shall be lifted up, and 40.04
and e. mountain and hill be made 40.04
east whom victory meets at e. step? 41.02
E. one helps his neighbor, and says 41.06
e. one who is called by my name, 43.07
O forest, and e. tree in it! 44.23
'To me e. knee shall bow, e. tongue 45.23
at the head of e. street like an 51.20
we have turned e. one to his own 53.06
shall confute e. tongue that rises 54.17
"Ho, e. one who thirsts, come to the 55.01
e. one who keeps the sabbath, and 56.06
the oaks, under e. green tree; 57.05
remove e. obstruction from my 57.14
go free, and to break e. yoke? 58.06
shall come and e. one shall set Jer 1.15
upon e. high hill and under e. green tree 2.20
up on e. high hill and under e. green tree, 3.06
strangers under e. green tree, 3.13
and archer e. city takes to flight 4.29
e. one who goes out of them shall 5.06
e. one is greedy for unjust gain; 6.13
e. one deals falsely. 6.13
has a sword, terror is on e. side. 6.25
E. one turns to his own course, 8.06
to the greatest e. one is greedy 8.10
to priest e. one deals falsely. 8.10
Let e. one beware of his neighbor, 9.04
for e. brother is a supplanter, and 9.04

EVERY (cont.)
and e. neighbor goes about as a Jer 9.04
E. one deceives his neighbor, and no 9.05
E. man is stupid and without 10.14
e. goldsmith is put to shame by his 10.14
but e. one walked in the stubbornness 11.08
and the grass of e. field wither? 12.04
"E. jar shall be filled with wine."' 13.12
know that e. jar will be filled 13.12
e. one of you follows his stubborn 16.12
hunt them from e. mountain and e. hill, 16.16
beside e. green tree, and on the 17.02
to give to e. man according to his 17.10
Return, e. one from his evil way, and 18.11
and will e. one act according to 18.12
E. one who passes by it is horrified 18.16
the ears of e. one who hears of it 19.03
e. one who passes by it will be 19.08
and e. one shall eat the flesh of 19.09
Pashhur, but Terror on e. side. 20.03
all the day; e. one mocks me. 20.07
Terror is on e. side! "Denounce 20.10
and e. man will say to his neighbor, 22.08
and to e. one who stubbornly 23.17
e. one to his neighbor and e. one 23.35
the burden is e. man's own word, 23.36
e. one of you, from his evil way and 25.05
and e. one turn from his evil way, 26.03
the LORD over e. madman who prophesies, 29.26
then do I see e. man with his hands 30.06
Why has e. face turned pale? 30.06
e. one of them, shall go into 30.16
and e. languishing soul I will 31.25
But e. one shall die for his own 31.30
rewarding e. man according to his 32.19
that e. one should set free his 34.09
covenant that e. one would set 34.10
e. one to his brother and to his 34.17
'Turn now e. one of you from his 35.15
so that e. one may turn from his 36.03
and that e. one will turn from his 36.07
e. man in his tent, they would rise 37.10
and e. person whom Nebuzaradan the 43.06
look not back—terror on e. side! 46.05
and e. inhabitant of the land shall 47.02
Tyre and Sidon e. helper that 47.04
The destroyer shall come upon e. city, 48.08
"For e. head is shaved and e. beard 48.37
e. man straight before him, with 49.05
e. one who passes by it will be 49.17
cry to them: 'Terror on e. side!' 49.29
will scatter to e. wind those who 49.32
calamity from e. side of them, 49.32
e. one who passes by Babylon shall 50.13
e. one shall turn to his own people, 50.16
and e. one shall flee to his own 50.16
Come against her from e. quarter; 50.26
her from e. side on the day of 51.02
let e. man save his life! Be not 51.06
E. man is stupid and without 51.17
e. goldsmith is put to shame by his 51.17
and e. land under their dominion. 51.28
that his city is taken on e. side; 51.31
Let e. man save his life from the 51.45
e. great house he burned down. 52.13
And e. day of his life he dined 52.33
hunger at the head of e. street. Lam 2.19
feast my terrors on e. side; and on 2.22
they are new e. morning; great is 3.23
scattered at the head of e. street. 4.01
they went e. one straight forward, Eze 1.09
upon e. high hill, on all the 6.13
under e. green tree, and under e. leafy 6.13
moaning, e. one over his iniquity. 7.16
e. man in his room of pictures? 8.12
e. man with his weapon for slaughter 9.02
And e. one had four faces: the first 10.14
They went e. one straight forward. 10.22
scatter toward e. wind all who are 12.14
and e. vision comes to naught'? 12.22
and the fulfilment of e. vision. 12.23
the heads of persons of e. stature, 13.18
yourself a lofty place in e. square; 16.24
at the head of e. street you built 16.25
chamber at the head of e. street, 16.31
your lofty place in e. square. 16.31
to you from e. side for your harlotries. 16.33
them against you from e. side, 16.37
Behold, e. one who uses proverbs 16.44
shall be scattered to e. wind; 17.21
branches birds of e. sort will nest. 17.23
e. one according to his ways, says 18.30
set against him snares on e. side; 19.08
e. one of you, and do not defile 20.07
they did not e. man cast away the 20.08
Go serve e. one of you his idols, 20.39
it shall devour e. green tree in 20.47
green tree in you and e. dry tree; 20.47
e. heart will melt and all hands 21.07
e. spirit will faint and all knees 21.07
e. one according to his power, have 22.06
the idols of e. one on whom she doted. 23.07
bring them against you from e. side: 23.22
against you on e. side with 23.24
the ground and tremble e. moment, 26.16
of your great wealth of e. kind; 27.12
of your great wealth of e. kind; 27.18
e. precious stone was your covering, 28.13
that is against her on e. side. Then they 28.23
e. head was made bald and e. shoulder 29.18
they shall tremble e. moment, 32.10
e. one for his own life, on the day 32.10
the mountains and on e. high hill; 34.06
and e. wall shall tumble to the 38.20
I will summon e. kind of terror 38.21
e. man's sword will be against his 38.21
of prey of e. sort and to the wild 39.04
to the birds of e. sort and to all 39.17
round about the temple on e. side. 41.10
and cherub. E. cherub had two faces: 41.18
and e. devoted thing in Israel 44.29
and e. offering of all kinds from 44.30
and one sheep from e. flock of two 45.15
the river goes e. living creature 47.09
will bear fresh fruit e. month, 47.12
And in e. matter of wisdom and Dan 1.20
and e. kind of music, you are to 3.05
and e. kind of music, all the 3.07
that e. man who hears the sound of 3.10
and e. kind of music, shall fall 3.10
and e. kind of music, to fall down 3.15
and magnify himself above e. god, 11.36
e. one whose name shall be found 12.01
E. evil of theirs is in Gilgal; Hos 9.15
his treasury of e. precious thing. 13.15
down beside e. altar upon garments Amo 2.08
e. one straight before her; and you 4.03
bring your sacrifices e. morning, 4.04
morning, your tithes e. three days; 4.04
in e. place they shall be cast out 8.03
and e. one mourn who dwells in it, 8.08
all loins, and baldness on e. head; 8.10
so that e. man from Mount Esau will Ob 1.09
yea, let e. one turn from his evil Jon 3.08
but they shall sit e. man under his Mic 4.04
or wealth of e. precious thing. Nah 2.09
in pieces at the head of e. street; 3.10
They laugh at e. fortress, for they Hab 1.10
I will punish e. one who leaps Zep 1.09
E. one who passes by her hisses and 2.15
e. morning he shows forth his 3.05
and so with e. work of their hands; Hag 2.14
e. one by the sword of his fellow. 2.22
e. one of you will invite his Zec 3.10

EVERY (cont.)
for e. one who steals shall be cut Zec 5.03
and e. one who swears falsely shall 5.03
for I set e. man against his fellow 8.10
the nations of e. tongue shall 8.23
to e. one the vegetation in the 10.01
battle bow, out of them e. ruler. 10.04
I will strike e. horse with panic, 12.04
when I strike e. horse of the 12.04
On that day e. prophet will be 13.04
Then e. one that survives of all 14.16
and e. pot in Jerusalem and Judah 14.21
and in e. place incense is offered Mal 1.11
By saying, "E. one who does evil 2.17
e. tree therefore that does not Mt 3.10
but by e. word that proceeds from 4.04
and healing e. disease and e. infirmity 4.23
say to you that e. one who is 5.22
say to you that e. one who looks 5.28
say to you that e. one who divorces 5.32
For e. one who asks receives, and he 7.08
So, e. sound tree bears good fruit, 7.17
E. tree that does not bear good 7.19
"Not e. one who says to me, 'Lord, 7.21
"E. one then who hears these words 7.24
And e. one who hears these words of 7.26
and healing e. disease and e. infirmity. 9.35
and to heal e. disease and e. infirmity. 10.01
So e. one who acknowledges me 10.32
"E. kingdom divided against itself 12.25
e. sin and blasphemy will be 12.31
account for e. careless word they 12.36
sea and gathered fish of e. kind; 13.47
"Therefore e. scribe who has been 13.52
He answered, "E. plant which my 15.13
he will repay e. man for what he 16.27
that e. word may be confirmed by 18.16
Father will do to e. one of you, 18.35
And e. one who has left houses or 19.29
For to e. one who has will more be 25.29
"E. one is searching for you." Mk 1.37
people came to him from e. quarter. 1.45
For e. one will be salted with fire 9.49
"E. male that opens the womb shall Lk 2.23
to Jerusalem e. year at the feast 2.41
E. valley shall be filled, and e. 3.05
and e. mountain and hill shall be 3.05
e. tree therefore that does not 3.09
the devil had ended e. temptation, 4.13
went out into e. place in the 4.37
his hands on e. one of them and 4.40
had come from e. village of 5.17
Give to e. one who begs from you; 6.30
but e. one when he is fully taught 6.40
E. one who comes to me and hears my 6.47
into e. town and place where he 10.01
ourselves forgive e. one who is 11.04
For e. one who asks receives, and he 11.10
"E. kingdom divided against itself 11.17
you tithe mint and rue and e. herb, 11.42
e. one who acknowledges me before 12.08
And e. one who speaks a word 12.10
E. one to whom much is given, of him 12.48
For e. one who exalts himself will 14.11
and e. one enters it violently. 16.16
"E. one who divorces his wife and 16.18
and who feasted sumptuously e. day. 16.19
for e. one who exalts himself will 18.14
that to e. one who has will more be 19.26
you, and hem you in on e. side, 19.43
E. one who falls on that stone will 20.18
And e. day he was teaching in the 21.37
that enlightens e. man was coming Jn 1.09
"E. man serves the good wine first; 2.10
so it is with e. one who is born of 3.08
For e. one who does evil hates the 3.20
"E. one who drinks of this water 4.13
that e. one who sees the Son and 6.40
E. one who has heard and learned 6.45
e. one who commits sin is a slave 8.34
e. one will believe in him, and the 11.48
E. branch of mine that bears no 15.02
and e. branch that does bear fruit 15.02
e. man to his home, and will leave 16.32
E. one who is of the truth hears my 18.37
e. one who makes himself a king 19.12
were e. one of them to be written, I 21.25
devout men from e. nation under Ac 2.05
and be baptized e. one of you in 2.38
e. one whom the Lord our God calls 2.39
And fear came upon e. soul; and many 2.43
shall be that e. soul that does 3.23
you in turning e. one of you from 3.26
And e. day in the temple and at 5.42
but in e. nation any one who fears 10.35
witness that e. one who believes 10.43
e. one according to his ability, to 11.29
prophets which are read e. sabbath, 13.27
and by him e. one that believes is 13.39
elders for them in e. church, with prayer 14.23
has had in e. city those who preach 15.21
for he is read e. sabbath in the 15.21
the brethren in e. city where we 15.36
were opened and e. one's fetters 16.26
market place e. day with those who 17.17
perceive that in e. way you are 17.22
made from one e. nation of men to 17.26
argued in the synagogue e. sabbath, 18.04
to me in e. city that imprisonment 20.23
day to admonish e. one with tears. 20.31
presented for e. one of them. 21.26
know that in e. synagogue I imprisoned 22.19
in e. way and everywhere we accept 24.03
salvation to e. one who has faith, Rom 1.16
will render to e. man according to 2.06
distress for e. human being who 2.09
and peace for e. one who does good, 2.10
Much in e. way. To begin with, 3.02
God be true though e. man be false, 3.04
so that e. mouth may be stopped, and 3.19
that e. one who has faith may be 10.04
For, "e. one who calls upon the name 10.13
to me I bid e. one among you not 12.03
Let e. person be subject to the 13.01
Let e. one be fully convinced in 14.05
e. knee shall bow to me, and e. 14.11
and e. tongue shall give praise to 14.11
those who in e. place call on the 1Co 1.02
that in e. way you were enriched in 1.05
Then e. man will receive his commendation 4.05
teach them everywhere in e. church. 4.17
E. other sin which a man commits is 6.18
Only, let e. one lead the life which 7.17
E. one should remain in the state 7.20
E. athlete exercises self-control 9.25
that the head of e. man is Christ, 11.03
who inspires them all in e. one. 12.06
destroying e. rule and e. authority 15.24
God may be everything to e. one. 15.28
Why am I in peril e. hour? 15.30
Jesus our Lord, I die e. day! 15.31
On the first day of e. week, 16.02
such men and to e. fellow worker 16.16
ourselves to e. man's conscience in 2Co 4.02
We are afflicted in e. way, 4.08
nature is being renewed e. day. 4.16
God we commend ourselves in e. way: 6.04
ourselves from e. defilement of 7.01
but we were afflicted at e. turn— 7.05
At e. point you have proved yourselves 7.11
you with e. blessing in abundance, 9.08
in abundance for e. good work. 9.08
be enriched in e. way for great 9.11
arguments and e. proud obstacle to 10.05

EVERY (cont.)

and take e. thought captive to obey 2Co 10.05
being ready to punish e. disobedience, 10.06
in e. way we have made this plain 11.06
"Cursed be e. one who does not abide Gal 3.10
"Cursed be e. one who hangs on a 3.13
again to e. man who receives 5.03
in Christ with e. spiritual Eph 1.03
and above e. name that is named, not 1.21
from whom e. family in heaven and 3.15
about with e. wind of doctrine, by 4.14
to grow up in e. way into him who 4.15
together by e. joint with which it 4.16
to practice e. kind of uncleanness 4.19
let e. one speak the truth with his 4.25
always in e. prayer of mine for you Php 1.04
Only that in e. way, whether in 1.18
the name which is above e. name, 2.09
name of Jesus e. knee should bow, 2.10
and e. tongue confess that Jesus 2.11
God will supply e. need of yours 4.19
Greet e. saint in Christ Jesus. 4.21
fruit in e. good work and increasing Col 1.10
preached to e. creature under 1.23
warning e. man and teaching e. man in all 1.28
we may present e. man mature in 1.28
how you ought to answer e. one. 4.06
abstain from e. form of evil. 1Th 5.22
and the love of e. one of you for 2Th 1.03
and may fulfil e. good resolve and 1.11
himself against e. so-called god 2.04
establish them in e. good work and 2.17
is the mark in e. letter of mine; 3.17
godly and respectful in e. way. 1Ti 2.02
then that in e. place the men 2.08
submissive and respectful in e. way; 3.04
godliness is of value in e. way, 4.08
herself to doing good in e. way. 5.10
"Let e. one who names the name of 2Ti 2.19
quarrelsome but kindly to e. one, 2.24
complete, equipped for e. good work. 3.17
rescue me from e. evil and save me 4.18
elders in e. town as I directed Tit 1.05
to give satisfaction in e. respect; 2.09
was valid and e. transgression or Heb 2.02
he might taste death for e. one. 2.09
like his brethren in e. respect, 2.17
(For e. house is built by some one, 3.04
But exhort one another e. day, 3.13
but one who in e. respect has been 4.15
For e. high priest chosen from 5.01
for e. one who lives on milk is 5.13
For e. high priest is appointed to 8.03
shall not teach e. one his fellow 8.11
his fellow or e. one his brother, 8.11
For when e. commandment of the law 9.19
And e. priest stands daily at his 10.11
let us also lay aside e. weight, 12.01
and chastises e. son whom he 12.06
E. good endowment and e. perfect Jas 1.17
Let e. man be quick to hear, slow to 1.19
For e. kind of beast and bird, of 3.07
be disorder and e. vile practice. 3.16
Lord's sake to e. human institution, 1Pe 2.13
reason make e. effort to supplement 2Pe 1.05
be sure that e. one who does right 1Jn 2.29
And e. one who thus hopes in him 3.03
E. one who commits sin is guilty of 3.04
Beloved, do not believe e. spirit, 4.01
e. spirit which confesses that 4.02
and e. spirit which does not confess 4.03
E. one who believes that Jesus is 5.01
and e. one who loves the parent 5.01
Demetrius has testimony from e. one, 3Jn 1.12
greet the friends, e. one of them. 1.15
and e. eye will see him, e. one who Rev 1.07
for God from e. tribe and tongue 5.09
And I heard e. creature in heaven 5.13
and e. mountain and island was 6.14
and e. one, slave and free, hid in 6.15
out of e. tribe of the sons of 7.04
from e. nation, from all tribes and 7.09
will wipe away e. tear from their 7.17
to smite the earth with e. plague, 11.06
given it over e. tribe and people 13.07
e. one whose name has not been 13.08
to e. nation and tribe and tongue 14.06
and e. living thing died that was 16.03
And e. island fled away, and no 16.20
a haunt of e. foul spirit, a haunt 18.02
a haunt of e. foul and hateful bird 18.02
he will wipe away e. tear from 21.04
city were adorned with e. jewel; 21.19
to repay e. one for what he has 22.12
and e. one who loves and practices 22.15
I warn e. one who hears the words 22.18

EVERYBODY

who wounds e. is he who hires a Pro 26.10

EVERYTHING

and e. that creeps upon the ground Gen 1.25
and to e. that creeps in the earth, 1.30
e. that has the breath of life, I 1.30
And God saw e. that he had made, and 1.31
e. that is on the earth shall die. 6.17
and of e. that creeps on the ground, 7.08
e. on the dry land in whose nostrils 7.22
e. that moves upon the earth, went 8.19
upon e. that creeps on the ground 9.02
the green plants, I give you e. 9.03
and Abram gave him a tenth of e. 14.20
and likewise e. that he had. 32.23
and he has put e. that he has in 39.08
struck down e. that was in the Ex 9.25
E. in the waters that has fins and Lev 11.09
E. in the waters that has not fins 11.12
And e. upon which any part of their 11.35
and e. on which he sits shall be 15.04
And e. upon which she lies during 15.20
e. also upon which she sits shall 15.20
and e. on which she sits shall be 15.26
E. that opens the womb of all flesh, Num 18.15
of Israel e. just as the LORD had 29.40
e. that can stand the fire, you 31.23
man lives by e. that proceeds out Deu 8.03
"E. that I command you you shall be 12.32
and e. else in the city, all its 20.14
until e. was finished that the LORD Jos 4.10
So Samuel told him e. and hid 1Sa 3.18
as e. that the king did pleased all 2Sa 3.36
you shall send to me e. you hear." 15.36
he took away e. He also took 1Ki 14.26
let the field exult, and e. in it! 1Ch 16.32
Manassites for e. pertaining to 26.32
he took away e. He also took 2Ch 12.09
in abundantly the tithe of e. 31.05
and the weight of e. was recorded. Ez 8.34
Thus I cleansed them from e. foreign, Neh 13.30
away and did e. as Esther had ordered Est 4.17
all his friends e. that had befallen 6.13
and sees e. under the heavens. Job 28.24
He beholds e. that is high; he is 41.34
the seas and e. that moves therein. Ps 69.34
has destroyed e. in the sanctuary! 74.03
let the field exult, and e. in it! 96.12
exalted above e. thy name and thy 138.02
Let e. that breathes praise the 150.06
In e. a prudent man acts with Pro 13.16
The simple believes e., but the 14.15
The LORD has made e. for its 16.04
get e. ready for you in the field; 24.27
who is hungry e. bitter is sweet. 27.07
I have seen e. that is done under Ecc 1.14

EVERYTHING (cont.)

For e. there is a season, and a time Ecc 3.01
He has made e. beautiful in its 3.11
In my vain life I have seen e.; 7.15
not know. E. before them is vanity, 9.01
gladdens life, and money answers e. 10.19
know the work of God who makes e. 11.05
and say to them e. that I command Jer 1.17
e. written in this book, which 25.13
But we will do e. that we have 44.17
we have lacked e. and have been 44.18
the rod, my son, with e. of wood. Eze 21.10
desolation upon the land and e. in it, 30.12
so e. will live where the river 47.09
sweep away e. from the face of the Zep 1.02
going into the city they told e., Mt 8.33
with me, and I will pay you e.' 18.26
we have left e. and followed you. 19.27
calves are killed, and e. is ready; 22.04
swears by it and by e. on it; 23.20
those outside e. is in parables; Mk 4.11
his own disciples he explained e. 4.34
was restored, and saw e. clearly. 8.25
we have left e. and followed you." 10.28
and when he had looked round at e., 11.11
her poverty has put in e. she had, 12.44
had performed e. according to the Lk 2.39
they left e. and followed him. 5.11
And he left e., and rose and 5.28
were all marveling at e. he did, 9.43
and behold, e. is clean for you. 11.41
And when he had spent e., a great 15.14
and e. that is written of the Son 18.31
that e. written about me in the law 24.44
but e. that John said about this Jn 10.41
Now they know that e. that thou 17.07
he said to him, "Lord, you know e.; 21.17
earth and the sea and e. in them, Ac 4.24
his own, but they had e. in common. 4.32
and having related e. to them, 10.08
is freed from e. from which you 13.39
who made the world and e. in it, 17.24
to all men life and breath and e. 17.25
from him about e. of which we 24.08
believing e. laid down by the law 24.14
We know that in e. God works for Rom 8.28
E. is indeed clean, but it is wrong 14.20
For the Spirit searches e., even the 1Co 2.10
earth is the Lord's, and e. in it. 10.26
I try to please all men in e. I do, 10.33
remember me in e. and maintain the 11.02
that God may be e. to every one. 15.28
whether you are obedient in e. 2Co 2.09
nothing, and yet possessing e. 6.10
but just as e. we said to you was 7.14
Now as you excel in e.—in faith, 8.07
have enough of e. and may provide 9.08
always and for e. giving thanks in Eph 5.20
be subject in e. to their husbands. 5.24
in the Lord will tell you e. 6.21
Indeed I count e. as loss because Php 3.08
but in e. by prayer and supplication 4.06
that in e. he might be pre-eminent. Col 1.18
which binds e. together in perfect 3.14
do e. in the name of the Lord Jesus, 3.17
Children, obey your parents in e., 3.20
obey in e. those who are your 3.22
tell you of e. that has taken 4.09
but test e.; hold fast what 1Th 5.21
For e. created by God is good, and 1Ti 4.04
furnishes us with e. to enjoy. 6.17
will grant you understanding in e. 2Ti 2.07
Therefore I endure e. for the sake 2.10
so that in e. they may adorn the Tit 2.10
putting e. in subjection under his Heb 2.08
Now in putting e. in subjection 2.08
do not yet see e. in subjection to 2.08
apportioned a tenth part of e. 7.02
that you make e. according to the 8.05
the law almost e. is purified with 9.22
equip you with e. good that you may 13.21
order that in e. God may be glorified 1Pe 4.11
his anointing teaches you about e., 1Jn 2.27
than our hearts, and he knows e. 3.20

EVERYWHERE

well watered e. like the garden of Gen 13.10
his fame spread e. throughout all Mk 1.28
preaching the gospel and healing e. Lk 9.06
he commands all men e. to repent, Ac 17.30
is teaching men e. against the 21.28
in every way and e. we accept this 24.03
we know that e. it is spoken 28.22
as I teach them e. in every church 1Co 4.17
fragrance of the knowledge of him e. 2Co 2.14
faith in God has gone forth e., 1Th 1.08

EVI

E., Rekem, Zur, Hur, and Reba, the five Num 31.08
E. and Rekem and Zur and Hur and Jos 13.21

EVICTIONS

cease your e. of my people, says the Eze 45.09

EVIDENCE

by beasts, let him bring it as e.; Ex 22.13
to death on the e. of witnesses; Num 35.30
On the e. of two witnesses or of Deu 17.06
to death on the e. of one witness. 17.06
only on the e. of two witnesses, or 19.15
speaks the truth gives honest e., Pro 12.17
confirmed by the e. of two or three Mt 18.16
sustained by the e. of two or three 2Co 13.01
This is e. of the righteous judgment 2Th 1.05
except on the e. of two or three 1Ti 5.19
rust will be e. against you and Jas 5.03

EVIDENT

Now it is e. that no man is justified Gal 3.11
For it is e. that our Lord was Heb 7.14
even more e. when another priest 7.15

EVIL

of the knowledge of good and e. Gen 2.09
of good and e. you shall not eat, 2.17
be like God, knowing good and e." 3.05
one of us, knowing good and e.; 3.22
his heart was only e. continually. 6.05
man's heart is e. from his youth; 8.21
'Why have you returned e. for good? 44.04
fear to see the e. that would come 44.34
few and e. have been the days of 47.09
who has redeemed me from all e., 48.16
for all the e. which we did to him 50.15
sin, because they did e. to you.' 50.17
As for you, you meant e. against me; 50.20
saw that they were in e. plight, Ex 5.19
hast thou done e. to this people? 5.22
he has done e. to this people, and 5.23
you have some e. purpose in mind. 10.10
not follow a multitude to do e.; 23.02
'With e. intent did he bring them 32.12
repent of this e. against thy 32.12
repented of the e. which he thought 32.14
people, that they are set on e. 32.22
When the people heard these e. tidings, 33.04
a rash oath to do e. or to do good, Lev 5.04
I will remove e. beasts from the 26.06
of Israel an e. report of the land Num 13.32
bringing up an e. report against 14.36
brought up an e. report of the 14.37
to bring us to this e. place? 20.05
if it is e. in thy sight, I will go 22.34
that had done e. in the sight of 32.13
men of this e. generation shall Deu 1.35

EVIL (cont.)

have no knowledge of good or e.,	Deu 1.39
doing what is e. in the sight of	4.25
and none of the e. diseases of	7.15
doing what was e. in the sight of	9.18
shall purge the e. from the midst	13.05
does what is e. in the sight of	17.02
woman who has done this e. thing,	17.05
shall purge the e. from the midst	17.07
you shall purge the e. from Israel.	17.12
shall purge the e. from the midst	19.19
again commit any such e. among you.	19.20
shall purge the e. from your midst	21.21
and brings an e. name upon her,	22.14
has brought an e. name upon a	22.19
shall purge the e. from the midst	22.21
you shall purge the e. from Israel.	22.22
shall purge the e. from the midst	22.24
keep yourself from every e. thing.	23.09
shall purge the e. from the midst	24.07
account of the e. of your doings,	28.20
day life and good, death and e.	30.15
of all the e. which they have done,	31.18
days to come e. will befall you,	31.29
will do what is e. in the sight of	31.29
bring upon you all the e. things,	Jos 23.15
did what was e. in the sight of	Ju 2.11
the LORD was against them for e.,	2.15
did what was e. in the sight of	3.07
did what was e. in the sight of	3.12
done what was e. in the sight of	3.12
did what was e. in the sight of	4.01
did what was e. in the sight of	6.01
And God sent an e. spirit between	9.23
did what was e. in the sight of	10.06
did what was e. in the sight of	13.01
death, and put away e. from Israel."	20.13
I hear of your e. dealings from	1Sa 2.23
have added to all our sins this e.,	12.19
you have done all this e., yet do not	12.20
and do what was e. in the sight of	15.19
and an e. spirit from the LORD	16.14
an e. spirit from God is tormenting	16.15
and when the e. spirit from God is	16.16
And whenever the e. spirit from God	16.23
and the e. spirit departed from him	16.23
presumption, and the e. of your heart;	17.28
the morrow an e. spirit from God	18.10
Then an e. spirit from the LORD	19.09
then know that e. is determined by	20.07
my father that e. should come upon	20.09
Saul was plotting e. against him;	23.09
good, whereas I have repaid you e.	24.17
for e. is determined against our	25.17
and he has returned me e. for good.	25.21
who seek to do e. to my lord be as	25.26
and e. shall not be found in you so	25.28
has kept back his servant from e.;	25.39
to do what is e. in his sight?	2Sa 12.09
I will raise up e. against you out	12.11
of God to discern good and e.	14.17
quickly, and bring down e. upon us,	15.14
LORD might bring e. upon Absalom.	17.14
all who rise up against you for e.,	18.32
than all the e. that has come upon	19.07
it, the LORD repented of the e.,	24.16
heart all the e. that you did to	1Ki 2.44
bring back your e. upon your own	2.44
I may discern between good and e.;	3.09
has brought all this e. upon them.' "	9.09
did what was e. in the sight of	11.06
did not turn from his e. way,	13.33
but you have done e. above all that	14.09
I will bring e. upon the house of	14.10
did what was e. in the sight of	14.22
He did what was e. in the sight of	15.26
He did what was e. in the sight of	15.34
of all the e. that he did in the	16.07
doing e. in the sight of the LORD,	16.19
Omri did what was e. in the sight	16.25
and did more e. than all who were	16.25
son of Omri did e. in the sight of	16.30
to do what is e. in the sight of	21.20
Behold, I will bring e. upon you;	21.21
to do what was e. in the sight of	21.25
will not bring the e. in his days;	21.29
I will bring the e. upon his house."	21.29
prophesies good concerning me, but e."	22.08
prophesy good concerning me, but e.?"	22.18
LORD has spoken e. concerning you."	22.23
He did what was e. in the sight of	22.52
He did what was e. in the sight of	2Ki 3.02
I know the e. that you will do to	8.12
he did what was e. in the sight of	8.18
did what was e. in the sight of	8.27
He did what was e. in the sight of	13.02
did what was e. in the sight of	13.11
And he did what was e. in the sight	14.24
And he did what was e. in the sight	15.09
And he did what was e. in the sight	15.18
And he did what was e. in the sight	15.24
And he did what was e. in the sight	15.28
And he did what was e. in the sight	17.02
"Turn from your e. ways and keep my	17.13
themselves to do e. in the sight of	17.17
And he did what was e. in the sight	21.02
He did much e. in the sight of the	21.06
them to do more e. than the	21.09
and Judah such e. that the ears of	21.12
done what is e. in my sight and	21.15
did what was e. in the sight of	21.16
And he did what was e. in the sight	21.20
I will bring e. upon this place and	22.16
not see all the e. which I will	22.20
And he did what was e. in the sight	23.32
And he did what was e. in the sight	23.37
And he did what was e. in the sight	24.09
And he did what was e. in the sight	24.19
because e. had befallen his house.	1Ch 7.23
saw, and he repented of the e.;	21.15
has brought all this e. upon them.	2Ch 7.22
And he did e., for he did not set	12.14
good concerning me, but always e."	18.07
prophesy good concerning me, but e.?"	18.17
LORD has spoken e. concerning you."	18.22
'If e. comes upon us, the sword,	20.09
he did what was e. in the sight of	21.06
He did what was e. in the sight of	22.04
done what was e. in the sight of	29.06
He did what was e. in the sight of	33.02
He did much e. in the sight of the	33.06
they did more e. than the nations	33.09
He did what was e. in the sight of	33.22
I will bring e. upon this place and	34.24
not see all the e. which I will	34.28
He did what was e. in the sight of	36.05
He did what was e. in the sight of	36.09
He did what was e. in the sight of	36.12
upon us for our e. deeds and for	Ez 9.13
so they could give me an e. name,	Neh 6.13
rest they did e. again before thee,	9.28
discovered the e. that Eliashib	13.07
"What is this e. thing which you	13.17
bring all this e. on us and on	13.18
all this great e. and act treacherously	13.27
for he saw that e. was determined	Est 7.07
to avert the e. design of Haman	8.03
feared God, and turned away from e.	Job 1.01
fears God and turns away from e?"	1.08
fears God and turns away from e.?	2.03
God, and shall we not receive e.?"	2.10
of all this e. that had come upon	2.11
seven there shall no e. touch you.	5.19
and bring forth e. and their heart	15.35

EVIL (cont.)
to depart from e. is understanding.'" Job 28.28
But when I looked for good, e. came; 30.26
or exulted when e. overtook him 31.29
because of the pride of e. men. 35.12
him for all the e. that the LORD 42.11
e. may not sojourn with thee. Ps 5.04
Depart from me, all you workers of e.; 6.08
my friend with e. or plundered my 7.04
O let the e. of the wicked come to 7.09
Behold, the wicked man conceives e., 7.14
and does no e. to his friend, nor 15.03
If they plan e. against you, if they 21.11
the shadow of death, I fear no e.; 23.04
men in whose hands are e. devices, 26.10
with those who are workers of e., 28.03
according to the e. of their deeds; 28.04
Keep your tongue from e., and your 34.13
Depart from e., and do good; seek 34.14
E. shall slay the wicked; 34.21
confounded who devise e. against me! 35.04
They requite me e. for good; my soul 35.12
is not good; he spurns not e. 36.04
the man who carries out e. devices! 37.07
yourself; it tends only to e. 37.08
they are not put to shame in e. times, 37.19
Depart from e., and do good; so shall 37.27
Those who render me e. for good are 38.20
"You give your mouth free rein for e., 50.19
done that which is e. in thy sight, 51.04
You love e. more than good, and 52.03
Have those who work e. no understanding, 53.04
He will requite my enemies with e.; 54.05
their thoughts are against me for e. 56.05
deliver me from those who work e., 59.02
of those who treacherously plot e. 59.05
They hold fast to their e. purpose; 64.05
as many years as we have seen e. 90.15
no e. shall befall you, no scourge 91.10
heard the doom of my e. assailants. 92.11
The LORD loves those who hate e.; 97.10
from me; I will know nothing of e. 101.04
melted away in their e. plight; 107.26
So they reward me e. for good, 109.05
those who speak e. against my life 109.20
He is not afraid of e. tidings; 112.07
back my feet from every e. way, 119.101
who persecute me with e. purpose; 119.150
The LORD will keep you from all e.; 121.07
themselves up against thee for e.! 139.20
Deliver me, O LORD, from e. men; 140.01
who plan e. things in their heart, 140.02
wicked; do not further his e. plot! 140.08
let e. hunt down the violent man 140.11
Incline not my heart to any e., 141.04
for their feet run to e., and they Pro 1.16
be at ease, without dread of e. 1.33
delivering you from the way of e., 2.12
in doing e. and delight in the 2.14
delight in the perverseness of e.; 2.14
the LORD, and turn away from e. 3.07
Do not plan e. against your neighbor 3.29
do not walk in the way of e. men. 4.14
the left; turn your foot away from e. 4.27
with perverted heart devises e., 6.14
feet that make haste to run to e., 6.18
to preserve you from the e. woman, 6.24
The fear of the LORD is hatred of e. 8.13
and the way of e. and perverted 8.13
but he who pursues e. will die. 11.19
Be assured, an e. man will not go 11.21
but e. comes to him who searches 11.27
but a man of e. devices he condemns 12.02
An e. man is ensnared by the transgression 12.13
the heart of those who devise e., 12.20
A righteous man turns away from e., 12.26
turn away from e. is an abomination 13.19
is cautious and turns away from e., 14.16
The e. bow down before the good, the 14.19
Do they not err that devise e.? 14.22
keeping watch on the e. and the good. 15.03
All the days of the afflicted are e., 15.15
of the wicked pours out e. things. 15.28
fear of the LORD a man avoids e. 16.06
an abomination to kings to do e., 16.12
of the upright turns aside from e.; 16.17
A worthless man plots e., and his 16.27
compresses his lips brings e. to pass. 16.30
An e. man seeks only rebellion, and 17.11
If a man returns e. for good, 17.13
e. will not depart from his house. 17.13
winnows all e. with his eyes. 20.08
Do not say, "I will repay e."; 20.22
Blows that wound cleanse away e.; 20.30
The soul of the wicked desires e.; 21.10
when he brings it with e. intent. 21.27
Be not envious of e. men, nor desire 24.01
He who plans to do e. will be called 24.08
for the e. man has no future; the lamp 24.20
are smooth lips with an e. heart. 26.23
E. men do not understand justice, 28.05
upright into an e. way will fall 28.10
An e. man is ensnared in his 29.06
or if you have been devising e., 30.32
This also is vanity and a great e. Ecc 2.21
not seen the e. deeds that are 4.03
do not know that they are doing e. 5.01
There is a grievous e. which I have 5.13
This also is a grievous e.: just as 5.16
There is an e. which I have seen 6.01
against an e. deed is not executed 8.11
sons of men is fully set to do e. 8.11
Though a sinner does e. a hundred 8.12
the wicked, to the good and the e., 9.02
This is an e. in all that is done 9.03
the hearts of men are full of e., 9.03
fish which are taken in an e. net, 9.12
of men are snared at an e. time, 9.12
ointment give off an e. odor; 10.01
There is an e. which I have seen 10.05
know not what e. may happen on 11.02
before the e. days come, and the 12.01
secret thing, whether good or e. 12.14
remove the e. of your doings from Is 1.16
before my eyes; cease to do e., 1.16
have brought e. upon themselves. 3.09
those who call e. good and good e., 5.20
has devised e. against you, saying, 7.05
to refuse the e. and choose the 7.15
to refuse the e. and choose the 7.16
I will punish the world for its e., 13.11
who watch to do e. shall be cut 29.20
The knaveries of the knave are e.; 32.07
his eyes from looking upon e. 33.15
But e. shall come upon you, for 47.11
keeps his hand from doing any e. 56.02
Their feet run to e., and they 59.07
departs from e. makes himself a 59.15
but you did what was e. in my eyes, 65.12
they did what was e. in my eyes, 66.04
of the north e. shall break forth Jer 1.14
e. came upon them, says the LORD. 2.03
see that it is e. and bitter for 2.19
done all the e. that you could." 3.05
stubbornly follow their own e. heart. 3.17
because of the e. of your doings. 4.04
for I bring e. from the north, and 4.06
long shall your e. thoughts lodge 4.14
and proclaims e. from Mount Ephraim. 4.15
They are skilled in doing e., 4.22
no e. will come upon us, nor shall 5.12
for e. looms out of the north, and 6.01
I am bringing e. upon this people, 6.19
stubbornness of their e. hearts, 7.24

EVIL (cont.)
of Judah have done e. in my sight, Jer 7.30
remains of this e. family in all 8.03
for they proceed from e. to e., 9.03
of them, for they cannot do e., 10.05
the stubbornness of his e. heart. 11.08
I am bringing e. upon them which 11.11
you, has pronounced e. against you, 11.17
because of the e. which the house 11.17
thou didst show me their e. deeds. 11.18
I will bring e. upon the men of 11.23
concerning all my e. neighbors who 12.14
This e. people, who refuse to hear 13.10
good who are accustomed to do e. 13.23
all this great e. against us? 16.10
you follows his stubborn e. will, 16.12
I have not pressed thee to send e., 17.16
art my refuge in the day of e. 17.17
bring upon them the day of e.; 17.18
I have spoken, turns from its e., 18.08
repent of the e. that I intended 18.08
and if it does e. in my sight, not 18.10
I am shaping e. against you and 18.11
return, every one from his e. way, 18.11
the stubbornness of his e. heart.' 18.12
Is e. a recompense for good? Yet 18.20
bringing such e. upon this place 19.03
towns all the e. that I have 19.15
this city for e. and not for good, 21.10
it, because of your e. doings. 21.12
attend to you for your e. doings, 23.02
Their course is e., and their 23.10
I will bring e. upon them in the 23.12
'No e. shall come upon you.'" 23.17
have turned them from their e. way, 23.22
and from the e. of their doings. 23.22
from his e. way and wrong doings, 25.05
I begin to work e. at the city 25.29
e. is going forth from nation to 25.32
and every one turn from his e. way, 26.03
repent of the e. which I intend to 26.03
to them because of their e. doings. 26.03
repent of the e. which he has 26.13
repent of the e. which he had 26.19
to bring great e. upon ourselves." 26.19
plans for welfare and not for e., 29.11
and bring e., so I will watch over 31.28
made all this e. come upon them. 32.23
nothing but e. in my sight from 32.30
because of all the e. of the sons 32.32
all this great e. upon this people, 32.42
every one of you from his e. way, 35.15
Jerusalem all the e. that I have 35.17
hear all the e. which I intend to 36.03
every one may turn from his e. way, 36.03
one will turn from his e. way, for great 36.07
all the e. that I have pronounced 36.31
men have done e. in all that they 38.09
this city for e. and not for good, 39.16
pronounced this e. against this 40.02
of all the e. which Ishmael the 41.11
Whether it is good or e., we will 42.06
I repent of the e. which I did to 42.10
from the e. which I will bring 42.17
seen all the e. that I brought 44.02
this great e. against yourselves, 44.07
set my face against you for e., 44.11
food, and prospered, and saw no e. 44.17
bear your e. doings and the abominations 44.22
that this e. has befallen you, as at 44.23
over them for e. and not for good; 44.27
surely stand against you for e.: 44.29
I am bringing e. upon all flesh, 45.05
they planned e. against her: 48.02
for they have heard e. tidings; 49.23
I will bring e. upon them my fierce 49.37
for all the e. that they have done 51.24
a book all the e. that should come 51.60
because of the e. that I am bringing 51.64
And he did what was e. in the sight 52.02
"Let all their e. doing come before Lam 1.22
Most High that good and e. come? 3.38
that I would do this e. to them." Eze 6.10
of all the e. abominations of the 6.11
e. beasts, and pestilence, to cut off 14.21
consoled for the e. that I have 14.22
not according to your e. ways, 20.44
the land into the hand of e. men; 30.12
back, turn back from your e. ways; 33.11
the talk and e. gossip of the 36.03
Then you will remember your e. ways, 36.31
and you will devise an e. scheme 38.10
that I remember all their e. works. Hos 7.02
yet they devise e. against me. 7.15
Every e. of theirs is in Gilgal; 9.15
steadfast love, and repents of e. Joe 2.13
Does e. befall a city, unless the Amo 3.06
such a time; for it is an e. time. 5.13
and not e., that you may live; 5.14
Hate e., and love good, and establish 5.15
O you who put far away the e. day, 6.03
upon them for e. and not for good." 9.04
'E. shall not overtake or meet us.' 9.10
account this e. has come upon us." Jon 1.07
account this e. has come upon us? 1.08
turn from his e. way and from the 3.08
how they turned from their e. way, 3.10
repented of the e. which he had 3.10
steadfast love, and repentest of e. 4.02
because e. has come down from the Mic 1.12
and work e. upon their beds! When the 2.01
this family I am devising e., from which 2.03
haughtily, for it will be an e. time. 2.03
You who hate the good and love the e., 3.02
they have made their deeds e. 3.04
midst of us? No e. shall come upon us." 3.11
Their hands are upon what is e., 7.03
man utters the e. desire of his 7.03
who plotted e. against the LORD, and Nah 1.11
has not come your unceasing e.? 3.19
than to behold e. and canst not Hab 1.13
Woe to him who gets e. gain for his 2.09
your midst; you shall fear e. no more. Zep 3.15
from your e. ways and from your e. deeds.' Zec 1.04
of you devise e. against his brother 7.10
"As I purposed to do e. to you, when 8.14
do not devise e. in your hearts against 8.17
in sacrifice, is that no e.? And when Mal 1.08
are lame or sick, is that no e.? 1.08
one who does e. is good in the 2.17
all kinds of e. against you falsely Mt 5.11
more than this comes from e. 5.37
you, Do not resist one who is e. 5.39
sun rise on the e. and on the good, 5.45
temptation, But deliver us from e. 6.13
who are e., know how to give good 7.11
but the bad tree bears e. fruit. 7.17
A sound tree cannot bear e. fruit, 7.18
"Why do you think e. in your hearts? 9.04
you speak good, when you are e.? 12.34
and the e. man out of his e. 12.35
man out of his e. treasure brings forth e. 12.35
"An e. and adulterous generation 12.39
other spirits more e. than himself, 12.45
it be also with this e. generation." 12.45
the e. one comes and snatches away 13.19
weeds are the sons of the e. one, 13.38
separate the e. from the righteous, 13.49
'He who speaks e. of father or mother, 15.04
For out of the heart come e. thoughts, 15.19
An e. and adulterous generation seeks 16.04
And he said, "Why, what e. has he done?" 27.23
'He who speaks e. of father or mother, Mk 7.10
come e. thoughts, fornication, theft, 7.21

EVIL (cont.)
All these e. things come from within, Mk 7.23
able soon after to speak e. of me. 9.39
to them, "Why, what e. has he done?" 15.14
and for all the e. things that Herod Lk 3.19
you, and cast out your name as e., 6.22
and the e. man out of his e. treasure 6.45
produces e.; for out of the abundance 6.45
diseases and plagues and e. spirits, 7.21
been healed of e. spirits and 8.02
who are e., know how to give good 11.13
other spirits more e. than himself, 11.26
generation is an e. generation; 11.29
Lazarus in like manner e. things; 16.25
to them, "Why, what e. has he done? 23.22
light, because their deeds were e. Jn 3.19
one who does e. hates the light, 3.20
life, and those who have done e., 5.29
of it that its works are e. 7.07
shouldst keep them from the e. one. 17.15
how much e. he has done to thy Ac 9.13
speaking e. of the Way before the 19.09
them and the e. spirits came out 19.12
over those who had e. spirits, 19.13
But the e. spirit answered them, 19.15
man in whom the e. spirit was 19.16
shall not speak e. of a ruler of 23.05
reported or spoken any e. about you. 28.21
e., covetousness, malice. Full of Rom 1.29
inventors of e., disobedient to 1.30
for every human being who does e., 2.09
And why not do e. that good may 3.08
but the e. I do not want is what I 7.19
do right, e. lies close at hand. 7.21
hate what is e., hold fast to what 12.09
Repay no one e. for e., but take 12.17
overcome by e., but overcome e. with 12.21
is good to you be spoken of as e. 14.16
and guileless as to what is e.; 16.19
the leaven of malice and e., but with 1Co 5.08
us, not to desire e. as they did. 10.06
be babes in e., but in thinking be 14.20
each one may receive good or e., 2Co 5.10
deliver us from the present e. age, Gal 1.04
Let no e. talk come out of your Eph 4.29
the time, because the days are e. 5.16
be able to withstand in the e. day, 6.13
the flaming darts of the e. one. 6.16
hostile in mind, doing e. deeds, Col 1.21
e. desire, and covetousness, which is 3.05
none of you repays e. for e., 1Th 5.15
abstain from every form of e. 5.22
delivered from wicked and e. men; 2Th 3.02
strengthen you and guard you from e. 3.03
while e. men and impostors will go 2Ti 3.13
me from every e. and save me for 4.18
liars, e. beasts, lazy gluttons." Tit 1.12
having nothing e. to say of us. 2.08
to speak e. of no one, to avoid 3.02
lest there be in any of you an e., Heb 3.12
practice to distinguish good from e. 5.14
clean from an e. conscience and 10.22
be tempted with e. and he himself Jas 1.13
and become judges with e. thoughts? 2.04
a restless e., full of deadly poison. 3.08
Do not speak e. against one another, 4.11
He that speaks e. against a brother 4.11
speaks e. against the law and 4.11
arrogance. All such boasting is e. 4.16
your freedom as a pretext for e.; 1Pe 2.16
Do not return e. for e. or reviling 3.09
his tongue from e. and his lips 3.10
him turn away from e. and do right; 3.11
Lord is against those that do e." 3.12
you have overcome the e. one. 1Jn 2.13
and you have overcome the e. one. 2.14
who was of the e. one and murdered 3.12
own deeds were e. and his brother's 3.12
and the e. one does not touch him. 5.18
is in the power of the e. one. 5.19
prating against me with e. words. 3Jn 1.10
Beloved, do not imitate e. but 1.11
he who does e. has not seen God. 1.11
you cannot bear e. men but have Rev 2.02
and foul and e. sores came upon the 16.02
Let the evildoer still do e., 22.11

EVILDOER
requite the e. according to his 2Sa 3.39
Break thou the arm of the wicked and e.; Ps 10.15
An e. listens to wicked lips; Pro 17.04
for every one is godless and an e., Is 9.17
him, "If this man were not an e., Jn 18.30
Let the e. still do evil, and the Rev 22.11

EVILDOERS
man, nor take the hand of e. Job 8.20
in company with e. and walks with 34.08
darkness where e. may hide themselves 34.22
thy eyes; thou hatest all e. Ps 5.05
all the e. who eat up my people as 14.04
a company of e. encircle me; 22.16
I hate the company of e., and I will 26.05
When e. assail me, uttering slanders 27.02
The face of the LORD is against e., 34.16
There the e. lie prostrate, they are 36.12
wicked, from the scheming of e., 64.02
like grass and all e. flourish, 92.07
perish; all e. shall be scattered. 92.09
words, they boast, all the e. 94.04
Who stands up for me against e.? 94.16
off all the e. from the city of 101.08
you e., that I may keep the commandments 119.115
the LORD will lead away with e.! 125.05
for me, and from the snares of e.! 141.09
is upright, but destruction to e. Pro 10.29
to the righteous, but dismay to e. 21.15
Fret not yourself because of e., 24.19
offspring of e., sons who deal Is 1.04
descendants of e. nevermore be 14.20
arise against the house of the e., 31.02
of the needy from the hand of e. Jer 20.13
they strengthen the hands of e., 23.14
Gilead is a city of e., tracked Hos 6.08
e. not only prosper but when they Mal 3.15
arrogant and all e. will be stubble 4.01
knew you; depart from me, you e.' Mt 7.23
all causes of sin and all e., 13.41

EVIL-DOING
returned the e. of Nabal upon his 1Sa 25.39
is overthrown through his e., Pro 14.32
who prolongs his life in his e. Ecc 7.15

EVILMERODACH
E. king of Babylon, in the year that 2Ki 25.27
E. king of Babylon, in the year that Jer 52.31

EVILS
and many e. and troubles will come Deu 31.17
'Have not these e. come upon us 31.17
And when many e. and troubles have 31.21
" 'And I will heap e. upon them; 32.23
For e. have encompassed me without Ps 40.12
for my people have committed two e.: Jer 2.13
sight for the e. which they have Eze 6.09
for all the e. that you have committed. 20.43
his case of such e. as I supposed; Ac 25.18
of money is the root of all e.; 1Ti 6.10

EVIL-WORKERS
for the dogs, look out for the e., Php 3.02

EWE
Abraham set seven e. lambs of the Gen 21.28
of these seven e. lambs which you 21.29

EWE (cont.)

"These seven e. lambs you will take Gen 21.30
and one e. lamb a year old without Lev 14.10
the mother is a cow or a e., you shall 22.28
and one e. lamb a year old without Num 6.14
had nothing but one little e. lamb, 2Sa 12.03

EWES

your e. and your she-goats have not Gen 31.38
two hundred e. and twenty rams, 32.14
from tending the e. that had young Ps 78.71
flock of shorn e. that have come Sol 4.02
Your teeth are like a flock of e., 6.06

EXACT

you shall not e. interest from him Ex 22.25
he shall not e. it of his neighbor, Deu 15.02
Of a foreigner you may e. it; but 15.03
its pattern, e. in all its details. 2Ki 16.10
and the e. sum of money that Haman Est 4.07

EXACTED

Menahem e. the money from Israel, 2Ki 15.20
He e. the silver and the gold of 23.35
For you have e. pledges of your Job 22.06

EXACTING

"You are e. interest, each from his Neh 5.07
oil which you have been e. of them." 5.11

EXACTION

year and the e. of every debt. Neh 10.31
ready not as an e. but as a 2Co 9.05

EXACTIONS

poor and take from him e. of wheat, Amo 5.11

EXACTLY

to determine his case more e. Ac 23.15
that it will be e. as I have been 27.25

EXACTOR

shall send an e. of tribute through Dan 11.20

EXACTS

then that God e. of you less than Job 11.06
but one who e. gifts ruins it. Pro 29.04
e. no pledge, commits no robbery, but Eze 18.16

EXALT

my father's God, and I will e. him. Ex 15.02
why then do you e. yourselves above Num 16.03
I will begin to e. you in the Jos 3.07
and e. the power of his anointed." 1Sa 2.10
thou didst e. me above my adversaries, 2Sa 22.49
to the promise of God to e. him; 1Ch 25.05
thou didst e. me above my adversaries; Ps 18.48
and let us e. his name together! 34.03
and he will e. you to possess the 37.34
not the rebellious e. themselves. 66.07
E. thyself, O God, above the heavens! 108.05
Prize her highly, and she will e. you; Pro 4.08
I will e. thee, I will praise thy Is 25.01
e. that which is low, and abase that Eze 21.26
and never again e. itself above 29.15
he shall e. himself and magnify Dan 11.36
Christ did not e. himself to be Heb 5.05
before the Lord and he will e. you. Jas 4.10
that in due time he may e. you. 1Pe 5.06

EXALTATION

the lowly brother boast in his e., Jas 1.09

EXALTED

Agag, and his kingdom shall be e. Num 24.07
day the LORD e. Joshua in the Jos 4.14
my strength is e. in the LORD. 1Sa 2.01
and that he had e. his kingdom for 2Sa 5.12
and e. be my God, the rock of my 22.47
the son of Haggith e. himself, 1Ki 1.05
I have built thee an e. house, 8.13
"Because I e. you from among the 14.07
"Since I e. you out of the dust and 16.02
was highly e. for the sake of his 1Ch 14.02
and thou art e. as head above all. 29.11
I have built thee an e. house, 2Ch 6.02
which is e., every one passing by 7.21
so that he was e. in the sight of 32.23
name which is e. above all blessing Neh 9.05
They are e. a little while, and then Job 24.24
them for ever, and they are e. 36.07
Behold, God is e. in his power; 36.22
as vileness is e. among the sons Ps 12.08
long shall my enemy be e. over me 13.02
and e. be the God of my salvation, 18.46
Be e., O LORD, in thy strength! 21.13
e. among the nations, I am e. in the earth!" 46.10
to God; he is highly e.! 47.09
Be e., O God, above the heavens! 57.05
Be e., O God, above the heavens! 57.11
horns of the righteous shall be e. 75.10
by thy favor our horn is e. 89.17
I have e. one chosen from the 89.19
in my name shall his horn be e. 89.24
Thou hast e. the right hand of his 89.42
But thou hast e. my horn like that 92.10
thou art e. far above all gods. 97.09
he is e. over all the peoples. 99.02
for ever; his horn is e. in honor. 112.09
the right hand of the LORD is e., 118.16
for thou hast e. above everything 138.02
the LORD, for his name alone is e.; 148.13
of the upright a city is e., but it is Pro 11.11
LORD alone will be e. in that day. Is 2.11
LORD alone will be e. in that day. 2.17
the LORD of hosts is e. in justice, 5.16
proclaim that his name is e. 12.04
The LORD is e., for he dwells on 33.05
lift myself up; now I will be e. 33.10
he shall be e. and lifted up, and 52.13
and e. the might of your foes. Lam 2.17
is taken, his heart shall be e., Dan 11.12
he was e. in Israel; but he Hos 13.01
may not be e. over that of Judah. Zec 12.07
Capernaum, will you be e. to heaven? Mt 11.23
whoever humbles himself will be e. 23.12
thrones, and e. those of low degree; Lk 1.52
Capernaum, will you be e. to heaven? 10.15
he who humbles himself will be e. 14.11
for what is e. among men is an 16.15
he who humbles himself will be e. 18.14
Being therefore e. at the right Ac 2.33
God e. him at his right hand as 5.31
myself so that you might be e., 2Co 11.07
Therefore God has highly e. him and Php 2.09
from sinners, e. above the heavens. Heb 7.26
with unutterable and e. joy. 1Pe 1.08

EXALTING

You are still e. yourself against Ex 9.17
e. yourself, or if you have been Pro 30.32

EXALTS

makes rich; he brings low, he also e. 1Sa 2.07
he who has a hasty temper e. folly. Pro 14.29
Righteousness e. a nation, but sin 14.34
therefore he e. himself to show Is 30.18
whoever e. himself will be humbled, Mt 23.12
For every one who e. himself will Lk 14.11
every one who e. himself will be 18.14
who opposes and e. himself against 2Th 2.04

EXAMINATION

and the priest shall make an e., Lev 13.08
and the priest shall make an e., 13.10
then the priest shall make an e., 13.13
and the priest shall make an e., 13.20

EXAMINATION (cont.)
the priest shall make an e., and if Lev 13.39
and the priest shall make an e. 14.03
the priest comes and makes an e., 14.48

EXAMINE
priest shall e. the diseased spot Lev 13.03
priest shall e. him on the seventh 13.05
priest shall e. him again on the 13.06
And the priest shall e. the raw flesh, 13.15
and the priest shall e. him, and if 13.17
the priest shall e. it, and if the 13.25
priest shall e. him the seventh 13.27
the priest shall e. the disease; 13.30
the priest shall e. the disease; 13.32
day the priest shall e. the itch, 13.34
then the priest shall e. him, 13.36
Then the priest shall e. him, 13.43
And the priest shall e. the disease, 13.50
then he shall e. the disease on the 13.51
priest shall e. the diseased thing 13.55
the priest goes to e. the disease, 14.36
And he shall e. the disease; 14.37
they sat down to e. the matter; Ez 10.16
or send to Kedar and e. with care; Jer 2.10
Let us test and e. our ways, Lam 3.40
yoke of oxen, and I go to e. them; Lk 14.19
were about to e. him withdrew from Ac 22.29
defense to those who would e. me. 1Co 9.03
Let a man e. himself, and so eat of 11.28
E. yourselves, to see whether you 2Co 13.05

EXAMINED
the priest has e. him he shall Lev 13.03
if we are being e. today concerning Ac 4.09
he e. the sentries and ordered that 12.19
ordered him to be e. by scourging, 22.24
after we have e. him, I may have 25.26
When they had e. me, they wished to 28.18

EXAMINES
But if the priest e. it, and the hair Lev 13.21
But if the priest e. it, and the hair 13.26
And if the priest e. the itching 13.31
"And if the priest e., and the 13.53
"But if the priest e., and the 13.56
until the other comes and e. him. Pro 18.17

EXAMINING
e. it all, how the righteous and the Ecc 9.01
and after e. him before you, behold, Lk 23.14
e. the scriptures daily to see if Ac 17.11
By e. him yourself you will be able 24.08

EXAMPLE
also seen this e. of wisdom under Ecc 9.13
For I have given you an e., that you Jn 13.15
also follow the e. of the faith Rom 4.12
To give a human e., brethren: Gal 3.15
so live as you have an e. in us. Php 3.17
and made a public e. of them, Col 2.15
you became an e. to all the believers 1Th 1.07
in our conduct an e. to imitate. 2Th 3.09
patience for an e. to those who 1Ti 1.16
believers an e. in speech and conduct, 4.12
As an e. of suffering and patience, Jas 5.10
suffered for you, leaving you an e., 1Pe 2.21
made them an e. to those who were 2Pe 2.06
serve as an e. by undergoing a Jud 1.07

EXAMPLES
charge but being e. to the flock. 1Pe 5.03

EXCEED
righteousness must far e. it in splendor. 2Co 3.09
your latter works e. the first. Rev 2.19

EXCEEDING
the altar of God, to God my e. joy; Ps 43.04
him according to his e. greatness! 150.02
mighty and of e. brightness, stood Dan 2.31

EXCEEDINGLY
and you, and will multiply you e." Gen 17.02
I will make you e. fruitful; 17.06
him fruitful and multiply him e.; 17.20
out with an e. great and bitter 27.34
Thus the man grew e. rich, and had 30.43
were fruitful and multiplied e. 47.27
they multiplied and grew e. strong; Ex 1.07
to spy it out, is an e. good land. Num 14.07
for it is e. bitter to me for your Ru 1.13
played the fool, and have erred e." 1Sa 26.21
But they were e. afraid, and said, 2Ki 10.04
the LORD must be e. magnificent, 1Ch 22.05
was with him and made him e. great. 2Ch 1.01
huge army with e. many chariots 16.08
people likewise were e. unfaithful, 36.14
who rejoice e., and are glad, when Job 3.22
but thy commandment is e. broad. Ps 119.96
testimonies; I love them e. 119.167
are small, but they are e. wise: Pro 30.24
aged you made your yoke e. heavy. Is 47.06
Be not e. angry, O LORD, and remember 64.09
rejected us? Art thou e. angry with us? Lam 5.22
of Israel and Judah is e. great; Eze 9.09
You grew e. beautiful, and came to 16.13
upon their feet, an e. great host. 37.10
Then the king was e. glad, and Dan 6.23
terrible and dreadful and e. strong; 7.07
e. terrible, with its teeth of iron 7.19
Then the he-goat magnified himself e.; 8.08
which grew e. great toward the south, 8.09
war with an e. great and mighty army; 11.25
his army, for his host is e. great; Joe 2.11
Then the men were e. afraid, Jon 1.10
Then the men feared the LORD e., 1.16
Now Nineveh was an e. great city, 3.03
But it displeased Jonah e., and he 4.01
So Jonah was e. glad because of the 4.06
I am e. jealous for Jerusalem and Zec 1.14
they rejoiced e. with great joy; Mt 2.10
And the king was e. sorry; but because Mk 6.26
to say, for they were e. afraid. 9.06
And they were e. astonished, and 10.26

EXCEEDS
righteousness e. that of the scribes Mt 5.20

EXCEL
strive to e. in building up the 1Co 14.12
Now as you e. in everything—in 2Co 8.07
see that you e. in this gracious 8.07

EXCELLED
Thus King Solomon e. all the kings 1Ki 10.23
Thus King Solomon e. all the kings 2Ch 9.22

EXCELLENCE
is gracious, if there is any e., Php 4.08
called us to his own glory and e., 2Pe 1.03

EXCELLENCY
"Claudius Lysias to his E. the Ac 23.26

EXCELLENT
in counsel, and e. in wisdom. Is 28.29
because an e. spirit, knowledge, and Dan 5.12
understanding and e. wisdom are 5.14
because an e. spirit was in him; 6.03
for you, most e. Theophilus, Lk 1.03
most e. Felix, reforms are introduced Ac 24.02
most e. Festus, but I am speaking 26.25
his will and approve what is e., Rom 2.18
will show you a still more e. way. 1Co 12.31

EXCELLENT (cont.)
so that you may approve what is e., Php 1.10
these are e. and profitable to men. Tit 3.08
obtained is more e. than theirs. Heb 1.04
is as much more e. than the old as 8.06

EXCELLENTLY
"Many women have done e., but you Pro 31.29

EXCELS
wisdom e. folly as light e. darkness. Ecc 2.13

EXCEPT
back anything from me e. yourself, Gen 39.09
e. for his nearest of kin, his Lev 21.02
e. Caleb the son of Jephunneh and Num 14.30
e. Caleb the son of Jephunneh and 26.65
none e. Caleb the son of Jephunneh 32.12
e. by the blood of him who shed it. 35.33
e. Caleb the son of Jephunneh; Deu 1.36
did Israel burn, e. Hazor only; Jos 11.13
e. the Hivites, the inhabitants of 11.19
marriage present e. a hundred 1Sa 18.25
e. four hundred young men, who 30.17
e. that each man may lead away his 30.22
And who is a rock, e. our God? 2Sa 22.32
in the ark e. the two tables of 1Ki 8.09
e. in the matter of Uriah the 15.05
rain these years, e. by my word. 17.01
in the house, e. a jar of oil. 2Ki 4.02
e. the poorest people of the land. 24.14
e. as a place to burn incense 2Ch 2.06
in the ark e. the two tables which 5.10
no son was left to him e. Jehoahaz, 21.17
of the LORD e. the priests and 23.06
e. those enrolled by genealogy, 31.16
for nothing e. what Hegai the Est 2.15
e. the one to whom the king holds 4.11
And who is a rock, e. our God? Ps 18.31
not return, e. some fugitives. Jer 44.14
show it to the king e. the gods, Dan 2.11
worship any god e. their own God. 3.28
e. to you, O king, shall be cast into 6.07
man within thirty days e. to you, 6.12
my side against these e. Michael, 10.21
e. that I will not utterly destroy Amo 9.08
for anything e. to be thrown out Mt 5.13
e. on the ground of unchastity, 5.32
no one knows the Son e. the Father, 11.27
the Father e. the Son and any one 11.27
be given to it e. the sign of the 12.39
without honor e. in his own 13.57
be given to it e. the sign of 16.04
never comes out e. by prayer and * 17.21
e. for unchastity, and marries 19.09
e. to be made manifest; nor is anything Mk 4.22
e. to come to light. 4.22
to follow him e. Peter and James 5.37
e. in his own country, and among his 6.04
e. that he laid his hands upon a 6.05
for their journey e. a staff; 6.08
e. Peter and John and James, and the Lk 8.51
knows who the Son is e. the Father, 10.22
the Father is e. the Son and any 10.22
be given to it e. the sign of 11.29
praise to God e. this foreigner?" 17.18
anything e. what is given him from Jn 3.27
seen the Father e. him who is from 6.46
e. for his feet, but he is clean all 13.10
Judea and Samaria, e. the apostles. Ac 8.01
speaking the word to none e. Jews. 11.19
time in nothing e. telling or hearing 17.21
e. that the Holy Spirit testifies 20.23
e. this one thing which I cried out 24.21
such as I am—e. for these chains." 26.29
there is no authority e. from God, Rom 13.01
e. to love one another; for he who 13.08
of anything e. what Christ has 15.18
none of you e. Crispus and Gaius; 1Co 1.14
among you e. Jesus Christ and him 2.02
man's thoughts e. the spirit of 2.11
thoughts of God e. the Spirit of 2.11
one another e. perhaps by agreement 7.05
"Jesus is Lord" e. by the Holy 12.03
I will not boast, e. of my weaknesses. 2Co 12.05
e. that I myself did not burden you? 12.13
other apostles e. James the Lord's Gal 1.19
me to glory e. in the cross of our 6.14
giving and receiving e. you only; Php 4.15
an elder e. on the evidence of two 1Ti 5.19
no one knows e. him who receives Rev 2.17
learn that song e. the hundred and 14.03

EXCEPTED
that he is e. who put all things 1Co 15.27

EXCESS
by which the e. number of them is Num 3.48

EXCESSIVE
he may be overwhelmed by e. sorrow. 2Co 2.07

EXCHANGE
you food in e. for your cattle, if Gen 47.16
them food in e. for the horses, 47.17
with food in e. for all their 47.17
substitute anything for it or e. it, Lev 27.10
if he makes any e. of beast for 27.10
or bad, neither shall he e. it; 27.33
Ethiopia and Seba in e. for you. Is 43.04
you, peoples in e. for your life. 43.04
They shall not sell or e. any of it; Eze 48.14
and make merry and e. presents, Rev 11.10

EXCHANGED
for which it is e. shall be holy. Lev 27.10
for which it is e. shall be holy; 27.33
nor can it be e. for jewels of fine Job 28.17
They e. the glory of God for the Ps 106.20
and lead they e. for your wares. Eze 27.12
they e. the persons of men and 27.13
Bethtogarmah e. for your wares 27.14
they e. for your wares emeralds, 27.16
they e. for your merchandise wheat, 27.17
from Uzal they e. for your wares; 27.19
they e. for your wares the best of 27.22
and e. the glory of the immortal Rom 1.23
because they e. the truth about God 1.25
Their women e. natural relations 1.26

EXCHANGES
and if he e. it, then both it and Lev 27.33

EXCHANGING
Israel concerning redeeming and e.: Ru 4.07

EXCITED
to be quickly shaken in mind or e., 2Th 2.02

EXCLAIMED
and she e. with a loud cry, "Blessed Lk 1.42

EXCLUDE
and when they e. you and revile you, Lk 6.22

EXCLUDED
for he was e. from the house of the 2Ch 26.21
so they were e. from the priesthood Ez 2.62
so they were e. from the priesthood Neh 7.64
who are to be e. from the sanctuary Eze 44.05
It is e. On what principle? Rom 3.27

EXCLUSION
destruction and e. from the 2Th 1.09

EXCREMENT
and turn back and cover up your e. Deu 23.13

EXCUSE
now they have no e. for their sin. Jn 15.22
have been made. So they are without e.; Rom 1.20
Therefore you have no e., O man, whoever 2.01
thoughts accuse or perhaps e. them 2.15

EXCUSED
and see it; I pray you, have me e.' Lk 14.18
examined them; I pray you, have me e.' 14.19

EXCUSES
But they all alike began to make e. Lk 14.18

EXECRATION
make you an e. and an oath among Num 5.21
shall become an e. among her 5.27
You shall become an e., a horror, Jer 42.18
and they shall become an e., 44.12

EXECUTE
gods of Egypt I will e. judgments: Ex 12.12
that shall e. vengeance for the Lev 26.25
priest shall e. upon her all this Num 5.30
to e. the LORD's vengeance on Midian 31.03
that you may e. justice and righteousness 1Ki 10.09
engraving and e. any design that 2Ch 2.14
that you may e. justice and righteousness 9.08
wilt thou not e. judgment upon them? 20.12
He will e. judgment among the nations, Ps 110.06
to e. on them the judgment written! 149.09
my mighty men to e. my anger, my proudly Is 13.03
For by fire will the LORD e. judgment, 66.16
if you truly e. justice one with Jer 7.05
"'E. justice in the morning, and 21.12
and shall e. justice and righteousness 23.05
and he shall e. justice and righteousness 33.15
when I will e. judgment upon her 51.52
and I will e. judgments in the Eze 5.08
and I will e. judgments on you, and 5.10
when I e. judgments on you in anger 5.15
of foreigners, and e. judgments upon you. 11.09
your houses and e. judgments upon 16.41
and I will e. judgments upon Moab. 25.11
I will e. great vengeance upon them 25.17
the LORD when I e. judgments in 28.22
when I e. judgments upon all their 28.26
and will e. acts of judgment upon 30.14
Thus I will e. acts of judgment 30.19
and e. justice and righteousness; 45.09
I will not e. my fierce anger, I Hos 11.09
wrath I will e. vengeance upon the Mic 5.15
given him authority to e. judgment, Jn 5.27
for the Lord will e. his sentence Rom 9.28
of God to e. his wrath on the 13.04
to e. judgment on all, and to Jud 1.15

EXECUTED
gods also the LORD e. judgments. Num 33.04
with Israel he e. the commands and Deu 33.21
Thus they e. judgment on Joash. 2Ch 24.24
judgment be strictly e. upon him, Ez 7.26
and edict were about to be e., Est 9.01
himself known, he has e. judgment; Ps 9.16
thou hast e. justice and righteousness 99.04
an evil deed is not e. speedily, Ecc 8.11
until he has e. and accomplished Jer 23.20
until he has e. and accomplished 30.24
nor e. my ordinances, but have acted Eze 11.12
because they had not e. my ordinances, 20.24
when judgment had been e. upon her. 23.10
see my judgment which I have e., 39.21

EXECUTES
He e. justice for the fatherless Deu 10.18
but it is God who e. judgment, Ps 75.07
and e. justice for the needy. 140.12
who e. justice for the oppressed; 146.07
e. true justice between man and man, Eze 18.08

he that e. his word is powerful. Joe 2.11
my cause and e. judgment for me. Mic 7.09

EXECUTING
And when Jehu was e. judgment upon 2Ch 22.08

EXECUTIONERS
you e. of the city, each with his Eze 9.01

EXEMPT
none was e., and they carried away 1Ki 15.22

EXERCISE
does not e. his right of redemption, Lev 25.33
their great men e. authority over Mt 20.25
their great men e. authority over Mk 10.42
of the Gentiles e. lordship over Lk 22.25
But if they cannot e. self-control, 1Co 7.09
was allowed to e. authority for Rev 13.05

EXERCISED
By Jacob shall dominion be e., Num 24.19
who e. authority over the people. 2Ch 8.10

EXERCISES
Every athlete e. self-control in 1Co 9.25
It e. all the authority of the Rev 13.12

EXERTION
depends not upon man's will or e., Rom 9.16

EXHAUSTED
who were too e. to cross the brook 1Sa 30.10
had been too e. to follow David, 30.21
weary, and young men shall fall e.; Is 40.30

EXHIBITED
that God has e. us apostles as 1Co 4.09

EXHORT
you in your faith and to e. you, 1Th 3.02
we beseech and e. you in the Lord 4.01
But we e. you, brethren, to do so 4.10
And we e. you, brethren, admonish the 5.14
we command and e. in the Lord 2Th 3.12
older man but e. him as you would 1Ti 5.01
and e., be unfailing in patience 2Ti 4.02
e. and reprove with all authority. Tit 2.15
But e. one another every day, as Heb 3.13
So I e. the elders among you, as a 1Pe 5.01

EXHORTATION
have any word of e. for the people, Ac 13.15
read it, they rejoiced at the e. 15.31
he who exhorts, in his e.; he who Rom 12.08
forgotten the e. which addresses Heb 12.05
brethren, bear with my word of e., 13.22

EXHORTATIONS
So, with many other e., he preached Lk 3.18

EXHORTED
with many other words and e. them, Ac 2.40
and he e. them all to remain faithful 11.23
e. the brethren with many words and 15.32
brethren, they e. them and departed. 16.40
and having e. them took leave of 20.01
we e. each one of you and encouraged 1Th 2.11

EXHORTING
e. them to continue in the faith, Ac 14.22
e. and declaring that this is the 1Pe 5.12

EXHORTS
he who e., in his exhortation; Rom 12.08

EXILE
and also an e. from your home. 2Sa 15.19
of the guard carried into e. 2Ki 25.11

EXILE (cont.)

was taken into e. out of its land. 2Ki 25.21
year of the e. of Jehoiachin king 25.27
of Assyria carried away into e.; 1Ch 5.06
dwelt in their place until the e. 5.22
went into e. when the LORD sent 6.15
Jerusalem into e. by the hand of 6.15
were carried into e. to Manahath): 8.06
was taken into e. in Babylon 9.01
He took into e. in Babylon those 2Ch 36.20
of Israel who had returned from e., Ez 6.21
that survived, who had escaped e., Neh 1.02
who escaped e. are in great trouble 1.03
of Babylon had carried into e.; 7.06
people go into e. for want of Is 5.13
by e. thou didst contend with them; 27.08
taken into e., wholly taken into e. Jer 13.19
had taken into e. from Jerusalem 24.01
he took into e. from Jerusalem to 27.20
had taken into e. from Jerusalem 29.01
have sent into e. from Jerusalem 29.04
city where I have sent you into e., 29.07
from which I sent you into e. 29.14
did not go out with you into e.: 29.16
saying, "Your e. will be long; 29.28
carried into e. to Babylon the rest 39.09
not been taken into e. to Babylon, 40.07
us or take us into e. in Babylon." 43.03
Prepare yourselves baggage for e., 46.19
and Chemosh shall go forth into e., 48.07
to vessel, nor has he gone into e.; 48.11
For Milcom shall go into e. 49.03
Judah has gone into e. because of Lam 1.03
he will keep you in e. no longer; 4.22
year of the e. of King Jehoiachin), Eze 1.02
and go into e. by day in their 12.03
go like an e. from your place to 12.03
in their sight, as baggage for e.; 12.04
as men do who must go into e. 12.04
baggage by day, as baggage for e., 12.07
they shall go into e., into captivity.' 12.11
of Judah when it went into e.; 25.03
In the twelfth year of our e., 33.21
sent them into e. among the nations, 39.28
In the twenty-fifth year of our e., 40.01
of Syria shall go into e. to Kir, Amo 1.05
carried into e. a whole people to 1.06
and their king shall go into e., 1.15
for Gilgal shall surely go into e., 5.05
take you into e. beyond Damascus," 5.27
the first of those to go into e., 6.07
must go into e. away from his land 7.11
surely go into e. away from its 7.17
for they shall go from you into e. Mic 1.16
half of the city shall go into e., Zec 14.02
and became an e. in the land of Ac 7.29
throughout the time of your e. 1Pe 1.17

EXILED

So Israel was e. from their own 2Ki 17.23
e. and put away, but who has brought Is 49.21
Judah who were being e. to Babylon. Jer 40.01

EXILE'S

prepare for yourself an e. baggage, Eze 12.03

EXILES

when the e. were brought up from Ez 1.11
of those e. whom Nebuchadnezzar 2.01
the returned e. were building a 4.01
and the rest of the returned e., 6.16
the returned e. kept the passover. 6.19
lamb for all the returned e., 6.20
the returned e., offered burnt 8.35
faithlessness of the returned e., 9.04
over the faithlessness of the e. 10.06
the returned e. that they should 10.07
from the congregation of the e. 10.08
Then the returned e. did so. 10.16
of those e. whom Nebuchadnezzar Neh 7.06
captives and the Ethiopians e., Is 20.04
build my city and set my e. free, 45.13
regard as good the e. from Judah, Jer 24.05
and all the e. from Judah who went 28.04
house of the LORD, and all the e. 28.06
Jerusalem to the elders of the e., 29.01
to all the e. whom I have sent into 29.04
all you e. whom I sent away from 29.20
used by all the e. from Judah in 29.22
"Send to all the e., saying 'Thus 29.31
I was among the e. by the river Eze 1.01
And go, get you to the e., to your 3.11
and I came to the e. at Telabib, 3.15
your fellow e., the whole house of 11.15
of God into Chaldea, to the e. Then 11.24
And I told the e. all the things 11.25
found among the e. from Judah a Dan 2.25
one of the e. of Judah, whom the 5.13
who is one of the e. from Judah, 6.13
The e. in Halah who are of the Ob 1.20
and the e. of Jerusalem who are in 1.20
"Take from the e. Heldai, Tobijah, Zec 6.10
were strangers and e. on the earth. Heb 11.13
To the e. of the dispersion in 1Pe 1.01
as aliens and e. to abstain from 2.11

EXIST

existence the things that do not e. Rom 4.17
and those that e. have been instituted 13.01
are all things and for whom we e., 1Co 8.06
all things and through whom we e. 8.06
for whom and by whom all things e., Heb 2.10
jealousy and selfish ambition e., Jas 3.16
earth that now e. have been stored 2Pe 3.07

EXISTED

word of God heavens e. long ago, 2Pe 3.05
world that then e. was deluged 3.06
thy will they e. and were created." Rev 4.11

EXISTENCE

and calls into e. the things that Rom 4.17
know that "an idol has no real e.," 1Co 8.04

EXISTS

believe that he e. and that he Heb 11.06

EXITS

with the same e. and arrangements Eze 42.11
its e. and its entrances, and its 43.11
"These shall be the e. of the city: 48.30

EXODUS

mention of the e. of the Israelites Heb 11.22

EXORCISTS

itinerant Jewish e. undertook to Ac 19.13

EXPANSE

comprehended the e. of the earth? Job 38.18

EXPECT

and yet they e. him to fulfil their Eze 13.06
is coming at an hour you do not e. Mt 24.44
he does not e. him and at an hour 24.50
is coming at an hour you do not e." Lk 12.40
he does not e. him and at an hour 12.46

EXPECTATION

but the e. of the wicked comes to Pro 10.28
and the e. of the godless comes to 11.07
the e. of the wicked in wrath. 11.23
my glory, and my e. from the LORD." Lam 3.18
As the people were in e., and all Lk 3.15
as it is my eager e. and hope that Php 1.20

EXPECTED
all Israel fully e. me to reign; 1Ki 2.15
not as we e., but first they gave 2Co 8.05

EXPECTING
e. nothing in return; and your Lk 6.35
e. to receive something from them. Ac 3.05
Cornelius was e. them and had 10.24
all that the Jewish people were e. 12.11
They waited, e. him to swell up or 28.06
for I am e. him with the brethren. 1Co 16.11

EXPEDIENT
his wife, it is not e. to marry. Mt 19.10
that it is e. for you that one man Jn 11.50
that it was e. that one man should 18.14

EXPEDITION
us as always when I go on an e.; 1Sa 21.05
from Keilah, he gave up the e. 23.13

EXPELLED
So Solomon e. Abiathar from being 1Ki 2.27

EXPENSE
we eaten at all at the king's e.? 2Sa 19.42
two whole years at his own e., Ac 28.30
Who serves as a soldier at his own e.? 1Co 9.07

EXPENSES
along with them and pay their e., Ac 21.24

EXPENSIVE
alabaster jar of very e. ointment, Mt 26.07

EXPERIENCE
who had no e. of any war in Canaan Ju 3.01
has had great e. of wisdom and Ecc 1.16
which you e. when you patiently 2Co 1.06
Did you e. so many things in vain? Gal 3.04
that the same e. of suffering is 1Pe 5.09

EXPERIENCED
and e. men, according to your tribes, Deu 1.13
wise and e. men, and set them as 1.15
wilderness mighty and e. warriors, 1Ch 12.08
of the affliction we e. in Asia; 2Co 1.08

EXPERT
and became an e. with the bow. Gen 21.20
besides, your father is e. in war; 2Sa 17.08
e. in war, forty-four thousand seven 1Ch 5.18
e. with shield and spear, whose 12.08
all girt with swords and e. in war, Sol 3.08
magician and the e. in charms. Is 3.03

EXPIATE
which you will not be able to e.; Is 47.11

EXPIATED
shall not be e. by sacrifice or 1Sa 3.14
this the guilt of Jacob will be e., Is 27.09

EXPIATION
sprinkle the water of e. upon them, Num 8.07
and no e. can be made for the land, 35.33
and makes e. for the land of his Deu 32.43
And how shall I make e., that you may 2Sa 21.03
put forward as an e. by his blood, Rom 3.25
to make e. for the sins of the Heb 2.17
and he is the e. for our sins, and 1Jn 2.02
his Son to be the e. for our sins. 4.10

EXPIRE
come forth from the womb and e. Job 3.11

EXPIRED
son-in-law. Before the time had e., 1Sa 18.26

EXPLAIN
was no one who could e. it to me." Gen 41.24
Moses undertook to e. this law, Deu 1.05
and e. his case to the elders of Jos 20.04
king which he could not e. to her. 1Ki 10.03
which he could not e. to her. 2Ch 9.02
to Esther and e. it to her and Est 4.08
and to whom will he e. the message Is 28.09
e. riddles, and solve problems were Dan 5.12
"E. to us the parable of the weeds Mt 13.36
said to him, "E. the parable to us." 15.15
much to say which is hard to e., Heb 5.11

EXPLAINED
his own disciples he e. everything. Mk 4.34
But Peter began and e. to them in Ac 11.04

EXPLAINING
e. and proving that it was necessary Ac 17.03

EXPLOIT
greed they will e. you with false 2Pe 2.03

EXPLORE
that they may e. the land for us, Deu 1.22
to spy out the land and to e. it; Ju 18.02
said to them, "Go and e. the land." 18.02

EXPLORED
of the earth below can be e., Jer 31.37

EXPORTED
they were e. to all the kings of 1Ki 10.29
them these were e. to all the 2Ch 1.17

EXPOSE
our fathers to e. their infants, Ac 7.19
of darkness, but instead e. them. Eph 5.11

EXPOSED
your nakedness be not e. on it.' Ex 20.26
wickedness will be e. in the Pro 26.26
they have not e. your iniquity to Lam 2.14
I e. you before kings, to feast Eze 28.17
light, lest his deeds should be e. Jn 3.20
and when he was e., Pharaoh's Ac 7.21
anything is e. by the light it Eph 5.13
sometimes being publicly e. to Heb 10.33
may not go naked and be seen e.!" Rev 16.15

EXPOSING
in them, e. the white of the rods. Gen 30.37

EXPOSURE
often without food, in cold and e. 2Co 11.27

EXPOUNDED
took him and e. to him the way of Ac 18.26
And he e. the matter to them from 28.23

EXPRESSED
For if I have e. to him some pride 2Co 7.14

EXPRESSES
But if her father e. disapproval to Num 30.05
he e. disapproval, then he shall 30.08

EXPRESSING
understanding, but only in e. his opinion. Pro 18.02

EXPRESSION
and the e. of his face was changed Dan 3.19

EXPRESSLY
who were e. named to come and make 1Ch 12.31
chosen and e. named to give thanks 16.41
Now the Spirit e. says that in 1Ti 4.01

EXTEND
the net shall e. half way down the Ex 27.05
then the boundary shall e. to Ziphron, Num 34.09
be none to e. kindness to him, nor Ps 109.12
the Lord will e. his hand yet a Is 11.11
I will e. prosperity to her like a 66.12
that day shall e. from one end of Jer 25.33

EXTENDED
of the Canaanites e. from Sidon, Gen 10.19
they lived e. from Mesha in the 10.30
Their region e. from Mahanaim, Jos 13.30
cherubim together e. twenty cubits: 2Ch 3.11
of these cherubim e. twenty cubits; 3.13
and who e. to me his steadfast love Ez 7.28
but has e. to us his steadfast love 9.09
day the boundary shall be far e. Mic 7.11

EXTENDING
under its ledge, e. halfway down. Ex 38.04
and e. from the western to the Eze 45.07
and e. from the east side to the 48.01
E. from the twenty-five thousand 48.21

EXTENDS
that e. from the boundary of the Num 21.13
valleys that e. to the seat of Ar, 21.15
then the boundary e. from the top Jos 15.09
e. to the heavens, thy faithfulness Ps 36.05
that as grace e. to more and more 2Co 4.15

EXTENT
land of Canaan in its full e.), Num 34.02
be holy throughout its whole e. Eze 45.01

EXTERMINATE
great fury to e. and utterly destroy Dan 11.44

EXTERMINATED
should receive no mercy but be e., Jos 11.20
father Asa, he e. from the land. 1Ki 22.46
and e. them to this day, and settled 1Ch 4.41

EXTERNAL
circumcision something e. and physical. Rom 2.28

EXTINCT
my days are e., the grave is ready Job 17.01

EXTINCTION
condemned them to e. and made them 2Pe 2.06

EXTINGUISHED
they are e., quenched like a wick: Is 43.17

EXTOL
"For this I will e. thee, O LORD, 2Sa 22.50
"Remember to e. his work, of which Job 36.24
For this I will e. thee, O LORD, Ps 18.49
I will e. thee, O LORD, for thou hast 30.01
all the day, and e. thy righteousness. 89.16
E. the LORD our God; worship at 99.05
E. the LORD our God, and worship at 99.09
Let them e. him in the congregation 107.32
all nations! E. him, all peoples! 117.01
thou art my God, I will e. thee. 118.28
I will e. thee, my God and King, and 145.01
we will e. your love more than wine Sol 1.04
praise and e. and honor the King of Dan 4.37

EXTOLLED
him, and he was e. with my tongue. Ps 66.17
the name of the Lord Jesus was e. Ac 19.17

EXTOLLING
speaking in tongues and e. GOD. Ac 10.46

EXTORTED
and have e. from the sojourner Eze 22.29

EXTORTION
Put no confidence in e., set no vain Ps 62.10
father, because he practiced e., Eze 18.18
sojourner suffers e. in your midst; 22.07
make gain of your neighbors by e.; 22.12
have practiced e. and committed 22.29
they are full of e. and rapacity. Mt 23.25
you are full of e. and wickedness. Lk 11.39

EXTORTIONERS
e., unjust, adulterers, or even like Lk 18.11

EXTRAORDINARY
and your offspring e. afflictions, Deu 28.59
And God did e. miracles by the Ac 19.11

EXTREME
people of Judah in the e. South, Jos 15.21
a place at the e. western end of Eze 46.19
joy and their e. poverty have 2Co 8.02

EXTREMELY
so e. zealous was I for the traditions Gal 1.14

EXTREMITY
by the Arnon, at the e. of the boundary. Num 22.36

EXULT
daughters of the uncircumcised e. 2Sa 1.20
let the field e., and everything in 1Ch 16.32
I would even e. in pain unsparing; Job 6.10
who love thy name may e. in thee. Ps 5.11
I will be glad and e. in thee, 9.02
let not my enemies e. over me. 25.02
let them e. before God; let them be 68.03
name is the LORD, e. before him! 68.04
who e. in thy name all the day, and 89.16
how long shall the wicked e.? 94.03
let the field e., and everything in 96.12
Let the faithful e. in glory; 149.05
We will e. and rejoice in you; Sol 1.04
will no more e. O oppressed virgin Is 23.12
among men shall e. in the Holy One 29.19
joy, O heavens, and e., O earth; 49.13
LORD, my soul shall e. in my God; 61.10
avert your doom? Can you then e.? Jer 11.15
though you e., O plunderers of my 50.11
E. not like the peoples; for you have Hos 9.01
Rejoice and e. with all your heart, Zep 3.14
he will e. over you with loud singing 3.17
their hearts shall e. in the LORD. Zec 10.07
Let us rejoice and e. and give him Rev 19.07

EXULTANT
shoutings, tumultuous city, e. town? Is 22.02
Is this your e. city whose origin 23.07
This is the e. city that dwelt secure, Zep 2.15
your midst your proudly e. ones, 3.11

EXULTATION
"With e. I will divide up Shechem Ps 60.06
"With e. I will divide up Shechem, 108.07

EXULTED
or e. when evil overtook him Job 31.29

EXULTING
that the e. of the wicked is short, Job 20.05
in the LORD, e. in his deliverance. Ps 35.09
my anger, my proudly e. ones. Is 13.03

EXULTS
and said, "My heart e. in the LORD; 1Sa 2.01
and e. in his strength; he goes out Job 39.21
and in thy help how greatly he e.! Ps 21.01
and my heart e., and with my song I 28.07
her throng and he who e. in her. Is 5.14
in his seine; so he rejoices and e. Hab 1.15

EYE

e. for e., tooth for tooth, hand for Ex 21.24
"When a man strikes the e. of his slave, 21.26
e. for e., tooth for tooth; Lev 24.20
of the man whose e. is opened, Num 24.03
of the man whose e. is opened, 24.15
your e. shall not pity them; Deu 7.16
to him, nor shall your e. pity him, 13.08
and your e. be hostile to your 15.09
Your e. shall not pity him, but you 19.13
Your e. shall not pity; it shall be 19.21
e. for e., tooth for tooth, hand for 19.21
off her hand; your e. shall have no pity. 25.12
he kept him as the apple of his e. 32.10
his e. was not dim, nor his natural 34.07
you go is under the e. of the LORD." Ju 18.06
with greedy e. at my sacrifices 1Sa 2.29
with envious e. on all the prosperity 2.32
But the e. of their God was upon Ez 5.05
my e. will never again see good. Job 7.07
The e. of him who sees me will 7.08
died before any e. had seen me, 10.18
"Lo, my e. has seen all this, my ear 13.01
my e. pours out tears to God, 16.20
and my e. dwells on their provocation 17.02
My e. has grown dim from grief, and 17.07
The e. which saw him will see him 20.09
The e. of the adulterer also waits 24.15
saying, 'No e. will see me'; 24.15
the falcon's e. has not seen it. 28.07
and his e. sees every precious 28.10
and when the e. saw, it approved; 29.11
the ear, but now my e. sees thee; 42.05
My e. wastes away because of grief, Ps 6.07
Keep me as the apple of the e.; 17.08
my e. is wasted from grief, my soul 31.09
counsel you with my e. upon you. 32.08
Behold, the e. of the LORD is on 33.18
those wink the e. who hate me 35.19
and my e. has looked in triumph on 54.07
my e. grows dim through sorrow. 88.09
He who formed the e., does he not 94.09
teachings as the apple of your e.; Pro 7.02
He who winks the e. causes trouble, 10.10
The hearing ear and the seeing e., 20.12
has a bountiful e. will be blessed, 22.09
The e. that mocks a father and 30.17
the e. is not satisfied with seeing, Ecc 1.08
for e. to e. they see the return Is 52.08
no e. has seen a God besides thee, 64.04
face to face and see him e. to e. Jer 32.04
king of Babylon e. to e. and speak with 34.03
my e. will not spare, and I will Eze 5.11
And my e. will not spare you, nor 7.04
And my e. will not spare, nor will I 7.09
my e. will not spare, nor will I 8.18
your e. shall not spare, and you 9.05
As for me, my e. will not spare, nor 9.10
No e. pitied you, to do any of these 16.05
Nevertheless my e. spared them, 20.17
you touches the apple of his e.: Zec 2.08
smite his arm and his right e.! 11.17
his right e. utterly blinded!" 11.17
If your right e. causes you to sin, Mt 5.29
'An e. for an e. and a tooth for a 5.38
"The e. is the lamp of the body. 6.22
So, if your e. is sound, your whole 6.22
but if your e. is not sound, your 6.23
speck that is in your brother's e., 7.03
the log that is in your own e.? 7.03
me take the speck out of your e.,' 7.04
there is the log in your own e.? 7.04
take the log out of your own e., 7.05
the speck out of your brother's e. 7.05
And if your e. causes you to sin, 18.09
life with one e. than with two 18.09
go through the e. of a needle than 19.24
And if your e. causes you to sin, Mk 9.47
of God with one e. than with two 9.47
go through the e. of a needle than 10.25
speck that is in your brother's e., Lk 6.41
the log that is in your own e.? 6.41
out the speck that is in your e.,' 6.42
see the log that is in your own e.? 6.42
take the log out of your own e., 6.42
speck that is in your brother's e. 6.42
Your e. is the lamp of your body; 11.34
when your e. is sound, your whole 11.34
go through the e. of a needle than 18.25
"What no e. has seen, nor ear heard, 1Co 2.09
should say, "Because I am not an e., 12.16
If the whole body were an e., where would 12.17
The e. cannot say to the hand, "I 12.21
moment, in the twinkling of an e., 15.52
and every e. will see him, every one Rev 1.07

EYEBROWS

his beard and his e., all his hair. Lev 14.09

EYED

And Saul e. David from that day on. 1Sa 18.09

EYELASHES

let her capture you with her e.; Pro 6.25

EYELIDS

nor see the e. of the morning; Job 3.09
and on my e. is deep darkness; 16.16
eyes are like the e. of the dawn. 41.18
his e. test, the children of men. Ps 11.04
Thou dost hold my e. from closing; 77.04
to my eyes or slumber to my e., 132.04
no sleep and your e. no slumber; Pro 6.04
their eyes, how high their e. lift! 30.13
with tears, and our e. gush with water. Jer 9.18

EYE'S

the slave go free for the e. sake. Ex 21.26

EYES

eat of it your e. will be opened, Gen 3.05
that it was a delight to the e., 3.06
Then the e. of both were opened, and 3.07
found favor in the e. of the LORD. 6.08
And Lot lifted up his e., and saw 13.10
"Lift up your e., and look from the 13.14
He lifted up his e. and looked, 18.02
vindication in the e. of all who 20.16
Then God opened her e., and she saw 21.19
lifted up his e. and saw the place 22.04
lifted up his e. and looked, and behold, 22.13
and he lifted up his e. and looked, 24.63
And Rebekah lifted up her e., 24.64
was old and his e. were dim so 27.01
Leah's e. were weak, but Rachel was 29.17
runnels before the e. of the flock, 30.41
of the flock I lifted up my e., 31.10
'Lift up your e. and see, all the 31.12
and my sleep fled from my e. 31.40
And Jacob lifted up his e. and looked, 33.01
Esau raised his e. and saw the 33.05
"Let me find favor in your e., 34.11
wife cast her e. upon Joseph, 39.07
them and bound him before their e. 42.24
And he lifted up his e., and saw his 43.29
me, that I may set my e. upon him.' 44.21
And now your e. see, and the e. of my brother 45.12
Joseph's hand shall close your e." 46.04
why should we die before your e.? 47.15
Why should we die before your e., 47.19
Now the e. of Israel were dim with 48.10
his e. shall be red with wine, and 49.12
now I have found favor in your e., 50.04
to the Egyptians before their e., Ex 8.26
and as a memorial between your e., 13.09

EYES (cont.)
hand or frontlets between your e.; Ex 13.16
of Israel lifted up their e., 14.10
do that which is right in his e., 15.26
fear of him may be before your e., 20.20
hidden from the e. of the assembly, Lev 4.13
and if in his e. the disease is 13.05
But if in his e. the itch is 13.37
at all hide their e. from that man, 20.04
that waste the e. and cause life 26.16
hidden from the e. of her husband, Num 5.13
and you will serve as e. for us. 10.31
your own heart and your own e., 15.39
you put out the e. of these men? 16.14
before their e. to yield its water 20.08
me in the e. of the people of 20.12
Then the LORD opened the e. of Balaam, 22.31
And Balaam lifted up his e., 24.02
down, but having his e. uncovered: 24.04
down, but having his e. uncovered: 24.16
me at the waters before their e." 27.14
pricks in your e. and thorns in 33.55
for you in Egypt before your e., Deu 1.30
'Your e. have seen all that the 3.21
lift up your e. westward and northward 3.27
eastward, and behold it with your e.; 3.27
Your e. have seen what the LORD did 4.03
the things which your e. have seen, 4.09
lest you lift up your e. to heaven, 4.19
for you in Egypt before your e.? 4.34
be as frontlets between your e. 6.08
all his household, before our e.; 6.22
the great trials which your e. saw, 7.19
and broke them before your e. 9.17
things which your e. have seen. 10.21
for your e. have seen all the great 11.07
the e. of the LORD your God are 11.12
be as frontlets between your e. 11.18
whatever is right in his own e.; 12.08
blinds the e. of the wise and 16.19
neither did our e. see it shed. 21.07
no favor in his e. because he has 24.01
Your ox shall be slain before your e., 28.31
while your e. look on and fail with 28.32
the sight which your e. shall see. 28.34
and failing e., and a languishing 28.65
the sights which your e. shall see. 28.67
did before your e. in the land of 29.02
the great trials which your e. saw, 29.03
or e., to see, or ears to hear. 29.04
I have let you see it with your e., 34.04
he lifted up his e. and looked, Jos 5.13
your sides, and thorns in your e., 23.13
and your e. saw what I did to Egypt 24.07
seized him and gouged out his e., Ju 16.21
Philistines for one of my two e." 16.28
did what was right in his own e. 17.06
And he lifted up his e., and saw the 19.17
did what was right in his own e. 21.25
Let your e. be upon the field which Ru 2.09
"Why have I found favor in your e., 2.10
maidservant find favor in your e." 1Sa 1.18
to weep out his e. and grieve his 2.33
years old and his e. were set, 4.15
lifted up their e. and saw the ark, 6.13
that I gouge out all your right e., 11.02
a bribe to blind my e. with it? 12.03
the LORD will do before your e. 12.16
to his mouth; and his e. became bright. 14.27
see how my e. have become bright, 14.29
you are little in your own e., 15.17
he was ruddy, and had beautiful e., 16.12
that I have found favor in your e.; 20.03
if I have found favor in your e., 20.29
this day your e. have seen how the 24.10
my young men find favor in your e.; 25.08
was precious in your e. this day; 26.21
"If I have found favor in your e., 27.05
before the e. of his servants' 2Sa 6.20
and I will be abased in your e.; 6.22
small thing in thy e., O Lord GOD; 7.19
take your wives before your e., 12.11
kept the watch lifted up his e., 13.34
I find favor in the e. of the LORD, 15.25
he lifted up his e. and looked, 18.24
but thy e. are upon the haughty to 22.28
while the e. of my lord the king 24.03
the e. of all Israel are upon you, 1Ki 1.20
this day, my own e. seeing it.'" 1.48
that thy e. may be open night and 8.29
Let thy e. be open to the supplication 8.52
my e. and my heart will be there 9.03
I came and my own e. had seen it; 10.07
is right in my e. by keeping my 11.38
for his e. were dim because of his 14.04
that which was right in my e., 14.08
was right in the e. of the LORD, 15.05
was right in the e. of the LORD, 15.11
himself with a bandage over his e. 20.38
take the bandage away from his e.; 20.41
his e. upon his e., and his hands 2Ki 4.34
times, and the child opened his e. 4.35
open his e. that he may see. 6.17
LORD opened the e. of the young 6.17
open the e. of these men, that they 6.20
LORD opened their e., and they saw; 6.20
"You shall see it with your own e., 7.02
"You shall see it with your own e., 7.19
and she painted her e., and adorned 9.30
do whatever is good in your e." 10.05
carrying out what is right in my e., 10.30
right in the e. of the LORD all 12.02
was right in the e. of the LORD, 14.03
was right in the e. of the LORD, 15.03
was right in the e. of the LORD, 15.34
right in the e. of the LORD his 16.02
was right in the e. of the LORD, 18.03
open thy e., O LORD, and see; 19.16
voice and haughtily lifted your e.? 19.22
was right in the e. of the LORD, 22.02
and your e. shall not see all the 22.20
the sons of Zedekiah before his e., 25.07
and put out the e. of Zedekiah, 25.07
right in the e. of all the people. 1Ch 13.04
was a small thing in thy e., O God; 17.17
lifted his e. and saw the angel of 21.16
that thy e. may be open day and 2Ch 6.20
let thy e. be open and thy ears 6.40
Now my e. will be open and my ears 7.15
my e. and my heart will be there 7.16
I came and my own e. had seen it; 9.06
right in the e. of the LORD his 14.02
For the e. of the LORD run to and 16.09
to do, but our e. are upon thee." 20.12
right in the e. of the LORD all 24.02
was right in the e. of the LORD, 25.02
was right in the e. of the LORD, 26.04
right in the e. of the LORD 27.02
was right in the e. of the LORD, 28.01
was right in the e. of the LORD, 29.02
as you see with your own e. 29.08
was right in the e. of the LORD, 34.02
and your e. shall not see all the 34.28
brighten our e. and grant us a Ez 9.08
and thy e. open, to hear the prayer Neh 1.06
favor in the e. of all who saw her Est 2.15
king, and I be pleasing in his e., 8.05
womb, nor hide trouble from my e. Job 3.10
A form was before my e.; there was 4.16
while thy e. are upon me, I shall be 7.08
Hast thou e. of flesh? Dost thou see 10.04
pure, and I am clean in God's e." 11.04
But the e. of the wicked will fail; 11.20
thou open thy e. upon such a one 14.03

EYES (cont.)

away, and why do your e. flash, Job 15.12
adversary sharpens his e. against me. 16.09
the e. of his children will fail. 17.05
I have become an alien in their e. 19.15
and my e. shall behold, and not 19.27
their offspring before their e. 21.08
Let their own e. see their destruction, 21.20
and his e. are upon their ways. 24.23
he opens his e., and his wealth is 27.19
It is hid from the e. of all living, 28.21
I was e. to the blind, and feet to 29.15
"I have made a covenant with my e.; 31.01
and my heart has gone after my e., 31.07
have caused the e. of the widow to 31.16
he was righteous in his own e. 32.01
"For his e. are upon the ways of a 34.21
withdraw his e. from the righteous, 36.07
out the prey; his e. behold it afar off. 39.29
and his e. are like the eyelids of 41.18
may not stand before thy e.; thou hatest Ps 5.05
His e. stealthily watch for the 10.08
his e. behold, his eyelids test, the 11.04
lighten my e., lest I sleep the 13.03
in whose e. a reprobate is despised, 15.04
come! Let thy e. see the right! 17.02
they set their e. to cast me to the 17.11
but the haughty e. thou dost bring 18.27
LORD is pure, enlightening the e.; 19.08
My e. are ever toward the LORD, for 25.15
thy steadfast love is before my e., 26.03
The e. of the LORD are toward the 34.15
they say, "Aha, Aha! our e. have seen it!" 35.21
is no fear of God before his e. 36.01
in his own e. that his iniquity 36.02
and the light of my e.—it also 38.10
whose e. keep watch on the nations— 66.07
My e. grow dim with waiting for my 69.03
Let their e. be darkened, so that 69.23
Their e. swell out with fatness, 73.07
among the nations before our e.! 79.10
look with your e. and see the 91.08
My e. have seen the downfall of my 92.11
set before my e. anything that is 101.03
do not speak; e., but do not see. 115.05
my e. from tears, my feet from 116.08
it is marvelous in our e. 118.23
having my e. fixed on all thy 119.06
precepts, and fix my e. on thy ways. 119.15
Open my e., that I may behold 119.18
Turn my e. from looking at vanities 119.37
My e. fail with watching for thy 119.82
My e. fail with watching for thy 119.123
My e. shed streams of tears, because 119.136
My e. are awake before the watches 119.148
I lift up my e. to the hills. 121.01
To thee I lift up my e., O thou who 123.01
Behold, as the e. of servants look 123.02
as the e. of a maid to the hand of 123.02
so our e. look to the LORD our God, 123.02
my e. are not raised too high; 131.01
sleep to my e. or slumber to my 132.04
they have e., but they see not, 135.16
Thy e. beheld my unformed substance 139.16
But my e. are toward thee, O LORD 141.08
The e. of all look to thee, and thou 145.15
the LORD opens the e. of the blind. 146.08
Be not wise in your own e.; fear the Pro 3.07
Let your e. look directly forward, 4.25
ways are before the e. of the LORD, 5.21
Give your e. no sleep and your eyelids 6.04
winks with his e., scrapes with his 6.13
haughty e., a lying tongue, and hands 6.17
to the teeth, and smoke to the e., 10.26
of a fool is right in his own e., 12.15
The e. of the LORD are in every 15.03
The light of the e. rejoices the 15.30
of a man are pure in his own e., 16.02
He who winks his e. plans perverse 16.30
stone in the e. of him who gives 17.08
but the e. of a fool are on the 17.24
winnows all evil with his e. 20.08
open your e., and you will have 20.13
of a man is right in his own e., 21.02
Haughty e. and a proud heart, the 21.04
neighbor finds no mercy in his e. 21.10
The e. of the LORD keep watch over 22.12
When your e. light upon it, it is 23.05
and let your e. observe my ways. 23.26
without cause? Who has redness of e.? 23.29
Your e. will see strange things, and 23.33
of the prince. What your e. have seen 25.07
lest he be wise in his own e. 26.05
a man who is wise in his own e.? 26.12
in his own e. than seven men who 26.16
never satisfied are the e. of man. 27.20
A rich man is wise in his own e., 28.11
who hides his e. will get many a 28.27
LORD gives light to the e. of both. 29.13
in their own e. but are not cleansed 30.12
There are those—how lofty are their e., 30.13
And whatever my e. desired I did Ecc 2.10
The wise man has his e. in his head, 2.14
and his e. are never satisfied with 4.08
owner but to see them with his e.? 5.11
sight of the e. than the wandering 6.09
day nor night one's e. see sleep; 8.16
pleasant for the e. to behold the 11.07
heart and the sight of your e. 11.09
are beautiful; your e. are doves. Sol 1.15
Your e. are doves behind your veil. 4.01
my heart with a glance of your e., 4.09
His e. are like doves beside springs 5.12
Turn away your e. from me, for they 6.05
Your e. are pools in Heshbon, by the 7.04
I was in his e. as one who brings 8.10
hands, I will hide my e. from you; Is 1.15
of your doings from before my e.; 1.16
glancing wantonly with their e., 3.16
and the e. of the haughty are humbled. 5.15
those who are wise in their own e., 5.21
for my e. have seen the King, the 6.05
shut their e.; lest they see with their e., 6.10
shall not judge by what his e. see, 11.03
dashed in pieces before their e.; 13.16
their e. will not pity children. 13.18
and their e. will look to the Holy 17.07
deep sleep, and has closed your e., 29.10
darkness the e. of the blind shall 29.18
but your e. shall see your Teacher. 30.20
Then the e. of those who see will 32.03
and shuts his e. from looking upon 33.15
Your e. will see the king in his 33.17
Your e. will see Jerusalem, a quiet 33.20
Then the e. of the blind shall be 35.05
open thy e., O LORD, and see; and hear 37.17
voice and haughtily lifted your e.? 37.23
My e. are weary with looking upward 38.14
Lift up your e. on high and see: who 40.26
to open the e. that are blind, to 42.07
Because you are precious in my e., 43.04
yet have e., who are deaf, yet have 43.08
for he has shut their e., so that they 44.18
I am honored in the e. of the LORD, 49.05
Lift up your e. round about and see 49.18
Lift up your e. to the heavens, and 51.06
arm before the e. of all the 52.10
we grope like those who have no e.; 59.10
Lift up your e. round about, and see 60.04
but you did what was evil in my e., 65.12
forgotten and are hid from my e. 65.16
they did what was evil in my e., 66.04
Lift up your e. to the bare heights, Jer 3.02
you enlarge your e. with paint? 4.30

EYES (cont.)
LORD, do not thy e. look for truth? Jer 5.03
who have e., but see not, who have 5.21
become a den of robbers in your e.? 7.11
and my e. a fountain of tears, that 9.01
that our e. may run down with tears, 9.18
my e. will weep bitterly and run 13.17
"Lift up your e. and see those who 13.20
their e. fail because there is no 14.06
'Let my e. run down with tears 14.17
before your e. and in your days, the 16.09
For my e. are upon all their ways; 16.17
iniquity concealed from my e. 16.17
But you have e. and heart only for 22.17
I will set my e. upon them for good, 24.06
he shall slay them before your e. 29.21
weeping, and your e. from tears; 31.16
whose e. are open to all the ways 32.19
was right in my e. by proclaiming 34.15
Zedekiah at Riblah before his e.; 39.06
He put out the e. of Zedekiah, and 39.07
a few of many, as your e. see us), 42.02
your very e. for all the evil that 51.24
the sons of Zedekiah before his e., 52.10
He put out the e. of Zedekiah, and 52.11
my e. flow with tears; for a Lam 1.16
pride of our e. in the tent of the 2.04
My e. are spent with weeping; 2.11
no rest, your e. no respite! 2.18
my e. flow with rivers of tears 3.48
"My e. will flow without ceasing, 3.49
my e. cause me grief at the fate of 3.51
Our e. failed, ever watching vainly 4.17
these things our e. have grown dim, 5.17
rims were full of e. round about. Eze 1.18
blinded their e. which turn wantonly 6.09
lift up your e. now in the direction 8.05
I lifted up my e. toward the north, 8.05
And he went in before my e. 10.02
were full of e. round about— 10.12
who have e. to see, but see not, who 12.02
may not see the land with his e. 12.12
or lift up his e. to the idols of 18.06
lifts up his e. to the idols, commits 18.12
or lift up his e. to the idols of 18.15
detestable things your e. feast on, 20.07
detestable things their e. feasted on, 20.08
and their e. were set on their 20.24
and bitter grief before their e. 21.06
lift up your e. to the Egyptians 23.27
painted your e., and decked yourself 23.40
delight of your e. away from you 24.16
your power, the delight of your e., 24.21
of their e. and their heart's desire, 24.25
kings, to feast their e. on you. 28.17
and lift up your e. to your idols, 33.25
my holiness before their e. 36.23
are in your hand before their e., 37.20
my holiness before their e. 38.16
known in the e. of many nations. 38.23
me, "Son of man, look with your e., 40.04
see with your e., and hear with 44.05
lifted my e. to heaven, and my Dan 4.34
this horn were e. like the e. of a man, 7.08
horn which had e. and a mouth that 7.20
I raised my e. and saw, and behold, a 8.03
had a conspicuous horn between his e. 8.05
between his e. is the first king. 8.21
open thy e. and behold our desolations, 9.18
I lifted up my e. and looked, and 10.05
his e. like flaming torches, his arms 10.06
destruction? Compassion is hid from my e. Hos 13.14
not the food cut off before our e., Joe 1.16
I will set my e. upon them for Amo 9.04
Behold, the e. of the Lord GOD are 9.08
and let our e. gaze upon Zion. Mic 4.11
My e. will gloat over her; now she 7.10
art of purer e. than to behold Hab 1.13
your fortunes before your e.," says the Zep 3.20
And I lifted my e. and saw, and behold, Zec 1.18
And I lifted my e. and saw, and behold, 2.01
"These seven are the e. of the LORD, 4.10
Again I lifted my e. and saw, and behold, 5.01
"Lift your e., and see what this is 5.05
Then I lifted my e. and saw, and behold, 5.09
And again I lifted my e. and saw, 6.01
them, for now I see with my own e. 9.08
house of Judah I will open my e., 12.04
their e. shall rot in their sockets, 14.12
Your own e. shall see this, and you Mal 1.05
Then he touched their e., saying, Mt 9.29
And their e. were opened. And Jesus 9.30
and their e. they have closed, lest 13.15
they should perceive with their e., 13.15
But blessed are your e., for they see, 13.16
And when they lifted up their e., 17.08
than with two e. to be thrown into 18.09
to him, "Lord, let our e. be opened." 20.33
And Jesus in pity touched their e., 20.34
doing, and it is marvelous in our e.'? 21.42
sleeping, for their e. were heavy. 26.43
Having e. do you not see, and having Mk 8.18
had spit on his e. and laid his 8.23
he laid his hands upon his e.; and he 8.25
than with two e. to be thrown into 9.47
doing, and it is marvelous in our e.'?" 12.11
for their e. were very heavy; and they 14.40
for mine e. have seen thy salvation Lk 2.30
and the e. of all in the synagogue 4.20
lifted up his e. on his disciples, 6.20
"Blessed are the e. which see what 10.23
in torment, he lifted up his e., 16.23
not even lift up his e. to heaven, 18.13
but now they are hid from your e. 19.42
But their e. were kept from recognizing 24.16
And their e. were opened and they 24.31
lift up your e., and see how the Jn 4.35
Lifting up his e., then, and seeing 6.05
anointed the man's e. with the clay, 9.06
him, "Then how were your e. opened?" 9.10
and anointed my e. and said to me, 9.11
made the clay and opened his e. 9.14
said to them, "He put clay on my e., 9.15
him, since he has opened your e.?" 9.17
nor do we know who opened his e. 9.21
do to you? How did he open your e.?" 9.26
from, and yet he opened my e. 9.30
one opened the e. of a man born 9.32
a demon open the e. of the blind?" 10.21
who opened the e. of the blind man 11.37
Jesus lifted up his e. and said, 11.41
blinded their e. and hardened their 12.40
see with their e. and perceive 12.40
lifted up his e. to heaven and 17.01
and when his e. were opened, he Ac 9.08
fell from his e. and he regained 9.18
And she opened her e., and when 9.40
to open their e., that they may 26.18
and their e. they have closed; 28.27
they should perceive with their e., 28.27
"There is no fear of God before their e." Rom 3.18
e. that should not see and ears 11.08
let their e. be darkened so that 11.10
Look at what is before your e. If any 2Co 10.07
before whose e. Jesus Christ was Gal 3.01
out your e. and given them to me. 4.15
having the e. of your hearts Eph 1.18
bare to the e. of him with whom we Heb 4.13
For the e. of the Lord are upon the 1Pe 3.12
They have e. full of adultery, 2Pe 2.14
which we have seen with our e., 1Jn 1.01
the darkness has blinded his e. 2.11
the lust of the e. and the pride 2.16
his e. were like a flame of fire, Rev 1.14

EYES (cont.)
who has e. like a flame of fire, and Rev 2.18
seen, and salve to anoint your e., 3.18
full of e. in front and behind: 4.06
are full of e. all round and within, 4.08
with seven horns and with seven e., 5.06
wipe away every tear from their e. 7.17
His e. are like a flame of fire, and 19.12
wipe away every tear from their e. 21.04
doing, and it is marvelous in our e.? Mt 21.42
doing and it is marvelous in our e.'?" Mk 12.11

EYESERVICE
not in the way of e., as men-pleasers, Eph 6.06
not with e., as men-pleasers, but in Col 3.22

EYESIGHT
whose e. had begun to grow dim, so 1Sa 3.02

EYEWITNESSES
beginning were e. and ministers of Lk 1.02
but we were e. of his majesty. 2Pe 1.16

EZBAI
Hezro of Carmel, Naarai the son of E., 1Ch 11.37

EZBON
Shuni, E., Eri, Arodi, and Areli. Gen 46.16
E., Uzzi, Uzziel, Jerimoth, and Iri, 1Ch 7.07

EZEKIEL
of the LORD came to E. the priest, Eze 1.03
Thus shall E. be to you a sign; 24.24

EZEM
Baalah, Iim, E., Jos 15.29
Hazarshual, Balah, E., 19.03
Bilhah, E., Tolad, 1Ch 4.29

EZER
Dishon, E., and Dishan; these are Gen 36.21
These are the sons of E.: Bilhan, 36.27
Dishon, E., and Dishan; these are 36.30
Anah, Dishon, E., and Dishan. 1Ch 1.38
The sons of E.: Bilhan, Zaavan, and 1.42
and E. the father of Hushah. These were 4.04
and E. and Elead, whom the men of 7.21
E. the chief, Obadiah second, Eliab 12.09

next to him E. the son of Jeshua, Neh 3.19
Jehohanan, Malchijah, Elam, and E. 12.42

EZIONGEBER
from Abronah, and encamped at E. Num 33.35
And they set out from E., and 33.36
the Arabah road from Elath and E. Deu 2.08
built a fleet of ships at E., which 1Ki 9.26
for the ships were wrecked at E. 22.48
Then Solomon went to E. and Eloth 2Ch 8.17
Tarshish, and they built the ships in E. 20.36

EZRA
Persia, E. the son of Seraiah, son of Ez 7.01
this E. went up from Babylonia. 7.06
for E. had set his heart to study 7.10
Artaxerxes gave to E. the priest, 7.11
to E. the priest, the scribe of the 7.12
Whatever E. the priest, the scribe 7.21
"And you, E., according to the wisdom 7.25
While E. prayed and made confession, 10.01
addressed E.: "We have broken faith 10.02
Then E. arose and made the leading 10.05
Then E. withdrew from before the 10.06
And E. the priest stood up and said 10.10
E. the priest selected men, heads of 10.16
and they told E. the scribe to bring Neh 8.01
And E. the priest brought the law 8.02
And E. the scribe stood on a wooden 8.04
And E. opened the book in the sight 8.05
And E. blessed the LORD, the great 8.06
and E. the priest and scribe, and 8.09
together to E. the scribe in order 8.13
And E. said: "Thou art the LORD, thou 9.06
and Jeshua: Seraiah, Jeremiah, E., 12.01
of E., Meshullam; of Amariah, 12.13
governor and of E. the priest the 12.26
and Azariah, E., Meshullam, 12.33
and E. the scribe went before them. 12.36

EZRAH
The sons of E.: Jether, Mered, Epher, 1Ch 4.17

EZRAHITE
other men, wiser than Ethan the E., 1Ki 4.31

EZRI
the soil was E. the son of Chelub; 1Ch 27.26

F

FABRICS
crimson, and blue f., trained also in 2Ch 2.07
and crimson f. and fine linen, and 2.14
and crimson f. and fine linen, and 3.14

FACE
was upon the f. of the deep; Gen 1.02
moving over the f. of the waters. 1.02
is upon the f. of all the earth, 1.29
watered the whole f. of the ground— 2.06
sweat of your f. you shall eat 3.19
and from thy f. I shall be hidden; 4.14
multiply on the f. of the ground, 6.01
created from the f. of the ground, 6.07
alive upon the f. of all the earth. 7.03
blot out from the f. of the ground." 7.04
floated on the f. of the waters. 7.18
that was upon the f. of the ground, 7.23
subsided from the f. of the ground; 8.08
still on the f. of the whole earth 8.09
behold, the f. of the ground was dry. 8.13
abroad upon the f. of the whole 11.04
there over the f. of all the earth, 11.08
abroad over the f. of all the 11.09
Then Abram fell on his f.; and God 17.03
Abraham fell on his f. and laughed, 17.17

himself with his f. to the earth, 19.01
and set his f. toward the hill country 31.21
and afterwards I shall see his f.; 32.20
"For I have seen God f. to f., 32.30
to see your f. is like seeing the f. of God, 33.10
harlot, for she had covered her f. 38.15
saying, 'You shall not see my f., 43.03
to us, 'You shall not see my f., 43.05
Then he washed his f. and came out; 43.31
you, you shall see my f. no more.' 44.23
see the man's f. unless our youngest 44.26
have seen your f. and know that 46.30
"I had not thought to see your f.; 48.11
himself with his f. to the earth. 48.12
Then Joseph fell on his father's f., 50.01
And Moses hid his f., for he was Ex 3.06
shall cover the f. of the land, 10.05
covered the f. of the whole land, 10.15
never see my f. again; for in the 10.28
day you see my f. you shall die." 10.28
"As you say! I will not see your f. again." 10.29
was on the f. of the wilderness a 16.14
them from the f. of the earth'? 32.12
used to speak to Moses f. to f., 33.11
that are upon the f. of the earth?" 33.16
But," he said, "you cannot see my f.; 33.20

FACE (cont.)
back; but my f. shall not be seen." Ex 33.23
the skin of his f. shone because 34.29
behold, the skin of his f. shone, 34.30
with them, he put a veil on his f.; 34.33
of Israel saw the f. of Moses, that 34.35
that the skin of Moses' f. shone; 34.35
put the veil upon his f. again, 34.35
I will set my f. against that person Lev 17.10
and honor the f. of an old man, and 19.32
will set my f. against that man. 20.03
then I will set my f. against that 20.05
I will set my f. against that person, 20.06
has a mutilated f. or a limb too 21.18
I will set my f. against you, and 26.17
The LORD make his f. to shine upon Num 6.25
cubits deep on the f. of the earth. 11.31
that were on the f. of the earth. 12.03
her father had but spit in her f., 12.14
art seen f. to f., and thy cloud 14.14
When Moses heard it, he fell on his f.; 16.04
they cover the f. of the earth, and they 22.05
and it covers the f. of the earth; 22.11
bowed his head, and fell on his f. 22.31
but set his f. toward the wilderness. 24.01
not be afraid of the f. of man, Deu 1.17
spoke with you f. to f. at the 5.04
you from off the f. of the earth. 6.15
that are on the f. of the earth. 7.06
to their f. those who hate him, by 7.10
him, he will requite him to his f. 7.10
that are on the f. of the earth. 14.02
off his foot, and spit in his f.; 25.09
violently taken away before your f., 28.31
them and hide my f. from them, 31.17
surely hide my f. in that day on 31.18
said, 'I will hide my f. from them, 32.20
Moses, whom the LORD knew f. to f., 34.10
Joshua fell on his f. to the earth, Jos 5.14
earth upon his f. before the ark 7.06
have you thus fallen upon your f.? 7.10
seen the angel of the LORD f. to f." Ju 6.22
Then she fell on her f., bowing to Ru 2.10
had fallen f. downward on the ground 1Sa 5.03
had fallen f. downward on the ground 5.04
he fell on his f. to the ground. 17.49
of David from the f. of the earth, 20.15
and fell on his f. to the ground, 20.41
bowed with his f. to the earth, 24.08
and fell before David on her f., 25.23
bowed with her f. to the ground, 25.41
he bowed with his f. to the ground, 28.14
I lift up my f. to your brother 2Sa 2.22
that is, you shall not see my f., 3.13
daughter, when you come to see my f." 3.13
and fell on his f. and did obeisance. 9.06
she fell on her f. to the ground, 14.04
remnant upon the f. of the earth. 14.07
And Joab fell on his f. to the ground, 14.22
himself on his f. to the ground 14.33
spread over the f. of all the 18.08
the king with his f. to the earth, 18.28
The king covered his f., and the king 19.04
David sought the f. of the LORD. 21.01
the king with his f. to the ground. 24.20
king with his f. to the ground. 1Ki 1.23
bowed with her f. to the ground, 1.31
destroy it from the f. of the earth. 13.34
recognized him, and fell on his f., 18.07
and put his f. between his knees. 18.42
he wrapped his f. in his mantle 19.13
on his bed, and turned away his f., 21.04
my staff upon the f. of the child." 2Ki 4.29
the staff upon the f. of the child, 4.31
it over his f., till he died. And Hazael 8.15
And he lifted up his f. to the window, 9.32
dung upon the f. of the field in 9.37
Hazael set his f. to go up against 12.17
let us look one another in the f." 14.08
Hezekiah turned his f. to the wall, 20.02
to David with his f. to the ground. 1Ch 21.21
turn away the f. of thy anointed 2Ch 6.42
themselves, and pray and seek my f., 7.14
his head with his f. to the ground, 20.18
let us look one another in the f." 25.17
will not turn away his f. from you, 30.09
with shame of f. to his own land. 32.21
and blush to lift my f. to thee, Ez 9.06
"Why is your f. sad, seeing you are Neh 2.02
Why should not my f. be sad, when the 2.03
and Media, who saw the king's f., Est 1.14
the king, they covered Haman's f. 7.08
and he will curse thee to thy f." Job 1.11
and he will curse thee to thy f." 2.05
A spirit glided past my f.; the hair 4.15
at me; for I will not lie to your f. 6.28
lift up your f. without blemish; 11.15
I will defend my ways to his f. 13.15
will not hide myself from thy f.: 13.20
Why dost thou hide thy f., and count 13.24
he has covered his f. with his fat, 15.27
against me, it testifies to my f. 16.08
My f. is red with weeping, and on my 16.16
Who declares his way to his f., 21.31
Almighty, and lift up your f. to God. 22.26
and thick darkness covers my f. 23.17
will see me'; and he disguises his f. 24.15
away upon the f. of the waters; 24.18
He covers the f. of the moon, and 26.09
circle upon the f. of the waters 26.10
When he hides his f., who can 34.29
them on the f. of the habitable 37.12
and the f. of the deep is frozen. 38.30
Who can open the doors of his f.? 41.14
forgotten, he has hidden his f., Ps 10.11
the upright shall behold his f. 11.07
long wilt thou hide thy f. from me? 13.01
behold thy f. in righteousness; when 17.15
and he has not hid his f. from him, 22.24
who seek the f. of the God of Jacob 24.06
Thou hast said, "Seek ye my f." My heart 27.08
"Thy f., LORD, do I seek." 27.08
Hide not thy f. from me. Turn not 27.09
Thou didst hide thy f., I was 30.07
Let thy f. shine on thy servant; 31.16
The f. of the LORD is against 34.16
I come and behold the f. of God? 42.02
me, and shame has covered my f., 44.15
Why dost thou hide thy f.? Why dost 44.24
Hide thy f. from my sins, and blot 51.09
us and make his f. to shine upon 67.01
reproach, that shame has covered my f. 69.07
Hide not thy f. from thy servant; 69.17
let thy f. shine, that we may be 80.03
let thy f. shine, that we may be 80.07
let thy f. shine, that we may be 80.19
look upon the f. of thine anointed! 84.09
why dost thou hide thy f. from me? 88.14
Do not hide thy f. from me in the 102.02
of man, oil to make his f. shine, 104.15
When thou hidest thy f., they are 104.29
thou renewest the f. of the ground. 104.30
Make thy f. shine upon thy servant, 119.135
turn away the f. of thy anointed 132.10
Hide not thy f. from me, lest I be 143.07
with impudent f. she says to him: Pro 7.13
a circle on the f. of the deep, 8.27
light of a king's f. there is life, 16.15
understanding sets his f. toward wisdom, 17.24
A wicked man puts on a bold f., 21.29
As in water f. answers to f., so the 27.19
a man's wisdom makes his f. shine, Ecc 8.01
of the cliff, let me see your f., let me Sol 2.14
is sweet, and your f. is comely. 2.14

FACE (cont.)

by grinding the f. of the poor?" Is 3.15
wings: with two he covered his f., 6.02
is hiding his f. from the house of 8.17
and fill the f. of the world with 14.21
the world upon the f. of the earth. 23.17
no more shall his f. grow pale. 29.22
Hezekiah turned his f. to the wall, 38.02
I hid not my f. from shame and 50.06
I have set my f. like a flint, 50.07
for a moment I hid my f. from you, 54.08
him, I hid my f. and was angry; 57.17
have hid his f. from you so that 59.02
for thou hast hid thy f. from us, 64.07
provoke me to my f. continually, 65.03
their back to me, and not their f. Jer 2.27
lift up your skirts over your f., 13.26
out of my lips was before thy f. 17.16
not my f., in the day of their 18.17
For I have set my f. against this 21.10
which are on the f. of the earth. 25.26
you from the f. of the earth. This very 28.16
in labor? Why has every f. turned pale? 30.06
speak with him f. to f. and see him 32.04
to me their back and not their f.; 32.33
have hidden my f. from this city because 33.05
eye and speak with him f. to f.; and you 34.03
I will set my f. against you for evil, 44.11
dishonor has covered our f., for aliens 51.51
herself groans, and turns her f. away. Lam 1.08
right hand in the f. of the enemy; 2.03
each had the f. of a man in front; Eze 1.10
four had the f. of a lion on the 1.10
four had the f. of an ox on the 1.10
four had the f. of an eagle at the 1.10
when I saw it, I fell upon my f., and 1.28
have made your f. hard against their 3.08
river Chebar; and I fell on my f. 3.23
and set your f. toward it, and let 4.03
shall set your f. toward the siege 4.07
set your f. toward the mountains of 6.02
I will turn my f. from them, that 7.22
was left alone, I fell upon my f., 9.08
the first f. was the f. of the herub, 10.14
and the second f. was the f. of a man, 10.14
and the third the f. of a lion, 10.14
and the fourth the f. of an eagle. 10.14
Then I fell down upon my f., and cried 11.13
you shall cover your f., that you may 12.06
he shall cover his f., that he may 12.12
set your f. against the daughters 13.17
of his iniquity before his f., and yet 14.04
of his iniquity before his f.. and yet 14.07
and I will set my f. against that 14.08
And I will set my f. against them; 15.07
when I set my f. against them. 15.07
into judgment with you f. to f. 20.35
set your f. toward the south, preach 20.46
set your f. toward Jerusalem and 21.02
set your f. toward the Ammonites, 25.02
set your f. toward Sidon, and prophesy 28.21
set your f. against Pharaoh king of 29.02
over all the f. of the earth, with none 34.06
set your f. against Mount Seir, and 35.02
set your f. toward Gog, of the land 38.02
that are upon the f. of the earth, 38.20
remaining upon the f. of the land, 39.14
that I hid my f. from them and gave them 39.23
transgressions, and hid my f. from them. 39.24
not hide my f. any more from them, when I 39.29
the f. of a man toward the palm tree 41.19
and the f. of a young lion toward 41.19
river Chebar; and I fell upon my f. 43.03
steps of the altar shall f. east. 43.17
the LORD; and I fell upon my f. 44.04
Nebuchadnezzar fell upon his f., Dan 2.46
expression of his f. was changed 3.19
west across the f. of the whole earth, 8.05
was frightened and fell upon my f. 8.17
sleep with my f. to the ground; but he 8.18
Then I turned my f. to the Lord God, 9.03
righteousness, but to us confusion of f., 9.07
O Lord, belongs confusion of f., to our 9.08
Lord, cause thy f. to shine upon thy 9.17
beryl, his f. like the appearance of 10.06
on my f. in a deep sleep with my f. 10.09
I turned my f. toward the ground 10.15
He shall set his f. to come with 11.17
shall turn his f. to the coastlands, 11.18
shall turn his f. back toward the 11.19
put away her harlotry from her f., Hos 2.02
of Israel testifies to his f.; Ephraim 5.05
acknowledge their guilt and seek my f., 5.15
encompass them, they are before my f. 7.02
like a chip on the f. of the waters. 10.07
will hide his f. from them at that Mic 3.04
lift up your skirts over your f.; Nah 3.05
everything from the f. of the earth, Zep 1.02
mankind from the f. of the earth, 1.03
out over the f. of the whole land; Zec 5.03
anoint your head and wash your f., Mt 6.17
I send my messenger before thy f., 11.10
and his f. shone like the sun, and 17.02
behold the f. of my Father who is 18.10
he fell on his f. and prayed, "My 26.39
Then they spat in his f., and struck 26.67
I send my messenger before thy f., Mk 1.02
spit on him, and to cover his f., 14.65
he fell on his f. and besought him, Lk 5.12
I send my messenger before thy f., 7.27
he set his f. to go to Jerusalem. 9.51
him, because his f. was set toward 9.53
and he fell on his f. at Jesus' feet, 17.16
dwell upon the f. of the whole earth. 21.35
and his f. wrapped with a cloth. Jn 11.44
saw that his f. was like the f. of an angel. Ac 6.15
to live on all the f. of the earth, 17.26
the kingdom will see my f. no more. 20.25
they should see his f. no more. And they 20.38
met the accusers f. to f., and had 25.16
caught and could not f. the wind, 27.15
mirror dimly, but then f. to f. Now I 1Co 13.12
and so, falling on his f., he will 14.25
look at Moses' f. because of its 2Co 3.07
who put a veil over his f. so that the 3.13
with unveiled f., beholding the glory 3.18
glory of God in the f. of Christ. 4.06
am humble when f. to f. with you, but 10.01
puts on airs, or strikes you in the f. 11.20
to Antioch I opposed him to his f., Gal 2.11
for all who have not seen my f., Col 2.01
of God in the f. of great opposition 1Th 2.02
with great desire to see you f. to f.; 2.17
we may see you f. to f. and supply 3.10
observes his natural f. in a mirror; Jas 1.23
But the f. of the Lord is against 1Pe 3.12
you and talk with you f. to f., 2Jn 1.12
we will talk together f. to f. 3Jn 1.14
and his f. was like the sun shining Rev 1.16
creature with the f. of a man, and the 4.07
us from the f. of him who is seated 6.16
and his f. was like the sun, and his 10.01
they shall see his f., and his 22.04

FACED

Then the king f. about, and blessed 1Ki 8.14
king of Judah f. one another in 2Ki 14.11
Then the king f. about, and blessed 2Ch 6.03
king of Judah f. one another in 25.21
of what they had f. in this matter, Est 9.26
I could not have f. his majesty. Job 31.23
the front wheel f. the others Eze 10.11
a gate which f. toward the north, 40.20
the gate which f. toward the east; 40.22

FACED (cont.)

Its vestibule f. the outer court, Eze 40.31
Its vestibule f. the outer court, 40.34
Its vestibule f. the outer court, 40.37
me out by the gate which f. east., 42.15
the east (for the temple f. east); 47.01

FACES

their f. were turned away, and they Gen 9.23
and set the f. of the flocks toward 30.40
"Why are your f. downcast today?" 40.07
him with their f. to the ground. 42.06
wings, their f. one to another; Ex 25.20
seat shall the f. of the cherubim 25.20
with their f. one to another; toward 37.09
seat were the f. of the cherubim. 37.09
they shouted, and fell on their f. Lev 9.24
fell on their f. before all the Num 14.05
And they fell on their f., and said, 16.22
moment." And they fell on their f. 16.45
of meeting, and fell on their f. 20.06
from the bay that f. southward; Jos 15.02
fell on their f. to the ground. Ju 13.20
with shame the f. of all your 2Sa 19.05
saw it, they fell on their f.; 1Ki 18.39
whose f. were like the f. of lions, 1Ch 12.08
in sackcloth, fell upon their f. 21.16
down with their f. to the earth on 2Ch 7.03
away their f. from the habitation 29.06
LORD with their f. to the ground. Neh 8.06
he covers the f. of its judges—if Job 9.24
bind their f. in the world below. 40.13
aim at their f. with your bows. Ps 21.12
so your f. shall never be ashamed. 34.05
Fill their f. with shame, that they 83.16
God, and turn their f. upward; Is 8.21
one another; their f. will be aflame. 13.08
will wipe away tears from all f., 25.08
With their f. to the ground they 49.23
men hide their f. he was despised, 53.03
have made their f. harder than Jer 5.03
If you set your f. to enter Egypt 42.15
who set their f. to go to Egypt to 42.17
have set their f. to come to the 44.12
with f. turned toward it, saying, 50.05
but each had four f., and each of Eze 1.06
four had their f. and their wings 1.08
As for the likeness of their f., 1.10
Such were their f. And their 1.11
your face hard against their f., 3.08
shame is upon all f., and baldness 7.18
of the inner court that f. north, 8.03
and their f. toward the east, 8.16
which f. north, every man with his 9.02
And every one had four f.: the first 10.14
Each had four f., and each four 10.21
And as for the likeness of their f., 10.22
were the very f. whose appearance 10.22
house of the LORD, which f. east. 11.01
of their iniquity before their f.; 14.03
turn away your f. from all your 14.06
and all f. from south to north 20.47
afraid, their f. are convulsed. 27.35
chamber which f. south is for the 40.45
chamber which f. north is for the 40.46
and cherub. Every cherub had two f.: 41.18
of the sanctuary, which f. east; 44.01
court that f. east shall be shut 46.01
outer gate, that f. toward the east; 47.02
are in anguish, all f. grow pale. Joe 2.06
is on all loins, all f. grow pale! Nah 2.10
and spread dung upon your f., Mal 2.03
disfigure their f. that their Mt 6.16
heard this, they fell on their f., 17.06
and bowed their f. to the ground, Lk 24.05
fell on their f. before the throne Rev 7.11
their f. were like human f., 9.07
fell on their f. and worshiped God, 11.16

FACETS

upon a single stone with seven f., Zec 3.09

FACING

shall encamp f. the tent of meeting Num 2.02
three f. north, three f. west, 1Ki 7.25
three f. south, and three f. east; 7.25
up in his chariot f. the Syrians, 22.35
stood on their feet, f. the nave. 2Ch 3.13
three f. north, three f. west, 4.04
three f. south, and three f. east; 4.04
in his chariot f. the Syrians until 18.34
And he read from it f. the square Neh 8.03
boiling pot, f. away from the north." Jer 1.13
Then he went into the gateway f. east, Eze 40.06
side of the north gate f. south, 40.44
side of the south gate f. north. 40.44
that was f. the temple yard on the 41.12
of the building f. the yard which 41.15
and f. the pavement which belonged 42.03
me to the gate, the gate f. east. 43.01
the temple by the gate f. east, 43.04
the gate f. east shall be opened 46.12
who stood f. him, saw that he thus Mk 15.39
the secret of f. plenty and hunger, Php 4.12

FACT

for by the f. that I cut off the 1Sa 24.11
yourselves the f. that you have no Mt 16.08
you discuss the f. that you have Mk 8.17
And as for the f. that he raised Ac 13.34
But in f. Christ has been raised 1Co 15.20
They deliberately ignore this f., 2Pe 3.05
But do not ignore this one f., beloved, 3.08

FACTIONS

for there must be f. among you in 1Co 11.19

FACTIOUS

those who are f. and do not obey Rom 2.08
As for a man who is f., after Tit 3.10

FACTS

not learn the f. because of the Ac 21.34

FACULTIES

those who have their f. trained by Heb 5.14

FADE

they wither and f. like the mallow; Job 24.24
For they will soon f. like the grass, Ps 37.02
We all f. like a leaf, and our Is 64.06
the rich man f. away in the midst Jas 1.11

FADED

For if what f. away came with 2Co 3.11

FADES

As the cloud f. and vanishes, so he Job 7.09
in the evening it f. and withers. Ps 90.06
the flower f., when the breath of Is 40.07
The grass withers, the flower f.; 40.08
wither, the bloom of Lebanon f. Nah 1.04

FADING

and to the f. flower of its glorious Is 28.01
and the f. flower of its glorious 28.04
of its brightness, f. as this was, 2Co 3.07
not see the end of the f. splendor. 3.13

FAIL

he will not f. you or destroy you Deu 4.31
look on and f. with longing for 28.32
he will not f. you or forsake you." 31.06
he will not f. you or forsake you; 31.08

FAIL (cont.)

I will not f. you or forsake you.	Jos 1.05
he will without f. drive out from	3.10
no man's heart f. because of him;	1Sa 17.32
I should not f. to sit at table	20.05
there shall not f. you a man on	1Ki 2.04
shall never f. you a man before me	8.25
'There shall not f. you a man upon	9.05
and the cruse of oil shall not f.,	17.14
neither did the cruse of oil f.,	17.16
He will not f. you or forsake you,	1Ch 28.20
shall never f. you a man before me	2Ch 6.16
'There shall not f. you a man to	7.18
to them day by day without f.,	Ez 6.09
that without f. they would keep	Est 9.27
But the eyes of the wicked will f.;	Job 11.20
As waters f. from a lake, and a	14.11
the eyes of his children will f.	17.05
Their bull breeds without f.; their	21.10
caused the eyes of the widow to f.,	31.16
My flesh and my heart may f., but God	Ps 73.26
My eyes f. with watching for thy	119.82
My eyes f. with watching for thy	119.123
and the rod of his fury will f.	Pro 22.08
for the vintage will f., the fruit	Is 32.10
He will not f. or be discouraged	42.04
Pit, neither shall his bread f.	51.14
spring of water, whose waters f. not.	58.11
courage shall f. both king and	Jer 4.09
their eyes f. because there is no	14.06
deceitful brook, like waters that f.?	15.18
he caused my strength to f.; the Lord	Lam 1.14
will not wither nor their fruit f.,	Eze 47.12
the vision; but they shall f.	Dan 11.14
and the new wine shall f. them.	Hos 9.02
is not upright in him shall f.,	Hab 2.04
of the olive f. and the fields	3.17
justice, each dawn he does not f.;	Zep 3.05
in the field shall not f. to bear,	Mal 3.11
How is it that you f. to perceive	Mt 16.11
in the heavens that does not f.,	Lk 12.33
for you that your faith may not f.;	22.32
undertaking is of men, it will f.;	Ac 5.38
indeed you f. to meet the test!	2Co 13.05
For time would f. me to tell of Gideon,	Heb 11.32
it that no one f. to obtain the grace	12.15
"I will never f. you nor forsake	13.05

FAILED

At this their hearts f. them,	Gen 42.28
made to the house of Israel had f.;	Jos 21.45
one thing has f. of all the good	23.14
for you, not one of them has f.	23.14
his courage f., and all Israel was	2Sa 4.01
one word has f. of all his good	1Ki 8.56
and my close friends have f. me;	Job 19.14
My soul f. me when he spoke. I sought	Sol 5.06
their strength has f., they have	Jer 51.30
Our eyes f., ever watching vainly	Lam 4.17
ruined because the grain has f.	Joe 1.17
while the sun's light f.; and the	Lk 23.45
When the wine f., the mother of	Jn 2.03
as though the word of God had f.	Rom 9.06
Israel f. to obtain what it sought.	11.07
will find out that we have not f.	2Co 13.06
though we may seem to have f.	13.07
be judged to have f. to reach it.	Heb 4.01
the good news f. to enter because	4.06

FAILING

and f. eyes, and a languishing soul;	Deu 28.65
of the burden-bearers is f., and there	Neh 4.10

FAILINGS

to bear with the f. of the weak,	Rom 15.01

FAILS

my strength f. because of my misery,	Ps 31.10
My heart throbs, my strength f. me;	38.10
of my head; my heart f. me.	40.12
My spirit f.! Hide not thy	143.07
drags itself along and desire f.;	Ecc 12.05
is withered, the new growth f.,	Is 15.06
becomes hungry and his strength f.,	44.12
the wine f., the oil languishes.	Joe 1.10
and gladness f. from the sons of	1.12
so that when it f. they may	Lk 16.09
whole law but f. in one point has	Jas 2.10
is right to do and f. to do it,	4.17

FAILURE

no mischance or f. in bearing;	Ps 144.14
and if their f. means riches for	Rom 11.12

FAINT

enemies: let not your heart f.; do not	Deu 20.03
when you were f. and weary, and cut	25.18
who were with him, f. yet pursuing.	Ju 8.04
for they are f., and I am pursuing	8.05
give bread to your men who are f.?"	8.15
food this day.' " And the people were f.	1Sa 14.28
Aijalon: And the people were very f.;	14.31
for those who f. in the wilderness	2Sa 16.02
God has made my heart f.; the Almighty	Job 23.16
call to thee, when my heart is f.	Ps 61.02
When my spirit is f., thou knowest	142.03
If you f. in the day of adversity,	Pro 24.10
is sick, and the whole heart f.	Is 1.05
your heart be f. because of these	7.04
he is drinking and awakes f., with his	29.08
He does not f. or grow weary, his	40.28
He gives power to the f., and to him	40.29
Even youths shall f. and be weary,	40.30
weary, they shall walk and not f.	40.31
fails, he drinks no water and is f.	44.12
your strength, and so you were not f.	57.10
of praise instead of a f. spirit; that they	61.03
Let not your heart f., and be not	Jer 51.46
me stunned, f. all the day long.	Lam 1.13
groans are many and my heart is f.	1.22
and babes f. in the streets of the	2.11
as they f. like wounded men in the	2.12
who f. for hunger at the head of	2.19
spirit will f. and all knees will	Eze 21.07
the field shall f. because of it.	31.15
the young men shall f. for thirst.	Amo 8.13
head of Jonah so that he was f.;	Jon 4.08
Hearts f. and knees tremble, anguish	Nah 2.10
hungry, lest they f. on the way."	Mt 15.32
homes, they will f. on the way; and	Mk 8.03

FAINTED

And his heart f., for he did not	Gen 45.26
thirsty, their soul f. within them.	Ps 107.05
Your sons have f., they lie at the	Is 51.20
When my soul f. within me. I remembered	Jon 2.07

FAINTHEARTED

is there that is fearful and f.?	Deu 20.08
of the land are f. because of us."	Jos 2.24
encourage the f., help the weak, be	1Th 5.14
that you may not grow weary or f.	Heb 12.03

FAINTING

"Woe is me! I am f. before murderers."	Jer 4.31
men f. with fear and with foreboding	Lk 21.26

FAINTNESS

I will send f. into their hearts in	Lev 26.36

FAINTS

not another. My heart f. within me!	Job 19.27
my flesh f. for thee, as in a dry	Ps 63.01
I moan; I meditate, and my spirit f.	77.03

FAINTS (cont.)
f. for the courts of the LORD; my heart Ps 84.02
Therefore my spirit f. within me; 143.04

FAIR
that the daughters of men were f.; Gen 6.02
The maiden was very f. to look upon, 24.16
because she was f. to look upon. 26.07
how f. are your tents, O Jacob, your Num 24.05
her beauty; for she was f. to behold. Est 1.11
By his wind the heavens were made f.; Job 26.13
no women so f. as Job's daughters; 42.15
for they are a f. garland for your Pro 1.09
place on your head a f. garland; she will 4.09
"Arise, my love, my f. one, and come away; Sol 2.10
Arise, my love, my f. one, and come away." 2.13
You are all f., my love; there is no 4.07
f. as the moon, bright as the sun, 6.10
How f. and pleasant you are, O loved 7.06
f. with goodly fruit'; but with the Jer 11.16
though they speak f. words to you." 12.06
You also took your f. jewels of my Eze 16.17
clothes and take your f. jewels, 16.39
with f. branches and forest shade, 31.03
Its leaves were f. and its fruit Dan 4.12
whose leaves were f. and its fruit 4.21
thresh, and I spared her f. neck; Hos 10.11
"In that day the f. virgins and the Amo 8.13
Yea, how good and how f. it shall be! Zec 9.17
"It is not f. to take the children's Mt 15.26
you say, 'It will be f. weather; for the 16.02
came to a place called F. Havens, Ac 27.08
and by f. and flattering words they Rom 16.18

FAIRER
not her younger sister f. than she? Ju 15.02

FAIREST
your f. wives and children also are 1Ki 20.03
You are the f. of the sons of men; Ps 45.02
O f. among women, follow in the Sol 1.08
another beloved, O f. among women? 5.09
beloved gone, O f. among women? 6.01

FAIRLY
Masters, treat your slaves justly and f., Col 4.01

FAITH
a breach of f. and sins unwittingly Lev 5.15
a breach of f. against the LORD by 6.02
by breaking f. with the LORD, and that Num 5.06
because you broke f. with me in the Deu 32.51
of Israel broke f. in regard to Jos 7.01
of Zerah break f. in the matter of 22.20
or in breach of f. toward the LORD, 22.22
'If in good f. you are anointing me Ju 9.15
acted in good f. and honor when 9.16
acted in good f. and honor with 9.19
"We have broken f. with our God and Ez 10.02
Do you have f. in him that he will Job 39.12
because they had no f. in God, Ps 78.22
land, having no f. in his promise. 106.24
I kept my f., even when I said, "I 116.10
is in them; who keeps f. for ever; 146.06
nation which keeps f. may enter in. Is 26.02
the righteous shall live by his f. Hab 2.04
clothe you, O men of little f.? Mt 6.30
in Israel have I found such f. 8.10
are you afraid, O men of little f.?" 8.26
Jesus saw their f. he said to the 9.02
your f. has made you well." And 9.22
"According to your f. be it done to 9.29
saying to him, "O man of little f., 14.31
her, "O woman, great is your f.! 15.28
of this, said, "O men of little f., 16.08
to them, "Because of your little f. 17.20
if you have f. as a grain of mustard 17.20
if you have f. and never doubt, you 21.21
you will receive, if you have f." 21.22
the law, justice and mercy and f.; 23.23
And when Jesus saw their f., he said Mk 2.05
are you afraid? Have you no f.?" 4.40
your f. has made you well; go in peace, 5.34
"Go your way; your f. has made you well." 10.52
answered them, "Have f. in God. 11.22
And when he saw their f. he said, Lk 5.20
in Israel have I found such f." 7.09
the woman, "Your f. has saved you; 7.50
He said to them, "Where is your f.?" 8.25
your f. has made you well; go in 8.48
he clothe you, O men of little f.? 12.28
said to the Lord, "Increase our f.!" 17.05
"If you had f. as a grain of mustard 17.06
your way; your f. has made you well." 17.19
comes, will he find f. on earth?" 18.08
your sight; your f. has made you well." 18.42
for you that your f. may not fail; 22.32
by f. in his name, has made this man Ac 3.16
and the f. which is through Jesus 3.16
a man full of f. and of the Holy 6.05
priests were obedient to the f. 6.07
full of the Holy Spirit and of f. 11.24
away the proconsul from the f. 13.08
that he had f. to be made well, 14.09
exhorting them to continue in the f., 14.22
opened a door of f. to the Gentiles. 14.27
but cleansed their hearts by f. 15.09
were strengthened in the f., and they 16.05
to God and of f. in our Lord Jesus 20.21
him speak upon f. in Christ Jesus. 24.24
who are sanctified by f. in me." 26.18
for I have f. in God that it will 27.25
obedience to the f. for the sake of Rom 1.05
because your f. is proclaimed in 1.08
encouraged by each other's f., both 1.12
salvation to every one who has f., 1.16
is revealed through f. for f.; 1.17
"He who through f. is righteous 1.17
of God through f. in Jesus Christ 3.22
by his blood, to be received by f. 3.25
justifies him who has f. in Jesus. 3.26
No, but on the principle of f. 3.27
is justified by f. apart from works 3.28
ground of their f. and the uncircumcised 3.30
uncircumcised because of their f. 3.30
then overthrow the law by this f.? 3.31
his f. is reckoned as righteousness. 4.05
We say that f. was reckoned to Abraham 4.09
which he had by f. while he was still 4.11
example of the f. which our father 4.12
through the righteousness of f. 4.13
f. is null and the promise is void. 4.14
That is why it depends on f., in order 4.16
those who share the f. of Abraham, 4.16
not weaken in f. when he considered 4.19
strong in his f. as he gave glory 4.20
That is why his f. was "reckoned to 4.22
Therefore, since we are justified by f., 5.01
that is, righteousness through f.; 9.30
they did not pursue it through f., 9.32
one who has f. may be justified. 10.04
the righteousness based on f. says, 10.06
the word of f. which we preach); 10.08
So f. comes from what is heard, and 10.17
but you stand fast only through f. 11.20
the measure of f. which God has 12.03
prophecy, in proportion to our f.; 12.06
As for the man who is weak in f., 14.01
The f. that you have, keep between 14.22
because he does not act from f.; 14.23
does not proceed from f. is sin. 14.23
bring about obedience to the f.— 16.26
that your f. might not rest in the 1Co 2.05
to another f. by the same Spirit, to 12.09
knowledge, and if I have all f., 13.02

FAITH (cont.)

So f., hope, love abide, these three; 1Co 13.13
is in vain and your f. is in vain. 15.14
your f. is futile and you are still 15.17
Be watchful, stand firm in your f., 16.13
Not that we lord it over your f.; 2Co 1.24
joy, for you stand firm in your f. 1.24
same spirit of f. as he had who 4.13
for we walk by f., not by sight. 5.07
in f., in utterance, in knowledge, in 8.07
hope is that as your f. increases, 10.15
whether you are holding to your f. 13.05
preaching the f. he once tried to Gal 1.23
law but through f. in Jesus Christ, 2.16
to be justified by f. in Christ, 2.16
flesh I live by f. in the Son of 2.20
of the law, or by hearing with f.? 3.02
of the law, or by hearing with f.? 3.05
it is men of f. who are the sons 3.07
would justify the Gentiles by f., 3.08
who are men of f. are blessed with 3.09
blessed with Abraham who had f. 3.09
"He who through f. is righteous 3.11
but the law does not rest on f., 3.12
promise of the Spirit through f. 3.14
was promised to f. in Jesus Christ 3.22
Now before f. came, we were confined 3.23
restraint until f. should be 3.23
that we might be justified by f. 3.24
But now that f. has come, we are no 3.25
are all sons of God, through f. 3.26
Spirit, by f., we wait for the hope of 5.05
any avail, but f. working through love. 5.06
to those who are of the household of f. 6.10
heard of your f. in the Lord Jesus Eph 1.15
you have been saved through f.; 2.08
of access through our f. in him. 3.12
dwell in your hearts through f.; 3.17
one Lord, one f., one baptism, 4.05
unity of the f. and of the knowledge 4.13
above all taking the shield of f., 6.16
and love with f., from God the 6.23
your progress and joy in the f., Php 1.25
by side for the f. of the gospel, 1.27
sacrificial offering of your f., 2.17
that which is through f. in Christ, 3.09
from God that depends on f.; 3.09
heard of your f. in Christ Jesus Col 1.04
provided that you continue in the f., 1.23
the firmness of your f. in Christ. 2.05
in him and established in the f., 2.07
him through f. in the working of 2.12
your work of f. and labor of love 1Th 1.03
but your f. in God has gone forth 1.08
you in your f. and to exhort you, 3.02
I sent that I might know your f., 3.05
the good news of your f. and love and 3.06
comforted about you through your f.; 3.07
supply what is lacking in your f.? 3.10
on the breastplate of f. and love, 5.08
because your f. is growing abundantly, 2Th 1.03
steadfastness and f. in all your 1.04
and work of f. by his power, 1.11
and evil men; for not all have f. 3.02
To Timothy, my true child in the f.: 1Ti 1.02
the divine training that is in f.; 1.04
a good conscience and sincere f. 1.05
for me with the f. and love that 1.14
holding f. and a good conscience. 1.19
have made shipwreck of their f., 1.19
of the Gentiles in f. and truth. 2.07
continues in f. and love and 2.15
mystery of the f. with a clear 3.09
confidence in the f. which is in 3.13
depart from the f. by giving heed 4.01
words of the f. and of the good 4.06
conduct, in love, in f., in purity. 4.12
disowned the f. and is worse than 5.08
away from the f. and pierced their 6.10
f., love, steadfastness, gentleness. 6.11
Fight the good fight of the f.; 6.12
missed the mark as regards the f. 6.21
I am reminded of your sincere f., 2Ti 1.05
a f. that dwelt first in your 1.05
in the f. and love which are in 1.13
they are upsetting the f. of some. 2.18
f., love, and peace, along with those 2.22
of corrupt mind and counterfeit f.; 3.08
my f., my patience, my love, my 3.10
for salvation through f. in Christ 3.15
finished the race, I have kept the f. 4.07
to further the f. of God's elect Tit 1.01
my true child in a common f.: Grace 1.04
sharply, that they may be sound in the f., 1.13
sound in f., in love, and in steadfastness. 2.02
greet those who love us in the f. Grace 3.15
love and of the f. which you have Phm 1.05
sharing of your f. may promote the 1.06
not meet with f. in the hearers. Heb 4.02
dead works and of f. toward God, 6.01
who through f. and patience inherit 6.12
true heart in full assurance of f., 10.22
but my righteous one shall live by f., 10.38
those who have f. and keep their 10.39
Now f. is the assurance of things 11.01
By f. we understand that the world 11.03
By f. Abel offered to God a more 11.04
but through his f. he is still 11.04
By f. Enoch was taken up so that he 11.05
And without f. it is impossible to 11.06
By f. Noah, being warned by God 11.07
righteousness which comes by f. 11.07
By f. Abraham obeyed when he was 11.08
By f. he sojourned in the land of 11.09
By f. Sarah herself received power 11.11
These all died in f., not having 11.13
By f. Abraham, when he was tested, 11.17
By f. Isaac invoked future blessings 11.20
By f. Jacob, when dying, blessed each 11.21
By f. Joseph, at the end of his life, 11.22
By f. Moses, when he was born, was 11.23
By f. Moses, when he was grown up, 11.24
By f. he left Egypt, not being afraid 11.27
By f. he kept the Passover and sprinkled 11.28
By f. the people crossed the Red 11.29
By f. the walls of Jericho fell 11.30
By f. Rahab the harlot did not perish 11.31
who through f. conquered kingdoms, 11.33
though well attested by their f., 11.39
pioneer and perfecter of our f., 12.02
their life, and imitate their f., 13.07
that the testing of your f. produces Jas 1.03
But let him ask in f., with no 1.06
as you hold the f. of our Lord 2.01
to be rich in f. and heirs of the 2.05
man says he has f. but has not 2.14
Can his f. save him? 2.14
So f. by itself, if it has no works, 2.17
"You have f. and I have works." Show 2.18
Show me your f. apart from your 2.18
I by my works will show you my f. 2.18
that f. apart from works is barren? 2.20
You see that f. was active along 2.22
and f. was completed by works, 2.22
by works and not by f. alone. 2.24
so f. apart from works is dead. 2.26
and the prayer of f. will save the 5.15
guarded through f. for a salvation 1Pe 1.05
so that the genuineness of your f., 1.07
outcome of your f. you obtain the 1.09
so that your f. and hope are in God 1.21
firm in your f., knowing that the 5.09
have obtained a f. of equal standing 2Pe 1.01
to supplement your f. with virtue, 1.05

FAITH (cont.)
that overcomes the world, our f. 1Jn 5.04
contend for the f. which was once Jud 1.03
yourselves up on your most holy f.; 1.20
did not deny my f. even in the Rev 2.13
your love and f. and service and 2.19
the endurance and f. of the saints. 13.10
commandments of God and the f. of Jesus. 14.12

FAITHFUL
the f. God who keeps covenant and Deu 7.09
Deborah, and Issachar f. to Barak; Ju 5.15
will guard the feet of his f. ones; 1Sa 2.09
raise up for myself a f. priest, 2.35
your servants is so f. as David, 22.14
who are peaceable and f. in Israel; 2Sa 20.19
for they were f. in keeping themselves 2Ch 31.18
and right and f. before the LORD 31.20
he was a more f. and God-fearing Neh 7.02
find his heart f. before thee, 9.08
Mattaniah, for they were counted f.; 13.13
for the f. have vanished from among Ps 12.01
hast redeemed me, O LORD, f. God. 31.05
the LORD preserves the f., but 31.23
"Gather to me my f. ones, who made 50.05
With thy f. help rescue me from 69.14
whose spirit was not f. to God. 78.08
speak in a vision to thy f. one, 89.19
with favor on the f. in the land, 101.06
works of his hands are f. and just; 111.07
The LORD is f. in all his words, and 145.13
praise in the assembly of the f.! 149.01
Let the f. exult in glory; let them 149.05
this is glory for all his f. ones. 149.09
but a f. envoy brings healing. Pro 13.17
A f. witness does not lie, but a 14.05
loyalty, but a f. man who can find? 20.06
of harvest is a f. messenger to 25.13
F. are the wounds of a friend; 27.06
A f. man will abound with blessings, 28.20
How the f. city has become a harlot, Is 1.21
city of righteousness, the f. city." 1.26
plans formed of old, f. and sure. 25.01
who is f., the Holy One of Israel, 49.07
be a true and f. witness against Jer 42.05
or any fault, because he was f., Dan 6.04
by God, and is f. to the Holy One. Hos 11.12
shall be called the f. city, and the Zec 8.03
"Who then is the f. and wise servant, Mt 24.45
'Well done, good and f. servant; you 25.21
you have been f. over a little, 25.21
'Well done, good and f. servant; 25.23
you have been f. over a little, 25.23
"Who then is the f. and wise steward, Lk 12.42
"He who is f. in a very little is f. also 16.10
have not been f. in the unrighteous 16.11
have not been f. in that which is 16.12
you have been f. in a very little, 19.17
all to remain f. to the Lord with Ac 11.23
judged me to be f. to the Lord, 16.15
God is f., by whom you were called 1Co 1.09
my beloved and f. child in the 4.17
God is f., and he will not let you 10.13
As surely as God is f., our word 2Co 1.18
who are also f. in Christ Jesus: Eph 1.01
brother and f. minister in the 6.21
To the saints and f. brethren in Col 1.02
He is a f. minister of Christ on 1.07
brother and f. minister and fellow 4.07
the f. and beloved brother, who is 4.09
He who calls you is f., and he will 1Th 5.24
But the Lord is f.; he will 2Th 3.03
he judged me f. by appointing me 1Ti 1.12
but temperate, f. in all things. 3.11
entrust to f. men who will be able 2Ti 2.02
he remains f.—for he cannot deny 2.13
a merciful and f. high priest in Heb 2.17
He was f. to him who appointed him, 3.02
Moses also was f. in God's house. 3.02
Now Moses was f. in all God's house 3.05
but Christ was f. over God's house 3.06
wavering, for he who promised is f.; 10.23
considered him f. who had promised 11.11
entrust their souls to a f. creator. 1Pe 4.19
By Silvanus, a f. brother as I regard 5.12
he is f. and just, and will forgive 1Jn 1.09
and from Jesus Christ the f. witness, Rev 1.05
Be f. unto death, and I will give 2.10
my f. one, who was killed among you, 2.13
the f. and true witness, the beginning 3.14
him are called and chosen and f." 17.14
sat upon it is called F. and True, 19.11

FAITHFULLY
deal kindly and f. with you when Jos 2.14
and serve him f. with all your 1Sa 12.24
And they f. brought in the contributions, 2Ch 31.12
Shecaniah were f. assisting him in 31.15
And the men did the work f. Over them 34.12
thou hast dealt f. and we have Neh 9.33
those who act f. are his delight. Pro 12.22
he will f. bring forth justice. Is 42.03
I will f. give them their recompense, 61.08
who has my word speak my word f. Jer 23.28

FAITHFULNESS
love and his f. toward my master. Gen 24.27
and all the f. which thou hast 32.10
abounding in steadfast love and f., Ex 34.06
A God of f. and without iniquity, Deu 32.04
generation, children in whom is no f. 32.20
serve him in sincerity and in f.; Jos 24.14
for his righteousness and his f.; 1Sa 26.23
show steadfast love and f. to you! 2Sa 2.06
show steadfast love and f. to you. 15.20
before me in f. with all their 1Ki 2.04
because he walked before thee in f., 3.06
before thee in f. and with a whole 2Ki 20.03
in f., and with your whole heart: 2Ch 19.09
these acts of f. Sennacherib king 32.01
the LORD are steadfast love and f., Ps 25.10
my eyes, and I walk in f. to thee. 26.03
praise thee? Will it tell of thy f.? 30.09
and all his work is done in f. 33.04
the heavens, thy f. to the clouds. 36.05
spoken of thy f. and thy salvation; 40.10
love and thy f. from the great 40.10
love and thy f. ever preserve me! 40.11
with evil; in thy f. put an end to them. 54.05
forth his steadfast love and his f.! 57.03
the heavens, thy f. to the clouds. 57.10
steadfast love and f. watch over him! 61.07
with the harp for thy f., O my God; 71.22
Steadfast love and f. will meet; 85.10
F. will spring up from the ground, 85.11
abounding in steadfast love and f. 86.15
in the grave, or thy f. in Abaddon? 88.11
proclaim thy f. to all generations 89.01
thy f. is firm as the heavens. 89.02
thy f. in the assembly of the holy 89.05
O LORD, with thy f. round about thee? 89.08
steadfast love and f. go before thee. 89.14
My f. and my steadfast love shall 89.24
steadfast love, or be false to my f. 89.33
which by thy f. thou didst swear to 89.49
his f. is a shield and buckler. 91.04
the morning, and thy f. by night, 92.02
love and f. to the house of Israel. 98.03
for ever, and his f. to all generations. 100.05
heavens, thy f. reaches to the clouds. 108.04
performed with f. and uprightness. 111.08
of thy steadfast love and thy f.! 115.01
and the f. of the LORD endures for 117.02
I have chosen the way of f., I set 119.30

FAITHFULNESS (cont.)
and that in f. thou hast afflicted Ps 119.75
Thy f. endures to all generations; 119.90
in righteousness and in all f. 119.138
for thy steadfast love and thy f.; 138.02
In thy f. answer me, in thy righteousness 143.01
Let not loyalty and f. forsake you; Pro 3.03
who devise good meet loyalty and f. 14.22
By loyalty and f. iniquity is atoned 16.06
Loyalty and f. preserve the king, 20.28
waist, and f. the girdle of his loins. Is 11.05
it will sit in f. in the tent of 16.05
before thee in f. and with a whole 38.03
to the pit cannot hope for thy f. 38.18
makes known to the children thy f. 38.19
I have continued my f. to you. Jer 31.03
will plant them in this land in f., 32.41
every morning; great is thy f. Lam 3.23
I will betroth you to me in f.; Hos 2.20
There is no f. or kindness, and no 4.01
Thou wilt show f. to Jacob and Mic 7.20
their God, in f. and in righteousness." Zec 8.08
faithlessness nullify the f. of God? Rom 3.03
patience, kindness, goodness, f., Gal 5.22

FAITHLESS
Judah and had been f. to the LORD. 2Ch 28.19
he became yet more f. to the LORD— 28.22
in his reign when he was f., we have 29.19
who were f. to the LORD God of 30.07
I look at the f. with disgust, Ps 119.158
the way of the f. is their ruin. Pro 13.15
righteous, and the f. for the upright. 21.18
he overthrows the words of the f. 22.12
and increases the f. among men. 23.28
Trust in a f. man in time of trouble 25.19
that f. one, Israel, how she went up Jer 3.06
all the adulteries of that f. one, 3.08
"F. Israel has shown herself less 3.11
f. Israel. says the LORD. I will not 3.12
Return, O f. children, says the LORD; 3.14
Surely, as a f. wife leaves her 3.20
husband, so have you been f. to me, 3.20
"Return, O f. sons, I will heal your 3.22
Judah have been utterly f. to me, 5.11
long will you waver, O f. daughter? 31.22
O f. daughter, who trusted in her 49.04
why dost thou look on f. men, and art Hab 1.13
Her prophets are wanton, f. men; Zep 3.04
why then are we f. to one another, Mal 2.10
Judah has been f., and abomination 2.11
youth, to whom you have been f., 2.14
and let none be f. to the wife of 2.15
to yourselves and do not be f." 2.16
"O f. and perverse generation, how Mt 17.17
"O f. generation, how long am I to Mk 9.19
"O f. and perverse generation, how Lk 9.41
my sde; do not be f., but believing." Jn 20.27
foolish, f., heartless, ruthless. Rom 1.31
if we are f., he remains faithful— 2Ti 2.13
the f., the polluted, as for murderers, Rev 21.08

FAITHLESSLY
since he has dealt f. with her. Ex 21.08
land sins against me by acting f., Eze 14.13
desolate, because they have acted f., 15.08
They have dealt f. with the LORD; Hos 5.07
there they dealt f. with me. 6.07

FAITHLESSNESS
and shall suffer for your f., until the last Num 14.33
entreaty, and all his sin and his f., 2Ch 33.19
And in this f. the hand of the Ez 9.02
because of the f. of the returned 9.04
mourning over the f. of the exiles. 10.06
faithless sons, I will heal your f. Jer 3.22
I will heal their f.; I will love Hos 14.04
Does their f. nullify the faithfulness Rom 3.03

FALCON
the kite, the f. according to its Lev 11.14

FALCON'S
and the f. eye has not seen it. Job 28.07

FALL
a deep sleep to f. upon the man, Gen 2.21
occasion against us and f. upon us, 43.18
lest he f. upon us with pestilence Ex 5.03
the LORD will f. with a very severe 9.03
I will cause very heavy hail to f., 9.18
no plague shall f. upon you to 12.13
Terror and dread f. upon them; 15.16
but God let him f. into his hand, 21.13
lest the land f. into harlotry and Lev 19.29
and they shall f. before you by 26.07
enemies shall f. before you by the 26.08
sword, and they shall f. when none 26.36
your thigh f. away and your body Num 5.21
body swell and your thigh f. away.' 5.22
swell, and her thigh shall f. away, 5.27
and let them f. beside the camp, 11.31
into this land, to f. by the sword? 14.03
bodies shall f. in this wilderness; 14.29
bodies shall f. in this wilderness. 14.32
you, and you shall f. by the sword; 14.43
land that shall f. to you for an 34.02
your house, if any one f. from it. Deu 22.08
wall of the city will f. down flat, Jos 6.05
f. upon their rear, do not let them 10.19
"Rise yourself, and f. upon us; Ju 8.21
men of Shechem f. back upon their 9.57
you will not f. upon me yourselves." 15.12
of thirst, and f. into the hands of the 15.18
us, lest angry fellows f. upon you, 18.25
none of his words f. to the ground. 1Sa 3.19
hair of his head f. to the ground; 14.45
to make David f. by the hand of 18.25
"You turn and f. upon the priests." 22.18
not my blood f. to the earth away 26.20
men and said, "Go, f. upon him." 2Sa 1.15
May it f. upon the head of Joab, and 3.29
of your son shall f. to the ground. 2Sa 14.11
of the people f. at the first attack, 17.09
let us f. into the hand of the LORD, 24.14
but let me not f. into the hand of 24.14
of his hairs shall f. to the earth; 1Ki 1.52
may go up and f. at Ramothgilead?' 22.20
man of God said, "Where did it f.?" 2Ki 6.06
there shall f. to the earth nothing 10.10
you provoke trouble so that you f., 14.10
cause him to f. by the sword in 19.07
let me f. into the hand of the 1Ch 21.13
but let me not f. into the hand of 21.13
may go up and f. at Ramothgilead?' 2Ch 18.19
you provoke trouble so that you f., 25.19
before whom you have begun to f., Est 6.13
him but will surely f. before him." 6.13
should never f. into disuse among 9.28
and the dread of him f. upon you? Job 13.11
shoulder blade f. from my shoulder, 31.22
snow he says, 'F. on the earth'; 37.06
let them f. by their own counsels; Ps 5.10
They will collapse and f.; but we 20.08
foes, they shall stumble and f. 27.02
let them f. therein to ruin! 35.08
though he f., he shall not be cast 37.24
For I am ready to f., and my pain 38.17
enemies; the peoples f. under you. 45.05
May all kings f. down before him, 72.11
thou dost make them f. to ruin. 73.18
he let them f. in the midst of 78.28
like men, and f. like any prince." 82.07
A thousand may f. at your side, ten 91.07
hate the work of those who f. away; 101.03
would make them f. in the wilderness, 106.26

FALL (cont.)

Let burning coals f. upon them!	Ps 140.10
wicked together f. into their own	141.10
people to whom such blessings f.!	144.15
and a haughty spirit before a f.	Pro 16.18
the LORD is angry will f. into it.	22.14
He who digs a pit will f. into it,	26.27
evil way will f. into his own pit;	28.10
his heart will f. into calamity.	28.14
in his ways will f. into a pit.	28.18
For if they f., one will lift up	Ecc 4.10
He who digs a pit will f. into it;	10.08
Your men shall f. by the sword and	Is 3.25
they shall f. and be broken;	8.15
prisoners or f. among the slain.	10.04
with its majestic trees will f.	10.34
is caught will f. by the sword.	13.15
and it will be cut down and f.,	22.25
the terror shall f. into the pit;	24.18
of the shades thou wilt let it f.	26.19
and f. backward, and be broken, and	28.13
great slaughter, when the towers f.	30.25
and he who is helped will f., and they	31.03
"And the Assyrian shall f. by a sword,	31.08
All their host shall f., as leaves f.	34.04
Wild oxen shall f. with them,	34.07
I will make him f. by the sword in	37.07
and young men shall f. exhausted;	40.30
Shall I f. down before a block of	44.19
then they f. down and worship!	46.06
disaster shall f. upon you, which you	47.11
with you shall f. because of you.	54.15
they shall f. among those who f.	Jer 6.15
of it, our hands f. helpless; anguish	6.24
When men f., do they not rise again?	8.04
they shall f. among the fallen;	8.12
of men shall f. like dung upon the	9.22
and if in a safe land you f. down,	12.05
and terror f. upon them suddenly.	15.08
their people to f. by the sword	19.07
They shall f. by the sword of their	20.04
friends, watching for my f. "Perhaps	20.10
which they shall be driven and f.;	23.12
f. and rise no more, because of the	25.27
and you shall f. like choice rams.	25.34
and you shall not f. by the sword;	39.18
in the land of Egypt they shall f.;	44.12
the terror shall f. into the pit,	48.44
sound of their f. the earth shall	49.21
young men shall f. in her squares,	49.26
young men shall f. in her squares,	50.30
The proud one shall stumble and f.,	50.32
They shall f. down slain in the	51.04
her slain shall f. in the midst of	51.47
Babylon must f. for the slain of	51.49
therefore her f. is terrible, she	Lam 1.09
part shall f. by the sword round	Eze 5.12
And the slain shall f. in the midst	6.07
for they shall f. by the sword,	6.11
that is near shall f. by the sword;	6.12
You shall f. by the sword; I will	11.10
it with whitewash that it shall f.!	13.11
of rain, great hailstones will f.,	13.11
his troops shall f. by the sword,	17.21
and many f. at all their gates.	21.15
survivors shall f. by the sword.	23.25
left behind shall f. by the sword.	24.21
Dedan they shall f. by the sword.	25.13
pillars will f. to the ground.	26.11
shake at the sound of your f.,	26.15
tremble on the day of your f.;	26.18
the slain shall f. in the midst of	28.23
you shall f. upon the open field,	29.05
Ethiopia, when the slain f. in Egypt,	30.04
shall f. with them by the sword.	30.05
Those who support Egypt shall f.,	30.06
they shall f. within her by the	30.06
of Pibeseth shall f. by the sword;	30.17
make the sword f. from his hand.	30.22
but the arms of Pharaoh shall f.;	30.25
the valleys its branches will f.,	31.12
quake at the sound of its f., when I	31.16
multitude to f. by the swords of	32.12
They shall f. amid those who are	32.20
he shall not f. by it when he turns	33.12
waste places shall f. by the sword;	33.27
those slain with the sword shall f.	35.08
I will f. upon the quiet people who	38.11
down, and the cliffs shall f., and	38.20
You shall f. upon the mountains of	39.04
You shall f. in the open field;	39.05
this land shall f. to you as your	47.14
you are to f. down and worship the	Dan 3.05
does not f. down and worship shall	3.06
shall f. down and worship the golden	3.10
does not f. down and worship shall	3.11
to f. down and worship the image	3.15
but he shall stumble and f., and shall	11.19
away, and many shall f. down slain.	11.26
they shall f. by sword and flame,	11.33
When they f., they shall receive a	11.34
of those who are wise shall f.,	11.35
And tens of thousands shall f.,	11.41
princes shall f. by the sword	Hos 7.16
us, and to the hills, F. upon us.	10.08
I will f. upon them like a bear	13.08
they shall f. by the sword, their	13.16
Does a bird f. in a snare on the	Amo 3.05
be cut off and f. to the ground.	3.14
daughters shall f. by the sword,	7.17
they shall f., and never rise	8.14
no pebble shall f. upon the earth.	9.09
when I f., I shall rise; when I sit	Mic 7.08
if shaken they f. into the mouth	Nah 3.12
cause men to f. each into the hand	Zec 11.06
from the LORD shall f. on them,	14.13
this plague shall f. on the horses,	14.15
if you will f. down and worship me."	Mt 4.09
upon that house, but it did not f.,	7.25
it fell; and great was the f. of it."	7.27
of them will f. to the ground without	10.29
blind man, both will f. into a pit.	15.14
the crumbs that f. from their	15.27
And then many will f. away, and betray	24.10
and the stars will f. from heaven,	24.29
"You will all f. away because of me	26.31
"Though they all f. away because of	26.33
of you, I will never f. away."	26.33
the word, immediately they f. away.	Mk 4.17
said to them, "You will all f. away;	14.27
him, "Even though they all f. away,	14.29
is set for the f. and rising of	Lk 2.34
Will they not both f. into a pit?	6.39
and in time of temptation f. away.	8.13
"I saw Satan f. like lightning from	10.18
they will f. by the edge of the	21.24
say to the mountains, 'F. on us';	23.30
shadow might f. on some of them.	Ac 5.15
swell up or suddenly f. down dead;	28.06
have sinned and f. short of the	Rom 3.23
of slavery to f. back into fear,	8.15
a rock that will make them f.;	9.33
have they stumbled so as to f.?	11.11
to make others f. by what he eats;	14.20
lest I cause my brother to f.	1Co 8.13
he stands take heed lest he f.	10.12
Who is made to f., and I am not	2Co 11.29
conceit and f. into the condemnation	1Ti 3.06
or he may f. into reproach and the	3.07
to be rich f. into temptation, into	6.09
leading you to f. away from the	Heb 3.12
that no one f. by the same sort of	4.11
thing to f. into the hands of the	10.31
you may not f. under condemnation.	Jas 5.12

FALL (cont.)
a rock that will make them f."; for they 1Pe 2.08
for if you do this you will never f.; 2Pe 1.10
twenty-four elders f. down before Rev 4.10
"F. on us and hide us from the face 6.16
no rain may f. during the days of 11.06

FALLEN
and why has your countenance f.? Gen 4.06
"If a man's hair has f. from his head, Lev 13.40
man's hair has f. from his forehead 13.41
you gather the f. grapes of your 19.10
ass or his ox f. down by the way, Deu 22.04
the fear of you has f. upon us, Jos 2.09
have you thus f. upon your face? 7.10
very last had f. by the edge of 8.24
for there had f. a hundred and Ju 8.10
tribes of Israel had f. to them. 18.01
Dagon had f. face downward on the 1Sa 5.03
Dagon had f. face downward on the 5.04
from the LORD had f. upon them. 26.12
his three sons f. on Mount Gilboa. 31.08
people also have f. and are dead; 2Sa 1.04
he could not live after he had f.; 1.10
because they had f. by the sword. 1.12
high places! How are the mighty f.! 1.19
"How are the mighty f. in the midst 1.25
"How are the mighty f., and the 1.27
place where Asahel had f. and died, 2.23
before the wicked you have f." 3.34
a great man has f. this day in 3.38
in a pit on a day when snow had f. 23.20
of Elijah that had f. from him, 2Ki 2.13
of Elijah that had f. from him, 2.14
Now when Elisha had f. sick with 13.14
and his sons f. on Mount Gilboa. 1Ch 10.08
in a pit on a day when snow had f. 11.22
fathers have f. by the sword and 2Ch 29.09
fear of the Jews had f. upon them. Est 8.17
of them had f. upon all peoples. 9.02
fear of Mordecai had f. upon them. 9.03
The lines have f. for me in pleasant Ps 16.06
They have all f. away; they are all 53.03
terrors of death have f. upon me. 55.04
but they have f. into it themselves 57.06
who insult thee have f. on me. 69.09
for dread of them had f. upon it. 105.38
This blessing has f. to me, that I 119.56
has stumbled, and Judah has f.; Is 3.08
"The bricks have f., but we will 9.10
"How you are f. from heaven, O Day 14.12
harvest the battle shout has f. 16.09
"F., f. is Babylon; and all 21.09
inhabitants of the world have not f. 26.18
for truth has f. in the public squares, 59.14
they shall fall among the f.; when I Jer 8.12
against warrior; they have both f. together." 46.12
your vintage the destroyer has f. 48.32
her bulwarks have f., her walls are 50.15
Suddenly Babylon has f. and been 51.08
flow to him; the wall of Babylon has f. 51.44
Babylon have f. the slain of all 51.49
my young men have f. by the sword; Lam 2.21
The crown has f. from our head; 5.16
all of them slain, f. by the sword; Eze 32.22
f. by the sword, who spread terror 32.23
f. by the sword, who went down 32.24
lie with the f. mighty men of old 32.27
to me and said, "The city has f." 33.21
All their kings have f.; and none Hos 7.07
"F., no more to rise, is the virgin Amo 5.02
David that is f. and repair its 9.11
Wail, O cypress, for the cedar has f., Zec 11.02
of the saints who had f. asleep were Mt 27.52
or an ox that has f. into a well, Lk 14.05
"Our friend Lazarus has f. asleep, Jn 11.11
if he has f. asleep, he will recover." 11.12
for it had not yet f. on any of them, Ac 8.16
dwelling of David, which has f.; 15.16
And when we had all f. to the ground, 26.14
severity toward those who have f., Rom 11.22
alive, though some have f. asleep. 1Co 15.06
also who have f. asleep in Christ 15.18
fruits of those who have f. asleep. 15.20
by the law; you have f. away from grace. Gal 5.04
with him those who have f. asleep. 1Th 4.14
precede those who have f. asleep. 4.15
Remember then from what you have f., Rev 2.05
I saw a star f. from heaven to earth, 9.01
"F., f. is Babylon the great, she who 14.08
seven kings, five of whom have f., 17.10
"F., f. is Babylon the great! 18.02

FALLING
f. down, but having his eyes uncovered: Num 24.04
f. down, but having his eyes uncovered: 24.16
as Haman was f. on the couch where Est 7.08
my feet from f., that I may walk Ps 56.13
so that I was f., but the LORD 118.13
The LORD upholds all who are f., 145.14
like leaves f. from the fig tree. Is 34.04
and the stars will be f. from heaven, Mk 13.25
and f. at Jesus' feet he besought Lk 8.41
and f. down before him declared in 8.47
drops of blood f. down upon the 22.44
to you to keep you from f. away. Jn 16.01
and f. headlong he burst open in Ac 1.18
food is a cause of my brother's f., 1Co 8.13
and so, f. on his face, he will 14.25
keep you from f. and to present Jud 1.24

FALLOW
you shall let it rest and lie f., Ex 23.11
The f. ground of the poor yields Pro 13.23
Jerusalem: "Break up your f. ground, Jer 4.03
break up your f. ground, for it is Hos 10.12

FALLS
so that his rider f. backward. Gen 49.17
and an ox or an ass f. into it, Ex 21.33
any of them f. when they are dead Lev 11.32
And if any of them f. into any earthen 11.33
their carcass f. shall be unclean; 11.35
their carcass f. upon any seed for 11.37
any part of their carcass f. on it, 11.38
wherever the lot f. to any man, that shall Num 33.54
makes war with you, until it f. Deu 20.20
as one f. before the wicked you 2Sa 3.34
him as the dew f. on the ground; 17.12
night, when deep sleep f. on men, Job 4.13
"But the mountain f. and crumbles 14.18
My skin turns black and f. from me, 30.30
night, when deep sleep f. upon men, 33.15
and f. into the hole which he has Ps 7.15
sinks down, and f. by his might. 10.10
like rain that f. on the mown 72.06
which f. on the mountains of Zion! 133.03
straight, but the wicked f. by his own Pro 11.05
Where there is no guidance, a people f.; 11.14
but his wrath f. on one who acts 14.35
a perverse tongue f. into calamity. 17.20
for a righteous man f. seven times, 24.16
Do not rejoice when your enemy f., 24.17
alone when he f. and has not another Ecc 4.10
when it suddenly f. upon them. 9.12
and if a tree f. to the south or to 11.03
in the place where the tree f., 11.03
and it f., and will not rise again. Is 24.20
graven image and f. down before it. 44.15
and f. down to it and worships it; 44.17
and when the wall f., will it not be Eze 13.12
when it f., you shall perish in the 13.14
sheep and it f. into a pit on the Mt 12.11
the word, immediately he f. away. 13.21
for often he f. into the fire, and 17.15

FALLS (cont.)

"And he who f. on this stone will Mt *21.44
but when it f. on any one, it will *21.44
waste, and house f. upon house. Lk 11.17
share of property that f. to me. 15.12
Every one who f. on that stone will 20.18
but when it f. on any one it will 20.18
grain of wheat f. into the earth Jn 12.24
of God rightly f. upon those who Rom 2.02
own master that he stands or f. 14.04
the rain that often f. upon it, Heb 6.07
grass; its flower f., and its beauty Jas 1.11
grass withers, and the flower f., 1Pe 1.24

FALSE

"You shall not bear f. witness against Ex 20.16
"You shall not utter a f. report. 23.01
Keep far from a f. charge, and do 23.07
shall you bear f. witness against Deu 5.20
witness is a f. witness and has 19.18
They went after f. idols, and became f., 2Ki 17.15
For he was f. to the LORD his God, 2Ch 26.16
I should have been f. to God above. Job 31.28
For truly my words are not f.; 36.04
not lift up his soul to what is f., Ps 24.04
I do not sit with f. men, nor do I 26.04
for f. witnesses have risen against 27.12
those who go astray after f. gods! 40.04
thee, or been f. to thy covenant. 44.17
an end to those who are f. to thee. 73.27
love, or be f. to my faithfulness. 89.33
Put f. ways far from me; and graciously 119.29
therefore I hate every f. way. 119.104
thy precepts; I hate every f. way. 119.128
a f. witness who breathes out lies, Pro 6.19
A f. balance is an abomination to 11.01
but a f. witness utters deceit. 12.17
but a f. witness breathes out lies. 14.05
still less is f. speech to a prince. 17.07
A f. witness will not go unpunished, 19.05
A f. witness will not go unpunished, 19.09
the LORD, and f. scales are not good. 20.23
A f. witness will perish, but the 21.28
A man who bears f. witness against 25.18
and his insolence—his boasts are f. Is 16.06
return, and her f. sister Judah saw it. Jer 3.07
yet her f. sister Judah did not fear, 3.08
all this her f. sister Judah did not 3.10
herself less guilty than f. Judah. 3.11
the f. pen of the scribes has made 8.08
for the customs of the peoples are f. 10.03
for his images are f., and there 10.14
any among the f. gods of the 14.22
me, they burn incense to f. gods; 18.15
And Jeremiah said, "It is f.; I am not 37.14
boasts are f., his deeds are f. 48.30
for his images are f., and there 51.17
seen for you f. and deceptive Lam 2.14
for you oracles f. and misleading. 2.14
shall be no more any f. vision or Eze 12.24
it will seem like a f. divination; 21.23
while they see for you f. visions, 21.29
seeing f. visions and divining lies 22.28
Their heart is f.; now they Hos 10.02
in whose hands are f. balances, 12.07
deal deceitfully with f. balances, Amo 8.05
and love no f. oath, for all these Zec 8.17
the dreamers tell f. dreams, 10.02
"Beware of f. prophets, who come to Mt 7.15
theft, f. witness, slander. 15.19
You shall not bear f. witness, 19.18
And many f. prophets will arise and 24.11
For f. Christs and f. prophets 24.24
council sought f. testimony against 26.59
though many f. witnesses came 26.60
Do not bear f. witness, Do not Mk 10.19
F. Christs and f. prophets will 13.22
For many bore f. witness against 14.56
up and bore f. witness against him, 14.57
by violence or by f. accusation, Lk 3.14
fathers did to the f. prophets. 6.26
Do not bear f. witness, Honor your 18.20
and set up f. witnesses who said, Ac 6.13
a Jewish f. prophet, named Bar-Jesus 13.06
God be true though every man be f., Rom 3.04
For such men are f. apostles, 2Co 11.13
at sea, danger from f. brethren; 11.26
But because of f. brethren secretly Gal 2.04
to make them believe what is f., 2Th 2.11
impossible that God should prove f., Heb 6.18
not boast and be f. to the truth. Jas 3.14
But f. prophets also arose among 2Pe 2.01
there will be f. teachers among 2.01
they will exploit you with f. words; 2.03
for many f. prophets have gone out 1Jn 4.01
are not, and found them to be f.; Rev 2.02
from the mouth of the f. prophet, 16.13
and with it the f. prophet who in 19.20
the beast and the f. prophet were, 20.10

FALSEHOOD

nothing left of your answers but f." Job 21.34
my lips will not speak f., and my 27.04
"If I have walked with f., and my 31.05
They take pleasure in f. They bless Ps 62.04
they persecute me with f.; help me! 119.86
I hate and abhor f., but I love 119.163
right hand is a right hand of f. 144.08
right hand is a right hand of f. 144.11
A righteous man hates f., but a wicked Pro 13.05
If a ruler listens to f., all his 29.12
Remove far from me f. and lying; 30.08
who draw iniquity with cords of f., Is 5.18
and in f. we have taken shelter"; 28.15
f. and not truth has grown strong Jer 9.03
They have spoken f. and divined a Eze 13.06
long; they multiply f. and violence; Hos 12.01
is true, and in him there is no f. Jn 7.18
But if through my f. God's truthfulness Rom 3.07
putting away f., let every one speak Eph 4.25
who practices abomination or f., but only Rev 21.27
every one who loves and practices f. 22.15

FALSELY

will not deal f. with me or with my Gen 21.23
Pharaoh deal f. again by not letting Ex 8.29
swearing f.—in any of all the things Lev 6.03
about which he has sworn f.; he shall 6.05
nor deal f., nor lie to one another 19.11
And you shall not swear by my name f., 19.12
witness and has accused his brother f., Deu 19.18
you, lest you deal f. with your God." Jos 24.27
Will you speak f. for God, and speak Job 13.07
people, sons who will not deal f.; Is 63.08
the LORD lives," yet they swear f. Jer 5.02
They have spoken f. of the LORD, 5.12
the prophets prophesy f., and the 5.31
prophet to priest, every one deals f. 6.13
swear f., burn incense to Baal, and 7.09
prophet to priest every one deals f. 8.10
friends, to whom you have prophesied f." 20.06
they are prophesying f. in my name, 27.15
for you are speaking f. of Ishmael." 40.16
have disheartened the righteous f., Eze 13.22
for they deal f., the thief breaks Hos 7.01
one who swears f. shall be cut off Zec 5.03
of him who swears f. by my name; and it 5.04
adulterers, against those who swear f., Mal 3.05
evil against you f. on my account. Mt 5.11
of old, 'You shall not swear f., but 5.33
of what is f. called knowledge, 1Ti 6.20

FAME

who have heard thy f. will say, Num 14.15
in praise and in f. and in honor, Deu 26.19

FAME (cont.)
and his f. was in all the land. Jos 6.27
and his f. was in all the nations 1Ki 4.31
heard of the f. of Solomon concerning 10.01
And the f. of David went out into 1Ch 14.17
of f. and glory throughout all lands; 22.05
heard of the f. of Solomon she came 2Ch 9.01
and his f. spread even to the 26.08
And his f. spread far, for he was 26.15
and his f. spread throughout all Est 9.04
his f. continue as long as the sun! Ps 72.17
pour forth the f. of thy abundant 145.07
not heard my f. or seen my glory; Is 66.19
So his f. spread throughout all Mt 4.24
and spread his f. through all that 9.31
tetrarch heard about the f. of Jesus; 14.01
And at once his f. spread everywhere Mk 1.28

FAMILIAR
seamen who were f. with the sea, 1Ki 9.27
and his f. friends, and his priests, 2Ki 10.11
ships and servants f. with the sea, 2Ch 8.18
equal, my companion, my f. friend. Ps 55.13
say all my f. friends, watching Jer 20.10
are especially f. with all customs Ac 26.03

FAMILIES
went forth by f. out of the ark. Gen 8.19
by their f., in their nations. 10.05
Afterward the f. of the Canaanites 10.18
by their f., their languages, their 10.20
by their f., their languages, their 10.31
These are the f. of the sons of 10.32
by you all the f. of the earth 12.03
shall all the f. of the earth 28.14
to their f. and their dwelling 36.40
midwives feared God he gave them f. Ex 1.21
Carmi; these are the f. of Reuben. 6.14
woman; these are the f. of Simeon. 6.15
Libni and Shimei, by their f. 6.17
These are the f. of the Levites 6.19
these are the f. of the Korahites. 6.24
houses of the Levites by their f. 6.25
yourselves according to your f., 12.21
you and their f. that are with you, Lev 25.45
by f., by fathers' houses, according Num 1.02
who registered themselves by f., 1.18
by their f., by their fathers' houses, 1.20
by their f., by their fathers' houses, 1.22
by their f., by their fathers' houses, 1.24
by their f., by their fathers' houses, 1.26
by their f., by their fathers' houses, 1.28
by their f., by their fathers' houses, 1.30
by their f., by their fathers' houses, 1.32
by their f., by their fathers' houses, 1.34
by their f., by their fathers' houses, 1.36
by their f., by their fathers' houses, 1.38
by their f., by their fathers' houses, 1.40
by their f., by their fathers' houses, 1.42
Levi, by fathers' houses and by f.; 3.15
of the sons of Gershon by their f.: 3.18
And the sons of Kohath by their f.: 3.19
And the sons of Merari by their f.: 3.20
These are the f. of the Levites, by 3.20
these were the f. of the Gershonites. 3.21
The f. of the Gershonites were to 3.23
these are the f. of the Kohathites. 3.27
The f. of the sons of Kohath were 3.29
house of the f. of the Kohathites. 3.30
Mushites: these are the f. of Merari. 3.33
house of the f. of Merari was 3.35
by f., all the males from a month 3.39
by their f. and their fathers' 4.02
tribe of the f. of the Kohathites 4.18
by their f. and their fathers' 4.22
service of the f. of the Gershonites, 4.24
service of the f. of the sons of 4.28
them by their f. and their fathers' 4.29
service of the f. of the sons of 4.33
by their f. and their fathers' houses, 4.34
and their number by f. was two 4.36
number of the f. of the Kohathites, 4.37
by their f. and their fathers' 4.38
their number by their f. and their 4.40
number of the f. of the sons of 4.41
The number of the f. of the sons of 4.42
by their f. and their fathers' 4.42
their number by f. was three 4.44
numbered of the f. of the sons of 4.45
by their f. and their fathers' 4.46
people weeping throughout their f., 11.10
These are the f. of the Reubenites; 26.07
of Simeon according to their f.: 26.12
These are the f. of the Simeonites, 26.14
The sons of Gad according to their f.: 26.15
These are the f. of the sons of Gad 26.18
Judah according to their f. were: 26.20
These are the f. of Judah according 26.22
of Issachar according to their f.: 26.23
These are the f. of Issachar according 26.25
of Zebulun, according to their f.: 26.26
These are the f. of the Zebulunites 26.27
of Joseph according to their f.: 26.28
These are the f. of Manasseh; and their 26.34
of Ephraim according to their f.: 26.35
These are the f. of the sons of 26.37
of Joseph according to their f. 26.37
of Benjamin according to their f.: 26.38
of Benjamin according to their f.; 26.41
sons of Dan according to their f.: 26.42
These are the f. of Dan according 26.42
of Dan according to their f. 26.42
All the f. of the Shuhamites, according 26.43
of Asher according to their f.: 26.44
These are the f. of the sons of 26.47
of Naphtali according to their f.: 26.48
These are the f. of Naphtali according 26.50
of Naphtali according to their f.; 26.50
as numbered according to their f.: 26.57
These are the f. of Levi: the family 26.58
from the f. of Manasseh the son of 27.01
land by lot according to your f.; 33.54
houses of the f. of the sons of 36.01
into the f. of the sons of Manasseh 36.12
LORD takes shall come near by f.; Jos 7.14
and he brought near the f. of Judah, 7.17
Reubenites according to their f. 13.15
to their f. with their cities and 13.23
the Gadites, according to their f. 13.24
the Gadites according to their f., 13.28
Manassites according to their f. 13.29
Machirites according to their f. 13.31
to their f. reached southward to 15.01
of Judah according to their f. 15.12
of Judah according to their f. 15.20
Ephraimites by their f. was as follows: 16.05
of the Ephraimites by their f., 16.08
by their f., Abiezer, Helek, Asriel, 17.02
the son of Joseph, by their f. 17.02
according to its f. came up, and the 18.11
of Benjamin, according to its f., 18.20
according to their f. were Jericho, 18.21
of Benjamin according to its f. 18.28
of Simeon, according to its f.; 19.01
of Simeon according to its f. 19.08
of Zebulun, according to its f. 19.10
of Zebulun, according to its f.— 19.16
of Issachar, according to its f. 19.17
of Issachar, according to its f.— 19.23
tribe of Asher according to its f. 19.24
of Asher according to its f.—these 19.31
of Naphtali, according to its f. 19.32
of Naphtali according to its f.— 19.39
tribe of Dan, according to its f. 19.40

FAMILIES (cont.)
of Dan, according to their f.—these Jos 19.48
out for the f. of the Kohathites. 21.04
by lot from the f. of the tribe of 21.05
by lot from the f. of the tribe of 21.06
to their f. received from the tribe 21.07
one of the f. of the Kohathites who 21.10
to the Kohathite f. of the Levites, 21.20
The cities of the f. of the rest of 21.26
one of the f. of the Levites, were 21.27
of the several f. of the Gershonites 21.33
the Merarite f., were given out of 21.34
cities of the several Merarite f., 21.40
remainder of the f. of the Levites, 21.40
each of the tribal f. of Israel, 22.14
to the heads of the f. of Israel, 22.21
heads of the f. of Israel who were 22.30
of all the f. of the tribe of 1Sa 9.21
tribe of Benjamin near by its f., 10.21
And the f. of Kiriathjearim: the 1Ch 2.53
The f. also of the scribes that 2.55
These were the f. of the Zorathites. 4.02
and the f. of Aharhel the son of 4.08
and the f. of the house of linen 4.21
by name were princes in their f., 4.38
And his kinsmen by their f., when 5.07
These are the f. of the Levites 6.19
of Aaron of the f. of Kohathites, 6.54
throughout their f. were thirteen. 6.60
to their f. were allotted thirteen 6.62
to their f. were allotted twelve 6.63
And some of the f. of the sons of 6.66
the rest of the f. of the Kohathites 6.70
to all the f. of Issachar were in 7.05
O f. of the peoples, ascribe to the 16.28
priests and heads of f. of Israel, 2Ch 19.08
Some of the heads of f., when they Ez 2.68
the people according to their f., Neh 4.13
the contempt of f. terrified me, Job 31.34
and all the f. of the nations shall Ps 22.27
O f. of the peoples, ascribe to the 96.07
and makes their f. like flocks. 107.41
and all the f. of the house of Jer 2.04
be the God of all the f. of Israel, 31.01
rejected the two f. which he chose'? 33.24
two hundred, from the f. of Israel. Eze 45.15
I known of all the f. of the earth; Amo 3.02
and all the f. that are left, each Zec 12.14
And if any of the f. of the earth 14.17
shall all the f. of the earth be Ac 3.25
upsetting whole f. by teaching for Tit 1.11

FAMILY
was the most honored of all his f. Gen 34.19
This is the history of the f. of Jacob. 37.02
that man and against his f., and will Lev 20.05
each of you shall return to his f. 25.10
him, and go back to his own f., 25.41
to a member of the stranger's f., 25.47
belonging to his f. may redeem him; 25.49
they set out, every one in his f., Num 2.34
were the f. of the Libnites and 3.21
Libnites and the f. of the Shimeites; 3.21
Of Kohath were the f. of the 3.27
and the f. of the Izharites, and the 3.27
and the f. of the Hebronites, and 3.27
and the f. of the Uzzielites; 3.27
Of Merari were the f. of the Mahlites 3.33
Mahlites and the f. of the Mushites: 3.33
a Midianite woman to his f., in the 25.06
of Hanoch, the f. of the Hanochites; 26.05
of Pallu, the f. of the Palluites; 26.05
of Hezron, the f. of the Hezronites; 26.06
of Carmi, the f. of the Carmites. 26.06
of Nemuel, the f. of the Nemuelites; 26.12
of Jamin, the f. of the Jaminites; 26.12
of Jachin, the f. of the Jachinites; 26.12
of Zerah, the f. of the Zerahites; 26.13
of Shaul, the f. of the Shaulites. 26.13
of Zephon, the f. of the Zephonites; 26.15
of Haggi, the f. of the Haggites; 26.15
of Shuni, the f. of the Shunites; 26.15
of Ozni, the f. of the Oznites; 26.16
of Eri, the f. of the Erites; 26.16
of Arod, the f. of the Arodites; 26.17
of Areli, the f. of the Arelites. 26.17
of Shelah, the f. of the Shelanites; 26.20
of Perez, the f. of the Perezites; 26.20
of Zerah, the f. of the Zerahites. 26.20
of Hezron, the f. of the Hezronites; 26.21
of Hamul, the f. of the Hamulites. 26.21
of Tola, the f. of the Tolaites; 26.23
of Puvah, the f. of the Punites; 26.23
of Jashub, the f. of the Jashubites; 26.24
of Shimron, the f. of the Shimronites. 26.24
of Sered, the f. of the Seredites; 26.26
of Elon, the f. of the Elonites; 26.26
Jahleel, the f. of the Jahleelites. 26.26
of Machir, the f. of the Machirites; 26.29
Gilead, the f. of the Gileadites. 26.29
of Iezer, the f. of the Iezerites; 26.30
of Helek, the f. of the Helekites; 26.30
of Asriel, the f. of the Asrielites; and 26.31
of Shechem, the f. of the Shechemites; 26.31
of Shemida, the f. of the Shemidaites; and 26.32
of Hepher, the f. of the Hepherites. 26.32
Shuthelah, the f. of the Shuthelahites; 26.35
of Becher, the f. of the Becherites; 26.35
of Tahan, the f. of the Tahanites. 26.35
of Eran, the f. of the Eranites. 26.36
of Bela, the f. of the Belaites; 26.38
of Ashbel, the f. of the Ashbelites; 26.38
Ahiram, the f. of the Ahiramites; 26.38
Shephupham, the f. of the Shuphamites; 26.39
of Hupham, the f. of the Huphamites. 26.39
of Ard, the f. of the Ardites; 26.40
of Naaman, the f. of the Naamites. 26.40
of Shuham, the f. of the Shuhamites. 26.42
of Imnah, the f. of the Imnites; 26.44
of Ishvi, the f. of the Ishvites; 26.44
of Beriah, the f. of the Beriites. 26.44
of Heber, the f. of the Heberites; 26.45
of Malchiel, the f. of the Malchielites. 26.45
of Jahzeel, the f. of the Jahzeelites; 26.48
of Guni, the f. of the Gunites; 26.48
of Jezer, the f. of the Jezerites; 26.49
Shillem, the f. of the Shillemites. 26.49
Gershon, the f. of the Gershonites; 26.57
of Kohath, the f. of the Kohathites; 26.57
of Merari, the f. of the Merarites. 26.57
the f. of the Libnites, the f. of the 26.58
the f. of the Hebronites, the f. 26.58
the f. of the Mahlites, the f. 26.58
the f. of the Mushites, the f. 26.58
the f. of the Korahites. 26.58
father be taken away from his f., 27.04
that is next to him of his f., 27.11
within the f. of the tribe of 36.06
to one of the f. of the tribe of 36.08
in the tribe of the f. of their father. 36.12
outside the f. to a stranger; her Deu 25.05
you a man or woman or f. or tribe, 29.18
and the f. which the LORD takes Jos 7.14
and the f. of the Zerahites was 7.17
near the f. of the Zerahites man 7.17
the head of a f. among the clans 22.14
they let the man and all his f. go. Ju 1.25
Manasseh, and I am the least in my f." 6.15
afraid of his f. and the men of 6.27
a snare to Gideon and to his f. 8.27
kindness to the f. of Jerubbaal 8.35
the whole clan of his mother's f., 9.01
and all his f. came down and took 16.31
of the f. of Judah, who was a Levite 17.07

FAMILY (cont.)

priest to a tribe and f. in Israel?" Ju 18.19
every man to his tribe and f., and they 21.24
of the f. of Elimelech, whose name Ru 2.01
who was of the f. of Elimelech. 2.03
And is not my f. the humblest of 1Sa 9.21
and the f. of the Matrites was 10.21
he brought the f. of the Matrites 10.21
priest to a tribe and f. in Israel?" 18.19
sacrifice there for all the f.' 20.06
for our f. holds a sacrifice in the 20.29
And now the whole f. has risen 2Sa 14.07
a man of the f. of the house of 16.05
and destroyed all the royal f. 2Ki 11.01
of the royal f., came with ten men, 25.25
did all their f. multiply like the 1Ch 4.27
by lot out of the f. of the tribe, 6.61
all the royal f. of the house of 2Ch 22.10
in every f., province, and city, and Est 9.28
of the f. of Ram, became angry. Job 32.02
one from a city and two from a f., Jer 3.14
of this evil f. in all the places 8.03
of the royal f., one of the chief 41.01
Levitical priests of the f. of Zadok, Eze 43.19
of the royal f. and of the nobility, Dan 1.03
the whole f. which I brought up Amo 3.01
against this f. I am devising evil, Mic 2.03
shall mourn, each f. by itself; Zec 12.12
the f. of the house of David by 12.12
the f. of the house of Nathan by 12.12
the f. of the house of Levi by 12.13
the f. of the Shimeites by itself, 12.13
And if the f. of Egypt do not go up 14.18
who were of the high-priestly f. Ac 4.06
and Joseph's f. became known to 7.13
sons of the f. of Abraham, and those 13.26
baptized at once, with all his f. 16.33
belong to the f. of Aristobulus. Rom 16.10
who belong to the f. of Narcissus. 16.11
from whom every f. in heaven and on Eph 3.15
to their own f. and make some return 1Ti 5.04
and especially for his own f., he has 5.08

FAMINE

Now there was a f. in the land. So Gen 12.10
for the f. was severe in the land. 12.10
Now there was a f. in the land, besides 26.01
the former f. that was in the days 26.01
the east wind are also seven years of f. 41.27
there will arise seven years of f., 41.30
the f. will consume the land, 41.30
reason of that f. which will follow, 41.31
seven years of f. which are to befall 41.36
land may not perish through the f." 41.36
Before the year of f. came, Joseph 41.50
seven years of f. began to come, 41.54
There was f. in all lands; 41.54
So when the f. had spread over all 41.56
for the f. was severe in the land 41.56
because the f. was severe over all 41.57
for the f. was in the land of Canaan. 42.05
grain for the f. of your households, 42.19
grain for the f. of your households, 42.33
Now the f. was severe in the land. 43.01
For the f. has been in the land 45.06
are yet five years of f. to come; 45.11
for the f. is severe in the land of 47.04
for the f. was very severe, so that 47.13
languished by reason of the f. 47.13
because the f. was severe upon them 47.20
ruled there was a f. in the land, Ru 1.01
Now there was a f. in the days of 2Sa 21.01
three years of f. come to you in 24.13
"If there is f. in the land, if 1Ki 8.37
Now the f. was severe in Samaria. 18.02
when there was a f. in the land. 2Ki 4.38
And there was a great f. in Samaria, 6.25
the f. is in the city, and we 7.04
for the LORD has called for a f., 8.01
month the f. was so severe in the 25.03
either three years of f.; or three 1Ch 21.12
"If there is f. in the land, if 2Ch 6.28
or f., we will stand before this 20.09
over to die by f. and by thirst, 32.11
houses to get grain because of the f." Neh 5.03
In f. he will redeem you from death, Job 5.20
At destruction and f. you shall 5.22
death, and keep them alive in f. Ps 33.19
times, in the days of f. they have 37.19
When he summoned a f. on the land, 105.16
but I will kill your root with f., Is 14.30
and destruction, f. and sword; 51.19
us, nor shall we see sword or f. Jer 5.12
their daughters shall die by f.; 11.22
sword, by f., an by pestilence." 14.12
the sword, nor shall you have f., 14.13
'Sword and f. shall not come on 14.15
By sword and f. those prophets 14.15
victims of f. and sword, with none 14.16
city, behold, the diseases of f.! 14.18
those who are for f., to f., and those 15.02
perish by the sword and by f., and 16.04
Therefore deliver up their children to f.; 18.21
and f., into the hand of Nebuchadrezzar 21.07
by f., and by pestilence; but he who 21.09
f., and pestilence upon them, until 24.10
with f., and with pestilence, says 27.08
by f., and by pestilence, as the 27.13
f., and pestilence against many 28.08
f., and pestilence, and I will make 29.17
f., and pestilence, and will make 29.18
of sword and f. and pestilence the 32.24
by sword, by f., and by pestilence': 32.36
pestilence, and to f., says the LORD. 34.17
by f., and by pestilence; but he who 38.02
and the f. of which you are afraid 42.16
by f., and by pestilence; they shall 42.17
by f., and by pestilence in the 42.22
sword and by f. they shall be 44.12
shall die by the sword and by f.; 44.12
sword, with f., and with pestilence, 44.13
consumed by the sword and by f. 44.18
be consumed by the sword and by f.," 44.27
month the f. was so severe in the 52.06
oven with the burning heat of f. Lam 5.10
consumed with f. in the midst of Eze 5.12
against you my deadly arrows of f., 5.16
I bring more and more f. upon you, 5.16
I will send f. and wild beasts 5.17
the sword, by f., and by pestilence. 6.11
and is preserved shall die of f. 6.12
pestilence and f. are within; he 7.15
is in the city f. and pestilence 7.15
from f. and pestilence, that they 12.16
staff of bread and send f. upon it, 14.13
f., evil beasts, and pestilence, to 14.21
it abundant and lay no f. upon you. 36.29
the disgrace of f. among the nations. 36.30
"when I will send a f. on the land; Amo 8.11
not a f. of bread, nor a thirst for 8.11
came a great f. over all the land; Lk 4.25
a great f. arose in that country, 15.14
Now there came a f. throughout all Ac 7.11
be a great f. over all the world; 11.28
or f., or nakedness, or peril, or Rom 8.35
sword and with f. and with pestilence Rev 6.08
pestilence and mourning and f., 18.08

FAMINES

there will be f. and earthquakes Mt 24.07
various places, there will be f.; Mk 13.08
various places f. and pestilences; Lk 21.11

FAMISH

yea, he will f. all the gods of the Zep 2.11

FAMISHED
in from the field, and he was f. Gen 25.29
of that red pottage, for I am f.!" 25.30
When all the land of Egypt was f., 41.55

FAMOUS
name of Solomon more f. than yours, 1Ki 1.47
f. men, heads of their fathers' 1Ch 5.24
f. men in their fathers' houses. 12.30
and slew f. kings, for his steadfast Ps 136.18
How the f. city is forsaken, the Jer 49.25
brother who is f. among all the 2Co 8.18

FANCIES
lay in bed the f. and the visions Dan 4.05

FANCY
my f. set me in a chariot beside my Sol 6.12

FANGS
I broke the f. of the unrighteous, Job 29.17
tear out the f. of the young lions, Ps 58.06
teeth, and it has the f. of a lioness. Joe 1.06

FAR
as f. as Gaza, and in the direction Gen 10.19
Admah, and Zeboiim, as f. as Lasha. 10.19
on from the Negeb as f. as Bethel, 13.03
and moved his tent as f. as Sodom. 13.12
Mount Seir as f. as Elparan on the 14.06
and went in pursuit as f. as Dan. 14.14
F. be it from thee to do such a 18.25
F. be that from thee! 18.25
F. be it from your servants that 44.07
But he said, "F. be it from me that 44.17
only you shall not go very f. away. Ex 8.28
Keep f. from a false charge, and do 23.07
f. off from the camp; and he called 33.07
to foot, so f. as the priest can see, Lev 13.12
said to them, "You have gone too f.! Num 16.03
You have gone too f., sons of Levi!" 16.07
then scatter the fire f. and wide. 16.37
as f. as to the Ammonites; for Jazer 21.24
of his hand, as f. as the Arnon. 21.26
as f. as Dibon, and we laid waste 21.30
Bethjeshimoth as f. as Abelshittim 33.49
as f. as the great river, the river Deu 1.07
you down in Seir as f. as Hormah. 1.44
lived in villages as f. as Gaza, 2.23
as f. as Gilead, there was not a 2.36
as f. as Salecah and Edrei, cities 3.10
as f. as the border of the Geshurites 3.14
from Gilead as f. as the valley of 3.16
as f. over as the river Jabbok, the 3.16
Chinnereth as f. as the sea of the 3.17
as f. as Mount Sirion (that is, 4.48
the Jordan as f. as the Sea of the 4.49
his name there is too f. from you, 12.21
near you or f. off from you, from the 13.07
the place is too f. from you, which the 14.24
cities which are very f. from you, 20.15
foreigner who comes from a f. land, 29.22
hard for you, neither is it f. off. 30.11
all the land, Gilead as f. as Dan, 34.01
of Judah as f. as the Western Sea, 34.02
city of palm trees, as f. as Zoar. 34.03
this Lebanon as f. as the great Jos 1.04
to the Jordan as f. as the fords; 2.07
stood and rose up in a heap f. off, 3.16
before the gate as f. as Shebarim, 7.05
do not go very f. from the city, 8.04
"We have come from a f. country; 9.06
"From a very f. country your servants 9.09
'We are very f. from you,' when you 9.22
smote them as f. as Azekah and 10.10
heaven upon them as f. as Azekah, 10.11
country of Goshen, as f. as Gibeon. 10.41
chased them as f. as Great Sidon 11.08
and eastward as f. as the valley 11.08
as f. as Baalgad in the valley of 11.17
the valley as f. as the river Jabbok, 12.02
tableland of Medeba as f. as Dibon: 13.09
Heshbon, as f. as the boundary of the 13.10
as f. as the territory of lower 16.03
was Atarothaddar as f. as upper 16.05
these cities as f. as Baalathbeer, 19.08
inheritance reached as f. as Sarid; 19.10
Kanah, as f. as Sidon the Great; 19.28
and Jabneel, as f. as Lakkum; and it 19.33
F. be it from us that we should 22.29
"F. be it from us that we should 24.16
Baalhermon as f. as the entrance Ju 3.03
his tent as f. away as the oak in 4.11
as f. as the neighborhood of Gaza, 6.04
army fled as f. as Bethshittah 7.22
as f. as the border of Abelmeholah, 7.22
as f. as Bethbarah, and also the 7.24
the waters as f. as Bethbarah, 7.24
and as f. as Abelkeramim, with a 11.33
how they were f. from the Sidonians 18.07
because it was f. from Sidon, 18.28
the day was f. spent, and the 19.11
from Nohah as f. as opposite 20.43
LORD declares: 'F. be it from me; 1Sa 2.30
after them as f. as the border of 6.12
smote them as f. as below Bethcar. 7.11
f. be it from me that I should sin 12.23
F. from it! As the LORD 14.45
Amalekites, from Havilah as f. as Shur, 15.07
Philistines as f. as Gath and the 17.52
Shaaraim as f. as Gath and Ekron. 17.52
And he said to him, "F. from it! 20.02
And Jonathan said, "F. be it from you! 20.09
as f. as Shur, to the land of Egypt. 27.08
that thou hast brought me thus f.? 2Sa 7.18
"F. be it from me, f. be it, that I 20.20
and said, "F. be it from me, O LORD, 23.17
as f. as the other side of Jokmean; 1Ki 4.12
comes from a f. country for thy 8.41
land of the enemy, f. off or near; 8.46
and to the other as f. as Dan. 12.30
LORD has sent me as f. as Bethel." 2Ki 2.02
after them as f. as the Jordan; 7.15
of Hamath as f. as the Sea of the 14.25
Philistines as f. as Gaza and its 18.08
to the f. recesses of Lebanon; 19.23
"They have come from a f. country, 20.14
about these cities as f. as Baal. 1Ch 4.33
Aroer, as f. as Nebo and Baalmeon. 5.08
to the east as f. as the entrance 5.09
land of Bashan as f. as Salecah: 5.11
and said, "F. be it from me before 11.19
from as f. as Issachar and Zebulun 12.40
that thou hast brought me thus f.? 17.16
so f. as I was able, the gold for 29.02
comes from a f. country for the 2Ch 6.32
away captive to a land f. or near; 6.36
Judah and came as f. as Jerusalem. 12.04
chariots, and came as f. as Mareshah. 14.09
him pursued them as f. as Gerar, 14.13
And his fame spread f., for he was 26.15
and Manasseh, and as f. as Zebulun; 30.10
and as f. as Naphtali, in their 34.06
consecrated it as f. as the Tower Neh 3.01
Jerusalem as f. as the Broad Wall. 3.08
of the wall, as f. as the Dung Gate. 3.13
as f. as the stairs that go down 3.15
tower as f. as the wall of Ophel. 3.27
repaired as f. as the house of the 3.31
on the wall, f. from one another. 4.19
as f. as we are able, have bought 5.08
King Ahasuerus, both near and f., Est 9.20
His sons are f. from safety, they Job 5.04
put it f. away, and let not wickedness 11.14

FAR (cont.)
withdraw thy hand f. from me, Job 13.21
"He has put my brethren f. from me, 19.13
counsel of the wicked is f. from me. 21.16
counsel of the wicked is f. from me. 22.18
unrighteousness f. from your tents, 22.23
F. be it from me to say that you 27.05
f. be it from God that he should do 34.10
'Thus f. shall you come, and no 38.11
Why art thou so f. from helping me, Ps 22.01
Be not f. from me, for trouble is 22.11
But thou, O LORD, be not f. off! 22.19
"I am driven f. from thy sight." 31.22
be not silent! O Lord, be not f. from me! 35.22
O LORD! O my God, be not f. from me! 38.21
in the f. north, the city of the 48.02
O God, be not f. from me; O my God, 71.12
those who are f. from thee shall 73.27
thou art exalted f. above all gods. 97.09
Perverseness of heart shall be f. from me; 101.04
as f. as the east is from the west, 103.12
so f. does he remove our transgressions 103.12
blessing; may it be f. from him! 109.17
who looks f. down upon the heavens 113.06
Put false ways f. from me; and 119.29
purpose; they are f. from thy law. 119.150
Salvation is f. from the wicked, for 119.155
and put devious talk f. from you. Pro 4.24
Keep your way f. from her, and do 5.08
The LORD is f. from the wicked, but 15.29
more do his friends go f. from him! 19.07
himself will keep f. from them. 22.05
discipline drives it f. from him. 22.15
so is good news from a f. country. 25.25
near than a brother who is f. away. 27.10
Remove f. from me falsehood and 30.08
She is f. more precious than jewels 31.10
will be wise"; but it was f. from me. Ecc 7.23
is f. off, and deep, very deep; 7.24
and the LORD removes men f. away, Is 6.12
give ear, all you f. countries; 8.09
mount of assembly in the f. north; 14.13
voice is heard as f. as Jahaz; 15.04
them, and they will flee f. away, 17.13
to a people feared near and f., 18.02
from a people feared near and f., 18.07
though they had fled f. away. 22.03
while their hearts are f. from me, 29.13
the name of the LORD comes from f., 30.27
you who are f. off, what I have done 33.13
to the f. recesses of Lebanon; 37.24
have come to me from a f. country, 39.03
of my counsel from a f. country. 46.11
you who are f. from deliverance: 46.12
it is not f. off, and my salvation 46.13
swallowed you up will be f. away. 49.19
you shall be f. from oppression, for 54.14
you sent your envoys f. off, and sent 57.09
to the f. and to the near, says the 57.19
Therefore justice is f. from us, 59.09
salvation, but it is f. from us. 59.11
your sons shall come from f., 60.04
first, to bring your sons from f., 60.09
in me that they went f. from me, Jer 2.05
their mouth and f. from their 12.02
f. and near, one after another, and 25.26
will be removed f. from your land, 27.10
the fields as f. as the brook 31.40
a cry is heard as f. as Zoar. 48.04
of the land of Moab, f. and near. 48.24
the sea, reached as f. as Jazer; 48.32
as f. as Jahaz they utter their 48.34
Thus f. is the judgment on Moab. 48.47
Flee, wander f. away, dwell in the 49.30
Thus f. are the words of Jeremiah. 51.64
for a comforter is f. from me, Lam 1.16
He that is f. off shall die of Eze 6.12
to drive me f. from my sanctuary? 8.06
was heard as f. as the outer court, 10.05
'They have gone f. from the LORD; 11.15
I removed them f. off among the 11.16
and he prophesies of times f. off.' 12.27
those who are f. from you will 22.05
They even sent for men to come from f., 23.40
as f. as the border of Ethiopia. 29.10
bodies of their kings f. from me, 43.09
But the Levites who went f. from me, 44.10
as f. as Hazerhatticon, which is on 47.16
the eastern sea and as f. as Tamar. 47.18
from Tamar as f. as the waters of 47.19
as f. as Hazarenon (which is on the 48.01
near and those that are f. away, Dan 9.07
fourth shall be f. richer than all 11.02
the war as f. as his fortress. 11.10
remove the northerner f. from you, Joe 2.20
removing them f. from their own 3.06
to the Sabeans, to a nation f. off; 3.08
O you who put f. away the evil day, Amo 6.03
Phoenicia as f. as Zarephath; Ob 1.20
the boundary shall be f. extended. Mic 7.11
"And those who are f. off shall Zec 6.15
yet in f. countries they shall 10.09
but their heart is f. from me; Mt 15.08
east and shines as f. as the west, 24.27
as f. as the courtyard of the high 26.58
but their heart is f. from me; Mk 7.06
"You are not f. from the kingdom of 12.34
when he was not f. from the house, Lk 7.06
took his journey into a f. country, 15.13
and saw Abraham f. off and Lazarus 16.23
standing f. off, would not even lift 18.13
went into a f. country to receive 19.12
and the day is now f. spent." So he 24.29
Then he led them out as f. as Bethany, 24.50
for they were not f. from the land, Jn 21.08
children and to all that are f. off., Ac 2.39
traveled as f. as Phoenicia and 11.19
the whole island as f. as Paphos, 13.06
Paul brought him as f. as Athens; 17.15
Yet he is not f. from each one of 17.27
I will send you f. away to the 22.21
spearmen to go as f. as Caesarea. 23.23
came as f. as the Forum of Appius 28.15
to you (but thus f. have been Rom 1.13
so f. as it depends upon you, live 12.18
the night is f. gone, the day is at 13.12
Jerusalem and as f. round as 15.19
righteousness must f. exceed it in 2Co 3.09
with f. greater labors, f. more 11.23
But f. be it from me to glory except Gal 6.14
f. above all rule and authority and Eph 1.21
who once were f. off have been 2.13
to you who were f. off and peace 2.17
is able to do f. more abundantly 3.20
also ascended f. above all the 4.10
with Christ, for that is f. better. Php 1.23
but they will not get very f., 2Ti 3.09
But rejoice in so f. as you share 1Pe 4.13
they will stand f. off, in fear of Rev 18.10
will stand f. off, in fear of her 18.15
trade is on the sea, stood f. off 18.17

FARE
the righteous f. as the wicked! Gen 18.25
said, "How did you f., my daughter?" Ru 3.16
See how your brothers f., and bring 1Sa 17.18
him with scant f. of bread and 1Ki 22.27
left here will f. like the whole 2Ki 7.13
him with scant f. of bread and 2Ch 18.26
so he paid the f., and went on Jon 1.03
temple of the LORD, how did you f.? Hag 2.15

FARED
how your cattle have f. with me. Gen 30.29
was doing, and how the people f., 2Sa 11.07

FARED (cont.)
how Esther was and how she f. Est 2.11
of hosts: Consider how you have f. Hag 1.05
of hosts: Consider how you have f. 1.07
we would have f. like Sodom and Rom 9.29

FARES
household, since he f. well with you, Deu 15.16

FAREWELL
kiss my sons and my daughters f.? Gen 31.28
me first say f. to those at my Lk 9.61
you will do well. F." Ac 15.29
we prayed and bade one another f. 21.05
Finally, brethren, f. Mend your 2Co 13.11

FARM
one to his f., another to his Mt 22.05

FARMER
in pieces the f. and his team; Jer 51.23
hard-working f. who ought to have 2Ti 2.06
Behold, the f. waits for the precious Jas 5.07

FARMERS
and he had f. and vinedressers in 2Ch 26.10
the f. are ashamed, they cover their Jer 14.04
and the f. and those who wander 31.24
shall call the f. to mourning and Amo 5.16

FARTHER
and no f., and here shall your Job 38.11
the measuring line shall go out f., Jer 31.39
And going a little f. he fell on Mt 26.39
And going on a little f., he saw Mk 1.19
And going a little f., he fell on 14.35
a little f. on they sounded again Ac 27.28

FARTHEST
wilderness of Zin at the f. south. Jos 15.01
and possess it to its f. borders; 17.18
I entered its f. retreat, its 2Ki 19.23
dispersed be under the f. skies, Neh 1.09
out to the f. bound the ore in Job 28.03
of the earth, and of the f. seas; Ps 65.05
at earth's f. bounds are afraid at 65.08
and called from its f. corners, Is 41.09
from the f. parts of the earth. Jer 6.22
from the f. parts of the earth! 25.32
them from the f. parts of the 31.08
from the f. parts of the earth. 50.41

FASHION
you or mislead you in this f., 2Ch 32.15
and did not one f. us in the womb? Job 31.15
suspect us of acting in worldly f. 2Co 10.02

FASHIONED
and f. it with a graving tool, and Ex 32.04
Thy hands f. and made me; and now thou Job 10.08
Thy hands have made and f. me; Ps 119.73
no weapon that is f. against you Is 54.17

FASHIONS
he who f. the hearts of them all, Ps 33.15
Who f. a god or casts an image, that Is 44.10
The ironsmith f. it and works it 44.12
he f. it with planes, and marks it 44.13
Does the clay say to him who f. it, 45.09

FAST
and hold him f. with your hand; Gen 21.18
but you who held f. to the LORD Deu 4.04
as he was lying f. asleep from Ju 4.21
why should I f.? Can I bring 2Sa 12.23
and his head caught f. in the oak, 18.09
"Proclaim a f., and set Naboth on 1Ki 21.09
they proclaimed a f., and set Naboth 21.12
and hold the door f. against him. 2Ki 6.32
For he held f. to the LORD; 18.06
proclaimed a f. throughout all 2Ch 20.03
Then I proclaimed a f. there, at the Ez 8.21
and hold a f. on my behalf, and Est 4.16
my maids will also f. as you do. 4.16
He still holds f. his integrity, Job 2.03
you still hold f. your integrity? 2.09
My foot has held f. to his steps; 23.11
I hold f. my righteousness, and will 27.06
and the broad waters are frozen f. 37.10
and the clods cleave f. together? 38.38
My steps have held f. to thy paths, Ps 17.05
They hold f. to their evil purpose; 64.05
established the earth, and it stands f. 119.90
who hold her f. are called happy. Pro 3.18
"Let your heart hold f. my words; 4.04
or as a stag is caught f. 7.22
Stand f. in your enchantments and Is 47.12
and the son of man who holds it f., 56.02
please me and hold f. my covenant, 56.04
profane it, and holds f. my covenant— 56.06
the day of your f. you seek your 58.03
Behold, you f. only to quarrel and 58.04
Is such the f. that I choose, a day 58.05
Will you call this a f., 58.05
"Is not this the f. that I choose: 58.06
They hold f. to deceit, they refuse Jer 8.05
Though they f., I will not hear 14.12
and on a f. day in the hearing of 36.06
proclaimed a f. before the LORD. 36.09
them captive have held them f., 50.33
king answered, "The thing stands f., Dan 6.12
hold f. to love and justice, and Hos 12.06
Sanctify a f., call a solemn Joe 1.14
sanctify a f.; call a solemn 2.15
had lain down, and was f. asleep. Jon 1.05
they proclaimed a f., and put on 3.05
is near, near and hastening f.; Zep 1.14
I mourn and f. in the fifth month, Zec 7.03
The f. of the fourth month, and the 8.19
and the f. of the fifth, and the 8.19
and the f. of the seventh, and the 8.19
and the f. of the tenth, shall be to 8.19
"And when you f., do not look dismal, Mt 6.16
But when you f., anoint your head 6.17
"Why do we and the Pharisees f., 9.14
but your disciples do not f.?" 9.14
from them, and then they will f. 9.15
the disciples of the Pharisees f., Mk 2.18
but your disciples do not f.?" 2.18
wedding guests f. while the bridegroom 2.19
bridegroom with them, they cannot f. 2.19
and then they will f. in that day. 2.20
and hold f. the tradition of men. 7.08
disciples of John f. often and Lk 5.33
you make wedding guests f. while the 5.34
then they will f. in those days." 5.35
hold it f. in an honest and good 8.15
I f. twice a week, I give tithes of 18.12
because the f. had already gone by, Ac 27.09
but you stand f. only through faith Rom 11.20
is evil, hold f. to what is good; 12.09
you are saved, if you hold it f.— 1Co 15.02
stand f. therefore, and do not Gal 5.01
holding f. the word of life, so that Php 2.16
and not holding f. to the Head, Col 2.19
live, if you stand f. in the Lord. 1Th 3.08
everything; hold f. what is good, 5.21
if we hold f. our confidence and Heb 3.06
God, let us hold f. our confession. 4.14
Let us hold f. the confession of 10.23
grace of God; stand f. in it. 1Pe 5.12
you hold f. my name and you did not Rev 2.13
only hold f. what you have, until I 2.25
hold f. what you have, so that no 3.11

FASTED
and f. that day until evening, and Ju 20.26
and f. on that day, and said there, 1Sa 7.06
tree in Jabesh, and f. seven days. 31.13
and wept and f. until evening for 2Sa 1.12
and David f., and went in and lay 12.16
You f. and wept for the child while 12.21
was still alive, I f. and wept; 12.22
and f. and lay in sackcloth, and 1Ki 21.27
oak in Jabesh, and f. seven days. 1Ch 10.12
So we f. and besought our God for Ez 8.23
'Why have we f., and thou seest it Is 58.03
When you f. and mourned in the Zec 7.05
years, was it for me that you f.? 7.05
And he f. forty days and forty Mt 4.02

FASTEN
and f. the rings to the four corners Ex 25.26
And you shall f. it on the turban 28.37
to f. it on the turban above; as the 39.31
And I will f. him like a peg in a Is 22.23
and they f. it with nails so that 41.07
they f. it with hammer and nails so Jer 10.04

FASTENED
and f. the rings to the four corners Ex 37.13
which has no cover f. upon it, Num 19.15
and they f. his body to the wall of 1Sa 31.10
in its sheath f. upon his loins, 2Sa 20.08
and f. his head in the temple of 1Ch 10.10
"A deadly thing has f. upon him; Ps 41.08
peg that was f. in a sure place Is 22.25
by his hand they were f. together; Lam 1.14
were f. round about within. And on Eze 40.43
great millstone f. round his neck Mt 18.06
prison and f. their feet in the Ac 16.24
of the heat and f. on his hand. 28.03

FASTING
sacrifice I rose from my f., with my Ez 9.05
and I continued f. and praying before Neh 1.04
assembled with f. and in sackcloth, 9.01
with f. and weeping and lamenting, Est 4.03
sackcloth, I afflicted myself with f. Ps 35.13
When I humbled my soul with f., it became 69.10
My knees are weak through f.; my body 109.24
F. like yours this day will not Is 58.04
his palace, and spent the night f.; Dan 6.18
supplications with f. and sackcloth 9.03
with f., with weeping, and with Joe 2.12
that their f. may be seen by men. Mt 6.16
that your f. may not be seen by men 6.18
comes out except by prayer and f. * 17.21
disciples and the Pharisees were f.; Mk 2.18
worshiping with f. and prayer Lk 2.37
were worshiping the Lord and f., Ac 13.02
Then after f. and praying they laid 13.03
every church, with prayer and f., 14.23

FASTNESS
his home in the f. of the rocky Job 39.28

FASTNESSES
and came trembling out of their f. 2Sa 22.46
and came trembling out of their f. Ps 18.45

FASTS
with regard to their f. and their Est 9.31

FAT
his flock and of their f. portions. Gen 4.04
the Nile seven cows sleek and f., 41.02
ate up the seven sleek and f. cows. 41.04
f. and sleek, came up out of the 41.18
ate up the first seven f. cows, 41.20
you shall eat the f. of the land.' 45.18
or let the f. of my feast remain Ex 23.18
take all the f. that covers the 29.13
with the f. that is on them, and 29.13
"You shall also take the f. of the ram, 29.22
the f. tail, and the f. that covers 29.22
with the f. that is on them, and 29.22
and the f., in order upon the wood Lev 1.08
pieces, with its head and its f., 1.12
shall offer the f. covering the 3.03
and all the f. that is on the 3.03
with the f. that is on them at the 3.04
to the LORD he shall offer its f., 3.09
the f. tail entire, taking it away 3.09
and the f. that covers the entrails, 3.09
and all the f. that is on the 3.09
with the f. that is on them at the 3.10
the f. covering the entrails, and 3.14
and all the f. that is on the 3.14
with the f. that is on them at the 3.15
pleasing odor. All f. is the LORD'S. 3.16
that you eat neither f. nor blood." 3.17
And all the f. of the bull of the 4.08
the f. that covers the entrails and 4.08
and all the f. that is on the 4.08
with the f. that is on them at the 4.09
And all its f. he shall take from 4.19
And all its f. he shall burn on the 4.26
like the f. of the sacrifice of 4.26
And all its f. he shall remove, as 4.31
as the f. is removed from the peace 4.31
And all its f. he shall remove as 4.35
remove as the f. of the lamb is 4.35
burn on it the f. of the peace 6.12
And all its f. shall be offered, the 7.03
the f. tail, the f. that covers the 7.03
with the f. that is on them at the 7.04
of Israel, You shall eat no f., 7.23
The f. of an animal that dies of 7.24
and the f. of one that is torn by 7.24
who eats of the f. of an animal of 7.25
shall bring the f. with the breast, 7.30
shall burn the f. on the altar, 7.31
offerings and the f. shall have the 7.33
And he took all the f. that was on 8.16
and the two kidneys with their f., 8.16
the head and the pieces and the f. 8.20
Then he took the f., and the f. tail, 8.25
and all the f. that was on the 8.25
and the two kidneys with their f., 8.25
them on the f. and on the right 8.26
but the f. and the kidneys and the 9.10
and the f. of the ox and of the ram, 9.19
the f. tail, and that which covers 9.19
and they put the f. upon the breasts, 9.20
he burned the f. upon the altar, 9.20
offering and the f. upon the altar; 9.24
the offerings by fire of the f., 10.15
And the f. of the sin offering he 16.25
and burn the f. for a pleasing odor 17.06
burn their f. as an offering by Num 18.17
eaten and are full and grown f., Deu 31.20
with f. of lambs and rams, herds of 32.14
"But Jeshurun waxed f., and kicked; 32.15
you waxed f., you grew thick, you 32.15
who ate the f. of their sacrifices, 32.38
of Moab. Now Eglon was a very f. man. Ju 3.17
and the f. closed over the blade, 3.22
before the f. was burned, the priest's 1Sa 2.15
to him, "Let them burn the f. first, 2.16
and to hearken than the f. of rams. 15.22
from the f. of the mighty, the bow 2Sa 1.22
ten f. oxen, and twenty pasture-fed 1Ki 4.23
offering and the f. pieces of the 8.64
offering and the f. of the peace 2Ch 7.07
and the cereal offering and the f. 7.07
there was the f. of the peace offerings, 29.35
offerings and the f. parts until 35.14
eat the f. and drink sweet wine and Neh 8.10
ate, and were filled and became f., 9.25

FAT (cont.)

has covered his face with his f., Job 15.27
and gathered f. upon his loins, 15.27
his body full of f. and the marrow 21.24
is feasted as with marrow and f., Ps 63.05
their heart is gross like f., 119.70
of rams and the f. of fed beasts; Is 1.11
Make the heart of this people f., 6.10
and the f. of his flesh will grow 17.04
all peoples a feast of f. things, 25.06
of f. things full of marrow, of wine 25.06
with blood, it is gorged with f., 34.06
with the f. of the kidneys of rams. 34.06
and their soil made rich with f. 34.07
me with the f. of your sacrifices. 43.24
they have grown f. and sleek. They Jer 5.28
You eat the f., you clothe yourselves Eze 34.03
and on f. pasture they shall feed 34.14
and the f. and the strong I will 34.16
between the f. sheep and the lean 34.20
And you shall eat f. till you are 39.19
me my food, the f. and the blood. 44.07
to offer me the f. and the blood, 44.15
devours the flesh of the f. ones, Zec 11.16
my oxen and my f. calves are Mt 22.04

FATE

are visited by the f. of all men, Num 16.29
This is the f. of those who have Ps 49.13
and their f. would last for ever. 81.15
that one f. comes to all of them. Ecc 2.14
For the f. of the sons of men and 3.19
of men and the f. of beasts is the 3.19
since one f. comes to all, to the 9.02
the sun, that one f. comes to all; 9.03
fold shall be appalled at their f. Jer 49.20
fold shall be appalled at their f. 50.45
cause me grief at the f. of all the Lam 3.51

FATHER

man leaves his f. and his mother Gen 2.24
and Irad was the f. of Mehujael, 4.18
and Mehujael the f. of Methushael, 4.18
and Methushael the f. of Lamech. 4.18
he was the f. of those who dwell in 4.20
he was the f. of all those who play 4.21
he became the f. of a son in his 5.03
after he became the f. of Seth were 5.04
years, he became the f. of Enosh. 5.06
years, he became the f. of Kenan. 5.09
he became the f. of Mahalalel. 5.12
years, he became the f. of Jared. 5.15
years he became the f. of Enoch. 5.18
he became the f. of Methuselah. 5.21
years, he became the f. of Lamech. 5.25
years, he became the f. of a son, 5.28
old, Noah became the f. of Shem, 5.32
Japheth. Ham was the f. of Canaan. 9.18
and Ham, the f. of Canaan, saw the 9.22
saw the nakedness of his f., 9.22
covered the nakedness of their f.; 9.23
Cush became the f. of Nimrod; he was 10.08
Egypt became the f. of Ludim, Anamim, 10.13
Canaan became the f. of Sidon his 10.15
the f. of all the children of Eber, 10.21
Arpachshad became the f. of Shelah; 10.24
and Shelah became the f. of Eber. 10.24
Joktan became the f. of Almodad, 10.26
he became the f. of Arpachshad two 11.10
years he became the f. of Shelah; 11.12
years, he became the f. of Eber; 11.14
years, he became the f. of Peleg; 11.16
years, he became the f. of Reu; 11.18
years, he became the f. of Serug; 11.20
years, he became the f. of Nahor; 11.22
years, he became the f. of Terah; 11.24
he became the f. of Abram, Nahor, and 11.26
Terah was the f. of Abram, Nahor, and 11.27
and Haran was the f. of Lot. 11.27
Haran died before his f. Terah in 11.28
of Haran the f. of Milcah and Iscah. 11.29
shall be the f. of a multitude of 17.04
made you the f. of a multitude of 17.05
he shall be the f. of twelve princes, 17.20
"Our f. is old, and there is not a 19.31
Come, let us make our f. drink wine, 19.32
preserve offspring through our f." 19.32
So they made their f. drink wine 19.33
went in, and lay with her f.; 19.33
I lay last night with my f.; let us 19.34
preserve offspring through our f." 19.34
So they made their f. drink wine 19.35
of Lot were with child by their f. 19.36
he is the f. of the Moabites to 19.37
he is the f. of the Ammonites to 19.38
daughter of my f. but not the 20.12
And Isaac said to his f. Abraham, "My f.!" 22.07
brother, Kemuel the f. of Aram, 22.21
Bethuel became the f. of Rebekah. 22.23
Jokshan was the f. of Sheba and 25.03
son: Abraham was the f. of Isaac, 25.19
which I swore to Abraham your f., 26.03
dug in the days of Abraham his f. 26.15
dug in the days of Abraham his f.; 26.18
names which his f. had given them. 26.18
"I am the God of Abraham your f.; 26.24
"I heard your f. speak to your 27.06
from them savory food for your f., 27.09
shall bring it to your f. to eat, 27.10
Perhaps my f. will feel me, and I 27.12
savory food, such as his f. loved. 27.14
So he went in to his f., and said, "My f."; 27.18
Jacob said to his f., "I am Esau 27.19
So Jacob went near to Isaac his f., 27.22
Then his f. Isaac said to him, "Come 27.26
from the presence of Isaac his f., 27.30
brought it to his f. And he said to his f., 27.31
"Let my f. arise, and eat of his 27.31
His f. Isaac said to him, "Who are 27.32
When Esau heard the words of his f., 27.34
and bitter cry, and said to his f., 27.34
"Bless me, even me also, O my f.!" 27.34
Esau said to his f., "Have you but one 27.38
"Have you but one blessing, my f.? 27.38
Bless me, even me also, O my f." 27.38
Then Isaac his f. answered him: 27.39
with which his f. had blessed him, 27.41
mourning for my f. are approaching; 27.41
house of Bethuel your mother's f.; 28.02
had obeyed his f. and his mother 28.07
women did not please Isaac his f., 28.08
of Abraham your f. and the God of 28.13
son; and she ran and told her f. 29.12
"I see that your f. does not regard 31.05
the God of my f. has been with me. 31.05
served your f. with all my strength 31.06
yet your f. has cheated me and 31.07
taken away the cattle of your f., 31.09
away from our f. belongs to us and 31.16
the land of Canaan to his f. Isaac. 31.18
the God of your f. spoke to me last 31.29
And she said to her f., "Let not my 31.35
If the God of my f., the God of 31.42
God of Nahor, the God of their f., 31.53
swore by the Fear of his f. Isaac, 31.53
"O God of my f. Abraham and God of 32.09
Abraham and God of my f. Isaac, 32.09
Shechem's f., he bought for a hundred 33.19
So Shechem spoke to his f. Hamor, 34.04
And Hamor the f. of Shechem went 34.06
said to her f. and to her brothers, 34.11
Shechem and his f. Hamor deceitfully, 34.13
but his f. called his name Benjamin. 35.18
Jacob came to his f. Isaac at Mamre, 35.27

FATHER (cont.)
of Esau the f. of the Edomites in Gen 36.09
pastured the asses of Zibeon his f. 36.24
the f. of Edom), according to their 36.43
an ill report of them to their f. 37.02
saw that their f. loved him more 37.04
told it to his f. and to his 37.10
his f. rebuked him, and said to him, 37.10
but his f. kept the saying in mind. 37.11
hand, to restore him to his f. 37.22
sleeves and brought it to their f., 37.32
mourning." Thus his f. wept for him. 37.35
youngest is this day with our f., 42.13
to Jacob their f. in the land of 42.29
twelve brothers, sons of our f.; 42.32
day with our f. in the land of 42.32
they and their f. saw their bundles 42.35
And Jacob their f. said to them, 42.36
Then Reuben said to his f., "Slay 42.37
their f. said to them, "Go again, buy 43.02
saying, 'Is your f. still alive? 43.07
And Judah said to Israel his f., 43.08
Then their f. Israel said to them, 43.11
the God of your f. must have put 43.23
"Is your f. well, the old man of 43.27
They said, "Your servant our f. is well, 43.28
for you, go up in peace to your f." 44.17
'Have you a f., or a brother?' 44.19
'We have a f., an old man, and a 44.20
and his f. loves him.' 44.20
lord, 'The lad cannot leave his f., 44.22
he should leave his f., his f. would 44.22
your servant my f. we told him the 44.24
And when our f. said, 'Go again, buy 44.25
Then your servant my f. said to us, 44.27
when I come to your servant my f., 44.30
servant our f. with sorrow to Sheol. 44.31
became surety for the lad to my f., 44.32
in the sight of my f. all my life.' 44.32
I go back to my f. if the lad is 44.34
evil that would come upon my f." 44.34
is my f. still alive?" But his 45.03
and he has made me a f. to Pharaoh, 45.08
and go up to my f. and say to him, 45.09
You must tell my f. of all my 45.13
haste and bring my f. down here." 45.13
and take your f. and your households, 45.18
wives, and bring your f., and come. 45.19
To his f. he sent as follows: ten 45.23
provision for his f. on the journey. 45.23
land of Canaan to their f. Jacob. 45.25
spirit of their f. Jacob revived; 45.27
sacrifices to the God of his f. Isaac. 46.01
said, "I am God, the God of your f.; 46.03
of Israel carried Jacob their f., 46.05
up to meet Israel his f. in Goshen; 46.29
"My f. and my brothers, with their 47.01
"Your f. and your brothers have 47.05
settle your f. and your brothers in 47.06
Then Joseph brought in Jacob his f., 47.07
settled his f. and his brothers, 47.11
And Joseph provided his f., his 47.12
was told, "Behold, your f. is ill"; 48.01
Joseph said to his f., "They are 48.09
saw that his f. laid his right 48.17
And Joseph said to his f., "Not so, my f.; 48.18
But his f. refused, and said, "I know, 48.19
Jacob, and hearken to Israel your f. 49.02
by the God of your f. who will help 49.25
blessings of your f. are mighty 49.26
is what their f. said to them as 49.28
the physicians to embalm his f. 50.02
My f. made me swear, saying, 'I am 50.05
go up, I pray you, and bury my f.; 50.05
and bury your f., as he made you 50.06
So Joseph went up to bury his f.; 50.07
a mourning for his f. seven days. 50.10
After he had buried his f., Joseph 50.14
gone up with him to bury his f. 50.14
brothers saw that their f. was dead, 50.15
"Your f. gave this command before 50.16
the servants of the God of your f." 50.17
When they came to their f. Reuel, Ex 2.18
And he said, "I am the God of your f., 3.06
said, "The God of my f. was my help, 18.04
"Honor your f. and your mother, that 20.12
"Whoever strikes his f. or his mother 21.15
"Whoever curses his f. or his mother 21.17
If her f. utterly refuses to give 22.17
them, as you anointed their f., that 40.15
uncover the nakedness of your f., Lev 18.07
daughter of your f. or the daughter 18.09
daughter, begotten by your f., since 18.11
shall revere his mother and his f., 19.03
who curses his f. or his mother 20.09
he has cursed his f. or his mother, 20.09
daughter of his f. or a daughter 20.17
his f., his son, his daughter, his 21.02
the harlot, profanes her f.; she shall 21.09
even for his f. or for his mother; 21.11
whose f. was an Egyptian, went out 24.10
in the lifetime of Aaron their f. Num 3.04
Neither for his f. nor for his 6.07
"If her f. had but spit in her face, 12.14
of Levi, the tribe of your f., that 18.02
and Machir was the f. of Gilead; 26.29
And Kohath was the f. of Amram. 26.58
"Our f. died in the wilderness; 27.03
the name of our f. be taken away 27.04
of their f. to pass to them. 27.07
And if his f. has no brothers, then 27.11
and her f. hears of her vow and of 30.04
But if her f. expresses disapproval 30.05
her, because her f. opposed her. 30.05
and between a f. and his daughter, 30.16
inheritance of the tribe of our f." 36.04
family of the tribe of their f. 36.06
the family of the tribe of her f., 36.08
tribe of the family of their f. 36.12
" 'Honor your f. and your mother, as Deu 5.16
and bewail her f. and her mother a 21.13
voice of his f. or the voice of his 21.18
then his f. and his mother shall take 21.19
then the f. of the young woman and 22.15
and the f. of the young woman shall 22.16
them to the f. of the young woman, 22.19
give to the f. of the young woman 22.29
'A wandering Aramean was my f.; 26.05
who dishonors his f. or his mother. 27.16
daughter of his f. or the daughter 27.22
Is not he your f., who created 32.06
ask your f., and he will show you; 32.07
who said of his f. and mother, 33.09
and save alive my f. and mother, Jos 2.13
into your house your f. and mother, 2.18
and her f. and mother and brothers 6.23
Hebron (Arba was the f. of Anak). 15.13
him to ask her f. for a field; 15.18
the f. of Gilead, were allotted 17.01
among the brethren of their f. 17.04
Arba being the f. of Anak (that is, 21.11
the f. of Abraham and of Nahor; 24.02
Then I took your f. Abraham from 24.03
of Hamor the f. of Shechem for a 24.32
him to ask her f. for a field; Ju 1.14
altar of Baal which your f. has, 6.25
buried in the tomb of Joash his f., 8.32
for my f. fought for you, and risked 9.17
the men of Hamor the f. of Shechem? 9.28
against his f. in killing his 9.56
Gilead was the f. of Jephthah. 11.01
"My f., if you have opened your 11.36
And she said to her f., "Let this 11.37
two months, she returned to her f., 11.39

FATHER (cont.)

and told his f. and mother, "I saw Ju 14.02
But his f. and mother said to him, 14.03
But Samson said to his f., 14.03
His f. and mother did not know that 14.04
down with his f. and mother to 14.05
not tell his f. or his mother what 14.06
and he came to his f. and mother, 14.09
And his f. went down to the woman, 14.10
have not told my f. nor my mother, 14.16
But her f. would not allow him to 15.01
And her f. said, "I really thought 15.02
burned her and her f. with fire. 15.06
in the tomb of Manoah his f. He had 16.31
me, and be to me a f. and a priest, 17.10
us, and be to us a f. and a priest. 18.19
and when the girl's f. saw him, 19.03
the girl's f., made him stay, and he 19.04
but the girl's f. said to his son-in-law, 19.05
and the girl's f. said to the man, 19.06
and the girl's f. said, "Strengthen 19.08
the girl's f., said to him, "Behold, 19.09
you left your f. and mother and Ru 2.11
he was the f. of Jesse, the f. of David. 4.17
Perez: Perez was the f. of Hezron, 4.18
listen to the voice of their f.; 1Sa 2.25
house of your f. when they were in 2.27
house of your f. all my offerings 2.28
house of your f. should go in and 2.30
of Kish, Saul's f., were lost. So Kish 9.03
lest my f. cease to care about the 9.05
and now your f. has ceased to care 10.02
answered, "And who is their f.?" 10.12
side." But he did not tell his f. 14.01
not heard his f. charge the people 14.27
"Your f. strictly charged the people 14.28
"My f. has troubled the land; see how 14.29
Kish was the f. of Saul, and Ner the f. 14.51
used to keep sheep for his f.; and when 17.34
David, "Saul my f. seeks to kill you; 19.02
stand beside my f. in the field where 19.03
I will speak to my f. about you; 19.03
spoke well of David to Saul his f., 19.04
and what is my sin before your f., 20.01
Behold, my f. does nothing either 20.02
why should my f. hide this from me? 20.02
"Your f. knows well that I have 20.03
If your f. misses me at all, then 20.06
why should you bring me to your f.?" 20.08
determined by my f. that evil 20.09
tell me if your f. answers you 20.10
When I have sounded my f., about this 20.12
it please my f. to do you harm, 20.13
you, as he has been with my f. 20.13
Then Jonathan answered Saul his f., 20.32
knew that his f. was determined to 20.33
because his f. had disgraced him. 20.34
"Pray let my f. and my mother stay 22.03
or to all the house of my f.; for your 22.15
hand of Saul my f. shall not find 23.17
to you; Saul my f. also knows this." 23.17
See, my f., see the skirt of your 24.11
buried him in the tomb of his f., 2Sa 2.32
to the house of Saul your f., to his 3.08
LORD, who chose me above your f., 6.21
I will be his f., and he shall be 7.14
for the sake of your f. Jonathan, 9.07
you all the land of Saul your f.; 9.07
as his f. dealt loyally with me." 10.02
to console him concerning his f. 10.02
you, that he is honoring your f.? 10.03
and when your f. comes to see you, 13.05
give me back the kingdom of my f.'" 16.03
As I have served your f., so I will 16.19
made yourself odious to your f., and 16.21
know that your f. and his men are 17.08
Besides, your f. is expert in war; 17.08
knows that your f. is a mighty man, 17.10
was buried in the tomb of his f. 17.23
the grave of my f. and my mother. 19.37
Zela, in the tomb of Kish his f.; 21.14
His f. had never at any time displeased 1Ki 1.06
upon the throne of David his f.; 2.12
me on the throne of David my f., 2.24
of the LORD GOD before David my f., 2.26
in all the affliction of my f." 2.26
the knowledge of my f. David, he attacked 2.32
evil that you did to David my f.; 2.44
in the statutes of David his f.; 3.03
love to thy servant David my f., 3.06
king in place of David my f., although 3.07
as your f. David walked, then I will 3.14
him king in place of his f.; for Hiram 5.01
that David my f. could not build a 5.03
as the LORD said to David my f., 5.05
which I spoke to David your f. 6.12
and his f. was a man of Tyre, a 7.14
which David his f. had dedicated, 7.51
his mouth to David my f., saying, 8.15
of David my f. to build a house 8.17
But the LORD said to David my f., 8.18
risen in the place of David my f., 8.20
David my f. what thou didst declare 8.24
David my f. what thou hast promised 8.25
spoken to thy servant David my f. 8.26
as David your f. walked, with integrity 9.04
ever, as I promised David your f., 9.05
as was the heart of David his f. 11.04
the LORD, as David his f. had done. 11.06
of David your f. I will not do it 11.12
breach of the city of David his f. 11.27
my ordinances, as David his f. did. 11.33
buried in the city of David his f.; 11.43
"Your f. made our yoke heavy. Now 12.04
service of your f. and his heavy 12.04
Solomon his f. while he was yet 12.06
the yoke that your f. put upon us'?" 12.09
'Your f. made our yoke heavy, but do 12.10
whereas my f. laid upon you a heavy 12.11
My f. chastised you with whips, but 12.11
"My f. made your yoke heavy, but I 12.14
my f. chastised you with whips, but 12.14
to the king, they told to their f. 13.11
And their f. said to them, "Which 13.12
sins which his f. did before him; 15.03
God, as the heart of David his f. 15.03
the LORD, as David his f. had done. 15.11
gifts of his f. and his own votive 15.15
as between my f. and your f.: 15.19
in the city of David his f.; and 15.24
the way of his f. and in his sin 15.26
"Let me kiss my f. and my mother, 19.20
cities which my f. took from your f. 20.34
Damascus, as my f. did in Samaria." 20.34
in all the way of Asa his f.; he did 22.43
remained in the days of his f. Asa, 22.46
in the city of David his f.; and 22.50
and walked in the way of his f., 22.52
in every way that his f. had done. 22.53
it and he cried, "My f., my f.! 2Ki 2.12
though not like his f. and mother, 3.02
of Baal which his f. had made. 3.02
prophets of your f. and the prophets 3.13
one day to his f. among the reapers. 4.18
And he said to his f., "Oh, my head, 4.19
The f. said to his servant, "Carry 4.19
"My f., if the prophet had commanded 5.13
"My f., shall I slay them? Shall I 6.21
side by side behind Ahab his f., 9.25
him, crying, "My f., my f.! 13.14
taken from Jehoahaz his f. in war. 13.25
LORD, yet not like David his f.; 14.03
things as Joash his f. had done. 14.03
servants who had slain the king his f. 14.05

FATHER (cont.)

him king instead of his f. Amaziah. 2Ki 14.21
to all that his f. Amaziah had 15.03
to all that his f. Uzziah had done. 15.34
in the city of David his f.; and Ahaz 15.38
his God, as his f. David had done, 16.02
to all that David his f. had done. 18.03
the LORD the God of David your f.: 20.05
Hezekiah his f. had destroyed; 21.03
LORD, as Manasseh his f. had done. 21.20
all the way in which his f. walked, 21.21
the idols that his f. served, 21.21
in all the way of David his f., 22.02
king in the place of Josiah his f., 23.34
according to all that his f. had done. 24.09
Cush was the f. of Nimrod; he began 1Ch 1.10
Egypt was the f. of Ludim, Anamim, 1.11
Canaan was the f. of Sidon his first-born 1.13
Arpachshad was the f. of Shelah; and 1.18
and Shelah was the f. of Eber. 1.18
Joktan was the f. of Almodad, Sheleph 1.20
Abraham was the f. of Isaac. The sons 1.34
Ram was the f. of Amminadab, and 2.10
Amminadab was the f. of Nahshon, 2.10
Nahshon was the f. of Salma, Salma 2.11
Jesse was the f. of Eliab his first 2.13
and the f. of Amasa was Jether the 2.17
Hur was the f. of Uri, and Uri was the f. 2.20
daughter of Machir the f. of Gilead, 2.21
and Segub was the f. of Jair, who had 2.22
of Machir, the f. of Gilead. 2.23
Ephrathah, the wife of Hezron his f., 2.24
bore him Ashhur, the f. of Tekoa. 2.24
Attai was the f. of Nathan and 2.36
Zabad was the f. of Ephlal, and 2.37
Obed was the f. of Jehu, and Jehu of 2.38
Azariah was the f. of Helez, 2.39
Eleasah was the f. of Sismai, and 2.40
Shallum was the f. of Jekamiah, 2.41
first-born, who was the f. of Ziph. 2.42
Shema was the f. of Raham, the f. 2.44
and Rekem was the f. of Shammai. 2.44
and Maon was the f. of Bethzur. 2.45
and Haran was the f. of Gazez. 2.46
bore Shaaph the f. of Madmannah, 2.49
Sheva the f. of Machbenah and the f. 2.49
Shobal the f. of Kiriathjearim, 2.50
Salma, the f. of Bethlehem, and 2.51
and Hareph the f. of Bethgader. 2.51
Shobal the f. of Kiriathjearim had 2.52
the f. of the house of Rechab. 2.55
son of Shobal was the f. of Jahath, 4.02
Jahath was the f. of Ahumai and 4.02
and Penuel was the f. of Gedor, 4.04
Gedor, and Ezer the f. of Hushah. 4.04
of Ephrathah the f. of Bethlehem. 4.04
Ashhur, the f. of Tekoa, had two 4.05
Koz was the f. of Anub, Zobebah, and 4.08
was the f. of Mehir, who was the f. 4.11
Eshton was the f. of Bethrapha, 4.12
and Tehinnah the f. of Irnahash. 4.12
Meonothai was the f. of Ophrah; 4.14
Seraiah was the f. of Joab the f. 4.14
and Ishbah, the f. of Eshtemoa. 4.17
wife bore Jered the f. of Gedor, 4.18
Heber the f. of Soco, and Jekuthiel the f. 4.18
Er the f. of Lecah, Laadah the f. 4.21
Eleazar was the f. of Phinehas, 6.04
Azariah was the f. of Amariah, 6.11
she bore Machir the f. of Gilead. 7.14
And Ephraim their f. mourned many 7.22
Malchiel, who was the f. of Birzaith. 7.31
Heber was the f. of Japhlet, Shomer, 7.32
Benjamin was the f. of Bela his 8.01
who was the f. of Uzza and Ahihud. 8.07
Jeiel the f. of Gibeon dwelt in 8.29
and Mikloth (he was the f. of Shimeah). 8.32
Ner was the f. of Kish, Kish of Saul, 8.33
and Meribbaal was the f. of Micah. 8.34
Ahaz was the f. of Jehoaddah; 8.36
Jehoaddah was the f. of Alemeth, 8.36
Zimri was the f. of Moza. 8.36
Moza was the f. of Binea: Raphah 8.37
In Gibeon dwelt the f. of Gibeon, 9.35
and Mikloth was the f. of Shimeam; 9.38
Ner was the f. of Kish, Kish of Saul, 9.39
and Meribbaal was the f. of Micah. 9.40
and Ahaz was the f. of Jarah, 9.42
and Zimri was the f. of Moza. 9.42
Moza was the f. of Binea; and Rephaiah 9.43
I will be his f., and he shall be 17.13
for his f. dealt loyally with me." 19.02
to console him concerning his f. 19.02
you, that he is honoring your f.? 19.03
be my son, and I will be his f., 22.10
and Abihu died before their f., 24.02
established for them by Aaron their f., 24.19
the direction of their f. Jeduthun, 25.03
of their f. in the music in the 25.06
the first-born, his f. made him chief), 26.10
to be my son, and I will be his f. 28.06
my son, know the God of your f., 28.09
O LORD, the God of Israel our f., 29.10
as king instead of David his f.; 29.23
and steadfast love to David my f., 2Ch 1.08
to David my f. be now fulfilled, 1.09
with David my f. and sent him cedar 2.03
Jerusalem, whom David my f. provided. 2.07
and his f. was a man of Tyre. 2.14
craftsmen of my lord, David your f. 2.14
them which David his f. had taken; 2.17
LORD had appeared to David his f., 3.01
which David his f. had dedicated, 5.01
his mouth to David my f., saying, 6.04
of David my f. to build a house 6.07
But the LORD said to David my f., 6.08
risen in the place of David my f., 6.10
David my f. what thou didst declare 6.15
David my f. what thou hast promised 6.16
before me, as David your f. walked, doing 7.17
as I covenanted with David your f., 7.18
According to the ordinance of David his f., 8.14
buried in the city of David his f.; 9.31
"Your f. made our yoke heavy. Now 10.04
service of your f. and his heavy 10.04
Solomon his f. while he was yet 10.06
the yoke that your f. put upon us'?" 10.09
'Your f. made our yoke heavy, but do 10.10
whereas my f. laid upon you a heavy 10.11
My f. chastised you with whips, but 10.11
"My f. made your yoke heavy, but I 10.14
my f. chastised you with whips, 10.14
gifts of his f. and his own votive 15.18
as between my f. and your f.; 16.03
Ephraim which Asa his f. had taken. 17.02
in the earlier ways of his f.; he did 17.03
the God of his f. and walked in 17.04
way of Asa his f. and did not turn 20.32
Their f. gave them great gifts, of 21.03
throne of his f. and was established, 21.04
the LORD, the God of David your f., 21.12
in the ways of Jehoshaphat your f., 21.12
for after the death of his f. they were his 22.04
Zechariah's f., had shown him, but 24.22
servants who had slain the king his f. 25.03
him king instead of his f. Amaziah. 26.01
to all that his f. Amaziah had done. 26.04
to all that his f. Uzziah had done— 27.02
of the LORD, like his f. David, 28.01
to all that David his f. had done. 29.02
which his f. Hezekiah had broken 33.03
LORD, as Manasseh his f. had done. 33.22
that Manasseh his f. had made, 33.22
as Manasseh his f. had humbled himself, 33.23

FATHER (cont.)
walked in the ways of David his f.; 2Ch 34.02
to seek the God of David his f.; 34.03
And Jeshua was the f. of Joiakim, Neh 12.10
the f. of Eliashib, Eliashib the f. 12.10
the f. of Jonathan, and Jonathan the f. 12.11
for she had neither f. nor mother; Est 2.07
and when her f. and her mother died, 2.07
are among us, older than your f. Job 15.10
'You are my f.,' and to the worm, 17.14
I was a f. to the poor, and I 29.16
his youth I reared him as a f., 31.18
"Has the rain a f., or who has 38.28
and their f. gave them inheritance 42.15
For my f. and my mother have Ps 27.10
F. of the fatherless and protector 68.05
'Thou art my F., my God, and the 89.26
As a f. pities his children, so the 103.13
as a f. the son in whom he delights Pro 3.12
When I was a son with my f., tender, 4.03
A wise son makes a glad f., but a 10.01
A wise son makes a glad f., but a 15.20
A stupid son is a grief to a f.; 17.21
and the f. of a fool has no joy. 17.21
a grief to his f. and bitterness 17.25
A foolish son is ruin to his f., 19.13
violence to his f. and chases away 19.26
If one curses his f. or his mother, 20.20
Hearken to your f. who begot you, 23.22
The f. of the righteous will greatly 23.24
Let your f. and mother be glad, let 23.25
companion of gluttons shames his f. 28.07
He who robs his f. or his mother 28.24
who loves wisdom makes his f. glad, 29.03
that mocks a f. and scorns to obey 30.17
and he is f. of a son, but he has Ecc 5.14
his brother in the house of his f., Is 3.06
how to cry 'My f.' or 'My mother,' 8.04
Everlasting F., Prince of Peace." 9.06
he shall be a f. to the inhabitants 22.21
the LORD, the God of David your f.: 38.05
the f. makes known to the children 38.19
Your first f. sinned, and your 43.27
Woe to him who says to a f., 'What 45.10
Look to Abraham your f. and to 51.02
with the heritage of Jacob your f., 58.14
For thou art our F., though Abraham 63.16
art our F., our Redeemer from of 63.16
Yet, O LORD, thou art our F.; we are 64.08
'You are my f.,' and to a stone, Jer 2.27
'My f., thou art the friend of my 3.04
My F., and would not turn from 3.19
brothers and the house of your f., 12.06
to drink for his f. or his mother. 16.07
man who brought the news to my f., 20.15
reigned instead of Josiah his f., 22.11
Did not your f. eat and drink and 22.15
for I am a f. to Israel, and Ephraim 31.09
our f., commanded us, 'You shall not 35.06
our f., in all that he commanded us, 35.08
that Jonadab our f. commanded us. 35.10
command which their f. gave them, 35.16
the command of Jonadab your f., 35.18
your f. was an Amorite, and your Eze 16.03
a Hittite and your f. an Amorite. 16.45
the soul of the f. as well as the 18.04
all the sins which his f. has done, 18.14
As for his f., because he practiced 18.18
suffer for the iniquity of the f.?' 18.19
suffer for the iniquity of the f., 18.20
nor the f. suffer for the iniquity 18.20
F. and mother are treated with 22.07
however, for f. or mother, for son or 44.25
Nebuchadnezzar his f. had taken out Dan 5.02
days of your f. light and understanding 5.11
your f., made him chief of the 5.11
the king my f. brought from Judah. 5.13
Nebuchadnezzar your f. kingship and 5.18
a man and his f. go in to the same Amo 2.07
son treats the f. with contempt, Mic 7.06
his f. and mother who bore him will Zec 13.03
f. and mother who bore him shall 13.03
"A son honors his f., and a servant Mal 1.06
If then I am a f., where is 1.06
Have we not all one f.? Has not one 2.10
Abraham was the f. of Isaac, and Isaac Mt 1.02
and Isaac the f. of Jacob, and Jacob 1.02
and Jacob the f. of Judah and his 1.02
and Judah the f. of Perez and Zerah 1.03
and Perez the f. of Hezron, and 1.03
Hezron, and Hezron the f. of Ram, 1.03
and Ram the f. of Amminadab, and 1.04
and Amminadab the f. of Nahshon, 1.04
and Nahshon the f. of Salmon, 1.04
and Salmon the f. of Boaz by Rahab, 1.05
and Boaz the f. of Obed by Ruth, and 1.05
by Ruth, and Obed the f. of Jesse, 1.05
and Jesse the f. of David the king. 1.06
David was the f. of Solomon by the 1.06
and Solomon the f. of Rehoboam, 1.07
and Rehoboam the f. of Abijah, 1.07
Abijah, and Abijah the f. of Asa, 1.07
and Asa the f. of Jehoshaphat, and 1.08
and Jehoshaphat the f. of Joram, 1.08
Joram, and Joram the f. of Uzziah, 1.08
and Uzziah the f. of Jotham, and 1.09
Jotham, and Jotham the f. of Ahaz, 1.09
Ahaz, and Ahaz the f. of Hezekiah, 1.09
and Hezekiah the f. of Manasseh, 1.10
and Manasseh the f. of Amos, 1.10
Amos, and Amos the f. of Josiah, 1.10
and Josiah the f. of Jechoniah and 1.11
Jechoniah was the f. of Shealtiel, 1.12
Shealtiel the f. of Zerubbabel, 1.12
and Zerubbabel the f. of Abiud, 1.13
and Abiud the f. of Eliakim, and 1.13
and Eliakim the f. of Azor, 1.13
and Azor the f. of Zadok, and Zadok 1.14
and Zadok the f. of Achim, and Achim 1.14
Achim, and Achim the f. of Eliud, 1.14
and Eliud the f. of Eleazar, and 1.15
and Eleazar the f. of Matthan, 1.15
and Matthan the f. of Jacob. 1.15
and Jacob the f. of Joseph the husband 1.16
Judea in place of his f. Herod, he was 2.22
'We have Abraham as our f.'; for I tell 3.09
in the boat with Zebedee their f., 4.21
Immediately they left the boat and their f., 4.22
glory to your F. who is in heaven. 5.16
be sons of your F. who is in heaven; 5.45
as your heavenly F. is perfect. 5.48
reward from your F. who is in heaven. 6.01
and your F. who sees in secret will 6.04
pray to your F. who is in secret; 6.06
and your F. who sees in secret will 6.06
for your F. knows what you need 6.08
Our F. who art in heaven, Hallowed 6.09
your heavenly F. also will forgive 6.14
will your F. forgive your trespasses. 6.15
men but by your F. who is in secret 6.18
and your F. who sees in secret will 6.18
yet your heavenly F. feeds them. Are you 6.26
and your heavenly F. knows that you 6.32
more will your F. who is in heaven 7.11
the will of my F. who is in heaven. 7.21
let me first go and bury my f." 8.21
Spirit of your F. speaking through 10.20
and the f. his child, and children 10.21
acknowledge before my F. who is in heaven; 10.32
deny before my F. who is in heaven. 10.32
come to set a man against his f., 10.35
He who loves f. or mother more than 10.37
F., Lord of heaven and earth, that 11.25
yea, F., for such was thy gracious 11.26

FATHER (cont.)
have been delivered to me by my F.; Mt 11.27
no one knows the Son except the F., 11.27
one knows the F. except the Son 11.27
the will of my F. in heaven is my 12.50
the sun in the kingdom of their F. 13.43
'Honor your f. and your mother,' and, 15.04
'He who speaks evil of f. or mother, 15.04
any one tells his f. or his mother, 15.05
to God, he need not honor his f.' 15.05
my heavenly F. has not planted will be 15.13
to you, but my F. who is in heaven. 16.17
his angels in the glory of his F., 16.27
the face of my F. who is in heaven 18.10
the will of my F. who is in heaven 18.14
done for them by my F. in heaven. 18.19
my heavenly F. will do to every 18.35
shall leave his f. and mother and 19.05
Honor your f. and mother, and, You 19.19
or sisters or f. or mother or children 19.29
whom it has been prepared by my F." 20.23
Which of the two did the will of his f.?" 21.31
And call no man your f. on earth, 23.09
on earth, for you have one F., 23.09
heaven, nor the Son, but the F. only. 24.36
hand, 'Come, O blessed of my F., inherit 25.34
"My F., if it be possible, let this 26.39
"My F., if this cannot pass unless 26.42
that I cannot appeal to my F., and he 26.53
the name of the F. and of the Son 28.19
they left their f. Zebedee in the Mk 1.20
the child's f. and mother and those 5.40
'Honor your f. and your mother'; and, 7.10
He who speaks evil of f. or mother, 7.10
a man tells his f. or his mother, 7.11
do anything for his f. or mother, 7.12
glory of his F. with the holy angels." 8.38
And Jesus asked his f. "How long has 9.21
Immediately the f. of the child 9.24
shall leave his f. and mother and 10.07
defraud, Honor your f. and mother.'" 10.19
or mother or f. or children or 10.29
kingdom of our f. David that is 11.10
so that your F. also who is in 11.25
not forgive, neither will your F. * 11.26
and the f. his child, and children 13.12
heaven, nor the Son, but only the F. 13.32
F., all things are possible to thee; 14.36
the f. of Alexander and Rufus, to 15.21
to him the throne of his f. David, Lk 1.32
named him Zechariah after his f., 1.59
And they made signs to his f., imquiring 1.62
And his f. Zechariah was filled 1.67
which he swore to our f. Abraham, 1.73
And his f. and his mother marveled 2.33
Behold, your f. and I have been 2.48
'We have Abraham as our f.'; for I tell 3.08
merciful, even as your F. is merciful. 6.36
and the f. and mother of the child. 8.51
glory of the F. and of the holy 9.26
boy, and gave him back to his f. 9.42
"Lord, let me first go and bury my f." 9.59
F., Lord of heaven and earth, that 10.21
yea, F., for such was thy gracious 10.21
have been delivered to me by my F.; 10.22
knows who the Son is except the F., 10.22
or who the F. is except the Son and 10.22
"F., hallowed be thy name. Thy kingdom 11.02
What f. among you, if his son asks 11.11
the heavenly F. give the Holy 11.13
and your F. knows that you need 12.30
f. against son and son against f., 12.53
hate his own f. and mother and 14.26
the younger of them said to his f., 15.12
'F., give me the share of property 15.12
I will arise and go to my f., and I will 15.18
"F., I have sinned against heaven 15.18
And he arose and came to his f. 15.20
his f. saw him and had compassion, 15.20
'F., I have sinned against heaven 15.21
But the f. said to his servants, 15.22
and your f. has killed the fatted 15.27
His f. came out and entreated him, 15.28
but he answered his f., 'Lo, these many 15.29
'F. Abraham, have mercy upon me, and 16.24
f., to send him to my father's house, 16.27
And he said, 'No, f. Abraham; but if some 16.30
witness, Honor your f. and mother.'" 18.20
as my F. appointed a kingdom for me, 22.29
"F., if thou art willing, remove 22.42
And Jesus said, "F., forgive them; 23.34
"F., into thy hands I commit my 23.46
send the promise of my F. upon you; 24.49
glory as of the only Son from the F. Jn 1.14
Son, who is in the bosom of the F., 1.18
the F. loves the Son, and has given 3.35
Are you greater than our f. Jacob, 4.12
Jerusalem will you worship the F. 4.21
worship the F. in spirit and truth, 4.23
for such the F. seeks to worship 4.23
The f. knew that was the hour when 4.53
"My F. is working still, and I am 5.17
sabbath but also called God his F., 5.18
but only what he sees the F. doing; 5.19
For the F. loves the Son, and shows 5.20
For as the F. raises the dead and 5.21
The F. judges no one, but has given 5.22
the Son, even as they honor the F. 5.23
does not honor the F. who sent him. 5.23
For as the F. has life in himself, 5.26
works which the F. has granted me 5.36
me witness that the F. has sent me. 5.36
And the F. who sent me has himself 5.37
that I shall accuse you to the F.; 5.45
on him has God the F. set his seal." 6.27
my F. gives you the true bread from 6.32
All that the F. gives me will come 6.37
For this is the will of my F., 6.40
whose f. and mother we know? How does 6.42
me unless the F. who sent me draws 6.44
learned from the F. comes to me. 6.45
has seen the F. except him who is 6.46
he has seen the F. 6.46
As the living F. sent me, and I live 6.57
me, and I live because of the F., 6.57
unless it is granted him by the F." 6.65
and the F. who sent me bears witness 8.18
to him therefore, "Where is your F.?" 8.19
"You know neither me nor my F.; 8.19
knew me, you would know my F. also." 8.19
that he spoke to them of the F. 8.27
but speak thus as the F. taught me. 8.28
of what I have seen with my F., and you 8.38
what you have heard from your f." 8.38
They answered him, "Abraham is our f." 8.39
You do what your f. did." They said 8.41
we have one F., even God." 8.41
Jesus said to them, "If God were your F., 8.42
You are of your f. the devil, and your 8.44
he is a liar and the f. of lies. 8.44
but I honor my F., and you dishonor 8.49
Are you greater than our f. Abraham, 8.53
it is my F. who glorifies me, of 8.54
Your f. Abraham rejoiced that he 8.56
as the F. knows me and I know the F.; 10.15
For this reason the F. loves me, 10.17
charge I have received from my F." 10.18
My F., who has given them to me, is 10.29
I and the F. are one." 10.30
you many good works from the F.; 10.32
of him whom the F. consecrated and 10.36
If I am not doing the works of my F., 10.37
that the F. is in me and I am in the F. 10.38
"F., I thank thee that thou hast 11.41

FATHER (cont.)

serves me, the F. will honor him. Jn 12.26
'F., save me from this hour'? No, for 12.27
F., glorify thy name." Then a voice came 12.28
the F. who sent me has himself given 12.49
I say as the F. has bidden me." 12.50
depart out of this world to the F., 13 01
that the F. had given all things 13.03
no one comes to the F., but by me. 14.06
you would have known my F. also; 14.07
show us the F., and we shall be 14.08
He who has seen me has seen the F.; 14.09
how can you say, 'Show us the F.'? 14.09
I am in the F. and the F. in me? 14.10
but the F. who dwells in me does 14.10
I am in the F. and the F. in me; 14.11
will he do, because I go to the F. 14.12
that the F. may be glorified in the 14.13
And I will pray the F., and he will 14.16
you will know that I am in my F., 14.20
loves me will be loved by my F., 14.21
and my F. will love him, and we will 14.23
whom the F. will send in my name, he 14.26
rejoiced, because I go to the F.; 14.28
for the F. is greater than I. 14.28
but I do as the F. has commanded me, 14.31
world may know that I love the F. 14.31
and my F. is the vinedresser. 15.01
By this my F. is glorified, that you 15.08
As the F. has loved me, so have I 15.09
heard from my F. I have made known 15.15
whatever you ask the F. in my name, 15.16
He who hates me hates my F. also. 15.23
seen and hated both me and my F. 15.24
I shall send to you from the F., even 15.26
of truth, who proceeds from the F., 15.26
they have not known the F., nor me. 16.03
righteousness, because I go to the F., 16.10
All that the F. has is mine; therefore 16.15
see me'; and, 'because I go to the F.'?" 16.17
you, if you ask anything of the F., 16.23
figures but tell you plainly of the F. 16.25
that I shall pray the F. for you; 16.26
for the F. himself loves you, because 16.27
believed that I came from the F. 16.27
I came from the F. and have come 16.28
the world and going to the F." 16.28
not alone, for the F. is with me. 16.32
"F., the hour has come; glorify 17.01
and now, F., glorify thou me in thy 17.05
Holy F., keep them in thy name which 17.11
even as thou, F., art in me, and I in 17.21
F., I desire that they also, whom 17.24
O righteous F., the world has not 17.25
the cup which the F. has given me?" 18.11
I have not yet ascended to the F.; 20.17
ascending to my F. and your F., 20.17
As the F. has sent me, even so I 20.21
to wait for the promise of the F., Ac 1.04
which the F. has fixed by his own 1.07
from the F. the promise of the 2.33
who by the mouth of our f. David, 4.25
glory appeared to our f. Abraham, 7.02
And after his f. died, God removed 7.04
so Abraham became the f. of Isaac, 7.08
and Isaac became the f. of Jacob, 7.08
him Jacob his f. and all his kindred, 7.14
where he became the f. of two sons. 7.29
a believer; but his f. was a Greek. 16.01
all knew that his f. was a Greek. 16.03
that the f. of Publius lay sick 28.08
from God our F. and the Lord Jesus Rom 1.07
to make him the f. of all who 4.11
and likewise the f. of the circumcised 4.12
faith which our f. Abraham had 4.12
Abraham, for he is the f. of us all, 4.16
made you the f. of many nations"— 4.17

become the f. of many nations; 4.18
the dead by the glory of the F., 6.04
When we cry, "Abba! F.!" 8.15
the God and F. of our Lord Jesus 15.06
from God our F. and the Lord Jesus 1Co 1.03
I became your f. in Christ Jesus 4.15
the F., from whom are all things 8.06
to God the F. after destroying 15.24
from God our F. and the Lord Jesus 2Co 1.02
Blessed be the God and F. of our 1.03
the F. of mercies and God of all 1.03
and I will be a f. to you, and you 6.18
The God and F. of the Lord Jesus, he 11.31
Jesus Christ and God the F., Gal 1.01
from God the F. and our Lord Jesus 1.03
to the will of our God and F.; 1.04
trustees until the date set by the f. 4.02
into our hearts, crying, "Abba! F.!" 4.06
from God our F. and the Lord Jesus Eph 1.02
Blessed be the God and F. of our 1.03
the F. of glory, may give you a 1.17
access in one Spirit to the F. 2.18
I bow my knees before the F., 3.14
one God and F. of us all, who is 4.06
Lord Jesus Christ to God the F. 5.20
shall leave his f. and mother and 5.31
"Honor your f. and mother" (this is 6.02
from God the F. and the Lord Jesus 6.23
from God our F. and the Lord Jesus Php 1.02
Lord, to the glory of God the F. 2.11
as a son with a f. he has served 2.22
To our God and F. be glory for ever 4.20
to you and peace from God our F. Col 1.02
the F. of our Lord Jesus Christ, 1.03
giving thanks to the F., who has 1.12
thanks to God the F. through him. 3.17
in God the F. and the Lord Jesus 1Th 1.01
our God and F. your work of faith 1.03
like a f. with his children, we 2.11
Now may our God and F. himself, 3.11
in holiness before our God and F., 3.13
in God our F. and the Lord Jesus 2Th 1.01
from God the F. and the Lord Jesus 1.02
and God our F., who loved us and 2.16
from God the F. and Christ Jesus 1Ti 1.02
but exhort him as you would a f.; 5.01
from God the F. and Christ Jesus 2Ti 1.02
from God the F. and Christ Jesus Tit 1.04
from God our F. and the Lord Jesus Phm 1.03
whose f. I have become in my 1.10
Or again, "I will be to him a f., Heb 1.05
He is without f. or mother or 7.03
there whom his f. does not discipline? 12.07
subject to the F. of spirits and 12.09
down from the F. of lights with Jas 1.17
before God and the F. is this: 1.27
Was not Abraham our f. justified by 2.21
With it we bless the Lord and F., 3.09
by God the F. and sanctified by 1Pe 1.02
Blessed be the God and F. of our 1.03
you invoke as F. him who judges 1.17
from God the F. and the voice was 2Pe 1.17
was with the F. and was made 1Jn 1.02
is with the F. and with his Son 1.03
we have an advocate with the F., 2.01
children, because you know the F. 2.13
love for the F. is not in him. 2.15
is not of the F. but is of the 2.16
he who denies the F. and the Son. 2.22
No one who denies the Son has the F. 2.23
confesses the Son has the F. also. 2.23
abide in the Son and in the F. 2.24
See what love the F. has given us, 3.01
that the F. has sent his Son as 4.14
from God the F. and from Jesus 2Jn 1.03
we have been commanded by the F. 1.04
Christ has both the F. and the Son. 1.09

FATHER (cont.)
in God the F. and kept for Jesus Jud 1.01
kingdom, priests to his God and F., Rev 1.06
have received power from my F.; 2.27
name before my F. and before his 3.05
sat down with my F. on his throne. 3.21

FATHER-IN-LAW
"Your f. is going up to Timnah to Gen 38.13
out, she sent word to her f., 38.25
was keeping the flock of his f., Ex 3.01
to Jethro his f. and said to him, 4.18
Moses' f., heard of all that God 18.01
Moses' f., had taken Zipporah, 18.02
Moses' f., came with his sons and 18.05
your f. Jethro is coming to you 18.06
Moses went out to meet his f., 18.07
Then Moses told his f. all that the 18.08
Moses' f., offered a burnt offering 18.12
bread with Moses' f. before God. 18.12
When Moses' f. saw all that he was 18.14
And Moses said to his f., "Because the people 18.15
Moses' f. said to him, "What you are 18.17
voice of his f. and did all that 18.24
Then Moses let his f. depart, 18.27
Moses' f., "We are setting out for Num 10.29
Moses' f., went up with the people Ju 1.16
descendants of Hobab the f. of Moses, 4.11
And his f., the girl's father, made 19.04
his f. urged him, till he lodged 19.07
his f., the girl's father, said to 19.09
and that her f. and her husband 1Sa 4.19
because of her f. and her husband. 4.21
for he was the f. of Caiaphas, Jn 18.13

FATHERLESS
become widows and your children f. Ex 22.24
justice for the f. and the widow, Deu 10.18
the f., and the widow, who are 14.29
the f., and the widow who are among 16.11
the f., and the widow who are 16.14
due to the sojourner or to the f., 24.17
sojourner, the f., and the widow; 24.19
sojourner, the f., and the widow. 24.20
sojourner, the f., and the widow. 24.21
the f., and the widow, that they may 26.12
the f., and the widow, according to 26.13
sojourner, the f., and the widow.' 27.19
But he saves the f. from their Job 5.15
You would even cast lots over the f., 6.27
the arms of the f. were crushed. 22.09
They drive away the ass of the f.; 24.03
who snatch the f. child from the 24.09
and the f. who had none to help him. 29.12
and the f. has not eaten of it 31.17
have raised my hand against the f., 31.21
hast been the helper of the f. Ps 10.14
justice to the f. and the oppressed, 10.18
Father of the f. and protector of 68.05
Give justice to the weak and the f.; 82.03
the sojourner, and murder the f.; 94.06
May his children be f., and his wife 109.09
nor any to pity his f. children! 109.12
he upholds the widow and the f.; 146.09
or enter the fields of the f., Pro 23.10
defend the f., plead for the widow. Is 1.17
They do not defend the f., 1.23
compassion on their f. and widows; 9.17
they may make the f. their prey! 10.02
with justice the cause of the f., Jer 5.28
the f. or the widow, or shed innocent 7.06
the f., and the widow, nor shed 22.03
Leave your f. children, I will keep 49.11
We have become orphans, f.; Lam 5.03
the f. and the widow are wronged in Eze 22.07
the f., the sojourner, or the poor; Zec 7.10

FATHER'S
did not see their f. nakedness. Gen 9.23
and your f. house to the land that 12.01
me to wander from my f. house, 20.13
took me from my f. house and from 24.07
room in your f. house for us to 24.23
shall go to my f. house and to my 24.38
my kindred and from my f. house; 24.40
wells which his f. servants had 26.15
come again to my f. house in peace, 28.21
Rachel came with her f. sheep; 29.09
Rachel that he was her f. kinsman, 29.12
has taken all that was our f.; 31.01
what was our f. he has gained all 31.01
inheritance left to us in our f. house? 31.14
Rachel stole her f. household gods. 31.19
longed greatly for your f. house, 31.30
lay with Bilhah his f. concubine; 35.22
in the land of his f. sojournings, 37.01
of Bilhah and Zilpah, his f. wives; 37.02
pasture their f. flock near 37.12
"Remain a widow in your f. house, 38.11
went and dwelt in her f. house. 38.11
my hardship and all my f. house." 41.51
brothers and to his f. household, 46.31
'My brothers and my f. household, 46.31
and all his f. household with food, 47.12
and he took his f. hand, 48.17
because you went up to your f. bed; 49.04
your f. sons shall bow down before 49.08
Then Joseph fell on his f. face, 50.01
his brothers, and his f. household; 50.08
in Egypt, he and his f. house; 50.22
troughs to water their f. flock. Ex 2.16
Jochebed his f. sister and she 6.20
my f. God, and I will exalt him. 15.02
priest in his f. place shall make Lev 16.32
the nakedness of your f. wife; 18.08
it is your f. nakedness. 18.08
nakedness of your f. wife's daughter, 18.11
the nakedness of your f. sister; 18.12
she is your f. near kinswoman. 18.12
the nakedness of your f. brother, 18.14
lies with his f. wife has uncovered 20.11
has uncovered his f. nakedness; 20.11
sister or of your f. sister, 20.19
child, and returns to her f. house, 22.13
youth, she may eat of her f. food; 22.13
a possession among our f. brethren." Num 27.04
among their f. brethren and cause 27.07
his inheritance to his f. brothers. 27.10
pledge, while within her f. house, 30.03
in her youth, within her f. house. 30.16
to sons of their f. brothers. 36.11
woman to the door of her f. house, Deu 22.21
playing the harlot in her f. house; 22.21
"A man shall not take his f. wife, 22.30
shall he uncover her who is his f. 22.30
be he who lies with his f. wife, 27.20
he has uncovered her who is his f. 27.20
will deal kindly with my f. house, Jos 2.12
brothers, and all your f. household. 2.18
and her f. household, and all who 6.25
"Take your f. bull, the second bull Ju 6.25
And he went to his f. house at 9.05
up against my f. house this day, 9.18
shall not inherit in our f. house; 11.02
and drive me out of my f. house? 11.07
you and your f. house with fire. 14.15
anger he went back to his f. house. 14.19
from him to her f. house at 19.02
And he came to her f. house; 19.03
and the strength of your f. house, 1Sa 2.31
for you and for all your f. house?" 9.20
to feed his f. sheep at Bethlehem. 17.15
and make his f. house free in 17.25
not let him return to his f. house. 18.02

FATHER'S (cont.)
my f. family in Israel, that I 1Sa 18.18
and all his f. house heard it, 22.01
and all his f. house, the priests 22.11
Ahimelech, you and all your f. house." 22.16
all the persons of your f. house. 22.22
destroy my name out of my f. house." 24.21
you gone in to my f. concubine?" 2Sa 3.07
of Joab, and upon all his f. house; 3.29
lord the king, and on my f. house; 14.09
have been your f. servant in time 15.34
"Go in to your f. concubines, 16.21
went in to his f. concubines in 16.22
For all my f. house were but men 19.28
against me and against my f. house." 24.17
me and from my f. house the guilt 1Ki 2.31
Edomites of his f. servants, Hadad being 11.17
finger is thicker than my f. loins. 12.10
and your f. house, because you have 18.18
sons and set him on his f. throne, 2Ki 10.03
and made him king in his f. stead. 23.30
because he polluted his f. couch, 1Ch 5.01
commanders from his own f. house. 12.28
against me and against my f. house; 21.17
they became a f. house in one 23.11
one f. house being chosen for 24.06
head of each f. house and his 24.31
me from all my f. house to be king 28.04
in the house of Judah my f. house, 28.04
and among my f. sons he took 28.04
finger is thicker than my f. loins. 2Ch 10.10
of your f. house, who were better 21.13
a part of a f. house of the Levites. 35.05
him king in his f. stead in Jerusalem, 36.01
Yea, I and my f. house have sinned. Neh 1.06
you and your f. house will perish. Est 4.14
your people and your f. house; Ps 45.10
your f. instruction, and reject not Pro 1.08
a f. instruction, and be attentive, 4.01
keep your f. commandment, and 6.20
A wise son hears his f. instruction, 13.01
A fool despises his f. instruction, 15.05
and your f. friend, do not forsake; 27.10
and upon your f. house such days Is 7.17
a throne of honor to his f. house. 22.23
the whole weight of his f. house, 22.24
they have obeyed their f. command. Jer 35.14
shall not die for his f. iniquity; Eze 18.17
in you defiles his sister, his f. daughter. 22.11
to the ground without your f. will. Mt 10.29
it new with you in my F. kingdom." 26.29
know that I must be in my F. house?" Lk 2.49
'How many of my f. hired servants 15.17
you, father, to send him to my f. house, 16.27
not make my F. house a house of Jn 2.16
I have come in my F. name, and you do 5.43
your will is to do your f. desires. 8.44
the works that I do in my F. name, 10.25
to snatch them out of the F. hand. 10.29
In my F. house are many rooms; 14.02
is not mine but the F. who sent me. 14.24
I have kept my F. commandments and 15.10
for three months in his f. house; Ac 7.20
a man is living with his f. wife. 1Co 5.01
and from Jesus Christ the F. Son, 2Jn 1.03
name and his F. name written on Rev 14.01

FATHERS
you shall go to your f. in peace; Gen 15.15
land of your f. and to your 31.03
even until now, both we and our f., 46.34
are shephreds, as our f. were." 47.03
the life of my f. in the days of 47.09
but let me lie with my f.; 47.30
before whom my f. Abraham and 48.15
the name of my f. Abraham and Isaac; 48.16
you again to the land of your f. 48.21
bury me with my f. in the cave that 49.29
'The God of your f. has sent me to Ex 3.13
'The LORD, the God of your f., 3.15
'The LORD, the God of your f., 3.16
that the LORD, the God of their f., 4.05
as neither your f. nor your grandfathers 10.06
he swore to your f. to give you, 13.05
as he swore to you and your f., 13.11
iniquity of the f. upon the 20.05
iniquity of the f. upon the 34.07
return to the possession of his f. Lev 25.41
of their f. they shall pine away 26.39
of their f. in their treachery 26.40
the head of the house of his f. Num 1.04
thou didst swear to give their f.?' 11.12
tribe of their f. shall you send a 13.02
the iniquity of f. upon children, 14.18
which I swore to give to their f.; 14.23
how our f. went down to Egypt, and 20.15
dealt harshly with us and our f.; 20.15
tribes of their f. they shall 26.55
Thus did your f., when I sent them 32.08
tribes of your f. you shall 33.54
from the inheritance of our f., 36.03
inheritance of the tribe of his f. 36.07
possess the inheritance of his f. 36.08
which the LORD swore to your f., Deu 1.08
May the LORD the God of your f., 1.11
the God of your f., has told you; 1.21
which I swore to give to your f., 1.35
the God of your f., gives you. 4.01
with your f. which he swore to 4.31
he loved your f. and chose their 4.37
Not with our f. did the LORD make 5.03
iniquity of the f. upon the 5.09
as the LORD, the God of your f., 6.03
the land which he swore to your f., 6.10
LORD swore to give to your f. 6.18
which he swore to give to our f. 6.23
the oath which he swore to your f., 7.08
which he swore to your f. to keep; 7.12
he swore to your f. to give you. 7.13
the LORD swore to give to your f. 8.01
did not know, nor did your f. know; 8.03
manna which your f. did not know, 8.16
covenant which he swore to your f., 8.18
which the LORD swore to your f., 9.05
I swore to their f. to give them.' 10.11
love upon your f. and chose their 10.15
Your f. went down to Egypt seventy 10.22
swore to your f. to give to them 11.09
LORD swore to your f. to give them, 11.21
which the LORD, the God of your f., 12.01
which neither you nor your f. have known, 13.06
you, as he swore to your f., 13.17
border, as he has sworn to your f., 19.08
he promised to give to your f.— 19.08
"The f. shall not be put to death 24.16
children be put to death for the f.; 24.16
LORD swore to our f. to give us.' 26.03
to the LORD the God of our f., 26.07
us, as thou didst swear to our f., 26.15
as the LORD, the God of your f., 27.03
LORD swore to your f. to give you. 28.11
neither you nor your f. have known; 28.36
neither you nor your f. have known. 28.64
you, and as he swore to your f., 29.13
of the LORD, the God of their f., 29.25
the land which your f. possessed, 30.05
prosperous and numerous than your f. 30.05
prospering you, as he took delight in your f., 30.09
which the LORD swore to your f., to Abraham, 30.20
has sworn to their f. to give them; 31.07
are about to sleep with your f.; 31.16
which I swore to give to their f., 31.20
whom your f. had never dreaded. 32.17
I swore to their f. to give them. Jos 1.06

FATHERS (cont.)
ask their f. in time to come, 'What Jos 4.21
had sworn to their f. to give us, 5.06
the God of your f., has given you? 18.03
which he swore to give to their f.; 21.43
just as he had sworn to their f.; 21.44
which our f. made, not for burnt 22.28
'Your f. lived of old beyond the 24.02
Then I brought your f. out of Egypt, 24.06
pursued your f. with chariots and 24.06
gods which your f. served beyond 24.14
the gods your f. served in the 24.15
us and our f. up from the land of 24.17
which I swore to give to your f. Ju 2.01
also were gathered to their f.; 2.10
the LORD, the God of their f., 2.12
way in which their f. had walked, 2.17
and behaved worse than their f., 2.19
covenant which I commanded their f., 2.20
the LORD as their f. did, or not." 2.22
he commanded their f. by Moses. 3.04
deeds which our f. recounted to us, 6.13
And when their f. or their brothers 21.22
brought your f. up out of the land 1Sa 12.06
performed for you and for your f. 12.07
then your f. cried to the LORD and 12.08
brought forth your f. out of Egypt, 12.08
and you lie down with your f., 2Sa 7.12
lord the king sleeps with his f., 1Ki 1.21
Then David slept with his f., and was 2.10
the LORD which he made with our f., 8.21
land which thou gavest to their f. 8.34
land which thou gavest to our f. 8.40
which thou gavest to their f., the city 8.48
didst bring our f. out of Egypt, 8.53
be with us, as he was with our f.; 8.57
ordinances, which he commanded our f. 8.58
brought their f. out of the land 9.09
slept with his f. and that Joab 11.21
And Solomon slept with his f., 11.43
not come to the tomb of your f.'" 13.22
land which he gave to their f., 14.15
and he slept with his f., and Nadab 14.20
than all that their f. had done. 14.22
slept with his f. and was buried 14.31
buried with his f. in the city of 14.31
And Abijam slept with his f.; 15.08
all the idols that his f. had made. 15.12
And Asa slept with his f., and was 15.24
buried with his f. in the city of 15.24
And Baasha slept with his f., and was 16.06
And Omri slept with his f.. and was 16.28
for I am no better than my f." 19.04
give you the inheritance of my f." 21.03
give you the inheritance of my f." 21.04
So Ahab slept with his f.; and Ahaziah 22.40
And Jehoshaphat slept with his f., 22.50
buried with his f. in the city of 22.50
So Joram slept with his f., 2Ki 8.24
buried with his f. in the city of 8.24
tomb with his f. in the city of 9.28
So Jehu slept with his f., and they 10.35
his f., the kings of Judah, had 12.18
him with his f. in the city of 12.21
So Jehoahaz slept with his f., and they 13.09
So Joash slept with his f., and Jeroboam 13.13
"The f. shall not be put to death 14.06
children be put to death for the f.; 14.06
And Jehoash slept with his f., and was 14.16
with his f. in the city of David. 14.20
after the king slept with his f. 14.22
And Jeroboam slept with his f., 14.29
And Azariah slept with his f., 15.07
him with his f. in the city of 15.07
of the LORD, as his f. had done. 15.09
And Menahem slept with his f., 15.22
Jotham slept with his f., and was 15.38
buried with his f. in the city of 15.38
And Ahaz slept with his f., and was 16.20
buried with his f. in the city of 16.20
the law which I commanded your f., 17.13
as their f. had been, who did not 17.14
covenant that he made with their f., 17.15
as their f. did, so they do to this 17.41
the nations which my f. destroyed, 19.12
that which your f. have stored up 20.17
And Hezekiah slept with his f.; and Manasseh 20.21
the land which I gave to their f., 21.08
the day their f. came out of Egypt, 21.15
And Manasseh slept with his f., 21.18
the LORD, the God of his f., and did not 21.22
because our f. have not obeyed the 22.13
I will gather you to your f., and you 22.20
according to all that his f. had done. 23.32
according to all that his f. had done. 23.37
So Jehoiakim slept with his f., 24.06
were the f. of Keilah the Garmite 1Ch 4.19
against the God of their f., and played 5.25
the Levites according to their f. 6.19
as their f. had been in charge of 9.19
the God of our f. see and rebuke 12.17
fulfilled to go to be with your f., 17.11
and sojourners, as all our f. were; 29.15
our f., keep for ever such purposes 29.18
the LORD, the God of their f., 29.20
gavest to them and to their f. 2Ch 6.25
land which thou gavest to our f. 6.31
which thou gavest to their f., 6.38
God of their f. who brought them 7.22
And Solomon slept with his f., 9.31
to the LORD, the God of their f. 11.16
And Rehoboam slept with his f., 12.16
the LORD, the God of your f.; 13.12
upon the LORD, the God of their f. 13.18
So Abijah slept with his f., and they 14.01
seek the LORD, the God of their f., 14.04
seek the LORD, the God of their f., 15.12
And Asa slept with his f., dying in 16.13
to the LORD, the God of their f. 19.04
God of our f., art thou not God in 20.06
hearts upon the God of their f. 20.33
Jehoshaphat slept with his f., and was 21.01
buried with his f. in the city of 21.01
forsaken the LORD, the God of his f. 21.10
like the fires made for his f. 21.19
of the LORD, the God of their f., 24.18
the LORD, the God of their f. 24.24
"The f. shall not be put to death 25.04
children be put to death for the f.; 25.04
buried with his f. in the city of 25.28
after the king slept with his f. 26.02
And Uzziah slept with his f., and they 26.23
him with his f. in the burial field which 26.23
And Jotham slept with his f., and they 27.09
the LORD, the God of their f. 28.06
the LORD, the God of your f., 28.09
anger the LORD, the God of his f. 28.25
And Ahaz slept with his f., and they 28.27
of the LORD, the God of your F., 29.05
For our f. have been unfaithful and 29.06
For lo, our f. have fallen by the 29.09
be like your f. and your brethren, 30.07
to the LORD God of their f., so that 30.07
be stiff-necked as your f. were, 30.08
God, the LORD the God of his f., 30.19
to the LORD the God of their f. 30.22
what I and my f. have done to all 32.13
which my f. utterly destroyed was 32.14
my hand or from the hand of my f. 32.15
And Hezekiah slept with his f., 32.33
land which I appointed for your f., 33.08
greatly before the God of his f. 33.12
So Manasseh slept with his f., 33.20
because our f. have not kept the 34.21

FATHERS (cont.)

Behold, I will gather you to your f., 2Ch 34.28
covenant of God, the God of their f. 34.32
following the LORD the God of their f. 34.33
was buried in the tombs of his f. 35.24
The LORD, the God of their f., sent 36.15
the book of the records of your f. Ez 4.15
But because our f. had angered the 5.12
Blessed be the LORD, the God of our f., 7.27
offering to the LORD, the God of your f. 8.28
From the days of our f. to this day 9.07
to the LORD the God of your f., and do 10.11
their sins and the iniquities of their f. Neh 9.02
affliction of our f. in Egypt and 9.09
acted insolently against our f.; and thou 9.10
"But they and our f. acted presumptuously 9.16
thou hadst told their f. to enter and possess. 9.23
our f., and all thy people, since the time 9.32
and our f. have not kept thy law or 9.34
gavest to our f. to enjoy its fruit 9.36
Did not your f. act in this way, and 13.18
consider what the f. have found; Job 8.08
and their f. have not hidden, 15.18
whose f. I would have disdained to 30.01
In thee our f. trusted; they trusted, Ps 22.04
guest, a sojourner, like all my f. 39.12
our f. have told us, what deeds thou 44.01
Instead of your f. shall be your 45.16
go to the generation of his f., 49.19
known, that our f. have told us. 78.03
commanded our f. to teach to their 78.05
they should not be like their f., 78.08
sight of their f. he wrought marvels 78.12
acted treacherously like their f.; 78.57
when your f. tested me, and put me 95.09
Both we and our f. have sinned; 106.06
Our f., when they were in Egypt, did 106.07
iniquity of his f. be remembered 109.14
and the glory of sons is their f. Pro 17.06
House and wealth are inherited from f., 19.14
landmark which your f. have set. 22.28
who curse their f. and do not bless 30.11
because of the guilt of their f., Is 14.21
the nations which my f. destroyed, 37.12
that which your f. have stored up 39.06
Kings shall be your foster f., and their 49.23
where our f. praised thee, has been 64.11
wrong did your f. find in me that Jer 2.05
that I gave your f. for a heritage. 3.18
all for which our f. labored, their flocks 3.24
we and our f., from our youth even 3.25
f. and sons together, neighbor and 6.21
I gave of old to your f. for ever. 7.07
which I gave to you and to your f., 7.14
the f. kindle fire, and the women 7.18
speak to your f. or command them 7.22
day that your f. came out of the 7.25
their necks. They did worse than their f. 7.26
the Baals, as their f. taught them. 9.14
they nor their f. have known; and I will 9.16
commanded your f. when I brought 11.04
I swore to your f. to give them a 11.05
warned your f. when I brought them 11.07
covenant which I made with their f. 11.10
f. and sons together, says the LORD. 13.14
O LORD, and the iniquity of our f., 14.20
them and the f. who begot them in 16.03
'Because your f. have forsaken me, 16.11
you have done worse than your f., 16.12
neither you nor your f. have known, 16.13
own land which I gave to their f. 16.15
"Our f. have inherited nought but 16.19
day holy, as I commanded your f. 17.22
they nor their f. nor the kings of 19.04
even as their f. forgot my name for 23.27
which I gave to you and your f. 23.39
which I gave to them and their f." 24.10

to you and your f. from of old and 25.05
the land which I gave to their f., 30.03
'The f. have eaten sour grapes, and 31.29
made with their f. when I took them by 31.32
the guilt of f. to their children 32.18
swear to their f. to give them, 32.22
as spices were burned for your f., 34.05
with your f. when I brought them 34.13
But your f. did not listen to me 34.14
which I gave to you and your f.' 35.15
neither they, nor you, nor your f. 44.03
forgotten the wickedness of your f., 44.09
set before you and before your f. 44.10
her, as we did, both we and our f., 44.17
you and your f., your kings and 44.21
the f. look not back to their 47.03
the LORD, the hope of their f. 50.07
Our f. sinned, and are no more; Lam 5.07
they and their f. have transgressed Eze 2.03
Therefore f. shall eat their sons 5.10
you, and sons shall eat their f.; 5.10
'The f. have eaten sour grapes, and 18.02
know the abominations of their f., 20.04
walk in the statutes of your f., 20.18
this again your f. blasphemed me, 20.27
manner of your f. and go astray 20.30
with your f. in the wilderness of 20.36
which I swore to give to your f. 20.42
the land which I gave to your f.; 36.28
land where your f. dwelt that I 37.25
I swore to give it to your f., 47.14
O God of my f., I give thanks and Dan 2.23
and our f., and to all the people 9.06
and to our f., because we have 9.08
and for the iniquities of our f., 9.16
neither his f. nor his fathers' f. 11.24
give no heed to the gods of his f., 11.37
a god whom his f. did not know he 11.38
in its first season, I saw your f. Hos 9.10
days, or in the days of your f.? Joe 1.02
them astray, after which their f. walked. Amo 2.04
sworn to our f. from the days of Mic 7.20
"The LORD was very angry with your f. Zec 1.02
Be not like your f., to whom the 1.04
Your f., where are they? And the prophets, 1.05
did they not overtake your f.? 1.06
when your f. provoked me to wrath, 8.14
profaning the covenant of our f.? Mal 2.10
days of your f. you have turned 3.07
the hearts of f. to their children 4.06
the hearts of children to their f., 4.06
we had lived in the days of our f., Mt 23.30
Fill up, then, the measure of your f. 23.32
hearts of the f. to the children, Lk 1.17
as he spoke to our f., to Abraham and 1.55
the mercy promised to our f., and to 1.72
for so their f. did to the prophets 6.23
for so their f. did to the false 6.26
the prophets whom your f. killed. 11.47
consent to the deeds of your f.; 11.48
Our f. worshiped on this mountain; Jn 4.20
Our f. ate the manna in the wilderness; 6.31
Your f. ate the manna in the wilderness, 6.49
not such as the f. ate and died; 6.58
but from the f.), and you circumcise 7.22
and of Jacob, the God of our f., Ac 3.13
covenant which God gave to your f., 3.25
The God of our f. raised Jesus whom 5.30
said: "Brethren and f., hear me. 7.02
and our f. could find no food. 7.11
sent forth our f. the first time. 7.12
And he died, himself and our f., 7.15
and forced our f. to expose their 7.19
'I am the God of your f., the God of 7.32
at Mount Sinai, and with our f.; 7.38
Our f. refused to obey him, but 7.39
"Our f. had the tent of witness in 7.44

FATHERS (cont.)

Our f. in turn brought it in with Ac 7.45
which God thrust out before our f. 7.45
Holy Spirit. As your f. did, so do you. 7.51
prophets did not your f. persecute? 7.52
chose our f. and made the people 13.17
that what God promised to the f., 13.32
asleep, and was laid with his f., 13.36
neither our f. nor we have been 15.10
"Brethren and f., hear the defense 22.01
strict manner of the law of our f., 22.03
'The God of our f. appointed you 22.14
sect, I worship the God of our f., 24.14
the promise made by God to our f., 26.06
people or the customs of our f., 28.17
saying to your f. through Isaiah 28.25
in Christ, you do not have many f. 1Co 4.15
that our f. were all under the 10.01
was I for the traditions of my f. Gal 1.14
F., do not provoke your children to Eph 6.04
F., do not provoke your children, Col 3.21
murderers of f. and murderers of 1Ti 1.09
as did my f., when I remember you 2Ti 1.03
of old to our f. by the prophets; Heb 1.01
where your f. put me to the test 3.09
made with their f. on the day when 8.09
had earthly f. to discipline us 12.09
futile ways inherited from your f., 1Pe 1.18
for ever since the f. fell asleep, 2Pe 3.04
f., because you know him who is 1Jn 2.13
f., because you know him who is 2.14

FATHERS'

These are the heads of their f. houses: Ex 6.14
heads of the f. houses of the Levites 6.25
lamb according to their f. houses, 12.03
by f. houses, according to the number Num 1.02
by f. houses, according to the number 1.18
by their f. houses, according to the 1.20
by their f. houses, those of them 1.22
by their f. houses, according to the 1.24
by their f. houses, according to the 1.26
by their f. houses, according to the 1.28
by their f. houses, according to the 1.30
by their f. houses, according to the 1.32
by their f. houses, according to the 1.34
by their f. houses, according to the 1.36
by their f. houses, according to the 1.38
by their f. houses, according to the 1.40
by their f. houses, according to the 1.42
twelve men, each representing his f. house. 1.44
by their f. houses, from twenty years old 1.45
the ensigns of their f. houses; they shall 2.02
as numbered by their f. houses; all in the 2.32
family, according to his f. house. 2.34
by f. houses and by families; every male 3.15
of the Levites, by their f. houses. 3.20
of Lael as head of the f. house of the 3.24
as head of the f. house of the families 3.30
And the head of the f. house of the 3.35
of Levi, by their families and their f. houses, 4.02
their families and their f. houses; 4.22
their families and their f. houses; 4.29
by their families and their f. houses, 4.34
by their families and their f. houses, 4.38
families and their f. houses was two 4.40
by their families and their f. houses, 4.42
by their families and their f. houses, 4.46
Israel, heads of their f. houses, 7.02
one for each f. house, from all 17.02
according to their f. houses, 17.02
rod for the head of each f. house. 17.03
according to their f. houses, 17.06
sons and your f. house with you 18.01
head of a f. house belonging to the 25.14
the people of a f. house in Midian 25.15
by their f. houses, all in Israel 26.02
and the heads of the f. houses of the 31.26
you have risen in your f. stead, a brood 32.14
heads of the f. houses of the tribes 32.28
of Reuben by f. houses and the tribe 34.14
of Gad by their f. houses have received 34.14
The heads of the f. houses of the 36.01
of the f. houses of the sons of Joseph, 36.01
heads of the f. houses of the people 36.01
heads of the f. houses of the tribes Jos 14.01
heads of the f. houses of the tribes 19.51
heads of the f. houses of the Levites 21.01
heads of the f. houses of the tribes 21.01
leaders of the f. houses of the 1Ki 8.01
and their f. houses increased greatly 1Ch 4.38
according to their f. houses: Michael, 5.13
Guni, was chief in their f. houses; 5.15
These were the heads of their f. houses: 5.24
famous men, heads of their f. houses. 5.24
Shemuel, heads of their f. houses, 7.02
according to their f. houses, were 7.04
heads of f. houses, mighty warriors; 7.07
as heads of their f. houses, mighty 7.09
to the heads of their f. houses, 7.11
heads of f. houses, approved, mighty 7.40
were heads of f. houses of the 8.06
were his sons, heads of f. houses. 8.10
were heads of f. houses of the 8.13
These were the heads of f. houses, 8.28
were heads of f. houses according to their f. 9.09
kinsmen, heads of their f. houses, 9.13
and his kinsmen of his f. house, 9.19
the heads of f. houses of the Levites, 9.33
These were heads of f. houses of 9.34
of valor, famous men in their f. houses. 12.30
heads of the f. houses of the 15.12
heads of the f. houses of Ladan. 23.09
sons of Levi by their f. houses, 23.24
the heads of f. houses as they were 23.24
heads of f. houses of the sons of 24.04
heads of the f. houses of the 24.06
the Levites according to their f. houses. 24.30
the heads of f. houses of the priests 24.31
who were rulers in their f. houses, 26.06
and they cast lots by f. houses, small 26.13
heads of the f. houses belonging 26.21
and the heads of the f. houses, 26.26
of whatever genealogy or f. houses. 26.31
heads of f. houses, to have the 26.32
the heads of f. houses, the commanders 27.01
Then the heads of f. houses made 29.06
all Israel, the heads of f. houses. 2Ch 1.02
leaders of the f. houses of the 5.02
the muster of them by f. houses: 17.14
the heads of f. houses of Israel, 23.02
and set them by f. houses under 25.05
of the heads of f. houses of mighty 26.12
was according to their f. houses; 31.17
according to your f. houses by your 35.04
groupings of the f. houses of your 35.05
groupings of the f. houses of the 35.12
heads of the f. houses of Judah Ez 1.05
not prove their f. houses or their 2.59
and Levites and heads of f. houses, 3.12
the heads of f. houses and said to 4.02
of the heads of f. houses in Israel 4.03
These are the heads of their f. houses, 8.01
the heads of f. houses in Israel 8.29
heads of f. houses, according to their f. 10.16
the place of my f. sepulchres, Neh 2.03
to the city of my f. sepulchres, 2.05
not prove their f. houses nor 7.61
of the heads of f. houses gave to 7.70
of the heads of f. houses gave 7.71
the heads of f. houses of all the 8.13
God, according to our f. houses, 10.34
heads of f. houses, two hundred and 11.13
heads of f. houses: of Seraiah, 12.12

FATHERS' (cont.)
recorded the heads of f. houses; Neh 12.22
heads of f. houses, were written in 12.23
and their f. iniquities together, Is 65.07
eyes were set on their f. idols. Eze 20.24
you men uncover their f. nakedness; 22.10
fathers nor his f. fathers have Dan 11.24

FATHOMS
So they sounded and found twenty f.; Ac 27.28
sounded again and found fifteen f. 27.28

FATLING
six paces, he sacrificed an ox and a f. 2Sa 6.13
and the lion and the f. together, Is 11.06

FATLINGS
and of the oxen and of the f., 1Sa 15.09
and f. by the Serpent's Stone, which 1Ki 1.09
f., and sheep in abundance, and has 1.19
f., and sheep in abundance, and has 1.25
to thee burnt offerings of f., Ps 66.15
f. and kids shall feed among the Is 5.17
the wool, you slaughter the f.; Eze 34.03
of bulls, all of them f. of Bashan. 39.18

FATNESS
and of the f. of the earth, and Gen 27.28
away from the f. of the earth shall 27.39
said to them, 'Shall I leave my f., Ju 9.09
set on your table was full of f. Job 36.16
tracks of thy chariot drip with f. Ps 65.11
Their eyes swell out with f., 73.07
good, and delight yourselves in f. Is 55.02

FATTED
Now the woman had a f. calf in the 1Sa 28.24
gazelles, roebucks, and f. fowl. 1Ki 4.23
love is than a f. ox and hatred Pro 15.17
in her midst are like f. calves; Jer 46.21
offerings of your f. beasts I will Amo 5.22
and bring the f. calf and kill it, Lk 15.23
your father has killed the f. calf, 15.27
you killed for him the f. calf!' 15.30

FATTENED
you have f. your hearts in a day of Jas 5.05

FATTENING
above me by f. yourselves upon the 1Sa 2.29

FATTER
appearance and f. in flesh than Dan 1.15

FAULT
but the f. is in your own people." Ex 5.16
Therefore the people found f. with Moses, 17.02
them, "Why do you find f. with me? 17.02
I have found no f. in him to this 1Sa 29.03
me today with a f. concerning a 2Sa 3.08
for no f. of mine, they run and make Ps 59.04
praise them; and find no f. in them. 73.10
no ground for complaint or any f., Dan 6.04
and no error or f. was found in 6.04
you, go and tell him his f., Mt 18.15
me then, "Why does he still find f.? Rom 9.19
so that no f. may be found with our 2Co 6.03
For he finds f. with them when he Heb 8.08

FAULTFINDER
"Shall a f. contend with the Job 40.02

FAULTFINDING
because of the f. of the children Ex 17.07

FAULTLESS
if that first covenant had been f., Heb 8.07

FAULTS
to Pharaoh, "I remember my f. today. Gen 41.09
his errors? Clear thou me from hidden f. Ps 19.12

FAVOR
But Noah found f. in the eyes of Gen 6.08
if I have found f. in your sight, 18.03
servant has found f. in your sight, 19.19
"Behold, I grant you this f. also, 19.21
not regard him with f. as before. 31.02
regard me with f. as he did before. 31.05
that I may find f. in your sight.'" 32.05
"To find f. in the sight of my lord." 33.08
if I have found f. in your sight, 33.10
with such f. have you received me. 33.10
Let me find f. in the sight of my 33.15
"Let me find f. in your eyes, and 34.11
So Joseph found f. in his sight and 39.04
and gave him f. in the sight of the 39.21
now I have found f. in your sight, 47.29
now I have found f. in your eyes, 50.04
this people f. in the sight of the Ex 3.21
gave the people f. in the sight of 11.03
the people f. in the sight of the 12.36
you have also found f. in my sight." 33.12
if I have found f. in thy sight, 33.13
know thee and find f. in thy sight. 33.13
that I have found f. in thy sight, 33.16
or you have found f. in my sight, 33.17
now I have found f. in thy sight, 34.09
have I not found f. in thy sight, Num 11.11
if I find f. in thy sight, that I 11.15
"If we have found f. in your sight, 32.05
she finds no f. in his eyes because Deu 24.01
the old or show f. to the young, 28.50
and the f. of him that dwelt in the 33.16
"O Naphtali, satisfied with f., 33.23
"If now I have found f. with thee, Ju 6.17
him in whose sight I shall find f." Ru 2.02
"Why have I found f. in your eyes, 2.10
maidservant find f. in your eyes." 1Sa 1.18
stature and in f. with the LORD 2.26
not entreated the f. of the LORD'; 13.12
for he has found f. in my sight." 16.22
that I have found f. in your eyes; 20.03
if I have found f. in your eyes, 20.29
my young men find f. in your eyes; 25.08
"If I have found f. in your eyes, 27.05
that I have found f. in your sight, 2Sa 14.22
If I find f. in the eyes of the 15.25
let me ever find f. in your sight, 16.04
found great f. in the sight of 1Ki 11.19
"Entreat now the f. of the LORD 13.06
man with his master and in high f., 2Ki 5.01
entreated the f. of the LORD his 2Ch 33.12
a brief moment f. has been shown Ez 9.08
servant has found f. in your sight, Neh 2.05
Remember this also in my f., O my God, 13.22
maiden pleased him and won his f.; Est 2.09
Esther found f. in the eyes of all 2.15
found grace and f. in his sight 2.17
she found f. in his sight and he 5.02
If I have found f. in the sight of 5.08
"If I have found f. in your sight, 7.03
if I have found f. in his sight, 8.05
thy hands and f. the designs of Job 10.03
you afraid; many will entreat your f. 11.19
will seek the f. of the poor, 20.10
cover him with f. as with a shield. Ps 5.12
offerings, and regard with f. your burnt 20.03
and his f. is for a lifetime. Weeping 30.05
By the f., O LORD, thou hadst 30.07
Tyre will sue your f. with gifts, 45.12
and shield; he bestows f. and honor. 84.11
Show me a sign of thy f., that those 86.17
by thy f. our horn is exalted. 89.17
Let the f. of the Lord our God be 90.17

FAVOR (cont.)
I will look with f. on the faithful Ps 101.06
it is the time to f. her; the appointed 102.13
when thou showest f. to thy people; 106.04
I entreat thy f. with all my heart; 119.58
in David's f., all the hardships he 132.01
So you will find f. and good repute Pro 3.04
scornful, but to the humble he shows f. 3.34
life and obtains f. from the LORD; 8.35
who diligently seeks good seeks f., 11.27
A good man obtains f. from the LORD, 12.02
Good sense wins f., but the way 13.15
but the upright enjoy his f. 14.09
who deals wisely has the king's f., 14.35
and his f. is like the clouds that 16.15
and obtains f. from the LORD. 18.22
Many seek the f. of a generous man, 19.06
but his f. is like dew upon the 19.12
and f. is better than silver or 22.01
find more f. than he who flatters 28.23
Many seek the f. of a ruler, but 29.26
nor f. to the men of skill; but time Ecc 9.11
of a wise man's mouth win him f., 10.12
If f. is shown to the wicked, he Is 26.10
formed them will show them no f. 27.11
"In a time of f. I have answered 49.08
but in my f. I have had mercy on 60.10
proclaim the year of the LORD's f., 61.02
night, for I will show you no f.' Jer 16.13
and entreat the f. of the LORD, 26.19
the priests, no f. to the elders. Lam 4.16
And God gave Daniel f. and compassion Dan 1.09
entreated the f. of the LORD our 9.13
prevailed, he wept and sought his f. Hos 12.04
to entreat the f. of the LORD, Zec 7.02
once to entreat the f. of the LORD, 8.21
and to entreat the f. of the LORD. 8.22
be pleased with you or show you f.? Mal 1.08
And now entreat the f. of God, 1.09
will he show f. to any of you? 1.09
or accepts it with f. at your hand. 2.13
for you have found f. with God. Lk 1.30
and the f. of God was upon him. 2.40
in stature, and in f. with God and man. 2.52
praising God and having f. with all Ac 2.47
and gave him f. and wisdom before 7.10
who found f. in the sight of God 7.46
and desiring to do the Jews a f., 24.27
asking as a f. to have the man sent 25.03
wishing to do the Jews a f., said to 25.09
be puffed up in f. of one against 1Co 4.06
earnestly for the f. of taking part 2Co 8.04
Am I now seeking the f. of men, Gal 1.10
you to keep these rules without f., 1Ti 5.21

FAVORABLE
saw that the interpretation was f., Gen 40.16
god will give Pharaoh a f. answer. 41.16
with one accord are f. to the king; 1Ki 22.13
with one accord are f. to the king; 2Ch 18.12
for ever, and never again be f.? Ps 77.07
LORD, thou wast f. to thy land; 85.01
made judgment f. to your sisters; Eze 16.52

FAVORABLY
sword of one of them, and speak f." 1Ki 22.13
word of one of them, and speak f." 2Ch 18.12

FAVORED
the land, and the f. man dwelt in it. Job 22.08
Kedar were your f. dealers in Eze 27.21
O f. one, the LORD is with you!" Lk 1.28
were you less f. than the rest of 2Co 12.13

FAVORITE
let him be the f. of his brothers, Deu 33.24

FAVORS
"Whoever f. Joab, and whoever is for 2Sa 20.11
scattered your f. among strangers Jer 3.13

FAWNING
your enemies shall come f. to you; Deu 33.29

FAWNS
let loose, that bears comely f. Gen 49.21
Your two breasts are like two f., Sol 4.05
Your two breasts are like two f., 7.03

FEAR
The f. of you and the dread of you Gen 9.02
"F. not, Abram, I am your shield; 15.01
There is no f. of God at all in 20.11
F. not; for God has heard the 21.17
for now I know that you f. God, 22.12
f. not, for I am with you and will 26.24
God of Abraham and the F. of Isaac, 31.42
swore by the F. of his father 31.53
for I f. him, lest he come and slay 32.11
the midwife said to her, "F. not; 35.17
and you will live, for I f. God: 42.18
I f. to see the evil that would 44.34
"F. not, for am I in the place of 50.19
So do not f.; I will provide 50.21
you do not yet f. the LORD God." Ex 9.30
and they were in great f. 14.10
"F. not, stand firm, and see the 14.13
such as f. God, men who are trustworthy 18.21
said to the people, "Do not f.; 20.20
and that the f. of him may be 20.20
but you shall f. your God: I am the Lev 19.14
and you shall f. your God: I am the 19.32
another, but you shall f. your God; 25.17
him or increase, but f. your God; 25.36
harshness, but shall f. your God. 25.43
and do not f. the people of the Num 14.09
LORD is with us; do not f. them." 14.09
LORD said to Moses, "Do not f. him; 21.34
overcome with f. of the people of 22.03
do not f. or be dismayed." Deu 1.21
the dread and f. of you upon the 2.25
LORD said to me, 'Do not f. him; 3.02
You shall not f. them; for it is the 3.22
may learn to f. me all the days 4.10
to f. me and to keep all my commandments, 5.29
that you may f. the LORD your God, 6.02
You shall f. the LORD your God; 6.13
to f. the LORD our God, for our good 6.24
but to f. the LORD your God, to walk 10.12
You shall f. the LORD your God; 10.20
will lay the f. of you and the 11.25
after the LORD your God and f. him, 13.04
and f., and never again do any such 13.11
may learn to f. the LORD your God 14.23
and f., and not act presumptuously 17.13
he may learn to f. the LORD his 17.19
and f., and shall never again 19.20
do not f., or tremble, or be in 20.03
and all Israel shall hear, and f. 21.21
behind you; and he did not f. God. 25.18
that you may f. this glorious and 28.58
dread which your heart shall f., 28.67
do not f. or be in dread of them: 31.06
do not f. or be dismayed." 31.08
and learn to f. the LORD your God, 31.12
and learn to f. the LORD your God, 31.13
and that the f. of you has fallen Jos 2.09
that you may f. the LORD your God 4.24
Joshua, "Do not f. or be dismayed; 8.01
"Do not f. them, for I have given 10.08
we did it from f. that in time to 22.24
"Now therefore f. the LORD, and 24.14
have no f." So he turned Ju 4.18
do not f., you shall not die." 6.23

FEAR (cont.)
But if you f. to go down, go down to Ju 7.10
for f. of Abimelech his brother. 9.21
do not f., I will do for you all Ru 3.11
"F. not, for you have borne a son." 1Sa 4.20
If you will f. the LORD and serve 12.14
And Samuel said to the people, "F. not; 12.20
Only f. the LORD, and serve him 12.24
Stay with me, f. not; for he that seeks 22.23
And he said to him, "F. not; 23.17
The king said to her "Have no f.; 28.13
filled with f. because of the words 28.20
And David said to him, "Do not f.; 2Sa 9.07
F. not; have I not commanded 13.28
a lion, will utterly melt with f.; 17.10
over men ruling in the f. of God, 23.03
that they may f. thee all the days 1Ki 8.40
may know thy name and f. thee, 8.43
And Elijah said to her, "F. not; 17.13
He said, "F. not, for those who are 2Ki 6.16
there, they did not f. the LORD; 17.25
them how they should f. the LORD. 17.28
They do not f. the LORD, and they do 17.34
"You shall not f. other gods or bow 17.35
but you shall f. the LORD, who brought 17.36
careful to do. You shall not f. other gods, 17.37
made with you. You shall not f. other gods, 17.38
but you shall f. the LORD your God, 17.39
brought the f. of him upon all 1Ch 14.17
F. not; be not dismayed. 22.13
F. not, be not dismayed; 28.20
that they may f. thee and walk in 2Ch 6.31
may know thy name and f. thee, 6.33
for the f. of the LORD was upon 14.14
And the f. of the LORD fell upon 17.10
let the f. of the LORD be upon you; 19.07
you shall do in the f. of the LORD, 19.09
'F. not, and be not dismayed at this 20.15
F. not, and be not dismayed; tomorrow 20.17
And the f. of God came on all the 20.29
instructed him in the f. of God; 26.05
for f. was upon them because of the Ez 3.03
servants who delight to f. thy name; Neh 1.11
to walk in the f. of our God to 5.09
do so, because of the f. of God. 5.15
for the f. of the Jews had fallen Est 8.17
for the f. of them had fallen upon 9.02
for the f. of Mordecai had fallen 9.03
LORD, "Does Job f. God for nought? Job 1.09
For the thing that I f. comes upon me, 3.25
Is not your f. of God your confidence, 4.06
and shall not f. destruction when 5.21
and shall not f. the beasts of the 5.22
forsakes the f. of the Almighty. 6.14
Then I would speak without f. of him, 9.35
will be secure, and will not f. 11.15
are doing away with the f. of God, 15.04
Their houses are safe from f., 21.09
Is it for your f. of him that he 22.04
"Dominion and f. are with God; 25.02
the f. of the Lord, that is wisdom; 28.28
stood in great f. of the multitude, 31.34
Behold, no f. of me need terrify you; 33.07
Therefore men f. him; he does not 37.24
be in vain, yet she has no f.; 39.16
He laughs at f., and is not dismayed; 39.22
his like, a creature without f. 41.33
Serve the LORD with f., with trembling Ps 2.11
thy holy temple in the f. of thee. 5.07
Put them in f., O LORD! 9.20
who honors those who f. the LORD; 15.04
the f. of the LORD is clean, enduring 19.09
You who f. the LORD, praise him! 22.23
I will pay before those who f. him. 22.25
the shadow of death, I f. no evil; 23.04
the LORD is for those who f. him, 25.14
whom shall I f.? The LORD is 27.01
against me, my heart shall not f.; 27.03
hast laid up for those who f. thee, 31.19
Let all the earth f. the LORD, 33.08
of the LORD is on those who f. him, 33.18
encamps around those who f. him, 34.07
O f. the LORD, you his saints, for 34.09
for those who f. him have no want! 34.09
will teach you the f. of the LORD. 34.11
there is no f. of God before his 36.01
Many will see and f., and put their 40.03
Therefore we will not f. though the 46.02
Why should I f. in times of trouble, 49.05
and f., and shall laugh at him, 52.06
F. and trembling come upon me, and 55.05
keep no law, and do not f. God. 55.19
in God I trust without a f. What can 56.04
in God I trust without a f. What can 56.11
up a banner for those who f. thee, 60.04
heritage of those who f. thy name. 61.05
at him suddenly and without f. 64.04
Then all men will f.; they will tell 64.09
all you who f. God, and I will tell 66.16
all the ends of the earth f. him! 67.07
is at hand for those who f. him, 85.09
unite my heart to f. thy name. 86.11
wrath according to the f. of thee? 90.11
You will not f. the terror of the 91.05
The nations will f. the name of the 102.15
love toward those who f. him; 103.11
the LORD pities those who f. him. 103.13
everlasting upon those who f. him. 103.17
provides food for those who f. him; 111.05
The f. of the LORD is the beginning 111.10
You who f. the LORD, trust in the 115.11
he will bless those who f. the LORD, 115.13
Let those who f. the LORD say, "His 118.04
With the LORD on my side I do not f. 118.06
which is for those who f. thee. 119.38
I am a companion of all who f. thee, 119.63
Those who f. thee shall see me and 119.74
Let those who f. thee turn to me, 119.79
My flesh trembles for f. of thee, 119.120
You that f. the LORD, bless the LORD 135.20
the desire of all who f. him, 145.19
takes pleasure in those who f. him, 147.11
The f. of the LORD is the beginning Pro 1.07
did not choose the f. of the LORD, 1.29
understand the f. of the LORD and 2.05
f. the LORD, and turn away from evil. 3.07
The f. of the LORD is hatred of 8.13
The f. of the LORD is the beginning 9.10
The f. of the LORD prolongs life, 10.27
In the f. of the LORD one has 14.26
The f. of the LORD is a fountain of 14.27
little with the f. of the LORD 15.16
The f. of the LORD is instruction 15.33
and by the f. of the LORD a man 16.06
The f. of the LORD leads to life; 19.23
humility and f. of the LORD is 22.04
continue in the f. of the LORD all 23.17
My son, f. the LORD and the king, and 24.21
The f. of man lays a snare, but he 29.25
that men should f. before him. Ecc 3.14
words grow many: but do you f. God. 5.07
will be well with those who f. God, 8.12
God, because they f. before him; 8.12
because he does not f. before God. 8.13
F. God, and keep his commandments; 12.13
do not f., and do not let your Is 7.04
come there for f. of briers and 7.25
and melt in f. before Rezin and the 8.06
and do not f. what they f., nor be 8.12
let him be your f., and let him 8.13
knowledge and the f. of the LORD. 11.02
shall be in the f. of the LORD. 11.03
melt in f., O Philistia, all of you! 14.31
tremble with f. before the hand 19.16

FEAR (cont.)

mentioned will f. because of the Is 19.17
of ruthless nations will f. thee. 25.03
and their f. of me is a commandment 29.13
the f. of the LORD is his treasure. 33.06
a fearful heart, "Be strong, f. not! 35.04
good tidings, lift it up, f. not; 40.09
f. not, for I am with you, be not 41.10
say to you, "F. not, I will help you." 41.13
F. not, you worm Jacob, you men of 41.14
"F. not, for I have redeemed you; 43.01
F. not, for I am with you; I will bring 43.05
F. not, O Jacob my servant, Jeshurun 44.02
F. not, nor be afraid; have I not 44.08
f. not the reproach of men, and be 51.07
and f. continually all the day 51.13
"F. not, for you will not be ashamed; 54.04
oppression, for you shall not f.; 54.14
long time, and so you do not f. me? 57.11
long time, and so you do not f. me? 57.11
So they shall f. the name of the 59.19
our heart, so that we f. thee not? 63.17
the f. of me is not in you, says the Jer 2.19
her false sister Judah did not f., 3.08
Do you not f. me? says the LORD; 5.22
'Let us f. the LORD our God, who 5.24
Who would not f. thee, O King of the 10.07
and does not f. when heat comes, for 17.08
them, and they shall f. no more, 23.04
Did he not f. the LORD and entreat 26.19
"Then f. not, O Jacob my servant, 30.10
that they may f. me for ever, for 32.39
I will put the f. of me in their 32.40
they shall f. and tremble because 33.09
Jerusalem for f. of the army of 35.11
they turned one to another in f.; 36.16
Do not f. the king of Babylon, of 42.11
do not f. him, says the LORD, for I 42.11
sword which you f. shall overtake 42.16
"But f. not, O Jacob my servant, nor 46.27
F. not, O Jacob my servant, says the 46.28
they melt in f., they are troubled 49.23
thou didst say, 'Do not f.!' Lam 3.57
f. them not, nor be dismayed at Eze 3.09
so I will put f. in the land of 30.13
"I f. lest my lord the king, who Dan 1.10
men tremble and f. before the God 6.26
"F. not, Daniel, for from the first 10.12
f. not, peace be with you; be strong and of 10.19
shall come in f. to the LORD and Hos 3.05
for we f. not the LORD, and a king, 10.03
"F. not, O land; be glad and rejoice, Joe 2.21
F. not, you beasts of the field, for 2.22
who will not f.? Amo 3.08
and I f. the LORD, the God of heaven, Jon 1.09
it is sound wisdom to f. thy name: Mic 6.09
and they shall f. because of thee. 7.17
and thy work, O LORD, do I f. In the midst Hab 3.02
I said, 'Surely she will f. me, Zep 3.07
you shall f. evil no more. 3.15
to Jerusalem: "Do not f., O Zion; 3.16
My Spirit abides among you; f. not. Hag 2.05
F. not, but let your hands be strong." Zec 8.13
to the house of Judah; f. not. 8.15
if I am a master, where is my f.? Mal 1.06
gave them to him, that he might f.; 2.05
and do not f. me, says the LORD of 3.05
But for you who f. my name the sun 4.02
do not f. to take Mary your wife, Mt 1.20
"So have no f. of them; for nothing is 10.26
And do not f. those who kill the 10.28
rather f. him who can destroy both 10.28
F. not, therefore; you are of more 10.31
And they cried out for f. 14.26
"Take heart, it is I; have no f." 14.27
them, saying, "Rise, and have no f." 17.07
And for f. of him the guards 28.04
the tomb with f. and great joy, 28.08
came in f. and trembling and fell Mk 5.33
synagogue, "Do not f., only believe." 5.36
"Take heart, it is I; have no f." 6.50
he saw him, and f. fell upon him. Lk 1.12
is on those who f. him from generation 1.50
And f. came on all their neighbors. 1.65
hand of our enemies, might serve him without f., 1.74
them, and they were filled with f. 2.09
F. seized them all; and they glorified 7.16
for they were seized with great f.; 8.37
this answered him, "Do not f.; 8.50
do not f. those who kill the body, 12.04
But I will warn you whom to f.: 12.05
f. him who, after he has killed, has 12.05
yes, I tell you, f. him! 12.05
F. not; you are of more value 12.07
"F. not, little flock, for it is your 12.32
I neither f. God nor regard man, 18.04
men fainting with f. and with 21.26
"Do you not f. God, since you are 23.40
Yet for f. of the Jews no one spoke Jn 7.13
"F. not, daughter of Zion; behold, 12.15
but for f. of the Pharisees they 12.42
for f. of the Jews, asked Pilate 19.38
for f. of the Jews, Jesus came and 20.19
And f. came upon every soul; and many Ac 2.43
And great f. came upon all who 5.05
And great f. came upon the whole 5.11
walking in the f. of the Lord and 9.31
"Men of Israel, and you that f. God, listen. 13.16
and those among you that f. God, 13.26
trembling with f. he fell down 16.29
and f. fell upon them all; and the name 19.17
"There is no f. of God before their Rom 3.18
of slavery to fall back into f., 8.15
you have no f. of him who is in 13.03
and in much f. and trembling; 1Co 2.03
knowing the f. of the Lord, we 2Co 5.11
holiness perfect in the f. of God. 7.01
turn—fighting without and f. within. 7.05
and the f. and trembling with which 7.15
For I f. that perhaps I may come 12.20
I f. that when I come again my God 12.21
with f. and trembling, in singleness Eph 6.05
speak the word of God without f. Php 1.14
salvation with f. and trembling; 2.12
for f. that somehow the tempter had 1Th 3.05
so that the rest may stand in f. 1Ti 5.20
who through f. of death were Heb 2.15
let us f. lest any of you be judged 4.01
and he was heard for his godly f. 5.07
that Moses said, "I tremble with f." 12.21
yourselves with f. throughout the 1Pe 1.17
F. God. Honor the emperor. 2.17
Have no f. of them, nor be troubled, 3.14
There is no f. in love, but perfect 1Jn 4.18
but perfect love casts out f. 4.18
For f. has to do with punishment, 4.18
on some have mercy with f., Jud 1.23
"F. not, I am the first and the last, Rev 1.17
Do not f. what you are about to 2.10
and great f. fell on those who saw 11.11
and those who f. thy name, both 11.18
"F. God and give him glory, for the 14.07
Who shall not f. and glorify thy 15.04
in f. of her torment, and say, "Alas! 18.10
in f. of her torment, weeping and 18.15
you who f. him, small and great." 19.05

FEARED

for he f. to say, "My wife," thinking, Gen 26.07
for he f. that he would die, like 38.11
for he f. that harm might befall 42.04
But the midwives f. God, and did not Ex 1.17
the midwives f. God he gave them 1.21
Then he who f. the word of the LORD 9.20

FEARED (cont.)
Egyptians, and the people f. the LORD; Ex 14.31
had I not f. provocation by the Deu 32.27
so we f. greatly for our lives Jos 9.24
he f. greatly, because Gibeon was a 10.02
people greatly f. the LORD and 1Sa 12.18
his mouth; for the people f. the oath. 14.26
because I f. the people and obeyed 15.24
for he f. greatly. Therefore Saul 31.04
another word, because he f. him. 2Sa 3.11
So the Syrians f. to help the 10.19
of David f. to tell him that the 12.18
And Adonijah f. Solomon; and he arose 1Ki 1.50
know that your servant f. the LORD, 2Ki 4.01
of Egypt, and had f. other gods 17.07
They also f. the LORD, and appointed 17.32
So they f. the LORD but also served 17.33
So these nations f. the LORD, and also 17.41
for he f. greatly. Therefore Saul took 1Ch 10.04
Then Jehoshaphat f., and set himself 2Ch 20.03
one who f. God, and turned away from Job 1.01
judgment; the earth f. and was still, Ps 76.08
gifts to him who is to be f., 76.11
a God f. in the council of the holy 89.07
he is to be f. above all gods. 96.04
with thee, that thou mayest be f. 130.04
to a people f. near and far, a Is 18.02
from a people f. near and far, a 18.07
nor have they f., nor walked in my Jer 44.10
You have f. the sword; and I will bring Eze 11.08
languages trembled and f. before him; Dan 5.19
Then the men f. the LORD exceedingly, Jon 1.16
and the people f. before the LORD. Hag 1.12
of hosts, and my name is f. among the Mal 1.14
and he f. me, he stood in awe of my 2.05
Then those who f. the LORD spoke 3.16
of those who f. the LORD and 3.16
he f. the people, because they held Mt 14.05
they f. the multitudes, because they 21.46
for Herod f. John, knowing that he Mk 6.20
for they f. him, because all the 11.18
but f. the multitude, for they 12.12
who neither f. God nor regarded Lk 18.02
very hour, but they f. the people; 20.19
put him to death; for they f. the people. 22.02
said this because they f. the Jews, Jn 9.22
a devout man who f. God with all Ac 10.02

FEARFUL
there that is f. and fainthearted? Deu 20.08
'Whoever is f. and trembling, let Ju 7.03
for thou art f. and wonderful. Ps 139.14
Say to those who are of a f. heart, Is 35.04
and be not f. at the report heard Jer 51.46
and he shall cause f. destruction, Dan 8.24
but a f. prospect of judgment, and a Heb 10.27
It is a f. thing to fall into the 10.31
plague of the hail, so f. was that plague. Rev 16.21

FEARFULLY
radiant appearance was f. changed, Dan 10.08

FEARFULNESS
eat bread by weight and with f.; Eze 4.16
water with trembling and with f.; 12.18
They shall eat their bread with f., 12.19

FEARING
walking in his ways and by f. him. Deu 8.06
then, f. that they should run on the Ac 27.17
And f. that we might run on the 27.29
himself, f. the circumcision party. Gal 2.12
singleness of heart, f. the Lord. Col 3.22

FEARS
"Behold, Adonijah f. King Solomon; 1Ki 1.51
who f. God and turns away from evil?" Job 1.08
who f. God and turns away from evil? 2.03
Who is the man that f. the LORD? Ps 25.12
and delivered me from all my f. 34.04
Blessed is the man who f. the LORD, 112.01
Blessed is every one who f. the LORD, 128.01
the man be blessed who f. the LORD. 128.04
walks in uprightness f. the LORD, Pro 14.02
Blessed is the man who f. the LORD 28.14
but a woman who f. the LORD is to 31.30
for he who f. God shall come forth Ecc 7.18
Who among you f. the LORD and obeys Is 50.10
them, and bring their f. upon them; 66.04
and f., and does not do likewise, Eze 18.14
any one who f. him and does what Ac 10.35
and he who f. is not perfected in 1Jn 4.18

FEAST
and he made them a f., and baked Gen 19.03
made a great f. on the day that 21.08
So he made them a f., and they ate 26.30
the men of the place and made a f. 29.22
he made a f. for all his servants, 40.20
they may hold a f. to me in the Ex 5.01
for we must hold a f. to the LORD." 10.09
shall keep it as a f. to the LORD; 12.14
observe the f. of unleavened bread, 12.17
there shall be a f. to the LORD. 13.06
the year you shall keep a f. to me. 23.14
You shall keep the f. of unleavened 23.15
You shall keep the f. of harvest, 23.16
shall keep the f. of ingathering 23.16
the fat of my f. remain until the 23.18
"Tomorrow shall be a f. to the LORD." 32.05
"The f. of unleavened bread you 34.18
And you shall observe the f. of weeks, 34.22
and the f. of ingathering at the 34.22
sacrifice of the f. of the passover 34.25
month is the f. of unleavened Lev 23.06
days is the f. of booths to the 23.34
shall keep the f. of the LORD 23.39
keep it as a f. to the LORD seven 23.41
fifteenth day of this month is a f.; Num 28.17
to the LORD at your f. of weeks, 28.26
shall keep a f. to the LORD seven 29.12
shall keep the f. of weeks to the Deu 16.10
"You shall keep the f. of booths 16.13
you shall rejoice in your f., 16.14
shall keep the f. to the LORD your 16.15
at the f. of unleavened bread, at 16.16
f. of weeks, and at the f. of booths. 16.16
of release, at the f. of booths, 31.10
woman, and Samson made a f. there; Ju 14.10
within the seven days of the f., 14.12
seven days that their f. lasted; 14.17
is the yearly f. of the LORD at 21.19
for we come on a f. day. Pray, give 1Sa 25.08
he was holding a f. in his house, 25.36
his house, like the f. of a king. 25.36
David made a f. for Abner and the 2Sa 3.20
and made a f. for all his servants. 1Ki 3.15
Solomon at the f. in the month 8.02
So Solomon held the f. at that time, 8.65
appointed a f. on the fifteenth 12.32
month like the f. that was in 12.32
he ordained a f. for the people of 12.33
So he prepared fro them a great f.; 2Ki 6.23
and f. days, according to the number 1Ch 23.31
the king at the f. which is in the 2Ch 5.03
Solomon held the f. for seven days, 7.08
seven days and the f. seven days. 7.09
the f. of unleavened bread, the 8.13
f. of weeks, and the f. of tabernacles. 8.13
to keep the f. of unleavened bread 30.13
kept the f. of unleavened bread 30.21
to keep the f. for another seven 30.23
and the f. of unleavened bread 35.17
And they kept the f. of booths, Ez 3.04
And they kept the f. of unleavened 6.22
during the f. of the seventh month, Neh 8.14

FEAST (cont.)
They kept the f. seven days; Neh 8.18
went in to f. with Queen Esther. Est 7.01
rose from the f. in wrath and went 7.07
among the Jews, a f. and a holiday. 8.17
go and hold a f. in the house of Job 1.04
the days of the f. had run their 1.05
They f. on the abundance of thy Ps 36.08
at the full moon, on our f. day. 81.03
cheerful heart has a continual f. Pro 15.15
and your princes f. in the morning! Ecc 10.16
your princes f. at the proper time, 10.17
for all peoples a f. of fat things, Is 25.06
a f. of wine on the lees, of fat 25.06
the night when a holy f. is kept; 30.29
I will f. the soul of the priests Jer 31.14
prepare them a f. and make them 51.39
in Zion appointed f. and sabbath, Lam 2.06
as on the day of an appointed f. 2.07
of an appointed f. my terrors on 2.22
detestable things your eyes f. on, Eze 20.07
before kings, to f. their eyes on you. 28.17
the sacrificial f. which I am 39.17
sacrificial f. upon the mountains 39.17
the sacrificial f. which I am 39.19
celebrate the f. of the passover, 45.21
and for the seven days of the f., 45.25
made a great f. for a thousand of Dan 5.01
her for the f. days of the Baals Hos 2.13
on the day of the f. of the LORD? 9.05
as in the days of the appointed f. 12.09
and to keep the f. of booths. Zec 14.16
not go up to keep the f. of booths. 14.18
not go up to keep the f. of booths. 14.19
gave a marriage f. for his son, Mt 22.02
were invited to the marriage f.; 22.03
is ready; come to the marriage f.' 22.04
to the marriage f. as many as you 22.09
in with him to the marriage f.; 25.10
But they said, "Not during the f., 26.05
Now at the f. the governor was 27.15
Passover and the f. of Unleavened Mk 14.01
for they said, "Not during the f., 14.02
Now at the f. he used to release 15.06
year at the f. of the Passover. Lk 2.41
and when the f. was ended, as they 2.43
made him a great f. in his house; 5.29
to come home from the marriage f., 12.36
by any one to a marriage f., do not sit 14.08
But when you give a f., invite the poor, 14.13
Now the f. of Unleavened Bread drew 22.01
take it to the steward of the f." Jn 2.08
steward of the f. tasted the water 2.09
steward of the f. called the 2.09
in Jerusalem at the Passover f., 2.23
he had done in Jerusalem at the f., 4.45
for they too had gone to the f. 4.45
After this there was a f. of the Jews, 5.01
the f. of the Jews, was at hand. 6.04
Now the Jews' f. of Tabernacles was 7.02
Go to the f. yourselves; 7.08
I am not going up to the f., 7.08
his brothers had gone up to the f., 7.10
were looking for him at the f., 7.11
middle of the f. Jesus went up 7.14
On the last day of the f., 7.37
It was the f. of the Dedication at 10.22
That he will not come to the f.?" 11.56
had come to the f. heard that 12.12
worship at the f. were some Greeks. 12.20
Now before the f. of the Passover, 13.01
him, "Buy what we need for the f."; 13.29
"Let their f. become a snare and a Rom 11.09

FEASTED
My soul is f. as with marrow and Ps 63.05
Those who f. on dainties perish in Lam 4.05
detestable things their eyes f. on, Eze 20.08
linen and who f. sumptuously every Lk 16.19

FEASTING
him heard it as they finished f. 1Ki 1.41
made that a day of f. and gladness. Est 9.17
that a day of f. and gladness. 9.18
gladness and f. and holiday-making, 9.19
make them days of f. and gladness, 9.22
a house full of f. with strife. Pro 17.01
than to go to the house of f.; Ecc 7.02
the house of f. to sit with them, Jer 16.08

FEASTS
The appointed f. of the LORD which Lev 23.02
convocations, my appointed f., are these. 23.02
"These are the appointed f. of the LORD, 23.04
"These are the appointed f. of the LORD, 23.37
of Israel the appointed f. of the LORD. 23.44
also, and at your appointed f., Num 10.10
offering or at your appointed f., 15.03
to the LORD at your appointed f., 29.39
the appointed f. of the LORD our 2Ch 2.04
moons, and the three annual f.— 8.13
new moons, and the appointed f., 31.03
all the appointed f. of the LORD, Ez 3.05
the appointed f., the holy things, Neh 10.33
let their sacrificial f. be a trap. Ps 69.22
your appointed f. my soul hates; Is 1.14
and flute and wine at their f.; 5.12
to year; let the f. run their round. 29.01
Zion, the city of our appointed f.! 33.20
for none come to the appointed f.; Lam 1.04
the place of his appointed f.; 2.06
Jerusalem during her appointed f., Eze 36.38
my statutes in all my appointed f., 44.24
at the f., the new moons, and the 45.17
the appointed f. of the house of 45.17
the LORD at the appointed f., he who 46.09
"At the f. and the appointed seasons 46.11
her f., her new moons, her sabbaths, Hos 2.11
sabbaths, and all her appointed f. 2.11
"I hate, I despise your f., and I take Amo 5.21
I will turn your f. into mourning, 8.10
Keep your f., O Judah, fulfil your Nah 1.15
joy and gladness, and cheerful f.; Zec 8.19
of honor at f. and the best seats Mt 23.06
and the places of honor at f., Mk 12.39
and the places of honor at f., Lk 20.46
These are blemishes on your love f., Jud 1.12

FEATHERS
take away its crop with the f., Lev 1.16
hair grew as long as eagles' f., Dan 4.33

FED
and Jacob f. the rest of Laban's Gen 30.36
and fat, and they f. in the reed grass. 41.02
out of the Nile and f. in the reed 41.18
with which I f. you in the wilderness, Ex 16.32
you hunger and f. you with manna, Deu 8.03
who f. you in the wilderness with 8.16
and f. them with bread and water.) 1Ki 18.04
and f. them with bread and water? 18.13
Thou hast f. them with the bread of Ps 80.05
of rams and the fat of f. beasts; Is 1.11
When I f. them to the full, they Jer 5.07
I f. you with fine flour and oil Eze 16.19
the shepherds have f. themselves, 34.08
themselves, and have not f. my sheep; 34.08
branches, and all flesh was f. from it. Dan 4.12
he was f. grass like an ox, and his 5.21
I bent down to them and f. them. Hos 11.04
but when they had f. to the full, 13.06
her, "Let the children first be f., Mk 7.27
gladly have f. on the pods that Lk 15.16
who desired to be f. with what fell 16.21
I f. you with milk, not solid food; 1Co 3.02

FEEBLE

broken, but the f. gird on strength. 1Sa 2.04
carrying all the f. among them on 2Ch 28.15
"What are these f. Jews doing? Neh 4.02
you have made firm the f. knees. Job 4.04
Therefore all hands will be f., Is 13.07
survive will be very few and f. 16.14
hands, and make firm the f. knees. 35.03
their children, so f. are their hands, Jer 47.03
Damascus has become f., 49.24
All hands are f., and all knees Eze 7.17
will melt and all hands will be f., 21.07

FEEBLER

but for the f. of the flock he did Gen 30.42
so the f. were Laban's, and the 30.42

FEEBLEST

so that the f. among them on that Zec 12.08

FEED

I will again f. your flock and keep Gen 30.31
flocks or herds f. before that Ex 34.03
from Saul to f. his father's sheep 1Sa 17.15
commanded the ravens to f. you there." 1Ki 17.04
commanded a widow there to f. you." 17.09
and f. him with scant fare of bread 22.27
and f. him with scant fare of bread 2Ch 18.26
"They f. on the barren childless Job 24.21
that move in the field f. on it. Ps 80.13
I would f. you with the finest of 81.16
The lips of the righteous f. many, Pro 10.21
the mouths of fools f. on folly. 15.14
f. me with the food that is needful 30.08
of a gazelle, that f. among the lilies. Sol 4.05
and kids shall f. among the ruins. Is 5.17
The cow and the bear shall f.; 11.07
the first-born of the poor will f., 14.30
He will f. his flock like a shepherd, 40.11
They shall f. along the ways, on 49.09
I will f. you with the heritage of 58.14
Aliens shall stand and f. your flocks, 61.05
and the lamb shall f. together, 65.25
who will f. you with knowledge and Jer 3.15
I will f. this people with wormwood, 9.15
I will f. them with wormwood, and 23.15
and he shall f. on Carmel and in 50.19
should not shepherds f. the sheep? Eze 34.02
fatlings; but you do not f. the sheep. 34.03
shall the shepherds f. themselves. 34.10
and I will f. them on the mountains 34.13
I will f. them with good pasture, 34.14
they shall f. on the mountains of 34.14
watch over; I will f. them in justice. 34.16
for you to f. on the good pasture, 34.18
and he shall f. them: he shall f. them 34.23
They f. on the sin of my people; Hos 4.08
the LORD now f. them like a lamb 4.16
and winevat shall not f. them, 9.02
let them not f., or drink water, Jon 3.07
shall stand and f. his flock in Mic 5.04
let them f. in Bashan and Gilead as 7.14
the desert to f. so great a crowd?" Mt 15.33
did we see thee hungry and f. thee, 25.37
"How can one f. these men with Mk 8.04
him into his fields to f. swine. Lk 15.15
He said to him, "F. my lambs." Jn 21.15
Jesus said to him, "F. my sheep. 21.17
to f. the church of the Lord which Ac 20.28
No, "if your enemy is hungry, f. him; Rom 12.20

FEEDING

and the asses f. beside them; Job 1.14
Israel who have been f. yourselves! Eze 34.02
put a stop to their f. the sheep; 34.10
many swine was f. at some distance Mt 8.30
of swine was f. there on the hillside; Mk 5.11
of swine was f. there on the hillside; Lk 8.32

FEEDS

loose and it f. in another man's Ex 22.05
He f. on ashes; a deluded mind Is 44.20
yet your heavenly Father f. them. Mt 6.26
nor barn, and yet God f. them. Lk 12.24

FEEL

Perhaps my father will f. me, Gen 27.12
that I may f. you, my son, to know 27.21
"Let me f. the pillars on which the Ju 16.26
your pots can f. the heat of Ps 58.09
They have hands, but do not f.; 115.07
they beat me, but I did not f. it. Pro 23.35
on them, that they may f. it." Jer 10.18
to those who f. secure on the Amo 6.01
that they might f. after him and Ac 17.27
I f. a divine jealousy for you, for 2Co 11.02
right for me to f. thus about you Php 1.07
joy which we f. for your sake 1Th 3.09
we f. sure of better things that Heb 6.09

FEELS

He f. only the pain of his own body, Job 14.22

FEES

with the f. for divination in Num 22.07

FEET

and wash your f., and rest yourselves Gen 18.04
spend the night, and wash your f.; 19.02
to wash his f. and the f. of the men 24.32
and they had washed their f., 43.24
ruler's staff from between his f., 49.10
he drew up his f. into the bed, 49.33
put off your shoes from your f., Ex 3.05
and touched Moses' f. with it, 4.25
girded, your sandals on your f., 12.11
was under his f. as it were a 24.10
for it and put them on its four f., 25.12
the great toes of their right f., 29.20
wash their hands and their f. 30.19
wash their hands and their f., 30.21
washed their hands and their f.; 40.31
the great toes of their right f.; Lev 8.24
which have legs above their f., 11.21
which have four f. are an abomination 11.23
all fours, or whatever has many f., 11.42
seed and watered it with your f., Deu 11.10
between her f. and her children 28.57
sandals have not worn off your f.; 29.05
soles of the f. of the priests who Jos 3.13
and the f. of the priests bearing 3.15
place where the priests' f. stood, 4.03
place where the f. of the priests 4.09
of the priests' f. were lifted up 4.18
"Put off your shoes from your f.; 5.15
patched sandals on their f., 9.05
put your f. upon the necks of these 10.24
and put their f. on their necks. 10.24
he fell, he lay still at her f.; Ju 5.27
at her f. he sank, he fell; where he 5.27
and they washed their f., and ate 19.21
go and uncover his f. and lie down; Ru 3.04
and uncovered his f., and lay down. 3.07
and behold, a woman lay at his f.! 3.08
So she lay at his f. until the 3.14
"He will guard the f. of his 1Sa 2.09
climbed up on his hands and f., 14.13
She fell at his f. and said, 25.24
to wash the f. of the servants of 25.41
your f. were not fettered; 2Sa 3.34
a son who was crippled in his f. 4.04
and cut off their hands and f., 4.12
he is crippled in his f." 9.03
Now he was lame in both his f. 9.13
to your house, and wash your f." 11.08
he had neither dressed his f., 19.24

FEET (cont.)
thick darkness was under his f. 2Sa 22.10
He made my f. like hinds' f., and 22.34
under me, and my f. did not slip; 22.37
did not rise; they fell under my f. 22.39
and upon the sandals of my f. 1Ki 2.05
put them under the soles of his f. 5.03
Ahijah heard the sound of her f., 14.06
When your f. enter the city, the 14.12
old age he was diseased in his f. 15.23
of God, she caught hold of his f. 2Ki 4.27
She came and fell at his f., bowing 4.37
of his master's f. behind him?" 6.32
skull and the f. and the palms of 9.35
he revived, and stood on his f. 13.21
not cause the f. of Israel to 21.08
King David rose to his f. and said: 1Ch 28.02
the cherubim stood on their f., facing 2Ch 3.13
reign Asa was diseased in his f., 16.12
wear out and their f. did not swell. Neh 9.21
she fell at his f. and besought him Est 8.03
is ready for those whose f. slip. Job 12.05
Thou puttest my f. in the stocks, 13.27
a bound to the soles of my f. 13.27
is cast into a net by his own f., 18.08
to the blind, and f. to the lame. 29.15
he puts my f. in the stocks, and 33.11
kiss his f., lest he be angry, and Ps 2.12
hast put all things under his f., 8.06
thy paths, my f. have not slipped. 17.05
thick darkness was under his f. 18.09
He made my f. like hinds' f., and 18.33
under me, and my f. did not slip. 18.36
able to rise; they fell under my f. 18.38
have pierced my hands and f.— 22.16
he will pluck my f. out of the net. 25.15
hast set my f. in a broad place. 31.08
and set my f. upon a rock, making my 40.02
under us, and nations under our f. 47.03
my f. from falling, that I may walk 56.13
will bathe his f. in the blood of 58.10
living, and has not let our f. slip. 66.09
that you may bathe your f. in blood, 68.23
my f. had almost stumbled, my steps 73.02
His f. were hurt with fetters, his 105.18
f., but do not walk; and they do 115.07
from tears, my f. from stumbling; 116.08
I turn my f. to thy testimonies; 119.59
I hold back my f. from every evil 119.101
is a lamp to my f. and a light to 119.105
Our f. have been standing within 122.02
who have planned to trip up my f. 140.04
for their f. run to evil, and they Pro 1.16
Take heed to the path of your f., 4.26
Her f. go down to death; her steps 5.05
with his eyes, scrapes with his f., 6.13
f. that make haste to run to evil, 6.18
coals and his f. not be scorched? 6.28
wayward, her f. do not stay at home; 7.11
haste with his f. misses his way. 19.02
off his own f. and drinks violence. 26.06
neighbor spreads a net for his f. 29.05
I had bathed my f., how could I Sol 5.03
How graceful are your f. in sandals, 7.01
as they go, tinkling with their f.; Is 3.16
and with two he covered his f., 6.02
the head and the hair of the f., 7.20
take off your shoes from your f., 20.02
whose f. carried her to settle afar? 23.07
the f. of the poor, the steps of the 26.06
who let the f. of the ox and the 32.20
by paths his f. have not trod. 41.03
you, and lick the dust of your f. 49.23
mountains are the f. of him who 52.07
Their f. run to evil, and they make 59.07
make the place of my f. glorious. 60.13
you shall bow down at your f.; 60.14
Keep your f. from going unshod and Jer 2.25
before your f. stumble on the 13.16
they have not restrained their f.; 14.10
take me, and laid snares for my f. 18.22
now that your f. are sunk in the 38.22
he spread a net for my f.; he turned Lam 1.13
soles of their f. were like the Eze 1.07
me, "Son of man, stand upon your f., 2.01
into me and set me upon my f.; 2.02
into me, and set me upon my f.; 3.24
and put your shoes on your f.; 24.17
heads and your shoes on your f.; 24.23
stamped your f. and rejoiced with 25.06
trouble the waters with your f., 32.02
down with your f. the rest of your 34.18
must foul the rest with your f.? 34.18
what you have trodden with your f., 34.19
what you have fouled with your f.? 34.19
lived, and stood upon their f., 37.10
the place of the soles of my f., 43.07
its f. partly of iron and partly of Dan 2.33
image on its f. of iron and clay, 2.34
And as you saw the f. and toes 2.41
the toes of the f. were partly 2.42
to stand upon two f. like a man; 7.04
stamped the residue with its f. 7.07
stamped the residue with its f.; 7.19
he touched me and set me on my f. 8.18
the clouds are the dust of his f. Nah 1.03
mountains the f. of him who brings 1.15
he makes my f. like hinds' f., he Hab 3.19
On that day his f. shall stand on Zec 14.04
while they are still on their f., 14.12
ashes under the soles of your f., Mal 4.03
dust from your f. as you leave Mt 10.14
and they put them at his f., and he 15.30
hands or two f. to be thrown into 18.08
I put thy enemies under thy f.'? 22.44
hold of his f. and worshiped him. 28.09
and seeing him, he fell at his f., Mk 5.22
that is on your f. for a testimony 6.11
and came and fell down at his f. 7.25
than with two f. to be thrown into 9.45
I put thy enemies under thy f.' 12.36
to guide our f. into the way of Lk 1.79
and standing behind him at his f., 7.38
began to wet his f. with her tears, 7.38
of her head, and kissed his f., 7.38
you gave me no water for my f., 7.44
she has wet my f. with her tears 7.44
she has not ceased to kiss my f. 7.45
has anointed my f. with ointment. 7.46
gone, sitting at the f. of Jesus, 8.35
at Jesus' f. he besought him to 8.41
dust from your f. as a testimony 9.05
of your town that clings to our f., 10.11
at the Lord's f. and listened to 10.39
on his hand, and shoes on his f.; 15.22
and he fell on his face at Jesus' f., 17.16
thy enemies a stool for thy f.' 20.43
See my hands and my f., that it is I 24.39
he showed them his hands and his f. * 24.40
and wiped his f. with her hair, Jn 11.02
fell at his f., saying to him, "Lord, 11.32
his hands and f. bound with bandages, 11.44
the f. of Jesus and wiped his f. 12.03
began to wash the disciples' f., 13.05
to him, "Lord, do you wash my f.?" 13.06
to him, "You shall never wash my f." 13.08
not my f. only but also my hands 13.09
need to wash, except for his f., 13.10
When he had washed their f., and taken 13.12
and Teacher, have washed your f., 13.14
ought to wash one another's f. 13.14
one at the head and one at the f. 20.12
thy enemies a stool for thy f.' Ac 2.35
immediately his f. and ankles were 3.07

FEET (cont.)

and laid it at the apostles' f.; Ac 4.35
and laid it at the apostles' f. 4.37
and laid it at the apostles' f. 5.02
Hark, the f. of those that have 5.09
Immediately she fell down at his f. and died. 5.10
'Take off the shoes from your f., 7.33
garments at the f. of a young man 7.58
down at his f. and worshiped him. 10.25
of whose f. I am not worthy to 13.25
dust from their f. against them, 13.51
sitting, who could not use his f.; 14.08
voice, "Stand upright on your f." 14.10
fastened their f. in the stocks. 16.24
and bound his own f. and hands, 21.11
in this city at the f. of Gamaliel, 22.03
But rise and stand upon your f.; 26.16
"Their f. are swift to shed blood, Rom 3.15
beautiful are the f. of those who 10.15
soon crush Satan under your f. 16.20
you," nor again the head to the f., 1Co 12.21
put all his enemies under his f. 15.25
things in subjection under his f. 15.27
under his f. and has made him the Eph 1.22
shod your f. with the equipment of 6.15
washed the f. of the saints, relieved 1Ti 5.10
thy enemies a stool for thy f."? Heb 1.13
everything in subjection under his f. 2.08
should be made a stool for his f. 10.13
and make straight paths for your f., 12.13
"Stand there," or, "Sit at my f.," Jas 2.03
his f. were like burnished bronze, Rev 1.15
I fell at his f. as though dead. 1.17
and whose f. are like burnished 2.18
come and bow down before your f., 3.09
and they stood up on their f., and great 11.11
sun, with the moon under her f., 12.01
its f. were like a bear's, and its 13.02
fell down at his f. to worship him, 19.10
worship at the f. of the angel who 22.08

FEIGNED

and f. himself mad in their hands, 1Sa 21.13

FELIX

him safely to F. the governor. Ac 23.24
Excellency the governor F., greeting. 23.26
your provision, most excellent F., 24.02
But F., having a rather accurate 24.22
After some days F. came with his 24.24
F. was alarmed and said, "Go away 24.25
F. was succeeded by Porcius Festus; 24.27
a favor F. left Paul in prison. 24.27
"There is a man left prisoner by F.; 25.14

FELL

very angry, and his countenance f. Gen 4.05
And rain f. upon the earth forty 7.12
some f. into them, and the rest fled 14.10
down, a deep sleep f. on Abram; 15.12
and great darkness f. upon him. 15.12
Then Abram f. on his face; and God 17.03
Then Abraham f. on his face and 17.17
and f. on his neck and kissed him, 33.04
terror from God f. upon the cities 35.05
And he f. asleep and dreamed a 41.05
and they f. before him to the 44.14
Then he f. upon his brother Benjamin's 45.14
and f. on his neck, and wept on his 46.29
Then Joseph f. on his father's face, 50.01
also came and f. down before him, 50.18
and there f. of the people that day Ex 32.28
shouted, and f. on their faces. Lev 9.24
on which the lot f. for the LORD, 16.09
which the lot f. for Azazel shall 16.10
When the dew f. upon the camp in Num 11.09
in the night, the manna f. with it. 11.09
Then Moses and Aaron f. on their 14.05
When Moses heard it, he f. on his face; 16.04
And they f. on their faces, and said, 16.22
a moment." And they f. on their faces. 16.45
of meeting, and f. on their faces. 20.06
bowed his head, and f. on his face. 22.31
And Joshua f. on his face to the Jos 5.14
and the wall f. down flat, so that 6.20
and f. to the earth upon his face 7.06
And all who f. that day, both men 8.25
waters of Merom, and f. upon them. 11.07
Thus there f. to Manasseh ten portions, 17.05
allotted to it f. between the tribe of 18.11
since the lot f. to them first. 21.10
and wrath f. upon all the congregation 22.20
army of Sisera f. by the edge of Ju 4.16
He sank, he f., he lay still at her 5.27
at her feet he sank, he f.; 5.27
where he sank, there he f. dead. 5.27
tent, and struck it so that it f., 7.13
and many f. wounded, up to the 9.40
And there f. at that time forty-two 12.06
and they f. on their faces to the 13.20
and the house f. upon the lords and 16.30
woman came and f. down at the door 19.26
Eighteen thousand men of Benjamin f., 20.44
So all who f. that day of Benjamin 20.46
Then she f. on her face, bowing to Ru 2.10
for there f. of Israel thirty 1Sa 4.10
Eli f. over backward from his seat 4.18
of the LORD f. upon the people, and 11.07
And they f. before Jonathan, and his 14.13
and he f. on his face to the ground. 17.49
wounded Philistines f. on the way from 17.52
stone heap and f. on his face to 20.41
turned and f. upon the priests, and 22.18
and f. before David on her face, and 25.23
She f. at his feet and said, "Upon 25.24
Then Saul f. at once full length 28.20
because I f. sick three days ago. 30.13
Philistines, and f. slain on Mount Gilboa. 31.01
took his own sword, and f. upon it. 31.04
he also f. upon his sword, and died 31.05
he f. to the ground and did obeisance 2Sa 1.02
so they f. down together. Therefore 2.16
and he f. there, and died where he 2.23
he f., and became lame. And his name 4.04
and f. on his face and did obeisance. 9.06
of David among the people f. 11.17
she f. on her face to the ground, 14.04
And Joab f. on his face to the 14.22
the son of Gera f. down before the 19.18
and as he went forward it f. out. 20.08
until rain f. upon them from the 21.10
and they f. by the hand of David 21.22
did not rise; they f. under my feet. 22.39
Abijah the son of Jeroboam f. sick. 1Ki 14.01
and f. on his face, and said, "Is it 18.07
Then the fire of the LORD f., and consumed 18.38
saw it, they f. on their faces; 18.39
and the wall f. upon twenty-seven 20.30
Now Ahaziah f. through the lattice 2Ki 1.02
and came and f. on his knees before 1.13
and shall f. every good tree, and 3.19
She came and f. at his feet, bowing 4.37
his axe head f. into the water; 6.05
the Hagrites, who f. by their hand; 1Ch 5.10
For many f. slain, because the war 5.22
Philistines, and f. slain on Mount Gilboa. 10.01
took his own sword, and f. upon it. 10.04
he also f. upon his sword, and died. 10.05
and they f. by the hand of David 20.08
and there f. seventy thousand men 21.14
in sackcloth, f. upon their faces. 21.16
The first lot f. to Jehoiarib, the 24.07
The first lot f. for Asaph to 25.09
The lot for the east f. to Shelemiah. 26.14

FELL (cont.)
so there f. slain of Israel five 2Ch 13.17
the Ethiopians f. until none remained 14.13
of the LORD f. upon all the kingdoms 17.10
of Jerusalem f. down before the 20.18
f. upon the cities of Judah, from 25.13
and f. upon my knees and spread out Ez 9.05
were afraid and f. greatly in Neh 6.16
she f. at his feet and besought him Est 8.03
and the Sabeans f. upon them and Job 1.15
"The fire of God f. from heaven and 1.16
and it f. upon the young people, and 1.19
and f. upon the ground, and worshiped. 1.20
able to rise; they f. under my feet. Ps 18.38
kings there, snow f. on Zalmon. 68.14
Their priests f. by the sword, and 78.64
they f. down, with none to help. 107.12
Your multitude stumbled and f., Jer 46.16
with axes, like those who f. trees. 46.22
of them, and his hands f. helpless; 50.43
When her people f. into the hand of Lam 1.07
I f. upon my face, and I heard the Eze 1.28
river Chebar; and I f. on my face. 3.23
of the Lord GOD f. there upon me. 8.01
I f. upon my face, and cried, "Ah 9.08
And the Spirit of the LORD f. upon me, 11.05
Then I f. down upon my face, and 11.13
and they all f. by the sword. 39.23
river Chebar; and I f. upon my face. 43.03
of the LORD; and I f. upon my face. 44.04
Nebuchadnezzar f. upon his face, Dan 2.46
and languages f. down and worshiped 3.07
f. bound into the burning fiery 3.23
there f. a voice from heaven, "O 4.31
and before which three of them f., 7.20
was frightened and f. upon my face. 8.17
I f. into a deep sleep with my face 8.18
but a great trembling f. upon them, 10.07
I f. on my face in a deep sleep 10.09
lots, and the lot f. upon Jonah. Jon 1.07
and they f. down and worshiped him. Mt 2.11
and the rain f., and the floods 7.25
and the rain f., and the floods 7.27
beat against that house, and it f.; 7.27
some seeds f. along the path, and 13.04
Other seeds f. on rocky ground, 13.05
Other seeds f. upon thorns, and the 13.07
Other seeds f. on good soil and 13.08
they f. on their faces, and were 17.06
So the servant f. on his knees, 18.26
fellow servant f. down and besought 18.29
farther he f. on his face and 26.39
they f. down before him and cried Mk 3.11
some seed f. along the path, and the 4.04
Other seed f. on rocky ground, where 4.05
Other seed f. among thorns and the 4.07
And other seeds f. into good soil 4.08
and seeing him, he f. at his feet, 5.22
trembling and f. down before him, 5.33
and came and f. down at his feet. 7.25
and he f. on the ground and rolled 9.20
At that saying his countenance f., 10.22
he f. on the ground and prayed that, 14.35
it f. to him by lot to enter the Lk 1.09
he saw him, and fear f. upon him. 1.12
he f. down at Jesus' knees, saying, 5.08
he f. on his face and besought him, 5.12
broke, and immediately it f., and the ruin 6.49
some f. along the path, and was 8.05
And some f. on the rock; and as it grew 8.06
And some f. among thorns; and the thorns 8.07
And some f. into good soil and grew, 8.08
And as for what f. among the thorns, 8.14
and as they sailed he f. asleep 8.23
cried out and f. down before him, 8.28
and he f. among robbers, who stripped 10.30
to the man who f. among the robbers?" 10.36
tower in Siloam f. and killed them, 13.04
fed with what f. from the rich 16.21
and he f. on his face at Jesus' 17.16
f. at his feet, saying to him, "Lord, Jn 11.32
drew back and f. to the ground. 18.06
them, and the lot f. on Matthias; Ac 1.26
these words, he f. down and died. 5.05
Immediately she f. down at his feet 5.10
he had said this, he f. asleep. 7.60
And he f. to the ground and heard a 9.04
like scales f. from his eyes and 9.18
In those days she f. sick and died; 9.37
preparing it, he f. into a trance 10.10
met him and f. down at his feet 10.25
the Holy Spirit f. on all who 10.44
the Holy Spirit f. on them just as 11.15
And the chains f. off his hands. 12.07
and darkness f. upon him and he 13.11
f. asleep, and was laid with his 13.36
with fear he f. down before Paul 16.29
and fear f. upon them all; and the 19.17
sacred stone that f. from the sky? 19.25
he f. down from the third story and 20.09
And I f. to the ground and heard a 22.07
in the temple, I f. into a trance 22.17
those who reproached thee f. on me. Rom 15.03
twenty-three thousand f. in a single day. 1Co 10.08
whose bodies f. in the wilderness? Heb 3.17
of Jericho f. down after they had 11.30
ever since the fathers f. asleep, 2Pe 3.04
I f. at his feet as though dead. Rev 1.17
twenty-four elders f. down before 5.08
and the elders f. down and 5.14
of the sky f. to the earth as the 6.13
and they f. on their faces before 7.11
with blood, which f. on the earth; 8.07
and a great star f. from heaven, 8.10
and it f. on a third of the rivers 8.10
and great fear f. on those who saw 11.11
earthquake, and a tenth of the city f.; 11.13
before God f. on their faces and 11.16
and the cities of the nations f., 16.19
creatures f. down and worshiped 19.04
Then I f. down at his feet to 19.10
I f. down to worship at the feet of 22.08

FELLED
and f. to the ground on that day Ju 20.21
and f. to the ground eighteen 20.25
and f. all the good trees; till only 2Ki 3.25
I f. its tallest cedars, its 19.23
remains standing when it is f. Is 6.13
I f. its tallest cedars, its choicest 37.24
for the thick forest has been f.! Zec 11.02

FELLING
But as one was f. a log, his axe 2Ki 6.05

FELLOW
"This f. came to sojourn, and he Gen 19.09
wrong, "Why do you strike your f.?" Ex 2.13
like all his f. Levites who stand to Deu 18.07
against his f. and against all the Ju 7.22
for all my f. townsmen know that Ru 3.11
man's sword was against his f., 1Sa 14.20
brought this f. to play the madman 21.15
Shall this f. come into my house?" 21.15
guarded all that this f. has in the 25.21
regard this ill-natured f., Nabal; 25.25
how could this f. reconcile himself 29.04
you man of blood, you worthless f.! 2Sa 16.07
happened to be there a worthless f., 20.01
said to his f. at the command of 1Ki 20.35
"Put this f. in prison, and feed him 22.27
Why did this mad f. come to you?" 2Ki 9.11
them, "You know the f. and his talk." 9.11

FELLOW (cont.)
Put this f. in prison, and feed him 2Ch 18.26
with his f. priests, and Zerubbabel Ez 3.02
for their f. priests, and for themselves; 6.20
they fall, one will lift up his f.; Ecc 4.10
every man his f. and every man his Is 3.05
and the base f. to the honorable. 3.05
the satyr shall cry to his f.; yea, there 34.14
set free the f. Hebrew who has been sold Jer 34.14
your f. exiles, the whole house of Eze 11.15
every one by the sword of his f. Hag 2.22
for I set every man against his f. Zec 8.10
lay hold on the hand of his f., and the 14.13
upon one of his f. servants who Mt 18.28
So his f. servant fell down and 18.29
When his f. servants saw what had 18.31
have had mercy on your f. servant, 18.33
and begins to beat his f. servants, 24.49
"This f. said, 'I am able to destroy 26.61
said to his f. disciples, "Let us Jn 11.16
"Away with such a f. from the earth! Ac 22.22
have found this man a pestilent f., 24.05
of God and f. heirs with Christ, Rom 8.17
in order to make my f. Jews jealous, 11.14
Aquila, my f. workers in Christ Jesus, 16.03
my kinsmen and my f. prisoners; they are 16.07
our f. worker in Christ, and my beloved 16.09
Timothy, my f. worker, greets you; 16.21
For we are f. workmen for God; you are 1Co 3.09
and to every f. worker and laborer. 16.16
my partner and f. worker in your 2Co 8.23
but you are f. citizens with the Eph 2.19
that is, how the Gentiles are f. heirs, 3.06
my brother and f. worker and f. soldier, Php 2.25
and the rest of my f. workers, whose names 4.03
Epaphras our beloved f. servant. He is Col 1.07
minister and f. servant in the Lord. 4.07
Aristarchus my f. prisoner greets 4.10
among my f. workers for the kingdom 4.11
To Philemon our beloved f. worker Phm 1.01
and Archippus our f. soldier, 1.02
Epaphras, my f. prisoner in Christ 1.23
Demas, and Luke, my f. workers. 1.24
every one his f. or every one his Heb 8.11
you foolish f., that faith apart Jas 2.20
as a f. elder and a witness of the 1Pe 5.01
that we may be f. workers in the 3Jn 1.08
number of their f. servants and Rev 6.11
I am a f. servant with you and your 19.10
I am a f. servant with you and your 22.09

FELLOWS
that certain base f. have gone out Deu 13.13
heart of his f. melt as his heart.' 20.08
hired worthless and reckless f., Ju 9.04
and worthless f. collected round 11.03
lest angry f. fall upon you, and you 18.25
base f., beset the house round 19.22
the base f. in Gibeah, that we may 20.13
But some worthless f. said, "How can 1Sa 10.27
wicked and base f. among the men 30.22
of the vulgar f. shamelessly uncovers 2Sa 6.20
and set two base f. opposite him, 1Ki 21.10
And the two base f. came in and sat 21.13
and the base f. brought a charge 21.13
and bid him rise from among his f., 2Ki 9.02
the oil of gladness above your f.; Ps 45.07
all his f. shall be put to shame, Is 44.11
which seemed greater than its f. Dan 7.20
some wicked f. of the rabble, they Ac 17.05

FELLOWSHIP
within God's house we walked in f. Ps 55.14
to the apostles' teaching and f., Ac 2.42
were called into the f. of his Son, 1Co 1.09
Or what f. has light with darkness? 2Co 6.14
of God and the f. of the Holy 13.14
and Barnabas the right hand of f., Gal 2.09
so that you may have f. with us; 1Jn 1.03
and our f. is with the Father and 1.03
If we say we have f. with him while 1.06
we have f. with one another, and the 1.07

FELT
who f. him and said, "The voice is Gen 27.22
Laban f. all about the tent, but did 31.34
Although you have f. through all my 31.37
land of Egypt, a darkness to be f." Ex 10.21
"Even if I f. in my hand the weight 2Sa 18.12
You f. secure in your wickedness, Is 47.10
them, but they f. no anguish; thou hast Jer 5.03
and she f. in her body that she was Mk 5.29
Why, we f. that we had received the 2Co 1.09
for I f. sure of all of you, that my 2.03
for you f. a godly grief, so that 7.09
become of the satisfaction you f.? Gal 4.15

FEMALE
male and f. he created them. Gen 1.27
Male and f. he created them, and he 5.02
with you, they shall be male and f. 6.19
male and f., to keep their kind 7.03
male and f., went into the ark with 7.09
male and f. of all flesh, went in as 7.16
and male and f. slaves, and gave 20.14
his wife and f. slaves so that 20.17
male or f., with a rod and the Ex 21.20
male or f., and destroys it, he 21.26
male or f., he shall let the slave 21.27
male or f., the owner shall give to 21.32
male or f., he shall offer it Lev 3.01
male or f., he shall offer it 3.06
a f. without blemish, for his sin 4.28
shall bring a f. without blemish, 4.32
a f. from the flock, a lamb or a 5.06
But if she bears a f. child, 12.05
bears a child, either male or f. 12.07
male or f., who has a discharge, and 15.33
your male and f. slaves and for 25.06
your male and f. slaves whom you 25.44
buy male and f. slaves from among 25.44
If the person is a f., your valuation 27.04
shekels, and for a f. ten shekels. 27.05
and for a f. your valuation shall 27.06
shekels, and for a f. ten shekels. 27.07
you shall put out both male and f., Num 5.03
shall offer a f. goat a year old 15.27
any figure, the likeness of male or f., Deu 4.16
not be male or f. barren among you, 7.14
your enemies as male and f. slaves, 28.68
male and f., as your slaves. Have you 2Ch 28.10
two hundred male and f. singers. Ez 2.65
forty-five singers, male and f. Neh 7.67
I bought male and f. slaves, and had Ecc 2.07
LORD's and as male and f. slaves; Is 14.02
male and f., so that no one should Jer 34.09
male or f., so that they would not 34.10
the male and f. slaves they had 34.11
took back his male and f. slaves, 34.16
beginning made them male and f., Mt 19.04
creation, 'God made them male and f.' Mk 10.06
free, there is neither male nor f.; Gal 3.28

FENCE
a leaning wall, a tottering f.? Ps 62.03

FENCES
settling on the f. in a day of Nah 3.17

FERMENTS
a little leaven f. the whole lump 1Co 5.06

FERTILE
land, and behold, it is very f. Ju 18.09
in the hills and in the f. lands, 2Ch 26.10

FERTILE (cont.)
had a vineyard on a very f. hill. Is 5.01
the land and planted it in f. soil; Eze 17.05

FERVENT
and being f. in spirit, he spoke and Ac 18.25

FERVENTLY
and he prayed f. that it might not Jas 5.17

FESTAL
all of them he gave f. garments; but to Gen 45.22
shekels of silver and five f. garments. 45.22
garments and thirty f. garments; Ju 14.12
garments and thirty f. garments. 14.13
and gave the f. garments to those 14.19
of gold, and ten f. garments. 2Ki 5.05
of silver and two f. garments. 5.22
with two f. garments, and laid them 5.23
the people who know the f. shout, Ps 89.15
Bind the f. procession with branches, 118.27
the f. robes, the mantles, the cloaks, Is 3.22
innumerable angels in f. gathering, Heb 12.22

FESTER
grow foul and f. because of my Ps 38.05

FESTIVAL
and held f., and went into the house Ju 9.27
the food of the f. for seven days, 2Ch 30.22
thanksgiving, a multitude keeping f. Ps 42.04
days of the f. he shall provide as Eze 45.23
you do on the day of appointed f., Hos 9.05
as on a day of f. "I will remove Zep 3.18
release one man to them at the f. *Lk 23.17
celebrate the f., not with the old 1Co 5.08
regard to a f. or a new moon or a Col 2.16

FESTUS
Felix was succeeded by Porcius F.; Ac 24.27
Now when F. had come into his province, 25.01
F. replied that Paul was being kept 25.04
But F., wishing to do the Jews a 25.09
Then F., when he had conferred with 25.12
arrived at Caesarea to welcome F. 25.13
F. laid Paul's case before the king, 25.14
And Agrippa said to F., "I should like 25.22
by command of F. Paul was brought 25.23
And F. said, "King Agrippa and all 25.24
F. said with a loud voice, "Paul, you 26.24
"I am not mad, most excellent F., 26.25
And Agrippa said to F., "This man 26.32

FETCH
while I f. a morsel of bread, that Gen 18.05
and f. me two good kids, that I may 27.09
my word, and go, f. them to me." 27.13
I will send, and f. you from there. 27.45
reeds and sent her maid to f. it. Ex 2.05
shall send and f. him from there, Deu 19.12
go into his house to f. his pledge. 24.10
you, and from there he will f. you; 30.04
said to Jesse, "Send and f. him; 1Sa 16.11
Therefore send and f. him to me, 20.31
the young men come over and f. it. 26.22
I will f. my knowledge from afar, Job 36.03

FETCHED
Then they ran and f. him from there; 1Sa 10.23
and f. from there a wise woman, and 2Sa 14.02
and f. from there four hundred and 2Ch 8.18
and he sent and f. his friends and Est 5.10
and they f. Uriah from Egypt and Jer 26.23

FETTERED
not bound, your feet were not f.; 2Sa 3.34
But the word of God is not f. 2Ti 2.09

FETTERS
Gaza, and bound him with bronze f.; Ju 16.21
of Zedekiah, and bound him in f., 2Ki 25.07
bound him with f. of bronze and 2Ch 33.11
bound him in f. to take him to 36.06
are bound in f. and caught in the Job 36.08
His feet were hurt with f., his neck Ps 105.18
and their nobles with f. of iron, 149.08
and nets, and whose hands are f.; Ecc 7.26
bound him in f. to take him to Jer 39.07
of Zedekiah, and bound him in f., 52.11
been bound with f. and chains, Mk 5.04
and the f. he broke in pieces; 5.04
and bound with chains and f., Lk 8.29
and every one's f. were unfastened Ac 16.26
with my own hand. Remember my f. Col 4.18
I am suffering and wearing f., 2Ti 2.09

FEUD
had a great f. with the Ammonites; Ju 12.02

FEVER
and f. that waste the eyes and Lev 26.16
and with f., inflammation, and fiery Deu 28.22
mother-in-law lying sick with a f.; Mt 8.14
and the f. left her, and she rose 8.15
mother-in-law lay sick with a f., Mk 1.30
lifted her up, and the f. left her; 1.31
mother-in law was ill with a high f., Lk 4.38
stood over her and rebuked the f., 4.39
the seventh hour the f. left him. Jn 4.52
lay sick with f. and dysentery; Ac 28.08

FEW
had one language and f. words. Gen 11.01
to him but a f. days because of 29.20
my numbers are f., and if they 34.30
f. and evil have been the days of 47.09
the years are f. you shall diminish Lev 25.16
remain but a f. years until the 25.52
and make you f. in number, so that 26.22
Sometimes the cloud was a f. days Num 9.20
weak, whether they are f. or many, 13.18
smaller tribes you shall take f.; 35.08
will be left f. in number among Deu 4.27
and sojourned there, f. in number; 26.05
you shall be left f. in number; 28.62
and not die, nor let his men be f." 33.06
toil up there, for they are but f." Jos 7.03
LORD from saving by many or by f." 1Sa 14.06
you left those f. sheep in the 17.28
empty vessels and not too f. 2Ki 4.03
When they were f. in number, and of 1Ch 16.19
the Syrians had come with f. men, 2Ch 24.24
were too f. and could not flay all 29.34
Only a f. men of Asher, of Manasseh, 30.11
the night, I and a f. men with me; Neh 2.12
within it were f. and no houses 7.04
Are not the days of my life f.? Job 10.20
is born of a woman is of f. days, 14.01
For when a f. years have come I 16.22
made my days a f. handbreadths, Ps 39.05
When they were f. in number, of 105.12
May his days be f.; and may another 109.08
during the f. days of their life. Ecc 2.03
therefore let your words be f. 5.02
the sun the f. days of his life 5.18
he lives the f. days of his vain 6.12
a little city with f. men in it; 9.14
grinders cease because they are f., 12.03
had not left us a f. survivors, Is 1.09
and to cut off nations not a f.; 10.07
will be so f. that a child can 10.19
survive will be very f. and feeble. 16.14
of the sons of Kedar will be f.; 21.17
are scorched, and f. men are left. 24.06
an infant that lives but a f. days, 65.20

FEW (cont.)
them, and they shall not be f.; Jer 30.19
(for we are left but a f. of many, 42.02
to the land of Judah, f. in number; 44.28
But I will let a f. of them escape Eze 12.16
but within a f. days he shall be Dan 11.20
life, and those who find it are f. Mt 7.14
plentiful, but the laborers are f.; 9.37
said, "Seven, and a f. small fish. 15.34
many are called, but f. are chosen." 22.14
hands upon a f. sick people and Mk 6.05
And they had a f. small fish; and having 8.07
plentiful, but the laborers are f.; Lk 10.02
will those who are saved be f.?" 13.23
there they stayed for a f. days. Jn 2.12
and not a f. of the leading women. Ac 17.04
with not a f. Greek women of high 17.12
in which a f., that is, eight persons, 1Pe 3.20
But I have a f. things against you: Rev 2.14
have still a f. names in Sardis, 3.04

FEWEST
for you were the f. of all peoples; Deu 7.07

FIDELITY
but to show entire and true f., so that Tit 2.10

FIELD
when no plant of the f. was yet in Gen 2.05
no herb of the f. had yet sprung 2.05
beast of the f. and every bird of 2.19
air, and to every beast of the f.; 2.20
you shall eat the plants of the f. 3.18
brother, "Let us go out to the f." 4.08
And when they were in the f., Cain rose 4.08
it is at the end of his f. For the full 23.09
I give you the f.. and I give you 23.11
I will give the price of the f.; 23.13
So the f. of Ephron in Machpelah, 23.17
the f. with the cave which was in 23.17
all the trees that were in the f., 23.17
the cave of the f. of Machpelah 23.19
The f. and the cave that is in it 23.20
meditate in the f. in the evening; 24.63
walking in the f. to meet us?" 24.65
in the f. of Ephron the son of 25.09
the f. which Abraham purchased from 25.10
a man of the f., while Jacob was a 25.27
pottage, Esau came in from the f., 25.29
and your bow, and go out to the f., 27.03
went to the f. to hunt for game 27.05
the smell of a f. which the LORD 27.27
he looked, he saw a well in the f., 29.02
went and found mandrakes in the f., 30.14
came from the f. in the evening, 30.16
Leah into the f. where his flock 31.04
were with his cattle in the f., 34.05
in from the f. when they heard of 34.07
was in the city and in the f.; 34.28
behold, we were binding sheaves in the f., 37.07
all that he had, in house and f. 39.05
as seed for the f. and as food for 47.24
that is in the f. of Ephron the 49.29
that is in the f. at Machpelah, 49.30
bought with the f. from Ephron the 49.30
the f. and the cave that is in it 49.32
in the cave of the f. at Machpelah, 50.13
bought with the f. from Ephron the 50.13
and in all kinds of work in the f.; Ex 1.14
your cattle which are in the f., 9.03
you have in the f. into safe 9.19
that is in the f. and is not 9.19
slaves and his cattle in the f. 9.21
beast and every plant of the f., 9.22
that was in the f. throughout all 9.25
struck down every plant of the f., 9.25
and shattered every tree of the f. 9.25
of yours which grows in the f., 10.05
neither tree nor plant of the f., 10.15
you will not find it in the f." 16.25
"When a man causes a f. or vineyard 22.05
and it feeds in another man's f., 22.05
best in his own f. and in his own 22.05
grain or the f. is consumed, he that 22.06
that is torn by beasts in the f.; 22.31
labor, of what you sow in the f. 23.16
in from the f. the fruit of your 23.16
living bird go into the open f. Lev 14.07
out of the city into the open f.; 14.53
which they slay in the open f., 17.05
not reap your f. to its very border, 19.09
not sow your f. with two kinds of 19.19
not reap your f. to its very border, 23.22
Six years you shall sow your f., 25.03
shall not sow your f. or prune your 25.04
eat what it yields out of the f. 25.12
trees of the f. shall yield their 26.04
dedicates his f. from the year of 27.17
dedicates his f. after the jubilee, 27.18
dedicates the f. wishes to redeem 27.19
he does not wish to redeem the f., 27.20
he has sold the f. to another man, 27.20
but the f., when it is released in 27.21
as a f. that has been devoted; the priest 27.21
to the LORD a f. which he has bought, 27.22
of jubilee the f. shall return to 27.24
or beast, or of his inherited f., 27.28
Whoever in the open f. touches one Num 19.16
not pass through f. or vineyard, 20.17
not turn aside into f. or vineyard; 21.22
ox licks up the grass of the f." 22.04
of the road, and went into the f.; 22.23
And he took him to the f. of Zophim, 23.14
his f., or his manservant, or his Deu 5.21
comes forth from the f. year by year. 14.22
trees in the f. men that they should 20.19
"When you reap your harvest in your f., 24.19
have forgotten a sheaf in the f., 24.19
and blessed shall you be in the f. 28.03
and cursed shall you be in the f. 28.16
You shall carry much seed into the f., 28.38
and he ate the produce of the f.; 32.13
him to ask her father for a f.; Jos 15.18
him to ask her father for a f.; Ju 1.14
too, on the heights of the f. 5.18
And they went out into the f., 9.27
to the woman as she sat in the f.; 13.09
from his work in the f. at evening; 19.16
said to Naomi, "Let me go to the f., Ru 2.02
gleaned in the f. after the reapers; 2.03
the part of the f. belonging to 2.03
in another f. or leave this one, 2.08
be upon the f. which they are reaping, 2.09
gleaned in the f. until evening; 2.17
lest in another f. you be molested." 2.22
day you buy the f. from the hand 4.05
thousand men on the f. of battle. 1Sa 4.02
the cart came into the f. of Joshua of 6.14
this day in the f. of Joshua of 6.18
coming from the f. behind the oxen; 11.05
in the f., and among all the people; 14.15
air and to the beasts of the f." 17.44
my father in the f. where you are, 19.03
myself in the f. till the third 20.05
"Come, let us go out into the f." 20.11
So they both went out into the f. 20.11
So David hid himself in the f.; 20.24
out into the f. to the appointment 20.35
my lord are camping in the open f.; 2Sa 11.11
and came out against us in the f.; 11.23
quarreled with one another in the f.; 14.06
Joab's f. is next to mine, and he has 14.30
Absalom's servants set the f. on fire. 14.30
your servants set my f. on fire?" 14.31

FIELD (cont.)
bear robbed of her cubs in the f. 2Sa 17.08
out into the f. against Israel; 18.06
out of the highway into the f., 20.12
or the beasts of the f. by night. 21.10
who dies in the f. the birds of 1Ki 16.04
out into the f. to gather herbs, 2Ki 4.39
the face of the f. in the territory 9.37
on the highway to the fuller's f. 18.17
have become like plants of the f., 19.26
let the f. exult, and everything in 1Ch 16.32
the work of the f. for tilling the 27.26
in the burial f. which belonged to 2Ch 26.23
and of all the produce of the f.; 31.05
the work, had fled each to his f. Neh 13.10
league with the stones of the f., Job 5.23
beasts of the f. shall be at peace 5.23
fodder in the f. and they glean 24.06
oxen, and also the beasts of the f., Ps 8.07
all that moves in the f. is mine. 50.11
cities like the grass of the f.! 72.16
all that move in the f. feed on it. 80.13
let the f. exult, and everything in 96.12
flourishes like a flower of the f.; 103.15
drink to every beast of the f.; 104.11
everything ready for you in the f.; Pro 24.27
I passed by the f. of a sluggard by 24.30
and the goats the price of a f.; 27.26
She considers a f. and buys it; 31.16
gazelles or the hinds of the f., Sol 2.07
gazelles or the hinds of the f., 3.05
like a lodge in a cucumber f., like a Is 1.08
who add f. to f., until there is 5.08
on the highway to the fuller's f., 7.03
taken away from the fruitful f.; 16.10
shall be turned into a fruitful f., 29.17
the fruitful f. shall be regarded 29.17
wilderness becomes a fruitful f., 32.15
the fruitful f. is deemed a forest 32.15
righteousness abide in the fruitful f. 32.16
on the highway to the fuller's f. 36.02
plants of the f. and like tender 37.27
beauty is like the flower of the f. 40.06
trees of the f. shall clap their 55.12
All you beasts of the f., come to 56.09
Like keepers of a f. are they Jer 4.17
Go not forth into the f., nor walk 6.25
trees of the f. and the fruit of 7.20
fall like dung upon the open f., 9.22
like scarecrows in a cucumber f., 10.05
and the grass of every f. wither? 12.04
harlotries, on the hills in the f. 13.27
Even the hind in the f. forsakes 14.05
If I go out into the f., behold, 14.18
Zion shall be plowed as a f.; 26.18
the beasts of the f. to serve him. 27.06
to him even the beasts of the f. 28.14
'Buy my f. which is at Anathoth, for 32.07
'Buy my f. which is at Anathoth in 32.08
"And I bought the f. at Anathoth 32.09
"Buy the f. for money and get 32.25
we have no vineyard or f. or seed; 35.09
by want of the fruits of the f. Lam 4.09
that is in the f. dies by the Eze 7.15
you were cast out on the open f., 16.05
and grow up like a plant of the f.' 16.07
trees of the f. shall know that I 17.24
you shall fall upon the open f., 29.05
beasts of the f. brought forth 31.06
will be all the beasts of the f. 31.13
trees of the f. shall faint because 31.15
on the open f. I will fling you, and 32.04
is in the open f. I will give to 33.27
trees of the f. shall yield their 34.27
the increase of the f. abundant, 36.30
the air, and the beasts of the f., 38.20
You shall fall in the open f.; for I have 39.05
wood out of the f. or cut down any 39.10
sort and to all beasts of the f., 39.17
sons of men. the beasts of the f., Dan 2.38
beasts of the f. found shade under 4.12
amid the tender grass of the f. 4.15
which beasts of the f. found shade, 4.21
in the tender grass of the f.; and let 4.23
lot be with the beasts of the f., 4.23
shall be with the beasts of the f.; 4.25
shall be with the beasts of the f.; 4.32
beasts of the f. shall devour them Hos 2.12
that day with the beasts of the f., 2.18
and also the beasts of the f., and the 4.03
weeds in the furrows of the f. 10.04
heaps on the furrows of the f. 12.11
the harvest of the f. has perished. Joe 1.11
the trees of the f. are withered; 1.12
has burned all the trees of the f. 1.19
Fear not, you beasts of the f., 2.22
one f. would be rained upon, and the Amo 4.07
and the f. on which it did not rain 4.07
you Zion shall be plowed as a f.; Mic 3.12
of her, all the beasts of the f.; Zep 2.14
every one the vegetation in the f. Zec 10.01
vine in the f. shall not fail to Mal 3.11
lilies of the f., how they grow; Mt 6.28
God so clothes the grass of the f., 6.30
man who sowed good seed in his f.; 13.24
you not sow good seed in your f.? 13.27
a man took and sowed in his f.; 13.31
the parable of the weeds of the f. 13.36
the f. is the world, and the good 13.38
is like treasure hidden in a f., 13.44
all that he has and buys that f. 13.44
who is in the f. not turn back to 24.18
Then two men will be in the f.; 24.40
bought with them the potter's f., 27.07
Therefore that f. has been called 27.08
been called the F. of Blood to 27.08
they gave them for the potter's f., 27.10
who is in the f. not turn back to Mk 13.16
there were shepherds out in the f. Lk 2.08
is alive in the f. today and tomorrow 12.28
said to him, 'I have bought a f., 14.18
"Now his elder son was in the f.; 15.25
when he has come in from the f., 17.07
him who is in the f. not turn back. 17.31
"Two men will be in the f.; one will * 17.36
near the f. that Jacob gave to his Jn 4.05
man bought a f. with the reward of Ac 1.18
so that the f. was called in their 1.19
Akeldama, that is, F. of Blood. 1.19
sold a f. which belonged to him, and 4.37
you are God's f., God's building. 1Co 3.09
out f. among you may be greatly 2Co 10.15
work already done in another's f. 10.16

FIELDS
man found him wandering in the f.; Gen 37.15
the food from the f. around it. 41.48
all the Egyptians sold their f., 47.20
and courtyards and out of the f. Ex 8.13
reckoned with the f. of the country; Lev 25.31
But the f. of common land belonging 25.34
us inheritance of f. and vineyards. Num 16.14
grass in your f. for your cattle, Deu 11.15
Sodom, and from the f. of Gomorrah; 32.32
But the f. of the city and its Jos 21.12
you, and lie in wait in the f. Ju 9.32
day the men went out into the f. 9.42
companies, and laid wait in the f.; 9.43
who were in the f. and slew them. 9.44
best of your f. and vineyards and 1Sa 8.14
every one of you f. and vineyards, 22.07
anything when we were in the f., 25.15
produce of the f. from the day 2Ki 8.06
Jerusalem in the f. of the Kidron, 23.04
but the f. of the city and its 1Ch 6.56

FIELDS (cont.)
who were in the f. of common land 2Ch 31.19
who said, "We are mortgaging our f., Neh 5.03
tax upon our f. and our vineyards. 5.04
men have our f. and our vineyards." 5.05
Return to them this very day their f., 5.11
with their f., some of the people 11.25
their villages, Lachish and its f., 11.30
according to the f. of the towns; 12.44
earth and sends waters upon the f.; Job 5.10
land of Egypt, in the f. of Zoan. Ps 78.12
and his miracles in the f. of Zoan. 78.43
they sow f., and plant vineyards, 107.37
we found it in the f. of Jaar. 132.06
and ten thousands in our f.; 144.13
before he had made the earth with its f., Pro 8.26
or enter the f. of the fatherless; 23.10
to a land with cultivated f. Ecc 5.09
let us go forth into the f., and lodge Sol 7.11
For the f. of Heshbon languish, and Is 16.08
your breasts for the pleasant f., 32.12
their f. and wives together; for I will Jer 6.12
others and their f. to conquerors, 8.10
and all the f. as far as the brook 31.40
Houses and f. and vineyards shall 32.15
F. shall be bought in this land of 32.43
F. shall be bought for money, and 32.44
vineyards and f. at the same time. 39.10
oil, and honey hidden in the f. 41.08
shall devour them with their f. Hos 5.07
The f. are laid waste, the ground Joe 1.10
They covet f., and seize them; and Mic 2.02
Among our captors he divides our f." 2.04
fail and the f. yield no food, Hab 3.17
which they had cut from the f. Mk 11.08
sent him into his f. to feed swine. Lk 15.15
and see how the f. are already Jn 4.35
of the laborers who mowed your f., Jas 5.04

FIERCE
Cursed be their anger, for it is f.; Gen 49.07
Turn from thy f. wrath, and repent Ex 32.12
that the f. anger of the LORD may Num 25.04
still more the f. anger of the 32.14
the table in f. anger and ate no 1Sa 20.34
carry out his f. wrath against 28.18
And the battle was very f. that day; 2Sa 2.17
and returned home in f. anger. 2Ch 25.10
for the f. wrath of the LORD is 28.11
and there is f. wrath against Israel." 28.13
that his f. anger may turn away from us. 29.10
that his f. anger may turn away from you. 30.08
till the f. wrath of our God over Ez 10.14
the lion, the voice of the f. lion, Job 4.10
will send his f. anger into him, 20.23
No one is so f. that he dares to 41.10
f. men band themselves against me. Ps 59.03
He let loose on them his f. anger, 78.49
at the f. anger of Rezin and Syria Is 7.04
cruel, with wrath and f. anger, 13.09
hosts in the day of his f. anger. 13.13
and a f. king will rule over them, 19.04
them with his f. blast in the day 27.08
for the f. anger of the LORD has Jer 4.08
the LORD, before his f. anger. 4.26
because of the f. anger of the 12.13
because of the f. anger of the 25.37
LORD, and because of his f. anger." 25.38
The f. anger of the LORD will not 30.24
upon them, my f. anger, says the LORD. 49.37
life from the f. anger of the LORD! 51.45
inflicted on the day of his f. anger. Lam 1.12
He has cut down in f. anger all the 2.03
and in his f. indignation has 2.06
I will not execute my f. anger, Hos 11.09
repent and turn from his f. anger, Jon 3.09
more f. than the evening wolves; Hab 1.08
upon you the f. anger of the LORD, Zep 2.02
so f. that no one could pass that Mt 8.28
my departure f. wolves will come Ac 20.29
profligates, f., haters of good, 2Ti 3.03
men were scorched by the f. heat, Rev 16.09

FIERCELY
The archers f. attack him, shot at Gen 49.23
The bellows blow f., the lead is Jer 6.29

FIERCENESS
may turn from the f. of his anger, Deu 13.17
turn from the f. of his great wrath, 2Ki 23.26
With f. and rage he swallows the Job 39.24

FIERCER
of Judah were f. than the words of 2Sa 19.43

FIERY
Then the LORD send f. serpents Num 21.06
"Make a f. serpent, and set it on a 21.08
with its f. serpents and scorpions Deu 8.15
and f. heat, and with drought, and 28.22
weapons, making his arrows f. shafts. Ps 7.13
and all the night with a f. light. 78.14
be cast into a burning f. furnace. Dan 3.06
be cast into a burning f. furnace. 3.11
be cast into a burning f. furnace; 3.15
us from the burning f. furnace; and he 3.17
them into the burning f. furnace. 3.20
cast into the burning f. furnace. 3.21
bound into the burning f. furnace. 3.23
of the burning f. furnace and said, 3.26
his throne was f. flames, its wheels 7.09
surprised at the f. ordeal which 1Pe 4.12

FIFTEEN
Kenan eight hundred and f. years, Gen 5.10
covering them f. cubits deep. 7.20
of the gate shall be f. cubits, Ex 27.14
the hangings shall be f. cubits, 27.15
side of the gate were f. cubits, 38.14
court were hangings of f. cubits, 38.15
for a male shall be f. shekels, Lev 27.07
about f. thousand men, all who were Ju 8.10
Now Ziba had f. sons and twenty 2Sa 9.10
with his f. sons and his twenty 19.17
forty-five pillars, f. in each row. 1Ki 7.03
lived f. years after the death of 2Ki 14.17
And I will add f. years to your 20.06
of Judah lived f. years after the 2Ch 25.25
I will add f. years to your life. Is 38.05
bought her for f. shekels of silver Hos 3.02
sounded again and found f. fathoms. Ac 27.28
and remained with him f. days. Gal 1.18

FIFTEENTH
on the f. day of the second month Ex 16.01
And on the f. day of the same month Lev 23.06
On the f. day of this seventh month 23.34
"On the f. day of the seventh month, 23.39
And on the f. day of this month is Num 28.17
"On the f. day of the seventh month 29.12
on the f. day of the first month; 33.03
a feast on the f. day of the eighth 1Ki 12.32
Bethel on the f. day in the eighth 12.33
In the f. year of Amaziah the son 2Ki 14.23
the f. to Bilgah, the sixteenth to 1Ch 24.14
to the f., to Jeremoth, his sons and 25.22
month of the f. year of the reign 2Ch 15.10
fourteenth, and rested on the f. day, Est 9.18
and also the f. day of the same, 9.21
on the f. day of the month, the word Eze 32.17
on the f. day of the month and for 45.25
In the f. year of the reign of Lk 3.01

FIFTH
and there was morning, a f. day. Gen 1.23
conceived and bore Jacob a f. son. 30.17

FIFTH (cont.)
and take the f. part of the produce Gen 41.34
you shall give a f. to Pharaoh, 47.24
that Pharaoh should have the f.; 47.26
and shall add a f. to it and give Lev 5.16
in full, and shall add a f. to it, 6.05
But in the f. year you may eat of 19.25
shall add the f. of its value to 22.14
he shall add a f. to the valuation. 27.13
he shall add a f. of the valuation 27.15
he shall add a f. of the valuation 27.19
your valuation, and add a f. to it; 27.27
his tithe, he shall add a f. to it. 27.31
adding a f. to it, and giving it to Num 5.07
On the f. day Shelumiel the son of 7.36
"On the f. day nine bulls, two rams, 29.26
on the first day of the f. month. 33.38
The f. lot came out for the tribe Jos 19.24
And on the f. day he arose early in Ju 19.08
and the f., Shephatiah the son of 2Sa 3.04
In the f. year of King Rehoboam, 1Ki 14.25
In the f. year of Joram the son of 2Ki 8.16
In the f. month, on the seventh day 25.08
Nethanel the fourth, Raddai the f., 1Ch 2.14
the f. Shephatiah, by Abital; 3.03
Nohah the fourth, and Rapha the f. 8.02
Mishmannah fourth, Jeremiah f., 12.10
the f. to Malchijah, the sixth to 24.09
the f. to Nethaniah, his sons and 25.12
Elam the f., Jehohanan the sixth, 26.03
the fourth, Nethanel the f., 26.04
The f. commander, for the f. month, 27.08
In the f. year of King Rehoboam, 2Ch 12.02
came to Jerusalem in the f. month, Ez 7.08
day of the f. month he came to 7.09
Sanballat for the f. time sent his Neh 6.05
of Jerusalem in the f. month. Jer 1.03
in the f. month of the fourth year, 28.01
In the f. year of Jehoiakim the son 36.09
In the f. month, on the tenth day of 52.12
on the f. day of the month, as I was Eze 1.01
On the f. day of the month (it was 1.02
(it was the f. year of the exile of 1.02
on the f. day of the month, as I sat 8.01
in the f. month, on the tenth day of 20.01
on the f. day of the month, a man 33.21
I mourn and fast in the f. month, Zec 7.03
mourned in the f. month and in the 7.05
month, and the fast of the f., 8.19
When he opened the f. seal, Rev 6.09
And the f. angel blew his trumpet, 9.01
The f. angel poured his bowl on the 16.10
the f. onyx, the sixth carnelian, the 21.20

FIFTHS
and four f. shall be your own, as Gen 47.24

FIFTIES
of hundreds, of f., and of tens. Ex 18.21
of hundred, of f., and of tens. 18.25
commanders of f., commanders of Deu 1.15
of thousands and commanders of f., 1Sa 8.12
and hid them by f. in a cave, 1Ki 18.04
LORD's prophets by f. in a cave, 18.13
captains of fifty men with their f.; 2Ki 1.14
in groups, by hundreds and by f. Mk 6.40

FIFTIETH
And you shall hallow the f. year, Lev 25.10
shall that f. year be to you; 25.11
In the f. year of Azariah king of 2Ki 15.23

FIFTY
its breadth f. cubits, and its Gen 6.15
the earth a hundred and f. days. 7.24
a hundred and f. days the waters 8.03
lived three hundred and f. years. 9.28
were nine hundred and f. years; 9.29
Suppose there are f. righteous 18.24
it for the f. righteous who are in 18.24
I find at Sodom f. righteous in 18.26
Suppose five of the f. righteous 18.28
F. loops you shall make on the one Ex 26.05
and f. loops you shall make on the 26.05
And you shall make f. clasps of gold, 26.06
And you shall make f. loops on the 26.10
and f. loops on the edge of the 26.10
"And you shall make f. clasps of 26.11
shall be hangings for f. cubits, 27.12
to the east shall be f. cubits. 27.13
the breadth f., and the height five 27.18
much, that is, two hundred and f., 30.23
aromatic cane two hundred and f., 30.23
he made f. loops on the one curtain, 36.12
and he made f. loops on the edge of 36.12
And he made f. clasps of gold, and 36.13
And he made f. loops on the edge of 36.17
and f. loops on the edge of the 36.17
And he made f. clasps of bronze to 36.18
side were hangings of f. cubits, 38.12
the front to the east, f. cubits. 38.13
thousand, five hundred and f. men. 38.26
counting f. days to the morrow Lev 23.16
old shall be f. shekels of silver, 27.03
be valued at f. shekels of silver. 27.16
thousand six hundred and f. Num 1.25
three thousand five hundred and f. 1.46
forty-five thousand six hundred and f. 2.15
thousand four hundred and f. They shall 2.16
three thousand five hundred and f. 2.32
years old up to f. years old, all who 4.03
years old up to f. years old, 4.23
years old up to f. years old, 4.30
years old up to f. years old, 4.35
two thousand seven hundred and f. 4.36
years old up to f. years old, 4.39
years old up to f. years old, 4.43
years old up to f. years old, 4.47
and from the age of f. years they 8.25
two hundred and f. leaders of the 16.02
censer, two hundred and f. censers; 16.17
two hundred and f. men offering 16.35
devoured two hundred and f. men; 26.10
take one drawn out of every f., 31.30
half Moses took one of every f., 31.47
seven hundred and f. shekels. 31.52
the young woman f. shekels of Deu 22.29
a bar of gold weighing f. shekels, Jos 7.21
and f. men to run before him. 2Sa 15.01
the oxen for f. shekels of silver. 24.24
and f. men to run before him. 1Ki 1.05
cubits, and its breadth f. cubits, 7.02
its length was f. cubits, and its 7.06
Solomon's work: five hundred and f., 9.23
and a horse for a hundred and f.; 10.29
hundred and f. prophets of Baal 18.19
prophets are four hundred and f. men. 18.22
a captain of f. men with his f. 2Ki 1.09
But Elijah answered the captain of f., 1.10
heaven and consume you and your f." 1.10
heaven, and consumed him and his f. 1.10
captain of f. men with his f. And he 1.11
heaven and consume you and your f." 1.12
heaven and consumed him and his f. 1.12
of a third f. with his f. And the 1.13
the third captain of f. went up, 1.13
life of these f. servants of yours, 1.13
captains of f. men with their 1.14
F. men of the sons of the prophets 2.07
with your servants f. strong men; 2.16
They sent therefore f. men; and for 2.17
of more than f. horsemen and ten 13.07
f. shekels of silver from every man, 15.20
him with f. men of the Gileadites, 15.25

FIFTY (cont.)

f. thousand of their camels, two 1Ch 5.21
two hundred and f. thousand sheep, 5.21
and grandsons, one hundred and f. 8.40
Of Zebulun f. thousand seasoned 12.33
and a horse for a hundred and f.; 2Ch 1.17
one shekel to f. shekels of gold. 3.09
King Solomon, two hundred and f., 8.10
hundred and f. talents of gold and 8.18
registered one hundred and f. men. Ez 8.03
of Jonathan, and with him f. men. 8.06
six hundred and f. talents of 8.26
at my table a hundred and f. men, Neh 5.17
f. basins, five hundred and thirty 7.70
"Let a gallows f. cubits high be Est 5.14
in Haman's house, f. cubits high." 7.09
the captain of f. and the man of Is 3.03
vestibule of the gate was f. cubits, Eze 40.15
its length was f. cubits, and its 40.21
its length was f. cubits, and its 40.25
its length was f. cubits, and its 40.29
its length was f. cubits, and its 40.33
its length was f. cubits, and its 40.36
cubits, and the breadth f. cubits. 42.02
the chambers, f. cubits long. 42.07
outer court were f. cubits long, 42.08
with f. cubits for an open space 45.02
and your mina shall be f. shekels. 45.12
north two hundred and f. cubits, 48.17
on the south two hundred and f., 48.17
on the east two hundred and f., 48.17
and on the west two hundred and f. 48.17
to the winevat to draw f. measures, Hag 2.16
hundred denarii, and the other f. Lk 7.41
down in companies, about f. each." 9.14
and sit down quickly and write f.' 16.06
him, "You are not yet f. years old, Jn 8.57
about four hundred and f. years. Ac 13.19
it came to f. thousand pieces of 19.19

FIFTY-FIVE

and he reigned f. years in Jerusalem 2Ki 21.01
and he reigned f. years in Jerusalem 2Ch 33.01
The sons of Adin, six hundred and f. Neh 7.20

FIFTY-FOUR

of Issachar was f. thousand four Num 1.29
numbered being f. thousand four 2.06
one thousand two hundred and f. Ez 2.07
The sons of Adin, four hundred and f. 2.15
one thousand two hundred and f. 2.31
a thousand two hundred and f. Neh 7.12
a thousand two hundred and f. 7.34

FIFTY-NINE

of Simeon was f. thousand three Num 1.23
numbered being f. thousand three 2.13

FIFTY-ONE

a hundred and f. thousand four Num 2.16

FIFTY-SECOND

In the f. year of Azariah king of 2Ki 15.27

FIFTY-SEVEN

of Zebulun was f. thousand four Num 1.31
numbered being f. thousand four 2.08
a hundred and f. thousand six 2.31

FIFTY-SIX

generations, nine hundred and f. 1Ch 9.09
of Bigvai, two thousand and f. Ez 2.14
The men of Netophah, f. 2.22
of Magbish, one hundred and f. 2.30

FIFTY-THREE

of Naphtali was f. thousand four Num 1.43
numbered being f. thousand four 2.30
number, f. thousand four hundred. 26.47
a hundred and f. thousand six 2Ch 2.17
fish, a hundred and f. of them; Jn 21.11

FIFTY-TWO

number was f. thousand seven Num 26.43
and he reigned f. years in Jerusalem 2Ki 15.02
and he reigned f. years in Jerusalem 2Ch 26.03
The sons of Nebo, f. Ez 2.29
sons of Immer, one thousand and f. 2.37
sons of Nekoda, six hundred and f. 2.60
day of the month Elul, in f. days. Neh 6.15
The sons of Arah, six hundred and f. 7.10
The men of the other Nebo, f. 7.33
The sons of Immer, a thousand and f. 7.40

FIG

and they sewed f. leaves together Gen 3.07
of vines and f. trees and pomegranates, Deu 8.08
And the trees said to the f. tree, Ju 9.10
But the f. tree said to them, 'Shall 9.11
his vine and under his f. tree, 1Ki 4.25
and every one of his own f. tree, 2Ki 18.31
He smote their vines and f. trees, Ps 105.33
He who tends a f. tree will eat its Pro 27.18
The f. tree puts forth its figs, and Sol 2.13
a first-ripe f. before the summer: Is 28.04
leaves falling from the f. tree. 34.04
and every one of his own f. tree, 36.16
up your vines and your f. trees; Jer 5.17
the vine, nor figs on the f. tree; 8.13
waste her vines and her f. trees, Hos 2.12
the first fruit on the f. tree, 9.10
vines, and splintered my f. trees; Joe 1.07
the f. tree languishes. Pomegranate, 1.12
the f. tree and vine give their 2.22
your f. trees and your olive trees Amo 4.09
his vine and under his f. tree, Mic 4.04
no first-ripe f. which my soul 7.01
are like f. trees with first ripe Nah 3.12
Though the f. tree do not blossom, Hab 3.17
the f. tree, the pomegranate, and the Hag 2.19
his vine and under his f. tree." Zec 3.10
And seeing a f. tree by the wayside Mt 21.19
And the f. tree withered at once. 21.19
"How did the f. tree wither at once?" 21.20
what has been done to the f. tree, 21.21
"From the f. tree learn its lesson: 24.32
in the distance a f. tree in leaf, Mk 11.13
they saw the f. tree withered away 11.20
The f. tree which you cursed has 11.21
"From the f. tree learn its lesson: 13.28
"A man had a f. tree planted in his Lk 13.06
come seeking fruit on this f. tree, 13.07
"Look at the f. tree, and all the 21.29
when you were under the f. tree, Jn 1.48
you, I saw you under the f. tree. 1.50
Can a f. tree. my brethren yield Jas 3.12
earth as the f. tree sheds its Rev 6.13

FIGHT

our enemies and f. against us and Ex 1.10
The LORD will f. for you, and you 14.14
us men, and go out, f. with Amalek; 17.09
be able to f. against them and Num 22.11
before you will himself f. for you. Deu 1.30
we will go up and f., just as the 1.41
'Say to them, Do not go up or f., 1.42
to f. for you against your enemies, 20.04
near to a city to f. against it, 20.10
"When men f. with one another, and 25.11
one accord to f. Joshua and Israel Jos 9.02
your enemies against whom you f." 10.25
waters of Merom, to f. with Israel. 11.05
the Canaanites, to f. against them?" Ju 1.01
that we may f. against the Canaanites 1.03
went down to f. against the Canaanites 1.09
us when you went to f. with Midian?" 8.01

FIGHT (cont.)

despised? Go out now and f. with them." Ju 9.38
the Jordan to f. also against Judah 10.09
man that will begin to f. against the 10.18
that we may f. with the Ammonites. 11.06
go with us and f. with the Ammonites, 11.08
home again to f. with the Ammonites, 11.09
come to me to f. against my land?" 11.12
the Ammonites to f. against them; 11.32
did you cross over to f. against the 12.01
to me this day, to f. against me?" 12.03
acquit yourselves like men and f." 1Sa 4.09
out before us and f. our battles." 8.20
Philistines mustered to f. with Israel, 13.05
and f. against them until they are 15.18
If he is able to f. with me and 17.09
me a man, that we may f. together." 17.10
will go and f. with this Philistine 17.32
this Philistine to f. with him; 17.33
for me and f. the LORD's battles." 18.17
for war, to f. against Israel. 28.01
may not go and f. against the enemies 29.08
no more, nor did they f. any more. 2Sa 2.28
did you go so near the city to f.? 11.20
to f. against the house of Israel, 1Ki 12.21
not go up or f. against your kinsmen 12.24
but let us f. against them in the 20.23
then we will f. against them in the 20.25
up to Aphek, to f. against Israel. 20.26
"F. with neither small nor great, 22.31
so they turned to f. against him; 22.32
had come up to f. against them, 2Ki 3.21
and f. for your master's house." 10.03
For you shall f. the Syrians in 13.17
he has set out to f. against you, 19.09
to f. against Israel, to restore the 2Ch 11.01
not go up or f. against your brethren. 11.04
do not f. against the LORD, the God 13.12
"F. with neither small nor great, 18.30
so they turned to f. against him; 18.31
will not need to f. in this battle; 20.17
and intended to f. against Jerusalem, 32.02
to help us and to f. our battles. 32.08
went up to f. at Carchemish on the 35.20
himself in order to f. with him. 35.22
to come and f. against Jerusalem Neh 4.08
and f. for your brethren, your sons, 4.14
to us there. Our God will f. for us." 4.20
f. against those who f. against me Ps 35.01
for many f. against me proudly. 56.02
and they will f., every man against Is 19.02
the nations that f. against Ariel, 29.07
all that f. against her and her 29.07
nations be that f. against Mount 29.08
brandished arm he will f. with them. 30.32
come down to f. upon Mount Zion 31.04
"He has set out to f. against you." 37.09
quarrel and to f. and to hit with 58.04
They will f. against you; but they Jer 1.19
they will f. against you, but they 15.20
I myself will f. against you with 21.05
though you f. against the Chaldeans, 32.05
coming in to f. and to fill them 33.05
and they will f. against it, and 34.22
come back and f. against this city 37.08
men and went to f. against Ishmael 41.12
will return to f. against the Dan 10.20
come out and f. with the king of 11.11
they shall f. because the LORD is Zec 10.05
go forth and f. against those 14.03
even Judah will f. against Jerusalem. 14.14
this world, my servants would f., Jn 18.36
F. the good f. of the faith; 1Ti 6.12
I have fought the good f., I have 2Ti 4.07
so you f. and wage war. You do not Jas 4.02
beast, and who can f. against it?" Rev 13.04

FIGHTING

take all the f. men with you, and Jos 8.01
and all the f. men, to go up to Ai; 8.03
And all the f. men were with 8.11
There was hard f. against the 1Sa 14.52
of Elah, f. with the Philistines. 17.19
Philistines are f. against Keilah, 23.01
my lord is f. the battles of the 25.28
Then Joab returned from f. against the 2Sa 10.14
in the forefront of the hardest f., 11.15
David all the news about the f.; 11.18
the news about the f. to the king, 11.19
king of Assyria f. against Libnah; 2Ki 19.08
king of Assyria f. against Libnah; Is 37.08
which you are f. against the king Jer 21.04
Chaldeans who are f. against it. 32.24
Chaldeans who are f. against this 32.29
peoples were f. against Jerusalem 34.01
of Babylon was f. against Jerusalem 34.07
Chaldeans who are f. against you, 37.10
warriors of Babylon have ceased f., 51.30
every turn—f. without and fear within. 2Co 7.05
and his angels f. against the Rev 12.07

FIGHTINGS

wars, and what causes f. among you? Jas 4.01

FIGHTS

for the LORD f. for them against Ex 14.25
the LORD your God who f. for you.' Deu 3.22
the LORD your God who f. for you, Jos 23.10
as when he f. on a day of battle. Zec 14.03

FIGS

also some pomegranates and f. Num 13.23
or f., or vines, or pomegranates; 20.05
and two hundred cakes of f., and laid 1Sa 25.18
of a cake of f. and two clusters 30.12
And Isaiah said, "Bring a cake of f. 2Ki 20.07
cakes of f., clusters of raisins, 1Ch 12.40
f., and all kinds of burdens, which Neh 13.15
The fig tree puts forth its f., Sol 2.13
said, "Let them take a cake of f., Is 38.21
nor f. on the fig tree; even the Jer 8.13
two baskets of f. placed before 24.01
basket had very good f., like first-ripe f., 24.02
the other basket had very bad f., 24.02
I said, "F., the good f. very good, 24.03
and the bad f. very bad, so bad that 24.03
God of Israel: Like these good f., 24.05
Like the bad f. which are so bad 24.08
them like vile f. which are so bad 29.17
merchandise wheat, olives and early f., Eze 27.17
like fig trees with first-ripe f.— Nah 3.12
from thorns, or f. from thistles? Mt 7.16
for it was not the season for f. Mk 11.13
For f. are not gathered from thorns, Lk 6.44
yield olives, or a grapevine f.? Jas 3.12

FIGURATIVELY

hence, f. speaking, he did receive Heb 11.19

FIGURE

yourselves, in the form of any f., Deu 4.16
to understand a proverb and a f., Pro 1.06
he shapes it into the f. of a man. Is 44.13
This f. Jesus used with them, but Jn 10.06
speaking plainly, not in any f.! 16.29

FIGURED

not set up a f. stone in your land, Lev 26.01
and destroy all their f. stones, Num 33.52

FIGUREHEAD

with the Twin Brothers as f. Ac 28.11

FIGURES

a box at its side the f. of gold, 1Sa 6.08
it, in which were the golden f., 6.15

FIGURES (cont.)
with carved f. of cherubim and 1Ki 6.29
Under it were f. of gourds, for 2Ch 4.03
"I have said this to you in f.; Jn 16.25
speak to you in f. but tell you 16.25
the f. which you made to worship; Ac 7.43

FILIGREE
enclose them in settings of gold f. Ex 28.11
shall make settings of gold f., 28.13
they shall be set in gold f. 28.20
attach to the two settings of f., 28.25
settings of gold f. and engraved 39.06
enclosed in settings of gold f. 39.13
settings of gold f. and two gold 39.16
attached to the two settings of f.; 39.18

FILL
multiply and f. the waters in the Gen 1.22
and f. the earth and subdue it; 1.28
and multiply, and f. the earth. 9.01
gave orders to f. their bags with 42.25
"F. the men's sacks with food, as 44.01
and they shall f. your houses, and Ex 10.06
desire shall have its f. of them. 15.09
fruit, and you will eat your f., Lev 25.19
good things, which you did not f., Deu 6.11
you may eat your f. of grapes, 23.24
the fleece to f. a bowl with water. Ju 6.38
F. your horn with oil, and go; 1Sa 16.01
And he said, "F. four jars with 1Ki 18.33
He will yet f. your mouth with Job 8.21
and f. himself with the east wind? 15.02
To f. his belly to the full God 20.23
before him and f. my mouth with 23.04
Can you f. his skin with harpoons, 41.07
F. me with joy and gladness; let the Ps 51.08
growl if they do not get their f. 59.15
may his glory f. the whole earth! 72.19
your mouth wide, and I will f. it. 81.10
F. their faces with shame, that they 83.16
reaper does not f. his hand or the 129.07
we shall f. our houses with spoil; Pro 1.13
take their f. of your strength, and 5.10
her affection f. you at all times 5.19
Come, let us take our f. of love 7.18
wings will f. the breadth of your Is 8.08
and f. the face of the world with 14.21
and f. the whole world with fruit. 27.06
he will f. Zion with justice and 33.05
has drunk its f. in the heavens; 34.05
let us f. ourselves with strong 56.12
for Fortune and f. cups of mixed 65.11
man who does not f. out his days, 65.20
I will f. with drunkenness all the Jer 13.13
Do I not f. heaven and earth? says the 23.24
to fight and to f. them with the 33.05
and drink its f. of their blood. 46.10
Surely I will f. you with men, as 51.14
I give you and f. your stomach Eze 3.03
their hunger or f. their stomachs 7.19
they should f. the land with violence, 8.17
and f. the courts with the slain. 9.07
f. your hands with burning coals 10.02
the shoulder; f. it with choice bones. 24.04
and f. the land with the slain. 30.11
and f. the valleys with your 32.05
And I will f. your mountains with 35.08
and those who f. their master's Zep 1.09
drink, but you never have your fill; Hag 1.06
and I will f. this house with 2.07
F. up, then, the measure of your Mt 23.32
"F. the jars with water." And they Jn 2.07
And when they had eaten their f., 6.12
you ate your f. of the loaves. 6.26
May the God of hope f. you with all Rom 15.13
heavens, that he might f. all things.) Eph 4.10
so as always to f. up the measure of their 1Th 2.16

FILLED
and the earth was f. with violence. Gen 6.11
the earth is f. with violence through 6.13
and f. the skin with water, and gave 21.19
spring, and f. her jar, and came up. 24.16
had stopped and f. with earth all 26.15
so that the land was f. with them. Ex 1.07
and f. the troughs to water their 2.16
shall be f. with swarms of flies, 8.21
morning you shall be f. with bread; 16.12
and I have f. him with the Spirit 31.03
and he has f. him with the Spirit 35.31
He has f. them with ability to do 35.35
glory of the LORD f. the tabernacle. 40.34
glory of the LORD f. the tabernacle. 40.35
and f. his hand from it, and burned Lev 9.17
earth shall be f. with the glory Num 14.21
shall come and eat and be f.; Deu 14.29
eat within your towns and be f., 26.12
wineskins were new when we f. them, Jos 9.13
f. with fear because of the words 1Sa 28.20
a cloud f. the house of the LORD, 1Ki 8.10
of the LORD f. the house of the 8.11
and f. the trench also with water. 18.35
but the Syrians f. the country. 20.27
stream-bed shall be f. with water, 2Ki 3.17
till the country was f. with water. 3.20
of Baal was f. from one end to the 10.21
till he had f. Jerusalem from one 21.16
and f. their places with the bones 23.14
for he f. Jerusalem with innocent 24.04
of the LORD, was f. with a cloud, 2Ch 5.13
of the LORD f. the house of God. 5.14
glory of the LORD f. the temple. 7.01
of the LORD f. the LORD's house. 7.02
which had been f. with various kinds of 16.14
which have f. it from end to end Ez 9.11
and were f. and became fat, and Neh 9.25
to him, Haman was f. with fury. Est 3.05
he was f. with wrath against 5.09
who f. their houses with silver. Job 3.15
for I am f. with disgrace and look 10.15
Yet he f. their houses with good 22.18
that has not been f. with his meat?" 31.31
His mouth is f. with cursing and Ps 10.07
their belly be f. with what thou 17.14
For my loins are f. with burning, 38.07
thy right hand is f. with victory; 48.10
My mouth is f. with thy praise, and 71.08
And they ate and were well f., 78.29
it took deep root and f. the land. 80.09
they are f. with good things. 104.28
Then our mouth was f. with laughter, 126.02
then your barns will be f. with plenty, Pro 3.10
but the wicked are f. with trouble. 12.21
man will be f. with the fruit of 14.14
the rooms are f. with all precious 24.04
and a fool when he is f. with food; 30.22
nor the ear f. with hearing. Ecc 1.08
Their land is f. with silver and Is 2.07
their land is f. with horses, and 2.07
Their land is f. with idols; 2.08
and his train f. the temple. 6.01
and the house was f. with smoke. 6.04
Therefore my loins are f. with anguish; 21.03
"Every jar shall be f. with wine." ' Jer 13.12
every jar will be f. with wine?' 13.12
for thou hadst f. me with indignation 15.17
and have f. my inheritance with 16.18
they have f. this place with the 19.04
of Nethaniah f. it with the slain. 41.09
he has f. his belly with my delicacies, 51.34
He has f. me with bitterness, he has Lam 3.15
the smiter, and be f. with insults. 3.30

FILLED (cont.)

and a cloud f. the inner court. Eze 10.03
the house was f. with the cloud, 10.04
and have f. its streets with the 11.06
you will be f. with drunkenness and 23.33
"So you were f. and heavily laden 27.25
trade you were f. with violence, 28.16
waste cities be f. with flocks of 36.38
And you shall eat fat till you are f., 39.19
And you shall be f. at my table 39.20
glory of the LORD f. the temple. 43.05
of the LORD f. the temple of the 44.04
mountain and f. the whole earth. Dan 2.35
they were f., and their heart was Hos 13.06
I am f. with power, with the Spirit Mic 3.08
he f. his caves with prey and his Nah 2.12
earth will be f. with the knowledge Hab 2.14
their faces. and were f. with awe. Mt 17.06
wedding hall was f. with guests. 22.10
f. it with vinegar, and put it on a 27.48
they were f. with awe, and said, 27.54
And they were f. with awe, and said Mk 4.41
and he will be f. with the Holy Lk 1.15
Elizabeth was f. with the Holy 1.41
he has f. the hungry with good 1.53
Zechariah was f. with the Holy 1.67
them, and they were f. with fear. 2.09
and became strong, f. with wisdom; 2.40
Every valley shall be f.. and every 3.05
the synagogue were f.. with wrath. 4.28
they came and f. both the boats, 5.07
glorified God and were f. with awe, 5.26
But they were f. with fury and 6.11
come in, that my house may be f. 14.23
And they f. them up to the brim. Jn 2.07
them up and f. twelve baskets with 6.13
the house was f. with the fragrance 12.03
to you, sorrow has f. your hearts. 16.06
and it f. all the house where they Ac 2.02
And they were all f. with the Holy 2.04
said, "They are f. with new wine." 2.13
and they were f. with wonder and 3.10
Then Peter, f. with the Holy Spirit, 4.08
they were all f. with the Holy 4.31
why has Satan f. your heart to lie 5.03
Sadducees, and f. with jealousy 5.17
here you have f. Jerusalem with 5.28
sight and be f. with the Holy 9.17
f. with the Holy Spirit, looked 13.09
they were f. with jealousy, and 13.45
disciples were f. with joy and 13.52
So the city was f. with the confusion 19.29
They were f. with all manner of Rom 1.29
f. with all knowledge, and able to 15.14
Already you are f.! Already you have 1Co 4.08
I am f. with comfort. With all our 2Co 7.04
that you may be f. with all the Eph 3.19
debauchery; but be f. with the Spirit, 5.18
f. with the fruits of righteousness Php 1.11
and more; I am f., having received from 4.18
that you may be f. with the knowledge Col 1.09
see you, that I may be f. with joy. 2Ti 1.04
be warmed and f.," without giving Jas 2.16
the censer and f. it with fire Rev 8.05
and the temple was f. with smoke 15.08

FILLETED

the court shall be f. with silver; Ex 27.17
of the court were f. with silver. 38.17

FILLETS

and their f. shall be of silver. Ex 27.10
and their f. shall be of silver. 27.11
and their f. were of gold, but their 36.38
of the pillars and their f. were of silver. 38.10
the pillars and their f. of silver. 38.11
of the pillars and their f. were of silver. 38.12
and their f. were of silver: the overlaying 38.17
capitals and their f. of silver. 38.19
their capitals and made f. for them. 38.28

FILLING

f. them with corpses; he will shatter Ps 110.06
who love me, and f. their treasuries. Pro 8.21
f. you with vain hopes; they speak Jer 23.16
so that the boat was already f. Mk 4.37
f. a sponge full of vinegar, put it 15.36
and they were f. with water, and Lk 8.23

FILLS

and all that f. it, let the field 1Ch 16.32
my breath, but f. me with bitterness. Job 9.18
the sea roar, and all that f. it; Ps 96.11
Let the sea roar, and all that f. it; 98.07
the hungry he f. with good things. 107.09
he f. you with the finest of the 147.14
earth listen, and all that f. it; Is 34.01
the sea roar and all that f. it, 42.10
devour the land and all that f. it, Jer 8.16
the land and all that f. it, the city 47.02
land is stripped of all that f. it, Eze 32.15
fulness of him who f. all in all. Eph 1.23

FILTH

carry out the f. from the holy 2Ch 29.05
but are not cleansed of their f. Pro 30.12
washed away the f. of the daughters Is 4.04
I will throw f. at you and treat Nah 3.06

FILTHINESS

of vomit, no place is without f. Is 28.08
I will consume your f. out of you. Eze 22.15
that its f. may be melted in it, its 24.11
you were not cleansed from your f., 24.13
Let there be no f., nor silly talk, Eph 5.04
Therefore put away all f. and rank Jas 1.21

FILTHY

grievously, therefore she became f.; Lam 1.08
has become a f. thing among them. 1.17
Its rust is your f. lewdness. Because Eze 24.13
angel, clothed with f. garments. Zec 3.03
"Remove the f. garments from him." 3.04
and the f. still be f. and the Rev 22.11

FINAL

the time of your f. punishment, Eze 21.25
the time of their f. punishment. 21.29
at the time of their f. punishment; 35.05
an oath is f. for confirmation. Heb 6.16

FINALLY

f. he brought the family of the 1Sa 10.21
f. he sent him to them, saying, 'They Mk 12.06
F., brethren, farewell. Mend your ways, 2Co 13.11
F., be strong in the Lord and in Eph 6.10
F., my brethren, rejoice in the Lord Php 3.01
F., brethren, whatever is true, 4.08
F., brethren, we beseech and exhort 1Th 4.01
F., brethren, pray for us, that the 2Th 3.01
F., all of you, have unity of spirit, 1Pe 3.08

FIND

"If I f. at Sodom fifty righteous Gen 18.26
"I will not destroy it if I f. forty-five 18.28
not do it, if I f. thirty there." 18.30
with whom you f. your gods shall 31.32
maidservants, but he did not f. them. 31.33
the tent, but did not f. them. 31.34
but did not f. the household gods. 31.35
that I may f. favor in your sight.'" 32.05
"To f. favor in the sight of my 33.08
Let me f. favor in the sight of my 33.15
"Let me f. favor in your eyes, and 34.11
woman's hand, he could not f. her. 38.20

FIND (cont.)

this kid, and you could not f. her."	Gen 38.23
"Can we f. such a man as this, in	41.38
your straw wherever you can f. it;	Ex 5.11
you will not f. it in the field.	16.25
them, "Why do you f. fault with me?	17.02
know thee and f. favor in thy sight.	33.13
LORD, that you may f. acceptance;	Lev 23.11
if I f. favor in thy sight, that I	Num 11.15
be sure your sin will f. you out.	32.23
and you will f. him, if you search	Deu 4.29
brother's, which he loses and you f.;	22.03
I did not f. in her the tokens of	22.14
"I did not f. in your daughter the	22.17
these nations you shall f. no ease,	28.65
and f. it out, then I will give you	Ju 14.12
to live where he could f. a place;	17.08
to sojourn where I may f. a place."	17.09
The LORD grant that you may f. a home,	Ru 1.09
in whose sight I shall f. favor."	2.02
maidservant f. favor in your eyes."	1Sa 1.18
Shalisha, but they did not f. them.	9.04
of Benjamin, but did not f. them.	9.04
you will f. him before he goes up	9.13
lad, saying, 'Go, f. the arrows.'	20.21
"Run and f. the arrows which I	20.36
of Saul my father shall not f. you;	23.17
my young men f. favor in your eyes;	25.08
If I f. favor in the eyes of the	2Sa 15.25
let me ever f. favor in your sight,	16.04
had sought and could not f. them,	17.20
perhaps we may f. grass and save	1Ki 18.05
and tell Ahab and he cannot f. you,	18.12
they sought him but did not f. him.	2Ki 2.17
you will f. them at the end of	2Ch 20.16
children will f. compassion with	30.09
of Assyria come and f. much water?"	32.04
You will f. in the book of the	Ez 4.15
which you shall f. in the whole	7.16
and could not f. a word to say.	Neh 5.08
and thou didst f. his heart faithful	9.08
are glad, when they f. the grave?	Job 3.22
that I may f. a little comfort	10.20
"Can you f. out the deep things of	11.07
Can you f. out the limit of the	11.07
and let my cry f. no resting place	16.18
and I shall not f. a wise man	17.10
Oh, that I knew where I might f. him,	23.03
I must speak, that I may f. relief;	32.20
The Almighty—we cannot f. him;	37.23
his wickedness till thou f. none.	Ps 10.15
thou wilt f. no wickedness in me;	17.03
Your hand will f. out all your	21.08
right hand will f. out those who	21.08
and by night, but f. no rest.	22.02
I would haste to f. me a shelter	55.08
praise them; and f. no fault in them.	73.10
under his wings you will f. refuge;	91.04
for I f. my delight in thy commandments,	119.47
until I f. a place for the LORD, a	132.05
we shall f. all precious goods, we	Pro 1.13
me diligently but will not f. me.	1.28
of the LORD and f. the knowledge	2.05
So you will f. favor and good	3.04
right to those who f. knowledge.	8.09
and I f. knowledge and discretion.	8.12
those who seek me diligently f. me.	8.17
but a faithful man who can f.?	20.06
kindness will f. life and honor.	21.21
if you f. it, there will be a future,	24.14
has understanding will f. him out.	28.11
will afterward f. more favor than	28.23
will in the end f. him his heir.	29.21
A good wife who can f.? She is far	31.10
and f. enjoyment in his toil.	Ecc 2.24
that he cannot f. out what God has	3.11
and drink and f. enjoyment in all	5.18
his lot and f. enjoyment in his	5.19
man may not f. out anything that	7.14
very deep; who can f. it out?	7.24
thing to another to f. the sum,	7.27
that man cannot f. out the work	8.17
in seeking, he will not f. it out;	8.17
to know, he cannot f. it out.	8.17
for you will f. it after many days.	11.01
sought to f. pleasing words,	12.10
if you f. my beloved, that you tell	Sol 5.08
afflicted of his people f. refuge.	Is 14.32
and f. for herself a resting place.	34.14
you, but you shall not f. them;	41.12
your fathers f. in me that they	Jer 2.05
in her month they will f. her.	2.24
you did not f. them breaking in.	2.34
squares to see if you can f. a man,	5.01
and f. rest for your souls. But they	6.16
they f. no water, they return with	14.03
welfare you will f. your welfare.	29.07
You will seek me and f. me; when you	29.13
with my groaning, and I f. no rest.	45.03
like harts that f. no pasture;	Lam 1.06
sought to f. a ground for complaint	Dan 6.04
but they could f. no ground for	6.04
"We shall not f. any ground for	6.05
unless we f. it in connection with	6.05
so that she cannot f. her paths.	Hos 2.06
seek them, but shall not f. them.	2.07
the LORD, but they will not f. him;	5.06
the LORD, but they shall not f. it.	Amo 8.12
seek, and you will f.; knock,	Mt 7.07
life, and those who f. it are few.	7.14
f. out who is worthy in it, and stay	10.11
his life for my sake will f. it.	10.39
and you will f. rest for your souls.	11.29
his life for my sake will f. it.	16.25
its mouth you will f. a shekel;	17.27
immediately you will f. an ass tied.	21.01
marriage feast as many as you f.'	22.09
when he comes will f. so doing.	24.46
enter it you will f. a colt tied,	Mk 11.02
see if he could f. anything on it.	11.13
he come suddenly and f. you asleep.	13.36
you will f. a babe wrapped in	Lk 2.12
and when they did not f. him,	2.45
that they might f. an accusation	6.07
seek, and you will f.; knock,	11.09
when he comes will f. so doing.	12.43
on this fig tree, and I f. none.	13.07
comes, will he f. faith on earth?"	18.08
entering you will f. a colt tied.	19.30
but they did not f. anything they	19.48
"I f. no crime in this man."	23.04
I did not f. this man guilty of any	23.14
went in they did not f. the body.	24.03
and did not f. his body; and they	24.23
seek me and you will not f. me;	Jn 7.34
to go that we shall not f. him?	7.35
seek me and you will not f. me,'	7.36
will go in and out and f. pasture.	10.09
told them, "I f. no crime in him."	18.38
may know that I f. no crime in him."	19.04
crucify him, for I f. no crime in him."	19.06
of the boat, and you will f. some."	21.06
they did not f. them in the prison,	Ac 5.22
and our fathers could f. no food.	7.11
asked leave to f. a habitation for	7.46
for him and could not f. him,	12.19
And when they could not f. them,	17.06
might feel after him and f. him.	17.27
to f. out why they shouted thus	22.24
"We f. nothing wrong in this man.	23.09
and they did not f. me disputing	24.12
So I f. it to be a law that when I	Rom 7.21
then, "Why does he still f. fault?	9.19
and I will f. out not the talk of	1Co 4.19

FIND (cont.)
promises of God f. their Yes in 2Co 1.20
I did not f. my brother Titus 2.13
with me and f. that you are not 9.04
I may come and f. you not what I 12.20
that you may f. me not what you 12.20
I hope you will f. out that we have 13.06
grant him to f. mercy from the 2Ti 1.18
mercy and f. grace to help in time Heb 4.16
greatly to f. some of your children 2Jn 1.04
will seek death and will not f. it; Rev 9.06

FINDING
'Are they not f. and dividing the Ju 5.30
f. no way to a city to dwell in; Ps 107.04
who, on f. one pearl of great value, Mt 13.46
but f. no way to bring him in, Lk 5.19
and f. none he says, 'I will return 11.24
f. no way to punish them, because of Ac 4.21
But sin, f. opportunity in the Rom 7.08
For sin, f. opportunity in the 7.11

FINDS
and whoever f. me will slay me." Gen 4.14
prosperous and f. sufficient means Lev 25.26
of blood f. him outside the bounds Num 35.27
if then she f. no favor in his eyes Deu 24.01
do whatever your hand f. to do. 1Sa 10.07
For if a man f. his enemy, will he 24.19
Behold, he f. occasions against me, Job 33.10
Even the sparrow f. a home, and the Ps 84.03
word like one who f. great spoil. 119.162
Happy is the man who f. wisdom, Pro 3.13
For they are life to him who f. them, 4.22
For he who f. me f. life and 8.35
the righteous f. refuge through 14.32
He who f. a wife f. a good thing, and 18.22
his neighbor f. no mercy in his 21.10
yet it f. rest rather than he. Ecc 6.05
Whatever your hand f. to do, 9.10
but f. no resting place; her pursuers Lam 1.03
In thee the orphan f. mercy. Hos 14.03
asks receives, and he who seeks f., Mt 7.08
He who f. his life will lose it, and 10.39
seeking rest, but he f. none. 12.43
and when he comes he f. it empty, 12.44
And if he f. it, truly, I say to you, 18.13
asks receives, and he who seeks f., Lk 11.10
he comes he f. it swept and put in 11.25
whom the master f. awake when he 12.37
and f. them so, blessed are those 12.38
one which is lost, until he f. it? 15.04
seek diligently until she f. it? 15.08
because my word f. no place in you. Jn 8.37
For he f. fault with them when he Heb 8.08

FINE
quickly three measures of f. meal, Gen 18.06
him in garments of f. linen, 41.42
And it shall become f. dust over Ex 9.09
on the face of the wilderness a f., 16.14
f. as hoarfrost on the ground. 16.14
scarlet stuff and f. twined linen, 25.04
ten curtains of f. twined linen 26.01
scarlet stuff and f. twined linen; 26.31
scarlet stuff and f. twined linen, 26.36
hangings of f. twined linen a 27.09
scarlet stuff and f. twined linen, 27.16
hangings of f. twined linen and 27.18
scarlet stuff, and f. twined linen. 28.05
and of f. twined linen, skilfully 28.06
scarlet stuff, and f. twined linen. 28.08
and f. twined linen shall you make 28.15
coat in checker work of f. linen, 28.39
shall make a turban of f. linen, 28.39
shall make them of f. wheat flour. 29.02
measure of f. flour mingled with a 29.40
scarlet stuff and f. twined linen; 35.06
stuff or f. linen or goats' hair 35.23
scarlet stuff and f. twined linen; 35.25
scarlet stuff and f. twined linen, 35.35
were made of f. twined linen and 36.08
scarlet stuff and f. twined linen; 36.35
scarlet stuff and f. twined linen, 36.37
the court were of f. twined linen, 38.09
the court were of f. twined linen. 38.16
scarlet stuff and f. twined linen; 38.18
scarlet stuff and f. twined linen. 38.23
scarlet stuff, and f. twined linen. 39.02
and into the f. twined linen, in 39.03
scarlet stuff, and f. twined linen; 39.05
scarlet stuff, and f. twined linen. 39.08
scarlet stuff and f. twined linen. 39.24
woven of f. linen, for Aaron and his 39.27
and the turban of f. linen, and the 39.28
linen, and the caps of f. linen, 39.28
linen breeches of f. twined linen, 39.28
and the girdle of f. twined linen 39.29
his offering shall be of f. flour; Lev 2.01
a handful of the f. flour and oil, 2.02
cakes of f. flour mixed with oil, 2.04
it shall be of f. flour unleavened. 2.05
shall be made of f. flour with oil. 2.07
of an ephah of f. flour for a sin 5.11
handful of the f. flour of the 6.15
of an ephah of f. flour as a 6.20
and cakes of f. flour well mixed 7.12
of an ephah of f. flour mixed with 14.10
of an ephah of f. flour mixed with 14.21
of an ephah of f. flour mixed with 23.13
they shall be of f. flour, they shall 23.17
"And you shall take f. flour, 24.05
cakes of f. flour mixed with oil, Num 6.15
of them full of f. flour mixed with 7.13
of them full of f. flour mixed with 7.19
of them full of f. flour mixed with 7.25
of them full of f. flour mixed with 7.31
of them full of f. flour mixed with 7.37
of them full of f. flour mixed with 7.43
of them full of f. flour mixed with 7.49
of them full of f. flour mixed with 7.55
of them full of f. flour mixed with 7.61
of them full of f. flour mixed with 7.67
of them full of f. flour mixed with 7.73
of them full of f. flour mixed with 7.79
offering of f. flour mixed with 8.08
of a tenth of an ephah of f. flour, 15.04
of an ephah of f. flour mixed with 15.06
tenths of an ephah of f. flour, 15.09
of an ephah of f. flour for a cereal 28.05
of an ephah of f. flour for a cereal 28.09
of an ephah of f. flour for a cereal 28.12
two tenths of f. flour for a cereal 28.12
and a tenth of f. flour mixed with 28.13
offering of f. flour mixed with 28.20
offering of f. flour mixed with 28.28
offering of f. flour mixed with 29.03
offering of f. flour mixed with 29.09
offering of f. flour mixed with 29.14
small, until it was as f. as dust; Deu 9.21
and they shall f. him a hundred 22.19
I beat them f. as the dust of the 2Sa 22.43
was thirty measures of f. flour, 1Ki 4.22
a measure of f. meal shall be sold 2Ki 7.01
So a measure of f. meal was sold 7.16
a measure of f. meal for a shekel, 7.18
also over the f. flour, the wine, the 1Ch 9.29
clothed with a robe of f. linen, 15.27
and crimson fabrics and f. linen, 2Ch 2.14
and covered it with f. gold, and made 3.05
six hundred talents of f. gold 3.08
and crimson fabrics and f. linen, 3.14
arrayed in f. linen, with cymbals, 5.12
two vessels of f. bright bronze as Ez 8.27

FINE (cont.)
with cords of f. linen and purple Est 1.06
and a mantle of f. linen and purple 8.15
be exchanged for jewels of f. gold. Job 28.17
or called f. gold my confidence; 31.24
I beat them f. as dust before the Ps 18.42
they than gold, even much f. gold; 19.10
set a crown of f. gold upon his 21.03
commandments above gold, above f. gold. 119.127
even f. gold, and my yield than Pro 8.19
F. speech is not becoming to a fool; 17.07
To impose a f. on a righteous man 17.26
her clothing is f. linen and purple 31.22
make men more rare than f. gold, Is 13.12
food and f. clothing for those who 23.18
he takes up the isles like f. dust. 40.15
worth their weight in f. gold, how they Lam 4.02
swathed you in f. linen and covered Eze 16.10
and your raiment was of f. linen, 16.13
you ate f. flour and honey and oil. 16.13
I fed you with f. flour and oil and 16.19
clothes and take away your f. jewels. 23.26
Of f. embroidered linen from Egypt 27.07
work, f. linen, coral, and agate. 27.16
The head of this image was of f. gold, Dan 2.32
a merchant in search of f. pearls, Mt 13.45
"You have a f. way of rejecting the Mk 7.09
in purple and f. linen and who Lk 16.19
rings and in f. clothing comes Jas 2.02
who wears the f. clothing and say, 2.03
f. linen, purple, silk and scarlet, Rev 18.12
f. flour and wheat, cattle and sheep, 18.13
city that was clothed in f. linen, 18.16
her to be clothed with f. linen, 19.08
for the f. linen is the righteous 19.08
arrayed in f. linen, white and pure, 19.14

FINED
the one who hurt her shall be f., Ex 21.22
the wine of those who have been f. Amo 2.08

FINELY
and the f. worked garments, the holy Ex 31.10
the f. wrought garments for ministering 35.19
stuff they made f. wrought garments, 39.01
the f. worked garments for ministering 39.41

FINERY
take away the f. of the anklets, Is 3.18

FINEST
"Take the f. spices: of liquid myrrh Ex 30.23
with the f. of the wheat—and of Deu 32.14
with the f. produce of the ancient 33.15
and overlaid it with the f. gold. 1Ki 10.18
feed you with the f. of the wheat, Ps 81.16
fills you with the f. of the wheat 147.14
His head is the f. gold; his locks Sol 5.11
anoint themselves with the f. oils, Amo 6.06

FINGER
to Pharaoh, "This is the f. of God." Ex 8.19
horns of the altar with your f., 29.12
stone, written with the f. of God. 31.18
shall dip his f. in the blood and Lev 4.06
shall dip his f. in the blood and 4.17
with his f. and put it on the 4.25
blood with his f. and put it on 4.30
with his f. and put it on the 4.34
and with his f. put it on the horns 8.15
he dipped his f. in the blood and 9.09
and dip his right f. in the oil 14.16
oil with his f. seven times before 14.16
with his right f. some of the oil 14.27
it with his f. on the front of the 16.14
the blood with his f. seven times. 16.14
upon it with his f. seven times, 16.19
take some of her blood with his f., Num 19.04
stone written with the f. of God; Deu 9.10
'My little f. is thicker than my 1Ki 12.10
'My little f. is thicker than my 2Ch 10.10
with his feet, points with his f., Pro 6.13
the yoke, the pointing of the f., Is 58.09
will not move them with their f. Mt 23.04
But if it is by the f. of God that Lk 11.20
the end of his f. in water and 16.24
wrote with his f. on the ground. *Jn 8.06
wrote with his f. on the ground. *8.08
and place my f. in the mark of the 20.25
"Put your f. here, and see my hands; 20.27

FINGERS
who had six f. on each hand, and six 2Sa 21.20
and its thickness was four f.; 1Ki 7.15
who had six f. on each hand, and six 1Ch 20.06
at thy heavens, the work of thy f., Ps 8.03
for war, and my f. for battle; 144.01
bind them on your f., write them Pro 7.03
my f. with liquid myrrh, upon the Sol 5.05
to what their own f. have made. Is 2.08
to what their own f. have made, 17.08
blood and your f. with iniquity; 59.03
and its thickness was four f., Jer 52.21
Immediately the f. of a man's hand Dan 5.05
he put his f. into his ears, and he Mk 7.33
the burdens with one of your f. Lk 11.46

FINISH
and f. it to a cubit above; and set Gen 6.16
began to number, but did not f.; 1Ch 27.24
house and to f. this structure?" Ez 5.03
house and to f. this structure?' 5.09
Will they f. up in a day? Will they Neh 4.02
When you f. reading this book, bind Jer 51.63
to f. the transgression, to put an Dan 9.24
and the third day I f. my course. Lk 13.32
foundation, and is not able to f., 14.29
to build, and was not able to f.' 14.30

FINISHED
Thus the heavens and the earth were f., Gen 2.01
seventh day God f. his work which 2.02
When he had f. talking with him, God 17.22
when he had f. speaking to Abraham; 18.33
When she had f. giving him a drink, 24.19
as Isaac had f. blessing Jacob, 27.30
When Jacob f. charging his sons, he 49.33
And when Moses had f. speaking with Ex 34.33
of the tent of meeting was f.; 39.32
of the court. So Moses f. the work 40.33
his sons have f. covering the Num 4.15
when Moses had f. setting up the 7.01
And as he f. speaking all these 16.31
"When you have f. paying all the Deu 26.12
When Moses had f. writing the words 31.24
of this song until they were f., 31.30
And when Moses had f. speaking all 32.45
all the nation f. passing over the Jos 3.17
the nation had f. passing over the 4.01
everything was f. that the Lord 4.10
all the people had f. passing over, 4.11
When Israel had f. slaughtering all 8.24
of Israel had f. slaying them with 10.20
When they had f. distributing the 19.49
So they f. dividing the land. 19.51
And when Ehud had f. presenting the Ju 3.18
When he had f. speaking, he threw 15.17
till they have f. all my harvest.'" Ru 2.21
until he has f. eating and drinking. 3.03
When he had f. prophesying, he came 1Sa 10.13
As soon as he had f. offering the 13.10
When he had f. speaking to Saul, the 18.01
When David had f. speaking these 24.16
And when David had f. offering the 2Sa 6.18
"When you have f. telling all the 11.19
And as soon as he had f. speaking, 13.36

FINISHED (cont.)

him heard it as they f. feasting. 1Ki 1.41
until he had f. building his own 3.01
So he built the house, and f. it; 6.09
Solomon built the house, and f. it. 6.14
gold, until all the house was f. 6.22
the house was f. in all its parts, 6.38
years, and he f. his entire house. 7.01
it was f. with cedar from floor to 7.07
the work of the pillars was f. 7.22
So Hiram f. all the work that he 7.40
on the house of the LORD was f. 7.51
Now as Solomon f. offering all this 8.54
When Solomon had f. building the 9.01
before the LORD. So he f. the house. 9.25
And when David had f. offering the 1Ch 16.02
of the house of the LORD is f. 28.20
So Huram f. the work that he did 2Ch 4.11
for the house of the LORD was f. 5.01
Thus Solomon f. the house of the 7.11
the LORD was laid until it was f. 8.16
into the chest until they had f. 24.10
And when they had f., they brought 24.14
day of the first month they f. 29.17
until the burnt offering was f. 29.28
When the offering was f., the king 29.29
them, until the work was f.— for the 29.34
Now when all this was f., all Israel 31.01
and f. them in the seventh month. 31.07
city is rebuilt and the walls f., Ez 4.13
city is rebuilt and its walls f., 4.16
great king of Israel built and f. 5.11
in building, and it is not yet f.' 5.16
They f. their building by command 6.14
and this house was f. on the third 6.15
So the wall was f. on the twenty-fifth Neh 6.15
When the Lord has f. all his work Is 10.12
Jeremiah had f. speaking all that Jer 26.08
When Jeremiah f. speaking to all 43.01
Now when he had f. measuring the Eze 42.15
When you have f. cleansing it, you 43.23
When they had f. eating the grass Amo 7.02
And when Jesus f. these sayings, the Mt 7.28
And when Jesus had f. instructing 11.01
And when Jesus had f. these parables, 13.53
Now when Jesus had f. these sayings, 19.01
When Jesus had f. all these sayings, 26.01
Jesus, knowing that all was now f., Jn 19.28
the vinegar, he said, "It is f."; 19.30
When they had f. breakfast, Jesus 21.15
After they f. speaking, James replied, Ac 15.13
When we had f. the voyage from Tyre, 21.07
I have f. the race, I have kept the 2Ti 4.07
his works were f. from the foundation Heb 4.03
And when they have f. their testimony, Rev 11.07

FINISHING

they are f. the walls and repairing Ez 4.12
And as John was f. his course, Ac 13.25

FINS

the waters that has f. and scales, Lev 11.09
rivers that has not f. and scales, 11.10
that has not f. and scales is an 11.12
whatever has f. and scales you may Deu 14.09
does not have f. and scales you 14.10

FIR

stork has her home in the f. trees. Ps 104.17
your planks of f. trees from Senir Eze 27.05
nor the f. trees equal its boughs; 31.08

FIRE

a smoking f. pot and a flaming Gen 15.17
brimstone and f. from the LORD out 19.24
in his hand the f. and the knife. 22.06
said, "Behold, the f. and the wood; 22.07
in a flame of f. out of the midst Ex 3.02
and f. ran down to the earth. 9.23
and f. flashing continually in the 9.24
in a pillar of f. to give them 13.21
the pillar of f. by night did not 13.22
the pillar of f. and of cloud 14.24
the LORD descended upon it in f.; 19.18
"When f. breaks out and catches in 22.06
kindled the f. shall make full 22.06
a devouring f. on the top of the 24.17
and basins and forks and f. pans; 27.03
shall burn with f. outside the 29.14
an offering by f. to the LORD. 29.18
is an offering by f. to the LORD. 29.25
shall burn the remainder with f.; 29.34
an offering by f. to the LORD. 29.41
burn an offering by f. to the LORD, 30.20
had made, and burnt it with f., 32.20
to me, and I threw it into the f., 32.24
you shall kindle no f. in all your 35.03
and the f. pans: all its utensils he 38.03
and f. was in it by night, in the 40.38
priest shall put f. on the altar, Lev 1.07
and lay wood in order upon the f.; 1.07
that is on the f. upon the altar; 1.08
burnt offering, an offering by f., 1.09
that is on the f. upon the altar; 1.12
burnt offering, an offering by f., 1.13
upon the wood that is on the f.; 1.17
burnt offering, and offering by f., 1.17
upon the altar, an offering by f., 2.02
of the offerings by f. to the LORD. 2.03
on the altar, an offering by f., 2.09
of the offerings by f. to the LORD. 2.10
as an offering by f. to the LORD. 2.11
from fresh ears, parched with f. 2.14
is an offering by f. to the LORD. 2.16
as an offering by f. to the LORD, 3.03
which is upon the wood on the f.; 3.05
it is an offering by f., a pleasing 3.05
an offering by f. to the LORD he 3.09
as food offered by f. to the LORD. 3.11
for an offering by f. to the LORD, 3.14
food offered by f. for a pleasing 3.16
and shall burn it on a f. of wood; 4.12
the offerings by f. to the LORD; 4.35
the offerings by f. to the LORD; 5.12
and the f. of the altar shall be 6.09
to which the f. has consumed the 6.10
The f. on the altar shall be kept 6.12
F. shall be kept burning upon the 6.13
portion of my offerings by f.; 6.17
from the LORD's offerings by f.; 6.18
it shall be burned with f. 6.30
as an offering by f. to the LORD; 7.05
third day shall be burned with f. 7.17
it shall be burned with f. 7.19
an offering by f. is made to the 7.25
the offerings by f. to the LORD; 7.30
offerings made by f. to the LORD, 7.35
he burned with f. outside the camp, 8.17
an offering by f. to the LORD, 8.21
an offering by f. to the LORD. 8.28
the bread you shall burn with f. 8.32
he burned with f. outside the camp. 9.11
And f. came forth from before the 9.24
and put f. in it, and laid incense 10.01
offered unholy f. before the LORD, 10.01
And f. came forth from the presence 10.02
of the offerings by f. to the LORD, 10.12
the offerings by f. to the LORD; 10.13
the offerings by f. of the fat, 10.15
leprosy; it shall be burned in the f. 13.52
you shall burn it in the f., whether 13.55
shall burn with f. that in which 13.57
of coals of f. from the altar 16.12
incense on the f. before the LORD, 16.13
their dung shall be burned with f. 16.27

FIRE (cont.)
to devote them by f. to Molech, Lev 18.21
third day shall be burned with f. 19.06
they shall be burned with f., both he 20.14
the offerings by f. to the LORD, 21.06
father; she shall be burned with f. 21.09
offer the LORD's offerings by f.; 21.21
an offering by f. upon the altar 22.22
as an offering by f. to the LORD. 22.27
an offering by f. to the LORD seven 23.08
to be offered by f. to the LORD, 23.13
drink offerings, an offering by f., 23.18
present an offering by f. to the LORD." 23.25
present an offering by f. to the LORD. 23.27
offerings by f. to the LORD; on the 23.36
an offering by f. to the LORD; it is 23.36
to the LORD offerings by f., burnt 23.37
to be offered by f. to the LORD. 24.07
of the offerings by f. the LORD, 24.09
offered unholy f. before the LORD Num 3.04
put it on the f. which is under 6.18
the appearance of f. until morning. 9.15
and the appearance of f. by night. 9.16
and the f. of the LORD burned among 11.01
to the LORD, and the f. abated. 11.02
because the f. of the LORD burned 11.03
day and in a pillar of f. by night. 14.14
an offering by f. or a burnt offering 15.03
hin of wine, as an offering by f., 15.10
way, in offering an offering by f., 15.13
wishes to offer an offering by f., 15.14
an offering by f. to the LORD, and 15.25
put f. in them and put incense upon 16.07
and they put f. in them and laid 16.18
And f. came forth from the LORD, and 16.35
then scatter the f. far and wide. 16.37
and put f. therein from off the 16.46
holy things, reserved from the f.; 18.09
their fat as an offering by f., 18.17
For f. went forth from Heshbon, 21.28
waste until f. spread to Medeba." 21.30
when the f. devoured two hundred 26.10
offered unholy f. before the LORD. 26.61
my food for my offerings by f., 28.02
the offering by f. which you shall 28.03
an offering by f. to the LORD. 28.06
offer it as an offering by f., 28.08
an offering by f. to the LORD. 28.13
but offer an offering by f., a burnt 28.19
the food of an offering by f., 28.24
an offering by f. to the LORD. 29.06
burnt offering, an offering by f., 29.13
burnt offering, an offering by f., 29.36
encampments, they burned with f., 31.10
everything that can stand the f., 31.23
you shall pass through the f., and it 31.23
and whatever cannot stand the f., 31.23
in f. by night, to show you by what Deu 1.33
burned with f. to the heart of 4.11
to you out of the midst of the f.; 4.12
Horeb out of the midst of the f., 4.15
is a devouring f., a jealous God. 4.24
speaking out of the midst of the f., 4.33
earth he let you see his great f., 4.36
words out of the midst of the f. 4.36
mountain, out of the midst of the f., 5.04
you were afraid because of the f., 5.05
mountain out of the midst of the f., 5.22
the mountain was burning with f., 5.23
voice out of the midst of the f.; 5.24
For this great f. will consume us; 5.25
speaking out of the midst of f., 5.26
burn their graven images with f. 7.05
their gods you shall burn with f.; 7.25
as a devouring f. is the LORD your 9.03
midst of the f. on the day of the 9.10
the mountain was burning with f.; 9.15
burned it with f. and crushed it, 9.21
midst of the f. on the day of the 10.04
and burn their Asherim with f.; 12.03
daughters in the f. to their gods. 12.31
the city and all its spoil with f., 13.16
the offerings by f. to the LORD, 18.01
God, or see this great f. any more, 18.16
For a f. is kindled by my anger, and 32.22
and sets on f. the foundations of 32.22
with flaming f. at his right hand. 33.02
And they burned the city with f., Jos 6.24
things shall be burned with f., 7.15
they burned them with f., and stoned 7.25
city, you shall set the city on f., 8.08
made haste to set the city on f. 8.19
and burn their chariots with f. 11.06
and burned their chariots with f. 11.09
breathed, and he burned Hazor with f. 11.11
offerings by f. to the LORD God of 13.14
the sword, and set the city on f. Ju 1.08
there sprang up f. from the rock 6.21
let f. come out of the bramble and 9.15
let f. come out from Abimelech, and 9.20
and let f. come out from the citizens 9.20
set the stronghold on f. over them, 9.49
of the tower to burn it with f." 9.52
burn your house over you with f." 12.01
and your father's house with f. 14.15
And when he had set f. to the torches, 15.05
burned her and her father with f. 15.06
became as flax that has caught f., 15.14
tow snaps when it touches the f. 16.09
sword, and burned the city with f. 18.27
which they found they set on f. 20.48
my offerings by f. from the people 1Sa 2.28
Ziklag, and burned it with f., 30.01
city, they found it burned with f., 30.03
and we burned Ziklag with f." 30.14
there; go and set it on f." 2Sa 14.30
servants set the field on f. 14.30
your servants set my field on f.?" 14.31
and devouring f. from his mouth; 22.09
him coals of f. flamed forth. 22.13
they are utterly consumed with f. 23.07
captured Gezer and burnt it with f., 1Ki 9.16
house over him with f., and died, 16.18
on the wood, but put no f. to it; 18.23
on the wood, and put no f. to it." 18.23
God who answers by f., he is God." 18.24
of your god, but put no f. to it." 18.25
Then the f. of the LORD fell, and 18.38
and after the earthquake a f., 19.12
but the LORD was not in the f.; 19.12
and after the f. a still small 19.12
let f. come down from heaven and 2Ki 1.10
Then f. came down from heaven, and 1.10
let f. come down from heaven and 1.12
Then the f. of God came down from 1.12
Lo, f. came down from heaven, and 1.14
a chariot of f. and horses of f. 2.11
and chariots of f. round about Elisha. 6.17
you will set on f. their fortresses, 8.12
children in the f. to Adrammelech 17.31
and have cast their gods into the f.; 19.18
the chariots of the sun with f. 23.11
him with f. from heaven upon the 1Ch 21.26
f. came down from heaven and consumed 2Ch 7.01
Israel saw the f. come down and 7.03
made a very great f. in his honor. 16.14
His people made no f. in his honor, 21.19
lamb with f. according to the 35.13
and burned all its palaces with f., 36.19
and its gates are destroyed by f. Neh 1.03
gates have been destroyed by f.?" 2.03
which had been destroyed by f. 2.13
by a pillar of f. in the night to 9.12
the pillar of f. by night which 9.19

FIRE (cont.)
"The f. of God fell from heaven and Job 1.16
and f. consumes the tents of 15.34
the flame of his f. does not shine. 18.05
a f. not blown upon will devour him; 20.26
what they left the f. has consumed.' 22.20
underneath it is turned up as by f. 28.05
for that would be a f. which 31.12
flaming torches; sparks of f. leap forth. 41.19
rain coals of f. and brimstone; Ps 11.06
and devouring f. from his mouth; 18.08
clouds hailstones and coals of f. 18.12
voice, hailstones and coals of f. 18.13
his wrath; and f. will consume them. 21.09
LORD flashes forth flames of f. 29.07
As I mused, the f. burned; then I 39.03
he burns the chariots with f.! 46.09
before him is a devouring f., 50.03
we went through f. and through 66.12
as wax melts before f., let the 68.02
They set thy sanctuary on f.; 74.07
a f. was kindled against Jacob, his 78.21
F. devoured their young men, and 78.63
thy jealous wrath burn like f.? 79.05
They have burned it with f., 80.16
As f. consumes the forest, as the 83.14
long will thy wrath burn like f.? 89.46
F. goes before him, and burns up his 97.03
f. and flame thy ministers. 104.04
and f. to give light by night. 105.39
F. also broke out in their company; 106.18
they blazed like a f. of thorns; 118.12
f. and hail, snow and frost, stormy 148.08
Can a man carry f. in his bosom and Pro 6.27
his speech is like a scorching f. 16.27
will heap coals of f. on his head, 25.22
For lack of wood the f. goes out; 26.20
to hot embers and wood to f., so is a 26.21
and the f. which never says, "Enough." 30.16
Its flashes are flashes of f., in a Sol 8.06
your cities are burned with f.; Is 1.07
shining of a flaming f. by night; 4.05
the tongue of f. devours the stubble, 5.24
will be burned as fuel for the f. 9.05
For wickedness burns like a f., 9.18
people are like fuel for the f.; 9.19
be kindled, like the burning of f. 10.16
The light of Israel will become a f., 10.17
Let the f. for thy adversaries 26.11
women come and make a f. of them. 27.11
and the flame of a devouring f. 29.06
which to take f. from the hearth, 30.14
his tongue is like a devouring f.; 30.27
anger and a flame of devouring f., 30.30
with f. and wood in abundance; 30.33
whose f. is in Zion, and whose 31.09
breath is a f. that will consume 33.11
down, that are burned in the f. 33.12
us can dwell with the devouring f.? 33.14
and have cast their gods into the f.; 37.19
it set him on f. round about, but he 42.25
walk through f. you shall not be 43.02
he kindles a f. and bakes bread; 44.15
Half of it he burns in the f.; 44.16
"Aha, I am warm, I have seen the f.!" 44.16
say, Half of it I burned in the f., 44.19
like stubble, the f. consumes them; 47.14
is this, no f. to sit before! 47.14
Behold, all you who kindle a f., 50.11
Walk by the light of your f., and by 50.11
smith who blows the f. of coals, 54.16
as when f. kindles brushwood and 64.02
brushwood and the f. causes water 64.02
thee, has been burned by f., and all 64.11
a f. that burns all the day. 65.05
"For behold, the LORD will come in f., 66.15
and his rebuke with flames of f. 66.15
For by f. will the LORD execute 66.16
their f. shall not be quenched, and 66.24
lest my wrath go forth like f., Jer 4.04
making my words in your mouth a f., 5.14
wood, and the f. shall devour them. 5.14
the lead is consumed by the f.; 6 29
gather wood, the fathers kindle f., 7.18
sons and their daughters in the f.; 7.31
great tempest he will set f. to it, 11.16
in my anger a f. is kindled which 15.14
in my anger a f. is kindled which 17.04
I will kindle a f. in its gates, 17.27
sons in the f. as burnt offerings 19.05
were a burning f. shut up in my 20.09
and he shall burn it with f. 21.10
lest my wrath go forth like f., 21.12
I will kindle a f. in her forest, 21.14
cedars, and cast them into the f. 22.07
Is not my word like f., says the LORD, 23.29
of Babylon roasted in the f.," 29.22
shall come and set this city on f., 32.29
and he shall burn it with f. 34.02
and take it, and burn it with f. 34.22
and there was a f. burning in the 36.22
them into the f. in the brazier, 36.23
consumed in the f. that was in the 36.23
king of Judah had burned in the f.; 36.32
shall take it and burn it with f. 37.08
rise up and burn this city with f. 37.10
city shall not be burned with f., 38.17
and they shall burn it with f., 38.18
this city shall be burned with f. 38.23
He shall kindle a f. in the temples 43.12
of Egypt he shall burn with f. 43.13
for a f. has gone forth from 48.45
villages shall be burned with f.; 49.02
And I will kindle a f. in the wall 49.27
I will kindle a f. in his cities, 50.32
her dwellings are on f., her bars are 51.30
the bulwarks are burned with f., 51.32
high gates shall be burned with f. 51.58
weary themselves only for f." 51.58
"From on high he sent f.; into my Lam 1.13
burned like a flaming f. in Jacob, 2.03
he has poured out his fury like f. 2.04
and he kindled a f. in Zion, which 4.11
and f. flashing forth continually, Eze 1.04
continually, and in the midst of the f., 1.04
looked like burning coals of f., 1.13
and the f. was bright, and out of the f. 1.13
appearance of f. enclosed round 1.27
as it were the appearance of f., 1.27
burn in the f. in the midst of the 5.02
the f., and burn them in the f.; 5.04
from there a f. will come forth 5.04
appeared to be his loins it was f., 8.02
"Take f. from between the whirling 10.06
cherubim to the f. that was between 10.07
Lo, it is given the f. for fuel; 15.04
when the f. has consumed both ends 15.04
when the f. has consumed it and it 15.05
I have given to the f. for fuel, 15.06
though they escape from the f., 15.07
the f. shall yet consume them; 15.07
up as an offering by f. to them? 16.21
was withered; the f. consumed it. 19.12
And f. has gone out from its stem, 19.14
them offer by f. all their first-born, 20.26
and sacrifice your sons by f., 20.31
Behold, I will kindle a f. in you, 20.47
upon you with the f. of my wrath; 21.31
You shall be fuel for the f.; 21.32
to blow the f. upon it in order to 22.20
upon you with the f. of my wrath, 22.21
them with the f. of my wrath; 22.31
survivors shall be devoured by f. 23.25
kindle the f., boil well the flesh, 24.10

FIRE (cont.)
rust does not go out of it by f. Eze 24.12
of the stones of f. you walked. 28.14
from the midst of the stones of f. 28.16
I brought forth f. from the midst 28.18
LORD, when I have set f. to Egypt, 30.08
and will set f. to Zoan, and will 30.14
And I will set f. to Egypt; Pelusium 30.16
and hailstones, f. and brimstone. 38.22
I will send f. on Magog and on 39.06
flame of the f. slew those men who Dan 3.22
cast three men bound into the f.?" 3.24
walking in the midst of the f., 3.25
and Abednego came out from the f. 3.26
saw that the f. had not had any 3.27
and no smell of f. had come upon 3.27
flames, its wheels were burning f. 7.09
A stream of f. issued and came 7.10
given over to be burned with f. 7.11
whose baker ceases to stir the f., Hos 7.04
morning it blazes like a flaming f. 7.06
I will send a f. upon his cities, 8.14
For f. has devoured the pastures of Joe 1.19
and f. has devoured the pastures of 1.20
F. devours before them, and behind 2.03
of a flame of f. devouring the 2.05
blood and f. and columns of smoke. 2.30
So I will send a f. upon the house Amo 1.04
So I will send a f. upon the wall 1.07
So I will send a f. upon the wall 1.10
So I will send a f. upon Teman, 1.12
So I will kindle a f. in the wall 1.14
So I will send a f. upon Moab, 2.02
So I will send a f. upon Judah, 2.05
break out like f. in the house of 5.06
was calling for a judgment by f., 7.04
The house of Jacob shall be a f., Ob 1.18
be cleft, like wax before the f., Mic 1.04
her hires shall be burned with f., 1.07
His wrath is poured out like f., Nah 1.06
your foes; f. has devoured your bars. 3.13
There will the f. devour you, the 3.15
that peoples labor only for f., Hab 2.13
In the f. of his jealous wrath, all Zep 1.18
for in the f. of my jealous wrath 3.08
be to her a wall of f. round about, Zec 2.05
this a brand plucked from the f.?" 3.02
and she shall be devoured by f. 9.04
that the f. may devour your cedars! 11.01
And I will put this third into the f., 13.09
not kindle f. upon my altar in Mal 1.10
a refiner's f. and like fullers' 3.02
is cut down and thrown into the f. Mt 3.10
with the Holy Spirit and with f. 3.11
he will burn with unquenchable f." 3.12
shall be liable to the hell of f. 5.22
is cut down and thrown into the f. 7.19
are gathered and burned with f., 13.40
and throw them into the furnace of f.; 13.42
and throw them into the furnace of f.; 13.50
for often he falls into the f., 17.15
to be thrown into the eternal f. 18.08
to be thrown into the hell of f. 18.09
the eternal f. prepared for the 25.41
him into the f. and into the water, Mk 9.22
go to hell, to the unquenchable f. 9.43
die and the f. is not quenched. * 9.44
die and the f. is not quenched. * 9.46
does not die, and the f. is not quenched. 9.48
For every one will be salted with f. 9.49
and warming himself at the f. 14.54
is cut down and thrown into the f. Lk 3.09
with the Holy Spirit and with f. 3.16
he will burn with unquenchable f. 3.17
want us to bid f. come down from 9.54
"I came to cast f. upon the earth; 12.49
out from Sodom f. and brimstone 17.29
had kindled a f. in the middle of 22.55
thrown into the f. and burned. Jn 15.06
officers had made a charcoal f., 18.18
land, they saw a charcoal f. there, 21.09
appeared to them tongues as of f., Ac 2.03
blood, and f., and vapor of smoke; 2.19
Sinai, in a flame of f. in a bush. 7.30
they kindled a f. and welcomed us 28.02
of sticks and put them on the f., 28.03
into the f. and suffered no harm. 28.05
because it will be revealed with f., 1Co 3.13
and the f. will test what sort of 3.13
be saved, but only as through f. 3.15
his mighty angels in flaming f., 2Th 1.07
and his servants flames of f. Heb 1.07
and a fury of f. which will consume 10.27
quenched raging f., escaped the 11.34
a blazing f., and darkness, and 12.18
for our God is a consuming f. 12.29
forest is set ablaze by a small f.! Jas 3.05
And the tongue is a f. The tongue 3.06
setting on f. the cycle of nature, 3.06
of nature, and set on f. by hell. 3.06
and will eat your flesh like f. 5.03
though perishable is tested by f., 1Pe 1.07
exist have been stored up for f., 2Pe 3.07
elements will be dissolved with f., 3.10
and the elements will melt with f.! 3.12
undergoing a punishment of eternal f. Jud 1.07
by snatching them out of the f.; 1.23
his eyes were like a flame of f., Rev 1.14
who has eyes like a flame of f., 2.18
to buy from me gold refined by f., 3.18
throne burn seven torches of f., 4.05
filled it with f. from the altar 8.05
and there followed hail and f., 8.07
burning with f., was thrown into 8.08
the color of f. and of sapphire 9.17
and f. and smoke and sulphur issued 9.17
by the f. and smoke and suplhur 9.18
and his legs like pillars of f. 10.01
f. pours from their mouth and 11.05
even making f. come down from 13.13
tormented with f. and brimstone in 14.10
the angel who has power over f., 14.18
be a sea of glass mingled with f., 15.02
was allowed to scorch men with f.; 16.08
her flesh and burn her up with f., 17.16
and she shall be burned with f.; 18.08
His eyes are like a flame of f., 19.12
the lake of f. that burns with 19.20
but f. came down from heaven and 20.09
the lake of f. and brimstone where 20.10
were thrown into the lake of f. 20.14
the second death, the lake of f.; 20.14
he was thrown into the lake of f. 20.15
that burns with f. and brimstone, 21.08

FIREBRANDS
Like a madman who throws f., arrows, Pro 26.18
these two smoldering stumps of f., Is 7.04

FIREPANS
the f., the forks, the shovels, and Num 4.14
for incense, and f., of pure gold; 1Ki 7.50
the f. also, and the bowls. What was of 2Ki 25.15
for incense, and f., of pure gold; 2Ch 4.22
and the f., and the basins, and the Jer 52.19

FIRES
like the f. made for his fathers. 2Ch 21.19
forth and make f. of the weapons Eze 39.09
they will make f. of them for 39.09
will make their f. of the weapons; 39,10

FIRM
stand f., and see the salvation of Ex 14.13
yea, the world stands f., never to be 1Ch 16.30

FIRM (cont.)

this we make a f. covenant and Neh 9.38
you have made f. the feeble knees. Job 4.04
faithfulness is f. as the heavens. Ps 89.02
my covenant will stand f. for him. 89.28
it shall stand f. while the skies 89.37
his heart is f., trusting in the 112.07
when he made f. the skies above, Pro 8.28
root of the righteous stands f. 12.12
He will seize f. hold on you, Is 22.17
hold the mast f. in its place, 33.23
and make f. the feeble knees. 35.03
God shall stand f. and take action. Dan 11.32
stand f. in your faith, be courageous, 1Co 16.13
for you stand f. in your faith. 2Co 1.24
that you stand f. in one spirit, Php 1.27
stand f. thus in the Lord, my 4.01
stand f. and hold to the traditions 2Th 2.15
But God's f. foundation stands, 2Ti 2.19
he must hold f. to the sure word as Tit 1.09
first confidence f. to the end, Heb 3.14
Resist him, f. in your faith, knowing 1Pe 5 09

FIRMAMENT

"Let there be a f. in the midst of Gen 1.06
And God made the f. and separated 1.07
were under the f. from the waters 1.07
the waters which were above the f. 1.07
And God called the f. Heaven. 1.08
lights in the f. of the heavens to 1.14
lights in the f. of the heavens to 1.15
set them in the f. of the heavens 1.17
earth across the f. of the heavens. 1.20
and the f. proclaims his handiwork. Ps 19.01
sanctuary; praise him in his mighty f.! 150.01
there was the likeness of a f., Eze 1.22
And under the f. their wings were 1.23
from above the f. over their heads; 1.25
And above the f. over their heads 1.26
on the f. that was over the heads 10.01
like the brightness of the f.; and those Dan 12.03

FIRMLY

and his kingdom was f. established. 1Ki 2.12
royal power was f. in his hand he 2Ki 14.05
royal power was f. in his hand he 2Ch 25.03
f. cast upon him and immovable. Job 41.23
thy word is f. fixed in the heavens. Ps 119.89
a city which is bound f. together, 122.03
and like nails f. fixed are the Ecc 12.11
But whoever is f. established in 1Co 7.37
have learned and have f. believed, 2Ti 3.14

FIRMNESS

but some of the f. of iron shall be Dan 2.41
order and the f. of your faith in Col 2.05

FIRST

The name of the f. is Pishon; Gen 2.11
on the f. day of the month, the tops 8.05
In the six hundred and f. year, 8.13
in the f. month, the f. day of 8.13
Noah was the f. tiller of the soil. 9.20
he was the f. on earth to be a 10.08
he had made an altar at the f.; 13.04
The f. came forth red, all his body 25.25
Jacob said, "F. sell me your birthright." 25.31
Jacob said, "Swear to me f." So he swore 25.33
name of the city was Luz at the f. 28.19
thread, saying, "This came out f." 38.28
cows ate up the f. seven fat cows, 41.20
replaced in our sacks the f. time, 43.18
came down the f. time to buy food; 43.20
and the f. fruits of my strength, 49.03
"or heed the f. sign, they may believe Ex 4.08
it shall be the f. month of the 12.02
on the f. day you shall put away 12.15
from the f. day until the seventh 12.15
On the f. day you shall hold a holy 12.16
In the f. month, on the fourteenth 12.18
whatever is the f. to open the womb 13.02
LORD all that f. opens the womb. 13.12
the males that f. open the womb; 13.15
of the f. fruits of your labor, of 23.16
"The f. of the f. fruits of your 23.19
the outmost curtain in the f. set; 26.04
joined at the top, at the f. ring; 26.24
and carbuncle shall be the f. row; 28.17
and with the f. lamb a tenth measure 29.40
two tables of stone like the f.; 34.01
words that were on the f. tables, 34.01
two tables of stone like the f.; 34.04
the f. fruits of wheat harvest, and 34.22
The f. of the f. fruits of your ground 34.26
the outmost curtain of the f. set; 36.11
joined at the top, at the f. ring; 36.29
and carbuncle was the f. row; 39.10
"On the f. day of the f. month you 40.02
And in the f. month in the second 40.17
on the f. day of the month, the 40.17
As an offering of f. fruits you may Lev 2.12
offering of f. fruits to the LORD, 2.14
offering of your f. fruits crushed 2.14
burn it as he burned the f. bull; 4.21
who shall offer f. the one for the 5.08
for sin, like the f. sin offering. 9.15
In the f. month, on the fourteenth 23.05
On the f. day you shall have a holy 23.07
sheaf of the f. fruits of your 23.10
leaven, as f. fruits to the LORD. 23.17
bread of the f. fruits as a wave 23.20
on the f. day of the month, you 23.24
On the f. day shall be a holy 23.35
on the f. day shall be a solemn 23.39
take on the f. day the fruit of 23.40
on the f. day of the second month, Num 1.01
and on the f. day of the second 1.18
They shall set out f. on the march. 2.09
offering the f. day was Nahshon 7.12
in the f. month of the second year 9.01
kept the passover in the f. month, 9.05
They set out for the f. time at the 10.13
Judah set out f. by their companies; 10.14
Of the f. of your coarse meal you 15.20
Of the f. of your coarse meal you 15.21
the f. fruits of what they give to 18.12
The f. ripe fruits of all that is 18.13
wilderness of Zin in the f. month, 20.01
"Amalek was the f. of the nations, 24.20
day of the f. month is the LORD's 28.16
On the f. day there shall be a holy 28.18
"On the day of the f. fruits, 28.26
"On the f. day of the seventh month 29.01
out from Rameses in the f. month, 33.03
the fifteenth day of the f. month; 33.03
on the f. day of the fifth month. 33.38
on the f. day of the eleventh month, Deu 1.03
two tables of stone like the f., 10.01
were on the f. tables which you 10.02
two tables of stone like the f., 10.03
as at the f. writing, the ten 10.04
as at the f. time, forty days and 10.10
hand shall be f. against him to 13.09
evening of the f. day remain all 16.04
the time you f. put the sickle to 16.09
shall be f. against him to put him 17.07
The f. fruits of your grain, of your 18.04
and the f. of the fleece of your 18.04
for he is the f. issue of his strength; 21.17
And the f. son whom she bears shall 25.06
some of the f. of all the fruit of 26.02
now I bring the f. of the fruit of 26.10
on the tenth day of the f. month, Jos 4.19
the LORD had commanded at the f., 8.33
Levites; since the lot fell to them f. 21.10

FIRST (cont.)

"Who shall go up f. for us against Ju 1.01
of the city was Laish at the f. 18.29
us shall go up f. to battle against 20.18
LORD said, "Judah shall go up f." 20.18
they had formed it on the f. day. 20.22
are routed before us, as at the f." 20.32
before us, as in the f. battle." 20.39
last kindness greater than the f., Ru 3.10
to him, "Let them burn the fat f., 1Sa 2.16
and that f. slaughter, which Jonathan 14.14
it was the f. altar that he built 14.35
Is today the f. time that I have 22.15
unless you f. bring Michal, Saul's 2Sa 3.13
the people fall at the f. attack, 17.09
the f. of all the house of Joseph 19.20
Were we not the f. to speak of 19.43
to death in the f. days of harvest, 21.09
swear to me f. that he will not 1Ki 1.51
The f. said, "No, the dead child is 3.22
the living child to the f. woman, 3.27
but f. make me a little cake of it 17.13
yourselves one bull and prepare it f., 18.25
'All that you f. demanded of your 20.09
of the districts went out f. And 20.17
"Inquire f. for the word of the 22.05
man of God bread of the f. fruits, 2Ki 4.42
Now the f. to dwell again in their 1Ch 9.02
the Jebusites f. shall be chief 11.06
Joab the son of Zeruiah went up f., 11.06
crossed the Jordan in the f. month, 12.15
Because you did not carry it the f. time, 15.13
that day David f. appointed that 16.07
The f. lot fell to Jehoiarib, the 24.07
The f. lot fell for Asaph to Joseph 25.09
charge of the f. division in the f. 27.02
of the army for the f. month. 27.03
from f. to last, are written in the 29.29
joined to the wing of the f. cherub. 2Ch 3.12
from f. to last, are they not written 9.29
from f. to last, are they not written 12.15
from f. to last, are written in the 16.11
"Inquire f. for the word of the 18.04
from f. to last, are written in the 20.34
from f. to last, are they not written 25.26
from f. to last, Isaiah the prophet 26.22
from f. to last, behold, they are 28.26
In the f. year of his reign, in the 29.03
in the f. month, he opened the doors 29.03
sanctify on the f. day of the f. month, 29.17
day of the f. month they finished. 29.17
abundance the f. fruits of grain, 31.05
the fourteenth day of the f. month. 35.01
and his acts, f. and last, behold, 35.27
Now in the f. year of Cyrus king of 36.22
In the f. year of Cyrus king of Ez 1.01
From the f. day of the seventh 3.06
old men who had seen the f. house, 3.12
However in the f. year of Cyrus 5.13
In the f. year of Cyrus the king, 6.03
day of the f. month the returned 6.19
for on the f. day of the f. month 7.09
and on the f. day of the fifth 7.09
on the twelfth day of the f. month, 8.31
on the f. day of the tenth month 10.16
and by the f. day of the f. month 10.17
of those who came up the f., Neh 7.05
on the f. day of the seventh month. 8.02
from the f. day to the last day, he 8.18
to bring the f. fruits of our 10.35
ground and the f. fruits of all 10.35
and to bring the f. of our coarse 10.37
the f. fruits, and the tithes, to 12.44
times, and for the f. fruits. Remember 13.31
face, and sat f. in the kingdom—: Est 1.14
In the f. month, which is the month 3.07
the thirteenth day of the f. month, 3.12
"Are you the f. man that was born? Job 15.07
"He is the f. of the works of God; 40.19
called the name of the f. Jemimah; 42.14
the f. issue of their strength in Ps 78.51
the f. issue of all their strength. 105.36
and with the f. fruits of all your Pro 3.09
the f. of his acts of old. 8.22
at the f., before the beginning of 8.23
or the f. of the dust of the world. 8.26
who states his case f. seems right, 18.17
restore your judges as at the f., Is 1.26
the f., and with the last; I am He. 41.04
I f. have declared it to Zion, and I 41.27
Your f. father sinned, and your 43.27
"I am the f. and I am the last; 44.06
I am the f., and I am the last. 48.12
down at the f. into Egypt to 52.04
for me, the ships of Tarshish f., 60.09
the f. fruits of his harvest. Jer 2.03
of one bringing forth her f. child, 4.31
where I made my name dwell at f., 7.12
(that was the f. year of Nebuchadrezzar 25.01
rebuild them as they were at f. 33.07
the land as at f., says the LORD. 33.11
words that were in the f. scroll, 36.28
F. the king of Assyria devoured him, 50.17
the f. face was the face of the Eze 10.14
on the f. day of the month, the word 26.01
in the f. month, on the f. day of 29.17
in the f. month, on the seventh day 30.20
on the f. day of the month, the word 31.01
on the f. day of the month, the word 32.01
in the f. month, on the fifteenth 32.17
same size as those of the f. gate; 40.21
And the f. of all the f. fruits 44.30
the priests the f. of your coarse 44.30
In the f. month, on the f. day of 45.18
"In the f. month, on the fourteenth 45.21
until the f. year of King Cyrus. Dan 1.21
In the f. year of Belshazzar king 7.01
The f. was like a lion and had 7.04
three of the f. horns were plucked 7.08
which appeared to me at the f. 8.01
between his eyes is the f. king. 8.21
In the f. year of Darius the son of 9.01
in the f. year of his reign, I, 9.02
I had seen in the vision at the f., 9.21
twenty-fourth day of the f. month, 10.04
for from the f. day that you set 10.12
in the f. year of Darius the Mede, I 11.01
When the LORD f. spoke through Hos 1.02
go and return to my f. husband, 2.07
Like the f. fruit on the fig tree, 9.10
in its f. season, I saw your fathers 9.10
men of the f. of the nations, Amo 6.01
now be the f. of those to go into 6.07
on the f. day of the month, the word Hag 1.01
The f. chariot had red horses, the Zec 6.02
victory to the tents of Judah f., 12.07
f. be reconciled to your brother, Mt 5.24
But seek f. his kingdom and his 6.33
You hypocrite, f. take the log out 7.05
let me f. go and bury my father." 8.21
f., Simon, who is called Peter, and 10.02
unless he f. binds the strong man? 12.29
that man becomes worse than the f. 12.45
the weeds f. and bind them in 13.30
say that f. Elijah must come?" 17.10
came home, Jesus spoke to him f., 17.25
and take the f. fish that comes up, 17.27
But many that are f. will be last, 19.30
will be last, and the last f. 19.30
with the last, up to the f.' 20.08
Now when the f. came, they thought 20.10
the last will be f., and the f. last." 20.16
would be f. among you must be your 20.27
and he went to the f. and said, 21.28

FIRST (cont.)

They said, "The f." Jesus said to them, Mt 21.31
other servants, more than the f.; 21.36
the f. married, and died, and having 22.25
This is the great and f. commandment. 22.38
f. cleanse the inside of the cup 23.26
Now on the f. day of Unleavened 26.17
fraud will be worse than the f." 27.64
the dawn of the f. day of the week, 28.01
unless he f. binds the strong man; Mk 3.27
f. the blade, then the ear, then the 4.28
to her, "Let the children f. be fed, 7.27
say that f. Elijah must come?" 9.11
does come f. to restore all things; 9.12
to them, "If any one would be f., 9.35
But many that are f. will be last, 10.31
will be last, and the last f. 10.31
would be f. among you must be 10.44
the f. took a wife, and when he died 12.20
"Which commandment is the f. of all?" 12.28
"The f. is 'Hear, O Israel: The Lord 12.29
And the gospel must f. be preached 13.10
And on the f. day of Unleavened 14.12
early on the f. day of the week 16.02
This was the f. enrollment, when Lk 2.02
f. take the log out of your own eye, 6.42
let me f. go and bury my father." 9.59
but let me f. say farewell to those 9.61
f. say, 'Peace be to this house!' 10.05
that man becomes worse than the f." 11.26
that he did not f. wash before 11.38
began to say to his disciples f., 12.01
some are last who will be f., 13.30
and some are f. who will be last." 13.30
The f. said to him, 'I have bought a 14.18
does not f. sit down and count the 14.28
not sit down f. and take counsel 14.31
one by one, he said to the f., 16.05
But f. he must suffer many things 17.25
The f. came before him, saying, 'Lord, 19.16
the f. took a wife, and died without 20.29
for this must f. take place, but the 21.09
But on the f. day of the week, at 24.01
He f. found his brother Simon, and Jn 1.41
"Every man serves the good wine f.; 2.10
This, the f. of his signs, Jesus did 2.11
whoever stepped in f. after the troubling * 5.04
knew from the f. who those were that did 6.64
a man without f. giving him a hearing 7.51
be the f. to throw a stone at her." * 8.07
place where John at f. baptized, 10.40
did not understand this at f.; 12.16
F. they led him to Annas; for he was the 18.13
came and broke the legs of the f., 19.32
who had at f. come to him by night, 19.39
Now on the f. day of the week Mary 20.01
outran Peter and reached the tomb f.; 20.04
disciple, who reached the tomb f., 20.08
the f. day of the week, the doors 20.19
In the f. book, O Theophilus, I have Ac 1.01
up his servant, sent him to you f., 3.26
sent forth our fathers the f. time. 7.12
were for the f. time called Christians. 11.26
had passed the f. and the second 12.10
of God should be spoken f. to you. 13.46
related how God f. visited the 15.14
On the f. day of the week, when we 20.07
time from the f. day that I set 20.18
but declared f. to those at Damascus, 26.20
by being the f. to rise from the 26.23
overboard f. and make for the land, 27.43
F., I thank my God through Jesus Rom 1.08
to the Jew f. and also to the Greek. 1.16
the Jew f. and also the Greek, 2.09
the Jew f. and also the Greek. 2.10
who have the f. fruits of the 8.23
F. Moses says, "I will make you 10.19
dough offered as f. fruits is holy, 11.16
to us now than when we f. believed; 13.11
who was the f. convert in Asia for 16.05
For, in the f. place, when you 1Co 11.18
appointed in the church f. apostles, 12.28
sitting by, let the f. be silent. 14.30
to you as of f. importance what I 15.03
the f. fruits of those who have 15.20
Christ the f. fruits, then at his 15.23
"The f. man Adam became a living 15.45
which is f. but the physical, and 15.46
The f. man was from the earth, a man 15.47
On the f. day of every week, each of 16.02
were the f. converts in Achaia, and 16.15
this, I wanted to come to you f., 2Co 1.15
but f. they gave themselves to the 8.05
we were the f. to come all the way 10.14
I preached the gospel to you at f.; Gal 4.13
we who f. hoped in Christ have been Eph 1.12
(this is the f. commandment with a 6.02
gospel from the f. day until now. Php 1.05
the dead in Christ will rise f.; 1Th 4.16
unless the rebellion comes f., and the 2Th 2.03
F. of all, then, I urge that supplications, 1Ti 2.01
For Adam was formed f., then Eve; 2.13
And let them also be tested f.; then if 3.10
let them f. learn their religious 5.04
having violated their f. pledge. 5.12
that dwelt f. in your grandmother 2Ti 1.05
to have the f. share of the crops. 2.06
At my f. defense no one took my 4.16
it was declared at f. by the Lord, Heb 2.03
we hold our f. confidence firm to 3.14
you again the f. principles of 5.12
He is f., by translation of his 7.02
f. for his own sins and then for 7.27
For if that f. covenant had been 8.07
he treats the f. as obsolete. 8.13
Now even the f. covenant had 9.01
transgressions under the f. covenant. 9.15
Hence even the f. covenant was not 9.18
abolishes the f. in order to 10.09
be a kind of f. fruits of his Jas 1.18
But the wisdom from above is f. pure., 3.17
F. of all you must understand this, 2Pe 1.20
become worse for them than the f. 2.20
F. of all you must understand this, 3.03
We love, because he f. loved us. 1Jn 4.19
who likes to put himself f., 3Jn 1.09
not, I am the f. and the last, Rev 1.17
abandoned the love you had at f. 2.04
and do the works you did at f. 2.05
'The words of the f. and the last, 2.08
your latter works exceed the f. 2.19
And the f. voice, which I had heard 4.01
the f. living creature like a lion, 4.07
The f. angel blew his trumpet, and 8.07
The f. woe has passed; behold, two 9.12
authority of the f. beast in its 13.12
inhabitants worship the f. beast, 13.12
from mankind as f. fruits for God 14.04
So the f. angel went and poured his 16.02
were ended. This is the f. resurrection. 20.05
who shares in the f. resurrection! 20.06
for the f. heaven and the f. earth 21.01
the f. was Jasper, the second 21.19
the f. and the last, the beginning 22.13

FIRST-BORN

father of Sidon his f., and Heth, Gen 10.15
And the f. said to the younger, "Our 19.31
and the f. went in, and lay with her 19.33
the f. said to the younger, "Behold, 19.34
The f. bore a son, and called his 19.37
Uz the f., Buz his brother, Kemuel 22.21
birth: Nebaioth, the f. of Ishmael; 25.13
to his father, "I am Esau your f. 27.19

FIRST-BORN (cont.)
"I am your son, your f., Esau." Gen 27.32
to give the younger before the f. 29.26
The sons of Leah: Reuben (Jacob's f.), 35.23
The sons of Eliphaz the f. of Esau: 36.15
And Judah took a wife for Er his f., 38.06
Judah's f., was wicked in the sight 38.07
called the name of the f. Manasseh, 41.51
the f. according to his birthright 43.33
Jacob and his sons. Reuben, Jacob's f., 46.08
his hands, for Manasseh was the f. 48.14
for this one is the f.; put your right 48.18
you are my f., my might, and the 49.03
the LORD, Israel is my f. son, Ex 4.22
behold, I will slay your f. son.'" 4.23
the f. of Israel: Hanoch, Pallu, 6.14
and all the f. in the land of Egypt 11.05
from the f. of Pharaoh who sits 11.05
even to the f. of the maidservant 11.05
and all the f. of the cattle. 11.05
smite all the f. in the land of 12.12
smote all the f. in the land of 12.29
from the f. of Pharaoh who sat on 12.29
throne to the f. of the captive 12.29
and all the f. of the cattle. 12.29
"Consecrate to me all the f.; 13.02
Every f. of man among your sons you 13.13
slew all the f. in the land of 13.15
both the f. of man and the f. of cattle. 13.15
but all the f. of my sons I redeem,' 13.15
"The f. of your sons you shall give 22.29
All the f. of your sons you shall 34.20
Israel's f., their generations, by Num 1.20
Nadab the f., and Abihu, Eleazar, and 3.02
of every f. that opens the womb 3.12
for all the f. are mine; on the day 3.13
I slew all the f. in the land of 3.13
for my own all the f. in Israel, 3.13
"Number all the f. males of the 3.40
of all the f. among the people of 3.41
numbered all the f. among the 3.42
And all the f. males, according to 3.43
of all the f. among the people of 3.45
seventy-three of the f. of the 3.46
from the f. of the people of Israel 3.50
the f. of all the people of Israel, 8.16
For all the f. among the people of 8.17
I slew all the f. in the land of 8.17
of all the f. among the people of 8.18
nevertheless the f. of man you 18.15
Reuben, the f. of Israel; the sons of 26.05
Egyptians were burying all their f., 33.04
and if the f. son is hers that is Deu 21.15
loved as the f. in preference to 21.16
of the disliked, who is the f., 21.16
but he shall acknowledge the f., 21.17
the right of the f. is his. 21.17
the cost of his f. shall he lay Jos 6.26
for he was the f. of Joseph. 17.01
To Machir the f. of Mannasseh, the 17.01
And he said to Jether his f., Ju 8.20
The name of his f. son was Joel, 1Sa 8.02
the name of the f. was Merab, 14.49
to the battle were Eliab the f., 17.13
his f. was Amnon, of Ahinoam of 2Sa 3.02
at the cost of Abiram his f., 1Ki 16.34
father of Sidon his f., and Heth, 1Ch 1.13
the f. of Ishmael, Nebaioth; 1.29
Judah's f., was wicked in the sight 2.03
Jesse was the father of Eliab his f., 2.13
the f. of Hezron: Ram, his first-born, 2.25
his f., Bunah, Oren, Ozem, and Ahijah 2.25
the f. of Jerahmeel: Maaz, Jamin, and 2.27
Mareshah his f., who was the father 2.42
sons of Hur the f. of Ephrathah: 2.50
the f. Amnon, by Ahinoam the Jezreelitess 3.01
Johanan the f., the second Jehoiakim, 3.15
the f. of Ephrathah the father of 4.04
Reuben the f. of Israel (for he was the f.; 5.01
the f. of Israel: Hanoch, Pallu, 5.03
Joel his f., the second Abijah. 6.28
Benjamin was the father of Bela his f., 8.01
His f. son: Abdon, then Zur, Kish, Baal, 8.30
Ulam his f., Jeush the second, and 8.39
Asaiah the f., and his sons. 9.05
the f. of Shallum the Korahite, was 9.31
and his f. son Abdon, then Zur, Kish, 9.36
Zechariah the f., Jediael the 26.02
Shemaiah the f., Jehozabad the 26.04
chief (for though he was not the f., 26.10
to Jehoram, because he was the f. 2Ch 21.03
the f. of our sons and of our Neh 10.36
the f. of death consumes his limbs. Job 18.13
He smote all the f. in Egypt, Ps 78.51
And I will make him the f., the highest 89.27
He smote all the f. in their land, 105.36
He it was who smote the f. of Egypt, 135.08
to him who smote the f. of Egypt, 136.10
And the f. of the poor will feed, Is 14.30
to Israel, and Ephraim is my f. Jer 31.09
them offer by fire all their f., Eze 20.26
Shall I give my f. for my transgression, Mic 6.07
over him, as one weeps over a f. Zec 12.10
birth to her f. son and wrapped Lk 2.07
he might be the f. among many Rom 8.29
invisible God, the f. of all creation; Col 1.15
the f. from the dead, that in 1.18
he brings the f. into the world, Heb 1.06
Destroyer of the f. might not touch 11.28
assembly of the f. who are enrolled 12.23
the f. of the dead, and the ruler of Rev 1.05

FIRSTLING
Every f. of an ass you shall redeem Ex 13.13
The f. of an ass you shall redeem 34.20
"But a f. of animals, which as a Lev 27.26
which as a f. belongs to the LORD, 27.26
and the f. of unclean beasts you Num 18.15
f. of a cow, or the f. of a sheep. 18.17
or the f. of a goat, you shall not 18.17
"All the f. males that are born of Deu 15.19
no work with the f. of your herd, 15.19
nor shear the f. of your flock. 15.19
His f. bull has majesty, and his 33.17

FIRSTLINGS
brought of the f. of his flock and Gen 4.04
All the f. of your cattle that are Ex 13.12
your male cattle, the f. of cow and sheep. 34.19
of all the f. among the cattle of Num 3.41
and the f. of your herd and of your Deu 12.06
or the f. of your herd or of your 12.17
and the f. of your herd and flock; 14.23
and the f. of our herds and of our Neh 10.36

FIRST-RIPE
the season of the f. grapes. Num 13.20
will be like a f. fig before the Is 28.04
like f. figs, but the other basket Jer 24.02
no f. fig which my soul desires. Mic 7.01
are like fig trees with f. figs— Nah 3.12

FISH
dominion over the f. of the sea, Gen 1.26
over the f. of the sea and over 1.28
ground and all the f. of the sea; 9.02
and the f. in the Nile shall die, Ex 7.18
And the f. in the Nile died; 7.21
We remember the f. we ate in Egypt Num 11.05
shall all the f. of the sea be 11.22
likeness of any f. that is in the Deu 4.18
birds, and of reptiles, and of f. 1Ki 4.33
to the entrance by the F. Gate, 2Ch 33.14
of Hassenaah built the F. Gate; Neh 3.03
and by the F. Gate and the Tower of 12.39

FISH (cont.)
brought in f. and all kinds of Neh 13.16
and the f. of the sea will declare Job 12.08
and the f. of the sea, whatever Ps 8.08
blood, and caused their f. to die. 105.29
Like f. which are taken in an evil Ecc 9.12
their f. stink for lack of water, Is 50.02
and make the f. of your streams Eze 29 04
with all the f. of your streams 29.04
you and all the f. of your streams; 29.05
the f. of the sea, and the birds of 38.20
and there will be very many f.; 47.09
its f. will be of very many kinds, 47.10
like the f. of the Great Sea. 47.10
and even the f. of the sea are Hos 4.03
appointed a great f. to swallow up Jon 1.17
belly of the f. three days and 1.17
his God from the belly of the f., 2.01
And the LORD spoke to the f., 2.10
makest men like the f. of the sea, Hab 1.14
of the air and the f. of the sea. Zep 1.03
cry will be heard from the F. Gate, 1.10
Or if he asks for a f., will give him Mt 7.10
sea and gathered f. of every kind; 13.47
only five loaves here and two f." 14.17
and the two f. he looked up to 14.19
said, "Seven, and a few small f." 15.34
he took the seven loaves and the f., 15.36
take the first f. that comes up, 17.27
out, they said, "Five, and two f." Mk 6.38
and the two f. he looked up to 6.41
divided the two f. among them all. 6.41
of broken pieces and of the f. 6.43
And they had a few small f.; and having 8.07
they enclosed a great shoal of f.; Lk 5.06
at the catch of f. which they had 5.09
more than five loaves and two f.— 9.13
and the two f. he looked up to heaven, 9.16
you, if his son asks for a f., 11.11
instead of a f give him a serpent 11.11
They gave him a piece of broiled f., 24.42
has five barley loaves and two f.; Jn 6.09
so also the f., as much as they 6.11
to them, "Children, have you any f.?" 21.05
haul it in, for the quantity of f. 21.06
boat, dragging the net full of f., 21.08
with f. lying on it, and bread. 21.09
some of the f. that you have just 21.10
full of large f., a hundred and 21.11
it to them, and so with the f. 21.13
for birds, and another for f. 1Co 15.39

FISHERMEN
The f. will mourn and lament, all Is 19.08
F. will stand beside the sea; Eze 47.10
into the sea; for they were f. Mt 4.18
in the sea; for they were f. Mk 1.16
but the f. had gone out of them and Lk 5.02

FISHERS
"Behold, I am sending for many f., Jer 16.16
me, and I will make you f. of men." Mt 4.19
I will make you become f. of men." Mk 1.17

FISHHOOK
"Can you draw out Leviathan with a f., Job 41.01

FISHHOOKS
with hooks, even the last of you with f. Amo 4.02

FISHING
harpoons, or his head with f. spears? Job 41.07
Simon Peter said to them, "I am going f." Jn 21.03

FIST
or with his f. and the man does Ex 21.18
will shake his f. at the mount of Is 10.32
to fight and to hit with wicked f. 58.04
by her hisses and shakes his f. Zep 2.15

FISTS
has gathered the wind in his f.? Pro 30.04

FIT
will make him a helper f. for him." Gen 2.18
was not found a helper f. for him. 2.20
all of them strong and f. for war. 2Ki 24.16
f. for war, able to handle spear and 2Ch 25.05
f. for war, in divisions according 26.11
looks back is f. for the kingdom Lk 9.62
It is f. neither for the land nor 14.35
did not see f. to acknowledge God, Rom 1.28

FITLY
A word f. spoken is like apples of Pro 25.11
of water, bathed in milk, f. set. Sol 5.12

FITS
as f. the occasion, that it may impart Eph 4.29

FITTED
they have f. their arrow to the string, Ps 11.02

FITTEST
select the best and f. of your master's 2Ki 10.03

FITTING
in each frame, for f. together; Ex 26.17
had two tenons, for f. together; 36.22
and it is not f. for us to witness Ez 4.14
It is not f. for a fool to live in Pro 19.10
so honor is not f. for a fool. 26.01
good and to be f. is to eat and Ecc 5.18
for thus it is f. for us to fulfil Mt 3.15
It was f. to make merry and be glad, Lk 15.32
among you, as is f. among saints. Eph 5.03
talk, nor levity, which are not f.; 5.04
husbands, as is f. in the Lord. Col 3.18
as is f., because your faith is 2Th 1.03
For it was f. that he, for whom and Heb 2.10
For it was f. that we should have 7.26

FIVE
had lived a hundred and f. years, Gen 5.06
were nine hundred and f. years; 5.11
birth of Noah f. hundred and 5.30
After Noah was f. hundred years old, 5.32
of Arpachshad f. hundred years, 11.11
were two hundred and f. years; 11.32
of Ellasar, four kings against f. 14.09
Suppose f. of the fifty righteous 18.28
the whole city for lack of f.?" 18.28
portion was f. times as much as 43.34
there are yet f. years in which 45.06
there are yet f. years of famine 45.11
of silver and f. festal garments. 45.22
brothers he took f. men and presented 47.02
he shall pay f. oxen for an ox, and Ex 22.01
F. curtains shall be coupled to one 26.03
and the other f. curtains shall be 26.03
shall couple f. curtains by 26.09
f. for the frames of the one side 26.27
and f. bars for the frames of the other 26.27
and f. bars for the frames of the side 26.27
for the screen f. pillars of 26.37
you shall cast f. bases of bronze 26.37
f. cubits long and f. cubits broad; 27.01
fifty, and the height f. cubits, 27.18
of liquid myrrh f. hundred shekels. 30.23
and of cassia f. hundred, according 30.24
And he coupled f. curtains to one 36.10
and the other f. curtains he coupled 36.10
He coupled f. curtains by themselves, 36.16
f. for the frames of the one side 36.31
and f. bars for the frames of the other 36.32

FIVE (cont.)
and f. bars for the frames of the Ex 36.32
and its f. pillars with their hooks. 36.38
but their f. bases were of bronze. 36.38
f. cubits was its length, and f. 38.01
and f. cubits its breadth; it was 38.01
cubits long and f. cubits high in 38.18
f. hundred and fifty men. 38.26
F. of you shall chase a hundred, and Lev 26.08
person is from f. years old up to 27.05
a month old up to f. years old, 27.06
be for a male f. shekels of silver, 27.06
was forty-six thousand f. hundred. Num 1.21
was forty thousand f. hundred. 1.33
was forty-one thousand f. hundred. 1.41
three thousand f. hundred and 1.46
forty-six thousand f. hundred. 2.11
being forty thousand f. hundred. 2.19
forty-one thousand f. hundred. 2.28
three thousand f. hundred and 2.32
was seven thousand f. hundred. 3.22
you shall take f. shekels apiece; 3.47
eight thousand f. hundred and 4.48
f. rams, f. male goats, and f. 7.17
and f. male lambs a year old. 7.17
f. rams, f. male goats. and f. 7.23
and f. male lambs a year old. 7.23
f. rams, f. male goats, and f. 7.29
and f. male lambs a year old. 7.29
f. rams. f. male goats, and f. 7.35
and f. male lambs a year old. 7.35
f. rams, f. male goats, and f. 7.41
and f. male lambs a year old. 7.41
f. rams, f. male goats, and f. 7.47
and f. male lambs a year old. 7.47
f. rams, f. male goats, and f. 7.53
and f. male lambs a year old. 7.53
f. rams, f. male goats, and f. 7.59
and f. male lambs a year old. 7.59
f. rams, f. male goats, and f. 7.65
and f. male lambs a year old. 7.65
f. rams, f. male goats, and f. 7.71
and f. male lambs a year old. 7.71
f. rams, f. male goats, and f. 7.77
and f. male lambs a year old. 7.77
f. rams, f. male goats, and f. 7.83
and f. male lambs a year old. 7.83
or f. days, or ten days, or twenty 11.19
shall fix at f. shekels in silver, 18.16
number, forty thousand f. hundred. 26.18
seventy-six thousand f. hundred. 26.22
number, sixty thousand f. hundred. 26.27
thirty-two thousand f. hundred. 26.37
the f. kings of Midian; and they also 31.08
one out of f. hundred, of the 31.28
thirty-seven thousand f. hundred sheep, 31.36
were thirty thousand f. hundred, 31.39
thirty-seven thousand f. hundred sheep, 31.43
and thirty thousand f. hundred asses, 31.45
And he took about f. thousand men, Jos 8.12
Then the f. kings of the Amorites, 10.05
These f. kings fled, and hid themselves 10.16
"The f. kings have been found, hidden 10.17
and bring those f. kings out to me 10.22
brought those f. kings out to him 10.23
and he hung them on f. trees. And they 10.26
there are f. rulers of the Philistines, 13.03
the f. lords of the Philistines, and Ju 3.03
Danites sent f. able men from the 18.02
Then the f. men departed, and came 18.07
Then the f. men who had gone to spy 18.14
and the f. men who had gone to spy 18.17
f. thousand men of them were cut 20.45
"F. golden tumors and f. golden mice, 1Sa 6.04
And when the f. lords of the 6.16
Philistines belonging to the f. lords, 6.18
of the coat was f. thousand 17.05
and chose f. smooth stones from the 17.40
Give me f. loaves of bread, or 21.03
f. sheep ready dressed, and f. measures 25.18
and her f. maidens attended her; 25.42
He was f. years old when the news 2Sa 4.04
and the f. sons of Merob the 21.08
of Judah were f. hundred thousand. 24.09
his songs were a thousand and f. 1Ki 4.32
The lowest story was f. cubits broad, 6.06
each story f. cubits high, and it 6.10
F. cubits was the length of one 6.24
and f. cubits the length of the 6.24
of the one capital was f. cubits, 7.16
of the other capital was f. cubits. 7.16
and f. cubits high, and a line of 7.23
f. on the south side of the house, 7.39
land f. on the north side of the 7.39
f. on the south side and f. on the north, 7.49
f. hundred and fifty, who had charge 9.23
dove's dung for f. shekels of 2Ki 6.25
some men take f. of the remaining 7.13
should have struck f. or six times; 13.19
and f. men of the king's council who 25.19
Judah had f. sons in all. 1Ch 2.04
Heman, Calcol, and Dara, f. in all. 2.06
Hasadiah, and Jushabhesed, f. 3.20
Tochen, and Ashan, f. cities, 4.32
f. hundred men of the Simeonites, 4.42
f., all of them chief men; 7.03
f., heads of fathers' houses, mighty 7.07
of great stature, f. cubits tall. 11.23
house of God f. thousand talents 29.07
of f. cubits, touched the wall of 2Ch 3.11
of f. cubits, touched the wing of 3.11
of f. cubits, touched the wall of 3.12
also of f. cubits, was joined to the 3.12
a capital of f. cubits on the top 3.15
and f. cubits high, and a line of 4.02
and set f. on the south side, and 4.06
and f. on the north side. In these 4.06
f. on the south side and f. on 4.07
f. on the south side and f. on 4.08
a bronze platform f. cubits long, 6.13
f. cubits wide, and three cubits 6.13
slain of Israel f. hundred thousand 13.17
and seven thousand f. hundred, 26.13
offerings f. thousand lambs and 35.09
and kids and f. hundred bulls. 35.09
of silver were f. thousand four Ez 1.11
f. thousand minas of silver, and one 2.69
f. hundred and thirty priests' Neh 7.70
slew and destroyed f. hundred men. Est 9.06
Jews have slain f. hundred men and 9.12
f. hundred yoke of oxen, and f. Job 1.03
and f. hundred she-asses, and very 1.03
four or f. on the branches of a Is 17.06
there will be f. cities in the 19.18
at the threat of f. you shall flee, 30.17
of the one capital was f. cubits; Jer 52.22
between the side rooms, f. cubits; Eze 40.07
a breadth of f. and twenty cubits, 40.13
cubits long and f. cubits broad. 40.30
f. cubits on either side; 40.48
entrance were f. cubits on either 41.02
of the side chambers was f. cubits; 41.09
which was left free was f. cubits. 41.09
left free was f. cubits round 41.11
building was f. cubits thick round 41.12
f. hundred cubits by the measuring 42.16
f. hundred cubits by the measuring 42.17
f. hundred cubits by the measuring 42.18
f. hundred cubits by the measuring 42.19
f. hundred cubits long and f. 42.20
cubits long and f. hundred cubits 42.20
square plot of f. hundred by f. 45.02
city an area f. thousand cubits 45.06
f. shekels shall be f. shekels, 45.12

FIVE (cont.)
f. thousand cubits in breadth and Eze 48.15
four thousand f. hundred cubits, 48.16
side four thousand f. hundred, 48.16
east side four thousand f. hundred, 48.16
west side four thousand f. hundred. 48.16
four thousand f. hundred cubits by 48.30
be four thousand f. hundred cubits, 48.32
four thousand f. hundred cubits by 48.33
be four thousand f. hundred cubits, 48.34
"We have only f. loaves here and Mt 14.17
and taking the f. loaves and the 14.19
who ate were about f. thousand men, 14.21
remember the f. loaves of the f. 16.09
F. of them were foolish, and f. were 25.02
to one he gave f. talents, to 25.15
received the f. talents went at 25.16
and he made f. talents more. 25.16
received the f. talents came 25.20
bringing f. talents more, saying, 25.20
you delivered to me f. talents; 25.20
here I have made f. talents more.' 25.20
out, they said, "F., and two fish." Mk 6.38
And taking the f. loaves and the 6.41
the loaves were f. thousand men. 6.44
When I broke the f. loaves for the f. 8.19
and for f. months she hid herself, Lk 1.24
one owed f. hundred denarii, and the 7.41
no more than f. loaves and two 9.13
For there were about f. thousand men. 9.14
And taking the f. loaves and the 9.16
Are not f. sparrows sold for two 12.06
one house there will be f. divided, 12.52
'I have bought f. yoke of oxen, 14.19
for I have f. brothers, so that he 16.28
your pound has made f. pounds.' 19.18
'And you are to be over f. cities.' 19.19
for you have had f. husbands, Jn 4.18
Bethzatha, which has f. porticoes. 5.02
here who has f. barley loaves and 6.09
down, in number about f. thousand. 6.10
fragments from the f. barley loaves, 6.13
the men came to about f. thousand. Ac 4.04
and in f. days we came to them at 20.06
And after f. days the high priest 24.01
rather speak f. words with my mind, 1Co 14.19
to more than f. hundred brethren 15.06
F. times I have received at the 2Co 11.24
to torture them for f. months, Rev 9.05
hurting men for f. months lies in 9.10
f. of whom have fallen, one is, the 17.10

FIX
them) you shall f. at five shekels Num 18.16
and f. my eyes on thy ways. Ps 119.15

FIXED
means that the thing is f. by God, Gen 41.32
priests had a f. allowance from 47.22
he f. the bounds of the peoples Deu 32.08
And he f. his gaze and stared at 2Ki 8.11
of Queen Esther f. these practices Est 9.32
Thou hast f. all the bounds of the Ps 74.17
having my eyes f. on all thy 119.06
word is firmly f. in the heavens. 119.89
he f. their bounds which cannot be 148.06
nails firmly f. are the collected Ecc 12.11
by day and the f. order of the Jer 31.35
"If this f. order departs from 31.36
and as the f. portion of oil, one Eze 45.14
in the synagogue were f. on him. Lk 4.20
and you a great chasm has been f., 16.26
the Father has f. by his own Ac 1.07
And he f. his attention upon them, 3.05
because he has f. a day on which he 17.31

FLAG
Never f. in zeal, be aglow with the Rom 12.11

FLAGONS
and its f. and bowls with which to Ex 25.29
its bowls and f. with which to 37.16
and the f. for the drink offering; Num 4.07
from the cups to all the f. Is 22.24

FLAGRANT
is great, because your sins are f. Jer 30.14
is great, because your sins are f., 30.15

FLAGSTAFF
are left like a f. on the top of a Is 30.17

FLAIL
I will f. your flesh with the Ju 8.07

FLAKE-LIKE
f. thing, fine as hoarfrost on the Ex 16.14

FLAME
to him in a f. of fire out of the Ex 3.02
f. from the city of Sihon. Num 21.28
And when the f. went up toward Ju 13.20
ascended in the f. of the altar 13.20
the f. will dry up his shoots, and Job 15.30
and the f. of his fire does not 18.05
and a f. comes forth from his mouth 41.21
as the f. sets the mountains ablaze, Ps 83.14
messengers, fire and f. thy ministers. 104.04
company; the f. burned up the wicked. 106.18
of fire, a most vehement f. Sol 8.06
as dry grass sinks down in the f., Is 5.24
a fire, and his Holy One a f.; 10.17
and the f. of a devouring fire. 29.06
anger and a f. of devouring fire, 30.30
and the f. shall not consume you. 43.02
themselves from the power of the f. 47.14
a f. from the house of Sihon; Jer 48.45
the blazing f. shall not be quenched, Eze 20.47
the f. of the fire slew those men Dan 3.22
they shall fall by sword and f., 11.33
and f. has burned all the trees of Joe 1.19
them, and behind them a f. burns. 2.03
crackling of a f. of fire devouring 2.05
fire, and the house of Joseph a f., Ob 1.18
flash like f. when mustered in Nah 2.03
for I am in anguish in this f.' Lk 16.24
in a f. of fire in a bush. Ac 7.30
his eyes were like a f. of fire, Rev 1.14
who has eyes like a f. of fire. 2.18
His eyes are like a f. of fire, 19.12

FLAMED
glowing coals f. forth from him. 2Sa 22.09
before him coals of fire f. forth. 22.13
glowing coals f. forth from him. Ps 18.08

FLAMES
the LORD flashes forth f. of fire. Ps 29.07
and his rebuke with f. of fire. Is 66.15
his throne was fiery f., its wheels Dan 7.09
winds, and his servants f. of fire. Heb 1.07

FLAMING
and a f. sword which turned every Gen 3.24
fire pot and a f. torch passed 15.17
with f. fire at his right hand. Deu 33.02
Out of his mouth go f. torches; Job 41.19
the shining of a f. fire by night; Is 4.05
has burned like a f. fire in Jacob, Lam 2.03
his eyes like f. torches, his arms Dan 10.06
morning it blazes like a f. fire. Hos 7.06
like a f. torch among sheaves; Zec 12.06
quench all the f. darts of the Eph 6.16
with his mighty angels in f. fire, 2Th 1.07

FLANK
lay open the f. of Moab from the Eze 25.09

FLASH
you away, and why do your eyes f., Job 15.12
His sneezings f. forth light, and 41.18
F. forth the lightning and scatter Ps 144.06
to and fro, like a f. of lightning. Eze 1.14
polished to f. like lightning! 21.10
glitter and to f. like lightning— 21.28
destruction f. forth against the Amo 5.09
The chariots f. like flame when Nah 2.03
at the f. of thy glittering spear. Hab 3.11

FLASHED
he f. forth lightnings, and routed Ps 18.14
thunder; thy arrows f. on every side. 77.17
lightning that f. through their 105.32
the light, rays f. from his hand; Hab 3.04
a light from heaven f. about him. Ac 9.03

FLASHES
of the LORD f. forth flames of Ps 29.07
Its f. are f. of fire, a most Sol 8.06
the lightning f. and lights up the Lk 17.24
From the throne issue f. of lightning, Rev 4.05
f. of lightning, and an earthquake. 8.05
and there were f. of lightning, 11.19
And there were f. of lightning, loud 16.18

FLASHING
and fire f. continually in the Ex 9.24
the f. spear and the javelin. Job 39.23
There he broke the f. arrows, Ps 76.03
and fire f. forth continually, and Eze 1.04
f. sword and glittering spear, hosts Nah 3.03

FLASK
and take this f. of oil in your 2Ki 9.01
Then take the f. of oil, and pour it 9.03
"Go, buy a potter's earthen f., Jer 19.01
shall break the f. in the sight of 19.10
brought an alabaster f. of ointment, Lk 7.37

FLASKS
but the wise took f. of oil with Mt 25.04

FLAT
wall of the city will fall down f., Jos 6.05
shout, and the wall fell down f., 6.20
down, so that the tent lay f. Ju 7.13
in charge of making the f. cakes. 1Ch 9.31

FLATTER
For I do not know how to f., Job 32.22
they f. with their tongue. Ps 5.09

FLATTERED
But they f. him with their mouths; Ps 78.36

FLATTERIES
and obtain the kingdom by f. Dan 11.21

FLATTERING
with f. lips and a double heart Ps 12.02
May the LORD cut off all f. lips, 12.03
and a f. mouth works ruin. Pro 26.28
false vision or f. divination Eze 12.24
and by fair and f. words they Rom 16.18
f. people to gain advantage. Jud 1.16

FLATTERS
For he f. himself in his own eyes Ps 36.02
than he who f. with his tongue. Pro 28.23
A man who f. his neighbor spreads a 29.05

FLATTERY
person or use f. toward any man. Job 32.21
seduce with f. those who violate Dan 11.32
join themselves to them with f.; 11.34
For we never used either words of f., 1Th 2.05

FLAUNTED
so openly and f. her nakedness, Eze 23.18

FLAUNTS
knowledge, but a fool f. his folly. Pro 13.16

FLAW
my love; there is no f. in you. Sol 4.07

FLAWLESS
f. to her that bore her. The maidens Sol 6.09

FLAX
(The f. and the barley were ruined, Ex 9.31
in the ear and the f. was in bud. 9.31
the stalks of f. which she had Jos 2.06
arms became as f. that has caught Ju 15.14
She seeks wool and f., and works Pro 31.13
in combed f. will be in despair, Is 19.09
with a line of f. and a measuring Eze 40.03
and my water, my wool and my f., Hos 2.05
I will take away my wool and my f., 2.09

FLAY
And he shall f. the burnt offering Lev 1.06
and could not f. all the burnt 2Ch 29.34
and f. their skin from off them, and Mic 3.03

FLAYED
while the Levites f. the victims. 2Ch 35.11

FLEA
After a dead dog! After a f.! 1Sa 24.14

FLED
the kings of Sodom and Gomorrah f., Gen 14.10
and the rest f. to the mountain. 14.10
with her, and she f. from her. 16.06
He f. with all that he had, and 31.21
the third day that Jacob had f., 31.22
and my sleep f. from my eyes. 31.40
to you when you f. from your 35.01
to him when he f. from his brother. 35.07
and f. and got out of the house. 39.12
and had f. out of the house, 39.13
and f. and got out of the house." 39.15
with me, and f. out of the house." 39.18
But Moses f. from Pharaoh, and Ex 2.15
a serpent; and Moses f. from it. 4.03
was told that the people had f., 14.05
and the Egyptians f. into it, 14.27
round about them f. at their cry; Num 16.34
city of refuge, to which he had f., 35.25
his city of refuge to which he f., 35.26
for him who has f. to his city of 35.32
and they f. before the men of Ai, Jos 7.04
and f. in the direction of the 8.15
the people that f. to the wilderness 8.20
And as they f. before Israel, while 10.11
These five kings f., and hid themselves 10.16
home, to the town from which he f. 20.06
Adonibezek f.; but they pursued Ju 1.06
his chariot and f. away on foot. 4.15
But Sisera f. away on foot to the 4.17
the army ran; they cried out and f. 7.21
and the army f. as far as Bethshittah 7.22
And Zebah and Zalmunna f.; 8.12
And Jotham ran away and f., 9.21
chased him, and he f. before him; 9.40
the people of the city f. to it, 9.51
Then Jephthah f. from his brothers, 11.03
And they turned and f. toward the 20.45
men turned and f. toward the 20.47
and they f., every man to his home; 1Sa 4.10
I f. from the battle today." 4.16
"Israel has f. before the Philistines, 4.17
f. from him, and were much afraid. 17.24
their champion was dead, they f. 17.51

FLED (cont.)
them, so that they f. before him. 1Sa 19.08
And David f., and escaped. 19.10
and he f. away and escaped. 19.12
Now David f. and escaped, and he 19.18
Then David f. from Naioth in Ramah, 20.01
And David rose and f. that day from 21.10
David, and they knew that he f., 22.17
Abiathar, escaped and f. after David. 22.20
of Ahimelech f. to David to Keilah, 23.06
Saul that David had f. to Gath, 27.04
men, who mounted camels and f. 30.17
men of Israel f. before the 31.01
of Israel had f. and that Saul and 31.07
they forsook their cities and f.; 31.07
"The people have f. from the battle, 2Sa 1.04
the Beerothites f. to Gittaim, 4.03
and his nurse took him up, and f.; 4.04
and, as she f. in her haste, he fell, 4.04
the Syrians; and they f. before him. 10.13
Ammonites saw that the Syrians f., 10.14
they likewise f. before Abishai, and 10.14
And the Syrians f. before Isarel; 10.18
and each mounted his mule and f. 13.29
But Absalom f. And the young 13.34
But Absalom f., and went to Talmai 13.37
So Absalom f., and went to Geshur, 13.38
and all Israel f. every one to his 18.17
Now Israel had f. every man to his 19.08
and now he has f. out of the land 19.09
and the men f. from the Philistines 23.11
met me when I f. from Absalom your 1Ki 2.07
Joab f. to the tent of the LORD 2.28
"Joab has f. to the tent of the 2.29
but Hadad f. to Egypt, together with 11.17
who had f. from his master Hadadezer 11.23
and f. into Egypt, to Shishak king 11.40
whither he had f. from King 12.02
the Syrians f. and Israel pursued 20.20
And the rest f. into the city of 20.30
Benhadad also f., and entered an 20.30
Moabites, till they f. before them; 2Ki 3.24
So they f. away in the twilight and 7.07
as it was, and f. for their lives. 7.07
surrounded him; but his army f. home. 8.21
Then he opened the door, and f. 9.10
Then Joram reined about and f., 9.23
he f. in the direction of Bethhaggan 9.27
And he f. to Megiddo, and died there. 9.27
and every man f. to his home. 14.12
in Jerusalem, and he f. to Lachish. 14.19
the men of war f. by night by the 25.04
men of Israel f. before the 1Ch 10.01
the army had f. and that Saul and 10.07
they forsook their cities and f.; 10.07
and the men f. from the Philistines. 11.13
for battle; and they f. before him. 19.14
Ammonites saw that the Syrians f., 19.15
they likewise f. before Abishai, 19.15
And the Syrians f. before Israel; 19.18
whither he had f. from King 2Ch 10.02
The men of Israel f. before Judah, 13.16
Judah, and the Ethiopians f. 14.12
and every man f. to his home. 25.22
in Jerusalem, and he f. to Lachish. 25.27
the work, had f. each to his field. Neh 13.10
At thy rebuke they f.; at the sound Ps 104.07
The sea looked and f., Jordan turned 114.03
I have f. to thee for refuge! 143.09
trembles, Gibeah of Saul has f. Is 10.29
and to whom we f. for help to be 20.06
For they have f. from the swords, 21.15
All your rulers have f. together, 22.03
though they had f. far away. 22.03
my sleep has f. because of the 38.15
all the birds of the air had f. Jer 4.25
the beasts have f. and are gone. 9.10
was afraid and f. and escaped to 26.21
they f., going out of the city at 39.04
beaten down, and have f. in haste; 46.05
Why has Apis f.? Why did not 46.15
they have turned and f. together, 46.21
the men of war f. and went out 52.07
they f. without strength before the Lam 1.06
to him, and sleep f. from him. Dan 6.18
and they f. to hide themselves. 10.07
(Jacob f. to the land of Aram, there Hos 12.12
as if a man f. from a lion, and a Amo 5.19
flee as you f. from the earthquake Zec 14.05
The herdsmen f., and going into the Mt 8.33
the disciples forsook him, and f. 26.56
The herdsmen f., and told it in the Mk 5.14
And they all forsook him, and f. 14.50
they went out and f. from the tomb; 16.08
they f., and told it in the city Lk 8.34
At this retort Moses f., and became Ac 7.29
of it and f. to Lystra and Derbe, 14.06
so that they f. out of that house 19.16
we who have f. for refuge might Heb 6.18
and the woman f. into the wilderness, Rev 12.06
And every island f. away, and no 16.20
his presence earth and sky f. away, 20.11

FLEE
forth, they said, "F. for your life; Gen 19.17
f. to the hills, lest you be consumed." 19.17
but I cannot f. to the hills, lest 19.19
city is near enough to f. to, 19.20
arise, f. to Laban my brother in 27.43
tell him that he intended to f. 31.20
Why did you f. secretly, and cheat 31.27
and his cattle f. into the houses; Ex 9.20
"Let us f. from before Israel; 14.25
for you a place to which he may f. 21.13
and you shall f. when none pursues Lev 26.17
and they shall f. as one flees 26.36
them that hate thee f. before thee." Num 10.35
Therefore now f. to your place; 24.11
shall permit the manslayer to f., 35.06
person without intent may f. there. 35.11
person without intent may f. there. 35.15
that the manslayer might f. there, Deu 4.42
that any manslayer can f. to them. 19.03
he may f. to one of these cities 19.05
and f. before you seven ways. 28.07
and f. seven ways before them; 28.25
before, we shall f. before them; Jos 8.05
as before.' So we will f. from them; 8.06
had no power to f. this way or 8.20
intent or unwittingly may f. there; 20.03
He shall f. to one of these cities 20.04
without intent could f. there, 20.09
"Let us f., and draw them away from Ju 20.32
at Jerusalem, "Arise, and let us f.; 2Sa 15.14
people who are with him will f. 17.02
For if we f., they will not care 18.03
are ashamed when they f. in battle. 19.03
Or will you f. three months before 24.13
his chariot, to f. to Jerusalem. 1Ki 12.18
Then open the door and f.; do not 2Ki 9.03
his chariot, to f. to Jerusalem. 2Ch 10.18
But I said, "Should such a man as I f.? Neh 6.11
they f. away, they see no good. Job 9.25
He will f. from an iron weapon; 20.24
When she rouses herself to f., 39.18
The arrow cannot make him f.; 41.28
"F. like a bird to the mountains; Ps 11.01
see me in the street f. from me. 31.11
those who hate him f. before him! 68.01
of the armies, they f., they f.!" 68.12
What ails you, O sea, that you f.? 114.05
whither shall I f. from thy presence? 139.07
The wicked f. when no one pursues, Pro 28.01
day breathes and the shadows f., Sol 2.17

FLEE (cont.)
day breathes and the shadows f., Sol 4.06
To whom will you f. for help, Is 10.03
inhabitants of Gebim f. for safety. 10.31
every man will f. to his own land. 13.14
his fugitives f. to Zoar, to Eglathshelishiyah. 15.05
harvest will f. away in a day of 17.11
and they will f. far away, chased 17.13
A thousand shall f. at the threat 30.17
at the threat of five you shall f., 30.17
and he shall f. from the sword, and 31.08
At the thunderous noise peoples f., 33.03
sorrow and sighing shall f. away. 35.10
f. from Chaldea, declare this with a 48.20
sorrow and sighing shall f. away. 51.11
f. for safety, stay not, for I bring Jer 4.06
F. for safety, O people of Benjamin, 6.01
The swift cannot f. away, nor the 46.06
F.! Save yourselves! Be like a 48.06
F., turn back, dwell in the depths, O 49.08
she turned to f., and panic seized 49.24
F., wander far away, dwell in the 49.30
both man and beast shall f. away. 50.03
"F. from the midst of Babylon, and 50.08
every one shall f. to his own land 50.16
they f. and escape from the land of 50.28
"F. from the midst of Babylon, let 51.06
let the beasts f. from under it and Dan 4.14
mighty shall f. away naked in that Amo 2.16
f. away to the land of Judah, and 7.12
not one of them shall f. away, 9.01
But Jonah rose to f. to Tarshish Jon 1.03
why I made haste to f. to Tarshish; 4.02
F. from the land of the north, says Zec 2.06
and you shall f. as you fled from 14.05
and f. to Egypt, and remain there Mt 2.13
warned you to f. from the wrath to 3.07
you in one town, f. to the next; 10.23
are in Judea f. to the mountains; 24.16
are in Judea f. to the mountains; Mk 13.14
warned you to f. from the wrath to Lk 3.07
are in Judea f. to the mountains, 21.21
but they will f. from him, for they Jn 10.05
the devil and he will f. from you. Jas 4.07

FLEECE
the first of the f. of your sheep, Deu 18.04
I am laying a f. of wool on the Ju 6.37
if there is dew on the f. alone, 6.37
next morning and squeezed the f., 6.38
dew from the f. to fill a bowl 6.38
trial only this once with the f.; 6.39
pray, let it be dry only on the f., 6.39
for it was dry on the f. only, 6.40
not warmed with the f. of my sheep; Job 31.20

FLEEING
"I am f. from my mistress Sarai." Gen 16.08
and that by f. to one of these Deu 4.42
who by f. there may save his life. 19.04
'They are f. from us, as before.' Jos 8.06
heard that the Philistines were f., 1Sa 14.22
his hand pierced the f. serpent. Job 26.13
punish Leviathan the f. serpent, Is 27.01
that he was f. from the presence Jon 1.10

FLEES
flee as one f. from the sword, Lev 26.36
and the man f. into one of these Deu 19.11
he f. like a shadow, and continues Job 14.02
he f. from its power in headlong 27.22
He who f. at the sound of the Is 24.18
Ask him who f. and her who escapes; Jer 48.19
He who f. from the terror shall 48.44
coming and leaves the sheep and f.; Jn 10.12
He f. because he is a hireling and 10.13

FLEET
King Solomon built a f. of ships at 1Ki 9.26
sent with the f. his servants, 9.27
Moreover the f. of Hiram, which 10.11
For the king had a f. of ships of 10.22
at sea with the f. of Hiram. 10.22
three years the f. of ships of 10.22

FLEETING
let me know how f. my life is! Ps 39.04
tongue is a f. vapor and a snare Pro 21.06
to enjoy the f. pleasures of sin. Heb 11.25

FLESH
and closed up its place with f.; Gen 2.21
of my bones and f. of my f.; 2.23
his wife, and they become one f. 2.24
for he is f., but his days shall be 6.03
for all f. had corrupted their way 6.12
determined to make an end of all f.; 6.13
to destroy all f. in which is the 6.17
And of every living thing of all f., 6.19
and two of all f. in which there 7.15
entered, male and female of all f., 7.16
And all f. died that moved upon the 7.21
thing that is with you of all f.— 8.17
you shall not eat f. with its life, 9.04
again shall all f. be cut off by 9.11
every living creature of all f.; 9.15
become a flood to destroy all f. 9.15
creature of all f. that is upon 9.16
me and all f. that is upon the 9.17
circumcised in the f. of your 17.11
be in your f. an everlasting 17.13
circumcised in the f. of his 17.14
circumcised the f. of their 17.23
circumcised in the f. of his 17.24
circumcised in the f. of his 17.25
"Surely you are my bone and my f.!" 29.14
for he is our brother, our own f. 37.27
the birds will eat the f. from you. 40.19
restored like the rest of his f. Ex 4.07
They shall eat the f. that night, 12.08
any of the f. outside the house; 12.46
in the evening f. to eat and in 16.08
'At twilight you shall eat f., 16.12
and its f. shall not be eaten; 21.28
not eat any f. that is torn by 22.31
breeches to cover their naked f.; 28.42
But the f. of the bull, and its skin, 29.14
and boil its f. in a holy place; 29.31
shall eat the f. of the ram and 29.32
And if any of the f. for the 29.34
skin of the bull and all its f., Lev 4.11
Whatever touches its f. shall be holy; 6.27
And the f. of the sacrifice of his 7.15
remains of the f. of the sacrifice 7.17
If any of the f. of the sacrifice 7.18
"F. that touches any unclean thing 7.19
All who are clean may eat f., 7.19
who eats of the f. of the sacrifice 7.20
eats of the f. of the sacrifice of 7.21
and its f., and its dung, he burned 8.17
"Boil the f. at the door of the 8.31
remains of the f. and the bread 8.32
The f. and the skin he burned with 9.11
Of their f. you shall not eat, and 11.08
of their f. you shall not eat, and 11.11
eighth day the f. of his foreskin 12.03
is quick raw f. in the swelling, 13.10
But when raw f. appears on him, he 13.14
priest shall examine the raw f., 13.15
raw f. is unclean, for it is leprosy. 13.15
But if the raw f. turns again and 13.16
and the raw f. of the burn becomes 13.24
skin and their f. and their dung 16.27
For the life of the f. is in the 17.11

FLESH (cont.)
does not wash them or bathe his f., Lev 17.16
not eat any f. with the blood in 19.26
cuttings in your f. on accout of 19.28
nor make any cuttings in their f. 21.05
You shall eat the f. of your sons, 26.29
shall eat the f. of your daughters. 26.29
of whom the f. is half consumed Num 12.12
the God of the spirits of all f., 16.22
Everything that opens the womb of all f., 18.15
but their f. shall be yours, as the 18.18
her skin, her f., and her blood, with 19.05
the God of the spirits of all f., 27.16
For who is there of all f., that has Deu 5.26
slaughter and eat f. within any of 12.15
'I will eat f.,' because you crave f., 12.20
may eat as much f. as you desire. 12.20
shall not eat the life with the f. 12.23
the f. and the blood, on the altar 12.27
your God, but the f. you may eat. 12.27
Their f. you shall not eat, and 14.08
any of the f. which you sacrifice 16.04
the f. of your sons and daughters, 28.53
them any of the f. of his children 28.55
and my sword shall devour f.— 32.42
consumed the f. and the unleavened Ju 6.21
will flail your f. with the thorns 8.07
that I am your bone and your f." 9.02
will give your f. to the birds of 1Sa 17.44
"Behold, we are your bone and f. 2Sa 5.01
kinsmen, you are my bone and my f.; 19.12
'Are you not my bone and my f.? 19.13
boiled their f. with the yokes of 1Ki 19.21
and put sackcloth upon his f., 21.27
the f. of the child became warm. 2Ki 4.34
and your f. shall be restored, and 5.10
and his f. was restored like the 5.14
like the f. of a little child, and 5.14
dogs shall eat the f. of Jezebel; 9.36
"Behold, we are your bone and f. 1Ch 11.01
With him is an arm of f.; but with us 2Ch 32.08
Now our f. is as the f. of our Neh 5.05
now, and touch his bone and his f., Job 2.05
my face; the hair of my f. stood up. 4.15
of stones, or is my f. bronze? 6.12
My f. is clothed with worms and 7.05
Hast thou eyes of f.? Dost thou see 10.04
Thou didst clothe me with skin and f., 10.11
I will take my f. in my teeth, and 13.14
cleave to my skin and to my f., 19.20
are you not satisfied with my f.? 19.22
then without my f. I shall see God, 19.26
am dismayed, and shuddering seizes my f. 21.06
His f. is so wasted away that it 33.21
let his f. become fresh with youth; 33.25
all f. would perish together, and 34.15
The folds of his f. cleave together, 41.23
soundness in my f. because of thy Ps 38.03
and there is no soundness in my f. 38.07
Do I eat the f. of bulls, or drink 50.13
without a fear. What can f. do to me? 56.04
my f. faints for thee, as in a dry 63.01
hearest prayer! To thee shall all f. come 65.02
My f. and my heart may fail, but God 73.26
he rained f. upon them like dust, 78.27
He remembered that they were but f., 78.39
the f. of thy saints to the beasts 79.02
my heart and f. sing for joy to the 84.02
groaning my bones cleave to my f. 102.05
My f. trembles for fear of thee, and 119.120
he who gives food to all f., for his 136.25
and let all f. bless his holy name 145.21
healing to your f. and refreshment Pro 3.08
them, and healing to all his f. 4.22
when your f. and body are consumed, 5.11
tranquil mind gives life to the f., 14.30
his hands, and eats his own f. Ecc 4.05
study is a weariness of the f. 12.12
each devours his neighbor's f., Is 9.20
the fat of his f. will grow lean. 17.04
eating f. and drinking wine. 22.13
and their horses are f., and not 31.03
and all f. shall see it together, 40.05
All f. is grass, and all its 40.06
over the half he eats f., he roasts 44.16
coals, I roasted f. and have eaten; 44.19
your oppressors eat their own f., 49.26
Then all f. shall know that I am 49.26
to hide yourself from your own f.? 58.07
who eat swine's f., and broth of 65.04
and by his sword, upon all f.; 66.16
eating swine's f. and the abomination 66.17
all f. shall come to worship before 66.23
shall be an abhorrence to all f. 66.24
to your sacrifices, and eat the f. Jer 7.21
and sacrificial f. avert your doom? 11.15
to the other; no f. has peace. 12.12
trusts in man and makes f. his arm, 17.05
them eat the f. of their sons and 19.09
shall eat the f. of his neighbor 19.09
entering into judgment with all f., 25.31
"Behold, I am the LORD, the God of all f.; 32.27
evil upon all f., says the LORD; 45.05
He has made my f. and my skin waste Lam 3.04
nor has foul f. come into my mouth." Eze 4.14
is the caldron, and we are the f.' 11.03
they are the f., and this city is 11.07
you be the f. in the midst of it; 11.11
out of their f. and give them a 11.19
flesh and give them a heart of f., 11.19
All f. shall see that I the LORD 20.48
against all f. from south to north; 21.04
and all f. shall know that I the 21.05
put in it the pieces of f., all the good 24.04
boil well the f., and empty out the 24.10
I will strew your f. upon the 32.05
You eat f. with the blood, and lift 33.25
out of your f. the heart of stone 36.26
stone and give you a heart of f. 36.26
and will cause f. to come upon you, 37.06
and f. had come upon them, and skin 37.08
you shall eat f. and drink blood. 39.17
You shall eat the f. of the mighty, 39.18
the tables the f. of the offering 40.43
uncircumcised in heart and f., to be in 44.07
uncircumcised in heart and f., of all the 44.09
and fatter in f. than all the Dan 1.15
whose dwelling is not with f." 2.11
branches, and all f. was fed from it. 4.12
was told, 'Arise, devour much f.' 7.05
they sacrifice f. and eat it; Hos 8.13
will pour out my spirit on all f.; Joe 2.28
and their f. from off their bones; Mic 3.02
who eat the f. of my people, and 3.03
in a kettle, like f. in a caldron. 3.03
prey and his dens with torn f. Nah 2.12
like dust, and their f. like dung. Zep 1.17
carries holy f. in the skirt of Hag 2.12
Be silent, all f., before the LORD; Zec 2.13
left devour the f. of one another." 11.09
but devours the f. of the fat ones, 11.16
their f. shall rot while they are 14.12
and boil the f. of the sacrifice 14.21
For f. and blood has not revealed Mt 16.17
is willing, but the f. is weak." 26.41
is willing, but the f. is weak." Mk 14.38
and all f. shall see the salvation Lk 3.06
spirit has not f. and bones as you 24.39
the will of the f. nor of the will Jn 1.13
And the Word became f. and dwelt 1.14
That which is born of the f. is f., 3.06
for the life of the world is my f." 6.51
can this man give us his f. to eat?" 6.52
you eat the f. of the Son of man 6.53

FLESH (cont.)

he who eats my f. and drinks my Jn 6.54
For my f. is food indeed, and my 6.55
He who eats my f. and drinks my 6.56
gives life, the f. is of no avail; 6.63
You judge according to the f., 8.15
hast given him power over all f., 17.02
pour out my Spirit upon all f., Ac 2.17
moreover my f. will dwell in hope. 2.26
nor did his f. see corruption. 2.31
from David according to the f. Rom 1.03
our forefather according to the f.? 4.01
While we were living in the f., 7.05
within me, that is, in my f. 7.18
but with my f. I serve the law of 7.25
what the law, weakened by the f., 8.03
likeness of sinful f. and for sin, 8.03
sin, he condemned sin in the f., 6.03
according to the f. but according 8.04
according to the f. set their minds 8.05
minds on the things of the f., 8.05
To set the mind on the f. is death, 8.06
is set on the f. is hostile to God 8.07
who are in the f. cannot please 8.08
But you are not in the f., 8.09
not to the f., to live according to the f.— 8.12
according to the f. you will die, 8.13
according to the f., is the Christ. 9.05
children of the f. who are the 9.08
and make no provision for the f., 13.14
spiritual men, but as men of the f., 1Co 3.01
for you are still of the f. 3.03
among you, are you not of the f., 3.03
for the destruction of the f., 5.05
For not all f. is alike, but there 15.39
f. and blood cannot inherit the 15.50
may be manifested in our mortal f. 2Co 4.11
a thorn was given me in the f., 12.07
did not confer with f. and blood, Gal 1.16
now live in the f. I live by faith 2.20
are you now ending with the f.? 3.03
slave was born according to the f., 4.23
according to the f. persecuted him 4.29
as an opportunity for the f., 5.13
not gratify the desires of the f. 5.16
desires of the f. are against the 5.17
of the Spirit are against the f.; 5.17
Now the works of the f. are plain: 5.19
crucified the f. with its passions 5.24
sows to his own f. will from the 6.08
will from the f. reap corruption; 6.08
showing in the f. that would 6.12
that they may glory in your f. 6.13
lived in the passions of our f., Eph 2.03
at one time you Gentiles in the f., 2.11
which is made in the f. by hands— 2.11
abolishing in his f. the law of 2.15
For no man ever hates his own f., 5.29
contending against f. and blood, 6.12
If it is to be life in the f., Php 1.22
remain in the f. is more necessary 1.24
out for those who mutilate the f. 3.02
and put no confidence in the f. 3.03
for confidence in the f. also. 3.04
confidence in the f., I have more: 3.04
in his body of f. by his death, Col 1.22
and in my f. I complete what is 1.24
off the body of f. in the circumcision 2.11
and the uncircumcision of your f., 2.13
checking the indulgence of the f. 2.23
He was manifested in the f., 1Ti 3.16
both in the f. and in the Lord. Phm 1.16
the children share in f. and blood, Heb 2.14
In the days of his f., Jesus 5.07
for the purification of the f., 9.13
curtain, that is, through his f., 10.20
you and will eat your f. like fire. Jas 5.03
for "All f. is like grass and all 1Pe 1.24
passions of the f. that wage war 2.11
to death in the f. but made alive 3.18
therefore Christ suffered in the f., 4.01
suffered in the f. has ceased from 4.01
the time in the f. no longer by 4.02
though judged in the f. like men, 4.06
passions of the f. men who have 2Pe 2.18
the lust of the f. and the lust of 1Jn 2.16
has come in the f. is of God, 4.02
coming of Jesus Christ in the f.; 2Jn 1.07
in their dreamings defile the f., Jud 1.08
even the garment spotted by the f. 1.23
and devour her f. and burn her up Rev 17.16
to eat the f. of kings, the f. of captains, 19.18
the f. of mighty men, the f. of horses 19.18
and the f. of all men, both free and 19.18
birds were gorged with their f. 19.21

FLESHPOTS

we sat by the f. and ate bread to Ex 16.03

FLEW

The people f. upon the spoil, and 1Sa 14.32
He rode on a cherub, and f.; he was 2Sa 22.11
He rode on a cherub, and f.; he came Ps 18.10
his feet, and with two he f. Is 6.02
Then f. one of the seraphim to me, 6.06
as it f. in midheaven, "Woe, woe, woe Rev 8.13

FLIES

send swarms of f. on you and your Ex 8.21
shall be filled with swarms of f., 8.21
no swarms of f. shall be there; 8.22
great swarms of f. into the house 8.24
was ruined by reason of the f. 8.24
the swarms of f. may depart from 8.29
the swarms of f. from Pharaoh, 8.31
winged bird that f. in the air, Deu 4.17
earth, as swift as the eagle f., 28.49
He sent among them swarms of f., Ps 78.45
nor the arrow that f. by day, 91.05
spoke, and there came swarms of f., 105.31
Dead f. make the perfumer's ointment Ecc 10.01
spreads its wings and f. away. Nah 3.16
to die, and death f. from them. Rev 9.06

FLIGHT

a driven leaf shall put them to f., Lev 26.36
the land of Egypt in hurried f.— Deu 16.03
and two put ten thousand to f., 32.30
One man of you puts to f. a thousand, Jos 23.10
who put to f. the inhabitants of 1Ch 8.13
and put to f. all those in the 12.15
from its power in headlong f. Job 27.22
For you will put them to f.; Ps 21.12
were in panic, they took to f.; 48.05
of thy thunder they took to f. 104.07
Madmenah is in f., the inhabitants Is 10.31
haste, and you shall not go in f., 52.12
and archer every city takes to f.; Jer 4.29
to me in swift f. at the time of Dan 9.21
F. shall perish from the swift, and Amo 2.14
Pray that your f. may not be in Mt 24.20
in war, put foreign armies to f. Heb 11.34

FLING

on the open field I will f. you, Eze 32.04

FLINT

Then Zipporah took a f. and cut off Ex 4.25
"Make f. knives and circumcise the Jos 5.02
So Joshua made f. knives, and 5.03
the f. into a spring of water. Ps 114.08
their horses' hoofs seem like f., Is 5.28
I have set my face like a f., 50.07
harder than f. have I made your Eze 3.09

FLINTY
you water out of the f. rock, Deu 8.15
rock, and oil out of the f. rock. 32.13
"Man puts his hand to the f. rock, Job 28.09

FLITTING
Like a sparrow in its f., like a Pro 26.02

FLOAT
it in there, and made the iron f. 2Ki 6.06

FLOATED
and the ark f. on the face of the Gen 7.18

FLOCK
firstlings of his f. and of their Gen 4.04
seven ewe lambs of the f. apart. 21.28
Go to the f., and fetch me two good 27.09
and watered the f. of Laban his 29.10
again feed your f. and keep it: 30.31
let me pass through all your f. today, 30.32
Jacob fed the rest of Laban's f. 30.36
all the black in the f. of Laban; 30.40
did not put them with Laban's f. 30.40
stronger of the f. were breeding 30.41
runnels before the eyes of the f., 30.41
feebler of the f. he did not lay 30.42
into the field where his f. was, 31.04
then all the f. bore spotted; and if he 31.08
your wages,' then all the f. bore striped. 31.08
season of the f. I lifted up my 31.10
leaped upon the f. were striped, 31.10
that leap upon the f. are striped, 31.12
daughters, and six years for your f., 31.41
shepherding the f. with his brothers; 37.02
pasture their father's f. near Shechem. 37.12
pasturing the f. at Shechem? 37.13
your brothers, and with the f.; 37.14
where they are pasturing the f. 37.16
"I will send you a kid from the f." 38.17
troughs to water their father's f. Ex 2.16
helped them, and watered their f. 2.17
water for us and watered the f." 2.19
was keeping the f. of his father-in-law, 3.01
and he led his f. to the west side 3.01
from the herd or from the f. Lev 1.02
a burnt offering is from the f., 1.10
the LORD is an animal from the f., 3.06
committed, a female from the f., 5.06
ram without blemish out of the f., 5.15
ram without blemish out of the f., 5.18
ram without blemish out of the f., 6.06
from the herd or from the f., 22.21
or from the f. an offering by fire Num 15.03
cattle and the young of your f., Deu 7.13
of your herd and of your f.; 12.06
firstlings of your herd or of your f., 12.17
kill any of your herd or your f., 12.21
the firstlings of your herd and f.; 14.23
him liberally out of your f., out of your 15.14
your herd and f. you shall consecrate 15.19
nor shear the firstling of your f. 15.19
from the f. or the herd, at the 16.02
cattle, and the young of your f. 28.04
cattle, and the young of your f. 28.18
cattle or the young of your f., 28.51
the herd, and milk from the f., 32.14
bear, and took a lamb from the f., 1Sa 17.34
one of his own f. or herd to 2Sa 12.04
kids from the f. to the number of 2Ch 35.07
a ram of the f. for their guilt. Ez 10.19
forth their little ones like a f., Job 21.11
to set with the dogs of my f. 30.01
thy f. found a dwelling in it; Ps 68.10
people like a f. by the hand of 77.20
them in the wilderness like a f. 78.52
the f. of thy pasture, will give 79.13
thou who leadest Joseph like a f.! 80.01
loves, where you pasture your f., Sol 1.07
follow in the tracks of the f., 1.08
he pastures his f. among the 2.16
Your hair is like a f. of goats, 4.01
are like a f. of shorn ewes that 4.02
to pasture his f. in the gardens, 6.02
he pastures his f. among the lilies 6.03
me—Your hair is like a f. of goats, 6.05
Your teeth are like a f. of ewes, 6.06
He will feed his f. like a shepherd, Is 40.11
of the sea the shepherds of his f.? 63.11
prospered, and all their f. is scattered. Jer 10.21
the LORD's f. has been taken captive. 13.17
Where is the f. that was given you, 13.20
was given you, your beautiful f.? 13.20
people: "You have scattered my f., 23.02
remnant of my f. out of all the 23.03
roll in ashes, you lords of the f., 25.34
nor escape for the lords of the f. 25.35
the wail of the lords of the f.! 25.36
him as a shepherd keeps his f. 31.10
the young of the f. and the herd; 31.12
ones of the f. shall be dragged 49.20
and be as he-goats before the f. 50.08
ones of their f. shall be dragged 50.45
in pieces the shepherd and his f.; 51.23
Take the choicest one of the f., Eze 24.05
seeks out his f. when some of his 34.12
my f., thus says the Lord GOD: 34.17
I will save my f., they shall no 34.22
to increase their men like a f. 36.37
Like the f. for sacrifices, like the 36.38
like the f. at Jerusalem during her 36.38
a ram from the f. without blemish. 43.23
also a bull and a ram from the f., 43.25
sheep from every f. of two hundred, 45.15
couches, and eat lambs from the f., Amo 6.04
LORD took me from following the f., 7.15
herd nor f., taste anything; Jon 3.07
like a f. in its pasture, a noisy Mic 2.12
And you, O tower of the f., hill of the 4.08
and feed his f. in the strength of 5.04
the f. of thy inheritance, who dwell 7.14
the f. be cut off from the fold and Hab 3.17
for they are the f. of his people; Zec 9.16
the LORD of hosts cares for his f., 10.03
shepherd of the f. doomed to 11.04
shepherd of the f. doomed to be 11.07
shepherd, who deserts the f.! 11.17
the cheat who has a male in his f., Mal 1.14
sheep of the f. will be scattered.' Mt 26.31
watch over their f. by night. Lk 2.08
little f., for it is your Father's 12.32
shall be one f., one shepherd. Jn 10.16
to yourselves and to all the f., Ac 20.28
in among you, not sparing the f.; 20.29
Who tends a f. without getting some 1Co 9.07
Tend the f. of God that is your 1Pe 5.02
but being examples to the f. 5.03

FLOCKS
also had f. and herds and tents, Gen 13.05
he has given him f. and herds, 24.35
He had possessions of f. and herds, 26.14
three f. of sheep lying beside it; 29.02
of that well the f. were watered. 29.02
and when all the f. were gathered 29.03
until all the f. are gathered 29.08
in front of the f. in the runnels, 30.38
troughs, where the f. came to drink. 30.38
the f. bred in front of the rods 30.39
rods and so the f. brought forth 30.39
faces of the f. toward the striped 30.40
and had large f., maidservants and 30.43
have not eaten the rams of your f. 31.38
the f. are my f., and all that 31.43
f., menservants, and maidservants; 32.05

FLOCKS (cont.)

and the f. and herds and camels, Gen 32.07
and that the f. and herds giving 33.13
for one day, all the f. will die. 33.13
they took their f. and their herds, 34.28
and your f., your herds, and all 45.10
and they have brought their f., 46.32
with their f. and herds and all 47.01
no pasture for your servants' f., 47.04
the f., the herds, and the asses: and 47.17
their f., and their herds were left 50.08
the camels, the herds, and the f. Ex 9.03
daughters and with our f. and herds, 10.09
only let your f. and your herds 10.24
Take your f. and your herds, as you 12.32
many cattle, both f. and herds. 12.38
let no f. or herds feed before that 34.03
And all the tithe of herds and f., Lev 27.32
Shall f. and herds be slaughtered Num 11.22
their f., and all their goods. 31.09
and of the asses and of the f.; 31.28
and of the f., of all the cattle., 31.30
build sheepfolds here for our f., 32.16
our f., and all our cattle, shall 32.26
and when your herds and f. multiply, Deu 8.13
to hear the piping for the f.? Ju 5.16
He will take the tenth of your f., 1Sa 8.17
also captured all the f. and herds; 30.20
man had very many f. and herds; 2Sa 12.02
them like two little f. of goats, 1Ki 20.27
to seek pasture there for their f., 1Ch 4.39
was pasture there for their f. 4.41
Over the f. was Jaziz the Hagrite. 27.30
and f. and herds in abundance; 2Ch 32.29
firstlings of our herds and of our f.; Neh 10.36
they seize f. and pasture them. Job 24.02
the meadows clothe themselves with f., Ps 65.13
to the hail, and their f. to thunderbolts. 78.48
and makes their families like f. 107.41
Know well the condition of your f., Pro 27.23
great possessions of herds and f., Ecc 2.07
beside the f. of your companions? Sol 1.07
will make their f. lie down there. Is 13.20
they will be for f., which will lie 17.02
joy of wild asses, a pasture of f.; 32.14
All the f. of Kedar shall be 60.07
Aliens shall stand and feed your f., 61.05
Sharon shall become a pasture for f., 65.10
their f. and their herds, their sons Jer 3.24
eat up your f. and your herds; 5.17
Shepherds with their f. shall come 6.03
and those who wander with their f. 31.24
of shepherds resting their f. 33.12
f. shall again pass under the hands 33.13
Their tents and their f. shall be taken, 49.29
of the Ammonites a fold for f. Eze 25.05
cities be filled with f. of men. 36.38
With their f. and herds they shall Hos 5.06
even the f. of sheep are dismayed. Joe 1.18
a young lion among the f. of sheep, Mic 5.08
for shepherds and folds for f. Zep 2.06

FLOG

is not good; to f. noble men is wrong. Pro 17.26
and f. you in their synagogues, Mt 10.17

FLOGGING

strife, and his mouth invites a f. Pro 18.06
and f. for the backs of fools. 19.29

FLOOD

I will bring a f. of waters upon Gen 6.17
old when the f. of waters came 7.06
to escape the waters of the f. 7.07
waters of the f. came upon the 7.10
The f. continued forty days upon 7.17
be cut off by the waters of a f., 9.11
there be a f. to destroy the earth." 9.11
again become a f. to destroy all 9.15
After the f. Noah lived three 9.28
were born to them after the f. 10.01
abroad on the earth after the f. 10.32
Arpachshad two years after the f.; 11.10
before me, like a bursting f." 2Sa 5.20
by my hand, like a bursting f." 1Ch 14.11
and a f. of water covers you. Job 22.11
Terrors overtake him like a f.; 27.20
that a f. of waters may cover you? 38.34
every night I f. my bed with tears; Ps 6.06
The LORD sits enthroned over the f.; 29.10
waters, and the f. sweeps over me. 69.02
Let not the f. sweep over me, or the 69.15
surround me like a f. all day long; 88.17
then the f. would have swept us 124.04
Its end shall come with a f., Dan 9.26
and the f. was round about me; Jon 2.03
an overflowing f. he will make a Nah 1.08
days before the f. they were Mt 24.38
know until the f. came and swept 24.39
and when a f. arose, the stream Lk 6.48
and the f. came and destroyed them 17.27
he brought a f. upon the world of 2Pe 2.05
to sweep her away with the f. Rev 12.15

FLOODS

The f. cover them; they went down Ex 15.05
the f. stood up in a heap; the deeps 15.08
The f. have lifted up, O LORD, the Ps 93.03
the f. have lifted up their voice, 93.03
the f. lift up their roaring. 93.03
Let the f. clap their hands; let the hills 98.08
love, neither can f. drown it. Sol 8.07
and the f. came, and the winds blew Mt 7.25
and the f. came, and the winds blew 7.27

FLOOR

came to the threshing f. of Atad, Gen 50.10
on the threshing f. of Atad, 50.11
that is on the f. of the tabernacle Num 5.17
an offering from the threshing f., 15.20
were the grain of the threshing f., 18.27
as produce of the threshing f., 18.30
flock, out of your threshing f., Deu 15.14
your threshing f. and your wine 16.13
lay their lord dead on the f. Ju 3.25
fleece of wool on the threshing f.; 6.37
barley tonight at the threshing f. Ru 3.02
and go down to the threshing f.; 3.03
the threshing f. and did just as 3.06
the woman came to the threshing f." 3.14
came to the threshing f. of Nacon, 2Sa 6.06
the threshing f. of Araunah the 24.16
the threshing f. of Araunah the 24.18
"To buy the threshing f. of you, 24.21
the threshing f. and the oxen for 24.24
from the f. of the house to the 1Ki 6.15
he covered the f. of the house 6.15
cedar from the f. to the rafters, 6.16
The f. of the house he overlaid 6.30
with cedar from f. to rafters. 7.07
the threshing f. at the entrance 22.10
From the threshing f., or from the 2Ki 6.27
came to the threshing f. of Chidon, 1Ch 13.09
the threshing f. of Ornan the 21.15
the threshing f. of Ornan the 21.18
went forth from the threshing f., 21.21
the threshing f. that I may build 21.22
the threshing f. of Ornan the 21.28
the threshing f. of Ornan the 2Ch 3.01
the threshing f. at the entrance 18.09
to the threshing f. in its season. Job 5.26
your grain to your threshing f.? 39.12
a threshing f. at the time when it Jer 51.33
from the f. up to the windows (now Eze 41.16
from the f. to above the door 41.20
Threshing f. and winevat shall not Hos 9.02

FLOOR (cont.)
the threshing f. or like smoke Hos 13.03
as sheaves to the threshing f. Mic 4.12
his threshing f. and gather his Mt 3.12
hand, to clear his threshing f., Lk 3.17

FLOORS
and are robbing the threshing f." 1Sa 23.01
chaff of the summer threshing f.; Dan 2.35
harlot's hire upon all threshing f. Hos 9.01
"The threshing f. shall be full of Joe 2.24

FLOUR
shall make them of fine wheat f. Ex 29.02
measure of fine f. mingled with a 29.40
his offering shall be of fine f.; Lev 2.01
a handful of the fine f. and oil, 2.02
cakes of fine f. mixed with oil, 2.04
it shall be of fine f. unleavened, 2.05
shall be made of fine f. with oil. 2.07
ephah of fine f. for a sin offering; 5.11
of the fine f. of the cereal offering 6.15
ephah of fine f. as a regular cereal 6.20
cakes of fine f. well mixed with 7.12
an ephah of fine f. mixed with oil, 14.10
ephah of fine f. mixed with oil 14.21
an ephah of fine f. mixed with oil, 23.13
they shall be of fine f., 23.17
"And you shall take fine f., 24.05
cakes of fine f. mixed with oil, and Num 6.15
full of fine f. mixed with oil for 7.13
full of fine f. mixed with oil for 7.19
full of fine f. mixed with oil for 7.25
full of fine f. mixed with oil for 7.31
full of fine f. mixed with oil for 7.37
full of fine f. mixed with oil for 7.43
full of fine f. mixed with oil for 7.49
full of fine f. mixed with oil for 7.55
full of fine f. mixed with oil for 7.61
full of fine f. mixed with oil for 7.67
full of fine f. mixed with oil for 7.73
full of fine f. mixed with oil for 7.79
offering of fine f. mixed with oil, 8.08
of a tenth of an ephah of fine f., 15.04
ephah of fine f. mixed with a 15.06
tenths of an ephah of fine f., 15.09
ephah of fine f. for a cereal 28.05
ephah of fine f. for a cereal 28.09
ephah of fine f. for a cereal 28.12
tenths of fine f. for a cereal 28.12
and a tenth of fine f. mixed with 28.13
offering of fine f. mixed with oil; 28.20
offering of fine f. mixed with oil, 28.28
offering of fine f. mixed with oil, 29.03
offering of fine f. mixed with oil, 29.09
offering of fine f. mixed with oil, 29.14
unleavened cakes from an ephah of f.; Ju 6.19
an ephah of f., and a skin of wine; 1Sa 1.24
and she took f., and kneeded it and 28.24
day was thirty measures of fine f., 1Ki 4.22
untensils, also over the fine f., 1Ch 9.29
the f. for the cereal offering, the 23.29
you ate fine f. and honey and oil. Eze 16.13
you with fine f. and oil and honey 16.19
of a hin of oil to moisten the f., 46.14
fine f. and wheat, cattle and sheep, Rev 18.13

FLOURISH
Can reeds f. where there is no Job 8.11
In his days may righteousness f., Ps 72.07
like grass and all evildoers f., 92.07
The righteous f. like the palm tree, 92.12
they f. in the courts of our God. 92.13
righteous will f. like a green Pro 11.28
the tent of the upright will f. 14.11
your bones shall f. like the grass; Is 66.14
tree, and make the dry tree f. Eze 17.24

Though he may f. as the reed plant, Hos 13.15
shadow, they shall f. as a garden; 14.07
grain shall make the young men f., Zec 9.17

FLOURISHES
in the morning it f. and is renewed; Ps 90.06
he f. like a flower of the field; 103.15

FLOUTED
"The Lord f. all my mighty men in Lam 1.15

FLOW
to its wonted f. when the morning Ex 14.27
be clean from the f. of her blood. Lev 12.07
Water shall f. from his buckets, and Num 24.07
and caused waters to f. down like rivers. Ps 78.16
valleys; they f. between the hills, 104.10
his wind blow, and the waters f. 147.18
for from it f. the springs of life. Pro 4.23
to the place where the streams f., Ecc 1.07
streams f., there they f. again. 1.07
all the nations shall f. to it, Is 2.02
waters of Shiloah that f. gently, 8.06
mountains shall f. with their 34.03
he made water f. for them from the 48.21
nations shall no longer f. to him; Jer 51.44
my eyes f. with tears; for a comforter Lam 1.16
my eyes f. with rivers of tears 3.48
"My eyes will f. without ceasing, 3.49
its rivers f. round the place of Eze 31.04
and the hills shall f. with milk, Joe 3.18
beds of Judah shall f. with water; 3.18
and all the hills shall f. with it. Amo 9.13
the hills; and peoples shall f. to it, Mic 4.01
waters shall f. out from Jerusalem, Zec 14.08
who had had a f. of blood for Mk 5.25
who had had a f. of blood for Lk 8.43
immediately her f. of blood ceased. 8.44
his heart shall f. rivers of Jn 7.38

FLOWED
A river f. out of Eden to water the Gen 2.10
of the wound f. into the bottom of 1Ki 22.35
the brook that f. through the land, 2Ch 32.04
it f. through the desert like a Ps 105.41
and blood f. from the wine press, as Rev 14.20

FLOWER
each with capital and f., on one branch, Ex 25.33
almonds, each with capital and f., 25.33
almonds, each with capital and f., on one 37.19
almonds, each with capital and f., on the 37.19
of a cup, like the f. of a lily; 1Ki 7.26
of a cup, like the f. of a lily; 2Ch 4.05
While yet in f. and not cut down, Job 8.12
comes forth like a f., and withers; 14.02
flourishes like a f. of the field; Ps 103.15
and the f. becomes a ripening grape, Is 18.05
to the fading f. of its glorious 28.01
and the fading f. of its glorious 28.04
beauty is like the f. of the field. 40.06
the f. fades, when the breath of the 40.07
The grass withers, the f. fades; 40.08
like the f. of the grass he will Jas 1.10
its f. falls, and its beauty perishes. 1.11
all its glory like the f. of grass. 1Pe 1.24
grass withers, and the f. falls, 1.24

FLOWERS
and its f. shall be of one piece Ex 25.31
almonds, with their capitals and f., 25.34
and its f. were of one piece with 37.17
almonds, with their capitals and f., 37.20
from its base to its f., it was Num 8.04
in the form of gourds and open f.; 1Ki 6.18
cherubim and palm trees and open f., 6.29
cherubim, palm trees, and open f.; 6.32
cherubim and palm trees and open f.; 6.35

FLOWERS (cont.)
the f., the lamps, and the tongs, of 1Ki 7.49
the f., the lamps, and the tongs, of 2Ch 4.21
The f. appear on the earth, the time Sol 2.12

FLOWING
a land f. with milk and honey, to Ex 3.08
a land f. with milk and honey."' 3.17
a land f. with milk and honey, you 13.05
Go up to a land f. with milk and 33.03
a land f. with milk and honey.' Lev 20.24
out of a land f. with milk and Num 16.13
us into a land f. with milk and 16.14
in a land f. with milk and honey. Deu 6.03
f. forth in valleys and hills, 8.07
a land f. with milk and honey. 11.09
a land f. with milk and honey. 26.09
a land f. with milk and honey.' 26.15
a land f. with milk and honey, as 27.03
into the land f. with milk and 31.20
Jordan shall be stopped from f., Jos 3.13
and those f. down toward the sea of 3.16
a land f. with milk and honey. 5.06
another." Then the oil stopped f. 2Ki 4.06
the streams f. with honey and curds Job 20.17
As a hart longs for f. streams, Ps 42.01
f. water from your own well. Pro 5.15
and f. streams from Lebanon. Sol 4.15
and your f. locks are like purple; 7.05
waters, like willows by f. streams. Is 44.04
them a land f. with milk and honey, Jer 11.05
waters run dry, the cold f. streams? 18.14
give them, a land f. with milk and honey; 32.22
a land f. with milk and honey, the Eze 20.06
a land f. with milk and honey, the 20.15
with f. turbans on their heads, all 23.15
the mountains with your f. blood; 32.06
the water was f. down from below 47.01
f. from the throne of God and of Rev 22.01

FLOWS
the one which f. around the whole Gen 2.11
the one which f. around the whole 2.13
which f. east of Assyria. And the 2.14
it f. with milk and honey, and this Num 13.27
a land which f. with milk and honey 14.08
"This water f. toward the eastern Eze 47.08
water for them f. from the sanctuary. 47.12

FLUNG
threw stones at him and f. dust. 2Sa 16.13
they f. me alive into the pit and Lam 3.53

FLUTE
f., and lyre before them, prophesying. 1Sa 10.05
timbrel and f. and wine at their Is 5.12
sound of the f. to go to the 30.29
Therefore my heart moans for Moab like a f., Jer 48.36
moans like a f. for the men of 48.36
and saw the f. players, and the Mt 9.23
such as the f. or the harp, do not 1Co 14.07
of f. players and trumpeters, shall Rev 18.22

FLUTTERING
Like f. birds, like scattered Is 16.02

FLUTTERS
that f. over its young, spreading Deu 32.11

FLY
and let birds f. above the earth Gen 1.20
to trouble as the sparks f. upward. Job 5.07
He will f. away like a dream, and 20.08
I would f. away and be at rest; Ps 55.06
they are soon gone, and we f. away. 90.10
whistle for the f. which is at the Is 7.18
Who are these that f. like a cloud, 60.08
to Moab, for she would f. away; Jer 48.09
one shall f. swiftly like an eagle, 48.40
mount up and f. swiftly like an 49.22
Ephraim's glory shall f. away like a Hos 9.11
when the sun rises, they f. away; Nah 3.17
they f. like an eagle swift to Hab 1.08
that she might f. from the serpent Rev 12.14
all the birds that f. in midheaven, 19.17

FLYING
creeping things and f. birds! Ps 148.10
f. like an eagle toward heaven Pro 23.05
flitting, like a swallow in its f., 26.02
and its fruit will be a f. serpent. Is 14.29
lion, the viper and the f. serpent, 30.06
and saw, and behold, a f. scroll! Zec 5.01
I answered, "I see a f. scroll; 5.02
living creature like a f. eagle. Rev 4.07
saw another angel f. in midheaven, 14.06

FOAL
Binding his f. to the vine and his Gen 49.11
an ass, on a colt the f. of an ass. Zec 9.09
and on a colt, the f. of an ass." Mt 21.05

FOAM
though its waters roar and f., Ps 46.03
casting up the f. of their own Jud 1.13

FOAMING
with f. wine, well mixed; and he will Ps 75.08
and rolled about, f. at the mouth. Mk 9.20

FOAMS
and he f. and grinds his teeth and Mk 9.18
it convulses him till he f., and shatters Lk 9.39

FODDER
grass, or the ox low over his f.? Job 6.05
They gather their f. in the field 24.06

FOE
And Esther said, "A f. and enemy! Est 7.06
hast made us turn back from the f.; Ps 44.10
O grant us help against the f., 60.11
may have their portion from the f. 68.23
How long, O God, is the f. to scoff? 74.10
when he redeemed them from the f.; 78.42
his glory to the hand of the f. 78.61
saved them from the hand of the f., 106.10
O grant us help from the f., for vain 108.12
the punishment of a merciless f., Jer 30.14
gone away, captives before the f. Lam 1.05
fell into the hand of the f., and there 1.07
the f. gloated over her, mocking at 1.07
with his right hand set like a f.; 2.04
that f. or enemy could enter the 4.12
safety from the f. for him who Zec 8.10
trampling the f. in the mud of the 10.05

FOEMEN
all day long f. oppress me; Ps 56.01

FOES
upon your f. and enemies who Deu 30.07
before your f. while they pursue 2Sa 24.13
months of devastation by your f., 1Ch 21.12
get the mastery over their f., Est 9.01
O LORD, how many are my f.! Ps 3.01
it grows weak because of all my f. 6.07
a bulwark because of thy f., 8.02
as for all his f., he puffs at 10.05
lest my f. rejoice because I am 13.04
Consider how many are my f., 25.19
against me, my adversaries and f., 27.02
hast not let my f. rejoice over me. 30.01
over me who are wrongfully my f., 35.19
Those who are my f. without cause 38.19
Through thee we push down our f.; 44.05

FOES (cont.)
But thou hast saved us from our f., Ps 44.07
is he who will tread down our f. 60.12
dishonor; my f. are all known to thee. 69.19
May his f. bow down before him, and 72.09
Thy f. have roared in the midst of 74.04
Do not forget the clamor of thy f., 74.23
and turn my hand against their f. 81.14
I will crush his f. before him and 89.23
exalted the right hand of his f.; 89.42
made them stronger than their f. 105.24
is he who will tread down our f. 108.13
Rule in the midst of your f.! 110.02
because my f. forget thy words. 119.139
and rescued us from our f., for his 136.24
enemies, and avenge myself on my f. Is 1.24
multitude of your f. shall be like 29.05
himself mighty against his f. 42.13
and all your f., every one of them, Jer 30.16
to avenge himself on his f. 46.10
Her f. have become the head, her Lam 1.05
his neighbors should be his f.; 1.17
and exalted the might of your f. 2.17
not take vengeance twice on his f. Nah 1.09
your land are wide open to your f.; 3.13
and a man's f. will be those of his Mt 10.36
their mouth and consumes their f.; Rev 11.05
sight of their f. they went up to 11.12

FOLD
inspect your f. and miss nothing. Job 5.24
I will bring them back to their f., Jer 23.03
will roar mightily against his f., 25.30
surely their f. shall be appalled 49.20
gone, they have forgotten their f. 50.06
surely their f. shall be appalled at 50.45
of the Ammonites a f. for flocks. Eze 25.05
them together like sheep in a f., Mic 2.12
off from the f. and there be no Hab 3.17
sheep, that are not of this f.; Jn 10.16

FOLDING
two leaves of the one door were f., 1Ki 6.34
leaves of the other door were f. 6.34
a little f. of the hands to rest, Pro 6.10
a little f. of the hands to rest," 24.33

FOLDS
little ones, and f. for your sheep; Num 32.24
fortified cities, and f. for sheep. 32.26
The f. of his flesh cleave together, Job 41.23
house, nor he-goat from your f. Ps 50.09
The fool f. his hands, and eats his Ecc 4.05
and the peaceful f. are devastated, Jer 25.37
for shepherds and f. for flocks. Zep 2.06

FOLIAGE
forth branches and put forth f. Eze 17.06

FOLK
taken, the old f. and the very aged. Jer 6.11
and all the foreign f. among them; 25.20

FOLLIES
fatness, their hearts overflow with f. Ps 73.07

FOLLOW
be willing to f. me to this land; Gen 24.05
the woman is not willing to f. you, 24.08
'Perhaps the woman will not f. me.' 24.39
of that famine which will f., 41.31
his steward, "Up, f. after the men; 44.04
out, and all the people who f. you.' Ex 11.08
him and all who f. him in playing Lev 20.05
not to f. after your own heart and Num 15.39
you be not ensnared to f. them, Deu 12.30
you shall f., that you may live and 16.20
not learn to f. the abominable 18.09
set out from your place and f. it, Jos 3.03
And he said to them, "F. after me; Ju 3.28
Abiezrites were called out to f. him. 6.34
they too were called out to f. him. 6.35
of bread to the people who f. me; 8.05
hearts inclined to f. Abimelech, 9.03
over you will f. the LORD your God, 1Sa 12.14
to the young men who f. my lord. 25.27
had been too exhausted to f. David, 30.21
among the people who f. Absalom. 2Sa 17.09
is for David, let him f. Joab." 20.11
and did not wholly f. the LORD, 1Ki 11.06
If the LORD is God, f. him; 18.21
but if Baal, then f. him." 18.21
my mother, and then I will f. you." 19.20
for all the people who f. me." 20.10
f. me, and I will bring you to the 2Ki 6.19
and they do not f. the statutes or 17.34
all men f. after him, and those who Job 21.33
and mercy shall f. me all the days Ps 23.06
adversaries because I f. after good. 38.20
to f. their own counsels. 81.12
the upright in heart will f. it. 94.15
f. in the tracks of the flock, and Sol 1.08
f. in the tracks of the flock, and Sol 1.08
and be yours, they shall f. you; Is 45.14
more stubbornly f. their own evil Jer 3.17
who stubbornly f. their own heart 13.10
We will f. our own plans, and will 18.12
afraid shall f. hard after you to 42.16
prophets who f. their own spirit, Eze 13.03
They shall f. my ordinances and be 37.24
Ethiopians shall f. in his train. Dan 11.43
"F. me, and I will make you fishers Mt 4.19
I will f. you wherever you go." 8.19
"F. me, and leave the dead to bury 8.22
and he said to him, "F. me." 9.09
his cross and f. me is not worthy 10.38
and take up his cross and f. me. 16.24
in heaven; and come, f. me." 19.21
"F. me and I will make you become Mk 1.17
office, and he said to him, "F. me." 2.14
no one to f. him except Peter and 5.37
and take up his cross and f. me. 8.34
in heaven; and come, f. me." 10.21
will meet you; f. him, 14.13
and he said to him, "F. me." Lk 5.27
take up his cross daily and f. me." 9.23
because he does not f. with us." 9.49
"I will f. you wherever you go." 9.57
To another he said, "F. me." 9.59
Another said, "I will f. you, Lord; 9.61
Do not go, do not f. them. 17.23
in heaven; and come, f. me." 18.22
f. him into the house which he 22.10
were about him saw what would f., 22.49
Philip and said to him, "F. me." Jn 1.43
and the sheep f. him, for they know 10.04
A stranger they will not f., 10.05
and I know them, and they f. me; 10.27
If any one serves me, he must f. me; 12.26
I am going you cannot f. me now; 13.36
but you shall f. afterward." 13.36
him, "Lord, why cannot I f. you now? 13.37
after this he said to him, "F. me." 21.19
until I come, what is that to you? F. me!" 21.22
your mantle around you and f. me." Ac 12.08
but also f. the example of the Rom 4.12
F. the pattern of the sound words 2Ti 1.13
that you should f. in his steps. 1Pe 2.21
For we did not f. cleverly devised 2Pe 1.16
And many will f. their licentiousness, 2.02
that we f. his commandments; 2Jn 1.06
the beginning, that you f. love. 1.06
as indeed you do f. the truth. 3Jn 1.03
hear that my children f. the truth. 1.04
it is these who f. the Lamb wherever Rev 14.04
labors, for their deeds f. them!" 14.13

FOLLOWED

upon the camels and f. the man; Gen 24.61
seven days and f. close after him 31.23
third and all who f. the droves, 32.19
that had f. them into the sea; Ex 14.28
different spirit and has f. me fully, Num 14.24
and the elders of Israel f. him. 16.25
because they have not wholly f. me; 32.11
for they have wholly f. the LORD.' 32.12
because he has wholly f. the LORD!' Deu 1.36
all the men who f. the Baal of 4.03
every living thing that f. them, 11.06
so they f. in thy steps, receiving 33.03
yet I wholly f. the LORD my God. Jos 14.08
you have wholly f. the LORD my God." 14.09
day, because he wholly f. the LORD, 14.14
and reckless fellows, who f. him. Ju 9.04
all the people f. him trembling. 1Sa 13.07
they too f. hard after them in the 14.22
of Jesse had f. Saul to the battle; 17.13
the youngest; the three eldest f. Saul, 17.14
But the house of Judah f. David. 2Sa 2.10
Abner." And King David f. the bier. 3.31
and there f. him a present from the 11.08
Gittites who had f. him from Gath, 15.18
saw that his counsel was not f., 17.23
and f. Sheba the son of Bichri; 20.02
men of Judah f. their king steadfastly 20.02
Bichrites assembled, and f. him in. 20.14
and they f. Adonijah and helped him. 1Ki 1.07
was none that f. the house of 12.20
and f. me with all his heart, doing 14.08
of the people f. Tibni the son of 16.21
to make him king, and half f. Omri. 16.21
But the people who f. Omri overcame 16.22
the people who f. Tibni the son of 16.22
of the LORD and f. the Baals. 18.18
districts, and the army which f. them. 20.19
or for the beasts which f. them. 2Ki 3.09
leave you." So he arose and f. her. 4.30
So Gehazi f. Naaman. And when Naaman 5.21
and f. the sins of Jeroboam the son 13.02
and they f. the nations that were 17.15
He even f. their counsel, and went 2Ch 22.05
people still f. corrupt practices. 27.02
nor the men of the guard who f. me, Neh 4.23
and I f. them with half of the 12.38
how you f. me in the wilderness, in Jer 2.02
but have stubbornly f. their own 9.14
the others f. without turning as Eze 10.11
pestilence, and plague f. close behind. Hab 3.05
Immediately they left their nets and f. him. Mt 4.20
boat and their father, and f. him. 4.22
And great crowds f. him from 4.25
the mountain, great crowds f. him; 8.01
and said to those who f. him, 8.10
the boat, his disciples f. him. 8.23
"Follow me." And he rose and f. him. 9.09
And Jesus rose and f. him, 9.19
two blind men f. him, crying aloud, 9.27
And many f. him, and he healed them 12.15
they f. him on foot from the towns. 14.13
and large crowds f. him, and he healed 19.02
we have left everything and f. you. 19.27
you who have f. me will also sit on 19.28
of Jericho, a great crowd f. him. 20.29
received their sight and f. him. 20.34
before him and that f. him shouted, 21.09
But Peter f. him at a distance, as 26.58
who had f. Jesus from Galilee, 27.55
they left their nets and f. him. Mk 1.18
the hired servants, and f. him. 1.20
those who were with him f. him, 1.36
"Follow me." And he rose and f. him. 2.14
for there were many who f. him. 2.15
a great multitude from Galilee f.; 3.07
a great crowd f. him and thronged 5.24
and his disciples f. him. 6.01
we have left everything and f. you." 10.28
and those who f. were afraid. 10.32
his sight and f. him on the way. 10.52
before and those who f. cried out, 11.09
And a young man f. him, with nothing 14.51
And Peter had f. him at a distance, 14.54
f. him, and ministered to him; 15.41
having f. all things closely for Lk 1.03
they left everything and f. him. 5.11
everything, and rose and f. him. 5.28
said to the multitude that f. him, 7.09
the crowds learned it, they f. him; 9.11
we have left our homes and f. you." 18.28
he received his sight and f. him, 18.43
of Olives; and the disciples f. him. 22.39
priest's house. Peter f. at a distance; 22.54
And there f. him a great multitude 23.27
women who had f. him from Galilee 23.49
had come with him from Galilee f., 23.55
him say this, and they f. Jesus. Jn 1.37
and f. him, was Andrew, Simon Peter's 1.40
And a multitude f. him, because they 6.02
they f. her, supposing that she was 11.31
Simon Peter f. Jesus, and so did 18.15
and all who f. him were dispersed Ac 5.36
and all who f. him were scattered. 5.37
And he went out and f. him; 12.09
to Judaism f. Paul and Barnabas, 13.43
She f. Paul and us, crying, "These 16.17
for the mob of the people f., 21.36
supernatural Rock which f. them, 1Co 10.04
good doctrine which you have f. 1Ti 4.06
they have f. the way of Balaam, the 2Pe 2.15
name was Death, and Hades f. him; Rev 6.08
and there f. hail and fire, mixed 8.07
the whole earth f. the beast with 13.03
f., saying, "Fallen, fallen is 14.08
f., saying with a loud voice, "If 14.09
and pure, f. him on white horses. 19.14

FOLLOWING

they came to him the f. year, Gen 47.18
have turned back from f. the LORD, Num 14.43
For if you turn away from f. him, 32.15
turn away your sons from f. me, Deu 7.04
the covenant of the LORD f. them. Jos 6.08
the Levites the f. cities and 21.03
they gave the f. cities mentioned 21.09
away this day from f. the LORD, 22.16
away this day from f. the LORD? 22.18
to turn away from f. the LORD; 22.23
this day from f. the LORD by 22.29
Tabor with ten thousand men f. him. Ju 4.14
f. you, Benjamin, with your kinsmen; 5.14
On the f. day the men went out into 9.42
his bundle and f. Abimelech put it 9.49
leave you or to return from f. you; Ru 1.16
do not turn aside from f. the LORD, 1Sa 12.20
for he has turned back from f. me, 15.11
returned from f. the Philistines, 24.01
hand nor to the left from f. Abner. 2Sa 2.19
would not turn aside from f. him. 2.21
to Asahel, "Turn aside from f. me; 2.22
from f. the sheep, that you should 7.08
But if you turn aside from f. me, 1Ki 9.06
And he returned from f. him, 19.21
son about that time the f. spring, 2Ki 4.17
Israel from f. the LORD and made 17.21
he did not depart from f. him, 18.06
from f. the sheep, that you should 1Ch 17.07
turn away from f. the LORD the God 2Ch 34.33
f. the directions of David king of 35.04
f. all the abominations of the 36.14
The f. were those who came up from Ez 2.59
The f. were those who came up from Neh 7.61
because they turned aside from f. him, Job 34.27

FOLLOWING (cont.)
and turning away from f. our God, Is 59.13
is not good, f. their own devices; 65.02
f. one in the midst, eating swine's 66.17
and would not turn from f. me. Jer 3.19
of the LORD our God by f. his laws, Dan 9.10
the LORD took me from f. the flock. Amo 7.15
have turned back from f. the LORD, Zep 1.06
him, because he was not f. us." Mk 9.38
On the f. day, when they came from 11.12
today and tomorrow and the day f.; Lk 13.33
and saw them f., and said to them, Jn 1.38
f. him, and he went into the tomb; 20.06
Peter turned and saw f. them the 21.20
And on the f. day he appeared to Ac 7.26
And on the f. day they entered 10.24
with the f. letter. "The brethren, 15.23
and the f. day to Neapolis, 16.11
we came the f. day opposite Chios; 20.15
On the f. day Paul went in with us 21.18
The f. night the Lord stood by him 23.11
the judgment f. one trespass Rom 5.16
the free gift f. many trespasses 5.16
But in the f. instructions I do not 1Co 11.17
f. the course of this world, f. the prince Eph 2.02
f. the desires of body and mind, and 2.03
with scoffing, f. their own passions 2Pe 3.03
some of your children f. the truth, 2Jn 1.04
f. their own passions, loud-mouthed Jud 1.16
f. their own ungodly passions." 1.18

FOLLOWS
To his father he sent as f.: Gen 45.23
a miscarriage, and yet no harm f., Ex 21.22
If any harm f., then you shall give 21.23
by their families was as f.: Jos 16.05
with the sword any one who f. her." 2Ki 11.15
any one who f. her is to be slain 2Ch 23.14
to Artaxerxes the king as f.— Ez 4.08
report, in which was written as f.: 5.07
All at once he f. her, as an ox goes Pro 7.22
but he who f. worthless pursuits 12.11
but he who f. worthless pursuits 28.19
Disaster f. hard on disaster, the Jer 4.20
one of you f. his stubborn evil 16.12
who stubbornly f. his own heart, 23.17
upon disaster, rumor f. rumor; Eze 7.26
all bounds and murder f. murder. Hos 4.02
he who f. me will not walk in Jn 8.12

FOLLY
he had wrought f. in Israel by Gen 34.07
she has wrought f. in Israel by Deu 22.21
is his name, and f. is with him; 1Sa 25.25
done in Israel; do not do this wanton f. 2Sa 13.12
deal with you according to your f.; Job 42.08
O God, thou knowest my f.; the wrongs Ps 69.05
because of his great f. he is lost. Pro 5.23
knowledge, but fools proclaim their f. 12.23
knowledge, but a fool flaunts his f. 13.16
but f. with her own hands tears it 14.01
but the f. of fools is deceiving. 14.08
The simple acquire f., but the prudent 14.18
but f. is the garland of fools. 14.24
who has a hasty temper exalts f. 14.29
the mouths of fools pour out f. 15.02
but the mouths of fools feed on f. 15.14
F. is a joy to him who has no sense, 15.21
but f. is the chastisement of fools. 16.22
cubs, rather than a fool in his f. 17.12
he hears it is his f. and shame. 18.13
When a man's f. brings his way to 19.03
F. is bound up in the heart of a 22.15
The devising of f. is sin, and the scoffer 24.09
Answer not a fool according to his f., 26.04
Answer a fool according to his f., 26.05
is a fool that repeats his f. 26.11
yet his f. will not depart from him 27.22
wisdom and to know madness and f. Ecc 1.17
wisdom—and how to lay hold on f., 2.03
consider wisdom and madness and f.; 2.12
wisdom excels f. as light excels 2.13
wickedness of f. and the foolishness 7.25
so a little f. outweighs wisdom and 10.01
f. is set in many high places, and 10.06
evildoer, and every mouth speaks f. Is 9.17
For the fool speaks f., and his mind 32.06
because they have committed f. in Israel, Jer 29.23
of the cross is f. to those who 1Co 1.18
God through the f. of what we 1.21
block to Jews and f. to Gentiles, 1.23
for they are f. to him, and he is 2.14
of this world is f. with God. 3.19
for their f. will be plain to all, 2Ti 3.09
For, uttering loud boasts of f., 2Pe 2.18

FONDLING
and saw Isaac f. Rebekah his wife. Gen 26.08

FOOD
fruit; you shall have them for f. Gen 1.29
given every green plant for f. 1.30
to the sight and good for f., 2.09
saw that the tree was good for f., 3.06
you every sort of f. that is eaten, 6.21
shall serve as f. for you and for 6.21
that lives shall be f. for you; 9.03
Then f. was set before him to eat; 24.33
and prepare for me savory f., 27.04
game, and prepare for me savory f., 27.07
them savory f. for you father, 27.09
and his mother prepared savory f., 27.14
gave the savory f. and the bread, 27.17
He also prepared savory f., 27.31
anything but the f. which he ate. 39.06
all sorts of baked f. for Pharaoh, 40.17
gather all the f. of these good 41.35
of Pharaoh for f. in the cities, 41.35
that f. shall be a reserve for the 41.36
up all the f. of the seven years 41.48
and stored up f. in the cities; 41.48
every city the f. from the fields 41.48
"From the land of Canaan, to buy f." 42.07
but to buy f. have your servants 42.10
them, "Go again, buy us a little f." 43.02
us, we will go down and buy you f.; 43.04
came down the first time to buy f.; 43.20
money down in our hand to buy f. 43.22
himself he said, "Let f. be served." 43.31
"Fill the men's sacks with f., 44.01
'Go again, buy us a little f.,' 44.25
all his father's household with f., 47.12
Now there was no f. in all the land 47.13
to Joseph, and said, "Give us f.; 47.15
I will give you f. in exchange for 47.16
gave them f. in exchange for the horses, 47.17
them with f. in exchange for all their 47.17
Buy us and our land for f., and we with 47.19
field and as f. for yourselves and 47.24
and as f. for your little ones." 47.24
Asher's f. shall be rich, and he 49.20
he shall not diminish her f., her Ex 21.10
on the altar as f. offered by fire Lev 3.11
on the altar as f. offered by fire 3.16
Any f. in it which may be eaten, Lev 11.34
plant all kinds of trees for f., 19.23
things, because such are his f. 22.07
in his house may eat of his f.; 22.11
she may eat of her father's f.; 22.13
the land shall provide f. for you, 25.06
land all its yield shall be for f. 25.07
nor give him your f. for profit. 25.37
when you eat of the f. of the land, Num 15.19
For there is no f. and no water, 21.05
and we loathe this worthless f." 21.05

FOOD (cont.)
my f. for my offerings by fire, my Num 28.02
the f. of an offering by fire, a 28.24
You shall purchase f. from them for Deu 2.06
You shall sell me f. for money, 2.28
sojourner, giving him f. and clothing. 10.18
not trees for f. you may destroy 20.20
body shall be f. for all birds of 28.26
you will grudge f. to his brother, 28.54
houses as our f. for the journey, Jos 9.12
me, I will not eat of your f.; Ju 13.16
his people and given them f. Ru 1.06
gave her what f. she had left over 2.18
man who eats f. until it is 1Sa 14.24
So none of the people tasted f. 14.24
be the man who eats f. this day.'" 14.28
came, the king sat down to eat f. 20.24
and ate no f. the second day of 20.34
not, nor did he eat f. with them. 2Sa 12.17
they set f. before him, and he ate. 12.20
child died, you arose and ate f." 12.21
and prepare the f. in my sight, 13.05
house, and prepare f. for him." 13.07
"Bring the f. into the chamber, that 13.10
the king with f. while he stayed 19.32
who provided f. for the king and 1Ki 4.07
by providing f. for my household." 5.09
of wheat as f. for his household, 5.11
the f. of his table, the seating of 10.05
assigned him an allowance of f., 11.18
strength of that f. forty days and 19.08
away his face, and would eat no f. 21.04
spirit so vexed that you eat no f.?" 21.05
who urged him to eat some f. So whenever 2Ki 4.08
he would turn in there to eat f. 4.08
there was no f. for the people of 25.03
came bringing f. on asses and on 1Ch 12.40
the f. of his table, the seating of 2Ch 9.04
and stores of f., oil, and wine. 11.11
provided them with f. and drink. 28.15
people ate the f. of the festival 30.22
not to partake of the most holy f., Ez 2.63
and f., drink, and oil to the 3.07
brethren at the f. allowance of Neh 5.14
and took from them f. and wine, 5.15
not demand the f. allowance of the 5.18
not to partake of the most holy f., 7.65
them on the day when they sold f. 13.15
ointments and her portion of f.. Est 2.09
they are as f. that is loathsome to Job 6.07
try words as the palate tastes f.? 12.11
yet his f. is turned in his stomach; 20.14
and rain it upon him as his f. 20.23
wilderness as f. for their children. 24.05
bread, and his appetite dainty f. 33.20
words as the palate tastes f. 34.03
judges peoples; he gives f. in abundance. 36.31
and wander about for lack of f.? 38.41
mountains yield f. for him where 40.20
have been my f. day and night, Ps 42.03
They roam about for f.. and growl if 59.15
They gave me poison for f., and for 69.21
give him as f. for the creatures 74.14
by demanding the f. they craved. 78.18
he sent them f. in abundance. 78.25
while the f. was still in their 78.30
to the birds of the air for f., 79.02
may bring forth f. from the earth, 104.14
prey, seeking their f. from God. 104.21
give them their f. in due season. 104.27
they loathed any kind of f., and they 107.18
He provides f. for those who fear 111.05
he who gives f. to all flesh, for 136.25
givest them their f. in due season. 145.15
the oppressed; who gives f. to the hungry. 146.07
He gives to the beasts their f., 147.09
she prepares her f. in summer, Pro 6.08
ground of the poor yields much f., 13.23
delicacies, for they are deceptive f. 23.03
be enough goats' milk for your f., 27.27
for the f. of your household and 27.27
a beating rain that leaves no f. 28.03
me with the f. that is needful for 30.08
a fool when he is filled with f.; 30.22
provide their f. in the summer; 30.25
merchant, she brings her f. from afar. 31.14
and provides f. for her household 31.15
supply abundant f. and fine clothing Is 23.18
grain to be f. for your enemies, 62.08
and dust shall be the serpent's f. 65.25
eat up your harvest and your f.; Jer 5.17
people will be f. for the birds of 7.33
bodies shall be f. for the birds 16.04
dead bodies for f. to the birds of 19.07
bodies shall be f. for the birds 34.20
an allowance of f. and a present, 40.05
for then we had plenty of f., 44.17
there was no f. for the people of 52.06
treasures for f. to revive their Lam 1.11
they sought f. to revive their 1.19
the children beg for f., but no one 4.04
became their f. in the destruction 4.10
And the f. which you eat shall be Eze 4.10
surfeit of f., and prosperous ease, 16.49
up to them for f. the sons whom 23.37
of the air I have given you as f. 29.05
and they became f. for all the wild 34.05
Have become f. for all the wild 34.08
that they may not be f. for them. 34.10
it, when you offer to me my f., 44.07
grow all kinds of trees for f. 47.12
Their fruit will be for f., and their 47.12
shall be f. for the workers of the 48.18
of the rich f. which the king ate, Dan 1.05
himself with the king's rich f., 1.08
appointed your f. and your drink, 1.10
the king's rich f. be observed by 1.13
youths who ate the king's rich f. 1.15
away their rich f. and the wine 1.16
abundant, and in it was f. for all. 4.12
and in which was f. for all; 4.21
eat his rich f. shall be his 11.26
shall eat unclean f. in Assyria. Hos 9.03
Is not the f. cut off before our Joe 1.16
in luxury, and his f. is rich. Hab 1.16
fail and the fields yield no f., 3.17
or wine. or oil, or any kind of f., Hag 2.12
offering polluted f. upon my altar. Mal 1.07
and the f. for it may be despised. 1.12
that there may be f. in my house; 3.10
and his f. was locusts and wild Mt 3.04
Is not life more than f., and the body 6.25
for the laborer deserves his f. 10.10
villages and buy f. for themselves. 14.15
give them their f. at the proper 24.45
for I was hungry and you gave me f., 25.35
I was hungry and you gave me no f., 25.42
and he who has f., let him do Lk 3.11
to go and buy f. for all these 9.13
For life is more than f., and the body 12.23
portion of f. at the proper time? 12.42
gone away into the city to buy f. Jn 4.08
"I have f. to eat of which you do 4.32
another, "Has any one brought him f.?" 4.33
"My f. is to do the will of him who 4.34
labor for the f. which perishes, 6.27
but for the f. which endures to 6.27
For my flesh is f. indeed. and my blood 6.55
they partook of f. with glad and Ac 2.46
and our fathers could find no f. 7.11
and took f. and was strengthened. 9.19
depended on the king's country for f. 12.20
your hearts with f. and gladness." 14.17
his house, and set f. before them; 16.34

FOOD (cont.)

to taste no f. till we have killed Ac 23.14
As they had been long without f., 27.21
urged them all to take some f., 27.33
continued in suspense and without f., 27.33
Therefore I urge you to take some f.; 27.34
encouraged and ate some f. themselves. 27.36
does not mean f. and drink but Rom 14.17
Do not, for the sake of f., 14.20
I fed you with milk, not solid f.; 1Co 3.02
"F. is meant for the stomach 6.13
and the stomach for f."—and God 6.13
Now concerning f. offered to idols: 8.01
the eating of f. offered to idols, 8.04
eat f. as really offered to an idol; 8.07
F. will not commend us to God. 8.08
is weak to eat f. offered to idols? 8.10
Therefore, if f. is a cause of my 8.13
have the right to our f. and drink? 9.04
get their f. from the temple, and 9.13
all ate the same supernatural f. 10.03
That f. offered to idols is anything, 10.19
and bread for f. will supply and 2Co 9.10
often without f., in cold and 11.27
in questions of f. and drink or Col 2.16
but if we have f. and clothing, with 1Ti 6.08
You need milk, not solid f.; Heb 5.12
But solid f. is for the mature, for 5.14
but deal only with f. and drink and 9.10
ill-clad and in lack of daily f., Jas 2.15
they might eat f. sacrificed to Rev 2.14
and to eat f. sacrificed to idols. 2.20

FOODS

(Thus he declared all f. clean.) Mk 7.19
abstinence from f. which God 1Ti 4.03
not by f., which have not benefited Heb 13.09

FOOL

behold, I have played the f., 1Sa 26.21
"Should Abner die as a f. dies? 2Sa 3.33
Surely vexation kills the f., Job 5.02
I have seen the f. taking root, 5.03
The f. says in his heart, "There is Ps 14.01
Make me not the scorn of the f.! 39.08
the f. and the stupid alike must 49.10
The f. says in his heart, "There is 53.01
but a prating f. will come to ruin. Pro 10.08
babbling of a f. brings ruin near. 10.14
and he who utters slander is a f. 10.18
It is like sport to a f. to do wrong, 10.23
and the f. will be servant to the 11.29
The way of a f. is right in his own 12.15
The vexation of a f. is known at 12.16
knowledge, but a f. flaunts his folly. 13.16
The talk of a f. is a rod for his 14.03
Leave the presence of a f., for there 14.07
but a f. throws off restraint and 14.16
A f. despises his father's instruction, 15.05
Fine speech is not becoming to a f.; 17.07
than a hundred blows into a f. 17.10
rather than a f. in his folly. 17.12
Why should a f. have a price in his 17.16
and the father of a f. has no joy. 17.21
the eyes of a f. are on the ends 17.24
Even a f. who keeps silent is 17.28
A f. takes no pleasure in understanding, 18.02
is perverse in speech, and is a f. 19.01
fitting for a f. to live in luxury, 19.10
but every f. will be quarreling. 20.03
Do not speak in the hearing of a f., 23.09
Wisdom is too high for a f.; in the gate 24.07
so honor is not fitting for a f. 26.01
Answer not a f. according to his 26.04
Answer a f. according to his folly, 26.05
the hand of a f. cuts off his own 26.06
is he who gives honor to a f. 26.08
who hires a passing f. or drunkard. 26.10
his vomit is a f. that repeats his 26.11
is more hope for a f. than for him. 26.12
Crush a f. in a mortar with a pestle 27.22
who trusts in his own mind is a f.; 28.26
wise man has an argument with a f., 29.09
the f. only rages and laughs, and 29.09
A f. gives full vent to his anger, 29.11
is more hope for a f. than for him. 29.20
and a f. when he is filled with food; 30.22
but the f. walks in darkness; and yet Ecc 2.14
befalls the f. will befall me also; 2.15
man as of the f. there is no 2.16
the wise man dies just like the f.! 2.16
he will be a wise man or a f.? 2.19
The f. folds his hands, and eats his 4.05
has the wise man over the f.? 6.08
wicked overmuch, neither be a f.; 7.17
Even when the f. walks on the road, 10.03
says to every one that he is a f. 10.03
but the lips of a f. consume him. 10.12
A f. multiplies words, though no man 10.14
The toil of a f. wearies him, so 10.15
The f. will no more be called noble, Is 32.05
For the f. speaks folly, and his 32.06
and at his end he will be a f. Jer 17.11
The prophet is a f., the man of Hos 9.07
council, and whoever says, 'You f.!' Mt 5.22
But God said to him, 'F.! This night Lk 12.20
him become a f. that he may become 1Co 3.18
even if you do, accept me as a f., 2Co 11.16
the Lord's authority but as a f., 11.17
to boast of—I am speaking as a f.— 11.21
wish to boast. I shall not be a f., 12.06
I have been a f.! You forced me 12.11

FOOLISH

you f. and senseless people? Deu 32.06
will provoke them with a f. nation. 32.21
as one of the f. women would speak. Job 2.10
of those who have f. confidence, Ps 49.13
prudence; O f. men, pay attention. Pro 8.05
A f. woman is noisy; she is wanton 9.13
but a f. son is a sorrow to his 10.01
but a f. man despises his mother. 15.20
A f. son is a grief to his father 17.25
A f. son is ruin to his father, and 19.13
dwelling, but a f. man devours it. 21.20
If you have been f., exalting yourself, 30.32
wise youth than an old and f. king, Ecc 4.13
Surely oppression makes the wise man f., 7.07
The princes of Zoan are utterly f.; Is 19.11
back, and makes their knowledge f.; 44.25
"For my people are f., they know me Jer 4.22
"Hear this, O f. and senseless 5.21
They are both stupid and f.; the instruction 10.08
Woe to the f. prophets who follow Eze 13.03
will be like a f. man who built Mt 7.26
Five of them were f., and five were 25.02
For when the f. took their lamps, 25.03
And the f. said to the wise, 'Give 25.08
"O f. men, and slow of heart to Lk 24.25
both to the wise and to the f.: Rom 1.14
f., faithless, heartless, ruthless. 1.31
a corrector of the f., a teacher 2.20
with a f. nation I will make you 10.19
not God made f. the wisdom of the 1Co 1.20
chose what is f. in the world to 1.27
You f. man! What you sow 15.36
I repeat, let no one think me f.; 2Co 11.16
O f. Galatians! Who has bewitched Gal 3.01
Are you so f.? Having begun with the Gal 3.03
Therefore do not be f., but understand Eph 5.17
For we ourselves were once f., Tit 3.03
you f. fellow, that faith apart from Jas 2.20
to silence the ignorance of f. men. 1Pe 2.15

FOOLISHLY

daughters farewell? Now you have done f. Gen 31.28
we have done f. and have sinned. Num 12.11
said to Saul, "You have done f.; 1Sa 13.13
thy servant; for I have done very f." 2Sa 24.10
thy servant; for I have done very f." 1Ch 21.08
You have done f. in this; for from now on 2Ch 16.09
A man of quick temper acts f., Pro 14.17
associate with one who speaks f. 20.19

FOOLISHNESS

the counsel of Ahithophel into f." 2Sa 15.31
foul and fester because of my f., Ps 38.05
folly and the f. which is madness. Ecc 7.25
of the words of his mouth is f., 10.13
licentiousness, envy, slander, pride, f. Mk 7.22
For the f. of God is wiser than men, 1Co 1.25
would bear with me in a little f. 2Co 11.01

FOOL'S

A f. lips bring strife, and his Pro 18.06
A f. mouth is his ruin, and his lips 18.07
but a f. provocation is heavier 27.03
and a f. voice with many words. Ecc 5.03
but a f. heart toward the left. 10.02

FOOLS

as one of the wanton f. in Israel. 2Sa 13.13
stripped, and judges he makes f. Job 12.17
of the people! F., when will you be wise? Ps 94.08
f. despise wisdom and instruction. Pro 1.07
scoffing and f. hate knowledge? 1.22
complacence of f. destroys them; 1.32
inherit honor, but f. get disgrace. 3.35
feed many, but f. die for lack of sense. 10.21
his knowledge, but f. proclaim their folly. 12.23
from evil is an abomination to f. 13.19
companion of f. will suffer harm. 13.20
but the folly of f. is deceiving. 14.08
but folly is the garland of f. 14.24
it is not known in the heart of f. 14.33
the mouths of f. pour out folly. 15.02
knowledge; not so the minds of f. 15.07
but the mouths of f. feed on folly. 15.14
folly is the chastisement of f. 16.22
and flogging for the backs of f. 19.29
ass, and a rod for the back of f. 26.03
is a proverb in the mouth of f. 26.07
is a proverb in the mouth of f. 26.09
than to offer the sacrifice of f.; Ecc 5.01
for he has no pleasure in f. 5.04
the heart of f. is in the house of 7.04
wise than to hear the song of f. 7.05
pot, so is the laughter of the f.; 7.06
anger lodges in the bosom of f. 7.09
the shouting of a ruler among f. 9.17
The princes of Zoan have become f., Is 19.13
and f. shall not err therein. 35.08
of liars, and makes f. of diviners; 44.25
diviners, that they may become f.! Jer 50.36
You blind f.! for which is greater, Mt 23.17
You f.! Did not he who Lk 11.40
Claiming to be wise, they became f., Rom 1.22
We are f. for Christ's sake, but you 1Co 4.10
For you gladly bear with f., being wise 2Co 11.19

FOOT

dove found no place to set her f., Gen 8.09
lift up hand or f. in all the land 41.44
six hundred thousand men on f., Ex 12.37
stand at the f. of the mountain. 19.17
tooth, hand for hand, f. for f., 21.24
an altar as the f. of the mountain, 24.04
them at the f. of the mountain. 32.19
on the great toe of his right f. Lev 8.23
diseased person from head to f., 13.12
on the great toe of his right f. 14.14
on the great toe of his right f., 14.17
on the great toe of his right f. 14.25
and the great toe of his right f., 14.28
has an injured f. or an injured 21.19
number six hundred thousand on f.; Num 11.21
pass through on f., nothing more." 20.19
Balaam's f. against the wall; 22.25
for the sole of the f. to tread on, Deu 2.05
only let me pass through on f., 2.28
stood at the f. of the mountain, 4.11
and your f. did not swell, these 8.04
sole of your f. treads shall be 11.24
tooth, hand for hand, f. for f. 19.21
and pull his sandal off his f., 25.09
sole of your f. to the crown of 28.35
the sole of her f. upon the ground 28.56
be no rest for the sole of your f.; 28.65
the time when their f. shall slip; 32.35
and let him dip his f. in oil. 33.24
sole of your f. will tread upon I Jos 1.03
southward to the f. of the slopes 12.03
on which your f. has trodden shall 14.09
his chariot and fled away on f. Ju 4.15
fled away on f. to the tent of 4.17
thousand men on f. that drew the 20.02
Israel thirty thousand f. soldiers. 1Sa 4.10
two hundred thousand men on f., 15.04
was as swift of f. as a wild gazelle; 2Sa 2.18
and twenty thousand f. soldiers; 8.04
Zobah, twenty thousand f. soldiers, 10.06
the sole of his f. to the crown of 14.25
each hand, and six toes on each f., 21.20
thousand f. soldiers in one day. 1Ki 20.29
the sole of my f. all the streams 2Ki 19.24
and twenty thousand f. soldiers; 1Ch 18.04
and forty thousand f. soldiers, 19.18
each hand, and six toes on each f., 20.06
more remove the f. of Israel from 2Ch 33.08
the sole of his f. to the crown of Job 2.07
My f. has held fast to his steps; 23.11
and my f. has hastened to deceit; 31.05
forgetting that a f. may crush them, 39.15
hid has their own f. been caught. Ps 9.15
My f. stands on level ground; 26.12
Let not the f. of arrogance come 36.11
boast against me when my f. slips! 38.16
men passed through the river on f. 66.06
Trample under f. those who lust 68.30
you dash your f. against a stone. 91.12
serpent you will trample under f. 91.13
"My f. slips," thy steadfast love, O 94.18
He will not let your f. be moved, 121.03
hold back your f. from their paths; Pro 1.15
and your f. will not stumble. 3.23
will keep your f. from being 3.26
turn your f. away from evil. 4.27
Let your f. be seldom in your 25.17
a bad tooth or a f. that slips. 25.19
princes walking on f. like slaves. Ecc 10.07
From the sole of the f. even to the Is 1.06
like a dead body trodden under f. 14.19
my mountains trample him under f.; 14.25
tramples under f. has vanished 16.04
The f. tramples it, the feet of the 26.06
Ephraim will be trodden under f.; 28.03
the sole of my f. all the streams 37.25
so that he tramples kings under f.; 41.02
turn back your f. from the sabbath, 58.13
"If you have raced with men on f., Jer 12.05
To crush under f. all the prisoners Lam 3.34
were like the sole of a calf's f.; Eze 1.07
and stamp your f., and say, Alas! 6.11
No f. of man shall pass through it, 29.11
and no f. of beast shall pass 29.11
and no f. of man shall trouble them 32.13
and host to be trampled under f.?" Dan 8.13
who is swift of f. shall not save Amo 2.15

FOOT (cont.)
will tread our iniquities under f. Mic 7.19
you strike your f. against a stone.'" Mt 4.06
out and trodden under f. by men. 5.13
followed him on f. from the towns. 14.13
hand or your f. causes you to sin, 18.08
attendants, 'Bind him hand and f., 22.13
ran there on f. from all the towns, Mk 6.33
And if your f. causes you to sin, 9.45
you strike your f. against a stone.'" Lk 4.11
the path, and was trodden under f., 8.05
first day that I set f. in Asia, Ac 20.18
If the f. should say, "Because I am 1Co 12.15
And he set his right f. on the sea, Rev 10.02
sea, and his left f. on the land, 10.02

FOOTHOLD
in deep mire, where there is no f.; Ps 69.02

FOOTMEN
ten chariots and ten thousand f.; 2Ki 13.07

FOOTPRINTS
great waters; yet thy f. were unseen. Ps 77.19

FOOT'S
not even a f. length, but promised Ac 7.05

FOOTSTEPS
before him. and make his f. a way. Ps 85.13
they mock the f. of thy anointed. 89.51

FOOTSTOOL
LORD. and for the f. of our God; 1Ch 28.02
had six steps and a f. of gold, 2Ch 9.18
worship at his f.! Holy is he! Ps 99.05
till I make your enemies your f. 110.01
dwelling place; let us worship at his f.!" 132.07
my throne and the earth is my f.; Is 66.01
remembered his f. in the day of Lam 2.01
for it is his f., or by Jerusalem. Mt 5.35
'Heaven is my throne, and earth my f. Ac 7.49

FORASMUCH
f. as we have sworn both of us in 1Sa 20.42

FORBADE
wherever the LORD our God f. us. Deu 2.37
and we f. him, because he was not Mk 9.38
and we f. him, because he does not Lk 9.49

FOREBEAR
Ramothgilead, or shall I f.?" And they said, 1Ki 22.06
Ramothgilead to battle, or shall we f.?" 22.15
Ramothgilead, or shall I f.?" And they said, 2Ch 18.05
Ramothgilead to battle, or shall I f.?" 18.14
and if I f., how much of it leaves Job 16.06
and f. threatening, knowing that he Eph 6.09

FOREBEARANCE
In thy f. take me not away; know that Jer 15.15
his kindness and f. and patience? Rom 2.04
in his divine f. he had passed 3.25
f., kindness, the Holy Spirit, 2Co 6.06
Let all men know your f. The Lord Php 4.05
And count the f. of our Lord as 2Pe 3.15

FOREBEARING
with patience, f. one another in love, Eph 4.02
f. one another and, if one has a Col 3.13
to every one, an apt teacher, f., 2Ti 2.24
but is f. toward you, not wishing 2Pe 3.09

FORBID
men, said, "My lord Moses, f. them." Num 11.28
"The LORD f. that I should do this 1Sa 24.06
The LORD f. that I should put forth 26.11
"The LORD f. that I should give you 1Ki 21.03
whom thou didst f. to enter thy Lam 1.10
rebuke him. saying, "God f., Lord! Mt 16.22
But Jesus said, "Do not f. him; Mk 9.39
But Jesus said to him, "Do not f. him; Lk 9.50
they heard this, they said, "God f.!" 20.16
"Can any one f. water for baptizing Ac 10.47
and do not f. speaking in tongues; 1Co 14.39
who f. marriage and enjoin abstinence 1Ti 4.03

FORBIDDEN
you shall count their fruit as f.; Lev 19.23
three years it shall be f. to you, 19.23
which the LORD your God has f. you. Deu 4.23
host of heaven, which I have f., 17.03
having been f. by the Holy Spirit Ac 16.06

FORBIDDING
and f. us to give tribute to Caesar, Lk 23.02

FORCE
take your daughters from me by f. Gen 31.31
many men, and with a strong f. Num 20.20
not dim, nor his natural f. abated. Deu 34.07
and if not, I will take it by f." 1Sa 2.16
him, "No, my brother, do not f. me; 2Sa 13.12
come on duty in f. on the sabbath 2Ki 11.07
Jerusalem and by f. and power made Ez 4.23
any armed f. of any people or Est 8.11
all the f. of misery will come upon Job 20.22
or all the f. of your strength? 36.19
for her enemies march in f., Jer 46.22
and with f. and harshness you have Eze 34.04
and men of violence take it by f. Mt 11.12
and take him by f. to make him Jn 6.15
and take him by f. from among them Ac 23.10
it is not in f. as long as the one Heb 9.17

FORCED
and became a slave at f. labor. Gen 49.15
in it shall do f. labor for you Deu 20.11
have become slaves to do f. labor. Jos 16.10
put the Canaanites to f. labor, 17.13
put the Canaanites to f. labor, Ju 1.28
and became subject to f. labor. 1.30
subject to f. labor for them. 1.33
they became subject to f. labor. 1.35
so I f. myself, and offered the 1Sa 13.12
he f. her, and lay with her. 2Sa 13.14
because he had f. his sister Tamar. 13.22
from the day he f. his sister 13.32
was in charge of the f. labor; 20.24
Abda was in charge of the f. labor. 1Ki 4.06
a levy of f. labor out of all 5.13
account of the f. labor which King 9.15
Solomon made a f. levy of slaves, 9.21
over all the f. labor of the house 11.28
was taskmaster over the f. labor, 12.18
Solomon made a f. levy and so they 2Ch 8.08
was taskmaster over the f. labor, 10.18
slothful will be put to f. labor. Pro 12.24
young men shall be put to f. labor. Is 31.08
our race and f. our fathers to Ac 7.19
You f. me to it, for I ought to have 2Co 12.11

FORCEFUL
How f. are honest words! But what does Job 6.25

FORCES
these joined f. in the Valley of Gen 14.03
And he divided his f. against them 14.15
So they stationed the f., the main Jos 8.13
king of Eglon, gathered their f., 10.05
And all these kings joined their f., 11.05
Philistines gathered their f. for war, 1Sa 28.01
gathered all their f. at Aphek; 29.01
captains of the f. in the open 2Ki 25.23
and the captains of the f. arose, 25.26
and drew up his f. against them. 1Ch 19.17
He placed f. in all the fortified 2Ch 17.02

FORCES (cont.)
besieging Lachish with all his f., 2Ch 32.09
captains of the f. in the open Jer 40.07
leaders of the f. in the open 40.13
leaders of the f. with him heard 41.11
all the leaders of the f. with him, 41.13
leaders of the f. with him took 41.16
Then all the commanders of the f., 42.01
commanders of the f. who were with 42.08
commanders of the f. and all the 43.04
commanders of the f. took all the 43.05
assemble a multitude of great f., Dan 11.10
And the f. of the south shall not 11.15
F. from him shall appear and 11.31
and if any one f. you to go one Mt 5.41

FORCING
yet we are f. our sons and our Neh 5.05

FORD
and crossed the f. of the Jabbok. Gen 32.22
crossed the f. to bring over the 2Sa 19.18

FORDS
way to the Jordan as far as the f.; Jos 2.07
and seized the f. of the Jordan Ju 3.28
took the f. of the Jordan against 12.05
slew him at the f. of the Jordan. 12.06
or crossed the f. of the Jordan to 1Sa 13.07
wait at the f. of the wilderness, 2Sa 15.28
tonight at the f. of the wilderness, 17.16
of Moab at the f. of the Arnon. Is 16.02
the f. have been seized, the bulwarks Jer 51.32

FOREBODING
fear and with f. of what is coming Lk 21.26

FOREFATHER
our f. according to the flesh? Rom 4.01
children by one man, our f. Isaac, 9.10

FOREFATHERS
remember the covenant with their f., Lev 26.45
us the iniquities of our f.; let thy Ps 79.08
back to the iniquities of their f., Jer 11.10
beloved for the sake of their f. Rom 11.28

FOREFRONT
Uriah in the f. of the hardest 2Sa 11.15

FOREGO
and we will f. the crops of the Neh 10.31

FOREHEAD
It shall be upon Aaron's f., and Aaron Ex 28.38
it shall always be upon his f., 28.38
has fallen from his f. and temples, Lev 13.41
baldness of the f. but he is clean. 13.41
or the bald f. a reddish-white 13.42
on his bald head or his bald f. 13.42
on his bald head or on his bald f., 13.43
it shall crush the f. of Moab, Num 24.17
struck the Philistine on his f.; 1Sa 17.49
the stone sank into his f., and he fell 17.49
leprosy broke out on his f., in the 2Ch 26.19
behold, he was leprous in his f.! 26.20
an iron sinew and your f. brass, Is 48.04
it has destroyed the f. of Moab, Jer 48.45
are of a hard f. and of a stubborn Eze 3.07
and your f. hard against their 3.08
than flint have I made your f.; 3.09
marked on the right hand or the f., Rev 13.16
a mark on his f. or on his hand, 14.09
and on her f. was written a name of 17.05

FOREHEADS
baldness on your f. for the dead. Deu 14.01
forehead hard against their f. Eze 3.08
a mark upon the f. of the men who 9.04
servants of our God upon their f. Rev 7.03
not the seal of God upon their f.; 9.04
Father's name written on their f. 14.01
mark on their f. or their hands. 20.04
and his name shall be on their f. 22.04

FOREIGN
"Put away the f. gods that are Gen 35.02
Jacob all the f. gods that they 35.04
have been a sojourner in a f. land." Ex 2.22
been a sojourner in a f. land"), 18.03
right to sell her to a f. people, 21.08
and there was no f. god with him. Deu 32.12
forsake the LORD and serve f. gods, Jos 24.20
put away the f. gods which are 24.23
put away the f. gods from among Ju 10.16
then put away the f. gods and the 1Sa 7.03
Now King Solomon loved many f. women: 1Ki 11.01
And so he did for all his f. wives, 11.08
I dug wells and drank f. waters, 2Ki 19.24
He took away the f. altars and the 2Ch 14.03
took away the f. gods and the idol 33.15
have married f. women from the Ez 10.02
trespassed and married f. women, 10.10
of the land and from the f. wives. 10.11
who have taken f. wives come at 10.14
the men who had married f. women. 10.17
who had married f. women were 10.18
All these had married f. women, 10.44
Israel all those of f. descent. Neh 13.03
nevertheless f. women made even him 13.26
our God by marrying f. women?" 13.27
I cleansed them from everything f., 13.30
you shall not bow down to a f. god. Ps 81.09
sing the LORD's song in a f. land? 137.04
me and served f. gods in your land, Jer 5.19
images, and with their f. idols?" 8.19
and all the f. folk among them; 25.20
upon all the f. troops in her 50.37
to a people of f. speech and a Eze 3.05
many peoples of f. speech and a 3.06
fortresses by the help of a f. god; Dan 11.39
who array themselves in f. attire. Zep 1.08
married the daughter of a f. god. Mal 2.11
be a preacher of f. divinities"— Ac 17.18
persecuted them even to f. cities. 26.11
as in a f. land, living in tents Heb 11.09
in war, put f. armies to flight. 11.34

FOREIGNER
money from any f. who is not of Gen 17.12
those bought with money from a f., 17.27
passover; no f. shall eat of it; Ex 12.43
any such animals gotten from a f. Lev 22.25
eat it, or you may sell it to a f.; Deu 14.21
Of a f. you may exact it; but whatever 15.03
you may not put a f. over you, 17.15
To a f. you may lend upon interest, 23.20
and the f. who comes from a far 29.22
take notice of me, when I am a f.?" Ru 2.10
for you are a f., and also an exile 2Sa 15.19
"Likewise when a f.. who is not 1Ki 8.41
all for which the f. calls to thee; 8.43
"Likewise when a f., who is not 2Ch 6.32
all for which the f. calls to thee; 6.33
Let not the f. who has joined Is 56.03
No f., uncircumcised in heart and Eze 44.09
give praise to God except this f.?" Lk 17.18
I shall be a f. to the speaker and 1Co 14.11
speaker and the speaker a f. to me. 14.11

FOREIGNERS
Are we not regarded by him as f.? Gen 31.15
not turn aside into the city of f., Ju 19.12
F. came cringing to me; as soon as 2Sa 22.45
F. lost heart, and came trembling 22.46

FOREIGNERS (cont.)
separated themselves from all f., Neh 9.02
obeyed me; f. came cringing to me. Ps 18.44
F. lost heart, and came trembling 18.45
pledge when he gives surety for f. Pro 20.16
pledge when he gives surety for f. 27.13
and they strike hands with f. Is 2.06
"And the f. who join themselves to 56.06
F. shall build up your walls, and 60.10
f. shall be your plowmen and 61.05
and f. shall not drink your wine 62.08
it into the hands of f. for a prey, Eze 7.21
and give you into the hands of f., 11.09
uncircumcised by the hand of f.; 28.10
everything in it, by the hand of f.; 30.12
F., the most terrible of the 31.12
in admitting f., uncircumcised in 44.07
you have set f. to keep my charge 44.08
of all the f. who are among the 44.09
and f. entered his gates and cast Ob 1.11
Athenians and the f. who lived Ac 17.21
by the lips of f. will I speak to 1Co 14.21

FOREKNEW
For those whom he f. he also Rom 8.29
not rejected his people whom he f. 11.02

FOREKNOWLEDGE
to the definite plan and f. of God, Ac 2.23

FOREMEN
of the people and their f., Ex 5.06
taskmasters and the f. of the 5.10
And the f. of the people of Israel, 5.14
Then the f. of the people of Israel 5.15
The f. of the people of Israel saw 5.19

FOREMOST
He instructed the f., "When Esau my Gen 32.17
running of the f. is like the 2Sa 18.27
officials and chief men has been f. Ez 9.02
sinners. And I am the f. of sinners; 1Ti 1.15
as the f., Jesus Christ might display 1.16

FORENOON
the whole f. they came to Mahanaim. 2Sa 2.29

FORERUNNER
has gone as a f. on our behalf, Heb 6.20

FORESAIL
hoisting the f. to the wind they Ac 27.40

FORESAW
he f. and spoke of the resurrection Ac 2.31

FORESEEING
f. that God would justify the Gal 3.08

FORESEEN
since God had f. something better Heb 11.40

FORESKIN
flesh of his f. shall be cut off Gen 17.14
curcumcised in the flesh of his f.; 17.24
curcumcised in the flesh of his f. 17.25
a flint and cut off her son's f., Ex 4.25
flesh of his f. shall be circumcised. Lev 12.03
Circumcise therefore the f. of your heart, Deu 10.16
remove the f. of your hearts, O men Jer 4.04

FORESKINS
circumcised in the flesh of your f., Gen 17.11
flesh of their f. that very day, 17.23
a hundred f. of the Philistines, 1Sa 18.25
and David brought their f., which were 18.27
of a hundred f. of the Philistines." 2Sa 3.14

FOREST
goes into the f. with his neighbor Deu 19.05
go up to the f., and there clear Jos 17.15
be yours, for though it is a f., 17.18
And all the people came into the f.; 1Sa 14.25
And when the people entered the f., 14.26
and went into the f. of Hereth. 22.05
was fought in the f. of Ephraim. 2Sa 18.06
and the f. devoured more people 18.08
him into a great pit in the f., 18.17
the House of the F. of Lebanon; 1Ki 7.02
in the House of the F. of Lebanon. 10.17
House of the F. of Lebanon were of 10.21
farthest retreat, its densest f. 2Ki 19.23
in the House of the F. of Lebanon. 2Ch 9.16
House of the F. of Lebanon were of 9.20
Asaph, the keeper of the king's f., Neh 2.08
For every beast of the f. is mine, Ps 50.10
The boar from the f. ravages it, 80.13
As fire consumes the f., as the flame 83.14
the beasts of the f. creep forth. 104.20
to water the f. of growing trees. Ecc 2.06
trees of the f. shake before the Is 7.02
it kindles the thickets of the f., 9.18
The glory of his f. and of his 10.18
trees of his f. will be so few 10.19
the thickets of the f. with an axe, 10.34
weapons of the house of the f., 22.08
field shall be regarded as a f.? 29.17
the fruitful field is deemed a f. 32.15
And the f. will utterly go down, and 32.19
remotest height, its densest f. 37.24
strong among the trees of the f.; 44.14
O f., and every tree in it! For the 44.23
to devour—all you beasts in the f. 56.09
Therefore a lion from the f. shall Jer 5.06
A tree from the f. is cut down, 10.03
become to me like a lion in the f., 12.08
I will kindle a fire in her f., 21.14
They shall cut down her f., says the LORD, 46.23
which is among the trees of the f.? Eze 15.02
the vine among the trees of the f., 15.06
against the f. land in the Negeb; 20.46
say to the f. of the Negeb, Hear the 20.47
with fair branches and f. shade, 31.03
streams to all the trees of the f. 31.04
high above all the trees of the f.; 31.05
I will make them a f., and the beasts Hos 2.12
Does a lion roar in the f., Amo 3.04
a lion among the beasts of the f., Mic 5.08
alone in a f. in the midst of a 7.14
for the thick f. has been felled! Zec 11.02
How great a f. is set ablaze by a Jas 3.05

FORESTS
to whirl, and strips the f. bare; Ps 29.09
or cut down any out of the f., Eze 39.10

FORETOLD
had made, as the LORD had f. 2Ki 24.13
But what God f. by the mouth of all Ac 3.18
stood up and f. by the Spirit that 11.28

FOREWARNED
things, as we solemnly f. you. 1Th 4.06

FORFEIT
hands to escape shall f. his life." 2Ki 10.24
the whole world and f. his life? Mk 8.36

FORFEITED
whole yield be f. to the sanctuary, Deu 22.09
all his property should be f., and he Ez 10.08
many peoples; you have f. your life. Hab 2.10

FORFEITS
provokes him to anger f. his life. Pro 20.02
the whole world and f. his life? Mt 16.26
world and loses or f. himself? Lk 9.25

FORGAVE

f. their iniquity, and did not Ps 78.38
released him and f. him the debt. Mt 18.27
I f. you all that debt because you 18.32
could not pay, he f. them both. Lk 7.42
one, I suppose, to whom he f. more." 7.43
another, as God in Christ f. you. Eph 4.32

FORGER

he was the f. of all instruments of Gen 4.22

FORGES

and f. it with his strong arm; Is 44.12

FORGET

"God has made me f. all my hardship Gen 41.51
lest you f. the things which you Deu 4.09
lest you f. the covenant of the 4.23
destroy you or f. the covenant 4.31
then take heed lest you f. the LORD, 6.12
"Take heed lest you f. the LORD 8.11
and you f. the LORD your God, who 8.14
And if you f. the LORD your God and 8.19
Remember and do not f. how you 9.07
under heaven; you shall not f. 25.19
and not f. thy maidservant, but wilt 1Sa 1.11
and you shall not f. the covenant 2Ki 17.38
Such are the paths of all who f. God; Job 8.13
'I will f. my complaint, I will put 9.27
You will f. your misery; you will 11.16
The squares of the town f. them; 24.20
because God has made her f. wisdom, 39.17
he does not f. the cry of the Ps 9.12
Sheol, all the nations that f. God. 9.17
thy hand; f. not the afflicted. 10.12
Wilt thou f. me for ever? How long 13.01
Why dost thou f. our affliction and 44.24
f. your people and your father's 45.10
you who f. God, lest I rend, and 50.22
Slay them not, lest my people f.; 59.11
do not f. the life of thy poor for 74.19
Do not f. the clamor of thy foes, 74.23
and not f. the works of God, but 78.07
and withered; I f. to eat my bread. 102.04
and f. not all his benefits, 103.02
thy statutes; I will not f. thy word. 119.16
ensnare me, I do not f. thy law. 119.61
I will never f. thy precepts; 119.93
continually, but I do not f. thy law. 119.109
me, because my foes f. thy words. 119.139
yet I do not f. thy precepts. 119.141
me, for I do not f. thy law. 119.153
for I do not f. thy commandments. 119.176
If I f. you, O Jerusalem, let my 137.05
My son, do not f. my teaching, but Pro 3.01
do not f., and do not turn away 4.05
lest they drink and f. what has 31.05
let them drink and f. their poverty, 31.07
"Can a woman f. her sucking child, Is 49.15
Even these may f., yet I will not f. you. 49.15
for you will f. the shame of your 54.04
who f. my holy mountain, who set a 65.11
Can a maiden f. her ornaments, or a Jer 2.32
make my people f. my name by their 23.27
Why dost thou f. us for ever, why Lam 5.20
They shall f. their shame, and all Eze 39.26
God, I also will f. your children. Hos 4.06
I will never f. any of their deeds. Amo 8.07
Can I f. the treasures of wickedness Mic 6.10

FORGETFULNESS

thy saving help in the land of f.? Ps 88.12

FORGETS

and he f. what you have done to him; Gen 27.45
her youth and f. the covenant of Pro 2.17
and at once f. what he was like. Jas 1.24
no hearer that f. but a doer that 1.25

FORGETTING

f. the LORD their God, and serving Ju 3.07
f. that a foot may crush them, and Job 39.15
f. what lies behind and straining Php 3.13

FORGIVE

F., I pray you, the transgression of Gen 50.17
f. the transgression of the servants 50.17
Now therefore, f. my sin, I pray you, Ex 10.17
if thou wilt f. their sin—and if 32.32
and the LORD will f. her, because her Num 30.05
herself; and the LORD will f. her. 30.08
void, and the LORD will f. her. 30.12
F., O LORD, thy people Israel, whom Deu 21.08
he will not f. your transgressions Jos 24.19
Pray f. the trespass of your handmaid; 1Sa 25.28
dwelling place; and when thou hearest, f. 1Ki 8.30
and f. the sin of thy people Israel. 8.34
and f. the sin of thy servants, thy 8.36
and f., and act, and render to each 8.39
and f. thy people who have sinned 8.50
dwelling place; and when thou hearest, f. 2Ch 6.21
and f. the sin of thy people Israel, 6.25
and f. the sin of thy servants, thy 6.27
and f., and render to each whose 6.30
their cause and f. thy people who 6.39
and will f. their sin and heal 7.14
But thou art a God ready to f., Neh 9.17
and my trouble, and f. all my sins. Ps 25.18
then thou didst f. the guilt of my 32.05
prevail over us, thou dost f. them. 65.03
and f. our sins, for thy name's sake! 79.09
Thou didst f. the iniquity of thy 85.02
and men are brought low—f. them not! Is 2.09
F. not their iniquity, nor blot out Jer 18.23
for I will f. their iniquity, and I 31.34
and I will f. all the guilt of 33.08
and that I may f. their iniquity 36.03
when I f. you all that you have Eze 16.63
O LORD, f.; O LORD, give heed Dan 9.19
house of Israel, to f. them at all. Hos 1.06
f., I beseech thee! How can Jacob Amo 7.02
And f. us our debts, As we also have Mt 6.12
For if you f. men their trespasses, 6.14
heavenly Father also will f. you; 6.14
but if you do not f. men their 6.15
your Father f. your trespasses. 6.15
authority on earth to f. sins"— 9.06
sin against me, and I f. him? 18.21
if you do not f. your brother from 18.35
Who can f. sins but God alone?" Mk 2.07
authority on earth to f. sins"— 2.10
f., if you have anything against 11.25
in heaven may f. you your trespasses 11.25
"But if you do not f., neither will *11.26
your Father who is in heaven f. your * 11.26
Who can f. sins but God only?" Lk 5.21
authority on earth to f. sins"— 5.24
f., and you will be forgiven; 6.37
and f. us our sins, for we ourselves 11.04
we ourselves f. every one who is 11.04
him, and if he repents, f. him; 17.03
says, 'I repent,' you must f. him." 17.04
And Jesus said, "Father, f. them; 23.34
If you f. the sins of any, they are Jn 20.23
rather turn to f. and comfort him, 2Co 2.07
Any one whom you f., I also f. 2.10
F. me this wrong! 12.13
forgiven you, so you also must f. Col 3.13
and will f. our sins and cleanse us 1Jn 1.09

FORGIVEN

for them, and they shall be f. Lev 4.20
for his sin, and he shall be f. 4.26
for him, and he shall be f. 4.31

FORGIVEN (cont.)
has committed, and he shall be f. Lev 4.35
has committed, and he shall be f. 5.10
these things, and he shall be f. 5.13
guilt offering, and he shall be f. 5.16
unwittingly, and he shall be f. 5.18
and he shall be f. for any of the 6.07
he has committed shall be f. him. 19.22
as thou hast f. this people, Num 14.19
of Israel, and they shall be f.; 15.25
the people of Israel shall be f., 15.26
atonement for him; and he shall be f. 15.28
let the guilt of blood be f. them.' Deu 21.08
Blessed is he whose transgression is f., Ps 32.01
is taken away, and your sin f." Is 6.07
will not be f. you till you die," 22.14
there will be f. their iniquity. 33.24
and rebelled, and thou hast not f. Lam 3.42
As we also have f. our debtors; Mt 6.12
"Take heart, my son; your sins are f." 9.02
easier, to say, 'Your sins are f.,' 9.05
sin and blasphemy will be f. men, 12.31
against the Spirit will not be f. 12.31
against the Son of man will be f.; 12.32
the Holy Spirit will not be f., 12.32
paralytic, "My son, your sins are f." Mk 2.05
the parlaytic, 'Your sins are f.,' 2.09
sins will be f. the sons of men, 3.28
they should turn again, and be f." 4.12
he said, "Man, your sins are f. you." Lk 5.20
to say, 'Your sins are f. you,' 5.23
forgive, and you will be f.; 6.37
are f., for she loved much; 7.47
but he who is f. little, loves 7.47
And he said to her, "Your sins are f." 7.48
against the Son of man will be f.; 12.10
the Holy Spirit will not be f. 12.10
the sins of any, they are f.; Jn 20.23
intent of your heart may be f. you. Ac 8.22
"Blessed are those whose iniquities are f., Rom 4.07
What I have f., if I have f. anything, 2Co 2.10
having f. us all our trespasses, Col 2.13
as the Lord has f. you, so you also 3.13
has committed sins, he will be f. Jas 5.15
your sins are f. for his sake. 1Jn 2.12

FORGIVENESS
But there is f. with thee, that thou Ps 130.04
Lord our God belong mercy and f.; Dan 9.09
out for many for the f. of sins. Mt 26.28
of repentance for the f. of sins. Mk 1.04
the Holy Spirit never has f., 3.29
people in the f. of their sins, Lk 1.77
of repentance for the f. of sins. 3.03
repentance and f. of sins should 24.47
Christ for the f. of your sins; Ac 2.38
repentance to Israel and f. of sins. 5.31
in him receives f. of sins through 10.43
this man f. of sins is proclaimed 13.38
may receive f. of sins and a place 26.18
the f. of our trespasses, according Eph 1.07
we have redemption, the f. of sins. Col 1.14
of blood there is no f. of sins. Heb 9.22
Where there is f. of these, there is 10.18

FORGIVES
who f. all your iniquity, who heals Ps 103.03
He who f. an offense seeks love, but Pro 17.09
"Who is this, who even f. sins?" Lk 7.49

FORGIVING
f. iniquity and transgression and Ex 34.07
f. iniquity and transgression, but Num 14.18
art good and f., abounding in Ps 86.05
thou wast a f. God to them, but an 99.08
f. one another, as God in Christ Eph 4.32
against another, f. each other; Col 3.13

FORGOT
not remember Joseph, but f. him. Gen 40.23
and you f. the God who gave you Deu 32.18
But they f. the LORD their God; 1Sa 12.09
They f. what he had done, and the Ps 78.11
But they soon f. his works; they did not 106.13
They f. God, their Savior, who had 106.21
their fathers f. my name for Baal? Jer 23.27
her lovers, and f. me, says the LORD. Hos 2.13
was lifted up; therefore they f. me. 13.06

FORGOTTEN
plenty will be f. in the land of Gen 41.30
and have f. a sheaf in the field, Deu 24.19
commandments. neither have I f. them; 26.13
the guests in my house have f. me; Job 19.15
they are f. by travelers, they hang 28.04
For the needy shall not always be f., Ps 9.18
"God has f., he has hidden his face, 10.11
"Why hast thou f. me? Why go I 42.09
us, though we have not f. thee, 44.17
If we had f. the name of our God, or 44.20
Has God f. to be gracious? Has he in 77.09
yet I have not f. thy statutes. 119.83
to come all will have been long f. Ecc 2.16
For you have f. the God of your Is 17.10
Tyre will be f. for seventy years, 23.15
go about the city, O f. harlot! 23.16
O Israel, you will not be f. by me. 44.21
has forsaken me, my Lord has f. me. 49.14
and have f. the LORD, your Maker, who 51.13
troubles are f. and are hid from 65.16
my people have f. me days without Jer 2.32
they have f. the LORD their God. 3.21
you have f. me and trusted in lies. 13.25
But my people have f. me, 18.15
eternal dishonor will never be f. 20.11
shame, which shall not be f. 23.40
All your lovers have f. you; 30.14
Have you f. the wickedness of your 44.09
covenant which will never be f.' 50.05
have gone, they have f. their fold. 50.06
I have f. what happiness is; Lam 3.17
and you have f. me, says the Lord Eze 22.12
you have f. me and cast me behind 23.35
since you have f. the law of your Hos 4.06
For Israel has f. his Maker, and 8.14
they had f. to bring any bread. Mt 16.05
Now they had f. to bring bread; Mk 8.14
not one of them is f. before God. Lk 12.06
And have you f. the exhortation Heb 12.05
shortsighted and has f. that he was 2Pe 1.09

FORK
a three-ponged f. in his hand, 1Sa 2.13
all that the f. brought up the 2.14
been winnowed with shovel and f. Is 30.24
a winnowing f. in the gates of the Jer 15.07
His winnowing f. is in his hand, and Mt 3.12
His winnowing f. is in his hand, to Lk 3.17

FORKS
and basins and f. and fire pans; Ex 27.03
the f., and the fire pans: all its 38.03
the f., the shovels, and the basins, Num 4.14
and pure gold for the f., the basins, 1Ch 28.17
the f., and all the equipment for 2Ch 4.16

FORLORN
she who has many children is f. 1Sa 2.05
evil for good; my soul is f. Ps 35.12

FORM
the earth was without f. and void, Gen 1.02
they shall f. the two corners. Ex 26.24
and he beholds the f. of the LORD. Num 26.24
the sound of words, but saw no f.; Deu 4.12
you saw no f. on the day that the 4.15

FORM (cont.)
in the f. of any figure, the likeness Deu 4.16
image in the f. of anything which 4.23
graven image in the f. of anything, 4.25
carved in the f. of gourds and 1Ki 6.18
the same measure and the same f. 6.25
olivewood, in the f. of a square, 6.33
the same measure and the same f. 7.37
A f. was before my eyes; there was silence, Job 4.16
be satisfied with beholding thy f. Ps 17.15
and their f. shall waste away; 49.14
which thou didst f. to sport in it. 104.26
For thou didst f. my inward parts, 139.13
I f. light and create darkness, I Is 45.07
and his f. beyond that of the sons 52.14
he had no f. or comeliness that we 53.02
beauty of their f. was like Lam 4.07
appearance: they had the f. of men, Eze 1.05
likeness as it were of a human f. 1.26
a f. that had the appearance of a 8.02
He put forth the f. of a hand, and took 8.03
sapphire, in f. resembling a throne. 10.01
to have the f. of a human hand 10.08
its entrances, and its whole f.; 43.11
descended upon him in bodily f., Lk 3.22
his f. you have never seen; Jn 5.37
For the f. of this world is passing 1Co 7.31
who, though he was in the f. of God, Php 2.06
taking the f. of a servant, being 2.07
found in human f. he humbled 2.08
abstain from every f. of evil. 1Th 5.22
holding the f. of religion but 2Ti 3.05
of the true f. of these realities, Heb 10.01

FORMED
then the LORD God f. man of dust Gen 2.07
he put the man whom he had f. 2.08
the LORD God f. every beast of the 2.19
on the boundary f. by the Arnon, Num 22.36
tribe of Simeon f. part of the Jos 19.09
and again f. the battle line in the Ju 20.22
where they had f. it on the first 20.22
and the doorposts f. a pentagon. 1Ki 6.31
"The Chaldeans f. three companies, Job 1.17
I too was f. from a piece of clay. 33.06
ever thou hadst f. the earth and Ps 90.02
He who f. the eye, does he not see? 94.09
for his hands f. the dry land. 95.05
them, the days that were f. for me, 139.16
plans f. of old, faithful and sure. Is 25.01
he that f. them will show them no 27.11
or the thing f. say of him who f. it, 29.16
he who f. you., O Israel: "Fear not, 43.01
for my glory, whom I f. and made," 43.07
Before me no god was f., nor shall 43.10
the people whom I f. for myself 43.21
who f. you from the womb and will 44.02
I f. you, you are my servant; 44.21
who f. you from the womb: "I am the 44.24
who f. the earth and made it (he 45.18
a chaos, he f. it to be inhabited!): 45.18
who f. me from the womb to be his 49.05
"Before I f. you in the womb I knew Jer 1.05
he is the one who f. all things, 10.16
the LORD who f. it to establish it— 33.02
which he has f. against the inhabitants 49.20
and f. a purpose against you. 49.30
which he has f. against the land 50.45
he is the one who f. all things, 51.19
your breasts were f., and your hair Eze 16.07
the earth and f. the spirit of man Zec 12.01
travail until Christ be f. in you! Gal 4.19
For Adam was f. first, then Eve; 1Ti 2.13
and an earth f. out of water and by 2Pe 3.05

FORMER
besides the f. famine that was in Gen 26.01
but the f. time shall be void, Num 6.12
against the f. king of Moab and 21.26
then her f. husband, who sent her Deu 24.04
the custom in f. times in Israel Ru 4.07
consumed the two f. captains of 2Ki 1.14
they do according to the f. manner. 17.34
did according to their f. manner. 17.40
for the f. inhabitants there 1Ch 4.40
The f. governors who were before me Neh 5.15
There is no remembrance of f. things, Ecc 1.11
"Why were the f. days better than 7.10
In the f. time he brought into Is 9.01
Tell us the f. things, what they are, 41.22
Behold, the f. things have come to 42.09
this, and show us the f. things? 43.09
"Remember not the f. things, 43.18
remember the f. things of old; 46.09
"The f. things I declared of old, 48.03
shall raise up the f. devastations; 61.04
bosom payment for their f. doings. 65.07
because the f. troubles are forgotten 65.16
and the f. things shall not be 65.17
the f. kings who were before you, so Jer 34.05
on it all the f. words that were 36.28
shall return to their f. estate, Eze 16.55
shall return to your f. estate. 16.55
be inhabited as in your f. times, 36.11
whom I spoke in f. days by my 38.17
be different from the f. ones, Dan 7.24
a multitude, greater than the f.; 11.13
the f. dominion shall come, the Mic 4.08
saw this house in its f. glory? Hag 2.03
house shall be greater than the f., 2.09
to whom the f. prophets cried out, Zec 1.04
LORD proclaimed by the f. prophets?" 7.07
his Spirit through the f. prophets. 7.12
of this people as in the f. days, 8.11
to the place of the f. gate, 14.10
the days of old and as in f. years. Mal 3.04
forbearance he had passed over f. sins; Rom 3.25
was written in f. days was written 15.04
heard of my f. life in Judaism, how Gal 1.13
belongs to your f. manner of life Eph 4.22
the f. proclaim Christ out of Php 1.17
a f. commandment is set aside Heb 7.18
The f. priests were many in number, 7.23
But recall the f. days when, after 10.32
the passions of your f. ignorance, 1Pe 1.14
for the f. things have passed away." Rev 21.04

FORMERLY
Pharaoh's cup in his hand as f., Gen 40.13
(The Emim f. lived there, a people Deu 2.10
The Horites also lived in Seir f., 2.12
Rephaim f. lived there, but the 2.20
for Hazor f. was the head of all Jos 11.10
name of Hebron f. was Kiriatharba); 14.15
name of Debir f. was Kiriathsepher 15.15
name of Hebron f. was Kiriatharba); Ju 1.10
name of Debir was f. Kiriathsepher. 1.11
the name of the city was f. Luz. 1.23
(F. in Israel, when a man went to 1Sa 9.09
a prophet was f. called a seer.) 9.09
shall afflict them no more, as f., 2Sa 7.10
Israel dwelt in their homes as f. 2Ki 13.05
shall waste them no more, as f., 1Ch 17.09
the man who had f. been blind. Jn 9.13
F., when you did not know God, you Gal 4.08
though I f. blasphemed and persecuted 1Ti 1.13
(F. he was useless to you, but now Phm 1.11
and those who f. received the good Heb 4.06
Those who f. became priests took 7.21
who f. did not obey., when God's 1Pe 3.20

FORMING
purposes which they are already f., Deu 31.21
with the sea f. its boundary; Jos 17.10
he was f. locusts in the beginning Amo 7.01

FORMS

of Judah. This f. the western side. Jos 18.14
The Jordan f. its boundary on the 18.20
For lo, he who f. the mountains, and Amo 4.13

FORNICATION

f., theft, false witness, slander. Mt 15.19
f.. theft, murder, adultery, Mk 7.21
to him, "We were not born of f.; Jn 8.41
of the earth have committed f., Rev 17.02
wine of whose f. the dwellers on 17.02
and the impurities of her f.; 17.04
earth have committed f. with her, 18.03
who committed f. and were wanton 18.09
corrupted the earth with her f., 19.02

FORNICATORS

f., sorcerers, idolaters., and all Rev 21.08
sorcerers and f. and murders and 22.15

FORSAKE

that you do not f. the Levite as Deu 12.19
And you shall not f. the Levite who 14.27
he will not fail you or f. you." 31.06
he will not fail you or f. you; 31.08
and they will f. me and break my 31.16
and I will f. them and hide my face 31.17
I will not fail you or f. you. Jos 1.05
from us that we should f. the LORD, 24.16
If you f. the LORD and serve 24.20
and will not f. my people Israel." 1Ki 6.13
may he not leave us or f. us; 8.57
but if you f. him, he will cast 1Ch 28.09
He will not fail you or f. you, 28.20
turn aside and f. my statutes and 2Ch 7.19
if you f. him, he will f. you. 15.02
wrath is against all that f. him." Ez 8.22
love, and didst not f. them. Neh 9.17
didst not f. them in the wilderness; 9.19
not make an end of them or f. them; 9.31
f. me not, O God of my salvation! Ps 27.09
Refrain from anger, and f. wrath! 37.08
justice; he will not f. his saints. 37.28
Do not f. me, O LORD! O my God, 38.21
f. me not when my strength is spent. 71.09
do not f. me, till I proclaim thy 71.18
If his children f. my law and do 89.30
For the LORD will not f. his people; 94.14
thy statutes; O f. me not utterly! 119.08
of the wicked, who f. thy law. 119.53
Do not f. the work of thy hands. 138.08
who f. the paths of uprightness to Pro 2.13
loyalty and faithfulness f. you; 3.03
precepts: do not f. my teaching. 4.02
Do not f. her, and she will keep you 4.06
and f. not your mother's teaching. 6.20
your father's friend, do not f.; 27.10
Those who f. the law praise the 28.04
and those who f. the LORD shall be Is 1.28
the God of Israel will not f. them. 41.17
I will do, and I will not f. them. 42.16
let the wicked f. his way, and the 55.07
But you who f. the LORD, who forget 65.11
for you to f. the LORD your God; Jer 2.19
all who f. thee shall be put to 17.13
F. her, and let us go each to his 51.09
ever, why dost thou so long f. us? Lam 5.20
nor did they f. the idols of Egypt. Eze 20.08
to those who f. the holy covenant. Dan 11.30
to vain idols f. their true Jon 2.08
are among the Gentiles to f. Moses, Ac 21.21
"I will never fail you nor f. you." Heb 13.05

FORSAKEN

who has not f. his steadfast love Gen 24.27
doings, because you have f. me. Deu 28.20
you have not f. your brethren these Jos 22.03
because we have f. our God and Ju 10.10
Yet you have f. me and served other 10.13
kindness has not f. the living or Ru 2.20
because we have f. the LORD, 1Sa 12.10
because he has f. me, and worshiped 1Ki 11.33
you have f. the commandments of 18.18
of Israel have f. thy covenant, 19.10
of Israel have f. thy covenant, 19.14
Because they have f. me and have 2Ki 22.17
is our God, and we have not f. him. 2Ch 13.10
LORD our God, but you have f. him. 13.11
rule, because he had f. the LORD, 21.10
have f. the LORD he has f. you.'" 24.20
army, because they had f. the LORD, 24.24
because they had f. the LORD, 28.06
they have f. him, and have turned 29.06
Because they have f. me and have 34.25
our God has not f. us in our Ez 9.09
For we have f. thy commandments, 9.10
said, "Why is the house of God f.?" Neh 13.11
shall the earth be f. for you, Job 18.04
hast not f. those who seek thee. Ps 9.10
My God, my God, why hast thou f. me? 22.01
my father and my mother have f. me, 27.10
the righteous f. for his children 37.25
and say, "God has f. him; pursue and 71.11
like one f. among the dead, like the 88.05
but I have not f. thy precepts. 119.87
They have f. the LORD, they have Is 1.04
and the f. places are many in the 6.12
that have been f. so I have gathered 10.14
a habitation deserted and f., like the 27.10
For the palace will be f., the populous 32.14
"The LORD has f. me, my Lord has 49.14
you like a wife f. and grieved in 54.06
Whereas you have been f. and hated, 60.15
You shall no more be termed F., 62.04
called Sought out, a city not f. 62.12
they have f. me, the fountain of Jer 2.13
all the cities are f., and no man 4.29
Your children have f. me, and have 5.07
'As you have f. me and served 5.19
rejected and f. the generation of 7.29
they have f. my law which I set 9.13
"I have f. my house, I have abandoned 12.07
'Because your fathers have f. me, 16.11
and have f. me and have not kept my 16.11
for they have f. the LORD, the 17.13
Because the people have f. me, 19.04
How the famous city is f., the joyful 49.25
have not been f. by their God, 51.05
see us, the LORD has f. the land.'" Eze 8.12
'The LORD has f. the land, and the 9.09
they have f. the LORD to cherish Hos 4.10
f. on her land, with none to raise Amo 5.02
Behold, your house is f. and desolate. Mt 23.38
God, my God, why hast thou f. me?" 27.46
God, my God, why hast thou f. me?" Mk 15.34
Behold, your house is f. And I tell Lk 13.35
persecuted, but not f.; struck down, 2Co 4.09

FORSAKES

from a friend f. the fear of the Job 6.14
who f. the companion of her youth Pro 2.17
discipline for him who f. the way; 15.10
confesses and f. them will obtain 28.13
in the field f. her newborn calf Jer 14.05

FORSAKING

f. me and serving other gods, so 1Sa 8.08
and f. the counsel which the old 1Ki 12.13
and f. the counsel of the old men, 2Ch 10.13
for all their wickedness in f. me; Jer 1.16
yourself by f. the LORD your God, 2.17
great harlotry by f. the LORD. Hos 1.02
played the harlot, f. your God. 9.01
F. the right way they have gone 2Pe 2.15

FORSOOK

is because they f. the covenant of Deu 29.25
then he f. God who made him, and 32.15
and they f. the LORD, the God of Ju 2.12
They f. the LORD, and served the 2.13
and they f. the Lord, and did not 10.06
they f. their cities and fled; 1Sa 31.07
'Because they f. the LORD their God 1Ki 9.09
But he f. the counsel which the old 12.08
in the twilight and f. their tents, 2Ki 7.07
And they f. all the commandments of 17.16
he f. the LORD, the God of his 21.22
they f. their cities and fled; 1Ch 10.07
'Because they f. the LORD the God 2Ch 7.22
But he f. the counsel which the old 10.08
he f. the law of the LORD, and all 12.01
And they f. the house of the LORD, 24.18
He f. his dwelling at Shiloh, the Ps 78.60
For a brief moment I f. you, but with Is 54.07
"Because they f. the covenant of Jer 22.09
all the disciples f. him and fled. Mt 26.56
And they all f. him, and fled. Mk 14.50

FORTH

"Let the earth put f. vegetation, Gen 1.11
The earth brought f. vegetation, 1.12
waters bring f. swarms of living 1.20
the earth bring f. living creatures 1.24
pain you shall bring f. children, 3.16
thistles it shall bring f. to you; 3.18
lest he put f. his hand and take 3.22
God sent him f. from the garden of 3.23
fountains of the great deep burst f., 7.11
and sent f. a raven; and it went 8.07
Then he sent f. a dove from him, to 8.08
So he put f. his hand and took her 8.09
again he sent f. the dove out of 8.10
seven days, and sent f. the dove; 8.12
"Go f. from the ark, you and your 8.16
Bring f. with you every living 8.17
So Noah went f., and his sons and 8.18
went f. by families out of the ark. 8.19
bring f. abundantly on the earth 9.07
Noah who went f. from the ark were 9.18
and they went f. together from Ur 11.31
and they set f. to go to the land 12.05
he led f. his trained men, born in 14.14
and kings shall come f. from you. 17.06
But the men put f. their hands and 19.10
brought him f. and set him outside 19.16
And when they had brought them f., 19.17
Then Abraham put f. his hand, 22.10
servant brought f. jewelry of 24.53
The first came f. red, all his body 25.25
Afterward his brother came f., 25.26
so the flocks brought f. striped, 30.39
Now arise, go f. from this land, and 31.13
as it budded, its blossoms shot f., 40.10
the earth brought f. abundantly. 41.47
that you may bring f. my people, Ex 3.10
have brought f. the people out of 3.12
them, as they came f. from Pharaoh; 5.20
upon Egypt and bring f. my hosts, 7.04
when I stretch f. my hand upon 7.05
secret arts to bring f. gnats, 8.18
could have put f. my hand and struck 9.15
"Stretch f. your hand toward heaven, 9.22
Then Moses stretched f. his rod 9.23
So Moses stretched f. his rod over 10.13
I will go f. in the midst of Egypt 11.04
go f. from among my people, both you 12.31
shall not carry f. any of the 12.46
This day you are to go f., in the month 13.04
Israel as they went f. defiantly. 14.08
So Moses stretched f. his hand over 14.27
thou sendest f. thy fury, it consumes 15.07
Israel had gone f. out of the land 19.01
brought them f. out of the land of 29.46
hast brought f. out of the land of 32.11
evil intent did he bring them f., 32.12
he shall carry f. outside the camp Lev 4.12
And he shall carry f. the bull 4.21
and carry f. the ashes outside the 6.11
And fire came f. from before the 9.24
And fire came f. from the presence 10.02
carry them f. out of the city to 14.45
and come f., and offer his burnt 16.24
be carried f. outside the camp; 16.27
shall not stand f. against the 19.16
it will bring f. fruit for three 25.21
who brought you f. out of the land 25.38
whom I brought f. out of the land 25.42
whom I brought f. out of the land 25.55
who brought you f. out of the land 26.13
whom I brought f. out of the land 26.45
who are able to go f. to war, Num 1.03
all who were able to go f. to war: 1.20
all who were able to go f. to war: 1.22
all who were able to go f. to war: 1.24
every man able to go f. to war: 1.26
every man able to go f. to war: 1.28
every man able to go f. to war: 1.30
every man able to go f. to war: 1.32
every man able to go f. to war: 1.34
every man able to go f. to war: 1.36
every man able to go f. to war: 1.38
every man able to go f. to war: 1.40
every man able to go f. to war: 1.42
man able to go f. to war in Israel— 1.45
Did I bring them f., that thou shouldst 11.12
"Why did we come f. out of Egypt?"'" 11.20
And there went f. a wind from the 11.31
And fire came f. from the LORD, and 16.35
wrath has gone f. from the LORD, 16.46
Levi had sprouted and put f. buds, 17.08
shall we bring f. water for you out 20.10
and water came f. abundantly, and the 20.11
and brought us f. out of Egypt; 20.16
For fire went f. from Heshbon, flame 21.28
I have come f. to withstand you, 22.32
a star shall come f. out of Jacob, 24.17
who are able to go f. to war. 26.02
who came f. out of the land of 26.04
went f. to meet them outside the 31.13
when they went f. out of the land 33.01
has brought us f. out of the land Deu 1.27
and brought you f. out of the iron 4.20
flowing f. in valleys and hills, 8.07
which comes f. from the field year 14.22
you shall bring f. all the tithe 14.28
then you shall bring f. to your 17.05
"When you go f. to war against your 20.01
and your judges shall come f., 21.02
"When you go f. to war against your 21.10
when you came f. out of Egypt, and 23.04
"When you go f. against your 23.09
way as you came f. out of Egypt. 24.09
he shone f. from Mount Paran, he 33.02
whelp, the leaps f. from Bashan." 33.22
"Bring f. the men that have come to Jos 2.03
of war that came f. out of Egypt, 5.06
valor, and sent them f. by night. 8.03
So Joshua sent them f.; and they went 8.09
And the others came f. from the 8.22
the day we set f. to come to you, 9.12
"LORD, when thou didst go f. from Seir, Ju 5.04
valley they rushed f. at his heels. 5.15
The trees once went f. to anoint a 9.08
then whoever comes f. from the 11.31
what has gone f. from your mouth, 11.36
set f. from Zorah and Eshtaol, 18.11
of the LORD had gone f. against me." Ru 1.13
So she set f. and went and gleaned 2.03
And the LORD came and stood f., 1Sa 3.10
who brought f. your fathers out of 12.08

FORTH (cont.)

so he put f. the tip of the staff 1Sa 14.27
went back and f. from Saul to feed 17.15
host was going f. to the battle 17.20
Saul saw David go f. against the 17.55
would not put f. their hand to 22.17
to put f. my hand against him, 24.06
'I will not put f. my hand against 24.10
of the wicked comes f. wickedness'; 24.13
for who can put f. his hand against 26.09
I should put f. my hand against 26.11
I would not put f. my hand against 26.23
afraid to put f. your hand to 2Sa 1.14
because he put f. his hand to the 6.07
the LORD had broken f. upon Uzzah; 6.08
who shall come f. from your body, 7.12
time when kings go f. to battle, 11.01
And he brought f. the spoil of the 12.30
And he brought f. the people who 12.31
king longed to go f. to Absalom; 13.39
So the king went f., and all his 15.16
And the king went f., and all the 15.17
And David sent f. the army, one 18.02
I would not put f. my hand against 18.12
glowing coals flamed f. from him. 22.09
before him coals of fire flamed f. 22.13
He brought me f. into a broad place 22.20
the sun shining f. upon a cloudless 23.04
angel stretched f. his hand toward 24.16
and Araunah went f., and did obeisance 24.20
him, "The king commands, 'Come f.'" 1Ki 2.30
and do not go f. from there to any 2.36
For on the day you go f., and cross 2.37
the day you go f. and go to any 2.42
and spread f. his hands toward 8.22
"Go f., and stand upon the mount 19.11
Then Benhadad came f. to him; 20.33
'I will go f., and will be a lying 22.22
you shall succeed; go f. and do so.' 22.22
she went f. to appeal to the king 2Ki 8.03
wherever he went f., he prospered. 18.07
is no strength to bring them f. 19.03
of Jerusalem shall go f. a remnant, 19.31
the angel of the LORD went f., 19.35
because he put f. his hand to the 1Ch 13.10
the LORD had broken f. upon Uzzah; 13.11
the LORD our God broke f. upon us, 15.13
time when kings go f. to battle, 20.01
And he brought f. the spoil of the 20.02
And he brought f. the people who 20.03
David and went f. from the threshing 21.21
of Israel, and spread f. his hands. 2Ch 6.12
and spread f. his hands toward 6.13
'I will go f., and will be a lying 18.21
you shall succeed; go f. and do so.' 18.21
that shall put f. a hand to alter Ez 6.12
and bring him f. out of Ur of the Neh 9.07
and bring f. water for them from 9.15
let a royal order go f. from him, Est 1.19
But put f. thy hand now, and touch Job 1.11
himself do not put f. your hand." 1.12
So Satan went f. from the presence 1.12
But put f. thy hand now, and touch 2.05
So Satan went f. from the presence 2.07
come f. from the womb and expire? 3.11
thou bring me f. from the womb? 10.18
He comes f. like a flower, and 14.02
bud and put f. branches like a 14.09
you brought f. before the hills? 15.07
has stretched f. his hand against 15.25
and bring f. evil and their heart 15.35
It is drawn f. and comes out of his 20.25
They send f. their little ones like 21.11
tried me, I shall come f. as gold. 23.10
desert they go f. to their toil, 24.05
whose spirit has come f. from you? 26.04
that is hid he brings f. to light. 28.11
they drive me f., they cast up 30.12
when it burst f. from the womb; 38.08
to make the ground put f. grass? 38.27
From whose womb did the ice come f., 38.29
Can you lead f. the Mazzaroth in 38.32
Can you send f. lightnings, that 38.35
when the mountain goats bring f.? 39.01
know the time when they bring f., 39.02
bring f. their offspring, and are 39.03
they go f., and do not return to 39.04
Pour f. the overflowings of your 40.11
His sneezings flash f. light, 41.18
torches; sparks of fire leap f. 41.19
Out of his nostrils comes f. smoke, 41.20
a flame comes f. from his mouth. 41.21
with mischief, and brings f. lies. Ps 7.14
glowing coals flamed f. from him. 18.08
he flashed f. lightnings, and routed 18.14
He brought me f. into a broad place; 18.19
Day to day pours f. speech, and night 19.02
which comes f. like a bridegroom 19.05
the LORD flashes f. flames of fire. 29.07
he commanded, and it stood f. 33.09
he looks f. on all the inhabitants 33.14
He will bring f. your vindication 37.06
or spread f. our hands to a strange 44.20
majesty ride f. victoriously for 45.04
perfection of beauty, God shines f. 50.02
I was brought f. in iniquity, and in 51.05
my mouth shall show f. thy praise. 51.15
God will send f. his steadfast love 57.03
Thou dost not go f., O God, with 60.10
hast brought us f. to a spacious 66.12
thou didst go f. before thy people, 68.07
lo, he sends f. his voice, his mighty 68.33
may men blossom f. from the cities 72.16
the skies gave f. thunder; thy arrows 77.17
Then he led f. his people like 78.52
enthroned upon the cherubim, shine f. 80.01
the word that went f. from my lips. 89.34
Before the mountains were brought f., 90.02
They still bring f. fruit in old 92.14
thou God of vengeance, shine f.! 94.01
break f. into joyous song and sing 98.04
springs gush f. in the valleys; 104.10
he may bring f. food from the earth, 104.14
the beasts of the forest creep f. 104.20
Man goes f. to his work and to his 104.23
When thou sendest f. thy Spirit, 104.30
Then he led f. Israel with silver 105.37
the rock, and water gushed f.; 105.41
So he led f. his people with joy, 105.43
LORD, or show f. all his praise? 106.02
he sent f. his word, and healed them, 107.20
Thou dost not go f., O God, with 108.11
is tried, let him come f. guilty; 109.07
The LORD sends f. from Zion your 110.02
from this time f. and for evermore! 113.02
When Israel went f. from Egypt, 114.01
from this time f. and for evermore. 115.18
My lips will pour f. praise that 119.171
from this time f. and for evermore. 121.08
from this time f. and for evermore. 125.02
righteous put f. their hands to do 125.03
He that goes f. weeping, bearing the 126.06
from this time f. and for evermore. 131.03
rain and brings f. the wind from 135.07
Flash f. the lightning and scatter 144.06
Stretch f. thy hand from on high, 144.07
our sheep bring f. thousands and 144.13
They shall pour f. the fame of thy 145.07
He sends f. his command to the 147.15
He casts f. his ice like morsels; 147.17
He sends f. his word, and melts them; 147.18
by his knowledge the deeps broke f., Pro 3.20
were no depths I was brought f., 8.24
before the hills, I was brought f.; 8.25

FORTH (cont.)

of the righteous brings f. wisdom, Pro 10.31
The north wind brings f. rain; 25.23
not know what a day may bring f. 27.01
God shall come f. from them all. Ecc 7.18
edge, he must put f. more strength; 10.10
my nard gave f. its fragrance. Sol 1.12
The fig tree puts f. its figs, 2.13
in blossom; they give f. fragrance. 2.13
Go f., O daughters of Zion, and 3.11
this that looks f. like the dawn, 6.10
let us go f. into the fields, and 7.11
The mandrakes give f. fragrance, 7.13
When you spread f. your hands, Is 1.15
out of Zion shall go f. the law, 2.03
men will cast f. their idols of 2.20
"Go f. to meet Ahaz, you and Shearjashub 7.03
from this time f. and for evermore. 9.07
There shall come f. a shoot from 11.01
They shall put f. their hand against 11.14
and quiet; they break f. into singing. 14.07
serpent's root will come f. an adder, 14.29
we have as it were brought f. wind. 26.18
Lord is coming f. out of his place 26.21
shall blossom and put f. shoots, 27.06
is called f. against him is not 31.04
conceive chaff, you bring f. stubble; 33.11
shall break f. in the wilderness, 35.06
is no strength to bring them f. 37.03
of Jerusalem shall go f. a remnant, 37.32
And the angel of the Lord went f., 37.36
Set f. your case, says the Lord; 41.21
he will bring f. justice to the 42.01
will faithfully bring f. justice. 42.03
who spread f. the earth and what 42.05
they spring f. I tell you of them." 42.09
The Lord goes f. like a mighty man, 42.13
Bring f. the people who are blind, 43.08
who brings f. chariot and horse, 43.17
now it springs f., do you not 43.19
set f. your case, that you may be 43.26
declare and set it f. before me. 44.07
all assemble, let them stand f., 44.11
break f. into singing, O mountains, O 44.23
open, that salvation may sprout f., 45.08
mouth has gone f. in righteousness 45.23
let them stand f. and save you, 47.13
and who came f. from the loins of 48.01
they went f. from my mouth and I 48.03
From this time f. I make you hear 48.06
to them, they stand f. together. 48.13
Go f. from Babylon, flee from 48.20
send it f. to the end of the earth; 48.20
'Come f.,' to those who are in 49.09
break f., O mountains, into singing! 49.13
who laid you waste go f. from you. 49.17
for a law will go f. from me, 51.04
speedily, my salvation has gone f., 51.05
Break f. together into singing, you 52.09
break f. into singing and cry aloud, 54.01
making it bring f. and sprout, 55.10
word be that goes f. from my mouth; 55.11
out in joy, and be led f. in peace; 55.12
you shall break f. into singing, 55.12
your light break f. like the dawn, 58.08
mischief and bring f. iniquity. 59.04
from this time f. and for evermore." 59.21
For as the earth brings f. its shoots, 61.11
to spring f. before all the nations. 61.11
vindication goes f. as brightness, 62.01
I will bring f. descendants from 65.09
nation be brought f. in one moment? 66.08
in labor she brought f. her sons. 66.08
birth and not cause to bring f.? 66.09
cause to bring f., shut the womb? 66.09
"And they shall go f. and look on 66.24
Then the Lord put f. his hand and Jer 1.09
evil shall break f. upon all the 1.14
lest my wrath go f. like fire, 4.04
he has gone f. from his place to 4.07
of one bringing f. her first child, 4.31
Go not f. into the field, nor walk 6.25
and he brings f. the wind from his 10.13
they grow and bring f. fruit; 12.02
Why did I come f. from the womb to 20.18
lest my wrath go f. like fire, 21.12
and cast f. beyond the gates of 22.19
has gone f. into all the land." 23.15
Wrath has gone f., a whirling 23.19
evil is going f. from nation to 25.32
shall come f. from their midst; 30.21
Wrath has gone f., a whirling 30.23
and shall go f. in the dance of the 31.04
Branch to spring f. for David; 33.15
were poured f. and kindled in the 44.06
Let the warriors go f.: men of 46.09
and Chemosh shall go f. into exile, 48.07
a fire has gone f. from Heshbon, 48.45
has brought f. our vindication; 51.10
and he brings f. the wind from his 51.16
and fire flashing f. continually, Eze 1.04
out of the fire went f. lightning. 1.13
go f. into the plain, and there I 3.22
I arose and went f. into the plain; 3.23
fire will come f. into all the house 5.04
He put f. the form of a hand, and 8.03
courts with the slain. Go f." 9.07
So they went f., and smote in the 9.07
stretched f. his hand from between 10.07
the Lord went f. from the threshold 10.18
earth in my sight as they went f., 10.19
be brought f. out of the midst of 11.07
will bring you f. out of the midst 11.09
you shall go f. yourself at evening 12.04
I went f. in the dark, carrying my 12.07
in the dark, and shall go f.; 12.12
daughters, when they come f. to you, 14.22
renown went f. among the nations 16.14
brought f. branches and put f. foliage. 17.06
and shot f. its branches toward him 17.07
that it might bring f. branches, 17.08
it may bring f. boughs and bear 17.23
and will draw f. my sword out of 21.03
them shall come f. from the same 21.19
so I brought f. fire from the midst 28.18
And I will cast you f. into the 29.05
horn to spring f. to the house of 29.21
shall go f. from me to terrify the 30.09
sending f. its streams to all the 31.04
the field brought f. their young; 31.06
you burst f. in your rivers, trouble 32.02
is that comes f. from the Lord. 33.30
shall shoot f. your branches, and 36.08
your jaws, and I will bring you f., 38.04
Israel will go f. and makes fires 39.09
Then he brought me f. to the outer 46.21
So the decree went f. that the wise Dan 2.13
High God, come f., and come here!" 3.26
issued and came f. from before him. 7.10
one of them came f. a little horn, 8.09
your supplications a word went f., 9.23
from the going f. of the word to 9.25
and he shall go f. with great fury 11.44
his going f. is sure as the dawn; Hos 6.03
my judgment goes f. as the light. 6.05
must lead f. his sons to slaughter. 9.13
Even though they bring f., I will slay 9.16
shall come f. from the house of Joe 3.18
you shall be cast f. into Harmon," Amo 4.03
city that went f. a thousand shall 5.03
that which went f. a hundred shall 5.03
destruction flash f. against the 5.09
Lord is coming f. out of his place, Mic 1.03
inhabitants of Zaanan do not come f.; 1.11

FORTH (cont.)
out of Zion shall go f. the law, Mic 4.02
from this time f. and for evermore. 4.07
you shall go f. from the city and 4.10
you shall come f. for me one who 5.02
who is in travail has brought f.; 5.03
He will bring me f. to the light; 7.09
slacked and justice never goes f. Hab 1.04
so justice goes f. perverted. 1.04
and look f. to see what he will say 2.01
the deep gave f. its voice, it 3.10
Thou wentest f. for the salvation 3.13
morning he shows f. his justice, Zep 3.05
upon what the ground brings f., Hag 1.11
I will send it f., says the LORD of Zec 5.04
and see what this is that goes f. 5.05
"This is the ephah that goes f." 5.06
"These are going f. to the four 6.05
and his arrow go f. like lightning; 9.14
and march f. in the whirlwinds of 9.14
LORD will go f. and fight against 14.03
You shall go f. leaping like calves Mal 4.02
his good treasure brings f. good, Mt 12.35
his evil treasure brings f. evil. 12.35
on good soil and brought f. grain, 13.08
tender and puts f. its leaves, you 24.32
good soil and brought f. grain, Mk 4.08
and puts f. large branches, so that 4.32
that power had gone f. from him, 5.30
tender and puts f. its leaves, 13.28
for power came f. from him and Lk 6.19
and bring f. fruit with patience. 8.15
that power has gone f. from me." 8.46
a rich man brought f. plentifully; 12.16
and come f., those who have done Jn 5.29
I proceeded and came f. from God; 8.42
he is cast f. as a branch and 15.06
he went f. with his disciples 18.01
he sent f. our fathers the first Ac 7.12
God sent f. his Son, born of woman, Gal 4.04
break f. and shout, thou who are not 4.27
purpose which he set f. in Christ Eph 1.09
Lord sounded f. from you in 1Th 1.08
in God has gone f. everywhere, 1.08
ministering spirits sent f. to serve, Heb 1.14
and brings f. vegetation useful to 6.07
Therefore let us go f. to him outside 13.13
it is full-grown brings f. death. Jas 1.15
he brought us f. by the word of 1.18
Does a spring pour f. from the same 3.11
and the earth brought f. its fruit. 5.18
her child when she brought it f.; Rev 12.04
she brought f. a male child, one who 12.05

FORTIETH
in the f. year after the people of Num 33.38
And in the f. year, on the first day Deu 1.03
(In the f. year of David's reign 1Ch 26.31

FORTIFICATIONS
And the high f. of his walls he will Is 25.12

FORTIFIED
the cities are f. and very large; Num 13.28
live in the f. cities because of 32.17
f. cities, and folds for sheep. 32.36
are great and f. up to heaven; Deu 1.28
were cities f. with high walls, 3.05
cities great and f. up to heaven, 9.01
until your high and f. walls, 28.52
had entered into the f. cities, Jos 10.20
with great f. cities: it may be that 14.12
reaching to the f. city of Tyre; 19.29
The f. cities are Ziddim, Zer, 19.35
both f. cities and unwalled villages. 1Sa 6.18
him, lest he get himself f. cities, 2Sa 20.06
and he f. the hill, and called the 1Ki 16.24
and you shall conquer every f. city, 2Ki 3.19
horses, f. cities also, and weapons, 10.02
towns, from watch tower to f. city; 17.09
territory, from watchtower to f. city. 18.08
against all the f. cities of Judah 18.13
you should turn f. cities into 19.25
f. cities with walls, gates, and bars, 2Ch 8.05
f. cities which are in Judah and in 11.10
and Benjamin, in all the f. cities; 11.23
And he took the f. cities of Judah 12.04
He built f. cities in Judah, for the 14.06
in all the f. cities of Judah, and 17.02
placed in the f. cities throughout 17.19
land in all the f. cities of Judah, 19.05
together with f. cities in Judah; 21.03
Gate and at the Angle, and f. them. 26.09
and encamped against the f. cities, 32.01
army in all the f. cities in Judah. 33.14
And they captured f. cities and a Neh 9.25
Who will bring me to the f. city? Ps 60.09
Who will bring me to the f. city? 108.10
tower, and against every f. wall; Is 2.15
city a heap, the f. city a ruin; 25.02
For the f. city is solitary, a 27.10
against all the f. cities of Judah 36.01
you should make f. cities crash 37.26
I make you this day a f. city, Jer 1.18
and let us go into the f. cities! 4.05
your f. cities in which you trust 5.17
let us go into the f. cities and 8.14
to this people a f. wall of bronze; 15.20
were the only f. cities of Judah 34.07
to Judah and to Jerusalem the f. Eze 21.20
cities are now inhabited and f. 36.35
and Judah has multiplied f. cities; Hos 8.14
cry against the f. cities and Zep 1.16

FORTIFY
down the houses to f. the wall. Is 22.10
she should f. her strong height, Jer 51.53

FORTRESS
rock, and my f., and my deliverer, 2Sa 22.02
and came to the f. of Tyre and to 24.07
the gates of the f. of the temple, Neh 2.08
and my f., and my deliverer, my God, Ps 18.02
for me, a strong f. to save me! 31.02
Yea, thou art my rock and my f.; 31.03
to thee; for thou, O God, art my f. 59.09
been to me a f. and a refuge in 59.16
art my f., the God who shows me 59.17
is my rock and my salvation, my f.; 62.02
is my rock and my salvation my f.; 62.06
a strong f., to save me, for thou 71.03
me, for thou art my rock and my f. 71.03
to the LORD, "My refuge and my f.; 91.02
my rock and my f., my stronghold 144.02
The f. will disappear from Ephraim, Is 17.03
the f. is put to shame and broken Jer 48.01
and enter the f. of the king of Dan 11.07
carry the war as far as his f. 11.10
and profane the temple and f., 11.31
that destruction comes upon the f. Amo 5.09
They laught at every f., for they heap Hab 1.10

FORTRESSES
you will set on fire their f., 2Ki 8.12
He made the f. strong, and put 2Ch 11.11
built in Judah f. and store-cities, 17.12
of defense will be the f. of rocks; Is 33.16
nettles and thistles in its f. 34.13
back toward the f. of his own land; Dan 11.19
the god of f. instead of these; 11.38
the strongest f. by the help of a 11.39
and all your f. shall be destroyed, Hos 10.14
gates, and devour them in their f. 11.06
All your f. are like fig trees with Nah 3.12

FORTS
and f. and towers on the wooded 2Ch 27.04
for the siege, strengthen your f.; Nah 3.14

FORTUNATE
dead more f. than the living who Ecc 4.02
"I think myself f. that it is before Ac 26.02

FORTUNATUS
of Stephanas and F. and Achaicus, 1Co 16.17

FORTUNE
And Leah said, "Good f.!" so she Gen 30.11
set a table for F. and fill cups Is 65.11

FORTUNES
LORD your God will restore your f., Deu 30.03
And the LORD restored the f. of Job, Job 42.10
LORD restores the f. of his people, Ps 14.07
God restores the f. of his people, 53.06
thou didst restore the f. of Jacob. 85.01
When the LORD restored the f. of Zion, 126.01
Restore our f., O LORD, like the 126.04
restore your f. and gather you from all Jer 29.14
I will restore the f. of my people, 30.03
restore the f. of the tents of Jacob, 30.18
cities, when I restore their f.: 31.23
restore their f., says the LORD. 32.44
restore the f. of Judah and the f. of 33.07
restore the f. of the land as at 33.11
For I will restore their f., and will 33.26
restore the f. of Moab in the 48.47
restore the f. of the Ammonites, 49.06
days I will restore the f. of Elam, 49.39
your iniquity to restore your f., Lam 2.14
their f., both the f. of Sodom and her Eze 16.53
and the f. of Samaria and her 16.53
your own f. in the midst of them, 16.53
and I will restore the f. of Egypt, 29.14
Now I will restore the f. of Jacob, 39.25
would restore the f. of my people, Hos 6.11
I restore the f. of Judah and Joe 3.01
restore the f. of my people Israel, Amo 9.14
of them and restore their f. Zep 2.07
I restore your f. before your eyes, 3.20

FORTY
Mahalalel eight hundred and f. years, Gen 5.13
upon the earth f. days and f. nights; 7.04
upon the earth f. days and f. nights. 7.12
The flood continued f. days upon 7.17
At the end of f. days Noah opened 8.06
"Suppose f. are found there." He 18.29
"For the sake of f. I will not do 18.29
and Isaac was f. years old when he 25.20
When Esau was f. years old, he took 26.34
colts, f. cows and ten bulls, twenty 32.15
f. days were required for it, for so 50.03
of Israel ate the manna f. years. Ex 16.35
the mountain f. days and f. nights. 24.18
and f. bases of silver you shall 26.19
and their f. bases of silver, two 26.21
with the LORD f. days and f. nights; 34.28
and he made f. bases of silver 36.24
and their f. bases of silver, two 36.26
of Ephraim was f. thousand five Num 1.33
numbered being f. thousand five 2.19
At the end of f. days they returned 13.25
shepherds in the wilderness f. years, 14.33
f. days, for every day a year, you 14.34
f. years, and you shall know my 14.34
number, f. thousand five hundred. 26.18
wander in the wilderness f. years, 32.13
these f. years the LORD your God Deu 2.07
led you these f. years in the 8.02
foot did not swell, these f. years. 8.04
on the mountain f. days and f. nights; 9.09
at the end of f. days and f. nights 9.11
as before, f. days and f. nights; 9.18
LORD for these f. days and f. nights, 9.25
time, f. days and f. nights, and the 10.10
F. stripes may be given him, but not 25.03
I have led you f. years in the 29.05
about f. thousand ready armed for Jos 4.13
Israel walked f. years in the 5.06
I was f. years old when Moses the 14.07
So the land had rest f. years. Ju 3.11
be seen among f. thousand in 5.08
And the land had rest for f. years. 5.31
land had rest f. years in the days 8.28
He had f. sons and thirty grandsons, 12.14
of the Philistines for f. years. 13.01
He had judged Israel f. years. 1Sa 4.18
For f. days the Philistine came 17.16
was f. years old when he began to 2Sa 2.10
to reign, and he reigned f. years. 5.04
and f. thousand horsemen, and 10.18
reigned over Israel was f. years; 1Ki 2.11
Solomon also had f. thousand stalls 4.26
inner sanctuary, was f. cubits long. 6.17
each laver held f. baths, each laver 7.38
over all Israel was f. years. 11.42
f. days and f. nights to Horeb 19.08
goods of Damascus, f. camel loads. 2Ki 8.09
and he reigned f. years in Jerusalem 12.01
Of Asher f. thousand seasoned troops 1Ch 12.36
and f. thousand foot soldiers, and 19.18
reigned over Israel was f. years; 29.27
Jerusalem over all Israel f. years. 2Ch 9.30
and he reigned f. years in Jerusalem; 24.01
and wine, besides f. shekels of silver. Neh 5.15
F. years didst thou sustain them in 9.21
Job lived a hundred and f. years, Job 42.16
For f. years I loathed that generation Ps 95.10
f. days I assign you, a day for each Eze 4.06
it shall be uninhabited f. years. 29.11
be a desolation f. years among cities 29.12
At the end of f. years I will gather 29.13
the length of the nave f. cubits, 41.02
f. cubits long and thirty broad; 46.22
and led you f. years in the wilderness, Amo 2.10
and offerings the f. years in the 5.25
"Yet f. days, and Nineveh shall be Jon 3.04
he fasted f. days and f. nights, Mt 4.02
And he was in the wilderness f. days, Mk 1.13
f. days in the wilderness, tempted Lk 4.02
appearing to them during f. days, Ac 1.03
performed was more than f. years old. 4.22
"When he was f. years old, it came 7.23
"Now when f. years had passed, an 7.30
and in the wilderness for f. years. 7.36
f. years in the wilderness, O house 7.42
And for about f. years he bore with 13.18
tribe of Benjamin, for f. years. 13.21
There were more than f. who made 23.13
for more than f. of their men lie 23.21
of the Jews the f. lashes less one 2Co 11.24
test and saw my works for f. years. Heb 3.09
with whom was he provoked f. years? 3.17

FORTY-EIGHT
you give to the Levites shall be f., Num 35.07
were in all f. cities with their Jos 21.41
sons of Binnui, six hundred and f. Neh 7.15
sons of Asaph, a hundred and f. 7.44

FORTY-FIRST
dying in the f. year of his reign. 2Ch 16.13

FORTY-FIVE
not destroy it if I find f. there. Gen 18.28
of Gad was f. thousand six hundred Num 1.25
as numbered being f. thousand six 2.15
number was f. thousand six hundred 26.41
number was f. thousand four hundred. 26.50
these f. years since the time that Jos 14.10

FORTY-FIVE (cont.)
that were upon the f. pillars, 1Ki 7.03
sons of Zattu, nine hundred and f. Ez 2.08
of Jericho, three hundred and f. 2.34
their mules were two hundred and f., 2.66
of Zattu, eight hundred and f. Neh 7.13
of Jericho, three hundred and f. 7.36
had two hundred and f. singers, 7.67
their mules two hundred and f., 7.68
Jews seven hundred and f. persons; Jer 52.30

FORTY-FOUR
f. thousand seven hundred and sixty, 1Ch 5.18
a hundred and f. thousand sealed, Rev 7.04
a hundred and f. thousand who had 14.01
the hundred and f. thousand who 14.03
a hundred and f. cubits by a man's 21.17

FORTY-NINE
of years shall be to you f. years. Lev 25.08

FORTY-ONE
of Asher was f. thousand five Num 1.41
numbered being f. thousand five 2.28
Rehoboam was f. years old when he 1Ki 14.21
and he reigned f. years in Jerusalem 15.10
Samaria, and he reigned f. years. 2Ki 14.23
Rehoboam was f. years old when he 2Ch 12.13

FORTY-SEVEN
life, were a hundred and f. years. Gen 47.28
one thousand two hundred and f. Ez 2.38
a thousand two hundred and f. Neh 7.41

FORTY-SIX
of Reuben was f. thousand five Num 1.21
numbered being f. thousand five 2.11
"It has taken f. years to build Jn 2.20

FORTY-THREE
number was f. thousand seven Num 26.07
and Beeroth, seven hundred and f. Ez 2.25
and Beeroth, seven hundred and f. Neh 7.29

FORTY-TWO
to them you shall give f. cities. Num 35.06
at that time f. thousand of the Ju 12.06
the woods and tore f. of the boys. 2Ki 2.24
f. persons, and he spared none of 10.14
Ahaziah was f. years old when he 2Ch 22.02
The sons of Bani, six hundred and f. Ez 2.10
The sons of Azmaveth, f. 2.24
together was f. thousand three 2.64
The men of Bethazmaveth, f. Neh 7.28
sons of Nekoda, six hundred and f. 7.62
together was f. thousand three 7.66
fathers' houses, two hundred and f.; 11.13
over the holy city for f. months. Rev 11.02
exercise authority for f. months; 13.05

FORUM
as far as the F. of Appius and Ac 28.15

FORWARD
Tell the people of Israel to go f. Ex 14.15
and Miriam; and they both came f. Num 12.05
shall come f. and speak to the Deu 20.02
the sons of Levi shall come f., 21.05
And he said to the people, "Go f.; Jos 6.07
horns before the LORD went f., 6.08
with him rushed f. and stood at Ju 9.44
upon David from that day f. 1Sa 16.13
Philistine came f. and took his 17.16
And from that day f. he made it a 30.25
and as he went f. it fell out. 2Sa 20.08
Then a spirit came f. and stood 1Ki 22.21
and they went f., slaughtering the 2Ki 3.24
shall the shadow go f. ten steps, 20.09
Then a spirit came f. and stood 2Ch 18.20
repairing went f. in their hands, 24.13
came f. with trumpets, and the Ez 3.10
was going f. and that the breaches Neh 4.07
"Behold, I go f., but he is not Job 23.08
Let your eyes look directly f., Pro 4.25
put yourself f. in the king's 25.06
and went backward and not f. Jer 7.24
they went every one straight f., Eze 1.09
And each went straight f.; wherever 1.12
They went every one straight f. 10.22
turn you about and drive you f., 39.02
LORD their God, from that day f. 39.22
Chaldeans came f. and maliciously Dan 3.08
angel who talked with me came f., Zec 2.03
another angel came f. to meet him, 2.03
he shall bring f. the top stone 4.07
with me came f. and said to me, 5.05
and behold, two women coming f.! 5.09
Capernaum, a centurion came f. to him, Mt 8.05
received the five talents came f., 25.20
who had the two talents came f., 25.22
received the one talent came f., 25.24
witnesses came f. At last two came f. 26.60
came f. to him, and said to him, Mk 10.35
came f. and said to them, "Whom do Jn 18.04
And they put f. two, Joseph called Ac 1.23
Alexander, whom the Jews had put f. 19.33
Paul then came f. among them and 27.21
whom God put f. as an expiation by Rom 3.25
and straining f. to what lies Php 3.13
For he looked f. to the city which Heb 11.10

FORSAKE
and did not f. the ordinance of Is 58.02

FOSTER
Kings shall be your f. fathers, Is 49.23

FOUGHT
Then came Amalek and f. with Israel Ex 17.08
Moses told him, and f. with Amalek; 17.10
he f. against Israel, and took some Num 21.01
to Jahaz, and f. against Israel. 21.23
who had f. against the former king 21.26
for the LORD f. for Israel. Jos 10.14
to Libnah, and f. against Libnah; 10.29
LORD God of Israel f. for Israel. 10.42
went up and f. against Leshem, 19.47
LORD your God who has f. for you. 23.03
they f. with you, and I gave them 24.08
Moab, arose and f. against Israel; 24.09
the men of Jericho f. against you, 24.11
and f. against him, and defeated the Ju 1.05
men of Judah f. against Jerusalem, 1.08
they f.; then f. the kings of Canaan, 5.19
From heaven f. the stars, from their 5.20
courses they f. against Sisera. 5.20
for my father f. for you, and risked 9.17
of Shechem, and f. with Abimelech. 9.39
And Abimelech f. against the city 9.45
and f. against it, and drew near to 9.52
at Jahaz, and f. with Israel. 11.20
men of Gilead and f. with Ephraim; 12.04
So the Philistines f., and Israel 1Sa 4.10
of Moab; and they f. against them. 12.09
he f. against all his enemies on 14.47
went out and f. with the Philistines, 19.08
and f. with the Philistines, and 23.05
Now the Philistines f. against Israel; 31.01
because he had f. against Hadadezer 2Sa 8.10
against David, and f. with him. 10.17
the city came out and f. with Joab; 11.17
Now Joab f. against Rabbah of the 12.26
and said, "I have f. against Rabbah; 12.27
and f. against it and took it. 12.29
the battle was f. in the forest of 18.06
and they f. against the Philistines; 21.15
besieged Samaria, and f. against it. 1Ki 20.01

FOUGHT (cont.)
the kings have surely f. together, 2Ki 3.23
when he f. against Hazael king of 8.29
when he f. with Hazael king of 9.15
Syria went up and f. against Gath, 12.17
with which he f. against Amaziah 13.12
and how he f. with Amaziah king of 14.15
how he f., and how he recovered for 14.28
Now the Philistines f. against Israel; 1Ch 10.01
because he had f. against Hadadezer 18.10
the Syrians, they f. with him. 19.17
the LORD had f. against the enemies 2Ch 20.29
when he f. against Hazael king of 22.06
He f. with the king of the Ammonites 27.05
to Ashdod and f. against it and Is 20.01
enemy, and himself f. against them. 63.10
I f. with beasts at Ephesus? If the 1Co 15.32
I have f. the good fight, I have 2Ti 4.07
and the dragon and his angels f., Rev 12.07

FOUL
die, and the Nile shall become f., Ex 7.18
and the Nile became f., so that the 7.21
and it bred worms and became f.; 16.20
and it did not become f., and there 16.24
and f. weeds instead of barley. Job 31.40
My wounds grow f. and fester Ps 38.05
and its canals will become f., Is 19.06
nor has f. flesh come into my mouth Eze 4.14
your feet, and f. their rivers. 32.02
that you must f. the rest with your 34.18
the stench and f. smell of him will Joe 2.20
slander, and f. talk from your mouth. Col 3.08
and f. and evil sores came upon the Rev 16.02
three f. spirits like frogs; 16.13
demons, a haunt of every f. spirit, 18.02
haunt of every f. and hateful bird 18.02

FOULED
what you have f. with your feet? Eze 34.19

FOUND
there was not f. a helper fit for Gen 2.20
But Noah f. favor in the eyes of 6.08
but the dove f. no place to set her 8.09
they f. a plain in the land of 11.02
of the LORD f. her by a spring of 16.07
if I have f. favor in your sight, do 18.03
said, "Suppose forty are f. there." 18.29
speak. Suppose thirty are f. there." 18.30
Lord. Suppose twenty are f. there." 18.31
this once. Suppose ten are f. there." 18.32
servant has f. favor in your sight, 19.19
the valley and f. there a well of 26.19
and said to him, "We have f. water." 26.32
it that you have f. it so quickly, 27.20
Reuben went and f. mandrakes in 30.14
if f. with me, shall be counted 30.33
what have you f. of all your household 31.37
if I have f. favor in your sight, 33.10
is the Anah who f. the hot springs 36.24
And a man f. him wandering in the 37.15
brothers, and f. them at Dothan. 37.17
father, and said, "This we have f.; 37.32
Judah, and said, "I have not f. her; 38.22
So Joseph f. favor in his sight and 39.04
money which we f. in the mouth of 44.08
whomever of your servants it be f., 44.09
with whom it is f. shall be my 44.10
and the cup was f. in Benjamin's 44.12
God has f. out the guilt of your 44.16
in whose hand the cup has been f." 44.16
the cup was f. shall be my slave; 44.17
money that was f. in the land of 47.14
him, "If now I have f. favor in your 47.29
"If now I have f. favor in your eyes, 50.04
leaven shall be f. in your houses; Ex 12.19
in the wilderness and f. no water. 15.22
out to gather, and they f. none. 16.27
Therefore the people f. fault with 17.02
sells him or is f. in possession 21.16
If a thief is f. breaking in, and is 22.02
stolen beast is f. alive in his 22.04
house, then, if the thief is f., 22.07
If the thief is not f., the owner 22.08
you have also f. favor in my sight.' 33.12
if I have f. favor in thy sight, 33.13
that I have f. favor in thy sight, 33.16
for you have f. favor in my sight, 33.17
"If now I have f. favor in thy 34.09
with whom was f. blue or purple or 35.23
with whom was f. acacia wood of 35.24
or has f. what was lost and lied Lev 6.03
or the lost thing which he f., 6.04
why have I not f. favor in thy Num 11.11
they f. a man gathering sticks on 15.32
And those who f. him gathering 15.33
what each man f., articles of gold, 31.50
"If we have f. favor in your sight, 32.05
"If there is f. among you, within Deu 17.02
There shall not be f. among you any 18.10
people who are f. in it shall do 20.11
any one is f. slain, lying in the 21.01
were not f. in the young woman, 22.20
"If a man is f. lying with the wife 22.22
lies with her, and they are f., 22.28
because he has f. some indecency 24.01
"If a man is f. stealing one of his 24.07
"He f. him in a desert land, and in 32.10
all along the way and f. nothing. Jos 2.22
"The five kings have been f., 10.17
"If now I have f. favor with thee, Ju 6.17
would not have f. out my riddle." 14.18
And he f. a fresh jawbone of an ass, 15.15
and beasts and all that they f. 20.48
which they f. they set on fire. 20.48
And they f. among the inhabitants 21.12
"Why have I f. favor in your eyes, Ru 2.10
on them, for they have been f. 1Sa 9.20
which you went to seek are f., 10.02
when we saw they were not to be f., 10.14
plainly that the asses had been f." 10.16
sought him, he could not be f. 10.21
you have not f. anything in my 12.05
no smith to be f. throughout all 13.19
sword nor spear f. in the hand of 13.22
of their enemies which they f.; 14.30
for he has f. favor in my sight." 16.22
that I have f. favor in your eyes; 20.03
if I have f. favor in your eyes, let 20.29
shall not be f. in you so long as 25.28
"If I have f. favor in your eyes, 27.05
to me I have f. no fault in him to 29.03
for I have f. nothing wrong in you 29.06
What have you f. in your servant 29.08
they f. it burned with fire, and 30.03
They f. an Egyptian in the open 30.11
upon Saul, and the archers f. him; 31.03
they f. Saul and his three sons 31.08
thy servant has f. courage to pray 2Sa 7.27
that I have f. favor in your sight, 14.22
in some place where he is to be f., 17.12
even a pebble is to be f. there." 17.13
and f. Abishag the Shunammite, and 1Ki 1.03
but if wickedness is f. in him, 1.52
of the bronze was not f. out. 7.47
And Hadad f. great favor in the 11.19
the Shilonite f. him on the road. 11.29
and f. him sitting under an oak; 13.14
And he went and f. his body thrown 13.28
because in him there is f. something 14.13
nation, that they had not f. you. 18.10
and f. Elisha the son of Shaphat, 19.19
Then he f. another man, and said, 20.37
Elijah, "Have you f. me, O my enemy?" 21.20

FOUND (cont.)
"I have f. you, because you have 1Ki 21.20
and f. a wild vine and gathered 2Ki 4.39
they f. no more of her than the 9.35
money that was f. in the house of 12.10
gold that was f. in the treasuries 12.18
that were f. in the house of the 14.14
gold that was f. in the house of 16.08
king of Assyria f. treachery in 17.04
silver that was f. in the house of 18.15
and f. the king of Assyria fighting 19.08
all that was f. in his storehouses; 20.13
"I have f. the book of the law in 22.08
the money that was f. in the house, 22.09
of this book that has been f.; 22.13
which had been f. in the house of 23.02
the priest f. in the house of the 23.24
council who were f. in the city; 25.19
the land who were f. in the city. 25.19
where they f. rich, good pasture, and 1Ch 4.40
and the Meunim who were f. there, 4.41
upon Saul, and the archers f. him; 10.03
they f. Saul and his sons fallen on 10.08
thy servant has f. courage to pray 17.25
he f. that it weighed a talent of 20.02
chief men were f. among the sons 24.04
among them were f. at Jazer in 26.31
you seek him, he will be f. by you; 28.09
and there were f. a hundred and 2Ch 2.17
he will be f. by you, but if you 15.02
and sought him, he was f. by them. 15.04
and he was f. by them, and the LORD 15.15
Nevertheless some good is f. in you, 19.03
they f. cattle in great numbers, 20.25
possessions they f. that belonged 21.17
and f. that they were three hundred 25.05
that were f. in the house of God, 25.24
that they f. in the temple of the 29.16
the priest f. the book of the law 34.14
"I have f. the book of the law in 34.15
money that was f. in the house of 34.17
words of the book that has been f.; 34.21
which had been f. in the house of 34.30
and what was f. against him, behold, 36.08
genealogies, but they were not f. there, Ez 2.62
and it has been f. that this city 4.19
a scroll was f. on which this was 6.02
I f. there none of the sons of Levi. 8.15
foreign women were f. Maaseiah, 10.18
servant has f. favor in your sight, Neh 2.05
And I f. the book of the genealogy 7.05
the first, and I f. written in it: 7.05
genealogies, but it was not f. there, 7.64
And they f. it written in the law 8.14
and in it was f. written that no 13.01
I also f. out that the portions of 13.10
Now Esther f. favor in the eyes of Est 2.15
and she f. grace and favor in his 2.17
was investigated and f. to be so, 2.23
all the Jews to be f. in Susa, 4.16
she f. favor in his sight and he 5.02
If I have f. favor in the sight of 5.08
And it was f. written how Mordecai 6.02
"If I have f. favor in your sight, O 7.03
and if I have f. favor in his sight, 8.05
consider what the fathers have f.; Job 8.08
root of the matter is f. in him'; 19.28
away like a dream, and not be f.; 20.08
"But where shall wisdom be f.? And 28.12
and it is not f. in the land of the 28.13
because they had f. no answer, although 32.03
Beware lest you say, 'We have f. wisdom; 32.13
into the Pit, I have f. a ransom; 33.24
iniquity cannot be f. out and hated. Ps 36.02
I sought him, he could not be f. 37.36
thy flock f. a dwelling in it; in thy 68.10
and for comforters, but I f. none. 69.20

I have f. David, my servant; with my 89.20
we f. it in the fields of Jaar. 132.06
you eagerly, and I have f. you. Pro 7.15
perverts his ways will be f. out. 10.09
who had understanding wisdom is f., 10.13
If you have f. honey, eat only 25.16
rebuke you, and you be f. a liar. 30.06
for my heart f. pleasure in all my Ecc 2.10
And I f. more bitter than death the 7.26
Behold, this is what I f., says the 7.27
repeatedly, but I have not f. 7.28
One man among a thousand I f., 7.28
among all these I have not f. 7.28
this alone I f., that God made man 7.29
But there was f. in it a poor wise 9.15
I sought him, but f. him not; I called Sol 3.01
loves." I sought him, but f. him not. 3.02
The watchmen f. me, as they went 3.03
when I f. him whom my soul loves. 3.04
I sought him, but f. him not; I called 5.06
The watchmen f. me, as they went 5.07
My hand has f. like a nest the wealth Is 10.14
Whoever is f. will be thrust through, 13.15
of you who were f. were captured, 22.03
not a sherd is f. with which to 30.14
they shall not be f. there, 35.09
and f. the king of Assyria fighting 37.08
all that was f. in his storehouses. 39.02
joy and gladness will be f. in her, 51.03
"Seek the LORD while he may be f., 55.06
you f. new life for your strength, 57.10
was ready to be f. by those who 65.01
"As the wine is f. in the cluster, 65.08
your skirts is f. the lifeblood of Jer 2.34
For wicked men are f. among my 5.26
Thy words were f., and I ate them, 15.16
my house I have f. their wickedness, 23.11
I will be f. by you, says the LORD, 29.14
the sword f. grace in the wilderness, 31.02
to you? Was he f. among thieves, that 48.27
All who f. them have devoured them, 50.07
sin in Judah, and none shall be f.; 50.20
you were f. and caught, because you 50.24
council, who were f. in the city; 52.25
who were f. in the midst of the 52.25
should not destroy it; but I f. none. Eze 22.30
for, you will never be f. again, 26.21
till iniquity was f. in you. 28.15
them all none was f. like Daniel, Dan 1.19
he f. them ten times better than 1.20
"I have f. among the exiles from 2.25
not a trace of them could be f. 2.35
of the field f. shade under it, 4.12
which beasts of the field f. shade, 4.21
were f. in him, and King Nebuchadnezzar, 5.11
problems were f. in this Daniel, 5.12
and excellent wisdom are f. in you. 5.14
in the balances and f. wanting; 5.27
no error or fault was f. in him. 6.04
agreement and f. Daniel making 6.11
because I was f. blameless before 6.22
no kind of hurt was f. upon him, 6.23
and fall, and shall not be f. 11.19
name shall be f. written in the 12.01
in the wilderness, I f. Israel. Hos 9.10
to Joppa and f. a ship going to Jon 1.03
for in you were f. the transgressions Mic 1.13
shall there be f. in their mouth a Zep 3.13
and no wrong was f. on his lips. Mal 2.06
together she was f. to be with Mt 1.18
when you have f. him bring me word, 2.08
in Israel have I f. such faith. 8.10
which a man f. and covered up; 13.44
he went out and f. others standing; 20.06
and f. nothing on it but leaves 21.19
and gathered all whom they f., 22.10
the disciples and f. them sleeping; 26.40

FOUND (cont.)

again he came and f. them sleeping, Mt 26.43
but they f. none, though many false 26.60
and they f. him and said to him, Mk 1.37
And when they had f. out, they said, 6.38
and f. the child lying in bed, and 7.30
and f. a colt tied at the door out 11.04
he f. nothing but leaves, for it was 11.13
and f. it as he had told them; 14.16
And he came and f. them sleeping, 14.37
again he came and f. them sleeping, 14.40
put him to death; but they f. none. 14.55
for you have f. favor with God. Lk 1.30
and f. Mary and Joseph, and the babe 2.16
After three days they f. him in the 2.46
the book and f. the place where it 4.17
in Israel have I f. such faith." 7.09
the house, they f. the slave well. 7.10
and f. the man from whom the demons 8.35
had spoken, Jesus was f. alone. And 9.36
seeking fruit on it and f. none. 13.06
And when he has f. it, he lays it on 15.05
for I have f. my sheep which was 15.06
And when she has f. it, she calls 15.09
for I have f. the coin which I had 15.09
he was lost, and is f.' And they 15.24
alive; he was lost, and is f.'" 15.32
Was no one f. to return and give 17.18
went away and f. it as he had told 19.32
and f. it as he had told them; 22.13
disciples and f. them sleeping for 22.45
"We f. this man perverting our 23.02
I have f. in him no crime deserving 23.22
And they f. the stone rolled away 24.02
and f. it just as the women had 24.24
and they f. the eleven gathered 24.33
He first f. his brother Simon, and Jn 1.41
"We have f. the Messiah" (which 1.41
And he f. Philip and said to him, 1.43
Philip f. Nathanael, and said to him, 1.45
"We have f. him of whom Moses in 1.45
In the temple he f. those who were 2.14
Jesus f. him in the temple, and said 5.14
When they f. him on the other side 6.25
and having f. him he said, "Do you 9.35
he f. that Lazarus had already been 11.17
And Jesus f. a young ass and sat 12.14
young men came in they f. her dead, Ac 5.10
"We f. the prison securely locked 5.23
we opened it we f. no one inside." 5.23
you might even be f. opposing God!" 5.39
who f. favor in the sight of God 7.46
But Philip was f. at Azotus, and 8.40
so that if he f. any belonging to 9.02
There he f. a man named Aeneas, who 9.33
he went in and f. many persons 10.27
and when he had f. him, he brought 11.26
'I have f. in David the son of 13.22
I f. also an altar with this 17.23
And he f. a Jew named Aquila, a 18.02
Ephesus. There he f. some disciples. 19.02
of them and f. it came to fifty 19.19
And having f. a ship crossing to 21.02
I f. that he was accused about 23.29
For we have f. this man a pestilent 24.05
they f. me purified in the temple, 24.18
wrongdoing they f. when I stood 24.20
But I f. that he had done nothing 25.25
There the centurion f. a ship of 27.06
they sounded and f. twenty fathoms; 27.28
again and f. fifteen fathoms. 27.28
There we f. brethren, and were 28.14
"I have been f. by those who did Rom 10.20
that they be f. trustworthy. 1Co 4.02
that is not f. even among pagans; 5.01
We are even f. to be misrepresenting 15.15
putting it on we may not be f. naked. 2Co 5.03
no fault may be f. with our ministry, 6.03
tested and f. earnest in many 8.22
we ourselves were f. to be sinners, Gal 2.17
of light is f. in all that is good Eph 5.09
And being f. in human form he Php 2.08
and be f. in him, not having a 3.09
searched for me eagerly and f. me— 2Ti 1.17
didst f. the earth in the beginning, Heb 1.10
and he was not f., because God 11.05
for he f. no chance to repent, 12.17
no guile was f. on his lips. 1Pe 2.22
zealous to be f. by him without 2Pe 3.14
I f. it necessary to write appealing Jud 1.03
but are not, and f. them to be false; Rev 2.02
for I have not f. your works 3.02
that no one was f. worthy to open 5.04
and in their mouth no lie was f., 14.05
and no mountains were to be f.; 16.20
lost to thee, never to be f. again!" 18.14
violence, and shall be f. no more; 18.21
craft shall be f. in thee no more; 18.22
And in her was f. the blood of 18.24
away, and no place was f. for them. 20.11
name was not f. written in the 20.15

FOUNDATION

his first-born shall he lay its f., Jos 6.26
to lay the f. of the house with 1Ki 5.17
fourth year the f. of the house of 6.37
even from the f. to the coping, and 7.09
The f. was of costly stones, huge 7.10
he laid its f. at the cost of 16.34
the day the f. of the house of the 2Ch 8.16
one third at the Gate of the F.; 23.05
But the f. of the temple of the Ez 3.06
laid the f. of the temple of the 3.10
because the f. of the house of the 3.11
they saw the f. of this house 3.12
whose f. is in the dust, who are Job 4.19
their time; their f. was washed away. 22.16
when I laid the f. of the earth 38.04
justice are the f. of thy throne; Ps 89.14
justice are the f. of his throne. 97.02
thou didst lay the f. of the earth, 102.25
am laying in Zion for a f. a stone, Is 28.16
of a sure f.: 'He who believes will 28.16
the temple, 'Your f. shall be laid.'" 44.28
My hand laid the f. of the earth, 48.13
for a corner and no stone for a f., Jer 51.26
so that its f. will be laid bare; Eze 13.14
the day that the f. of the LORD's Hag 2.18
have laid the f. of this house; Zec 4.09
day that the f. of the house of 8.09
hidden since the f. of the world." Mt 13.35
for you from the f. of the world; 25.34
deep, and laid the f. upon rock; Lk 6.48
a house on the ground without a f.; 6.49
shed from the f. of the world, may 11.50
Otherwise, when he has laid a f., 14.29
for me before the f. of the world. Jn 17.24
lest I build on another man's f., Rom 15.20
skilled master builder I laid a f., 1Co 3.10
For no other f. can any one lay 3.11
any one builds on the f. with gold, 3.12
man has built on the f. survives, 3.14
in him before the f. of the world, Eph 1.04
built upon the f. of the apostles 2.20
themselves a good f. for the future, 1Ti 6.19
But God's firm f. stands, bearing 2Ti 2.19
finished from the f. of the world. Heb 4.03
laying again a f. of repentance 6.01
repeatedly since the f. of the world. 9.26
before the f. of the world but was 1Pe 1.20
written before the f. of the world Rev 13.08
of life from the f. of the world, 17.08

FOUNDATIONS
on fire the f. of the mountains. Deu 32.32
the f. of the heavens trembled and 2Sa 22.08
the f. of the world were laid bare, 22.16
the walls and repairing the f. Ez 4.12
and laid the f. of the house of 5.16
if the f. are destroyed, what can Ps 11.03
the f. also of the mountains 18.07
and the f. of the world were laid 18.15
all the f. of the earth are shaken. 82.05
Thou didst set the earth on its f., 104.05
"Rase it, rase it! Down to its f.!" 137.07
he marked out the f. of the earth, Pro 8.29
And the f. of the thresholds shook Is 6.04
and the f. of the earth tremble. 24.18
understood from the f. of the earth? 40.21
heavens and laid the f. of the earth, 51.13
and laying the f. of the earth, and 51.16
and lay your f. with sapphires. 54.11
raise up the f. of many generations; 58.12
and the f. of the earth below can Jer 31.37
in Zion, which consumed its f. Lam 4.11
away, and her f. are torn down. Eze 30.04
the f. of the side chambers measured 41.08
the valley, and uncover her f. Mic 1.06
and you enduring f. of the earth; 6.02
so that the f. of the prison were Ac 16.26
forward to the city which has f., Heb 11.10
the wall of the city had twelve f., Rev 21.14
The f. of the wall of the city were 21.19

FOUNDED
from the day it was f. until now. Ex 9.18
thou hast f. a bulwark because of Ps 8.02
for he has f. it upon the seas, and 24.02
earth, which he has f. for ever. 78.69
holy mount stands the city he f.; 87.01
that is in it, thou hast f. them. 89.11
that thou hast f. them for ever. 119.152
The LORD by wisdom f. the earth; Pro 3.19
"The LORD has f. Zion, and in her Is 14.32
the heavens and f. the earth and Zec 12.01
because it had been f. on the rock. Mt 7.25

FOUNDS
and f. his vault upon the earth; Amo 9.06
blood, and f. a city on iniquity! Hab 2.12

FOUNTAIN
nakedness, he has made naked her f., Lev 20.18
has uncovered the f. of her blood; 20.18
the f. of Jacob alone, in a land of Deu 33.28
encamped by the f. which is in 1Sa 29.01
went on to the F. Gate and to the Neh 2.14
of Mizpah, repaired the F. Gate; 3.15
At the F. Gate they went up straight 12.37
For with thee is the f. of life; Ps 36.09
LORD, O you who are of Israel's f.! 68.26
Let your f. be blessed, and rejoice Pro 5.18
of the righteous is a f. of life, 10.11
of the wise is a f. of life, 13.14
The fear of the LORD is a f. of life, 14.27
Wisdom is a f. of life to him who 16.22
the f. of wisdom is a gushing 18.04
or a polluted f. is a righteous 25.26
or the pitcher is broken at the f., Ecc 12.06
bride, a garden locked, a f. sealed. Sol 4.12
a garden f., a well of living water, 4.15
the f. of living waters, and hewed Jer 2.13
and my eyes a f. of tears, that I 9.01
the LORD, the f. of living water. 17.13
dry up her sea and make her f. dry; 51.36
and his f. shall dry up, his spring Hos 13.15
and a f. shall come forth from the Joe 3.18
shall be a f. opened for the house Zec 13.01
price from the f. of the water of Rev 21.06

FOUNTAINS
day all the f. of the great deep Gen 7.11
the f. of the deep and the windows 8.02
of f. and springs, flowing forth in Deu 8.07
he established the f. of the deep, Pro 8.28
and f. in the midst of the valleys; Is 41.18
by the f., and in all the inhabited Eze 34.13
the rivers and on the f. of water. Rev 8.10
earth, the sea and the f. of water." 14.07
the rivers and the f. of water, 16.04

FOUR
it divided and became f. rivers. Gen 2.10
birth of Shelah f. hundred and 11.13
birth of Eber f. hundred and three 11.15
birth of Peleg f. hundred and 11.17
of Ellasar, f. kings against five. 14.09
be oppressed for f. hundred years; 15.13
of land worth f. hundred shekels 23.15
f. hundred shekels of silver, 23.16
you, and f. hundred men with him." 32.06
coming, and f. hundred men with him. 33.01
and f. fifths shall be your own, as 47.24
in Egypt was f. hundred and thirty Ex 12.40
And at the end of f. hundred and 12.41
for an ox, and f. sheep for a sheep. 22.01
And you shall cast f. rings of gold 25.12
for it and put them on its f. feet, 25.12
shall make for it f. rings of gold, 25.26
to the f. corners at its f. legs. 25.26
lampstand itself f. cups made like 25.34
breadth of each curtain f. cubits; 26.02
breadth of each curtain f. cubits; 26.08
hang it upon f. pillars of acacia 26.32
of gold, upon f. bases of silver. 26.32
horns for it on its f. corners; 27.02
f. bronze rings at its f. corners. 27.04
have f. pillars and with them f. bases. 27.16
shall set in it f. rows of stones. 28.17
breadth of each curtain f. cubits; 36.09
breadth of each curtain f. cubits; 36.15
And for it he made f. pillars of 36.36
cast for them f. bases of silver. 36.36
f. rings of gold for its f. corners. 37.03
He cast for it f. rings of gold, and 37.13
to the f. corners at its f. legs. 37.13
itself were f. cups made like 37.20
horns for it on its f. corners; 38.02
He cast f. rings on the f. corners 38.05
And their pillars were f.; their 38.19
their f. bases were of bronze, their 38.19
thousand and f. hundred shekels; 38.29
And they set in it f. rows of stones. 39.10
which have f. feet are an abomination Lev 11.23
was fifty-four thousand f. hundred. Num 1.29
fifty-seven thousand f. hundred. 1.31
thirty-five thousand f. hundred. 1.37
fifty-three thousand f. hundred. 1.43
fifty-four thousand f. hundred. 2.06
fifty-seven thousand f. hundred. 2.08
and eighty-six thousand f. hundred. 2.09
thousand f. hundred and fifty. 2.16
thirty-five thousand f. hundred. 2.23
fifty-three thousand f. hundred. 2.30
Two wagons and f. oxen he gave to 7.07
and f. wagons and eight oxen he 7.08
two thousand f. hundred shekels 7.85
sixty-four thousand f. hundred. 26.43
fifty-three thousand f. hundred. 26.47
was forty-five thousand f. hundred. 26.50
and f. cubits its breadth, according Deu 3.11
tassels on the f. corners of your 22.12
f. cities with their villages; Jos 19.07
with its pasture lands—f. cities. 21.18
with its pasturelands—f. cities; 21.22
with its pasture lands—f. cities; 21.24
with its pasture lands—f. cities; 21.29

FOUR (cont.)

with its pasture lands—f. cities; Jos 21.31
with its pasture lands—f. cities; 21.35
with its pasture lands—f. cities; 21.37
its pasture lands—f. cities in all. 21.39
against Shechem in f. companies. Ju 9.34
the Gileadite f. days in the year. 11.40
Judah, and was there some f. months. 19.02
f. hundred thousand men on foot 20.02
mustered f. hundred thousand men 20.17
at the rock of Rimmon f. months. 20.47
of Jabeshgilead f. hundred young 21.12
who slew about f. thousand men on 1Sa 4.02
were with him about f. hundred men. 22.02
and about f. hundred men went up 25.13
Philistines was a year and f. months. 27.07
the pursuit, he and f. hundred men; 30.10
except f. hundred young men, who 30.17
And at the end of f. years Absalom 2Sa 15.07
These f. were descended from the 21.22
In the f. hundred and eightieth year 1Ki 6.01
and its thickness was f. fingers; 7.15
were of lily-work, f. cubits. 7.19
each stand was f. cubits long, 7.27
f. cubits wide, and three cubits 7.27
Moreover each stand had f. bronze 7.30
and at the f. corners were supports 7.30
And the f. wheels were underneath 7.32
f. supports at the f. corners of each 7.34
each laver measured f. cubits, and 7.38
and the f. hundred pomegranates for 7.42
the amount of f. hundred and twenty 9.28
and the f. hundred and fifty prophets 18.19
of Baal and the f. hundred prophets 18.19
prophets are f. hundred and fifty 18.22
"Fill f. jars with water, and pour 18.33
about f. hundred men, and said to 22.06
Now there were f. men who were 2Ki 7.03
of Jerusalem for f. hundred cubits, 14.13
f. by Bathshua, the daughter of 1Ch 3.05
Tola, Puah, Jashub, and Shimron, f. 7.01
The gatekeepers were on the f. sides, 9.24
for the f. chief gatekeepers, who 9.26
Of the Levites f. thousand six hundred. 12.26
and in Judah f. hundred and seventy 21.05
and his f. sons who were with him 21.20
f. thousand gatekeepers, and f. 23.05
and f. thousand shall offer praises 23.05
These f. were the sons of Shimei. 23.10
Amram, Izhar, Hebron, and Uzziel, f. 23.12
on the north f. each day, on the 26.17
on the south f. each day, as well as 26.17
west there were f. at the road and 26.18
and the f. hundred pomegranates for 2Ch 4.13
from there f. hundred and fifty 8.18
And Solomon had f. thousand stalls 9.25
f. hundred thousand picked men; 13.03
f. hundred men, and said to them, 18.05
of Jerusalem for f. hundred cubits, 25.23
two thousand f. hundred and ten Ez 1.10
five thousand f. hundred and sixty 1.11
of Adin, f. hundred and fifty-four. 2.15
their camels were f. hundred and 2.67
f. hundred lambs, and as a sin 6.17
And they sent to me f. times in Neh 6.04
their camels f. hundred and thirty-five, 7.69
lived in Jerusalem were f. hundred and 11.06
and struck the f. corners of the Job 1.19
and his sons' sons, f. generations. 42.16
satisfied; f. never say, "Enough": Pro 30.15
for me; f. I do not understand: 30.18
trembles; under f. it cannot bear up: 30.21
F. things on earth are small, but 30.24
f. are stately in their stride: 30.29
Judah from the f. corners of the Is 11.12
f. or five on the branches of a 17.06
over them f. kinds of destroyers, Jer 15.03
As Jehudi read three or f. columns, 36.23
Elam the f. winds from the f. quarters 49.36
and its thickness was f. fingers, 52.21
persons were f. thousand and six 52.30
the likeness of f. living creatures. Eze 1.05
f. faces, and each of them had f. wings. 1.06
wings on their f. sides they had 1.08
And the f. had their faces and 1.08
the f. had the face of a lion on 1.10
the f. had the face of an ox on the 1.10
and the f. had the face of an eagle 1.10
one for each of the f. of them. 1.15
and the f. had the same likeness, 1.16
in any of their f. directions 1.17
The f. wheels had rims and they had 1.18
come upon the f. corners of the 7.02
there were f. wheels beside the 10.09
the f. had the same likeness, as if 10.10
went in any of their f. directions 10.11
the wheels that the f. of them had. 10.12
And every one had f. faces: the first 10.14
Each had f. faces, and each f. wings, 10.21
upon Jerusalem my f. sore acts of 14.21
Come from the f. winds, O breath, and 37.09
F. tables were on the inside 40.41
and f. tables on the outside of the 40.41
And there were also f. tables of 40.42
f. cubits, round about the temple. 41.05
He measured it on the f. sides. 42.20
f. cubits, with a breadth of one 43.14
and the altar hearth, f. cubits; 43.15
upward, f. horns, one cubit high. 43.15
put it on the f. horns of the altar, 43.20
and on the f. corners of the ledge, 43.20
the f. corners of the ledge of the 45.19
led me to the f. corners of the 46.21
in the f. corners of the court were 46.22
broad; the f. were of the same size. 46.22
each of the f. courts was a row of 46.23
the north side f. thousand five 48.16
the south side f. thousand five 48.16
the east side f. thousand five 48.16
the west side f. thousand five 48.16
which is to be f. thousand five 48.30
which is to be f. thousand five 48.32
which is to be f. thousand five 48.33
which is to be f. thousand five 48.34
As for these f. youths, God gave Dan 1.17
"But I see f. men loose, walking in 3.25
the f. winds of heaven were stirring 7.02
And f. great beasts came up out of 7.03
with f. wings of a bird on its back; 7.06
and the beast had f. heads; and 7.06
'These f. great beasts are f. kings 7.17
there came up f. conspicuous horns 8.08
toward the f. winds of heaven. 8.08
in place of which f. others arose, 8.22
f. kingdoms shall arise from his 8.22
toward the f. winds of heaven, but 11.04
and for f., I will not revoke the Amo 1.03
and for f., I will not revoke the 1.06
and for f., I will not revoke the 1.09
and for f., I will not revoke the 1.11
and for f., I will not revoke the 1.13
and for f., I will not revoke the 2.01
and for f., I will not revoke the 2.04
and for f., I will not revoke the 2.06
eyes and saw, and behold, f. horns! Zec 1.18
Then the LORD showed me f. smiths. 1.20
abroad as the f. winds of the 2.06
f. chariots came out from between 6.01
forth to the f. winds of heaven, 6.05
Those who ate were f. thousand men, Mt 15.38
seven loaves of the f. thousand, 16.10
gather his elect from the f. winds, 24.31
him a paralytic carried by f. men. Mk 2.03
there were about f. thousand people. 8.09

FOUR (cont.)

“And the seven for the f. thousand, Mk 8.20
gather his elect from the f. winds, 13.27
not say, ‘There are yet f. months, Jn 4.35
had rowed about three or f. miles, 6.19
already been in the tomb f. days. 11.17
odor, for he has been dead f. days.” 11.39
his garments and made f. parts, 19.23
about f. hundred joined him; Ac 5.36
ill-treat them f. hundred years. 7.06
let down by f. corners upon the 10.11
“F. days ago, about this hour, I was 10.30
let down from heaven by f. corners; 11.05
delivered him to f. squads of 12.04
for about f. hundred and fifty 13.19
And he had f. unmarried daughters, 21.09
We have f. men who are under a vow; 21.23
and led the f. thousand men of the 21.38
they let out f. anchors from the 27.29
which came f. hundred and thirty Gal 3.17
are f. living creatures, full of Rev 4.06
And the f. living creatures, each of 4.08
throne and the f. living creatures 5.06
the f. living creatures and the 5.08
And the f. living creatures said, 5.14
one of the f. living creatures say, 6.01
midst of the f. living creatures 6.06
I saw f. angels standing at the f. corners 7.01
back the f. winds of the earth, 7.01
voice to the f. angels who had 7.02
elders and the f. living creatures, 7.11
voice from the f. horns of the 9.13
“Release the f. angels who are 9.14
So the f. angels were released, who 9.15
and before the f. living creatures 14.03
And one of the f. living creatures 15.07
elders and the f. living creatures 19.04
are at the f. corners of the earth, 20.08

FOURFOLD

and he shall restore the lamb f., 2Sa 12.06
one of anything, I restore it f. Lk 19.08

FOURS

go upon all f. are an abomination Lev 11.20
that go on all f. you may eat 11.21
the animals that go on all f., 11.27
belly, and whatever goes on all f., 11.42

FOURSCORE

or even by reason of strength f.; Ps 90.10

FOURSQUARE

and a hundred cubits broad, f.; Eze 40.47
The city lies f., its length the Rev 21.16

FOURTEEN

I served you f. years for your two Gen 31.41
born to Jacob—f. persons in all). 46.22
the plague were f. thousand seven Num 16.49
two rams, f. male lambs a year old; 29.13
and a tenth for each of the f. lambs; 29.15
f. male lambs a year old without 29.17
f. male lambs a year old without 29.20
f. male lambs a year old without 29.23
f. male lambs a year old without 29.26
f. male lambs a year old without 29.29
f. male lambs a year old without 29.32
f. cities with their villages. Jos 15.36
f. cities with their villages. 18.28
he had f. hundred chariots and 1Ki 10.26
had given Heman f. sons and three 1Ch 25.05
he had f. hundred chariots and 2Ch 1.14
And he took f. wives, and had twenty 13.21
and he had f. thousand sheep, six Job 42.12
breadth of the gate was f. cubits; Eze 40.48
square, f. cubits long by f. broad, 43.17
to David were f. generations, and from Mt 1.17
deportation to Babylon f. generations, 1.17
Babylon to the Christ f. generations. 1.17
in Christ who f. years ago was 2Co 12.02
Then after f. years I went up again Gal 2.01

FOURTEENTH

In the f. year Chedorlaomer and the Gen 14.05
it until the f. day of this month, Ex 12.06
on the f. day of the month at 12.18
on the f. day of the month in the Lev 23.05
On the f. of this month, in the Num 9.03
on the f. day of the month, in the 9.05
month on the f. day in the evening 9.11
“On the f. day of the first month 28.16
passover on the f. day of the Jos 5.10
In the f. year of King Hezekiah 2Ki 18.13
to Huppah, the f. to Jeshebeab, 1Ch 24.13
to the f., Mattithiah, his sons and 25.21
lamb on the f. day of the second 2Ch 30.15
lamb on the f. day of the first 35.01
On the f. day of the first month Ez 6.19
also on the f. day of the month of Est 9.15
and on the f. day they rested and 9.17
the thirteenth day and on the f., 9.18
hold the f. day of the month of 9.19
should keep the f. day of the 9.21
In the f. year of King Hezekiah, Is 36.01
in the f. year after the city was Eze 40.01
on the f. day of the month, you 45.21
When the f. night had come, as we Ac 27.27
“Today is the f. day that you have 27.33

FOURTH

and there was morning, a f. day. Gen 1.19
And the f. river is the Euphrates. 2.14
back here in the f. generation; 15.16
third and the f. generation of Ex 20.05
and the f. row a beryl, an onyx, and 28.20
mingled with a f. of a hin of 29.40
and a f. of a hin of wine for a 29.40
to the third and the f. generation.” 34.07
and the f. row, a beryl, an onyx, and 39.13
And in the f. year all their fruit Lev 19.24
it shall be of wine, a f. of a hin. 23.13
On the f. day Elizur the son of Num 7.30
third and upon the f. generation.” 14.18
mixed with a f. of a hin of oil; 15.04
a f. of a hin, you shall prepare 15.05
or number the f. part of Israel? 23.10
mixed with a f. of a hin of beaten 28.05
shall be a f. of a hin for each 28.07
and a f. of a hin for a lamb; 28.14
“On the f. day ten bulls, two rams, 29.23
the third and f. generation of Deu 5.09
The f. lot came out for Issachar, Jos 19.17
On the f. day they said to Samson’s Ju 14.15
On the f. day they arose early 19.05
with me the f. part of a shekel of 1Sa 9.08
and the f., Adonijah the son of 2Sa 3.04
in the f. year of Solomon’s reign 1Ki 6.01
In the f. year the foundation of 6.37
Judah in the f. year of Ahab king 22.41
and the f. part of a kab of dove’s 2Ki 6.25
sons of the f. generation shall 10.30
of Israel to the f. generation.” 15.12
In the f. year of King Hezekiah, 18.09
day of the f. month the famine was 25.03
Nethanel the f., Raddai the fifth, 1Ch 2.14
the f. Adonijah, whose mother was 3.02
the third Zedekiah, the f. Shallum. 3.15
Nohah the f., and Rapha the fifth. 8.02
Mishmannah f., Jeremiah fifth, 12.10
the third, and Jekameam the f. 23.19
the third to Harim, the f. to Seorim, 24.08
Jahaziel the third, Jekameam the f. 24.23
the f. to Izri, his sons and his 25.11
the third, Jathniel the f., 26.02

FOURTH (cont.)
Sachar the f., Nethanel the fifth, 1Ch 26.04
Zechariah the f.: all the sons and 26.11
Asahel the brother of Joab was f., 27.07
for the f. month, and his son 27.07
month of the f. year of his reign. 2Ch 3.02
On the f. day they assembled in the 20.26
On the f. day, within the house of Ez 8.33
LORD their God for a f. of the day; Neh 9.03
for another f. of it they made 9.03
in the f. year of Jehoiakim the son Jer 25.01
in the fifth month of the f. year, 28.01
In the f. year of Jehoiakim the son 36.01
in the f. month, on the ninth day of 39.02
in the f. year of Jehoiakim the son 45.01
defeated on the f. year of Jehoiakim 46.02
Babylon, in the f. year of his reign. 51.59
day of the f. month the famine was 52.06
in the f. month, on the fifth day of Eze 1.01
and the f. the face of an eagle. 10.14
And there shall be a f. kingdom, Dan 2.40
appearance of the f. is like a son 3.25
a f. beast, terrible and dreadful 7.07
the truth concerning the f. beast, 7.19
'As for the f. beast, there shall be 7.23
shall be a f. kingdom on earth, 7.23
and a f. shall be far richer than 11.02
and the f. chariot dappled gray Zec 6.03
In the f. year of King Darius, the 7.01
Zechariah in the f. day of the 7.01
of hosts: The fast of the f. month, 8.19
And in the f. watch of the night he Mt 14.25
And about the f. watch of the night Mk 6.48
and the f. living creature like a Rev 4.07
When he opened the f. seal, I heard 6.07
voice of the f. living creature say, 6.07
given power over a f. of the earth, 6.08
The f. angel blew his trumpet, and a 8.12
The f. angel poured his bowl on the 16.08
the third agate, the f. emerald, 21.19

FOWL
whether of f. or of animal, in any Lev 7.26
gazelles, roebucks, and fatted f. 1Ki 4.23

FOWLER
snare of the f. and from the deadly Ps 91.03
like a bird from the hand of the f. Pro 6.05

FOWLER'S
yet a f. snare is on all his ways, Hos 9.08

FOWLERS
as a bird from the snare of the f.; Ps 124.07
they lurk like f. lying in wait. Jer 5.26

FOWLS
f. likewise were prepared for me, Neh 5.18

FOX
if a f. goes up on it he will break Neh 4.03
said to them, "Go and tell that f., Lk 13.32

FOXES
went and caught three hundred f., Ju 15.04
he let the f. go into the standing 15.05
Catch us the f., the little f., that Sol 2.15
have been like f. among ruins, Eze 13.04
"F. have holes, and birds of the air Mt 8.20
"F. have holes, and birds of the air Lk 9.58

FRACTURE
f. for f., eye for eye, tooth for Lev 24.20

FRAGMENTS
that among its f. not a sherd is Is 30.14
house shall be smitten into f., Amo 6.11
disciples, "Gather up the f. left over, Jn 6.12
baskets with f. from the five barley 6.13

FRAGRANCE
couch, my nard gave forth its f. Sol 1.12
in blossom; they give forth f. 2.13
and the f. of your oils than any 4.10
let its f. be wafted abroad. 4.16
like beds of spices, yielding f. 5.13
The mandrakes give forth f., 7.13
the olive, and his f. like Lebanon. Hos 14.06
their f. shall be like the wine of 14.07
filled with the f. of the ointment. Jn 12.03
us spreads the f. of the knowledge 2Co 2.14
to one a f. from death to death, to 2.16
to the other a f. from a life to 2.16

FRAGRANT
anointing oil and for the f. incense, Ex 25.06
And Aaron shall burn f. incense on it; 30.07
oil and the f. incense for the holy 31.11
anointing oil and for the f. incense, 35.08
anointing oil and the f. incense, 35.15
anointing oil, and for the f. incense. 35.28
and the pure f. incense, blended as 37.29
anointing oil and the f. incense, 39.28
and burnt f. incense upon it; 40.27
of the altar of f. incense before Lev 4.07
the f. incense, the continual cereal Num 4.16
your robes are all f. with myrrh Ps 45.08
your anointing oils are f., your name Sol 1.03
with all the f. powders of the 3.06
a f. offering and sacrifice to God. Eph 5.02
a f. offering, a sacrifice acceptable Php 4.18

FRAIL
knows that the children are f., Gen 33.13

FRAME
around it a f. a handbreadth wide, Ex 25.25
a molding of gold around the f. 25.25
Close to the f. the rings shall lie, 25.27
cubits shall be the length of a f., 26.16
and a half the breadth of each f. 26.16
There shall be two tenons in each f., 26.17
two bases under one f. for its two 26.19
under another f. for its two tenons; 26.19
of silver, two bases under one f., 26.21
and two bases under another f.; 26.21
bases; two bases under one f., and 26.25
and two bases under another f. 26.25
Ten cubits was the length of a f. 36.21
and a half the breadth of each f. 36.21
Each f. had two tenons, for fitting 36.22
two bases under one f. for its two 36.24
under another f. for its two tenons. 36.24
bases under one f. and two bases 36.26
and two bases under another f. 36.26
bases, under every f. two bases. 36.30
around it a f. a handbreadth wide, 37.12
a molding of a gold around the f. 37.12
Close to the f. were the rings, as 37.14
and put it upon the carrying f. Num 4.10
and put them on the carrying f. 4.12
mighty strength, or his goodly f. Job 41.12
thee, who f. mischief by statute? Ps 94.20
For he knows our f.; he remembers 103.14
my f. was not hidden from thee, when 139.15

FRAMES
make upright f. for the tabernacle Ex 26.15
do for all the f. of the tabernacle. 26.17
You shall make the f. for the 26.18
twenty f. for the south side; 26.18
you shall make under the twenty f., 26.19
on the north side twenty f., 26.20
westward you shall make six f. 26.22
shall make two f. for corners of 26.23
And there shall be eight f., with 26.25
five for the f. of the one side of 26.27
bars for the f. of the other side 26.27

FRAMES (cont.)
bars for the f. of the side of the Ex 26.27
The middle bar, halfway up the f., 26.28
You shall overlay the f. with gold, 26.29
its covering, its hooks and its f., 35.11
the upright f. for the tabernacle 36.20
for all the f. of the tabernacle. 36.22
The f. for the tabernacle he made 36.23
thus: twenty f. for the south side; 36.23
bases of silver under the twenty f., 36.24
on the north side, he made twenty f. 36.25
tabernacle westward he made six f. 36.27
And he made two f. for corners of 36.28
There were eight f. with their 36.30
five for the f. of the one side of 36.31
bars for the f. of the other side 36.32
bars for the f. of the tabernacle 36.32
from end to end halfway up the f. 36.33
And he overlaid the f. with gold, 36.34
its f., its bars, its pillars, and 39.33
laid its bases, and set up its f., 40.18
was to be the f. of the tabernacle, Num 3.36
the f. of the tabernacle, with its 4.31
the house windows with recessed f. 1Ki 6.04
There were window f. in three rows, 7.04
doorways and windows had square f., 7.05
the panels were set in the f. 7.28
that were set in the f. were lions, 7.29
Upon the f., both above and below 7.29
Ahaz cut off the f. of the stands, 2Ki 16.17
evil, and your tongue f. deceit. Ps 50.19
three had windows with recessed f. Eze 41.16

FRANKINCENSE
with pure f. (of each shall there Ex 30.34
oil upon it, and put f. on it, Lev 2.01
flour and oil, with all of its f.; 2.02
put oil upon it, and lay f. on it; 2.15
and of the oil with all of its f.; 2.16
upon it, and shall put no f. on it, 5.11
oil and all the f. which is on the 6.15
shall put pure f. with each row, 24.07
no oil upon it and put no f. on it, Num 5.15
the f., the vessels, and the tithes Neh 13.05
the cereal offering and the f. 13.09
smoke, perfumed with myrrh and f., Sol 3.06
of myrrh and the hill of f. 4.06
and cinnamon, with all trees of f., 4.14
offerings, or wearied you with f. Is 43.23
They shall bring gold and f., 60.06
makes a memorial offering of f., 66.03
purpose does f. come to me from Jer 6.20
sacrifices, cereal offerings and f., 17.26
him gifts, gold and f. and myrrh. Mt 2.11
f., wine, oil, fine flour and wheat, Rev 18.13

FRAUD
oppression and f. do not depart Ps 55.11
master's house with violence and f." Zep 1.09
and the last f. will be worse than Mt 27.64
which you kept back by f., cry out; Jas 5.04

FREE
you will be f. from this oath of Gen 24.08
then you will be f. from my oath, 24.41
you, will be f. from my oath.,' 24.41
he shall go out f., for nothing. Ex 21.02
children; I will not go out f.,' 21.05
the slave go f. for the eye's sake. 21.26
the slave go f. for the tooth's 21.27
to death, because she was not f.; Lev 19.20
be f. from this water of bitterness Num 5.19
she shall be f. and shall conceive 5.28
The man shall be f. from iniquity, 5.31
return and be f. of obligation to 32.22
you shall let him go f. from you, Deu 15.12
And when you let him go f. from you, 15.13
when you let him go f. from you; 15.18
he shall be f. at home one year, to 24.05
is none remaining, bond or f. 32.36
other times, and shake myself f." Ju 16.20
his father's house f. in Israel." 1Sa 17.25
both bond and f. in Israel, and will 1Ki 14.10
every male, bond or f., in Israel; 21.21
every male, bond or f., in Israel. 2Ki 9.08
bond or f., and there was none to 14.26
of the temple f. from other service, 1Ch 9.33
the slave is f. from his master. Job 3.19
I will give f. utterance to my 10.01
"Who has let the wild ass go f.? 39.05
my prayer from lips f. of deceit! Ps 17.01
peoples, but them thou didst set f.; 44.02
"You give your mouth f. rein for evil, 50.19
set me f. because of my enemies! 69.18
to set f. those who were doomed to 102.20
ruler of the peoples set him f.; 105.20
the LORD answered me and set me f. 118.05
The LORD sets the prisoners f.; 146.07
your king is the son of f. men, Ecc 10.17
of the ox and the ass range f. Is 32.20
build my city and set my exiles f., 45.13
yoke, to let the oppressed go f., 58.06
'We are f., we will come no more to Jer 2.31
one should set f. his Hebrew 34.09
every one would set f. his slave, 34.10
again; they obeyed and set them f. 34.10
and female slaves they had set f., 34.11
of you must set f. the fellow 34.14
must set him f. from your service. 34.14
you had set f. according to their 34.16
that you hunt go f. like birds. Eze 13.20
which was left f. was five cubits. 41.09
of the platform that was left f., 41.11
that was left f. was five cubits 41.11
your captives f. from the waterless Zec 9.11
said to him, "Then the sons are f. Mt 17.26
and the truth will make you f." Jn 8.32
you say, 'You will be made f.'?" 8.33
So if the Son makes you f., 8.36
you free, you will be f. indeed. 8.36
have been set f. if he had not Ac 26.32
But the f. gift is not like the Rom 5.15
of God and the f. gift in the 5.15
And the f. gift is not like the 5.16
but the f. gift following many 5.16
grace and the f. gift of righteousness 5.17
and, having been set f. from sin, 6.18
you were f. in regard to righteousness. 6.20
have been set f. from sin and have 6.22
but the f. gift of God is eternal 6.23
dies she is f. from that law, 7.03
has set me f. from the law of sin 8.02
will be set f. from its bondage to 8.21
he who was f. when called is a 1Co 7.22
seek to be f. Are you f. from a wife? 7.27
I want you to be f. from anxieties. 7.32
she is f. to be married to whom she 7.39
Am I not f.? Am I not an apostle? 9.01
I may make the gospel f. of charge, 9.18
For though I am f. from all men, 9.19
slaves or f.—and all were made to 12.13
their means, of their own f. will, 2Co 8.03
there is neither slave nor f., Gal 3.28
by a slave and one by a f. woman. 4.22
the son of the f. woman through 4.23
But the Jerusalem above is f., 4.26
with the son of the f. woman. 4.30
of the slave but of the f. woman. 4.31
For freedom Christ has set us f.; 5.01
Lord, whether he is a slave or f. Eph 6.08
f. man, but Christ is all, and in all. Col 3.11
unstained and f. from reproach 1Ti 6.14
compulsion but of your own f. will. Phm 1.14
Keep your life f. from love of Heb 13.05
Live as f. men, yet without using 1Pe 2.16

FREE (cont.)
slave and f., hid in the caves and Rev 6.15
both f. and slave, to be marked on 13.16
both f. and slave, both small and 19.18

FREED
graciously f. Jehoiachin king of 2Ki 25.27
your hands were f. from the basket. Ps 81.06
you are f. from your infirmity." Lk 13.12
believes is f. from everything Ac 13.39
could not be f. by the law of 13.39
For he who has died is f. from sin. Rom 6.07
us and has f. us from our sins by Rev 1.05

FREEDMAN
as a slave is a f. of the Lord. 1Co 7.22

FREEDMEN
synagogue of the F. (as it was Ac 6.09

FREEDOM
not yet ransomed or given her f., Lev 19.20
But if you can gain your f., 1Co 7.21
Spirit of the Lord is, there is f. 2Co 3.17
to spy out our f. which we have in Gal 2.04
For f. Christ has set us free; 5.01
For you were called to f., brethren; 5.13
do not use your f. as an opportunity 5.13
using your f. as a pretext for 1Pe 2.16
They promise them f., but they 2Pe 2.19

FREELY
"You may f. eat of every tree of Gen 2.16
You shall give to him f., and your Deu 15.10
had eaten f. today of the spoil of 1Sa 14.30
not move about f. because of Saul 1Ch 12.01
they had offered f. to the LORD; 29.09
my heart I have f. offered all 29.17
offering f. and joyously to thee. 29.17
besides all that was f. offered. Ez 1.06
who f. offers to go to Jerusalem, 7.13
counselors have f. offered to the 7.15
themselves f. on the day you lead Ps 110.03
He has distributed f., he has given 112.09
One man gives f., yet grows all the Pro 11.24
I will love them f., for my anger Hos 14.04
out and began to talk f. about it, Mk 1.45
and when men have drunk f., then Jn 2.10
things, and to him I speak f.; Ac 26.26
grace which he f. bestowed on us Eph 1.06

FREEWILL
it as their f. offering to the Ex 35.29
Moses all the f. offering which 36.03
bringing him f. offerings every 36.03
a votive offering or a f. offering, Lev 7.16
a vow or as a f. offering which is 22.18
fulfil a vow or as a f. offering, 22.21
you may present for a f. offering; 22.23
and besides all your f. offerings, 23.38
a vow or as a f. offering or at Num 15.03
offerings and your f. offerings, 29.39
your f. offerings, and the firstlings Deu 12.06
or your f. offerings, or the offering 12.17
tribute of a f. offering from your 16.10
houses made their f. offerings, 1Ch 29.06
was over the f. offerings to God, to 2Ch 31.14
besides f. offerings for the house Ez 1.04
made f. offerings for the house of 2.68
one who made a f. offering to the 3.05
and with the f. offerings of the 7.16
the gold are a f. offering to the 8.28
With a f. offering I will sacrifice Ps 54.06
When the prince provides a f. offering, Eze 46.12
offerings as a f. offering to the 46.12
and proclaim f. offerings, publish Amo 4.05

FREQUENT
those days; there was no f. vision. 1Sa 3.01
on f. journeys, in danger from 2Co 11.26
your stomach and your f. ailments. 1Ti 5.23

FRESH
Then Jacob took f. rods of poplar Gen 30.37
crushed a new grain from f. ears, Lev 2.14
parched or f. until this same day, 23.14
grapes or eat grapes, f. or dried. Num 6.03
And he found a f. jawbone of an ass, Ju 15.15
me with seven f. bowstrings which 16.07
her seven f. bowstrings which had 16.08
and f. ears of grain in his sack. 2Ki 4.42
thou dost bring f. hosts against me. Job 10.17
my glory f. with me, and my bow ever 29.20
let his flesh become f. with youth; 33.25
thou hast poured over me f. oil. Ps 92.10
shall obtain f. joy in the LORD, Is 29.19
As a well keeps its water f., Jer 6.07
so she keeps f. her wickedness; 6.07
so that all its f. sprouting Eze 17.09
the sea, the water will become f. 47.08
waters of the sea may become f.; 47.09
and marshes will not become f.; 47.11
they will bear f. fruit every 47.12
new wine is put into f. wineskins, Mt 9.17
but new wine is for f. skins." Mk 2.22
wine must be put into f. wineskins. Lk 5.38
leaven that you may be f. dough, 1Co 5.07
same opening f. water and brackish? Jas 3.11
No more can salt water yield f. 3.12

FRESHETS
torrent-bed, as f. that pass away, Job 6.15

FRESHLY
in her mouth a f. plucked olive Gen 8.11

FRET
F. not yourself because of the Ps 37.01
f. not yourself over him who 37.07
F. not yourself; it tends only 37.08
F. not yourself because of evildoers, Pro 24.19

FRETFUL
with a contentious and f. woman. Pro 21.19

FRIEND
he and his f. Hirah the Adullamite. Gen 38.12
the kid by his f. the Adullamite, 38.20
to face, as a man speaks to his f. Ex 33.11
or your f. who is as your own soul, Deu 13.06
So Boaz said, "Turn aside, f.; Ru 4.01
But Amnon had a f., whose name was 2Sa 13.03
David's f., came into the city, just 15.37
David's f., came to Absalom, Hushai 16.16
"Is this your loyalty to your f.? 16.17
Why did you not go with your f.?" 16.17
of Nathan was priest and king's f.; 1Ki 4.05
the Archite was the king's f. 1Ch 27.33
the descendants of Abraham thy f.? 2Ch 20.07
kindness from a f. forsakes the Job 6.14
fatherless, and bargain over your f. 6.27
I have requited my f. with evil or Ps 7.04
tongue, and does no evil to his f., 15.03
I grieved for my f. or my brother; 35.14
Even my bosom f. in whom I trusted, 41.09
see a thief, you are a f. of his; 50.18
my companion, my familiar f. 55.13
caused lover and f. to shun me; 88.18
and call insight your intimate f.; Pro 7.04
repeats a matter alienates a f. 17.09
A f. loves at all times, and a 17.17
but there is a f. who sticks 18.24
a poor man is deserted by his f. 19.04
every one is a f. to a man who 19.06
will have the king as his f. 22.11

FRIEND (cont.)
Faithful are the wounds of a f.; Pro 27.06
Your f., and your father's f., do not 27.10
is my beloved and this is my f., Sol 5.16
the offspring of Abraham, my f.; Is 41.08
thou art the f. of my youth— Jer 3.04
neighbor and f. hall perish.'" 6.21
neighbor, have no confidence in a f.; Mic 7.05
a f. of tax collectors and sinners!' Mt 11.19
'F., I am doing you no wrong; did you 20.13
'F., how did you get in here without 22.12
said to him, "F., why are you here?" 26.50
a f. of tax collectors and sinners!' Lk 7.34
you who has a f. will go to him at 11.05
'F., lend me three loaves; 11.05
for a f. of mine has arrived on a 11.06
him anything because he is his f., 11.08
may say to you, 'F., go up higher'; 14.10
the f. of the bridegroom, who stands Jn 3.29
"Our f. Lazarus has fallen asleep, 11.11
this man, you are not Caesar's f.; 19.12
and he was called the f. of God. Jas 2.23
wishes to be a f. of the world 4.04

FRIENDLY
"These men are f. with us; let them Gen 34.21
she had given f. welcome to the Heb 11.31

FRIENDS
But thy f. be like the sun as he Ju 5.31
sent part of the spoil to his f., 1Sa 30.26
and to his f., and have not given 2Sa 3.08
male of his kinsmen or his f. 1Ki 16.11
his great men, and his familiar f., 2Ki 10.11
and fetched his f. and his wife Est 5.10
Zeresh and all his f. said to him, 5.14
and all his f. everything that had 6.13
Job's three f. heard of all this Job 2.11
I am a laughingstock to my f.; 12.04
My f. scorn me; my eye pours out 16.20
against his f. to get a share of 17.05
and my close f. have failed me; 19.14
All my intimate f. abhor me, 19.19
O you my f., for the hand of God 19.21
for they are f. with the terrors of 24.17
at Job's three f. because they had 32.03
answer you and your f. with you. 35.04
you and against your two f.; 42.07
Job, when he had prayed for his f.; 42.10
My f. and companions stand aloof Ps 38.11
out his hand against his f., 55.20
neighbor, but the rich has many f. Pro 14.20
and a whisperer separates close f. 16.28
There are f. who pretend to be f., 18.24
Wealth brings many new f., but a poor 19.04
more do his f. go far from him! 19.07
Eat, O f., and drink: drink deeply, O Sol 5.01
have taught to be f. to you? Jer 13.21
to yourself and to all your f. 20.04
be buried, you and all your f. 20.06
say all my familiar f., watching 20.10
'Your trusted f. have deceived you 38.22
all her f. have dealt treacherously Lam 1.02
your trusted f. have set a trap Ob 1.07
you and your f. who sit before you, Zec 3.08
I received in the house of my f. 13.06
Make f. quickly with your accuser, Mt 5.25
And when his f. heard it, they went Mk 3.21
said to him, "Go home to your f., 5.19
the centurion sent f. to him, Lk 7.06
my f., do not fear those who kill 12.04
not invite your f. or your brothers 14.12
together his f. and his neighbors, 15.06
together her f. and neighbors, 15.09
that I might make merry with my f. 15.29
make f. for yourselves by means of 16.09
and brothers and kinsmen and f., 21.16
Pilate became f. with each other 23.12
a man lay down his life for his f. Jn 15.13
You are my f. if you do what I 15.14
but I have called you f., for all 15.15
went to their f. and reported what Ac 4.23
together his kinsmen and close f. 10.24
who were f. of his, sent to him and 19.31
none of his f. should be prevented 24.23
to go to his f. and be cared for. 27.03
The f. greet you. Greet the f., 3Jn 1.15

FRIENDSHIP
have come to me in f. to help me, 1Ch 12.17
when the f. of God was upon my tent; Job 29.04
The f. of the Lord is for those who Ps 25.14
Make no f. with a man given to Pro 22.24
not know that f. with the world is Jas 4.04

FRIGHTEN
shall be none to f. them away. Deu 28.26
to f. and terrify them, in order 2Ch 32.18
For they all wanted to f. us, Neh 6.09
Wilt thou f. a driven leaf and Job 13.25
Terrors f. him on every side, and 18.11
earth; and none will f. them away. Jer 7.33

FRIGHTENED
be not f., neither be dismayed; Jos 1.09
river is turbulent he is not f.; Job 40.23
I was f. and fell upon my face. Dan 8.17
and as they were f. and bowed their Lk 24.05
But they were startled and f., 24.37
near to the boat. They were f., Jn 6.19
and not f. in anything by your Php 1.28

FRIGHTENING
you, and its appearance was f. Dan 2.31
not seem to be f. you with letters 2Co 10.09

FRINGE
and touched the f. of his garment; Mt 9.20
only touch the f. of his garment; 14.36
touch even the f. of his garment; Mk 6.56
and touched the f. of his garment; Lk 8.44

FRINGES
phylacteries broad and their f. long, Mt 23.05

FRO
it went to and f. until the waters Gen 8.07
and go to and f. from gate to gate Ex 32.27
walked once to and f. in the house, 2Ki 4.35
Lord run to and f. throughout the 2Ch 16.09
"From going to and f. on the earth, Job 1.07
"From going to and f. on the earth, 2.02
from men, they swing to and f. 28.04
and all the hills moved to and f. Jer 4.24
Run to and f. through the streets 5.01
and run to and f. among the hedges 49.03
moving to and f. among the living Eze 1.13
living creatures darted to and f., 1.14
of the end. Many shall run to and f., Dan 12.04
they shall run to and f., to seek the Amo 8.12
rush to and f. through the squares; Nah 2.04
so that no one went to and f., Zec 7.14
so that none shall march to and f.; 9.08
tossed to and f. and carried about Eph 4.14

FROGS
plague all your country with f.; Ex 8.02
swarm with f. which shall come up 8.03
the f. shall come up on you and on 8.04
and cause f. to come upon the land 8.05
and the f. came up and covered the 8.06
and brought f. upon the land of 8.07
take away the f. from me and from 8.08
that the f. be destroyed from you 8.09
The f. shall depart from you and 8.11

FROGS (cont.)
to the LORD concerning the f., Ex 8.12
the f. died out of the houses and 8.13
and f., which destroyed them. Ps 78.45
Their land swarmed with f., even in 105.30
prophet, three foul spirits like f.; Rev 16.13

FRONT
three men stood in f. of him. Gen 18.02
had peeled in f. of the flocks in 30.38
the flocks bred in f. of the rods 30.39
maids with their children in f., 33.02
and encamp in f. of Pihahiroth, Ex 14.02
and the sea, in f. of Baalzephon; 14.02
by Pihahiroth, in f. of Baalzephon. 14.09
light upon the space in f. of it. 25.37
double over at the f. of the tent. 26.09
court on the f. to the east shall 27.13
so attach it in f. to the shoulder-pieces 28.25
attach them in f. to the lower 28.27
shall be on the f. of the turban. 28.37
And for the f. to the east, fifty 38.13
it in f. to the shoulder-pieces 39.18
attached them in f. to the lower 39.20
the LORD in f. of the veil of the Lev 4.06
before the LORD in f. of the veil. 4.17
before the LORD, in f. of the altar. 6.14
in f., he set the golden plate, the 8.09
spot is on the back or on the f. 13.55
finger on the f. of the mercy seat, 16.14
give light in f. of the lampstand. Num 8.02
give light in f. of the lampstand, 8.03
came to the f. of the tent of 16.43
blood toward the f. of the tent of 19.04
half of them in f. of Mount Gerizim Jos 8.33
half of them in f. of Mount Ebal, 8.33
cattle and the goods in f. of them. Ju 18.21
on the north in f. of Michmash, 1Sa 14.05
other on the south in f. of Geba. 14.05
his shield-bearer in f. of him. 17.41
and his men in f. of the Wildgoats' 24.02
him both in f. and in the rear, he 2Sa 10.09
The vestibule in f. of the nave of 1Ki 6.03
ten cubits deep in f. of the house. 6.03
the nave in f. of the inner sanctuary, 6.17
in f. of the inner sanctuary, and 6.21
was a porch in f. with pillars, 7.06
back and f., even from the foundation 7.09
removed from the f. of the house, 2Ki 16.14
him both in f. and in the rear, he 1Ch 19.10
The vestibule in f. of the nave of 2Ch 3.04
In f. of the house he made two 3.15
up the pillars in f. of the temple, 3.17
his troops were in f. of Judah, 13.13
that was in f. of the vestibule of 15.08
walked in f. of the court of the Est 2.11
of the city in f. of the king's 4.06
the singers in f., the minstrels Ps 68.25
beside the gates in f. of the town, Pro 8.03
each had the face of a man in f.; Eze 1.10
writing on the f. and on the back, 2.10
direction the f. wheel faced the 10.11
From the f. of the gate at the 40.15
from the inner f. of the lower 40.19
to the outer f. of the inner court, 40.19
the altar was in f. of the temple. 40.47
of the east f. of the temple and 41.14
and in f. of the holy place was 41.21
of wood in f. of the vestibule 41.25
with a passage in f. of them; 42.11
north gate to the f. of the temple; 44.04
drank wine in f. of the thousand. Dan 5.01
his f. into the eastern sea, and his Joe 2.20
And those who were in f. rebuked him, Lk 18.39
and beat him in f. of the tribunal. 18.17
full of eyes in f. and behind: Rev 4.06

FRONTED
thirty chambers f. on the pavement. Eze 40.17

FRONTIER
approach the f. of the sons of Deu 2.19
an altar at the f. of the land of Jos 22.11
out, and were drawn up at the f. 2Ki 3.21
of Moab from the cities on its f., Eze 25.09

FRONTLETS
on your hand or f. between your Ex 13.16
shall be as f. between your eyes. Deu 6.08
shall be as f. between your eyes. 11.18

FROST
hail, and their sycamores with f. Ps 78.47
snow and f., stormy wind fulfilling 148.08
heat by day and the f. by night. Jer 36.30
there shall be neither cold nor f. Zec 14.06

FROZEN
and the broad waters are f. fast. Job 37.10
and the face of the deep is f. 38.30

FRUIT
and f. trees bearing f. in which is Gen 1.11
trees bearing f. in which is their 1.12
and every tree with seed in its f.; 1.29
may eat of the f. of the trees of 3.02
shall not eat of the f. of the tree 3.03
wise, she took of its f. and ate; 3.06
she gave me f. of the tree, and I 3.12
offering of the f. of the ground, 4.03
from you the f. of the womb?" 30.02
and all the f. of the trees which Ex 10.15
the field the f. of your labor. 23.16
shall count their f. as forbidden; Lev 19.23
year all their f. shall be holy, 19.24
fifth year you may eat of their f., 19.25
first day the f. of goodly trees, 23.40
The land will yield its f., and you 25.19
bring forth f. for three years. 25.21
of the field shall yield their f. 26.04
the land shall not yield their f. 26.20
the land or of the f. of the trees, 27.30
bring some of the f. of the land. Num 13.20
and showed them the f. of the land. 13.26
milk and honey, and this is its f. 13.27
some of the f. of the land and Deu 1.25
also bless the f. of your body and 7.13
body and the f. of your ground, 7.13
no rain, and the land yield no f. 11.17
vineyard and has not enjoyed its f.? 20.06
and another man enjoy its f. 20.06
first of all the f. of the ground, 26.02
the first of the f. of the ground, 26.10
Blessed shall be the f. of your body, 28.04
and the f. of your ground, and the 28.04
and the f. of your beasts, the increase 28.04
in the f. of your body, and in the 28.11
and in the f. of your cattle, and in 28.11
and in the f. of your ground, within 28.11
Cursed shall be the f. of your body, 28.18
and the f. of your ground, the increase 28.18
and you shall not use the f. of it. 28.30
eat up the f. of your ground and 28.33
trees and the f. of your ground 28.42
cattle and the f. of your ground, 28.51
bearing poisonous and bitter f., 29.18
in the f. of your body, and in the 30.09
and in the f. of your cattle, and in 30.09
and in the f. of your ground; for the 30.09
but ate of the f. of the land of Jos 5.12
you eat the f. of vineyards and 24.13
leave my sweetness and my good f., Ju 9.11
and summer f. for the young men to 2Sa 16.02
plant vineyards, and eat their f. 2Ki 19.29
root downward, and bear f. upward; 19.30

FRUIT (cont.)
orchards and f. trees in abundance; Neh 9.25
to enjoy its f. and its good gifts, 9.36
fruits of all f. of every tree, 10.35
the f. of every tree, the wine and 10.37
He will give back the f. of his toil, Job 20.18
that yields its f. in its season, Ps 1.03
may its f. be like Lebanon; 72.16
and the f. of their labor to the 78.46
pass along the way pluck its f.? 80.12
They still bring forth f. in old age, 92.14
satisfied with the f. of thy work. 104.13
and ate up the f. of their ground. 105.35
possession of the f. of the peoples' 105.44
the LORD, the f. of the womb a reward. 127.03
You shall eat the f. of the labor 128.02
all hills, f. trees and all cedars! 148.09
shall eat the f. of their way and Pro 1.31
My f. is better than gold, even fine 8.19
The f. of the righteous is a tree 11.30
From the f. of his words a man is 12.14
From the f. of his mouth a good man 13.02
be filled with the f. of his ways, 14.14
good man with the f. of his deeds. 14.14
From the f. of his mouth a man is 18.20
tends a fig tree will eat its f., 27.18
with the f. of her hands she plants 31.16
Give her of the f. of her hands, 31.31
in them all kinds of f. trees. Ecc 2.05
and his f. was sweet to my taste. Sol 2.03
bring for its f. a thousand pieces 8.11
the keepers of the f. two hundred. 8.12
shall eat the f. of their deeds. Is 3.10
and the f. of the land shall be the 4.02
no mercy on the f. of the womb; 13.18
and its f. will be flying serpent. 14.29
for upon your f. and your harvest 16.09
five on the branches of a f. tree, 17.06
and fill the whole world with f. 27.06
be the full f. of the removal of 27.09
the f. harvest will not come. 32.10
plant vineyards, and eat their f. 37.30
root downward, and bear f. upward; 37.31
he shall see the f. of the travail 53.11
his mourners the f. of the lips. 57.18
plant vineyards and eat their f. 65.21
the f. of their devices, because Jer 6.19
the field and the f. of the ground; 7.20
olive tree, fair with goodly f.'; 11.16
us destroy the tree with its f., 11.19
they grow and bring forth f.; 12.02
for it does not cease to bear f. 17.08
according to the f. of his doings. 17.10
according to the f. of your doings, 21.14
plant, and shall enjoy the f. 31.05
according to the f. of his doings; 32.19
and bear f., and become a noble Eze 17.08
may bring forth boughs and bear f., 17.23
its f. was stripped off, its strong 19.12
has consumed its branches and f., 19.14
take away all the f. of your labor, 23.29
they shall eat your f., and they 25.04
of the field shall yield their f., 34.27
and yield your f. to my people 36.08
I will make the f. of the tree and 36.30
will not wither nor their f. fail, 47.12
will bear fresh f. every month, 47.12
Their f. will be for food, and their 47.12
were fair and its f. abundant, Dan 4.12
off its leaves and scatter its f.; 4.14
were fair and its f. abundant, 4.21
Like the first f. on the fig tree, Hos 9.10
is dried up, they shall bear no f. 9.16
luxuriant vine that yields its f. 10.01
The more his f. increased the more 10.01
reap the f. of steadfast love; 10.12
you have eaten the f. of lies. 10.13
we will render the f. of our lips. 14.02
cypress, from me comes your f. 14.08
the tree bears its f., the fig tree Joe 2.22
I destroyed his f. above, and his Amo 2.09
poison and the f. of righteousness 6.12
me: behold, a basket of summer f. 8.01
And I said, "A basket of summer f." 8.02
make gardens and eat their f. 9.14
the f. of my body for the sin of my Mic 6.07
when the summer f. has been gathered, 7.01
for the f. of their doings. 7.13
nor f. be on the vines, the produce Hab 3.17
the vine shall yield its f., Zec 8.12
Bear f. that befits repentance, Mt 3.08
not bear good f. is cut down and 3.10
So, every sound tree bears good f., 7.17
but the bad tree bears evil f. 7.17
A sound tree cannot bear evil f., 7.18
nor can a bad tree bear good f. 7.18
not bear good f. is cut down and 7.19
the tree good, and its f. good; 12.33
make the tree bad, and its f. bad; 12.33
for the tree is known by its f. 12.33
he indeed bears f., and yields, in 13.23
"May no f. ever come from you again!" 21.19
When the season of f. drew near, 21.34
to the tenants, to get his f.; 21.34
again of this f. of the vine until 26.29
the word and accept it and bear f., Mk 4.20
no one ever eat f. from you again." 11.14
some of the f. of the vineyard. 12.02
again of the f. of the vine until 14.25
and blessed is the f. of your womb! Lk 1.42
not bear good f. is cut down and 3.09
"For no good tree bears bad f., 6.43
again does a bad tree bear good f.; 6.43
for each tree is known by its own f. 6.44
and their f. does not mature. 8.14
and bring forth f. with patience. 8.15
he came seeking f. on it and found 13.06
come seeking f. on this fig tree, 13.07
And if it bears f. next year, 13.09
him some of the f. of the vineyard, 20.10
drink of the f. of the vine until 22.18
and gathers f. for eternal life, so Jn 4.36
but if it dies, it bears much f. 12.24
Every branch of mine that bears no f., 15.02
branch that does bear f. he prunes, 15.02
prunes, that it may bear more f. 15.02
branch cannot bear f. by itself, 15.04
him, he it is that bears much f., 15.05
glorified, that you bear much f., 15.08
go and bear f. and that your f. 15.16
order that we may bear f. for God. Rom 7.04
our members to bear f. for death. 7.05
without eating any of its f.? 1Co 9.07
But the f. of the Spirit is love, Gal 5.22
(for the f. of light is found in Eph 5.09
but I seek the f. which increases Php 4.17
it is bearing f. and growing— Col 1.06
bearing f. in every good work and 1.10
the peaceful f. of righteousness Heb 12.11
the f. of lips that acknowledge his 13.15
for the precious f. of the earth, Jas 5.07
and the earth brought forth its f. 5.18
its winter f. when shaken by a Rev 6.13
"The f. for which thy soul longed 18.14
twelve kinds of f., yielding its f. 22.02

FRUITFUL
"Be f. and multiply and fill the Gen 1.22
"Be f. and multiply, and fill the 1.28
and be f. and multiply upon the 8.17
"Be f. and multiply, and fill the 9.01
And you be f. and multiply, bring 9.07
I will make you exceedingly f.; 17.06
and make him f. and multiply him 17.20

FRUITFUL (cont.)

us, and we shall be f. in the land." Gen 26.22
and make you f. and multiply you, 28.03
God Almighty: be f. and multiply; 35.11
God has made me f. in the land of 41.52
and were f. and multiplied exceedingly. 47.27
to me, 'Behold I will make you f., 48.04
Joseph is a f. bough, a f. bough by a 49.22
of Israel were f. and increased Ex 1.07
and make you f. and multiply you, Lev 26.09
And the Lord made his people very f., Ps 105.24
a f. land into a salty waste, 107.34
vineyards, and get a f. yield. 107.37
will be like a f. vine within your 128.03
and of his f. land the LORD will Is 10.18
are taken away from the f. field; 16.10
turned into a f. field, and the f. 29.17
pleasant fields, for the f. vine, 32.12
the wilderness becomes a f. field, 32.15
and the f. field is deemed a forest. 32.15
righteousness abide in the f. field. 32.16
the f. land was a desert, and all Jer 4.26
and they shall be f. and multiply. 23.03
away from the f. land of Moab; 48.33
f. and full of branches by reason Eze 19.10
and they shall increase and be f.; 36.11
from heaven rains and f. seasons, Ac 14.17
flesh, that means f. labor for me. Php 1.22

FRUITLESS

f. trees in late autumn, twice dead, Jud 1.12

FRUITS

of the choice f. of the land in Gen 43.11
and the first f. of my strength, 49.03
of the first f. of your labor, of Ex 23.16
of the first f. of your ground you 23.19
the first f. of wheat harvest, and 34.22
of the first f. of your ground you 34.26
of first f. you may bring them to Lev 2.12
offering of first f. to the LORD, 2.14
of your first f. crushed new grain 2.14
of the first f. of your harvest to 23.10
leaven, as first f. to the LORD. 23.17
of the first f. as a wave offering 23.20
vineyard, and gather in its f.; 25.03
the first f. of what they give to Num 18.12
The first ripe f. of all that is in 18.13
"On the day of the first f., when 28.26
The first f. of your grain, of your Deu 18.04
with the choicest f. of the sun, 33.14
of raisins, a hundred of summer f., 2Sa 16.01
man of God bread of the first f., 2Ki 4.42
in abundance the first f. of grain, 2Ch 31.05
bring the first f. of our ground Neh 10.35
and the first f. of all fruit of 10.35
the first f., and the tithes, to 12.44
times, and for the first f. 13.31
strangers plunder the f. of his toil! Ps 109.11
with the first f. of all your Pro 3.09
those who love it will eat its f. 18.21
pomegranates with all choicest f., Sol 4.13
garden, and eat its choicest f. 4.16
over our doors are all choice f., 7.13
LORD, the first f. of his harvest. Jer 2.03
to enjoy its f. and its good 2.07
gather wine and summer f. and oil, 40.10
wine and summer f. in great 40.12
your summer f. and your vintage 48.32
by want of the f. of the field. Lam 4.09
of all the first f. of all kinds, Eze 44.30
not destroy the f. of your soil; Mal 3.11
You will know them by their f. Mt 7.16
Thus you will know them by their f. 7.20
give him the f. in their seasons." 21.41
to a nation producing the f. of it. 21.43
Bear f. that befit repentance, and Lk 3.08
have the first f. of the Spirit, Rom 8.23
dough offered as first f. is holy, 11.16
the first f. of those who have 1Co 15.20
his own order: Christ the first f., 15.23
filled with the f. of righteousness Php 1.11
a kind of first f. of his creatures Jas 1.18
reason, full of mercy and good f., 3.17
as first f. for God and the Lamb, Rev 14.04

FRUSTRATE

against them to f. their purpose, Ez 4.05

FRUSTRATED

us and that God had f. their plan, Neh 4.15

FRUSTRATES

He f. the devices of the crafty, so Job 5.12
he f. the plans of the peoples. Ps 33.10
who f. the omens of liars, and makes Is 44.25

FRUSTRATION

and f., in all that you undertake Deu 28.20

FUEL

will be burned as f. for the fire. Is 9.05
people are like f. for the fire; 9.19
Lebanon would not suffice for f., 40.16
Then it becomes f. for a man; 44.15
Lo, it is given the fire for f.; Eze 15.04
I have given to the fire for f., 15.06
You shall be f. for the fire; 21.32

FUGITIVE

you shall be a f. and a wanderer on Gen 4.12
I shall be a f. and a wanderer on 4.14
let him be a f. until death; let no Pro 28.17
the outcasts, betray not the f.; Is 16.03
meet the f. with bread, O inhabitants 21.14
on that day a f. will come to you Eze 24.26
mouth will be opened to the f., 24.27
me the evening before the f. came; 33.22

FUGITIVES

He has made his sons f., and his Num 21.29
"You are f. of Ephraim, you Gileadites, Ju 12.04
when any of the f. of Ephraim said, 12.05
his f. flee to Zoar, to Eglathshelishiyah. Is 15.05
shall not return, except some f." Jer 44.14
of Heshbon f. stop without strength 48.45
him, with none to gather the f. 49.05
So they became f. and wanderers; Lam 4.15
of the ways to cut off his f.; Ob 1.14

FULFIL

and I will f. the oath which I Gen 26.03
I will f. the number of your days. Ex 23.26
to f. a vow or as a freewill Lev 22.21
to f. a vow or as a freewill Num 15.03
to f. a vow, or for peace offerings 15.08
he spoken, and will he not f. it? 23.19
On that day I will f. against Eli 1Sa 3.12
the LORD that he might f. his word. 1Ki 12.15
that the LORD might f. his word, 2Ch 10.15
to f. the word of the LORD by the 36.21
kept sabbath, to f. seventy years. 36.21
my petition and f. my request, Est 5.08
you number the months that they f., Job 39.02
desire, and f. all your plans! Ps 20.04
May the LORD f. all your petitions! 20.05
The LORD will f. his purpose for me; 138.08
and he shall f. all my purpose'; Is 44.28
and I will f. to you my promise and Jer 29.10
when I will f. the promise I made 33.14
Behold I will f. my words against 39.16
they expect him to f. their word. Eze 13.06
up in order to f. the vision; Dan 11.14
f. your vows, for never again shall Nah 1.15
took place to f. what the Lord had Mt 1.22

FULFIL (cont.)

This was to f. what the Lord had Mt 2.15
for us to f. all righteousness. 3.15
not to abolish them but to f. them. 5.17
This was to f. what was spoken by 8.17
This was to f. what was spoken by 12.17
This was to f. what was spoken by 13.35
This took place to f. what was 21.04
vengeance, to f. all that is written. Lk 21.22
It is to f. the word that is Jn 15.25
This was to f. the word which he 18.09
This was to f. the word which Jesus 18.32
This was to f. the scripture. 19.24
said (to f. the scripture), "I 19.28
and so f. the law of Christ. Gal 6.02
"See that you f. the ministry which Col 4.17
and may f. every good resolve and 2Th 1.11
of an evangelist, f. your ministry. 2Ti 4.05
If you really f. the royal law, Jas 2.08

FULFILLED

When her days to be delivered were f., Gen 25.24
concerning you have been f. for you, Jos 23.15
When your days are f. and you lie 2Sa 7.12
his hand has f. what he promised 1Ki 8.15
Now the LORD has f. his promise 8.20
with thy hand hast f. it this day. 8.24
When your days are f. to go to be 1Ch 17.11
to David my father be now f., 2Ch 1.09
his hand has f. what he promised 6.04
Now the LORD has f. his promise 6.10
with thy hand hast f. it this day. 6.15
and thou hast f. thy promise, for Neh 9.08
half of my kingdom, it shall be f." Est 5.06
half of my kingdom, it shall be f." 7.02
is your request? It shall be f." 9.12
but a desire f. is a tree of life. Pro 13.12
A desire f. is sweet to the soul; 13.19
and have f. it with your hands, Jer 44.25
Behold, it comes and it will be f., Eze 21.07
Immediately the word was f. upon Dan 4.33
Then was f. what was spoken by the Mt 2.17
spoken by the prophets might be f., 2.23
by the prophet Isaiah might be f.: 4.14
With them indeed is f. the prophecy 13.14
then should the scriptures be f., 26.54
of the prophets might be f." 26.56
Then was f. what had been spoken by 27.09
"The time is f., and the kingdom of Mk 1.15
But let the scriptures be f." 14.49
scripture was f. which says, "He * 15.28
which will be f. in their time. Lk 1.20
has been f. in your hearing. 4.21
the times of the Gentiles are f. 21.24
it until it is f. in the kingdom 22.16
this scripture must be f. in me, 22.37
prophets and the psalms must be f." 24.44
by the prophet Isaiah might be f.: Jn 12.38
it is that the scripture may be f., 13.18
that the scripture might be f. 17.12
may have my joy f. in themselves. 17.13
that the scripture might be f., 19.36
"Brethren, the scripture had to be f., Ac 1.16
Christ should suffer, he thus f. 3.18
when they had f. their mission, 12.25
f. these by condemning him. 13.27
And when they had f. all that was 13.29
this he has f. to us their children 13.33
God for the work which they had f. 14.26
would be f. and the offering 21.26
of the law might be f. in us, Rom 8.04
loves his neighbor has f. the law. 13.08
For the whole law is f. in one word, Gal 5.14
and the scripture was f. which says, Jas 2.23
servants the prophets, should be f. Rev 10.07
until the words of God shall be f. 17.17

FULFILLING

thus f. the word of the LORD which 1Ki 2.27
frost, stormy wind f. his command! Ps 148.08
law did not succeed in f. that law. Rom 9.31
therefore love is the f. of the law. 13.10

FULFILMENT

and for the f. of thy righteous Ps 119.123
at hand, and the f. of every vision. Eze 12.23
would be a f. of what was spoken Lk 1.45
is written about me has its f." 22.37

FULFILS

to God who f. his purpose for me. Ps 57.02
He f. the desire of all who fear 145.19

FULL

of Siddim was f. of bitumen pits; Gen 14.10
For the f. price let him give it to 23.09
age, an old man and f. of years, 25.08
to his people, old and f. of days; 35.29
up the seven plump and f. ears. 41.07
growing on one stalk, f. and good; 41.22
his sack, our money in f. weight; 43.21
fleshpots and ate bread to the f.; Ex 16.03
and in the morning bread to the f., 16.08
the fire shall make f. restitution. 22.06
it, he shall make f. restitution. 22.14
he shall restore it in f., and shall Lev 6.05
take a censer f. of coals of fire 16.12
the land become f. of wickedness. 19.29
seven f. weeks shall they be, 23.15
for a f. year he shall have the 25.29
is not redeemed within a f. year, 25.30
you shall eat your bread to the f., 26.05
shall stand at your f. valuation; 27.17
he shall make f. restitution for Num 5.07
both of them f. of fine flour mixed 7.13
dish of ten shekels, f. of incense; 7.14
both of them f. of fine flour mixed 7.19
dish of ten shekels, f. of incense; 7.20
both of them f. of fine flour mixed 7.25
dish of ten shekels, f. of incense; 7.26
both of them f. of fine flour mixed 7.31
dish of ten shekels, f. of incense; 7.32
both of them f. of fine flour mixed 7.37
dish of ten shekels, f. of incense; 7.38
both of them f. of fine flour mixed 7.43
dish of ten shekels, f. of incense; 7.44
both of them f. of fine flour mixed 7.49
dish of ten shekels, f. of incense; 7.50
both of them f. of fine flour mixed 7.55
dish of ten shekels, f. of incense; 7.56
both of them f. of fine flour mixed 7.61
dish of ten shekels, f. of incense; 7.62
both of them f. of fine flour mixed 7.67
dish of ten shekels, f. of incense; 7.68
both of them f. of fine flour mixed 7.73
dish of ten shekels, f of incense; 7.74
both of them f. of fine flour mixed 7.79
dish of ten shekels, f. of incense; 7.80
f. of incense, weighing ten shekels 7.86
they shall come to a f. end. 14.35
me his house f. of silver and gold, 22.18
me his house f. of silver and gold. 24.13
land of Canaan in its f. extent), 34.02
and houses f. of all good things, Deu 6.11
plant, and when you eat and are f., 6.11
And you shall eat and be f., and you 8.10
lest, when you have eaten and are f., 8.12
cattle, and you shall eat and be f. 11.15
father and her mother a f. month; 21.13
A f. and just weight you shall have, 25.15
a f. and just measure you shall have; 25.15
eaten and are f. and grown fat, 31.20
and f. of the blessing of the LORD, 33.23
son of Nun was f. of the spirit of 34.09
Now the house was f. of men and Ju 16.27

FULL (cont.)
I went away f., and the LORD has Ru 1.21
and a f. reward be given you by the 2.12
Those who were f. have hired 1Sa 2.05
were given in f. number to the 18.27
fell at once f. length upon the 28.20
and one f. line to be spared. 2Sa 8.02
After two f. years Absalom had 13.23
dwelt two f. years in Jerusalem, 14.28
was a plot of ground f. of lentils; 23.11
and he was f. of wisdom, understanding, 1Ki 7.14
this dry stream-bed f. of pools.' 2Ki 3.16
and when one is f., set it aside." 4.04
When the vessels were f., she said 4.06
from it his lap f. of wild gourds, 4.39
mountain was f. of horses and 6.17
drew his bow with his f. strength, 9.24
was a plot of ground f. of barley, 1Ch 11.13
to Hebron with f. intent to make 12.38
give it to me at its f. price— 21.22
but I will buy it for the f. price; 21.24
When David was old and f. of days, 23.01
f. of days, riches, and honor; 29.28
But Jehoiada grew old and f. of days, 2Ch 24.15
to these men in f. and without Ez 6.08
it be done in f. for the house of 7.23
of houses f. of all good things, Neh 9.25
the Jew gave f. written authority, Est 9.29
and the f. account of the high 10.02
and I am f. of tossing till the Job 7.04
and a man f. of talk be vindicated? 11.02
is of few days, and f. of trouble. 14.01
It will be paid in f. before his 15.32
His bones are f. of youthful vigor, 20.11
belly to the f. God will send his 20.23
One dies in f. prosperity, being 21.23
his body f. of fat and the marrow 21.24
For I am f. of words, the spirit 32.18
on your table was f. of fatness. 36.16
"But you are f. of the judgment on 36.17
died, an old man, and f. of days. 42.17
whose right hands are f. of bribes. Ps 26.10
voice of the LORD is f. of majesty. 29.04
the earth is f. of the steadfast 33.05
the river of God is f. of water; 65.09
of the land are f. of the habitations 74.20
the LORD heard, he was f. of wrath; 78.21
he was f. of wrath, and he utterly 78.59
them tears to drink in f. measure. 80.05
at the f. moon, on our feast day. 81.03
For my soul is f. of troubles and 88.03
thou art f. of wrath against thy 89.38
they are ever f. of sap and green, 92.14
the earth is f. of thy creatures. 104.24
F. of honor and majesty is his work, 111.03
is f. of thy steadfast love; teach me 119.64
man who has his quiver f. of them! 127.05
youth be like plants f. grown, 144.12
may our garners be f., providing 144.13
brighter and brighter until f. day. Pro 4.18
at f. moon he will come home. 7.20
than a house f. of feasting with 17.01
his mouth will be f. of gravel. 20.17
A fool gives f. vent to his anger, 29.11
lest I be f., and deny thee, and say, 30.09
to the sea, but the sea is not f.; Ecc 1.07
All things are f. of weariness; 1.08
For all his days are f. of pain, 2.23
than two hands f. of toil and a 4.06
the hearts of men are f. of evil, 9.03
If the clouds are f. of rain, they 11.03
listen; your hands are f. of blood. Is 1.15
harlot, she that was f. of justice! 1.21
they are f. of diviners from the 2.06
the whole earth is f. of his glory." 6.03
will make a f. end, as decreed, in 10.23
earth shall be f. of the knowledge 11.09
houses will be f. of howling 13.21
waters of Dibon are f. of blood; 15.09
you who are f. of shoutings, tumultuous 22.02
valleys were f. of chariots, 22.07
of fat things f. of marrow, of wine 25.06
will be the f. fruit of the 27.09
For all tables are f. of vomit, 28.08
his lips are f. of indignation, and 30.27
shall come upon you in f. measure, 47.09
they are f. of the wrath of the 51.20
among those in f. vigor we are 59.10
a wind too f. for this comes for me Jer 4.12
yet I will not make a f. end. 4.27
When I fed them to the f., 5.07
and destroy, but make not a f. end; 5.10
I will not make a f. end of you. 5.18
Like a basket f. of birds, their 5.27
their houses are f. of treachery, 5.27
Therefore I am f. of the wrath of 6.11
they are in f. cry after you; 12.06
For the land is f. of adulterers; 23.10
I will make a f. end of all the 30.11
of you I will not make a f. end. 30.11
the Rechabites pitchers f. of wine, 35.05
and the earth is f. of your cry; 46.12
I will make a f. end of all the 46.28
of you I will not make a f. end. 46.28
Chaldeans is f. of guilt against 51.05
the city that was f. of people! Lam 1.01
The LORD gave f. vent to his wrath, 4.11
their rims were f. of eyes round Eze 1.18
the land is f. of bloody crimes 7.23
and the city is f. of violence, 7.23
the land is f. of blood, and the 9.09
and the city f. of injustice; 9.09
the court was f. of the brightness 10.04
the wheels were f. of eyes round 10.12
thou make a f. end of the remnant 11.13
tall and arrived at f. maidenhood; 16.07
fruitful and f. of branches by 19.10
wilderness, to make a f. end of them. 20.13
them or make a f. end of them in 20.17
you infamous one, f. of tumult. 22.05
warriors clothed in f. armor, 23.12
f. of wisdom and perfect in beauty. 28.12
the watercourses will be f. of you. 32.06
of the valley; it was f. of bones. 37.01
all of them clothed in f. armor, 38.04
measured a f. reed of six long 41.08
Then Nebuchadnezzar was f. of fury, Dan 3.19
have reached their f. measure, 8.23
at all, for the f. three weeks. 10.03
but when they had fed to the f., Hos 13.06
tree and vine give their f. yield. Joe 2.22
floors shall be f. of grain, 2.24
tread, for the wine press is f. 3.13
as a cart f. of sheaves presses Amo 2.13
Your rich men are f. of violence; Mic 6.12
he will make a f. end of his Nah 1.08
He will make a f. end; he will not 1.09
all f. of lies and booty—no end 3.01
and the earth was f. of his praise. Hab 3.03
for a f., yea, sudden end he will Zep 1.18
city shall be f. of boys and girls Zec 8.05
and be f. like a bowl, drenched like 9.15
Bring the f. tithes into the storehouse, Mal 3.10
whole body will be f. of light; Mt 6.22
whole body will be f. of darkness. 6.23
when it was f., men drew it ashore 13.48
twelve baskets f. of the broken 14.20
seven baskets f. of the broken 15.37
inside they are f. of extortion 23.25
within they are f. of dead men's 23.27
within you are f. of hypocrisy and 23.28
then the f. grain in the ear. Mk 4.28
twelve baskets f. of broken pieces 6.43
pieces left over, seven baskets f. 8.08

FULL (cont.)
many baskets f. of broken pieces Mk 8.19
many baskets f. of broken pieces 8.20
filling a sponge f. of vinegar, 15.36
And Jesus, f. of the Holy Spirit, Lk 4.01
there came a man f. of leprosy; 5.12
"Woe to you that are f. now, 6.25
your whole body is f. of light; 11.34
sound, your body is f. of darkness. 11.34
your whole body is f. of light, 11.36
inside you are f. of extortion and 11.39
man named Lazarus, f. of sores, 16.20
f. of grace and truth; we once beheld Jn 1.14
therefore this joy of mine is now f. 3.29
you, and that your joy may be f. 15.11
receive, that your joy may be f. 16.24
A bowl f. of vinegar stood there; 19.29
put a sponge f. of the vinegar on 19.29
boat, dragging the net f. of fish, 21.08
f. of large fish, a hundred and 21.11
wilt make me f. of gladness with Ac 2.28
f. of the Spirit and of wisdom, whom 6.03
a man f. of faith and of the Holy 6.05
And Stephen, f. of grace and power, 6.08
But he, f. of the Holy Spirit, gazed 7.55
She was f. of good works and acts 9.36
f. of the Holy Spirit and of faith. 11.24
f. of all deceit and villainy, will 13.10
saw that the city was f. of idols. 17.16
F. of envy, murder, strife, deceit, Rom 1.29
"Their mouth is f. of curses and 3.14
more will their f. inclusion mean! 11.12
until the f. number of the Gentiles 11.25
how it is f. time now for you to 13.11
you yourselves are f. of goodness, 15.14
not making f. use of my right in 1Co 9.18
but that with f. courage now as Php 1.20
being in f. accord and of one mind. 2.02
I have received f. payment, and more 4.18
Holy Spirit and with f. conviction. 1Th 1.05
sure and worthy of f. acceptance, 1Ti 1.15
sure and worthy of f. acceptance. 4.09
realizing the f. assurance of hope Heb 6.11
a true heart in f. assurance of 10.22
steadfastness have its f. effect, Jas 1.04
a restless evil, f. of deadly posion. 3.08
f. of mercy and good fruits, without 3.17
They have eyes f. of adultery, 2Pe 2.14
for, but may win a f. reward. 2Jn 1.08
the sun shining in f. strength. Rev 1.16
f. of eyes in front and behind: 4.06
are f. of eyes all round and within, 4.08
with golden bowls f. of incense, 5.08
the f. moon became like blood, 6.12
golden bowls f. of the wrath of 15.07
beast which was f. of blasphemous 17.03
a golden cup f. of abominations 17.04
the seven bowls f. of the seven 21.09

FULLER
as no f. on earth could bleach them. Mk 9.03

FULLER'S
is on the highway to the f. field. 2Ki 18.17
on the highway to the f. field, Is 7.03
on the highway to the f. field. 36.02

FULLERS'
a refiner's fire and like f. soap; Mal 3.02

FULL-GROWN
sin when it is f. brings forth Jas 1.15

FULLY
spirit and has followed me f., Num 14.24
your husband has been f. told me, Ru 2.11
that all Israel f. expected me to 1Ki 2.15
sons of men is f. set to do evil. Ecc 8.11
one when he is f. taught will be Lk 6.40
f. armed, guards his own palace, his 11.21
and could not f. straighten herself. 13.11
for my time has not yet f. come. Jn 7.08
f. convinced that God was able to Rom 4.21
every one be f. convinced in his 14.05
Illyricum I have f. preached the 15.19
know in part; then I shall understand f., 1Co 13.12
even as I have been f. understood. 13.12
I hope you will understand f., 2Co 1.13
But when the time had f. come, Gal 4.04
f. pleasing to him, bearing fruit in Col 1.10
to make the word of God f. known, 1.25
mature and f. assured in all the 4.12
strength to proclaim the word f., 2Ti 4.17
set your hope f. upon the grace 1Pe 1.13
you were once for all f. informed, Jud 1.05
harvest of the earth is f. ripe. Rev 14.15

FULNESS
offer from the f. of your harvest Ex 22.29
and as the f. of the wine press. Num 18.27
best gifts of the earth and its f., Deu 33.16
In the f. of his sufficiency he Job 20.22
in thy presence there is f. of joy, Ps 16.11
is the LORD's and the f. thereof, Ps 24.01
And from his f. have we all received, Jn 1.16
come in the f. of the blessing of Rom 15.29
as a plan for the f. of time, to unite Eph 1.10
the f. of him who fills all in all. 1.23
be filled with all the f. of God. 3.19
of the stature of the f. of Christ; 4.13
For in him all the f. of God was Col 1.19
him the whole f. of deity dwells 2.09
you have come to f. of life in him, 2.10

FUNCTION
members do not have the same f., Rom 12.04

FURIOUS
For jealousy makes a man f., and he will Pro 6.34
in f. anger and a flame of devouring Is 30.30
and f. against all their host, he 34.02
and with f. chastisements—I, the Eze 5.15
the king was angry and very f., Dan 2.12
Nebuchadnezzar in f. rage commanded 3.13
was in a f. rage, and he sent and Mt 2.16

FURIOUSLY
son of Nimshi; for he drives f." 2Ki 9.20

FURLONGS
time was many f. distant from the Mt 14.24

FURNACE
went up like the smoke of a f. Gen 19.28
you forth out of the iron f., Deu 4.20
from the midst of the iron f.). 1Ki 8.51
refined in a f. on the ground, Ps 12.06
smoke, and my bones burn like a f. 102.03
and the f. is for gold, and the LORD Pro 17.03
and the f. is for gold, and a man is 27.21
and whose f. is in Jerusalem. Is 31.09
tried you in the f. of affliction. 48.10
from the iron f., saying, Listen to Jer 11.04
tin and iron and lead in the f., Eze 22.18
iron and lead and tin into a f., 22.20
As silver is melted in a f., 22.22
be cast into a burning fiery f." Dan 3.06
be cast into a burning fiery f. 3.11
be cast into a burning fiery f.; 3.15
us from the burning fiery f.; and he will 3.17
He ordered the f. heated seven 3.19
them into the burning fiery f. 3.20
cast into the burning fiery f. 3.21
was strict and the f. very hot, 3.22
bound into the burning fiery f. 3.23
of the burning fiery f. and said, 3.26
and throw them into the f. of fire; Mt 13.42
and throw them into the f. of fire; 13.50

FURNACE (cont.)
burnished bronze, refined as in a f., Rev 1.15
smoke like the smoke of a great f., 9.02

FURNACES
all, above the Tower of the F., Neh 12.38

FURNISH
you shall f. him liberally out of Deu 15.14
prince's duty to f. the burnt Eze 45.17

FURNISHED
a large upper room f. and ready; Mk 14.15
show you a large upper room f.; Lk 22.12

FURNISHES
God who richly f. us with everything 1Ti 6.17

FURNISHINGS
is thereon, and all the f. of the tent, Ex 31.07
the testimony, and over all its f., Num 1.50
the tabernacle and all its f., 1.50
of all the f. of the tent of 3.08
and all the f. of the sanctuary, as 4.15
and consecrated it with all its f., 7.01
upon the tent. and upon all the f., 19.18

FURNITURE
the tabernacle, and of all its f., Ex 25.09
and consecrate it and all its f.; 40.09
of them were appointed over the f., 1Ch 9.29
the household f. of Tobiah out of Neh 13.08

FURROW
Can you bind him in the f. with ropes, Job 39.10

FURROW'S
as it were half a f. length in an 1Sa 14.14

FURROWS
and its f. have wept together; Job 31.38
Thou waterest its f. abundantly, Ps 65.10
upon my back; they made long their f." 129.03
weeds in the f. of the field. Hos 10.04
stone heaps on the f. of the field. 12.11

FURTHER
shall speak f. to the people, and say, Deu 20.08
on from there f. and come to the 1Sa 10.03
What f. right have I, then, to cry to 2Sa 19.28
and f. reported to the king, "All 2Ch 34.16
And what f. is your request? It shall Est 9.12
twice, but I will proceed no f." Job 40.05
the wicked; do not f. his evil plot! Ps 140.08
violence, and provoke me f. to anger? Eze 8.17
But she carried her harlotry f.; 23.14
Why trouble the Teacher any f.?" Mk 5.35
But Jesus made no f. answer, 15.05
"What f. testimony do we need? Lk 22.71
were going. He appeared to be going f., 24.28
may spread no f. among the people, Ac 4.17
And when they had f. threatened 4.21
But if you seek anything f., 19.39
But, to detain you no f., I beg you 24.04
and f. Isaiah says, "The root of Rom 15.12
but that we would be f. clothed, 2Co 5.04
to f. the faith of God's elect and Tit 1.01
what f. need would there have been Heb 7.11
entreat that no f. messages be 12.19

FURTHERED
but a little they f. the disaster. Zec 1.15

FURTHERMORE
F. the LORD was angry with me on Deu 4.21
"F. the LORD said to me, 'I have 9.13
and f. he took the high places 2Ch 17.06

FURY
until your brother's f. turns away; Gen 27.44
thou sendest forth thy f., it consumes Ex 15.07
then I will walk contrary to you in f., Lev 26.28
in anger and f. and great wrath, Deu 29.28
to him, Haman was filled with f. Est 3.05
terrify them in his f., saying, Ps 2.05
up against the f. of my enemies; 7.06
and the rod of his f. will fail. Pro 22.08
of my anger, the staff of my f.! Is 10.05
has ceased, the insolent f. ceased! 14.04
a man of war he stirs up his f.; 42.13
because of the f. of the oppressor, 51.13
where is the f. of the oppressor? 51.13
wrapped himself in f. as a mantle. 59.17
stormwind, to render his anger in f., 66.15
and in f., and in great wrath. Jer 21.05
he has poured out his f. like fire. Lam 2.04
I will vent my f. upon them and Eze 5.13
when I spend my f. upon them. 5.13
judgments on you in anger and f., 5.15
thus I will spend my f. upon them. 6.12
So will I satisfy my f. on you, 16.42
But the vine was plucked up in f., 19.12
my hands, and I will satisfy my f.; 21.17
that they may deal with you in f. 23.25
I have satisfied my f. upon you. 24.13
Then Nebuchadnezzar was full of f., Dan 3.19
with great f. to exterminate and 11.44
Thou didst bestride the earth in f., Hab 3.12
filled with f. and discussed with Lk 6.11
and in raging f. against them, I Ac 26.11
wickedness, there will be wrath and f. Rom 2.08
and a f. of fire which will consume Heb 10.27
the cup of the f. of his wrath. Rev 16.19
press of the f. of the wrath of 19.15

FUTILE
but they became f. in their thinking Rom 1.21
the thoughts of the wise are f. 1Co 3.20
your faith is f. and you are still 15.17
for they are unprofitable and f. Tit 3.09
from the f. ways inherited from 1Pe 1.18

FUTILITY
for the creation was subjected to f., Rom 8.20
do, in the f. of their minds; Eph 4.17

FUTURE
with you, for all f. generations: Gen 9.12
and hast shown me f. generations, 2Sa 7.19
and hast shown me f. generations, 1Ch 17.17
you may gain wisdom for the f. Pro 19.20
Surely there is a f., and your hope 23.18
if you find it, there will be a f., 24.14
for the evil man has no f.; the lamp 24.20
evil, to give you a f. and a hope. Jer 29.11
There is hope for your f., says the LORD, 31.17
and self-control and f. judgment, Ac 24.25
present or the f., all are yours; 1Co 3.22
a good foundation for the f., so that 1Ti 6.19
Isaac invoked f. blessings on Jacob Heb 11.20

G

GAAL
And G. the son of Ebed moved into Ju 9.26
And G. the son of Ebed said, "Who is 9.28
the words of G. the son of Ebed, 9.30
G. the son of Ebed and his kinsmen 9.31
And G. the son of Ebed went out and 9.35
And when G. saw the men, he said to 9.36
G. spoke again and said, "Look, men 9.37
And G. went out at the head of the 9.39
Zebul drove out G. and his kinsmen, 9.41

GAASH
Ephraim, north of the mountain of G. Jos 24.30
of Ephraim, north of Mount G. Ju 2.09
Hiddai of the brooks of G., 2Sa 23.30
Hurai of the brooks of G., Abiel 1Ch 11.32

GABBAI
And after him G., Sallai, nine Neh 11.08

GABBATHA
The Pavement, and in Hebrew, G. Jn 19.13

GABRIEL
"G., make this man understand the Dan 8.16
the man G., whom I had seen in the 9.21
"I am G., who stand in the presence Lk 1.19
month the angel G. was sent from 1.26

GAD
"Good fortune!" so she called his name G. Gen 30.11
Zilpah, Leah's maid: G. and Asher. 35.26
The sons of G.: Ziphion, Haggi, Shuni, 46.16
Raiders shall raid G., but he shall 49.19
Dan and Naphtali, G. and Asher. Ex 1.04
from G., Eliasaph the son of Deuel; Num 1.14
Of the people of G., their generations, 1.24
of the tribe of G. was forty-five 1.25
Then the tribe of G., the leader 2.14
the people of G. being Eliasaph 2.14
the leader of the men of G.: 7.42
of the men of G. was Eliasaph the 10.20
from the tribe of G., Geuel the son 13.15
The sons of G. according to their 26.15
of the sons of G. according to 26.18
and the sons of G. had a very 32.01
So the sons of G. and the sons of 32.02
to the sons of G. and to the sons 32.06
And the sons of G. and the sons of 32.25
"If the sons of G. and the sons of 32.29
And the sons of G. and the sons of 32.31
to the sons of G. and to the sons 32.33
And the sons of G. built Dibon, 32.34
of the sons of G. by their fathers' 34.14
G., Asher, Zebulun, Dan, and Naphtali. Deu 27.13
And of G. he said, "Blessed be he 33.20
"Blessed be he who enlarges G.! 33.20
G. couches like a lion, he tears the 33.20
and the sons of G. and the half Jos 4.12
and G. and Reuben and half the 18.07
in Gilead, from the tribe of G., 20.08
the tribe of G., and the tribe of 21.07
and out of the tribe of G., Ramoth 21.38
to the land of G. and Gilead. 1Sa 13.07
Then the prophet G. said to David, 22.05
the valley, toward G. and on to Jazer. 2Sa 24.05
of the LORD came to the prophet G., 24.11
So G. came to David and told him, 24.13
Then David said to G., "I am in 24.14
And G. came that day to David, and 24.18
Benjamin, Naphtali, G., and Asher. 1Ch 2.02
The sons of G. dwelt over against 5.11
tribes of Reuben, G., and Zebulun. 6.63
and out of the tribe of G.: Ramoth 6.80
And the LORD spoke to G., David's seer, 21.09
So G. came to David and said to him, 21.11
Then David said to G., "I am in 21.13
LORD commanded G. to say to David 21.18
in the Chronicles of G. the seer, 29.29
of David and of G. the king's seer 2Ch 29.25
How lightly you g. about, changing Jer 2.36
then has Milcom dispossessed G., 49.01
side to the west, G., one portion. Eze 48.27
the territory of G. to the south, 48.28
the gate of G., the gate of Asher, 48.34
twelve thousand of the tribe of G., Rev 7.05

GADARENES
side, to the country of the G., Mt 8.28

GADDI
Manasseh), G. the son of Susi; Num 13.11

GADDIEL
of Zebulun, G. the son of Sodi; Num 13.10

GADDING
g. about from house to house, and 1Ti 5.13

GADFLY
but a g. from the north has come Jer 46.20

GADI
the son of G. came up from Tirzah 2Ki 15.14
the son of G. began to reign over 15.17

GADITE
of Nathan of Zobah, Bani the G., 2Sa 23.36

GADITES
Reubenites and the G. the territory Deu 3.12
Reubenites and the G. I gave the 3.16
and Ramoth in Gilead for the G., 4.43
the G., and the half-tribe of the 29.08
the G., and the half-tribe of Manasseh Jos 1.12
Reubenites and the G. and the 12.06
Reubenites and the G. received 13.08
also to the tribe of the G., 13.24
inheritance of the G. according to 13.28
and the G., and the half-tribe of 22.01
Reubenites and the G. and the half-tribe 22.09
Reubenites and the G. and the half-tribe 22.10
Reubenites and the G. and the half-tribe 22.11
Reubenites and the G. and the half-tribe 22.13
the G., and the half-tribe of 22.15
the G., and the half-tribe of 22.21
us and you, you Reubenites and G.; 22.25
Reubenites and the G. and the 22.30
Reubenites and the G. and the 22.31
Reubenites and the G. in the land 22.32
Reubenites and the G. were settled. 22.33
Reubenites and the G. called the 22.34
the G., and the Reubenites, and the 2Ki 10.33
the G., and the half-tribe of 1Ch 5.18
the G., and the half-tribe of 5.26
From the G. there went over to 12.08
These G. were officers of the army, 12.14
Reubenites and G. and the half-tribe 12.37
the G., and the half-tribe of the 26.32

GAD'S
So David went up at G. word, as the LORD 2Sa 24.19
So David went up at G. word, which he had 1Ch 21.19

GAHAM
bore Tebah, G., Tahash, and Maacah. Gen 22.24

GAHAR
the sons of G., the sons of Reaiah, Ez 2.47
sons of Giddel, the sons of G., Neh 7.49

GAILY
for yourself g. decked shrines, Eze 16.16

GAIN
ways, but turned aside after g.; 1Sa 8.03
or is it g. to him if you make your Job 22.03
What could I g. from the strength 30.02
man greedy for g. curses and Ps 10.03
to thy testimonies, and not to g.! 119.36
ways of all who get g. by violence; Pro 1.19
for the g. from it is better than 3.14
is better than g. from silver and 3.14
attentive, that you may g. insight; 4.01
to life, the g. of the wicked to sin. 10.16
for unjust g. makes trouble for 15.27
that you may g. wisdom for the 19.20
understanding, and he will g. knowledge. 19.25

GAIN (cont.)
hates unjust g. will prolong his Pro 28.16
and he will have no lack of g. 31.11
What does man g. by all the toil at Ecc 1.03
What g. has the worker from his 3.09
wealth, with g.: this also is vanity. 5.10
and what g. has their owner but to 5.11
and what g. has he that he toiled 5.16
who despises the g. of oppressions, Is 33.15
each to his own g., one and all. 56.11
And now what do you g. by going to Jer 2.18
Or what do you g. by going to 2.18
every one is greedy for unjust g.; 6.13
every one is greedy for unjust g.; 8.10
heart only for your dishonest g., 22.17
and make g. of your neighbors by Eze 22.12
the dishonest g. which you have 22.13
destroying lives to get dishonest g. 22.27
but their heart is set on their g. 33.31
that you are trying to g. time, Dan 2.08
shall devote their g. to the LORD, Mic 4.13
him who gets evil g. for his house, Hab 2.09
to g. the whole world and forfeit Mk 8.36
Whoever seeks to g. his life will Lk 17.33
endurance you will g. your lives. 21.19
her owners much g. by soothsaying. Ac 16.16
saw that their hope of g. was gone, 16.19
But if you can g. your freedom, avail 1Co 7.21
burned, but have not love, I g. nothing. 13.03
What do I g. if, humanly speaking, I 15.32
live is Christ, and to die is g. Php 1.21
But whatever g. I had, I counted as 3.07
as refuse, in order that I may g. Christ 3.08
to much wine, not greedy for g.; 1Ti 3.08
well as deacons g. a good standing 3.13
that godliness is a means of g. 6.05
There is great g. in godliness with 6.06
drunkard or violent or greedy for g., Tit 1.07
for base g. what they have no 1.11
a year there and trade and get g."; Jas 4.13
not for shameful g. but eagerly, 1Pe 5.02
of Beor, who loved g. from wrongdoing, 2Pe 2.15
for the sake of g. to Balaam's error, Jud 1.11
flattering people to g. advantage. 1.16

GAINED
and g. more and more until he Gen 26.13
father's he has g. all this wealth 31.01
all his livestock which he had g., 31.18
which they had g. in the land of 46.06
and they g. possessions in it, and 47.27
"The men g. an advantage over us, 2Sa 11.23
Treasures g. by wickedness do not Pro 10.02
glory; it is g. in a righteous life. 16.31
Bread g. by deceit is sweet to a 20.17
was nothing to be g. under the sun. Ecc 2.11
they have g. and what they have Is 15.07
the riches they g. have perished. Jer 48.36
I have g. wealth for myself"; but Hos 12.08
you would have g. from me is given Mt 15.05
to you, you have g. your brother. 18.15
you would have g. from me is Corban' Mk 7.11
know what they had g. by trading. Lk 19.15
there is nothing to be g. by it, 2Co 12.01
been secretly g. by some who long Jud 1.04
who g. wealth from her, will stand Rev 18.15

GAINING
Pilate saw that he was g. nothing, Mt 27.24
to keep Satan from g. the advantage 2Co 2.11

GAINS
heeds admonition g. understanding. Pro 15.32
man is instructed, he g. knowledge. 21.11
all its g., all its prized belongings, Jer 20.05
if he g. the whole world and forfeits Mt 16.26
a man if he g. the whole world and Lk 9.25

GAIUS
dragging with them G. and Aristarchus, Ac 19.29
and G. of Derbe, and Timothy; and the 20.04
G., who is host to me and to the Rom 16.23
none of you except Crispus and G.; 1Co 1.14
The elder to the beloved G., whom I 3Jn 1.01

GALAL
G., and Mattaniah the son of Mica, 1Ch 9.15
son of G., son of Jeduthun, and 9.16
son of G., son of Jeduthun. Neh 11.17

GALATIA
the region of Phrygia and G., having Ac 16.06
through the region of G. and Phrygia, 18.23
as I directed the churches of G., 1Co 16.01
with me, To the churches of G.: Gal 1.02
Crescens has gone to G., Titus to 2Ti 4.10
G., Cappadocia, Asia, and Bithynia, 1Pe 1.01

GALATIANS
O foolish G.! Who has bewitched Gal 3.01

GALBANUM
and g., sweet spices with pure Ex 30.34

GALE
winter fruit when shaken by a g.; Rev 6.13

GALEED
Jegarsahadutha; but Jacob called it G. Gen 31.47
today." Therefore he named it G., 31.48

GALILEAN
"You also were with Jesus the G." Mt 26.69
one of them; for you are a G." Mk 14.70
was with them; for he is a G." Lk 22.59
he asked whether the man was a G. 23.06
After him Judas the G. arose in the Ac 5.37

GALILEANS
told him of the G. whose blood Lk 13.01
that these G. were worse sinners 13.02
sinners than all the other G., 13.02
the G. welcomed him, having seen all Jn 4.45
not all these who are speaking G.? Ac 2.07

GALILEE
the king of Goiim in G., one; Jos 12.23
apart Kedesh in G. in the hill 20.07
Kedesh in G. with its pasture lands, 21.32
twenty cities in the land of G. 1Ki 9.11
and G., all the land of Naphtali; 2Ki 15.29
Kedesh in G. with its pasture lands, 1Ch 6.76
the Jordan, G. of the nations. Is 9.01
he withdrew to the district of G. Mt 2.22
Then Jesus came from G. to the 3.13
been arrested, he withdrew into G.; 4.12
the Jordan, G. of the Gentiles— 4.15
As he walked by the Sea of G., 4.18
And he went about all G., teaching 4.23
him from G. and the Decapolis and 4.25
and passed along the Sea of G. 15.29
As they were gathering in G., 17.22
went away from G. and entered the 19.01
prophet Jesus from Nazareth of G." 21.11
up, I will go before you to G." 26.32
who had followed Jesus from G., 27.55
he is going before you to G.; 28.07
and tell my brethren to go to G., 28.10
Now the eleven disciples went to G., 28.16
Nazareth of G. and was baptized by Mk 1.09
was arrested, Jesus came into G., 1.14
And passing along by the Sea of G., 1.16
all the surrounding region of G. 1.28
And he went throughout all G., preaching 1.39
a great multitude from G. followed; 3.07
officers and the leading men of G. 6.21

GALILEE (cont.)
through Sidon to the Sea of G., Mk 7.31
from there and passed through G. 9.30
up, I will go before you to G." 14.28
who, when he was in G., followed him, 15.41
that he is going before you to G.; 16.07
God to a city of G. named Nazareth, Lk 1.26
And Joseph also went up from G., 2.04
of the Lord, they returned into G., 2.39
and Herod being tetrarch of G., 3.01
in the power of the Spirit into G., 4.14
down to Capernaum, a city of G. 4.31
village of G. and Judea and from 5.17
Gerasenes, which is opposite G. 8.26
passing along between Samaria and G. 17.11
all Judea, from G. even to this place. 23.05
him from G. stood at a distance 23.49
had come with him from G. followed, 23.55
told you, while he was still in G., 24.06
next day Jesus decided to go to G. Jn 1.43
there was a marriage at Cana in G., 2.01
his signs, Jesus did at Cana in G., 2.11
Judea and departed again to G. 4.03
After the two days he departed to G. 4.43
So when he came to G., the Galileans 4.45
So he came again to Cana in G., 4.46
Jesus had come from Judea to G., 4.47
when he had come from Judea to G. 4.54
to the other side of the Sea of G., 6.01
After this Jesus went about in G.; 7.01
So saying, he remained in G. 7.09
"Is the Christ to come from G.? 7.41
They replied, "Are you from G. too? 7.52
that no prophet is to rise from G." 7.52
who was from Bethsaida in G., and said 12.21
the Twin, Nathanael of Cana in G., 21.02
"Men of G., why do you stand looking Ac 1.11
all Judea and G. and Samaria had 9.31
beginning from G. after the baptism 10.37
up with him from G. to Jerusalem, 13.31

GALL
he pours out my g. on the ground. Job 16.13
it is the g. of asps within him. 20.14
glittering point comes out of his g.; 20.25
bitterness, the wormwood and the g.! Lam 3.19
him wine to drink, mingled with g.; Mt 27.34
you are in the g. of bitterness and in Ac 8.23

GALLERIES
for the g. took more away from them Eze 42.05

GALLERY
was g. against g. in three stories. Eze 42.03

GALLEY
where no g. with oars can go, nor Is 33.21

GALLIM
the son of Laish, who was of G. 1Sa 25.44
Cry aloud, O daughter of G.! Hearken Is 10.30

GALLIO
But when G. was proconsul of Achaia, Ac 18.12
G. said to the Jews, "If it were a 18.14
But G. paid no attention to this. 18.17

GALLONS
each holding twenty or thirty g. Jn 2.06

GALLOPING
horses' hoofs with the g., g. of his steeds. Ju 5.22
of wheel, g. horse and bounding chariot! Nah 3.02

GALLOWS
the men were both hanged on the g. Est 2.23
"Let a g. fifty cubits high be made, 5.14
pleased Haman, and he had the g. made. 5.14
hanged on the g. that he had prepared 6.04
the g. which Haman has prepared for 7.09
Haman on the g. which he had prepared 7.10
and they have hanged him on the g., 8.07
sons of Haman be hanged on the g." 9.13
sons should be hanged on the g. 9.25

GAMAD
and men of G. were in your towers; Eze 27.11

GAMALIEL
Manasseh, G. the son of Pedahzur; Num 1.10
Manasseh being G. the son of 2.20
On the eighth day G. the son of 7.54
the offering of G. the son of 7.59
of Manasseh was G. the son of 10.23
a Pharisee in the council named G., Ac 5.34
up in this city at the feet of G., 22.03

GAME
Esau, because he ate of his g.; Gen 25.28
to the field, and hunt g. for me, 27.03
field to hunt for g. and bring it, 27.05
'Bring me g., and prepare for me 27.07
now sit up and eat of my g., that you may 27.19
eat of my son's g. and bless you." 27.25
arise, and eat of his son's g., that you may 27.31
that hunted g. and brought it to 27.33

GAMUL
Jachin, the twenty-second to G., 1Ch 24.17

GANGRENE
talk will eat its way like g. Among them 2Ti 2.17

GAPED
Men have g. at me with their mouth, Job 16.10

GARB
she shall put off her captive's g., Deu 21.13

GARDEN
And the LORD God planted a g. in Eden, Gen 2.08
life also in the midst of the g., 2.09
flowed out of Eden to water the g., 2.10
put him in the g. of Eden to till 2.15
freely eat of every tree of the g.; 2.16
'You shall not eat of any tree of the g.'?" 3.01
the fruit of the trees of the g.; 3.02
which is in the midst of the g., 3.03
walking in the g. in the cool of 3.08
LORD God among the trees of the g. 3.08
heard the sound of thee in the g., 3.10
sent him forth from the g. of Eden, 3.23
the east of the g. of Eden he placed 3.24
everywhere like the g. of the LORD, 13.10
your feet, like a g. of vegetables; Deu 11.10
I may have it for a vegetable g., 1Ki 21.02
was buried in the g. of his house, 2Ki 21.18
of his house, in the g. of Uzza; 21.18
in his tomb in the g. of Uzza; and Josiah 21.26
by the king's g., though the Chaldeans 25.04
Pool of Shelah of the king's g., Neh 3.15
court of the g. of the king's palace. Est 1.05
wrath and went into the palace g.; 7.07
from the palace g. to the place where 7.08
and his shoots spread over his g. Job 8.16
A g. locked is my sister, my bride, a Sol 4.12
a g. locked, a fountain sealed. 4.12
a g. fountain, a well of living water, 4.15
Blow upon my g., let its fragrance 4.16
Let my beloved come to his g., and eat 4.16
I come to my g., my sister, my bride, 5.01
My beloved has gone down to his g., 6.02
withers, and like a g. without water. Is 1.30
her desert like the g. of the LORD; 51.03
and you shall be like a watered g., 58.11
and as a g. causes what is sown in 61.11

GARDEN (cont.)
life shall be like a watered g., and they Jer 31.12
of the king's g. through the gate 39.04
by the king's g., while the Chaldeans 52.07
down his booth like that of a g., laid in Lam 2.06
You were in Eden, the g. of God; every Eze 28.13
The cedars in the g. of God could 31.08
no tree in the g. of God was like 31.08
envied it, that were in the g. of God. 31.09
has become like the g. of Eden; and the 36.35
they shall flourish as a g.; they shall Hos 14.07
is like the g. of Eden before them, Joe 2.03
a forest in the midst of a g. land; Mic 7.14
a man took and sowed in his g.; Lk 13.19
valley, where there was a g., which he Jn 18.01
I not see you in the g. with him?" 18.26
he was crucified there was a g., 19.41
and in the g. a new tomb where no 19.41

GARDENER
Supposing him to be the g., she said Jn 20.15

GARDENS
like g. beside a river, like aloes Num 24.06
I made myself g. and parks, and planted Ecc 2.05
to pasture his flock in the g., and to Sol 6.02
O you who dwell in the g., my companions 8.13
blush for the g. which you have Is 1.29
sacrificing in g. and burning incense. 65.03
themselves to go into the g., following 66.17
plant g. and eat their produce. Jer 29.05
and plant g. and eat their produce. 29.28
laid waste your g. and your vineyards; Amo 4.09
they shall make g. and eat their 9.14

GAREB
Ira the Ithrite, G. the Ithrite, 2Sa 23.38
Ira the Ithrite, G. the Ithrite, 1Ch 11.40
farther, straight to the hill G., and shall Jer 31.39

GARLAND
for they are a fair g. for your head, Pro 1.09
She will place on your head a fair g.; 4.09
their wisdom, but folly is the g. of fools. 14.24
to give them a g. instead of ashes, Is 61.03
bridegroom decks himself with a g., 61.10

GARLANDS
oxen and g. to the gates and wanted Ac 14.13

GARLIC
the leeks, the onions, and the g.; Num 11.05

GARMENT
Then Shem and Japheth took a g., Gen 9.23
she caught him by his g., saying, 39.12
But he left his g. in her hand, 39.12
he had left his g. in her hand, 39.13
he left his g. with me, and fled and 39.15
Then she laid up his g. by her 39.16
he left his g. with me, and fled out 39.18
take your neighbor's g. in pledge, Ex 22.26
opening, like the opening in a g., 28.32
in it was like the opening in a g., 39.23
priest shall put on his linen g., Lev 6.10
of its blood is sprinkled on a g., 6.27
of wood or a g. or a skin or a 11.32
there is a leprous disease in a g., 13.47
whether a woolen or a linen g., 13.47
greenish or reddish in the g., 13.49
the disease has spread in the g., 13.51
And he shall burn the g., whether 13.52
spread in the g. in warp or woof 13.53
spot out of the g. or the skin or 13.56
then if it appears again in the g., 13.57
But the g., warp or woof, or anything 13.58
disease in a g. of wool or linen, 13.59
for leprosy in a g. or in a house, 14.55
And every g. and every skin on 15.17
come upon you a g. of cloth made 19.19
You shall purify every g., every Num 31.20
so you shall do with his g.; Deu 22.03
shall a man put on a woman's g.; 22.05
spread the g. before the elders of 22.17
or take a widow's g. in pledge; 24.17
And they spread a g., and every man Ju 8.25
Joab was wearing a soldier's g., 2Sa 20.08
the field, and threw a g. over him. 20.12
had clad himself with a new g.; 1Ki 11.29
hold of the new g. that was on him, 11.30
"He wore a g. of haircloth, with a 2Ki 1.08
every man of them took his g., 9.13
like a g. that is moth-eaten. Job 13.28
With violence it seizes my g.; 30.18
when I made clouds its g., and thick 38.09
the seal, and it is dyed like a g. 38.14
Who can strip off his outer g.? 41.13
violence covers them as a g. Ps 73.06
they will all wear out like a g. 102.26
thyself with light as with a g., 104.02
it with the deep as with a g.; 104.06
May it be like a g. which he wraps 109.19
Take a man's g. when he has given Pro 20.16
who takes off a g. on a cold day, 25.20
Take a man's g. when he has given 27.13
has wrapped up the waters in a g.? 30.04
I had put off my g., how could I Sol 5.03
and every g. rolled in blood will Is 9.05
of them will wear out like a g.; 50.09
the earth will wear out like a g., 51.06
moth will eat them up like a g., 51.08
deeds are like a polluted g. 64.06
and covers the naked with a g., Eze 18.07
and covers the naked with a g., 18.16
holy flesh in the skirt of his g., Hag 2.12
covering one's g. with violence, Mal 2.16
Now John wore a g. of camel's hair, Mt 3.04
of unshrunk cloth on an old g., 9.16
the patch tears away from the g., 9.16
and touched the fringe of his g.; 9.20
to herself, "If I only touch his g., 9.21
only touch the fringe of his g.; 14.36
there a man who had no wedding g.; 22.11
get in here without a wedding g.?' 22.12
of unshrunk cloth on an old g.; if he Mk 2.21
in the crowd and touched his g. 5.27
touch even the fringe of his g.; 6.56
from a new g. and puts it upon an old g.; Lk 5.36
and touched the fringe of his g.; 8.44
they will all grow old like a g., Heb 1.11
hating even the g. spotted by the Jud 1.23

GARMENTS
Adam and for his wife g. of skins, Gen 3.21
took the best g. of Esau her older 27.15
and he smelled the smell of his g., 27.27
purify yourselves, and change your g.; 35.02
Then Jacob rent his g., and put 37.34
she put off her widow's g., and put 38.14
she put on the g. of her widowhood. 38.19
arrayed him in g. of fine linen, 41.42
and all of them he gave festal g.; 45.22
shekels of silver and five festal g. 45.22
he washes his g. in wine and his 49.11
tomorrow, and let them wash their g., Ex 19.10
the people; and they washed their g. 19.14
shall make holy g. for Aaron your 28.02
make Aaron's g. to consecrate him 28.03
These are the g. which they shall 28.04
shall make holy g. for Aaron your 28.04
And you shall take the g., and put on 29.05
sprinkle it upon Aaron and his g., 29.21
his sons and his sons' g. with him; 29.21
and he and his g. shall be holy, 29.21
his sons and his sons' g. with him. 29.21

GARMENTS (cont.)

“The holy g. of Aaron shall be for Ex 29.29
and the finely worked g., 31.10
the holy g. for Aaron the priest 31.10
and the g. of his sons, for their service 31.10
the finely wrought g. for ministering 35.19
the holy g. for Aaron the priest, 35.19
and the g. of his sons, for their 35.19
its service, and for the holy g. 35.21
stuff they made finely wrought g., 39.01
they made the holy g. for Aaron; 39.01
the finely worked g. for ministering 39.41
the holy g. for Aaron the priest, 39.41
and the g. of his sons to serve as 39.41
and put upon Aaron the holy g., 40.13
Then he shall put off his g., Lev 6.11
and put on other g., and carry 6.11
and the g., and the anointing oil, 8.02
sprinkled it upon Aaron and his g., 8.30
upon his sons and his sons' g.; 8.30
so he consecrated Aaron and his g., 8.30
his sons and his sons' g. with him. 8.30
these are the holy g. He shall bathe 16.04
off the linen g. which he put on 16.23
in a holy place, and put on his g., 16.24
atonement, wearing the holy linen g.; 16.32
been consecrated to wear the g., 21.10
of their g. throughout their generations, Num 15.38
and strip Aaron of his g., and put them 20.26
And Moses stripped Aaron of his g., 20.28
and these g. and shoes of ours are Jos 9.13
and the purple g. worn by the kings of Ju 8.26
thirty linen g. and thirty festal g.; 14.12
me thirty linen g. and thirty festal g. 14.13
gave the festal g. to those who 14.19
and the g., and came back to Achish. 1Sa 27.09
himself and put on other g., and went 28.08
and cut off their g. in the middle, 2Sa 10.04
and rent his g., and lay on the 13.31
who were standing by rent their g. 13.31
a mourner, and put on mourning g.; 14.02
g., myrrh, spices, horses, and mules, 1Ki 10.25
shekels of gold, and ten festal g. 2Ki 5.05
talent of silver and two festal g. 5.22
in two bags, with two festal g., 5.23
it a time to accept money and g., 5.26
littered with g. and equipment 7.15
So Jehoiachin put off his prison g. 25.29
and cut off their g. in the middle, 1Ch 19.04
g., myrrh, spices, horses, and mules, 2Ch 9.24
of silver, and one hundred priests' g. Ez 2.69
I rent my g. and my mantle, and 9.03
with my g. and my mantle rent, and 9.05
five hundred and thirty priests' g. Neh 7.70
of silver, and sixty-seven priests' g. 7.72
she sent g. to clothe Mordecai, so Est 4.04
you whose g. are hot when the earth Job 37.17
they divide my g. among them, and Ps 22.18
She makes linen g. and sells them; Pro 31.24
Let your g. be always white; Ecc 9.08
scent of your g. is like the scent Sol 4.11
the g. of gauze, the linen g., the Is 3.23
put on your beautiful g., O Jerusalem, 52.01
he put on g. of vengeance for 59.17
me with the g. of salvation, 61.10
in crimsoned g. from Bozrah, he that 63.01
and thy g. like his that treads in 63.02
lifeblood is sprinkled upon my g., 63.03
afraid, nor did they rend their g. Jer 36.24
So Jehoiachin put off his prison g. 52.33
that none could touch their g. Lam 4.14
You took some of your g., and made Eze 16.16
your embroidered g. to cover them, 16.18
and strip off their embroidered g.; 26.16
These traded with you in choice g., 27.24
there the g. in which they minister, 42.14
put on other g. before they go 42.14
court, they shall wear linen g.; 44.17
put off the g. in which they have 44.19
and they shall put on other g., 44.19
holiness to the people with their g. 44.19
their hats, and their other g., Dan 3.21
and rend your hearts and not your g.” Joe 2.13
altar upon g. taken in pledge; Amo 2.08
the angel, clothed with filthy g. Zec 3.03
him, “Remove the filthy g. from him.” 3.04
his head and clothed him with g.; 3.05
silver, and g. in great abundance. 14.14
and his g. became white as light. Mt 17.02
and put their g. on them, and he sat 21.07
crowd spread their g. on the road, 21.08
divided his g. among them by 27.35
For she said, “If I touch even his g., Mk 5.28
crowd, and said, “Who touched my g.?” 5.30
and his g. became glistening, 9.03
to Jesus, and threw their g. on it; 11.07
And many spread their g. on the road, 11.08
him, and divided his g. among them, 15.24
throwing their g. on the colt they Lk 19.35
they spread their g. on the road. 19.36
they cast lots to divide his g. 23.34
rose from supper, laid aside his g., Jn 13.04
and taken his g., and resumed his 13.12
they took his g. and made four parts, 19.23
“They parted my g. among them, and for 19.24
laid down their g. at the feet of Ac 7.58
coats and g. which Dorcas made while 9.39
they tore their g. and rushed out 14.14
tore the g. off them and gave orders 16.22
shook out his g. and said to them, 18.06
and keeping the g. of those who 22.20
and waved their g. and threw dust 22.23
rotted and your g. are moth-eaten. Jas 5.02
who have not soiled their g.; and they Rev 3.04
shall be clad thus in white g., and I 3.05
and white g. to clothe you and to 3.18
clad in white g., with golden crowns 4.04
keeping his g. that he may not go 16.15

GARMITE

of Keilah the G. and Eshtemoa the 1Ch 4.19

GARNER

but those who g. it shall eat it Is 62.09

GARNERS

may our g. be full, providing all Ps 144.13

GARRISON

there is a g. of the Philistines; 1Sa 10.05
Jonathan defeated the g. of the 13.03
defeated the g. of the Philistines, 13.04
And the g. of the Philistines went 13.23
the Philistine g. on yonder side.” 14.01
to go over to the Philistine g., 14.04
go over to the g. of these uncircumcised; 14.06
themselves to the g. of the Philistines 14.11
And the men of the g. hailed Jonathan 14.12
the g. and even the raiders trembled; 14.15
and the g. of the Philistines was 2Sa 23.14
and the g. of the Philistines was 1Ch 11.16

GARRISONS

Then David put g. in Aram of 2Sa 8.06
And he put g. in Edom; 8.14
throughout all Edom he put g., 8.14
Then David put g. in Syria of 1Ch 18.06
And he put g. in Edom; and all the 18.13
and set g. in the land of Judah, and 2Ch. 17.02

GASH

how long will you g. yourselves? Jer 47.05
grain and wine they g. themselves, Hos 7.14

GASHED

clothes torn, and their bodies g., Jer 41.05

GASHES
upon all the hands are g., and on the Jer 48.37

GASP
in travail, I will g. and pant. Is 42.14

GASPING
the daughter of Zion g. for breath, Jer 4.31

GATAM
Teman, Omar, Zepho, G., and Kenaz. Gen 36.11
Korah, G., and Amalek; these are 36.16
G., Kenaz, Timna, and Amalek. 1Ch 1.36

GATE
Lot was sitting in the g. of Sodom. Gen 19.01
possess the g. of their enemies, 22.17
who went in at the g. of his city, 23.10
who went in at the g. of his city. 23.18
possess the g. of those who hate 24.60
God, and this is the g. of heaven." 28.17
came to the g. of their city and 34.20
went out of the g. of his city hearkened 34.24
who went out of the g. of his city. 34.24
for the one side of the g. shall be Ex 27.14
For the g. of the court there shall 27.16
then Moses stood in the g. of the camp, 32.26
to and fro from g. to g. throughout 32.27
the screen for the g. of the court; 35.17
one side of the g. were fifteen cubits, 38.14
hand by the g. of the court were 38.15
screen for the g. of the court was 38.18
the bases of the g. of the court, 38.31
the screen for the g. of the court, 39.40
the screen for the g. of the court. 40.08
the screen of the g. of the court. 40.33
entrance of the g. of the court Num 4.26
his city at the g. of the place Deu 21.19
the elders of the city in the g.; 22.15
both out to the g. of that city, 22.24
go up to the g. to the elders, 25.07
and when the g. was to be closed, at Jos 2.05
had gone out, the g. was shut. 2.07
chased them before the g. as far as 7.05
the entrance of the g. of the city, 8.29
the entrance of the g. of the city, 20.04
the entrance of the g. of the city; Ju 9.35
up to the entrance of the g. 9.40
the entrance of the g. of the city, 9.44
all night at the g. of the city. 16.02
doors of the g. of the city and 16.03
stood by the entrance of the g.; 18.16
entrance of the g. with the six 18.17
went up to the g. and sat down Ru 4.01
and from the g. of his native 4.10
Then all the people who were at the g., 4.11
his seat by the side of the g.; 1Sa 4.18
Then Saul approached Samuel in the g., 9.18
made marks on the doors of the g., 21.13
midst of the g. to speak with him 2Sa 3.27
array at the entrance of the g.; 10.08
back to the entrance of the g. 11.23
and stand beside the way of the g.; 15.02
king stood at the side of the g., 18.04
to the roof of the g. by the wall, 18.24
watchman called to the g. and said, 18.26
the chamber over the g., and wept; 18.33
arose, and took his seat in the g. 19.08
"Behold, the king is sitting in the g."; 19.08
of Bethlehem which is by the g.!" 23.15
of Bethlehem which was by the g., 23.16
when he came to the g. of the city, 1Ki 17.10
the entrance of the g. of Samaria; 22.10
for a shekel, at the g. of Samaria. 2Ki 7.01
lepers at the entrance to the g.; 7.03
he leaned to have charge of the g.; 7.17
the people trod upon him in the g., 7.17
tomorrow in the g. of Samaria," 7.18
upon him in the g. and he died. 7.20
And as Jehu entered the g., she said, 9.31
entrance of the g. until the morning." 10.08
being at the g. Sur and a third at 11.06
a third at the g. behind the guards), 11.06
through the g. of the guards to 11.19
the Ephraim G. to the Corner G. 14.13
built the upper g. of the house of 15.35
entrance of the g. of Joshua the 23.08
one's left at the g. of the city. 23.08
the way of the g. between the two 25.04
in the king's g. on the east side. 1Ch 9.18
of Bethlehem which is by the g.!" 11.17
of Bethlehem which was by the g., 11.18
Jeduthun were appointed to the g. 16.42
at the g. of Shallecheth on the 26.16
the entrance of the g. of Samaria; 2Ch 18.09
third at the G. of the Foundation; 23.05
of the horse g. of the king's house, 23.15
the upper g. to the king's house. 23.20
it outside the g. of the house of 24.08
the Ephraim G. to the Corner G. 25.23
at the Corner G. and at the Valley G. 26.09
He built the upper g. of the house 27.03
the Levite, keeper of the east g., 31.14
square at the g. of the city and 32.06
to the entrance by the Fish G., 33.14
the gatekeepers were at each g.; 35.15
by the Valley G. to the Jackal's Neh 2.13
Jackal's Well and to the Dung G., 2.13
to the Fountain G. and to the 2.14
back and entered by the Valley G., 2.15
and they built the Sheep G. They 3.01
of Hassenaah built the Fish G.; 3.03
of Besodeiah repaired the Old G.; 3.06
of Zanoah repaired the Valley G.; 3.13
of the wall, as far as the Dung G. 3.13
Bethhaccherem, repaired the Dung G.; 3.14
Mizpah, repaired the Fountain G.; 3.15
the Water G. on the east and the 3.26
Above the Horse G. the priests 3.28
keeper of the East G., repaired. 3.29
merchants, opposite the Muster G., 3.31
and the Sheep G. the goldsmiths 3.32
the square before the Water G.; 8.01
the Water G. from early morning 8.03
at the Water G. and in the square 8.16
in the square at the G. of Ephraim. 8.16
right upon the wall to the Dung G.; 12.31
At the Fountain G. they went up 12.37
David, to the Water G. on the east. 12.37
and above the G. of Ephraim, and by 12.39
Old G., and by the Fish G. and the Tower 12.39
of the Hundred, to the Sheep G.; 12.39
to a halt at the G. of the Guard. 12.39
was sitting at the king's g. Est 2.19
was sitting at the king's g., 2.21
at the king's g. bowed down and 3.02
at the king's g. said to Mordecai, 3.03
to the entrance of the king's g., 4.02
the king's g. clothed with sackcloth. 4.02
city in front of the king's g., 4.06
saw Mordecai in the king's g., 5.09
the Jew sitting at the king's g." 5.13
the Jew who sits at the king's g. 6.10
Mordecai returned to the king's g. 6.12
safety, they are crushed in the g., Job 5.04
When I went out to the g. of the city, 29.07
because I saw help in the g.; 31.21
talk of those who sit in the g., Ps 69.12
This is the g. of the LORD; 118.20
speaks with his enemies in the g. 127.05
or crush the afflicted at the g.; Pro 22.22
in the g. he does not open his 24.07
Heshbon, by the g. of Bathrabbim. Sol 7.04
Wail, O g.; cry, O city; melt Is 14.31

GATE (ocnt.)
who turn back the battle at the g. Is 28.06
for him who reproves in the g., 29.21
"Stand in the g. of the LORD's house, Jer 7.02
"Go and stand in the Benjamin G., 17.19
at the entry of the Potsherd G., 19.02
upper Benjamin G. of the house of 20.02
of the New G. of the house of the 26.10
tower of Hananel to the Corner G. 31.38
of the Horse G. toward the east, 31.40
of the New G. of the LORD's house. 36.10
When he was at the Benjamin G., 37.13
was sitting in the Benjamin G.— 38.07
came and sat in the middle g.: 39.03
through the g. between the two 39.04
by the way of a g. between the two 52.07
The old men have quit the city g., Lam 5.14
and behold, north of the altar g., Eze 8.05
of the north g. of the house of 8.14
from the direction of the upper g., 9.02
of the east g. of the house of the 10.19
me to the east g. of the house of 11.01
the g. of the peoples is broken, it 26.02
threshold of the g., one reed deep; 40.06
threshold of the g. by the vestibule of the g. 40.07
vestibule of the g. was at the 40.09
on either side of the east g.; 40.10
Then he measured the g. from the 40.13
front of the g. at the entrance to 40.15
vestibule of the g. was fifty 40.15
of the lower g. to the outer front 40.19
there was a g. which faced toward 40.20
same size as those of the first g.; 40.21
as those of the g. which faced 40.22
And opposite the g. on the north, 40.23
was a g. to the inner court; 40.23
and he measured from g. to g., 40.23
there was a g. on the south; 40.24
And there was a g. on the south of 40.27
measured from g. to g. toward the south, 40.27
to the inner court by the south g., 40.28
and he measured the south g.; it was 40.28
east side, and he measured the g.; 40.32
Then he brought me to the north g., 40.35
door in the vestibule of the g., 40.38
vestibule of the g. were two tables 40.39
of the north g. were two tables; 40.40
vestibule of the g. were two tables. 40.40
the outside of the side of the g., 40.41
side of the north g. facing south, 40.44
side of the south g. facing north. 40.44
breadth of the g. was fourteen cubits; 40.48
sidewalls of the g. were three 40.48
me out by the g. which faced east, 42.15
brought me to the g., the g. facing east. 43.01
the temple by the g. facing east, 43.04
to the outer g. of the sanctuary, 44.01
"This g. shall remain shut; it shall 44.02
by way of the vestibule of the g., 44.03
of the north g. to the front of 44.04
posts of the g. of the inner court. 45.19
The g. of the inner court that 46.01
vestibule of the g. from without, 46.02
his stand by the post of the g. 46.02
worship at the threshold of the g. 46.02
but the g. shall not be shut until 46.02
entrance of that g. before the LORD 46.03
go in by the vestibule of the g., 46.08
by the north g. to worship shall 46.09
shall go out by the south g.; 46.09
by the south g. shall go out by the north g.: 46.09
by way of the g. by which he 46.09
the g. facing east shall be opened 46.12
has gone out the g. shall be shut. 46.12
which was at the side of the g., 46.19
me out by way of the north g., 47.02
on the outside to the outer g., 47.02
the g. of Reuben, the g. of Judah, 48.31
and the g. of Levi, the gates of the city 48.31
the g. of Joseph, the g. of Benjamin, 48.32
of Benjamin, and the g. of Dan. 48.32
the g. of Simeon, the g. of Issachar, 48.33
of Issachar, and the g. of Zebulun. 48.33
the g. of Gad, the g. of Asher, and 48.34
of Asher, and the g. of Naphtali. 48.34
They hate him who reproves in the g., Amo 5.10
and turn aside the needy in the g. 5.12
and establish justice in the g.; 5.15
entered the g. of my people in the Ob 1.13
has reached to the g. of my people, Mic 1.09
the LORD to the g. of Jerusalem. 1.12
will break through and pass the g., 2.13
cry will be heard from the Fish G., Zep 1.10
site from the G. of Benjamin to Zec 14.10
to the place of the former g., 14.10
to the Corner G., and from the 14.10
"Enter by the narrow g.; Mt 7.13
for the g. is wide and the way is 7.13
For the g. is narrow and the way is 7.14
he drew near to the g. of the city, Lk 7.12
And at his g. lay a poor man named 16.20
Jerusalem by the sheep g. a pool, Jn 5.02
daily at that g. of the temple Ac 3.02
at the Beautiful G. of the temple; 3.10
Simon's house, stood before the g. 10.17
to the iron g. leading into the 12.10
not open the g. but ran in and 12.14
that Peter was standing at the g. 12.14
outside the g. to the riverside, 16.13
outside the g. in order to sanctify Heb 13.12

GATEKEEPER
Meshelemiah was g. at the entrance 1Ch 9.21
To him the g. opens; the sheep Jn 10.03

GATEKEEPERS
and called to the g. of the city, 2Ki 7.10
Then the g. called out, and it was 7.11
The g. were: Shallum, Akkub, Talmon, 1Ch 9.17
These were the g. of the camp of 9.18
were chosen as g. at the thresholds, 9.22
The g. were on the four sides, east, 9.24
for the four chief g., who were 9.26
and the g. Obededom and Jeiel. 15.18
Elkanah were to be g. for the ark. 15.23
also were to be g. for the ark. 15.24
Jeduthun, and Hosah were to be g. 16.38
four thousand g., and four thousand 23.05
As for the divisions of the g.: 26.01
These divisions of the g., corresponding 26.12
divisions of the g. among the 26.19
and the g. in their divisions for 2Ch 8.14
sabbath, one third shall be g., 23.04
He stationed the g. at the gates of 23.19
scribes, and officials, and g. 34.13
and the g. were at each gate; 35.15
The sons of the g.: the sons of Ez 2.42
the g., and the temple servants 2.70
and Levites, the singers and g., 7.07
Of the g.: Shallum, Telem, and Uri. 10.24
and the g., the singers, and the Neh 7.01
The g.: the sons of Shallum, the sons 7.45
the g., the singers, some of the 7.73
the g., the singers, the temple 10.28
and the g. and the singers. 10.39
The g., Akkub, Talmon and their 11.19
and Akkub were g. standing guard 12.25
as did the singers and the g., 12.45
portions for the singers and the g.; 12.47
and g., and the contributions for 13.05

GATES
sojourner who is within your g.; Ex 20.10
g., and bars, besides very many Deu 3.05
scjourner who is within your g., 5.14

GATES (cont.)

of your house and on your g. Deu 6.09
of your house and upon your g., 11.20
forth to your g. that man or woman 17.05
youngest son shall he set up its g." Jos 6.26
chosen, then war was in the g. Ju 5.08
down to the g. marched the people 5.11
as far as Gath and the g. of Ekron, 1Sa 17.52
entering a town that has g. and bars." 23.07
was sitting between the two g.; 2Sa 18.24
and set up its g. at the cost of 1Ki 16.34
places of the g. that were at the 2Ki 23.08
charge of the g. of the house of 1Ch 9.23
the doors of the g. and for clamps, 22.03
and great alike, for their g. 26.13
cities with walls, g., and bars, 2Ch 8.05
their divisions for the several g.; 8.14
with walls and towers, g. and bars; 14.07
gatekeepers at the g. of the house 23.19
minister in the g. of the camp of 31.02
and its g. are destroyed by fire." Neh 1.03
and its g. have been destroyed by 2.03
beams for the g. of the fortress 2.08
down and its g. which had been 2.13
lies in ruins with its g. burned. 2.17
not set up the doors in the g.), 6.01
"Let not the g. of Jerusalem be 7.03
brethren, who kept watch at the g., 11.19
guard at the storehouses of the g. 12.25
the people and the g. and the wall. 12.30
be dark at the g. of Jerusalem 13.19
some of my servants over the g., 13.19
themselves and come and guard the g., 13.22
Have the g. of death been revealed Job 38.17
you seen the g. of deep darkness? 38.17
liftest me up from the g. of death, Ps 9.13
that in the g. of the daughter of 9.14
Lift up your heads, O g.! and be lifted 24.07
Lift up your heads, O g.! and be lifted 24.09
the LORD loves the g. of Zion more 87.02
Enter his g. with thanksgiving, and 100.04
they drew near to the g. of death. 107.18
Open to me the g. of righteousness, 118.19
standing within your g., O Jerusalem! 122.02
he strengthens the bars of your g.; 147.13
entrance of the city g. she speaks: Pro 1.21
beside the g. in front of the town, 8.03
to me, watching daily at my g., 8.34
wicked at the g. of the righteous. 14.19
Her husband is known in the g., 31.23
let her works praise her in the g. 31.31
And her g. shall lament and mourn; Is 3.26
them to enter the g. of the nobles. 13.02
horsemen took their stand at the g. 22.07
city, the g. are battered into ruins. 24.12
Open the g., that the righteous nation 26.02
consigned to the g. of Sheol for 38.10
before him that g. may not be 45.01
your g. of carbuncles, and all your 54.12
Your g. shall be open continually; 60.11
Salvation, and your g. Praise. 60.18
Go through, go through the g., 62.10
entrance of the g. of Jerusalem, Jer 1.15
who enter these g. to worship the 7.02
"Judah mourns and her g. languish; 14.02
winnowing fork in the g. of the land; 15.07
and in all the g. of Jerusalem, 17.19
Jerusalem, who enter by these g. 17.20
bring it in by the g. of Jerusalem. 17.21
burden by the g. of this city on 17.24
enter by the g. of this city kings 17.25
enter by the g. of Jerusalem on 17.27
I will kindle a fire in its g., 17.27
and your people who enter these g. 22.02
shall enter the g. of this house 22.04
forth beyond the g. of Jerusalem." 22.19
that has no g. or bars, that dwells 49.31
and her high g. shall be burned 51.58
all her g. are desolate, her priests Lam 1.04
Her g. have sunk into the ground; 2.09
could enter the g. of Jerusalem. 4.12
and many fall at all their g. Eze 21.15
set battering rams against the g., 21.22
he enters your g. as one enters a 26.10
walls, and having no bars or g.'; 38.11
ran along the side of the g., 40.18
corresponding to the length of the g.; 40.18
oversight at the g. of the temple, 44.11
When they enter the g. of the inner 44.17
minister at the g. of the inner 44.17
three g., the gate of Reuben, the 48.31
the g. of the city being named 48.31
three g., the gate of Joseph, the 48.32
three g., the gate of Simeon, the 48.33
three g., the gate of Gad, the gate 48.34
consume the bars of their g., Hos 11.06
entered his g. and cast lots for Ob 1.11
The river g. are opened, the palace Nah 2.06
The g. of your land are wide open 3.13
render in your g. judgments that Zec 8.16
that he is near, at the very g. Mt 24.33
that he is near, at the very g. Mk 13.29
were watching the g. day and night, Ac 9.24
garlands to the g. and wanted to 14.13
and at once the g. were shut. 21.30
twelve g., and at the g. twelve angels, Rev 21.12
and on the g. the names of the 21.12
east three g., on the north three g., 21.13
south three g., and on the west three g. 21.13
the city and its g. and walls. 21.15
And the twelve g. were twelve 21.21
each of the g. made of a single 21.21
and its g. shall never be shut by 21.25
they may enter the city by the g. 22.14

GATEWAY

entrance of the g. of the inner Eze 8.03
the door of the g. there were 11.01
and he was standing in the g. 40.03
Then he went into the g. facing east, 40.06
vestibule of the g., eight cubits; 40.08
the opening of the g., ten cubits; 40.11
and the breadth of the g., thirteen 40.11
vestibule of the g. was the court. 40.14
And the g. had windows round about, 40.16
mean." And he went out into the g. Mk 14.68
he knocked at the door of the g., Ac 12.13

GATH

in G., and in Ashdod, did some Jos 11.22
G., and Ekron, and those of the 13.03
of Israel he brought around to G. 1Sa 5.08
Ashkelon, one for G., one for Ekron; 6.17
to Israel, from Ekron to G.; and Israel 7.14
of G., whose height was six cubits 17.04
the champion, the Philistine of G., 17.23
as far as G. and the gates of 17.52
Shaaraim as far as G. and Ekron. 17.52
and went to Achish the king of G. 21.10
afraid of Achish the king of G. 21.12
the son of Maoch, king of G. 27.02
And David dwelt with Achish at G., 27.03
Saul that David had fled to G., 27.04
alive, to bring tidings to G., 27.11
Tell it not in G., publish it not 2Sa 1.20
who had followed him from G., 15.18
And there was again war at G., 21.20
descended from the giants in G.; 21.22
Achish, son of Maacah, king of G. 1Ki 2.39
"Behold, your slaves are in G.," 2.39
and went to G. to Achish, to seek 2.40
and brought his slaves from G. 2.40
from Jerusalem to G. and returned, 2.41
and fought against G., and took it. 2Ki 12.17

GATH (cont.)
whom the men of G. who were born 1Ch 7.21
to flight the inhabitants of G.); 8.13
and he took G. and its villages out 18.01
And there was again war at G., 20.06
descended from the giants in G.; 20.08
G., Mareshah, Ziph, 2Ch 11.08
the wall of G. and the wall of 26.06
then go down to G. of the Philistines. Amo 6.02
Tell it not in G., weep not at all; Mic 1.10

GATHER
"G. stones," and they took stones, Gen 31.46
and if they g. themselves against 34.30
And let them g. all the food of 41.35
"G. yourselves together, that I may 49.01
Go and g. the elders of Israel Ex 3.16
let them go and g. straw for 5.07
of Egypt, to g. stubble for straw. 5.12
go out and g. a day's portion every 16.04
be twice as much as they g. daily." 16.05
'G. of it, every man of you, as much 16.16
Six days you shall g. it; 16.26
some of the people went out to g., 16.27
sow your land and g. in its yield; 23.10
when you g. in from the field the 23.16
shall you g. the gleanings after Lev 19.09
shall you g. the fallen grapes of 19.10
nor shall you g. the gleanings 23.22
vineyard, and g. in its fruits; 25.03
undressed vine you shall not g.; 25.05
nor g. the grapes from the undressed 25.11
we may not sow or g. in our crop?' 25.20
and if you g. within your cities I 26.25
congregation shall g. themselves to Num 10.03
of Israel, shall g. themselves to you. 10.04
"G. for me seventy men of the 11.16
is clean shall g. up the ashes of 19.09
"G. the people together, and I will 21.16
'G. the people to me, that I may let Deu 4.10
that you may g. in your grain and 11.14
You shall g. all its spoil into the 13.16
When you g. the grapes of your 24.21
the field, and shall g. little in; 28.38
of the wine nor g. the grapes; 28.39
and he will g. you again from all 30.03
the LORD your God will g. you, 30.04
and you shall g. into your house Jos 2.18
g. your men at Mount Tabor, taking Ju 4.06
me glean and g. among the sheaves Ru 2.07
"G. all Israel at Mizpah, and I will 1Sa 7.05
and will g. all Israel to my lord 2Sa 3.21
Now, then, g. the rest of the people 12.28
send and g. all Israel to me at 1Ki 18.19
out into the field to g. herbs, 2Ki 4.39
I will g. you to your fathers, and 22.20
and g. and save us from among the 1Ch 16.35
David commanded to g. together the 22.02
and g. from all Israel money to 2Ch 24.05
Behold, I will g. you to your 34.28
I will g. them thence and bring Neh 1.09
to g. into them the portions 12.44
his kingdom to g. all the beautiful Est 2.03
"Go, g. all the Jews to be found in 4.16
every city to g. and defend their 8.11
They g. their fodder in the field Job 24.06
and g. to himself his breath, 34.14
up, and knows not who will g.! Ps 39.06
of the peoples g. as the people of 47.09
"G. to me my faithful ones, who made 50.05
when peoples g. together, and 102.22
thou givest to them, they g. it up; 104.28
and g. us from among the nations, 106.47
and a time to g. stones together; Ecc 3.05
I g. my myrrh with my spice, I eat Sol 5.01
in the gardens, and to g. lilies. 6.02
and as men g. eggs that have been Is 10.14
and g. the dispersed of Judah from 11.12
or like sheep with none to g. them, 13.14
and hatch and g. her young in her 34.15
he will g. the lambs in his arms, he 40.11
and from the west I will g. you; 43.05
Let all the nations g. together, 43.09
they all g., they come to you. 49.18
great compassion I will g. you. 54.07
I will g. yet others to him besides 56.08
they all g. together, they come to 60.04
and those who g. it shall drink it 62.09
I am coming to g. all nations and 66.18
and all nations shall g. to it, Jer 3.17
The children g. wood, the fathers 7.18
When I would g. them, says the LORD, 8.13
G. together, let us go into the 8.14
the reaper, and none shall g. them.'" 9.22
G. up your bundle from the ground, O 10.17
Then I will g. the remnant of my 23.03
fortunes and g. you from all the 29.14
and g. them from the farthest parts 31.08
who scattered Israel will g. him, 31.10
Behold, I will g. them from all the 32.37
g. wine and summer fruits and oil, 40.10
him, with none to g. the fugitives. 49.05
"G. yourselves together and come 49.14
I will g. you from the peoples, and Eze 11.17
I will g. all your lovers, with whom 16.37
I will g. them against you from 16.37
the peoples and g. you out of the 20.34
and g. you out of the countries 20.41
I will g. you into the midst of 22.19
As men g. silver and bronze and 22.20
so I will g. you in my anger and in 22.20
I will g. you and blow upon you 22.21
When I g. the house of Israel from 28.25
years I will g. the Egyptians from 29.13
and g. them from the countries, and 34.13
and g. you from all the countries, 36.24
and will g. them from all sides, and 37.21
g. from all sides to the sacrificial 39.17
nations, I will soon g. them up. Hos 8.10
Egypt shall g. them, Memphis shall 9.06
G. the elders and all the inhabitants Joe 1.14
g. the people. Sanctify the 2.16
g. the children, even nursing 2.16
I will g. all the nations and bring 3.02
round about, g. yourselves there. 3.11
I will surely g. all of you, O Jacob, Mic 2.12
I will g. the remnant of Israel; 2.12
the lame and g. those who have 4.06
the mountains with none to g. them. Nah 3.18
They g. captives like sand. Hab 1.09
For my decision is to g. nations, Zep 3.08
save the lame and g. the outcast, 3.19
at the time when I g. you together; 3.20
signal for them and g. them in, Zec 10.08
and g. them from Assyria; and I will 10.10
For I will g. all the nations against 14.02
floor and g. his wheat into the Mt 3.12
sow nor reap nor g. into barns, 6.26
he who does not g. with me scatters 12.30
do you want us to go and g. them?' 13.28
G. the weeds first and bind them in 13.30
but g. the wheat into my barn.'" 13.30
and they will g. out of his kingdom 13.41
and they will g. his elect from the 24.31
and g. where I have not winnowed? 25.26
and g. his elect from the four Mk 13.27
and to g. the wheat into his Lk 3.17
he who does not g. with me scatters 11.23
"G. up the fragments left over, that Jn 6.12
but to g. into one the children of 11.52
and g. the clusters of the vine of Rev 14.18
g. for the great supper of God, 19.17
to g. them for battle; their number 20.08

GATHERED
the heavens be g. together into Gen 1.09
that were g. together he called 1.10
possessions which they had g., 12.05
of years, and was g. to his people. 25.08
died, and was g. to his kindred. 25.17
and when all the flocks were g. there, 29.03
for the animals to be g. together; 29.07
all the flocks are g. together, 29.08
So Laban g. together all the men of 29.22
he died and was g. to his people, 35.29
your sheaves g. round it, and bowed 37.07
and he g. up all the food of the 41.48
And Joseph g. up all the money that 47.14
them, "I am to be g. to my people; 49.29
his last, and was g. to his people. 49.33
Aaron went and g. together all the Ex 4.29
And they g. them together in heaps, 8.14
they g., some more, some less. 16.17
he that g. much had nothing over, 16.18
and he that g. little had no lack; 16.18
each g. according to what he could 16.18
Morning by morning they g. it, 16.21
sixth day they g. twice as much 16.22
the people g. themselves together 32.01
sons of Levi g. themselves together 32.26
when you have g. in the produce of Lev 23.39
the assembly is to be g. together, Num 10.07
The people went about and g. it, 11.08
of the sea be g. together for them, 11.22
and he g. seventy men of the elders 11.24
the next day, and g. the quails; 11.32
he who g. least g. ten homers; and 11.32
that are g. together against me: in 14.35
all your company have g. together; 16.11
And Moses and Aaron g. the assembly 20.10
"Aaron shall be g. to his people; 20.24
Aaron shall be g. to his people, 20.26
He g. all his men together, and went 21.23
of those who g. themselves together 27.03
also shall be g. to your people, 27.13
your brother Aaron was g., because 27.13
you shall be g. to your people." 31.02
and be g. to your people, as Aaron Deu 32.50
Mount Hor and was g. to his people; 32.50
the heads of the people were g., 33.05
they g. together with one accord to Jos 9.02
g. their forces, and went up with 10.05
the hill country are g. against us." 10.06
the people of Israel g. at Shiloh, 22.12
Then Joshua g. all the tribes of 24.01
also were g. to their fathers; Ju 2.10
He g. to himself the Ammonites and 3.13
and g. the grapes from their 9.27
Tower of Shechem were g. together. 9.47
so Sihon g. all his people together, 11.20
Then Jephthah g. all the men of 12.04
the Philistines g. to offer a 16.23
men of Israel g. against the city, 20.11
So they sent and g. together all 1Sa 5.08
therefore and g. together all the 5.11
So they g. at Mizpah, and drew water 7.06
people of Israel had g. at Mizpah, 7.07
of Israel g. together and came to 8.04
Now the Philistines g. their armies 17.01
and they were g. at Soco, which 17.01
Saul and the men of Israel were g., 17.02
So Jonathan's lad g. up the arrows, 20.38
who was discontented, g. to him; 22.02
the Philistines g. their forces 28.01
and Saul g. all Israel, and they 28.04
Now the Philistines g. all their 29.01
Benjaminites g. themselves together 2Sa 2.25
and when he had g. all the people 2.30
David again g. all the chosen men 6.01
Israel, they g. themselves together. 10.15
he g. all Israel together, and 10.17
So David g. all the people together 12.29
which cannot be g. up again; but God 14.14
is that all Israel be g. to you, 17.11
and they g. the bones of those who 21.13
who were g. there for battle, and 23.09
The Philistines g. together at Lehi, 23.11
And Solomon g. together chariots 1Ki 10.26
And he g. men about him and became 11.24
and g. the prophets together at 18.20
king of Syria g. all his army 20.01
king of Israel g. the prophets 22.06
a wild vine and g. from it his lap 2Ki 4.39
you shall be g. to your grave in 22.20
Judah and Jerusalem were g. to him. 23.01
Then all Israel g. together to 1Ch 11.01
Philistines were g. there for 11.13
And David g. together the sons of 15.04
he g. all Israel together, and 19.17
Solomon g. together chariots and 2Ch 1.14
who had g. at Jerusalem because of 12.05
scoundrels g. about him and defied 13.07
And he g. all Judah and Benjamin, 15.09
They were g. at Jerusalem in the 15.10
king of Israel g. the prophets 18.05
Judah and g. the Levites from all 23.02
And he g. the priests and the 24.05
And Ahaz g. together the vessels of 28.24
They g. their brethren, and sanctified 29.15
rose early and g. the officials of 29.20
A great many people were g., and they 32.04
and g. them together to him in the 32.06
you shall be g. to your grave in 34.28
king sent and g. together all the 34.29
the people g. as one man to Jerusalem. Ez 3.01
and I g. leading men from Israel to 7.28
I g. them to the river that runs to 8.15
g. round me while I sat appalled 9.04
g. to him out of Israel; for the 10.01
servants were g. there for the Neh 5.16
And all the people g. as one man 8.01
of the singers g. together from 12.28
And I g. them together and set 13.11
maidens were g. in Susa the capital Est 2.08
virgins were g. together the second 2.19
the Jews g. in their cities throughout 9.02
were in Susa g. also on the fourteenth 9.15
provinces also g. to defend their 9.16
were in Susa g. on the thirteenth 9.18
his fat, and g. fat upon his loins, Job 15.27
of the peoples be g. about thee; Ps 7.07
He g. the waters of the sea as in a 33.07
But at my stumbling they g. in glee, 35.15
they g. together against me; cripples 35.15
and g. in from the lands, from the 107.03
herbage of the mountains is g., Pro 27.25
Who has g. the wind in his fists? 30.04
I also g. for myself silver and Ecc 2.08
forsaken so I have g. all the earth; Is 10.14
They will be g. together as prisoners 24.22
and you will be g. one by one, 27.12
and spoil is g. as the caterpillar 33.04
yea, there shall the kites be g., 34.15
commanded, and his Spirit has g. them. 34.16
and that Israel might be g. to him, 49.05
to him besides those already g. 56.08
flocks of Kedar shall be g. to you, 60.07
and they shall not be g. or buried; Jer 8.02
not be lamented, or g., or buried; 25.33
all the people g. about Jeremiah 26.09
and they g. wine and summer fruits 40.12
Jews who are g. about you would be 40.15
and have g. gold and silver into Eze 28.04
field, and not be g. and buried. 29.05
people were g. from many nations 38.08
people who were g. from the nations, 38.12
the peoples and g. them from their 39.27
and then g. them into their own 39.28

GATHERED (cont.)
counselors g. together and saw Dan 3.27
of Israel shall be g. together, Hos 1.11
shall be g. against them when they 10.10
the hire of a harlot she g. them, Mic 1.07
that he has g. them as sheaves to 4.12
when the summer fruit has been g., 7.01
Are grapes g. from thorns, or figs Mt 7.16
And great crowds g. about him, 13.02
the weeds are g. and burned with 13.40
the sea and g. fish of every kind; 13.47
and how many baskets you g.? 16.09
and how many baskets you g.? 16.10
two or three are g. in my name, 18.20
the streets and g. all whom they 22.10
the Pharisees were g. together, 22.41
would I have g. your children 23.37
the eagles will be g. together. 24.28
Before him will be g. all the 25.32
of the people g. in the palace of 26.03
the scribes and the elders had g. 26.57
So when they had g., Pilate said 27.17
and they g. the whole battalion 27.27
and the Pharisees g. before Pilate 27.62
whole city was g. together about Mk 1.33
And many were g. together, so that 2.02
and all the crowd g. about him, 2.13
a very large crowd g. about him, 4.01
side, a great crowd g. about him; 5.21
the Pharisees g. together to him, 7.01
when again a great crowd had g., 8.01
Jordan, and crowds g. to him again; 10.01
multitudes g. to hear and to be Lk 5.15
For figs are not g. from thorns, 6.44
multitude had g. together that 12.01
would I have g. your children 13.34
the younger son g. all he had and 15.13
the eagles will be g. together." 17.37
elders of the people g. together, 22.66
the eleven g. together and those 24.33
So they g. them up and filled Jn 6.13
So the Jews g. round him and said 10.24
and the Pharisees g. the council, 11.47
and the branches are g., thrown into 15.06
elders and scribes were g. together in Ac 4.05
and the rulers were g. together, 4.26
city there were g. together 4.27
which they were g. together was 4.31
The people also g. from the towns 5.16
went in and found many persons g.; 10.27
where many were g. together and 12.12
the whole city g. together to hear 13.44
But when the disciples g. about him, 14.20
they g. the church together and 14.27
the elders were g. together to 15.06
and having g. the congregation 15.30
they g. a crowd, set the city in an 17.05
These he g. together, with the 19.25
when we were g. together to break 20.07
the upper chamber where we were g. 20.08
Paul had g. a bundle of sticks and 28.03
and when they had g., he said 28.17
"He who g. much had nothing over, 2Co 8.15
and he who g. little had no lack." 8.15
the earth and g. the vintage of Rev 14.19
their armies g. to make war 19.19

GATHERING
found a man g. sticks on the Num 15.32
who found him g. sticks brought 15.33
thick clouds, a g. of water. 2Sa 22.12
a widow was there g. sticks; 1Ki 17.10
and now, I am g. a couple of sticks, 17.12
gives the work of g. and heaping, Ecc 2.26
kingdoms, of nations g. together! Is 13.04
lest in g. the weeds you root up Mt 13.29
As they were g. in Galilee, Jesus 17.22
and g. where you did not winnow; 25.24
innumerable angels in festal g., Heb 12.22

GATHERINGS
and upon the g. of young men, also; Jer 6.11

GATHERS
And he who g. the ashes of the Num 19.10
words, while his heart g. mischief; Ps 41.06
he g. the outcasts of Israel. 147.02
and g. her sustenance in harvest. Pro 6.08
A son who g. in summer is prudent, 10.05
but he who g. little by little will 13.11
and increase g. it for him who is 28.08
when the reaper g. standing grain Is 17.05
is gathered as the caterpillar g.; 33.04
who g. the outcasts of Israel, I 56.08
partridge that g. a brood which Jer 17.11
he g. them in his seine; so he rejoices Hab 1.15
He g. for himself all nations, and 2.05
as a hen g. her brood under her Mt 23.37
as a hen g. her brood under her Lk 13.34
and g. fruit for eternal life, so Jn 4.36

GATHHEPHER
the east toward the sunrise to G., Jos 19.13
the prophet, who was from G. 2Ki 14.25

GATHRIMMON
Jehud, Beneberak, G., Jos 19.45
G. with its pasture lands—four 21.24
and G. with its pasture lands—two 21.25
lands, G. with its pasture lands, 1Ch 6.69

GAUNT
g. and thin, came up out of the Nile Gen 41.03
And the g. and thin cows ate up the 41.04
poor and very g. and thin, such as I 41.19
And the thin and g. cows ate up the 41.20
were still as g. as at the beginning 41.21
The seven lean and g. cows that 41.27
fasting; my body has become g. Ps 109.24

GAUZE
the garments of g., the linen garments, Is 3.23

GAVE
The man g. names to all cattle, and Gen 2.20
and she also g. some to her husband, 3.06
she g. me fruit of the tree, and I 3.12
and as I g. you the green plants, I 9.03
And Pharaoh g. men orders concerning 12.20
And Abram g. him a tenth of everything 14.20
and g. her to Abram her husband as 16.03
I g. my maid to your embrace, and 16.05
and g. it to the servant, who 18.07
and g. them to Abraham, and restored 20.14
and g. it to Hagar, putting it on 21.14
with water, and g. the lad a drink. 21.19
and oxen and g. them to Abimelech, 21.27
upon her hand, and g. him a drink. 24.18
and g. him straw and provender for 24.32
and she g. the camels drink also. 24.46
and raiment, and g. them to Rebekah; 24.53
he also g. to her brother and to 24.53
Abraham g. all he had to Isaac. 25.05
of his concubines Abraham g. gifts, 25.06
Then Jacob g. Esau bread and 25.34
and he g. them the names which his 26.18
and she g. the savory food and the 27.17
sojournings which God g. to Abraham!" 28.04
(Laban g. his maid Zilpah to his 29.24
then Laban g. him his daughter 29.28
(Laban g. his maid Bilhah to his 29.29
So she g. him her maid Bilhah as a 30.04
maid Zilpah and g. her to Jacob as 30.09
hire because I g. my maid to my 30.18
So they g. to Jacob all the foreign 35.04

GAVE (cont.)

The land which I g. to Abraham and	Gen 35.12
So he g. them to her, and went in to	38.18
and g. him favor in the sight of	39.21
and he g. him in marriage Asenath,	41.45
And Joseph g. orders to fill their	42.25
and Joseph g. them wagons, according	45.21
and g. them provisions for the journey.	45.21
all of them he g. festal garments;	45.22
to Benjamin he g. three hundred shekels	45.22
whom Laban g. to Leah his daughter;	46.18
whom Laban g. to Rachel his daughter,	46.25
and g. them a possession in the	47.11
and Joseph g. them food in exchange	47.17
allowance which Pharaoh g. them;	47.22
"Your father g. this command before	50.16
midwives feared God he g. them families.	Ex 1.21
and he g. Moses his daughter	2.21
and g. them a charge to the people	6.13
And the LORD g. the people favor in	11.03
So Moses g. heed to the voice of	18.24
And he g. to Moses, when he had made	31.18
so they g. it to me, and I threw it	32.24
and he g. them in commandment all	34.32
So Moses g. command, and word was	36.06
and Moses g. the redemption money	Num 3.51
the oxen, and g. them to the Levites.	7.06
four oxen he g. to the sons of	7.07
eight oxen he g. to the sons of	7.08
But to the sons of Kohath he g. none,	7.09
day that the LORD g. commandment,	15.23
and all their leaders g. him rods,	17.06
and g. over the Canaanites; and they	21.03
to Balaam, and g. him Balak's message.	22.07
And Moses g. the tribute, which was	31.41
and g. them to the Levites who had	31.47
So Moses g. command concerning them	32.28
And Moses g. to them, to the sons of	32.33
and they g. other names to the	32.38
And Moses g. Gilead to Machir the	32.40
possession, which the LORD g. to them.)	Deu 2.12
the LORD our God g. him over to us;	2.33
LORD our God g. all into our hands.	2.36
LORD our God g. into our hand Og	3.03
I g. to the Reubenites and the	3.12
I g. to the half-tribe of Manasseh.	3.13
To Machir I g. Gilead,	3.15
the Gadites I g. the territory	3.16
tables of stone, and g. them to me.	5.22
And the LORD g. me the two tables	9.10
nights the LORD g. me the two	9.11
and the LORD g. them to me.	10.04
'I g. my daughter to this man to	22.16
this place and g. us this land,	26.09
and g. it for an inheritance to the	29.08
and g. it to the priests the sons	31.09
When the Most High g. to the	32.08
forgot the God who g. you birth.	32.18
which Moses g. you beyond the	Jos 1.14
of the LORD g. you beyond the	1.15
when the LORD g. the Amorites over	10.12
and the LORD g. it also and its	10.30
and the LORD g. Lachish into the	10.32
And the LORD g. them into the hand	11.08
and Joshua g. it for an inheritance	11.23
of the LORD g. their land for a	12.06
Seir (and Joshua g. their land to	12.07
which Moses g. them, beyond the	13.08
the servant of the LORD g. them:	13.08
Levi alone Moses g. no inheritance;	13.14
And Moses g. an inheritance to the	13.15
And Moses g. an inheritance also to	13.24
And Moses g. an inheritance to the	13.29
of Levi Moses g. no inheritance;	13.33
the Levites he g. no inheritance	14.03
and he g. Hebron to Caleb the son	14.13
he g. to Caleb the son of Jephunneh	15.13
and he g. him Achsah his daughter	15.17
And Caleb g. her the upper springs	15.19
of the LORD he g. them an inheritance	17.04
the servant of the LORD g. them."	18.07
of Israel g. an inheritance among	19.49
the LORD they g. him the city	19.50
of Israel g. to the Levites the	21.03
of Israel g. by lot to the Levites,	21.08
of Simeon they g. the following	21.09
They g. them Kiriatharba, Arba being	21.11
of Aaron the priest they g. Hebron,	21.13
Thus the LORD g. to Israel all the	21.43
And the LORD g. them rest on every	21.44
of the LORD g. you on the other	22.04
offspring many. I g. him Isaac;	24.03
and to Isaac I g. Jacob and Esau.	24.04
And I g. Esau the hill country of	24.04
and I g. them into your hand, and	24.08
and I g. them into your hand.	24.11
I g. you a land on which you had	24.13
up and the LORD g. the Canaanites	Ju 1.04
and he g. him Achsah his daughter	1.13
And Caleb g. her the upper springs	1.15
and he g. them over to plunderers,	2.14
daughters they g. to their sons;	3.06
and the LORD g. Cushanrishathaim	3.10
of milk and g. him a drink and	4.19
He asked water and she g. him milk,	5.25
and the LORD g. them into the hand	6.01
before you, and g. you their land;	6.09
And they g. him seventy pieces of	9.04
g. Sihon and all his people into	11.21
and the LORD g. them into his hand.	11.32
and the LORD g. them into my hand;	12.03
daughters he g. in marriage outside	12.09
and the LORD g. them into the hand	13.01
and g. some to them, and they ate.	14.09
their spoil and g. the festal	14.19
so I g. her to your companion.	15.02
and g. it to the silversmith, who	17.04
and g. the asses provender;	19.21
men of Israel g. ground to Benjamin,	20.36
and they g. them the women whom	21.14
brought out and g. her what food	Ru 2.18
six measures of barley he g. to me,	3.17
his sandal and g. it to the other,	4.07
and the LORD g. her conception, and	4.13
of the neighborhood g. him a name,	4.17
and I g. to the house of your	1Sa 2.28
all Israel g. a mighty shout, so	4.05
were dead, she bowed and g. birth;	4.19
the hall and g. them a place at	9.22
cook, "Bring the portion I g. you,	9.23
God g. him another heart; and all these	10.09
and g. it to David, and his armor,	18.04
And Saul g. him his daughter Michal	18.27
And Jonathan g. his weapons to his	20.40
So the priest g. him the holy bread;	21.06
and g. him provisions, and gave him	22.10
and g. him the sword of Goliath the	22.10
from Keilah, he g. up the expedition.	23.13
how the LORD g. you today into my	24.10
for the LORD g. you into my hand	26.23
So that day Achish g. him Ziklag;	27.06
and they g. him bread and he ate,	30.11
they g. him water to drink,	30.11
and they g. him a piece of a cake	30.12
the reward I g. him for his news.	2Sa 4.10
And the LORD g. victory to David	8.06
And the LORD g. victory to David	8.14
and I g. you your master's house, and	12.08
and g. you the house of Israel and	12.08
not go but g. him his blessing.	13.25
Ahithophel g. was as if one	16.23
when the king g. orders to all the	18.05
And the king g. him his oath.	19.23
and he g. them into the hands of	21.09

GAVE (cont.)
the God who g. me vengeance and 2Sa 22.48
And Joab g. the sum of the numbering 24.09
and I g. birth to a child while she 1Ki 3.17
delivered, this woman also g. birth; 3.18
And God g. Solomon wisdom and 4.29
while Solomon g. Hiram twenty 5.11
Solomon g. this to Hiram year by 5.11
And the LORD g. Solomon wisdom, as 5.12
King Solomon g. to Hiram twenty 9.11
Then she g. the king a hundred and 10.10
queen of Sheba g. to King Solomon. 10.10
And King Solomon g. to the queen of 10.13
who g. him a house, and assigned him 11.18
allowance of food, and g. him land. 11.18
so that he g. him in marriage the 11.19
industrious he g. him charge over 11.28
counsel which the old men g. him, 12.08
And he g. a sign the same day, 13.03
house of David and g. it to you; 14.08
land which he g. to their fathers, 14.15
LORD his God g. him a lamp in 15.04
and g. them into the hands of his 15.18
and g. it to the people, and they 19.21
So he g. him his hand. And Jehu took 2Ki 10.15
and g. him the testimony; and they 11.12
and he g. them continually into the 13.03
(Therefore the LORD g. Israel a 13.05
of the LORD which he g. to Jehu, 15.12
and Menahem g. Pul a thousand 15.19
and the warnings which he g. them. 17.15
and g. them into the hand of 17.20
And Hezekiah g. him all the silver 18.15
overlaid and g. it to the king of 18.16
land which I g. to their fathers, 21.08
And Hilkiah g. the book to 22.08
And Jehoiakim g. the silver and the 23.35
king of Judah g. himself up to the 24.12
and g. him a seat above the seats 25.28
So Sheshan g. his daughter in 1Ch 2.35
to them they g. Hebron in the land 6.55
villages they g. to Caleb the son 6.56
of Aaron they g. the cities of 6.57
of Israel g. the Levites the 6.64
They also g. them by lot out of the 6.65
who g. him strong support in his 11.10
and David g. command, and they were 14.12
And the LORD g. victory to David 18.06
And the LORD g. victory to David 18.13
And Joab g. the sum of the numbering 21.05
it not I who g. command to number 21.17
Then David g. Solomon his son the 28.11
They g. for the service of the 29.07
precious stones g. them to the 29.08
And the LORD g. Solomon great 29.25
worshiped and g. thanks to the 2Ch 7.03
Then she g. the king a hundred and 9.09
queen of Sheba g. to King Solomon. 9.09
And King Solomon g. to the queen of 9.12
counsel which the old men g. him, 10.08
and he g. them abundant provisions, 11.23
God of Israel g. the kingship over 13.05
and God g. them into their hand. 13.16
years, for the LORD g. him peace. 14.06
and the LORD g. them rest round 15.15
he g. them into your hand. 16.08
for his God g. him rest round about. 20.30
Their father g. them great gifts, of 21.03
but he g. the kingdom to Jehoram, 21.03
and g. him the testimony; and they 23.11
and Jehoiada g. it to those who 24.12
the Ammonites g. him that year a 27.05
LORD his God g. him into the hand 28.05
he g. them into your hand, but you 28.09
g. them sandals, provided them with 28.15
and g. tribute to the king of 28.21
king of Judah g. the assembly a 30.24
and the princes g. the assembly a 30.24
of Israel g. in abundance the 31.05
and he g. them rest on every side. 32.22
he answered him and g. him a sign. 32.24
to his people, but they g. no heed. 33.10
of the LORD g. it for repairing 34.10
They g. it to the carpenters and 34.11
the LORD"; and Hilkiah g. the book to 34.15
g. to the priests for the passover 35.08
g. to the Levites for the passover 35.09
he g. them all into his hand. 36.17
ability they g. to the treasury of Ez 2.69
So they g. money to the masons and 3.07
"Who g. you a decree to build this 5.03
'Who g. you a decree to build this 5.09
he g. them into the hand of Nebuchadnezzar 5.12
King Artaxerxes g. to Ezra the 7.11
up the wine and g. it to the king. Neh 2.01
and g. them the king's letters. 2.09
I g. my brother Hanani and Hananiah 7.02
of fathers' houses g. to the work. 7.70
The governor g. to the treasury a 7.70
fathers' houses g. into the treasury 7.71
of the people g. was twenty thousand 7.72
and they g. the sense, so that the 8.08
companies which g. thanks and went 12.31
of those who g. thanks went to the 12.38
of those who g. thanks stood in 12.40
of Nehemiah g. the daily portions 12.47
Then I g. orders and they cleansed 13.09
be shut and g. orders that they 13.19
of his reign he g. a banquet for Est 1.03
the king g. for all the people 1.05
Queen Vashti also g. a banquet for 1.09
Then the king g. a great banquet to 2.18
and g. gifts with royal liberality. 2.18
his hand and g. it to Haman the 3.10
Mordecai also g. him a copy of the 4.08
to Hathach and g. him a message 4.10
and he g. orders to bring the book 6.01
King Ahasuerus g. to Queen Esther 8.01
from Haman, and g. it to Mordecai. 8.02
he g. orders in writing that his 9.25
Mordecai the Jew g. full written 9.29
the LORD g., and the LORD has taken Job 1.21
When he g. to the wind its weight, 28.25
I g. you my attention, and, behold, 32.12
Who g. him charge over the earth 34.13
and the LORD g. Job twice as much 42.10
each of them g. him a piece of 42.11
their father g. them inheritance 42.15
the God who g. me vengeance and Ps 18.47
They g. me poison for food, and for 69.21
my thirst they g. me vinegar to 69.21
the skies g. forth thunder; thy arrows 77.17
and g. them drink abundantly as 78.15
and g. them the grain of heaven. 78.24
for he g. them what they craved. 78.29
He g. their crops to the caterpillar, 78.46
He g. over their cattle to the hail, 78.48
but g. their lives over to the 78.50
He g. his people over to the sword, 78.62
So I g. them over to their stubborn 81.12
and the statutes that he g. them. 99.07
He g. them hail for rain, and 105.32
and g. them bread from heaven in 105.40
And he g. them the lands of the 105.44
he g. them what they asked, but sent 106.15
he g. them into the hand of the 106.41
and g. their land as a heritage, a 135.12
and g. their land as a heritage, for 136.21
about and g. my heart up to Ecc 2.20
spirit returns to God who g. it. 12.07
my nard g. forth its fragrance. Sol 1.12
I called him, but he g. no answer. 3.01
I called him, but he g. no answer. 5.06
Who g. up Jacob to the spoiler, and Is 42.24

GAVE (cont.)
I g. them into your hand, you showed Is 47.06
I g. my back to the smiters, and my 50.06
Spirit of the LORD g. them rest. 63.14
"Before she was in labor she g. birth; 66.07
and to a stone, 'You g. me birth.' Jer 2.27
the land that I g. your fathers 3.18
the land that I g. of old to your 7.07
place which I g. to you and to 7.14
But this command I g. them, 'Obey my 7.23
and what I g. them has passed away 8.13
land which I g. to their fathers. 16.15
your heritage which I g. to you, 17.04
city which I g. to you and your 23.39
land which I g. to them and their 24.10
land which I g. to their fathers, 30.03
and I g. the deed of purchase to 32.12
the son of Rechab g. to his sons, 35.14
land which I g. to you and your 35.15
command which their father g. them, 35.16
scroll and g. it to Baruch the 36.32
So King Zedekiah g. orders, 37.21
and g. them vineyards and fields at 39.10
Nebuchadrezzar king of Babylon g. 39.11
of the guard g. him an allowance 40.05
as I g. Zedekiah king of Judah into 44.30
and g. him a seat above the seats 52.32
the LORD g. me into the hands of Lam 1.14
The LORD g. full vent to his wrath, 4.11
and he g. me the scroll to eat. Eze 3.02
Also my bread which I g. you— 16.19
but you g. your gifts of all your 16.33
and you g. hire, while no hire was 16.34
your children that you g. to them, 16.36
because he g. his hand and yet did 17.18
I g. them my statutes and showed 20.11
Moreover I g. them my sabbaths, as a 20.12
Moreover I g. them statutes that 20.25
helmet in you; they g. you splendor. 27.10
land which I g. to my servant 28.25
and g. over the people of Israel to 35.05
who g. my land to themselves as a 36.05
land which I g. to your fathers; 36.28
dwelt that I g. to my servant 37.25
from them and g. them into the 39.23
And the Lord g. Jehoiakim king of Dan 1.02
chief of the eunuchs g. them names: 1.07
And God g. Daniel favor and compassion 1.09
to drink, and g. them vegetables. 1.16
God g. them learning and skill in 1.17
Then the king g. Daniel high honors 2.48
his limbs g. way, and his knees 5.06
Most High God g. Nebuchadnezzar 5.18
of the greatness that he g. him, 5.19
and prayed and g. thanks before 6.10
that it was I who g. her the grain, Hos 2.08
through the prophets g. parables. 12.10
"I g. you cleanness of teeth in all Amo 4.06
the deep g. forth its voice, it Hab 3.10
and I g. them to him, that he might Mal 2.05
he g. orders to go over to the Mt 8.18
disciples and g. them authority 10.01
and broke and g. the loaves to the 14.19
the disciples g. them to the 14.19
broke them and g. them to the 15.36
the disciples g. them to the 15.36
and who g. you this authority?" 21.23
to a king who g. a marriage feast 22.02
to one he g. five talents, to 25.15
for I was hungry and you g. me food, 25.35
I was thirsty and you g. me drink, 25.35
I was hungry and you g. me no food, 25.42
thirsty and you g. me no drink, 25.42
and g. it to the disciples and said, 26.26
had given thanks he g. it to them, 26.27
and they g. them for the potter's 27.10
But he g. him no answer, not even to 27.14
on a reed, and g. it to him to drink. 27.48
they g. a sum of money to the 28.12
and also g. it to those who were Mk 2.26
So he g. them leave. And the unclean 5.13
and g. them authority over the 6.07
on his birthday g. a banquet for 6.21
the guard and g. orders to bring 6.27
a platter, and g. it to the girl; 6.28
and the girl g. it to her mother. 6.28
and g. them to the disciples to set 6.41
broke them and g. them to his 8.06
or who g. you this authority to do 11.28
and g. it to them, and said, "Take; 14.22
had given thanks he g. it to them, 14.23
on a reed and g. it to him to drink, 15.36
delivered, and she g. birth to a son. Lk 1.57
And she g. birth to her first-born 2.07
very hour she g. thanks to God, 2.38
and g. it back to the attendant, and 4.20
and also g. it to those with him?" 6.04
And he g. him to his mother. 7.15
you g. me no water for my feet, but 7.44
You g. me no kiss, but from the time 7.45
enter these. So he g. them leave. 8.32
together and g. them power and 9.01
and g. them to the disciples to set 9.16
and g. him back to his father. 9.42
two denarii and g. them to the 10.35
"A man once g. a great banquet, and 14.16
and no one g. him anything. 15.16
yet you never g. me a kid, that I 15.29
when they saw it, g. praise to God. 18.43
he g. them ten pounds, and said to 19.13
who it is that g. you this authority." 20.02
he broke it and g. it to them, 22.19
So Pilate g. sentence that their 23.24
and the breasts that never g. suck!' 23.29
and broke it, and g. it to them. 24.30
They g. him a piece of broiled fish, 24.42
he g. power to become children of Jn 1.12
the world that he g. his only Son, 3.16
that Jacob g. to his son Joseph. 4.05
who g. us the well, and drank from 4.12
'He g. them bread from heaven to 6.31
not Moses who g. you the bread 6.32
Moses g. you circumcision (not that 7.22
he g. it to Judas, the son of Simon 13.26
you from?" But Jesus g. no answer. 19.09
his head and g. up his spirit. 19.30
of Jesus, and Pilate g. him leave. 19.38
took the bread and g. it to them, 21.13
as the Spirit g. them utterance. Ac 2.04
which God g. to your fathers, 3.25
the apostles g. their testimony to 4.33
yet he g. him no inheritance in it, 7.05
And he g. him the covenant of 7.08
and g. him favor and wisdom before 7.10
But God turned and g. them over to 7.42
with one accord g. heed to what 8.06
They all g. heed to him, from the 8.10
And they g. heed to him, because for 8.11
And he g. her his hand and lifted 9.41
g. alms liberally to the people, and 10.02
If then God g. the same gift to 11.17
to them as he g. to us when we 11.17
he g. them their land as an inheritance, 13.19
And after that he g. them judges 13.20
and God g. them Saul the son of 13.21
he did good and g. you from heaven 14.17
and they g. great joy to all the 15.03
although we g. them no instructions, 15.24
off them and g. orders to beat 16.22
Then he g. orders to the centurion 24.23
of the Jews g. information about 25.15
and g. him leave to go to his 27.03
we g. way to it and were driven. 27.15
Therefore God g. them up in the Rom 1.24

GAVE (cont.)
For this reason God g. them up to Rom 1.26
men likewise g. up natural relations 1.27
God g. them up to a base mind and 1.28
his faith as he g. glory to God, 4.20
his own Son but g. him up for us 8.32
"God g. them a spirit of stupor, 11.08
watered, but God g. the growth. 1Co 3.06
became a man, I g. up childish ways. 13.11
to himself and g. us the ministry 2Co 5.18
For they g. according to their 8.03
but first they g. themselves to 8.05
which the Lord g. for building you 10.08
who g. himself for our sins to Gal 1.04
g. to me and Barnabas the right 2.09
who loved me and g. himself for me. 2.20
but God g. it to Abraham by a 3.18
captives, and he g. gifts to men. Eph 4.08
loved us and g. himself up for us, 5.02
the church and g. himself up for 5.25
instructions we g. you through the 1Th 4.02
loved us and g. us eternal comfort 2Th 2.16
we g. you this command: If any one 3.10
who g. himself as a ransom for all, 1Ti 2.06
grace which he g. us in Christ 2Ti 1.09
stood by me and g. me strength to 4.17
who g. himself for us to redeem us Tit 2.14
the patriarch g. him a tithe of Heb 7.04
Israelites and g. directions 11.22
again and the heaven g. rain, Jas 5.18
him from the dead and g. him glory, 1Pe 1.21
that God g. us eternal life, and 1Jn 5.11
which God g. him to show to his Rev 1.01
I g. her time to repent, but she 2.21
terrified and g. glory to the God 11.13
it the dragon g. his power and his 13.02
creatures g. the seven angels 15.07
And the sea g. up the dead in it, 20.13
Death and Hades g. up the dead in 20.13

GAVEST
woman whom thou g. to be with me, Gen 3.12
again to the land which thou g. to their 1Ki 8.34
land which thou g. to our fathers. 8.40
which thou g. to their fathers, the 8.48
land which thou g. to them and to 2Ch 6.25
land which thou g. to our fathers. 6.31
which thou g. to their fathers, the 6.38
Thou g. thy good Spirit to instruct Neh 9.20
and g. them water for their thirst. 9.20
great goodness which thou g. them, 9.35
land that thou g. to our fathers 9.36
thou g. it to him, length of days Ps 21.04
and thou g. them this land, which Jer 32.22
the work which thou g. me to do; Jn 17.04
men whom thou g. me out of the 17.06
and thou g. them to me, and they 17.06
them the words which thou g. me, 17.08
those whom thou g. me I lost not 18.09

GAZA
as far as G., and in the direction Gen 10.19
who lived in villages as far as G., Deu 2.23
them from Kadeshbarnea to G., and all the Jos 10.41
only in B., in Gath, and in Ashdod, 11.22
those of G., Ashdod, Ashkelon, Gath, 13.03
G., its towns and its villages; 15.47
Judah also took G. with its territory, Ju 1.18
as far as the neighborhood of G., 6.04
Samson went to G., and there he saw 16.01
eyes, and brought him down to G., 16.21
one for G., one for Ashkelon, one 1Sa 6.17
the Euphrates from Tiphsah to G., 1Ki 4.24
as far as G. and its territory, 2Ki 18.08
G., Ekron, and the remnant of Ashdod); Jer 25.20
Philistines, before Pharaoh smote G. 47.01
Baldness has come upon G., Ashkelon 47.05
"For three transgressions of G., Amo 1.06
send a fire upon the wall of G., 1.07
For G. shall be deserted, and Zep 2.04
G. too, and shall writhe in anguish; Zec 9.05
The king shall perish from G.; 9.05
goes down from Jerusalem to G. Ac 8.26

GAZE
to the LORD to g. and many of them Ex 19.21
And he fixed his g. and stared at 2Ki 8.11
and your g. be straight before you. Pro 4.25
Do not g. at me because I am swarthy, Sol 1.06
who g. at the stars, who at the new Is 47.13
and let our eyes g. upon Zion. Mic 4.11
them drunk, to g. on their shame! Hab 2.15
And Peter directed his g. at him, Ac 3.04
and nations g. at their dead bodies Rev 11.09

GAZED
The man g. at her in silence to Gen 24.21
of Sisera g. through the lattice: Ju 5.28
g. into heaven and saw the glory of Ac 7.55

GAZELLE
as of the g. and as of the hart. Deu 12.15
Just as the g. or the hart is eaten, 12.22
the hart, the g., the roebuck, the 14.05
as though it were a g. or a hart. 15.22
was as swift of foot as a wild g.; 2Sa 2.18
save yourself like a g. from the Pro 6.05
My beloved is like a g., or a young Sol 2.09
be like a g., or a young stag upon 2.17
twins of a g., that fed among the 4.05
are like two fawns, twins of a g. 7.03
and be like a g. or a young stag 8.14
And like a hunted g., or like a Is 13.14
Tabitha, which means Dorcas or G. Ac 9.36

GAZELLES
g., roebucks, and batted fowl. 1Ki 4.23
were swift as g. upon the mountains: 1Ch 12.08
by the g. or the hinds of the field, Sol 2.07
by the g. or the hinds of the field, 3.05

GAZEZ
concubine, bore Haran, Moza, and G.; 1Ch 2.46
and Haran was the father of G. 2.46

GAZING
g. in at the windows, looking Sol 2.09
he sat in the light and g. at him, Lk 22.56
And while they were g. into heaven Ac 1.10
And g. at him, all who sat in the 6.15

GAZINGSTOCK
with contempt, and make you a g. Nah 3.06

GAZITES
The G. were told, "Samson has come Ju 16.02

GAZZAM
Sons of Nekoda, the sons of G., Ez 2.48
the sons of G., the sons of Uzza, Neh 7.51

GEAR
on the Syrtis, they lowered the g., Ac 27.17

GEBA
G.—twelve cities with their villages: Jos 18.24
lands, G. with its pasture lands, 21.17
out of their place west of G. Ju 20.33
of the Philistines which was at G.; 1Sa 13.03
them, stayed in G. of Benjamin; 13.16
other on the south in front of G. 14.05
the Philistines from G. to Gezer. 2Sa 5.25
King Asa built G. of Benjamin and 1Ki 15.22
incense, from G. to Beersheba; 2Ki 23.08
G. with its pasture lands, Alemeth, 1Ch 6.60
houses of the inhabitants of G., 8.06

GEBA (cont.)
with them he built G. and Mizpah. 2Ch 16.06
The sons of Ramah and G., six hundred Ez 2.26
The men of Ramah and G., six hundred Neh 7.30
Benjamin also lived from G. onward, 11.31
from the region of G. and Azmaveth; 12.29
at G. they lodge for the night; Is 10.29
a plain from G. to Rimmon south of Zec 14.10

GEBAL
and the men of G. did the hewing 1Ki 5.18
G. and Ammon and Amalek, Philistia Ps 83.07
The elders of G. and her skilled Eze 27.09

GEBALITES
and the land of the G., and all Jos 13.05

GEBER
G. the son of Uri, in the land of 1Ki 4.19

GEBIM
inhabitants of G. flee for safety. Is 10.31

GECKO
the g., the land crocodile, the Lev 11.30

GEDALIAH
he appointed G. the son of Ahikam, 2Ki 25.22
Babylon had appointed G. governor, 25.23
with their men to G. at Mizpah, 25.23
And G. swore to them and their men, 25.24
and killed G. and the Jews and the 25.25
G., Zeri, Jeshaiah, Shimei, Hashabiah, 1Ch 25.03
the second to G., to him and his 25.09
and G., of the sons of Jeshua the Ez 10.18
G. the son of Pashhur, Jucal the son Jer 38.01
entrusted him to G. the son of 39.14
then return to G. the son of 40.05
Jeremiah went to G. the son of 40.06
had appointed G. the son of Ahikam 40.07
they went to G. at Mizpah—Ishmael 40.08
G. the son of Ahikam, son of Shaphan, 40.09
had appointed G. the son of Ahikam, 40.11
the land of Judah, to G. at Mizpah; 40.12
open country came to G. at Mizpah 40.13
But G. the son of Ahikam would 40.14
spoke secretly to G. at Mizpah, 40.15
But G. the son of Ahikam said to 40.16
with ten men to G. the son of 41.01
and struck down G. the son of 41.02
Jews who were with G. at Mizpah, 41.03
On the day after the murder of G., 41.04
"Come in to G. the son of Ahikam." 41.06
committed to G. the son of Ahikam. 41.10
he had slain G. the son of Ahikam— 41.16
had slain G. the son of Ahikam, 41.18
had left with G. the son of Ahikam, 43.06
son of G., son of Amariah, son of Zep 1.01

GEDER
Debir, one; the king of G., one; Jos 12.13

GEDERAH
G., Gederothaim: fourteen cities Jos 15.36
and inhabitants of Netaim and G.; 1Ch 4.23
Jahaziel, Johanan, Jozabad of G., 12.04

GEDERITE
the Shephelah was Baalhanan the G.; 1Ch 27.28

GEDEROTH
G., Bethdagon, Naamah, and Makkedah; Jos 15.41
G., Soco with its villages, Timnah 2Ch 28.18

GEDEROTHAIM
G.: fourteen cities with their Jos 15.36

GEDOR
Halhul, Bethzur, G., Jos 15.58
and Penuel was the father of G., 1Ch 4.04
wife bore Jered the father of G., 4.18
They journeyed to the entrance of G., 4.39
G., Ahio, Zecher, 8.31
G., Ahio, Zechariah, and Mikloth; 9.37
Zebadiah, the sons of Jeroham of G. 12.07

GEHARASHIM
father of Joab the father of G., 1Ch 4.14

GEHAZI
And he said to G. his servant, 2Ki 4.12
G. answered, "Well, she has no son, 4.14
he said to G. his servant, "Look, 4.25
And G. came to thrust her away. 4.27
He said to G., "Gird up your loins, 4.29
G. went on ahead and laid the staff 4.31
Then he summoned G. and said, 4.36
G., the servant of Elisha the man 5.20
So G. followed Naaman. And when 5.21
and they carried them before G. 5.23
to him, "Where have you been, G.?" 5.25
talking with G. the servant of the 8.04
And G. said, "My lord, O king, here is 8.05

GELILOTH
Enshemesh, and thence goes to G., Jos 18.17

GEMALLI
tribe of Dan, Ammiel the son of G.; Num 13.12

GEMARIAH
of Shaphan and G. the son of Jer 29.03
the chamber of G. the son of 36.10
When Micaiah the son of G., 36.11
G. the son of Shaphan, Zedekiah the 36.12
and Delaiah and G. urged the king 36.25

GENEALOGICAL
settlements, and they kept a g. record. 1Ch 4.33

GENEALOGIES
of Noah, according to their g., Gen 10.32
These are their g.: the first-born 1Ch 1.29
enrolled by g. in the days of 5.17
enrollment by g. was twenty-two 7.07
and their enrollment by g., 7.09
Their number enrolled by g., 7.40
So all Israel was enrolled by g.; 9.01
enrolled by g. in their villages. 9.22
among those enrolled in the g., Ez 2.62
among those enrolled in the g., Neh 7.64
and endless g. which promote 1Ti 1.04
g., dissensions, and quarrels over Tit 3.09

GENEALOGY
enrolled in the g. according to 1Ch 5.01
when the g. of their generations 5.07
mighty warriors, enrolled by g. 7.05
of whatever g. or fathers' houses. 26.31
except those enrolled by g., 2Ch 31.16
and this is the g. of those who Ez 8.01
the people to be enrolled by g. Neh 7.05
the book of the g. of those who 7.05
The book of the g. of Jesus Christ, Mt 1.01
He is without father or mother or g., Heb 7.03
has not their g. received tithes 7.06

GENERAL
the g. of Jabin's army, to meet you Ju 4.07

GENERALS
men and the g. and the rich and Rev 6.15

GENERATION
righteous man, blameless in his g.; Gen 6.09
are righteous before me in this g. 7.01

GENERATION (cont.)
come back here in the fourth g.; Gen 15.16
Ephraim's children of the third g.; 50.23
all his brothers, and all that g. Ex 1.06
have war with Amalek from g. to g." 17.16
and the fourth g. of those who 20.05
to the third and the fourth g." 34.07
the third and upon the fourth g.' Num 14.18
until all the g. that had done evil 32.13
of this evil g. shall see the good Deu 1.35
thirty-eight years, until the entire g., 2.14
and fourth g. of those who hate me, 5.09
to the tenth g. none of his 23.02
to the tenth g. none belonging to 23.03
of the third g. that are born to 23.08
And the g. to come, your children 29.22
they are a perverse and crooked g. 32.05
be, for they are a perverse g., 32.20
And all that g. also were gathered Ju 2.10
there arose another g. after them, 2.10
of the fourth g. shall sit on the 2Ki 10.30
throne of Israel to the fourth g." 15.12
and kept throughout every g., in every Est 9.28
us, guard us ever from this g. Ps 12.07
GOD is with the g. of the righteous. 14.05
tell of the LORD to the coming g., 22.30
Such is the g. of those who seek 24.06
that you may tell the next g. 48.13
he will go to the g. of his fathers, 49.19
untrue to the g. of thy children. 73.15
to the coming g. the glorious 78.04
that the next g. might know them, 78.06
a stubborn and rebellious g., 78.08
a g. whose heart was not steadfast, 78.08
from g. to g. we will recount 79.13
years I loathed that g. and said, 95.10
Let this be recorded for a g. to come, 102.18
righteousness from g. to g. for ever. 106.31
be blotted out in the second g.! 109.13
the g. of the upright will be 112.02
One g. shall laud thy works to 145.04
A g. goes, and a g. comes, but the Ecc 1.04
From g. to g. it shall lie waste; Is 34.10
from g. to g. they shall dwell 34.17
and as for his g., who considered 53.08
And you, O g., heed the word of the Jer 2.31
and forsaken the g. of his wrath.' 7.29
his dominion is from g. to g. Dan 4.03
kingdom endures from g. to g.; 4.34
and their children another g. Joe 1.03
"But to what shall I compare this g.? Mt 11.16
and adulterous g. seeks for a sign; 12.39
with this g. and condemn it; for they 12.41
with this g. and condemn it; for she 12.42
shall it be also with this evil g." 12.45
and adulterous g. seeks for a sign, 16.04
"O faithless and perverse g., 17.17
all this will come upon this g. 23.36
this g. will not pass away till all 24.34
said, "Why does this g. seek a sign? Mk 8.12
no sign shall be given to this g." 8.12
in this adulterous and sinful g., 8.38
"O faithless g., how long am I to 9.19
this g. will not pass away before 13.30
those who fear him from g. to g. Lk 1.50
shall I compare the men of this g., 7.31
"O faithless and perverse g., 9.41
began to say, "This g. is an evil g.; 11.29
will the Son of man be to this g. 11.30
the men of this g. and condemn 11.31
with this g. and condemn it; 11.32
world, may be required of this g., 11.50
it shall be required of this g. 11.51
in their own g. than the sons of 16.08
things and be rejected by this g. 17.25
this g. will not pass away till all 21.32
yourselves from this crooked g." Ac 2.40
Who can describe his g.? For his life 8.33
the counsel of God in his own g., 13.36
midst of a crooked and perverse g., Php 2.15
Therefore I was provoked with that g., Heb 3.10
in the seventh g. from Adam prophesied, Jud 1.14

GENERATIONS
These are the g. of the heavens and Gen 2.04
This is the book of the g. of Adam. 5.01
These are the g. of Noah. Noah was 6.09
is with you, for all future g.: 9.12
These are the g. of the sons of 10.01
throughout their g. for an everlasting 17.07
after you throughout their g. 17.09
every male throughout your g., 17.12
to be remembered throughout all g. Ex 3.15
sons of Levi according to their g.: 6.16
the Levites according to their g. 6.19
throughout your g. you shall observe 12.14
this day, throughout your g., as an 12.17
people of Israel throughout their g. 12.42
of it be kept throughout your g., 16.32
the LORD, to be kept throughout your g." 16.33
throughout their g. by the people 27.21
throughout your g. at the door of 29.42
before the LORD throughout your g. 30.08
in the year throughout your g.; 30.10
descendants throughout their g." 30.21
anointing oil throughout your g. 30.31
me and you throughout your g., 31.13
the sabbath throughout their g., 31.16
priesthood throughout their g." 40.15
perpetual statute throughout your g., Lev 3.17
for ever throughout your g., from the 6.18
perpetual due throughout their g." 7.36
statute for ever throughout your g. 10.09
ever to them throughout their g. 17.07
throughout their g. who has a 21.17
throughout your g. approaches the 22.03
throughout your g. in all your 23.14
your dwellings throughout your g. 23.21
throughout your g. in all your 23.31
for ever throughout your g.; you shall 23.41
that your g. may know that I made 23.43
statute for ever throughout your g. 24.03
who bought it, throughout his g.; 25.30
their g., by their families by Num 1.20
their g., by their families, by 1.22
their g., by their families, by 1.24
their g., by their families, by 1.26
their g., by their families, by 1.28
their g., by their families, by 1.30
their g., by their families, by 1.32
their g., by their families, by 1.34
their g., by their families, by 1.36
their g., by their families, by 1.38
their g., by their families, by 1.40
their g., by their families, by 1.42
These are the g. of Aaron and Moses 3.01
perpetual statute throughout your g. 10.08
is among you throughout your g., 15.14
perpetual statute throughout your g.; 15.15
an offering throughout your g. 15.21
and onward throughout your g., 15.23
their garments throughout their g., 15.38
perpetual statute throughout your g.; 18.23
throughout your g. in all your 35.29
commandments, to a thousand g., Deu 7.09
old, consider the years of many g.; 32.07
you, and between the g. after us, Jos 22.27
only that the g. of the people of Ju 3.02
shown me future g., O Lord GOD! 2Sa 7.19
genealogy of their g. was reckoned: 1Ch 5.07
Tola, mighty warriors of their g., 7.02
by their g., according to their 7.04
genealogies, according to their g., 7.09
according to their g., chief men. 8.28

GENERATIONS (cont.)
kinsmen according to their g., 1Ch 9.09
the Levites, according to their g., 9.34
he commanded, for a thousand g., 16.15
shown me future g., O LORD God! 17.17
sons, and his sons' sons, four g. Job 42.16
throughout all g. I shall not meet Ps 10.06
thoughts of his heart to all g. 33.11
name to be celebrated in all g.; 45.17
their dwelling places to all g., 49.11
may his years endure to all g.! 61.06
thy might to all the g. to come. 71.18
as the moon, throughout all g.! 72.05
thou prolong thy anger to all g.? 85.05
proclaim thy faithfulness to all g. 89.01
and build your throne for all g. 89.04
been our dwelling place in all g. 90.01
and his faithfulness to all g. 100.05
thy name endures to all g. 102.12
years endure throughout all g.! 102.24
he commanded, for a thousand g., 105.08
Thy faithfulness endures to all g.; 119.90
dominion endures throughout all g. 145.13
ever, thy God, O Zion, to all g. 146.10
and does a crown endure to all g.? Pro 27.24
inhabited or dwelt in for all g.; Is 13.20
calling the g. from the beginning? 41.04
ever, and my salvation to all g." 51.08
in days of old, the g. of long ago. 51.09
up the foundations of many g.; 58.12
cities, the devastations of many g. 61.04
for ever, nor inhabited for all g. Jer 50.39
thy throne endures to all g. Lam 5.19
them through the years of all g. Joe 2.02
for ever, and Jerusalem to all g. 3.20
So all the g. from Abraham to David Mt 1.17
Abraham to David were fourteen g., 1.17
deportation to Babylon fourteen g., 1.17
Babylon to the Christ fourteen g. 1.17
henceforth all g. will call me Lk 1.48
In past g. he allowed all the Ac 14.16
For from early g. Moses has had in 15.21
of men in other g. as it has now Eph 3.05
and in Christ Jesus to all g., 3.21
for ages and g. but now made Col 1.26

GENEROSITY
Or do you begrudge my g.?' Mt 20.15
enriched in every way for great g., 2Co 9.11
and by the g. of your contribution 9.13

GENEROUS
whoever is of a g. heart, let him Ex 35.05
but the righteous is g. and gives; Ps 37.21
Many seek the favor of a g. man, Pro 19.06
of food with glad and g. hearts, Ac 2.46
in good deeds, liberal and g., 1Ti 6.18

GENEROUSLY
the man who deals g. and lends, Ps 112.05
to all men g. and without reproaching, Jas 1.05

GENNESARET
over, they came to land at G. Mt 14.34
over, they came to land at G., Mk 6.53
he was standing by the lake of G. Lk 5.01

GENTILE
be to you as a G. and a tax Mt 18.17
live like a G. and not like a Jew, Gal 2.14
Jews by birth and not G. sinners, 2.15

GENTILES
the Jordan, Galilee of the G.— Mt 4.15
Do not even the G. do the same? 5.47
heap up empty phrases as the G. do; 6.07
For the G. seek all these things; 6.32
them, "Go nowhere among the G., 10.05
testimony before them and the G. 10.18
shall proclaim justice to the G. 12.18
and in his name will the G. hope." 12.21
him to the G. to be mocked and 20.19
rulers of the G. lord it over them, 20.25
death, and deliver him to the G.; Mk 10.33
rule over the G. lord it over them, 10.42
a light for revelation to the G., Lk 2.32
For he will be delivered to the G., 18.32
will be trodden down by the G., 21.24
the times of the G. are fulfilled. 21.24
kings of the G. exercise lordship 22.25
"Why did the G. rage, and the Ac 4.25
with the G. and the peoples of 4.27
name before the G. and kings and 9.15
had been poured out even on the G. 10.45
heard that the G. also had received 11.01
"Then to the G. also God has 11.18
life, behold, we turn to the G. 13.46
set you to be a light for the G., 13.47
And when the G. heard this, they 13.48
stirred up the G. and poisoned 14.02
was made by both G. and Jews, 14.05
opened a door of faith to the G. 14.27
reporting the conversion of the G., 15.03
by my mouth the G. should hear the 15.07
had done through them among the G. 15.12
how God first visited the G., 15.14
and all the G. who are called by my 15.17
those of the G. who turn to God, 15.19
who are the G. in Antioch and 15.23
From now on I will go to the G." 18.06
him into the hands of the G.'" 21.11
done among the G. through his 21.19
are among the G. to forsake Moses, 21.21
But as for the G. who have believed, 21.25
I will send you far away to the G.'" 22.21
from the people and from the G.— 26.17
of Judea, and also to the G., 26.20
both to the people and to the G." 26.23
of God has been sent to the G.; 28.28
well as among the rest of the G. Rom 1.13
When G. who have not the law do by 2.14
among the G. because of you." 2.24
Is he not the God of G. also? Yes, of G. also, 3.29
the Jews only but also from the G.? 9.24
That G. who did not pursue righteousness 9.30
salvation has come to the G., 11.11
failure means riches for the G., 11.12
Now I am speaking to you G. 11.13
then as I am an apostle to the G., 11.13
the full number of the G. come in, 11.25
order that the G. might glorify 15.09
I will praise thee among the G., 15.09
"Rejoice, O G., with his people"; 15.10
all G., and let all the peoples 15.11
come, he who rises to rule the G.; 15.12
in him shall the G. hope." 15.12
Jesus to the G. in the priestly 15.16
offering of the G. may be acceptable, 15.16
me to win obedience from the G., 15.18
for if the G. have come to share in 15.27
the churches of the G. give thanks; 16.04
block to Jews and folly to G., 1Co 1.23
danger from G., danger in the city, 2Co 11.26
I might preach him among the G., Gal 1.16
gospel which I preach among the G., 2.02
through me also for the G.), 2.08
go to the G. and they to the 2.09
from James, he ate with the G.; 2.12
you compel the G. to live like 2.14
God would justify the G. by faith, 3.08
of Abraham might come upon the G., 3.14
at one time you G. in the flesh, Eph 2.11
Christ Jesus on behalf of you G.— 3.01
how the G. are fellow heirs, members 3.06
preach to the G. the unsearchable 3.08

GENTILES (cont.)
must no longer live as the G. do, Eph 4.17
great among the G. are the riches Col 1.27
speaking to the G. that they may 1Th 2.16
teacher of the G. in faith and 1Ti 2.07
that all the G. might hear it. 2Ti 4.17
Maintain good conduct among the G., 1Pe 2.12
for doing what the G. like to do, 4.03

GENTLE
as the g. rain upon the tender Deu 32.02
A g. tongue is a tree of life, but Pro 15.04
But I was like a g. lamb led to the Jer 11.19
for I am g. and lowly in heart, and Mt 11.29
But we were g. among you, like a 1Th 2.07
no drunkard, not violent but g., 1Ti 3.03
to be g., and to show perfect Tit 3.02
g., open to reason, full of mercy Jas 3.17
to the kind and g. but also to the 1Pe 2.18
jewel of a g. and quiet spirit, 3.04

GENTLENESS
or with love in a spirit of g.? 1Co 4.21
by the meekness and g. of Christ— 2Co 10.01
g., self-control; against such Gal 5.23
restore him in a spirit of g. 6.01
faith, love, steadfastness, g. 1Ti 6.11
correcting his opponents with g. 2Ti 2.25
yet do it with g. and reverence; 1Pe 3.15

GENTLY
"Deal g. for my sake with the young 2Sa 18.05
or the word that deals g. with you? Job 15.11
the waters of Shiloah that flow g., Is 8.06
and g. lead those that are with 40.11
And when the south wind blew g., Ac 27.13
He can deal g. with the ignorant Heb 5.02

GENUBATH
of Tahpenes bore him G. his son, 1Ki 11.20
and G. was in Pharaoh's house among 11.20

GENUINE
Let love be g.; hate what is Rom 12.09
those who are g. among you may be 1Co 11.19
kindness, the Holy Spirit, g. love, 2Co 6.06
others that your love also is g. 8.08

GENUINELY
who will be g. anxious for your Php 2.20

GENUINENESS
so that the g. of your faith, more 1Pe 1.07

GERA
G., Naaman, Ehi, Rosh, Muppim, Huppim, Gen 46.21
the son of G., the Benjaminite, a Ju 3.15
name was Shimei, the son of G.; 2Sa 16.05
And Shimei the son of G., 19.16
the son of G. fell down before the 19.18
also with you Shimei the son of G., 1Ki 2.08
And Bela had sons: Addar, G., Abihud, 1Ch 8.03
G., Shephuphan, and Huram. 8.05
and G., that is, Heglam, who was the 8.07

GERAHS
sanctuary (the shekel is twenty g.), Ex 30.13
twenty g. shall make a shekel. Lev 27.25
sanctuary, the shekel of twenty g., Num 3.47
the sanctuary, which is twenty g. 18.16
The shekel shall be twenty g.; Eze 45.12

GERAR
from Sidon, in the direction of G., Gen 10.19
and Shur; and he sojourned in G. 20.01
Abimelech king of G. sent and took 20.02
And Isaac went to G., to Abimelech 26.01
So Isaac dwelt in G. 26.06
the valley of G. and dwelt there. 26.17
the herdsmen of G. quarreled with 26.20
to him from G. with Ahuzzath his 26.26
with him pursued them as far as G., 2Ch 14.13
all the cities round about G., 14.14

GERASENES
the sea, to the country of the G. Mk 5.01
arrived at the country of the G., Lk 8.26
country of the G. asked him to 8.37

GERIZIM
on Mount G. and the curse on Mount Deu 11.29
upon Mount G. to bless the people: 27.12
front of Mount G. and half of them Jos 8.33
and stood on the top of Mount G., Ju 9.07

GERSHOM
a son, and he called his name G.; Ex 2.22
name of the one was G. (for he said, 18.03
and Jonathan the son of G., Ju 18.30
of Levi: G., Kohath, and Berari. 1Ch 6.01
of Levi: G., Kohath, and Merari. 6.16
are the names of the sons of G.: 6.17
Of G.: Libni his son, Jahath his son, 6.20
son of Jahath, son of G., son of Levi. 6.43
of the sons of G., Joel the chief, 15.07
of Levi: G.. Kohath, and Merari. 23.06
The sons of G. were Ladan and 23.07
The sons of Moses: G. and Eliezer. 23.15
The sons of G.: Shebuel the chief. 23.16
and Shebuel the son of G., son of 26.24
Of the sons of Phinehas, G. Of the Ez 8.02

GERSHOMITES
To the G. according to their families 1Ch 6.62
To the G. were given out of the 6.71

GERSHON
of Levi: G., Kohath, and Merari. Gen 46.11
G., Kohath, and Merari, the years of Ex 6.16
The sons of G.: Libni and Shimei, by 6.17
their names: G. and Kohath and Merari. Num 3.17
of the sons of G. by their families: 3.18
Of G. were the family of the 3.21
of the sons of G. in the tent of 3.25
"Take a census of the sons of G. also, 4.22
The number of the sons of G., 4.38
of the families of the sons of G.. 4.41
oxen he gave to the sons of G., 7.07
the sons of G. and the sons of 10.17
of G., the family of the Gershonites; 26.57

GERSHONITE
belonging to Ladan the G.: Jehieli. 1Ch 26.21
LORD, in the care of Jehiel the G. 29.08

GERSHONITES
these were the families of the G. Num 3.21
The families of the G. were to 3.23
of the fathers' house of the G. 3.24
service of the families of the G. 4.24
the sons of the G. shall be at the 4.27
the sons of the G. in the tent of 4.28
of Gershon, the family of the G.; 26.57
The G. received by lot from the Jos 21.06
And to the G., one of the families 21.27
families of the G. were in all 21.33
the sons of the G. belonging to 1Ch 26.21
and of the G., Joah the son of 2Ch 29.12

GERUTH
and stayed at G. Chimham near Jer 41.17

GESHAN
G., Pelet, Ephah, and Shaaph. 1Ch 2.47

GESHEM
and G. the Arab heard of it, they Neh 2.19
Tobiah and to G. the Arab and to 6.01

GESHEM (cont.)
Sanballat and G. sent to me, saying, Neh 6.02
and G. also says it, that you and 6.06

GESHUR
but G. and Maacath dwell in the Jos 13.13
the daughter of Talmai king of G.; 2Sa 3.03
the son of Ammihud, king of G. 13.37
and went to G., and was there three 13.38
So Joab arose and went to G., 14.23
to ask, "Why have I come from G.? 14.32
a vow while I dwelt at G. in Aram, 15.08
But G. and Aram took from them 1Ch 2.23
the daughter of Talmai, king of G.; 3.02

GESHURITES
border of the G and the Maacathites, Deu 3.14
boundary of the G. and the Maacathites, Jos 12.05
Philistines, and all those of the G. 13.02
region of the G. and Maacathites, 13.11
drive out the G. or the Maacathites; 13.13
up, and made raids upon the G., 1Sa 27.08

GET
g. out of this place; for the LORD Gen 19.14
"G. me this maiden for my wife." 34.04
trade in it, and g. property in it." 34.10
and so g. me out of this house. 40.14
their work? G. to your burdens." Ex 5.04
Go yourselves, g. your straw wherever 5.11
g. your cattle and all that you 9.19
said to him, "G. away from me; 10.28
'G. you out, and all the people who 11.08
them and I will g. glory over 14.04
them and I will g. glory over 14.17
means to g. it back for himself, Lev 25.28
Where am I to g. meat to give to Num 11.13
G. away from about the dwelling of 16.24
"G. away from the midst of this 16.45
and g. from them rods, one for each 17.02
who gives you power to g. wealth; Deu 8.18
you shall not go back to g. it; 24.19
now g. her for me as my wife." Ju 14.02
said to his father, "G. her for me; 14.03
"G. up, let us be going." But there was 19.28
let me g. away, and see my brothers.' 1Sa 20.29
making haste to g. away from Saul, 23.26
let him g. up the water shaft to 2Sa 5.08
lest he g. himself fortified cities, 20.06
with clothes, he could not g. warm. 1Ki 1.01
and g. something from him." 2Ki 5.20
and each of us g. there a log, 6.02
them alive and g. into the city.'" 7.12
let us g. grain, that we may eat and Neh 5.02
our houses to g. grain because of 5.03
and thou didst g. thee a name, 9.10
Jews hoped to g. the mastery over Est 9.01
the Jews should g. the mastery 9.01
he will not let me g. my breath, Job 9.18
a stupid man will g. understanding, 11.12
his friends to g. a share of their 17.05
trading he will g. no enjoyment. 20.18
profit do we g. if we pray to him?' 21.15
growl if they do not g. their fill. Ps 59.15
that we may g. at heart of wisdom. 90.12
they g. them away and lie down in 104.22
vineyards, and g. a fruitful yield. 107.37
Through thy precepts I g. understanding; 119.104
let no iniquity g. dominion over 119.133
enter my house or g. into my bed; 132.03
ways of all who g. gain by violence Pro 1.19
honor, but fools g. disgrace. 3.35
of my mouth. G. wisdom; g. insight. 4.05
G. wisdom, and whatever you g., g. insight. 4.07
Wounds and dishonor will he g., 6.33
honor, and violent men g. riches. 11.16
man will g. precious wealth. 12.27
To g. wisdom is better than gold; 16.16
to g. understanding is to be chosen 16.16
g. everything ready for you in the 24.27
his eyes will g. many a curse. 28.27
G. you up to a high mountain, O Zion, Is 40.09
"let us g. wine, let us fill ourselves 56.12
field for money and g. witnesses"— Jer 32.25
king sent Jehudi to g. the scroll, 36.21
the wood we g. must be bought. Lam 5.04
and to Assyria, to g. bread enough. 5.06
We g. our bread at the peril of our 5.09
g. you to the house of Israel, and Eze 3.04
And go, g. you to the exiles, to your 3.11
and g. yourselves a new heart and a 18.31
destroying lives to g. dishonest gain. 22.27
impatient to g. off and patrol the Zec 6.07
you will never g. out till you Mt 5.26
give will be the measure you g. 7.02
did this man g. this wisdom and 13.54
then did this man g. all this?" 13.56
the disciples g. into the boat and 14.22
"Where are we to g. bread enough in 15.33
"G. behind me, Satan! You are a hindrance 16.23
to the tenants, to g. his fruit; 21.34
how did you g. in here without a 22.12
they could not g. near him because Mk 2.04
give will be the measure you g., 4.24
"Where did this man g. all this? 6.02
his disciples g. into the boat and 6.45
"G. behind me, Satan! For you are not 8.33
to g. from them some of the fruit 12.02
will be the measure you g. back." Lk 6.38
about, to lodge and g. provisions; 9.12
I cannot g. up and give you anything'? 11.07
he will not g. up and give him 11.08
and to eat and drink and g. drunk, 12.45
you will never g. out till you 12.59
"G. away from here, for Herod wants 13.31
I give tithes of all that I g.' 18.12
where do you g. that living water? Jn 4.11
for each of them to g. a little." 6.07
woke him, saying, "G. up quickly." Ac 12.07
'Make haste and g. quickly out of 22.18
of the night g. ready two hundred 23.23
return did you g. from the things Rom 6.21
the return you g. is sanctification 6.22
temple service g. their food from 1Co 9.13
gospel should g. their living by 9.14
who will g. ready for battle? 14.08
And do not g. drunk with wine, for Eph 5.18
and those who g. drunk are drunk at 1Th 5.07
but they will not g. very far, 2Ti 3.09
G. Mark and bring him with you; 4.11
year there and trade and g. gain"; Jas 4.13

GETHER
of Aram: Uz, Hul, G., and Mash. Gen 10.23
Aram. Uz, Hul, G., and Meshech. 1Ch 1.17

GETHSEMANE
with them to a place called G., Mt 26.36
to a place which was called G.; Mk 14.32

GETS
though a man g. praise when he Ps 49.18
and the man who g. understanding, Pro 3.13
corrects a scoffer g. himself abuse, 9.07
and the wicked g. into it instead. 11.08
A gracious woman g. honor, and violent 11.16
righteousness g. a sure reward. 11.18
and g. nothing, while the soul of 13.04
He who g. wisdom loves himself; 19.08
but from the LORD a man g. justice. 29.26
woman when she g. a husband, and a maid 30.23
so is he who g. riches but not by Jer 17.11
Woe to him who g. evil gain for his Hab 2.09
on service g. entangled in civilian 2Ti 2.04

GETTING
The g. of treasures by a lying Pro 21.06
And g. into a boat he crossed over Mt 9.01
And as he was g. into the boat, the Mk 5.18
and g. into the boat again he 8.13
G. into one of the boats, which was Lk 5.03
a flock without g. some of the 1Co 9.07

GEUEL
tribe of Gad, G. the son of Machi. Num 13.15

GEZER
Then Horam king of G. came up to Jos 10.33
Eglon, one; the king of G., one; 12.12
then to G., and it ends at the sea. 16.03
the Canaanites that dwelt in G.: 16.10
of Ephraim, G. with its pasture lands, 21.21
out the Canaanites who dwelt in G.; Ju 1.29
Canaanites dwelt in G. among them. 1.29
the Philistines from Geba to G. 2Sa 5.25
and Hazor and Megiddo and G. 1Ki 9.15
up and captured G. and burnt it 9.16
so Solomon rebuilt G.) and Bethhoron 9.17
of Ephraim, G. with its pasture lands, 1Ch 6.67
and westward G. and its towns, 7.28
Philistine army from Gibeon to G. 14.16
war with the Philistines at G.; 20.04

GHOST
the ground like the voice of a g., Is 29.04
were terrified, saying. "It is a g.!" Mt 14.26
thought it was a g., and cried out; Mk 6.49

GIAH
lies before G. on the way to the 2Sa 2.24

GIANTS
one of the descendants of the g., 2Sa 21.16
one of the descendants of the g. 21.18
he also was descended from the g. 21.20
were descended from the g. of Gath; 21.22
one of the descendants of the g.; 1Ch 20.04
he also was descended from the g. 20.06
were descended from the g. in Gath; 20.08

GIBBAR
the sons of G., ninety-five. Ez 2.20

GIBBETHON
Eltekeh, G., Baalath, Jos 19.44
pasture lands, G. with its pasture lands, 21.23
and Baasha struck him down at G., 1Ki 15.27
all Israel were laying siege to G. 15.27
troops were encamped against G., 16.15
So Omri went up from G., and all 16.17

GIBEA
of Machbenah and the father of G.; 1Ch 2.49

GIBEAH
Kain, G., and Timnah: ten cities with Jos 15.57
G. and Kiriathjearim—fourteen 18.28
and they buried him at G., the town of 24.33
of Israel, but we will pass on to G." Ju 19.12
spend the night at G. or at Ramah. 19.13
the sun went down on them near G., 19.14
to go in and spend the night at G. 19.15
and he was sojourning in G.; 19.16
"I came to G. that belongs to 20.04
And the men of G. rose against me, 20.05
But now this is what we will do to G.: 20.09
they may requite G. of Benjamin, 20.10
up the men, the base fellows in G., 20.13
together out of the cities of G., 20.14
besides the inhabitants of G., 20.15
morning, and encamped against G. 20.19
the battle line against them at G. 20.20
The Benjaminites came out of G., 20.21
them out of G. the second day, 20.25
set men in ambush round about G. 20.29
set themselves in array against G., 20.30
up to Bethel and the other to G., 20.31
came against G. ten thousand 20.34
whom they had set against G. 20.36
made haste and rushed upon G.; 20.37
as far as opposite G. on the east. 20.43
When they came to G., behold, a band 1Sa 10.10
Saul also went to his home at G., 10.26
When the messengers came to G. of Saul, 11.04
with Jonathan in G. of Benjamin; 13.02
up from Gilgal to G. of Benjamin. 13.15
outskirts of G. under the pomegranate 14.02
of Saul in G. of Benjamin looked; 14.16
went up to his house in G. of Saul. 15.34
Saul was sitting at G., under the 22.06
the Ziphites went up to Saul at G., 23.19
Then the Ziphites came to Saul at G., 26.01
son of Ribai of G. of the Benjaminites, 2Sa 23.29
son of Ribai of G. of the Benjaminites, 1Ch 11.31
Joash, both sons of Shemaah of G.; 12.03
the daughter of Uriel of G. 2Ch 13.02
Ramah trembles, G. of Saul has fled. Is 10.29
Blow the horn in G., the trumpet Hos 5.08
themselves as in the days of G.: 9.09
From the days of G., you have 10.09
Shall not war overtake them in G.? 10.09

GIBEATHELOHIM
After that you shall come to G., 1Sa 10.05

GIBEATH-HAARALOTH
circumcised the people of Israel at G. Jos 5.03

GIBEON
inhabitants of G. heard what Joshua Jos 9.03
Now their cities were G., Chephirah, 9.17
inhabitants of G. had made peace 10.01
because G. was a great city, like 10.02
and help me, and let us smite G.; 10.04
armies and encamped against G., 10.05
And the men of G. sent to Joshua at 10.06
them with a great slaughter at G., 10.10
"Sun, stand thou still at G., 10.12
country of Goshen, as far as G. 10.41
the Hivites, the inhabitants of G.; 11.19
G., Ramah, Beeroth, 18.25
G. with its pasture lands, Geba with 21.17
Saul, went out from Mahanaim to G. 2Sa 2.12
out and met them at the pool of G.; 2.13
Helkathhazzurim, which is at G. 2.16
on the way to the wilderness of G. 2.24
brother Asahel in the battle at G. 3.30
at the great stone which is in G., 20.08
the LORD at G. on the mountain of 21.06
king went to G. to sacrifice there, 1Ki 3.04
At G. the LORD appeared to Solomon 3.05
as he had appeared to him at G. 9.02
Jeiel the father of G. dwelt in G., 1Ch 8.29
In G. dwelt the father of G., Jeiel, 9.35
Ishmaiah of G., a mighty man among 12.04
Philistine army from G. to Gezer. 14.16
in the high place that was at G., 16.39
that time in the high place at G.; 21.29
to the high place that was at G.; 2Ch 1.03
came from the high place at G., 1.13
the men of G. and of Mizpah, who Neh 3.07
The sons of G., ninety-five. 7.25
be wroth as in the valley of G.; Is 28.21
son of Azzur, the prophet from G., Jer 28.01
at the great pool which is in G. 41.12
whom Johanan brought back from G. 41.16

GIBEONITE
Melatiah the G. and Jadon the Neh 3.07

GIBEONITES
because he put the G. to death. 2Sa 21.01
king called the G. Now the G. were 21.02
And David said to the G., "What 21.03
The G. said to him, "It is not a 21.04
gave them into the hands of the G., 21.09

GIDDALTI
G., and Romamtiezer, Joshbekashah, 1Ch 25.04
to G., his sons and his brethren, 25.29

GIDDEL
the sons of G., the sons of Gahar, Ez 2.47
sons of Darkon, the sons of G., 2.56
the sons of G., the sons of Gahar, Neh 7.49
sons of Darkon, the sons of G., 7.58

GIDEON
as his son G. was beating out wheat Ju 6.11
And G. said to him, "Pray, sir, if the 6.13
So G. went into his house and prepared 6.19
Then G. perceived that he was the 6.22
and G. said, "Alas, O Lord GOD! 6.22
Then G. built an altar there to the 6.24
So G. took ten men to his servants, 6.27
"G. the son of Joash has done this 6.29
of the LORD took possession of G.; 6.34
Then G. said to God, "If thou wilt 6.36
Then G. said to God, "Let not thy 6.39
is, G.) and all the people who were 7.01
The LORD said to G., "The people 7.02
And G. tested them; twenty-two 7.03
And the LORD said to G., "The people 7.04
and the LORD said to G., "Every one 7.05
And the LORD said to G., "With the 7.07
When G. came, behold a man was 7.13
the sword of G. the son of Joash, a 7.14
When G. heard the telling of the 7.15
shout, 'For the LORD and for G.'" 7.18
So G. and the hundred men who were 7.19
"A sword for the LORD and for G.!" 7.20
And G. sent messengers throughout 7.24
and Zeeb to G. beyond the Jordan. 7.25
And G. came to the Jordan and 8.04
And G. said, "Well then, when the 8.07
And G. went up by the caravan route 8.11
Then G. the son of Joash returned 8.13
And G. arose and slew Zebah and 8.21
Then the men of Israel said to G., 8.22
G. said to them, "I will not rule 8.23
And G. said to them, "Let me make a 8.24
And G. made an ephod of it and put 8.27
a snare to G. and to his family. 8.27
rest forty years in the days of G. 8.28
Now G. had seventy sons, his own 8.30
And G. the son of Joash died in a 8.32
As soon as G. died, the people of 8.33
G.) in return for all the good that 8.35
time would fail me to tell of G., Heb 11.32

GIDEONI
from Benjamin, Abidan the son of G.; Num 1.11
Benjamin being Abidan the son of G., 2.22
the ninth day Abidan the son of G., 7.60
offering of Abidan the son of G. 7.65
Benjamin was Abidan the son of G. 10.24

GIDOM
and they were pursued hard to G., Ju 20.45

GIFT
my g. that is brought to you, Gen 33.11
so much as marriage present and g., 34.12
"If his g. for a burnt offering is Lev 1.10
offer it as a g. to the LORD 17.04
and he shall offer his g. to the LORD, Num 6.14
Levites as a g. to Aaron and his 8.19
they are a g. to you, given to the 18.06
I give your priesthood as a g., 18.07
is yours, the offering of their g., 18.11
Or has he given us any g.?" 2Sa 19.42
Have I said, 'Make me a g.'? Job 6.22
A man's g. makes room for him and Pro 18.16
A g. in secret averts anger; 21.14
who boasts of a g. he does not 25.14
it is God's g. to man that every Ecc 3.13
in his toil—this is the g. of God. 5.19
prince makes a g. to any of his Eze 46.16
But if he makes a g. out of his 46.17
sons may keep a g. from his 46.17
With such a g. from your hand, will Mal 1.09
are offering your g. at the altar, Mt 5.23
leave your g. there before the 5.24
and then come and off your g. 5.24
and offer the g. that Moses commanded, 8.04
swears by the g. that is on the 23.18
the g. or the altar that makes the g. 23.19
her, "If you knew the g. of God, Jn 4.10
receive the g. of the Holy Spirit. Ac 2.38
obtain the g. of God with money! 8.20
because the g. of the Holy Spirit 10.45
gave the same g. to them as he 11.17
some spiritual g. to strengthen Rom 1.11
are justified by his grace as a g., 3.24
reckoned as a g. but as his due. 4.04
But the free g. is not like the 5.15
and the free g. in the grace of 5.15
And the free g. is not like the 5.16
but the free g. following many 5.16
and the free g. of righteousness 5.17
but the free g. of God is eternal 6.23
"Or who has given a g. to him that 11.35
not lacking in any spiritual g., 1Co 1.07
you boast as if it were not a g.? 4.07
has his own special g. from God, 7.07
to carry your g. to Jerusalem. 16.03
this liberal g. which we are 2Co 8.20
for this g. you have promised, so 9.05
as an exaction but as a willing g. 9.05
be to God for his inexpressible g.! 9.15
own doing, it is the g. of God— Eph 2.08
according to the g. of God's grace 3.07
to the measure of Christ's g. 4.07
Not that I seek the g.; but I seek Php 4.17
Do not neglect the g. you have, 1Ti 4.14
to rekindle the g. of God that is 2Ti 1.06
who have tasted the heavenly g., Heb 6.04
and every perfect g. is from above, Jas 1.17
As each has received a g., employ it 1Pe 4.10

GIFTS
sorts of choice g. from his master; Gen 24.10
of his concubines Abraham gave g., 25.06
of Israel hallow as their holy g.; Ex 28.38
of the LORD, and besides your g., Lev 23.38
Out of all the g. to you, you shall Num 18.29
the choicest g. of heaven above, Deu 33.13
with the best g. of the earth and 33.16
LORD the votive g. of his father 1Ki 15.15
his father and his own votive g., 15.15
all the votive g. that Jehoshaphat 2Ki 12.18
dedicated, and his own votive g., 12.18
the treasuries of the dedicated g. 1Ch 26.20
the dedicated g. which David the 26.26
they dedicated g. for the maintenance 26.27
all dedicated g. were in the care 26.28
the treasuries for dedicated g.; 28.12
God the votive g. of his father 2Ch 15.18
his father and his own votive g., 15.18
Their father gave them great g., 21.03
And many brought g. to the LORD to 32.23
to enjoy its fruit and its good g., Neh 9.36
and gave g. with royal liberality. Est 2.18
to one another and g. to the poor. 9.22

GIFTS (cont.)

Tyre will sue your favor with g., Ps 45.12
and receiving g. among men, even 68.18
at Jerusalem kings bear g. to thee. 68.29
kings of Sheba and Seba bring g.! 72.10
him bring g. to him who is to be 76.11
be appeased though you multiply g. Pro 6.35
is a friend to a man who gives g. 19.06
but one who exacts g. ruins it. 29.04
loves a bribe and runs after g. Is 1.23
At that time g. will be brought to 18.07
Men give g. to all harlots; but Eze 16.33
you gave your g. to all your lovers, 16.33
their very g. in making them offer 20.26
When you offer your g. and sacrifice 20.31
profane with your g. and your idols. 20.39
and the choicest of your g., with all 20.40
receive from me g. and rewards and Dan 2.06
high honors and many great g., 2.48
"Let your g. be for yourself, and 5.17
with precious stones and costly g. 11.38
give parting g. to Moreshethgath; Mic 1.14
treasures, they offered him g., Mt 2.11
to give good g. to your children, 7.11
to give good g. to your children, Lk 11.13
putting their g. into the treasury; 21.01
They presented many g. to us; Ac 28.10
For the g. and the call of God are Rom 11.29
Having g. that differ according to 12.06
understand the g. bestowed on us 1Co 2.12
not receive the g. of the Spirit 2.14
Now concerning spiritual g., 12.01
Now there are varieties of g., 12.04
to another g. of healing by the one 12.09
Do all possess g. of healing? 12.30
But earnestly desire the higher g. 12.31
earnestly desire the spiritual g., 14.01
of captives, and he gave g. to men." Eph 4.08
And his g. were that some should be 4.11
from Epaphroditus the g. you sent, Php 4.18
miracles and by g. of the Holy Heb 2.04
to offer g. and sacrifices for sins. 5.01
appointed to offer g. and sacrifices; 8.03
who offer g. according to the law. 8.04
g. and sacrifices are offered which 9.09
witness by accepting his g.; he died, 11.04

GIHON

The name of the second river is G.; Gen 2.13
own mule, and bring him down to G.; 1Ki 1.33
David's mule, and brought him to G. 1.38
have anointed him king at G.; and 1.45
the waters of G. and directed them 2Ch 32.30
to the city of David west of G., 33.14

GILALAI

G., Maai Nethanel, Judah, and Hanani, Neh 12.36

GILBOA

all Israel, and they encamped at G. 1Sa 28.04
Philistines, and fell slain on Mount G. 31.01
his three sons fallen on Mount G. 31.08
I happened to be on Mount G.; and there 2Sa 1.06
"Ye mountains of G., let there be no 1.21
the Philistines killed Saul on G.; 21.12
Philistines, and fell slain on Mount G. 1Ch 10.01
and his sons fallen on Mount G. 10.08

GILEAD

face toward the hill country of G. Gen 31.21
him into the hill country of G. 31.23
encamped in the hill country of G. 31.25
of Ishmaelites coming from G., 37.25
and Machir was the father of G.; Num 26.29
of G., the family of the Gileadites. 26.29
These are the sons of G.: of Iezer, 26.30
son of G., son of Machir, son of 27.01
land of Jazer and the land of G., 32.01
remain there in the cities of G.; 32.26
the land of G. for a possession; 32.29
of Manasseh went to G. and took it, 32.39
And Moses gave G. to Machir the son 32.40
of the sons of G. the son of Machir, 36.01
as far as G., there was not a city Deu 2.36
tableland and all G. and all Bashan, 3.10
hill country of G. with its cities 3.12
the rest of G., and all Bashan, the 3.13
To Machir I gave G., 3.15
territory from G. as far as the 3.16
and Ramoth in G. for the Gadites, 4.43
all the land, G. as far as Dan, 34.01
Ammonites, that is, half of G., Jos 12.02
over half of G. to the boundary of 12.05
and G., and the region of the 13.11
Jazer, and all the cities of G., 13.25
and half G., and Ashtaroth, and 13.31
the father of G., were allotted G. 17.01
son of G., son of Machir, son of 17.03
besides the land of G. and Bashan, 17.05
The land of G. was allotted to the 17.06
and Ramoth in G., from the tribe of 20.08
Ramoth in G. with its pasture lands, 21.38
of Canaan, to go to the land of G., 22.09
of Manasseh, in the land of G., 22.13
of Manasseh, in the land of G., 22.15
in the land of G. to the land of 22.32
G. stayed beyond the Jordan; Ju 5.17
day, which are in the land of G. 10.04
of the Amorites, which is in G. 10.08
to arms, and they encamped in G.; 10.17
And the people, the leaders of G., 10.18
over all the inhabitants of G." 10.18
G. was the father of Jephthah. 11.01
the elders of G. went to bring 11.05
But Jephthah said to the elders of G., 11.07
And the elders of G. said to 11.08
over all the inhabitants of G." 11.08
Jephthah said to the elders of G., 11.09
And the elders of G. said to 11.10
Jephthah went with the elders of G., 11.11
he passed through G. and Manasseh, 11.29
and passed on to Mizpah of G., 11.29
from Mizpah of G. he passed on to 11.29
all the men of G. and fought with 12.04
and the men of G. smote Ephraim, 12.04
the men of G. said to him, "Are 12.05
and was buried in his city in G. 12.07
Beersheba, including the land of G., 20.01
Jordan to the land of Gad and G. 1Sa 13.07
him king over G. and the Ashurites 2Sa 2.09
Absalom encamped in the land of G. 17.26
Then they came to G., and to Kadesh 24.06
which are in G., and he had the 1Ki 4.13
Geber the son of Uri, in the land of G., 4.19
of Tishbe in G., said to Ahab, "As 17.01
eastward, all the land of G., 2Ki 10.33
the Arnon, that is, G. and Bashan. 10.33
G., and Galilee, all the land of 15.29
daughter of Machir the father of G., 1Ch 2.21
twenty-three cities in the land of G. 2.22
descendants of Machir, the father of G. 2.23
had multiplied in the land of G. 5.09
throughout all the region east of G. 5.10
son of G., son of Michael, son of 5.14
and they dwelt in G., in Bashan and 5.16
Ramoth in G. with its pasture lands, 6.80
she bore Machir the father of G. 7.14
the sons of G. the son of Machir, 7.17
them were found at Jazer in G.) 26.31
for the half tribe of Manasseh in G., 27.21
G. is mine; Manasseh is mine; Ps 60.07
G. is mine; Manasseh is mine; 108.08
goats, moving down the slopes of G. Sol 4.01
goats, moving down the slopes of G. 6.05

GILEAD (cont.)
Is there no balm in G.? Is there no Jer 8.22
"'You are as G. to me, as the summit 22.06
Go up to G., and take balm, O virgin 46.11
on the hills of Ephraim and in G. 50.19
Jordan between G. and the land of Eze 47.18
G. is a city of evildoers, tracked Hos 6.08
is iniquity in G. they shall 12.11
have threshed G. with threshing Amo 1.03
ripped up women with child in G., 1.13
and Benjamin shall possess G. Ob 1.19
in Bashan and G. as in the days of Mic 7.14
to the land of G. and to Lebanon, Zec 10.10

GILEADITE
After him arose Jair the G., who Ju 10.03
Now Jephthah the G. was a mighty 11.01
of Jephthah the G. four days in 11.40
Then Jephthah the G. died, and was 12.07
and Barzillai the G. from Rogelim, 2Sa 17.27
Now Barzillai the G. had come down 19.31
with the sons of Barzillai the G., 1Ki 2.07
the daughters of Barzillai the G., Ez 2.61
Barzillai the G. and was called by Neh 7.63

GILEADITES
of Gilead, the family of the G. Num 26.29
you G., in the midst of Ephraim and Ju 12.04
And the G. took the fords of the 12.05
him with fifty men of the G., 2Ki 15.25

GILEAD'S
And G. wife also bore him sons; Ju 11.02

GILGAL
over against G., beside the oak of Deu 11.30
encamped in G. on the east border Jos 4.19
of the Jordan, Joshua set up in G. 4.20
place is called G. to this day. 5.09
encamped in G. they kept the 5.10
went to Joshua in the camp at G., 9.06
sent to Joshua at the camp in G., 10.06
So Joshua went up from G., 10.07
marched up all night from G. 10.09
Israel with him, to the camp at G. 10.15
Israel with him, to the camp at G. 10.43
of Judah came to Joshua at G.; 14.06
so northward, turning toward G., 15.07
the LORD went up from G. to Bochim. Ju 2.01
at the sculptured stones near G., 3.19
by year to Bethel, G., and Mizpah; 1Sa 7.16
And you shall go down before me to G.; 10.08
let us go to G. and there renew the 11.14
So all the people went to G., 11.15
Saul king before the LORD in G. 11.15
were called out to join Saul at G. 13.04
Saul was still at G., and all the 13.07
but Samuel did not come to G., 13.08
will come down upon me at G., 13.12
went up from G. to Gibeah of 13.15
and passed on, and went down to G." 15.12
sacrifice to the LORD you God in G." 15.21
in pieces before the LORD in G. 15.33
Judah came to G. to meet the king 2Sa 19.15
The king went on to G., and Chimham 19.40
Elisha were on their way from G. 2Ki 2.01
came again to G. when there was a 4.38
Enter not into G., nor go up to Hos 4.15
Every evil of theirs is in G.; 9.15
if in G. they sacrifice bulls, their 12.11
to G., and multiply transgression; Amo 4.04
not enter into G. or cross over to 5.05
for G. shall surely go into exile, 5.05
what happened from Shittim to G., Mic 6.05

GILO
Eliam the son of Ahithophel of G., 2Sa 23.34

GILOH
and G.: eleven cities with their Jos 15.51
counselor, from his city G. 2Sa 15.12

GILONITE
he sent for Ahithophel the G., David's 2Sa 15.12

GIMZO
and G. with its villages; and they 2Ch 28.18

GINATH
followed Tibni the son of G., 1Ki 16.21
who followed Tibni the son of G.; 16.22

GINNETHOI
Iddo, G., Abijah, Neh 12.04

GINNETHON
Daniel, G., Baruch, Neh 10.06
of Iddo, Zechariah; of G., Meshullam; 12.16

GIRD
to g. it on, shall be of the same Ex 28.08
and g. him with the skilfully woven 29.05
and you shall g. them with girdles 29.09
to g. it on, was of the same materials 39.05
but the feeble g. on strength. 1Sa 2.04
his men, "Every man g. on his sword!" 25.13
and g. on sackcloth, and mourn 2Sa 3.31
For thou didst g. me with strength 22.40
"G. up your loins, and take my staff 2Ki 4.29
"G. up your loins, and take this 9.01
G. up your loins like a man, I will Job 38.03
"G. up your loins like a man; 40.07
For thou didst g. me with strength Ps 18.39
G. your sword upon your thigh, O 45.03
the hills g. themselves with joy, 65.12
of wrath thou wilt g. upon thee. 76.10
all you far countries; g. yourselves Is 8.09
g. yourselves and be dismayed. 8.09
in the streets they g. on sackcloth; 15.03
and g. sackcloth upon your loins. 32.11
I g. you, though you do not know me, 45.05
But you, g. up your loins; arise, and Jer 1.17
For this g. you with sackcloth, 4.08
g. on sackcloth, and roll in ashes; 6.26
G. yourselves with sackcloth, lament, 49.03
They g. themselves with sackcloth, Eze 7.18
and g. themselves with sackcloth, 27.31
they shall not g. themselves with 44.18
G. on sackcloth and lament, O priests, Joe 1.13
g. your loins; collect all your Nah 2.01
he will g. himself and have them Lk 12.37
and g. yourself and serve me, till I 17.08
another will g. you and carry you Jn 21.18
Therefore g. up your minds, be sober, 1Pe 1.13

GIRDED
your loins g., your sandals on your Ex 12.11
and g. him with the girdle, and Lev 8.07
and g. him with the skilfully woven 8.07
and g. them with girdles, and bound 8.13
be g. with the linen girdle, and 16.04
man of you g. on his weapons of Deu 1.41
and he g. it on his right thigh Ju 3.16
LORD, a boy g. with a linen ephod. 1Sa 2.18
And David g. his sword over his 17.39
every man of them g. on his sword; 25.13
David also g. on his sword; 25.13
and David was g. with a linen ephod. 2Sa 6.14
and who was g. with a new sword, 21.16
and he g. up his loins and ran 1Ki 18.46
So they g. sackcloth on their loins, 20.32
had his sword g. at his side while Neh 4.18
the God who g. me with strength, and Ps 18.32
sackcloth and g. me with gladness, 30.11
the mountains, being g. with might; 65.06

GIRDED (cont.)
is robed, he is g. with strength. Ps 93.01
g. with belts on their loins, with Eze 23.15
loins were g. with gold of Uphaz. Dan 10.05
Lament like a virgin g. with Joe 1.08
"Let your loins be g. and your Lk 12.35
and g. himself with a towel. Jn 13.04
the towel with which he was g. 13.05
you g. yourself and walked where 21.18
having g. your loins with truth, and Eph 6.14
their breasts g. with golden girdles. Rev 15.06

GIRDING
of a rich robe, a g. of sackcloth; Is 3.24
to baldness and g. with sackcloth; 22.12

GIRDLE
checker work, a turban, and a g; Ex 28.04
shall make a g. embroidered with 28.39
and the g. of fine twined linen and 39.29
coat, and girded him with the g., Lev 8.07
body, be girded with the linen g., 16.04
his sword and his bow and his g. 1Sa 18.04
you ten pieces of silver and a g." 2Sa 18.11
over it was a g. with a sword in 20.08
blood upon the g. about my loins, 1Ki 2.05
with a g. of leather about his 2Ki 1.08
and instead of a g., a rope; Is 3.24
Righteousness shall be the g. of his waist, 11.05
faithfulness the g. of his loins. 11.05
robe, and will bind your g. on him, 22.21
and a leather g. around his waist; Mt 3.04
had a leather g. around his waist, Mk 1.06
he took Paul's g. and bound his Ac 21.11
who owns this g. and deliver him 21.11
with a golden g. round his breast; Rev 1.13

GIRDLES
shall make coats and g. and caps; Ex 28.40
gird them with g. and bind caps on 29.09
coats, and girded them with g., Lev 8.13
she delivers g. to the merchant. Pro 31.24
their breasts girded with golden g. Rev 15.06

GIRDS
not him that g. on his armor boast 1Ki 20.11
with which he daily g. himself! Ps 109.19
She g. her loins with strength and Pro 37.17

GIRGASHITE
Perizzite, the Jebusite, and the G.; Neh 9.08

GIRGASHITES
Jebusites, the Amorites, the G., Gen 10.16
Canaanites, the G. and the Jebusites. 15.21
the G., the Amorites, the Canaanites, Deu 7.01
the G., the Amorites, and the Jos 3.10
the G., the Hivites, and the Jebusites; 24.11
Jebusites, the Amorites, the G., 1Ch 1.14

GIRL
So the g. went and called the Ex 2.08
and have sold a g. for wine, Joe 3.03
for the g. is not dead but sleeping." Mt 9.24
her by the hand, and the g. arose. 9.25
on a platter and given to the g., 14.11
"Little g., I say to you, arise." Mk 5.41
And immediately the g. got up and 5.42
and the king said to the g., 6.22
a platter, and gave it to the g.; 6.28
and the g. gave it to her mother. 6.28
met by a slave g. and who had a spirit Ac 16.16
and if a g. marries she does not 1Co 7.28
woman or g. is anxious about the 7.34

GIRL'S
and when the g. father saw him, he Ju 19.03
the g. father, made him stay, and he 19.04
to go; but the g. father said to his 19.05
and the g. father said to the man, 19.06
and the g. father said, "Strengthen 19.08
the g. father, said to him, "Behold, 19.09

GIRLS
But all the young g. who have not Num 31.18
of boys and g. playing in its Zec 8.05

GIRT
all g. with swords and expert in Sol 3.08

GIRZITES
the G., and the Amalekites; for these 1Sa 27.08

GISHPA
and Ziha and G. were over the temple Neh 11.21

GITTAIM
the Beerothites fled to G., and have 2Sa 4.03
Hazor, Ramah, G., Neh 11.33

GITTITE
to the house of Obededom the G. 2Sa 6.10
of Obededom the G. three months; 6.11
Then the king said to Ittai the G., 15.19
So Ittai the G. passed on, with all 15.22
under the command of Ittai the G. 18.02
Bethlehemite, slew Goliath the G., 21.19
to the house of Obededom the G. 1Ch 13.13
the brother of Goliath the G., 20.05

GITTITES
the six hundred G. who had followed 2Sa 15.18

GIVE
the heavens to g. light upon the Gen 1.15
the heavens to g. light upon the 1.17
green plants, I g. you everything. 9.03
descendants I will g. this land." 12.07
you see I will g. to you and to 13.15
the land, for I will g. it to you." 13.17
"G. me the persons, but take the 14.21
"O Lord God, what wilt thou g. me, 15.02
to g. you this land to possess." 15.07
"To your descendants I g. this land, 15.18
And I will g. to you, and to your 17.08
moreover I will g. you a son by 17.16
g. me property among you for a 23.04
that he may g. me the cave of 23.09
price let him g. it to me in your 23.09
I g. you the field, and I g. you 23.11
and I g. you the cave that is in it; 23.11
sons of my people I g. it to you; 23.11
I will g. the price of the field; 23.13
descendants I will g. this land, 24.07
"Pray g. me a little water to drink 24.17
and if they will not g. her to you, 24.41
"Pray g. me a little water from 24.43
and I will g. your camels drink 24.46
descendants I will g. all these 26.03
and will g. to your descendants all 26.04
May God g. you of the dew of heaven, 27.28
May he g. the blessing of Abraham 28.04
you lie I will g. to you and to 28.13
and will g. me bread to eat and 28.20
me I will g. the tenth to thee." 28.22
better that I g. her to you than 29.19
that I should g. her to any other 29.19
"G. me my wife that I may go in to 29.21
to g. the younger before the 29.26
and we will g. you the other also 29.27
"G. me children, or I shall die!" 30.01
"G. me, I pray, some of your son's 30.14
G. me my wives and my children for 30.26
name your wages, and I will g. it." 30.28
He said, "What shall I g. you?" 30.31
said, "You shall not g. me anything; 30.31

GIVE (cont.)
I pray you, g. her to him in marriage. Gen 34.08
g. your daughters to us, and take 34.09
whatever you say to me I will g. 34.11
and I will g. according as you say 34.12
only g. me the maiden to be my wife." 34.12
to g. our sister to one who is 34.14
Then we will g. our daughters to 34.16
and let us g. them our daughters. 34.21
Abraham and Isaac I will g. to you, 35.12
and I will g. the land to your 35.12
lest he should g. offspring to his 38.09
She said, "What will you g. me, 38.16
"Will you g. me a pledge, till you 38.17
He said, "What pledge shall I g. you?" 38.18
as I did not g. her to my son 38.26
God will g. Pharaoh a favorable 41.16
and to g. them provisions for the 42.25
his sack to g. his ass provender 42.27
and I will g. you the best of the 45.18
G. no thought to your goods, for the 45.20
to Joseph, and said, "G. us food; 47.15
"G. your cattle, and I g. you food 47.16
and g. us seed, that we may live, and 47.19
you shall g. a fifth to Pharaoh, 47.24
peoples, and will g. this land to your 48.04
me, and I will g. you your wages." Ex 2.09
And I will g. this people favor in 3.21
"You shall no longer g. the people 5.07
Pharaoh, 'I will not g. you straw. 5.10
to g. them the land of Canaan, the 6.04
which I swore to g. to Abraham, 6.08
I will g. it to you for a possession. 6.08
land which the LORD will g. you, 12.25
he swore to your fathers to g. you, 13.05
fathers, and shall g. it to you, 13.11
a pillar of fire to g. them light, 13.21
and g. heed to his commandments and 15.26
"G. us water to drink." And Moses 17.02
I will g. you counsel, and God be 18.19
then you shall g. life for life, 21.23
then he shall g. for the redemption 21.30
the owner shall g. to their master 21.32
he shall g. money to its owner, and 21.34
he shall g. the marriage present 22.16
utterly refuses to g. her to him, 22.17
of your sons you shall g. to me. 22.29
eighth day you shall g. it to me. 22.30
G. heed to him and hearken to his 23.21
and I will g. you the tables of 24.12
the testimony which I shall g. you. 25.16
the testimony that I shall g. you. 25.21
all that I will g. you in commandment 25.22
set up so as to g. light upon the 25.37
then each shall g. a ransom for 30.12
in the census shall g. this: half a 30.13
upward, shall g. the LORD's offering. 30.14
The rich shall not g. more, and the 30.15
and the poor shall not g. less, 30.15
when you g. the LORD's offering to 30.15
promised I will g. to your descendants, 32.13
'To your descendants I will g. it.' 33.01
with you, and I will g. you rest." 33.14
fifth to it and g. it to the Lev 5.16
and g. it to him to whom it belongs, 6.05
thigh you shall g. to the priest 7.32
which I g. you for a possession, and 14.34
and g. them to the priest; 15.14
You shall not g. any of your 18.21
shall any woman g. herself to a 18.23
and I will g. it to you to possess, 20.24
and g. the holy thing to the priest. 22.14
land which I g. you and reap its 23.10
offerings, which you g. to the LORD. 23.38
come into the land which I g. you, 25.02
nor g. him your food for profit. 25.37
of Egypt to g. you the land of 25.38
then I will g. you your rains in 26.04
And I will g. peace in the land, and 26.06
the man shall g. the amount of the 27.23
And you shall g. the Levites to Num 3.09
and g. the money by which the excess 3.48
countenance upon you, and g. you peace. 6.26
and g. them to the Levites, to each 7.05
lamps shall g. light in front of 8.02
up its lamps to g. light in front 8.03
LORD said, 'I will g. it to you'; 10.29
didst swear to g their fathers?' 11.12
to get meat to g. to all this 11.13
'G. us meat, that we may eat.' 11.13
saying, "Who will g. us meat to eat? 11.18
Therefore the LORD will g. you meat, 11.18
'I will g. them meat, that they may 11.21
which I g. to the people of Israel; 13.02
us into this land and g. it to us, 14.08
land which he swore to g. to them, 14.16
I swore to g. to their fathers; 14.23
are to inhabit, which I g. you, 15.02
meal you shall g. to the LORD an 15.21
I g. your priesthood as a gift, and 18.07
what they g. to the LORD, I g. to you. 18.12
present to the LORD I g. to you, 18.19
it you shall g. the LORD's offering 18.28
And you shall g. her to Eleazar the 19.03
them; so you shall g. drink to the 20.08
Thus Edom refused to g. Israel 20.21
wilt indeed g. this people into my 21.02
together, and I will g. them water." 21.16
Balak were to g. me his house full 22.18
'If Balak should g. me his house 24.13
I g. to him my covenant of peace; 25.12
tribe you shall g. a large inheritance, 26.54
tribe you shall g. a small inheritance; 26.54
G. to us a possession among our 27.04
you shall g. them possession of an 27.07
then you shall g. his inheritance 27.09
then you shall g. his inheritance 27.10
then you shall g. his inheritance 27.11
and g. it to Eleazar the priest as 31.29
and g. them to the Levites who have 31.30
which I swore to g. to Abraham, 32.11
then you shall g. them the land of 32.29
tribe you shall g. a large inheritance, 33.54
tribe you shall g. a small inheritance; 33.54
commanded to g. to the nine tribes 34.13
that they g. to the Levites, from 35.02
and you shall g. to the Levites 35.02
which you shall g. to the Levites, 35.04
which you g. to the Levites shall 35.06
them you shall g. forty-two cities. 35.06
which you g. to the Levites shall 35.07
which you shall g. from the possession 35.08
shall g. of its cities to the 35.08
which you g. shall be your six 35.13
You shall g. three cities beyond 35.14
my lord to g. the land for inheritance 36.02
by the LORD to g. the inheritance 36.02
to g. to them and to their descendants Deu 1.08
to g. us into the hand of the 1.27
I swore to g. to your fathers, 1.35
children I will g. the land upon 1.36
in there, and to them I will g. it, 1.39
to your voice or g. ear to you. 1.45
for I will not g. you any of their 2.05
for I will not g. you any of their 2.09
for I will not g. you any of the 2.19
and g. me water for money, that I 2.28
that he might g. him into your hand, 2.30
I have begun to g. Sihon and his 2.31
g. heed to the statutes and the 4.01
to g. you their land for an inheritance, 4.38
land which I g. them to possess.' 5.31
to g. you, with great and goodly 6.10
LORD swore to g. to your fathers 6.18

GIVE (cont.)

bring us in and g. us the land Deu 6.23
he swore to g. to our fathers. 6.23
he swore to your fathers to g. you. 7.13
LORD your God will g. over to you, 7.16
your God will g. them over to you, 7.23
And he will g. their kings into 7.24
LORD swore to g. to your fathers. 8.01
swore to their fathers to g. them.' 10.11
your fathers to g. to them and to 11.09
he will g. the rain for your land 11.14
And he will g. grass in your fields 11.15
swore to your fathers to g. them, 11.21
you may g. it to the alien who is 14.21
and you g. him nothing, and he cry 15.09
You shall g. to him freely, and your 15.10
not be grudging when you g. to him; 15.10
blessed you, you shall g. to him. 15.14
which you shall g. as the LORD 16.10
every man shall g. as he is able, 16.17
the instructions which they g. you, 17.11
they shall g. to the priest the 18.03
of your sheep, you shall g. him. 18.04
g. heed to soothsayers and to 18.14
will not g. need to my words which 18.19
he promised to g. to your fathers— 19.08
your enemies, to g. you the victory.) 20.04
him, will not g. heed to them, 21.18
and g. them to the father of the 22.19
with her shall g. to the father of 22.29
save you and to g. up your enemies 23.14
"You shall not g. up to his master 23.15
you shall g. him his hire on the 24.15
LORD swore to our fathers to g. us.' 26.03
swore to your fathers to go to you. 28.11
to g. the rain of your land in its 28.12
he will not g. to any of them any 28.55
but the LORD will g. you there a 28.65
to Isaac, and to Jacob, to g. them," 30.20
And the LORD will g. them over to 31.05
sworn to their fathers to g. them; 31.07
I swore to g. to their fathers, and 31.20
into the land that I swore to g." 31.21
the land which I swore to g. them: 31.23
"G. ear, O heavens, and I will speak; 32.01
which I g. to the people of Israel 32.49
land which I g. to the people of 32.52
"G. to Levi thy Thummim, and thy 33.08
'I will g. it to your descendants.' 34.04
swore to their fathers to g. them. Jos 1.06
of rest, and will g. you this land.' 1.13
father's house, and g. me a sure sign, 2.12
sworn to their fathers to g. us, 5.06
to g. us into the hands of the 7.07
g. glory to the LORD God of Israel, 7.19
your God will g. it into your hand. 8.07
for I will g. it into your hand." 8.18
Moses to g. you all the land, and 9.24
time I will g. over all of them, 11.06
So now g. me this hill country of 14.12
to him will I g. Achsah my daughter 15.16
She said to him, "G. me a present; 15.19
g. me also springs of water." 15.19
Moses to g. us an inheritance 17.04
and g. him a place, and he shall 20.04
they shall not g. up the slayer 20.05
he swore to g. to their fathers; 21.43
I will g. him Achsah my daughter as Ju 1.12
She said to him, "G. me a present; 1.15
g. me also springs of water." 1.15
I swore to g. to your fathers. 2.01
and he did not g. them into the 2.23
and I will g. him into your hand.'" 4.07
g. me a little water to drink; 4.19
"Hear, O kings, g. ear, O princes; 5.03
many for me to g. the Midianites 7.02
and g. the Midianites into your 7.07
g. loaves of bread to the people 8.05
that we should g. bread to your 8.06
that we should g. bread to your 8.15
g. me every man of you the earrings 8.24
answered, "We will willingly g. them." 8.25
"If thou wilt g. the Ammonites into 11.30
then I will g. you thirty linen 14.12
then you shall g. me thirty linen 14.13
that we may g. you into the hands 15.12
bind you and g. you into their 15.13
we will each g. you eleven hundred 16.05
and I will g. you ten pieces of 17.10
g. your advice and counsel here." 20.07
Now therefore g. up the men, the 20.13
tomorrow I will g. them into your 20.28
one of us shall g. his daughter in 21.01
we will not g. them any of our 21.07
Yet we cannot g. them wives of our 21.18
neither did you g. them to them, 21.22
the LORD will g. you by this young Ru 4.12
he would g. portions to Peninnah 1Sa 1.04
he would g. Hannah only one portion, 1.05
but wilt g. to thy maidservant a 1.11
then I will g. him to the LORD all 1.11
he will g. strength to his king, and 2.10
"G. meat for the priest to roast; 2.15
would say, "No, you must g. it now; 2.16
"The LORD g. you children by this 2.20
was with child, about to g. birth. 4.19
But she did not answer or g. heed. 4.20
and g. glory to the God of Israel; 6.05
"G. us a king to govern us." And 8.06
olive orchards and g. them to his 8.14
vineyards and g. it to his officers 8.15
and I will g. it to the man of God, 9.08
greet you and g. you two loaves of 10.04
"G. us seven days respite that we 11.03
we will g. ourselves up to you." 11.03
"Tomorrow we will g. ourselves up to 11.10
Wilt thou g. them into the hand of 14.37
O LORD, God of Israel, g. Urim; 14.41
in thy people Israel, g. Thummim." 14.41
g. me a man, that we may fight 17.10
and will g. him his daughter, and 17.25
and I will g. your flesh to the 17.44
and I will g. the dead bodies of 17.46
and he will g. you into our hand." 17.47
I will g. her to you for a wife; 18.17
"Let me g. her to him, that she may 18.21
G. me five loaves of bread, or 21.03
is none like that; g. it to me." 21.09
son of Jesse g. every one of you 22.07
for I will g. the Philistines into 23.04
but God did not g. him into his 23.14
I will g. your enemy into your hand, 24.04
and g. sentence between me and you, 24.15
Pray, g. whatever you have at hand 25.08
and g. it to men who come from I do 25.11
Moreover the LORD will g. Israel 28.19
the LORD will g. the army of Israel 28.19
we will not g. them any of the 30.22
"G. me my wife Michal, whom I 2Sa 3.14
Wilt thou g. them into my hand 5.19
will certainly g. the Philistines 5.19
and I will g. you rest from all 7.11
and g. them to your neighbor, and he 12.11
Tamar come and g. me bread to eat, 13.05
'G. up the man who struck his 14.07
and I will g. orders concerning you." 14.08
to me, and I would g. him justice." 15.04
of Israel will g. me back the 16.03
to Ahithophel, "G. your counsel; 16.20
been glad to g. you ten pieces of 18.11
g. up him alone, and I will withdraw 20.21
And the king said, "I will g. them." 21.06
Thou didst g. a wide place for my 22.37
some one would g. me water to drink 23.15

GIVE (cont.)

let me g. you counsel, that you may 1Ki 1.12
to g. me Abishag the Shunammite as 2.17
God said, "Ask what I shall g. you." 3.05
G. thy servant therefore an understanding 3.09
Behold, I g. you a wise and discerning 3.12
I g. you also what you have not 3.13
and g. half to the one, and half to 3.25
g. her the living child, and by no 3.26
"G. the living child to the first 3.27
and dost g. them to an enemy, so 8.46
you and will g. it to your servant. 11.11
but I will g. one tribe to your son, 11.13
Solomon, and will g. you ten tribes 11.31
and will g. it to you, ten tribes. 11.35
Yet to his son I will g. one tribe, 11.36
David, and I will g. Israel to you. 11.38
yourself, and I will g. you a reward." 13.07
"If you g. me half your house, I 13.08
And he will g. Israel up because of 14.16
And he said to her, "G. me your son." 17.19
that you would g. your servant 18.09
I will g. it into your hand this 20.13
therefore I will g. all this great 20.28
"G. me your vineyard, that I may 21.02
and I will g. you a better vineyard 21.02
I will g. you its value in money." 21.02
that I should g. you the inheritance 21.03
"I will not g. you the inheritance 21.04
'G. me your vineyard for money; 21.06
I will g. you another vineyard for 21.06
'I will not g. you my vineyard.'" 21.06
I will g. you the vineyard of 21.07
he refused to g. you for money; 21.15
the LORD will g. it into the hand 22.06
the LORD will g. it into the hand 22.12
the LORD will g. it into the hand 22.15
three kings to g. them into the 2Ki 3.10
three kings to g. them into the 3.13
he will also g. the Moabites into 3.18
"G. to the men, that they may eat." 4.42
"G. them to the men, that they may 4.43
pray, g. them a talent of silver and 5.22
'G. your son, that we may eat him 6.28
'G. your son, that we may eat him'; 6.29
he promised to g. a lamp to him 8.19
said, "If it is, g. me your hand." 10.15
of those whom I g. into your hands 10.24
Then they would g. the money that 12.11
'G. your daughter to my son for a 14.09
to g. to the king of Assyria. 15.20
I will g. you two thousand horses, 18.23
and g. them into the hand of their 21.14
and let them g. it to the workmen 22.05
the land to g. the money according 23.35
to g. it to Pharaoh Neco. 23.35
some one would g. me water to 1Ch 11.17
Wilt thou g. them into my hand?" 14.10
and I will g. them into your hand." 14.10
O g. thanks to the LORD, call on his 16.08
saying, "To you I will g. the land 16.18
O g. thanks to the LORD, for he is 16.34
that we may g. thanks to thy holy 16.35
named to g. thanks to the LORD, for 16.41
"G. me the site of the threshing 21.22
g. it to me at its full price—that 21.22
see, I g. the oxen for burnt 21.23
cereal offering. I g. it all." 21.23
I will g. him peace from all his 22.09
and I will g. peace and quiet to 22.09
of my God I g. it to the house of 29.03
great and to g. strength to all. 29.12
to him, "Ask what I shall g. you." 2Ch 1.07
G. me now wisdom and knowledge to 1.10
I will also g. you riches, possessions, 1.12
I will g. for your servants, the 2.10
and dost g. them to an enemy, so 6.36
for God will g. it into the hand 18.05
the LORD will g. it into the hand 18.11
to g. judgment for the LORD and to 19.08
and g. it for ever to the descendants 20.07
"G. thanks to the Lord, for his 20.21
had promised to g. a lamp to him 21.07
them, but they would not g. heed. 24.19
LORD is able to g. you much more 25.09
'G. your daughter to my son for a 25.18
that he might g. them into the 25.20
upon Judah to g. them one heart to 30.12
the LORD and to g. thanks and 31.02
in Jerusalem to g. the portion due 31.04
that they might g. themselves to 31.04
that he may g. you over to die by 32.11
and to g. us to secure hold within Ez 9.08
and to g. us protection in Judea 9.09
Therefore g. not your daughters to 9.12
and g. success to thy servant today, Neh 1.11
that he may g. me timber to make 2.08
and g. them up to be plundered in a 4.04
so they could g. me an evil name, 6.13
Chaldees and g. him the name 9.07
the covenant to g. to his descendants 9.08
from heaven and g. them right 9.13
Thou didst g. them bread from 9.15
which thou hadst sworn to g. them. 9.15
And thou didst g. them kingdoms and 9.22
and didst g. them into their hands, 9.24
Therefore thou didst g. them into 9.27
thou didst g. them saviors who 9.27
yet they would not g. ear. 9.30
thou didst g. them into the hand 9.30
warnings which thou didst g. them. 9.34
We will not g. our daughters to the 10.30
them, to praise and to g. thanks, 12.24
"You shall not g. your daughters to 13.25
let the king g. her royal position Est 1.19
all women will g. honor to their 1.20
a man has he will g. for his life. Job 2.04
I will g. free utterance to my 10.01
there that will g. surety for me? 17.03
his hands will g. back his wealth. 20.10
He will g. back the fruit of his 20.18
he would g. heed to me. 23.06
I would g. him an account of all my 31.37
I also will g. my answer; 32.17
G. heed, O Job, listen to me; 33.31
and g. ear to me, you who know; 34.02
righteous, what do you g. to him; 35.07
"Do you g. the horse his might? 39.19
own right hand can g. you victory. 40.14
G. ear to my words, O LORD; Ps 5.01
g. heed to my groaning. 5.01
in Sheol who can g. thee praise? 6.05
I will g. to the LORD the thanks 7.17
I will g. thanks to the LORD with 9.01
For thou dost not g. me up to Sheol, 16.10
G. ear to my prayer from lips free 17.01
Thou didst g. a wide place for my 18.36
and g. you support from Zion! 20.02
G. victory to the king, O LORD; 20.09
G. me not up to the will of my 27.12
with my song I g. thanks to him. 28.07
May the LORD g. strength to his 29.11
and g. thanks to his holy name. 30.04
I will g. thanks to thee for ever. 30.12
and he will g. you the desires of 37.04
O LORD, and g. ear to my cry; 39.12
thou dost not g. him up to the will 41.02
did their own arm g. them victory; 44.03
and we will g. thanks to thy name 44.08
G. ear, all inhabitants of the world, 49.01
or g. to God the price of his life, 49.07
"You g. your mouth free rein for 50.19
were I to g. a burnt offering, thou 51.16
g. ear to the words of my mouth. 54.02

GIVE (cont.)
I will g. thanks to thy name, O LORD, Ps 54.06
G. ear to my prayer, O God; 55.01
God will g. ear, and humble them, he 55.19
I will g. thanks to thee, O Lord, 57.09
g. victory by thy right hand and 60.05
g. to him glorious praise! 66.02
G. the king thy justice, O God, and 72.01
g. deliverance to the needy, and 72.04
thou didst g. him as food for the 74.14
We g. thanks to thee, O God; 75.01
we g. thanks; we call on thy 75.01
G. ear, O my people, to my teaching; 78.01
Can he also g. bread, or provide 78.20
will g. thanks to thee for ever; 79.13
G. ear, O Shepherd of Israel, thou 80.01
g. us life, and we will call on thy 80.18
G. justice to the weak and the 82.03
prayer; g. ear, O God of Jacob! 84.08
the LORD will g. what is good, and 85.12
G. ear, O LORD, to my prayer; 86.06
I g. thanks to thee, O Lord my God, 86.12
g. thy strength to thy servant, and 86.16
For he will g. his angels charge of 91.11
It is good to g. thanks to the LORD, 92.01
to g. him respite from days of 94.13
and g. thanks to his holy name! 97.12
G. thanks to him, bless his name! 100.04
I will g. heed to the way that is 101.02
they g. drink to every beast of the 104.11
to g. them their food in due season 104.27
O g. thanks to the LORD, call on his 105.01
saying, "To you I will g. the land 105.11
and fire to g. light by night. 105.39
O g. thanks to the LORD, for he is 106.01
that he may g. thanks to thy holy 106.47
O g. thanks to the LORD, for he is 107.01
let him g. heed to these things; 107.43
I will g. thanks to thee, O Lord, 108.03
g. help by thy right hand, and 108.06
With my mouth I will g. great 109.30
I will g. thanks to the LORD with 111.01
to us, but to thy name g. glory, 115.01
May the LORD g. you increase, you 115.14
O g. thanks to the LORD, for he is 118.01
them and g. thanks to the LORD. 118.19
we beseech thee, g. us success! 118.25
God, and I will g. thanks to thee; 118.28
O g. thanks to the LORD, for he is 118.29
G. me understanding, that I may keep 119.34
and g. me life in thy ways. 119.37
in thy righteousness g. me life! 119.40
g. me understanding that I may 119.73
g. me life, O LORD, according to thy 119.107
g. me understanding, that I may know 119.125
g. me understanding that I may live. 119.144
g. me life according to thy promise. 119.154
g. me life according to thy justice. 119.156
g. me understanding according to 119.169
to g. thanks to the name of the 122.04
I will not g. sleep to my eyes or 132.04
g. praise, O servants of the LORD, 135.01
O g. thanks to the LORD, for he is 136.01
O g. thanks to the God of gods, for 136.02
O g. thanks to the Lord of lords, 136.03
O g. thanks to the God of heaven, 136.26
I g. thee thanks, O LORD, with my 138.01
holy temple and g. thanks to thy 138.02
g. ear to the voice of my supplications, 140.06
righteous shall g. thanks to thy 140.13
G. ear to my voice, when I call to 141.01
G. heed to my cry; for I am brought 142.06
that I may g. thanks to thy name! 142.07
g. ear to my supplications! 143.01
All thy works shall g. thanks to thee, 145.10
G. heed to my reproof; behold, I will Pro 1.23
abundant welfare will they g. you. 3.02
again, tomorrow I will g. it"— 3.28
for I g. you good precepts: do not 4.02
lest you g. your honor to others 5.09
G. your eyes no sleep and your 6.04
he will g. all the goods of his 6.31
G. instruction to a wise man, and he 9.09
withholds what he should g., 11.24
that you may g. a true answer to 22.21
Be not one of those who g. pledges, 22.26
My son, g. me your heart, and let 23.26
boasts of a gift he does not g. 25.14
is hungry, g. him bread to eat; 25.21
is thirsty, g. him water to drink; 25.21
and g. attention to your herds; 27.23
The rod and reproof g. wisdom, 29.15
Discipline your son, and he will g. you rest; 29.17
he will g. delight to your heart. 29.17
understands, he will not g. heed. 29.19
g. me neither poverty nor riches; 30.08
two daughters; "G., g.," they cry. 30.15
G. not your strength to women, your 31.03
G. strong drink to him who is 31.06
G. her of the fruit of her hands, 31.31
only to g. to one who pleases God. Ecc 2.26
God does not g. him power to enjoy 6.02
Do not g. heed to all the things 7.21
ointment g. off an evil odor; 10.01
G. a portion to seven, or even to 11.02
in blossom; they g. forth fragrance. Sol 2.13
There I will g. you my love. 7.12
The mandrakes g. forth fragrance, 7.13
I would g. you spiced wine to drink, 8.02
Hear, O heavens, and g. ear, O earth; Is 1.02
G. ear to the teaching of our God, 1.10
Lord himself will g. you a sign. 7.14
abundance of milk which they g., 7.22
g. ear, all you far countries; 8.09
"I will g. thanks to thee, O LORD, 12.01
"G. thanks to the LORD, call upon 12.04
constellations will not g. their light; 13.10
"G. counsel, grant justice; 16.03
and I will g. over the Egyptians 19.04
of Pharaoh g. stupid counsel. 19.11
in a sure place will g. way; 22.25
Therefore in the east g. glory to 24.15
is rest; g. rest to the weary; 28.12
G. ear, and hear my voice; 28.23
When men g. it to one who can read, 29.11
And when they g. the book to one 29.12
And though the Lord g. you the 30.20
And he will g. rain for the seed 30.23
daughters, g. ear to my speech. 32.09
I will g. you two thousand horses, 36.08
and I g. to Jerusalem a herald of 41.27
my glory I g. to no other, nor my 42.08
Let them g. glory to the LORD, and 42.12
Who among you will g. ear to this, 42.23
I g. Egypt as your ransom, Ethiopia 43.03
I g. men in return for you, peoples 43.04
G. up, and to the south, Do not 43.06
for I g. water in the wilderness, 43.20
to g. drink to my chosen people, 43.20
I will g. you the treasures of 45.03
my glory I will not g. to another. 48.11
I will g. you as a light to the 49.06
and g. ear to me, my nation; 51.04
I will g. in my house and within my 56.05
I will g. them an everlasting name 56.05
me, did not g. me a thought? 57.11
shall the moon g. light to you by 60.19
to g. them a garland instead of 61.03
will faithfully g. them their 61.08
the mouth of the LORD will g. 62.02
and g. him no rest until he establishes 62.07
will not again g. your grain to be 62.08
" 'And I will g. you shepherds after Jer 3.15
and g. you a pleasant land, a 3.19

GIVE (cont.)

To whom shall I speak and g. warning, Jer 6.10
'G. heed to the sound of the 6.17
they said, 'We will not g. heed.' 6.17
Therefore I will g. their wives to 8.10
and g. them poisonous water to 9.15
your fathers to g. them a land 11.05
Hear and g. ear; be not proud, 13.15
G. glory to the LORD your God 13.16
but I will g. you assured peace in 14.13
Or can the heavens g. showers? 14.22
of them I will g. to the sword 15.09
your treasures I will g. as spoil, 15.13
shall any one g. him the cup of 16.07
treasures I will g. for spoil as 17.03
to g. to every man according to his 17.10
G. heed to me, O LORD, and hearken to 18.19
g. them over to the power of the 18.21
I will g. their dead bodies for 19.07
And I will g. all Judah into the 20.04
I will g. all the wealth of the 20.05
and does not g. him his wages; 22.13
and g. you into the hand of those 22.25
and g. them poisoned water to drink; 23.15
I will g. them a heart to know that 24.07
G. them this charge for their 27.04
and I g. it to whomever it seems 27.05
the day when I g. attention to 27.22
and g. your daughters in marriage, 29.06
to g. you a future and a hope. 29.11
proclaim, g. praise, and say, 'The 31.07
and g. them gladness for sorrow. 31.13
swear to their fathers to g. them, 32.22
I will g. them one heart and one 32.39
'G. thanks to the LORD of hosts, for 33.11
and I will g. them into the hand of 34.20
princes I will g. into the hand of 34.21
And if I g. you counsel, you will 38.15
Behold I will g. Pharaoh Hophra 44.30
but I will g. you your life as a 45.05
"G. wings to Moab, for she would fly 48.09
that he may g. rest to the earth, 50.34
G. yourself no rest, your eyes no Lam 2.18
let him g. his cheek to the smiter, 3.30
Thou wilt g. them dullness of heart; 3.65
Even the jackals g. the breast and 4.03
your mouth, and eat what I g. you." Eze 2.08
scroll that I g. you and fill your 3.03
you shall g. them warning from me. 3.17
and you g. him no warning, nor 3.18
And I will g. it into the hands of 7.21
iniquity and who g. wicked counsel 11.02
and g. you into the hands of 11.09
and I will g. you the land of 11.17
And I will g. them one heart, and 11.19
their flesh and g. them a heart of 11.19
visions and who g. lying divinations; 13.09
so will I g. up the inhabitants of 15.06
Men g. gifts to all harlots; 16.33
And I will g. you into the hand of 16.39
and you shall also g. hire no more. 16.41
and g. them to you as daughters, but 16.61
that they might g. him horses and 17.15
the land which I swore to g. them, 20.28
I swore to g. to your fathers. 20.42
right it is; and to him I will g. it. 21.27
She did not g. up her harlotry 23.08
therefore I will g. her cup into 23.31
I will g. it along with the Ammonites 25.10
I will g. the land of Egypt to 29.19
I will g. it into the hand of a 31.11
the moon shall not g. its light. 32.07
you shall g. them warning from me. 33.07
field I will g. to the beasts to 33.27
A new heart I will g. you, 36.26
of stone and g. you a heart of 36.26
I will g. you to birds of prey of 39.04
"On that day I will g. to Gog a 39.11
you shall g. to the Levitical 43.19
and you shall g. them no possession 44.28
you shall also g. to the priests 44.30
the land shall g. this offering to 45.16
lambs as much as one is able to g., 46.11
he shall g. his sons their inheritance 46.18
I swore to g. it to your fathers, 47.14
I g. thanks and praise, for thou Dan 2.23
that you can g. interpretations 5.16
and g. your rewards to another; 5.17
these satraps should g. account, 6.02
O LORD, g. heed and act; delay not, 9.19
now come out to g. you wisdom and 9.22
g. heed to the words that I speak 10.11
He shall g. him the daughter of 11.17
turn back and g. heed to those who 11.30
He shall g. no heed to the gods of 11.37
he shall not g. heed to any other 11.37
who g. me my bread and my water, my Hos 2.05
And there I will g. her her vineyards. 2.15
they g. themselves to harlotry; 4.18
G. heed, O house of Israel! 5.01
G. them, O LORD—what wilt thou g.? 9.14
G. them a miscarrying womb and dry 9.14
How can I g. you up, O Ephraim! 11.08
"G. me a king and princes"? 13.10
g. ear, all inhabitants of the land! Joe 1.02
tree and vine g. their full yield. 2.22
"And I will g. portents in the 2.30
the god will g. a thought to us, Jon 1.06
Therefore you shall g. parting Mic 1.14
Its heads g. judgment for a bribe, 3.11
Therefore he shall g. them up until 5.03
Shall I g. my first-born for my 6.07
you save I will g. to the sword. 6.14
Can this g. revelation? Behold, Hab 2.19
in this place I will g. prosperity, Hag 2.09
and I will g. you the right of Zec 3.07
the ground shall g. its increase, 8.12
and the heavens shall g. their dew; 8.12
false dreams, and g. empty consolation. 10.02
seems right to you, g. me my wages; 11.12
"And the LORD will g. victory to 12.07
it to heart to g. glory to my name, Mal 2.02
'He will g. his angels charge of Mt 4.06
to him, "All these I will g. you, 4.09
good works and g. glory to your 5.16
let him g. her a certificate of 5.31
G. to him who begs from you, and do 5.42
when you g. alms, sound no trumpet 6.02
But when you g. alms, do not let 6.03
G. us this day our daily bread; 6.11
the measure you g. will be the 7.02
"Do not g. dogs what is holy; 7.06
for a loaf, will g. him a stone? 7.09
for a fish, will g. him a serpent? 7.10
know how to g. good gifts to your 7.11
is in heaven g. good things to 7.11
without pay, g. without pay. 10.08
heavy-laden, and I will g. you rest. 11.28
with an oath to g. her whatever 14.07
"G. me the head of John the Baptist 14.08
you g. them something to eat." 14.16
I will g. you the keys of the 16.19
shall a man g. in return for his 16.26
not to g. offense to them, go to the 17.27
take that and g. it to them for me 17.27
command one to g. a certificate of 19.07
you possess and g. to the poor, 19.21
whatever is right I will g. you.' 20.04
I choose to g. to this last as I g. to 20.14
and to g. his life as a ransom for 20.28
who will g. him the fruits in 21.41
for those who g. suck in those 24.19
and the moon will not g. its light, 24.29
to g. them their food at the proper 24.45

GIVE (cont.)
'G. us some of your oil, for our Mt 25.08
and g. it to him who has the ten 25.28
thee, or thirsty and g. thee drink? 25.37
"What will you g. me if I deliver 26.15
the measure you g. will be the Mk 4.24
told them to g. her something to 5.43
I will g. you, even half of my 6.23
"I want you to g. me at once the 6.25
"You g. them something to eat." 6.37
bread, and g. it to them to eat?" 6.37
For what can a man g. in return for 8.37
and g. to the poor, and you will 10.21
and to g. his life as a ransom for 10.45
and g. the vineyard to others. 12.09
for those who g. suck in those 13.17
the moon will not g. its light, 13.24
glad, and promised to g. him money. 14.11
Lord God will g. to him the throne Lk 1.32
to g. knowledge of salvation to his 1.77
to g. light to those who sit in 1.79
"To you I will g. all this authority 4.06
and I g. it to whom I will. 4.06
'He will g. his angels charge of 4.10
G. to every one who begs from you; 6.30
g., and it will be given to you; 6.38
the measure you g. will be the 6.38
"You g. them something to eat." 9.13
G. us each day our daily bread; 11.03
cannot get up and g. you anything'? 11.07
not get up and g. him anything 11.08
will rise and g. him whatever he 11.08
instead of a fish g. him a serpent; 11.11
for an egg, will g. him a scorpion? 11.12
know how to g. good gifts to your 11.13
heavenly Father g. the Holy Spirit 11.13
But g. for alms those things which 11.41
pleasure to g. you the kingdom. 12.32
Sell your possessions, and g. alms; 12.33
to g. them their portion of food at 12.42
I have come to g. peace on earth? 12.51
'G. place to this man,' and then you 14.09
"When you g. a dinner or a banquet, 14.12
But when you g. a feast, invite the 14.13
g. me the share of property that 15.12
who will g. you that which is your 16.12
to return and g. praise to God 17.18
I g. tithes of all that I get.' 18.12
half of my goods I g. to the poor; 19.08
and g. it to him who has the ten 19.24
they should g. him some of the 20.10
and g. the vineyard to others." 20.16
for us to g. tribute to Caesar, or 20.22
for I will g. you a mouth and 21.15
for those who g. suck in those 21.23
glad, and engaged to g. him money. 22.05
forbidding us to g. tribute to 23.02
Jesus said to her, "G. me a drink." Jn 4.07
'G. me a drink,' you would have 4.10
that I shall g. him will never 4.14
that I shall g. him will become in 4.14
g. me this water, that I may not 4.15
the Son of man will g. to you; 6.27
"Lord, g. us this bread always." 6.34
which I shall g. for the life of 6.51
can this man g. us his flesh to 6.52
Did not Moses g. you the law? 7.19
and said to him, "G. God the praise; 9.24
and I g. them eternal life, and they 10.28
you ask from God, God will g. you." 11.22
to whom I shall g. this morsel 13.26
that he should g. something to the 13.29
A new commandment I g. to you, 13.34
and he will g. you another Counselor, 14.16
my peace I g. to you; not as the 14.27
as the world gives do I g. to you. 14.27
in my name, he may g. it to you. 15.16
he will g. it to you in my name. 16.23
to g. eternal life to all whom thou 17.02
known to you, and g. ear to my words. Ac 2.14
but I g. you what I have; 3.06
to g. repentance to Israel and 5.31
that we should g. up preaching the 6.02
but promised to g. it to him in 7.05
received living oracles to g. to us. 7.38
saying, "G. me also this power, that 8.19
he did not g. God the glory; 12.23
'I will g. you the holy and sure 13.34
her heart to g. heed to what was 16.14
that we can g. to justify this 19.40
you up and to g. you the inheritance 20.32
more blessed to g. than to receive.'" 20.35
to g. notice when the days of 21.26
g. notice now to the tribune to 23.15
me, no one can g. me up to them. 25.11
the Romans to g. up any one before 25.16
it will g. you strength, since not a 27.34
him as God or g. thanks to him, Rom 1.21
immortality, he will g. eternal life; 2.07
the dead will g. life to your 8.11
he not also g. us all things with 8.32
if he is thirsty, g. him drink; 12.20
tongue shall g. praise to God." 14.11
of us shall g. account of himself 14.12
churches of the Gentiles g. thanks; 16.04
I g. thanks to God always for you 1Co 1.04
The husband should g. to his wife 7.03
To the married I g. charge, 7.10
but I g. my opinion as one who by 7.25
of that for which I g. thanks? 10.30
G. no offense to Jews or to Greeks 10.32
things I will g. directions when I 11.34
If I g. away all I have, and if I 13.03
do not g. distinct notes, how will 14.07
For you may g. thanks well enough, 14.17
G. recognition to such men. 16.18
that many will g. thanks on our 2Co 1.11
our hearts to g. the light of the 4.06
And in this matter I g. my advice: 8.10
So g. proof, before the churches, of 8.24
To g. a human example, brethren: no Gal 3.15
I do not cease to g. thanks for you, Eph 1.16
may g. you a spirit of wisdom and 1.17
and g. no opportunity to the devil. 4.27
may be able to g. to those in need. 4.28
and Christ shall g. you light." 5.14
G. my greetings to the brethren at Col 4.15
We g. thanks to God always for you 1Th 1.02
g. thanks in all circumstances; 5.18
We are bound to g. thanks to God 2Th 1.03
But we are bound to g. thanks to 2.13
but to g. you in our conduct an 3.09
peace himself g. you peace at all 3.16
and g. the enemy no occasion to 1Ti 5.14
for God did not g. us a spirit of 2Ti 1.07
may be able to g. instruction in Tit 1.09
masters and to g. satisfaction in 2.09
as men who will have to g. account. Heb 13.17
but they will g. account to him who 1Pe 4.05
and God will g. him life for those 1Jn 5.16
the house or g. him any greeting; 2Jn 1.10
and I will g. you the crown of life. Rev 2.10
conquers I will g. some of the 2.17
and I will g. him a white stone, 2.17
and I will g. to each of you as 2.23
I will g. him power over the 2.26
and I will g. him the morning star. 2.28
creatures g. glory and honor and 4.09
their hands nor g. up worshiping 9.20
and told him to g. me the little 10.09
saying, "We g. thanks to thee, Lord 11.17
was allowed to g. breath to the 13.15
"Fear God and g. him glory, for the 14.07
did not repent and g. him glory. 16.09

GIVE (cont.)
of one mind and g. over their Rev 17.13
so g. her a like measure of torment 18.07
and exult and g. him the glory, 19.07
thirsty I will g. water without 21.06

GIVEN
I have g. you every plant yielding Gen 1.29
I have g. every green plant for 1.30
thou hast g. me no offspring; 15.03
the LORD has g. heed to your 16.11
I gave g. your brother a thousand 20.16
he has g. him flocks and herds, 24.35
to him he has g. all that he has. 24.36
names which his father had g. them. 26.18
brothers I have g. to him for 27.37
he has g. me this son also"; and she 29.33
heard my voice and g. me a son"; 30.06
"God has g. me my hire because I 30.18
the service which I have g. you." 30.26
of your father, and g. them to me. 31.09
been using up the money g. for us. 31.15
God has graciously g. your servant." 33.05
had not been g. to him in marriage. 38.14
and g. them water, and they had 43.24
and when he had g. their asses 43.24
my sons, whom God has g. me here." 48.09
Moreover I have g. to you rather 48.22
No straw is g. to your servants, yet Ex 5.16
for no straw shall be g. you, 5.18
and the LORD had g. the people 12.36
which the LORD has g. you to eat. 16.15
The LORD has g. you the sabbath, 16.29
and I have g. to all able men 31.06
I have g. it as their portion of my Lev 6.17
and have g. them to Aaron the 7.34
this to be g. them by the people 7.36
for they are g. as your due and 10.14
and has been g. to you that you 10.17
and I have g. it for you upon the 17.11
not yet ransomed or g. her freedom, 19.20
because he has g. one of his 20.03
they are wholly g. to him from Num 3.09
For they are wholly g. to me from 8.16
And I have g. the Levites as a gift 8.19
nor g. us inheritance of fields and 16.14
g. to the LORD, to do the service of 18.06
I have g. you whatever is kept of 18.08
I have g. them to you as a portion, 18.08
I have g. them to you, and to your 18.11
Levites I have g. every tithe in 18.21
I have g. to the Levites for an 18.24
which I have g. you from them for 18.26
into the land which I have g. them." 20.12
which I have g. to the people of 20.24
for I have g. him into your hand, 21.34
tribe shall be g. its inheritance 26.54
no inheritance g. to them among 26.62
which I have g. to the people of 27.12
this land be g. to your servants 32.05
land which the LORD has g. them? 32.07
land which the LORD had g. them. 32.09
for I have g. the land to you to 33.53
the LORD had g. him in commandment Deu 1.03
because I have g. Mount Seir to 2.05
because I have g. Ar to the sons 2.09
because I have g. it to the sons 2.19
I have g. into your hand Sihon the 2.24
for I have g. him and all his 3.02
your God has g. you this land to 3.18
in the cities which I have g. you, 3.19
his possession which I have g. you.' 3.20
for the good land he has g. you. 8.10
of the land which I have g. you, 9.23
has g. you to possess, all the days 12.01
LORD your God which he has g. you; 12.15
flock, which the LORD has g. you, 12.21
LORD your God which he has g. you. 16.17
which the LORD your God has g. you. 20.14
Forty stripes may be g. him, 25.03
your God has g. you rest from all 25.19
which thou, O LORD, hast g. me.' 26.10
your God has g. to you and to your 26.11
Moreover I have g. it to the 26.13
the ground which thou hast g. us, 26.15
sheep shall be g. to your enemies, 28.31
shall be g. to another people, 28.32
which the LORD your God has g. you. 28.52
whom the LORD your God has g. you, 28.53
LORD has not g. you a mind to 29.04
them, and the LORD had g. them up? 32.30
will tread upon I have g. to you, Jos 1.03
that the LORD has g. you the land, 2.09
the LORD has g. all the land into 2.24
I have g. into your hand Jericho, 6.02
for the LORD has g. you the city. 6.16
see, I have g. into your hand the 8.01
for I have g. them into your hands; 10.08
your God has g. them into your 10.19
For Moses had g. an inheritance to 14.03
no portion was g. to the Levites 14.04
"Why have you g. me but one lot and 17.14
God of your fathers, has g. you? 18.03
that we be g. cities to dwell in, 21.02
had been g. to Caleb the son of 21.12
To them were g. Shechem, the city of 21.21
were g. out of the half-tribe of 21.27
were g. out of the tribe of Zebulun, 21.34
the LORD had g. all their enemies 21.44
your God has g. rest to your 22.04
Moses had g. a possession in 22.07
half Joshua had g. a possession 22.07
the LORD had g. rest to Israel 23.01
which the LORD your God has g. you. 23.13
the LORD your God has g. you. 23.15
good land which he has g. to you." 23.16
which had been g. him in the hill 24.33
I have g. the land into his hand." Ju 1.02
And Hebron was g. to Caleb, as Moses 1.20
the LORD has g. your enemies the 3.28
the LORD has g. Sisera into your 4.14
you have not g. heed to my voice." 6.10
and g. us into the hand of Midian." 6.13
for I have g. it into your hand. 7.09
hand God has g. Midian and all the 7.14
the LORD has g. the host of Midian 7.15
God has g. into your hands the 8.03
the LORD has g. Zebah and Zalmunna 8.07
wife was g. to his companion, who 14.20
his wife and g. her to his companion." 15.06
"Our god has g. Samson our enemy 16.23
"Our god has g. our enemy into our 16.24
yea, God has g. it into your hands, a 18.10
his people and g. them food. Ru 1.06
full reward be g. you by the LORD, 2.12
the LORD has g. them into our hand. 1Sa 14.10
the LORD has g. them into the hand 14.12
and has g. it to a neighbor of 15.28
should have been g. to David, 18.19
she was g. to Adriel the Meholathite 18.19
which were g. in full number to the 18.27
that you have g. him bread and a 22.13
"God has g. him into my hand; 23.07
to my lord be g. to the young men 25.27
Saul had g. Michal his daughter, 25.44
"God has g. your enemy into your 26.08
let a place be g. me in one of the 27.05
and g. it to your neighbor, David. 28.17
with what the LORD has g. us; 30.23
preserved us and g. into our hand 30.23
men would have g. up the pursuit 2Sa 2.27
and have not g. you into the hand 3.08
the LORD had g. him rest from all 7.01
house I have g. to your master's 9.09

GIVEN (cont.)

the LORD has g. the kingdom into 2Sa 16.08
Ahithophel has g. is not good." 17.07
Or has he g. us any gift 19.42
let seven of his sons be g. to us, 21.06
Thou hast g. me the shield of thy 22.36
Shunammite be g. to Adonijah your 1Ki 2.21
and hast g. him a son to sit on his 3.06
LORD my God has g. me rest on 5.04
who has g. to David a wise son to 5.07
which thou hast g. to thy people 8.36
LORD who has g. rest to his people 8.56
from the land which I have g. them; 9.07
cities which Solomon had g. him, 9.12
which you have g. me, my brother?" 9.13
and had g. it as dowry to his 9.16
what was g. her by the bounty of 10.13
which the old men had g. him, 12.13
man of God had g. by the word of 13.05
the LORD has g. him to the lion, 13.26
Let two bulls be g. to us; 18.23
took the bull which was g. them, 18.26
the LORD had g. victory to Syria. 2Ki 5.01
let there be g. to your servant two 5.17
the Syrians had g. him at Ramah, 8.29
which the Syrians had g. him, 9.15
for that was g. to the workmen who 12.14
will not be g. into the hand of 18.30
will not be g. into the hand of 19.10
and let it be g. into the hand of 22.05
the priest has g. me a book." 22.10
allowance was g. him by the king, 25.30
birthright was g. to the sons of 1Ch 5.01
with them were g. into their hands, 5.20
Kohathites were g. by lot out of 6.61
They were g. the cities of refuge: 6.67
Gershomites were g. out of the half 6.71
And has he not g. you peace on 22.18
has g. peace to his people; 23.25
for God had g. Heman fourteen 25.05
the LORD has g. me many sons) he 28.05
because these had g. willingly, 29.09
and of thy own have we g. thee. 29.14
who has g. King David a wise son, 2Ch 2.12
which thou hast g. to thy people 6.27
from the land which I have g. you; 7.20
cities which Huram had g. to him, 8.02
and he has g. us peace on every 14.07
they will be g. into your hand." 18.14
which thou hast g. us to inherit. 20.11
which I have g. to the army of 25.09
He was also g. into the hand of the 28.05
for God had g. him very great 32.29
the ordinances g. through Moses." 33.08
law of the LORD g. through Moses. 34.14
the priest has g. me a book." 34.18
has g. me all the kingdoms of the 36.23
has g. me all the kingdoms of the Ez 1.02
let that be g. to them day by day 6.09
the LORD the God of Israel had g.; 7.06
that have been g. you for the 7.19
have been g. into the hand of the 9.07
and hast g. us such a remnant as 9.13
let letters be g. me to the Neh 2.07
which the LORD had g. to Israel. 8.01
law which was g. by Moses the 10.29
which were g. by commandment to the 13.05
Levites had not been g. to them; 13.10
the king had g. orders to all the Est 1.08
let their ointments be g. them. 2.03
way she was g. whatever she 2.13
"The money is g. to you, the people 3.11
It shall be g. you, even to the half 5.03
let my life be g. me at my petition, 7.03
I have g. Esther the house of Haman, 8.07
"Why is light g. to him that is in Job 3.20
Why is light g. to a man whose way 3.23
The earth is g. into the hand of 9.24
to whom alone the land was g., 15.19
You have g. no water to the weary 22.07
By the breath of God ice is g., 37.10
and who has g. birth to the hoarfrost 38.29
or g. understanding to the mists? 38.36
to whom I have g. the steppe for 39.06
and g. her no share in understanding. 39.17
Who has g. to me, that I should 41.11
Thou hast g. me room when I was in Ps 4.01
Thou hast g. him dominion over the 8.06
Thou hast g. me the shield of thy 18.35
Thou hast g. him his heart's desire, 21.02
but thou hast g. me an open ear. 40.06
thou hast g. us wine to drink that 60.03
thou hast g. me the heritage of 61.05
they shall be g. over to the power 63.10
he has g. heed to the voice of my 66.19
may gold of Sheba be g. to him! 72.15
They have g. the bodies of thy 79.02
and g. them tears to drink in full 80.05
freely, he has g. to the poor; 112.09
earth he has g. to the sons of men. 115.16
but he has not g. me over to death. 118.18
is God, and he has g. us light. 118.27
for by them thou hast g. me life. 119.93
What shall be g. to you? And what 120.03
who has not g. us as prey to their 124.06
When they are g. over to those who 141.06
that prudence may be g. to the simple, Pro 1.04
have g. your pledge for a stranger; 6.01
when he has g. surety for a 20.16
friendship with a man g. to anger, 22.24
if you are a man g. to appetite. 23.02
when he has g. surety for a 27.13
and a man g. to anger causes much 29.22
that God has g. to the sons of men Ecc 1.13
that God has g. to the sons of men 3.10
of his life which God has g. him, 5.18
to whom God has g. wealth and 5.19
deliver those who are g. to it. 8.08
which he has g. you under the sun, 9.09
which are g. by one Shepherd. 12.11
the LORD has g. me are signs and Is 8.18
a child is born, to us a son is g.; 9.06
When the LORD has g. you rest from 14.03
neither travailed nor g. birth, 23.04
the LORD has g. command concerning 23.11
his bread will be g. him, 33.16
has g. them over for slaughter. 34.02
glory of Lebanon shall be g. to it, 35.02
will not be g. into the hand of 36.15
will not be g. into the hand of 37.10
I have g. you as a covenant to the 42.06
kept you and g. you as a covenant 49.08
The Lord GOD has g. me the tongue 50.04
they have not g. heed to my words; Jer 6.19
I have g. heed and listened, but 8.06
and has g. us poisoned water to 8.14
I have g. the beloved of my soul 12.07
which I have g. my people Israel 12.14
Where is the flock that was g. you, 13.20
it shall be g. into the hand of the 21.10
or who has g. heed to his word and 23.18
the LORD has g. to you and your 25.05
that he was not g. over to the 26.24
Now I have g. all these lands into 27.06
and I have g. him also the beasts 27.06
for I have g. to him even the 28.14
shall surely be g. into the hand 32.04
"After I had g. the deed of purchase 32.16
the city is g. into the hands of 32.24
the city is g. into the hands of 32.25
'It is g. into the hand of the king 32.36
it is g. into the hands of the 32.43
of bread was g. him daily from the 37.21
shall surely be g. into the hand 38.03

GIVEN (cont.)

city shall be g. into the hand of Jer 38.18
Jeremiah said, "You shall not be g. to them. 38.20
shall not be g. into the hand of 39.17
people who had g. him this answer: 44.20
when the LORD has g. it a charge? 47.07
allowance was g. him by the king 52.34
we are weary, we are g. no rest. Lam 5.05
We have g. the hand to Egypt, and to 5.06
us this land is g. for a possession Eze 11.15
Lo, it is g. the fire for fuel; 15.04
which I have g. to the fire for 15.06
which I had g. you, and made for 16.17
hire, while no hire was g. to you; 16.34
into the land which I had g. them, 20.15
So the sword is g. to be polished, 21.11
polished to be g. into the hand of 21.11
I have g. the glittering sword; 21.15
of the air I have g. you as food. 29.05
I have g. him the land of Egypt as 29.20
or they are all g. over to death, 31.14
land is surely g. us to possess.' 33.24
desolate, they are g. us to devour. 35.12
let us be g. vegetables to eat and Dan 1.12
for thou hast g. me wisdom and 2.23
God of heaven has g. the kingdom, 2.37
and into whose hand he has g., 2.38
let a beast's mind be g. to him; 4.16
is divided and g. to the Medes and 5.28
and the mind of a man was g. to it. 7.04
and dominion was g. to it. 7.06
destroyed and g. over to be burned 7.11
And to him was g. dominion and 7.14
judgment was g. for the saints of 7.22
they shall be g. into his hand for 7.25
heaven shall be g. to the people 7.27
And the host was g. over to it 8.12
but she shall be g. up, and her 11.06
but it shall be g. into his hand. 11.11
whom royal majesty has not been g.; 11.21
hire, which my lovers have g. me.' Hos 2.12
Ephraim has g. bitter provocation; 12.14
I have g. you kings in my anger, and 13.11
for he has g. the early rain for Joe 2.23
and have g. a boy for a harlot, and 3.03
of the land which I have g. them, Amo 9.15
The LORD has g. commandment about Nah 1.14
"Ask, and it will be g. you; Mt 7.07
who had g. such authority to men. 9.08
to say will be g. to you in that 10.19
sign shall be g. to it except the 12.39
you it has been g. to know the 13.11
but to them it has not been g. 13.11
For to him who has will more be g., 13.12
guests he commanded it to be g.; 14.09
on a platter and g. to the girl, 14.11
have gained from me is g. to God, 15.05
and having g. thanks he broke them 15.36
sign shall be g. to it except the 16.04
but only those to whom it is g. 19.11
from you and g. to a nation 21.43
marry nor are g. in marriage, 22.30
every one who has will more be g., 25.29
a large sum, and g. to the poor." 26.09
and when he had g. thanks he gave 26.27
Now the betrayer had g. them a sign, 26.48
Pilate ordered it to be g. to him. 27.58
and on earth has been g. to me. 28.18
"To you has been g. the secret of Mk 4.11
get, and still more will be g. you. 4.24
For to him who has will more be g.; 4.25
What is the wisdom g. to him? 6.02
is Corban' (that is, g. to God)— 7.11
and having g. thanks he broke them 8.06
sign shall be g. to this generation." 8.12
marry nor are g. in marriage, 12.25
say whatever is g. you in that 13.11
denarii, and g. to the poor." 14.05
and when he had g. thanks he gave 14.23
Now the betrayer had g. them a sign, 14.44
the name g. by the angel before he Lk 2.21
and there was g. to him the book of 4.17
give, and it will be g. to you; 6.38
you it has been g. to know the 8.10
for to him who has will more be g. 8.18
something should be g. her to eat. 8.55
Behold, I have g. you authority to 10.19
you, Ask, and it will be g. you; 11.09
sign shall be g. to it except the 11.29
Every one to whom much is g., 12.48
they were g. in marriage, until the 17.27
to whom he had g. the money, 19.15
every one who has will more be g.; 19.26
age marry and are g. in marriage; 20.34
marry nor are g. in marriage, 20.35
and when he had g. thanks he said, 22.17
and when he had g. thanks he broke 22.19
which is g. for you. Do this in *22.19
For the law was g. through Moses; Jn 1.17
except what is g. him from heaven. 3.27
and has g. all things into his hand. 3.35
he would have g. you living water." 4.10
but has g. all judgment to the Son, 5.22
and has g. him authority to execute 5.27
loaves, and when he had g. thanks, 6.11
bread after the Lord had g. thanks. 6.23
nothing of all that he has g. me, 6.39
as yet the Spirit had not been g., 7.39
who has g. them to me, is greater 10.29
Pharisees had g. orders that if 11.57
hundred denarii and g. to the poor?" 12.05
me has himself g. me commandment 12.49
the Father had g. all things into 13.03
For I have g. you an example, that 13.15
since thou hast g. him power over 17.02
life to all whom thou hast g. him. 17.02
that thou hast g. me is from thee; 17.07
for I have g. them the words which 17.08
but for those whom thou hast g. me, 17.09
in thy name which thou hast g. me, 17.11
in thy name which thou hast g. me; 17.12
I have g. them thy word; and the 17.14
thou hast g. me I have g. to them, 17.22
they also, whom thou hast g. me, 17.24
which thou hast g. me in thy love 17.24
the cup which the Father has g. me?" 18.11
Caiaphas who had g. counsel to the 18.14
it had been g. you from above; 19.11
after he had g. commandment through Ac 1.02
Jesus has g. the man this perfect 3.16
under heaven g. among men by which 4.12
whom God has g. to those who obey 5.32
the Spirit was g. through the 8.18
of this he has g. assurance to all 17.31
parts and had g. them much encouragement, 20.02
And when he had g. him leave, 21.40
that money would be g. him by Paul. 24.26
Spirit which has been g. to us. Rom 5.05
in the world before the law was g., 5.13
"Or who has g. a gift to him that 11.35
For by the grace g. to me I bid 12.03
according to the grace g. to us, 12.06
the promises g. to the patriarchs, 15.08
because of the grace g. me by God 15.15
God which was g. you in Christ 1Co 1.04
According to the commission of God g. to me, 3.10
For her hair is g. to her for a 11.15
and when he had g. thanks, he broke 11.24
To each is g. the manifestation of 12.07
To one is g. through the Spirit the 12.08
upon us and g. us his Spirit in 2Co 1.22
always being g. up to death for 4.11
who has g. us the Spirit as a 5.05
a thorn was g. me in the flesh, a 12.07

GIVEN (cont.)
the Lord has g. me for building up 2Co 13.10
the grace that was g. to me, Gal 2.09
a law had been g. which could make 3.21
Christ might be g. to those who 3.22
out your eyes and g. them to me. 4.15
grace that was g. to me for you, Eph 3.02
grace which was g. me by the 3.07
all the saints, this grace was g., 3.08
But grace was g. to each of us 4.07
and have g. themselves up to 4.19
utterance may be g. me in opening 6.19
office which was g. to me for you, Col 1.25
him who has g. me strength for 1Ti 1.12
which was g. you by prophetic 4.14
I, and the children God has g. me." Heb 2.13
For if Joshua had g. them rest, 4.08
because she had g. friendly 11.31
not endure the order that was g., 12.20
reproaching, and it will be g. him. Jas 1.05
according to the wisdom g. him, 2Pe 3.15
See what love the Father has g. us, 1Jn 3.01
by the Spirit which he has g. us. 3.24
because he has g. us of his own 4.13
come and has g. us understanding, 5.20
and a crown was g. to him, and he Rev 6.02
and he was g. a great sword. 6.04
and they were g. power over a 6.08
Then they were each g. a white robe 6.11
who had been g. power to harm 7.02
and seven trumpets were g. to them. 8.02
and he was g. much incense to 8.03
and he was g. the key of the shaft 9.01
and they were g. power like the 9.03
Then I was g. a measuring rod like 11.01
for it is g. over to the nations, 11.02
But the woman was g. the two wings 12.14
for he had g. his authority to the 13.04
And the beast was g. a mouth 13.05
authority was g. it over every 13.07
and thou hast g. them blood to 16.06
for God has g. judgment for you 18.20

GIVER
for God loves a cheerful g. 2Co 9.07

GIVES
"When the LORD g. you in the Ex 16.08
sixth day he g. you bread for two 16.29
which the LORD your God g. you. 20.12
If his master g. him a wife and she 21.04
who g. any of his children to Lev 20.02
when he g. one of his children to 20.04
that any man g. to the LORD is 27.09
whatever any man g. to the priest Num 5.10
which the LORD our God g. us. Deu 1.20
land which the LORD our God g. us.' 1.25
which the LORD our God g. to us.' 2.29
until the LORD g. rest to your 3.20
LORD your God g. them beyond the 3.20
the God of your fathers, g. you. 4.01
LORD your God g. you for an 4.21
the LORD your God g. you for ever." 4.40
which the LORD your God g. you. 5.16
LORD your God g. them over to you, 7.02
it is he who g. you power to get 8.18
good land which the LORD g. you. 11.17
which the LORD your God g. you; 11.31
which the LORD your God g. you. 12.09
LORD your God g. you to inherit, 12.10
and when he g. you rest from all 12.10
and g. you a sign or a wonder, 13.01
LORD your God g. you to dwell 13.12
LORD your God g. you for an 15.04
which the LORD your God g. you, 15.07
which the LORD your God g. you; 16.05
which the LORD your God g. you, 16.18
which the LORD your God g. you. 16.20
which the LORD your God g. you, 17.02
which the LORD your God g. you, 17.14
which the LORD your God g. you, 18.09
land the LORD your God g. you, 19.01
LORD your God g. you to possess. 19.02
LORD your God g. you as a possession, 19.03
and g. you all the land which he 19.08
LORD your God g. you for an 19.10
LORD your God g. you to possess, 19.14
LORD your God g. it into your hand 20.13
LORD your G. g. you for an 20.16
LORD your God g. you to possess, 21.01
LORD your God g. them into your 21.10
LORD your God g. you for an 21.23
LORD your God g. you for an 24.04
which the LORD your God g. you. 25.15
LORD your God g. you for an 25.19
LORD your God g. you for an 26.01
land that the LORD your God g. you, 26.02
which the LORD your God g. you, 27.02
which the LORD your God g. you, 27.03
which the LORD your God g. you. 28.08
LORD your God g. you to possess.'" Jos 1.11
until the LORD g. rest to your 1.15
you when the LORD g. us the land." 2.14
nay, she g. answer to herself, Ju 5.29
and the LORD g. them over to me, I 11.09
Chemosh your god g. you to possess? 11.24
be he who g. a wife to Benjamin." 21.18
Great triumphs he g. to his king, 2Sa 22.51
O king, Araunah g. to the king." 24.23
that when he g. you charge over 1Ch 22.12
he g. rain upon the earth and sends Job 5.10
God g. me up to the ungodly, and 16.11
my servant, but he g. me no answer; 19.16
He g. them security, and they are 24.23
breath of the Almighty g. me life. 33.04
who g. songs in the night, 35.10
but g. the afflicted their right. 36.06
peoples; he g. food in abundance. 36.31
I bless the LORD who g. me counsel; Ps 16.07
Great triumphs he g. to his king, 18.50
the righteous is generous and g.; 37.21
God g. the desolate a home to dwell 68.06
The Lord g. the command; great is 68.11
he g. power and strength to his 68.35
He g. the barren woman a home, 113.09
that thy promise g. me life. 119.50
The unfolding of thy words g. light; 119.130
for he g. to his beloved in sleep. 127.02
he who g. food to all flesh, for his 136.25
who g. food to the hungry. 146.07
he g. to all of them their names. 147.04
He g. to the beasts their food, and 147.09
He g. snow like wool; he scatters 147.16
For the LORD g. wisdom; from Pro 2.06
He who g. surety for a stranger 11.15
One man g. freely, yet grows all the 11.24
the truth g. honest evidence, but a 12.17
A tranquil mind g. life to the 14.30
He who g. heed to the word will 16.20
and a liar g. heed to a mischievous 17.04
stone in the eyes of him who g. it; 17.08
A man without sense g. a pledge, 17.18
If one g. answer before he hears, it 18.13
is a friend to a man who g. gifts. 19.06
pledge when he g. surety for 20.16
the righteous g. and does not hold 21.26
or g. to the rich, will only come to 22.16
He who g. a right answer kisses the 24.26
righteous man who g. way before the 25.26
sling is he who g. honor to a fool. 26.08
pledge when he g. surety for 27.13
He who g. to the poor will not want, 28.27
By justice a king g. stability to 29.04
A fool g. full vent to his anger, 29.11

GIVES (cont.)

the LORD g. light to the eyes of Pro 29.13
pleases him God g. wisdom and Ecc 2.26
the sinner he g. the work of 2.26
a man to whom God g. wealth, 6.02
Wisdom g. strength to the wise man 7.19
life which God g. him under the 8.15
He g. power to the faint, and to him Is 40.29
He g. up nations before him, so that 41.02
who, when I ask, g. an answer. 41.28
who g. breath to the people upon it 42.05
who g. the rain in its season, the Jer 5.24
who g. the sun for light by day and 31.35
for food, but no one g. to them. Lam 4.04
g. his bread to the hungry and Eze 18.07
but g. his bread to the hungry and 18.16
g. back what he had taken by 33.15
he g. wisdom to the wise and Dan 2.21
and g. it to whom he will, and sets 4.17
of men, and g. it to whom he will. 4.25
of men and g. it to whom he will." 4.32
and their staff g. them oracles. Hos 4.12
midst, a warrior who g. victory; Zep 3.17
who g. men showers of rain, to every Zec 10.01
and it g. light to all in the house. Mt 5.15
And whoever g. to one of these 10.42
whoever g. you a cup of water to Mk 9.41
a lamp with its rays g. you light." Lk 11.36
by measure that he g. the Spirit; Jn 3.34
raises the dead and g. them life, 5.21
so also the Son g. life to whom he 5.21
my Father g. you the true bread 6.32
and g. life to the world." 6.33
All that the Father g. me will come 6.37
It is the spirit that g. life, 6.63
as the world g. do I give to you. 14.27
he himself g. to all men life and Ac 17.25
who g. life to the dead and calls Rom 4.17
he who g. aid, with zeal; 12.08
Lord, since he g. thanks to God; 14.06
of the Lord and g. thanks to God. 14.06
but only God who g. the growth. 1Co 3.07
that g. me no ground for boasting. 9.16
And if the bugle g. an indistinct 14.08
But God g. it a body as he has 15.38
who g. us the victory through our 15.57
code kills, but the Spirit g. life. 2Co 3.06
scatters abroad, he g. to the poor; 9.09
who g. his Holy Spirit to you. 1Th 4.08
of God who g. life to all things, 1Ti 6.13
him ask God who g. to all men Jas 1.05
it has conceived g. birth to sin; 1.15
But he g. more grace; therefore 4.06
but g. grace to the humble." 4.06
but g. grace to the humble." 1Pe 5.05

GIVEST

all that thou g. me I will give Gen 28.22
and thou g. them drink from the Ps 36.08
When thou g. to them, they gather it 104.28
who g. victory to kings, who rescuest 144.10
and thou g. them their food in due 145.15

GIVING

When she had finished g. him a drink, Gen 24.19
and herds g. suck are a care to me; 33.13
g. an interpretation to each man 41.12
and g. it to him to whom he did the Num 5.07
g. the hallowed part from them.' 18.29
g. your daughters to their sons or Deu 7.03
your God is not g. you this good 9.06
g. him food and clothing. 10.18
by g. him a double portion of all 21.17
g. it to the Levite, the sojourner, 26.12
the land which I am g. to them, Jos 1.02
which the LORD your God is g. them; 1.15
For in g. this decision the king 2Sa 14.13
g. ear to them whenever thy call 1Ki 8.52
had made for g. thanks to the LORD— 2Ch 7.06
he is with you in g. judgment. 19.06
offerings and g. thanks to the 30.22
praising and g. thanks to the LORD, Ez 3.11
on the throne g. righteous judgment. Ps 9.04
He is ever g. liberally and lending, 37.26
in g. them the heritage of the 111.06
they stumble in g. judgment. Is 28.07
g. seed to the sower and bread to 55.10
Behold I am g. this city into the Jer 32.03
I am g. this city into the hands of 32.28
I am g. this city into the hand of 34.02
g. to the pestilence those who are 43.11
and the g. over of the sanctuary Dan 8.13
iniquities and g. heed to thy 9.13
marrying and g. in marriage, until Mt 24.38
face at Jesus' feet, g. him thanks. Lk 17.16
without first g. him a hearing and Jn 7.51
g. himself out to be somebody, and a Ac 5.36
that God was g. them deliverance 7.25
g. them the Holy Spirit just as he 15.08
and g. thanks to God in the presence 27.35
the g. of the law, the worship, and Rom 9.04
g. the greater honor to the inferior 1Co 12.24
you again but g. you cause to be 2Co 5.12
for everything g. thanks in the Eph 5.20
with me in g. and receiving except Php 4.15
g. thanks to the Father, who has Col 1.12
g. thanks to God the Father through 3.17
the faith by g. heed to deceitful 1Ti 4.01
instead of g. heed to Jewish myths Tit 1.14
without g. them the things needed Jas 2.16
of one mind and g. over their Rev 17.17

GIZONITE

Hashem the G., Jonathan the son of 1Ch 11.34

GLAD

you he will be g. in his heart. Ex 4.14
And the priest's heart was g.; Ju 18.20
the men of Jabesh, they were g. 1Sa 11.09
would have been g. to give you ten 2Sa 18.11
joyful and g. of heart for all the 1Ki 8.66
Let the heavens be g., and let the 1Ch 16.31
joyful and g. of heart for the 2Ch 7.10
that day joyful and g. of heart. Est 5.09
and are g., when they find the Job 3.22
The righteous see it and are g.; 22.19
I will be g. and exult in thee, I Ps 9.02
shall rejoice, Israel shall be g. 14.07
Therefore my heart is g., 16.09
dost make him g. with the joy of 21.06
rejoice and be g. for thy steadfast 31.07
Be g. in the LORD, and rejoice, O 32.11
our heart is g. in him, because we 33.21
let the afflicted hear and be g. 34.02
vindication shout for joy and be g., 35.27
I have told the g. news of deliverance 40.09
thee rejoice and be g. in thee; 40.16
with g. shouts and songs of thanksgiving, 42.04
stringed instruments make you g.; 45.08
streams make g. the city of God, 46.04
let Mount Zion be g.! Let the 48.11
will rejoice and Israel be g. 53.06
Let the nations be g. and sing for 67.04
Let the oppressed see it and be g.; 69.32
thee rejoice and be g. in thee! 70.04
may rejoice and be g. all our days. 90.14
Make us g. as many days as thou 90.15
LORD, hast made me g. by thy work; 92.04
Let the heavens be g., and let the 96.11
let the many coastlands be g.! 97.01
Zion hears and is g., and the 97.08
Egypt was g. when they departed, for 105.38
Then they were g. because they had 107.30
The upright see it and are g.; 107.42

GLAD (cont.)

shame; may thy servant be g.! Ps 109.28
Hark, g. songs of victory in the 118.15
let us rejoice and be g. in it. 118.24
I was g. when they said to me, "Let 122.01
done great things for us; we are g. 126.03
Let Israel be g. in his Maker, let 149.02
A wise son makes a g. father, Pro 10.01
down, but a good word makes him g. 12.25
A g. heart makes a cheerful countenance, 15.13
A wise son makes a g. father, 15.20
he who is g. at calamity will not 17.05
is wise, my heart too will be g. 23.15
a wise son will be g. in him. 23.24
Let your father and mother be g., 23.25
your heart be g. when he stumbles; 24.17
Oil and perfume make the heart g., 27.09
wise, my son, and make my heart g., 27.11
loves wisdom makes his father g., 29.03
countenance the heart is made g. Ecc 7.03
let us be g. and rejoice in his Is 25.09
and the dry land shall be g., 35.01
But be g. and rejoice for ever in Is 65.18
Jerusalem, and be g. in my people; 65.19
and be g. for her, all you who love 66.10
born to you," making him very g. Jer 20.15
they are g. that thou hast done it. Lam 1.21
Rejoice and be g., O daughter of 4.21
Then the king was exceedingly g., Dan 6.23
wickedness they make the king g., Hos 7.03
be g. and rejoice, for the LORD has Joe 2.21
"Be g., O sons of Zion, and rejoice 2.23
was exceedingly g. because of the Jon 4.06
hearts shall be g. as with wine. Zec 10.07
Rejoice and be g., for your reward Mt 5.12
And when they heard it they were g., Mk 14.11
fitting to make merry and be g., Lk 15.32
And they were g., and engaged to 22.05
he was very g., for he had long 23.08
Then they were g. to take him into Jn 6.21
see my day; he saw it and was g." 8.56
your sake I am g. that I was not 11.15
disciples were g. when they saw 20.20
therefore my heart was g., Ac 2.26
of food with g. and generous 2.46
saw the grace of God, he was g.; 11.23
they were g. and glorified the word 13.48
to make me g. but the one whom I 2Co 2.02
For we are g. when we are weak and 13.09
I am g. and rejoice with you all. Php 2.17
also should be g. and rejoice with 2.18
I would have been g. to keep him Phm 1.13
rejoice and be g. when his glory 1Pe 4.13

GLADDEN

G. the soul of thy servant, for to Ps 86.04
and wine to g. the heart of man, oil 104.15

GLADDENS

and wine g. life, and money answers Ecc 10.19

GLADLY

perplexed; and yet he heard him g. Mk 6.20
And the great throng heard him g. 12.37
And he would g. have fed on the Lk 15.16
the brethren received us g. Ac 21.17
For you g. bear with fools, being 2Co 11.19
all the more g. boast of my 12.09
I will most g. spend and be spent 12.15

GLADNESS

On the day of your g. also, Num 10.10
with joyfulness and g. of heart, Deu 28.47
the LORD on that day with great g. 1Ch 29.22
And they sang praises with g., 2Ch 29.30
bread seven days with great g.; 30.21
it for another seven days with g. 30.23
celebrate the dedication with g., Neh 12.27
had light and g. and joy and honor. Est 8.16
there was g. and joy among the Jews, 8.17
made that a day of feasting and g. 9.17
that a day of feasting and g. 9.18
as a day for g. and feasting and 9.19
sorrow into g. and from mourning 9.22
make them days of feasting and g., 9.22
sackcloth and girded me with g., Ps 30.11
Look away from me, that I may know g., 39.13
with the oil of g. above your 45.07
With joy and g. they are led along 45.15
Fill me with joy and g.; let the 51.08
Serve the LORD with g.! Come into 100.02
rejoice in the g. of thy nation, 106.05
The hope of the righteous ends in g., Pro 10.28
perish there are shouts of g. 11.10
on the day of the g. of his heart. Sol 3.11
And joy and g. are taken away from Is 16.10
joy and g., slaying oxen and 22.13
the g. of the earth is banished. 24.11
and g. of heart, as when one sets 30.29
they shall obtain joy and g., 35.10
joy and g. will be found in her, 51.03
they shall obtain joy and g., 51.11
the oil of g. instead of mourning, 61.03
servants shall sing for g. of heart, 65.14
voice of mirth and the voice of g., Jer 7.34
voice of mirth and the voice of g., 16.09
voice of mirth and the voice of g., 25.10
LORD: "Sing aloud with g. for Jacob, 31.07
them, and give them g. for sorrow. 31.13
voice of mirth and the voice of g., 33.11
G. and joy have been taken away 48.33
and g. fails from the sons of men. Joe 1.12
joy and g. from the house of our 1.16
he will rejoice over you with g., Zep 3.17
of Judah seasons of joy and g., Zec 8.19
And you will have joy and g., Lk 1.14
make me full of g. with thy Ac 2.28
your hearts with food and g." 14.17
with the oil of g. beyond thy Heb 1.09

GLANCE

my heart with a g. of your eyes, Sol 4.09

GLANCING

g. wantonly with their eyes, mincing Is 3.16

GLASS

Gold and g. cannot equal it, nor can Job 28.17
it were a sea of g., like crystal. Rev 4.06
to be a sea of g. mingled with 15.02
the sea of g. with harps of God in 15.02
city was pure gold, clear as g. 21.18
was pure gold, transparent as g. 21.21

GLAZE

Like the g. covering an earthen Pro 26.23

GLEAM

legs like the g. of burnished Dan 10.06
they g. like torches, they dart like Nah 2.04

GLEAMING

of the fire, as it were g. bronze. Eze 1.04
was like the g. of a chrysolite; 1.16
loins I saw as it were g. bronze, 1.27
of brightness, like g. bronze. 8.02

GLEAN

you shall not g. it afterward; Deu 24.21
and g. among the ears of grain Ru 2.02
let me g. and gather among the 2.07
do not go to g. in another field or 2.08
When she rose to g., Boaz instructed 2.15
"Let her g. even among the sheaves, 2.15
her, and leave it for her to g., 2.16
to her, "Where did you g. today? 2.19

GLEAN (cont.)
field and they g. the vineyard of Job 24.06
"G. thoroughly as a vine the Jer 6.09

GLEANED
and went and g. in the field after Ru 2.03
So she g. in the field until 2.17
then she beat out what she had g., 2.17
her mother-in-law what she had g., 2.18
as when the vintage has been g.: Mic 7.01

GLEANING
Is not the g. of the grapes of Ju 8.02
g. until the end of the barley and Ru 2.23
as at the g. when the vintage is Is 24.13

GLEANINGS
you gather the g. after your Lev 19.09
you gather the g. after your 23.22
G. will be left in it, as when an Is 17.06
to you, would they not leave g.? Jer 49.09
to you, would they not leave g.? Ob 1.05

GLEANS
and as when one g. the ears of Is 17.05

GLEE
my stumbling they gathered in g., Ps 35.15

GLEN
among the myrtle trees in the g.; Zec 1.08

GLIDED
A spirit g. past my face; Job 4.15

GLIDING
smoothly, g. over lips and teeth. Sol 7.09
a sound like a serpent g. away; Jer 46.22

GLISTENING
and his garments became g., intensely Mk 9.03

GLITTER
is polished to g. and to flash Eze 21.28

GLITTERING
if I whet my g. sword, and my hand Deu 32.41
the g. point comes out of his gall; Job 20.25
I have given the g. sword; Eze 21.15
flashing sword and g. spear, Nah 3.03
sped, at the flash of thy g. spear. Hab 3.11

GLOAT
my bones—they stare and g. over me; Ps 22.17
My eyes will g. over her; now she Mic 7.10

GLOATED
the foe g. over her, mocking at her Lam 1.07
should not have g. over the day of Ob 1.12
should not have g. over his 1.13

GLOOM
wrapped in darkness, cloud, and g. Deu 4.11
and the deep g., with a loud voice; 5.22
Let g. and deep darkness claim it. Job 3.05
to the land of g. and deep darkness, 10.21
the land of g. and chaos, where 10.22
the ore in g. and deep darkness. 28.03
There is no g. or deep darkness 34.22
Some sat in darkness and in g., Ps 107.10
them out of darkness and g., 107.14
and darkness, the g. of anguish; Is 8.22
will be no g. for her that was in 9.01
out of their g. and darkness the 29.18
and your g. be as the noonday. 58.10
for brightness, but we walk in g. 59.09
turns it into g. and makes it deep Jer 13.16
I will clothe Lebanon in g. for it, Eze 31.15
a day of darkness and g., Joe 2.02
and g. with no brightness in it? Amo 5.20
devastation, a day of darkness and g., Zep 1.15
darkness, and g., and a tempest, Heb 12.18
pits of nether g. to be kept until 2Pe 2.04
them the nether g. of darkness has 2.17
in the nether g. until the judgment Jud 1.06
whom the nether g. of darkness has 1.13

GLORIES
but let him who g. glory in this, Jer 9.24

GLORIFICATION
decreed before the ages for our g. 1Co 2.07

GLORIFIED
before all the people I will be g.' " Lev 10.03
thou art g.; thou hast enlarged Is 26.15
Jacob, and will be g. in Israel. 44.23
Israel, in whom I will be g." 49.03
One of Israel, for he has g. you. 55.05
of Israel, because he has g. you. 60.09
of my hands, that I might be g. 60.21
of the LORD, that he may be g. 61.03
have said, 'Let the LORD be g., 66.05
and they g. God, who had given such Mt 9.08
and they g. the God of Israel. 15.31
they were all amazed and g. God, Mk 2.12
their synagogues, being g. by all. Lk 4.15
and they g. God and were filled 5.26
and they g. God, saying, "A great 7.16
because Jesus was not yet g. Jn 7.39
of God may be g. by means of it." 11.04
but when Jesus was g., then they 12.16
come for the Son of man to be g. 12.23
"I have g. it, and I will glorify it 12.28
said, "Now is the Son of man g., 13.31
man g., and in him God is g.; 13.31
if God is g. in him, God will also 13.32
the Father may be g. in the Son; 14.13
By this my Father is g., that you 15.08
I g. thee on earth, having accomplished 17.04
are mine, and I am g. in them. 17.10
g. his servant Jesus, whom you Ac 3.13
And they g. God, saying, "Then to the 11.18
were glad and g. the word of God; 13.48
And when they heard it, they g. God. 21.20
that we may also be g. with him. Rom 8.17
those whom he justified he also g. 8.30
And they g. God because of me. Gal 1.24
on that day to be g. in his saints, 2Th 1.10
of our Lord Jesus may be g. in you, 1.12
God may be g. through Jesus Christ. 1Pe 4.11
As she g. herself and played the Rev 18.07

GLORIFIES
it is my Father who g. me, of whom Jn 8.54

GLORIFY
g. him, and stand in awe of him, all Ps 22.23
deliver you, and you shall g. me." 50.15
O Lord, and shall g. thy name. 86.09
and I will g. thy name for ever. 86.12
Therefore strong peoples will g. thee; Is 25.03
and I will g. my glorious house. 60.07
"If I g. myself, my glory is nothing; Jn 8.54
Father, g. thy name." Then a voice 12.28
glorified it, and I will g. it again." 12.28
God will also g. him in himself, and g. 13.32
He will g. me, for he will take what 16.14
g. thy Son that the Son may g. thee, 17.01
g. thou me in thy own presence with 17.05
by what death he was to g. God.) 21.19
with one voice g. the God and Rom 15.06
Gentiles might g. God for his 15.09
a price. So g. God in your body. 1Co 6.20
you will g. God by your obedience 2Co 9.13
good deeds and g. God on the day 1Pe 2.12

GLORIFY (cont.)
but under that name let him g. God. 1Pe 4.16
Who shall not fear and g. thy name, Rev 15.04

GLORIFYING
g. and praising God for all they Lk 2.20
he lay, and went home, g. God. 5.25
his sight and followed him, g. God; 18.43

GLORIOUS
g. in power, thy right hand, O LORD, Ex 15.06
terrible in g. deeds, doing wonders? 15.11
may fear this g. and awful name, Deu 28.58
our God, and praise thy g. name. 1Ch 29.13
Blessed be thy g. name which is Neh 9.05
his name; give to him g. praise! Ps 66.02
Blessed be his g. name for ever; 72.19
G. art thou, more majestic than the 76.04
generation the g. deeds of the 78.04
G. things are spoken of you, O city 87.03
and thy g. power to their children. 90.16
Of the g. splendor of thy majesty, 145.05
and the g. splendor of thy kingdom. 145.12
the LORD, defying his g. presence. Is 3.08
the LORD shall be beautiful and g., 4.02
he will make g. the way of the sea, 9.01
and his dwellings shall be g. 11.10
the fading flower of its g. beauty, 28.01
the fading flower of its g. beauty, 28.04
to magnify his law and make it g. 42.21
and I will glorify my g. house. 60.07
will make the place of my feet g. 60.13
he that is g. in his apparel, 63.01
who caused his g. arm to go at the 63.12
to make for thyself a g. name. 63.14
from thy holy and g. habitation. 63.15
do not dishonor thy g. throne; Jer 14.21
A g. throne set on high from the 17.12
scepter is broken, the g. staff.' 48.17
honey, the most g. of all lands. Eze 20.06
honey, the most g. of all lands, 20.15
the east, and toward the g. land. Dan 8.09
and he shall stand in the g. land, 11.16
He shall come into the g. land. 11.41
the sea and the g. holy mountain; 11.45
for the g. trees are ruined! Zec 11.02
of man shall sit on his g. throne, Mt 19.28
then he will sit on his g. throne. 25.31
at all the g. things that were Lk 13.17
and obtain the g. liberty of the Rom 8.21
praise of his g. grace which he Eph 1.06
riches of his g. inheritance in 1.18
lowly body to be like his g. body, Php 3.21
power, according to his g. might, Col 1.11
with the g. gospel of the blessed 1Ti 1.11
not afraid to revile the g. ones, 2Pe 2.10
authority, and revile the g. ones. Jud 1.08

GLORIOUSLY
the LORD, for he has triumphed g.; Ex 15.01
the LORD, for he has triumphed g.; 15.21
to the LORD, for he has done g.; Is 12.05

GLORY
and I will get g. over Pharaoh and Ex 14.04
and I will get g. over Pharaoh and 14.17
when I have gotten g. over Pharaoh, 14.18
you shall see the g. of the LORD, 16.07
the g. of the LORD appeared in the 16.10
The g. of the LORD settled on Mount 24.16
appearance of the g. of the LORD 24.17
brother, for g. and for beauty. 28.02
shall make them for g. and beauty. 28.40
it shall be sanctified by my g.; 29.43
Moses said, "I pray thee, show me thy g." 33.18
and while my g. passes by I will 33.22
and the g. of the LORD filled the 40.34
and the g. of the LORD filled the 40.35
and the g. of the LORD will appear Lev 9.06
and the g. of the LORD appeared to 9.23
Then the g. of the LORD appeared at Num 14.10
be filled with the g. of the LORD, 14.21
have seen my g. and my signs which 14.22
And the g. of the LORD appeared to 16.19
and the g. of the LORD appeared. 16.42
And the g. of the LORD appeared to 20.06
has shown us his g. and greatness, Deu 5.24
give g. to the LORD God of Israel, Jos 7.19
are going will not lead to your g., Ju 4.09
"The g. has departed from Israel!" 1Sa 4.21
"The g. has departed from Israel, 4.22
and give g. to the God of Israel; 6.05
And also the G. of Israel will not 15.29
"Thy g., O Israel, is slain upon thy 2Sa 1.19
for the g. of the LORD filled the 1Ki 8.11
Be content with your g., and stay 2Ki 14.10
G. in his holy name; let the hearts 1Ch 16.10
Declare his g. among the nations, 16.24
to the LORD g. and strength! 16.28
Ascribe to the LORD the g. due his name; 16.29
holy name, and g. in thy praise. 16.35
of fame and g. throughout all lands; 22.05
and the g., and the victory, and the 29.11
for the g. of the LORD filled the 2Ch 5.14
and the g. of the LORD filled the 7.01
because the g. of the LORD filled 7.02
down and the g. of the LORD upon 7.03
of his royal g. and the splendor Est 1.04
He has stripped from me my g., Job 19.09
my g. fresh with me, and my bow ever 29.20
yourself with g. and splendor. 40.10
my g., and the lifter of my head. Ps 3.03
Thou whose g. above the heavens is 8.01
dost crown him with g. and honor. 8.05
The heavens are telling the g. of God; 19.01
His g. is great through thy help; 21.05
that the King of g. may come in. 24.07
Who is the King of g.? The LORD, 24.08
that the King of g. may come in! 24.09
Who is this King of g.? The LORD 24.10
of hosts, he is the King of g.! 24.10
and the place where thy g. dwells. 26.08
to the LORD g. and strength. 29.01
Ascribe to the LORD the g. of his name; 29.02
the God of g. thunders, the LORD, 29.03
and in his temple all cry, "G.!" 29.09
are like the g. of the pastures, 37.20
mighty one, in your g. and majesty! 45.03
when the g. of his house increases. 49.16
his g. will not go down after him. 49.17
Let thy g. be over all the earth! 57.05
Let thy g. be over all the earth! 57.11
sanctuary, beholding thy power and g. 63.02
all who swear by him shall g.; 63.11
Let all the upright in heart g.! 64.10
sing the g. of his name; give to him 66.02
and with thy g. all the day. 71.08
may his g. fill the whole earth! 72.19
afterward thou wilt receive me to g. 73.24
his g. to the hand of the foe. 78.61
salvation, for the g. of thy name; 79.09
that g. may dwell in our land. 85.09
For thou art the g. of their 89.17
Declare his g. among the nations, 96.03
to the LORD g. and strength! 96.07
Ascribe to the LORD the g. due his name; 96.08
and all the peoples behold his g. 97.06
all the kings of the earth thy g. 102.15
up Zion, he will appear in his g.; 102.16
May the g. of the LORD endure for 104.31
G. in his holy name; let the hearts 105.03
that I may g. with thy heritage. 106.05
They exchanged the g. of God for 106.20
thy holy name and g. in thy praise. 106.47

GLORY (cont.)

Let thy g. be over all the earth! Ps 108.05
and his g. above the heavens! 113.04
not to us, but to thy name give g., 115.01
for great is the g. of the LORD. 138.05
speak of the g. of thy kingdom, 145.11
his g. is above earth and heaven. 148.13
Let the faithful exult in g.; 149.05
This is g. for all his faithful 149.09
of people is the g. of a king, Pro 14.28
A hoary head is a crown of g.; 16.31
and the g. of sons is their fathers. 17.06
and it is his g. to overlook an 19.11
The g. of young men is their 20.29
It is the g. of God to conceal 25.02
but the g. of kings is to search 25.02
righteous triumph, there is great g.; 28.12
and from the g. of his majesty. Is 2.10
and from the g. of his majesty, when 2.19
and from the g. of his majesty, when 2.21
the pride and g. of the survivors 4.02
over all the g. there will be a 4.05
the whole earth is full of his g." 6.03
the king of Assyria and all his g.; 8.07
and under his g. a burning will be 10.16
The g. of his forest and of his 10.18
the g. of kingdoms, the splendor and 13.19
the kings of the nations lie in g., 14.18
the g. of Moab will be brought into 16.14
be like the g. of the children of 17.03
And in that day the g. of Jacob 17.04
all the g. of Kedar will come to an 21.16
it, to defile the pride of all g., 23.09
Therefore in the east give g. to the LORD; 24.15
of g. to the Righteous One. 24.16
his elders he will manifest his g. 24.23
of hosts will be a crown of g., 28.05
The g. of Lebanon shall be given to 35.02
they shall see the g. of the LORD, 35.02
And the g. of the LORD shall be 40.05
Holy One of Israel you shall g. 41.16
my g. I give to no other, nor my 42.08
Let them give g. to the LORD, and 42.12
my name, whom I created for my g., 43.07
of Israel shall triumph and g." 45.25
salvation in Zion, for Israel my g. 46.13
My g. I will not give to another. 48.11
the g. of the LORD shall be your 58.08
and his g. from the rising of the 59.19
and the g. of the LORD has risen 60.01
and his g. will be seen upon you. 60.02
The g. of Lebanon shall come to you, 60.13
and your God will be your g. 60.19
and in their riches you shall g. 61.06
vindication, and all the kings your g.; 62.02
from the abundance of her g." 66.11
shall come and shall see my g., 66.18
not heard my fame or seen my g.; 66.19
declare my g. among the nations. 66.19
changed their g. for that which Jer 2.11
in him, and in him shall they g." 4.02
not the wise man g. in his wisdom, 9.23
not the mighty man g. in his might, 9.23
not the rich man g. in his riches; 9.23
but let him who glories g. in this, 9.24
and a g., but they would not listen. 13.11
Give g. to the LORD your God before 13.16
a praise and a g. before all the 33.09
"Come down from your g., and sit 48.18
"Gone is my g., and my expectation Lam 3.18
the likeness of the g. of the LORD. Eze 1.28
and as the g. of the LORD arose 3.12
and, lo, the g. of the LORD stood 3.23
like the g. which I had seen by the 3.23
the g. of the God of Israel was 8.04
Now the g. of the God of Israel had 9.03
And the g. of the LORD went up from 10.04
brightness of the g. of the LORD. 10.04
Then the g. of the LORD went forth 10.18
and the g. of the God of Israel was 10.19
and the g. of the God of Israel was 11.22
And the g. of the LORD went up from 11.23
their joy and g., the delight of 24.25
the g. of the country, Bethjeshimoth, 25.09
manifest my g. in the midst of you. 28.22
thus like in g. and in greatness 31.18
honor on the day that I show my g., 39.13
"And I will set my g. among the 39.21
the g. of the God of Israel came 43.02
and the earth shone with his g. 43.02
As the g. of the LORD entered the 43.04
the g. of the LORD filled the 43.05
the g. of the LORD filled the 44.04
power, and the might, and the g., Dan 2.37
and for the g. of my majesty?" 4.30
and for the g. of my kingdom, my 4.36
and greatness and g. and majesty; 5.18
and his g. was taken from him; 5.20
given dominion and g. and kingdom, 7.14
through the g. of the kingdom; 11.20
I will change their g. into shame. Hos 4.07
they love shame more than their g. 4.18
Ephraim's g. shall fly away like a 9.11
over its g. which has departed from 10.05
the g. of Israel shall come to Mic 1.15
you take away my g. for ever. 2.09
knowledge of the g. of the LORD, Hab 2.14
sated with contempt instead of g. 2.16
and shame will come upon your g.! 2.16
His g. covered the heavens, and the 3.03
may appear in my g., says the LORD. Hag 1.08
saw this house in its former g.? 2.03
and I will be the g. within her.'" Zec 2.05
after his g. sent me to the nations 2.08
LORD and they shall g. in his name, 10.12
shepherds, for their g. is despoiled! 11.03
that the g. of the house of David 12.07
David and the g. of the inhabitants 12.07
it to heart to give g. to my name, Mal 2.02
of the world and the g. of them; Mt 4.08
works and give g. to your Father 5.16
kingdom and the power and the g., * 6.13
in all his g. was not arrayed like 6.29
his angels in the g. of his Father, 16.27
of heaven with power and great g.; 24.30
"When the Son of man comes in his g., 25.31
he comes in the g. of his Father Mk 8.38
and one at your left, in your g." 10.37
in clouds with great power and g. 13.26
and the g. of the Lord shone around Lk 2.09
"G. to God in the highest, and on 2.14
and for g. to thy people Israel." 2.32
all this authority and their g.; 4.06
his g. and the g. of the Father 9.26
who appeared in g. and spoke of his 9.31
they saw his g. and the two men 9.32
in all his g. was not arrayed like 12.27
in heaven and g. in the highest!" 19.38
in a cloud with power and great g. 21.27
these things and enter into his g.?" 24.26
these things; we have beheld his g.," Jn 1.14
g. as of the only Son from the 1.14
in Galilee, and manifested his g.; 2.11
I do not receive g. from men. 5.41
who receive g. from one another and 5.44
do not seek the g. that comes from 5.44
his own authority seeks his own g.; 7.18
who seeks the g. of him who sent 7.18
Yet I do not seek my own g.; 8.50
I glorify myself, my g. is nothing; 8.54
it is for the g. of God, so that the 11.04
you would see the g. of God?" 11.40
he saw his g. and spoke of him. 12.41
with the g. which I had with thee 17.05

GLORY (cont.)

The g. which thou hast given me I Jn 17.22
to behold my g. which thou hast 17.24
The God of g. appeared to our Ac 7.02
into heaven and saw the g. of God, 7.55
because he did not give God the g.; 12.23
and exchanged the g. of the immortal Rom 1.23
seek for g. and honor and immortality, 2.07
but g. and honor and peace for 2.10
truthfulness abounds to his g., 3.07
and fall short of the g. of God, 3.23
in his faith as he gave g. to God, 4.20
our hope of sharing the g. of God. 5.02
the dead by the g. of the Father, 6.04
with the g. that is to be revealed 8.18
the g., the covenants, the giving of 9.04
riches of his g. for the vessels 9.23
he has prepared beforehand for g., 9.23
all things. To him be g. for ever. 11.36
welcomed you, for the g. of God. 15.07
wise God be g. for evermore 16.27
not have crucified the Lord of g. 1Co 2.08
you do, do all to the g. of God. 10.31
he is the image and g. of God; 11.07
but woman is the g. of man. 11.07
but the g. of the celestial is one, 15.40
and the g. of the terrestrial is 15.40
There is one g. of the sun, and 15.41
and another g. of the moon, and 15.41
moon, and another g. of the stars; 15.41
for star differs from star in g. 15.41
in dishonor, it is raised in g. 15.43
Amen through him, to the g. of God. 2Co 1.20
beholding the g. of the Lord, are 3.18
from one degree of g. to another; 3.18
of the gospel of the g. of Christ, 4.04
knowledge of the g. of God in the 4.06
thanksgiving, to the g. of God. 4.15
weight of g. beyond all comparison, 4.17
for the g. of the Lord and to show 8.19
of the churches, the g. of Christ. 8.23
to whom be the g. for ever and ever. Gal 1.05
that they may g. in your flesh. 6.13
it from me to g. except in the 6.14
to live for the praise of his g. Eph 1.12
of it, to the praise of his g. 1.14
the Father of g., may give you a 1.17
suffering for you, which is your g. 3.13
riches of his g. he may grant you 3.16
to him be g. in the church and in 3.21
to the g. and praise of God. Php 1.11
ample cause to g. in Christ Jesus, 1.26
to the g. of God the Father. 2.11
and g. in Christ Jesus, and put no 3.03
and they g. in their shame, with 3.19
his riches in g. in Christ Jesus. 4.19
and Father be g. for ever and ever. 4.20
riches of the g. of this mystery, Col 1.27
is Christ in you, the hope of g. 1.27
also will appear with him in g. 3.04
nor did we seek g. from men, 1Th 2.06
you into his own kingdom and g. 2.12
For you are our g. and joy. 2.20
Lord and from the g. of his might, 2Th 1.09
may obtain the g. of our Lord 2.14
be honor and g. for ever and ever. 1Ti 1.17
on in the world, taken up in g. 3.16
Christ Jesus goes with eternal g. 2Ti 2.10
To him be the g. for ever and ever. 4.18
appearing of the g. of our great Tit 2.13
He reflects the g. of God and bears Heb 1.03
crowned him with g. and honor, 2.07
crowned with g. and honor because 2.09
exist, in bringing many sons to g., 2.10
of as much more g. than Moses as 3.03
the cherubim of g. overshadowing 9.05
to whom be g. for ever and ever. 13.21
Lord Jesus Christ, the Lord of g. Jas 2.01
to praise and g. and honor at the 1Pe 1.07
of Christ and the subsequent g. 1.11
him from the dead and gave him g., 1.21
and all its g. like the flower of 1.24
To him belong g. and dominion for 4.11
be glad when his g. is revealed. 4.13
the spirit of g. and of God rests 4.14
partaker in the g. that is to be 5.01
obtain the unfading crown of g. 5.04
you to his eternal g. in Christ, 5.10
us to his own g. and excellence, 2Pe 1.03
honor and g. from God the Father 1.17
borne to him by the Majestic G., 1.17
To him be the g. both now and to 3.18
presence of his g. with rejoicing, Jud 1.24
be g., majesty, dominion, and authority, 1.25
to him be g. and dominion for ever Rev 1.06
creatures give g. and honor and 4.09
to receive g. and honor and power. 4.11
and honor and g. and blessing!" 5.12
and honor and g. and might for 5.13
Blessing and g. and wisdom and 7.12
and gave g. to the God of heaven. 11.13
voice, "Fear God and give him g., 14.07
smoke from the g. of God and from 15.08
did not repent and give him g. 16.09
Salvation and g. and power belong 19.01
and exult and give him the g., 19.07
having the g. of God, its radiance 21.11
for the g. of God is its light, and 21.23
shall bring their g. into it, 21.24
into it the g. and the honor of 21.26

GLOWING

g. coals flamed forth from him. 2Sa 22.09
g. coals flamed forth from him. Ps 18.08
with g. coals of the broom tree! 120.04

GLUTTON

he is a g. and a drunkard.' Deu 21.20
drunkard and the g. will come to Pro 23.21
a g. and a drunkard, a friend of tax Mt 11.19
a g. and a drunkard, a friend of tax Lk 7.34

GLUTTONOUS

winebibbers, or among g. eaters of meat; Pro 23.20

GLUTTONS

a companion of g. shames his Pro 28.07
always liars, evil beasts, lazy g." Tit 1.12

GNASH

they g. their teeth, they cry: "We Lam 2.16
men will weep and g. their teeth." Mt 8.12
men will weep and g. their teeth. 13.42
men will weep and g. their teeth. 13.50
men will weep and g. their teeth.' 22.13
men will weep and g. their teeth. 24.51
men will weep and g. their teeth.' 25.30
There you will weep and g. your teeth, Lk 13.28

GNASHED

he has g. his teeth at me; my adversary Job 16.09

GNASHES

the righteous, and g. his teeth at him; Ps 37.12
he g. his teeth and melts away; 112.10

GNASHING

and more, g. at me with their teeth. Ps 35.16

GNAT

straining out a g. and swallowing Mt 23.24

GNATS

it may become g. throughout all Ex 8.16
and there came g. on man and beast; 8.17
earth became g. throughout all the 8.17

GNATS (cont.)
secret arts to bring forth g., Ex 8.18
So there were g. on man and beast. 8.18
and g. throughout their country. Ps 105.31
who dwell in it will die like g.; Is 51.06

GNAW
hunger they g. the dry and desolate Job 30.03

GNAWED
king of Babylon has g. his bones. Jer 50.17
men g. their tongues in anguish Rev 16.10

GNAWS
the pain that g. me takes no rest. Job 30.17

GOADS
the axes and for setting the g. 1Sa 13.21
The sayings of the wise are like g., Ecc 12.11
hurts you to kick against the g.' Ac 26.14

GOAH
Gareb, and shall then turn to G. Jer 31.39

GOAL
on toward the g. for the prize of Php 3.14

GOAT
and killed a g., and dipped the Gen 37.31
"If his offering is a g., then he Lev 3.12
shall bring as his offering a g., 4.23
his hand upon the head of the g., 4.24
shall bring for his offering a g., 4.28
a lamb or a g., for a sin offering; 5.06
eat no fat, of ox, or sheep, or g. 7.23
'Take a male g. for a sin offering, 9.03
and took the g. of the sin offering 9.15
about the g. of the sin offering. 10.16
present the g. on which the lot 16.09
but the g. on which the lot fell 16.10
shall kill the g. of the sin 16.15
bull and of the blood of the g., 16.18
he shall present the live g.; 16.20
hands upon the head of the live g., 16.21
put them upon the head of the g., 16.21
The g. shall bear all their iniquities 16.22
shall let the g. go in the wilderness. 16.22
And he who lets the g. go to Azazel 16.26
offering and the g. for the sin 16.27
ox or a lamb or a g. in the camp, 17.03
"When a bull or sheep or g. is born. 22.27
offer one male g. for a sin offering, 23.19
one male g. for a sin offering; Num 7.16
one male g. for a sin offering; 7.22
one male g. for a sin offering; 7.28
one male g. for a sin offering; 7.34
one male g. for a sin offering; 7.40
one male g. for a sin offering; 7.46
one male g. for a sin offering; 7.52
one male g. for a sin offering; 7.58
one male g. for a sin offering; 7.64
one male g. for a sin offering; 7.70
one male g. for a sin offering; 7.76
one male g. for a sin offering; 7.82
and one male g. for a sin offering. 15.24
offer a female g. a year old for a 15.27
a sheep, or the firstling of a g., 18.17
Also one male g. for a sin offering 28.15
also one male g. for a sin offering, 28.22
with one male g., to make atonement 28.30
with one male g. for a sin offering, 29.05
also one male g. for a sin offering, 29.11
also one male g. for a sin offering, 29.16
also one male g. for a sin offering, 29.19
also one male g. for a sin offering, 29.22
also one male g. for a sin offering, 29.25
also one male g. for a sin offering; 29.28
also one male g. for a sin offering; 29.31
also one male g. for a sin offering; 29.34
also one male g. for a sin offering; 29.38
eat: the ox, the sheep, the g., Deu 14.04
the wild g., the ibex, the antelope, 14.05
provide daily a g. for a sin Eze 43.25
and the g. had a conspicuous horn Dan 8.05

GOATS
spotted the speckled among the g.; Gen 30.32
among the g. and black among the 30.33
all the g. that leap upon the flock 31.12
it from the sheep or from the g.; Ex 12.05
the flock, from the sheep or g., Lev 1.10
Israel two male g. for a sin 16.05
Then he shall take the two g., 16.07
shall cast lots upon the two g., 16.08
the bulls or the sheep or the g. 22.19
five male g., and five male lambs a Num 7.17
five male g., and five male lambs a 7.23
five male g., and five male lambs a 7.29
five male g., and five male lambs a 7.35
five male g., and five male lambs a 7.41
five male g., and five male lambs a 7.47
five male g., and five male lambs a 7.53
five male g., and five male lambs a 7.59
five male g., and five male lambs a 7.65
five male g., and five male lambs a 7.71
five male g., and five male lambs a 7.77
five male g., and five male lambs a 7.83
and twelve male g. for a sin 7.87
the male g. sixty, the male lambs a 7.88
and rams, herds of Bashan and g., Deu 32.14
thousand sheep and a thousand g. 1Sa 25.02
them like two little flocks of g., 1Ki 20.27
when the mountain g. bring forth? Job 39.01
of bulls, or drink the blood of g.? Ps 50.13
make an offering of bulls and g. 66.15
high mountains are for the wild g.; 104.18
and the g. the price of a field; Pro 27.26
Your hair is like a flock of g., Sol 4.01
me—Your hair is like a flock of g., 6.05
with the blood of lambs and g., Is 34.06
dealers in lambs, rams, and g.; Eze 27.21
and of g., of bulls, all of them 39.18
separates the sheep from the g., Mt 25.32
right hand, but the g. at the left. 25.33
the blood of g. and calves but his Heb 9.12
the blood of g. and bulls and with 9.13
he took the blood of calves and g., 9.19
of bulls and g. should take away 10.04
about in skins of sheep and g., 11.37

GOATS'
and fine twined linen, g. hair, Ex 25.04
curtains of g. hair for a tent 26.07
fine twined linen; g. hair, 35.06
fine linen or g. hair or tanned 35.23
with ability spun the g. hair. 35.26
curtains of g. hair for a tent 36.14
all work of g. hair, and every Num 31.20
put a pillow of g. hair at its 1Sa 19.13
the pillow of g. hair at its head. 19.16
there will be enough g. milk for Pro 27.27

GOATSKIN
shall put on it a covering of g., Num 4.06
the same with a covering of g., 4.08
a covering of g. and put it upon 4.10
and cover it with a covering of g., 4.11
cover them with a covering of g., 4.12
spread upon it a covering of g., 4.14

GOATSKINS
tanned rams' skins, g., acacia wood, Ex 25.05
of tanned rams' skins and g. 26.14
tanned rams' skins, and g.; 35.07
rams' skins or g., brought them. 35.23

GOATSKINS (cont.)
of tanned rams' skins and g. Ex 36.19
of tanned rams' skins and g., 39.34

GOB
war with the Philistines at G.; 2Sa 21.18
war with the Philistines at G.; 21.19

GOBBETS
Drinks were served in golden g., Est 1.07
g. of different kinds, and the royal 1.07

GOD
In the beginning G. created the Gen 1.01
the Spirit of G. was moving over 1.02
And G. said, "Let there be light"; 1.03
And G. saw that the light was good; 1.04
and G. separated the light from the 1.04
G. called the light Day, and the 1.05
And G. said, "Let there be a firmament 1.06
And G. made the firmament and 1.07
And G. called the firmament Heaven. 1.08
And G. said, "Let the waters under 1.09
G. called the dry land Earth, and 1.10
And G. saw that it was good. 1.10
And G. said, "Let the earth put 1.11
And G. saw that it was good. 1.12
And G. said, "Let there be lights in 1.14
And G. made the two great lights, 1.16
And G. set them in the firmament of 1.17
And G. saw that it was good. 1.18
And G. said, "Let the waters bring 1.20
So G. created the great sea monsters 1.21
And G. saw that it was good. 1.21
And G. blessed them, saying, "Be 1.22
And G. said, "Let the earth bring 1.24
And G. made the beasts of the earth 1.25
And G. saw that it was good. 1.25
Then G. said, "Let us make man in 1.26
So G. created man in his own image, 1.27
in the image of G. he created him; 1.27
And G. blessed them, and God said to 1.28
and G. said to them, "Be fruitful 1.28
And G. said, "Behold, I have given 1.29
And G. saw everything that he had 1.31
the seventh day G. finished his 2.02
So G. blessed the seventh day and 2.03
because on it G. rested from all 2.03
that the LORD G. made the earth 2.04
for the LORD G. had not caused it 2.05
then the LORD G. formed man of dust 2.07
And the LORD G. planted a garden in 2.08
ground the LORD G. made to grow 2.09
The LORD G. took the man and put 2.15
And the LORD G. commanded the man, 2.16
Then the LORD G. said, "It is not 2.18
ground the LORD G. formed every 2.19
So the LORD G. caused a deep sleep 2.21
which the LORD G. has taken from 2.22
creature that the LORD G. had made. 3.01
"Did G. say, 'You shall not eat of 3.01
but G. said, 'You shall not eat of 3.03
For G. knows that when you eat of 3.05
be opened, and you will be like G., 3.05
of the LORD G. walking in the 3.08
of the LORD G. among the trees of 3.08
But the LORD G. called to the man, 3.09
Then the LORD G. said to the woman, 3.13
The LORD G. said to the serpent, 3.14
And the LORD G. made for Adam and 3.21
Then the LORD G. said, "Behold, the 3.22
therefore the LORD G. sent him 3.23
"G. has appointed for me another 4.25
When G. created man, he made him in 5.01
he made him in the likeness of G. 5.01
Enoch walked with G. after the 5.22
Enoch walked with G.; and he was 5.24
and he was not, for G. took him. 5.24
the sons of G. saw that the daughters 6.02
the sons of G. came in to the 6.04
generation; Noah walked with G. 6.09
And G. saw the earth, and behold, it 6.12
And G. said to Noah, "I have determined 6.13
he did all that G. commanded him. 6.22
with Noah, as G. had commanded Noah. 7.09
went in as G. had commanded him; 7.16
But G. remembered Noah and all the 8.01
And G. made a wind blow over the 8.01
Then G. said to Noah, 8.15
And G. blessed Noah and his sons, 9.01
for G. made man in his own image. 9.06
Then G. said to Noah and to his 9.08
And G. said, "This is the sign of 9.12
covenant between G. and every 9.16
G. said to Noah, "This is the sign 9.17
"Blessed by the LORD my G. be Shem; 9.26
G. enlarge Japheth, and let him 9.27
he was priest of G. Most High. 14.18
"Blessed be Abram by G. Most High, 14.19
and blessed be G. Most High, who has 14.20
sworn to the LORD G. Most High, 14.22
"O LORD G., what wilt thou give me, 15.02
"O LORD G., how am I to know that 15.08
to her, "Thou art a G. of seeing"; 16.13
"Have I really seen G. and remained 16.13
and said to him, "I am G. Almighty; 17.01
fell on his face; and G. said to him, 17.03
to be G. to you and to your descendants 17.07
possession; and I will be their G." 17.08
And G. said to Abraham, "As for you, 17.09
And G. said to Abraham. "As for 17.15
And Abraham said to G., "Oh that 17.18
G. said, "No, but Sarah your wife 17.19
with him, G. went up from Abraham. 17.22
that very day, as G. had said to him. 17.23
when G. destroyed the cities of the 19.29
G. remembered Abraham, and sent Lot 19.29
But G. came to Abimelech in a dream 20.03
Then G. said to him in the dream, 20.06
is no fear of G. at all in this 20.11
And when G. caused me to wander 20.13
Then Abraham prayed to G.; 20.17
and G. healed Abimelech, and also 20.17
time of which G. had spoken to him. 21.02
days old, as G. had commanded him. 21.04
"G. has made laughter for me; 21.06
But G. said to Abraham, "Be not 21.12
And G. heard the voice of the lad; 21.17
the angel of G. called to Hagar 21.17
for G. has heard the voice of the 21.17
Then G. opened her eyes, and she saw 21.19
And G. was with the lad, and he grew 21.20
"G. is with you in all that you do; 21.22
to me here by G. that you will not 21.23
of the LORD, the Everlasting G. 21.33
After these things G. tested Abraham, 22.01
the place of which G. had told him. 22.03
Abraham said, "G. will provide 22.08
the place of which G. had told him, 22.09
for now I know that you fear G., 22.12
the G. of heaven and of the earth, 24.03
The LORD, the G. of heaven, who took 24.07
G. of my master Abraham, grant me 24.12
the G. of my master Abraham, who 24.27
the G. of my master Abraham, if now 24.42
the G. of my master Abraham, who had 24.48
of Abraham G. blessed Isaac his 25.11
"I am the G. of Abraham your father; 26.24
the LORD your G. granted me success." 27.20
May G. give you of the dew of 27.28
G. Almighty bless you and make you 28.03
sojournings which G. gave to 28.04
the angels of G. were ascending and 28.12
the G. of Abraham your father and 28.13

GOD (cont.)
your father and the G. of Isaac; Gen 28.13
is none other than the house of G., 28.17
"If G. will be with me, and will 28.20
then the LORD shall be my G., 28.21
he said, "Am I in the place of G., 30.02
"G. has judged me, and has also 30.06
And G. hearkened to Leah, and she 30.17
Leah said, "G. has given me my hire 30.18
"G. has endowed me with a good 30.20
Then G. remembered Rachel, and God 30.22
and G. hearkened to her and opened 30.22
"G. has taken away my reproach"; 30.23
But the G. of my father has been 31.05
but G. did not permit him to harm 31.07
Thus G. has taken away the cattle 31.09
Then the angel of G. said to me in 31.11
I am the G. of Bethel, where you 31.13
property which G. has taken away 31.16
whatever G. has said to you, do." 31.16
But G. came to Laban the Aramean in 31.24
but the G. of your father spoke to 31.29
If the G. of my father, the G. of 31.42
the G. of Abraham and the Fear of 31.42
G. saw my affliction and the labor 31.42
G. is witness between you and me." 31.50
G. of Abraham and the G. of Nahor, 31.53
the G. of their father, judge 31.53
way and the angels of G. met him; 32.01
"O G. of my father Abraham and G. 32.09
and G. of my father Isaac, O LORD 32.09
have striven with G. and with men, 32.28
"For I have seen G. face to face, 32.30
children whom G. has graciously 33.05
face is like seeing the face of G., 33.10
because G. has dealt graciously 33.11
G. said to Jacob, "Arise, go up to 35.01
an altar to the G. who appeared to 35.01
an altar to the G. who answered me 35.03
a terror from G. fell upon the 35.05
because there G. had revealed 35.07
G. appeared to Jacob again, when he 35.09
And G. said to him, "Your name is 35.10
And G. said to him, "I am G. 35.11
"I am G. Almighty: be fruitful and 35.11
Then G. went up from him in the 35.13
the place where G. had spoken with 35.15
wickedness, and sin against G.?" 39.09
not interpretations belong to G.? 40.08
G. will give Pharaoh a favorable 41.16
G. has revealed to Pharaoh what he 41.25
G. has shown to Pharaoh what he is 41.28
that the thing is fixed by G., 41.32
and G. will shortly bring it to 41.32
this, in whom is the Spirit of G.?" 41.38
"Since G. has shown you all this, 41.39
"G. has made me forget all my 41.51
For G. has made me fruitful in the 41.52
and you will live, for I fear G.: 42.18
is this that G. has done to us?" 42.28
may G. Almighty grant you mercy 43.14
your G. and the G. of your father must 43.23
G. be gracious to you, my son!" 43.29
G. has found out the guilt of your 44.16
for G. sent me before you to preserve 45.05
And G. sent me before you to preserve 45.07
not you who sent me here, but G.; 45.08
G. has made me lord of all Egypt; 45.09
sacrifices to the G. of his father 46.01
And G. spoke to Israel in visions 46.02
"I am G., the G. of your father; 46.03
"G. Almighty appeared to me at Luz 48.03
are my sons, whom G. has given me here." 48.09
and lo, G. has let me see your 48.11
"The G. before whom my fathers Abraham 48.15
the G. who has led me all my life 48.15
'G. make you as Ephraim and as 48.20
but G. will be with you, and will 48.21
by the G. of your father who will 49.25
by G. Almighty who will bless you 49.25
servants of the G. of your father." 50.17
not, for am I in the place of G.? 50.19
but G. meant it for good, to bring 50.20
but G. will visit you, and bring you 50.24
"G. will visit you, and you shall 50.25
But the midwives feared G., and did not Ex 1.17
So G. dealt well with the midwives; 1.20
midwives feared G. he gave them 1.21
cry under bondage came up to G. 2.23
And G. heard their groaning, and 2.24
and G. remembered his covenant with 2.24
And G. saw the people of Israel, and 2.25
and G. knew their condition. 2.25
came to Horeb, the mountain of G. 3.01
G. called to him out of the bush, 3.04
"I am the G. of your father, the G. 3.06
the G. of Abraham, the G. of Isaac, 3.06
and the G. of Jacob." And Moses hid 3.06
for he was afraid to look at G. 3.06
But Moses said to G., "Who am I 3.11
you shall serve G. upon this 3.12
Then Moses said to G., "If I come 3.13
'The G. of your fathers has sent me 3.13
G. said to Moses, "I AM WHO I AM." 3.14
G. also said to Moses, "Say this to 3.15
the G. of your fathers, the G. of Abraham; 3.15
the G. of Isaac, and the G. of Jacob, has sent 3.15
the G. of your fathers, the G. of 3.16
the G. of Abraham, of Isaac, and of 3.16
the G. of the Hebrews, has met with 3.18
may sacrifice to the LORD our G.' 3.18
the G. of their fathers, the G. of 4.05
the G. of Abraham, the G. of Isaac, 4.05
and the G. of Jacob, has appeared to 4.05
Then G. said, "Put your hand back 4.07
G. said, "or heed the first sign, 4.08
you, and you shall be to him as G. 4.16
his hand Moses took the rod of G. 4.20
the mountain of G. and kissed him. 4.27
the G. of Israel, 'Let my people go, 5.01
"The G. of the Hebrews has met with 5.03
and sacrifice to the LORD our G., 5.03
go and offer sacrifice to our G.' 5.08
And G. said to Moses, "I am the LORD. 6.02
as G. Almighty, but by my name the 6.03
my people, and I will be your G.; 6.07
know that I am the LORD your G., 6.07
"See, I make you as G. to Pharaoh; 7.01
the G. of the Hebrews, sent me to 7.16
is no one like the LORD our G. 8.10
Pharaoh, "This is the finger of G." 8.19
sacrifice to your G. within the 8.25
to the LORD our G. offerings abominable 8.26
to the LORD our G. as he will command 8.27
the LORD your G. in the wilderness; 8.28
the G. of the Hebrews, "Let my people 9.01
the G. of the Hebrews, "Let my people 9.13
you do not yet fear the LORD G." 9.30
the G. of the Hebrews, 'How long 10.03
they may serve the LORD their G.; 10.07
them, "Go, serve the LORD your G.; 10.08
sinned against the LORD your G., 10.16
the LORD your G. only to remove 10.17
may sacrifice to the LORD our G. 10.25
of them to serve the LORD our G., 10.26
G. did not lead them by way of the 13.17
for G. said, "Lest the people repent 13.17
But G. led the people round by the 13.18
Israel, saying, "G. will visit you; 13.19
Then the angel of G. who went before 14.19
this is my G., and I will praise 15.02
my father's G., and I will exhalt him. 15.02
to the voice of the LORD your G., 15.26
know that I am the LORD your G.'" 16.12

GOD (cont.)
hill with the rod of G. in my hand." Ex 17.09
of all that G. had done for Moses 18.01
"The G. of my father was my help, 18.04
was encamped at the mountain of G. 18.05
offering and sacrifices to G.; 18.12
Moses' father-in-law before G. 18.12
people come to me to inquire of G.; 18.15
the statutes of G. and his decisions." 18.16
you counsel, and G. be with you! 18.19
represent the people before G., 18.19
G., and bring their cases to G.; 18.19
such as fear G., men who are 18.21
and G. so commands you, then you 18.23
And Moses went up to G., and the LORD 19.03
people out of the camp to meet G.; 19.17
and G. answered him in thunder. 19.19
And G. spoke all these words, saying, 20.01
"I am the LORD your G., who brought 20.02
I the LORD your G. am a jealous G., 20.05
name of the LORD your G. in vain; 20.07
is a sabbath to the LORD your G.; 20.10
which the LORD your G. gives you. 20.12
but let not G. speak to us, lest we 20.19
for G. has come to prove you, and 20.20
to the thick cloud where G. was. 20.21
then his master shall bring him to G., 21.06
but G. let him fall into his hand, 21.13
of the house shall come near to G., 22.08
both parties shall come before G.; 22.09
he whom G. shall condemn shall pay 22.09
"Whoever sacrifices to any g., 22.20
"You shall not revile G., nor curse 22.28
males appear before the Lord G. 23.17
into the house of the LORD your G. 23.19
You shall serve the LORD your G., 23.25
and they saw the G. of Israel; 24.10
they beheld G., and ate and drank. 24.11
went up into the mountain of G. 24.13
of Israel, and will be their G. 29.45
know that I am the LORD their G., 29.46
among them; I am the LORD their G. 29.46
filled him with the Spirit of G., 31.03
written with the finger of G. 31.18
But Moses besought the LORD his G., 32.11
And the tables were the work of G., 32.16
the writing was the writing of G., 32.16
"Thus says the LORD G. of Israel, 32.27
a G. merciful and gracious, slow to 34.06
(for you shall worship no other g., 34.14
name is Jealous, is a jealous G.), 34.14
appear before the LORD G., the G. of Israel. 34.23
the LORD your G. three times in 34.24
to the house of the LORD your G. 34.26
he had been talking with G. 34.29
filled him with the Spirit of G., 35.31
with your G. be lacking from your Lev 2.13
the LORD his G. has commanded not 4.22
For I am the LORD your G.; 11.44
the land of Egypt, to be your G.; 11.45
of Israel, I am the LORD your G. 18.02
walk in them. I am the LORD your G. 18.04
the name of your G.: I am the LORD. 18.21
by them: I am the LORD your G." 18.30
for I the LORD your G. am holy. 19.02
my sabbaths: I am the LORD your G. 19.03
molten gods: I am the LORD your G. 19.04
sojourner: I am the LORD your G. 19.10
the name of your G.: I am the LORD. 19.12
shall fear your G.: I am the LORD. 19.14
for you: I am the LORD your G 19.25
by them: I am the LORD your G. 19.31
shall fear your G.: I am the LORD. 19.32
of Egypt: I am the LORD your G. 19.34
a just hin: I am the LORD your G., 19.36
for I am the LORD your G. 20.07
I am the LORD your G., who have 20.24
They shall be holy to their G., 21.06
not profane the name of their G.; 21.06
to the LORD, the bread of their G.; 21.06
for the priest is holy to his G. 21.07
for he offers the bread of your G.; 21.08
profane the sanctuary of his G.; 21.12
anointing oil of his G. is upon him: 21.12
to offer the bread of his G. 21.17
near to offer the bread of his G. 21.21
He may eat the bread of his G., 21.22
bread of your G. any such animals 22.25
Egypt to be your G.: I am the LORD." 22.33
brought the offering of your G.: 23.14
stranger: I am the LORD your G." 23.22
for you before the LORD your G. 23.28
before the LORD your G. seven days. 23.40
of Egypt: I am the LORD your G." 23.43
curses his G. shall bear his sin. 24.15
the native; for I am the LORD your God." 24.22
another, but you shall fear your G.; 25.17
for I am the LORD your G. 25.17
him or increase, but fear your G.; 25.36
I am the LORD your G., who brought 25.38
land of Canaan, and to be your G. 25.38
harshness, but shall fear your G. 25.43
of Egypt: I am the LORD your G. 25.55
to them; for I am the LORD your G. 26.01
among you, and will be your G., 26.12
I am the LORD your G.. who brought 26.13
for I am the LORD their G.; 26.44
I might be their G.: I am the LORD." 26.45
separation to G. is upon his head. Num 6.07
remembered before the LORD your G., 10.09
you for remembrance before your G.: 10.10
your G.: I am the LORD your G." 10.10
"Heal her, O G., I beseech thee." 12.13
commandments, and be holy to your G. 15.40
I am the LORD your G., who brought 15.41
to be your G.: I am the LORD your 15.41
be your G.: I am the LORD your G." 15.41
you that the G. of Israel has 16.09
"O G., the G. of the spirits of all flesh, 16.22
spoke against G. and against Moses, 21.05
And G. came to Balaam and said, "Who 22.09
And Balaam said to G., "Balah, the son 22.10
G. said to Balaam, "You shall not go 22.12
the command of the LORD my G., 22.18
And G. came to Balaam at night and 22.20
The word that G. puts in my mouth, 22.38
And G. met Balaam; and Balaam said 23.04
can I curse whom G. has not cursed? 23.08
G. is not man, that he should lie, or 23.19
The LORD their G. is with them, 23.21
G. brings them out of Egypt; 23.22
and Israel, 'What has G. wrought!' 23.23
it will please G. that you may 23.27
the Spirit of G. came upon him, 24.02
of him who hears the words of G., 24.04
G. brings him out of Egypt; he has 24.08
of him who hears the words of G., 24.16
who shall live when G. does this? 24.23
because he was jealous for his G., 25.13
the G. of the spirits of all flesh, 27.16
"The LORD our G. said to us in Deu 1.06
the LORD your G. has multiplied you, 1.10
the G. of your fathers, make you a 1.11
as the LORD our G. commanded us; 1.19
which the LORD our G. gives us. 1.20
the LORD your G. has set the land 1.21
the G. of your fathers, has told you 1.21
which the LORD our G. gives us.' 1.25
the command of the LORD your G.; 1.26
The LORD your G. who goes before 1.30
seen how the LORD your G. bore you, 1.31
did not believe the LORD your G., 1.32
as the LORD our G. commanded us.' 1.41
For the LORD your G. has blessed 2.07

GOD (cont.)

the LORD your G. has been with you; Deu 2.07
which the LORD our G. gives to us.' 2.29
the LORD your G. hardened his 2.30
And the LORD our G. gave him over 2.33
the LORD our G. gave all into our 2.36
wherever the LORD our G. forbade us. 2.37
So the LORD our G. gave into our 3.03
'The LORD your G. has given you 3.18
the LORD your G. gives them beyond 3.20
the LORD your G. has done to these 3.21
the LORD your G. who fights for 3.22
'O Lord G., thou hast only begun to 3.24
for what g. is there in heaven or 3.24
the G. of your fathers, gives you. 4.01
the LORD your G. which I command 4.02
the LORD your G. destroyed from 4.03
the LORD your G. are all alive 4.04
as the LORD my G. commanded me, 4.05
that has a g. so near to it as the 4.07
to it as the LORD our G. is to us, 4.07
before the LORD your G. at Horeb, 4.10
the LORD your G. has allotted to 4.19
the LORD your G. gives you for an 4.21
the covenant of the LORD your G., 4.23
the LORD your G. has forbidden you 4.23
For the LORD your G. is a devouring 4.24
is a devouring fire, a jealous G. 4.24
in the sight of the LORD your G., 4.25
you will seek the LORD your G., 4.29
the LORD your G. and obey his 4.30
for the LORD your G. is a merciful G.; 4.31
the day that G. created man upon 4.32
the voice of a g. speaking out of 4.33
Or has any g. ever attempted to go 4.34
the LORD your G. did for you in 4.34
you might know that the LORD is G.; 4.35
the LORD is G. in heaven above and 4.39
the LORD your G. gives you for 4.40
The LORD our G. made a covenant 5.02
" 'I am the LORD your G., who brought 5.06
I the LORD your G. am a jealous G., 5.09
name of the LORD your G. in vain: 5.11
as the LORD your G. commanded you. 5.12
is a sabbath to the LORD your G.; 5.14
the LORD your G. brought you out 5.15
the LORD your G. commanded you to 5.15
as the LORD your G. commanded you; 5.16
which the LORD your G. gives you. 5.16
the LORD our G. has shown us his 5.24
this day seen G. speak with man 5.24
voice of the LORD our G. any more, 5.25
of the living G. speaking out of 5.26
all that the LORD our G. will say; 5.27
the LORD our G. will speak to you; 5.27
the LORD your G. has commanded you; 5.32
the LORD your G. has commanded you, 5.33
the LORD your G. commanded me to 6.01
that you may fear the LORD your G., 6.02
the G. of your fathers, has promised 6.03
The LORD our G. is one LORD; 6.04
the LORD your G. with all your 6.05
the LORD your G. brings you into 6.10
You shall fear the LORD your G.; 6.13
for the LORD your G. is the midst 6.15
the midst of you is a jealous G.; 6.15
the anger of the LORD your G. be kindled 6.15
put the LORD your G. to the test, 6.16
commandments of the LORD your G., 6.17
the LORD our G. has commanded you?' 6.20
statutes, to fear the LORD our G., 6.24
commandment before the LORD our G., 6.25
"When the LORD your G. brings you 7.01
the LORD your G. gives them over 7.02
a people holy to the LORD your G.; 7.06
the LORD your G. has chosen you to 7.06
that the LORD your G. is G., 7.09
the faithful G. who keeps covenant 7.09
the LORD your G. will keep with you 7.12
the LORD your G. will give over to 7.16
the LORD your G. did to Pharaoh 7.18
the LORD your G. brought you out; 7.19
the LORD your G. do to all the 7.19
Moreover the LORD your G. will send 7.20
the LORD your G. is in the midst 7.21
of you, a great and terrible G. 7.21
The LORD your G. will clear away 7.22
But the LORD your G. will give them 7.23
an abomination to the LORD your G. 7.25
the LORD your G. has led you these 8.02
the LORD your G. disciplines you. 8.05
commandments of the LORD your G., 8.06
For the LORD your G. is bringing 8.07
the LORD your G. for the good land 8.10
lest you forget the LORD your G., 8.11
and you forget the LORD your G., 8.14
You shall remember the LORD your G., 8.18
the LORD your G. and go after 8.19
obey the voice of the LORD your G. 8.20
devouring fire is the LORD your G.; 9.03
the LORD your G. has thrust them 9.04
the LORD your G. is driving them 9.05
the LORD your G. is not giving you 9.06
the LORD your G. to wrath in the 9.07
written with the finger of G.; 9.10
sinned against the LORD your G.; 9.16
commandment of the LORD your G., 9.23
'O Lord G., destroy not thy people 9.26
as the LORD your G. said to him.) 10.09
the LORD your G. require of you, 10.12
you, but to fear the LORD your G., 10.12
the LORD your G. with all your heart 10.12
the LORD your G. belong heaven and 10.14
the LORD your G. is G. of gods and Lord of 10.17
the mighty, and the terrible G., 10.17
You shall fear the LORD your G.; 10.20
he is your G., who has done for you 10.21
the LORD your G. has made you as 10.22
therefore love the LORD your G., 11.01
the discipline of the LORD your G., 11.02
which the LORD your G. cares for; 11.12
the LORD your G. are always upon 11.12
this day, to love the LORD your G., 11.13
you to do, loving the LORD your G., 11.22
the LORD your G. will lay the fear 11.25
commandments of the LORD your G., 11.27
commandments of the LORD your G., 11.28
the LORD your G. brings you into 11.29
which the LORD your G. gives you; 11.31
the G. of your fathers, has given 12.01
not do so to the LORD your G. 12.04
the LORD your G. will choose out 12.05
shall eat before the LORD your G., 12.07
the LORD your G. has blessed you. 12.07
which the LORD your G. gives you. 12.09
the LORD your G. gives you to 12.10
which the LORD your G. will choose, 12.11
rejoice before the LORD your G., 12.12
the LORD your G. which he has 12.15
the LORD your G. in the place 12.18
which the LORD your G. will choose, 12.18
the LORD your G. in all that you 12.18
"When the LORD your G. enlarges 12.20
the LORD your G. will choose to 12.21
on the altar of the LORD your G.; 12.27
your G., but the flesh you may eat. 12.27
in the sight of the LORD your G. 12.28
"When the LORD your G. cuts off 12.29
not do so to the LORD your G.; 12.31
the LORD your G. is testing you, 13.03
the LORD your G. with all your 13.03
the LORD your G. and fear him, 13.04
rebellion against the LORD your G., 13.05
the LORD your G. commanded you to 13.05

GOD (cont.)

you away from the LORD your G., Deu 13.10
the LORD your G. gives you to 13.12
burnt offering to the LORD your G.; 13.16
obey the voice of the LORD your G., 13.18
in the sight of the LORD your G. 13.18
"You are the sons of the LORD your G.; 14.01
a people holy to the LORD your G., 14.02
a people holy to the LORD your G. 14.21
And before the LORD your G., in the 14.23
to fear the LORD your G. always. 14.23
when the LORD your G. blesses you, 14.24
which the LORD your G. chooses, 14.24
which the LORD your G. chooses, 14.25
the LORD your G. and rejoice, 14.26
the LORD your G. may bless you in 14.29
the LORD your G. gives you for an 15.04
obey the voice of the LORD your G., 15.05
For the LORD your G. will bless you, 15.06
which the LORD your G. gives you, 15.07
the LORD your G. will bless you in 15.10
the LORD your G. has blessed you, 15.14
and the LORD your G. redeemed you; 15.15
the LORD your G. will bless you in 15.18
consecrate to the LORD your G.; 15.19
the LORD your G. year by year at 15.20
sacrifice it to the LORD your G. 15.21
the passover to the LORD your G.; 16.01
the LORD your G. brought you out 16.01
sacrifice to the LORD your G., 16.02
which the LORD your G. gives you; 16.05
which the LORD your G. will choose, 16.06
which the LORD your G. will choose; 16.07
assembly to the LORD your G.; 16.08
the LORD your G. with the tribute 16.10
as the LORD your G. blesses you; 16.10
rejoice before the LORD your G., 16.11
which the LORD your G. will choose, 16.11
the LORD your G. at the place 16.15
the LORD your G. will bless you in 16.15
the LORD your G. at the place 16.16
the LORD your G. which he has 16.17
which the LORD your G. gives you, 16.18
which the LORD your G. gives you. 16.20
the LORD your G. which you shall 16.21
which the LORD your G. hates. 16.22
the LORD your G. an ox or a sheep 17.01
an abomination to the LORD your G. 17.01
which the LORD your G. gives you, 17.02
in the sight of the LORD your G., 17.02
the LORD your G. will choose, 17.08
there before the LORD your G., 17.12
which the LORD your G. gives you, 17.14
whom the LORD your G. will choose. 17.15
may learn to fear the LORD his G., 17.19
For the LORD your G. has chosen him 18.05
in the name of the LORD his G., 18.07
which the LORD your G. gives you, 18.09
the LORD your G. is driving them 18.12
blameless before the LORD your G. 18.13
the LORD your G. has not allowed 18.14
"The LORD your G. will raise up for 18.15
the LORD your G. at Horeb on the 18.16
again the voice of the LORD my G., 18.16
"When the LORD your G. cuts off the 19.01
land the LORD your G. gives you, 19.01
the LORD your G. gives you to 19.02
the LORD your G. gives you as a 19.03
the LORD your G. enlarges your 19.08
the LORD your G. and by walking 19.09
the LORD your G. gives you for an 19.10
the LORD your G. gives you to 19.14
for the LORD your G. is with you, 20.01
for the LORD your G. is he that 20.04
the LORD your G. gives it into 20.13
the LORD your G. has given you. 20.14
the LORD your G. gives you for an 20.16
as the LORD your G. has commanded; 20.17
so to sin against the LORD your G. 20.18
the LORD your G. gives you to 21.01
the LORD your G. has chosen them 21.05
the LORD your G. gives them into 21.10
for a hanged man is accursed by G.; 21.23
the LORD your G. gives you for an 21.23
an abomination to the LORD your G. 22.05
Nevertheless the LORD your G. would 23.05
the LORD your G. turned the curse 23.05
because the LORD your G. loved you. 23.05
Because the LORD your G. walks in 23.14
the LORD your G. in payment for 23.18
an abomination to the LORD your G. 23.18
the LORD your G. may bless you in 23.20
you make a vow to the LORD your G., 23.21
the LORD your G. will surely 23.21
the LORD your G. what you have 23.23
the LORD your G. gives you for an 24.04
the LORD your G. did to Miriam on 24.09
to you before the LORD your G. 24.13
the LORD your G. redeemed you from 24.18
the LORD your G. may bless you in 24.19
which the LORD your G. gives you. 25.15
an abomination to the LORD your G. 25.16
behind you; and he did not fear G. 25.18
the LORD your G. has given you 25.19
the LORD your G. gives you for an 25.19
the LORD your G. gives you for an 26.01
that the LORD your G. gives you, 26.02
which the LORD your G. will choose, 26.02
the LORD your G. that I have come 26.03
the altar of the LORD your G. 26.04
response before the LORD your G., 26.05
to the LORD the G. of your fathers, 26.07
it down before the LORD your G., 26.10
worship before the LORD your G.; 26.10
the LORD your G. has given to you 26.11
shall say before the LORD your G., 26.13
obeyed the voice of the LORD my G., 26.14
the LORD your G. commands you to 26.16
the LORD that he is your G., 26.17
a people holy to the LORD your G., 26.19
which the LORD your G. gives you, 27.02
which the LORD your G. gives you, 27.03
the G. of your fathers, has promised 27.03
build an altar to the LORD your G., 27.05
the LORD your G. of unhewn stones; 27.06
offerings on it to the LORD your G.; 27.06
rejoice before the LORD your G. 27.07
the people of the LORD your G. 27.09
obey the voice of the LORD your G., 27.10
obey the voice of the LORD your G., 28.01
the LORD your G. will set you high 28.01
obey the voice of the LORD your G. 28.02
which the LORD your G. gives you. 28.08
commandments of the LORD your G., 28.09
commandments of the LORD your G., 28.13
the LORD your G. or be careful to 28.15
obey the voice of the LORD your G., 28.45
the LORD your G. with joyfulness 28.47
the LORD your G. has given you. 28.52
the LORD your G. has given you, 28.53
and awful name, the LORD your G., 28.58
obey the voice of the LORD your G. 28.62
know that I am the LORD your G. 29.06
all of you before the LORD your G.; 29.10
sworn covenant of the LORD your G., 29.12
the LORD your G. makes with you 29.12
people, and that he may be your G., 29.13
us this day before the LORD our G. 29.15
the LORD our G. to go and serve 29.18
the G. of their fathers, which he 29.25
things belong to the LORD our G.; 29.29
the LORD your G. has driven you, 30.01
and return to the LORD your G., 30.02
then the LORD your G. will restore 30.03
the LORD your G. has scattered you. 30.03
the LORD your G. will gather you, 30.04

GOD (cont.)

and the LORD your G. will bring you Deu 30.05
And the LORD your G. will circumcise 30.06
the LORD your G. with all your 30.06
And the LORD your G. will put all 30.07
The LORD your G. will make you 30.09
obey the voice of the LORD your G., 30.10
the LORD your G. with all your 30.10
the LORD your G. which I command 30.16
day, by loving the LORD your G., 30.16
the LORD your G. will bless you in 30.16
loving the LORD your G., obeying 30.20
The LORD your G. himself will go 31.03
the LORD your G. who goes with you 31.06
the LORD your G. at the place 31.11
and learn to fear the LORD your G., 31.12
and learn to fear the LORD your G., 31.13
us because our G. is not among us?' 31.17
the covenant of the LORD your G., 31.26
Ascribe greatness to our G.! 32.03
A G. of faithfulness and without 32.04
to the number of the sons of G. 32.08
there was no foreign g. with him. 32.12
then he forsook G. who made him, 32.15
you forgot the G. who gave you 32.18
me to jealousy with what is no g.; 32.21
he, and there is no g. beside me; 32.39
the man of G. blessed the children 33.01
"There is none like G., O Jeshurun, 33.26
The eternal G. is your dwelling 33.27
the LORD your G. is with you wherever Jos 1.09
the LORD your G. gives you to possess." 1.11
'The LORD your G. is providing you 1.13
the LORD your G. is giving them; 1.15
may the LORD your G. be with you, 1.17
the LORD your G. is he who is 2.11
is he who is G. in heaven above 2.11
the LORD your G. being carried by 3.03
hear the words of the LORD your G." 3.09
that the living G. is among you, 3.10
the LORD your G. into the midst of 4.05
For the LORD your G. dried up the 4.23
the LORD your G. did to the Red 4.23
may fear the LORD your G. for ever." 4.24
O Lord G., why hast thou brought 7.07
G. of Israel, "There are devoted 7.13
glory to the LORD G. of Israel, 7.19
against the LORD G. of Israel, 7.20
the LORD your G. will give it into 8.07
to the LORD, the G. of Israel, 8.30
of the name of the LORD your G.; 9.09
them by the LORD, the G. of Israel. 9.18
the G. of Israel, and now we may not 9.19
of water for the house of my G." 9.23
the LORD your G. had commanded his 9.24
the LORD your G. has given them 10.19
as the LORD G. of Israel commanded. 10.40
the LORD G. of Israel fought for 10.42
to the LORD G. of Israel are their 13.14
the LORD G. of Israel is their 13.33
the man of G. in Kadeshbarnea 14.06
I wholly followed the LORD my G. 14.08
wholly followed the LORD my G.' 14.09
followed the LORD, the G. of Israel. 14.14
the G. of your fathers, has given 18.03
you here before the LORD our G. 18.06
the charge of the LORD your G. 22.03
the LORD your G. has given rest to 22.04
you, to love the LORD your G., 22.05
against the G. of Israel in turning 22.16
than the altar of the LORD our G. 22.19
"The Mighty One, G., the LORD! 22.22
do with the LORD, the G. of Israel? 22.24
of the LORD our G. that stands 22.29
Israel blessed G. and spoke no 22.33
between us that the LORD is G." 22.34
the LORD your G. has done to all 23.03
the LORD your G. who has fought 23.03
The LORD your G. will push them 23.05
as the LORD your G. promised you. 23.05
the LORD your G. as you have done 23.08
the LORD your G. who fights for 23.10
therefore, to love the LORD your G. 23.11
the LORD your G. will not continue 23.13
the LORD your G. has given you. 23.13
the LORD your G. promised concerning 23.14
the LORD your G. promised concerning 23.15
the LORD your G. has given you, 23.15
the covenant of the LORD your G., 23.16
presented themselves before G. 24.01
the G. of Israel, 'Your fathers 24.02
is the LORD our G. who brought us 24.17
serve the LORD, for he is our G." 24.18
for he is a holy G.; he is a jealous G.; 24.19
to the LORD, the G. of Israel." 24.23
"The LORD our G. we will serve, and 24.24
words in the book of the law of G.; 24.26
lest you deal falsely with your G." 24.27
so G. has requited me." And they Ju 1.07
the G. of their fathers, who had 2.12
LORD, forgetting the LORD their G., 3.07
"I have a message from G. for you." 3.20
the G. of Israel, command you, 'Go, 4.06
So on that day G. subdued Jabin the 4.23
to the LORD, the G. of Israel. 5.03
before the LORD, the G. of Israel. 5.05
the G. of Israel: I led you up from 6.08
to you, 'I am the LORD your G.; 6.10
And the angel of G. said to him, 6.20
and Gideon said, "Alas, O Lord G.! 6.22
the LORD your G. on the top of the 6.26
If he is a g., let him contend for 6.31
Then Gideon said to G., "If thou wilt 6.36
Then Gideon said to G., "Let not the 6.39
And G. did so that night; for it was 6.40
into his hand G. has given Midian 7.14
G. has given into your hands the 8.03
and made Baalberith their g. 8.33
did not remember the LORD their G., 8.34
of Shechem, that G. may listen to you. 9.07
And G. sent an evil spirit between 9.23
went into the house of their g., 9.27
Thus G. requited the crime of 9.56
and G. also made all the wickedness 9.57
forsaken our G. and have served 10.10
the G. of Israel, gave Sihon and all 11.21
the G. of Israel, dispossessed the 11.23
Chemosh your g. gives you to possess? 11.24
the LORD our G. has dispossessed 11.24
be a Nazirite to G. from birth; 13.05
"A man of G. came to me, and his 13.06
of the angel of G., very terrible; 13.06
a Nazirite to G. from birth to the 13.07
let the man of G. whom thou didst 13.08
And G. listened to the voice of 13.09
the angel of G. came again to the 13.09
surely die, for we have seen G." 13.22
And G. split open the hollow place 15.19
a Nazirite to G. from my mother's 16.17
great sacrifice to Dagon their g., 16.23
"Our g. has given Samson our enemy 16.23
saw him, they praised their g.; 16.24
"Our g. has given our enemy into 16.24
"O Lord G., remember me, I pray thee, 16.28
O G, that I may be avenged upon 16.28
"Inquire of G., we pray thee, that 18.05
yea, G. has given it into your hands, 18.10
as the house of G. was at Shiloh. 18.31
the assembly of the people of G., 20.02
up to Bethel, and inquired of G., 20.18
the covenant of G. was there in 20.27
sat there till evening before G., 21.02
the G. of Israel, why has this come 21.03
be my people, and your G. my G.; Ru 1.16

GOD (cont.)
the G. of Israel, under whose wings Ru 2.12
and the G. of Israel grant your 1Sa 1.17
besides thee; there is no rock like our G. 2.02
or the LORD is a G. of knowledge, 2.03
G. will mediate for him; but if a 2.25
And there came a man of G. to Eli, 2.27
Therefore the LORD the G. of Israel 2.30
the lamp of G. had not yet gone out, 3.03
the LORD, where the ark of G. was. 3.03
his sons were blaspheming G., and he did 3.13
May G. do so to you and more also, 3.17
with the ark of the covenant of G. 4.04
And the ark of G. was captured; 4.11
heart trembled for the ark of G. 4.13
and the ark of G. has been captured." 4.17
When he mentioned the ark of G., 4.18
that the ark of G. was captured, 4.19
the ark of G. had been captured 4.21
for the ark of G. has been captured." 4.22
Philistines captured the ark of G., 5.01
took the ark of G. and brought it 5.02
"The ark of the G. of Israel must 5.07
upon us and upon Dagon our g." 5.07
with the ark of the G. of Israel?" 5.08
the ark of the G. of Israel be 5.08
they brought the ark of the G. of 5.08
So they sent the ark of G. to Ekron. 5.10
when the ark of G. came to Ekron, 5.10
the ark of the G. of Israel to slay 5.10
away the ark of the G. of Israel, 5.11
The hand of G. was very heavy there; 5.11
away the ark of the G. of Israel, 6.03
and give glory to the G. of Israel; 6.05
before the LORD, this holy G.? 6.20
to cry to the LORD our G. for us, 7.08
there is a man of G. in this city, 9.06
present to bring to the man of G. 9.07
I will give it to the man of G., 9.08
when a man went to inquire of G., 9.09
the city where the man of G. was. 9.10
make known to you the word of G." 9.27
men going up to G. at Bethel will 10.03
finds to do, for G. is with you. 10.07
G. gave him another heart; and all 10.09
the spirit of G. came mightily 10.10
the G. of Israel, 'I brought up 10.18
you have this day rejected your G., 10.19
valor whose hearts G. had touched. 10.26
And the spirit of G. came mightily 11.06
But they forgot the LORD their G.; 12.09
the LORD your G. was your king. 12.12
you will follow the LORD your G., 12.14
your servants to the LORD your G., 12.19
commandment of the LORD your G., 13.13
Ahijah, "Bring hither the ark of G." 14.18
For the ark of G. went at that time 14.18
"Let us draw near hither to G." 14.36
And Saul inquired of G., "Shall I go 14.37
"O LORD G. of Israel, why hast thou 14.41
G. of Israel, give Urim; but if 14.41
"G. do so to me and more also; 14.44
he has wrought with G. this day." 14.45
to sacrifice to the LORD your G.; 15.15
to the LORD your G. in Gilgal." 15.21
I may worship the LORD your G." 15.30
spirit from G. is tormenting you. 16.15
evil spirit from G. is upon you, 16.16
evil spirit from G. was upon Saul, 16.23
defy the armies of the living G.?" 17.26
defied the armies of the living G." 17.36
the G. of the armies of Israel, whom 17.45
know that there is a G. in Israel, 17.46
spirit from G. rushed upon Saul, 18.10
the Spirit of G. came upon the 19.20
the Spirit of G. came upon him 19.23
the G. of Israel, be witness! 20.12
till I know what G. will do for me." 22.03
and have inquired of G. for him. 22.13
that I have inquired of G. for him? 22.15
"G. has given him into my hand; 23.07
the G. of Israel, thy servant has 23.10
O LORD, the G. of Israel, I beseech 23.11
but G. did not give him into his 23.14
and strengthen his hand in G. 23.16
G. do so to David and more also, if 25.22
in the care of the LORD your G.; 25.29
the G. of Israel, who sent you this 25.32
as the LORD the G. of Israel lives, 25.34
"G. has given your enemy into your 26.08
"I see a g. coming up out of the 28.13
and G. has turned away from me and 28.15
in my sight as an angel of G.; 29.09
strengthened himself in the LORD his G. 30.06
And he said, "Swear to me by G., 30.15
"As G. lives, if you had not spoken, 2Sa 2.27
G. do so to Abner, and more also, if 3.09
"G. do so to me and more also, if I 3.35
the G. of hosts, was with him. 5.10
bring up from there the ark of G., 6.02
the ark of G. upon a new cart, and 6.03
with the ark of G.; and Ahio went 6.04
to the ark of G. and took hold of 6.06
and G. smote him there because he 6.07
he died there beside the ark of G. 6.07
to him, because of the ark of G." 6.12
up the ark of G. from the house of 6.12
but the ark of G. dwells in a tent 7.02
O Lord G., and what is my house, 7.18
small thing in thy eyes, O Lord G.; 7.19
me future generations, O LORD G.! 7.19
knowest thy servant, O Lord G.! 7.20
Therefore thou art great, O LORD G.; 7.22
and there is no G. besides thee, 7.22
whom G. went to redeem to be his 7.23
O LORD, didst become their G. 7.24
O LORD G., confirm for ever the 7.25
LORD of hosts is G. over Israel, 7.26
the G. of Israel, hast made this 7.27
O Lord G., thou art G., and thy 7.28
O Lord G., hast spoken, and with thy 7.29
may show the kindness of G. to him? 9.03
and for the cities of our G.; 10.12
the G. of Israel, 'I anointed you 12.07
therefore besought G. for the child; 12.16
the king invoke the LORD your G., 14.11
a thing against the people of G.? 14.13
but G. will not take away the life 14.14
together from the heritage of G.' 14.16
the angel of G. to discern good 14.17
The LORD your G. be with you!" 14.17
of the angel of G. to know all 14.20
the ark of the covenant of G.; 15.24
and they set down the ark of G., 15.24
the ark of G. back into the city. 15.25
the ark of G. back to Jerusalem; 15.29
where G. was worshiped, behold, 15.32
if one consulted the oracle of G.; 16.23
said, "Blessed be the LORD your G., 18.28
G. do so to me, and more also, if you 19.13
the king is like the angel of G.; 19.27
And after that G. heeded supplications 21.14
my G., my rock, in whom I take 22.03
to my G. I called. From his temple 22.07
not wickedly departed from my G. 22.22
and my G. lightens my darkness. 22.29
and by my G. I can leap over a wall. 22.30
This G.—his way is perfect; the promise 22.31
"For who is G., but the LORD? And who 22.32
And who is a rock, except our G.? 22.32
This G. is my strong refuge, and has 22.33
be my rock, and exalted be my G., 22.47
the G. who gave me vengeance and 22.48

GOD (cont.)
the anointed of the G. of Jacob, 2Sa 23.01
The G. of Israel has spoken, the 23.03
over men ruling in the fear of G., 23.03
does not my house stand so with G.? 23.05
the LORD your G. add to the people 24.03
king, "The LORD your G. accept you." 24.23
to the LORD my G. which cost me 24.24
maidservant by the LORD your G., 1Ki 1.17
the G. of Israel, saying, 'Solomon 1.30
the G. of my lord the king, say so. 1.36
'Your G. make the name of Solomon 1.47
the G. of Israel, who has granted 1.48
the charge of the LORD your G., 2.03
"G. do so to me and more also if 2.23
ark of the LORD G. before David my 2.26
and G. said, "Ask what I shall give 3.05
O LORD my G., thou hast made thy 3.07
And G. said to him, "Because you 3.11
that the wisdom of G. was in him, 3.28
And G. gave Solomon wisdom and 4.29
of the LORD his G. because of the 5.03
But now the LORD my G. has given me 5.04
for the name of the LORD my G., 5.05
the G. of Israel, who with his hand 8.15
name of the LORD, the G. of Israel. 8.17
name of the LORD, the G. of Israel. 8.20
G. of Israel, there is no G. like thee, 8.23
G. of Israel, keep with thy servant 8.25
O G. of Israel, let thy word be 8.26
"But will G. indeed dwell on the 8.27
O LORD my G., hearkening to the cry 8.28
fathers out of Egypt, O Lord G." 8.53
The LORD our G. be with us, as he 8.57
to the LORD our G. day and night, 8.59
earth may know that the LORD is G.; 8.60
be wholly true to the LORD our G., 8.61
before the LORD our G., seven days. 8.65
the LORD their G. who brought their 9.09
Blessed be the LORD your G., who has 10.09
which G. had put into his mind. 10.24
not wholly true to the LORD his G., 11.04
the G. of Israel, who had appeared 11.09
G. also raised up as an adversary 11.23
the G. of Israel, 'Behold, I am about 11.31
Chemosh the g. of Moab, and Milcom 11.33
and Milcom the g. of the Ammonites, 11.33
But the word of G. came to Shemaiah 12.22
came to Shemaiah the man of G.: 12.22
a man of G. came out of Judah by 13.01
heard the saying of the man of G., 13.04
the man of G. had given by the 13.05
And the king said to the man of G., 13.06
now the favor of the LORD your G., 13.06
And the man of G. entreated the 13.06
And the king said to the man of G., 13.07
And the man of G. said to the king, 13.08
that the man of G. had done that 13.11
the man of G. who came from Judah 13.12
And he went after the man of G., 13.14
you the man of G. who came from 13.14
to the man of G. who came from 13.21
the LORD your G. commanded you, 13.21
it, he said, "It is the man of G., 13.26
of the man of G. and laid it upon 13.29
in which the man of G. is buried; 13.31
the G. of Israel: "Because I exalted 14.07
the G. of Israel, in the house of 14.13
not wholly true to the LORD his G., 15.03
the LORD his G. gave him a lamp in 15.04
provoked the LORD, the G. of Israel. 15.30
the LORD G. of Israel to anger 16.13
the G. of Israel, to anger by their 16.26
the G. of Israel, to anger than all 16.33
"As the LORD the G. of Israel lives, 17.01
said, "As the LORD your G. lives, 17.12
says the LORD the G. of Israel, 17.14
have you against me, O man of G.? 17.18
"O LORD my G., hast thou brought 17.20
"O LORD my G., let this child's soul 17.21
I know that you are a man of G., 17.24
As the LORD your G. lives, there is 18.10
If the LORD is G., follow him; 18.21
name of your g. and I will call on 18.24
and the G. who answers by fire, he is G." 18.24
and call on the name of your g., 18.25
saying, "Cry aloud, for he is a g.; 18.27
G. of Abraham, Isaac, and Israel, let 18.36
day that thou art G. in Israel, 18.36
art G., and that thou hast turned 18.37
"The LORD, he is G.; the LORD, he is G." 18.39
nights to Horeb the mount of G. 19.08
for the LORD, the G. of hosts; 19.10
for the LORD, the G. of hosts; 19.14
And a man of G. came near and said 20.28
"The LORD is a g. of the hills but 20.28
but he is not a g. of the valleys," 20.28
'You have cursed G. and the king.' 21.10
"Naboth cursed G. and the king." 21.13
the G. of Israel, to anger in every 22.53
the g. of Ekron, whether I shall 2Ki 1.02
there is no G. in Israel that you 1.03
of Baalzebub, the g. of Ekron?' 1.03
there is no G. in Israel that you 1.06
of Baalzebub, the g. of Ekron? 1.06
"O man of G., the king says, 'Come 1.09
of fifty, "If I am a man of G., 1.10
"O man of G., this is the king's 1.11
answered them, "If I am a man of G., 1.12
the fire of G. came down from 1.12
"O man of G., I pray you, let my 1.13
the g. of Ekron,—is it because 1.16
there is no G. in Israel to 1.16
is the LORD, the G. of Elijah?" 2.14
She came and told the man of G., 4.07
that this is a holy man of G., 4.09
she said, "No, my lord, O man of G.; 4.16
him on the bed of the man of G., 4.21
I may quickly go to the man of G., 4.22
to the man of G. at Mount Carmel. 4.25
when the man of G. saw her coming, 4.25
to the mountain to the man of G., 4.27
But the man of G. said, "Let her 4.27
"O man of G., there is death in the 4.40
the man of G. bread of the first 4.42
"Am I G., to kill and to make alive, 5.07
the man of G. heard that the king 5.08
on the name of the LORD his G., 5.11
to the word of the man of G.; 5.14
Then he returned to the man of G., 5.15
there is no G. in all the earth 5.15
sacrifice to any g. but the LORD. 5.17
servant of Elisha the man of G., 5.20
Then the man of G. said, "When did it 6.06
But the man of G. sent word to the 6.09
of which the man of G. told him. 6.10
of the man of G. rose early in the 6.15
"May G. do so to me, and more also, 6.31
king leaned said to the man of G., 7.02
as the man of G. had said when the 7.17
For when the man of G. had said to 7.18
captain had answered the man of G., 7.19
to the word of the man of G.; 8.02
the servant of the man of G., 8.04
"The man of G. has come here," 8.07
you and go to meet the man of G., 8.08
was ashamed. And the man of G. wept. 8.11
says the LORD the G. of Israel, 9.06
of the LORD the G. of Israel with 10.31
Then the man of G. was angry with 13.19
the G. of Israel, which he spoke by 14.25
in the eyes of the LORD his G., 16.02
sinned against the LORD their G., 17.07
the LORD their G. things that were 17.09

GOD (cont.)
not believe in the LORD their G. 2Ki 17.14
commandments of the LORD their G., 17.16
commandments of the LORD their G., 17.19
know the law of the g. of the land; 17.26
because they do not know the law of the g. 17.26
them the law of the g. of the land. 17.27
but you shall fear the LORD your G., 17.39
in the LORD the G. of Israel; so that 18.05
the LORD their G. but transgressed 18.12
to me, "We rely on the LORD our G.," 18.22
the LORD your G. heard all the 19.04
has sent to mock the living G., 19.04
which the LORD your G. has heard; 19.04
'Do not let your G. on whom you 19.10
"O LORD the G. of Israel, who art 19.15
thou art the G., thou alone, of all 19.15
he has sent to mock the living G. 19.16
O LORD our G., save us, I beseech 19.19
that thou, O LORD, art G. alone." 19.19
the G. of Israel: Your prayer to me 19.20
in the house of Nisroch his g., 19.37
the G. of David your father: I have 20.05
the G. of Israel, Behold. I am 21.12
the G. of his fathers, and did not 21.22
the G. of Israel: 'Tell the man who 22.15
the G. of Israel: Regarding the 22.18
which the man of G. proclaimed, 23.16
of the man of G. who came from 23.17
the passover to the LORD your G., 23.21
Jabez called on the G. of Israel, 1Ch 4.10
And G. granted what he asked. 4.10
for they cried to G. in the battle, 5.20
slain, because the war was of G. 5.22
against the G. of their fathers, 5.25
whom G. had destroyed before them. 5.25
So the G. of Israel stirred up the 5.26
the tabernacle of the house of G. 6.48
the servant of G. had commanded. 6.49
chief officer of the house of G.; 9.11
of the service of the house of G. 9.13
the treasures of the house of G. 9.26
lodged round about the house of G.; 9.27
and the LORD your G. said to you, 11.02
me before my G. that I should do 11.19
then may the G. of our fathers see 12.17
For your G. helps you." Then David 12.18
a great army, like an army of G. 12.22
it is the will of the LORD our G., 13.02
again the ark of our G. to us; 13.03
the ark of G. from Kiriathjearim. 13.05
bring up from there the ark of G., 13.06
the ark of G. upon a new cart, from 13.07
merry before G. with all their 13.08
the ark; and he died there before G. 13.10
And David was afraid of G. that day; 13.12
I bring the ark of G. home to me?" 13.12
And the ark of G. remained with the 13.14
And David inquired of G., "Shall I go 14.10
"G. has broken through my enemies 14.11
And when David again inquired of G., 14.14
G. said to him, "You shall not go up 14.14
for G. has gone out before you to 14.15
And David did as G. commanded him, 14.16
prepared a place for the ark of G., 15.01
Levites may carry the ark of G., 15.02
the G. of Israel, to the place that 15.12
the LORD our G. broke forth upon us, 15.13
ark of the LORD, the G. of Israel. 15.14
the ark of G. upon their shoulders 15.15
the trumpets before the ark of G. 15.24
And because G. helped the Levites 15.26
And they brought in the ark of G., 16.01
offerings and peace offerings before G. 16.01
praise the LORD, the G. of Israel. 16.04
the ark of the covenant of G. 16.06
He is the LORD our G.; his judgments 16.14
O G. of our salvation, and gather 16.35
the G. of Israel, from everlasting 16.36
in your heart, for G. is with you." 17.02
O LORD G., and what is my house, 17.16
a small thing in thy eyes, O G.; 17.17
me future generations, O LORD G.! 17.17
and there is no G. besides thee, 17.20
whom G. went to redeem to be his 17.21
and thou, O LORD, didst become their G. 17.22
of hosts, the G. of Israel, is Israel's G.,' 17.24
For thou, my G., hast revealed to 17.25
thou art G., and thou hast promised 17.26
and for the cities of our G.; 19.13
But G. was displeased with this 21.07
And David said to G., "I have sinned 21.08
And G. sent the angel to Jerusalem 21.15
And David said to G., "Was it not I 21.17
O LORD my G., be against me and 21.17
not go before it to inquire of G., 21.30
of the LORD G. and here the altar 22.01
for building the house of G. 22.02
for the LORD, the G. of Israel. 22.06
to the name of the LORD my G. 22.07
the house of the LORD your G., 22.11
keep the law of the LORD your G. 22.12
"Is not the LORD your G. with you? 22.18
and heart to seek the LORD your G. 22.19
build the sanctuary of the LORD G., 22.19
holy vessels of G. may be brought 22.19
the man of G. were named among the 23.14
the G. of Israel, has given peace to 23.25
for the service of the house of G.; 23.28
and officers of G. among both the 24.05
as the LORD G. of Israel had commanded 24.19
to the promise of G. to exalt him; 25.05
for G. had given Heman fourteen 25.05
for the service of the house of G. 25.06
the eighth; for G. blessed him. 26.05
of the house of G. and the treasuries 26.20
pertaining to G. and for the 26.32
and for the footstool of our G.; 28.02
But G. said to me, 'You may not 28.03
Yet the LORD G. of Israel chose me 28.04
LORD, and in the hearing of our G., 28.08
commandments of the LORD your G.; 28.08
know the G. of your father, and 28.09
the treasuries of the house of G., 28.12
the LORD G., even my G., is with you. 28.20
all the service of the house of G.; 28.21
whom alone G. has chosen, is young 29.01
not be for man but for the LORD G. 29.01
provided for the house of my G., 29.02
the house of my G. I give it to 29.03
I give it to the house of my G.: 29.03
of the house of G. five thousand 29.07
the G. of Israel our father, for 29.10
our G., and praise thy glorious 29.13
O LORD our G., all this abundance 29.16
I know, my G., that thou triest the 29.17
O LORD, the G. of Abraham, Isaac, and 29.18
assembly, "Bless the LORD your G." 29.20
the G. of their fathers, and bowed 29.20
the LORD his G. was with him and 2Ch 1.01
for the tent of meeting of G., 1.03
up the ark of G. from Kiriathjearim 1.04
In that night G. appeared to 1.07
And Solomon said to G., "Thou hast 1.08
O LORD G., let thy promise to David 1.09
G. answered Solomon, "Because this 1.11
of the LORD my G. and dedicate it 2.04
appointed feasts of the LORD our G., 2.04
for our G. is greater than all gods. 2.05
"Blessed be the LORD G. of Israel, 2.12
for building the house of G.: 3.03
King Solomon on the house of G.: 4.11
that were in the house of G.: 4.19
the treasures of the house of G. 5.01

GOD (cont.)

of the LORD filled the house of G. 2Ch 5.14
the G. of Israel, who with his hand 6.04
name of the LORD, the G. of Israel. 6.07
name of the LORD, the G. of Israel. 6.10
G. of Israel, there is no G. like thee, 6.14
G. of Israel, keep with thy servant 6.16
G. of Israel, let thy word be 6.17
"But will G. dwell indeed with man 6.18
O LORD my G., hearkening to the cry 6.19
Now, O my G., let thy eyes be open 6.40
O LORD G., and go to thy resting 6.41
O LORD G., be clothed with salvation, 6.41
O LORD G., do not turn away the 6.42
people dedicated the house of G. 7.05
the LORD the G. of their fathers 7.22
David the man of G. had commanded. 8.14
Blessed be the LORD your G., 9.08
as king for the LORD your G.! 9.08
Because your G. loved Israel and 9.08
which G. had put into his mind. 9.23
about by G. that the LORD might 10.15
came to Shemaiah the man of G.: 11.02
seek the LORD G. of Israel came 11.16
the LORD, the G. of their fathers. 11.16
that the LORD G. of Israel gave 13.05
But as for us, the LORD is our G., 13.10
keep the charge of the LORD our G., 13.11
Behold, G. is with us at our head, 13.12
the G. of your fathers; for you cannot 13.12
G. defeated Jeroboam and all Israel 13.15
and G. gave them into their hand. 13.16
the LORD, the G. of their fathers. 13.18
in the eyes of the LORD his G. 14.02
the G. of their fathers, and to keep 14.04
we have sought the LORD our G.; 14.07
And Asa cried to the LORD his G., 14.11
O LORD our G., for we rely on thee, 14.11
O LORD, thou art our G.; let not 14.11
The spirit of G. came upon Azariah 15.01
Israel was without the true G., 15.03
the G. of Israel, and sought him, he 15.04
for G. troubled them with every 15.06
that the LORD his G. was with him. 15.09
the G. of their fathers, with all 15.12
the G. of Israel, should be put to 15.13
the house of G. the votive gifts 15.18
did not rely on the LORD your G., 16.07
but sought the G. of his father and 17.04
for G. will give it into the hand 18.05
what my G. says, that I will speak." 18.13
helped him. G. drew them away from him, 18.31
and have set your heart to seek G." 19.03
to the LORD, the G. of their fathers. 19.04
of justice with the LORD our G., 19.07
G. of our fathers, art thou not 20.06
fathers, art thou not G. in heaven? 20.06
O our G., drive out the inhabitants 20.07
O our G., wilt thou not execute 20.12
the G. of Israel, with a very loud 20.19
Believe in the LORD your G., 20.20
And the fear of G. came on all the 20.29
for his G. gave him rest round 20.30
hearts upon the G. of their 20.33
the LORD, the G. of his fathers. 21.10
the G. of David your father, 'Because 21.12
was ordained by G. that the 22.07
six years, hid in the house of G., 22.12
with the king in the house of G. 23.03
which were in the house of G.; 23.09
house of your G. from year to year; 24.05
had broken into the house of G.; 24.07
the servant of G. laid upon Israel 24.09
the house of G. to its proper 24.13
and toward G. and his house. 24.16
the G. of their fathers, and served 24.18
Then the Spirit of G. took possession 24.20
"Thus says G., 'Why do you transgress 24.20
the G. of their fathers. Thus they 24.24
of the house of G. are written in 24.27
But a man of G. came to him and 25.07
G. will cast you down before the 25.08
for G. has power to help or to 25.08
And Amaziah said to the man of G., 25.09
The man of G. answered, "The LORD 25.09
"I know that G. has determined to 25.16
for it was of G., in order that 25.20
that were found in the house of G., 25.24
himself to seek G. in the days of 26.05
instructed him in the fear of G.; 26.05
the LORD, G. made him prosper. 26.05
G. helped him against the Philistines, 26.07
he was false to the LORD his G., 26.16
you no honor from the LORD G." 26.18
his ways before the LORD his G. 27.06
Therefore the LORD his G. gave him 28.05
the LORD, the G. of their fathers. 28.06
the G. of your fathers, was angry 28.09
your own against the LORD your G.? 28.10
of the house of G. and cut in 28.24
the vessels of the house of G., 28.24
the LORD, the G. of his fathers. 28.25
the G. of your fathers, and carry 29.05
in the sight of the LORD our G.; 29.06
the holy place to the G. of Israel. 29.07
the G. of Israel, that his fierce 29.10
because of what G. had done for 29.36
to the LORD the G. of Israel. 30.01
to the LORD the G. of Israel, 30.05
the G. of Abraham, Isaac, and Israel, 30.06
to the LORD G. of their fathers, so 30.07
ever, and serve the LORD your G., 30.08
the LORD your G. is gracious and 30.09
The hand of G. was also upon Judah 30.12
to the law of Moses the man of G.; 30.16
who sets his heart to seek G., 30.19
the LORD the G. of his fathers, even 30.19
to the LORD the G. of their 30.22
consecrated to the LORD their G., 31.06
chief officer of the house of G. 31.13
over the freewill offerings to G., 31.14
faithful before the LORD his G. 31.20
of the house of G. and in accordance 31.21
seeking his G., he did with all his 31.21
but with us is the LORD our G., 32.08
"The LORD our G. will deliver us 32.11
that your G. should be able to 32.14
for no g. of any nation or kingdom 32.15
less will your G. deliver you out 32.15
the Lord G. and against his 32.16
on the LORD the G. of Israel and 32.17
so the G. of Hezekiah will not 32.17
spoke of the G. of Jerusalem as 32.19
he came into the house of his g., 32.21
for G. had given him very great 32.29
G. left him to himself, in order to 32.31
had made he set in the house of G., 33.07
of which G. said to David and to 33.07
of the LORD his G. and humbled 33.12
before the G. of his fathers. 33.12
and G. received his entreaty and 33.13
Manasseh knew that the LORD was G. 33.13
to serve the LORD the G. of Israel. 33.16
but only to the LORD their G. 33.17
Manasseh, and his prayer to his G., 33.18
name of the LORD the G. of Israel, 33.18
and how G. received his entreaty, 33.19
to seek the G. of David his father; 34.03
the house of the LORD his G. 34.08
been brought in to the house of G., 34.09
the G. of Israel: 'Tell the man who 34.23
the G. of Israel: Regarding the 34.26
yourself before G. when you heard 34.27
according to the covenant of G., 34.32

GOD (cont.)
the G. of their fathers. 2Ch 34.32
in Israel serve the Lord their G. 34.33
the Lord the G. of their fathers. 34.33
the Lord your G. and his people 35.03
chief officers of the house of G., 35.08
and G. has commanded me to make 35.21
Cease opposing G., who is with 35.21
words of Neco from the mouth of G., 35.22
in the sight of the Lord his G. 36.05
in the sight of the Lord his G. 36.12
who had made him swear by G.; 36.13
to the Lord, the G. of Israel. 36.13
The Lord, the G. of their fathers, 36.15
kept mocking the messengers of G., 36.16
all the vessels of the house of G., 36.18
And they burned the house of G., 36.19
the G. of heaven, has given me all 36.23
may the Lord his G. be with him. 36.23
the G. of heaven, has given me all Ez 1.02
may his G. be with him, and let him 1.03
the house of the Lord, the G. of Israel— 1.03
he is the G. who is in Jerusalem; 1.03
the house of G. which is in 1.04
whose spirit G. had stirred to go 1.05
offerings for the house of G., 2.68
the altar of the G. of Israel, 3.02
in the law of Moses the man of G. 3.02
to the house of G. at Jerusalem, 3.08
of the workmen in the house of G., 3.09
to the Lord, the G. of Israel, 4.01
for we worship your G. as you do, 4.02
us in building a house to our G.; 4.03
the G. of Israel, as King Cyrus the 4.03
on the house of G. which is in 4.24
the name of the G. of Israel who 5.01
the house of G. which is in 5.02
the prophets of G., helping them. 5.02
eye of their G. was upon the 5.05
to the house of the great G. 5.08
servants of the G. of heaven and 5.11
had angered the G. of heaven, 5.12
this house of G. should be rebuilt. 5.13
silver vessels of the house of G., 5.14
the house of G. be rebuilt on its 5.15
of the house of G. which is in 5.16
of this house of G. in Jerusalem. 5.17
the house of G. at Jerusalem, 6.03
silver vessels of the house of G., 6.05
shall put them in the house of G." 6.05
the work on this house of G. alone; 6.07
this house of G. on its site. 6.07
the rebuilding of this house of G.; 6.08
offerings to the G. of heaven, 6.09
sacrifices to the G. of heaven, 6.10
May the G. who has caused his name 6.12
this house of G. which is in 6.12
command of the G. of Israel and by 6.14
of this house of G. with joy. 6.16
this house of G. one hundred bulls, 6.17
for the service of G. at Jerusalem, 6.18
worship the Lord, the G. of Israel. 6.21
in the work of the house of G., 6.22
the house of God, the G. of Israel. 6.22
the Lord the G. of Israel had 7.06
of the Lord his G. was upon him. 7.06
good hand of his G. was upon him. 7.09
of the law of the G. of heaven. 7.12
according to the law of your G., 7.14
freely offered to the G. of Israel, 7.15
house of their G. which is in 7.16
house of your G. which is in 7.17
according to the will of your G. 7.18
service of the house of your G., 7.19
deliver before the G. of Jerusalem. 7.19
required for the house of your G., 7.20
of the law of the G. of heaven, 7.21
Whatever is commanded by the G. of heaven, 7.23
for the house of the G. of heaven, 7.23
other servants of this house of G. 7.24
wisdom of your G. which is in your 7.25
such as know the laws of your G.; 7.25
the law of your G. and the law of 7.26
the G. of our fathers, who put such 7.27
hand of the Lord my G. was upon me, 7.28
ministers for the house of our G. 8.17
by the good hand of our G. upon us, 8.18
humble ourselves before our G., 8.21
"The hand of our G. is for good 8.22
and besought our G. for this, 8.23
house of our G. which the king and 8.25
to the Lord, the G. of your fathers. 8.28
Jerusalem, to the house of our G. 8.30
the hand of our G. was upon us, 8.31
day, within the house of our G., 8.33
offerings to the G. of Israel. 8.35
the people and the house of G. 8.36
at the words of the G. of Israel, 9.04
out my hands to the Lord my G., 9.05
saying: "O my G., I am ashamed and 9.06
my G., for our iniquities have 9.06
has been shown by the Lord our G., 9.08
that our G. may brighten our eyes 9.08
yet our G. has not forsaken us in 9.09
to set up the house of our G., 9.09
O our G., what shall we say after 9.10
our G., hast punished us less than 9.13
O Lord the G. of Israel, thou art 9.15
down before the house of G., 10.01
faith with our G. and have married 10.02
with our G. to put away all these 10.03
at the commandment of our G.; 10.03
from before the house of G., 10.06
open square before the house of G., 10.09
to the Lord the G. of your fathers, 10.11
wrath of our G. over this matter 10.14
praying before the G. of heaven. Neh 1.04
"O Lord G. of heaven, the great and 1.05
and terrible G. who keeps covenant 1.05
So I prayed to the G. of heaven. 2.04
the good hand of my G. was upon me. 2.08
no one what my G. had put into my 2.12
the hand of my G. which had been 2.18
"The G. of heaven will make us 2.20
Hear, O our G., for we are despised; 4.04
And we prayed to our G., and set a 4.09
to us and that G. had frustrated 4.15
to us there. Our G. will fight for us." 4.20
the fear of our G. to prevent the 5.09
"So may G. shake out every man from 5.13
do so, because of the fear of G. 5.15
O my G., all that I have done for 5.19
But now, O G., strengthen thou my 6.09
meet together in the house of G., 6.10
and saw that G. had not sent him, 6.12
O my G., according to these things 6.14
accomplished with the help of our G. 6.16
Then G. put it into my mind to 7.05
blessed the Lord, the great G.; 8.06
book, from the law of G., clearly; 8.08
day is holy to the Lord your G.; 8.09
in the courts of the house of G., 8.16
from the book of the law of G. 8.18
the Lord their G. for a fourth of 9.03
and worshiped the Lord their G. 9.03
a loud voice to the Lord their G. 9.04
the Lord your G. from everlasting 9.05
the G. who didst choose Abram and 9.07
But thou art a G. ready to forgive, 9.17
'This is your G. who brought you up 9.18
art a gracious and merciful G. 9.31
our G., the great and mighty and 9.32
great and mighty and terrible G., 9.32
of the lands to the law of G., 10.28

GOD (cont.)
given by Moses the servant of G., Neh 10.29
service of the house of our G.: 10.32
the work of the house of our G. 10.33
bring it into the house of our G., 10.34
upon the altar of the LORD our G., 10.34
also to bring to the house of our G., 10.36
minister in the house of our G., 10.36
chambers of the house of our G.; 10.37
the tithes to the house of our G., 10.38
not neglect the house of our G. 10.39
Ahitub, ruler of the house of G., 11.11
outside work of the house of G.; 11.16
over the work of the house of G. 11.22
commandment of David the man of G., 12.24
instruments of David the man of G.; 12.36
thanks stood in the house of G., 12.40
for G. had made them rejoice with 12.43
of their G. and the service of 12.45
of praise and thanksgiving to G. 12.46
ever enter the assembly of G.; 13.01
yet our G. turned the curse into a 13.02
chambers of the house of our G., 13.04
in the courts of the house of G. 13.07
the vessels of the house of G., 13.09
"Why is the house of G. forsaken?" 13.11
O my G., concerning this, and wipe 13.14
the house of my G. and for his 13.14
and did not our G. bring all this 13.18
O my G., and spare me according to 13.22
them take oath in the name of G., 13.25
him, and he was beloved by his G., 13.26
and G. make him king over all 13.26
against our G. by marrying foreign 13.27
O my G., because they have defiled 13.29
Remember me, O my G., for good. 13.31
and upright, one who feared G., Job 1.01
and cursed G. in their hearts." 1.05
the sons of G. came to present 1.06
who fears G. and turns away from 1.08
LORD, "Does Job fear G. for nought? 1.09
"The fire of G. fell from heaven 1.16
not sin or charge G. with wrong. 1.22
the sons of G. came to present 2.01
who fears G. and turns away from 2.03
your integrity. Curse G., and die." 2.09
we receive good at the hand of G., 2.10
May G. above not seek it, nor light 3.04
way is hid, whom G. has hedged in? 3.23
your fear of G. your confidence, 4.06
By the breath of G. they perish, 4.09
'Can mortal man be righteous before G.? 4.17
I would seek G., and to G. would I 5.08
and to G. would I commit my cause; 5.08
"Behold, happy is the man whom G. reproves; 5.17
the terrors of G. are arrayed 6.04
and that G. would grant my desire; 6.08
that it would please G. to crush me, 6.09
Does G. pervert justice? Or does the 8.03
If you will seek G. and make 8.05
are the paths of all who forget G.; 8.13
"Behold, G. will not reject a 8.20
how can a man be just before G.? 9.02
"G. will not turn back his anger; 9.13
I will say to G., Do not condemn me 10.02
But oh, that G. would speak, and open 11.05
Know then that G. exacts of you 11.06
you find out the deep things of G.? 11.07
who called upon G. and he answered 12.04
those who provoke G. are secure, 12.06
who bring their g. in their hand. 12.06
"With G. are wisdom and might; 12.13
I desire to argue my case with G. 13.03
Will you speak falsely for G., 13.07
will you plead the case for G.? 13.08
are doing away with the fear of G., 15.04
hindering meditation before G., 15.04
Have you listened in the council of G.? 15.08
consolations of G. too small for 15.11
that you turn your spirit against G., 15.13
Behold, G. puts no trust in his holy 15.15
stretched forth his hand against G., 15.25
Surely now G. has worn me out; 16.07
G. gives me up to the ungodly, and 16.11
my eye pours out tears to G., 16.20
maintain the right of a man with G., 16.21
the place of him who knows not G. 18.21
know then that G. has put me in the 19.06
for the hand of G. has touched me! 19.21
Why do you, like G., pursue me? 19.22
without my flesh I shall see G., 19.26
G. casts them out of his belly. 20.15
to the full G. will send his 20.23
the wicked man's portion from G., 20.29
the heritage decreed for him by G." 20.29
and no rod of G. is upon them. 21.09
They say to G., 'Depart from us! 21.14
That G. distributes pains in his 21.17
You say, 'G. stores up their iniquity 21.19
Will any teach G. knowledge, seeing 21.22
"Can a man be profitable to G.? 22.02
"Is not G. high in the heavens? 22.12
Therefore you say, 'What does G. know? 22.13
They said to G., 'Depart from us,' 22.17
"Agree with G., and be at peace; 22.21
and lift up your face to G. 22.26
For G. abases the proud, but he 22.29
G. has made my heart faint; 23.16
yet G. pays no attention to their 24.12
Yet G. prolongs the life of the 24.22
"Dominion and fear are with G.; 25.02
can man be righteous before G.? 25.04
Sheol is naked before G., and Abaddon 26.06
"As G. lives, who has taken away my 27.02
the spirit of G. is in my nostrils; 27.03
the godless when G. cuts him off, 27.08
when G. takes away his life? 27.08
Will G. hear his cry, when trouble 27.09
will he call upon G. at all times? 27.10
you concerning the hand of G.; 27.11
portion of a wicked man with G., 27.13
"G. understands the way to it, and 28.23
the days when G. watched over me; 29.02
friendship of G. was upon my tent; 29.04
Because G. has loosed my cord and 30.11
G. has cast me into the mire, and I 30.19
What would be my portion from G. above, 31.02
and let G. know my integrity!) 31.06
what then shall I do when G. rises up? 31.14
was in terror of calamity from G., 31.23
should have been false to G. above. 31.28
justified himself rather than G.; 32.02
G. may vanquish him, not man.' 32.13
The spirit of G. has made me, and 33.04
Behold, I am toward G. as you are; 33.06
answer you. G. is greater than man. 33.12
For G. speaks in one way, and in two, 33.14
Then man prays to G., and he accepts 33.26
"Behold, G. does all these things, 33.29
and G. has taken away my right; 34.05
that he should take delight in G.' 34.09
far be it from G. that he should 34.10
Of a truth, G. will not do wickedly, 34.12
man to go before G. in judgment. 34.23
"For has any one said to G., 34.31
multiplies his words against G." 34.37
say, 'It is my right before G.,' 35.02
'Where is G. my Maker, who gives 35.10
Surely G. does not hear an empty 35.13
"Behold, G. is mighty, and does not 36.05
Behold, G. is exalted in his power; 36.22
Behold, G. is great, and we know him 36.26
G. thunders wondrously with his 37.05
By the breath of G. ice is given, 37.10

GOD (cont.)

consider the wondrous works of G. Job 37.14
Do you know how G. lays his command 37.15
G. is clothed with terrible majesty. 37.22
all the sons of G. shouted for joy? 38.07
when its young ones cry to G., 38.41
because G. has made her forget 39.17
He who argues with G., let him 40.02
Have you an arm like G., and can you 40.09
"He is the first of the works of G.; 40.19
me, there is no help for him in G. Ps 3.02
Deliver me, O my G.! For thou dost 3.07
Answer me when I call, O G. of my right! 4.01
sound of my cry, my King and my G., 5.02
For thou art not a G. who delights 5.04
Make them bear their guilt, O G.; 5.10
O LORD my G., in thee do I take 7.01
O LORD my G., if I have done this, 7.03
awake, O my G.; thou hast 7.06
and hearts, thou righteous G. 7.09
My shield is with G., who saves 7.10
G. is a righteous judge, and a 7.11
and a G. who has indignation every 7.11
not repent, G. will whet his sword; 7.12
hast made him little less than G., 8.05
all the nations that forget G. 9.17
his thoughts are, "There is no G." 10.04
"G. has forgotten, he has hidden his 10.11
O G., lift up thy hand; forget not 10.12
Why does the wicked renounce G., 10.13
Consider and answer me, O LORD my G.; 13.03
says in his heart, "There is no G." 14.01
act wisely, that seek after G. 14.02
for G. is with the generation of 14.05
Preserve me, O G., for in thee I 16.01
choose another g. multiply their 16.04
for thou wilt answer me, O G.; 17.06
my G., my rock, in whom I take 18.02
to my G. I cried for help. 18.06
not wickedly departed from my G. 18.21
the LORD my G. lightens my darkness. 18.28
and by my G. I can leap over a wall. 18.29
This G.—his way is perfect; the promise 18.30
For who is G., but the LORD? And who 18.31
And who is a rock, except our G.? 18.31
the G. who girded me with strength, 18.32
exalted be the G. of my salvation, 18.46
the G. who gave me vengeance and 18.47
are telling the glory of G.; 19.01
The name of the G. of Jacob protect 20.01
the name of our G. set up our 20.05
of the name of the LORD our G. 20.07
My G., my G., why hast thou forsaken 22.01
O my G., I cry by day, but thou dost 22.02
bore me thou hast been my G. 22.10
from the G. of his salvation. 24.05
seek the face of the G. of Jacob. 24.06
O my G., in thee I trust, let me not 25.02
thou art the G. of my salvation; 25.05
O G., out of all his troubles. 25.22
me not, O G. of my salvation! 27.09
the G. of glory thunders, the LORD, 29.03
O LORD my G., I cried to thee for 30.02
O LORD my G., I will give thanks to 30.12
redeemed me, O LORD, faithful G. 31.05
O LORD, I say, "Thou art my G." 31.14
is the nation whose G. is the LORD, 33.12
for my cause, my G. and my Lord! 35.23
my G., according to thy righteousness; 35.24
is no fear of G. before his eyes. 36.01
is like the mountains of G., 36.06
is thy steadfast love, O G.! 36.07
The law of his G. is in his heart; 37.31
O LORD my G., who wilt answer. 38.15
O my G., be not far from me! 38.21
mouth, a song of praise to our G. 40.03
O LORD my G., thy wondrous deeds 40.05
I delight to do thy will, O my G.; 40.08
my deliverer, do not tarry, O my G.! 40.17
the G. of Israel, from everlasting 41.13
so longs my soul for thee, O G. 42.01
thirsts for G., for the living G. 42.02
I come and behold the face of G.? 42.02
me continually, "Where is your G.?" 42.03
in procession to the house of G., 42.04
Hope in G.; for I shall 42.05
praise him, my help and my G. 42.05
me, a prayer to the G. of my life. 42.08
I say to G., my rock; "Why hast 42.09
me continually, "Where is your G.?" 42.10
Hope in G.; for I shall 42.11
praise him, my help and my G. 42.11
O G., and defend my cause against 43.01
For thou art the G. in whom I take 43.02
Then I will go to the altar of G., 43.04
to G. my exceeding joy; 43.04
thee with the lyre, O G., my G. 43.04
within me? Hope in G.; 43.05
praise him, my help and my G. 43.05
O G., our fathers have told us, what 44.01
Thou art my King and my G., 44.04
In G. we have boasted continually, 44.08
had forgotten the name of our G., 44.20
forth our hands to a strange g., 44.20
would not G. discover this? 44.21
therefore G. has blessed you for 45.02
Therefore G., your G., has anointed 45.07
G. is our refuge and strength, a 46.01
streams make glad the city of G., 46.04
G. is in the midst of her, she shall 46.05
G. will help her right early. 46.05
the G. of Jacob is our refuge. 46.07
"Be still, and know that I am G. 46.10
the G. of Jacob is our refuge. 46.11
Shout to G. with loud songs of joy! 47.01
G. has gone up with a shout, the 47.05
Sing praises to G., sing praises! 47.06
For G. is the king of all the earth; 47.07
G. reigns over the nations; 47.08
G. sits on his holy throne. 47.08
as the people of the G. of Abraham. 47.09
shields of the earth belong to G.; 47.09
be praised in the city of our G.! 48.01
Within her citadels G. has shown 48.03
of hosts, in the city of our G., 48.08
which G. establishes for ever. 48.08
O G., in the midst of thy temple. 48.09
As thy name, O G., so thy praise 48.10
that this is G., our G. for ever 48.14
or give to G. the price of his life, 49.07
But G. will ransom my soul from the 49.15
G. the LORD, speaks and summons the 50.01
perfection of beauty, G. shines forth. 50.02
Our G. comes, he does not keep 50.03
for G. himself is judge! 50.06
testify against you. I am G., your G. 50.07
Offer to G. a sacrifice of thanksgiving, 50.14
But to the wicked G. says: 50.16
"Mark this, then, you who forget G., 50.22
I will show the salvation of G.!" 50.23
O G., according to thy steadfast 51.01
O G., and put a new and right 51.10
O G., thou G. of my salvation, and 51.14
acceptable to G. is a broken 51.17
O G., thou wilt not despise. 51.17
But G. will break you down for ever; 52.05
who would not make G. his refuge, 52.07
olive tree in the house of G. 52.08
steadfast love of G. for ever and 52.08
says in his heart, "There is no G." 53.01
G. looks down from heaven upon the 53.02
that are wise, that seek after G. 53.02
eat bread, and do not call upon G.? 53.04
For G. will scatter the bones of 53.05

GOD (cont.)
put to shame, for G. has rejected them. Ps 53.05
When G. restores the fortunes of 53.06
Save me, O G., by thy name, and 54.01
Hear my prayer, O G.; give ear to 54.02
they do not set G. before them. 54.03
Behold, G. is my helper; the Lord is 54.04
Give ear to my prayer, O G.; 55.01
But I call upon G.; and the LORD 55.16
G. will give ear, and humble them, he 55.19
keep no law, and do not fear G. 55.19
But thou, O G., wilt cast them down 55.23
O G., for men trample upon me; 56.01
In G., whose word I praise, in 56.04
in G. I trust without a fear. 56.04
wrath cast down the peoples, O G.! 56.07
This I know, that G. is for me. 56.09
In G., whose word I praise, in the 56.10
in G. I trust without a fear. 56.11
My vows to thee I must perform, O G.; 56.12
may walk before G. in the light of 56.13
O G., be merciful to me, for in thee 57.01
I cry to G. Most High, to G. who 57.02
to G. who fulfils his purpose for 57.02
G. will send forth his steadfast 57.03
Be exalted, O G., above the heavens! 57.05
O G., my heart is steadfast! 57.07
Be exalted, O G., above the heavens! 57.11
O G., break the teeth in their 58.06
there is a G. who judges on earth." 58.11
O my G., protect me from those who 59.01
LORD G. of hosts, art G. of Israel. 59.05
for thou, O G., art my fortress. 59.09
My G. in his steadfast love will 59.10
my G. will let me look in triumph 59.10
may know that G. rules over Jacob 59.13
for thou, O G., art my fortress, 59.17
the G. who shows me steadfast love. 59.17
O G., thou hast rejected us, broken 60.01
G. has spoken in his sanctuary: 60.06
Hast thou not rejected us, O G.? 60.10
go forth, O G., with our armies. 60.10
With G. we shall do valiantly; 60.12
Hear my cry, O G., listen to my 61.01
For thou, O G., hast heard my vows, 61.05
he be enthroned for ever before G.; 61.07
For G. alone my soul waits in 62.01
For G. alone my soul waits in 62.05
On G. rests my deliverance and my 62.07
my mighty rock, my refuge is G. 62.07
before him; G. is a refuge for us. 62.08
Once G. has spoken; twice have I 62.11
this: that power belongs to G.; 62.11
O G., thou art my G., I seek thee, 63.01
But the king shall rejoice in G.; 63.11
O G., in my complaint; 64.01
But G. will shoot his arrow at them; 64.07
they will tell what G. has wrought, 64.09
Praise is due to thee, O G., in Zion; 65.01
O G. of our salvation, who art the 65.05
the river of G. is full of water; 65.09
joyful noise to G., all the earth; 66.01
Say to G., "How terrible are thy 66.03
Come and see what G. has done: 66.05
Bless our G., O peoples, let the 66.08
For thou, O G., hast tested us; 66.10
Come and hear, all you who fear G., 66.16
But truly G. has listened; 66.19
Blessed be G., because he has not 66.20
May G. be gracious to us and bless 67.01
Let the peoples praise thee, O G.; 67.03
Let the peoples praise thee, O G.; 67.05
G., our G., has blessed us. 67.06
G. has blessed us; let all the 67.07
Let G. arise, let his enemies be 68.01
let the wicked perish before G.! 68.02
let them exult before G.; 68.03
Sing to G., sing praises to his 68.04
of widows is G. in his holy 68.05
G. gives the desolate a home to 68.06
O G., when thou didst go forth 68.07
down rain, at the presence of G.; 68.08
at the presence of G., the G. of Israel. 68.08
O G., thou didst shed abroad; 68.09
O G., thou didst provide for the 68.10
the mount which G. desired for his 68.16
that the LORD G. may dwell there. 68.18
G. is our salvation. 68.19
Our G. is a G. of salvation; 68.20
and to G., the Lord, belongs escape 68.20
But G. will shatter the heads of 68.21
O G., the processions of my G., my 68.24
"Bless G. in the great congregation, 68.26
Summon thy might, O G., show thy strength, 68.28
O G., thou who hast wrought for us. 68.28
to stretch out her hands to G. 68.31
Sing to G., O kingdoms of the earth; 68.32
Ascribe power to G., whose majesty 68.34
Terrible is G. in his sanctuary, the 68.35
the G. of Israel, he gives power and 68.35
Blessed be G.! 68.35
Save me, O G.! For the waters 69.01
grow dim with waiting for my G. 69.03
O G., thou knowest my folly; 69.05
through me, O Lord G. of hosts; 69.06
dishonor through me, O G. of Israel. 69.06
O G., in the abundance of thy 69.13
salvation, O G., set me on high! 69.29
praise the name of G. with a song; 69.30
you who seek G., let your hearts 69.32
For G. will save Zion and rebuild 69.35
Be pleased, O G., to deliver me! 70.01
salvation say evermore, "G. is great!" 70.04
hasten to me, O G.! Thou art my 70.05
O my G., from the hand of the 71.04
and say, "G. has forsaken him; 71.11
O G., be not far from me; 71.12
O my G., make haste to help me! 71.12
deeds of the Lord G. I will come, 71.16
O G., from my youth thou hast 71.17
O G., do not forsake me, till I 71.18
O G., reach the high heavens. 71.19
O G., who is like thee? 71.19
harp for thy faithfulness, O my G.; 71.22
O G., and thy righteousness to the 72.01
the G. of Israel, who alone does 72.18
Truly G. is good to the upright, to 73.01
And they say, "How can G. know? 73.11
until I went into the sanctuary of G.; 73.17
but G. is the strength of my heart 73.26
But for me it is good to be near G.; 73.28
I have made the Lord G. my refuge, 73.28
O G., why dost thou cast us off for 74.01
meeting places of G. in the land. 74.08
How long, O G., is the foe to scoff? 74.10
Yet G. my King is from of old, 74.12
Arise, O G., plead thy cause; 74.22
We give thanks to thee, O G.; 75.01
but it is G. who executes judgment, 75.07
sing praises to the G. of Jacob. 75.09
In Judah G. is known, his name is 76.01
O G. of Jacob, both rider and horse 76.06
when G. arose to establish judgment 76.09
Make your vows to the LORD your G., 76.11
I cry aloud to G., aloud to G., that 77.01
I think of G., and I moan; I meditate 77.03
Has G. forgotten to be gracious? 77.09
Thy way, O G., is holy. 77.13
What g. is great like our G.? 77.13
Thou art the G. who workest wonders, 77.14
O G., when the waters saw thee, they 77.16
they should set their hope in G., 78.07
and not forget the works of G., 78.07
spirit was not faithful to G. 78.08

GOD (cont.)

They tested G. in their heart by Ps 78.18
They spoke against G., saying, 78.19
"Can G. spread a table in the 78.19
because they had no faith in G., 78.22
the anger of G. rose against them 78.31
repented and sought G. earnestly. 78.34
They remembered that G. was their rock, 78.35
the Most High G. their redeemer. 78.35
rebelled against the Most High G., 78.56
When G. heard, he was full of wrath, 78.59
O G., the heathen have come into 79.01
Help us, O G. of our salvation, for 79.09
the nations say, "Where is their G.?" 79.10
Restore us, O G.; let thy face 80.03
O LORD G. of hosts, how long wilt 80.04
Restore us, O G. of hosts; 80.07
Turn again, O G. of hosts! 80.14
Restore us, O LORD G. of hosts! 80.19
Sing aloud to G. our strength; 81.01
shout for joy to the G. of Jacob! 81.01
an ordinance of the G. of Jacob. 81.04
There shall be no strange g. among you; 81.09
shall not bow down to a foreign g. 81.09
I am the LORD your G., who brought 81.10
G. has taken his place in the 82.01
Arise, O G., judge the earth; 82.08
O G., do not keep silence; 83.01
hold thy peace or be still, O G.! 83.01
ourselves of the pastures of G." 83.12
O my G., make them like whirling 83.13
sing for joy to the living G. 84.02
O LORD of hosts, my king and my G. 84.03
the G. of gods will be seen in Zion. 84.07
O LORD G. of hosts, hear my prayer; 84.08
give ear, O G. of Jacob! 84.08
Behold our shield, O G.; look upon 84.09
the house of my G. than dwell in 84.10
For the LORD G. is a sun and shield; 84.11
O G. of our salvation, and put away 85.04
Let me hear what G. the LORD will 85.08
Thou art my G.; be gracious to me, 86.03
wondrous things, thou alone art G. 86.10
O Lord my G., with my whole heart, 86.12
O G., insolent men have risen up 86.14
art a G. merciful and gracious, slow 86.15
are spoken of you, O city of G. 87.03
O LORD, my G., I call for help by 88.01
a G. feared in the council of the 89.07
O LORD G. of hosts, who is mighty as 89.08
my G., and the Rock of my salvation.' 89.26
everlasting to everlasting thou art G. 90.02
of the Lord our G. be upon us, 90.17
my fortress; my G., in whom I trust." 91.02
flourish in the courts of our G. 92.13
O LORD, thou G. of vengeance, thou 94.01
thou G. of vengeance, shine forth! 94.01
the G. of Jacob does not perceive." 94.07
and my G. the rock of my refuge. 94.22
the LORD our G. will wipe them out. 94.23
For the LORD is a great G., 95.03
For he is our G., and we are the 95.07
because of thy judgments, O G. 97.08
have seen the victory of our G. 98.03
Extol the LORD our G.; worship at 99.05
O LORD our G., thou didst answer 99.08
thou wast a forgiving G. to them, 99.08
Extol the LORD our G., and worship at 99.09
for the LORD our G. is holy! 99.09
Know that the LORD is G.! It is he 100.03
"O my G.," I say, "take me not hence 102.24
O LORD my G., thou art very great! 104.01
prey, seeking their food from G. 104.21
praise to my G. while I have being 104.33
He is the LORD our G., his judgments 105.07
and put G. to the test in the 106.14
the glory of G. for the image of 106.20
They forgot G., their Savior, who 106.21
O LORD our G., and gather us from 106.47
the G. of Israel, from everlasting 106.48
rebelled against the words of G., 107.11
O G., my heart is ready! I will sing 108.01
O G., above the heavens! Let thy glory 108.05
G. has promised in his sanctuary: 108.07
Hast thou not rejected us, O G.? 108.11
go forth, O G., with our armies. 108.11
With G. we shall do valiantly; 108.13
Be not silent, O G. of my praise! 109.01
But thou, O G. my Lord, deal on my 109.21
Help me, O LORD my G.! Save me 109.26
Who is like the LORD our G., 113.05
the presence of the G. of Jacob, 114.07
the nations say, "Where is their G.?" 115.02
Our G. is in the heavens; he does 115.03
and righteous; our G. is merciful. 116.05
The LORD is G., and he has given us 118.27
Thou art my G., and I will give 118.28
thou art my G., I will extol thee. 118.28
may keep the commandments of my G. 119.115
of the house of the LORD our G., 122.09
our eyes look to the LORD our G., 123.02
the courts of the house of our G.! 135.02
O give thanks to the G. of gods, 136.02
O give thanks to the G. of heaven, 136.26
to me are thy thoughts, O G.! 139.17
O G., and that men of blood would 139.19
Search me, O G., and know my heart! 139.23
I say to the LORD, Thou art my G.; 140.06
my eyes are toward thee, O LORD G.; 141.08
to do thy will, for thou art my G.! 143.10
will sing a new song to thee, O G.; 144.09
the people whose G. is the LORD! 144.15
my G. and King, and bless thy name 145.01
praises to my G. while I have 146.02
he whose help is the G. of Jacob, 146.05
whose hope is in the LORD his G., 146.05
thy G., O Zion, to all generations. 146.10
is good to sing praises to our G.; 147.01
melody to our G. upon the lyre! 147.07
O Jerusalem! Praise your G., O Zion! 147.12
high praises of G. be in their 149.06
Praise G. in his sanctuary; praise him 150.01
LORD and find the knowledge of G. Pro 2.05
and forgets the covenant of her G.; 2.17
repute in the sight of G. and man. 3.04
G. scorns the wicked, but the 14.09
It is the glory of G. to conceal 25.02
Every word of G. proves true; 30.05
and profane the name of my G. 30.09
business that G. has given to the Ecc 1.13
I saw, is from the hand of G.; 2.24
who pleases him G. gives wisdom 2.26
only to give to one who pleases G. 2.26
business that G. has given to the 3.10
find out what G. has done from the 3.11
that whatever G. does endures for 3.14
G. has made it so, in order that men 3.14
and G. seeks what has been driven 3.15
G. will judge the righteous and the 3.17
of men that G. is testing them to 3.18
when you go to the house of G.; 5.01
be hasty to utter a word before G., 5.02
for G. is in heaven, and you upon 5.02
When you vow a vow to G., do not 5.04
why should G. be angry at your 5.06
grow many: but do you fear G. 5.07
of his life which G. has given him, 5.18
also to whom G. has given wealth 5.19
in his toil—this is the gift of G. 5.19
life because G. keeps him occupied 5.20
a man to whom G. gives wealth, 6.02
yet G. does not give him power to 6.02
Consider the work of G.; who can 7.13
G. has made the one as well as the 7.14

GOD (cont.)
he who fears G. shall come forth Ecc 7.18
he who pleases G. escapes her, 7.26
that G. made man upright, but they 7.29
be well with those who fear G., 8.12
because he does not fear before G. 8.13
of life which G. gives him under 8.15
then I saw all the work of G., 8.17
their deeds are in the hand of G.; 9.01
for G. has already approved what 9.07
the work of G. who makes everything. 11.05
these things G. will bring you 11.09
spirit returns to G. who gave it. 12.07
Fear G., and keep his commandments; 12.13
For G. will bring every deed into 12.14
Give ear to the teaching of our G., Is 1.10
to the house of the G. of Jacob; 2.03
of the poor?" says the Lord G. of hosts. 3.15
and the Holy G. shows himself holy 5.16
thus says the Lord G.: It shall not 7.07
"Ask a sign of the LORD your G.; 7.11
men, that you weary my G. also? 7.13
will not stand, for G. is with us. 8.10
not a people consult their G.? 8.19
will curse their king and their G., 8.21
Mighty G., Everlasting Father, 9.06
remnant of Jacob, to the mighty G. 10.21
"Behold, G. is my salvation; 12.02
for the LORD G. is my strength and 12.02
Gomorrah when G. overthrew them. 13.19
the stars of G. I will set my 14.13
tree, says the LORD G. of Israel. 17.06
forgotten the G. of your salvation, 17.10
and set out slips of an alien g., 17.10
the G. of Israel, I announce to you. 21.10
the G. of Israel, has spoken." 21.17
For the Lord G. of hosts has a day 22.05
In that day the Lord G. of hosts, 22.12
die," says the Lord G. of hosts. 22.14
Thus says the Lord G. of hosts, 22.15
name of the LORD, the G. of Israel. 24.15
O LORD, thou art my G.; I will exalt 25.01
and the Lord G. will wipe away 25.08
on that day, "Lo, this is our G.; 25.09
for the LORD G. is an everlasting 26.04
O LORD our G., others lords besides 26.13
therefore thus says the Lord G., 28.16
from the Lord G. of hosts upon the 28.22
instructed aright; his G. teaches him. 28.26
stand in awe of the G. of Israel. 29.23
For thus said the Lord G., 30.15
For the LORD is a G. of justice; 30.18
The Egyptians are men, and not G.; 31.03
of the LORD, the majesty of our G. 35.02
Behold, your G. will come with 35.04
vengeance, with the recompense of G. 35.04
to me, "We rely on the LORD our G.," 36.07
the LORD your G. heard the words 37.04
has sent to mock the living G., 37.04
which the LORD your G. has heard; 37.04
'Do not let your G. on whom you 37.10
G. of Israel, who art enthroned 37.16
thou art the G., thou alone, of all 37.16
he has sent to mock the living G. 37.17
O LORD our G., save us from his 37.20
the G. of Israel: Because you have 37.21
in the house of Nisroch his g., 37.38
the G. of David your father: I have 38.05
Comfort, comfort my people, says your G. 40.01
in the desert a highway for our G. 40.03
the word of our G. will stand for 40.08
cities of Judah, "Behold your G.!" 40.09
the Lord G. comes with might, and 40.10
To whom then will you liken G., 40.18
my right is disregarded by my G."? 40.27
The LORD is the everlasting G., 40.28
be not dismayed, for I am your G.; 41.10
the LORD your G., hold your right 41.13
I the G. of Israel will not forsake 41.17
Thus says G., the LORD, who created 42.05
For I am the LORD your G., the Holy One 43.03
Before me no g. was formed, nor 43.10
there was no strange g. among you; 43.12
"I am G., and also henceforth I am 43.13
besides me there is no g. 44.06
Is there a G. besides me? 44.08
Who fashions a g. or casts an image, 44.10
also he makes a g. and worships it, 44.15
of it he makes into a g., his idol; 44.17
"Deliver me, for thou art my g.!" 44.17
the G. of Israel, who call you by 45.03
other, besides me there is no G.; 45.05
'G. is with you only, and there is 45.14
is no other, no g. besides him.'" 45.14
thou art a G. who hidest thyself, O 45.15
O G. of Israel, the Savior. 45.15
who created the heavens (he is G.!), 45.18
on praying to a g. that cannot 45.20
there is no other g. besides me, 45.21
me, a righteous G. and a Savior; 45.21
For I am G., and there is no other. 45.22
goldsmith, and he makes it into a g.; 46.06
for I am G., and there is no other; 46.09
I am G., and there is none like me, 46.09
LORD, and confess the G. of Israel, 48.01
themselves on the G. of Israel; 48.02
now the Lord G. has sent me and 48.16
of Israel: "I am the LORD your G., 48.17
LORD, and my recompense with my G." 49.04
and my G. has become my strength— 49.05
Thus says the Lord G.: "Behold, 49.22
The Lord G. has given me the tongue 50.04
The Lord G. has opened my ear, and I 50.05
For the Lord G. helps me; therefore 50.07
Behold, the Lord G. helps me; 50.09
of the LORD and relies upon his G.? 50.10
For I am the LORD your G., 51.15
of the LORD, the rebuke of your G. 51.20
your G. who pleads the cause of his 51.22
For thus says the Lord G.: 52.04
who says to Zion, "Your G. reigns." 52.07
shall see the salvation of our G. 52.10
and the G. of Israel will be your 52.12
smitten by G., and afflicted. 53.04
the G. of the whole earth he is 54.05
when she is cast off, says your G. 54.06
you, because of the LORD your G., 55.05
and to our G., for he will abundantly 55.07
Thus says the Lord G., who gathers the 56.08
no peace, says my G., for the wicked." 57.21
forsake the ordinance of their G.; 58.02
they delight to draw near to G. 58.02
separation between you and your G., 59.02
turning away from following our G., 59.13
for the name of the LORD your G., 60.09
and your G. will be your glory. 60.19
The Spirit of the Lord G. is upon me, 61.01
and the day of vengeance of our G., 61.02
of you as the ministers of our G.; 61.06
LORD, my soul shall exult in my G.; 61.10
so the Lord G. will cause righteousness 61.11
diadem in the hand of your G. 62.03
so shall your G. rejoice over you. 62.05
no eye has seen a G. besides thee, 64.04
Therefore thus says the Lord G.: 65.13
and the Lord G. will slay you; 65.15
bless himself by the G. of truth, 65.16
shall swear by the G. of truth; 65.16
shut the womb? says your G. 66.09
Then I said, "Ah, Lord G.! Jer 1.06
by forsaking the LORD your G., 2.17
you to forsake the LORD your G.; 2.19
in you, says the Lord G. of hosts. 2.19
the LORD your G. and scattered 3.13

GOD (cont.)
have forgotten the LORD their G. Jer 3.21
for thou art the LORD our G. 3.22
in the LORD our G. is the salvation 3.23
sinned against the LORD our G., 3.25
the voice of the LORD our G." 3.25
Lord G., surely thou hast utterly 4.10
of the LORD, the law of their G. 5.04
of the LORD, the law of their G." 5.05
the G. of hosts: "Because they have 5.14
the LORD our G. done all these 5.19
'Let us fear the LORD our G., 5.24
the G. of Israel, Amend your ways 7.03
Therefore thus says the Lord G.: 7.20
the G. of Israel: "Add your burnt 7.21
my voice, and I will be your G., 7.23
the voice of the LORD their G., 7.28
the LORD our G. has doomed us to 8.14
the G. of Israel: Behold, I will feed 9.15
But the LORD is the true G.; 10.10
is the living G. and the everlasting 10.10
the G. of Israel: Cursed be the man 11.03
my people, and I will be your G., 11.04
the G. of Israel, "Every jar shall 13.12
the LORD your G. before he brings 13.16
Lord G., behold, the prophets say to 14.13
Art thou not he, O LORD our G.? 14.22
by thy name, O LORD, G. of hosts. 15.16
the G. of Israel: Behold, I will make 16.09
committed against the LORD our G.?' 16.10
the G. of Israel, Behold, I am 19.03
the G. of Israel, Behold, I am 19.15
the G. of Israel: Behold, I will turn 21.04
the covenant of the LORD their G., 22.09
the G. of Israel, concerning the 23.02
"Am I a G. at hand, says the LORD, 23.23
the LORD, and not a G. afar off? 23.23
pervert the words of the living G., 23.36
the LORD of hosts, our G. 23.36
the G. of Israel: Like these good 24.05
my people and I will be their G., 24.07
the G. of Israel, said to me: "Take 25.15
the G. of Israel: Drink, be drunk and 25.27
obey the voice of the LORD your G., 26.13
us in the name of the LORD our G." 26.16
the G. of Israel: This is what you 27.04
the G. of Israel, concerning the 27.21
the G. of Israel: I have broken the 28.02
the G. of Israel: I have put upon 28.14
the G. of Israel, to all the exiles 29.04
the G. of Israel: Do not let your 29.08
the G. of Israel, concerning Ahab 29.21
the G. of Israel: You have sent 29.25
the G. of Israel: Write in a book 30.02
the LORD their G. and David their 30.09
my people, and I will be your G." 30.22
I will be the G. of all the families 31.01
go up to Zion, to the LORD our G." 31.06
for thou art the LORD my G. 31.18
the G. of Israel: "Once more they 31.23
and I will be their G., and they shall be 31.33
the G. of Israel: Take these deeds, 32.14
the G. of Israel: Houses and fields 32.15
'Ah Lord G.! It is thou who 32.17
and mighty G. whose name is the 32.18
O Lord G., hast said to me, "Buy the 32.25
I am the LORD, the G. of all flesh; 32.27
the G. of Israel, concerning this 32.36
my people, and I will be their G. 32.38
the G. of Israel, concerning the 33.04
the G. of Israel: Go and speak to 34.02
the G. of Israel: I made a covenant 34.13
the man of G., which was near the 35.04
the G. of Israel: Go and say to the 35.13
the G. of hosts, the G. of Israel: 35.17
the G. of Israel: Because you have 35.18
the G. of Israel: Jonadab the son of 35.19
"Pray for us to the LORD our G." 37.03
G. of Israel: Thus shall you say to 37.07
the G. of hosts, the G. of Israel, 38.17
the G. of Israel: Behold I will 39.16
"The LORD your G. pronounced this 40.02
pray to the LORD your G. for us, 42.02
that the LORD your G. may show us 42.03
the LORD your G. according to your 42.04
the LORD your G. sends you to us. 42.05
of the LORD our G. to whom we are 42.06
obey the voice of the LORD our G." 42.06
the G. of Israel, to whom you sent 42.09
the voice of the LORD your G. 42.13
the G. of Israel: If you set your 42.15
the G. of Israel: As my anger and my 42.18
you sent me to the LORD your G., 42.20
'Pray for us to the LORD our G., 42.20
the LORD our G. says declare to us 42.20
the LORD your G. in anything that 42.21
these words of the LORD their G., 43.01
the LORD their G. had sent him to 43.01
The LORD our G. did not send you to 43.02
the G. of Israel: Behold, I will send 43.10
the G. of Israel: You have seen all 44.02
now thus says the LORD G. of hosts, 44.07
the G. of Israel: Why do you commit 44.07
the G. of Israel: Behold, I will set 44.11
the G. of Israel: You and your wives 44.25
saying, 'As the Lord G. lives.' 44.26
the G. of Israel, to you, O Baruch: 45.02
is the day of the Lord G. of hosts, 46.10
For the Lord G. of hosts holds a 46.10
the G. of Israel, said: "Behold, I am 46.25
the G. of Israel: "Woe to Nebo, for 48.01
place and burns incense to his g. 48.35
says the Lord G. of hosts, from all 49.05
they shall seek the LORD their G. 50.04
the G. of Israel: Behold, I am 50.18
for the Lord G. of hosts has a work 50.25
the vengeance of the LORD our G., 50.28
one, says the Lord G. of hosts; 50.31
As when G. overthrew Sodom and 50.40
have not been forsaken by their G., 51.05
Zion the work of the LORD our G. 51.10
the G. of Israel: The daughter of 51.33
for the LORD is a G. of recompense, 51.56
hearts and hands to G. in heaven: Lam 3.41
opened, and I saw visions of G. Eze 1.01
to them, 'Thus says the Lord G.' 2.04
to them, 'Thus says the Lord G.'; 3.11
to them, 'Thus says the Lord G.'; 3.27
Then I said, "Ah Lord G.! behold, I have 4.14
Thus says the Lord G.: This is Jerusalem; 5.05
Therefore thus says the Lord G.: 5.07
therefore thus says the Lord G.: 5.08
says the Lord G., surely, because 5.11
hear the word of the Lord G.! 6.03
says the Lord G. to the mountains 6.03
Thus says the Lord G.: "Clap your 6.11
says the Lord G. to the land of 7.02
"Thus says the LORD G.: Disaster after 7.05
of the Lord G. fell there upon me. 8.01
me in visions of G. to Jerusalem, 8.03
glory of the G. of Israel was 8.04
glory of the G. of Israel had gone 9.03
my face, and cried, "Ah Lord G.! 9.08
the voice of G. Almighty when he 10.05
glory of the G. of Israel was over 10.19
underneath the G. of Israel by the 10.20
Therefore thus says the Lord G.: 11.07
sword upon you, says the Lord G. 11.08
a loud voice, and said, "Ah Lord G.! 11.13
Therefore say, 'Thus says the Lord G.: 11.16
my people, and I will be their G. 11.20
their own heads, says the Lord G." 11.21
glory of the G. of Israel was over 11.22
by the Spirit of G. into Chaldea, 11.24

GOD (cont.)
Say to them, 'Thus says the Lord G.: Eze 12.10
says the Lord G. concerning the 12.19
therefore, 'Thus says the Lord G.: 12.23
and perform it, says the Lord G." 12.25
say to them, Thus says the Lord G.: 12.28
be performed, says the Lord G." 12.28
Thus says the Lord G., Woe to the 13.03
Therefore thus says the Lord G.: 13.08
I am against you, says the Lord G. 13.08
shall know that I am the Lord G. 13.09
Therefore thus says the Lord G.: 13.13
was no peace, says the Lord G. 13.16
and say, Thus says the Lord G.: 13.18
"Wherefore thus says the Lord G.: 13.20
say to them, Thus says the Lord G.: 14.04
of Israel, Thus says the Lord G.: 14.06
I may be their G., says the Lord G." 14.11
righteousness, says the Lord G. 14.14
says the Lord G., they would deliver 14.16
says the Lord G., they would deliver 14.18
says the Lord G., they would deliver 14.20
"For thus says the Lord G.: How much 14.21
have done in it, says the Lord G." 14.23
Therefore thus says the Lord G.: 15.06
acted faithlessly, says the Lord G." 15.08
Thus says the Lord G. to Jerusalem: 16.03
says the Lord G., and you became 16.08
bestowed upon you, says the Lord G. 16.14
a pleasing odor, says the Lord G. 16.19
(woe, woe to you! says the Lord G.), 16.23
says the Lord G., seeing you did 16.30
Thus says the Lord G., Because 16.36
upon your head, says the Lord G. 16.43
says the Lord G., your sister Sodom 16.48
"Yea, thus says the Lord G.: 16.59
you have done, says the Lord G." 16.63
say, Thus says the Lord G.: 17.03
Say, Thus says the Lord G.: 17.09
says the Lord G., surely in the 17.16
Therefore thus says the Lord G.: 17.19
Thus says the Lord G.: "I myself will 17.22
says the Lord G., this proverb 18.03
surely live, says the Lord G. 18.09
says the Lord G., and not rather 18.23
to his ways, says the Lord G. 18.30
death of any one, says the Lord G.; 18.32
say to them, Thus says the Lord G., 20.03
says the Lord G., I will not be 20.03
say to them, Thus says the Lord G.: 20.05
saying, I am the LORD your G. 20.05
idols of Egypt; I am the LORD your G. 20.07
I the LORD am your G.; I walk in my 20.19
know that I the LORD am your G. 20.20
say to them, Thus says the Lord G.: 20.27
of Israel, Thus says the Lord G.: 20.30
says the Lord G., I will not be 20.31
says the Lord G., surely with a 20.33
judgment with you, says the Lord G. 20.36
of Israel, thus says the Lord G.: 20.39
says the Lord G., there all the 20.40
house of Israel, says the Lord G." 20.44
of the LORD: Thus says the Lord G., 20.47
Then I said, "Ah Lord G.! 20.49
be fulfilled,' " says the Lord G. 21.07
despise the rod?" says the Lord G." 21.13
"Therefore thus says the Lord G.: 21.24
thus says the Lord G.: 21.26
says the Lord G. concerning the 21.28
You shall say, Thus says the Lord G. : 22.03
forgotten me, says the Lord G. 22.12
Therefore thus says the Lord G: 22.19
saying, 'Thus says the Lord G.,' 22.28
upon their heads, says the Lord G." 22.31
Therefore, O Oholibah, thus says the Lord G.: 23.22
For thus says the Lord G.: 23.28
Thus says the Lord G.: "You shall drink 23.32
I have spoken, says the Lord G. 23.34
Therefore thus says the Lord G.: 23.35
For thus says the Lord G.: 23.46
shall know that I am the Lord G." 23.49
say to them, Thus says the Lord G.: 24.03
"Therefore thus says the Lord G.: 24.06
Therefore thus says the Lord G.: 24.09
I will judge you, says the Lord G." 24.14
of Israel, Thus says the Lord G.: 24.21
will know that I am the Lord G." 24.24
Thus says the Lord G., Because you 25.03
For thus says the Lord G.: 25.06
"Thus says the Lord G.: 25.08
"Thus says the Lord G.: 25.12
therefore thus says the Lord G., 25.13
my vengeance, says the Lord G. 25.14
"Thus says the Lord G.: 25.15
therefore thus says the Lord G., 25.16
therefore thus says the Lord G.: 26.03
I have spoken, says the Lord G.; 26.05
"For thus says the Lord G.: 26.07
LORD have spoken, says the Lord G. 26.14
"Thus says the Lord G. to Tyre: 26.15
"For thus says the Lord G.: 26.19
be found again, says the Lord G." 26.21
coastlands, thus says the Lord G.: 27.03
of Tyre, Thus says the Lord G.: 28.02
'I am a g., I sit in the seat of 28.02
and no g., though you consider 28.02
consider yourself as wise as a g.— 28.02
therefore thus says the Lord G.: 28.06
consider yourself as wise as a g., 28.06
'I am a g.,' in the presence of 28.09
and no g., in the hands of those 28.09
I have spoken, says the Lord G." 28.10
say to him, Thus says the Lord G.: 28.12
You were in Eden, the garden of G.; 28.13
were on the holy mountain of G.; 28.14
thing from the mountain of G., 28.16
and say, Thus says the Lord G.: 28.22
will know that I am the Lord G. 28.24
"Thus says the Lord G.: When I gather 28.25
know that I am the LORD their G. 28.26
speak, and say, Thus says the Lord G.: 29.03
therefore thus says the Lord G.: 29.08
"For thus says the Lord G.: 29.13
will know that I am the Lord G." 29.16
Therefore thus says the Lord G.: 29.19
worked for me, says the Lord G. 29.20
and say, Thus says the Lord G.: 30.02
her by the sword, says the Lord G. 30.06
"Thus says the Lord G.: I will put an 30.10
"Thus says the Lord G.: I will destroy 30.13
Therefore thus says the Lord G.: 30.22
the garden of G. could not rival 31.08
the garden of G. was like it in 31.08
it, that were in the garden of G. 31.09
"Therefore thus says the Lord G.: 31.10
"Thus says the Lord G.: When it goes 31.15
his multitude, says the Lord G." 31.18
Thus says the Lord G.: I will throw 32.03
upon your land, says the Lord G. 32.08
For thus says the Lord G: The sword 32.11
to run like oil, says the Lord G. 32.14
they chant it, says the Lord G." 32.16
by the sword, says the Lord G. 32.31
his multitude, says the Lord G.", 32.32
says the Lord G., I have no pleasure 33.11
say to them, Thus says the Lord G.: 33.25
to them, Thus says the Lord G.: 33.27
shepherds, Thus says the Lord G.: 34.02
says the Lord G., because my sheep 34.08
Thus says the Lord G., Behold, I am 34.10
"For thus says the Lord G.: 34.11
them lie down, says the Lord G. 34.15
my flock, thus says the Lord G.: 34.17
"Therefore, thus says the Lord G. to them: 34.20

GOD (cont.)

will be their G., and my servant Eze 34.24
know that I, the LORD their G., 34.30
are my people, says the Lord G. 34.30
and I am your G., says the Lord G." 34.31
and say to it, Thus says the Lord G.: 35.03
says the Lord G., I will prepare 35.06
says the Lord G., I will deal with 35.11
Thus says the Lord G.: For the 35.14
Thus says the Lord G.: Because the 36.02
and say, Thus says the Lord G.: 36.03
hear the word of the Lord G.: 36.04
says the Lord G. to the mountains 36.04
therefore thus says the Lord G.: 36.05
and valleys, Thus says the Lord G.: 36.06
therefore thus says the Lord G.: 36.07
Thus says the Lord G.: Because men 36.13
of children, says the Lord G.; 36.14
to stumble, says the Lord G." 36.15
of Israel, Thus says the Lord G.: 36.22
says the Lord G., when through you 36.23
my people, and I will be your G. 36.28
that I will act, says the Lord G.; 36.32
"Thus says the Lord G.: On the day 36.33
"Thus says the Lord G.: This also 36.37
answered, "O Lord G., thou knowest." 37.03
Thus says the Lord G. to these bones: 37.05
the breath, Thus says the Lord G.: 37.09
say to them, Thus says the Lord G.: 37.12
say to them, Thus says the Lord G.: 37.19
say to them, Thus says the Lord G.: 37.21
my people, and I will be their G. 37.23
and I will be their G., and they shall 37.27
and say, Thus says the Lord G.: 38.03
"Thus says the Lord G.: On that day 38.10
say to Gog, Thus says the Lord G.: 38.14
"Thus says the Lord G.: Are you he 38.17
says the Lord G., my wrath will be 38.18
against Gog, says the Lord G.; 38.21
and say, Thus says the Lord G.: 39.01
I have spoken, says the Lord G. 39.05
be brought about, says the Lord G. 39.08
plundered them, says the Lord G. 39.10
I show my glory, says the Lord G. 39.13
son of man, thus says the Lord G.: 39.17
of warriors,' says the Lord G. 39.20
know that I am the LORD their G., 39.22
"Therefore thus says the Lord G.: 39.25
the LORD their G. because I sent 39.28
house of Israel, says the Lord G." 39.29
the visions of G. into the land of 40.02
glory of the G. of Israel came 43.02
"Son of man, thus says the Lord G.: 43.18
says the Lord G., a bull for a sin 43.19
will accept you, says the Lord G." 43.27
the G. of Israel, has entered by it; 44.02
of Israel, Thus says the Lord G.: 44.06
"Therefore thus says the Lord G.: 44.09
says the Lord G., that they shall 44.12
and the blood, says the Lord G.; 44.15
his sin offering, says the Lord G. 44.27
"Thus says the Lord G.: Enough, 45.09
of my people, says the Lord G. 45.09
atonement for them, says the Lord G. 45.15
"Thus says the Lord G.: In the first 45.18
"Thus says the Lord G.: The gate of 46.01
"Thus says the Lord G.: If the prince 46.16
Thus says the Lord G.: "These are the 47.13
his inheritance, says the Lord G. 47.23
several portions, says the Lord G. 48.29
of the vessels of the house of G.; Dan 1.02
of Shinar, to the house of his g., 1.02
vessels in the treasury of his g. 1.02
And G. gave Daniel favor and 1.09
G. gave them learning and skill in 1.17
mercy of the G. of heaven concerning 2.18
Daniel blessed the G. of heaven. 2.19
be the name of G. for ever and 2.20
To thee, O G. of my fathers, I give 2.23
but there is a G. in heaven who 2.28
to whom the G. of heaven has given 2.37
those kings the G. of heaven will 2.44
A great G. has made known to the 2.45
your G. is G. of gods and Lord of 2.47
and who is the g. that will deliver 3.15
our G. whom we serve is able to 3.17
servants of the Most High G., 3.26
"Blessed be the G. of Shadrach, 3.28
and worship any g. except their own G. 3.28
anything against the G. of Shadrach, 3.29
is no other g. who is able to 3.29
the Most High G. has wrought 4.02
Belteshazzar after the name of my g., 4.08
the house of G. in Jerusalem; 5.03
the Most High G. gave Nebuchadnezzar 5.18
the Most High G. rules the kingdom 5.21
but the G. in whose hand is your 5.23
G. has numbered the days of your 5.26
connection with the law of his G." 6.05
petition to any g. or man for 6.07
and gave thanks before his G., 6.10
and supplication before his G. 6.11
petition to any g. or man within 6.12
"May your G., whom you serve 6.16
"O Daniel, servant of the living G., 6.20
has your G., whom you serve continually, 6.20
My G. sent his angel and shut the 6.22
because he had trusted in his G. 6.23
and fear before the G. of Daniel, 6.26
of Daniel, for he is the living G., 6.26
Then I turned my face to the Lord G., 9.03
to the LORD my G. and made confession, 9.04
"O Lord, the great and terrible G., 9.04
To the Lord our G. belong mercy and 9.09
of the LORD our G. by following 9.10
the servant of G. have been poured 9.11
the favor of the LORD our G., 9.13
the LORD our G. is righteous in 9.14
O Lord our G., who didst bring thy 9.15
O our G., hearken to the prayer of 9.17
O my G., incline thy ear and hear; 9.18
O my G, because thy city and thy 9.19
LORD my G. for the holy hill of my G.; 9.20
humbled yourself before your G., 10.12
who know their G. shall stand firm 11.32
and magnify himself above every g., 11.36
things against the G. of gods. 11.36
not give heed to any other g., 11.37
He shall honor the g. of fortresses 11.38
a g. whom his fathers did not know 11.38
by the help of a foreign g.; 11.39
deliver them by the LORD their G.; Hos 1.07
not my people and I am not your G." 1.09
to them, "Sons of the living G." 1.10
and he shall say, 'Thou art my G.'" 2.23
return and seek the LORD their G., 3.05
and no knowledge of G. in the land; 4.01
have forgotten the law of your G., 4.06
have left their G. to play the 4.12
permit them to return to their G. 5.04
not sacrifice, the knowledge of G., 6.06
do not return to the LORD their G., 7.10
My G., we Israel know thee. 8.02
it is not G. The calf of Samaria 8.06
the harlot, forsaking your G. 9.01
of Ephraim, the people of my G., 9.08
and hatred in the house of his G. 9.08
My G. will cast them off, because 9.17
for I am G. and not man, the Holy 11.09
but Judah is still known by G., 11.12
in his manhood he strove with G. 12.03
met G. at Bethel, and there G. spoke 12.04
the LORD the G. of hosts, the LORD 12.05
"So you, by the help of your G., 12.06

GOD (cont.)

and wait continually for your G." Hos 12.06
the LORD your G. from the land of 12.09
the LORD your G. from the land of 13.04
you know no G. but me, and besides 13.04
she has rebelled against her G; 13.16
Return, O Israel, to the LORD your G., 14.01
'Our G.,' to the work of our hands. 14.03
in sackcloth, O ministers of my G.! Joe 1.13
withheld from the house of your G. 1.13
to the house of the LORD your G.; 1.14
gladness from the house of our G.? 1.16
your G., for he is gracious and 2.13
offering for the LORD, your G.? 2.14
the peoples, 'Where is their G.?'" 2.17
and rejoice in the LORD, your G.; 2.23
the name of the LORD your G., 2.26
am your G. and there is none else. 2.27
know that I am the LORD your G., 3.17
shall perish," says the Lord G. Amo 1.08
house of their G. they drink the 2.08
Surely the Lord G. does nothing, 3.07
The Lord G. has spoken; who can but 3.08
Therefore thus says the Lord G.: 3.11
says the Lord G., the G. of hosts, 3.13
The Lord G. has sworn by his 4.02
people of Israel!" says the Lord G. 4.05
as when G. overthrew Sodom and 4.11
prepare to meet your G., O Israel!" 4.12
the G. of hosts, is his name! 4.13
For thus says the Lord G.: 5.03
the G. of hosts, will be with you, as 5.14
the G. of hosts, will be gracious to 5.15
the G. of hosts, the Lord: "In all 5.16
whose name is the G. of hosts. 5.27
The Lord G. has sworn by himself 6.08
the G. of hosts): "I abhor the pride 6.08
says the LORD, the G. of hosts; 6.14
Thus the Lord G. showed me: behold, 7.01
"O Lord G., forgive, I beseech thee! 7.02
Thus the Lord G. showed me: behold, 7.04
the Lord G. was calling for a 7.04
"O Lord G., cease, I beseech thee! 7.05
shall not be," said the Lord G. 7.06
Thus the Lord G. showed me: behold, a 8.01
in that day," says the Lord G.; 8.03
"And on that day," says the Lord G., 8.09
days are coming," says the Lord G., 8.11
'As thy g. lives, O Dan,' and, 'As the 8.14
The Lord, G. of hosts, he who touches 9.05
of the Lord G. are upon the sinful 9.08
given them," says the LORD your G. 9.15
says the Lord G. concerning Edom: Ob 1.01
afraid, and each cried to his g.; Jon 1.05
Arise, call upon your g.! 1.06
Perhaps the g. will give a thought 1.06
the G. of heaven, who made the sea 1.09
to the LORD his G. from the belly 2.01
my life from the Pit, O LORD my G. 2.06
And the people of Nineveh believed G.; 3.05
and let them cry mightily to G.; 3.08
Who knows, G. may yet repent and 3.09
When G. saw what they did, how they 3.10
G. repented of the evil which he 3.10
art a gracious G. and merciful, 4.02
And the LORD G. appointed a plant, 4.06
G. appointed a worm which attacked 4.07
G. appointed a sultry east wind, and 4.08
But G. said to Jonah, "Do you do 4.09
let the Lord G. be a witness Mic 1.02
for there is no answer from G. 3.07
to the house of the G. of Jacob; 4.02
walk each in the name of its g., 4.05
of the LORD our G. for ever and 4.05
of the name of the LORD his G. 5.04
and bow myself before G. on high? 6.06
and to walk humbly with your G.? 6.08
wait for the G. of my salvation; my G. 7.07
to me, "Where is the LORD your G.?" 7.10
turn in dread to the LORD our G., 7.17
Who is a G. like thee, pardoning 7.18
The LORD is a jealous G. and avenging, Nah 1.02
The oracle of G. which Habakkuk the Hab 1.01
men, whose own might is their g.! 1.11
everlasting, O LORD my G., my Holy One? 1.12
G. came from Teman, and the Holy One 3.03
will joy in the G. of my salvation. 3.18
G., the Lord, is my strength; he makes 3.19
Be silent before the Lord G.! For the day Zep 1.07
the LORD their G. will be mindful 2.07
the G. of Israel, "Moab shall become 2.09
she does not draw near to her G. 3.02
The LORD, your G., is in your midst, 3.17
the voice of the LORD their G., Hag 1.12
as the LORD their G. had sent him; 1.12
of the LORD of hosts, their G., 1.14
obey the voice of the LORD your G. Zec 6.15
my people and I will be their G., 8.08
we have heard that G. is with you.'" 8.23
too shall be a remnant for our G.; 9.07
the Lord G. will sound the trumpet, 9.14
the LORD their G. will save them 9.16
the LORD their G. and I will answer 10.06
Thus said the LORD my G.: "Become 11.04
through the LORD of hosts, their G.' 12.05
house of David shall be like G., 12.08
they will say, 'The LORD is my G.'" 13.09
Then the LORD your G. will come, 14.05
And now entreat the favor of G., Mal 1.09
Has not one G. created us? Why then 2.10
the daughter of a foreign g. 2.11
Has not the one G. made and sustained 2.15
says the LORD the G. of Israel, and 2.16
asking, "Where is the G. of justice?" 2.17
Will man rob G.? Yet you are 3.08
have said, 'It is vain to serve G. 3.14
when they put G. to the test they 3.15
one who serves G. and one who does 3.18
Emmanuel" (which means, G. with us). Mt 1.23
G. is able from these stones to 3.09
the Spirit of G. descending like a 3.16
to him, "If you are the Son of G., 4.03
that proceeds from the mouth of G.'" 4.04
to him, "If you are the Son of G., 4.06
shall not tempt the Lord your G.'" 4.07
the Lord your G. and him only 4.10
in heart, for they shall see G. 5.08
they shall be called sons of G. 5.09
for it is the throne of G., 5.34
You cannot serve G. and mammon. 6.24
But if G. so clothes the grass of 6.30
you to do with us, O Son of G.? 8.29
were afraid, and they glorified G., 9.08
the house of G. and ate the bread 12.04
the Spirit of G. that I cast out 12.28
the kingdom of G. has come upon 12.28
"Truly you are the Son of G." 14.33
commandment of G. for the sake of 15.03
For G. commanded, 'Honor your father 15.04
have gained from me is given to G., 15.05
you have made void the word of G. 15.06
they glorified the G. of Israel. 15.31
Christ, the Son of the living G." 16.16
him, saying, "G. forbid, Lord! 16.22
not on the side of G., but of men." 16.23
What therefore G. has joined 19.06
man to enter the kingdom of G." 19.24
but with G. all things are possible." 19.26
the temple of G. and drove out all 21.12
into the kingdom of G. before you. 21.31
the kingdom of G. will be taken 21.43
and teach the way of G. truthfully, 22.16
and to G. the things that are God's." 22.21
the scriptures nor the power of G. 22.29

GOD (cont.)
read what was said to you by G., Mt 22.31
'I am the G. of Abraham, and the 22.32
the G. of Isaac, and the G. of Jacob'? 22.32
He is not G. of the dead, but of the 22.32
the Lord your G. with all your 22.37
the throne of G. and by him who 23.22
able to destroy the temple of G., 26.61
him, "I adjure you by the living G., 26.63
you are the Christ, the Son of G." 26.63
If you are the Son of G., come down 27.40
He trusts in G.; let G. deliver him now, 27.43
for he said, 'I am the Son of G.' 27.43
"My G., my G., why hast thou forsaken 27.46
said, "Truly this was a son of G.!" 27.54
of Jesus Christ, the Son of G. Mk 1.01
preaching the gospel of G., 1.14
and the kingdom of G. is at hand; 1.15
who you are, the Holy One of G." 1.24
who can forgive sins but G. alone?" 2.07
were all amazed and glorified G., 2.12
how he entered the house of G., 2.26
cried out, "You are the Son of G." 3.11
Whoever does the will of G. is my brother, 3.35
the secret of the kingdom of G., 4.11
"The kingdom of G. is as if a man 4.26
can we compare the kingdom of G., 4.30
me, Jesus, Son of the Most High G.? 5.07
I adjure you by G., do not torment 5.07
You leave the commandment of G., 7.08
of rejecting the commandment of G., 7.09
is Corban' (that is, given to G.)— 7.11
the word of G. through your 7.13
not on the side of G., but of men." 8.33
the kingdom of G. come with power." 9.01
the kingdom of G. with one eye 9.47
'G. made them male and female.' 10.06
What therefore G. has joined 10.09
to such belongs the kingdom of G. 10.14
the kingdom of G. like a child 10.15
call me good? No one is good but G. alone. 10.18
riches to enter the kingdom of G.!" 10.23
it is to enter the kingdom of G.! 10.24
man to enter the kingdom of G." 10.25
it is impossible, but not with G.; 10.27
all things are possible with G." 10.27
answered them, "Have faith in G. 11.22
men, but truly teach the way of G. 12.14
and to G. the things that are God's." 12.17
the scriptures nor the power of G.? 12.24
how G. said to him, 'I am the God of 12.26
'I am the G. of Abraham, and the 12.26
the G. of Isaac, and the G. of Jacob'? 12.26
He is not G. of the dead, but of the 12.27
The Lord our G., the Lord is one; 12.29
the Lord your G. with all your 12.30
are not far from the kingdom of G." 12.34
creation which G. created until 13.19
drink it new in the kingdom of G." 14.25
"My G., my G., why hast thou forsaken me?" 15.34
"Truly this man was a son of G.!" 15.39
looking for the kingdom of G., 15.43
they were both righteous before G., Lk 1.06
priest before G. when his division 1.08
of Israel to the Lord their G., 1.16
who stand in the presence of G.; 1.19
was sent from G. to a city of 1.26
for you have found favor with G. 1.30
and the Lord G. will give to him 1.32
will be called holy, the Son of G. 1.35
For with G. nothing will be impossible." 1.37
spirit rejoices in G. my Savior, 1.47
loosed, and he spoke, blessing G. 1.64
"Blessed be the Lord G. of Israel, 1.68
through the tender mercy of our G., 1.78
host praising G. and saying, 2.13
"Glory to G. in the highest, and on 2.14
and praising G. for all they had 2.20
his arms and blessed G. and said, 2.28
very hour she gave thanks to G., 2.38
and the favor of G. was upon him. 2.40
and in favor with G. and man. 2.52
the word of G. came to John the son 3.02
shall see the salvation of G." 3.06
G. is able from these stones to 3.08
the son of Adam, the son of G. 3.38
to him, "If you are the Son of G., 4.03
You shall worship the Lord your G., 4.08
to him, "If you are the Son of G., 4.09
shall not tempt the Lord your G.' " 4.12
who you are, the Holy One of G." 4.34
crying, "You are the Son of G.!" 4.41
the kingdom of G. to the other 4.43
upon him to hear the word of G., 5.01
Who can forgive sins but G. only?" 5.21
lay, and went home, glorifying G. 5.25
they glorified G. and were filled 5.26
how he entered the house of G., 6.04
night he continued in prayer to G. 6.12
for yours is the kingdom of G. 6.20
and they glorified G., saying, "A great 7.16
and "G. has visited his people!" 7.16
the kingdom of G. is greater than 7.28
the tax collectors justified G., 7.29
the purpose of G. for themselves, 7.30
the good news of the kingdom of G. 8.01
the secrets of the kingdom of G.; 8.10
this: The seed is the word of G. 8.11
who hear the word of G. and do it." 8.21
me, Jesus, Son of the Most High G.? 8.28
how much G. has done for you." 8.39
the kingdom of G. and to heal. 9.02
spoke to them of the kingdom of G., 9.11
Peter answered, "The Christ of G." 9.20
before they see the kingdom of G." 9.27
astonished at the majesty of G. 9.43
go and proclaim the kingdom of G." 9.60
back is fit for the kingdom of G." 9.62
'The kingdom of G. has come near 10.09
the kingdom of G. has come near.' 10.11
the Lord your G. with all your 10.27
the finger of G. that I cast out 11.20
the kingdom of G. has come upon 11.20
hear the word of G. and keep it!" 11.28
neglect justice and the love of G.; 11.42
Therefore also the Wisdom of G. said, 11.49
one of them is forgotten before G. 12.06
acknowledge before the angels of G.; 12.08
be denied before the angels of G. 12.09
But G. said to him, 'Fool! 12.20
himself, and is not rich toward G." 12.21
nor barn, and yet G. feeds them. 12.24
But if G. so clothes the grass 12.28
made straight, and she praised G. 13.13
"What is the kingdom of G. like? 13.18
shall I compare the kingdom of G.? 13.20
the kingdom of G. and you yourselves 13.28
sit at table in the kingdom of G. 13.29
eat bread in the kingdom of G.!" 14.15
the angels of G. over one sinner 15.10
You cannot serve G. and mammon." 16.13
but G. knows your hearts; 16.15
an abomination in the sight of G. 16.15
of the kingdom of G. is preached, 16.16
praising G. with a loud voice; 17.15
give praise to G. except this 17.18
when the kingdom of G. was coming, 17.20
"The kingdom of G. is not coming 17.20
the kingdom of G. is in the midst 17.21
neither feared G. nor regarded man; 18.02
I neither fear G. nor regard man, 18.04
And will not G. vindicate his elect, 18.07
'G., I thank thee that I am not 18.11

GOD (cont.)
'G., be merciful to me a sinner!' Lk 18.13
to such belongs the kingdom of G. 18.16
the kingdom of G. like a child 18.17
No one is good but G. alone. 18.19
riches to enter the kingdom of G.! 18.24
man to enter the kingdom of G." 18.25
with men is possible with G." 18.27
for the sake of the kingdom of G., 18.29
and followed him, glorifying G.; 18.43
they saw it, gave praise to G. 18.43
the kingdom of G. was to appear 19.11
and praise G. with a loud voice 19.37
heard this, they said, "G. forbid!" 20.16
but truly teach the way of G. 20.21
and to G. the things that are God's." 20.25
equal to angels and are sons of G., 20.36
the Lord the G. of Abraham and the 20.37
the G. of Isaac and the G. of Jacob. 20.37
Now he is not G. of the dead, but of 20.38
that the kingdom of G. is near. 21.31
is fulfilled in the kingdom of G." 22.16
vine until the kingdom of G. comes." 22.18
the right hand of the power of G." 22.69
said, "Are you the Son of G., then?" 22.70
himself, if he is the Christ of G., 23.35
him, saying, "Do you not fear G., 23.40
he praised G., and said, "Certainly 23.47
was looking for the kingdom of G. 23.51
and word before G. and all the 24.19
continually in the temple blessing G. 24.53
Word was with G., and the Word was G. Jn 1.01
He was in the beginning with G.; 1.02
There was a man sent from G., 1.06
power to become children of G.; 1.12
nor of the will of man, but of G. 1.13
No one has ever seen G.; 1.18
the Lamb of G., who takes away the 1.29
witness that this is the Son of G." 1.34
and said, "Behold, the Lamb of G.!" 1.36
him, "Rabbi, you are the Son of G.! 1.49
the angels of G. ascending and 1.51
you are a teacher come from G.; 3.02
that you do, unless G. is with him." 3.02
he cannot see the kingdom of G." 3.03
he cannot enter the kingdom of G. 3.05
For G. so loved the world that he 3.16
For G. sent the Son into the world, 3.17
in the name of the only Son of G. 3.18
his deeds have been wrought in G. 3.21
his seal to this, that G. is true. 3.33
For he whom G. has sent utters the 3.34
has sent utters the words of G., 3.34
but the wrath of G. rests upon him. 3.36
her, "If you knew the gift of G., 4.10
G. is spirit, and those who worship 4.24
but also called G. his Father, 5.18
making himself equal with G. 5.18
hear the voice of the Son of G., 5.25
have not the love of G. within you. 5.42
glory that comes from the only G.? 5.44
for on him has G. the Father set 6.27
we do, to be doing the work of G.?" 6.28
them, "This is the work of G., 6.29
For the bread of G. is that which 6.33
'And they shall all be taught by G.' 6.45
Father except him who is from G.; 6.46
that you are the Holy One of G." 6.69
teaching is from G. or whether I am 7.17
the truth which I heard from G.; 8.40
we have one Father, even G." 8.41
"If G. were your Father, you would 8.42
I proceeded and came forth from G.; 8.42
He who is of G. hears the words of 8.47
is of God hears the words of G.; 8.47
them is that you are not of G." 8.47
of whom you say that he is your G. 8.54
the works of G. might be made 9.03
said, "This man is not from G., 9.16
said to him, "Give G. the praise; 9.24
We know that G. has spoken to Moses, 9.29
We know that G. does not listen to 9.31
a worshiper of G. and does his 9.31
does his will, G. listens to him. 9.31
If this man were not from G., 9.33
you, being a man, make yourself G." 10.33
the word of G. came (and scripture 10.35
I said, 'I am the Son of G.'? 10.36
it is for the glory of G., 11.04
that the Son of G. may be glorified 11.04
you ask from G., G. will give you." 11.22
the Son of G., he who is coming 11.27
you would see the glory of G.?" 11.40
the children of G. who are scattered 11.52
of men more than the praise of G. 12.43
had come from G. and was going to G., 13.03
glorified, and in him G. is glorified; 13.31
if G. is glorified in him, G. will 13.32
G. will also glorify him in himself, 13.32
believe in G., believe also in me. 14.01
think he is offering service to G. 16.02
we believe that you came from G." 16.30
they know thee the only true G., 17.03
he has made himself the Son of G." 19.07
your Father, to my G. and your G." 20.17
Thomas answered him, "My Lord and my G.!" 20.28
the Son of G., and that believing 20.31
by what death he was to glorify G.) 21.19
and speaking of the kingdom of G. Ac 1.03
own tongues the mighty works of G." 2.11
G. declares, that I will pour out my 2.17
to you by G. with mighty works and 2.22
and signs which G. did through him 2.22
plan and foreknowledge of G., 2.23
But G. raised him up, having loosed 2.24
knowing that G. had sworn with an 2.30
This Jesus G. raised up, and of that 2.32
exalted at the right hand of G., 2.33
assuredly that G. has made him 2.36
whom the Lord our G. calls to him." 2.39
praising G. and having favor with 2.47
and leaping and praising G. 3.08
saw him walking and praising G., 3.09
The G. of Abraham and of Isaac and 3.13
the G. of our fathers, glorified his 3.13
whom G. raised from the dead. 3.15
But what G. foretold by the mouth 3.18
all that G. spoke by the mouth of 3.21
'The Lord G. will raise up for you 3.22
covenant which G. gave to your 3.25
G., having raised up his servant, 3.26
whom G. raised from the dead, by him 4.10
in the sight of G. to listen to 4.19
to listen to you rather than to G., 4.19
all men praised G. for what had 4.21
voices together to G. and said, 4.24
spoke the work of G. with boldness. 4.31
You have not lied to men but to G." 5.04
"We must obey G. rather than men. 5.29
The G. of our fathers raised Jesus 5.30
G. exalted him at his right hand as 5.31
Spirit whom G. has given to those 5.32
but if it is of G., you will not 5.39
might even be found opposing G.!" 5.39
the word of G. to serve tables. 6.02
And the word of G. increased; 6.07
blasphemous words against Moses and G." 6.11
The G. of glory appeared to our 7.02
G. removed him from there into this 7.04
And G. spoke to this effect, that 7.06
said G., 'and after that they 7.07
him into Egypt; but G. was with him, 7.09
which G. had granted to Abraham, the 7.17
born, and was beautiful before G. 7.20

GOD (cont.)
understood that G. was giving them Ac 7.25
'I am the G. of your fathers, the 7.32
the G. of Abraham and of Isaac and 7.32
G. sent as both ruler and deliverer 7.35
'G. will raise up for your a prophet 7.37
But G. turned and gave them over to 7.42
and the star of the g. Rephan, 7.43
nations which G. thrust out before 7.45
in the sight of G. and asked leave 7.46
a habitation for the G. of Jacob. 7.46
heaven and saw the glory of G., 7.55
standing at the right hand of G.; 7.55
standing at the right hand of G." 7.56
that power of G. which is called 8.10
the kingdom of G. and the name of 8.12
had received the word of G., 8.14
obtain the gift of G. with money! 8.20
your heart is not right before G. 8.21
that Jesus Christ is the Son of G." * 8.37
Jesus, saying, "He is the Son of G." 9.20
man who feared G. with all his 10.02
and prayed constantly to G. 10.02
an angel of G. coming in and 10.03
ascended as a memorial before G. 10.04
"What G. has cleansed, you must not 10.15
but G. has shown me that I should 10.28
have been remembered before G. 10.31
here present in the sight of G., 10.33
I perceive that G. shows no 10.34
how G. anointed Jesus of Nazareth 10.38
by the devil, for G. was with him. 10.38
but G. raised him on the third day 10.40
who were chosen by G. as witnesses, 10.41
one ordained by G. to be judge of 10.42
in tongues and extolling G. 10.46
also had received the word of G. 11.01
'What G. has cleansed you must not 11.09
If then G. gave the same gift to 11.17
was I that I could withstand G.?" 11.17
And they glorified G., 11.18
Gentiles also G. has granted 11.18
saw the grace of G., he was glad; 11.23
him was made to G. by the church. 12.05
people shouted, "The voice of a g., 12.22
he did not give G. the glory; 12.23
But the word of G. grew and multiplied. 12.24
the word of G. in the synagogues 13.05
and sought to hear the word of G. 13.07
and you that fear G., listen. 13.16
The G. of this people Israel chose 13.17
and G. gave them Saul the son of 13.21
man's posterity G. has brought to 13.23
and those among you that fear G., 13.26
But G. raised him from the dead; 13.30
news that what G. promised to the 13.32
the counsel of G. in his own 13.36
but he whom G. raised up saw no 13.37
to continue in the grace of G. 13.43
together to hear the word of G. 13.44
the word of G. should be spoken 13.46
glad and glorified the word of G.; 13.48
to a living G. who made the heaven 14.15
we must enter the kingdom of G. 14.22
to the grace of G. for the work 14.26
all that G. had done with them, and 14.27
all that G. had done with them. 15.04
the early days G. made choice 15.07
And G. who knows the heart bore 15.08
make trial of G. by putting a yoke 15.10
and wonders G. had done through 15.12
Symeon has related how G. first 15.14
of the Gentiles who turn to G., 15.19
concluding that G. had called us 16.10
goods, who was a worshiper of G. 16.14
are servants of the Most High G., 16.17
praying and singing hymns to G., 16.25
household that he had believed in G. 16.34
the word of G. was proclaimed by 17.13
inscription, 'To an unknown g.' 17.23
The G. who made the world and 17.24
that they should seek G., in the hope 17.27
The times of ignorance G. overlooked, 17.30
Titius Justus, a worshiper of G.; 18.07
teaching the word of G. among them. 18.11
men to worship G. contrary to the 18.13
"I will return to you if G. wills, 18.21
him the way of G. more accurately. 18.26
pleading about the kingdom of G.; 19.08
And G. did extraordinary miracles 19.11
repentance to G. and of faith in 20.21
to the gospel of the grace of G. 20.24
to you the whole counsel of G. 20.27
commend you to G. and to the word 20.32
the things that G. had done among 21.19
they heard it, they glorified G. 21.20
zealous for G. as you all are this 22.03
'The G. of our fathers appointed 22.14
lived before G. in all good conscience 23.01
"G. shall strike you, you whitewashed 23.03
I worship the G. of our fathers, 24.14
having a hope in G. which these 24.15
conscience toward G. and toward men. 24.16
promise made by G. to our fathers, 26.06
any of you that G. raises the dead? 26.08
and from the power of Satan to G., 26.18
and turn to G. and perform deeds 26.20
had the help that comes from G., 26.22
I would to G. that not only you but 26.29
an angel of the G. to whom I 27.23
and lo, G. has granted you all those 27.24
I have faith in G. that it will be 27.25
thanks to G. in the presence of 27.35
minds and said that he was a g. 28.06
Paul thanked G. and took courage. 28.15
the kingdom of G. and trying to 28.23
salvation of G. has been sent to 28.28
preaching the kingdom of G. and 28.31
set apart for the gospel of G. Rom 1.01
designated Son of G. in power 1.04
and peace from G. our Father and 1.07
I thank my G. through Jesus Christ 1.08
For G. is my witness, whom I serve 1.09
is the power of G. for salvation 1.16
righteousness of G. is revealed 1.17
For the wrath of G. is revealed 1.18
be known about G. is plain to them, 1.19
because G. has shown it to them. 1.19
they knew G. they did not honor 1.21
honor him as G. or give thanks to 1.21
of the immortal G. for images 1.23
Therefore G. gave them up in the 1.24
the truth about G. for a lie and 1.25
For this reason G. gave them up to 1.26
did not see fit to acknowledge G., 1.28
G. gave them up to a base mind and 1.28
haters of G., insolent, haughty, 1.30
the judgment of G. rightly falls 2.02
you will escape the judgment of G.? 2.03
For G. shows no partiality. 2.11
law who are righteous before G., 2.13
G. judges the secrets of men by 2.16
and boast of your relation to G. 2.17
do you dishonor G. by breaking the 2.23
"The name of G. is blasphemed among 2.24
praise is not from men but from G. 2.29
entrusted with the oracles of G. 3.02
nullify the faithfulness of G.? 3.03
Let G. be true though every man be 3.04
serves to show the justice of G., 3.05
That G. is unjust to inflict wrath 3.05
then how could G. judge the world? 3.06
understands, no one seeks for G. 3.11
"There is no fear of G. before 3.18

GOD (cont.)

world may be held accountable to G. Rom 3.19
righteousness of G. has been manifested 3.21
righteousness of G. through faith 3.22
and fall short of the glory of G., 3.23
whom G. put forward as an expiation 3.25
Or is G. the G. of Jews only? 3.29
Is he not the G. of Gentiles also? 3.29
since G. is one; and he will 3.30
to boast about, but not before G. 4.02
"Abraham believed G., 4.03
the man to whom G. reckons righteousness 4.06
presence of the G. in whom he 4.17
waver concerning the promise of G., 4.20
his faith as he gave glory to G., 4.20
fully convinced that G. was able to 4.21
have peace with G. through our 5.01
hope of sharing the glory of G. 5.02
But G. shows his love for us in 5.08
saved by him from the wrath of G. 5.09
reconciled to G. by the death of 5.10
also rejoice in G. through our 5.11
the grace of G. and the free gift 5.15
the life he lives he lives to G. 6.10
and alive to G. in Christ Jesus. 6.11
yourselves to G. as men who have 6.13
your members to G. as instruments 6.13
But thanks be to G., that you who 6.17
sin and have become slaves of G., 6.22
free gift of G. is eternal life in 6.23
that we may bear fruit for G. 7.04
For I delight in the law of G., 7.22
Thanks be to G. through Jesus 7.25
serve the law of G. with my mind, 7.25
For G. has done what the law, 8.03
set on the flesh is hostile to G.; 8.07
are in the flesh cannot please G. 8.08
the Spirit of G. really dwells in 8.09
the Spirit of G. are sons of G. 8.14
spirit that we are children of G., 8.16
heirs of G. and fellow heirs with 8.17
the revealing of the sons of G.; 8.19
liberty of the children of G. 8.21
saints according to the will of G. 8.27
in everything G. works for good 8.28
If G. is for us, who is against us? 8.31
elect? It is G. who justifies; 8.33
who is at the right hand of G., 8.34
the love of G. in Christ Jesus our 8.39
G. who is over all be blessed for 9.05
though the words of G. had failed. 9.06
flesh who are the children of G., 9.08
you, a man, to answer back to G.? 9.20
What if G., desiring to show his 9.22
be called 'sons of the living G.'" 9.26
and prayer to G. for them is that 10.01
that they have a zeal for G., 10.02
righteousness that comes from G., 10.03
your heart that G. raised him from 10.09
has G. rejected his people? By no means! 11.01
G. has not rejected his people whom 11.02
he pleads with G. against Israel? 11.02
"G. gave them a spirit of stupor, 11.08
For if G. did not spare the natural 11.21
kindness and the severity of G.: 11.22
for G. has the power to graft them 11.23
are enemies of G., for your sake; 11.28
and the call of G. are irrevocable. 11.29
disobedient to G. but now have 11.30
For G. has consigned all men to 11.32
and wisdom and knowledge of G.! 11.33
brethren, by the mercies of G., 12.01
sacrifice, holy and acceptable to G., 12.01
may prove what is the will of G., 12.02
of faith which G. has assigned him. 12.03
but leave it to the wrath of G.; 12.19
is no authority except from G., 13.01
exist have been instituted by G. 13.01
resists what G. has appointed, 13.02
the servant of G. to execute his 13.04
authorities are ministers of G., 13.06
who eats; for G. has welcomed him. 14.03
Lord, since he gives thanks to G.; 14.06
of the Lord and gives thanks to G. 14.06
before the judgment seat of G.; 14.10
tongue shall give praise to G." 14.11
give account of himself to G. 14.12
For the kingdom of G. does not mean 14.17
acceptable to G. and approved by 14.18
of food, destroy the work of G. 14.20
have, keep between yourself and G.; 14.22
May the G. of steadfastness and 15.05
glorify the G. and Father of our 15.06
welcomed you, for the glory of G. 15.07
might glorify G. for his mercy. 15.09
May the G. of hope fill you with 15.13
of the grace given me by G. 15.15
service of the gospel of G., 15.16
to be proud of my work for G. 15.17
your prayers to G. on my behalf, 15.30
The G. of peace be with you all. 15.33
then the G. of peace will soon 16.20
to the command of the eternal G., 16.26
to the only wise G. be glory for 16.27
by the will of G. to be an apostle 1Co 1.01
To the church of G. which is at 1.02
and peace from G. our Father and 1.03
I give thanks to G. always for you 1.04
of the grace of G. which was given 1.04
G. is faithful, by whom you were 1.09
being saved it is the power of G. 1.18
Has not G. made foolish the wisdom 1.20
For since, in the wisdom of G., 1.21
did not know G. through wisdom, 1.21
it pleased G. through the folly of 1.21
the power of G. and the wisdom of G. 1.24
foolishness of G. is wiser than 1.25
the weakness of G. is stronger 1.25
but G. chose what is foolish in the 1.27
G. chose what is weak in the world 1.27
G. chose what is low and despised 1.28
might boast in the presence of G. 1.29
whom G. made our wisdom, our righteousness 1.30
testimony of G. in lofty words or 2.01
of men but in the power of G. 2.05
a secret and hidden wisdom of G., 2.07
which G. decreed before the ages 2.07
what G. has prepared for those who 2.09
G. has revealed to us through the 2.10
everything, even the depths of G. 2.10
thoughts of G. except the Spirit of G. 2.11
but the Spirit which is from G., 2.12
the gifts bestowed on us by G. 2.12
the gifts of the Spirit of G., 2.14
watered, but G. gave the growth. 3.06
but only G. who gives the growth. 3.07
For we are fellow workmen for G.; 3.09
the commission of G. given to me, 3.10
temple, G. will destroy him. 3.17
of this world is folly with G. 3.19
stewards of the mysteries of G. 4.01
receive his commendation from G. 4.05
For I think that G. has exhibited 4.09
For the kingdom of G. does not 4.20
G. judges those outside. Drive 5.13
will not inherit the kingdom of G.? 6.09
will inherit the kingdom of G. 6.10
Christ and in the Spirit of our G. 6.11
and G. will destroy both one and 6.13
And G. raised the Lord and will 6.14
within you, which you have from G.? 6.19
a price. So glorify G. in your body. 6.20
has his own special gift from G., 7.07
For G. has called us to peace. 7.15

GOD (cont.)

and in which G. has called him. 1Co 7.17
but keeping the commandments of G. 7.19
there let him remain with G. 7.24
think that I have the Spirit of G. 7.40
But if one loves G., one is known 8.03
and that "there is no G. but one." 8.04
yet for us there is one G., 8.06
Food will not commend us to G. 8.08
it for oxen that G. is concerned? 9.09
law toward G. but under the law of 9.21
most of them G. was not pleased; 10.05
G. is faithful, and he will not let 10.13
they offer to demons and not to G. 10.20
you do, do all to the glory of G. 10.31
to Greeks or to the church of G., 10.32
and the head of Christ is G. 11.03
he is the image and glory of G.; 11.07
And all things are from G.) 11.12
to pray to G. with her head 11.13
practice, nor do the churches of G. 11.16
the church of G. and humiliate 11.22
the Spirit of G. ever says "Jesus 12.03
it is the same G. who inspires 12.06
But as it is, G. arranged the organs 12.18
But G. has so adjusted the body, 12.24
And G. has appointed in the church 12.28
tongue speaks not to men but to G.; 14.02
I thank G. that I speak in tongues 14.18
he will worship G. and declare 14.25
declare that G. is really among 14.25
and speak to himself and to G. 14.28
For G. is not a G. of confusion 14.33
Did the word of G. originate with 14.36
I persecuted the church of G. 15.09
But by the grace of G. I am what I am, 15.10
the grace of G. which is with me. 15.10
found to be misrepresenting G., 15.15
we testified of G. that he raised 15.15
the kingdom to G. the Father after 15.24
"For G. has put all things in 15.27
that G. may be everything to every 15.28
For some have no knowledge of G. 15.34
But G. gives it a body as he has 15.38
cannot inherit the kingdom of G., 15.50
But thanks be to G., who gives us 15.57
of Christ Jesus by the will of G., 2Co 1.01
the church of G. which is at 1.01
and peace from G. our Father and 1.02
Blessed be the G. and Father of our 1.03
of mercies and G. of all comfort, 1.03
we ourselves are comforted by G. 1.04
ourselves but on G. who raises the 1.09
wisdom but by the grace of G. 1.12
As surely as G. is faithful, our 1.18
For the Son of G., Jesus Christ, 1.19
promises of G. find their Yes in 1.20
through him, to the glory of G. 1.20
But it is G. who establishes us 1.21
But I call G. to witness against me— 1.23
But thanks be to G., who in Christ 2.14
of Christ to G. among those who 2.15
sincerity, as commissioned by G., 2.17
in the sight of G. we speak in 2.17
with the Spirit of the living G., 3.03
we have through Christ toward G. 3.04
our sufficiency is from G., 3.05
this ministry by the mercy of G., 4.01
conscience in the sight of G. 4.02
In their case the g. of this world 4.04
Christ, who is the likeness of G. 4.04
For it is the G. who said, "Let 4.06
of the glory of G. in the face of 4.06
power belongs to G. and not to us. 4.07
thanksgiving, to the glory of G. 4.15
destroyed, we have a building from G., 5.01
us for this very thing is G., 5.05
but what we are is known to G., 5.11
are beside ourselves, it is for G.; 5.13
All this is from G., who through 5.18
that is, G. was in Christ reconciling 5.19
G. making his appeal through us. 5.20
of Christ, be reconciled to G. 5.20
become the righteousness of G. 5.21
to accept the grace of G. in vain. 6.01
but as servants of G. we commend 6.04
truthful speech, and the power of G.; 6.07
has the temple of G. with idols? 6.16
we are the temple of the living G.; 6.16
as G. said, "I will live in them and 6.16
among them, and I will be their G., 6.16
holiness perfect in the fear of G. 7.01
But G., who comforts the downcast, 7.06
revealed to you in the sight of G. 7.12
the grace of G. which has been 8.01
Lord and to us by the will of G. 8.05
But thanks be to G. who puts the 8.16
for G. loves a cheerful giver. 9.07
And G. is able to provide you with 9.08
us will produce thanksgiving to G.; 9.11
overflows in many thanksgivings to G. 9.12
will glorify G. by your obedience 9.13
the surpassing grace of G. in you. 9.14
Thanks be to G. for his inexpressible 9.15
obstacle to the knowledge of G., 10.05
to the limits G. has apportioned 10.13
I do not love you? G. knows I do! 11.11
The G. and Father of the Lord Jesus, 11.31
the body I do not know, G. knows. 12.02
the body I do not know, G. knows— 12.03
in the sight of G. that we have 12.19
I come again my G. may humble me 12.21
but lives by the power of G. 13.04
live with him by the power of G. 13.04
But we pray G. that you may not do 13.07
and the G. of love and peace will 13.11
and the love of G. and the fellowship 13.14
Jesus Christ and G. the Father, Gal 1.01
and peace from G. the Father and 1.03
to the will of our G. and Father; 1.04
seeking the favor of men, or of G.? 1.10
the church of G. violently and 1.13
to you, before G., I do not lie!) 1.20
And they glorified G. because of me. 1.24
G. shows no partiality)—those, I say, 2.06
the law, that I might live to G. 2.19
I live by faith in the Son of G., 2.20
I do not nullify the grace of G.; 2.21
Thus Abraham "believed G., and it was 3.06
foreseeing that G. would justify 3.08
is justified before G. by the law; 3.11
covenant previously ratified by G., 3.17
but G. gave it to Abraham by a 3.18
more than one; but G. is one. 3.20
then against the promises of G.? 3.21
are all sons of G., through faith. 3.26
G. sent forth his Son, born of woman, 4.04
G. has sent the Spirit of his Son 4.06
So through G. you are no longer a 4.07
Formerly, when you did not know G., 4.08
but now that you have come to know G., 4.09
or rather to be known by G., how 4.09
but received me as an angel of G., 4.14
not inherit the kingdom of G. 5.21
G. is not mocked, for whatever a man 6.07
this rule, upon the Israel of G. 6.16
of Christ Jesus by the will of G., Eph 1.01
and peace from G. our Father and 1.02
Blessed be the G. and Father of our 1.03
that the G. of our Lord Jesus 1.17
But G., who is rich in mercy, out of 2.04
own doing, it is the gift of G.— 2.08
which G. prepared beforehand, that 2.10
hope and without G. in the world. 2.12

GOD (cont.)
us both to G. in one body through Eph 2.16
members of the household of G., 2.19
dwelling place of G. in the Spirit. 2.22
for ages in G. who created all 3.09
wisdom of G. might now be made 3.10
filled with all the fulness of G. 3.19
one G. and Father of us all, who is 4.06
of the knowledge of the Son of G., 4.13
the life of G. because of the 4.18
the likeness of G. in true righteousness 4.24
not grieve the Holy Spirit of G., 4.30
as G. in Christ forgave you. 4.32
Therefore be imitators of G., 5.01
offering and sacrifice to G. 5.02
in the kingdom of Christ and of G. 5.05
the wrath of G. comes upon the 5.06
Lord Jesus Christ to G. the Father. 5.20
the will of G. from the heart, 6.06
Put on the whole armor of G., 6.11
Therefore take the whole armor of G., 6.13
Spirit, which is the word of G. 6.17
from G. the Father and the Lord 6.23
and peace from G. our Father and Php 1.02
I thank my G. in all my remembrance 1.03
For G. is my witness, how I yearn 1.08
to the glory and praise of G. 1.11
speak the word of G. without fear. 1.14
your salvation, and that from G. 1.28
who, though he was in the form of G., 2.06
equality with G. a thing to be 2.06
Therefore G. has highly exalted him 2.09
to the glory of G. the Father. 2.11
for G. is at work in you, both to 2.13
children of G. without blemish in 2.15
But G. had mercy on him, and not 2.27
who worship G. in spirit, and glory 3.03
righteousness from G. that depends 3.09
upward call of G. in Christ Jesus. 3.14
G. will reveal that also to you. 3.15
their g. is the belly, and they 3.19
your requests be made known to G. 4.06
And the peace of G., which passes 4.07
and the G. of peace will be with 4.09
acceptable and pleasing to G. 4.18
And my G. will supply every need of 4.19
To our G. and Father be glory for 4.20
of Christ Jesus by the will of G., Col 1.01
you and peace from G. our Father. 1.02
We always thank G., the Father of 1.03
understood the grace of G. in truth, 1.06
increasing in the knowledge of G. 1.10
He is the image of the invisible G., 1.15
the fulness of G. was pleased to 1.19
make the word of G. fully known, 1.25
To them G. chose to make known how 1.27
through faith in the working of G., 2.12
G. made alive together with him, 2.13
with a growth that is from G. 2.19
is, seated at the right hand of G. 3.01
your life is hid with Christ in G. 3.03
of these the wrath of G. is coming. 3.06
thankfulness in your hearts to G. 3.16
thanks to G. the Father through 3.17
that G. may open to us a door for 4.03
workers for the kingdom of G., 4.11
assured in all the will of G. 4.12
Thessalonians in G. the Father and 1Th 1.01
We give thanks to G. always for you 1.02
remembering before our G. and 1.03
For we know, brethren beloved by G., 1.04
your faith in G. has gone forth 1.08
how you turned to G. from idols, 1.09
to serve a living and true G., 1.09
courage in our G. to declare to 2.02
the gospel of G. in the face of 2.02
approved by G. to be entrusted 2.04
but to please G. who tests our 2.04
cloak for greed, as G. is witness; 2.05
the gospel of G. but also our own 2.08
preached to you the gospel of G. 2.09
and G. also, how holy and righteous 2.10
to lead a life worthy of G., 2.12
And we also thank G. constantly for 2.13
the word of G. which you heard 2.13
the word of G., which is at work in 2.13
the churches of G. in Christ Jesus 2.14
and displease G. and oppose all men 2.15
can we render to G. for you, 3.09
feel for your sake before our G., 3.09
Now may our G. and Father himself, 3.11
holiness before our G. and Father, 3.13
you ought to live and to please G., 4.01
For this is the will of G., 4.03
like heathen who do not know G.; 4.05
For G. has not called us for 4.07
this, disregards not man but G., 4.08
been taught by G. to love one 4.09
G. will bring with him those who 4.14
the sound of the trumpet of G. 4.16
For G. has not destined us for 5.09
is the will of G. in Christ Jesus 5.18
May the G. of peace himself sanctify 5.23
Thessalonians in G. our Father and 2Th 1.01
and peace from G. the Father and 1.02
give thanks to G. always for you, 1.03
the churches of G. for your 1.04
of the righteous judgment of G., 1.05
made worthy of the kingdom of G., 1.05
since indeed G. deems it just to 1.06
who do not know G. and upon those 1.08
that our G. may make you worthy of 1.11
grace of our G. and the Lord Jesus 1.12
every so-called g. or object of 2.04
takes his seat in the temple of G., 2.04
proclaiming himself to be G. 2.04
Therefore G. sends upon them a 2.11
give thanks to G. always for you, 2.13
because G. chose you from the 2.13
and G. our Father, who loved us and 2.16
to the love of G. and to the 3.05
by command of G. our Savior and of 1Ti 1.01
and peace from G. the Father and 1.02
of the blessed G. with which I 1.11
the only G., be honor and glory for 1.17
in the sight of G. our Savior, 2.03
For there is one G., and there 2.05
is one mediator between G. and men, 2.05
to behave in the household of G., 3.15
is the church of the living G., 3.15
foods which G. created to be 4.03
For everything created by G. is good, 4.04
by the word of G. and prayer. 4.05
have our hope set on the living G., 4.10
is acceptable in the sight of G. 5.04
set her hope on G. and continues 5.05
In the presence of G. and of Christ 5.21
the name of G. and the teaching 6.01
for you, man of G., shun all this; 6.11
In the presence of G. who gives 6.13
riches but on G. who richly 6.17
by the will of G. according to the 2Ti 1.01
and peace from G. the Father and 1.02
I thank G. whom I serve with a 1.03
the gift of G. that is within you 1.06
for G. did not give us a spirit of 1.07
for the gospel in the power of G., 1.08
But the word of G. is not fettered. 2.09
yourself to G. as one approved, a 2.15
G. may perhaps grant that they will 2.25
pleasure rather than lovers of G., 3.04
is inspired by G. and profitable 3.16
that the man of G. may be complete, 3.17
the presence of G. and of Christ 4.01

GOD (cont.)
a servant of G. and an apostle of Tit 1.01
in hope of eternal life which G., 1.02
by command of G. our Savior; 1.03
and peace from G. the Father and 1.04
They profess to know G., but they 1.16
the word of G. may not be discredited. 2.05
the doctrine of G. our Savior. 2.10
For the grace of G. has appeared 2.11
of our great G. and Savior Jesus 2.13
kindness of G. our Savior appeared, 3.04
believed in G. may be careful to 3.08
and peace from G. our Father and Phm 1.03
I thank my G. always when I remember 1.04
various ways G. spoke of old to Heb 1.01
the glory of G. and bears the very 1.03
For to what angel did G. ever say, 1.05
O G., is for ever and ever, the 1.08
therefore G., thy G., has anointed 1.09
while G. also bore witness by signs 2.04
to angels that G. subjected the 2.05
by the grace of G. he might taste 2.09
and the children G. has given me." 2.13
high priest in the service of G., 2.17
the builder of all things is G.) 3.04
to fall away from the living G. 3.12
"And G. rested on the seventh day 4.04
G. would not speak later of another 4.08
sabbath rest for the people of G.; 4.09
from his labors as G. did from his. 4.10
For the word of G. is living and 4.12
the Son of G., let us hold fast our 4.14
on behalf of men in relation to G., 5.01
himself, but he is called by G., 5.04
being designated by G. a high 5.10
dead works and of faith toward G., 6.01
And this we will do if G. permits. 6.03
of the word of G. and the powers 6.05
the Son of G. on their own account 6.06
receives a blessing from G. 6.07
For G. is not so unjust as to 6.10
For when G. made a promise to 6.13
So when G. desired to show more 6.17
impossible that G. should prove 6.18
Salem, priest of the Most High G., 7.01
the Son of G. he continues a 7.03
through which we draw near to G. 7.19
who draw near to G. through him, 7.25
the tent, he was instructed by G., 8.05
hearts, and I will be their G., 8.10
himself without blemish to G., 9.14
dead works to serve the living G. 9.14
covenant which G. commanded you." 9.20
the presence of G. on our behalf. 9.24
O G.,' as it is written of me in 10.07
sat down at the right hand of G., 10.12
great priest over the house of G., 10.21
man who has spurned the Son of G., 10.29
into the hands of the living G. 10.31
do the will of G. and receive what 10.36
was created by the word of G., 11.03
Abel offered to G. a more acceptable 11.04
G. bearing witness by accepting his 11.04
found, because G. had taken him. 11.05
was attested as having pleased G. 11.05
draw near to G. must believe that 11.06
being warned by G. concerning 11.07
whose builder and maker is G. 11.10
Therefore G. is not ashamed to be 11.16
not ashamed to be called their G., 11.16
He considered that G. was able to 11.19
the people of G. than to enjoy the 11.25
since G. had foreseen something 11.40
the right hand of the throne of G. 12.02
G. is treating you as sons; 12.07
one fail to obtain the grace of G.; 12.15
and to the city of the living G., 12.22
and to a judge who is G. of all, 12.23
let us offer to G. acceptable 12.28
for our G. is a consuming fire. 12.29
for G. will judge the immoral and 13.04
who spoke to you the word of G.; 13.07
up a sacrifice of praise to G., 13.15
such sacrifices are pleasing to G. 13.16
Now may the G. of peace who brought 13.20
a servant of G. and of the Lord Jas 1.01
let him ask G. who gives to all men 1.05
of life which G. has promised to 1.12
he is tempted, "I am tempted by G."; 1.13
for G. cannot be tempted with evil 1.13
not work the righteousness of G. 1.20
undefiled before G. and the Father 1.27
Has not G. chosen those who are 2.05
You believe that G. is one; 2.19
which says, "Abraham believed G., 2.23
and he was called the friend of G. 2.23
who are made in the likeness of G. 3.09
with the world is enmity with G.? 4.04
world makes himself an enemy of G. 4.04
"G. opposes the proud, but gives 4.06
Submit yourselves therefore to G. 4.07
Draw near to G. and he will draw 4.08
chosen and destined by G. the 1Pe 1.02
Blessed be the G. and Father of our 1.03
Through him you have confidence in G., 1.21
that your faith and hope are in G. 1.21
the living and abiding word of G.; 1.23
acceptable to G. through Jesus 2.05
and glorify G. on the day of 2.12
evil; but live as servants of G. 2.16
Fear G. Honor the emperor. 2.17
mindful of G., he endures pain 2.19
who hoped in G. used to adorn 3.05
that he might bring us to G., 3.18
as an appeal to G. for a clear 3.21
and is at the right hand of G., 3.22
passions but by the will of G. 4.02
might live in the spirit like G. 4.06
as one who utters oracles of G.; 4.11
by the strength which G. supplies; 4.11
in everything G. may be glorified 4.11
of glory and of G. rests upon you. 4.14
under that name let him glorify G. 4.16
to begin with the household of G.; 4.17
who do not obey the gospel of G.? 4.17
Tend the flock of G. that is your 5.02
for "G. opposes the proud, but gives 5.05
under the mighty hand of G., 5.06
the G. of all grace, who has called 5.10
that this is the true grace of G.; 5.12
righteousness of our G. and Savior 2Pe 1.01
knowledge of G. and of Jesus our 1.02
and glory from G. the Father and 1.17
by the Holy Spirit spoke from G. 1.21
For if G. did not spare the angels 2.04
by the word of G. heavens existed 3.05
the coming of the day of G., 3.12
that G. is light and in him is no 1Jn 1.05
him truly love for G. is perfected. 2.05
and the word of G. abides in you, 2.14
the will of G. abides for ever. 2.17
we should be called children of G.; 3.01
the Son of G. appeared was to 3.08
No one born to G. commits sin; 3.09
sin because he is born of G. 3.09
be seen who are the children of G., 3.10
does not do right is not of G., 3.10
for G. is greater than our hearts, 3.20
us, we have confidence before G.; 3.21
to see whether they are of G.; 4.01
By this you know the Spirit of G.: 4.02
has come in the flesh is of G., 4.02
not confess Jesus is not of G. 4.03
you are of G., and have overcome 4.04

GOD (cont.)
We are of G. Whoever knows G. listens 1Jn 4.06
who is not of G. does not listen 4.06
one another; for love is of G., 4.07
loves is born of G. and knows G. 4.07
who does not love does not know G.; 4.08
not know G.; for G. is love. 4.08
the love of G. was made manifest 4.09
that G. sent his only Son into the 4.09
that we loved G. but that he loved 4.10
Beloved, if G. so loved us, we also 4.11
No man has ever seen G.; if we love 4.12
G. abides in us and his love is 4.12
that Jesus is the Son of G., 4.15
G. abides in him, and he in G. 4.15
and believe the love G. has for us. 4.16
G. is love, and he who abides in 4.16
abides in G., and G. abides in him. 4.16
"I love G.," and hates his brother, 4.20
cannot love G. whom he has not seen 4.20
he who loves G. should love his 4.21
is the Christ is a child of G., 5.01
that we love the children of G., 5.02
when we love G. and obey his 5.02
For this is the love of G., 5.03
is born of G. overcomes the world; 5.04
that Jesus is the Son of G.? 5.05
the testimony of G. is greater; 5.09
testimony of G. that he has borne 5.09
in the Son of G. has the testimony 5.10
He who does not believe G., 5.10
testimony that G. has borne to his 5.10
that G. gave us eternal life, and 5.11
in the name of the Son of G., 5.13
and G. will give him life for those 5.16
any one born of G. does not sin, 5.18
He who was born of G. keeps him, 5.18
We know that we are of G., 5.19
that the Son of G. has come and 5.20
is the true G. and eternal life. 5.20
from G. the Father and from Jesus 2Jn 1.03
doctrine of Christ does not have G.; 1.09
He who does good is of G.; 3Jn 1.11
he who does evil has not seen G. 1.11
beloved in G. the Father and kept Jud 1.01
grace of our G. into licentiousness 1.04
keep yourselves in the love of G.; 1.21
to the only G., our Savior through 1.25
which G. gave him to show to his Rev 1.01
to the word of G. and to the 1.02
priests to his G. and Father, 1.06
and the Omega," says the Lord G., 1.08
of the word of G. and the testimony 1.09
which is in the paradise of G. 2.07
write: 'The words of the Son of G., 2.18
spirits of G. and the seven stars. 3.01
perfect in the sight of my G. 3.02
a pillar in the temple of my G.; 3.12
write on him the name of my G., 3.12
and the name of the city of my G., 3.12
down from my G. out of heaven, 3.12
which are the seven spirits of G.; 4.05
is the Lord G. Almighty, who was and 4.08
our Lord and G., to receive glory 4.11
spirits of G. sent out into all 5.06
ransom men for G. from every tribe 5.09
a kingdom and priests to our G., 5.10
for the word of G. and for the 6.09
with the seal of the living G., 7.02
servants of our G. upon their 7.03
belongs to our G. who sits upon 7.10
the throne and worshiped G., 7.11
might be to our G. for ever and 7.12
Therefore are they before the throne of G., 7.15
and G. will wipe away every tear 7.17
seven angels who stand before G., 8.02
the hand of the angel before G. 8.04
not the seal of G. upon their 9.04
of the golden altar before G., 9.13
seventh angel, the mystery of G., 10.07
the temple of G. and the altar and 11.01
of life from G. entered them, 11.11
and gave glory to the G. of heaven. 11.13
thrones before G. fell on their 11.16
on their faces and worshiped G., 11.16
Lord G. Almighty, who art and who 11.17
caught up to G. and to his throne, 12.05
she has a place prepared by G., 12.06
kingdom of our G. and the authority 12.10
them day and night before out G. 12.10
commandments of G. and bear 12.17
to utter blasphemies against G., 13.06
first fruits for G. and the Lamb, 14.04
"Fear G. and give him glory, for the 14.07
commandments of G. and the faith 14.12
wine press of the wrath of G.; 14.19
with them the wrath of G. is ended. 15.01
with harps of G. in their hands. 15.02
song of Moses, the servant of G., 15.03
thy deeds, O Lord G. the Almighty! 15.03
of the wrath of G. who lives for 15.07
the glory of G. and from his power, 15.08
the seven bowls of the wrath of G." 16.01
Lord G. the Almighty, true and just 16.07
the name of G. who had power over 16.09
and cursed the G. of heaven for 16.11
the great day of G. the Almighty. 16.14
and G. remembered great Babylon, to 16.19
till men cursed G. for the plague 16.21
for G. has put it into their hearts 17.17
the words of G. shall be fulfilled 17.17
and G. has remembered her iniquities. 18.05
is the Lord G. who judges her." 18.08
for G. has given judgment for you 18.20
glory and power belong to our G., 19.01
and worshiped G. who is seated on 19.04
"Praise our G., all you his servants, 19.05
the Lord our G. the Almighty 19.06
to me, "These are true words of G." 19.09
testimony of Jesus. Worship G." 19.10
he is called is The Word of G. 19.13
of the wrath of G. the Almighty. 19.15
gather for the great supper of G., 19.17
to Jesus and for the word of G., 20.04
be priests of G. and of Christ, 20.06
coming down out of heaven from G., 21.02
the dwelling of G. is with men. 21.03
and G. himself will be with them; 21.03
I will be his G. and he shall be 21.07
coming down out of heaven from G., 21.10
having the glory of G., its radiance 21.11
is the Lord G. the Almighty and 21.22
for the glory of G. is its light, 21.23
the throne of G. and of the Lamb 22.01
the throne of G. and of the Lamb 22.03
for the Lord G. will be their light, 22.05
the G. of the spirits of the 22.06
words of this book. Worship G." 22.09
G. will add to him the plagues 22.18
G. will take away his share in the 22.19

GODDESS
Ashtoreth the g. of the Sidonians, 1Ki 11.05
Ashtoreth the g. of the Sidonians, 11.33
of the great g. Artemis may count Ac 19.27
sacrilegious nor blasphemers of our g. 19.37

GOD-FEARING
more faithful and G. man than many. Neh 7.02
a centurion, an upright and G. man, Ac 10.22

GODLESS
But g. men are all like thorns that 2Sa 23.06
the hope of the g. man shall perish. Job 8.13
that a g. man shall not come before 13.16

GODLESS (cont.)
For the company of the g. is barren, Job 15.34
stirs himself up against the g. 17.08
the joy of the g. but for a moment? 20.05
the hope of the g. when God cuts 27.08
that a g. man should not reign, that 34.30
"The g. in heart cherish anger; 36.13
G. men utterly deride me, but I do Ps 119.51
The g. besmear me with lies, but 119.69
Let the g. be put to shame, because 119.78
G. men have dug pitfalls for me, men 119.85
let not the g. oppress me. 119.122
expectation of the g. comes to Pro 11.07
With his mouth the g. man would 11.09
every one is g. and an evildoer, Is 9.17
Against a g. nation I send him, and 10.06
trembling has seized the g.: 33.14
to do with g. and silly myths. 1Ti 4.07
Avoid the g. chatter and contradictions 6.20
Avoid such g. chatter, for it will 2Ti 2.16

GODLINESS
silly myths. Train yourself in g.; 1Ti 4.07
g. is of value in every way, as it 4.08
teaching which accords with g., 6.03
imagining that g. is a means of 6.05
great gain in g. with contentment; 6.06
g., faith, love, steadfastness, 6.11
the truth which accords with g., Tit 1.01
things that pertain to life and g., 2Pe 1.03
steadfastness, and steadfastness with g., 1.06
and g. with brotherly affection, and 1.07
to be in lives of holiness and g., 3.11

GODLY
Thummim, and thy Urim to thy g. one, Deu 33.08
has set apart the g. for himself; Ps 4.03
there is no longer any that is g.; 12.01
or let thy g. one see the Pit. 16.10
one who is g. offer prayer to thee; 32.06
of mischief done against the g.? 52.01
is good, in the presence of the g. 52.09
Preserve my life, for I am g.; 86.02
The g. man has perished from the Mic 7.02
what does he desire? G. offspring. Mal 2.15
with holiness and g. sincerity, 2Co 1.12
for you felt a g. grief, 7.09
For g. grief produces a repentance 7.10
earnestness this g. grief has 7.11
g. and respectful in every way. 1Ti 2.02
to live a g. life in Christ Jesus 2Ti 3.12
and g. lives in this world, Tit 2.12
and he was heard for his g. fear. Heb 5.07
how to rescue the g. from trial, 2Pe 2.09

GOD'S
Now the earth was corrupt in G. sight, Gen 6.11
up for a pillar, shall be G. house; 28.22
saw them he said, "This is G. army!" 32.02
But G. anger was kindled because he Num 22.22
of man, for the judgment is G.; Deu 1.17
for the battle is not yours but G. 2Ch 20.15
oath to walk in G. law which was Neh 10.29
is pure, and I am clean in G. eyes.' Job 11.04
dragged off in the day of G. wrath. 20.28
yet something to say on G. behalf. 36.02
within G. house we walked in Ps 55.14
They did not keep G. covenant, 78.10
also that it is G. gift to man that Ecc 3.13
and to God the things that are G." Mt 22.21
and to God the things that are G." Mk 12.17
and to God the things that are G." Lk 20.25
Being then G. offspring, we ought Ac 17.29
"Would you revile G. high priest?" 23.04
To all G. beloved in Rome, who are Rom 1.07
asking that somehow by G. will I 1.10
Though they know G. decree that 1.32
not know that G. kindness is meant 2.04
of wrath when G. righteous judgment 2.05
my falsehood G. truthfulness 3.07
this was to show G. righteousness, 3.25
because G. love has been poured 5.05
it does not submit to G. law, 8.07
bring any charge against G. elect? 8.33
in order that G. purpose of election 9.11
Is there injustice on G. part? 9.14
or exertion, but upon G. mercy. 9.16
did not submit to G. righteousness. 10.03
But what is G. reply to him? 11.04
but G. kindness to you, provided you 11.22
for he is G. servant for your good. 13.04
only to avoid G. wrath but also 13.05
circumcised to show G. truthfulness, 15.08
so that by G. will I may come to 15.32
you are G. field, G. building. 1Co 3.09
that you are G. temple and that 3.16
and that G. Spirit dwells in you? 3.16
If any one destroys G. temple, 3.17
For G. temple is holy, and that 3.17
you are Christ's; and Christ is G. 3.23
was not at all G. will for him to 16.12
like so many, peddlers of G. word; 2Co 2.17
cunning or to tamper with G. word, 4.02
I preached G. gospel without cost 11.07
stewardship of G. grace that was Eph 3.02
to the gift of G. grace which was 3.07
and the knowledge of G. mystery, Col 2.02
as G. chosen ones, holy and beloved, 3.12
But G. wrath has come upon them at 1Th 2.16
our brother and G. servant in the 3.02
how can he care for G. church? 1Ti 3.05
But G. firm foundation stands, 2Ti 2.19
the faith of G. elect and their Tit 1.01
as G. steward, must be blameless; 1.07
"Let all G. angels worship him." Heb 1.06
also was faithful in G. house. 3.02
faithful in all G. house as a 3.05
faithful over G. house as a son. 3.06
for whoever enters G. rest also 4.10
the first principles of G. word. 5.12
who by G. power are guarded through 1Pe 1.05
by men but in G. sight chosen and 2.04
G. own people, that you may declare 2.09
people but now you are G. people; 2.10
For it is G. will that by doing 2.15
it patiently, you have G. approval. 2.20
which in G. sight is very precious. 3.04
right, if that should be G. will, 3.17
when G. patience waited in the days 3.20
good stewards of G. varied grace: 4.10
according to G. will do right and 4.19
Beloved, we are G. children now; 1Jn 3.02
for G. nature abides in him, and he 3.09
how does G. love abide in him? 3.17
their journey as befits G. service. 3Jn 1.06
the beginning of G. creation. Rev 3.14
Then G. temple in heaven was opened, 11.19
shall drink the wine of G. wrath, 14.10

GODS
stole her father's household g. Gen 31.19
house, but why did you steal my g.?" 31.30
you find your g. shall not live. 31.32
the household g. and put them in 31.34
but did not find the household g. 31.35
the foreign g. that are among you, 35.02
all the foreign g. that they had, 35.04
and on all the g. of Egypt I will Ex 12.12
is like thee, O LORD, among the g.? 15.11
the LORD is greater than all g., 18.11
"You shall have no other g. before me. 20.03
You shall not make g. of silver to 20.23
you make for yourselves g. of gold. 20.23
mention of the names of other g., 23.13
you shall not bow down to their g., 23.24

GODS (cont.)
covenant with them or with their g. Ex 23.32
for if you serve their g., it will 23.33
make us g., who shall go before us; 32.01
and they said, "These are your g., 32.04
it, and said, 'These are your g., 32.08
'Make us g., who shall go before us; 32.23
made for themselves g. of gold. 32.31
after their g. and sacrifice to 34.15
to their g. and one invites you, 34.15
after their g. and make your sons 34.16
play the harlot after their g. 34.16
make for yourself no molten g. 34.17
or make for yourselves molten g.: Lev 19.04
to the sacrifices of their g., Num 25.02
ate, and bowed down to their g. 25.02
upon their g. also the LORD executed 33.04
you will serve g. of wood and Deu 4.28
shall have no other g. before me. 5.07
You shall not go after other g., 6.14
of the g. of the peoples who are 6.14
following me, to serve other g.; 7.04
neither shall you serve their g., 7.16
images of their g. you shall burn 7.25
go after other g. and serve them 8.19
God is God of g. and Lord of lords, 10.17
and serve other g. and worship 11.16
go after other g. which you have 11.28
shall dispossess served their g., 12.02
down the graven images of their g., 12.03
you do not inquire about their g., 12.30
did these nations serve their g.?— 12.30
hates they have done for their g.; 12.31
daughters in the fire to their g. 12.31
he says, 'Let us go after other g.,' 13.02
'Let us go and serve other g., 13.06
some of the g. of the peoples that 13.07
'Let us go and serve other g.,' 13.13
served other g. and worshiped them, 17.03
who speaks in the name of other g., 18.20
done in the service of their g., 20.18
to go after other g. to serve them. 28.14
and there you shall serve other g., 28.36
and there you shall serve other g., 28.64
and serve the g. of those nations; 29.18
served other g. and worshiped them, 29.26
g. whom they had not known and whom 29.26
to worship other g. and serve them, 30.17
after the strange g. of the land, 31.16
they have turned to other g. 31.18
turn to other g. and serve them, 31.20
him to jealousy with strange g.; 32.16
sacrificed to demons which were no g., 32.17
to g. they had never known, to new g. 32.17
Then he will say, 'Where are their g., 32.37
mention of the names of their g., Jos 23.07
and serve other g. and bow down to 23.16
and they served other g. 24.02
put away the g. which your fathers 24.14
whether the g. your fathers served 24.15
or the g. of the Amorites in whose 24.15
the LORD, to serve other g.; 24.16
the LORD and serve foreign g., 24.20
the foreign g. which are among you, 24.23
and their g. shall be a snare to Ju 2.03
of Egypt; they went after other g., 2.12
from among the g. of the peoples 2.12
after other g. and bowed down to 2.17
fathers, going after other g., 2.19
their sons; and they served their g. 3.06
When new g. were chosen, then war 5.08
reverence to the g. of the Amorites, 6.10
by which g. and men are honored, and 9.09
my wine which cheers g. and men, 9.13
the g. of Syria, the g. of Sidon, the 10.06
g. of Moab, the g. of the Ammonites, 10.06
and the g. of the Philistines; 10.06
forsaken me and served other g.; 10.13
Go and cry to the g. whom you have 10.14
the foreign g. from among them and 10.16
"You take my g. which I made, and 18.24
back to her people and to her g.; Ru 1.15
"The g. have come into the camp." 1Sa 4.07
from the power of these mighty g.? 4.08
These are the g. who smote the 4.08
off you and your g. and your land. 6.05
the foreign g. and the Ashtaroth 7.03
forsaking me and serving other g., 8.08
Philistine cursed David by his g. 17.43
LORD, saying, 'Go, serve other g.' 26.19
his people a nation and its g.? 2Sa 7.23
and serve other g. and worship 1Ki 9.06
Egypt, and laid hold on other g., 9.09
away your heart after their g."; 11.02
away his heart after other g.; 11.04
incense and sacrificed to their g. 11.08
he should not go after other g.; 11.10
Behold your g., O Israel, who 12.28
and made for yourself other g., 14.09
"So may the g. do to me, and more 19.02
"The g. do so to me, and more also, 20.10
"Their g. are g. of the hills, and 20.23
Egypt, and had feared other g. 2Ki 17.07
nation still made g. of its own, 17.29
Anammelech, the g. of Sepharvaim. 17.31
LORD but also served their own g., 17.33
not fear other g. or bow yourselves 17.35
You shall not fear other g., 17.37
You shall not fear other g., 17.38
Has any of the g. of the nations 18.33
Where are the g. of Hamath and 18.34
Where are the g. of Sepharvaim, Hena, 18.34
Who among all the g. of the countries 18.35
Have the g. of the nations delivered 19.12
and have cast their g. into the fire; 19.18
for they were no g., but the work 19.18
have burned incense to other g., 22.17
after the g. of the peoples of the 1Ch 5.25
armor in the temple of their g., 10.10
And they left their g. there, 14.12
is to be held in awe above all g. 16.25
For all the g. of the peoples are 16.26
for our God is greater than all g. 2Ch 2.05
and serve other g. and worship 7.19
Egypt, and laid hold on other g., 7.22
which Jeroboam made you for g. 13.08
becomes a priest of what are no g. 13.09
he brought the g. of the men of 25.14
of Seir, and set them up as his g., 25.14
you resorted to the g. of a people, 25.15
they had sought the g. of Edom. 25.20
sacrificed to the g. of Damascus 28.23
"Because the g. of the kings of 28.23
places to burn incense to other g., 28.25
Were the g. of the nations of those 32.13
Who among all the g. of those 32.14
"Like the g. of the nations of the 32.17
spoke of the g. of the peoples of 32.19
the foreign g. and the idol from 33.15
have burned incense to other g., 34.25
and placed in the house of his g. Ez 1.07
those who g. astray after false g.! Ps 40.04
decree what is right, you g.? 58.01
midst of the g. he holds judgment: 82.01
"You are g., sons of the Most High, 82.06
the God of g. will be seen in Zion. 84.07
There is none like thee among the g., 86.08
God, and a great King above all g. 95.03
he is to be feared above all g. 96.04
For all the g. of the peoples are 96.05
all g. bow down before him. 97.07
thou art exalted far above all g. 97.09
and that our Lord is above all g. 135.05
O give thanks to the God of g., 136.02
before the g. I sing thy praise; 138.01

GODS (cont.)
images of her g. he has shattered Is 21.09
Has any of the g. of the nations 36.18
Where are the g. of Hamath and 36.19
Where are the g. of Sepharvaim? 36.19
Who among all the g. of these 36.20
Have the g. of the nations delivered 37.12
and have cast their g. into the fire; 37.19
for they were no g., but the work 37.19
that we may know that you are g.; 41.23
to molten images, "You are our g." 42.17
have burned incense to other g., Jer 1.16
Has a nation changed its g., even 2.11
though they are no g.? But my 2.11
But where are your g. that you made 2.28
your cities are your g., O Judah. 2.28
have sworn by those who are no g. 5.07
and served foreign g. in your land, 5.19
go after other g. to your own hurt, 7.06
go after other g. that you have 7.09
out drink offerings to other g., 7.18
"The g. who did not make the 10.11
gone after other g. to serve them; 11.10
and cry to the g. to whom they 11.12
For your g. have become as many as 11.13
after other g. to serve them and 13.10
among the false g. of the nations 14.22
after other g. and have served and 16.11
shall serve other g. day and night, 16.13
make for himself g.? Such are no g.!" 16.20
me, they burn incense to false g.; 18.15
in it to other g. whom neither 19.04
have been poured out to other g.— 19.13
worshiped other g. and served them."'" 22.09
go after other g. to serve and 25.06
have been poured out to other g., 32.29
go after other g. to serve them, 35.15
in the temples of the g. of Egypt; 43.12
temples of the g. of Egypt he 43.13
and serve other g. that they knew 44.03
and burn no incense to other g. 44.05
to other g. in the land of Egypt 44.08
had offered incense to other g., 44.15
and Egypt and her g. and her kings, 46.25
a god, I sit in the seat of the g., Eze 28.02
show it to the king except the g., Dan 2.11
God is God of g. and Lord of kings, 2.47
not serve your g. or worship the 3.12
do not serve my g. or worship the 3.14
not serve your g. or worship the 3.18
the fourth is like a son of the g." 3.25
whom is the spirit of the holy g.— 4.08
of the holy g. is in you and that 4.09
spirit of the holy g. is in you." 4.18
and praised the g. of gold and 5.04
whom is the spirit of the holy g. 5.11
wisdom, like the wisdom of the g., 5.11
spirit of the holy g. is in you, 5.14
praised the g. of silver and gold. 5.23
to Egypt their g. with their 11.08
things against the God of g. 11.36
no heed to the g. of his fathers, 11.37
turn to other g. and love cakes of Hos 3.01
house of your g. I will cut off Nah 1.14
famish all the g. of the earth, Zep 2.11
in your law, 'I said, you are g.'? Jn 10.34
If he called them g. to whom the 10.35
'Make for us g. to go before us; Ac 7.40
"The g. have come down to us in the 14.11
that g. made with hands are not g. 19.26
be so-called g. in heaven or on 1Co 8.05
there are many "g." and many 8.05
to beings that by nature are no g.; Gal 4.08

GOG
G. his son, Shimei his son, 1Ch 5.04
"Son of man, set your face toward G., Eze 38.02
O G., chief prince of Meshech and 38.03
and say to G., Thus says the Lord 38.14
O G., I vindicate my holiness 38.16
when G. shall come against the land 38.18
every kind of terror against G., 38.21
son of man, prophesy against G., 39.01
O G., chief prince of Meshech and 39.01
I will give to G. a place for 39.11
for there G. and all his multitude 39.11
G. and Magog, to gather them for Rev 20.08

GOIIM
of Elam, and Tidal king of G., Gen 14.01
Tidal king of G., Amraphel king of 14.09
the king of G. in Galilee, one; Jos 12.23

GOLAN
and G. in Bashan for the Manassites. Deu 4.43
and G. in Bashan, from the tribe of Jos 20.08
G. in Bashan with its pasture lands, 21.27
G. in Bashan with its pasture lands 1Ch 6.71

GOLD
land of Havilah, where there is g.; Gen 2.11
and the g. of that land is good; 2.12
in cattle, in silver, and in g. 13.02
the man took a g. ring weighing a 24.22
her arms weighing ten g. shekels, 24.22
silver and g., menservants and 24.35
forth jewelry of silver and of g., 24.53
and put a g. chain about her neck; 41.42
steal silver or g. from your lord's 44.08
house, jewelry of silver and of g., Ex 3.22
jewelry of silver and of g. 11.02
of silver and of g., and clothing; 12.35
you make for yourselves gods of g. 20.23
from them: g., silver, and bronze, 25.03
And you shall overlay it with pure g., 25.11
it a molding of g. round about. 25.11
four rings of g. for it and put 25.12
wood, and overlay them with g. 25.13
shall make a mercy seat of pure g.; 25.17
And you shall make two cherubim of g.; 25.18
You shall overlay it with pure g., 25.24
and make a molding of g. around it. 25.24
a molding of g. around the frame. 25.25
shall make for it four rings of g., 25.26
wood, and overlay them with g., 25.28
of pure g. you shall make them. 25.29
shall make a lampstand of pure g. 25.31
piece of hammered work of pure g. 25.36
their trays shall be of pure g. 25.38
talent of pure g. shall it be made, 25.39
And you shall make fifty clasps of g., 26.06
You shall overlay the frames with g., 26.29
their rings of g. for holders for 26.29
you shall overlay the bars with g. 26.29
pillars of acacia overlaid with g., 26.32
with hooks of g., upon four bases 26.32
acacia, and overlay them with g.; 26.37
their hooks shall be of g., and you 26.37
"They shall receive g., blue and 28.05
And they shall make the ephod of g., 28.06
of g., blue and purple and scarlet 28.08
them in settings of g. filigree. 28.11
make settings of g. filigree, 28.13
and two chains of pure g., twisted 28.14
of g., blue and purple and scarlet 28.15
they shall be set in g. filigree. 28.20
chains like cords, of pure g.; 28.22
the breastpiece two rings of g., 28.23
two cords of g. in the two rings 28.24
And you shall make two rings of g., 28.26
And you shall make two rings of g., 28.27
with bells of g. between them, 28.33
"And you shall make a plate of pure g., 28.36
And you shall overlay it with pure g., 30.03
for it a molding of g. round about. 30.03
wood, and overlay them with g. 30.05

GOLD (cont.)

to work in g., silver, and bronze, Ex 31.04
the rings of g. which are in the 32.02
the rings of g. which were in 32.03
And he received the g. at their hand, 32.04
'Let any who have g. take it off'; 32.24
made for themselves gods of g. 32.31
offering; g., silver, and bronze; 35.05
all sorts of g. objects, every man 35.22
an offering of g. to the LORD. 35.22
to work in g. and silver and bronze, 35.32
And he made fifty clasps of g., 36.13
And he overlaid the frames with g., 36.34
their rings of g. for holders for 36.34
and overlaid the bars with g. 36.34
acacia, and overlaid them with g.; 36.36
their hooks were of g., and he cast 36.36
and their fillets were of g., 36.38
it with pure g. within and without, 37.02
and made a molding of g. around it. 37.02
four rings of g. for its four 37.03
wood, and overlaid them with g., 37.04
And he made a mercy seat of pure g.; 37.06
made two cherubim of hammered g.; 37.07
and he overlaid it with pure g., 37.11
and made a molding of g. around it. 37.11
a molding of g. around the frame. 37.12
He cast for it four rings of g., 37.13
table, and overlaid them with g. 37.15
vessels of pure g. which were to 37.16
also made the lampstand of pure g. 37.17
piece of hammered work of pure g. 37.22
snuffers and its trays of pure g. 37.23
utensils of a talent of pure g. 37.24
He overlaid it with pure g., 37.26
a molding of g. round about it, 37.26
two rings of g. on it under its 37.27
wood, and overlaid them with g. 37.28
All the g. that was used for the 38.24
the g. from the offering, was twenty 38.24
And he made the ephod of g., 39.02
And g. leaf was hammered out and 39.03
of g., blue and purple and scarlet 39.05
in settings of g. filigree and 39.06
of g., blue and purple and scarlet 39.08
enclosed in settings of g. filigree. 39.13
chains like cords, of pure g.; 39.15
settings of g. filigree and two g. rings, 39.16
two cords of g. in the two rings 39.17
Then they made two rings of g., 39.19
And they made two rings of g., 39.20
They also made bells of pure g., 39.25
plate of the holy crown of pure g., 39.30
lampstand of pure g. and its lamps 39.37
lampstand of pure g. before the Lev 24.04
a row, upon the table of pure g. 24.06
all the g. of the dishes being a Num 7.86
the lampstand, hammered work of g.; 8.04
me his house full of silver and g., 22.18
me his house full of silver and g., 24.13
only the g., the silver, the bronze, 31.22
articles of g., armlets and bracelets, 31.50
priest received from them the g., 31.51
And all the g. of the offering that 31.52
received the g. from the commanders 31.54
silver or the g. that is on them, Deu 7.25
your silver and g. is multiplied, 8.13
multiply for himself silver and g. 17.17
of silver and g., which were among 29.17
But all silver and g., and vessels Jos 6.19
only the silver and g., and the 6.24
and a bar of g. weighing fifty 7.21
and the mantle and the bar of g., 7.24
g., bronze, and iron, and with much 22.08
seven hundred shekels of g.; Ju 8.26
box at its side the figures of g., 1Sa 6.08
ornaments of g. upon your apparel. 2Sa 1.24
the shields of g. which were 8.07
of silver, and g., and of bronze; 8.10
the silver and g. which he dedicated 8.11
weight of it was a talent of g., 12.30
of silver and g. between us and 21.04
and he overlaid it with pure g. 1Ki 6.20
inside of the house with pure g., 6.21
and he drew chains of g. across, 6.21
sanctuary, and overlaid it with g. 6.21
overlaid the whole house with g., 6.22
sanctuary he overlaid with g. 6.22
And he overlaid the cherubim with g. 6.28
overlaid with g. in the inner and 6.30
flowers; he overlaid them with g., 6.32
and spread g. upon the cherubim and 6.32
them with g. evenly applied upon 6.35
the lampstands of pure g., five 7.49
the lamps, and the tongs, of g.; 7.49
incense, and firepans, of pure g.; 7.50
and the sockets of g., for the doors 7.50
the g., and the vessels, and stored 7.51
cedar and cypress timber and g., 9.11
hundred and twenty talents of g. 9.14
Ophir, and brought from there g., 9.28
and very much g., and precious 10.02
a hundred and twenty talents of g., 10.10
which brought g. from Ophir, brought 10.11
Now the weight of g. that came to 10.14
and sixty-six talents of g., 10.14
hundred large shields of beaten g.; 10.16
shekels of g. went into each 10.16
three hundred shields of beaten g.; 10.17
three minas of g. went into each 10.17
and overlaid it with the finest g. 10.18
drinking vessels were of g., 10.21
Forest of Lebanon were of pure g.; 10.21
Tarshish used to come bringing g., 10.22
present, articles of silver and g., 10.25
counsel, and made two calves of g. 12.28
the shields of g. which Solomon 14.26
gifts, silver, and g., and vessels. 15.15
silver and the g. that were left 15.18
to you a present of silver and g.; 15.19
'Your silver and your g. are mine; 20.03
to me your silver and your g., 20.05
and for my silver and my g., 20.07
of Tarshish to go to Ophir for g.; 22.48
silver, six thousand shekels of g., 2Ki 5.05
off silver and g. and clothing, 7.08
trumpets, or any vessels of g., 12.13
and all the g. that was found in 12.18
And he seized all the g. and silver, 14.14
the silver and g. that was found 16.08
of silver and thirty talents of g. 18.14
stripped the g. from the doors of 18.16
the g., the spices, the precious oil, 20.13
talents of silver and a talent of g. 23.33
the silver and the g. to Pharaoh, 23.35
silver and the g. of the people of 23.35
the vessels of g. in the temple of 24.13
What was of g. the captain of the 25.15
of the guard took away as g., 25.15
the shields of g. which were 1Ch 18.07
sent all sorts of articles of g., 18.10
the silver and g. which he had 18.11
that it weighed a talent of g., 20.02
shekels of g. by weight for the 21.25
a hundred thousand talents of g., 22.14
g., silver, bronze, and iron. 22.16
the weight of g. for all golden 28.14
the weight of g. for each lampstand 28.15
the weight of g. for each table for 28.16
and pure g. for the forks, the 28.17
of incense made of refined g., 28.18
the g. for the things of g., the 29.02
treasure of my own of g. and silver, 29.03
three thousand talents of g., 29.04

GOLD (cont.)
of the g. of Ophir, and seven 1Ch 29.04
g. for the things of g. and silver 29.05
and ten thousand darics of g., 29.07
made silver and g. as common in 2Ch 1.15
me a man skilled to work in g., 2.07
He is trained to work in g., 2.14
it on the inside with pure g. 3.04
and covered it with fine g., 3.05
stones. The g. was g. of Parvaim. 3.06
So he lined the house with g.— 3.07
six hundred talents of fine g. 3.08
one shekel to fifty shekels of g. 3.09
overlaid the upper chambers with g. 3.09
of wood and overlaid them with g. 3.10
And he made a hundred basins of g. 4.08
lamps of pure g. to burn before 4.20
lamps, and the tongs, of purest g.; 4.21
incense, and firepans, of pure g.; 4.22
the nave of the temple were of g. 4.22
the g., and all the vessels in the 5.01
talents of g. and brought it to 8.18
and very much g. and precious 9.01
a hundred and twenty talents of g., 9.09
who brought g. from Ophir, brought 9.10
Now the weight of g. that came to 9.13
and sixty-six talents of g., 9.13
land brought g. and silver to 9.14
hundred large shields of beaten g.; 9.15
of beaten g. went into each shield 9.15
three hundred shields of beaten g.; 9.16
shekels of g. went into each 9.16
and overlaid it with pure g. 9.17
six steps and a footstool of g., 9.18
drinking vessels were of g., 9.20
Forest of Lebanon were of pure g.; 9.20
Tarshish used to come bringing g., 9.21
articles of silver and of g., 9.24
the shields of g. which Solomon 12.09
showbread on the table of pure g., 13.11
gifts, silver, and g., and vessels. 15.18
took silver and g. from the 16.02
I am sending to you silver and g.; 16.03
g., and valuable possessions, 21.03
and vessels of g. and silver. 24.14
And he seized all the g. and silver, 25.24
for g., for precious stones, for 32.27
of silver and a talent of g. 36.03
of his place with silver and g., Ez 1.04
with g., with goods, with beasts, and 1.06
of them: a thousand basins of g., 1.09
thirty bowls of g., two thousand 1.10
all the vessels of g. and of silver 1.11
sixty-one thousand darics of g., 2.69
And the g. and silver vessels of 5.14
And also let the g. and silver 6.05
the silver and g. which the king 7.15
the silver and g. which you shall 7.16
with the rest of the silver and g., 7.18
silver and the g. and the vessels, 8.25
and a hundred talents of g., 8.26
twenty bowls of g. worth a thousand 8.27
bright bronze as precious as g. 8.27
silver and the g. are a freewill 8.28
silver and the g. and the vessels, 8.30
silver and the g. and the vessels 8.33
treasure a thousand darics of g., Neh 7.70
darics of g. and two thousand two 7.71
was twenty thousand darics of g., 7.72
also couches of g. and silver on a Est 1.06
or with princes who had g., Job 3.15
g. in the dust, and g. of Ophir among 22.24
and if the Almighty is your g., 22.25
tried me, I shall come forth as g. 23.10
and a place for g. which they 28.01
sapphires, and it has dust of g. 28.06
It cannot be gotten for g., 28.15
be valued in the g. of Ophir, 28.16
G. and glass cannot equal it, nor 28.17
be exchanged for jewels of fine g. 28.17
nor can it be valued in pure g. 28.19
"If I have made g. my trust, 31.24
or called fine g. my confidence; 31.24
a piece of money and a ring of g. 42.11
More to be desired are they than g., Ps 19.10
even much fine g.; sweeter also than 19.10
a crown of fine g. upon his head. 21.03
stands the queen in g. of Ophir. 45.09
silver, its pinions with green g. 68.13
may g. of Sheba be given to him! 72.15
forth Israel with silver and g., 105.37
Their idols are silver and g., 115.04
thousands of g. and silver pieces. 119.72
commandments above g., above fine g. 119.127
of the nations are silver and g., 135.15
and its profit better than g. Pro 3.14
knowledge rather than choice g.; 8.10
My fruit is better than g., even fine g., 8.19
Like a g. ring in a swine's snout is 11.22
To get wisdom is better than g.; 16.16
silver, and the furnace is for g., 17.03
There is g., and abundance of 20.15
favor is better than silver or g. 22.01
like apples of g. in a setting of 25.11
Like a g. ring or an ornament of g. 25.12
silver, and the furnace is for g., 27.21
silver and g. and the treasure of Ecc 2.08
We will make you ornaments of g., Sol 1.11
its back of g., its seat of purple; 3.10
His head is the finest g.; his locks 5.11
His arms are rounded g., set with 5.14
columns, set upon bases of g. 5.15
Their land is filled with silver and g., Is 2.07
of silver and their idols of g., 2.20
make men more rare than fine g., 13.12
and mankind than the g. of Ophir. 13.12
silver and do not delight in g. 13.17
of silver and his idols of g., 31.07
the g., the spices, the precious oil, 39.02
a goldsmith overlays it with g., 40.19
Those who lavish g. from the purse, 46.06
shall bring g. and frankincense, 60.06
far, their silver and g. with them, 60.09
Instead of bronze I will bring g., 60.17
deck yourself with ornaments of g., Jer 4.30
Men deck it with silver and g.; 10.04
from Tarshish, and g. from Uphaz. 10.09
What was of g. the captain of the 52.19
of the guard took away as g., 52.19
How the g. has grown dim, how the Lam 4.01
dim, how the pure g. is changed! 4.01
worth their weight in fine g., 4.02
and their g. is like an unclean Eze 7.19
silver and g. are not able to 7.19
you were decked with g. and silver; 16.13
jewels of my g. and of my silver, 16.17
and all precious stones, and g. 27.22
have gathered g. and silver into 28.04
and wrought in g. were your settings 28.13
to carry away silver and g., 38.13
The head of this image was of fine g., Dan 2.32
and the g., all together were 2.35
them all—you are the head of g. 2.38
the clay, the silver, and the g. 2.45
Nebuchadnezzar made an image of g., 3.01
the vessels of g. and of silver 5.02
praised the gods of g. and silver, 5.04
have a chain of g. about his neck, 5.07
have a chain of g. about your neck, 5.16
praised the gods of silver and g., 5.23
a chain of g. was put about his 5.29
loins were girded with g. of Uphaz. 10.05
vessels of silver and of g.; 11.08
he shall honor with g. and silver, 11.38

GOLD (cont.)

the treasures of g. and of silver, Dan 11.43
her silver and g. which they used Hos 2.08
silver and g. they made idols for 8.04
you have taken my silver and my g., Joe 3.05
Plunder the silver, plunder the g.! Nah 2.09
it is overlaid with g. and silver, Hab 2.19
nor their g. shall be able to Zep 1.18
and the g. is mine, says the LORD of Hag 2.08
and behold, a lampstand all of g., Zec 4.02
Take from them silver and g., 6.11
and g. like the dirt of the streets. 9.03
and test them as g. is tested. 13.09
g., silver, and garments in great 14.14
and refine them like g. and silver, Mal 3.03
g. and frankincense and myrrh. Mt 2.11
Take no g., nor silver, nor copper 10.09
one swears by the g. of the temple, 23.16
the g. or the temple that has made 23.17
temple that has made the g. sacred? 23.17
said, "I have no silver and g., Ac 3.06
to think that the Deity is like g., 17.29
no one's silver or g. or apparel. 20.33
builds on the foundation with g., 1Co 3.12
braided hair or g. or pearls or 1Ti 2.09
only vessels of g. and silver but 2Ti 2.20
covered on all sides with g., Heb 9.04
For if a man with g. rings and in Jas 2.02
Your g. and silver have rusted, and 5.03
precious than g. which though 1Pe 1.07
things such as silver or g., 1.18
decoration of g., and wearing of 3.03
to buy from me g. refined by fire, Rev 3.18
were what looked like crowns of g.; 9.07
and idols of g. and silver and 9.20
bedecked with g. and jewels and 17.04
cargo of g., silver, jewels and 18.12
bedecked with g., with jewels, and 18.16
measuring rod of g. to measure the 21.15
jasper, while the city was pure g., 21.18
the street of the city was pure g., 21.21

GOLDEN

a g. bell and a pomegranate, a Ex 28.34
a g. bell and a pomegranate, round 28.34
And two g. rings shall you make for 30.04
the g. altar, the anointing oil and 39.38
shall put the g. altar for incense 40.05
And he put the g. altar in the tent 40.26
he set the g. plate, the holy crown, Lev 8.09
And over the g. altar they shall Num 4.11
one g. dish of ten shekels, full of 7.14
one g. dish of ten shekels, full of 7.20
one g. dish of ten shekels, full of 7.26
one g. dish of ten shekels, full of 7.32
one g. dish of ten shekels, full of 7.38
one g. dish of ten shekels, full of 7.44
one g. dish of ten shekels, full of 7.50
one g. dish of ten shekels, full of 7.56
one g. dish of ten shekels, full of 7.62
one g. dish of ten shekels, full of 7.68
one g. dish of ten shekels, full of 7.74
one g. dish of ten shekels, full of 7.80
silver basins, twelve g. dishes, 7.84
the twelve g. dishes, full of 7.86
(For they had g. earrings, Ju 8.24
weight of the g. earrings that he 8.26
"Five g. tumors and five g. mice, 1Sa 6.04
box with the g. mice and the 6.11
it, in which were the g. figures, 6.15
These are the g. tumors, which the 6.17
also the g. mice, according to the 6.18
the g. altar, the g. table for the 1Ki 7.48
the g. calves that were in Bethel, 2Ki 10.29
of gold for all g. vessels for 1Ch 28.14
the weight of the g. lampstands and 28.15
for the g. bowls and the weight 28.17
plan for the g. chariot of the 28.18
And he made ten g. lampstands as 2Ch 4.07
the g. altar, the tables for the 4.19
with you the g. calves which 13.08
care for the g. lampstand that its 13.11
Drinks were served in g. goblets, Est 1.07
holds out the g. scepter that he 4.11
to Esther the g. scepter that was 5.02
held out the g. scepter to Esther, 8.04
with a great g. crown and a mantle 8.15
Out of the north comes g. splendor; Job 37.22
or the g. bowl is broken, or the Ecc 12.06
Babylon was a g. cup in the LORD's Jer 51.07
and worship the g. image that King Dan 3.05
worshiped the g. image which King 3.07
fall down and worship the g. image; 3.10
or worship the g. image which you 3.12
or worship the g. image which I 3.14
or worship the g. image which you 3.18
brought in the g. and silver 5.03
beside the two g. pipes from which Zec 4.12
having the g. altar of incense and Heb 9.04
contained a g. urn holding the 9.04
turning I saw seven g. lampstands, Rev 1.12
robe and with a g. girdle round 1.13
and the seven g. lampstands, the 1.20
among the seven g. lampstands. 2.01
with g. crowns upon their heads. 4.04
and with g. bowls full of incense, 5.08
at the altar with a g. censer; 8.03
saints upon the g. altar before 8.03
horns of the g. altar before God, 9.13
with a g. crown on his head, and a 14.14
breasts girded with g. girdles. 15.06
angels seven g. bowls full of the 15.07
in her hand a g. cup full of 17.04

GOLD-PLATED

images and your g. molten images. Is 30.22

GOLDSMITH

and a g. overlays it with gold, and Is 40.19
The craftsman encourages the g., 41.07
hire a g., and he makes it into a 46.06
craftsman and of the hands of the g.; Jer 10.09
every g. is put to shame by his 10.14
every g. is put to shame by his 51.17

GOLDSMITHS

the son of Harhaiah, g., repaired. Neh 3.08
one of the g., repaired as far as 3.31
Sheep Gate the g. and the merchants 3.32

GOLD-WOVEN

in her chamber with g. robes; Ps 45.13

GOLGOTHA

a place called G. (which means the Mt 27.33
place called G. (which means the Mk 15.22
which is called in Hebrew G. Jn 19.17

GOLIATH

Philistines a champion named G., 1Sa 17.04
G. by name, came up out of the ranks 17.23
"The sword of G. the Philistine, 21.09
him the sword of G. the Philistine." 22.10
slew G. the Gittite, the shaft of 2Sa 21.19
the brother of G. the Gittite, 1Ch 20.05

GOMER

G., Magog, Madai, Javan, Tubal, Meshech, Gen 10.02
The sons of G.: Ashkenaz, Riphath, and 10.03
G., Magog, Madai, Javan, Tubal, Meshech, 1Ch 1.05
The sons of G.: Ashkenaz, Diphath, and 1.06
G. and all his hordes; Bethtogarmah Eze 38.06
went and took G. the daughter of Hos 1.03

GOMORRAH

G., Admah, and Zeboiim, as far as Gen 10.19
the LORD destroyed Sodom and G. 13.10
king of Sodom, Birsha king of G., 14.02
the king of G., the king of Admah, 14.08
as the kings of Sodom and G. fled, 14.10
took all the goods of Sodom and G., 14.11
Sodom and G. is great and their 18.20
on Sodom and G. brimstone and fire 19.24
Sodom and G. and toward all the 19.28
overthrow like that of Sodom and G., Deu 29.23
Sodom, and from the fields of G.; 32.32
like Sodom, and become like G. Is 1.09
of our God, you people of G.! 1.10
like Sodom and G. when God overthrew 13.19
to me, and its inhabitants like G." Jer 23.14
As when Sodom and G. and their 49.18
Sodom and G. and their neighbor 50.40
as when God overthrew Sodom and G., Amo 4.11
Sodom, and the Ammonites like G., Zep 2.09
of Sodom and G. than for that town. Mt 10.15
like Sodom and been made like G." Rom 9.29
of Sodom and G. to ashes he 2Pe 2.06
just as Sodom and G. and the Jud 1.07

GONG

I am a noisy g. or a clanging 1Co 13.01

GOOD

And God saw that the light was g.; Gen 1.04
And God saw that it was g. 1.10
And God saw that it was g. 1.12
And God saw that it was g. 1.18
And God saw that it was g. 1.21
And God saw that it was g. 1.25
made, and behold, it was very g. 1.31
to the sight and g. for food, 2.09
of the knowledge of g. and evil. 2.09
and the gold of that land is g.; 2.12
knowledge of g. and evil you shall 2.17
"It is not g. that the man should 2.18
be like God, knowing g. and evil." 3.05
saw that the tree was g. for food, 3.06
one of us, knowing g. and evil; 3.22
shall be buried in a g. old age. 15.15
tender and g., and gave it to the 18.07
down over against him a g. way off, 21.16
we cannot speak to you bad or g. 24.50
his last and died in a g. old age, 25.08
you nothing but g. and have sent 26.29
flock, and fetch me two g. kids, 27.09
what g. will my life be to me?" 27.46
And Leah said, "G. fortune!" 30.11
"God has endowed me with a g. dowry; 30.20
Laban said, "G.! Let it be as 30.34
a word to Jacob, either g. or bad." 31.24
speak to Jacob neither g. nor bad.' 31.29
kindred, and I will do you g.,' 32.09
But thou didst say, 'I will do you g., 32.12
plump and g., were growing on one 41.05
growing on one stalk, full and g.; 41.22
swallowed up the seven g. ears. 41.24
The seven g. cows are seven years, 41.26
and the seven g. ears are seven 41.26
food of these g. years that are 41.35
This proposal seemed g. to Pharaoh 41.37
'Why have you returned evil for g.? 44.04
loaded with the g. things of Egypt, 45.23
and wept on his neck a g. while. 46.29
he saw that a resting place was g., 49.15
but God meant it for g., to bring 50.20
that land to a g. and broad land, Ex 3.08
for all the g. which the LORD had 18.09
him, "What you are doing is not g. 18.17
the owner of the pit shall make it g.; 21.34
a rash oath to do evil or to do g., Lev 5.04
shall make it g., life for life. 24.18
who kills a beast shall make it g.; 24.21
a g. for a bad, or a bad for a g.; 27.10
shall value it as either g. or bad; 27.12
shall value it as either g. or bad; 27.14
inquire whether it is g. or bad, 27.33
with us, and we will do you g.; Num 10.29
the LORD has promised g. to Israel." 10.29
whatever g. the LORD will do to us, 10.32
that they dwell in is g. or bad, 13.19
Be of g. courage, and bring some of 13.20
it out, is an exceedingly g. land. 14.07
to do either g. or bad of my own 24.13
you have spoken is g. for us to do.' Deu 1.14
The thing seemed g. to me, and I took 1.23
'It is a g. land which the LORD our 1.25
shall see the g. land which I 1.35
have no knowledge of g. or evil, 1.39
afraid of you. So take g. heed; 2.04
and see the g. land beyond the 3.25
"Therefore take g. heed to yourselves. 4.15
not enter the g. land which the 4.21
take possession of that g. land. 4.22
and houses full of all g. things, 6.11
is right and g. in the sight of 6.18
possession of the g. land which the 6.18
for our g. always, that he might 6.24
God is bringing you into a g. land, 8.07
God for the g. land he has given 8.10
test you, to do you g. in the end. 8.16
giving you this g. land to possess 9.06
I command you this day for your g.? 10.13
quickly off the g. land which the 11.17
you do what is g. and right in the 12.28
in all the g. which the LORD your 26.11
open to you his g. treasury the 28.12
in doing you g. and multiplying 28.63
before you this day life and g., 30.15
Be strong and of g. courage, 31.06
"Be strong and of g. courage; 31.07
said, "Be strong and of g. courage; 31.23
Be strong and of g. courage; Jos 1.06
you may have g. success wherever 1.07
and then you shall have g. success. 1.08
Be strong and of g. courage; 1.09
Only be strong and of g. courage." 1.18
do as it seems g. and right in 9.25
be strong and of g. courage; 10.25
Not one of all the g. promises 21.45
Take g. care to observe the commandment 22.05
Take g. heed to yourselves, therefore, 23.11
from off this g. land which the 23.13
of all the g. things which the 23.14
But just as all the g. things which 23.15
from off this g. land which the 23.15
from off the g. land which he has 23.16
you, after having done you g." 24.20
son of Joash died in a g. old age, Ju 8.32
for all the g. that he had done to 8.35
leave my sweetness and my g. fruit, 9.11
'If in g. faith you are anointing 9.15
if you acted in g. faith and honor 9.16
have acted in g. faith and honor 9.19
do to us whatever seems g. to thee; 10.15
When they were a g. way from the 18.22
do with them what seems g. to you; 19.24
it is no g. report that I hear the 1Sa 2.24
let him do what seems g. to him." 3.18
do to us whatever seems g. to you." 11.10
you in the g. and the right way. 12.23
said, "Do whatever seems g. to you." 14.36
to Saul, "Do what seems g. to you." 14.40
and the lambs, and all that was g., 15.09
speech, and a man of g. presence; 16.18
And this was g. in the sight of all 18.05
have been of g. service to you; 19.04
If he says, 'G.!' it will be well 20.07
to him as it shall seem g. to you.'" 24.04
for you have repaid me g., 24.17
reward you with g. for what you 24.19

GOOD (cont.)

woman was of g. understanding and 1Sa 25.03
Yet the men were very g. to us, 25.15
and he has returned me evil for g. 25.21
to all the g. that he has spoken 25.30
thing that you have done is not g. 26.16
to carry the g. news to their idols 31.09
And I will do g. to you because you 2Sa 2.06
And he said, "G.; I will make 3.13
house of Benjamin thought g. to do. 3.19
thought he was bringing g. news, 4.10
promised this g. thing to thy 7.28
Be of g. courage, and let us play 10.12
the LORD do what seems g. to him. 10.12
spoke to Amnon neither g. nor bad; 13.22
of God to discern g. and evil. 14.17
"See, your claims are g. and right; 15.03
him do to me what seems g. to him." 15.26
repay me with g. for this cursing 16.12
Ahithophel has given is not g." 17.07
to defeat the g. counsel of 17.14
king said, "He is a g. man, and comes 18.27
man, and comes with g. tidings." 18.27
"G. tidings for my lord the king! 18.31
do therefore what seems g. to you. 19.27
for him whatever seems g. to you." 19.37
for him whatever seems g. to you; 19.38
and offer up what seems g. to him; 24.22
are a worthy man and bring g. news." 1Ki 1.42
to the king, "What you say is g.; 2.38
said to me, 'What you say is g.; 2.42
I may discern between g. and evil; 3.09
teach them the g. way in which 8.36
has failed of all his g. promise, 8.56
and speak g. words to them when you 12.07
out of this g. land which he gave 14.15
if it seems g. to you, I will give 21.02
never prophesies g. concerning me, 22.08
not prophesy g. concerning me, 22.18
city, and shall fell every g. tree, 2Ki 3.19
and ruin every g. piece of land 3.19
and on every g. piece of land every 3.25
water, and felled all the g. trees; 3.25
This day is a day of g. news; 7.09
do whatever is g. in your eyes." 10.05
have done what is g. in thy sight." 20.03
LORD which you have spoken is g." 20.19
g. pasture, and the land was very 1Ch 4.40
to carry the g. news to their idols 10.09
"If it seems g. to you, and if it is 13.02
thanks to the LORD, for he is g.; 16.34
promised this g. thing to thy 17.26
Be of g. courage, and let us play 19.13
the LORD do what seems g. to him." 19.13
the king do what seems g. to him; 21.23
Be strong, and of g. courage. 22.13
that you may possess this g. land, 28.08
son, "Be strong and of g. courage, 28.20
Then he died in a g. old age, 29.28
"For he is g., for his steadfast 2Ch 5.13
teach them the g. way in which 6.27
"For he is g., for his steadfast 7.03
and speak g. words to them, then 10.07
conditions were g. in Judah. 12.12
did what was g. and right in the 14.02
never prophesies g. concerning me, 18.07
not prophesy g. concerning me, 18.17
Nevertheless some g. is found in 19.03
because he had done g. in Israel, 24.16
"The g. LORD pardon every one 30.18
who showed g. skill in the service 30.22
he did what was g. and right and 31.20
"Be strong and of g. courage. 32.07
and his g. deeds, behold, they are 32.32
and his g. deeds according to what 35.26
"For he is g., for his steadfast Ez 3.11
if it seem g. to the king, let 5.17
for the g. hand of his God was upon 7.09
Whatever seems g. to you and your 7.18
And by the g. hand of our God upon 8.18
our God is for g. upon all that 8.22
and eat the g. of the land, and 9.12
for the g. hand of my God was upon Neh 2.08
God which had been upon me for g., 2.18
their hands for the g. work. 2.18
thing that you are doing is not g. 5.09
Remember for my g., O my God, all 5.19
spoke of his g. deeds in my 6.19
g. statutes and commandments, 9.13
Thou gavest thy g. Spirit to 9.20
of houses full of all g. things, 9.25
enjoy its fruit and its g. gifts, 9.36
wipe not out my g. deeds that I 13.14
Remember me, O my God, for g. 13.31
do with them as it seems g. to you." Est 3.11
Yet all this does me no g., 5.13
we receive g. at the hand of God, Job 2.10
Hear, and know it for your g." 5.27
my eye will never again see g. 7.07
they flee away, they see no g. 9.25
countenance, and be of g. cheer,' 9.27
Does it seem g. to thee to oppress, 10.03
words with which he can do no g.? 15.03
of soul, never having tasted of g. 21.25
their houses with g. things— 22.18
thereby g. will come to you. 22.21
woman, and do no g. to the widow. 24.21
But when I looked for g., evil came; 30.26
determine among ourselves what is g. 34.04
say, "O that we might see some g.! Ps 4.06
deeds, there is none that does g. 14.01
is none that does g., no, not one. 14.03
I have no g. apart from thee." 16.02
G. and upright is the LORD; 25.08
O taste and see that the LORD is g.! 34.08
who seek the LORD lack no g. thing. 34.10
many days, that he may enjoy g.? 34.12
Depart from evil, and do g.; 34.14
They requite me evil for g.; 35.12
has ceased to act wisely and do g. 36.03
himself in a way that is not g.; 36.04
Trust in the LORD, and do g.; 37.03
Depart from evil, and do g.; 37.27
me evil for g. are my adversaries 38.20
adversaries because I follow after g. 38.20
Do g. to Zion in thy g. pleasure; 51.18
You love evil more than g., 52.03
for it is g., in the presence of 52.09
there is none that does g. 53.01
is none that does g., no, not one. 53.03
to thy name, O LORD, for it is g. 54.06
LORD, for thy steadfast love is g.; 69.16
Truly God is g. to the upright, to 73.01
But for me it is g. to be near God; 73.28
No g. thing does the LORD withhold 84.11
Yea, the LORD will give what is g., 85.12
art g. and forgiving, abounding in 86.05
It is g. to give thanks to the LORD, 92.01
For the LORD is g.; his steadfast 100.05
you with g. as long as you live so 103.05
they are filled with g. things. 104.28
thanks to the LORD, for he is g.; 106.01
thanks to the LORD, for he is g.; 107.01
the hungry he fills with g. things. 107.09
So they reward me evil for g., 109.05
steadfast love is g., deliver me! 109.21
a g. understanding have all those 111.10
thanks to the LORD, for he is g.; 118.01
thanks to the LORD, for he is g.; 118.29
for thy ordinances are g. 119.39
Teach me g. judgment and knowledge, 119.66
Thou art g. and doest g.; teach 119.68
It is g. for me that I was afflicted, 119.71
Be surety for thy servant for g.; 119.122

GOOD (cont.)
LORD our God, I will seek your g. Ps 122.09
Do g., O LORD, to those who are g., 125.04
Behold, how g. and pleasant it is 133.01
Praise the LORD, for the LORD is g.; 135.03
for he is g., for his steadfast 136.01
Let a g. man strike or rebuke me in 141.05
Let thy g. spirit lead me on a 143.10
The LORD is g. to all, and his 145.09
For it is g. to sing praises to our 147.01
justice and equity, every g. path; Pro 2.09
in the way of g. men and keep to 2.20
find favor and g. repute in the 3.04
Do not withhold g. from those to 3.27
for I give you g. precepts: do not 4.02
of the righteous ends only in g.; 11.23
diligently seeks g. seeks favor, 11.27
A g. man obtains favor from the 12.02
A g. wife is the crown of her 12.04
commended according to his g. sense, 12.08
words a man is satisfied with g., 12.14
but those who plan g. have joy. 12.20
but a g. word makes him glad. 12.25
of his mouth a g. man eats g., 13.02
G. sense wins favor, but the way of 13.15
A g. man leaves an inheritance to 13.22
and a g. man with the fruit of his 14.14
The evil bow down before the g., 14.19
who devise g. meet loyalty and 14.22
watch on the evil and the g. 15.03
and a word in season, how g. it is! 15.23
and g. news refreshes the bones. 15.30
leads him in a way that is not g. 16.29
If a man returns evil for g., 17.13
A cheerful heart is a g. medicine, 17.22
fine on a righteous man is not g.; 17.26
It is not g. to be partial to a 18.05
He who finds a wife finds a g. thing, 18.22
It is not g. for a man to be 19.02
G. sense makes a man slow to anger, 19.11
LORD, and false scales are not g. 20.23
A g. name is to be chosen rather 22.01
for it is g., and the drippings of 24.13
Partiality in judging is not g. 24.23
and a g. blessing will be upon them. 24.25
so is g. news from a far country. 25.25
It is not g. to eat much honey, so 25.27
To show partiality is not g.; 28.21
A g. wife who can find? She is 31.10
She does him g., and not harm, all 31.12
see what was g. for the sons of Ecc 2.03
they have a g. reward for their 4.09
have seen to be g. and to be 5.18
he does not enjoy life's g. things, 6.03
yet enjoy no g.—do not all go to 6.06
knows what is g. for man while he 6.12
A g. name is better than precious 7.01
Wisdom is g. with an inheritance, an 7.11
It is g. that you should take hold 7.18
earth who does g. and never sins. 7.20
for man has no g. thing under the 8.15
to the g. and the evil, to the clean 9.02
As is the g. man, so is the sinner; 9.02
but one sinner destroys much g. 9.18
or whether both alike will be g. 11.06
secret thing, whether g. or evil. 12.14
learn to do g.; seek justice, Is 1.17
you shall eat the g. of the land; 1.19
who call evil g. and g. evil, 5.20
refuse the evil and choose the g. 7.15
refuse the evil and choose the g., 7.16
of the rash will have g. judgment, 32.04
have done what is g. in thy sight." 38.03
LORD which you have spoken is g." 39.08
O Zion, herald of g. tidings; 40.09
herald of g. tidings, lift it up, 40.09
saying of the soldering, "It is g."; 41.07
do g., or do harm, that we may be 41.23
Jerusalem a herald of g. tidings. 41.27
feet of him who brings g. tidings, 52.07
who brings g. tidings of g., who 52.07
diligently to me, and eat what is g., 55.02
satisfy your desire with g. things, 58.11
me to bring g. tidings to the 61.01
who walk in a way that is not g., 65.02
enjoy its fruits and its g. things. Jer 2.07
but how to do g. they know not." 4.22
your sins have kept g. from you. 5.25
ancient paths, where the g. way is; 6.16
but no g. came, for a time of 8.15
neither is it in them to do g." 10.05
was spoiled; it was g. for nothing. 13.07
waistcloth, which is g. for nothing. 13.10
also you can do g. who are accustomed 13.23
looked for peace, but no g. came; 14.19
not entreated thee for their g., 15.11
and shall not see any g. come. 17.06
as it seemed g. to the potter to do 18.04
repent of the g. which I had 18.10
Is evil a recompense for g.? 18.20
before thee to speak g. for them, 18.20
this city for evil and not for g., 21.10
One basket had very g. figs, 24.02
said, "Figs, the g. figs very g., and 24.03
Like these g. figs, so I will regard 24.05
will regard as g. the exiles from 24.05
I will set my eyes upon them for g., 24.06
me as seems g. and right to you. 26.14
to see the g. that I will do to my 29.32
own g. and the g. of their children 32.39
turn away from doing g. to them; 32.40
I will rejoice in doing them g., 32.41
them all the g. that I promise 32.42
hear of all the g. that I do for 33.09
of all the g. and all the prosperity 33.09
LORD of hosts, for the LORD is g., 33.11
this city for evil and not for g., 39.16
If it seems g. to you to come with 40.04
you think it g. and right to go. 40.04
Whether it is g. or evil, we will 42.06
over them for evil and not for g.; 44.27
The LORD is g. to those who wait Lam 3.25
It is g. that one should wait 3.26
It is g. for a man that he bear the 3.27
Most High that g. and evil come? 3.38
transplanted it to g. soil by Eze 17.08
did what is not g. among his 18.18
that were not g. and ordinances by 20.25
all the g. pieces, the thigh and the 24.04
I will feed them with g. pasture, 34.14
shall lie down in g. grazing land, 34.14
for you to feed on the g. pasture, 34.18
will do more g. to you than ever 36.11
and your deeds that were not g.; 36.31
which I have made, well and g.; Dan 3.15
It has seemed g. to me to show the 4.02
be strong and of g. courage." 10.19
terebinth, because their shade is g. Hos 4.13
Israel has spurned the g.; 8.03
that which is g. and we will 14.02
Seek g., and not evil, that you may Amo 5.14
and love g., and establish justice 5.15
upon them for evil and not for g. 9.04
of Maroth wait anxiously for g., Mic 1.12
not my words do g. to him who 2.07
You who hate the g. and love the 3.02
He has showed you, O man, what is g.; 6.08
The LORD is g., a stronghold in the Nah 1.07
feet of him who brings g. tidings, 1.15
hearts, 'The LORD will not do g., Zep 1.12
you, for they are men of g. omen: Zec 3.08
days to do g. to Jerusalem and to 8.15
Yea, how g. and how fair it shall be 9.17
does evil is g. in the sight of Mal 2.17
What is the g. of our keeping his 3.14

GOOD (cont.)
does not bear g. fruit is cut down Mt 3.10
It is no longer g. for anything 5.13
may see your g. works and give 5.16
sun rise on the evil and on the g., 5.45
how to give g. gifts to your 7.11
in heaven give g. things to those 7.11
So, every sound tree bears g. fruit, 7.17
nor can a bad tree bear g. fruit. 7.18
does not bear g. fruit is cut down 7.19
the poor have g. news preached to 11.05
is lawful to do g. on the sabbath." 12.12
make the tree g., and its fruit g.; 12.33
how can you speak g., when you are 12.34
The g. man out of his g. treasure 12.35
brings forth g., and the evil man 12.35
Other seeds fell on g. soil and 13.08
As for what was sown on g. soil, 13.23
a man who sowed g. seed in his 13.24
did you not sow g. seed in your 13.27
"He who sows the g. seed is the Son 13.37
and the g. seed means the sons of 13.38
and sorted the g. into vessels but 13.48
what g. deed must I do, to have 19.16
"Why do you ask me about what is g.? 19.17
One there is who is g. If you would 19.17
whom they found, both bad and g.; 22.10
'Well done, g. and faithful servant; 25.21
'Well done, g. and faithful servant; 25.23
the sabbath to do g. or to do harm, Mk 3.04
seeds fell into g. soil and 4.08
sown upon the g. soil are the ones 4.20
Salt is g.; but if the salt has 9.50
"G. Teacher, what must I do to 10.17
said to him, "Why do you call me g.? 10.18
No one is g. but God alone. 10.18
you will, you can do g. to them; 14.07
it seemed g. to me also, having Lk 1.03
you, and to bring you this g. news. 1.19
filled the hungry with g. things, 1.53
I bring you g. news of a great joy 2.10
does not bear g. fruit is cut down 3.09
he preached g. news to the people. 3.18
me to preach g. news to the poor. 4.18
must preach the g. news of the 4.43
new; for he says, 'The old is g.'" 5.39
the sabbath to do g. or to do harm, 6.09
do g. to those who hate you, 6.27
do g. to those who do g. to you, 6.33
and do g., and lend, expecting 6.35
g. measure, pressed down, shaken 6.38
"For no g. tree bears bad fruit, nor 6.43
does a bad tree bear g. fruit; 6.43
The g. man out of the g. treasure of 6.45
treasure of his heart produces g., 6.45
the poor have g. news preached to 7.22
bringing the g. news of the 8.01
And some fell into g. soil and grew, 8.08
And as for that in the g. soil, 8.15
it fast in an honest and g. heart, 8.15
Mary has chosen the g. portion, 10.42
how to give g. gifts to your 11.13
your Father's g. pleasure to give 12.32
bears fruit next year, well and g.; 13.09
"Salt is g.; but if salt has 14.34
since then the g. news of the 16.16
lifetime received your g. things, 16.25
"G. Teacher, what shall I do to 18.18
said to him, "Why do you call me g.? 18.19
No one is g. but God alone. 18.19
to him, 'Well done, g. servant! 19.17
council, a g. and righteous man, 23.50
"Can anything g. come out of Jn 1.46
"Every man serves the g. wine first; 2.10
have kept the g. wine until now." 2.10
come forth, those who have done g., 5.29
"He is a g. man," others said, "No, he 7.12
I am the g. shepherd. The g. shepherd 10.11
I am the g. shepherd; I know my 10.14
shown you many g. works from the 10.32
you for no g. work but for blasphemy; 10.33
but be of g. cheer, I have overcome 16.33
concerning a g. deed done to a Ac 4.09
among you seven men of g. repute, 6.03
as he preached g. news about the 8.12
he told him the g. news of Jesus. 8.35
She was full of g. works and acts 9.36
preaching g. news of peace by Jesus 10.36
about doing g. and healing all 10.38
for he was a g. man, full of the 11.24
bring you the g. news that what 13.32
and bring you g. news, that you 14.15
for he did g. and gave you from 14.17
Then it seemed g. to the apostles 15.22
it has seemed g. to us in assembly 15.25
For it has seemed g. to the Holy 15.28
God in all g. conscience up to 23.01
peace for every one who does g., Rom 2.10
And why not do evil that g. may come? 3.08
no one does g., not even one." 3.12
which was as g. as dead because he 4.19
perhaps for a g. man one will dare 5.07
commandment is holy and just and g. 7.12
Did that which is g., then, bring 7.13
death in me through what is g., 7.13
want, I agree that the law is g. 7.16
that nothing g. dwells within me, 7.18
For I do not do the g. I want, 7.19
God works for g. with those who 8.28
had done nothing either g. or bad, 9.11
feet of those who preach g. news!" 10.15
what is g. and acceptable and 12.02
is evil, hold fast to what is g.; 12.09
by evil, but overcome evil with g. 12.21
are not a terror to g. conduct, 13.03
Then do what is g., and you will 13.03
for he is God's servant for your g. 13.04
not let what is g. to you be 14.16
neighbor for his g., to edify him. 15.02
as to what is g. and guileless as 16.19
Your boasting is not g. Do you not 1Co 5.06
but to promote g. order and to 7.35
have sown spiritual g. among you, 9.11
Let no one seek his own g., 10.24
but the g. of his neighbor. 10.24
of the Spirit for the common g. 12.07
"Bad company ruins g. morals." 15.33
So we are always of g. courage; 2Co 5.06
We are of g. courage, and we would 5.08
each one may receive g. or evil, 5.10
in ill repute and g. repute. 6.08
the Lord and to show our g. will. 8.19
in abundance for every g. work. 9.08
much of you, but for no g. purpose; Gal 4.17
For a g. purpose it is always g. to be 4.18
word share all g. things with him 6.06
let us do g. to all men, and especially 6.10
want to make a g. showing in the 6.12
in Christ Jesus for g. works, Eph 2.10
only such as is g. for edifying, 4.29
in all that is g. and right and 5.09
rendering service with a g. will as 6.07
knowing that whatever g. any one does, 6.08
he who began a g. work in you will Php 1.06
rivalry, but others from g. will. 1.15
and to work for his g. pleasure. 2.13
fruit in every g. work and increasing Col 1.10
to see your g. order and the 2.05
brought us the g. news of your 1Th 3.06
seek to do g. to one another and 5.15
everything; hold fast what is g., 5.21
fulfil every g. resolve and work 2Th 1.11
comfort and g. hope through grace, 2.16
them in every g. work and word. 2.17
heart and a g. conscience and 1Ti 1.05

GOOD (cont.)
Now we know that the law is g., 1Ti 1.08
them you may wage the g. warfare, 1.18
holding faith and a g. conscience. 1.19
This is g., and it is acceptable in 2.03
but by g. deeds, as befits women who 2.10
deacons gain a g. standing for 3.13
For everything created by God is g., 4.04
you will be a g. minister of Christ 4.06
and of the g. doctrine which you 4.06
be well attested for her g. deeds, 5.10
herself to doing g. in every way. 5.10
So also g. deeds are conspicuous; 5.25
Fight the g. fight of the faith; 6.12
you made the g. confession in the 6.12
Pilate made the g. confession, 6.13
are to do g., to be rich in g. deeds, 6.18
themselves a g. foundation for the 6.19
suffering as a g. soldier of 2Ti 2.03
which does no g., but only ruins 2.14
the house, ready for any g. work. 2.21
profligates, fierce, haters of g., 3.03
complete, equipped for every g. work. 3.17
I have fought the g. fight, I have 4.07
disobedient, unfit for any g. deed. Tit 1.16
they are to teach what is g., 2.03
all respects a model of g. deeds, 2.07
own who are zealous for g. deeds. 2.14
to apply themselves to g. deeds; 3.08
to apply themselves to g. deeds, 3.14
of all the g. that is ours in Phm 1.06
For g. news came to us just as to Heb 4.02
received the g. news failed to 4.06
to distinguish g. from evil. 5.14
priest of the g. things that have 9.11
a shadow of the g. things to come 10.01
one another to love and g. works, 10.24
and him as g. as dead, were born 11.12
but he disciplines us for our g., 12.10
neglect to do g. and to share what 13.16
with everything g. that you may do 13.21
Every g. endowment and every perfect Jas 1.17
By his g. life let him show his 3.13
full of mercy and g. fruits, 3.17
preached the g. news to you 1Pe 1.12
word is the g. news which was 1.25
Maintain g. conduct among the 2.12
may see your g. deeds and glorify 2.12
would love life and see g. days, 3.10
who revile your g. behavior in 3.16
as g. stewards of God's varied grace: 4.10
do not imitate evil but imitate g. 3Jn 1.11
He who does g. is of God; 1.11

GOOD-LOOKING
Now Joseph was handsome and g. Gen 39.06

GOODLY
she saw that he was a g. child, Ex 2.02
first day the fruit of g. trees, Lev 23.40
that g. hill country, and Lebanon.' Deu 3.25
give you, with great and g. cities, 6.10
and have built g. houses and live 8.12
mighty strength, or his g. frame. Job 41.12
places; yea, I have a g. heritage. Ps 16.06
dost meet him with g. blessings; 21.03
My heart overflows with a g. theme; 45.01
blameless will have a g. inheritance. Pro 28.10
olive tree, fair with g. fruit'; Jer 11.16

GOODNESS
make all my g. pass before you, and Ex 33.19
for all the g. that the LORD had 1Ki 8.66
let thy saints rejoice in thy g. 2Ch 6.41
heart for the g. that the LORD had 7.10
delighted themselves in thy great g. Neh 9.25
in thy great g. which thou gavest 9.35
Surely g. and mercy shall follow me Ps 23.06
I shall see the g. of the LORD in 27.13
O how abundant is thy g., which 31.19
satisfied with the g. of thy house, 65.04
in thy g., O God, thou didst provide 68.10
forth the fame of thy abundant g., 145.07
and the great g. to the house of Is 63.07
be radiant over the g. of the LORD, Jer 31.12
satisfied with my g., says the LORD." 31.14
LORD and to his g. in the latter Hos 3.05
that you yourselves are full of g., Rom 15.14
kindness, g., faithfulness, Gal 5.22
a lover of g., master of himself, Tit 1.08
but when the g. and loving kindness 3.04
order that your g. might not be by Phm 1.14
and have tasted the g. of the word Heb 6.05

GOODNESS'
me, for thy g. sake. O LORD! Ps 25.07

GOODS
took all the g. of Sodom and Gen 14.11
in Sodom, and his g., and departed. 14.12
Then he brought back all the g., 14.16
back his kinsman Lot with his g., 14.16
but take the g. for yourself." 14.21
Although you have felt through all my g., 31.37
you found of all your household g.? 31.37
Give no thought to your g., 45.20
took their cattle and their g., 46.06
his neighbor money or g. to keep, Ex 22.07
put his hand to his neighbor's g. 22.08
belonged to Korah and all their g. Num 16.32
their flocks, and all their g. 31.09
cattle and the g. in front of them. Ju 18.21
all kinds of g. of Damascus, forty 2Ki 8.09
g., clothing, and precious things, 2Ch 20.25
with g. and with beasts, besides Ez 1.04
with g., with beasts, and with 1.06
confiscation of his g. or for 7.26
our children, and all our g. 8.21
of Adar, and to plunder their g. Est 3.13
women, and to plunder their g., 8.11
may another seize his g.! Ps 109.08
we shall find all precious g., Pro 1.13
will give all the g. of his house. 6.31
When g. increase, they increase who Ecc 5.11
their curtains and all their g.; Jer 49.29
you because of your abundant g.; Eze 27.16
with you for your abundant g., 27.18
who have gotten cattle and g., 38.12
gold, to take away cattle and g., 38.13
among them plunder, spoil, and g. Dan 11.24
have looted his g. in the day of Ob 1.13
Their g. shall be plundered, and Zep 1.13
man's house and plunder his g., Mt 12.29
man's house and plunder his g., Mk 3.27
and of him who takes away your g., Lk 6.30
own palace, his g. are in peace; 11.21
will store all my grain and my g. 12.18
you have ample g. laid up for many 12.19
that this man was wasting his g. 16.01
with his g. in the house, not come 17.31
the half of my g. I give to the 19.08
possessions and g. and distributed Ac 2.45
of Thyatira, a seller of purple g., 16.14
who buy as though they had no g., 1Co 7.30
has the world's g. and sees his 1Jn 3.17

GOPHER
Make yourself an ark of g. wood; Gen 6.14

GORE
been accustomed to g. in the past, Ex 21.29
been accustomed to g. in the past, 21.36

GORES
"When an ox g. a man or a woman to Ex 21.28
If it g. a man's son or daughter, he 21.31
If the ox g. a slave, male or female, 21.32

GORGE
in the sides of the mouth of a g. Jer 48.28
and I will g. the beasts of the Eze 32.04

GORGED
it is g. with fat, with the blood of Is 34.06
the birds were g. with their flesh Rev 19.21

GORGEOUS
then, arraying him in g. apparel, Lk 23.11

GORGEOUSLY
those who are g. appareled and live Lk 7.25

GOSHEN
you shall dwell in the land of G., Gen 45.10
Joseph, to appear before him in G.; 46.28
and they came into the land of G. 46.28
up to meet Israel his father in G.; 46.29
you may dwell in the land of G.; 46.34
they are now in the land of G." 47.01
servants dwell in the land of G." 47.04
let them dwell in the land of G.; 47.06
land of Egypt, in the land of G.; 47.27
herds were left in the land of G. 50.08
I will set apart the land of G., Ex 8.22
Only in the land of G., where the 9.26
to Gaza, and all the country of G., Jos 10.41
all the land of G. and the lowland 11.16
G., Holon, and Giloh: eleven cities 15.51

GOSPEL
preaching the g. of the kingdom Mt 4.23
preaching the g. of the kingdom, 9.35
And this g. of the kingdom will be 24.14
wherever this g. is preached in the 26.13
beginning of the g. of Jesus Christ, Mk 1.01
Galilee, preaching the g. of God, 1.14
repent, and believe in the g." 1.15
lands, for my sake and for the g., 10.29
And the g. must first be preached 13.10
wherever the g. is preached in the 14.09
preaching the g. and healing Lk 9.06
in the temple and preaching the g., 20.01
preaching the g. to many villages Ac 8.25
he preached the g. to all the 8.40
and there they preached the g. 14.07
preached the g. to that city and 14.21
the word of the g. and believe. 15.07
called us to preach the g. to them. 16.10
testify to the g. of the grace of 20.24
set apart for the g. of God Rom 1.01
the g. concerning his Son, who was 1.03
my spirit in the g. of his Son, 1.09
to preach the g. to you also who 1.15
For I am not ashamed of the g.: 1.16
on that day when, according to my g., 2.16
But they have not all heeded the g.; 10.16
As regards the g. they are enemies 11.28
priestly service of the g. of God, 15.16
fully preached the g. of Christ, 15.19
it my ambition to preach the g., 15.20
according to my g. and the preaching 16.25
me to baptize but to preach the g., 1Co 1.17
in Christ Jesus through the g. 4.15
in the way of the g. of Christ. 9.12
proclaim the g. should get their 9.14
should get their living by the g. 9.14
For if I preach the g., that gives 9.16
to me if I do not preach the g.! 9.16
I may make the g. free of charge, 9.18
full use of my right in the g. 9.18
I do it all for the sake of the g., 9.23
terms I preached to you the g., 15.01
Troas to preach the g. of Christ, 2Co 2.12
And even if our g. is veiled, 4.03
light of the g. of the glory of 4.04
for his preaching of the g.; 8.18
in acknowledging the g. of Christ, 9.13
way to you with the g. of Christ. 10.14
may preach the g. in lands beyond 10.16
a different g. from the one you 11.04
preached God's g. without cost to 11.07
and turning to a different g.— Gal 1.06
not that there is another g., 1.07
want to pervert the g. of Christ. 1.07
preach to you a g. contrary to 1.08
to you a g. contrary to that which 1.09
that the g. which was preached by 1.11
was preached by me is not man's g. 1.11
of repute) the g. which I preach 2.02
truth of the g. might be preserved 2.05
with the g. to the uncircumcised, 2.07
with the g. to the circumcised 2.07
straightforward about the truth of the g., 2.14
preached the g. beforehand to 3.08
I preached the g. to you at first; 4.13
the g. of your salvation, and have Eph 1.13
in Christ Jesus through the g. 3.06
Of this g. I was made a minister 3.07
the equipment of the g. of peace; 6.15
to proclaim the mystery of the g., 6.19
partnership in the g. from the Php 1.05
defense and confirmation of the g. 1.07
really served to advance the g., 1.12
put here for the defense of the g.; 1.16
life be worthy of the g. of Christ, 1.27
by side for the faith of the g., 1.27
he has served with me in the g. 2.22
with me in the g. together with 4.03
that in the beginning of the g., 4.15
in the word of the truth, the g. Col 1.05
the hope of the g. which you heard, 1.23
for our g. came to you not only in 1Th 1.05
to you the g. of God in the face 2.02
by God to be entrusted with the g., 2.04
not only the g. of God but also 2.08
we preached to you the g. of God. 2.09
God's servant in the g. of Christ, 3.02
do not obey the g. of our Lord 2Th 1.08
To this he called you through our g., 2.14
the glorious g. of the blessed God 1Ti 1.11
suffering for the g. in the power 2Ti 1.08
immortality to light through the g. 1.10
For this g. I was appointed a 1.11
from David, as preached in my g., 2.08
the g. for which I am suffering and 2.09
during my imprisonment for the g.; Phm 1.13
For this is why the g. was preached 1Pe 4.06
who do not obey the g. of God? 4.17
with an eternal g. to proclaim to Rev 14.06

GOSPEL'S
my sake and the g. will save it. Mk 8.35

GOSSIP
the talk and evil g. of the people; Eze 36.03
slander, g., conceit, and disorder. 2Co 12.20

GOSSIPING
He who goes about g. reveals secrets; Pro 20.19

GOSSIPS
deceit, malignity, they are g., Rom 1.29
only idlers but g. and busybodies, 1Ti 5.13

GOT
and fled and g. out of the house. Gen 39.12
and fled and g. out of the house." 39.15
or what he g. by oppression, or the Lev 6.04
So they g. away from about the Num 16.27
they g. no spoils of silver. Ju 5.19
After this Absalom g. himself a 2Sa 15.01
Then he g. up again, and walked once 2Ki 4.35
Jehoiada g. for him two wives, and 2Ch 24.03
and g. relief from their enemies, Est 9.16

GOT (cont.)
which the Jews g. relief from Est 9.22
I g. singers, both men and women, and Ecc 2.08
And I g. reliable witnesses, Uriah Is 8.02
g. witnesses, and weighed the money Jer 32.10
he nor his army g. anything from Eze 29.18
yet he g. possession of the land; 33.24
and he g. down upon his knees three Dan 6.10
and he who g. possession of her. 11.06
And when he g. into the boat, his Mt 8.23
so that he g. into a boat and sat 13.02
So Peter g. out of the boat and 14.29
And when they g. into the boat, the 14.32
he g. into the boat and went to the 15.39
so that he g. into a boat and sat Mk 4.01
immediately the girl g. up and walked; 5.42
and g. there ahead of them. 6.33
And he g. into the boat with them 6.51
And when they g. out of the boat, 6.54
immediately he g. into the boat 8.10
One day he g. into a boat with his Lk 8.22
so he g. into the boat and returned. 8.37
returned, and she g. up at once; 8.55
g. into a boat, and started across Jn 6.17
they themselves g. into the boats 6.24
They went out and g. into the boat; 21.03
When they g. out on land, they saw a 21.09
and g. the better of you by guile. 2Co 12.16

GOTTEN
"I have g. a man with the help of Gen 4.01
persons that they had g. in Haran; 12.05
when I have g. glory over Pharaoh, Ex 14.18
such animals g. from a foreigner. Lev 22.25
of my hand have g. me this wealth.' Deu 8.17
It cannot be g. for gold, and silver Job 28.15
or because my hand had g. much; 31.25
and our enemies have g. spoil. Ps 44.10
congregation, which thou hast g. of old, 74.02
his holy arm have g. him victory. 98.01
Wealth hastily g. will dwindle, but Pro 13.11
An inheritance g. hastily in the 20.21
you have g. wealth for yourself, Eze 28.04
who have g. cattle and goods, who 38.12

GOUGE
that I g. out all your right eyes, 1Sa 11.02

GOUGED
seized him and g. out his eyes, and Ju 16.21

GOURDS
in the form of g. and open flowers; 1Ki 6.18
Under its brim were g., for thirty 7.24
the g. were in two rows, cast with 7.24
from it his lap full of wild g., 2Ki 4.39
Under it were figures of g., 2Ch 4.03
the g. were in two rows, cast with 4.03

GOVERN
us a king to g. us like all the 1Sa 8.05
they said, "Give us a king to g. us." 8.06
our king may g. us and go out 8.20
understanding mind to g. thy people, 1Ki 3.09
who is able to g. this thy great 3.09
said to him, "Do you now g. Israel? 21.07
Shall one who hates justice g.? Job 34.17
rule, and nobles g. the earth. Pro 8.16
ruler who will g. my people Israel.' " Mt 2.06

GOVERNING
household, g. the people of the land. 2Ki 15.05
household, g. the people of the land. 2Ch 26.21
be subject to the g. authorities. Rom 13.01

GOVERNMENT
and the g. will be upon his shoulder, Is 9.06
increase of his g. and of peace 9.07

GOVERNOR
Now Joseph was g. over the land; Gen 42.06
to Amon the g. of the city and to 1Ki 22.26
gate of Joshua the g. of the city, 2Ki 23.08
son of Ahikam, son of Shaphan, g., 25.22
Babylon had appointed Gedaliah g., 25.23
to Amon the g. of the city and to 2Ch 18.25
the g. of the house of Judah, in all 19.11
and Maaseiah the g. of the city, 34.08
the g. told them that they were not Ez 2.63
Tattenai the g. of the province 5.03
Tattenai the g. of the province 5.06
Sheshbazzar, whom he had made g.; 5.14
g. of the province Beyond the River, 6.06
let the g. of the Jews and the 6.07
the g. of the province Beyond the 6.13
jurisdiction of the g. of the Neh 3.07
to be their g. in the land of 5.14
ate the food allowance of the g. 5.14
the food allowance of the g., 5.18
Hananiah the g. of the castle 7.02
the g. told them that they were not 7.65
The g. gave to the treasury a 7.70
who was the g., and Ezra the priest 8.09
set their seal are Nehemiah the g., 10.01
of Nehemiah the g. and of Ezra the 12.26
appointed g. of the cities of Jer 40.05
the son of Ahikam g. in the land, 40.07
son of Shaphan, as g. over them, 40.11
had appointed g. in the land. 41.02
Babylon had made g. over the land. 41.18
g. of Judah, and to Joshua the son Hag 1.01
g. of Judah, and the spirit of 1.14
g. of Judah, and to Joshua the son 2.02
g. of Judah, saying, I am about to 2.21
Present that to your g.; Mal 1.08
and delivered him to Pilate the g. Mt 27.02
Now Jesus stood before the g.; 27.11
and the g. asked him, "Are you the 27.11
so that the g. wondered greatly. 27.14
the feast the g. was accustomed to 27.15
The g. again said to them, "Which of 27.21
soldiers of the g. took Jesus into 27.27
when Quirinius was g. of Syria. Lk 2.02
Pontius Pilate being g. of Judea, 3.01
authority and jurisdiction of the g. 20.20
who made him g. over Egypt and over Ac 7.10
bring him safely to Felix the g." 23.24
to his Excellency the g. Felix, 23.26
and delivered the letter to the g., 23.33
laid before the g. their case 24.01
And when the g. had motioned to him 24.10
and the g. and Bernice and those 26.30
the g. under King Aretas guarded 2Co 11.32

GOVERNOR'S
And if this comes to the g. ears, Mt 28.14

GOVERNORS
Arabia and from the g. of the land. 1Ki 10.15
servants of the g. of the districts." 20.14
servants of the g. of the districts, 20.15
The servants of the g. of the 20.17
servants of the g. of the districts, 20.19
Arabia and the g. of the land 2Ch 9.14
the g. of the people, and all the 23.20
the g., the officials, the Persians, Ez 4.09
associates the g. who were in the 5.06
associates the g. who are in the 6.06
and to the g. of the province 8.36
given me to the g. of the province Neh 2.07
Then I came to the g. of the 2.09
The former g. who were before me 5.15
the nobles and g. of the provinces Est 1.03
and to the g. over all the provinces 3.12
satraps and the g. and the princes 8.09
satraps and the g. and the royal 9.03
break in pieces g. and commanders. Jer 51.23

GOVERNORS (cont.)
with their g. and deputies, and Jer 51.28
her g., her commanders, and her 51.57
g. and commanders, all of them Eze 23.06
g. and commanders, warriors clothed 23.12
g. and commanders all of them, 23.23
and the g., the counselors, the Dan 3.02
and the g., the counselors, the 3.03
the g., and the king's counselors 3.27
counselors and the g. are agreed 6.07
dragged before g. and kings for my Mt 10.18
stand before g. and kings for my Mk 13.09
kings and g. for my name's sake. Lk 21.12
or to g. as sent by him to punish 1Pe 2.14

GOZAN
the river of G., and in the cities 2Ki 17.06
the river of G., and in the cities 18.11
G., Haran, Rezeph, and the people of 19.12
and the river G., to this day. 1Ch 5.26
G., Haran, Rezeph, and the people of Is 37.12

GRACE
and she found g. and favor in his Est 2.17
g. is poured upon your lips; Ps 45.02
the sword found g. in the wilderness; Jer 31.02
stone amid shouts of 'G., g. to it!'" Zec 4.07
one I named G., the other I named 11.07
And I took my staff G., and I broke 11.10
among us, full of g. and truth; Jn 1.14
have we all received, g. upon g. 1.16
g. and truth came through Jesus 1.17
and great g. was upon them all. Ac 4.33
full of g. and power, did great 6.08
When he came and saw the g. of God, 11.23
them to continue in the g. of God. 13.43
bore witness to the word of his g., 14.03
commended to the g. of God for the 14.26
through the g. of the Lord Jesus, 15.11
the brethren to the g. of the Lord. 15.40
those who through g. had believed, 18.27
to the gospel of the g. of God. 20.24
to God and to the word of his g., 20.32
have received g. and apostleship Rom 1.05
G. to you and peace from God our 1.07
they are justified by his g. as a gift, 3.24
may rest on g. and be guaranteed 4.16
access to this g. in which we 5.02
more have the g. of God and the 5.15
gift in the g. of that one man 5.15
abundance of g. and the free gift 5.17
increased, g. abounded all the more, 5.20
g. also might reign through righteousness 5.21
continue in sin that g. may abound? 6.01
you are not under law but under g. 6.14
we are not under law but under g.? 6.15
there is a remnant, chosen by g. 11.05
But if it is by g., it is no longer 11.06
otherwise g. would no longer be g. 11.06
For by the g. given to me I bid 12.03
according to the g. given to us, 12.06
because of the g. given me by God 15.15
The g. of our Lord Jesus Christ be 16.20
The g. of our Lord Jesus Christ *16.24
G. to you and peace from God our 1Co 1.03
because of the g. of God which was 1.04
But by the g. of God I am what I am, 15.10
and his g. toward me was not in 15.10
but the g. of God which is with me. 15.10
The g. of the Lord Jesus be with 16.23
G. to you and peace from God our 2Co 1.02
wisdom but by the g. of God. 1.12
so that as g. extends to more and 4.15
to accept the g. of God in vain. 6.01
about the g. of God which has been 8.01
For you know the g. of our Lord 8.09
of the surpassing g. of God in you. 9.14
"My g. is sufficient for you, for my 12.09
The g. of the Lord Jesus Christ and 13.14
G. to you and peace from God the Gal 1.03
you in the g. of Christ and 1.06
and had called me through his g., 1.15
perceived the g. that was given to 2.09
I do not nullify the g. of God; 2.21
you have fallen away from g. 5.04
The g. of our Lord Jesus Christ be 6.18
G. to you and peace from God our Eph 1.02
of his glorious g. which he freely 1.06
according to the riches of his g. 1.07
with Christ (by g. you have been 2.05
riches of his g. in kindness 2.07
For by g. you have been saved 2.08
of God's g. that was given to me 3.02
gift of God's g. which was given 3.07
this g. was given, to preach to the 3.08
But g. was given to each of us 4.07
it may impart g. to those who hear 4.29
G. be with all who love our Lord 6.24
G. to you and peace from God our Php 1.02
are all partakers with me of g., 1.07
The g. of the Lord Jesus Christ be 4.23
G. to you and peace from God our Col 1.02
understood the g. of God in truth, 1.06
Remember my fetters. G. be with you. 4.18
Jesus Christ: G. to you and peace. 1Th 1.01
The g. of our Lord Jesus Christ be 5.28
G. to you and peace from God the 2Th 1.02
according to the g. of our God and 1.12
comfort and good hope through g., 2.16
The g. of our Lord Jesus Christ be 3.18
G., mercy, and peace from God the 1Ti 1.02
and the g. of our Lord overflowed 1.14
as regards the faith. G. be with you. 6.21
G., mercy, and peace from God the 2Ti 1.02
purpose and the g. which he gave 1.09
strong in the g. that is in Christ 2.01
with your spirit. G. be with you. 4.22
G. and peace from God the Father Tit 1.04
For the g. of God has appeared for 2.11
justified by his g. and become 3.07
in the faith. G. be with you all. 3.15
G. to you and peace from God our Phm 1.03
The g. of the Lord Jesus Christ be 1.25
so that by the g. of God he might Heb 2.09
draw near to the throne of g., 4.16
mercy and find g. to help in time 4.16
and outraged the Spirit of g.? 10.29
one fail to obtain the g. of God; 12.15
the heart be strengthened by g., 13.09
G. be with all of you. Amen. 13.25
But he gives more g.; therefore Jas 4.06
proud, but gives g. to the humble." 4.06
May g. and peace be multiplied to 1Pe 1.02
prophesied of the g. that was to be 1.10
fully upon the g. that is coming 1.13
are joint heirs of the g. of life, 3.07
good stewards of God's varied g.: 4.10
proud, but gives g. to the humble." 5.05
a little while, the God of all g., 5.10
that this is the true g. of God; 5.12
May g. and peace be multipled to 2Pe 1.02
But grow in the g. and knowledge of 3.18
G., mercy, and peace will be with us, 2Jn 1.03
who pervert the g. of our God into Jud 1.04
G. to you and peace from him who is Rev 1.04
The g. of the Lord Jesus be with 22.21

GRACEFUL
a lovely hind, a g. doe. Let her Pro 5.19
How g. are your feet in sandals, O Sol 7.01
g. and of deadly charms, who betrays Nah 3.04

GRACIOUS
to me? God be g. to you, my son!" Gen 43.29
and I will be g. to whom I will be g., Ex 33.19
the LORD, a God merciful and g., 34.06

GRACIOUS (cont.)
shine upon you, and be g. to you: Num 6.25
"You are most g. to me, my lord, for Ru 2.13
whether the LORD will be g. to me, 2Sa 12.22
But the LORD was g. to them and had 2Ki 13.23
LORD your God is g. and merciful, 2Ch 30.09
g. and merciful, slow to anger and Neh 9.17
for thou art a g. and merciful God. 9.31
and he is g. to him, and says, Job 33.24
Be g. to me, and hear my prayer. Ps 4.01
Be g. to me, O LORD, for I am languishing; 6.02
Be g. to me, O LORD! Behold what 9.13
Turn thou to me, and be g. to me; 25.16
redeem me, and be g. to me. 26.11
be g. to me and answer me! 27.07
Hear, O LORD, and be g. to me! 30.10
Be g. to me, O LORD, for I am in 31.09
me, I said, "O LORD, be g. to me; 41.04
be g. to me, and raise me up, that I 41.10
Be g. to me, O God, for men trample 56.01
May God be g. to us and bless us 67.01
Has God forgotten to be g.? Has he in 77.09
be g. to me, O Lord, for to thee do I 86.03
O Lord, art a God merciful and g., 86.15
The LORD is merciful and g., slow to 103.08
the LORD is g. and merciful. 111.04
the LORD is g., merciful, and 112.04
G. is the LORD, and righteous; 116.05
be g. to me according to thy 119.58
Turn to me and be g. to me, 119.132
sing to his name, for he is g.! 135.03
The LORD is g. and merciful, slow to 145.08
his words, and g. in all his deeds. 145.13
for he is g., and a song of praise 147.01
A g. woman gets honor, and violent Pro 11.16
of heart, and whose speech is g., 22.11
Therefore the LORD waits to be g. to you; Is 30.18
will surely be g. to you at the 30.19
O LORD, be g. to us; we wait for 33.02
for he is g. and merciful, slow to Joe 2.13
will be g. to the remnant of Joseph. Amo 5.15
that thou art a g. God and merciful, Jon 4.02
LORD answered g. and comforting Zec 1.13
of God, that he may be g. to us. Mal 1.09
yea, Father, for such was thy g. will. Mt 11.26
wondered at the g. words which Lk 4.22
Father, for such was thy g. will. 10.21
complete among you this g. work. 2Co 8.06
you excel in this g. work also. 8.07
with us in this g. work which we 8.19
whatever is g., if there is any Php 4.08
Let your speech always be g., Col 4.06

GRACIOUSLY
whom God has g. given your servant." Gen 33.05
because God has dealt g. with me, 33.11
say to them, 'Grant them g. to us; Ju 21.22
g. freed Jehoiachin king of Judah 2Ki 25.27
from me; and g. teach me thy law! Ps 119.29
when he speaks g., believe him not, Pro 26.25
speaks more g. than the blood of Heb 12.24

GRAFT
has the power to g. them in again. Rom 11.23

GRAFTED
were g. in their place to share the Rom 11.17
off so that I might be g. in." 11.19
will be g. in, for God has the power 11.23
and g., contrary to nature, into a 11.24
branches be g. back into their own 11.24

GRAIN
earth, and plenty of g. and wine. Gen 27.28
and with g. and wine I have sustained 27.37
seven ears of g., plump and good, 41.05
and lay up g. under the authority 41.35
stored up g. in great abundance, 41.49
came to Egypt to Joseph to buy g., 41.57
learned that there was g. in Egypt, 42.01
heard that there is g. in Egypt; 42.02
go down and buy g. for us there, 42.02
went down to buy g. in Egypt. 42.03
go and carry g. for the famine of 42.19
orders to fill their bags with g., 42.25
asses with their g., and departed. 42.26
and take g. for the famine of your 42.33
had eaten the g. which they had 43.02
youngest, with his money for the g." 44.02
and ten she-asses loaded with g., 45.23
for the g. which they bought; 47.14
the stacked g. or the standing Ex 22.06
or the standing g. or the field is 22.06
crushed new g. from fresh ears, Lev 2.14
of the crushed g. and of the oil 2.16
bread nor g. parched or fresh 23.14
offering of new g. to the LORD. 23.16
the best of the wine and of the g., Num 18.12
it were the g. of the threshing 18.27
It is no place for g., or figs, or 20.05
offering of new g. to the LORD at 28.26
your g. and your wine and your oil, Deu 7.13
gather in your g. and your wine 11.14
tithe of your g. or of your wine 12.17
you shall eat the tithe of your g., 14.23
put the sickle to the standing g. 16.09
The first fruits of your g., of your 18.04
into your neighbor's standing g., 23.25
sickle to your neighbor's standing g. 23.25
an ox when it treads out the g. 25.04
who also shall not leave you g., 28.51
alone, in a land of g. and wine; 33.28
unleavened cakes and parched g. Jos 5.11
the standing g. of the Philistines, Ju 15.05
up the shocks and the standing g., 15.05
the ears of g. after him in whose Ru 2.02
and he passed to her parched g.; 2.14
down at the end of the heap of g. 3.07
tenth of your g. and of your 1Sa 8.15
an ephah of this parched g., 17.17
and five measures of parched g., 25.18
mouth, and scattered g. upon it; 2Sa 17.19
parched g., beans and lentils, 17.28
and fresh ears of g. in his sack. 2Ki 4.42
a land of g. and wine, a land of 18.32
abundance the first fruits of g., 2Ch 31.05
for the yeild of g., wine, and oil; 32.28
let us get g., that we may eat and Neh 5.02
houses to get g. because of the 5.03
are leanding them money and g. 5.10
g., wine, and oil which you have 5.11
in wares or any g. on the sabbath 10.31
shall bring the contribution of g., 10.39
the vessels, and the tithes of g., 13.05
Judah brought the tithe of g., 13.12
in heaps of g. and loading them on 13.15
as a shock of g. comes up to the Job 5.26
are cut off like the heads of g. 24.24
and bring your g. to your threshing 39.12
have when their g. and wine abound. Ps 4.07
thou providest their g., for so thou 65.09
valleys deck themselves with g., 65.13
be abundance of g. in the land; 72.16
and gave them the g. of heaven. 78.24
people curse him who holds back g., Pro 11.26
Where there are no oxen, there is no g.; 14.04
a pestle along with crushed g., 27.22
standing g. and his arm harvests Is 17.05
the ears of g. in the Valley of 17.05
your revenue was the g. of Shihor, 23.03
the LORD will thresh out the g., 27.12
Does one crush bread g.? No, he 28.28
and g., the produce of the ground, 30.23
a land of g. and wine, a land of 36.17
again give your g. to be food for 62.08
over the g., the wine, and the oil, Jer 31.12

GRAIN (cont.)
pile her up like heaps of g., Jer 50.26
will summon the g. and make it Eze 36.29
that it was I who gave her the g., Hos 2.08
I will take back my g. in its time, 2.09
and the earth shall answer the g., 2.22
for g. and wine they gash themselves, 7.14
The standing g. has no heads, it 8.07
because the g. is destroyed, the Joe 1.10
ruined because the g. has failed. 1.17
"Behold, I am sending to you g., 2.19
threshing floors shall be full of g., 2.24
moon be over, that we may sell g.? Amo 8.05
upon the g., the new wine, the oil, Hag 1.11
G. shall make the young men flourish, Zec 9.17
to pluck ears of g. and to eat. Mt 12.01
on good soil and brought forth g., 13.08
the plants came up and bore g., 13.26
is like a g. of mustard seed which 13.31
have faith as a g. of mustard seed, 17.20
disciples began to pluck ears of g. Mk 2.23
choked it, and it yielded no g. 4.07
good soil and brought forth g., 4.08
ear, then the full g. in the ear. 4.28
But when the g. is ripe, at once he 4.29
It is like a g. of mustard seed, 4.31
plucked and ate some ears of g., Lk 6.01
will store all my g. and my goods. 12.18
It is like a g. of mustard seed 13.19
had faith as a g. of mustard seed, 17.06
unless a g. of wheat falls into the Jn 12.24
heard that there was g. in Egypt, Ac 7.12
ox when it is treading out the g." 1Co 9.09
of wheat or of some other g. 15.37
ox when it is treading out the g., 1Ti 5.18

GRAINFIELDS
went through the g. on the sabbath; Mt 12.01
he was going through the g.; Mk 2.23
while he was going through the g., Lk 6.01

GRAINS
and your descendants like its g.; Is 48.19
the innumerable g. of sand by the Heb 11.12

GRANARIES
open her g.; pile her up like heaps Jer 50.26
the g. are ruined because the grain Joe 1.17

GRANARY
and gather his wheat into the g., Mt 3.12
to gather the wheat into his g., Lk 3.17

GRANDCHILDREN
and kissed his g. and his daughters Gen 31.55
G. are the crown of the aged, and Pro 17.06
If a widow has children or g., 1Ti 5.04

GRANDDAUGHTER
she was a g. of Omri king of Israel. 2Ki 8.26
name was Athaliah, the g. of Omri. 2Ch 22.02

GRANDFATHERS
your fathers nor your g. have seen, Ex 10.06

GRANDMOTHER
first in your g. Lois and your mother 2Ti 1.05

GRANDSON
his g., and Sarai his daughter-in-law, Gen 11.31
you and your son and your g. also; Ju 8.22
"He is the g. of Jehoshaphat, who 2Ch 22.09
serve him and his son and his g., Jer 27.07

GRANDSONS
He had forty sons and thirty g., Ju 12.14
bowmen, having many sons and g., 1Ch 8.40

GRANT
I g. you this favor also, that I Gen 19.21
g. me success today, I pray thee, and 24.12
may God Almighty g. you mercy 43.14
you shall g. a redemption of the Lev 25.24
seven years you shall g. a release. Deu 15.01
'G. them graciously to us; because Ju 21.22
The LORD g. that you may find a Ru 1.09
God of Israel g. your petition 1Sa 1.17
to Joab, "Behold now, I g. this; 2Sa 14.21
and g. rain upon thy land, which 1Ki 8.36
and g. them compassion in the sight 8.50
may the LORD g. you discretion and 1Ch 22.12
G. to Solomon my son that with a 29.19
and g. rain upon thy land, which 2Ch 6.27
but I will g. them some deliverance, 12.07
according to the g. which they had Ez 3.07
our eyes and g. us a little reviving 9.08
to g. us some reviving to set up 9.09
and g. him mercy in the sight of Neh 1.11
the king to g. my petition and Est 5.08
and that God would g. my desire; Job 6.08
Only g. two things to me, then I 13.20
May he g. you your heart's desire, Ps 20.04
O g. us help against the foe, for 60.11
O LORD, and g. us thy salvation. 85.07
O g. us help from the foe, for vain 108.12
G. not, O LORD, the desires of the 140.08
"Give counsel, g. justice; make your Is 16.03
to g. to those who mourn in Zion— 61.03
I will g. you mercy, that he may Jer 42.12
and at my left is not mine to g., Mt 20.23
whatever you wish, and I will g. it." Mk 6.22
"G. us to sit, one at your right 10.37
or at my left is not mine to g., 10.40
to g. us that we, being delivered Lk 1.74
and g. to thy servants to speak thy Ac 4.29
encouragement g. you to live in Rom 15.05
glory he may g. you to be strengthened Eph 3.16
and to g. rest with us to you who 2Th 1.07
May the Lord g. mercy to the 2Ti 1.16
may the Lord g. him to find mercy 1.18
the Lord will g. you understanding 2.07
God may perhaps g. that they will 2.25
conquers I will g. to eat of the Rev 2.07
I will g. him to sit with me on my 3.21
And I will g. my two witnesses 11.03

GRANTED
and the LORD g. his prayer, and Gen 25.21
the LORD your God g. me success." 27.20
"Thou hast g. this great deliverance Ju 15.18
the LORD has g. me my petition 1Sa 1.27
voice, and I have g. your petition." 25.35
the king has g. the request of his 2Sa 14.22
who has g. one of my offspring to 1Ki 1.48
me!" And God g. what he asked. 1Ch 4.10
and he g. their entreaty because 5.20
wisdom and knowledge are g. to you. 2Ch 1.12
and the king g. him all that he Ez 7.06
And the king g. me what I asked, Neh 2.08
He also g. a remission of taxes to Est 2.18
It shall be g. you. And what is 5.06
It shall be g. you. And what is 7.02
is your petition? It shall be g. you. 9.12
Thou hast g. me life and steadfast Job 10.12
desire of the righteous will be g. Pro 10.24
to all that the LORD has g. us, Is 63.07
which he has g. them according to 63.07
was dead, he g. the body to Joseph. Mk 15.45
And why is this g. me, that the Lk 1.43
that their demand should be g. 23.24
so he has g. the Son also to have Jn 5.26
the Father has g. me to accomplish, 5.36
me unless it is g. him by the 6.65
for a murderer to be g. to you, Ac 3.14
which God had g. to Abraham, the 7.17

GRANTED (cont.)
also God has g. repentance unto Ac 11.18
God has g. you all those who sail 27.24
the blessing g. us in answer to 2Co 1.11
For it has been g. to you that for Php 1.29
your prayers to be g. to you. Phm 1.22
power has g. to us all things that 2Pe 1.03
by which he has g. to us his 1.04
it was g. her to be clothed with Rev 19.08

GRANTING
g. signs and wonders to be done by Ac 14.03
But g. that I myself did not burden 2Co 12.16

GRAPE
the blood of the g. you drank wine. Deu 32.14
He will shake off his unripe g., Job 15.33
whether the g. blossoms have opened Sol 7.12
the flower becomes a ripening g., Is 18.05

GRAPE-GATHERER
like a g. pass your hand again over Jer 6.09

GRAPE-GATHERERS
If g. came to you, would they not Jer 49.09
If g. came to you, would they not Ob 1.05

GRAPES
and the clusters ripened into g. Gen 40.10
and I took the g. and pressed them 40.11
and his vesture in the blood of g.; 49.11
the fallen g. of your vineyard; Lev 19.10
and the g. of your undressed vine 25.05
nor gather the g. from the undressed 25.11
not drink any juice of g. or eat g., Num 6.03
the season of the first-ripe g. 13.20
branch with a single cluster of g., 13.23
you may eat your fill of g., Deu 23.24
When you gather the g. of your 24.21
of the wine nor gather the g.; 28.39
their g. are g. of poison, their 32.32
gleaning of the g. of Ephraim Ju 8.02
gathered the g. from their vineyards 9.27
g., figs, and all kinds of burdens, Neh 13.15
and he looked for it to yield g., Is 5.02
yield g., but it yielded wild g. 5.02
When I looked for it to yield g., 5.04
yield g., why did it yield wild g.? 5.04
there are no g. on the vine, nor Jer 8.13
and shout, like those who tread g., 25.30
'The fathers have eaten sour g., 31.29
each man who eats sour g., his teeth 31.30
'The fathers have eaten sour g., Eze 18.02
Like g. in the wilderness, I found Hos 9.10
the treader of g. him who sows the Amo 9.13
you shall tread g., but not drink Mic 6.15
Are g. gathered from thorns, or figs Mt 7.16
nor are g. picked from a bramble Lk 6.44
of the earth, for its g. are ripe." Rev 14.18

GRAPEVINE
nothing that is produced by the g., Num 6.04
brethren, yield olives, or a g. figs? Jas 3.12

GRASP
from the g. of the unjust and cruel Ps 71.04
the wind or to g. oil in his right Pro 27.16
you from the g. of the ruthless. Jer 15.21
and they did not g. what was said. Lk 18.34

GRASPED
And Samson g. the two middle Ju 16.29
Cyrus, whose right hand I have g., Is 45.01
when they g. you with the hand, you Eze 29.07
equality with God a thing to be g., Php 2.06

GRASS
fat, and they fed in the reed g. Gen 41.02
of the Nile and fed in the reed g.; 41.18
ox licks up the g. of the field." Num 22.04
And he will give g. in your fields Deu 11.15
where no g. can sprout, an overthrow 29.23
the gentle rain upon the tender g., 32.02
rain that makes g. to sprout from 2Sa 23.04
we may find g. and save the horses 1Ki 18.05
tender g., like g. on the housetops; 2Ki 19.26
offspring as the g. of the earth. Job 5.25
Does the wild ass bray when he has g., 6.05
to make the ground put forth g.? 38.27
I made you; he eats g. like an ox. 40.15
For they will soon fade like the g., Ps 37.02
like g. let them be trodden down 58.07
rain that falls on the mown g., 72.06
cities like the g. of the field! 72.16
like g. which is renewed in the 90.05
sprout like g. and all evildoers 92.07
is smitten like g., and withered; 102.04
shadow; I wither away like g. 102.11
As for man, his days are like g.; 103.15
Thou dost cause the g. to grow for 104.14
the image of an ox that eats g. 106.20
be like the g. on the housetops, 129.06
he makes g. grow upon the hills. 147.08
his favor is like dew upon the g. Pro 19.12
When the g. is gone, and the new 27.25
and as dry g. sinks down in the Is 5.24
the g. is withered, the new growth 15.06
the g. shall become reeds and 35.07
of the field and like tender g., 37.27
like g. on the housetops, blighted 37.27
All flesh is g., and all its 40.06
The g. withers, the flower fades, 40.07
upon it; surely the people is g. 40.07
The g. withers, the flower fades; 40.08
spring up like g. amid waters, 44.04
son of man who is made like g., 51.12
bones shall flourish like the g.; 66.14
and the g. of every field wither? Jer 12.04
calf because there is no g. 14.05
you are wanton as a heifer at g., 50.11
amid the tender g. of the field. Dan 4.15
the beasts in the g. of the earth; 4.15
in the tender g. of the field; 4.23
shall be made to eat g. like an ox, 4.25
shall be made to eat g. like an ox; 4.32
and ate g. like an ox, and his body 4.33
he was fed g. like an ox, and his 5.21
finished eating the g. of the land, Amo 7.02
the LORD, like showers upon the g., Mic 5.07
God so clothes the g. of the field, Mt 6.30
the crowds to sit down on the g.; 14.19
by companies upon the green g. Mk 6.39
so clothes the g. which is alive Lk 12.28
Now there was much g. in the place; Jn 6.10
flower of the g. he will pass away. Jas 1.10
scorching heat and withers the g.; 1.11
flesh is like g. and all its glory 1Pe 1.24
the flower of g. The g. withers, 1.24
up, and all green g. was burnt up. Rev 8.07
not to harm the g. of the earth or 9.04

GRASSHOPPER
and the g. according to its kind. Lev 11.22
the g. drags itself along and Ecc 12.05
the locust, multiply like the g.! Nah 3.15

GRASSHOPPERS
and we seemed to ourselves like g., Num 13.33
and its inhabitants are like g.; Is 40.22
Your princes are like g., your scribes Nah 3.17

GRATEFUL
Therefore let us be g. for receiving Heb 12.28

GRATIFY
for the flesh, to g. its desires. Rom 13.14
and do not g. the desires of the Gal 5.16

GRATING

You shall also make for it a g., Ex 27.04
with its g. of bronze, its poles, and 35.16
And he made for the altar a g., 38.04
of the bronze g. as holders for 38.05
and the bronze g. for it and all 38.30
and its g. of bronze, its poles, and 39.39

GRATITUDE

everywhere we accept this with all g. Ac 24.03

GRAVE

is great and their sin is very g., Gen 18.20
and Jacob set up a pillar upon her g.; 35.20
or a g., shall be unclean seven Num 19.16
the slain, or the dead, or the g.; 19.18
voice and wept at the g. of Abner; 2Sa 3.32
near the g. of my father and my 19.37
his head down with blood to the g." 1Ki 2.09
And he laid the body in his own g.; 13.30
bury me in the g. in which the man 13.31
of Jeroboam shall come to the g., 14.13
man was cast into the g. of Elisha; 2Ki 13.21
be gathered to your g. in peace, 22.20
be gathered to your g. in peace, 2Ch 34.28
are glad, when they find the g.? Job 3.22
come to your g. in ripe old age, as 5.26
carried from the womb to the g. 10.19
are extinct, the g. is ready for me. 17.01
When he is borne to the g., 21.32
straight to the g. they descend, Ps 49.14
like the slain that lie in the g., 88.05
steadfast love declared in the g., 88.11
death, jealousy is cruel as the g. Sol 8.06
And they made his g. with the Is 53.09
so my mother would have been my g., Jer 20.17
her company is round about her g.; Eze 32.23
and all her multitude about her g.; 32.24
I will make your g., for you are Nah 1.14
"Their throat is an open g., Rom 3.13

GRAVEL

his mouth will be full of g. Pro 20.17
He has made my teeth grind on g., Lam 3.16

GRAVEN

shall not make yourself a g. image, Ex 20.04
writing of God, g. upon the tables. 32.16
and erect no g. image or pillar, Lev 26.01
by making a g. image for yourselves, Deu 4.16
and make a g. image in the form of 4.23
by making a g. image in the form 4.25
not make for yourself a g. image, 5.08
and burn their g. images with fire. 7.05
The g. images of their gods you 7.25
hew down the g. images of their 12.03
man who makes a g. or molten image, 27.15
to make a g. image and a molten Ju 17.03
made it into a g. image and a 17.04
a g. image, and a molten image? 18.14
and entered and took the g. image, 18.17
house and took the g. image, 18.18
and the g. image, and went in the 18.20
set up the g. image for themselves; 18.30
set up Micah's g. image which he 18.31
and also served their g. images; 2Ki 17.41
And the g. image of Asherah that he 21.07
and the g. and the molten images. 2Ch 34.03
Asherim and the g. and the molten 34.04
lead they were g. in the rock for Job 19.24
to jealousy with their g. images. Ps 78.58
the idols whose g. images were Is 10.10
silver-covered g. images and your 30.22
other, nor my praise to g. images. 42.08
who trust in g. images, who say to 42.17
he makes it a g. image and falls 44.15
my g. image and my molten image 48.05
Behold, I have g. you on the palms 49.16
me to anger with their g. images, Jer 8.19
cut off the g. image and the molten Nah 1.14

GRAVES

there are no g. in Egypt that you Ex 14.11
of it upon the g. of the common 2Ki 23.06
it over the g. of those who had 2Ch 34.04
Their g. are their homes for ever, Ps 49.11
go away in terror into their g. 55.15
their g. round about her, all of Eze 32.22
whose g. are set in the uttermost 32.23
their g. round about her, all of 32.25
their g. round about them, all of 32.26
God: Behold, I will open your g., 37.12
you from your g., O my people; 37.12
I am the Lord, when I open your g., 37.13
you from your g., O my people. 37.13
you are like g. which are not seen, Lk 11.44

GRAVING

and fashioned it with a g. tool, Ex 32.04

GRAVITY

your teaching show integrity, g., Tit 2.07

GRAY

bring down my g. hairs with sorrow Gen 42.38
bring down my g. hairs in sorrow 44.29
bring down the g. hairs of your 44.31
child with the man of g. hairs. Deu 32.25
and I am old and g., and behold, 1Sa 12.02
So even to old age and g. hairs, Ps 71.18
beauty of old men is their g. hair. Pro 20.29
and to g. hairs I will carry you. Is 46.04
g. hairs are sprinkled upon him, and Hos 7.09
fourth chariot dappled g. horses. Zec 6.03

GRAYHAIRED

Both the g. and the aged are among Job 15.10

GRAZE

Then shall the lambs g. as in their Is 5.17
cattle will g. in large pastures; 30.23

GRAZED

a field or vineyard to be g. over, Ex 22.05

GRAZES

there the calf g., there he lies down, Is 27.10

GRAZING

shall lie down in good g. land, Eze 34.14

GREAT

And God made the two g. lights, Gen 1.16
wickedness of man was g. in the earth, 6.05
fountains of the g. deep burst 7.11
and Calah; that is the g. city. 10.12
And I will make of you a g. nation, 12.02
bless you, and make your name g., 12.02
his house with g. plagues because 12.17
possessions were so g. that they 13.06
g. sinners against the Lord. 13.13
your reward shall be very g." 15.01
a dread and g. darkness fell upon 15.12
shall come out with g. possessions. 15.14
the river of Egypt to the g. river, 15.18
and I will make him a g. nation. 17.20
shall become a g. and mighty 18.18
and Gomorrah is g. and their sin 18.20
of the house, both small and g., 19.11
has become g. before the Lord, and 19.13
have shown me g. kindness in 19.19
on me and my kingdom a g. sin? 20.09
Abraham made a g. feast on the day 21.08
for I will make him a g. nation." 21.18
my master, and he has become g.; 24.35
and a g. household, so that the 26.14
an exceedingly g. and bitter cry, 27.34

GREAT (cont.)
were too g. for them to dwell Gen 36.07
then can I do this g. wickedness, 39.09
seven years of g. plenty throughout 41.29
stored up grain in g. abundance, 41.49
will there make of you a g. nation. 46.03
a people, and he also shall be g.; 48.19
and horsemen; it was a very g. company. 50.09
with a very g. and sorrowful lamentation; 50.10
turn aside and see this g. sight, Ex 3.03
arm and with g. acts of judgment, 6.06
of Egypt by g. acts of judgment. 7.04
there came g. swarms of flies into 8.24
Moses was very g. in the land of 11.03
shall be a g. cry throughout all 11.06
and there was a g. cry in Egypt, 12.30
and they were in g. fear. And then the 14.10
And Israel saw the g. work which 14.31
every g. matter they shall bring to 18.22
and upon the g. toes of their right 29.20
but of you I will make a g. nation." 32.10
of Egypt with g. power and with a 32.11
have brought a g. sin upon them?" 32.21
people, "You have sinned a g. sin. 32.30
this people have sinned a g. sin; 32.31
hand and on the g. toe of his Lev 8.23
and on the g. toes of their right 8.24
the g. lizard according to its kind, 11.29
and on the g. toe of his right foot, 14.14
and on the g. toe of his right foot, 14.17
and on the g. toe of his right foot. 14.25
and the g. of his right foot, in 14.28
to the poor or defer to the g., 19.15
the people with a very g. plague. Num 11.33
we saw in it are men of g. stature. 13.32
of the LORD be g. as thou hast 14.17
And Moab was in g. dread of the 22.03
for I will surely do you g. honor, 22.17
Gad had a very g. multitude of 32.01
shall have the G. Sea and its 34.06
from the G. Sea you shall mark out 34.07
as far as the g. river, the river Deu 1.07
hear the small and the g. alike; 1.17
all that g. and terrible wilderness 1.19
the cities are g. and fortified up 1.28
going through this g. wilderness; 2.07
a people g. and many, and tall as 2.10
a people g. and many, and tall as 2.21
'Surely this g. nation is a wise 4.06
For what g. nation is there that 4.07
And what g. nation is there that 4.08
whether such a g. thing as this 4.32
and by g. terrors, according to all 4.34
earth he let you see his g. fire, 4.36
his own presence, by his g. power, 4.37
For this g. fire will consume us; 5.25
with g. and goodly cities, which you 6.10
g. and grievous, against Egypt and 6.22
the g. trials which your eyes saw, 7.19
midst of you, a g. and terrible God. 7.21
and throw them into g. confusion, 7.23
you through the g. and terrible 8.15
cities g. and fortified up to heaven, 9.01
a people g. and tall, the sons of 9.02
out by thy g. power and by thy 9.29
the g., the mighty, and the terrible 10.17
for you these g. and terrible 10.21
seen all the g. work of the LORD 11.07
the little owl and the g. owl, 14.16
or see this g. fire any more, lest I 18.16
a nation, g., mighty, and populous. 26.05
with g. terror, with signs and 26.08
the g. trials which your eyes saw, 29.03
the signs, and those g. wonders; 29.03
means the heat of this g. anger?' 29.24
in anger and fury and g. wrath, 29.28
and all the g. and terrible deeds 34.12
Lebanon as far as the g. river, Jos 1.04
Hittites to the G. Sea toward the 1.04
people shall shout with a g. shout; 6.05
the people raised a g. shout, 6.20
what wilt thou do for thy g. name?" 7.09
over him a g. heap of stones that 7.26
raised over it a g. heap of stones, 8.29
coast of the G. Sea toward Lebanon, 9.01
because Gibeon was a g. city, 10.02
them with a g. slaughter at Gibeon, 10.10
LORD threw down g. stones from 10.11
"Roll g. stones against the mouth 10.18
them with a very g. slaughter, 10.20
and they set g. stones against the 10.27
a g. host, in number like the sand 11.04
and chased them as far as G. Sidon and 11.08
with g. fortified cities: it may be 14.12
boundary was the G. Sea with its 15.12
and the g. sea with its coast-line. 15.47
numerous people, and have g. power; 17.17
Kanah, as far as Sidon the G.; 19.28
by the Jordan, an altar of g. size. 22.10
Jordan to the G. Sea in the west. 23.04
out before you g. and strong 23.09
who did those g. signs in our 24.17
and he took a g. stone, and set it 24.26
cut off his thumbs and his g. toes. Ju 1.06
and their g. toes cut off used to 1.07
seen all the g. work which the 2.07
there were g. searchings of heart. 5.15
there were g. searchings of heart. 5.16
Abelkeramim, with a very g. slaughter. 11.33
the cause of g. trouble to me; for I have 11.35
my people had a g. feud with the 12.02
hip and thigh with g. slaughter; 15.08
granted this g. deliverance by the 15.18
see wherein his g. strength lies, 16.05
me wherein your g. strength lies, 16.06
me wherein your g. strength lies. 16.15
to offer a g. sacrifice to Dagon 16.23
they made a g. cloud of smoke rise 20.38
had taken a g. oath concerning him 21.05
out of my g. anxiety and vexation." 1Sa 1.16
men was very g. in the sight of 2.17
"What does this g. shouting in the 4.06
and there was a very g. slaughter, 4.10
has also been a g. slaughter among 4.17
the city, causing a very g. panic, 5.09
is he who has done us this g. harm; 6.09
A g. stone was there; and they split 6.14
and set them upon the g. stone; 6.15
The g. stone, beside which they set 6.18
LORD had made a g. slaughter among 6.19
stand still and see this g. thing, 12.16
and see that your wickedness is g., 12.17
for his g. name's sake, because it 12.22
consider what g. things he has 12.24
and it became a very g. panic. 14.15
and there was very g. confusion. 14.20
the Philistines has not been g." 14.30
treacherously; roll a g. stone to me here." 14.33
wrought this g. victory in Israel? 14.45
"Has the LORD as g. delight in 15.22
king will enrich with g. riches, 17.25
Saul saw that he had g. success, 18.15
LORD wrought a g. victory for all 19.05
and made a g. slaughter among them, 19.08
and came to the g. well that is in 19.22
nothing either g. or small without 20.02
and made a g. slaughter among them. 23.05
the mountain, with a g. space between them; 26.13
Saul answered. "I am in g. distress; 28.15
who were in it, both small and g.; 30.02
of all the g. spoil they had taken 30.16
Nothing was missing, whether small or g., 30.19
a prince and a g. man has fallen 2Sa 3.38
and I will make for you a g. name, 7.09
the name of the g. ones of the 7.09
house for a g. while to come, 7.19

GREAT (cont.)
Therefore thou art g., O LORD God; 2Sa 7.22
doing for them g. and terrible 7.23
of the city, a very g. amount. 12.30
hated her with very g. hatred; 13.15
slaughter there was g. on that day, 18.07
the thick branches of a g. oak, 18.09
him into a g. pit in the forest, 18.17
over him a very g. heap of stones; 18.17
I saw a g. tumult, but I do not know 18.29
were at the g. stone which is in 20.08
there was a man of g. stature, who had 21.20
salvation, and thy help made me g. 22.36
G. triumphs he gives to his king, 22.51
LORD wrought a g. victory that day; 23.10
and the LORD wrought a g. victory. 23.12
man of Kabzeel, a doer of g. deeds; 23.20
said to Gad, "I am in g. distress; 24.14
of the LORD, for his mercy is g.; 24.14
pipes, and rejoicing with g. joy, 1Ki 1.40
for that was the g. high place; 3.04
"Thou hast shown g. and steadfast 3.06
for him this g. and steadfast love, 3.06
a g. people, that cannot be numbered 3.08
able to govern this thy g. people?" 3.09
sixty g. cities with walls and 4.13
wise son to be over this g. people." 5.07
command, they quarried out g., 5.17
house of the LORD to the g. court. 7.09
The g. court had three courses of 7.12
(for they shall hear of thy g. name, 8.42
a g. assembly, from the entrance of 8.65
Jersualem with a very g. retinue, 10.02
and a very g. quantity of spices, 10.10
Ophir a very g. amount of almug 10.11
The king also made a g. ivory throne, 10.18
And Hadad found g. favor in the 11.19
as g. as would contain two measures 18.32
and wind, and there was a g. rain. 18.45
the journey will be too g. for you." 19.07
and a g. and strong wind rent the 19.11
you seen all this g. multitude? Behold 20.13
the Syrians with a g. slaughter. 20.21
give all this g. multitude into 20.28
"Fight with neither small nor g., 22.31
And there came g. wrath upon Israel; 2Ki 3.27
"Set on the g. pot, and boil pottage 4.38
was a g. man with his master and in 5.01
commanded you to do some g. thing, 5.13
horses and chariots and a g. army; 6.14
So he prepared for them a g. feast; 6.23
And there was a g. famine in Samaria, 6.25
of horses, the sound of a g. army, 7.06
"Tell me all the g. things that 8.04
that he should do this g. thing?" 8.13
were with the g. men of the city, 10.06
all his g. men, and his familiar 10.11
for I have a g. sacrifice to offer 10.19
"Upon the g. altar burn the morning 16.15
LORD and made them commit g. sin. 17.21
of Egypt with g. power and with an 17.36
Rabshakeh with a g. army from Lachish 18.17
Hezekiah, 'Thus says the g. king, 18.19
"Hear the word of the g. king, 18.28
for g. is the wrath of the LORD 22.13
all the people, both small and g.; 23.02
the fierceness of his g. wrath, 23.26
every g. house he burned down. 25.09
Then all the people, both small and g., 25.26
LORD saved them by a g. victory. 1Ch 11.14
man of Kabzeel. a doer of g. deeds; 11.22
a man of g. stature, five cubits 11.23
him, until there was a g. army, 12.22
For g. is the LORD, and greatly to 16.25
the name of the g. ones of the 17.08
house for a g. while to come, and hast 17.17
making known all these g. things. 17.19
a name for g. and terrible things, 17.21
the spoil of the city, a very g. amount. 20.02
there was a man of g. stature, who had 20.06
said to Gad, "I am in g. distress; 21.13
the LORD, for his mercy is very g.; 21.13
David also provided g. stores of 22.03
Tyrians brought g. quantities of 22.04
materials in g. quantity before 22.05
much blood and have waged g. wars; 22.08
With g. pains I have provided for 22.14
small and g., teacher and pupil 25.08
for they were men of g. ability. 26.06
small and g. alike, for their gates. 26.13
made and men of g. ability among 26.31
inexperienced, and the work is g.; 29.01
besides g. quantities of onyx and 29.02
it is to make g. and to give strength 29.12
LORD on that day with g. gladness. 29.22
gave Solomon g. repute in the sight 29.25
him and made him exceedingly g. 2Ch 1.01
"Thou hast shown g. and steadfast 1.08
this thy people, that is so g.?" 1.10
which I am to build will be g., 2.05
to build will be g. and wonderful. 2.09
and the g. court, and doors for the 4.09
all these things in g. quantities, 4.18
for the sake of thy g. name, 6.32
a very g. congregation, from the 7.08
having a very g. retinue and camels 9.01
and a very g. quantity of spices, 9.09
The king also made a g. ivory throne, 9.17
you are a g. multitude and have 13.08
slew them with a g. slaughter; 13.17
for g. disturbances afflicted all 15.05
for g. numbers had deserted to him 15.09
made a very g. fire in his honor. 16.14
and he had g. riches and honor. 17.05
and he had g. stores in the cities 17.13
Now Jehoshaphat had g. riches and 18.01
"Fight with neither small nor g., 18.30
"A g. multitude is coming against 20.02
against this g. multitude that is 20.12
not dismayed at this g. multitude; 20.15
they found cattle in g. numbers, 20.25
Their father gave them g. gifts, 21.03
will bring a g. plague on your 21.14
disease, and he died in g. agony. 21.19
into their hand a very g. army, 24.24
to shoot arrows and g. stones. 26.15
took captive a g. number of his 28.05
who defeated him with g. slaughter. 28.05
For our guilt is already g., 28.13
Besides the g. number of burnt 29.35
not kept it in g. numbers as 30.05
second month, a very g. assembly. 30.13
bread seven days with g. gladness; 30.21
sanctified themselves in g. numbers. 30.24
So there was g. joy in Jerusalem, 30.26
so that we have this g. store left." 31.10
A g. many people were gathered, and 32.04
had very g. riches and honor; and he made 32.27
had given him very g. possessions. 32.29
and raised it to a very g. height; 33.14
for g. is the wrath of the LORD 34.21
all the people both g. and small; 34.30
g. and small, and the treasures of 36.18
the people shouted with a g. shout, Ez 3.11
the people shouted with a g. shout, 3.13
whom the g. and noble Osnappar deported 4.10
Judah, to the house of the g. God. 5.08
which a g. king of Israel built and 5.11
courses of g. stones and one course of 6.04
this day we have been in g. guilt; 9.07
evil deeds and for our g. guilt, 9.13
a very g. assembly of men, women, and 10.01
exile are in g. trouble and shame; Neh 1.03
the g. and terrible God who keeps 1.05

GREAT (cont.)

redeemed by thy g. power and by Neh 1.10
opposite the g. projecting tower 3.27
who is g. and terrible, and fight 4.14
"The work is g. and widely spread, 4.19
Now there arose a g. outcry of the 5.01
And I held a g. assembly against 5.07
"I am doing a g. work and I cannot 6.03
and Ezra blessed the LORD, the g. God; 8.06
portions and to make g. rejoicing, 8.12
And there was very g. rejoicing. 8.17
and had committed g. blasphemies, 9.18
thou in thy g. mercies didst not 9.19
delighted themselves in thy g. goodness. 9.25
and they committed g. blasphemies. 9.26
according to thy g. mercies thou 9.27
Nevertheless in thy g. mercies thou 9.31
the g. and mighty and terrible God, 9.32
and in thy g. goodness which thou 9.35
pleasure, and we are in g. distress." 9.37
appointed two g. companies which 12.31
And they offered g. sacrifices that 12.43
had made them rejoice with g. joy; 12.43
and do all this g. evil and act 13.27
both g. and small, a banquet lasting Est 1.05
Then the king gave a g. banquet to 2.18
there was g. mourning among the 4.03
with a g. golden crown and a mantle 8.15
For Mordecai was g. in the king's 9.04
and he was g. among the Jews and 10.03
and behold, a g. wind came across Job 1.19
saw that his suffering was very g. 2.13
The small and the g. are there, 3.19
who does g. things and unsearchable, 5.09
words of your mouth be a g. wind? 8.02
your latter days will be very g. 8.07
who does g. things beyond understanding, 9.10
He makes nations g., and he destroys 12.23
Is not your wickedness g.? There is no 22.05
rejoiced because my wealth was g., 31.25
because I stood in g. fear of the 31.34
Behold, God is g., and we know him 36.26
he does g. things which we cannot 37.05
he is g. in power and justice, and 37.23
and the number of your days is g.! 38.21
on him because his strength is g., 39.11
the tongue that makes g. boasts, Ps 12.03
There they shall be in g. terror, 14.05
me, and thy help made me g. 18.35
G. triumphs he gives to his king, 18.50
in keeping them there is g. reward. 19.11
and innocent of g. transgression. 19.13
His glory is g. through thy help; 21.05
my praise in the g. congregation; 22.25
pardon my guilt, for it is g. 25.11
in the g. congregation I will bless 26.12
distress, in the rush of g. waters, 32.06
A king is not saved by his g. army; 33.16
not delivered by his g. strength. 33.16
and by its g. might it cannot save. 33.17
thank thee in the g. congregation; 35.18
"G. is the LORD, who delights in the 35.27
thy judgments are like the g. deep; 36.06
deliverance in the g. congregation; 40.09
faithfulness from the g. congregation. 40.10
say continually, "G. is the LORD!" 40.16
is terrible, a g. king over all the earth. 47.02
G. is the LORD and greatly to be 48.01
far north, the city of the g. King. 48.02
in g. terror, in terror such as has 53.05
steadfast love is g. to the heavens, 57.10
So g. is thy power that thy enemies 66.03
g. is the host of those who bore 68.11
"Bless God in the g. congregation, 68.26
salvation say evermore, "God is g.!" 70.04
Thou who hast done g. things, O God, 71.19
is known, his name is g. in Israel. 76.01
is holy. What god is g. like our God? 77.13
thy path through the g. waters; 77.19
according to thy g. power preserve 79.11
For thou art g. and doest wondrous 86.10
For g. is thy steadfast love toward 86.13
g. and terrible above all that are 89.07
How g. are thy works, O LORD! Thy thoughts 92.05
For the LORD is a g. God, and a g. King 95.03
For g. is the LORD, and greatly to 96.04
The LORD is g. in Zion; he is exalted 99.02
Let them praise thy g. and terrible 99.03
so g. is his steadfast love toward 103.11
O LORD my God, thou art very g.! 104.01
g. and wide, which teems with things 104.25
living things both small and g. 104.25
who had done g. things in Egypt, 106.21
doing business on the g. waters; 107.23
steadfast love is g. above the 108.04
I will give g. thanks to the LORD; 109.30
G. are the works of the LORD, studied 111.02
fear the LORD, both small and g. 115.13
For g. is his steadfast love toward 117.02
G. is thy mercy, O LORD; give me life 119.156
word like one who finds g. spoil. 119.162
G. peace have those who love thy 119.165
LORD has done g. things for them." 126.02
The LORD has done g. things for us; 126.03
with things too g. and too marvelous 131.01
For I know that the LORD is g., 135.05
to him who alone does g. wonders, 136.04
to him who made the g. lights, 136.07
to him who smote g. kings, 136.17
for g. is the glory of the LORD. 138.05
G. is our LORD, and greatly to be 145.03
G. is our LORD, and abundant in 147.05
because of his g. folly he is lost. Pro 5.23
who plays the g. man but lacks 12.09
to be poor, yet has g. wealth. 13.07
slow to anger has g. understanding, 14.29
the LORD then g. treasure and trouble 15.16
righteousness than g. revenues with 16.08
him and brings him before g. men. 18.16
A man of g. wrath will pay the 19.19
to be chosen rather than g. riches, 22.01
or stand in the place of the g.; 25.06
righteous triumph, there is g. glory; 28.12
myself, "I have acquired g. wisdom, Ecc 1.16
my mind has had g. experience of 1.16
I made g. works; I built houses, 2.04
I had also g. possessions of herds 2.07
So I became g. and surpassed all 2.09
this also is vanity and a g. evil. 2.21
the sun, and it seemed g. to me. 9.13
and a g. king came against it and 9.14
building g. siegeworks against it. 9.14
will make amends for g. offences. 10.04
arranging proverbs with g. care. 12.09
With g. delight I sat in his shadow, Sol 2.03
in darkness have seen a g. light; Is 9.02
the g. in height will be hewn down, 10.33
for g. in your midst is the Holy 12.06
the mountains as of a g. multitude! 13.04
in spite of all his g. multitude, 16.14
his hard and g. and strong sword 27.01
And in that day a g. trumpet will 27.13
and with earthquake and g. noise, 29.06
in the day of the g. slaughter, 30.25
the shade of a g. rock in a weary 32.02
a g. slaughter in the land of Edom. 34.06
at Jerusalem, with a g. army. And he stood 36.02
Hezekiah, 'Thus says the g. king, 36.04
"Hear the words of the g. king, 36.13
welfare that I had g. bitterness; 38.17
sorceries and the g. power of your 47.09
the sea, the waters of the g. deep; 51.10
divide him a portion with the g., 53.12
but with g. compassion I will 54.07
and g. shall be the prosperity of 54.13

GREAT (cont.)

like this day, g. beyond measure." Is 56.12
and the g. goodness to the house of 63.07
from the north, and g. destruction. Jer 4.06
I will go to the g., 5.05
are many, their apostasies are g. 5.06
they have become g. and rich, 5.27
of the north, and g. destruction. 6.01
a g. nation is stirring from the 6.22
thou art g., and thy name is g. 10.06
a g. commotion out of the north 10.22
the roar of a g. tempest he will 11.16
Judah and the g. pride of Jerusalem. 13.09
people is smitten with a g. wound, 14.17
Both g. and small shall die in this 16.06
all this g. evil against us? What is our 16.10
my grave, and her womb for ever g. 20.17
in anger, and in fury, and in g. wrath. 21.05
they shall die of a g. pestilence. 21.06
LORD dealt thus with this g. city?" 22.08
build myself a g. house with spacious 22.14
nations and g. kings shall make slaves 25.14
and a g. tempest is stirring from 25.32
about to bring g. evil upon ourselves." 26.19
"It is I who by my g. power and my 27.05
nations and g. kings shall make 27.07
many countries and g. kingdoms. 28.08
that day is so g. there is none 30.07
foe, because your guilt is g., 30.14
Because your guilt is g., because your sins 30.15
a g. company, they shall return here. 31.08
earth by thy g. power and by thy 32.17
O g. and mighty God whose name is 32.18
g. in counsel and mighty in deed; 32.19
outstretched arm, and with g. terror; 32.21
and my wrath and in g. indignation; 32.37
all this g. evil upon this people, 32.42
will tell you g. and hidden things 33.03
for g. is the anger and wrath that 36.07
and summer fruits in g. abundance. 40.12
upon him at the g. pool which is 41.12
you commit this g. evil against 44.07
a g. assembly, all the people who 44.15
Behold, I have sworn by my g. name, 44.26
And do you seek g. things for 45.05
'Desolation and g. destruction!' 48.03
Babylon a company of g. nations, 50.09
is in the land, and g. destruction! 50.22
The noise of g. destruction from 51.54
every g. house he burned down. 52.13
she that was g. among the nations! Lam 1.01
every morning; g. is thy faithfulness. 3.23
and a g. cloud, with brightness Eze 1.04
me the sound of a g. earthquake; 3.12
that sounded like a g. earthquake. 3.13
the g. abominations that the house 8.06
Israel and Judah is exceedingly g.; 9.09
g. hailstones will fall, and a stormy 13.11
and g. hailstones in wrath to destroy it. 13.13
A g. eagle with g. wings and long 17.03
was another g. eagle with g. wings 17.07
mighty army and g. company will 17.17
is the sword for the g. slaughter, 21.14
city! I also will make the pile g. 24.09
I will execute g. vengeance upon 25.17
deep over you, and the g. waters cover you, 26.19
because of your g. wealth of every 27.12
because of your g. wealth of every 27.18
by your g. wisdom in trade you have 28.05
the g. dragon that lies in the midst 29.03
Pelusium shall be in g. agony; Thebes 30.16
and of g. height, its top among the 31.03
and under its shadow dwelt all g. nations. 31.06
vindicate the holiness of my g. name, 36.23
their feet, an exceedingly g. host. 37.10
a g. company, all of them with buckler 38.04
cattle and goods, to seize g. spoil?' 38.13
riding on horses, a g. host, a mighty army; 38.15
shall be a g. shaking in the land 38.19
a g. sacrificial feast upon the 39.17
kinds, like the fish of the G. Sea. 47.10
from the G. Sea by way of Hethlon 47.15
the Brook of Egypt to the G. Sea. 47.19
the G. Sea shall be the boundary to 47.20
the Brook of Egypt to the G. Sea. 48.28
me gifts and rewards and g. honor. Dan 2.06
for no g. and powerful king has 2.10
O king, and behold, a g. image. 2.31
image became a g. mountain and 2.35
A g. God has made known to the king 2.45
high honors and many g. gifts, 2.48
How g. are his signs, how mighty his 4.03
of the earth; and its height was g. 4.10
"Is not this g. Babylon, which I 4.30
Belshazzar made a g. feast for a 5.01
heaven were stirring up the g. sea. 7.02
And four g. beasts came up out of 7.03
and it had g. iron teeth; it devoured 7.07
and a mouth speaking g. things. 7.08
sound of the g. words which the 7.11
'These four g. beasts are four 7.17
and a mouth that spoke g. things, 7.20
the g. horn was broken, and instead 8.08
exceedingly g. toward the south, 8.09
It grew g., even to the host of 8.10
and the g. horn between his eyes is 8.21
His power shall be g., and he shall 8.24
the g. and terrible God, who keepest 9.04
by bringing upon us a g. calamity; 9.12
but on the ground of thy g. mercy. 9.18
was true, and it was a g. conflict. 10.01
on the bank of the g. river, that is, the 10.04
but a g. trembling fell upon them, 10.07
left alone and saw this g. vision, 10.08
shall rule with g. dominion and do 11.03
dominion shall be a g. dominion. 11.05
assemble a multitude of g. forces, 11.10
and he shall raise a g. multitude, 11.11
come on with a g. army and abundant 11.13
king of the south with a g. army; 11.25
an exceedingly g. and mighty army; 11.25
to his land with g. substance, but his 11.28
go forth with g. fury to exterminate 11.44
the g. prince who has charge of 12.01
land commits g. harlotry by forsaking Hos 1.02
for g. shall be the day of Jezreel. 1.11
Assyria, and sent to the g. king. 5.13
because of your g. iniquity and g. hatred. 9.07
Assyria, as tribute to the g. king. 10.06
because of your g. wickedness. In the storm 10.15
the mountains a g. and powerful Joe 2.02
for his host is exceedingly g.; 2.11
of the LORD is g. and very terrible; 2.11
rise, for he has done g. things. 2.20
for the LORD has done g. things! 2.21
my g. army, which I sent among you. 2.25
before the g. and terrible day of 2.31
overflow, for their wickedness is g. 3.13
and see the g. tumults within her, Amo 3.09
and the g. houses shall come to an 3.15
and how g. are your sins—you who 5.12
and thence go to Hamath the g.; 6.02
and the g. house shall be smitten 6.11
it devoured the g. deep and was 7.04
the ephah small and the shekel g., 8.05
that g. city, and cry against it; Jon 1.02
LORD hurled a g. wind upon the sea, 1.04
of me that this g. tempest has 1.12
appointed a g. fish to swallow up 1.17
that g. city, and proclaim to it the 3.02
Nineveh was an exceedingly g. city, 3.03
that g. city, in which there are 4.11
now he shall be g. to the ends of Mic 5.04
and the g. man utters the evil 7.03

GREAT (cont.)

is slow to anger and of g. might, Nah 1.03
and all her g. men were bound in 3.10
The g. day of the LORD is near, near Zep 1.14
What are you, O g. mountain? Before Zec 4.07
Therefore g. wrath came from the 7.12
jealous for Zion with g. jealousy, 8.02
I am jealous for her with g. wrath. 8.02
will be as g. as the mourning for 12.11
And on that day a g. panic from the 14.13
silver, and garments in g. abundance. 14.14
"G. is the LORD, beyond the border Mal 1.05
my name is g. among the nations, 1.11
for I am a g. King, says the LORD of 1.14
before the g. and terrible day of 4.05
rejoiced exceedingly with g. joy; Mt 2.10
in darkness have seen a g. light, 4.16
And g. crowds followed him from 4.25
for your reward is g. in heaven, 5.12
shall be called g. in the kingdom 5.19
for it is the city of the g. King. 5.35
is darkness, how g. is the darkness! 6.23
it fell; and g. was the fall of it." 7.27
mountain, g. crowds followed him; 8.01
Now when Jesus saw g. crowds around 8.18
there arose a g. storm on the sea, 8.24
and the sea; and there was a g. calm. 8.26
And g. crowds gathered about him, so 13.02
who, on finding one pearl of g. value, 13.46
As he went ashore he saw a g. throng; 14.14
her, "O woman, g. is your faith! 15.28
And g. crowds came to him, bringing 15.30
the desert to feed so g. a crowd?" 15.33
him to have a g. millstone fastened 18.06
sorrowful; for he had g. possessions. 19.22
and their g. men exercise authority 20.25
would be g. among you must be your 20.26
of Jericho, a g. crowd followed him. 20.29
which is the g. commandment in the 22.36
This is the g. and first commandment. 22.38
For then there will be g. tribulation, 24.21
arise and show g. signs and 24.24
of heaven with power and g. glory; 24.30
and with him a g. crowd with swords 26.47
and he rolled a g. stone to the 27.60
And behold, there was a g. earthquake; 28.02
from the tomb with fear and g. joy, 28.08
a g. while before day, he rose and Mk 1.35
and a g. multitude from Galilee followed; 3.07
Tyre and Sidon a g. multitude, hearing all 3.08
And a g. storm of wind arose, and 4.37
ceased, and there was a g. calm. 4.39
Now a g. herd of swine was feeding 5.11
a g. crowd gathered about him; 5.21
And a g. crowd followed him and 5.24
As he landed he saw a g. throng, 6.34
when again a g. crowd had gathered, 8.01
they saw a g. crowd about them, and 9.14
for him if a g. millstone were hung round 9.42
sorrowful; for he had g. possessions. 10.22
and their g. men exercise authority 10.42
would be g. among you must be your 10.43
his disciples and a g. multitude, 10.46
And the g. throng heard him gladly. 12.37
him, "Do you see these g. buildings? 13.02
in clouds with g. power and glory. 13.26
for he will be g. before the Lord, Lk 1.15
He will be g., and will be called 1.32
mighty has done g. things for me, 1.49
the Lord had shown g. mercy to her, 1.58
good news of a g. joy which will 2.10
she was of a g. age, having lived 2.36
there came a g. famine over all 4.25
they enclosed a g. shoal of fish; 5.06
and g. multitudes gathered to hear 5.15
And Levi made him a g. feast in his 5.29
with a g. crowd of his disciples 6.17
and a g. multitude of people from 6.17
your reward is g. in heaven; for so their 6.23
and your reward will be g., and you will 6.35
and the ruin of that house was g." 6.49
disciples and a g. crowd went with 7.11
"A g. prophet has arisen among us!" 7.16
And when a g. crowd came together 8.04
or they were seized with g. fear; 8.37
the mountain, a g. crowd met him. 9.37
among you all is the one who is g." 9.48
him, "A man once gave a g. banquet, 14.16
Now g. multitudes accompanied him; 14.25
the other is yet a g. way off, 14.32
a g. famine arose in that country, 15.14
us and you a g. chasm has been 16.26
there will be g. earthquakes, and in 21.11
be terrors and g. signs from heaven. 21.11
For g. distress shall be upon the 21.23
in a cloud with power and g. glory. 21.27
became like g. drops of blood falling 22.44
followed him a g. multitude of the 23.27
returned to Jerusalem with g. joy, 24.52
the g. day, Jesus stood up and Jn 7.37
When the g. crowd of the Jews 12.09
The next day a g. crowd who had 12.12
Lord comes, the g. and manifest day. Ac 2.20
And with g. power the apostles gave 4.33
and g. grace was upon them all. 4.33
And g. fear came upon all who heard 5.05
And g. fear came upon the whole 5.11
and a g. many of the priests were 6.07
did g. wonders and signs among the 6.08
and g. affliction, and our fathers 7.11
on that day a g. persecution arose 8.01
and made g. lamentation over him. 8.02
that he himself was somebody g. 8.09
power of God which is called G." 8.10
signs and g. miracles performed, he 8.13
like a g. sheet, let down by four 10.11
like a g. sheet, let down from 11.05
and a g. number that believed 11.21
would be a g. famine over all the 11.28
made the people g. during their 13.17
so spoke that a g. company believed, 14.01
and they gave g. joy to all the 15.03
suddenly there was a g. earthquake, 16.26
as did a g. many of the devout 17.04
temple of the g. goddess Artemis 19.27
"G. is Artemis of the Ephesians!" 19.28
"G. is Artemis of the Ephesians!" 19.34
is temple keeper of the g. Artemis, 19.35
and when there was a g. hush, 21.40
about noon a g. light from heaven 22.06
Then a g. clamor arose; and some of 23.09
Lysias came and with g. violence * 24.07
and Bernice came with g. pomp, 25.23
testifying both to small and g., 26.22
your g. learning is turning you mad." 26.24
him at his lodging in g. numbers. 28.23
that I have g. sorrow and unceasing Rom 9.02
through g. endurance, in afflictions, 2Co 6.04
I have g. confidence in you; 7.04
I have g. pride in you; I am filled 7.04
because of his g. confidence in 8.22
in every way for g. generosity, 9.11
to the working of his g. might Eph 1.19
out of the g. love with which he 2.04
This is a g. mystery, and I take it 5.32
make known how g. among the riches of Col 1.27
God in the face of g. opposition. 1Th 2.02
and with g. desire to see you face 2.17
and also g. confidence in the 1Ti 3.13
G. indeed, we confess, is the mystery 3.16
There is g. gain in godliness with 6.06
In a g. house there are not only 2Ti 2.20
Alexander the coppersmith did me g. harm; 4.14

GREAT (cont.)
glory of our g. God and Savior Tit 2.13
if we neglect such a g. salvation? Heb 2.03
Since then we have a g. high priest 4.14
See how g. he is! Abraham the 7.04
and since we have a g. priest over 10.21
confidence, which has a g. reward. 10.35
surrounded by so g. a cloud of 12.01
the g. shepherd of the sheep, by the 13.20
they are so g. and are driven by Jas 3.04
member and boasts of g. things. 3.05
How g. a forest is set ablaze by a 3.05
righteous man has g. power in its 5.16
By his g. mercy we have been born 1Pe 1.03
his precious and very g. promises, 2Pe 1.04
until the judgment of the g. day; Jud 1.06
I will throw into g. tribulation, Rev 2.22
another; and he was given a g. sword. 6.04
behold, there was a g. earthquake; 6.12
earth and the g. men and the 6.15
for the g. day of their wrath has 6.17
a g. multitude which no man could 7.09
come out of the g. tribulation; 7.14
and something like a g. mountain, 8.08
and a g. star fell from heaven, 8.10
like the smoke of a g. furnace, 9.02
bound at the g. river Euphrates." 9.14
street of the g. city which is 11.08
and g. fear fell on those who saw 11.11
hour there was a g. earthquake, 11.13
hast taken thy g. power and begun 11.17
fear thy name, both small and g., 11.18
And a g. portent appeared in heaven, 12.01
behold a g. red dragon, with seven 12.03
And the g. dragon was thrown down, 12.09
has come down to you in g. wrath, 12.12
wings of the g. eagle that she 12.14
and his throne and g. authority. 13.02
It works g. signs, even making fire 13.13
Also it causes all, both small and g., 13.16
"Fallen, fallen is Babylon the g., 14.08
it into the g. wine press of the 14.19
g. and wonderful, seven angels with 15.01
"G. and wonderful are thy deeds, O 15.03
his bowl on the g. river Euphrates, 16.12
battle on the g. day of God the 16.14
and a g. voice came out of the 16.17
and a g. earthquake such as had 16.18
the earth, so g. was that earthquake. 16.18
The g. city was split into three 16.19
and God remembered g. Babylon, 16.19
and g. hailstones, heavy as a hundredweight, 16.21
judgment of the g. harlot who is 17.01
"Babylon the g., mother of harlots 17.05
you saw is the g. city which has 17.18
from heaven, having g. authority; 18.01
"Fallen, fallen is Babylon the g.! 18.02
thou g. city, thou mighty city, Babylon! 18.10
for the g. city that was clothed in 18.16
"What city was like the g. city?" 18.18
for the g. city where all who had 18.19
a stone like a g. millstone and 18.21
Babylon the g. city be thrown down 18.21
were the g. men of the earth, and 18.23
voice of a g. multitude in heaven, 19.01
has judged the g. harlot who corrupted 19.02
you who fear him, small and g." 19.05
to be the voice of a g. multitude, 19.06
gather for the g. supper of God, 19.17
free and slave, both small and g." 19.18
the bottomless pit and a g. chain. 20.01
Then I saw a g. white throne and 20.11
g. and small, standing before the 20.12
and I heard a g. voice from the 21.03
Spirit he carried me away to a g., 21.10
It had a g., high wall, with twelve 21.12

GREATER
the g. light to rule the day, and Gen 1.16
punishment is g. than I can bear. 4.13
he is not g. in this house than I 39.09
the throne will I be g. than you." 41.40
brother shall be g. than he, and his 48.19
that the LORD is g. than all gods, Ex 18.11
of you a nation g. and mightier Num 14.12
"The people are g. and taller than Deu 1.28
you nations g. and mightier than 4.38
seven nations g. and mightier than 7.01
'These nations are g. than I; 7.17
dispossess nations g. and mightier 9.01
a nation mightier and g. than they.' 9.14
dispossess nations g. and mightier 11.23
and because it was g. than Ai, Jos 10.02
last kindness g. than the first, Ru 3.10
And David became g. and g., for the LORD, 2Sa 5.10
hated her was g. than the love 13.15
me away is g. than the other which 13.16
make his throne g. than the throne 1Ki 1.37
make his throne g. than your 1.47
And David became g. and g., for 1Ch 11.09
hundred and the g. over a thousand. 12.14
for our God is g. than all gods. 2Ch 2.05
And Jehoshaphat grew steadily g. 17.12
there is one g. with us than with 32.07
answer you. God is g. than man. Job 33.12
images were g. than those of Is 10.10
people has been g. than the Lam 4.06
you will see still g. abominations." Eze 8.06
will see still g. abominations 8.13
will see still g. abominations 8.15
which seemed g. than its fellows. Dan 7.20
g. than the former; and after some 11.13
their territory g. than your Amo 6.02
house shall be g. than the former, Hag 2.09
risen no one g. than John the Mt 11.11
kingdom of heaven is g. than he. 11.11
something g. than the temple is 12.06
something g. than Jonah is here. 12.41
something g. than Solomon is here. 12.42
you will receive g. condemnation. * 23.14
For which is g., the gold or the 23.17
For which is g., the gift or the 23.19
no other commandment g. than these." Mk 12.31
will receive the g. condemnation." 12.40
born of women none is g. than John; Lk 7.28
the kingdom of God is g. than he." 7.28
something g. than Solomon is here. 11.31
something g. than Jonah is here. 11.32
will receive the g. condemnation." 20.47
For which is the g., one who sits 22.27
You shall see g. things than these." Jn 1.50
Are you g. than our father Jacob, 4.12
and g. works than these will he 5.20
which I have is g. than that of 5.36
Are you g. than our father Abraham, 8.53
is g. than all, and no one is able 10.29
servant is not g. than his master; 13.16
he who is sent g. than he who sent 13.16
and g. works than these will he do, 14.12
for the Father is g. than I. 14.28
G. love has no man than this, that a 15.13
servant is not g. than his master.' 15.20
delivered me to you has the g. sin." 19.11
lay upon you no g. burden than Ac 15.28
impurity and to g. and g. iniquity, Rom 6.19
we invest with the g. honor, 1Co 12.23
parts are treated with g. modesty, 12.23
giving the g. honor to the inferior 12.24
prophesies is g. than he who 14.05
be attended with g. splendor? 2Co 3.08
with far g. labors, far more imprisonments, 11.23
he had no one g. by whom to swear, Heb 6.13
swear by a g. than themselves, and 6.16
through the g. and more perfect 9.11

GREATER (cont.)
for the Christ g. wealth than the Heb 11.26
shall be judged with g. strictness. Jas 3.01
though g. in might and power, do not 2Pe 2.11
for God is g. than our hearts, and 1Jn 3.20
is in you is g. than he who is in 4.04
of men, the testimony of God is g.; 5.09
No g. joy can I have than this, to 3Jn 1.04

GREATEST
Arba was the g. man among the Anakim. Jos 14.15
man was the g. of all the people Job 1.03
"For from the least to the g. of them, Jer 6.13
least to the g. every one is greedy 8.10
of them to the g., says the LORD; 31.34
the least to the g., came near 42.01
people from the least to the g., 42.08
from the least to the g., they shall 44.12
from the g. of them to the least of Jon 3.05
grown it is the g. of shrubs and Mt 13.32
"Who is the g. in the kingdom of 18.01
he is the g. in the kingdom of 18.04
He who is g. among you shall be 23.11
and becomes the g. of all shrubs, Mk 4.32
with one another who was the g. 9.34
as to which of them was the g. Lk 9.46
them was to be regarded as the g. 22.24
rather let the g. among you become 22.26
to him, from the least to the g., Ac 8.10
but the g. of these is love. 1Co 13.13
from the least of them to the g. Heb 8.11

GREATLY
"I will g. multiply your pain in Gen 3.16
and increased g. upon the earth; 7.18
"I will so g. multiply your descendants 16.10
The LORD has g. blessed my master, 24.35
you longed g. for your father's 31.30
Then Jacob was g. afraid and distressed; 32.07
were fruitful and increased g.; Ex 1.07
and the whole mountain quaked g. 19.18
Israel, and the people mourned g. Num 14.39
you, and that you may multiply g., Deu 6.03
nor shall he g. multiply for himself 17.17
so we feared g. for our lives because Jos 9.24
he feared g., because Gibeon was a 10.02
there words, and his anger was g. kindled. 1Sa 11.06
all the men of Israel rejoiced g. 11.15
all the people g. feared the LORD 12.18
And Saul loved him g., 16.21
they were dismayed and g. afraid. 17.11
third day you will be g. missed; 20.19
afraid, and his heart trembled g. 28.05
And David was g. distressed; for the people 30.06
for he feared g. Therefore Saul 31.04
them, for the men were g. ashamed. 2Sa 10.05
anger was g. kindled against the 12.05
"I have sinned g. in what I have 24.10
he rejoiced g., and said, "Blessed 1Ki 5.07
(Now Obadiah revered the LORD g.; 18.03
of Syria was g. troubled because 2Ki 6.11
their fathers' houses increased g. 1Ch 4.38
for he feared g. Therefore Saul 10.04
and g. to be praised, and he is to 16.25
them, for the men were g. ashamed. 19.05
"I have sinned g. in that I have 21.08
David the king also rejoiced g. 29.09
humbled himself g. before the God 2Ch 33.12
for we have g. transgressed in this Ez 10.13
displeased them g. that some one Neh 2.10
wall, he was angry and g. enraged, 4.01
afraid and fell g. in their own 6.16
and he does not g. heed transgression, Job 35.15
and in thy help how g. he exults! Ps 21.01
Great is the LORD and g. to be 48.01
my fortress; I shall not be g. moved. 62.02
waterest it, thou g. enrichest it; 65.09
is the LORD, and g. to be praised; 96.04
By his blessing they multiply g.; 107.38
who g. delights in his commandments! 112.01
when I said, "I am g. afflicted"; 116.10
and g. to be praised, and his 145.03
of the righteous will g. rejoice; Pro 23.24
g. distressed and hungry; and when they Is 8.21
I will g. rejoice in the LORD, my 61.10
Would not that land be g. polluted? Jer 3.01
They will be g. shamed, for they 20.11
and my sabbaths they g. profaned. Eze 20.13
Then King Belshazzar was g. alarmed, Dan 5.09
my thoughts g. alarmed me, and my 7.28
it to you, for you are g. beloved; 9.23
man g. beloved, give heed to the 10.11
"O man g. beloved, fear not, peace be 10.19
Rejoice g., O daughter of Zion! Zec 9.09
the third day." And they were g. distressed. Mt 17.23
they were g. distressed, and they 18.31
heard this they were g. astonished, 19.25
so that the governor wondered g. 27.14
were g. amazed, and ran up to him Mk 9.15
and began to be g. distressed and 14.33
But she was g. troubled at the Lk 1.29
rejoices g. at the bridegroom's Jn 3.29
disciples multiplied g. in Jerusalem, Ac 6.07
he g. helped those who through 18.27
among you may be g. enlarged, 2Co 10.15
in the Lord g. that now at length Php 4.10
you to know now g. I strive for Col 2.10
g. distressed by the licentiousness 2Pe 2.07
I rejoiced g. to find some of your 2Jn 1.04
For I g. rejoiced when some of the 3Jn 1.03
When I saw her I marveled g. Rev 17.06

GREATNESS
In the g. of thy majesty thou Ex 15.07
because of the g. of thy arm, 15.16
according to the g. of thy steadfast Num 14.19
thy servant thy g. and thy mighty Deu 3.24
God has shown us his glory and g., 5.24
thou hast redeemed through thy g., 9.26
his g., his mighty hand and his 11.02
of the LORD. Ascribe g. to our God! 32.03
thou hast wrought all this g., 2Sa 7.21
thou hast wrought all this g., 1Ch 17.19
is the g., and the power, and the 29.11
half the g. of your wisdom was not 2Ch 9.06
according to the g. of thy steadfast Neh 13.22
with me in the g. of his power? Job 23.06
and let not the g. of the ransom 36.18
and his g. is unsearchable. Ps 145.03
acts, and I will declare thy g. 145.06
him according to his exceeding g.! 150.02
by the g. of his might, and because Is 40.26
marching in the g. of his strength? 63.01
it is for the g. of your iniquity Jer 13.22
"Whom are you like in your g.? Eze 31.02
It was beautiful in its g., 31.07
in glory and in g. among the trees 31.18
So I will show my g. and my holiness 38.23
Your g. has grown and reaches to Dan 4.22
and still more g. was added to me. 4.36
kingship and g. and glory and 5.18
and because of the g. that he gave 5.19
dominion and the g. of the kingdoms 7.27
immeasurable g. of his power in us Eph 1.19

GREAVES
And he had g. of bronze upon his 1Sa 17.06

GREECE
And the he-goat is the king of G.; Dan 8.21
lo, the prince of G. will come. 10.20
up all against the kingdom of G. 11.02
O G., and wield you like a warrior's Zec 9.13
much encouragement, he came to G. Ac 20.02

GREED
"Because his g. knew no rest, he Job 20.20
you to the g. of your enemies, the Eze 16.27
His g. is as wide as Sheol; Hab 2.05
he is guilty of immorality or g., 1Co 5.11
as you know, or a cloak for g., 1Th 2.05
And in their g. they will exploit 2Pe 2.03
They have hearts trained in g. 2.14

GREEDILY
of lions that g. devour the sons Ps 57.04

GREEDY
Why then look with g. eye at my 1Sa 2.29
and the man g. for gain curses and Ps 10.03
He who is g. for unjust gain makes Pro 15.27
A g. man stirs up strife, but he who 28.25
every one is g. for unjust gain; Jer 6.13
every one is g. for unjust gain; 8.10
they are g. for their iniquity. Hos 4.08
or the g. and robbers, or idolaters, 1Co 5.10
nor the g., nor drunkards, nor 6.10
g. to practice every kind of Eph 4.19
to much wine, not g. for gain; 1Ti 3.08
drunkard or violent or g. for gain, Tit 1.07

GREEK
Now the woman was a G., Mk 7.26
in Hebrew, in Latin, and in G. Jn 19.20
a believer; but his father was a G. Ac 16.01
all knew that his father was a G. 16.03
with not a few G. women of high 17.12
And he said, "Do you know G.? 21.37
the Jew first and also to the G. Rom 1.16
the Jew first and also the G., 2.09
the Jew first and also the G. 2.10
no distinction between Jew and G.; 10.12
be circumcised, though he was a G. Gal 2.03
There is neither Jew nor G., 3.28
Here there cannot be G. and Jew, Col 3.11
and in G. he is called Apollyon. Rev 9.11

GREEKS
of Judah and Jerusalem to the G., Joe 3.06
among the G. and teach the G.? Jn 7.35
worship at the feast were some G. 12.20
to Antioch spoke to the G. also, Ac 11.20
believed, both of Jews and of G. 14.01
of the devout G. and not a few of 17.04
sabbath, and persuaded Jews and G. 18.04
word of the Lord, both Jews and G. 19.10
of Ephesus, both Jews and G.; 19.17
to Jews and to G. of repentance to 20.21
he also brought G. into the temple, 21.28
obligation both to G. and to Rom 1.14
both Jews and G., are under the 3.09
demand signs and G. seek wisdom, 1Co 1.22
both Jews and G., Christ the power 1.24
to Jews or to G. or to the church 10.32
Jews or G., slaves or free—and all 12.13

GREEN
have given every g. plant for food. Gen 1.30
and as I gave you the g. plants, 9.03
not a g. thing remained, neither Ex 10.15
the hills and under every g. tree; Deu 12.02
high hill and under every g. tree; 1Ki 14.23
the hills, and under every g. tree. 2Ki 16.04
high hill and under every g. tree; 17.10
the hills, and under every g. tree. 2Ch 28.04
and his branch will not be g. Job 15.32
he searches after every g. thing. 39.08
he makes me lie down in g. pastures. Ps 23.02
grass, and wither like the g. herb. 37.02
But I am like a g. olive tree in 52.08
whether g. or ablaze, may he sweep 58.09
silver, its pinions with g. gold. 68.13
they are ever full of sap and g., 92.14
will flourish like a g. leaf. Pro 11.28
truly lovely. Our couch is g.; Sol 1.16
the oaks, under every g. tree; Is 57.05
and under every g. tree you bowed Jer 2.20
high hill and under every g. tree, 3.06
strangers under every g. tree, 3.13
'A g. olive tree, fair with goodly 11.16
beside every g. tree, and on the 17.02
comes, for its leaves remain g., 17.08
under every g. tree, and under every Eze 6.13
dry up the g. tree, and make the dry 17.24
devour every g. tree in you and 20.47
pastures of the wilderness are g.; Joe 2.22
by companies upon the g. grass. Mk 6.39
they do this when the wood is g., Lk 23.31
and all g. grass was burnt up. Rev 8.07
earth or any g. growth or any tree, 9.04

GREENISH
disease shows g. or reddish in the Lev 13.49
the house with g. or reddish spots, 14.37

GREET
And they will g. you and give you 1Sa 10.04
go to Nabal, and g. him in my name. 25.05
to g. him, and to congratulate him 2Sa 8.10
to g. him, and to congratulate him 1Ch 18.10
it rouses the shades to g. you, Is 14.09
G. Prisca and Aquila, my fellow Rom 16.03
g. also the church in their house. 16.05
G. my beloved Epaenetus, who was the 16.05
G. Mary, who has worked hard among 16.06
G. Andronicus and Junias, my kinsmen 16.07
G. Ampliatus, my beloved in the Lord. 16.08
G. Urbanus. our fellow worker in 16.09
G. Apelles, who is approved in 16.10
G. those who belong to the family 16.10
G. my kinsman Herodion. G. those in 16.11
G. those workers in the Lord, 16.12
G. the beloved Persis, who has 16.12
G. Rufus, eminent in the Lord, also 16.13
G. Asyncritus, Phlegon, Hermes, 16.14
G. Philologus, Julia, Nereus and his 16.15
G. one another with a holy kiss. 16.16
all the churches of Christ g. you. 16.16
of this letter, g. you in the Lord. 16.22
and our brother Quartus, g. you. 16.23
G. one another with a holy kiss. 1Co 16.20
G. one another with a holy kiss. 2Co 13.12
All the saints g. you. 13.13
G. every saint in Christ Jesus. Php 4.21
brethren who are with me g. you. 4.21
All the saints g. you, especially 4.22
beloved physician and Demas g. you. Col 4.14
G. all the brethren with a holy 1Th 5.26
G. Prisca and Aquila, and the 2Ti 4.19
G. those who love us in the faith. Tit 3.15
G. all your leaders and all the Heb 13.24
G. one another with the kiss of 1Pe 5.14
children of your elect sister g. you. 2Jn 1.13
The friends g. you. G. the friends, 3Jn 1.15

GREETED
and went and g. his brothers. 1Sa 17.22
and he g. him, and said to him, "Is 2Ki 10.15
and ran up to him and g. him. Mk 9.15
of Zechariah and g. Elizabeth. Lk 1.40
he went up and g. the church, Ac 18.22
and we g. the brethren and stayed 21.07
having seen it and g. it from afar, Heb 11.13

GREETING
province Beyond the River, send g. Ez 4.11
the province Beyond the River, g. 4.17
mind what sort of g. this might be. Lk 1.29
Elizabeth heard the g. of Mary, 1.41
voice of your g. came to my ears, 1.44
Antioch and Syria and Cilicia, g. Ac 15.23

GREETING (cont.)
After g. them, he related one by one Ac 21.19
Excellency the governor Felix, g. 23.36
write this g. with my own hand. 1Co 16.21
write this g. with my own hand. Col 4.18
write this g. with my own hand. 2Th 3.17
tribes in the dispersion: G. Jas 1.01
into the house or give him any g.; 2Jn 1.10

GREETINGS
The churches of Asia send g. 1Co 16.19
send you hearty g. in the Lord. 16.19
All the brethren send g. Greet one 16.20
Give my g. to the brethren at Col 4.15
Eubulus sends g. to you, as do 2Ti 4.21
All who are with me send g. to you. Tit 3.15
in Christ Jesus, sends g. to you, Phm 1.23
who come from Italy send you g. Heb 13.24
is likewise chosen, sends you g.; 1Pe 5.13

GREETS
Timothy, my fellow worker, g. you; Rom 16.21
me and to the whole church, g. you 16.23
Aristarchus my fellow prisoner g. you, Col 4.10
g. you, always remembering you 4.12
for he who g. him shares his wicked 2Jn 1.11

GREW
cities, and what g. on the ground. Gen 19.25
And the child g., and was weaned; 21.08
God was with the lad, and he g. up; 21.20
When the boys g. up, Esau was a 25.27
Thus the man g. exceedingly rich, 30.43
multiplied and g. exceedingly Ex 1.07
multiplied and g. very strong. 1.20
And the child g., and she brought 2.10
but when the sun g. hot, it melted. 16.21
But Moses' hands g. weary; 17.12
of the trumpet g. louder and 19.19
you g. thick, you became sleek; Deu 32.15
the people of Israel g. strong, Jos 17.13
When Israel g. strong, they put the Ju 1.28
and when his wife's sons g. up, 11.02
and the boy g., and the LORD 13.24
the boy Samuel g. in the presence 1Sa 2.21
And Samuel g., and the LORD was 3.19
and David g. stronger and stronger, 2Sa 3.01
but she g. drowsy and slept; 4.06
and it g. up with him and with his 12.03
And the conspiracy g. strong, 15.12
the Philistines; and David g. weary. 21.15
the heavens g. black with clouds 1Ki 18.45
And the battle g. hot that day, and 22.35
But Abijah g. mighty. And he took 2Ch 13.21
And Jehoshaphat g. steadily greater. 17.12
And the battle g. hot that day, and 18.34
But Jehoiada g. old and full of 24.15
But when he was strong he g. proud, 26.16
man Mordecai g. more and more Est 9.04
to no avail; my distress g. worse, Ps 39.02
For he g. up before him like a Is 53.02
And you g. up and became tall and Eze 16.07
You g. exceedingly beautiful, and 16.13
wither away on the bed where it g.?" 17.10
its boughs g. large and its branches 31.05
The tree g. and became strong, and Dan 4.11
which g. and became strong, so that 4.20
till his hair g. as long as eagles' 4.33
which g. exceedingly great toward 8.09
It g. great, even to the host of 8.10
For the sea g. more and more Jon 1.11
for the sea g. more and more 1.13
and the thorns g. up and choked Mt 13.07
and the thorns g. up and choked it, Mk 4.07
was no better but rather g. worse. 5.26
And when it g. late, his disciples 6.35
And the child g. and became strong Lk 1.80
And the child g. and became strong, 2.40
and as it g. up, it withered away, 8.06
and the thorns g. with it and 8.07
And some fell into good soil and g., 8.08
and it g. and became a tree, and the 13.19
the people g. and multiplied in Ac 7.17
But the word of God g. and multiplied. 12.24
of the Lord g. and prevailed 19.20
but he g. strong in his faith as he Rom 4.20
ships at sea g. rich by her wealth! Rev 18.19

GRIDDLE
is a cereal offering baked on a g., Lev 2.05
It shall be made with oil on a g.; 6.21
on a pan or a g. shall belong to 7.09

GRIEF
my lord shall have no cause of g., 1Sa 25.31
My eye has grown dim from g., Job 17.07
My eye wastes away because of g., Ps 6.07
my eye is wasted from g., 31.09
"It is my g. that the right hand of 77.10
is sad, and the end of joy is g. Pro 14.13
A stupid son is a g. to a father; 17.21
son is a g. to his father and 17.25
all his days in darkness and g., Ecc 5.17
in a day of g. and incurable pain. Is 17.11
of sorrows, and acquainted with g.; 53.03
he has put him to g.; when he 53.10
My g. is beyond healing, my heart is Jer 8.18
poured out in g. because of the Lam 2.11
but, though he cause g., he will have 3.32
my eyes cause me g. at the fate of 3.51
and bitter g. before their eyes. Eze 21.06
for you felt a godly g., so that you 2Co 7.09
For godly g. produces a repentance 7.10
but worldly g. produces death. 7.10
this godly g. has produced in you, 7.11

GRIEFS
has borne our g. and carried our Is 53.04

GRIEVANCE
of you has a g. against a brother, 1Co 6.01

GRIEVE
weep out his eyes and g. his heart; 1Sa 2.33
"How long will you g. over Saul, 16.01
afflict or g. the sons of men. Lam 3.33
And do not g. the Holy Spirit of Eph 4.30
you may not g. as others do who 1Th 4.13

GRIEVED
and it g. him to his heart. Gen 6.06
his death, but Samuel g. over Saul. 1Sa 15.35
Jonathan know this, lest he be g.' 20.03
for he was g. for David, because his 20.34
and do not be g., for the joy of Neh 8.10
day is holy; do not be g." 8.11
Was not my soul g. for the poor? Job 30.25
as though I g. for my friend or my Ps 35.14
wilderness and g. him in the 78.40
all who work for hire will be g. Is 19.10
a wife forsaken and g. in spirit, 54.06
rebelled and g. his holy Spirit; 63.10
but are not g. over the ruin of Amo 6.06
g. at their hardness of heart, and Mk 3.05
Peter was g. because he said to Jn 21.17
for I see that that letter g. you, 2Co 7.08
I rejoice, not because you were g., 7.09
because you were g. into repenting; 7.09

GRIEVING
day, "The king is g. for his son." 2Sa 19.02

GRIEVOUS
follow, for it will be very g. Gen 41.31
"This is a g. mourning to the 50.11
great and g., against Egypt and Deu 6.22
the legs with g. boils of which 28.35

GRIEVOUS (cont.)

and sicknesses g. and lasting. Deu 28.59
me with a g. curse on the day when 1Ki 2.08
is done under the sun was g. to me; Ecc 2.17
There is a g. evil which I have 5.13
This also is a g. evil: just as he 5.16
My wound is g. But I said, "Truly Jer 10.19
a great wound, with a very g. blow. 14.17
is incurable, and your wound is g. 30.12
destroys with a g. destruction. Mic 2.10
your hurt, your wound is g. All who hear Nah 3.19

GRIEVOUSLY

Jerusalem sinned g., therefore she became Lam 1.08
Judah and has g. offended in Eze 25.12
lift it shall g. hurt themselves. Zec 12.03

GRIND

then let my wife g. for another, Job 31.10
Take the millstones and g. meal, Is 47.02
He has made my teeth g. on gravel, Lam 3.16
are compelled to g. at the mill; 5.13

GRINDERS

and the g. cease because they are Ecc 12.03

GRINDING

g. it very small, until it was as Deu 9.21
when the sound of the g. is low, Ecc 12.04
by g. the face of the poor?" Is 3.15
the g. of the millstones and the Jer 25.10
Two women will be g. at the mill; Mt 24.41
There will be two women g. together; Lk 17.35

GRINDS

he foams and g. his teeth and Mk 9.18

GROAN

From out of the city the dying g., Job 24.12
despoiled, because the needy g., Ps 12.05
I g. because of the tumult of my 38.08
and at the end of your life you g., Pro 5.11
the wicked rule, the people g. 29.02
how you will g. when pangs come Jer 22.23
all her land the wounded shall g. 51.52
gates are desolate, her priests g.; Lam 1.04
All her people g. as they search 1.11
"Hear how I g.; there is none 1.21
who sigh and g. over all the Eze 9.04
iniquities and g. to one another. 24.23
of your fall, when the wounded g., 26.15
and he will g. before him like a 30.24
How the beasts g.! The herds of Joe 1.18
Writhe and g., O daughter of Zion, Mic 4.10
g. inwardly as we wait for adoption Rom 8.23
Here indeed we g., and long to put 2Co 5.02

GROANED

of Israel g. under their bondage, Ex 2.23

GROANING

And God heard their g., and God Ex 2.24
have heard the g. of the people of 6.05
pity by their g. because of those Ju 2.18
hand is heavy in spite of my g. Job 23.02
words, O LORD; give heed to my g. Ps 5.01
me, from the words of my g.? 22.01
away through my g. all day long. 32.03
Because of my loud g. my bones 102.05
I am weary with my g., Jer 45.03
weeping and g. because he no Mal 2.13
are in Egypt and heard their g., Ac 7.34
has been g. in travail together Rom 8.22

GROANINGS

and my g. are poured out like water. Job 3.24

GROANS

Let the g. of the prisoners come Ps 79.11
to hear the g. of the prisoners, to 102.20
she herself g., and turns her face Lam 1.08
for my g. are many and my heart is 1.22

GROPE

and you shall g. at noonday, as the Deu 28.29
as the blind g. in darkness, and you 28.29
and g. at noonday as in the night. Job 5.14
They g. in the dark without light; 12.25
We g. for the wall like the blind, Is 59.10
we g. like those who have no eyes; 59.10

GROPING

wearied themselves g. for the door. Gen 19.11

GROSS

their heart is g. like fat, but I Ps 119.70

GROUND

creeps upon the g. according to Gen 1.25
there was no man to till the g.; 2.05
watered the whole face of the g.— 2.06
God formed man of dust from the g., 2.07
And out of the g. the LORD God made 2.09
So out of the g. the LORD God 2.19
cursed is the g. because of you; 3.17
bread till you return to the g., 3.19
to till the g. from which he was 3.23
sheep, and Cain a tiller of the g. 4.02
offering of the fruit of the g., 4.03
blood is crying to me from the g. 4.10
And now you are cursed from the g., 4.11
When you till the g., it shall no longer 4.12
me this day away from the g.; 4.14
"Out of the g. which the LORD has 5.29
to multiply on the face of the g., 6.01
created from the face of the g., 6.07
thing of the g. according to its 6.20
blot out from the face of the g." 7.04
everything that creeps on the g., 7.08
that was upon the face of the g., 7.23
subsided from the face of the g.; 8.08
behold, the face of the g. was dry. 8.13
again curse the g. because of man, 8.21
creeps on the g. and all the fish 9.02
cities, and what grew on the g. 19.25
himself to the g. seven times, 33.03
bow ourselves to the g. before you?" 37.10
he spilled the semen on the g., 38.09
him with their faces to the g. 42.06
and bowed down to him to the g. 43.26
quickly lowered his sack to the g., 44.11
and they fell before him to the g. 44.14
which you are standing is holy g." Ex 3.05
And he said, "Cast it on the g." 4.03
So he cast it on the g., and it became 4.03
Nile and pour it upon the dry g.; 4.09
will become blood upon the dry g." 4.09
and also the g. on which they stand. 8.21
may go on dry g. through the sea. 14.16
the midst of the sea on dry g., 14.22
walked on dry g. through the sea, 14.29
walked on dry g. in the midst of 15.19
thing, fine as hoarfrost on the g. 16.14
fruits of your g. you shall bring 23.19
and g. it to powder, and scattered 32.20
fruits of your g. you shall bring 34.26
anything with which the g. teems, Lev 20.25
and g. it in mills or beat it in Num 11.08
and the g. opens its mouth, and 16.30
the g. under them split asunder; 16.31
of anything that creeps on the g., Deu 4.18
your body and the fruit of your g., 7.13
and thirsty g. where there was no 8.15
pour it out on the g. like water. 15.23
nest, in any tree or on the g., 22.06

GROUND (cont.)
first of all the fruit of the g., Deu 26.02
the first of the fruit of the g., 26.10
Israel and the g. which thou hast 26.15
body, and the fruit of your g., 28.04
and in the fruit of your g., 28.11
body, and the fruit of your g., 28.18
fruit of your g. and of all your 28.33
fruit of your g. the locust shall 28.42
cattle and the fruit of your g., 28.51
foot upon the g. because she is so 28.56
and in the fruit of your g.; 30.09
Israel were passing over on dry g., Jos 3.17
stood on dry g. in the midst of 3.17
feet were lifted up on dry g., 4.18
passed over this Jordan on dry g.' 4.22
and there clear g. for yourselves 17.15
the portion of g. which Jacob 24.32
till it went down into the g., Ju 4.21
alone, and it is dry on all the g., 6.37
and on all the g. let there be dew." 6.39
and on all the g. there was dew. 6.40
they fell on their faces to the g. 13.20
and he g. at the mill in the prison. 16.21
felled to the g. on that day 20.21
felled to the g. eighteen thousand 20.25
men of Israel gave g. to Benjamin, 20.36
bowing to the g., and said to him, Ru 2.10
none of his words fall to the g. 1Sa 3.19
downward on the g. before the ark 5.03
downward on the g. before the ark 5.04
to plow his g. and to reap his 8.12
and there was honey on the g. 14.25
calves, and slew them on the g.; 14.32
hair of his head fall to the g.; 14.45
and he fell on his face to the g. 17.49
and fell on his face to the g.. 20.41
on her face, and bowed to the g. 25.23
and bowed with her face to the g., 25.41
spear stuck in the g. at his head; 26.07
he bowed with his face to the g., 28.14
at once full length upon the g., 28.20
he fell to the g. and did obeisance. 2Sa 1.02
why should I smite you to the g.? 2.22
making them lie down on the g.; 8.02
in and lay all night upon the g. 12.16
him, to raise him from the g.; 12.17
she fell on her face to the g., 14.04
of your son shall fall to the g." 14.11
we are like water split on the g., 14.14
And Joab fell on his face to the g., 14.22
his face to the g. before the king; 14.33
him as the dew falls on the g.; 17.12
you not strike him there to the g.? 18.11
and shed his bowels to the g., 20.10
was a plot of g. full of lentils; 23.11
the king with his face to the g. 24.20
the king, with his face to the g. 1Ki 1.23
bowed with her face to the g., 1.31
in the clay g. between Succoth and 7.46
of them could go over on dry g. 2Ki 2.08
and bowed to the g. before him. 2.15
fell at his feet, bowing to the g.; 4.37
on the plot of g. belonging to 9.25
requite you on this plot of g.' 9.26
up and cast him on the plot of g., 9.26
Israel, "Strike the g. with them"; 13.18
was a plot of g. full of barley, 1Ch 11.13
to David with his face to the g. 21.21
in the clay g. between Succoth and 2Ch 4.17
his head with his face to the g., 20.18
were dead bodies lying on the g.; 20.24
LORD with their faces to the g. Neh 8.06
fruits of our g. and the first 10.35
the Levites the tithes from our g., 10.37
fell upon the g., and worshiped. Job 1.20
with him on the g. seven days and 2.13
does trouble sprout from the g.; 5.06
and its stump die in the g., 14.08
he pours out my gall on the g. 16.13
A rope is hid for him in the g., 18.10
they gnaw the dry and desolate g.; 30.03
and to make the g. put forth grass? 38.27
and lets them be warmed on the g., 39.14
and rage he swallows the g.; 39.24
let him trample my life to the g., Ps 7.05
refined in a furnace on the g., 12.06
their eyes to cast me to the g. 17.11
My foot stands on level g.; 26.12
our body cleaves to the g. 44.25
to the g. they desecrated the 74.07
Thou didst clear the g. for it; 80.09
Endor, who became dung for the g. 83.10
Faithfulness will spring up from the g., 85.11
and cast his throne to the g. 89.44
thou renewest the face of the g. 104.30
and ate up the fruit of their g. 105.35
springs of water into thirsty g., 107.33
he has crushed my life to the g.; 143.03
he casts the wicked to the g. 147.06
The fallow g. of the poor yields Pro 13.23
the g. was covered with nettles, and 24.31
the rocks and the holes of the g., Is 2.19
ravaged, she shall sit upon the g. 3.26
How you are cut down to the g., 14.12
gods he has shattered to the g." 21.09
down, lay low, and cast to the g., 25.12
lays it low, lays it low to the g., 26.05
continually open and harrow his g.? 28.24
come from the g. like the voice of 29.04
the seed with which you sow the g., 30.23
and grain, the produce of the g., 30.23
that till the g. will eat salted 30.24
and the thirsty g. springs of 35.07
the uneven g. shall become level, 40.04
the rough places into level g. 42.16
land, and streams on the dry g.; 44.03
sit on the g. without a throne, O 47.01
faces to the g. they shall bow 49.23
back like the g. and like the 51.23
and like a root out of dry g.; 53.02
Jerusalem: "Break up your fallow g., Jer 4.03
the field and the fruit of the g.; 7.20
as dung on the surface of the g. 8.02
Gather up your bundle from the g., 10.17
her people lament on the g., 14.02
Because of the g. which is dismayed, 14.04
as dung on the surface of the g. 16.04
be dung on the surface of the g. 25.33
glory, and sit on the parched g., 48.18
leveled to the g. and her high 51.58
down to the g. in dishonor the Lam 2.02
Her gates have sunk into the g.; 2.09
of Zion sit on the g. in silence; 2.10
have bowed their heads to the g. 2.10
and bring it down to the g., Eze 13.14
up in fury, cast down to the g.; 19.12
it upon the g. to cover it with 24.07
mighty pillars will fall to the g. 26.11
sit upon the g. and tremble every 26.16
I cast you to the g.; I exposed you 28.17
And I will cast you on the g., 32.04
things that creep on the g., 38.20
every wall shall tumble to the g. 38.20
back from the g. more than the 42.06
the base on the g. to the lower 43.14
to find a g. for complaint against Dan 6.04
could find no g. for complaint or 6.04
not find any g. for complaint 6.05
up from the g. and made to stand 7.04
earth, without touching the g.; 8.05
him down to the g. and trampled 8.07
the stars it cast down to the g., 8.10
and truth was cast down to the g., 8.12
deep sleep with my face to the g.; 8.18
thee on the g. of our righteousness, 9.18

GROUND (cont.)
but on the g. of thy great mercy. Dan 9.18
deep sleep with my face to the g. 10.09
my face toward the g. and was dumb. 10.15
and the creeping things of the g.; Hos 2.18
break up your fallow g., 10.12
are laid waste, the g. mourns; Joe 1.10
Does a snare spring up from the g., Amo 3.05
be cut off and fall to the g. 3.14
it from the surface of the g.; 9.08
"Who will bring me down to the g.?" Ob 1.03
upon what the g. brings forth, upon Hag 1.11
and the g. shall give its increase, Zec 8.12
except on the g. of unchastity, Mt 5.32
fall to the g. without your Father's 10.29
Other seeds fell on rocky g., where they 13.05
As for what was sown on rocky g., 13.20
the crowd to sit down on the g., 15.35
and dug in the g. and hid his 25.18
went and hid your talent in the g. 25.25
Other seed fell on rocky g., where it Mk 4.05
are the ones sown upon rocky g., 4.16
should scatter seed upon the g., 4.26
seed, which, when sown upon the g., 4.31
the crowd to sit down on the g.; 8.06
he fell on the g. and rolled about, 9.20
he fell on the g. and prayed that, 14.35
a house on the g. without a foundation; Lk 6.49
down; why should it use up the g.?' 13.07
and dash you to the g., you and your 19.44
of blood falling down upon the g. 22.44
and bowed their faces to the g., 24.05
and wrote with his finger on the g. *Jn 8.06
wrote with his finger on the g. *8.08
he spat on the g. and made clay of 9.06
they drew back and fell to the g. 18.06
where you are standing is holy g. Ac 7.33
and they g. their teeth against him. 7.54
And he fell to the g. and heard a 9.04
Saul arose from the g.; and when 9.08
And I fell to the g. and heard a 22.07
And when we had all fallen to the g. 26.14
circumcised on the g. of their Rom 3.30
deprive me of my g. for boasting. 1Co 9.15
that gives me no g. for boasting. 9.16
question on the g. of conscience. 10.25
question on the g. of conscience. 10.27
disrespectful on the g. that they 1Ti 6.02

GROUNDED
you, being rooted and g. in love, Eph 3.17

GROUPINGS
according to the g. of the fathers' 2Ch 35.05
according to the g. of the fathers' 35.12

GROUPS
So they sat down in g., by hundreds Mk 6.40

GROW
God made to g. every tree that is Gen 2.09
and let them g. into a multitude in 48.16
locks of hair of his head g. long. Num 6.05
the wild beasts g. too numerous Deu 7.22
head began to g. again after it Ju 16.22
continued to g. both in stature 1Sa 2.26
whose eyesight had begun to g. dim, 3.02
should damage g. to the hurt of Ez 4.22
"Can papyrus g. where there is no Job 8.11
Though its root g. old in the earth, 14.08
reach old age, and g. mighty in power? 21.07
let thorns g. instead of wheat, and 31.40
strong, they g. up in the open; 39.04
My wounds g. foul and fester because Ps 38.05
My eyes g. dim with waiting for my 69.03
and g. like a cedar in Lebanon. 92.12
the grass to g. for the cattle, 104.14
he makes grass g. upon the hills. 147.08
empty words g. many: but do you fear Ecc 5.07
and briers and thorns shall g. up; Is 5.06
a branch shall g. out of his roots. 11.01
the fat of his flesh will g. lean. 17.04
though you make them g. on the day 17.11
no more shall his face g. pale. 29.22
Thorns shall g. over its strongholds, 34.13
He does not faint or g. weary, 40.28
oak and lets it g. strong among 44.14
they g. and bring forth fruit; Jer 12.02
'The days g. long, and every vision Eze 12.22
and g. up like a plant of the field.' 16.07
it, the deep made it g. tall, 31.04
the waters may g. to lofty height 31.14
heads or let their locks g. long; 44.20
there will g. all kinds of trees 47.12
thistle shall g. up on their Hos 10.08
are in anguish, all faces g. pale. Joe 2.06
not labor, nor did you make it g., Jon 4.10
is on all loins, all faces g. pale! Nah 2.10
let not your hands g. weak. Zep 3.16
for he shall g. up in his place, and Zec 6.12
lilies of the field, how they g.; Mt 6.28
Let both g. together until the 13.30
most men's love will g. cold. 24.12
and the seed should sprout and g., Mk 4.27
Consider the lilies, how they g.; Lk 12.27
with purses that do not g. old, 12.33
And let us not g. weary in well-doing, Gal 6.09
we are to g. up in every way into Eph 4.15
for when they g. wanton against 1Ti 5.11
they will all g. old like a garment, Heb 1.11
you may not g. weary or fainthearted. 12.03
by it you may g. up to salvation; 1Pe 2.02
But g. in the grace and knowledge 2Pe 3.18

GROWING
and good, were g. on one stalk. Gen 41.05
dream seven ears g. on one stalk, 41.22
and g. nothing, where no grass can Deu 29.23
to water the forest of g. trees. Ecc 2.06
of my people g. up in thorns and Is 32.13
g. up and increasing and yielding Mk 4.08
world it is bearing fruit and g.— Col 1.06
your faith is g. abundantly, 2Th 1.03
obsolete and g. old is ready to Heb 8.13

GROWL
man or beast, not a dog shall g.; Ex 11.07
and g. if they do not get their Ps 59.15
they g. and seize their prey, they Is 5.29
They will g. over it on that day, 5.30
We all g. like bears, we moan and 59.11
they shall g. like lions' whelps. Jer 51.38

GROWLING
wrath is like the g. of a lion, Pro 19.12
of a king is like the g. of a lion; 20.02

GROWLS
or a young lion g. over his prey, Is 31.04

GROWN
"After I have g. old, and my husband Gen 18.12
or she saw that Shelah was g. up, 38.14
One day, when Moses had g. up, Ex 2.11
and black hair has g. in it, Lev 13.37
and have g. old in the land, if you Deu 4.25
have eaten and are full and g. fat, 31.20
therefore wait till they were g.? Ru 1.13
Jericho until your beards have g., 2Sa 10.05
men who had g. up with him and 1Ki 12.08
men who had g. up with him said to 12.10
When the child had g., he went out 2Ki 4.18
on the housetops; blighted before it is g.? 19.26
Jericho until your beards have g., 1Ch 19.05
men who had g. up with him and 2Ch 10.08
men who had g. up with him said to 10.10

GROWN (cont.)
My eye has g. dim from grief, and Job 17.07
their youth be like plants full g., Ps 144.12
housetops, blighted before it is g. Is 37.27
they have g. fat and sleek. Jer 5.28
not truth has g. strong in the 9.03
How the gold has g. dim, how the pure Lam 4.01
these things our eyes have g. dim, 5.17
Violence has g. up into a rod of Eze 7.11
were formed, and your hair had g.; 16.07
who have g. and become strong. Dan 4.22
greatness has g. and reaches to 4.22
For this people's heart has g. dull, Mt 13.15
but when it has g. it is the 13.32
For this people's heart has g. dull, Ac 28.27
appointed time has g. very short; 1Co 7.29
when he has g. up, refused to be Heb 11.24
sake, and you have not g. weary. Rev 2.03
the earth have g. rich with the 18.03

GROWS
house, till Shelah my son g. up"— Gen 38.11
of yours which g. in the field, Ex 10.05
What g. of itself in your harvest Lev 25.05
nor reap what g. of itself, nor 25.11
or if he g. rich he may redeem 25.49
the hyssop that g. out of the wall; 1Ki 4.33
you shall eat what g. of itself, 2Ki 19.29
has clean hands g. stronger and Job 17.09
and let what g. for me be rooted 31.08
it g. weak because of all my foes. Ps 6.07
my eye g. dim through sorrow. 88.09
which withers before it g. up, 129.06
freely, yet g. all the richer; Pro 11.24
this year eat what g. of itself, Is 37.30
my compassion g. warm and tender. Hos 11.08
it is sown it g. up and becomes Mk 4.32
together and g. into a holy temple Eph 2.21
g. with a growth that is from God. Col 2.19

GROWTH
with showers, and blessing its g. Ps 65.10
and the new g. appears, and the Pro 27.25
the new g. fails, the verdure is no Is 15.06
the shooting up of the latter g.; Amo 7.01
was the latter g. after the king's 7.01
watered, but God gave the g. 1Co 3.06
but only God who gives the g. 3.07
makes bodily g. and upbuilds itself Eph 4.16
grows with a g. that is from God. Col 2.19
and rank g. of wickedness and Jas 1.21
earth or any green g. or any tree, Rev 9.04

GRUDGE
or bear any g. against the sons of Lev 19.18
among you will g. food to his Deu 28.54
will g. to the husband of her bosom, 28.56
And Herodias had a g. against him, Mk 6.19

GRUDGING
shall not be g. when you give to Deu 15.10

GRUMBLE
nor g., as some of them did and 1Co 10.10
Do not g., brethren, against one Jas 5.09

GRUMBLED
receiving it they g. at the householder, Mt 20.11

GRUMBLERS
These are g., malcontents, following Jud 1.16

GRUMBLING
things without g. or questioning, Php 2.14

GUARANTEE
his Spirit in our hearts as a g. 2Co 1.22
has given us the Spirit as a g. 5.05
which is the g. of our inheritance Eph 1.14

GUARANTEED
on grace and be g. to all his Rom 4.16

GUARD
to g. the way to the tree of life. Gen 3.24
of Pharaoh, the captain of the g. 37.36
of Pharaoh, the captain of the g., 39.01
the house of the captain of the g., 40.03
The captain of the g. charged Joseph 40.04
house of the captain of the g., 41.10
a servant of the captain of the g.; 41.12
to g. you on the way and to bring Ex 23.20
as the rear g. of all the camps, Num 10.25
and the rear g. came after the ark, Jos 6.09
and the rear g. came after the ark 6.13
and its rear g. west of the city. 8.13
cave, and set men by it to g. them; 10.18
the army; for the army was off its g. Ju 8.11
"He will g. the feet of his faithful 1Sa 2.09
said to the g. who stood about him, 22.17
and put them in a house under g., 2Sa 20.03
hands of the officers of the g., 1Ki 14.27
the g. bore them and brought them 14.28
had been on g. at Ramothgilead 2Ki 9.14
said to the g. and to the officers, 10.25
the g. and the officers cast them 10.25
the sabbath and g. the king's house 11.05
the guards), shall g. the palace; 11.06
the sabbath and g. the house of 11.07
noise of the g. and of the people. 11.13
were with the captain of the g., 25.10
captain of the g. carried into 25.11
captain of the g. left some of the 25.12
captain of the g. took away as 25.15
captain of the g. took Seraiah the 25.18
the captain of the g. took them, 25.20
hands of the officers of the g., 2Ch 12.10
the g. came and bore them, and 12.11
the people as a g. for the king, 23.10
G. them and keep them until you Ez 8.29
of the king at the court of the g. Neh 3.25
and set a g. as a protection 4.09
they may be a g. for us by night 4.22
the men of the g. who followed me, 4.23
still standing g. let them shut 7.03
standing g. at the storehouses of 12.25
to a halt at the Gate of the G. 12.39
themselves and come and g. the gates, 13.22
that thou settest a g. over me? Job 7.12
g. us ever from this generation. Ps 12.07
Oh g. my life, and deliver me; 25.20
"I will g. my ways, that I may not 39.01
of you to g. you in all your ways. 91.11
G. me, O LORD, from the hands of the 140.04
Set a g. over my mouth, O LORD, keep 141.03
understanding will g. you; Pro 2.11
love her, and she will g. you. 4.06
g. her, for she is your life. 4.13
and your lips may g. knowledge. 5.02
G. your steps when you go to the Ecc 5.01
any one harm it, I g. it night and day; Is 27.03
God of Israel will be your rear g. 52.12
of the LORD shall be your rear g. 58.08
court of the g. which was in the Jer 32.02
came to me in the court of the g., 32.08
sitting in the court of the g. 32.12
shut up in the court of the g.: 33.01
Jeremiah to the court of the g.; 37.21
remained in the court of the g. 37.21
which was in the court of the g., 38.06
remained in the court of the g. 38.13
court of the g. until the day that 38.28
Nebuzaradan, the captain of the g., 39.09
Nebuzaradan, the captain of the g., 39.10
the captain of the g., saying, 39.11
So Nebuzaradan the captain of the g., 39.13
Jeremiah from the court of the g. 39.14
shut up in the court of the g.: 39.15

GUARD (cont.)
captain of the g. had let him go Jer 40.01
The captain of the g. took Jeremiah 40.02
captain of the g. gave him an 40.05
Nebuzaradan, the captain of the g., 41.10
captain of the g. had left with 43.06
were with the captain of the g., 52.14
captain of the g. carried away 52.15
captain of the g. left some of the 52.16
captain of the g. took away as 52.19
captain of the g. took Seraiah the 52.24
the captain of the g. took them, 52.26
captain of the g. carried away 52.30
about you, and be a g. for them. Eze 38.07
the captain of the king's g., Dan 2.14
g. the doors of your mouth from her Mic 7.05
Then I will encamp at my house as a g., Zec 9.08
of a priest should g. knowledge, Mal 2.07
the judge, and the judge to the g., Mt 5.25
to them, "You have a g. of soldiers; 27.65
sealing the stone and setting a g. 27.66
some of the g. went into the city 28.11
soldier of the g. and gave orders Mk 6.27
angels charge of you, to g. you,' Lk 4.10
he was kept under g., and bound 8.29
four squads of soldiers to g. him, Ac 12.04
passed the first and the second g., 12.10
praetorian g. and to all the rest Php 1.13
strengthen you and g. you from evil. 2Th 3.03
O Timothy, g. what has been entrusted 1Ti 1.12
he is able to g. until that Day 2Ti 1.12
g. the truth that has been entrusted 1.14

GUARDED
in vain have I g. all that this 1Sa 25.21
the priests who g. the threshold 2Ki 12.09
who g. the threshold, became angry Est 2.21
who g. the threshold, and who had 6.02
I have g. them, and none of them is Jn 17.12
him to be g. in Herod's praetorium. Ac 23.35
by himself, with the soldier that g. him. 28.16
King Aretas g. the city of Damascus 2Co 11.32
God's power are g. through faith 1Pe 1.05

GUARDIAN
With an anointed g. cherub I placed Eze 28.14
and the g. cherub drove you out 28.16
the Shepherd and G. of your souls. 1Pe 2.25

GUARDIANS
and to the g. of the sons of Ahab, 2Ki 10.01
together with the elders and the g., 10.05
the Holy Spirit has made you g., Ac 20.28
but he is under g. and trustees Gal 4.02

GUARDING
By g. it according to thy word. Ps 119.09
g. the paths of justice and preserving Pro 2.08
before the door were g. the prison; Ac 12.06

GUARDROOM
and brought them back to the g. 1Ki 14.28
and brought them back to the g. 2Ch 12.11

GUARDS
of the Carites and of the g., 2Ki 11.04
a third at the gate behind the g.), 11.06
and the g. stood, every man with his 11.11
the g., and all the people of the 11.19
the gate of the g. to the king's 11.19
is, the house of the tent, as g. 1Ch 9.23
Appoint g. from among the inhabitants Neh 7.03
He who g. his mouth preserves his Pro 13.03
Righteousness g. him whose way is 13.06
he who g. his way preserves his 16.17
he who g. himself will keep far 22.05
and he who g. his master will be 27.18
he sat with the g. to see the end. Mt 26.58
fear of him the g. trembled and 28.04
and he was sitting with the g., Mk 14.54
And the g. received him with 14.65
g. his own palace, his goods are in Lk 11.21

GUDGODAH
From there they journeyed to G., Deu 10.07
and from G. to Jotbathah, a land 10.07

GUEST
For I am thy passing g., Ps 39.12
Where is my g. room, where I am to Mk 14.14
in to be the g. of a man who is a Lk 19.07
Where is the g. room, where I am to 22.11
prepare a g. room for me, for I am Phm 1.22

GUESTS
that you might eat with the g." 1Sa 9.24
from Jerusalem who were invited g., 2Sa 15.11
Adonijah and all the g. who were 1Ki 1.41
Then all the g. of Adonijah trembled, 1.49
the g. in my house have forgotten Job 19.15
that her g. are in the depths of Pro 9.18
a sacrifice and consecrated his g. Zep 1.07
"Can the wedding g. mourn as long Mt 9.15
oaths and his g. he commanded it 14.09
wedding hall was filled with g. 22.10
the king came in to look at the g., 22.11
"Can the wedding g. fast while the Mk 2.19
she pleased Herod and his g.; 6.22
oaths and his g. he did not want 6.26
make wedding g. fast while the Lk 5.34
So he called them in to be his g. Ac 10.23

GUIDANCE
consulted a medium, seeking g., 1Ch 10.13
and did not seek g. from the LORD. 10.14
They turn round and round by his g., Job 37.12
Where there is no g., a people falls; Pro 11.14
by counsel; by wise g. wage war. 20.18
for by wise g. you can wage your 24.06

GUIDE
or can you g. the Bear with its Job 38.32
thy name's sake lead me and g. me, Ps 31.03
ever and ever. He will be our g. for ever. 48.14
with equity and g. the nations 67.04
Thou dost g. me with thy counsel, 73.24
they have not known I will g. them. Is 42.16
by springs of water will g. them. 49.10
There is none to g. her among all 51.18
And the LORD will g. you continually, 58.11
to g. our feet into the way of Lk 1.79
he will g. you into all the truth; Jn 16.13
Judas who was g. to those who Ac 1.16
that you are a g. to the blind, Rom 2.19
may obey us, we g. their whole bodies. Jas 3.03
and he will g. them to springs of Rev 7.17

GUIDED
thou hast g. them by thy strength Ex 15.13
from his mother's womb I g. him); Job 31.18
and g. them in the wilderness like Ps 78.52
and g. them with skilful hand. 78.72
they are g. by a very small rudder Jas 3.04

GUIDEPOSTS
for yourself, make yourself g.; Jer 31.21

GUIDES
The integrity of the upright g. them, Pro 11.03
they are blind g. And if a blind Mt 15.14
blind g., who say, 'If any one 23.16
You blind g., straining out a gnat 23.24
"How can I, unless some one g. me?" Ac 8.31
you have countless g. in Christ, 1Co 4.15

GUIDING
my mind still g. me with wisdom— Ecc 2.03

GUILE

he said, "Your brother came with g., Gen 27.35
they have subverted me with g.; Ps 119.78
though his hatred be covered with g., Pro 26.26
Israelite indeed, in whom is no g.! Jn 1.47
and got the better of you by g. 2Co 12.16
uncleanness, nor is it made with g.; 1Th 2.03
malice and all g. and insincerity and envy 1Pe 2.01
committed no sin; no g. was found on his lips. 2.22
evil and his lips from speaking g.; 3.10

GUILELESS

is good and g. as to what is evil; Rom 16.19

GUILT

you would have brought g. upon us." Gen 26.10
found out the g. of your servants; 44.16
himself any g. incurred in the Ex 28.38
lest they bring g. upon themselves 28.43
thus bringing g. on the people, then Lev 4.03
shall bring his g. offering to the 5.06
as his g. offering to the LORD for 5.07
as his g. offering to the LORD, a 5.15
the sanctuary; it is a g. offering. 5.15
with the ram of the g. offering, 5.16
you at the price for a g. offering, 5.18
It is a g. offering; he is guilty 5.19
on the day of his g. offering. 6.05
the priest his g. offering to the 6.06
you at the price for a g. offering; 6.06
sin offering and the g. offering. 6.17
"This is the law of the g. offering. 7.01
they shall kill the g. offering, 7.02
to the LORD; it is a g. offering. 7.05
The g. offering is like the sin 7.07
of the g. offering, of the consecration, 7.37
and offer it for a g. offering, 14.12
for the g. offering, like the sin 14.13
of the blood of the g. offering, 14.14
upon the blood of the g. offering; 14.17
male lamb for a g. offering to be 14.21
take the lamb of the g. offering, 14.24
kill the lamb of the g. offering; 14.25
of the blood of the g. offering, 14.25
blood of the g. offering was put; 14.28
shall bring a g. offering for 19.21
meeting, a ram for a g. offering. 19.21
the ram of the g. offering before 19.22
cause them to bear iniquity and g., 22.16
lamb a year old for a g. offering; Num 6.12
and every g. offering of theirs, 18.09
and so the g. of bloodshed be upon Deu 19.10
shall purge the g. of innocent 19.13
and set not the g. of innocent 21.08
but let the g. of blood be forgiven 21.08
shall purge the g. of innocent 21.09
not bring the g. of blood upon 22.08
shall not bring g. upon the land 24.04
means return him a g. offering. 1Sa 6.03
"What is the g. offering that we 6.04
returning to him as a g. offering. 6.08
returned as a g. offering to the 6.17
If this g. is in me or in Jonathan 14.41
but if this g. is in thy people 14.41
What is my g.? And what is my 20.01
But if there is g. in me, slay me 20.08
"Upon me alone, my lord, be the g.; 25.24
have I done? What g. is on my hands? 26.18
"On me be the g., my lord the king, 2Sa 14.09
and if there is g. in me, 14.32
"There is blood g. on Saul and on 21.01
him, and I kept myself from g. 22.24
house the g. for the blood which 1Ki 2.31
The money from the g. offerings and 2Ki 12.16
Why should he bring g. upon Israel?" 1Ch 21.03
may not incur g. before the LORD 2Ch 19.10
do, and you will not incur g. 19.10
and Jerusalem for this their g. 24.18
bring upon us g. against the LORD 28.13
addition to our present sins and g. 28.13
For our g. is already great, and 28.13
Amon incurred g. more and more. 33.23
and our g. has mounted up to the Ez 9.06
this day we have been in great g.; 9.07
evil deeds and for our great g., 9.13
we are before thee in our g., 9.15
and so increased the g. of Israel. 10.10
and their g. offering was a ram of 10.19
a ram of the flock for their g. 10.19
Do not cover their g., and let not Neh 4.05
of you less than your g. deserves. Job 11.06
Make them bear their g., O God; Ps 5.10
him, and I kept myself from g. 18.23
pardon my g., for it is great. 25.11
didst forgive the g. of my sin. 32.05
your g. is taken away, and your sin Is 6.07
because of the g. of their fathers, 14.21
inhabitants suffer for their g.; 24.06
Therefore by this the g. of Jacob 27.09
stain of your g. is still before Jer 2.22
Only acknowledge your g., that you 3.13
because your g. is great, because 30.14
Because your g. is great, because 30.15
requite the g. of fathers to their 32.18
from all the g. of their sin 33.08
forgive all the g. of their sin 33.08
is full of g. against the Holy One 51.05
"The g. of the house of Israel and Eze 9.09
this was the g. of your sister 16.49
he brings their g. to remembrance, 21.23
have made your g. to be remembered, 21.24
offering and the g. offering were 40.39
and the g. offering, for the place 42.13
sin offering, and the g. offering; 44.29
shall boil the g. offering and the 46.20
Ephraim shall stumble in his g.; Hos 5.05
acknowledge their g. and seek my 5.15
now they must bear their g. The LORD will 10.02
offset the g. he has incurred. 12.08
but he incurred g. through Baal and 13.01
Samaria shall bear her g., because she has 13.16
will remove the g. of this land in Zec 3.09
were blind, you would have no g.; Jn 9.41
you say, 'We see,' your g. remains. 9.41

GUILTLESS

not hold him g. who takes his name Ex 20.07
not hold him g. who takes his name Deu 5.11
"We will be g. with respect to this Jos 2.17
upon his head, and we shall be g.; 2.19
we shall be g. with respect to 2.20
the LORD's anointed, and be g.?" 1Sa 26.09
are for ever g. before the LORD 2Sa 3.28
let the king and his throne be g." 14.09
Now therefore hold him not g. 1Ki 2.09
is found the lifeblood of g. poor; Jer 2.34
profane the sabbath, and are g.? Mt 12.05
would not have condemned the g. 12.07
g. in the day of our Lord Jesus 1Co 1.08
proved yourselves g. in the matter. 2Co 7.11

GUILTY

"In truth we are g. concerning our Gen 42.21
who will by no means clear the g., Ex 34.07
commanded not to be done and are g.; Lev 4.13
commanded not to be done, and is g., 4.22
commanded not to be done, and is g., 4.27
has become unclean, he shall be g. 5.02
he comes to know it he shall be g. 5.03
it he shall in any of these be g. 5.04
When a man is g. in any of these, he 5.05
yet he is g. and shall bear his 5.17
offering; he is g. before the LORD." 5.19
when one has sinned and become g., 6.04
one may do and thereby become g." 6.07
the LORD, and that person is g., Num 5.06

GUILTY (cont.)
he will by no means clear the g., Num 14.18
he shall not be g. of blood. 35.27
of a murderer who is g. of death; 35.31
innocent and condemning the g., Deu 25.01
then if the g. man deserves to be 25.02
to them, else you would now be g.' " Ju 21.22
my lord hold me g. or remember how 2Sa 19.19
condemning the g. by bringing his 1Ki 8.32
requiting the g. by bringing his 2Ch 6.23
although thou knowest that I am not g., Job 10.07
of him who walks in his g. ways. Ps 68.21
he is tried, let him come forth g.; 109.07
The way of the g. is crooked, but Pro 21.08
he curse you, and you be held g. 30.10
who acquit the g. for a bribe, and Is 5.23
who will declare me g.? Behold, all of 50.09
All who ate of it became g.; Jer 2.03
herself less g. than false Judah. 3.11
'We are not g., for they have 50.07
of which he is g. and the sin he Eze 18.24
You have become g. by the blood 22.04
because you are g. of blood, 35.06
O Israel, let not Judah become g. Hos 4.15
blood, and I will not clear the g., Joe 3.21
Lord will by no means clear the g. Nah 1.03
g. men, whose own might is their god! Hab 1.11
but is g. of an eternal sin"— Mk 3.29
find this man g. of any of your Lk 23.14
if he is g. of immorality or greed, 1Co 5.11
manner will be g. of profaning the 11.27
point has become g. of all of it. Jas 2.10
commits sin is g. of lawlessness; 1Jn 3.04

GULL
the sea g., the hawk according to Lev 11.16
the sea g., the hawk, after their Deu 14.15

GULLIES
In the g. of the torrents they must Job 30.06

GUM
with their camels bearing g., Gen 37.25
g., myrrh, pistachio nuts, and 43.11

GUNI
Jahzeel, G., Jezer, and Shillem Gen 46.24
of G., the family of the Gunites; Num 26.48
son of G., was chief in their 1Ch 5.15
G., Jezer, and Shallum, the offspring 7.13

GUNITES
of Guni, the family of the G.; Num 26.48

GUR
in the chariot at the ascent of G., 2Ki 9.27

GURBAAL
against the Arabs that dwelt in G., 2Ch 26.07

GUSH
Thou makest springs g. forth in the Ps 104.10
and our eyelids g. with water. Jer 9.18

GUSHED
until the blood g. out upon them. 1Ki 18.28
so that water g. out and streams Ps 78.20
the rock, and water g. forth; 105.41
the rock and the water g. out. Is 48.21
middle and all his bowels g. out. Ac 1.18

GUSHING
fountain of wisdom is a g. stream, Pro 18.04

H

HAAHASHTARI
Ahuzzam, Hepher, Temeni, and H. These 1Ch 4.06

HABAIAH
the sons of H., the sons of Hakkoz, Ez 2.61

HABAKKUK
of God which H. the prophet saw. Hab 1.01
A prayer of H. the prophet, according 3.01

HABAZZINIAH
son of H., and his brothers, and all Jer 35.03

HABIT
as is the h. of some, but encouraging Heb 10.25

HABITABLE
years, till they came to a h. land; Ex 16.35
them on the face of the h. world. Job 37.12

HABITATION
alone in a h. outside the camp. Lev 13.46
put his name and make his h. there; Deu 12.05
Look down from thy holy h., 26.15
and let me see both it and his h.; 2Sa 15.25
faces from the h. of the Lord, 2Ch 29.06
came to his holy h. in heaven. 30.27
and reward you with a rightful h. Job 8.06
brimstone is scattered upon his h. 18.15
I love the h. of thy house, and the Ps 26.08
the holy h. of the Most High. 46.04
of widows is God in his holy h. 68.05
Jacob, and laid waste his h. 79.07
refuge, the Most High your h., 91.09
the birds of the air have their h.; 104.12
he has desired it for his h.: 132.13
and carve a h. for yourself in the Is 22.16
a h. deserted and forsaken, like the 27.10
people will abide in a peaceful h., 32.18
a quiet h., an immovable tent, whose 33.20
see, from thy holy and glorious h. 63.15
him, and have laid waste his h. Jer 10.25
from his holy h. utter his voice; 25.30
O h. of righteousness, O holy hill!' 31.23
their true h., the Lord, the hope of 50.07
still in their h. at the light of Hab 3.11
'Let his h. become desolate, and let Ac 1.20
leave to find a h. for the God of 7.46
and the boundaries of their h., 17.26

HABITATIONS
in all your h. on the sabbath day." Ex 35.03
are full of the h. of violence. Ps 74.20
of their camp, all around their h. 78.28
curtains of your h. be stretched Is 54.02
us, or who shall enter our h.?' Jer 21.13
shall again be h. of shepherds 33.12
without mercy all the h. of Jacob; Lam 2.02
and waste, throughout all their h., Eze 6.14
earth, to seize h. not their own. Hab 1.06
receive you into the eternal h. Lk 16.09

HABOR
and on the H., the river of Gozan, 2Ki 17.06
and on the H., the river of Gozan, 18.11
H., Hara, and the river Gozan, to 1Ch 5.26

HACALIAH
The words of Nehemiah the son of H. Neh 1.01
governor, the son of H., Zedekiah, 10.01

HACHILAH
at Horesh, on the hill of H., 1Sa 23.19

HACHILAH (cont.)
hiding himself on the hill of H., 1Sa 26.01
And Saul encamped on the hill of H., 26.03

HACHMONI
the son of H. attended the king's 1Ch 27.32

HACHMONITE
a H., was chief of the three; 1Ch 11.11

HACKED
entrance they h. the wooden Ps 74.05

HAD
And they h. brick for stone, and Gen 11.03
and he h. sheep, oxen, he-asses, 12.16
also h. flocks and herds and tents, 13.05
and h. large flocks, maidservants 30.43
him in charge of all that he h. 39.04
all that he h. the LORD blessed 39.05
the LORD was upon all that he h., 39.05
of Israel h. light where they Ex 10.23
for the stuff they h. was sufficient 36.07
him because she has h. no husband; Lev 21.03
and they h. no children. Num 3.04
the son of Hepher h. no sons, 26.33
his own sin; and he h. no sons. 27.03
the sons of Gad h. a very great 32.01
people of Israel h. manna no more, Jos 5.12
h. no sons, but only daughters; 17.03
Asher Manasseh h. Bethshean and 17.11
And it h. for its inheritance 19.02
Now Gideon h. seventy sons, his own Ju 8.30
offspring, for he h. many wives. 8.30
And he h. thirty sons who rode on 10.04
and they h. thirty cities, called 10.04
He h. thirty sons; and thirty daughters 12.09
He h. forty sons and thirty grandsons, 12.14
And taking what Micah h. made, 18.27
He h. two wives; the name of the 1Sa 1.02
And Peninnah h. children, but Hannah 1.02
children, but Hannah h. no children. 1.02
and he h. a son whose name was Saul, 9.02
Now Saul's son h. two men who were 2Sa 4.02
Now Ziba h. fifteen sons and twenty 9.10
The rich man h. very many flocks 12.02
when any man h. a suit to come 15.02
The Philistines h. war again with 21.15
For he h. dominion over all the 1Ki 4.24
and he h. peace on all sides round 4.24
Solomon also h. seventy thousand 5.15
the store-cities that Solomon h., 9.19
He h. seven hundred wives, princesses, 11.03
the Jezreelite h. a vineyard in 12.01
of the LORD which Elijah h. spoken. 2Ki 1.17
Judah, because Ahaziah h. no son. 1.17
who h. twenty-three cities in the 1Ch 2.22
Now Sheshan h. no sons, only daughters 2.34
but Sheshan h. an Egyptian slave, 2.34
h. two wives, Helah and Naarah; 4.05
sons of Kohath h. cities of their 6.66
and Zelophehad h. daughters. 7.15
children whom he h. in Jerusalem: 14.04
him because he h. fought against 18.10
for Hadadezer h. often been at 18.10
Eliezer h. no other sons, but the 23.17
and h. no children, so Eleazar and 24.02
Of Mahli: Eleazar, who h. no sons. 24.28
majesty as h. not been on any king 29.25
of the LORD h. made in the wilderness, 2Ch 1.03
of the kings h. who were before 1.12
he h. fourteen hundred chariots 1.14
the store-cities that Solomon h., 8.06
And Solomon h. four thousand stalls 9.25
who h. stood before Solomon his 10.06
And Asa h. an army of three hundred 14.08
and he h. great riches and honor. 17.05
and he h. great stores in the 17.13
He h. soldiers, mighty men of valor, 17.13
Now Jehoshaphat h. great riches and 18.01
as the house of Ahab h. done; 21.06
for he h. large herds, both in the 26.10
and he h. farmers and vinedressers 26.10
And Hezekiah h. very great riches 32.27
For the people h. a mind to work. Neh 4.06
and he h. fourteen thousand sheep, Job 42.12
He h. also seven sons and three 42.13
h. not Moses, his chosen one, stood Ps 106.23
and h. slaves who were born in my Ecc 2.07
I h. also great possessions of 2.07
than any who h. been before me in 2.07
for then we h. plenty of food, and Jer 44.17
the four h. the same likeness, as if Eze 10.10
labor that he h. performed against 29.18
Daniel h. a dream and visions of Dan 7.01
them as one who h. authority, Mt 7.29
he h. compassion for them, because 9.36
where they h. not much soil, and 13.05
since they h. no depth of soil, 13.05
and since they h. no root they 13.06
sold all that he h. and bought it. 13.46
and children and all that he h., 18.25
sorrowful; for he h. great possessions. 19.22
A man h. two sons; and he went to 21.28
there a man who h. no wedding 22.11
will she be wife? For they all h. her." 22.28
And they h. then a notorious 27.16
them as one who h. authority, Mk 1.22
was there who h. a withered hand. 3.01
to the man who h. the withered 3.03
for he h. healed many, so that all 3.10
so that all who h. diseases pressed 3.10
for they h. said, "He has an unclean 3.30
where it h. not much soil, and 4.05
sprang up, since it h. no depth of soil; 4.05
and since it h. no root it withered 4.06
the man who h. the legion; 5.15
was a woman who h. a flow of 5.25
and who h. suffered much under many 5.26
and h. spent all that she h., and 5.26
and he h. compassion on them, 6.34
And when they h. found out, they said, 6.38
again a great crowd h. gathered, 8.01
and they h. nothing to eat, he 8.01
And they h. a few small fish; 8.07
Now they h. forgotten to bring 8.14
and they h. only one loaf with them 8.14
sorrowful; for he h. great possessions. 10.22
He h. still one other, a beloved son; 12.06
For the seven h. her as wife." 12.23
has put in everything she h., 12.44
But they h. no child, because Lk 1.07
was a man who h. the spirit of an 4.33
all those who h. any that were sick 4.40
to the man who h. the withered 6.08
"A certain creditor h. two debtors; 7.41
a man from the city who h. demons; 8.27
a long time he h. worn no clothes, 8.27
for he h. an only daughter, about 8.42
And a woman who h. a flow of 8.43
cured those who h. need of healing. 9.11
And she h. a sister called Mary, who 10.39
"A man h. a fig tree planted in his 13.06
was a woman who h. had a spirit of 13.11
"There was a man who h. two sons; 15.11
was a rich man who h. a steward, 16.01
"If you h. faith as a grain of 17.06
For the seven h. her as wife." 20.33
put in all the living that she h." 21.04
for you have h. five husbands, and Jn 4.18
was healed of whatever disease he h. * 5.04
and as he h. the money box he used 12.06
When Jesus h. said this, he 12.36
because Judas h. the money box, 13.29
If I h. not come and spoken to them, 15.22

HAD (cont.)
If I h. not done among them the Jn 15.24
glory which I h. with thee before 17.05
me unless it h. been given you 19.11
together and h. all things in Ac 2.44
them to all, as any h. need. 2.45
but they h. everything in common. 4.32
was made to each as any h. need. 4.35
after him, though he h. no child. 7.05
"Our fathers h. the tent of witness 7.44
to the pattern that he h. seen. 7.44
and Samaria h. peace and was built 9.31
And they h. John to assist them. 13.05
seeing that he h. faith to be made 14.09
and Barnabas h. no small dissension 15.02
Moses has h. in every city those 15.21
he cut his hair, for he h. a vow. 18.18
over those who h. evil spirits, 19.13
And he h. four unmarried daughters, 21.09
and h. opportunity to make his 25.16
but they h. certain points of 25.19
And when this h. taken place, the 28.09
the island who h. diseases also 28.09
though I h. no charge to bring 28.19
wives live as though they h. none, 1Co 7.29
Why, we felt that we h. received the 2Co 1.09
spirit of faith as he h. who wrote, 4.13
our bodies h. no rest but we were 7.05
written that Abraham h. two sons, Gal 4.22
But God h. mercy on him, and not Ph 2.27
us what a welcome we h. among you, 1Th 1.09
blessed him who h. the promises. Heb 7.06
first covenant h. regulations for 9.01
the worshipers h. once been 10.02
For you h. compassion on the 10.34
you yourselves h. a better possession 10.34
If they h. been thinking of that 11.15
land from which they h. gone out, 11.15
they would have h. opportunity to 11.15
we have h. earthly fathers to 12.09
which you h. from the beginning; 1Jn 2.07
the one we have h. from the 2Jn 1.05
I h. much to write to you, but I 3Jn 1.13
abandoned the love you h. at first. Rev 2.04
as though it h. been slain, with 5.06
And when he h. taken the scroll, the 5.08
horse, and its rider h. a bow; 6.02
and its rider h. a balance in his 6.05
four angels who h. been given 7.02
angels who h. the seven trumpets 8.06
they h. scales like iron breastplates, 9.09
the sixth angel who h. the trumpet, 9.14
He h. a little scroll open in his 10.02
it h. two horns like a lamb and it 13.11
thousand who h. his name and his 14.01
and he too h. a sharp sickle. 14.17
to him who h. the sharp sickle, 14.18
and those who h. conquered the 15.02
name of God who h. power over 16.09
angels who h. the seven bowls came 17.01
and it h. seven heads and ten horns 17.03
where all who h. ships at sea grew 18.19
angels who h. the seven bowls full 21.09
It h. a great, high wall, with twelve 21.12
of the city h. twelve foundations, 21.14
talked to me h. a measuring rod of 21.15

HADAD
H., Tema, Jetur, Naphish, and Kedemah. Gen 25.15
and H. the son of Bedad, who defeated 36.35
H. died, and Samlah of Masrekah 36.36
against Solomon, H. the Edomite; 1Ki 11.14
but H. fled to Egypt, together with 11.17
H. being yet a little child. 11.17
And H. found great favor in the 11.19
But when H. heard in Egypt that 11.21
H. said to Pharaoh, "Let me depart, 11.21
Solomon, doing mischief as H. did; 11.25
Mishma, Dumah, Massa, H., Tema, 1Ch 1.30
H. the son of Bedad, who defeated 1.46
When H. died, Samlah of Masrekah 1.47
H. reigned in his stead; and the name 1.50
And H. died. The chiefs of 1.51

HADADEZER
David also defeated H. the son of 2Sa 8.03
came to help H. king of Zobah, 8.05
were carried by the servants of H., 8.07
cities of H., King David took very 8.08
had defeated the whole army of H., 8.09
fought against H. and defeated him; 8.10
for H. had often been at war with 8.10
the spoil of H. the son of Rehob, 8.12
And H. sent, and brought out the 10.16
of the army of H. at their head. 10.16
servants of H. saw that they had 10.19
from his master H. king of Zobah. 1Ki 11.23
David also defeated H. king of Zobah, 1Ch 18.03
came to help H. king of Zobah, 18.05
were carried by the servants of H., 18.07
cities of H., David took very much 18.08
had defeated the whole army of H., 18.09
fought against H. and defeated him; 18.10
for H. had often been at war with 18.10
of the army of H. at their head. 19.16
the servants of H. saw that they 19.19

HADADRIMMON
mourning for H. in the plain of Zec 12.11

HADAR
and H. reigned in his stead, the Gen 36.39

HADASHAH
Zenan, H., Migdalgad, Jos 15.37

HADASSAH
He had brought up H., that is Esther, Est 2.07

HADES
You shall be brought down to H. Mt 11.23
You shall be brought down to H. Lk 10.15
and in H., being in torment, he 16.23
wilt not abandon my soul to H., Ac 2.27
that he was not abandoned to H., 2.31
I have the keys of Death and H. Rev 1.18
was Death, and H. followed him; 6.08
Death and H. gave up the dead in 20.13
Then Death and H. were thrown into 20.14

HADID
H., and Ono, seven hundred and Ez 2.33
H., and Ono, seven hundred and Neh 7.37
H., Zeboim, Neballat, 11.34

HADLAI
Shallum, and Amasa the son of H., 2Ch 28.12

HADORAM
H., Uzal, Diklah, Gen 10.27
H., Uzal, Diklah, 1Ch 1.21
he sent his son H. to King David, 18.10
Then King Rehoboam sent H., 2Ch 10.18

HADRACH
the land of H. and will rest upon Zec 9.01

HADST
land which thou h. sword to give Neh 9.15
land which thou h. told their 9.23
thou h. established me as a strong Ps 30.07
or ever thou h. formed the earth 90.02
for thou h. filled me with indignation. Jer 15.17

HAELEPH
Zela, H., Jebus (that is, Jerusalem), Jos 18.28

HAG
there shall the night h. alight, Is 34.14

HAGAB
the sons of H., the sons of Shamlai, Ez 2.46

HAGABA
the sons of H., the sons of Shalmai, Neh 7.48

HAGABAH
the sons of H., the sons of Akkub, Ez 2.45

HAGAR
an Egyptian maid whose name was H.; Gen 16.01
took H. the Egyptian her maid, and 16.03
And he went in to H., and she conceived; 16.04
And he said, "H., maid of Sarai, 16.08
And H. bore Abram a son; and Abram 16.15
of his son, whom H. bore, Ishmael. 16.15
years old when H. bore Ishmael to 16.16
saw the son of H. the Egyptian, 21.09
a skin of water, and gave it to H., 21.14
of God called to H. from heaven, 21.17
said to her, "What troubles you, H.? 21.17
whom H. the Egyptian, Sarah's maid, 25.12
children for slavery; she is H. Gal 4.24
Now H. is Mount Sinai in Arabia; 4.25

HAGGAI
H. and Zechariah the son of Iddo, Ez 5.01
prophesying of H. the prophet and 6.14
LORD came by H. the prophet to Hag 1.01
the LORD came by H. the prophet, 1.03
and the words of H. the prophet, 1.12
Then H., the messenger of the LORD, 1.13
the LORD came by H the prophet, 2.01
the LORD came by H. the prophet, 2.10
Then said H., "If one who is 2.13
Then H. said, "So is it with this 2.14
came a second time to H. on the 2.20

HAGGARD
why are you so h. morning after 2Sa 13.04

HAGGEDOLIM
overseer was Zabdiel the son of H. Neh 11.14

HAGGI
H., Shuni, Ezbon, Eri, Arodi, and Areli. Gen 46.16
of H., the family of the Haggites; Num 26.15

HAGGIAH
H. his son, and Asaiah his son. 1Ch 6.30

HAGGITES
of Haggi, the family of the H.; Num 26.15

HAGGITH
the fourth, Adonijah the son of H. 2Sa 3.04
the son of H. exalted himself, 1Ki 1.05
the son of H. has become king and 1.11
the son of H. came to Bathsheba 2.13
Adonijah, whose mother was H.; 1Ch 3.02

HAGRI
of Nathan, Mibhar the son of H., 1Ch 11.38

HAGRITE
Over the flocks was Jaziz the H. 1Ch 27.30

HAGRITES
of Saul they made war on the H., 1Ch 5.10
They made war upon the H., 5.19
the H. and all who were with them 5.20
the Ishmaelites, Moab and the H., Ps 83.06

HAHANIAH
of Shaphan, Zedekiah the son of H., Jer 36.12

HAHIROTH
And they set out from before H., Num 33.08

HAIL
I will cause very heavy h. to fall, Ex 9.18
for the h. shall come down upon 9.19
there may be h. in all the land of 9.22
and the LORD sent thunder and h., 9.23
the LORD rained h. upon the land 9.23
there was h., and fire flashing 9.24
continually in the midst of the h., 9.24
very heavy h., such as had never 9.24
The h. struck down everything that 9.25
and the h. struck down every plant 9.25
of Israel were, there was no h. 9.26
been enough of this thunder and h.; 9.28
and there will be no more h., 9.29
and the thunder and the h. ceased, 9.33
rain and the h. and the thunder 9.34
what is left to you after the h., 10.05
the land, all that the h. has left." 10.12
of the trees which the h. had left; 10.15
seen the storehouses of the h., Job 38.22
He destroyed their vines with h., Ps 78.47
He gave over their cattle to the h., 78.48
He gave them h. for rain, and 105.32
fire and h., snow and frost, stormy 148.08
like a storm of h., a destroying Is 28.02
and h. will sweep away the refuge 28.17
toil with blight and mildew and h.; Hag 2.17
Jesus at once and said, "H. Master!" Mt 26.49
him, saying, "H., King of the Jews!" 27.29
Jesus met them and said, "H.!" 28.09
salute him, "H., King of the Jews!" Mk 15.18
"H., O favored one, the Lord is with Lk 1.28
him, saying, "H., King of the Jews!" Jn 19.03
and there followed h. and fire, Rev 8.07
an earthquake, and heavy h. 11.19
God for the plague of the h., 16.21

HAILED
of the garrison h. Jonathan and 1Sa 14.12

HAILSTONES
because of the h. than the men of Jos 10.11
his clouds h. and coals of fire. Ps 18.12
uttered his voice, h. and coals of fire. 18.13
a cloudburst and tempest and h. Is 30.30
great h. will fall, and a stormy Eze 13.11
and great h. in wrath to destroy it. 13.13
with him, torrential rains and h., 38.22
and great h., heavy as a hundredweight, Rev 16.21

HAIR
and fine twined linen, goats' h., Ex 25.04
of goats' h. for a tent over the 26.07
fine twined linen; goats' h., 35.06
linen or goats' h. or tanned rams' 35.23
with ability spun the goats' h. 35.26
of goats' h. for a tent over the 36.14
"Do not let the h. of your heads Lev 10.06
and if the h. in the diseased spot 13.03
and the h. in it has not turned 13.04
which has turned the h. white, 13.10
skin and its h. has turned white, 13.20
and the h. on it is not white and 13.21
and if the h. in the spot has 13.25
and the h. in the spot is not white 13.26
and the h. in it is yellow and thin, 13.30
and there is no black h. in it, 13.31
and there is in it no yellow h., 13.32
need not seek for the yellow h.; 13.36
and black h. has grown in it, the 13.37
"If a man's h. has fallen from his 13.40
And if a man's h. has fallen from 13.41
and let the h. of his head hang 13.45
clothes, and shave off all his h., 14.08
shave all his h. off his head; 14.09
beard and his eyebrows, all his h. 14.09
round off the h. on your temples 19.27
not let the h. of his head hang 21.10

HAIR (cont.)
and unbind the h. of the woman's Num 5.18
the locks of h. of his head grow 6.05
shall take the h. from his consecrated 6.18
has shaven the h. of his consecration, 6.19
of skin, all work of goats' h., 31.20
But the h. of his head began to Ju 16.22
a stone at a h., and not miss. 20.16
shall not one h. of his head fall 1Sa 14.45
a pillow of goats' h. at its head, 19.13
pillow of goats' h. at its head. 19.16
not one h. of your son shall fall 2Sa 14.11
And when he cut the h. of his head 14.26
it), he weighed the h. of his head, 14.26
and pulled h. from my head and Ez 9.03
of them and pulled out their h.; Neh 13.25
the h. of my flesh stood up. Job 4.15
beauty of old men is their gray h. Pro 20.29
Your h. is like a flock of goats, Sol 4.01
Your h. is like a flock of goats, 6.05
instead of well-set h., baldness; Is 3.24
the head and the h. of the feet, 7.20
Cut off your h. and cast it away; Jer 7.29
that cut the corners of their h.; 9.26
who cut the corners of their h.; 25.23
who cut the corners of their h., 49.32
for weighing, and divide the h. Eze 5.01
were formed, and your h. had grown; 16.07
it out, and pluck out your h., 23.34
only trim the h. of their heads. 44.20
the h. of their heads was not Dan 3.27
heaven till his h. grew as long as 4.33
and the h. of his head like pure 7.09
yourselves bald and cut off your h., Mic 1.16
Now John wore a garment of camel's h., Mt 3.04
cannot make one h. white or black. 5.36
Now John was clothed with camel's h., Mk 1.06
wiped them with the h. of her head, Lk 7.38
tears and wiped them with her h. 7.44
But not a h. of your head will 21.18
and wiped his feet with her h., Jn 11.02
and wiped his feet with her h.; 12.03
At Cenchreae he cut his h., Ac 18.18
since not a h. is to perish from 27.34
then she should cut off her h.; 1Co 11.06
to wear long h. is degrading to 11.14
but if a woman has long h., 11.15
For her h. is given to her for a 11.15
with braided h. or gold or pearls 1Ti 2.09
adorning with braiding of h., 1Pe 3.03
his head and his h. were white as Rev 1.14
their h. like women's h., and their 9.08

HAIRCLOTH
him. "He wore a garment of h., 2Ki 1.08

HAIRS
down my gray h. with sorrow to Gen 42.38
down my gray h. in sorrow to Sheol.' 44.29
down the gray h. of your servant 44.31
child with the man of gray h. Deu 32.25
not one of his h. shall fall to 1Ki 1.52
are more than the h. of my head; Ps 40.12
number than the h. of my head are 69.04
So even to old age and gray h., 71.18
and to gray h. I will carry you. Is 46.04
gray h. are sprinkled upon him, and Hos 7.09
But even the h. of your head are Mt 10.30
Why, even the h. of your head are Lk 12.07

HAIRY
red, all his body like a h. mantle; Gen 25.25
my brother Esau is a h. man, 27.11
his hands were h. like his brother 27.23
the h. crown of him who walks in Ps 68.21
not put on a h. mantle in order to Zec 13.04

HAKKATAN
of Azgad, Johanan the son of H., Ez 8.12

HAKKOZ
the seventh to H., the eighth to 1Ch 24.10
the sons of H., and the sons of Ez 2.61
son of Uriah, son of H. repaired. Neh 3.04
son of H. repaired another section 3.21
the sons of H., the sons of Barzillai 7.63

HAKUPHA
the sons of H., the sons of Harhur, Ez 2.51
the sons of H., the sons of Harhur, Neh 7.53

HALAH
to Assyria, and placed them in H., 2Ki 17.06
to Assyria, and put them in H., 18.11
Manasseh, and brought them to H., 1Ch 5.26
The exiles in H. who are of the Ob 1.20

HALAK
from Mount H., that rises toward Jos 11.17
the valley of Lebanon to Mount H., 12.07

HALF
and laid each h. over against the Gen 15.10
a gold ring weighing a h. shekel, 24.22
And Moses took h. of the blood and Ex 24.06
and h. of the blood he threw 24.06
cubits and a h. shall be its 25.10
a cubit and a h. its breadth, and a 25.10
and a cubit and a h. its height. 25.10
cubits and a h. shall be its 25.17
and a cubit and a h. its breadth. 25.17
and a cubit and a h. its height. 25.23
the h. curtain that remains, shall 26.12
a cubit and a h. the breadth of 26.16
h. a shekel according to the shekel 30.13
h. a shekel as an offering to the 30.13
than the h. shekel, when you give 30.15
sweet-smelling cinnamon h. as much, 30.23
a cubit and a h. the breadth of 36.21
two cubits and a h. was its length, 37.01
a cubit and a h. its breadth, and a 37.01
and a cubit and a h. its height. 37.01
two cubits and a h. was its length, 37.06
and a cubit and a h. its breadth. 37.06
and a cubit and a h. its height; 37.10
h. a shekel, by the shekel of the 38.26
h. of it in the morning and h. in Lev 6.20
the flesh is h. consumed when he Num 12.12
flour, mixed with h. a hin of oil, 15.09
drink offering h. a hin of wine, 15.10
shall be h. a hin of wine for a 28.14
take it from their h., and give it to 31.29
of Israel's h. you shall take one 31.30
And the h., the portion of those 31.36
From the people of Israel's h., 31.42
congregation's h. was three 31.43
of Israel's h. Moses took one of 31.47
and h. the hill country of Gilead Deu 3.12
for at h. the cost of a hired 15.18
of Gad and the h. tribe of Manasseh Jos 4.12
h. of them in front of Mount 8.33
Gerizim and h. of them in front of 8.33
Ammonites, that is, h. of Gilead, 12.02
and over h. of Gilead to the 12.05
nine tribes and h. the tribe of 13.07
With the other h. of the tribe of 13.08
and h. the land of the Ammonites, to 13.25
and h. Gilead, and Ashtaroth, and 13.31
Manasseh for the h. of the Machirites 13.31
and Reuben and h. the tribe of 18.07
Now to the one h. of the tribe of 22.07
to the other h. Joshua had given a 22.07
as it were h. a furrow's length in 1Sa 14.14
and shaved off h. the beard of 2Sa 10.04
If h. of us die, they will not care 18.03
and also h. the people of Israel, 19.40
h. to the one, and h. to the other. 1Ki 3.25
is made, a cubit and a h. deep. 7.31

HALF (cont.)
of a wheel was a cubit and a h. 1Ki 7.32
was a round band h. a cubit high; 7.35
the h. was not told me; your wisdom 10.07
king, "If you give me h. your house, 13.08
commander of h. his chariots, 16.09
h. of the people followed Tibni the 16.21
him king, and h. followed Omri. 16.21
Haroeh, h. of the Menuhoth. 1Ch 2.52
and h. of the Manahathites, the 2.54
the h. of Manasseh, ten cities. 6.61
for the h. tribe of Manasseh, Joel 27.20
for the h. tribe of Manasseh in 27.21
and behold, h. the greatness of 2Ch 9.06
ruler of h. the district of Jerusalem, Neh 3.09
ruler of h. the district of Jerusalem, 3.12
ruler of h. the district of Bethzur, 3.16
ruler of h. the district of Keilah, 3.17
ruler of h. the district of Keilah; 3.18
joined together to h. its height. 4.06
h. of my servants worked on construction, 4.16
and h. held the spears, shields, bows, 4.16
and h. of them held the spears from 4.21
Hoshaiah and h. of the princes of 12.32
followed them with h. of the people, 12.38
and I and h. of the officials with 12.40
and h. of their children spoke the 13.24
you, even to the h. of my kingdom." Est 5.03
Even to the h. of my kingdom, it 5.06
Even to the h. of my kingdom, it 7.02
shall not live out h. their days. Ps 55.23
H. of it he burns in the fire; Is 44.16
over the h. he eats flesh, he roasts 44.16
H. of it I burned in the fire, I 44.19
Samaria has not committed h. your sins; Eze 16.51
a cubit and a h. long, and a cubit 40.42
long, and a cubit and a h. broad, 40.42
a rim around it h. a cubit broad, 43.17
a time, two times, and h. a time. Dan 7.25
and for h. of the week he shall 9.27
a time, two times, and h. a time; 12.07
h. of the city shall go into exile, Zec 14.02
so that one h. of the Mount shall 14.04
northward, and the other h. southward. 14.04
h. of them to the eastern sea and 14.08
and h. of them to the western sea; 14.08
give you, even h. of my kingdom." Mk 6.23
him, and departed, leaving him h. dead. Lk 10.30
the h. of my goods I give to the 19.08
in heaven for about h. an hour. Rev 8.01
days and a h. men from the peoples 11.09
the three and a h. days a breath 11.11
a time, and times, and h. a time. 12.14

HALF-SHEKEL
collectors of the h. tax went up to Mt 17.24

HALF-TRIBE
and to the h. of Manasseh the son Num 32.33
to the nine tribes and to the h.; 34.13
and also the h. of Manasseh; 34.14
tribes and the h. have received 34.15
I gave to the h. of Manasseh. Deu 3.13
and the h. of the Manassites. 29.08
and the h. of Manasseh Joshua said, Jos 1.12
the Gadites and the h. of Manasseh. 12.06
inheritance to the h. of Manasseh; 13.29
allotted to the h. of the Manassites 13.29
of Dan and the h. of Manasseh, 21.05
and from the h. of Manasseh in 21.06
and out of the h. of Manasseh, 21.25
given out of the h. of Manasseh, 21.27
Gadites, and the h. of Manasseh, 22.01
Gadites and the h. of Manasseh 22.09
Gadites and the h. of Manasseh 22.10
Gadites and the h. of Manasseh 22.11
the Gadites and the h. of Manasseh, 22.13
and the h. of Manasseh, in the land 22.15
and the h. of Manasseh said in 22.21
and the h. of Manasseh had valiant 1Ch 5.18
The members of the h. of Manasseh 5.23
and the h. of Manasseh, and brought 5.26
out of the h., the half of Manasseh, 6.61
and out of the h. of Manasseh, Aner 6.70
given out of the h. of Manasseh: 6.71
Of the h. of Manasseh eighteen 12.31
Gadites and the h. of Manasseh 12.37
and the h. of the Manassites for 26.32

HALFWAY
h. up the frames, shall pass through Ex 26.28
shall extend h. down the altar. 27.05
from end to end h. up the frames. 36.33
under its ledge, extending h. down. 38.04

HALHUL
H., Bethzur, Gedor, Jos 15.58

HALI
Helkath, H., Beten, Achshaph, Jos 19.25

HALL
them into the h. and gave them a 1Sa 9.22
And he made the H. of Pillars; 1Ki 7.06
And he made the H. of the Throne 7.07
judgment, even the H. of Judgment; 7.07
in the other court back of the h., 7.08
house like this h. for Pharaoh's 7.08
palace, opposite the king's h. Est 5.01
lords, came into the banqueting h.; Dan 5.10
so the wedding h. was filled with Mt 22.10
argued daily in the h. of Tyrannus. Ac 19.09
the audience h. with the military 25.23

HALLELUJAH
multitude in heaven, crying, "H.! Rev 19.01
Once more they cried, "H.! 19.03
on the throne, saying, "Amen. H.!" 19.04
of mighty thunderpeals, crying, "H.! 19.06

HALLOHESH
Next to him Shallum the son of H., Neh 3.12
H., Pilha, Shobek, 10.24

HALLOW
of Israel h. as their holy gifts; Ex 28.38
cleanse it and h. it from the Lev 16.19
And you shall h. the fiftieth year, 25.10
and h. my sabbaths that they may be Eze 20.20

HALLOWED
blessed the seventh day and h. it, Gen 2.03
blessed the sabbath day and h. it. Ex 20.11
she shall not touch any h. thing, Lev 12.04
but I will be h. among the people 22.32
them, giving the h. part from them.' Num 18.29
LORD which he had h. in Jerusalem. 2Ch 36.14
who art in heaven, H. be thy name. Mt 6.09
pray, say: "Father, h. be thy name. Lk 11.02

HALT
they came to a h. at the Gate of Neh 12.39
This very day he will h. at Nob, Is 10.32
"H.! H.!" they cry; but none Nah 2.08

HALTED
and they h. at the last house. 2Sa 15.17
and h. at the door of Eisha's house. 2Ki 5.09
through the weapons and are not h. Joe 2.08

HALVES
cheeks are like h. of a pomegranate Sol 4.03
Your cheeks are like h. of a 6.07

HAM
father of Shem, H., and Japheth. Gen 5.32
three sons, Shem, H., and Japheth. 6.10

HAM (cont.)
Shem and H. and Japheth, and Noah's Gen 7.13
the ark were Shem, H., and Japheth. 9.18
H. was the father of Canaan. 9.18
And H., the father of Canaan, saw 9.22
of Noah, Shem, H., and Japheth; 10.01
The sons of H.: Cush, Egypt, Put, and 10.06
These are the sons of H., 10.20
the Zuzim in H., the Emim in 14.05
Noah, Shem, H., and Japheth. 1Ch 1.04
The sons of H.: Cush, Egypt, Put, and 1.08
inhabitants there belonged to H. 4.40
their strength in the tents of H. Ps 78.51
Jacob sojourned in the land of H. 105.23
and miracles in the land of H. 105.27
wondrous works in the land of H., 106.22

HAMAN
promoted H. the son of Hammedatha Est 3.01
bowed down and did obeisance to H.; 3.02
they told H., in order to see 3.04
And when H. saw that Mordecai did 3.05
to him, H. was filled with fury. 3.05
H. sought to destroy all the Jews, 3.06
the lot, before H. day after day; 3.07
Then H. said to King Ahasuerus, 3.08
hand and gave it to H. the Agagite, 3.10
And the king said to H., "The money 3.11
according to all that H. commanded, 3.12
the king and H. sat down to drink; 3.15
of money that H. had promised to 4.07
the king and H. come this day to a 5.04
"Bring H. quickly, that we may do as 5.05
So the king and H. came to the 5.05
the king and H. come tomorrow to 5.08
And H. went out that day joyful and 5.09
But when H. saw Mordecai in the 5.09
Nevertheless H. restrained himself, 5.10
And H. recounted to them the 5.11
And H. added, "Even Queen Esther let 5.12
This counsel pleased H., and he had 5.14
Now H. had just entered the outer 6.04
"H. is there, standing in the court." 6.05
So H. came in, and the king said to 6.06
And H. said to himself, "Whom 6.06
And H. said to the king, "For the 6.07
Then the king said to H., "Make haste, 6.10
So H. took the robes and the horse, 6.11
But H. hurried to his house, mourning 6.12
And H. told his wife Zeresh and all 6.13
and brought H. in haste to the 6.14
So the king and H. went in to feast 7.01
"A foe and enemy! This wicked H.!" 7.06
Then H. was in terror before the 7.06
but H. stayed to beg his life from 7.07
as H. was falling on the couch 7.08
gallows which H. has prepared for 7.09
So they hanged H. on the gallows 7.10
to Queen Esther the house of H., 8.01
ring, which he had taken from H., 8.02
set Mordecai over the house of H. 8.02
evil design of H. the Agagite and 8.03
letters devised by H. the Agagite, 8.05
have given Esther the house of H., 8.07
the ten sons of H. the son of 9.10
men and also the ten sons of H. 9.12
the ten sons of H. be hanged on 9.13
and the ten sons of H. were hanged. 9.14
For H. the Agagite, the son of 9.24

HAMAN'S
of the king, they covered H. face. Est 7.08
the king, is standing in H. house, 7.09

HAMATH
to Rehob, near the entrance of H. Num 13.21
mark it out to the entrance of H., 34.08
Mount Hermon to the entrance of H., Jos 13.05
as far as the entrance of H. Ju 3.03
When Tou king of H. heard that 2Sa 8.09
the entrance of H. to the Brook of 1Ki 8.65
the entrance of H. as far as the 2Ki 14.25
recovered for Israel Damascus and H., 14.28
H., and Sepharvaim, and placed them 17.24
Nergal, the men of H. made Ashima, 17.30
Where are the gods of H. and Arpad? 18.34
Where is the king of H., the king of 19.13
bonds at Riblah in the land of H., 23.33
death at Riblah in the land of H. 25.21
of Egypt to the entrance of H., 1Ch 13.05
toward H., as he went to set up his 18.03
When Tou king of H. heard that 18.09
the entrance of H. to the Brook of 2Ch 7.08
store-cities which he built in H. 8.04
Is not H. like Arpad? Is not Samaria Is 10.09
from H., and from the coastlands of 11.11
Where are the gods of H. and Arpad? 36.19
Where are the king of H., the king of 37.13
at Riblah, in the land of H.; Jer 39.05
"H. and Arpad are confounded, for 49.23
at Riblah in the land of H., 52.09
death at Riblah in the land of H. 52.27
of Hethlon to the entrance of H., Eze 47.15
border between Damascus and of H.), 47.16
with the border of H. to the north. 47.17
point opposite the entrance of H. 47.20
of Hethlon to the entrance of H., 48.01
of Damascus over against H.), 48.01
and thence go to H. the great; Amo 6.02
the entrance of H. to the Brook of 6.14
H. also, which borders thereon, Tyre Zec 9.02

HAMATHITES
Arvadites, the Zemarites, and the H. Gen 10.18
Arvadites, the Zemarites, and the H. 1Ch 1.16

HAMATHZOBAH
And Solomon went to H., and took it. 2Ch 8.03

HAMMATH
Ziddim, Zer, H., Rakkath, Chinnereth, Jos 19.35
are the Kenites who came from H., 1Ch 2.55

HAMMEDATHA
Haman the son of H. the Agagite, Est 3.01
the son of H., the enemy of the 3.10
the son of H., which he wrote to 8.05
the ten sons of Haman the son of H., 9.10
the son of H., the enemy of all the 9.24

HAMMER
and took a h. in her hand, and went Ju 4.21
so that neither h. nor axe nor any 1Ki 6.07
with the h. him who strikes the Is 41.07
fasten it with h. and nails so Jer 10.04
and like a h. which breaks the rock 23.29
How the h. of the whole earth is 50.23
"You are my h. and weapon of war: 51.20

HAMMERED
of h. work shall you make them, on Ex 25.18
lampstand shall be made of h. work; 25.31
it one piece of h. work of pure 25.36
And he made two cherubim of h. gold; 37.07
the lampstand were made of h. work; 37.17
one piece of h. work of pure gold. 37.22
And gold leaf was h. out and cut 39.03
of the lampstand, h. work of gold; Num 8.04
to its flowers, it was h. work; 8.04
of h. work you shall make them; 10.02
be made into h. plates as a covering 16.38
and they were h. out as a covering 16.39

HAMMERS
broke down with hatchets and h. Ps 74.06
he shapes it with h., and forges it Is 44.12

HAMMOLECHETH
And his sister H. bore Ishhod, 1Ch 7.18

HAMMON
Ebron, Rehob, H., Kanah, as far as Jos 19.28
H. with its pasture lands, and 1Ch 6.76

HAMMOTHDOR
H. with its pasture lands, and Jos 21.32

HAMMUEL
H. his son, Zaccur his son, Shimei 1Ch 4.26

HAMONAH
(A city H. is there also.) Thus shall they Eze 39.16

HAMONGOG
it will be called the Valley of H. Eze 39.11
have buried it in the Valley of H. 39.15

HAMOR
And from the sons of H., Shechem's Gen 33.19
Shechem the son of H. the Hivite, 34.02
So Shechem spoke to his father H., 34.04
And H. the father of Shechem went 34.06
But H. spoke with them, saying, "The 34.08
and his father H. deceitfully, 34.13
Their words pleased H. and Hamor's 34.18
So H. and his son Shechem came to 34.20
hearkened to H. and his son 34.24
They slew H. and his son Shechem 34.26
the sons of H. the father of Jos 24.32
the men of H. the father of Ju 9.28
from the sons of H. in Shechem. Ac 7.16

HAMOR'S
pleased Hamor and H. son Shechem. Gen 34.18

HAMPERED
you walk, your step will not be h.; Pro 4.12

HAMRAN
H., Eshban, Ithran, and Cheran. 1Ch 1.41

HAMSTRING
in their wantonness they h. oxen. Gen 49.06
you shall h. their horses, and burn Jos 11.06

HAMSTRUNG
he h. their horses, and burned their Jos 11.09
and David h. all the chariot horses, 2Sa 8.04
and David h. all the chariot horses, but 1Ch 18.04

HAMUL
sons of Perez were Hezron and H. Gen 46.12
of H., the family of the Hamulites. Num 26.21
The sons of Perez: Hezron and H. 1Ch 2.05

HAMULITES
of Hamul, the family of the H. Num 26.21

HAMUTAL
name was H. the daughter of Jeremiah 2Ki 23.31
name was H. the daughter of Jeremiah 24.18
name was H. the daughter of Jeremiah Jer 52.01

HANAMEL
Behold, H. the son of Shallum your Jer 32.07
Then H. my cousin came to me in the 32.08
at Anathoth from H. my cousin, 32.09
in the presence of H. my cousin, 32.12

HANAN
Abdon, Zichri, H., 1Ch 8.23
Ishmael, Sheariah, Obadiah, and H. 8.38
Ishmael, Sheariah, Obadiah, and H.; 9.44
H. the son of Maacah, and Joshaphat 11.43
sons of Shamlai, the sons of H., Ez 2.46
the sons of H., the sons of Giddel, Neh 7.49
H., Pelaiah, the Levites, helped the 8.07
Hodiah, Kelita, Pelaiah, H., 10.10
Pelatiah, H., Anaiah, 10.22
Ahiah, H., Anan, 10.26
their assistant H. the son of 13.13
of the sons of H. the son of Jer 35.04

HANANEL
Hundred, as far as the Tower of H. Neh 3.01
the Tower of H. and the Tower of 12.39
the tower of H. to the Corner Gate. Jer 31.38
the Tower of H. to the king's wine Zec 14.10

HANANI
Jehu the son of H. against Baasha, 1Ki 16.01
Jehu the son of H. against Baasha 16.07
H., Eliathah, Giddalti, and Romamtiezer, 1Ch 25.04
to H., his sons and his brethren, 25.25
At that time H. the seer came to 2Ch 16.07
But Jehu the son of H. the seer 19.02
chronicles of Jehu the son of H., 20.34
the sons of Immer: H. and Zebadiah. Ez 10.20
that H., one of my brethren, came Neh 1.02
I gave my brother H. and Hananiah 7.02
and H., with the musical instruments 12.36

HANANIAH
Meshullam and H., and Shelomith was 1Ch 3.19
The sons of H.: Pelatiah and Jeshaiah, 3.21
H., Elam, Anthothijah, 8.24
H., Hanai, Eliathah, Giddalti, and 25.04
to H., his sons and his brethren, 25.23
officer, under the direction of H., 2Ch 26.11
Jehohanan, H., Zabbai, and Athlai. Ez 10.28
Next to him H., one of the perfumers, Neh 3.08
After him H. the son of Shelemiah 3.30
Hanani and H. the governor of the 7.02
Hoshea, H., Hasshub, 10.23
of Seraiah, Meraiah; of Jeremiah, H.; 12.12
Zechariah, and H., with trumpets, 12.41
H. the son of Azzur, the prophet Jer 28.01
spoke to H. the prophet in the 28.05
Then the prophet H. took the yoke-bars 28.10
And H. spoke in the presence of all 28.11
the prophet H. had broken the yoke-bars 28.12
"Go, tell H., 'Thus says the LORD: 28.13
the prophet said to the prophet H., 28.15
H., the LORD has not sent you, and 28.15
seventh month, the prophet H. died. 28.17
son of H., seized Jeremiah the prophet, 37.13
H., Mishael, and Azariah of the Dan 1.06
H. he called Shadrach, Mishael he 1.07
over Daniel, H., Mishael, and Azariah; 1.11
H., Mishael, and Azariah; therefore 1.19
and made the matter known to H., 2.17

HAND
put forth his h. and take also of Gen 3.22
your brother's blood from your h. 4.11
put forth his h. and took her and 8.09
into your h. they are delivered. 9.02
If you take the left h., then I will go 13.09
or if you take the right h., then I will go 13.09
delivered your enemies into your h.!" 14.20
his h. against every man and every 16.12
man and every man's h. against him; 16.12
and his two daughters by the h., 19.16
and hold him fast with your h.; 21.18
ewe lambs you will take from my h., 21.30
he took in his h. the fire and the 22.06
Then Abraham put forth his h., 22.10
"Do not lay your h. on the lad or 22.12
"Put your h. under my thigh, 24.02
servant put his h. under the thigh 24.09
let down her jar upon her h., 24.18
to the right h. or to the left." 24.49
and his h. had taken hold of Esau's 25.26
into the h. of her son Jacob. 27.17
of my h. your required it, whether 31.39

HAND (cont.)
from the h. of my brother, from the Gen 32.11
from the h. of Esau, for I fear him, 32.11
into the h. of his servants, every 32.16
then accept my present from my h.; 33.10
but lay no h. upon him"—that he 37.22
might rescue him out of their h., 37.22
and let not our h. be upon him, 37.27
and your staff that is in your h." 38.18
the pledge from the woman's h., 38.20
she was in labor, one put out a h.; 38.28
bound on his h. a scarlet thread, 38.28
But as he drew back his h., 38.29
the scarlet thread upon his h.; 38.30
everything that he has in my h.; 39.08
But he left his garment in her h., 39.12
he had left his garment in her h., 39.13
Pharaoh's cup was in my h.; 40.11
and placed the cup in Pharaoh's h." 40.11
Pharaoh's cup in his h. as formerly, 40.13
he placed the cup in Pharaoh's h.; 41.42
ring from is h. and put it on 41.42
put it on Joseph's h., and arrayed 41.42
shall lift up h. or foot in all 41.44
of my h. you shall require him. 43.09
money down in our h. to buy food. 43.22
also in whose h. the cup has been 44.16
man in whose h. the cup was found 44.17
and Joseph's h. shall close your 46.04
put your h. under my thigh, and 47.29
his right h. toward Israel's left h., 48.13
his left h. toward Israel's right h., 48.13
out his right h. and laid it upon 48.14
and his left h. upon the head of 48.14
laid his right h. upon the head of 48.17
and he took his father's h., 48.17
put your right h. upon his head." 48.18
I took from the h. of the Amorites 48.22
your h. shall be on the neck of 49.08
us out of the h. of the shepherds, Ex 2.19
them out of the h. of the Egyptians, 3.08
go unless compelled by a mighty h. 3.19
stretch out my h. and smite Egypt 3.20
to him, "What is that in your h.?" 4.02
"Put out your h., and take it by 4.04
so he put out his h. and caught it, 4.04
and it became a rod in his h.— 4.04
"Put your h. into your bosom." 4.06
and he put his h. into his bosom; 4.06
his h. was leprous, as white as snow. 4.06
"Put your h. back into your bosom." 4.07
So he put his h. back into his 4.07
you shall take in your h. this rod, 4.17
and in his h. Moses took the rod of 4.20
put a sword in their h. to kill us." 5.21
with a strong h. he will send them 6.01
with a strong h. he will drive them 6.01
I will lay my h. upon Egypt and 7.04
forth my h. upon Egypt and bring 7.05
take in your h. the rod which was 7.15
Nile with the rod that is in my h., 7.17
out your h. over the waters of 7.19
out your h. with your rod over the 8.05
stretched out his h. over the 8.06
stretched out his h. with his rod, 8.17
behold, the h. of the LORD will fall 9.03
put forth my h. and struck you and 9.15
forth your h. toward heaven, 9.22
out your h. over the land of Egypt 10.12
out your h. toward heaven that 10.21
stretched out his h. toward heaven, 10.22
feet, and your staff in your h.; 12.11
by strength of h. the LORD brought 13.03
a sign on your h. and as a memorial 13.09
with a strong h. the LORD has 13.09
'By strength of h. the LORD 13.14
a mark on your h. or frontlets 13.16
for by a strong h. the LORD brought 13.16
out your h. over the sea and 14.16
stretched out his h. over the sea; 14.21
on their right h. and on their 14.22
"Stretch out your h. over the sea, 14.26
stretched forth his h. over the sea, 14.27
on their right h. and on their 14.29
day from the h. of the Egyptians; 14.30
Thy right h., O LORD, glorious in 15.06
thy right h., O LORD, shatters the 15.06
my h. shall destroy them." 15.09
Thou didst stretch out thy right h., 15.12
of Aaron, took a timbrel in her h.; 15.20
had died by the h. of the LORD in 16.03
take in your h. the rod with which 17.05
hill with the rod of God in my h." 17.09
Whenever Moses held up his h., 17.11
and whenever he lowered his h., 17.11
saying, "A h. upon the banner of the 17.16
them out of the h. of the Egyptians 18.09
you out of the h. of the Egyptians 18.10
and out of the h. of Pharaoh. 18.10
from under the h. of the Egyptians, 18.11
no h. shall touch him, but he shall 19.13
but God let him fall into his h., 21.13
and the slave dies under his h., 21.20
tooth, h. for h., foot for foot, 21.24
he has put his h. to his neighbor's 22.08
has not put his h. to his neighbor's 22.11
inhabitants of the land into your h., 23.31
did not lay his h. on the chief 24.11
And he received the gold at their h., 32.04
great power and with a mighty h.? 32.11
you with my h. until I have passed 33.22
then I will take away my h., 33.23
and took in his h. two tables of 34.04
testimony in his h. as he came down 34.29
on this h. and that h. by the gate 38.15
he shall lay his h. upon the head Lev 1.04
shall lay his h. upon the head of 3.02
laying his h. upon the head of his 3.08
and lay his h. upon its head, and 3.13
and lay his h. on the head of the 4.04
and shall lay his h. upon the head 4.24
shall lay his h. on the head of 4.29
and lay his h. upon the head of the 4.33
of his right h. and on the great 8.23
offering, and filled his h. from it, 9.17
and on the thumb of his right h., 14.14
into the palm of his own left h., 14.15
in the oil that is in his left h., 14.16
remains in his h. the priest shall 14.17
and on the thumb of his right h., 14.17
in the priest's h. he shall put on 14.18
and on the thumb of his right h., 14.25
into the palm of his own left h.; 14.26
is in his left h. seven times 14.27
is in his right h. on the tip of 14.28
and on the thumb of his right h., 14.28
in the priest's h. he shall put on 14.29
wilderness by the h. of a man who 16.21
an injured foot or an injured h., 21.19
remain in the h. of him who bought 25.28
delivered into the h. of the enemy. 26.25
under the h. of Ithamar the son of Num 4.33
And in his h. the priest shall have 5.18
of jealousy out of the woman's h., 5.25
Moses, "Is the LORD's h. shortened? 11.23
who does anything with a high h., 15.30
lifted up his h. and struck the 20.11
to the right h. or to the left, 20.17
indeed give this people into my h., 21.02
taken all his land out of his h., 21.26
or I have given him into your h., 21.34
fees for divination in their h.; 22.07
road, with a drawn sword in his h.; 22.23
I wish I had a sword in my h., 22.29

HAND (cont.)

with his drawn sword in his h.; Num 22.31
congregation, and took a spear in his h. 25.07
spirit, and lay your h. upon him; 27.18
trumpets for the alarm in his h. 31.06
him down with a stone in the h., 35.17
with a weapon of wood in the h., 35.18
enmity struck him down with his h., 35.21
from the h. of the avenger of 35.25
us into the h. of the Amorites, to Deu 1.27
For indeed the h. of the LORD was 2.15
given into your h. Sihon the 2.24
he might give him into your h., 2.30
people and his land into your h.; 3.02
our God gave into our h. Og also, 3.03
time out of the h. of the two 3.08
thy greatness and thy mighty h.; 3.24
by a mighty h. and an outstretched 4.34
with a mighty h. and an outstretched 5.15
to the right h. or to the left. 5.32
bind them as a sign upon your h., 6.08
us out of Egypt with a mighty h.; 6.21
brought you out with a mighty h., 7.08
from the h. of Pharaoh king of 7.08
the mighty h., and the outstretched 7.19
will give their kings into your h., 7.24
the might of my h. have gotten me 8.17
out of Egypt with a mighty h. 9.26
with the two tables in my h. 10.03
his mighty h. and his outstretched 11.02
bind them as a sign upon your h., 11.18
your h. shall be first against him 13.09
afterwards the h. of all the 13.09
things shall cleave to your h.; 13.17
and bind up the money in your h., 14.25
your brother your h. shall release. 15.03
or shut your h. against your poor 15.07
but you shall open your h. to him, 15.08
open wide your h. to your brother, 15.11
a freewill offering from your h., 16.10
The h. of the witnesses shall be 17.07
afterward the h. of all the people. 17.07
to the right h. or to the left. 17.11
to the right h. or to the left; 17.20
and his h. swings the axe to cut 19.05
and h. him over to the avenger of 19.12
tooth, h. for h., foot for foot. 19.21
it into your h. you shall put all 20.13
may pluck the ears with your h., 23.25
puts it in her h. and sends her 24.01
puts it in her h. and sends her 24.03
from the h. of him who is beating 25.11
puts out her h. and seizes him by 25.11
then you shall cut off her h.; 25.12
shall take the basket from your h., 26.04
with a mighty h. and an outstretched 26.08
to the right h. or to the left, to 28.14
the power of your h. to prevent it. 28.32
prosperous in all the work of your h., 30.09
"Our h. is triumphant, the LORD has 32.27
the day of their calamity is at h., 32.35
none that can deliver out of my h. 32.39
For I lift up my h. to heaven, 32.40
and my h. takes hold on judgment, I 32.41
with flaming fire at his right h. 33.02
consecrated to him were in his h.; 33.03
it to the right h. or to the left, Jos 1.07
but if a h. is laid upon any one 2.19
know that the h. of the LORD is 4.24
him with his drawn sword in his h.; 5.13
I have given into your h. Jericho, 6.02
given into your h. the king of Ai, 8.01
your God will give it into your h. 8.07
that is in your h. toward Ai; 8.18
for I will give it into your h." 8.18
that was in his h. toward the city. 8.18
as he had stretched out his h., 8.19
For Joshua did not draw back his h., 8.26
provisions in your h. for the 9.11
And now, behold, we are in your h.: 9.25
them out of the h. of the people 9.26
not relax your h. from your 10.06
God has given them into your h." 10.19
and its king into the h. of Israel; 10.30
gave Lachish into the h. of Israel, 10.32
gave them into the h. of Israel, 11.08
not give up the slayer into his h.; 20.05
not die by the h. of the avenger 20.09
of Israel from the h. of the LORD." 22.31
to the right h. nor to the left, 23.06
you, and I gave them into your h., 24.08
so I delivered you out of his h. 24.10
and I gave them into your h. 24.11
I have given the land into his h." Ju 1.02
and the Perizzites into their h.; 1.04
but the h. of the house of Joseph 1.35
the h. of the LORD was against them 2.15
them from the h. of their enemies 2.18
them into the h. of Cushanrishathaim 3.08
king of Mesopotamia into his h.; 3.10
and his h. prevailed over Cushanrishathaim. 3.10
And Ehud reached with his left h., 3.21
enemies the Moabites into your h." 3.28
that day under the h. of Israel. 3.30
them into the h. of Jabin king of 4.02
and I will give him into your h.'" 4.07
sell Sisera into the h. of a woman." 4.09
LORD has given Sisera into your h. 4.14
peg, and took a hammer in her h., 4.21
And the h. of the people of Israel 4.24
She put her h. to the tent peg and 5.26
and her right h. to the workmen's 5.26
them into the h. of Midian seven 6.01
And the h. of Midian prevailed over 6.02
you from the h. of the Egyptians, 6.09
and from the h. of all who oppressed 6.09
and given us into the h. of Midian." 6.13
Israel from the h. of Midian; 6.14
of the staff that was in his h., 6.21
thou wilt deliver Israel by my h., 6.36
thou wilt deliver Israel by my h., 6.37
give the Midianites into their h., 7.02
'My own h. has delivered me.' 7.02
give the Midianites into your h.; 7.07
for I have given it into your h. 7.09
into his h. God has given Midian 7.14
the host of Midian into your h." 7.15
and Zalmunna already in your h., 8.06
Zebah and Zalmunna into my h., 8.07
and Zalmunna already in your h., 8.15
delivered us out of the h. of Midian." 8.22
them from the h. of all their 8.34
rescued you from the h. of Midian; 9.17
Would that this people were under my h.! 9.29
Abimelech took an axe in his h., 9.48
them into the h. of the Philistines 10.07
and into the h. of the Ammonites, 10.07
I delivered you out of their h. 10.12
his people into the h. of Israel, 11.21
give the Ammonites into my h., 11.30
and the LORD gave them into his h. 11.32
did not deliver me from their h. 12.02
me, I took my life in my h., 12.03
and the LORD gave them into my h.; 12.03
them into the h. of the Philistines 13.01
Israel from the h. of the Philistines." 13.05
and he had nothing in his h. 14.06
and put out his h. and seized it, 15.15
away the jawbone out of his h.; 15.17
deliverance by the h. of thy servant; 15.18
given Samson our enemy into our h." 16.23
has given our enemy into our h., 16.24
to the lad who held him by the h., 16.26
his right h. on the one and his 16.29

HAND (cont.)
one and his left h. on the other. Ju 16.29
to the LORD from my h. for my son, 17.03
put your h. upon your mouth, and 18.19
I will give them into your h." 20.28
sake that the h. of the LORD has Ru 1.13
buy the field from the h. of Naomi, 4.05
bought from the h. of Naomi all 4.09
a three-pronged fork in his h., 1Sa 2.13
The h. of the LORD was heavy upon 5.06
for his h. is heavy upon us and 5.07
the h. of the LORD was against the 5.09
The h. of God was very heavy there; 5.11
to you why his h. does not turn 6.03
lighten his h. from off you and 6.05
it is not his h. that struck us, 6.09
you out of the h. of the Philistines." 7.03
us from the h. of the Philistines." 7.08
And the h. of the LORD was against 7.13
from the h. of the Philistines. 7.14
people from the h. of the Philistines; 9.16
them from the h. of their enemies 10.01
you shall accept from their h. 10.04
do whatever your h. finds to do, 10.07
you from the h. of the Egyptians 10.18
and from the h. of all the kingdoms 10.18
of Israel by the h. of messengers, 11.07
Or from whose h. have I taken a 12.03
taken anything from any man's h." 12.04
have not found anything in my h." 12.05
he sold them into the h. of Sisera, 12.09
and into the h. of the Philistines, 12.09
and into the h. of the king of Moab; 12.09
us out of the h. of our enemies, 12.10
you out of the h. of your enemies 12.11
then the h. of the LORD will be 12.15
found in the h. of any of the 13.22
LORD has given them into our h. 14.10
given them into the h. of Israel." 14.12
to the priest, "Withdraw your h." 14.19
but no man put his h. to his mouth; 14.26
of the staff that was in his h., 14.27
and put his h. to his mouth; 14.27
give them into the h. of Israel?" 14.37
tip of the staff that was in my h.; 14.43
the lyre and played it with his h.; 16.23
me from the h. of this Philistine." 17.37
Then he took his staff in his h., 17.40
his sling was in his h., 17.40
LORD will deliver you into my h., 17.46
and he wll give you into our h." 17.47
And David put his h. in his bag and 17.49
was no sword in the h. of David. 17.50
head of the Philistine in his h. 17.57
Saul had his spear in his h.; 18.10
"Let not my h. be upon him, but let 18.17
but let the h. of the Philistines 18.17
and that the h. of the Philistines 18.21
fall by the h. of the Philistines. 18.25
his life in his h. and he slew the 19.05
his house with his spear in his h.; 19.09
yourself when the matter was in h., 20.19
Now then, what have you at h.? 21.03
"I have no common bread at h., 21.04
not here a spear or a sword at h.? 21.08
height, with his spear in his h., 22.06
because their h. also is with David, 22.17
put forth their h. to fall upon 22.17
give the Philistines into your h." 23.04
came down with an ephod in his h. 23.06
said, "God has given him into my h.; 23.07
of Keilah surrender me into his h.? 23.11
me and my men into the h. of Saul?" 23.12
God did not give him into his h. 23.14
and strengthened his h. in God. 23.16
for the h. of Saul my father shall 23.17
surrender him into the king's h." 23.20
will give your enemy into your h., 24.04
to put forth my h. against him, 24.06
you today into my h. in the cave; 24.10
put forth my h. against my lord; 24.10
the skirt of your robe in my h.; 24.11
but my h. shall not be against you. 24.12
but my h. shall not be against you. 24.13
cause, and deliver me from your h." 24.15
shall be established in your h. 24.20
you have at h. to your servants 25.08
taking vengeance with your own h., 25.26
avenging myself with my own h.! 25.33
from her h. what she had brought 25.35
I received at the h. of Nabal, 25.39
your enemy into your h. this day; 26.08
put forth his h. against the LORD's 26.09
put forth my h. against the LORD's 26.11
the LORD gave you into my h. today, 26.23
put forth my h. against the LORD's 26.23
perish one day by the h. of Saul; 27.01
and I shall escape out of his h." 27.01
torn the kingdom out of your h., 28.17
you into the h. of the Philistines; 28.19
also into the h. of the Philistines." 28.19
I have taken my life in my h., 28.21
given into our h. the band that 30.23
put forth your h. to destroy the 2Sa 1.14
to the right h. nor to the left 2.19
to your right h. or to your left, 2.21
not given you into the h. of David; 3.08
my h. shall be with you to bring 3.12
'By the h. of my servant David I 3.18
Israel from the h. of the Philistines, 3.18
and from the h. of all their 3.18
now require his blood at your h., 4.11
Wilt thou give them into my h.?" 5.19
give the Philistines into your h." 5.19
put out his h. to the ark of God 6.06
he put forth his h. to the ark; 6.07
out of the h. of the Philistines. 8.01
and sent it by the h. of Uriah. 11.14
delivered you out of the h. of Saul; 12.07
may see it, and eat it from her h.'" 13.05
sight, that I may eat from her h." 13.06
that I may eat from your h." 13.10
and she laid her h. on her head, 13.19
from the h. of the man who would 14.16
"Is the h. of Joab with you in all 14.19
to the right h. or to the left 14.19
to him, he would put out his h., 15.05
on his right h. and on his left. 16.06
into the h. of your son Absalom. 16.08
if I felt in my h. the weight of a 18.12
put forth my h. against the king's 18.12
On the other h., if I had dealt 18.13
And he took three darts in his h., 18.14
raised their h. against my lord 18.28
us from the h. of our enemies, 19.09
us from the h. of the Philistines; 19.09
with his right h. to kiss him. 20.09
the sword which was in Joab's h.; 20.10
lifted up his h. against King 20.21
who had six fingers on each h., 21.20
fell by the h. of David and by the 21.22
and by the h. of his servants. 21.22
him from the h. of all his enemies, 22.01
enemies, and from the h. of Saul. 22.01
they cannot be taken with the h.; 23.06
Philistines until his h. was weary, 23.10
and his h. clove to the sword; 23.10
The Egyptian had a spear in his h.; 23.21
the spear out of the Egyptian's h., 23.21
us fall into the h. of the LORD, 24.14
let me not fall into the h. of man." 24.14
forth his h. toward Jerusalem to 24.16
"It is enough; now stay your h." 24.16
Let thy h., I pray thee, be against 24.17

HAND (cont.)
established in the h. of Solomon. 1Ki 2.46
who with his h. has fulfilled what 8.15
and with thy h. hast fulfilled it 8.24
thy great name, and thy mighty h., 8.42
tear it out of the h. of your son. 11.12
lifted up his h. against the king. 11.26
lifted up his h. against the king. 11.27
the kingdom from the h. of Solomon, 11.31
the whole kingdom out of his h.; 11.34
the kingdom out of his son's h., 11.35
stretched out his h. from the altar, 13.04
And his h., which he stretched out 13.04
that my h. may be restored to me." 13.06
and the king's h. was restored to 13.06
me a morsel of bread in your h." 17.11
your servant into the h. of Ahab, 18.09
like a man's h. is rising out of 18.44
And the h. of the LORD was on 18.46
will give it into your h. this day; 20.13
this great multitude into your h., 20.28
go out of your h. the man whom I 20.42
it out of the h. of the king of 22.03
give it into the h. of the king." 22.06
give it into the h. of the king." 22.12
give it into the h. of the king." 22.15
on his right h. and on his left; 22.19
to give them into the h. of Moab." 2Ki 3.10
to give them into the h. of Moab." 3.13
give the Moabites into your h., 3.18
take my staff in your h., and go. 4.29
and wave his h. over the place, and 5.11
from his h. what he brought. 5.20
hill, he took them from their h., 5.24
he reached out his h. and took it. 6.07
on whose h. the king leaned said 7.02
on whose h. he leaned to have 7.17
take his flask of oil in your h., 9.01
said, "If it is, give me your h." 10.15
So he gave him his h. And Jehu 10.15
each with his weapons in his h.; 11.08
man with his weapons in his h., 11.11
but h. it over for the repair of 12.07
men into whose h. they delivered 12.15
into the h. of Hazael king of 13.03
and into the h. of Benhadad the 13.03
escaped from the h. of the Syrians; 13.05
firmly in his h. he killed his 14.05
them by the h. of Jeroboam the son 14.27
me from the h. of the king of 16.07
and from the h. of the king of 16.07
from under the h. of Pharaoh king 17.07
gave them into the h. of spoilers, 17.20
you out of the h. of all your 17.39
will pierce the h. of any man who 18.21
able to deliver you out of my h. 18.29
given into the h. of the king of 18.30
land out of the h. of the king of 18.33
delivered Samaria out of my h.? 18.34
their countries out of my h., 18.35
deliver Jerusalem out of my h.?'" 18.35
given into the h. of the king of 19.10
letter from the h. of the messengers, 19.14
from his h., that all the kingdoms 19.19
city out of the h. of the king of 20.06
them into the h. of their enemies, 21.14
to the right h. or to the left. 22.02
given into the h. of the workmen 22.05
which is delivered into their h., 22.07
it into the h. of the workmen who 22.09
and that thy h. might be with me, 1Ch 4.10
the Hagrites, who fell by their h.; 5.10
exile by the h. of Nebuchadnezzar. 6.15
Asaph, who stood on his right h., 6.39
On the left h. were their brethren 6.44
had in his h. a spear like a 11.23
the spear out of the Egyptian's h., 11.23
either the right or the left h.; 12.02
put out his h. to hold the ark, for 13.09
he put forth his h. to the ark; 13.10
Wilt thou give them into my h.?" 14.10
and I will give them into your h." 14.10
broken through my enemies by my h., 14.11
out of the h. of the Philistines. 18.01
who had six fingers on each h., 20.06
fell by the h. of David and by the 20.08
and by the h. of his servants. 20.08
me fall into the h. of the LORD, 21.13
let me not fall into the h. of man." 21.13
"It is enough; now stay your h." 21.15
and in his h. a drawn sword stretched 21.16
Let thy h., I pray thee, O LORD my 21.17
inhabitants of the land into my h.; 22.18
from the h. of the LORD concerning 28.19
In thy h. are power and might; 29.12
and in thy h. it is to make great 29.12
comes from thy h. and is all thy 29.16
who with his h. was fulfilled what 2Ch 6.04
and with thy h. hast fulfilled it 6.15
thy great name, and thy mighty h., 6.32
abandoned you to the h. of Shishak.'" 12.05
Jerusalem by the h. of Shishak. 12.07
the LORD in the h. of the sons of 13.08
and God gave them into their h. 13.16
LORD, he gave them into your h. 16.08
established the kingdom in his h.; 17.05
give it into the h. of the king." 18.05
give it into the h. of the king." 18.11
they will be given into your h." 18.14
on his right h. and on his left; 18.18
In thy h. are power and might, so 20.06
each with his weapons in his h.; 23.07
man with his weapon in his h., 23.10
into their h. a very great army, 24.24
firmly in his h. he killed his 25.03
their own people from your h.?" 25.15
them into the h. of their enemies, 25.20
a censer in his h. to burn incense, 26.19
him into the h. of the king of 28.05
given into the h. of the king of 28.05
Judah, he gave them into your h., 28.09
from the h. of the kings of 30.06
The h. of God was also upon Judah 30.12
received from the h. of the Levites. 30.16
us from the h. of the king of 32.11
deliver their lands out of my h.? 32.13
to deliver his people from my h., 32.14
be able to deliver you from my h.? 32.14
my h. or from the h. of my fathers. 32.15
your God deliver you out of my h.!" 32.15
not deliver his people from my h." 32.17
from the h. of Sennacherib king of 32.22
and from the h. of all his enemies; 32.22
it into the h. of the overseers 34.17
he gave them all into his h. 36.17
them into the h. of Nebuchadnezzar Ez 5.12
shall put forth a h. to alter this, 6.12
for the h. of the LORD his God was 7.06
for the good h. of his God was upon 7.09
of your God, which is in your h., 7.14
of your God which is in your h., 7.25
for the h. of the LORD my God was 7.28
And by the good h. of our God upon 8.18
"The h. of our God is for good upon 8.22
out into their h. six hundred and 8.26
the h. of our God was upon us, and 8.31
us from the h. of the enemy and 8.31
faithlessness the h. of the officials 9.02
given into the h. of the kings of 9.07
great power and by thy strong h. Neh 1.10
for the good h. of my God was upon 2.08
them of the h. of my God which had 2.18
each with one h. labored on the 4.17
each kept his weapon in his h. 4.23

HAND (cont.)

me with an open letter in his h. Neh 6.05
and Maaseiah on his right h.; 8.04
and Meshullam on his left h. 8.04
them into the h. of their enemies, 9.27
them from the h. of their enemies. 9.27
them to the h. of their enemies, so 9.28
them into the h. of the peoples of 9.30
at the king's h. in all matters 11.24
ring from his h. and gave it to Est 3.10
golden scepter that was in his h. 5.02
but they laid no h. on the plunder. 9.10
But put forth thy h. now, and touch Job 1.11
himself do not put forth your h." 1.12
But put forth thy h. now, and touch 2.05
we receive good at the h. of God, 2.10
needy from the h. of the mighty. 5.15
let loose his h. and cut me off! 6.09
me from the adversary's h.'? 6.23
me from the h. of oppressors'? 6.23
man, nor take the h. of evildoers. 8.20
is given into the h. of the wicked; 9.24
who might lay his h. upon us both. 9.33
is none to deliver out of thy h.? 10.07
If iniquity is in your h., put it 11.14
who bring their god in their h. 12.06
know that the h. of the LORD has 12.09
In his h. is the life of every 12.10
my teeth, and put my life in my h. 13.14
withdraw thy h. far from me, and let 13.21
day of darkness is ready at his h.; 15.23
stretched forth his h. against God, 15.25
for the h. of God has touched me! 19.21
and lay your h. upon your mouth. 21.05
not their prosperity in their h.? 21.16
his h. is heavy in spite of my 23.02
on the left h. I seek him, but I 23.09
I turn to the right h., but I 23.09
his h. pierced the fleeing serpent. 26.13
teach you concerning the h. of God; 27.11
"Man puts his h. to the flinty rock, 28.09
and laid their h. on their mouth; 29.09
me, and my bow ever new in my h.' 29.20
On my right h. the rabble rise, they 30.12
might of thy h. thou dost persecute 30.21
a heap of ruins stretch out his h., 30.24
have raised my h. against the 31.21
or because my h. had gotten much; 31.25
and my mouth has kissed my h.; 31.27
are taken away by no human h. 34.20
what does he receive from your h.? 35.07
He seals up the h. of every man, 37.07
thee? I lay my h. on my mouth. 40.04
your own right h. can give you 40.14
O God, lift up thy h.; forget Ps 10.12
because he is at my right h., 16.08
in thy right h. are pleasures for 16.11
their adversaries at thy right h. 17.07
from men by thy h., O LORD, from 17.14
and thy right h. supported me, and 18.35
mighty victories by his right h. 20.06
Your h. will find out all your 21.08
your right h. will find out those 21.08
Into thy h. I commit my spirit; 31.05
me into the h. of the enemy; 31.08
My times are in thy h.; deliver 31.15
me from the h. of my enemies and 31.15
and night thy h. was heavy upon me; 32.04
nor the h. of the wicked drive me 36.11
for the LORD is the stay of his h. 37.24
and thy h. has come down on me. 38.02
I am spent by the blows of thy h. 39.10
thou with thy own h. didst drive 44.02
but thy right h., and thy arm, and 44.03
let your right h. teach you dread 45.04
at your right h. stands the queen 45.09
Thy right h. is filled with victory; 48.10
stretched out his h. against his 55.20
by thy right h. and answer us! 60.05
to thee; thy right h. upholds me. 63.08
from the h. of the wicked, from the 71.04
thou dost hold my right h. 73.23
Why dost thou hold back thy h., 74.11
keep thy right h. in thy bosom? 74.11
For in the h. of the LORD there is 75.08
in the night my h. is stretched out 77.02
that the right h. of the Most High 77.10
a flock by the h. of Moses and 77.20
mountain which his right h. had won. 78.54
his glory to the h. of the foe. 78.61
and guided them with skilful h. 78.72
the stock which thy right h. planted. 80.15
But let thy h. be upon the man of 80.17
be upon the man of thy right h., 80.17
and turn my h. against their foes. 81.14
them from the h. of the wicked." 82.04
salvation is at h. for those who 85.09
for they are cut off from thy h. 88.05
strong is thy h., high thy right h. 89.13
so that my h. shall ever abide with 89.21
I will set his h. on the sea and 89.25
sea and his right h. on the rivers. 89.25
exalted the right h. of his foes; 89.42
removed the scepter from his h., 89.44
ten thousand at your right h., 91.07
In his h. are the depths of the 95.04
pasture, and the sheep of his h. 95.07
them from the h. of the wicked. 97.10
His right h. and his holy arm have 98.01
when thou openest thy h., 104.28
saved them from the h. of the foe, 106.10
Therefore he raised his h. and 106.26
them into the h. of the nations, 106.41
by thy right h., and answer me! 108.06
Let them know that this is thy h.; 109.27
at the right h. of the needy, 109.31
to my lord: "Sit at my right h., 110.01
The Lord is at your right h.; 110.05
"The right h. of the LORD does 118.15
the right h. of the LORD is exalted, 118.16
the right h. of the LORD does 118.16
I hold my life in my h. continually, 119.109
Let thy h. be ready to help me, for 119.173
is your shade on your right h. 121.05
look to the h. of their master, as 123.02
a maid to the h. of her mistress, 123.02
Like arrows in the h. of a warrior 127.04
not fill his h. or the binder of 129.07
with a strong h. and an outstretched 136.12
Jerusalem, let my right h. wither! 137.05
stretch out thy h. against the 138.07
and thy right h. delivers me. 138.07
before, and layest thy h. upon me. 139.05
even there thy h. shall lead me, and 139.10
me, and thy right h. shall hold me. 139.10
Stretch forth thy h. from on high, 144.07
waters, from the h. of aliens, 144.07
right h. is a right h. of falsehood. 144.08
deliver me from the h. of aliens, 144.11
right h. is a right h. of falsehood. 144.11
Thou openest thy h., thou satisfiest 145.16
stretched out my h. and no one has Pro 1.24
Long life is in her right h.; 3.16
in her left h. are riches and honor. 3.16
a bird from the h. of the fowler. 6.05
A slack h. causes poverty, but the 10.04
but the h. of the diligent makes 10.04
work of a man's h. comes back to 12.14
The h. of the diligent will rule, 12.24
a price in his h. to buy wisdom, 17.16
sluggard buries his h. in the dish, 19.24
of water in the h. of the LORD; 21.01
message by the h. of a fool cuts 26.06
up into the h. of a drunkard is a 26.09

HAND (cont.)

sluggard buries his h. in the dish;	Pro	26.15
or to grasp oil in his right h.		27.16
evil, put your h. on your mouth.		30.32
She opens her h. to the poor, and		31.20
also, I saw, is from the h. of God;	Ecc	2.24
son, but he has nothing in his h.		5.14
which he may carry away in his h.		5.15
and from that withhold not your h.;		7.18
their deeds are in the h. of God;		9.01
Whatever your h. finds to do, do it		9.10
at evening withhold not your h.;		11.06
O that his left h. were under my	Sol	2.06
and that his right h. embraced me!		2.06
My beloved put his h. to the latch,		5.04
jewels, the work of a master h.		7.01
O that his left h. were under my		8.03
and that his right h. embraced me!		8.03
I will turn my h. against you and	Is	1.25
stretched out his h. against them		5.25
away and his h. is stretched out		5.25
having in his h. a burning coal		6.06
to me with his strong h. upon me,		8.11
away and his h. is stretched out		9.12
away and his h. is stretched out		9.17
away and his h. is stretched out		9.21
away and his h. is stretched out		10.04
As my h. has reached to the kingdoms		10.10
strength of my h. I have done it,		10.13
My h. has found like a nest the		10.14
shall put his h. on the adder's den.		11.08
will extend his h. yet a second		11.11
put forth their h. against Edom		11.14
will wave his h. over the River		11.15
wave the h. for them to enter the		13.02
is close at h. and its days will		13.22
and this is the h. that is stretched		14.26
His h. is stretched out, and who		14.27
into the h. of a hard master;		19.04
fear before the h. which the LORD		19.16
commit your authority to his h.;		22.21
stretched out his h. over the sea,		23.11
For the h. of the LORD will rest on		25.10
O LORD, thy h. is lifted up, but they		26.11
it up as soon as it is in his h.		28.04
When the LORD stretches out his h.,		31.03
his h. has portioned it out to them		34.17
will pierce the h. of any man who		36.06
given into the h. of the king of		36.15
land out of the h. of the king of		36.18
delivered Samaria out of my h.?		36.19
their countries out of my h.,		36.20
deliver Jerusalem out of my h.?'"		36.20
given into the h. of the king of		37.10
letter from the h. of the messengers,		37.14
LORD our God, save us from his h.,		37.20
city out of the h. of the king of		38.06
from the LORD's h. double for all		40.02
hollow of his h. and marked off		40.12
you with my victorious right h.		41.10
LORD your God, hold your right h.;		41.13
that the h. of the LORD has done		41.20
taken you by the h. and kept you;		42.06
is none who can deliver from my h.;		43.13
and another will write on his h.,		44.05
"Is there not a lie in my right h.?"		44.20
whose right h. I have grasped, to		45.01
I gave them into your h.,		47.06
My h. laid the foundation of the		48.13
and my right h. spread out the		48.13
in the shadow of his h. he hid me;		49.02
will lift up my h. to the nations,		49.22
Is my h. shortened, that it cannot		50.02
This shall you have from my h.:		50.11
and hid you in the shadow of my h.,		51.16
drunk at the h. of the LORD the		51.17
take her by the h. among all the		51.18
taken from your h. the cup of		51.22
put it into the h. of your tormentors,		51.23
the LORD shall prosper in his h.;		53.10
and keeps his h. from doing any		56.02
the LORD's h. is not shortened, that		59.01
of beauty in the h. of the LORD,		62.03
royal diadem in the h. of your God.		62.03
by his right h. and by his mighty		62.08
arm to go to the right h. of Moses,		63.12
us into the h. of our iniquities.		64.07
we are all the work of thy h.		64.08
All these things my h. has made,		66.02
known that the h. of the LORD is		66.14
put forth his h. and touched my	Jer	1.09
pass your h. again over its		6.09
stretch out my h. against the		6.12
LORD, or you will die by our h."—		11.21
stretched out my h. against you and		15.06
because thy h. was upon me, for thou		15.17
you out of the h. of the wicked,		15.21
loosen your h. from your heritage		17.04
was spoiled in the potter's h.,		18.04
like the clay in the potter's h.,		18.06
so are you in my h., O house of		18.06
and by the h. of those who seek		19.07
Judah into the h. of the king of		20.04
Judah into the h. of their enemies,		20.05
the needy from the h. of evildoers.		20.13
outstretched h. and strong arm,		21.05
into the h. of Nebuchadrezzar king		21.07
and into the h. of their enemies,		21.07
into the h. of those who seek their		21.07
given into the h. of the king of		21.10
from the h. of the oppressor him		21.12
from the h. of the oppressor him		22.03
the signet ring of my right h.,		22.24
you into the h. of those who seek		22.25
into the h. of those of whom you		22.25
even into the h. of Nebuchadrezzar		22.25
and into the h. of the Chaldeans.		22.25
"Am I a God at h., says the LORD,		23.23
"Take from my h. this cup of the		25.15
So I took the cup from the LORD's h.,		25.17
the cup from your h. to drink,		25.28
But the h. of Ahikam the son of		26.24
of Sidon by the h. of the envoys		27.03
lands into the h. of Nebuchadnezzar,		27.06
until I have consumed it by his h.		27.08
was sent by the h. of Elasah the		29.03
them into the h. of Nebuchadrezzar		29.21
them by the h. to bring them out		31.32
city into the h. of the king of		32.03
out of the h. of the Chaldeans, but		32.04
given into the h. of the king of		32.04
with a strong h. and outstretched		32.21
and into the h. of Nebuchadrezzar		32.28
given into the h. of the king of		32.36
city into the h. of the king of		34.02
You shall not escape from his h.		34.03
captured and delivered into his h.;		34.03
them into the h. of their enemies		34.20
and into the h. of those who seek		34.20
give into the h. of their enemies		34.21
and into the h. of those who seek		34.21
into the h. of the army of the king		34.21
"Take in your h. the scroll that		36.14
scroll in his h. and came to them.		36.14
into the h. of the king of Babylon."		37.17
given into the h. of the army of		38.03
you into the h. of these men who		38.16
given into the h. of the Chaldeans,		38.18
you shall not escape from their h."		38.18
shall not escape from their h.,		38.23
given into the h. of the men of		39.17
you and to deliver you from his h.		42.11
us into the h. of the Chaldeans,		43.03
Egypt into the h. of his enemies		44.30

HAND (cont.)

and into the h. of those who seek Jer 44.30
Judah into the h. of Nebuchadrezzar 44.30
into the h. of a people from the 46.24
them into the h. of those who seek 46.26
into the h. of Nebuchadrezzar king 46.26
Moab is near at h. and his affliction 48.16
Babylon was a golden cup in the LORD's h., 51.07
will stretch out my h. against you, 51.25
people fell into the h. of the foe, Lam 1.07
by his h. they were fastened 1.14
them his right h. in the face of 2.03
with his right h. set like a foe; 2.04
into the h. of the enemy the walls 2.07
restrained not his h. from destroying; 2.08
me he turns his h. again and again 3.03
a moment, no h. being laid on it. 4.06
We have given the h. to Egypt, 5.06
none to deliver us from their h. 5.08
and the h. of the LORD was upon him Eze 1.03
a h. was stretched out to me, and, lo, 2.09
the h. of the LORD being strong 3.14
blood I will require at your h. 3.18
blood I will require at your h. 3.20
And the h. of the LORD was there 3.22
stretch out my h. against them, 6.14
the h. of the Lord GOD fell there 8.01
He put forth the form of a h., 8.03
Each had his censer in his h., 8.11
his destroying weapon in his h." 9.01
his weapon for slaughter in his h., 9.02
forth his h. from between the 10.07
form of a human h. under their 10.08
say to them, The days are at h., 12.23
My h. will be against the prophets 13.09
deliver my people out of your h., 13.21
be no more in your h. as prey; 13.21
deliver my people out of your h. 13.23
will stretch out my h. against him, 14.09
and I stretch out my h. against it, 14.13
I stretched out my h. against you, 16.27
you into the h. of your lovers, 16.39
he gave his h. and yet did all 17.18
withholds his h. from iniquity, 18.08
withholds his h. from iniquity, 18.17
But I withheld my h., and acted 20.22
with a mighty h. and an outstretched 20.33
with a mighty h. and an outstretched 20.34
be given into the h. of the slayer. 21.11
Into his right h. comes the lot for 21.22
I will give her cup into your h. 23.31
stretched out my h. against you, 25.07
and will h. you over as spoil to 25.07
stretch out my h. against Edom, 25.13
Edom by the h. of my people Israel; 25.14
stretch out my h. against the 25.16
uncircumcised by the h. of foreigners; 28.10
when they grasped you with the h., 29.07
by the h. of Nebuchadrezzar king of 30.10
the land into the h. of evil men; 30.12
it it, by the h. of foreigners; 30.12
make the sword fall from his h. 30.22
Babylon, and put my sword in his h.: 30.24
sword into the h. of the king of 30.25
it into the h. of a mighty one of 31.11
will require at the watchman's h. 33.06
blood I will require at your h. 33.08
Now the h. of the LORD had been 33.22
will require my sheep at their h., 34.10
them from the h. of those who 34.27
will stretch out my h. against you, 35.03
The h. of the LORD was upon me, and 37.01
they may become one in your h. 37.17
(which is in the h. of Ephraim) and 37.19
that they may be one in my h. 37.19
are in your h. before their eyes, 37.20
strike your bow from your left h., 39.03
arrows drop out of your right h. 39.03
and my h. which I have laid on them. 39.21
them into the h. of their adversaries, 39.23
the h. of the LORD was upon me, 40.01
and a measuring reed in his h.; 40.03
in the man's h. was six long 40.05
Going on eastward with a line in his h., 47.03
Jehoiakim king of Judah into his h., Dan 1.02
a stone was cut out by no human h., 2.34
and into whose h. he has given, 2.38
cut from a mountain by no human h., 2.45
deliver us out of your h., O king. 3.17
none can stay his h. or say to him, 4.35
of a man's h. appeared and wrote 5.05
the king saw the h. as it wrote. 5.05
the God in whose h. is your breath, 5.23
"Then from his presence the h. was sent, 5.24
be given into his h. for a time, 7.25
make deceit prosper under his h., 8.25
by no human h., he shall be broken. 8.25
the land of Egypt with a mighty h., 9.15
And behold, a h. touched me and set 10.10
but it shall be given into his h. 11.11
shall be delivered out of his h.: 11.41
stretch out his h. against the 11.42
his right h. and his left h. toward 12.07
one shall rescue her out of my h. Hos 2.10
stretched out his h. with mockers. 7.05
How can I h. you over, O Israel! 11.08
into the h. of the sons of Judah, Joe 3.08
I will turn my h. against Ekron; Amo 1.08
leaned with his h. against the 5.19
line, with a plumb line in his h. 7.07
from there shall my h. take them; 9.02
their right h. from their left, and Jon 4.11
it is in the power of their h. Mic 2.01
you from the h. of your enemies. 4.10
Your h. shall be lifted up over 5.09
cut off sorceries from your h., 5.12
now their confusion is at h. 7.04
LORD's right h. will come around Hab 2.16
light, rays flashed from his h.; 3.04
stretch out my h. against Judah, Zep 1.04
For the day of the LORD is at h.; 1.07
stretch out his h. against the 2.13
with a measuring line in his h.! Zec 2.01
"Behold, I will shake my h. over them, 2.09
at his right h. to accuse him. 3.01
plummet in the h. of Zerubbabel. 4.10
each with staff in h. for very age. 8.04
each into the h. of his shepherd, 11.06
and each into the h. of his king; 11.06
I will deliver none from their h." 11.06
I will turn my h. against the 13.07
lay hold on the h. of his fellow, 14.13
and the h. of the one will be 14.13
raised against the h. of the other; 14.13
With such a gift from your h., Mal 1.09
accept an offering from your h. 1.10
Shall I accept that from your h.? 1.13
accepts it with favor at your h. 2.13
for the kingdom of heaven is at h." Mt 3.02
His winnowing fork is in his h., 3.12
for the kingdom of heaven is at h." 4.17
your accuser h. you over to the 5.25
And if your right h. causes you to 5.30
let your left h. know what your 6.03
know what your right h. is doing, 6.03
stretched out his h. and touched 8.03
he touched her h., and the fever 8.15
but come and lay your h. on her, 9.18
he went in and took her by the h., 9.25
'The kingdom of heaven is at h.' 10.07
there was a man with a withered h. 12.10
to the man, "Stretch out your h." 12.13
stretching out his h. toward his 12.49
reached out his h. and caught him, 14.31

HAND (cont.)
And if your h. or your foot causes Mt 18.08
at your right h. and one at your 20.21
sit at my right h. and at my left 20.23
'Bind him h. and foot, and cast him 22.13
to my Lord, Sit at my right h., 22.44
place the sheep at his right h., 25.33
will say to those at his right h., 25.34
will say to those at his left h., 25.41
The Teacher says, My time is at h.; 26.18
has dipped his h. in the dish with 26.23
Behold, the hour is at h., 26.45
see, my betrayer is at h." 26.46
stretched out his h. and drew his 26.51
seated at the right h. of Power, 26.64
and put a reed in his right h. 27.29
and the kingdom of God is at h.; Mk 1.15
took her by the h. and lifted her 1.31
stretched out his h. and touched 1.41
was there who had a withered h. 3.01
who had the withered h., "Come here." 3.03
to the man, "Stretch out your h." 3.05
it out, and his h. was restored. 3.05
Taking her by the h. he said to her, 5.41
your tradition which you h. on. 7.13
besought him to lay his h. upon him. 7.32
And he took the blind man by the h., 8.23
took him by the h. and lifted him 9.27
And if your h. causes you to sin, 9.43
at your right h. and one at your 10.37
sit at my right h. or at my left 10.40
to my Lord, Sit at my right h., 12.36
see, my betrayer is at h." 14.42
sitting at the right h. of Power, 14.62
For the h. of the LORD was with Lk 1.66
and from the h. of all who hate us; 1.71
delivered from the h. of our enemies, 1.74
His winnowing fork is in his h., 3.17
And he stretched out his h., 5.13
there whose right h. was withered. 6.06
to the man who had the withered h., 6.08
said to him, "Stretch out your h." 6.10
he did so, and his h. was restored. 6.10
But taking her by the h. he called, 8.54
who puts his h. to the plow and 9.62
and the judge h. you over to the 12.58
and put a ring on his h., and 15.22
to my LORD, Sit at my right h., 20.42
and, 'The time is at h.!' Do 21.08
But behold the h. of him who 22.21
at the right h. of the power of 22.69
The Passover of the Jews was at h., Jn 2.13
has given all things into his h. 3.35
the feast of the Jews, was at h. 6.04
feast of Tabernacles was at h. 7.02
one shall snatch them out of my h. 10.28
snatch them out of the Father's h. 10.29
the Passover of the Jews was at h., 11.55
by struck Jesus with his h., 18.22
as the tomb was close at h., 19.42
and place my h. in his side, I will 20.25
and put out your h., and place it 20.27
is at my right h. that I may not Ac 2.25
exalted at the right h. of God, 2.33
to my Lord, Sit at my right h., 2.34
by the right h. and raised him up; 3.07
to do whatever thy h. and thy plan 4.28
thou stretchest out thy h. to heal, 4.30
at his right h. as Leader and 5.31
giving them deliverance by his h., 7.25
deliverer by the h. of the angel 7.35
Did not my h. make all these things?' 7.50
standing at the right h. of God; 7.55
standing at the right h. of God. 7.56
led him by the h. and brought him 9.08
And he gave her his h. and lifted 9.41
And the h. of the Lord was with 11.21
elders by the h. of Barnabas and 11.30
me from the h. of Herod and from 12.11
to them with his h. to be silent, 12.17
the h. of the Lord is upon you, and 13.11
people to lead him by the h. 13.11
up, and motioning with his h. said: 13.16
And Alexander motioned with his h., 19.33
motioned with his h. to the people; 21.40
was led by the h. by those who 22.11
The tribune took him by the h., 23.19
stretched out his h. and made his 26.01
of the heat and fastened on his h. 28.03
the creature hanging from his h., 28.04
to do right, evil lies close at h. Rom 7.21
who is at the right h. of God, 8.34
is far gone, the day is at h. 13.12
should say, "Because I am not a h., 1Co 12.15
The eye cannot say to the h., 12.21
On the other h., he who prophesies 14.03
write this greeting with my own h. 16.21
for the right h. and for the left; 2Co 6.07
Barnabas the right h. of fellowship, Gal 2.09
I am writing to you with my own h. 6.11
at his right h. in the heavenly Eph 1.20
forbearance. The Lord is at h. Php 4.05
is seated at the right h. of God. Col 3.01
write this greeting with my own h. 4.18
write this greeting with my own h. 2Th 3.17
I, Paul, write this with my own h., Phm 1.19
at the right h. of the Majesty on Heb 1.03
he ever said, "Sit at my right h., 1.13
On the one h., a former commandment 7.18
on the other h., a better hope is 7.19
at the right h. of the throne of 8.01
them by the h. to lead them out of 8.09
sat down at the right h. of God, 10.12
at the right h. of the throne of 12.02
the coming of the Lord is at h. Jas 5.08
and is at the right h. of God, 1Pe 3.22
The end of all things is at h.; 4.07
therefore under the mighty h. of God, 5.06
in his right h. he held seven stars, Rev 1.16
But he laid his right h. upon me, 1.17
stars which you saw in my right h., 1.20
the seven stars in his right h., 2.01
in the right h. of him who was 5.01
from the right h. of him who was 5.07
its rider had a balance in his h.; 6.05
saints from the h. of the angel 8.04
had a little scroll open in his h. 10.02
lifted up his right h. to heaven 10.05
is open in the h. of the angel who 10.08
scroll from the h. of the angel 10.10
on the right h. or the forehead, 13.16
mark on his forehead or on his h., 14.09
head, and a sharp sickle in his h. 14.14
holding in her h. a golden cup 17.04
holding in his h. the key of the 20.01

HANDBAGS
mantles, the cloaks, and the h.; Is 3.22

HANDBREADTH
make around it a frame a h. wide, Ex 25.25
made around it a frame a h. wide, 37.12
Its thickness was a h.; and its 1Ki 7.26
Its thickness was a h.; and its 2Ch 4.05
being a cubit and a h. in length; Eze 40.05
And hooks, a h. long, were fastened 40.43
(the cubit being a cubit and a h.): 43.13

HANDBREADTHS
Behold, thou hast made my days a few h., Ps 39.05

HANDED
the horse be h. over to one of the Est 6.09
lest I be h. over to them and they Jer 38.19
we would not have h. him over." Jn 18.30

HANDED (cont.)
priests have h. you over to me; Jn 18.35
I might not be h. over to the Jews; 18.36
Then he h. him over to them to be 19.16

HANDFUL
take from it a h. of the fine Lev 2.02
shall take a h. of it as its 5.12
take from it a h. of the fine 6.15
shall take a h. of the cereal Num 5.26
shall take a h. of the cereal in a jar, and a 1Ki 17.12
Better is a h. of quietness than Ecc 4.06

HANDFULS
"Take h. of ashes from the kiln, and Ex 9.08
and two h. of sweet incense beaten Lev 16.12
suffice for h. for all the people 1Ki 20.10
my people for h. of barley and for Eze 13.19

HANDING
therefore I am h. over to the Eze 25.04

HANDIWORK
and the firmament proclaims his h. Ps 19.01

HANDKERCHIEFS
so that h. or aprons were carried Ac 19.12

HANDLE
slips from the h. and strikes his Deu 19.05
able to h. spear and shield. 2Ch 25.05
Those who h. the law did not know Jer 2.08
Ethiopia and Put who h. the shield, 46.09
ships come all that h. the oar. Eze 27.29
h. me, and see; for a spirit Lk 24.39
"Do not h., Do not taste, Do not Col 2.21

HANDLED
to be polished, that it may be h.; Eze 21.11
pressed and their virgin bosoms h. 23.03
and her and h. her virgin bosom 23.08
the Egyptians h. your bosom and 23.21

HANDLES
myrrh, upon the h. of the bolt. Sol 5.05
or 'Your work has no h.'? Is 45.09
and the one who h. the sickle in Jer 50.16
he who h. the bow shall not stand, Amo 2.15

HANDLING
men of Lud, skilled in h. the bow. Jer 46.09
rightly h. the word of truth. 2Ti 2.15

HANDMAID
pray let your h. speak in your ears, 1Sa 25.24
and hear the words of your h. 25.24
but I your h. did not see the young 25.25
Pray forgive the trespass of your h.; 25.28
my lord, then remember your h." 25.31
your h. is a servant to wash the 25.41
your h. has hearkened to you; 28.21
you also hearken to your h.; 28.22
And your h. had two sons, and they 2Sa 14.06
family has risen against your h., 14.07
"Pray let your h. speak a word to 14.12
and your h. thought, 'I will speak 14.15
And your h. thought. 'The word of my 14.17
words in the mouth of your h. 14.19
servant, and save the son of thy h. Ps 86.16
am thy servant, the son of thy h. 116.16
"Behold I am the h. of the Lord; Lk 1.38

HANDMAIDEN
regarded the low estate of his h. Lk 1.48

HANDPIKES
h. and spears, and they will make Eze 39.09

HANDS
work and from the toil of our h." Gen 5.29
put forth their h. and brought Lot 19.10
innocence of my h. I have done 20.05
put upon his h. and upon the 27.16
voice, but the h. are the h. of Esau." 27.22
because his h. were hairy like his 27.23
hairy like his brother Esau's h.; 27.23
affliction and the labor of my h., 31.42
he delivered him out of their h., 37.21
that he did to prosper in his h. 39.03
put him in my h., and I will bring 42.37
crossing his h., for Manasseh was 48.14
agile by the h. of the Mighty One 49.24
will stretch out my h. to the LORD; Ex 9.29
stretched out his h. to the LORD; 9.33
which thy h. have established. 15.17
But Moses' h. grew weary; so they 17.12
and Aaron and Hur held up his h., 17.12
so his h. were steady until the 17.12
shall not join h. with a wicked 23.01
shall lay their h. upon the head 29.10
shall lay their h. upon the head 29.15
shall lay their h. upon the head 29.19
upon the thumbs of their right h., 29.20
these in the h. of Aaron and in 29.24
of Aaron and in the h. of his sons, 29.24
Then you shall take them from their h., 29.25
shall wash their h. and their feet. 30.19
shall wash their h. and their feet, 30.21
tables of the testimony in his h., 32.15
out of his h. and broke them at 32.19
who had ability spun with their h., 35.25
washed their h. and their feet; 40.31
shall lay their h. upon the head Lev 4.15
with his own h. the offerings by 7.30
sons laid their h. upon the head 8.14
sons laid their h. on the head of 8.18
sons laid their h. on the head of 8.22
of their right h. and on the great 8.24
these in the h. of Aaron and in 8.27
of Aaron and in the h. of his sons, 8.27
Then Moses took them from their h., 8.28
lifted up his h. toward the people 9.22
rinsed his h. in water shall wash 15.11
lay both his h. upon the head of 16.21
him lay their h. upon his head, 24.14
place in her h. the cereal offering Num 5.18
them upon the h. of the Nazirite, 6.19
shall lay their h. upon the 8.10
shall lay their h. upon the heads 8.12
and he struck his h. together; 24.10
and he laid his h. upon him, 27.23
took in their h. some of the fruit Deu 1.25
you in all the work of your h.; 2.07
LORD our God gave all into our h. 2.36
and stone, the work of men's h., 4.28
of the covenant were in my two h. 9.15
and cast them out of my two h., 9.17
the work of your h. that you do. 14.29
and in all the work of your h., 16.15
wash their h. over the heifer 21.06
'Our h. did not shed this blood, 21.07
your God gives them into your h., 21.10
you in all the work of your h. 24.19
made by the h. of a craftsman, 27.15
to bless all the work of your h.; 28.12
anger through the work of your h." 31.29
With thy h. contend for him, and be 33.07
and accept the work of his h.; 33.11
for Moses had laid his h. upon him; 34.09
has given all the land into our h.; Jos 2.24
us into the h. of the Amorites, to 7.07
for I have given them into your h.; 10.08
all their enemies into their h. 21.44
putting their h. to their mouths, Ju 7.06
jars of the people from their h., 7.08

HANDS (cont.)
afterward your h. shall be strengthened Ju 7.11
into the h. of all of them and 7.16
the jars that were in their h. 7.19
in their left h. the torches, 7.20
in their right h. the trumpets to 7.20
given into your h. the princes of 8.03
strengthened his h. to slay his 9.24
and a cereal offering at our h., 13.23
He scraped it out into his h., 14.09
you into the h. of the Philistines." 15.12
you and give you into their h.; 15.13
and his bonds melted off his h. 15.14
fall into the h. of the uncircumcised?" 15.18
and brought the money in their h. 16.18
yea, God has given it into your h., 18.10
with her h. on the threshold. 19.27
and both his h. were lying cut off 1Sa 5.04
climbed up on his h. and feet, 14.13
out of the h. of those who plundered 14.48
feigned himself mad in their h., 21.13
is no wrong or treason in my h. 24.11
when the LORD put me into your h. 24.18
What guilt is on my h.? 26.18
me into the h. of my master, 30.15
Now therefore let your h. be strong, 2Sa 2.07
Your h. were not bound, your feet 3.34
and cut off their h. and feet, 4.12
and the h. of all who are with you 16.21
them into the h. of the Gibeonites, 21.09
cleanness of my h. he recompensed 22.21
He trains my h. for war, so that my 22.35
spread forth his h. toward heaven; 1Ki 8.22
stretching out his h. toward this 8.38
had knelt with h. outstretched 8.54
them to the h. of the officers of 14.27
them into the h. of his servants; 15.18
to anger with the work of his h., 16.07
and lay h. on whatever pleases them, 20.06
poured water on the h. of Elijah." 2Ki 3.11
his eyes, and his h. upon his h.; 4.34
the feet and the palms of her h. 9.35
give into your h. to escape shall 10.24
and they clapped their h., 11.12
So they laid h. on her; and she 11.16
out into the h. of the workmen who 12.11
Elisha laid his h. upon the king's h. 13.16
no gods, but the work of men's h., 19.18
with all the work of their h., 22.17
with them were given into their h., 1Ch 5.20
although there is no wrong in my h., 12.17
of Israel, and spread forth his h. 2Ch 6.12
spread forth his h. toward heaven; 6.13
stretching out his h. toward this 6.29
them to the h. of the officers of 12.10
Do not let your h. be weak, 15.07
So they laid h. on her; and she 23.15
repairing went forward in their h., 24.13
and they laid their h. upon them, 29.23
delivered their people from my h., 32.17
which are the work of men's h. 32.19
with all the works of their h., 34.25
diligently and prospers in their h. Ez 5.08
into the h. of Meremoth the priest, 8.33
spread out my h. to the LORD my 9.05
strengthened their h. for the good Neh 2.18
"Their h. will drop from the work, 6.09
now, O God, strengthen thou my h. 6.09
"Amen, Amen," lifting up their h.; 8.06
and didst give them into their h., 9.24
do so again I will lay h. on you." 13.21
sought to lay h. on King Ahasuerus. Est 2.21
disdained to lay h. on Mordecai 3.06
silver into the h. of those who 3.09
sought to lay h. upon King Ahasuerus. 6.02
he would lay h. on the Jews. 8.07
Ahasuerus to lay h. on such as 9.02
but they laid no h. on the plunder. 9.15
but they laid no h. on the plunder. 9.16
hast blessed the work of his h., Job 1.10
you have strengthened the weak h. 4.03
so that their h. achieve no success. 5.12
he smites, but his h. heal. 5.18
snow, and cleanse my h. with lye, 9.30
the work of thy h. and favor the 10.03
Thy h. fashioned and made me; 10.08
stretch out your h. toward him. 11.13
long for the work of thy h. 14.15
casts me into the h. of the wicked. 16.11
although there is no violence in my h., 16.17
that has clean h. grows stronger 17.09
and his h. will give back his 20.10
through the cleanness of your h." 22.30
It claps its h. at him, and hisses 27.23
gain from the strength of their h., 30.02
if any spot has cleaved to my h.; 31.07
they are all the work of his h.? 34.19
he claps his h. among us, and 34.37
He covers his h. with the lightning, 36.32
Lay h. on him; think of the 41.08
this, if there is wrong in my h., Ps 7.03
dominion over the works of thy h.; 8.06
snared in the work of their own h. 9.16
thou mayest take it into thy h.; 10.14
cleanness of my h. he recompensed 18.20
cleanness of my h. in his sight. 18.24
He trains my h. for war, so that my 18.34
they have pierced my h. and feet— 22.16
He who has clean h. and a pure 24.04
I wash my h. in innocence, and go 26.06
men in whose h. are evil devices, 26.10
and whose right h. are full of 26.10
as I lift up my h. toward thy most 28.02
according to the work of their h.; 28.04
of the LORD, or the work of his h., 28.05
forth our h. to a strange god, 44.20
Clap your h., all peoples! 47.01
your h. deal out violence on earth. 58.02
will lift up my h. and call on thy 63.04
to stretch out her h. to God. 68.31
and washed my h. in innocence. 73.13
of war were unable to use their h. 76.05
your h. were freed from the basket. 81.06
I spread out my h. to thee. 88.09
thou the work of our h. upon us, 90.17
the work of our h. establish thou 90.17
On their h. they will bear you up, 91.12
the works of thy h. I sing for joy. 92.04
for his h. formed the dry land. 95.05
Let the floods clap their h.; 98.08
the heavens are the work of thy h. 102.25
The works of his h. are faithful 111.07
and gold, the work of men's h. 115.04
They have h., but do not feel; 115.07
Thy h. have made and fashioned me; 119.73
put forth their h. to do wrong. 125.03
the fruit of the labor of your h.; 128.02
Lift up your h. to the holy place, 134.02
and gold, the work of men's h. 135.15
do not forsake the work of thy h. 138.08
O LORD, from the h. of the wicked; 140.04
up of my h. as an evening sacrifice! 141.02
I muse on what thy h. have wrought. 143.05
I stretch out my h. to thee; 143.06
who trains my h. for war, and my 144.01
and two-edged swords in their h., 149.06
little folding of the h. to rest, Pro 6.10
and h. that shed innocent blood, 6.17
with her own h. tears it down. 14.01
him for his h. refuse to labor. 21.25
little folding of the h. to rest," 24.33
the lizard you can take in your h., 30.28
flax, and works with willing h. 31.13
fruit of her h. she plants a 31.16

HANDS (cont.)

She puts her h. to the distaff, and Pro 31.19
and her h. hold the spindle. 31.19
reaches out her h. to the needy. 31.20
Give her of the fruit of her h., 31.31
all that my h. had done and the Ecc 2.11
The fool folds his h., 4.05
than two h. full of toil and a 4.06
and destroy the work of your h.? 5.06
and nets, and whose h. are fetters; 7.26
and my h. dripped with myrrh, my Sol 5.05
When you spread forth your h., Is 1.15
your h. are full of blood. 1.15
and they strike h. with foreigners. 2.06
bow down to the work of their h., 2.08
for what his h. have done shall be 3.11
LORD, or see the work of his h. 5.12
Therefore all h. will be feeble, and 13.07
the altars, the work of their h., 17.08
and Assyria the work of my h., 19.25
spread out his h. in the midst of 25.11
swimmer spreads his h. out to swim; 25.11
together with the skill of his h. 25.11
his children, the work of my h., 29.23
which your h. have sinfully made 31.07
of oppressions, who shakes his h., 33.15
Strengthen the weak h., 35.03
no gods, but the work of men's h., 37.19
me concerning the work of my h.? 45.11
it was my h. that stretched out the 45.12
graven you on the palms of my h.; 49.16
of the field shall clap their h. 55.12
For your h. are defiled with blood 59.03
deeds of violence are in their h. 59.06
of my planting, the work of my h., 60.21
I spread out my h. all the day to a 65.02
long enjoy the work of their h. 65.22
worshiped the works of their own h. Jer 1.16
away with your h. upon your head, 2.37
stretching out her h., "Woe is me! 4.31
report of it, our h. fall helpless; 6.24
an axe by the h. of a craftsman. 10.03
and of the h. of the goldsmith; 10.09
my soul into the h. of her enemies. 12.07
are in your h. and with which you 21.04
strengthen the h. of evildoers, 23.14
to anger with the work of your h.; 25.06
work of your h. to your own harm. 25.07
deeds and the work of their h." 25.14
as for me, behold, I am in your h. 26.14
man with his h. on his loins like 30.06
him from h. too strong for him. 31.11
given into the h. of the Chaldeans 32.24
given into the h. of the Chaldeans.'" 32.25
city into the h. of the Chaldeans 32.28
work of their h., says the LORD. 32.30
given into the h. of the Chaldeans. 32.43
pass under the h. of the one who 33.13
weakening the h. of the soldiers 38.04
and the h. of all the people, by 38.04
said, "Behold, he is in your h.; 38.05
today from the chains on your h. 40.04
"Take in your h. large stones, and 43.09
to anger with the works of your h., 44.08
and have fulfilled it with your h., 44.25
children, so feeble are their h., 47.03
upon all the h. are gashes, and on 48.37
of them, and his h. fell helpless; 50.43
stretched out his h. over all her Lam 1.10
me into the h. of those whom I 1.14
Zion stretches out her h., 1.17
along the way clap their h. at you; 2.15
Lift your h. to him for the lives 2.19
our hearts and h. to God in heaven: 3.41
according to the work of their h. 3.64
pots, the work of a potter's h.! 4.02
The h. of compassionate women have 4.10
Princes are hung up by their h.; 5.12
their four sides they had human h. Eze 1.08
"Clap your h., and stamp your foot, 6.11
All h. are feeble, and all knees 7.17
it into the h. of foreigners for a 7.21
and the h. of the people of the 7.27
fill your h. with burning coals 10.02
put it into the h. of the man 10.07
wings the semblance of human h. 10.21
give you into the h. of foreigners, 11.09
through the wall with my own h. 12.07
melt and all h. will be feeble, 21.07
clap your h. and let the sword come 21.14
I also will clap my h., and I will 21.17
you into the h. of brutal men, 21.31
I strike my h. together at the 22.13
or can your h. be strong, in the 22.14
her into the h. of her lovers, 23.09
into the h. of the Assyrians, upon 23.09
you into the h. of those whom you 23.28
into the h. of those from whom you 23.28
adultery, and blood is upon their h.; 23.37
bracelets upon the h. of the women, 23.42
adulteresses, and blood is upon their h." 23.45
clapped your h. and stamped your 25.06
in the h. of those who wound you? 28.09
that will deliver you out of my h.?" Dan 3.15
me trembling on my h. and knees. 10.10
in whose h. are false balances, he Hos 12.07
'Our God,' to the work of our h. 14.03
the violence which is in his h. Jon 3.08
no more to the work of your h.; Mic 5.13
Their h. are upon what is evil, to 7.03
shall lay their h. on their mouths; 7.16
news of you clap their h. over you. Nah 3.19
voice, it lifted its h. on high. Hab 3.10
let not your h. grow weak. Zep 3.16
and so with every work of their h.; Hag 2.14
"The h. of Zerubbabel have laid the Zec 4.09
his h. shall also complete it. 4.09
"Let your h. be strong, you who in 8.09
not, but let your h. be strong." 8.13
and 'On their h. they will bear Mt 4.06
do not wash their h. when they eat." 15.02
with unwashed h. does not defile a 15.20
Son of man will suffer at their h." 17.12
be delivered into the h. of men, 17.22
than with two h. or two feet to be 18.08
might lay his h. on them and pray. 19.13
And he laid his h. on them and went 19.15
is betrayed into the h. of sinners. 26.45
up and laid h. on Jesus and seized 26.50
and washed his h. before the crowd, 27.24
Come and lay your h. on her, Mk 5.23
mighty works are wrought by his h.! 6.02
he laid his h. upon a few sick 6.05
his disciples ate with h. defiled, 7.02
not eat unless they wash their h., 7.03
elders, but eat with h. defiled?" 7.05
his eyes and laid his h. upon him, 8.23
again he laid his h. upon his eyes; 8.25
be delivered into the h. of men, 9.31
than with two h. to go to hell, 9.43
them, laying his h. upon them. 10.16
is betrayed into the h. of sinners. 14.41
And they laid h. on him and seized 14.46
this temple that is made with h., 14.58
build another, not made with h.'" 14.58
and 'On their h. they will bear you Lk 4.11
and he laid his h. on every one of 4.40
of grain, rubbing them in their h. 6.01
to be delivered into the h. of men." 9.44
And he laid his h. upon her, 13.13
tried to lay h. on him at that 20.19
will lay their h. on you and 21.12
temple, you did not lay h. on me." 22.53
into thy h. I commit my spirit!" 23.46

HANDS (cont.)

delivered into the h. of sinful men,	Lk 24.07
See my h. and my feet, that it is I	24.39
he showed them his h. and his feet.	* 24.40
lifting up his h. he blessed them.	24.50
but no one laid h. on him,	Jn 7.30
him, but no one laid h. on him.	7.44
him, but he escaped from their h.	10.39
his h. and feet bound with bandages,	11.44
had given all things into his h.,	13.03
only but also my h. and my head!"	13.09
and struck him with their h.	19.03
he showed them his h. and his side.	20.20
I see in his h. the print of the	20.25
your finger here, and see my h.;	20.27
old, you will stretch out your h.,	21.18
killed by the h. of lawless men.	Ac 2.23
people by the h. of the apostles.	5.12
prayed and laid their h. upon them.	6.06
rejoiced in the works of their h.	7.41
not dwell in houses made with h.;	7.48
Then they laid their h. on them and	8.17
the laying on of the apostles' h.,	8.18
whom I lay my h. may receive the	8.19
in and lay his h. on him so that	9.12
And laying his h. on him he said,	9.17
laid violent h. upon some who	12.01
And the chains fell off his h.	12.07
they laid their h. on them and	13.03
and wonders to be done by their h.	14.03
nor is he served by human h.,	17.25
Paul had laid his h. upon them,	19.06
miracles by the h. of Paul,	19.11
gods made with h. are not gods.	19.26
know that these h. ministered to	20.34
and bound his own feet and h.,	21.11
him into the h. of the Gentiles.'"	21.11
all the crowd, and laid h. on him,	21.27
violence took him out of our h.,	* 24.07
with their own h. the tackle of	27.19
and putting his h. on him healed	28.08
Jerusalem into the h. of the Romans.	28.17
held out my h. to a disobedient	Rom 10.21
and we labor, working with our own h.	1Co 4.12
from God, a house not made with h.,	2Co 5.01
received at the h. of the Jews the	11.24
in the wall, and escaped his h.	11.33
which is made in the flesh by h.—	Eph 2.11
doing honest work with his h.,	4.28
a circumcision made without h.,	Col 2.11
affairs, and to work with your h.,	1Th 4.11
lifting holy h. without anger or	1Ti 2.08
the elders laid their h. upon you.	4.14
be hasty in the laying on of h.,	5.22
you through the laying on of my h.;	2Ti 1.06
the heavens are the work of thy h.;	Heb 1.10
ablutions, the laying on of h.,	6.02
more perfect tent (not made with h.,	9.11
not into a sanctuary made with h.,	9.24
fall into the h. of the living God.	10.31
your drooping h. and strengthen	12.12
Cleanse your h., you sinners, and	Jas 4.08
upon and touched with our h.,	1Jn 1.01
with palm branches in their h.,	Rev 7.09
works of their h. nor give up	9.20
with harps of God in their h.	15.02
on their foreheads or their h.	20.04

HANDSOME

Now Joseph was h. and good-looking.	Gen 39.06
name was Saul, a h. young man.	1Sa 9.02
people of Israel more h. than he;	9.02
and had beautiful eyes, and was h.	16.12
And he slew an Egyptian, a h. man.	2Sa 23.21
He was also a very h. man;	1Ki 1.06
h. and skilful in all wisdom,	Dan 1.04

HANES

at Zoan and his envoys reach H.,	Is 30.04

HANG

h. you on a tree; and the birds	Gen 40.19
shall h. over the back of the	Ex 26.12
the tent shall h. over the sides	26.13
and you shall h. it upon four	26.32
And you shall h. the veil from the	26.33
and h. up the screen for the gate	40.08
the hair of your heads h. loose,	Lev 10.06
let the hair of his head h. loose,	13.45
let the hair of his head h. loose,	21.10
and h. them in the sun before the	Num 25.04
death, and you h. him on a tree,	Deu 21.22
your life shall h. in doubt before	28.66
so that we may h. them up before	2Sa 21.06
And the king said, "H. him on that."	Est 7.10
they h. afar from men, they swing to	Job 28.04
which h. useless, is a proverb in	Pro 26.07
whereon h. a thousand bucklers, all	Sol 4.04
And they will h. on him the whole	Is 22.24
a peg from it to h. any vessel on?	Eze 15.03

HANGED

but he h. the chief baker, as Joseph	Gen 40.22
to my office, and the baker was h."	41.13
for a h. man is accursed by God;	Deu 21.23
And he h. the king of Ai on a tree	Jos 8.29
and h. them beside the pool at	2Sa 4.12
his house in order, and h. himself;	17.23
and they h. them on the mountain	21.09
where the Philistines had h. them,	21.12
the bones of those who were h.	21.13
men were both h. on the gallows.	Est 2.23
king to have Mordecai h. upon it;	5.14
having Mordecai h. on the gallows	6.04
So they h. Haman on the gallows	7.10
and they have h. him on the gallows,	8.07
sons of Haman be h. on the gallows."	9.13
and the ten sons of Haman were h.	9.14
sons should be h. on the gallows.	9.25
and he went and h. himself.	Mt 27.05
criminals who were h. railed at him,	Lk 23.39

HANGING

and he left h. between heaven	2Sa 18.09
"Behold, I saw Absalom h. in an oak."	18.10
you killed by h. him on a tree.	Ac 5.30
him to death by h. him on a tree;	10.39
saw the creature h. from his hand,	28.04

HANGINGS

shall have h. of fine twined linen	Ex 27.09
there shall be h. a hundred cubits	27.11
there shall be h. for fifty cubits,	27.12
The h. for the one side of the gate	27.14
other side the h. shall be fifteen	27.15
with h. of fine twined linen and	27.18
the h. of the court, its pillars and	35.17
south side the h. of the court	38.09
west side were h. of fifty cubits,	38.12
The h. for one side of the gate	38.14
the court were h. of fifteen	38.15
All the h. round about the court	38.16
corresponding to the h. of the court.	38.18
the h. of the court, its pillars, and	39.40
the h. of the court, the screen for	Num 3.26
and the h. of the court, and the	4.26
the women wove h. for the Asherah.	2Ki 23.07
and blue h. caught up with cords	Est 1.06

HANGS

and h. the earth upon nothing.	Job 26.07
Your tackle h. loose; it cannot	Is 33.23
be every one who h. on a tree"—	Gal 3.13

HANNAH
the name of the one was H., and the 1Sa 1.02
children, but H. had no children. 1.02
and, although he loved H., he would 1.05
he would give H. only one portion, 1.05
Therefore H. wept and would not eat 1.07
"H., why do you weep? And why do 1.08
eaten and drunk in Shiloh, H. rose. 1.09
H. was speaking in her heart; 1.13
But H. answered, "No, my lord, I am a 1.15
And Elkanah knew H. his wife, 1.19
and in due time H. conceived and 1.20
But H. did not go up, for she said 1.22
H. also prayed and said, "My heart 2.01
And the LORD visited H., 2.21

HANNATHON
the boundary turns about to H., Jos 19.14

HANNIEL
a leader, H. the son of Ephod. Num 34.23
the sons of Ulla: Arah, H., and Rizia. 1Ch 7.39

HANOCH
Ephah, Epher, H., Abida, and Eldaah. Gen 25.04
H., Pallu, Hezron, and Carmi. 46.09
H., Pallu, Hezron and Carmi; Ex 6.14
of H., the family of the Hanochites; Num 26.05
H., Abida, and Eldaah. All these were 1Ch 1.33
H., Pallu, Hezron, and Carmi. 5.03

HANOCHITES
of Hanoch, the family of the H.; Num 26.05

HANUN
and H. his son reigned in his stead. 2Sa 10.01
loyally with H. the son of Nahash, 10.02
Ammonites said to H. their lord, 10.03
So H. took David's servants, and 10.04
loyally with H. the son of Nahash, 1Ch 19.02
servants came to H. in the land of 19.02
of the Ammonites said to H., 19.03
So H. took David's servants, and 19.04
H. and the Ammonites sent a thousand 19.06
H. and the inhabitants of Zanoah Neh 3.13
Shelemiah and H. the sixth son of 3.30

HAPHARAIM
H., Shion, Anaharath, Jos 19.19

HAPLESS
eyes stealthily watch for the h., Ps 10.08
The h. is crushed, sinks down, and 10.10
the h. commits himself to thee; 10.14

HAPPEN
you what shall h. to the child." 1Ki 14.03
or for love, he causes it to h. Job 37.13
things yet to h. among those who Ecc 1.11
but time and chance h. to them all. 9.11
know not what evil may h. on earth. 11.02
it will h. to Tyre as in the song Is 23.15
them, and tell us what is to h. 41.22
congregation, what will h. to them. Jer 6.18
"What is in your mind shall never h.— Eze 20.32
This shall never h. to you." Mt 16.22
tell them what was to h. to him, Mk 10.32
Pray that it may not h. in winter. 13.18
green, what will h. when it is dry?" Lk 23.31

HAPPENED
It h. at that time that Judah went Gen 38.01
this has ever h. or was ever heard Deu 4.32
thing has never h. or been seen Ju 19.30
and she h. to come to the part of Ru 2.03
nothing like this has h. before. 1Sa 4.07
struck us, it h. to us by chance." 6.09
"By chance I h. to be on Mount 2Sa 1.06
It h., late one afternoon, when 11.02
Now there h. to be there a worthless 20.01
But it h. at the end of three years 1Ki 2.39
And so it h. to him, for the people 2Ki 7.20
Now it h. in the month of Chislev, Neh 1.01
told him all that had h. to him, Est 4.07
is what has h. to those in whom we Is 20.06
horrible thing has h. in the land: Jer 5.30
soldiers who h. to be there. 41.03
who escapes; say, 'What has h.?' 48.19
Has such a thing h. in your days, Joe 1.02
and what h. from Shittim to Gilgal, Mic 6.05
and what had h. to the demoniacs. Mt 8.33
to see what it was that had h. Mk 5.14
told what had h. to the demoniac 5.16
and see this thing that has h., Lk 2.16
When the herdsmen saw what had h., 8.34
people went out to see what had h., 8.35
them to tell no one what had h. 8.56
Now it h. that as he was praying 9.18
went home wondering at what had h. * 24.12
about all these things that had h. 24.14
that have h. there in these days?" 24.18
is now the third day since this h. 24.21
Then they told what had h. on the road, 24.35
amazement at what had h. to him. Ac 3.10
men praised God for what had h. 4.21
came in, not knowing what had h. 5.07
This h. three times, and the thing 10.16
This h. three times, and all was 11.10
It h. that the father of Publius 28.08
Now these things h. to them as a 1Co 10.11
that what has h. to me has really Php 1.12
It has h. to them according to the 2Pe 2.22

HAPPENING
something strange were h. to you. 1Pe 4.12

HAPPENS
h. according to the deeds of the wicked, Ecc 8.14
h. according to the deeds of the righteous. 8.14
shower is coming'; and so it h. Lk 12.54
will be scorching heat'; and so it h. 12.55

HAPPIER
H. were the victims of the sword Lam 4.09
judgment she is h. if she remains. 1Co 7.40

HAPPINESS
peace, I have forgotten what h. is; Lam 3.17

HAPPIZZEZ
to Hezir, the eighteenth to H., 1Ch 24.15

HAPPY
And Leah said, "H. am I! For the Gen 30.13
For the women will call me h."; 30.13
to be h. with his wife whom he has Deu 24.05
H. are you, O Israel! Who is like 33.29
they ate and drank and were h. 1Ki 4.20
H. are your wives! 10.08
H. are these your servants, who 10.08
H. are your wives! 2Ch 9.07
H. are these your servants, who 9.07
"Behold, h. is the man whom God Job 5.17
H. is the man who takes refuge in Ps 34.08
he lives, he counts himself h., 49.18
H. is the man who has his quiver 127.05
you shall be h., and it shall be 128.02
H. shall he be who requites you 137.08
H. shall he be who takes your 137.09
H. the people to whom such blessings 144.15
H. the people whose God is the LORD 144.15
H. is he whose help is the God of 146.05
H. is the man who finds wisdom, and Pro 3.13
who hold her fast are called h. 3.18
h. are those who keep my ways. 8.32
H. is the man who listens to me, 8.34

HAPPY (cont.)

but h. is he who is kind to the Pro 14.21
and h. is he who trusts in the LORD. 16.20
them than to be h. and enjoy Ecc 3.12
H. are you, O land, when your king is 10.17
maidens saw her and called her h.; Sol 6.09
H. are you who sow beside all Is 32.20
h. is he who has no reason to judge Rom 14.22
we call those h. who were steadfast. Jas 5.11

HARA

H., and the river Gozan, to this day. 1Ch 5.26

HARADAH

Mount Shepher, and encamped at H. Num 33.24
And they set out from H., 33.25

HARAN

the father of Abram, Nahor, and H. Gen 11.26
the father of Abram, Nahor, and H.; 11.27
and H. was the father of Lot. 11.27
H. died before his father Terah in 11.28
the daughter of H. the father of 11.29
his son and Lot the son of H., 11.31
but when they came to H., 11.31
five years; and Terah died in H. 11.32
years old when he departed from H. 12.04
persons that they had gotten in H.; 12.05
flee to Laban my brother in H., 27.43
left Beersheba, and went toward H. 28.10
They said, "We are from H." 29.04
H., Rezeph, and the people of Eden 2Ki 19.12
bore H., Moza, and Gazez; 1Ch 2.46
and H. was the father of Gazez. 2.46
Shelomoth, Haziel, and H., three. 23.09
H., Rezeph, and the people of Eden Is 37.12
H., Canneh, Eden, Asshur, and Chilmad Eze 27.23
Mesopotamia, before he lived in H., Ac 7.02
of the Chaldeans, and lived in H. 7.04

HARARITE

Shammah, the son of Agee the H. 2Sa 23.11
Shammah the H., Ahiam the son of 23.33
Ahiam the son of Sharar the H., 23.33
Jonathan the son of Shagee the H., 1Ch 11.34
Ahiam the son of Sachar the H., 11.35

HARASS

"H. the Midianites, and smite them; Num 25.17
'Do not h. Moab or contend with Deu 2.09
do not h. them or contend with them, 2.19
and those who h. Judah shall be cut Is 11.13
and Judah shall not h. Ephraim. 11.13
to h. me, to keep me from being too 2Co 12.07

HARASSED

shot at him, and h. him sorely; Gen 49.23
for they have h. you with their Num 25.18
because they were h. and helpless, Mt 9.36

HARBONA

H., Bigtha and Abagtha, Zethar and Est 1.10
Then said H., one of the eunuchs in 7.09

HARBOR

And because the h. was not suitable Ac 27.12
a h. of Crete, looking northeast and 27.12

HARBORS

his lips and h. deceit in his Pro 26.24

HARD

Is anything too h. for the LORD? Gen 18.14
they pressed h. against the man 19.09
travailed, and she had h. labor. 35.16
And when she was in her h. labor, 35.17
their lives bitter with h. service, Ex 1.14
h. cases they brought to Moses, but 18.26
the case that is too h. for you, Deu 1.17
It shall not seem h. to you, 15.18
us, and laid upon us h. bondage. 26.06
you this day is not too h. for you, 30.11
her, because she pressed him h. Ju 14.17
she pressed him h. with her words 16.16
all Israel, and the battle was h.; 20.34
and they were pursued h. to Gidom, 20.45
(for the people were h. pressed), 1Sa 13.06
too followed h. after them in the 14.22
There was h. fighting against the 14.52
The battle pressed h. upon Saul, 31.03
sons of Zeruiah are too h. for me. 2Sa 3.39
came to test him with h. questions. 1Ki 10.01
lighten the h. service of your 12.04
he said, "You have asked a h. thing; 2Ki 2.10
The battle pressed h. upon Saul, 1Ch 10.03
to test him with h. questions, 2Ch 9.01
lighten the h. service of your 10.04
"Has not man a h. service upon Job 7.01
Through want and h. hunger they 30.23
I weep for him whose day was h.? 30.25
the skies, h. as a molten mirror? 37.18
The waters become h. like stone, 38.30
His heart is h. as a stone, 41.24
h. as the nether millstone. 41.24
made thy people suffer h. things; Ps 60.03
were bowed down with h. labor; 107.12
I was pushed h., so that I was 118.13
turmoil and the h. service with Is 14.03
into the hand of a h. master; 19.04
LORD with his h. and great and 27.01
Disaster follows h. on disaster, Jer 4.20
Nothing is too h. for thee, 32.17
is anything too h. for me? 32.27
shall follow h. after you to Egypt; 42.16
of affliction and h. servitude; Lam 1.03
yoke on our necks we are h. driven; 5.05
foreign speech and a h. language, Eze 3.05
foreign speech and a h. language, 3.06
Israel are of a h. forehead and of 3.07
made your face h. against their 3.08
your forehead h. against their 3.08
his army labor h. against Tyre; 29.18
Nevertheless the men rowed h. to Jon 1.13
gate is narrow and the way is h., Mt 7.14
it will be h. for a rich man to 19.23
h. to bear, and lay them on men's 23.04
'Master, I knew you to be a h. man, 25.24
"How h. it will be for those who Mk 10.23
how h. it is to enter the kingdom 10.24
load men with burdens h. to bear, Lk 11.46
Pharisees began to press him h., 11.53
"How h. it is for those who have 18.24
it, said, "This is a h. saying; Jn 6.60
But by your h. and impenitent heart Rom 2.05
Greet Mary, who has worked h. among you. 16.06
who has worked h. in the Lord. 16.12
I am h. pressed between the two. Php 1.23
he has worked h. for you and for Col 4.13
much to say which is h. to explain, Heb 5.11
you endured a h. struggle with 10.32
things in them h. to understand, 2Pe 3.16

HARDEN

but I will h. his heart, so that he Ex 4.21
But I will h. Pharaoh's heart, and 7.03
And I will h. Pharaoh's heart, and he 14.04
And I will h. the hearts of the 14.17
you shall not h. your heart or shut Deu 15.07
LORD's doing to h. their hearts Jos 11.20
Why should you h. your hearts as 1Sa 6.06
H. not your hearts, as at Meribah, as Ps 95.08
err from thy ways and h. our heart, Is 63.17
do not h. your hearts as in the Heb 3.08
voice do not h. your hearts as in 3.15
his voice, do not h. your hearts." 4.07

HARDENED
Still Pharaoh's heart was h., Ex 7.13
to Moses, "Pharaoh's heart is h., 7.14
so Pharaoh's heart remained h., 7.22
he h. his heart, and would not 8.15
But Pharaoh's heart was h., 8.19
But Pharaoh h. his heart this time 8.32
But the heart of Pharaoh was h., 9.07
But the LORD h. the heart of 9.12
and h. his heart, he and his servants. 9.34
So the heart of Pharaoh was h., 9.35
for I have h. his heart and the 10.01
But the LORD h. Pharaoh's heart, and 10.20
But the LORD h. Pharaoh's heart, and 10.27
and the LORD h. Pharaoh's heart, and 11.10
And the LORD h. the heart of 14.08
LORD your God h. his spirit and Deu 2.30
and Pharaoh h. their hearts? 1Sa 6.06
his neck and h. his heart against 2Ch 36.13
who has h. himself against him, and Job 9.04
his spirit was h. so that he dealt Dan 5.20
loaves, but their hearts were h. Mk 6.52
or understand? Are your hearts h.? 8.17
their eyes and h. their heart, Jn 12.40
obtained it, but the rest were h., Rom 11.07
But their minds were h.; 2Co 3.14
of you may be h. by the deceitfulness Heb 3.13

HARDENING
a h. has come upon part of Israel, Rom 11.25

HARDENS
my skin h., then breaks out afresh. Job 7.05
but he who h. his heart will fall Pro 28.14
and he h. the heart of whomever he Rom 9.18

HARDER
of Israel bore h. and h. on Jabin Ju 4.24
have made their faces h. than rock; Jer 5.03
Like adamant h. than flint have I Eze 3.09
I worked h. than any of them, though 1Co 15.10

HARDEST
the forefront of the h. fighting, 2Sa 11.15

HARDLY
shatters him, and will h. leave him. Lk 9.39
Why, one will h. die for a righteous Rom 5.07

HARDNESS
and the h. of his countenance is Ecc 8.01
"For your h. of heart Moses allowed Mt 19.08
grieved at their h. of heart, Mk 3.05
"For your h. of heart he wrote you 10.05
in them, due to their h. of heart; Eph 4.18

HARDSHIP
forget all my h. and all my Gen 41.51
all the h. that had come upon them Ex 18.08
let not all the h. seem little to Neh 9.32
in toil and h., through many a 2Co 11.27

HARDSHIPS
favor, all the h. he endured; Ps 132.01
in afflictions, h., calamities, 2Co 6.04
h., persecutions, and calamities; 12.10

HARD-WORKING
It is the h. farmer who ought to 2Ti 2.06

HARE
And the h., because it chews the Lev 11.06
the h., and the rock badger, because Deu 14.07

HAREM
virgins to the h. in Susa the Est 2.03
maids to the best place in the h. 2.09
in front of the court of the h., 2.11
her from the h. to the king's 2.13
to the second h. in custody of 2.14

HAREPH
and H. the father of Bethgader. 1Ch 2.51

HARHAIAH
Next to them Uzziel the son of H., Neh 3.08

HARHAS
son of H., keeper of the wardrobe 2Ki 22.14

HARHERES
Amorites persisted in dwelling in H., Ju 1.35

HARHUR
sons of Hakupha, the sons of H., Ez 2.51
sons of Hakupha, the sons of H., Neh 7.53

HARIM
the third to H., the fourth to 1Ch 24.08
The sons of H., three hundred and Ez 2.32
The sons of H., one thousand and 2.39
Of the sons of H.: Maaseiah, Elijah, 10.21
Of the sons of H.: Eliezer, Isshijah, 10.31
Malchijah the son of H. and Hasshub Neh 3.11
The sons of H., three hundred and 7.35
The sons of H., a thousand and 7.42
H., Meremoth, Obadiah, 10.05
Malluch, H., Baanah. 10.27
of H., Adna; of Meraioth, Helkai; 12.15

HARIPH
The sons of H., a hundred and Neh 7.24
H., Anathoth, Nebai, 10.19

HARK
H., glad songs of victory in the Ps 118.15
H.! my beloved is knocking. Sol 5.02
H., a tumult on the mountains as of Is 13.04
H., an uproar of kingdoms, of 13.04
H., your watchmen lift up their 52.08
"H., an uproar from the city! 66.06
H., the cry of the daughter of my Jer 8.19
H., a rumor! Behold, it comes!— 10.22
H., the cry of the shepherds, and 25.36
"H.! a cry from Horonaim, 48.03
"H.! they flee and escape from the 50.28
"H.! a cry from Babylon! The noise of 51.54
H., the wail of the shepherds, for Zec 11.03
H., the roar of the lions, for the 11.03
H., the feet of those that have Ac 5.09

HARLOT
"Should he treat our sister as a h.?" Gen 34.31
saw her, he thought her to be a h., 38.15
"Where is the h. who was at Enaim 38.21
And they said, "No h. has been here." 38.21
place said, 'No h. has been here.'" 38.22
daughter-in-law has played the h.; 38.24
they play the h. after their gods Ex 34.15
play the h. after their gods and 34.16
sons play the h. after their gods. 34.16
after whom they play the h. Lev 17.07
your daughter by making her a h., 19.29
him in playing the h. after Molech. 20.05
playing the h. after them, I will 20.06
not marry a h. or a woman who has 21.07
profanes herself by playing the h., 21.09
or a h., these he shall not marry; 21.14
to play the h. with the daughters Num 25.01
by playing the h. in her father's Deu 22.21
You shall not bring the hire of a h., 23.18
and play the h. after the strange 31.16
the house of a h. whose name was Jos 2.01
only Rahab the h. and all who are 6.17
But Rahab the h., and her father's 6.25
they played the h. after other Ju 2.17
played the h. after it there, 8.27

HARLOT (cont.)
and played the h. after the Baals, Ju 8.33
warrior, but he was the son of a h. 11.01
to Gaza, and there he saw a h., 16.01
and played the h. after the gods 1Ch 5.25
and played the h. in their doings. Ps 106.39
for a h. may be hired for a loaf of Pro 6.26
dressed as a h., wily of heart. 7.10
For a h. is a deep pit; 23.27
How the faithful city has become a h., Is 1.21
to Tyre as in the song of the h.: 23.15
go about the city, O forgotten h.! 23.16
will play the h. with all the 23.17
of the adulterer and the h. 57.03
green tree you bowed down as a h. Jer 2.20
have played the h. with many 3.01
tree, and there played the h.? 3.06
but she too went and played the h. 3.08
and played the h. because of your Eze 16.15
shrines, and on them played the h.; 16.16
men, and with them played the h.; 16.17
You also played the h. with the 16.26
You played the h. also with the 16.28
yea, you played the h. with them, 16.28
things, the deeds of a brazen h.; 16.30
Yet you were not like a h., 16.31
none solicited you to play the h.; 16.34
"Wherefore, O h., hear the word of 16.35
will make you stop playing the h., 16.41
they played the h. in Egypt; 23.03
they played the h. in their youth; 23.03
"Oholah played the h. while she was 23.05
she played the h. in the land of Egypt 23.19
you played the h. with the nations, 23.30
in to her, as men go in to a h. 23.44
For their mother has played the h.; Hos 2.05
you shall not play the h., 3.03
they shall play the h., but not 4.10
have left their God to play the h. 4.12
Therefore your daughters play the h., 4.13
daughters when they play the h., 4.14
Though you play the h., O Israel, 4.15
O Ephraim, you have played the h., 5.03
for you have played the h., 9.01
and have given a boy for a h., Joe 3.03
wife shall be a h. in the city, Amo 7.17
the hire of a h. she gathered them, Mic 1.07
the hire of a h. they shall return. 1.07
the countless harlotries of the h., Nah 3.04
By faith Rahab the h. did not Hab 11.31
also Rahab the h. justified by Jas 2.25
of the great h. who is seated upon Rev 17.01
where the h. is seated, are peoples 17.15
and the beast will hate the h.; 17.16
the great h. who corrupted the 19.02

HARLOTRIES
so long as the h. and the sorceries 2Ki 9.22
your lewd h., on the hills in the Jer 13.27
lavished your h. on any passer-by. Eze 16.15
Were your h. so small a matter 16.20
and your h. you did not remember 16.22
to you from every side for your h. 16.33
from other women in your h.: 16.34
uncovered in your h. with your 16.36
She bestowed her h. upon them, 23.07
for the countless h. of the harlot, Nah 3.04
who betrays nations with her h., 3.04

HARLOTRY
moreover she is with child by h." Gen 38.24
land fall into h. and the land Lev 19.29
polluted the land with your vile h. Jer 3.02
Because h. was so light to her, she 3.09
passer-by, and multiplying your h. Eze 16.25
neighbors, multiplying your h., 16.26
You multiplied your h. also with 16.29
not give up her h. which she had 23.08
she in her doting and in her h., 23.11
But she carried her h. further; 23.14
carried on her h. so openly and 23.18
Yet she increased her h., 23.19
and your h. brought from the land 23.27
nakedness of your h. shall be 23.29
Your lewdness and your h. 23.29
consequences of your lewdness and h." 23.25
when they practice h. with her? 23.43
by their h., and by the dead bodies 43.07
a wife of h. and have children of h., Hos 1.02
commits great h. by forsaking the 1.02
she put away her h. from her face, 2.02
because they are children of h. 2.04
forsaken the LORD to cherish h. 4.10
For a spirit of h. has led them 4.12
drunkards, they give themselves to h.; 4.18
the spirit of h. is within them, 5.04
Ephraim's h. is there, Israel is 6.10

HARLOT'S
"Go into the h. house, and bring out Jos 6.22
yet you have a h. brow, Jer 3.03
have loved a h. hire upon all Hos 9.01

HARLOTS
Then two h. came to the king, and 1Ki 3.16
and the h. washed themselves in it, 22.38
company with h. squanders his Pro 29.03
and trooped to the houses of h. Jer 5.07
Men give gifts to all h.; Eze 16.33
men themselves go aside with h., Hos 4.14
collectors and the h. go into the Mt 21.31
collectors and the h. believed him; 21.32
has devoured your living with h., Lk 15.30
mother of h. and of earth's abominations." Rev 17.05

HARM
that you will do us no h., Gen 26.29
God did not permit him to h. me. 31.07
It is in my power to do you h.; 31.29
heap and this pillar to me, for h. 31.52
he feared that h. might befall him. 42.04
If h. should befall him on the 42.38
and h. befalls him, you will bring 44.29
and yet no h. follows, the one who Ex 21.22
If any h. follows, then you shall 21.23
his enemy, and did not seek his h.; Num 35.23
then he will turn and do you h., Jos 24.20
he who has done us this great h.; 1Sa 6.09
it please my father to do you h., 20.13
with us, and we did them no h., 25.07
good to us, and we suffered no h., 25.15
for I will no more do you h., 26.21
He may do himself some h." 2Sa 12.18
will do us more h. than Absalom; 20.06
And there was no h. in the pot. 2Ki 4.41
keep me from h. so that it might 1Ch 4.10
anointed ones, do my prophets no h.!" 16.22
But they intended to do me h. Neh 6.02
anointed ones, do my prophets no h.!" Ps 105.15
reason, when he has done you no h. Pro 3.30
companion of fools will suffer h. 13.20
he will not be visited by h. 19.23
and not h., all the days of her 31.12
obeys a command will meet no h., Ecc 8.05
Lest any one h. it, I guard it night Is 27.03
or do h., that we may be dismayed 41.23
Then I will do you no h.' Jer 25.06
work of your hands to your own h. 25.07
of this people, but their h." 38.04
after him well and do him no h., 39.12
to be safe from the reach of h.! Hab 2.09
the sabbath to do good or to do h., Mk 3.04
out of him, having done him no h. Lk 4.35
the sabbath to do good or to do h., 6.09
"Do not h. yourself, for we are all Ac 16.28

HARM (cont.)
no man shall attack you to h. you; Ac 18.10
into the fire and suffered no h. 28.05
Alexander the coppersmith did me great h.; 2Ti 4.14
Now who is there to h. you if you 1Pe 3.13
but do not h. oil and wine!" Rev 6.06
given power to h. earth and sea, 7.02
"Do not h. the earth or the sea or 7.03
told not to h. the grass of the 9.04
And if any one would h. them, fire 11.05
if any one would h. them, thus he 11.05

HARMED
and I have not h. one of them." Num 16.15
singed, their mantels were not h., Dan 3.27

HARMON
you shall be cast forth into H., Amo 4.03

HARMONY
Live in h. with one another; Rom 12.16
to live in such h. with one 15.05
everything together in perfect h. Col 3.14

HARNEPHER
Zophah: Suah, H., Shual, Beri, Imrah, 1Ch 7.36

HARNESS
H. the horses; mount, O horsemen! Jer 46.04
H. the steeds to the chariots, Mic 1.13

HAROD
encamped beside the spring of H.; Ju 7.01
Shammah of H., Elika of H., 2Sa 23.25
Shammoth of H., Helez the Pelonite, 1Ch 11.27

HAROEH
other sons: H., half of the Menuhoth. 1Ch 2.52

HAROSHETHHAGOIIM
army was Sisera, who dwelt in H. Ju 4.02
with him, from H. to the river Kishon. 4.13
the chariots and the army to H., 4.16

HARP
down from the high place with h., 1Sa 10.05
to him with the h. of ten strings! Ps 33.02
Awake, O h. and lyre! I will awake 57.08
thee with the h. for thy faithfulness, 71.22
timbrel, the sweet lyre with the h. 81.02
to the music of the lute and the h., 92.03
Awake, O h. and lyre! I will awake 108.02
a ten-stringed h. I will play to 144.09
praise him with lute and h.! 150.03
They have lyre and h., timbrel and Is 5.12
"Take a h., go about the city, O 23.16
h., bagpipe, and every kind of music, Dan 3.05
h., bagpipe, and every kind of music, 3.07
h., bagpipe, and every kind of music, 3.10
h., bagpipe, and every kind of music, 3.15
idle songs to the sound of the h., Amo 6.05
such as the flute or the h., 1Co 14.07
before the Lamb, each holding a h., Rev 5.08

HARPERS
the sound of h. playing on their Rev 14.02
and the sound of h. and minstrels, 18.22

HARPOONS
Can you fill his skin with h., Job 41.07

HARPS
and lyres and h. and tambourines 2Sa 6.05
lyres also and h. for the singers; 1Ki 10.12
and lyres and h. and tambourines 1Ch 13.08
on h. and lyres and cymbals, to 15.16
were to play h. according to 15.20
made loud music on h. and lyres. 15.28
who were to play h. and lyres; 16.50
with h., and with cymbals. 25.01
h., and lyres for the service of 25.06
h., and lyres, stood east of the 2Ch 5.12
lyres also and h. for the singers; 9.11
with h. and lyres and trumpets, to 20.28
h., and lyres, according to the 29.25
with cymbals, h., and lyres. Neh 12.27
to Sheol, the sound of your h.; Is 14.11
melody of your h. I will not Amo 5.23
of harpers playing on their h., Rev 14.02
of glass with h. of God in their 15.02

HARROW
or will he h. the valleys after you? Job 39.10
continually open and h. his ground? Is 28.24
plow, Jacob must h. for himself. Hos 10.11

HARSH
but a h. word stirs up anger. Pro 15.01
wives, and do not be h. with them. Col 3.19
and of all the h. things which Jud 1.15

HARSHA
sons of Mehida, the sons of H., Ez 2.52
sons of Mehida, the sons of H., Neh 7.54

HARSHLY
Then Sarai dealt h. with her, Gen 16.06
Egyptians dealt h. with us and our Num 20.15
And the Egyptians treated us h., Deu 26.06
And the king answered the people h., 1Ki 12.13
And the king answered them h., 2Ch 10.13

HARSHNESS
You shall not rule over him with h., Lev 25.43
rule, one over another, with h. 25.46
not rule with h. over him in your 25.53
with force and h. you have ruled Eze 34.04

HART
as of the gazelle and as of the h. Deu 12.15
Just as the gazelle or the h. is eaten, 12.22
the h., the gazelle, the roebuck, the 14.05
though it were a gazelle or a h. 15.22
As a h. longs for flowing streams, Ps 42.01
then shall the lame man leap like a h., Is 35.06

HARTS
besides h., gazelles, roebucks, and 1Ki 4.23
become like h. that find no pasture; Lam 1.06

HARUM
famlies of Aharhel the son of H. 1Ch 4.08

HARUMAPH
the son of H. repaired opposite Neh 3.10

HARUPHITE
Bealiah, Shemariah, Shephatiah the H.; 1Ch 12.05

HARUZ
the daughter of H. of Jotbah. 2Ki 21.19

HARVEST
seedtime and h., cold and heat, Gen 8.22
days of wheat h. Reuben went and 30.14
will be neither plowing nor h. 45.06
fulness of your h. and from the Ex 22.29
You shall keep the feast of h., 23.16
time and in h. you shall rest. 34.21
the first fruits of wheat h., 34.22
"When you reap the h. of your land, Lev 19.09
gather the gleanings after your h. 19.09
which I give you and reap its h., 23.10
fruits of your h. to the priest; 23.10
"And when you reap the h. of your land, 23.22
gather the gleanings after your h.; 23.22
itself in your h. you shall not 25.05
"When you reap your h. in your field, Deu 24.19

HARVEST (cont.)
which you h. from your land that Deu 26.02
banks throughout the time of h.), Jos 3.15
After a while, at the time of wheat h., Ju 15.01
at the beginning of barley h. Ru 1.22
till they have finished all my h.'" 2.21
their wheat h. in the valley; 1Sa 6.13
plow his ground and to reap his h., 8.12
Is it not wheat h. today? I will 12.17
to death in the first days of h., 2Sa 21.09
at the beginning of barley h. 21.09
beginning of h. until rain fell 21.10
and came about h. time to David at 23.13
His h. the hungry eat, and he takes Job 5.05
and gathers her sustenance in h. Pro 6.08
son who sleeps in h. brings shame. 10.05
he will seek at h. and have nothing. 20.04
in the time of h. is a faithful 25.13
Like snow in summer or rain in h., 26.01
before thee as with joy at the h., Is 9.03
fruit and your h. the battle shout 16.09
yet the h. will flee away in a day 17.11
a cloud of dew in the heat of h." 18.04
For before the h., when the blossom 18.05
of Shihor, the h. of the Nile; 23.03
fail, the fruit h. will not come. 32.10
LORD, the first fruits of his h. Jer 2.03
shall eat up your h. and your food; 5.17
us the weeks appointed for the h.' 5.24
"The h. is past, the summer is ended, 8.20
handles the sickle in time of h.; 50.16
and the time of her h. will come." 51.33
also, O Judah, a h. is appointed. Hos 6.11
because the h. of the field has Joe 1.11
Put in the sickle, for the h. is ripe. 3.13
were yet three months to the h.; Amo 4.07
"The h. is plentiful, but the Mt 9.37
pray therefore the Lord of the h. to 9.38
to send out laborers into his h." 9.38
Let both grow together until the h.; 13.30
and at h. time I will tell the 13.30
the h. is the close of the age, and 13.39
sickle, because the h. has come." Mk 4.29
"The h. is plentiful, but the Lk 10.02
pray therefore the Lord of the h. to 10.02
to send out laborers into his h. 10.02
four months, then comes the h.'? Jn 4.35
fields are already white for h. 4.35
I may reap some h. among you as Rom 1.13
increase the h. of your righteousness. 2Co 9.10
And the h. of righteousness is sown Jas 3.18
for the h. of the earth is fully Rev 14.15

HARVESTED
You have sown much, and h. little; Hag 1.06

HARVESTERS
cries of the h. have reached the Jas 5.04

HARVESTS
And at the h. you shall give a Gen 47.24
the end of the barley and wheat h.; Ru 2.23
grain and his arm h. the ears, Is 17.05
of their h. because of the fierce Jer 12.13

HAS
because God h. dealt graciously Gen 33.11
me my master h. no concern about 39.08
and he h. put everything that he h. 39.08
burnt offering which he h. offered. Lev 7.08
"When a man h. on the skin of his 13.02
when the body h. a burn on its skin 13.24
"When a man or woman h. a disease 13.29
man or a woman h. spots on the 13.38
When any man h. a discharge from 15.02
"When a woman h. a discharge of 15.19
"If a woman h. a discharge of blood 15.25
or if she h. a discharge beyond the 15.25
him because she h. had no husband; 21.03
generations who h. a blemish may 21.17
If a man h. no one to redeem it, and 25.26
because he h. a different spirit Num 14.24
spirit and h. followed me fully, I 14.24
Therefore Levi h. no portion or Deu 10.09
"If a man h. two wives, the one 21.15
a double portion of all that he h., 21.17
"If a man h. a stubborn and rebellious 21.18
maidservant h. nothing in the 2Ki 4.02
for God h. power to help or to 2Ch 25.08
"H. the rain a father, or who Job 38.28
or who h. begotten the drops of dew? 38.28
This blessing h. fallen to me, that Ps 119.56
of the LORD one h. strong confidence, Pro 14.26
fountain of life to him who h. it, 16.22
What h. a man from all the toil and Ecc 2.22
and also h. no burial, I say that an 6.03
preserves the life of him who h. it. 7.12
the sword h. reached their very Jer 4.10
for he h. talked rebellion against 29.32
all the living h. this mystery Dan 2.30
your brother h. something against Mt 5.23
the Son of man h. nowhere to lay 8.20
the Son of man h. authority on 9.06
He who h. ears to hear, let him hear. 11.15
and they say, "He h. a demon'; 11.18
if he h. one sheep and it falls 12.11
He who h. ears, let him hear. 13.09
For to him who h. will more be 13.12
but from him who h. not, 13.12
even what he h. will be taken away. 13.12
yet he h. no root in himself, but 13.21
your field? How then h. it weeds?' 13.27
He who h. ears, let him hear. 13.43
all that he h. and buys that field. 13.44
If a man h. a hundred sheep, and one 18.12
and one of them h. gone astray, 18.12
'The Lord h. need of them,' and he 21.03
only do what h. been done to the 21.21
it to him who h. the ten talents. 25.28
every one who h. will more be 25.29
but from him who h. not, 25.29
even what he h. will be taken away. 25.29
"He h. uttered blasphemy. Why do 26.65
the Son of man h. authority on Mk 2.10
And if Satan h. risen up against 3.26
Holy Spirit never h. forgiveness, 3.29
"He h. an unclean spirit." 3.30
"He who h. ears to hear, let him 4.09
If any man h. ears to hear, let him 4.23
For to him who h. will more be 4.25
and from him who h. not, 4.25
even what he h. will be taken away." 4.25
"If any man h. ears to hear, * 7.16
to you, for he h. a dumb spirit; 9.17
but if the salt h. lost its saltness, 9.50
'The Lord h. need of it and will 11.03
of her poverty h. put in everything 12.44
"He who h. two coats, let him share Lk 3.11
let him share with him who h. none; 3.11
and he who h. food, let him do 3.11
the Son of man h. authority on 5.24
the Baptist h. come eating no 7.33
and you say, 'He h. a demon.' 7.33
"He who h. ears to hear, let him 8.08
for to him who h. will more be 8.18
be given, and from whom who h. not, 8.18
thinks that he h. will be taken 8.18
the Son of man h. nowhere to lay 9.58
of you who h. a friend will go to 11.05
friend of mine h. arrived on a 11.06
after he h. killed, h. power to cast 12.05
whether he h. enough to complete it? 14.28
all that he h. cannot be my 14.33
He who h. ears to hear, let him hear." 14.35
if he h. lost one of them, does not 15.04

HAS (cont.)
who h. a servant plowing or keeping Lk 17.07
to him when he h. come in from the 17.07
it to him who h. the ten pounds.' 19.24
to him, 'Lord, he h. ten pounds!') 19.25
every one who h. will more be 19.26
but from him who h. not, 19.26
even what he h. will be taken away. 19.26
say this, 'The Lord h. need of it.' " 19.31
And they said, "The Lord h. need of it." 19.34
likeness and inscription h. it?" 20.24
let him who h. a purse take it, and 22.36
And let him who h. no sword sell 22.36
written about me h. its fulfilment." 22.37
for a spirit h. not flesh and bones 24.39
He who h. the bride is the bridegroom; Jn 3.29
believes in the Son h. eternal life; 3.36
that a prophet h. no honor in his 4.44
Bethzatha, which h. five porticoes. 5.02
him who sent me, h. eternal life; 5.24
but h. passed from death to life. 5.24
For as the Father h. life in 5.26
so he h. granted the Son also to 5.26
the Father h. granted me to 5.36
witness that the Father h. sent me. 5.36
do not believe him whom he h. sent. 5.38
a lad here who h. five barley 6.09
he who believes h. eternal life. 6.47
drinks my blood h. eternal life, 6.54
"He h. a demon, and he is mad; 10.20
not receive my sayings h. a judge; 12.48
He who h. my commandments and keeps 14.21
He h. no power over me; 14.30
Greater love h. no man than this, 15.13
All that the Father h. is mine; 16.15
woman is in travail she h. sorrow, 16.21
because her hour h. come; but when 16.21
because he h. made himself the Son 19.07
me to you h. the greater sin." 19.11
and here he h. authority from the Ac 9.14
generations Moses h. had in every 15.21
for he h. something to tell him." 23.17
as he h. something to say to you." 23.18
he h. something to boast about, but Rom 4.02
H. the potter no right over the 9.21
happy is he who h. no reason to 14.22
"For who h. known the mind of the 1Co 2.16
When one of you h. a grievance 6.01
But each h. his own special gift 7.07
if any brother h. a wife who is an 7.12
If any woman h. a husband who is an 7.13
appointed time h. grown very short; 7.29
and h. determined this in his heart, 7.37
body is one and h. many members, 12.12
But God h. so adjusted the body, 12.24
each one h. a hymn, a lesson, a 14.26
acceptable according to what a man h., 2Co 8.12
not according to what he h. not. 8.12
h. any inheritance in the kingdom Eph 5.05
man thinks he h. reason for Php 3.04
if one h. a complaint against Col 3.13
as the Lord h. forgiven you, so you 3.13
witness that he h. worked hard for 4.13
that Timothy h. come to us from 1Th 3.06
and h. brought us the good news of 3.06
If a widow h. children or grandchildren, 1Ti 5.04
believing woman h. relatives who 5.16
who alone h. immortality and dwells 6.16
whom no man h. ever seen or can see. 6.16
destroy him who h. the power of Heb 2.14
Yet Jesus h. been counted worthy of 3.03
of a house h. more honor than the 3.03
high priest who h. passed through 4.14
every respect h. been tempted as 4.15
and h. neither beginning of days 7.03
But this man who h. not their 7.06
a Son who h. been made perfect for 7.28
For since the law h. but a shadow 10.01
confidence, which h. a great reward. 10.35
to the city which h. foundations, 11.10
for he h. said, "I will never fail 13.05
man says he h. faith but h. not works? Jas 2.14
if it h. no works, is dead. 2.17
who denies the Son h. the Father. 1Jn 2.23
confesses the Son h. the Father 2.23
no murderer h. eternal life 3.15
But if any one h. the world's goods 3.17
and believe the love God h. for us. 4.16
For fear h. to do with punishment, 4.18
the Son of God h. the testimony in 5.10
not believe God, h. made him a liar, 5.10
because he h. not believed in the 5.10
that God h. borne to his Son. 5.10
He who h. the Son h. life; 5.12
he who h. not the Son h. not life. 5.12
of Christ h. both the Father and 2Jn 1.09
He who h. an ear, let him hear what Rev 2.07
of him who h. the sharp two-edged 2.12
He who h. an ear, let him hear what 2.17
who h. eyes like a flame of fire, 2.18
He who h. an ear, let him hear what 2.29
of him who h. the seven spirits of 3.01
He who h. an ear, let him hear what 3.06
who h. the key of David, who opens 3.07
He who h. an ear, let him hear what 3.13
He who h. an ear, let him hear what 3.22
where she h. a place prepared by 12.06
for the devil h. come down to you 12.12
If any one h. an ear, let him hear: 13.09
buy or sell unless he h. the mark, 13.17
let him who h. understanding reckon 13.18
the angel who h. power over fire, 14.18
In one hour she h. been laid waste. 18.19
and he h. a name inscribed which no 19.12
on his thigh he h. a name inscribed, 19.16
such the second death h. no power, 20.06
And the city h. no need of sun or 21.23

HASADIAH
Berechiah, H., and Jushabhesed, five. 1Ch 3.20

HASHABIAH
son of H., son of Amaziah, son of 1Ch 6.45
son of H., of the sons of Merari; 9.14
H., and Mattithiah, six, under the 25.03
the twelfth to H., his sons and his 25.19
H. and his brethren, one thousand 26.30
for Levi, H. the son of Kemuel; 27.17
and H. and Jeiel and Jozabad, the 2Ch 35.09
also H. and with him Jeshaiah of Ez 8.19
H., and ten of their kinsmen with 8.24
Mijamin, Eleazar, H., and Benaiah. 10.25
next to him H., ruler of half the Neh 3.17
Mica, Rehob, H., 10.11
Azrikam, son of H., son of Bunni; 11.15
son of H., son of Mattaniah, son of 11.22
of Hilkiah, H.; of Jedaiah, Nethanel. 12.21
H., Sherebiah, and Jeshua the son of 12.24

HASHABNAH
Rehum, H., Maaseiah, Neh 10.25

HASHABNEIAH
him Hattush the son of H. repaired. Neh 3.10
H., Sherebiah, Hodiah, Shebaniah, and 9.05

HASHBADDANAH
H., Zechariah, and Meshullam on his Neh 8.04

HASHEM
H. the Gizonite, Jonathan the son of 1Ch 11.34

HASHMONAH
from Mithkah, and encamped at H. Num 33.29
And they set out from H., and 33.30

HASHUBAH
and H., Ohel, Berechiah, Hasadiah, and 1Ch 3.20

HASHUM
The sons of H., two hundred and Ez 2.19
Of the sons of H.: Mattenai, Mattattah, 10.33
The sons of H., three hundred and Neh 7.22
H., Hashbaddanah, Zechariah, and 8.04
Hodiah, H., Bezai, 10.18

HASRAH
son of H., keeper of the wardrobe 2Ch 34.22

HASSENAAH
And the sons of H. built the Fish Neh 3.03

HASSENUAH
son of Hodaviah, son of H., 1Ch 9.07
the son of H. was second over the Neh 11.09

HASSHUB
Levites: Shemaiah the son of H., 1Ch 9.14
of Harim and H. the son of Pahathmoab Neh 3.11
Benjamin and H. repaired opposite 3.23
Hoshea, Hananiah, H., 10.23
Levites: Shemaiah the son of H., 11.15

HASSOPHERETH
the sons of H., the sons of Peruda, Ez 2.55

HAST
Behold, thou h. driven me this day Gen 4.14
thou h. given me no offspring; 15.03
one whom thou h. appointed for thy 24.14
know that thou h. shown steadfast 24.14
which thou h. shown to thy servant, 32.10
or since thou h. spoken to thy Ex 4.10
why h. thou done evil to this 5.22
and thou h. not delivered thy 5.23
"Thou h. led in thy steadfast love 15.13
the people whom thou h. redeemed, 15.13
thou h. guided them by thy strength 15.13
pass by whom thou h. purchased. 15.16
which thou h. made for thy abode, 15.17
whom thou h. brought forth out of 32.11
of thy book which thou h. written." 32.32
but thou h. not let me know whom 33.12
Yet thou h. said, 'I know you by 33.12
"Why h. thou dealt ill with thy Num 11.11
and thou h. said, 'I will give them 11.21
LORD be great as thou h. promised, 14.17
according as thou h. forgiven this 14.19
thou h. only begun to show thy Deu 3.24
whom thou h. redeemed through thy 9.26
whom thou h. brought out of Egypt 9.26
whom thou h. redeemed, and set not 21.08
which thou, O LORD, h. given me.' 26.10
commandment which thou h. commanded me; 26.13
to all that thou h. commanded me. 26.14
the ground which thou h. given us, 26.15
why h. thou brought this people Jos 7.07
by my hand, as thou h. said, Ju 6.36
Israel by my hand, as thou h. said." 6.37
"Thou h. granted this great deliverance 15.18
why h. thou not answered thy 1Sa 14.41
that thou h. brought me thus far 2Sa 7.18
thou h. spoken also of thy servant's 7.19
and h. shown me future generations, 7.19
thou h. wrought all this greatness, 7.21
word which thou h. spoken concerning 7.25
house, and do as thou h. spoken; 7.25
h. made this revelation to thy 7.27
and thou h. promised this good 7.28
h. spoken, and with thy blessing 7.29
Thou h. given me the shield of thy 22.36
"Thou h. shown great and steadfast 1Ki 3.06
and thou h. kept for him this great 3.06
and h. given him a son to sit on 3.06
thou h. made thy servant king in 3.07
of thy people whom thou h. chosen, 3.08
who h. kept with thy servant David 8.24
with thy hand h. fulfilled it this 8.24
father what thou h. promised him, 8.25
which thou h. spoken to thy servant 8.26
the place of which thou h. said, 8.29
which thou h. given to thy people 8.36
city which thou h. chosen and the 8.44
the city which thou h. chosen, 8.48
h. thou brought calamity even upon 17.20
and that thou h. turned their 18.37
thou h. made heaven and earth. 2Ki 19.15
that thou h. brought me thus far? 1Ch 17.16
thou h. also spoken of thy 17.17
and h. shown me future generations, 17.17
thou h. wrought all this greatness, 17.19
word which thou h. spoken concerning 17.23
for ever, and do as thou h. spoken; 17.23
h. revealed to thy servant that 17.25
and thou h. promised this good 17.26
h. blessed is blessed for ever." 17.27
and h. pleasure in uprightness; 29.17
"Thou h. shown great and steadfast 2Ch 1.08
and h. made me king in his stead. 1.08
for thou h. made me king over a 1.09
who h. kept with thy servant David 6.15
with thy hand h. fulfilled it this 6.15
father what thou h. promised him, 6.16
which thou h. spoken to thy servant 6.17
where thou h. promised to set thy 6.20
which thou h. given to thy people 6.27
city which thou h. chosen and the 6.34
the city which thou h. chosen, 6.38
which thou h. given us to inherit. 20.11
h. punished us less than our Eze 9.13
deserved and h. given us such a 9.13
whom thou h. redeemed by thy great Neh 1.10
thou h. made heaven, the heaven of 9.06
and thou h. fulfilled thy promise, 9.08
Yet thou h. been just in all that 9.33
for thou h. dealt faithfully and we 9.33
kings whom thou h. set over us 9.37
H. thou not put a hedge about him Job 1.10
Thou h. blessed the work of his 1.10
Why h. thou made me thy mark? 7.20
H. thou eyes of flesh? Dost thou 10.04
Remember that thou h. made me of 10.09
Thou h. granted me life and steadfast 10.12
and thou h. appointed his bounds 14.05
Since thou h. closed their minds to 17.04
Thou h. turned cruel to me; 30.21
who can say, 'Thou h. done wrong'? 36.23
Thou h. give me room when I was in Ps 4.01
Thou h. put more joy in my heart 4.07
thou h. appointed a judgment. 7.06
thou h. founded a bulwark because 8.02
stars which thou h. established; 8.03
Yet thou h. made him little less 8.05
Thou h. given him dominion over the 8.06
thou h. put all things under his 8.06
For thou h. maintained my just 9.04
thou h. sat on the throne giving 9.04
Thou h. rebuked the nations, thou 9.05
thou h. destroyed the wicked; 9.05
thou h. blotted out their name for 9.05
their cities thou h. rooted out; 9.06
h. not forsaken those who seek thee. 9.10
thou h. been the helper of the 10.14
with what thou h. stored up for 17.14
Thou h. given me the shield of thy 18.35
Thou h. given him his heart's desire, 21.02
and h. not withheld the request of 21.02
my God, why h. thou forsaken me? 22.01
mother bore me thou h. been my God. 22.10
Thou h. said, "Seek ye my face." 27.08
in anger, thou who h. been my help. 27.09

HAST (cont.)
LORD, for thou h. drawn me up, and Ps 30.01
and h. not let my foes rejoice over 30.01
for help, and thou h. healed me. 30.02
O LORD, thou h. brought up my soul 30.03
Thou h. turned for me my mourning 30.11
thou h. loosed my sackcloth and 30.11
thou h. redeemed me, O LORD, faithful 31.05
because thou h. seen my affliction, 31.07
thou h. taken heed of my adversities, 31.07
and h. not delivered me into the 31.08
thou h. set my feet in a broad 31.08
which thou h. laid up for those who 31.19
Thou h. seen, O LORD; be not silent! 35.22
Behold, thou h. made my days a few 39.05
for it is thou who h. done it. 39.09
Thou h. multiplied, O LORD my God, 40.05
but thou h. given me an open ear. 40.06
sin offering thou h. not required. 40.06
But thou h. upheld me because of my 41.12
"Why h. thou forgotten me? 42.09
why h. thou cast me off? 43.02
But thou h. saved us from our foes, 44.07
and h. put to confusion those who 44.07
Yet thou h. cast us off and abased 44.09
and h. not gone out with our armies. 44.09
Thou h. made us turn back from the 44.10
Thou h. made us like sheep for 44.11
and h. scattered us among the 44.11
Thou h. sold thy people for a 44.12
Thou h. made us the taunt of our 44.13
Thou h. made us a byword among the 44.14
bones which thou h. broken rejoice. 51.08
For thou h. no delight in sacrifice; 51.16
for ever, because thou h. done it. 52.09
For thou h. delivered me from every 54.07
Thou h. kept count of my tossings; 56.08
For thou h. delivered my soul from 56.13
For thou h. been to me a fortress 59.16
O God, thou h. rejected us, broken 60.01
thou h. been angry; oh, restore us. 60.01
Thou h. made the land to quake, thou 60.02
thou h. rent it open; repair its 60.02
Thou h. made thy people suffer hard 60.03
thou h. given us wine to drink that 60.03
Thou h. set up a banner for those 60.04
H. thou not rejected us, O God? 60.10
For thou, O God, h. heard my vows, thou 61.05
thou h. given me the heritage of 61.05
for thou h. been my help, and in the 63.07
who by thy strength h. established 65.06
grain, for so thou h. prepared it. 65.09
For thou, O God, h. tested us; 66.10
thou h. tried us as silver is tried. 66.10
yet thou h. brought us forth to a 66.12
O God, thou who h. wrought for us. 68.28
persecute him whom thou h. smitten, 69.26
and him whom thou h. wounded, they 69.26
from my youth thou h. taught me, 71.17
Thou who h. done great things, O God, 71.19
Thou who h. made me see many sore 71.20
soul also, which thou h. rescued. 71.23
which thou h. gotten of old, which 74.02
which thou h. redeemed to be the 74.02
Mount Zion, where thou h. dwelt. 74.02
thou h. established the luminaries 74.16
Thou h. fixed all the bounds of the 74.17
thou h. made summer and winter. 74.17
who h. manifested thy might among 77.14
Thou h. fed them with the bread of 80.05
Why then h. thou broken down its 80.12
man whom thou h. made strong for 80.17
nations thou h. made shall come 86.09
thou h. delivered my soul from the 86.13
h. helped me and comforted me. 86.17
Thou h. put me in the depths of the 88.06
Thou h. caused my companions to 88.08
thou h. made me a thing of horror 88.08
Thou h. caused lover and friend to 88.18
Thou h. said, "I have made a covenant 89.03
is in it, thou h. founded them. 89.11
the south, thou h. created them; 89.12
Thou h. a mighty arm; strong is thy 89.13
But now thou h. cast off and 89.38
Thou h. renounced the covenant with 89.39
thou h. defiled his crown in the 89.39
Thou h. breached all his walls; 89.40
thou h. laid his strongholds in 89.40
Thou h. exalted the right hand of 89.42
thou h. made all his enemies 89.42
Yea, thou h. turned back the edge of 89.43
and thou h. not made him stand in 89.43
Thou h. removed the scepter from 89.44
Thou h. cut short the days of his 89.45
thou h. covered him with shame. 89.45
vanity thou h. created all the 89.47
Lord, thou h. been our dwelling 90.01
Thou h. set our iniquities before 90.08
many days as thou h. afflicted us, 90.15
h. made me glad by thy work; 92.04
But thou h. exalted my horn like 92.10
thou h. poured over me fresh oil. 92.10
thou h. established equity; 99.04
thou h. executed justice and 99.04
for thou h. taken me up and thrown 102.10
who h. stretched out the heavens 104.02
who h. laid the beams of thy 104.03
Thou h. made the moon to mark the 104.19
In wisdom h. thou made them all; 104.24
H. thou not rejected us, O God? 108.11
thou, O LORD, h. done it! 109.27
For thou h. delivered my soul from 116.08
handmaid. Thou h. loosed my bonds. 116.16
thee that thou h. answered me and 118.21
answered me and h. become my salvation. 118.21
Thou h. commanded thy precepts to 119.04
in which thou h. made me hope. 119.49
Thou h. dealt well with thy servant, 119.65
faithfulness thou h. afflicted me. 119.75
thou h. established the earth, and 119.90
or by them thou h. given me life. 119.93
ordinances, for thou h. taught me. 119.102
Thou h. appointed thy testimonies 119.138
that thou h. founded them for ever. 119.152
for thou h. exalted above everything 138.02
O LORD, thou h. searched me and 139.01
thou h. covered my head in the day 140.07
meditate on all that thou h. done; 143.05
For thou h. rejected thy people, the Is 2.06
Thou h. multiplied the nation, thou 9.03
thou h. increased its joy; 9.03
thou h. broken as on the day of 9.04
for thou h. done wonderful things, 25.01
For thou h. made the city a heap, 25.02
For thou h. been a stronghold to 25.04
thou h. wrought for us all our 26.12
that end thou h. visited them with 26.14
But thou h. increased the nation, O 26.15
thou h. increased the nation; 26.15
thou h. enlarged all the borders of 26.15
thou h. made heaven and earth. 37.16
but thou h. held back my life from 38.17
for thou h. cast all my sins behind 38.17
over whom thou h. never ruled, 63.19
for thou h. hid thy face from us, 64.07
and h. delivered us into the hand 64.07
surely thou h. utterly deceived Jer 4.10
Thou h. smitten them, but they felt 5.03
thou h. consumed them, but they 5.03
H. thou utterly rejected Judah? 14.19
Why h. thou smitten us so that 14.19
O LORD, thou h. deceived me, and I 20.07
than I, and thou h. prevailed. 20.07
'Thou h. chastened me, and I was 31.18

HAST (cont.)
It is thou who h. made the heavens Jer 32.17
who h. shown signs and wonders in 32.20
and h. made thee a name, as at this 32.20
Therefore thou h. made all this 32.23
h. said to me, "Buy the field for 32.25
thou h. said concerning this place 51.62
they are glad that thou h. done it. Lam 1.21
thou the day thou h. announced, 1.21
them as thou h. dealt with me 1.22
With whom h. thou dealt thus? 2.20
of thy anger thou h. slain them, 2.21
rebelled, and thou h. not forgiven. 3.42
"Thou h. wrapped thyself with anger 3.43
thou h. wrapped thyself with a 3.44
Thou h. made us offscouring and 3.45
"Thou h. taken up my cause, O Lord, 3.58
O Lord, thou h. redeemed my life. 3.58
Thou h. seen the wrong done to me, O 3.59
Thou h. seen all their vengeance, 3.60
"Thou h. heard their taunts, O LORD, 3.61
Or h. thou utterly rejected us? 5.22
for thou h. given me wisdom and Dan 2.23
and h. now made known to me what we 2.23
for thou h. made known to us the 2.23
lands to which thou h. driven them, 9.07
and h. made thee a name, as at this 9.15
h. done as it pleased thee." Jon 1.14
as thou h. sworn to our fathers Mic 7.20
O LORD, thou h. ordained them as a Hab 1.12
h. established them for chastisement. 1.12
which thou h. had indignation Zec 1.12
but you say, "How h. thou loved us?" Mal 1.02
that thou h. hidden these things Mt 11.25
sucklings thou h. brought perfect 21.16
my God, why h. thou forsaken me?" 27.46
my God, why h. thou forsaken me?" Mk 15.34
which thou h. prepared in the Lk 2.31
that thou h. hidden these things 10.21
I thank thee that thou h. heard me. Jn 11.41
since thou h. given him power over 17.02
life to all whom thou h. given him. 17.02
and Jesus Christ whom thou h. sent. 17.03
that thou h. given me is from thee; 17.07
for those whom thou h. given me, 17.09
in thy name which thou h. given me, 17.11
in thy name which thou h. given me; 17.12
may believe that thou h. sent me. 17.21
which thou h. given me I have 17.22
world may know that thou h. sent me 17.23
h. loved them even as thou h. loved me. 17.23
whom thou h. given me, may be with 17.24
which thou h. given me in thy love 17.24
these know that thou h. sent me. 17.25
with which thou h. loved me may be 17.26
one of these two thou h. chosen Ac 1.24
Thou h. made known to me the ways 2.28
Thou h. loved righteousness and Heb 1.09
thou h. crowned him with glory and 2.07
and offerings thou h. not desired, 10.05
but a body h. thou prepared for me; 10.05
offerings thou h. taken no pleasure. 10.06
"Thou h. neither desired nor taken 10.08
and h. made them a kingdom and Rev 5.10
that thou h. taken thy great power 11.17
and thou h. given them blood to 16.06

HASTE
Make h., escape there; for I can do Gen 19.22
Then Joseph made h., for his heart 43.30
Make h. and go up to my father and 45.09
Make h. and bring my father down 45.13
called Moses and Aaron in h., Ex 10.16
and you shall eat it in h. 12.11
to send them out of the land in h.; 12.33
And Moses made h. to bow his head 34.08
The people passed over in h.; Jos 4.10
made h. and went out early to the 8.14
and they made h. to set the city on 8.19
make h. to do, as I have done." Ju 9.48
woman ran in h. and told her 13.10
in ambush made h. and rushed upon 20.37
Make h.; he has come just now 1Sa 9.12
the lad, "Hurry, make h., stay not." 20.38
the king's business required h." 21.08
was making h. to get away from 23.26
to Saul, saying, "Make h. and come; 23.27
Then Abigail made h., and took two 25.18
she made h., and alighted from the 25.23
you had made h. and come to meet 25.34
And Abigail made h. and rose and 25.42
and, as she fled in her h., 2Sa 4.04
go in h., lest he overtake us 15.14
made h. to come down with the men 19.16
Rehoboam made h. to mount his 1Ki 12.18
Then he made h. to take the bandage 20.41
had thrown away in their h. 2Ki 7.15
Then in h. every man of them took 9.13
Rehoboam made h. to mount his 2Ch 10.18
God has commanded me to make h. 35.21
they went in h. to the Jews at Ez 4.23
couriers went in h. by order of the Est 3.15
"Make h., take the robes and the 6.10
Haman in h. to the banquet that 6.14
rode out in h., urged by the king's 8.14
me, because of my h. within me. Job 20.02
Make h. to help me, O Lord, my Ps 38.22
O LORD, make h. to help me! 40.13
I would h. to find me a shelter 55.08
in distress, make h. to answer me. 69.17
O LORD, make h. to help me! 70.01
O my God, make h. to help me! 71.12
make h. to me! Give ear to my voice, 114.01
Make h. to answer me, O LORD! 143.07
and they make h. to shed blood. Pro 1.16
feet that make h. to turn to evil, 6.18
he who makes h. with his feet 19.02
Draw me after you, let us make h. Sol 1.04
Make h., my beloved, and be like a 8.14
"Let him make h., let him speed his Is 5.19
'He who believes will not be in h.' 28.16
For you shall not go out in h., 52.12
and they make h. to shed innocent 59.07
let them make h. and raise a Jer 9.18
beaten down, and have fled in h.; 46.05
in Daniel before the king in h., Dan 2.25
was astonished and rose up in h. 3.24
and went in h. to the den of lions. 6.19
is why I made h. to flee to Jon 4.02
in immediately with h. to the king, Mk 6.25
and went with h. into the hill Lk 1.39
And they went with h., and found 2.16
"Zacchaeus, make h. and come down; 19.05
So he made h. and came down, and 19.06
'Make h. and get quickly out of Ac 22.18

HASTEN
and did not h. to go down for about Jos 10.13
and see that you h. the matter." 2Ch 24.05
But the Levites did not h. it. 24.05
O thou my help, h. to my aid! Ps 22.19
let Ethiopia h. to stretch out her 68.31
h. to me, O God! Thou art my help 70.05
I h. and do not delay to keep thy 119.60
h., and importune your neighbor. Pro 6.03
in its time I will h. it. Is 60.22
H. and come, all you nations round Joe 3.11
they h. to the wall, the mantelet is Nah 2.05

HASTENED
And Abraham h. into the tent to Gen 18.06
the servant, who h. to prepare it. 18.07
Then the man h. and came and told 1Sa 4.14
and he himself h. to go out, 2Ch 26.20
and my foot has h. to deceit; Job 31.05

HASTENING
the LORD is near, near and h. fast; Zep 1.14
for he was h. to be at Jerusalem, if Ac 20.16
waiting for and h. the coming of 2Pe 3.12

HASTENS
but he who h. to be rich will not Pro 28.20
A miserly man h. after wealth, and 28.22
and h. to the place where it rises. Ecc 1.05
hand and his affliction h. apace. Jer 48.16
it h. to the end—it will not lie. Hab 2.03

HASTILY
brought him h. out of the dungeon; Gen 41.14
Then he called h. to the young man Ju 9.54
Wealth h. gotten will dwindle, but Pro 13.11
inheritance gotten h. in the 20.21
do not h. bring into court; for what 25.08

HASTY
he who has a h. temper exalts Pro 14.29
one who is h. comes only to want. 21.05
see a man who is h. in his words? 29.20
your heart be h. to utter a word Ecc 5.02
Chaldeans, that bitter and h. nation, Hab 1.06
Do not be h. in the laying on of 1Ti 5.22

HASUPHA
the sons of H., the sons of Tabbaoth, Ez 2.43
the sons of H., the sons of Tabbaoth, Neh 7.46

HATCH
and lay and h. and gather her young Is 34.15
They h. adders' eggs, they weave the 59.05
a brood which she did not h., Jer 17.11

HATCHED
one which is crushed a viper is h. Is 59.05

HATCHETS
broke down with h. and hammers. Ps 74.06

HATE
the gate of those who h. them!" Gen 24.60
seeing that you h. me and have 26.27
Joseph will h. us and pay us back 50.15
are trustworthy and who h. a bribe; Ex 18.21
generation of those who h. me, 20.05
"You shall not h. your brother in Lev 19.17
those who h. you shall rule over 26.17
let them that h. thee flee before Num 10.35
generation of those who h. me, Deu 5.09
to their face those who h. him, 7.10
will lay them upon all who h. you. 7.15
and will requite those who h. me. 32.41
of those that h. him, that they rise 33.11
"Did you not h. me, and drive me out Ju 11.07
"You only h. me, you do not love me; 14.16
because you love those who h. you 2Sa 19.06
and h. those who love you. 19.06
but I h. him, for he never prophesies 1Ki 22.08
or the life of those who h. you, 2Ch 1.11
but I h. him, for he never prophesies 18.07
and love those who h. the LORD? 19.02
Those who h. you will be clothed Job 8.22
what I suffer from those who h. me, Ps 9.13
will find out those who h. you. 21.08
what violent hatred they h. me. 25.19
I h. the company of evildoers, and I 26.05
and those who h. the righteous will 34.21
the eye who h. me without cause. 35.19
are those who h. me wrongfully. 38.19
All who h. me whisper together 41.07
put to confusion those who h. us. 44.07
righteousness and h. wickedness. 45.07
For you h. discipline, and you cast 50.17
let those who h. him flee before 68.01
are those who h. me without cause; 69.04
Those who h. the LORD would cringe 81.15
those who h. thee have raised their 83.02
that those who h. me may see and 86.17
and strike down those who h. him. 89.23
The LORD loves those who h. evil; 97.10
I h. the work of those who fall 101.03
their hearts to h. his people, 105.25
They beset me with words of h., 109.03
look in triumph on those who h. me. 118.07
therefore I h. every false way. 119.104
I h. double-minded men, but I love 119.113
thy precepts; I h. every false way. 119.128
I h. and abhor falsehood, but I love 119.163
dwelling among those who h. peace. 120.06
May all who h. Zion be put to shame 129.05
Do I not h. them that h. thee, O LORD? 139.21
I h. them with perfect hatred; 139.22
scoffing and fools h. knowledge? Pro 1.22
of evil and perverted speech I h. 8.13
all who h. me love death." 8.36
a scoffer, or he will h. you; 9.08
All a poor man's brothers h. him; 19.07
he become weary of you and h. you. 25.17
Bloodthirsty men h. one who is 29.10
a time to love, and a time to h.; Ecc 3.08
it is love or h. man does not know. 9.01
Their love and their h. and their 9.06
I h. robbery and wrong; I will Is 61.08
brethren who h. you and cast you 66.05
against me; therefore I h. her. Jer 12.08
do this abominable thing that I h.!' 44.04
the hands of those whom you h., Eze 23.28
for those who h. you and its Dan 4.19
there I began to h. them. Hos 9.15
They h. him who reproves in the Amo 5.10
H. evil, and love good, and establish 5.15
"I h., I despise your feasts, and I 5.21
of Jacob, and h. his strongholds; 6.08
You who h. the good and love the Mic 3.02
these things I h., says the LORD. Zec 8.17
"For I h. divorce, says the LORD the Mal 2.16
your neighbor and h. your enemy.' Mt 5.43
either he will h. the one and love 6.24
one another, and h. one another. 24.10
and from the hand of all who h. us; Lk 1.71
"Blessed are you when men h. you, 6.22
do good to those who h. you, 6.27
me and does not h. his own father 14.26
either he will h. the one and love 16.13
The world cannot h. you, but it Jn 7.07
want, but I do the very thing I h. Rom 7.15
h. what is evil, hold fast to what 12.09
you h. the works of the Nicolaitans, Rev 2.06
the Nicolaitans, which I also h. 2.06
and the beast will h. the harlot; 17.16

HATED
Now Esau h. Jacob because of the Gen 27.41
When the LORD saw that Leah was h., 29.31
the LORD has heard that I am h., 29.33
they h. him, and could not speak 37.04
brothers they only h. him the more. 37.05
So they h. him yet more for his 37.08
the LORD h. us he has brought us Deu 1.27
them, and because he h. them, 9.28
thought that you utterly h. her; Ju 15.02
who are h. by David's soul." 2Sa 5.08
Then Amnon h. her with very great 13.15
with which he h. her was greater 13.15
for Absalom h. Amnon, because he had 13.22
strong enemy, from those who h. me; 22.18
those who h. me, and I destroyed 22.41
they pleased to those who h. them. Est 9.05
thousand of those who h. them; 9.16
torn me in his wrath, and h. me; Job 16.09
at the ruin of him that h. me, 31.29
enemy, and from those who h. me; Ps 18.17
and those who h. me I destroyed. 18.40

HATED (cont.)
iniquity cannot be found out and h. Ps 36.02
that those who h. them ruled over 106.41
Because they h. knowledge and did Pro 1.29
"How I h. discipline, and my heart 5.12
So I h. life, because what is done Ecc 2.17
I h. all my toil in which I had 2.18
Whereas you have been forsaken and h., Is 60.15
but I have h. Esau; I have laid waste Mal 1.03
and you will be h. by all for my Mt 10.22
and you will be h. by all nations 24.09
and you will be h. by all for my Mk 13.13
But his citizens h. him and sent an Lk 19.14
you will be h. by all for my name's 21.17
that it has h. me before it h. you. Jn 15.18
have seen and h. both me and my 15.24
in their law, 'They h. me without a cause.' 15.25
the world has h. them because they 17.14
is written, "Jacob I loved, but Esau I h." Rom 9.13
h. by men and hating one another; Tit 3.03
righteousness and h. lawlessness; Heb 1.09

HATEFUL
a haunt for every foul and h. bird; Rev 18.02

HATERS
slanderers, h. of God, insolent, Rom 1.30
profligates, fierce, h. of good, 2Ti 3.03

HATES
ass of one who h. you lying under Ex 23.05
not be slack with him who h. him, Deu 7.10
which the LORD h. they have done 12.31
pillar, which the LORD your God h. 16.22
"But if any man h. his neighbor, and lies 19.11
Shall one who h. justice govern? Will you Job 34.17
and his soul h. him that loves violence. Ps 11.05
There are six things which the LORD h., Pro 6.16
but he who h. suretyship is secure. 11.15
knowledge, but he who h. reproof is stupid. 12.01
A righteous man h. falsehood, but a wicked 13.05
He who spares the rod h. his son, 13.24
the way; he who h. reproof will die. 15.10
but he who h. bribes will live. 15.27
He who h., dissembles with his lips 26.24
A lying tongue h. its victims, and a 26.28
but he who h. unjust gain will prolong 28.16
partner of a thief h. his own life; 29.24
your appointed feasts my soul h.; Is 1.14
one who does evil h. the light, and does not Jn 3.20
but it h. me because I testify of it 7.07
and he who h. his life in this world 12.25
"If the world h. you, know that it 15.18
world, therefore the world h. you. 15.19
He who h. me h. my Father also. 15.23
For no man ever h. his own flesh, Eph 5.29
the light and h. his brother is in 1Jn 2.09
But he who h. his brother is in the 2.11
brethren, that the world h. you. 3.13
Any one who h. his brother is a 3.15
and h. his brother, he is a liar; 4.20

HATEST
thy eyes; thou h. all evildoers. Ps 5.05
Thou h. those who pay regard to 31.06

HATH
the desolate h. more children than Gal 4.27
children than she who h. a husband." 4.27

HATHACH
Then Esther called for H., one of the Est 4.05
H. went out to Mordecai in the open 4.06
And H. went and told Esther what 4.09
Then Esther spoke to H. and gave 4.10

HATHATH
sons of Othniel: H. and Meonothai. 1Ch 4.13

HATING
hated by men and h. one another; Tit 3.03
h. even the garment spotted by the Jud 1.23

HATIPHA
sons of Neziah, and the sons of H. Ez 2.54
the sons of Neziah, the sons of H. Neh 7.56

HATITA
The sons of H., and the sons of Ez 2.42
the sons of H., the sons of Shobai, Neh 7.45

HATRED
And if he stabbed him from h., or hurled Num 35.20
Amnon hated her with very great h.; 2Sa 13.15
so that the h. with which he hated 13.15
with what violent h. they hate me. Ps 25.19
evil for good, and h. for my love. 109.05
I hate them with perfect h.; I count them 139.22
The fear of the LORD is h. of evil. Pro 8.13
H. stirs up strife, but love covers 10.12
He who conceals h. was lying lips, 10.18
is than a fatted ox and h. with it. 15.17
though his h. be covered with guile, 26.26
and they shall deal with you in h., Eze 23.29
because of your h. against them; and I will 35.11
because of your great iniquity and great h. Hos 9.07
his ways, and h. in the house of his God. 9.08

HATS
their h., and their other garments, Dan 3.21

HATTIL
sons of H., the sons of Pocherethhazzebaim, Ez 2.57
sons of H., the sons of Pocherethhazzebaim, Neh 7.59

HATTUSH
H., Igal, Bariah, Neariah, and Shaphat, 1Ch 3.22
Daniel. Of the sons of David, H., Ez 8.02
and next to him H. the son of Neh 3.10
H., Shebaniah, Malluch, 10.04
Amariah, Malluch, H., 12.02

HAUGHTILY
your voice and h. lifted your eyes? 2Ki 19.22
requites him who acts h. Ps 31.23
your voice and h. lifted your eyes? Is 37.23
and you shall not walk h., for it will be Mic 2.03

HAUGHTINESS
And the h. of man shall be humbled, Is 2.17
and lay low the h. of the ruthless. 13.11
arrogance, and the h. of his heart. Jer 48.29

HAUGHTY
are upon the h. to bring them down. 2Sa 22.28
but the h. eyes thou dost bring Ps 18.27
The man of h. looks and arrogant 101.05
the lowly; but the h. he knows from afar. 138.06
h. eyes, a lying tongue, and hands Pro 6.17
and a h. spirit before a fall. 16.18
Before destruction a man's heart is h., 18.12
H. eyes and a proud heart, the lamp 21.04
h. man who acts with arrogant pride. 21.24
The h. looks of man shall be brought low, Is 2.11
of Zion are h. and walk with outstretched 3.16
and the eyes of the h. are humbled. 5.15
king of Assyria and his h. pride. 10.12
They were h., and did abominable Eze 16.50
no longer be h. in my holy mountain. Zep 3.11
h., boastful, inventors of evil, Rom 1.30
do not be h., but associate with 12.16
world, charge them not to be h., 1Ti 6.17
mouth uttering h. and blasphemous Rev 13.05

HAUL
and I will h. you up in my dragnet. Eze 32.03
now they were not able to h. it in, Jn 21.06

HAULED
went abroad and h. the net ashore, Jn 21.11
HAUNT
and see the place where his h. is, 1Sa 23.22
It shall be the h. of jackals, an abode Is 34.13
the h. of jackals shall become a 35.07
Hazor shall become a h. of jackals, Jer 49.33
the h. of jackals, a horror and a 51.37
of demons, a h. of every foul spirit, Rev 18.02
a h. of every foul and hateful bird; 18.02

HAURAN
which is on the border of H. Eze 47.16
Hazarenon between H. and Damascus; 47.18
HAVE
"After I h. grown old, and my husband Gen 18.12
is old, shall I h. pleasure?" 18.12
and I h. oxen, asses, flocks, menservants, 32.05
and I h. sent to tell my lord, in 32.05
Esau said, "I h. enough, my brother; 33.09
keep what you h. for yourself." 33.09
with me, and because I h. enough." 33.11
H. you another brother?' What we 43.07
'H. you a father, or a brother?' 44.19
'We h. a father, an old man, and a 44.20
It shall h. two shoulder-pieces Ex 28.07
It shall h. in it an opening for 28.32
atonement with it shall h. it. Lev 7.07
offering shall h. for himself the 7.08
the fat shall h. the right thigh 7.33
and shall h. the linen breeches on 16.04
You shall h. just balances, just 19.36
day you shall h. a holy convocation; 23.07
You shall h. one law for the sojourner 24.22
and female slaves whom you may h.: 25.44
and you shall h. no power to stand 26.37
priest shall h. the water of bitterness Num 5.18
you shall h. one statute, both for 9.14
You shall h. one law for him who 15.29
"You shall h. no inheritance in 18.20
shall you h. any portion among 18.20
day you shall h. a holy convocation; 28.25
you shall h. a holy convocation; 28.26
month you shall h. a holy convocation; 29.01
month you shall h. a holy convocation, 29.07
month you shall h. a holy convocation; 29.12
day you shall h. a solemn assembly: 29.35
they shall h. possessions among you 32.30
you shall h. the Great Sea and its 34.06
"'You shall h. no other gods before Deu 5.07
and they h. borne him children, both 21.15
"You shall h. a place outside the 23.12
"You shall not h. in your bag two 25.13
You shall not h. in your house two 25.14
A full and just weight you shall h., 25.15
full and just measure you shall h.; 25.15
numerous people, and h. great power; Jos 17.17
you shall not h. one lot only, 17.17
because I h. a Levite as priest." Ju17.13
but we will h. a king over us, 1Sa 8.19
I h. with me the fourth part of a 9.08
master's son may h. bread to eat; 2Sa 9.10
What further right h. I, then, to cry 19.28
(but he shall h. one tribe, for the 1Ki 11.32
city which I h. chosen out of all 11.32
I h. nothing baked, only a handful 17.12
that I may h. it for a vegetable 21.02
what h. you in the house?" And she said, 2Ki 4.02
to all that I h. provided for the 1Ch 29.03
I h. a treasure of my own of gold 29.03
none after you shall h. the like." 2Ch 1.12
You h. done foolishly in this; 16.09
for from now on you will h. wars." 16.09
you will then h. no possession in Ez 4.16
And mighty kings h. been over 4.20
So the poor h. hope, and injustice Job 5.16
"O that I might h. my request, 6.08
for I h. not denied the words of 6.10
If you h. anything to say, answer me; 33.32
The lines h. fallen for me in Ps 16.06
places; yea, I h. a goodly heritage. 16.06
fallen to me, that I h. kept thy precepts. 119.56
us, we will all h. one purse"— Pro 1.14
give it"—when you h. it with you. 3.28
and his children will h. a refuge. 14.26
because they h. a good reward for Ecc 4.09
You shall h. a song as in the night Is 30.29
yet h. eyes, who are deaf, yet h. ears! 43.08
by the brands which you h. kindled! 50.11
This shall you h. from my hand: 50.11
The dogs h. a mighty appetite; 56.11
they never h. enough. 56.11
shepherds also h. no understanding; 56.11
they h. all turned to their own way, 56.11
he shall not h. any one living Jer 29.32
he shall not h. a son to reign on 33.21
We h. no vineyard or field or seed; 35.09
He shall h. none to sit upon the 36.30
for we h. stores of wheat, barley, 41.08
of Judah who h. come to live in 44.14
do everything that we h. vowed, 44.17
When you h. among the nations some Eze 6.08
and they shall all h. one shepherd. 37.24
They shall h. linen turbans upon 44.18
"You shall h. just balances, a just 45.10
among you and h. begotten children 47.22
wisdom that I h. more than all the Dan 2.30
Therefore you will h. none to cast Mic 2.05
and you shall h. no more soothsayers; 5.12
'We h. Abraham as our father'; for I Mt 3.09
John would h. prevented him, saying, 3.14
who love you, what reward h. you? 5.46
then you will h. no reward from 6.01
I say to you, they h. their reward. 6.02
I say to you, they h. their reward. 6.05
I say to you, they h. their reward. 6.16
"Foxes h. holes, and birds of the air h. nests; 8.20
be given, and he will h. abundance; 13.12
"It is not lawful for you to h. her." 14.04
"We h. only five loaves here and 14.17
"I h. compassion on the crowd, 15.32
because they h. been with me now 15.32
three days, and h. nothing to eat; 15.32
to them, "How many loaves h. you?" 15.34
if you h. faith as a grain of 17.20
deed must I do, to h. eternal life?" 19.16
and you will h. treasure in heaven; 19.21
we h. left everything and followed 19.27
you. What then shall we h.?" 19.27
if you h. faith and never doubt, you 21.21
ground. Here you h. what is yours.' 25.25
be given, and he will h. abundance; 25.29
For you always h. the poor with you, 26.11
you, but you will not always h. me. 26.11
You h. now heard his blasphemy. 26.65
"You h. a guard of soldiers; 27.65
who are well h. no need of a Mk 2.17
As long as they h. the bridegroom 2.19
and h. authority to cast out demons: 3.15
and they h. no root in themselves, 4.17
you afraid? H. you no faith?" 4.40
for you to h. your brother's wife." 6.18
to them, "How many loaves h. you? 6.38
"I h. compassion on the crowd, 8.02
because they h. been with me now 8.02
three days, and h. nothing to eat; 8.02
asked them, "How many loaves h. you?" 8.05
another, saying, "We h. no bread." 8.16
the fact that you h. no bread? 8.17
H. salt in yourselves, and be at 9.50
sell what you h., and give to the 10.21
and you will h. treasure in heaven; 10.21
for those who h. riches to enter 10.23
answered them, "H. faith in God. 11.22

HAVE (cont.)

if you h. anything against any one; Mk 11.25
For you always h. the poor with you, 14.07
but you will not always h. me. 14.07
And you will h. joy and gladness, Lk 1.14
'We h. Abraham as our father'; for I 3.08
I h. something to say to you." 7.40
but these h. no root, they believe 8.13
nor money; and do not h. two tunics. 9.03
"We h. no more than five loaves and 9.13
"Foxes h. holes, and birds of the air h. nests; 9.58
and I h. nothing to set before him'; 11.06
and after that h. no more that 12.04
for I h. nowhere to store my crops?' 12.17
you h. ample goods laid up for many 12.19
they h. neither storehouse nor barn, 12.24
I h. a baptism to be baptized with; 12.50
'I h. bought a field, and I must go 14.18
and see it; I pray you, h. me excused.' 14.18
'I h. bought five yoke of oxen, and 14.19
examine them; I pray you, h. me excused.' 14.19
for I h. five brothers, so that he 16.28
'They h. Moses and the prophets; 16.29
all that you h. and distribute to 18.22
and you will h. treasure in heaven; 18.22
for those who h. riches to enter 18.24
Because you h. been faithful in a 19.17
you shall h. authority over ten 19.17
and bones as you see that I h." 24.39
"H. you anything here to eat?" 24.41
Jesus said to him, "They h. no wine." Jn 2.03
believes in him may h. eternal life." 3.15
not perish but h. eternal life. 3.16
you h. nothing to draw with, and the 4.11
answered him, "I h. no husband." 4.17
right in saying, 'I h. no husband'; 4.17
for you h. had five husbands, and he 4.18
he whom you now h. is not your 4.18
"I h. food to eat of which you do 4.32
I h. no man to put me into the pool 5.07
the Son also to h. life in himself, 5.26
testimony which I h. is greater 5.36
and you do not h. his word abiding 5.38
that in them you h. eternal life; 5.39
to come to me that you may h. life. 5.40
But I know that you h. not the love 5.42
in him should h. eternal life; 6.40
his blood, you h. no life in you; 6.53
You h. the words of eternal life; 6.68
The people answered, "You h. a demon! 7.20
that they might h. some charge to *8.06
but will h. the light of life." 8.12
I h. much to say about you and much 8.26
the world what I h. heard from him." 8.26
fornications; we h. one Father, even God." 8.41
you are a Samaritan and h. a demon?" 8.48
Jesus answered, "I h. not a demon; 8.49
"Now we know that you h. a demon. 8.52
were blind, you would h. no guilt; 9.41
that they may h. life, and h. it 10.10
And I h. other sheep, that are not 10.16
I h. power to lay it down, and I 10.18
and I h. power to take it again; 10.18
this charge I h. received from my 10.18
The poor you always h. with you, 12.08
you, but you do not always h. me." 12.08
Walk while you h. the light, lest the 12.35
While you h. the light, believe in 12.36
the word that I h. spoken will be 12.48
not wash you, you h. no part in me." 13.08
if you h. love for one another." 13.35
to them, they would not h. sin; 15.22
but now they h. no excuse for their 15.22
else did, they would not h. sin; 15.24
but now they h. seen and hated both 15.24
"I h. yet many things to say to you, 16.12
So you h. sorrow now, but I will see 16.22
I h. said this to you, that in me 16.33
you, that in me you may h. peace. 16.33
In the world you h. tribulation; 16.33
good cheer, I h. overcome the world." 16.33
that they may h. my joy fulfilled 17.13
But you h. a custom that I should 18.39
will you h. me release for you the 18.39
"We h. a law, and by that law he 19.07
not know that I h. power to 19.10
"You would h. no power over me 19.11
answered, "We h. no king but Caesar." 19.15
believing you may h. life in his 20.31
to them, "Children, h. you any fish?" 21.05
"I h. no silver and gold, but I give Ac 3.06
and gold, but I give you what I h.; 3.06
You h. neither part nor lot in this 8.21
if you h. any word of exhortation 13.15
for I h. many people in this city." 18.10
this business we h. our wealth. 19.25
with him h. a complaint against 19.38
We h. four men who are under a vow; 21.23
"What is it that you h. to tell me?" 23.19
take pains to h. a clear conscience 24.16
if they h. anything against me. 24.19
custody but should h. some liberty, 24.23
when I h. an opportunity I will 24.25
But I h. nothing definite to write 25.26
Therefore I h. brought him before 25.26
after we h. examined him, I may h. 25.26
that I h. often intended to come to Rom 1.13
(but thus far h. been prevented), in 1.13
When Gentiles who h. not the law do 2.14
even though they do not h. the law. 2.14
we h. peace with God through our 5.01
Through him we h. obtained access 5.02
But now that you h. been set free 6.22
from sin and h. becomes slaves of 6.22
who does not h. the Spirit of 8.09
who h. the first fruits of the 8.23
that I h. great sorrow and unceasing 9.02
return and Sarah shall h. a son." 9.09
that they h. a zeal for God, but it is 10.02
For as in one body we h. many members, 12.04
members do not h. the same function, 12.04
Would you h. no fear of him who is 13.03
The faith that you h., keep between 14.22
of the scriptures we might h. hope. 15.04
I h. reason to be proud of my work 15.17
I no longer h. any room for work 15.23
and since I h. longed for many 15.23
But we h. the mind of Christ. 1Co 2.16
What h. you that you did not 4.07
For though you h. countless guides 4.15
Christ, you do not h. many fathers. 4.15
If then you h. such cases, why do 6.04
within you, which you h. from God? 6.19
each man should h. his own wife 7.02
I h. no command of the Lord, but I 7.25
who marry will h. worldly troubles, 7.28
let those who h. wives live as 7.29
I think that I h. the Spirit of 7.40
Do we not h. the right to our food 9.04
Do we not h. the right to be 9.05
and I who h. no right to refrain 9.06
this of my own will, I h. a reward; 9.17
woman ought to h. a veil on her 11.10
Do you not h. houses to eat and 11.22
and humiliate those who h. nothing? 11.22
"I h. no need of you," nor again the 12.21
to the feet, "I h. no need of you." 12.21
but h. not love, I am a noisy gong 13.01
And if I h. prophetic powers, and 13.02
and if I h. all faith, so as to 13.02
but h. not love, I am nothing. 13.02
If I give away all I h., and if I 13.03
but h. not love, I gain nothing. 13.03
we who are in Christ h. only hope, 15.19
in you which I h. in Christ Jesus 15.31

HAVE (cont.)

For some h. no knowledge of God. 1Co 15.34
that you might h. a double pleasure; 2Co 1.15
who should h. made me rejoice, for 2.03
abundant love that I h. for you. 2.04
confidence that we h. through 3.04
Since we h. such a hope, we are very 3.12
But we h. this treasure in earthen 4.07
Since we h. the same spirit of 4.13
we h. a building from God, a house 5.01
Since we h. these promises, beloved, 7.01
completing it out of what you h. 8.11
so that you may always h. enough of 9.08
which we h. in Christ Jesus, that Gal 2.04
So then, as we h. opportunity, let us 6.10
In him we h. redemption through his Eph 1.07
him we both h. access in one 2.18
in whom we h. boldness and confidence 3.12
I h. no one like him, who will be Php 2.20
lest I should h. sorrow upon sorrow. 2.27
Though I myself h. reason for 3.04
confidence in the flesh, I h. more: 3.04
so live as you h. an example in us. 3.17
I h. received full payment, and more; 4.18
in whom we h. redemption, the Col 1.14
and for all who h. not seen my 2.01
These h. indeed an appearance of 2.23
that you also h. a Master in 4.01
But we would not h. you ignorant, 1Th 4.13
grieve as others do who h. no hope. 4.13
you h. no need to h. anything 5.01
not because we h. not that right, 2Th 3.09
but if we h. food and clothing, with 1Ti 6.08
faith which you h. toward the Lord Phm 1.05
For I h. derived much joy and 1.07
of the saints h. been refreshed 1.07
Since then we h. a great high Heb 4.14
For we h. not a high priest who is 4.15
for those who h. their faculties 5.14
we who h. fled for refuge might 6.18
refuge might h. strong encouragement 6.18
We h. this as a sure and steadfast 6.19
priestly office h. a commandment 7.05
we h. such a high priest, one who is 8.01
priest also to h. something to 8.03
Otherwise, would they not h. ceased 10.02
would no longer h. any consciousness 10.02
since we h. confidence to enter the 10.19
they would h. had opportunity to 11.15
we h. had earthly fathers to discipline 12.09
and be content with what you h.; 13.05
We h. an altar from which those who 13.10
serve the tent h. no right to eat. 13.10
For here we h. no lasting city, but 13.14
steadfastness h. its full effect, Jas 1.04
say, "You have faith and I h. works." 2.18
But if you h. bitter jealousy and 3.14
You desire and do not h.; so you kill. 4.02
You do not h., because you do not 4.02
And we h. the prophetic word made 2Pe 1.19
They h. eyes full of adultery, 2.14
They h. hearts trained in greed. 2.14
that which we h. seen and heard we 1Jn 1.03
so that you may h. fellowship with 1.03
If we say we h. fellowship with him 1.06
we h. fellowship with one another, 1.07
If we say we h. no sin, we deceive 1.08
we h. an advocate with the Father, 2.01
is the word which you h. heard. 2.07
But you h. been anointed by the 2.20
appears we may h. confidence and 2.28
condemn us, we h. confidence before God; 3.21
that we may h. confidence for the 4.17
And this commandment we h. from him, 4.21
may know that you h. eternal life. 5.13
the confidence which we h. in him, 5.14
we know that we h. obtained the 5.15
but the one we h. had from the 2Jn 1.05
not lose what you h. worked for, 1.08
doctrine of Christ does not h. God; 1.09
Though I h. much to write to you, I 1.12
and I h. the keys of Death and Rev 1.18
name's sake, and you h. not grown weary. 2.03
But I h. this against you, that you 2.04
that you h. abandoned the love you 2.04
Yet this you h., you hate the works 2.06
ten days you will h. tribulation. 2.10
But I h. a few things against you: 2.14
you h. some there who hold the 2.14
So you also h. some who hold the 2.15
But I h. this against you, that you 2.20
who h. not learned what some call 2.24
fast what you h., until I come. 2.25
you h. the name of being alive, and 3.01
Yet you h. still a few names in 3.04
people who h. not soiled their 3.04
Behold, I h. set before you an open 3.08
I know that you h. but little power, 3.08
and yet you h. kept my word and 3.08
my word and h. not denied my name. 3.08
hold fast what you h., so that no 3.11
I h. prospered, and I need nothing; 3.17
of mankind who h. not the seal of 9.04
they h. tails like scorpions, and 9.10
They h. as king over them the angel 9.11
They h. power to shut the sky, that 11.06
and they h. power over the waters 11.06
and they h. no rest, day or night, 14.11
that they may h. the right to the 22.14

HAVEN

he shall become a h. for ships, Gen 49.13
brought them to their desired h. Ps 107.03
is laid waste, without house or h.! Is 23.01

HAVENS

we came to a place called Fair H., Ac 27.08

HAVILAH

flows around the whole land of H., Gen 2.11
H., Sabtah, Raamah, and Sabteca. 10.07
Ophir, H., and Jobab; all these 10.29
They dwelt from H. to Shur, 25.18
from H. as far as Shur, which is 1Sa 15.07
H., Sabta, Raama, and Sabteca. 1Ch 1.09
Ophir, H., and Jobab; all these 1.23

HAVING

h. me my master has no concern Gen 39.08
Eleazar died h. no sons, but only 1Ch 23.22
sledge, new, sharp, and h. teeth; Is 41.15
h. no children, his brother must Mt 22.24
and h. no children left his wife to 22.25
and h. blessed them, he commanded Mk 8.07
H. eyes do you not see, and having 8.18
and h. ears do you not hear? 8.18
h. no part dark, it will be wholly Lk 11.36
h. a hundred sheep, if he has lost 15.04
h. ten silver coins, if she loses 15.08
h. a wife but no children, the man 20.28
h. a sword, drew it and struck the Jn 18.10
praising God and h. favor with all Ac 2.47
h. a hope in God which these 24.15
h. in the law the embodiment of Rom 2.20
H. gifts that differ according to 12.06
necessity but h. his desire under 1Co 7.37
Therefore, h. this ministry by the 2Co 4.01
as h. nothing, and yet possessing 6.10
h. no hope and without God in the Eph 2.12
h. girded your loins with truth, and 6.14
and h. put on the breastplate of 6.14
h. the same love, being in full Php 2.02
not h. a righteousness of my own, 3.09
I am filled, h. received from 4.18
condemnation for h. violated their 1Ti 5.12

HAVING (cont.)
h. nothing evil to say of us. Tit 2.08
h. the golden altar of incense and Heb 9.04
h. great authority; and the earth Rev 18.01
h. the glory of God, its radiance 21.11

HAVOC
man who made h. in Jerusalem of Ac 9.21

HAVVOTHJAIR
their villages, and called them H. Num 32.41
H., as it is to this day.) Deu 3.14
called H. to this day, which are in Ju 10.04
But Geshur and Aram took from them H., 1Ch 2.23

HAWK
sea gull, the h. according to its kind, Lev 11.16
the sea gull, the h., after their kinds; Deu 14.15
by your wisdom that the h. soars, Job 39.26
But the h. and the porcupine shall Is 34.11

HAY
precious stones, wood, h., stubble— 1Co 3.12

HAZAEL
shall anoint H. to be king over 1Ki 19.15
the sword of H. shall Jehu slay; 19.17
the king said to H., "Take a 2Ki 8.08
So H. went to meet him, and took a 8.09
And H. said, "Why does my lord weep?" 8.12
And H. said, "What is your servant, 8.13
And H. became king in his stead. 8.15
war against H. king of Syria at 8.28
he fought against H. king of Syria. 8.29
Ramothgilead against H. king of Syria; 9.14
he fought with H. king of Syria.) 9.15
H. defeated them throughout the 10.32
At that time H. king of Syria went 12.17
But when H. set his face to go up 12.17
and sent these to H. king of Syria. 12.13
Then H. went away from Jerusalem. 12.18
the hand of H. king of Syria and 13.03
the hand of Benhadad the son of H. 13.03
Now H. king of Syria oppressed 13.22
When H. king of Syria died, Benhadad 13.24
the son of H. the cities which he 13.25
war against H. king of Syria at 2Ch 22.05
he fought against H. king of Syria. 22.06
send a fire upon the house of H., Amo 1.04

HAZAIAH
son of H., son of Adaiah, son of Neh 11.05

HAZARADDAR
then it shall go on to H., Num 34.04

HAZARENAN
Ziphron, and its end shall be at H.; Num 34.09
boundary from H. to Shepham; 34.10

HAZARENON
shall run from the sea to H., Eze 47.17
shall run from H. between Hauran 47.18
as far as H. (which is on the 48.01

HAZARGADDAH
H., Heshmon, Bethpelet, Jos 15.27

HAZARMAVETH
of Almodad, Sheleph, H., Jerah, Gen 10.26
of Almodad, Sheleph, H., Jerah, 1Ch 1.20

HAZARSHUAL
H., Beersheba, Biziothiah, Jos 15.28
H., Balah, Ezem, 19.03
They dwelt in Beersheba, Moladah, H., 1Ch 4.28
in H., in Beersheba and its villages, Neh 11.27

HAZARSUSAH
Ziklag, Bethmarcaboth, H., Jos 19.05

HAZARSUSIM
Bethmarcaboth, H., Bethbiri, and 1Ch 4.31

HAZAZONTAMAR
also the Amorites who dwelt in H. Gen 14.07
they are in H." (that is, Engedi). 2Ch 20.02

HAZERHATTICON
as far as H., which is on the Eze 47.16

HAZEROTH
Kibrothhattaavah the people journeyed to H.; Num 11.35
and they remained at H. 11.35
After that the people set out from H., 12.16
Kibrothhattaavah, and encamped at H. 33.17
And they set out from H., 33.18
and Tophel, Laban, H., and Dizahab. Deu 1.01

HAZIEL
Shelomoth, H., and Haran, three. 1Ch 23.09

HAZO
Chesed, H., Pildash, Jidlaph, and Gen 22.22

HAZOR
When Jabin king of H. heard of this, Jos 11.01
and took H., and smote its king 11.10
for H. formerly was the head of all 11.10
breathed, and he burned H. with fire. 11.11
did Israel burn, except H. only; 11.13
of Madon, one; the king of H., one; 12.19
Kedesh, H., Ithnan, 15.23
Hazorhadattah, Keriothhezron (that is, H.), 15.25
Adamah, Ramah, H., 19.36
king of Canaan, who reigned in H.; Ju 4.02
the king of H. and the house of 4.17
of the army of Jabin king of H., 1Sa 12.09
Jerusalem and H. and Megiddo and 1Ki 9.15
H., Gilead, and Galilee, all the land 2Ki 15.29
H., Ramah, Gittaim, Neh 11.33
the kingdoms of H. which Nebuchadrezzar Jer 49.28
in the depths, O inhabitants of H.! 49.30
H. shall become a haunt of jackals, 49.33

HAZORHADATTAH
H., Keriothhezron (that is, Hazor), Jos 15.25

HAZZELELPONI
the name of their sister was H., 1Ch 4.03

HEAD
he shall bruise your h., and you shall Gen 3.15
The man bowed his h. and worshiped 24.26
Then I bowed my h. and worshiped 24.48
it under his h. and lay down in 28.11
put under his h. and set it up for 28.18
lift up your h. and restore you to 40.13
were three cake baskets on my h., 40.16
it out of the basket on my h." 40.17
will lift up your h.—from you!— 40.19
lifted up the h. of the chief butler 40.20
and the h. of the chief baker. 40.20
himself upon the h. of his bed. 47.31
and laid it upon the h. of Ephraim, 48.14
left hand upon the h. of Manasseh, 48.14
right hand upon the h. of Ephraim, 48.17
from Ephraim's h. to Manasseh's 48.17
Ephraim's head to Manasseh's h. 48.17
put your right hand upon his h." 48.18
may they be on the h. of Joseph, 49.26
its h. with its legs and its inner Ex 12.09
have in it an opening for the h., 28.32
you shall set the turban on his h., 29.06
pour it on his h. and anoint him. 29.07
hands upon the h. of the bull, 29.10
hands upon the h. of the ram, 29.15

HEAD (cont.)

them with its pieces and its h., Ex 29.17
hands upon the h. of the ram, 29.19
to bow his h. toward the earth, and 34.08
a beka a h. (that is, half a shekel, 38.26
hand upon the h. of the burnt Lev 1.04
the h., and the fat, in order upon 1.08
with its h. and its fat, and the 1.12
to the altar and wring off its h., 1.15
hand upon the h. of his offering 3.02
hand upon the h. of his offering 3.08
and lay his hand upon its h., 3.13
lay his hand on the h. of the bull, 4.04
with its h., its legs, its entrails, 4.11
hands upon the h. of the bull 4.15
his hand upon the h. of the goat, 4.24
his hand on the h. of the sin 4.29
hand upon the h. of the sin 4.33
shall wring its h. from its neck, 5.08
And he set the turban upon his h., 8.09
of the anointing oil on Aaron's h., 8.12
hands upon the h. of the bull of 8.14
their hands on the h. of the ram. 8.18
burned the h. and the pieces and 8.20
their hands on the h. of the ram. 8.22
to him, piece by piece, and the h.; 9.13
diseased person from h. to foot, 13.12
a disease on the h. or the beard, 13.29
a leprosy of the h. or the beard. 13.30
man's hair has fallen from his h., 13.40
is on the bald h. or the bald 13.42
out on his bald h. or his bald 13.42
on his bald h. or on his bald 13.43
unclean; his disease is on his h. 13.44
let the hair of his h. hang loose, 13.45
shave all his hair off his h.; 14.09
put on the h. of him who is to be 14.18
put on the h. of him who is to be 14.29
hands upon the h. of the live goat, 16.21
put them upon the h. of the goat, 16.21
"You shall rise up before the hoary h., 19.32
upon whose h. the anointing oil is 21.10
let the hair of his h. hang loose, 21.10
him lay their hands upon his h., 24.14
of names, every male, h. by h.; Num 1.02
man being the h. of the house of 1.04
years old and upward, h. by h., 1.18
h. by h., every male from twenty 1.20
h. by h., every male from twenty 1.22
son of Lael as h. of the fathers' 3.24
of Uzziel as h. of the fathers' 3.30
And the h. of the fathers' house of 3.35
unbind the hair of the woman's h., 5.18
no razor shall come upon his h.; 6.05
locks of hair of his h. grow long. 6.05
separation to God is upon his h. 6.07
and he defiles his consecrated h., 6.09
shall shave his h. on the day of 6.09
consecrate his h. that same day, 6.11
his consecrated h. at the door of 6.18
his consecrated h. and put it on 6.18
one rod for the h. of each fathers' 17.03
and he bowed his h., and fell on 22.31
h. of a fathers' house belonging to 25.14
who was the h. of the people of a 25.15
go over at the h. of this people, Deu 3.28
journey at the h. of the people, 10.11
and the h. slips from the handle 19.05
appointed at the h. of the people. 20.09
shall shave her h. and pare her 21.12
And the LORD will make you the h., 28.13
over your h. shall be brass, 28.23
your foot to the crown of your h. 28.35
he shall be the h., and you shall 28.44
and Joshua will go over at your h., 31.03
these come upon the h. of Joseph, 33.16
crown of the h. of him that is 33.16
the arm, and the crown of the h. 33.20
his blood shall be upon his h., Jos 2.19
his blood shall be on our h. 2.19
formerly was the h. of all those 11.10
one of them the h. of a family 22.14
country, having him at their h. Ju 3.27
Sisera a blow, she crushed his h., 5.26
went out at the h. of the men of 9.39
millstone upon Abimelech's h., 9.53
He shall be h. over all the inhabitants 10.18
and be our h. over all the inhabitants 11.08
them over to me, I will be your h." 11.09
people made him h. and leader over 11.11
No razor shall come upon his h., 13.05
locks of my h. with the web and 16.13
locks of his h. and wove them into 16.14
"A razor has never come upon my h.; 16.17
off the seven locks of his h. 16.19
But the hair of his h. began to 16.22
and no razor shall touch his h." 1Sa 1.11
rent and with earth upon his h. 4.12
and the h. of Dagon and both his 5.04
a place at the h. of those who had 9.22
of oil and poured it on his h., 10.01
one hair of his h. fall to the 14.45
are you not the h. of the tribes 15.17
He had a helmet of bronze on his h., 17.05
and his spear's h. weighed six 17.07
put a helmet of bronze on his h., 17.38
you down, and cut off your h.; 17.46
him, and cut off his h. with it. 17.51
And David took the h. of the 17.54
Saul with the h. of the Philistine 17.57
a pillow of goats' hair at its h., 19.13
pillow of goats' hair at its h. 19.16
Samuel standing as h. over them, 19.20
evil-doing of Nabal upon his own h." 25.39
stuck in the ground at his h.; 26.07
now the spear that is at his h., 26.11
the jar of water from Saul's h.; 26.12
jar of water that was at his h." 26.16
And they cut off his h., and stripped 31.09
clothes rent and earth upon his h. 2Sa 1.02
was on his h. and the armlet which 1.10
to him, "Your blood be upon your h.; 1.16
each caught his opponent by the h., 2.16
and said, "Am I a dog's h. of Judah? 3.08
May it fall upon the h. of Joab, 3.29
They took his h., and went by the 4.07
and brought the h. of Ishbosheth to 4.08
"Here is the h. of Ishbosheth, the 4.08
But they took the h. of Ishbosheth, 4.12
the army of Hadadezer at their h. 10.16
crown of their king from his h.; 12.30
and it was placed on David's h. 12.30
And Tamar put ashes on her h., 13.19
and she laid her hand on her h., 13.19
crown of his h. there was no 14.25
the hair of his h. (for at the end 14.26
it), he weighed the hair of his h., 14.26
barefoot and with his h. covered; 15.30
coat rent and earth upon his h. 15.32
Let me go over and take off his h." 16.09
and his h. caught fast in the oak, 18.09
his h. shall be thrown to you over 20.21
cut the h. of Sheba the son of 20.22
keep me as the h. of the nations; 22.44
do not let his h. go down to Sheol 1Ki 2.06
shall bring his h. down with blood 2.09
his bloody deeds upon his own h., 2.32
back upon the h. of Joab and upon 2.33
and upon the h. of his descendants 2.33
blood shall be upon your own h." 2.37
back your evil upon your own h. 2.44
his conduct upon his own h., 8.32
back of the throne was a calf's h., 10.19
was at his h. a cake baked on hot 19.06
to his father, "Oh, my h., my h.!" 2Ki 4.19

HEAD (cont.)

his axe h. fell into the water; 2Ki 6.05
until an ass's h. was sold for 6.25
if the h. of Elisha the son of 6.31
murderer has sent to take off my h.? 6.32
of oil, and pour it on his h., 9.03
young man poured the oil on his h., 9.06
her eyes, and adorned her h., 9.30
she wags her h. behind you—the 19.21
him and took his h. and his armor, 1Ch 10.09
fastened his h. in the temple of 10.10
the army of Hadadezer at their h. 19.16
crown of their king from his h.; 20.02
and it was placed on David's h. 20.02
the h. of each father's house and 24.31
thou art exalted as h. above all. 29.11
his conduct upon his own h., 2Ch 6.23
Behold, God is with us at our h., 13.12
bowed his h. with his face to the 20.18
and Jehoshaphat at their h., 20.27
the names of the men at their h. Ez 5.10
pulled hair from my h. and beard, 9.03
crown on her h. and made her queen Est 2.17
and on whose h. a royal crown is 6.08
mourning and with his h. covered. 6.12
Jews should come upon his own h., 9.25
rent his robe, and shaved his h., Job 1.20
of his foot to the crown of his h. 2.07
righteous, I cannot lift up my h., 10.15
you, and shake my h. at you. 16.04
and taken the crown from my h. 19.09
and his h. reach to the clouds, 20.06
when his lamp shone upon my h., 29.03
or his h. with fishing spears? 41.07
my glory, and the lifter of my h. Ps 3.03
His mischief returns upon his own h., 7.16
make me the h. of the nations; 18.43
a crown of fine gold upon his h. 21.03
thou anointest my h. with oil, 23.05
And now my h. shall be lifted up 27.06
I prayed with h. bowed on my bosom, 35.13
my iniquities have gone over my h.; 38.04
are more than the hairs of my h.; 40.12
they lie at the h. of every street 51.20
the hairs of my h. are those who 69.04
therefore he will lift up his h. 110.07
like the precious oil upon the h., 133.02
hast covered my h. in the day of 140.07
Those who surround me lift up their h., 140.09
of the wicked never anoint my h.; 141.05
are a fair garland for your h., Pro 1.09
place on your h. a fair garland; 4.09
Blessings are on the h. of the 10.06
is on the h. of him who sells it. 11.26
A hoary h. is a crown of glory; 16.31
will heap coals of fire on his h., 25.22
The wise man has his eyes in his h., Ecc 2.14
let not oil be lacking on your h. 9.08
his left hand were under my h., Sol 2.06
for my h. is wet with dew, my locks 5.02
His h. is the finest gold; 5.11
Your h. crowns you like Carmel, and 7.05
his left hand were under my h., 8.03
The whole h. is sick, and the whole Is 1.05
sole of the foot even to the h., 1.06
For the h. of Syria is Damascus, and 7.08
and the h. of Damascus is Rezin. 7.08
And the h. of Ephraim is Samaria, 7.09
and the h. of Samaria is the son of 7.09
cut off from Israel h. and tail, 9.14
the elder and honored man is the h., 9.15
the h. and the hair of the feet, and 7.20
On every h. is baldness, every beard 15.02
nothing for Egypt which h. or tail, 19.15
which is on the h. of the rich 28.01
which is on the h. of the rich 28.04
she wags her h. behind you—the 37.22
it to bow down his h. like a rush, 58.05
a helmet of salvation upon his h.; 59.17
have broken the crown of your h. Jer 2.16
away with your hands upon your h., 2.37
O that my h. were waters, and my 9.01
crown has come down from your h." 13.18
they set as h. over you those whom 13.21
it is horrified and shakes his h. 18.16
burst upon the h. of the wicked. 23.19
burst upon the h. of the wicked. 30.23
spoke of him you wagged your h.? 48.27
"For every h. is shaved and every 48.37
lifted up the h. of Jehoiachin king 52.31
Her foes have become the h., her enemies Lam 1.05
hunger at the h. of every street. 2.19
water closed over my h.; I said, 3.54
scattered at the h. of every street. 4.01
The crown has fallen from our h.; 5.16
it over your h. and your beard; Eze 5.01
and took me by a lock of my h.; 8.03
and a beautiful crown upon your h. 16.12
at the h. of every street you built 16.25
chamber at the h. of every street, 16.31
requite your deeds upon your h., 16.43
broke, I will requite upon his h. 17.19
make it at the h. of the way to a 21.19
at the h. of the two ways, to use 21.21
every h. was made bald and every 29.18
his blood shall be upon his own h. 33.04
would endanger my h. with the king." Dan 1.10
visions of your h. as you lay in 2.28
The h. of this image was of fine 2.32
them all—you are the h. of gold. 2.38
the visions of my h. alarmed me. 4.05
The visions of my h. as I lay in 4.10
visions of my h. as I lay in bed, 4.13
visions of his h. as he lay in his 7.01
the hair of his h. like pure wool; 7.09
the visions of my h. alarmed me. 7.15
the ten horns that were on its h., 7.20
appoint for themselves one h.; Hos 1.11
upon your own h. swiftly and Joe 3.04
requite your deed upon your own h. 3.07
trample the h. of the poor into Amo 2.07
loins, and baldness on every h.; 8.10
deeds shall return on your own h. Ob 1.15
weeds were wrapped about my h. Jon 2.05
it might be a shade over his h., 4.06
beat upon the h. of Jonah so that 4.08
before them, the LORD at their h. Mic 2.13
pieces at the h. of every street; Nah 3.10
didst crush the h. of the wicked, Hab 3.13
thy shafts the h. of his warriors, 3.14
so that no man raised his h.; Zec 1.21
them put a clean turban on his h." 3.05
turban on his h. and clothed him 3.05
and set it upon the h. of Joshua, 6.11
the angel of the LORD, at their h. 12.08
And do not swear by your h., Mt 5.36
anoint your h. and wash your face, 6.17
of man has nowhere to lay his h." 8.20
hairs of your h. are all numbered. 10.30
"Give me the h. of John the Baptist 14.08
and his h. was brought on a platter 14.11
has become the h. of the corner; 21.42
and she poured it on his h., as he sat 26.07
of thorns they put it on his h., 27.29
the reed and struck him on the h. 27.30
And over his h. they put the charge 27.37
"The h. of John the baptizer." Mk 6.24
me at once the h. of John the 6.25
and gave orders to bring his h. 6.27
and brought his h. on a platter, 6.28
and they wounded him in the h., 12.04
has become the h. of the corner; 12.10
the jar and poured it over his h. 14.03
And they struck his h. with a reed, 15.19
wiped them with the hair of her h., Lk 7.38

HEAD (cont.)
You did not anoint my h. with oil, Lk 7.46
man has nowhere to lay his h." 9.58
hairs of your h. are all numbered. 12.07
has become the h. of the corner'? 20.17
But not a hair of your h. will perish. 21.18
only but also my hands and my h.!" Jn 13.09
of thorns, and put it on his h., 19.02
he bowed his h. and gave up his 19.30
napkin, which had been on his h., 20.07
one at the h. and one at the feet. 20.12
has become the h. of the corner. Ac 4.11
perish from the h. of any of you." 27.34
heap burning coals upon his h." Rom 12.20
that the h. of every man is Christ, 1Co 11.03
the h. of a woman is her husband, 11.03
and the h. of Christ is God. 11.03
with his h. covered dishonors his h., 11.04
with her h. unveiled dishonors her h.— 11.05
the same as if her h. were shaven. 11.05
For a man ought not to cover his h., 11.07
ought to have a veil on her h., 11.10
pray to God with her h. uncovered? 11.13
you," nor again the h. to the feet, 12.21
made him the h. over all things Eph 1.22
him who is the h., into Christ, 4.15
husband is the h. of the wife as 5.23
as Christ is the h. of the church, 5.23
He is the h. of the body, the church; Col 1.18
who is the h. of all rule and 2.10
and not holding fast to the H., 2.19
worship over the h. of his staff. Heb 11.21
has become the h. of the corner, 1Pe 2.07
his h. and his hair were white as Rev 1.14
cloud, with a rainbow over his h., 10.01
and on her h. a crown of twelve 12.01
man, with a golden crown on his h., 14.14
and on his h. are many diadems; 19.12

HEADBANDS
the h., and the crescents; Is 3.18

HEADDRESSES
the h., the armlets, the sashes, the Is 3.20

HEADLONG
flees from its power in h. flight. Job 27.22
though he fall, he shall not be cast h., Ps 37.24
a horse plunging h. into battle. Jer 8.06
that they might throw him down h. Lk 4.29
and falling h. he burst open in the Ac 1.18

HEADS
bowed their h. and made obeisance. Gen 43.28
they bowed their h. and worshiped. Ex 4.31
These are the h. of their fathers' 6.14
These are the h. of the fathers' 6.25
bowed their h. and worshiped. 12.27
and made them h. over the people, 18.25
let the hair of your h. hang loose, Lev 10.06
not make tonsures upon their h., 21.05
the h. of the clans of Israel. Num 1.16
h. of their fathers' houses, the 7.02
hands upon the h. of the bulls; 8.12
the h. of the tribes of Israel, 10.04
men who were h. of the people of 13.03
Moses said to the h. of the tribes 30.01
priest and the h. of the fathers' 31.26
and to the h. of the fathers' 32.28
The h. of the fathers' houses of 36.01
and before the leaders, the h. of 36.01
and I will appoint them as your h.' Deu 1.13
So I took the h. of your tribes, 1.15
men, and set them as h. over you, 1.15
all the h. of your tribes, and your 5.23
the h. of your tribes, your elders, 29.10
the long-haired h. of the enemy." 32.42
when the h. of the people were 33.05
he came to the h. of the people, 33.21
and they put dust upon their h. Jos 7.06
and the h. of the fathers' houses 14.01
of Nun and the h. of the fathers' 19.51
Then the h. of the fathers' houses 21.01
Nun and to the h. of the fathers' 21.01
answer to the h. of the families 22.21
the h. of the families of Israel 22.30
all Israel, their elders and h., 23.02
the h., the judges, and the officers 24.01
brought the h. of Oreb and Zeeb to Ju 7.25
they lifted up their h. no more. 8.28
of Shechem fall back upon their h., 9.57
not be with the h. of the men here? 1Sa 29.04
who were with him covered their h., 2Sa 15.30
and all the h. of the tribes, 1Ki 8.01
on our loins and ropes upon our h., 20.31
loins, and put ropes on their h., 20.32
take the h. of your master's sons, 2Ki 10.06
and put their h. in baskets, and 10.07
brought the h. of the king's sons," 10.08
These were the h. of their fathers' 1Ch 5.24
mighty warriors, famous men, h. of 5.24
h. of their fathers' houses, namely 7.02
h. of fathers' houses, mighty 7.07
as h. of their fathers' houses, 7.09
according to the h. of their 7.11
h. of fathers' houses, approved, 7.40
Ehud (they were h. of fathers' 8.06
were his sons, h. of fathers' houses. 8.10
Shema (they were h. of fathers' 8.13
These were the h. of fathers' 8.28
All these were h. of fathers' 9.09
h. of their fathers' houses, one 9.13
the h. of fathers' houses of the 9.33
These were h. of fathers' houses of 9.34
"At peril to our h. he will desert 12.19
You are the h. of the fathers' 15.12
These were the h. of the fathers' 23.09
the h. of fathers' houses as they 23.24
under sixteen h. of fathers' 24.04
and the h. of the fathers' houses 24.06
and the h. of fathers' houses of 24.31
the h. of the fathers' houses 26.21
and the h. of the fathers' houses, 26.26
h. of fathers' houses, to have the 26.32
the h. of fathers' houses, the 27.01
Then the h. of fathers' houses made 29.06
their fathers, and bowed their h., 29.20
in all Israel, the h. of fathers' houses. 2Ch 1.02
and all the h. of the tribes, 5.02
and priests and h. of families of 19.08
and the h. of fathers' houses of 23.02
number of the h. of fathers' 26.12
Then rose up the h. of the fathers' Ez 1.05
Some of the h. of families, when 2.68
and Levites and h. of fathers' 3.12
Zerubbabel and the h. of fathers' 4.02
the rest of the h. of fathers' 4.03
These are the h. of their fathers' 8.01
Levites and the h. of fathers' 8.29
have risen higher than our h., 9.06
h. of fathers' houses, according to 10.16
back their taunt upon their own h., Neh 4.04
Now some of the h. of fathers' 7.70
And some of the h. of fathers' 7.71
bowed their h. and worshiped the 8.06
second day the h. of fathers' 8.13
and with earth upon their h. 9.01
h. of fathers' houses, two hundred 11.13
h. of fathers' houses: of Seraiah, 12.12
recorded the h. of fathers' houses; 12.22
h. of fathers' houses, were written 12.23
dust upon their h. toward heaven. Job 2.12
are cut off like the h. of grain. 24.24
mouths at me, they wag their h.; Ps 22.07
Lift up your h., O gates! and be lifted 24.07

HEADS (cont.)
Lift up your h., O gates! and be lifted Ps 24.09
all who see them will wag their h. 64.08
thou didst let men ride over our h.; 66.12
will shatter the h. of his enemies, 68.21
didst break the h. of the dragons 74.13
Thou didst crush the h. of Leviathan, 74.14
who hate thee have raised their h. 83.02
they see me, they wag their h. 109.25
with a scab the h. of the daughters Is 3.17
and covered your h., the seers. 29.10
with everlasting joy upon their h.; 35.10
everlasting joy shall be upon their h.; 51.11
and confounded and cover their h. Jer 14.03
are ashamed, they cover their h. 14.04
dust on their h. and put on Lam 2.10
have bowed their h. to the ground. 2.10
and wag their h. at the daughter 2.15
Over the h. of the living creatures Eze 1.22
crystal, spread out above their h. 1.22
above the firmament over their h.; 1.25
over their h. there was the 1.26
and baldness on all their h. 7.18
requite their deeds upon their h." 9.10
was over the h. of the cherubim 10.01
their deeds upon their own h., 11.21
veils for the h. of persons of 13.18
way have I requited upon their h., 22.31
with flowing turbans on their h., 23.15
and beautiful crowns upon their h. 23.42
be on your h. and your shoes on 24.23
dust on their h. and wallow in 27.30
swords were laid under their h., 32.27
have linen turbans upon their h., 44.18
not shave their h. or let their 44.20
only trim the hair of their h. 44.20
hair of their h. was not singed, Dan 3.27
and the beast had four h.; and dominion 7.06
The standing grain has no h., it shall Hos 8.07
them on the h. of all the people; Amo 9.01
you h. of Jacob and rulers of the Mic 3.01
Hear this, you h. of the house of 3.09
Its h. give judgment for a bribe, 3.11
derided him, wagging their h. Mt 27.39
wagging their h., and saying, "Aha! Mk 15.29
place, look up and raise your h., Lk 21.28
them, "Your blood be upon your h.! Ac 18.06
so that they may shave their h. 21.24
with golden crowns upon their h. Rev 4.04
on their h. were what looked like 9.07
and the h. of the horses were like 9.17
of the horses were like lions' h., 9.17
with h., and by means of them they 9.19
with seven h. and ten horns, and 12.03
and seven diadems upon his h. 12.03
sea, with ten horns and seven h., 13.01
and a blasphemous name upon its h. 13.01
One of its h. seemed to have a 13.03
and it had seven h. and ten horns. 17.03
with seven h. and ten horns that 17.07
the seven h. are seven hills on 17.09
And they threw dust on their h., 18.19

HEAL
"H. her, O God, I beseech thee." Num 12.13
I wound and I h.; and there is none Deu 32.39
behold, I will h. you; on the third 2Ki 20.05
the sign that the LORD will h. me, 20.08
forgive their sin and h. their land. 2Ch 7.14
he binds up; he smites, but his hands h. Job 5.18
O LORD, h. me, for my bones are Ps 6.02
h. me, for I have sinned against 41.04
a time to kill, and a time to h.; Ec 3.03
their supplications and h. them. Is 19.22
seen his ways, but I will h. him; 57.18
says the LORD; and I will h. him. 57.19
I will h. your faithlessness." Jer 3.22
H. me, O LORD, and I shall be healed; 17.14
to you, and your wounds I will h., 30.17
and I will h. them and reveal to 33.06
to h. it by binding it with a Eze 30.21
able to cure you or h. your wound. Hos 5.13
for he has torn, that he may h. us; 6.01
when I would h. Israel, the corruption 7.01
I will h. their faithlessness; 14.04
or h. the maimed, or nourish the Zec 11.16
to him, "I will come and h. him." Mt 8.07
and to h. every disease and every 10.01
H. the sick, raise the dead, cleanse 10.08
"Is it lawful to h. on the sabbath?" 12.10
heart, and turn for me to h. them.' 13.15
disciples, and they could not h. him." 17.16
he would h. him on the sabbath, so Mk 3.02
proverb, 'Physician, h. yourself; Lk 4.23
of the Lord was with him to h. 5.17
whether he would h. on the sabbath, 6.07
him to come and h. his slave. 7.03
the kingdom of God and to h. 9.02
h. the sick in it and say to them, 10.09
"Is it lawful to h. on the sabbath, 14.03
him to come down and h. his son, Jn 4.47
heart, and turn for me to h. them." 12.40
thou stretchest out thy hand to h., Ac 4.30
heart, and turn for me to h. them.' 28.27

HEALED
and God h. Abimelech, and also Gen 20.17
and also h. his wife and female 20.17
and shall have him thoroughly h. Ex 21.19
of one's body a boil that has h., Lev 13.18
in it, the itch is h., he is clean; 13.37
leprous disease is h. in the leper, 14.03
house clean, for the disease is h. 14.48
itch, of which you cannot be h. Deu 28.27
boils of which you cannot be h., 28.35
in the camp till they were h. Jos 5.08
Then you will be h., and it will be 1Sa 6.03
returned to be h. in Jezreel of 2Ki 8.29
returned to be h. in Jezreel of 9.15
returned to be h. in Jezreel of 2Ch 22.06
heard Hezekiah, and h. the people, 30.20
thee for help, and thou hast h. me. Ps 30.02
and h. them, and delivered them from 107.20
their hearts, and turn and be h." Is 6.10
and with his stripes we are h. 53.05
They have h. the wound of my people Jer 6.14
They have h. the wound of my people 8.11
wound incurable, refusing to be h.? 15.18
Heal me, O LORD, and I shall be h.; 17.14
for her pain; perhaps she may be h. 51.08
We would have h. Babylon, but she was not h. 51.09
strengthened, the sick you have not h., Eze 34.04
they did not know that I h. them. Hos 11.03
and paralytics, and he h. them. Mt 4.24
word, and my servant will be h. 8.08
the servant was h. at that very 8.13
with a word, and h. all who were sick. 8.16
followed him, and he h. them all, 12.15
and he h. him, so that the dumb man 12.22
compassion on them, and h. their sick. 14.14
And her daughter was h. instantly. 15.28
them at his feet, and he h. them, 15.30
followed him, and he h. them there. 19.02
him in the temple, and he h. them. 21.14
And he h. many who were sick with Mk 1.34
for he had h. many, so that all who 3.10
that she was h. of her disease. 5.29
in peace, and be h. of your disease." 5.34
upon a few sick people and h. them. 6.05
many that were sick and h. them. 6.13
on every one of them and h. them. Lk 4.40
hear and to be h. of their infirmities. 5.15
him and to be h. of their diseases; 6.17
forth from him and h. them all. 6.19
the word, and let my servant be h. 7.07
who had been h. of evil spirits 8.02

HEALED (cont.)
been possessed with demons was h. Lk 8.36
and could not be h. by any one, 8.43
how she had been immediately h. 8.47
and h. the boy, and gave him back to 9.42
Jesus had h. on the sabbath, said to the 13.14
come on those days and be h., and not on 13.14
Then he took him and h. him, and let him 14.04
them, when he saw that he was h., 17.15
And he touched his ear and h. him. 22.51
troubling of the water was h. of Jn* 5.04
said to him, "Do you want to be h.?" 5.06
And at once the man was h., and he took 5.09
"The man who h. me said to me, 'Take 5.11
who had been h. did not know who 5.13
that it was Jesus who had h. him. 5.15
what means this man has been h., Ac 4.09
that had been h. standing beside 4.14
spirits, and they were all h. 5.16
who were paralyzed or lame were h. 8.07
putting his hands on him h. him. 28.08
put out of joint but rather be h. Heb 12.13
one another, that you may be h. Jas 5.16
By his wounds you have been h. 1Pe 2.24
wound, but its mortal wound was h., Rev 13.03
beast, whose mortal wound was h. 13.12

HEALER
Egyptians; for I am the LORD, your h." Ex 15.26
out, saying: "I will not be a h.; Is 3.07

HEALERS
then h., helpers, administrators, 1Co 12.28

HEALEST
illness thou h. all his infirmities. Ps 41.03

HEALING
It will be h. to your flesh and Pro 3.08
finds them, and h. to all his flesh. 4.22
moment he will be broken beyond h. 6.15
the tongue of the wise brings h. 12.18
but a faithful envoy brings h. 13.17
will suddenly be broken beyond h. 29.01
smiting and h., and they will Is 19.22
and your h. shall spring up speedily 58.08
for a time of h., but behold, terror Jer 8.15
My grief is beyond h., my heart 8.18
us so that there is no h. for us? 14.19
for a time of h., but behold, terror 14.19
for your wound, no h. for you. 30.13
Behold, I will bring to it health and h., 33.06
many medicines; there is no h. for you. 46.11
for food, and their leaves for h." Eze 47.12
shall rise, with h. in its wings. Mal 4.02
the kingdom and h. every disease Mt 4.23
and h. every disease and every 9.35
the gospel and h. everywhere. Lk 9.06
and cured those who had need of h. 9.11
this sign of h. was performed was Ac 4.22
doing good and h. all that were 10.38
gifts of h. by the one Spirit, 1Co 12.09
Do all possess gifts of h.? 12.30
were for the h. of the nations. Rev 22.02

HEALS
iniquity, who h. all your diseases, Ps 103.03
He h. the brokenhearted, and binds 147.03
and h. the wounds inflicted by his Is 30.26
him, "Aeneas, Jesus Christ h. you; Ac 9.34

HEALTH
there is no h. in my bones because Ps 38.03
to the soul and h. to the body. Pro 16.24
restore me to h. and make me live! Is 38.16
then has the h. of the daughter of Jer 8.22
For I will restore h. to you, 30.17
Behold, I will bring to it h. and healing, 33.06

this perfect h. in the presence of Ac 3.16
with you and that you may be in h.; 3Jn 1.02

HEAP
they took stones, and made a h.; Gen 31.46
and they ate there by the h. 31.46
"This h. is a witness between you 31.48
"See this h. and the pillar, which I 31.51
This h. is a witness, and the pillar 31.52
will not pass over this h. to you, 31.52
pass over this h. and this pillar 31.52
up, the floods stood up in a h.; Ex 15.08
it shall be a h. for ever, it shall Deu 13.16
"'And I will h. evils upon them; 32.23
from above shall stand in one h." Jos 3.13
stood and rose up in a h. far off, 3.16
him a great h. of stones that 7.26
and made it for ever a h. of ruins, 8.28
over it a great h. of stones, 8.29
down at the end of the h. of grain. Ru 3.07
he lifts the needy from the ash h., 1Sa 2.08
and remain beside yonder stone h. 20.19
the stone h. and fell on his face 20.41
over him a very great h. of stones; 2Sa 18.17
house will become a h. of ruins; 1Ki 9.08
Though he h. up silver like dust, Job 27.16
not one in a h. of ruins stretch 30.24
made the waters stand like a h. Ps 78.13
lifts the needy from the ash h., 113.07
for you will h. coals of fire on Pro 25.22
Your belly is a h. of wheat, Sol 7.02
and this h. of ruins shall be under Is 3.06
and will become a h. of ruins. 17.01
For thou hast made the city a h., 25.02
I will make Jerusalem a h. of ruins, Jer 9.11
Jerusalem shall become a h. of ruins, 26.18
Babylon shall become a h. of ruins, 51.37
H. on the logs, kindle the fire, boil Eze 24.10
make Samaria a h. in the open Mic 1.06
Jerusalem shall become a h. of ruins, 3.12
for they h. up earth and take it. Hab 1.10
When one came to a h. of twenty Hag 2.16
praying do not h. up empty phrases Mt 6.07
doing you will h. burning coals Rom 12.20

HEAPED
and h. up silver like dust, and gold Zec 9.03
for her sins are h. high as heaven, Rev 18.05

HEAPING
gives the work of gathering and h., Ecc 2.26
H. oppression upon oppression, and Jer 9.06

HEAPS
And they gathered them together in h., Ex 8.14
h. upon h., with the jawbone of Ju 15.16
"Lay them in two h. at the entrance 2Ki 10.08
fortified cities into h. of ruins, 19.25
their God, and laid them in h. 2Ch 31.06
month they began to pile up the h., 31.07
the princes came and saw the h., 31.08
and the Levites about the h. 31.09
stones out of the h. of rubbish, Neh 4.02
and bringing in h. of grain and 13.15
destined to become h. of ruins; Job 15.28
man h. up, and knows not who will Ps 39.06
cities crash into h. of ruins, Is 37.26
pile her up like h. of grain, Jer 50.26
brought up in purple lie on ash h. Lam 4.05
be like stone h. on the furrows of Hos 12.11
h. of corpses, dead bodies without Nah 3.03
"Woe to him who h. up what is not Hab 2.06

HEAR
"Adah and Zillah, h. my voice; Gen 4.23
"H. us, my lord; you are a mighty 23.06
h. me, and entreat for me Ephron the 23.08
"No, my lord, h. me; I gave you the 23.11

HEAR (cont.)

the land, "But if you will, h. me; Gen 23.13
"H. this dream which I have dreamed: 37.06
that when you h. a dream you can 41.15
Assemble and h., O sons of Jacob, 49.02
the people may h. when I speak Ex 19.09
"You speak to us, and we will h.; 20.19
to me, I will surely h. their cry; 22.23
I will h., for I am compassionate. 22.27
but the sound of singing that I h." 32.18
that I may h. what the LORD will Num 9.08
And he said, "H. my words: If there 12.06
"Then the Egyptians will h. of it, 14.13
said to Korah, "H. now, you sons of Levi: 16.08
"H. now, you rebels; shall we bring 20.10
and said, "Rise, Balak, and h.; 23.18
that her husband comes to h. of it, 30.08
'H. the cases between your brethren, Deu 1.16
you shall h. the small and the 1.17
bring to me, and I will h. it.' 1.17
who shall h. the report of you and 2.25
when they h. all these statutes, 4.06
that I may let them h. my words, 4.10
nor h., nor eat, nor smell. 4.28
Did any people ever h. the voice of 4.33
Out of heaven he let you h. his voice, 4.36
"H., O Israel, the statutes and the 5.01
if we h. the voice of the LORD our 5.25
Go near, and h. all that the LORD 5.27
and we will h. and do it.' 5.27
H. therefore, O Israel, and be 6.03
"H., O Israel: The LORD our God is 6.04
"H., O Israel; you are to pass 9.01
And all Israel shall h., and fear, and 13.11
"If you h. in one of your cities, 13.12
and it is told you and you h. of it; 17.04
And all the people shall h., 17.13
'Let me not h. again the voice of 18.16
And the rest shall h., and fear, and 19.20
'H., O Israel, you draw near this 20.03
and all Israel shall h., and fear. 21.21
to all Israel, "Keep silence and h., 27.09
or eyes to see, or ears to h. 29.04
to us, that we may h. it and do it?' 30.12
to us, that we may h. it and do it?' 30.13
turns away, and you will not h., 30.17
that they may h. and learn to fear 31.12
may h. and learn to fear the LORD 31.13
let the earth h. the words of my 32.01
"H., O LORD, the voice of Judah, and 33.07
and h. the words of the LORD your Jos 3.09
as soon as you h. the sound of the 6.05
inhabitants of the land will h. of it, 7.09
"H., O kings; give ear, O princes; Ju 5.03
to h. the piping for the flocks? 5.16
and you shall h. what they say, and 7.11
"Put your riddle, that we may h. it." 14.13
For I h. of your evil dealings from 1Sa 2.23
report that I h. the people of the 2.24
land, saying, "Let the Hebrews h." 13.03
the lowing of the oxen which I h.?" 15.14
"H. now, you Benjaminites; will the son 22.07
"H. now, son of Ahitub." And he answered, 22.12
I h. that you have shearers; 25.07
and h. the words of your handmaid. 25.24
lord the king h. the words of his 26.19
And when you h. the sound of marching 2Sa 5.24
For the king will h., and deliver his 14.16
man deputed by the king to h. you." 15.03
"As soon as you h. the sound of the 15.10
So whatever you h. from the king's 15.35
shall send to me everything you h." 15.36
all Israel will h. that you have 16.21
and let us h. what he has to say." 17.05
woman called from the city, "H.! H.! 20.16
all peoples to h. the wisdom of 1Ki 4.34
yea, h. thou in heaven thy dwelling 8.30
then h. thou in heaven, and act, and 8.32
then h. thou in heaven, and forgive 8.34
then h. thou in heaven, and forgive 8.36
then h. thou in heaven thy dwelling 8.39
(for they shall h. of thy great 8.42
h. thou in heaven thy dwelling 8.43
then h. thou in heaven their prayer 8.45
then h. thou in heaven thy dwelling 8.49
before you and h. your wisdom! 10.08
of Solomon to h. his wisdom, 10.24
"Therefore h. the word of the LORD: 22.19
And he said, "H., all you peoples!" 22.28
"H. the word of the LORD: thus says 2Ki 7.01
of the Syrians h. the sound of 7.06
"H. the word of the great king, the 18.28
that he shall h. a rumor and 19.07
Incline thy ear, O LORD, and h.; 19.16
and h. the words of Sennacherib, 19.16
Hezekiah, "H. the word of the LORD: 20.16
And when you h. the sound of 1Ch 14.15
"H. me, my brethren and my people. 28.02
yea, h. thou from heaven thy 2Ch 6.21
then h. thou from heaven, and act, 6.23
then h. thou from heaven, and 6.25
then h. thou in heaven, and forgive 6.27
then h. thou from heaven thy 6.30
h. thou from heaven thy dwelling 6.33
then h. thou from heaven their 6.35
then h. thou from heaven thy 6.39
then I will h. from heaven, and will 7.14
before you and h. your wisdom! 9.07
of Solomon to h. his wisdom, 9.23
"H. me, O Jeroboam and all Israel! 13.04
"H. me, Asa, and all Judah and 15.02
"Therefore h. the word of the LORD: 18.18
And he said, "H., all you peoples!" 18.27
affliction, and thou wilt h. and save.' 20.09
"H. me, Judah and inhabitants of 20.20
Now h. me, and send back the captives 28.11
and said to them, "H. me, Levites! 29.05
to h. the prayer of thy servant Neh 1.06
H., O our God, for we are despised; 4.04
place where you h. the sound of 4.20
all who could h. with understanding, 8.02
in Egypt and h. their cry at the 9.09
and thou didst h. them from heaven; 9.27
to thee thou didst h. from heaven, 9.28
they h. not the voice of the Job 3.18
H., and know it for your good." 5.27
H. now my reasoning, and listen to 13.06
"I will show you, h. me; and what I have seen 15.17
I h. censure which insults me, and 20.03
prayer to him, and he will h. you; 22.27
small a whisper do we h. of him! 26.14
Will God h. his cry, when trouble 27.09
Oh, that I had one to h. me! 31.35
"But now, h. my speech, O Job, and 33.01
"H. my words, you wise men, and give 34.02
"Therefore, h. me, you men of understanding, 34.10
"If you have understanding, h. this; 34.16
Surely God does not h. an empty cry, 35.13
"H. this, O Job; stop and consider 37.14
'H., and I will speak; I will question 42.04
gracious to me, and h. my prayer. Ps 4.01
the morning thou dost h. my voice; 5.03
thou wilt h. the desire of the meek; 10.17
H. a just cause, O LORD; attend to my 17.01
incline thy ear to me, h. my words. 17.06
H., O LORD, when I cry aloud, be 27.07
H. the voice of my supplication, as 28.02
H., O LORD, and be gracious to me! 30.10
Yea, I h. the whispering of many— 31.13
But thou didst h. my supplications, 31.22
let the afflicted h. and be glad. 34.02
I do not h., like a dumb man who 38.13
Yea, I am like a man who does not h., 38.14
"H. my prayer, O LORD, and give ear 39.12

HEAR (cont.)

H., O daughter, consider, and incline Ps 45.10
H. this, all peoples! Give ear, all 49.01
"H., O my people, and I will speak, O 50.07
H. my prayer, O God; give ear to the words 54.02
and moan, and he will h. my voice. 55.17
it does not h. the voice of charmers 58.05
for "Who," they think, "will h. us?" 59.07
H. my cry, O God. listen to my prayer; 61.01
H. my voice, O God, in my complaint; 64.01
Come and h., all you who fear God, 66.16
aloud to God, that he may h. me. 77.01
I h. a voice I had not known: 81.05
H., O my people, while I admonish 81.08
O LORD God of hosts, h. my prayer; 84.08
Let me h. what God the LORD will 85.08
planted the ear, does he not h.? 94.09
H. my prayer, O LORD; let my cry come 102.01
to h. the groans of the prisoners, 102.20
They have ears, but do not h.; 115.06
H. my voice in thy steadfast love; 119.149
Lord, h. my voice! Let thy ears be 130.02
but they h. not, nor is there any 135.17
H. my prayer, O LORD; give ear to my 143.01
Let me h. in the morning of thy 143.08
man also may h. and increase in Pro 1.05
H., my son, your father's instruction, 1.08
H., O sons, a father's instruction, 4.01
H., my son, and accept my words, that 4.10
H., for I will speak noble things, 8.06
H. instruction and be wise, and do 8.33
to h. instruction only to stray 19.27
and h. the words of the wise, and 22.17
H., my son, and be wise, and direct 23.19
for a man to h. the rebuke of the Ecc 7.05
wise than to h. the song of fools. 7.05
lest you h. your servant cursing 7.21
let me h. your voice, for your voice Sol 2.14
listening for your voice; let me h. it. 8.13
H., O heavens, and give ear, O earth; Is 1.02
H. the word of the LORD, you rulers 1.10
'H. and h., but do not understand; 6.09
and h. with their ears, and understand 6.10
And he said, "H. then, O house of 7.13
see, or decide by what his ears h.; 11.03
When a trumpet is blown, h.! 18.03
am bowed down so that I cannot h., 21.03
of the earth we h. songs of praise, 24.16
is repose"; yet they would not h. 28.12
Therefore h. the word of the LORD, 28.14
Give ear, and h. my voice; 28.23
hearken, and h. my speech. 28.23
the deaf shall h. the words of a 29.18
who will not h. the instruction of 30.09
let us h. no more of the Holy One 30.11
And your ears shall h. a word 30.21
ears of those who h. will hearken. 32.03
women who are at ease, h. my voice; 32.09
H., you who are far off, what I have 33.13
to h., and hearken, O peoples! 34.01
"H. the words of the great king, the 36.13
him, so that he shall h. a rumor, 37.07
Incline thy ear, O LORD, and h.; 37.17
and h. all the words of Sennacherib, 37.17
"H. the word of the LORD of hosts: 39.05
H., you deaf; and look, you blind, 42.18
ears are open, but he does not h. 42.20
and let them h. and say, It is true. 43.09
"But now h., O Jacob my servant, 44.01
Now therefore h. this, you lover of 47.08
H. this, O house of Jacob, who are 48.01
forth I make you h. new things, 48.06
"Assemble, all of you, and h.! 48.14
h. this: from the beginning I have 48.16
my ear to h. as those who are 50.04
Therefore h. this, you who are 51.21
h., that your soul may live; 55.03
or his ear dull, that it cannot h.; 59.01
from you so that he does not h. 59.02
they are yet speaking I will h. 65.24
H. the word of the LORD, you who 66.05
H. the word of the LORD, O house of Jer 2.04
for I h. the sound of the trumpet, 4.19
and h. the sound of the trumpet? 4.21
"H. this, O foolish and senseless 5.21
see not, who have ears, but h. not. 5.21
and give warning, that they may h.? 6.10
Therefore h., O nations, and know, O 6.18
H., O earth; behold, I am bringing 6.19
H. the word of the LORD, all you men 7.02
with me, for I do not h. you. 7.16
H., O women, the word of the LORD, 9.20
H. the word which the LORD speaks 10.01
"H. the words of this covenant, and 11.02
H. the words of this covenant and 11.06
forefathers, who refused to h. my words; 11.10
who refuse to h. my words, who 13.10
H. and give ear; be not proud, 13.15
I will not h. their cry, and though 14.12
and say: 'H. the word of the LORD, 17.20
they might not h. and receive 17.23
there I will let you h. my words." 18.02
'H. the word of the LORD, O kings of 19.03
neck, refusing to h. my words." 19.15
For I h. many whispering. Terror is on 20.10
let him h. a cry in the morning and 20.16
of Judah say, 'H. the word of the LORD, 21.11
and say, 'H. the word of the LORD, O 22.02
land, land, h. the word of the LORD! 22.29
to perceive and to h. his word, 23.18
nor inclined your ears to h., 25.04
Yet h. now this word which I speak 28.07
and pray to me, and I will h. you. 29.12
H. the word of the LORD, all you 29.20
"H. the word of the LORD, O nations, 31.10
earth who shall h. of all the good 33.09
Yet h. the word of the LORD, O 34.04
of Judah will h. all the evil 36.03
against them, but they would not h.'" 36.31
Now h., I pray you, O my lord the 37.20
If the princes h. that I have 38.25
or h. the sound of the trumpet, or 42.14
then h. the word of the LORD, O 42.15
"H. the word of the LORD, all you of 44.24
Therefore h. the word of the LORD, 44.26
Therefore h. the plan which the 49.20
Therefore h. the plan which the 50.45
but h., all you peoples, and behold Lam 1.18
"H. how I groan; there is none to 1.21
thou didst h. my plea, 'Do not close 3.56
And whether they h. or refuse to Eze 2.05
or refuse to h. (for they are a 2.05
whether they h. or refuse to h.; 2.07
h. what I say to you; 2.08
your heart, and h. with your ears. 3.10
whether they h. or refuse to h." 3.11
whenever you h. a word from my 3.17
he that will h., let him h.; 3.27
and he that will refuse to h., 3.27
h. the word of the Lord GOD! 6.03
a loud voice, I will not h. them." 8.18
who have ears to h., but h. not; 12.02
own minds: 'H. the word of the LORD!' 13.02
O harlot, h. the word of the LORD: 16.35
H. now, O house of Israel: Is my 18.25
H. the word of the LORD: Thus says 20.47
H. the word of the Lord GOD: Thus 25.03
whenever you h. a word from my 33.07
and h. what the word is that comes 33.30
and they h. what you say but they 33.31
for they h. what you say, but they 33.32
you shepherds, h. the word of the LORD: 34.07
you shepherds, h. the word of the LORD: 34.09
of Israel, h. the word of the LORD. 36.01

HEAR (cont.)

h. the word of the Lord GOD: Thus Eze 36.04
not let you h. any more the 36.15
O dry bones, h. the word of the LORD. 37.04
and h. with your ears, and set your 40.04
and h. with your ears all that I 44.05
that when you h. the sound of the Dan 3.05
ready when you h. the sound of the 3.15
which do not see or h. or know, 5.23
O my God, incline thy ear and h.; 9.18
O LORD, h.; O LORD, forgive; 9.19
H. the word of the LORD, O people of Hos 4.01
H. this, O priests! Give heed, O house 5.01
H. this, you aged men, give ear, all Joe 1.02
H. this word that the LORD has Amo 3.01
"H., and testify against the house 3.13
"H. this word, you cows of Bashan, 4.01
H. this word which I take up over 5.01
"Now therefore h. the word of the 7.16
H. this, you who trample upon the 8.04
cried, and thou didst h. my voice. Jon 2.02
H., you peoples, all of you; Mic 1.02
And I said: H., you heads of Jacob 3.01
H. this, you heads of the house of 3.09
H. what the LORD says: Arise, plead 6.01
and let the hills h. your voice. 6.01
H., you mountains, the controversy 6.02
"H., O tribe and assembly of the 6.09
of my salvation; my God will h. me. 7.07
All who h. the news of you clap Nah 3.19
cry for help, and thou wilt not h.? Hab 1.02
I h., and my body trembles, my lips 3.16
But they did not h. or heed me, Zec 1.04
H. now, O Joshua the high priest, you 3.08
their ears that they might not h. 7.11
they should h. the law and the 7.12
"As I called, and they would not h., 7.13
so they called, and I would not h., 7.13
and what you h. whispered, proclaim Mt 10.27
and tell John what you h. and see: 11.04
are cleansed and the deaf h., 11.05
He who has ears to h., let him h. 11.15
will any one h. his voice in the 12.19
of the earth to h. the wisdom of 12.42
He who has ears, let him h." 13.09
see, and hearing they do not h., 13.13
shall indeed h. but never understand, 13.14
and h. with their ears, and understand 13.15
see, and your ears, for they h. 13.16
to h. what you h., and did not h. it. 13.17
"H. then the parable of the sower. 13.18
Father. He who has ears, let him h. 13.43
and said to them, "H. and understand: 15.10
"Do you h. what these are saying?" 21.16
"H. another parable. There was a 21.33
And you will h. of wars and rumors 24.06
"Do you not h. how many things they 27.13
"He who has ears to h., let him h." Mk 4.09
and may indeed h. but not understand; 4.12
when they h., Satan immediately 4.15
when they h. the word, immediately 4.16
they are those who h. the word, 4.18
the ones who h. the word and 4.20
any man has ears to h., let him h." 4.23
to them, "Take heed what you h.; 4.24
them, as they were able to h. it; 4.33
you and they refuse to h. you, 6.11
"H. me, all of you, and understand: 7.14
man has ears to h., let him h. *7.16
makes the deaf h. and the dumb 7.37
see, and having ears do you not h.? 8.18
'H., O Israel: The Lord our God, the 12.29
And when you h. of wars and rumors 13.07
upon him to h. the word of God, he Lk 5.01
gathered to h. and to be healed of 5.15
who came to h. him and to be healed 6.17
"But I say to you that h., Love your 6.27
and the deaf h., the dead are 7.22
"He who has ears to h., let him h." 8.08
when they h. the word, receive it 8.13
the thorns, they are those who h., 8.14
Take heed then how you h.; 8.18
are those who h. the word of God 8.21
this about whom I h. such things?" 9.09
and to h. what you h., and did not h. it." 10.24
are those who h. the word of God 11.28
of the earth to h. the wisdom of 11.31
He who has ears to h., let him h." 14.35
were all drawing near to h. him. 15.01
'What is this that I h. about you? 16.02
and the prophets; let them h. them.' 16.29
'If they do not h. Moses and the 16.31
"H. what the unrighteous judge says 18.06
And when you h. of wars and tumults, 21.09
to him in the temple to h. him. 21.38
and you h. the sound of it, but you Jn 3.08
the dead will h. the voice of the 5.25
of God, and those who h. will live. 5.25
are in the tombs will h. his voice 5.28
as I h., I judge; and my judgment 5.30
you cannot bear to h. my word. 8.43
why you do not h. them is that you 8.47
Why do you want to h. it again? 9.27
the sheep h. his voice, and he calls 10.03
My sheep h. my voice, and I know 10.27
word which you h. is not mine but 14.24
And how is it that we h., Ac 2.08
we h. them telling in our own 2.11
h. these words: Jesus of Nazareth, a 2.22
out this which you see and h. 2.33
said: "Brethren and fathers, h. me. 7.02
and to h. what you have to say." 10.22
to h. all that you have been 10.33
and sought to h. the word of God. 13.07
together to h. the word of God. 13.44
Gentiles should h. the word of the 15.07
"We will h. you again about this." 17.32
And you see and h. that not only at 19.26
will certainly h. that you have 21.22
h. the defense which I now make 22.01
but did not h. the voice of the 22.09
Just One and to h. a voice from 22.14
"I will h. you when your accusers 23.35
in your kindness to h. us briefly. 24.04
"I should like to h. the man myself." 25.22
"Tomorrow," said he, "you shall h. him." 25.22
also all who h. me this day might 26.29
But we desire to h. from you what 28.22
shall indeed h. but never understand, 28.26
and h. with their ears, and understand 28.27
how are they to h. without a preacher? Rom 10.14
see and ears that should not h., 11.08
I h. that there are divisions among 1Co 11.18
under law, do you not h. the law? Gal 4.21
may impart grace to those who h. Eph 4.29
I may h. of you that you stand firm Php 1.27
you saw and now h. to be mine 1.30
For we h. that some of you are 2Th 3.11
that all the Gentiles might h. it 2Ti 4.17
because I h. of your love and of Phm 1.05
"Today, when you h. his voice, Heb 3.07
when you h. his voice do not harden 3.15
when you h. his voice, do not harden 4.07
Let every man be quick to h., Jas 1.19
to h. that my children follow the 3Jn 1.04
and blessed are those who h., Rev 1.03
let him h. what the Spirit says to 2.07
let him h. what the Spirit says to 2.11
let him h. what the Spirit says to 2.17
let him h. what the Spirit says to 2.29
let him h. what the Spirit says to 3.06
let him h. what the Spirit says to 3.13
let him h. what the Spirit says to 3.22
cannot either see or h. or walk; 9.20
If any one has an ear, let him h.: 13.09

HEARD

And they h. the sound of the LORD Gen 3.08
"I h. the sound of thee in the 3.10
When Abram h. that his kinsman had 14.14
As for Ishmael, I have h. you; 17.20
And God h. the voice of the lad; 21.17
for God has h. the voice of the lad 21.17
and I have not h. of it until 21.26
and when he h. the words of Rebekah 24.30
When Abraham's servant h. their words, 24.52
"I h. your father speak to your 27.06
When Esau h. the words of his 27.34
When Laban h. the tidings of Jacob 29.13
the LORD has h. that I am hated, he 29.33
and has also h. my voice and given 30.06
Now Jacob h. that the sons of Laban 31.01
Now Jacob h. that he had defiled 34.05
from the field when they h. of it; 34.07
and Israel h. of it. Now the sons of 35.22
for I h. them say, 'Let us go to 37.17
But when Reuben h. it, he delivered 37.21
and when he h. that I lifted up my 39.15
When his master h. the words which 39.19
and I have h. it said of you that 41.15
I have h. that there is grain in 42.02
for they h. that they should eat 43.25
aloud, so that the Egyptians h. it, 45.02
and the household of Pharaoh h. it. 45.02
When the report was h. in Pharaoh's 45.16
When Pharaoh h. of it, he sought to Ex 2.15
And God h. their groaning, and God 2.24
and have h. their cry because of 3.07
and when they h. that the LORD had 4.31
Moreover I have h. the groaning of 6.05
The peoples have h., they tremble; 15.14
because he has h. your murmurings 16.07
the LORD has h. your murmurings 16.08
for he has h. your murmurings.'" 16.09
"I have h. the murmurings of the 16.12
h. of all that God had done for 18.01
nor let such be h. out of your 23.13
sound shall be h. when he goes 28.35
When Joshua h. the noise of the 32.17
When the people h. these evil 33.04
And when Moses h. that, he was Lev 10.20
and let all who h. him lay their 24.14
he h. the voice speaking to him Num 7.89
and when the LORD h. it, his anger was 11.01
Moses h. the people weeping throughout 11.10
through us also?" And the LORD h. it. 12.02
They have h. that thou, O LORD, art 14.14
who have h. thy fame will say, 14.15
I have h. the murmurings of the 14.27
When Moses h. it, he fell on his 16.04
he h. our voice, and sent an angel 20.16
h. that Israel was coming by the 21.01
When Balak h. that Balaam had come. 22.36
and her husband h. of it, and said 30.11
her on the day that he h. of them. 30.14
and void after he has h. of them, 30.15
h. of the coming of the people of 33.40
"And the LORD h. your words, and was Deu 1.34
you h. the sound of words, but saw 4.12
ever happened or was ever h. of. 4.32
as you have h., and still live? 4.33
and you h. his words out of the 4.36
And when you h. the voice out of 5.23
and we have h. his voice out of the 5.24
that has h. the voice of the living 5.26
"And the LORD h. your words, when 5.28
'I have h. the words of this people, 5.28
and of whom you have h. it said, 9.02
and the LORD h. our voice, and saw 26.07
For we have h. how the LORD dried Jos 2.10
And as soon as we h. it, our hearts 2.11
h. that the LORD had dried up the 5.01
not shout or let your voice be h., 6.10
as the people h. the sound of the 6.20
and the Jebusites, h. of this, 9.01
of Gibeon h. what Joshua had done 9.03
for we have h. a report of him, and 9.09
they h. that they were their 9.16
of Jerusalem h. how Joshua had 10.01
When Jabin king of Hazor h. of this, 11.01
for you h. on that day how the 14.12
And the people of Israel h. say, 22.11
when the people of Israel h. of it, 22.12
h. the words that the Reubenites 22.30
for it has h. all the words of the 24.27
When Gideon h. the telling of the Ju 7.15
of the city h. the words of Gaal 9.30
of the Tower of Shechem h. of it, 9.46
not let your voice be h. among us, 18.25
Benjaminites h. that the people of 20.03
for she had h. in the country of Ru 1.06
moved, and her voice was not h.; 1Sa 1.13
and he h. all that his sons were 2.22
the Philistines h. the noise of 4.06
When Eli h. the sound of the outcry, 4.14
And when she h. the tidings that 4.19
the Philistines h. that the people 7.07
of Israel h. of it they were 7.07
And when Samuel had h. all the 8.21
upon Saul when he h. these words, 11.06
and the Philistines h. of it. 13.03
And all Israel h. it said that Saul 13.04
of Ephraim h. that the Philistines 14.22
Jonathan had not h. his father 14.27
and all Israel h. these words of 17.11
same words as before. And David h. him. 17.23
eldest brother h. when he spoke to 17.28
words which David spoke were h., 17.31
and all his father's house h. it, 22.01
Now Saul h. that David was discovered, 22.06
has surely h. that Saul seeks to 23.10
come down, as thy servant has h.? 23.11
And when Saul h. that, he pursued 23.25
David h. in the wilderness that 25.04
When David h. that Nabal was dead, 25.39
of Jabeshgilead h. what the 31.11
when David h. of it, he said, "I and 2Sa 3.28
h. that Abner had died at Hebron, 4.01
When the Philistines h. that David 5.17
but David h. of it and went down to 5.17
all that we have h. with our ears. 7.22
king of Hamath h. that David had 8.09
And when David h. of it, he sent 10.07
wife of Uriah h. that Uriah her 11.26
When King David h. of all these 13.21
all the people h. when the king 18.05
for the people h. that day, "The king 19.02
From his temple he h. my voice, 22.07
as soon as they h. of me, they obeyed 22.45
"Have you not h. that Adonijah the 1Ki 1.11
were with him h. it as they 1.41
And when Joab h. the sound of the 1.41
This is the noise that you have h. 1.45
And all Israel h. of the judgment 3.28
earth, who had h. of his wisdom. 4.34
when he h. that they had anointed 5.01
When Hiram h. the words of Solomon, 5.07
"I have h. the message which you 5.08
tool of iron was h. in the temple, 6.07
'I have h. your prayer and your 9.03
queen of Sheba h. of the fame of 10.01
true which I h. in my own land of 10.06
surpass the report which I h. 10.07
But when Hadad h. in Egypt that 11.21
son of Nebat h. of it (for he was 12.02
And when all Israel h. that Jeroboam 12.20
And when the king h. the saying of 13.04
him back from the way h. of it, 13.26
But when Ahijah h. the sound of her 14.06
And when Baasha h. of it, he stopped 15.21
who were encamped h. it said, 16.16

HEARD (cont.)

And when Elijah h. it, he wrapped his 1Ki 19.13
When Benhadad h. this message as he 20.12
we have h. that the kings of the 20.31
As soon as Jezebel h. that Naboth 21.15
And as soon as Ahab h. that Naboth 21.16
And when Ahab h. those words, he 21.27
the Moabites h. that the kings had 2Ki 3.21
the man of God h. that the king of 5.08
When the king h. the words of the 6.30
was no one to be seen or h. there, 7.10
came to Jezreel, Jezebel h. of it; 9.30
When Athaliah h. the noise of the 11.13
When King Hezekiah h. it, he rent 19.01
LORD your God h. all the words of 19.04
which the LORD your God has h.; 19.04
of the words that you have h., 19.06
for he h. that the king had left 19.08
And when the king h. concerning 19.09
you have h. what the kings of 19.11
Sennacherib king of Assyria I have h. 19.20
"Have you not h. that I determined 19.25
I have h. your prayer, I have seen 20.05
for he h. that Hezekiah had been 20.12
And when the king h. the words of 22.11
Regarding the words which you have h., 22.18
when you h. how I spoke against 22.19
I also have h. you, says the LORD. 22.19
and their men h. that the king of 25.23
Jabeshgilead h. all that the 1Ch 10.11
When the Philistines h. that David 14.08
and David h. of it and went out 14.08
all that we have h. with our ears. 17.20
king of Hamath h. that David had 18.09
When David h. of it, he sent Joab 19.08
make themselves h. in unison in 2Ch 5.13
"I have h. your prayer, and have 7.12
queen of Sheba h. of the fame of 9.01
true which I h. in my own land of 9.05
you surpass the report which I h. 9.06
son of Nebat h. of it (for he was 10.02
When Asa h. these words, the prophecy 15.08
And when Baasha h. of it, he stopped 16.05
when they h. that the LORD had 20.29
When Athaliah h. the noise of the 23.12
And the LORD h. Hezekiah, and healed 30.20
the people, and their voice was h., 30.27
entreaty and h. his supplication 33.13
When the king h. the words of the 34.19
the words which you have h., 34.26
God when you h. his words against 34.27
I also have h. you, says the LORD. 34.27
shout, and the sound was h. afar. Ez 3.13
and Benjamin h. that the returned 4.01
When I h. this, I rent my garments 9.03
When I h. these words I sat down Neh 1.04
h. this, it displeased them greatly 2.10
and Geshem the Arab h. of it, 2.19
Now when Sanballat h. that we were 4.01
the Ashdodites h. that the repairing 4.07
When our enemies h. that it was 4.15
angry when I h. their outcry and 5.06
And when all our enemies h. of it, 6.16
wept when they h. the words of the 8.09
joy of Jerusalem was h. afar off 12.43
When the people h. the law, 13.03
Media who have h. of the queen's Est 1.18
three friends h. of all this evil Job 2.11
let no joyful cry be h. in it. 3.07
was silence, then I h. a voice: 4.16
my ear has h. and understood it. 13.01
"I have h. many such things; 16.02
'We have h. a rumor of it with our 28.22
When the ear h., it called me 29.11
and I have h. the sound of your 33.08
and he h. the cry of the afflicted— 34.28
lightnings when his voice is h. 37.04
I had h. of thee by the hearing of 42.05
the LORD has h. the sound of my Ps 6.08
The LORD has h. my supplication; 6.09
From his temple he h. my voice, 18.06
As soon as they h. of me they 18.44
are there words; their voice is not h.; 19.03
but has h., when he cried to him. 22.24
for he has h. the voice of my 28.06
and the LORD h. him and saved him 34.06
he inclined to me and h. my cry. 40.01
We have h. with our ears, O God, our 44.01
As we have h., so have we seen in 48.08
hast h. my vows, thou hast given me 61.05
twice have I h. this: that power 62.11
let the sound of his praise be h., 66.08
things that we have h. and known, 78.03
when the LORD h., he was full of 78.21
When God h., he was full of wrath, 78.59
my ears have h. the doom of my evil 92.11
distress, when he h. their cry. 106.44
because he has h. my voice and my 116.01
Lo, we h. of it in Ephrathah. we 132.06
for they have h. the words of thy 138.04
will himself cry out and not be h. Pro 21.13
of the wise h. in quiet are better Ecc 9.17
end of the matter; all has been h. 12.13
the turtledove is h. in our land. Sol 2.12
And I h. the voice of the Lord Is 6.08
their voice is h. as far as Jahaz; 15.04
We have h. of the pride of Moab, how 16.06
what I have h. from the LORD of 21.10
for I have h. a decree of destruction 28.22
voice to be h. and the descending 30.30
When King Hezekiah h. it, he rent his 37.01
LORD your God h. the words of the 37.04
which the LORD your God has h.; 37.04
of the words that you have h., 37.06
for he had h. that the king had 37.08
Now the king h. concerning Tirhakah 37.09
And when he h. it, he sent messengers 37.09
you have h. what the kings of 37.11
'Have you not h. that I determined 37.26
I have h. your prayer, I have seen 38.05
for he h. that he had been sick and 39.01
Have you not h.? Has it not been 40.21
Have you not h.? The LORD is the 40.28
proclaimed, none who h. your words. 41.26
voice, or make it h. in the street; 42.02
"You have h.; now see all this; 48.06
today you have never h. of them, 48.07
You have never h., you have never 48.08
they have not h. they shall 52.15
Who has believed what we have h.? 53.01
make your voice to be h. on high. 58.04
Violence shall no more be h. in your land, 60.18
old no one has h. or perceived by 64.04
more shall be h. in it the sound 65.19
Who has h. such a thing? Who has seen such 66.08
that have not h. my fame or seen my 66.19
A voice on the bare heights is h., Jer 3.21
For I h. a cry as of a woman in 4.31
and destruction are h. within her; 6.07
We have h. the report of it, our 6.24
of their horses is h. from Dan; 8.16
and the lowing of cattle is not h.; 9.10
a sound of wailing is h. from Zion: 9.19
who has h. the like of this? 18.13
May a cry be h. from their houses, 18.22
h. Jeremiah prophesying these 20.01
I have h. what the prophets have 23.25
all the people h. Jeremiah speaking 26.07
princes of Judah h. these things, 26.10
as you have h. with your own ears." 26.11
city all the words you have h. 26.12
h. his words, the king sought to put 26.21
but when Uriah h. of it, he was afraid 26.21
We have h. a cry of panic, of terror, 30.05
"A voice is h. in Ramah, lamentation 31.15
I have h. Ephraim bemoaning, 'Thou 31.18

HEARD (cont.)
there shall be h. again the voice Jer 33.11
h. all the words of the LORD from 36.11
them all the words that he had h., 36.13
When they h. all the words, they 36.16
servants who h. all these words, 36.24
besieging Jerusalem h. news of them, 37.05
son of Malchiah h. the words that 38.01
h. that they had put Jeremiah into 38.07
and their men h. that the king of 40.07
in other lands h. that the king of 40.11
forces with him h. of all the evil 41.11
said to them, "I have h. you; 42.04
The nations have h. of your shame, 46.12
a cry is h. as far as Zoar. 48.04
they have h. the cry of destruction. 48.05
We have h. of the pride of Moab—he 48.29
cry to be h. against Rabbah of the 49.02
I have h. tidings from the LORD, and 49.14
cry shall be h. at the Red Sea. 49.21
for they have h. evil tidings; 49.23
"The king of Babylon h. the report 50.43
cry shall be h. among the nations." 50.46
at the report h. in the land, 51.46
to shame, for we have h. reproach; 51.51
my enemies have h. of my trouble; Lam 1.21
"Thou hast h. their taunts, O LORD, 3.61
I h. the sound of their wings like Eze 1.24
and I h. the voice of one speaking. 1.28
and I h. him speaking to me. 2.02
I h. behind me the sound of a great 3.12
cherubim was h. as far as the 10.05
no more be h. upon the mountains 19.09
of your lyres shall be h. no more. 26.13
He h. the sound of the trumpet, and 33.05
have h. all the revilings which you 35.12
words against me; I h. it. 35.13
I h. one speaking to me out of the 43.06
all the peoples h. the sound of Dan 3.07
I have h. of you that the spirit of 5.14
But I have h. that you can give 5.16
when he h. these words, was much 6.14
Then I h. a holy one speaking; 8.13
And I h. a man's voice between the 8.16
Then I h. the sound of his words; 10.09
and when I h. the sound of his 10.09
your God, your words have been h., 10.12
and I h. him swear by him who lives 12.07
I h., but I did not understand. 12.08
We have h. tidings from the LORD, Ob 1.01
messengers shall no more be h. Nah 2.13
O LORD, I have h. the report of thee, Hab 3.02
"a cry will be h. from the Fish Zep 1.10
"I have h. the taunts of Moab and 2.08
for we have h. that God is with you.'" Zec 8.23
the LORD heeded and h. them, Mal 3.16
When Herod the king h. this, Mt 2.03
When they had h. the king they went 2.09
"A voice was h. in Ramah, wailing 2.18
But when he h. that Archelaus 2.22
Now when he h. that John had been 4.12
"You have h. that it was said to 5.21
"You have h. that it was said, 'You 5.27
"Again you have h. that it was said 5.33
"You have h. that it was said, 'An 5.38
"You have h. that it was said, 'You 5.43
they will be h. for their many 6.07
When Jesus h. him, he marveled, and 8.10
But when he h. it, he said, "Those 9.12
Now when John h. in prison about 11.02
when the Pharisees h. it they said, 12.24
the tetrarch h. about the fame of 14.01
Now when Jesus h. this, he withdrew 14.13
But when the crowds h. it, 14.13
offended when they h. this saying?" 15.12
When the disciples h. this, 17.06
When the young man h. this he went 19.22
When the disciples h. this they 19.25
And when the ten h. it, they were 20.24
when they h. that Jesus was passing 20.30
and the Pharisees h. his parables, 21.45
When they h. it, they marveled; 22.22
And when the crowd h. it, they were 22.33
the Pharisees h. that he had 22.34
You have now h. his blasphemy. 26.65
And when Jesus h. it, he said to Mk 2.17
And when his friends h. it, 3.21
She had h. the reports about Jesus, 5.27
and many who h. him were astonished, 6.02
King Herod h. of it; for Jesus' 6.14
But when Herod h. of it he said, 6.16
When he h. him, he was much perplexed; 6.20
and yet he h. him gladly. 6.20
When his disciples h. of it, 6.29
to any place where they h. he was. 6.55
h. of him, and came and fell down at 7.25
And when the ten h. it, they began 10.41
And when he h. that it was Jesus of 10.47
from you again." And his disciples h. it. 11.14
and the scribes h. it and sought a 11.18
came up and h. them disputing with 12.28
And the great throng h. him gladly. 12.37
And when they h. it they were glad, 14.11
"We h. him say, 'I will destroy this 14.58
You have h. his blasphemy. 14.64
Zechariah, for your prayer is h., Lk 1.13
And when Elizabeth h. the greeting 1.41
and kinsfolk h. that the Lord had 1.58
and all who h. them laid them up in 1.66
and all who h. it wondered at what 2.18
God for all they had h. and seen, 2.20
and all who h. him were amazed at 2.47
what we have h. you did at Capernaum, 4.23
When they h. this, all in the 4.28
When he h. of Jesus, he sent to him 7.03
When Jesus h. this he marveled at 7.09
John what you have seen and h.: 7.22
(When they h. this all the people 7.29
the path are those who have h.; 8.12
the tetrarch h. of all that was 9.07
the dark shall be h. in the light, 12.03
who sat at table with him h. this, 14.15
to the house, he h. music and dancing. 15.25
h. all this, and they scoffed at him. 16.14
And when Jesus h. it, he said to him, 18.22
But when he h. this he became sad, 18.23
Those who h. it said, "Then who can 18.26
As they h. these things. he proceeded 19.11
When they h. this, they said, "God 20.16
We have h. it ourselves from his 22.71
When Pilate h. this, he asked 23.06
him, because he had h. about him, 23.08
The two disciples h. him say this, Jn 1.37
One of the two who h. John speak, 1.40
witness to what he has seen and h., 3.32
Pharisees had h. that Jesus was 4.01
for we have h. for ouselves, and we 4.42
When he h. that Jesus had come from 4.47
His voice you have never h., 5.37
one who has h. and learned from 6.45
when they h. it, said, "This is a 6.60
The Pharisees h. the crowd thus 7.32
When they h. these words, some of 7.40
But when they h. it, they went * 8.09
the world what I have h. from him." 8.26
what you have h. from your father." 8.38
you the truth which I h. from God; 8.40
has it been h. that any one opened 9.32
Jesus h. that they had cast him out, 9.35
Some of the Pharisees near him h. this, 9.40
But when Jesus h. it he said, "This 11.04
So when he h. that he was ill, he 11.06
When Martha h. that Jesus was 11.20
And when she h. it, she rose quickly 11.29
I thank thee that thou hast h. me. 11.41
to the feast h. that Jesus was 12.12

HEARD (cont.)

was that they h. he had done this Jn 12.18
standing by h. it and said that it 12.29
"We have h. from the law that the 12.34
You h. me say to you, 'I go away, and 14.28
all that I have h. from my Father 15.15
Ask those who have h. me, 18.21
When Pilate h. these words, he was 19.08
When Pilate h. these words, he 19.13
Simon Peter h. that it was the 21.07
which, he said, "you h. from me, Ac 1.04
each one h. them speaking in his 2.06
Now when they h. this they were cut 2.37
of those who h. the word believed; 4.04
speak of what we have seen and h." 4.20
And when they h. it, they lifted 4.24
When Ananias h. these words, he fell 5.05
fear came upon all who h. of it. 5.05
upon all who h. of these things. 5.11
And when they h. this, they entered 5.21
the chief priests h. these words, 5.24
When they h. this they were enraged 5.33
"We have h. him speak blasphemous 6.11
for we have h. him say that this 6.14
But when Jacob h. that there was 7.12
are in Egypt and h. their groaning, 7.34
Now when they h. these things they 7.54
when they h. him and saw the signs 8.06
at Jerusalem h. that Samaria had 8.14
and h. him reading Isaiah the 8.30
the ground and h. a voice saying 9.04
I have h. from many about this man, 9.13
And all who h. him were amazed, and 9.21
prayer has been h. and your alms 10.31
Spirit fell on all who h. the word. 10.44
For they h. them speaking in 10.46
were in Judea h. that the Gentiles 11.01
And I h. a voice saying to me, 'Rise, 11.07
When they h. this they were silenced. 11.18
And when the Gentiles h. this, 13.48
apostles Barnabas and Paul h. of it, 14.14
Since we have h. that some persons 15.24
One who h. us was a woman named 16.14
when they h. that they were Roman 16.38
were disturbed when they h. this. 17.08
Now when they h. of the resurrection 17.32
when Priscilla and Aquila h. him, 18.26
have never even h. that there is a 19.02
residents of Asia h. the word of 19.10
When they h. this they were enraged, 19.28
When we h. this, we and the people 21.12
And when they h. it, they glorified 21.20
And when they h. that he addressed 22.02
the ground and h. a voice saying 22.07
men of what you have seen and h. 22.15
When the centurion h. that, 22.26
Paul's sister h. of their ambush; 23.16
for Paul and h. him speak upon 24.24
I h. a voice saying to me in the 26.14
when they h. of us, came as far as 28.15
in him of whom they have never h.? Rom 10.14
believed what he has h. from us?" 10.16
So faith comes from what is h., 10.17
and what is h. comes by the preaching 10.17
But I ask, have they not h.? 10.18
understand who have never h. of him." 15.21
nor ear h., nor the heart of man 1Co 2.09
and he h. things that cannot be 2Co 12.04
For you have h. of my former life Gal 1.13
they only h. it said, "He who once 1.23
who have h. the word of truth, the Eph 1.13
because I have h. of your faith in 1.15
assuming that you have h. of the 3.02
assuming that you have h. about him 4.21
because you h. that he was ill. Php 2.26
and received and h. and seen in me, 4.09
because we have h. of your faith in Col 1.04
this you have h. before in the 1.05
the day you h. and understood the 1.06
And so, from the day we h. of it, 1.09
hope of the gospel which you h., 1.23
word of God which you h. from us, 1Th 2.13
words which you have h. from me, 2Ti 1.13
and what you have h. from me before 2.02
attention to what we have h., Heb 2.01
attested to us by those who h. him, 2.03
Who were they that h. and yet were 3.16
which they h. did not benefit them, 4.02
and he was h. for his godly fear. 5.07
You have h. of the steadfastness of Jas 5.11
we h. this voice borne from heaven, 2Pe 1.18
man saw and h. as he lived among 2.08
which we have h., which we have 1Jn 1.01
have seen and h. we proclaim also 1.03
message we have h. from him and 1.05
is the word which you have h. 2.07
and as you have h. that antichrist 2.18
Let what you h. from the beginning 2.24
If what you h. from the beginning 2.24
which you have h. from the beginning, 3.11
of which you h. that it was coming, 4.03
as you have h. from the beginning, 2Jn 1.06
and I h. behind me a loud voice Rev 1.10
Remember then what you received and h.; 3.03
which I had h. speaking to me like 4.01
and I h. around the throne and the 5.11
And I h. every creature in heaven 5.13
and I h. one of the four living 6.01
I h. the second living creature say, 6.03
I h. the third living creature say, 6.05
and I h. what seemed to be a voice 6.06
I h. the voice of the fourth living 6.07
And I h. the number of the sealed, a 7.04
and I h. an eagle crying with a 8.13
and I h. a voice from the four 9.13
ten thousand; I h. their number. 9.16
but I h. a voice from heaven saying, 10.04
which I had h. from heaven spoke 10.08
Then they h. a loud voice from 11.12
And I h. a loud voice in heaven, 12.10
And I h. a voice from heaven like 14.02
the voice I h. was like the sound 14.02
And I h. a voice from heaven saying, 14.13
Then I h. a loud voice from the 16.01
And I h. the angel of water say, 16.05
And I h. the altar cry, "Yea, Lord 16.07
Then I h. another voice from heaven 18.04
players and trumpeters shall be h. in 18.22
sound of the millstone shall be h. 18.22
bride shall be h. in thee no more; 18.23
After this I h. what seemed to be 19.01
Then I h. what seemed to be the 19.06
and I h. a great voice from the 21.03
I John am he who h. and saw these 22.08
And when I h. and saw them, I fell 22.08

HEARER

For if any one is a h. of the word Jas 1.23
being no h. that forgets but a doer 1.25

HEARERS

For it is not the h. of the law who Rom 2.13
save both yourself and your h. 1Ti 4.16
no good, but only ruins the h. 2Ti 2.14
did not meet with faith in the h. Heb 4.02
words made the h. entreat that no 12.19
and not h. only, deceiving yourselves. Jas 1.22

HEAREST

dwelling place; and when thou h., forgive. 1Ki 8.30
dwelling place; and when thou h., forgive. 2Ch 6.21
O thou who h. prayer! To thee shall Ps 65.02
I knew that thou h. me always, Jn 11.42

HEARING
Abraham in the h. of the Hittites, Gen 23.10
Ephron in the h. of the people of 23.13
named in the h. of the Hittites, 23.16
may tell in the h. of your son and Ex 10.02
Speak now in the h. of the people, 11.02
read it in the h. of the people; 24.07
complained in the h. of the LORD Num 11.01
have wept in the h. of the LORD, 11.18
have said in my h. I will do to 14.28
which I speak in your h. this day, Deu 5.01
law before all Israel in their h. 31.11
this song in the h. of the people, 32.44
for in our h. the king commanded 2Sa 18.12
within the h. of the people who 2Ki 18.26
read in their h. all the words of 23.02
and in the h. of our God, observe 1Ch 28.08
read in their h. all the words of 2Ch 34.30
of Moses in the h. of the people; Neh 13.01
"Surely, you have spoken in my h., Job 33.08
heard of thee by the h. of the ear, 42.05
The h. ear and the seeing eye, the Pro 20.12
Do not speak in the h. of a fool, 23.09
turns away his ear from h. the law, 28.09
seeing, nor the ear filled with h. Ecc 1.08
The LORD of hosts has sworn in my h.: Is 5.09
his ears from h. of bloodshed, 33.15
within the h. of the people who 36.11
proclaim in the h. of Jerusalem, Jer 2.02
I speak in your h. and in the 28.07
and in the h. of all the people. 28.07
letter in the h. of Jeremiah the 29.29
fast day in the h. of all the 36.06
also in the h. of all the men of 36.06
Then, in the h. of all the people, 36.10
the scroll in the h. of the people. 36.13
you read in the h. of the people, 36.14
And to the others he said in my h., Eze 9.05
called in my h. the whirling 10.13
but of h. the words of the LORD. Amo 8.11
days have been h. these words from Zec 8.09
and h. they do not hear, nor do they Mt 13.13
and their ears are heavy of h., 13.15
And some of the bystanders h. it said, 27.47
h. all that he did, came to him. Mk 3.08
And some of the bystanders h. it said, 15.35
has been fulfilled in your h." Lk 4.21
sayings in the h. of the people he 7.01
and h. they may not understand. 8.10
h. the word, hold it fast in an 8.15
But Jesus on h. this answered him, 8.50
and h. a multitude going by, he 18.36
And in the h. of all the people he 20.45
giving him a h. and learning what Jn 7.51
h. the voice but seeing no one. Ac 9.07
h. that Peter was there, sent two 9.38
except telling or h. something new. 17.21
the Corinthians h. Paul believed 18.08
On h. this, they were baptized in 19.05
and their ears are heavy of h., 28.27
were an eye, where would be the h.? 1Co 12.17
of the law, or by h. with faith? Gal 3.02
of the law, or by h. with faith? 3.05
since you have become dull of h. Heb 5.11

HEARKEN
h. to what I say: I have slain a man Gen 4.23
and h. to Israel your father. 49.02
And they will h. to your voice; Ex 3.18
will diligently h. to the voice of 15.26
Give heed to him and h. to his voice, 23.21
"But if you h. attentively to his 23.22
"But if you will not h. to me, Lev 26.14
of this you will not h. to me, 26.18
and will not h. to me, I will bring 26.21
of this you will not h. to me, 26.27
h. to me, O son of Zippor: Num 23.18
spoke to you, and you would not h.; Deu 1.43
LORD did not h. to your voice or 1.45
account, and would not h. to me; 3.26
"And because you h. to these 7.12
your God would not h. to Balaam; 23.05
they did not h. to the voice of Jos 5.06
"H. to the voice of the people in 1Sa 8.07
Now then, h. to their voice; 8.09
"H. to their voice, and make them a 8.22
serve him and h. to his voice and 12.14
but if you will not h. to the voice 12.15
now therefore h. to the words of 15.01
and to h. than the fat of rams. 15.22
you also h. to your handmaid; 28.22
thou mayest h. to the prayer which 1Ki 8.29
And h. thou to the supplication of 8.30
And if you will h. to all that I 11.38
So the king did not h. to the people; 12.15
that the king did not h. to them, 12.16
thou mayest h. to the prayer which 2Ch 6.20
And h. thou to the supplications of 6.21
So the king did not h. to the people; 10.15
that the king did not h. to them, 10.16
And he said, "H., all Judah and 20.15
If they h. and serve him, they Job 36.11
But if they do not h., they perish 36.12
H. to the thunder of his voice and 37.02
H. to the sound of my cry, my King Ps 5.02
h. to my cry of supplication. 86.06
today you would h. to his voice! 95.07
H. to your father who begot you, and Pro 23.22
H., O Laishah! Answer her, Is 10.30
hear my voice; h., and hear my speech. 28.23
the ears of those who hear will h. 32.03
nations, to hear, and h., O peoples! 34.01
"H. to me, O house of Jacob, all the 46.03
"H. to me, you stubborn of heart, you 46.12
"H. to me, O Jacob, and Israel, whom I 48.12
and h., you peoples from afar. 49.01
"H. to me, you who pursue deliverance. 51.01
"H. to me, you who know righteousness, 51.07
H. diligently to me, and eat what is 55.02
to me, O LORD, and h. to my plea. Jer 18.19
h. to the prayer of thy servant and Dan 9.17
H., O house of the king! For the judgment Hos 5.01
h., O earth, and all that is in it; Mic 1.02
But they refused to h., and turned a Zec 7.11

HEARKENED
And Abram h. to the voice of Sarai. Gen 16.02
And God h. to Leah, and she conceived 30.17
and God h. to her and opened her 30.22
of his city h. to Hamor and his 34.24
times and have not h. to my voice, Num 14.22
And the LORD h. to the voice of 21.03
But the LORD h. to me that time Deu 9.19
and the LORD h. to me that time 10.10
when the LORD h. to the voice of a Jos 10.14
I have h. to your voice in all that 1Sa 12.01
And Saul h. to the voice of Jonathan; 19.06
see, I have h. to your voice, and I 25.35
your handmaid has h. to you; 28.21
and have h. to what you have said 28.21
and he h. to their words. 28.23
So they h. to the word of the LORD, 1Ki 12.24
And Benhadad h. to King Asa, and 15.20
And the LORD h. to the voice of 17.22
And he h. to their voice, and did so 20.25
the LORD, and the LORD h. to him; 2Ki 13.04
And the king of Assyria h. to him; 16.09
So they h. to the word of the 2Ch 11.04
And Benhadad h. to King Asa, and 16.04
to the king; then the king h. to them. 24.17
O that you had h. to my commandments! Is 48.18
So he h. to them in this matter, and Dan 1.14
because they have not h. to him; Hos 9.17

HEARKENING

h. to the cry and to the prayer 1Ki 8.28
h. to the cry and to the prayer 2Ch 6.19
h. to the voice of his word! Ps 103.20

HEARS

every one who h. will laugh over me." Gen 21.06
sins in that he h. a public Lev 5.01
of him who h. the words of God, who Num 24.04
of him who h. the words of God, and 24.16
and her father h. of her vow and of 30.04
to her on the day that he h. of it, 30.05
and her husband h. of it, 30.07
to her on the day that he h.; 30.07
void on the day that he h. them, 30.12
when he h. the words of this sworn Deu 29.19
'Speak, LORD, for thy servant h.'" 1Sa 3.09
said, "Speak, for thy servant h." 3.10
every one that h. it will tingle. 3.11
If Saul h. it, he will kill me." 16.02
whoever h. it will say, 'There has 2Sa 17.09
every one who h. of it will tingle. 2Ki 21.12
the wise man who h. me will say: Job 34.34
he h. not the shouts of the driver. 39.07
the LORD h. when I call to him. Ps 4.03
the LORD h., and delivers them out 34.17
For the LORD h. the needy, and does 69.33
Zion h. and is glad, and the daughters 97.08
he also h. their cry, and saves them 145.19
A wise son h. his father's instruction, Pro 13.01
but he h. the prayer of the righteous. 15.29
If one gives answer before he h., 18.13
word of a man who h. will endure. 21.28
lest he who h. you bring shame upon 25.10
he h. the curse, but discloses 29.24
when he h. it, he will answer you. Is 30.19
every one who h. of it will tingle. Jer 19.03
then if any one who h. the sound of Eze 33.04
every man who h. the sound of the Dan 3.10
"Every one then who h. these words Mt 7.24
And every one who h. these words of 7.26
When any one h. the word of the 13.19
this is he who h. the word and 13.20
thorns, this is he who h. the word, 13.22
this is he who h. the word and 13.23
comes to me and h. my words and Lk 6.47
But he who h. and does not do them 6.49
"He who h. you h. me, and he who 10.16
bridegroom, who stands and h. him, Jn 3.29
he who h. my word and believes him 5.24
He who is of God h. the words of 8.47
If any one h. my sayings and does 12.47
but whatever he h. he will speak, 16.13
who is of the truth h. my voice." 18.37
Than he sees in me or h. from me. 2Co 12.06
according to his will he h. us. 1Jn 5.14
we know that he h. us in whatever 5.15
if any one h. my voice and opens Rev 3.20
And let him who h. say, "Come." 22.17
every one who h. the words of the 22.18

HEART

thoughts of his h. was only evil Gen 6.05
and it grieved him to his h. 6.06
odor, the LORD said in his h., 8.21
of man's h. is evil from his youth; 8.21
integrity of my h. and the innocence 20.05
this in the integrity of your h., 20.06
"Before I had done speaking in my h., 24.45
for his h. yearned for his brother, 43.30
And his h. fainted, for he did not 45.26
sees you he will be glad in his h. Ex 4.14
but I will harden his h., 4.21
But I will harden Pharaoh's h., 7.03
Still Pharaoh's h. was hardened, 7.13
"Pharaoh's h. is hardened, he refuses 7.14
so Pharaoh's h. remained hardened, 7.22
and he did not lay even this to h. 7.23
was a respite, he hardened his h., 8.15
But Pharaoh's h. was hardened, 8.19
harden his h. this time also, 8.32
But the h. of Pharaoh was hardened, 9.07
LORD hardened the h. of Pharaoh, 9.12
send all my plagues upon your h., 9.14
yet again, and hardened his h., 9.34
So the h. of Pharaoh was hardened, 9.35
hardened his h. and the h. of 10.01
But the LORD hardened Pharaoh's h., 10.20
But the LORD hardened Pharaoh's h., 10.27
and the LORD hardened Pharaoh's h., 11.10
And I will harden Pharaoh's h., 14.04
hardened the h. of Pharaoh king of 14.08
congealed in the h. of the sea. 15.08
you know the h. of a stranger, for 23.09
every man whose h. makes him 25.02
breastpiece of judgment upon his h., 28.29
and they shall be upon Aaron's h., 28.30
Israel upon his h. before the LORD 28.30
whoever is of a generous h., 35.05
every one whose h. stirred him, 35.21
of a willing h. brought brooches 35.22
whose h. moved them to bring 35.29
every one whose h. stirred him up 36.02
not hate your brother in your h., Lev 19.17
uncircumcised h. is humbled and 26.41
after your own h. and your own Num 15.39
discourage the h. of the people of 32.07
discouraged the h. of the people 32.09
spirit and made his h. obstinate, Deu 2.30
from your h. all the days of your 4.09
with fire to the h. of heaven, 4.11
with all your h. and with all your 4.29
this day, and lay it to your h., 4.39
the LORD your God with all your h., 6.05
you this day shall be upon your h.; 6.06
"If you say in your h., 'These nations 7.17
you to know what was in your h., 8.02
Know then in your h. that, as a man 8.05
then your h. be lifted up, and you 8.14
Beware lest you say in your h., 8.17
"Do not say in your h., after the LORD 9.04
uprightness of your h. are you 9.05
with all your h. and with all your 10.12
LORD set his h. in love upon your 10.15
Circumcise therefore the foreskin of your h., 10.16
with all your h. and with all your 11.13
Take heed lest your h. be deceived, 11.16
of mine in your h. and in your 11.18
with all your h. and with all your 13.03
not harden your h. or shut your 15.07
there be a base thought in your h., 15.09
and your h. shall not be grudging 15.10
for himself, lest his h. turn away; 17.17
that his h. may not be lifted up 17.20
And if you say in your h., 'How may we 18.21
enemies: let not your h. faint; 20.03
lest the h. of his fellows melt as his h.' 20.08
is poor, and sets his h. upon it); 24.15
with all your h. and with all your 26.16
with joyfulness and gladness of h., 28.47
will give you there a trembling h., 28.65
the dread which your h. shall fear, 28.67
whose h. turns away this day from 29.18
covenant, blesses himself in his h., 29.19
walk in the stubbornness of my h.' 29.19
with all your h. and with all your 30.02
circumcise your h. and the h. of your 30.06
with all your h. and with all your 30.06
with all your h. and with all your 30.10
it is in your mouth and in your h., 30.14
But if your h. turns away, and you 30.17
"Lay to h. all the words which I 32.46
their h. melted, and there was no Jos 5.01
him word again as it was in my h. 14.07
me made the h. of the people melt; 14.08

HEART (cont.)

with all your h. and with all your Jos 22.05
and incline your h. to the LORD, 24.23
My h. goes out to the commanders of Ju 5.09
there were great searchings of h. 5.15
there were great searchings of h. 5.16
you,' when your h. is not with me? 16.15
And the priest's h. was glad; 18.20
"Strengthen your h. with a morsel 19.05
night, and let your h. be merry." 19.06
father said, "Strengthen your h., 19.08
here and let your h. be merry; 19.09
and his h. was merry, he went to lie Ru 3.07
And why is your h. sad? Am I not more 1Sa 1.08
Hannah was speaking in her h.; 1.13
"My h. exults in the LORD; 2.01
out his eyes and grieve his h.; 2.33
to what is in my h. and in my mind; 2.35
for his h. trembled for the ark of 4.13
to the LORD with all your h., 7.03
and direct your h. to the LORD, 7.03
Samuel, God gave him another h.; 10.09
serve the LORD with all your h.; 12.20
him faithfully with all your h.; 12.24
sought out a man after his own h.; 13.14
but the LORD looks on the h." 16.07
presumption, and the evil of your h.; 17.28
"Let no man's h. fail because of him; 17.32
And David took these words to h., 21.12
And afterward David's h. smote him, 24.05
And Nabal's h. was merry within him, 25.36
and his h. died within him, and he 25.37
And David said in his h., "I shall now 27.01
and his h. trembled greatly. 28.05
over all that your h. desires." 2Sa 3.21
and she despised him in her h. 6.16
"Go, do all that is in your h.; 7.03
and according to thy own h., 7.21
do not take this to h." So Tamar dwelt 13.20
when Amnon's h. is merry with wine, 13.28
so take it to h. as to suppose 13.33
that the king's h. went out to 14.01
whose h. is like the h. of a lion, 17.10
thrust them into the h. of Absalom, 18.14
And he swayed the h. of all the men 19.14
Foreigners lost h., and came trembling 22.46
But David's h. smote him after he 24.10
with all their h. and with all 1Ki 2.04
in your own h. all the evil that 2.44
in uprightness of h. toward thee; 3.06
because her h. yearned for her son, 3.26
Now it was in the h. of David my 8.17
it was in your h. to build a house 8.18
did well that it was in your h.; 8.18
walk before thee with all their h.; 8.23
of his own h. and stretching out 8.38
to each whose h. thou knowest, 8.39
they lay it to h. in the land to 8.47
with all their h. in the land of 8.48
Let your h. therefore be wholly 8.61
and glad of h. for all the goodness 8.66
my eyes and my h. will be there for 9.03
integrity of h. and uprightness, 9.04
turn away your h. after their gods'; 11.02
and his wives turned away his h. 11.03
turned away his h. after other 11.04
and his h. was not wholly true to 11.04
as was the h. of David his father. 11.04
because his h. had turned away from 11.09
And Jeroboam said in his h., 12.26
then the h. of this people will 12.27
which he had devised of his own h.; 12.33
and followed me with all his h., 14.08
and his h. was not wholly true to 15.03
as the h. of David his father. 15.03
Nevertheless the h. of Asa was 15.14
bread, and let your h. be cheerful; 21.07
so that the arrow pierced his h., 2Ki 9.24
"Is your h. true to my h. as mine 10.15
according to all that was in my h., 10.30
the God of Israel with all his h.; 10.31
which a man's h. prompts him to 12.04
and your h. has lifted you up. 14.10
faithfulness and with a whole h., 20.03
because your h. was penitent, and 22.19
with all his h. and all his soul, to 23.03
with all his h. and with all his 23.25
my h. will be knit to you; 1Ch 12.17
and she despised him in her h. 15.29
David, "Do all that is in your h., 17.02
LORD, and according to thy own h., 17.19
I had it in my h. to build a house 22.07
your mind and h. to seek the LORD 22.19
I had it in my h. to build a house 28.02
with a whole h. and with a willing 28.09
with a whole h. they had offered 29.09
my God, that thou triest the h., 29.17
uprightness of my h. I have freely 29.17
with a whole h. he may keep thy 29.19
"Because this was in your h., 2Ch 1.11
Now it was in the h. of David my 6.07
it was in your h. to build a house 6.08
did well that it was in your h.; 6.08
walk before thee with all their h.; 6.14
to each whose h. thou knowest, 6.30
they lay it to h. in the land to 6.37
with all their h. in the land of 6.38
and glad of h. for the goodness 7.10
my eyes and my h. will be there for 7.16
did not set his h. to seek the 12.14
with all their h. and with all 15.12
they had sworn with all their h., 15.15
Nevertheless the h. of Asa was 15.17
of those whose h. is blameless 16.09
His h. was courageous in the ways 17.06
and have set your h. to seek God." 19.03
faithfulness, and with your whole h.: 19.09
sought the LORD with all his h." 22.09
LORD, yet not with a blameless h. 25.02
and your h. has lifted you up in 25.19
Now it is in my h. to make a 29.10
of a willing h. brought burnt 29.31
more upright in h. than the 29.34
give them one h. to do what the 30.12
who sets his h. to seek God, the 30.19
did with all his h., and prospered. 31.21
done to him, for his h. was proud. 32.25
himself for the pride of his h., 32.26
and to know all that was in his h. 32.31
because your h. was penitent and 34.27
with all his h. and all his soul, to 34.31
hardened his h. against turning to 36.13
had turned the h. of the king of Ez 6.22
had set his h. to study the law of 7.10
as this into the h. of the king, 7.27
nothing else but sadness of the h." Neh 2.02
had put into my h. to do for 2.12
didst find his h. faithful before 9.08
when the h. of the king was merry Est 1.10
out that day joyful and glad of h. 5.09
He is wise in h., and mighty in Job 9.04
things thou didst hide in thy h.; 10.13
"If you set your h. aright, 11.13
Why does your h. carry you away, and 15.12
evil and their h. prepares deceit." 15.35
broken off, the desires of my h. 17.11
and not another. My h. faints within me! 19.27
and lay up his words in your h. 22.22
God has made my h. faint; 23.16
my h. does not reproach me for any 27.06
the widow's h. to sing for joy. 29.13
My h. is in turmoil, and is never 30.27
and my h. has gone after my eyes, 31.07
"If my h. has been enticed to a 31.09
and my h. has been secretly enticed, 31.27
Behold, my h. is like wine that has 32.19

HEART (cont.)
declare the uprightness of my h., Job 33.03
"The godless in h. cherish anger; 36.13
"At this also my h. trembles, 37.01
His h. is hard as a stone, hard as 41.24
more joy in my h. than they have Ps 4.07
their h. is destruction, their 5.09
God, who saves the upright in h. 7.10
to the LORD with my whole h.; 9.01
boasts of the desires of his h., 10.03
He thinks in his h., "I shall not be 10.06
He thinks in his h., "God has forgotten, 10.11
renounce God, and say in his h., 10.13
thou wilt strengthen their h., 10.17
in the dark at the upright in h.; 11.02
lips and a double h. they speak. 12.02
have sorrow in my h. all the day? 13.02
my h. shall rejoice in thy salvation. 13.05
The fool says in his h., "There is no God." 14.01
and speaks truth from his h.; 15.02
the night also my h. instructs me. 16.07
Therefore my h. is glad, and my soul 16.09
If thou triest my h., if thou visitest 17.03
Foreigners lost h., and came trembling 18.45
LORD are right, rejoicing the h.; 19.08
meditation of my h. be acceptable 19.14
my h. is like wax, it is melted 22.14
He who has clean hands and a pure h., 24.04
Relieve the troubles of my h., 25.17
and try me; test my h. and my mind. 26.02
against me, my h. shall not fear; 27.03
My h. says to thee, "Thy face, LORD, 27.08
and let your h. take courage; 27.14
in him my h. trusts; so I am helped, 28.07
and my h. exults, and with my song I 28.07
and let your h. take courage, 31.24
for joy, all you upright in h.! 32.11
thoughts of his h. to all generations. 33.11
Yea, our h. is glad in him, because 33.21
to the wicked deep in his h.; 36.01
thy salvation to the upright of h.! 36.10
give you the desires of your h. 37.04
their sword shall enter their own h., 37.15
The law of his God is in his h.; 37.31
because of the tumult of my h. 38.08
My h. throbs, my strength fails me; 38.10
my h. became hot within me. As I mused, 39.03
O my God; thy law is within my h." 40.08
hid thy saving help within my h., 40.10
hairs of my head; my h. fails me. 40.12
while his h. gathers mischief; 41.06
Our h. has not turned back, nor have 44.18
For he knows the secrets of the h. 44.21
My h. overflows with a goodly theme; 45.01
sharp in the h. of the king's 45.05
mountains shake in the h. of the sea; 46.02
meditation of my h. shall be 49.03
teach me wisdom in my secret h. 51.06
Create in me a clean h., O God, 51.10
a broken and contrite h., O God, 51.17
The fool says in his h., "There is no 53.01
My h. is in anguish within me, the 55.04
than butter, yet war was in his h.; 55.21
My h. is steadfast, O God, my h. is 57.07
call to thee, when my h. is faint. 61.02
pour out your h. before him; God is a 62.08
increase, set not your h. on them. 62.10
inward mind and h. of a man are 64.06
Let all the upright in h. glory! 64.10
If I had cherished iniquity in my h., 66.18
Insults have broken my h., so that I am 69.20
upright, to those who are pure in h. 73.01
have I kept my h. clean and washed 73.13
embittered, when I was pricked in h., 73.21
My flesh and my h. may fail, 73.26
strength of my h. and my portion 73.26
I commune with my h. in the night; 77.06
generation whose h. was not steadfast, 78.08
God in their h. by demanding the 78.18
Their h. was not steadfast toward 78.37
With upright h. he tended them, and 78.72
my h. and flesh sing for joy to the 84.02
in whose h. are the highways to 84.05
unite my h. to fear thy name. 86.11
with my whole h., and I will 86.12
that we may get a h. of wisdom. 90.12
the upright in h. will follow it. 94.15
When the cares of my h. are many, 94.19
"They are a people who err in h., 95.10
and joy for the upright in h. 97.11
integrity of h. within my house; 101.02
Perverseness of h. shall be far 101.04
and arrogant h. I will not endure. 101.05
My h. is smitten like grass, and 102.04
and wine to gladden the h. of man, 104.15
and bread to strengthen man's h. 104.15
My h. is ready, O God, my h. is 108.01
and my h. is stricken within me. 109.22
to the LORD with my whole h., 111.01
his h. is firm, trusting in the LORD. 112.07
his h. is steady, he will not be 112.08
who seek him with their whole h., 119.02
praise thee with an upright h., 119.07
With my whole h. I seek thee; 119.10
I have laid up thy word in my h., 119.11
and observe it with my whole h. 119.34
Incline my h. to thy testimonies, 119.36
I entreat thy favor with all my h.; 119.58
with my whole h. I keep thy 119.69
their h. is gross like fat, but I 119.70
May my h. be blameless in thy 119.80
yea, they are the joy of my h. 119.111
I incline my h. to perform thy 119.112
With my whole h. I cry; answer me, 119.145
but my h. stands in awe of thy 119.161
O LORD, my h. is not lifted up, my 131.01
thanks, O LORD, with my whole h.; 138.01
Search me, O God, and know my h.! 139.23
who plan evil things in their h., 140.02
Incline not my h. to any evil, to 141.04
my h. within me is appalled. 143.04
inclining your h. to understanding; Pro 2.02
for wisdom will come into your h., 2.10
but let your h. keep my commandments; 3.01
them on the tablet of your h. 3.03
Trust in the LORD with all your h., 3.05
"Let your h. hold fast my words; 4.04
from your sight; keep them within your h. 4.21
Keep your h. with all vigilance; 4.23
and my h. despised reproof! 5.12
with perverted h. devises evil, 6.14
a h. that devises wicked plans, feet 6.18
Bind them upon your h. always; 6.21
Do not desire her beauty in your h., 6.25
them on the tablet of your h. 7.03
dressed as a harlot, wily of h. 7.10
Let not your h. turn aside to her 7.25
The wise of h. will heed commandments, 10.08
Deceit is in the h. of those who 12.20
Anxiety in a man's h. weighs him 12.25
Hope deferred makes the h. sick, 13.12
The h. knows its own bitterness, and 14.10
Even in laughter the h. is sad, 14.13
it is not known in the h. of fools. 14.33
A glad h. makes a cheerful countenance, 15.13
by sorrow of h. the spirit is 15.13
but a cheerful h. has a continual 15.15
The light of the eyes rejoices the h., 15.30
The wise of h. is called a man of 16.21
A cheerful h. is a good medicine, 17.22
Before destruction a man's h. is haughty, 18.12
his h. rages against the LORD. 19.03
do not set your h. on his destruction. 19.18
Who can say, "I have made my h. clean; 20.09
The king's h. is a stream of water 21.01

HEART (cont.)
eyes, but the LORD weighs the h. Pro 21.02
Haughty eyes and proud h., 21.04
He who loves purity of h., 22.11
Folly is bound up in the h. of a child, 22.15
but his h. is not with you. 23.07
if your h. is wise, my h. too will be 23.15
Let not your h. envy sinners, but 23.17
give me your h., and let your eyes 23.26
he who weighs the h. perceive it? 24.12
let not your h. be glad when he 24.17
to a heavy h. is like one who 25.20
are smooth lips with an evil h. 26.23
lips and harbors deceit in his h.; 26.24
are seven abominations in his h.; 26.25
Oil and perfume make the h. glad, 27.09
and make my h. glad, that I may 27.11
who hardens his h. will fall into 28.14
he will give delight to your h. 29.17
The h. of her husband trusts in her, 31.11
I kept my h. from no pleasure, for Ecc 2.10
for my h. found pleasure in all my 2.10
and gave my h. up to despair over 2.20
I said in my h., God will judge the 3.17
I said in my h. with regard to the 3.18
nor let your h. be hasty to utter a 5.02
him occupied with joy in his h. 5.20
and the living will lay it to h. 7.02
of countenance the h. is made glad. 7.03
The h. of the wise is in the house of mourning; 7.04
but the h. of fools is in the house of mirth. 7.04
your h. knows that many times you 7.22
the woman whose h. is snares and 7.26
the h. of the sons of men is fully 8.11
But all this I laid to h., 9.01
drink your wine with a merry h.; 9.07
A wise man's h. inclines him toward 10.02
but a fool's h. toward the left. 10.02
and let your h. cheer you in the 11.09
ways of your h. and the sight of 11.09
the day of the gladness of his h. Sol 3.11
You have ravished my h., my sister, 4.09
ravished my h. with a glance of 4.09
I slept, but my h. was awake. 5.02
and my h. was thrilled within me. 5.04
Set me as a seal upon your h., 8.06
is sick, and the whole h. faint. Is 1.05
Make the h. of this people fat, and 6.10
his h. and the h. of his people 7.02
do not let your h. be faint 7.04
in pride and in arrogance of h.: 9.09
and every man's h. will melt, 13.07
You said in your h., "I will ascend 14.13
My h. cries out for Moab; 15.05
for Moab, and my h. for Kirheres. 16.11
and the h. of the Egyptians will 19.01
and gladness of h., as when one 30.29
Say to those who are of a fearful h., 35.04
faithfulness and with a whole h., 38.03
him, but he did not take it to h. 42.25
"Hearken to me, you stubborn of h., 46.12
these things to h. or remember 47.07
sit securely, who say in your h., 47.08
astray, and you said in your h., 47.10
Then you will say in your h.: 49.21
the people in whose h. is my law; 51.07
perishes, and no one lays it to h.; 57.01
to revive the h. of the contrite. 57.15
backsliding in the way of his own h. 57.17
uttering from the h. lying words. 59.13
your h. shall thrill and rejoice; 60.05
For the day of vengeance was in my h., 63.04
yearning of thy h. and thy compassion 63.15
from thy ways and harden our h., 63.17
shall sing for gladness of h., 65.14
you shall cry out for pain of h., 65.14
see, and your h. shall rejoice; 66.14
not return to me with her whole h., Jer 3.10
give you shepherds after my own h., 3.15
stubbornly follow their own evil h. 3.17
wash your h. from wickedness, that 4.14
it has reached your very h." 4.18
I writhe pain! Oh, the walls of my h.! 4.19
My h. is beating wildly; I cannot keep 4.19
has a stubborn and rebellious h.; 5.23
beyond healing, my h. is sick within me. 8.18
of my people is my h. wounded, 8.21
but in his h. he plans an ambush 9.08
of Israel is uncircumcised in h." 9.26
in the stubbornness of his evil h. 11.08
who triest the h. and the mind, 11.20
their mouth and far from their h. 12.02
desolate, but no man lays it to h. 12.11
their own h. and have gone after 13.10
And if you say in your h., 'Why have 13.22
yet my h. would not turn toward 15.01
me a joy and the delight of my h.; 15.16
engraved on the tablet of their h., 17.01
whose h. turns away from the LORD. 17.05
The h. is deceitful above all 17.09
search the mind and try the h., 17.10
to the stubbornness of his evil h.' 18.12
there is in my h. as it were a 20.09
who seest the h. and the mind, let 20.12
have eyes and h. only for your 22.17
My h. is broken within me, all my 23.09
who stubbornly follows his own h., 23.17
be lies in the h. of the prophets 23.26
who prophesy the deceit of their own h., 23.26
give them a h. to know that I am 24.07
return to me with their whole h. 24.07
when you seek me with all your h., 29.13
Therefore my h. yearns for him; 31.20
I will give them one h. and one way, 32.39
with all my h. and all my soul. 32.41
and the haughtiness of his h. 48.29
Therefore my h. moans for Moab like 48.36
and my h. moans like a flute for 48.36
The h. of the warriors of Moab 48.41
day like the h. of a woman in her 48.41
you, and the pride of your h., 49.16
and the h. of the warriors of Edom 49.22
day like the h. of a woman in her 49.22
Let not your h. faint, and be not 51.46
my h. is wrung within me, because I Lam 1.20
groans are many and my h. is faint." 1.22
my h. is poured out in grief 2.11
Pour out your h. like water before 2.19
He drove into my h. the arrows of 3.13
Thou wilt give them dullness of h.; 3.65
For this our h. has become sick, for 5.17
hard forehead and of a stubborn h. Eze 3.07
speak to you receive in your h., 3.10
their wanton h. which has departed 6.09
And I will give them one h., 11.19
take the stony h. out of their 11.19
flesh and give them a h. of flesh, 11.19
for those whose h. goes after their 11.21
idols into his h. and sets the 14.04
idols into his h. and putting the 14.07
"How lovesick is your h., say the Lord 16.30
yourselves a new h. and a new 18.31
for their h. went after their idols. 20.16
with breaking h. and bitter grief 21.06
every h. will melt and all hands 21.07
with malice of h. to destroy in 25.15
Your borders are in the h. of the seas; 27.04
laden in the h. of the seas. 27.25
wrecked you in the h. of the seas. 27.26
sink into the h. of the seas on the 27.27
"Because your h. is proud, and you 28.02
in the h. of the seas,' yet you are 28.02
and your h. has become proud in 28.05
of the slain in the h. of the seas. 28.08
Your h. was proud because of your 28.17
and its h. was proud of its height, 31.10

HEART (cont.)
but their h. is set on their gain. Eze 33.31
A new h. I will give you, and a new 36.26
the h. of stone and give you a h. of flesh. 36.26
uncircumcised in h. and flesh, 44.07
uncircumcised in h. and flesh, 44.09
But when his h. was lifted up and Dan 5.20
Belshazzar, have not humbled your h., 5.22
his h. shall be exalted, and he 11.12
but his h. shall be set against the 11.28
They do not cry to me from the h., Hos 7.14
Their h. is false; now they must bear 10.02
My h. recoils within me, my compassion 11.08
filled, and their h. was lifted up; 13.06
"return to me with all your h., Joe 2.12
who is stout of h. among the Amo 2.16
The pride of your h. has deceived Ob 1.03
is high, who say in your h., 1.03
into the h. of the seas, and the Jon 2.03
Rejoice and exult with all your h., Zep 3.14
against his brother in your h." Zec 7.10
not lay it to h. to give glory to Mal 2.02
because you do not lay it to h. 2.02
"Blessed are the pure in h., Mt 5.08
adultery with her in his h. 5.28
is, there will your h. be also. 6.21
to the paralytic, "Take h., my son; 9.02
her he said, "Take h., daughter; 9.22
for I am gentle and lowly in h., 11.29
abundance of the h. the mouth 12.34
nights in the h. of the earth. 12.40
For this people's h. has grown dull, 13.15
ears, and understand with their h., 13.15
away what is sown in his h.; 13.19
to them, saying, "Take h., it is I; 14.27
lips, but their h. is far from me; 15.08
of the mouth proceeds from the h., 15.18
For out of the h. come evil thoughts, 15.19
forgive your brother from your h." 18.35
hardness of h. Moses allowed you 19.08
the Lord your God with all your h., 22.37
grieved at their hardness of h., Mk 3.05
to them and said, "Take h., it is I; 6.50
lips, but their h. is far from me; 7.06
not his h. but his stomach, and so 7.19
out of the h. of man, come evil 7.21
hardness of h. he wrote you this 10.05
blind man, saying to him, "Take h.; 10.49
sea,' and does not doubt in his h., 11.23
the Lord your God with all your h., 12.30
and to love him with all the h., 12.33
things, pondering them in her h. Lk 2.19
kept all these things in her h. 2.51
treasure of his h. produces good, 6.45
abundance of the h. his mouth 6.45
it fast in an honest and good h., 8.15
the Lord your God with all your h., 10.27
is, there will your h. be also. 12.34
always to pray and not lose h. 18.01
and slow of h. to believe all that 24.25
'Out of his h. shall flow rivers of Jn 7.38
their eyes and hardened their h., 12.40
eyes and perceive with their h., 12.40
put it into the h. of Judas 13.02
therefore my h. was glad, and my Ac 2.26
heard this they were cut to the h., 2.37
believed were of one h. and soul, 4.32
filled your h. to lie to the Holy 5.03
contrived this deed in your h.? 5.04
came into his h. to visit his 7.23
uncircumcised in h. and ears, 7.51
for your h. is not right before God. 8.21
intent of your h. may be forgiven 8.22
believe with all your h., you may." * 8.37
the son of Jesse a man after my h., 13.22
who knows the h. bore witness to 15.08
Lord opened her h. to give heed to 16.14
doing, weeping and breaking my h.? 21.13
I now bid you take h.; for there will 27.22
So take h., men, for I have faith in 27.25
For this people's h. has grown dull, 28.27
ears, and understand with their h., 28.27
and impenitent h. you are storing Rom 2.05
circumcision is a matter of the h., 2.29
from the h. to the standard of 6.17
and unceasing anguish in my h. 9.02
he hardens the h. of whomever he 9.18
faith says, Do not say in your h. 10.06
your lips and in your h. (that is, 10.08
believe in your h. that God raised 10.09
with his h. and so is justified, 10.10
nor the h. of man conceived, what 1Co 2.09
disclose the purposes of the h. 4.05
is firmly established in his h., 7.37
and has determined this in his h., 7.37
the secrets of his h. are disclosed; 14.25
and anguish of h. and with many 2Co 2.04
mercy of God, we do not lose h. 4.01
So we do not lose h. Though our 4.16
a man's position and not on his h. 5.12
to you, Corinthians; our h., is wide. 6.11
And his h. goes out all the more to 7.15
care for you into the h. of Titus. 8.16
shall reap, if we do not lose h. Gal 6.09
you not to lose h. over what I am Eph 3.13
them, due to their hardness of h.; 4.18
to the Lord with all your h., 5.19
in singleness of h., as to Christ; 6.05
doing the will of God from the h., 6.06
all, because I hold you in my h., Php 1.07
men-pleasers, but in singleness of h., Col 3.22
a short time, in person not in h., 1Th 2.17
from a pure h. and a good conscience 1Ti 1.05
call upon the Lord from a pure h. 2Ti 2.22
back to you, sending my very h. Phm 1.12
the Lord. Refresh my h. in Christ. 1.20
unbelieving h., leading you to fall Heb 3.12
thoughts and intentions of the h. 4.12
with a true h. in full assurance 10.22
well that the h. be strengthened 13.09
his tongue but deceives his h., Jas 1.26
one another earnestly from the h. 1Pe 1.22
person of the h. with the imperishable 3.04
a tender h. and a humble mind. 3.08
yet closes his h. against him, 1Jn 3.17
I am he who searches mind and h., Rev 2.23
Since in her h. she says, 'A queen I 18.07

HEARTH
shall be on the h. upon the altar Lev 6.09
which to take fire from the h., Is 30.14
and the altar h., four cubits; Eze 43.15
from the altar h. projecting 43.15
The altar h. shall be square, twelve 43.16

HEARTHS
with h. made at the bottom of the Eze 46.23

HEARTILY
work h., as serving the Lord and Col 3.23

HEARTLESS
foolish, faithless, h., ruthless. Rom 1.31

HEART'S
to all your h. desire to come down; 1Sa 23.20
May he grant you your h. desire, Ps 20.04
Thou hast given him his h. desire, 21.02
themselves, "Aha, we have our h. desire!" 35.25
of their eyes and their h. desire, Eze 24.25
Brethren, my h. desire and prayer to Rom 10.01

HEARTS
At this their h. failed them, Gen 42.28
will harden the h. of the Egyptians, Ex 14.17

HEARTS (cont.)
all the women whose h. were moved Ex 35.26
into their h. in the lands of Lev 26.36
Our brethren have made our h. melt, Deu 1.28
our h. melted, and there was no Jos 2.11
And the h. of the people melted, and 7.05
to harden their h. that they 11.20
and you know in your h. and souls, 23.14
and their h. inclined to follow Ju 9.03
And when their h. were merry, they 16.25
As they were making their h. merry, 19.22
you harden your h. as the Egyptians 1Sa 6.06
and Pharaoh hardened their h.? 6.06
of valor whose h. God had touched. 10.26
stole the h. of the men of Israel. 2Sa 15.06
"The h. of the men of Israel have 15.13
knowest the h. of all the children 1Ki 8.39
that he may incline our h. to him, 8.58
thou hast turned their h. back." 18.37
let the h. of those who seek the 1Ch 16.10
for the LORD searches all h., 28.09
thoughts in the h. of thy people, 29.18
and direct their h. toward thee. 29.18
knowest the h. of the children of 2Ch 6.30
had set their h. to seek the LORD 11.16
yet set their h. upon the God of 20.33
sinned, and cursed God in their h." Job 1.05
with your own h. on your beds, Ps 4.04
thou who triest the minds and h., 7.09
They close their h. to pity; 17.10
May your h. live for ever! 22.26
while mischief is in their h. 28.03
he who fashions the h. of them all. 33.15
Nay, in your h. you devise wrongs; 58.02
who seek God, let your h. revive. 69.32
their h. overflow with follies. 73.07
them over to their stubborn h., 81.12
those who turn to him in their h. 85.08
Harden not your h., as at Meribah, 95.08
let the h. of those who seek the 105.03
He turned their h. to hate his 105.25
Their h. were bowed down with hard 107.12
those who are upright in their h.! 125.04
LORD, how much more the h. of men! Pro 15.11
is for gold, and the LORD tries h. 17.03
also the h. of men are full of evil, Ecc 9.03
is in their h. while they live, and 9.03
ears, and understand with their h., Is 6.10
while their h. are far from me, and 29.13
remove the foreskin of your h., Jer 4.04
They do not say in their h., 5.24
the stubbornness of their evil h.. 7.24
their own h. and have gone after 9.14
and I will write it upon their h.; 31.33
put the fear of me in their h., 32.40
Let us lift up our h. and hands to Lam 3.41
The joy of our h. has ceased; 5.15
taken their idols into their h., Eze 14.03
lay hold of the h. of the house of 14.05
that their h. may melt, and many 21.15
trouble the h. of many peoples, 32.09
an oven their h. burn with intrigue; Hos 7.06
and rend your h. and not your Joe 2.13
H. faint and knees tremble, anguish Nah 2.10
lees, those who say in their h., Zep 1.12
They made their h. like adamant Zec 7.12
evil in your h. against one 8.17
and their h. shall be glad as with 10.07
their h. shall exult in the LORD. 10.07
will turn the h. of fathers to Mal 4.06
the h. of children to their fathers, 4.06
"Why do you think evil in your h.? Mt 9.04
there, questioning in their h., Mk 2.06
do you question thus in your h.? 2.08
loaves, but their h. were hardened. 6.52
or understand? Are your h. hardened? 8.17
to turn the h. of the fathers to Lk 1.17
in the imagination of their h., 1.51
them laid them up in their h., 1.66
out of many h. may be revealed." 2.35
in their h. concerning John. 3.15
"Why do you question in your h.? 5.22
takes away the word from their h., 8.12
perceived the thought of their h., 9.47
before men, but God knows your h.; 16.15
lest your h. be weighed down with 21.34
"Did not our h. burn within us 24.32
do questionings rise in your h.? 24.38
"Let not your h. be troubled; Jn 14.01
Let not your h. be troubled, neither 14.27
to you, sorrow has filled your h. 16.06
you again and your h. will rejoice, 16.22
who knowest the h. of all men, Ac 1.24
of food with glad and generous h., 2.46
and in their h. they turned to 7.39
satisfying your h. with food and 14.17
but cleansed their h. by faith. 15.09
the lusts of their h. to impurity, Rom 1.24
requires is written on their h., 2.15
poured into our h. through the 5.05
searches the h. of men knows what 8.27
deceive the h. of the simple-minded. 16.18
Spirit in our h. as a guarantee. 2Co 1.22
recommendation, written on your h., 3.02
stone but on tablets of human h. 3.03
shone in our h. to give the light 4.06
as to children—widen your h. also. 6.13
Open your h. to us; we have wronged 7.02
said before that you are in our h., 7.03
his Son into our h., crying, "Abba! Gal 4.06
having the eyes of your h. enlightened, Eph 1.18
may dwell in your h. through faith; 3.17
and that he may encourage your h. 6.22
will keep your h. and your minds Php 4.07
that their h. may be encouraged as Col 2.02
peace of Christ rule in your h., 3.15
thankfulness in your h. to God. 3.16
and that he may encourage your h., 4.08
but to please God who tests our h. 1Th 2.04
establish your h. unblamable in 3.13
comfort your h. and establish them 2Th 2.17
direct your h. to the love of God 3.05
pierced their h. with many pangs. 1Ti 6.10
because the h. of the saints have Phm 1.07
do not harden your h. as in the Heb 3.08
'They always go astray in their h.; 3.10
not harden your h. as in the 3.15
his voice, do not harden your h." 4.07
minds, and write them on their h., 8.10
I will put my laws on their h., 10.16
with our h. sprinkled clean from an 10.22
and selfish ambition in your h., Jas 3.14
you sinners, and purify your h., 4.08
fattened your h. in a day of 5.05
Establish your h., for the coming 5.08
but in your h. reverence Christ as 1Pe 3.15
the morning star rises in your h. 2Pe 1.19
They have h. trained in greed. 2.14
and reassure our h. before him 1Jn 3.19
whenever our h. condemn us; 3.20
for God is greater than our h., 3.20
if our h. do not condemn us, we have 3.21
it into their h. to carry out his Rev 17.17

HEARTY
send you h. greetings in the Lord. 1Co 16.19

HE-ASSES
h., menservants, maidservants, she-asses, Gen 12.16
bulls, twenty she-asses and ten h. 32.15

HEAT
cold and h., summer and winter, day Gen 8.22
of his tent in the h. of the day. 18.01
by day the h. consumed me, and the 31.40
and fiery h., and with drought, and Deu 28.22

HEAT (cont.)
What means the h. of this great Deu 29.24
with burning h. and poisonous 32.24
Ammonites until the h. of the day; 1Sa 11.11
and about the h. of the day they 2Sa 4.05
In time of h. they disappear; Job 6.17
Drought and h. snatch away the snow 24.19
from me, and my bones burn with h. 30.30
there is nothing hid from its h. Ps 19.06
dried up as by the h. of summer. 32.04
pots can feel the h. of thorns, 58.09
be for a shade by day from the h., Is 4.06
dwelling like clear h. in sunshine, 18.04
cloud of dew in the h. of harvest." 18.04
the storm and a shade from the h.; 25.04
like h. in a dry place. Thou dost 25.05
as h. by the shade of a cloud, so 25.05
upon him the h. of his anger and 42.25
in her h. sniffing the wind! Jer 2.24
and does not fear when h. comes, 17.08
cast out to the h. by day and the 36.30
oven with the burning h. of famine. Lam 5.10
bitterness in the h. of my spirit, Eze 3.14
became sick with the h. of wine; Hos 7.05
Who can endure the h. of his anger? Nah 1.06
indignation, all the h. of my anger; Zep 3.08
of the day and the scorching h.' Mt 20.12
say, 'There will be scorching h.'; Lk 12.55
because of the h. and fastened on Ac 28.03
its scorching h. and withers the Jas 1.11
strike them, nor any scorching h. Rev 7.16
men were scorched by the fierce h., 16.09

HEATED
the furnace h. seven times more Dan 3.19
more than it was wont to be h. 3.19
they are like a h. oven, whose Hos 7.04

HEATHEN
O God, the h. have come into thy Ps 79.01
You know that when you were h., 1Co 12.02
of lust like h. who do not know 1Th 4.05
have accepted nothing from the h. 3Jn 1.07

HEAVEN
And God called the firmament H. Gen 1.08
the breath of life from under h.; 6.17
under the whole h. were covered; 7.19
Most High, maker of h. and earth; 14.19
Most High, maker of h. and earth, 14.22
"Look toward h., and number the 15.05
and fire from the LORD out of h.; 19.24
of God called to Hagar from h., 21.17
of the LORD called to him from h., 22.11
to Abraham a second time from h., 22.15
as the stars of h. and as the sand 22.17
the God of h. and of the earth, 24.03
the God of h., who took me from 24.07
descendants as the stars of h., 26.04
May God give you of the dew of h., 27.28
away from the dew of h. on high. 27.39
and the top of it reached to h.; 28.12
of God, and this is the gate of h." 28.17
you with blessings of h. above, 49.25
them toward h. in the sight of Ex 9.08
and Moses threw them toward h., 9.10
"Stretch forth your hand toward h., 9.22
"Stretched forth his rod toward h.; 9.23
hand toward h. that there may be 10.21
stretched out his hand toward h., 10.22
I will rain bread from h. for you; 16.04
remembrance of Amalek from under h." 17.14
of anything that is in h. above, 20.04
days the LORD made h. and earth, 20.11
I have talked with you from h. 20.22
like the very h. for clearness. 24.10
days the LORD made h. and earth, 31.17
descendants as the stars of h., 32.13
as the stars of h. for multitude. Deu 1.10
are great and fortified up to h.; 1.28
that are under the whole h., 2.25
god is there in h. or on earth who 3.24
with fire to the heart of h., 4.11
lest you lift up your eyes to h., 4.19
and the stars, all the host of h., 4.19
all the peoples under the whole h. 4.19
I call h. and earth to witness 4.26
from one end of h. to the other, 4.32
Out of h. he let you hear his voice, 4.36
LORD is God in h. above and on the 4.39
of anything that is in h. above, 5.08
their name perish from under h.; 7.24
great and fortified up to h., 9.01
blot out their name from under h.; 9.14
God belong h. and the h. of heavens, 10.14
as the stars of h. for multitude. 10.22
drinks water by the rain from h., 11.11
the moon or any of the host of h., 17.03
remembrance of Amalek from under h.; 25.19
from h., and bless thy people 26.15
from h. it shall come down upon you 28.24
as the stars of h. for multitude, 28.62
blot out his name from under h. 29.20
are in the uttermost parts of h., 30.04
It is not in h., that you should 30.12
say, 'Who will go up for us to h., 30.12
I call h. and earth to witness 30.19
ears and call h. and earth to 31.28
For I lift up my hand to h., 32.40
the choicest gifts of h. above, 33.13
who is God in h. above and on Jos 2.11
smoke of the city went up to h.; 8.20
stones from h. upon them as far as 10.11
the sun stayed in the midst of h., 10.13
From h. fought the stars, from their Ju 5.20
went up toward h. from the altar, 13.20
of the city went up in smoke to h. 20.40
against them he will thunder in h. 1Sa 2.10
the cry of the city went up to h. 5.12
left hanging between h. and earth, 2Sa 18.09
The LORD thundered from h., 22.14
spread forth his hands toward h.; 1Ki 8.22
in h. above or on earth beneath, 8.23
h. and the highest h. cannot contain 8.27
hear thou in h. thy dwelling place; 8.30
then hear thou in h., and act, and 8.32
then hear thou in h., and forgive 8.34
"When h. is shut up and there is no 8.35
then hear thou in h., and forgive 8.36
then hear thou in h. thy dwelling 8.39
hear thou in h. thy dwelling place, 8.43
then hear thou in h. their prayer 8.45
then hear thou in h. thy dwelling 8.49
with hands outstretched toward h.; 8.54
all the host of h. standing beside 22.19
come down from h. and consume you 2Ki 1.10
Then fire came down from h., 1.10
come down from h. and consume you 1.12
came down from h. and consumed him 1.12
Lo, fire came down from h., 1.14
Elijah up to h. by a whirlwind, 2.01
went up by a whirlwind into h. 2.11
himself should make windows in h., 7.02
himself should make windows in h., 7.19
the name of Israel from under h., 14.27
and worshiped all the host of h., 17.16
thou hast made h. and earth. 19.15
and worshiped all the host of h., 21.03
all the host of h. in the two 21.05
Asherah, and for all the host of h.; 23.04
LORD standing between earth and h., 1Ch 21.16
with fire from h. upon the altar 21.26
Israel as many as the stars of h. 27.23
h., even highest h., cannot contain him? 2Ch 2.06
who made h. and earth, who has given 2.12

HEAVEN (cont.)
spread forth his hands toward h.; 2Ch 6.13
in h. or on earth, keeping covenant 6.14
h. and the highest h. cannot contain 6.18
hear thou from h. thy dwelling 6.21
then hear thou from h., and act, and 6.23
then hear thou from h., and forgive 6.25
"When h. is shut up and there is no 6.26
then hear thou in h., and forgive 6.27
then hear thou from h. thy dwelling 6.30
hear thou from h. thy dwelling 6.33
then hear thou from h. their prayer 6.35
then hear thou from h. thy dwelling 6.39
came down from h. and consumed the 7.01
ways, then I will hear from h., 7.14
all the host of h. standing on his 18.18
fathers, art thou not God in h.? 20.06
a rage which has reached up to h. 28.09
came to his holy habitation in h. 30.27
because of this and cried to h. 32.20
and worshiped all the host of h., 33.03
all the host of h. in the two 33.05
the God of h., has given me all the 36.23
the God of h., has given me all the Ez 1.02
servants of the God of h. and earth, 5.11
fathers had angered the God of h., 5.12
burnt offerings to the God of h., 6.09
sacrifices to the God of h., 6.10
scribe of the law of the God of h. 7.12
scribe of the law of the God of h., 7.21
Whatever is commanded by the God of h., 7.23
for the house of the God of h., 7.23
and praying before the God of h. Neh 1.04
And I said, "O LORD God of h., 1.05
So I prayed to the God of h. 2.04
"The God of h. will make us prosper, 2.20
thou hast made h., the h. of heavens, 9.06
and the host of h. worships thee. 9.06
with them from h. and give them 9.13
them bread from h. for their 9.15
descendants as the stars of h., 9.23
and thou didst hear them from h.; 9.27
to thee thou didst hear from h., 9.28
God fell from h. and burned up the Job 1.16
dust upon their heads toward h. 2.12
It is higher than h.—what can 11.08
Even now, behold, my witness is in h., 16.19
and he walks on the vault of h.' 22.14
he makes peace in his high h. 25.02
The pillars of h. tremble, and are 26.11
Under the whole h. he lets it go, 37.03
given birth to the hoarfrost of h.? 38.29
is under the whole h. is mine. 41.11
temple, the LORD's throne is in h.; Ps 11.04
looks down from h. upon the 14.02
from his holy h. with mighty 20.06
The LORD looks down from h., 33.13
God looks down from h. upon the 53.02
He will send from h. and save me, 57.03
Let h. and earth praise him, the 69.34
Whom have I in h. but thee 73.25
above, and opened the doors of h.; 78.23
eat, and gave them the grain of h. 78.24
Look down from h., and see; 80.14
from h. the LORD looked at the 102.19
them bread from h. in abundance. 105.40
They mounted up to h., they went 107.26
by the LORD, who made h. and earth! 115.15
the LORD, who made h. and earth. 121.02
of the LORD, who made h. and earth. 124.08
Zion, he who made h. and earth! 134.03
in h. and on earth, in the seas and 135.06
O give thanks to the God of h., 136.26
If I ascend to h., thou art there! 139.08
who made h. and earth, the sea, and 146.06
his glory is above earth and h. 148.13
flying like an eagle toward h. Pro 23.05
Who has ascended to h. and come down? 30.04
wisdom all that is done under h.; Ecc 1.13
men to do under h. during the few 2.03
a time for every matter under h.: 3.01
for God is in h., and you upon 5.02
it be deep as Sheol or high as h." Is 7.11
"How you are fallen from h., 14.12
your heart, 'I will ascend to h.; 14.13
For the windows of h. are opened, 24.18
LORD will punish the host of h., in h., 24.21
All the host of h. shall rot away, 34.04
thou hast made h. and earth. 37.16
and the snow come down from h., 55.10
Look down from h. and see, from thy 63.15
"H. is my throne and the earth is 66.01
"For as the new h. and the new 66.22
to make cakes for the queen of h.; Jer 7.18
the moon and all the host of h., 8.02
been burned to all the host of h., 19.13
Do I not fill h. and earth? 23.24
As the host of h. cannot be numbered 33.22
the ordinances of h. and earth, 33.25
to the queen of h. and pour out 44.17
to the queen of h. and pouring out 44.18
to the queen of h. and poured out 44.19
to the queen of h. and to pour out 44.25
winds from the four quarters of h.; 49.36
reached up to h. and has been 51.09
Though Babylon should mount up to h., 51.53
cast down from h. to earth the Lam 2.01
our hearts and hands to God in h.: 3.41
until the LORD from h. looks down 3.50
lifted me up between earth and h., Eze 8.03
lights of h. will I make dark over 32.08
of the God of h. concerning this Dan 2.18
then Daniel blessed the God of h. 2.19
is a God in h. who reveals mysteries, 2.28
whom the God of h. has given the 2.37
the God of h. will set up a 2.44
strong, and its top reached to h., 4.11
a holy one, came down from h. 4.13
let him be wet with the dew of h.; 4.15
so that its top reached to h., 4.20
has grown and reaches to h., 4.22
coming down from h. and saying, 4.23
let him be wet with the dew of h.; 4.23
shall be wet with the dew of h., 4.25
time that you know that H. rules. 4.26
mouth, there fell a voice from h., 4.31
with the dew of h. till his hair 4.33
Nebuchadnezzar, lifted my eyes to h., 4.34
in the host of h. and among the 4.35
and extol and honor the King of h.; 4.37
body was wet with the dew of h., 5.21
up yourself against the Lord of h., 5.23
and wonders in h. and on earth, 6.27
four winds of h. were stirring up 7.02
the clouds of h. there came one 7.13
under the whole h. shall be given 7.27
horns toward the four winds of h. 8.08
grew great, even to the host of h.; 8.10
under the whole h. there has not 9.12
toward the four winds of h., 11.04
hand and his left hand toward h.; 12.07
though they climb up to h., Amo 9.02
the God of h., who made the sea and Jon 1.09
up the ephah between earth and h. Zec 5.09
forth to the four winds of h., 6.05
the windows of h. for you and pour Mal 3.10
"Repent, for the kingdom of h. is at hand." Mt 3.02
a voice from h., saying, "This is my 3.17
for the kingdom of h. is at hand." 4.17
for theirs is the kingdom of h. 5.03
for theirs is the kingdom of h. 5.10
for your reward is great in h., 5.12
glory to your Father who is in h. 5.16
till h. and earth pass away, not an 5.18

HEAVEN (cont.)
called least in the kingdom of h.; Mt 5.19
called great in the kingdom of h. 5.19
will never enter the kingdom of h. 5.20
either by h., for it is the throne 5.34
sons of your Father who is in h.; 5.45
from your Father who is in h. 6.01
this: Our Father who art in h., 6.09
be done, On earth as it is in h. 6.10
up for yourselves treasures in h., 6.20
who is in h. give good things to 7.11
shall enter the kingdom of h., 7.21
the will of my Father who is in h. 7.21
and Jacob in the kingdom of h., 8.11
'The kingdom of h. is at hand.' 10.07
before my Father who is in h.; 10.32
deny before my Father who is in h. 10.33
the kingdom of h. is greater than 11.11
the kingdom of h. has suffered 11.12
Capernaum, will you be exalted to h.? 11.23
Lord of h. and earth, that thou hast 11.25
of my Father in h. is my brother, 12.50
the secrets of the kingdom of h., 13.11
"The kingdom of h. may be compared 13.24
"The kingdom of h. is like a grain 13.31
"The kingdom of h. is like leaven 13.33
"The kingdom of h. is like treasure 13.44
"Again, the kingdom of h. is like a 13.45
"Again, the kingdom of h. is like a 13.47
the kingdom of h. is like a 13.52
the two fish he looked up to h., 14.19
him to show them a sign from h. 16.01
to you, but my Father who is in h. 16.17
you the keys of the kingdom of h., 16.19
bind on earth shall be bound in h., 16.19
on earth shall be loosed in h." 16.19
the greatest in the kingdom of h.?" 18.01
will never enter the kingdom of h. 18.03
the greatest in the kingdom of h. 18.04
you that in h. their angels always 18.10
the face of my Father who is in h. 18.10
who is in h. that one of these 18.14
bind on earth shall be bound in h., 18.18
on earth shall be loosed in h. 18.18
done for them by my Father in h. 18.19
"Therefore the kingdom of h. may be 18.23
for the sake of the kingdom of h. 19.12
to such belongs the kingdom of h." 19.14
and you will have treasure in h.; 19.21
man to enter the kingdom of h. 19.23
"For the kingdom of h. is like a 20.01
From h. or from men?" And they 21.25
'From h.,' he will say to us, 'Why 21.25
"The kingdom of h. may be compared 22.02
marriage, but are like angels in h. 22.30
you have one Father, who is in h. 23.09
shut the kingdom of h. against men; 23.13
and he who swears by h., swears by 23.22
and the stars will fall from h., 24.29
the sign of the Son of man in h., 24.30
the clouds of h. with power and 24.30
from one end of h. to the other. 24.31
H. and earth will pass away, but my 24.35
knows, not even the angels of h., 24.36
"Then the kingdom of h. shall be 25.01
and coming on the clouds of h." 26.64
descended from h. and came and 28.02
authority in h. and on earth has 28.18
and a voice came from h., Mk 1.11
the two fish he looked up to h., 6.41
and looking up to h., he sighed, 7.34
him a sign from h., to test him. 8.11
and you will have treasure in h.; 10.21
also who is in h. may forgive you 11.25
neither will your Father in h. forgive * 11.26
of John from h. or from men? 11.30
'From h.,' he will say, 'Why then 11.31
marriage, but are like angels in h. 12.25
and the stars will be falling from h., 13.25
of the earth to the ends of h. 13.27
H. and earth will pass away, but my 13.31
knows, not even the angels in h., 13.32
and coming with the clouds of h." 14.62
angels went away from them into h., Lk 2.15
was praying, the h. was opened, 3.21
a dove, and a voice came from h., 3.22
when the h. was shut up three years 4.25
behold, your reward is great in h.; 6.23
the two fish he looked up to h., 9.16
come down from h. and consume them?" 9.54
Capernaum, will you be exalted to h.? 10.15
Satan fall like lightning from h. 10.18
that your names are written in h." 10.20
Lord of h. and earth, that thou hast 10.21
sought from him a sign from h. 11.16
be more joy in h. over one sinner 15.07
sinned against h. and before you; 15.18
sinned against h. and before you; 15.21
is easier for h. and earth to pass 16.17
rained from h. and destroyed them 17.29
not even lift up his eyes to h., 18.13
and you will have treasure in h.; 18.22
Peace in h. and glory in the 19.38
of John from h. or from men?" 20.04
'From H.,' he will say, 'Why did you 20.05
be terrors and great signs from h. 21.11
H. and earth will pass away, but my 21.33
appeared to him an angel from h., 22.43
Spirit descend as a dove from h., Jn 1.32
you will see h. opened, and the 1.51
ascended into h. but he who 3.13
but he who descended from h., 3.13
except what is given him from h. 3.27
he who comes from h. is above all. 3.31
'He gave them bread from h. to eat.'" 6.31
who gave you the bread from h.; 6.32
gives you the true bread from h. 6.32
is that which comes down from h., 6.33
For I have come down from h., 6.38
the bread which came down from h." 6.41
say, 'I have come down from h.'?" 6.42
the bread which comes down from h., 6.50
bread which came down from h.; 6.51
bread which came down from h., 6.58
Then a voice came from h., 12.28
lifted up his eyes to h. and said, 17.01
were gazing into h. as he went, Ac 1.10
why do you stand looking into h.? 1.11
who was taken up from you into h., 1.11
same way as you saw him go into h." 1.11
sound came from h. like the rush 2.02
men from every nation under h. 2.05
wonders in the h. above and signs 2.19
whom h. must receive until the time 3.21
name under h. give among men by 4.12
didst make the h. and the earth 4.24
over to worship the host of h., 7.42
'H. is my throne, and earth my 7.49
gazed into h. and saw the glory of 7.55
a light from h. flashed about him. 9.03
and saw the h. opened, and something 10.11
thing was taken up at once to h. 10.16
let down from h. by four corners; 11.05
answered a second time from h., 11.09
and all was drawn up again into h. 11.10
who made the h. and the earth and 14.15
gave you from h. rains and fruitful 14.17
being Lord of h. and earth, does not 17.24
light from h. suddenly shone about 22.06
I saw on the way a light from h., 26.13
revealed from h. against all Rom 1.18
heart, "Who will ascend into h.?" 10.06
so-called gods in h. or on earth— 1Co 8.05
of dust; the second man is from h. 15.47

HEAVEN (cont.)
and as is the man of h., so are 1Co 15.48
h., so are those who are of h. 15.48
bear the image of the man of h. 15.49
ago was caught up to the third h.— 2Co 12.02
But even if we, or an angel from h., Gal 1.08
things in h. and things on earth. Eph 1.10
every family in h. and on earth is 3.15
their Master and yours is in h., 6.09
in h. and on earth and under the Php 2.10
But our commonwealth is in h., 3.20
because of the hope laid up for you in h. Col 1.05
in h. and on earth, visible and 1.16
things, whether on earth or in h., 1.20
preached to every creature under h., 1.23
that you also have a Master in h. 4.01
and to wait for his Son from h., 1Th 1.10
descend from h. with a cry of 4.16
revealed from h. with his mighty 2Th 1.07
the throne of the Majesty in h., Heb 8.01
but into h. itself, now to appear in 9.24
as the stars of h. and as the 11.12
first-born who are enrolled in h., 12.23
if we reject him who warns from h. 12.25
not only the earth but also the h." 12.26
either by h. or by earth or with Jas 5.12
prayed again and the h. gave rain, 5.18
and unfading, kept in h. for you, 1Pe 1.04
the Holy Spirit sent from h., 1.12
who has gone into h. and is at the 3.22
we heard this voice borne from h., 2Pe 1.18
comes down from my God out of h., Rev 3.12
looked, and lo, in h. an open door! 4.01
and lo, a throne stood in h., 4.02
And no one in h. or on earth or 5.03
creature in h. and on earth and 5.13
was silence in h. for about half 8.01
and a great star fell from h., 8.10
saw a star fallen from h. to earth, 9.01
mighty angel coming down from h., 10.01
but I heard a voice from h. saying, 10.04
lifted up his right hand to h. 10.05
who created h. and what is in it, 10.06
had heard from h. spoke to me 10.08
loud voice from h. saying to them, 11.12
foes they went up to h. in a cloud. 11.12
and gave glory to the God of h. 11.13
and there were loud voices in h., 11.15
Then God's temple in h. was opened, 11.19
And a great portent appeared in h., 12.01
And another portent appeared in h.; 12.03
down a third of the stars of h., 12.04
Now war arose in h., Michael and his 12.07
no longer any place for them in h. 12.08
And I heard a loud voice in h., 12.10
O h. and you that dwell therein! 12.12
that is, those who dwell in h. 13.06
come down from h. to earth in the 13.13
a voice from h. like the sound of 14.02
worship him who made h. and earth, 14.07
And I heard a voice from h. saying, 14.13
angel came out of the temple in h., 14.17
Then I saw another portent in h., 15.01
tent of witness in h. was opened, 15.05
the God of h. for their pain and 16.11
hundredweight, dropped on men from h., 16.21
another angel coming down from h., 18.01
heard another voice from h. saying, 18.04
for her sins are heaped high as h., 18.05
O h., O saints and apostles and 18.20
voice of a great multitude in h., 19.01
Then I saw h. opened, and behold, a 19.11
And the armies of h., arrayed in 19.14
I saw an angel coming down from h., 20.01
came down from h. and consumed 20.09
Then I saw a new h. and a new earth; 21.01
for the first h. and the first 21.01
coming down out of h. from God, 21.02
coming down out of h. from God, 21.10

HEAVENLY
O h. beings, ascribe to the LORD Ps 29.01
Who among the h. beings is like the 89.06
as your h. Father is perfect. Mt 5.48
your h. Father also will forgive 6.14
and yet your h. Father feeds them. 6.26
and your h. Father knows that you 6.32
plant which my h. Father has not 15.13
So also my h. Father will do to 18.35
multitude of the h. host praising Lk 2.13
more will the h. Father give the 11.13
believe if I tell you h. things? Jn 3.12
not disobedient to the h. vision, Ac 26.19
long to put on our h. dwelling, 2Co 5.02
spiritual blessing in the h. places, Eph 1.03
his right hand in the h. places, 1.20
with him in the h. places in 2.06
and powers in the h. places. 3.10
of wickedness in the h. places. 6.12
and save me for his h. kingdom. 2Ti 4.18
brethren, who share in a h. call, Heb 3.01
who have tasted the h. gift, 6.04
and shadow of the h. sanctuary; 8.05
copies of the h. things to be 9.23
but the h. things themselves with 9.23
better country, that is, a h. one. 11.16
the h. Jerusalem, and to innumerable 12.22

HEAVENS
God created the h. and the earth. Gen 1.01
under the h. be gathered together 1.09
firmament of the h. to separate the 1.14
firmament of the h. to give light 1.15
firmament of the h. to give light 1.17
across the firmament of the h." 1.20
Thus the h. and the earth were 2.01
generations of the h. and the earth 2.04
God made the earth and the h., 2.04
the windows of the h. were opened. 7.11
the windows of the h. were closed, 8.02
rain from the h. was restrained, 8.02
and a tower with its top in the h., 11.04
will make your h. like iron and Lev 26.19
belong heaven and the heaven of h., Deu 10.14
against you, and he shut up the h., 11.17
as long as the h. are above the 11.21
to you his good treasury the h., 28.12
And the h. over your head shall be 28.23
"Give ear, O h., and I will speak; 32.01
rides through the h. to your help, 33.26
yea, his h. drop down dew. 33.28
and the h. dropped, yea, the clouds Ju 5.04
rain fell upon them from the h.; 2Sa 21.10
foundations of the h. trembled and 22.08
He bowed the h., and came down; 22.10
"The LORD has set the sun in the h., 1Ki 8.12
while the h. grew black with 18.45
constellations, and all the host of the h. 2Ki 23.05
are idols; but the LORD made the h. 1Ch 16.26
Let the h. be glad, and let the 16.31
that is in the h. and in the earth 29.11
When I shut up the h. so that there 2Ch 7.13
our guilt has mounted up to the h. Ez 9.06
the heaven of h., with all their Neh 9.06
who alone stretched out the h., Job 9.08
till the h. are no more he will not 14.12
and the h. are not clean in his 15.15
Though his height mount up to the h., 20.06
The h. will reveal his iniquity, and 20.27
"Is not God high in the h.? 22.12
By his wind the h. were made fair; 26.13
and sees everything under the h. 28.24
Look at the h., and see; and behold 35.05
Do you know the ordinances of the h.? 38.33

HEAVENS (cont.)
can tilt the waterskins of the h., Job 38.37
He who sits in the h. laughs; Ps 2.04
glory above the h. is changed 8.01
When I look at thy h., the work of 8.03
He bowed the h., and came down; 18.09
The LORD also thundered in the h., 18.13
The h. are telling the glory of God; 19.01
Its rising is from the end of the h., 19.06
word of the LORD the h. were made, 33.06
love, O LORD, extends to the h., 36.05
He calls to the h. above and to the 50.04
The h. declare his righteousness, 50.06
Be exalted, O God, above the h.! 57.05
steadfast love is great to the h., 57.10
Be exalted, O God, above the h.! 57.11
the h. poured down rain, at the 68.08
to him who rides in the h., 68.33
in the heavens, the ancient h.; 68.33
righteousness, O God, reach the high h. 71.19
They set their mouths against the h., 73.09
From the h. thou didst utter 76.08
the east wind to blow in the h., 78.26
his sanctuary like the high h., 78.69
thy faithfulness is firm as the h. 89.02
Let the h. praise thy wonders, O 89.05
The h. are thine, the earth also is 89.11
his throne as the days of the h. 89.29
are idols; but the LORD made the h. 96.05
Let the h. be glad, and let the 96.11
The h. proclaim his righteousness; 97.06
and the h. are the work of thy 102.25
For as the h. are high above the 103.11
established his throne in the h., 103.19
stretched out the h. like a tent, 104.02
steadfast love is great above the h., 108.04
Exalt thyself, O God, above the h.! 108.05
nations, and his glory above the h.! 113.04
far down upon the h. and the earth? 113.06
Our God is in the h.; he does 115.03
The h. are the LORD's h., but the earth 115.16
thy word is firmly fixed in the h. 119.89
O thou who art enthroned in the h.! 123.01
who by understanding made the h., 136.05
Bow thy h., O LORD, and come down! 144.05
He covers the h. with clouds, he 147.08
Praise the LORD from the h., 148.01
you highest h., and you waters 148.04
and you waters above the h.! 148.04
understanding he established the h.; Pro 3.19
When he established the h., 8.27
As the h. for height, and the earth 25.03
Hear, O h., and give ear, O earth; Is 1.02
land, from the end of the h., 13.05
stars of the h. and their constellations 13.10
Therefore I will make the h. tremble, 13.13
the h. languish together with the 24.04
sword has drunk its fill in the h.; 34.05
and marked off the h. with a span, 40.12
stretches out the h. like a curtain, 40.22
who created the h. and stretched 42.05
Sing, O h., for the LORD has done it 44.23
who stretched out the h. alone, 44.24
"Shower, O h., from above, and let 45.08
my hands that stretched out the h., 45.12
who created the h. (he is God!), 45.18
save you, those who divide the h., 47.13
my right hand spread out the h.; 48.13
O h., and exult, O earth; 49.13
I clothe the h. with blackness, and 50.03
Lift up your eyes to the h., 51.06
for the h. will vanish like smoke, 51.06
stretched out the h. and laid the 51.13
stretching out the h. and laying the 51.16
For as the h. are higher than the 55.09
wouldst rend the h. and come down, 64.01
I create new h. and a new earth; 65.17
Be appalled, O h., at this, be Jer 2.12
and to the h., and they had no 4.23
mourn, and the h. above be black; 4.28
stork in the h. knows her times; 8.07
signs of the h. because the 10.02
not make the h. and the earth 10.11
the earth and from under the h." 10.11
understanding stretched out the h. 10.12
is a tumult of waters in the h., 10.13
Or can the h. give showers? 14.22
"If the h. above can be measured, 31.37
hast made the h. and the earth by 32.17
understanding stretched out the h. 51.15
is a tumult of waters in the h., 51.16
Then the h. and the earth, and all 51.48
them from under thy h., O LORD. Lam 3.66
than the vultures in the h.; 4.19
the h. were opened, and I saw Eze 1.01
blot you out, I will cover the h., 32.07
will answer the h. and they shall Hos 2.21
quakes before them, the h. tremble. Joe 2.10
portents in the h. and on the 2.30
and the h. and the earth shake. 3.16
his upper chambers in the h., Amo 9.06
more than the stars of the h. Nah 3.16
His glory covered the h., and the Hab 3.03
on the roofs to the host of the h.; Zep 1.05
Therefore the h. above you have Hag 1.10
will shake the h. and the earth 2.06
to shake the h. and the earth, 2.21
winds of the h., says the LORD. Zec 2.06
and the h. shall give their dew; 8.12
stretched out the h. and founded 12.01
the h. were opened and he saw the Mt 3.16
powers of the h. will be shaken; 24.29
he saw the h. opened and the Mk 1.10
powers in the h. will be shaken. 13.25
treasure in the h. that does not Lk 12.33
powers of the h. will be shaken. 21.26
For David did not ascend into the h.; Ac 2.34
I see the h. opened, and the Son of 7.56
made with hands, eternal in the h. 2Co 5.01
also ascended far above all the h., Eph 4.10
and the h. are the work of thy Heb 1.10
who has passed through the h., 4.14
from sinners, exalted above the h. 7.26
the word of God h. existed long 2Pe 3.05
same word the h. and earth that 3.07
and then the h. will pass away with 3.10
of which the h. will be kindled 3.12
we wait for new h. and a new earth 3.13

HEAVIER
Let h. work be laid upon the men Ex 5.09
it would be h. than the sand of Job 6.03
fool's provocation is h. than both. Pro 27.03

HEAVILY
wheels so that they drove h.; Ex 14.25
of Joseph rested h. upon them, Ju 1.35
were filled and h. laden in the Eze 27.25

HEAVY
to afflict them with h. burdens; Ex 1.11
I will cause very h. hail to fall, 9.18
very h. hail, such as had never been 9.24
for the thing is too h. for you; 18.18
alone, the burden is too h. for me. Num 11.14
for he was an old man, and h. 1Sa 4.18
of the LORD was h. upon the people 5.06
for his hand is h. upon us and upon 5.07
the hand of God was very h. there; 5.11
when it was h. on him, he cut it), he 2Sa 14.26
"Your father made our yoke h. 1Ki 12.04
father and his h. yoke upon us, 12.04
you, 'Your father made our yoke h., 12.10
my father laid upon you a h. yoke, 12.11
"My father made your yoke h., 12.14

HEAVY (cont.)
am charged with h. tidings for you. 1Ki 14.06
"Your father made our yoke h. 2Ch 10.04
father and his h. yoke upon us, 10.04
you, 'Your father made our yoke h., 10.10
my father laid upon you a h. yoke, 10.11
'My father made your yoke h., 10.14
matter and because of the h. rain. Ez 10.09
many, and it is a time of h. rain; 10.13
before me laid h. burdens upon the Neh 5.15
servitude was h. upon this people. 5.18
his hand is h. in spite of my Job 23.02
pressure will not be h. upon you. 33.07
and night thy hand was h. upon me; Ps 32.04
weigh like a burden too h. for me. 38.04
Thy wrath lies h. upon me, and thou 88.07
may our cattle be h. with young, 144.14
songs to a h. heart is like one Pro 25.20
A stone is h., and sand is weighty, 27.03
the sun, and it lies h. upon men: Ecc 6.01
man's trouble lies h. upon him. 8.06
this people fat, and their ears h., Is 6.10
its transgression lies h. upon it, 24.20
you made your yoke exceedingly h. 47.06
he has put h. chains on me; Lam 3.07
Jerusalem a h. stone for all the Zec 12.03
to me, all who labor and are h. laden, Mt 11.28
and their ears are h. of hearing, 13.15
They bind h. burdens, hard to bear, 23.04
sleeping, for their eyes were h. 26.43
for their eyes were very h.; Mk 14.40
with him were h. with sleep but Lk 9.32
and their ears are h. of hearing, Ac 28.27
thunder, an earthquake, and h. hail. Rev 11.19
h. as a hundredweight, dropped on 16.21

HEBER
sons of Beriah: H. and Malchiel Gen 46.17
of H., the family of the Heberites; Num 26.45
Now H. the Kenite had separated Ju 4.11
of Jael, the wife of H. the Kenite; 4.17
and the house of H. the Kenite. 4.17
the wife of H. took a tent peg, and 4.21
the wife of H. the Kenite, of 5.24
H. the father of Soco, and Jekuthiel 1Ch 4.18
H. and Malchiel, who was the father 7.31
H. was the father of Japhlet, Shomer, 7.32
Zebadiah, Meshullam, Hizki, H., 8.17

HEBERITES
of Heber, the family of the H.; Num 26.45

HEBREW
came, and told Abram the H., Gen 14.13
brought among us a H. to insult us; 39.14
"The H. servant, whom you have 39.17
A young H. was there with us, a 41.12
of Egypt said to the H. midwives, Ex 1.15
serve as midwife to the H. women, 1.16
"Because the H. women are not like 1.19
nurse from the H. women to nurse 2.07
he saw an Egyptian beating a H., 2.11
When you buy a H. slave, he shall 21.02
a H. man, or a H. woman, is sold to Deu 15.12
one should set free his H. slaves, Jer 34.09
free the fellow H. who has been 34.14
And he said to them, "I am a H.; Jon 1.09
in H. called Bethzatha, which has Jn 5.02
The Pavement, and in H., Gabbatha. 19.13
which is called in H. Golgotha. 19.17
and it was written in H., in Latin, 19.20
and said to him in H., "Rabboni!" 20.16
spoke to them in the H. language, Ac 21.40
addressed them in the H. language, 22.02
saying to me in the H. language, 26.14
a H. born of Hebrews; as to the Php 3.05
his name in H. is Abaddon, and in Rev 9.11
which is called in H. Armageddon. 16.16

HEBREWS
stolen out of the land of the H.; Gen 40.15
might not eat bread with the H., 43.32
is born to the H. you shall cast Ex 1.22
two H. were struggling together; 2.13
him, 'The LORD, the God of the h., 3.18
"The God of the H. has met with us; 5.03
him, 'The LORD, the God of the H., 7.16
says the LORD, the God of the H., 9.01
says the LORD, the God of the H., 9.13
says the LORD, the God of the H., 10.03
shouting in the camp of the H. mean?" 1Sa 4.06
slaves to the H. as they have been 4.09
the land, saying, "Let the H. hear." 13.03
"Lest the H. make themselves swords 13.19
H. are coming out of the holes 14.11
Now the H. who had been with the 14.21
said, "What are these H. doing here?" 29.03
against the H. because their Ac 6.01
Are they H.? So am I. Are they 2Co 11.22
of Benjamin, a Hebrew born of H.; Php 3.05

HEBREWS'
"This is one of the H. children." Ex 2.06

HEBRON
the oaks of Mamre, which are at H.; Gen 13.18
H.) in the land of Canaan; 23.02
H.) in the land of Canaan. 23.19
H.), where Abraham and Isaac had 35.27
he sent him from the valley of H., 37.14
H. and Uzziel, the years of the life Ex 6.18
Amram, Izhar, H., and Uzziel. Num 3.19
up into the Negeb, and came to H.; 13.22
(H. was built seven years before 13.22
Jerusalem sent to Hoham king of H., Jos 10.03
the king of H., the king of Jarmuth, 10.05
the king of H., the king of Jarmuth, 10.23
with all Israel from Eglon to H.; 10.36
he had done to H. and to Libnah 10.39
from H., from Debir, from Anab, and 11.21
Jerusalem, one; the king of H., one; 12.10
and he gave H. to Caleb the son of 14.13
So H. became the inheritance of 14.14
Now the name of H. formerly was 14.15
H. (Arba was the father of Anak). 15.13
H.), and Zior: nine cities with 15.54
H.) in the hill country of Judah. 20.07
H.), in the hill country of Judah, 21.11
of Aaron the priest they gave H., 21.13
dwelt in H. (now the name of H. was Ju 1.10
And H. was given to Caleb, as Moses 1.20
top of the hill that is before H. 16.03
in H., for all the places where 1Sa 30.31
I go up?" And he said, "To H." 2Sa 2.01
and they dwelt in the towns of H. 2.03
was king in H. over the house of 2.11
and the day broke upon them at H. 2.32
And sons were born to David at H.: 3.02
These were born to David in H. 3.05
sent messengers to David at H., 3.12
tell David at H. all that Israel 3.19
with twenty men to David at H., 3.20
But Abner was not with David at H., 3.22
And when Abner returned to H., 3.27
They buried Abner at H.; and the 3.32
heard that Abner had died at H., 4.01
head of Ishbosheth to David at H. 4.08
hanged them beside the pool at H. 4.12
it in the tomb of Abner at H. 4.12
of Israel came to David at H., 5.01
of Israel came to the king at H.; 5.03
with them at H. before the LORD, 5.03
At H. he reigned over Judah seven 5.05
Jerusalem, after he came from H.; 5.13
I have vowed to the LORD, in H. 15.07
So he arose, and went to H. 15.09
then say, 'Absalom is king at H.!'" 15.10

HEBRON (cont.)
he reigned seven years in H., 1Ki 2.11
of Ziph. The sons of Mareshah: H. 1Ch 2.42
The sons of H.: Korah, Tappuah, Rekem, 2.43
David that were born to him in H.: 3.01
six were born to him in H., where he 3.04
Amram, Izhar, H., and Uzziel. 6.02
Amram, Izhar, H., and Uzziel. 6.18
to them they gave H. in the land of 6.55
H., Libnah with its pasture lands, 6.57
gathered together to David at H., 11.01
of Israel came to the king at H.; 11.03
with them at H. before the LORD, 11.03
troops, who came to David in H., 12.23
came to H. with full intent to make 12.38
of the sons of H., Eliel the chief, 15.09
Amram, Izhar, H., and Uzziel, four. 23.12
The sons of H.: Jeriah the chief, 23.19
The sons of H.: Jeriah the chief, 24.23
he reigned seven years in H., 29.27
and H., fortified cities which are 2Ch 11.10

HEBRONITES
Izharites, and the family of the H., Num 3.27
the Libnites, the family of the H., 26.58
the H., and the Uzzielites— 1Ch 26.23
Of the H., Hashabiah and his 26.30
Of the H., Jerijah was chief of the 26.31
chief of the H. of whatever 26.31

HEDGE
Hast thou not put a h. about him Job 1.10
I will remove its h., and it shall Is 5.05
Therefore I will h. up her way with Hos 2.06
most upright of them a thorn h. Mic 7.04
and set a h. around it, and dug a Mt 21.33
and set a h. around it, and dug a Mk 12.01

HEDGED
way is hid, whom God has h. in? Job 3.23

HEDGEHOG
make it a possession of the h., Is 14.23
vulture and the h. shall lodge in Zep 2.14

HEDGES
and run to and fro among the h.! Jer 49.03
'Go out to the highways and h., Lk 14.23

HEED
LORD has given h. to your affliction. Gen 16.11
"Take h. that you say not a word to 31.24
'Take h. that you speak to Jacob 31.29
prison paid no h. to anything that 39.23
"or h. the first sign, they may Ex 4.08
these two signs or h. your voice, 4.09
that I should h. his voice and let 5.02
take h. to yourself; never see my 10.28
and give h. to his commandments and 15.26
So Moses gave h. to the voice of 18.24
'Take h. that you do not go up into 19.12
Take h. to all that I have said to 23.13
Give h. to him and hearken to his 23.21
Take h. to yourself, lest you make a 34.12
"Must I not take h. to speak what Num 23.12
you shall take h. to offer to me 28.02
afraid of you. So take good h.; Deu 2.04
give h. to the statutes and the 4.01
"Only take h., and keep your soul 4.09
"Therefore take good h. to yourselves. 4.15
Take h. to yourselves, lest you 4.23
then take h. lest you forget the 6.12
"Take h. lest you forget the LORD 8.11
Take h. lest your heart be deceived, 11.16
Take h. that you do not offer your 12.13
Take h. that you do not forsake the 12.19
Be careful to h. all these words 12.28
take h. that you be not ensnared to 12.30
Take h. lest there be a base 15.09
give h. to soothsayers and to 18.14
your brethren—him you shall h.— 18.15
will not give h. to my words which 18.19
him, will not give h. to them, 21.18
"Take h., in an attack of leprosy, 24.08
Take good h. to yourselves, therefore, Jos 23.11
you have not given h. to my voice." Ju 6.10
Ammonites did not h. the message of 11.28
But she did not answer or give h. 1Sa 4.20
therefore take h. to yourself in 19.02
'If your sons take h. to their way, 1Ki 2.04
your sons take h. to their way, 8.25
said to him, "Do not h. or consent." 20.08
Take h. now, for the LORD has chosen 1Ch 28.10
your sons take h. to their way, 2Ch 6.16
take h. what you do, for there is 19.07
them, but they would not give h. 24.19
to his people, but they gave no h. 33.10
power? No; he would give h. to me. Job 23.06
I stand, and thou dost not h. me. 30.20
Give h., O Job, listen to me; 33.31
does not greatly h. transgression, 35.15
Take h., do not turn to iniquity, 36.21
O LORD; give h. to my groaning. Ps 5.01
thou hast taken h. of my adversities, 31.07
he has given h. to the voice of my 66.19
I will give h. to the way that is 101.02
let him give h. to these things; 107.43
Give h. to my cry; for I am brought 142.06
Give h. to my reproof; behold, Pro 1.23
Take h. to the path of your feet, 4.26
she does not take h. to the path of 5.06
wise of heart will h. commandments, 10.08
He who gives h. to the word will 16.20
a liar gives h. to a mischievous 17.04
understands, he will not give h. 29.19
Do not give h. to all the things Ecc 7.21
'Take h., be quiet, do not fear, and Is 7.04
and he will h. their supplications 19.22
generation, h. the word of the LORD. Jer 2.31
'Give h. to the sound of the 6.17
they said, 'We will not give h.' 6.17
they have not given h. to my words; 6.19
I have given h. and listened, but 8.06
who does not h. the words of this 11.03
Take h. for the sake of your lives, 17.21
and let us not h. any of his words." 18.18
Give h. to me, O LORD, and hearken to 18.19
But if you will not h. these words, 22.05
who has given h. to his word and 23.18
and to h. the words of my servants 26.05
because they did not h. my words, 29.19
men, O king, pay no h. to you; Dan 3.12
pays no h. to you, O king, or the 6.13
iniquities and giving h. to thy truth. 9.13
O LORD, give h. and act; delay not, 9.19
give h. to the words that I speak 10.11
back and give h. to those who 11.30
He shall give no h. to the gods of 11.37
shall not give h. to any other god, 11.37
Give h., O house of Israel! Hos 5.01
But they did not hear or h. me, Zec 1.04
So take h. to yourselves, and let Mal 2.15
So take h. to yourselves and do not 2.16
"Take h. and beware of the leaven Mt 16.06
"Take h. that no one leads you 24.04
to them, "Take h. what you hear; Mk 4.24
"Take h., beware of the leaven of 8.15
"Take h. that no one leads you 13.05
"But take h. to yourselves; for they 13.09
But take h.; I have told you all 13.23
Take h., watch; for you do not know 13.33
Take h. then how you hear; for to him Lk 8.18
"Take h., and beware of all covetousness; 12.15
Take h. to yourselves; if your brother 17.03
"Take h. that you are not led astray; 21.08
"But take h. to yourselves lest 21.34

HEED (cont.)
but the sheep did not h. them. Jn 10.08
also, and they will h. my voice. 10.16
one accord gave h. to what was Ac 8.06
They all gave h. to him, from the 8.10
And they gave h. to him, because for 8.11
heart to give h. to what was said 16.14
Take h. to yourselves and to all 20.28
he stands take h. lest he fall. 1Co 10.12
h. my appeal, agree with one another, 2Co 13.11
another take h. that you are not Gal 5.15
faith by giving h. to deceitful 1Ti 4.01
Take h. to yourself and to your 4.16
instead of giving h. to Jewish Tit 1.14
and so I paid no h. to them, says Heb 8.09
took h. and constructed an ark for 11.07

HEEDED
And his brothers h. him. Gen 37.27
after that God h. supplications 2Sa 21.14
So the LORD h. supplications for 24.25
no one answered, no one h. 1Ki 18.29
kept thy law or h. thy commandments Neh 9.34
out my hand and no one has h., Pro 1.24
despised, and his words are not h. Ecc 9.16
urgently, though you have not h., Jer 26.05
the LORD h. and heard them, and a Mal 3.16
But they have not all h. the gospel; Rom 10.16

HEEDLESS
By insolence the h. make strife, Pro 13.10

HEEDS
He who h. instruction is on the Pro 10.17
but he who h. reproof is honored. 13.18
but he who h. admonition is prudent. 15.05
He whose ear h. wholesome admonition 15.31
but he who h. admonition gains 15.32

HEEL
head, and you shall bruise his h." Gen 3.15
hand had taken hold of Esau's h.; 25.26
A trap seizes him by the h., Job 18.09
has lifted his h. against me. Ps 41.09
womb he took his brother by the h., Hos 12.03
bread has lifted his h. against me.' Jn 13.18

HEELS
the horse's h. so that his rider Gen 49.17
Gad, but he shall raid at their h. 49.19
ten thousand men went up at his h.; Ju 4.10
valley they rushed forth at his h. 5.15
side, and chase him at his h. Job 18.11

HEGAI
custody of H. the king's eunuch who Est 2.03
Susa the capital in custody of H., 2.08
in custody of H. who had charge of 2.08
except what H. the king's eunuch, 2.15

HEGLAM
H., who was the father of Uzza and 1Ch 8.07

HE-GOAT
from your house, nor h. from your folds. Ps 50.09
the h., and a king striding before Pro 30.31
shall offer a h. without blemish Eze 43.22
and a h. daily for a sin offering. 45.23
a h. came from the west across the Dan 8.05
Then the h. magnified himself 8.08
And the h. is the king of Greece; 8.21

HE-GOATS
removed the h. that were striped Gen 30.35
dream that the h. which leaped 31.10
two hundred she-goats and twenty h., 32.14
seven thousand seven hundred h. 2Ch 17.11
and seven h. for a sin offering for 29.21
Then the h. for the sin offering 29.23

offering for all Israel twelve h., Ez 6.17
and as a sin offering twelve h.; 8.35
of bulls, or of lambs, or of h. Is 1.11
and be as h. before the flock. Jer 50.08
to the slaughter, like rams and h. 51.40
sheep and sheep, rams and h. Eze 34.17

HEIFER
"Bring me a h. three years old, a Gen 15.09
bring you a red h. without defect, Num 19.02
And the h. shall be burned in his 19.05
the midst of the burning of the h. 19.06
He who burns the h. shall wash his 19.08
gather up the ashes of the h., 19.09
ashes of the h. shall wash his 19.10
shall take a h. which has never Deu 21.03
shall bring the h. down to a 21.04
hands over the h. whose neck was 21.06
"If you had not plowed with my h., Ju 14.18
"Take a h. with you, and say, 'I have 1Sa 16.02
"A beautiful h. is Egypt, but a Jer 46.20
you are wanton as a h. at grass, 50.11
Like a stubborn h., Israel is Hos 4.16
Ephraim was a trained h. that loved 10.11
the ashes of a h. sanctifies for Heb 9.13

HEIFER'S
shall break the h. neck there in Deu 21.04

HEIGHT
cubits, and its h. thirty cubits. Gen 6.15
and a cubit and a half its h. Ex 25.10
and a cubit and a half its h. 25.23
and its h. shall be three cubits. 27.01
and the h. five cubits, with hangings 27.18
and two cubits shall be its h.; 30.02
and a cubit and a half its h. 37.01
and a cubit and a half its h.; 37.10
square, and two cubits was its h.; 37.25
and three cubits was its h. 38.01
tell you." And he went to a bare h. Num 23.03
or on the h. of his stature, 1Sa 16.07
whose h. was six cubits and a span. 17.04
under the tamarisk tree on the h., 22.06
The h. of one cherub was ten cubits, 1Ki 6.26
and its h. thirty cubits, and it was 7.02
cubits was the h. of one pillar, 7.15
the h. of the one capital was five 7.16
and the h. of the other capital was 7.16
and the h. of a wheel was a cubit 7.32
The h. of the one pillar was 2Ki 25.17
the h. of the capital was three 25.17
and its h. was a hundred and 2Ch 3.04
and raised it to a very great h.; 33.14
its h. shall be sixty cubits and Ez 6.03
was joined together to half its h. Neh 4.06
Though his h. mount up to the Job 20.06
that he looked down from his holy h., Ps 102.19
As the heavens for h., and the earth Pro 25.03
the great in h. will be hewn down, Is 10.33
shade like night at the h. of noon; 16.03
you who hew a tomb on the h., 22.16
low the inhabitants of the h., 26.05
I came to its remotest h., its densest 37.24
mountain of the house a wooded h.' Jer 26.18
and sing aloud on the h. of Zion, 31.12
rock, who hold the h. of the hill. 49.16
she should fortify her strong h., 51.53
the h. of the one pillar was 52.21
the h. of the one capital was five 52.22
on the mountain h. of Israel will I Eze 17.23
was seen in its h. with the mass 19.11
the mountain h. of Israel, says the 20.40
and of great h., its top among the 31.03
and its heart was proud of its h., 31.10
grow to lofty h. or set their tops 31.14
water may reach up to them in h.; 31.14
wall, one reed; and the h., one reed. 40.05

HEIGHT (cont.)
And this shall be the h. of the altar: Eze 43.14
whose h. was sixty cubits and its Dan 3.01
of the earth; and its h. was great. 4.10
h. was like the h. of the cedars, Amo 2.09
mountain of the house a wooded h. Mic 3.12
nor h., nor depth, nor anything else Rom 8.39
and length and h. and depth, Eph 3.18
and breadth and h. are equal. Rev 21.16

HEIGHTS
went up to the h. of the hill Num 14.40
to go up to the h. of the hill 14.44
the lords of the h. of the Arnon. 21.28
too, on the h. of the field. Ju 5.18
feet, and set me secure on the h. 2Sa 22.34
gone up the h. of the mountains, to 2Ki 19.23
feet, and set me secure on the h. Ps 18.33
the h. of the mountains are his 95.04
the heavens, praise him in the h.! 148.01
On the h. beside the way, in the Pro 8.02
ascend above the h. of the clouds, Is 14.14
He will dwell on the h.; his place 33.16
gone up the h. of the mountains, to 37.24
I will open rivers on the bare h., 41.18
on all bare h. shall be their 49.09
you ride upon the h. of the earth; 58.14
your eyes to the bare h., and see! Jer 3.02
A voice on the bare h. is heard, 3.21
from the bare h. in the desert 4.11
raise a lamentation on the bare h., 7.29
Upon all the bare h. in the desert 12.12
The wild asses stand on the bare h., 14.06
the mountain h. of Israel shall be Eze 34.14
'The ancient h. have become our 36.02
and treads on the h. of the earth— Amo 4.13

HEINOUS
For that would be a h. crime; Job 31.11

HEIR
and the h. of my house is Eliezer Gen 15.02
born in my house will be my h." 15.03
him, "This man shall not be your h.; 15.04
your own son shall be your h." 15.04
shall not be h. with my son Isaac." 21.10
so they would destroy the h. also. 2Sa 14.07
will in the end find him his h. Pro 29.21
"Has Israel no sons? Has he no h.? Jer 49.01
to themselves, 'This is the h.; Mt 21.38
to one another, 'This is the h.; Mk 12.07
to themselves, 'This is the h.; Lk 20.14
I mean that the h., as long as he Gal 4.01
but a son, and if a son then an h. 4.07
he appointed the h. of all things, Heb 1.02
and became an h. of the righteousness 11.07

HEIRS
of the law who are to be the h., Rom 4.14
and if children, then h., h. of God 8.17
h. of God and fellow h. with Christ, 8.17
offspring, h. according to promise. Gal 3.29
is, how the Gentiles are fellow h., Eph 3.06
and become h. in hope of eternal Tit 3.07
convincingly to the h. of the Heb 6.17
h. with him of the same promise. 11.09
in faith and h. of the kingdom Jas 2.05
you are joint h. of the grace of 1Pe 3.07

HELAH
had two wives, H. and Naarah; 1Ch 4.05
The sons of H.: Zereth, Izhar, and 4.07

HELAM
and they came to H., with Shobach 2Sa 10.16
crossed the Jordan, and came to H. 10.17

HELBAH
or of H., or of Aphik, or of Rehob; Ju 1.31

HELBON
every kind; wine of H., and white wool, Eze 27.18

HELD
so Jacob h. his peace until they Gen 34.05
Whenever Moses h. up his hand, Ex 17.11
and Aaron and Hur h. up his hands, 17.12
glorified.'" And Aaron h. his peace. Lev 10.03
freedom, an inquiry shall be h. 19.20
the LORD has h. you back from Num 24.11
but you who h. fast to the LORD Deu 4.04
and h. festival, and went into the Ju 9.27
to the lad who h. him by the hand, 16.26
So she h. it, and he measured out Ru 3.15
he is a man that is h. in honor; 1Sa 9.06
no present. But he h. his peace. 10.27
by them I shall be h. in honor." 2Sa 6.22
it h. two thousand baths. 1Ki 7.26
each laver h. forty baths, each 7.38
So Solomon h. the feast at that 8.65
For he h. fast to the LORD; 2Ki 18.06
and he is to be h. in awe above 1Ch 16.25
it h. over three thousand baths. 2Ch 4.05
time Solomon h. the feast for 7.08
eighth day they h. a solemn 7.09
So he h. Judah and Benjamin. 11.12
and half h. the spears, shields, bows, Neh 4.16
and with the other h. his weapon. 4.17
half of them h. the spears from 4.21
And I h. a great assembly against 5.07
I also h. to the work on this wall, 5.16
sight and he h. out to Esther the Est 5.02
women, I would have h. my peace; 7.04
And the king h. out the golden 8.04
My foot has h. fast to his steps; Job 23.11
My steps have h. fast to thy paths, Ps 17.05
I h. my peace to no avail; 39.02
steadfast love, O LORD, h. me up. 94.18
by all those who h. them captive. 106.46
he curse you, and you be h. guilty. Pro 30.10
I h. him, and would not let him go Sol 3.04
a king is h. captive in the tresses 7.05
but thou hast h. back my life from Is 38.17
For a long time I have h. my peace, 42.14
Have I not h. my peace, even for a 57.11
and he too shall be h. in derision. Jer 48.26
them captive have h. them fast, 50.33
be laughed at and h. in derision, Eze 23.32
because they h. him to be a prophet. Mt 14.05
because they h. him to be a prophet. 21.46
and immediately h. counsel with Mk 3.06
for all h. that John was a real 11.32
whole council h. a consultation; 15.01
on hyssop and h. it to his mouth. Jn 19.29
possible for him to be h. by it. Ac 2.24
but the people h. them in high 5.13
h. in honor by all the people, stood 5.34
him to be h. until I could send 25.21
world may be h. accountable to God. Rom 3.19
dead to that which h. us captive, 7.06
day long I have h. out my hands to 10.21
You are h. in honor, but we in 1Co 4.10
Let marriage be h. in honor among Heb 13.04
in his right hand he h. seven stars, Rev 1.16
who had been h. ready for the hour, 9.15

HELDAI
was H. the Netophathite, of Othniel; 1Ch 27.15
"Take from the exiles H., Zec 6.10
of the LORD as a reminder to H., 6.14

HELEB
H. the son of Baanah of Netophah, 2Sa 23.29

HELECH
of Arvad and H. were upon your Eze 27.11

HELED
H. the son of Baanah of Netophah, 1Ch 11.30

HELEK
of H., the family of the Helekites; Num 26.30
H., Asriel, Shechem, Hepher, and Jos 17.02

HELEKITES
of Helek, the family of the H.; Num 26.30

HELEPH
And its boundary ran from H., from the Jos 19.33

HELER
The sons of H. his brother: Zophah, 1Ch 7.35

HELEZ
H. the Paltite, Ira the son of 2Sa 23.26
Azariah was the father of H., and H. of 1Ch 2.39
Shammoth of Harod, H. the Pelonite, 11.27
was H. the Pelonite, of the sons of 27.10

HELI
supposed) of Joseph, the son of H., Lk 3.23

HELIOPOLIS
the obelisks of H. which is in the Jer 43.13

HELKAI
of Harim, Adna; of Meraioth, H.; Neh 12.15

HELKATH
Its territory included H., Hali, Beten, Jos 19.25
H. with its pasture lands, and Rehob 21.31

HELKATHHAZZURIM
Therefore that place was called H., 2Sa 2.16

HELL
shall be liable to the h. of fire. Mt 5.22
your whole body be thrown into h. 5.29
that your whole body go into h. 5.30
destroy both soul and body in h. 10.28
to be thrown into the h. of fire. 18.09
much a child of h. as yourselves. 23.15
to escape being sentenced to h.? 23.33
than with two hands to go to h., Mk 9.43
with two feet to be thrown into h. 9.45
two eyes to be thrown into h., 9.47
killed, has power to cast into h.; Lk 12.05
of nature, and set on fire by h. Jas 3.06
cast them into h. and committed 2Pe 2.04

HELLENISTS
the H. murmured against the Hebrews Ac 6.01
spoke and disputed against the H.; 9.29

HELMET
He had a h. of bronze on his head, 1Sa 17.05
he put a h. of bronze on his head, 17.38
Ephraim is my h.; Judah is my Ps 60.07
Ephraim is my h.; Judah my 108.08
and a h. of salvation upon his head; Is 59.17
and h., and I will commit the Eze 23.24
they hung the shield and h. in you; 27.10
all of them with shield and h.; 38.05
And take the h. of salvation, and Eph 6.17
and for a h. the hope of salvation. 1Th 5.08

HELMETS
h., coats of mail, bows, and stones 2Ch 26.14
Take your stations with your h., Jer 46.04

HELON
from Zebulun, Eliab the son of H.; Num 1.09
Zebulun being Eliab the son of H., 2.07
On the third day Eliab the son of H., 7.24
offering of Eliab the son of H. 7.29
of Zebulun was Eliab the son of H. 10.16

HELP
a man with the h. of the LORD." Gen 4.01
God of your father who will h. you, 49.25
bondage, and cried out for h., Ex 2.23
"The God of my father was my h., 18.04
you shall h. him to lift it up. 23.05
with the h. of the leaders of Num 1.44
and withhold your h. from them; Deu 22.01
you may not withhold your h. 22.03
and withhold your h. from them; 22.04
you shall h. him to lift them up 22.04
did not cry for h. though she was 22.24
woman cried for h. there was no 22.27
and there shall be none to h. you. 28.29
and there shall be none to h. you. 28.31
Let them rise up and h. you, 32.38
and be a h. against his adversaries." 33.07
through the heavens to your h., 33.26
by the LORD, the shield of your h., 33.29
your brethren and shall h. them, Jos 1.14
and h. me, and let us smite Gibeon; 10.04
us quickly, and save us, and h. us; 10.06
of Gezer came up to h. Lachish; 10.33
of Israel cried to the LORD for h.; Ju 4.03
came not to the h. of the LORD, 5.23
to the h. of the LORD against the 5.23
of Israel cried for h. to the LORD. 6.06
Damascus came to h. Hadadezer king 2Sa 8.05
for me, then you shall h. me; 10.11
you, then I will come and h. you. 10.11
feared to h. the Ammonites any 10.19
obeisance, and said, "H., O king." 14.04
that you send us h. from the city." 18.03
salvation, and thy h. made me great. 22.36
to prosper all my h. and my desire? 23.05
saying, "H., my lord, O king!" 2Ki 6.26
said, "If the LORD will not h. you, 6.27
whence shall I h. you? From the 6.27
and there was none to h. Israel. 14.26
that he might h. him to confirm his 15.19
when they received h. against them, 1Ch 5.20
come to me in friendship to h. me, 12.17
(Yet he did not h. them, for the 12.19
men kept coming to David to h. him, 12.22
to h. David with singleness of 12.33
Damascus came to h. Hadadezer king 18.05
for me, then you shall h. me; 19.12
strong for you, then I will h. you. 19.12
not willing to h. the Ammonites 19.19
of Israel to h. Solomon his son, 22.17
With the h. of Zadok of the sons of 24.03
there is none like thee to h., 2Ch 14.11
H. us, O LORD our God, for we rely on 14.11
but sought h. from physicians. 16.12
"Should you h. the wicked and love 19.02
assembled to seek h. from the LORD; 20.04
has power to h. or to cast down." 25.08
to h. the king against the enemy. 26.13
sent to the king of Assyria for h. 28.16
of Assyria; but it did not h. him. 28.21
to them that they may h. me." 28.23
to h. us and to fight our battles." 32.08
it is not in our power to h. it, Neh 5.05
accomplished with the h. of our God. 6.16
In truth I have no h. in me, Job 6.13
soul of the wounded cries for h.; 24.12
With whose h. have you uttered 26.04
fatherless who had none to h. him. 29.12
and in his disaster cry for h.? 30.24
up in the assembly, and cry for h. 30.28
because I saw h. in the gate; 31.21
they call for h. because of the arm 35.09
do not cry for h. when he binds 36.13
me, there is no h. for him in God. Ps 3.02

HELP (cont.)

H., LORD; for there is no longer any Ps 12.01
the LORD; to my God I cried for h. 18.06
me, and thy h. made me great. 18.35
They cried for h., but there was 18.41
May he send you h. from the sanctuary, 20.02
that the LORD will h. his anointed; 20.06
and in thy h. how greatly he exults 21.01
His glory is great through thy h.; 21.05
is near and there is none to h. 22.11
O thou my h., hasten to my aid! 22.19
in anger, thou who hast been my h. 27.09
supplication, as I cry to thee for h., 28.02
my God, I cried to thee for h., 30.02
when I cried to thee for h. 31.22
for the LORD; he is our h. and shield. 33.20
When the righteous cry for h., 34.17
and buckler, and rise for my h.! 35.02
Make haste to h. me, O Lord, my 38.22
hid thy saving h. within my heart, 40.10
O LORD, make haste to h. me! 40.13
Thou art my h. and my deliverer; 40.17
again praise him, my h. and my God. 42.05
again praise him, my h. and my God. 42.11
again praise him, my h. and my God. 43.05
Rise up, come to our h.! 44.26
a very present h. in trouble. 46.01
God will h. her right early. 46.05
thyself, come to my h., and see! 59.04
O grant us h. against the foe, for 60.11
the foe, for vain is the h. of man! 60.11
for thou hast been my h., and in the 63.07
With thy faithful h. rescue me from 69.14
O LORD, make haste to h. me! 70.01
Thou art my h. and my deliverer; 70.05
O my God, make haste to h. me! 71.12
thy righteous h. all the day long, 71.24
H. us, O God of our salvation, for 79.09
LORD, my God, I call for h. by day; 88.01
or thy saving h. in the land of 88.12
If the LORD had not been my h., 94.17
h. me when thou deliverest them; 106.04
they fell down, with none to h. 107.12
give h. by thy right hand, and 108.06
O grant us h. from the foe, for vain 108.12
the foe, for vain is the h. of man! 108.12
H. me, O LORD my God! Save me 109.26
He is their h. and their shield. 115.09
He is their h. and their shield. 115.10
He is their h. and their shield. 115.11
The LORD is on my side to h. me; 118.07
me with falsehood; h. me! 119.86
I rise before dawn and cry for h.; 119.147
Let thy hand be ready to h. me, 119.173
thee, and let thy ordinance h. me. 119.175
From whence does my h. come? 121.01
My h. comes from the LORD, who made 121.02
Our h. is in the name of the LORD, 124.08
son of man, in whom there is no h. 146.03
Happy is he whose h. is the God of 146.05
for the LORD, and he will h. you. Pro 20.22
until death; let no one h. him. 28.17
To whom will you flee for h., Is 10.03
we fled for h. to be delivered 20.06
that brings neither h. nor profit, 30.05
For Egypt's h. is worthless and 30.07
to Egypt for h. and rely on horses, 31.01
I cry for h. until morning; 38.13
I will h. you, I will uphold you 41.10
to you, "Fear not, I will h. you." 41.13
I will h. you, says the LORD; 41.14
you from the womb and will h. you: 44.02
doings, but they will not h. you. 57.12
looked, but there was no one to h.; 63.05
which came to h. you is about to Jer 37.07
foe, and there was none to h. her, Lam 1.07
though I call and cry for h., 3.08
close thine ear to my cry for h.!' 3.56
ever watching vainly for h.; 4.17
company will not h. him in war, Eze 17.17
came to h. me, so I left him there Dan 10.13
they shall receive a little h. 11.34
fortresses by the h. of a foreign 11.39
to his end, with none to h. him. 11.45
by the h. of your God, return, hold Hos 12.06
you, O Israel; who can h. you? 13.09
O LORD, how long shall I cry for h., Hab 1.02
shall come and h. to build the Zec 6.15
before him, saying, "Lord, h. me." Mt 15.25
anything, have pity on us and h. us." Mk 9.22
and said, "I believe; h. my unbelief! 9.24
the other boat to come and h. them. Lk 5.07
serve alone? Tell her then to h. me." 10.40
"Come over to Macedonia and h. us." Ac 16.09
by so toiling one must h. the weak, 20.35
crying out, "Men of Israel, h.! 21.28
I have had the h. that comes from 26.22
and h. her in whatever she may Rom 16.02
You also must h. us by prayer, so 2Co 1.11
prayers and the h. of the Spirit Php 1.19
h. these women, for they have 4.03
you sent me h. once and again. 4.16
h. the weak, be patient with them 1Th 5.14
so as to h. cases of urgent need, Tit 3.14
he is able to h. those who are Heb 2.18
find grace to h. in time of need. 4.16
earth came to the h. of the woman, Rev 12.16

HELPED

but Moses stood up and h. them, Ex 2.17
said, "Hitherto the LORD has h. us." 1Sa 7.12
they followed Adonijah and h. him. 1Ki 1.07
the thirty-two kings who h. him. 20.16
the mighty men who h. him in war. 1Ch 12.01
They h. David against the band of 12.21
And because God h. the Levites who 15.26
cried out, and the LORD h. him. 2Ch 18.31
they all h. to destroy one another. 20.23
God h. him against the Philistines, 26.07
far, for he was marvelously h., 26.15
gods of the kings of Syria h. them, 28.23
their brethren the Levites h. them, 29.34
outside the city; and they h. him. 32.03
h. the people to understand the law, Neh 8.07
royal officials also h. the Jews, Est 9.03
"How you have h. him who has no Job 26.02
so I am h., and my heart exults, and Ps 28.07
hast h. me and comforted me. 86.17
I was falling, but the LORD h. me. 118.13
A brother h. is like a strong city, Pro 18.19
and he who is h. will fall, and they Is 31.03
a day of salvation I have h. you; 49.08
He has h. his servant Israel, in Lk 1.54
he greatly h. those who through Ac 18.27
and h. you on the day of salvation." 2Co 6.02

HELPER

I will make him a h. fit for him." Gen 2.18
was not found a h. fit for him. 2.20
hast been the h. of the fatherless Ps 10.14
to me! O LORD, be thou my h.!" 30.10
Behold, God is my h.; the Lord is 54.04
the poor and him who has no h. 72.12
the h. will stumble, and he who is Is 31.03
and Sidon every h. that remains. Jer 47.04
she has been a h. of many and of Rom 16.02
confidently say, "The Lord is my h., Heb 13.06

HELPERS

peace to you, and peace to your h.! 1Ch 12.18
beneath him bowed the h. of Rahab. Job 9.13
and against the h. of those who Is 31.02
his h. and all his troops; Eze 12.14
Egypt, and all her h. are broken. 30.08
with their h., out of the midst of 32.21
Put and the Libyans were her h. Nah 3.09

HELPERS (cont.)
sent into Macedonia two of his h., Ac 19.22
h., administrators, speakers in 1Co 12.28

HELPFUL
for me," but not all things are h. 1Co 6.12
lawful," but not all things are h. 10.23

HELPING
were the prophets of God, h. them. Ez 5.02
Why art thou so far from h. me, Ps 22.01

HELPLESS
I suffer thy terrors; I am h. Ps 88.15
report of it, our hands fall h.; Jer 6.24
of them, and his hands fell h.; 50.43
because they were harassed and h., Mt 9.36
While we were yet h., at the right Rom 5.06

HELPS
your helpers! For your God h. you." 1Ch 12.18
The LORD h. them and delivers them; Ps 37.40
but wisdom h. one to succeed. Ecc 10.10
Every one h. his neighbor, and says Is 41.06
For the Lord GOD h. me; therefore I 50.07
Behold, the Lord GOD h. me; 50.09
Likewise the Spirit h. us in our Rom 8.26

HEM
and h. you in on every side, Lk 19.43

HEMAN
The sons of Lotan were Hori and H.; Gen 36.22
and H., Calcol, and Darda, the sons 1Ki 4.31
H., Calcol, and Dara, five in all. 1Ch 2.06
H. the singer the son of Joel, son 6.33
appointed H. the son of Joel; 15.17
The singers, H., Asaph, and Ethan, 15.19
With them were H. and Jeduthun, and 16.41
H. and Jeduthun had trumpets and 16.42
and of H., and of Jeduthun, who 25.01
Of H., the sons of H.: Bukkiah, 25.04
the sons of H. the king's seer, 25.05
God had given h. fourteen sons and 25.05
and H. were under the order of the 25.06
H., and Jeduthun, their sons and 2Ch 5.12
and of the sons of H., Jehuel and 29.14
and H., and Jeduthun the king's seer; 35.15

HEMDAN
H., Eshban, Ithran, and Cheran. Gen 36.26

HEMMED
for I am h. in by darkness, and Job 23.17

HEMORRHAGE
suffered from a h. for twelve years Mt 9.20
And immediately the h. ceased; and Mk 5.29

HEN
the water h., the pelican, the Lev 11.18
and the great owl, the water h. Deu 14.16
together as a h. gathers her brood Mt 23.37
together as a h. gathers her brood Lk 13.34

HENA
gods of Sepharvaim, H., and Ivvah? 2Ki 18.34
the king of H., or the king of 19.13
the king of H., or the king of Is 37.13

HENADAD
the sons of H. and the Levites, Ez 3.09
repaired: Bavvai the son of H., Neh 3.18
the son of H. repaired another 3.24
Binnui of the sons of H., Kadmiel; 10.09

HENCE
afterwards he will let you go h.; Ex 11.01
go up h., you and the people whom 33.01
H. it is said, "Is Saul also among 1Sa 19.24
"take me not h. in the midst of my Ps 102.24
that he sees is for many days h., Eze 12.27
h. the upper chambers were set back 42.06
for it pertains to many days h." Dan 8.26
'Move h. to yonder place,' and it Mt 17.20
the Father. Rise, let us go h. Jn 14.31
H., as to the eating of food 1Co 8.04
H. I remind you to rekindle the 2Ti 1.06
h. it is necessary for this priest Heb 8.03
H. even the first covenant was not 9.18
h., figuratively speaking, he did 11.19
H. we can confidently say, "The Lord 13.06

HENCEFORTH
And h. the people of Israel shall Num 18.22
I will not h. drive out before them Ju 2.21
of my army h. in place of Joab.'" 2Sa 19.13
house of Jeroboam today. And h. 1Ki 14.14
h. neither death nor miscarriage 2Ki 2.21
for h. your servant will not offer 5.17
"I am God, and also h. I am He; Is 43.13
the name of the city h. shall be, Eze 48.35
steals shall be cut off h. according Zec 5.03
who swears falsely shall be cut off h. 5.03
H. we deem the arrogant blessed; Mal 3.15
For behold, h. all generations will Lk 1.48
h. you will be catching men." 5.10
for h. in one house there will be 12.52
h. you know him and have seen him." Jn 14.07
H. let no man trouble me; Gal 6.17
H. there is laid up for me the 2Ti 4.08
the dead who die in the Lord h." Rev 14.13

HENNA
me a cluster of h. blossoms in the Sol 1.14
all choicest fruits, h. with nard, 4.13

HEPHER
and of H., the family of the Num 26.32
Zelophehad the son of H. had no sons, 26.33
of Zelophehad the son of H., son of 27.01
of Tappuah, one; the king of H., one; Jos 12.17
Asriel, Shechem, H., and Shemida; 17.02
Now Zelophehad the son of H., 17.03
Soco and all the land of H.; 1Ki 4.10
H., Temeni, and Haahashtari. 1Ch 4.06
H. the Mecherathite, Ahijah the 11.36

HEPHERITES
of Hepher, the family of the H. Num 26.32

HEPHZIBAH
Jerusalem. His mother's name was H. 2Ki 21.01

HERALD
h. of good tidings; lift up your voice Is 40.09
h. of good tidings, lift it up, fear 40.09
to Jerusalem a h. of good tidings. 41.27
And the h. proclaimed aloud, "You Dan 3.04
a h. of righteousness, with seven 2Pe 2.05

HERB
earth and no h. of the field had Gen 2.05
and as the showers upon the h. Deu 32.02
and wither like the green h. Ps 37.02
tithe the mint and rue and every h., Lk 11.42

HERBAGE
and the h. of the mountains is Pro 27.25
and hills, and dry up all their h.; Is 42.15
eyes fail because there is no h. Jer 14.06

HERBS
and bitter h. they shall eat it. Ex 12.08
unleavened bread and bitter h. Num 9.11
out into the field to gather h., 2Ki 4.39
Better is a dinner of h. where love Pro 15.17

HERD

And Abraham ran to the h., and took Gen 18.07
cattle from the h. or from the Lev 1.02
is a burnt offering from the h., 1.03
if he offers an animal from the h., 3.01
from the h. or from the flock, to be 22.21
LORD from the h. or from the flock Num 15.03
firstlings of your h. and of your Deu 12.06
firstlings of your h. or of your 12.17
kill any of your h. or your flock, 12.21
firstlings of your h. and flock; 14.23
born of your h. and flock you 15.19
work with the firstling of your h., 15.19
your God, from the flock or the h., 16.02
Curds from the h., and milk from 32.14
own flock or h. to prepare for the 2Sa 12.04
and sheep and cheese from the h., 17.29
the h. of bulls with the calves of Ps 68.30
the young of the flock and the h.; Jer 31.12
h. nor flock, taste anything; Jon 3.07
and there be no h. in the stalls, Hab 3.17
Now a h. of many swine was feeding Mt 8.30
send us away into the h. of swine." 8.31
the whole h. rushed down the steep 8.32
Now a great h. of swine was feeding Mk 5.11
and the h., numbering about two 5.13
Now a large h. of swine was feeding Lk 8.32
and the h. rushed down the steep 8.33

HERDED

a wife, and for a wife he h. sheep.) Hos 12.12

HERDS

also had flocks and h. and tents, Gen 13.05
he has given him flocks and h., 24.35
He had possessions of flocks and h., 26.14
and the flocks and h. and camels, 32.07
the flocks and h. giving suck are 33.13
they took their flocks and their h., 34.28
your h., and all that you have; 45.10
and their h., and all that they 46.32
flocks and h. and all that they 47.01
the h., and the asses: and he 47.17
and the h. of cattle are my lord's; 47.18
and their h. were left in the land 50.08
the camels, the h., and the flocks. Ex 9.03
daughters and with your flocks and h., 10.09
flocks and your h. remain behind." 10.24
Take your flocks and your h., 12.32
many cattle, both flocks and h. 12.38
no flocks or h. feed before that 34.03
And all the tithe of h. and flocks, Lev 27.32
Shall flocks and h. be slaughtered Num 11.22
and when your h. and flocks multiply, Deu 8.13
h. of Bashan and goats, with the 32.14
captured all the flocks and h.; 1Sa 30.20
man had very many flocks and h.; 2Sa 12.02
Over the h. that pastured in Sharon 1Ch 27.29
over the h. in the valleys was 27.29
many cisterns, for he had large h., 2Ch 26.10
and flocks and h. in abundance; 32.29
firstlings of your h. and of our Neh 10.36
and give attention to your h.; Pro 27.23
great possessions of h. and flocks, Ecc 2.07
Achor a place for h. to lie down, Is 65.10
labored, their flocks and their h., Jer 3.24
eat up your flocks and your h.; 5.17
booty, their h. of cattle a spoil. 49.32
flocks and h. they shall go to Hos 5.06
Ephraim h. the wind, and pursues the 12.01
The h. of cattle are perplexed Joe 1.18
H. shall lie down in the midst of Zep 2.14

HERDSMAN

but I am a h., and a dresser of Amo 7.14

HERDSMAN'S

all that pass under the h. staff, Lev 27.32

HERDSMEN

between the h. of Abram's cattle Gen 13.07
cattle and the h. of Lot's cattle. 13.07
between your h. and my h.; for we are 13.08
h. of Gerar quarreled with Isaac's h., 26.20
Edomite, the chief of Saul's h. 1Sa 21.07
The h. fled, and going into the city Mt 8.33
The h. fled, and told it in the city Mk 5.14
When the h. saw what had happened, Lk 8.34

HERE

Now then, h. is your wife, take her, Gen 12.19
shall come back h. in the fourth 15.16
to Lot, "Have you any one else h.? 19.12
and your two daughters who are h., 19.15
swear to me h. by God that you 21.23
"Abraham!" And he said, "H. am I." 22.01
young men, "Stay h. with the ass; 22.05
And he said, "H. am I, my son." 22.07
Abraham!" And he said, "H. am I." 22.11
son"; and he answered, "H. I am." 27.01
and he said, "H. I am; who are you, my 27.18
"H. is my maid Bilhah; go in to her, 30.03
'Jacob,' and I said, 'H. I am!' 31.11
Set it h. before my kinsmen and 31.37
And he said to him, "H. I am." 37.13
one another, "H. comes this dreamer. 37.19
into this pit h. in the wilderness, 37.22
they said, "No harlot has been h." 38.21
place said, 'No harlot has been h.' " 38.22
and h. also I have done nothing 40.15
your youngest brother comes h. 42.15
h. it is in the mouth of my sack!" 42.28
yourselves, because you sold me h.; 45.05
not you who sent me h., but God; 45.08
haste and bring my father down h." 45.13
Jacob." And he said, "H. am I." 46.02
Now h. is seed for you, and you 47.23
My sons, whom God has given me h." 48.09
shall carry up my bones from h." 50.25
Moses!" And he said, "H. am I." Ex 3.04
carry my bones with you from h." 13.19
"Tarry h. for us, until we come to 24.14
me, do not carry us up from h. 33.15
we are h., we will go up to the Num 14.40
wilderness, that we should die h., 20.04
and h. we are in Kadesh, a city on 20.16
"Lodge h. this night, and I will 22.08
tarry h. this night also, that I may 22.19
"Build for me h. seven altars, and 23.01
provide for me h. seven bulls and 23.01
"Stand h. beside your burnt offering, 23.15
"Build for me h. seven altars, and 23.29
provide for me h. seven bulls and 23.29
go to the war while you sit h.? 32.06
build sheepfolds h. for our flocks, 32.16
are all of us h. alive this day. Deu 5.03
But you, stand h. by me, and I will 5.31
'Arise, go down quickly from h.; 9.12
all that we are doing h. this day, 12.08
are not cities of the nations h. 20.15
him who is not h. with us this day 29.15
him who stands h. with us this day 29.15
have come h. tonight to search out Jos 2.02
stones from h. out of the midst of 4.03
H. is our bread; it was still warm 9.12
The cities h., to the south of the 17.09
and bring the description h. to me; 18.06
lots for you h. before the LORD 18.06
lots for you h. before the LORD in 18.08
these nations left h. among you, 23.07
of these nations left h. among you, 23.12
comes and asks you, 'Is any one h.?' Ju 4.20
Do not depart from h., I pray thee, 6.18
on the top of the stronghold h., 6.26
you invited us h. to impoverish us?" 14.15
were told, "Samson has come h.," 16.02
said to him, "Who brought you h.? 18.03

HERE (cont.)
What is your business h.?" Ju 18.03
lodge h. and let your heart be 19.09
Behold, h. are my virgin daughter 19.24
give your advice and counsel h." 20.07
"Come h., and eat some bread, and Ru 2.14
sit down h."; and he turned aside 4.01
the city, and said, "Sit down h."; 4.02
the presence of those sitting h., 4.04
was standing h. in your presence, 1Sa 1.26
Samuel!" and he said, "H. I am!" 3.04
"H. I am, for you called me." But he 3.05
"H. I am, for you called me." But he 3.06
"H. I am, for you called me." Then Eli 3.08
my son." And he said, "H. I am." 3.16
covenant of the LORD h. from Shiloh, 4.03
"H., I have with me the fourth part 9.08
and said to them, "Is the seer h.?" 9.11
"H. is the man of whom I spoke to 9.17
passed on stop h. yourself for a 9.27
H. I am; testify against me before the 12.03
"Bring the burnt offering h. to me, 13.09
roll a great stone to me h." 14.33
sheep, and slay them h., and eat; 14.34
in my hand; h. I am, I will die." 14.43
"Bring h. to me Agag the king of 15.32
to Jesse, "Are all your sons h.?" 16.11
will not sit down till he comes h." 16.11
"H. is my elder daughter Merab; 18.17
loaves of bread, or whatever is h." 21.03
have you not h. a spear or a sword 21.08
it is h. wrapped in a cloth behind 21.09
it, for there is none but that h." 21.09
And he answered, "H. I am, my lord." 22.12
"Behold, we are afraid h. in Judah; 23.03
the priest, "Bring the ephod h." 23.09
"H. is the day of which the LORD 24.04
"H. is the spear, O king! Let one 26.22
"What are these Hebrews doing h.?" 29.03
be with the heads of the men h.?" 29.04
"H. is a present for you from the 30.26
to me. And I answered, 'H. I am.' 2Sa 1.07
I have brought them h. to my lord." 1.10
"H. is the head of Ishbosheth, the 4.08
to David, "You will not come in h., 5.06
thinking, "David cannot come in h." 5.06
"Remain h. today also, and tomorrow 11.12
'Come h., that I may send you to 14.32
h. I am, let him do to me what seems 15.26
said, "Turn aside, and stand h." 18.30
But h. is your servant Chimham; 19.37
three days. and be h. yourself." 20.04
'Come h., that I may speak to you.'" 20.16
h. are the oxen for the burnt 24.22
"H. is Nathan the prophet." And when 1Ki 1.23
But he said, "No, I will die h." 2.30
"Depart from h. and turn eastward, 17.03
your lord, 'Behold, Elijah is h.'" 18.08
'He is not h.,' he would take an 18.10
your lord, "Behold Elijah is h.,"' 18.11
your lord, "Behold, Elijah is h."'; 18.14
him, "What are you doing h., Elijah?" 19.09
"What are you doing h., Elijah?" 19.13
your servant was busy h. and there, 20.40
"Is there not h. another prophet of 22.07
to Elisha, "Tarry h., I pray you; 2Ki 2.02
him, "Elisha, tarry h., I pray you; 2.04
said to him, "Tarry h., I pray you; 2.06
"Is there no prophet of the LORD h., 3.11
"Elisha the son of Shaphat is h., 3.11
"Why do we sit h. till we die? 7.03
and if we sit h., we die also. 7.04
who are left h. will fare like the 7.13
h. is the woman, and here is her son 8.05
and h. is her son whom Elisha 8.05
him, "The man of God has come h.," 8.07
servant of the LORD h. among you, 10.23
to David, "You will not come in h." 1Ch 11.05
"H. shall be the house of the LORD 22.01
LORD God and h. the altar of burnt 22.01
thy people, who are present h., 29.17
"Is there not h. another prophet of 2Ch 18.06
shall not bring the captives in h., 28.13
king of Assyria who brought us h." Ez 4.02
(H. is my signature! let the Almighty Job 31.35
and h. shall your proud waves be 38.11
may go and say to you, 'H. we are'? 38.35
h. I will dwell, for I have desired Ps 132.14
"Whoever is simple, let him turn in h.!" Pro 9.04
"Whoever is simple, let him turn in h.!" 9.16
"Come up h.," than to be put lower 25.07
Then I said, "H. I am! Send me." Is 6.08
And, behold, h. come riders, horsemen 21.09
have you to do h. and whom have you h., 22.16
you have hewn h. a tomb for 22.16
h. a little, there a little." 28.10
h. a little, there a little; 28.13
Now therefore what have I h., 52.05
it is I who speak; h. am I." 52.06
cry, and he will say, H. I am. 58.09
I said, "H. am I, h. am I," to a nation 65.01
place: "He shall return h. no more, Jer 22.11
company, they shall return h. 31.08
"Take three men with you from h., 38.10
house of Israel are committing h., Eze 8.06
that they are committing h." 8.09
abominations which they commit h., 8.17
were brought h. in order that I 40.04
High God, come forth, and come h.!" Dan 3.26
h. is the dream which I saw; 4.09
"H. is the end of the matter. 7.28
among those who are standing h. Zec 3.07
Have you come h. to torment us Mt 8.29
greater than the temple is h. 12.06
something greater than Jonah is h. 12.41
something greater than Solomon is h. 12.42
"H. are my mother and my brothers! 12.49
John the Baptist h. on a platter." 14.08
only five loaves h. and two fish." 14.17
And he said, "Bring them h. to me." 14.18
some standing h. who will not 16.28
"Lord, it is well that we are h.; 17.04
wish, I will make three booths h., 17.04
bear with you? Bring him h. to me." 17.17
'Why do you stand h. idle all day?' 20.06
did you get in h. without a 22.12
not be left h. one stone upon 24.02
says to you, 'Lo, h. is the Christ!' 24.23
h. I have made five talents more.' 25.20
h. I have made five talents more.' 25.22
H. you have what is yours.' 25.25
"Sit h., while I go yonder and pray." 26.36
remain h., and watch with me." 26.38
to him, "Friend, why are you h.?" 26.50
He is not h.; for he has risen, as 28.06
who had the withered hand, "Come h." Mk 3.03
"H. are my mother and my brothers! 3.34
and are not his sisters h. with us?" 6.03
men with bread h. in the desert?" 8.04
some standing h. who will not 9.01
"Master, it is well that we are h.; 9.05
will send it back h. immediately.'" 11.03
not be left h. one stone upon 13.02
to you, 'Look, h. is the Christ!' 13.21
disciples, "Sit h., while I pray." 14.32
even to death; remain h., and watch." 14.34
He has risen, he is not h.; 16.06
God, throw yourself down from h.; Lk 4.09
do h. also in your own country.'" 4.23
withered hand, "Come and stand h." 6.08
for we are h. in a lonely place." 9.12
some standing h. who will not 9.27
"Master, it is well that we are h.; 9.33
and bear with you? Bring your son h." 9.41
something greater than Solomon is h. 11.31
something greater than Jonah is h. 11.32

HERE (cont.)
and said to him, "Get away from h., Lk 13.31
spare, but I perish h. with hunger! 15.17
but now he is comforted h., 16.25
would pass from h. to you may not 16.26
nor will they say, 'Lo, h. it is!' 17.21
or 'Lo, h.!' Do not go, do not follow 17.23
h. is your pound, which I kept laid 19.20
bring them h. and slay them before 19.27
yet sat; untie it and bring it h. 19.30
not be left h. one stone upon 21.06
"Look, Lord, h. are two swords." 22.38
them, "Have you anything h. to eat?" 24.41
h. he is, baptizing, and all are Jn 3.26
not thirst, nor come h. to draw." 4.15
"Go, call your husband, and come h." 4.16
For h. the saying holds true, 'One 4.37
"There is a lad h. who has five 6.09
him, "Rabbi, when did you come h.?" 6.25
"Leave h. and go to Judea, that your 7.03
come, but your time is always h. 7.06
And h. he is, speaking openly, and 7.26
to Jesus, "Lord, if you had been h., 11.21
"The Teacher is h. and is calling 11.28
to him, "Lord, if you had been h., 11.32
Pilate said to them, "H. is the man!" 19.05
said to the Jews, "H. is your King!" 19.14
said to Thomas, "Put your finger h., 20.27
yet h. you have filled Jerusalem Ac 5.28
the eunuch said, "See, h. is water! 8.36
And he said, "H. I am, Lord." 9.10
and h. he has authority from the 9.14
And he has come h. for this purpose, 9.21
Now as Peter went h. and there 9.32
we are all h. present in the sight 10.33
harm yourself, for we are all h." 16.28
upside down have come h. also, 17.06
these men h. who are neither 19.37
they ought to be h. before you and 24.19
When therefore they came together h., 25.17
me, both at Jerusalem and h., 25.24
And now I stand h. on trial for 26.06
and so I stand h. testifying both 26.22
brethren coming h. has reported or 28.21
H. indeed we groan, and long to put 2Co 5.02
H. for the third time I am ready to 12.14
that I am put h. for the defense Php 1.16
H. there cannot be Greek and Jew, Col 3.11
everything that has taken place h. 4.09
And again, "H. am I, and the Heb 2.13
H. tithes are received by mortal 7.08
For h. we have no lasting city, but 13.14
"Have a seat h., please," while you Jas 2.03
H. is a call for the endurance and Rev 13.10
H. is a call for the endurance of 14.12

HEREAFTER
Tell us what is to come h., Is 41.23
now and h., if you will not listen Eze 20.39
came thoughts of what would be h., Dan 2.29
known to the king what shall be h. 2.45
h. you will see the Son of man Mt 26.64
is and what is to take place h. Rev 1.19

HEREBY
"H. you shall know that the LORD Num 16.28
"H. you shall know that the living Jos 3.10

HERES
from the battle by the ascent of H. Ju 8.13

HERESH
and Bakbakkar, H., Galal, and Mattaniah 1Ch 9.15

HERESIES
secretly bring in destructive h., 2Pe 2.01

HERETH
and went into the forest of H. 1Sa 22.05

HERETOFORE
either h. or since thou hast spoken Ex 4.10
people straw to make bricks, as h.; 5.07
which they made h. you shall lay 5.08

HERITAGE
destroy not thy people and thy h., Deu 9.26
For they are thy people and thy h., 9.29
his people, Jacob his allotted h. 32.09
priesthood of the LORD is their h.; Jos 18.07
you to be prince over his h. 1Sa 10.01
no share in the h. of the LORD, 26.19
my son together from the h. of God.' 2Sa 14.16
you swallow up the h. of the LORD?" 20.19
you may bless the h. of the LORD?" 21.03
and thy h., which thou didst bring 1Ki 8.51
to be thy h., as thou didst declare 8.53
will cast off the remnant of my h., 2Ki 21.14
the h. decreed for him by God." Job 20.29
and the h. which oppressors receive 27.13
and my h. from the Almighty on high? 31.02
I will make the nations your h., Ps 2.08
places; yea, I have goodly h. 16.06
O save thy people, and bless thy h.; 28.09
whom he has chosen as his h.! 33.12
and their h. will abide for ever; 37.18
He chose our h. for us, the pride of 47.04
given me the h. of those who fear 61.05
restore thy h. as it languished; 68.09
redeemed to be the tribe of thy h.! 74.02
and vented his wrath on his h. 78.62
people, O LORD, and afflict thy h. 94.05
he will not abandon his h.; 94.14
that I may glory with thy h. 106.05
his people, and he abhorred his h.; 106.40
giving them the h. of the nations. 111.06
Thy testimonies are my h. for ever; 119.111
Lo, sons are a h. from the LORD, the 127.03
and gave their land as a h., 135.12
a h. to his people Israel. 135.12
and gave their land as a h., 136.21
a h. to Israel his servant, for his 136.22
work of my hands, and Israel my h." Is 19.25
with my people, I profaned my h.; 47.06
This is the h. of the servants of 54.17
you with the h. of Jacob your 58.14
thy servants, the tribes of thy h. 63.17
and made my h. an abomination. Jer 2.07
that I gave your fathers for a h. 3.18
a h. most beauteous of all nations. 3.19
my house, I have abandoned my h.; 12.07
My h. has become to me like a lion 12.08
Is my h. to me like a speckled bird 12.09
who touch the h. which I have 12.14
each to his h. and each to his 12.15
hand from your h. which I gave to 17.04
you exult, O plunderers of my h., 50.11
and make not thy h. a reproach, Joe 2.17
of my people and my h. Israel, 3.02
and left his h. to jackals of the Mal 1.03
He who conquers shall have this h., Rev 21.07

HERITAGES
land, to apportion the desolate h.; Is 49.08

HERMAS
H., and the brethren who are with Rom 16.14

HERMES
the chief speaker, they called H. Ac 14.12
H., Patrobas, Hermas, and the brethren Rom 16.14

HERMOGENES
me, and among them Phygelus and H. 2Ti 1.15

HERMON
valley of the Arnon to Mount H. Deu 3.08
(the Sidonians call H. Sirion, 3.09

HERMON (cont.)
far as Mount Sirion (that is, H.), Deu 4.48
Hivites under H. in the land of Jos 11.03
valley of Lebanon below Mount H. 11.17
valley of the Arnon to Mount H., 12.01
over Mount H. and Salecah and all 12.05
below Mount H. to the entrance of 13.05
and all Mount H., and all Bashan to 13.11
to Baalhermon, Senir, and Mount H. 1Ch 5.23
from the land of Jordan and of H., Ps 42.06
Tabor and H. joyously praise thy 89.12
It is like the dew of H., 133.03
from the peak of Senir and H., Sol 4.08

HEROD
Judea in the days of H. the king, Mt 2.01
When H. the king heard this, he was 2.03
Then H. summoned the wise men 2.07
in a dream not to return to H., 2.12
for H. is about to search for the 2.13
there until the death of H. 2.15
Then H., when he saw that he had 2.16
But when H. died, behold, an angel of 2.19
Judea in place of his father H., 2.22
At that time H. the tetrarch heard 14.01
For H. had seized John and bound 14.03
the company, and pleased H., 14.06
King H. heard of it; for Jesus' Mk 6.14
But when H. heard of it he said, 6.16
For H. had sent and seized John, and 6.17
For John said to H., "It is not lawful 6.18
for H. feared John, knowing that he 6.20
came when H. on his birthday gave 6.21
she pleased H. and his guests; 6.22
the Pharisees and the leaven of H." 8.15
In the days of H., king of Judea, Lk 1.05
and H. being tetrarch of Galilee, 3.01
But H. the tetrarch, who had been 3.19
the evil things that H. had done, 3.19
Now H. the tetrarch heard of all 9.07
H. said, "John I beheaded; but who 9.09
for H. wants to kill you." 13.31
jurisdiction, he sent him over to H., 23.07
When H. saw Jesus, he was very glad, 23.08
And H. with his soldiers treated 23.11
And H. and Pilate became friends 23.12
neither did H., for he sent him 23.15
both H. and Pontius Pilate, with the Ac 4.27
About that time H. the king laid 12.01
The very night when H. was about to 12.06
the hand of H. and from all that 12.11
And when H. had sought for him and 12.19
Now H. was angry with the people of 12.20
appointed day H. put on his royal 12.21
of the court of H. the tetrarch, 13.01

HERODIANS
disciples to him, along with the H., Mt 22.16
counsel with the H. against him, Mk 3.06
the Pharisees and some of the H., 12.13

HERODIAS
him in prison, for the sake of H., Mt 14.03
the daughter of H. danced before 14.06
him in prison for the sake of H., Mk 6.17
And H. had a grudge against him, and 6.19
had been reproved by him for H., Lk 3.19

HERODIAS'
For when H. daughter came in and Mk 6.22

HERODION
Greet my kinsman H. Greet those in Rom 16.11

HEROD'S
But when H. birthday came, the Mt 14.06
H. steward, and Susanna, and many Lk 8.03
he belonged to H. jurisdiction, 23.07
him to be guarded in H. praetorium. Ac 23.35

HEROES
those who are h. at drinking wine, Is 5.22
'We are h. and mighty men of war'? Jer 48.14

HERON
the stork, the h. according to its Lev 11.19
the stork, the h., after their kinds Deu 14.18

HERSELF
So Sarah laughed to h., saying, Gen 18.12
And she h. said, 'He is my brother.' 20.05
she took her veil and covered h. 24.65
wrapping h. up, and sat at the 38.14
she shall count for h. seven days, Lev 15.28
any woman give h. to a beast to 18.23
if she profanes h. by playing the 21.09
undetected though she has defiled h., Num 5.13
of his wife who has defiled h.; 5.14
though she has not defiled h.; 5.14
she has defiled h. and has acted 5.27
she not defiled h. and is clean, 5.28
goes astray and defiles h., 5.29
and binds h. by a pledge, while 30.03
pledge by which she has bound h., 30.04
which she has bound h. shall stand. 30.04
she has bound h., shall stand; 30.05
lips by which she has bound h., 30.06
which she has bound h. shall stand. 30.07
of her lips, by which she bound h.; 30.08
anything by which she has bound h., 30.09
or bound h. by a pledge with an 30.10
by which she bound h. shall stand. 30.11
or concerning her pledge of h., 30.12
and any binding oath to afflict h., 30.13
nay, she gives answer to h., Ju 5.29
was purifying h. from her uncleanness.) 2Sa 11.04
and spread it for h. on the rock, 21.10
shut the door upon h. and her sons; 2Ki 4.05
When she rouses h. to flee, Job 39.18
and the swallow a nest for h., Ps 84.03
She makes h. coverings; her clothing Pro 31.22
and find for h. a resting place. Is 34.14
a bride adorns h. with her jewels. 61.10
has shown h. less guilty than Jer 3.11
and she h. suffers bitterly. Lam 1.04
yea, she h. groans, and turns her 1.08
and that makes idols to defile h.! Eze 22.03
and she defiled h. with all the 23.07
them and decked h. with her ring Hos 2.13
that said to h., "I am and there is Zep 2.15
Tyre has built h. a rampart, and Zec 9.03
for she said to h., "If I only touch Mt 9.21
five months she hid h., saying, Lk 1.24
and could not fully straighten h. 13.11
For if a woman will not veil h., 1Co 11.06
and devoted h. to doing good in 1Ti 5.10
By faith Sarah h. received power to Heb 11.11
who calls h. a prophetess and is Rev 2.20
Render to her as she h. has rendered, 18.06
As she glorified h. and played the 18.07
and his Bride has made h. ready; 19.07

HESHBON
in H., and in all its villages. Num 21.25
For H. was the city of Sihon the 21.26
'Come to H., let it be built, let 21.27
For fire went forth from H., 21.28
So their posterity perished from H., 21.30
of the Amorites, who dwelt at H. 21.34
H., Elealeh, Sebam, Nebo, and Beon, 32.03
And the sons of Reuben built H., 32.37
who lived in H., and Og the king of Deu 1.04
Amorite, king of H., and his land; 2.24
Kedemoth to Sihon the king of H., 2.26
the king of H. would not let us 2.30
of the Amorites, who dwelt at H.,' 3.02
as we did to Sihon the king of H., 3.06
who lived at H., whom Moses and the 4.46

HESHBON (cont.)
the king of H. and Og the king of Deu 29.07
the Jordan, Sihon the king of H., Jos 9.10
of the Amorites who dwelt at H., 12.02
the boundary of Sihon king of H. 12.05
of the Amorites, who reigned in H., 13.10
with H., and all its cities that 13.17
of the Amorites, who reigned in H., 13.21
and from H. to Ramathmizpeh and 13.26
of the kingdom of Sihon king of H., 13.27
H. with its pasture lands, Jazer 21.39
king of the Amorites, king of H.; Ju 11.19
While Israel dwelt in H. and its 11.26
H. with its pasture lands, and Jazer 1Ch 6.81
Sihon king of H. and the land of Neh 9.22
Your eyes are pools in H., Sol 7.04
H. and Elealeh cry out, their voice Is 15.04
For the fields of H. languish, 16.08
with my tears, O H. and Elealeh; 16.09
In H. they planned evil against her: Jer 48.02
"H. and Elealeh cry out; 48.34
"In the shadow of H. fugitives stop 48.45
or a fire has gone forth from H., 48.45
"Wail, O H., for Ai is laid waste! 49.03

HESHMON
Hazargaddah, H., Bethpelet, Jos 15.27

HESITATE
they do not h. to spit at the sight Job 30.10

HESITATION
and accompany them without h.; Ac 10.20
told me to go with them without h. 11.12

HETH
of Sidon his first-born, and H., Gen 10.15
of Sidon his first-born, and H., 1Ch 1.13

HETHLON
Sea by way of H. to the entrance Eze 47.15
sea by way of H. to the entrance 48.01

HEW
hewn out, which you did not h., Deu 6.11
and h. down their Asherim, and burn 7.05
'H. two tables of stone like the 10.01
you shall h. down the graven images 12.03
spreading branches he will h. away. Is 18.05
you who h. a tomb on the height, and 22.16
LORD of hosts: "H. down her trees; Jer 6.06
'H. down the tree and cut off its Dan 4.14
'H. down the tree and destroy it, 4.23

HEWED
my tomb which I h. out for myself Gen 50.05
and h. two tables of stone like the Deu 10.03
And Samuel h. Agag in pieces before 1Sa 15.33
the pillars and h. down the Asherim, 2Ch 14.03
and h. out many cisterns, for he had 26.10
the pillars and h. down the Asherim 31.01
and he h. down the incense altars 34.04
and h. down all the incense altars 34.07
and h. out a wine vat in it; Is 5.02
and h. out cisterns for themselves, Jer 2.13

HEWER
laid low, no h. comes up against us.' Is 14.08

HEWERS
So they became h. of wood and Jos 9.21
h. of wood and drawers of water for 9.23
them that day h. of wood and 9.27
eighty thousand h. of stone in the 1Ki 5.15
the h. who cut timber, twenty 2Ch 2.10

HEWING
Gebal did the h. and prepared the 1Ki 5.18

HEWN
shall not build it of h. stones; Ex 20.25
and cisterns h. out, which you did Deu 6.11
courses of h. stone and one course 1Ki 6.36
h. according to measure, sawed with 7.09
h. according to measurement, and 7.11
courses of h. stone round about, 7.12
which he had h. out for himself in 2Ch 16.14
cisterns h. out, vineyards, olive Neh 9.25
great in height will be h. down, Is 10.33
that you have h. here a tomb for 22.16
to the rock from which you were h., 51.01
has blocked my ways with h. stones, Lam 3.09
four tables of h. stone for the Eze 40.42
Therefore I have h. them by the Hos 6.05
you have built houses of h. stone, Amo 5.11
tomb, which he had h. in the rock; Mt 27.60
which had been h. out of the rock; Mk 15.46

HEWS
both he who h. your wood and he who Deu 29.11
itself over him who h. with it, Is 10.15

HEZEKIAH
and H. his son reigned in his 2Ki 16.20
H. the son of Ahaz, king of Judah, 18.01
In the fourth year of King H., 18.09
In the sixth year of H., 18.10
year of King H. Sennacherib king 18.13
And H. king of Judah sent to the 18.14
required of H. king of Judah three 18.14
And H. gave him all the silver that 18.15
At that time H. stripped the gold 18.16
doorposts which H. king of Judah 18.16
Lachish to King H. at Jerusalem. 18.17
"Say to H., 'Thus says the great 18.19
places and altars H. has removed, 18.22
'Do not let H. deceive you, for he 18.29
Do not let H. make you to rely on 18.30
Do not listen to H.; for thus says 18.31
not listen to H. when he misleads 18.32
came to H. with their clothes rent, 18.37
When King H. heard it, he rent his 19.01
"Thus says H., This day is a day of 19.03
servants of King H. came to Isaiah, 19.05
messengers again to H., saying, 19.09
you speak to H. king of Judah: 19.10
H. received the letter from the 19.14
and H. went up to the house of 19.14
And H. prayed before the LORD, and 19.15
Then Isaiah the son of Amoz sent to H., 19.20
In those days H. became sick and 20.01
Then H. turned his face to the wall, 20.02
in thy sight." And H. wept bitterly. 20.03
and say to H. the prince of my 20.05
And H. said to Isaiah, "What shall 20.08
And H. answered, "It is an easy 20.10
with letters and a present to H.; 20.12
for he heard that H. had been sick. 20.12
And H. welcomed them, and he showed 20.13
his realm that H. did not show 20.13
Isaiah the prophet came to King H., 20.14
And H. said, "They have come from 20.14
And H. answered, "They have seen all 20.15
Then Isaiah said to H., "Hear the word 20.16
Then said H. to Isaiah, "The word of 20.19
The rest of the deeds of H., and all 20.20
And H. slept with his fathers; 20.21
places which H. his father had 21.03
Ahaz his son, H. his son, Manasseh 1Ch 3.13
by name, came in the days of H., 4.41
And H. his son reigned in his stead 2Ch 28.27
H. began to reign when he was 29.01
Then they went in to H. the king 29.18
Then H. the king rose early and 29.20
Then H. commanded that the burnt 29.27
And H. the king and the princes 29.30

HEZEKIAH (cont.)

Then H. said, "You have now consecrated 2Ch 29.31
And H. and all the people rejoiced 29.36
H. sent to all Israel and Judah, and 30.01
For H. had prayed for them, saying, 30.18
And the LORD heard H., and healed 30.20
And H. spoke encouragingly to all 30.22
For H. king of Judah gave the 30.24
And H. appointed the divisions of 31.02
When H. and the princes came and 31.08
And H. questioned the priests and 31.09
Then H. commanded them to prepare 31.11
appointment of H. the king and 31.13
Thus H. did throughout all Judah; 31.20
And when H. saw that Sennacherib 32.02
from the words of H. king of Judah. 32.08
to Jerusalem to H. king of Judah 32.09
Is not H. misleading you, that he 32.11
Has not this same H. taken away his 32.12
do not let H. deceive you or 32.15
GOD and against his servant H. 32.16
so the God of H. will not deliver 32.17
Then H. the king and Isaiah the 32.20
So the LORD saved H. and the 32.22
precious things to H. king of Judah, 32.23
In those days H. became sick and 32.24
But H. did not make return according 32.25
But H. humbled himself for the 32.26
come upon them in the days of H. 32.26
And H. had very great riches and 32.27
This same H. closed the upper 32.30
And H. prospered in all his works. 32.30
Now the rest of the acts of H., 32.32
And H. slept with his fathers, and 32.33
his father H. had broken down, and 33.03
Ater, namely of H., ninety-eight. Ez 2.16
Ater, namely of H., ninety-eight. Neh 7.21
Ater, H., Azzur, 10.17
the men of H. king of Judah copied Pro 25.01
Jotham, Ahaz, and H., kings of Judah. Is 1.01
In the fourteenth year of King H., 36.01
Lachish to King H. at Jerusalem, 36.02
"Say to H., 'Thus says the great 36.04
places and altars H. has removed, 36.07
'Do not let H. deceive you, for he 36.14
Do not let H. make you rely on the 36.15
Do not listen to H.; for thus says 36.16
Beware lest H. mislead you by 36.18
came to H. with their clothes rent, 36.22
When King H. heard it, he rent his 37.01
"Thus says H., 'This day is a day 37.03
servants of King H. came to Isaiah, 37.05
he sent messengers to H., saying, 37.09
you speak to H. king of Judah: 37.10
H. received the letter from the 37.14
and H. went up to the house of the 37.14
And H. prayed to the LORD: 37.15
Then Isaiah the son of Amoz sent to H., 37.21
In those days H. became sick and 38.01
Then H. turned his face to the wall, 38.02
in thy sight." And H. wept bitterly. 38.03
"Go and say to H., Thus says the 38.05
A writing of H. king of Judah, after 38.09
H. also had said, "What is the sign 38.22
with letters and a present to H., 39.01
And H. welcomed them; and he showed 39.02
his realm that H. did not show 39.02
Isaiah the prophet came to King H., 39.03
H. said, "They have come to me 39.03
H. answered, "They have seen all 39.04
Then Isaiah said to H., "Hear the word 39.05
Then said H. to Isaiah, "The word of 39.08
of what Manasseh the son of H., Jer 15.04
in the days of H. the king of Judah, 26.18
Did H. king of Judah and all Judah 26.19
and H., kings of Judah, and in the Hos 1.01
and H., kings of Judah, which he saw Mic 1.01
son of H., in the days of Josiah Zep 1.01
Ahaz, and Ahaz the father of H., Mt 1.09
and H. the father of Manasseh, and 1.10

HEZION

the son of H., king of Syria, who 1Ki 15.18

HEZIR

the seventeenth to H., the eighteenth 1Ch 24.15
Magpiash, Meshullam, H., Neh 10.20

HEZRO

H. of Carmel, Paarai the Arbite, 2Sa 23.35
H. of Carmel, Naarai the son of 1Ch 11.37

HEZRON

Hanoch, Pallu, H., and Carmi. Gen 46.09
sons of Perez were H. and Hamul. 46.12
Hanoch, Pallu, H. and Carmi; Ex 6.14
of H., the family of the Hezronites; Num 26.06
of H., the family of the Hezronites; 26.21
along by H., up to Addar, turns Jos 15.03
Perez: Perez was the father of H., Ru 4.18
H. of Ram, Ram of Amminadab, 4.19
The sons of Perez: H. and Hamul. 1Ch 2.05
The sons of H., that were born to 2.09
Caleb the son of H. had children by 2.18
Afterward H. went in to the daughter 2.21
After the death of H., Caleb went 2.24
the wife of H. his father, and she 2.24
of Jerahmeel, the first-born of H.: 2.25
H., Carmi, Hur, and Shobal. 4.01
Hanoch, Pallu, H., and Carmi. 5.03
Tamar, and Perez the father of H., Mt 1.03
and H. the father of Ram, 1.03
the son of H., the son of Perez, the Lk 3.33

HEZRONITES

of Hezron, the family of the H.; Num 26.06
of Hezron, the family of the H.; 26.21

HID

and his wife h. themselves from Gen 3.08
I was naked; and I h. myself." 3.10
and Jacob h. them under the oak 35.04
goodly child, she h. him three months. Ex 2.02
Egyptian and h. him in the sand. 2.12
And Moses h. his face, for he was 3.06
and h. them with the stalks of flax Jos 2.06
because she h. the messengers that 6.17
because she h. the messengers whom 6.25
and h. themselves in the cave at 10.16
was left, for he h. himself. Ju 9.05
everything and h. nothing from him. 1Sa 3.18
the people h. themselves in caves 13.06
where they have h. themselves." 14.11
Israel who had h. themselves in 14.22
place where you h. yourself when 20.19
So David h. himself in the field; 20.24
prophets and h. them by fifties in 1Ki 18.04
how I h. a hundred men of the LORD's 18.13
and clothing, and went and h. them; 2Ki 7.08
from it, and went and h. them. 7.08
Thus she h. him from Athaliah, so 11.02
h. in the house of the LORD, while 11.03
who were with him h. themselves. 1Ch 21.20
h. him from Athaliah, so that she 2Ch 22.11
h. in the house of God, while 22.12
for it more than for h. treasures; Job 3.21
given to a man whose way is h., 3.23
You shall be h. from the scourge of 5.21
A rope is h. for him in the ground, 18.10
thing that is h. he brings forth 28.11
It is h. from the eyes of all 28.21
net which they h. has their own Ps 9.15
there is nothing h. from its heat. 19.06
and he has not h. his face from him, 22.24
cause they h. their net for me; 35.07

HID (cont.)

the net which they h. ensnare them; Ps 35.08
I have not h. thy saving help 40.10
their discerning men shall be h." Is 29.14
"My way is h. from the LORD, and my 40.27
in the shadow of his hand he h. me; 49.02
arrow, in his quiver he h. me away. 49.02
I h. not my face from shame and 50.06
and h. you in the shadow of my hand, 51.16
for a moment I h. my face from you, 54.08
I h. my face and was angry; 57.17
your sins have h. his face from 59.02
for thou hast h. thy face from us, 64.07
forgotten and are h. from my eyes. 65.16
So I went, and h. it by the Euphrates, Jer 13.05
they are not h. from me, nor is 16.17
the prophet, but the LORD h. them. 36.26
above these stones which I have h., 43.10
with me that I h. my face from Eze 39.23
and h. my face from them. 39.24
and Israel is not h. from me; Hos 5.03
Compassion is h. from my eyes. 13.14
a city set on a hill cannot be h. Mt 5.14
woman took and h. in three measures 13.33
the ground and h. his master's 25.18
and I went and h. your talent in 25.25
For there is nothing h., except to Mk 4.22
one know it; yet he could not be h. 7.24
and for five months she h. herself, Lk 1.24
For nothing is h. that shall not be 8.17
woman took and h. in three measures 13.21
this saying was h. from them, 18.34
But now they are h. from your eyes. 19.42
but Jesus h. himself, and went out Jn 8.59
he departed and h. himself from 12.36
in whom are h. all the treasures of Col 2.03
your life is h. with Christ in God. 3.03
was h. for three months by his Heb 11.23
h. in the caves and among the rocks Rev 6.15

HIDDAI

of Pirathon, H. of the brooks of Gaash, 2Sa 23.30

HIDDEKEL

And the name of the third river is H., Gen 2.14

HIDDEN

and from thy face I shall be h.; Gen 4.14
the thing is h. from the eyes of Lev 4.13
and it is h. from him, and he has 5.02
and it is h. from him, when he comes 5.03
and it is h. from him, when he comes 5.04
and it is h. from the eyes of her Num 5.13
seas and the h. treasures of the Deu 33.19
had taken the two men and h. them; Jos 2.04
they are h. in the earth inside my 7.21
it was h. in his tent with the 7.22
h. in the cave at Makkedah." 10.17
cave where they had h. themselves, 10.27
he had h. himself among the baggage." 1Sa 10.22
Behold, even now he has h. himself 2Sa 17.09
there is nothing h. from the king), 18.13
was nothing h. from the king which 1Ki 10.03
and the LORD has h. it from me, 2Ki 4.27
but she has h. her son." 6.29
was nothing h. from Solomon which 2Ch 9.02
was I not as a h. untimely birth, Job 3.16
and their fathers have not h., 15.18
he has h. his face, he will never Ps 10.11
Clear thou me from h. faults. 19.12
out of the net which is h. for me, 31.04
my sighing is not h. from thee. 38.09
I have done are not h. from thee. 69.05
my frame was not h. from thee, 139.15
Arrogant men have h. a trap for me, 140.05
I walk they have h. a trap for me. 142.03
search for it as for h. treasures; Pro 2.04
trustworthy in spirit keeps a thing h. 11.13
Better is open rebuke than h. love. 27.05
trapped in holes and h. in prisons; Is 42.22
h. things which you have not known. 48.06
from the place where I had h. it. Jer 13.07
you great and h. things which you 33.03
for I have h. my face from this 33.05
oil, and honey h. in the fields." 41.08
no secret is h. from you; Eze 28.03
you may be h. on the day of the Zep 2.03
or h. that will not be known. Mt 10.26
that thou hast h. these things 11.25
what has been h. since the foundation 13.35
is like treasure h. in a field, 13.44
the woman saw that she was not h., Lk 8.47
that thou hast h. these things 10.21
or h. that will not be known. 12.02
a secret and h. wisdom of God, 1Co 2.07
the things now h. in darkness and 4.05
of the mystery h. for ages in God Eph 3.09
the mystery h. for ages and generations Col 1.26
are not, they cannot remain h. 1Ti 5.25
And before him no creature is h., Heb 4.13
but let it be the h. person of the 1Pe 3.04
I will give some of the h. manna, Rev 2.17

HIDE

"Shall I h. from Abraham what I am Gen 18.17
"We will not h. from my lord that 47.18
And when she could h. him no longer Ex 2.03
land do at all h. their eyes from Lev 20.04
are left and h. themselves from Deu 7.20
them and h. my face from them, and 31.17
And I will surely h. my face in 31.18
'I will h. my face from them, I will 32.20
and h. yourselves there three days, Jos 2.16
you have done; do not h. it from me." 7.19
to h. it from the Midianites. Ju 6.11
Do not h. it from me. May God do so 1Sa 3.17
if you h. anything from me of all 3.17
in a secret place and h. yourself; 19.02
should my father h. this from me? 20.02
that I may h. myself in the field 20.05
"Does not David h. among us in the 23.19
"Do not h. from me anything I ask 2Sa 14.18
and h. yourself by the brook 1Ki 17.03
an inner chamber to h. yourself. 22.25
of the camp to h. themselves in 2Ki 7.12
an inner chamber to h. yourself." 2Ch 18.24
nor h. trouble from my eyes. Job 3.10
things thou didst h. in thy heart; 10.13
then I will not h. myself from thy 13.20
Why dost thou h. thy face, and count 13.24
Oh that thou wouldest h. me in Sheol, 14.13
of the earth all h. themselves. 24.04
where evildoers may h. themselves. 34.22
H. them all in the dust together; 40.13
Why dost thou h. thyself in times Ps 10.01
long wilt thou h. thy face from me? 13.01
h. me in the shadow of thy wings, 17.08
For he will h. me in his shelter in 27.05
H. not thy face from me. 27.09
thou didst h. thy face, I was 30.07
thee, and I did not h. my iniquity; 32.05
Why dost thou h. thy face? 44.24
H. thy face from my sins, and blot 51.09
and h. not thyself from my supplication! 55.01
with me—then I could h. from him. 55.12
h. me from the secret plots of the 64.02
H. not thy face from thy servant; 69.17
We will not h. them from their 78.04
Why dost thou h. thy face from me? 88.14
Wilt thou h. thyself for ever? 89.46
Do not h. thy face from me in the 102.02
h. not thy commandments from me! 119.19
H. not thy face from me, lest I be 143.07
the wicked rise, men h. themselves. Pro 28.12
men h. themselves, but when they 28.28

HIDE (cont.)

I will h. my eyes from you; Is 1.15
and h. in the dust from before the 2.10
sin like Sodom, they do not h. it. 3.09
h. the outcasts, betray not the 16.03
h. yourselves for a little while 26.20
Woe to those who h. deep from the 29.15
will not h. himself any more, but 30.20
from whom men h. their faces he 53.03
and not to h. yourself from your 58.07
and h. it there in a cleft of the Jer 13.04
which I commanded you to h. there." 13.06
Can a man h. himself in secret 23.24
"Go and h., you and Jeremiah, and 36.19
a question; h. nothing from me." 38.14
h. nothing from us and we will not 38.25
and h. them in the mortar in the 43.09
and I will not h. my face any more Eze 39.29
and they fled to h. themselves. Dan 10.07
Though they h. themselves on the Amo 9.03
and though they h. from my sight at 9.03
he will h. his face from them at Mic 3.04
"Fall on us and h. us from the face Rev 6.16

HIDES

all the lurking places where he h., 1Sa 23.23
ice, and where the snow h. itself. Job 6.16
though he h. it under his tongue, 20.12
When he h. his face, who can behold 34.29
'Who is this that h. counsel 42.03
man sees danger and h. himself; Pro 22.03
man sees danger and h. himself; 27.12
but he who h. his eyes will get 28.27

HIDEST

presence thou h. them from the Ps 31.20
When thou h. thy face, they are 104.29
Truly, thou art a God who h. thyself, Is 45.15

HIDING

"Is not David h. himself on the 1Sa 26.01
was captured while h. in Samaria, 2Ch 22.09
by h. my iniquity in my bosom, Job 31.33
in h. places he murders the innocent. Ps 10.08
Thou art a h. place for me, thou 32.07
Thou art my h. place and my shield; 119.114
who is h. his face from the house Is 8.17
will be like a h. place from the wind, 32.02
I have uncovered his h. places, Jer 49.10
lying in wait, like a lion in h.; Lam 3.10

HIE

I will h. me to the mountain of Sol 4.06

HIEL

In his days H. of Bethel built 1Ki 16.34

HIERAPOLIS

for those in Laodicea and in H. Col 4.13

HIGH

and it rose h. above the earth. Gen 7.17
that all the h. mountains under 7.19
he was priest of God Most H. 14.18
"Blessed be Abram by God Most H., 14.19
and blessed be God Most H., 14.20
have sworn to the LORD Most H., 14.22
away from the dew of heaven on h. 27.38
it is still h. day, it is not time 29.07
and five cubits h. in its breadth, Ex 38.18
And I will destroy your h. places, Lev 26.30
who does anything with a h. hand, Num 15.30
knows the knowledge of the Most H., 24.16
and demolish all their h. places, 33.52
death of the h. priest who was 35.25
until the death of the h. priest; 35.28
death of the h. priest the manslayer 35.28
before the death of the h. priest. 35.32
there was not a city too h. for us; Deu 2.36
cities fortified with h. walls, 3.05
upon the h. mountains and upon the 12.02
that he will set you h. above all 26.19
will set you h. above all the 28.01
until your h. and fortified walls, 28.52
When the Most H. gave to the 32.08
him ride on the h. places of the 32.13
shall tread upon their h. places." 33.29
of him who is h. priest at the Jos 20.06
a sacrifice today on the h. place. 1Sa 9.12
he goes up to the h. place to eat; 9.13
them on his way up to the h. place. 9.14
go up before me to the h. place, 9.19
down from the h. place into the 9.25
down from the h. place with harp, 10.05
prophesying, he came to the h. place. 10.13
is slain upon thy h. places! 2Sa 1.19
lies slain upon thy h. places. 1.25
and the Most H. uttered his voice. 22.14
"He reached from on h., he took me, 22.17
of the man who was raised on h., 23.01
were sacrificing at the h. places, 1Ki 3.02
and burnt incense at the h. places. 3.03
for that was the great h. place; 3.04
and these were his h. officials: 4.02
cubits wide, and thirty cubits h. 6.02
house, each story five cubits h., 6.10
cubits wide, and twenty cubits h.; 6.20
of olivewood, each ten cubits h. 6.23
brim to brim, and five cubits h., 7.23
cubits wide, and three cubits h. 7.27
was a round band half a cubit h.; 7.35
Then Solomon built a h. place for 11.07
He also made houses on h. places, 12.31
priests of the h. places that he 12.32
priests of the h. places who burn 13.02
houses of the h. places which are 13.32
priests for the h. places again 13.33
to be priests of the h. places. 13.33
built for themselves h. places, 14.23
on every h. hill and under every 14.23
But the h. places were not taken 15.14
set Naboth on h. among the people; 21.09
set Naboth on h. among the people. 21.12
yet the h. places were not taken 22.43
burned incense on the h. places. 22.43
with his master and in h. favor, 2Ki 5.01
Nevertheless the h. places were not 12.03
and burn incense on the h. places. 12.03
secretary and the h. priest came up 12.10
But the h. places were not removed; 14.04
and burned incense on the h. places. 14.04
Nevertheless the h. places were not 15.04
burned incense on the h. places. 15.04
Nevertheless the h. places were not 15.35
burned incense on the h. places. 15.35
burned incense on the h. places, 16.04
for themselves h. places at all 17.09
on every h. hill and under every 17.10
incense on all the h. places, 17.11
shrines of the h. places which the 17.29
people as priests of the h. places, 17.32
in the shrines of the h. places. 17.32
He removed the h. places, and broke 18.04
it not he whose h. places and 18.22
For he rebuilt the h. places which 21.03
"Go up to Hilkiah the h. priest, 22.04
And Hilkiah the h. priest said to 22.08
the h. priest, and the priests of 23.04
incense in the h. places at the 23.05
and defiled the h. places where 23.08
broke down the h. places of the 23.08
priests of the h. places did not 23.09
defiled the h. places that were 23.13

HIGH (cont.)
the h. place erected by Jeroboam 2Ki 23.15
altar with the h. place he pulled 23.15
also of the h. places that were in 23.19
priests of the h. places who were 23.20
the LORD in the h. place that was 1Ch 16.39
time in the h. place at Gibeon; 21.29
went to the h. place that was at 2Ch 1.03
came from the h. place at Gibeon, 1.13
two pillars thirty-five cubits h., 3.15
cubits wide, and ten cubits h. 4.01
brim to brim, and five cubits h., 4.02
cubits wide, and three cubits h., 6.13
his own priests for the h. places, 11.15
foreign altar and the h. places, 14.03
of Judah the h. places and the 14.05
But the h. places were not taken 15.17
he took the h. places and the 17.06
The h. places, however, were not 20.33
Moreover he made h. places in the 21.11
burned incense on the h. places, 28.04
Judah he made h. places to burn 28.25
broke down the h. places and the 31.01
taken away his h. places and his 32.12
For he rebuilt the h. places which 33.03
still sacrificed at the h. places, 33.17
which he built h. places and set 33.19
and Jerusalem of the h. places, 34.03
to Hilkiah the h. priest and 34.09
Then Eliashib the h. priest rose up Neh 3.01
house of Eliashib the h. priest. 3.20
the son of Eliashib the h. priest, 13.28
to their husbands, h. and low." Est 1.20
a gallows fifty cubits h. be made, 5.14
in Haman's house, fifty cubits h. 7.09
account of the h. honor of Mordecai, 10.02
he sets on h. those who are lowly, Job 5.11
he that vouches for me is on h. 16.19
he judges those that are on h.? 21.22
"Is not God h. in the heavens? 22.12
he makes peace in his h. heaven. 25.02
heritage from the Almighty on h.? 31.02
mounts up and makes his nest on h.? 39.27
He beholds everything that is h.; 41.34
and over it take thy seat on h. Ps 7.07
the name of the LORD, the Most H. 7.17
sing praise to thy name, O Most H. 9.02
thy judgments are on h., 10.05
and the Most H. uttered his voice, 18.13
He reached from on h., he took me, 18.16
of the Most H. he shall not be 21.07
he will set me h. upon a rock. 27.05
demanding no h. price for them. 44.12
the holy habitation of the Most H. 46.04
the Most H., is terrible, a great 47.02
both low and h., rich and poor 49.02
and pay your vows to the Most H.; 50.14
I cry to God Most H., to God who 57.02
men of h. estate are a delusion; 62.09
Thou didst ascend the h. mount, 68.18
thy salvation, O God, set me on h.! 69.29
O God, reach the h. heavens. 71.19
is there knowledge in the Most H.?" 73.11
do not lift up your horn on h., 75.05
hand of the Most H. has changed." 77.10
against the Most H. in the desert. 78.17
the Most H. God their redeemer. 78.35
rebelled against the Most H. God, 78.56
him to anger with their h. places; 78.58
his sanctuary like the h. heavens, 78.69
sons of the Most H., all of you; 82.06
art the Most H. over all the earth. 83.18
for the Most H. himself will 87.05
is thy hand, h. thy right hand. 89.13
in the shelter of the Most H., 91.01
the Most H. your habitation, 91.09
praises to thy name, O Most H.; 92.01
but thou, O LORD, art on h. for ever. 92.08
the sea, the LORD on h. is mighty! 93.04
art most h. over all the earth; 97.09
the heavens are h. above the earth, 103.11
The h. mountains are for the wild 104.18
against the Most H. at the Red Sea. 106.07
spurned the counsel of the Most H. 107.11
The LORD is h. above all nations, 113.04
LORD our God, who is seated on h., 113.05
up, my eyes are not raised too h.; 131.01
For though the LORD is h., 138.06
it is h., I cannot attain it. 139.06
Stretch forth thy hand from on h., 144.07
Let the h. praises of God be in 149.06
a seat on the h. places of the Pro 9.14
makes his door h. seeks destruction. 17.19
and like a h. wall protecting him. 18.11
Wisdom is too h. for a fool; 24.07
how h. their eyelids lift! 30.13
the way of a ship on the h. seas, 30.19
for the h. official is watched by a Ecc 5.08
folly is set in many h. places, 10.06
they are afraid also of what is h., 12.05
all that is lifted up and h.; Is 2.12
against all the h. mountains, 2.14
against every h. tower, and against 2.15
upon a throne, h. and lifted up; 6.01
be deep as Sheol or h. as heaven." 7.11
of God I will set my throne on h.; 14.13
will make myself like the Most H. 14.14
gone up to the h. places to weep; 15.02
wearies himself upon the h. place, 16.12
And the h. fortifications of his 25.12
to you like a break in a h. wall, 30.13
and every h. hill there will be 30.25
is poured upon us from on h., 32.15
is exalted, for he dwells on h.; 33.05
it not he whose h. places and 36.07
Get you up to a h. mountain, 40.09
Lift up your eyes on h. and see: 40.26
lifted up, and shall be very h. 52.13
Upon a h. and lofty mountain you 57.07
For thus says the h. and lofty One 57.15
"I dwell in the h. and holy place, 57.15
make your voice to be heard on h. 58.04
upon every h. hill and under every Jer 2.20
up on every h. hill and under 3.06
have built the h. place of Topheth, 7.31
green tree, and on the h. hills, 17.02
throne set on h. from the beginning 17.12
and have built the h. places of 19.05
'The LORD will roar from on h., 25.30
They built the h. places of Baal in 32.35
sacrifice in the h. place and burns 48.35
your nest as h. as the eagle's, 49.16
ground and her h. gates shall be 51.58
"From on h. he sent fire; Lam 1.13
in the presence of the Most H., 3.35
of the Most H. that good and evil 3.38
and I will destroy your h. places. Eze 6.03
be waste and your h. places ruined, 6.06
upon every h. hill, on all the 6.13
plant it upon a h. and lofty 17.22
I the LORD bring low the h. tree, 17.24
and make h. the low tree, dry up the 17.24
they saw any h. hill or any leafy 20.28
What is the h. place to which you 20.29
is low, and abase that which is h. 21.26
brought you out into the h. seas. 27.26
So it towered h. above all the 31.05
it towered h. and set its top 31.10
the mountains and on every h. hill; 34.06
me down upon a very h. mountain, 40.02
and one cubit h., on which the 40.42
three cubits h., two cubits long, 41.22
its base shall be one cubit h., 43.13
upward, four horns, one cubit h. 43.15

HIGH (cont.)
gave Daniel h. honors and many Dan 2.48
servants of the Most H. God, 3.26
that the Most H. God has wrought 4.02
that the Most H. rules the kingdom 4.17
It is a decree of the Most H., 4.24
that the Most H. rules the kingdom 4.25
that the Most H. rules the kingdom 4.32
to me, and I blessed the Most H., 4.34
the Most H. God gave Nebuchadnezzar 5.18
that the Most H. God rules the 5.21
of the Most H. shall receive the 7.18
for the saints of the Most H., 7.22
speak words against the Most H., 7.25
wear out the saints of the Most H., 7.25
of the saints of the Most H.; 7.27
and both horns were h., 8.03
The h. places of Aven, the sin of Hos 10.08
the h. places of Isaac shall be Amo 7.09
of the rock, whose dwelling is h., Ob 1.03
tread upon the h. places of the Mic 1.03
and bow myself before God on h.? 6.06
his house, to set his nest on h., Hab 2.09
voice, it lifted its hands on h. 3.10
makes me tread upon my h. places. 3.19
son of Jehozadak, the h. priest, Hag 1.01
the h. priest, with all the remnant 1.12
the h. priest, and the spirit of all 1.14
the h. priest, and to all the 2.02
son of Jehozadak, the h. priest; 2.04
me Joshua the h. priest standing Zec 3.01
O Joshua the h. priest, you and your 3.08
son of Jehozadak, the h. priest; 6.11
took him to a very h. mountain, Mt 4.08
led them up a h. mountain apart. 17.01
in the palace of the h. priest, 26.03
struck the slave of the h. priest, 26.51
led him to Caiaphas the h. priest, 26.57
as the courtyard of the h. priest, 26.58
And the h. priest stood up and said, 26.62
And the h. priest said to him, "I 26.63
Then the h. priest tore his robes, 26.65
God, when Abiathar was h. priest, Mk 2.26
me, Jesus, Son of the Most H. God? 5.07
led them up a h. mountain apart by 9.02
slave of the h. priest and cut off 14.47
And they led Jesus to the h. priest; 14.53
the courtyard of the h. priest; 14.54
And the h. priest stood up in the 14.60
Again the h. priest asked him, "Are 14.61
And the h. priest tore his mantle, 14.63
of the maids of the h. priest came; 14.66
be called the Son of the Most H.; Lk 1.32
of the Most H. will overshadow you; 1.35
called the prophet of the Most H.; 1.76
the day shall dawn upon us from on h. 1.78
mother-in-law was ill with a h. fever, 4.38
you will be sons of the Most H.; 6.35
me, Jesus, Son of the Most H. God? 8.28
slave of the h. priest and cut off 22.50
him into the h. priest's house. 22.54
are clothed with power from on h." 24.49
who was h. priest that year, said to Jn 11.49
but being h. priest that year he 11.51
and struck the h. priest's slave 18.10
who was h. priest that year. 18.13
disciple was known to the h. priest, 18.15
court of the h. priest along with 18.15
who was known to the h. priest, 18.16
The h. priest then questioned Jesus 18.19
that how you answer the h. priest?" 18.22
bound to Caiaphas the h. priest. 18.24
One of the servants of the h. priest, 18.26
(for that sabbath was a h. day), 19.31
with Annas the h. priest and Caiaphas Ac 4.06
the people held them in h. honor. 5.13
But the h. priest rose up and all 5.17
Now the h. priest came and those 5.21
And the h. priest questioned them, 5.27
And the h. priest said, "Is this so?" 7.01
Yet the Most H. does not dwell in 7.48
of the Lord, went to the h. priest 9.01
devout women of h. standing and 13.50
are servants of the Most H. God, 16.17
Greek women of h. standing as well 17.12
of a Jewish h. priest named Sceva 19.14
as the h. priest and the whole 22.05
And the h. priest Ananias commanded 23.02
"Would you revile God's h. priest?" 23.04
brethren, that he was the h. priest; 23.05
five days the h. priest Ananias 24.01
he ascended on h. he led a host of Eph 4.08
and all who are in h. positions, 1Ti 2.02
right hand of the Majesty on h., Heb 1.03
and faithful h. priest in the 2.17
the apostle and h. priest of our 3.01
we have a great h. priest who has 4.14
For we have not a h. priest who is 4.15
For every h. priest chosen from 5.01
himself to be made a h. priest, 5.05
by God a h. priest after the order 5.10
having become a h. priest for ever 6.20
Salem, priest of the Most H. God, 7.01
we should have such a h. priest, 7.26
like those h. priests, to offer 7.27
in their weakness as h. priests, 7.28
is this: we have such a h. priest, 8.01
For every h. priest is appointed to 8.03
the second only the h. priest goes, 9.07
appeared as a h. priest of the 9.11
as the h. priest enters the Holy 9.25
sanctuary by the h. priest as a 13.11
as h. as a horse's bridle, for one Rev 14.20
for her sins are heaped h. as heaven, 18.05
h. mountain, and showed me the holy 21.10
h. wall, with twelve gates, and at 21.12

HIGHER
his king shall be h. than Agag, Num 24.07
shall mount above you h. and h.; Deu 28.43
have risen h. than our heads, and our Ez 9.06
It is h. than heaven—what can you Job 11.08
the clouds, which are h. than you. 35.05
me to the rock that is h. than I; Ps 61.02
high official is watched by a h., Ecc 5.08
there are yet h. ones over them. 5.08
the heavens are h. than the earth, Is 55.09
so are my ways h. than your ways 55.09
but one was h. than the other, and Dan 8.03
and the h. one came up last. 8.03
may say to you, 'Friend, go up h.'; Lk 14.10
But earnestly desire the h. gifts. 1Co 12.31

HIGHEST
heaven and the h. heaven cannot 1Ki 8.27
even h. heaven, cannot contain him? 2Ch 2.06
heaven and the h. heaven cannot 6.18
See the h. stars, how lofty they are Job 22.12
the h. of the kings of the earth. Ps 89.27
not set Jerusalem above my h. joy! 137.06
you h. heavens, and you waters above 148.04
call from the h. places in the Pro 9.03
established as the h. of the mountains, Is 2.02
berries in the top of the h. bough, 17.06
established as the h. of the mountains, Mic 4.01
name of the Lord! Hosanna in the h.!" Mt 21.09
is coming! Hosanna in the h!" Mk 11.10
"Glory to God in the h., and on earth Lk 2.14
Peace in heaven and glory in the h.!" 19.38

HIGHLY
so that his name was h. esteemed. 1Sa 18.30
his kingdom was h. exalted for the 1Ch 14.02
belong to God; he is h. exalted! Ps 47.09
Prize her h., and she will exalt Pro 4.08

HIGHLY (cont.)
of himself more h. than he ought Rom 12.03
Therefore God has h. exalted him Php 2.09
them very h. in love because of 1Th 5.13

HIGH-PRIESTHOOD
in the h. of Annas and Caiaphas, the Lk 3.02

HIGH-PRIESTLY
and all who were of the h. family. Ac 4.06

HIGHWAY
we will go along the King's H., Num 20.17
to him, "We will go up by the h.; 20.19
we will go by the King's H., until we 21.22
the east of the h. that goes up Ju 21.19
of Bethshemesh along one h., lowing 1Sa 6.12
wallowing in his blood in the h. 2Sa 20.12
Amasa out of the h. into the field, 20.12
When he was taken out of the h., 20.13
which is on the h. to the fuller's 2Ki 18.17
path of the upright is a level h. Pro 15.19
The h. of the upright turns aside 16.17
pool on the h. to the fuller's Is 7.03
And there will be a h. from Assyria 11.16
there will be a h. from Egypt to 19.23
And a h. shall be there, and it 35.08
pool on the h. to the fuller's 36.02
in the desert a h. for our God. 40.03
build up the h., clear it of stones, 62.10
gone into bypaths, not the h., Jer 18.15
consider well the h., the road by 31.21

HIGHWAYS
in the h., one of which goes up to Ju 20.31
them away from the city to the h." 20.32
of them were cut down in the h., 20.45
in whose heart are the h. to Zion. Ps 84.05
The h. lie waste, the wayfaring man Is 33.08
and my h. shall be raised up. 49.11
and destruction are in their h. 59.07
'Go out to the h. and hedges, Lk 14.23

HILEN
H. with its pasture lands, Debir 1Ch 6.58

HILKIAH
out to them Eliakim the son of H., 2Ki 18.18
Then Eliakim the son of H., 18.26
Then Eliakim the son of H., 18.37
"Go up to H. the high priest, that 22.04
And H. the priest said to 22.08
And H. gave the book to Shaphan, 22.08
"H. the priest has given me a book." 22.10
And the king commanded H. the priest, 22.12
So H. the priest, and Ahikam, and 22.14
And the king commanded H., 23.04
the book that H. the priest found 23.24
Shallum of H., H. of Azariah, 1Ch 6.13
Hashabiah, son of Amaziah, son of H., 6.45
and Azariah the son of H., son of 9.11
H. the second, Tebaliah the third, 26.11
They came to H. the high priest and 2Ch 34.09
H. the priest found the book of the 34.14
Then H. said to Shaphan the secretary, 34.15
and H. gave the book to Shaphan. 34.15
"H. the priest has given me a book." 34.18
And the king commanded H., Ahikam 34.20
So H. and those whom the king had 34.22
H., Zechariah, and Jehiel, the chief 35.08
Seraiah, son of Azariah, son of H., Ez 7.01
H., and Maaseiah on his right hand; Neh 8.04
Seraiah the son of H., son of 11.11
Sallu, Amok, H., Jedaiah. These were 12.07
of H., Hashabiah; of Jedaiah, 12.21
my servant Eliakim the son of H., Is 22.20
out to him Eliakim the son of H., 36.03
Then Eliakim the son of H., 36.22
the son of H., of the priests who Jer 1.01
Shaphan and Gemariah the son of H., 29.03

HILL
Sephar to the h. country of the Gen 10.30
face toward the h. country of 31.21
him into the h. country of Gilead. 31.23
pitched his tent in the h. country, 31.25
encamped in the h. country of 31.25
dwelt in the h. country of Seir; 36.08
Edomites in the h. country of Seir. 36.09
the top of the h. with the rod of Ex 17.09
Hur went up to the top of the h. 17.10
and go up into the h. country, Num 13.17
Amorites dwell in the h. country; 13.29
to the heights of the h. country, 14.40
to the heights of the h. country, 14.44
dwelt in that h. country came down, 14.45
and go to the h. country of the Deu 1.07
in the h. country and in the lowland, 1.07
the way to the h. country of the 1.19
come to the h. country of the 1.20
and went up into the h. country, 1.24
easy to go up into the h. country. 1.41
and went up into the h. country. 1.43
lived in that h. country came out 1.44
and the cities of the h. country, 2.37
and half the h. country of Gilead 3.12
that goodly h. country, and Lebanon. 3.25
Jordan in the h. country and in Jos 9.01
dwell in the h. country are gathered 10.06
the h. country and the Negeb and 10.40
were in the northern h. country, 11.02
the Jebusites in the h. country, 11.03
the h. country and all the Negeb 11.16
Arabah and the h. country of Israel 11.16
out the Anakim from the h. country, 11.21
from all the h. country of Judah, 11.21
from all the h. country of Israel; 11.21
in the h. country, in the lowland, in 12.08
inhabitants of the h. country from 13.06
Zerethshahar on the h. of the valley, 13.19
give me this h. country of which 14.12
shoulder of the h. north of Ekron, 15.11
And in the h. country, Shamir, Jattir, 15.48
Jericho into the h. country to Bethel; 16.01
since the h. country of Ephraim is 17.15
"The h. country is not enough for 17.16
but the h. country shall be yours, 17.18
up through the h. country westward 18.12
Timnathserah in the h. country of 19.50
Galilee in the h. country of Naphtali, 20.07
Shechem in the h. country of Ephraim, 20.07
Hebron) in the h. country of Judah. 20.07
in the h. country of Judah, along 21.11
lands in the h. country of Ephraim, 21.21
I gave Esau the h. country of Seir 24.04
which is in the h. country of Ephraim, 24.30
him in the h. country of Ephraim. 24.33
who dwelt in the h. country, in the Ju 1.09
took possession of the h. country, 1.19
Danites back into the h. country, 1.34
in the h. country of Ephraim, north 2.09
trumpet in the h. country of Ephraim; 3.27
down with him from the h. country, 3.27
Bethel in the h. country of Ephraim; 4.05
by the h. of Moreh, in the valley. 7.01
throughout all the h. country of 7.24
Shamir in the h. country of Ephraim. 10.01
in the h. country of the Amalekites. 12.15
the top of the h. that is before 16.03
a man of the h. country of Ephraim, 17.01
he came to the h. country of Ephraim 17.08
came to the h. country of Ephraim, 18.02
there to the h. country of Ephraim, 18.13
parts of the h. country of Ephraim, 19.01
was from the h. country of Ephraim, 19.16

HILL (cont.)
parts of the h. country of Ephraim, Ju 19.18
Ramathaimzophim of the h. country 1Sa 1.01
to the house of Abinadab on the h.; 7.01
through the h. country of Ephraim 9.04
As they went up the h. to the city, 9.11
Michmash and the h. country of Bethel, 13.02
themselves in the h. country of Ephraim 14.22
in the h. country of the Wilderness 23.14
on the h. of Hachilah, which is south 23.19
himself on the h. of Hachilah, which is 26.01
encamped on the h. of Hachilah, which is 26.03
down they came to the h. of Ammah, 2Sa 2.24
and took their stand on the top of a h. 2.25
of Abinadab which was on the h.; 6.03
a man of the h. country of Ephraim, 20.21
Benhur, in the h. country of Ephraim; 1Ki 4.08
hewers of stone in the h. country, 5.15
Shechem in the h. country of Ephraim, 12.25
on every high h. and under every 14.23
He bought the h. of Samaria from 16.24
and he fortified the h., and called the 16.24
of Shemer, the owner of the h. 16.24
who was sitting on the top of a h., 2Ki 1.09
to me from the h. country of Ephraim 5.22
And when he came to the h., he took 5.24
on every high h. and under every 17.10
lands in the h. country of Ephraim, 1Ch 6.67
to quarry in the h. country, and 2Ch 2.02
to quarry in the h. country, and 2.18
which is in the h. country of 13.04
taken in the h. country of Ephraim, 15.08
Beersheba to the h. country of 19.04
places in the h. country of Judah, 21.11
cities in the h. country of Judah, 27.04
set my king on Zion, my holy h." Ps 2.06
and he answers me from his holy h. 3.04
Who shall dwell on thy holy h.? 15.01
Who shall ascend the h. of the LORD? 24.03
me to thy holy h. and to thy 43.03
myrrh and the h. of frankincense. Sol 4.06
a vineyard on a very fertile h. Is 5.01
of Zion, the h. of Jerusalem. 10.32
On a bare h. raise a signal, cry 13.02
a mountain, like a signal on a h. 30.17
and every high h. there will be 30.25
upon Mount Zion and upon its h. 31.04
the h. and the watchtower will 32.14
every mountain and h. be made low; 40.04
upon every high h. and under every Jer 2.20
on every high h. and under every 3.06
from every mountain and every h., 16.16
from the h. country, and from the 17.26
call in the h. country of Ephraim: 31.06
habitation of righteousness, O holy h.!' 31.23
farther, straight to the h. Gareb, 31.39
in the cities of the h. country, 32.44
In the cities of the h. country, 33.13
who hold the height of the h. 49.16
from mountain to h. they have gone, 50.06
their altars, upon every high h., Eze 6.13
saw any high h. or any leafy tree, 20.28
the mountains and on every high h.; 34.06
round about my h. a blessing; and I will 34.26
thy city Jerusalem, thy holy h.; Dan 9.16
my God for the holy h. of my God; 9.20
h. of the daughter of Zion, to you Mic 4.08
laid waste his h. country and left Mal 1.03
A city set on a h. cannot be hid. Mt 5.14
with haste into the h. country, to a city Lk 1.39
through all the h. country of Judea; 1.65
mountain and h. shall be brought 3.05
the brow of the h. on which their 4.29

HILLEL
the son of H. the Pirathonite judged Ju 12.13
the son of H. the Pirathonite died, 12.15

HILLS
flee to the h., lest you be consumed." Gen 19.17
but I cannot flee to the h., lest the 19.19
dwelt in the h. with his two daughters, 19.30
the bounties of the everlasting h.; 49.26
see him, from the h. I behold him; Num 23.09
flowing forth in valleys and h., Deu 8.07
out of whose h. you can dig copper. 8.09
is a land of h. and valleys, which drinks 11.11
and upon the h. and under every 12.02
abundance of the everlasting h., 33.15
"Go into the h., lest the pursuers Jos 2.16
They departed, and went into the h., 2.22
men came down again from the h., 2.23
him, "Their gods are gods of the h., 1Ki 20.23
is a god of the h. but he is not a 20.28
and on the h., and under every 2Ki 16.04
vinedressers in the h. and in the 2Ch 26.10
forts and towers on the wooded h. 27.04
and on the h., and under every 28.04
"Go out to the h. and bring branches Neh 8.15
you brought forth before the h.? Job 15.07
mine, the cattle on a thousand h. Ps 50.10
the h. gird themselves with joy, 65.12
the people, and the h., in righteousness! 72.03
let the h. sing for joy together 98.08
the valleys; they flow between the h., 104.10
like rams, the h. like lambs. 114.04
you skip like rams? O h., like lambs? 114.06
I lift up my eyes to the h. 121.01
he makes grass grow upon the h. 147.08
Mountains and all h., fruit trees 148.09
before the h., I was brought forth; Pro 8.25
mountains, bounding over the h. Sol 2.08
and shall be raised above the h.; Is 2.02
and against all the lofty h.; 2.14
and as for all the h. which used to 7.25
in scales and the h. in a balance? 40.12
you shall make the h. like chaff; 41.15
I will lay waste mountains and h., 42.15
may depart and the h. be removed, 54.10
mountains and the h. before you 55.12
mountains and reviled me upon the h., 65.07
Truly the h. are a delusion, the Jer 3.23
and all the h. moved to and fro. 4.24
harlotries, on the h. in the field. 13.27
green tree, and on the high h., 17.02
satisfied on the h. of Ephraim and 50.19
GOD to the mountains and the h., Eze 6.03
on your h. and in your valleys and 35.08
GOD to the mountains and the h., 36.04
and say to the mountains and h., 36.06
and make offerings upon the h., Hos 4.13
us, and to the h., Fall upon us. 10.08
and the h. shall flow with milk, and Joe 3.18
and all the h. shall flow with it. Amo 9.13
shall be raised up above the h.; Mic 4.01
and let the h. hear your voice. 6.01
quake before him, the h. melt; Nah 1.05
the everlasting h. sank low. Hab 3.06
Quarter, a loud crash from the h. Zep 1.10
Go up to the h. and bring wood and Hag 1.08
a drought upon the land and the h., 1.11
up into the h. by himself to pray. Mt 14.23
And he went up into the h., 15.29
ninety-nine on the h. and go in 18.12
And he went up into the h., Mk 3.13
them, he went into the h. to pray. 6.46
he went out into the h. to pray; Lk 6.12
'Fall on us'; and to the h., 'Cover us.' 23.30
Jesus went up into the h., Jn 6.03
withdrew again to the h. by himself. 6.15
heads are seven h. on which the Rev 17.09

HILLSIDE
along on the h. opposite him and 2Sa 16.13

HILLSIDE (cont.)
swine was feeding there on the h.; Mk 5.11
swine was feeding there on the h.; Lk 8.32

HILT
and the h. also went in after the Ju 3.22

HIMSELF
So Lot chose for h. all the Jordan Gen 13.11
and said to h., "Shall a child be 17.17
them, and bowed h. to the earth, 18.02
and bowed h. with his face to the 19.01
Did he not h. say to me, 'She is my 20.05
will provide h. the lamb for a 22.08
he bowed h. to the earth before the 24.52
blessed him, and Esau said to h., 27.41
Esau comforts h. by planning to 27.42
days' journey between h. and Jacob; 30.36
and he h. lodged that night in the 32.21
He h. went on before them, bowing 33.03
bowing h. to the ground seven times, 33.03
and built h. a house, and made 33.17
had revealed h. to him when he 35.07
he had shaved h. and changed his 41.14
and controlling h. he said, "Let food be 43.31
They served him by h., and them by 43.32
for you are like Pharaoh h. 44.18
not control h. before all those 45.01
Joseph made h. known to his 45.01
and he presented h. to him, 46.29
Israel bowed h. upon the head of 47.31
and he bowed h. with his face to 48.12
who has designated her for h., Ex 21.08
If he takes another wife to h., 21.10
shall take upon h. any guilt 28.38
a ransom for h. to the LORD when 30.12
shall have for h. the skin of the Lev 7.08
the sin offering, which was for h. 9.08
he has shown h. to the priest for 13.07
then he shall shave h., but the itch 13.33
and bathe h. in water, and he shall 14.08
and bathe h. in water, and be 15.05
and bathe h. in water, and be 15.06
and bathe h. in water, and be 15.07
and bathe h. in water, and be 15.08
and bathe h. in water, and be 15.10
and bathe h. in water, and be 15.11
shall count for h. seven days for 15.13
and bathe h. in water, and be 15.21
and bathe h. in water, and be 15.22
and bathe h. in water, and be 15.27
the bull as a sin offering for h., 16.06
atonement for h. and for his house. 16.06
the bull as a sin offering for h., 16.11
atonement for h. and for his house; 16.11
the bull as a sin offering for h. 16.11
atonement for h. and for his house 16.17
atonement for h. and for the 16.24
and bathe h. in water, and be 17.15
guilt offering for h. to the LORD, 19.21
shall defile h. for the dead among 21.01
no husband; for her he may defile h.). 21.03
not defile h. as a husband among 21.04
among his people and so profane h. 21.04
nor defile h., even for his father 21.11
defiling h. by it: I am the LORD.' 22.08
and then h. becomes prosperous and 25.26
means to get it back for h., then what 25.28
and cannot maintain h. with you, 25.35
and sells h. to you, you shall not 25.39
poor and sells h. to the stranger 25.47
if he grows rich he may redeem h. 25.49
when he sold h. to him until the 25.50
a Nazirite, to separate h. to the LORD, Num 6.02
he shall separate h. from wine and 6.03
which he separates h. to the LORD, 6.05
he separates h. to the LORD he 6.06
they die, shall he make h. unclean; 6.07
and separate h. to the LORD for the 6.12
of Israel, to bring you near to h., 16.09
he shall cleanse h. with the water 19.12
not cleanse h. on the third day 19.12
has died, and does not cleanse h., 19.13
his clothes and bathe h. in water, 19.19
is unclean and does not cleanse h., 19.20
and he showed h. holy among them. 20.13
So Israel yoked h. to Baal of Peor. 25.03
an oath to bind h. by a pledge, 30.02
had taken booty, every man for h.) 31.53
of blood shall h. put the murderer 35.19
before you will h. fight for you, Deu 1.30
a nation for h. from the midst of 4.34
he must not multiply horses for h., 17.16
he shall not multiply wives for h., 17.17
multiply for h. silver and gold. 17.17
shall write for h. in a book a 17.18
on, he shall bathe h. in water, 23.11
establish you as a people holy to h., 28.09
blesses h. in his heart, saying, 'I 29.19
The LORD your God h. will go over 31.03
He chose the best of the land for h., 33.21
it, may the LORD h. take vengeance. Jos 22.23
He gathered to h. the Ammonites and Ju 3.13
And Ehud made for h. a sword with 3.16
But he h. turned back at the 3.19
only relieving h. in the closet of 3.24
is a god, let him contend for h., 6.31
as a dog laps, you shall set by h.; 7.05
Jerubbaal was left, for he hid h. 9.05
who took to h. a concubine from 19.01
up the priest would take for h. 1Sa 2.14
LORD revealed h. to Samuel at 3.21
appoint for h. commanders of thousands 8.12
he has hidden h. among the baggage." 10.22
LORD to make you a people for h. 12.22
valiant man, he attached him to h. 14.52
up a monument for h. and turned, 15.12
stripped h. of the robe that was 18.04
Then he h. went to Ramah, and came 19.22
So David hid h. in the field; and when 20.24
another, until David recovered h. 20.41
and feigned h. mad in their hands, 21.13
for he has shut h. in by entering a 23.07
and Saul went in to relieve h. Now David 24.03
or for my lord taking vengeance h. 25.31
David hiding h. on the hill of Hachilah, 26.01
"He has made h. utterly abhorred by 27.12
So Saul disguised h. and put on 28.08
fellow reconcile h. to his lord? 29.04
strengthened h. in the LORD his 30.06
was making h. strong in the house 2Sa 3.06
king of Israel honored h. today, 6.20
uncovering h. today before the eyes 6.20
fellows shamelessly uncovers h.!" 6.20
making h. a name, and doing for them 7.23
And David won a name for h. When he 8.13
is dead? He may do h. some harm." 12.18
and anointed h., and changed his 12.20
that he made h. ill because of his 13.02
this decision the king convicts h., 14.13
and bowed h. on his face to the 14.33
Absalom got h. a chariot and 15.01
the Jordan; and there he refreshed h. 16.14
he has hidden h. in one of the 17.09
his house in order, and hanged h.; 17.23
and set up for h. the pillar which 18.18
lest he get h. fortified cities, and 20.06
them arms h. with iron and the 23.07
the son of Haggith exalted h., 1Ki 1.05
he prepared for h. chariots and 1.05
And the king bowed h. upon the bed. 1.47
more righteous and better than h., 2.32
Ahijah had clad h. with a new 11.29
he could not draw it back to h. 13.04

HIMSELF (cont.)
raise up for h. a king over Israel, 1Ki 14.14
drinking h. drunk in the house of 16.09
as he had seated h. on his throne, 16.11
Then he stretched h. upon the child 17.21
So Elijah went to show h. to Ahab. 18.02
Ahab went in one direction by h., 18.06
went in another direction by h. 18.06
and he bowed h. down upon the earth, 18.42
But he h. went a day's journey into 19.04
his armor boast h. as he that puts 20.11
was drinking h. drunk in the booths, 20.16
disguising h. with a bandage over 20.38
none who sold h. to do what was 21.25
how Ahab has humbled h. before me? 21.29
Because he has humbled h. before me, 21.29
Chenaanah made for h. horns of iron, 22.11
disguised h. and went into battle. 22.30
and as he stretched h. upon him, 2Ki 4.34
went up, and stretchel h. upon him; 4.35
down and dipped h. seven times in 5.14
that he saved h. there more than 6.10
"If the LORD h. should make windows 7.02
"If the LORD h. should make windows 7.19
and covered h. with sackcloth, and 19.01
of Judah gave h. up to the king of 24.12
h., and his mother, and his servants, 24.12
houses for h. in the city of David; 1Ch 15.01
consecrating h. today to the LORD?" 29.05
established h. in his kingdom, 2Ch 1.01
LORD, and a royal palace for h. 2.01
cedar to build h. a house to dwell 2.03
LORD, and a royal palace for h. 2.12
And when he humbled h. the wrath of 12.12
established h. in Jerusalem and 12.13
to consecrate h. with a young bull 13.09
hewn out for h. in the city of 16.14
and strengthened h. against Israel. 17.01
Chenaanah made for h. horns of iron, 18.10
the king of Israel disguised h.; 18.29
Israel propped h. up in his 18.34
and set h. to seek the LORD, and 20.03
covenant between h. and all the 23.16
He set h. to seek God in the days 26.05
and he h. hastened to go out, 26.20
and he made h. altars in every 28.24
fortified cities, thinking to win them for h. 32.01
Hezekiah humbled h. for the pride 32.26
and he made for h. treasuries for 32.27
He likewise provided cities for h., 32.29
in the land, God left him to h., 32.31
God and humbled h. greatly before 33.12
the images, before he humbled h., 33.19
did not humble h. before the LORD, 33.23
Manasseh his father had humbled h., 33.23
but disguised h. in order to fight 35.22
did not humble h. before Jeremiah 36.12
and separated h. from the pollutions Ez 6.21
and casting h. down before the 10.01
and he h. banned from the congregation 10.08
Haman restrained h., and went home; Est 5.10
And Haman said to h., "Whom would 6.06
only upon h. do not put forth your Job 1.12
them to present h. before the LORD. 2.01
a potsherd with which to scrape h., 2.08
he will rouse h. for you and reward you 8.06
who has hardened h. against him, 9.04
body, and he mourns only for h." 14.22
and fill h. with the east wind? 15.02
trust in emptiness, deceiving h.; 15.31
innocent stirs h. up against the 17.08
he who is wise is profitable to h. 22.02
he justified h. rather than God; 32.02
should take back his spirit to h., 34.14
and gather to h. his breath, 34.14
When he raises h. up the mighty are 41.25
he spreads h. like a threshing 41.30
has set apart the godly for h.; Ps 4.03
The LORD has made h. known, he has 9.16
the hapless commits h. to thee; 10.14
and he who cannot keep h. alive. 22.29
He h. shall abide in prosperity, and 25.13
For he flatters h. in his own eyes 36.02
he sets h. in a way that is not 36.04
God has shown h. a sure defense. 48.03
Truly no man can ransom h., or give to 49.07
he counts h. happy, and though a man 49.18
praise when he does well for h., 49.18
righteousness, for God h. is judge! 50.06
the Most High h. will establish 87.05
He clothed h. with cursing as his 109.18
belt with which he daily girds h.! 109.19
but upon h. his crown will shed its 132.18
For the LORD has chosen Jacob for h., 135.04
has no sense; he who does it destroys h. Pro 6.32
but he who misses me injures h.; 8.36
corrects a scoffer gets h. abuse, 9.07
A man who is kind benefits h., 11.17
but a cruel man hurts h. 11.17
one who waters will h. be watered. 11.25
who works for h. than one who plays 12.09
the word brings destruction on h., 13.13
ignores instruction despises h., 15.32
and his lips are a snare to h. 18.07
He who gets wisdom loves h.; he who 19.08
Even a child makes h. known by his 20.11
the poor will h. cry out and not 21.13
his tongue keeps h. out of trouble. 21.23
prudent man sees danger and hides h.; 22.03
he who guards h. will keep far from 22.05
Argue your case with your neighbor h., 25.09
prudent man sees danger and hides h.; 27.12
a child left to h. brings shame to 29.15
how to conduct h. before the living? Ecc 6.08
and enjoy h., for this will go with 8.15
King Solomon made h. a palanquin Sol 3.09
Holy God shows h. holy in righteousness. Is 5.16
Therefore the Lord h. will give you 7.14
And when Moab presents h., 16.12
when he wearies h. upon the high 16.12
LORD will make h. known to the 19.21
hosts has revealed h. in my ears: 22.14
he exalts h. to show mercy to you. 30.18
Teacher will not hide h. any more, 30.20
and covered h. with sackcloth, and 37.01
to me, and he h. has done it. 38.15
he shows h. mighty against his foes. 42.13
will call h. by the name of Jacob, 44.05
and surname h. by the name of 44.05
he takes a part of it and warms h., 44.15
also he warms h. and says, "Aha, I am 44.16
and he cannot deliver h. or say, 44.20
oppressor, when he sets h. to destroy? 51.13
when he makes h. an offering for 53.10
who has joined h. to the LORD say, 56.03
a day for a man to humble h.? 58.05
departs from evil makes h. a prey. 59.15
and wrapped h. in fury as a mantle. 59.17
bridegroom decks h. with a garland, 61.10
and h. fought against them. 63.10
to make for h. an everlasting name, 63.12
that bestirs h. to take hold of 64.07
he who blesses h. in the land 65.16
shall bless h. by the God of truth, 65.16
that the way of man is not in h., Jer 10.23
for them or cut h. or make h. bald for them. 16.06
Can man make for h. gods? Such are 16.20
Can a man hide h. in secret places 23.24
would dare of h. to approach me? 30.21
vengeance, to avenge h. on his foes. 46.10
he magnified h. against the LORD; 48.26
he magnified h. against the LORD. 48.42
and he is not able to conceal h. 49.10
The LORD of hosts has sworn by h.: 51.14

HIMSELF (cont.)

The LORD h. has scattered them, he Lam 4.16
who separates h. from me, taking his Eze 14.07
a prophet to inquire for h. of me, 14.07
his blood shall be upon h. 18.13
of the righteous shall be upon h., 18.20
of the wicked shall be upon h. 18.20
he will comfort h. for all his 32.31
his blood shall be upon h. 33.05
he shall count for h. seven days, 44.26
provide for h. and all the people 45.22
not defile h. with the king's rich Dan 1.08
to allow him not to defile h. 1.08
did as he pleased and magnified h. 8.04
he-goat magnified h. exceedingly; 8.08
his own mind he shall magnify h. 8.25
exhalt h. and magnify h. above every god, 11.36
for he shall magnify h. above all. 11.37
Ephraim mixes h. with the peoples; Hos 7.08
plow, Jacob must harrow for h. 10.11
not present h. at the mouth of the 13.13
is swift of foot shall not save h. Amo 2.15
GOD has sworn by h. (says the LORD, 6.08
and covered h. with sackcloth, and Jon 3.06
and made a booth for h. there. 4.05
He gathers for h. all nations, Hab 2.05
and loads h. with pledges!" 2.06
he has roused h. from his holy Zec 2.13
Satan, he is divided against h.; Mt 12.26
other spirits more evil than h., 12.45
yet he has no root in h., but endures 13.21
up into the hills by h. to pray. 14.23
let him deny h. and take up his 16.24
Whoever humbles h. like this child, 18.04
whoever exalts h. will be humbled, 23.12
whoever humbles h. will be exalted. 23.12
But if that wicked servant says to h., 24.48
invoke a curse on h. and to swear, 26.74
he departed; and he went and hanged h. 27.05
he cannot save h. He is the 27.42
for they said, "He is beside h." Mk 3.21
risen up against h. and is divided, 3.26
out, and bruising h. with stones. 5.05
perceiving in h. that power had 5.30
let him deny h. and take up his 8.34
David h., inspired by the Holy 12.36
David h. calls him Lord; so how is 12.37
guards, and warming h. at the fire. 14.54
and seeing Peter warming h., she looked 14.67
invoke a curse on h. and to swear, 14.71
"He saved others; he cannot save h. 15.31
who was also h. looking for the 15.43
he said to h., "If this man were a Lk 7.39
let him deny h. and take up his 9.23
world and loses or forfeits h.? 9.25
place where he h. was about to 10.01
But he, desiring to justify h., 10.29
Satan also is divided against h., 11.18
other spirits more evil than h., 11.26
and he thought to h., 'What shall I do, 12.17
So is he who lays up treasure for h., 12.21
he will gird h. and have them sit 12.37
But if that servant says to h., 12.45
one who exalts h. will be humbled, 14.11
he who humbles h. will be exalted." 14.11
went and joined h. to one of the 15.15
But when he came to h. he said, 15.17
And the steward said to h., 'What shall I do, 16.03
but afterward he said to h., 'Though I neither 18.04
stood and prayed thus with h., 18.11
one who exalts h. will be humbled, 18.14
he who humbles h. will be exalted." 18.14
For David h. says in the Book of 20.42
saying that he h. is Christ a king." 23.02
who was h. in Jerusalem at that 23.07
let him save h., if he is the 23.35
Jesus h. drew near and went with 24.15
scriptures the things concerning h. 24.27
saying this, Jesus h. stood among them. 24.36
but Jesus did not trust h. to them, Jn 2.24
for he h. knew what was in man. 2.25
(although Jesus h. did not baptize, 4.02
us the well, and drank from it h., 4.12
For Jesus h. testified that a 4.44
and he h. believed, and all his 4.53
Father, making h. equal with God. 5.18
shows him all that he h. is doing; 5.20
For as the Father has life in h., 5.26
the Son also to have life in h., 5.26
who sent me has h. borne witness 5.37
for he h. knew what he would do. 6.06
withdrew again to the hills by h. 6.15
knowing in h. that his disciples 6.61
"Will he kill h., since he says, 8.22
but Jesus hid h., and went out of 8.59
he is of age, he will speak for h." 9.21
he departed and hid h. from them. 12.36
the Father who sent me has h. given me 12.49
garments, and girded h. with a towel. 13.04
God will also glorify him in h., 13.32
for the Father h. loves you, because 16.27
with them, standing and warming h. 18.18
Peter was standing and warming h. 18.25
he has made h. the Son of God." 19.07
who makes h. a king sets h. against Caesar." 19.12
Jesus revealed h. again to the 21.01
and he revealed h. in this way. 21.01
he presented h. alive after his Ac 1.03
but he h. says, 'The Lord said to my 2.34
giving h. out to be somebody, and a 5.36
Joseph made h. known to his brothers, 7.13
And he died, h. and our fathers, 7.15
saying that he h. was somebody 8.09
Even Simon h. believed, and after 8.13
about h. or about some one else?" 8.34
And Peter came to h., and said, 12.11
did not leave h. without witness, 14.17
his sword and was about to kill h., 16.27
since he h. gives to all men life 17.25
but he h. went into the synagogue 18.19
he h. stayed in Asia for a while. 19.22
arranged, intending h. to go by land. 20.13
day he purified h. with them and 21.26
and that he h. intended to go there 25.04
and as he h. appealed to the emperor, 25.25
Paul was allowed to stay by h., 28.16
time that he h. is righteous and Rom 3.26
it is the Spirit h. bearing witness 8.16
but the Spirit h. intercedes for 8.26
not to think of h. more highly 12.03
None of us lives to h., 14.07
and none of us dies to h. 14.07
us shall give account of h. to God. 14.12
reason to judge h. for what he 14.22
For Christ did not please h.; 15.03
but is h. to be judged by no one. 1Co 2.15
though he h. will be saved, but only 3.15
Let no one deceive h. If any one 3.18
he who joins h. to a prostitute 6.16
Let a man examine h., and so eat 11.28
eats and drinks judgment upon h. 11.29
He who speaks in a tongue edifies h., 14.04
church and speak to h. and to God. 14.28
then the Son h. will also be 15.28
reconciled us to h. and gave us the 2Co 5.18
Christ reconciling the world to h., 5.19
but being h. very earnest he is 8.17
let him remind h. that as he is 10.07
who commends h. that is accepted, 10.18
Satan disguises h. as an angel of 11.14
who gave h. for our sins to deliver Gal 1.04
came he drew back and separated h., 2.12
who loved me and gave h. for me. 2.20
when he is nothing, he deceives h. 6.03

HIMSELF (cont.)

will be in h. alone and not in his Gal 6.04
might create in h. one new man in Eph 2.15
Christ Jesus h. being the chief 2.20
loved us and gave h. up for us, 5.02
God of peace h. sanctify you wholly; 5.23
the church and gave h. up for her, 5.25
He who loves his wife loves h. 5.28
one of you love his wife as h., 5.33
but emptied h., taking the form of Php 2.07
form he humbled h. and became 2.08
even to subject all things to h. 3.21
him to reconcile to h. all things, Col 1.20
Now may our God and Father h., 1Th 3.11
take a wife for h. in holiness and 4.04
For the Lord h. will descend from 4.16
God of peace h. sanctify you wholly; 5.23
and exalts h. against every so-called 2Th 2.04
of God, proclaiming h. to be God. 2.04
Now may our Lord Jesus Christ h., 2.16
Lord of peace h. give you peace at 3.16
who gave h. as a ransom for all, the 1Ti 2.06
faithful—for he cannot deny h. 2Ti 2.13
one purifies h. from what is 2.21
master of h., upright, holy, and Tit 1.08
who gave h. for us to redeem us 2.14
to purify for h. a people of his 2.14
he h. likewise partook of the same Heb 2.14
For because he h. has suffered and 2.18
since he h. is beset with weakness. 5.02
does not take the honor upon h., 5.04
did not exalt h. to be made a high 5.05
by whom to swear, he swore by h., 6.13
One might even say that Levi h., 7.09
once for all when he offered up h. 7.27
he offers for h. and for the 9.07
Spirit offered h. without blemish 9.14
Nor was it to offer h. repeatedly, 9.25
away sin by the sacrifice of h. 9.26
sinners such hostility against h., 12.03
with evil and he h. tempts no one; Jas 1.13
for he observes h. and goes away 1.24
the world makes h. an enemy of God. 4.04
He h. bore our sins in his body on 1Pe 2.24
will h. restore, establish, and 5.10
in him purifies h. as he is pure. 1Jn 3.03
Son of God has the testimony in h. 5.10
Diotrephes, who likes to put h. first, 3Jn 1.09
he refuses h. to welcome the brethren, 1.10
inscribed which no one knows but h. Rev 19.12
and God h. will be with them; 21.03

HIN

a fourth of a h. of beaten oil, Ex 29.40
a fourth of a h. of wine for a 29.40
sanctuary, and of olive oil a h.; 30.24
and a just h.: I am the LORD your Lev 19.36
shall be of wine, a fourth of a h. 23.13
mixed with a fourth of a h. of oil; Num 15.04
a fourth of a h., you shall prepare 15.05
mixed with a third of a h. of oil; 15.06
offer a third of a h. of wine, 15.07
mixed with half a h. of oil, 15.09
drink offering half a h. of wine, 15.10
a fourth of a h. of beaten oil. 28.05
be a fourth of a h. for each lamb; 28.07
shall be half a h. of wine for a 28.14
a third of a h. for a ram, and a 28.14
and a fourth of a h. for a lamb; 28.14
by measure, the sixth part of a h.; Eze 4.11
and a h. of oil to each ephah. 45.24
together with a h. of oil to each 46.05
together with a h. of oil to each 46.07
together with a h. of oil to an 46.11
one third of a h. of oil to 46.14

HIND

Naphtali is a h. let loose, that Gen 49.21
a lovely h., a graceful doe. Pro 5.19
Even the h. in the field forsakes Jer 14.05

HINDER

or h. you from burying your dead." Gen 23.06
'Let nothing h. you from coming to Num 22.16
for nothing can h. the LORD from 1Sa 14.06
and all their h. parts were inward. 1Ki 7.25
and all their h. parts were inward. 2Ch 4.04
who can h. him? Who will say Job 9.12
calls to judgment, who can h. him? 11.10
my hand; I work and who can h. it?" Is 43.13
come to me, and do not h. them; Mt 19.14
children come to me, do not h. them; Mk 10.14
come to me, and do not h. them; Lk 18.16

HINDERED

and you h. those who were entering." Lk 11.52
so often been h. from coming to Rom 15.22
who h. you from obeying the truth? Gal 5.07
again and again—but Satan h. us. 1Th 2.18
that your prayers may not be h. 1Pe 3.07

HINDERING

and h. meditation before God, Job 15.04
by h. us from speaking to the 1Th 2.16

HINDRANCE

You are a h. to me; for you are Mt 16.23
block or h. in the way of a Rom 14.13

HINDS

you observe the calving of the h.? Job 39.01
gazelles or the h. of the field, Sol 2.07
gazelles or the h. of the field, 3.05

HINDS'

He made my feet like h. feet, 2Sa 22.34
He made my feet like h. feet, Ps 18.33
he makes my feet like h. feet, Hab 3.19

HINGES

As a door turns on its h., so does a Pro 26.14

HINNOM

of the son of H. at the southern Jos 15.08
lies over against the valley of H., 15.08
the valley of the son of H., 18.16
it then goes down the valley of H., 18.16
is in the valley of the sons of H., 2Ki 23.10
in the valley of the son of H., 2Ch 28.03
in the valley of the son of H., 33.06
from Beersheba to the valley of H. Neh 11.30
is in the valley of the son of H., Jer 7.31
or the valley of the son of H., 7.32
in the valley of the son of H., 32.35

HIP

sinew of the h. which is upon the Gen 32.32
thigh on the sinew of the h. 32.32
And he smote them h. and thigh with Ju 15.08
you shall be carried upon her h., Is 66.12

HIPS

at their h., and sent them away. 2Sa 10.04
at their h., and sent them away; 1Ch 19.04

HIRAH

Adullamite, whose name was H. Gen 38.01
and his friend H. the Adullamite. 38.12

HIRAM

And H. King of Tyre sent messengers 2Sa 5.11
Now H. king of Tyre sent his 1Ki 5.01
his father; for H. always loved David. 5.01
And Solomon sent word to H., 5.02
When H. heard the words of Solomon, 5.07

HIRAM (cont.)
And H. sent to Solomon, saying, "I 1Ki 5.08
So H. supplied Solomon with all the 5.10
while Solomon gave H. twenty 5.11
gave this to H. year by year. 5.11
was peace between H. and Solomon; 5.12
sent and brought H. from Tyre. 7.13
H. also made the pots, the shovels, 7.40
So H. finished all the work that he 7.40
which H. made for King Solomon, were 7.45
and H. king of Tyre had supplied 9.11
Solomon gave to H. twenty cities 9.11
But when H. came from Tyre to see 9.12
H. had sent to the king one hundred 9.14
And H. sent with the fleet his 9.27
Moreover the fleet of H., 10.11
at sea with the fleet of H.. 10.22
And H. king of Tyre sent messengers 1Ch 14.01

HIRAM'S
builders and H. builders and the 1Ki 5.18

HIRE
has given me my h. because I gave Gen 30.18
it was hired, it came for its h. Ex 22.15
shall not bring the h. of a harlot, Deu 23.18
give him his h. on the day he 24.15
of silver to h. chariots and 1Ch 19.06
who work for h. will be grieved. Is 19.10
and she will return to her h., 23.17
merchandise and her h. will be 23.18
h. a goldsmith, and he makes it into 46.06
a harlot, because you scorned h. Eze 16.31
you gave h., while no h. was given to 16.34
and you shall also give h. no more. 16.41
'These are my h., which my lovers Hos 2.12
Though they h. allies among the 8.10
a harlot's h. upon all threshing 9.01
for from the h. of a harlot she Mic 1.07
and to the h. of a harlot they 1.07
a bribe, its priests teach for h., 3.11
the morning to h. laborers for his Mt 20.01

HIRED
for I have h. you with my son's Gen 30.16
No sojourner or h. servant may eat Ex 12.45
if it was h., it came for its hire. 22.15
The wages of a h. servant shall not Lev 19.13
the priest or a h. servant shall 22.10
and for your h. servant and the 25.06
with you as a h. servant and as a 25.40
rated as the time of a h. servant. 25.50
As a servant h. year by year shall 25.53
the cost of a h. servant he has Deu 15.18
because they h. against you Balaam 23.04
not oppress a h. servant who is 24.14
which Abimelech h. worthless and Ju 9.04
he has h. me, and I have become his 18.04
were full have h. themselves out 1Sa 2.05
sent and h. the Syrians of Bethrehob, 2Sa 10.06
of Israel has h. against us the 2Ki 7.06
They h. thirty-two thousand chariots 1Ch 19.07
and they h. masons and carpenters 2Ch 24.12
He h. also a hundred thousand 25.06
and h. counselors against them to Ez 4.05
Tobiah and Sanballat had h. him. Neh 6.12
For this purpose he was h., 6.13
but h. Balaam against them to curse 13.02
for a harlot may be h. for a loaf Pro 6.26
razor which is h. beyond the River Is 7.20
Even her h. soldiers in her midst Jer 46.21
wandering alone; Ephraim has h. lovers. Hos 8.09
to him, 'Because no one has h. us.' Mt 20.07
And when those h. about the eleventh 20.09
in the boat with the h. servants, Mk 1.20
of my father's h. servants have Lk 15.17
me as one of your h. servants."' 15.19

HIRELING
not his days like the days of a h.? Job 7.01
and like a h. who looks for his 7.02
he may enjoy, like a h., his day. 14.06
years, like the years of a h., Is 16.14
according to the years of a h., 21.16
who oppress the h. in his wages, Mal 3.05
He who is a h. and not a shepherd, Jn 10.12
because he is a h. and cares 10.13

HIRES
is he who h. a passing fool or Pro 26.10
all her h. shall be burned with Mic 1.07

HISS
it will be astonished, and will h.; 1Ki 9.08
and will h. because of all its Jer 19.08
and will h. because of all its 49.17
and h. because of all her wounds. 50.13
they h. and wag their heads at the Lam 2.15
they h., they gnash their teeth, 2.16
merchants among the peoples h. at you; Eze 27.36

HISSED
a thing to be h. at for ever. Jer 18.16
city a horror, a thing to be h. at; 19.08

HISSES
and h. at him from its place. Job 27.23
passes by her h. and shakes his Zep 2.15

HISSING
and of h., as you see with your own 2Ch 29.08
a h., and an everlasting reproach. Jer 25.09
a h. and a curse, as at this day; 25.18
a h., and a reproach among all the 29.18
of jackals, a horror and a h., 51.37
desolation, and your inhabitants a h.; Mic 6.16

HISTORY
This is the h. of the family of Gen 37.02
written in the h. of Nathan the 2Ch 9.29

HIT
to fight and to h. with wicked Is 58.04

HITHER
"Come h., and hear the words of the Jos 3.09
of the LORD, "Did the man come h.?" 1Sa 10.22
multitude was surging h. and thither. 14.16
to Ahijah, "Bring h. the ark of God." 14.18
said, "Let us draw near h. to God." 14.36
"Come h., all you leaders of the 14.38
draw near h., sons of the sorceress, Is 57.03
"Come up h., and I will show you Rev 4.01
heaven saying to them, "Come up h.!" 11.12

HITHERTO
task of making bricks today, as h.?" Ex 5.14
since h. the LORD has blessed me?" Jos 17.14
for he said, "H. the LORD has helped 1Sa 7.12
stationed h. in the king's gate on 1Ch 9.18
majority had h. kept their allegiance 12.29
H. you have asked nothing in my Jn 16.24
through being h. accustomed to 1Co 8.07

HITTITE
and Ephron the H. answered Abraham Gen 23.10
of Ephron the son of Zohar the H., 25.09
the daughter of Beeri the H., 26.34
the daughter of Elon the H.; 26.34
of my life because of the H. women. 27.46
one of the H. women such as these, 27.46
Adah the daughter of Elon the H., 36.02
is in the field of Ephron the H., 49.29
from Ephron the H. to possess as a 49.30
with the field from Ephron the H., 50.13
Canaanite, and H. from before you. Ex 23.28

HITTITE (cont.)
Then David said to Ahimelech the H., 1Sa 26.06
of Eliam, the wife of Uriah the H.?" 2Sa 11.03
word to Joab, "Send me Uriah the H." 11.06
Uriah the H. was slain also. 11.17
servant Uriah the H. is dead also.'" 11.21
servant Uriah the H. is dead also." 11.24
Uriah the H. with the sword, 12.09
of Uriah the H. to be your wife.' 12.10
Uriah the H.: thirty-seven in all. 23.39
Edomite, Sidonian, and H. women, 1Ki 11.01
in the matter of Uriah the H. 15.05
Uriah the H., Zabad the son of 1Ch 11.41
the H., the Amorite, the Perizzite, Neh 9.08
an Amorite, and your mother a H. Eze 16.03
mother was a H. and your father an 16.45

HITTITES
the H., the Perizzites, the Rephaim, Gen 15.20
his dead, and said to the H., 23.03
The H. answered Abraham, 23.05
Abraham rose and bowed to the H., 23.07
Now Ephron was sitting among the H.; 23.10
Abraham in the hearing of the H., 23.10
had named in the hearing of the H., 23.16
possession in the presence of the H., 23.18
for a burying place by the H. 23.20
Abraham purchased from the H. 25.10
in it were purchased from the H." 49.32
the H., the Amorites, the Perizzites, Ex 3.08
the H., the Amorites, the Perizzites, 3.17
the H., the Amorites, the Hivites, 13.05
and the H., and the Perizzites, and 23.23
the H., the Perizzites, the Hivites, 33.02
the H., the Perizzites, the Hivites, 34.11
the H., the Jebusites, and the Num 13.29
the H., the Girgashites, the Amorites, Deu 7.01
the H. and the Amorites, the Canaanites 20.17
the land of the H. to the Great Jos 1.04
the H., the Hivites, the Perizzites, 3.10
the H., the Amorites, the Canaanites, 9.01
the H., the Perizzites, and the 11.03
in the Negeb, the land of the H., 12.08
the H., the Girgashites, the Hivites, 24.11
the land of the H. and built a Ju 1.26
the H., the Amorites, the Perizzites, 3.05
to Kadesh in the land of the H.; 2Sa 24.06
the H., the Perizzites, the Hivites, 1Ki 9.20
kings of the H. and the kings of 10.29
kings of the H. and the kings of 2Ki 7.06
kings of the H. and the kings of 2Ch 1.17
the people who were left of the H., 8.07
the H., the Perizzites, the Jebusites, Ez 9.01

HIVITE
Shechem the son of Hamor the H., Gen 34.02
of Anah the son of Zibeon the H., 36.02
you, which shall drive out H., Ex 23.28

HIVITES
the H., the Arkites, the Sinites, Gen 10.17
the H., and the Jebusites. Ex 3.08
the H., and the Jebusites, a land 3.17
the H., and the Jebusites, which he 13.05
the H., and the Jebusites, and I 23.23
the H., and the Jebusites. 33.02
the H., and the Jebusites. 34.11
the H., and the Jebusites, seven Deu 7.01
the H. and the Jebusites, as the 20.17
the H., the Perizzites, the Girgashites, Jos 3.10
the H., and the Jebusites, heard of 9.01
But the men of Israel said to the H., 9.07
and the H. under Hermon in the land 11.03
except the H., the inhabitants of 11.19
the H., and the Jebusites): 12.08
the H., and the Jebusites; 24.11
and the H. who dwelt on Mount Ju 3.03
the H., and the Jebusites; 3.05
cities of the H. and Canaanites; 2Sa 24.07
the H., and the Jebusites, who were 1Ki 9.20
the H., the Arkites, the Sinites, 1Ch 1.15
the H., and the Jebusites, who were 2Ch 8.07
places of the H. and the Amorites, Is 17.09

HIZKI
Zebadiah, Meshullam, H., Heber, 1Ch 8.17

HIZKIAH
Elioenai, H., and Azrikam, three. 1Ch 3.23

HO
H. Ariel, Ariel, the city where David Is 29.01
"H., every one who thirsts, come to 55.01
H., shepherds of Israel who have Eze 34.02
H.! h.! Flee from the land Zec 2.06
H.! Escape to Zion, you who dwell 2.07

HOARDED
it will not be stored or h., Is 23.18

HOARDS
darkness and the h. in secret Is 45.03

HOARFROST
thing, fine as h. on the ground. Ex 16.14
given birth to the h. of heaven? Job 38.29
he scatters h. like ashes. Ps 147.16

HOARY
"You shall rise up before the h. head, Lev 19.32
one would think the deep to be h. Job 41.32
A h. head is a crown of glory; Pro 16.31

HOBAB
And Moses said to H. the son of Num 10.29
descendants of H. the father-in-law Ju 4.11

HOBAH
routed them and pursued them to H., Gen 14.15

HOBAIAH
the sons of H., the sons of Hakkoz, Neh 7.63

HOD
Bezer, H., Shamma, Shilshah, Ithran, 1Ch 7.37

HODAVIAH
H., Eliashib, Pelaiah, Akkub, Johanan, 1Ch 3.24
H., and Jahdiel, mighty warriors, 5.24
son of H., son of Hassenuah, 9.07
of the sons of H., seventy-four. Ez 2.40

HODESH
He had sons by H. his wife: Jobab, 1Ch 8.09

HODEVAH
of the sons of H., seventy-four. Neh 7.43

HODIAH
The sons of the wife of H., the sister 1Ch 4.19
H., Maaseiah, Kelita, Azariah, Jozabad, Neh 8.07
H., Shebaniah, and Pethahiah, said, 9.05
H., Kelita, Pelaiah, Hanan, 10.10
H., Bani, Beninu. 10.13
H., Hashum, Bezai, 10.18

HOE
which used to be hoed with a h., Is 7.25

HOED
it shall not be pruned or h., Is 5.05
which used to be h. with a hoe, 7.25

HOGLAH
Mahlah, Noah, H., Milcah, and Tirzah. Num 26.33
Mahlah, Noah, H., Milcah, and Tirzah. 27.01
H., Milcah, and Noah, the daughters 36.11
Mahlah, Noah, H., Milcah, and Tirzah. Jos 17.03

HOHAM
Jerusalem sent to H. king of Hebron, Jos 10.03

HOISTING
after h. it up, they took measures Ac 27.17
then h. the foresail to the wind 27.40

HOLD
and h. him fast with your hand; Gen 21.18
hand had taken h. of Esau's heel; 25.26
that they may h. a feast to me in Ex 5.01
the Egyptians h. in bondage and I 6.05
to let them go and still h. them, 9.02
for we must h. a feast to the LORD." 10.09
day you shall h. a holy assembly, 12.16
LORD will not h. him guiltless who 20.07
set apart for you to h. unclean. Lev 20.25
you shall h. a holy convocation; 23.21
day you shall h. a holy convocation 23.36
LORD will not h. him guiltless who Deu 5.11
So I took h. of the two tables, and 9.17
which you will h. in the land that 19.14
shall take h. of him and bring him 21.19
and my hand takes h. on judgment, 32.41
but h. yourselves all in readiness; Jos 8.04
arose and took h. of the doors of Ju 16.03
and laying h. of his concubine he 19.29
you are wearing and h. it out." Ru 3.15
Saul laid h. upon the skirt of his 1Sa 15.27
Then David took h. of his clothes, 2Sa 1.11
the ark of God and took h. of it, 6.06
he took h. of her, and said to her, 13.11
Now h. your peace, my sister; 13.20
and take h. of him, and kiss him. 15.05
"Let not my lord h. me guilty or 19.19
and caught h. of the horns of the 1Ki 1.50
he has laid h. of the horns of the 1.51
Now therefore h. him not guiltless, 2.09
LORD and caught h. of the horns of 2.28
and laid h. on other gods, and 9.09
Then Ahijah laid h. of the new 11.30
the altar, saying, "Lay h. of him." 13.04
"Yes, I know it; h. your peace." 2Ki 2.03
"Yes, I know it; h. your peace." 2.05
Then he took h. of his own clothes 2.12
of God, she caught h. of his feet. 4.27
and h. the door fast against him. 6.32
to confirm his h. of the royal 15.19
put out his hand to h. the ark, 1Ch 13.09
made could not h. the burnt 2Ch 7.07
and laid h. on other gods, and 7.22
us a secure h. within his holy Ez 9.08
and h. a fast on my behalf, and Est 4.16
h. the fourteenth day of the month 9.19
used to go and h. a feast in the Job 1.04
"Do you still h. fast your integrity? 2.09
he lays h. of it, but it does not 8.15
know thou wilt not h. me innocent. 9.28
the heel, a snare lays h. of him. 18.09
I h. fast my righteousness, and will 27.06
of affliction have taken h. of me. 30.16
that it might take h. of the skirts 38.13
Take h. of shield and buckler, and Ps 35.02
h. not thy peace at my tears! 39.12
trembling took h. of them there, 48.06
We used to h. sweet converse 55.14
thou dost h. all the nations in 59.08
They h. fast to their evil purpose; 64.05
with thee; thou dost h. my right hand. 73.23
Why dost thou h. back thy hand, why 74.11
Thou dost h. my eyelids from 77.04
do not h. thy peace or be still, O 83.01
For thy servants h. her stones dear, 102.14
the pangs of Sheol laid h. on me; 116.03
I h. back my feet from every evil 119.101
I h. my life in my hand continually, 119.109
H. me up, that I may be safe and 119.117
me, and thy right hand shall h. me. 139.10
h. back your foot from their paths; Pro 1.15
of life to those who lay h. of her; 3.18
those who h. her fast are called 3.18
"Let your heart h. fast my words; 4.04
Keep h. of instruction, do not let 4.13
and h. him in pledge when he gives 20.16
righteous gives and does not h. back. 21.26
h. back those who are stumbling to 24.11
and h. him in pledge when he gives 27.13
the distaff, and her hands h. the spindle. 31.19
and how to lay h. on folly, till I Ecc 2.03
that you should take h. of this, 7.18
tree and lay h. of its branches. Sol 7.08
When a man takes h. of his brother Is 3.06
shall take h. of one man in that 4.01
He will seize firm h. on you, 22.17
Or let them lay h. of my protection, 27.05
lest they h. a bribe, who stops his 33.15
it cannot h. the mast firm in its 33.23
h. your right hand; it is I who say 41.13
h. not back, lengthen your cords and 54.02
please me and h. fast my covenant, 56.04
bestirs himself to take h. of thee; 64.07
cisterns, that can h. no water. Jer 2.13
They lay h. on bow and spear, they 6.23
anguish has taken h. of us, 6.24
They h. fast to deceit, they refuse 8.05
and dismay has taken h. on me. 8.21
Will not pangs take h. of you, 13.21
speak to them; do not h. back a word. 26.02
and all the people laid h. of him, 26.08
who h. the height of the hill. 49.16
and sorrows have taken h. of her, 49.24
They lay h. of bow and spear; 50.42
that I may lay h. of the hearts of Eze 14.05
but they will not h. together, Dan 2.43
h. fast to love and justice, and Hos 12.06
take h. of the brick mold! Nah 3.14
Come together and h. assembly, Zep 2.01
shall take h. of the robe of a Jew, Zec 8.23
each will lay h. on the hand of 14.13
that my covenant with Levi may h., Mal 2.04
will not lay h. of it and lift it Mt 12.11
for all h. that John was a prophet." 21.26
up and took h. of his feet and 28.09
and h. fast the tradition of men." Mk 7.08
h. it fast in an honest and good Lk 8.15
they might take h. of what he said, 20.20
"Do not h. me, for I have not yet Jn 20.17
do not h. this sin against them." Ac 7.60
And they took h. of him and brought 17.19
For we h. that a man is justified Rom 3.28
is evil, h. fast to what is good; 12.09
if you h. it fast—unless you 1Co 15.02
because I h. you in my heart, for Php 1.07
Only let us h. true to what we have 3.16
and in him all things h. together. Col 1.17
everything; h. fast what is good, 1Th 5.21
stand firm and h. to the traditions 2Th 2.15
they must h. the mystery of the 1Ti 3.09
h. to that, for by so doing you will 4.16
take h. of the eternal life to 6.12
they may take h. of the life which 6.19
he must h. firm to the sure word as Tit 1.09
his house if we h. fast our Heb 3.06
if only we h. our first confidence 3.14
let us h. fast our confession. 4.14
own account and h. him up to 6.06
Let us h. fast the confession of 10.23
partiality as you h. the faith of Jas 2.01
Above all h. unfailing your love 1Pe 4.08
you h. fast my name and you did not Rev 2.13
some there who h. the teaching of 2.14
have some who h. the teaching of 2.15
who do not h. this teaching, who 2.24
only h. fast what you have, until I 2.25

HOLD (cont.)
h. fast what you have, so that no Rev 3.11
brethren who h. the testimony of 19.10

HOLDERS
as h. for the poles to carry the Ex 25.27
rings of gold for h. for the bars; 26.29
they shall be h. for poles with 30.04
rings of gold for h. for the bars, 36.34
as h. for the poles to carry the 37.14
as h. for the poles with which to 37.27
bronze grating as h. for the poles; 38.05

HOLDEST
and my cup; thou h. my lot. Ps 16.05
thou h. them safe under thy shelter 31.20

HOLDING
or a cistern h. water shall be Lev 11.36
h. in their left hands the torches, Ju 7.20
he was h. a feast in his house, like 1Sa 25.36
I am weary of h. it in. Jer 6.11
and I am weary with h. it in, 20.09
men who were h. Jesus mocked him Lk 22.63
which you are h. with each other 24.17
each h. twenty or thirty gallons. Jn 2.06
h. much dispute among themselves. * Ac 28.29
whether you are h. to your faith. 2Co 13.05
h. fast the word of life, so that in Php 2.16
and not h. fast to the Head, from Col 2.19
h. faith and a good conscience. 1Ti 1.19
the truth by h. that the resurrection 2Ti 2.18
h. the form of religion but denying 3.05
contained a golden urn h. the manna, Heb 9.04
each h. a harp, and with golden Rev 5.08
h. back the four winds of the earth, 7.01
h. in her hand a golden cup full of 17.04
h. in his hand the key of the 20.01

HOLDINGS
lands and their h. and came to 2Ch 11.14

HOLDS
for our family h. a sacrifice in 1Sa 20.29
or who h. a spindle, or who is slain 2Sa 3.29
whom the king h. out the golden Est 4.11
He still h. fast his integrity, Job 2.03
Yet the righteous h. to his way, 17.09
let it go, and h. it in his mouth, 20.13
midst of the gods he h. judgment: Ps 82.01
people curse him who h. back grain, Pro 11.26
but a wise man quietly h. it back. 29.11
and the son of man who h. it fast, Is 56.02
profane it, and h. fast my covenant— 56.06
God of hosts h. a sacrifice in the Jer 46.10
and him that h. the scepter from Amo 1.05
and him that h. the scepter from 1.08
For here the saying h. true, Jn 4.37
as it h. promise for the present 1Ti 4.08
but he h. his priesthood permanently, Heb 7.24
of him who h. the seven stars in Rev 2.01

HOLE
outside, you shall dig a h. with it, Deu 23.13
and bored a h. in the lid on it, and 2Ki 12.09
falls into the h. which he has Ps 7.15
shall play over the h. of the asp, Is 11.08
behold, there was a h. in the wall. Eze 8.07

HOLES
in caves and in h. and in rocks 1Sa 13.06
out of the h. where they have hid 14.11
in h. of the earth and of the rocks. Job 30.06
the rocks and the h. of the ground, Is 2.19
them trapped in h. and hidden in 42.22
to put them into a bag with h. Hag 1.06
"Foxes have h., and birds of the Mt 8.20
"Foxes have h., and birds of the Lk 9.58

HOLIDAY
among the Jews, a feast and a h. Est 8.17
and from mourning into a h.; 9.22

HOLIDAY-MAKING
for gladness and feasting and h., Est 9.19

HOLIES
a tent called the Holy of H., Heb 9.03

HOLINESS
majestic in h., terrible in glorious Ex 15.11
Once for all I have sworn by my h.; Ps 89.35
h. befits thy house, O LORD, for 93.05
manifest my h. among you in the Eze 20.41
in her, and manifest my h. in her; 28.22
and manifest my h. in them in the 28.25
vindicate the h. of my great name, 36.23
I vindicate my h. before their 36.23
I vindicate my h. before their 38.16
greatness and my h. and make myself 38.23
vindicated my h. in the sight of 39.27
communicate h. to the people with 44.19
so communicate h. to the people." 46.20
The Lord GOD has sworn by his h. that, Amo 4.02
in h. and righteousness before him Lk 1.75
the Spirit of h. by his resurrection Rom 1.04
with h. and godly sincerity, not by 2Co 1.12
and make h. perfect in the fear of 7.01
God in true righteousness and h. Eph 4.24
unblamable in h. before our God 1Th 3.13
wife for himself in h. and honor, 4.04
us for uncleanness, but in h. 4.07
and love and h., with modesty. 1Ti 2.15
our good, that we may share his h. Heb 12.10
and for the h. without which no one 12.14
be in lives of h. and godliness, 2Pe 3.11

HOLLOW
he touched the h. of his thigh; Gen 32.25
which is upon the h. of the thigh, 32.32
he touched the h. of Jacob's thigh 32.32
You shall make it h., with boards; Ex 27.08
he made it h., with boards. 38.07
split open the h. place that is at Ju 15.19
out as from the h. of a sling. 1Sa 25.29
it was h., and its thickness was 1Ki 7.15
waters in the h. of his hand and Is 40.12
was four fingers, and it was h. Jer 52.21

HOLM
or he chooses a h. tree or an oak Is 44.14

HOLON
Goshen, H., and Giloh: eleven cities Jos 15.51
H. with its pasture lands, Debir 21.15
upon H., and Jahzah, and Mephaath, Jer 48.21

HOLY
you are standing is h. ground." Ex 3.05
day you shall hold a h. assembly, 12.16
on the seventh day a h. assembly; 12.16
by thy strength to thy h. abode. 15.13
a h. sabbath to the LORD; bake what you 16.23
kingdom of priests and a h. nation. 19.06
"Remember the sabbath day, to keep it h. 20.08
for you the h. place from the most h. 26.33
the testimony in the most h. place. 26.34
And you shall make h. garments for 28.02
they shall make h. garments for 28.04
when he goes into the h. place, 28.29
goes into the h. place before the 28.35
of a signet, 'H. to the LORD.' 28.36
incurred in the h. offering which 28.38
of Israel hallow as their h. gifts; 28.38
altar to minister in the h. place; 28.43
and put the h. crown upon the 29.06
he and his garments shall be h., 29.21

HOLY (cont.)
"The h. garments of Aaron shall be Ex 29.29
to minister in the h. place. 29.30
and boil its flesh in a h. place; 29.31
eat of them, because they are h. 29.33
not be eaten, because it is h. 29.34
it, and the altar shall be most h.; 29.37
touches the altar shall become h. 29.37
it is most h. to the LORD." 30.10
a h. anointing oil it shall be. 30.25
them, that they may be most h.; 30.29
touches them will become h. 30.29
shall be my h. anointing oil 30.31
it is h., and it shall be h. to you. 30.32
seasoned with salt, pure and h.; 30.35
it shall be for you most h. 30.36
it shall be for you h. to the LORD. 30.37
the h. garments for Aaron the 31.10
fragrant incense for the h. place. 31.11
sabbath, because it is h. for you; 31.14
of solemn rest, h. to the LORD; 31.15
shall have a h. sabbath of solemn 35.02
for ministering in the h. place, 35.19
the h. garments for Aaron the 35.19
service, and for the h. garments. 35.21
He made the h. anointing oil also, 37.29
for ministering in the h. place; 39.01
they made the h. garments for Aaron; 39.01
plate of the h. crown of pure gold, 39.30
of a signet, "H. to the LORD." 39.30
for ministering in the h. place, 39.41
the h. garments for Aaron the 39.41
furniture; and it shall become h. 40.09
and the altar shall be most h. 40.10
and put upon Aaron the h. garments, 40.13
it is a most h. part of the offerings Lev 2.03
it is a most h. part of the offerings 2.10
in any of the h. things of the 5.15
he has done amiss in the h. thing, 5.16
be eaten unleavened in a h. place; 6.16
it is a thing most h., 6.17
touches them shall become h." 6.18
before the LORD; it is most h. 6.25
in a h. place it shall be eaten, in 6.26
Whatever touches its flesh shall be h.; 6.27
it was sprinkled in a h. place. 6.27
may eat of it; it is most h. 6.29
to make atonement in the h. place; 6.30
guilt offering. It is most h.; 7.01
be eaten in a h. place; it is most h. 7.06
the h. crown, as the LORD commanded 8.09
show myself h. among those who are 10.03
between the h. and the common, 10.10
the altar, for it is most h.; 10.12
you shall eat it in a h. place, 10.13
is a thing most h. and has been 10.17
therefore, and be h., for I am h. 11.44
you shall therefore be h., for I am h." 11.45
burnt offering, in the h. place; 14.13
to the priest; it is most h. 14.13
times into the h. place within the 16.02
shall Aaron come into the h. place: 16.03
He shall put on the h. linen coat, 16.04
linen turban; these are the h. garments. 16.04
make atonement for the h. place, 16.16
atonement in the h. place until he 16.17
atoning for the h. place and the 16.20
on when he went into the h. place, 16.23
his body in water in a h. place, 16.24
to make atonement in the h. place, 16.27
wearing the h. linen garments; 16.32
people of Israel, You shall be h.; 19.02
for I the LORD your God am h. 19.02
has profaned a h. thing of the 19.08
year all their fruit shall be h., 19.24
sanctuary and profaning my h. name. 20.03
Consecrate yourselves therefore, and be h.; 20.07
You shall be h. to me; for I the LORD am h., 20.26
They shall be h. to their God, and 21.06
their God; therefore they shall be h. 21.06
for the priest is h. to his God. 21.07
your God, he shall be h. to you; 21.08
your God; he shall be h. to you; 21.08
of the most h. and of the h. things, 21.22
away from the h. things of the 22.02
they may not profane my h. name; 22.02
generations approaches the h. things, 22.03
may eat of the h. things until he 22.04
not eat of the h. things unless he 22.06
he may eat of the h. things, because such 22.07
outsider shall not eat of a h. thing. 22.10
servant shall not eat of a h. thing; 22.10
of the offering of the h. things. 22.12
a man eats of a h. thing unwittingly, 22.14
and give the h. thing to the priest. 22.14
not profane the h. things of the 22.15
guilt, by eating their h. things: 22.16
And you shall not profane my h. name, 22.32
shall proclaim as h. convocations, 23.02
of solemn rest, a h. convocation; 23.03
the h. convocations, which you shall 23.04
you shall have a h. convocation; 23.07
seventh day is a h. convocation; 23.08
they shall be h. to the LORD for 23.20
you shall hold a h. convocation; 23.21
blast of trumpets, a h. convocation. 23.24
for you a time of h. convocation, 23.27
first day shall be a h. convocation; 23.35
shall hold a h. convocation and 23.36
proclaim as times of h. convocation, 23.37
they shall eat it in a h. place, 24.09
for him a most h. portion out of 24.09
it shall be h. to you; you shall eat 25.12
any man gives to the LORD is h. 27.09
which it is exchanged shall be h. 27.10
his house to be h. to the LORD, 27.14
shall be h. to the LORD, as a field 27.21
that day as a h. thing to the LORD. 27.23
thing is most h. to the LORD. 27.28
is the LORD's; it is h. to the LORD. 27.30
staff, shall be h. to the LORD. 27.32
which it is exchanged shall be h.; 27.33
of meeting: the most h. things. Num 4.04
they must not touch the h. things, 4.15
come near to the most h. things: 4.19
look upon the h. things even for a 4.20
all the h. things of the people of 5.09
and every man's h. things shall be 5.10
shall take h. water in an earthen 5.17
to the LORD, he shall be h.; 6.05
separation he is h. to the LORD. 6.08
they are a h. portion for the 6.20
the care of the h. things which 7.09
carrying the h. things, and the 10.21
commandments, and be h. to your God. 15.40
For all the congregation are h., 16.03
and who is h., and will cause him 16.05
LORD chooses shall be the h. one. 16.07
far and wide. For they are h., 16.37
therefore they are h. Thus they shall 16.38
be yours of the most h. things, 18.09
shall be most h. to you and to your 18.09
In a most h. place shall you eat of 18.10
may eat of it; it is h. to you. 18.10
they are h. You shall sprinkle 18.17
All the h. offerings which the 18.19
not profane the h. things of the 18.32
he showed himself h. among them. 20.13
in the h. place you shall pour out 28.07
there shall be a h. convocation: 28.18
you shall have a h. convocation; 28.25
you shall have a h. convocation; 28.26
you shall have a h. convocation; 29.01
you shall have a h. convocation, 29.07
you shall have a h. convocation; 29.12

HOLY (cont.)
who was anointed with the h. oil. Num 35.25
to keep it h., as the LORD your God Deu 5.12
are a people h. to the LORD your 7.06
But the h. things which are due 12.26
are a people h. to the LORD your 14.02
are a people h. to the LORD your 14.21
therefore your camp must be h., 23.14
Look down from thy h. habitation, 26.15
be a people h. to the LORD your 26.19
you as a people h. to himself, 28.09
revere me as h. in the midst of 32.51
from the ten thousands of h. ones, 33.02
the place where you stand is h." Jos 5.15
for he is a h. God; he is a jealous 24.19
"There is none h. like the LORD, 1Sa 2.02
stand before the LORD, this h. God? 6.20
at hand, but there is h. bread; 21.04
today will their vessels be h.?" 21.05
today will their vessels be h.? 21.05
So the priest gave him the h. bread; 21.06
sanctuary, as the most h. place. 1Ki 6.16
the most h. place, and for the doors 7.50
and all the h. vessels that were in 8.04
in the most h. place, underneath the 8.06
seen from the h. place before the 8.08
priests came out of the h. place, 8.10
that this is a h. man of God, 2Ki 4.09
money of the h. things which is 12.04
Against the H. One of Israel! 19.22
all the work of the most h. place, 1Ch 6.49
and over all the h. utensils, 9.29
Glory in his h. name; let the hearts 16.10
Worship the LORD in h. array; 16.29
we may give thanks to thy h. name, 16.35
LORD and the h. vessels of God may 22.19
to consecrate the most h. things, 23.13
the cleansing of all that is h., 23.28
I have provided for the h. house, 29.03
a house for thy h. name comes from 29.16
And he made the most h. place; 2Ch 3.08
In the most h. place he made two 3.10
to the most h. place and for the 4.22
and all the h. vessels that were in 5.05
in the most h. place, underneath the 5.07
seen from the h. place before the 5.09
came out of the h. place (for all 5.11
ark of the LORD has come are h." 8.11
LORD and praise him in h. array, 20.21
for they are h., but all the people 23.06
out the filth from the h. place. 29.05
offerings in the h. place to the 29.07
clean, to make it h. to the LORD. 30.17
came to his h. habitation in 30.27
the LORD and the most h. offerings. 31.14
faithful in keeping themselves h. 31.18
Israel and who were h. to the LORD, 35.03
"Put the h. ark in the house which 35.03
And stand in the h. place according 35.05
they boiled the h. offerings in 35.13
not to partake of the most h. food, Ez 2.63
"You are h. to the LORD, and the 8.28
the LORD, and the vessels are h.; 8.28
so that the h. race has mixed 9.02
a secure hold within his h. place, 9.08
not to partake of the most h. food, Neh 7.65
"This day is h. to the LORD your 8.09
for this day is h. to our Lord; 8.10
"Be quiet, for this day is h.; 8.11
to them thy h. sabbath and command 9.14
them on the sabbath or on a h. day; 10.31
the h. things, and the sin offerings 10.33
to live in Jerusalem the h. city, 11.01
Levites in the h. city were two 11.18
gates, to keep the sabbath day h. 13.22
To which of the h. ones will you Job 5.01
not denied the words of the H. One. 6.10
Behold, God puts no trust in his h. ones, 15.15
set my king on Zion, my h. hill." Ps 2.06
and he answers me from his h. hill. 3.04
toward thy h. temple in the fear 5.07
The LORD is in his h. temple, 11.04
Who shall dwell on thy h. hill? 15.01
him from his h. heaven with mighty 20.06
Yet thou art h., enthroned on the 22.03
who shall stand in his h. place? 24.03
hands toward thy most h. sanctuary. 28.02
worship the LORD in h. array. 29.02
and give thanks to his h. name. 30.04
because we trust in his h. name. 33.21
bring me to thy h. hill and to thy 43.03
the h. habitation of the Most High. 46.04
God sits on his h. throne. 47.08
His h. mountain, beautiful in 48.02
and take not thy h. Spirit from me. 51.11
of thy house, thy h. temple! 65.04
widows is God in his h. habitation. 68.05
came from Sinai into the h. place. 68.17
with the lyre, O H. One of Israel. 71.22
in the midst of thy h. place; 74.04
Thy way, O God, is h. 77.13
and provoked the H. One of Israel. 78.41
And he brought them to his h. land, 78.54
they have defiled thy h. temple; 79.01
On the h. mount stands the city he 87.01
in the assembly of the h. ones! 89.05
in the council of the h. ones, 89.07
our king to the H. One of Israel. 89.18
with my h. oil I have anointed him; 89.20
Worship the LORD in h. array; 96.09
and give thanks to his h. name! 97.12
hand and his h. arm have gotten 98.01
and terrible name! H. is he! 99.03
at his footstool! H. is he! 99.05
and worship at his h. mountain; 99.09
for the LORD our God is h.! 99.09
that he looked down from his h. height, 102.19
is within me, bless his h. name! 103.01
Glory in his h. name; 105.03
For he remembered his h. promise, 105.42
and Aaron, the h. one of the LORD, 106.16
thanks to thy h. name and glory in 106.47
your host upon the h. mountains. 110.03
H. and terrible is his name! 111.09
Lift up your hands to the h. place, 134.02
down toward thy h. temple and give 138.02
flesh bless his h. name for ever 145.21
knowledge of the H. One is insight. Pro 9.10
"It is h.," and to reflect only 20.25
nor have I knowledge of the H. One. 30.03
to go in and out of the h. place, Ecc 8.10
have despised the H. One of Israel, Is 1.04
in Jerusalem will be called h., 4.03
H. God shows himself h. in righteousness. 5.16
purpose of the H. One of Israel 5.19
the word of the H. One of Israel. 5.24
"H., h., h., is the LORD of hosts; 6.03
is felled." The h. seed is its stump. 6.13
hosts, him you shall regard as h.; 8.13
a fire, and his H. One a flame; 10.17
the H. One of Israel, in truth. 10.20
or destroy in all my h. mountain; 11.09
your midst is the H. One of Israel." 12.06
will look to the H. One of Israel; 17.07
the LORD on the h. mountain at 27.13
exult in the H. One of Israel. 29.19
will sanctify the H. One of Jacob, 29.23
no more of the H. One of Israel." 30.11
Therefore thus says the H. One of Israel, 30.12
the H. One of Israel, "In returning 30.15
the night when a h. feast is kept; 30.29
not look to the H. One of Israel 31.01
and it shall be called the H. Way; 35.08
Against the H. One of Israel! 37.23
be like him? says the H. One. 40.25
Redeemer is the H. One of Israel. 41.14

HOLY (cont.)

in the H. One of Israel you shall Is 41.16
the H. One of Israel has created it. 41.20
the H. One of Israel, your Savior. 43.03
the H. One of Israel: "For your sake 43.14
your H. One, the Creator of Israel, 43.15
the H. One of Israel, and his Maker: 45.11
is his name—is the H. One of Israel. 47.04
call themselves after the h. city, 48.02
the H. One of Israel: "I am the LORD 48.17
Redeemer of Israel and his H. One, 49.07
the H. One of Israel, who has chosen 49.07
garments, O Jerusalem, the h. city; 52.01
has bared his h. arm before the 52.10
and the H. One of Israel is your 54.05
and of the H. One of Israel, for he 55.05
these I will bring to my h. mountain, 56.07
and shall inherit my h. mountain. 57.13
whose name is H.: "I dwell in the 57.15
"I dwell in the high and h. place, 57.15
doing your pleasure on my h. day, 58.13
delight and the h. day of the LORD 58.13
and for the H. One of Israel, 60.09
the Zion of the H. One of Israel. 60.14
they shall be called The h. people, 62.12
rebelled and grieved his h. Spirit; 63.10
the midst of them his h. Spirit, 63.11
from thy h. and glorious habitation 63.15
Thy h. people possessed thy sanctuary 63.18
Thy h. cities have become a wilderness, 64.10
Our h. and beautiful house, where 64.11
who forget my h. mountain, who set a 65.11
or destroy in all my h. mountain, 65.25
to my h. mountain Jerusalem, says 66.20
Israel was h. to the LORD, the first Jer 2.03
work, but keep the sabbath day h., 17.22
the sabbath day h. and do no work 17.24
to me, to keep the sabbath day h., 17.27
LORD and because of his h. words. 23.09
and from his h. habitation utter 25.30
of righteousness, O h. hill!' 31.23
the LORD, the H. One of Israel. 50.29
guilt against the H. One of Israel. 51.05
come into the h. places of the 51.51
The h. stones lie scattered at the Lam 4.01
and their h. places shall be Eze 7.24
but my h. name you shall no more 20.39
"For on my h. mountain, the mountain 20.40
You have despised my h. things, 22.08
law and have profaned my h. things; 22.26
between the h. and the common, 22.26
you were on the h. mountain of God; 28.14
came, thy profaned my h. name, 36.20
But I had concern for my h. name, 36.21
but for the sake of my h. name, 36.22
"And my h. name I will make known 39.07
will not let my h. name be profaned 39.07
am the LORD, the H. One in Israel. 39.07
I will be jealous for my h. name. 39.25
to me, This is the most h. place. 41.04
in front of the h. place was 41.21
The nave and the h. place had each 41.23
the yard are the h. chambers, 42.13
shall eat the most h. offerings; 42.13
shall put the most h. offerings— 42.13
offering, for the place is h. 42.13
When the priests enter the h. place, 42.14
they minister, for these are h.; 42.14
between the h. and the common. 42.20
shall no more defile my h. name, 43.07
have defiled my h. name by their 43.08
of the mountain shall be most h. 43.12
not kept charge of my h. things; 44.08
and lay them in the h. chambers; 44.19
between the h. and the common, 44.23
and they shall keep my sabbaths h. 44.24
day that he goes into the h. place, 44.27
court, to minister in the h. place, 44.27
of the land as a h. district, 45.01
it shall be h. throughout its whole 45.01
And in the h. district you shall 45.03
the sanctuary, the most h. place. 45.03
It shall be the h. portion of the 45.04
houses and a h. place for the 45.04
apart as the h. district you shall 45.06
sides of the h. district and the 45.07
alongside the h. district and the 45.07
row of the h. chambers for the 46.19
the allotments of the h. portion: 48.10
from the h. portion of the land, a 48.12
a most h. place, adjoining the 48.12
the land, for it is h. to the LORD. 48.14
alongside the h. portion shall be 48.18
shall be alongside the h. portion. 48.18
the h. portion together with the 48.20
sides of the h. portion and of the 48.21
cubits of the h. portion to the 48.21
The h. portion with the sanctuary 48.21
whom is the spirit of the h. gods— Dan 4.08
spirit of the h. gods is in you 4.09
a h. one, came down from heaven. 4.13
decision by the word of the h. ones, 4.17
spirit of the h. gods is in you." 4.18
a h. one, coming down from heaven 4.23
whom is the spirit of the h. gods. 5.11
spirit of the h. gods is in you, 5.14
Then I heard a h. one speaking; 8.13
and another h. one said to the one 8.13
thy city Jerusalem, thy h. hill; 9.16
my God for the h. hill of my God; 9.20
your people and your h. city, 9.24
and to anoint a most h. place. 9.24
be set against the h. covenant. 11.28
action against the h. covenant. 11.30
those who forsake the h. covenant. 11.30
sea and the glorious h. mountain; 11.45
power of the h. people comes to an 12.07
the H. One in your midst, and I will Hos 11.09
God, and is faithful to the H. One. 11.12
sound the alarm on my h. mountain! Joe 2.01
who dwell in Zion, my h. mountain. 3.17
shall be h. and strangers shall 3.17
so that my h. name is profaned; Amo 2.07
you have drunk upon my h. mountain, Ob 1.16
that escape, and it shall be h.; 1.17
I again look upon thy h. temple?' Jon 2.04
came to thee, into thy h. temple. 2.07
you, the Lord from his h. temple. Mic 1.02
everlasting, O LORD my God, my H. One? Hab 1.12
But the LORD is in his h. temple; 2.20
and the H. One from Mount Paran. 3.03
be haughty in my h. mountain. Zep 3.11
'If one carries h. flesh in the Hag 2.12
kind of food, does it become h.?'" 2.12
as his portion in the h. land, Zec 2.12
himself from his h. dwelling. 2.13
the LORD of hosts, the h. mountain. 8.03
come, and all the h. ones with him. 14.05
of the horses, "H. to the LORD." 14.20
to be with child of the H. Spirit; Mt 1.18
conceived in her is of the H. Spirit; 1.20
you with the H. Spirit and with 3.11
Then the devil took him to the h. city, 4.05
"Do not give dogs what is h.; 7.06
against the H. Spirit will not be 12.32
standing in the h. place (let the 24.15
went into the h. city and appeared 27.53
of the Son and of the H. Spirit, 28.19
baptize you with the H. Spirit." Mk 1.08
who you are, the H. One of God." 1.24
against the H. Spirit never has 3.29
that he was a righteous and h. man, 6.20
of his Father with the h. angels." 8.38
himself, inspired by the H. Spirit, 12.36
you who speak, but the H. Spirit. 13.11
will be filled with the H. Spirit, Lk 1.15

HOLY (cont.)

"The H. Spirit will come upon you, Lk 1.35
child to be born will be called h., 1.35
was filled with the H. Spirit 1.41
things for me, and h. is his name. 1.49
was filled with the H. Spirit, 1.67
mouth of his h. prophets from of 1.70
and to remember his h. covenant, 1.72
shall be called h. to the Lord") 2.23
and the H. Spirit was upon him. 2.25
to him by the H. Spirit that he 2.26
you with the H. Spirit and with 3.16
and the H. Spirit descended upon 3.22
full of the H. Spirit, returned from 4.01
who you are, the H. One of God." 4.34
of the Father and of the h. angels. 9.26
rejoiced in the H. Spirit and said, 10.21
Father give the H. Spirit to those 11.13
against the H. Spirit will not be 12.10
for the H. Spirit will teach you in 12.12
he who baptizes with the H. Spirit.' Jn 1.33
that you are the H. One of God." 6.69
both our h. place and our nation." 11.48
the H. Spirit, whom the Father will 14.26
H. Father, keep them in thy name 17.11
to them, "Receive the H. Spirit. 20.22
through the H. Spirit to the Ac 1.02
be baptized with the H. Spirit." 1.05
power when the H. Spirit has come 1.08
which the H. Spirit spoke beforehand 1.16
filled with the H. Spirit and 2.04
nor let thy H. One see corruption. 2.27
the promise of the H. Spirit, 2.33
receive the gift of the H. Spirit. 2.38
But you denied the H. and Righteous 3.14
mouth of his h. prophets from of 3.21
Then Peter, filled with the H. Spirit, 4.08
servant, didst say by the H. Spirit, 4.25
against thy h. servant Jesus, 4.27
the name of thy h. servant Jesus." 4.30
filled with the H. Spirit and 4.31
to lie to the H. Spirit and to 5.03
and so is the H. Spirit whom God 5.32
full of faith and of the H. Spirit, 6.05
against this h. place and the law; 6.13
you are standing is h. ground. 7.33
you always resist the H. Spirit. 7.51
full of the H. Spirit, gazed into 7.55
they might receive the H. Spirit; 8.15
and they received the H. Spirit. 8.17
my hands may receive the H. Spirit." 8.19
and be filled with the H. Spirit." 9.17
comfort of the H. Spirit it was 9.31
directed by a h. angel to send for 10.22
with the H. Spirit and with power; 10.38
the H. Spirit fell on all who heard 10.44
the gift of the H. Spirit had been 10.45
received the H. Spirit just as we 10.47
the H. Spirit fell on them just as 11.15
be baptized with the H. Spirit.' 11.16
full of the H. Spirit and of faith. 11.24
the H. Spirit said, "Set apart for 13.02
So, being sent out by the H. Spirit, 13.04
Paul, filled with the H. Spirit, 13.09
give you the h. and sure blessings 13.34
not let thy H. One see corruption.' 13.35
with joy and with the H. Spirit. 13.52
giving them the H. Spirit just as 15.08
good to the H. Spirit and to us to 15.28
forbidden by the H. Spirit to speak 16.06
you receive the H. Spirit when you 19.02
heard that there is a H. Spirit." 19.02
the H. Spirit came on them; 19.06
except that the H. Spirit testifies 20.23
in which the H. Spirit has made you 20.28
and said, "Thus says the H. Spirit, 21.11
and he has defiled this h. place." 21.28
"The H. Spirit was right in saying 28.25
his prophets in the h. scriptures, Rom 1.02
through the H. Spirit which has 5.05
law is h., and the commandment is h. 7.12
bears me witness in the H. Spirit, 9.01
offered as first fruits is h., 11.16
and if the root is h., so are the 11.16
h. and acceptable to God, which is 12.01
and peace and joy in the H. Spirit; 14.17
power of the H. Spirit you may 15.13
sanctified by the H. Spirit. 15.16
by the power of the H. Spirit, 15.19
Greet one another with a h. kiss. 16.16
For God's temple is h., and that 1Co 3.17
a temple of the H. Spirit within 6.19
unclean, but as it is they are h. 7.14
how to be h. in body and spirit; 7.34
is Lord" except by the H. Spirit. 12.03
Greet one another with a h. kiss. 16.20
the H. Spirit, genuine love, 2Co 6.06
Greet one another with a h. kiss. 13.12
fellowship of the H. Spirit be with 13.14
we should be h. and blameless Eph 1.04
with the promised H. Spirit, 1.13
grows into a h. temple in the Lord; 2.21
revealed to his h. apostles and 3.05
do not grieve the H. Spirit of God, 4.30
she might be h. and without 5.27
to present you h. and blameless Col 1.22
h. and beloved, compassion, kindness, 3.12
and in the H. Spirit and with full 1Th 1.05
with joy inspired by the H. Spirit; 1.06
how h. and righteous and blameless 2.10
who gives his H. Spirit to you. 4.08
Greet all the brethren with a h. kiss. 5.26
lifting h. hands without anger or 1Ti 2.08
us and called us with a h. calling, 2Ti 1.09
to you by the H. Spirit who dwells 1.14
upright, h., and self-controlled; Tit 1.08
and renewal in the H. Spirit, 3.05
by gifts of the H. Spirit distributed Heb 2.04
Therefore, h. brethren, who share in 3.01
as the H. Spirit says, "Today, when 3.07
become partakers of the H. Spirit, 6.04
h., blameless, unstained, separated 7.26
it is called the H. Place. 9.02
a tent called the H. of Holies, 9.03
By this the H. Spirit indicates 9.08
once for all into the H. Place, 9.12
enters the H. Place yearly with 9.25
And the H. Spirit also bears 10.15
you through the H. Spirit sent 1Pe 1.12
but as he who called you is h., 1.15
be h. yourselves in all your 1.15
written, "You shall be h., for I am h." 1.16
to be a h. priesthood, to offer 2.05
a h. nation, God's own people, that 2.09
So once the h. women who hoped in 3.05
were with him on the h. mountain. 2Pe 1.18
moved by the H. Spirit spoke from 1.21
back from the h. commandment 2.21
predictions of the h. prophets and 3.02
have been anointed by the H. One, 1Jn 2.20
the Lord came with his h. myriads, Jud 1.14
yourselves up on your most h. faith; 1.20
pray in the H. Spirit; 1.20
write: 'The words of the h. one, Rev 3.07
"H., h., h., is the Lord God Almighty, 4.08
h. and true, how long before thou 6.10
over the h. city for forty-two 11.02
presence of the h. angels and in 14.10
For thou alone art h. All nations 15.04
thou who art and wast, O H. One. 16.05
Blessed and h. is he who shares in 20.06
And I saw the h. city, new Jerusalem, 21.02
showed me the h. city Jerusalem 21.10
still do right, and the h. still be h." 22.11
tree of life and in the h. city, 22.19

HOMAGE
and did h. to Daniel, and commanded Dan 2.46
and they knelt down in h. to him. Mk 15.19

HOMAM
The sons of Lotan: Hori and H.; 1Ch 1.39

HOME
I may go to my own h. and country. Gen 30.25
then he departed and returned h. 31.55
by her until his master came h., 39.16
When Joseph came h., they brought into 43.26
in the field and is not brought h., Ex 9.19
whether born at h. or born abroad. Lev 18.09
shall bring her h. to your house, Deu 21.12
shall bring it h. to your house, 22.02
he shall be free at h. one year, 24.05
to his own town and his own h., Jos 20.06
and go to your h. in the land 22.04
half-tribe of Manasseh returned h., 22.09
and trembling, let him return h.'" Ju 7.03
the others go every man to his h." 7.07
they departed every man to his h. 9.55
"If you bring me h. again to fight 11.09
Then Jephthah came to his h. at Mizpah; 11.34
at the h. of Micah, and asked him of 18.15
a good way from the h. of Micah, 18.22
he turned and went back to his h. 18.26
for your journey, and go h." 19.09
and I am going to my h.; and nobody takes 19.18
rose up and went away to his h. 19.28
The LORD grant that you may find a h., Ru 1.09
should I not seek a h. for you, 3.01
Then Elkanah went h. to Ramah. 1Sa 2.11
then they would return to their h. 2.20
and they fled, every man to his h.; 4.10
the cart, but take their calves h., 6.07
and shut up their calves at h. 6.10
for his h. was there, and there also 7.17
people away, each one to his h. 10.25
Saul also went to his h. at Gibeah, 10.26
the rest of the people he sent h., 13.02
As they were coming h., when David 18.06
at Horesh, and Jonathan went h. 23.18
Then Saul went h.; but David and 24.22
Then David sent h. to Tamar, 2Sa 13.07
bring his banished one h. again. 14.13
and also an exile from your h. 15.19
as a bride comes h. to her husband. 17.03
and went off h. to his own city. 17.23
fled every one to his own h. 18.17
had fled every man to his own h. 19.08
lord the king has come safely h.' 19.30
him, and he returned to his own h. 19.39
from the city, every man to his h. 20.22
in Lebanon and two months at h.; 1Ki 5.14
Return every man to his h., 12.24
and went h. again, according to the 12.24
"Come h. with me, and refresh 13.07
"Come h. with me and eat bread." 13.15
let each return to his h. in peace.'" 22.17
surrounded him; but his army fled h. 2Ki 8.21
with your glory, and stay at h.; 14.10
and every man fled to his h. 14.12
and went h., and dwelt at Nineveh. 19.36
I bring the ark of God h. to me?" 1Ch 13.12
take the ark h. into the city of 13.13
and David went h. to bless his 16.43
Return every man to his h., 2Ch 11.04
let each return to his h. in peace.'" 18.16
him from Ephraim, to go h. again. 25.10
and returned h. in fierce anger. 25.10
But now stay at h.; why should you 25.19
and every man fled to his h. 25.22
restrained himself, and went h.; Est 5.10
may discern the paths to its h.? Job 38.20
I have given the steppe for his h., 39.06
and makes his h. in the fastness 39.28
waste away; Sheol shall be their h. Ps 49.14
the desolate a h. to dwell in; 68.06
The women at h. divide the spoil, 68.12
Even the sparrow finds a h., 84.03
stork has her h. in the fir trees. 104.17
He gives the barren woman a h., 113.09
shall come h. with shouts of joy, 126.06
wayward, her feet do not stay at h.; Pro 7.11
For my husband is not at h.; 7.19
at full moon he will come h." 7.20
do not violence to his h.; 24.15
is a man who strays from his h. 27.08
because man goes to his eternal h., Ecc 12.05
did not let his prisoners go h.?' Is 14.17
and went h. and dwelt at Nineveh. 37.37
Shaphan, that he should take him h. Jer 39.14
for they will soon come h. Eze 36.08
will bring you h. into the land of 37.12
At that time I will bring you h., Zep 3.20
and when you brought it h., Hag 1.09
I will bring them h. from the land Zec 10.10
servant is lying paralyzed at h., Mt 8.06
"Rise, take up your bed and go h." 9.06
And he rose and went h. 9.07
And when he came h., Jesus spoke to 17.25
it was reported that he was at h. Mk 2.01
take up your pallet and go h." 2.11
who betrayed him. Then he went h.; 3.19
"Go h. to your friends, and tell 5.19
And she went h., and found the 7.30
And he sent him away to his h., 8.26
when he leaves h. and puts his 13.34
was ended, he went to his h. Lk 1.23
months, and returned to her h. 1.56
rise, take up your bed and go h." 5.24
and went h., glorifying God. 5.25
"Return to your h., and declare how 8.39
say farewell to those at my h." 9.61
master to come h. from the marriage 12.36
And when he comes h., he calls together 15.06
returned h. beating their breasts. 23.48
he went h. wondering at what had *24.12
He came to his own h., Jn 1.11
to him and make our h. with him. 14.23
be scattered, every man to his h., 16.32
disciple took her to his own h. 19.27
temple and at h. they did not Ac 5.42
the ship, and they returned h. 21.06
one is hungry, let him eat at h.— 1Co 11.34
let them ask their husbands at h. 14.35
while we are at h. in the body we 2Co 5.06
the body and at h. with the Lord. 5.08
So whether we are at h. or away, 5.09

HOMEBORN
Israel, sojourner as well as h., Jos 8.33
Is he a h. servant? Why then has he Jer 2.14

HOMELAND
clear that they are seeking a h. Heb 11.14

HOMELESS
and bring the h. poor into your Is 58.07
are ill-clad and buffeted and h., 1Co 4.11

HOMER
a sowing of a h. of barley shall be Lev 27.16
and a h. of seed shall yield but an Is 5.10
bath containing one tenth of a h., Eze 45.11
and the ephah one tenth of a h.; 45.11
the h. shall be the standard 45.11
of an ephah from each h. of wheat, 45.13
an ephah from each h. of wheat, 45.13
like the h., contains ten baths); 45.14
of silver and a h. and a lethech Hos 3.02

HOMERS
who gathered least gathered ten h.; Num 11.32

HOMES
return to our h. until the people Num 32.18
and they went to their h. Jos 22.06
away to their h. and blessed them, 22.07
"Go back to your h. with much 22.08
went to their h. joyful and glad 1Ki 8.66
dwelt in their h. as formerly. 2Ki 13.05
sent the people away to their h., 2Ch 7.10
daughters, your wives, and your h." Neh 4.14
Their graves are their h. for ever, Ps 49.11
they make their h. in the rocks; Pro 30.26
to strangers, our h. to aliens. Lam 5.02
them to their h., says the LORD. Hos 11.11
send them away hungry to their h., Mk 8.03
have left our h. and followed you." Lk 18.28
disciples went back to their h. Jn 20.10
and breaking bread in their h., Ac 2.46

HOMICIDE
between one kind of h. and another, Deu 17.08

HOMOSEXUALS
idolaters, nor adulterers, nor h., 1Co 6.09

HONEST
we are h. men, your servants are not Gen 42.11
if you are h. men, let one of your 42.19
'We are h. men, we are not spies; 42.31
I shall know that you are h. men: 42.33
that you are not spies but h. men, 42.34
you have been h., and to me it 1Sa 29.06
How forceful are h. words! Job 6.25
speaks the truth gives h. evidence, Pro 12.17
it fast in an h. and good heart, Lk 8.15
doing h. work with his hands, so Eph 4.28
obedient, to be ready for any h. work, Tit 3.01

HONESTLY
to the workmen, for they dealt h. 2Ki 12.15
into their hand, for they deal h." 22.07
suit justly, no one goes to law h.; Is 59.04

HONESTY
So my h. will answer for me later, Gen 30.33

HONEY
a little balm and a little h., Gen 43.11
a land flowing with milk and h., Ex 3.08
a land flowing with milk and h." ' 3.17
a land flowing with milk and h., 13.05
of it was like wafers made with h. 16.31
to a land flowing with milk and h.; 33.03
leaven nor any h. as an offering Lev 2.11
a land flowing with milk and h.' 20.24
it flows with milk and h., Num 13.27
land which flows with milk and h. 14.08
of a land flowing with milk and h., 16.13
a land flowing with milk and h., 16.14
in a land flowing with milk and h. Deu 6.03
a land of olive trees and h., 8.08
a land flowing with milk and h. 11.09
a land flowing with milk and h. 26.09
a land flowing with milk and h.' 26.15
a land flowing with milk and h., 27.03
the land flowing with milk and h., 31.20
made him suck h. out of the rock, 32.13
a land flowing with milk and h. Jos 5.06
in the body of the lion, and h. Ju 14.08
had taken the h. from the carcass 14.09
went down, "What is sweeter than h.? 14.18
and there was h. on the ground. 1Sa 14.25
the h. was dropping, but no man put 14.26
I tasted a little of this h. 14.29
tasted a little h. with the tip of 14.43
h. and curds and sheep and cheese 2Sa 17.29
and a jar of h., and go to him; 1Ki 14.03
a land of olive trees and h., 2Ki 18.32
h., and of all the produce of the 2Ch 31.05
streams flowing with h. and curds. Job 20.17
also than h. and drippings of the Ps 19.10
and with h. from the rock I would 81.16
taste, sweeter than h. to my mouth! 119.103
For the lips of a loose woman drip h., Pro 5.03
My son, eat h., for it is good, and 24.13
If you have found h., eat only enough 25.16
It is not good to eat much h., 25.27
He who is sated loathes h., 27.07
h. and milk are under your tongue; Sol 4.11
I eat my honeycomb with my h., 5.01
eat curds and h. when he knows how Is 7.15
in the land will eat curds and h. 7.22
a land flowing with milk and h., Jer 11.05
a land flowing with milk and h.; 32.22
and h. hidden in the fields." 41.08
it was in my mouth as sweet as h. Eze 3.03
you ate fine flour and h. and oil. 16.13
with fine flour and oil and h.— 16.19
a land flowing with milk and h., 20.06
a land flowing with milk and h., 20.15
and early figs, h., oil, and balm. 27.17
his food was locusts and wild h. Mt 3.04
waist, and ate locusts and wild h. Mk 1.06
but sweet as h. in your mouth. Rev 10.09
it was sweet as h. in my mouth, 10.10

HONEYCOMB
his hand, and dipped it in the h., 1Sa 14.27
than honey and drippings of the h. Ps 19.10
Pleasant words are like a h., Pro 16.24
drippings of the h. are sweet to 24.13
I eat my h. with my honey, I drink Sol 5.01

HONOR
now my husband will h. me, Gen 30.20
"H. your father and your mother, Ex 20.12
and h. the face of an old man, and Lev 19.32
for I will surely do you great h., Num 22.17
come to me? Am I not able to h. you?" 22.37
I said, 'I will certainly h. you.' 24.11
the LORD has held you back from h." 24.11
" 'H. your father and your mother, as Deu 5.16
in praise and in fame and in h., 26.19
good faith and h. when you made Ju 9.16
good faith and h. with Jerubbaal 9.19
words come true, we may h. you?" 13.17
princes and inherit a seat of h. 1Sa 2.08
and h. your sons above me by 2.29
for those who h. me I will h., 2.30
and he is a man that is held in h.; 9.06
yet h. me now before the elders of 15.30
by them I shall be held in h." 2Sa 6.22
have not asked, both riches and h., 1Ki 3.13
H. and majesty are before him; 1Ch 16.27
Both riches and h. come from thee, 29.12
age, full of days, riches, and h.; 29.28
h., or the life of those who hate 2Ch 1.11
and h., such as none of the kings 1.12
made a very great fire in his h. 16.14
and he had great riches and h. 17.05
Jehoshaphat had great riches and h.; 18.01
his people made no fire in his h., 21.19
bring you no h. from the LORD God." 26.18
had very great riches and h.; 32.27
Jerusalem did him h. at his death. 32.33
women will give h. to their Est 1.20
"What h. or dignity has been 6.03
man whom the king delights to h.?" 6.06
king delight to h. more than me?" 6.06
man whom the king delights to h., 6.07
delights to h., and let him conduct 6.09
man whom the king delights to h.' " 6.09
man whom the king delights to h." 6.11
light and gladness and joy and h. 8.16
account of the high h. of Mordecai, 10.02
His sons come to h., and he does not Job 14.21
my h. is pursued as by the wind, and 30.15

HONOR (cont.)
how long shall my h. suffer shame? Ps 4.02
dost crown him with glory and h. 8.05
kings are among your ladies of h.; 45.09
God rests my deliverance and my h.; 62.07
Thou wilt increase my h., and comfort 71.21
he bestows favor and h. No good thing 84.11
I will rescue him and h. him. 91.15
H. and majesty are before him; 96.06
art clothed with h. and majesty, 104.01
Full of h. and majesty is his work, 111.03
for ever; his horn is exalted in h. 112.09
H. the LORD with your substance and Pro 3.09
in her left hand are riches and h. 3.16
The wise will inherit h., but fools get 3.35
she will h. you if you embrace her. 4.08
lest you give your h. to others and 5.09
Riches and h. are with me, enduring 8.18
A gracious woman gets h., and violent 11.16
and humility goes before h. 15.33
but humility goes before h. 18.12
It is an h. for a man to keep aloof 20.03
and kindness will find life and h. 21.21
the LORD is riches and h. and life. 22.04
so h. is not fitting for a fool. 26.01
sling is he who gives h. to a fool. 26.08
is lowly in spirit will obtain h. 29.23
and h., so that he lacks nothing of Ecc 6.02
folly outweighs wisdom and h. 10.01
a throne of h. to his father's Is 22.23
their mouth and h. me with their 29.13
The wild beasts will h. me, 43.20
if you h. it, not going your own 58.13
no h. was shown to the priests, no Lam 4.16
to their h. on the day that I show Eze 39.13
me gifts and rewards and great h. Dan 2.06
and extol and h. the King of 4.37
He shall h. the god of fortresses 11.38
know he shall h. with gold and 11.38
him he shall magnify with h. He shall 11.39
the LORD, and shall bear royal h., Zec 6.13
then I am a father, where is my h.? Mal 1.06
is not without h. except in his Mt 13.57
'H. your father and your mother,' 15.04
to God, he need not h. his father.' 15.05
H. your father and mother, and, You 19.19
the place of h. at feasts and the 23.06
them, "A prophet is not without h., Mk 6.04
'H. your father and your mother'; 7.10
H. your father and mother.'" 10.19
and the places of h. at feasts, 12.39
how they chose the places of h., Lk 14.07
do not sit down in a place of h., 14.08
H. your father and mother.'" 18.20
and the places of h. at feasts, 20.46
prophet has no h. in his own Jn 4.44
that all may h. the Son, even as 5.23
Son, even as they h. the Father. 5.23
He who does not h. the Son does not 5.23
Son does not h. the Father who 5.23
but I h. my Father, and you dishonor 8.49
serves me, the Father will h. him. 12.26
the people held them in high h. Ac 5.13
held in h. by all the people, stood 5.34
they did not h. him as God or give Rom 1.21
for glory and h. and immortality, 2.07
but glory and h. and peace for 2.10
outdo one another in showing h. 12.10
respect is due, h. to whom h. is due. 13.07
day, observes it in h. of the Lord. 14.06
eats in h. of the Lord, since he 14.06
abstains in h. of the Lord and 14.06
You are held in h., but we in 1Co 4.10
we invest with the greater h., 12.23
the greater h. to the inferior 12.24
in h. and dishonor, in ill repute 2Co 6.08
"H. your father and mother" (this is Eph 6.02
with all joy; and h. such men, Php 2.29
for himself in holiness and h., 1Th 4.04
be h. and glory for ever and ever. 1Ti 1.17
H. widows who are real widows. 5.03
be considered worthy of double h., 5.17
their masters as worthy of all h., 6.01
To him be h. and eternal dominion. 6.16
crowned him with glory and h., Heb 2.07
with glory and h. because of the 2.09
a house has more h. than the house. 3.03
does not take the h. upon himself, 5.04
Let marriage be held in h. among all, 13.04
and glory and h. at the revelation 1Pe 1.07
H. all men. Love the brotherhood. 2.17
Fear God. H. the emperor. 2.17
bestowing h. on the woman as the 3.07
he received h. and glory from God 2Pe 1.17
give glory and h. and thanks to Rev 4.09
to receive glory and h. and power, 4.11
and might and h. and glory and 5.12
be blessing and h. and glory and 5.13
thanksgiving and h. and power and 7.12
glory and the h. of the nations. 21.26

HONORABLE
in number and more h. than they. Num 22.15
Jabez was more h. than his brothers; 1Ch 4.09
and the base fellow to the h. Is 3.05
noble, nor the knave said to be h. 32.05
and the holy day of the LORD h.; 58.13
we think less h. we invest with 1Co 12.23
aim at what is h. not only in the 2Co 8.21
whatever is h., whatever is just, Php 4.08
blaspheme that h. name by which Jas 2.07

HONORABLY
desiring to act h. in all things. Heb 13.18

HONORED
he was the most h. of all his Gen 34.19
by which gods and men are h., Ju 9.09
bodyguard, and h. in your house? 1Sa 22.14
king of Israel h. himself today, 2Sa 6.20
with which the king had h. him, Est 5.11
but he who heeds reproof is h. Pro 13.18
who guards his master will be h. 27.18
their h. men are dying of hunger, Is 5.13
the elder and h. man is the head, 9.15
traders were the h. of the earth? 23.08
dishonor all the h. of the earth. 23.09
and h., and I love you, I give men 43.04
or h. me with your sacrifices. 43.23
for I am h. in the eyes of the LORD, 49.05
I will make them h., and they shall Jer 30.19
all who h. her despise her, for they Lam 1.08
and praised and h. him who lives Dan 4.34
are all your ways, you have not h. 5.23
for her h. men lots were cast, and Nah 3.10
you will be h. in the presence of Lk 14.10
if one member is h., all rejoice 1Co 12.26
Christ will be h. in my body, Php 1.20

HONORING
to you, that he is h. your father? 2Sa 10.03
say to thee for h. thy servant? 1Ch 17.18
to you, that he is h. your father? 19.03

HONORS
but who h. those who fear the LORD; Ps 15.04
thanksgiving as his sacrifice h. me; 50.23
he who is kind to the needy h. him. Pro 14.31
Daniel high h. and many great Dan 2.48
"A son h. his father, and a servant Mal 1.06
'This people h. me with their lips, Mt 15.08
'This people h. me with their lips, Mk 7.06

HOOF
not a h. shall be left behind, for Ex 10.26
Whatever parts the h. and is Lev 11.03

HOOF (cont.)

that chew the cud or part the h.,	Lev 11.04
the cud but does not part the h.,	11.04
the cud but does not part the h.,	11.05
the cud but does not part the h.,	11.06
it parts the h. and is cloven-footed	11.07
which parts the h. but is not	11.26
parts the h. and has the h. cloven	Deu 14.06
cud or have the h. cloven you	14.07
the cud but do not part the h.,	14.07
it parts the h. but does not chew	14.08

HOOFBEATS

Why tarry the h. of his chariots?'	Ju 5.28

HOOFS

the horses' h. with the galloping,	Ju 5.22
an ox or a bull with horns and h.	Ps 69.31
their horses' h. seem like flint,	Is 5.28
stamping of the h. of his stallions,	Jer 47.03
With the h. of his horses he will	Eze 26.11
nor shall the h. of beasts trouble	32.13
your horn iron and your h. bronze;	Mic 4.13
ones, tearing off even their h.	Zec 11.16

HOOK

I will put my h. in your nose and	2Ki 19.28
nose, or pierce his jaw with a h.?	Job 41.02
all who cast h. in the Nile;	Is 19.08
I will put my h. in your nose and	37.29
He brings all of them up with a h.,	Hab 1.15
them, go to the sea and cast a h.,	Mt 17.27

HOOKS

with h. of gold, upon four bases of	Ex 26.32
their h. shall be of gold, and you	26.37
but the h. of the pillars and their	27.10
but the h. of the pillars and their	27.11
their h. shall be of silver, and	27.17
its h. and its frames, its bars, its	35.11
their h. were of gold, and he cast	36.36
and its five pillars with their h.	36.38
but the h. of the pillars and their	38.10
but the h. of the pillars and their	38.11
the h. of the pillars and their	38.12
but the h. of the pillars and their	38.17
their h. of silver, and the overlaying	38.19
shekels he made h. for the pillars,	38.28
its h., its frames, its bars, its	39.33
Manasseh with h. and bound him	2Ch 33.11
Can one take him with h., or pierce	Job 40.24
and their spears into pruning h.;	Is 2.04
cut off the shoots with pruning h.,	18.05
him with h. to the land of Egypt.	Eze 19.04
With h. they put him in a cage, and	19.09
I will put h. in your jaws, and make	29.04
and put h. into your jaws, and I	38.04
And h., a handbreadth long, were	40.43
and your pruning h. into spears;	Joe 3.10
they shall take you away with h.,	Amo 4.02
and their spears into pruning h.;	Mic 4.03

HOOPOE

to its kind, the h., and the bat.	Lev 11.19
after their kinds; the h. and the bat.	Deu 14.18

HOOT

the owl shall h. in the window, the	Zep 2.14

HOPE

If I should say I have h., even if	Ru 1.12
now there is h. for Israel in	Ez 10.02
let it h. for light, but have none,	Job 3.09
the integrity of your ways your h.?	4.06
So the poor have h., and injustice	5.16
look, the travelers of Sheba h.	6.19
and come to their end without h.	7.06
the h. of the godless man shall	8.13
confidence, because there is h.;	11.18
and their h. is to breathe their	11.20
I have no h.; yet I will defend	13.15
"For there is h. for a tree, if it	14.07
so thou destroyest the h. of man.	14.19
where then is my h.? Who will see my h.?	17.15
and my h. has he pulled up like a	19.10
For what is the h. of the godless	27.08
Behold, the h. of a man is disappointed;	41.09
and the h. of the poor shall not	Ps 9.18
war horse is a vain h. for victory,	33.17
on those who h. in his steadfast	33.18
be upon us, even as we h. in thee.	33.22
for what do I wait? My h. is in thee.	39.07
H. in God; for I shall again	42.05
H. in God; for I shall again	42.11
H. in God; for I shall again	43.05
in silence, for my h. is from him.	62.05
who art the h. of all the ends of	65.05
Let not those who h. in thee be put	69.06
art my h., my trust. O LORD, from my	71.05
But I will h. continually, and will	71.14
they should set their h. in God,	78.07
consternation, "Men are all a vain h."	116.11
for my h. is in thy ordinances.	119.43
in which thou hast made me h.	119.49
for thy salvation; I h. in thy word.	119.81
and my shield; I h. in thy word.	119.114
me not be put to shame in my h.!	119.116
cry for help; I h. in thy words.	119.147
I h. for thy salvation, O LORD, and I	119.166
soul waits, and in his word I h.;	130.05
O Israel, h. in the LORD!	130.07
O Israel, h. in the LORD from this	131.03
whose h. is in the LORD his God,	146.05
in those who h. in his steadfast	147.11
The h. of the righteous ends in	Pro 10.28
his h. perishes, and the expectation	11.07
H. deferred makes the heart sick,	13.12
Discipline your son while there is h.;	19.18
and your h. will not be cut off.	23.18
and your h. will not be cut off.	24.14
There is more h. for a fool than	26.12
There is more h. for a fool than	29.20
joined with all the living has h.,	Ecc 9.04
of Jacob, and I will h. in him.	Is 8.17
Ethiopia their h. and of Egypt	20.05
the pit cannot h. for thy faithfulness.	38.18
for me, and for my arm they h.	51.05
O thou h. of Israel, its savior in	Jer 14.08
We set our h. on thee, for thou	14.22
O LORD, the h. of Israel, all who	17.13
to give you a future and a h.	29.11
There is h. for your future, says	31.17
the LORD, the h. of their fathers.'	50.07
to mind, and therefore I have h.:	Lam 3.21
soul, "therefore I will h. in him."	3.24
in the dust—there may yet be h.;	3.29
that her h. was lost, she took	Eze 19.05
are dried up, and our h. is lost;	37.11
the Valley of Achor a door of h.	Hos 2.15
your stronghold, O prisoners of h.;	Zec 9.12
and in his name will the Gentiles h."	Mt 12.21
those from whom you h. to receive,	Lk 6.34
you, on whom you set your h.	Jn 5.45
moreover my flesh will dwell in h.	Ac 2.26
saw that their h. of gain was gone,	16.19
in the h. that they might feel	17.27
respect to the h. and the resurrection	23.06
having a h. in God which these	24.15
on trial for h. in the promise	26.06
our twelve tribes h. to attain,	26.07
And for this h. I am accused by	26.07
all h. of our being saved was at	27.20
because of the h. of Israel that I	28.20
In h. he believed against h., that	Rom 4.18
rejoice in our h. of sharing the	5.02

HOPE (cont.)
character, and character produces h., Rom 5.04
and h. does not disappoint us, 5.05
will of him who subjected it in h.; 8.20
For in this h. we were saved. 8.24
Now h. that is seen is not h. 8.24
But if we h. for what we do not see, 8.25
Rejoice in your h., be patient in 12.12
of the scriptures we might have h. 15.04
in him shall the Gentiles h." 15.12
May the God of h. fill you with all 15.13
Holy Spirit you may abound in h. 15.13
I h. to see you in passing as I go 15.24
should plow in h. and the thresher 1Co 9.10
thresh in h. of a share in the 9.10
So faith, h., love abide, these three 13.13
we who are in Christ have only h., 15.19
I h. to spend some time with you, if 16.07
Our h. for you is unshaken; 2Co 1.07
we have set our h. that we will 1.10
I h. you will understand fully, 1.13
Since we have such a h., 3.12
and I h. it is known also to your 5.11
but our h. is that as your faith 10.15
I h. you will find out that we have 13.06
we wait for the h. of righteousness. Gal 5.05
what is the h. to which he has Eph 1.18
having no h. and without God in the 2.12
to the one h. that belongs to your 4.04
expectation and h. that I shall Php 1.20
I h. in the Lord Jesus to send 2.19
I h. therefore to send him just as 2.23
because of the h. laid up for you Col 1.05
from the h. of the gospel which 1.23
is Christ in you, the h. of glory. 1.27
steadfastness of h. in our Lord 1Th 1.03
For what is our h. or joy or crown 2.19
grieve as others do who have no h. 4.13
for a helmet the h. of salvation. 5.08
comfort and good h. through grace, 2Th 2.16
Savior and of Christ Jesus our h., 1Ti 1.01
I h. to come to you soon, but I am 3.14
we have our h. set on the living 4.10
has set her h. on God and continues 5.05
in h. of eternal life which God, who Tit 1.02
awaiting our blessed h., the appearing 2.13
become heirs in h. of eternal life. 3.07
our confidence and pride in our h. Heb 3.06
assurance of h. until the end, 6.11
to seize the h. set before us. 6.18
a h. that enters into the inner 6.19
a better h. is introduced, through 7.19
confession of our h. without 10.23
to a living h. through the resurrection 1Pe 1.03
set your h. fully upon the grace 1.13
that your faith and h. are in God. 1.21
account for the h. that is in you, 3.15
but I h. to come to see you and 2Jn 1.12
I h. to see you soon, and we will 3Jn 1.14

HOPED
of the Jews h. to get the mastery Est 9.01
because I have h. in thy word. Ps 119.74
in whom we h. and to whom we fled Is 20.06
But we had h. that he was the one Lk 24.21
same time he h. that money would Ac 24.26
we who first h. in Christ have been Eph 1.12
is the assurance of things h. for, Heb 11.01
holy women who h. in God used to 1Pe 3.05

HOPELESS
but you did not say, "It is h."; Is 57.10
'It is h., for I have loved strangers, Jer 2.25

HOPES
extortion, set no vain h. on robbery; Ps 62.10
to you, filling you with vain h.; Jer 23.16
because its h. are confounded. Zec 9.05

For who h. for what he sees? Rom 8.24
h. all things, endures all things. 1Co 13.07
to set their h. on uncertain 1Ti 6.17
one who thus h. in him purifies 1Jn 3.03

HOPHNI
H. and Phinehas, were priests of the 1Sa 1.03
H. and Phinehas, shall be the sign 2.34
H. and Phinehas, were there with the 4.04
H. and Phinehas, were slain. 4.11
H. and Phinehas, are dead, and the 4.17

HOPHRA
give Pharaoh H. king of Egypt into Jer 44.30

HOPING
and he was h. to see some sign done Lk 23.08
for I am h. through your prayers to Phm 1.22

HOPPER
the h., the destroyer, and the Joe 2.25

HOPPING
the h. locust has eaten, and what Joe 1.04
and what the h. locust left, the 1.04

HOR
congregation, came to Mount H. Num 20.22
to Moses and Aaron at Mount H., 20.23
son, and bring them up to Mount H.; 20.25
went up Mount H. in the sight of 20.27
From Mount H. they set out by the 21.04
Kadesh, and encamped at Mount H., 33.37
went up Mount H. at the command of 33.38
years old when he died on Mount H. 33.39
And they set out from Mount H., 33.41
mark out your line to Mount H.; 34.07
from Mount H. you shall mark it out 34.08
died in Mount H. and was gathered Deu 32.50

HORAM
Then H. king of Gezer came up to Jos 10.33

HORDE
"This h. will now lick up all that Num 22.04
and all the h. that is with him; 2Ch 32.07

HORDES
Gomer and all his h.; Bethtogarmah Eze 38.06
of the north with all his h.— 38.06
the land, you and all your h., 38.09
him and his h. and the many 38.22
and all your h. and the peoples 39.04

HOREB
and came to H., the mountain of God. Ex 3.01
before you there on the rock at H.; 17.06
ornaments, from Mount H. onward. 33.06
journey from H. by the way of Deu 1.02
"The LORD our God said to us in H., 1.06
"And we set out from H., and went 1.19
before the LORD your God at H, 4.10
spoke to you at H. out of the 4.15
God made a covenant with us in H. 5.02
Even at H. you provoked the LORD to 9.08
your God at H. on the day of the 18.16
which he had made with them at H. 29.01
stone which Moses put there at H., 1Ki 8.09
forty nights to H. the mount of 19.08
tables which Moses put there at H., 2Ch 5.10
They made a calf in H. and worshiped Ps 106.19
command him at H. for all Israel. Mal 4.04

HOREM
H., Bethanath, and Bethshemesh— Jos 19.38

HORESH
in the Wilderness of Ziph at H. 1Sa 23.15
son, rose, and went to David at H., 23.16

HORESH (cont.)
David remained at H., and Jonathan 1Sa 23.18
among us in the strongholds at H., 23.19

HORHAGGIDGAD
Benejaakan, and encamped at H. Num 33.32
And they set out from H., 33.33

HORI
The sons of Lotan were H. and Heman; Gen 36.22
of Simeon, Shaphat the son of H.; Num 13.05
The sons of Lotan: H. and Homam; 1Ch 1.39

HORITE
These are the sons of Seir the H., Gen 36.20

HORITES
and the H. in their Mount Seir as Gen 14.06
these are the chiefs of the H.; 36.21
These are the chiefs of the H.: 36.29
these are the chiefs of the H., 36.30
The H. also lived in Seir formerly, Deu 2.12
he destroyed the H. before them, 2.22

HORMAH
them and pursued them, even to H. Num 14.45
name of the place was called H. 21.03
beat you down in Seir as far as H. Deu 1.44
the king of H., one; the king of Arad, Jos 12.14
Eltolad, Chesil, H., 15.30
Eltolad, Bethul, H., 19.04
the name of the city was called H. Ju 1.17
in H., in Borashan, in Athach, 1Sa 30.30
Bethuel, H., Ziklag, 1Ch 4.30

HORN
a long blast with the ram's h., Jos 6.05
Fill your h. with oil, and go; 1Sa 16.01
Then Samuel took the h. of oil, 16.13
and with the sound of the h. 2Sa 6.15
shield and the h. of my salvation, 22.03
priest took the h. of oil from the 1Ki 1.39
shouting, to the sound of the h., 1Ch 15.28
and the h. of my salvation, my Ps 18.02
the wicked, "Do not lift up your h.; 75.04
do not lift up your h. on high, 75.05
by thy favor our h. is exalted. 89.17
in my name shall his h. be exalted. 89.24
hast exalted my h. like that of 92.10
sound of the h. make a joyful 98.06
his h. is exalted in honor. 112.09
There I will make a h. to sprout 132.17
He has raised up a h. for his people, 148.14
The h. of Moab is cut off, and his Jer 48.25
I will cause a h. to spring forth Eze 29.21
that when you hear the sound of the h., Dan 3.05
peoples heard the sound of the h., 3.07
man who hears the sound of the h., 3.10
when you hear the sound of the h., 3.15
came up among them another h., 7.08
in this h. were eyes like the eyes 7.08
words which the h. was speaking. 7.11
and the other h. which came up and 7.20
the h. which had eyes and a mouth 7.20
this h. made war with the saints, 7.21
a conspicuous h. between his eyes. 8.05
the great h. was broken, and instead 8.08
one of them came forth a little h., 8.09
and the h. acted and prospered. 8.12
and the great h. between his eyes 8.21
As for the h. that was broken, in 8.22
Blow the h. in Gibeah, the trumpet Hos 5.08
will make your h. iron and your Mic 4.13
and has raised up a h. of salvation Lk 1.69

HORNET
And I sent the h. before you, which Jos 24.12

HORNETS
And I will send h. before you, Ex 23.28
your God will send h. among them, Deu 7.20

HORNS
ram, caught in a thickets by his h.; Gen 22.13
And you shall make h. for it on its Ex 27.02
its h. shall be of one piece with 27.02
put it upon the h. of the altar 29.12
its h. shall be of one piece with 30.02
its sides round about and its h.; 30.03
atonement upon its h. once a year; 30.10
its h. were of one piece with it. 37.25
its sides round about, and its h.; 37.26
He made h. for it on its four 38.02
its h. were of one piece with it, 38.02
blood on the h. of the altar of Lev 4.07
blood on the h. of the altar which 4.18
put it on the h. of the altar of 4.25
put it on the h. of the altar of 4.30
put it on the h. of the altar of 4.34
put it on the h. of the altar 8.15
and put it on the h. of the altar, 9.09
put it on the h. of the altar 16.18
as it were the h. of the wild ox. Num 23.22
as it were the h. of the wild ox, 24.08
and his h. are the h. of a wild ox; Deu 33.17
trumpets of rams' h. before the ark; Jos 6.04
of rams' h. before the ark of the 6.06
of rams' h. before the LORD went 6.08
of rams' h. before the ark of the 6.13
caught hold of the h. of the altar. 1Ki 1.50
laid hold of the h. of the altar, 1.51
caught hold of the h. of the altar. 2.28
made for himself h. of iron, 22.11
and with trumpets, and with h. 2Ch 15.14
made for himself h. of iron, 18.10
soul from the h. of the wild oxen! Ps 22.21
an ox or a bull with h. and hoofs. 69.31
All the h. of the wicked he will 75.10
but the h. of the righteous shall 75.10
branches, up to the h. of the altar! 118.27
and on the h. of their altars, Jer 17.01
at all the weak with your h., Eze 34.21
upward, four h., one cubit high. 43.15
put it on the four h. of the altar, 43.20
were before it; and it had ten h. Dan 7.07
I considered the h., and behold, 7.08
of the first h. were plucked up by 7.08
concerning the ten h. that were on 7.20
As for the ten h., out of this 7.24
It had two h.; and both h. were high, 8.03
He came to the ram with the two h., 8.06
the ram and broke his two h.; 8.07
conspicuous h. toward the four 8.08
ram which you saw with the two h., 8.20
and the h. of the altar shall be Amo 3.14
eyes and saw, and behold, four h.! Zec 1.18
"These are the h. which have 1.19
"These are the h. which scattered 1.21
cast down the h. of the nations 1.21
lifted up their h. against the 1.21
with seven h. and with seven eyes, Rev 5.06
from the four h. of the golden 9.13
with seven heads and ten h., 12.03
with ten h. and seven heads, with 13.01
upon its h. and a blasphemous name 13.01
it had two h. like a lamb and it 13.11
and it had seven heads and ten h. 17.03
heads and ten h. that carries her. 17.07
And the ten h. that you saw are ten 17.12
And the ten h. that you saw, they 17.16

HORONAIM
coming from the H. road by the 2Sa 13.34
on the road to H. they raise a cry Is 15.05
a cry from H., 'Desolation and Jer 48.03

HORONAIM (cont.)
the descent of H. they have heard Jer 48.05
from Zoar to H. and Eglathshelishiyah. 48.34

HORONITE
Sanballat the H. and Tobiah the Neh 2.10
Sanballat the H. and Tobiah the 2.19
the son-in-law of Sanballat the H.; 13.28

HORRIBLE
An appalling and h. thing has Jer 5.30
Israel has done a very h. thing. 18.13
Jerusalem I have seen a h. thing: 23.14
of Israel I have seen a h. thing; Hos 6.10

HORRIBLY
and their kings are h. afraid, Eze 27.35

HORRIFIED
passes by it is h. and shakes his Jer 18.16
by it will be h. and will hiss 19.08
by it will be h. and will hiss 49.17

HORRIFY
first-born, that I might h. them; Eze 20.26

HORROR
you shall be a h. to all the kingdoms Deu 28.25
And you shall become a h., a proverb, 28.37
he has made them an object of h., 2Ch 29.08
and h. seizes them of the east. Job 18.20
a h. to my neighbors, an object of Ps 31.11
come upon me, and h. overwhelms me. 55.05
hast made me a thing of h. to them. 88.08
My mind reels, h. has appalled me; Is 21.04
make them a h. to all the kingdoms Jer 15.04
making their land a h., a thing to be 18.16
And I will make this city a h., 19.08
make them a h. to all the kingdoms 24.09
destroy them, and make them a h., 25.09
make them a h. to all the kingdoms 29.18
will make you a h. to all the 34.17
a h., a curse, and a taunt. You shall see 42.18
an execration, a h., a curse, and a taunt. 44.12
derision and a h. to all that are 48.39
that Bozrah shall become a h., 49.13
The h. you inspire has deceived you, 49.16
"Edom shall become a h.; every one 49.17
has become a h. among the nations! 50.23
a h. and a hissing, without inhabitant. 51.37
has become a h. among the nations! 51.41
Her cities have become a h., a land of 51.43
and a taunt, a warning and a h., Eze 5.15
with sackcloth, and h. covers them; 7.18
A cup of h. and desolation, is the 23.33

HORSE
the h. and his rider he has thrown Ex 15.01
the h. and his rider he has thrown 15.21
and a h. for a hundred and fifty; 1Ki 10.29
escaped on a h. with horsemen. 20.20
h. for h., and chariot for chariot; 20.25
and a h. for a hundred and fifty; 2Ch 1.17
entrance of the h. gate of the 23.15
Above the H. Gate the priests Neh 3.28
and the h. which the king has Est 6.08
robes and the h. be handed over to 6.09
haste, take the robes and the h., 6.10
So Haman took the robes and the h., 6.11
she laughs at the h. and his rider. Job 39.18
"Do you give the h. his might? 39.19
Be not like a h. or a mule, without Ps 32.09
The war h. is a vain hope for 33.17
both rider and h. lay stunned. 76.06
is not in the strength of the h., 147.10
The h. is made ready for the day of Pro 21.31
A whip for the h., a bridle for the 26.03
who brings forth chariot and h., Is 43.17
Like a h. in the desert, they did 63.13
like a h. plunging headlong into Jer 8.06
corner of the H. Gate toward the 31.40
in pieces the h. and his rider; 51.21
he who rides the h. save his life; Amo 2.15
galloping h. and bounding chariot! Nah 3.02
behold, a man riding upon a red h.! Zec 1.08
and the war h. from Jerusalem; 9.10
I will strike every h. with panic, 12.04
I strike every h. of the peoples 12.04
a white h., and its rider had a bow Rev 6.02
And out came another h., bright red; 6.04
a black h., and its rider had a 6.05
a pale h., and its rider's name was 6.08
opened, and behold, a white h.! 19.11
sits upon the h. and against his 19.19
sword of him who sits upon the h., 19.21

HORSEBACK
So a man on h. went to meet him, and 2Ki 9.18
the man on h. through the open Est 6.09

HORSEMAN
"Take a h., and send to meet them, 2Ki 9.17
Then he sent out a second h., 9.19
At the noise of h. and archer every Jer 4.29

HORSEMEN
up with him both chariots and h.; Gen 50.09
chariots and his h. and his army, Ex 14.09
his host, his chariots, and his h. 14.17
Pharaoh, his chariots, and his h." 14.18
horses, his chariots, and his h. 14.23
their chariots, and upon their h." 14.26
chariots and the h. and all the 14.28
chariots and his h. went into the 15.19
chariots and h. to the Red Sea. Jos 24.06
to his chariots and to be his h., 1Sa 8.11
chariots, and six thousand h., 13.05
chariots and the h. were close upon 2Sa 1.06
a thousand and seven hundred h., 8.04
chariots, and forty thousand h., 10.18
for himself chariots and h., 1Ki 1.05
chariots, and twelve thousand h. 4.26
chariots, and the cities for his h., 9.19
his chariot commanders and his h. 9.22
gathered together chariots and h.; 10.26
chariots and twelve thousand h., 10.26
Syria escaped on a horse with h. 20.20
the chariots of Israel and its h.!" 2Ki 2.12
more than fifty h. and ten chariots 13.07
the chariots of Israel and its h.!" 13.14
on Egypt for chariots and for h.? 18.24
chariots, seven thousand h., 1Ch 18.04
chariots and h. from Mesopotamia, 19.06
Solomon gathered together chariots and h.; 2Ch 1.14
chariots and twelve thousand h., 1.14
chariots, and the cities for his h., 8.06
of his chariots, and his h. 8.09
chariots, and twelve thousand h., 9.25
chariots and sixty thousand h. 12.03
exceedingly many chariots and h.? 16.08
of soldiers and h. to protect us Ez 8.22
me officers of the army and h. Neh 2.09
h. in pairs, riders on asses, riders Is 21.07
here come riders, h. in pairs!" 21.09
the quiver with chariots and h., 22.06
and the h. took their stand at the 22.07
are many and in h. because they 31.01
on Egypt for chariots and for h.? 36.09
mount, O h.! Take your stations Jer 46.04
young men, h. riding on horses. Eze 23.06
h. riding on horses, all of them 23.12
and with h. and a host of many 26.07
noise of the h. and wagons and 26.10
horses and h., all of them clothed 38.04
a whirlwind, with chariots and h., Dan 11.40
by war, nor by horses, nor by h." Hos 1.07
H. charging, flashing sword and Nah 3.03

HORSEMEN (cont.)
their h. press proudly on. Hab 1.08
Yea, their h. come from afar; 1.08
with seventy h. and two hundred Ac 23.23
leaving the h. to go on with him. 23.32

HORSE'S
that bites the h. heels so that Gen 49.17
as high as a h. bridle, for one Rev 14.20

HORSES
them food in exchange for the h., Gen 47.17
the h., the asses, the camels, the Ex 9.03
all Pharaoh's h. and chariots and 14.09
all Pharaoh's h., his chariots, and 14.23
For when the h. of Pharaoh with his 15.19
to their h. and to their chariots; Deu 11.04
must not multiply h. for himself, 17.16
to Egypt in order to multiply h., 17.16
and see h. and chariots and an army 20.01
with very many h. and chariots. Jos 11.04
you shall hamstring their h., 11.06
he hamstrung their h., and burned 11.09
David hamstrung all the chariot h., 2Sa 8.04
got himself a chariot and h., 15.01
stalls of h. for his chariots, and 1Ki 4.26
straw for the h. and swift steeds 4.28
h., and mules, so much year by year. 10.25
import of h. was from Egypt and 10.28
and save the h. and mules alive, 18.05
were with him, and h. and chariots; 20.01
and captured the h. and chariots, 20.21
people as your people, my h. as your h." 22.04
of fire and h. of fire separated 2Ki 2.11
people as your people, my h. as your h." 3.07
came with his h. and chariots, 5.09
So he sent there h. and chariots 6.14
an army with h. and chariots was 6.15
was full of h. and chariots of 6.17
and of h., the sound of a great 7.06
their h., and their asses, leaving 7.07
there, nothing but the h. tied, 7.10
men take five of the remaining h., 7.13
spattered on the wall and on the h., 9.33
there are with you chariots and h., 10.02
And they brought him upon h.; 14.20
I will give you two thousand h., 18.23
And he removed the h. that the 23.11
David hamstrung all the chariot h., 1Ch 18.04
import of h. was from Egypt and 2Ch 1.16
h., and mules, so much year by year. 9.24
thousand stalls for h. and chariots, 9.25
And h. were imported for Solomon 9.28
And they brought him upon h.; 25.28
Their h. were seven hundred and Ez 2.66
Their h. were seven hundred and Neh 7.68
riding on swift h. that were used Est 8.10
on their swift h. that were used 8.14
Some boast of chariots, and some of h.; Ps 20.07
I have seen slaves on h., and princes Ecc 10.07
their land is filled with h., Is 2.07
his cart wheel over it with his h., 28.28
We will speed upon h.," therefore you 30.16
to Egypt for help and rely on h., 31.01
and their h. are flesh, and not 31.03
I will give you two thousand h., 36.08
upon h., and in chariots, and in 66.20
his h. are swifter than eagles—woe Jer 4.13
they ride upon h., set in array as a 6.23
of their h. is heard from Dan; 8.16
you, how will you compete with h.? 12.05
riding in chariots and on h., 17.25
riding in chariots and on h., 22.04
Harness the h.; mount, O horsemen! 46.04
Advance, O h., and rage, O chariots! 46.09
A sword upon her h. and upon her 50.37
they ride upon h., arrayed as a man 50.42
bring up h. like bristling locusts. 51.27
might give him h. and a large army. Eze 17.15
young men, horsemen riding on h. 23.06
full armor, horsemen riding on h., 23.12
whose issue was like that of h. 23.20
warriors, all of them riding on h. 23.23
with h. and chariots, and with 26.07
His h. will be so many that their 26.10
hoofs of his h. he will trample 26.11
for your wares h., war h., and mules. 27.14
h. and horsemen, all of them clothed 38.04
with you, all of them riding on h., 38.15
at my table with h. and riders, 39.20
nor by war, nor by h., nor by horsemen." Hos 1.07
save us, we will not ride upon h.; 14.03
the appearance of h., and like war h. Joe 2.04
I carried away your h.; and I made Amo 4.10
Do h. run upon rocks? Does one plow 6.12
cut off your h. from among you and Mic 5.10
Their h. are swifter than leopards, Hab 1.08
when thou didst ride upon thy h., 3.08
Thou didst trample the sea with thy h., 3.15
and the h. and their riders shall Hag 2.22
him were red, sorrel, and white h. Zec 1.08
chariot had red h., the second black h., 6.02
the third white h., and 6.03
the fourth chariot dappled gray h. 6.03
with the black h. goes toward the 6.06
shall confound the riders on h. 10.05
this plague shall fall on the h., 14.15
inscribed on the bells of the h., 14.20
the mouths of h. that they may Jas 3.03
were like h. arrayed for battle; Rev 9.07
chariots with h. rushing into 9.09
was how I saw the h. in my vision: 9.17
heads of the h. were like lions' 9.17
power of the h. is in their mouths 9.19
h. and chariots, and slaves, that is, 18.13
and pure, followed him on white h. 19.14
the flesh of h. and their riders, 19.18

HORSES'
"Then loud beat the h. hoofs with Ju 5.22
through the h. entrance to the 2Ki 11.16
their h. hoofs seem like flint, and Is 5.28

HOSAH
then the boundary turns to H., Jos 19.29
and H. were to be gatekeepers. 1Ch 16.38
And H., of the sons of Merari, had 26.10
and brethren of H. were thirteen. 26.11
For Shuppim and H. it came out for 26.16

HOSANNA
"H. to the Son of David! Blessed be he Mt 21.09
name of the Lord! H. in the highest!" 21.09
"H. to the Son of David!" they were 21.15
those who followed cried out, "H.! Mk 11.09
that is coming! H. in the highest!" 11.10
went out to meet him, crying, "H.! Jn 12.13

HOSEA
that came to H. the son of Beeri, Hos 1.01
When the LORD first spoke through H., 1.02
the LORD said to H., "Go, take to 1.02
As indeed he says in H., Rom 9.25

HOSHAIAH
and after them went H. and half of Neh 12.32
Kareah and Azariah the son of H., Jer 42.01
Azariah the son of H. and Johanan 43.02

HOSHAMA
Shenazzar, Jekamiah, H., and Nedabiah; 1Ch 3.18

HOSHEA
of Ephraim, H. the son of Nun; Num 13.08
Moses called H. the son of Nun 13.16
Then H. the son of Elah made a 2Ki 15.30

HOSHEA (cont.)
king of Judah H. the son of Elah 2Ki 17.01
and H. became his vassal, and paid 17.03
of Assyria found treachery in H.; 17.04
ninth year of H. the king of 17.06
In the third year of H. son of Elah, 18.01
the seventh year of H. son of Elah, 18.09
ninth year of H. king of Israel, 18.10
H. the son of Azaziah; 1Ch 27.20
H., Hananiah, Hasshub, Neh 10.23

HOSPITABLE
sensible, dignified, h., an apt teacher, 1Ti 3.02
but h., a lover of goodness, master Tit 1.08

HOSPITABLY
entertained us h. for three days. Ac 28.07

HOSPITALITY
needs of the saints, practice h. Rom 12.13
shown h., washed the feet of the 1Ti 5.10
neglect to show h. to strangers, Heb 13.02
Practice h. ungrudgingly to one 1Pe 4.09

HOST
finished, and all the h. of them. Gen 2.01
glory over Pharaoh and all his h.; Ex 14.04
glory over Pharaoh and all his h., 14.17
went before the h. of Israel moved 14.19
the h. of Egypt and the h. of Israel. 14.20
down upon the h. of the Egyptians, 14.24
discomfited the h. of the Egyptians, 14.24
and all the h. of Pharaoh that had 14.28
chariots and his h. he cast into 15.04
his h. as numbered being seventy-four Num 2.04
his h. as numbered being fifty-four 2.06
his h. as numbered being fifty-seven 2.08
his h. as numbered being forty-six 2.11
his h. as numbered being fifty-nine 2.13
his h. as numbered being forty-five 2.15
his h. as numbered being forty 2.19
his h. as numbered being thirty-two 2.21
his h. as numbered being thirty-five 2.23
his h. as numbered being sixty-two 2.26
his h. as numbered being forty-one 2.28
his h. as numbered being fifty-three 2.30
and over their h. was Nahshon the 10.14
And over the h. of the tribe of the 10.15
And over the h. of the tribe of the 10.16
and over their h. was Elizur the 10.18
And over the h. of the tribe of the 10.19
And over the h. of the tribe of the 10.20
and over their h. was Elishama the 10.22
And over the h. of the tribe of the 10.23
And over the h. of the tribe of the 10.24
and over their h. was Ahiezer the 10.25
And over the h. of the tribe of the 10.26
And over the h. of the tribe of the 10.27
all the h. of heaven, you be drawn Deu 4.19
moon or any of the h. of heaven, 17.03
a great h., in number like the sand Jos 11.04
has given Midian and all the h." Ju 7.14
has given the h. of Midian into 7.15
encampment as the h. was going 1Sa 17.20
bodies of the h. of the Philistines 17.46
and all the h. of the mighty men. 2Sa 10.07
and all the h. of heaven standing 1Ki 22.19
and worshiped all the h. of heaven, 2Ki 17.16
and worshiped all the h. of heaven, 21.03
for all the h. of heaven in the 21.05
and for all the h. of heaven; 23.04
and all the h. of the heavens. 23.05
and all the h. of heaven standing 2Ch 18.18
and worshiped all the h. of heaven, 33.03
for all the h. of heaven in the 33.05
of heavens, with all their h., Neh 9.06
and the h. of heaven worships thee. 9.06
Though a h. encamp against me, my Ps 27.03
and all their h. by the breath of 33.06
great is the h. of those who bore 68.11
you lead your h. upon the holy 110.03
Pharaoh and his h. in the Red Sea, 136.15
his angels, praise him, all his h.! 148.02
yea, all her slain are a mighty h. Pro 7.26
hosts is mustering a h. for battle. Is 13.04
LORD will punish the h. of heaven, 24.21
and furious against all their h., 34.02
All the h. of heaven shall rot away, 34.04
All their h. shall fall, as leaves 34.04
who brings out their h. by number, 40.26
and I commanded all their h. 45.12
the moon and all the h. of heaven, Jer 8.02
burned to all the h. of heaven, 19.13
As the h. of heaven cannot be 33.22
utterly destroy all her h. 51.03
of tumult like the sound of a h.; Eze 1.24
They shall bring up a h. against you, 16.40
and wagons and a h. of peoples; 23.24
"Bring up a h. against them, and 23.46
And the h. shall stone them and 23.47
horsemen and a h. of many soldiers. 26.07
over you with a h. of many peoples; 32.03
feet, an exceedingly great h. 37.10
horses, a great h., a mighty army; 38.15
his will in the h. of heaven and Dan 4.35
great, even to the h. of heaven; 8.10
and some of the h. of the stars it 8.10
even up to the Prince of the h.; 8.11
And the h. was given over to it 8.12
sanctuary and h. to be trampled 8.13
for his h. is exceedingly great; Joe 2.11
the roofs to the h. of the heavens; Zep 1.05
of the heavenly h. praising God Lk 2.13
that when your h. comes he may say 14.10
over to worship the h. of heaven, Ac 7.42
Gaius, who is h. to me and to the Rom 16.23
on high he led a h. of captives, Eph 4.08

HOSTAGES
also h., and he returned to Samaria. 2Ki 14.14
and h., and he returned to Samaria. 2Ch 25.24

HOSTILE
and your eye be h. to your poor Deu 15.09
is set on the flesh is h. to God; Rom 8.07
once were estranged and h. in mind, Col 1.21

HOSTILITY
down the dividing wall of h., Eph 2.14
thereby bringing the h. to an end. 2.16
sinners such h. against himself, so Heb 12.03

HOSTS
from the land of Egypt by their h." Ex 6.26
upon Egypt and bring forth my h., 7.04
I brought your h. out of the land 12.17
all the h. of the LORD went out 12.41
of the land of Egypt by their h. 12.51
of Israel according to their h., Num 10.28
Egypt by their h. under the 33.01
to the LORD of h. at Shiloh, 1Sa 1.03
"O LORD of h., if thou wilt indeed 1.11
of the covenant of the LORD of h., 4.04
Thus says the LORD of h., 15.02
you in the name of the LORD of h., 17.45
LORD, the God of h., was with him. 2Sa 5.10
of the LORD of h. who sits enthroned 6.02
in the name of the LORD of h., 6.18
David, 'Thus says the LORD of h., 7.08
'The LORD of h. is God over Israel, 7.26
O LORD of h., the God of Israel, 7.27
said, "As the LORD of h. lives, 1Ki 18.15
for the LORD, the God of h.; 19.10
for the LORD, the God of h.; 19.14
said, "As the LORD of h. lives, 2Ki 3.14
for the LORD of h. was with him. 1Ch 11.09

HOSTS (cont.)

David, 'Thus says the LORD of h., 1Ch 17.07
'The LORD of h., the God of Israel, 17.24
dost bring fresh h. against me. Job 10.17
The LORD of h., he is the King of Ps 24.10
The LORD of h. is with us; 46.07
The LORD of h. is with us; 46.11
seen in the city of the LORD of h., 48.08
LORD God of h., art God of Israel. 59.05
shame through me, O Lord GOD of h.; 69.06
O LORD God of h., how long wilt 80.04
Restore us, O God of h.; 80.07
Turn again, O God of h.! 80.14
Restore us, O LORD God of h.! 80.19
thy dwelling place, O LORD of h.! 84.01
O LORD of h., my king and my God. 84.03
O LORD God of h., hear my prayer; 84.08
O LORD of h., blessed is the man 84.12
O LORD God of h., who is mighty as 89.08
all his h., his ministers that do 103.21
If the LORD of h. had not left us a Is 1.09
the LORD of h., the Mighty One of 1.24
For the LORD of h. has a day 2.12
the LORD of h., is taking away from 3.01
says the Lord GOD of h. 3.15
of the LORD of h. is the house of 5.07
The LORD of h. has sworn in my 5.09
But the LORD of h. is exalted in 5.16
rejected the law of the LORD of h., 5.24
"Holy, holy, holy is the LORD of h.; 6.03
have seen the King, the LORD of h.!" 6.05
But the LORD of h., him you shall 8.13
in Israel from the LORD of h., 8.18
of the LORD of h. will do this. 9.07
them, nor seek the LORD of h. 9.13
of the LORD of h. the land is 9.19
the LORD of h., will send wasting 10.16
the LORD of h., will make a full 10.23
the LORD of h.: "O my people, who 10.24
And the LORD of h. will wield 10.26
the LORD of h. will lop the boughs 10.33
The LORD of h. is mustering a host 13.04
of the LORD of h. in the day of 13.13
against them," says the LORD of h., 14.22
destruction, says the LORD of h." 14.23
The LORD of h. has sworn: "As I have 14.24
For the LORD of h. has purposed, 14.27
of Israel, says the LORD of h. 17.03
to the LORD of h. from a people 18.07
of the name of the LORD of h. 18.07
says the Lord, the LORD of h. 19.04
the LORD of h. has purposed 19.12
the LORD of h. shakes over them. 19.16
the LORD of h. has purposed 19.17
swear allegiance to the LORD of h. 19.18
to the LORD of h. in the land of 19.20
whom the LORD of h. has blessed, 19.25
I have heard from the LORD of h., 21.10
For the Lord GOD of h. has a day of 22.05
In that day the Lord GOD of h., 22.12
The LORD of h. has revealed himself 22.14
you die," says the Lord GOD of h. 22.14
Thus says the Lord GOD of h., 22.15
In that day, says the LORD of h., 22.25
The LORD of h. has purposed it, to 23.09
for the LORD of h. will reign on 24.23
the LORD of h. will make for all 25.06
day the LORD of h. will be a crown 28.05
the Lord GOD of h. upon the whole 28.22
This also comes from the LORD of h.; 28.29
by the LORD of h. with thunder and 29.06
so the LORD of h. will come down 31.04
so the LORD of h. will protect 31.05
"O LORD of h., God of Israel, who 37.16
of the LORD of h. will accomplish 37.32
"Hear the word of the LORD of h.: 39.05
the LORD of h.: "I am the first and 44.06
or reward," says the LORD of h. 45.13
the LORD of h. is his name—is the 47.04
the LORD of h. is his name. 48.02
roar—the LORD of h. is his name. 51.15
husband, the LORD of h. is his name; 54.05
in you, says the Lord GOD of h. Jer 2.19
the God of h.: "Because they have 5.14
For thus says the LORD of h.: 6.06
Thus says the LORD of h.: 6.09
Thus says the LORD of h., 7.03
Thus says the LORD of h., 7.21
driven them, says the LORD of h. 8.03
Therefore thus says the LORD of h.: 9.07
Therefore thus says the LORD of h., 9.15
Thus says the LORD of h.: 9.17
the LORD of h. is his name. 10.16
The LORD of h., who planted you, has 11.17
But, O LORD of h., who judgest 11.20
therefore thus says the LORD of h.: 11.22
by thy name, O LORD, God of h. 15.16
For thus says the LORD of h., 16.09
Thus says the LORD of h., 19.03
to them, 'Thus says the LORD of h.: 19.11
"Thus says the LORD of h., 19.15
O LORD of h., who triest the 20.12
the LORD of h. concerning the 23.15
Thus says the LORD of h.: 23.16
God, the LORD of h., our God. 23.36
"Therefore thus says the LORD of h.: 25.08
to them, 'Thus says the LORD of h., 25.27
to them, 'Thus says the LORD of h.: 25.28
of the earth, says the LORD of h.' 25.29
"Thus says the LORD of h.: 25.32
Judah: 'Thus says the LORD of h., 26.18
masters: 'Thus says the LORD of h., 27.04
them intercede with the LORD of h., 27.18
the LORD of h. concerning the 27.19
thus says the LORD of h., 27.21
"Thus says the LORD of h., 28.02
For thus says the LORD of h., 28.14
"Thus says the LORD of h., 29.04
For thus says the LORD of h., 29.08
'Thus says the LORD of h., 29.17
Thus says the LORD of h., 29.21
"Thus says the LORD of h., 29.25
in that day, says the LORD of h., 30.09
Thus says the LORD of h., 31.23
roar—the LORD of h. is his name: 31.35
'Thus says the LORD of h., 32.14
For thus says the LORD of h., 32.15
God whose name is the LORD of h., 32.18
'Give thanks to the LORD of h., 33.11
"Thus says the LORD of h.: 33.12
"Thus says the LORD of h., 35.13
the God of h., the God of Israel: 35.17
said, "Thus says the LORD of h., 35.18
therefore thus says the LORD of h., 35.19
the God of h., the God of Israel, If 38.17
Ethiopian, 'Thus says the LORD of h., 39.16
Thus says the LORD of h., 42.15
"For thus says the LORD of h., 42.18
to them, 'Thus says the LORD of h., 43.10
"Thus says the LORD of h., 44.02
And now thus says the LORD God of h., 44.07
"Therefore thus says the LORD of h., 44.11
Thus says the LORD of h., 44.25
is the day of the Lord GOD of h., 46.10
the Lord GOD of h. holds a sacrifice 46.10
King, whose name is the LORD of h., 46.18
The LORD of h., the God of Israel, 46.25
Thus says the LORD of h., 48.01
King, whose name is the LORD of h. 48.15
upon you, says the Lord GOD of h., 49.05
Thus says the LORD of h.: 49.07
in that day, says the LORD of h. 49.26
Thus says the LORD of h.: 49.35
Therefore, thus says the LORD of h., 50.18
the Lord GOD of h. has a work to 50.25
proud one, says the Lord GOD of h.; 50.31

HOSTS (cont.)

"Thus says the LORD of h.:	Jer 50.33
the LORD of h. is his name.	50.34
by their God, the LORD of h.;	51.05
The LORD of h. has sworn by himself:	51.14
the LORD of h. is his name.	51.19
For thus says the LORD of h.,	51.33
King, whose name is the LORD of h.	51.57
"Thus says the LORD of h.:	51.58
you and all the h. that are	Eze 38.07
assembled your h. to carry off	38.13
the LORD the God of h.,	Hos 12.05
says the Lord GOD, the God of h.,	Amo 3.13
LORD, the God of h., is his name!	4.13
the God of h., will be with you, as	5.14
the God of h., will be gracious to	5.15
the God of h., the Lord: "In all the	5.16
LORD, whose name is the God of h.	5.27
the God of h.): "I abhor the pride	6.08
says the LORD, the God of h.;	6.14
GOD of h., he who touches the earth	9.05
mouth of the LORD of h. has spoken.	Mic 4.04
am against you, says the LORD of h.,	Nah 2.13
h. of slain, heaps of corpses, dead	3.03
against you, says the LORD of h.,	3.05
the LORD of h. that peoples labor	Hab 2.13
Therefore, as I live," says the LORD of h.,	Zep 2.09
the people of the LORD of h.	2.10
"Thus says the LORD of h.:	Hag 1.02
therefore thus says the LORD of h.:	1.05
"Thus says the LORD of h.:	1.07
says the LORD of h.	1.09
of the LORD of h., their God,	1.14
am with you, says the LORD of h.,	2.04
For thus says the LORD of h.:	2.06
with splendor, says the LORD of h.	2.07
gold is mine, says the LORD of h.	2.08
prosperity, says the LORD of h.'"	2.09
the former, says the LORD of h.;	2.09
the LORD of h.; Ask the priests to	2.11
On that day, says the LORD of h.,	2.23
chosen you, says the LORD of h."	2.23
to them, Thus says the LORD of h.:	Zec 1.03
Return to me, says the LORD of h.,	1.03
return to you, says the LORD of h.	1.03
out, 'Thus says the LORD of h.,	1.04
As the LORD of h. purposed to deal	1.06
'O LORD of h., how long wilt thou	1.12
'Cry out, Thus says the LORD of h.:	1.14
built in it, says the LORD of h.,	1.16
Cry again, Thus says the LORD of h.:	1.17
For thus said the LORD of h.,	2.08
that the LORD of h. has sent me.	2.09
the LORD of h. has sent me to you.	2.12
"Thus says the LORD of h.:	3.07
inscription, says the LORD of h.,	3.09
In that day, says the LORD of h.,	3.10
by my Spirit, says the LORD of h.	4.06
the LORD of h. has sent me to you.	4.09
send it forth, says the LORD of h.,	5.04
to him, 'Thus says the LORD of h.,	6.12
the LORD of h. has sent me to you.	6.15
of the LORD of h. and the prophets,	7.03
word of the LORD of h. came to me;	7.04
"Thus says the LORD of h.,	7.09
the LORD of h. had sent by his	7.12
wrath came from the LORD of h.	7.12
not hear," says the LORD of h.,	7.13
word of the LORD of h. came to me,	8.01
"Thus says the LORD of h.:	8.02
and the mountain of the LORD of h.,	8.03
Thus says the LORD of h.:	8.04
Thus says the LORD of h.:	8.06
in my sight, says the LORD of h.?	8.06
Thus says the LORD of h.:	8.07
Thus says the LORD of h.:	8.09
house of the LORD of h. was laid,	8.09
former days, says the LORD of h.	8.11
For thus says the LORD of h.:	8.14
not relent, says the LORD of h.,	8.14
word of the LORD of h. came to me,	8.18
"Thus says the LORD of h.:	8.19
"Thus says the LORD of h.:	8.20
LORD, and to seek the LORD of h.;	8.21
seek the LORD of h. in Jerusalem,	8.22
Thus says the LORD of h.:	8.23
The LORD of h. will protect them,	9.15
for the LORD of h. cares for his	10.03
through the LORD of h., their God.'	12.05
"And on that day, says the LORD of h.,	13.02
next to me," says the LORD of h.	13.07
the LORD of h., and to keep the	14.16
the LORD of h., there will be no	14.17
shall be sacred to the LORD of h.,	14.21
of the LORD of h. on that day.	14.21
the LORD of h. says, "They may	Mal 1.04
says the LORD of h. to you,	1.06
show you favor? says the LORD of h.	1.08
to any of you? says the LORD of h.	1.09
in you, says the LORD of h.,	1.10
the nations, says the LORD of h.	1.11
sniff at me, says the LORD of h.	1.13
a great King, says the LORD of h.,	1.14
to my name, says the LORD of h.,	2.02
Levi may hold, says the LORD of h.	2.04
is the messenger of the LORD of h.	2.07
of Levi, says the LORD of h.,	2.08
an offering to the LORD of h.!	2.12
with violence, says the LORD of h.	2.16
he is coming, says the LORD of h.	3.01
not fear me, says the LORD of h.	3.05
return to you, says the LORD of h.	3.07
to the test, says the LORD of h.,	3.10
fail to bear, says the LORD of h.	3.11
of delight, says the LORD of h.	3.12
in mourning before the LORD of h.?	3.14
shall be mine, says the LORD of h.,	3.17
burn them up, says the LORD of h.,	4.01
when I act, says the LORD of h.	4.03
"If the Lord of h. had not left us	Rom 9.29
the spiritual h. of wickedness in	Eph 6.12
reached the ears of the Lord of h.	Jas 5.04

HOT

who found the h. springs in the	Gen 36.24
went out from Pharaoh in h. anger.	Ex 11.08
when the sun grew h., it melted.	16.21
wrath may burn h. against them and	32.10
thy wrath burn h. against thy	32.11
dancing, Moses' anger burned h.,	32.19
not the anger of my lord burn h.;	32.22
the anger and h. displeasure which	Deu 9.19
of blood in h. anger pursue the	19.06
In h. anger he went back to his	Ju 14.19
Tomorrow, by the time the sun is h.,	1Sa 11.09
be replaced by h. bread on the day	21.06
a cake baked on h. stones and a	1Ki 19.06
And the battle grew h. that day,	22.35
And the battle grew h. that day,	2Ch 18.34
be opened until the sun is h.;	Neh 7.03
when it is h., they vanish from	Job 6.17
garments are h. when the earth is	37.17
my heart became h. within me.	Ps 39.03
thou didst turn from thy h. anger.	85.03
H. indignation seizes me because of	119.53
one walk upon h. coals and his	Pro 6.28
As charcoal to h. embers and wood	26.21
"A h. wind from the bare heights in	Jer 4.11
wrath, he poured out his h. anger;	Lam 4.11
Our skin is h. as an oven with the	5.10
the coals, that it may become h.,	Eze 24.11
I speak in my h. jealousy against	36.05
was strict and the furnace very h.,	Dan 3.22
All of them are h. as an oven,	Hos 7.07
"My anger is h. against the shepherds,	Zec 10.03
works: you are neither cold nor h.	Rev 3.15

HOT (cont.)
Would that you were cold or h.! Rev 3.15
lukewarm, and neither cold nor h., 3.16

HOTHAM
H., and their sister Shua. 1Ch 7.32
Jeiel the sons of H. the Aroerite, 11.44

HOTHIR
Joshbekashah, Mallothi, H., Mahazioth. 1Ch 25.04
to H., his sons and his brethren, 25.28

HOTLY
sin, that you have h. pursued me? Gen 31.36
the anger of the LORD blazed h., Num 11.10
the wicked h. pursue the poor; Ps 10.02

HOT-TEMPERED
A h. man stirs up strife, but he who Pro 15.18

HOUR
for you until the h. appointed, 1Sa 9.24
'Noisy one who lets the h. go by.' Jer 46.17
will be given to you in that h.; Mt 10.19
about the third h. he saw others 20.03
about the sixth h. and the ninth h., 20.05
the eleventh h. he went out and 20.06
hired about the eleventh h. came, 20.09
saying, 'These last worked only one h., 20.12
"But of that day and h. no one knows, 24.36
is coming at an h. you do not 24.44
him and at an h. he does not know, 24.50
know neither the day nor the h. 25.13
could you not watch with me one h.? 26.40
Behold, the h. is at hand, and the 26.45
At that h. Jesus said to the crowds, 26.55
Now from the sixth h. there was 27.45
all the land until the ninth h. 27.45
And about the ninth h. Jesus cried 27.46
place, and the h. is now late; Mk 6.35
whatever is given you in that h., 13.11
that day or that h. no one knows, 13.32
the h. might pass from him. 14.35
Could you not watch one h.? 14.37
the h. has come; the Son of man is 14.41
And it was the third h., 15.25
And when the sixth h. had come, 15.33
the whole land until the ninth h. 15.33
And at the ninth h. Jesus cried 15.34
outside at the h. of incense. Lk 1.10
up at that very h. she gave thanks 2.38
In that h. he cured many of diseases 7.21
In that same h. he rejoiced in the 10.21
in that very h. what you ought to 12.12
known at what h. the thief was 12.39
is coming at an h. you do not 12.40
him and at an h. he does not know, 12.46
At that very h. some Pharisees came, 13.31
lay hands on him at that very h., 20.19
And when the h. came, he sat at 22.14
But this is your h., and the power of 22.53
of about an h. still another 22.59
It was now about the sixth h. 23.44
the whole land until the ninth h., 23.44
rose that same h. and returned to 24.33
day, for it was about the tenth h. Jn 1.39
My h. has not yet come." 2.04
It was about the sixth h. 4.06
the h. is coming when neither on 4.21
But the h. is coming, and now is, 4.23
asked them the h. when he began to 4.52
at the seventh h. the fever left 4.52
that was the h. when Jesus had 4.53
the h. is coming, and now is, when 5.25
for the h. is coming when all who 5.28
because his h. had not yet come. 7.30
because his h. had not yet come. 8.20
"The h. has come for the Son of man 12.23
'Father, save me from this h.'? 12.27
purpose I have come to this h. 12.27
knew that his h. had come to 13.01
indeed, the h. is coming when 16.02
that when their h. comes you may 16.04
sorrow, because her h. has come; 16.21
the h. is coming when I shall no 16.25
The h. is coming, indeed it has come, 16.32
and said, "Father, the h. has come; 17.01
it was about the sixth h. 19.14
And from that h. the disciple took 19.27
it is only the third h. of the day; Ac 2.15
at the h. of prayer, the ninth h. 3.01
About the ninth h. of the day he 10.03
to pray, about the sixth h. 10.09
about this h., I was keeping the 10.30
the ninth h. of prayer in my house; 10.30
And it came out that very h. 16.18
took them the same h. of the night, 16.33
in that very h. I received my 22.13
"At the third h. of the night get 23.23
Besides this you know what h. it is, Rom 13.11
To the present h. we hunger and 1Co 4.11
Why am I in peril every h.? 15.30
Children, it is the last h.; 1Jn 2.18
we know that it is the last h. 2.18
know at what h. I will come upon Rev 3.03
you from the h. of trial which is 3.10
in heaven for about half an h. 8.01
who had been held ready for the h., 9.15
And at that h. there was a great 11.13
for the h. of his judgment has come; 14.07
for the h. to reap has come, for the 14.15
authority as kings for one h., 17.12
In one h. has thy judgment come." 18.10
In one h. all this wealth has been 18.17
In one h. she has been laid waste. 18.19

HOURS
"Are there not twelve h. in the day? Jn 11.09
of about three h. his wife came in, Ac 5.07
for about two h. they all with one 19.34

HOUSE
your father's h. to the land that Gen 12.01
woman was taken into Pharaoh's h. 12.15
Pharaoh and his h. with great 12.17
born in his h., three hundred and 14.14
the heir of my h. is Eliezer of 15.02
born in my h. will be my heir." 15.03
generations, whether born in your h., 17.12
is born in your h. and he that is 17.13
born in his h. or bought with his 17.23
male among the men of Abraham's h., 17.23
and all the men of his h., 17.27
born in the h. and those bought 17.27
your servant's h. and spend the 19.02
aside to him and entered his h.; 19.03
to the last man, surrounded the h.; 19.04
brought Lot into the h. to them, 19.10
men who were at the door of the h., 19.11
me to wander from my father's h., 20.13
wombs of the h. of Abimelech 20.18
his servant, the oldest of his h., 24.02
my father's h. and from the land 24.07
your father's h. for us to lodge 24.23
the way to the h. of my master's 24.27
prepared the h. and a place for 24.31
So the man came into the h.; 24.32
to my father's h. and to my 24.38
my kindred and from my father's h.; 24.40
son, which were with her in the h., 27.15
Paddan-aram to the h. of Bethuel your 28.02
is none other than the h. of God, 28.17
again to my father's h. in peace, 28.21
up for a pillar, shall be God's h.; 28.22
him, and brought him to his h. 29.13
left to us in our father's h.? 31.14

HOUSE (cont.)
greatly for your father's h., Gen 31.30
years I have been in your h.; 31.41
to Succoth, and built himself a h., 33.17
out of Shechem's h., and went away. 34.26
"Remain a widow in your father's h., 38.11
went and dwelt in her father's h. 38.11
he was in the h. of his master the 39.02
overseer of his h. and put him in 39.04
overseer in his h. and over all 39.05
the Egyptian's h. for Joseph's sake; 39.05
all that he had, in h. and field. 39.05
concern about anything in the h., 39.08
not greater in this h. than I am; 39.09
went into the h. to do his work 39.11
the men of the h. was there in the h., 39.11
and fled and got out of the h. 39.12
hand, and had fled out of the h., 39.13
me, and fled and got out of the h." 39.15
with me, and fled out of the h." 39.18
custody in the h. of the captain 40.03
him in custody in his master's h., 40.07
and so get me out of this h. 40.14
custody in the h. of the captain 41.10
you shall be over my h., 41.40
my hardship and all my father's h." 41.51
he said to the steward of his h., 43.16
"Bring the men into the h., and 43.16
and brought the men to Joseph's h. 43.17
they were brought to Joseph's h., 43.18
up to the steward of Joseph's h., 43.19
with him at the door of the h., 43.19
brought the men into Joseph's h., 43.24
into the h. to him the present 43.26
he commanded the steward of his h., 44.01
silver or gold from your lord's h.? 44.08
his brothers came to Joseph's h., 44.14
lord of all his h. and ruler over 45.08
report was heard in Pharaoh's h., 45.16
all the persons of the h. of Jacob, 46.27
the money into Pharaoh's h. 47.14
in Egypt, he and his father's h.; 50.22
Now a man from the h. of Levi went Ex 2.01
and of her who sojourns in her h., 3.22
Pharaoh turned and went into his h., 7.23
which shall come up into your h., 8.03
flies into the h. of Pharaoh and 8.24
next to his h. shall take according 12.04
the door of his h. until the 12.22
there was not a h. where one was 12.30
In one h. shall it be eaten; 12.46
any of the flesh outside the h.; 12.46
out of the h. of bondage, for by 13.03
of Egypt, from the h. of bondage. 13.14
Now the h. of Israel called its 16.31
you shall say to the h. of Jacob, 19.03
of Egypt, out of the h. of bondage. 20.02
shall not covet your neighbor's h.; 20.17
it is stolen out of the man's h., 22.07
owner of the h. shall come near to 22.08
bring into the h. of the LORD your 23.19
bring to the h. of the LORD your 34.26
the sight of all the h. of Israel. 40.38
the whole h. of Israel, may bewail Lev 10.06
disease in a h. in the land of 14.34
then he who owns the h. shall come 14.35
be some sort of disease in my h.' 14.35
they empty the h. before the 14.36
that is in the h. be declared 14.36
priest shall go in to see the h. 14.36
walls of the h. with greenish or 14.37
go out of the h. to the door of the h., 14.38
and shut up the h. seven days. 14.38
has spread in the walls of the h., 14.39
inside of the h. to be scraped 14.41
other plaster and plaster the h. 14.42
disease breaks out again in the h., 14.43
and scraped the h. and plastered 14.43
the disease has spread in the h., 14.44
is a malignant leprosy in the h.; 14.44
And he shall break down the h., 14.45
and all the plaster of the h.; 14.45
who enters the h. while it is shut 14.46
down in the h. shall wash his 14.47
who eats in the h. shall wash his 14.47
in the h. after the h. was plastered, 14.48
shall pronounce the h. clean, 14.48
cleansing of the h. he shall take 14.49
and sprinkle the h. seven times. 14.51
cleanse the h. with the blood of 14.52
he shall make atonement for the h., 14.53
for leprosy in a garment or in a h., 14.55
atonement for himself and for his h. 16.06
atonement for himself and for his h.; 16.11
and for his h. and for all the 16.17
If any man of the h. of Israel 17.03
them, Any man of the h. of Israel, 17.08
"If any man of the h. of Israel or 17.10
are born in his h. may eat of his 22.11
and returns to her father's h., 22.13
any one of the h. of Israel or of 22.18
a dwelling h. in a walled city, he 25.29
then the h. that is in the walled 25.30
then the h. that was sold in a city 25.33
dedicates his h. to be holy to the 27.14
dedicates it wishes to redeem his h., 27.15
the head of the h. of his fathers. Num 1.04
each representing his fathers' h. 1.44
according to his fathers' h. 2.34
of the fathers' h. of the Gershonites. 3.24
of the fathers' h. of the families 3.30
of the fathers' h. of the families 3.35
he is entrusted with all my h. 12.07
rods, one for each fathers' h., 17.02
for the head of each fathers' h. 17.03
Aaron for the h. of Levi had 17.08
your fathers' h. with you shall 18.01
is clean in your h. may eat of it. 18.11
is clean in your h. may eat of it. 18.13
all the h. of Israel wept for Aaron 20.29
to give me his h. full of silver 22.18
give me his h. full of silver and 24.13
of a fathers' h. belonging to the 25.14
people of a fathers' h. in Midian. 25.15
her father's h., in her youth, 30.03
And if she vowed in her husband's h., 30.10
her youth, within her father's h. 30.16
of Egypt, out of the h. of bondage. Deu 5.06
not desire your neighbor's h., 5.21
of them when you sit in your h., 6.07
doorposts of your h. and on your 6.09
of Egypt, out of the h. of bondage. 6.12
redeemed you from the h. of bondage, 7.08
an abominable thing into your h., 7.26
Egypt, out of the h. of bondage, 8.14
when you are sitting in your h., 11.19
doorposts of your h. and upon your 11.20
you out of the h. of bondage, 13.05
of Egypt, out of the h. of bondage. 13.10
has built a new h. and has not 20.05
Let him go back to his h., lest he 20.05
Let him go back to his h., lest he 20.06
Let him go back to his h., lest he 20.07
Let him go back to his h., lest the 20.08
shall bring her home to your h., 21.12
remain in your h. and bewail her 21.13
you shall bring it home to your h., 22.02
"When you build a new h., you shall 22.08
the guilt of blood upon your h., 22.08
to the door of her father's h., 22.21
the harlot in her father's h.; 22.21
into the h. of the LORD your God in 23.18
hand and sends her out of his h., 24.01
and she departs out of his h., 24.01
hand and sends her out of his h., 24.03
not go into his h. to fetch his 24.10

HOUSE (cont.)
does not build up his brother's h.' Deu 25.09
And the name of his h. shall be 25.10
The h. of him that had his sandal 25.10
have in your h. two kinds of 25.14
has given to you and to your h., 26.11
the sacred portion out of my h., 26.13
you shall build a h., and you shall 28.30
came into the h. of a harlot whose Jos 2.01
come to you, who entered your h.; 2.03
deal kindly with my father's h., 2.12
for her h. was built into the city 2.15
into your h. your father and 2.18
doors of your h. into the street, 2.19
any one who is with you in the h., 2.19
are with her in her h. shall live, 6.17
the land, "Go into the harlot's h., 6.22
the treasury of the h. of the LORD. 6.24
of water for the h. of my God." 9.23
Then Joshua said to the h. of Joseph, 17.17
and the h. of Joseph in their 18.05
had made to the h. of Israel had 21.45
but as for me and my h., we will 24.15
out of the h. of bondage, and who 24.17
The h. of Joseph also went up Ju 1.22
And the h. of Joseph sent to spy 1.23
the hand of the h. of Joseph 1.35
Hazor and the h. of Heber the 4.17
you out of the h. of bondage; 6.08
went into his h. and prepared a 6.19
Joash went and dwelt in his own h. 8.29
out of the h. of Baalberith with 9.04
went to his father's h. at Ophrah, 9.05
well with Jerubbaal and his h., 9.16
up against my father's h. this day, 9.18
Jerubbaal and with his h. this day, 9.19
and went into the h. of their god, 9.27
stronghold of the h. of Elberith. 9.46
and against the h. of Ephraim; 10.09
not inherit in our father's h.; 11.02
and drive me out of my father's h.? 11.07
from the doors of my h. to meet me, 11.31
will burn your h. over you with 12.01
you and your father's h. with fire. 14.15
he went back to his father's h. 14.19
the pillars on which the h. rests, 16.26
Now the h. was full of men and 16.27
pillars upon which the h. rested, 16.29
and the h. fell upon the lords and 16.30
and it was in the h. of Micah. 17.04
of Ephraim to the h. of Micah. 17.08
priest, and was in the h. of Micah. 17.12
to the h. of Micah, and lodged there 18.02
When they were by the h. of Micah, 18.03
and came to the h. of Micah. 18.13
and came to the h. of the young 18.15
into Micah's h. and took the 18.18
to be priest to the h. of one man, 18.19
near Micah's h. were called out, 18.22
as long as the h. of God was at 18.31
to her father's h. at Bethlehem in 19.02
And he came to her father's h.; 19.03
them into his h. to spend the 19.15
and nobody takes me into his h. 19.18
So he brought him into his h., 19.21
beset the h. round about, beating on 19.22
the old man, the master of the h., 19.22
out the man who came into your h., 19.22
And the man, the master of the h., 19.23
that this man has come into my h., 19.23
of the man's h. where her master 19.26
doors of the h. and went out to go 19.27
lying at the door of the h., 19.27
And when he entered his h., 19.29
and beset the h. round about me by 20.05
none of us will return to his h. 20.08
each of you to her mother's h. Ru 1.08
of you in the h. of her husband!" 1.09
woman, who is coming into your h., 4.11
together built up the h. of Israel. 4.11
your h. be like the h. of Perez, 4.12
she went up to the h. of the LORD, 1Sa 1.07
went back to their h. at Ramah. 1.19
and all his h. went up to offer to 1.21
him to the h. of the LORD at 1.24
myself to the h. of your father 2.27
Egypt subject to the h. of Pharaoh. 2.27
I gave to the h. of your father 2.28
your h. and the h. of your father 2.30
the strength of your father's h., 2.31
will not be an old man in your h. 2.31
be an old man in your h. for ever. 2.32
increase of your h. shall die by 2.33
and I will build him a sure h., 2.35
is left in your h. shall come to 2.36
I have spoken concerning his h., 3.12
am about to punish his h. for ever, 3.13
Therefore I swear to the h. of Eli 3.14
of Eli's h. shall not be expiated 3.14
the doors of the h. of the LORD. 3.15
it into the h. of Dagon and set it 5.02
who enter the h. of Dagon do not 5.05
it to the h. of Abinadab on the 7.01
and all the h. of Israel lamented 7.02
said to all the h. of Israel, 7.03
me where is the h. of the seer?" 9.18
you and for all your father's h.?" 9.20
went up to his h. in Gibeah of 15.34
his father's h. free in Israel." 17.25
let him return to his father's h. 18.02
Saul, and he raved within his h., 18.10
he sat in his h. with his spear in 19.09
messengers to David's h. to watch him, 19.11
your loyalty from my h. for ever. 20.15
be cut off from the h. of David. 20.16
shall this fellow come into my h.?" 21.15
and all his father's h. heard it, 22.01
of Ahitub, and all his father's h., 22.11
bodyguard, and honored in your h.? 22.14
or to all the h. of my father; 22.15
you and all your father's h." 22.16
the persons of your father's h. 22.22
my name out of my father's h." 24.21
they buried him in his h. at Ramah. 25.01
be to you, and peace be to your h., 25.06
our master and against all his h., 25.17
certainly make my lord a sure h., 25.28
to her, "Go up in peace to your h.; 25.35
he was holding a feast in his h., 25.36
woman had a fatted calf in the h., 28.24
the LORD and for the h. of Israel, 2Sa 1.12
David king over the h. of Judah. 2.04
and the h. of Judah has anointed me 2.07
But the h. of Judah followed David. 2.10
Hebron over the h. of Judah was 2.11
war between the h. of Saul and the 3.01
of Saul and the h. of David; and 3.01
while the h. of Saul became weaker 3.01
war between the h. of Saul and the 3.06
of Saul and the h. of David, Abner 3.06
himself strong in the h. of Saul. 3.06
loyalty to the h. of Saul your 3.08
the kingdom from the h. of Saul, 3.10
and the whole h. of Benjamin 3.19
Joab, and upon all his father's h.; 3.29
and may the h. of Joab never be 3.29
they came to the h. of Ishbosheth, 4.05
doorkeeper of the h. had been 4.06
When they came into the h., 4.07
man in his own h. upon his bed, 4.11
lame shall not come into the h." 5.08
and masons who built David a h. 5.11
it out of the h. of Abinadab which 6.03
and all the h. of Israel were 6.05
it aside to the h. of Obededom the 6.10
remained in the h. of Obededom the 6.11

HOUSE (cont.)
of God from the h. of Obededom to 2Sa 6.12
and all the h. of Israel brought 6.15
people departed, each to his h. 6.19
your father, and above all his h., 6.21
Now when the king dwelt in his h., 7.01
I dwell in a h. of cedar, but the 7.02
you build me a h. to dwell in? 7.05
not dwelt in a h. since the day I 7.06
you not built me a h. of cedar?"' 7.07
that the LORD will make you a h. 7.11
He shall build a h. for my name, 7.13
And your h. and your kingdom shall 7.16
I, O Lord GOD, and what is my h., 7.18
thy servant's h. for a great while 7.19
thy servant and concerning his h., 7.25
and the h. of thy servant David will 7.26
saying, 'I will build you a h.'; 7.27
to bless the h. of thy servant, 7.29
shall the h. of thy servant be 7.29
any one left of the h. of Saul, 9.01
servant of the h. of Saul whose 9.02
still some one of the h. of Saul, 9.03
"He is in the h. of Machir the son 9.04
him from the h. of Machir the son 9.05
and to all his h. I have given to 9.09
dwelt in Ziba's h. became Mephibosheth's 9.12
upon the roof of the king's h., 11.02
Then she returned to her h. 11.04
said to Uriah, "Go down to your h., 11.08
Uriah went out of the king's h., 11.08
of the king's h. with all the 11.09
and did not go down to his h. 11.09
"Uriah did not go down to his h.," 11.10
Why did you not go down to your h.?" 11.10
shall I then go to my h., to eat and 11.11
but he did not go down to his h. 11.13
sent and brought her to his h., 11.27
and I gave you your master's h., 12.08
gave you the h. of Israel and of 12.08
shall never depart from your h., 12.10
against you out of your own h.; 12.11
Then Nathan went to his h. 12.15
elders of his h. stood beside him, 12.17
he went into the h. of the LORD, 12.20
he then went to his own h.; 12.20
"Go to your brother Amnon's h., 13.07
went to her brother Amon's h., 13.08
woman, in her brother Absalom's h. 13.20
"Go to your h., and I will give 14.08
the king, and on my father's h.; 14.09
"Let him dwell apart in his own h.; 14.24
Absalom dwelt apart in his own h., 14.24
and went to Absalom at his h., 14.31
left ten concubines to keep the h. 15.16
and they halted at the last h. 15.17
you hear from the king's h., 15.35
'Today the h. of Israel will give 16.03
of the family of the h. of Saul, 16.05
all the blood of the h. of Saul, 16.08
whom he has left to keep the h.; 16.21
and came to the h. of a man at 17.18
came to the woman at the h., 17.20
And he set his h. in order, 17.23
Then Joab came into the h. to the king, 19.05
to bring the king back to his h., 19.11
Ziba the servant of the h. of Saul, 19.17
of all the h. of Joseph to come 19.20
For all my father's h. were but men 19.28
And David came to his h. at Jerusalem; 20.03
he had left to care for the h., 20.03
and put them in a h. under guard, 20.03
blood guilt on Saul and on his h., 21.01
gold between us and Saul or his h.; 21.04
does not my h. stand so with God? 23.05
me and against my father's h." 24.17
Solomon said to him, "Go to your h." 1Ki 1.53
father, and who has made me a h., 2.24
concerning the h. of Eli in Shiloh. 2.27
my father's h. the guilt for the 2.31
and to his h., and to his throne, 2.33
in his own h. in the wilderness. 2.34
"Build yourself a h. in Jerusalem, 2.36
his own h. and the h. of the LORD 3.01
because no h. had yet been built 3.02
woman and I dwell in the same h.; 3.17
to a child while she was in the h. 3.17
was no one else with us in the h., 3.18
only we two were in the h. 3.18
not build a h. for the name of the 5.03
to build a h. for the name of the 5.05
shall build the h. for my name.' 5.05
foundation of the h. with dressed 5.17
and the stone to build the h. 5.18
began to build the h. of the LORD. 6.01
The h. which King Solomon built for 6.02
the nave of the h. was twenty 6.03
long, equal to the width of the h., 6.03
ten cubits deep in front of the h. 6.03
And he made for the h. windows with 6.04
structure against the wall of the h., 6.05
running round the walls of the h., 6.05
outside of the h. he made offsets 6.06
inserted into the walls of the h. 6.06
When the h. was built, it was with 6.07
was on the south side of the h.; 6.08
So he built the h., and finished it 6.09
ceiling of the h. of beams and 6.09
the structure against the whole h., 6.10
joined to the h. with timbers of 6.10
"Concerning this h. which you are 6.12
So Solomon built the h., and finished 6.14
walls of the h. on the inside with 6.15
floor of the h. to the rafters of 6.15
floor of the h. with boards of 6.15
the rear of the h. with boards of 6.16
The h., that is, the nave in front 6.17
within the h. was carved in the 6.18
in the innermost part of the h., 6.19
inside of the h. with pure gold, 6.21
he overlaid the whole h. with gold, 6.22
until all the h. was finished. 6.22
in the innermost part of the h.; 6.27
each other in the middle of the h. 6.27
walls of the h. round about with 6.29
The floor of the h. he overlaid 6.30
foundation of the h. of the LORD 6.37
the h. was finished in all its 6.38
building his own h. thirteen years, 7.01
and he finished his entire h. 7.01
He built the H. of the Forest of 7.02
His own h. where he was to dwell, in 7.08
also made a h. like this hall for 7.08
court of the h. of the LORD to the 7.09
inner court of the h. of the LORD, 7.12
LORD, and the vestibule of the h. 7.12
five on the south side of the h., 7.39
five on the north side of the h.; 7.39
on the southeast corner of the h. 7.39
Solomon on the h. of the LORD: 7.40
vessels in the h. of the LORD, 7.45
that were in the h. of the LORD: 7.48
of the innermost part of the h., 7.50
did on the h. of the LORD was 7.51
treasuries of the h. of the LORD. 7.51
in the inner sanctuary of the h., 8.06
a cloud filled the h. of the LORD, 8.10
the LORD filled the h. of the LORD. 8.11
I have built thee an exalted h., 8.13
of Israel in which to build a h., 8.16
to build a h. for the name of the 8.17
heart to build a h. for my name, 8.18
nevertheless you shall not build the h., 8.19
you shall build the h. for my name.' 8.19

HOUSE (cont.)

have built the h. for the name of 1Ki 8.20
much less this h. which I have 8.27
open night and day toward this h., 8.29
before thine altar in this h., 8.31
supplication to thee in this h.; 8.33
out his hands toward this h.; 8.38
he comes and prays toward this h., 8.42
know that this h. which I have 8.43
chosen and the h. which I have 8.44
and the h. which I have built for 8.48
dedicated the h. of the LORD. 8.63
that was before the h. of the LORD; 8.64
building the h. of the LORD and 9.01
and the king's h. and all that 9.01
consecrated this h. which you have 9.03
and the h. which I have consecrated 9.07
And this h. will become a heap of 9.08
thus to this land and to this h.?' 9.08
the h. of the LORD and the king's h., 9.10
to build the h. of the LORD and 9.15
and his own h. and the Millo and 9.15
to her own h. which Solomon had 9.24
the LORD. So he finished the h. 9.25
the h. that he had built, 10.04
he offered at the h. of the LORD, 10.05
supports for the h. of the LORD, 10.12
of the LORD, and for the king's h., 10.12
put them in the H. of the Forest 10.17
vessels of the H. of the Forest of 10.21
he was of the royal h. in Edom. 11.14
king of Egypt, who gave him a h., 11.18
Tahpenes weaned in Pharaoh's h.; 11.20
in Pharaoh's h. among the sons of 11.20
forced labor of the h. of Joseph. 11.28
you, and will build you a sure h., 11.38
Look now to your own h., David." 12.16
against the h. of David to this 12.19
none that followed the h. of David, 12.20
he assembled all the h. of Judah, 12.21
to fight against the h. of Israel, 12.21
and to all the h. of Judah and 12.23
will turn back to the h. of David; 12.26
sacrifices in the h. of the LORD at 12.27
shall be born to the h. of David, 13.02
king, "If you give me half your h., 13.08
you into your h. that he may eat 13.18
with him, and ate bread in his h., 13.19
became sin to the h. of Jeroboam, 13.34
and came to the h. of Ahijah. 14.04
away from the h. of David and gave 14.08
bring evil upon the h. of Jeroboam, 14.10
utterly consume the h. of Jeroboam, 14.10
Arise therefore, go to your h. 14.12
of Israel, in the h. of Jeroboam. 14.13
cut off the h. of Jeroboam today. 14.14
came to the threshold of the h., 14.17
treasures of the h. of the LORD and 14.26
and the treasures of the king's h.; 14.26
who kept the door of the king's h. 14.27
king went into the h. of the LORD, 14.28
into the h. of the LORD the votive 15.15
treasures of the h. of the LORD and 15.18
and the treasures of the king's h., 15.18
of the h. of Issachar, conspired 15.27
he killed all the h. of Jeroboam; 15.29
he left to the h. of Jeroboam not 15.29
sweep away Baasha and his h., 16.03
make your h. like the h. of Jeroboam 16.03
Hanani against Baasha and his h., 16.07
in being like the h. of Jeroboam, 16.07
himself drunk in the h. of Arza, 16.09
he killed all the h. of Baasha; 16.11
destroyed all the h. of Baasha, 16.12
into the citadel of the king's h., 16.18
the king's h. over him with fire, 16.18
altar for Baal in the h. of Baal, 16.32

the mistress of the h., became ill; 17.17
from the upper chamber into the h., 17.23
but you have, and your father's h., 18.18
search your h. and the houses of 20.06
kings of the h. of Israel are 20.31
went to his h. resentful and 20.43
garden, because it is near my h.; 21.02
went into his h. vexed and sullen 21.04
make your h. like the h. of Jeroboam 21.22
and like the h. of Baasha the son 21.22
I will bring the evil upon his h." 21.29
and the ivory h. which he built, and 22.39
what have you in the h.?" 2Ki 4.02
maidservant has nothing in the h., 4.02
When Elisha came into the h., 4.32
walked once to and fro in the h., 4.35
halted at the door of Elisha's h. 5.09
goes into the h. of Rimmon to 5.18
I bow myself in the h. of Rimmon, 5.18
I bow myself in the h. of Rimmon, 5.18
their hand, and put them in the h.; 5.24
Elisha was sitting in his h., 6.32
the king for her h. and her land. 8.03
the king for her h. and her land. 8.05
as the h. of Ahab had done, for the 8.18
in the way of the h. of Ahab, 8.27
as the h. of Ahab had done, for he 8.27
was son-in-law to the h. of Ahab. 8.27
So he arose, and went into the h.; 9.06
strike down the h. of Ahab your 9.07
For the whole h. of Ahab shall 9.08
And I will make the h. of Ahab like 9.09
Ahab like the h. of Jeroboam the 9.09
and like the h. of Baasha the son 9.09
and fight for your master's h." 10.03
spoke concerning the h. of Ahab; 10.10
remained of the h. of Ahab in 10.11
And they entered the h. of Baal, 10.21
and the h. of Baal was filled from 10.21
went into the h. of Baal with 10.23
the inner room of the h. of Baal 10.25
pillar that was in the h. of Baal, 10.26
and demolished the h. of Baal, 10.27
done to the h. of Ahab according 10.30
hid in the h. of the LORD, while 11.03
come to him in the h. of the LORD; 11.04
under oath in the h. of the LORD, 11.04
sabbath and guard the king's h. 11.05
and guard the h. of the LORD, 11.07
which were in the h. of the LORD; 11.10
from the south side of the h. to 11.11
to the north side of the h., 11.11
around the altar and the h. 11.11
went into the h. of the LORD to 11.13
not be slain in the h. of the LORD." 11.15
horses' entrance to the king's h., 11.16
of the land went to the h. of Baal, 11.18
watchmen over the h. of the LORD. 11.18
king down from the h. of the LORD, 11.19
of the guards to the king's h. 11.19
with the sword at the king's h. 11.20
is brought into the h. of the LORD, 12.04
to bring into the h. of the LORD, 12.04
them repair the h. wherever any 12.05
had made no repairs on the h. 12.06
"Why are you not repairing the h.? 12.07
it over for the repair of the h." 12.07
that they should not repair the h. 12.08
as one entered the h. of the LORD; 12.09
brought into the h. of the LORD. 12.09
was found in the h. of the LORD. 12.10
oversight of the h. of the LORD; 12.11
worked upon the h. of the LORD, 12.11
repairs on the h. of the LORD, 12.12
outlay upon the repairs of the h. 12.12
made for the h. of the LORD basins 12.13
brought into the h. of the LORD, 12.13

HOUSE (cont.)
repairing the h. of the LORD with 2Ki 12.14
brought into the h. of the LORD; 12.16
treasuries of the h. of the LORD 12.18
of the LORD and of the king's h., 12.18
and slew Joash in the h. of Millo, 12.20
the sins of the h. of Jeroboam, 13.06
found in the h. of the LORD and in 14.14
in the treasuries of the king's h., 14.14
and he dwelt in a separate h. 15.05
in the citadel of the king's h.; 15.25
upper gate of the h. of the LORD. 15.35
found in the h. of the LORD and in 16.08
in the treasures of the king's h., 16.08
removed from the front of the h., 16.14
his altar and the h. of the LORD, 16.14
he removed from the h. of the LORD, 16.18
Israel from the h. of David they 17.21
was found in the h. of the LORD, 18.15
in the treasuries of the king's h. 18.15
and went into the h. of the LORD. 19.01
went up to the h. of the LORD, 19.14
remnant of the h. of Judah shall 19.30
worshiping in the h. of Nisroch his 19.37
the LORD, 'Set your h. in order; 20.01
shall go up to the h. of the LORD. 20.05
go up to the h. of the LORD on the 20.08
he showed them all his treasure h., 20.13
nothing in his h. or in all his 20.13
"What have they seen in your h." 20.15
have seen all that is in my h.; 20.15
when all that is in your h., 20.17
built altars in the h. of the LORD, 21.04
two courts of the h. of the LORD. 21.05
he set in the h. of which the LORD 21.07
"In this h., and in Jerusalem, which 21.07
and the plummet of the h. of Ahab; 21.13
was buried in the garden of his h., 21.18
him, and killed the king in his h. 21.23
to the h. of the LORD, saying, 22.03
brought into the h. of the LORD, 22.04
oversight of the h. of the LORD; 22.05
who are at the h. of the LORD, 22.05
of the LORD, repairing the h., 22.05
quarried stone to repair the h. 22.06
of the law in the h. of the LORD." 22.08
the money that was found in the h., 22.09
oversight of the h. of the LORD." 22.09
king went up to the h. of the LORD, 23.02
been found in the h. of the LORD. 23.02
Asherah from the h. of the LORD, 23.06
which were in the h. of the LORD, 23.07
the entrance to the h. of the LORD, 23.11
two courts of the h. of the LORD, 23.12
priest found in the h. of the LORD. 23.24
and the h. of which I said, My name 23.27
treasures of the h. of the LORD, 24.13
and the treasures of the king's h., 24.13
And he burned the h. of the LORD, 25.09
and the king's h. and all the 25.09
every great h. he burned down. 25.09
that were in the h. of the LORD, 25.13
that were in the h. of the LORD, 25.13
had made for the h. of the LORD, 25.16
the father of the h. of Rechab. 1Ch 2.55
families of the h. of linen workers 4.21
priest in the h. that Solomon 6.10
of song in the h. of the LORD, 6.31
had built the h. of the LORD in 6.32
of the tabernacle of the h. of God. 6.48
because evil had befallen his h. 7.23
the chief officer of the h. of God; 9.11
of the service of the h. of God. 9.13
and his kinsmen of his fathers' h., 9.19
of the gates of the h. of the LORD, 9.23
the h. of the tent, as guards. 9.23
and the treasures of the h. of God. 9.26
lodged round about the h. of God; 9.27
sons and all his h. died together. 10.06
of the h. of Aaron, and with him 12.27
commanders from his own father's h. 12.28
their allegiance to the h. of Saul. 12.29
from the h. of Abinadab, and Uzzah 13.07
it aside to the h. of Obededom the 13.13
of Obededom in his h. three months; 13.14
carpenters to build a h. for him. 14.01
LORD from the h. of Obededom with 15.25
the people departed each to his h., 16.43
Now when David dwelt in his h., 17.01
I dwell in a h. of cedar, but the 17.01
not build me a h. to dwell in. 17.04
not dwelt in a h. since the day I 17.05
you not built me a h. of cedar?"' 17.06
that the LORD will build you a h. 17.10
He shall build a h. for me, 17.12
him in my h. and in my kingdom for 17.14
I, O LORD God, and what is my h., 17.16
thy servant's h. for a great while 17.17
concerning his h. be established 17.23
and the h. of thy servant David 17.24
that thou wilt build a h. for him; 17.25
to bless the h. of thy servant, 17.27
me and against my father's h.; 21.17
shall be the h. of the LORD God 22.01
stones for building the h. of God. 22.02
and the h. that is to be built for 22.05
him to build a h. for the LORD, 22.06
to build a h. to the name of the 22.07
shall not build a h. to my name, 22.08
He shall build a h. for my name. 22.10
in building the h. of the LORD 22.11
provided for the h. of the LORD a 22.14
brought into a h. built for the 22.19
of the work in the h. of the LORD, 23.04
a father's h. on one reckoning. 23.11
the service of the h. of the LORD. 23.24
the service of the h. of the LORD, 23.28
for the service of the h. of God; 23.28
the service of the h. of the LORD." 23.32
one father's h. being chosen for 24.06
come into the h. of the LORD 24.19
each father's h. and his younger 24.31
music in the h. of the LORD with 25.06
for the service of the h. of God. 25.06
ministering in the h. of the LORD; 26.12
treasuries of the h. of God and the 26.20
treasuries of the h. of the LORD. 26.22
maintenance of the h. of the LORD. 26.27
to build a h. of rest for the ark 28.02
You may not build a h. for my name, 28.03
all my father's h. to be king over 28.04
and in the h. of Judah my father's h., 28.04
shall build my h. and my courts, 28.06
you to build a h. for the sanctuary; 28.10
the courts of the h. of the LORD, 28.12
the treasuries of the h. of God, 28.12
the service in the h. of the LORD; 28.13
the service in the h. of the LORD, 28.13
service of the h. of the LORD is 28.20
all the service of the h. of God; 28.21
have provided for the h. of my God, 29.02
I have provided for the holy h., 29.03
devotion to the h. of my God I 29.03
God I give it to the h. of my God; 29.03
overlaying the walls of the h., 29.04
service of the h. of God five 29.07
the treasury of the h. of the LORD, 29.08
building thee a h. for thy holy 29.16
to build himself a h. to dwell in, 2Ch 2.03
to build a h. for the name of the 2.04
The h. which I am to build will be 2.05
But who is able to build him a h., 2.06
Who am I to build a h. for him, 2.06
for the h. I am to build will be 2.09

HOUSE (cont.)
to build the h. of the LORD in 2Ch 3.01
measurements for building the h. of God: 3.03
the nave of the h. was twenty 3.04
long, equal to the width of the h.; 3.04
He adorned the h. with settings of 3.06
So he lined the h. with gold— 3.07
corresponding to the breadth of the h., 3.08
cubits, touched the wall of the h., 3.11
cubits, touched the wall of the h., 3.12
In front of the h. he made two 3.15
at the southeast corner of the h. 4.10
for King Solomon on the h. of God: 4.11
Solomon for the h. of the LORD. 4.16
things that were in the h. of God: 4.19
did for the h. of the LORD was 5.01
in the treasuries of the h. of God. 5.01
in the inner sanctuary of the h., 5.07
the h., the h. of the LORD, was filled 5.13
of the LORD filled the h. of God. 5.14
I have built thee an exalted h., 6.02
of Israel in which to build a h., 6.05
to build a h. for the name of the 6.07
heart to build a h. for my name, 6.08
nevertheless you shall not build the h., 6.09
you shall build the h. for my name.' 6.09
have built the h. for the name of 6.10
much less this h. which I have 6.18
open day and night toward this h., 6.20
oath before thy altar in this h., 6.22
supplication to thee in this h., 6.24
out his hands toward this h.; 6.29
he comes and prays toward this h., 6.32
know that this h. which I have 6.33
chosen and the h. which I have 6.34
and the h. which I have built for 6.38
could not enter the h. of the LORD, 7.02
of the LORD filled the LORD's h. 7.02
the people dedicated the h. of God. 7.05
that was before the h. of the LORD; 7.07
finished the h. of the LORD and 7.11
of the LORD and the king's h.; 7.11
to do in the h. of the LORD and in 7.11
and in his own h. he successfully 7.11
for myself as a h. of sacrifice. 7.12
consecrated this h. that my name 7.16
and this h., which I have consecrated 7.20
And at this h., which is exalted, 7.21
thus to this land and to this h.?' 7.21
had built the h. of the LORD and 8.01
of the LORD and his own h., 8.01
of David to the h. which he had 8.11
not live in the h. of David king 8.11
foundation of the h. of the LORD 8.16
So the h. of the LORD was completed. 8.16
the h. that he had built, 9.03
he offered at the h. of the LORD, 9.04
steps for the h. of the LORD and 9.11
of the LORD and for the king's h., 9.11
put them in the H. of the Forest 9.16
vessels of the H. of the Forest of 9.20
Look now to your own h., David." 10.16
against the h. of David to this 10.19
he assembled the h. of Judah, 11.01
treasures of the h. of the LORD and 12.09
and the treasures of the king's h.; 12.09
who kept the door of the king's h. 12.10
king went into the h. of the LORD, 12.11
vestibule of the h. of the LORD. 15.08
into the h. of God the votive 15.18
treasures of the h. of the LORD and 16.02
of the LORD and the king's h., 16.02
in safety to his h. in Jerusalem. 19.01
the governor of the h. of Judah, 19.11
in the h. of the LORD, before the 20.05
we will stand before this h., 20.09
thee, for thy name is in this h., 20.09
trumpets, to the h. of the LORD. 20.28
as the h. of Ahab had done; 21.06
would not destroy the h. of David, 21.07
as the h. of Ahab led Israel into 21.13
your brothers, of your father's h., 21.13
that belonged to the king's h., 21.17
in the ways of the h. of Ahab, 22.03
as the h. of Ahab had done; 22.04
anointed to destroy the h. of Ahab. 22.07
judgment upon the h. of Ahab, 22.08
And the h. of Ahaziah had no one 22.09
royal family of the h. of Judah. 22.10
hid in the h. of God, while Athaliah 22.12
with the king in the h. of God. 23.03
at the king's h. and one third at 23.05
the courts of the h. of the LORD. 23.05
one enter the h. of the LORD 23.06
enters the h. shall be slain. 23.07
which were in the h. of God; 23.09
side of the h. to the north side of the h., 23.10
around the altar and the h. 23.10
went into the h. of the LORD to 23.12
not slay her in the h. of the LORD." 23.14
of the horse gate of the king's h., 23.15
the people went to the h. of Baal, 23.17
watchmen for the h. of the LORD 23.18
be in charge of the h. of the LORD, 23.18
gates of the h. of the LORD so 23.19
king down from the h. of the LORD, 23.20
the upper gate to the king's h. 23.20
to restore the h. of the LORD. 24.04
to repair the h. of your God from 24.05
had broken into the h. of God; 24.07
things of the h. of the LORD for 24.07
the gate of the h. of the LORD. 24.08
of the work of the h. of the LORD, 24.12
to restore the h. of the LORD, 24.12
to repair the h. of the LORD. 24.12
restored the h. of God to its 24.13
utensils for the h. of the LORD, 24.14
offerings in the h. of the LORD 24.14
Israel, and toward God and his h. 24.16
And they forsook the h. of the LORD, 24.18
in the court of the h. of the LORD. 24.21
rebuilding of the h. of God are 24.27
that were found in the h. of God, 25.24
the treasuries of the king's h., 25.24
the priests in the h. of the LORD, 26.19
a leper dwelt in a separate h., 26.21
excluded from the h. of the LORD. 26.21
upper gate of the h. of the LORD, 27.03
took from the h. of the LORD and 28.21
LORD and the h. of the king and of 28.21
vessels of the h. of God and cut 28.24
the vessels of the h. of God, 28.24
up the doors of the h. of the LORD; 28.24
the doors of the h. of the LORD, 29.03
and sanctify the h. of the LORD, 29.05
to cleanse the h. of the LORD. 29.15
part of the h. of the LORD to 29.16
the court of the h. of the LORD; 29.16
they sanctified the h. of the LORD, 29.17
cleansed all the h. of the LORD, 29.18
and went up to the h. of the LORD. 29.20
Levites in the h. of the LORD with 29.25
offerings to the h. of the LORD." 29.31
service of the h. of the LORD was 29.35
come to the h. of the LORD at 30.01
offerings into the h. of the LORD. 30.15
priest, who was of the h. of Zadok, 31.10
into the h. of the LORD we have 31.10
chambers in the h. of the LORD; 31.11
the chief officer of the h. of God. 31.13
who entered the h. of the LORD as 31.16
service of the h. of God and in 31.21
he came into the h. of his god, 32.21
built altars in the h. of the LORD, 33.04

HOUSE (cont.)
two courts of the h. of the LORD. 2Ch 33.05
had made he set in the h. of God, 33.07
"In this h., and in Jerusalem, which 33.07
the idol from the h. of the LORD, 33.15
mountain of the h. of the LORD and 33.15
and they buried him in his h.; 33.20
him and killed him in his h. 33.24
he had purged the land and the h., 34.08
to repair the h. of the LORD his 34.08
been brought in to the h. of God, 34.09
oversight of the h. of the LORD; 34.10
working in the h. of the LORD gave 34.10
for repairing and restoring the h. 34.10
brought into the h. of the LORD, 34.14
of the law in the h. of the LORD"; 34.15
found in the h. of the LORD and 34.17
king went up to the h. of the LORD, 34.30
been found in the h. of the LORD. 34.30
the service of the h. of the LORD. 35.02
holy ark in the h. which Solomon 35.03
of a father's h. of the Levites. 35.05
chief officers of the h. of God, 35.08
but against the h. with which I am 35.21
vessels of the h. of the LORD to 36.07
vessels of the h. of the LORD, 36.10
polluted the h. of the LORD which 36.14
sword in the h. of their sanctuary, 36.17
And all the vessels of the h. of God, 36.18
treasures of the h. of the LORD, 36.18
And they burned the h. of God, 36.19
me to build him a h. at Jerusalem, 36.23
me to build him a h. at Jerusalem, Ez 1.02
and rebuild the h. of the LORD, 1.03
offerings for the h. of God which 1.04
to rebuild the h. of the LORD 1.05
vessels of the h. of the LORD 1.07
and placed in the h. of his gods. 1.07
of the h. of Jeshua, nine hundred 2.36
came to the h. of the LORD which 2.68
offerings for the h. of God, 2.68
coming to the h. of God at Jerusalem, 3.08
of the work of the h. of the LORD. 3.08
of the workmen in the h. of God, 3.09
foundation of the h. of the LORD 3.11
old men who had seen the first h., 3.12
foundation of this h. being laid, 3.12
us in building a h. to our God; 4.03
Then the work on the h. of God 4.24
to rebuild the h. of God which is 5.02
to build this h. and to finish 5.03
to the h. of the great God. 5.08
to build this h. and to finish 5.09
rebuilding the h. that was built 5.11
destroyed this h. and carried away 5.12
that this h. of God should be 5.13
silver vessels of the h. of God, 5.14
and let the h. of God be rebuilt on 5.15
foundations of the h. of God which 5.16
rebuilding of this h. of God in 5.17
in the h. of the archives where the 6.01
Concerning the h. of God at 6.03
let the h. be rebuilt, the place 6.03
silver vessels of the h. of God, 6.05
shall put them in the h. of God." 6.05
let the work on this h. of God alone; 6.07
rebuild this h. of God on its site. 6.07
the rebuilding of this h. of God; 6.08
beam shall be pulled out of his h., 6.11
and his h. shall be made a dunghill. 6.11
to destroy this h. of God which is 6.12
and this h. was finished on the 6.15
dedication of this h. of God with 6.16
dedication of this h. of God one 6.17
them in the work of the h. of God, 6.22
willingly for the h. of their God 7.16
altar of the h. of your God which 7.17
the service of the h. of your God, 7.19
is required for the h. of your God, 7.20
in full for the h. of the God of 7.23
other servants of this h. of God. 7.24
to beautify the h. of the LORD 7.27
us ministers for the h. of our God. 8.17
offering for the h. of our God 8.25
the chambers of the h. of the LORD." 8.29
to Jerusalem, to the h. of our God. 8.30
within the h. of our God, the silver 8.33
aided the people and the h. of God. 8.36
to set up the h. of our God, 9.09
himself down before the h. of God, 10.01
withdrew from before the h. of God, 10.06
open square before the h. of God, 10.09
I and my father's h. have sinned. Neh 1.06
and for the h. which I shall occupy." 2.08
Harumaph repaired opposite his h.; 3.10
and to the h. of the mighty men. 3.16
the door of the h. of Eliashib the 3.20
the door of the h. of Eliashib to 3.21
to the end of the h. of Eliashib. 3.21
Hasshub repaired opposite their h. 3.23
Ananiah repaired beside his own h. 3.23
from the h. of Azariah to the Angle 3.24
from the upper h. of the king at 3.25
each one opposite his own h. 3.28
Immer repaired opposite his own h. 3.29
as far as the h. of the temple 3.31
stood behind all the h. of Judah, 4.16
man from his h. and from his labor 5.13
I went into the h. of Shemaiah the 6.10
us meet together in the h. of God, 6.10
and each opposite his own h." 7.03
namely the h. of Jeshua, nine 7.39
and in the courts of the h. of God, 8.16
the service of the h. of our God: 10.32
all the work of the h. of our God. 10.33
to bring it into the h. of our God, 10.34
by year, to the h. of the LORD; 10.35
also to bring to the h. of our God, 10.36
who minister in the h. of our God, 10.36
the chambers of the h. of our God; 10.37
of the tithes to the h. of our God, 10.38
will not neglect the h. of our God. 10.39
of Ahitub, ruler of the h. of God, 11.11
brethren who did the work of the h., 11.12
the outside work of the h. of God; 11.16
over the work of the h. of God. 11.22
above the h. of David, to the Water 12.37
gave thanks stood in the h. of God, 12.40
the chambers of the h. of our God, 13.04
in the courts of the h. of God. 13.07
the vessels of the h. of God, 13.09
"Why is the h. of God forsaken?" 13.11
done for the h. of my God and for 13.14
lord in his own h. and speak Est 1.22
and your father's h. will perish. 4.14
But Haman hurried to his h., 6.12
queen in my presence, in my own h." 7.08
king, is standing in Haman's h., 7.09
to Queen Esther the h. of Haman, 8.01
set Mordecai over the h. of Haman. 8.02
have given Esther the h. of Haman, 8.07
Mordecai was great in the king's h., 9.04
a feast in the h. of each on his Job 1.04
him and his h. and all that he has, 1.10
wine in their eldest brother's h.; 1.13
wine in their eldest brother's h.; 1.18
struck the four corners of the h., 1.19
he returns no more to his h., 7.10
He leans against his h., 8.15
If I look for Sheol as my h., 17.13
the guests in my h. have forgotten 19.15
he has seized a h. which he did 20.19
possessions of his h. will be 20.28
'Where is the h. of the prince? 21.28

HOUSE (cont.)

The h. which he builds is like a Job 27.18
and to the h. appointed for all 30.23
and ate bread with him in his h.; 42.11
steadfast love will enter thy h., Ps 5.07
dwell in the h. of the LORD for 23.06
I love the habitation of thy h., 26.08
dwell in the h. of the LORD all 27.04
They feast on the abundance of thy h., 36.08
in procession to the h. of God, 42.04
your people and your father's h.; 45.10
when the glory of his h. increases. 49.16
I will accept no bull from your h., 50.09
green olive tree in the h. of God. 52.08
within God's h. we walked in fellowship 55.14
with the goodness of thy h., 65.04
come into thy h. with burnt 66.13
For zeal for thy h. has consumed me, 69.09
Blessed are those who dwell in thy h., 84.04
doorkeeper in the h. of my God than 84.10
They are planted in the h. of the LORD, 92.13
holiness befits thy h., 93.05
faithfulness to the h. of Israel. 98.03
integrity of heart within my h.; 101.02
deceit shall dwell in my h.; 101.07
he made him lord of his h., 105.21
Wealth and riches are in his h.; 112.03
the h. of Jacob from a people of 114.01
O h. of Aaron, put your trust in the 115.10
he will bless the h. of Israel; 115.12
he will bless the h. of Aaron; 115.12
in the courts of the h. of the LORD, 116.19
Let the h. of Aaron say, "His 118.03
bless you from the h. of the LORD. 118.26
my songs in the h. of my pilgrimage. 119.54
"Let us go to the h. of the LORD!" 122.01
the thrones of the h. of David. 122.05
For the sake of the h. of the LORD 122.09
Unless the LORD builds the h., 127.01
a fruitful vine within your h.; 128.03
not enter my h. or get into my bed; 132.03
by night in the h. of the LORD! 134.01
you that stand in the h. of the LORD, 135.02
in the courts of the h. of our God! 135.02
O h. of Israel, bless the LORD! 135.19
O h. of Aaron, bless the LORD! 135.19
O h. of Levi, bless the LORD! 135.20
for her h. sinks down to death, and Pro 2.18
curse is on the h. of the wicked, 3.33
do not go near the door of her h.; 5.08
labors go to the h. of an alien; 5.10
will give all the goods of his h. 6.31
window of my h. I have looked out 7.06
corner, taking the road to her h. 7.08
Her h. is the way to Sheol, going 7.27
Wisdom has built her h., she has 9.01
She sits at the door of her h., 9.14
but the h. of the righteous will 12.07
Wisdom builds her h., but folly 14.01
The h. of the wicked will be 14.11
In the h. of the righteous there is 15.06
tears down the h. of the proud, 15.25
quiet than a h. full of feasting 17.01
evil will not depart from his h. 17.13
H. and wealth are inherited from 19.14
than in a h. shared with a contentious 21.09
observes the h. of the wicked; 21.12
By wisdom a h. is built, and by 24.03
and after that build your h. 24.27
be seldom in your neighbor's h., 25.17
than in a h. shared with a contentious 25.24
your brother's h. in the day of 27.10
had slaves who were born in my h.; Ecc 2.07
steps when you go to the h. of God; 5.01
to go to the h. of mourning than 7.02
than to go to the h. of feasting; 7.02
the wise is in the h. of mourning; 7.04
of fools is in the h. of mirth. 7.04
and through indolence the h. leaks. 10.18
when the keepers of the h. tremble, 12.03
the beams of our h. are cedar, Sol 1.17
He brought me to the banqueting h., 2.04
brought him into my mother's h., 3.04
bring you into the h. of my mother, 8.02
for love all the wealth of his h., 8.07
mountain of the h. of the LORD Is 2.02
to the h. of the God of Jacob; 2.03
O h. of Jacob, come, let us walk in 2.05
the h. of Jacob, because they are 2.06
brother in the h. of his father, 3.06
in my h. there is neither bread nor 3.07
LORD of hosts is the h. of Israel, 5.07
Woe to those who join h. to h., 5.08
and the h. was filled with smoke. 6.04
When the h. of David was told, 7.02
And he said, "Hear then, O h. of David! 7.13
your father's h. such days as have 7.17
his face from the h. of Jacob, 8.17
survivors of the h. of Jacob will 10.20
and will cleave to the h. of Jacob. 14.01
and the h. of Israel will possess 14.02
weapons of the h. of the forest, 22.08
you shame of your master's h. 22.18
Jerusalem and to the h. of Judah. 22.21
shoulder the key of the h. of David; 22.22
throne of honor to his father's h. 22.23
whole weight of his father's h., 22.24
is laid waste, without h. or haven! 23.01
every h. is shut up so that none 24.10
Abraham, concerning the h. of Jacob: 29.22
against the h. of the evildoers, 31.02
and went into the h. of the LORD. 37.01
went up to the h. of the LORD, 37.14
remnant of the h. of Judah shall 37.31
worshiping in the h. of Nisroch his 37.38
the LORD: Set your h. in order; 38.01
of our life, at the h. of the LORD. 38.20
shall go up to the h. of the LORD?" 38.22
and he showed them his treasure h., 39.02
nothing in his h. or in all his 39.02
"What have they seen in your h.?" 39.04
have seen all that is in my h.; 39.04
when all that is in your h., 39.06
beauty of a man, to dwell in a h. 44.13
O h. of Jacob, all the remnant of 46.03
the remnant of the h. of Israel, 46.03
Hear this, O h. of Jacob, who are 48.01
I will give in my h. and within my 56.05
them joyful in my h. of prayer; 56.07
my h. shall be called a h. of prayer 56.07
to the h. of Jacob their sins. 58.01
the homeless poor into your h.; 58.07
and I will glorify my glorious h. 60.07
goodness to the h. of Israel which 63.07
Our holy and beautiful h., 64.11
what is the h. which you would 66.01
clean vessel to the h. of the LORD. 66.20
O h. of Jacob, and all the families Jer 2.04
the families of the h. of Israel. 2.04
so the h. of Israel shall be shamed: 2.26
h. of Judah shall join the h. of Israel, 3.18
O h. of Israel, says the LORD.'" 3.20
the h. of Israel and the h. of Judah 5.11
O h. of Israel, says the LORD. 5.15
Declare this in the h. of Jacob, 5.20
"Stand in the gate of the LORD's h., 7.02
and stand before me in this h., 7.10
Has this h., which is called by my 7.11
will do to the h. which is called 7.14
abominations in the h. which is 7.30
and all the h. of Israel is uncircumcised 9.26
LORD speaks to you, O h. of Israel. 10.01
the h. of Israel and the h. of Judah 11.10
What right has my beloved in my h., 11.15

HOUSE (cont.)
the h. of Israel and the h. of Judah Jer 11.17
brothers and the h. of your father, 12.06
"I have forsaken my h., 12.07
pluck up the h. of Judah from 12.14
made the whole h. of Israel and 13.11
and the whole h. of Judah cling to 13.11
Do not enter the h. of mourning, 16.05
not go into the h. of feasting to 16.08
offerings to the h. of the LORD. 17.26
"Arise, and go down to the potter's h., 18.02
So I went down to the potter's h., 18.03
"O h. of Israel, can I not do with 18.06
are you in my hand, O h. of Israel. 18.06
in the court of the LORD's h., 19.14
officer in the h. of the LORD, 20.01
Benjamin Gate of the h. of the LORD. 20.02
and all who dwell in your h., 20.06
"And to the h. of the king of Judah 21.11
O h. of David! Thus says the LORD: 21.12
"Go down to the h. of the king of 22.01
gates of this h. kings who sit on 22.04
that this h. shall become a desolation. 22.05
concerning the h. of the king of 22.06
who builds his h. by unrighteousness, 22.13
myself a great h. with spacious 22.14
descendants of the h. of Israel out 23.08
even in my h. I have found their 23.11
in the court of the LORD's h., 26.02
worship in the h. of the LORD all 26.02
then I will make this h. like Shiloh, 26.06
these words in the h. of the LORD. 26.07
'This h. shall be like Shiloh, and 26.09
Jeremiah in the h. of the LORD. 26.09
came up from the king's h. to the 26.10
to the h. of the LORD and took their 26.10
the New Gate of the h. of the LORD. 26.10
against this h. and this city all 26.12
mountain of the h. a wooded height.' 26.18
of the LORD's h. will now shortly 27.16
are left in the h. of the LORD, 27.18
in the h. of the king of Judah, and 27.18
are left in the h. of the LORD, 27.21
in the h. of the king of Judah, and 27.21
spoke to me in the h. of the LORD, 28.01
all the vessels of the LORD's h., 28.03
standing in the h. of the LORD; 28.05
the vessels of the h. of the LORD, 28.06
charge in the h. of the LORD over 29.26
sow the h. of Israel and the h. of Judah 31.27
with the h. of Israel and the h. of Judah, 31.31
make with the h. of Israel after 31.33
abominations in the h. which is 32.34
offerings to the h. of the LORD: 33.11
to the h. of Israel and the h. of Judah. 33.14
on the throne of the h. of Israel, 33.17
out of the h. of bondage, saying, 34.13
me in the h. which is called by my 34.15
"Go to the h. of the Rechabites, and 35.02
bring them to the h. of the LORD, 35.02
and the whole h. of the Rechabites. 35.03
them to the h. of the LORD into 35.04
you shall not build a h.; 35.07
But to the h. of the Rechabites 35.18
It may be that the h. of Judah will 36.03
from going to the h. of the LORD; 36.05
in the LORD's h. you shall read 36.06
words of the LORD in the LORD's h. 36.08
in the h. of the LORD, in the 36.10
of the New Gate of the LORD's h. 36.10
he went down to the king's h., 36.12
in the winter h. and there was a 36.22
him in the h. of Jonathan the 37.15
questioned him secretly in his h., 37.17
me back to the h. of Jonathan the 37.20
a eunuch, who was in the king's h., 38.07
from the king's h. and said to the 38.08
him and went to the h. of the king, 38.11
and you and your h. shall live. 38.17
left in the h. of the king of 38.22
me back to the h. of Jonathan to 38.26
king's h. and the h. of the people, 39.08
as the h. of Israel was ashamed of 48.13
a flame from the h. of Sihon; 48.45
the holy places of the LORD's h.' 51.51
And he burned the h. of the LORD, 52.13
and the king's h. and all the 52.13
every great h. he burned down. 52.13
pillars of bronze that were in the h. 52.17
sea that were in the h. of the LORD, 52.17
had made for the h. of the LORD, 52.20
in the h. it is like death. Lam 1.20
raised in the h. of the LORD as on 2.07
a rebellious h.) they will know Eze 2.05
for they are a rebellious h. 2.06
for they are a rebellious h. 2.07
rebellious like that rebellious h.; 2.08
and go, speak to the h. of Israel." 3.01
go, get you to the h. of Israel, 3.04
language, but to the h. of Israel— 3.05
But the h. of Israel will not 3.07
because all the h. of Israel are of 3.07
for they are a rebellious h." 3.09
a watchman for the h. of Israel; 3.17
"Go, shut yourself within your h. 3.24
for they are a rebellious h. 3.26
for they are a rebellious h. 3.27
is a sign for the h. of Israel. 4.03
punishment of the h. of Israel upon 4.04
the punishment of the h. of Israel. 4.05
the punishment of the h. of Judah; 4.06
forth into all the h. of Israel. 5.04
abominations of the h. of Israel; 6.11
of the month, as I sat in my h., 8.01
that the h. of Israel are committing 8.06
all the idols of the h. of Israel. 8.10
of the elders of the h. of Israel, 8.11
elders of the h. of Israel are 8.12
north gate of the h. of the LORD; 8.14
inner court of the h. of the LORD; 8.16
a thing for the h. of Judah to 8.17
rested to the threshold of the h.; 9.03
the elders who were before the h. 9.06
"Defile the h., and fill the courts 9.07
guilt of the h. of Israel and 9.09
on the south side of the h., 10.03
cherubim to the threshold of the h.; 10.04
and the h. was filled with the 10.04
forth from the threshold of the h., 10.18
east gate of the h. of the LORD; 10.19
east gate of the h. of the LORD, 11.01
LORD: So you think, O h. of Israel; 11.05
the whole h. of Israel, all of them, 11.15
in the midst of a rebellious h., 12.02
for they are a rebellious h. 12.03
though they are a rebellious h. 12.03
you a sign for the h. of Israel." 12.06
the h. of Israel, the rebellious h., 12.09
and all the h. of Israel who are 12.10
divination within the h. of Israel. 12.24
O rebellious h., I will speak the 12.25
they of the h. of Israel say, 'The 12.27
up a wall for the h. of Israel, 13.05
the register of the h. of Israel, 13.09
Any man of the h. of Israel who 14.04
of the hearts of the h. of Israel, 14.05
"Therefore say to the h. of Israel, 14.06
For any one of the h. of Israel, 14.07
that the h. of Israel may go no 14.11
an allegory to the h. of Israel; 17.02
"Say now to the rebellious h., 17.12
to the idols of the h. of Israel, 18.06
to the idols of the h. of Israel, 18.15
Hear now, O h. of Israel: Is my way 18.25

HOUSE (cont.)
Yet the h. of Israel says, 'The way Eze 18.29
O h. of Israel, are my ways not 18.29
O h. of Israel, every one according 18.30
Why will you die, O h. of Israel? 18.31
to the seed of the h. of Jacob, 20.05
But the h. of Israel rebelled 20.13
speak to the h. of Israel and say 20.27
Wherefore say to the h. of Israel, 20.30
inquired of by you, O h. of Israel? 20.31
"As for you, O h. of Israel, thus 20.39
there all the h. of Israel, all of 20.40
O h. of Israel, says the Lord GOD." 20.44
the h. of Israel has become dross 22.18
lo, this is what they did in my h. 23.39
the rebellious h. and say to them, 24.03
'Say to the h. of Israel, Thus says 24.21
and over the h. of Judah when it 25.03
the h. of Judah is like all the 25.08
against the h. of Judah and has 25.12
"And for the h. of Israel there 28.24
I gather the h. of Israel from the 28.25
staff of reed to the h. of Israel; 29.06
the reliance of the h. of Israel, 29.16
spring forth to the h. of Israel, 29.21
a watchman for the h. of Israel; 33.07
say to the h. of Israel, Thus have 33.10
why will you die, O h. of Israel? 33.11
O h. of Israel, I will judge each 33.20
the h. of Israel, are my people, says 34.30
inheritance of the h. of Israel, 35.15
the whole h. of Israel, all of it; 36.10
when the h. of Israel dwelt in 36.17
which the h. of Israel caused to be 36.21
"Therefore say to the h. of Israel, 36.22
O h. of Israel, that I am about to 36.22
for your ways, O h. of Israel. 36.32
I will let the h. of Israel ask me 36.37
bones are the whole h. of Israel. 37.11
and all the h. of Israel associated 37.16
months the h. of Israel will be 39.12
The h. of Israel shall know that I 39.22
know that the h. of Israel went 39.23
mercy upon the whole h. of Israel; 39.25
my Spirit upon the h. of Israel, 39.29
that you see to the h. of Israel." 40.04
And the h. of Israel shall no more 43.07
describe to the h. of Israel the 43.10
And say to the rebellious h., 44.06
to the h. of Israel, Thus says the 44.06
O h. of Israel, let there be an end 44.06
of iniquity to the h. of Israel, 44.12
of the stock of the h. of Israel, 44.22
a blessing may rest on your h. 44.30
belong to the whole h. of Israel. 45.06
shall let the h. of Israel have 45.08
appointed feasts of the h. of Israel: 45.17
atonement for the h. of Israel. 45.17
of the vessels of the h. of God; Dan 1.02
to the h. of his god, and placed the 1.02
went to his h. and made the matter 2.17
at ease in my h. and prospering in 4.04
the h. of God in Jerusalem; 5.03
vessels of his h. have been 5.23
he went to his h. where he had 6.10
will punish the h. of Jehu for the Hos 1.04
to the kingdom of the h. of Israel. 1.04
more have pity on the h. of Israel, 1.06
will have pity on the h. of Judah, 1.07
Give heed, O h. of Israel! 5.01
Hearken, O h. of the king! 5.01
like dry rot to the h. of Judah. 5.12
a young lion to the h. of Judah. 5.14
In the h. of Israel I have seen a 6.10
vulture is over the h. of the LORD, 8.01
not come to the h. of the LORD. 9.04
and hatred in the h. of his God. 9.08

I will drive them out of my h. 9.15
O h. of Israel, because of your 10.15
and the h. of Israel with deceit; 11.12
cut off from the h. of the LORD. Joe 1.09
withheld from the h. of your God. 1.13
the land to the h. of the LORD 1.14
gladness from the h. of our God? 1.16
forth from the h. of the LORD and 3.18
send a fire upon the h. of Hazael, Amo 1.04
and in the h. of their God they 2.08
testify against the h. of Jacob, 3.13
the winter h. with the summer h.; 3.15
in lamentation, O h. of Israel: 5.01
have ten left to the h. of Israel." 5.03
says the LORD to the h. of Israel: 5.04
out like fire in the h. of Joseph, 5.06
went into the h. and leaned with 5.19
in the wilderness, O h. of Israel? 5.25
to whom the h. of Israel come! 6.01
And if ten men remain in one h., 6.09
to bring the bones out of the h., 6.10
in the innermost parts of the h., 6.10
and the great h. shall be smitten 6.11
and the little h. into bits. 6.11
O h. of Israel," says the LORD, the 6.14
against the h. of Jeroboam with 7.09
in the midst of the h. of Israel; 7.10
not preach against the h. of Isaac.' 7.16
utterly destroy the h. of Jacob, 9.08
and shake the h. of Israel among 9.09
and the h. of Jacob shall possess Ob 1.17
The h. of Jacob shall be a fire, and 1.18
and the h. of Joseph a flame, and 1.18
and the h. of Esau stubble; 1.18
be no survivor to the h. of Esau; 1.18
for the sins of the h. of Israel. Mic 1.05
what is the sin of the h. of Judah? 1.05
they oppress a man and his h., 2.02
Should this be said, O h. of Jacob? 2.07
and rulers of the h. of Israel! 3.01
heads of the h. of Jacob and 3.09
and rulers of the h. of Israel, 3.09
mountain of the h. a wooded height. 3.12
mountain of the h. of the LORD 4.01
to the h. of the God of Jacob; 4.02
redeemed you from the h. of bondage; 6.04
wickedness in the h. of the wicked, 6.10
all the works of the h. of Ahab; 6.16
enemies are the men of his own h. 7.06
from the h. of your gods I will cut Nah 1.14
him who gets evil gain for his h., Hab 2.09
shame to your h. by cutting off 2.10
their master's h. with violence Zep 1.09
of the remnant of the h. of Judah, 2.07
come to rebuild the h. of the LORD." Hag 1.02
while this h. lies in ruins? 1.04
and bring wood and build the h., 1.08
Because of my h. that lies in ruins, 1.09
yourselves each with his own h. 1.09
worked on the h. of the LORD of 1.14
that saw this h. in its former 2.03
I will fill this h. with splendor, 2.07
splendor of this h. shall be 2.09
my h. shall be built in it, says the Zec 1.16
shall rule my h. and have charge 3.07
laid the foundation of this h.; 4.09
it shall enter the h. of the thief, 5.04
and the h. of him who swears 5.04
abide in his h. and consume it, 5.04
of Shinar, to build a h. for it; 5.11
the same day to the h. of Josiah, 6.10
priests of the h. of the LORD of 7.03
foundation of the h. of the LORD of 8.09
O h. of Judah and h. of Israel, so will 8.13
Jerusalem and to the h. of Judah; 8.15
shall be to the h. of Judah 8.19
Then I will encamp at my h. as a guard, 9.08

HOUSE (cont.)
the h. of Judah, and will make them Zec 10.03
"I will strengthen the h. of Judah, 10.06
and I will save the h. of Joseph. 10.06
the treasury in the h. of the LORD. 11.13
But upon the h. of Judah I will 12.04
glory of the h. of David and the 12.07
and the h. of David shall be like 12.08
pour out on the h. of David and 12.10
family of the h. of David by 12.12
family of the h. of Nathan by 12.12
the family of the h. of Levi by 12.13
opened for the h. of David and the 13.01
I received in the h. of my friends.'" 13.06
the pots in the h. of the LORD 14.20
a trader in the h. of the LORD of 14.21
that there may be food in my h.; Mal 3.10
and going into the h. they saw the Mt 2.11
it gives light to all in the h. 5.15
man who built his h. upon the rock; 7.24
winds blew and beat upon that h., 7.25
man who built his h. upon the sand; 7.26
beat against that h., and it fell; 7.27
And when Jesus entered Peter's h., 8.14
And as he sat at table in the h., 9.10
And when Jesus came to the ruler's h., 9.23
When he entered the h., 9.28
the lost sheep of the h. of Israel. 10.06
As you enter the h., salute it. 10.12
And if the h. is worthy, let your 10.13
feet as you leave that h. or town. 10.14
the master of the h. Beelzebul, 10.25
how he entered the h. of God and 12.04
and no city or h. divided against 12.25
a strong man's h. and plunder his 12.29
then indeed he may plunder his h. 12.29
return to my h. from which I came.' 12.44
went out of the h. and sat beside 13.01
the crowds and went into the h. 13.36
his own country and in his own h." 13.57
the lost sheep of the h. of Israel." 15.24
'My h. shall be called a h. of prayer'; 21.13
Behold, your h. is forsaken and 23.38
go down to take what is in his h.; 24.17
not have let his h. be broken into. 24.43
Bethany in the h. of Simon the 26.06
passover at your h. with my disciples.'" 26.18
and entered the h. of Simon and Mk 1.29
And as he sat at table in his h., 2.15
how he entered the h. of God, 2.26
And if a h. is divided against 3.25
that h. will not be able to stand. 3.25
a strong man's h. and plunder his 3.27
then indeed he may plunder his h. 3.27
from the ruler's h. some who said, 5.35
came to the h. of the ruler of the 5.38
his own kin, and in his own h." 6.04
said to them, "Where you enter a h., 6.10
And when he had entered the h., 7.17
And he entered a h., and would not 7.24
And when he had entered the h., 9.28
he was in the h. he asked them, 9.33
And in the h. the disciples asked 10.10
who has left h. or brothers or 10.29
'My h. shall be called a h. of prayer 11.17
nor enter his h., to take anything 13.15
the master of the h. will come, 13.35
Bethany in the h. of Simon the 14.03
was Joseph, of the h. of David; Lk 1.27
reign over the h. of Jacob for 1.33
and she entered the h. of Zechariah 1.40
for us in the h. of his servant 1.69
he was of the h. and lineage of 2.04
that I must be in my Father's h.?" 2.49
synagogue, and entered Simon's h. 4.38
made him a great feast in his h.; 5.29
how he entered the h. of God, 6.04
he is like a man building a h., 6.48
the stream broke against that h., 6.48
man who built a h. on the ground 6.49
and the ruin of that h. was great." 6.49
When he was not far from the h., 7.06
had been sent returned to the h., 7.10
and he went into the Pharisee's h., 7.36
at table in the Pharisee's h., 7.37
I entered your h., you gave me no 7.44
lived not in a h. but among the 8.27
he besought him to come to his h., 8.41
from the ruler's h. came and said, 8.49
And when he came to the h., 8.51
And whatever h. you enter, stay 9.04
Whatever h. you enter, first say, 10.05
first say, 'Peace be to this h.!' 10.05
And remain in the same h., 10.07
his wages; do not go from h. to h. 10.07
Martha received him into her h. 10.38
is laid waste, and h. falls upon h. 11.17
return to my h. from which I came.' 11.24
have left his h. to be broken into. 12.39
henceforth in one h. there will be 12.52
Behold, your h. is forsaken. 13.35
to dine at the h. of a ruler who 14.01
come in, that my h. may be filled. 14.23
and sweep the h. and seek diligently 15.08
as he came and drew near to the h., 15.25
to send him to my father's h., 16.27
housetop, with his goods in the h., 17.31
down to his h. justified rather 18.14
who has left h. or wife or brothers 18.29
for I must stay at your h. today." 19.05
salvation has come to this h., 19.09
'My h. shall be a h. of prayer'; but 19.46
him into the h. which he enters, 22.10
him into the high priest's h. 22.54
not make my Father's h. a h. of trade." Jn 2.16
"Zeal for thy h. will consume me." 2.17
They went each to his own h., * 7.53
not continue in the h. for ever; 8.35
met him, while Mary sat in the h. 11.20
Jews who were with her in the h., 11.31
and the h. was filled with the 12.03
In my Father's h. are many rooms; 14.02
Jesus from the h. of Caiaphas to 18.28
his disciples were again in the h., 20.26
filled all the h. where they were Ac 2.02
Let all the h. of Israel therefore 2.36
three months in his father's h.; 7.20
in the wilderness, O h. of Israel? 7.42
was Solomon who built a h. for him. 7.47
What h. will you build for me, says 7.49
and entering h. after h. he dragged 8.03
inquire in the h. of Judas for a 9.11
departed and entered the h. 9.17
whose h. is by the seaside." 10.06
having made inquiry for Simon's h., 10.17
to send for you to come to his h., 10.22
the ninth hour of prayer in my h.; 10.30
he is lodging in the h. of Simon, 10.32
arrived at the h. in which we were, 11.11
me, and we entered the man's h. 11.12
standing in his h. and saying, 11.13
this, he went to the h. of Mary, 12.12
the Lord, come to my h. and stay." 16.15
him and to all that were in his h. 16.32
Then he brought them up into his h., 16.34
and attacked the h. of Jason, 17.05
and went to the h. of a man named 18.07
his h. was next door to the synagogue. 18.07
out of that h. naked and wounded. 19.16
teaching you in public and from h. to h., 20.20
we entered the h. of Philip the 21.08
us to the h. of Mnason of Cyprus, 21.16
greet also the church in their h. Rom 16.05
with the church in their h., 1Co 16.19

HOUSE (cont.)
a h. not made with hands, eternal in 2Co 5.01
to Nympha and the church in her h. Col 4.15
gadding about from h. to h., and not 1Ti 5.13
In a great h. there are not only 2Ti 2.20
and useful to the master of the h., 2.21
soldier, and the church in your h.: Phm 1.02
also was faithful in God's h. Heb 3.02
builder of a h. has more honor 3.03
has more honor than the h. 3.03
(For every h. is built by some one, 3.04
in all God's h. as a servant, 3.05
faithful over God's h. as a son. 3.06
And we are his h. if we hold fast 3.06
h. of Israel and with the h. of Judah; 8.08
make with the h. of Israel after 8.10
a great priest over the h. of God, 10.21
yourselves built into a spiritual h., 1Pe 2.05
him into the h. or give him any 2Jn 1.10

HOUSEHOLD
into the ark, you and all your h., Gen 7.01
children and his h. after him to 18.19
her mother's h. about these things. 24.28
and a great h., so that the Philistines 26.14
shall I provide for my own h. also?" 30.30
Rachel stole her father's h. gods. 31.19
had taken the h. gods and put them 31.34
but did not find the h. gods. 31.35
you found of all your h. goods? 31.37
be destroyed, both I and my h." 34.30
said to his h. and to all who were 35.02
and all the members of his h., 36.06
the men of her h. and said to them, 39.14
and the h. of Pharaoh heard it. 45.02
lest you and your h., and all that 45.11
brothers and to his father's h., 46.31
'My brothers and my father's h., 46.31
and all his father's h. with food, 47.12
Joseph spoke to the h. of Pharaoh, 50.04
of Pharaoh, the elders of his h., 50.07
as well as all the h. of Joseph, 50.08
his brothers, and his father's h.; 50.08
with Jacob, each with his h.: Ex 1.01
fathers' houses, a lamb for a h.; 12.03
and if the h. is too small for a 12.04
and against Pharaoh and all his h., Deu 6.22
God and rejoice, you and your h. 14.26
because he loves you and your h., 15.16
you and your h., before the LORD 15.20
brothers, and all your father's h. Jos 2.18
the harlot, and her father's h., 6.25
and the h. which the LORD takes 7.14
and he brought near his h. man by man, 7.18
life with the lives of your h." Ju 18.25
and his men, every man with his h., 1Sa 27.03
with him, every one with his h.; 2Sa 2.03
blessed Obededom and all his h. 6.11
has blessed the h. of Obededom and 6.12
And David returned to bless his h. 6.20
forth, and all his h. after him. 15.16
are for the king's h. to ride on, 16.02
ford to bring over the king's h., 19.18
king and his h. over the Jordan, 19.41
food for the king and his h.; 1Ki 4.07
wishes by providing food for my h." 5.09
cors of wheat as food for his h., 5.11
who was over the h. in Tirzah, 16.09
and her h. ate for many days. 17.15
Obadiah, who was over the h. 18.03
let us go and tell the king's h." 2Ki 7.09
it was told within the king's h. 7.11
"Arise, and depart with your h., 8.01
went with her h. and sojourned in 8.02
the king's son was over the h., 15.05
of Hilkiah, who was over the h., 18.18
of Hilkiah, who was over the h., 18.37
sent Eliakim, who was over the h., 19.02
with the h. of Obededom in his 1Ch 13.14
blessed the h. of Obededom and all 13.14
David went home to bless his h. 16.43
his son was over the king's h., 2Ch 26.21
I threw all the h. furniture of Neh 13.08
troubles his h. will inherit wind, Pro 11.29
gain makes trouble for his h., 15.27
food of your h. and maintenance 27.27
food for her h. and tasks for her 31.15
She is not afraid of snow for her h., 31.21
for all her h. are clothed in 31.21
She looks well to the ways of her h., 31.27
to Shebna, who is over the h., Is 22.15
of Hilkiah, who was over the h., 36.03
of Hilkiah, who was over the h., 36.22
sent Eliakim, who was over the h., 37.02
I will punish that man and his h. Jer 23.34
will they malign those of his h. Mt 10.25
foes will be those of his own h. 10.36
his master has set over his h., 24.45
his master will set over his h., Lk 12.42
himself believed, and all his h. Jn 4.53
over Egypt and over all his h. Ac 7.10
man who feared God with all his h., 10.02
will be saved, you and all your h.' 11.14
with her h., she besought us, saying, 16.15
you will be saved, you and your h." 16.31
with all his h. that he had 16.34
the Lord, together with all his h.; 18.08
baptize also the h. of Stephanas. 1Co 1.16
know that the h. of Stephanas were 16.15
those who are of the h. of faith. Gal 6.10
and members of the h. of God, Eph 2.19
especially those of Caesar's h. Php 4.22
He must manage his own h. well, 1Ti 3.04
not know how to manage his own h., 3.05
ought to behave in the h. of God, 3.15
mercy to the h. of Onesiphorus, 2Ti 1.16
Aquila, and the h. of Onesiphorus. 4.19
an ark for the saving of his h.; Heb 11.07
to begin with the h. of God; 1Pe 4.17

HOUSEHOLDER
servants of the h. came and said Mt 13.27
is like a h. who brings out of his 13.52
is like a h. who went out early in 20.01
receiving it they grumbled at the h., 20.11
There was a h. who planted a 21.33
that if the h. had known in what 24.43
say to the h., 'The Teacher says, Mk 14.14
that if the h. had known at what Lk 12.39
When once the h. has risen up and 13.25
Then the h. in anger said to his 14.21
and tell the h., 'The Teacher says 22.11

HOUSEHOLDS
grain for the famine of your h., Gen 42.19
grain for the famine of your h., 42.33
and take your father and your h., 45.18
as food for yourselves and your h., 47.24
with their h. and all the men that Num 16.32
it in any place, you and your h.; 18.31
with their h., their tents, and Deu 11.06
you and your h., in all that you 12.07
LORD takes shall come near by h.; Jos 7.14
their children and their h. well; 1Ti 3.12
rule their h., and give the enemy 5.14
their way into h. and capture weak 2Ti 3.06

HOUSES
wives, all that was in the h., Gen 34.29
are the heads of their fathers' h.: Ex 6.14
of the fathers' h. of the Levites 6.25
and into the h. of your servants 8.03
you and your h. and be left only 8.09
you and your h. and your servants 8.11

HOUSES (cont.)
died out of the h. and courtyards Ex 8.13
and your people, and into your h.; 8.21
and the h. of the Egyptians shall 8.21
Pharaoh and into his servants' h., 8.24
and his cattle flee into the h.; 9.20
and they shall fill your h., 10.06
and the h. of all your servants and 10.06
according to their fathers' h., 12.03
lintel of the h. in which they eat 12.07
for you, upon the h. where you are; 12.13
put away leaven out of your h., 12.15
leaven shall be found in your h.; 12.19
to enter your h. to slay you. 12.23
passed over the h. of the people 12.27
the Egyptians but spared our h.' " 12.27
But the h. of the villages which Lev 25.31
the h. in the cities of their 25.32
for the h. in the cities of the 25.33
by fathers' h., according to the Num 1.02
by fathers' h., according to the 1.18
families, by their fathers' h., 1.20
families, by their fathers' h., 1.22
families, by their fathers' h., 1.24
families, by their fathers' h., 1.26
families, by their fathers' h., 1.28
families, by their fathers' h., 1.30
families, by their fathers' h., 1.32
families, by their fathers' h., 1.34
families, by their fathers' h., 1.36
families, by their fathers' h., 1.38
families, by their fathers' h., 1.40
families, by their fathers' h., 1.42
of Israel, by their fathers' h., 1.45
the ensigns of their father's h.; 2.02
as numbered by their father's h.; 2.32
by fathers' h. and by families; 3.15
the Levites, by their fathers' h. 3.20
families and their fathers' h., 4.02
families and their fathers' h.; 4.22
families and their fathers' h.; 4.29
families and their fathers' h., 4.34
families and their fathers' h., 4.38
their fathers' h. was two thousand 4.40
families and their fathers' h., 4.42
families and their fathers' h., 4.46
Israel, heads of their fathers' h., 7.02
to their fathers' h., twelve rods. 17.02
to their fathers' h., twelve rods; 17.06
and upward, by their fathers' h., 26.02
of the fathers' h. of the congregation; 31.26
of the fathers' h. of the tribes 32.28
by fathers' h. and the tribe of 34.14
their fathers' h. have received 34.14
of the fathers' h. of the families 36.01
of the fathers' h. of the sons of 36.01
of the fathers' h. of the people 36.01
and h. full of all good things, Deu 6.11
built goodly h. and live in them, 8.12
in their cities and in their h., 19.01
it from our h. as our food for the Jos 9.12
of the fathers' h. of the tribes 14.01
of the fathers' h. of the tribes 19.51
of the fathers' h. of the Levites 21.01
of the fathers' h. of the tribes 21.01
that in these h. there are an Ju 18.14
who were in the h. near Micah's 18.22
of the fathers' h. of the people 1Ki 8.01
which Solomon had built the two h., 9.10
He also made h. on high places, and 12.31
against all the h. of the high 13.32
house and the h. of your servants, 20.06
broke down the h. of the cult 2Ki 23.07
house and all the h. of Jerusalem; 25.09
their fathers' h. increased 1Ch 4.38
according to their fathers' h.: 5.13
was chief in their fathers' h.; 5.15
the heads of their fathers' h.: 5.24
men, heads of their fathers' h. 5.24
Shemuel, heads of their fathers' h., 7.02
according to their fathers' h., 7.04
Iri, five, heads of fathers' h., 7.07
as heads of their fathers' h., 7.09
to the heads of their fathers' h., 7.11
men of Asher, heads of fathers' h., 7.40
of fathers' h. of the inhabitants 8.06
his sons, heads of fathers' h. 8.10
of fathers' h. of the inhabitants 8.13
These were the heads of fathers' h., 8.28
of fathers' h. according to their 9.09
according to their fathers' h. 9.09
kinsmen, heads of their fathers' h., 9.13
of fathers' h. of the Levites, 9.33
of fathers' h. of the Levites, 9.34
famous men in their fathers' h. 12.30
David built h. for himself in the 15.01
of the fathers' h. of the Levites; 15.12
heads of the fathers' h. of Ladan. 23.09
sons of Levi by their fathers' h., 23.24
of fathers' h. as they were 23.24
of fathers' h. of the sons of 24.04
of the fathers' h. of the priests 24.06
according to their fathers' h. 24.30
of fathers' h. of the priests and 24.31
were rulers in their fathers' h., 26.06
and they cast lots by fathers' h., 26.13
of the fathers' h. belonging to 26.21
and the heads of the fathers' h., 26.26
whatever genealogy or fathers' h. 26.31
of ability, heads of fathers' h., 26.32
Israel, the heads of fathers' h., 27.01
and of its h., its treasuries, its 28.11
of fathers' h. made their freewill 29.06
Israel, the heads of fathers' h. 2Ch 1.02
of the fathers' h. of the people 5.02
the muster of them by fathers' h.: 17.14
the heads of fathers' h. of Israel, 23.02
by fathers' h. under commanders of 25.05
of fathers' h. of mighty men of 26.12
was according to their fathers' h.; 31.17
your fathers' h. by your divisions, 35.04
of the fathers' h. of your brethren 35.05
of the fathers' h. of the lay 35.12
of the fathers' h. of Judah and Ez 1.05
their fathers' h. or their descent, 2.59
Levites and heads of fathers' h., 3.12
of fathers' h. and said to them, 4.02
of fathers' h. in Israel said to 4.03
are the heads of their fathers' h., 8.01
of fathers' h. in Israel at 8.29
selected men, heads of fathers' h., 10.16
according to their fathers' h., 10.16
and our h. to get grain because of Neh 5.03
and their h., and the hundredth of 5.11
were few and no h. had been built. 7.04
their fathers' h. nor their 7.61
of fathers' h. gave to the work. 7.70
of fathers' h. gave into the 7.71
of fathers' h. of all the people, 8.13
possession of h. full of all good 9.25
God, according to our fathers' h., 10.34
his brethren, heads of fathers' h. 11.13
were priests, heads of fathers' h.: 12.12
recorded the heads of fathers' h.; 12.22
sons of Levi, heads of fathers' h.; 12.23
who filled their h. with silver. Job 3.15
more those who dwell in h. of clay, 4.19
in h. which no man should inhabit, 15.28
Their h. are safe from fear, and no 21.09
they care for their h. after them, 21.21
Yet he filled their h. with good 22.18
In the dark they dig through h.; 24.16
we shall fill our h. with spoil; Pro 1.13
I built h. and planted vineyards Ecc 2.04

HOUSES (cont.)

spoil of the poor is in your h. Is 3.14
"Surely many h. shall be desolate, 5.09
desolate, large and beautiful h., 5.09
and h. without men, and the land is 6.11
of stumbling to both h. of Israel, 8.14
their h. will be plundered and 13.16
and its h. will be full of howling 13.21
and you counted the h. of Jerusalem, 22.10
broke down the h. to fortify the 22.10
all the joyous h. in the joyful 32.13
They shall build h. and inhabit 65.21
and trooped to the h. of harlots. Jer 5.07
their h. are full of treachery; 5.27
Their h. shall be turned over to 6.12
out of your h. on the sabbath or 17.22
May a cry be heard from their h., 18.22
The h. of Jerusalem and the 19.13
and the h. of the kings of Judah— 19.13
all the h. upon whose roofs incense 19.13
Build h. and live in them; 29.05
build h. and live in them, and plant 29.28
H. and fields and vineyards shall 32.15
with the h. on whose roofs incense 32.29
h. of this city and the h. of the kings 33.04
and not to build h. to dwell in. 35.09
house and all the h. of Jerusalem; 52.13
to take possession of their h.; Eze 7.24
'The time is not near to build h.; 11.03
shall burn your h. and execute 16.41
daughters, and burn up their h. 23.47
walls and destroy your pleasant h.; 26.12
shall build h. and plant vineyards. 28.26
walls and at the doors of the h., 33.30
place for their h. and a holy 45.04
and your h. shall be laid in ruins. Dan 2.05
limb, and their h. laid in ruins; 3.29
they climb up into the h., Joe 2.09
and the h. of ivory shall perish, Amo 3.15
and the great h. shall come to an 3.15
you have built h. of hewn stone, 5.11
the h. of Achzib shall be a deceitful Mic 1.14
and h., and take them away; 2.02
drive out from their pleasant h.; 2.09
plundered, and their h. laid waste. Zep 1.13
Though they build h., they shall not 1.13
and in the h. of Ashkelon they 2.07
to dwell in your paneled h., Hag 1.04
taken and the h. plundered and the Zec 14.02
wear soft raiment are in kings' h. Mt 11.08
who has left h. or brothers or 19.29
you devour widows' h. and for a * 23.14
h. and brothers and sisters and Mk 10.30
who devour widows' h. and for a 12.40
me into their h. when I am put out Lk 16.04
who devour widows' h. and for a 20.47
possessors of lands or h. sold them, Ac 4.34
not dwell in h. made with hands; 7.48
Do you not have h. to eat and drink 1Co 11.22

HOUSETOP

I am like a lonely bird on the h. Ps 102.07
a corner of the h. than in a house Pro 21.09
a corner of the h. than in a house 25.24
who is on the h. not go down to Mt 24.17
let him who is on the h. not go down, Mk 13.15
that day, let him who is on the h., Lk 17.31
Peter went up on the h. to pray, Ac 10.09

HOUSETOPS

tender grass, like grass on the h.; 2Ki 19.26
Let them be like the grass on the h., Ps 129.06
on the h. and in the squares every Is 15.03
gone up, all of you, to the h., 22.01
tender grass, like grass on the h., 37.27
On all the h. of Moab and in the Jer 48.38
whispered, proclaim upon the h. Mt 10.27
shall be proclaimed upon the h. Lk 12.03

HOVERING

Like birds h., so the LORD of hosts Is 31.05

HOW

This is h. you are to make it: the Gen 6.15
h. am I to know that I shall 15.08
And h. have I sinned against you, 20.09
h. then could you say, 'She is my 26.09
"H. is it that you have found it so 27.20
"H. awesome is this place! 28.17
yourself know h. I have served you, 30.29
and h. your cattle have fared with 30.29
h. then can I do this great wickedness, 39.09
h. then should we steal silver or 44.08
Or h. can we clear ourselves? 44.16
For h. can I go back to my father 44.34
"H. many are the days of the years 47.08
"H. is it that you have come so Ex 2.18
h. then shall Pharaoh listen to me, 6.12
h. then shall Pharaoh listen to me?" 6.30
your son's son h. I have made 10.02
'H. long will you refuse to humble 10.03
"H. long shall this man be a snare 10.07
"H. long do you refuse to keep my 16.28
h. the LORD had brought Israel out 18.01
and h. the LORD had delivered them. 18.08
and h. I bore you on eagles' wings 19.04
For h. shall it be known that I 33.16
intelligence to know h. to do any 36.01
for you know h. we are to encamp in Num 10.31
"H. long will this people despise 14.11
And h. long will they not believe 14.11
"H. long shall this wicked congregation 14.27
h. our fathers went down to Egypt, 20.15
H. can I curse whom God has not 23.08
H. can I denounce whom the LORD has 23.08
h. fair are your tents, O Jacob, your 24.05
H. long shall Asshur take you away 24.22
H. can I bear alone the weight and Deu 1.12
you have seen h. the LORD your God 1.31
h. on the day that you stood before 4.10
h. can I dispossess them?' 7.17
do not forget h. you provoked the 9.07
h. he made the water of the Red Sea 11.04
and h. the LORD has destroyed them 11.04
h. the earth opened its mouth and 11.06
'H. did these nations serve their 12.30
'H. may we know the word which the 18.21
h. he attacked you on the way, when 25.18
"You know h. we dwelt in the land of 29.16
and h. we came through the midst of 29.16
For I know h. rebellious and 31.27
h. much more after my death! 31.27
H. should one chase a thousand, and 32.30
For we have heard h. the LORD dried Jos 2.10
then h. can we make a covenant with 9.07
Jerusalem heard h. Joshua had 10.01
and h. the inhabitants of Gibeon 10.01
on that day h. the Anakim were 14.12
"H. long will you be slack to go in 18.03
h. can I deliver Israel? Ju 6.15
and h. you might be bound, that one 16.06
please tell me h. you might be 16.10
tell me h. you might be bound." 16.13
"H. can you say, 'I love you,' when 16.15
h. they dwelt in security, after the 18.07
and h. they were far from the 18.07
H. then do you ask me, 'What ails 18.24
h. was this wickedness brought to 20.03
and h. you left your father and Ru 2.11
"H. did you fare, my daughter?" 3.16
until you learn h. the matter 3.18
"H. long will you be drunken? 1Sa 1.14
and h. they lay with the women who 2.22
And he said, "H. did it go, my son?" 4.16
men of Ashdod saw h. things were, 5.07
him before saw h. he prophesied 10.11

HOW (cont.)
said, "H. can this man save us?" 1Sa 10.27
see h. my eyes have become bright, 14.29
H. much better if the people had 14.30
know and see h. this sin has 14.38
"H. long will you grieve over Saul, 16.01
And Samuel said, "H. can I go? 16.02
See h. your brothers fare, and bring 17.18
h. much more today will their 21.05
h. much more then if we go to 23.03
eyes have seen h. the LORD gave 24.10
this day h. you have dealt well 24.18
h. he has cut off the mediums and 28.09
For h. could this fellow reconcile 29.04
And David said to him, "H. did it go? 2Sa 1.04
"H. do you know that Saul and his 1.05
"H. is it you were not afraid to 1.14
H. are the mighty fallen! 1.19
"H. are the mighty fallen in the 1.25
"H. are the mighty fallen, and the 1.27
H. then could I lift up my face to 2.22
H. long will it be before you bid 2.26
H. much more, when wicked men have 4.11
and he said, "H. can the ark of the 6.09
"H. the king of Israel honored 6.20
David asked h. Joab was doing, and 11.07
and h. the people fared, and 11.07
and h. the war prospered. 11.07
h. then can we say to him the child 12.18
h. much more now may this Benjaminite! 16.11
or remember h. your servant did 19.19
"H. many years have I still to live, 19.34
And h. shall I make expiation, that 21.03
h. he dealt with the two commanders 1Ki 2.05
I do not know h. to go out or come 3.07
us who knows h. to cut timber like 5.06
h. much less this house which I 8.27
"H. do you advise me to answer this 12.06
h. he warred and h. he reigned, 14.19
h. I hid a hundred men of the LORD's 18.13
"H. long will you go limping with 18.21
and h. he had slain all the prophets 19.01
and see h. this man is seeking 20.07
"Have you seen h. Ahab has humbled 21.29
"H. many times shall I adjure you 22.16
"H. did the Spirit of the LORD go 22.24
and h. he warred, are they not 22.45
"H. am I to set this before a 2Ki 4.43
and see h. he is seeking a quarrel 5.07
H. much rather, then, when he says to 5.13
"Do you see h. this murderer has 6.32
the king h. Elisha had restored 8.05
h. the LORD uttered this oracle 9.25
before him; h. then can we stand?" 10.04
h. the king of Syria oppressed them. 13.04
and h. he fought with Amaziah king 14.15
h. he fought, and h. he recovered for 14.28
and taught them h. they should 17.28
H. then can you repulse a single 18.24
h. I have walked before thee in 20.03
and h. he made the pool and the 20.20
when you heard h. I spoke against 22.19
and he said, "H. can I bring the 1Ch 13.12
servants know h. to cut timber in 2Ch 2.08
h. much less this house which I 6.18
"H. do you advise me to answer this 10.06
"H. many times shall I adjure you 18.15
H. much less will your God deliver 32.15
and h. God received his entreaty, 33.19
salt without prescribing h. much. Ez 7.22
"H. long will you be gone, and when Neh 2.06
h. Jerusalem lies in ruins with its 2.17
learn h. Esther was and h. she fared. Est 2.11
and h. he had advanced him above 5.11
found written h. Mordecai had told 6.02
For h. can I endure to see the 8.06
Or h. can I endure to see the 8.06
h. much more those who dwell in Job 4.19
make me understand h. I have erred. 6.24
H. forceful are honest words! 6.25
H. long wilt thou not look away 7.19
"H. long will you say these things, 8.02
But h. can a man be just before God? 9.02
H. then can I answer him, choosing 9.14
H. many are my iniquities and my 13.23
h. much less one who is abominable 15.16
h. much of it leaves me? 16.06
"H. long will you hunt for words? 18.02
"H. long will you torment me, and 19.02
If you say, 'H. we will pursue him!' 19.28
"H. often is it that the lamp of 21.17
H. then will you comfort me with 21.34
highest stars, h. lofty they are! 22.12
H. then can man be righteous before 25.04
H. can he who is born of woman be 25.04
h. much less man, who is a maggot, 25.06
"H. you have helped him who has no 26.02
H. you have saved the arm that has 26.02
H. you have counseled him who has 26.03
and h. small a whisper do we hear 26.14
h. then could I look upon a virgin? 31.01
For I do not know h. to flatter, 32.22
H. am I better off than if I had 35.03
H. much less when you say that you 35.14
Do you know h. God lays his command 37.15
O LORD, h. many are my foes! Ps 3.01
O men, h. long shall my honor suffer 4.02
H. long will you love vain words, 4.02
But thou, O LORD—h. long? 6.03
h. majestic is thy name in all the 8.01
h. majestic is thy name in all the 8.09
h. can you say to me, "Flee like a 11.01
H. long, O LORD? Wilt thou forget me 13.01
H. long wilt thou hide thy face 13.01
H. long must I bear pain in my soul, 13.02
H. long shall my enemy be exalted 13.02
and in thy help h. greatly he 21.01
Consider h. many are my foes, and 25.19
O h. abundant is thy goodness, which 31.19
H. long, O LORD, wilt thou look on? 35.17
H. precious is thy steadfast love, O 36.07
let me know h. fleeting my life is! 39.04
h. I went with the throng, and led 42.04
h. he has wrought desolations in 46.08
H. long will you set upon a man to 62.03
Say to God, "H. terrible are thy 66.03
And they say, "H. can God know? 73.11
But when I thought h. to understand 73.16
H. they are destroyed in a moment, 73.19
is none among us who knows h. long. 74.09
H. long, O God, is the foe to scoff? 74.10
h. the enemy scoffs, and an impious 74.18
remember h. the impious scoff at 74.22
H. often they rebelled against him 78.40
H. long, O LORD? Wilt thou be angry 79.05
h. long wilt thou be angry with thy 80.04
"H. long will you judge unjustly 82.02
H. lovely is thy dwelling place, O 84.01
H. long, O LORD? Wilt thou hide 89.46
H. long will thy wrath burn like 89.46
h. thy servant is scorned; 89.50
h. I bear in my bosom the insults 89.50
H. long? Have pity on thy servants! 90.13
H. great are thy works, O LORD! 92.05
O LORD, h. long shall the wicked, 94.03
h. long shall the wicked exult? 94.03
O LORD, h. manifold are thy works! 104.24
H. can a young man keep his way 119.09
H. long must thy servant endure? 119.84
Oh, h. I love thy law! 119.97
H. sweet are thy words to my taste, 119.103
Consider h. I love thy precepts! 119.159
h. he swore to the LORD and vowed 132.02
Behold, h. good and pleasant it is 133.01

HOW (cont.)
H. shall we sing the LORD's song in Ps 137.04
h. they said, "Rase it, rase it! 137.07
H. precious to me are thy thoughts, 139.17
H. vast is the sum of them! 139.17
"H. long, O simple ones, will you Pro 1.22
H. long will scoffers delight in 1.22
and you say, "H. I hated discipline, 5.12
H. long will you lie there, O 6.09
h. much more the wicked and the 11.31
h. much more the hearts of men! 15.11
a word in season, h. good it is! 15.23
the righteous ponders h. to answer, 15.28
h. much more do his friends go far 19.07
h. then can man understand his way? 20.24
h. much more when he brings it with 21.27
h. lofty are their eyes, 30.13
h. high their eyelids lift! 30.13
with my mind h. to cheer my body Ecc 2.03
and h. to lay hold on folly, till I 2.03
H. the wise man dies just like the 2.16
but h. can one be warm alone? 4.11
have who knows h. to conduct 6.08
for who can tell him h. it will be? 8.07
h. neither day nor night one's eyes 8.16
h. the righteous and the wise and 9.01
As you do not know h. the spirit 11.05
H. sweet is your love, my sister, my Sol 4.10
h. much better is your love than 4.10
my garment, h. could I put it on? 5.03
my feet, h. could I soil them? 5.03
H. graceful are your feet in 7.01
H. fair and pleasant you are, O 7.06
H. the faithful city has become a Is 1.21
Then I said, "H. long, O Lord?" 6.11
when he knows h. to refuse the 7.15
the child knows h. to refuse the 7.16
the child knows h. to cry 'My 8.04
"H. the oppressor has ceased, the 14.04
"H. you are fallen from heaven, O 14.12
H. you are cut down to the ground, 14.12
the pride of Moab, h. proud he was; 16.06
H. can you say to Pharaoh, "I am a 19.11
And we, h. shall we escape?'" 20.06
H. then can you repulse a single 36.09
h. I have walked before thee in 38.03
for h. should my name be profaned? 48.11
that I may know h. to sustain with 50.04
H. beautiful upon the mountains are 52.07
I do not know h. to speak, for I am Jer 1.06
h. you followed me in the wilderness, 2.02
H. then have you turned degenerate 2.21
H. can you say, 'I am not defiled, I 2.23
"H. well you direct your course to 2.33
H. lightly you gad about, changing 2.36
h. she went up on every high hill 3.06
"'I thought h. I would set you 3.19
H. long shall your evil thoughts 4.14
H. long must I see the standard, and 4.21
but h. to do good they know not." 4.22
"H. can I pardon you? Your children 5.07
they did not know h. to blush. 6.15
"H. can you say, 'We are wise, and 8.08
they did not know h. to blush. 8.12
heard from Zion: 'H we are ruined! 9.19
H. long will the land mourn, and the 12.04
h. will you compete with horses? 12.05
h. will you do in the jungle of the 12.05
H. long will it be before you are 13.27
Remember h. I stood before thee to 18.20
h. you will groan when pangs come 22.23
H. long shall there be lies in the 23.26
H. long will you waver, O faithless 31.22
h. did you write all these words? 36.17
h. long will you gash yourselves? 47.05
H. long till you are quiet? 47.06
H. can it be quiet, when the LORD 47.07
"H. do you say, 'We are heroes and 48.14
say, 'H. the mighty scepter is 48.17
H. it is broken! H. they wail! 48.39
H. Moab has turned his back in 48.39
H. the famous city is forsaken, the 49.25
H. the hammer of the whole earth is 50.23
H. Babylon has become a horror 50.23
"H. Babylon is taken, the praise of 51.41
H. Babylon has become a horror 51.41
H. lonely sits the city that was Lam 1.01
H. like a widow has she become, she 1.01
"Hear h. I groan; there is none to 1.21
H. the Lord in his anger has set 2.01
H. the gold has grown dim, how the 4.01
h. the pure gold is changed! 4.01
h. they are reckoned as earthen 4.02
H. much more when I send upon Eze 14.21
"Son of man, h. does the wood of the 15.02
h. much less, when the fire has 15.05
"H. lovesick is your heart, says the 16.30
'H. you have vanished from the seas, 26.17
of them; h. then can we live?' 33.10
and show them h. to distinguish 44.23
H. great are his signs, h. mighty his Dan 4.03
"For h. long is the vision concerning 8.13
H. can my lord's servant talk with 10.17
"H. long shall it be till the end 12.06
H. long will it be till they are Hos 8.05
H. can I give you up, O Ephraim! 11.08
H. can I hand you over, O Israel! 11.08
H. can I make you like Admah! 11.08
H. can I treat you like Zeboiim! 11.08
H. the beasts groan! The herds of Joe 1.18
"They do not know h. to do right, Amo 3.10
For I know h. many are your transgressions, 5.12
and h. great are your sins—you who 5.12
H. can Jacob stand? He is so small!" 7.02
H. can Jacob stand? He is so small!" 7.05
h. you have been destroyed!— Ob 1.05
H. Esau has been pillaged, his 1.06
h. shall I again look upon thy holy Jon 2.04
h. they turned from their evil way, 3.10
h. he removes it from me! Mic 2.04
O LORD, h. long shall I cry for help, Hab 1.02
up what is not his own—for h. long?— 2.06
h. they have taunted my people and Zep 2.08
hosts: Consider h. you have fared. Hag 1.05
hosts: Consider h. you have fared. 1.07
H. do you see it now? Is it not in 2.03
of the LORD, h. did you fare? 2.15
h. long wilt thou have no mercy on Zec 1.12
Yea, h. good and h. fair it shall 9.17
But you say, "H. hast thou loved us?" Mal 1.02
You say, 'H. have we despised thy 1.06
And you say, 'H. have we polluted it?' 1.07
Yet you say, "H. have we wearied him?" 2.17
But you say, 'H. shall we return?' 3.07
But you say, 'H. are we robbing thee?' 3.08
Yet you say, 'H. have we spoken 3.13
h. shall its saltness be restored? Mt 5.13
h. great is the darkness! 6.23
lilies of the field, h. they grow; 6.28
Or h. can you say to your brother, 7.04
know h. to give good gifts to your 7.11
h. much more will your Father who 7.11
not be anxious h. you are to speak 10.19
h. much more will they malign those 10.25
h. he entered the house of God and 12.04
read in the law h. on the sabbath 12.05
Of h. much more value is a man than 12.12
against him, h. to destroy him. 12.14
h. then will his kingdom stand? 12.26
Or h. can one enter a strong man's 12.29
h. can you speak good, when you are 12.34
in your field? H. then has it weeds?' 13.27
"H. many loaves have you?" They said 15.34
You know h. to interpret the 16.03

HOW (cont.)

and h. many baskets you gathered? Mt 16.09
and h. many baskets you gathered? 16.10
H. is it that you fail to perceive 16.11
h. long am I to be with you? 17.17
H. long am I to bear with you? 17.17
h. often shall my brother sin 18.21
"H. did the fig tree wither at once?" 21.20
h. did you get in here without a 22.12
took counsel h. to entangle him in 22.15
"H. is it then that David, inspired 22.43
calls him Lord, h. is he his son?" 22.45
h. are you to escape being sentenced 23.33
H. often would I have gathered your 23.37
But h. then should the scriptures 26.54
"Do you not hear h. many things 27.13
we remember h. that impostor said, 27.63
h. he entered the house of God, when Mk 2.26
against him, h. to destroy him. 3.06
"H. can Satan cast out Satan? 3.23
H. then will you understand all the 4.13
sprout and grow, he knows not h. 4.27
and tell them h. much the LORD has 5.19
and h. he has had mercy on you." 5.19
the Decapolis h. much Jesus had 5.20
"H. many loaves have you? Go and 6.38
"H. can one feed these men with 8.04
them, "H. many loaves have you?" 8.05
h. many baskets full of broken 8.19
h. many baskets full of broken 8.20
and h. is it written of the Son of 9.12
h. long am I to be with you? 9.19
H. long am I to bear with you? 9.19
"H. long has he had this?" 9.21
h. will you season it? 9.50
"H. hard it will be for those who 10.23
h. hard it is to enter the kingdom 10.24
h. God said to him, 'I am the God of 12.26
"H. can the scribes say that the 12.35
so h. is he his son?" And the great 12.37
were seeking h. to arrest him by 14.01
remembered h. Jesus had said to 14.72
See h. many charges they bring 15.04
"H. shall I know this? For I am Lk 1.18
"H. can this be since I have no 1.34
"H. is it that you sought me? 2.49
h. he entered the house of God, and 6.04
Or h. can you say to your brother, 6.42
Take heed then h. you hear; 8.18
it told them h. he who had been 8.36
and declare h. much God has done 8.39
the whole city h. much Jesus had 8.39
and h. she had been immediately 8.47
h. long am I to be with you and 9.41
written in the law? H. do you read?" 10.26
know h. to give good gifts to your 11.13
h. much more will the heavenly 11.13
h. will his kingdom stand? 11.18
not be anxious h. or what you are 12.11
Of h. much more value are you than 12.24
Consider the lilies, h. they grow; 12.27
h. much more will he clothe you, O 12.28
and h. I am constrained until it is 12.50
You know h. to interpret the 12.56
do you not know h. to interpret 12.56
H. often would I have gathered your 13.34
when he marked h. they chose the 14.07
h. shall its saltness be restored? 14.34
'H. many of my father's hired 15.17
'H. much do you owe my master?' 16.05
'And h. much do you owe?' 16.07
"H. hard it is for those who have 18.24
"H. can they say that the Christ is 20.41
him Lord; so h. is he his son?" 20.44
h. it was adorned with noble stones 21.05
meditate beforehand h. to answer; 21.14
were seeking h. to put him to 22.02
and captains h. he might betray 22.04
h. he had said to him, "Before the 22.61
and h. his body was laid; 23.55
Remember h. he told you, while he 24.06
and h. our chief priests and rulers 24.20
and h. he was known to them in the 24.35
said to him, "H. do you know me?" Jn 1.48
"H. can a man be born when he is 3.04
Nicodemus said to him, "H. can this be? 3.09
h. can you believe if I tell you 3.12
"H. is it that you, a Jew, ask a 4.09
and see h. the fields are already 4.35
H. can you believe, who receive 5.44
h. will you believe my words?" 5.47
"H. are we to buy bread, so that 6.05
H. does he now say, 'I have come 6.42
"H. can this man give us his flesh 6.52
"H. is it that this man has learning, 7.15
H. is it that you say, 'You will be 8.33
"Then h. were your eyes opened?" 9.10
again asked him h. he had received 9.15
"H. can a man who is a sinner do 9.16
H. then does he now see?" 9.19
but h. he now sees we do not know, 9.21
H. did he open your eyes?" 9.26
"H. long will you keep us in 10.24
the Jews said, "See h. he loved him!" 11.36
took counsel h. to put him to 11.53
H. can you say that the Son of man 12.34
h. can we know the way?" 14.05
h. can you say, 'Show us the Father'? 14.09
h. is it that you will manifest 14.22
"Is that h. you answer the high 18.22
And h. is it that we hear, each of Ac 2.08
H. is it that you have contrived 5.04
"H. is it that you have agreed 5.09
And he said, "H. can I, unless some 8.31
h. much evil he has done to thy 9.13
for I will show him h. much he must 9.16
declared to them h. on the road he 9.27
and h. at Damascus he had preached 9.27
yourselves know h. unlawful it is 10.28
h. God anointed Jesus of Nazareth 10.38
h. he went about doing good and 10.38
And he told us h. he had seen the 11.13
h. he said, 'John baptized with 11.16
described to them h. the Lord had 12.17
and h. he had opened a door of 14.27
Symeon has related h. God first 15.14
of the Lord, and see h. they are." 15.36
yourselves know h. I lived among 20.18
h. I did not shrink from declaring 20.20
h. he said, 'It is more blessed to 20.35
h. many thousands there are among 21.20
Being at a loss h. to investigate 25.20
For then h. could God judge the Rom 3.06
H. then was it reckoned to him? 4.10
H. can we who died to sin still 6.02
we do not know h. to pray as we 8.26
But h. are men to call upon him in 10.14
And h. are they to believe in him 10.14
And h. are they to hear without a 10.14
And h. can men preach unless they 10.15
"H. beautiful are the feet of those 10.15
h. he pleads with God against 11.02
h. much more will their full 11.12
h. much more will these natural 11.24
judgments and h. inscrutable his ways! 11.33
judgments and h. inscrutable his 11.33
h. it is full time now for you to 13.11
man take care h. he builds upon it. 1Co 3.10
This is h. one should regard us, as 4.01
H. much more, matters pertaining to 6.03
Wife, h. do you know whether you 7.16
Husband, h. do you know whether you 7.16
h. to please the Lord; 7.32
h. to please his wife, 7.33

HOW (cont.)

h. to be holy in body and spirit; 1Co 7.34
h. to please her husband. 7.34
h. shall I benefit you unless I 14.06
h. will any one know what is played? 14.07
h. will any one know what is said? 14.09
h. can any one in the position of 14.16
h. can some of you say that there 15.12
"H. are the dead raised? 15.35
h. I persecuted the church of God Gal 1.13
h. can you compel the Gentiles to 2.14
h. can you turn back again to the 4.09
h. the mystery was made known to me Eph 3.03
that is, h. the Gentiles are fellow 3.06
Look carefully then h. you walk, 5.15
also may know h. I am and what I 6.21
that you may know h. we are, 6.22
h. I yearn for you all with the Php 1.08
h. as a son with a father he has 2.22
soon as I see h. it will go with 2.23
h. to be abased, and I know h. to abound; 4.12
to make known h. great among the Col 1.27
you may know h. you ought to 4.06
you may know h. we are and that he 4.08
and h. you turned to God from idols, 1Th 1.09
h. holy and righteous and blameless 2.10
for you know h., like a father with 2.11
learned from us h. you ought to 4.01
one of you know h. to take a wife 4.04
yourselves know h. you ought to 2Th 3.07
does not know h. to manage his own 1Ti 3.05
h. can he care for God's church? 3.05
you may know h. one ought to behave 3.15
and h. from childhood you have been 2Ti 3.15
to me but h. much more to you, both Phm 1.16
h. shall we escape if we neglect Heb 2.03
See h. great he is! Abraham the 7.04
h. much more shall the blood of 9.14
and let us consider h. to stir up 10.24
H. much worse punishment do you 10.29
H. great a forest is set ablaze by Jas 3.05
h. the Lord is compassionate and 5.11
then the Lord knows h. to rescue 2Pe 2.09
h. does God's love abide in him? 1Jn 3.17
and h. you cannot bear evil men but Rev 2.02
h. long before thou wilt judge and 6.10
And this was h. I saw the horses in 9.17

HOWEVER

"H., you may slaughter and eat Deu 12.15
H. they did not drive out the Jos 16.10
h. the kingdom has turned about and 1Ki 2.15
h., because no house had yet been 3.02
H. I will not tear away all the 11.13
H. they would not listen, but they 2Ki 17.40
H., the priests of the high places 23.09
h., were not taken away; 2Ch 20.33
H. in the first year of Cyrus king Ez 5.13
H. much man may toil in seeking, he Ecc 8.17
h., for father or mother, for son or Eze 44.25
H., not to give offense to them, go Mt 17.27
H., boats from Tiberias came near Jn 6.23
He, h., shook off the creature into Ac 28.05
At present, h., I am going to Rom 15.25
H., not all possess this knowledge. 1Co 8.07
h. you may have been moved. 12.02
h., let each one of you love his Eph 5.33

HOWL

weep and h. for the miseries that Jas 5.01

HOWLING

and in the h. waste of the wilderness; Deu 32.10
h. like dogs and prowling about the Ps 59.06
h. like dogs and prowling about the 59.14
will be full of h. creatures; Is 13.21

HUBS

spokes, and their h., were all cast. 1Ki 7.33

HUDDLE

under the nettles they h. together. Job 30.07

HUGE

h. stones, stones of eight and ten 1Ki 7.10
the Libyans a h. army with exceedingly 2Ch 16.08
It is being built with h. stones, Ez 5.08

HUKKOK

Aznothtabor, and goes from there to H., Jos 19.34

HUKOK

H. with its pasture lands, and Rehob 1Ch 6.75

HUL

of Aram: Uz, H., Gether, and Mash. Gen 10.23
Lud, Aram, Uz, H., Gether, and Meshech. 1Ch 1.17

HULDAH

Asaiah went to H. the prophetess, 2Ki 22.14
had sent went to H. the prophetess, 2Ch 34.22

HUMAN

Or if he touches h. uncleanness, Lev 5.03
are taken away by no h. hand. Job 34.20
beyond h. semblance, and his form Is 52.14
their four sides they had h. hands. Eze 1.08
a likeness as it were of a h. form. 1.26
it in their sight on h. dung." 4.12
have cow's dung instead of h. dung, 4.15
the form of a h. hand under their 10.08
wings the semblance of h. hands. 10.21
they have devoured h. lives; 22.25
a stone was cut out by no h. hand, Dan 2.34
cut from a mountain by no h. hand, 2.45
but, by no h. hand, he shall be 8.25
no h. being would be saved; but for the Mt 24.22
no h. being would be saved; but for the Mk 13.20
nor is he served by h. hands, Ac 17.25
for every h. being who does evil, Rom 2.09
wrath on us? (I speak in a h. way.) 3.05
For no h. being will be justified 3.20
I am speaking in h. terms, because of your 6.19
so that no h. being might boast in 1Co 1.29
not taught by h. wisdom but taught 2.13
judged by you or by any h. court. 4.03
Do I say this on h. authority? 9.08
stone but on tablets of h. hearts. 2Co 3.03
no one from a h. point of view, 5.16
Christ from a h. point of view, 5.16
To give a h. example, brethren: no Gal 3.15
And being found in h. from he Php 2.08
according to h. tradition, according Col 2.08
according to h. precepts and 2.22
but no h. being can tame the tongue— Jas 3.08
sake to every h. institution, 1Pe 2.13
no longer by h. passions but by 4.02
ass spoke with h. voice and 2Pe 2.13
their faces were like h. faces, Rev 9.07
for it is a h. number, its number is 13.18
and slaves, that is, h. souls. 18.13

HUMANKIND

be tamed and has been tamed by h., Jas 3.07

HUMANLY

h. speaking, I fought with beasts at 1Co 15.32

HUMBLE

you refuse to h. yourself before Ex 10.03
that he might h. you, testing you to Deu 8.02
that he might h. you and test you, 8.16
Thou dost deliver a h. people, 2Sa 22.28
called by my name h. themselves, 2Ch 7.14
And he did not h. himself before 33.23

HUMBLE (cont.)
He did not h. himself before 2Ch 36.12
that we might h. ourselves before Ez 8.21
to the Almighty and h. yourself, Job 22.23
For thou dost deliver a h. people; Ps 18.27
He leads the h. in what is right, 25.09
right, and teaches the h. his way. 25.09
and h. them, he who is enthroned 55.19
him, the wicked shall not h. him. 89.22
he adorns the h. with victory. 149.04
but to the h. he shows favor. Pro 3.34
comes disgrace; but with the h. is wisdom. 11.02
Better is a man of h. standing who 12.09
who is of a contrite and h. spirit, Is 57.15
to revive the spirit of the h., 57.15
a day for a man to h. himself? 58.05
he that is h. and contrite in 66.02
let my h. plea come before you, and Jer 37.20
'I made a h. plea to the king that 38.26
might be h. and not lift itself up, Eze 17.14
in you they h. women who are unclean 22.10
all you h. of the land, who do his Zep 2.03
midst of you a people h. and lowly. 3.12
h. and riding on an ass, on a colt Zec 9.09
h., and mounted on an ass, and on a Mt 21.05
I who am h. when face to face with 2Co 10.01
again my God may h. me before you, 12.21
proud, but gives grace to the h." Jas 4.06
H. yourselves before the Lord and 4.10
the brethren, a tender heart and a h. mind. 1Pe 3.08
proud, but gives grace to the h." 5.05
H. yourselves therefore under the 5.06

HUMBLED
her and lay with her and h. her. Gen 34.02
heart is h. and they make amends Lev 26.41
And he h. you and let you hunger Deu 8.03
how Ahab has h. himself before me? 1Ki 21.29
Because he has h. himself before me, 21.29
and you h. yourself before the LORD, 2Ki 22.19
and the king h. themselves and 2Ch 12.06
LORD saw that they h. themselves, 12.07
Shemaiah: "They have h. themselves; 12.07
And when he h. himself the wrath of 12.12
and of Zebulun h. themselves and 30.11
But Hezekiah h. himself for the 32.26
his God and h. himself greatly 33.12
before he h. himself, behold, they 33.19
Manasseh his father had h. himself, 33.23
penitent and you h. yourself before 34.27
and you have h. yourself before me, 34.27
Because God has loosed my cord and h. me, Jos 30.11
When I h. my soul with fasting, it Ps 69.10
So man is h., and men are brought Is 2.09
and the pride of men shall be h.; 2.11
the haughtiness of man shall be h., 2.17
and the eyes of the haughty are h. 5.15
Why have we h. ourselves, and thou 58.03
They have not h. themselves even to Jer 44.10
have not h. your heart, though you Dan 5.22
understand and h. yourself before 10.12
whoever exalts himself will be h., Mt 23.12
one who exalts himself will be h., Lk 14.11
one who exalts himself will be h., 18.14
human form he h. himself and beame Php 2.08

HUMBLES
Whoever h. himself like this child, Mt 18.04
and whoever h. himself will be 23.12
and he who h. himself will be Lk 14.11
but he who h. himself will be 18.14

HUMBLEST
my family the h. of all the families 1Sa 9.21

HUMBLY
and to walk h. with your God? Mic 6.08

HUMILIATE
of God and h. those who have 1Co 11.22

HUMILIATED
as a slave, since you have h. her. Deu 21.14
we be h.—to say nothing of you— 2Co 9.04

HUMILIATION
and make my h. an argument against Job 19.05
in the shadow of Egypt to your h. Is 30.03
In his h. justice was denied him. Ac 8.33
and the rich in his h., Jas 1.10

HUMILITY
in wisdom, and h. goes before honor. Pro 15.33
is haughty, but h. goes before honor. 18.12
The reward for h. and fear of the 22.04
seek righteousness, seek h.; perhaps you Zep 2.03
Lord with all h. and with tears Ac 20.19
but in h. count others better than Php 2.03
with h. toward one another, for "God 1Pe 5.05

HUMPS
treasures on the h. of camels, Is 30.06

HUMTAH
H., Kiriatharba (that is, Hebron), Jos 15.54

HUNCHBACK
or a h., or a dwarf, or a man with a Lev 21.20

HUNDRED
had lived a h. and thirty years, he Gen 5.03
father of Seth were eight h. years; 5.04
lived were nine h. and thirty years; 5.05
Seth had lived a h. and five years, 5.06
of Enosh eight h. and seven years, 5.07
Seth were nine h. and twelve years; 5.08
of Kenan eight h. and fifteen years, 5.10
Enosh were nine h. and five years; 5.11
Mahalalel eight h. and forty years, 5.13
Kenan were nine h. and ten years; 5.14
of Jared eight h. and thirty years, 5.16
were eight h. and ninety-five 5.17
had lived a h. and sixty-two years 5.18
the birth of Enoch eight h. years, 5.19
Jared were nine h. and sixty-two 5.20
birth of Methuselah three h. years, 5.22
were three h. and sixty-five years. 5.23
had lived a h. and eighty-seven 5.25
of Lamech seven h. and eighty-two 5.26
were nine h. and sixty-nine years; 5.27
had lived a h. and eighty-two 5.28
of Noah five h. and ninety-five 5.30
were seven h. and seventy-seven 5.31
After Noah was five h. years old, 5.32
days shall be a h. and twenty years." 6.03
length of the ark three h. cubits, 6.15
Noah was six h. years old when the 7.06
upon the earth a h. and fifty days. 7.24
At the end of a h. and fifty days 8.03
In the six h. and first year, in the 8.13
lived three h. and fifty years. 9.28
Noah were nine h. and fifty years; 9.29
When Shem was a h. years old, 11.10
birth of Arpachshad five h. years, 11.11
of Shelah four h. and three years, 11.13
of Eber four h. and three years, 11.15
of Peleg four h. and thirty years, 11.17
birth of Reu two h. and nine years, 11.19
of Serug two h. and seven years, 11.21
the birth of Nahor two h. years, 11.23
of Terah a h. and nineteen years, 11.25
Terah were two h. and five years; 11.32
three h. and eighteen of them, and 14.14
be oppressed for four h. years; 15.13
be born to a man who is a h. years old? 17.17
Abraham was a h. years old when his 21.05

HUNDRED (cont.)

Sarah lived a h. and twenty-seven years; Gen 23.01
land worth four h. shekels of 23.15
four h. shekels of silver, according 23.16
life, a h. and seventy-five years. 25.07
a h. and thirty-seven years; he breathed 25.17
meet you, and four h. men with him." 32.06
two h. she-goats and twenty he-goats, 32.14
he-goats, two h. ewes and twenty rams, 32.14
coming, and four h. men with him. 33.01
he bought for a h. pieces of money 33.19
of Isaac were a h. and eighty years. 35.28
he gave three h. shekels of silver 45.22
sojourning are a h. and thirty 47.09
were a h. and forty-seven years. 47.28
Joseph lived a h. and ten years. 50.22
being a h. and ten years old; 50.26
of Levi being a h. and thirty-seven Ex 6.16
Kohath being a h. and thirty-three 6.18
Amram being one h. and thirty-seven 6.20
about six h. thousand men on foot, 12.37
Egypt was four h. and thirty years. 12.40
the end of four h. and thirty years, 12.41
and took six h. picked chariots and 14.07
twined linen a h. cubits long for 27.09
shall be hangings a h. cubits long, 27.11
of the court shall be a h. cubits, 27.18
of liquid myrrh five h. shekels, 30.23
two h. and fifty, and of aromatic 30.23
of aromatic cane two h. and fifty, 30.23
and of cassia five h., according to 30.24
of fine twined linen, a h. cubits; 38.09
And for the north side a h. cubits, 38.11
and seven h. and thirty shekels, by 38.24
numbered was a h. talents and a 38.25
thousand seven h. and seventy-five 38.25
for six h. and three thousand, five 38.26
thousand, five h. and fifty men. 38.26
The h. talents of silver were for 38.27
a h. bases for the h. talents, 38.27
thousand seven h. and seventy-five 38.28
two thousand and four h. shekels; 38.29
Five of you shall chase a h., Lev 26.08
and a h. of you shall chase ten 26.08
was forty-six thousand five h. Num 1.21
was fifty-nine thousand three h. 1.23
forty-five thousand six h. and fifty. 1.25
was seventy-four thousand six h. 1.27
was fifty-four thousand four h. 1.29
was fifty-seven thousand four h. 1.31
Ephraim was forty thousand five h. 1.33
was thirty-two thousand two h. 1.35
was thirty-five thousand four h. 1.37
was sixty-two thousand seven h. 1.39
was forty-one thousand five h. 1.41
was fifty-three thousand four h. 1.43
number was six h. and three thousand 1.46
three thousand five h. and fifty. 1.46
being seventy-four thousand six h. 2.04
being fifty-four thousand four h. 2.06
being fifty-seven thousand four h. 2.08
is a h. and eighty-six thousand four h. 2.09
being forty-six thousand five h. 2.11
being fifty-nine thousand three h. 2.13
forty-five thousand six h. and fifty. 2.15
is a h. and fifty-one thousand four h. 2.16
as numbered being forty thousand five h. 2.19
being thirty-two thousand two h. 2.21
being thirty-five thousand four h. 2.23
is a h. and eight thousand one h. 2.24
being sixty-two thousand seven h. 2.26
being forty-one thousand five h. 2.28
being fifty-three thousand four h. 2.30
is a h. and fifty-seven thousand six h. 2.31
were six h. and three thousand five h. and fifty. 2.32
upward was seven thousand five h. 3.22
there were eight thousand six h., 3.28
and upward was six thousand two h. 3.34
thousand two h. and seventy-three. 3.43
of the two h. and seventy-three of 3.46
thousand three h. and sixty-five 3.50
two thousand seven h. and fifty. 4.36
was two thousand six h. and thirty. 4.40
families was three thousand two h. 4.44
eight thousand five h. and eighty. 4.48
weight was a h. and thirty shekels, 7.13
weight was a h. and thirty shekels, 7.19
weight was a h. and thirty shekels, 7.25
weight was a h. and thirty shekels, 7.31
weight was a h. and thirty shekels, 7.37
weight was a h. and thirty shekels, 7.43
weight was a h. and thirty shekels, 7.49
weight was a h. and thirty shekels, 7.55
weight was a h. and thirty shekels, 7.61
weight was a h. and thirty shekels, 7.67
weight was a h. and thirty shekels, 7.73
weight was a h. and thirty shekels, 7.79
weighing a h. and thirty shekels 7.85
two thousand four h. shekels according 7.85
dishes being a h. and twenty 7.86
I am number six h. thousand on 11.21
two h. and fifty leaders of the 16.02
two h. and fifty censers; 16.17
consumed the two h. and fifty men 16.35
were fourteen thousand seven h., 16.49
thousand seven h. and thirty. 26.07
fire devoured two h. and fifty men; 26.10
Simeonites, twenty-two thousand two h. 26.14
number, forty thousand five h. 26.18
seventy-six thousand five h. 26.22
sixty-four thousand three h. 26.25
number, sixty thousand five h. 26.27
was fifty-two thousand seven h. 26.34
thirty-two thousand five h. 26.37
was forty-five thousand six h. 26.41
were sixty-four thousand four h. 26.43
fifty-three thousand four h. 26.47
was forty-five thousand four h. 26.50
six h. and one thousand seven h. 26.51
out to battle, one out of five h., 31.28
six h. and seventy-five thousand 31.32
in number three h. and thirty-seven 31.36
thirty-seven thousand five h. sheep, 31.36
sheep was six h. and seventy-five. 31.37
asses were thirty thousand five h., 31.39
half was three h. and thirty-seven 31.43
thirty-seven thousand five h. sheep, 31.43
and thirty thousand five h. asses, 31.45
sixteen thousand seven h. and fifty 31.52
And Aaron was a h. and twenty-three 33.39
fine him a h. shekels of silver, Deu 22.19
"I am a h. and twenty years old 31.02
Moses was a h. and twenty years old 34.07
and two h. shekels of silver, and a Jos 7.21
being a h. and ten years old. 24.29
Shehem for a h. pieces of money; 24.32
at the age of one h. and ten years. Ju 2.08
who killed six h. of the Philistines 3.31
for he had nine h. chariots of iron, 4.03
nine h. chariots of iron, and all 4.13
to their mouths, was three h. men; 7.06
"With the three h. men that lapped 7.07
but retained the three h. men; 7.08
the three h. men into three companies, 7.16
So Gideon and the h. men who were 7.19
When they blew the three h. trumpets, 7.22
and the three h. men who were with 8.04
had fallen a h. and twenty thousand 8.10
thousand seven h. shekels of gold; 8.26
three h. years, why did you not 11.26
went and caught three h. foxes, 15.04
give you eleven h. pieces of 16.05
"The eleven h. pieces of silver 17.02
the eleven h. pieces of silver to 17.03

HUNDRED (cont.)

mother took two h. pieces of Ju 17.04
And six h. men of the tribe of Dan, 18.11
Now the six h. men of the Danites, 18.16
with the six h. men armed with 18.17
four h. thousand men on foot that 20.02
ten men of a h. throughout all the 20.10
and a h. of a thousand, and a 20.10
who mustered seven h. picked men. 20.15
were seven h. picked men who were 20.16
mustered four h. thousand men that 20.17
thousand one h. men of Benjamin 20.35
But six h. men turned and fled 20.47
Jabeshgilead four h. young virgins 21.12
of Israel were three h. thousand, 1Sa 11.08
present with him, about six h. men. 13.15
with him were about six h. men, 14.02
two h. thousand men on foot, and ten 15.04
weighed six h. shekels of iron; 17.07
except a h. foreskins of the Philistines, 18.25
and killed two h. of the Philistines; 18.27
were with him about four h. men. 22.02
and his men, who were about six h., 23.13
and about four h. men went up after 25.13
while two h. remained with the 25.13
and took two h. loaves, and two 25.18
and a h. clusters of raisins, and 25.18
and two h. cakes of figs, and laid 25.18
he and the six h. men who were 27.02
and the six h. men who were with 30.09
the pursuit, he and four h. men; 30.10
two h. stayed behind, who were too 30.10
except four h. young men, who mounted 30.17
Then David came to the two h. men, 30.21
Benjamin three h. and sixty of 2Sa 2.31
the price of a h. foreskins of the 3.14
a thousand and seven h. horsemen, 8.04
but left enough for a h. chariots. 8.04
the Syrians the men of seven h. chariots, 10.18
two h. shekels by the king's weight. 14.26
went two h. men from Jerusalem who 15.11
and all the six h. Gittites who 15.18
bearing two h. loaves of bread, a 16.01
a h. bunches of raisins, a 16.01
a h. of summer fruits, and a skin of 16.01
weighed three h. shekels of bronze, 21.16
against eight h. whom he slew at 23.08
against three h. men and slew them, 23.18
to the people a h. times as many 24.03
were eight h. thousand valiant men 24.09
men of Judah were five h. thousand. 24.09
a h. sheep, besides harts, gazelles, 1Ki 4.23
three thousand three h. chief officers 5.16
In the four h. and eightieth year 6.01
its length was a h. cubits, and its 7.02
there were two h. pomegranates, 7.20
and the four h. pomegranates for 7.42
oxen and a h. and twenty thousand 8.63
to the king one h. and twenty talents 9.14
five h. and fifty, who had charge of 9.23
amount of four h. and twenty talents; 9.28
gave the king a h. and twenty talents 10.10
year was six h. and sixty-six talents 10.14
made two h. large shields of 10.16
six h. shekels of gold went into 10.16
And he made three h. shields of 10.17
he had fourteen h. chariots and 10.26
Egypt for six h. shekels of silver, 10.29
and a horse for a h. and fifty; 10.29
He had seven h. wives, princesses, 11.03
princesses, and three h. concubines; 11.03
a h. and eighty thousand chosen 12.21
Obadiah took a h. prophets and hid 18.04
how I hid a h. men of the LORD's 18.13
and the four h. and fifty prophets 18.19
and the four h. prophets of Asherah, 18.19
prophets are four h. and fifty men. 18.22
they were two h. and thirty-two; 20.15
the Syrians a h. thousand foot 20.29
about four h. men, and said to them, 22.06
king of Israel a h. thousand lambs, 2Ki 3.04
and the wool of a h. thousand rams. 3.04
with him seven h. swordsmen to break 3.26
am I to set this before a h. men?" 4.43
of Jerusalem for four h. cubits, 14.13
of Judah three h. talents of 18.14
and slew a h. and eighty-five 19.35
a tribute of a h. talents of 23.33
five h. men of the Simeonites, went 1Ch 4.42
forty-four thousand seven h. and sixty, 5.18
two h. and fifty thousand sheep, two 5.21
and a h. thousand men alive. 5.21
being twenty-two thousand six h. 7.02
warriors, was twenty thousand two h. 7.09
seventeen thousand and two h., 7.11
and grandsons, one h. and fifty. 8.40
their kinsmen, six h. and ninety. 9.06
generations, nine h. and fifty-six. 9.09
one thousand seven h. and sixty, 9.13
thresholds, were two h. and twelve. 9.22
against three h. whom he slew at 11.11
against three h. men and slew them, 11.20
lesser over a h. and the greater 12.14
six thousand eight h. armed troops. 12.24
for war, seven thousand one h. 12.25
Of the Levites four thousand six h. 12.26
with him three thousand seven h. 12.27
Ephraimites twenty thousand eight h., 12.30
two h. chiefs, and all their kinsmen 12.32
thousand six h. men equipped for 12.35
one h. and twenty thousand men 12.37
with a h. and twenty of his brethren; 15.05
with two h. and twenty of his 15.06
with a h. and thirty of his brethren; 15.07
with two h. of his brethren; 15.08
with a h. and twelve of his brethren. 15.10
but left enough for a h. chariots. 18.04
to his people a h. times as many 21.03
one million one h. thousand men 21.05
in Judah four h. and seventy thousand 21.05
paid Ornan six h. shekels of gold 21.25
of the LORD a h. thousand talents 22.14
skilful, was two h. and eighty-eight. 25.07
thousand seven h. men of ability, 26.30
thousand seven h. men of ability, 26.32
and a h. thousand talents of iron. 29.07
he had fourteen h. chariots and 2Ch 1.14
Egypt for six h. shekels of silver, 1.17
and a horse for a h. and fifty; 1.17
thousand six h. to oversee them. 2.02
a h. and fifty-three thousand six h. 2.17
thousand six h. as overseers to 2.18
height was a h. and twenty cubits. 3.04
it with six h. talents of fine gold. 3.08
and he made a h. pomegranates, and 3.16
And he made a h. basins of gold. 4.08
and the four h. pomegranates for 4.13
altar with a h. and twenty priests 5.12
oxen and a h. and twenty thousand 7.05
two h. and fifty, who exercised 8.10
from there four h. and fifty talents 8.18
gave the king a h. and twenty talents 9.09
year was six h. and sixty-six talents 9.13
made two h. large shields of 9.15
six h. shekels of beaten gold 9.15
And he made three h. shields of 9.16
three h. shekels of gold went 9.16
a h. and eighty thousand chosen 11.01
with twelve h. chariots and sixty 12.03
four h. thousand picked men; 13.03
him with eight h. thousand picked 13.03
of Israel five h. thousand picked 13.17
army of three h. thousand from 14.08
and two h. and eighty thousand men 14.08
million men and three h. chariots, 14.09

HUNDRED (cont.)

seven h. oxen and seven thousand 2Ch 15.11
thousand seven h. rams and seven h. he-goats. 17.11
with three h. thousand mighty men 17.14
with two h. and eighty thousand, 17.15
with two h. thousand mighty men of 17.16
with two h. thousand men armed with 17.17
Jehozabad with a h. and eighty 17.18
four h. men, and said to them, "Shall 18.05
he was a h. and thirty years old 24.15
they were three h. thousand picked 25.05
He hired also a h. thousand mighty 25.06
Israel for a h. talents of silver. 25.06
we do about the h. talents which I 25.09
of Jerusalem for four h. cubits, 25.23
of valor was two thousand six h. 26.12
three h. and seven thousand five h., 26.13
him that year a h. talents of 27.05
Remaliah slew a h. and twenty 28.06
captive two h. thousand of their 28.08
a h. rams, and two h. lambs; 29.32
were six h. bulls and three thousand 29.33
thousand six h. lambs and kids and three h. bulls. 35.08
lambs and kids and five h. bulls. 35.09
a tribute of a h. talents of silver 36.03
thousand four h. and ten bowls of Ez 1.10
thousand four h. and sixty-nine. 1.11
thousand one h. and seventy-two. 2.03
three h. and seventy-two. 2.04
seven h. and seventy-five. 2.05
two thousand eight h. and twelve. 2.06
one thousand two h. and fifty-four. 2.07
of Zattu, nine h. and forty-five. 2.08
sons of Zaccai, seven h. and sixty. 2.09
sons of Bani, six h. and forty-two. 2.10
six h. and twenty-three. 2.11
one thousand two h. and twenty-two. 2.12
of Adonikam, six h. and sixty-six. 2.13
of Adin, four h. and fifty-four. 2.15
three h. and twenty-three. 2.17
The sons of Jorah, one h. and twelve. 2.18
two h. and twenty-three. 2.19
one h. and twenty-three. 2.21
one h. and twenty-eight. 2.23
seven h. and forty-three. 2.25
and Geba, six h. and twenty-one. 2.26
of Michmas, one h. and twenty-two. 2.27
two h. and twenty-three. 2.28
of Magbish, one h. and fifty-six. 2.30
one thousand two h. and fifty-four. 2.31
sons of Harim, three h. and twenty. 2.32
seven h. and twenty-five. 2.33
Jericho, three h. and forty-five. 2.34
three thousand six h. and thirty. 2.35
nine h. and seventy-three. 2.36
thousand two h. and forty-seven. 2.38
one h. and twenty-eight. 2.41
in all one h. and thirty-nine. 2.42
were three h. and ninety-two. 2.58
of Nekoda, six h. and fifty-two. 2.60
thousand three h. and sixty, 2.64
thousand three h. and thirty-seven; 2.65
they had two h. male and female 2.65
were seven h. and thirty-six, 2.66
mules were two h. and forty-five, 2.66
were four h. and thirty-five, and 2.67
six thousand seven h. and twenty. 2.67
of silver, and one h. priests' garments. 2.69
of this house of God one h. bulls, 6.17
two h. rams, four h. lambs, and as a 6.17
h. talents of silver, a h. measures of wheat, 7.22
a h. baths of wine, a h. baths of oil, 7.22
registered one h. and fifty men. 8.03
Zerahiah, and with him two h. men. 8.04
Jahaziel, and with him three h. men. 8.05
with him two h. and eighteen men. 8.09
and with him a h. and sixty men. 8.10
and with him a h. and ten men. 8.12
besides two h. and twenty of the 8.20
their hand six h. and fifty 8.26
silver vessels worth a h. talents, 8.26
and a h. talents of gold, 8.26
it as far as the Tower of the H., Neh 3.01
at my table a h. and fifty men, 5.17
two thousand a h. and seventy-two. 7.08
three h. and seventy-two. 7.09
sons of Arah, six h. and fifty-two. 7.10
two thousand eight h. and eighteen. 7.11
a thousand two h. and fifty-four. 7.12
of Zattu, eight h. and forty-five. 7.13
sons of Zaccai, seven h. and sixty. 7.14
six h. and forty-eight. 7.15
six h. and twenty-eight. 7.16
thousand three h. and twenty-two. 7.17
six h. and sixty-seven. 7.18
of Adin, six h. and fifty-five. 7.20
three h. and twenty-eight. 7.22
three h. and twenty-four. 7.23
The sons of Hariph, a h. and twelve. 7.24
a h. and eighty-eight. 7.26
a h. and twenty-eight. 7.27
seven h. and forty-three. 7.29
and Geba, six h. and twenty-one. 7.30
of Michmas, a h. and twenty-two. 7.31
a h. and twenty-three. 7.32
a thousand two h. and fifty-four. 7.34
sons of Harim, three h. and twenty. 7.35
Jericho, three h. and forty-five. 7.36
and Ono, seven h. and twenty-one. 7.37
three thousand nine h. and thirty. 7.38
nine h. and seventy-three. 7.39
a thousand two h. and forty-seven. 7.41
a h. and forty-eight. 7.44
a h. and thirty-eight. 7.45
were three h. and ninety-two. 7.60
of Nekoda, six h. and forty-two. 7.62
thousand three h. and sixty, 7.66
thousand three h. and thirty-seven; 7.67
they had two h. and forty-five 7.67
were seven h. and thirty-six, 7.68
their mules two h. and forty-five, 7.68
their camels four h. and thirty-five, 7.69
six thousand seven h. and twenty. 7.69
five h. and thirty priests' garments. 7.70
thousand two h. minas of silver. 7.71
were four h. and sixty-eight 11.06
nine h. and twenty-eight. 11.08
the house, eight h. and twenty-two; 11.12
houses, two h. and forty-two; 11.13
a h. and twenty-eight; 11.14
city were two h. and eighty-four. 11.18
were a h. and seventy-two. 11.19
of Hananel and the Tower of the H., 12.39
over one h. and twenty-seven Est 1.01
many days, a h. and eighty days. 1.04
a h. and twenty-seven provinces, to 8.09
slew and destroyed five h. men, 9.06
have slain five h. men and also 9.12
and they slew three h. men in Susa; 9.15
to the h. and twenty-seven provinces 9.30
five h. yoke of oxen, and five Job 1.03
and five h. she-asses, and very many 1.03
Job lived a h. and forty years, and 42.16
understanding than a h. blows into Pro 17.10
If a man begets a h. children, Ecc 6.03
does evil a h. times and prolongs 8.12
the keepers of the fruit two h. Sol 8.12
and slew a h. and eighty-five Is 37.36
the child shall die a h. years old, 65.20
the sinner a h. years old shall be 65.20
pomegranates were a h. upon the Jer 52.23
Jerusalem eight h. and thirty-two 52.29
the Jews seven h. and forty-five 52.30
were four thousand and six h. 52.30
three h. and ninety days, equal to Eze 4.05
three h. and ninety days, you shall 4.09

HUNDRED (cont.)
of the inner court, a h. cubits. Eze 40.19
from gate to gate, a h. cubits. 40.23
gate toward the south, a h. cubits. 40.27
a h. cubits long, and a h. cubits broad, 40.47
the temple, a h. cubits long; 41.13
with its walls, a h. cubits long; 41.13
temple and the yard, a h. cubits. 41.14
walls on either side, a h. cubits. 41.15
on the north side was a h. cubits, 42.02
cubits wide and a h. cubits long, 42.04
the temple were a h. cubits long. 42.08
five h. cubits by the measuring 42.16
five h. cubits by the measuring 42.17
five h. cubits by the measuring 42.18
five h. cubits by the measuring 42.19
five h. cubits long and five h. cubits broad, 42.20
plot of five h. by five h. cubits shall 45.02
sheep from every flock of two h., 45.15
north side four thousand five h. cubits, 48.16
south side four thousand five h., 48.16
east side four thousand five h., 48.16
west side four thousand five h. 48.16
the north two h. and fifty cubits, 48.17
on the south two h. and fifty, 48.17
on the east two h. and fifty, 48.17
and on the west two h. and fifty. 48.17
thousand five h. cubits by measure, 48.30
to be four thousand five h. cubits, 48.32
thousand five h. cubits by measure, 48.33
to be four thousand five h. cubits, 48.34
the kingdom a h. and twenty satraps, Dan 6.01
and three h. evenings and mornings; 8.14
a thousand two h. and ninety days. 12.11
thousand three h. and thirty-five 12.12
a thousand shall have a h. left, Amo 5.03
went forth a h. shall have ten 5.03
are more than a h. and twenty Jon 4.11
If a man has a h. sheep, and one of Mt 18.12
servants who owed him a h. denarii; 18.28
go and buy two h. denarii worth of Mk 6.37
for more than three h. denarii, 14.05
one owed five h. denarii, and the Lk 7.41
having a h. sheep, if he has lost 15.04
He said, 'A h. measures of oil.' 16.06
He said, 'A h. measures of wheat.' 16.07
"Two h. denarii would not buy Jn 6.07
sold for three h. denarii and 12.05
aloes, about a h. pounds' weight. 19.39
the land, but about a h. yards off. 21.08
a h. and fifty-three of them; 21.11
was in all about a h. and twenty), Ac 1.15
of men, about four h. joined him; 5.36
and ill-treat them four h. years. 7.06
for about four h. and fifty years. 13.19
get ready two h. soldiers with 23.23
horsemen and two h. spearmen to go 23.23
(We were in all two h. and seventy-six 27.37
he was about a h. years old, Rom 4.19
more than five h. brethren at one 1Co 15.06
which came four h. and thirty Gal 3.17
a h. and forty-four thousand sealed, Rev 7.04
one thousand two h. and sixty days, 11.03
one thousand two h. and sixty days. 12.06
its number is six h. and sixty-six. 13.18
and with him a h. and forty-four 14.01
song except the h. and forty-four 14.03
for one thousand six h. stadia. 14.20
a h. and forty-four cubits by a 21.17

HUNDREDFOLD
and reaped in the same year a h. Gen 26.12
some a h., some sixty, some thirty. Mt 13.08
in one case a h., in another sixty, 13.23
my name's sake, will receive a h., 19.29
thirtyfold and sixtyfold and a h." Mk 4.08
thirtyfold and sixtyfold and a h." 4.20

not receive a h. now in this time, 10.30
soil and grew, and yielded a h. Lk 8.08

HUNDREDS
of h., of fifties, and of tens. Ex 18.21
of h., of fifties, and of tens. 18.25
thousands and the commanders of h., Num 31.14
thousands and the captains of h., 31.48
thousands and the commanders of h., 31.52
commanders of thousands and of h., 31.54
commanders of h., commanders of Deu 1.15
of thousands and commanders of h., 1Sa 22.07
passing on by h. and by thousands, 29.02
of thousands and commanders of h. 2Sa 18.01
marched out by h. and by thousands. 18.04
commanders of thousands and of h., 1Ch 13.01
of the thousands and the h., 26.26
the commanders of thousands and h., 27.01
of thousands, the commanders of h., 28.01
commanders of thousands and of h., 29.06
commanders of thousands and of h., 2Ch 1.02
compact with the commanders of h., 23.01
thousands and of h. for all Judah 25.05
in groups, by h. and by fifties. Mk 6.40

HUNDREDTH
In the six h. year of Noah's life, in Gen 7.11
and the h. of money, grain, wine, and Neh 5.11

HUNDREDWEIGHT
heavy as a h., dropped on men from Rev 16.21

HUNG
and he h. them on five trees. Jos 10.26
And they h. upon the trees until 10.26
willows there we h. up our lyres. Ps 137.02
Princes are h. up by their hands; Lam 5.12
they h. the shiled and helmet in Eze 27.10
they h. their shields upon your 27.11
millstone were h. round his neck Mk 9.42
millstone were h. round his neck Lk 17.02
all the people h. upon his words. 19.48

HUNGER
kill this whole assembly with h." Ex 16.03
you and let you h. and fed you Deu 8.03
in h. and thirst, in nakedness, and 28.48
they shall be wasted with h., 32.24
who were hungry have ceased to h. 1Sa 2.05
for their h. and bring forth water Neh 9.15
Through want and hard h. they gnaw Job 30.03
The young lions suffer want and h.; Ps 34.10
and an idle person will suffer h. Pro 19.15
their honored men are dying of h., Is 5.13
awakes with his h. not satisfied, 29.08
they shall not h. or thirst, neither 49.10
and he will die there of h., Jer 38.09
who faint for h. at the head of Lam 2.19
the sword than the victims of h., 4.09
satisfy their h. or fill their Eze 7.19
be consumed with h. in the land, 34.29
bread shall be for their h. only; Hos 9.04
there shall be h. in your inward Mic 6.14
"Blessed are those who h. and Mt 5.06
"Blessed are you that h. now, Lk 6.21
are full now, for you shall h. 6.25
spare, but I perish here with h.! 15.17
he who comes to me shall not h., Jn 6.35
To the present hour we h. and thirst, 1Co 4.11
tumults, labors, watching, h.; 2Co 6.05
in h. and thirst, often without food, 11.27
the secret of facing plenty and h., Php 4.12
They shall h. no more, neither Rev 7.16

HUNGER-BITTEN
His strength is h., and calamity Job 18.12

HUNGRY
those who were h. have ceased to 1Sa 2.05
"The people are h. and weary and 2Sa 17.29

HUNGRY (cont.)

They know that we are h.; therefore 2Ki 7.12
His harvest the h. eat, and he takes Job 5.05
have withheld bread from the h. 22.07
h., they carry the sheaves; 24.10
"If I were h., I would not tell you; Ps 50.12
h. and thirsty, their soul fainted 107.05
and the h. he fills with good 107.09
And there he lets the h. dwell, 107.36
the oppressed; who gives food to the h. 146.07
satisfy his appetite when he is h.? Pro 6.30
does not let the righteous go h., 10.03
If your enemy is h., give him 25.21
to one who is h. everything bitter 27.07
land, greatly distressed and h.; Is 8.21
and when they are h., they will be 8.21
but are still h., and they devour 9.20
As when a h. man dreams he is 29.08
the craving of the h. unsatisfied, 32.06
he becomes h. and his strength 44.12
to share your bread with the h., 58.07
out for the h. and satisfy the 58.10
shall eat, but you shall be h.; 65.13
or be h. for bread, and we will Jer 42.14
bread to the h. and covers the Eze 18.07
bread to the h. and covers the 18.16
nights, and afterward he was h. Mt 4.02
his disciples were h., and they began 12.01
when he was h.. and those who were 12.03
am unwilling to send them away h., 15.32
returning to the city, he was h. 21.18
for I was h. and you gave me food, I 25.35
did we see thee h. and feed thee, 25.37
for I was h. and you gave me no 25.42
did we see thee h. or thirsty or a 25.44
when he was in need and was h., Mk 2.25
I send them away h. to their homes, 8.03
they came from Bethany, he was h. 11.12
he has filled the h. with good Lk 1.53
when they were ended, he was h. 4.02
read what David did when he was h., 6.03
And he became h. and desired Ac 10.10
No, "if your enemy is h., feed him; Rom 12.20
and one is h. and another is drunk. 1Co 11.21
if any one is h., let him eat at 11.34

HUNT

to the field, and h. game for me, Gen 27.03
to the field to h. for game and 27.05
though you h. my life to take it. 1Sa 24.11
thou dost h. me like a lion, and Job 10.16
"How long will you h. for words? 18.02
"Can you h. the prey for the lion, 38.39
let evil h. down the violent man Ps 140.11
and they shall h. them from every Jer 16.16
every stature, in the h. for souls! Eze 13.18
Will you h. down souls belonging to 13.18
bands with which you h. the souls, 13.20
souls that you h. go free like 13.20

HUNTED

it then that h. game and brought Gen 27.33
And like a h. gazelle, or like sheep Is 13.14
"Israel is a h. sheep driven away Jer 50.17
"I have been h. like a bird by Lam 3.52

HUNTER

He was a mighty h. before the LORD; Gen 10.09
Nimrod a mighty h. before the LORD." 10.09
grew up, Esau was a skilful h., 25.27
yourself like a gazelle from the h., Pro 6.05

HUNTERS

afterwards I will send for many h., Jer 16.16

HUNTING

his brother came in from his h. Gen 27.30
who takes in h. any beast or bird Lev 17.13

HUNTS

like one who h. a partridge in the 1Sa 26.20
and each h. his brother with a net. Mic 7.02

HUPHAM

of H., the family of the Huphamites. Num 26.39

HUPHAMITES

of Hupham, the family of the H. Num 26.39

HUPPAH

the thirteenth to H., the fourteenth 1Ch 24.13

HUPPIM

Ehi, Rosh, Muppim, H., and Ard Gen 46.21
And Shuppim and H. were the sons of 1Ch 7.12
took a wife for H. and for Shuppim. 7.15

HUR

and H. went up to the top of the Ex 17.10
and Aaron and H. held up his hands, 17.12
behold, Aaron and H. are with you; 24.14
son of H., of the tribe of Judah: 31.02
son of H., of the tribe of Judah; 35.30
son of H., of the tribe of Judah, 38.22
H., and Reba, the five kings of Num 31.08
and Rekem and Zur and H. and Reba, Jos 13.21
married Ephrath, who bore him H. 1Ch 2.19
H. was the father of Uri, and Uri 2.20
The sons of H. the first-born of 2.50
Hezron, Carmi, H., and Shobal. 4.01
These were the sons of H. 4.04
son of H., had made, was there 2Ch 1.05
Next to them Rephaiah the son of H., Neh 3.09

HURAI

H. of the brooks of Gaash, Abiel the 1Ch 11.32

HURAM

Gera, Shephuphan, and H. 1Ch 8.05
sent word to H. the king of Tyre: 2Ch 2.03
Then H. the king of Tyre answered 2.11
H. also said, "Blessed be the LORD 2.12
H. also made the pots, the shovels, 4.11
So H. finished the work that he did 4.11
cities which H. had given to him, 8.02
And H. sent him by his servants 8.18
Moreover the servants of H. and the 9.10
Tarshish with the servants of H.; 9.21

HURAMABI

endued with understanding, H., 2Ch 2.13
for these H. made of burnished 4.16

HURI

the sons of Abihail the son of H., 1Ch 5.14

HURL

the LORD will h. you away violently, Is 22.17
therefore I will h. you out of this Jer 16.13
I will h. you and the mother who 22.26
possessions and h. her wealth into Zec 9.04

HURLED

or h. at him, lying in wait, so that Num 35.20
or h. anything on him without lying 35.22
his children h. and cast into a Jer 22.28
But the LORD h. a great wind upon Jon 1.04

HURLS

It h. at him without pity; he flees Job 27.22

HURRICANE

and terrify them with thy h.! Ps 83.15

HURRIED

of the land of Egypt in h. flight— Deu 16.03
But Haman h. to his house, mourning Est 6.12

HURRY
"H., make haste, stay not." 1Sa 20.38

HURT
and h. a woman with child, so that Ex 21.22
the one who h. her shall be fined, 21.22
it dies or is h. or is driven away, 22.10
and it is h. or dies, the owner not 22.14
say, 'Behold, David seeks your h.'? 1Sa 24.09
harm so that it might not h. me!" 1Ch 4.10
damage grow to the h. of the king?" Ez 4.22
hands on such as sought their h. Est 9.02
to his own h. and does not change; Ps 15.04
those who seek my h. speak of ruin, 38.12
to dishonor who desire my h.! 40.14
to dishonor who desire my h.! 70.02
may they be covered who seek my h. 71.13
disgraced who sought to do me h. 71.24
His feet were h. with fetters, his 105.18
you will say, "but I was not h.; Pro 23.35
kept by their owner to his h., Ecc 5.13
man lords it over man to his h. 8.09
He who quarries stones is h. by them; 10.09
They shall not h. or destroy in all Is 11.09
LORD binds up the h. of his people, 30.26
They shall not h. or destroy in all 65.25
after other gods to your own h., Jer 7.06
Woe is me because of my h.! 10.19
Your h. is incurable, and your wound 30.12
Why do you cry out over your h.? 30.15
or a thorn to h. them among all Eze 28.24
of the fire, and they are not h.; Dan 3.25
mouths, and they have not h. me, 6.22
and no kind of h. was found upon 6.23
There is no assuaging your h., Nah 3.19
it shall grievously h. themselves. Zec 12.03
the enemy; and nothing shall h. you. Lk 10.19
shall not be h. by the second Rev 2.11

HURTFUL
h. to kings and provinces, and that Ez 4.15
senseless and h. desires that 1Ti 6.09

HURTING
who has restrained me from h. you, 1Sa 25.34
their power of h. men for five Rev 9.10

HURTS
"When one man's ox h. another's, Ex 21.35
himself, but a cruel man h. himself. Pro 11.17
It h. you to kick against the goads.' Ac 26.14

HUSBAND
gave some to her h., and he ate. Gen 3.06
your desire shall be for your h., 3.16
gave her to Abram her h. as a wife. 16.03
and my h. is old, shall I have 18.12
surely now my h. will love me." 29.32
this time my h. will be joined to 29.34
that you have taken away my h.? 30.15
because I gave my maid to my h."; 30.18
now my h. will honor me, because I 30.20
as the woman's h. shall lay upon Ex 21.22
to him because she has had no h.; Lev 21.03
himself as a h. among his people 21.04
marry a woman divorced from her h.; 21.07
is hidden from the eyes of her h., Num 5.13
other than your h. has lain with 5.20
acted unfaithfully against her h., 5.27
And if she is married to a h., 30.06
and her h. hears of it, and says 30.07
day that her h. comes to hear of 30.08
and her h. heard of it, and said 30.11
But if her h. makes them null and 30.12
her h. has made them void, and the 30.12
to afflict herself, her h. may establish, 30.13
establish, or her h. may make void. 30.13
But if her h. says nothing to her 30.14
and be her h., and she shall be Deu 21.13
and the latter h. dislikes her and 24.03
house, or if the latter h. dies, 24.03
then her former h., who sent 24.04
to rescue her h. from the hand of 25.11
will grudge to the h. of her bosom, 28.56
Then the woman came and told her h., Ju 13.06
but Manoah her h. was not with her. 13.09
woman ran in haste and told her h., 13.10
"Entice your h. to tell us what the 14.15
Then her h. arose and went after 19.03
the h. of the woman who was murdered, 20.04
Elimelech, the h. of Naomi, died, and Ru 1.03
bereft of her two sons and her h. 1.05
each of you in the house of her h.!" 1.09
way, for I am too old to have a h. 1.12
I should have a h. this night and 1.12
death of your h. has been fully 2.11
her h., said to her, "Hannah, why do 1Sa 1.08
not go up, for she said to her h., 1.22
Elkanah her h. said to her, "Do what 1.23
up with her h. to offer the yearly 2.19
father-in-law and her h. were dead, 4.19
of her father-in-law and her h. 4.21
But she did not tell her h. Nabal. 25.19
her from her h. Paltiel the son of 2Sa 3.15
But her h. went with her, weeping 3.16
heard that Uriah her h. was dead, 11.26
she made lamentation for her h. 11.26
I am a widow; my h. is dead. 14.05
and leave to my h. neither name 14.07
as a bride comes home to her h. 17.03
Elisha, "Your servant my h. is dead; 2Ki 4.01
And she said to her h., "Behold 4.09
she has no son, and her h. is old." 4.14
Then she called to her h., and said, 4.22
Is it well with your h.? Is it well 4.26
For my h. is not at home; he has gone Pro 7.19
A good wife is the crown of her h., 12.04
an unloved woman when she gets a h., 30.23
The heart of her h. trusts in her, 31.11
Her h. is known in the gates, when 31.23
her h. also, and he praises her: 31.28
For your Maker is your h., the LORD Is 54.05
Surely, as a faithless wife leaves her h., Jer 3.20
both h. and wife shall be taken, the 6.11
I was their h., says the LORD. 31.32
strangers instead of her h.! Eze 16.32
who loathed her h. and her children; 16.45
not my wife, and I am not her h.— Hos 2.02
will go and return to my first h., 2.07
'My h.,' and no longer will you 2.16
father of Joseph the h. of Mt 1.16
and her h. Joseph, being a just man 1.19
divorces her h. and marries Mk 10.12
can this be, since I have no h.?" Lk 1.34
lived with her h. seven years from 2.36
divorced from her h. commits adultery. 16.18
"Go, call your h., and come here." Jn 4.16
The woman answered him, "I have no h." 4.17
right in saying, 'I have no h.'; 4.17
whom you now have is not your h.; 4.18
buried your h. are at the door, and Ac 5.09
out and buried her beside her h. 5.10
by law to her h. as long as he Rom 7.02
but if her h. dies she is discharged 7.02
from the law concerning the h. 7.02
another man while her h. is alive. 7.03
But if her h. dies she is free from 7.03
own wife and each woman her own h. 1Co 7.02
The h. should give to his wife her 7.03
and likewise the wife to her h. 7.03
over her own body, but the h. does; 7.04
likewise the h. does not rule over 7.04
should not separate from her h. 7.10
or else be reconciled to her h.)— 7.11
and that the h. should not divorce 7.11
If any woman has a h. who is an 7.13

HUSBAND (cont.)
For the unbelieving h. is consecrated 1Co 7.14
wife is consecrated through her h. 7.14
know whether you will save your h.? 7.16
H., how do you know whether you 7.16
affairs, how to please her h. 7.34
is bound to her h. as long as he 7.39
If the h. dies, she is free to be 7.39
the head of a woman is her h., 11.03
you as a pure bride to her one h. 2Co 11.02
children than she who hath a h." Gal 4.27
For the h. is the head of the wife Eph 5.23
wife see that she respects her h. 5.33
as a bride adorned for her h.; Rev 21.02

HUSBAND'S
you were under your h. authority, Num 5.19
you are under your h. authority, 5.20
though under her h. authority, 5.29
And if she vowed in her h. house, 30.10
her h. brother shall go in to her, Deu 25.05
the duty of a h. brother to her. 25.05
'My h. brother refuses to perpetuate 25.07
the duty of a h. brother to me.' 25.07
Now Naomi had a kinsman of her h., Ru 2.01

HUSBANDS
womb that they may become your h.? Ru 1.11
look with contempt upon their h., Est 1.17
honor to their h., high and low." 1.20
loathed their h. and their children. Eze 16.45
the needy, who say to their h., Amo 4.01
for you have had five h., Jn 4.18
let them ask their h. at home. 1Co 14.35
Wives, be subject to your h., Eph 5.22
subject in everything to their h. 5.24
H., love your wives, as Christ loved 5.25
Even so h. should love their wives 5.28
Wives, be subject to your h., Col 3.18
H., love your wives, and do not be 3.19
to love their h. and children, Tit 2.04
kind, and submissive to their h., 2.05
wives, be submissive to your h., 1Pe 3.01
and were submissive to their h., 3.05
Likewise you h., live considerately 3.07

HUSBANDS'
it without our h. approval that we Jer 44.19

HUSH
and he shall say, "H.! We must not Amo 6.10
and when there was a great h., Ac 21.40

HUSHAH
Gedor, and Ezer the father of H. 1Ch 4.04

HUSHAI
H. the Archite came to meet him 2Sa 15.32
So H., David's friend, came into the 15.37
And when H. the Archite, David's 16.16
H. said to Absalom, "Long live the 16.16
And Absalom said to H., "Is this your 16.17
And H. said to Absalom, "No; 16.18
"Call H. the Archite also, and let 17.05
And when H. came to Absalom, Absalom 17.06
Then H. said to Absalom, "This time 17.07
H. said moreover, "You know that 17.08
"The counsel of H. the Archite is 17.14
Then H. said to Zadok and Abiathar 17.15
Baana the son of H., 1Ki 4.16
and H. the Archite was the king's 1Ch 27.33

HUSHAM
and H. of the land of the Temanites Gen 36.34
H. died, and Hadad the son of Bedad, 36.35
H. of the land of the Temanites 1Ch 1.45
When H. died, Hadad the son of Bedad, 1.46

HUSHATHITE
then Sibbecai the H. slew Saph, 2Sa 21.18
Abiezer, of Anathoth, Mebunnai the H., 23.27
Sibbecai the H., Ilai the Ahohite, 1Ch 11.29
then Sibbecai the H. slew Sippai, 20.04
eighth month, was Sibbecai the H., 27.11

HUSHED
the voice of the nobles was h., Job 29.10
and the waves of the sea were h. Ps 107.29
the vintage shout is h. Is 16.10

HUSHIM
The sons of Dan: H. Gen 46.23
the sons of Ir, H. the sons of Aher. 1Ch 7.12
had sent away H. and Baara his 8.08
He also had sons by H.: Abitub and 8.11

HUT
a drunken man, it sways like a h.; Is 24.20

HYENAS
H. will cry in its towers, and Is 13.22
And wild beasts shall meet with h., 34.14

HYMENAEUS
among them H. and Alexander, whom I 1Ti 1.20
Among them are H. and Philetus, 2Ti 2.17

HYMN
And when they had sung a h., Mt 26.30
And when they had sung a h., Mk 14.26
come together, each one has a h., 1Co 14.26

HYMNS
were praying and singing h. to God, Ac 16.25
in psalms and h. and spiritual Eph 5.19
sing psalms and h. and spiritual Col 3.16

HYPOCRISY
you are full of h. and iniquity. Mt 23.28
But knowing their h., he said to Mk 12.15
of the Pharisees, which is h. Lk 12.01

HYPOCRITE
You h., first take the log out of Mt 7.05
You h., first take the log out of Lk 6.42

HYPOCRITES
as the h. do in the synagogues and Mt 6.02
pray, you must not be like the h.; 6.05
like the h., for they disfigure 6.16
You h.! Well did Isaiah 15.07
"Why put me to the test, you h.? 22.18
to you, scribes and Pharisees, h.! 23.13
you, scribes and Pharisees, h.! *23.14
Woe to you, scribes and Pharisees, h.! 23.15
"Woe to you, scribes and Pharisees, h.! 23.23
"Woe to you, scribes and Pharisees, h.! 23.25
"Woe to you, scribes and Pharisees, h.! 23.27
"Woe to you, scribes and Pharisees, h.! 23.29
him, and put him with the h.; 24.51
"Well did Isaiah prophesy of you h., Mk 7.06
You h.! You know how Lk 12.56
Then the Lord answered him, "You h.! 13.15

HYSSOP
Take a bunch of h. and dip it in Ex 12.22
cedarwood and scarlet stuff and h.; Lev 14.04
and the scarlet stuff and the h., 14.06
cedarwood and scarlet stuff and h., 14.49
cedarwood and the h. and the 14.51
cedarwood and h. and scarlet stuff; 14.52
cedarwood and h. and scarlet Num 19.06
then a clean person shall take h., 19.18
Lebanon to the h. that grows out 1Ki 4.33
Purge me with h., and I shall be Ps 51.07
the vinegar on h. and held it to Jn 19.29
with water and scarlet wool and h., Heb 9.19

IBEX
the i., the antelope, and the Deu 14.05

IBHAR
I., Elishua, Nepheg, Japhia, 2Sa 5.11
then I., Elishama, Eliphelet, 1Ch 3.06
I., Elishua, Elpelet, 14.05

IBIS
the owl, the cormorant, the i. Lev 11.17

IBLEAM
and I. and its villages, and the Jos 17.11
inhabitants of I. and its villages, Ju 1.27
the ascent of Gur, which is by I. 2Ki 9.27
him, and struck him down at I., 11.10

IBNEIAH
I. the son of Jeroham, Eliah the son 1Ch 9.08

IBNIJAH
Shephatiah, son of Reuel, son of I.; 1Ch 9.08

IBRI
Beno, Shoham, Zaccur, and I. 1Ch 24.27

IBSAM
I., and Shemuel, heads of their fathers' 1Ch 7.02

IBZAN
After him I. of Bethlehem judged Ju 12.08
Then I. died, and was buried at 12.10

ICE
which are dark with i. and where the Job 6.16
By the breath of God i. is given, 37.10
From whose womb did the i. come forth, 38.29
He casts forth his i. like morsels; Ps 147.17

ICHABOD
And she named the child I., 1Sa 4.21

ICHABOD'S
I. brother, son of Phinehas, son of 1Sa 14.03

ICONIUM
feet against them, and went to I. Ac 13.51
Now at I. they entered together 14.01
came there from Antioch and I.; 14.19
to Lystra and to I. and to Antioch, 14.21
by the brethren at Lystra and I. 16.02
at I., and at Lystra, what persecutions 2Ti 3.11

IDALAH
I., and Bethlehem—twelve cities Jos 19.15

IDBASH
of Etam: Jezreel, Ishma, and I.; 1Ch 4.03

IDDO
Ahinadab the son of I., in Mahanaim; 1Ki 4.14
Joah his son, I. his son, Zerah his 1Ch 6.21
I. the son of Zechariah; for Benjamin, 27.21
the visions of I. the seer concerning 2Ch 9.29
the prophet and of I. the seer? 12.15
in the story of the prophet I. 13.22
Haggai and Zechariah the son of I., Ez 5.01
and Zechariah the son of I. 6.14
and sent them to I., 8.17
what to say to I. and his brethren 8.17
I., Ginnethoi, Abijah, Neh 12.04
of I., Zechariah; 12.16
son of I., the prophet, saying, Zec 1.01
Berechiah, son of I., the prophet; 1.07

IDLE
for they are i.; therefore they cry, Ex 5.08
But he said, "You are i., you are i.; 5.17
and an i. person will suffer hunger. Pro 19.15
who sing i. songs to the sound of Amo 6.05
others standing i. in the market Mt 20.03
'Why do you stand here i. all day?' 20.06
words seemed to them an i. tale, Lk 24.11
admonish the i., encourage the 1Th 5.14
we were not i. when we were with 2Th 3.07
their condemnation has not been i., 2Pe 2.03

IDLENESS
and does not eat the bread of i. Pro 31.27
is living in i. and not in accord 2Th 3.06
that some of you are living in i., 3.11

IDLERS
Besides that, they learn to be i., 1Ti 5.13
and not only i. but gossips and 5.13

IDLY
your own pleasure, or talking i.; Is 58.13

IDOL
image of the i. which he had made 2Ch 33.07
gods and the i. from the house of 33.15
The i.! a workman casts it, Is 40.19
of it he makes into a god, his i.; 44.17
'My i. did them, my graven image and 48.05
frankincense, like him who blesses an i. 66.03
Israel shall be ashamed of his i. Hos 10.06
What profit is an i. when its maker Hab 2.18
sacrifice to the i. and rejoiced in Ac 7.41
we know that "an i. has no real 1Co 8.04
food as really offered to an i.; 8.07
anything, or that an i. is anything? 10.19

IDOLATER
or is an i., reviler, drunkard, or 1Co 5.11
an i.), has any inheritance in the Eph 5.05

IDOLATERS
or i., since then you would need to 1Co 5.10
nor i., nor adulterers, nor homosexuals, 6.09
Do not be i. as some of them were; 10.07
i., and all liars, their lot shall Rev 21.08
fornicators and murderers and i., 22.15

IDOLATROUS
And he deposed the i. priests whom 2Ki 23.05
and its i. priests shall wail over Hos 10.05
and the name of the i. priests; Zep 1.04

IDOLATRY
stubbornness is as iniquity and i. 1Sa 15.23
the penalty for your sinful i.; Eze 23.49
put away their i. and the dead 43.09
i., sorcery, enmity, strife, jealousy, Gal 5.20
and covetousness, which is i. Col 3.05
revels, carousing, and lawless i. 1Pe 4.03

IDOL'S
knowledge, at table in an i. temple, 1Co 8.10

IDOLS
Do not turn to i. or make for Lev 19.04
yourselves no i. and erect no 26.01
upon the dead bodies of your i.; 26.30
their i. of wood and stone, of Deu 29.17
have provoked me with their i. 32.21
news to their i. and to the people. 1Sa 31.09
Philistines left their i. there, 2Sa 5.21
removed all the i. that his 1Ki 15.12
of Israel to anger with their i. 16.13
of Israel, to anger by their i. 16.26
very abominably in going after i., 21.26
and they served i., of which the 2Ki 17.12
They went after false i., and became 17.15
made Judah also to sin with his i.; 21.11
and served the i. that his father 21.21
teraphim and the i. and all the 23.24

IDOLS (cont.)

news to their i. and to the people. 1Ch 10.09
all the gods of the peoples are i.; 16.26
the abominable i. from all the 2Ch 15.08
and served the Asherim and the i. 24.18
those who pay regard to vain i.; Ps 31.06
all the gods of the peoples are i.; 96.05
make their boast in worthless i.; 97.07
They served their i., which became 106.36
sacrificed to the i. of Canaan; 106.38
Their i. are silver and gold, the 115.04
The i. of the nations are silver 135.15
Their land is filled with i.; Is 2.08
And the i. shall utterly pass away. 2.18
forth their i. of silver and their 2.20
of silver and their i. of gold, 2.20
kingdoms of the i. whose graven 10.10
Jerusalem and her i. as I have done 10.11
and the i. of Egypt will tremble at 19.01
consult the i. and the sorcerers, 19.03
cast away his i. of silver and his i. of 31.07
All who make i. are nothing, and the 44.09
the makers of i. go in confusion 45.16
who carry about their wooden i., 45.20
their i. are on beasts and cattle; 46.01
your collection of i. deliver you! 57.13
images, and with their foreign i.?" Jer 8.19
Their i. are like scarecrows in a 10.05
the instruction of i. is but wood! 10.08
goldsmith is put to shame by his i.; 10.14
carcasses of their detestable i., 16.18
put to shame, her i. are dismayed.' 50.02
images, and they are mad over i. 50.38
goldsmith is put to shame by his i.; 51.17
down your slain before your i. Eze 6.04
people of Israel before their i.; 6.05
your i. broken and destroyed, your 6.06
which turn wantonly after their i.; 6.09
lie among their i. round about 6.13
pleasing odor to all their i. 6.13
and all the i. of the house of 8.10
taken their i. into their hearts, 14.03
who takes his i. into his heart 14.04
of the multitude of his i., 14.04
estranged from me through their i. 14.05
Repent and turn away from your i.; 14.06
taking his i. into his heart and 14.07
lovers, and because of all your i., 16.36
his eyes to the i. of the house of 18.06
lifts up his eyes to the i., 18.12
his eyes to the i. of the house of 18.15
yourselves with the i. of Egypt; 20.07
did they forsake the i. of Egypt. 20.08
their heart went after their i. 20.16
defile yourselves with their i. 20.18
eyes were set on their fathers' i. 20.24
with all your i. to this day. 20.31
Go serve every one of you his i., 20.39
with your gifts and your i. 20.39
and that makes i. to defile 22.03
defiled by the i. which you have 22.04
with all the i. of every one on 23.07
polluted yourself with their i. 23.30
with their i. they have committed 23.37
children in sacrifice to their i., 23.39
Lord GOD: I will destroy the i., 30.13
and lift up your eyes to your i., 33.25
for the i. with which they had 36.18
from all your i. I will cleanse 36.25
more with their i. and their 37.23
me after their i. when Israel went 44.10
before their i. and became a 44.12
Ephraim is joined to i., let him alone. Hos 4.17
gold they made i. for their own 8.04
Baals, and burning incense to i. 11.02
i. skillfully made of their silver, 13.02
Ephraim, what have I to do with i.? 14.08
regard to vain i. forsake their Jon 2.08
and all her i. I will lay waste; Mic 1.07
own creation when he makes dumb i.! Hab 2.18
the names of the i. from the land, Zec 13.02
pollutions of i. and from unchastity Ac 15.20
sacrificed to i. and from blood 15.29
saw that the city was full of i. 17.16
sacrificed to i. and from blood 21.25
You who abhor i., do you rob Rom 2.22
Now concerning food offered to i.: 1Co 8.01
the eating of food offered to i., 8.04
being hitherto accustomed to i., 8.07
is weak, to eat food offered to i.? 8.10
my beloved, shun the worship of i. 10.14
food offered to i. is anything, 10.19
you were led astray to dumb i., 12.02
has the temple of God with i.? 2Co 6.16
and how you turned to God from i., 1Th 1.09
Little children, keep youselves from i. 1Jn 5.21
sacrificed to i. and practice Rev 2.14
and to eat food sacrificed to i. 2.20
demons and i. of gold and silver 9.20

IDUMEA

and Jerusalem and I. and from Mk 3.08

IEZER

of I., the family of the Iezerites; Num 26.30

IEZERITES

of Iezer, the family of the I.; Num 26.30

IGAL

Issachar, I. the son of Joseph; Num 13.07
I. the son of Nathan of Zobah, Bani 2Sa 23.36
I., Bariah, Neariah, and Shaphat, six. 1Ch 3.22

IGDALIAH

of the sons of Hanan the son of I., Jer 35.04

IGNOBLE

some for noble use, some for i. 1Ti 2.20
purifies himself from what is i., 2.21

IGNORANCE

who has sinned through error or i.; Eze 45.20
I know that you acted in i., Ac 3.17
The times of i. God overlooked, but 17.30
because of the i. that is in them, Eph 4.18
to the passions of your former i., 1Pe 1.14
to silence the i. of foolish men. 2.15

IGNORANT

I was stupid and i., I was like a Ps 73.22
For, being i. of the righteousness Rom 10.03
For we do not want you to be i., 2Co 1.08
for we are not i. of his designs. 2.11
But we would not have you i., 1Th 4.13
gently with the i. and wayward, Heb 5.02
in matters of which they are i., 2Pe 2.12
which the i. and unstable twist to 3.16

IGNORANTLY

I had acted i. in unbelief, 1Ti 1.13

IGNORE

They deliberately i. this fact, 2Pe 3.05
But do not i. this one fact, beloved, 3.08

IGNORED

his brothers, and i. his children. Deu 33.09
and you have i. all my counsel and Pro 1.25

IGNORES

but the prudent man i. an insult. Pro 12.16
come to him who i. instruction, 13.18
He who i. instruction despises 15.32

IGNORING

But i. what they said, Jesus said to Mk 5.36

IIM
Baalah, I., Ezem, Jos 15.29

IJON
and conquered I., Dan, Abelbethmaacah, 1Ki 15.20
of Assyria came and captured I., 2Ki 15.29
of Israel, and they conquered I., 2Ch 16.04

IKKESH
Ira the son of I. of Tekoa, 2Sa 23.26
Ira the son of I. of Tekoa, Abiezer 1Ch 11.28
was Ira, the son of I. the Tekoite; 27.09

ILAI
Sibbecai the Hushathite, I. the Ahohite, 1Ch 11.29

ILL
brought an i. report of them to Gen 37.02
you treat me so i. as to tell the 43.06
told, "Behold, your father is i."; 48.01
hast thou dealt i. with thy Num 11.11
he made himself i. because of his 2Sa 13.02
on your bed, and pretend to be i.; 13.05
lay down, and pretended to be i.; 13.06
mistress of the house, became i.; 1Ki 17.17
and it went i. with Moses on their Ps 106.32
No i. befalls the righteous, but the Pro 12.21
and your i. repute have no end. 25.10
It shall be i. with him, for what Is 3.11
not do good, nor will he do i.' Zep 1.12
mother-in-law was i. with a high Lk 4.38
was an official whose son was i. Jn 4.46
who had been i. for thirty-eight 5.05
Now a certain man was i., Lazarus 11.01
hair, whose brother Lazarus was i. 11.02
"Lord, he whom you love is i." 11.03
So when he heard that he was i., 11.06
is why many of you are weak and i., 1Co 11.30
in i. repute and good repute. 2Co 6.08
because you heard that he was i. Php 2.26
Indeed was i., near to death. 2.27
Trophimus I left i. at Miletus. 2Ti 4.20

ILL-BEHAVED
but the man was churlish and i.; 1Sa 25.03

ILL-CLAD
we are i. and buffeted and homeless, 1Co 4.11
or sister is i. and in lack of Jas 2.15

ILLEGITIMATE
then you are i. children and not Heb 12.08

ILL-NATURED
and he is so i. that one cannot 1Sa 25.17
lord regard this i. fellow, Nabal; 25.25

ILLNESS
and his i. was so severe that there 1Ki 17.17
sick with the i. of which he was 2Ki 13.14
in his i. thou healest all his Ps 41.03
"This i. is not unto death; it is for the Jn 11.04

ILL-TREAT
If you i. my daughters, or if you Gen 31.50
them and i. them four hundred Ac 7.06

ILL-TREATED
goats, destitute, afflicted, i.— Heb 11.37
and those who are i., 13.03

ILL-TREATMENT
surely seen the i. of my people Ac 7.34
choosing rather to share i. with Heb 11.25

ILLUSIONS
to us smooth things, prophesy i., Is 30.10

ILLYRICUM
as far round as I. I have fully Rom 15.19

IMAGE
said, "Let us make man in our i., Gen 1.26
So God created man in his own i., 1.27
in the i. of God he created him; 1.27
after his i., and named him Seth. 5.03
for God made man in his own i. 9.06
not make yourself a graven i., Ex 20.04
and erect no graven i. or pillar, Lev 26.01
making a graven i. for yourselves, Deu 4.16
make a graven i. in the form of 4.23
making a graven i. in the form of 4.25
not make for youself a graven i., 5.08
have made themselves a molten i.' 9.12
who makes a graven or molten i., 27.15
make a graven i. and a molten i.; Ju 17.03
into a graven i. and a molten i.; 17.04
a graven i., and a molten i.? 18.14
and entered and took the graven i., 18.17
the teraphim, and the molten i., 18.17
house and took the graven i., 18.18
the teraphim, and the molten i., 18.18
the teraphim, and the graven i., 18.20
up the graven i. for themselves; 18.30
up Micah's graven i. which he made, 18.31
Michal took an i. and laid it on 1Sa 19.13
the i. was in the bed, with the 19.16
an abominable i. made for Asherah; 1Ki 15.13
cut down her i. and burned it at 15.13
And the graven i. of Asherah that 2Ki 21.07
made an abominable i. for Asherah. 2Ch 15.16
Asa cut down her i., crushed it, 15.16
And the i. of the idol which he had 33.07
in Horeb and worshiped a molten i. Ps 106.19
of God for the i. of an ox that 106.20
to set up an i. that will not move. Is 40.20
Who fashions a god or casts an i., 44.10
it a graven i. and falls down 44.15
my graven i. and my molten i. 48.05
her bearing her i. and poured out Jer 44.19
was the seat of the i. of jealousy, Eze 8.03
entrance, was this i. of jealousy. 8.05
O king, and behold, a great i. Dan 2.31
This i., mighty and of exceeding 2.31
The head of this i. was of fine 2.32
it smote the i. on its feet of 2.34
that struck the i. became a great 2.35
King Nebuchadnezzar made an i. of gold, 3.01
dedication of the i. which King 3.02
dedication of the i. the King 3.03
before the i. that Nebuchadnezzar 3.03
the golden i. that King Nebuchadnezzar 3.05
the golden i. which King Nebuchadnezzar 3.07
down and worship the golden i.; 3.10
the golden i. which you have set 3.12
the golden i. which I have set up? 3.14
and worship the i. which I have 3.15
the golden i. which you have set 3.18
off the graven i. and the molten i. Nah 1.14
a metal i., a teacher of lies? Hab 2.18
be conformed to the i. of his Son, Rom 8.29
since he is the i. and glory of 1Co 11.07
have borne the i. of the man of 15.49
also bear the i. of the man of 15.49
He is the i. of the invisible God, Col 1.15
after the i. of its creator. 3.10
them make an i. for the beast Rev 13.14
breath to the i. of the beast so 13.15
so that the i. of the beast should 13.15
not worship the i. of the beast to 13.15
one worships the beast and its i., 14.09
worshipers of the beast and its i., 14.11
beast and its i. and the number of 15.02
of the beast and worshiped its i. 16.02

IMAGE (cont.)
and those who worshiped its i. Rev 19.20
beast or its i. and had not 20.04

IMAGES
and destroy all their molten i., Num 33.52
and burn their graven i. with fire. Deu 7.05
The graven i. of their gods you 7.25
down the graven i. of their gods, 12.03
So you must make i. of your tumors 1Sa 6.05
your tumors and i. of your mice 6.05
mice and the i. of their tumors. 6.11
and molten i., provoking me to 1Ki 14.09
altars and his i. they broke in 2Ki 11.18
themselves molten i. of two calves; 17.16
and also served their graven i.; 17.41
altars and his i. they broke in 2Ch 23.17
even made molten i. for the Baals; 28.02
and set up the Asherim and the i., 33.19
to all the i. that Manasseh his 33.22
and the graven and the molten i. 34.03
and the graven and the molten i., 34.04
the Asherim and the i. into powder, 34.07
to jealousy with their graven i. Ps 78.58
All worshipers of i. are put to 97.07
whose graven i. were greater than Is 10.10
I have done to Samaria and her i.?" 10.11
and all the i. of her gods he has 21.09
silver-covered graven i. and your 30.22
and your gold-plated molten i. 30.22
their molten i. are empty wind. 41.29
other, nor my praise to graven i. 42.08
to shame, who trust in graven i., 42.17
who say to molten i., "You are 42.17
me to anger with their graven i., Jer 8.19
for his i. are false, and there is 10.14
Her i. are put to shame, her idols 50.02
For it is a land of i., 50.38
for his i. are false, and there is 51.17
I will punish the i. of Babylon; 51.47
will execute judgment upon her i., 51.52
abominable i. and their detestable Eze 7.20
and made for yourself i. of men, 16.17
the i. of the Chaldeans portrayed 23.14
put an end to the i., in Memphis; 30.13
their molten i. and with their Dan 11.08
and make for themselves molten i., Hos 13.02
your i., which you made for yourselves; Amo 5.26
All her i. shall be beaten to Mic 1.07
cut off your i. and your pillars 5.13
immortal God for i. resembling Rom 1.23

IMAGINATION
and that every i. of the thoughts Gen 6.05
for the i. of man's heart is evil 8.21
proud in the i. of their hearts, Lk 1.51
representation by the art and i. of man. Ac 17.29

IMAGINE
they i. the worst for me. Ps 14.07
and the peoples i. vain things? Ac 4.25

IMAGINES
If any one i. that he knows something, 1Co 8.02

IMAGINING
i. that godliness is a means of 1Ti 6.05

IMITATE
know how you ought to i. us; 2Th 3.07
in our conduct an example to i. 3.09
of their life, and i. their faith. Heb 13.07
Beloved, do not i. evil but i. good 3Jn 1.11

IMITATING
join in i. me, and mark those who so Php 3.17

IMITATORS
I urge you, then, be i. of me. 1Co 4.16
Be i. of me, as I am of Christ. 11.01
Therefore be i. of God, as beloved Eph 5.01
And you became i. of us and of the 1Th 1.06
became i. of the churches of God in 2.14
but i. of those who through faith Heb 6.12

IMLAH
of the LORD, Micaiah the son of I.; 1Ki 22.08
quickly Micaiah the son of I. 22.09
of the LORD, Micaiah the son of I.; 2Ch 18.07
quickly Micaiah the son of I. 18.08

IMMANUEL
a son, and shall call his name I. Is 7.14
the breadth of your land, O I. 8.08

IMMEASURABLE
and what is the i. greatness of his Eph 1.19
might show the i. riches of his 2.07

IMMEDIATELY
go up, for you will meet him i." 1Sa 9.13
worship shall i. be cast into a Dan 3.06
you shall i. be cast into a burning 3.15
I. the word was fulfilled upon 4.33
I. the fingers of a man's hand 5.05
he went up i. from the water, and Mt 3.16
I. they left their nets and followed 4.20
I. they left the boat and their 4.22
And i. his leprosy was cleansed. 8.03
and i. they sprang up, since they 13.05
the word and i. receives it with 13.20
of the word, i. he falls away. 13.21
But i. he spoke to them, saying, 14.27
Jesus i. reached out his hand and 14.31
and i. they received their sight 20.34
and i. you will find an ass tied, 21.02
of them.' and he will send them i." 21.03
"I. after the tribulation of those 24.29
And i. the cock crowed. 26.74
i. he saw the heavens opened and Mk 1.10
The Spirit i. drove him out into 1.12
And i. they left their nets and 1.18
And i. he called them; and they left 1.20
and i. on the sabbath he entered 1.21
And i. there was in their synagogue 1.23
And i. he left the synagogue, and 1.29
with a fever, and i. they told him of her. 1.30
And i. the leprosy left him, and he 1.42
And i. Jesus, perceiving in his 2.08
and i. took up the pallet and went 2.12
and i. held counsel with the 3.06
and i. it sprang up, since it had no 4.05
Satan i. comes and takes away the 4.15
hear the word, i. receive it with joy; 4.16
of the word, i. they fall away. 4.17
And i. the hemorrhage ceased; 5.29
i. turned about in the crowd, and 5.30
And i. the girl got up and walked; 5.42
And i. they were overcome with 5.42
And she came in i. with haste to 6.25
And i. the king sent a soldier of 6.27
I. he made his disciples get into 6.45
But i. he spoke to them and said, 6.50
i. the people recognized him, 6.54
But i. a woman, whose little daughter 7.25
and i. he got into the boat with 8.10
And i. all the crowd, when they saw 9.15
i. it convulsed the boy, and he fell 9.20
I. the father of the child cried 9.24
And i. he received his sight and 10.52
and i. as you enter it you will 11.02
it and will send it back here i.'" 11.03
And i., while he was still speaking, 14.43
And i. the cock crowed a second 14.72

IMMEDIATELY (cont.)
And i. his mouth was opened and his Lk 1.64
and i. she rose and served them. 4.39
And i. the leprosy left him. 5.13
And i. he rose before them, and took 5.25
and i. it fell, and the ruin of that 6.49
and i. her flow of blood ceased. 8.44
and how she had been i. healed. 8.47
and i. she was made straight, and 13.13
will not i. pull him out on a 14.05
And i. he received his sight and 18.43
kingdom of God was to appear i. 19.11
And i., while he was still 22.60
and i. the boat was at the land to Jn 6.21
receiving the morsel, he i. went out; 13.30
and i. his feet and ankles were Ac 3.07
I. she fell down at his feet and 5.10
And i. something like scales fell 9.18
the synagogues i. he proclaimed 9.20
make your bed." And i. he rose. 9.34
and i. the angel left him. 12.10
I. an angel of the Lord smote him, 12.23
I. mist and darkness fell upon 13.11
i. we sought to go on into Macedonia, 16.10
and i. all the doors were opened 16.26
The brethren i. sent Paul and Silas 17.10
Then the brethren i. sent Paul off 17.14

IMMER
son of Meshillemith, son of I.; 1Ch 9.12
to Bilgah, the sixteenth to I., 24.14
The sons of I., one thousand and Ez 2.37
and I., though they could not prove 2.59
Of the sons of I.: Hanani and 10.20
the son of I. repaired opposite Neh 3.29
The sons of I., a thousand and 7.40
and I., but they could not prove 7.61
son of Meshillemoth, son of I., 11.13
the son of I., who was chief Jer 20.01

IMMORAL
not to associate with i. men; 1Co 5.09
all meaning the i. of this world. 5.10
neither the i., nor idolaters, nor 6.09
but the i. man sins against his own 6.18
that no i. or impure man, or one who Eph 5.05
i. persons, sodomites, kidnapers, 1Ti 1.10
that no one be i. or irreligious Heb 12.16
will judge the i. and adulterous. 13.04

IMMORALITY
reported that there is i. among you, 1Co 5.01
if he is guilty of i. or greed, 5.11
The body is not meant for i., 6.13
Shun i. Every other sin 6.18
But because of the temptation to i., 7.02
not indulge in i. as some of them 10.08
i., and licentiousness which they 2Co 12.21
i., impurity, licentiousness, Gal 5.19
But i. and all impurity and covetousness Eph 5.03
i., impurity, passion, evil desire, Col 3.05
sanctification: that you abstain from i.; 1Th 4.03
sacrificed to idols and practice i. Rev 2.14
to practice i. and to eat food 2.20
she refuses to repent of her i. 2.21
or their i. or their thefts. 9.21

IMMORALLY
likewise acted i. and indulged in Jud 1.07

IMMORTAL
glory of the i. God for images Rom 1.23
i., invisible, the only God, be honor 1Ti 1.17

IMMORTALITY
seek for glory and honor and i., Rom 2.07
this mortal nature must put on i. 1Co 15.53
imperishable, and the mortal puts on i., 15.54
who alone has i. and dwells in 1Ti 6.16
life and i. to light through the 2Ti 1.10

IMMOVABLE
firmly cast upon him and i. Job 41.23
an i. tent, whose stakes will never Is 33.20
the bow stuck and remained i., Ac 27.41
i., always abounding in the work of 1Co 15.58

IMNA
I., Shelesh, and Amal. 1Ch 7.35

IMNAH
I., Ishvah, Ishvi, Beriah, with Serah Gen 46.17
of I., the family of the Imnites; Num 26.44
I., Ishvah, Ishvi, Beriah, and their 1Ch 7.30
And Kore the son of I. the Levite, 2Ch 31.14

IMNITES
of Imnah, the family of the I.; Num 26.44

IMPAIR
lest I i. my own inheritance. Ru 4.06

IMPAIRED
and the royal revenue will be i. Ez 4.13

IMPALED
house, and he shall be i. upon it, Ez 6.11

IMPART
that I may i. to you some spiritual Rom 1.11
Yet among the mature we do i. wisdom, 1Co 2.06
But we i. a secret and hidden 2.07
And we i. this in words not taught 2.13
that it may i. grace to those who Eph 4.29

IMPARTIALLY
judges each one i. according to 1Pe 1.17

IMPARTS
it i. understanding to the simple. Ps 119.130

IMPATIENT
the people became i. on the way. Num 21.04
it has come to you, and you are i.; Job 4.05
against man? Why should I not be i.? 21.04
Is the Spirit of the LORD i.? Mic 2.07
they were i. to get off and patrol Zec 6.07
But I became i. with them, and they 11.08

IMPEDIMENT
deaf and had an i. in his speech; Mk 7.32

IMPENDING
in view of the i. distress it is 1Co 7.26

IMPENETRABLE
though it is i., because they are Jer 46.23

IMPENITENT
your hard and i. heart you are Rom 2.05

IMPERFECT
knowledge is i. and our prophecy is i.; 1Co 13.09
comes, the i. will pass away. 13.10

IMPERISHABLE
a perishable wreath, but we an i. 1Co 9.25
perishable, what is raised is i. 15.42
does the perishable inherit the i. 15.50
and the dead will be raised i., 15.52
perishable nature must put on the i., 15.53
When the perishable puts on the i., 15.54
and to an inheritance which is i., 1Pe 1.04
not of perishable seed but of i., 1.23
heart with the i. jewel of a 3.04

IMPIOUS
and an i. people reviles thy name. Ps 74.18
remember how the i. scoff at thee 74.22
where will the i. and sinner 1Pe 4.18

IMPIOUSLY
they i. mocked more and more, Ps 35.16

IMPLACABLE
inhuman, i., slanderers, profligates, 2Ti 3.03

IMPLANTED
receive with meekness the i. word, Jas 1.21

IMPLEMENTS
and to make his i. of war and the 1Sa 8.12
once more the i. of a worthless Zec 11.15

IMPLIES
Now an intermediary i. more than one; Gal 3.20

IMPLORE
shall come to i. him for a piece 1Sa 2.36

IMPLORING
i. him, 'Lord, have patience with me, Mt 18.26

IMPLY
What do I i. then? That food offered 1Co 10.19
No, I i. that what pagans sacrifice 10.20

IMPORT
And Solomon's i. of horses was from 1Ki 10.28
And Solomon's i. of horses was from 2Ch 1.16

IMPORTANCE
you as of first i. what I also 1Co 15.03

IMPORTED
could be i. from Egypt for six 1Ki 10.29
They i. a chariot from Egypt for 2Ch 1.17
And horses were i. for Solomon from 9.28

IMPORTUNE
go, hasten, and i. your neighbor. Pro 6.03

IMPORTUNITY
because of his i. he will rise and Lk 11.08

IMPOSE
whatever you i. on me I will bear." 2Ki 18.14
shall not be lawful to i. tribute, Ez 7.24
To i. a fine on a righteous man is Pro 17.26

IMPOSED
who i. your terror on all the Eze 26.17
for the body i. until the time of Heb 9.10

IMPOSSIBLE
to do will now be i. for them. Gen 11.06
and it seemed i. to Amnon to do 2Sa 13.02
and nothing will be i. to you." Mt 17.20
said to them, "With men this is i., 19.26
them and said, "With men it is i., Mk 10.27
For with God nothing will be i." Lk 1.37
"What is i. with men is possible 18.27
For it is i. to restore again to Heb 6.04
in which it is i. that God should 6.18
For it is i. that the blood of 10.04
faith it is i. to please him. 11.06

IMPOSTOR
"Sir, we remember how that i. said, Mt 27.63

IMPOSTORS
We are treated as i., and yet are true; 2Co 6.08
while evil men and i. will go on 2Ti 3.13

IMPOVERISH
have you invited us here to i. us?" Ju 14.15

IMPOVERISHED
He who is i. chooses for an offering Is 40.20

IMPRISONED
For Zedekiah king of Judah had i. him, Jer 32.03
beat him and i. him in the house 37.15
not only to be i. but even to die Ac 21.13
synagogue I i. and beat those who 22.19

IMPRISONMENT
confiscation of his goods or for i." Ez 7.26
every city that i. and afflictions Ac 20.23
with nothing deserving death or i. 23.29
nothing to deserve death or i." 26.31
both in my i. and in the defense Php 1.07
the rest that my i. is for Christ; 1.13
in the Lord because of my i., 1.14
thinking to afflict me in my i. 1.17
father I have become in my i. Phm 1.10
behalf during my i. for the gospel; 1.13
scourging, and even chains and i. Heb 11.36

IMPRISONMENTS
beatings, i., tumults, labors, watching, 2Co 6.05
far more i., with countless beatings, 11.23

IMPRISONS
and i., and calls to judgment, who Job 11.10

IMPROPER
to a base mind and to i. conduct. Rom 1.28

IMPROVED
as his country i. he i. his pillars. Hos 10.01

IMPROVEMENT
What we pray for is your i. 2Co 13.09

IMPUDENT
and with i. face she says to him: Pro 7.13
The people also are i. and stubborn: Eze 2.04

IMPULSE
prophecy ever came by the i. of man, 2Pe 1.21

IMPULSES
sins and swayed by various i., 2Ti 3.06

IMPURE
of this, that no immoral or i. man, Eph 5.05
drink the wine of her i. passion. Rev 14.08
drunk the wine of her i. passion, 18.03

IMPURITIES
abominations and the i. of her Rev 17.04

IMPURITY
shall be in her i. for seven days, Lev 15.19
lies during her i. shall be unclean, 15.20
and her i. is on him, he shall be 15.24
days, not at the time of her i., 15.25
discharge beyond the time of her i., 15.25
as in the days of her i., she shall be 15.25
be to her as the bed of her i.; 15.26
as in the uncleanness of her i. 15.26
also for her who is sick with her i.; 15.33
takes his brother's wife, it is i.; 20.21
of Israel for the water for i., Num 19.09
the water for i. was not thrown 19.13
the water for i. has not been 19.20
the water for i. shall wash his 19.21
the water for i. shall be unclean 19.21
be purified with the water of i.; 31.23
approach a woman in her time of i., Eze 18.06
women who are unclean in their i. 22.10
uncleanness of a woman in her i. 36.17
in the lusts of their hearts to i., Rom 1.24
your members to i. and to greater 6.19
and have not repented of the i., 2Co 12.21

IMPURITY (cont.)
immorality, i., licentiousness, Gal 5.19
immorality and all i. or covetousness Eph 5.03
i., passion, evil desire, and covetousness, Col 3.05

IMPUTE
not the king i. anything to his 1Sa 22.15

IMPUTED
bloodguilt shall be i. to that man; Lev 17.04

IMPUTES
to whom the LORD i. no iniquity, Ps 32.02

IMRAH
Suah, Harnepher, Shual, Beri, I., 1Ch 7.36

IMRI
son of I., son of Bani, from the 1Ch 9.04
to them Zaccur the son of I. built. Neh 3.02

INASMUCH
i. as I did not give her to my son Gen 38.26
i. as the king does not bring his 2Sa 14.13
i. as you have not kept my ways but Mal 2.09
I. as many have undertaken to Lk 1.01
I. then as I am an apostle to the Rom 11.13

INCENSE
oil and for the fragrant i., Ex 25.06
make its plates and dishes for i., 25.29
make an altar to burn i. upon; 30.01
Aaron shall burn fragrant i. on it; 30.07
a perpetual i. before the LORD 30.08
You shall offer an unholy i. thereon, 30.09
its utensils, and the altar of i., 30.27
and make an i. blended as by the 30.35
And the i. which you shall make 30.37
its utensils, and the altar of i., 31.08
the fragrant i. for the holy place. 31.11
oil and for the fragrant i., 35.08
and the altar of i., with its poles, 35.15
anointing oil and the fragrant i., 35.15
anointing oil, and for the fragrant i. 35.28
its plates and dishes for i., 37.16
the altar of i. of acacia wood; 37.25
oil also, and the pure fragrant i., 37.29
anointing oil and the fragrant i., 39.38
altar for i. before the ark of the 40.05
and burnt fragrant i. upon it; 40.27
of fragrant i. before the LORD Lev 4.07
and laid i. on it, and offered 10.01
handfuls of sweet i. beaten small; 16.12
and put the i. on the fire before 16.13
cloud of the i. may cover the 16.13
and cut down your i. altars, 26.30
it the plates, the dishes for i., Num 4.07
the fragrant i., the continual 4.16
dish of ten shekels, full of i.; 7.14
dish of ten shekels, full of i.; 7.20
dish of ten shekels, full of i.; 7.26
dish of ten shekels, full of i.; 7.32
dish of ten shekels, full of i.; 7.38
dish of ten shekels, full of i.; 7.44
dish of ten shekels, full of i.; 7.50
dish of ten shekels, full of i.; 7.56
dish of ten shekels, full of i.; 7.62
dish of ten shekels, full of i.; 7.68
dish of ten shekels, full of i.; 7.74
dish of ten shekels, full of i.; 7.80
full of i., weighing ten shekels 7.86
in them and put i. upon them before the 16.07
and put i. upon it, and every one of 16.17
fire in them and laid i. upon them, 16.18
and fifty men offering the i. 16.35
near to burn i. before the LORD, 16.40
and lay i. on it, and carry it 16.46
and he put on the i., and made 16.47
they shall put i. before thee, Deu 33.10
to burn i., to wear an ephod before 1Sa 2.28
and burnt i. at the high places. 1Ki 3.03
dishes for i., and firepans, of pure 7.50
burning i. before the LORD. So he finished 9.25
who burned i. and sacrificed to 11.08
went up to the altar to burn i. 12.33
standing by the altar to burn i. 13.01
high places who burn i. upon you, 13.02
and burned i. on the high places. 22.43
and burn i. on the high places. 2Ki 12.03
and burned i. on the high places. 14.04
and burned i. on the high places. 15.04
and burned i. on the high places. 15.35
and burned i. on the high places, 16.04
they burned i. on all the high 17.11
of Israel had burned i. to it; 18.04
and have burned i. to other gods, 22.17
ordained to burn i. in the high 23.05
those also who burned i. to Baal, 23.05
where the priests had burned i., 23.08
the dishes for i. and all the 25.14
the altar of i. for all the work 1Ch 6.49
the oil, the i., and the spices. 9.29
should burn i. before the LORD, and 23.13
for the altar of i. made of refined 28.18
the burning of i. of sweet spices 2Ch 2.04
as a place to burn i. before him? 2.06
dishes for i., and firepans, of pure 4.22
offerings and i. of sweet spices, 13.11
the high places and the i. altars. 14.05
burnt offerings, and dishes for i., 24.14
LORD to burn i. on the altar of i. 26.16
to burn i. to the LORD, but for the 26.18
who are consecrated to burn i. 26.18
a censer in his hand to burn i., 26.19
of the LORD, by the altar of i. 26.19
and he burned i. in the valley of 28.03
and burned i. on the high places, 28.04
places to burn i. to other gods, 28.25
have not burned i. or offered 29.07
his ministers and burn i. to him." 29.11
for burning i. they took away and 30.14
hewed down the i. altars which 34.04
down all the i. altars throughout 34.07
and have burned i. to other gods, 34.25
be counted as i. before thee, Ps 141.02
i. is an abomination to me. Is 1.13
the Asherim or the altars of i. 17.08
no Asherim or i. altars will remain 27.09
gardens and burning i. upon bricks; 65.03
they burned i. upon the mountains 65.07
they have burned i. to other gods, Jer 1.16
burn i. to Baal, and go after other 7.09
to the gods to whom they burn i., 11.12
shame, altars to burn i. to Baal. 11.13
me to anger by burning i. to Baal. 11.17
me, they burn i. to false gods; 18.15
by burning i. in it to other gods 19.04
whose roofs i. has been burned to 19.13
on whose roofs i. has been offered 32.29
offerings and i. to present at the 41.05
went to burn i. and serve other 44.03
and burn no i. to other gods. 44.05
burning i. to other gods in the 44.08
wives had offered i. to other gods, 44.15
burn i. to the queen of heaven and 44.17
off burning i. to the queen of 44.18
"When we burned i. to the queen of 44.19
"As for the i. that you burned in 44.21
It is because you burned i., and because 44.23
to burn i. to the queen of heaven 44.25
high place and burns i. to his god. 48.35
the basins, and the dishes for i., 52.18
lampstands, and the dishes for i., 52.19
and your i. altars shall be broken; Eze 6.04
your i. altars cut down, and your 6.06

INCENSE (cont.)
smoke of the cloud of i. went up. Eze 8.11
set my oil and my i. before them. 16.18
you had placed my i. and my oil. 23.41
an offering and i. be offered up Dan 2.46
when she burned i. to them and Hos 2.13
the Baals, and burning i. to idols. 11.02
his net and burns i. to his seine; Hab 1.16
in every place i. is offered to my Mal 1.11
the temple of the Lord and burn i. Lk 1.09
praying outside at the hour of i. 1.10
the right side of the altar of i. 1.11
golden altar of i. and the ark of Heb 9.04
and with golden bowls full of i., Rev 5.08
was given much i. to mingle with 8.03
smoke of the i. rose with the 8.04
i., myrrh, frankincense, wine, oil, 18.13

INCENSED
all who are i. against you shall be Is 41.11
all who were i. against him. 45.24

INCENTIVE
any i. of love, any participation in Php 2.01

INCEST
they have committed i., their blood Lev 20.12

INCITED
and he i. David against them, saying, 2Sa 24.01
Ahab, whom Jezebel his wife i. 1Ki 21.25
and i. David to number Israel. 1Ch 21.01
But the Jews i. the devout women of Ac 13.50

INCITING
too, stirring up and i. the crowds. Ac 17.13

INCLINE
and i. your heart to the LORD, the Jos 24.23
that he may i. our hearts to him, to 1Ki 8.58
I. thy ear. O LORD, and hear; 2Ki 19.16
their heart, thou wilt i. thy ear Ps 10.17
i. thy ear to me, hear my words. 17.06
I. thy ear to me, rescue me speedily! 31.02
daughter, consider, and i. your ear; 45.10
I will i. my ear to a proverb; 49.04
i. thy ear to me, and save me! 71.02
i. your ears to the words of my 78.01
I. thy ear, O LORD, and answer me, for 86.01
come before thee, i. thy ear to my cry! 88.02
I. thy ear to me; answer me 102.02
I. my heart to thy testimonies, and 119.36
I i. my heart to perform thy 119.112
I. not my heart to any evil, to busy 141.04
i. your ear to my sayings. Pro 4.20
i. your ear to my understanding; 5.01
my teachers or i. my ear to my 5.13
I. your ear, and hear the words of 22.17
I. thy ear, O LORD, and hear; Is 37.17
I. your ear, and come to me; 55.03
But they did not obey or i. their ear, Jer 7.24
or i. their ear, but stiffened their 7.26
Yet they did not obey or i. their ear, 11.08
did not listen or i. their ear, 17.23
listen to me or i. their ears to 34.14
But you did not i. your ear or 35.15
did not listen or i. their ear, 44.05
O my God, i. thy ear and hear; Dan 9.18

INCLINED
which you are i. to go after Num 15.39
their hearts i. to follow Abimelech, Ju 9.03
he i. to me and heard my cry. Ps 40.01
Because he i. his ear to me, therefore 116.02
listened nor i. your ears to hear, Jer 25.04

INCLINES
him, "Do all that your mind i. to; 1Sa 14.07
man's heart i. him toward the Ecc 10.02

INCLINING
to wisdom and i. your heart to Pro 2.02

INCLUDE
But he did not i. Levi and Benjamin 1Ch 21.06

INCLUDED
Its territory i. Jezreel, Chesulloth, Jos 19.18
Its territory i. Helkath, Hali, Beten, 19.25
of its inheritance i. Zorah, 19.41

INCLUDING
not i. Jacob's sons' wives, were Gen 46.26
i. the land of Gilead, and the Ju 20.01
i. yourselves who are called to Rom 1.06

INCLUSION
much more will their full i. mean! Rom 11.12

INCOME
befalls the i. of the wicked. Pro 15.06

INCOMPETENT
are you i. to try trivial cases? 1Co 6.02

INCREASE
are many you shall i. the price, Lev 25.16
Take no interest from him or i., 25.36
and the land shall yield its i., 26.04
your land shall not yield its i., 26.20
to i. still more the fierce anger Num 32.14
the i. of your cattle and the young Deu 7.13
the i. of your cattle, and the young 28.04
the i. of your cattle, and the young 28.18
the i. of your cattle or the young 28.51
devours the earth and its i., 32.22
say to Abimelech 'I. your army, Ju 9.29
and all the i. of your house shall 1Sa 2.33
and i. thy vexation toward me; Job 10.17
would burn to the root all my i. 31.12
if riches i., set not your heart on Ps 62.10
The earth has yielded its i.; 67.06
Thou wilt i. my honor, and comfort 71.21
always at ease, they i. in riches. 73.12
and our land will yield its i. 85.12
May the LORD give you i., 115.14
my strength of soul thou didst i. 138.03
also may hear and i. in learning, Pro 1.05
man and he will i. in learning. 9.09
little by little will i. it. 13.11
the poor to i. his own wealth, 22.16
by interest and i. gathers it for 28.08
when they perish, the righteous i. 28.28
For when dreams i., empty words Ecc 5.07
When goods i., they i. who eat them; 5.11
Of the i. of his government and of Is 9.07
lend at interest or take any i., Eze 18.08
lends at interest, and takes i.; 18.13
iniquity, takes no interest or i., 18.17
interest and i. and make gain of 22.12
and the earth shall yield its i., 34.27
and they shall i. and be fruitful; 36.11
tree and the i. of the field 36.30
to i. their men like a flock. 36.37
to and fro, and knowledge shall i. Dan 12.04
and the ground shall give its i., Zec 8.12
said to the Lord, "I. our faith!" Lk 17.05
He must i., but I must decrease." Jn 3.30
Law came in, to i. the trespass; Rom 5.20
more people it may i. thanksgiving, 2Co 4.15
resources and i. the harvest of 9.10
Lord make you i. and abound in 1Th 3.12

INCREASED
and the waters i., and bore up Gen 7.17
prevailed and i. greatly upon the 7.18
I came, and it has i. abundantly; 30.30
were fruitful and i. greatly; Ex 1.07

INCREASED (cont.)
until you are i. and possess the Ex 23.30
the Philistines i. more and more; 1Sa 14.19
their fathers' houses i. greatly. 1Ch 4.38
and so i. the guilt of Israel. Ez 10.10
possessions have i. in the land. Job 1.10
the nation, thou hast i. its joy; Is 9.03
But thou hast i. the nation, O LORD, 26.15
thou hast i. the nation; thou art 26.15
Yet she i. her harlotry, remembering Eze 23.19
in trade you have i. your wealth, 28.05
The more they i., the more they Hos 4.07
more his fruit i. the more altars 10.01
You i. your merchants more than the Nah 3.16
And Jesus i. in wisdom and in Lk 2.52
And the word of God i.; and the number Ac 6.07
But Saul i. all the more in strength, 9.22
and they i. in numbers daily. 16.05
but where sin i., grace abounded Rom 5.20

INCREASES
when the glory of his house i. Ps 49.16
pleasant speech i. persuasiveness. Pro 16.21
a robber and i. the faithless 23.28
are in authority, transgression i.; 29.16
and he who i. knowledge i. sorrow. Ecc 1.18
who has no might he i. strength. Is 40.29
our hope is that as your faith i., 2Co 10.15
the fruit which i. to your credit. Php 4.17

INCREASING
the people with Absalom kept i. 2Sa 15.12
growing up and i. and yielding Mk 4.08
When the crowds were i., Lk 11.29
the disciples were i. in number, Ac 6.01
good work and i. in the knowledge Col 1.10
one of you for one another is i. 2Th 1.03

INCREDIBLE
Why is it thought i. by any of you Ac 26.08

INCUR
they may not i. guilt before the 2Ch 19.10
do, and you will not i. guilt. 19.10
those who resist will i. judgment. Rom 13.02
and so they i. condemnation for 1Ti 5.12

INCURABLE
in his bowels with an i. disease. 2Ch 21.18
my wound is i., though I am without Job 34.06
away in a day of grief and i. pain. Is 17.11
my wound i., refusing to be healed? Jer 15.18
Your hurt is i., and your wound is 30.12
Your pain is i. Because your guilt 30.15
For her wound is i.; and it has come Mic 1.09

INCURRED
any guilt i. in the holy offering Ex 28.38
but this Amon i. guilt more and 2Ch 33.23
never offset the guilt he has i. Hos 12.08
but he i. guilt through Baal and 13.01
from Crete and i. this injury and Ac 27.21

INCURS
reproves a wicked man i. injury. Pro 9.07

INDEBTED
forgive every one who is i. to us; Lk 11.04

INDECENCY
he has found some i. in her, Deu 24.01

INDECENT
may not see anything i. among you, Deu 23.14

INDEED
'Shall I i. bear a child now that I Gen 18.13
"Wilt thou i. destroy the righteous 18.23
Besides she is i. my sister, the 20.12
I will i. bless you, and I will 22.17
"Are you i. to reign over us? 37.08
Or are you i. to have dominion over 37.08
your brothers i. come to bow 37.10
For I was i. stolen out of the land 40.15
that such a man as I can i. divine?" 44.15
"Has the LORD i. spoken only Num 12.02
"If thou wilt i. give this people 21.02
For i. the hand of the LORD was Deu 2.15
you may i. set as king over you him 17.15
if thou wilt i. look on the affliction 1Sa 1.11
the LORD will i. bring me back to 2Sa 15.08
"But will God i. dwell on the earth? 1Ki 8.27
You have i. smitten Edom, and your 2Ki 14.10
"But will God dwell i. with man on 2Ch 6.18
If i. you magnify yourselves Job 19.05
Do you i. decree what is right, you Ps 58.01
'Do we not i. know that every jar Jer 13.12
For if you will i. obey this word, 22.04
you are i. wiser than Daniel; Eze 28.03
i. he shall turn his insolence back Dan 11.18
Is it not i. so, O people of Israel?" Amo 2.11
i. I have already cursed them, Mal 2.02
Then i. he may plunder his house. Mt 12.29
With them i. is fulfilled the 13.14
'You shall i. hear but never 13.14
and you shall i. see but never 13.14
he i. bears fruit, and yields, in one 13.23
i. he said nothing to them without 13.34
the spirit i. is willing, but the 26.41
then i. he may plunder his house. Mk 3.27
so that they may i. see but not 4.12
and may i. hear but not understand; 4.12
the spirit i. is willing, but the 14.38
And we i. justly; for we are Lk 23.41
who said, "The Lord has risen i., 24.34
an Israelite i., in whom is no Jn 1.47
that this is i. the Savior of the 4.42
"This is i. the prophet who is to 6.14
For my flesh is food i., 6.55
and my blood is drink i. 6.55
you free, you will be free i. 8.36
i., the hour is coming when whoever 16.02
i. it has come, when you will be 16.32
said, 'For we are i. his offsprng.' Ac 17.28
You shall i. hear but never understand, 28.26
and you shall i. see but never 28.26
Circumcision i. is of value if you Rom 2.25
sin i. was in the world before the 5.13
submit to God's law, i. it cannot; 8.07
hand of God, who i. intercedes for us? 8.34
As i. he says in Hosea, "Those who 9.25
I. they have; for "Their voice 10.18
Everything is i. clean, but it is 14.20
and i. they are in debt to them, for 15.27
as i. there are many "gods" and many 1Co 8.05
I., in this case, what once had 2Co 3.10
Here i. we groan, and long to put on 5.02
unless i. you fail to meet the 13.05
righteousness would i. be by the law. Gal 3.21
Some i. preach Christ from envy and Php 1.15
I. he was ill, near to death. 2.27
I. I count everything as loss 3.08
you were i. concerned for me, but 4.10
as i. in the whole world it is Col 1.06
These have i. an appearance of 2.23
to which i. you were called in the 3.15
and i. you do love all the brethren 1Th 4.10
since i. God deems it just to repay 2Th 1.06
Great i., we confess, is the mystery 1Ti 3.16
hold of the life which is life i. 6.19
I. all who desire to live a godly 2Ti 3.12
but now he is i. useful to you and Phm 1.11
Men i. swear by a greater than Heb 6.16
I., the law appoints men in their 7.28
I., under the law almost everything 9.22
I., so terrifying was the sight 12.21

INDEED (cont.)
as i. you do follow the truth. 3Jn 1.03
"Blessed i.," says the Spirit, Rev 14.13

INDEPENDENT
woman is not i. of man nor man of 1Co 11.11

INDESTRUCTIBLE
but by the power of an i. life. Heb 7.16

INDIA
reigned from I. to Ethiopia over Est 1.01
the provinces from I. to Ethiopia, 8.09

INDICATE
not to i. the charges against him. Ac 25.27

INDICATED
or time was i. by the Spirit of 1Pe 1.11

INDICATES
the Holy Spirit i. that the way Heb 9.08
i. the removal of what is shaken, 12.27

INDICTMENT
that I had the i. written by my Job 31.35
the LORD has an i. against the Jer 25.31
The LORD has an i. against Judah, Hos 12.02

INDIGNANT
and the men were i. and very angry, Gen 34.07
and he became i. over the misery of Ju 10.16
for ever, will he be i. to the end?" Jer 3.05
they were i. at the two brothers. Mt 20.24
the Son of David!" they were i.; 21.15
they were i., saying, "Why this 26.08
But when Jesus saw it he was i., Mk 10.14
began to be i. at James and John. 10.41
i. because Jesus had healed on the Lk 13.14
is made to fall, and I am not i.? 2Co 11.29

INDIGNANTLY
some who said to themselves i., Mk 14.04

INDIGNATION
and a God who has i. every day. Ps 7.11
in my flesh because of thy i.; 38.03
Pour out thy i. upon them, and let 69.24
i., and distress, a company of 78.49
and put away thy i. toward us! 85.04
because of thy i. and anger; 102.10
Hot i. seizes me because of the 119.53
little while my i. will come to an Is 10.25
the LORD and the weapons of his i. 13.05
his lips are full of i., and his tongue 30.27
and his i. is against his enemies. 66.14
the nations cannot endure his i. Jer 10.10
for thou hadst filled me with i. 15.17
anger and my wrath and in great i.; 32.37
in his fierce i. has spurned king Lam 2.06
And I will pour out my i. upon you; Eze 21.31
or rained upon in the day of i. 22.24
Therefore I have poured out my i. upon them; 22.31
And I will direct my i. against you, 23.25
be at the latter end of the i.; Dan 8.19
till the i. is accomplished; 11.36
I will bear the i. of the LORD Mic 7.09
Who can stand before his i.? Nah 1.06
or thy i. against the sea, when thou Hab 3.08
to pour out upon them my i., Zep 3.08
thou hast had i. these seventy Zec 1.12
what i., what alarm, what longing, 2Co 7.11

INDISPENSABLE
which seem to be weaker are i., 1Co 12.22

INDISTINCT
And if the bugle gives an i. sound, 1Co 14.08

INDIVIDUALLY
and i. members one of another. Rom 12.05
apportions to each one i. as he wills. 1Co 12.11
of Christ and i. members of it. 12.27

INDIVIDUALS
names of the i. from twenty years 1Ch 23.24

INDOLENCE
and through i. the house leaks. Ecc 10.18

INDUCED
and i. him to go up against Ramothgilead. 2Ch 18.02

INDULGE
We must not i. in immorality as 1Co 10.08
those who i. in the lust of defiling 2Pe 2.10

INDULGED
immorally and i. in unnatural lust, Jud 1.07

INDULGENCE
in checking the i. of the flesh. Col 2.23

INDUSTRIOUS
young man was i. he gave him 1Ki 11.28

INEFFECTIVE
you from being i. or unfruitful in 2Pe 1.08

INEXPERIENCED
"Solomon my son is young and i., 1Ch 22.06
is young and i., and the work is 29.01

INEXPRESSIBLE
Thanks be to God for his i. gift! 2Co 9.15

INFAMOUS
mock you, you i. one, full of tumult. Eze 22.05

INFANT
i. and suckling, ox and sheep, camel 1Sa 15.03
take in pledge the i. of the poor. Job 24.09
be in it an i. that lives but a Is 65.20
i. and chld, from the midst of Jer 44.07

INFANTS
as i. that never see the light? Job 3.16
by the mouth of babes and i., Ps 8.02
Their i. will be dashed in pieces Is 13.16
because i. and babes faint in the Lam 2.11
the children, even nursing i. Joe 2.16
bringing even i. to him that he Lk 18.15
our fathers to expose their i., Ac 7.19

INFATUATED
with delight, be i. always with her love. Pro 5.19
Why should you be i., my son, with 5.20

INFERIOR
I am not i. to you. Who does not Job 12.03
I also know; I am not i. to you. 13.02
arise another kingdom i. to you, Dan 2.39
the greater honor to the i. part, 1Co 12.24
in the least i. to these superlative 2Co 11.05
I am not at all i. to these 12.11
that the i. is blessed by the Heb 7.07

INFIRMITIES
illness thou healest all his i. Ps 41.03
"He took our i. and bore our Mt 8.17
hear and to be healed of their i. Lk 5.15
been healed of evil spirits and i.: 8.02

INFIRMITY
and every i. among the people. Mt 4.23
healing every disease and every i. 9.35
to heal every disease and every i. 10.01

INFIRMITY (cont.)
had a spirit of i. for eighteen Lk 13.11
"Woman, you are freed from your i." 13.12

INFLAMED
While they are i. I will prepare Jer 51.39

INFLAMES
into the evening till wine i. them! Is 5.11

INFLAMMATION
i., and fiery heat and with drought, Deu 28.22

INFLICT
will he i. upon you, but he will lay Deu 7.15
God is unjust to i. wrath on us? Rom 3.05

INFLICTED
And Asa i. cruelties upon some of 2Ch 16.10
heals the wounds i. by his blow. Is 30.26
which the LORD i. on the day of Lam 1.12
And when they had i. many blows Ac 16.23

INFLICTING
i. vengeance upon those who do not 2Th 1.08

INFORM
until word comes from you to i. me. 2Sa 15.28
therefore we send and i. the king, Ez 4.14

INFORMATION
and come back to me with sure i. 1Sa 23.23
for your i., that we might write Ez 5.10
of the Jews gave i. about him, Ac 25.15

INFORMED
things of which you have been i. Lk 1.04
no one that you have i. me of this. Ac 23.22
men of the Jews i. him against 25.02
consideration for the man who i. you, 1Co 10.28
you were once for all fully i., Jud 1.05

INFORMS
He who i. against his friends to Job 17.05

INGATHERING
the feast of i. at the end of the Ex 23.16
the feast of i. at the year's end. 34.22
you make your i. from your threshing Deu 16.13

INHABIT
come into the land you are to i., Num 15.02
in houses which no man should i., Job 15.28
be driven out of the ruins they i.! Ps 109.10
For the upright will i. the land, Pro 2.21
They shall build houses and i. them; Is 65.21
They shall not build and another i.; 65.22
the ruined cities and i. them; Amo 9.14
houses, they shall not i. them; Zep 1.13

INHABITANT
and beautiful houses, without i. Is 5.09
"Until cities lie waste without i., 6.11
O i. of Zion, for great in your 12.06
are upon you, O i. of the earth! 24.17
And no i. will say, "I am sick"; the 33.24
cities are in ruins, without i. Jer 2.15
cities will be ruins without i. 4.07
of Judah a desolation, without i." 9.11
O i. of the valley, O rock of the 21.13
O i. of Lebanon, nested among the 22.23
shall be desolate, without i.'?" 26.09
without man or i. or beast, 33.10
of Judah a desolation without i. 34.22
without i., as it is this day. 44.22
become a waste, a ruin, without i. 46.19
and every i. of the land shall wail. 47.02
a desolation, with no i. in them. 48.09
the parched ground, O i. of Dibon! 48.18
the way and watch. O i. of Aroer! 48.19
snare are before you, O i. of Moab! 48.43
Babylon a desolation, without i. 51.29
Babylon," let the i. of Zion say. 51.35
a horror and a hissing without i. 51.37
has come to you, O i. of the land; Eze 7.07
destroy you till no i. is left. Zep 2.05
without a man, without an i. 3.06

INHABITANTS
and all the i. of the cities, and Gen 19.25
me odious to the i. of the land, 34.30
the i. of the land: Lotan, Shobal, 36.20
the i. of the land, the Canaanites, 50.11
have seized on the i. of Philistia. Ex 15.14
all the i. of Canaan have melted 15.15
deliver the i. of the land into 23.31
with the i. of the land whither 34.12
a covenant with the i. of the land, 34.15
and the land vomited out its i. Lev 18.25
throughout the land to all its i.; 25.10
out, is a land that devours its i.; Num 13.32
they will tell the i. of this land. 14.14
because of the i. of the land. 32.17
out all the i. of the land from 33.25
drive out the i. of the land from 33.55
have drawn away the i. of the city, Deu 13.13
surely put the i. of that city to 13.15
that all the i. of the land melt Jos 2.09
moreover all the i. of the land are 2.24
and all the i. of the land will 7.09
slaughtering all the i. of Ai in 8.24
utterly destroyed all the i. of Ai. 8.26
But when the i. of Gibeon heard 9.03
and all the i. of our country said 9.11
destroy all the i. of the land 9.24
and how the i. of Gibeon had made 10.01
the Hivites, the i. of Gibeon; 11.19
all the i. of the hill country from 13.06
from there against the i. of Debir; 15.15
the i. of Jerusalem, the people of 15.63
southward to the i. of Entappuah. 17.07
and the i. of Dor and its villages, 17.11
and the i. of Endor and its villages, 17.11
and the i. of Taanach and its villages, 17.11
and the i. of Megiddo and its villages; 17.11
they went against the i. of Debir. Ju 1.11
not drive out the i. of the plain, 1.19
drive out the i. of Bethshean and 1.27
or the i. of Dor and its villages, 1.27
or the i. of Ibleam and its villages, 1.27
or the i. of Megiddo and its 1.27
did not drive out the i. of Kitron, 1.30
of Kitron, or the i. of Nahalol; 1.30
Asher did not drive out the i. of Acco, 1.31
or the i. of Sidon, or of Ahlab, or 1.31
the Canaanites, the i. of the land; 1.32
drive out the i. of Bethshemesh, 1.33
or the i. of Bethanath, but dwelt 1.33
the Canaanites, the i. of the land; 1.33
nevertheless the i. of Bethshemesh 1.33
covenant with the i. of this land; 2.02
of the LORD, curse bitterly its i., 5.23
be head over all the i. of Gilead. 10.18
our head over all the i. of Gilead. 11.08
besides the i. of Gibeah, who 20.15
not one of the i. of Jabeshgilead 21.09
and smite the i. of Jabeshgilead 21.10
found among the i. of Jabeshgilead 21.12
messengers to the i. of Kiriathjearim, 1Sa 6.21
David delivered the i. of Keilah. 23.05
these were the i. of the land from 27.08
But when the i. of Jabeshgilead 31.11
the i. of the land, who said to 2Sa 5.06
while their i., shorn of strength, 2Ki 19.26
upon this place and upon its i. 22.16
this place, and against its i., 22.19
Judah and all the i. of Jerusalem, 23.02

INHABITANTS (cont.)
the potters and i. of Netaim and 1Ch 4.23
for the former i. there belonged to 4.40
fathers' houses of the i. of Geba, 8.06
houses of the i. of Aijalon, 8.13
who put to flight the i. of Gath); 8.13
Jebusites were, the i. of the land. 11.04
The i. of Jebus said to David, "You 11.05
delivered the i. of the land into 22.18
afflicted all the i. of the lands. 2Ch 15.05
drive out the i. of this land 20.07
all Judah and i. of Jerusalem, and 20.15
Judah and the i. of Jerusalem fell 20.18
"Hear me, Judah and i. of Jerusalem! 20.20
rose against the i. of Mount Seir, 20.23
had made an end of the i. of Seir, 20.23
and led the i. of Jerusalem into 21.11
Judah and the i. of Jerusalem into 21.13
And the i. of Jerusalem made 22.01
Hezekiah and the i. of Jerusalem 32.22
both he and the i. of Jerusalem, 32.26
Judah and the i. of Jerusalem did 32.33
Judah and the i. of Jerusalem, 33.09
and from the i. of Jerusalem. 34.09
upon this place and upon its i., 34.24
against this place and its i., 34.27
bring upon this place and its i. 34.28
Judah and the i. of Jerusalem and 34.30
And the i. of Jerusalem did according 34.32
present, and the i. of Jerusalem. 35.18
against the i. of Judah and Ez 4.06
Hanun and the i. of Zanoah repaired Neh 3.13
from among the i. of Jerusalem, 7.03
before them the i. of the land, 9.24
tremble, the waters and their i. Job 26.05
let all the i of the world stand Ps 33.08
forth on all the i. of the earth, 33.14
Give ear, all i. of the world, 49.01
and all its i., it is I who keep 75.03
Philistia with the i. of Tyre; 83.07
because of the wickedness of its i. 107.34
And now, O i. of Jerusalem and men Is 5.03
and a snare to the i. of Jerusalem. 8.14
Ephraim and the i. of Samaria, 9.09
and i. of Gebim flee for safety. 10.31
All you i. of the world, you who 18.03
And the i. of this coastland will 20.06
with bread, O i. of the land of Tema. 21.14
a father to the i. of Jerusalem 22.21
Be still, O i. of the coast, O 23.02
Tarshish, wail, O i. of the coast! 23.06
its surface and scatter its i. 24.01
The earth lies polluted under its i.; 24.05
and its i. suffer for their guilt; 24.06
therefore the i. of the earth are 24.06
brought low the i. of the height, 26.05
the i. of the world learn righteousness. 26.09
and the i. of the world have not 26.18
to punish the i. of the earth for 26.21
while their i., shorn of strength, 37.27
no more among the i. of the world. 38.11
and its i. are like grasshoppers; 40.22
it, the coastlands and their i. 42.10
let the i. of Sela sing for joy, let 42.11
you will be too narrow for your i., 49.19
forth upon all the i. of the land. Jer 1.14
Judah and to the i. of Jerusalem: 4.03
O men of Judah and i. of Jerusalem; 4.04
my hand against the i. of the land, 6.12
bones of the i. of Jerusalem shall 8.01
slinging out the i. of the land at 10.18
of Judah and the i. of Jerusalem. 11.02
of Judah and the i. of Jerusalem. 11.09
Judah and the i. of Jerusalem will 11.12
drunkenness all the i. of this land: 13.13
the prophets, and all the i. of Jerusalem. 13.13
and all the i. of Jerusalem, who 17.20
of Judah and the i. of Jerusalem; 17.25
of Judah and the i. of Jerusalem: 18.11
kings of Judah and i. of Jerusalem. 19.03
and to its i., making this city 19.12
And I will smite the i. of this city, 21.06
to me, and its i. like Gomorrah. 23.14
Judah and all the i. of Jerusalem: 25.02
them against this land and its i., 25.09
against all the i. of the earth, 25.29
against all the i. of the earth. 25.30
and upon this city and its i., 26.15
of Judah and the i. of Jerusalem. 32.32
of Judah and the i. of Jerusalem, 35.13
and all the i. of Jerusalem all 35.17
and upon the i. of Jerusalem, and 36.31
poured out on the i. of Jerusalem, 42.18
I will destroy cities and their i. 46.08
baggage for exile, O i. of Egypt! 46.19
dwell in the rock, O i. of Moab! 48.28
dwell in the depths, O i. of Dedan! 49.08
has formed against the i. of Teman: 49.20
dwell in the depths, O i. of Hazor! 49.30
and against the i. of Pekod. Slay, and 50.21
but unrest to the i. of Babylon. 50.34
and upon the i. of Babylon, and upon 50.35
Babylon, against the i. of Chaldea; 51.01
spoke concerning the i. of Babylon. 51.12
and all the i. of Chaldea before 51.24
"My blood be upon the i. of Chaldea," 51.35
or any of the i. of the world, that Lam 4.12
of whom the i. of Jerusalem have Eze 11.15
concerning the i. of Jerusalem in 12.19
will I give up the i. of Jerusalem. 15.06
you and your i., who imposed your 26.17
The i. of Sidon and Arvad were your 27.08
All the i. of the coastlands are 27.35
"Then all the i. of Egypt shall 29.06
the i. of these waste places in the 33.24
all the i. of the earth are accounted Dan 4.35
and among the i. of the earth; 4.35
to the i. of Jerusalem, and to all 9.07
controversy with the i. of the land. Hos 4.01
The i. of Samaria tremble for the 10.05
men, give ear. all i. of the land! Joe 1.02
and all the i. of the land to the 1.14
Let all the i. of the land tremble, 2.01
and cut off the i. from the Valley Amo 1.05
I will cut off the i. from Ashdod, 1.08
i. of Shaphir, in nakedness and Mic 1.11
and i. of Zaanan do not come forth; 1.11
For the i. of Maroth wait anxiously 1.12
to the chariots, i. of Lachish; 1.13
conqueror upon you, i. of Mareshah; 1.15
your i. speak lies, and their tongue 6.12
desolation, and your i. a hissing; 6.16
will be desolate because of its i., 7.13
against all the i. of Jerusalem; Zep 1.04
Wail, O i. of the Mortar! For all the 1.11
make of all the i. of the earth. 1.18
Woe to you i. of the seacoast, you 2.05
come, even the i. of many cities; Zec 8.20
the i. of one city shall go to 8.21
have pity on the i. of this land, 11.06
'The i. of Jerusalem have strength 12.05
glory of the i. of Jerusalem may 12.07
about the i. of Jerusalem so that 12.08
David and i. of Jerusalem a 12.10
David and the i. of Jerusalem to 13.01
known to all the i. of Jerusalem, Ac 1.19
manifest to all the i. of Jerusalem, 4.16
earth and its i. worship the first Rev 13.12

INHABITED
the Canaanites who i. Zephath, Ju 1.17
the Amorites, who i. that country. 11.21
rejoicing in his i. world and Pro 8.31
It will never be i. or dwelt in for Is 13.20
'She shall be i.,' and of the 44.26
it a chaos, he formed it to be i.! 45.18

INHABITED (cont.)
and this city shall be i. for ever. Jer 17.25
Egypt shall be i. as in the days 46.26
of the LORD she shall not be i., 50.13
nor i. for all generations. 50.39
And the i. cities shall be laid Eze 12.20
like the cities that are not i., 26.19
you will not be i. or have a place 26.20
and in all the i. places of the 34.13
and your cities shall not be i. 35.09
cities shall be i. and the waste 36.10
cause you to be i. as in your 36.11
I will cause the cities to be i., 36.33
cities are now i. and fortified. 36.35
the waste places which are now i., 38.12
But Judah shall be i. for ever, Joe 3.20
shall be i. as villages without Zec 2.04
When Jerusalem was i. and in 7.07
the South and the lowland were i., 7.07
shall still be i. in its place, 12.06
And it shall be i., for there shall 14.11

INHABITS
voice, the villages that Kedar i.; Is 42.11
high and lofty One who i. eternity, 57.15

INHERIT
and they shall i. it for ever.'" Ex 32.13
'You shall i. their land, and I will Lev 20.24
to i. as a possession for ever; 25.46
of their fathers they shall i. Num 26.55
For we will not i. with them on the 32.19
You shall i. the land by lot 33.54
of your fathers you shall i. 33.54
the land which you shall i. by lot, 34.13
for he shall cause Israel to i. it. Deu 1.38
the LORD your God gives you to i., 12.10
may live and i. the land which the 16.20
this people to i. the land which I Jos 1.06
"You shall not i. in our father's Ju 11.02
princes and i. a seat of honor. 1Sa 2.08
let me i. a double share of your 2Ki 2.09
which thou hast given us to i. 2Ch 20.11
and makest me i. the iniquities of Job 13.26
of his servants shall i. it, and those who Ps 69.36
The wise will i. honor, but fools Pro 3.35
troubles his household will i. wind, 11.29
and shall i. my holy mountain. Is 57.13
my chosen shall i. it, and my servants 65.09
have given my people Israel to i.: Jer 12.14
the LORD will i. Judah as his Zec 2.12
meek, for they shall i. the earth. Mt 5.05
a hundredfold, and i. eternal life. 19.29
i. the kingdom prepared for you 25.34
what must I do to i. eternal life?" Mk 10.17
what shall I do to i. eternal life?" Lk 10.25
what shall I do to i. eternal life?" 18.18
that they should i. the world, Rom 4.13
will not i. the kingdom of God? 1Co 6.09
nor robbers will i. the kingdom of God. 6.10
blood cannot i. the kingdom of God, 15.50
the perishable i. the imperishable. 15.50
slave shall not i. with the son of Gal 4.30
shall not i. the kingdom of God. 5.21
faith and patience i. the promises. Heb 6.12
when he desired to i. the blessing, 12.17

INHERITANCE
any portion or i. left to us in Gen 31.14
name of their brothers in their i. 48.06
our sin, and take us for thy i." Ex 34.09
of the land which is his by i., Lev 27.16
a part of his possession by i., 27.22
land belongs as a possession by i. 27.24
nor given us i. of fields and Num 16.14
"You shall have no i. in their land, 18.20
and your i. among the people of 18.20
every tithe in Israel for an i., 18.21
of Israel they shall have no i. 18.23
given to the Levites for an i.; 18.24
shall have no i. among the people 18.24
given you from them for your i., 18.26
be divided for i. according to the 26.53
tribe you shall give a large i., 26.54
tribe you shall give a small i.; 26.54
be given its i. according to its 26.54
Their i. shall be divided according 26.56
there was no i. given to them 26.62
possession of an i. among their 27.07
and cause the i. of their father 27.07
shall cause his i. to pass to his 27.08
shall give his i. to his brothers. 27.09
shall give his i. to his father's 27.10
shall give his i. to his kinsman 27.11
Israel have inherited each his i. 32.18
because our i. has come to us on 32.19
possession of our i. shall remain 32.32
tribe you shall give a large i., 33.54
tribe you shall give a small i.; 33.54
that shall fall to you for an i., 34.02
houses have received their i., 34.14
received their i. beyond the 34.15
divide the land to you for i.: 34.17
tribe, to divide the land for i. 34.18
to divide the i. for the people of 34.29
from the i. of their possession, 35.02
proportion to the i. which it 35.08
the land for i. by lot to the 36.02
to give the i. of Zelophehad our 36.02
then their i. will be taken from the i. of 36.03
added to the i. of the tribe to 36.03
taken away from the lot of our i. 36.03
then their i. will be added to the i. of 36.04
and their i. will be taken from the i. of 36.04
The i. of the people of Israel 36.07
cleave to the i. of the tribe of 36.07
possesses an i. in any tribe of 36.08
may possess the i. of his fathers. 36.08
So no i. shall be transferred from 36.09
Israel shall cleave to its own i.'" 36.09
and their i. remained in the tribe 36.12
LORD your God gives you for an i. Deu 4.21
to give you their land for an i., 4.38
no portion or i. with his brothers 10.09
the LORD is his i., as the LORD your 10.09
rest and to the i. which the LORD 12.09
he has no portion or i. with you. 12.12
he has no portion or i. with you. 14.27
he has no portion or i. with you, 14.29
gives you for an i. to possess), 15.04
have no portion or i. with Israel; 18.01
They shall have no i. among their 18.02
the LORD is their i., as he promised 18.02
LORD your God gives you for an i., 19.10
"In the i. which you will hold in 19.14
LORD your God gives you for an i., 20.16
possessions as an i. to his sons, 21.16
LORD your God gives you for an i. 21.23
LORD your God gives you for an i. 24.04
God give you for an i. to possess, 25.19
LORD your God gives you for an i., 26.01
gave it for an i. to the Reubenites, 29.08
High gave to the nations their i., 32.08
gave it for an i. to Israel according Jos 11.23
allot the land to Israel for an i., 13.06
land for an i. to the nine tribes 13.07
and the Gadites received their i., 13.08
of Levi alone Moses gave no i.; 13.14
LORD God of Israel are their i., 13.14
And Moses gave an i. to the tribe 13.15
This was the i. of the Reubenites, 13.23
And Moses gave an i. also to the 13.24
This is the i. of the Gadites 13.28
And Moses gave an i. to the half-tribe 13.29
the tribe of Levi Moses gave no i.; 13.33

INHERITANCE (cont.)

the LORD God of Israel is their i., Jos 13.33
Their i. was by lot, as the LORD had 14.02
had given an i. to the two and 14.03
Levites he gave no i. among them. 14.03
shall be an i. for you and your 14.09
the son of Jephunneh for an i. 14.13
became the i. of Caleb the son of 14.14
This is the i. of the tribe of the 15.20
and Ephraim, received their i. 16.04
of their i. on the east was 16.05
Such is the i. of the tribe of the 16.08
within the i. of the Manassites, 16.09
to give us an i. along with our 17.04
he gave them an i. among the 17.04
received an i. along with his sons. 17.06
one lot and one portion as an i., 17.14
tribes whose i. had not yet been 18.02
received their i. beyond the 18.07
This is the i. of the tribe of 18.20
This is the i. of the tribe of 18.28
and its i. was in the midst of the i. of 19.01
And it had for its i. Beersheba, 19.02
This was the i. of the tribe of 19.08
The i. of the tribe of Simeon 19.09
obtained an i. in the midst of their i. 19.09
territory of its i. reached as far 19.10
This is the i. of the tribe of 19.16
This is the i. of the tribe of 19.23
This is the i. of the tribe of 19.31
This is the i. of the tribe of 19.39
territory of its i. included Zorah, 19.41
This is the i. of the tribe of Dan, 19.48
Israel gave an i. among them to 19.49
and pasture lands out of their i. 21.03
to you as an i. for your tribes 23.04
people away, every man to his i. 24.28
him in his own i. at Timnathserah, 24.30
it became an i. of the descendants 24.32
each to his i. to take possession Ju 2.06
bounds of his i. in Timnathheres, 2.09
for itself an i. to dwell in; 18.01
until then no i. among the tribes 18.01
the country of the i. of Israel; 20.06
must be an i. for the survivors of 21.17
they went and returned to their i., 21.23
out from there every man to his i. 21.24
the name of the dead to his i. Ru 4.05
myself, lest I impair my own i. 4.06
the name of the dead in his i., 4.10
and we have no i. in the son of 2Sa 20.01
hast given to thy people as an i. 1Ki 8.36
We have no i. in the son of Jesse. 12.16
give you the i. of my fathers." 21.03
not give you the i. of my fathers." 21.04
Canaan, as your portion for an i." 1Ch 16.18
leave it for i. to your children 28.08
hast given to thy people as an i. 2Ch 6.27
We have no i. in the son of Jesse. 10.16
leave it for an i. to your children Ez 9.12
of Judah, every one in his i. Neh 11.20
gave them i. among their brothers. Job 42.15
Jacob his people, of Israel his i. Ps 78.71
the heathen have come into thy i.; 79.01
Canaan as your portion for an i. 105.11
man leaves an i. to his children's Pro 13.22
will share the i. as one of the 17.02
An i. gotten hastily in the beginning 20.21
blameless will have a goodly i. 28.10
Wisdom is good with an i., an advantage Ecc 7.11
and Israel is the tribe of his i.; Jer 10.16
have filled my i. with their abominations." 16.18
and Israel is the tribe of his i.; 51.19
Our i. has been turned over to strangers, Lam 5.02
over the i. of the house of Israel, Eze 35.15
you, and you shall be their i., 36.12
"They shall have no i.; I am their i.: 44.28
to any of his sons out of his i., 46.16
sons, it is their property by i. 46.16
gift out of his i. to one of his 46.17
sons may keep a gift from his i. 46.17
take any of the i. of the people, 46.18
his sons their i. out of his own 46.18
the land for i. among the twelve 47.13
land shall fall to you as your i. 47.14
allot it as an i. for yourselves 47.22
be allotted an i. among the tribes 47.22
there you shall assign him his i., 47.23
allot as an i. among the tribes of 48.29
and his house, a man and his i. Mic 2.02
thy staff, the flock of thy i., 7.14
transgression for the remnant of his i.? 7.18
let us kill him and have his i.' Mt 21.38
kill him, and the i. will be ours.' Mk 12.07
my brother divide the i. with me." Lk 12.13
kill him, that the i. may be ours.' 20.14
yet he gave him no i. in it, not even Ac 7.05
he gave them their land as an i., 13.19
to give you the i. among all those 20.32
For if the i. is by the law, it is Gal 3.18
guarantee of our i. until we acquire Eph 1.14
of his glorious i. in the saints, 1.18
has any i. in the kingdom of Christ 5.05
to share in the i. of the saints Col 1.12
will receive the i. as your reward; 3.24
receive the promised eternal i., Heb 9.15
which he was to receive as an i.; 11.08
and to an i. which is imperishable, 1Pe 1.04

INHERITANCES

These are the i. which Moses Jos 13.32
And these are the i. which the 14.01
of it with a view to their i., 18.04
territories of the land as i., 19.49
These are the i. which Eleazar the 19.51

INHERITED

or of his i. field, shall be sold or Lev 27.28
of Israel have i. each his inheritance. Num 32.18
House and wealth are i. from fathers, Pro 19.14
fathers have i. nought but lies, Jer 16.19
the futile ways i. from your fathers, 1Pe 1.18

INHERITORS

and from Judah i. of my mountains; Is 65.09

INHERITS

to the inheritance which it i., Num 35.08

INHUMAN

i., implacable, slanderers. profligates, 2Ti 3.03

INIQUITIES

him all the i. of the people of Lev 16.21
bear all their i. upon him to a 16.22
because of the i. of their fathers 26.39
for our i. have risen higher than Ez 9.06
and for our i. we, our kings, and 9.07
less than our i. deserved and hast 9.13
sins and the i. of their fathers. Neh 9.02
How many are my i. and my sins? Job 13.23
me inherit the i. of my youth. 13.26
great? There is no end to your i. 22.05
For my i. have gone over my head; Ps 38.04
my i. have overtaken me, till I 40.12
my sins, and blot out all my i. 51.09
against us the i. of our forefathers; 79.08
Thou hast set our i. before thee, 90.08
nor requite us according to our i. 103.10
of their i. suffered affliction; 107.17
shouldst mark i., Lord, who could 130.03
will redeem Israel from all his i. 130.08
The i. of the wicked ensnare him, Pro 5.22
you have wearied me with your i. Is 43.24
for your i. you were sold, and for 50.01

INIQUITIES (cont.)
transgressions, he was bruised for our i.; Is 53.05
righteous; and he shall bear their i. 53.11
but your i. have made a separation 59.02
are with us, and we know our i.: 59.12
and our i., like the wind, take us 64.06
delivered us into the hand of our i. 64.07
their i. and their fathers' i. 65.07
Your i. have turned these away, and Jer 5.25
back to the i. of their forefathers, 11.10
"Though our i. testify against us, 14.07
prophets and the i. of her priests, Lam 4.13
are no more; and we bear their i. 5.07
away in your i. and groan to one Eze 24.23
By the multitude of your i., in the 28.18
for your i. and your abominable 36.31
I cleanse you from all your i., 36.33
they may be ashamed of their i. 43.10
and your i. by showing mercy to the Dan 4.27
from our i. and giving heed to thy 9.13
and for the i. of our fathers, 9.16
I will punish you for all your i. Amo 3.02
he will tread our i. under foot. Mic 7.19
"Blessed are those whose i. are forgiven, Rom 4.07
I will be merciful toward their i., Heb 8.12
heaven, and God has remembered her i. Rev 18.05

INIQUITOUS
Woe to those who decree i. decrees, Is 10.01

INIQUITY
for the i. of the Amorites is not Gen 15.16
visiting the i. of the fathers upon Ex 20.05
forgiving i. and transgression and 34.07
visiting the i. of the fathers upon 34.07
and pardon our i. and our sin, 34.09
not speak, he shall bear his i. Lev 5.01
he is guilty and shall bear his i. 5.17
who eats of it shall bear his i. 7.18
may bear the i. of the congregation, 10.17
his flesh, he shall bear his i. 17.16
defiled, so that I punished its i., 18.25
one who eats it shall bear his i. 19.08
nakedness, he shall bear his i. 20.17
near kin; they shall bear their i. 20.19
so cause them to bear i. and guilt, 22.16
enemies' lands because of their i.; 26.39
confess their i. and the i. 26.40
and they make amends for their i.; 26.41
shall make amends for their i., 26.43
remembrance, bringing i. to remembrance. Num 5.15
The man shall be free from i., 5.31
but the woman shall bear her i." 5.31
forgiving i. and transgression, but 14.18
visiting the i. of fathers upon 14.18
Pardon the i. of this people, I pray 14.19
day a year, you shall bear your i., 14.34
cut off; his i. shall be upon him." 15.31
you shall bear i. in connection 18.01
and they shall bear their i.; it shall be 18.23
of them, then he shall bear her i. 30.15
visiting the i. of the fathers upon Deu 5.09
God of faithfulness and without i., 32.04
he did not perish alone for his i. Jos 22.20
for the i. which he knew, because 1Sa 3.13
of Eli that the i. of Eli's house 3.14
stubbornness is as i. and idolatry. 15.23
When he commits i., I will chasten 2Sa 7.14
take away the i. of thy servant; 24.10
take away the i. of thy servant; 1Ch 21.08
those who plow i. and sow trouble Job 4.08
transgression and take away my i.? 7.21
seek out my i. and search for my 10.06
and dost not acquit me of my i. 10.14
when he sees i., will he not 11.11
If i. is in your hand, put it far 11.14
and thou wouldest cover over my i. 14.17
For your i. teaches your mouth, and 15.05
a man who drinks i. like water! 15.16
The heavens will reveal his i., 20.27
stores up their i. for their sons. 21.19
and disaster the workers of i.? 31.03
would be an i. to be punished by 31.11
would be an i. to be punished by 31.28
men, by hiding my i. in my bosom, 31.33
am pure, and there is no i. in me. 33.09
if I have done i., I will do it 34.32
commands that they return from i. 36.10
Take heed, do not turn to i., 36.21
is jealous with anger against i. 36.33
his tongue are mischief and i. Ps 10.07
man to whom the LORD imputes no i., 32.02
to thee, and I did not hide my i.; 32.05
eyes that his i. cannot be found 36.02
I confess my i., I am sorry for my 38.18
when the i. of my persecutors surrounds 49.05
Wash me thoroughly from my i., and cleanse 51.02
Behold, I was brought forth in i., 51.05
are corrupt, doing abominable i.; 53.01
If I had cherished i. in my heart, 66.18
forgave their i., and did not destroy 78.38
didst forgive the i. of thy people; 85.02
the rod and their i. with scourges; 89.32
on them their i. and wipe them out 94.23
who forgives all your i., who heals 103.03
we have committed i, we have done 106.06
were brought low through their i. 106.43
May the i. of his fathers be 109.14
and let no i. get dominion over me. 119.133
in company with men who work i.; 141.04
and faithfulness i. is atoned for, Pro 16.06
the mouth of the wicked devours i. 19.28
nation, a people laden with i., Is 1.04
cannot endure i. and solemn 1.13
those who draw i. with cords of 5.18
evil, and the wicked for their i.; 13.11
"Surely this i. will not be forgiven 22.14
inhabitants of the earth for their i., 26.21
therefore this i. shall be to you 30.13
the helpers of those who work i. 31.02
folly, and his mind plots i.: 32.06
there will be forgiven their i. 33.24
that her i. is pardoned, that she 40.02
has laid on him the i. of us all. 53.06
Because of the i. of his covetousness 57.17
blood and your fingers with i.; 59.03
conceive mischief and bring forth i. 59.04
Their works are works of i., and deeds 59.06
their thoughts are thoughts of i., 59.07
LORD, and remember not i. for ever. 64.09
they commit i. and are too weary to Jer 9.05
greatness of your i. that your 13.22
remember their i. and punish their 14.10
and the i. of our fathers, for we 14.20
What is our i.? What is the 16.10
nor is their i. concealed from my 16.17
recompense their i. and their sin, 16.18
Forgive not their i., nor blot out 18.23
for their i., says the LORD, making 25.12
for I will forgive their i., 31.34
may forgive their i. and their sin. 36.03
and his servants for their i.; 36.31
i. shall be sought in Israel, and 50.20
exposed your i. to restore your Lam 2.14
The punishment of your i., 4.22
but your i., O daughter of Edom, he 4.22
wicked man shall die in his i.; Eze 3.18
wicked way, he shall die in his i.; 3.19
his righteousness and commits i., 3.20
and because of his i., none can 7.13
moaning, every one over his i. 7.16
the stumbling block of their i. 7.19
men who devise i. and who give 11.02
block of their i. before their 14.03
block of his i. before his face, 14.04
block of his i. before his face, 14.07

INIQUITY (cont.)
increase, withholds his hand from i., Eze 18.08
withholds his hand from i., 18.17
shall not die for his father's i.; 18.17
behold, he shall die for his i. 18.18
suffer for the i. of the father?' 18.19
suffer for the i. of the father, 18.20
suffer for the i. of the son; 18.20
and commits i. and does the same 18.24
his righteousness and commits i., 18.26
for the i. which he has committed 16.26
transgressions, lest i. be your ruin. 18.30
created, till i. was found in you. 28.15
of Israel, recalling their i., 29.16
that man is taken away in his i., 33.06
wicked man shall die in his i., 33.08
he shall die in his i., but you will 33.09
his righteousness and commits i., 33.13
but in the i. that he has committed 33.13
statutes of life, committing no i.; 33.15
and commits i., he shall die for it. 33.18
went into captivity for their i., 39.23
block of i. to the house of Israel, 44.12
an end to sin, and to atone for i., Dan 9.24
they are greedy for their i. Hos 4.08
Now he will remember their i., 8.13
of your great i. and great hatred. 9.07
Gibeah: he will remember their i., 9.09
are chastised for their double i. 10.10
You have plowed i., you have reaped 10.13
If there is i. in Gilead they shall 12.11
The i. of Ephraim is bound up, his 13.12
have stumbled because of your i. 14.01
say to him, "Take away all i.; 14.02
pardoning i. and passing over Mic 7.18
blood, and founds a city on i.! Hab 2.12
I have taken your i. away from you, Zec 3.04
"This is the i. in all the land." 5.06
uprightness, and he turned many from i. Mal 2.06
you are full of hypocrisy and i., Mt 23.28
from me, all you workers of i.!' Lk 13.27
bitterness and in the bond of i. Ac 8.23
and to greater and greater i., Rom 6.19
partnership have righteousness and i.? 2Co 6.14
name of the Lord depart from i. 2Ti 2.19
us from all i. and to purify for Tit 2.14

INJURE
All day long they seek to i. my cause; Ps 56.05

INJURED
man who has an i. foot or an i. hand, Lev 21.19
is being i. by what you eat, you Rom 14.15

INJURES
but he who misses me i. himself; Pro 8.36

INJURY
reproves a wicked man incurs i. Pro 9.07
will be with i. and much loss, Ac 27.10
and incurred this i. and loss. 27.21

INJUSTICE
"You shall do no i. in judgment; Lev 19.15
hope, and i. shuts her mouth. Job 5.16
but it is swept away through i. Pro 13.23
than great revenues with i. 16.08
He who sows i. will reap calamity, 22.08
unrighteousness, and his upper rooms by i.; Jer 22.13
i. has blossomed, pride has budded. Eze 7.10
of blood, and the city full of i.; 9.09
iniquity, you have reaped i., Hos 10.13
Is there i. on God's part? Rom 9.14

INK
I wrote them with i. on the scroll." Jer 36.18
not with i. but with the Spirit of 2Co 3.03
would rather not use paper and i., 2Jn 1.12
rather not write with pen and i.; 3Jn 1.13

INLAID
coasts of Cyprus, i. with ivory. Eze 27.06

INMOST
in the law of God, in my i. self, Rom 7.22

INN
was no place for them in the i. Lk 2.07
own beast and brought him to an i., 10.34

INNER
with its legs and its i. parts. Ex 12.09
into the i. part of the sanctuary. Lev 10.18
the man of Israel into the i. room, Num 25.08
men lying in wait in an i. chamber. Ju 16.09
in wait were in an i. chamber. 16.12
both the nave and the i. sanctuary; 1Ki 6.05
this within as an i. sanctuary, 6.16
nave in front of the i. sanctuary, 6.17
The i. sanctuary he prepared in the 6.19
The i. sanctuary was twenty cubits 6.20
in front of the i. sanctuary, 6.21
belonged to the i. sanctuary he 6.22
In the i. sanctuary he made two 6.23
flowers, in the i. and outer rooms. 6.29
gold in the i. and outer rooms. 6.30
entrance to the i. sanctuary he 6.31
He built the i. court with three 6.36
so had the i. court of the house of 7.12
the north, before the i. sanctuary; 7.49
in the i. sanctuary of the house, in 8.06
holy place before the i. sanctuary; 8.08
and entered an i. chamber in the 20.30
you go into an i. chamber to hide 22.25
and lead him to an i. chamber. 2Ki 9.02
went into the i. room of the house 10.25
and its i. chambers, and of the room 1Ch 28.11
to burn before the i. sanctuary, 2Ch 4.20
for the i. doors to the most holy 4.22
in the i. sanctuary of the house, in 5.07
holy place before the i. sanctuary; 5.09
you go into an i. chamber to hide 18.24
went into the i. part of the house 29.16
king inside the i. court without Est 4.11
stood in the i. court of the king's 5.01
down into the i. parts of the body. Pro 18.08
down into the i. parts of the body. 26.22
gateway of the i. court that faces Eze 8.03
me into the i. court of the house 8.16
and a cloud filled the i. court. 10.03
the gate at the i. end, one reed. 40.07
of the gate was at the i. end. 40.09
the end of the i. vestibule of the 40.15
from the i. front of the lower 40.19
to the outer front of the i. court, 40.19
east, was a gate to the i. court; 40.23
gate on the south of the i. court; 40.27
me to the i. court by the south 40.28
me to the i. court on the east 40.32
me from without into the i. court, 40.44
were two chambers in the i. court, 40.44
went into the i. room and measured 41.03
temple and the i. room and the 41.15
even to the i. room, and on the 41.17
about in the i. room and the nave 41.17
Then he led me out into the i. court, 42.01
which belonged to the i. court, 42.03
and brought me into the i. court; 43.05
enter the gates of the i. court, 44.17
minister at the gates of the i. court, 44.17
wine, when he enters the i. court. 44.21
into the i. court, to minister in 44.27
posts of the gate of the i. court. 45.19
The gate of the i. court that 46.01
down into the i. part of the ship Jon 1.05
he is in the i. rooms,' do not Mt 24.26
them into the i. prison and Ac 16.24
our i. nature is being renewed 2Co 4.16

INNER (cont.)
through his Spirit in the i. man, Eph 3.16
enters into the i. shrine behind Heb 6.19

INNERMOST
sitting in the i. parts of the 1Sa 24.03
prepared in the i. part of the 1Ki 6.19
cherubim in the i. part of the 6.27
doors of the i. part of the house, 7.50
LORD, searching all his i. parts. Pro 20.27
strokes make clean the i. parts. 20.30
who is in the i. parts of the Amo 6.10

INNKEEPER
denarii and gave them to the i., Lk 10.35

INNOCENCE
heart and the i. of my hands I Gen 20.05
I wash my hands in i., and go about Ps 26.06
clean and washed my hands in i. 73.13

INNOCENT
"Lord, wilt thou slay an i. people? Gen 20.04
do not slay the i. and righteous, Ex 23.07
lest i. blood be shed in your land Deu 19.10
the guilt of i. blood from Israel, 19.13
the guilt of i. blood in the midst 21.08
the guilt of i. blood from your 21.09
acquitting the i. and condemning 25.01
takes a bribe to slay an i. person. 27.25
you sin against i. blood by 1Sa 19.05
and putting i. blood upon the 1Ki 2.05
said to all the people, "You are i. 2Ki 10.09
Moreover Manasseh shed very much i. blood, 21.16
and also for the i. blood that he 24.04
he filled Jerusalem with i. blood, 24.04
now, who that was i. ever perished? Job 4.07
Though I am i., I cannot answer him; 9.15
Though I am i., my own mouth would 9.20
he mocks at the calamity of the i. 9.23
I know thou wilt not hold me i. 9.28
and the i. stirs himself up against 17.08
the i. laugh them to scorn, 22.19
He delivers the i. man; you will be 22.30
and the i. will divide the silver. 27.17
'I am i., and God has taken away my 34.05
in hiding places he murders the i. Ps 10.08
not take a bribe against the i. 15.05
and i. of great transgression. 19.13
and condemn the i. to death. 94.21
they poured out i. blood, the blood 106.38
let us wantonly ambush the i.; Pro 1.11
and hands that shed i. blood, 6.17
"You are i.," will be cursed by 24.24
and deprive the i. of his right! Is 5.23
they make haste to shed i. blood; 59.07
you say, 'I am i.; surely his anger Jer 2.35
or shed i. blood in this place, and 7.06
nor shed i. blood in this place. 22.03
for shedding i. blood, and for 22.17
you will bring i. blood upon 26.15
they have shed i. blood in their Joe 3.19
life, and lay not on us i. blood; Jon 1.14
wise as serpents and i. as doves. Mt 10.16
the blood of i. Abel to the blood 23.35
have sinned in betraying i. blood. 27.04
"I am i. of this man's blood; 27.24
said, "Certainly this man was i.!" Lk 23.47
I am i. From now on I will go to Ac 18.06
day that I am i. of the blood of 20.26
that you may be blameless and i., Php 2.15

INNOCENTS
this place with the blood of i., Jer 19.04

INNUMERABLE
and those who go before him are i. Job 21.33
wide, which teems with things i., Ps 104.25
and as the i. grains of sand by Heb 11.12
and to i. angels in festal gathering, 12.22

INQUIRE
So she went to i. of the LORD. Gen 25.22
the people come to me to i. of God; Ex 18.15
A man shall not i. whether it is Lev 27.33
who shall i. for him by the judgment Num 27.21
that you do not i. about their Deu 12.30
then you shall i. and make search 13.14
then you shall i. diligently, 17.04
the judges shall i. diligently, 19.18
"I. of God, we pray thee, that we may Ju 18.05
when a man went to i. of God, 1Sa 9.09
"I. whose son the stripling is." 17.56
that I may go to her and i. of her. 28.07
is coming to i. of you concerning 1Ki 14.05
"I. first for the word of the LORD." 22.05
of the LORD of whom we may i.?" 22.07
man by whom we may i. of the LORD, 22.08
i. of Baalzebub, the god of Ekron, 2Ki 1.02
you are going to i. of Baalzebub, 1.03
you are sending to i. of Baalzebub, 1.06
sent messengers to i. of Baalzebub, 1.16
no God in Israel to i. of his word? 1.16
through whom we may i. of the LORD?" 3.11
and i. of the LORD through him, 8.08
altar shall be for me to i. by." 16.15
"Go, i. of the LORD for me, and for 22.13
who sent you to i. of the LORD, 22.18
not go before it to i. of God, 1Ch 21.30
"I. first for the word of the LORD." 2Ch 18.04
of the LORD of whom we may i.?" 18.06
man by whom we may i. of the LORD, 18.07
sent to him to i. about the sign 32.31
"Go, i. of the LORD for me and for 34.21
Judah, who sent you to i. of the LORD, 34.26
"For i., I pray you, of bygone ages, Job 8.08
the LORD, and to i. in his temple. Ps 27.04
If you will i., i.; come back again." Is 21.12
stupid, and do not i. of the LORD; Jer 10.21
"I. of the LORD for us, for Nebuchadrezzar 21.02
who sent you to me to i. of me, 37.07
to a prophet to i. for himself of Eze 14.07
of Israel came to i. of the LORD, 20.01
Is it to i. of me that you come? 20.03
My people i. of a thing of wood, and Hos 4.12
do not seek the LORD or i. of him. Zep 1.06
and i. in the house of Judas for a Ac 9.11
were going to i. somewhat more 23.20

INQUIRED
And he i. about their welfare, and Gen 43.27
diligently i. about the goat of Lev 10.16
people of Israel i. of the LORD, Ju 1.01
after they had made search and i., 6.29
and i. of God, "Which of us shall go 20.18
and they i. of the LORD, "Shall we 20.23
of Israel i. of the LORD (for the 20.27
So they i. again of the LORD, "Did 1Sa 10.22
And Saul i. of God, "Shall I go down 14.37
and he i. of the LORD for him, and 22.10
and have i. of God for him, so that 22.13
time that I have i. of God for him? 22.15
Therefore David i. of the LORD, 23.02
Then David i. of the LORD again. 23.04
And when Saul i. of the LORD, the 28.06
And David i. of the LORD, "Shall I 30.08
After this David i. of the LORD, 2Sa 2.01
And David i. of the LORD, "Shall I 5.19
And when David i. of the LORD, he 5.23
And David sent and i. about the 11.03
And David i. of God, "Shall I go up 1Ch 14.10
And when David again i. of God, 14.14
I let myself be i. of at all by Eze 14.03
GOD, I will not be i. of by you. 20.03
And shall I be i. of by you, 20.31
GOD, I will not be i. of by you. 20.31

INQUIRED (cont.)
concerning which the king i. of them, Dan 1.20
he i. of them where the Christ was Mt 2.04
going by, he i. what this meant. Lk 18.36
they i., "By what power or by what Ac 4.07
He i. who he was and what he had 21.33
searched and i. about this salvation, 1Pe 1.10
they i. what person or time was 1.11

INQUIRER
punishment of the i. shall be alike Eze 14.10

INQUIRIES
counselors to make i. about Judah Ez 7.14

INQUIRING
i. what he would have him called. Lk 1.62

INQUIRY
her freedom, an i. shall be held. Lev 19.20
When he makes i., what shall I Job 31.14
having made i. for Simon's house, Ac 10.17

INSATIABLE
the Assyrians, because you were i.; Eze 16.28
eyes full of adultery, i. for sin. 2Pe 2.14

INSCRIBE
and i. it in a book, that it may be Is 30.08

INSCRIBED
Oh that they were i. in a book! Job 19.23
was sent, and this writing was i. Dan 5.24
And this is the writing that was i.: 5.25
you what is i. in the book of 10.21
there shall be i. on the bells of Zec 14.20
he has a name i. which no one Rev 19.12
and on his thigh he has a name i., 19.16
of the sons of Israel were i.; 21.12

INSCRIPTION
pure gold, and wrote upon it an i., Ex 39.30
facets, I will engrave its i., Zec 3.09
"Whose likeness and i. is this?" Mt 22.20
"Whose likeness and i. is this?" Mk 12.16
And the i. of the charge against 15.26
Whose likeness and i. has it?" Lk 20.24
There was also an i. over him, 23.38
I found also an altar with this i., Ac 17.23

INSCRUTABLE
his judgments and how i. his ways! Rom 11.33

INSECTS
"All winged i. that go upon all Lev 11.20
the winged i. that go on all fours 11.21
other winged i. which have four 11.23
And all winged i. are unclean for Deu 14.19

INSERTED
should not be i. into the walls of 1Ki 6.06

INSHORE
all sailed along Crete, close i. Ac 27.13

INSIDE
and cover it i. and out with pitch. Gen 6.14
on its i. edge next to the ephod. Ex 28.26
on its i. edge next to the ephod. 39.19
shall cause the i. of the house to Lev 14.41
are hidden in the earth i. my tent, Jos 7.21
jars, with torches i. the jars. Ju 7.16
i. the tent which David pitched 2Sa 6.17
house on the i. with boards of 1Ki 6.15
covered them on the i. with wood; 6.15
overlaid the i. of the house with 6.21
which had been built i. the palace, 2Ki 16.18
and set it i. the tent which David 1Ch 16.01
it on the i. with pure gold. 2Ch 3.04
to the king i. the inner court Est 4.11
royal throne i. the palace opposite 5.01
vestibule had windows round about i., Eze 40.16
and its vestibule was on the i. 40.22
and its vestibule was on the i.; 40.26
Four tables were on the i., and four 40.41
On the i., around each of the four 46.23
but i. they are full of extortion Mt 23.25
cleanse the i. of the cup and of 23.26
and going i. he sat with the guards 26.58
led him away i. the palace (that Mk 15.16
but i. you are full of extortion Lk 11.39
made the outside make the i. also? 11.40
those who are i. the city depart, 21.21
we opened it we found no one i." Ac 5.23
Is it not those i. the church whom 1Co 5.12

INSIGHT
and Elnathan, who were men of i., Ez 8.16
knowledge, his words are without i. Job 34.35
instruction, understand words of i., Pro 1.02
you cry out for i. and raise your 2.03
and do not rely on your own i. 3.05
be attentive, that you may gain i.; 4.01
of my mouth. Get wisdom; get i. 4.05
and whatever you get, get i. 4.07
and call i. your intimate friend; 7.04
I have i., I have strength. 8.14
live, and walk in the way of i. 9.06
knowledge of the Holy One is i. 9.10
all wisdom and i. the mystery of Eph 1.09
can perceive my i. into the 3.04

INSINCERELY
him the rest of the Jews acted i., Gal 2.13

INSINCERITY
was carried away by their i. Gal 2.13
fruits, without uncertainty or i. Jas 3.17
all guile and i. and envy and all 1Pe 2.01

INSIST
Love does not *i.* on its own way; 1Co 13.05
I desire you to i. on these things, Tit 3.08

INSISTED
of about an hour still another i., Lk 22.59
But she i. that it was so. Ac 12.15

INSISTING
i. on self-abasement and worship of Col 2.18

INSOLENCE
By i. the heedless make strife, but Pro 13.10
and his i.—his boasts are false. Is 16.06
I know his i., says the LORD; Jer 48.30
commander shall put an end to his i.; Dan 11.18
he shall turn his i. back upon him. 11.18
because of the i. of their tongue. Hos 7.16

INSOLENT
For i. men have risen against me, Ps 54.03
on high, or speak with i. neck. 75.05
O God, i. men have risen up against 86.14
Thou dost rebuke the i., accursed 119.21
the youth will be i. to the elder, Is 3.05
has ceased, the i. fury ceased! 14.04
You will see no more the i. people, 33.19
and all the i. men said to Jeremiah, Jer 43.01
i., haughty, boastful, inventors of Rom 1.30

INSOLENTLY
that they acted i. against our Neh 9.10
have struck me i. upon the cheek, Job 16.10
which speak i. against the righteous Ps 31.18
an adversary who deals i. with me— 55.12

INSPECT
and you shall i. your fold and miss Job 5.24

INSPECTED
and I i. the walls of Jerusalem Neh 2.13
by the valley and i. the wall; 2.15

INSPIRE
succeed, perhaps you may i. terror. Is 47.12
The horror you i. has deceived you, Jer 49.16

INSPIRED
And he has i. him to teach, both him Ex 35.34
I. decisions are on the lips of a Pro 16.10
i. by the Spirit, calls him Lord, Mt 22.43
David himself, i. by the Holy Spirit, Mk 12.36
And i. by the Spirit he came into Lk 2.27
All these are i. by one and the 1Co 12.11
with joy i. by the Holy Spirit; 1Th 1.06
that i. by them you may wage the 1Ti 1.18
All scripture is i. by God and 2Ti 3.16

INSPIRES
same God who i. them all in every 1Co 12.06
which he mightily i. within me. Col 1.29

INSTALLED
and i. one of his sons, who became Ju 17.05
And Micah i. the Levite, and the 17.12

INSTANT
passing chaff. And in an i., suddenly, Is 29.05
crash comes suddenly, in an i.; 30.13

INSTANTLY
And i. the woman was made well. Mt 9.22
And her daughter was healed i. 15.28
of him, and the boy was cured i. 17.18
examine him withdrew from him i.; Ac 22.29

INSTEAD
for me another child i. of Abel, Gen 4.25
as a burnt offering i. of his son. 22.13
remain i. of the lad as a slave to 44.33
of Israel i. of every first-born Num 3.12
i. of all the first-born among the 3.41
of the Levites i. of all the 3.41
"Take the Levites i. of all the 3.45
of the Levites i. of their cattle; 3.45
i. of all that open the womb, the 8.16
the Levites i. of all the first-born 8.18
fairer than she? Pray take her i." Ju 15.02
set Amasa over the army i. of Joab. 2Sa 17.25
Would I had died i. of you, 18.33
made him king i. of his father 2Ki 14.21
of Samaria i. of the people of 17.24
Lord as king i. of David his 1Ch 29.23
made him king i. of his father 2Ch 26.01
afflicted him i. of strengthening 28.20
the king be queen i. of Vashti. Est 2.04
and made her queen i. of Vashti. 2.17
let thorns grow i. of wheat, Job 31.40
wheat, and foul weeds i. of barley. 31.40
I. of your fathers shall be your Ps 45.16
Take my instruction i. of silver, Pro 8.10
and the wicked gets into it i. 11.08
I. of perfume there will be rottenness, Is 3.24
and i. of a girdle, a rope; 3.24
and i. of well-set hair, baldness; 3.24
and i. of a rich robe, a girding of 3.24
sackcloth; i. of beauty, shame. 3.24
i. of the thorn shall come up the 55.13
i. of the brier shall come up the 55.13
I. of bronze I will bring gold, and 60.17
and i. of iron I will bring silver; 60.17
i. of wood, bronze, i. of stones, iron. 60.17
to give them a garland i. of ashes, 61.03
the oil of gladness i. of mourning, 61.03
mantle of praise i. of a faint spirit; 61.03
I. of your shame you shall have a 61.07
i. of dishonor you shall rejoice in 61.07
who reigned i. of Josiah his father, Jer 22.11
made you priest i. of Jehoiada the 29.26
reigned i. of Coniah the son of 37.01
have cow's dung i. of human dung, Eze 4.15
strangers i. of her husband! 16.32
i. of being the desolation that it 36.34
and i. of it there came up four Dan 8.08
the god of fortresses i. of these; 11.38
be sated with contempt i. of glory. Hab 2.16
him release for them Barabbas i. Mk 15.11
will i. of a fish give him a Lk 11.11
I., seek his kingdom, and these 12.31
the unrighteous i. of the saints? 1Co 6.01
but i. let there be thanksgiving. Eph 5.04
of darkness, but i. expose them. 5.11
i. of giving heed to Jewish myths Tit 1.14
things to come i. of the true form Heb 10.01
I. you ought to say, "If the Lord Jas 4.15

INSTIGATED
Then they secretly i. men, who said, Ac 6.11

INSTINCT
creatures of i., born to be caught 2Pe 2.12
things they know by i. as irrational Jud 1.10

INSTITUTED
that exist have been i. by God. Rom 13.01

INSTITUTION
the Lord's sake to every human i., 1Pe 2.13

INSTRUCT
and I will i. you in the good and 1Sa 12.23
ordinances, then you shall i. them, 2Ch 19.10
Thou gavest thy good Spirit to i. them, Neh 9.20
Him will he i. in the way that he Ps 25.12
I will i. you and teach you the way 32.08
to i. his princes at his pleasure, 105.22
knowledge, and able to i. one another. Rom 15.14
mind of the Lord so as to i. him?" 1Co 2.16
in order to i. others, than ten 14.19
are able to i. you for salvation 2Ti 3.15

INSTRUCTED
He i. the foremost, "When Esau my Gen 32.17
He likewise i. the second and the 32.19
Boaz, i. his young men, saying, "Let Ru 2.15
and he i. the messenger, "When you 2Sa 11.19
because Jehoiada the priest i. him. 2Ki 12.02
who i. him in the fear of God; 2Ch 26.05
you have i. many, and you have Job 4.03
when a wise man is i., he gains Pro 21.11
For he is i. aright; his God teaches Is 28.26
or as his counselor has i. him? 40.13
and after I was i., I smote upon Jer 31.19
them as the king had i. him. So 38.27
And Moses was i. in all the wisdom Ac 7.22
He had been i. in the way of the 18.25
because you are i. in the law, Rom 2.18
he was i. by God, saying, "See that Heb 8.05

INSTRUCTING
i. them, "Thus you shall say to my Gen 32.04
had finished i. his twelve disciples, Mt 11.01

INSTRUCTION
which I have written for their i. Ex 24.12
Receive i. from his mouth, and lay Job 22.22
He opens their ears to i., 36.10
That men may know wisdom and i., Pro 1.02
receive i. in wise dealing righteousness, 1.03
fools despise wisdom and i. 1.07
your father's i., and reject not 1.08
your father's i., and be attentive, that 4.01
Keep hold of i., do not let go; 4.13
Take my i. instead of silver, and 8.10
Hear i. and be wise, and do not 8.33

INSTRUCTION (cont.)
Give i. to a wise man, and he will Pro 9.09
He who heeds i. is on the path to 10.17
A wise son hears his father's i., 13.01
disgrace come to him who ignores i., 13.18
A fool despises his father's i., 15.05
He who ignores i. despises himself, 15.32
The fear of the LORD is i. in wisdom, 15.33
Listen to advice and accept i., 19.20
to hear i. only to stray from the 19.27
Apply your mind to i. and your ear 23.12
buy wisdom, i., and understanding. 23.23
I looked and received i. 24.32
those who murmer will accept i." Is 29.24
will not hear the i. of the LORD; 30.09
the i. of idols is but wood! Jer 10.08
they might not hear and receive i. 17.23
have not listened to receive i. 32.33
you not receive i. and listen to 35.13
True i. was in his mouth, and no Mal 2.06
men should seek i. from his mouth, 2.07
caused many to stumble by your i.; 2.08
have shown partiality in your i. 2.09
former days was written for our i., Rom 15.04
they were written down for our i., 1Co 10.11
the discipline and i. of the Lord. Eph 6.04
be able to give i. in sound Tit 1.09
with i. about ablutions, the laying Heb 6.02

INSTRUCTIONS
according to the i. which they give Deu 17.11
although we gave them no i., Ac 15.24
soldiers, according to their i., 23.31
the following i. I do not commend 1Co 11.17
(concerning whom you have received i.— Col 4.10
For you know what i. we gave you 1Th 4.02
am writing these i. to you so that, 1Ti 3.14
If you put these i. before the 4.06

INSTRUCTORS
teachers or incline my ear to my i. Pro 5.13

INSTRUCTS
in the night also my heart i. me. Ps 16.07
therefore he i. sinners in the way. 25.08

INSTRUMENT
struck him down with an i. of iron, Num 35.16
voice and plays well on an i., Eze 33.32
he is a chosen i. of mine to carry Ac 9.15

INSTRUMENTS
forger of all i. of bronze and Gen 4.22
songs of joy, and with i. of music. 1Sa 18.06
should play loudly on musical i., 1Ch 15.16
the music and i. for sacred song. 16.42
LORD with the i. which I have made 23.05
and cymbals and other musical i., 2Ch 5.13
with the i. for music to the LORD 7.06
their musical i. leading in the 23.13
Levites stood with the i. of David, 29.26
accompanied by the i. of David king 29.27
who were skilful with i. of music, 34.12
the musical i. of Davd the man of Neh 12.36
palaces stringed i. make you glad; Ps 45.08
to stringed i. all the days of our Is 38.20
on which the i. were to be laid Eze 40.42
invent for themselves i. of music; Amo 6.05
members to sin as i. of wickedness, Rom 6.13
to God as i. of righteousness. 6.13
If even lifeless i., such as the flute 1Co 14.07

INSUBORDINATE
charge of being profligate or i. Tit 1.06
For there are many i. men, 1.10

INSULT
brought among us a Hebrew to i. us; Gen 39.14
among us, came in to me to i. me; 39.17
has avenged the i. I received at 1Sa 25.39
of those who i. thee have fallen Ps 69.09
but the prudent man ignores an i. Pro 12.16

INSULTED
blasphemed and persecuted and i. him; 1Ti 1.13

INSULTS
I hear censure which i. me, Job 20.03
and the i. of those who insult thee Ps 69.09
I. have broken my heart, so that I 69.20
in my bosom the i. of the peoples, 89.50
oppresses a poor man i. his Maker, Pro 14.31
He who mocks the poor i. his Maker; 17.05
the smiter, and be filled with i. Lam 3.30
whoever i. his brother shall be Mt 5.22
i., hardships, persecutions, and 2Co 12.10

INSURRECTION
who had committed murder in the i., Mk 15.07
prison for an i. started in the Lk 23.19
into prison for i. and murder, 23.25

INTEGRITY
In the i. of my heart and the Gen 20.05
done this in the i. of your heart, 20.06
with i. of heart and uprightness, 1Ki 9.04
He still holds fast his i., Job 2.03
"Do you still hold fast your i.? 2.09
and the i. of your ways your hope? 4.06
I will not put away my i. from me. 27.05
balance, and let God know my i.!) 31.06
according to the i. that is in me. Ps 7.08
May i. and uprightness preserve me, 25.21
O LORD, for I have walked in my i., 26.01
But as for me, I walk in my i.; 26.11
hast upheld me because of my i., 41.12
will walk with i. of heart within 101.02
a shield to those who walk in i., Pro 2.07
and men of i. will remain in it; 2.21
He who walks in i. walks securely, 10.09
The i. of the upright guides them, 11.03
finds refuge through his i. 14.32
walks in his i. than a man who is 19.01
righteous man who walks in his i.— 20.07
walks in his i. than a rich man 28.06
He who walks in i. will be delivered, 28.18
in your teaching show i., gravity, Tit 2.07

INTELLIGENCE
Spirit of God, with ability and i., Ex 31.03
with i., with knowledge, and with 35.31
put ability and i. to know how to 36.01
a man of i., who summoned Barnabas Ac 13.07

INTELLIGENT
closes his lips, he is deemed i. Pro 17.28
An i. mind acquires knowledge, and 18.15
to the wise, nor riches to the i., Ecc 9.11

INTELLIGIBLE
tongue utter speech that is not i., 1Co 14.09

INTEND
And now you i. to subjugate the 2Ch 28.10
that you and the Jews i. to rebel; Neh 6.06
But he does not so i., and his mind Is 10.07
evil which I i. to do to them Jer 26.03
the evil which I i. to do to them, 36.03
does this man i. to go that we Jn 7.35
Does he i. to go to the Dispersion 7.35
teaching and you i. to bring this Ac 5.28
for I i. to pass through Macedonia, 1Co 16.05
We i. that no one should blame us 2Co 8.20
Therefore I i. always to remind you 2Pe 1.12

INTENDED
not tell him that he i. to flee. Gen 31.20
for he i. to make him king. 2Ch 11.22
had come and i. to fight against 32.02
But they i. to do me harm. Neh 6.02
of the evil that I i. to do to it. Jer 18.08
good which I had i. to do to it. 18.10
that he himself i. to go there Ac 25.04
I have often i. to come to you Rom 1.13

INTENDING
near Bethlehem, i. to go to Egypt Jer 41.17
i. after the Passover to bring him Ac 12.04
i. to depart on the morrow; and he 20.07
i. to take Paul aboard there; for so 20.13
had arranged, i. himself to go by land. 20.13

INTENSELY
i. white, as no fuller on earth Mk 9.30

INTENT
'With evil i. did he bring them Ex 32.12
person without i. may flee there. Num 35.11
person without i. may flee there. 35.15
person without i. or unwittingly Jos 20.03
person without i. could flee there, 20.09
with full i. to make David king 1Ch 12.38
when he brings it with evil i. Pro 21.27
and i. of your heart may be forgiven Ac 8.22

INTENTIONS
the thoughts and i. of the heart. Heb 4.12

INTENTLY
and he looked i. and was restored, Mk 8.25
the Holy Spirit, looked i. at him Ac 13.09
looking i. at him and seeing that 14.09
looking i. at the council, said, 23.01

INTENTS
accomplished the i. of his mind. Jer 23.20
accomplished the i. of his mind. 30.24

INTERCEDE
The LORD, who can i. for him?" 1Sa 2.25
and do not i. with me, for I do not Jer 7.16
then let them i. with the LORD of 27.18

INTERCEDES
Spirit himself i. for us with Rom 8.26
the Spirit i. for the saints 8.27
hand of God, who indeed i. for us? 8.34

INTERCESSION
and made i. for the transgressors. Is 53.12
always lives to make i. for them. Heb 7.25

INTERCESSIONS
i., and thanksgivings be made for 1Ti 2.01

INTERDICT
an ordinance and enforce an i., Dan 6.07
establish the i. and sign the 6.08
Darius signed the document and i. 6.09
king, concerning the i., "O king! 6.12
Did you not sign an i., that any 6.12
or the i. you have signed, but makes 6.13
Persians that no i. or ordinance 6.15

INTEREST
you shall not exact i. from him. Ex 22.25
Take no i. from him or increase, but Lev 25.36
not lend him your money at i., 25.37
not lend upon i. to your brother, Deu 23.19
i. no money, i. on victuals, 23.19
i. on anything that is lent for i. 23.19
To a foreigner you may lend upon i., 23.20
brother you shall not lend upon i.; 23.20
said to them, "You are exacting i., Neh 5.07
Let us leave off this i. 5.10
who does not put out his money at i., Ps 15.05
his wealth by i. and increase Pro 28.08
does not lend at i. or take any Eze 18.08
lends at i., and takes increase; 18.13
takes no i. or increase, observes my 18.17
you take i. and increase and make 22.12
received what was my own with i. Mt 25.27
I should have collected with i.?' Lk 19.23

INTERESTS
and his i. are divided. And the 1Co 7.34
of you look not only to his own i., Php 2.04
but also to the i. of others. 2.04
They all look after their own i., 2.21

INTERIOR
measuring the i. of the temple Eze 42.15

INTERLACING
restive young camel i. her tracks, Jer 2.23

INTERMARRY
again and i. with the peoples who Ez 9.14

INTERMEDIARY
ordained by angels through an i. Gal 3.19
Now an i. implies more than one; 3.20

INTERPOSED
Then Phinehas stood up and i., Ps 106.30
his purpose, he i. with an oath, Heb 6.17

INTERPRET
and there is no one to i. them. Gen 40.08
none who could i. it to Pharaoh. 41.08
and there is no one who can i. it; 41.15
you hear a dream you can i. it. 41.15
and understanding to i. dreams, Dan 5.12
You know how to i. the appearance Mt 16.03
but you cannot i. the signs of the 16.03
You know how to i. the appearance Lk 12.56
not know how to i. the present 12.56
all speak with tongues? Do all i.? 1Co 12.30
should pray for the power to i. 14.13
and each in turn; and let one i. 14.27
But if there is no one to i., 14.28

INTERPRETATION
"This is its i.: the three branches Gen 40.12
saw that the i. was favorable, 40.16
"This is its i.: the three baskets 40.18
giving an i. to each man according 41.12
the dream and its i., he worshiped; Ju 7.15
And who knows the i. of a thing? Ecc 8.01
the dream, and we will show the i." Dan 2.04
known to me the dream and its i., 2.05
But if you show the dream and its i., 2.06
show me the dream and its i." 2.06
the dream, and we will show its i." 2.07
know that you can show me its i." 2.09
he might show to the king the i. 2.16
and I will show the king the i." 2.24
can make known to the king the i." 2.25
dream that I have seen and its i.?" 2.26
order that the i. may be made 2.30
now we will tell the king its i. 2.36
dream is certain, and its i. sure." 2.45
known to me the i. of the dream. 4.06
could not make known to me its i. 4.07
dream which I saw; tell me its i. 4.09
declare the i., because all the 4.18
able to make known to me the i., 4.18
not the dream or the i. alarm you." 4.19
you and its i. for your enemies! 4.19
this is the i., O king: It is a 4.24
this writing, and shows me its i., 5.07
or make known to the king the i. 5.08

INTERPRETATION (cont.)
be called, and he will show the i." Dan 5.12
and make known to me its i.; 5.15
not show the i. of the matter. 5.15
and make known to me its i., 5.16
king and make known to him the i. 5.17
This is the i. of the matter: MENE, 5.26
known to me the i. of the things. 7.16
to another the i. of tongues. 1Co 12.10
a revelation, a tongue, or an i. 14.26
is a matter of one's own i., 2Pe 1.20

INTERPRETATIONS
to them, "Do not i. belong to God? Gen 40.08
you can give i. and solve problems. Dan 5.16

INTERPRETED
baker, as Joseph had i. to them. Gen 40.22
he i. our dream to us, giving an 41.12
And as he i. to us, so it came to 41.13
he i. to them in all the scriptures Lk 24.27

INTERPRETER
for there was an i. between them. Gen 42.23

INTERPRETING
i. spiritual truths to those who 1Co 2.13

INTERPRETS
in tongues, unless some one i., 1Co 14.05

INTERVAL
And after an i. of about an hour Lk 22.59
After an i. of about three hours Ac 5.07

INTERVENE
wondered that there was no one to i.; Is 59.16

INTIMATE
All my i. friends abhor me, and Job 19.19
and call insight your i. friend; Pro 7.04

INTRICATELY
i. wrought in the depths of the Ps 139.15

INTRIGUE
an oven their hearts burn with i.; Hos 7.06

INTRODUCED
which the kings of Israel had i. 2Ki 17.08
in the customs which Israel had i. 17.19
reforms are i. on behalf of this Ac 24.02
other hand, a better hope is i., Heb 7.19

INVADE
Moabites used to i. the land in the 2Ki 13.20
not let Israel i. when they came 2Ch 20.10
only he did not i. the temple of 27.02
seen the nations i. her sanctuary, Lam 1.10
to come upon people who i. us. Hab 3.16

INVADED
king of Assyria i. all the land 2Ki 17.05
and i. it, and carried away all the 2Ch 21.17
had again i. and defeated Judah, 28.17
came and i. Judah and encamped 32.01

INVALIDS
In these lay a multitude of i., Jn 5.03

INVENT
and like David i. for themselves Amo 6.05

INVENTED
i. by skilful men, to be on the 2Ch 26.15

INVENTING
for you are i. them out of your own Neh 6.08

INVENTORS
i. of evil, disobedient to parents, Rom 1.30

INVEST
You shall i. him with some of your Num 27.20
honorable we i. with the greater 1Co 12.23

INVESTED
ought to have i. my money with the Mt 25.27

INVESTIGATE
a loss how to i. these questions, I Ac 25.20

INVESTIGATED
When the affair was i. and found to Est 2.23

INVESTIGATION
He shatters the mighty without i., Job 34.24

INVISIBLE
creation of the world his i. nature, Rom 1.20
He is the image of the i. God, Col 1.15
visible and i., whether thrones or 1.16
i., the only God, be honor and glory 1Ti 1.17
he endured as seeing him who is i. Heb 11.27

INVITE
And i. Jesse to the sacrifice, and I 1Sa 16.03
but he did not i. Nathan the 1Ki 1.10
would send and i. their three Job 1.04
Thou didst i. as to the day of an Lam 2.22
one of you will i. his neighbor Zec 3.10
and i. to the marriage feast as Mt 22.09
do not i. your friends or your Lk 14.12
lest they also i. you in return, 14.12
i. the poor, the maimed, the lame, the 14.13

INVITED
These i. the people to the sacrifices Num 25.02
and he sent and i. Balaam the son Jos 24.09
Have you i. us here to impoverish Ju 14.15
afterward those eat who are i. 1Sa 9.13
the head of those who had been i., 9.22
and i. them to the sacrifice. 16.05
And David i. him, and he ate in his 2Sa 11.13
and Absalom i. all the king's sons. 13.23
from Jerusalem who were i. guests, 15.11
and he i. all his brothers, the 1Ki 1.09
and has i. all the sons of the king, 1.19
Solomon your servant he has not i. 1.19
and has i. all the king's sons, Joab 1.25
servant Solomon, he has not i. 1.26
also I am i. by her together with Est 5.12
those who were i. to the marriage Mt 22.03
saying, 'Tell those who are i., 22.04
but those i. were not worthy. 22.08
the Pharisee who had i. him saw it, Lk 7.39
a parable to those who were i., 14.07
"When you are i. by any one to a 14.08
eminent man than you be i. by him; 14.08
and he who i. you both will come 14.09
But when you are i., go and sit in 14.10
also to the man who had i. him, 14.12
gave a great banquet, and i. many; 14.16
to those who had been i., 'Come; 14.17
men who were i. shall taste my 14.24
Jesus also was i. to the marriage, Jn 2.02
And he i. Philip to come up and Ac 8.31
and were i. to stay with them for 28.14
those who are i. to the marriage Rev 19.09

INVITES
to their gods and one i. you, Ex 34.15
and his mouth i. a flogging. Pro 18.06
the unbelievers i. you to dinner 1Co 10.27

INVOKE
let the king i. the LORD your God, 2Sa 14.11
to i., to thank, and to praise the 1Ch 16.04

INVOKE (cont.)
Then he began to i. a curse on Mt 26.74
But he began to i. a curse on Mk 14.71
And if you i. as Father him who 1Pe 1.17

INVOKED
and blessings i. for him all the Ps 72.15
no more be i. by the mouth of any Jer 44.26
By faith Isaac i. future blessings Heb 11.20

INVOLVED
population was i. in the error. Num 15.26
For where a will is i., the death Heb 9.16

INWARD
city round about from the Millo i. 2Sa 5.09
and all their hinder parts were i. 1Ki 7.25
and all their hinder parts were i. 2Ch 4.04
desirest truth in the i. being; Ps 51.06
For the i. mind and heart of a man 64.06
For thou didst form my i. parts, 139.13
narrowing i. into their jambs in Eze 40.16
the chambers was a passage i., 42.04
shall be hunger in your i. parts; Mic 6.14

INWARDLY
their mouths, but i. they curse. Ps 62.04
he is like one who is i. reckoning. Pro 23.07
clothing but i. are ravenous Mt 7.15
Now while Peter was i. perplexed as Ac 10.17
He is a Jew who is one i., and real Rom 2.29
groan i. as we wait for adoption as 8.23

IOB
Tola, Puvah, I., and Shimron. Gen 46.13

IOTA
not an i., not a dot, will pass from Mt 5.18

IPHDEIAH
I., and Penuel were the sons of 1Ch 8.25

IPHTAH
I., Ashnah, Nezib, Jos 15.43

IPHTAHEL
and it ends at the valley of I.; Jos 19.14
the valley of I. northward to 19.27

IR
and Huppim were the sons of I., 1Ch 7.12

IRA
and I. the Jairite was also David's 2Sa 20.26
I. the son of Ikkesh of Tekoa, 23.26
I. the Ithrite, Gareb the Ithrite, 23.38
I. the son of Ikkesh of Tekoa, 1Ch 11.28
I. the Ithrite, Gareb the Ithrite, 11.40
was I., the son of Ikkesh the 27.09

IRAD
To Enoch was born I.; Gen 4.18
and I. was the father of Mehujael, 4.18

IRAM
Magdiel, and I.; these are the chiefs Gen 36.43
Magdiel, and I.; these are the chiefs 1Ch 1.54

IRI
and I., five, heads of fathers' 1Ch 7.07

IRIJAH
there named I. the son of Shelemiah, Jer 37.13
But I. would not listen to him, 37.14

IRKSOME
same things to you is not i. to me, Php 3.01

IRNAHASH
and Tehinnah the father of I. These 1Ch 4.12

IRON
all instruments of bronze and i. Gen 4.22
heavens like i. and your earth Lev 26.19
the i., the tin, and the lead, Num 31.22
him down with an instrument of i., 35.16
his bedstead was a bedstead of i.; Deu 3.11
you forth out of the i. furnace, 4.20
nothing, a land whose stones are i., 8.09
shall lift up no i. tool upon them. 27.05
the earth under you shall be i. 28.23
put a yoke of i. upon your neck, 28.48
Your bars shall be i. and bronze; 33.25
gold, and vessels of bronze and i., Jos 6.19
the vessels of bronze and of i., 6.24
no man has lifted an i. tool"; 8.31
in the plain have chariots of i., 17.16
though they have chariots of i., 17.18
and i., and with much clothing; 22.08
because they had chariots of i. Ju 1.19
he had nine hundred chariots of i., 4.03
nine hundred chariots of i., 4.13
weighed six hundred shekels of i.; 1Sa 17.07
with saws and i. picks and i. axes, 2Sa 12.31
himself with i. and the shaft of a 23.07
nor any tool of i. was heard in 1Ki 6.07
from the midst of the i. furnace). 8.51
made for himself horns of i., 22.11
it in there, and made the i. float. 2Ki 6.06
with saws and i. picks and axes; 1Ch 20.03
great stores of i. for nails for 22.03
and bronze and i. beyond weighing, 22.14
gold, silver, bronze, and i. 22.16
the i. for the things of i., and wood 29.02
a hundred thousand talents of i. 29.07
and i., and in purple, crimson, and 2Ch 2.07
i., stone, and wood, and in purple, 2.14
made for himself horns of i., 18.10
also workers in i. and bronze to 24.12
Oh that with an i. pen and lead Job 19.24
He will flee from an i. weapon; 20.24
I. is taken out of the earth, and 28.02
bronze, his limbs like bars of i. 40.18
He counts i. as straw, and bronze as 41.27
You shall break them with a rod of i., Ps 2.09
his neck was put in a collar of i.; 105.18
and cuts in two the bars of i. 107.16
their nobles with fetters of i., 149.08
I. sharpens i., and one man sharpens Pro 27.17
If the i. is blunt, and one does not Ecc 10.10
and cut asunder the bars of i., Is 45.02
your neck is an i. sinnew and your 48.04
and instead of i. I will bring 60.17
bronze, instead of stones, i. 60.17
an i. pillar, and bronze walls, Jer 1.18
they are bronze and i., all of them 6.28
from the i. furnace, saying, Listen 11.04
Can one break i., i. from the north, 15.12
Judah is written with a pen of i.; 17.01
make in their place bars of i. 28.13
nations an i. yoke of servitude to 28.14
And take an i. plate, and place it Eze 4.03
place it as an i. wall between you 4.03
and tin and i. and lead in the 22.18
and bronze and i. and lead and tin 22.20
silver, i., tin, and lead they 27.12
wrought i., cassia, and calamus were 27.19
its legs of i., its feet partly of i. Dan 2.33
image on its feet of i. and clay, 2.34
then the i., the clay, the bronze, 2.35
strong as i., because i. breaks to 2.40
and like i. which crushes, it shall 2.40
of potter's clay and partly of i., 2.41
the firmness of i. shall be in it, 2.41
just as you saw i. mixed with the 2.41
were partly i. and partly clay, so 2.42
As you saw the i. mixed with miry 2.43
just as i. does not mix with clay. 2.43

IRON (cont.)
and that it broke in pieces of i., Dan 2.45
bound with a band of i. and bronze, 4.15
bound with a band of i. and bronze, 4.23
silver, bronze, i., wood, and stone. 5.04
i., wood, and stone, which do not see 5.23
and it had great i. teeth; 7.07
its teeth of i. and claws of 7.19
with threshing sledges of i. Amo 1.03
make your horn i. and your hoofs Mic 4.13
came to the i. gate leading into Ac 12.10
shall rule them with a rod of i., Rev 2.27
they had scales like i. breastplates, 9.09
all the nations with a rod of i., 12.05
wood, bronze, i. and marble, 18.12
he will rule them with a rod of i.; 19.15

IRONS
prisoners in affliction and in i., Ps 107.10

IRONSMITH
The i. fashions it and works it Is 44.12

IRPEEL
Rekem, I., Taralah, Jos 18.27

IRRATIONAL
lke i. animals, creatures of 2Pe 2.12
know by instinct as i. animals do, Jud 1.10

IRRELIGION
training us to renounce i. and Tit 2.12

IRRELIGIOUS
that no one be immoral or i. like Esau, Heb 12.16

IRREPROACHABLE
and blameless and i. before him, Col 1.22

IRRESOLUTE
was young and i. and could not 2Ch 13.07

IRREVOCABLE
gifts and the call of God are i. Rom 11.29

IRRITABLE
own way it is not i. or resentful; 1Co 13.05

IRRITATE
to i. her, because the LORD had 1Sa 1.06

IRSHEMESH
included Zorah, Eshtaol, I., Jos 19.41

IRU
I., Elah, and Naam; and the sons of 1Ch 4.15

ISAAC
and you shall call his name I. Gen 17.19
will establish my covenant with I., 17.21
to him, whom Sarah bore him, I. 21.03
circumcised his son I. when he was 21.04
when his son I. was born to him. 21.05
on the day that I. was weaned. 21.08
Abraham, playing with her son I. 21.09
shall not be heir with my son I." 21.10
for through I. shall your descendants 21.12
your only son I., whom you love, and 22.02
young men with him, and his son I.; 22.03
offering, and laid it on I. his son; 22.06
And I. said to his father Abraham, 22.07
and bound I. his son, and laid him 22.09
and take a wife for my son I." 24.04
hast appointed for thy servant I. 24.14
Now I. had come from Beerlahairoi, 24.62
And I. went out to meditate in the 24.63
up her eyes, and when she saw I., 24.64
servant told I. all the things 24.66
Then I. brought her into the tent, 24.67
So I. was comforted after his 24.67
Abraham gave all he had to I. 25.05
he sent them away from his son I., 25.06
I. and Ishmael his sons buried him 25.09
of Abraham God blessed I. his son. 25.11
And I. dwelt at Beerlahairoi. 25.11
These are the descendants of I., 25.19
son: Abraham was the father of I., 25.19
and I. was forty years old when he 25.20
And I. prayed to the LORD for his 25.21
I. was sixty years old when she 25.26
I. loves Esau, because he ate of his 25.28
And I. went to Gerar, to Abimelech 26.01
So I. dwelt in Gerar. 26.06
window and saw I. fondling Rebekah 26.08
So Abimelech called I., and said, 26.09
I. said to him, "Because I thought, 26.09
And I. sowed in that land, and 26.12
And Abimelech said to I., 26.16
So I. departed from there, and 26.17
And I. dug again the wells of water 26.18
I. said to them, "Why have you come 26.27
and I. set them on their way, and 26.31
life bitter for I. and Rebekah. 26.35
When I. was old and his eyes were 27.01
listening when I. spoke to his son 27.05
But I. said to his son, "How is it 27.20
me success." Then I. said to Jacob, 27.21
So Jacob went near to I. his father, 27.22
Then his father I. said to him, 27.26
As soon as I. had finished blessing 27.30
from the presence of I. his father, 27.30
His father I. said to him, "Who are 27.32
Then I. trembled violently, and said, 27.33
I. answered Esau, "Behold, I have 27.37
Then I. his father answered him: 27.39
Then Rebekah said to I., "I am weary 27.46
Then I. called Jacob and blessed 28.01
Thus I. sent Jacob away; and he 28.05
Now Esau saw that I. had blessed 28.06
did not please I. his father, 28.08
your father and the God of I.; 28.13
land of Canaan to his father I. 31.18
God of Abraham and the Fear of I., 31.42
by the Fear of his father I., 31.53
Abraham and God of my father I., 32.09
to Abraham and I. I will give to 35.12
came to his father I. at Mamre, 35.27
where Abraham and I. had sojourned. 35.27
Now the days of I. were a hundred 35.28
And I. breathed his last; 35.29
to the God of his father I. 46.01
my fathers Abraham and I. walked, 48.15
name of my fathers Abraham and I.; 48.16
they buried I. and Rebekah his 49.31
to Abraham, to I., and to Jacob. 50.24
with I., and with Jacob. Ex 2.24
the God of I., and the God of Jacob 3.06
the God of I., and the God of Jacob, 3.15
of I., and of Jacob, has appeared to 3.16
the God of I., and the God of Jacob, 4.05
to I., and to Jacob, as God Almighty, 6.03
to Abraham, to I., and to Jacob; 6.08
I., and Israel, thy servants, to whom 32.13
I., and Jacob saying, 'To your 33.01
covenant with I. and my covenant Lev 26.42
to I., and to Jacob, because they Num 32.11
to I., and to Jacob, to give to them Deu 1.08
to I., and to Jacob, to give you, 6.10
to Abraham, to I., and to Jacob. 9.05
servants, Abraham, I., and Jacob; 9.27
to Abraham, to I., and to Jacob. 29.13
to I., and to Jacob, to give them." 30.20
to I., and to Jacob, 'I will give it 34.04
offspring many. I gave him I.; Jos 24.03
and to I. I gave Jacob and Esau. 24.04
I., and Israel, let it be known this 1Ki 18.36

ISAAC (cont.)
I., and Jacob, and would not destroy 2Ki 13.23
The sons of Abraham: I. and Ishmael. 1Ch 1.28
Abraham was the father of I. 1.34
The sons of I.: Esau and Israel. 1.34
Abraham, his sworn promise to I., 16.16
I., and Israel, our fathers, keep for 29.18
I., and Israel, that he may turn 2Ch 30.06
Abraham, his sworn promise to I., Ps 105.09
the seed of Abraham, I., and Jacob. Jer 33.26
the high places of I. shall be made Amo 7.09
not preach against the house of I. 7.16
Abraham was the father of I., Mt 1.02
and I. the father of Jacob, and 1.02
I., and Jacob in the kingdom of 8.11
God of Abraham, and the God of I., 22.32
God of Abraham, and the God of I., Mk 12.26
the son of I., the son of Abraham, Lk 3.34
see Abraham and I. and Jacob and 13.28
and the God of I. and the God of 20.37
of Abraham and of I. and of Jacob, Ac 3.13
so Abraham became the father of I. 7.08
and I. became the father of Jacob, 7.08
of Abraham and of I. and of Jacob. 7.32
but "Through I. shall your descendants Rom 9.07
by one man, our forefather I., 9.10
like I., are children of promise. Gal 4.28
living in tents with I. and Jacob, Heb 11.09
offered up I., and he who had 11.17
"Through I. shall your descendants 11.18
By faith I. invoked future blessings 11.20
offered his son I. upon the altar? Jas 2.21

ISAAC'S
But when I. servants dug in the Gen 26.19
Gerar quarreled with I. herdsmen, 26.20
And there I. servants dug a well. 26.25
That same day I. servants came and 26.32

ISAIAH
to the prophet I. the son of Amoz. 2Ki 19.02
of King Hezekiah came to I., 19.05
I. said to them, "Say to your master, 19.06
Then I. the son of Amoz sent to 19.20
And I. the prophet the son of Amoz 20.01
And before I. had gone out of the 20.04
And I. said, "Bring a cake of figs. 20.07
And Hezekiah said to I., "What shall 20.08
And I. said, "This is the sign to 20.09
And I. the prophet cried to the 20.11
Then I. the prophet came to King 20.14
Then I. said to Hezekiah, "Hear the 20.16
Then said Hezekiah to I., "The word 20.19
I. the prophet the son of Amoz 2Ch 26.22
the king and I. the prophet, 32.20
the vision of I. the prophet the 32.32
The vision of I. the son of Amoz, Is 1.01
The word which I. the son of Amoz 2.01
And the LORD said to I., "Go forth 7.03
Babylon which I. the son of Amoz 13.01
had spoken by I. the son of Amoz, 20.02
"As my servant I. has walked naked 20.03
to the prophet I. the son of Amoz. 37.02
of King Hezekiah came to I., 37.05
I. said to them, "Say to your master, 37.06
Then I. the son of Amoz sent to 37.21
And I. the prophet the son of Amoz 38.01
Then the word of the LORD came to I.: 38.04
Now I. had said, "Let them take a 38.21
Then I. the prophet came to King 39.03
Then I. said to Hezekiah, "Hear the 39.05
Then said Hezekiah to I., "The word 39.08
of by the prophet I. when he said, Mt 3.03
by the prophet I. might be fulfilled: 4.14
what was spoken by the prophet I., 8.17
what was spoken by the prophet I.: 12.17
the prophecy of I. which says: 13.14
Well did I prophesy of you, when he 15.07
As it is written in I. the prophet, Mk 1.02
"Well did I. prophesy of you 7.06
of the words of I. the prophet, Lk 3.04
to him the book of the prophet I. 4.17
the Lord,' as the prophet I. said." Jn 1.23
by the prophet I. might be fulfilled: 12.38
could not believe. For I. again said, 12.39
I. said this because he saw his 12.41
he was reading the prophet I. Ac 8.28
heard him reading I. the prophet, 8.30
fathers through I. the prophet: 28.25
And I. cries out concerning Israel: Rom 9.27
And as I. predicted, "If the Lord of 9.29
for I. says, "Lord, who has believed 10.16
Then I. is so bold as to say, "I 10.20
and further I. says, "The root of 15.12

ISCAH
Haran the father of Milcah and I. Gen 11.29

ISCARIOT
and Judas I., who betrayed him. Mt 10.04
twelve, who was called Judas I., 26.14
and Judas I., who betrayed him. Mk 3.19
Then Judas I., who was one of the 14.10
and Judas I., who became a traitor. Lk 6.16
Satan entered into Judas called I., 22.03
spoke of Judas the son of Simon I., Jn 6.71
But Judas I., one of his disciples 12.04
put it into the heart of Judas I., 13.02
it to Judas, the son of Simon I. 13.26
Judas (not I.) said to him, "Lord, 14.22

ISHBAH
and I., the father of Eshtemoa. 1Ch 4.17

ISHBAK
Medan, Midian, I., and Shuah. Gen 25.02
Medan, Midian, I., and Shuah. 1Ch 1.32

ISHBIBENOB
And I., one of the descendants of 2Sa 21.16

ISHBOSHETH
had taken I. the son of Saul, and 2Sa 2.08
I., Saul's son, was forty years old 2.10
the servants of I. the son of Saul, 2.12
Benjamin and I. the son of Saul, 2.15
and I. said to Abner, "Why have you 3.07
very angry over the words of I., 3.08
And I. could not answer Abner 3.11
sent messengers to I. Saul's son, 3.14
And I. sent, and took her from her 3.15
When I., Saul's son, heard that Abner 4.01
day they came to the house of I., 4.05
the head of I. to David at Hebron. 4.08
the king, "Here is the head of I., 4.08
But they took the head of I., 4.12

ISHHOD
And his sister Hammolecheth bore I., 1Ch 2.31

ISHI
The sons of Appaim: I. 1Ch 2.31
The sons of I.: Sheshan. 2.31
The sons of I.: Zoheth and Benzoheth 4.20
Rephaiah, and Uzziel, the sons of I.; 4.42
I., Eliel, Azriel, Jeremiah, Hodaviah, 5.24

ISHMA
of Etam: Jezreel, I., and Idbash; 1Ch 4.03

ISHMAEL
you shall call his name I.; Gen 16.11
of his son, whom Hagar bore, I. 16.15
old when Hagar bore I. to Abram. 16.16
"Oh that I. might live in thy sight!" 17.18
As for I., I have heard you; 17.20

ISHMAEL (cont.)
Then Abraham took I. his son and Gen 17.23
And I. his son was thirteen years 17.25
and his son I. were circumcised: 17.26
Isaac and I. his sons buried him in 25.09
These are the descendants of I., 25.12
These are the names of the sons of I., 25.13
Nebaioth, the first-born of I.; 25.13
These are the sons of I. and these 25.16
(These are the years of the life of I., 25.17
Esau went to I. and took to wife, 28.09
the daughter of I. Abraham's son, 28.09
I. the son of Nethaniah, and Johanan 2Ki 25.23
I. the son of Nethaniah, son of 25.25
The sons of Abraham: Isaac and I. 1Ch 1.28
the first-born of I., Nebaioth; 1.29
These are the sons of I. 1.31
I., Sheariah, Obadiah, and Hanan. 8.38
I., Sheariah, Obadiah, and Hanan; 9.44
and Zebadiah the son of I., 2Ch 19.11
I. the son of Jehohanan, Azariah the 23.01
I., Nethanel, Jozabad, and Elasah. Ez 10.22
I. the son of Nethaniah, Jer 40.08
has sent I. the son of Nethaniah 40.14
me go and slay I. the son of 40.15
for you are speaking falsely of I." 40.16
I. the son of Nethaniah, son of 41.01
I. the son of Nethaniah and the ten 41.02
I. also slew all the Jews who were 41.03
And I. the son of Nethaniah came 41.06
I. the son of Nethaniah and the men 41.07
ten men among them who said to I., 41.08
into which I. cast all the bodies 41.09
I. the son of Nethaniah filled it 41.09
Then I. took captive all the rest 41.10
I. the son of Nethaniah took them 41.10
the evil which I. the son of 41.11
fight against I. the son of 41.12
who were with I. saw Johanan the 41.13
the people whom I. had carried 41.14
But I. the son of Nethaniah escaped 41.15
the people whom I. the son of 41.16
because I. the son of Nethaniah had 41.18

ISHMAELITE
son of a man named Ithra the I., 2Sa 17.25
father of Amasa was Jether the I. 1Ch 2.17
Over the camels was Obil the I.; 27.30

ISHMAELITES
a caravan of I. coming from Gilead, Gen 37.25
Come, let us sell him to the I., 37.27
sold him to the I. for twenty 37.28
him from the I. who had brought 39.01
earrings, because they were I. Ju 8.24
the tents of Edom and the I., Ps 83.06

ISHMAEL'S
and Basemath, I. daughter, the sister Gen 36.03

ISHMAIAH
I. of Gibeon, a mighty man among the 1Ch 12.04
for Zebulun, I. the son of Obadiah; 27.19

ISHMERAI
I., Izliah, and Jobab were the sons 1Ch 8.18

ISHPAH
Michael, I., and Joha were sons of 1Ch 8.16

ISHPAN
I., Eber, Eliel, 1Ch 8.22

ISHVAH
I., Ishvi, Beriah, with Serah their Gen 46.17
I., Ishvi, Beriah, and their sister 1Ch 7.30

ISHVI
I., Beriah, with Serah their sister. Gen 46.17
of I., the family of the Ishvites; Num 26.44
I., and Malchishua; 1Sa 14.49
I., Beriah, and their sister Serah. 1Ch 7.30

ISHVITES
of Ishvi, the family of the I.; Num 26.44

ISLAND
the whole i. as far as Paphos, they Ac 13.06
the lee of a small i. called Cauda, 27.16
But we shall have to run on some i. 27.26
that the i. was called Malta. 28.01
belonging to the chief man of the i., 28.07
people on the i. who had diseases 28.09
ship which had wintered in the i., 28.11
was on the i. called Patmos on Rev 1.09
mountain and i. was removed from 6.14
And every i. fled away, and no 16.20

ISLANDS
I will turn the rivers into i., Is 42.15

ISLES
and of the i. render him tribute, Ps 72.10
he takes up the i. like fine dust. Is 40.15
Now the i. tremble on the day of Eze 26.18
yea, the i. that are in the sea are 26.18

ISMACHIAH
I., Mahath, and Benaiah were overseers 2Ch 31.13

ISRAEL
but I., for you have striven with Gen 32.28
folly in I. by lying with Jacob's 34.07
but I. shall be your name." 35.10
So his name was called I. 35.10
I. journeyed on, and pitched his 35.21
While I. dwelt in that land Reuben 35.22
concubine; and I. heard of it. 35.22
Now I. loved Joseph more than any 37.03
And I. said to Joseph, "Are not your 37.13
Thus the sons of I. came to buy 42.05
I. said, "Why did you treat me so 43.06
And Judah said to I. his father, 43.08
Then their father I. said to them, 43.11
The sons of I. did so; and Joseph 45.21
and I. said, "It is enough; Joseph 45.28
So I. took his journey with all 46.01
And God spoke to I. in visions of 46.02
and the sons of I. carried Jacob 46.05
the names of the descendants of I., 46.08
went up to meet I. his father in 46.29
I. said to Joseph, "Now let me die, 46.30
Thus I. dwelt in the land of Egypt, 47.27
time drew near that I. must die, 47.29
Then I. bowed himself upon the head 47.31
then I. summoned his strength, and 48.02
When I. saw Joseph's sons, he said, 48.08
Now the eyes of I. were dim with 48.10
And I. said to Joseph, "I had not 48.11
And I. stretched out his right hand 48.14
"By you I. will pronounce blessings, 48.20
Then I. said to Joseph, "Behold, I am 48.21
and hearken to I. your father. 49.02
in Jacob and scatter them in I. 49.07
people as one of the tribes of I. 49.16
of the Shepherd, the Rock of I.), 49.24
All these are the twelve tribes of I.; 49.28
So the physicians embalmed I.; 50.02
took an oath of the sons of I., 50.25
of the sons of I. who came to Ex 1.01
descendants of I. were fruitful 1.07
the people of I. are too many and 1.09
were in dread of the people of I. 1.12
the people of I. serve with rigor, 1.13
the people of I. groaned under 2.23

ISRAEL (cont.)

And God saw the people of I., Ex 2.25
of the people of I. has come to me, 3.09
the sons of I., out of Egypt." 3.10
bring the sons of I. out of Egypt?" 3.11
the people of I. and say to them, 3.13
said, "Say this to the people of I., 3.14
"Say this to the people of I., 3.15
gather the elders of I. together, 3.16
the elders of I. shall go to the 3.18
I. is my first-born son, 4.22
all the elders of the people of I. 4.29
the people of I. and that he had 4.31
the God of I., 'Let my people go, 5.01
heed his voice and let I. go? 5.02
and moreover I will not let I. go." 5.02
And the foremen of the people of I., 5.14
the people of I. came and cried to 5.15
the people of I. saw that they 5.19
the people of I. whom the Egyptians 6.05
Say therefore to the people of I., 6.06
Moses spoke thus to the people of I.; 6.09
the people of I. go out of his 6.11
the people of I. have not listened 6.12
the people of I. and to Pharaoh 6.13
the people of I. out of the land 6.13
of Reuben, the first-born of I.: 6.14
the people of I. from the land of 6.26
out the people of I. from Egypt, 6.27
the people of I. go out of his 7.02
my hosts, my people the sons of I., 7.04
the people of I. from among them." 7.05
the cattle of I. and the cattle of 9.04
that belongs to the people of I."'" 9.04
of the people of I. not one died. 9.06
where the people of I. were, 9.26
he did not let the people of I. go; 9.35
did not let the children of I. go. 10.20
the people of I. had light where 10.23
But against any of the people of I., 11.07
between the Egyptians and I. 11.07
the people of I. go out of his 11.10
congregation of I. that on the 12.03
congregation of I. shall kill 12.06
person shall be cut off from I. 12.15
off from the congregation of I. 12.19
Then Moses called all the elders of I., 12.21
of the people of I. in Egypt, 12.27
Then the people of I. went and did 12.28
both you and the people of I.; 12.31
The people of I. had also done as 12.35
And the people of I. journeyed from 12.37
the people of I. dwelt in Egypt 12.40
the people of I. thoughout their 12.42
congregation of I. shall keep it. 12.47
Thus did all the people of I.; 12.50
the people of I. out of the land 12.51
the womb among the people of I., 13.02
the people of I. went up out of 13.18
solemnly sworn the people of I., 13.19
"Tell the people of I. to turn back 14.02
will say of the people of I., 14.03
we have let I. go from serving us?" 14.05
the people of I. as they went 14.08
the people of I. lifted up their 14.10
the people of I. cried out to the 14.10
the people of I. to go forward. 14.15
the people of I. may go on dry 14.16
the host of I. moved and went 14.19
host of Egypt and the host of I. 14.20
And the people of I. went into the 14.22
said, "Let us flee from before I.; 14.25
But the people of I. walked on dry 14.29
Thus the LORD saved I. that day 14.30
and I. saw the Egyptians dead upon 14.30
And I. saw the great work which the 14.31
the people of I. sang this song to 15.01
the people of I. walked on dry 15.19
Then Moses led I. onward from the 15.22
the people of I. came to the 16.01
the people I. murmured against 16.02
Aaron said to all the people of I., 16.06
congregation of the people of I., 16.09
congregation of the people of I., 16.10
the murmurings of the people of I.; 16.12
When the people of I. saw it, 16.15
And the people of I. did so; 16.17
Now the house of I. called its name 16.31
And the people of I. ate the manna 16.35
the people of I. moved on from the 17.01
with you some of the elders of I.; 17.05
in the sight of the elders of I. 17.06
faultfinding of the children of I., 17.07
and fought with I. at Rephidim. 17.08
held up his hand, I. prevailed; 17.11
for Moses and for I. his people, 18.01
LORD had brought I. out of Egypt. 18.01
good which the LORD had done to I., 18.09
the elders of I. to eat bread with 18.12
Moses chose able men out of all I., 18.25
the people of I. had gone forth 19.01
and there I. encamped before the 19.02
Jacob, and tell the people of I.: 19.03
shall speak to the children of I. 19.06
you shall say to the people of I.: 20.22
and seventy of the elders of I., 24.01
according to the twelve tribes of I. 24.04
sent young men of the people of I., 24.05
of the elders of I. went up, 24.09
and they saw the God of I.; 24.10
the chief men of the people of I.; 24.11
in the sight of the people of I. 24.17
"Speak to the people of I., 25.02
commandment for the people of I. 25.22
the people of I. that they bring 27.20
generations by the people of I. 27.21
him, from among the people of I., 28.01
them the names of the sons of I., 28.09
with the names of the sons of I.; 28.11
of remembrance for the sons of I.; 28.12
to the names of the sons of I.; 28.21
of the sons of I. in the breastpiece 28.29
the people of I. upon his heart 28.30
the people of I. hallow as their 28.38
perpetual due from the people of I., 29.28
the people of I. from their peace 29.28
There I will meet with the people of I., 29.43
will dwell among the people of I., 29.45
the census of the people of I., 30.12
money from the people of I., 30.16
the people of I. to remembrance 30.16
And you shall say to the people of I., 30.31
"Say to the people of I., 31.13
Wherefore the people of I. shall 31.16
the people of I. that in six days 31.17
O I., who brought you up out of the 32.04
O I., who brought you up out of the 32.08
and I., thy servants, to whom thou 32.13
and made the people of I. drink it. 32.20
them, "Thus says the LORD God of I., 32.27
to Moses, "Say to the people of I., 33.05
Therefore the people of I. stripped 33.06
before the LORD God, the God of I. 34.23
a covenant with you and with I." 34.27
and all the people of I. saw Moses, 34.30
all the people of I. came near, 34.32
the people of I. what he was 34.34
the people of I. saw the face of 34.35
congregation of the people of I., 35.01
congregation of the people of I., 35.04
the people of I. departed from the 35.20
the people of I., whose heart moved 35.29
And Moses said to the people of I., 35.30
the people of I. had brought for 36.03

ISRAEL (cont.)
to the names of the sons of I. Ex 39.06
of remembrance for the sons of I.; 39.07
to the names of the sons of I.; 39.14
the people of I. had done according 39.32
the people of I. had done all the 39.42
the people of I. would go onward; 40.36
the sight of all the house of I. 40.38
"Speak to the people of I., Lev 1.02
"Say to the people of I., 4.02
congregation of I. commits a sin 4.13
"Say to the people of I., 7.23
"Say to the people of I., 7.29
I have taken from the people of I., 7.34
perpetual due from the people of I. 7.34
be given them by the people of I., 7.36
the people of I. to bring their 7.38
and his sons and the elders of I.; 9.01
And say to the people of I., 9.03
brethren, the whole house of I., 10.06
the people of I. all the statutes 10.11
offerings of the people of I. 10.14
"Say to the people of I., These 11.02
"Say to the people of I., If a 12.02
"Say to the people of I., When 15.02
the people of I. separate from 15.31
the people of I. two male goats 16.05
uncleannesses of the people of I., 16.16
and for all the assembly of I. 16.17
uncleannesses of the people of I. 16.19
the iniquities of the people of I., 16.21
the people of I. once in the year 16.34
sons, and to all the people of I., 17.02
of the house of I. kills an ox or 17.03
the people of I. may bring their 17.05
them, Any man of the house of I., 17.08
of the house of I. or of the 17.10
Therefore I have said to the people of I., 17.12
Any man also of the people of I., 17.13
I have said to the people of I., 17.14
"Say to the people of I., 18.02
congregation of the people of I., 19.02
"Say to the people of I., 20.02
Any man of the people of I., 20.02
the strangers that sojourn in I., 20.02
sons and to all the people of I. 21.24
holy things of the people of I., 22.02
the people of I. dedicate to the 22.03
holy things of the people of I., 22.15
his sons and all the people of I., 22.15
his sons and all the people of I., 22.18
of the house of I. or of the 22.18
sojourners in I. presents his 22.18
be hallowed among the people of I.; 22.32
"Say to the people of I., The 23.02
"Say to the people of I., When 23.10
"Say to the people of I., In 23.24
"Say to the people of I., On 23.34
are native in I. shall dwell in 23.42
the people of I. dwell in booths 23.43
the people of I. the appointed 23.44
"Command the people of I. to bring 24.02
the people of I. as a covenant for 24.08
went out among the people of I.; 24.10
and a man of I. quarreled in the 24.10
And say to the people of I., 24.15
So Moses spoke to the people of I.; 24.23
the people of I. did as the LORD 24.23
"Say to the people of I., 25.02
possession among the people of I. 25.33
the people of I. you shall not 25.46
me the people of I. are servants, 25.55
the people of I. on Mount Sinai by 26.46
"Say to the people of I., 27.02
the people of I. on Mount Sinai. 27.34
congregation of the people of I., Num 1.02
all in I. who are able to go forth 1.03
the heads of the clans of I. 1.16
with the help of the leaders of I., 1.44
whole number of the people of I. 1.45
able to go forth to war in I.— 1.45
of them among the people of I.; 1.49
The people of I. shall pitch their 1.52
congregation of the people of I.; 1.53
Thus did the people of I.; 1.54
"The people of I. shall encamp each 2.02
the people of I. as numbered by 2.32
numbered among the people of I., 2.33
Thus did the people of I. 2.34
the people of I. as they minister 3.08
to him from among the people of I. 3.09
the people of I. instead of every 3.12
the womb among the people of I. 3.12
my own all the first-born in I., 3.13
to be done for the people of I.; 3.38
first-born males of the people of I., 3.40
first-born among the people of I., 3.41
the cattle of the people of I." 3.41
first-born among the people of I., 3.42
first-born among the people of I., 3.45
the first-born of the people of I., 3.46
the people of I. he took the money, 3.50
and the leaders of I. numbered, 4.46
"Command the people of I. that they 5.02
And the people of I. did so, 5.04
to Moses, so the people of I. did. 5.04
"Say to the people of I., 5.06
holy things of the people of I., 5.09
"Say to the people of I., 5.12
"Say to the people of I., 6.02
you shall bless the people of I.: 6.23
put my name upon the people of I., 6.27
the leaders of I., heads of their 7.02
anointed, from the leaders of I.: 7.84
from among the people of I., 8.06
congregation of the people of I. 8.09
the people of I. shall lay their 8.10
offering from the people of I., 8.11
from among the people of I., 8.14
to me from among the people of I.; 8.16
first-born of all the people of I., 8.16
among the people of I. are mine, 8.17
first-born among the people of I. 8.18
sons from among the people of I., 8.19
the people of I. at the tent of 8.19
atonement for the people of I., 8.19
the people of I. in case the 8.19
the people of I. should come near 8.19
of the people of I. to the Levites; 8.20
the people of I. did to them. 8.20
"Let the people of I. keep the 9.02
the people of I. that they should 9.04
Moses, so the people of I. did. 9.05
time among the people of I.? 9.07
"Say to the people of I., 9.10
that the people of I. set out; 9.17
there the people of I. encamped. 9.17
the LORD the people of I. set out, 9.18
the people of I. kept the charge of 9.19
the people of I. remained in camp 9.22
the heads of the tribes of I., 10.04
and the people of I. set out by 10.12
the people of I. according to 10.28
the LORD has promised good to I." 10.29
the ten thousand thousands of I." 10.36
the people of I. also wept again, 11.04
me seventy men of the elders of I., 11.16
the elders of I. returned to the 11.30
which I give to the people of I.; 13.02
who were heads of the people of I. 13.03
the men of I. cut down from there. 13.24
the people of I. in the wilderness 13.26
the people of I. an evil report of 13.32
the people of I. murmured against 14.02

ISRAEL (cont.)

congregation of the people of I. Num 14.05
congregation of the people of I., 14.07
of meeting to all the people of I. 14.10
the murmurings of the people of I., 14.27
words to all the people of I., 14.39
"Say to the people of I., 15.02
"Say to the people of I., 15.18
congregation of the people of I., 15.25
the people of I. shall be forgiven, 15.26
is native among the people of I., 15.29
While the people of I. were in the 15.32
"Speak to the people of I., 15.38
with a number of the people of I., 16.02
that the God of I. has separated 16.09
you from the congregation of I., 16.09
and the elders of I. followed him. 16.25
And all I. that were round about 16.34
be a sign to the people of I. 16.38
to be a reminder of the people of I., 16.40
the people of I. murmured against 16.41
"Speak to the people of I., 17.02
the murmurings of the people of I., 17.05
Moses spoke to the people of I.; 17.06
the LORD to all the people of I.; 17.09
And the people of I. said to Moses, 17.12
no more upon the people of I. 18.05
from among the people of I.; 18.06
consecrated things of the people of I.; 18.08
wave offerings of the people of I.; 18.11
devoted thing in I. shall be yours. 18.14
the people of I. present to the 18.19
inheritance among the people of I. 18.20
every tithe in I. for an inheritance, 18.21
the people of I. shall not come 18.22
the people of I. they shall have 18.23
For the tithe of the people of I., 18.24
inheritance among the people of I. 18.24
the people of I. the tithe which I 18.26
you receive from the people of I.; 18.28
of the people of I., lest you die.'" 18.32
the people of I. to bring you a 19.02
the people of I. for the water for 19.09
this shall be to the people of I., 19.10
person shall be cut off from I.; 19.13
And the people of I., 20.01
me in the eyes of the people of I., 20.12
the people of I. contended with 20.13
of Edom, "Thus says your brother I.: 20.14
And the people of I. said to him, 20.19
refused to give I. passage through 20.21
so I. turned away from him. 20.21
from Kadesh, and the people of I., 20.22
I have given to the people of I., 20.24
the house of I. wept for Aaron 20.29
heard that I. was coming by the way 21.01
of Atharim, he fought against I., 21.01
And I. vowed a vow to the LORD, and 21.02
LORD hearkened to the voice of I., 21.03
so that many people of I. died. 21.06
And the people of I. set out, 21.10
Then I. sang this song: "Spring up, O 21.17
Then I. sent messengers to Sihon 21.21
would not allow I. to pass through 21.23
out against I. to the wilderness, 21.23
to Jahaz, and fought against I. 21.23
And I slew him with the edge of 21.24
And I. took all these cities, and 21.25
and I. settled in all the cities of 21.25
Thus I. dwelt in the land of the 21.31
Then the people of I. set out, 22.01
saw all that I. had done to the 22.02
with fear of the people of I. 22.03
for me, and come, denounce I.!' 23.07
or number the fourth part of I.? 23.10
nor has he seen trouble in I. 23.21
Jacob, no divination against I.; 23.23
it shall be said of Jacob and I., 23.23
it pleased the LORD to bless I., 24.01
and saw I. encamping tribe by tribe. 24.02
O Jacob, your encampments, O I! 24.05
and a scepter shall rise out of I.; 24.17
dispossessed, while I. does valiantly. 24.18
While I. dwelt in Shittim the 25.01
So I. yoked himself to Baal of Peor. 25.03
of the LORD was kindled against I.; 25.03
of the LORD may turn away from I. 25.04
And Moses said to the judges of I., 25.05
the people of I. came and brought 25.06
congregation of the people of I., 25.06
the man of I. into the inner room, 25.08
the man of I. and the woman, through 25.08
was stayed from the people of I. 25.08
my wrath from the people of I., 25.11
the people of I. in my jealousy. 25.11
atonement for the people of I. 25.13
The name of the slain man of I., 25.14
congregation of the people of I., 26.02
all in I. who are able to go forth 26.02
The people of I., who came forth 26.04
Reuben, the first-born of I.; 26.05
was the number of the people of I., 26.51
numbered among the people of I., 26.62
to them among the people of I. 26.62
the people of I. in the plains of 26.63
the people of I. in the wilderness 26.64
And you shall say to the people of I., 27.08
the people of I. a statute and 27.11
I have given to the people of I. 27.12
of the people of I. may obey. 27.20
and all the people of I. with him, 27.21
"Command the people of I., 28.02
the people of I. everything just 29.40
of the tribes of the people of I., 30.01
"Avenge the people of I. on the 31.02
of the tribes of I. to the war." 31.04
provided, out of the thousands of I., 31.05
And the people of I. took captive 31.09
congregation of the people of I., 31.12
Behold, these caused the people of I., 31.16
the people of I. before the LORD. 31.54
before the congregation of I., 32.04
the people of I. from going over 32.07
the people of I. from going into 32.09
anger was kindled against I., 32.13
anger of the LORD against I.! 32.14
to go before the people of I., 32.17
the people of I. have inherited 32.18
obligation to the LORD and to I.; 32.22
of the tribes of the people of I. 32.28
are the stages of the people of I., 33.01
the people of I. went out triumphantly 33.03
So the people of I. set out from 33.05
the people of I. had come out of 33.38
of the coming of the people of I. 33.40
"Say to the people of I., 33.51
"Command the people of I., 34.02
Moses commanded the people of I., 34.13
the people of I. in the land of 34.29
"Command the people of I., 35.02
the possession of the people of I., 35.08
"Say to the people of I., 35.10
be for refuge for the people of I., 35.15
in the midst of the people of I." 35.34
fathers' houses of the people of I.; 36.01
inheritance by lot to the people of I.; 36.02
the people of I. then their 36.03
jubilee of the people of I. comes, 36.04
the people of I. according to the 36.05
the people of I. shall not be 36.07
the people of I. shall cleave to 36.07
in any tribe of the people of I., 36.08
the people of I. may possess the 36.08
the people of I. shall cleave to 36.09

ISRAEL (cont.)
the people of I. in the plains of Num 36.13
spoke to all I. beyond the Jordan Deu 1.01
the people of I. according to all 1.03
he shall cause I. to inherit it. 1.38
as I. did to the land of their 2.12
your brethren the people of I. 3.18
"And now, O I., give heed to the 4.01
set before the children of I.; 4.44
the children of I. when they came 4.45
the children of I. defeated when 4.46
And Moses summoned all I., 5.01
O I., the statutes and the ordinances 5.01
O I., and be careful to do them; 6.03
"Hear, O I.: The LORD our God is one 6.04
"Hear, O I.; you are to pass over the 9.01
(The people of I. journeyed from 10.06
"And now, I., what does the LORD 10.12
them, in the midst of all I.; 11.06
And all I. shall hear, and fear, and 13.11
abominable thing has been done in I., 17.04
you shall purge the evil from I. 17.12
kingdom, he and his children, in I. 17.20
no portion or inheritance with I.; 18.01
any of your towns out of all I., 18.06
guilt of innocent blood from I., 19.13
O I., you draw near this day to 20.03
thy people I., whom thou hast 21.08
in the midst of thy people I.; 21.08
and all I. shall hear, and fear. 21.21
an evil name upon a virgin of I.; 22.19
folly in I. by playing the harlot 22.21
you shall purge the evil from I. 22.22
prostitute of the daughters of I., 23.17
cult prostitute of the sons of I. 23.17
the people of I., and if he treats 24.07
name may not be blotted out of I. 25.06
perpetuate his brother's name in I.; 25.07
of his house shall be called in I., 25.10
thy people I. and the ground which 26.15
the elders of I. commanded the 27.01
Levitical priests said to all I., 27.09
O I.: this day you have become the 27.09
all the men of I. with a loud 27.14
the people of I. in the land of 29.01
summoned all I. and said to them: 29.02
your officers, all the men of I., 29.10
all the tribes of I. for calamity, 29.21
to speak these words to all I. 31.01
said to him in the sight of all I., 31.07
LORD, and to all the elders of I. 31.09
when all I. comes to appear before 31.11
law before all I. in their hearing. 31.11
and teach it to the people of I.; 31.19
for me against the people of I. 31.19
and taught it to the people of I. 31.22
the children of I. into the land 31.23
ears of all the assembly of I.: 31.30
speaking all these words to all I., 32.45
the people of I. for a possession; 32.49
the people of I. at the waters of 32.51
in the midst of the people of I. 32.51
which I give to the people of I. 32.52
the children of I. before his 33.01
all the tribes of I. together. 33.05
thy ordinances, and I. thy law; 33.10
with I. he executed the commands 33.21
So I. dwelt in safety, the fountain 33.28
Happy are you, O I.! 33.29
And the people of I. wept for Moses 34.08
so the people of I. obeyed him, 34.09
a prophet since in I. like Moses, 34.10
wrought in the sight of all I. 34.12
to them, to the people of I. Jos 1.02
certain men of I. have come here 2.02
Shittim, with all the people of I.; 3.01
exalt you in the sight of all I., 3.07
And Joshua said to the people of I., 3.09
twelve men from the tribes of I., 3.12
And while all I. were passing over 3.17
twelve men from the people of I., 4.04
of the tribes of the people of I., 4.05
the people of I. a memorial for 4.07
And the men of I. did as Joshua 4.08
of the tribes of the people of I., 4.08
over armed before the people of I., 4.12
Joshua in the sight of all I.; 4.14
And he said to the people of I., 4.21
'I. passed over this Jordan on dry 4.22
the people of I. until they had 5.01
them, because of the people of I. 5.01
the people of I. again the second 5.02
the people of I. at Gibeath-Haaraloth. 5.03
For the people of I. walked forty 5.06
While the people of I. were encamped 5.10
the people of I. had manna no more, 5.12
because of the people of I.; 6.01
the camp of I. a thing for destruction, 6.18
set them outside the camp of I. 6.23
and she dwelt in I. to this day, 6.25
But the people of I. broke faith in 7.01
burned against the people of I. 7.01
evening, he and the elders of I.; 7.06
when I. has turned their backs 7.08
I. has sinned; they have transgressed 7.11
Therefore the people of I. cannot 7.12
God of I., "There are devoted 7.13
things in the midst of you, O I.; 7.13
he has done a shameful thing in I.'" 7.15
and brought I. near tribe by tribe, 7.16
give glory to the LORD God of I., 7.19
sinned against the LORD God of I., 7.20
to Joshua and all the people of I.; 7.23
And Joshua and all I. with him took 7.24
And all I. stoned him with stones; 7.25
and went up, with the elders of I., 8.10
the Arabah to meet I. in battle; 8.14
And Joshua and all I. made a 8.15
who did not go out after I.; 8.17
left the city open, and pursued I. 8.17
Joshua and all I. saw that the 8.21
so they were in the midst of I., 8.22
and I. smote them, until there was 8.22
When I. had finished slaughtering 8.24
all I. returned to Ai, and smote it 8.24
of that city I. took as their 8.27
Ebal to the LORD, the God of I., 8.30
had commanded the people of I., 8.31
the presence of the people of I., 8.32
And all I., sojourner as well as 8.33
they should bless the people of I. 8.33
read before all the assembly of I., 8.35
one accord to fight Joshua and I. 9.02
said to him and to the men of I., 9.06
But the men of I. said to the 9.07
And the people of I. set out and 9.17
But the people of I. did not kill 9.18
to them by the LORD, the God of I. 9.18
the God of I., and now we may not 9.19
of the hand of the people of I.; 9.26
made peace with I. and were among 10.01
Joshua and with the people of I." 10.04
threw them into a panic before I., 10.10
And as they fled before I., 10.11
than the men of I. killed with the 10.11
the Amorites over to the men of I.; 10.12
and he said in the sight of I., 10.12
for the LORD fought for I. 10.14
and all I. with him, to the camp at 10.15
and the men of I. had finished 10.20
against any of the people of I. 10.21
Joshua summoned all the men of I., 10.24
and all I. with him, to Libnah, and 10.29
and its king into the hand of I.; 10.30

ISRAEL (cont.)
and all I. with him, to Lachish, and Jos 10.31
gave Lachish into the hand of I., 10.32
on with all I. from Lachish to 10.34
up with all I. from Eglon to 10.36
with all I., turned back to Debir 10.38
as the LORD God of I. commanded. 10.40
the LORD God of I. fought for I. 10.42
and all I. with him, to the camp at 10.43
waters of Merom, to fight with I. 11.05
over all of them, slain, to I.; 11.06
LORD gave them into the hand of I., 11.08
that stood on mounds did I. burn, 11.13
the people of I. took for their 11.14
hill country of I. and its lowland 11.16
made peace with the people of I., 11.19
should come against I. in battle, 11.20
from all the hill country of I.; 11.21
in the land of the people of I.; 11.22
inheritance to I. according to 11.23
whom the people of I. defeated, 12.01
and the people of I. defeated them; 12.06
the people of I. defeated on the 12.07
the tribes of I. as a possession 12.07
out from before the people of I.; 13.06
the land of I. for an inheritance, 13.06
Yet the people of I. did not drive 13.13
in the midst of I. to this day. 13.13
the LORD God of I. are their 13.14
the people of I. killed with the 13.22
the LORD God of I. is their inheritance, 13.33
the people of I. received in the 14.01
the people of I. distributed to 14.01
the people of I. did as the LORD 14.05
while I. walked in the wilderness; 14.10
followed the LORD, the God of I. 14.14
But when the people of I. grew strong, 17.13
the people of I. assembled at 18.01
the people of I. seven tribes 18.02
So Joshua said to the people of I., 18.03
the land of the people of I., 18.10
the people of I. gave an inheritance 19.49
the people of I. distributed by 19.51
"Say to the people of I., 20.02
designated for all the people of I., 20.09
of the tribes of the people of I.; 21.01
the people of I. gave to the 21.03
the people of I. gave by lot to 21.08
the people of I. were in all forty 21.41
LORD gave to I. all the land which 21.43
made to the house of I. had failed; 21.45
from the people of I. at Shiloh, 22.09
And the people of I. heard say, 22.11
that belongs to the people of I. 22.11
And when the people of I. heard of it, 22.12
the people of I. gathered at 22.12
Then the people of I. sent to the 22.13
each of the tribal families of I., 22.14
of the family among the clans of I. 22.14
the God of I. in turning away this 22.16
whole congregation of I. tomorrow. 22.18
upon all the congregation of I.? 22.20
the heads of the families of I., 22.21
he knows, and lets I. itself know! 22.22
to do with the LORD, the God of I. 22.24
the families of I. who were with 22.30
the people of I. from the hand of 22.31
of Canaan, to the people of I., 22.32
report pleased the people of I.; 22.33
the people of I. blessed God and 22.33
given rest to I. from all their 23.01
Joshua summoned all I., their elders 23.02
all the tribes of I. to Shechem, 24.01
the judges, and the officers of I.; 24.01
the God of I., 'Your fathers lived 24.02
Moab, arose and fought against I.; 24.09
heart to the LORD, the God of I." 24.23
And I. served the LORD all the days 24.31
the work which the LORD did for I. 24.31
the people of I. brought up from 24.32
the people of I. inquired of the Ju 1.01
When I. grew strong, they put the 1.28
words to all the people of I., 2.04
the people of I. went each to his 2.06
which the LORD had done for I. 2.07
the work which he had done for I. 2.10
And the people of I. did what was 2.11
of the LORD was kindled against I., 2.14
of the LORD was kindled against I.; 2.20
that by them I may test I., 2.22
to test I. by them, that is, all in I. 3.01
of the people of I. might know war, 3.02
They were for the testing of I., 3.04
to know whether I. would obey the 3.04
So the people of I. dwelt among the 3.05
And the people of I. did what was 3.07
of the LORD was kindled against I., 3.08
the people of I. served Cushanrishathaim 3.08
the people of I. cried to the LORD, 3.09
a deliverer for the people of I., 3.09
came upon him, and he judged I.; 3.10
And the people of I. again did what 3.12
Eglon the king of Moab against I., 3.12
Amalekites, and went and defeated I.; 3.13
And the people of I. served Eglon 3.14
the people of I. cried to the LORD, 3.15
The people of I. sent tribute by 3.15
the people of I. went down with 3.27
that day under the hand of I. 3.30
an oxgoad; and he too delivered I. 3.31
And the people of I. again did what 4.01
Then the people of I. cried to the 4.03
the people of I. cruelly for 4.03
was judging I. at that time. 4.04
the people of I. came up to her 4.05
the God of I., command you, 'Go, 4.06
of Canaan before the people of I. 4.23
the people of I. bore harder and 4.24
"That the leaders took the lead in I., 5.02
melody to the LORD, the God of I. 5.03
before the LORD, the God of I. 5.05
The peasantry ceased in I., they 5.07
Deborah, arose as a mother in I. 5.07
be seen among forty thousand in I.? 5.08
commanders of I. who offered 5.09
triumphs of his peasantry in I. 5.11
The people of I. did what was evil 6.01
hand of Midian prevailed over I.; 6.02
the people of I. made for themselves 6.02
and leave no sustenance in I., 6.04
And I. was brought very low because 6.06
the people of I. cried for help to 6.06
When the people of I. cried to the 6.07
sent a prophet to the people of I.; 6.08
the God of I.: I led you up from 6.08
and deliver I. from the hand of 6.14
"Pray, Lord, how can I deliver I.? 6.15
"If thou wilt deliver I. by my hand, 6.36
thou wilt deliver I. by my hand, 6.37
lest I. vaunt themselves against me, 7.02
all the rest of I. every man to 7.08
the son of Joash, a man of I.; 7.14
and he returned to the camp of I., 7.15
And the men of I. were called out 7.23
Then the men of I. said to Gideon, 8.22
and all I. played the harlot after 8.27
subdued before the people of I., 8.28
the people of I. turned again and 8.33
And the people of I. did not 8.34
the good that he had done to I. 8.35
Abimelech ruled over I. three years. 9.22
And when the men of I. saw that 9.55
to deliver I. Tola the son of Puah, 10.01
And he judged I. twenty-three years. 10.02

ISRAEL (cont.)
who judged I. twenty-two years. Ju 10.03
And the people of I. again did what 10.06
of the LORD was kindled against I., 10.07
the children of I. that year. 10.08
the people of I. that were beyond 10.08
so that I. was sorely distressed. 10.09
And the people of I. cried to the 10.10
And the LORD said to the people of I., 10.11
And the people of I. said to the 10.15
indignant over the misery of I. 10.16
and the people of I. came together, 10.17
the Ammonites made war against I. 11.04
the Ammonites made war against I., 11.05
"Because I. on coming from Egypt 11.13
I. did not take away the land of 11.15
I. went through the wilderness to 11.16
I. then sent messengers to the king 11.17
consent. So I. remained at Kadesh. 11.17
I. then sent messengers to Sihon 11.19
and I. said to him, 'Let us pass, we 11.19
did not trust I. to pass through 11.20
at Jahaz, and fought with I. 11.20
the God of I., gave Sihon and all 11.21
all his people into the hand of I., 11.21
so I. took possession of all the 11.21
the God of I., dispossessed the 11.23
Amorites from before his people I.; 11.23
Did he ever strive against I., 11.25
While I. dwelt in Heshbon and its 11.26
the people of I. and the people of 11.27
subdued before the people of I. 11.33
And it became a custom in I. 11.39
daughters of I. went year by year 11.40
Jephthah judged I. six years. 12.07
After him Ibzan of Bethlehem judged I. 12.08
And he judged I. seven years. 12.09
After him Elon the Zebulunite judged I.; 12.11
and he judged I. ten years. 12.11
Hillel the Pirathonite judged I. 12.13
and he judged I. eight years. 12.14
And the people of I. again did what 13.01
to deliver I. from the hand of the 13.05
Philistines had dominion over I. 14.04
And he judged I. in the days of the 15.20
He had judged I. twenty years. 16.31
those days there was no king in I.; 17.06
those days there was no king in I. 18.01
the tribes of I. had fallen to 18.01
priest to a tribe and family in I.?" 18.19
their ancestor, who was born to I.; 18.29
days, when there was no king in I., 19.01
do not belong to the people of I.; 19.12
throughout all the territory of I. 19.29
the people of I. came up out of 19.30
Then all the people of I. came out, 20.01
people, of all the tribes of I., 20.02
the people of I. had gone up to 20.03
And the people of I. said, 20.03
country of the inheritance of I.; 20.06
abomination and wantonness in I. 20.06
you people of I., all of you, give 20.07
throughout all the tribes of I., 20.10
which they have committed in I." 20.10
So all the men of I. gathered 20.11
And the tribes of I. sent men 20.12
death, and put away evil from I." 20.13
their brethren, the people of I. 20.13
to battle against the people of I. 20.14
And the men of I., apart from 20.17
The people of I. arose and went up 20.18
Then the people of I. rose in the 20.19
And the men of I. went out to 20.20
and the men of I. drew up the 20.20
the men of I., took courage, and 20.22
And the people of I. went up and 20.23
So the people of I. came near 20.24
thousand men of the people of I.; 20.25
Then all the people of I., 20.26
And the people of I. inquired of 20.27
So I. set men in ambush round about 20.29
And the people of I. went up 20.30
country, about thirty men of I. 20.31
But the men of I. said, 20.32
And all the men of I. rose up out 20.33
and the men of I. who were in 20.33
thousand picked men out of all I., 20.34
LORD defeated Benjamin before I.; 20.35
and the men of I. destroyed twenty-five 20.35
The men of I. gave ground to 20.36
the men of I. and the men in 20.38
the men of I. should turn in battle, 20.39
and kill about thirty men of I.; 20.39
Then the men of I. turned, 20.41
the men of I. in the direction of 20.42
And the men of I. turned back 20.48
Now the men of I. had sworn at 21.01
the God of I., why has this come to 21.03
why has this come to pass in I., 21.03
be today one tribe lacking in I.?" 21.03
And the people of I. said, 21.05
the tribes of I. did not come up 21.05
And the people of I. had compassion 21.06
tribe is cut off from I. this day. 21.06
the tribes of I. that did not come 21.08
made a breach in the tribes of I. 21.15
a tribe be not blotted out from I. 21.17
For the people of I. had sworn, 21.18
And the people of I. departed from 21.24
those days there was no king in I.; 21.25
the God of I., under whose wings Ru 2.12
former times in I. concerning 4.07
was the manner of attesting in I. 4.07
together built up the house of I. 4.11
and may his name be renowned in I.! 4.14
and the God of I. grant your 1Sa 1.17
that his sons were doing to all I., 2.22
the tribes of I. to be my priest, 2.28
by fire from the people of I. 2.28
of every offering of my people I.?" 2.29
Therefore the LORD the God of I. declares: 2.30
which shall be bestowed upon I.; 2.32
I am about to do a thing in I., 3.11
And all I. from Dan to Beersheba 3.20
And the word of Samuel came to all I. 4.01
Now I. went out to battle against 4.01
Philistines drew up in line against I., 4.02
I. was defeated by the Philistines, 4.02
the elders of I. said, "Why has the 4.03
all I. gave a mighty shout, so that 4.05
and I. was defeated, and they fled, 4.10
there fell of I. thirty thousand 4.10
"I. has fled before the Philistines, 4.17
He had judged I. forty years. 4.18
"The glory has departed from I.!" 4.21
"The glory has departed from I., 4.22
of the God of I. must not remain 5.07
do with the ark of the God of I.?" 5.08
of the God of I. be brought around 5.08
the ark of the God of I. there. 5.08
of the God of I. to slay us and 5.10
"Send away the ark of the God of I., 5.11
send away the ark of the God of I., 6.03
and give glory to the God of I.; 6.05
the house of I. lamented after the 7.02
Samuel said to all the house of I., 7.03
So I. put away the Baals and the 7.04
"Gather all I. at Mizpah, and I will 7.05
judged the people of I. at Mizpah. 7.06
the people of I. had gathered at 7.07
the Philistines went up against I. 7.07
the people of I. heard of it they 7.07
And the people of I. said to Samuel, 7.08
Samuel cried to the LORD for I., 7.09

ISRAEL (cont.)

Philistines drew near to attack I.;	1Sa 7.10
and they were routed before I.	7.10
And the men of I. went out of	7.11
again enter the territory of I.	7.13
had taken from I. were restored to I.	7.14
and I. rescued their territory from	7.14
also between I. and the Amorites.	7.14
Samuel judged I. all the days of	7.15
and he judged I. in all these	7.16
also he administered justice to I.	7.17
he made his sons judges over I.	8.01
the elders of I. gathered together	8.04
Samuel then said to the men of I.,	8.22
the people of I. more handsome	9.02
(Formerly in I., when a man went to	9.09
him to be prince over my people I.	9.16
is all that is desirable in I.?	9.20
from the least of the tribes of I.?	9.21
to be prince over his people I.?	10.01
and he said to the people of I.,	10.18
the God of I., 'I brought up I. out	10.18
brought all the tribes of I. near,	10.20
and thus put disgrace upon all I.	11.02
through all the territory of I.	11.03
territory of I. by the hand of	11.07
the men of I. were three hundred	11.08
LORD has wrought deliverance in I."	11.13
all the men of I. rejoiced greatly.	11.15
And Samuel said to all I.,	12.01
reigned . . . and two years over I.	13.01
Saul chose three thousand men of I.;	13.02
And all I. heard it said that Saul	13.04
and also that I. had become odious	13.04
Philistines mustered to fight with I.,	13.05
When the men of I. saw that they	13.06
your kingdom over I. for ever.	13.13
throughout all the land of I.;	13.19
has given them into the hand of I."	14.12
at that time with the people of I.	14.18
all the men of I. who had hid	14.22
So the LORD delivered I. that day;	14.23
And the men of I. were distressed	14.24
thou give them into the hand of I.?"	14.37
For as the LORD lives who saves I.,	14.39
Then he said to all I.,	14.40
Therefore Saul said, "O LORD God of I.,	14.41
son, O LORD, God of I., give Urim;	14.41
is in thy people I., give Thummim."	14.41
wrought this great victory in I.?	14.45
had taken the kingship over I.,	14.47
and delivered I. out of the hands	14.48
anoint you king over his people I.;	15.01
Amalek did to I. in opposing them	15.02
the people of I. when they came up	15.06
not the head of the tribes of I.?	15.17
The LORD anointed you king over I.	15.17
rejected you from being king over I."	15.26
the kingdom of I. from you this	15.28
the Glory of I. will not lie or	15.29
elders of my people and before I.,	15.30
that he had made Saul king over I.	15.35
him from being king over I.?	16.01
and the men of I. were gathered,	17.02
and I. stood on the mountain on the	17.03
and shouted to the ranks of I.,	17.08
"I defy the ranks of I. this day;	17.10
When Saul and all I. heard these	17.11
and they, and all the men of I.,	17.19
And I. and the Philistines drew up	17.21
All the men of I., when they saw	17.24
And the men of I. said, "Have you	17.25
Surely he has come up to defy I.;	17.25
make his father's house free in I."	17.25
takes away the reproach from I.?	17.26
hosts, the God of the armies of I.,	17.45
know that there is a God in I.,	17.46

And the men of I. and Judah rose	17.52
came out of all the cities of I.,	18.06
But all I. and Judah loved David;	18.16
kinsfolk, my father's family in I.,	18.18
David, and that all I. loved him,	18.28
wrought a great victory for all I.	19.05
LORD, the God of I., be witness!	20.12
the God of I., thy servant has	23.10
the God of I., I beseech thee, tell	23.11
you shall be king over I.,	23.17
thousand chosen men out of all I.,	24.02
After whom has the king of I. come out?	24.14
the kingdom of I. shall be established	24.20
and all I. assembled and mourned	25.01
has appointed you prince over I.,	25.30
the God of I., who sent you this	25.32
as the LORD the God of I. lives,	25.34
three thousand chosen men of I.,	26.02
Who is like you in I.?	26.15
for the king of I. has come out to	26.20
longer within the borders of I.,	27.01
utterly abhorred by his people I.;	27.12
for war, to fight against I.	28.01
and all I. had mourned for him and	28.03
and Saul gathered all I.,	28.04
LORD will give I. also with you	28.19
the army of I. also into the hand	28.19
king of I., who has been with me	29.03
an ordinance for I. to this day.	30.25
Now the Philistines fought against I.;	31.01
and the men of I. fled before the	31.01
And when the men of I. who were on	31.07
that the men of I. had fled and	31.07
"I have escaped from the camp of I."	2Sa 1.03
the LORD and for the house of I.,	1.12
"Thy glory, O I., is slain upon thy	1.19
"Ye daughters of I., weep over Saul,	1.24
Ephraim and Benjamin and all I.	2.09
old when he began to reign over I.,	2.10
and the men of I. were beaten	2.17
and pursued I. no more, nor did they	2.28
of David over I. and over Judah,	3.10
you to bring over all I. to you."	3.12
conferred with the elders of I.,	3.17
save my people I. from the hand of	3.18
Hebron all that I. and the whole	3.19
will gather all I. to my lord the	3.21
people and all I. understood that	3.37
man has fallen this day in I.?	3.38
failed, and all I. was dismayed.	4.01
the tribes of I. came to David at	5.01
you that led out and brought in I.;	5.02
shall be shepherd of my people I.,	5.02
and you shall be prince over I."	5.02
the elders of I. came to the king	5.03
they anointed David king over I.	5.03
over all I. and Judah thirty-three	5.05
had established him king over I.,	5.12
for the sake of his people I.	5.12
had been anointed king over I.,	5.17
gathered all the chosen men of I.,	6.01
the house of I. were making merry	6.05
the house of I. brought up the ark	6.15
people, the whole multitude of I.,	6.19
"How the king of I. honored himself	6.20
to appoint me as prince over I.,	6.21
the people of I. from Egypt to	7.06
moved with all the people of I.,	7.07
word with any of the judges of I.,	7.07
commanded to shepherd my people I.,	7.07
should be prince over my people I.;	7.08
appoint a place for my people I.,	7.10
appointed judges over my people I.;	7.11
on earth is like thy people I.,	7.23
thy people I. to be thy people for	7.24
'The LORD of hosts is God over I.,'	7.26
the God of I., has made this	7.27

ISRAEL (cont.)
So David reigned over all I.; 2Sa 8.15
chose some of the picked men of I., 10.09
that they had been defeated by I., 10.15
David, he gathered all I. together, 10.17
And the Syrians fled before I.; 10.18
that they had been defeated by I., 10.19
they made peace with I., and became 10.19
his servants with him, and all I.; 11.01
"The Ark and I. and Judah dwell in 11.11
the LORD, the God of I., 'I anointed 12.07
'I anointed you king over I., 12.07
you the house of I. and of Judah; 12.08
I will do this thing before all I., 12.12
for such a thing is not done in I.; 13.12
as one of the wanton fools in I. 13.13
Now in all I. there was no one so 14.25
of such and such a tribe in I.," 15.02
did to all of I. who came to the 15.06
stole the hearts of the men of I. 15.06
throughout all the tribes of I., 15.10
of the men of I. have gone after 15.13
the house of I. will give me back 16.03
the men of I., came to Jerusalem, 16.15
and all the men of I. have chosen, 16.18
and all I. will hear that you have 16.21
concubines in the sight of all I. 16.22
Absalom and all the elders of I. 17.04
for all I. knows that your father 17.10
is that all I. be gathered to you, 17.11
then all I. will bring ropes to 17.13
Absalom and all the men of I. said, 17.14
Absalom and the elders of I.; 17.15
the Jordan with all the men of I. 17.24
And I. and Absalom encamped in the 17.26
went out into the field against I.; 18.06
And the men of I. were defeated 18.07
troops came back from pursuing I.; 18.16
and all I. fled every one to his 18.17
Now I. had fled every man to his 19.08
throughout all the tribes of I., 19.09
the word of all I. has come to the 19.11
one be put to death in I. this day? 19.22
that I am this day king over I.?" 19.22
and also half the people of I., 19.40
Then all the men of I. came to the 19.41
of Judah answered the men of I., 19.42
And the men of I. answered the men 19.43
than the words of the men of I. 19.43
every man to his tents, O I.!" 20.01
So all the men of I. withdrew from 20.02
the tribes of I. to Abel of 20.14
are peaceable and faithful in I.; 20.19
a city which is a mother in I.; 20.19
in command of all the army of I.; 20.23
were not of the people of I., 21.02
the people of I. had sworn to 21.02
for the people of I. and Judah. 21.02
us to put any man to death in I." 21.04
place in all the territory of I., 21.05
The Philistines had war again with I., 21.15
lest you quench the lamp of I." 21.17
And when he taunted I., Jonathan 21.21
Jacob, the sweet psalmist of I.: 23.01
God of I. has spoken, the Rock of I. 23.03
battle, and the men of I. withdrew. 23.09
of the LORD was kindled against I., 24.01
saying, "Go, number I. and Judah." 24.01
"Go through all the tribes of I., 24.02
king to number the people of I. 24.04
in I. there were eight hundred 24.09
pestilence upon I. from the 24.15
and the plague was averted from I. 24.25
throughout all the territory of I., 1Ki 1.03
the eyes of all I. are upon you, 1.20
the God of I., saying, 'Solomon your 1.30
there anoint him king over I.; 1.34
to be ruler over I. and over Judah." 1.35
the God of I., who has granted one 1.48
fail you a man on the throne of I.' 2.04
two commanders of the armies of I., 2.05
reigned over I. was forty years; 2.11
and that all I. fully expected me 2.15
Ner, commander of the army of I., 2.32
And all I. heard of the judgment 3.28
King Solomon was king over all I., 4.01
Solomon had twelve officers over all I., 4.07
Judah and I. were as many as the 4.20
And Judah and I. dwelt in safety, 4.25
levy of forced labor out of all I.; 5.13
the people of I. came out of the 6.01
year of Solomon's reign over I., 6.01
dwell among the children of I., 6.13
and will not forsake my people I." 6.13
the elders of I. and all the heads 8.01
fathers' houses of the people of I., 8.01
And all the men of I. assembled to 8.02
And all the elders of I. came, 8.03
and all the congregation of I., 8.05
a covenant with the people of I., 8.09
and blessed all the assembly of I., 8.14
while all the assembly of I. stood. 8.14
the God of I., who with his hand 8.15
brought my people I. out of Egypt, 8.16
the tribes of I. in which to build 8.16
David to be over my people I.' 8.16
name of the LORD, the God of I. 8.17
and sit on the throne of I., 8.20
name of the LORD, the God of I. 8.20
presence of all the assembly of I., 8.22
God of I., there is no God like 8.23
God of I., keep with thy servant 8.25
me to sit upon the throne of I., 8.25
O God of I., let thy word be 8.26
thy servant and of thy people I., 8.30
"When thy people I. are defeated 8.33
forgive the sin of thy people I., 8.34
thy people I., when thou dost teach 8.36
by any man or by all thy people I., 8.38
who is not of thy people I., 8.41
and fear thee, as do thy people I., 8.43
the supplication of thy people I., 8.52
the assembly of I. with a loud 8.55
has given rest to his people I., 8.56
and the cause of his people I., 8.59
and all I. with him, offered sacrifice 8.62
the people of I. dedicated the 8.63
and all I. with him, a great assembly, 8.65
his servant and to I. his people. 8.66
your royal throne over I. for ever, 9.05
you a man upon the throne of I.' 9.05
then I will cut off I. from the 9.07
and I. will become a proverb and a 9.07
who were not of the people of I.— 9.20
the people of I. were unable to 9.21
the people of I. Solomon made no 9.22
and set you on the throne of I.! 10.09
Because the LORD loved I. for ever, 10.09
LORD had said to the people of I., 11.02
the God of I., who had appeared to 11.09
(for Joab and all I. remained there 11.16
an adversary of I. all the days of 11.25
and he abhorred I., and reigned over 11.25
the God of I., 'Behold, I am about 11.31
out of all the tribes of I.), 11.32
and you shall be king over I. 11.37
David, and I will give I. to you. 11.38
over all I. was forty years. 11.42
for all I. had come to Shechem to 12.01
the assembly of I. came and said 12.03
And when all I. saw that the king 12.16
To your tents, O I.! Look now to 12.16
So I. departed to their tents. 12.16
the people of I. who dwelt in the 12.17

ISRAEL (cont.)
and all I. stoned him to death with 1Ki 12.18
So I. has been in rebellion against 12.19
And when all I. heard that Jeroboam 12.20
and made him king over all I. 12.20
to fight against the house of I., 12.21
your kinsmen the people of I. 12.24
O I., who brought you up out of the 12.28
a feast for the people of I., 12.33
the God of I.: "Because I exalted 14.07
made you leader over my people I., 14.07
male, both bond and free in I., 14.10
And all I. shall mourn for him, and 14.13
the God of I., in the house of 14.13
up for himself a king over I., 14.14
the LORD will smite I., as a reed 14.15
and root up I. out of this good 14.15
And he will give I. up because of 14.16
sinned and which he made I. to sin." 14.16
And all I. buried him and mourned 14.18
the Chronicles of the Kings of I. 14.19
chosen out of all the tribes of I., 14.21
drove out before the people of I. 14.24
Jeroboam king of I. Asa began to 15.09
Baasha king of I. all their days. 15.16
Baasha king of I. went up against 15.17
your league with Baasha king of I., 15.19
armies against the cities of I., 15.20
to reign over I. in the second 15.25
and he reigned over I. two years. 15.25
in his sin which he made I. to sin. 15.26
Nadab and all I. were laying siege 15.27
sinned and which he made I. to sin, 15.30
provoked the LORD, the God of I. 15.30
the Chronicles of the Kings of I.? 15.31
Baasha king of I. all their days. 15.32
to reign over all I. at Tirzah, 15.33
in his sin which he made I. to sin. 15.34
made you leader over my people I., 16.02
and have made my people I. to sin, 16.02
the Chronicles of the Kings of I.? 16.05
began to reign over I. in Tirzah, 16.08
and which they made I. to sin, 16.13
the LORD God of I. to anger with 16.13
the Chronicles of the Kings of I.? 16.14
therefore all I. made Omri, the 16.16
king over I. that day in the camp. 16.16
and all I. with him, and they 16.17
he committed, making I. to sin. 16.19
the Chronicles of the Kings of I.? 16.20
Then the people of I. were divided 16.21
Judah, Omri began to reign over I., 16.23
the sins which he made I. to sin, 16.26
the God of I., to anger by their 16.26
the Chronicles of the Kings of I.? 16.27
son of Omri began to reign over I., 16.29
reigned over I. in Samaria twenty-two 16.29
the God of I., to anger than all 16.33
the kings of I. who were before 16.33
"As the LORD the God of I. lives, 17.01
For thus says the LORD the God of I., 17.14
him, "Is it you, you troubler of I.?" 18.17
answered, "I have not troubled I.; 18.18
and gather all I. to me at Mount 18.19
So Ahab sent to all the people of I., 18.20
"I. shall be your name"; 18.31
and I., let it be known this day 18.36
this day that thou art God in I., 18.36
the people of I. have forsaken thy 19.10
the people of I. have forsaken thy 19.14
shall anoint to be king over I.; 19.16
Yet I will leave seven thousand in I., 19.18
into the city to Ahab king of I., 20.02
And the king of I. answered, 20.04
Then the king of I. called all the 20.07
And the king of I. answered, 20.11
near to Ahab king of I. and said, 20.13
he mustered all the people of I., 20.15
Syrians fled and I. pursued them, 20.20
And the king of I. went out, 20.21
came near to the king of I., 20.22
up to Aphek, to fight against I. 20.26
And the people of I. were mustered, 20.27
the people of I. encamped before 20.27
near and said to the king of I., 20.28
the people of I. smote of the 20.29
of the house of I. are merciful 20.31
and go out to the king of I.; 20.31
went to the king of I. and said, 20.32
The king of I. said to him, "So 20.40
and the king of I. recognized him 20.41
And the king of I. went to his 20.43
said to him, "Do you now govern I.? 21.07
"Arise, go down to meet Ahab king of I., 21.18
every male, bond or free, in I.; 21.21
because you have made I. to sin. 21.22
cast out before the people of I. 21.26
years Syria and I. continued 22.01
Judah came down to the king of I. 22.02
And the king of I. said to his 22.03
Jehoshaphat said to the king of I., 22.04
Jehoshaphat said to the king of I., 22.05
Then the king of I. gathered the 22.06
And the king of I. said to Jehoshaphat, 22.08
Then the king of I. summoned an 22.09
Now the king of I. and Jehoshaphat 22.10
"I saw all I. scattered upon the 22.17
And the king of I. said to Jehoshaphat, 22.18
And the king of I. said, 22.26
So the king of I. and Jehoshaphat 22.29
And the king of I. said to Jehoshaphat, 22.30
And the king of I. disguised 22.30
but only with the king of I." 22.31
said, "It is surely the king of I." 22.32
saw that it was not the king of I., 22.33
the king of I. between the scale 22.34
the Chronicles of the Kings of I.? 22.39
the forth year of Ahab king of I. 22.41
made peace with the king of I. 22.44
to reign over I. in Samaria in the 22.51
and he reigned two years over I. 22.51
son of Nebat, who made I. to sin. 22.52
the God of I., to anger in every 22.53
of Ahab, Moab rebelled against I. 2Ki 1.01
is no God in I. that you are going 1.03
is no God in I. that you are 1.06
is no God in I. to inquire of his 1.16
the Chronicles of the Kings of I.? 1.18
the chariots of I. and its horsemen!" 2.12
became king over I. in Samaria, 3.01
of Nebat, which he made I. to sin; 3.03
to the king of I. a hundred 3.04
rebelled against the king of I. 3.05
at that time and mustered all I. 3.06
So the king of I. went with the 3.09
Then the king of I. said, "Alas! 3.10
So the king of I. and Jehoshaphat 3.12
And Elisha said to the king of I., 3.13
But the king of I. said to him, 3.13
But when they came to the camp of I., 3.24
And there came great wrath upon I.; 3.27
a little maid from the land of I., 5.02
the maiden from the land of I." 5.04
send a letter to the king of I." 5.05
the letter to the king of I., 5.06
the king of I. read the letter, he 5.07
the king of I. had rent his 5.08
know that there is a prophet in I." 5.08
better than all the waters of I.? 5.12
no God in all the earth but in I.; 5.15
of Syria was warring against I., 6.08
of God sent word to the king of I., 6.09
And the king of I. sent to the 6.10
me who of us is for the king of I.?" 6.11
Elisha, the prophet who is in I., 6.12

ISRAEL (cont.)
the king of I. the words that you 2Ki 6.12
When the king of I. saw them he 6.21
more on raids into the land of I. 6.23
Now as the king of I. was passing 6.26
the king of I. has hired against us 7.06
multitude of I. that have already 7.13
you will do to the people of I.; 8.12
king of I., Jehoram the son of 8.16
In the way of the kings of I., 8.18
king of I., Ahaziah the son of 8.25
a granddaughter of Omri king of I. 8.26
LORD, I anoint you king over I.' 9.03
"Thus says the LORD the God of I. 9.06
the people of the LORD, over I. 9.06
every male, bond or free, in I. 9.08
LORD, I anoint you king over I.'" 9.12
Joram with all I. had been on 9.14
Joram king of I. and Ahaziah king 9.21
And Jehu sent throughout all I.; 10.21
Thus Jehu wiped out Baal from I. 10.28
which he made I. to sin, the golden 10.29
shall sit on the throne of I." 10.30
LORD the God of I. with all his 10.31
Jeroboam, which he made I. to sin. 10.31
LORD began to cut off parts of I. 10.32
throughout the territory of I.: 10.32
the Chronicles of the Kings of I.? 10.34
reigned over I. in Samaria was 10.36
began to reign over I. in Samaria, 13.01
of Nebat, which he made I. to sin; 13.02
of the LORD was kindled against I., 13.03
for he saw the oppression of I., 13.04
(Therefore the LORD gave I. a savior, 13.05
the people of I. dwelt in their 13.05
which he made I. to sin, but walked 13.06
the Chronicles of the Kings of I.? 13.08
began to reign over I. in Samaria, 13.10
which he made I. to sin, but he 13.11
the Chronicles of the Kings of I.? 13.12
in Samaria with the kings of I. 13.13
Joash king of I. went down to him, 13.14
The chariots of I. and its horsemen!" 13.14
Then he said to the king of I., 13.16
And he said to the king of I., 13.18
Syria oppressed I. all the days of 13.22
him and recovered the cities of I. 13.25
king of I., Amaziah the son of 14.01
king of I., saying, "Come, let us 14.08
And Jehoash king of I. sent word to 14.09
So Jehoash king of I. went up, 14.11
And Judah was defeated by I., 14.12
And Jehoash king of I. captured 14.13
the Chronicles of the Kings of I? 14.15
in Samaria with the kings of I.; 14.16
son of Jehoahaz, king of I., 14.17
king of I., began to reign in 14.23
of Nebat, which he made I. to win. 14.24
the border of I. from the entrance 14.25
the God of I., which he spoke by 14.25
affliction of I. was very bitter, 14.26
and there was none to help I. 14.26
out the name of I. from under 14.27
recovered for I. Damascus and 14.28
and the Chronicles of the Kings of I.? 14.28
the kings of I., and Zechariah his 14.29
Jeroboam king of I. Azariah the son 15.01
reigned over I. in Samaria six 15.08
of Nebat, which he made I. to sin. 15.09
the Chronicles of the Kings of I. 15.11
the throne of I. to the fourth 15.12
the Chronicles of the Kings of I. 15.15
son of Gadi began to reign over I., 15.17
of Nebat, which he made I. to sin. 15.18
Menahem exacted the money from I., 15.20
the Chronicles of the Kings of I.? 15.21
began to reign over I. in Samaria, 15.23
of Nebat, which he made I. to sin. 15.24
the Chronicles of the Kings of I. 15.26
began to reign over I. in Samaria, 15.27
of Nebat, which he made I. to sin. 15.28
Pekah king of I. Tiglathpileser 15.29
the Chronicles of the Kings of I. 15.31
king of I., Jotham the son of 15.32
in the way of the kings of I., 16.03
drove out before the people of I. 16.03
king of I., came up to wage war on 16.05
from the hand of the king of I., 16.07
began to reign in Samaria over I., 17.01
as the kings of I. who were before 17.02
the people of I. had sinned 17.07
drove out before the people of I., 17.08
the kings of I. had introduced. 17.08
And the people of I. did secretly 17.09
Yet the LORD warned I. and Judah by 17.13
Therefore the LORD was very angry with I., 17.18
customs which I. had introduced. 17.19
rejected all the descendants of I., 17.20
When he had torn I. from the house 17.21
Jeroboam drove I. from following 17.21
The people of I. walked in all the 17.22
LORD removed I. out of his sight, 17.23
So I. was exiled from their own 17.23
instead of the people of I.; 17.24
children of Jacob, whom he named I. 17.34
king of I., Hezekiah the son of 18.01
the people of I. had burned 18.04
He trusted in the LORD the God of I.; 18.05
king of I., Shalmaneser king of 18.09
ninth year of Hoshea king of I., 18.10
and said: "O LORD the God of I., 19.15
the God of I.: Your prayer to me 19.20
Against the Holy One of I.! 19.22
drove out before the people of I. 21.02
as Ahab king of I. had done, 21.03
chosen out of all the tribes of I., 21.07
the feet of I. to wander any more 21.08
destroyed before the people of I. 21.09
the God of I., Behold, I am bringing 21.12
the God of I.: 'Tell the man who 22.15
the God of I.: Regarding the words 22.18
the king of I. had built for 23.13
who made I. to sin, that altar with 23.15
Samaria, which kings of I. had made, 23.19
days of the judges who judged I., 23.22
of the kings of I. or of the kings 23.22
of my sight, as I have removed I., 23.27
which Solomon king of I. had made, 24.13
The sons of Isaac: Esau and I. 1Ch 1.34
These are the sons of I.: 2.01
Carmi: Achar, the troubler of I., 2.07
Jabez called on the God of I., 4.10
first-born of I. (for he was the 5.01
the sons of Joseph the son of I., 5.01
of Reuben, the first-born of I.: 5.03
in the days of Jeroboam king of I. 5.17
So the God of I. stirred up the 5.26
of Kohath, son of Ievi, son of I.; 6.38
and to make atonement for I., 6.49
So the people of I. gave the 6.64
the sons of Joseph the son of I. 7.29
So all I. was enrolled by genealogies 9.01
in the Book of the Kings of I. 9.01
possessions in their cities were I., 9.02
Now the Philistines fought against I.; 10.01
and the men of I. fled before the 10.01
all the men of I. who were in the 10.07
Then all I. gathered together to 11.01
you that led out and brought in I.; 11.02
shall be shepherd of my people I., 11.02
shall be prince over my people I.'" 11.02
the elders of I. came to the king 11.03
they anointed David king over I., 11.03
And David and all I. went to 11.04

ISRAEL (cont.)
his kingdom, together with all I., 1Ch 11.10
the word of the LORD concerning I. 11.10
to know what I. ought to do, two 12.32
to make David king over all I.; 12.38
all the rest of I. were of a 12.38
and sheep, for there was joy in I. 12.40
said to all the assembly of I., 13.02
who remain in all the land of I., 13.02
assembled all I. from Shihor 13.05
And David and all I. went up to 13.06
And David and all I. were making 13.08
had established him king over I., 14.02
for the sake of his people I. 14.02
had been anointed king over all I., 14.08
assembled all I. at Jerusalem, 15.03
the God of I., to the place that I 15.12
the ark of the LORD, the God of I. 15.14
So David and the elders of I., 15.25
So all I. brought up the ark of the 15.28
and distributed to all I., 16.03
to praise the LORD, the God of I. 16.04
as an everlasting covenant to I., 16.17
the God of I., from everlasting to 16.36
of the LORD which he commanded I. 16.40
the day I led up I. to this day, 17.05
where I have moved with all I., 17.06
word with any of the judges of I., 17.06
should be prince over my people I.; 17.07
appoint a place for my people I., 17.09
appointed judges over my people I.; 17.10
on earth is like thy people I., 17.21
make thy people I. to be thy 17.22
the God of I., is Israel's God,' and 17.24
So David reigned over all I.; 18.14
chose some of the picked men of I., 19.10
that they had been defeated by I., 19.16
David, he gathered all I. together, 19.17
And the Syrians fled before I.; 19.18
that they had been defeated by I., 19.19
And when he taunted I., Jonathan 20.07
Satan stood up against I., and 21.01
and incited David to number I. 21.01
number I., from Beersheba to Dan, 21.02
why should he bring guilt upon I.?" 21.03
departed and went throughout all I., 21.04
In all I. there were one million 21.05
with this thing, and he smote I. 21.07
throughout all the territory of I.' 21.12
the LORD sent a pestilence upon I.; 21.14
fell seventy thousand men of I. 21.14
the altar of burnt offering for I." 22.01
aliens who were in the land of I., 22.02
house for the LORD, the God of I. 22.06
peace and quiet to I. in his days. 22.09
his royal throne in I. for ever.' 22.10
you charge over I. you may keep 22.12
the LORD commanded Moses for I. 22.13
the leaders of I. to help Solomon 22.17
made Solomon his son king over I. 23.01
the leaders of I. and the priests 23.02
the God of I., has given peace to 23.25
the LORD God of I. had commanded 24.19
appointed to outside duties for I., 26.29
oversight of I. westward of the 26.30
This is the list of the people of I., 27.01
Over the tribes of I., for the 27.16
the leaders of the tribes of I. 27.22
promised to make I. as many as the 27.23
yet wrath came upon I. for this, 27.24
Jerusalem all the officials of I., 28.01
Yet the LORD God of I. chose me 28.04
house to be king over I. for ever; 28.04
in me to make me king over all I. 28.04
of the kingdom of the LORD over I. 28.05
Now therefore in the sight of all I., 28.08
the God of I. our father, for ever 29.10
and I., our fathers, keep for ever 29.18
sacrifices in abundance for all I.; 29.21
prospered, and all I. obeyed him. 29.23
repute in the sight of all I., 29.25
been on any king before him in I. 29.25
son of Jesse reigned over all I. 29.26
he reigned over I. was forty years; 29.27
that came upon him and upon I., 29.30
Solomon spoke to all I., 2Ch 1.02
and to all the leaders in all I., 1.02
And he reigned over I. 1.13
God, as ordained for ever for I. 2.04
"Blessed be the LORD God of I., 2.12
aliens who were in the land of I., 2.17
the elders of I. and all the heads 5.02
fathers' houses of the people of I., 5.02
And all the men of I. assembled 5.03
And all the elders of I. came, 5.04
and all the congregation of I., 5.06
a covenant with the people of I., 5.10
and blessed all the assembly of I., 6.03
while all the assembly of I. stood. 6.03
the God of I., who with his hand 6.04
the tribes of I. in which to build 6.05
no man as prince over my people I.; 6.05
David to be over my people I.' 6.06
name of the LORD, the God of I. 6.07
and sit on the throne of I., 6.10
name of the LORD, the God of I. 6.10
he made with the people of I." 6.11
presence of all the assembly of I. 6.12
presence of all the assembly of I., 6.13
God of I., there is no God like 6.14
God of I., keep with thy servant 6.16
me to sit upon the throne of I., 6.16
God of I., let thy word be confirmed, 6.17
thy servant and of thy people I., 6.21
"If the people I. are defeated 6.24
forgive the sin of thy people I., 6.25
thy people I., when thou dost teach 6.27
by any man or by all thy people I., 6.29
who is not of thy people I., 6.32
and fear thee, as do thy people I., 6.33
the children of I. saw the fire 7.03
sounded trumpets; and all I. stood. 7.06
and all I. with him, a very great 7.08
to Solomon and to I. his people. 7.10
not fail you a man to rule I. 7.18
settled the people of I. in them. 8.02
the Jebusites, who were not of I., 8.07
the people of I. had not destroyed— 8.08
the people of I. Solomon made no 8.09
in the house of David king of I., 8.11
your God loved I. and would 9.08
Jerusalem over all I. forty years. 9.30
for all I. had come to Shechem to 10.01
Jeroboam and all I. came and said 10.03
And when all I. saw that the king 10.16
Each of you to your tents, O I.! 10.16
So all I. departed to their tents 10.16
the people of I. who dwelt in the 10.17
the people of I. stoned him to 10.18
So I. has been in rebellion against 10.19
warriors, to fight against I., 11.01
and to all I. in Judah and Benjamin, 11.03
were in all I. resorted to him 11.13
the LORD God of I. came after them 11.16
the tribes of I. to Jerusalem to 11.16
of the LORD, and all I. with him. 12.01
Then the princes of I. and the king 12.06
the tribes of I. to put his name 12.13
"Hear me, O Jeroboam and all I.! 13.04
the LORD God of I. gave the 13.05
kingship over I. for ever to David 13.05
O sons of I., do not fight against 13.12
Jeroboam and all I. before Abijah 13.15
The men of I. fled before Judah, and 13.16

ISRAEL (cont.)
fell slain of I. five hundred thousand 2Ch 13.17
Thus the men of I. were subdued at 13.18
For a long time I. was without the 15.03
the God of I., and sought him, he 15.04
to him from I. when they saw that 15.09
the God of I., should be put to 15.13
places were not taken out of I. 15.17
Baasha king of I. went up against 16.01
your league with Baasha king of I., 16.03
armies against the cities of I., 16.04
Book of the Kings of Judah and I. 16.11
strengthened himself against I. 17.01
not according to the ways of I. 17.04
Ahab king of I. said to Jehoshaphat 18.03
Jehoshaphat said to the king of I., 18.04
Then the king of I. gathered the 18.05
And the king of I. said to Jehoshaphat, 18.07
Then the king of I. summoned an 18.08
Now the king of I. and Jehoshaphat 18.09
"I saw all I. scattered upon the 18.16
And the king of I. said to Jehoshaphat, 18.17
will entice Ahab the king of I., 18.19
And the king of I. said, "Seize 18.25
So the king of I. and Jehoshaphat 18.28
And the king of I. said to Jehoshaphat, 18.29
And the king of I. disguised 18.29
but only with the king of I." 18.30
they said, "It is the king of I." 18.31
saw that it was not the king of I., 18.32
the king of I. between the scale 18.33
and the king of I. propped himself 18.34
and heads of families of I., 19.08
of this land before thy people I., 20.07
wouldest not let I. invade when 20.10
the God of I., with a very loud 20.19
fought against the enemies of I. 20.29
in the Book of the Kings of I. 20.34
joined with Ahaziah king of I., 20.35
in the way of the kings of I., 21.06
in the way of the kings of I., 21.13
of Ahab led I. into unfaithfulness, 21.13
of Ahab king of I. to make war 22.05
the heads of fathers' houses of I., 23.02
gather from all I. money to repair 24.05
congregation of I. for the tent of 24.06
God laid upon I. in the wilderness. 24.09
because he had done good in I., 24.16
of valor from I. for a hundred 25.06
not let the army of I. go with you, 25.07
you, for the LORD is not with I., 25.07
I have given to the army of I.?" 25.09
king of I., saying, "Come, let us 25.17
the king of I. sent word to 25.18
So Joash king of I. went up; 25.21
And Judah was defeated by I., 25.22
And Joash king of I. captured 25.23
the son of Jehoahaz, king of I. 25.25
Book of the Kings of Judah and I.? 25.26
Book of the Kings of I. and Judah. 27.07
in the ways of the kings of I. 28.02
drove out before the people of I. 28.03
into the hand of the king of I., 28.05
The men of I. took captive two 28.08
there is fierce wrath against I. 28.13
low because of Ahaz king of I., 28.19
the ruin of him and all I. 28.23
Book of the Kings of Judah and I. 28.26
into the tombs of the kings of I. 28.27
in the holy place to the God of I. 29.07
the God of I., that his fierce 29.10
to make atonement for all I. 29.24
offering should be made for all I. 29.24
instruments of David king of I. 29.27
Hezekiah sent to all I. and Judah, 30.01
passover to the LORD the God of I. 30.01
a proclamation throughout all I., 30.05
LORD the God of I., at Jerusalem; 30.05
throughout all I. and Judah with 30.06
"O people of I., return to the LORD, 30.06
and I., that he may turn again to 30.06
And the people of I. that were 30.21
whole assembly that came out of I., 30.25
who came out of the land of I., 30.25
David king of I. there had been 30.26
all I. who were present went out to 31.01
the people of I. returned to their 31.01
the people of I. gave in abundance 31.05
And the people of I. and Judah who 31.06
blessed the LORD and his people I. 31.08
LORD the God of I. and to speak 32.17
Book of the Kings of Judah and I. 32.32
drove out before the people of I. 33.02
chosen out of all the tribes of I., 33.07
the foot of I. from the land which 33.08
destroyed before the people of I. 33.09
to serve the LORD the God of I. 33.16
the name of the LORD the God of I., 33.18
the Chronicles of the Kings of I. 33.18
throughout all the land of I. 34.07
the remnant of I. and from all 34.09
who are left in I. and in Judah, 34.21
the God of I.: 'Tell the man who 34.23
the God of I.: Regarding the words 34.26
that belonged to the people of I., 34.33
all who were in I. serve the LORD 34.33
who taught all I. and who were 35.03
son of David, king of I., built; 35.03
LORD your God and his people I. 35.03
David king of I. and the directions 35.04
And the people of I. who were 35.17
been kept in I. since the days of 35.18
of the kings of I. had kept such a 35.18
all Judah and I. who were present, 35.18
They made these an ordinance in I.; 35.25
Book of the Kings of I. and Judah. 35.27
Book of the Kings of I. and Judah; 36.08
turning to the LORD, the God of I. 36.13
the God of I.—he is the God who is Ez 1.03
of the men of the people of I.: 2.02
whether they belonged to I.: 2.59
towns, and all I. in their towns. 2.70
and the sons of I. were in the 3.01
built the altar of the God of I., 3.02
the directions of David king of I.; 3.10
love endures for ever toward I. 3.11
temple of the LORD, the God of I., 4.01
fathers' houses in I. said to them, 4.03
the God of I., as King Cyrus the 4.03
of the God of I. who was over them. 5.01
a great king of I. built and 5.11
of the God of I. and by decree of 6.14
And the people of I., the priests 6.16
offering for all I. twelve he-goats, 6.17
to the number of the tribes of I. 6.17
the people of I. who had returned 6.21
to worship the LORD, the God of I. 6.21
of the house of God, the God of I. 6.22
the LORD the God of I. had given; 7.06
the king, some of the people of I., 7.07
his statutes and ordinances in I. 7.10
the LORD and his statutes for I.: 7.11
the people of I. or their priests 7.13
freely offered to the God of I., 7.15
men from I. to go up with me. 7.28
son of I., namely Sherebiah with 8.18
lords and all I. there present had 8.25
fathers' houses in I. at Jerusalem, 8.29
burnt offerings to the God of I., 8.35
of Israel, twelve bulls for all I., 8.35
"The people of I. and the priests 9.01
at the words of the God of I., 9.04
O LORD the God of I., thou art just, 9.15
children, gathered to him out of I.; 10.01

ISRAEL (cont.)
is hope for I. in spite of this. Ez 10.02
Levites and all I. take oath that 10.05
and so increased the guilt of I. 10.10
And of I.: of the sons of Parosh: 10.25
for the people of I. thy servants, Neh 1.06
the sins of the people of I., 1.06
the welfare of the children of I. 2.10
of the men of the people of I.: 7.07
whether they belonged to I.: 7.61
and all I., lived in their towns. 7.73
the children of I. were in their 7.73
which the LORD had given to I. 8.01
the people of I. should dwell in 8.14
the people of I. had not done so. 8.17
the people of I. were assembled 9.01
offerings to make atonement for I., 10.33
For the people of I. and the sons 10.39
I., the priests, the Levites, the 11.03
And the rest of I., and of the priests 11.20
And all I. in the days of Zerubbabel 12.47
the children of I. with bread and 13.02
separated from I. all those of 13.03
more wrath upon I. by profaning 13.18
Solomon king of I. sin on account 13.26
and God made him king over all I.; 13.26
deliverance for I. would come out Ps 14.07
shall rejoice, I. shall be glad. 14.07
enthroned on the praises of I. 22.03
in awe of him, all you sons of I.! 22.23
Redeem I., O God, out of all his 25.22
the God of I., from everlasting to 41.13
O I., I will testify against you. 50.07
deliverance for I. would come from 53.06
Jacob will rejoice and I. be glad. 53.06
Thou, LORD God of hosts, art God of I. 59.05
the presence of God, the God of I. 68.08
to God, whose majesty is over I., 68.34
the God of I., he gives power and 68.35
dishonor through me, O God of I. 69.06
with the lyre, O Holy One of I. 71.22
the God of I., who alone does 72.18
is known, his name is great in I. 76.01
Jacob, and appointed a law in I., 78.05
his anger mounted against I.; 78.21
and laid low the picked men of I. 78.31
and provoked the Holy One of I. 78.41
the tribes of I. in their tents. 78.55
wrath, and he utterly rejected I. 78.59
Jacob his people, of I. his inheritance. 78.71
O Shepherd of I., thou who leadest 80.01
For it is a statute for I., 81.04
O I., if you would but listen to me! 81.08
I would have none of me. 81.11
that I. would walk in my ways! 81.13
let the name of I. be remembered no 83.04
our king to the Holy One of I. 89.18
faithfulness to the house of I. 98.03
his acts to the people of I. 103.07
to I. as an everlasting covenant, 105.10
Then I. came to Egypt; Jacob sojourned 105.23
Then he led forth I. with silver 105.37
the God of I., from everlasting to 106.48
When I. went forth from Egypt, the 114.01
his sanctuary, I. his dominion. 114.02
O I., trust in the LORD! He is their 115.09
he will bless the house of I.; 115.12
Let I. say, "His steadfast love 118.02
he who keeps I. will neither 121.04
of the LORD, as was decreed for I., 122.04
was on our side, let I. now say— 124.01
with evildoers! Peace be in I.! 125.05
children's children! Peace be upon I.! 128.06
from my youth," let I. now say— 129.01
O I, hope in the LORD! 130.07
And he will redeem I. from all his 130.08
O I., hope in the LORD from this 131.03
for himself, I. as his own possession. 135.04
a heritage to his people I. 135.12
O house of I., bless the LORD! 135.19
and brought I. out from among them, 136.11
and made I. pass through the midst 136.14
a heritage to I. his servant, for 136.22
he gathers the outcasts of I. 147.02
his statutes and ordinances to I. 147.19
the people of I. who are near to 148.14
Let I. be glad in his Maker, let the 149.02
Solomon, son of David, king of I.: Pro 1.01
been king over I. in Jerusalem. Ecc 1.12
men of the mighty men of I., Sol 3.07
but I. does not know, my people does Is 1.03
have despised the Holy One of I., 1.04
of hosts, the Mighty One of I.: 1.24
and glory of the survivors of I. 4.02
LORD of hosts is the house of I., 5.07
of the Holy One of I. draw near, 5.19
the word of the Holy One of I. 5.24
the king of I. came up to Jerusalem 7.01
of stumbling to both houses of I., 8.14
and portents in I. from the LORD 8.18
Jacob, and it will light upon I.; 9.08
the west devour I. with open mouth. 9.12
LORD cut off from I. head and tail, 9.14
The light of I. will become a fire, 10.17
the remnant of I. and the survivors 10.20
LORD, the Holy One of I., in truth. 10.20
your people I. be as the sand of 10.22
will assemble the outcasts of I., 11.12
there was for I. when they came up 11.16
your midst is the Holy One of I. 12.06
on Jacob and will again choose I., 14.01
the house of I. will possess them 14.02
the glory of the children of I., 17.03
tree, says the LORD God of I. 17.06
will look to the Holy One of I.; 17.07
because of the children of I., 17.09
In that day I. will be the third 19.24
of my hands, and I. my heritage. 19.25
the God of I., I announce to you. 21.10
LORD, the God of I., has spoken. 21.17
name of the LORD, the God of I. 24.15
I. shall blossom and put forth 27.06
gathered one by one, O people of I. 27.12
shall exult in the Holy One of I. 29.19
will stand in awe of the God of I. 29.23
hear no more of the Holy One of I. 30.11
Therefore thus says the Holy One of I., 30.12
the Lord GOD, the Holy One of I., 30.15
of the LORD, to the Rock of I. 30.29
the Holy One of I. or consult the 31.01
deeply revolted, O people of I. 31.06
God of I., who art enthroned above 37.16
the God of I.: Because you have 37.21
Against the Holy One of I.! 37.23
O I., "My way is hid from the LORD, 40.27
But you, I., my servant, Jacob, whom I 41.08
not, you worm Jacob, you men of I.! 41.14
Redeemer is the Holy One of I. 41.14
the Holy One of I. you shall glory. 41.16
I the God of I. will not forsake 41.17
the Holy One of I. has created it. 41.20
the spoiler, and I. to the robbers? 42.24
O I.: "Fear not, for I have redeemed 43.01
the Holy One of I., your Savior. 43.03
your Redeemer, the Holy One of I.: 43.14
One, the Creator of I., your King. 43.15
you have been weary of me, O I.! 43.22
destruction and I. to reviling. 43.28
my servant, I. whom I have chosen! 44.01
surname himself by the name of I. 44.05
the King of I. and his Redeemer, the 44.06
and I., for you are my servant; 44.21
O I., you will not be forgotten by 44.21
Jacob, and will be glorified in I. 44.23

ISRAEL (cont.)

the God of I., who call you by Is 45.03
and I. my chosen, I call you by your 45.04
Thus says the LORD, the Holy One of I., 45.11
thyself, O God of I., the Savior. 45.15
But I. is saved by the LORD with 45.17
offspring of I. shall triumph and 45.25
all the remnant of the house of I., 46.03
salvation in Zion, for I. my glory. 46.13
is his name—is the Holy One of I. 47.04
who are called by the name of I., 48.01
LORD, and confess the God of I., 48.01
stay themselves on the God of I.; 48.02
me, O Jacob, and I., whom I called! 48.12
your Redeemer, the Holy One of I.: 48.17
I., in whom I will be glorified. 49.03
and that I. might be gathered to 49.05
and to restore the preserved of I.; 49.06
the Redeemer of I. and his Holy 49.07
is faithful, the Holy One of I., 49.07
and the God of I. will be your 52.12
the Holy One of I. is your Redeemer, 54.05
God, and of the Holy One of I., 55.05
who gathers the outcasts of I., 56.08
God, and for the Holy One of I., 60.09
the Zion of the Holy One of I. 60.14
to the house of I. which he has 63.07
not know us and I. does not acknowledge 63.16
I. was holy to the LORD, the first Jer 2.03
the families of the house of I. 2.04
"Is I. a slave? Is he a homeborn 2.14
so the house of I. shall be shamed: 2.26
Have I been a wilderness to I., 2.31
I, how she went up on every high 3.06
I., I had sent her away with a 3.08
"Faithless I. has shown herself 3.11
faithless I., says the LORD. 3.12
Judah shall join the house of I., 3.18
me, O house of I., says the LORD. 3.20
our God is the salvation of I. 3.23
O I., says the LORD, to me you 4.01
For the house of I. and the house 5.11
afar, O house of I., says the LORD. 5.15
as a vine the remnant of I.; 6.09
the God of I., Amend your ways and 7.03
for the wickedness of my people I. 7.12
the God of I.: "Add your burnt 7.21
the God of I.: Behold, I will feed 9.15
the house of I. is uncircumcised 9.26
LORD speaks to you, O house of I. 10.01
and I. is the tribe of his inheritance 10.16
the God of I.: Cursed be the man who 11.03
the house of I. and the house of 11.10
the house of I. and the house of 11.17
have given my people I. to inherit: 12.14
whole house of I. and the whole 13.11
the God of I., "Every jar shall be 13.12
O thou hope of I., its savior in 14.08
the God of I.: Behold, I will make to 16.09
the people of I. out of the land 16.14
the people of I. out of the north 16.15
the hope of I., all who forsake 17.13
"O house of I., can I not do with 18.06
are you in my hand, O house of I. 18.06
The virgin I. has done a very 18.13
the God of I., Behold, I am bringing 19.03
the God of I., Behold, I am bringing 19.15
the God of I.: Behold, I will turn 21.04
the God of I., concerning the 23.02
and I. will dwell securely. 23.06
the people of I. out of the land 23.07
of the house of I. out of the 23.08
Baal and led my people I. astray. 23.13
the God of I.: Like these good figs, 24.05
the God of I., said to me: "Take 25.15
the God of I.: Drink, be drunk and 25.27
the God of I.: This is what you 27.04
the God of I., concerning the 27.21
the God of I.: I have broken the 28.02
the God of I.: I have put upon the 28.14
the God of I., to all the exiles 29.04
the God of I.: Do not let your 29.08
the God of I., concerning Ahab the 29.21
because they have committed folly in I., 29.23
the God of I.: You have sent letters 29.25
the God of I.: Write in a book all 30.02
I. and Judah, says the LORD, and I 30.03
spoke concerning I. and Judah: 30.04
the LORD, nor be dismayed, O I.; 30.10
the God of all the families of I., 31.01
wilderness; when I. sought for rest, 31.02
you shall be built, O virgin I.! 31.04
his people, the remnant of I. 31.07
for I am a father to I., 31.09
who scattered I. will gather him, 31.10
O virgin, I., return to these your 31.21
the God of I.: "Once more they shall 31.23
the house of I. and the house of 31.27
the house of I. and the house of 31.31
the house of I. after those days, 31.33
descendants of I. cease from being 31.36
descendants of I. for all that 31.37
the God of I.: Take these deeds, both 32.14
the God of I.: Houses and fields and 32.15
to this day in I. and among all 32.20
thy people I. out of the land of 32.21
For the sons of I. and the sons of 32.30
the sons of I. have done nothing 32.30
of the sons of I. and the sons of 32.32
the God of I., concerning this city 32.36
the God of I., concerning the 33.04
of Judah and the fortunes of I., 33.07
to the house of I. and the house 33.14
on the throne of the house of I., 33.17
the God of I.: Go and speak to 34.02
the God of I.: I made a covenant 34.13
the God of I.: Go and say to the men 35.13
the God of I.: Behold, I am bringing 35.17
the God of I.: Because you have 35.18
the God of I.: Jonadab the son of 35.19
to you against I. and Judah and 36.02
God of I.: Thus shall you say to the 37.07
the God of I., If you will surrender 38.17
the God of I.: Behold I will fulfil 39.16
defense against Baasha king of I.; 41.09
the God of I., to whom you sent me 42.09
the God of I.: If you set your faces 42.15
the God of I.: As my anger and my 42.18
the God of I.: Behold, I will send 43.10
the God of I.: You have seen all the 44.02
the God of I.: Why do you commit 44.07
the God of I.: Behold, I will set my 44.11
the God of I.: You and your wives 44.25
the God of I., to you, O Baruch: 45.02
the God of I., said: "Behold, I am 46.25
my servant, nor be dismayed, O I.; 46.27
the God of I.: "Woe to Nebo, for it 48.01
as the house of I. was ashamed of 48.13
Was not I. a derision to you? 48.27
Thus says the LORD: "Has I. no sons? 49.01
then I. shall dispossess those who 49.02
the people of I. and the people of 50.04
"I. is a hunted sheep driven away 50.17
the God of I.: Behold, I am bringing 50.18
I will restore I. to his pasture, 50.19
iniquity shall be sought in I., 50.20
the LORD, the Holy One of I. 50.29
The people of I. are oppressed, and 50.33
For I. and Judah have not been 51.05
guilt against the Holy One of I. 51.05
and I. is the tribe of his inheritance; 51.19
the God of I.: The daughter of 51.33
Babylon must fall for the slain of I., 51.49
heaven to earth the splendor of I.; Lam 2.01

ISRAEL (cont.)
fierce anger all the might of I.; Lam 2.03
like an enemy, he has destroyed I.; 2.05
I send you to the people of I., Eze 2.03
and go, speak to the house of I. 3.01
go, get you to the house of I., 3.04
language, but to the house of I.— 3.05
But the house of I. will not listen 3.07
the house of I. are of a hard 3.07
you a watchman for the house of I.; 3.17
This is a sign for the house of I. 4.03
of the house of I. upon you; 4.04
the punishment of the house of I. 4.05
the people of I. eat their bread 4.13
forth into all the house of I. 5.04
face toward the mountains of I., 6.02
and say, You mountains of I., 6.03
the people of I. before their 6.05
abominations of the house of I.; 6.11
Lord God to the land of I.: An end! 7.02
glory of the God of I. was there, 8.04
the house of I. are committing 8.06
all the idols of the house of I. 8.10
of the elders of the house of I., 8.11
of the house of I. are doing in 8.12
of the God of I. had gone up from 9.03
that remains of I. in the outpouring 9.08
of the house of I. and Judah is 9.09
of the God of I. was over them. 10.19
the God of I. by the river Chebar; 10.20
Lord: So you think, O house of I.; 11.05
will judge you at the border of I.; 11.10
will judge you at the border of I.; 11.11
a full end of the remnant of I.? 11.13
exiles, the whole house of I., 11.15
and I will give you the land of I. 11.17
of the God of I. was over them. 11.22
you a sign for the house of I. 12.06
"Son of man, has not the house of I., 12.09
all the house of I. who are in it. 12.10
of Jerusalem in the land of I.: 12.19
that you have about the land of I., 12.22
no more use it as a proverb in I. 12.23
divination within the house of I. 12.24
they of the house of I. say, 12.27
prophesy against the prophets of I., 13.02
been like foxes among ruins, O I. 13.04
up a wall for the house of I., 13.05
in the register of the house of I., 13.09
shall they enter the land of I.; 13.09
the prophets of I. who prophesied 13.16
certain of the elders of I. to me, 14.01
of the house of I. who takes his 14.04
of the hearts of the house of I., 14.05
"Therefore say to the house of I., 14.06
For any one of the house of I., 14.07
the strangers that sojourn in I., 14.07
him from the midst of my people I. 14.09
that the house of I. may go no more 14.11
an allegory to the house of I.; 17.02
height of I. will I plant it, that 17.23
proverb concerning the land of I., 18.02
shall no more be used by you in I. 18.03
to the idols of the house of I., 18.06
to the idols of the house of I., 18.15
O house of I.: Is my way not just? 18.25
Yet the house of I. says, 18.29
O house of I., are my ways not 18.29
O house of I., every one according 18.30
Why will you die, O house of I.? 18.31
lamentation for the princes of I., 19.01
be heard upon the mountains of I. 19.09
the elders of I. came to inquire 20.01
"Son of man, speak to the elders of I., 20.03
God: On the day when I chose I., 20.05
But the house of I. rebelled 20.13
to the house of I. and say to them, 20.27
Wherefore say to the house of I., 20.30
inquired of by you, O house of I.? 20.31
shall not enter the land of I. 20.38
O house of I., thus says the Lord 20.39
mountain, the mountain height of I., 20.40
God, there all the house of I., 20.40
I bring you into the land of I., 20.42
O house of I., says the Lord God. 20.44
prophesy against the land of I. 21.02
and say to the land of I., Thus says 21.03
is against all the princes of I.; 21.12
prince of I., whose day has come, 21.25
"Behold, the princes of I. in you, 22.06
the house of I. has become dross to 22.18
'Say to the house of I., Thus says 24.21
the land of I. when it was made 25.03
within you against the land of I., 25.06
Edom by the hand of my people I.; 25.14
Judah and the land of I. traded 27.17
the house of I. there shall be no 28.24
the house of I. from the peoples 28.25
a staff of reed to the house of I.; 29.06
be the reliance of the house of I., 29.16
to spring forth to the house of I., 29.21
a watchman for the house of I.; 33.07
son of man, say to the house of I., 33.10
why will you die, O house of I.? 33.11
O house of I., I will judge each 33.20
in the land of I. keep saying, 33.24
mountains of I. shall be so desolate 33.28
prophesy against the shepherds of I., and say 34.02
shepherds of I. who have been 34.02
feed them on the mountains of I., 34.13
heights of I. shall be their 34.14
shall feed on the mountains of I. 34.14
the house of I., are my people, says 34.30
the people of I. to the power of 35.05
against the mountains of I., 35.12
the inheritance of the house of I., 35.15
prophesy to the mountains of I., 36.01
I., and say, O mountains of I., 36.01
therefore, O mountains of I., 36.04
prophesy concerning the land of I., 36.06
"But you, O mountains of I., 36.08
yield your fruit to my people I.; 36.08
the whole house of I., all of it; 36.10
walk upon you, even my people I.; 36.12
the house of I. dwelt in their own 36.17
the house of I. caused to be 36.21
"Therefore say to the house of I., 36.22
O house of I., that I am about to 36.22
for your ways, O house of I. 36.32
the house of I. ask me to do for 36.37
bones are the whole house of I. 37.11
bring you home into the land of I. 37.12
the children of I. associated with 37.16
the house of I. associated with 37.16
the tribes of I. associated with 37.19
the people of I. from the nations 37.21
the land, upon the mountains of I.; 37.22
know that I the Lord sanctify I., 37.28
nations upon the mountains of I., 38.08
when my people I. are dwelling 38.14
you will come up against my people I., 38.16
by my servants the prophets of I., 38.17
shall come against the land of I., 38.18
a great shaking in the land of I.; 38.19
you against the mountains of I.; 39.02
fall upon the mountains of I., 39.04
kown in the midst of my people I.; 39.07
I am the Lord, the Holy One in I. 39.07
the cities of I. will go forth and 39.09
to Gog a place for burial in I., 39.11
the house of I. will be burying 39.12
feast upon the mountains of I., 39.17
The house of I. shall know that I 39.22
the house of I. went into captivity 39.23

ISRAEL (cont.)
mercy upon the whole house of I.; Eze 39.25
out my Spirit upon the house of I., 39.29
visions of God into the land of I., 40.02
that you see to the house of I. 40.04
of the God of I. came from the 43.02
midst of the people of I. for ever. 43.07
the house of I. shall no more 43.07
to the house of I. the temple and 43.10
the God of I., has entered by it; 44.02
rebellious house, to the house of I., 44.06
O house of I., let there be an end 44.06
who are among the people of I., 44.09
their idols when I. went astray, 44.10
of iniquity to the house of I., 44.12
the people of I. went astray from 44.15
of the stock of the house of I., 44.22
give them no possession in I.; 44.28
thing in I. shall be theirs. 44.29
belong to the whole house of I. 45.06
It is to be his property in I. 45.08
the house of I. have the land 45.08
Lord God: Enough, O princes of I.! 45.09
hundred, from the families of I. 45.15
this offering to the prince in I. 45.16
appointed feasts of the house of I.: 45.17
make atonement for the house of I. 45.17
among the twelve tribes of I. 47.13
between Gilead and the land of I.; 47.18
you according to the tribes of I. 47.21
to you as native-born sons of I.; 47.22
inheritance among the tribes of I. 47.22
when the people of I. went astray, 48.11
the tribes of I., shall till it. 48.19
inheritance among the tribes of I., 48.29
being named after the tribes of I. 48.31
to bring some of the people of I., Dan 1.03
and to all I., those that are near 9.07
All I. has transgressed thy law and 9.11
my sin and the sin of my people I., 9.20
the son of Joash, king of I. Hos 1.01
to the kingdom of the house of I. 1.04
the bow of I. in the valley of 1.05
more have pity on the house of I., 1.06
the people of I. shall be like the 1.10
the people of I. shall be gathered 1.11
as the Lord loves the people of I., 3.01
For the children of I. shall dwell 3.04
Afterward the children of I. shall 3.05
word of the Lord, O people of I.; 4.01
O I., let not Judah become guilty. 4.15
Like a stubborn heifer, I. is stubborn; 4.16
Give heed, O house of I.! 5.01
and I. is not hid from me; 5.03
played the harlot, I. is defiled. 5.03
The pride of I. testifies to his 5.05
the tribes of I. I declare what is 5.09
In the house of I. I have seen a 6.10
harlotry is there, I. is defiled. 6.10
when I would heal I., the corruption 7.01
The pride of I. witnesses against 7.10
they cry, My God, we I. know thee. 8.02
I. has spurned the good; the enemy 8.03
in I.? A workman made it; 8.06
I. is swallowed up; already they are 8.08
For I. has forgotten his Maker, and 8.14
Rejoice not, O I.! Exult not 9.01
I. shall know it. The prophet is a fool, 9.07
in the wilderness, I found I. 9.10
I. is a luxuriant vine that yields 10.01
and I. shall be ashamed of his idol. 10.06
the sin of I., shall be destroyed. 10.08
of Gibeah, you have sinned, O I.; 10.09
O house of I., because of your 10.15
the king of I. shall be utterly 10.15
When I. was a child, I loved him, and 11.01
How can I hand you over, O I.! 11.08
and the house of I. with deceit; 11.12
there I. did service for a wife, and 12.12
the Lord brought I. up from Egypt, 12.13
he was exalted in I.; but he incurred 13.01
I will destroy you, O I.; who can 13.09
Return, O I., to the Lord your God, 14.01
I will be as the dew to I.; 14.05
know that I am in the midst of I., Joe 2.27
of my people and my heritage I., 3.02
a stronghold to the people of I. 3.16
saw concerning I. in the days of Amo 1.01
king of I., two years before the 1.01
"For three transgressions of I., 2.06
it not indeed so, O people of I.?" 2.11
O people of I., against the whole 3.01
the people of I. who dwell in 3.12
day I punish I. for his transgressions, 3.14
so you love to do, O people of I.!" 4.05
"Therefore thus I will do to you, O I.; 4.12
prepare to meet your God, O I.!" 4.12
you in lamentation, O house of I.: 5.01
"Fallen, no more to rise, is the virgin I.; 5.02
have ten left to the house of I." 5.03
says the Lord to the house of I.: 5.04
in the wilderness, O house of I.? 5.25
to whom the house of I. come! 6.01
O house of I.," says the Lord, the 6.14
line in the midst of my people I.; 7.08
sanctuaries of I. shall be laid 7.09
Bethel sent to Jeroboam king of I., 7.10
in the midst of the house of I.; 7.10
and I. must go into exile away from 7.11
me, "Go, prophesy to my people I.' 7.15
say, 'Do not prophesy against I., 7.16
and I. shall surely go into exile 7.17
"The end has come upon my people I.; 8.02
Ethiopians to me, O people of I.?" 9.07
I not bring up I. from the land of 9.07
the house of I. among all the 9.09
the fortunes of my people I., 9.14
the people of I. shall possess Ob 1.20
for the sins of the house of I. Mic 1.05
found the transgressions of I. 1.13
deceitful thing to the kings of I. 1.14
the glory of I. shall come to 1.15
I will gather the remnant of I.; 2.12
and rulers of the houe of I.! 3.01
transgression and to I. his sin. 3.08
and rulers of the house of I., 3.09
upon the cheek the ruler of I. 5.01
me one who is to be ruler in I., 5.02
shall return to the people of I. 5.03
and he will contend with I. 6.02
of Jacob as the majesty of I., Nah 2.02
the God of I., "Moab shall become Zep 2.09
those who are left in I.; 3.13
shout, O I.! Rejoice and exult 3.14
The King of I., the Lord, is in your 3.15
scattered Judah, I., and Jerusalem." Zec 1.19
O house of Judah and house of I., 8.13
Aram, even as all the tribes of I.; 9.01
brotherhood between Judah and I. 11.14
The word of the Lord concerning I.: 12.01
word of the Lord to I. by Malachi. Mal 1.01
the Lord, beyond the border of I.!" 1.05
committed in I. and in Jerusalem; 2.11
says the Lord the God of I., 2.16
commanded him at Horeb for all I. 4.04
ruler who will govern my people I.'" Mt 2.06
mother, and go to the land of I., 2.20
mother, and went to the land of I. 2.21
not even in I. have I found such 8.10
was anything like this seen in I." 9.33
the lost sheep of the house of I. 10.06
gone through all the towns of I., 10.23
the lost sheep of the house of I." 15.24
and they glorified the God of I. 15.31

ISRAEL (cont.)
judging the twelve tribes of I. Mt 19.28
set by some of the sons of I., 27.09
He is the King of I.; 27.42
O I.: The Lord our God, the Lord is Mk 12.29
the King of I., come down now from 15.32
of the sons of I. to the Lord Lk 1.16
He has helped his servant I., 1.54
"Blessed be the Lord God of I., 1.68
the day of his manifestation to I. 1.80
looking for the consolation of I., 2.25
and for glory to thy people I." 2.32
the fall and rising of many in I., 2.34
many widows in I. in the days of 4.25
many lepers in I. in the time of 4.27
not even in I. have I found such 7.09
judging the twelve tribes of I. 22.30
that he was the one to redeem I. 24.21
that he might be revealed to I. Jn 1.31
Son of God! You are the King of I.!" 1.49
him, "Are you a teacher of I., 3.10
of the Lord, even the King of I.!" 12.13
time restore the kingdom to I.?" Ac 1.06
"Men of I., hear these words: Jesus 2.22
the house of I. therefore know 2.36
"Men of I., why do you wonder at 3.12
all, and to all the people of I., 4.10
Gentiles and the peoples of I., 4.27
council and all the senate of I., 5.21
repentance to I. and forgiveness 5.31
"Men of I., take care what you do 5.35
visit his brethren, the sons of I. 7.23
in the wilderness, O house of I.? 7.42
and kings and the sons of I.; 9.15
You know the word which he sent to I., 10.36
"Men of I., and you that fear God, 13.16
of this people I. chose our 13.17
God has brought to I. a savior, 13.23
repentance to all the people of I. 13.24
crying out, "Men of I., help! 21.28
of the hope of I. that I am bound 28.20
descended from I. belong to I., Rom 9.06
And Isaiah cries out concerning I.: 9.27
of the sons of I. be as the sand 9.27
but that I. who pursued the righteousness 9.31
Again I ask, did I. not understand? 10.19
But of I. he says, "All day long I 10.21
how he pleads with God against I.? 11.02
I. failed to obtain what it sought. 11.07
Gentiles, so as to make I. jealous. 11.11
hardening has come upon part of I., 11.25
and so all I. will be saved; 11.26
Consider the practice of I.; 1Co 10.18
by this rule, upon the I. of God. Gal 6.16
from the commonwealth of I., Eph 2.12
eighth day, of the people of I., Php 3.05
the house of I. and with the house Heb 8.08
the house of I. after those days, 8.10
block before the sons of I., Rev 2.14
of every tribe of the sons of I., 7.04
of the sons of I. were inscribed; 21.12

ISRAELITE
Now an I. woman's son, whose father Lev 24.10
and the I. woman's son and a man of 24.10
and the I. woman's son blasphemed 24.11
an I. indeed, in whom is no guile!" Jn 1.47
I myself am an I., a descendant of Rom 11.01

ISRAELITES
Therefore to this day the I. do not Gen 32.32
any king reigned over the I. 36.31
of the cattle of the I. was dead. Ex 9.07
For whenever the I. put in seed the Ju 6.03
twenty-two thousand men of the I. 20.21
to all the I. who came there. 1Sa 2.14
one of the I. went down to the 13.20
to be with the I. who were with 14.21
And the I. came back from chasing 17.53
and the I. were encamped by the 29.01
the I. rose and attacked the 2Ki 3.24
he carried the I. away to Assyria, 17.06
carried the I. away to Assyria, and 18.11
any king reigned over the I.: 1Ch 1.43
And the I. separated themselves Neh 9.02
just as the I. bring their cereal Is 66.20
This is the Moses who said to the I., Ac 7.37
They are I., and to them belong the Rom 9.04
that the I. could not look at 2Co 3.07
so that the I. might not see the 3.13
Are they I.? 11.22
exodus of the I. and gave directions Heb 11.22

ISRAEL'S
his right hand toward I. left hand, Gen 48.13
his left hand toward I. right hand, 48.13
and to the Egyptians for I. sake, Ex 18.08
I. first-born, their generations, by Num 1.20
the people of I. half you shall 31.30
From the people of I. half, 31.42
from the people of I. half Moses 31.47
of the king of I. servants answered, 2Ki 3.11
is I. God,' and the house of thy 1Ch 17.24
LORD, O you who are of I. fountain! Ps 68.26
weeping and pleading of I. sons, Jer 3.21

ISSACHAR
my husband": so she called his name I. Gen 30.18
Levi, Judah, I., and Zebulun. 35.23
The sons of I.: Tola, Puvah, Iob, and 46.13
I. is a strong ass, crouching 49.14
I., Zebulun, and Benjamin, Ex 1.03
from I., Nethanel the son of Zuar; Num 1.08
Of the people of I., their generations, 1.28
of the tribe of I. was fifty-four 1.29
to him shall be the tribe of I., 2.05
the people of I. being Nethanel 2.05
the leader of I., made an offering; 7.18
of the men of I. was Nethanel the 10.15
from the tribe of I., Igal the son of 13.07
The sons of I. according to their 26.23
the families of I. according to 26.25
tribe of the sons of I. a leader, 34.26
Levi, Judah, I., Joseph, and Benjamin. Deu 27.12
your going out; and I., in your tents. 33.18
is reached, and on the east I. Jos 17.10
Also in I. and in Asher Manasseh 17.11
The fourth lot came out for I., 19.17
for I., for the tribe of I. 19.17
the inheritance of the tribe of I., 19.23
the families of the tribe of I., 21.06
and out of the tribe of I., 21.28
the princes of I. came with Deborah, Ju 5.15
and I. faithful to Barak; 5.15
of Puah, son of Dodo, a man of I.; 10.01
Jehoshaphat the son of Paruah, in I.; 1Ki 4.17
son of Ahijah, of the house of I., 15.27
Simeon, Levi, Judah, I., Zebulun, 1Ch 2.01
cities out of the tribes of I., 6.62
and out of the tribe of I.: 6.72
The sons of I.: Tola, Puah, Jashub, and 7.01
the families of I. were in all 7.05
Of I. men who had understanding of 12.32
from as far as I. and Zebulun and 12.40
I. the seventh, Peullethai the 26.05
for I., Omri the son of Michael; 27.18
I., and Zebulun, had not cleansed 2Ch 30.18
side to the west, I., one portion Eze 48.25
Adjoining the territory of I., 48.26
the gate of I., and the gate of 48.33
thousand of the tribe of I., Rev 7.07

ISSHIAH
and I., five, all of them chief men; 1Ch 7.03
Elkanah, I., Azarel, Joezer, and 12.06

ISSHIAH (cont.)
Micah the chief and I. the second. 1Ch 23.20
the sons of Rehabiah, I. the chief 24.21
The brother of Micah, I.; 24.25
of the sons of I., Zechariah. 24.25

ISSHIJAH
I., Malchijah, Shemaiah, Shimeon, Ez 10.31

ISSUE
he is the first i. of his strength; Deu 21.17
the first i. of their strength in Ps 78.51
the first of all their strength. 105.36
house, the offspring and i., Is 22.24
and whose i. was like that of Eze 23.20
shall be the i. of these things?" Dan 12.08
From the throne i. flashes of Rev 4.05

ISSUED
a decree was i. by Cyrus the king Ez 5.17
king, Cyrus the king i. a decree: 6.03
was to be i. as a decree in every Est 3.14
the decree was i. in Susa the 3.15
written decree i. in Susa for 4.08
was to be i. as a decree in every 8.13
the decree was i. in Susa the 8.14
a decree was i. in Susa, and the ten 9.14
A stream of fire i. and came forth Dan 7.10
from his mouth i. a sharp two-edged Rev 1.16
and sulphur i. from their mouths. 9.17

ISSUES
is love that i. from a pure heart 1Ti 1.05
From his mouth i. a sharp sword Rev 19.15
the sword that i. from his mouth; 19.21

ISSUING
water was i. from below the threshold Eze 47.01
and sulphur i. from their mouths. Rev 9.18
And I saw, i. from the mouth of the 16.13

ITALIAN
what was known as the I. Cohort, Ac 10.01

ITALY
come from I. with his wife Priscilla, Ac 18.02
decided that we should sail for I., 27.01
ship of Alexandria sailing for I., 27.06
who come from I. send you greetings. Heb 13.24

ITCH
it is an i., a leprosy of the head Lev 13.30
and if the i. has not spread, and 13.32
and the i. appears to be no deeper 13.32
but the i. he shall not shave; 13.33
the priest shall examine the i., 13.34
and if the i. has not spread in the 13.34
But if the i. spreads in the skin 13.35
and if the i. has spread in the 13.36
But if in his eyes the i. is checked, 13.37
the i. is healed, he is clean; 13.37
any leprous disease: for an i., 14.54
a discharge or an i. or scabs, 22.22
ulcers and the scurvy and the i., Deu 28.27

ITCHING
the priest examines the i. disease, Lev 13.31
person with the i. disease for 13.31
person with the i. disease for 13.33
his sight or an i. disease or 21.20
but having i. ears they will 2Ti 4.03

ITHAI
I. the son of Ribai of Gibeah of 1Ch 11.31

ITHAMAR
him Nadab, Abihu, Eleazar, and I. Ex 6.23
Nadab and Abihu, Eleazar and I. 28.01
direction of I. the son of Aaron 38.21
to Aaron and to Eleazar and I., Lev 10.06
to Aaron and to Eleazar and I., 10.12
he was angry with Eleazar and I., 10.16
first-born, and Abihu, Eleazar, and I.; Num 3.02
So Eleazar and I. served as priests 3.04
oversight of I. the son of Aaron 4.28
the hand of I. the son of Aaron 4.33
direction of I. the son of Aaron 7.08
born Nadab, Abihu, Eleazar and I. 26.60
Nadab, Abihu, Eleazar, and I. 1Ch 6.03
Nadab, Abihu, Eleazar, and I. 24.01
so Eleazar and I. became the 24.02
and Ahimelech of the sons of I., 24.03
Eleazar than among the sons of I., 24.04
and eight of the sons of I. 24.04
sons of Eleazar and the sons of I. 24.05
for Eleazar and one chosen for I. 24.06
Of the sos of I., Daniel. Ez 8.02

ITHIEL
son of I., son of Jeshaiah. Neh 11.07
The man says to I., to I. and Ucal: Pro 30.01

ITHLAH
Shaalabbin, Aijalon, I., Jos 19.42

ITHMAH
of Elnaam, and I. the Moabite, 1Ch 11.46

ITHNAN
Kedesh, Hazor, I., Jos 15.23

ITHRA
of a man named I. the Ishmaelite, 2Sa 17.25

ITHRAN
Hemdan, Eshban, I., and Cheran. Gen 36.26
Hamran, Eshban, I., and Cheran. 1Ch 1.41
Shamma, Shilshah, I., and Beera. 7.37

ITHREAM
and the sixth, I. of Eglah, David's 2Sa 3.05
the sixth I., by his wife Eglah; 1Ch 3.03

ITHRITE
Ira the I., Gareb the Ithrite, 2Sa 23.38
Ira the Ithrite, Gareb the I, 23.38
Ira the I., Gareb the Ithrite, 1Ch 11.40
Ira the Ithrite, Gareb the I., 11.40

ITHRITES
the I., the Puthrites, the Shumathites, 1Ch 2.53

ITINERANT
Then some of the i. Jewish exorcists Ac 19.13

ITSELF
of his servants, every drove by i., Gen 32.16
the lampstand i. four cups made Ex 25.34
the lampstand i. were four cups 37.20
The fat of an animal that dies of i. Lev 7.24
what dies of i. or what is torn by 17.15
That which dies of i. or is torn by 22.08
What grows of i. in your harvest 25.05
sow, nor reap what grows of i., 25.11
not reckoning i. among the nations Num 23.09
rises up and as a lion it lifts i.; 23.24
not eat anything that dies of i.; Deu 14.21
he knows, and lets Israel i. know! Jos 22.22
was seeking for i. an inheritance Ju 18.01
you shall eat what grows of i., 2Ki 19.29
race has mixed i. with the peoples Ez 9.02
the capital i. the Jews slew and Est 9.06
ice, and where the snow hides i. Job 6.16
or suddenly it takes to i. wings, Pro 23.05
grasshopper drags i. along and Ecc 12.05
Shall the axe vaunt i. over him who Is 10.15
the saw magnify i. against him who 10.15
this year eat what grows of i., 37.30

ITSELF (cont.)
go down, nor your moon withdraw i.; Is 60.20
what died of i. or was torn by Eze 4.14
"Thus shall my anger spend i., 5.13
might be humble and not lift i. up, 17.14
again exalt i. above the nations; 29.15
that has died of i. or is torn. 44.31
It magnified i., even up to the Dan 8.11
Yea, the thing i. shall be carried Hos 10.06
shall mourn, each family by i.; Zec 12.12
family of the house of David by i., 12.12
of the house of Nathan by i., 12.12
the family of the house of Levi by i., 12.13
the family of the Shimeites by i., 12.13
each by i., and their wives by 12.14
tomorrow will be anxious for i. Mt 6.34
divided against i. is laid waste, 12.25
divded aganst i. will stand; 12.25
If a kngdom is divided against i., Mk 3.24
And if a house is divided aganst i., 3.25
The earth produces of i., first the 4.28
divided against i. is laid waste, Lk 11.17
the branch cannot bear fruit by i., Jn 15.04
but rolled up in a place by i. 20.07
that the world i. could not contain 21.25
because the creation i. will be set Rom 8.21
that nothing is unclean in i.; 14.14
Does not nature i. teach you that 1Co 11.14
that we despaired of life i. 2Co 1.08
growth and upbuilds i. in love. Eph 4.16
both the book i. and all the Heb 9.19
the true one, but into heaven i., 9.24
So faith by i., if it has no works, Jas 2.17
every one, and from the truth i.; 3Jn 1.12

ITTAI
Then the king said to I. the Gittite, 2Sa 15.19
But I. answered the king, "As the 15.21
And David said to I., "Go then, pass on." 15.22
So I. the Gittite passed on, with 15.22
the command of I. the Gittite. 18.02
ordered Joab and Abishai and I., 18.05
commanded you and Abishai and I., 18.12
I. the son of Ribai of Gibeah of 23.29

ITURAEA
the region of I. and Trachonitis, Lk 3.01

IVORY
The king also made a great i. throne, 1Ki 10.18
gold, silver, i., apes, and peacocks. 10.22
and the i. house which he built, and 22.39
The king also made a great i. throne, 2Ch 9.17
gold, silver, i., apes, and peacocks. 9.21
From i. palaces stringed instruments Ps 45.08
His body is i. work, encrusted with Sol 5.14
Your neck is like an i. tower. 7.04
coasts of Cyprus, inlaid with i. Eze 27.06
you in payment i. tusks and ebony. 27.15
and the houses of i. shall perish, Amo 3.15
Woe to those who lie upon beds of i., 6.04
scented wood, all articles of i., Rev 18.12

IVVAH
gods of Sepharvaim, Hena, and I.? 2Ki 18.34
king of Hena, or the king of I.? 19.13
king of Hena, or the king of I.? Is 37.13

IYEABARIM
out from Oboth, and encamped at I., Num 21.11
out from Oboth, and encamped at I., 33.44

IYIM
And they set out from I., Num 33.45

IZHAR
I., Hebron and Uzziel, the years of Ex 6.18
The sons of I.: Korah, Nepheg, and 6.21
Amram, I., Hebron, and Uzziel. Num 3.19
Now Korah the son of I., 16.01
of Helah: Zereth, I., and Ethnan. 1Ch 4.07
Amram, I., Hebron, and Uzziel. 6.02
Amram, I., Hebron, and Uzziel. 6.18
son of I., son of Kohath, son of 6.38
I., Hebron, and Uzziel, four. 23.12
The sons of I.: Shelomith the chief. 23.18

IZHARITES
Amramites, and the family of the I., Num 3.27
Of the I., Shelomoth; of the sons of 1Ch 24.22
the I., the Hebronites, and the 26.23
Of the I., Chenaniah and his sons 26.29

IZLIAH
Ishmerai, I., and Jobab were the 1Ch 8.18

IZRAHIAH
The sons of Uzzi: I. And the sons of I.: 1Ch 7.03

IZRAHITE
fifth month, was Shamhuth, the I.; 1Ch 27.08

IZRI
the fourth to I., his sons and his 1Ch 25.11

IZZIAH
I., Malchijah, Mijamin, Eleazar, Ez 10.25

J

JAAKAN
of Ezer: Bilhan, Zaavan, and J. 1Ch 1.42

JAAKOBAH
Elioenai, J., Jeshohaiah, Asaiah, 1Ch 4.36

JAALA
the sons of J., the sons of Darkon, Neh 7.58

JAALAH
the sons of J., the sons of Darkon, Ez 2.56

JAAR
we found it in the fields of J. Ps 132.06

JAAREOREGIM
at God; and Elhanan the son of J., 2Sa 21.19

JAARESHIAH
J., Elijah, and Zichri were the sons 1Ch 8.27

JAASIEL
Eliel, and Obed, and J. the Mezobaite. 1Ch 11.47
for Benjamin, J. the son of Abner; 27.21

JAASU
Mattaniah, Mattenai, J. Ez 10.37

JAAZANIAH
and J. the son of the Maacathite. 2Ki 25.23
So I took J. the son of Jeremiah, Jer 35.03
with J. the son of Shaphan standing Eze 8.11
saw among them J. the son of Azzur, 11.01

JAAZIAH
and Mushi. The sons of J.: Beno. 1Ch 24.26
of J., Beno, Shoham, Zaccur, and Ibri. 24.27

JAAZIEL
J., Shemiramoth, Jehiel, Unni, Eliab, 1Ch 15.18

JABAL

Adah bore J.; he was the father Gen 4.20

JABBOK

and crossed the ford of the J. Gen 32.22
his land from the Arnon to the J., Num 21.24
of the river J. and the cities of Deu 2.37
as far over as the river J., 3.16
the valley as far as the river J., Jos 12.02
Arnon to the J. and to the Jordan; Ju 11.13
Arnon to the J. and from the 11.22

JABESH

all the men of J. said to Nahash, 1Sa 11.01
The elders of J. said to him, "Give 11.03
him the tidings of the men of J. 11.05
came and told the men of J., 11.09
Therefore the men of J. said, 11.10
they came to J. and burnt them 31.12
them under the tamarisk tree in J., 31.13
Shallum the son of J. conspired 2Ki 15.10
Shallum the son of J. began to 15.13
the son of J. in Samaria and slew 15.14
his sons, and brought them to J. 1Ch 10.12
their bones under the oak in J., 10.12

JABESHGILEAD

one had come to the camp from J., Ju 21.08
of the inhabitants of J. was there. 21.09
inhabitants of J. with the edge of 21.10
inhabitants of J. four hundred 21.12
had saved alive of the women of J.; 21.14
Ammonite went up and besieged J.; 1Sa 11.01
shall you say to the men of J.: 11.09
inhabitants of J. heard what the 31.11
was the men of J. who buried Saul, 2Sa 2.04
David sent messengers to the men of J., 2.05
son Jonathan from the men of J., 21.12
But when all J. heard all that the 1Ch 10.11

JABEZ

of the scribes that dwelt at J.: 1Ch 2.55
J. was more honorable than his 4.09
and his mother called his name J., 4.09
J. called on the God of Israel, 4.10

JABIN

When J. king of Hazor heard of this, Jos 11.01
into the hand of J. king of Canaan, Ju 4.02
peace between J. the king of Hazor 4.17
day God subdued J. the king of 4.23
and harder on J. the king of 4.24
they destroyed J. king of Canaan. 4.24
of the army of J. king of Hazor, 1Sa 12.09
to Sisera and J. at the river Ps 83.09

JABIN'S

out Sisera, the general of J. army, Ju 4.07

JABNEEL

Mount Baalah, and goes out to J.; Jos 15.11
And J., as far as Lakkum; 19.33

JABNEH

and the wall of J. and the wall of 2Ch 26.06

JACAN

J., Zia, and Eber, seven. 1Ch 5.13

JACHIN

J., Zohar, and Shaul, the son of a Gen 46.10
J., Zohar, and Shaul, the son of a Ex 6.15
of J., the family of the Jachinites; Num 26.12
the south and called its name J.; 1Ki 7.21
priests: Jedaiah, Jehoiarib, J., 1Ch 9.10
the twenty-first to J., the twenty-second 24.17
that on the south he called J., 2Ch 3.17
Jedaiah the son of Joiarib, J., Neh 11.10

JACHINITES

of Jachin, the family of the J.; Num 26.12

JACINTH

and the third row a j., Ex 28.19
a j., an agate, and an amethyst; 39.12
the eleventh j., the twelfth Rev 21.20

JACKAL'S

Gate to the J. Well and to the Neh 2.13

JACKALS

I am a brother of j., and a companion Job 30.29
have broken us in the place of j., Ps 44.19
sword, they shall be prey for j. 63.10
and j. in the pleasant palaces; Is 13.22
It shall be the haunt of j., 34.13
the haunt of j. shall become a 35.07
the j. and the ostriches; 43.20
a heap of ruins, a lair of j.; Jer 9.11
Judah a desolation, a lair of j. 10.22
heights, they pant for air like j.; 14.06
Hazor shall become a haunt of j., 49.33
"Therefore wild beasts and j. shall 50.39
the haunt of j., a horror and a 51.37
Even the j. give the breast and Lam 4.03
lies desolate; j. prowl over it. 5.18
will make lamentation like the j., Mic 1.08
his heritage to j. of the desert. Mal 1.03

JACOB

so his name was called J. Isaac was Gen 25.26
while J. was a quiet man, dwelling 25.27
ate of his game; but Rebekah loved J. 25.28
Once when J. was boiling pottage, 25.29
And Esau said to J., "Let me eat some 25.30
J. said, "First sell me your birthright." 25.31
J. said, "Swear to me first." 25.33
him, and sold his birthright to J. 25.33
Then J. gave Esau bread and pottage 25.34
Rebekah said to her son J., 27.06
But J. said to Rebekah his mother, 27.11
and put them on J. her younger son; 27.15
prepared, into the hand of her son J. 27.17
J. said to his father, "I am Esau 27.19
me success." Then Isaac said to J., 27.20
So J. went near to Isaac his father, 27.22
as Isaac had finished blessing J., 27.30
when J. had scarcely gone out from 27.30
Esau said, "Is he not rightly named J.? 27.36
Now Esau hated J. because of the 27.41
then I will kill my brother J." 27.41
sent and called J. her younger son, 27.42
If J. marries one of the Hittite 27.46
Then Isaac called J. and blessed 28.01
Thus Isaac sent J. away; and he went 28.05
had blessed J. and sent him away 28.06
and that J. had obeyed his father 28.07
J. left Beersheba, and went toward 28.10
Then J. awoke from his sleep and 28.16
So J. rose early in the morning, and 28.18
Then J. made a vow, saying, "If God 28.20
Then J. went on his journey, and 29.01
J. said to them, "My brothers, where 29.04
Now when J. saw Rachel the daughter 29.10
J. went up and rolled the stone 29.10
Then J. kissed Rachel, and wept 29.11
And J. told Rachel that he was her 29.12
the tidings of J. his sister's son, 29.13
J. told Laban all these things, 29.13
Then Laban said to J., "Because you are 29.15
J. loved Rachel; and he said, 29.18
So J. served seven years for Rachel, 29.20
Then J. said to Laban, "Give me my 29.21
daughter Leah and brought her to J.; 29.23
and J. said to Laban, "What is this 29.25
J. did so, and completed her week; 29.28

JACOB (cont.)
So J. went in to Rachel also, and he Gen 29.30
saw that she bore J. no children, 30.01
and she said to J., "Give me children, 30.01
as a wife; and J. went into her. 30.04
Bilhah conceived and bore J. a son. 30.05
again and bore J. a second son. 30.07
and gave her to J. as a wife. 30.09
Then Leah's maid Zilpah bore J. a son. 30.10
Leah's maid Zilpah bore J. a second son. 30.12
When J. came from the field in the 30.16
conceived and bore J. a fifth son. 30.17
again, and she bore J. a sixth son. 30.19
J. said to Laban, "Send me away, that 30.25
J. said to him, "You yourself know 30.29
J. said, "You shall not give me 30.31
journey between himself and J.; 30.36
and J. fed the rest of Laban's flock. 30.36
Then J. took fresh rods of poplar 30.37
And J. separated the lambs, and set 30.40
were breeding J. laid the rods in 30.41
Now J. heard that the sons of Laban 31.01
"J. has taken all that was our 31.01
And J. saw that Laban did not 31.02
Then the LORD said to J., "Return to the 31.03
So J. sent and called Rachel and 31.04
'J.,' and I said, 'Here I am!' 31.11
So J. arose, and set his sons and 31.17
And J. outwitted Laban the Aramean, 31.20
on the third day that J. had fled, 31.22
heed that you say not a word to J., 31.24
And Laban overtook J. Now J. had pitched 31.25
And Laban said to J., "What have you done, 31.26
you speak to J. neither good nor 31.29
J. answered Laban, "Because I was 31.31
Now J. did not know that Rachel had 31.32
Then J. became angry, and upbraided 31.36
J. said to Laban, "What is my 31.36
Then Laban answered and said to J., 31.43
So J. took a stone, and set it up as 31.45
And J. said to his kinsmen, "Gather 31.46
but J. called it Galeed. 31.47
Then Laban said to J., 31.51
So J. swore by the Fear of his 31.53
and J. offered a sacrifice on the 31.54
J. went on his way and the angels 32.01
and when J. saw them he said, "This 32.02
And J. sent messengers before him 32.03
Esau: Thus says your servant J., 32.04
And the messengers returned to J., 32.06
Then J. was greatly afraid and 32.07
And J. said, "O God of my father 32.09
'They belong to your servant J.; 32.18
your servant J. is behind us.'" 32.20
And J. was left alone; and a man wrestled 32.24
that he did not prevail against J., 32.25
But J. said, "I will not let you go, 32.26
is your name?" And he said, "J." 32.27
name shall no more be called J., 32.28
Then J. asked him, "Tell me, I pray, 32.29
So J. called the name of the place 32.30
And J. lifted up his eyes and 33.01
J. said, "The children whom God has 33.05
J. answered, "To find favor in the 33.08
J. said, "No, I pray you, if I have 33.10
But J. said to him, "My lord knows 33.13
But J. journeyed to Succoth, and 33.17
And J. came safely to the city of 33.18
of Leah, whom she had borne to J., 34.01
drawn to Dinah the daughter of J.; 34.03
Now J. heard that he had defiled 34.05
so J. held his peace until they 34.05
went out to J. to speak with him. 34.06
The sons of J. came in from the 34.07
The sons of J. answered Shechem and 34.13
were sore, two of the sons of J., 34.25
And the sons of J. came upon the 34.27
Then J. said to Simeon and Levi, 34.30
God said to J., "Arise, go up to 35.01
So J. said to his household and to 35.02
So they gave to J. all the foreign 35.04
and J. hid them under the oak which 35.04
they did not pursue the sons of J. 35.05
And J. came to Luz (that is, Bethel), 35.06
God appeared to J. again, when he came 35.09
And God said to him, "Your name is J.; 35.10
shall your name be called J., 35.10
And J. set up a pillar in the place 35.14
So J. called the name of the place 35.15
and J. set up a pillar upon her 35.20
Now the sons of J. were twelve. 35.22
the sons of J. who were born to 35.26
And J. came to his father Isaac at 35.27
his sons Esau and J. buried him. 35.29
a land away from his brother J. 36.06
J. dwelt in the land of his father's 37.01
is the history of the family of J. 37.02
Then J. rent his garments, and put 37.34
When J. learned that there was 42.01
But J. did not send Benjamin, 42.04
When they came to J. their father 42.29
And J. their father said to them, 42.36
land of Canaan to their father J. 45.25
spirit of their father J. revived; 45.27
visions of the night, and said "J., J." 46.02
Then J. set out from Beersheba; 46.05
of Israel carried J. their father, 46.05
J. and all his offspring with him, 46.06
came into Egypt, J. and his sons. 46.08
whom she bore to J. in Paddan-aram, 46.15
and these she bore to J.—sixteen 46.18
of Rachel, who were born to J.—fourteen 46.22
daughter, and these she bore to J.— 46.25
belonging to J. who came into 46.26
all the persons of the house of J., 46.27
Then Joseph brought in J. his father, 47.07
and J. blessed Pharaoh. 47.07
And Pharaoh said to J., "How many 47.08
And J. said to Pharaoh, "The days of 47.09
And J. blessed Pharaoh, and went out 47.10
And J. lived in the land of Egypt 47.28
so the days of J., the years of his 47.28
And it was told to J., "Your son Joseph 48.02
And J. said to Joseph, "God Almighty 48.03
Then J. called his sons, and said, 49.01
O sons of J., and hearken to Israel 49.02
divide them in J. and scatter them 49.07
Mighty One of J. (by the name of 49.24
When J. finished charging his sons, 49.33
to Abraham, to Isaac, and to J." 50.24
Israel who came to Egypt with J., Ex 1.10
offspring of J. were seventy 1.05
Abraham, with Isaac, and with J. 2.24
God of Isaac, and the God of J." 3.06
God of Isaac, and the God of J., 3.15
and of J., has appeared to me, 3.16
God of Isaac, and the God of J., 4.05
and to J., as God Almighty, but by 6.03
to Abraham, to Isaac, and to J.; 6.08
you shall say to the house of J., 19.03
and J., saying, 'To your descendants 33.01
will remember my covenant with J., Lev 26.42
curse J. for me, and come, denounce Num 23.07
Who can count the dust of J., 23.10
He has not beheld misfortune in J.; 23.21
there is no enchantment against J., 23.23
it shall be said of J. and Israel, 23.23
O J., your encampments, O Israel! 24.05
a star shall come forth out of J., 24.17
By J. shall dominion be exercised, 24.19
and to J., because they have not 32.11
and to J., to give to them and to Deu 1.08
and to J., to give you, with great 6.10
to Abraham, to Isaac, and to J. 9.05

JACOB (cont.)

servants, Abraham, Isaac, and J.; Deu 9.27
to Abraham, to Isaac, and to J. 29.13
to Isaac, and to J., to give them." 30.20
is his people, J. his allotted heritage. 32.09
possession for the assembly of J. 33.04
They shall teach J. thy ordinances, 33.10
safety, the fountain of J. alone, 33.28
and to J., 'I will give it to your 34.04
and to Isaac I gave J. and Esau. Jos 24.04
but J. and his children went down 24.04
of ground which J. bought from the 24.32
When J. went into Egypt and the 1Sa 12.08
the anointed of the God of J., 2Sa 23.01
of the tribes of the sons of J., 1Ki 18.31
and J., and would not destroy them; 2Ki 13.23
LORD commanded the children of J., 17.34
sons of J., his chosen ones! 1Ch 16.13
which he confirmed as a statute to J., 16.17
J. shall rejoice, Israel shall be Ps 14.07
name of the God of J. protect you! 20.01
all your sons of J., glorify him, 22.23
who seek the face of the God of J. 24.06
who ordainest victories for J. 44.04
is with us; the God of J. is our refuge. 46.07
is with us; the God of J. is our refuge. 46.11
us, the pride of J. whom he loves. 47.04
J. will rejoice and Israel be glad. 53.06
God rules over J. to the ends of 59.13
will sing praises to the God of J. 75.09
O God of J., both rider and horse 76.06
people, the sons of J. and Joseph. 77.15
He established a testimony in J., 78.05
a fire was kindled against J., 78.21
be the shepherd of J. his people, 78.71
For they have devoured J., and laid 79.07
shout for joy to the God of J.! 81.01
an ordinance of the God of J. 81.04
hear my prayer; give ear, O God of J.! 84.08
didst restore the fortunes of J. 85.01
than all the dwelling places of J. 87.02
the God of J. does not perceive." 94.07
justice and righteousness in J. 99.04
his servant, sons of J., his chosen ones! 105.06
which he confirmed to J. as a statute, 105.10
J. sojourned in the land of Ham. 105.23
the house of J. from a people of 114.01
at the presence of the God of J., 114.07
and vowed to the Mighty One of J., 132.02
place for the Mighty One of J." 132.05
the LORD has chosen J. for himself, 135.04
Happy is he whose help is the God of J., 146.05
He declares his word to J., his statutes 147.19
to the house of the God of J.; Is 2.03
O house of J., come, let us walk in 2.05
the house of J., because they are 2.06
his face from the house of J., 8.17
The Lord has sent a word against J., 9.08
of the house of J. will no more 10.20
will return, the remnant of J., 10.21
compassion on J. and will again 14.01
and will cleave to the house of J. 14.01
the glory of J. will be brought 17.04
In days to come J. shall take root, 27.06
the guilt of J. will be expiated, 27.09
Abraham, concerning the house of J.: 29.22
"J. shall no more be ashamed, no 29.22
will sanctify the Holy One of J., 29.23
O J., and speak, O Israel, "My way is 40.27
J., whom I have chosen, the offspring 41.08
you worm J., you men of Israel! 41.14
your proofs, says the King of J. 41.21
Who gave up J. to the spoiler, and 42.24
O J., he who formed you, O Israel: 43.01
"Yet you did not call upon me, O J.; 43.22
I delivered J. to utter destruction 43.28
O J. my servant, Israel whom I have 44.01
O J. my servant, Jeshurun whom I 44.02
call himself by the name of J., 44.05
O J., and Israel, for you are my 44.21
For the LORD has redeemed J., 44.23
For the sake of my servant J., 45.04
did not say to the offspring of J., 45.19
O house of J., all the remnant of 46.03
O house of J., who are called by 48.01
O J., and Israel, whom I called! 48.12
LORD has redeemed his servant J.!" 48.20
to bring J. back to him, that 49.05
the tribes of J. and to restore 49.06
Redeemer, the Mighty One of J. 49.26
to the house of J. their sins. 58.01
the heritage of J. your father, 58.14
to those in J. who turn from 59.20
Redeemer, the Mighty One of J. 60.16
bring forth descendants from J., 65.09
O house of J., and all the families Jer 2.04
Declare this in the house of J., 5.20
is he who is the portion of J., 10.16
for they have devoured J.; 10.25
it is a time of distress for J.; 30.07
O J. my servant, says the LORD, nor 30.10
J. shall return and have quiet and 30.10
the fortunes of the tents of J., 30.18
"Sing aloud with gladness for J., 31.07
For the LORD has ransomed J., 31.11
descendants of J. and David my 33.26
the seed of Abraham, Isaac, and J. 33.26
O J. my servant, nor be dismayed, O 46.27
J. shall return and have quiet and 46.27
Fear not, O J. my servant, says the 46.28
is he who is the portion of J., 51.19
commanded against J. that his Lam 1.17
mercy all the habitations of J.; 2.02
burned like a flaming fire in J., 2.03
to the seed of the house of J., Eze 20.05
land which I gave to my servant J. 28.25
dwelt that I gave to my servant J.; 37.25
I will restore the fortunes of J., 39.25
must plow, J. must harrow for himself. Hos 10.11
and will punish J. according to 12.02
(J. fled to the land of Aram, there 12.12
testify against the house of J., Amo 3.13
of hosts): "I abhor the pride of J., 6.08
How can J. stand? He is so small!" 7.02
How can J. stand? He is so small!" 7.05
The LORD has sworn by the pride of J.: 8.07
utterly destroy the house of J., 9.08
violence done to your brother j., Ob 1.10
the house of J. shall possess 1.17
The house of J. shall be a fire, and 1.18
transgression of J. and for the Mic 1.05
What is the transgression of J.? 1.05
Should this be said, O house of J.? 2.07
O J., I will gather the remnant of 2.12
you heads of J. and rulers of the 3.01
to declare to J. his transgression 3.08
of the house of J. and rulers of 3.09
to the house of the God of J.; 4.02
Then the remnant of J. shall be in 5.07
And the remnant of J. shall be 5.08
faithfulness to J. and steadfast 7.20
the majesty of J. as the majesty Nah 2.02
says the LORD, "Yet I have loved J. Mal 1.02
LORD cut off from the tents of J., 2.12
O sons of J., are not consumed. 3.06
Isaac, and Isaac the father of J., Mt 1.02
and J. the father of Judah and his 1.02
and Matthan the father of J., 1.15
and J. the father of Joseph the 1.16
and J. in the kingdom of heaven, 8.11
God of Isaac, and the God of J.'? 22.32
God of Isaac, and the God of J.'? Mk 12.26
over the house of J. for ever; Lk 1.33
the son of J., the son of Isaac, the 3.34

JACOB (cont.)
and Isaac and J. and all the Lk 13.28
the God of Isaac and the God of J. 20.37
the field that J. gave to his son Jn 4.05
Are you greater than our father J., 4.12
of Abraham and of Isaac and of J., Ac 3.13
and Isaac became the father of J., 7.08
and J. of the twelve patriarchs. 7.08
But when J. heard that there was 7.12
called to him J. his father and 7.14
and J. went down into Egypt. 7.15
of Abraham and of Isaac and of J.' 7.32
a habitation for the God of J. 7.46
"J. I loved, but Esau I hated." Rom 9.13
will banish ungodliness from J."; 11.26
living in tents with Isaac and J., Heb 11.09
future blessings on J. and Esau. 11.20
By faith J., when dying, blessed 11.21

JACOB'S
"The voice is J. voice, but the Gen 27.22
of Rebekah, J. and Esau's mother. 28.05
J. anger was kindled against Rachel, 30.02
were Laban's, and the stronger J. 30.42
So Laban went into J. tent, 31.33
and J. thigh was put out of joint 32.25
the hollow of J. thigh on the 32.32
Israel by lying with J. daughter, 34.07
he had delight in J. daughter. 34.19
Reuben (J. first-born), Simeon, Levi, 35.23
and his sons. Reuben, J. first-born, 46.08
J. wife: Joseph and Benjamin. 46.19
not including J. sons' wives, were 46.26
"Is not Esau J. brother?" says the LORD. Mal 1.02
J. well was there, and so Jesus, Jn 4.06

JADA
The sons of Onam: Shammai and J. 1Ch 2.28
The sons of J., Shammai's brother: 2.32

JADDAI
Zebina, J., Joel, and Benaiah. Ez 10.43

JADDUA
Meshezabel, Zadok, J., Neh 10.21
and Jonathan the father of J. 12.11
and J., there were recorded the 12.22

JADON
Gibeonite and J. the Meronothite, Neh 3.07

JAEL
away on foot to the tent of J., Ju 4.17
And J. came out to meet Sisera, and 4.18
But J. the wife of Heber took a 4.21
J. went out to meet him, and said to 4.22
son of Anath, in the days of J., 5.06
"Most blessed of women be J., 5.24

JAGUR
of Edom, were Kabzeel, Eder, J., Jos 15.21

JAHATH
son of Shobal was the father of J., 1Ch 4.02
and J. was the father of Ahumai and 4.02
J. his son, Zimmah his son, 6.20
son of J., son of Gershom, son of 6.43
J., Zina, and Jeush, and Beriah. 23.10
J. was the chief, and Zizah the 23.11
of the sons of Shelomoth, J. 24.22
them were set J. and Obadiah the 2Ch 34.12

JAHAZ
and came to J., and fought against Num 21.23
all his people, to battle at J. Deu 2.32
and J., and Kedemoth, and Mephaath, Jos 13.18
lands, J. with its pasture lands, 21.36
together, and encamped at J., Ju 11.20
their voice is heard as far as J.; Is 15.04
as far as J. they utter their voice, Jer 48.34

JAHAZIEL
Jeremiah, J., Johanan, Jozabad of 1Ch 12.04
and Benaiah and J. the priests were 16.06
J. the third, and Jekameam the 23.19
J. the third, Jekameam the fourth. 24.23
LORD came upon J. the son of 2Ch 20.14
of Zattu, Shecaniah the son of J., Ez 8.05

JAHDAI
The sons of J.: Regem, Jotham, Geshan, 1Ch 2.47

JAHDIEL
and J., mighty warriors, famous men, 1Ch 5.24

JAHDO
Jeshishai, son of J., son of Buz; 1Ch 5.14

JAHLEEL
Zebulun: Sered, Elon, and J. Gen 46.14
of J., the family of the Jahleelites. Num 26.26

JAHLEELITES
of Jahleel, the family of the J. Num 26.26

JAHMAI
J., Ibsam, and Shemuel, heads of 1Ch 7.02

JAHZAH
lands, J. with its pasture lands, 1Ch 6.78
upon Holon, and J., and Mephaath, Jer 48.21

JAHZEEL
J., Guni, Jezer, and Shillem Gen 46.24
of J., the family of the Jahzeelites; Num 26.48

JAHZEELITES
of Jahzeel, the family of the J.; Num 26.48

JEHZEIAH
of Asahel and J. the son of Tikvah Ez 10.15

JAHZERAH
son of J., son of Meshullam, son of 1Ch 9.12

JAHZIEL
J., Guni, Jezer, and Shallum, the 1Ch 7.13

JAILER
charging the j. to keep them safely. Ac 16.23
When the j. woke and saw that the 16.27
And the j. reported the words to 16.36

JAILERS
his lord delivered him to the j., Mt 18.34

JAIR
And J. the son of Manasseh went and Num 32.41
J. the Manassite took all the Deu 3.14
of Bashan, and all the towns of J., Jos 13.30
After him arose J. the Gileadite, Ju 10.03
And J. died, and was buried in Kamon. 10.05
the villages of J. the son of 1Ki 4.13
and Segub was the father of J., 1Ch 2.22
the son of J. slew Lahmi the 20.05
the son of J., son of Shimei, son of Est 2.05

JAIRITE
and Ira the J. was also David's 2Sa 20.26

JAIRUS
of the synagogue, J. by name; Mk 5.22
And there came a man named J., Lk 8.41

JAKEH
The words of Agur son of J. of Massa. Pro 30.01

JAKIM
J., Zichri, Zabdi, 1Ch 8.19
to Eliashib, the twelfth to J., 24.12

JALAM
Oholibamah bore Jeush, J., and Korah. Gen 36.05
bore to Esau Jeush, J., and Korah. 36.14
the chiefs Jeush, J., and Korah; 36.18
Reuel, Jeush, J., and Korah. 1Ch 1.35

JALON
Jether, Mered, Epher, and J. 1Ch 4.17

JAMBRES
As Jannes and J. opposed Moses, so 2Ti 3.08

JAMBS
and its j., two cubits; and the vestibule Eze 40.09
and the j. on either side were of 40.10
into their j. in the side rooms, 40.16
and on the j. were palm trees. 40.16
and its j. and its vestibule were 40.21
he measured its j. and its vestibule 40.24
and it had palm trees on its j., 40.26
its j., and its vestibule were of 40.29
and palm trees were on its j., 40.31
its j., and its vestibule were of 40.33
and it had palm trees on its j., 40.34
its j., and its vestibule were of 40.36
and it had palm trees on its j., 40.37
measured the j. of the vestibule, 40.48
beside the j. on either side. 40.49
to the nave, and measured the j.; 41.01
cubits was the breadth of the j. 41.01
measured the j. of the entrance, 41.03

JAMES
J. the son of Zebedee and John his Mt 4.21
J. the son of Zebedee, and John his 10.02
J. the son of Alphaeus, and Thaddaeus; 10.03
his brothers J. and Joseph and 13.55
him Peter and J. and John his 17.01
Mary the mother of J. and Joseph, 27.56
he saw J. the son of Zebedee and Mk 1.19
Simon and Andrew, with J. and John. 1.29
J. the son of Zebedee and John the 3.17
Zebedee and John the brother of J., 3.17
and J. the son of Alphaeus, and 3.18
Peter and J. and John the brother of J. 5.37
and brother of J. and Joses and 6.03
with him Peter and J. and John, 9.02
And J. and John, the sons of Zebedee, 10.35
to be indignant at J. and John. 10.41
Peter and J. and John and Andrew 13.03
with him Peter and J. and John, 14.33
the mother of J. the younger and 15.40
Magdalene, and Mary the mother of J., 16.01
and so also were J. and John, Lk 5.10
and J. and John, and Philip, and 6.14
and J. the son of Alphaeus, and 6.15
and Judas the son of J., and Judas Iscariot, 6.16
him, except Peter and John and J., 8.51
with him Peter and John and J., 9.28
his disciples J. and John saw it, 9.54
the mother of J. and the other 24.10
Peter and John and J. and Andrew, Ac 1.13
J. the son of Alphaeus and Simon 1.13
the Zealot and Judas the son of J. 1.13
He killed J. the brother of John 12.02
"Tell this to J. and to the brethren." 12.17
J. replied, "Brethren, listen to me. 15.13
day Paul went in with us to J.; 21.18
Then he appeared to J., then to all 1Co 15.07
apostles except J. the Lord's Gal 1.19
J. and Cephas and John, who were 2.09
For before certain men came from J., 2.12
J., a servant of God and of the Jas 1.01
of Jesus Christ and brother of J., Jud 1.01

JAMIN
J., Ohad, Jachin, Zohar, and Shaul, the Gen 46.10
J., Ohad, Jachin, Zohar, and Shaul, the Ex 6.15
of J., the family of the Jaminites; Num 26.12
of Jerahmeel: Maaz, J., and Eker. 1Ch 2.27
Nemuel, J., Jarib, Zerah, Shaul; 4.24
J., Akkub, Shabbethai, Hodiah, Maaseiah, Neh 8.07

JAMINITES
of Jamin, the family of the J.; Num 26.12

JAMLECH
Meshobab, J., Joshah the son of 1Ch 4.34

JANAI
the second, J., and Shaphat in Bashan. 1Ch 5.12

JANIM
J., Bethtappuah, Aphekah, Jos 15.53

JANNAI
the son of J., the son of Joseph, Lk 3.24

JANNES
As J. and Jambres opposed Moses, so 2Ti 3.08

JANOAH
along beyond it on the east to J., Jos 16.06
goes down from J. to Ataroth and 16.07
J., Kedesh, Hazor, Gilead, and Galilee, 2Ki 15.29

JAPHETH
the father of Shem, Ham, and J. Gen 5.32
had three sons, Shem, Ham, and J. 6.10
and his sons, Shem and Ham and J., 7.13
the ark were Shem, Ham, and J. 9.18
Then Shem and J. took a garment, 9.23
God enlarge J., and let him dwell 9.27
sons of Noah, Shem, Ham, and J.; 10.01
The sons of J.: Gomer, Magog, Madai, 10.02
are the sons of J. in their lands, 10.05
of Eber, the elder brother of J., 10.21
Noah, Shem, Ham, and J. 1Ch 1.04
The sons of J.: Gomer, Magog, Madai, 1.05

JAPHIA
to J. king of Lachish, and to Debir Jos 10.03
it goes to Daberath, then up to J.; 19.13
Ibhar, Elishua, Nepheg, J., 2Sa 5.15
Nogah, Nepheg, J., 1Ch 3.07
Nogah, Nepheg, J., 14.06

JAPHLET
Heber was the father of J., 1Ch 7.32
The sons of J.: Pasach, Bimhal, and 7.33
These are the sons of J. 7.33

JAPHLETITES
westward to the territory of the J., Jos 16.03

JAR
let down your j. that I may drink,' Gen 24.14
with her water j. upon her shoulder. 24.15
and filled her j., and came up. 24.16
little water to drink from your j." 24.17
let down her j. upon her hand, 24.18
emptied her j. into the trough and 24.20
water from your j. to drink," 24.43
with her water j. on her shoulder; 24.45
let down her j. from her shoulder, 24.46
"Take a j., and put an omer of Ex 16.33
and the j. of water, and let us go." 1Sa 26.11
spear and the j. of water from 26.12
and the j. of water that was at his 26.16
and a j. of honey, and go to him; 1Ki 14.03
only a handful of meal in a j., 17.12
The j. of meal shall not be spent, 17.14
The j. of meal was not spent, 17.16
on hot stones and a j. of water. 19.06

JAR (cont.)
in the house, except a j. of oil." 2Ki 4.02
"Every j. shall be filled with wine."' Jer 13.12
know that every j. will be filled 13.12
an alabaster j. of very expensive Mt 26.07
an alabaster j. of ointment of Mk 14.03
she broke the j. and poured it 14.03
man carrying a j. of water will 14.13
man carrying a j. of water will Lk 22.10
So the woman left her water j., Jn 4.28

JARAH
and Ahaz was the father of J., 1Ch 9.42
and J. of Alemeth, Azmaveth, and 9.42

JARED
years, he became the father of J. Gen 5.15
the birth of J. eight hundred and 5.16
When J. had lived a hundred and 5.18
J. lived after the birth of Enoch 5.19
Thus all the days of J. were nine 5.20
Kenan, Mahalalel, J.; 1Ch 1.02
the son of J., the son of Mahalaleel, Lk 3.37

JARHA
Egyptian slave, whose name was J. 1Ch 2.34
in marriage to J. his slave; 2.35

JARIB
Nemuel, Jamin, J., Zerah, Shaul; 1Ch 4.24
J., Elnathan, Nathan, Zechariah, and Ez 8.16
J., and Gedaliah, of the sons of 10.18

JARMUTH
of Hebron, to Piram king of J., Jos 10.03
the king of J., the king of Lachish, 10.05
the king of J., the king of Lachish, 10.23
the king of J., one; the king of 12.11
J., Adullam, Soco, Azekah, 15.35
J. with its pasture lands, Engannim 21.29
in Enrimmon, in Zorah, in J., Neh 11.29

JAROAH
son of J., son of Gilead, son of 1Ch 5.14

JARS
So he took the j. of the people Ju 7.08
empty j., with torches inside the j. 7.16
and smashed the j. that were in 7.19
blew the trumpets and broke the j., 7.20
"Fill four j. with water, and pour 1Ki 18.33
vessels, and break his j. in pieces. Jer 48.12
Now six stone j. were standing Jn 2.06
to them, "Fill the j. with water." 2.07

JASHAR
this not written in the Book of J.? Jos 10.13
it is written in the book of J. 2Sa 1.18

JASHEN
Shaalbon, the sons of J., Jonathan, 2Sa 23.32

JASHOBEAM
J., a Hachmonite, was chief of the 1Ch 11.11
Joezer, and J., the Korahites; 12.06
J. the son of Zabdiel was in charge 27.02

JASHUB
of J., the family of the Jashubites; Num 26.24
Tola, Puah, J., and Shimron, four. 1Ch 7.01
Malluch, Adaiah, J., Sheal, and Jeremoth. Ez 10.29

JASHUBITES
of Jashub, the family of the J.; Num 26.24

JASON
and attacked the house of J., Ac 17.05
they dragged J. and some of the 17.06
and J. has received them; 17.07
security from J. and the rest, 17.09
so do Lucius and J. and Sosipater, Rom 16.21

JASPER
row a beryl, an onyx, and a j.; Ex 28.20
row, a beryl, an onyx, and a j.; 39.13
and j., chrysolite, beryl, and onyx, Eze 28.13
appeared like j. and carnelian, Rev 4.03
like a j., clear as crystal. 21.11
The wall was built of j., 21.18
the first was j., the second 21.19

JATHNIEL
Zebadiah the third, J. the fourth, 1Ch 26.02

JATTIR
hill country, Shamir, J., Soco, Jos 15.48
J. with its pasture lands, Eshtemoa 21.14
in Ramoth of the Negeb, in J., 1Sa 30.27
J., Eshtemoa with its pasture lands, 1Ch 6.57

JAVAN
J., Tubal, Meshech, and Tiras. Gen 10.02
The sons of J.: Elishah, Tarshish, 10.04
J., Tubal, Meshech, and Tiras. 1Ch 1.05
The sons of J.: Elishah, Tarshish, 1.07
to Tubal and J., to the coastlands Is 66.19
J., Tubal, and Meshech traded with Eze 27.13

JAVELIN
"Stretch out the j. that is in your Jos 8.18
stretched out the j. that was in 8.18
with which he stretched out the j., 8.26
and a j. of bronze slung between 1Sa 17.06
and with a spear and with a j.; 17.45
the flashing spear and the j. Job 39.23
nor the spear, the dart, or the j. 41.26
Draw the spear and j. against my Ps 35.03

JAVELINS
he laughs at the rattle of j. Job 41.29

JAW
nose, or pierce his j. with a hook? Job 41.02

JAWBONE
And he found a fresh j. of an ass, Ju 15.15
"With the j. of an ass, heaps upon 15.16
with the j. of an ass have I slain 15.16
threw away the j. out of his hand; 15.17

JAWS
and my tongue cleaves to my j.; Ps 22.15
to place on the j. of the peoples Is 30.28
I will put hooks in your j., Eze 29.04
about, and put hooks into your j., 38.04
one who eases the yoke on their j., Hos 11.04

JAZER
for J. was the boundary of the Num 21.24
And Moses sent to spy out J.; 21.32
saw the land of J. and the land of 32.01
J., Nimrah, Heshbon, Elealeh, Sebam, 32.03
Atroth-Shophan, J., Jogbehah, 32.35
Their territory was J., and all the cities Jos 13.25
J. with its pasture lands—four 21.39
valley, toward Gad and on to J. 2Sa 24.05
and J. with its pasture lands. 1Ch 6.81
them were found at J. in Gilead. 26.31
reached to J. and strayed to the Is 16.08
the weeping of J. for the vine of 16.09
More than for J. I weep for you, O Jer 48.32
over the sea, reached as far as J.; 48.32

JAZIZ
Over the flocks was J. the Hagrite. 1Ch 27.30

JEALOUS
And his brothers were j. of him, Gen 37.11
I the LORD your God am a j. God, Ex 20.05
LORD whose name is J., is a j. God), 34.14
and he is j. of his wife who has Num 5.14
and he is j. of his wife, though she 5.14
a man and he is j. of his wife; 5.30
to him, "Are you j. for my sake? 11.29
in that he was j. with my jealousy 25.11
because he was j. for his God, 25.13
God is a devouring fire, a j. God. Deu 4.24
I the LORD your God am a j. God, 5.09
in the midst of you is a j. God; 6.15
he is a j. God; he will not forgive Jos 24.19
"I have been very j. for the LORD, 1Ki 19.10
"I have been very j. for the LORD, 19.14
who is j. with anger against Job 36.33
Will thy j. wrath burn like fire? Ps 79.05
the camp were j. of Moses and 106.16
Ephraim shall not be j. of Judah, Is 11.13
I speak in my j. wrath, because you Eze 36.06
and I will be j. for my holy name. 39.25
Then the LORD became j. for his land, Joe 2.18
The LORD is a j. God and avenging, Nah 1.02
In the fire of his j. wrath, Zep 1.18
the fire of my j. wrath all the 3.08
am exceedingly j. for Jerusalem Zec 1.14
I am j. for Zion with great jealousy, 8.02
and I am j. for her with great 8.02
j. of Joseph, sold him into Egypt; Ac 7.09
But the Jews were j., and taking some 17.05
"I will make you j. of those who Rom 10.19
Gentiles, so as to make Israel j. 11.11
in order to make my fellow Jews j., 11.14
love is not j. or boastful; 1Co 13.04

JEALOUSLY
"He yearns j. over the spirit which Jas 4.05

JEALOUSY
if the spirit of j. comes upon him, Num 5.14
if the spirit of j. comes upon him, 5.14
for it is a cereal offering of j., 5.15
which is the cereal offering of j. 5.18
offering of j. out of the woman's 5.25
"This is the law in cases of j., 5.29
the spirit of j. comes upon a man 5.30
was jealous with my j. among them, 25.11
the people of Israel in my j. 25.11
LORD and his j. would smoke against Deu 29.20
They stirred him to j. with strange 32.16
stirred me to j. with what is no 32.21
stir them to j. with those who are 32.21
provoked him to j. with their sins 1Ki 14.22
kills the fool, and j. slays the simple. Job 5.02
moved him to j. with their graven Ps 78.58
For j. makes a man furious, and he Pro 6.34
but who can stand before j.? 27.04
j. is cruel as the grave. Its flashes Sol 8.06
The j. of Ephraim shall depart, and Is 11.13
I, the LORD, have spoken in my j., Eze 5.13
image of j., which provokes to j. 8.03
the entrance, was this image of j. 8.05
upon you the blood of wrath and j. 16.38
and my j. shall depart from you; 16.42
speak in my hot j. against the 36.05
For in my j. and in my blazing 38.19
am jealous for Zion with great j., Zec 8.02
Sadducees, and filled with j., Ac 5.17
multitudes, they were filled with j., 13.45
licentiousness, not in quarreling and j. Rom 13.13
while there is j. and strife among 1Co 3.03
Shall we provoke the Lord to j.? 10.22
I feel a divine j. for you, 2Co 11.02
quarreling, j., anger, selfishness, 12.20
j., anger, selfishness, dissension, Gal 5.20

you have bitter j. and selfish Jas 3.14
For where j. and selfish ambition 3.16

JEARIM
of Mount J. (that is Chesalon), and Jos 15.10

JEATHERAI
his son, Zerah his son, J. his son. 1Ch 6.21

JEBERECHIAH
priest and Zechariah the son of J., Is 8.02

JEBUS
Zela, Haeleph, J. (that is, Jerusalem), Jos 18.28
and arrived opposite J. (that is, Ju 19.10
When they were near J., the day was 19.11
that is J., where the Jebusites 1Ch 11.04
The inhabitants of J. said to David, 11.05

JEBUSITE
southern shoulder of the J. (that is, Jos 15.08
threshing floor of Araunah the J. 2Sa 24.16
threshing floor of Araunah the J." 24.18
threshing floor of Ornan the J." 1Ch 21.15
threshing floor of Ornan the J. 21.18
threshing floor of Ornan the J., 21.28
threshing floor of Ornan the J. 2Ch 3.01
the J., and the Girgashite; Neh 9.08

JEBUSITES
and the J., the Amorites, the Gen 10.16
Canaanites, the Girgashites and the J." 15.21
Perizzites, the Hivites, and the J. Ex 3.08
and the J., a land flowing with 3.17
and the J., which he swore to your 13.05
and the J., and I blot them out, 23.23
Perizzites, the Hivites, and the J. 33.02
Perizzites, the Hivites, and the J. 34.11
the J., and the Amorites dwell in Num 13.29
and the J., seven nations greater Deu 7.01
Perizzites, the Hivites and the J., 20.17
Girgashites, the Amorites, and the J. Jos 3.10
and the J., heard of this, 9.01
and the J. in the hill country, and 11.03
Perizzites, the Hivites, and the J.); 12.08
But the J., the inhabitants of 15.63
so the J. dwell with the people of 15.63
south of the shoulder of the J., 18.16
Girgashites, the Hivites, and the J.; 24.11
drive out the J. who dwelt in Ju 1.21
so the J. have dwelt with the 1.21
Perizzites, the Hivites, and the J.; 3.05
turn aside to this city of the J., 19.11
went to Jerusalem against the J., 2Sa 5.06
day, "Whoever would smite the J., 5.08
and the J., who were not of the 1Ki 9.20
and the J., the Amorites, the 1Ch 1.14
where the J. were, the inhabitants 11.04
shall smite the J. first shall be 11.06
and the J., who were not of Israel, 2Ch 8.07
the J., the Ammonites, the Moabites, Ez 9.01
and Ekron shall be like the J. Zec 9.07

JECHONIAH
the father of J. and his brothers, Mt 1.11
J. was the father of Shealtiel, and 1.12

JECOLIAH
mother's name was J. of Jerusalem. 2Ki 15.02
mother's name was J. of Jerusalem. 2Ch 26.03

JECONIAH
J. his son, Zedekiah his son; 1Ch 3.16
and the sons of J., the captive: 3.17
carried away with J. king of Judah, Est 2.05
from Jerusalem J. the son of Jer 24.01
to Babylon J. the son of Jehoiakim, 27.20

JECONIAH (cont.)
to this place J. the son of Jer 28.04
This was after King J., and the queen 29.02

JEDAIAH
son of J., son of Shimri, son of 1Ch 4.37
the priests: J., Jehoiarib, Jachin, 9.10
to Jehoiarib, the second to J., 24.07
the sons of J., of the house of Ez 2.36
Next to them J. the son of Harumaph Neh 3.10
the sons of J., namely the house of 7.39
J. the son of Joiarib, Jachin, 11.10
Shemaiah, Joiarib, J., 12.06
Sallu, Amok, Hilkiah, J. These were 12.07
Mattenai; of J., Uzzi; 12.19
Hashabiah; of J., Nethanel. 12.21
and J., who have arrived from Zec 6.10
J., and Josiah the son of Zephaniah. 6.14

JEDIAEL
Bela, Becher, and J., three. 1Ch 7.06
The sons of J.: Bilhan. And the sons 7.10
the sons of J. according to the 7.11
J. the son of Shimri, and Joha his 11.45
J., Michael, Jozabad, Elihu, and 12.20
J. the second, Zebadiah the third, 26.02

JEDIDAH
name was J. the daughter of Adaiah 2Ki 22.01

JEDIDIAH
so he called his name J., 2Sa 12.25

JEDUTHUN
son of J., and Berechiah the son of 1Ch 9.16
the son of J., and Hosah were to be 16.38
With them were Heman and J., 16.41
Heman and J. had trumpets and 16.42
The sons of J. were appointed to 16.42
and of J., who should prophesy with 25.01
Of J., the sons of Jeduthun: Gedaliah, 25.03
the sons of J.: Gedaliah, Zeri, 25.03
the direction of their father J., 25.03
Asaph, J., and Heman were under the 25.06
and J., their sons and kinsmen, 2Ch 5.12
and of the sons of J., 29.14
and J. the king's seer; 35.15
Shammua, son of Galal, son of J. Neh 11.17

JEERED
came out of the city and j. at him, 2Ki 2.23

JEGARSAHADUTHA
Laban called it J.: but Jacob Gen 31.47

JEHALLELEL
The sons of J.: Ziph, Ziphah, Tiria, 1Ch 4.16
of Abdi, and Azariah the son of J.; 2Ch 29.12

JEHDEIAH
of the sons of Shubael, J. 1Ch 24.20
she-asses was J. the Meronothite. 27.30

JEHEZKEL
to Pethahiah, the twentieth to J., 1Ch 24.16

JEHIAH
Obededom and J. also were to be 1Ch 15.24

JEHIEL
J., Unni, Eliab, Benaiah, Maaseiah, 1Ch 15.18
J., Unni, Eliab, Maaseiah, and Benaiah 15.20
J., Mattithiah, Eliab, Benaiah, 16.05
J. the chief, and Zetham, and Joel, 23.08
he and J. the son of Hachmoni 27.32
in the care of J. the Gershonite. 29.08
J., Zechariah, Azariah, Michael, and 2Ch 21.02
while J., Azaziah, Nahath, Asahel, 31.13
and J., the chief officers of the 35.08
of Joab, Obadiah the son of J., Ez 8 09
And Shecaniah the son of J., 10 02
Elijah, Shemaiah, J., and Uzziah. 10.21
J., Abdi, Jeremoth, and Elijah. 10.26

JEHIELI
to Ladan the Gershonite: J. 1Ch 26.21
The sons of J., Zetham and Joel his 26.22

JEHIZKIAH
J. the son of Shallum, and Amasa the 2Ch 28.12

JEHOADDAH
Ahaz was the father of J.; 1Ch 8.36
and J. was the father of Alemeth, 8.36

JEHOADDAN
mother's name was J. of Jerusalem. 2Ch 25.01

JEHOADDIN
mother's name was J. of Jerusalem. 2Ki 14.02

JEHOAHAZ
And J. his son reigned in his stead. 2Ki 10.35
J. the son of Jehu began to reign 13.01
Then J. besought the LORD, and the 13.04
was not left to J. an army of more 13.07
of the acts of J. and all that he 13.08
So J. slept with his fathers, and 13.09
the son of J. began to reign over 13.10
oppressed Israel all the days of J. 13.22
the son of J. took again from 13.25
had taken from J. his father in 13.25
messengers to Jehoash the son of J., 14.08
the death of Jehoash son of J., 14.17
the land took J. the son of Josiah, 23.30
J. was twenty-three years old when 23.31
But he took J. away; and he came 23.34
no son was left to him except J., 2Ch 21.17
and sent to Joash the son of J., 25.17
the death of Joash the son of J., 25.25
the land took J. the son of Josiah 36.01
J. was twenty-three years old when 36.02
but Neco took J. his brother and 36.04

JEHOASH
J. was seven years old when he 2Ki 11.21
year of Jehu J. began to reign, 12.01
And J. did what was right in the 12.02
J. said to the priests, "All the 12.04
year of King J. the priests had 12.06
Therefore King J. summoned Jehoiada 12.07
J. king of Judah took all the 12.18
king of Judah J. the son of 13.10
Then J. the son of Jehoahaz took 13.25
messengers to J. the son of 14.08
And J. king of Israel sent word to 14.09
So J. king of Israel went up, and he 14.11
And J. king of Israel captured 14.13
the son of J., son of Ahaziah, at 14.13
of the acts of J. which he did, 14.15
And J. slept with his fathers, and 14.16
the death of J. son of Jehoahaz, 14.17

JEHOHANAN
J. the sixth, Eliehoenai the seventh. 1Ch 26.03
and next to him J. the commander, 2Ch 17.15
of Jeroham, Ishmael the son of J., 23.01
went to the chamber of J. the son of Ez 10.06
Of the sons of Bebai were J., 10.28
and his son J. had taken the Neh 6.18
Meshullam; of Amariah, J.; 12.13
J., Malchijah, Elam, and Ezer. 12.42

JEHOIACHIN
and J. his son reigned in his stead. 2Ki 24.06
J. was eighteen years old when he 24.08

JEHOIACHIN (cont.)
and J. the king of Judah gave 2Ki 24.12
And he carried away J. to Babylon; 24.15
of the exile of J. king of Judah, 25.27
graciously freed J. king of Judah 25.27
So J. put off his prison garments. 25.29
and J. his son reigned in his 2Ch 36.08
J. was eight years old when he 36.09
the captivity of J. king of Judah, Jer 52.31
up the head of J. king of Judah 52.31
So J. put off his prison garments. 52.33
year of the exile of King J.), Eze 1.02

JEHOIACHIN'S
J. uncle, king in his stead, and 2Ki 24.17

JEHOIADA
the son of J. was over the Cherethites 2Sa 8.18
the son of J. was in command of 20.23
the son of J. was a valiant man of 23.20
These things did Benaiah the son of J., 23.22
priest, and Benaiah the son of J., 1Ki 1.08
priest, and Benaiah the son of J., 1.26
prophet, and Benaiah the son of J." 1.32
the son of J. answered the king, 1.36
prophet, and Benaiah the son of J., 1.38
prophet, and Benaiah the son of J., 1.44
Solomon sent Benaiah the son of J.; 2.25
Solomon sent Benaiah the son of J., 2.29
Then Benaiah the son of J. went up, 2.34
the son of J. over the army in 2.35
commanded Benaiah the son of J.; 2.46
Benaiah the son of J. was in 4.04
seventh year J. sent and brought 2Ki 11.04
to all that J. the priest commanded, 11.09
sabbath, and came to J. the priest. 11.09
Then J. the priest commanded the 11.15
And J. made a covenant between the 11.17
because J. the priest instructed 12.02
summoned J. the priest and the 12.07
Then J. the priest took a chest, and 12.09
the son of J. was a valiant man of 1Ch 11.22
These things did Benaiah the son of J., 11.24
The prince J., of the house of 12.27
the son of J. was over the Cherethites 18.17
the son of J. the priest, as chief; 27.05
succeeded by J. the son of Benaiah, 27.34
Jehoram and wife of J. the priest, 2Ch 22.11
the seventh year J. took courage, 23.01
And J. said to them, "Behold, the 23.03
to all that J. the priest commanded. 23.08
for J. the priest did not dismiss 23.08
And J. the priest delivered to the 23.09
and J. and his sons anointed him, 23.11
Then J. the priest brought out the 23.14
And J. made a covenant between 23.16
And J. posted watchmen for the 23.18
LORD all the days of J. the priest. 24.02
J. got for him two wives, and he had 24.03
So the king summoned J. the chief, 24.06
And the king and J. gave it to 24.12
the money before the king and J., 24.14
continually all the days of J. 24.14
But J. grew old and full of days, 24.15
the death of J. the princes of 24.17
Zechariah the son of J. the priest; 24.20
not remember the kindness which J., 24.22
blood of the son of J. the priest, 24.25
And one of the sons of J., the son of Neh 13.28
priest instead of J. the priest, Jer 29.26

JEHOIAKIM
father, and changed his name to J. 2Ki 23.34
And J. gave the silver and the gold 23.35
J. was twenty-five years old when 23.36
and J. became his servant three 24.01
Now the rest of the deeds of J., 24.05
So J. slept with his fathers, and 24.06
according to all that J. had done. 24.19
the second J., the third Zedekiah, 1Ch 3.15
The descendants of J.: Jeconiah 3.16
Jerusalem, and changed his name to J.; 2Ch 36.04
J. was twenty-five years old when 36.05
Now the rest of the acts of J. 36.08
in the days of J. the son of Jer 1.03
LORD concerning J. the son of Josiah, 22.18
LORD, though Coniah the son of J., 22.24
Jerusalem Jeconiah the son of J., 24.01
fourth year of J. the son of Josiah, 25.01
of the reign of J. the son of Josiah, 26.01
And when King J., with all his 26.21
Then King J. sent to Egypt certain 26.22
Egypt and brought him to King J., 26.23
to Babylon Jeconiah the son of J., 27.20
this place Jeconiah the son of J., 28.04
in the days of J. the son of Josiah, 35.01
fourth year of J. the son of Josiah, 36.01
fifth year of J. the son of Josiah, 36.09
which J. the king of Judah has 36.28
And concerning J. king of Judah you 36.29
LORD concerning J. king of Judah, 36.30
scroll which J. king of Judah had 36.32
instead of Coniah the son of J. 37.01
fourth year of J. the son of Josiah, 45.01
fourth year of J. the son of Josiah, 46.02
according to all that J. had done. 52.02
of the reign of J. king of Judah, Dan 1.01
And the Lord gave J. king of Judah 1.02

JEHOIARIB
Of the priests: Jedaiah, J., Jachin, 1Ch 9.10
The first lot fell to J., the second 24.07

JEHONADAB
he met J. the son of Rechab coming 2Ki 10.15
And J. answered, "It is." 10.15
of Baal with J. the son of Rechab; 10.23

JEHONATHAN
J., Adonijah, Tobijah, and Tobadonijah; 2Ch 17.08
Shammua; of Shemaiah, J.; Neh 12.18

JEHORAM
and J. his son reigned in his stead. 1Ki 22.50
J., his brother, became king in his 2Ki 1.17
second year of J. the son of 1.17
J. the son of Ahab became king over 3.01
So King J. marched out of Samaria 3.06
J. answered, "By the way of the 3.08
J. the son of Jehoshaphat, king of 8.16
of Israel, Ahaziah the son of J., 8.25
the son of J. king of Judah went 8.29
Jehoshaphat and J. and Ahaziah, 12.18
the priests Elishama and J. 2Ch 17.08
and J. his son reigned in his 21.01
but he gave the kingdom to J., 21.03
When J. had ascended the throne of 21.04
J. was thirty-two years old when he 21.05
Then J. passed over with his 21.09
up against J. the anger of the 21.16
the son of J. king of Judah 22.01
and went with J. the son of Ahab 22.05
the son of J. king of Judah went 22.06
went out with J. to meet Jehu the 22.07
daughter of King J. and wife of 22.11

JEHOSHABEATH
But J., the daughter of the king, 2Ch 22.11
Thus J., the daughter of King 22.11

JEHOSHAPHAT
and J. the son of Ahilud was 2Sa 8.16
and J. the son of Ahilud was the 20.24
J. the son of Ahilud was recorder; 1Ki 4.03
J. the son of Paruah, in Issachar; 4.17

JEHOSHAPHAT (cont.)
and J. his son reigned in his stead. 1Ki 15.24
the third year J. the king of 22.02
And he said to J., "Will you go 22.04
And J. said to the king of Israel, 22.04
And J. said to the king of Israel, 22.05
But J. said, "Is there not here 22.07
And the king of Israel said to J., 22.08
And J. said, "Let not the king say 22.08
of Israel and J. the king of Judah 22.10
And the king of Israel said to J., 22.18
of Israel and J. the king of Judah 22.29
And the king of Israel said to J., 22.30
captains of the chariots saw J., 22.32
fight against him; and J. cried out. 22.32
J. the son of Asa began to reign 22.41
J. was thirty-five years old when 22.42
J. also made peace with the king of 22.44
Now the rest of the acts of J., 22.45
J. made ships of Tarshish to go to 22.48
Ahaziah the son of Ahab said to J., 22.49
in the ships," but J. was not willing. 22.49
And J. slept with his fathers, and 22.50
seventeenth year of J. king of Judah, 22.51
year of Jehoram the son of J., 2Ki 1.17
eighteenth year of J. king of Judah, 3.01
and sent word to J. king of Judah, 3.07
And J. said, "Is there no prophet of 3.11
And J. said, "The word of the LORD 3.12
of Israel and J. and the king of 3.12
have regard for J. the king of 3.14
of Israel, Jehoram the son of J., 8.16
Jehu the son of J., son of Nimshi; 9.02
Thus Jehu the son of J. the son of 9.14
gifts that J. and Jehoram and 12.18
his son, Asa his son, J. his son, 1Ch 3.10
and J. the son of Ahilud was 18.15
J. his son reigned in his stead, and 2Ch 17.01
The LORD was with J., because he 17.03
all Judah brought tribute to J.; 17.05
and they made no war against J. 17.10
Philistines brought J. presents, 17.11
And J. grew steadily greater. 17.12
Now J. had great riches and honor; 18.01
of Israel said to J. king of Judah, 18.03
And J. said to the king of Israel, 18.04
But J. said, "Is there not here 18.06
And the king of Israel said to J., 18.07
And J. said, "Let not the king say 18.07
of Israel and J. the king of Judah 18.09
And the king of Israel said to J., 18.17
of Israel and J. the king of Judah 18.28
And the king of Israel said to J., 18.29
captains of the chariots saw J., 18.31
and J. cried out, and the LORD 18.31
J. the king of Judah returned in 19.01
to meet him, and said to King J., 19.02
J. dwelt at Jerusalem; and he went 19.04
Moreover in Jerusalem J. appointed 19.08
Meunites, came against J. for battle. 20.01
Some men came and told J., "A great 20.02
Then J. feared, and set himself to 20.03
And J. stood in the assembly of 20.05
and King J.: Thus says the LORD to 20.15
Then J. bowed his head with his 20.18
J. stood and said, "Hear me, Judah 20.20
When J. and his people came to take 20.25
and J. at their head, returning to 20.27
So the realm of J. was quiet, for his 20.30
Thus J. reigned over Judah. He was 20.31
Now the rest of the acts of J., 20.34
After this J. king of Judah joined 20.35
of Mareshah prophesied against J., 20.37
J. slept with his fathers, and was 21.01
the sons of J.: Azariah, Jehiel, 21.02
were the sons of J. king of Judah. 21.02
in the ways of J. your father, 21.12
said, "He is the grandson of J., 22.09
them down to the valley of J., Joe 3.02
and come up to the valley of J.; 3.12
and Asa the father of J., Mt 1.08
and J. the father of Joram, and 1.08

JEHOSHEBA
But J., the daughter of King Joram, 2Ki 11.02

JEHOZABAD
of Shimeath and J. the son of 2Ki 12.21
J. the second, Joah the third, Sachar 1Ch 26.04
and next to him J. with a hundred 2Ch 17.18
and J. the son of Shimrith the 24.26

JEHOZADAK
Azariah of Seraiah, Seraiah of J.; 1Ch 6.14
and J. went into exile when the 6.15
Judah, and to Joshua the son of J., Hag 1.01
Shealtiel, and Joshua the son of J., 1.12
the spirit of Joshua the son of J., 1.14
Judah, and to Joshua the son of J., 2.02
son of J., the high priest; 2.04
the son of J., the high priest; Zec 6.11

JEHU
LORD came to J. the son of Hanai 1Ki 16.01
by the prophet J. the son of 16.07
against Baasha by J. the prophet, 16.12
and J. the son of Nimshi you shall 19.16
the sword of Hazael shall J. slay; 19.17
the sword of J. shall Elisha slay. 19.17
look there for J. the son of 2Ki 9.02
And J. said, "To which of us all?" 9.05
When J. came out to the servants of 9.11
trumpet, and proclaimed, "J. is king." 9.13
Thus J. the son of Jehoshaphat the 9.14
So J. said, "If this is your mind, 9.15
Then J. mounted his chariot, and 9.16
spied the company of J. as he came, 9.17
And J. said, "What have you to do 9.18
And J. answered, "What have you 9.19
the driving of J. the son of 9.20
his chariot, and went to meet J., 9.21
And when Joram saw J., 9.22
he said, "Is it peace, J.?" 9.22
And J. drew his bow with his full 9.24
J. said to Bidkar his aide, "Take 9.25
And J. pursued him, and said, "Shoot 9.27
When J. came to Jezreel, Jezebel 9.30
And as J. entered the gate, she said, 9.31
So J. wrote letters, and sent them 10.01
sent to J., saying, "We are your 10.05
So J. slew all that remained of the 10.11
J. met the kinsmen of Ahaziah king 10.13
J. said, "If it is, give me your 10.15
And J. took him up with him into 10.15
Then J. assembled all the people, 10.18
but J. will serve him much. 10.18
But J. did it with cunning in 10.19
And J. ordered, "Sanctify a solemn 10.20
And J. sent throughout all Israel; 10.21
Then J. went into the house of Baal 10.23
Now J. had stationed eighty men 10.24
J. said to the guard and to the 10.25
Thus J. wiped out Baal from Israel. 10.28
But J. did not turn aside from the 10.29
And the LORD said to J., 10.30
But J. was not careful to walk in 10.31
Now the rest of the acts of J., 10.34
So J. slept with his fathers, and 10.35
The time that J. reigned over 10.36
seventh year of J. Jehoash began 12.01
the son of J. began to reign over 13.01
son of J., king of Israel, saying, 14.08
of the LORD which he gave to J., 15.12
the father of J., and J. of Azariah. 1Ch 2.38
Joel, J. the son of Joshibiah, son of 4.35

JEHU (cont.)
Azmaveth; Beracah, J. of Anathoth, 1Ch 12.03
But J. the son of Hanani the seer 2Ch 19.02
chronicles of J. the son of Hanani, 20.34
Jehoram to meet J. the son of 22.07
And when J. was executing judgment 22.08
was brought to J. and put to death. 22.09
son of J., king of Israel, saying, 25.17
the house of J. for the blood of Hos 1.04

JEHUBBAH
his brother: Rohgah, J., and Aram. 1Ch 7.34

JEHUCAL
King Zedekiah sent J. the son of Jer 37.03

JEHUD
J., Beneberak, Gathrimmon, Jos 19.45

JEHUDI
princes sent J. the son of Nethaniah, Jer 36.14
Then the king sent J. to get the 36.21
and J. read it to the king and all 36.21
As J. read three or four columns, 36.23

JEHUEL
the sons of Heman, J. and Shimei; 2Ch 29.14

JEIEL
the chief, J., and Zechariah, 1Ch 5.07
J. the father of Gibeon dwelt in 8.29
J., and the name of his wife was 9.35
Shama and J. the sons of Hotham the 11.44
the gatekeepers Obededom and J. 15.18
J., and Azaziah were to lead with 15.21
J., Shemiramoth, Jehiel, Mattithiah, 16.05
and J., who were to play harps and 16.05
son of J., son of Mattaniah, a 2Ch 20.14
muster made by J. the secretary 26.11
and Hashabiah and J. and Jozabad, 35.09
J., Mattithiah, Zabad, Zebina, Jaddai, Ez 10.43

JEKABZEEL
and in J. and its villages, Neh 11.25

JEKAMEAM
the third, and J. the fourth. 1Ch 23.19
Jahaziel the third, J. the fourth. 24.23

JEKAMIAH
Shallum was the father of J., 1Ch 2.41
of Jekamiah, and J. of Elishama. 2.41
J., Hoshama, and Nedabiah; 3.18

JEKUTHIEL
and J. the father of Zanoah. 1Ch 4.18

JEMIMAH
he called the name of the first J.; Job 42.14

JEMUEL
J., Jamin, Ohad, Jachin, Zohar, and Gen 46.10
J., Jamin, Ohad, Jachin, Zohar, and Ex 6.15

JEOPARDED
a people that j. their lives to Ju 5.18

JEPHTHAH
Now J. the Gileadite was a mighty Ju 11.01
Gilead was the father of J. 11.01
they thrust J. out, and said to him, 11.02
Then J. fled from his brothers, and 11.03
worthless fellows collected round J., 11.03
went to bring J. from the land of 11.05
and they said to J., "Come and be 11.06
But J. said to the elders of Gilead, 11.07
And the elders of Gilead said to J., 11.08
J. said to the elders of Gilead, "If 11.09
And the elders of Gilead said to J., 11.10
So J. went with the elders of 11.11
and J. spoke all his words before 11.11
Then J. sent messengers to the king 11.12
answered the messengers of J., 11.13
And J. sent messengers again to the 11.14
"Thus says J.: Israel did not take 11.15
the message of J. which he sent to 11.28
Spirit of the LORD came upon J., 11.29
And J. made a vow to the LORD, and 11.30
So J. crossed over to the Ammonites 11.32
Then J. came to his home at Mizpah; 11.34
the daughter of J. the Gileadite 11.40
crossed to Zaphon and said to J., 12.01
And J. said to them, "I and my 12.02
Then J. gathered all the men of 12.04
J. judged Israel six years. 12.07
Then J. the Gileadite died, and was 12.07
and J., and Samuel, and delivered 1Sa 12.11
J., of David and Samuel and the Heb 11.32

JEPHUNNEH
of Judah, Caleb the son of J.; Num 13.06
son of Nun and Caleb the son of J., 14.06
the son of J. and Joshua the son 14.30
Caleb the son of J. remained alive, 14.38
the son of J. and Joshua the son 26.65
the son of J. the Kenizzite and 32.12
of Judah, Caleb the son of J. 34.19
except Caleb the son of J.; Deu 1.36
the son of J. the Kenizzite said Jos 14.06
the son of J. for an inheritance. 14.13
the son of J. the Kenizzite to 14.14
the son of J. a portion among the 15.13
the son of J. as his possession. 21.12
The sons of Caleb the son of J.: 1Ch 4.15
they gave to Caleb the son of J. 6.56
J., Pispa, and Ara. 7.38

JERAH
Almodad, Sheleph, Hazarmaveth, J., Gen 10.26
Almodad, Sheleph, Hazarmaveth, J., 1Ch 1.20

JERAHMEEL
born to him: J., Ram, and Chelubai. 1Ch 2.09
The sons of J., the first-born of 2.25
J. also had another wife, whose name 2.26
The sons of Ram, the first-born of J.: 2.27
These were the descendants of J. 2.33
The sons of Caleb the brother of J.: 2.42
Of Kish, the sons of Kish: J. 24.29
king commanded J. the king's son Jer 36.26

JERAHMEELITES
or "Against the Negeb of the J.," 1Sa 27.10
in Racal, in the cities of the J., 30.29

JERED
wife bore J. the father of Gedor, 1Ch 4.18

JEREMAI
J., Manasseh, and Shimei. Ez 10.33

JEREMIAH
the daughter of J. of Libnah. 2Ki 23.31
the daughter of J. of Libnah. 24.18
J., Hodaviah, and Jahdiel, mighty 1Ch 5.24
J., Jahaziel, Johanan, Jozabad of 12.04
Mishmannah fourth, J. fifth, 12.10
J. tenth, Machbannai eleventh. 12.13
J. also uttered a lament for Josiah; 2Ch 35.25
himself before J. the prophet, 36.12
of the LORD by the mouth of J., 36.21
by the mouth of J. might be 36.22
by the mouth of J. might be Ez 1.01
Seraiah, Azariah, J., Neh 10.01
and Jeshun; Seraiah, J., Ezra, 12.01
Meraiah; of J., Hananiah; 12.12
Judah, Benjamin, Shemaiah, and J., 12.34

JEREMIAH (cont.)

The words of J., the son of Hilkiah, Jer 1.01
"J., what do you see?" And I said, 1.11
that came to J. from the LORD: 7.01
that came to J. from the LORD: 11.01
which came to J. concerning the 14.01
that came to J. from the LORD: 18.01
"Come, let us make plots against J., 18.18
Then J. came from Topheth, where the 19.14
heard J. prophesying these things. 20.01
Then Pashhur beat J. the prophet, 20.02
released J. from the stocks, 20.03
J. said to him, "The LORD does not 20.03
which came to J. from the LORD, 21.01
Then J. said to them: 21.03
said to me, "What do you see, J.?" 24.03
that came to J. concerning all the 25.01
which J. the prophet spoke to all 25.02
which J. prophesied against all the 25.13
people heard J. speaking these 26.07
And when J. had finished speaking 25.08
gathered about J. in the house of 26.09
Then J. spoke to all the princes 26.12
land in words like those of J. 26.20
was with J. so that he was not 26.24
this word came to J. from the LORD. 27.01
Then the prophet J. spoke to 28.05
and the prophet J. said, "Amen! 28.06
from the neck of J. the prophet, 28.10
But J. the prophet went his way. 28.11
off the neck of J. the prophet, 28.12
the word of the LORD came to J.: 28.12
And J. the prophet said to the 28.15
letter which J. the prophet sent 29.01
you not rebuked J. of Anathoth who 29.27
in the hearing of J. the prophet. 29.29
Then the word of the LORD came to J.: 29.30
that came to J. from the LORD: 30.01
that came to J. from the LORD in 32.01
and J. the prophet was shut up in 32.02
J. said, "The word of the LORD came 32.06
The word of the LORD came to J.: 32.26
The LORD came to J. a second time, 33.01
The word of the LORD came to J.: 33.19
The word of the LORD came to J.: 33.23
which came to J. from the LORD, 34.01
Then J. the prophet spoke all these 34.06
which came to J. from the LORD, 34.08
the LORD came to J. from the LORD: 34.12
which came to J. from the LORD in 35.01
So I took Jaazaniah the son of J., 35.03
Then the word of the LORD came to J.: 35.12
house of the Rechabites J. said, 35.18
word came to J. from the LORD: 36.01
Then J. called Baruch the son of 36.04
dictation of J. all the words of 36.04
And J. ordered Baruch, saying, "I am 36.05
did all that J. the prophet 36.08
the words of J. from the scroll, in 36.10
you and J., and let no one know 36.19
the secretary and J. the prophet, 36.26
the word of the LORD came to J.: 36.27
Then J. took another scroll and 36.32
dictation of J. all the words of 36.32
he spoke through J. the prophet. 37.02
to J. the prophet saying, "Pray for 37.03
Now J. was still going in and out 37.04
the LORD came to J. the prophet: 37.06
J. set out from Jerusalem to go to 37.12
seized J. the prophet, saying, "You 37.13
And J. said, "It is false; 37.14
and seized J. and brought him to 37.14
And the princes were enraged at J., 37.15
When J. had come to the dungeon 37.16
J. said, "There is." Then he said, 37.17
J. also said to King Zedekiah, "What 37.18
they committed J. to the court of 37.21
So J. remained in the court of the 37.21
the words that J. was saying to 38.01
took J. and cast him into the cistern 38.06
guard, letting J. down by ropes. 38.06
and J. sank in the mire. 38.06
they had put J. into the cistern— 38.07
they did to J. the prophet by 38.09
and lift J. the prophet out of the 38.10
he let down to J. in the cistern 38.11
Ebedmelech the Ethiopian said to J., 38.12
and the ropes." J. did so. 38.12
Then they drew J. up with ropes and 38.13
And J. remained in the court of the 38.13
sent for J. the prophet and 38.14
The king said to J., "I will ask 38.14
J. said to Zedekiah, "If I tell you, 38.15
King Zedekiah swore secretly to J., 38.16
Then J. said to Zedekiah, "Thus says 38.17
King Zedekiah said to J., 38.19
J. said, "You shall not be given to 38.20
Then Zedekiah said to J., 38.24
princes came to J. and asked him, 38.27
And J. remained in the court of the 38.28
concerning J. through Nebuzaradan, 39.11
sent and took J. from the court of 39.14
LORD came to J. while he was shut 39.15
that came to J. from the LORD 40.01
the guard took J. and said to him, 40.02
Then J. went to Gedaliah the son of 40.06
and said to J. the prophet, "Let our 42.02
J. the prophet said to them, "I have 42.04
Then they said to J., "May the LORD 42.05
the word of the LORD came to J. 42.07
When J. finished speaking to all 43.01
all the insolent men said to J., 43.02
also J. the prophet and Baruch the 43.06
the LORD came to J. in Tahpanhes: 43.08
that came to J. concerning all the 44.01
in the land of Egypt, answered J.: 44.15
Then J. said to all the people, men 44.20
J. said to all the people and all 44.24
The word that J. the prophet spoke 45.01
in a book at the dictation of J., 45.01
which came to J. the prophet 46.01
LORD spoke to J. the prophet about 46.13
that came to J. the prophet 47.01
that came to J. the prophet 49.34
the Chaldeans, by J. the prophet: 50.01
The word which J. the prophet 51.59
J. wrote in a book all the evil 51.60
And J. said to Seraiah: "When you 51.61
Thus far are the words of J. 51.64
the daughter of J. of Libnah. 52.01
word of the LORD to J. the prophet, Dan 9.02
what was spoken by the prophet J.: Mt 2.17
and others J. or one of the prophets." 16.14
had been spoken by the prophet J., 27.09

JEREMIAH'S

which Baruch wrote at J. dictation, Jer 36.27

JEREMOTH

J., Abijah, Anathoth, and Alemeth. 1Ch 7.08
and Ahio, Shashak, and J. 8,14
Mushi: Mahli, Eder, and J., three. 23.23
to J., his sons and his brethren, 25.22
for Naphtali, J. the son of Azriel; 27.19
Jehiel, Abdi, J., and Elijah. Ez 10.26
Mattaniah, J., Zabad, and Aziza. 10.27
Adaiah, Jashub, Sheal, and J. 10.29

JERIAH

J. the chief, Amariah the second, 1Ch 23.19
J. the chief, Amariah the second, 24.23

JERIBAI

and J., and Joshaviah, the sons of 1Ch 11.46

JERICHO

of Moab beyond the Jordan at J. Num 22.01
Moab by the Jordan at J., saying, 26.03
plains of Moab by the Jordan at J. 26.63
plains of Moab by the Jordan at J. 31.12
plains of Moab by the Jordan at J.; 33.48
of Moab by the Jordan at J., 33.50
beyond the Jordan at J. eastward, 34.15
of Moab by the Jordan at J., 35.01
plains of Moab by the Jordan at J. 36.13
in the land of Moab, opposite J.; Deu 32.49
of Pisgah, which is opposite J. 34.01
the valley of J. the city of palm 34.03
"Go, view the land, especially J." Jos 2.01
And it was told the king of J., 2.02
Then the king of J. sent to Rahab, 2.03
the people passed over opposite J. 3.16
for battle, to the plains of J. 4.13
in Gilgal on the east border of J. 4.19
at evening in the plains of J. 5.10
When Joshua was by J., he lifted up 5.13
Now J. was shut up from within and 6.01
I have given into your hand J., 6.02
whom Joshua sent to spy out J. 6.25
up and rebuilds this city, J. 6.26
Joshua sent men from J. to Ai, 7.02
king as you did to J. and its king; 8.02
Joshua had done to J. and to Ai, 9.03
as he had done to J. and its king, 10.01
as he had done to the king of J. 10.28
as he had done to the king of J. 10.30
the king of J., one; the king of 12.09
Moab, beyond the Jordan east of J. 13.32
Jordan by J., east of the waters of J., 16.01
going up from J. into the hill 16.01
and touches J., ending at the 16.07
up to the shoulder north of J., 18.12
according to their families were J., 18.21
And beyond the Jordan east of J., 20.08
over the Jordan and came to J., 24.11
and the men of J. fought against 24.11
"Remain at J. until your beards 2Sa 10.05
In his days Hiel of Bethel built J.; 1Ki 16.34
for the LORD has sent me to J." 2Ki 2.04
will not leave you." So they came to J. 2.04
who were at J. drew near to Elisha, 2.05
who were at J. saw him over 2.15
to him, while he tarried at J., 2.18
overtook him in the plains of J.; 25.05
and beyond the Jordan at J., 1Ch 6.78
"Remain at J. until your beards 19.05
them to their kinsfolk at J., 2Ch 28.15
The sons of J., three hundred and Ez 2.34
And next to him the men of J. built. Neh 3.02
The sons of J., three hundred and 7.36
Zedekiah in the plains of J.; Jer 39.05
Zedekiah in the plains of J.; 52.08
And as they went out of J., Mt 20.29
And they came to J.; and as Mk 10.46
he was leaving J. with his disciples 10.46
going down from Jerusalem to J., Lk 10.30
As he drew near to J., a blind man 18.35
He entered J. and was passing 19.01
the walls of J. fell down after Heb 11.30

JERIEL

J., Jahmai, Ibsam, and Shemuel, heads 1Ch 7.02

JERIJAH

J. was chief of the Hebronites of 1Ch 26.31

JERIMOTH

J., and Iri, five, heads of fathers' 1Ch 7.07
Eluzai, J., Bealiah, Shemariah, 12.05
sons of Mushi: Mahli, Eder, and J. 24.30
and J., Hananiah, Hanani, Eliathah, 25.04
the daughter of J. the son of 2Ch 11.18
J., Jozabad, Eliel, Ismachiah, Mahath, 31.13

JERIOTH

by his wife Azubah, and by J.; 1Ch 2.18

JEROBOAM

J. the son of Nebat, an Ephraimite 1Ki 11.26
The man J. was very able, and when 11.28
when J. went out of Jerusalem, the 11.29
And he said to J., "Take for 11.31
Solomon sought therefore to kill J.; 11.40
but J. arose, and fled into Egypt, to 11.40
And when J. the son of Nebat heard 12.02
then J. returned from Egypt. 12.02
and J. and all the assembly of 12.03
So J. and all the people came to 12.12
Shilonite to J. the son of Nebat. 12.15
Israel heard that J. had returned, 12.20
Then J. built Shechem in the hill 12.25
And J. said in his heart, "Now the 12.26
And J. appointed a feast on the 12.32
J. was standing by the altar to 13.01
J. stretched out his hand from the 13.04
After this thing J. did not turn 13.33
became sin to the house of J., 13.34
Abijah the son of J. fell sick. 14.01
And J. said to his wife, "Arise, and 14.02
known that you are the wife of J., 14.02
the wife of J. is coming to inquire 14.05
door, he said, "Come in, wife of J.; 14.06
Go, tell J., 'Thus says the LORD, the 14.07
bring evil upon the house of J., 14.10
will cut off from J. every male, 14.10
utterly consume the house of J., 14.10
belonging to J. who dies in the 14.11
for he only of J. shall come to the 14.13
God of Israel, in the house of J. 14.13
cut off the house of J. today. 14.14
up because of the sins of J., 14.16
Now the rest of the acts of J., 14.19
And the time that J. reigned was 14.20
Rehoboam and J. continually. 14.30
year of King J. the son of Nebat, 15.01
Rehoboam and J. all the days of 15.06
was war between Abijam and J. 15.07
twentieth year of J. king of Israel 15.09
Nadab the son of J. began to reign 15.25
he killed all the house of J.; 15.29
to the house of J. not one that 15.29
for the sins of J. which he sinned 15.30
in the way of J. and in his sin 15.34
you have walked in the way of J., 16.02
the house of J. the son of Nebat. 16.03
in being like the house of J., 16.07
the LORD, walking in the way of J., 16.19
all the way of J. the son of Nebat, 16.26
in the sins of J. the son of Nebat, 16.31
the house of J. the son of Nebat, 21.22
in the way of J. the son of Nebat, 22.52
to the sin of J. the son of Nebat, 2Ki 3.03
the house of J. the son of Nebat, 9.09
the sins of J. the son of Nebat, 10.29
did not turn from the sins of J., 10.31
the sins of J. the son of Nebat, 13.02
from the sins of the house of J., 13.06
all the sins of J. the son of 13.11
and J. sat upon his throne; 13.13
and J. his son reigned in his 14.16
J. the son of Joash, king of Israel, 14.23
all the sins of J. the son of 14.24
by the hand of J. the son of Joash. 14.27
Now the rest of the acts of J., 14.28
And J. slept with his fathers: the 14.29
twenty-seventh year of J. king of 15.01
the son of J. reigned over Israel 15.08
the sins of J. the son of Nebat, 15.09
all the sins of J. the son of 15.18
the sins of J. the son of Nebat, 15.24
the sins of J. the son of Nebat, 15.28

JEROBOAM (cont.)
David they made J. the son of 2Ki 17.21
And J. drove Israel from following 17.21
in all the sins which J. did; 17.22
erected by J. the son of Nebat, who 23.15
in the days of J. king of Israel. 1Ch 5.17
seer concerning J. the son of 2Ch 9.29
And when J. the son of Nebat heard 10.02
then J. returned from Egypt. 10.02
and J. and all Israel came and 10.03
So J. and all the people came to 10.12
Shilonite to J. the son of Nebat. 10.15
returned and did not go against J. 11.04
because J. and his sons cast them 11.14
wars between Rehoboam and J. 12.15
year of King J. Abijah began to 13.01
was war between Abijah and J. 13.02
and J. drew up his line of battle 13.03
said, "Hear me, O J. and all Israel! 13.04
Yet J. the son of Nebat, a servant 13.06
calves which J. made you for gods. 13.08
J. had sent an ambush around to 13.13
God defeated J. and all Israel 13.15
And Abijah pursued J., 13.19
J. did not recover his power in the 13.20
in the days of J. the son of Joash, Hos 1.01
in the days of J. the son of Joash, Amo 1.01
the house of J. with the sword." 7.09
Bethel sent to J. king of Israel, 7.10
'J. shall die by the sword, and 7.11

JEROBOAM'S
J. wife did so; she arose 1Ki 14.04
Then J. wife arose, and departed, and 14.17

JEROHAM
name was Elkanah the son of J., 1Sa 1.01
Eliab his son, J. his son, Elkanah 1Ch 6.27
son of J., son of Eliel, son of Toah, 6.34
and Zichri were the sons of J. 8.27
Ibneiah the son of J., Elah the son 9.08
and Adaih the son of J., 9.12
Zebadiah, the sons of J. of Gedor. 12.07
for Dan, Azarel the son of J. 27.22
of hundreds, Azariah the son of J., 2Ch 23.01
and Adaiah the son of J., Neh 11.12

JERUBBAAL
Therefore on that day he was called J., Ju 6.32
Then J. (that is, Gideon' and all the 7.01
J. the son of Joash went and dwelt 8.29
to the family of J. (that is, 8.35
the son of J. went to Shechem to 9.01
of the sons of J. rule over you, 9.02
slew his brothers the sons of J., 9.05
the youngest son of J. was left, 9.05
dealt well with J. and his house, 9.16
and honor with J. and with his 9.19
seventy sons of J. might come and 9.24
not the son of J. and Zebul his 9.28
the curse of Jotham the son of J. 9.57
And the LORD sent J. and Barak, 1Sa 12.11

JERUBBESHETH
Who killed Abimelech the son of J.? 2Sa 11.21

JERUEL
east of the wilderness of J. 2Ch 20.16

JERUSALEM
Adonizedek king of J. heard how Jos 10.01
Adonizedek king of J. sent to Hoham 10.03
the king of J., the king of Hebron, 10.05
the king of J., the king of Hebron, 10.23
the king of J., one; the king of 12.10
of the Jebusite (that is, J.), 15.08
Jebusites, the inhabitants of J., 15.63
people of Judah at J. to this day. 15.63
J.), Gibeah and Kiriathjearim— 18.28
And they brought him to J. Ju 1.07
the men of Judah fought against J., 1.08
out the Jebusites who dwelt in J.; 1.21
of Benjamin in J. to this day. 1.21
opposite Jebus (that is, J.). 19.10
Philistine and brought it to J.; 1Sa 17.54
and at J. he reigned over all 2Sa 5.05
his men went to J. against the 5.06
more concubines and wives from J., 5.13
those who were born to him in J.: 5.14
Hadadezer, and brought them to J. 8.07
So Mephibosheth dwelt in J.; 9.13
the Ammonites, and came to J. 10.14
But David remained at J. 11.01
so Uriah remained in J. that day, 11.12
and all the people returned to J. 12.31
Geshur, and brought Absalom to J. 14.23
Absalom dwelt two full years in J., 14.28
will indeed bring me back to J., 15.08
men from J. who were invited 15.11
servants who were with him at J., 15.14
carried the ark of God back to J.; 15.29
just as Absalom was entering J. 15.37
the king, "Behold, he remains in J.; 16.03
came to J., and Ahithophel with him. 16.15
not find them, they returned to J. 17.20
the day my lord the king left J., 19.19
he came from J. to meet the king, 19.25
will provide for you with me in J." 19.33
I should go up with the king to J.? 19.34
steadfastly from the Jordan to J. 20.02
And David came to his house at J.; 20.03
went out from J. to pursue Sheba 20.07
Joab returned to J. to the king. 20.22
they came to J. at the end of nine 24.08
his hand toward J. to destroy it, 24.16
and thirty-three years in J. 1Ki 2.11
him, "Build yourself a house in J., 2.36
So Shimei dwelt in J. many days. 2.38
had gone from J. to Gath and 2.41
of the LORD and the wall around J. 3.01
Then he came to J., and stood before 3.15
Israel, before King Solomon in J., 8.01
and the wall of J. and Hazor and 9.15
Solomon desired to build in J., 9.19
She came to J. with a very great 10.02
cities and with the king in J. 10.26
silver as common in J. as stone, 10.27
Ammonites, on the mountain east of J. 11.07
for the sake of J. which I have 11.13
time, when Jeroboam went out of J., 11.29
David and for the sake of J., 11.32
always have a lamp before me in J., 11.36
reigned in J. over all Israel was 11.42
mount his chariot, to flee to J. 12.18
When Rehoboam came to J., 12.21
in the house of the LORD at J., 12.27
"You have gone up to J. long enough. 12.28
he reigned seventeen years in J., 14.21
king of Egypt came up against J.; 14.25
He reigned for three years in J. 15.02
LORD his God gave him a lamp in J., 15.04
son after him, and establishing J.; 15.04
and he reigned forty-one years in J. 15.10
he reigned twenty-five years in J. 22.42
and he reigned eight years in J. 2Ki 8.17
and he reigned one year in J. 8.26
carried him in a chariot to J., 9.28
and he reigned forty years in J. 12.01
set his face to go up against J., 12.17
Then Hazael went away from J. 12.18
he reigned twenty-nine years in J. 14.02
mother's name was Jehoaddin of J. 14.02
and came to J., and broke down the 14.13
the wall of J. for four hundred 14.13
a conspiracy against him in J., 14.19

JERUSALEM (cont.)
was buried in J. with his fathers 2Ki 14.20
he reigned fifty-two years in J. 15.02
mother's name was Jecoliah of J. 15.02
and he reigned sixteen years in J. 15.33
and he reigned sixteen years in J. 16.02
Israel, came up to wage war on J., 16.05
he reigned twenty-nine years in J. 18.02
Lachish to King Hezekiah at J. 18.17
And they went up and came to J. 18.17
removed, saying to Judah and to J., 18.22
worship before this altar in J."? 18.22
should deliver J. out of my hand?'" 18.35
promising that J. will not be 19.10
head behind you—the daughter of J. 19.21
for out of J. shall go forth a 19.31
he reigned fifty-five years in J. 21.01
"In J. will I put my name." 21.04
and in J., which I have chosen out 21.07
bringing upon J. and Judah such 21.12
stretch over J. the measuring line 21.13
and I will wipe J. as one wipes a 21.13
he had filled J. from one end to 21.16
and he reigned two years in J. 21.19
he reigned thirty-one years in J. 22.01
she dwelt in J. in the Second 22.14
of Judah and J. were gathered to 23.01
and all the inhabitants of J., 23.02
them outside J. in the fields of 23.04
cities of Judah and round about J.; 23.05
outside J., to the brook Kidron, and 23.06
up to the altar of the LORD in J., 23.09
high places that were east of J., 23.13
upon them. Then he returned to J. 23.20
passover was kept to the LORD in J. 23.23
in the land of Judah and in J., 23.24
J., and the house of which I said, 23.27
Megiddo, and brought him to J., 23.30
and he reigned three months in J. 23.31
that he might not reign in J., 23.33
and he reigned eleven years in J. 23.36
for he filled J. with innocent 24.04
and he reigned three months in J. 24.08
the daughter of Elnathan of J. 24.08
king of Babylon came up to J., 24.10
He carried away all J., 24.14
into captivity from J. to Babylon. 24.15
and he reigned eleven years in J. 24.18
to the point in J. and Judah that 24.20
came with all his army against J., 25.01
of the king of Babylon, came to J. 25.08
house and all the houses of J.; 25.09
broke down the walls around J. 25.10
reigned thirty-three years in J. 1Ch 3.04
These were born to him in J.: 3.05
house that Solomon built in J.). 6.10
sent Judah and J. into exile by 6.15
built the house of the LORD in J.; 6.32
chief men. These dwelt in J. 8.28
dwelt opposite their kinsmen in J., 8.32
Ephraim, and Manasseh dwelt in J.; 9.03
generations, leaders, who lived in J. 9.34
dwelt opposite their kinsmen in J., 9.38
And David and all Israel went to J., 11.04
And David took more wives in J., 14.03
of the children whom he had in J.: 14.04
And David assembled all Israel at J., 15.03
Hadadezer, and brought them to J. 18.07
entered the city. Then Joab came to J. 19.15
Rabbah. But David remained at J. 20.01
and all the people returned to J. 20.03
all Israel, and came back to J. 21.04
sent the angel to J. to destroy it; 21.15
drawn sword stretched out over J. 21.16
and he dwells in J. for ever. 23.25
David assembled at J. all the 28.01
and thirty-three years in J. 29.27
he had pitched a tent for it in J.) 2Ch 1.04
before the tent of meeting, to J. 1.13
cities and with the king in J. 1.14
and gold as common in J. as stone, 1.15
who are with me in Judah and J., 2.07
so that you may take it up to J." 2.16
of the LORD in J. on Mount Moriah, 3.01
in J., to bring up the ark of the 5.02
but I have chosen J. that my name 6.06
Solomon desired to build in J., 8.06
she came to J. to test him with 9.01
cities and with the king in J. 9.25
silver as common in J. as stone, 9.27
Solomon reigned in J. over all 9.30
mount his chariot, to flee to J. 10.18
When Rehoboam came to J., 11.01
Rehoboam dwelt in J., 11.05
holdings and came to Judah and J., 11.14
of Israel to J. to sacrifice to 11.16
of Egypt came up against J. 12.02
of Judah and came as far as J. 12.04
had gathered at J. because of 12.05
poured out upon J. by the hand of 12.07
king of Egypt came up against J.; 12.09
established himself in J. and reigned. 12.13
he reigned seventeen years in J., 12.13
He reigned for three years in J. 13.02
Then they returned to J. 14.15
gathered at J. in the third month 15.10
soldiers, mighty men of valor, in J. 17.13
in safety to his house in J. 19.01
Jehoshaphat dwelt at J.; 19.04
Moreover in J. Jehoshaphat appointed 19.08
They had their seat at J. 19.08
in the assembly of Judah and J., 20.05
all Judah and inhabitants of J., 20.15
on your behalf, O Judah and J.' 20.17
inhabitants of J. fell down before 20.18
me, Judah and inhabitants of J.! 20.20
returned, every man of Judah and J., 20.27
returning to J. with joy, for the 20.27
They came to J., with harps and 20.28
he reigned twenty-five years in J. 20.31
and he reigned eight years in J. 21.05
inhabitants of J. into unfaithfulness, 21.11
inhabitants of J. into unfaithfulness, 21.13
and he reigned eight years in J.; 21.20
inhabitants of J. made Ahaziah his 22.01
and he reigned one year in J. 22.02
of Israel, and they came to J. 23.02
and he reigned forty years in J.; 24.01
from Judah and J. the tax levied 24.06
was made throughout Judah and J., 24.09
upon Judah and J. for this their 24.18
They came to Judah and J., and destroyed 24.23
he reigned twenty-nine years in J. 25.01
mother's name was Jehoaddan of J. 25.01
Bethshemesh, and brought him to J., 25.23
the wall of J. for four hundred 25.23
a conspiracy against him in J., 25.27
he reigned fifty-two years in J. 26.03
mother's name was Jecoliah of J. 26.03
built towers in J. at the Corner 26.09
In J. he made engines, invented by 26.15
and he reigned sixteen years in J. 27.01
and he reigned sixteen years in J. 27.08
and he reigned sixteen years in J. 28.01
subjugate the people of Judah and J., 28.10
altars in every corner of J. 28.24
in J., for they did not bring him 28.27
he reigned twenty-nine years in J. 29.01
of the LORD came on Judah and J., 29.08
to the house of the LORD at J., 30.01
the assembly in J. had taken 30.02
had the people assembled in J.— 30.03
the LORD the God of Israel, at J.; 30.05
humbled themselves and came to J. 30.11

JERUSALEM (cont.)
together in J. to keep the feast 2Ch 30.13
removed the altars that were in J., 30.14
were present at J. kept the feast 30.21
So there was great joy in J., 30.26
had been nothing like this in J. 30.26
who lived in J. to give the 31.04
and intended to fight against J., 32.02
his servants to J. to Hezekiah 32.09
of Judah that were in J., saying, 32.09
relying, that you stand siege in J.? 32.10
altars and commanded Judah and J., 32.12
the people of J. who were upon the 32.18
of the God of J. as they spoke of 32.19
inhabitants of J. from the hand of 32.22
to the LORD to J. and precious 32.23
came upon him and Judah and J. 32.25
both he and the inhabitants of J., 32.26
inhabitants of J. did him honor at 32.33
he reigned fifty-five years in J. 33.01
"In J. shall my name be for ever." 33.04
and in J., which I have chosen out 33.07
Judah and the inhabitants of J., 33.09
him again to J. into his kingdom. 33.13
of the house of the LORD and in J., 33.15
and he reigned two years in J. 33.21
he reigned thirty-one years in J. 34.01
purge Judah and J. of the high 34.03
altars, and purged Judah and J. 34.05
land of Israel. Then he returned to J. 34.07
and from the inhabitants of J. 34.09
she dwelt in J. in the Second 34.22
all the elders of Judah and J. 34.29
inhabitants of J. and the priests 34.30
were present in J. and in Benjamin 34.32
inhabitants of J. did according to 34.32
Josiah kept a passover to the LORD in J.; 35.01
present, and the inhabitants of J. 35.18
chariot and brought him to J. 35.24
All Judah and J. mourned for Josiah. 35.24
king in his father's stead in J. 36.01
and he reigned three months in J. 36.02
deposed him in J. and laid upon 36.03
his brother king over Judah and J., 36.04
and he reigned eleven years in J. 36.05
three months and ten days in J. 36.09
Zedekiah king over Judah and J. 36.10
and he reigned eleven years in J. 36.11
LORD which he had hallowed in J. 36.14
God, and broke down the wall of J., 36.19
me to build him a house at J., which is 36.23
me to build him a house at J., which is Ez 1.02
with him, and let him go up to J., 1.03
Israel—he is the God who is in J.; 1.03
the house of God which is in J." 1.04
house of the LORD which is in J.; 1.05
away from J. and placed in the 1.07
brought up from Babylonia to J. 1.11
they returned to J. and Judah, 2.01
house of the LORD which is in J., 2.68
people lived in J. and its vicinity; 2.70
people gathered as one man to J. 3.01
coming to the house of God at J., 3.08
who had come to J. from the 3.08
the inhabitants of Judah and J. 4.06
letter against J. to Artaxerxes 4.08
up from you to us have gone to J. 4.12
And mighty kings have been over J., 4.20
to the Jews at J. and by force and 4.23
of God which is in J. stopped; 4.24
the Jews who were in Judah and J., 5.01
the house of God which is in J.; 5.02
that was in J. and brought into 5.14
them in the temple which is in J., 5.15
of the house of God which is in J.; 5.16
rebuilding of this house of God in J. 5.17
Concerning the house of God at J.: 6.03
that is in J. and brought to 6.05
back to the temple which is in J., 6.05
oil, as the priest at J. require— 6.09
this house of God which is in J. 6.12
for the service of God at J., 6.18
And there went up also to J., 7.07
And he came to J. in the fifth 7.08
of the fifth month he came to J., 7.09
who freely offers to go to J., 7.13
about Judah and J. according to 7.14
Israel, whose dwelling is in J., 7.15
house of their God which is in J. 7.16
house of your God which is in J. 7 17
shall deliver before the God of J. 7.19
house of the LORD which is in J., 7.27
of fathers' houses in Israel at J., 8.29
the vessels, to bring them to J., 8.30
of the first month, to go to J.; 8.31
We came to J., and there we remained 8.32
give us protection in Judea and J. 9.09
Judah and J. to all the returned 10.07
that they should assemble at J., 10.07
assembled at J. within the three 10.09
escaped exile, and concerning J. Neh 1.02
the wall of J. is broken down, and 1.03
So I came to J. and was there three 2.11
had put into my heart to do for J. 2.12
the walls of J. which were broken 2.13
how J. lies in ruins with its gates 2.17
come, let us build the wall of J., 2.17
portion or right or memorial in J." 2.20
they restored J. as far as the 3.08
half the district of J., repaired. 3.09
ruler of half the district of J., 3.12
of the walls of J. was going 4.07
fight against J. and to cause 4.08
servant pass the night within J., 4.22
to proclaim concerning you in J., 6.07
of the castle charge over J., 7.02
the gates of J. be opened until 7.03
from among the inhabitants of J., 7.03
they returned to J. and Judah, 7.06
in all their towns and in J., 8.15
leaders of the people lived in J.; 11.01
of ten to live in J. the holy city, 11.01
willingly offered to live in J. 11.02
of the province who lived in J.; 11.03
And in J. lived certain of the sons 11.04
who lived in J. were four hundred 11.06
the Levites in J. was Uzzi the son 11.22
of the wall of J. they sought the 12.27
bring them to J. to celebrate the 12.27
circuit round J. and from the 12.28
for themselves villages around J. 12.29
And the joy of J. was heard afar 12.43
was taking place I was not in J., 13.06
and came to J., and I then discovered 13.07
brought into J. on the sabbath day; 13.15
to the people of Judah, and in J. 13.16
at the gates of J. before the 13.19
lodged outside J. once or twice. 13.20
away from J. among the captives Est 2.06
pleasure; rebuild the walls of J., Ps 51.18
thy temple at J. kings bear gifts 68.29
they have laid J. in ruins. 79.01
blood like water round about J., 79.03
of the LORD, and in J. his praise, 102.21
of the LORD, in your midst, O J. 116.19
standing within your gates, O J.! 122.02
J., built as a city which is bound 122.03
Pray for the peace of J.! 122.06
As the mountains are round about J., 125.02
prosperity of J. all the days of 128.05
from Zion, he who dwells in J.! 135.21
O J., let my right hand wither! 137.05
if I do not set J. above my 137.06
against the Edomites the day of J., 137.07

JERUSALEM (cont.)
The LORD builds up J.; Ps 147.02
Praise the LORD, O J.! 147.12
the son of David, king in J. Ecc 1.01
have been king over Israel in J. 1.12
all who were over J. before me; 1.16
any who had been before me in J. 2.07
all who were before me in J.; 2.09
but comely, O daughters of J., Sol 1.05
I adjure you, O daughters of J., 2.07
I adjure you, O daughters of J., 3.05
within by the daughters of J. 3.10
I adjure you, O daughters of J., 5.08
is my friend, O daughters of J. 5.16
comely as J., terrible as an army 6.04
I adjure you, O daughters of J., 8.04
Judah and J. in the days of Uzziah, Is 1.01
Amoz saw concerning Judah and J. 2.01
and the word of the LORD from J. 2.03
away from J. and from Judah stay 3.01
For J. has stumbled, and Judah has 3.08
and remains in J. will be called 4.03
has been recorded for life in J., 4.03
bloodstains of J. from its midst 4.04
inhabitants of J. and men of Judah, 5.03
the nobility of J. and her multitude 5.14
came up to J. to wage war against 7.01
a snare to the inhabitants of J. 8.14
than those of J. and Samaria, 10.10
shall I not do to J. and her idols 10.11
Zion and on J. he will punish the 10.12
daughter of Zion, the hill of J. 10.32
and you counted the houses of J., 22.10
inhabitants of J. and to the house 22.21
Zion and in J. and before his 24.23
LORD on the holy mountain at J. 27.13
scoffers, who rule this people in J.! 28.14
Yea, O people in Zion who dwell at J.; 30.19
the LORD of hosts will protect J.; 31.05
Zion, and whose furnace is in J. 31.09
Your eyes will see J., a quiet 33.20
Lachish to King Hezekiah at J., 36.02
removed, saying to Judah and to J., 36.07
should deliver J. out of my hand?' " 36.20
promising that J. will not be 37.10
behind you—the daughter of J. 37.22
for out of J. shall go forth a 37.32
Speak tenderly to J., and cry to 40.02
O J., herald of good tidings, lift 40.09
and I give to J. a herald of good 41.27
who says of J., 'She shall be 44.26
saying of J., 'She shall be built,' 44.28
O J., you who have drunk at the 51.17
garments, O J., the holy city; 52.01
the dust, arise, O captive J.; 52.02
singing, you waste places of J.; 52.09
his people, he has redeemed J. 52.09
O J., I have set watchmen; 62.06
he establishes J. and makes it a 62.07
a wilderness, J. a desolation. 64.10
I create J. a rejoicing, and her 65.18
I will rejoice in J., and be glad 65.19
"Rejoice with J., and be glad for 66.10
you shall be comforted in J. 66.13
dromedaries, to my holy mountain J., 66.20
captivity of J. in the fifth month Jer 1.03
at the entrance of the gates of J., 1.15
"Go and proclaim in the hearing of J., 2.02
At that time J. shall be called the 3.17
to the presence of the LORD in J., 3.17
Judah and to the inhabitants of J.: 4.03
men of Judah and inhabitants of J.; 4.04
Declare in Judah, and proclaim in J., 4.05
deceived this people and J., 4.10
be said to this people and to J., 4.11
O J., wash your heart from wickedness, 4.14
announce to J., "Besiegers come 4.16
and fro through the streets of J., 5.01
of Benjamin, from the midst of J.! 6.01
cast up a siege mound against J. 6.06
Be warned, O J., lest I be alienated 6.08
of Judah and in the streets of J.? 7.17
the streets of J. the voice of 7.34
inhabitants of J. shall be brought 8.01
I will make J. a heap of ruins, a 9.11
of Judah and the inhabitants of J. 11.02
of Judah, and in the streets of J.: 11.06
of Judah and the inhabitants of J. 11.09
inhabitants of J. will go and cry 11.12
the streets of J. are the altars 11.13
of Judah and the great pride of J. 13.09
and all the inhabitants of J. 13.13
Woe to you, O J.! How long will 13.27
ground, and the cry of J. goes up. 14.02
be cast out in the streets of J., 14.16
Hezekiah, king of Judah, did in J. 15.04
O J., or who will bemoan you? 15.05
out, and in all the gates of J., 17.19
and all the inhabitants of J., 17.20
or bring it in by the gates of J. 17.21
of Judah and the inhabitants of J.; 17.25
and the places round about J., 17.26
by the gates of J. on the sabbath 17.27
the palaces of J. and shall not be 17.27
of Judah and the inhabitants of J.: 18.11
of Judah and inhabitants of J. 19.03
void the plans of Judah and J., 19.07
The houses of J. and the houses of 19.13
cast forth beyond the gates of J." 22.19
the prophets of J. I have seen a 23.14
the prophets of J. ungodliness has 23.15
into exile from J. Jeconiah the 24.01
the remnant of J. who remain in 24.08
and all the inhabitants of J.: 25.02
J. and the cities of Judah, its 25.18
J. shall become a heap of ruins, and 26.18
have come to J. to Zedekiah king 27.03
and in J. may not go to Babylon. 27.18
into exile from J. to Babylon 27.20
all the nobles of Judah and J.— 27.20
of the king of Judah, and in J.: 27.21
sent from J. to the elders of the 29.01
into exile from J. to Babylon. 29.01
the princes of Judah and J., 29.02
the smiths had departed from J. 29.02
into exile from J. to Babylon: 29.04
I sent away from J. to Babylon: 29.20
to all the people who are in J., 29.25
king of Babylon was besieging J., 32.02
of Judah and the inhabitants of J. 32.32
Benjamin, in the places about J., 32.44
the streets of J. that are desolate, 33.10
of Benjamin, the places about J., 33.13
be saved and J. will dwell securely. 33.16
fighting against J. and all of its 34.01
to Zedekiah king of Judah, in J., 34.06
fighting against J. and against all 34.07
the people in J. to make a proclamation 34.08
of Judah, the princes of J., 34.19
let us go to J. for fear of the 35.11
the Syrians.' So we are living in J. 35.11
of Judah and the inhabitants of J., 35.13
inhabitants of J. all the evil 35.17
the people in J. and all the 36.09
of Judah to J. proclaimed a fast 36.09
and upon the inhabitants of J., 36.31
were besieging J. heard news of 37.05
of them, they withdrew from J. 37.05
withdrawn from J. at the approach 37.11
Jeremiah set out from J. to go to 37.12
until the day that J. was taken. 38.28
came against J. and besieged it; 39.01
When J. was taken, all the princes 39.03
and broke down the walls of J. 39.08

JERUSALEM (cont.)
the captives of J. and Judah who Jer 40.01
out on the inhabitants of J., 42.18
I brought upon J. and upon all the 44.02
of Judah and in the streets of J.; 44.06
of Judah and in the streets of J.? 44.09
of Egypt, as I have punished J., 44.13
of Judah and in the streets of J.; 44.17
of Judah and in the streets of J., 44.21
inhabitants of Chaldea," let J. say. 51.35
and let J. come into your mind: 51.50
and he reigned eleven years in J. 52.01
such a pass in J. and Judah that 52.03
came with all his army against J., 52.04
the king of Babylon, entered J. 52.12
house and all the houses of J.; 52.13
down all the walls round about J. 52.14
captive from J. eight hundred and 52.29
J. remembers in the days of her Lam 1.07
J. sinned grievously, therefore she 1.08
J. has become a filthy thing among 1.17
the maidens of J. have bowed their 2.10
what compare you, O daughter of J.? 2.13
their heads at the daughter of J.; 2.15
enemy could enter the gates of J. 4.12
portray upon it a city, even J.; Eze 4.01
your face toward the siege of J., 4.07
break the staff of bread in J.; 4.16
Thus says the Lord GOD: This is J.; 5.05
brought me in visions of God to J., 8.03
through J., and put a mark upon the 9.04
outpouring of thy wrath upon J.?" 9.08
the inhabitants of J. have said, 11.15
the prince in J. and all the house 12.10
inhabitants of J. in the land of 12.19
concerning J. and saw visions of 13.16
I send upon J. my four sore acts 14.21
evil that I have brought upon J., 14.22
I give up the inhabitants of J. 15.06
make known to J. her abominations, 16.02
and say, Thus says the Lord GOD to J.: 16.03
the king of Babylon came to J., 17.12
face toward J. and preach against 21.02
to Judah and to J. the fortified. 21.20
right hand comes the lot for J., 21.22
gather you into the midst of J. 22.19
is Samaria, and Oholibah is J. 23.04
has laid siege to J. this very day. 24.02
because Tyre said concerning J., 26.02
escaped from J. came to me and 33.21
the flock at J. during her appointed 36.38
Babylon came to J. and besieged it. Dan 1.01
out of the temple in J. be brought, 5.02
the temple, the house of God in J.; 5.03
his upper chamber open toward J.; 6.10
the end of the desolations of J., 9.02
of Judah, to the inhabitants of J., 9.07
of what has been done against J. 9.12
from thy city J., thy holy hill; 9.16
J. and thy people have become a 9.16
and build J. to the coming of an 9.25
Zion and in J. there shall be Joe 2.32
the fortunes of Judah and J., 3.01
of Judah and J. to the Greeks, 3.06
Zion, and utters his voice from J., 3.16
And J. shall be holy and strangers 3.17
and J. to all generations. 3.20
Zion, and utters his voice from J.; Amo 1.02
shall devour the strongholds of J." 2.05
his gates and cast lots for J., Ob 1.11
the exiles of J. who are in 1.20
he saw concerning Samaria and J. Mic 1.01
house of Judah? Is it not J.? 1.05
to the gate of my people, to J. 1.09
from the LORD to the gate of J. 1.12
Zion with blood and J. with wrong. 3.10
J. shall become a heap of ruins, and 3.12
and the word of the LORD from J. 4.02
the kingdom of the daughter of J. 4.08
against all the inhabitants of J.; Zep 1.04
time I will search J. with lamps, 1.12
all your heart, O daughter of J.! 3.14
On that day it shall be said to J.: 3.16
no mercy on J. and the cities of Zec 1.12
jealous for J. and for Zion. 1.14
returned to J. with compassion; 1.16
shall be stretched out over J. 1.16
comfort Zion and again choose J.'" 1.17
scattered Judah, Israel, and J." 1.19
"To measure J., to see what is its 2.02
'J. shall be inhabited as villages 2.04
land, and will again choose J." 2.12
LORD who has chosen J. rebuke you! 3.02
When J. was inhabited and in 7.07
and will dwell in the midst of J., 8.03
and J. shall be called the faithful 8.03
again sit in the streets of J., 8.04
them to dwell in the midst of J.; 8.08
to do good to J. and to the house 8.15
to seek the LORD of hosts in J., 8.22
Shout aloud, O daughter of J.! 9.09
Ephraim and the war horse from J.; 9.10
about to make J. a cup of reeling 12.02
Judah also in the siege against J. 12.02
day I will make J. a heavy stone 12.03
inhabitants of J. have strength 12.05
while J. shall still be inhabited 12.06
be inhabited in its place, in J. 12.06
inhabitants of J. may not be 12.07
inhabitants of J. so that the 12.08
the nations that come against J. 12.09
inhabitants of J. a spirit of 12.10
the mourning in J. will be as 12.11
inhabitants of J. to cleanse them 13.01
the nations against J. to battle, 14.02
which lies before J. on the east; 14.04
waters shall flow out from J., 14.08
from Geba to Rimmon south of J. 14.10
But J. shall remain aloft upon its 14.10
J. shall dwell in security. 14.11
peoples that wage war against J.: 14.12
even Judah will fight against J. 14.14
come against J. shall go up year 14.16
do not go up to J. to worship the 14.17
and every pot in J. and Judah shall 14.21
been committed in Israel and in J.; Mal 2.11
of Judah and J. will be pleasing 3.04
from the East came to J., saying, Mt 2.01
was troubled, and all J. with him; 2.03
Then went out to him J. and all 3.05
Decapolis and J. and Judea and 4.25
or by J., for it is the city of the 5.35
came to Jesus from J. and said, 15.01
he must go to J. and suffer many 16.21
And as Jesus was going up to J., 20.17
"Behold, we are going up to J.; 20.18
drew near to J. and came to 21.01
And when he entered J., all the city 21.10
"O J., J., killing the prophets and 23.37
of Judea, and all the people of J.; Mk 1.05
and J. and Idumea and from beyond 3.08
scribes who came down from J. said, 3.22
the scribes, who had come from J., 7.01
going up to J., and Jesus was 10.32
saying, "Behold, we are going up to J.; 10.33
And when they drew near to J., 11.01
And he entered J., and went into 11.11
And they came to J. And he entered 11.15
And they came again to J. 11.27
women who came up with him to J. 15.41
him up to J. to present him to the Lk 2.22
Now there was a man in J., 2.25
looking for the redemption of J. 2.38
parents went to J. every year at 2.41

JERUSALEM (cont.)
the boy Jesus stayed behind in J. Lk 2.43
they returned to J., seeking him. 2.45
And he took him to J., and set him 4.09
of Galilee and Judea and from J.; 5.17
all Judea and J. and the seacoast 6.17
which he was to accomplish at J. 9.31
up, he set his face to go to J. 9.51
because his face was set toward J. 9.53
was going down from J. to Jericho, 10.30
all the others who dwelt in J.? 13.04
teaching, and journeying toward J. 13.22
prophet should perish away from J.' 13.33
O J., J., killing the prophets and 13.34
On the way to J. he was passing 17.11
"Behold, we are going up to J., 18.31
parable, because he was near to J., 19.11
he went on ahead, going up to J. 19.28
"But when you see J. surrounded by 21.20
and J. will be trodden down by the 21.24
who was himself in J. at that time. 23.07
"Daughters of J., do not weep for 23.28
Emmaus, about seven miles from J., 24.13
only visitor to J. who does not 24.18
that same hour and returned to J.; 24.33
to all nations, beginning from J. 24.47
they returned to J. with great joy, 24.52
and Levites from J. to ask him, Jn 1.19
at hand, and Jesus went up to J. 2.13
Now when he was in J. at the 2.23
you say that in J. is the place 4.20
mountain nor in J. will you 4.21
he had done in J. at the feast, 4.45
the Jews, and Jesus went up to J. 5.01
Now there is in J. by the sheep 5.02
of the people of J. therefore said, 7.25
the feast of the Dedication at J.; 10.22
Bethany was near J., about two miles 11.18
the country to J. before the 11.55
heard that Jesus was coming to J. 12.12
charged them not to depart from J., Ac 1.04
my witnesses in J. and in all 1.08
returned to J. from the mount 1.12
which is near J., a sabbath day's 1.12
known to all the inhabitants of J., 1.19
Now there were dwelling in J. Jews, 2.05
of Judea and all who dwell in J., 2.14
were gathered together in J., 4.05
to all the inhabitants of J., 4.16
gathered from the towns around J., 5.16
you have filled J. with your 5.28
disciples multiplied greatly in J., 6.07
arose against the church in J.; 8.01
the apostles at J. heard that 8.14
of the Lord, they returned to J., 8.25
that goes down from J. to Gaza." 8.26
treasure, had come to J. to worship 8.27
he might bring them bound to J. 9.02
he has done to thy saints at J.; 9.13
made havoc in J. of those who 9.21
he had come to J. he attempted to 9.26
went in and out among them at J., 9.28
the country of the Jews and in J. 10.39
So when Peter went up to J., 11.02
to the ears of the church in J., 11.22
came down from J. to Antioch. 11.27
returned from J. when they had 12.25
John left them and returned to J.; 13.13
who live in J. and their rulers, 13.27
up with him from Galilee to J., 13.31
to go up to J. to the apostles and 15.02
When they came to J., they were 15.04
apostles and elders who were at J. 16.04
Macedonia and Achaia and go to J., 19.21
for he was hastening to be at J., 20.16
I am going to J., bound in the 20.22
they told Paul not to go on to J. 21.04
the Jews at J. bind the man who 21.11
begged him not to go up to J. 21.12
even to die at J. for the name of 21.13
we made ready and went up to J. 21.15
When we had come to J., the brethren 21.17
cohort that all J. was in confusion. 21.31
them in bonds to J. to be punished. 22.05
had returned to J. and was praying 22.17
haste and get quickly out of J., 22.18
you have testified about me at J., 23.11
since I went up to worship at J.; 24.11
he went up to J. from Caesarea. 25.01
a favor to have the man sent to J., 25.03
gone down from J. stood about him, 25.07
Paul, "Do you wish to go up to J., 25.09
and when I was at J., the chief priests 25.15
wished to go to J. and be tried 25.20
both at J. and here, shouting that 25.24
among my own nation and at J., 26.04
And I did so in J.; I not only shut 26.10
then at J. and throughout all the 26.20
prisoner from J. into the hands of 28.17
so that from J. and as far round as Rom 15.19
I am going to J. with aid for the 15.25
the poor among the saints at J.; 15.26
my service for J. may be acceptable 15.31
by letter to carry your gift to J. 1Co 16.03
nor did I go up to J. to those who Gal 1.17
I went up to J. to visit Cephas, 1.18
went up again to J. with Barnabas, 2.01
she corresponds to the present J., 4.25
But the J. above is free, and she is 4.26
the heavenly J., and to innumerable Heb 12.22
the New J. which comes down from my Rev 3.12
new J., coming down out of heaven 21.02
the holy city J. coming down out 21.10

JERUSALEM'S
and for J. sake I will not rest, Is 62.01

JERUSHA
name was J. the daughter of Zadok. 2Ki 15.33

JERUSHAH
name was J. the daughter of Zadok. 2Ch 27.01

JESHAIAH
Pelatiah and J., his son Rephaiah, 1Ch 3.21
J., Shimei, Hasabiah, and Mattithiah, 25.03
the eighth to J., his sons and his 25.15
and his son J., and his son Joram, 26.25
J. the son of Athaliah, and with him Ez 8.07
and with him J. of the sons of 8.19
Maaseiah, son of Ithiel, son of J. Neh 11.07

JESHANAH
set it up between Mizpah and J., 1Sa 7.12
villages and J. with its villages 2Ch 13.19

JESHARELAH
the seventh to J., his sons and his 1Ch 25.14

JESHEBEAB
to Huppah, the fourteenth to J., 1Ch 24.13

JESHER
J., Shobab, and Ardon. 1Ch 2.18

JESHIMON
of Hachilah, which is south of J.? 1Sa 23.19
in the Arabah to the south of J. 23.24
Hachilah, which is on the east of J.?" 26.01
beside the road on the east of J. 26.03

JESHISHAI
son of J., son of Jahdo, son of Buz; 1Ch 5.14

JESHOHAIAH
J., Asaiah, Adiel, Jesimiel, Benaiah, 1Ch 4.36

JESHUA

the ninth to J., the tenth to 1Ch 24.11
J., Shemaiah, Amariah, and Shecaniah 2Ch 31.15
J., Nehemiah, Seraiah, Reelaiah, Ez 2.02
namely the sons of J. and Joab, 2.06
of Jedaiah, of the house of J., 2.36
the sons of J. and Kadmiel, of the 2.40
Then arose J. the son of Jozadak, 3.02
Shealtiel and J. the son of 3.08
And J. with his sons and his 3.09
J., and the rest of the heads of 4.03
Shealtiel and J. the son of 5.02
the son of J. and Noadiah the son 8.33
of the sons of J. the son of 10.18
next to him Ezer the son of J., Neh 3.19
J., Nehemiah, Azariah, Raamiah, 7.07
namely the sons of J. and Joab, 7.11
of Jedaiah, namely the house of J., 7.39
the sons of J., namely of Kadmiel 7.43
Also J., Bani, Sherebiah, Jamin, Akkub, 8.07
the days of J. the son of Nun to 8.17
the stairs of the Levites stood J., 9.04
J., Kadmiel, Bani, Hashabneiah, 9.05
J. the son of Azaniah, Binnui of the 10.09
and in J. and in Moladah and 11.26
and J.: Seraiah, Jeremiah, Ezra, 12.01
their brethren in the days of J. 12.07
J., Binnui, Kadmiel, Sherebiah, Judah, 12.08
And J. was the father of Joiakim, 12.10
and J. the son of Kadmiel, with 12.24
the son of J. son of Jozadak, 12.26

JESHURUN

"But J. waxed fat, and kicked; Deu 32.15
Thus the LORD became king in J., 33.05
O J., who rides through the heavens 33.26
my servant, J. whom I have chosen. Is 44.02

JESIMIEL

Asaiah, Adiel, J., Benaiah, 1Ch 4.36

JESSE

he was the father of J., the father Ru 4.17
Obed of J., and J. of David. 4.22
send you to J. the Bethlehemite, 1Sa 16.01
And invite J. to the sacrifice, and 16.03
And he consecrated J. and his sons, 16.05
Then J. called Abinadab, and made 16.08
Then J. made Shammah pass by. 16.09
And J. made seven of his sons pass 16.10
And Samuel said to J., "The LORD 16.10
And Samuel said to J., "Are all 16.11
And Samuel said to J., "Send and 16.11
seen a son of J. the Bethlehemite, 16.18
Therefore Saul sent messengers to J., 16.19
And J. took an ass laden with bread, 16.20
And Saul sent to J., saying, "Let 16.22
named J., who had eight sons. 17.12
eldest sons of J. had followed 17.13
And J. said to David his son, "Take 17.17
and went, as J. had commanded him; 17.20
of your servant J. the Bethlehemite." 17.58
not the son of J. come to the meal, 20.27
the son of J. to your own shame, 20.30
as the son of J. lives upon the 20.31
will the son of J. give every one 22.07
makes a league with the son of J., 22.08
"I saw the son of J. coming to Nob, 22.09
against me, you and the son of J., 22.13
Who is the son of J.? There are 25.10
no inheritance in the son of J.; 2Sa 20.01
the son of J., the oracle of the 23.01
no inheritance in the son of J. 1Ki 12.16
Boaz of Obed, Obed of J. 1Ch 2.12
J. was the father of Eliab his 2.13
over to David the son of J. 10.14
and with you, O son of J.! 12.18
the son of J. reigned over all 29.26
no inheritance in the son of J. 2Ch 10.16
daughter of Eliab the son of J.; 11.18
of David, the son of J., are ended. Ps 72.20
forth a shoot from the stump of J., Is 11.01
day the root of J. shall stand as 11.10
Ruth, and Obed the father of J., Mt 1.05
and J. the father of David the king. 1.06
the son of J., the son of Obed, the Lk 3.32
the son of J. a man after my heart, Ac 13.22
"The root of J. shall come, he who Rom 15.12

JESTING

seemed to his sons-in-law to be j. Gen 19.14

JESUS

book of the genealogy of J. Christ, Mt 1.01
of whom J. was born, who is called 1.16
Now the birth of J. Christ took 1.18
and you shall call his name J., 1.21
and he called his name J. 1.25
Now when J. was born in Bethlehem 2.01
Then J. came from Galilee to the 3.13
But J. answered him, "Let it be so 3.15
And when J. was baptized, he went up 3.16
Then J. was led up by the Spirit 4.01
J. said to him, "Again it is written, 4.07
Then J. said to him, "Begone, Satan! 4.10
From that time J. began to preach, 4.17
And when J. finished these sayings, 7.28
And J. said to him, "See that you 8.04
When J. heard him, he marveled, and 8.10
And to the centurion J. said, "Go; 8.13
And when J. entered Peter's house, he 8.14
Now when J. saw great crowds around 8.18
And J. said to him, "Foxes have 8.20
But J. said to him, "Follow me, and 8.22
all the city came out to meet J.; 8.34
and when J. saw their faith he said 9.02
But J., knowing their thoughts, said 9.04
As J. passed on from there, he saw a 9.09
sat down with J. and his disciples 9.10
And J. said to them, "Can the 9.15
And J. rose and followed him, with 9.19
J. turned, and seeing her he said, 9.22
And when J. came to the ruler's 9.23
And as J. passed on from there, two 9.27
and J. said to them, "Do you believe 9.28
And J. sternly charged them, "See 9.30
And J. went about all the cities 9.35
These twelve J. sent out, charging 10.05
And when J. had finished instructing 11.01
And J. answered them, "Go and tell 11.04
J. began to speak to the crowds 11.07
At that time J. declared, "I thank 11.25
At that time J. went through the 12.01
J., aware of this, withdrew from 12.15
That same day J. went out of the 13.01
All this J. said to the crowds in 13.34
And when J. had finished these 13.53
But J. said to them, "A prophet is 13.57
tetrarch heard about the fame of J.; 14.01
and they went and told J. 14.12
Now when J. heard this, he withdrew 14.13
J. said, "They need not go away; 14.16
walked on the water and came to J.; 14.29
J. immediately reached out his hand 14.31
scribes came to J. from Jerusalem 15.01
And J. went away from there and 15.21
Then J. answered her, "O woman, great 15.28
And J. went on from there and 15.29
Then J. called his disciples to him 15.32
And J. said to them, "How many 15.34
J. said to them, "Take heed and 16.06
But J., aware of this, said, "O men 16.08
Now when J. came into the district 16.13
And J. answered him, "Blessed are 16.17
From that time J. began to show his 16.21

JESUS (cont.)
Then J. told his disciples, "If any Mt 16.24
And after six days J. took with him 17.01
And Peter said to J., "Lord, it is 17.04
But J. came and touched them, saying, 17.07
eyes, they saw no one but J. only. 17.08
J. commanded them, "Tell no one the 17.09
And J. answered, "O faithless and 17.17
And J. rebuked him, and the demon 17.18
disciples came to J. privately and 17.19
J. said to them, "The Son of man is 17.22
J. spoke to him first, saying, "What 17.25
J. said to him, "Then the sons are 17.26
that time the disciples came to J., 18.01
J. said to him, "I do not say to you 18.22
Now when J. had finished these 19.01
but J. said, "Let the children come 19.14
And J. said, "You shall not kill. 19.18
J. said to him, "If you would be 19.21
And J. said to his disciples, "Truly, 19.23
But J. looked at them and said to 19.26
J. said to them, "Truly, I say to you, 19.28
And as J. was going up to Jerusalem, 20.17
But J. answered, "You do not know 20.22
But J. called them to him and said, 20.25
they heard that J. was passing by, 20.30
And J. stopped and called them, 20.32
And J. in pity touched their eyes, 20.34
then J. sent two disciples, 21.01
went and did as J. had directed 21.06
is the prophet J. from Nazareth of 21.11
And J. entered the temple of God 21.12
And J. said to them, "Yes; have you 21.16
And J. answered them, "Truly, I say 21.21
J. answered them, "I also will ask 21.24
So they answered J., "We do not know." 21.27
J. said to them, "Truly, I say to 21.31
J. said to them, "Have you never 21.42
And again J. spoke to them in 22.01
But J., aware of their malice, said, 22.18
And J. said to them, "Whose likeness 22.20
But J. answered them, "You are wrong, 22.29
together, J. asked them a question, 22.41
Then said J. to the crowds and to 23.01
J. left the temple and was going 24.01
And J. answered them, "Take heed 24.04
When J. had finished all these 26.01
order to arrest J. by stealth and 26.04
Now when J. was at Bethany in the 26.06
But J., aware of this, said to them, 26.10
the disciples came to J., saying, 26.17
disciples did as J. had directed 26.19
J. took bread, and blessed, and broke 26.26
Then J. said to them, "You will all 26.31
J. said to him, "Truly, I say to you, 26.34
Then J. went with them to a place 26.36
And he came up to J. at once and 26.49
J. said to him, "Friend, why are you 26.50
laid hands on J. and seized him. 26.50
who were with J. stretched out his 26.51
Then J. said to him, "Put your sword 26.52
At that hour J. said to the crowds, 26.55
those who had seized J. led him to 26.57
testimony against J. that they 26.59
But J. was silent. And the high 26.63
J. said to him, "You have said so. 26.64
"You also were with J. the Galilean." 26.69
"This man was with J. of Nazareth." 26.71
And Peter remembered the saying of J., 26.75
counsel against J. to put him to 27.01
Now J. stood before the governor; 27.11
J. said to him, "You have said so." 27.11
Barabbas or J. who is called Christ?" 27.17
to ask for Barabbas and destroy J. 27.20
shall I do with J. who is called 27.22
Barabbas, and having scourged J., 27.26
governor took J. into the praetorium, 27.27
"This is J. the King of the Jews." 27.37
the ninth hour J. cried with a 27.46
And J. cried again with a loud 27.50
with him, keeping watch over J., 27.54
who had followed J. from Galilee, 27.55
who also was a disciple of J. 27.57
and asked for the body of J. 27.58
that you seek J. who was crucified. 28.05
And behold, J. met them and said, 28.09
Then J. said to them, "Do not be 28.10
to which J. had directed them. 28.16
And J. came and said to them, "All 28.18
beginning of the gospel of J. Christ, Mk 1.01
In those days J. came from Nazareth 1.09
J. came into Galilee, preaching the 1.14
And J. said to them, "Follow me and 1.17
you to do with us, J. of Nazareth? 1.24
But J. rebuked him, saying, "Be 1.25
so that J. could no longer openly 1.45
And when J. saw their faith, he said 2.05
And immediately J., perceiving in his 2.08
sitting with J. and his disciples; 2.15
And when J. heard it, he said to 2.17
And J. said to them, "Can the 2.19
J. withdrew with his disciples to 3.07
And when he saw J. from afar, 5.06
J., Son of the Most High God? 5.07
And J. asked him, "What is your name?" 5.09
And they came to J., and saw the 5.15
began to beg J. to depart from 5.17
how much J. had done for him; 5.20
And when J. had crossed again in 5.21
She had heard the reports about J., 5.27
And J., perceiving in himself that 5.30
J. said to the ruler of the synagogue, 5.36
And J. said to them, "A prophet is 6.04
The apostles returned to J., and told 6.30
J. said to them, "Why do you discuss 8.17
And J. went on with his disciples, 8.27
And after six days J. took with him 9.02
Moses; and they were talking to J. 9.04
And Peter said to J., "Master, it is 9.05
saw any one with them but J. only. 9.08
And J. asked his father, "How long 9.21
And J. said to him, "If you can! 9.23
And when J. saw that a crowd came 9.25
But J. took him by the hand and 9.27
But J. said, "Do not forbid him; 9.39
But J. said to them, "For your 10.05
But when J. saw it he was indignant, 10.14
And J. said to him, "Why do you call 10.18
And J. looking upon him loved him, 10.21
And J. looked around and said to 10.23
But J. said to them again, "Children, 10.24
J. looked at them and said, "With 10.27
J. said, "Truly, I say to you, there 10.29
and J. was walking ahead of them; 10.32
But J. said to them, "You do not 10.38
And J. said to them, "The cup that 10.39
And J. called them to him and said 10.42
heard that it was J. of Nazareth, 10.47
"J., Son of David, have mercy on me!" 10.47
And J. stopped and said, "Call him." 10.49
mantle he sprang up and came to J. 10.50
And J. said to him, "What do you 10.51
And J. said to him, "Go your way; 10.52
And they told them what J. had said; 11.06
And they brought the colt to J., 11.07
And J. answered them, "Have faith in 11.22
J. said to them, "I will ask you a 11.29
So they answered J., "We do not know." 11.33
And J. said to them, "Neither will 11.33
J. said to them, "Render to Caesar 12.17
J. said to them, "Is not this why 12.24
J. answered, "The first is, 'Hear, O 12.29
And when J. saw that he answered 12.34
And as J. taught in the temple, he 12.35

JESUS (cont.)

And J. said to him, "Do you see	Mk 13.02
And J. began to say to them, "Take	13.05
But J. said, "Let her alone; why do	14.06
J. said, "Truly, I say to you, one of	14.18
And J. said to them, "You will all	14.27
And J. said to him, "Truly, I say to	14.30
And J. said to them, "Have you come	14.48
And they led J. to the high priest;	14.53
testimony against J. to put him to	14.55
and asked J., "Have you no answer	14.60
And J. said, "I am; and you will	14.62
also were with the Nazarene, J."	14.67
remembered how J. had said to him,	14.72
and they bound J. and led him away	15.01
But J. made no further answer, so	15.05
and having scourged J., he delivered	15.15
the ninth hour J. cried with a	15.34
And J. uttered a loud cry, and	15.37
and asked for the body of J.	15.43
you seek J. of Nazareth, who was	16.06
and you shall call his name J.	Lk 1.31
he was called J., the name given by	2.21
parents brought in the child J.,	2.27
the boy J. stayed behind in Jerusalem.	2.43
And J. increased in wisdom and in	2.52
and when J. also had been baptized	3.21
J., when he began his ministry, was	3.23
the son of J., the son of Eliezer,	3.29
And J., full of the Holy Spirit,	4.01
And J. answered him, "It is written,	4.04
And J. answered him, "It is written,	4.08
And J. answered him, "It is said,	4.12
And J. returned in the power of the	4.14
you to do with us, J. of Nazareth?	4.34
But J. rebuked him, saying, "Be	4.35
And J. said to Simon, "Do not be	5.10
and when he saw J., he fell on his	5.12
bring him in and lay him before J.;	5.18
the tiles into the midst before J.	5.19
When J. perceived their questionings,	5.22
And J. answered them, "Those who are	5.31
And J. said to them, "Can you make	5.34
And J. answered, "Have you not read	6.03
And J. said to them, "I ask you, is	6.09
another what they might do to J.	6.11
When he heard of J., he sent to him	7.03
And when they came to J., they	7.04
And J. went with them. When he was	7.06
When J. heard this he marveled at	7.09
And J. answering said to him, "Simon,	7.40
When he saw J., he cried out and	8.28
J., Son of the Most High God?	8.28
J. then asked him, "What is your	8.30
had happened, and they came to J.,	8.35
gone, sitting at the feet of J.,	8.35
city how much J. had done for him.	8.39
Now when J. returned, the crowd	8.40
and J. said, "Who was it that	8.45
But J. said, "Some one touched me;	8.46
But J. on hearing this answered him,	8.50
Peter said to J., "Master, it is	9.33
voice had spoken, J. was found alone.	9.36
J. answered, "O faithless and	9.41
But J. rebuked the unclean spirit,	9.42
But when J. perceived the thought	9.47
But J. said to him, "Do not forbid	9.50
And J. said to him, "Foxes have	9.58
J. said to him, "No one who puts his	9.62
said to J., "And who is my neighbor?"	10.29
J. replied, "A man was going down	10.30
And J. said to him, "Go and do	10.37
And when J. saw her, he called her	13.12
indignant because J. had healed on	13.14
And J. spoke to the lawyers and	14.03
"J., Master, have mercy on us."	17.13
Then said J., "Were not ten cleansed?	17.17
But J. called them to him, saying,	18.16
And J. said to him, "Why do you call	18.19
And when J. heard it, he said to him,	18.22
J. looking at him said, "How hard it	18.24
"J. of Nazareth is passing by."	18.37
And he cried, "J., Son of David, have	18.38
And J. stopped, and commanded him to	18.40
And J. said to him, "Receive your	18.42
And he sought to see who J. was,	19.03
And when J. came to the place, he	19.05
And J. said to him, "Today salvation	19.09
And they brought it to J., and throwing	19.35
on the colt they set J. upon it.	19.35
And J. said to them, "Neither will I	20.08
And J. said to them, "The sons of	20.34
So J. sent Peter and John, saying,	22.08
He drew near to J. to kiss him;	22.47
but J. said to him, "Judas, would you	22.48
But J. said, "No more of this!"	22.51
Then J. said to the chief priests	22.52
were holding J. mocked him and	22.63
When Herod saw J., he was very glad,	23.08
once more, desiring to release J.;	23.20
but J. he delivered up to their	23.25
the cross, to carry it behind J.	23.26
But J. turning to them said, "Daughters	23.28
And J. said, "Father, forgive them;	23.34
And he said, "J., remember me when	23.42
Then J., crying with a loud voice,	23.46
and asked for the body of J.	23.52
J. himself drew near and went with	24.15
"Concerning J. of Nazareth, who was	24.19
J. himself stood among them.	24.36
and truth came through J. Christ.	Jn 1.17
The next day he saw J. coming	1.29
and he looked at J. as he walked,	1.36
him say this, and they followed J.	1.37
J. turned, and saw them following,	1.38
He brought him to J.	1.42
J. looked at him, and said, "So you	1.42
The next day J. decided to go to	1.43
J. of Nazareth, the son of Joseph."	1.45
J. saw Nathanael coming to him, and	1.47
J. answered him, "Before Philip	1.48
J. answered him, "Because I said to	1.50
and the mother of J. was there;	2.01
J. also was invited to the marriage,	2.02
the mother of J. said to him, "They	2.03
And J. said to her, "O woman, what	2.04
J. said to them, "Fill the jars with	2.07
J. did at Cana in Galilee, and	2.11
and J. went up to Jerusalem.	2.13
J. answered them, "Destroy this	2.19
and the word which J. had spoken.	2.22
but J. did not trust himself to	2.24
This man came to J. by night and	3.02
J. answered him, "Truly, truly, I say	3.03
J. answered, "Truly, truly, I say to	3.05
J. answered him, "Are you a teacher	3.10
After this J. and his disciples	3.22
had heard that J. was making and	4.01
(although J. himself did not	4.02
and so J., wearied as he was with	4.06
J. said to her, "Give me a drink."	4.07
J. answered her, "If you knew the	4.10
J. said to her, "Every one who	4.13
J. said to her, "Go, call your	4.16
J. said to her, "You are right in	4.17
J. said to her, "Woman, believe me,	4.21
J. said to her, "I who speak to you	4.26
J. said to them, "My food is to do	4.34
For J. himself testified that a	4.44
When he heard that J. had come from	4.47
J. therefore said to him, "Unless	4.48
J. said to him, "Go; your son will	4.50
the word that J. spoke to him and	4.50
the hour when J. had said to him,	4.53

JESUS (cont.)
sign that J. did when he had come Jn 4.54
and J. went up to Jerusalem. 5.01
When J. saw him and knew that he 5.06
J. said to him, "Rise, take up your 5.08
for J. had withdrawn, as there was a 5.13
Afterward, J. found him in the 5.14
that it was J. who had healed him. 5.15
was why the Jews persecuted J., 5.16
But J. answered them, "My Father is 5.17
J. said to them, "Truly, truly, I say 5.19
After this J. went to the other 6.01
J. went up into the hills, and there 6.03
J. said to Philip, "How are we to 6.05
J. said, "Make the people sit down." 6.10
J. then took the loaves, and when he 6.11
J. withdrew again to the hills by 6.15
and J. had not yet come to them. 6.17
they saw J. walking on the sea and 6.19
and that J. had not entered the 6.22
people saw that J. was not there, 6.24
and went to Capernaum, seeking J. 6.24
J. answered them, "Truly, truly, I say 6.26
J. answered them, "This is the work 6.29
J. then said to them, "Truly, truly, I 6.32
J. said to them, "I am the bread of 6.35
"Is not this J., the son of Joseph, 6.42
J. answered them, "Do not murmur 6.43
So J. said to them, "Truly, truly, I 6.53
But J., knowing in himself that his 6.61
For J. knew from the first who those 6.64
J. said to the twelve, "Will you 6.67
J. answered them, "Did I not choose 6.70
After this J. went about in Galilee; 7.01
J. said to them, "My time has not 7.06
of the feast J. went up into the 7.14
So J. answered them, "My teaching is 7.16
J. answered them, "I did one deed, 7.21
So J. proclaimed, as he taught in 7.28
J. then said, "I shall be with you a 7.33
J. stood up and proclaimed, "If any 7.37
because J. was not yet glorified. 7.39
but J. went to the Mount of Olives. * 8.01
J. bent down and wrote with his * 8.06
J. was left alone with the woman * 8.09
J. looked up and said to her, * 8.10
and J. said, "Neither do I condemn * 8.11
Again J. spoke to them, saying, "I am 8.12
J. answered, "Even if I do bear 8.14
J. answered, "You know neither me 8.19
J. said to them, "Even what I have 8.25
So J. said, "When you have lifted up 8.28
J. then said to the Jews who had 8.31
J. answered them, "Truly, truly, I say 8.34
J. said to them, "If you were 8.39
J. said to them, "If God were your 8.42
J. answered, "I have not a demon; 8.49
J. answered, "If I glorify myself, my 8.54
J. said to them, "Truly, truly, I say 8.58
but J. hid himself, and went out of 8.59
J. answered, "It was not that this 9.03
"The man called J. made clay and 9.11
day when J. made the clay and 9.14
J. heard that they had cast him out, 9.35
J. said to him, "You have seen him, 9.37
J. said, "For judgment I came into 9.39
J. said to them, "If you were blind, 9.41
This figure J. used with them, but 10.06
So J. again said to them, "Truly, 10.07
and J. was walking in the temple, in 10.23
J. answered them, "I told you, and 10.25
J. answered them, "I have shown you 10.32
J. answered them, "Is it not written 10.34
But when J. heard it he said, "This 11.04
Now J. loved Martha and her sister 11.05
J. answered, "Are there not twelve 11.09
Now J. had spoken of his death, but 11.13
Then J. told them plainly, "Lazarus 11.14
Now when J. came, he found that 11.17
When Martha heard that J. was coming, 11.20
Martha said to J., "Lord, if you had 11.21
J. said to her, "Your brother will 11.23
J. said to her, "I am the resurrection 11.25
Now J. had not yet come to the 11.30
she came where J. was and saw him, 11.32
When J. saw her weeping, and the 11.33
J. wept. 11.35
Then J., deeply moved again, came to 11.38
J. said, "Take away the stone." 11.39
J. said to her, "Did I not tell you 11.40
And J. lifted up his eyes and said, 11.41
J. said to them, "Unbind him, and let 11.44
and told them what J. had done. 11.46
prophesied that J. should die for 11.51
J. therefore no longer went about 11.54
looking for J. and saying to one 11.56
J. came to Bethany, where Lazarus 12.01
whom J. had raised from the dead. 12.01
the feet of J. and wiped his feet 12.03
J. said, "Let her alone, let her keep 12.07
on account of J. but also to see 12.09
going away and believing in J. 12.11
heard that J. was coming to 12.12
And J. found a young ass and sat 12.14
but when J. was glorified, then they 12.16
to him, "Sir, we wish to see J." 12.21
went with Philip and they told J. 12.22
And J. answered them, "The hour has 12.23
J. answered, "This voice has come 12.30
J. said to them, "The light is with 12.35
When J. had said this, he departed 12.36
And J. cried out and said, "He who 12.44
when J. knew that his hour had come 13.01
J., knowing that the Father had 13.03
J. answered him, "What I am doing 13.07
J. answered him, "If I do not wash 13.08
J. said to him, "He who has bathed 13.10
When J. had thus spoken, he was 13.21
whom J. loved, was lying close to 13.23
lying close to the breast of J.; 13.23
thus, close to the breast of J., 13.25
J. answered, "It is he to whom I 13.26
J. said to him, "What you are going 13.27
J. was telling him, "Buy what we 13.29
J. said, "Now is the Son of man 13.31
J. answered, "Where I am going you 13.36
J. answered, "Will you lay down your 13.38
J. said to him, "I am the way, and 14.06
J. said to him, "Have I been with 14.09
J. answered him, "If a man loves me, 14.23
J. knew that they wanted to ask him; 16.19
J. answered them, "Do you now 16.31
When J. had spoken these words, he 17.01
and J. Christ whom thou hast sent. 17.03
When J. had spoken these words, he 18.01
for J. often met there with his 18.02
Then J., knowing all that was to 18.04
They answered him, "J. of Nazareth." 18.05
J. said to them, "I am he." 18.05
And they said, "J. of Nazareth." 18.07
J. answered, "I told you that I am 18.08
J. said to Peter, "Put your sword 18.11
the Jews seized J. and bound him. 18.12
Simon Peter followed J., and so did 18.15
of the high priest along with J., 18.15
then questioned J. about his 18.19
J. answered him, "I have spoken 18.20
standing by struck J. with his hand, 18.22
J. answered him, "If I have spoken 18.23
Then they led J. from the house of 18.28
the word which J. had spoken to 18.32
the praetorium again and called J., 18.33
J. answered, "Do you say this of 18.34
J. answered, "My kingship is not of 18.36

JESUS (cont.)

J. answered, "You say that I am a	Jn 18.37
Then Pilate took J. and scourged	19.01
So J. came out, wearing the crown of	19.05
praetorium again and said to J.,	19.09
you from?" But J. gave no answer.	19.09
J. answered him, "You would have no	19.11
he brought J. out and sat down on	19.13
So they took J., and he went out,	19.17
either side, and J. between them.	19.18
it read, "J. of Nazareth, the King of	19.19
the place where J. was crucified	19.20
had crucified J. they took his	19.23
by the cross of J. were his mother,	19.25
When J. saw his mother, and the	19.26
After this J., knowing that all was	19.28
When J. had received the vinegar, he	19.30
they came to J. and saw that he	19.33
Arimathea, who was a disciple of J.,	19.38
he might take away the body of J.,	19.38
They took the body of J., and bound	19.40
close at hand, they laid J. there.	19.42
the one whom J. loved, and said to	20.02
where the body of J. had lain,	20.12
turned round and saw J. standing,	20.14
she did not know that it was J.	20.14
J. said to her, "Woman, why are you	20.15
J. said to her, "Mary." She turned	20.16
J. said to her, "Do not hold me, for	20.17
J. came and stood among them and	20.19
J. said to them again, "Peace be	20.21
was not with them when J. came.	20.24
but J. came and stood among them,	20.26
J. said to him, "Have you believed	20.29
Now J. did many other signs in the	20.30
may believe that J. is the Christ,	20.31
After this J. revealed himself	21.01
J. stood on the beach; yet the	21.04
did not know that it was J.	21.04
J. said to them, "Children, have you	21.05
That disciple whom J. loved said to	21.07
J. said to them, "Bring some of the	21.10
J. said to them, "Come and have	21.12
J. came and took the bread and gave	21.13
third time that J. was revealed to	21.14
J. said to Simon Peter, "Simon, son	21.15
J. said to him, "Feed my sheep.	21.17
them the disciple whom J. loved,	21.20
he said to J., "Lord, what about	21.21
J. said to him, "If it is my will	21.22
yet J. did not say to him that he	21.23
many other things which J. did;	21.25
with all that J. began to do and	Ac 1.01
This J., who was taken up from you	1.11
women and Mary the mother of J.,	1.14
was guide to those who arrested J.	1.16
that the Lord J. went in and out	1.21
J. of Nazareth, a man attested to	2.22
this J., delivered up according to	2.23
This J. God raised up, and of that	2.32
Christ, this J. whom you crucified."	2.36
in the name of J. Christ for the	2.38
in the name of J. Christ of Nazareth,	3.06
fathers, glorified his servant J.,	3.13
is through J. has given the man	3.16
the Christ appointed for you, J.,	3.20
proclaiming in J. the resurrection	4.02
by the name of J. Christ of	4.10
recognized that they had been with J.	4.13
or teach at all in the name of J.	4.18
against thy holy servant J.,	4.27
the name of thy holy servant J."	4.30
to the resurrection of the Lord J.,	4.33
fathers raised J. whom you killed	5.30
not to speak in the name of J.,	5.40
and preaching J. as the Christ.	5.42
say that this J. of Nazareth will	6.14
and J. standing at the right hand	7.55
"Lord J., receive my spirit."	7.59
of God and the name of J. Christ,	8.12
baptized in the name of the Lord J.	8.16
he told him the good news of J.	8.35
"I believe that J. Christ is the	* 8.37
"I am J., whom you are persecuting;	9.05
the Lord J. who appeared to you on	9.17
immediately he proclaimed J.,	9.20
by proving that J. was the Christ.	9.22
preached boldly in the name of J.	9.27
J. Christ heals you; rise and make	9.34
of peace by J. Christ (he is Lord	10.36
how God anointed J. of Nazareth	10.38
baptized in the name of J. Christ.	10.48
we believed in the Lord J. Christ,	11.17
Greeks also, preaching the Lord J.	11.20
a Savior, J., as he promised.	13 23
to us their children by raising J.;	13.33
through the grace of the Lord J.,	15.11
for the sake of our Lord J. Christ.	15.26
the Spirit of J. did not allow	16.07
in the name of J. Christ to come	16.18
And they said, "Believe in the Lord J.,	16.31
"This J., whom I proclaim to you, is	17.03
that there is another king, J."	17.07
he preached J. and the resurrection.	17.18
to the Jews that the Christ was J.	18.05
accurately the things concerning J.,	18.25
scriptures that the Christ was J.	18.28
was to come after him, that is J."	19.04
baptized in the name of the Lord J.	19.05
of the Lord J. over those who had	19.13
you by the J. whom Paul preaches."	19.13
"J. I know, and Paul I know; but	19.15
name of the Lord J. was extolled.	19.17
and of faith in our Lord J. Christ.	20.21
which I received from the Lord J.,	20.24
remembering the words of the Lord J.,	20.35
for the name of the Lord J."	21.13
'I am J. of Nazareth whom you are	22.08
him speak upon faith in Christ J.	24.24
own superstition and about one J.,	25.19
opposing the name of J. of Nazareth.	26.09
'I am J. whom you are persecuting.	26.15
them about J. both from the law of	28.23
about the Lord J. Christ quite	28.31
a servant of J. Christ, called to be	Rom 1.01
from the dead, J. Christ our Lord,	1.04
are called to belong to J. Christ;	1.06
our Father and the Lord J. Christ.	1.07
my God through J. Christ for all	1.08
the secrets of men by Christ J.	2.16
faith in J. Christ for all who	3.22
redemption which is in Christ J.,	3.24
justifies him who has faith in J.	3.26
raised from the dead J. our Lord,	4.24
God through our Lord J. Christ.	5.01
in God through our Lord J. Christ,	5.11
of that one man J. Christ abounded	5.15
life through the one man J. Christ.	5.17
life through J. Christ our Lord.	5.21
into Christ J. were baptized into	6.03
sin and alive to God in Christ J.	6.11
eternal life in Christ J. our Lord.	6.23
to God through J. Christ our Lord!	7.25
for those who are in Christ J.	8.01
life in Christ J. has set me free	8.02
him who raised J. from the dead	8.11
raised Christ J. from the dead	8.11
Is it Christ J., who died, yes, who	8.34
love of God in Christ J. our Lord.	8.39
your lips that J. is Lord and	10.09
But put on the Lord J. Christ,	13.14
in the Lord J. that nothing is	14.14
another, in accord with Christ J.,	15.05
and Father of our Lord J. Christ.	15.06

JESUS (cont.)

of Christ J. to the Gentiles in	Rom	15.16
In Christ J., then, I have reason to		15.17
by our Lord J. Christ and by the		15.30
my fellow workers in Christ J.,		16.03
of our Lord J. Christ be with you.		16.20
The grace of our Lord J. Christ		* 16.24
and the preaching of J. Christ,		16.25
for evermore through J. Christ!		16.27
God to be an apostle of Christ J.,	1Co	1.01
to those sanctified in Christ J.,		1.02
on the name of our Lord J. Christ,		1.02
our Father and the Lord J. Christ.		1.03
which was given you in Christ J.,		1.04
revealing of our Lord J. Christ;		1.07
in the day of our Lord J. Christ.		1.08
of his Son, J. Christ our Lord.		1.09
by the name of our Lord J. Christ,		1.10
source of your life in Christ J.,		1.30
you except J. Christ and him		2.02
which is laid, which is J. Christ.		3.11
in Christ J. through the gospel.		4.15
of the Lord J. on the man who has		5.04
with the power of our Lord J.,		5.04
be saved in the day of the Lord J.		5.05
of the Lord J. Christ and in the		6.11
J. Christ, through whom are all		8.06
Have I not seen J. our Lord?		9.01
that the Lord J. on the night when		11.23
of God ever says "J. be cursed!"		12.03
no one can say "J. is Lord" except		12.03
which I have in Christ J. our Lord,		15.31
victory through our Lord J. Christ.		15.57
The grace of the Lord J. be with you.		16.23
My love be with you all in Christ J.		16.24
of Christ J. by the will of God,	2Co	1.01
our Father and the Lord J. Christ.		1.02
and Father of our Lord J. Christ,		1.03
of you, on the day of the Lord J.		1.14
J. Christ, whom we preached among		1.19
but J. Christ as Lord, with ourselves		4.05
in the body the death of J.,		4.10
the life of J. may also be manifested		4.10
the life of J. may be manifested		4.11
raised the Lord J. will raise us		4.14
us also with J. and bring us with		4.14
the grace of our Lord J. Christ,		8.09
preaches another J. than the one we		11.04
The God and Father of the Lord J.,		11.31
realize that J. Christ is in you?—		13.05
of the Lord J. Christ and the love		13.14
but through J. Christ and God the	Gal	1.01
the Father and our Lord J. Christ,		1.03
through a revelation of J. Christ.		1.12
freedom which we have in Christ J.,		2.04
law but through faith in J. Christ,		2.16
even we have believed in Christ J.,		2.16
whose eyes J. Christ was publicly		3.01
that in Christ J. the blessing of		3.14
to faith in J. Christ might be		3.22
for in Christ J. you are all sons		3.26
for you are all one in Christ J.		3.28
as an angel of God, as Christ J.		4.14
For in Christ J. neither circumcision		5.06
to Christ J. have crucified the		5.24
in the cross of our Lord J. Christ,		6.14
I bear on my body the marks of J.		6.17
of our Lord J. Christ be with your		6.18
of Christ J. by the will of God, To	Eph	1.01
are also faithful in Christ J.:		1.01
our Father and the Lord J. Christ.		1.02
and Father of our Lord J. Christ,		1.03
to be his sons through J. Christ,		1.05
in the Lord J. and your love		1.15
that the God of our Lord J. Christ,		1.17
the heavenly places in Christ J.,		2.06
in kindness toward us in Christ J.		2.07
in Christ J. for good works,		2.10
But now in Christ J. you who once		2.13
Christ J. himself being the chief		2.20
for Christ J. on behalf of you		3.01
in Christ J. through the gospel.		3.06
realized in Christ J. our Lord,		3.11
and in Christ J. to all generations,		3.21
in him, as the truth is in J.		4.21
of our Lord J. Christ to God the		5.20
the Father and the Lord J. Christ.		6.23
love our Lord J. Christ with love		6.24
and Timothy, servants of Christ J.,	Php	1.01
in Christ J. who are at Philippi,		1.01
our Father and the Lord J. Christ.		1.02
completion at the day of J. Christ.		1.06
with the affection of Christ J.		1.08
which come through J. Christ.		1.11
the Spirit of J. Christ this will		1.19
ample cause to glory in Christ J.,		1.26
which you have in Christ J.,		2.05
that at the name of J. every knee		2.10
confess that J. Christ is Lord,		2.11
in the Lord J. to send Timothy to		2.19
interests, not those of J. Christ.		2.21
in spirit, and glory in Christ J.,		3.03
worth of knowing Christ J. my Lord.		3.08
because Christ J. has made me his		3.12
upward call of God in Christ J.		3.14
a Savior, the Lord J. Christ,		3.20
hearts and your minds in Christ J.		4.07
his riches in glory in Christ J.		4.19
Greet every saint in Christ J.		4.21
of the Lord J. Christ be with your		4.23
of Christ J. by the will of God,	Col	1.01
the Father of our Lord J. Christ,		1.03
faith in Christ J. and of the love		1.04
you received Christ J. the Lord,		2.06
everything in the name of the Lord J.,		3.17
and J. who is called Justus.		4.11
yourselves, a servant of Christ J.,		4.12
the Father and the Lord J. Christ:	1Th	1.01
of hope in our Lord J. Christ.		1.03
J. who delivers us from the wrath		1.10
God in Christ J. which are in		2.14
both the Lord J. and the prophets,		2.15
before our Lord J. at his coming?		2.19
and our Lord J., direct our way to		3.11
of our Lord J. with all his saints		3.13
and exhort you in the Lord J.,		4.01
we gave you through the Lord J.		4.02
we believe that J. died and rose		4.14
through J., God will bring with him		4.14
through our Lord J. Christ,		5.09
will of God in Christ J. for you.		5.18
the coming of our Lord J. Christ.		5.23
of our Lord J. Christ be with you.		5.28
our Father and the Lord J. Christ:	2Th	1.01
the Father and the Lord J. Christ.		1.02
when the Lord J. is revealed from		1.07
not obey the gospel of our Lord J.		1.08
of our Lord J. may be glorified in		1.12
of our God and the Lord J. Christ.		1.12
of our Lord J. Christ and our		2.01
and the Lord J. will slay him with		2.08
the glory of our Lord J. Christ.		2.14
Now may our Lord J. Christ himself,		2.16
in the name of our Lord J. Christ,		3.06
in the Lord J. Christ to do their		3.12
of our Lord J. Christ be with you		3.18
of Christ J. by command of God our	1Ti	1.01
Savior and of Christ J. our hope,		1.01
the Father and Christ J. our Lord.		1.02
Christ J. our Lord, because he		1.12
and love that are in Christ J.		1.14
that Christ J. came into the world		1.15
J. Christ might display his perfect		1.16
God and men, the man Christ J.,		2.05

JESUS (cont.)
in the faith which is in Christ J. 1Ti 3.13
be a good minister of Christ J., 4.06
and of Christ J. and of the elect 5.21
of our Lord J. Christ and the 6.03
and of Christ J. who in his testimony 6.13
appearing of our Lord J. Christ; 6.14
of Christ J. by the will of God 2Ti 1.01
of the life which is in Christ J., 1.01
the Father and Christ J. our Lord. 1.02
he gave us in Christ J. ages ago, 1.09
appearing of our Savior Christ J., 1.10
and love which are in Christ J.; 1.13
in the grace that is in Christ J., 2.01
as a good soldier of Christ J. 2.03
Remember J. Christ, risen from the 2.08
which in Christ J. goes with 2.10
life in Christ J. will be persecuted, 3.12
salvation through faith in Christ J. 3.15
and of Christ J. who is to judge 4.01
of God and an apostle of J. Christ, Tit 1.01
Father and Christ J. our Savior. 1.04
great God and Savior J. Christ, 2.13
richly through J. Christ our 3.06
Paul, a prisoner for Christ J., Phm 1.01
our Father and the Lord J. Christ. 1.03
toward the Lord J. and all the 1.05
a prisoner also for Christ J.— 1.09
Epaphras, my fellow prisoner in Christ J., 1.23
of the Lord J. Christ be with your 1.25
But we see J., who for a little Heb 2.09
consider J., the apostle and high 3.01
Yet J. has been counted worthy of 3.03
J., the Son of God, let us hold fast 4.14
J. offered up prayers and supplications, 5.07
where J. has gone as a forerunner 6.20
This makes J. the surety of a 7.22
of the body of J. Christ once for 10.10
the sanctuary by the blood of J., 10.19
looking to J. the pioneer and 12.02
and to J., the mediator of a new 12.24
J. Christ is the same yesterday and 13.08
So J. also suffered outside the 13.12
again from the dead our Lord J., 13.20
in his sight, through J. Christ; 13.21
of God and of the Lord J. Christ, Jas 1.01
the faith of our Lord J. Christ, 2.01
an apostle of J. Christ, to the 1Pe 1.01
obedience to J. Christ and for 1.02
and Father of our Lord J. Christ! 1.03
resurrection of J. Christ from the 1.03
at the revelation of J. Christ. 1.07
you at the revelation of J. Christ. 1.13
acceptable to God through J. Christ. 2.05
the resurrection of J. Christ, 3.21
may be glorified through J. Christ. 4.11
a servant and apostle of J. Christ, 2Pe 1.01
of our God and Savior J. Christ: 1.01
knowledge of God and of J. our Lord. 1.02
knowledge of our Lord J. Christ. 1.08
of our Lord and Savior J. Christ. 1.11
as our Lord J. Christ showed me. 1.14
and coming of our Lord J. Christ, 1.16
of our Lord and Savior J. Christ, 2.20
of our Lord and Savior J. Christ. 3.18
Father and with his Son J. Christ. 1Jn 1.03
the blood of J. his Son cleanses 1.07
the Father, J. Christ the righteous; 2.01
who denies that J. is the Christ? 2.22
name of his Son J. Christ and love 3.23
confesses that J. Christ has come 4.02
does not confess J. is not of God. 4.03
Whoever confesses that J. is the 4.15
believes that J. is the Christ is 5.01
believes that J. is the Son of God? 5.05
J. Christ, not with the water only 5.06
who is true, in his Son J. Christ. 5.20
Father and from J. Christ the 2Jn 1.03
the coming of J. Christ in the 1.07
a servant of J. Christ and brother Jud 1.01
the Father and kept for J. Christ: 1.01
only Master and Lord, J. Christ. 1.04
the apostles of our Lord J. Christ; 1.17
of our Lord J. Christ unto eternal 1.21
Savior through J. Christ our Lord, 1.25
The revelation of J. Christ, Rev 1.01
and to the testimony of J. Christ, 1.02
and from J. Christ the faithful 1.05
with you in J. the tribulation and 1.09
of God and the testimony of J. 1.09
of God and bear testimony to J. 12.17
commandments of God and the faith of J. 14.12
and the blood of the martyrs of J. 17.06
who hold the testimony of J. 19.10
testimony of J. is the spirit of 19.10
testimony to J. and for the word 20.04
"I J. have sent my angel to you 22.16
soon." Amen. Come, Lord J.! 22.20
of the Lord J. be with all the 22.21

JESUS'
for J. name had become known. Mk 6.14
saw it, he fell down at J. knees, Lk 5.08
and falling at J. feet he besought 8.41
and he fell on his face at J. feet, 17.16
as your servants for J. sake. 2Co 4.05
given up to death for J. sake, 4.11

JETHER
And he said to J. his first-born, Ju 8.20
of Ner, and Amasa the son of J., 1Ki 2.05
of Israel, and Amasa the son of J., 2.32
of Amasa was J. the Ishmaelite. 1Ch 2.17
Shammai's brother: J. and Jonathan; 2.32
Jonathan; and J. died childless. 2.32
J., Mered, Epher, and Jalon. 4.17
The sons of J.: Jephunneh, Pispa, and 7.38

JETHETH
the chiefs Timna, Alvah, J., Gen 36.40
were: chiefs Timna, Aliah, J., 1Ch 1.51

JETHRO
J., the priest of Midian; and he Ex 3.01
Moses went back to J. his father-in-law 4.18
And J. said to Moses, "Go in peace." 4.18
J., the priest of Midian, Moses' 18.01
Now J., Moses' father-in-law, had 18.02
And J., Moses' father-in-law, came 18.05
father-in-law J. is coming to you 18.06
And J. rejoiced for all the good 18.09
And J. said, "Blessed be the LORD, 18.10
And J., Moses' father-in-law, offered 18.12

JETUR
Hadad, Tema, J., Naphish, and Kedemah. Gen 25.15
J. Naphish, and Kedemah. These are 1Ch 1.31
the Hagrites, J., Naphish, and Nodab; 5.19

JEUEL
J. and their kinsmen, six hundred 1Ch 9.06
sons of Elizaphan, Shimri and J.; 2Ch 29.13
J., and Shemaiah, and with them Ez 8.13

JEUSH
and Oholibamah bore J., Jalam, and Gen 36.05
Esau's wife: she bore to Esau J., 36.14
the chiefs, J., Jalam, and Korah; 36.18
Eliphaz, Reuel, J., Jalam, and Korah. 1Ch 1.35
J., Benjamin, Ehud, Chenaanah, Zethan, 7.10
J. the second, and Eliphelet the 8.39
Jahath, Zina, and J., and Beriah. 23.10
but J. and Beriah had not many 23.11
him sons, J., Shemariah, and Zaham. 2Ch 11.19

JEUZ
J., Sachia, and Mirmah. These were his 1Ch 8.10

JEW
Now there was a J. in Susa the Est 2.05
he had told them that he was a J. 3.04
Mordecai the J. sitting at the 5.13
to Mordecai the J. who sits at the 6.10
Esther and to Mordecai the J., 8.07
Mordecai the J. gave full written 9.29
as Mordecai the J. and Queen 9.31
For Mordecai the J. was next in 10.03
should enslave a J., his brother. Jer 34.09
take hold of the robe of a J., Zec 8.23
disciples and a J. over purifying. Jn 3.25
a J., ask a drink of me, a woman of 4.09
Pilate answered, "Am I a J.? Your 18.35
it is for a J. to associate with Ac 10.28
And he found a J. named Aquila, a 18.02
Now a J. named Apollos, a native of 18.24
they recognized that he was a J., 19.34
"I am a J., from Tarsus in Cilicia, 21.39
"I am a J., born at Tarsus in 22.03
to the J. first and also to the Rom 1.16
the J. first and also the Greek, 2.09
the J. first and also the Greek. 2.10
call yourself a J. and rely upon 2.17
is not a real J. who is one 2.28
He is a J. who is one inwardly, and 2.29
Then what advantage has the J.? 3.01
distinction between J. and Greek; 10.12
To the Jews I became as a J., 1Co 9.20
though a J., live like a Gentile Gal 2.14
like a Gentile and not like a J. 2.14
There is neither J. nor Greek, 3.28
Here there cannot be Greek and J., Col 3.11

JEWEL
lips of knowledge are a precious j. Pro 20.15
with one j. of your necklace. Sol 4.09
imperishable j. of a gentle and 1Pe 3.04
its radiance like a most rare j., Rev 21.11
city were adorned with every j.; 21.19

JEWELER
As a j. engraves signets, so shall Ex 28.11

JEWELRY
brought forth j. of silver and of Gen 24.53
j. of silver and of gold, and Ex 3.22
neighbor, j. of silver and of gold." 11.02
the Egyptians j. of silver and of 12.35
herself with her ring and j., Hos 2.13

JEWELS
be exchanged for j. of fine gold. Job 28.17
She is more precious than j., Pro 3.15
for wisdom is better than j., 8.11
She is far more precious than j. 31.10
your neck with strings of j. Sol 1.10
arms are rounded gold, set with j. 5.14
Your rounded thighs are like j., 7.01
a bride adorns herself with her j. Is 61.10
took your fair j. of my gold and Eze 16.17
your clothes and take your fair j., 16.39
clothes and take away your fine j. 23.26
for like the j. of a crown they Zec 9.16
with gold and j. and pearls, Rev 17.04
j. and pearls, fine linen, purple, 18.12
with j., and with pearls! 18.16

JEWESS
his wife Drusilla, who was a J.; Ac 24.24

JEWISH
And his J. wife bore Jered the 1Ch 4.18
wives against their J. brethren. Neh 5.01
bought back our J. brethren who 5.08
is of the J. people, you will not Est 6.13
Joseph from the J. town of Arimathea. Lk 23.50
for the J. rites of purification, Jn 2.06
So because of the J. day of Preparation, 19.42
spoken of by the whole J. nation, Ac 10.22
all that the J. people were 12.11
a J. false prophet, named Bar-Jesus. 13.06
together into the J. synagogue, 14.01
the son of a J. woman who was a 16.01
they went into the J. synagogue. 17.10
the itinerant J. exorcists undertook 19.13
Seven sons of a J. high priest 19.14
whom the whole J. people petitioned 25.24
giving heed to J. myths or to Tit 1.14

JEWS
Gedaliah and the J. and the Chaldeans 2Ki 25.25
king that the J. who came up from Ez 4.12
in haste to the J. at Jerusalem 4.23
prophesied to the J. who were in 5.01
God was upon the elders of the J., 5.05
governor of the J. and the elders 6.07
elders of the J. rebuild this 6.07
elders of the J. for the rebuilding 6.08
elders of the J. built and prospered, 6.14
concerning the J. that survived, Neh 1.02
and I had not yet told the J., 2.16
enraged, and he ridiculed the J. 4.01
"What are these feeble J. doing? 4.02
When the J. who lived by them came 4.12
J. and officials, besides those who 5.17
you and the J. intend to rebel; 6.06
also I saw the J. who had married 13.23
Haman sought to destroy all the J., Est 3.06
of Hammedatha, the enemy of the J. 3.10
to slay, and to annihilate all J., 3.13
was great mourning among the J., 4.03
for the destruction of the J. 4.07
any more than all the other J. 4.13
rise for the J. from another 4.14
"Go, gather all the J. to be found 4.16
of Haman, the enemy of the J. 8.01
he had devised against the J. 8.03
to destroy the J. who are in all 8.05
he would lay hands on the J. 8.07
you please with regard to the J., 8.08
concerning the J. to the satraps 8.09
and also to the J. in their script 8.09
allowed the J. who were in every 8.11
and the J. were to be ready on that 8.13
The J. had light and gladness and 8.16
was gladness and joy among the J., 8.17
the country declared themselves J., 8.17
the fear of the J. had fallen upon 8.17
enemies of the J. hoped to get the 9.01
a day when the J. should get the 9.01
the J. gathered in their cities 9.02
royal officials also helped the J., 9.03
So the J. smote all their enemies 9.05
itself the J. slew and destroyed 9.06
of Hammedatha, the enemy of the J.; 9.10
the capital the J. have slain five 9.12
let the J. who are in Susa be 9.13
The J. who were in Susa gathered 9.15
Now the other J. who were in the 9.16
But the J. who were in Susa gathered 9.18
Therefore the J. of the villages, 9.19
to all the J. who were in all the 9.20
on which the J. got relief from 9.22
So the J. undertook to do as they 9.23
Hammedatha, the enemy of all the J., 9.24
against the J. to destroy them, and 9.24
against the J. should come upon 9.25
the J. ordained and took it upon 9.27
fall into disuse among the J., 9.28
Letters were sent to all the J., 9.30
Queen Esther enjoined upon the J., 9.31

JEWS (cont.)
great among the J. and popular Est 10.03
of all the J. who were sitting in Jer 32.12
afraid of the J. who have deserted 38.19
when all the J. who were in Moab 40.11
then all the J. returned from all 40.12
so that all the J. who are gathered 40.15
slew all the J. who were with 41.03
concerning all the J. that dwelt in 44.01
three thousand and twenty-three J.; 52.28
captive of the J. seven hundred 52.30
and maliciously accused the J. Dan 3.08
There are certain J. whom you have 3.12
who has been born king of the J.? Mt 2.02
him, "Are you the King of the J.?" 27.11
him, saying, "Hail, King of the J.!" 27.29
"This is Jesus the King of the J." 27.37
spread among the J. to this day. 28.15
and all the J., do not eat unless Mk 7.03
him, "Are you the King of the J.?" 15.02
release for you the King of the J.?" 15.09
whom you call the King of the J.?" 15.12
salute him, "Hail, King of the J.!" 15.18
him read, "The King of the J." 15.26
he sent to him elders of the J., Lk 7.03
him, "Are you the King of the J.?" 23.03
the King of the J., save yourself!" 23.37
him, "This is the King of the J." 23.38
when the J. sent priest and Jn 1.19
The Passover of the J. was at hand, 2.13
The J. then said to him, "What sign 2.18
The J. then said, "It has taken 2.20
named Nicodemus, a ruler of the J. 3.01
For J. have no dealings with 4.09
know, for salvation is from the J. 4.22
After this there was a feast of the J., 5.01
So the J. said to the man who was 5.10
and told the J. that it was Jesus 5.15
was why the J. persecuted Jesus, 5.16
This was why the J. sought all the 5.18
the feast of the J., was at hand. 6.04
The J. then murmured at him, because 6.41
The J. then disputed among themselves, 6.52
because the J. sought to kill him. 7.01
The J. were looking for him at the 7.11
Yet for fear of the J. no one spoke 7.13
The J. marveled at it, saying, "How 7.15
The J. said to one another, "Where 7.35
Then said the J., "Will he kill 8.22
said to the J. who had believed in 8.31
The J. answered him, "Are we not 8.48
The J. said to him, "Now we know 8.52
The J. then said to him, "You are 8.57
The J. did not believe that he had 9.18
this because they feared the J., 9.22
for the J. had already agreed that 9.22
among the J. because of these 10.19
So the J. gathered round him and 10.24
The J. took up stones again to 10.31
The J. answered him, "We stone you 10.33
the J. were but now seeking to 11.08
and many of the J. had come to 11.19
When the J. who were with her in 11.31
and the J. who came with her also 11.33
So the J. said, "See how he loved 11.36
Many of the J. therefore, who had 11.45
went about openly among the J., 11.54
the Passover of the J. was at hand, 11.55
crowd of the J. learned that he 12.09
him many of the J. were going away 12.11
I said to the J. so now I say to 13.33
officers of the J. seized Jesus 18.12
counsel to the J. that it was 18.14
temple, where all J. come together; 18.20
The J. said to him, "It is not 18.31
to him, "Are you the King of the J.?" 18.33
might not be handed over to the J.; 18.36
this, he went out to the J. again, 18.38
release for you the King of the J.?" 18.39
him, saying, "Hail, King of the J.!" 19.03
The J. answered him, "We have a law, 19.07
but the J. cried out, "If you 19.12
He said to the J., "Here is your 19.14
of Nazareth, the King of the J." 19.19
Many of the J. read this title, for 19.20
priests of the J. then said to 19.21
"Do not write, 'The King of the J.,' 19.21
'This man said, I am King of the J.'" 19.21
the J. asked Pilate that their legs 19.31
but secretly, for fear of the J., 19.38
as is the burial custom of the J. 19.40
disciples were, for fear of the J., 20.19
were dwelling in Jerusalem J., Ac 2.05
from Rome, both J. and proselytes, 2.10
confounded the J. who lived in 9.22
passed, the J. plotted to kill him, 9.23
country of the J. and in Jerusalem. 10.39
speaking the word to none except J. 11.19
when he saw that it pleased the J., 12.03
of God in the synagogues of the J. 13.05
many J. and devout converts to 13.43
But when the J. saw the multitudes, 13.45
But the J. incited the devout women 13.50
believed, both of J. and of Greeks. 14.01
But the unbelieving J. stirred up 14.02
some sided with the J., and some 14.04
was made by both Gentiles and J., 14.05
But J. came there from Antioch and 14.19
because of the J. that were in 16.03
"These men are J. and they are 16.20
there was a synagogue of the J. 17.01
But the J. were jealous, and taking 17.05
Now these J. were more noble than 17.11
But when the J. of Thessalonica 17.13
with the J. and the devout persons, 17.17
commanded all the J. to leave Rome. 18.02
sabbath, and persuaded J. and Greeks. 18.04
testifying to the J. that the 18.05
the J. made a united attack upon 18.12
his mouth, Gallio said to the J., 18.14
have reason to bear with you, O J.; 18.14
synagogue and argued with the J. 18.19
powerfully confuted the J. in public, 18.28
of the Lord, both J. and Greeks. 19.10
of Ephesus, both J. and Greeks; 19.17
whom the J. had put forward. 19.33
him by the J. as he was about to 20.03
me through the plots of the J.; 20.19
testifying both to J. and to Greeks 20.21
'So shall the J. at Jerusalem bind 21.11
are among the J. of those who have 21.20
teach all the J. who are among the 21.21
the J. from Asia, who had seen him 21.27
of by all the J. who lived there, 22.12
real reason why the J. accused him, 22.30
the J. made a plot and bound 23.12
"The J. have agreed to ask you to 23.20
This man was seized by the J., 23.27
among all the J. throughout the 24.05
The J. also joined in the charge, 24.09
or tumult. But some J. from Asia— 24.18
and desiring to do the J. a favor, 24.27
men of the J. informed him against 25.02
the J. who had gone down from 25.07
"Neither against the law of the J., 25.08
wishing to do the J. a favor, 25.09
to the J. I have done no wrong, as 25.10
elders of the J. gave information 25.15
all the accusations of the J., 26.02
and controversies of the J.; 26.03
Jerusalem, is known by all the J. 26.04
hope I am accused by J., O king! 26.07
For this reason the J. seized me in 26.21
the local leaders of the J.; 28.17

JEWS (cont.)
But when the J. objected, I was Ac 28.19
J. departed, holding much dispute * 28.29
the J. are entrusted with the Rom 3.02
Are we J. any better off? No, not 3.09
both J. and Greeks, are under the 3.09
Or is God the God of J. only? 3.29
not from the J. only but also from 9.24
order to make my fellow J. jealous, 11.14
For J. demand signs and Greeks seek 1Co 1.22
block to J. and folly to Gentiles, 1.23
both J. and Greeks, Christ the power 1.24
To the J. I became as a Jew, in 9.20
as a Jew, in order to win J.; 9.20
Give no offense to J. or to Greeks 10.32
J. or Greeks, slaves or free—and 12.13
hands of the J. the forty lashes 2Co 11.24
the rest of the J. acted insincerely, Gal 2.13
the Gentiles to live like J.?" 2.14
who are J. by birth and not Gentile 2.15
countrymen as they did from the J., 1Th 2.14
say that they are J. and are not, Rev 2.09
say that they are J. and are not, 3.09

JEWS'
Now the J. feast of Tabernacles was Jn 7.02

JEZANIAH
J. the son of the Maacathite, they Jer 40.08

JEZEBEL
took for wife J. the daughter of 1Ki 16.31
and when J. cut off the prophets of 18.04
what I did when J. killed the 18.13
Ahab told J. all that Elijah had 19.01
Then J. sent a messenger to Elijah, 19.02
But J. his wife came to him, and 21.05
And J. his wife said to him, "Do you 21.07
did as J. had sent word to them. 21.11
Then they sent to J., saying, 21.14
As soon as J. heard that Naboth had 21.15
J. said to Ahab, "Arise, take possession 21.15
And of J. the LORD also said, 'The 21.23
dogs shall eat J. within the 21.23
like Ahab, whom J. his wife incited. 21.25
I may avenge on J. the blood of my 2Ki 9.07
dogs shall eat J. in the territory of 9.10
of your mother J. are so many?" 9.22
came to Jezreel, J. heard of it; 9.30
the dogs shall eat the flesh of J.; 9.36
and the corpse of J. shall be as 9.37
so that no one can say, This is J.'" 9.37
that you tolerate the woman J., Rev 2.20

JEZEBEL'S
of Asherah, who eat at J. table." 1Ki 18.19

JEZER
Jahzeel, Guni, J., and Shillem Gen 46.24
of J., the family of the Jezerites; Num 26.49
J., and Shallum, the offspring of 1Ch 7.13

JEZERITES
of Jezer, the family of the J.; Num 26.49

JEZIEL
also J. and Pelet the sons of 1Ch 12.03

JEZRAHIAH
singers sang with J. as their leader. Neh 12.42

JEZREEL
J., Jokdeam, Zanoah, Jos 15.56
villages and those in the Valley of J." 17.16
Its territory included J., Chesulloth, 19.18
they encamped in the Valley of J. Ju 6.33
David also took Ahinoam of J.; and 1Sa 25.43
Ahinoam of J., and Abigail of Carmel, 27.03
by the fountain which is in J. 29.01
but the Philistines went up to J. 29.11
Ahinoam of J., and Abigail the widow 30.05
Ahinoam of J., and Abigail the widow 2Sa 2.02
the Ashurites and J. and Ephraim and 2.09
was Amnon, of Ahinoam of J.; 3.02
Saul and Jonathan came from J.; 4.04
which is beside Zarethan below J., 1Ki 4.12
And Ahab rode and went to J. 18.45
before Ahab to the entrance of J. 18.46
Jezreelite had a vineyard in J., 21.01
Jezebel within the bounds of J.' 21.23
to be healed in J. of the wounds 2Ki 8.29
to see Joram the son of Ahab in J., 8.29
eat Jezebel in the territory of J., 9.10
to be healed in J. of the wounds 9.15
city to go and tell the news in J." 9.15
and went to J., for Joram lay there 9.16
was standing on the tower in J., 9.17
When Jehu came to J., Jezebel heard 9.30
territory of J. the dogs shall eat 9.36
the field in the territory of J., 9.37
come to me at J. tomorrow at this 10.06
baskets, and sent them to him at J. 10.07
remained of the house of Ahab in J., 10.11
sons of Etam: J., Ishma, and Idbash; 1Ch 4.03
to be healed in J. of the wounds 2Ch 22.06
to see Joram the son of Ahab in J., 22.06
LORD said to him, "Call his name J.; Hos 1.04
house of Jehu for the blood of J., 1.04
bow of Israel in the valley of J." 1.05
for great shall be the day of J. 1.11
the oil, and they shall answer J.; 2.22

JEZREELITE
Now Naboth the J. had a vineyard in 1Ki 21.01
what Naboth the J. had said to him; 21.04
"Because I spoke to Naboth the J., 21.06
you the vineyard of Naboth the J." 21.07
of the vineyard of Naboth the J., 21.15
to the vineyard of Naboth the J., 21.16
at the property of Naboth the J. 2Ki 9.21
ground belonging to Naboth the J.; 9.25

JEZREELITESS
first-born Amnon, by Ahinoam the J.; 1Ch 3.01

JIDLAPH
Chesed, Hazo, Pildash, J., and Bethuel. Gen 22.22

JOAB
And J. the son of Zeruiah, and the 2Sa 2.13
And Abner said to J., "Let the young 2.14
And J. said, "Let them arise." 2.14
were there, J., Abishai, and Asahel. 2.18
lift up my face to your brother J.?" 2.22
But J. and Abishai pursued Abner; 2.24
Then Abner called to J., "Shall the 2.26
And J. said, "As God lives, if you 2.27
So J. blew the trumpet; and all the 2.28
J. returned from the pursuit of 2.30
And J. and his men marched all 2.32
David arrived with J. from a raid, 3.22
When J. and all the army that was 3.23
it was told J., "Abner the son of 3.23
Then J. went to the king and said, 3.24
When J. came out from David's 3.26
J. took him aside into the midst of 3.27
May it fall upon the head of J., 3.29
the house of J. never be without 3.29
So J. and Abishai his brother slew 3.30
Then David said to J. and to all 3.31
And J. the son of Zeruiah was over 8.16
he sent J. and all the host of the 10.07
When J. saw that the battle was set 10.09
So J. and the people who were with 10.13
Then J. returned from fighting 10.14
David sent J., and his servants 11.01

JOAB (cont.)

So David sent word to J., "Send me 2Sa 11.06
And J. sent Uriah to David. 11.06
him, David asked how J. was doing, 11.07
and my lord J. and the servants of 11.11
morning David wrote a letter to J., 11.14
And as J. was besieging the city, he 11.16
city came out and fought with J.; 11.17
Then J. sent and told David all the 11.18
David all that J. had sent him to 11.22
messenger, "Thus shall you say to J., 11.25
Now J. fought against Rabbah of the 12.26
And J. sent messengers to David, and 12.27
Now J. the son of Zeruaih perceived 14.01
And J. sent to Tekoa, and fetched 14.02
So J. put the words in her mouth. 14.03
"Is the hand of J. with you in all 14.19
It was your servant J. who bade me; 14.19
affairs your servant J. did this. 14.20
Then the king said to J., "Behold now, 14.21
And J. fell on his face to the 14.22
and J. said, "Today your servant 14.22
So J. arose and went to Geshur, and 14.23
Then Absalom sent for J., to send 14.29
but J. would not come to him. 14.29
second time, but J. would not come. 14.29
Then J. arose and went to Absalom 14.31
Absalom answered J., "Behold, I sent 14.32
Then J. went to the king, and told 14.33
Amasa over the army instead of J. 17.25
one third under the command of J., 18.02
king ordered J. and Abishai and 18.05
and told J., "Behold, I saw Absalom 18.10
J. said to the man who told him, 18.11
But the man said to J., "Even if I felt 18.12
J. said, "I will not waste time like 18.14
Then J. blew the trumpet, and the 18.16
Israel; for J. restrained them. 18.16
And J. said to him, "You are not to 18.20
Then J. said to the Cushite, "Go, 18.21
Cushite bowed before J., and ran. 18.21
the son of Zadok said again to J., 18.22
And J. said, "Why will you run, my 18.22
"When J. sent your servant, I saw a 18.29
It was told J., "Behold, the king is 19.01
Then J. came into the house to the 19.05
my army henceforth in place of J.'" 19.13
J. and the Cherethites and the 20.07
Now J. was wearing a soldier's 20.08
And J. said to Amasa, "Is it well 20.09
And J. took Amasa by the beard with 20.09
so J. struck him with it in the 20.10
Then J. and Abishai his brother 20.10
Amasa, and said, "Whoever favors J., 20.11
is for David, let him follow J." 20.11
went on after J. to pursue Sheba 20.13
who were with J. came besieged 20.15
Tell J., 'Come here, that I may 20.16
and the woman said, "Are you J.?" 20.17
J. answered, "Far be it from me, far 20.20
And the woman said to J., "Behold, his 20.21
of Bichri, and threw it out to J. 20.22
And J. returned to Jerusalem to the 20.22
Now J. was in command of all the 20.23
Now Abishai, the brother of J., 23.18
Asahel the brother of J. was one of 23.24
armor-bearer of J. the son of 23.37
king said to J. and the commanders 24.02
But J. said to the king, "May the 24.03
prevailed against J. and the 24.04
So J. and the commanders of the 24.04
And J. gave the sum of the numbering 24.09
He conferred with J. the son of 1Ki 1.07
and J. the commander of the army; 1.19
J. the commander of the army, and 1.25
And when J. heard the sound of the 1.41
you know also what J. the son of 2.05
the priest and J. the son of Zeruiah." 2.22
When the news came to J.—for J. had 2.28
J. fled to the tent of the LORD 2.28
"J. has fled to the tent of the 2.29
"Thus said J., and thus he answered 2.30
the blood which J. shed without 2.31
the head of J. and upon the head 2.33
over the army in place of J., 2.35
and J. the commander of the army 11.15
(for J. and all Israel remained 11.16
and that J. the commander of the 11.21
Abishai, J., and Asahel, three. 1Ch 2.16
the father of J. the father of 4.14
And J. the son of Zeruiah went up 11.06
and J. repaired the rest of the 11.08
Now Abishai, the brother of J., 11.20
were Asahel the brother of J., 11.26
armor-bearer of J. the son of 11.39
And J. the son of Zeruiah was over 18.15
he sent J. and all the army of the 19.08
When J. saw that the battle was set 19.10
So J. and the people who were with 19.14
Then J. came to Jerusalem. 19.15
J. led out the army, and ravaged the 20.01
And J. smote Rabbah, and overthrew 20.01
So David said to J. and the commanders 21.02
But J. said, "May the LORD add to 21.03
king's word prevailed against J. 21.04
So J. departed and went throughout 21.04
And J. gave the sum of the numbering 21.05
king's command was abhorrent to J. 21.06
and J. the son of Zeruiah had 26.28
Asahel the brother of J. was fourth, 27.07
J. the son of Zeruiah began to 27.24
J. was commander of the king's army. 27.34
namely the sons of Jeshua and J., Ez 2.06
Of the sons of J., Obadiah the son 8.09
namely the sons of Jeshua and J., Neh 7.11

JOAB'S

and to J. brother Abishai the son 1Sa 26.06
J. field is next to mine, and he has 2Sa 14.30
sister of Zeruiah, J. mother. 17.25
J. brother, and one third under the 18.02
J. armor-bearers, surrounded Absalom 18.15
the sword which was in J. hand; 20.10
And one of J. men took his stand by 20.11
J. brother, and entered the city. 1Ch 19.15

JOAH

and J. the son of Asaph, the recorder. 2Ki 18.18
and J., said to the Rabshakeh, "Pray, 18.26
and J. the son of Asaph, the recorder, 18.37
J. his son, Iddo his son, Zerah his 1Ch 6.21
J. the third, Sachar the fourth, 26.04
J. the son of Zimmah, and Eden the 2Ch 29.12
of Zimmah, and Eden the son of J.; 29.12
and J. the son of Joahaz, the 34.08
and J. the son of Asaph, the recorder. Is 36.03
and J. said to the Rabshakeh, "Pray, 36.11
and J. the son of Asaph, the recorder, 36.22

JOAHAZ

second year of Joash the son of J., 2Ki 14.01
the city, and Joah the son of J., 2Ch 34.08

JOANAN

the son of J., the son of Rhesa, the Lk 3.27

JOANNA

and J., the wife of Chuza, Herod's Lk 8.03
Magdalene and J. and Mary the 24.10

JOASH

which belonged to J. the Abiezrite, Ju 6.11
the son of J. has done this thing." 6.29
Then the men of the town said to J., 6.30
But J. said to all who were arrayed 6.31

JOASH (cont.)

the sword of Gideon the son of J., Ju 7.14
the son of J. returned from the 8.13
Jerubbaal the son of J. went and 8.29
the son of J. died in a good old 8.32
in the tomb of J. his father, 8.32
the city and to J. the king's son; 1Ki 22.26
took J. the son of Ahaziah, and 2Ki 11.02
Now the rest of the acts of J., 12.19
and slew J. in the house of Millo, 12.20
twenty-third year of J. the son of 13.01
and J. his son reigned in his 13.09
thirty-seventh year of J. king of 13.10
Now the rest of the acts of J., 13.12
So J. slept with his fathers, and 13.13
and J. was buried in Samaria with 13.13
J. king of Israel went down to him, 13.14
Three times J. defeated him and 13.25
second year of J. the son of 14.01
of Israel, Amaziah the son of J., 14.01
all things as J. his father had 14.03
Amaziah the son of J., king of 14.17
year of Amaziah the son of J., 14.23
of Judah, Jeroboam the son of J., 14.23
the hand of Jeroboam the son of J. 14.27
son, Ahaziah his son, J. his son, 1Ch 3.11
and J., and Saraph, who ruled in 4.22
J., Eliezer, Elioenai, Omri, Jeremoth, 7.08
then J., both sons of Shemaah of 12.03
and over the stores of oil was J. 27.28
the city and to J. the king's son; 2Ch 18.25
took J. the son of Ahaziah, and 22.11
J. was seven years old when he 24.01
And J. did what was right in the 24.02
After this J. decided to restore 24.04
Thus J. the king did not remember 24.22
of the Syrians came up against J. 24.23
thus they executed judgment on J. 24.24
and sent to J. the son of Jehoahaz, 25.17
And J. the king of Israel sent word 25.18
So J. king of Israel went up; 25.21
And J. king of Israel captured 25.23
the son of J., son of Ahaziah, at 25.23
Amaziah the son of J. king of Judah 25.25
the death of J. the son of Jehoahaz, 25.25
the days of Jeroboam the son of J., Hos 1.01
the days of Jeroboam the son of J., Amo 1.01

JOB

the land of Uz, whose name was J.; Job 1.01
J. would send and sanctify them, and 1.05
for J. said, "It may be that my sons 1.05
hearts." Thus J. did continually. 1.05
"Have you considered my servant J., 1.08
"Does J. fear God for nought? 1.09
and there came a messenger to J., 1.14
Then J. arose, and rent his robe, and 1.20
In all this J. did not sin or 1.22
"Have you considered my servant J., 2.03
and afflicted J. with loathsome 2.07
In all this J. did not sin with 2.10
After this J. opened his mouth and 3.01
And J. said: 3.02
Then J. answered: 6.01
Then J. answered: 9.01
Then J. answered: 12.01
Then J. answered: 16.01
Then J. answered: 19.01
Then J. answered: 21.01
Then J. answered: 23.01
Then J. answered: 26.01
And J. again took up his discourse, 27.01
And J. again took up his discourse, 29.01
The words of J. are ended. 31.40
three men ceased to answer J., 32.01
He was angry at J. because he 32.02
had declared J. to be in the wrong. 32.03
to speak to J. because they were 32.04
there was none that confuted J., 32.12
O J., and listen to all my words. 33.01
Give heed, O J., listen to me; 33.31
For J. has said, 'I am innocent, and 34.05
What man is like J., who drinks up 34.07
'J. speaks without knowledge, his 34.35
Would that J. were tried to the end, 34.36
J. opens his mouth in empty talk, he 35.16
"Hear this, O J.; stop and consider the 37.14
LORD answered J. out of the whirlwind: 38.01
And the LORD said to J.: 40.01
Then J. answered the LORD: 40.03
LORD answered J. out of the whirlwind: 40.06
Then J. answered the LORD: 42.01
LORD had spoken these words to J., 42.07
is right, as my servant J. has. 42.07
rams, and go to my servant J., and 42.08
and my servant J. shall pray for 42.08
is right, as my servant J. has." 42.08
LORD restored the fortunes of J., 42.10
the LORD gave J. twice as much as 42.10
latter days of J. more than his 42.12
And after this J. lived a hundred 42.16
And J. died, an old man, and full of 42.17
and J., were in it, they would Eze 14.14
and J. were in it, as I live, says 14.20
heard of the steadfastness of J., Jas 5.11

JOBAB

Ophir, Havilah, and J.; all these Gen 10.29
Bela died, and J. the son of Zerah 36.33
J. died, and Husham of the land of 36.34
he sent to J. king of Madon, and to Jos 11.01
Ophir, Havilah, and J.; all these 1Ch 1.23
J. the son of Zerah of Bozrah 1.44
When J. died, Husham of the land of 1.45
his wife: J., Zibia, Mesha, Malcam, 8.09
and J. were the sons of Elpaal. 8.18

JOB'S

Now when J. three friends heard of Job 2.11
angry also at J. three friends 32.03
and the LORD accepted J. prayer. 42.09
no women so fair as J. daughters; 42.15

JOCHEBED

Amram took to wife J. his father's Ex 6.20
wife was J. the daughter of Levi, Num 26.59

JODA

the son of Josech, the son of J., Lk 3.26

JOED

son of J., son of Pedaiah, son of Neh 11.07

JOEL

The name of his first-born son was J., 1Sa 8.02
J., Jehu the son of Joshibiah, son 1Ch 4.35
The sons of J.: Shemaiah his son, Gog 5.04
son of J., who dwelt in Aroer, as 5.08
J. the chief, Shapham the second, 5.12
J. his first-born, the second Abijah. 6.28
Beman the singer the son of J., 6.33
son of J., son of Azariah, son of 6.36
J., and Isshiah, five, all of them 7.03
J. the brother of Nathan, Mibhar the 11.38
J. the chief, with a hundred and 15.07
J., Shemaiah, Eliel, and Amminadab, 15.11
appointed Heman the son of J.; 15.17
chief, and Zetham, and J., three. 23.08
Zetham and J. his brother, were in 26.22
of Manasseh, J. the son of Pedaiah; 27.20
and J. the son of Azariah, of the 2Ch 29.12
Zebina, Jaddai, J., and Benaiah. Ez 10.43
J. the son of Zichri was their Neh 11.09
The word of the LORD that came to J., Joe 1.01
what was spoken by the prophet J.: Ac 2.16

JOELAH
and J. and Zebadiah, the sons of 1Ch 12.07

JOEZER
J., and Jashobeam, the Korahites; 1Ch 12.06

JOGBEHAH
Atroth-Shophan, Jazer, J., Num 32.35
caravan route east of Nobah and J., Ju 8.11

JOGLI
Dan a leader, Bukki the son of J. Num 34.22

JOHA
Izliah, and J. were sons of Beriah. 1Ch 8.16
Shimri, and J. his brother, the Tizite, 11.45

JOHANAN
and J. the son of Kareah, and 2Ki 25.23
sons of Josiah: J. the first-born, the 1Ch 3.15
Akkub, J., Delaiah, and Anani, seven. 3.24
Ahimaaz of Azariah, Azariah of J., 6.09
and J. of Azariah (it was he who 6.10
Jahaziel, J., Jozabad of Gederah, 12.04
J. eighth, Elzabad ninth, 12.12
of Ephraim, Azariah the son of J., 2Ch 28.12
J. the son of Hakkatan, and with him Ez 8.12
J., and Jaddua, there were recorded Neh 12.22
the days of J. the son of Eliashib. 12.23
J. the son of Kareah, Seraiah the Jer 40.08
Now J. the son of Kareah and all 40.13
Then J. the son of Kareah spoke 40.15
Ahikam said to J. the son of 40.16
But when J. the son of Kareah and 41.11
Ishmael saw J. the son of Kareah 41.13
and went to J. the son of Kareah. 41.14
escaped from J. with eight men, 41.15
Then J. the son of Kareah and all 41.16
whom J. brought back from Gibeon. 41.16
and J. the son of Kareah and 42.01
Then he summoned J. the son of 42.08
of Hoshaiah and J. the son of 43.02
So J. the son of Kareah and all the 43.04
But J. the son of Kareah and all 43.05

JOHN
In those days came J. the Baptist, Mt 3.01
Now J. wore a garment of camel's 3.04
from Galilee to the Jordan to J., 3.13
J. would have prevented him, saying, 3.14
he heard that J. had been arrested, 4.12
son of Zebedee and J. his brother, 4.21
Then the disciples of J. came to him, 9.14
son of Zebedee, and J. his brother; 10.02
Now when J. heard in prison about 11.02
"Go and tell J. what you hear and 11.04
speak to the crowds concerning J.: 11.07
no one greater than J. the Baptist; 11.11
From the days of J. the Baptist 11.12
and the law prophesied until J.; 11.13
For J. came neither eating nor 11.18
"This is J. the Baptist, he has been 14.02
had seized J. and bound him and 14.03
because J. said to him, "It is not 14.04
me the head of J. the Baptist here 14.08
he sent and had J. beheaded in the 14.10
"Some say J. the Baptist, others say 16.14
Peter and James and J. his brother, 17.01
speaking to them of J. the Baptist. 17.13
The baptism of J., whence was it? 21.25
for all hold that J. was a prophet." 21.26
For J. came to you in the way of 21.32
J. the baptizer appeared in the Mk 1.04
Now J. was clothed with camel's hair, 1.06
was baptized by J. in the Jordan. 1.09
Now after J. was arrested, Jesus 1.14
son of Zebedee and J. his brother, 1.19
and Andrew, with James and J. 1.29
of Zebedee and J. the brother of 3.17
and James and J. the brother of 5.37
Some said, "J. the baptizer has been 6.14
"J., whom I beheaded, has been 6.16
For Herod had sent and seized J., 6.17
For J. said to Herod, "It is not 6.18
for Herod feared J., knowing that 6.20
said, "The head of J. the baptizer." 6.24
the head of J. the Baptist on a 6.25
And they told him, "J. the Baptist; 8.28
with him Peter and James and J., 9.02
J. said to him, "Teacher, we saw a 9.38
And James and J., the sons of 10.35
to be indignant at James and J. 10.41
Was the baptism of J. from heaven 11.30
all held that J. was a real 11.32
and James and J. and Andrew asked 13.03
with him Peter and James and J., 14.33
and you shall call his name J. Lk 1.13
"Not so; he shall be called J." 1.60
tablet, and wrote, "His name is J." 1.63
of God came to J. the son of 3.02
in their hearts concerning J., 3.15
J. answered them all, "I baptized you 3.16
all, that he shut up J. in prison. 3.20
and so also were James and J., 5.10
disciples of J. fast often and 5.33
and James and J., and Philip, and 6.14
The disciples of J. told him of all 7.18
And J., calling to him two of his 7.19
"J. the Baptist has sent us to you, 7.20
"Go and tell J. what you have seen 7.22
When the messengers of J. had gone, 7.24
speak to the crowds concerning J.: 7.24
of women none is greater than J.; 7.28
baptized with the baptism of J.; 7.29
For J. the Baptist has come eating 7.33
him, except Peter and J. and James, 8.51
by some that J. had been raised 9.07
Herod said, "J. I beheaded; 9.09
And they answered, "J. the Baptist; 9.19
with him Peter and J. and James, 9.28
J. answered, "Master, we saw a man 9.49
his disciples James and J. saw it, 9.54
pray, as J. taught his disciples." 11.01
law and the prophets were until J.; 16.16
Was the baptism of J. from heaven 20.04
convinced that J. was a prophet." 20.06
So Jesus sent Peter and J., saying, 22.08
sent from God, whose name was J. Jn 1.06
(J. bore witness to him, and cried, 1.15
And this is the testimony of J., 1.19
J. answered them, "I baptize with 1.26
the Jordan, where J. was baptizing. 1.28
And J. bore witness, "I saw the 1.32
The next day again J. was standing 1.35
One of the two who heard J. speak, 1.40
"So you are Simon the son of J.? 1.42
J. also was baptizing at Aenon near 3.23
For J. had not yet been put in 3.24
And they came to J., and said to 3.26
J. answered, "No one can receive 3.27
baptizing more disciples than J. 4.01
You sent to J., and he has borne 5.33
I have is greater than that of J.; 5.36
the place where J. at first 10.40
"J. did no sign, but everything that 10.41
everything that J. said about this 10.41
son of J., do you love me more than 21.15
"Simon, son of J., do you love me?" 21.16
"Simon, son of J., do you love me?" 21.17
for J. baptized with water, but Ac 1.05
Peter and J. and James and Andrew, 1.13
the baptism of J. until the day 1.22
Now Peter and J. were going up to 3.01
Seeing Peter and J. about to go 3.03
with J., and said, "Look at us." 3.04

JOHN (cont.)
While he clung to Peter and J., Ac 3.11
and Caiaphas and J. and Alexander, 4.06
saw the boldness of Peter and J., 4.13
But Peter and J. answered them, 4.19
they sent to them Peter and J., 8.14
the baptism which J. preached: 10.37
'J. baptized with water, but you 11.16
the brother of J. with the sword; 12.02
the mother of J. whose other name 12.12
with them J. whose other name was 12.25
And they had J. to assist them. 13.05
And J. left them and returned to 13.13
Before his coming J. had preached a 13.24
And as J. was finishing his course, 13.25
to take with them J. called Mark. 15.37
he knew only the baptism of J. 18.25
"J. baptized with the baptism of 19.04
to me, James and Cephas and J., Gal 2.09
his angel to his servant J., Rev 1.01
J. to the seven churches that are 1.04
I J., your brother, who share with 1.09
I J. am he who heard and saw these 22.08

JOHN'S
Now J. disciples and the Pharisees Mk 2.18
"Why do J. disciples and the 2.18
arose between J. disciples and a Jn 3.25
They said, "Into J. baptism." Ac 19.03

JOIADA
And J. the son of Paseah and Neh 3.06
Eliashib, Eliashib the father of J., 12.10
J. the father of Jonathan, and 12.11
J., Johanan, and Jaddua, there were 12.22

JOIAKIM
And Jeshua was the father of J., Neh 12.10
J. the father of Eliashib, Eliashib 12.10
And in the days of J. were priests, 12.12
in the days of J. the son of 12.26

JOIARIB
and for J. and Elnathan, who were Ez 8.16
son of J., son of Zechariah, son of Neh 11.05
Jedaiah the son of J., Jachin, 11.10
Shemaiah, J., Jedaiah, 12.06
of J., Mattenai; of Jedaiah, Uzzi; 12.19

JOIN
they j. our enemies and fight Ex 1.10
You shall not j. hands with a 23.01
that they may j. you, and minister Num 18.02
They shall j. you, and attend to the 18.04
and j. the remnant of these nations Jos 23.12
called out to j. Saul at Gilgal. 1Sa 13.04
my servants will j. your servants, 1Ki 5.06
j. with their brethren, their nobles, Neh 10.29
I could j. words together against Job 16.04
Woe to those who j. house to house, Is 5.08
and aliens will j. them and will 14.01
foreigners who j. themselves to 56.06
of Judah shall j. the house of Jer 3.18
let us j. ourselves to the LORD in 50.05
and j. them together into one stick, Eze 37.17
and I will j. with it the stick of 37.19
And many shall j. themselves to Dan 11.34
nations shall j. themselves to the Zec 2.11
None of the rest dared j. them, Ac 5.13
Philip, "Go up and j. this chariot." 8.29
he attempted to j. the disciples; 9.26
Brethren, j. in imitating me, and Php 3.17
you do not now j. them in the same 1Pe 4.04

JOINED
And all these j. forces in the Gen 14.03
and they j. battle in the Valley of 14.08
time my husband will be j. to me, 29.34
spirit, be not j. to their company; 49.06
but j. at the top, at the first ring Ex 26.24
edges, that it may be j. together. 28.07
but j. at the top, at the first ring; 36.29
j. to it at its two edges. 39.04
And all these kings j. their forces, Jos 11.05
and it was j. to the house with 1Ki 6.10
the seventh day the battle was j.; 20.29
all the people j. in the covenant. 2Ki 23.03
was j. to the wing of the first 2Ch 3.12
king of Judah j. with Ahaziah king 20.35
He j. him in building ships to go 20.36
"Because you have j. with Ahaziah, 20.37
but j. battle in the plain of 35.22
one who had j. them and separated Ez 6.21
the wall was j. together to half Neh 4.06
in Judah were j. to Benjamin. 11.36
descendants and all who j. them, Est 9.27
They are j. one to another; they Job 41.17
Assyria also has j. them; they are Ps 83.08
But he who is j. with all the Ecc 9.04
You will not be j. with them in Is 14.20
foreigner who has j. himself to the 56.03
Ephraim is j. to idols, let him Hos 4.17
and mother and be j. to his wife, Mt 19.05
What therefore God has j. together, 19.06
and mother and be j. to his wife, Mk 10.07
What therefore God has j. together, 10.09
So he went and j. himself to one of Lk 15.15
of men, about four hundred j. him; Ac 5.36
The crowd j. in attacking them; 16.22
persuaded, and j. Paul and Silas; 17.04
But some men j. him and believed, 17.34
The Jews also j. in the charge, 24.09
structure is j. together and grows Eph 2.21
j. and knit together by every joint 4.16
and mother and be j. to his wife, 5.31

JOINING
at its j. above the skilfully woven Ex 28.27
at its j. above the skilfully woven 39.20

JOINS
that he who j. himself to a prostitute 1Co 6.16

JOINT
was put out of j. as he wrestled Gen 32.25
and all my bones are out of j.; Ps 22.14
by every j. with which it is Eph 4.16
be put out of j. but rather be Heb 12.13
since you are j. heirs of the grace 1Pe 3.07

JOINTS
through its j. and ligaments, Col 2.19
of j. and marrow, and discerning the Heb 4.12

JOKDEAM
Jezreel, J., Zanoah, Jos 15.56

JOKIM
and J., and the men of Cozeba, and 1Ch 4.22

JOKING
his neighbor and says, "I am only j.!" Pro 26.19

JOKMEAM
as far as the other side of J.; 1Ki 4.12
J. with its pasture lands, Bethhoron 1Ch 6.68

JOKNEAM
the king of J. in Carmel, one; Jos 12.22
then the brook which is east of J.; 19.11
J. with its pasture lands, Kartah 21.34

JOKSHAN
J., Medan, Midian, Ishbak, and Shuah. Gen 25.02
J. was the father of Sheba and 25.03
J., Medan, Midian, Ishbak, and Shuah. 1Ch 1.32
The sons of J.: Sheba and Dedan. 1.32

JOKTAN
and his brother's name was J. Gen 10.25
J. became the father of Almodad, 10.26
all these were the sons of J. 10.29
and the name of his brother J. 1Ch 1.19
J. was the father of Almodad, 1.20
all these were the sons of J. 1.23

JOKTHEEL
Dilean, Mizpeh, J., Jos 15.38
and called it J., which is its name 2Ki 14.07

JONADAB
had a friend, whose name was J., 2Sa 13.03
and J. was a very crafty man. 13.03
J. said to him, "Lie down on your 13.05
But J. the son of Shimeah, David's 13.32
And J. said to the king, "Behold, the 13.35
for J. the son of Rechab, our father, Jer 35.06
the voice of J. the son of Rechab, 35.08
done all that J. our father 35.10
The command which J. the son of 35.14
The sons of J. the son of Rechab 35.16
the command of J. your father, 35.18
J. the son of Rechab shall never 35.19

JONAH
by his servant J. the son of 2Ki 14.25
LORD came to J. the son of Amittai, Jon 1.01
But J. rose to flee to Tarshish 1.03
But J. had gone down into the inner 1.05
lots, and the lot fell upon J. 1.07
So they took up J. and threw him 1.15
a great fish to swallow up J.; 1.17
and J. was in the belly of the fish 1.17
Then J. prayed to the LORD his God 2.01
it vomited out J. upon the dry 2.10
LORD came to J. the second time, 3.01
So J. arose and went to Nineveh, 3.03
J. began to go into the city, going 3.04
But it displeased J. exceedingly, 4.01
Then J. went out of the city and 4.05
plant, and made it come up over J., 4.06
So J. was exceedingly glad because 4.06
the head of J. so that he was 4.08
But God said to J., "Do you do well 4.09
except the sign of the prophet J. Mt 12.39
For as J. was three days and three 12.40
repented at the preaching of J., 12.41
something greater than J. is here. 12.41
given to it except the sign of J. 16.04
given to it except the sign of J. Lk 11.29
For as J. became a sign to the men 11.30
repented at the preaching of J., 11.32
something greater than J. is here. 11.32

JONAM
the son of J., the son of Eliakim, Lk 3.30

JONATHAN
and J. the son of Gershom, son of Ju 18.30
were with J. in Gibeah of Benjamin; 1Sa 13.02
J. defeated the garrison of the 13.03
And Saul, and J. his son, and the 13.16
any of the people with Saul and J.; 13.22
but Saul and J. his son had them. 13.22
One day J. the son of Saul said to 14.01
did not know that J. had gone. 14.03
by which J. sought to go over to 14.04
And J. said to the young man who 14.06
Then said J., "Behold, we will cross 14.08
garrison hailed J. and his armor-bearer, 14.12
And J. said to his armor-bearer, 14.12
Then J. climbed up on his hands and 14.13
And they fell before J., and his 14.13
which J. and his armor-bearer made, 14.14
J. and his armor-bearer were not 14.17
Israelites who were with Saul and J. 14.21
But J. had not heard his father 14.27
Then J. said, "My father has troubled 14.29
Israel, though it be in J. my son, 14.39
and I and J. my son will be on the 14.40
guilt is in me or in J. my son, 14.41
And J. and Saul were taken, but the 14.41
the lot between me and my son J." 14.42
And J. was taken. 14.42
Then Saul said to J., "Tell me what 14.43
And J. told him, "I tasted a little 14.43
also; you shall surely die, J." 14.44
"Shall J. die, who has wrought this 14.45
So the people ransomed J., 14.45
Now the sons of Saul were J., 14.49
the soul of J. was knit to the soul 18.01
and J. loved him as his own soul. 18.01
Then J. made a covenant with David, 18.03
And J. stripped himself of the robe 18.04
And Saul spoke to J. his son and to 19.01
But J., Saul's son, delighted much in 19.01
And J. told David, "Saul my father 19.02
And J. spoke well of David to Saul 19.04
And Saul hearkened to the voice of J.; 19.06
And J. called David, and J. showed 19.07
And J. brought David to Saul, and he 19.07
Ramah, and came and said before J., 20.01
'Let not J. know this, lest he be 20.03
Then said J. to David, "Whatever you 20.04
David said to J., "Behold, tomorrow 20.05
And J. said, "Far be it from you! 20.09
Then said David to J., "Who will tell 20.10
And J. said to David, "Come, let us 20.11
And J. said to David, "The LORD, the 20.12
do you harm, the LORD do so to J., 20.13
let not the name of J. be cut off 20.16
And J. made David swear again by 20.17
Then J. said to him, "Tomorrow is 20.18
J. sat opposite, and Abner sat by 20.25
And Saul said to J. his son, 20.27
J. answered Saul, "David earnestly 20.28
anger was kindled against J., 20.30
Then J. answered Saul his father, 20.32
so J. knew that his father was 20.33
And J. rose from the table in 20.34
In the morning J. went out into the 20.35
of the arrow which J. had shot, 20.37
J. called after the lad and said, 20.37
And J. called after the lad, "Hurry, 20.38
only J. and David knew the matter. 20.39
And J. gave his weapons to his lad, 20.40
Then J. said to David, "Go in peace, 20.42
and J. went into the city. 20.42
And J., Saul's son, rose, and went to 23.16
remained at Horesh, and J. went home. 23.18
Philistines slew J. and Abinadab 31.02
Saul and his son J. are also dead." 2Sa 1.04
that Saul and his son J. are dead?" 1.05
Saul and for J. his son and for 1.12
lamentation over Saul and J. his son, 1.17
the bow of J. turned not back, and 1.22
"Saul and J., beloved and lovely! 1.23
"J. lies slain upon thy high places. 1.25
distressed for you, my brother J.; 1.26
J., the son of Saul, had a son who 4.04
about Saul and J. came from Jezreel; 4.04
king, "There is still a son of J.; 9.03
And Mephibosheth the son of J., 9.06
for the sake of your father J., 9.07
your son, and J. the son of Abiathar. 15.27
Zadok's son, and J., Abiathar's son; 15.36
Now J. and Ahimaaz were waiting at 17.17
said, "Where are Ahimaaz and J.?" 17.20
Mephibosheth, the son of Saul's son J., 21.07
between David and J. the son of Saul. 21.07
bones of his son J. from the men of 21.12
Saul and the bones of his son J.; 21.13
Saul and his son J. in the land of 21.14

JONATHAN (cont.)

J. the son of Shimei, David's brother, 2Sa 21.21
Shaalbon, the sons of Jashen, J., 23.32
J. the son of Abiathar the priest 1Ki 1.42
J. answered Adonijah, "No, for our 1.43
Shammai's brother: Jether and J.; 1Ch 2.32
The sons of J.: Peleth and Zaza. 2.33
Saul of J., Malchishua, Abinadab, and 8.33
and the son of J. was Meribbaal; 8.34
Saul of J., Malchishua, Abinadab, and 9.39
and the son of J. was Meribbaal; 9.40
Philistines slew J. and Abinadab 10.02
J. the son of Shagee the Hararite, 11.34
J. the son of Shimea, David's brother, 20.07
the towers, was J. the son of Uzziah; 27.25
J., David's uncle, was a counselor, 27.32
sons of Adin, Ebed the son of J., Ez 8.06
Only J. the son of Asahel and 10.15
Joiada the father of J., Neh 12.11
and J. the father of Jaddua. 12.11
of Malluchi, J.; of Shebaniah, 12.14
trumpets: Zechariah the son of J., 12.35
in the house of J. the secretary, Jer 37.15
to the house of J. the secretary, 37.20
to the house of J. to die there.'" 38.26

JONATHAN'S

So J. lad gathered up the arrows, 1Sa 20.38
may show him kindness for J. sake?" 2Sa 9.01

JOPPA

with the territory over against J. Jos 19.46
it to you in rafts by sea to J., 2Ch 2.16
to J., according to the grant which Ez 3.07
He went down to J. and found a ship Jon 1.03
Now there was at J. a disciple Ac 9.36
Since Lydda was near J., the disciples, 9.38
And it became known throughout all J., 9.42
And he stayed in J. for many days 9.43
And now send men to J., and bring one 10.05
everything to them, he sent them to J. 10.08
brethren from J. accompanied him. 10.23
Send therefore to J. and ask for 10.32
"I was in the city of J. praying; 11.05
'Send to J. and bring Simon called 11.13

JORAH

The sons of J., one hundred and twelve. Ez 2.18

JORAI

Sheba, J., Jacan, Zia, and Eber, seven. 1Ch 5.13

JORAM

Tou sent his son J. to King David, 2Sa 8.10
And J. brought with him articles of 8.10
fifth year of J. the son of Ahab, 2Ki 8.16
Then J. passed over to Zair with 8.21
Now the rest of the acts of J., 8.23
So J. slept with his fathers, and 8.24
twelfth year of J. the son of Ahab, 8.25
He went with J. the son of Ahab to 8.28
where the Syrians wounded J. 8.28
And King J. returned to be healed 8.29
down to see J. the son of Ahab in 8.29
son of Nimshi conspired against J. 9.14
(Now J. with all Israel had been on 9.14
but King J. had returned to be 9.15
went to Jezreel, for J. lay there. 9.16
of Judah had come down to visit J. 9.16
And J. said, "Take a horseman, and 9.17
J. said, "Make ready." And they made 9.21
Then J. king of Israel and Ahaziah 9.21
And when J. saw Jehu, he said, "Is it 9.22
Then J. reined about and fled, 9.23
and shot J. between the shoulders, 9.24
eleventh year of J. the son of Ahab, 9.29
Jehosheba, the daughter of King J., 11.02
J. his son, Ahaziah his son, Joash 1Ch 3.11
and his son J., and his son Zichri, 26.25
And the Syrians wounded J., 2Ch 22.05
down to see J. the son of Ahab in 22.06
through his going to visit J. 22.07
and Jehoshaphat the father of J., Mt 1.08
and J. the father of Uzziah, 1.08

JORDAN

saw that the J. valley was well Gen 13.10
for himself all the J. valley, 13.11
only my staff I crossed this J.; 32.10
of Atad, which is beyond the J., 50.10
Abelmizraim; it is beyond the J. 50.11
dwell by the sea, and along the J. Num 13.29
of Moab beyond the J. at Jericho. 22.01
of Moab by the J. at Jericho, 26.03
of Moab by the J. at Jericho, 26.63
of Moab by the J. at Jericho, 31.12
do not take us across the J." 32.05
other side of the J. and beyond; 32.19
on this side of the J. to the east. 32.19
pass over the J. before the LORD, 32.21
you over the J. and the land shall 32.29
shall remain with us beyond the J." 32.32
of Moab by the J. at Jericho; 33.48
they encamped by the J. from 33.49
of Moab by the J. at Jericho, 33.50
pass over the J. into the land of 33.51
boundary shall go down to the J., 34.12
beyond the J. at Jericho eastward, 34.15
of Moab by the J. at Jericho, 35.01
you cross the J. into the land of 35.10
give three cities beyond the J., 35.14
of Moab by the J. at Jericho. 36.13
beyond the J. in the wilderness, in Deu 1.01
Beyond the J., in the land of Moab, 1.05
I go over the J. into the land 2.29
Amorites who were beyond the J., 3.08
with the J. as the boundary, from 3.17
your God gives them beyond the J.; 3.20
see the good land beyond the J., 3.25
or you shall not go over this J. 3.27
that I should not cross the J., 4.21
land, I must not go over the J.; 4.22
are going over the J. to possess; 4.26
cities in the east beyond the J., 4.41
beyond the J. in the valley opposite 4.46
lived to the east beyond the J.; 4.47
side of the J. as far as the Sea 4.49
are to pass over the J. this day, 9.01
Are they not beyond the J., 11.30
pass over the J. to go in to take 11.31
But when you go over the J., 12.10
pass over the J. to the land which 27.02
And when you have passed over the J., 27.04
"When you have passed over the J., 27.12
going over the J. to enter and 30.18
me, 'You shall not go over this J.' 31.02
are going over the J. to possess." 31.13
are going over the J. to possess." 32.47
go over this J., you and all this Jos 1.02
days you are to pass over this J., 1.11
which Moses gave you beyond the J.; 1.14
you beyond the J. toward the 1.15
the way to the J. as far as the 2.07
Amorites that were beyond the J., 2.10
and they came to the J., and lodged 3.01
the brink of the waters of the J. 3.08
you shall stand still in the J.'" 3.08
pass over before you into the J. 3.11
shall rest in the waters of the J., 3.13
waters of the J. shall be stopped 3.13
pass over the J. with the priests 3.14
bore the ark had come to the J., 3.15
the water (the J. overflows all its 3.15
dry ground in the midst of the J., 3.17
finished passing over the J. 3.17

JORDAN (cont.)

had finished passing over the J., Jos 4.01
here out of the midst of the J., 4.03
your God into the midst of the J., 4.05
waters of the J. were cut off 4.07
the LORD; when it passed over the J., 4.07
the waters of the J. were cut off. 4.07
stones out of the midst of the J., 4.08
stones in the midst of the J., 4.09
ark stood in the midst of the J., 4.10
testimony to come up out of the J." 4.16
the priests, "Come up out of the J." 4.17
came up from the midst of the J., 4.18
waters of the J. returned to their 4.18
up out of the J. on the tenth day 4.19
which they took out of the J., 4.20
passed over this J. on dry ground.' 4.22
waters of the J. for you until you 4.23
were beyond the J. to the west, 5.01
waters of the J. for the people of 5.01
this people over the J. at all, 7.07
content to dwell beyond the J.! 7.07
were beyond the J. in the hill 9.01
Amorites who were beyond the J., 9.10
land beyond the J. toward the 12.01
defeated on the west side of the J., 12.07
beyond the J. eastward, as Moses the 13.08
of Reuben was the J. as a boundary, 13.23
having the J. as a boundary, to the 13.27
Chinnereth, eastward beyond the J. 13.27
beyond the J. east of Jericho. 13.32
and one-half tribes beyond the J.; 14.03
Salt Sea, to the mouth of the J. 15.05
of the sea at the mouth of the J.; 15.05
Joseph went from the J. by Jericho, 16.01
touches Jericho, ending at the J. 16.07
is on the other side of the J.; 17.05
inheritance beyond the J. eastward, 18.07
their boundary began at the J.; 18.12
Sea, at the south end of the J.: 18.19
The J. forms its boundary on the 18.20
and its boundary ends at the J. 19.22
as Lakkum; and it ended at the J.; 19.33
and Judah on the east at the J. 19.34
And beyond the J. east of Jericho, 20.08
you on the other side of the J. 22.04
brethren in the land west of the J. 22.07
came to the region about the J., 22.10
built there an altar by the J., 22.10
Canaan, in the region about the J., 22.11
has made the J. a boundary between 22.25
from the J. to the Great Sea in the 23.04
lived on the other side of the J.; 24.08
went over the J. and came to 24.11
seized the fords of the J. against the Ju 3.28
Gilead stayed beyond the J.; 5.17
crossing the J. they encamped in 6.33
far as Bethbarah, and also the J." 7.24
and Zeeb to Gideon beyond the J. 7.25
came to the J. and passed over, he 8.04
were beyond the J. in the land of 10.08
crossed the J. to fight also 10.09
Arnon to the Jabbok and to the J.; 11.13
and from the wilderness to the J. 11.22
took fords of the J. against the 12.05
slew him at the fords of the J. 12.06
fords of the J. to the land of Gad 1Sa 13.07
beyond the J. saw that the men of 31.07
they crossed the J., and marching the 2Sa 2.29
together, and crossed the J., and 10.17
with him, arrived weary at the J.; 16.14
with him, and they crossed the J.; 17.22
left who had not crossed the J. 17.22
crossed the J. with all the men of 17.24
So the king came back to the J.; 19.15
and to bring the king over the J. 19.15
down to the J. before the king, 19.17
as he was about to cross the J., 19.18
to the J., to escort him over the J. 19.31
way over the J. with the king. 19.36
Then all the people went over the J., 19.39
king and his household over the J., 19.41
steadfastly from the J. to Jerusalem. 20.02
They crossed the J., and began from 24.05
he came down to meet me at the J., 1Ki 2.08
plain of the J. the king cast them, 7.46
Cherith, that is east of the J. 17.03
Cherith that is east of the J. 17.05
for the LORD has sent me to the J." 2Ki 2.06
they both were standing by the J. 2.07
and stood on the bank of the J. 2.13
"Go and wash in the J. seven times, 5.10
himself seven times in the J., 5.14
Let us go to the J. and each of us 6.02
And when they came to the J., they 6.04
went after them as far as the J.; 7.15
from the J. eastward, all the land 10.33
J. at Jericho, on the east side of the J., 1Ch 6.78
who crossed the J. in the first 12.15
of Manasseh from beyond the J., 12.37
together, and crossed the J., 19.17
westward of the J. for all the 26.30
plain of the J. the king cast them, 2Ch 4.17
confident though J. rushes against Job 40.23
from the land of J. and of Hermon, Ps 42.06
looked and fled, J. turned back. 114.03
you flee? O J., that you turn back? 114.05
of the sea, the land beyond the J., Is 9.01
you do in the jungle of the J.? Jer 12.05
jungle of the J. against a strong 49.19
jungle of the J. against a strong 50.44
along the J. between Gilead and the Eze 47.18
the jungle of the J. is laid waste! Zec 11.03
and all the region about the J., Mt 3.05
baptized by him in the river J., 3.06
from Galilee to the J. to John, 3.13
across the J., Galilee of the 4.15
and Judea and from beyond the J. 4.25
the region of Judea beyond the J.; 19.01
baptized by him in the river J., Mk 1.05
and was baptized by John in the J. 1.09
from beyond the J. and from about 3.08
region of Judea and beyond the J., 10.01
into all the region about the J., Lk 3.03
Holy Spirit, returned from the J., 4.01
place in Bethany beyond the J., Jn 1.28
he who was with you beyond the J., 3.26
across the J. to the place where 10.40

JORIM

the son of J., the son of Matthat, Lk 3.29

JORKEAM

father of Raham, the father of J.; 1Ch 2.44

JOSECH

the son of J., the son of Joda, Lk 3.26

JOSEPH

and she called his name J., saying, Gen 30.24
When Rachel had borne J., Jacob said 30.25
and Rachel and J. last of all. 33.02
and last J. and Rachel drew near, 33.07
The sons of Rachel: J. and Benjamin. 35.24
J., being seventeen years old, was 37.02
and J. brought an ill report of 37.02
Now Israel loved J. more than any 37.03
Now J. had a dream, and when he told 37.05
And Israel said to J., "Are not your 37.13
So J. went after his brothers, and 37.17
So when J. came to his brothers, 37.23
and they drew J. up and lifted him 37.28
of silver; and they took J. to Egypt. 37.28
and saw that J. was not in the pit, 37.29

JOSEPH (cont.)

J. is without doubt torn to pieces."	Gen 37.33
Now J. was taken down to Egypt, and	39.01
The LORD was with J., and he became	39.02
So J. found favor in his sight and	39.04
Now J. was handsome and good-looking.	39.06
master's wife cast her eyes upon J.,	39.07
she spoke to J. day after day,	39.10
LORD was with J. and showed him	39.21
the prison where J. was confined.	40.03
of the guard charged J. with them,	40.04
When J. came to them in the morning	40.06
And J. said to them, "Do not interpretations	40.08
chief butler told his dream to J.,	40.09
Then J. said to him, "This is its	40.12
he said to J., "I also had a dream:	40.16
And J. answered, "This is its	40.18
as J. had interpreted to them.	40.22
chief butler did not remember J.,	40.23
Then Pharaoh sent and called J.,	41.14
And Pharaoh said to J., "I have had	41.15
J. answered Pharaoh, "It is not in	41.16
Then Pharaoh said to J., "Behold, in	41.17
Then J. said to Pharaoh, "The dream	41.25
So Pharaoh said to J., "Since God	41.39
And Pharaoh said to J., "Behold, I	41.41
Moreover Pharaoh said to J.,	41.44
So J. went out over the land of	41.45
J. was thirty years old when he	41.46
And J. went out from the presence	41.46
And J. stored up grain in great	41.49
J. had two sons, whom Asenath, the	41.50
J. called the name of the first-born	41.51
began to come, as J. had said.	41.54
to all the Egyptians, "Go to J.;	41.55
J. opened all the storehouses, and	41.56
came to Egypt to J. to buy grain,	41.57
Now J. was governor over the land;	42.06
J. saw his brothers, and knew them,	42.07
Thus J. knew his brothers, but they	42.08
And J. remembered the dreams which	42.09
But J. said to them, "It is as I	42.14
On the third day J. said to them,	42.18
not know that J. understood them,	42.23
And J. gave orders to fill their	42.25
J. is no more, and Simeon is no more,	42.36
down to Egypt, and stood before J.	43.15
When J. saw Benjamin with them, he	43.16
The man did as J. bade him, and	43.17
When J. came home, they brought into	43.26
Then J. made haste, for his heart	43.30
And he did as J. told him.	44.02
J. said to his steward, "Up, follow	44.04
J. said to them, "What deed is this	44.15
Then J. could not control himself	45.01
with him when J. made himself	45.01
And J. said to his brothers, "I am J.;	45.03
So J. said to his brothers, "Come	45.04
J., whom you sold into Egypt.	45.04
say to him, 'Thus says your son J.,	45.09
And Pharaoh said to J., "Say to your	45.17
and J. gave them wagons, according	45.21
"J. is still alive, and he is ruler	45.26
they told him all the words of J.,	45.27
wagons which J. had sent to carry	45.27
J. my son is still alive; I will go	45.28
Jacob's wife: J. and Benjamin.	46.19
And to J. in the land of Egypt were	46.20
and the sons of J., who were born to	46.27
He sent Judah before him to J.,	46.28
Then J. made ready his chariot and	46.29
Israel said to J., "Now let me die,	46.30
J. said to his brothers and to his	46.31
So J. went in and told Pharaoh, "My	47.01
Then Pharaoh said to J., "Your father	47.05
Then J. brought in Jacob his father,	47.07
Then J. settled his father and his	47.11

And J. provided his father, his	47.12
And J. gathered up all the money	47.14
and J. brought the money into	47.14
all the Egyptians came to J.,	47.15
And J. answered, "Give your cattle,	47.16
So they brought their cattle to J.;	47.17
and J. gave them food in exchange	47.17
So J. bought all the land of Egypt	47.20
Then J. said to the people, "Behold,	47.23
So J. made it a statute concerning	47.26
called his son J. and said to him,	47.29
After this J. was told, "Behold, your	48.01
"Your son J. has come to you"; then	48.02
And Jacob said to J., "God Almighty	48.03
J. said to his father, "They are my	48.09
So J. brought them near him;	48.10
And Israel said to J., "I had not	48.11
Then J. removed them from his knees,	48.12
And J. took them both, Ephraim in	48.13
And he blessed J., and said, "The	48.15
When J. saw that his father laid	48.17
And J. said to his father, "Not so,	48.18
Then Israel said to J., "Behold, I am	48.21
J. is a frutiful bough, a fruitful	49.22
may they be on the head of J.,	49.26
Then J. fell on his father's face,	50.01
And J. commanded his servants the	50.02
J. spoke to the household of	50.04
So J. went up to bury his father;	50.07
as well as all the household of J.,	50.08
J. returned to Egypt with his	50.14
"It may be that J. will hate us and	50.15
So they sent a message to J.,	50.16
'Say to J., Forgive, I pray you, the	50.17
J. wept when they spoke to him.	50.17
But J. said to them, "Fear not, for	50.19
So J. dwelt in Egypt, he and his	50.22
and J. lived a hundred and ten	50.22
And J. saw Ephraim's children of the	50.23
And J. said to his brothers, "I am	50.24
Then J. took an oath of the sons of	50.25
So J. died, being a hundred and ten	50.26
persons; J. was already in Egypt.	Ex 1.05
Then J. died, and all his brothers,	1.06
over Egypt, who did not know J.	1.08
took the bones of J. with him;	13.19
for J. had solemnly sworn the	13.19
from the sons of J., from Ephraim,	Num 1.10
Of the people of J., namely, of the	1.32
of Issachar, Igal the son of J.;	13.07
from the tribe of J. (that is from	13.11
The sons of J. according to their	26.28
are the sons of J. according to	26.37
families of Manasseh the son of J.	27.01
half-tribe of Manasseh the son of J.,	32.33
Of the sons of J.: of the tribe of	34.23
fathers' houses of the sons of J.,	36.01
tribe of the sons of J. is right.	36.05
the sons of Manasseh the son of J.,	36.12
Judah, Issachar, J., and Benjamin.	Deu 27.12
And of J. he said, "Blessed by the	33.13
Let these come upon the head of J.,	33.16
For the people of J. were two	Jos 14.04
descendants of J. went from the	16.01
The people of J., Manasseh and	16.04
for he was the first-born of J.	17.01
descendants of Manasseh the son of J.,	17.02
And the tribe of J. spoke to Joshua,	17.14
The tribe of J. said, "The hill	17.16
Then Joshua said to the house of J.,	17.17
the house of J. in their territory	18.05
tribe of Judah and the tribe of J.	18.11
The bones of J. which the people of	24.32
inheritance of the descendants of J.	24.32
The house of J. also went up	Ju 1.22
And the house of J. sent to spy out	1.23
of the house of J. rested heavily	1.35

JOSEPH (cont.)
the house of J. to come down to 2Sa 19.20
forced labor of the house of J. 1Ki 11.28
Dan, J., Benjamin, Naphtali, Gad, and 1Ch 2.02
to the sons of J. the son of 5.01
the birthright belonged to J.), 5.02
the sons of J. the son of Israel. 7.29
J., Nethaniah, and Asharelah, sons of 25.02
The first lot fell for Asaph to J.; 25.09
Shallum, Amariah, and J. Ez 10.42
of Malluchi, Jonathan; of Shebaniah, J.; Neh 12.14
people, the sons of Jacob and J. Ps 77.15
He rejected the tent of J., he did 78.67
thou who leadest J. like a flock! 80.01
He made it a decree in J., when he 81.05
of them, J., who was sold as a slave. 105.17
'For J. (the stick of Ephraim) and Eze 37.16
the stick of J. (which is in the 37.19
J. shall have two portions. 47.13
the gate of J., the gate of Benjamin, 48.32
out like fire in the house of J., Amo 5.06
be gracious to the remnant of J. 5.15
not grieved over the ruin of J.! 6.06
fire, and the house of J. a flame, Ob 1.18
and I will save the house of J. Zec 10.06
the father of J. the husband of Mt 1.16
Mary had been betrothed to J., 1.18
and her husband J., being a just 1.19
"J., son of David, do not fear to 1.20
When J. woke from sleep, he did as 1.24
appeared to J. in a dream and said, 2.13
appeared in a dream to J. in Egypt, 2.19
James and J. and Simon and Judas? 13.55
Mary the mother of James and J., 27.56
named J., who also was a disciple 27.57
And J. took the body, and wrapped it 27.59
J. of Arimathea, a respected member Mk 15.43
dead, he granted the body to J. 15.45
betrothed to a man whose name was J., Lk 1.27
And J. also went up from Galilee, 2.04
with haste, and found Mary and J., 2.16
the son (as was supposed of J., 3.23
the son of Jannai, the son of J., 3.24
the son of J., the son of Jonam, the 3.30
was a man named J. from the Jewish 23.50
Jesus of Nazareth, the son of J." Jn 1.45
that Jacob gave to his son J. 4.05
the son of J., whose father and 6.42
After this J. of Arimathea, who was 19.38
J. called Barsabbas, who was surnamed Ac 1.23
Thus J. who was surnamed by the 4.36
jealous of J., sold him into Egypt; 7.09
second visit J. made himself known 7.13
And J. sent and called to him Jacob 7.14
another king who had not known J. 7.18
blessed each of the sons of J., Heb 11.21
By faith J., at the end of his life, 11.22
twelve thousand of the tribe of J., Rev 7.08

JOSEPH'S
Then they took J. robe, and killed a Gen 37.31
the Egyptian's house for J. sake; 39.05
left all that he had in J. charge; 39.06
And J. master took him and put him 39.20
prison committed to J. care all the 39.22
to anything that was in J. care, 39.23
his hand and put it on J. hand, 41.42
Pharaoh called J. name Zaphenathpaneah; 41.45
So ten of J. brothers went down to 42.03
J. brother, with his brothers, for he 42.04
And J. brothers came, and bowed 42.06
and brought the men to J. house. 43.17
they were brought to J. house, 43.18
went up to the steward of J. house, 43.19
had brought the men into J. house, 43.24
the present for J. coming at noon, 43.25
Portions were taken to them from J. table, 43.34
and his brothers came to J. house, 44.14
"J. brothers have come," it pleased 45.16
and J. hand shall close your eyes." 46.04
When Israel saw J. sons, he said, "Who 48.08
When J. brothers saw that their 50.15
Manasseh were born upon J. knees. 50.23
and they said, "Is not this J. son?" Lk 4.22
and J. family became known to Pharaoh. Ac 7.13

JOSES
of James and J. and Judas and Mk 6.03
the younger and of J., and Salome, 15.40
the mother of J. saw where he was 15.47

JOSHAH
Jamlech, J. the son of Amaziah, 1Ch 4.34

JOSHAPHAT
of Maacah, and J. the Mithnite, 1Ch 11.43
Shebaniah, J., Nethanel, Amasai, 15.24

JOSHAVIAH
and J., the sons of Elnaam, and 1Ch 11.46

JOSHBEKASHAH
J., Mallothi, Hothir, Mahazioth. 1Ch 25.04
to J., his sons and his brethren, 25.24

JOSHEBBASSHEBETH
whom David had: J. a Tahchemonite; 2Sa 23.08

JOSHIBIAH
Joel, Jehu the son of J., son of 1Ch 4.35

JOSHUA
And Moses said to J., "Choose for us Ex 17.09
So J. did as Moses told him, and 17.10
And J. mowed down Amalek and his 17.13
and recite it in the ears of J., 17.14
So Moses rose with his servant J., 24.13
When J. heard the noise of the 32.17
his servant J. the son of Nun, a 33.11
And J. the son of Nun, the minister Num 11.28
called Hoshea the son of Nun J. 13.16
And J. the son of Nun and Caleb the 14.06
of Jephunneh and J. the son of Nun. 26.65
But J. the son of Nun and Caleb the 14.38
of Jephunneh and J. the son of Nun. 26.65
"Take J. the son of Nun, a man in 27.18
he took J. and caused him to stand 27.22
Kenizzite and J. the son of Nun, 32.12
and to J. the son of Nun, and to the 32.28
the priest and J. the son of Nun. 34.17
J. the son of Nun, who stands before Deu 1.38
And I commanded J. at that time, 3.21
But charge J., and encourage and 3.28
and J. will go over at your head, as 31.03
Then Moses summoned J., and said to 31.07
call J., and present yourselves in 31.14
And Moses and J. went and presented 31.14
commissioned J. the son of Nun and 31.23
people, he and J. the son of Nun. 32.44
And J. the son of Nun was full of 34.09
the LORD said to J. the son of Nun, Jos 1.01
Then J. commanded the officers of 1.10
half-tribe of Manasseh J. said, 1.12
And they answered J., "All that you 1.16
And J. the son of Nun sent two men 2.01
over and came to J. the son of Nun; 2.23
And they said to J., "Truly the LORD 2.24
Early in the morning J. rose and 3.01
And J. said to the people, "Sanctify 3.05
And J. said to the priests, "Take up 3.06
And the LORD said to J., "This day I 3.07
And J. said to the people of Israel, 3.09
And J. said, "Hereby you shall know 3.10
the Jordan, the LORD said to J., 4.01
Then J. called the twelve men from 4.04

JOSHUA (cont.)

and J. said to them, "Pass on before Jos 4.05
men of Israel did as J. commanded, 4.08
of Israel, as the LORD told J.; 4.08
And J. set up twelve stones in the 4.09
LORD commanded J. to tell the 4.10
to all that Moses had commanded J. 4.10
LORD exalted J. in the sight of 4.14
And the LORD said to J., 4.15
J. therefore commanded the priests, 4.17
out of the Jordan, J. set up in Gilgal. 4.20
At that time the LORD said to J., 5.02
So J. made flint knives, and circumcised 5.03
the reason why J. circumcised them: 5.04
their stead, that J. circumcised; 5.07
And the LORD said to J., "This day I 5.09
When J. was by Jericho, he lifted up 5.13
and J. went to him and said to him, 5.13
And J. fell on his face to the 5.14
of the LORD's army said to J., 5.15
stand is holy." And J. did so. 5.15
And the LORD said to J., "See, I have 6.02
So J. the son of Nun called the 6.06
And as J. had commanded the people, 6.08
But J. commanded the people, "You 6.10
Then J. rose early in the morning, 6.12
J. said to the people, "Shout; 6.16
And J. said to the two men who had 6.22
belonged to her, J. saved alive; 6.25
messengers whom J. sent to spy out 6.25
J. laid an oath upon them at that 6.26
So the LORD was with J.; and his fame 6.27
J. sent men from Jericho to Ai, 7.02
And they returned to J., 7.03
Then J. rent his clothes, and fell 7.06
And J. said, "Alas, O Lord GOD, why 7.07
The LORD said to J., "Arise, why 7.10
So J. rose early in the morning, and 7.16
Then J. said to Achan, "My son, give 7.19
And Achan answered J., "Of a truth 7.20
So J. sent messengers, and they ran 7.22
brought them to J. and all the 7.23
And J. and all Israel with him took 7.24
And J. said, "Why did you bring 7.25
And the LORD said to J., "Do not fear 8.01
So J. arose, and all the fighting 8.03
and J. chose thirty thousand mighty 8.03
So J. sent them forth; and they went 8.09
but J. spent that night among the 8.09
And J. arose early in the morning 8.10
But J. spent that night in the 8.13
And J. and all Israel made a 8.15
as they pursued J. they were drawn 8.16
Then the LORD said to J., "Stretch out the 8.18
And J. stretched out the javelin 8.18
And when J. and all Israel saw that 8.21
took alive, and brought him to J. 8.23
For J. did not draw back his hand, 8.26
of the LORD which he commanded J. 8.27
So J. burned Ai, and made it for 8.28
going down of the sun J. commanded, 8.29
Then J. built an altar in Mount 8.30
commanded which J. did not read 8.35
one accord to fight J. and Israel. 9.02
heard what J. had done to Jericho 9.03
And they went to J. in the camp at 9.06
They said to J., "We are your servants." 9.08
And J. said to them, "Who are you? 9.08
And J. made peace with them, and 9.15
J. summoned them, and he said to 9.22
They answered J., "Because it was 9.24
But J. made them that day hewers of 9.27
Jerusalem heard how J. had taken Ai, 10.01
made peace with J. and with the 10.04
Gibeon sent to J. at the camp in 10.06
So J. went up from Gilgal, he and 10.07
And the LORD said to J., "Do not fear 10.08
So J. came upon them suddenly, 10.09
Then spoke J. to the LORD in the 10.12
Then J. returned, and all Israel 10.15
And it was told J., "The five kings 10.17
And J. said, "Roll great stones 10.18
When J. and the men of Israel had 10.20
returned safe to J. in the camp at 10.21
Then J. said, "Open the mouth of the 10.22
they brought those kings out to J., 10.24
J. summoned all the men of Israel, 10.24
And J. said to them, "Do not be 10.25
And afterward J. smote them and put 10.26
J. commanded, and they took them 10.27
And J. took Makkedah on that day, 10.28
Then J. passed on from Makkedah, and 10.29
And J. passed on from Libnah, and 10.31
and J. smote him and his people, 10.33
And J. passed on with all Israel 10.34
Then J. went up with all Israel 10.36
Then J., with all Israel, turned 10.38
So J. defeated the whole land, the 10.40
And J. defeated them from Kadeshbarnea 10.41
And J. took all these kings and 10.42
Then J. returned, and all Israel 10.43
And the LORD said to J., "Do not be 11.06
So J. came suddenly upon them with 11.07
And J. did to them as the LORD bade 11.09
And J. turned back at that time, and 11.10
J. took, and smote them with the 11.12
except Hazor only; that J. burned. 11.13
so Moses commanded J., and so J. did; 11.15
So J. took all that land, the hill 11.16
J. made war a long time with all 11.18
And J. came at that time, and wiped 11.21
J. utterly destroyed them with 11.21
So J. took the whole land, according 11.23
and J. gave it for an inheritance 11.23
the land whom J. and the people of 12.07
toward Seir (and J. gave their land 12.07
Now J. was old and advanced in 13.01
and J. the son of Nun, and the heads 14.01
of Judah came to J. at Gilgal; 14.06
Then J. blessed him; and he gave 14.13
the commandment of the LORD to J., 15.13
the priest and J. the son of Nun 17.04
And the tribe of Joseph spoke to J., 17.14
And J. said to them, "If you are a 17.15
Then J. said to the house of Joseph, 17.17
So J. said to the people of Israel, 18.03
and J. charged those who went to 18.08
they came to J. in the camp at 18.09
and J. cast lots for them in Shiloh 18.10
and there J. apportioned the land 18.10
among them to J. the son of Nun. 19.49
the priest and J. the son of Nun 19.51
Then the LORD said to J., 20.01
priest and to J. the son of Nun 21.01
Then J. summoned the Reubenites, and 22.01
So J. blessed them, and sent them 22.06
the other half J. had given a 22.07
And when J. sent them away to their 22.07
and J. was old and well advanced in 23.01
J. summoned all Israel, their elders 23.02
Then J. gathered all the tribes of 24.01
And J. said to all the people, "Thus 24.02
But J. said to the people, "You 24.19
And the people said to J., "Nay; 24.21
Then J. said to the people, "You are 24.22
And the people said to J., "The LORD our 24.24
So J. made a covenant with the 24.25
And J. wrote these words in the 24.26
And J. said to all of the people, 24.27
So J. sent the people away, every 24.28
After these things J. the son of Nun, 24.29
served the LORD all the days of J., 24.31
who outlived J. and had known all 24.31
After the death of J. the people of Ju 1.01

JOSHUA (cont.)

When J. dismissed the people, the Ju 2.06
served the LORD all the days of J., 2.07
days of the elders who outlived J., 2.07
And J. the son of Nun, the servant 2.08
nations that J. left when he died, 2.21
not give them into the power of J. 2.23
the field of J. of Bethshemesh, 1Sa 6.14
in the field of J. of Bethshemesh. 6.18
he spoke by J. the son of Nun. 1Ki 16.34
of the gate of J. the governor of 2Ki 23.08
Nun his son, J. his son. 1Ch 7.27
and to J. the son of Jehozadak, the Hag 1.01
and J. the son of Jehozadak, the 1.12
of Judah, and the spirit of J. the son 1.14
and to J. the son of Jehozadak, the 2.02
O J., son of Jehozadak, the high 2.04
Then he showed me J. the high Zec 3.01
Now J. was standing before the 3.03
the angel of the LORD enjoined J., 3.06
Hear now, O J. the high priest, you 3.08
stone which I have set before J., 3.09
and set it upon the head of J., 6.11
it in with J. when they dispossessed Ac 7.45
For if J. had given them rest, God Heb 4.08

JOSIAH

to the house of David, J. by name; 1Ki 13.02
the land made J. his son king in 2Ki 21.24
and J. his son reigned in his 21.26
J. was eight years old when he 22.01
In the eighteenth year of King J., 22.03
And as J. turned, he saw the tombs 23.16
the LORD to anger, J. removed; 23.19
year of King J. this passover was 23.23
Moreover J. put away the mediums 23.24
Now the rest of the acts of J., 23.28
King J. went to meet him; and Pharaoh 23.29
land took Jehoahaz the son of J., 23.30
made Eliakim the son of J. king 23.34
king in the place of J. his father, 23.34
Amon his son, J. his son. 1Ch 3.14
The sons of J.: Johanan the first-born, 3.15
the land made J. his son king in 2Ch 33.25
J. was eight years old when he 34.01
And J. took away all the abominations 34.33
J. kept a passover to the LORD in 35.01
Then J. contributed to the lay 35.07
according to the command of King J. 35.16
such a passover as was kept by J., 35.18
of the reign of J. this passover 35.19
when J. had prepared the temple, 35.20
Euphrates and J. went out against 35.20
Nevertheless J. would not turn away 35.22
And the archers shot King J.; 35.23
Judah and Jerusalem mourned for J. 35.24
Jeremiah also uttered a lament for J.; 35.25
have spoken of J. in their laments 35.25
Now the rest of the acts of J., 35.26
the son of J. and made him king in 36.01
in the days of J. the son of Amon, Jer 1.02
days of Jehoiakim the son of J., 1.03
the son of J., king of Judah, until 1.03
said to me in the days of King J.: 3.06
concerning Shallum the son of J., 22.11
reigned instead of J. his father, 22.11
concerning Jehoiakim the son of J., 22.18
year of Jehoiakim the son of J., 25.01
thirteenth year of J. the son of 25.03
reign of Jehoiakim the son of J., 26.01
reign of Zedekiah the son of J., 27.01
days of Jehoiakim the son of J., 35.01
year of Jehoiakim the son of J., 36.01
from the days of J. until today. 36.02
year of Jehoiakim the son of J., 36.09
Zedekiah the son of J., whom 37.01
year of Jehoiakim the son of J., 45.01
year of Jehoiakim the son of J., 46.02
in the days of J. the son of Amon, Zep 1.01
go the same day to the house of J., Zec 6.10
Jedaiah, and J. the son of Zephaniah. 6.14
Amos, and Amos the father of J., Mt 1.10
and J. the father of Jechoniah and 1.11

JOSIPHIAH

of Bani, Shelomith the son of J., Ez 8.10

JOSTLE

They do not j. one another, each Joe 2.08

JOTBAH

the daughter of Haruz of J. 2Ki 21.19

JOTBATHAH

Horhaggidgad, and encamped at J. Num 33.33
And they set out from J., and encamped 33.34
Gudgodah, and from Gudgodah to J., Deu 10.07

JOTHAM

but J. the youngest son of Jerubbaal Ju 9.05
When it was told to J., he went and 9.07
And J. ran away and fled, and went 9.21
the curse of J. the son of Jerubbaal. 9.57
And J. the king's son was over the 2Ki 15.05
and J. his son reigned in his stead. 15.07
twentieth year of J. the son of 15.30
J. the son of Uzziah, king of Judah, 15.32
Now the rest of the acts of J., 15.36
J. slept with his fathers, and was 15.38
of Remaliah, Ahaz the son of J., 16.01
J., Geshan, Pelet, Ephah, and Shaaph. 1Ch 2.47
son, Azariah his son, J. his son, 3.12
in the days of J. king of Judah, 5.17
And J. his son was over the king's 2Ch 26.21
And J. his son reigned in his 26.23
J. was twenty-five years old when 27.01
So J. became mighty, because he 27.06
Now the rest of the acts of J., 27.07
And J. slept with his fathers, and 27.09
J., Ahaz, and Hezekiah, kings of Is 1.01
In the days of Ahaz the son of J., 7.01
J., Ahaz, and Hezekiah, kings of Hos 1.01
of Moresheth in the days of J., Mic 1.01
and Uzziah the father of J., Mt 1.09
and J. the father of Ahaz, and Ahaz 1.09

JOURNEY

LORD had prospered his j. or not. Gen 24.21
Then Jacob went on his j., 29.01
of three days' j. between himself 30.36
"Let us j. on our way, and I will go 33.12
to give them provisions for the j. 42.25
him on the j. that you are to make, 42.38
gave them provisions for the j. 45.21
provision for his father on the j. 45.23
So Israel took his j. with all that 46.01
a three days' j. into the wilderness, Ex 3.18
a three days' j. into the wilderness, 5.03
go three days' j. into the wilderness 8.27
dead body, or is afar off on a j., Num 9.10
who is clean and is not on j., 9.13
mount of the LORD three days' j.; 10.33
went before them three days' j., 10.33
about a day's j. on this side and a 11.31
and a day's j. on the other side, 11.31
a three days' j. in the wilderness 33.08
It is eleven days' j. from Horeb by Deu 1.02
turn and take your j., and go to the 1.07
and j. into the wilderness in the 1.40
take your j., and go over the 2.24
go on your j. at the head of the 10.11
a j. which I promised that you 28.68
provisions in your hand for the j., Jos 9.11
our houses as our food for the j., 9.12
are worn out from the very long j." 9.13

JOURNEY (cont.)
whether the j. on which we are Ju 18.05
The j. on which you go is under the 18.06
morning for your j., and go home." 19.09
us about the j. on which we have 1Sa 9.06
holy, even when it is common j.; 21.05
Uriah, "Have you not come from a j.? 2Sa 11.10
or he is on a j., or perhaps he is 1Ki 18.27
went a days' j. into the wilderness, 19.04
else the j. will be too great for 19.07
not at home; he has gone on a long j.; Pro 7.19
city, three days' j. in breadth. Jon 3.03
go into the city, going a day's j. 3.04
no bag for your j., nor two tunics, Mt 10.10
man going on a j. called his 25.14
for their j. except a staff; Mk 6.08
And as he was setting out on his j., 10.17
It is like a man going on a j., 13.34
the company they went a day's j., Lk 2.44
to them, "Take nothing for your j., 9.03
friend of mine has arrived on a j., 11.06
and took his j. into a far country, 15.13
wearied as he was with his j., Jn 4.06
Jerusalem, a sabbath day's j. away; Ac 1.12
were on their j. and coming near 10.09
we departed and went on our j.; 21.05
"As I made my j. and drew near to 22.06
to be sped on my j. there by you, Rom 15.24
speed me on my j., wherever I go. 1Co 16.06
them on their j. as befits God's 3Jn 1.06

JOURNEYED
And Abram j. on, still going toward Gen 12.09
And he j. on from the Negeb as far 13.03
the Jordan valley, and Lot j. east; 13.11
From there Abraham j. toward the 20.01
But Jacob j. to Succoth, and built 33.17
And as they j., a terror from God 35.05
Then they j. from Bethel; and when they 35.16
Israel j. on, and pitched his tent 35.21
of Israel j. from Rameses to Ex 12.37
Kibrothhattaavah the people j. to Hazeroth; Num 11.35
And they j. from Kadesh, and the 20.22
and j. into the wilderness in the Deu 2.01
of Israel j. from Beeroth Benejaakan 10.06
From there they j. to Gudgodah, 10.07
Then they j. through the wilderness, Ju 11.18
and as he j., he came to the hill 17.08
The j. to the entrance of Gedor, to 1Ch 4.39
You j. to Molech with oil and Is 57.09
as he j., came to where he was; Lk 10.33
Now as he j. he approached Damascus, Ac 9.03
and I j. to Damascus to take those 22.05
"Thus I j. to Damascus with the 26.12
round me and those who j. with me. 26.13

JOURNEYING
teaching, and j. toward Jerusalem. Lk 13.22

JOURNEYS
Throughout all their j., whenever Ex 40.36
all their j. the cloud of the LORD 40.38
on frequent j., in danger from 2Co 11.26

JOY
him, he came with j. to meet him. Ju 19.03
with songs of j., and with instruments 1Sa 18.06
pipes, and rejoicing with great j., 1Ki 1.40
sheep, for there was j. in Israel. 1Ch 12.40
and cymbals, to raise sounds of j. 15.16
strength and j. are in his place. 16.27
wood sing for j. before the LORD, 16.33
returning to Jerusalem with j., 2Ch 20.27
So there was great j. in Jerusalem, 30.26
though many shouted aloud for j.; Ez 3.12
of this house of God with j. 6.16
unleavened bread seven days with j.; 6.22
for the j. of the LORD is your Neh 8.10
made them rejoice with great j.; 12.43
And the j. of Jerusalem was heard 12.43
and gladness and j. and honor. Est 8.16
was gladness and j. among the Jews, 8.17
Behold, this is the j. of his way; Job 8.19
and the j. of the godless but for a 20.05
the widow's heart to sing for j. 29.13
he comes into his presence with j. 33.26
all the sons of God shouted for j.? 38.07
Thou hast put more j. in my heart Ps 4.07
rejoice, let them ever sing for j.; 5.11
presence there is fullness of j., 16.11
strong man runs its course with j. 19.05
May we shout for j. over your victory, 20.05
glad with the j. of thy presence. 21.06
tent sacrifices with shouts of j.; 27.06
but j. comes with the morning. 30.05
and shout for j., all you upright 32.11
vindication shout for j. and be glad, 35.27
of God, to God my exceeding j.; 43.04
With j. and gladness they are led 45.15
Shout to God with loud songs of j.! 47.01
is the j. of all the earth, Mount 48.02
Fill me with j. and gladness; 51.08
Restore to me the j. of thy salvation, 51.12
shadow of thy wings I sing for j. 63.07
and the evening to shout for j. 65.08
the hills gird themselves with j., 65.12
shout and sing together for j. 65.13
nations be glad and sing for j., 67.04
let them be jubilant with j.! 68.03
My lips will shout for j., 71.23
shout for j. to the God of Jacob! 81.01
flesh sing for j. to the living 84.02
works of thy hands I sing for j. 92.04
the trees of the wood sing for j. 96.12
and j. for the upright in the heart. 97.11
let the hills sing for j. together 98.08
So he led forth his people with j., 105.43
tell of his deeds in songs of j.! 107.22
yea, they are the j. of my heart. 119.111
and our tongue with shouts of j.; 126.02
in tears reap with shouts of j.! 126.05
shall come home with shouts of j., 126.06
and let thy saints shout for j. 132.09
and her saints will shout for j. 132.16
set Jerusalem above my highest j.! 137.06
them sing for j. on their couches. 149.05
but those who plan good have j. Pro 12.20
and no stranger shares its j. 14.10
is sad, and the end of j. is grief. 14.13
Folly is a j. to him who has no 15.21
an apt answer is a j. to a man, 15.23
and the father of a fool has no j. 17.21
it is a j. to the righteous, but 21.15
gives wisdom and knowledge and j.; Ecc 2.26
him occupied with j. in his heart. 5.20
nation, thou hast increased its j.; Is 9.03
thee as with j. at the harvest, 9.03
With j. you will draw water from 12.03
and sing for j., O inhabitant of 12.06
And j. and gladness are taken away 16.10
and behold, j. and gladness, slaying 22.13
all j. has reached its eventide; 24.11
up their voices, they sing for j.; 24.14
in the dust, awake and sing for j.! 26.19
shall obtain fresh j. in the LORD, 29.19
a j. of wild asses, a pasture of 32.14
and rejoice with j. and singing. 35.02
the tongue of the dumb sing for j. 35.06
everlasting j. upon their heads; 35.10
they shall obtain j. and gladness, 35.10
inhabitants of Sela sing for j., 42.11
declare this with a shout of j., 48.20
Sing for j., O heavens, and exult, O 49.13
j. and gladness will be found in 51.03

JOY (cont.)

everlasting j. shall be upon their — Is 51.11
they shall obtain j. and gladness, — 51.11
voice, together they sing for j.; — 52.08
"For you shall go out in j., and be — 55.12
for ever. a j. from age to age. — 60.15
yours shall be everlasting j. — 61.07
a rejoicing, and her people a j. — 65.18
glorified, that we may see your j.'; — 66.05
rejoice with her in j., all you who — 66.10
became to me a j. and the delight — Jer 15.16
I will turn their mourning into j., — 31.13
city shall be to me a name of j., — 33.09
Gladness and j. have been taken — 48.33
one treads them with shouts of j.; — 48.33
shouting is not the shout of j. — 48.33
shall sing for j. over Babylon; — 51.48
of beauty, the j. of all the earth?" — Lam 2.15
The j. of our hearts has ceased; — 5.15
their j. and glory, the delight of — Eze 24.25
wholehearted j. and utter contempt, — 36.05
j. and gladness from the house of — Joe 1.16
I will j. in the God of my salvation. — Hab 3.18
Judah seasons of j. and gladness, — Zec 8.19
rejoiced exceedingly with great j.; — Mt 2.10
immediately receives it with j.; — 13.20
then in his j. he goes and sells — 13.44
enter into the j. of your master.' — 25.21
enter into the j. of your master.' — 25.23
the tomb with fear and great j., — 28.08
immediately receive it with j.; — Mk 4.16
And you will have j. and gladness, — Lk 1.14
the babe in my womb leaped for j. — 1.44
news of a great j. which will come — 2.10
and leap for j., for behold, your — 6.23
hear the word, receive it with j.; — 8.13
The seventy returned with j., — 10.17
will be more j. in heaven over one — 15.07
there is j. before the angels of — 15.10
they still disbelieved for j., — 24.41
to Jerusalem with great j., — 24.52
therefore this j. of mine is now — Jn 3.29
that my j. may be in you, and that — 15.11
you, and that your j. may be full. — 15.11
but your sorrow will turn into j. — 16.20
for j. that a child is born into — 16.21
no one will take your j. from you. — 16.22
receive, that your j. may be full. — 16.24
may have my j. fulfilled in — 17.13
So there was much j. in that city. — Ac 8.08
in her j. she did not open the gate — 12.14
filled with j. and with the Holy — 13.52
they gave great j. to all the — 15.03
and peace and j. in the Holy — Rom 14.17
you with all j. and peace in — 15.13
to you with j. and be refreshed in — 15.32
we work with you for your j., — 2Co 1.24
that my j. would be the j. of you all. — 2.03
still more at the j. of Titus, — 7.13
abundance of j. and their extreme — 8.02
j., peace, patience, kindness, goodness, — Gal 5.22
you all making my prayer with j., — Php 1.04
your progress and j. in the faith, — 1.25
complete my j. by being of the same — 2.02
him in the Lord with all j.; — 2.29
my j. and crown, stand firm thus in — 4.01
endurance and patience with j., — Col 1.11
with j. inspired by the Holy Spirit; — 1Th 1.06
is our hope or j. or crown of — 2.19
For you are our glory and j. — 2.20
for all the j. which we feel for — 3.09
you, that I may be filled with j. — 2Ti 1.04
derived much j. and comfort from — Phm 1.07
who for the j. that was set before — Heb 12.02
Count it all j., my brethren, when — Jas 1.02
mourning and your j. to dejection. — 4.09
with unutterable and exalted j. — 1Pe 1.08
this that our j. may be complete. — 1Jn 1.04
so that our j. may be complete. — 2Jn 1.12
No greater j. can I have than this, — 3Jn 1.04

JOYFUL

so that you will be altogether j. — Deu 16.15
to their homes j. and glad of — 1Ki 8.66
j. and glad of heart for the — 2Ch 7.10
sound of the j. shout from the — Ez 3.13
for the LORD had made them j., — 6.22
out that day j. and glad of heart. — Est 5.09
let no j. cry be heard in it. — Job 3.07
mouth praises thee with j. lips, — Ps 63.05
Make a j. noise to God, all the — 66.01
But let the righteous be j.; — 68.03
let us make a j. noise to the rock — 95.01
let us make a j. noise to him with — 95.02
Make a j. noise to the LORD, all the — 98.04
the horn make a j. noise before — 98.06
Make a j. noise to the LORD, all the — 100.01
In the day of prosperity be j., — Ecc 7.14
the joyous houses in the j. city. — Is 32.13
and make them j. in my house of — 56.07
city is forsaken, the j. city! — Jer 49.25
and not of j. shouting upon the — Eze 7.07

JOYFULLY

him that j. works righteousness, — Is 64.05
and came down, and received him j. — Lk 19.06
and you j. accepted the plundering — Heb 10.34
Let them do this j., and not sadly, — 13.17

JOYFULNESS

your God with j. and gladness of — Deu 28.47

JOYOUS

forth into j. song and sing — Ps 98.04
making her the j. mother of — 113.09
for all the j. houses in the joyful — Is 32.13

JOYOUSLY

offering freely and j. to thee. — 1Ch 29.17
and Hermon j. praise thy name. — Ps 89.12

JOZABAD

Jahaziel, Johanan, J. of Gederah, — 1Ch 12.04
J., Jediael, Michael, J., Elihu, — 12.20
J., Eliel, Ismachiah, Mahath, and — 2Ch 31.13
and Hashabiah and Jeiel and J., — 35.09
J. the son of Jeshua and Noadiah — Ez 8.33
Ishmael, Nethanel, J., and Elasah. — 10.22
J., Shimei, Kelaiah (that is, Kelita), — 10.23
J., Hanan, Pelaiah, the Levites, — Neh 8.07
and Shabbethai and J., of the chief — 11.16

JOZACAR

It was J. the son of Shimeath and — 2Ki 12.21

JOZADAK

Then arose Jeshua the son of J., — Ez 3.02
the son of J. made a beginning, — 3.08
the son of J. arose and began to — 5.02
the son of J. and his brethren, — 10.18
the son of Jeshua son of J., — Neh 12.26

JUBAL

His brother's name was J.; he was the — Gen 4.21

JUBILANT

exult before God; let them be j. with joy! — Ps 68.03
the noise of the j. has ceased, — Is 24.08

JUBILEE

it shall be a j. for you, when each — Lev 25.10
A j. shall that fiftieth year be to — 25.11
For it is a j.; it shall be — 25.12
"In this year of j. each of you — 25.13
the number of years after the j., — 25.15
who bought it until the year of j.; — 25.28

JUBILEE (cont.)

in the j. it shall be released, and Lev 25.28
it shall not be released in the j. 25.30
they shall be released in the j. 25.31
shall be released in the j.; for the houses 25.33
with you until the year of the j.; 25.40
to him until the year of j., and the 25.50
a few years until the year of j., 25.52
be released in the year of j., 25.54
his field from the year of j., 27.17
dedicates his field after the j., 27.18
that remain until the year of j., 27.18
when it is released in the j., 27.21
for it up to the year of j., 27.23
In the year of j. the field shall 27.24
And when the j. of the people of Num 36.04

JUCAL

J. the son of Shelemiah, and Pashhur Jer 38.01

JUDAH

therefore she called his name J.; Gen 29.35
Simeon, Levi, J., Issachar, and Zebulun. 35.23
Then J. said to his brothers, "What 37.26
that time that J. went down from 38.01
There J. saw the daughter of a 38.02
And J. took a wife for Er his 38.06
Then J. said to Onan, "Go in to your 38.08
Then J. said to Tamar his daughter-in-law, 38.11
In course of time the wife of J. 38.12
and when J. was comforted, he went 38.12
When J. saw her, he thought her to 38.15
When J. sent the kid by his friend 38.20
So he returned to J., and said, 38.22
And J. replied, "Let her keep the 38.23
About three months later J. was told, 38.24
And J. said, "Bring her out, and let 38.24
Then J. acknowledged them and said, 38.26
But J. said to him, "The man solemnly 43.03
And J. said to Israel his father, 43.08
When J. and his brothers came to 44.14
And J. said, "What shall we say to 44.16
Then J. went up to him and said, "O 44.18
The sons of J.: Er, Onan, Shelah, Perez, 46.12
He sent J. before him to Joseph, to 46.28
J., your brothers shall praise you; 49.08
J. is a lion's whelp; from the prey, 49.09
The scepter shall not depart from J., 49.10
Reuben, Simeon, Levi, and J., Ex 1.02
son of Hur, of the tribe of J.: 31.02
son of Hur, of the tribe of J.; 35.30
son of Hur, of the tribe of J., 38.22
from J., Nahshon the son of Amminadab; Num 1.07
Of the people of J., their generations, 1.26
of the tribe of J. was seventy-four 1.27
of the camp of J. by their companies, 2.03
the people of J. being Nahshon the 2.03
The whole number of the camp of J., 2.09
of Amminadab, of the tribe of J.; 7.12
of the men of J. set out first by 10.14
from the tribe of J., Caleb the son 13.06
The sons of J. were Er and Onan; 26.19
And the sons of J. according to 26.20
the families of J. according to 26.22
of the men: Of the tribe of J., 34.19
J., Issachar, Joseph, and Benjamin. Deu 27.12
And this he said of J.: "Hear, O LORD, 33.07
the voice of J., and bring him in 33.07
all the land of J. as far as the 34.02
son of Zerah, of the tribe of J., Jos 7.01
and the tribe of J. was taken; 7.16
he brought near the families of J., 7.17
of the tribe of J., was taken. 7.18
from all the hill country of J., 11.21
Then the people of J. came to 14.06
the people of J. according to 15.01
the people of J. according to 15.12
a portion among the people of J., 15.13
the people of J. according to 15.20
the people of J. in the extreme 15.21
the people of J. could not drive 15.63
the people of J. at Jerusalem to 15.63
J. continuing in his territory on 18.05
the tribe of J. and the tribe of 18.11
city belonging to the tribe of J. 18.14
the inheritance of the tribe of J. 19.01
formed part of the territory of J.; 19.09
of the tribe of J. was too large 19.09
and J. on the east at the Jordan. 19.34
Hebron) in the hill country of J. 20.07
by lot from the tribes of J., 21.04
Out of the tribe of J. and the 21.09
Hebron), in the hill country of J., 21.11
The LORD said, "J. shall go up; Ju 1.02
And J. said to Simeon his brother, 1.03
Then J. went up and the LORD gave 1.04
And the men of J. fought against 1.08
the men of J. went down to fight 1.09
And J. went against the Canaanites 1.10
the people of J. from the city of 1.16
of palms into the wilderness of J., 1.16
And J. went with Simeon his brother, 1.17
J. also took Gaza with its territory, 1.18
And the LORD was with J., and he took 1.19
also against J. and against 10.09
Philistines came up and encamped in J., 15.09
And the men of J. said, "Why have 15.10
thousand men of J. went down to 15.11
was a young man of Bethlehem in J., 17.07
in Judah, of the family of J., 17.07
from the town of Bethlehem in J., 17.08
"I am a Levite of Bethlehem in J., 17.09
encamped at Kiriathjearim in J. 18.12
a concubine from Bethlehem in J. 19.01
father's house at Bethlehem in J., 19.02
Bethlehem in J. to the remote 19.18
I went to Bethlehem in J.; and I am 19.18
LORD said, "J. shall go up first." 20.18
of Bethlehem in J. went to sojourn Ru 1.01
Ephrathites from Bethlehem in J. 1.02
way to return to the land of J. 1.07
of Perez, whom Tamar bore to J., 4.12
and the men of J. thirty thousand. 1Sa 11.08
foot, and ten thousand men of J. 15.04
at Soco, which belongs to J., 17.01
an Ephrathite of Bethlehem in J., 17.12
of Israel and J. rose with a shout 17.52
But all Israel and J. loved David; 18.16
depart, and go into the land of J." 22.05
"Behold, we are afraid here in J.; 23.03
out among all the thousands of J." 23.23
to the kings of J. to this day. 27.06
would say, "Against the Negeb of J., 27.10
belongs to J. and upon the Negeb 30.14
Philistines and from the land of J. 30.16
the elders of J., saying, "Here is a 30.26
be taught to the people of J.; 2Sa 1.18
go up into any of the cities of J.?" 2.01
And the men of J. came, and there 2.04
David king over the house of J. 2.04
the house of J. has anointed me 2.07
But the house of J. followed David. 2.10
the house of J. was seven years 2.11
and said, "Am I a dog's head of J.? 3.08
of David over Israel and over J., 3.10
he reigned over J. seven years and 5.05
all Israel and J. thirty-three 5.05
and Israel and J. dwell in booths; 11.11
you the house of Israel and of J.; 12.08
priests, "Say to the elders of J., 19.11
of all the men of J. as one man; 19.14
and J. came to Gilgal to meet the 19.15
with the men of J. to meet King 19.16
all the people of J., and also half 19.40

JUDAH (cont.)
the men of J. stolen you away, and 2Sa 19.41
All the men of J. answered the men 19.42
of Israel answered the men of J., 19.43
of the men of J. were fiercer than 19.43
but the men of J. followed their 20.02
"Call the men of J. together to me 20.04
So Amasa went to summon J.; 20.05
for the people of Israel and J. 21.02
saying, "Go, number Israel and J." 24.01
to the Negeb of J. at Beersheba. 24.07
and the men of J. were five 24.09
and all the royal officials of J., 1Ki 1.09
be ruler over Israel and over J. 1.35
commander of the army of J. 2.32
was one officer in the land of J. 4.19
J. and Israel were as many as the 4.20
And J. and Israel dwelt in safety, 4.25
the wilderness, in the land of J., 9.18
who dwelt in the cities of J. 12.17
of David, but the tribe of J. only. 12.20
he assembled all the house of J., 12.21
king of J., and to all the house of 12.23
all the house of J. and Benjamin, 12.23
their lord, to Rehoboam king of J., 12.27
and return to Rehoboam king of J." 12.27
like the feast that was in J., 12.32
God came out of J. by the word of 13.01
of God who came from J. had gone. 13.12
the man of God who came from J.?" 13.14
to the man of God who came from J., 13.21
the son of Solomon reigned in J. 14.21
And J. did what was evil in the 14.22
the Chronicles of the Kings of J.? 14.29
Abijam began to reign over J. 15.01
the Chronicles of the Kings of J.? 15.07
Israel Asa began to reign over J., 15.09
Baasha king of Israel went up against J., 15.17
out or come in to Asa king of J. 15.17
Asa made a proclamation to all J., 15.22
the Chronicles of the Kings of J.? 15.23
the second year of Asa king of J.; 15.25
the third year of Asa king of J., 15.28
In the third year of Asa king of J., 15.33
twenty-sixth year of Asa king of J., 16.08
twenty-seventh year of Asa king of J., 16.10
of Asa king of J. Zimri reigned 16.15
thirty-first year of Asa king of J., 16.23
thirty-eighth year of Asa king of J., 16.29
to Beersheba, which belongs to J., 19.03
the king of J. came down to the 22.02
the king of J. were sitting on 22.10
the king of J. went up to Ramothgilead. 22.29
to reign over J. in the fourth 22.41
the Chronicles of the Kings of J.? 22.45
year of Jehoshaphat king of J., 22.51
king of J., because Ahaziah had no 2Ki 1.17
year of Jehoshaphat king of J., 3.01
word to Jehoshaphat king of J., 3.07
the king of J. and the king of 3.09
for Jehoshaphat the king of J., 3.14
king of J., began to reign. 8.16
Yet the LORD would not destroy J., 8.19
Edom revolted from the rule of J., 8.20
from the rule of J. to this day. 8.22
the Chronicles of the Kings of J.? 8.23
king of J., began to reign. 8.25
Jehoram king of J. went down to 8.29
Ahaziah king of J. had come down 9.16
and Ahaziah king of J. set out, 9.21
When Ahaziah the king of J. saw this, 9.27
Ahaziah began to reign over J. 9.29
the kinsmen of Ahaziah king of J., 10.13
Jehoash king of J. took all the 12.18
the kings of J., had dedicated, and 12.18
the Chronicles of the Kings of J.? 12.19
king of J., Jehoahaz the son of 13.01
Joash king of J. Jehoash the son 13.10
fought against Amaziah king of J., 13.12
of Joash, king of J., began to reign. 14.01
sent word to Amaziah king of J., 14.09
that you fall, you and J. with you?" 14.10
Amaziah king of J. faced one another 14.11
Bethshemesh, which belongs to J. 14.11
And J. was defeated by Israel, and 14.12
Israel captured Amaziah king of J., 14.13
he fought with Amaziah king of J., 14.15
king of J., lived fifteen years 14.17
the Chronicles of the Kings of J.? 14.18
And all the people of J. took Azariah, 14.21
He built Elath and restored it to J., 14.22
king of J., Jeroboam the son of 14.23
Hamath, which had belonged to J., 14.28
king of J., began to reign. 15.01
the Chronicles of the Kings of J.? 15.06
Azariah king of J. Zechariah the 15.08
thirty-ninth year of Uzziah king of J., 15.13
Azariah king of J. Menahem the son 15.17
Azariah king of J. Pekahiah the 15.23
Azariah king of J. Pekah the son 15.27
of Uzziah, king of J., began to reign. 15.32
the Chronicles of the Kings of J.? 15.36
the son of Remaliah against J. 15.37
of Jotham, king of J., began to reign. 16.01
and drove the men of J. from Elath; 16.06
the Chronicles of the Kings of J.? 16.19
of Ahaz king of J. Hoshea the son 17.01
Israel and J. by every prophet and 17.13
was left but the tribe of J. only. 17.18
J. also did not keep the commandments 17.19
of Ahaz, king of J., began to reign. 18.01
all the kings of J. after him, 18.05
fortified cities of J. and took them. 18.13
Hezekiah king of J. sent to the 18.14
Hezekiah king of J. three hundred 18.14
Hezekiah king of J. had overlaid 18.16
saying to J. and to Jerusalem, "You 18.22
the language of J. within the 18.26
a loud voice in the language of J.: 18.28
you speak to Hezekiah king of J.: 19.10
of the house of J. shall again 19.30
the Chronicles of the Kings of J.? 20.20
Manasseh king of J. has committed 21.11
and has made J. also to sin with 21.11
Jerusalem and J. such evil that 21.12
which he made J. to sin so that 21.16
the Chronicles of the Kings of J.? 21.17
the Chronicles of the Kings of J.? 21.25
and for all J., concerning the 22.13
book which the king of J. has read. 22.16
But as to the king of J., who sent 22.18
the elders of J. and Jerusalem 23.01
all the men of J. and all the 23.02
the kings of J. had ordained to 23.05
the cities of J. and round about 23.05
priests out of the cities of J., 23.08
the kings of J. had dedicated to 23.11
which the kings of J. had made, 23.12
who came from J. and predicted 23.17
of Israel or of the kings of J.; 23.22
in the land of J. and in Jerusalem, 23.24
his anger was kindled against J., 23.26
"I will remove J. also out of my 23.27
the Chronicles of the Kings of J.? 23.28
sent them against J. to destroy it, 24.02
Surely this came upon J. at the 24.03
the Chronicles of the Kings of J.? 24.05
the king of J. gave himself up to 24.12
Jerusalem and J. that he cast them 24.20
So J. was taken into exile out of 25.21
who remained in the land of J., 25.22
the exile of Jehoiachin king of J., 25.27
Jehoiachin king of J. from prison; 25.27
Simeon, Levi, J., Issachar, Zebulun, 1Ch 2.01

JUDAH (cont.)

The sons of J.: Er, Onan, and Shelah; 1Ch 2.03
and Zerah. J. had five sons in all. 2.04
Nahshon, prince of the sons of J. 2.10
The sons of J.: Perez, Hezron, Carmi, 4.01
The sons of Shelah the son of J.; 4.21
family multiply like the men of J. 4.27
king of J., and destroyed their 4.41
though J. became strong among his 5.02
in the days of Jotham king of J., 5.17
the LORD sent J. and Jerusalem 6.15
in the land of J. and its surrounding 6.55
by lot out of the tribes of J., 6.65
And J. was taken into exile in 9.01
And some of the people of J., 9.03
the sons of Perez the son of J. 9.04
of Benjamin and J. came to the 12.16
The men of J. bearing shield and 12.24
Kiriathjearim which belongs to J., 13.06
and in J. four hundred and seventy 21.05
for J., Elihu, one of David's brothers; 27.18
for he chose J. as leader, and in 28.04
in the house of J. my father's 28.04
are with me in J. and Jerusalem, 2Ch 2.07
of them before in the land of J. 9.11
who dwelt in the cities of J. 10.17
he assembled the house of J., 11.01
the son of Solomon king of J., 11.03
to all Israel in J. and Benjamin, 11.03
he built cities for defense in J. 11.05
which are in J. and in Benjamin. 11.10
very strong. So he held J. and Benjamin. 11.12
and came to J. and Jerusalem, because 11.14
They strengthened the kingdom of J., 11.17
the districts of J. and Benjamin, 11.23
cities of J. and came as far as 12.04
Rehoboam and to the princes of J., 12.05
moreover, conditions were good in J. 12.12
Abijah began to reign over J. 13.01
his troops were in front of J., 13.13
And when J. looked, behold, the 13.14
Then the men of J. raised the 13.15
And when the men of J. shouted, 13.15
all Israel before Abijah and J. 13.15
The men of Israel fled before J., 13.16
time, and the men of J. prevailed, 13.18
and commanded J. to seek the LORD, 14.04
the cities of J. the high places 14.05
He built fortified cities in J., 14.06
And he said to J., "Let us build 14.07
of three hundred thousand from J., 14.08
Ethiopians before Asa and before J., 14.12
The men of J. carried away very 14.13
and all J. and Benjamin: The LORD is 15.02
all the land of J. and Benjamin 15.08
And he gathered all J. and Benjamin, 15.09
And all J. rejoiced over the oath; 15.15
king of Israel went up against J., 16.01
out or come in to Asa king of J. 16.01
Then King Asa took all J., and they 16.06
the seer came to Asa king of J., 16.07
Book of the Kings of J. and Israel. 16.11
in all the fortified cities of J., 17.02
set garrisons in the land of J., 17.02
and all J. brought tribute to 17.05
places and the Asherim out of J. 17.06
to teach in the cities of J.; 17.07
And they taught in J., having the 17.09
the cities of J. and taught among 17.09
the lands that were round about J., 17.10
built in J. fortresses and store-cities, 17.12
great stores in the cities of J. 17.13
Of J., the commanders of thousands: 17.14
fortified cities throughout all J. 17.19
said to Jehoshaphat king of J., 18.03
the king of J. were sitting on 18.09
the king of J. went up to Ramothgilead. 18.28
Jehoshaphat the king of J. returned 19.01
fortified cities of J., city by city, 19.05
the governor of the house of J., 19.11
proclaimed a fast throughout all J. 20.03
And J. assembled to seek help from 20.04
the cities of J. they came to seek 20.04
the assembly of J. and Jerusalem, 20.05
Meanwhile all the men of J. stood 20.13
all J. and inhabitants of Jerusalem, 20.15
on your behalf, O J. and Jerusalem. 20.17
and all J. and the inhabitants of 20.18
J. and inhabitants of Jerusalem! 20.20
Seir, who had come against J., 20.22
When J. came to the watchtower of 20.24
every man of J. and Jerusalem, and 20.27
Thus Jehoshaphat reigned over J. 20.31
Jehoshaphat king of J. joined with 20.35
the sons of Jehoshaphat king of J. 21.02
with fortified cities in J.; 21.03
and also some of the princes of J. 21.04
Edom revolted from the rule of J., 21.08
from the rule of J. to this day. 21.10
places in the hill country of J., 21.11
unfaithfulness, and made J. go astray. 21.11
or in the ways of Asa king of J., 21.12
and have led J. and the inhabitants 21.13
and they came up against J., and invaded 21.17
son of Jehoram king of J. reigned. 22.01
Jehoram king of J. went down to 22.06
the princes of J. and the sons of 22.08
royal family of the house of J. 22.10
about through J. and gathered the 23.02
Levites from all the cities of J., 23.02
The Levites and all J. did according 23.08
them, "Go out to the cities of J., 24.05
bring in from J. and Jerusalem the 24.06
made throughout J. and Jerusalem, 24.09
the princes of J. came and did 24.17
wrath came upon J. and Jerusalem 24.18
They came to J. and Jerusalem, and 24.23
Then Amaziah assembled the men of J., 25.05
hundreds for all J. and Benjamin. 25.05
And they became very angry with J., 25.10
The men of J. captured another ten 25.12
battle, fell upon the cities of J., 25.13
Then Amaziah king of J. took counsel 25.17
sent word to Amaziah king of J., 25.18
that you fall, you and J. with you?" 25.19
Amaziah king of J. faced one another 25.21
Bethshemesh, which belongs to J. 25.21
And J. was defeated by Israel, and 25.22
Israel captured Amaziah king of J., 25.23
Joash king of J. lived fifteen 25.25
Book of the Kings of J. and Israel? 25.26
And all the people of J. took Uzziah, 26.01
He built Eloth and restored it to J., 26.02
cities in the hill country of J., 27.04
Book of the Kings of Israel and J. 27.07
twenty thousand in J. in one day, 28.06
of your fathers, was angry with J., 28.09
the people of J. and Jerusalem, 28.10
had again invaded and defeated J., 28.17
the Shephelah and the Negeb of J., 28.18
LORD brought J. low because of Ahaz 28.19
wantonly in J. and had been faithless 28.19
In every city of J. he made high 28.25
Book of the Kings of J. and Israel. 28.26
the LORD came on J. and Jerusalem, 29.08
and for the sanctuary and for J. 29.21
Hezekiah sent to all Israel and J., 30.01
all Israel and J. with letters from the 30.06
was also upon J. to give them one 30.12
Hezekiah king of J. gave the 30.24
The whole assembly of J., and the 30.25
sojourners who dwelt in J., rejoiced. 30.25
the cities of J. and broke in pieces 31.01
throughout all J. and Benjamin, 31.01

JUDAH (cont.)
of Israel and J. who lived in the 2Ch 31.06
the cities of J. also brought in 31.06
Thus Hezekiah did throughout all J.; 31.20
and invaded J. and encamped against the 32.01
the words of Hezekiah king of J. 32.08
Hezekiah king of J. and to all the 32.09
the people of J. that were in 32.09
and commanded J. and Jerusalem, 32.12
the language of J. to the people 32.18
things to Hezekiah king of J., 32.23
came upon him and J. and Jerusalem. 32.25
Book of the Kings of J. and Israel. 32.32
and all J. and the inhabitants of 32.33
Manasseh seduced J. and the inhabitants 33.09
in all the fortified cities in J. 33.14
he commanded J. to serve the LORD 33.16
began to purge J. and Jerusalem of 34.03
their altars, and purged J. and Jerusalem. 34.05
and from all J. and Benjamin and 34.09
the kings of J. had let go to ruin. 34.11
who are left in Israel and in J., 34.21
was read before the king of J. 34.24
But to the king of J., who sent you 34.26
all the elders of J. and Jerusalem. 34.29
all the men of J. and the inhabitants 34.30
and all J. and Israel who were 35.18
to do with each other, king of J.? 35.21
All J. and Jerusalem mourned for 35.24
Book of the Kings of Israel and J. 35.27
brother king over J. and Jerusalem, 36.04
Book of the Kings of Israel and J.; 36.08
Zedekiah king over J. and Jerusalem. 36.10
house at Jerusalem, which is in J. 36.23
house at Jerusalem, which is in J. Ez 1.02
which is in J., and rebuild the 1.03
fathers' houses of J. and Benjamin, 1.05
to Sheshbazzar the prince of J. 1.08
they returned to Jerusalem and J., 2.01
the sons of J., together took the 3.09
adversaries of J. and Benjamin 4.01
land discouraged the people of J., 4.04
inhabitants of J. and Jerusalem. 4.06
Jews who were in J. and Jerusalem, 5.01
that we went to the province of J., 5.08
inquiries about J. and Jerusalem 7.14
made throughout J. and Jerusalem 10.07
Then all the men of J. and Benjamin 10.09
Kelita), Pethahiah, J., and Eliezer. 10.23
came with certain men out of J.; Neh 1.02
your sight, that you send me to J., 2.05
me pass through until I come to J.; 2.07
But J. said, "The strength of the 4.10
stood behind all the house of J., 4.16
their governor in the land of J., 5.14
Jerusalem, 'There is a king in J.' 6.07
the nobles of J. sent many letters 6.17
For many in J. were bound by oath 6.18
they returned to Jerusalem and J., 7.06
in the towns of J. every one lived 11.03
of the sons of J. and of the sons 11.04
Of the sons of J.: Athaiah 11.04
and J. the son of Hassenuah was 11.09
were in all the towns of J., 11.20
of the sons of Zerah the son of J., 11.24
the people of J. lived in Kiriatharba 11.25
the Levites in J. were joined to 11.36
J., and Mattaniah, who with his 12.08
up the princes of J. upon the wall, 12.31
and half of the princes of J., 12.32
J., Benjamin, Shemaiah, and Jeremiah, 12.34
J., and Hanani, with the musical 12.36
for J. rejoiced over the priests 12.44
Then all J. brought the tithe of 13.12
days I saw in J. men treading wine 13.15
on the sabbath to the people of J., 13.16
the nobles of J. and said to them, 13.17
could not speak the language of J., 13.24
away with Jeconiah king of J., Est 2.06
daughters of J. rejoice because of Ps 48.11
my helmet; J. is my scepter. 60.07
the princes of J. in their throng, 68.27
Zion and rebuild the cities of J.; 69.35
In J. God is known, his name is 76.01
but he chose the tribe of J., 78.68
and the daughters of J. rejoice, 97.08
is my helmet; J. my scepter. 108.08
J. becamse his sanctuary, Israel his 114.02
men of Hezekiah king of J. copied. Pro 25.01
saw concerning J. and Jerusalem in Is 1.01
Ahaz, and Hezekiah, kings of J. 1.01
saw concerning J. and Jerusalem. 2.01
Jerusalem and from J. stay and staff, 3.01
has stumbled, and J. has fallen; 3.08
inhabitants of Jerusalem and men of J., 5.03
and the men of J. are his pleasant 5.07
king of J., Rezin the king of Syria 7.01
us go up against J. and terrify it, 7.06
day the Ephraim departed from J.— 7.17
and it will sweep on into J., 8.08
and together they are against J. 9.21
dispersed of J. from the four 11.12
who harass J. shall be cut off; 11.13
Ephraim shall not be jealous of J., 11.13
and J. shall not harass Ephraim. 11.13
And the land of J. will become a 19.17
He has taken away the covering of J. 22.08
Jerusalem and to the house of J. 22.21
will be sung in the land of J.: 26.01
fortified cities of J. and took them. 36.01
saying to J. and to Jerusalem, "You 36.07
the language of J. within the 36.11
a loud voice in the language of J.: 36.13
you speak to Hezekiah king of J.: 37.10
of the house of J. shall again 37.31
A writing of Hezekiah king of J., 38.09
say to the cities of J., "Behold your 40.09
inhabited,' and of the cities of J., 44.26
came forth from the loins of J.; 48.01
and from J. inheritors of my mountains; 65.09
king of J., in the thirteenth year Jer 1.02
king of J., and until the end of 1.03
king of J., until the captivity of 1.03
and against all the cities of J. 1.15
land, against the kings of J., 1.18
as your cities are your gods, O J. 2.28
and her false sister J. saw it. 3.07
her false sister J. did not fear, 3.08
false sister J. did not return to 3.10
herself less guilty than false J. 3.11
the house of J. shall join the 3.18
to the men of J. and to the inhabitants 4.03
O men of J. and inhabitants of 4.04
Declare in J., and proclaim in 4.05
shout against the cities of J. 4.16
the house of J. have been utterly 5.11
house of Jacob, proclaim it in J.: 5.20
all you men of J. who enter these 7.02
the cities of J. and in the streets of 7.17
"For the sons of J. have done evil 7.30
the cities of J. and from the 7.34
LORD, the bones of the kings of J., 8.01
make the cities of J. a desolation, 9.11
Egypt, J., Edom, the sons of Ammon, 9.26
make the cities of J. a desolation, 10.22
to the men of J. and the inhabitants 11.02
these words in the cities of J., 11.06
the men of J. and the inhabitants 11.09
the house of J. have broken my covenant 11.10
Then the cities of J. and the inhabitants 11.12
as many as your cities, O J.; and as 11.13
and the house of J. have done, provoking 11.17
up the house of J. from among them. 12.14
the pride of J. and the great pride of 13.09

JUDAH (cont.)
the whole house of J. cling to me, Jer 13.11
all J. is taken into exile, wholly 13.19
"J. mourns and her gates languish; 14.02
Hast thou utterly rejected J.? Does thy 14.19
king of J., did in Jerusalem. 15.04
"The sin of J. is written with a 17.01
the kings of J. enter and by which 17.19
you kings of J., and all J., and all 17.20
the men of J. and the inhabitants 17.25
the cities of J. and the places 17.26
to the men of J. and the inhabitants 18.11
O kings of J. and inhabitants of 19.03
nor the kings of J. have known; 19.04
void the plans of J. and Jerusalem, 19.07
and the houses of the kings of J.— 19.13
I will give all J. into the hand 20.04
of the kings of J. into the hand 20.05
I will deliver Zedekiah king of J., 21.07
to the house of the king of J. say, 21.11
to the house of the king of J., 22.01
O King of J., who sit on the throne 22.02
the house of the king of J.: 22.06
king of J., who reigned instead of 22.11
king of J.: "They shall not lament 22.18
king of J., were the signet ring on 22.24
of David, and ruling again in J." 22.30
In his days J. will be saved, and 23.06
king of J., together with the 24.01
together with the princes of J., 24.01
regard as good the exiles from J., 24.05
I treat Zedekiah the king of J., 24.08
concerning all the people of J., 25.01
king of J. (that was the first year 25.01
the people of J. and all the inhabitants 25.02
king of J., to this day, the word of 25.03
Jerusalem and the cities of J., 25.18
king of J., this word came from the 26.01
the cities of J. which come to 26.02
When the princes of J. heard these 26.10
in the days of Hezekiah king of J., 26.18
and said to all the people of J.: 26.18
Hezekiah king of J. and all J. put 26.19
king of J. this word came to Jeremiah 27.01
Jerusalem to Zedekiah king of J. 27.03
Zedekiah king of J. I spoke in like 27.12
in the house of the king of J., 27.18
king of J., and all the nobles of 27.20
the nobles of J. and Jerusalem— 27.20
in the house of the king of J., 27.21
the reign of Zedekiah king of J., 28.01
king of J., and all the exiles from J. who 28.04
the princes of J. and Jerusalem, 29.02
Zedekiah king of J. sent to Babylon 29.03
all the exiles from J. in Babylon: 29.22
Israel and J., says the LORD, and I 30.03
spoke concerning Israel and J.: 30.04
in the land of J. and in its 31.23
And J. and all its cities shall 31.24
the house of J. with the seed of 31.27
of Israel and the house of J., 31.31
tenth year of Zedekiah king of J., 32.01
in the palace of the king of J., 32.02
Zedekiah king of J. had imprisoned 32.03
Zedekiah king of J. shall not escape 32.04
and the sons of J. have done nothing 32.30
and the sons of J. which they did 32.32
the men of J. and the inhabitants 32.32
abomination, to cause J. to sin. 32.35
Jerusalem, and in the cities of J., 32.44
of the kings of J. which were torn 33.04
the fortunes of J. and the fortunes 33.07
the cities of J. and the streets 33.10
Jerusalem, and in the cities of J., 33.13
of Israel and the house of J. 33.14
In those days J. will be saved and 33.16
Zedekiah king of J. and say to him, 34.02
of the LORD, O Zedekiah king of J.! 34.04
Zedekiah king of J., in Jerusalem, 34.06
the cities of J. that were left, 34.07
fortified cities of J. that remained. 34.07
the princes of J., the princes of 34.19
And Zedekiah king of J., and his princes 34.21
the cities of J. a desolation 34.22
the son of Josiah, king of J.: 35.01
to the men of J. and the inhabitants 35.13
am bringing on J. and all the inhabitants 35.17
king of J., this word came to Jeremiah 36.01
Israel and J. and all the nations, 36.02
the house of J. will hear all the 36.03
all the men of J. who come out of 36.06
king of J., in the ninth month, all 36.09
the cities of J. to Jerusalem proclaimed 36.09
Jehoiakim the king of J. has burned. 36.28
Jehoiakim king of J. you shall say, 36.29
concerning Jehoiakim king of J., 36.30
Jerusalem, and upon the men of J., 36.31
Jehoiakim king of J. had burned in 36.32
made king in the land of J., reigned 37.01
to the king of J. who sent you to 37.07
of the king of J. were being led 38.22
ninth year of Zedekiah king of J., 39.01
Zedekiah king of J. and all the 39.04
Babylon slew all the nobles of J. 39.06
in the land of J. some of the poor 39.10
Jerusalem and J. who were being 40.01
governor of the cities of J., 40.05
a remnant in J. and had appointed 40.11
driven and came to the land of J., 40.12
and the remnant of J. would perish?" 40.15
word of the LORD, O remnant of J. 42.15
O remnant of J., 'Do not go to 42.19
LORD, to remain in the land of J. 43.04
the remnant of J. who had returned 43.05
in the land of J. from all the 43.05
in the sight of the men of J., 43.09
and upon all the cities of J. 44.02
the cities of J. and in the streets 44.06
and child, from the midst of J., 44.07
the wickedness of the kings of J., 44.09
in the land of J. and in the 44.09
you for evil, to cut off all J. 44.11
the remnant of J. who have set 44.12
the remnant of J. who have come to 44.14
or return to the land of J., 44.14
the cities of J. and in the streets 44.17
the cities of J. and in the streets 44.21
all you of J. who are in the land 44.24
all you of J. who dwell in the land 44.26
of any man of J. in all the land 44.26
all the men of J. who are in the 44.27
to the land of J., few in number; 44.28
and all the remnant of J., 44.28
Zedekiah king of J. into the hand 44.30
the son of Josiah, king of J.: 45.01
the son of Josiah, king of J.: 46.02
the reign of Zedekiah king of J. 49.34
the people of J. shall come together, 50.04
and sin in J., and none shall be 50.20
and the people of J. with them; 50.33
For Israel and J. have not been 51.05
Zedekiah king of J. to Babylon, 51.59
Jerusalem and J. that he cast them 52.03
all the princes of J. at Riblah. 52.10
So J. was carried captive out of 52.27
captivity of Jehoiachin king of J., 52.31
Jehoiachin king of J. and brought 52.31
J. has gone into exile because of Lam 1.03
press the virgin daughter of J. 1.15
strongholds of the daughter of J.; 2.02
the daughter of J. mourning and 2.05
Zion, virgins in the towns of J. 5.11
the punishment of the house of J.; Eze 4.06
the elders of J. sitting before me, 8.01

JUDAH (cont.)
the house of J. to commit the abominations Eze 8.17
of Israel and J. is exceedingly 9.09
Ammonites and to J. and to Jerusalem 21.20
the house of J. when it went into 25.03
the house of J. is like all the 25.08
the house of J. and has grievously 25.12
J. and the land of Israel traded 27.17
'For J., and the children of Israel 37.16
will join with it the stick of J., 37.19
side to the west, J., one portion. 48.07
"Adjoining the territory of J., 48.08
territory of J. and the territory 48.22
the gate of J., and the gate of 48.31
the reign of Jehoiakim king of J., Dan 1.01
Jehoiakim king of J. into his hand, 1.02
and Azariah of the tribe of J. 1.06
the exiles from J. a man who can 2.25
Daniel, one of the exiles of J., 5.13
the king my father brought from J. 5.13
who is one of the exiles from J., 6.13
to the men of J., to the inhabitants 9.07
kings of J., and in the days of Hos 1.01
will have pity on the house of J., 1.07
And the people of J. and the people 1.11
O Israel, let not J. become guilty. 4.15
J. also shall stumble with them. 5.05
The princes of J. have become like 5.10
like dry rot to the house of J. 5.12
and J. his wound, then Ephraim went 5.13
a young lion to the house of J. 5.14
What shall I do with you, O J.? 6.04
you also, O J., a harvest is appointed. 6.11
and J. has multiplied fortified 8.14
J. must plow, Jacob must harrow for 10.11
but J. is still known by God, and is 11.12
The LORD has an indictment against J., 12.02
the fortunes of J. and Jerusalem, Joe 3.01
the people of J. and Jerusalem to 3.06
into the hand of the sons of J., 3.08
stream beds of J. shall flow with 3.18
violence done to the people of J., 3.19
But J. shall be inhabited for ever, 3.20
Uzziah king of J. and in the days Amo 1.01
"For three transgressions of J., 2.04
So I will send a fire upon J., 2.05
go, flee away to the land of J., 7.12
the people of J. in the day of Ob 1.12
kings of J., which he saw concerning Mic 1.01
what is the sin of the house of J.? 1.05
and it has come to J., it has reached 1.09
little to be among the clans of J., 5.02
O J., fulfil your vows, for never Nah 1.15
Josiah the son of Amon, king of J. Zep 1.01
stretch out my hand against J., 1.04
of the remnant of the house of J., 2.07
governor of J., and to Joshua the Hag 1.01
governor of J., and the spirit of 1.14
governor of J., and to Joshua the 2.02
governor of J., saying, I am about 2.21
on Jerusalem and the cities of J., Zec 1.12
the horns which have scattered J., 1.19
are the horns which scattered J., 1.21
the land of J. to scatter it. 1.21
will inherit J. as his portion in 2.12
O house of J. and house of Israel, 8.13
Jerusalem and to the house of J.; 8.15
to the house of J. seasons of joy 8.19
it shall be like a clan in J., 9.07
For I have bent J. as my bow; 9.13
the house of J., and will make them 10.03
"I will strengthen the house of J., 10.06
brotherhood between J. and Israel. 11.14
will be against J. also in the 12.02
the house of J. I will open my 12.04
Then the clans of J. shall say to 12.05
the clans of J. like a blazing pot 12.06
victory to the tents of J. first, 12.07
may not be exalted over that of J. 12.07
in the days of Uzziah king of J. 14.05
even J. will fight against Jerusalem. 14.14
Jerusalem and J. shall be sacred 14.21
J. has been faithless, and abomination Mal 2.11
for J. has profaned the sanctuary 2.11
Then the offering of J. and Jerusalem 3.04
the father of J. and his brothers, Mt 1.02
and J. the father of Perez and 1.03
O Bethlehem, in the land of J., 2.06
means least among the rulers of J.; 2.06
the hill country, to a city of J., Lk 1.39
the son of Perez, the son of J., 3.33
our Lord was descended from J., Heb 7.14
of Israel and with the house of J.; 8.08
lo, the Lion of the tribe of J., Rev 5.05
sealed out of the tribe of J., 7.05

JUDAH'S
But Er, J. first-born, was wicked in Gen 38.07
Now Er, J. first-born, was wicked in 1Ch 2.03

JUDAISM
converts to J. followed Paul and Ac 13.43
have heard of my former life in J., Gal 1.13
and I advanced in J. beyond many of 1.14

JUDAS
and J. Iscariot, who betrayed him. Mt 10.04
James and Joseph and Simon and J.? 13.55
twelve, who was called J. Iscariot, 26.14
J., who betrayed him, said, "Is it I, 26.25
J. came, one of the twelve, and with 26.47
When J., his betrayer, saw that he 27.03
and J. Iscariot, who betrayed him. Mk 3.19
James and Joses and J. and Simon, 6.03
Then J. Iscariot, who was one of the 14.10
J. came, one of the twelve, and with 14.43
the son of J., the son of Joseph, Lk 3.30
J. the son of James, and J. Iscariot, 6.16
entered into J. called Iscariot, 22.03
a crowd, and the man called J., 22.47
"J., would you betray the Son of 22.48
He spoke of J. the son of Simon Jn 6.71
But J. Iscariot, one of his disciples 12.04
it into the heart of J. Iscariot, 13.02
he gave it to J., the son of Simon 13.26
because J. had the money box, Jesus 13.29
J. (not Iscariot) said to him, "Lord, 14.22
Now J., who betrayed him, also knew 18.02
So J., procuring a band of soldiers 18.03
J., who betrayed him, was standing 18.05
the Zealot and J. the son of James. Ac 1.13
concerning J. who was guide to 1.16
apostleship from which J. turned aside, 1.25
After him J. the Galilean arose in 5.37
in the house of J. for a man of 9.11
They sent J. called Barsabbas, and 15.22
We have therefore sent J. and Silas, 15.27
And J. and Silas, who were themselves 15.32

JUDE
J., a servant of Jesus Christ and Jud 1.01

JUDEA
us protection in J. and Jerusalem. Ez 9.09
in Bethlehem of J. in the days of Mt 2.01
They told him, "In Bethlehem of J.; 2.05
reigned over J. in place of his 2.22
preaching in the wilderness of J., 3.01
Jerusalem and all J. and all the 3.05
Jerusalem and J. and from beyond 4.25
the region of J. beyond the Jordan 19.01
who are in J. flee to the mountains; 24.16
out to him all the country of J., Mk 1.05
Galilee followed; also from J. 3.07
the region of J. and beyond the 10.01

JUDEA (cont.)

who are in J. flee to the mountains; Mk 13.14
king of J., there was a priest Lk 1.05
through all the hill country of J.; 1.65
to J., to the city of David, which 2.04
Pilate being governor of J., 3.01
preaching in the synagogues of J. 4.44
of Galilee and J. and from Jerusalem; 5.17
people from all J. and Jerusalem 6.17
the whole of J. and all the 7.17
who are in J. flee to the mountains, 21.21
people, teaching throughout all J., 23.05
disciples went into the land of J.; Jn 3.22
he left J. and departed again to 4.03
Jesus had come from J. to Galilee, 4.47
he had come from J. to Galilee. 4.54
he would not go about in J., 7.01
to him, "Leave here and go to J., 7.03
disciples, "Let us go into J. again." 11.07
and in all J. and Samaria and to Ac 1.08
J. and Cappadocia, Pontus and Asia, 2.09
"Men of J. and all who dwell in 2.14
the region of J. and Samaria, 8.01
throughout all J. and Galilee and 9.31
was proclaimed throughout all J., 10.37
who were in J. heard that the 11.01
to the brethren who lived in J.; 11.29
he went down from J. to Caesarea, 12.19
came down from J. and were teaching 15.01
named Agabus came down from J. 21.10
throughout all the country of J., 26.20
no letters from J. about you, 28.21
delivered from the unbelievers in J., Rom 15.31
have you send me on my way to J. 2Co 1.16
to the churches of Christ in J.; Gal 1.22
in Christ Jesus which are in J.; 1Th 2.14

JUDGE

May the LORD j. between you and me!" Gen 16.05
Shall not the J. of all the earth 18.25
sojourn, and he would play the j.! 19.09
God of their father, j. between us." 31.53
Dan shall j. his people as one of 49.16
made you a prince and a j. over us? Ex 2.14
"The LORD look upon you and j., 5.21
morrow Moses sat to j. the people, 18.13
And let them j. the people at all 18.22
righteousness shall you j. your neighbor. Lev 19.15
congregation shall j. between the Num 35.24
and j. righteously between a man Deu 1.16
and they shall j. the people with 16.18
and to the j. who is in office in 17.09
or the j., that man shall die; 17.12
the j. shall cause him to lie down 25.02
their adversaries should j. amiss, 32.27
for them, the LORD was with the j., Ju 2.18
enemies all the days of the j.; 2.18
But whenever the j. died, they turned 2.19
the LORD, the J., decide this day 11.27
The LORD will j. the ends of the 1Sa 2.10
May the LORD j. between me and you, 24.12
May the LORD therefore be j., 24.15
"Oh that I were j. in the land! 2Sa 15.04
and j. thy servants, condemning the 1Ki 8.32
LORD, for he comes to j. the earth. 1Ch 16.33
and j. thy servants, requiting the 2Ch 6.23
for you j. not for man but for the 19.06
judges who may j. all the people Ez 7.25
Can he j. through the deep darkness? Job 22.13
be acquitted for ever by my j. 23.07
j. me, O LORD, according to my Ps 7.08
God is a righteous j., and a God 7.11
earth, that he may j. his people: 50.04
righteousness, for God himself is j.! 50.06
Do you j. the sons of men uprightly? 58.01
for thou dost j. the peoples with 67.04
May he j. thy people with righteousness, 72.02
I appoint I will j. with equity. 75.02
"How long will you j. unjustly and 82.02
Arise, O God, j. the earth; for to thee 82.08
Rise up, O j. of the earth; render 94.02
he will j. the peoples with equity." 96.10
for he comes to j. the earth. 96.13
He will j. the world with righteousness, 96.13
He will j. the world with righteousness, 98.09
When wilt thou j. those who persecute 119.84
j. righteously, maintain the rights Pro 31.09
God will j. the righteous and the Ecc 3.17
He shall j. between the nations, and Is 2.04
the j. and the prophet, the diviner 3.02
contend, he stands to j. his people. 3.13
j., I pray you, between me and my 5.03
He shall not j. by what his eyes 11.03
righteousness he shall j. the poor, 11.04
For the LORD is our j., the LORD is 33.22
they j. not with justice the cause Jer 5.28
me, O LORD; j. thou my cause. Lam 3.59
and will j. you according to your Eze 7.03
and j. you according to your ways; 7.08
their own judgments I will j. them; 7.27
I will j. you at the border of 11.10
I will j. you at the border of 11.11
And I will j. you as women who 16.38
"Therefore I will j. you, O house of 18.30
j. them, son of man, will you j. them? 20.04
land of your origin, I will j. you. 21.30
will you j., will you j. the bloody city? 22.02
and they shall j. you according to 23.24
will you j. Oholah and Oholibah? 23.36
ways and your doings I will j. you, 24.14
I will j. each of you according to 33.20
I j. between sheep and sheep, rams 34.17
I myself will j. between the fat 34.20
and I will j. between sheep and 34.22
known among you, when I j. you. 35.11
and they shall j. it according to 44.24
I will sit to j. all the nations Joe 3.12
He shall j. between many peoples, Mic 4.03
prince and the j. ask for a bribe, 7.03
accuser hand you over to the j., Mt 5.25
and the j. to the guard, and you be 5.25
"J. not, that you be not judged. 7.01
"J. not, and you will not be judged; Lk 6.37
who made me a j. or divider over 12.14
"And why do you not j. for yourselves 12.57
way, lest he drag you to the j., 12.58
and the j. hand you over to the 12.58
there was a j. who neither feared 18.02
"Hear what the unrighteous j. says. 18.06
as I hear, I j.; and my judgment Jn 5.30
Do not j. by appearances, but 7.24
but j. with right judgment." 7.24
"Does our law j. a man without 7.51
You j. according to the flesh, I j. no one. 8.15
Yet even if I do j., my judgment 8.16
for it is not I alone that j., 8.16
to say about you and much to j.; 8.26
who seeks it and he will be the j. 8.50
not keep them, I do not j. him; 12.47
did not come to j. the world but 12.47
not receive my sayings has a j.; 12.48
will be his j. on the last day. 12.48
yourselves and j. him by your own 18.31
rather than to God you must j.; Ac 4.19
'But I will j. the nation which 7.07
made you a ruler and a j. over us? 7.27
'Who made you a ruler and a j.? 7.35
by God to be j. of the living and 10.42
and j. yourselves unworthy of eternal 13.46
which he will j. the world in 17.31
refuse to be a j. of these things." 18.15
you sitting to j. me according to 23.03
you have been j. over this nation, 24.10
you are, when you j. another; Rom 2.01

JUDGE (cont.)
the j., are doing the very same Rom 2.01
that when you j. these who do such 2.03
then how could God j. the world? 3.06
no reason to j. himself for what 14.22
human court. I do not even j. myself. 1Co 4.03
the church whom you are to j.? 5.12
that the saints will j. the world? 6.02
not know that we are to j. angels? 6.03
.j for yourselves what I say. 10.15
J. for yourselves; is it proper 11.13
Jesus who is to j. the living and 2Ti 4.01
the righteous j., will award to me 4.08
again, "The Lord will j. his people." Heb 10.30
and to a j. who is God of all, and 12.23
for God will j. the immoral and 13.04
But if you j. the law, you are not a Jas 4.11
are not a doer of the law but a j. 4.11
There is one lawgiver and j., 4.12
are you that you j. your neighbor? 4.12
behold, the J. is standing at the 5.09
who is ready to j. the living and 1Pe 4.05
thou wilt j. and avenge our blood Rev 6.10

JUDGED
"God has j. me, and has also heard Gen 30.06
And they j. the people at all times; Ex 18.26
came upon him, and he j. Israel; Ju 3.10
And he j. Israel twenty-three years. 10.02
who j. Israel twenty-two years. 10.03
Jephthah j. Israel six years. 12.07
After him Ibzan of Bethlehem j. Israel. 12.08
And he j. Israel seven years. 12.09
After him Elon the Zebulunite j. Israel; 12.11
and he j. Israel ten years. 12.11
Hillel the Pirathonite j. Israel. 12.13
and he j. Israel eight years. 12.14
And he j. Israel in the days of the 15.20
He had j. Israel twenty years. 16.31
He had j. Israel forty years. 1Sa 4.18
And Samuel j. the people of Israel 7.06
Samuel j. Israel all the days of 7.15
and he j. Israel in all these 7.16
days of the judges who j. Israel, 2Ki 23.22
let the nations be j. before thee! Ps 9.19
and a man is j. by his praise. Pro 27.21
He j. the cause of the poor and Jer 22.16
wedlock and shed blood are j., Eze 16.38
conduct and their deeds I j. them. 36.19
"Judge not, that you be not j. Mt 7.01
you pronounce you will be j., and the 7.02
"Judge not, and you will not be j.; Lk 6.37
said to him, "You have j. rightly." 7.43
because the ruler of this world is j. Jn 16.11
"If you have j. me to be faithful Ac 16.15
and we would have j. him according * 24.06
the law will be j. by the law. Rom 2.12
and prevail when thou art j." 3.04
but is himself to be j. by no one. 1Co 2.15
I should be j. by your or by any 4.03
if the world is to be j. by you, 6.02
But if we j. ourselves truly, we 11.31
ourselves truly, we should not be j. 11.31
But when we are j. by the Lord, 11.32
because he j. me faithful by appointing 1Ti 1.12
any of you be j. to have failed to Heb 4.01
who are to be j. under the law of Jas 2.12
teach shall be j. with greater 3.01
another, that you may not be j.; 5.09
that though j. in the flesh like 1Pe 4.06
and the time for the dead to be j., Rev 11.18
he has j. the great harlot who 19.02
the dead were j. by what was written 20.12
and all were j. by what they had 20.13

JUDGES
he shall pay as the j. determine. Ex 21.22
And Moses said to the j. of Israel, Num 25.05
And I charged your j. at that time, Deu 1.16
"You shall appoint j. and officers 16.18
priests and the j. who are in office 19.17
the j. shall inquire diligently, and 19.18
elders and your j. shall come forth, 21.02
and the j. decide between them, 25.01
our enemies themselves being j. 32.31
elders and officers and their j., Jos 8.33
their j. and officers, and said to 23.02
the j., and the officers of Israel; 24.01
Then the LORD raised up j., who saved Ju 2.16
they did not listen to their j.; 2.17
Whenever the LORD raised up j. for them, 2.18
days when the j. ruled there was a Ru 1.01
he made his sons j. over Israel. 1Sa 8.01
Abijah; they were j. in Beersheba. 8.02
word with any of the j. of Israel, 2Sa 7.07
I appointed j. over my people 7.11
the days of the j. who judged 2Ki 23.22
word with any of the j. of Israel, 1Ch 17.06
I appointed j. over my people 17.10
thousand shall be officers and j., 23.04
for Israel, as officers and j. 26.29
to the j., and to all the leaders 2Ch 1.02
He appointed j. in the land in all 19.05
and said to the j., "Consider 19.06
the j., the governors, the officials, Ez 4.09
magistrates and j. who may judge 7.25
the elders and j. of every city, 10.14
he covers the faces of its j.— Job 9.24
stripped, and j. he makes fools. 12.17
seeing that he j. those that are 21.22
iniquity to be punished by the j.; 31.11
iniquity to be punished by the j., 31.28
For by these he j. peoples; 36.31
The LORD j. the peoples; judge me, Ps 7.08
and he j. the world with righteousness, 9.08
he j. the peoples with equity. 9.08
there is a God who j. on earth." 58.11
If a king j. the poor with equity Pro 29.14
restore your j. as at the first, Is 1.26
David one who j. and seeks justice 16.05
a controversy they shall act as j., Eze 44.24
her j. are evening wolves that Zep 3.03
Therefore they shall be your j. Mt 12.27
Therefore they shall be your j. Lk 11.19
The Father j. no one, but has given Jn 5.22
he gave them j. until Samuel the Ac 13.20
God j. the secrets of men by Christ Rom 2.16
The spiritual man j. all things, 1Co 2.15
It is the Lord who j. me. 4.04
God j. those outside. Drive out 5.13
and become j. with evil thoughts? Jas 2.04
a brother or j. his brother, 4.11
against the law and j. the law. 4.11
Father him who j. each one impartially 1Pe 1.17
he trusted to him who j. justly. 2.23
mighty is the Lord God who j. her." Rev 18.08
righteousness he j. and makes war. 19.11

JUDGEST
who j. righteously, who triest the Jer 11.20

JUDGING
was j. Israel at that time. Ju 4.04
Partiality in j. is not good. Pro 24.23
j. the twelve tribes of Israel. Mt 19.28
sit on thrones j. the twelve Lk 22.30
have I to do with j. outsiders? 1Co 5.12

JUDGMENT
but I will bring j. on the nation Gen 15.14
arm and with great acts of j., Ex 6.06
land of Egypt by great acts of j. 7.04
you shall make a breastpiece of j., 28.15
breastpiece of j. upon his heart, 28.29
breastpiece of j. you shall put 28.30
shall bear the j. of the people of 28.30

JUDGMENT (cont.)

"You shall do no injustice in j.;	Lev 19.15
"You shall do no wrong in j.,	19.35
for him by the j. of the Urim	Num 27.21
before the congregation for j.	35.12
You shall not be partial in j.;	Deu 1.17
face of man, for the j. is God's;	1.17
judge the people with righteous j.	16.18
and my hand takes hold on j.,	32.41
before the congregation for j.,	Jos 20.06
of Israel came up to her for j.	Ju 4.05
to come before the king for j.,	2Sa 15.02
Israel who came to the king for j.;	15.06
heard of the j. which the king had	1Ki 3.28
where he was to pronounce j.,	7.07
judgment, even the Hall of J.;	7.07
said to him, "So shall your j. be;	20.40
he is with you in giving j.	2Ch 19.06
to give j. for the LORD and to	19.08
j., or pestilence, or famine, we will	20.09
wilt thou not execute j. upon them?	20.12
was executing j. upon the house of	22.08
Thus they executed j. on Joash.	24.24
let j. be strictly executed upon	Ez 7.26
all who were versed in law and j.,	Est 1.13
and calls to j., who can hinder him?	Job 11.10
and bring him into j. with thee?	14.03
that you may know there is a j."	19.29
you, and enters into j. with you?	22.04
not times of j. kept by the Almighty,	24.01
for any man to go before God in j.	34.23
are full of the j. on the wicked;	36.17
j. and justice seize you.	36.17
wicked will not stand in the j.,	Ps 1.05
my God; thou hast appointed a j.	7.06
on the throne giving righteous j.	9.04
has established his throne for j.;	9.07
himself known, he has executed j.;	9.16
sentence and blameless in thy j.	51.04
but it is God who executes j.,	75.07
From the heavens thou didst utter j.;	76.08
to establish j. to save all the	76.09
the midst of the gods he holds j.:	82.01
He will execute j. among the	110.06
Teach me good j. and knowledge, for	119.66
There thrones for j. were set,	122.05
Enter not into j. with thy servant;	143.02
to execute on them the j. written!	149.09
his mouth does not sin in j.	Pro 16.10
to break out against all sound j.	18.01
the throne of j. winnows all evil	20.08
things God will bring you into j.	Ecc 11.09
For God will bring every deed into j.,	12.14
enters into j. with the elders and	Is 3.14
by a spirit of j. and by a spirit	4.04
of justice to him who sits in j.,	28.06
vision, they stumble in giving j.	28.07
mind of the rash will have good j.,	32.04
it descends for j. upon Edom,	34.05
let us together draw near for j.	41.01
By oppression and j. he was taken	53.08
that rises against you in j.	54.17
For by fire will the LORD execute j.,	66.16
I will bring you to j. for saying,	Jer 2.35
it is I who speak in j. upon them."	4.12
is entering into j. with all flesh,	25.31
"J. has come upon the tableland,	48.21
Thus far is the j. on Moab.	48.47
for her j. has reached up to heaven	51.09
I will execute j. upon her images,	51.52
Jerusalem my four sore acts of j.,	Eze 14.21
you have made j. favorable to your	16.52
and enter into j. with him there	17.20
will enter into j. with you face	20.35
As I entered into j. with your	20.36
so I will enter into j. with you,	20.36
when j. had been executed upon her.	23.10
and I will commit the j. to them,	23.24
men shall pass j. on them with the	23.45
execute acts of j. upon Thebes.	30.14
will execute acts of j. upon Egypt.	30.19
I will enter into j. with him;	38.22
shall see my j. which I have	39.21
the court sat in j., and the books	Dan 7.10
and j. was given for the saints of	7.22
But the court shall sit in j.,	7.26
For the j. pertains to you;	Hos 5.01
crushed in j., because he was	5.11
and my j. goes forth as the light.	6.05
so j. springs up like poisonous	10.04
will enter into j. with them there,	Joe 3.02
GOD was calling for a j. by fire,	Amo 7.04
Its heads give j. for a bribe, its	Mic 3.11
my cause and executes j. for me.	7.09
thou hast ordained them as a j.;	Hab 1.12
"Then I will draw near to you for j.;	Mal 3.05
whoever kills shall be liable to j.'	Mt 5.21
his brother shall be liable to j.;	5.22
For with the j. you pronounce you	7.02
on the day of j. for the land of	10.15
on the day of j. for Tyre and	11.22
on the day of j. for the land of	11.24
on the day of j. men will render	12.36
arise at the j. with this generation	12.41
arise at the j. with this generation	12.42
What is your j.?" They answered,	26.66
he was sitting on the j. seat,	27.19
tolerable in the j. for Tyre and	Lk 10.14
arise at the j. with the men of	11.31
arise at the j. with this generation	11.32
And this is the j., that the light	Jn 3.19
but has given all j. to the Son,	5.22
he does not come into j.,	5.24
given him authority to execute j.,	5.27
evil, to the resurrection of j.	5.29
and my j. is just, because I seek	5.30
appearances, but judge with right j."	7.24
my j. is true, for it is not I alone	8.16
"For j. I came into this world, that	9.39
Now is the j. of this world, now	12.31
and of righteousness and of j.:	16.08
of j., because the ruler of this	16.11
sat down on the j. seat at a place	19.13
Therefore my j. is that we should	Ac 15.19
letter with our j. that they	21.25
and self-control and future j.,	24.25
for in passing j. upon him you	Rom 2.01
We know that the j. of God rightly	2.02
you will escape the j. of God?	2.03
God's righteous j. will be revealed.	2.05
For the j. following one trespass	5.16
think, but to think with sober j.,	12.03
and those who resist will incur j.	13.02
abstains pass j. on him who eats;	14.03
Who are you to pass j. on the	14.04
Why do you pass j. on your brother?	14.10
stand before the j. seat of God;	14.10
us no more pass j. on one another,	14.13
in the same mind and the same j.	1Co 1.10
not pronounce j. before the time,	4.05
I have already pronounced j.	5.03
But in my j. she is happier if she	7.40
eats and drinks j. upon himself.	11.29
before the j. seat of Christ,	2Co 5.10
will bear his j., whoever he is.	Gal 5.10
Therefore let no one pass j. on you	Col 2.16
evidence of the righteous j. of God,	2Th 1.05
pointing to j., but the sins of	1Ti 5.24
of the dead, and eternal j.	Heb 6.02
die once, and after that comes j.,	9.27
but a fearful prospect of j.,	10.27
For j. is without mercy to one who	Jas 2.13
mercy; yet mercy triumphs over j.	2.13
has come for j. to begin with the	1Pe 4.17

JUDGMENT (cont.)
gloom to be kept until the j.; 2Pe 2.04
punishment until the day of j., 2.09
a reviling j. upon them before the 2.11
the day of j. and destruction of 3.07
have confidence for the day of j., 1Jn 4.17
gloom until the j. of the great Jud 1.06
pronounce a reviling j. upon him, 1.09
to execute j. on all, and to convict 1.15
for the hour of his j. has come; Rev 14.07
show you the j. of the great 17.01
In one hour has thy j. come." 18.10
God has given j. for you against 18.20
those to whom j. was committed. 20.04

JUDGMENTS
I will execute j.: I am the LORD. Ex 12.12
gods also the LORD executed j. Num 33.04
he wrought, the j. he uttered, 1Ch 16.12
his j. are in all the earth. 16.14
thy j. are on high, out of his sight; Ps 10.05
thy j. are like the great deep; 36.06
of Judah rejoice because of thy j.! 48.11
rejoice, because of thy j., O God. 97.08
miracles, and the j. he uttered, 105.05
his j. are in all the earth. 105.07
that thy j. are right, and that in 119.75
of thee, and I am afraid of thy j. 119.120
thou, O LORD, and right are thy j. 119.137
In the path of thy j., O LORD, we Is 26.08
For when thy j. are in the earth, 26.09
they ask of me righteous j., 58.02
And I will utter my j. against them, Jer 1.16
I will execute j. in the midst of Eze 5.08
and I will execute j. on you, 5.10
when I execute j. on you in anger 5.15
to their own j. I will judge them; 7.27
foreigners, and execute j. upon you. 11.09
and execute j. upon you in the 16.41
judge you according to their j. 23.24
and I will execute j. upon Moab. 25.11
the LORD when I execute j. in her, 28.22
when I execute j. upon all their 28.26
shall judge it according to my j. 44.24
has taken away the j. against you, Zep 3.15
Render true j., show kindness and Zec 7.09
in your gates j. that are true and 8.16
unsearchable are his j. and how Rom 11.33
for thy j. have been revealed." Rev 15.04
say, "Just art thou in these thy j., 16.05
Almighty, true and just are thy j.!" 16.07
for his j. are true and just; 19.02

JUDICIOUS
of the wise makes his speech j., Pro 16.23

JUDITH
he took to wife J. the daughter of Gen 26.34

JUICE
not drink any j. of grapes or eat Num 6.03
the j. of my pomegranates. Sol 8.02

JULIA
J., Nereus and his sister, and Rom 16.15

JULIUS
of the Augustan Cohort, named J. Ac 27.01
and J. treated Paul kindly, and gave 27.03

JUNGLE
you do in the j. of the Jordan? Jer 12.05
up from the j. of the Jordan 49.19
up from the j. of the Jordan 50.44
for the j. of the Jordan is laid Zec 11.03

JUNIAS
Greet Andronicus and J., my kinsmen Rom 16.07

JURISDICTION
were under the j. of the governor Neh 3.07
authority and j. of the governor. Lk 20.20
that he belonged to Herod's j., 23.07

JUSHABHESED
Berechiah, Hasadiah, and J., five. 1Ch 3.20

JUST
j. as we have not touched you and Gen 26.29
(j. as these are taken from the ox Lev 4.10
You shall have j. balances, j. 19.36
j. weights, a j. ephah, and a j. hin: 19.36
surely j. now I would have slain Num 22.33
everything j. as the LORD had 29.40
j. as he did for you in Egypt Deu 1.30
J. as the LORD our God commanded us.' 1.41
J. as the gazelle or the hart is 12.22
j. as you desired of the LORD your 18.16
A full and j. weight you shall have, 25.15
a full and j. measure you shall 25.15
without iniquity, j. and right is he. 32.04
commands and j. decrees of the 33.21
J. as we obeyed Moses in all things, Jos 1.17
on every side j. as he had sworn 21.44
But j. as all the good things which 23.15
when they had j. set the watch; Ju 7.19
floor and did j. as her mother-in-law Ru 3.06
behold, he is j. ahead of you. 1Sa 9.12
he has come j. now to the city, 9.12
J. then the servants of David 2Sa 3.22
j. as Absalom was entering Jerusalem. 15.37
'There have j. now come to me from 2Ki 5.22
j. as their brethren the sons of 1Ch 24.31
j. as their brethren did, ministering 26.12
thou art j., for we are left a Ez 9.15
Yet thou hast been j. in all that Neh 9.33
obeyed Mordecai j. as when she was Est 2.20
Now Haman had j. entered the 6.04
But how can a man be j. before God? Job 9.02
a j. and blameless man, am a laughingstock. 12.04
but the j. will wear it, and the 27.17
(Let me be weighed in a j. balance, 31.06
"Do you think this to be j.? 35.02
For thou hast maintained my j. cause; Ps 9.04
Hear a j. cause, O LORD; attend to my 17.01
of his hands are faithful and j.; 111.07
I have done what is j. and right; 119.121
The LORD is j. in all his ways, and 145.17
and rulers decree what is j.; Pro 8.15
but a j. weight is his delight. 11.01
The thoughts of the righteous are j.; 12.05
A j. balance and scales are the 16.11
because they refuse to do what is j. 21.07
the wise man dies j. like the fool! Ecc 2.16
j. as he came, so shall he go; 5.16
j. as the Israelites bring their Is 66.20
Have you not j. now called to me, Jer 3.04
Correct me, O LORD, but in j. measure; 10.24
I will chasten you in j. measure, 30.11
J. as I have brought all this great 32.42
I will chasten you in j. measure, 46.28
'The way of the Lord is not j.' Eze 18.25
house of Israel: Is my way not j.? 18.25
Is it not your ways that are not j.? 18.25
'The way of the Lord is not j.' 18.29
of Israel, are my ways not j.? 18.29
Is it not your ways that are not j.? 18.29
'The way of the Lord is not j.'; 33.17
it is their own way that is not j. 33.17
'The way of the Lord is not j.' 33.20
j. balances, a j. ephah, and a j. bath. 45.10
j. as you saw iron mixed with the Dan 2.41
j. as iron does not mix with clay. 2.43
j. as you saw that a stone was cut 2.45
are right and his ways are j.; 4.37
being a j. man and unwilling to put Mt 1.19

JUST (cont.)

rain on the j. and on the unjust. Mt 5.45
saying, "My daughter has j. died; 9.18
J. as the weeds are gathered and 13.40
j. as he was, in the boat. And other Mk 4.36
j. as they were delivered to us by Lk 1.02
disobedient to the wisdom of the j., 1.17
at the resurrection of the j." 14.14
and found it j. as the women had 24.24
J. then his disciples came. They marveled Jn 4.27
and my judgment is j., because I seek 5.30
j. as I have kept my Father's 15.10
J. as day was breaking, Jesus stood 21.04
the fish that you have j. caught." 21.10
the Holy Spirit j. as we have?" Ac 10.47
fell on them j. as on us at the 11.15
the Holy Spirit j. as he did to us; 15.08
of the Lord Jesus, J. as they will." 15.11
to see the J. One and to hear a 22.14
of both the j. and the unjust. 24.15
with saying. Their condemnation is j. Rom 3.08
For j. as you once yielded your 6.19
commandment is holy and j. and good. 7.12
in order that the j. requirement of 8.04
J. as you were once disobedient to 11.30
J. this: that in my preaching I may 1Co 9.18
j. as I try to please all men in 10.33
For j. as the body is one and has 12.12
J. as we have borne the image of 15.49
want to see you now j. in passing; 16.07
but j. as everything we said to you 2Co 7.14
j. as Peter had been entrusted with Gal 2.07
j. as you were called to the one Eph 4.04
to send him j. as soon as I see Php 2.23
whatever is j., whatever is pure, 4.08
j. as you were taught, abounding in Col 2.07
but j. as we have been approved by 1Th 2.04
j. as it has come to pass, and as 3.04
j. as you are doing, you do so more 4.01
one another up, j. as you are doing. 5.11
God deems it j. to repay with 2Th 1.06
down for the j. but for the 1Ti 1.09
disobedience received a j. retribution, Heb 2.02
j. as Moses also was faithful in 3.02
good news came to us j. as to them; 4.02
is called by God, j. as Aaron was. 5.04
And j. as it is appointed for men 9.27
the spirits of j. men made perfect, 12.23
j. as there will be false teachers 2Pe 2.01
our sins, he is faithful and j., 1Jn 1.09
j. as it has taught you, abide in 2.27
love one another, j. as he has commanded us. 3.23
j. as we have been commanded by the 2Jn 1.04
j. as Sodom and Gomorrah and the Jud 1.07
J. and true are thy ways, O King of Rev 15.03
"J. art thou in these thy judgments, 16.05
true and j. are thy judgments!" 16.07
for his judgments are true and j.; 19.02

JUSTICE

LORD by doing righteousness and j.; Gen 18.19
a multitude, so as to pervert j.; Ex 23.02
not pervert the j. due to your 23.06
He executes j. for the fatherless Deu 10.18
You shall not pervert j.; you shall not 16.19
J., and only j., you shall follow, 16.20
not pervert the j. due to the sojourner 24.17
perverts the j. due to the sojourner, 27.19
for all his ways are j. A God of 32.04
also he administered j. to Israel. 1Sa 7.17
they took bribes and perverted j. 8.03
administered j. and equity to all 2Sa 8.15
to me, and I would give him j." 15.04
of God was in him, to render j. 1Ki 3.28
you may execute j. and righteousness." 10.09
he administered j. and equity to 1Ch 18.14
you may execute j. and righteousness." 2Ch 9.08
perversion of j. with the LORD our 19.07
Does God pervert j.? Or does the Job 8.03
If it is a matter of j., who can 9.19
I call aloud, but there is no j. 19.07
my j. was like a robe and a turban. 29.14
the Almighty will not pervert j. 34.12
Shall one who hates j. govern? 34.17
the wicked; judgment and j. seize you. 36.17
he is great in power and j., and abundant 37.23
to do j. to the fatherless and the Ps 10.18
He loves righteousness and j.; 33.05
For the LORD loves j.; he will not 37.28
wisdom, and his tongue speaks j. 37.30
Give the king thy j., O God, 72.01
righteousness, and thy poor with j.! 72.02
Give j. to the weak and the fatherless; 82.03
Righteousness and j. are the foundation 89.14
for j. will return to the righteous, 94.15
righteousness and j. are the foundation 97.02
lover of j., thou hast established 99.04
hast executed j. and righteousness 99.04
I will sing of loyalty and of j.; 101.01
vindication and j. for all who are 103.06
Blessed are they who observe j., 106.03
who conducts his affairs with j. 112.05
O LORD, in thy j. preserve my life. 119.149
give me life according to thy j. 119.156
and executes j. for the needy. 140.12
who executes j. for the oppressed; 146.07
righteousness, j., and equity; Pro 1.03
guarding the paths of j. and 2.08
righteousness and j. and equity, 2.09
righteousness, in the paths of j., 8.20
bosom to pervert the ways of j. 17.23
to deprive a righteous man of j. 18.05
A worthless witness mocks at j., 19.28
righteousness and j. is more 21.03
When j. is done, it is a joy to the 21.15
Evil men do not understand j., 28.05
By j. a king gives stability to the 29.04
but from the LORD a man gets j. 29.26
the sun that in the place of j., Ecc 3.16
oppressed and j. and right violently 5.08
do good; seek j., correct oppression; Is 1.17
a harlot, she that was full of j.! 1.21
Zion shall be redeemed by j., 1.27
and he looked for j., but behold, 5.07
the LORD of hosts is exalted in j., 5.16
uphold it with j. and with righteousness 9.07
the needy from j. and to rob the 10.02
"Give counsel, grant j.; make your 16.03
and seeks j. and is swift to do 16.05
and a spirit of j. to him who sits 28.06
And I will make j. the line, 28.17
For the LORD is a God of j.; 30.18
and princes will rule in j. 32.01
Then j. will dwell in the wilderness, 32.16
fill Zion with j. and righteousness; 33.05
and who taught him the path of j., 40.14
will bring forth j. to the nations. 42.01
he will faithfully bring forth j. 42.03
he has established j. in the earth; 42.04
and my j. for a light to the 51.04
"Keep j., and do righteousness, for 56.01
and there is no j. in their paths; 59.08
Therefore j. is far from us, and 59.09
we look for j., but there is none; 59.11
J. is turned back, and righteousness 59.14
displeased him that there was no j. 59.15
For I the LORD love j., I hate 61.08
in j., and in uprightness, then Jer 4.02
one who does j. and seeks truth; 5.01
judge not with j. the cause of the 5.28
truly execute j. one with another, 7.05
j., and righteousness in the earth; 9.24
" 'Execute j. in the morning, and 21.12
Do j. and righteousness, and deliver 22.03

JUSTICE (cont.)
drink and do j. and righteousness Jer 22.15
shall execute j. and righteousness 23.05
shall execute j. and righteousness 33.15
executes true j. between man and Eze 18.08
watch over; I will feed them in j. 34.16
and execute j. and righteousness; 45.09
to me in righteousness and in j., Hos 2.19
return, hold fast to love and j., 12.06
O you who turn j. to wormwood, and Amo 5.07
good, and establish j. in the gate; 5.15
But let j. roll down like waters, 5.24
you have turned j. into poison and 6.12
of Israel! Is it not for you to know j.?— Mic 3.01
and with j. and might, to declare to 3.08
who abhor j. and pervert all equity, 3.09
LORD require of you but to do j., 6.08
is slacked and j. never goes forth Hab 1.04
righteous, so j. goes forth perverted. 1.04
their j. and dignity proceed from 1.07
morning he shows forth his j., Zep 3.05
by asking, "Where is the God of j.?" Mal 2.17
shall proclaim j. to the Gentiles. Mt 12.18
wick, till he brings j. to victory; 12.20
j. and mercy and faith; these you ought 23.23
and neglect j. and the love of God; Lk 11.42
In his humiliation j. was denied him. Ac 8.33
he argued about j. and self-control 24.25
j. has not allowed him to live." 28.04
serves to show the j. of God, Rom 3.05
enforced j., received promises, Heb 11.33

JUSTICES
the j., the magistrates, and all the Dan 3.02
the j., the magistrates, and all the 3.03

JUSTIFICATION
trespasses and raised for our j. Rom 4.25
following many trespasses brings j. 5.16
for if j. were through the law, then Gal 2.21

JUSTIFIED
Job because he j. himself rather Job 32.02
you condemn me that you may be j.? 40.08
that thou art j. in thy sentence Ps 51.04
Yet wisdom is j. by her deeds." Mt 11.19
for by your words you will be j., 12.37
and the tax collectors j. God, Lk 7.29
Yet wisdom is j. by all her children." 7.35
to his house j. rather than the 18.14
doers of the law who will be j. Rom 2.13
thou mayest be j. in thy words, 3.04
being will be j. in his sight by 3.20
they are j. by his grace as a gift, 3.24
that a man is j. by faith apart 3.28
For if Abraham was j. by works, 4.02
since we are j. by faith, we have 5.01
we are now j. by his blood, much 5.09
those whom he called he also j.; 8.30
those whom he j. he also glorified. 8.30
every one who has faith may be j. 10.04
with his heart and so is j., 10.10
you were j. in the name of the Lord 1Co 6.11
a man is not j. by works of the Gal 2.16
in order to be j. by faith in 2.16
of the law shall no one be j. 2.16
in our endeavor to be j. in Christ, 2.17
that no man is j. before God by 3.11
came, that we might be j. by faith. 3.24
you who would be j. by the law; 5.04
we might be j. by his grace and Tit 3.07
not Abraham our father j. by works, Jas 2.21
that a man is j. by works and not 2.24
the harlot j. by works when she 2.25

JUSTIFIES
He who j. the wicked and he who Pro 17.15
and that he j. him who has faith Rom 3.26
but trusts him who j. the ungodly, 4.05
God's elect? It is God who j.; 8.33

JUSTIFY
speak, for I desire to j. you. Job 33.32
bring their witnesses to j. them, Is 43.09
desiring to j. himself, said to Lk 10.29
are those who j. yourselves before 16.15
we can give to j. this commotion." Ac 19.40
and he will j. the circumcised on Rom 3.30
that God would j. the Gentiles by Gal 3.08

JUSTLY
When one rules j. over men ruling 2Sa 23.03
No one enters suit j., no one goes Is 59.04
And we indeed j.; for we are Lk 23.41
Masters, treat your slaves j. and fairly, Col 4.01
he trusted to him who judges j. 1Pe 2.23

JUSTUS
who was surnamed J., and Matthias. Ac 1.23
the house of a man named Titius J., 18.07
and Jesus who is called J. Col 4.11

JUTTAH
Maon, Carmel, Ziph, J., Jos 15.55
J. with its pasture lands, Bethshemesh 21.16

K

KAB
part of a k. of dove's dung for 2Ki 6.25

KABZEEL
of Edom. were K., Eder, Jagur, Jos 15.21
Jehoiada was a valiant man of K., 2Sa 23.20
Jehoiada was a valiant man of K., 1Ch 11.22

KADESH
K.), and subdued all the country of Gen 14.07
it lies between K. and Bered. 16.14
and dwelt between K. and Shur; 20.01
in the wilderness of Paran, at K.; Num 13.26
month, and the people stayed in K.; 20.01
messengers from K. to the king of 20.14
and here we are in K., a city on 20.16
And they journeyed from K., and the people 20.22
of Meribah of K. in the wilderness 27.14
the wilderness of Zin (that is, K.). 33.36
And they set out from K., and encamped 33.37
So you remained at K. many days, Deu 1.46
to the Red Sea and came to K. Ju 11.16
not consent. So Israel remained at K. 11.17
and to K. in the land of the 2Sa 24.06
LORD shakes the wilderness of K. Ps 29.08

KADESHBARNEA
sent them from K. to see the land. Num 32.08
and its end shall be south of K.; 34.04
by the way of Mount Seir to K. Deu 1.02
commanded us; and we came to K. 1.19
our leaving K. until we crossed 2.14
And when the LORD sent you from K., 9.23
defeated them from K. to Gaza, Jos 10.41
man of God in K. concerning you 14.06
sent me from K. to spy out the 14.07
to Zin, and goes up south of K., 15.03

KADMIEL
Levites: the sons of Jeshua and K., Ez 2.40
and K. and his sons, the sons of 3.09
namely of K. of the sons of Hodevah, Neh 7.43

KADMIEL (cont.)
K., Shebaniah, Bunni, Sherebiah, Bani, Neh 9.04
K., Bani, Hashabneiah, Sherebiah, 9.05
Binnui of the sons of Henadad, K.; 10.09
K., Sherebiah, Judah, and Mattaniah, 12.08
Sherebiah, and Jeshua the son of K., 12.24

KADMONITES
Kenites, the Kenizzites, the K., Gen 15.19

KAIN
nevertheless K. shall be wasted. Num 24.22
K., Gibeah, and Timnah: ten cities Jos 15.57

KAIWAN
and K. your star-god, your images, Amo 5.26

KALLAI
of Sallai, K.; of Amok, Eber; Neh 12.20

KAMON
And Jair died, and was buried in K. Ju 10.05

KANAH
goes westward to the brook K., Jos 16.08
went down to the brook of K. 17.09
K., as far as Sidon the Great; 19.28

KAREAH
Nethaniah, and Johanan the son of K., 2Ki 25.23
Nethaniah, Johanan the son of K., Jer 40.08
the son of K. and all the leaders 40.13
the son of K. spoke secretly to 40.15
said to Johanan the son of K., 40.16
the son of K. and all the leaders 41.11
the son of K. and all the leaders 41.13
and went to Johanan the son of K. 41.14
the son of K. and all the leaders 41.16
the son of K. and Azariah the son 42.01
the son of K. and all the commanders 42.08
the son of K. and all the insolent 43.02
the son of K. and all the commanders 43.04
the son of K. and all the commanders 43.05

KARKA
up to Addar, turns about to K., Jos 15.03

KARKOR
Zalmunna were in K. with their army, Ju 8.10

KARNAIM
own strength taken K. for ourselves?" Amo 6.13

KARTAH
lands, K. with its pasture lands, Jos 21.34

KARTAN
and K. with its pasture lands— Jos 21.32

KATTATH
and K., Nahalal, Shimron, Idalah, and Jos 19.15

KEDAR
of Ishmael, and K., Adbeel, Mibsam, Gen 25.13
Nebaioth; and K., Adbeel, Mibsam, 1Ch 1.29
that I dwell among the tents of K.! Ps 120.05
of Jerusalem, like the tents of K., Sol 1.05
the glory of K. will come to an Is 21.16
men of the sons of K. will be few; 21.17
the villages that K. inhabits; 42.11
All the flocks of K. shall be 60.07
or send to K. and examine with care Jer 2.10
Concerning K. and the kingdoms of 49.28
Lord: "Rise up, advance against K.! 49.28
the princes of K. were your Eze 27.21

KEDEMAH
Hadad, Tema, Jetur, Naphish, and K. Gen 25.15
Jetur, Naphish, and K. These are the 1Ch 1.31

KEDEMOTH
wilderness of K. to Sihon the king Deu 2.26
and Jahaz, and K., and Mephaath, Jos 13.18
K. with its pasture lands, and 21.37
K. with its pasture lands, and 1Ch 6.79

KEDESH
the king of K., one; the king of Jos 12.22
K., Hazor, Ithnan, 15.23
K., Edrei, Enhazor, 19.37
So they set apart K. in Galilee in 20.07
K. in Galilee with its pasture 21.32
son of Abinoam from K. in Naphtali, Ju 4.06
arose, and went with Barak to K. 4.09
summoned Zebulun and Naphtali to K.; 4.10
oak in Zaanannim, which is near K. 4.11
K., Hazor, Gilead, and Galilee, all 2Ki 15.29
K. with its pasture lands, Daberath 1Ch 6.72
K. in Galilee with its pasture 6.76

KEEP
of Eden to till it and k. it. Gen 2.15
to k. them alive with you; 6.19
come in to you, to k. them alive. 6.20
to k. their kind alive upon the 7.03
you shall k. my covenant, you and 17.09
is my covenant, which you shall k., 17.10
after him to k. the way of the 18.19
you and will k. you wherever you 28.15
and will k. me in this way that I 28.20
again feed your flock and k. it: 30.31
k. what you have for yourself." 33.09
"Let her k. the things as her own, 38.23
in the cities, and let them k. it. 41.35
and to k. alive for you many 45.07
and you shall k. it until the Ex 12.06
and you shall k. it as a feast to 12.14
promised, you shall k. this service. 12.25
congregation of Israel shall k. it. 12.47
you and would k. the passover to 12.48
then he may come near and k. it; 12.48
you shall k. this service in this 13.05
You shall therefore k. this ordinance 13.10
commandments and k. all his statutes, 15.26
you refuse to k. my commandments 16.28
obey my voice and k. my covenant, 19.05
who love me and k. my commandments 20.06
"Remember the sabbath day, to k. it holy. 20.08
his neighbor money or goods to k., 22.07
ox or a sheep or any beast to k., 22.10
K. far from a false charge, and do 23.07
year you shall k. a feast to me. 23.14
You shall k. the feast of unleavened 23.15
You shall k. the feast of harvest, 23.16
You shall k. the feast of ingathering 23.16
'You shall k. my sabbaths, for this 31.13
You shall k. the sabbath, because it 31.14
of Israel shall k. the sabbath, 31.16
of unleavened bread you shall k. 34.18
"Thus you shall k. the people of Lev 15.31
ordinances and k. my statutes and 18.04
You shall therefore k. my statutes 18.05
But you shall k. my statutes and my 18.26
So k. my charge never to practice 18.30
and you shall k. my sabbaths: I am 19.03
"You shall k. my statutes. You shall not 19.19
You shall k. my sabbaths and reverence 19.30
K. my statutes, and do them; I am the 20.08
"You shall therefore k. all my 20.22
and his sons to k. away from the 22.02
They shall therefore k. my charge, 22.09
"So you shall k. my commandments 22.31
evening shall you k. your sabbath." 23.32
you shall k. the feast of the Lord 23.39
You shall k. it as a feast to the 23.41
you shall k. it in the seventh 23.41
Aaron shall k. it in order from 24.03
He shall k. the lamps in order upon 24.04

KEEP (cont.)
the land shall k. a sabbath to the Lev 25.02
and k. my ordinances and perform 25.18
You shall k. my sabbaths and reverence 26.02
Levites shall k. charge of the Num 1.53
The LORD bless you and k. you: 6.24
to k. the charge, and they shall do 8.26
of Israel k. the passover at its 9.02
you shall k. it at its appointed 9.03
all its ordinances you shall k. it. 9.03
that they should k. the passover. 9.04
they could not k. the passover on 9.06
he shall still k. the passover to 9.10
in the evening they shall k. it; 9.11
for the passover they shall k. it. 9.12
and will k. the passover to the 9.14
and you shall k. a feast to the 29.12
with him, k. alive for yourselves. 31.18
that you may k. the commandments of Deu 4.02
K. them and do them; for that will 4.06
and k. your soul diligently, lest 4.09
Therefore you shall k. his statutes 4.40
who love me and k. my commandments. 5.10
to k. it holy, as the LORD your God 5.12
commanded you to k. the sabbath day. 5.15
fear me and to k. all my commandments, 5.29
diligently k. the commandments of 6.17
love him and k. his commandments, 7.09
and k. and do them, the LORD your 7.12
your God will k. with you the 7.12
he swore to your fathers to k.; 7.12
you would k. his commandments, or 8.02
So you shall k. the commandments of 8.06
and to k. the commandments and 10.13
and k. his charge, his statutes, his 11.01
"You shall therefore k. all the 11.08
and k. his commandments and obey 13.04
and k. the passover to the LORD 16.01
Then you shall k. the feast of 16.10
"You shall k. the feast of booths 16.13
days you shall k. the feast to the 16.15
are careful to k. all this commandment, 19.09
then you shall k. yourself from 23.09
and k. his statutes and his commandments 26.17
that you are to k. all his commandments, 26.18
"K. all the commandment which I command 27.01
"K. silence and hear, O Israel: this 27.09
if you k. the commandments of the 28.09
to k. his commandments and his 28.45
and k. all his commandments which I 30.08
to k. his commandments and his 30.10
But you, k. yourselves from the Jos 6.18
been careful to k. the charge of 22.03
and to k. his commandments, and to 22.05
steadfast to k. and do all that is 23.06
"K. quiet, put your hand upon your Ju 18.19
but k. close to my maidens. Ru 2.08
'You shall k. close by my servants, 2.21
servant used to k. sheep for his 1Sa 17.34
This day I k. showing loyalty to 2Sa 3.08
means not to k. his banished one 14.14
ten concubines to k. the house. 15.16
whom he has left to k. the house; 16.21
have no son to k. my name in 18.18
thou didst k. me as the head of the 22.44
and k. the charge of the LORD your 1Ki 2.03
ordinances and k. all my commandments 6.12
k. with thy servant David my father 8.25
and to k. his commandments, his 8.58
and do not k. my commandments and 9.06
but he did not k. what the LORD 11.10
man to me, and said, 'K. this man; 20.39
and we k. quiet and do not take it 22.03
evil ways and k. my commandments 2Ki 17.13
Judah also did not k. the commandments 17.19
the LORD and to k. his commandments 23.03
"K. the passover to the LORD your 23.21
thou wouldst k. me from harm so 1Ch 4.10
that he did not k. the command of 10.13
Israel you may k. the law of the 22.12
Thus they shall k. charge of the 23.32
k. for ever such purposes and 29.18
heart he may k. thy commandments, 29.19
k. with thy servant David my father 2Ch 6.16
for we k. the charge of the LORD 13.11
and to k. the law and the commandment. 14.04
people shall k. the charge of the 23.06
to k. the passover to the LORD the 30.01
counsel to k. the passover in the 30.02
for they could not k. it in its 30.03
should come and k. the passover to 30.05
in Jerusalem to k. the feast of 30.13
together to k. the feast for 30.23
the LORD and to k. his commandments 34.31
to k. the passover and to offer 35.16
province Beyond the River, k. away; Ez 6.06
Guard them and k. them until you 8.29
love him and k. his commandments; Neh 1.05
to me and k. my commandments and 1.09
that we may eat and k. alive." 5.02
to k. the sabbath day holy. 13.22
and they do not k. the king's laws, Est 3.08
For if you k. silence at such a 4.14
they should k. the fourteenth day 9.21
fail they would k. these two days 9.27
Yet who can k. from speaking? Job 4.02
Oh that you would k. silent, 13.05
wouldest not k. watch over my sin; 14.16
Will you k. to the old way which 22.15
They abhor me, they k. aloof from me; 30.10
He does not k. the wicked alive, but 36.06
cry avail to k. you from distress, 36.19
"I will not k. silence concerning 41.12
I k. the LORD always before me; Ps 16.08
K. me as the apple of the eye; 17.08
K. back thy servant also from 19.13
thou didst k. me safe upon my 22.09
and he who cannot k. himself alive. 22.29
for those who k. his covenant and 25.10
else it will not k. with you. 32.09
and k. them alive in famine. 33.19
K. your tongue from evil, and your 34.13
and k. to his way, and he will exalt 37.34
he does not k. silence, before him 50.03
and you k. company with adulterers. 50.18
because they k. no law, and do not 55.19
whose eyes k. watch on the nations— 66.07
why dost thou k. thy right hand in 74.11
it is I who k. steady its pillars. 75.03
works of God but k. his commandments; 78.07
They did not k. God's covenant, but 78.10
They did not k. in mind his power, 78.42
O God, do not k. silence; do not hold 83.01
love I will k. for him for ever, 89.28
and do not k. my commandments, 89.31
nor will he k. his anger for ever. 103.09
to those who k. his covenant and 103.18
that they should k. his statutes, 105.45
Blessed are those who k. his 119.02
How can a young man k. his way pure? 119.09
and I will k. it to the end. 119.33
that I may k. thy law and observe 119.34
I will k. thy law continually, for 119.44
the night, O LORD, and k. thy law. 119.55
my portion; I promise to k. thy words. 119.57
do not delay to k. thy commandments 119.60
thee, of those who k. thy precepts. 119.63
I went astray; but now I k. thy word. 119.67
my whole heart I k. thy precepts; 119.69
that I may k. the testimonies of 119.88
the aged, for I k. thy precepts. 119.100
evil way, in order to k. thy word. 119.101
that I may k. the commandments of 119.115
K. steady my steps according to thy 119.133
oppression, that I may k. thy precepts. 119.134

KEEP (cont.)
because men do not k. thy law. Ps 119.136
O LORD! I will k. thy statutes. 119.145
because they do not k. thy commands. 119.158
I k. thy precepts and testimonies, 119.168
The LORD will k. you from all evil; 121.07
he will k. your life. 121.07
The LORD will k. your going out and 121.08
If your sons k. my covenant and my 132.12
k. watch over the door of my lips! 141.03
K. me from the trap which they have 141.09
of good men and k. to the paths of Pro 2.20
let your heart k. my commandments; 3.01
My son, k. sound wisdom and discretion; 3.21
and will k. your foot from being 3.26
k. my commandments, and live; 4.04
forsake her, and she will k. you; 4.06
K. hold of instruction, do not let 4.13
your sight; k. them within your heart. 4.21
K. your heart with all vigilance; 4.23
that you may k. discretion, and your 5.02
K. your way far from her, and do not 5.08
My son, k. your father's commandment, 6.20
My son, k. my words and treasure up 7.01
k. my commandments and live, keep my 7.02
k. my teachings as the apple of 7.02
me: happy are those who k. my ways. 8.32
for a man to k. aloof from strife; 20.03
himself will k. far from them. 22.05
of the LORD k. watch over knowledge, 22.12
pleasant if you k. them within you, 22.18
but those who k. the law strive 28.04
desired I did not k. from them; Ecc 2.10
a time to k., and a time to cast 3.06
a time to k. silence, and a time to 3.07
K. the king's command, and because of 8.02
Fear God, and k. his commandments; 12.13
day a man will k. alive a young Is 7.21
the writers who k. writing oppression, 10.01
Thou dost k. him in perfect peace, 26.03
in its place, or k. the sail spread out. 33.23
and k. on praying to a god that 45.20
"K. justice, and do righteousness, 56.01
"To the eunuchs who k. my sabbaths, 56.04
For Zion's sake I will not k. silent, 62.01
Wilt thou k. silent, and afflict us 64.12
who, say, "K. to yourself, do not come 65.05
"I will not k. silent, but I will 65.06
K. your feet from going unshod and Jer 2.25
I cannot k. silent; for I hear 4.19
and crane k. the time of their 8.07
the LORD, you k. going backward; 15.06
but k. the sabbath day holy, as I 17.22
but k. the sabbath day holy and do 17.24
to k. the sabbath day holy, and not 17.27
and will k. him as a shepherd keeps 31.10
"K. your voice from weeping, and 31.16
and did not k. the terms of the 34.18
I will k. nothing back from you." 42.04
children, I will k. them alive; 49.11
he will k. you in exile no longer; Lam 4.22
my statutes and k. my ordinances Eze 11.20
and k. other souls alive for your 13.18
in the land of Israel k. saying, 33.24
"Be ready and k. ready, you and all 38.07
foreigners to k. my charge in my 44.08
appoint them to k. charge of the 44.14
to me, and they shall k. my charge. 44.16
They shall k. my laws and my 44.24
and they shall k. my sabbaths holy. 44.24
his sons may k. a gift from his 46.17
love him and k. his commandments, Dan 9.04
is prudent will k. silent in such Amo 5.13
K. your feasts, O Judah, fulfil your Nah 1.15
Is he then to k. on emptying his Hab 1.17
all the earth k. silence before 2.20
walk in my ways and k. my charge, Zec 3.07
my wages; but if not, k. them." 11.12
and to k. the feast of booths. 14.16
do not go up to k. the feast of 14.18
do not go up to k. the feast of 14.19
enter life, k. the commandments." Mt 19.17
I will k. the passover at your 26.18
satisfy him and k. you out of 28.14
God, in order to k. your tradition! Mk 7.09
who hear the word of God and k. it!" Lk 11.28
I do know him and I k. his word. Jn 8.55
for he does not k. the sabbath." 9.16
long will you k. us in suspense? 10.24
let her k. it for the day of my 12.07
this world will k. it for eternal 12.25
my sayings and does not k. them, 12.47
you will k. my commandments. 14.15
he will k. my word, and my Father 14.23
not love me does not k. my words; 14.24
If you k. my commandments, you will 15.10
my word, they will k. yours also. 15.20
this to you to k. you from falling 16.01
Holy Father, k. them in thy name 17.11
thou shouldst k. them from the 17.15
Spirit and to k. back part of the Ac 5.03
k. away from these men and let them 5.38
by angels and did not k. it." 7.53
charge them to k. the law of Moses." 15.05
If you k. yourselves from these, you 15.29
the jailer to k. them safely. 16.23
uncircumcised but k. the law will Rom 2.27
k. between yourself and God; 14.22
to k. her as his betrothed, he will 1Co 7.37
each of them k. silence in church 14.28
the women should k. silence in the 14.34
to k. Satan from gaining the 2Co 2.11
to k. them from seeing the light of 4.04
but will k. to the limits God has 10.13
And to k. me from being too elated 12.07
he is bound to k. the whole law. Gal 5.03
do not themselves k. the law, 6.13
To that end k. alert with all Eph 6.18
will k. your hearts and your minds Php 4.07
but let us k. awake and be sober. 1Th 5.06
that you k. away from any brother 2Th 3.06
over men; she is to k. silent. 1Ti 2.12
I charge you to k. these rules 5.21
man's sins; k. yourself pure. 5.22
I charge you to k. the commandment 6.14
have been glad to k. him with me, Phm 1.13
who have faith and k. their souls. Heb 10.39
K. your life free from love of 13.05
and to k. oneself unstained from Jas 1.27
let him k. his tongue from evil and 1Pe 3.10
and k. your conscience clear, so 3.16
therefore k. sane and sober for 4.07
they k. you from being ineffective 2Pe 1.08
and to k. the unrighteous under 2.09
we know him, if we k. his commandments. 1Jn 2.03
because we k. his commandments and 3.22
All who k. his commandments abide 3.24
love of God, that we k. his commandments. 5.03
k. yourselves from idols. 5.21
that did not k. their own position Jud 1.06
k. yourselves in the love of God; 1.21
who is able to k. you from falling 1.24
and who k. what is written therein; Rev 1.03
k. that, and repent. If you will not 3.03
I will k. you from the hour of 3.10
you and to k. the shame of your 3.18
on those who k. the commandments of 12.17
those who k. the commandments of 14.12
with those who k. the words of 22.09

KEEPER
Now Abel was a k. of sheep, Gen 4.02
"I do not know; am I my brother's k.?" 4.09
the sight of the k. of the prison. 39.21
And the k. of the prison committed 39.22

KEEPER (cont.)
the k. of the prison paid no heed Gen 39.23
and left the sheep with a k., 1Sa 17.20
in charge of the k. of the baggage, 17.22
k. of the wardrobe (now she dwelt 2Ki 22.14
k. of the east gate, was over the 2Ch 31.14
k. of the wardrobe (now she dwelt 34.22
the k. of the king's forest, that he Neh 2.08
the k. of the East Gate, repaired. 3.29
The LORD is your k.; the LORD is your Ps 121.05
they made me k. of the vineyards; Sol 1.06
I, the LORD, am its k.; every Is 27.03
of Shallum, k. of the threshold. Jer 35.04
is temple k. of the great Artemis, Ac 19.35

KEEPERS
for they have been k. of cattle; Gen 46.32
have been k. of cattle from our 46.34
which the k. of the threshold have 2Ki 22.04
and the k. of the threshold, to 23.04
and the three k. of the threshold; 25.18
k. of the thresholds of the tent, as 1Ch 9.19
of the LORD, k. of the entrance. 9.19
the k. of the threshold, had collected 2Ch 34.09
day when the k. of the house Ecc 12.03
he let out the vineyard to k.; Sol 8.11
and the k. of the fruit two hundred 8.12
Like k. of a field are they against Jer 4.17
and the three k. of the threshold; 52.24

KEEPEST
who k. covenant and steadfast love, Neh 9.32
who k. covenant and steadfast love Dan 9.04

KEEPING
Now Moses was k. the flock of his Ex 3.01
k. steadfast love for thousands, 34.07
yet refrains from k. the passover, Num 9.13
by k. all his statutes and his Deu 6.02
and is k. the oath which he swore 7.08
by not k. his commandments and his 8.11
k. all his commandments which I 13.18
by k. all the words of this law and 17.19
k. his commandments and his statutes, 27.10
and by k. his commandments and his 30.16
but behold, he is k. the sheep. 1Sa 16.11
we were with them k. the sheep. 25.16
in his ways and k. his statutes, 1Ki 2.03
k. my statutes and my commandments, 3.14
k. covenant and showing steadfast 8.23
statutes and k. his commandments, 8.61
and k. my statutes and my ordinances, 9.04
in my sight and k. my statutes and 11.33
in my eyes by k. my statutes and 11.38
resolute in k. my commandments and 1Ch 28.07
k. covenant and showing steadfast 2Ch 6.14
commanded you and k. my statutes 7.17
faithful in k. themselves holy. 31.18
in k. them there is great reward. Ps 19.11
thanksgiving, a multitude k. festival. 42.04
be steadfast in k. thy statutes! 119.05
k. watch on the evil and the good. Pro 15.03
not die and k. alive persons who Eze 13.19
and that by k. his covenant it 17.14
the good of our k. his charge or Mal 3.14
k. watch over Jesus, saw the earthquake Mt 27.54
k. watch over their flock by night. Lk 2.08
has a servant plowing or k. sheep, 17.07
I was k. the ninth hour of prayer Ac 10.30
and k. the garments of those who 22.20
but k. the commandments of God. 1Co 7.19
k. his children submissive and 1Ti 3.04
for they are k. watch over your Heb 13.17
k. his garments that he may not go Rev 16.15

KEEPS
man does not die but k. his bed, Ex 21.18
faithful God who k. covenant and Deu 7.09
terrible God who k. covenant and Neh 1.05
he k. back his soul from the Pit, Job 33.18
He k. all his bones; not one of them Ps 34.20
LORD protects him and k. him alive; 41.02
therefore my soul k. them. 119.129
My soul k. thy testimonies; 119.167
he who k. you will not slumber. 121.03
Behold, he who k. Israel will 121.04
is in them; who k. faith for ever; 146.06
the blameless k. his way straight, Pro 11.05
in spirit k. a thing hidden. 11.13
Even a fool who k. silent is 17.28
he who k. understanding will 19.08
He who k. the commandment k. his life; 19.16
He who k. his mouth and his tongue k. 21.23
Does not he who k. watch over your 24.12
He who k. the law is a wise son, but 28.07
but one who k. company with harlots 29.03
but blessed is he who k. the law. 29.18
because God k. him occupied with Ecc 5.20
nation which k. faith may enter in Is 26.02
who k. the sabbath, not profaning it, 56.02
and k. his hand from doing any evil 56.02
every one who k. the sabbath, and 56.06
and k. for us the weeks appointed Jer 5.24
As a well k. its water fresh, so she k. 6.07
him as a shepherd k. his flock. 31.10
is he who k. back his sword from 48.10
committed and k. all my statutes Eze 18.21
adversaries and k. wrath for his Nah 1.02
Yet none of you k. the law. Jn 7.19
if any one k. my word, he will never 8.51
'If any one k. my word, he will 8.52
has my commandments and k. them, 14.21
uncircumcised k. the precepts of Rom 2.26
For whoever k. the whole law but Jas 2.10
but whoever k. his word, in him 1Jn 2.05
but He who was born of God k. him, 5.18
conquers and who k. my works until Rev 2.26
is he who k. the words of the 22.07

KEHELATHAH
from Rissah, and encamped at K. Num 33.22
And they set out from K., 33.23

KEILAH
K., Achzib, and Mareshah: nine cities Jos 15.44
Philistines are fighting against K., 1Sa 23.01
attack the Philistines and save K. 23.02
if we go to K. against the armies 23.03
answered him, "Arise, go down to K.; 23.04
And David and his men went to K., 23.05
delivered the inhabitants of K. 23.05
of Ahimelech fled to David to K., 23.06
Saul that David had come to K. 23.07
to go down to K., to besiege David 23.08
that Saul seeks to come to K., 23.10
Will the men of K. surrender me 23.11
"Will the men of K. surrender me 23.12
hundred, arose and departed from K., 23.13
that David had escaped from K., 23.13
the fathers of K. the Garmite and 1Ch 4.19
ruler of half the district of K., Neh 3.17
ruler of half the district of K.; 3.18

KELAIAH
K. (that is, Kelita), Pethahiah, Judah, Ez 10.23

KELITA
K.), Pethahiah, Judah, and Eliezer. Ez 10.23
K., Azariah, Jozabad, Hanan, Pelaiah, Neh 8.07
Hodiah, K., Pelaiah, Hanan, 10.10

KEMUEL
his brother, K. the father of Aram, Gen 22.21
a leader, K. the son of Shiphtan. Num 34.24
for Levi, Hashabiah the son of K.; 1Ch 27.17

KENAN
years, he became the father of K. Gen 5.09
the birth of K. eight hundred and 5.10
When K. had lived seventy years, he 5.12
K. lived after the birth of Mahalalel 5.13
Thus all the days of K. were nine 5.14
K., Mahalalel, Jared; 1Ch 1.02

KENATH
went and took K. and its villages, Num 32.42
K. and its villages, sixty towns. 1Ch 2.23

KENAZ
Teman, Omar, Zepho, Gatam, and K. Gen 36.11
the chiefs Teman, Omar, Zepho, K., 36.15
K., Teman, Mibzar, 36.42
And Othniel the son of K., the brother Jos 15.17
And Othniel the son of K., Caleb's Ju 1.13
them, Othniel the son of K., 3.09
Then Othniel the son of K. died. 3.11
Gatam, K., Timma, and Amalek. 1Ch 1.36
K., Teman, Mibzar, 1.53
The sons of K.: Othniel and Seraiah; 4.13
and Naam; and the sons of Elah: K. 4.15

KENITE
And he looked on the K., and took up Num 24.21
And the descendants of the K., Ju 1.16
Now Heber the K. had separated from 4.11
of Jael, the wife of Heber the K.; 4.17
and the house of Heber the K. 4.17
be Jael, the wife of Heber the K., 5.24

KENITES
the land of the K., the Kenizzites, Gen 15.19
Kenite had separated from the K., Ju 4.11
And Saul said to the K., "Go, depart, 1Sa 15.06
So the K. departed from among the 15.06
or, "Against the Negeb of the K." 27.10
Jerahmeelites, in the cities of the K., 30.29
These are the K. who came from 1Ch 2.55

KENIZZITE
Jephunneh the K. and Joshua the Num 32.12
of Jephunneh the K. said to him, Jos 14.06
of Jephunneh the K. to this day, 14.14

KENIZZITES
the Kenites, the K., the Kadmonites, Gen 15.19

KEPT
it was I who k. you from sinning Gen 20.06
obeyed my voice and k. my charge, 26.05
father's sheep; for she k. them. 29.09
but his father k. the saying in 37.11
nor has he k. back anything from me 39.09
many people should be k. alive, 50.20
of watching k. to the LORD by all Ex 12.42
lay by to be k. till the morning. 16.23
omer of it be k. throughout your 16.32
to be k. throughout your generations." 16.33
it before the Testimony, to be k. 16.34
been warned but has not k. it in, 21.29
and its owner has not k. it in, 21.36
They still k. bringing him freewill 36.03
altar shall be k. burning on it. Lev 6.09
altar shall be k. burning on it, 6.12
Fire shall be k. burning upon the 6.13
a light may be k. burning continually. 24.02
And you shall eat old store long k., 26.10
And they k. the passover in the Num 9.05
why are we k. from offering the 9.07
of Israel k. the charge of the 9.19
they k. the charge of the LORD, at 9.23
to be k. as a sign for the rebels, 17.10
you whatever is k. of the offerings 18.08
they shall be k. for the congregation 19.09
he k. him as the apple of his eye. Deu 32.10
thy word, and k. thy covenant. 33.09
in Gilgal they k. the passover on Jos 5.10
the LORD has k. me alive, as he said, 14.10
"You have k. all that Moses the 22.02
and travelers k. to the byways. Ju 5.06
They k. quiet all night, saying, "Let 16.02
So she k. close to the maidens of Ru 2.23
what was k. is set before you. 1Sa 9.24
because it was k. for you until the 9.24
you have not k. the commandment of 13.13
you have not k. what the LORD 13.14
young men have k. themselves from 21.04
women have been k. from us as 21.05
who have k. me this day from 25.33
and has k. back his servant from 25.39
have you not k. watch over your 26.15
you have not k. watch over your 26.16
young man who k. the watch lifted 2Sa 13.34
people with Absalom k. increasing. 15.12
For I have k. the ways of the LORD, 22.22
and I k. myself from guilt. 22.24
have you not k. your oath to the 1Ki 2.43
and thou hast k. for him this great 3.06
who hast k. with thy servant David 8.24
you have not k. my covenant and my 11.11
who k. my commandments and my 11.34
and have not k. the commandment 13.21
who k. my commandments, and followed 14.08
who k. the door of the king's house. 14.27
but k. the commandments which the 2Ki 18.06
had been k. since the days of the 23.22
passover was k. to the LORD in 23.23
and they k. a genealogical record. 1Ch 4.33
day to day men k. coming to David 12.22
had hitherto k. their allegiance 12.29
who hast k. with thy servant David 2Ch 6.15
for they had k. the dedication of 7.09
who k. the door of the king's house. 12.10
they had not k. it in great 30.05
at Jerusalem k. the feast of 30.21
so they k. it for another seven 30.23
have not k. the word of the LORD, 34.21
Josiah k. a passover to the LORD in 35.01
were present k. the passover at 35.17
it had been k. in Israel since the 35.18
of Israel had k. such a passover 35.18
a passover as was k. by Josiah, 35.18
of Josiah this passover was k. 35.19
but they k. mocking the messengers 36.16
that it lay desolate it k. sabbath, 36.21
And they k. the feast of booths, as Ez 3.04
returned exiles k. the passover. 6.19
And they k. the feast of unleavened 6.22
and have not k. the commandments, Neh 1.07
each k. his weapon in his hand. 4.23
They k. the feast seven days; 8.18
have not k. thy law or heeded thy 9.34
who k. watch at the gates, were a 11.19
remembered and k. throughout every Est 9.28
grave, watch is k. over his tomb. Job 21.32
I have k. his way and have not 23.11
of judgment k. by the Almighty, and 24.01
and k. silence for my counsel. 29.21
so that I k. silence, and did not go 31.34
For I have k. the ways of the LORD, Ps 18.21
and I k. myself from guilt. 18.23
Thou hast k. count of my tossings; 56.08
who has k. us among the living, and 66.09
All in vain have I k. my heart 73.13
they k. his testimonies, and the 99.07
I k. my faith, even when I said, "I 116.10
thy precepts to be k. diligently. 119.04
for I have k. thy testimonies. 119.22
to me, that I have k. thy precepts. 119.56
I k. my heart from no pleasure, for Ecc 2.10
riches were k. by their owner to 5.13
but, my own vineyard I have not k.! Sol 1.06
the night when a holy feast is k.; Is 30.29

KEPT (cont.)
taken you by the hand and k. you; Is 42.06
I have k. still and restrained 42.14
I have k. you and given you as a 49.08
your sins have k. good from you. Jer 5.25
forsaken me and have not k. my law, 16.11
to drink no wine, has been k.; 35.14
of Rechab have k. the command 35.16
and k. all his precepts, and done 35.18
in my statutes or k. my ordinances, Eze 5.07
And you have not k. charge of my 44.08
who k. the charge of my sanctuary 44.15
who k. my charge, who did not go 48.11
and whom he would he k. alive; Dan 5.19
but I k. the matter in my mind. 7.28
Therefore the LORD has k. ready the 9.14
they k. sacrificing to the Baals, Hos 11.02
bound up, his sin is k. in store. 13.12
and he k. his wrath for ever. Amo 1.11
and have not k. his statutes, but 2.04
For you have k. the statutes of Mic 6.16
as you have not k. my ways but Mal 2.09
my statutes and have not k. them. 3.07
sat down and k. watch over him Mt 27.36
and holy man, and k. him safe. Mk 6.20
So they k. the matter to themselves, 9.10
But Mary k. all these things, Lk 2.19
and his mother k. all these things 2.51
and would have k. him from leaving 4.42
he was k. under guard, and bound 8.29
were heavy with sleep but k. awake, 9.32
And they k. silence and told no one 9.36
that city who k. coming to him and 18.03
which I k. laid away in a napkin; 19.20
But their eyes were k. from recognizing 24.16
but you have k. the good wine until Jn 2.10
blind man have k. this man from 11.37
just as I have k. my Father's 15.10
if they k. my word, they will keep 15.20
to me, and they have k. thy word. 17.06
I k. them in thy name which thou 17.12
spoke to the maid who k. the door, 18.16
The maid who k. the door said to 18.17
knowledge he k. back some of the Ac 5.02
that they might not be k. alive. 7.19
So Peter was k. in prison; 12.05
And all the assembly k. silence; 15.12
he should be k. in custody but 24.23
that Paul was being k. at Caesarea, 25.04
appealed to be k. in custody for 25.21
k. them from carrying out their 27.43
"I have k. for myself seven thousand Rom 11.04
which was k. secret for long ages 16.25
k. under restraint until faith Gal 3.23
and body be k. sound and blameless 1Th 5.23
the race, I have k. the faith. 2Ti 4.07
By faith he k. the Passover and Heb 11.28
which you k. back by fraud, cry out; Jas 5.04
k. in heaven for you, 1Pe 1.04
gloom to be k. until the judgment; 2Pe 2.04
being k. until the day of judgment 3.07
the Father and k. for Jesus Christ: Jud 1.01
have been k. by him in eternal 1.06
yet you have k. my word and have Rev 3.08
Because you have k. my word of 3.10
of the day was k. from shining, 8.12

KERENHAPPUCH
and the name of the third K. Job 42.14

KERIOTH
and K., and Bozrah, and all the Jer 48.24
shall devour the strongholds of K., Amo 2.02

KERIOTHHEZRON
Hazorhadattah, K. (that is, Hazor), Jos 15.25

KERNEL
but a bare k., perhaps of wheat or 1Co 15.37

KEROS
the sons of K., the sons of Siaha, Ez 2.44
the sons of K., the sons of Sia, the Neh 7.47

KETTLE
or k., or cauldron, or pot; 1Sa 2.14
and chop them up like meat in a k., Mic 3.03

KETURAH
another wife, whose name was K. Gen 25.01
all these were the children of K. 25.04
The sons of K., Abraham's concubine: 1Ch 1.32
these were the descendants of K. 1.33

KEY
they took the k. and opened them; Ju 3.25
shoulder the k. of the house of Is 22.22
taken away the k. of knowledge; Lk 11.52
who has the k. of David, who opens Rev 3.07
was given the k. of the shaft of 9.01
in his hand the k. of the bottomless 20.01

KEYS
give you the k. of the kingdom of Mt 16.19
and I have the k. of Death and Rev 1.18

KEZIAH
and the name of the second K.; Job 42.14

KIBROTHHATTAAVAH
name of that place was called K., Num 11.34
From K. the people journeyed to 11.35
of Sinai, and encamped at K. 33.16
And they set out from K., 33.17
and at K., you provoked the LORD to Deu 9.22

KIBZAIM
K. with its pasture lands, Bethhoron Jos 21.22

KICK
It hurts you to k. against the Ac 26.14

KICKED
"But Jeshurun waxed fat, and k.; Deu 32.15

KID
will send you a k. from the flock." Gen 38.17
When Judah sent the k. by his 38.20
I sent this k., and you could not 38.23
not boil a k. in its mother's milk. Ex 23.19
not boil a k. in its mother's milk." 34.26
not boil a k. in its mother's milk. Deu 14.21
into his house and prepared a k., Ju 6.19
you, and prepare a k. for you. 13.15
So Manoah took the k. with the 13.19
the lion asunder as one tears a k.; 14.06
went to visit his wife with a k.; 15.01
bread, and a skin of wine and a k., 1Sa 16.20
leopard shall lie down with the k., Is 11.06
yet you never gave me a k., Lk 15.29

KIDNAPERS
k., liars, perjurers, and whatever 1Ti 1.10

KIDNEYS
and the two k. with the fat that is Ex 29.13
and the two k. with the fat that is 29.22
and the two k. with the fat that is Lev 3.04
he shall take away with the k. 3.04
and the two k. with the fat that is 3.10
he shall take away with the k. 3.10
and the two k. with the fat that is 3.15
he shall take away with the k. 3.15
and the two k. with the fat that is 4.09
he shall take away with the k. 4.09
the two k. with the fat that is on 7.04
he shall take away with the k.; 7.04
and the two k. with their fat, and 8.16
and the two k. with their fat, and 8.25

KIDNEYS (cont.)
but the fat and the k. and the Lev 9.10
and the k., and the appendage of 9.19
He slashes open my k., and does not Job 16.13
with the fat of the k. of rams. Is 34.06

KIDRON
and the king crossed the brook K., 2Sa 15.23
go forth, and cross the brook K., 1Ki 2.37
and burned it at the brook K. 15.13
Jerusalem in the fields of the K., 2Ki 23.04
brook K., and burned it at the brook K., 23.06
the dust of them into the brook K. 23.12
it, and burned it at the brook K. 2Ch 15.16
and carried it out to the brook K. 29.16
away and threw into the K. valley. 30.14
the fields as far as the brook K., Jer 31.40
his disciples across the K. valley, Jn 18.01

KIDS
flock, and fetch me two good k., Gen 27.09
skins of the k. she put upon his 27.16
each of the male lambs or the k. Num 15.11
you there, one carrying three k., 1Sa 10.03
lambs and k. from the flock to the 2Ch 35.07
lambs and k. and three hundred 35.08
lambs and k. and five hundred 35.09
pasture your k. beside the shepherds' Sol 1.08
fatlings and k. shall feed among Is 5.17

KILL
who came upon him should k. him. Gen 4.15
then they will k. me. but they will 12.12
and they will k. me because of my 20.11
place should k. me for the sake of 26.07
then I will k. my brother Jacob." 27.41
himself by planning to k. you. 27.42
conspired against him to k. him. 37.18
let us k. him and throw him into 37.20
if it is a son, you shall k. him; Ex 1.16
Do you mean to k. me as you killed 2.14
heard of it, he sought to k. Moses. 2.15
LORD met him and sought to k. him. 4.24
put a sword in their hand to k. us. 5.21
of Israel shall k. their lambs in 12.06
and k. the passover lamb. 12.21
wilderness to k. this whole 16.03
to k. us and our children and our 17.03
"You shall not k. 20.13
another to k. him treacherously, 21.14
and I will k. you with the sword, 22.24
and you shall k. the bull before 29.11
and you shall k. the ram, and take 29.20
Then he shall k. the bull before Lev 1.05
and he shall k. it on the north 1.11
offering and k. it at the door of 3.02
and k. it before the tent of 3.13
and k. the bull before the LORD. 4.04
and k. it in the place where they 4.24
where they k. the burnt offering 4.24
and k. the sin offering in the 4.29
and k. it for a sin offering in the 4.33
where they k. the burnt offering. 4.33
where they k. the burnt offering 7.02
they shall k. the guilt offering, 7.02
command them to k. one of the 14.05
and he shall k. the lamb in the 14.13
where they k. the sin offering and 14.13
he shall k. the burnt offering; 14.19
And he shall k. the lamb of the 14.25
and shall k. one of the birds in an 14.50
he shall k. the bull as a sin 16.11
"Then he shall k. the goat of the 16.15
and you shall k. the beast. 20.15
you shall k. the woman and the 20.16
you shall not k. both her and her 22.28
k. me at once, if I find favor in Num 11.15
Now if thou dost k. this people as 14.15
to k. us in the wilderness, that you 16.13
my hand, for then I would k. you." 22.29
Now therefore, k. every male among 31.17
and k. every woman who has known 31.17
'You shall not k. Deu 5.17
then you may k. any of your herd or 12.21
but you shall k. him; your hand 13.09
I k. and I make alive; I wound and 32.39
people of Israel did not k. them, Jos 9.18
of Israel; and they did not k. them. 9.26
to him, "draw your sword and k. me, Ju 9.54
"If the LORD had meant to k. us, 13.23
into their hands; we will not k. you." 15.13
the morning; then we will k. him." 16.02
night; they meant to k. me, and they 20.05
to smite and k. some of the people, 20.31
to smite and k. about thirty men 20.39
but k. both man and woman, infant 1Sa 15.03
If Saul hears it, he will k. me." 16.02
is able to fight with me and k. me, 17.09
I prevail against him and k. him, 17.09
servants, that they should k. David. 19.01
"Saul my father seeks to k. you; 19.02
that he might k. him in the morning 19.11
me in the bed, that I may k. him." 19.15
'Let me go; why should I k. you?'" 19.17
"Turn and k. the priests of the 22.17
and some bade me k. you, but I 24.10
and did not k. you, you may know and 24.11
you did not k. me when the LORD 24.18
me by God, that you will not k. me, 30.15
you, 'Strike Amnon,' then k. him. 2Sa 13.28
that we may k. him for the life of 14.07
is guilt in me, let him k. me.'" 14.32
a new sword, thought to k. David. 21.16
Solomon sought therefore to k. Jeroboam; 1Ki 11.40
and they will k. me and return to 12.27
into the hand of Ahab, to k. me? 18.09
he will k. me, although I your 18.12
Elijah is here"'; and he will k. me." 18.14
gone from me, a lion shall k. you." 20.36
to k. and to make alive, that this 2Ki 5.07
and if they k. us we shall but die." 7.04
Levites had to k. the passover lamb 2Ch 30.17
And k. the passover, and sanctify 35.06
of them and k. them and stop the Neh 4.11
for they are coming to k. you, 6.10
at night they are coming to k. you." 6.10
the tongue of a viper will k. him. Job 20.16
that he may k. the poor and needy; 24.14
a time to k., and a time to heal; Ecc 3.03
but I will k. your root with famine, Is 14.30
because he did not k. me in the womb; Jer 20.17
"Do not k. us, for we have stores of 41.08
and did not k. them with their 41.08
that they may k. us or take us into 43.03
the men of old, 'You shall not k.; Mt 5.21
fear those who k. the body but 10.28
the body but cannot k. the soul; 10.28
and they will k. him, and he will be 17.23
and Jesus said, "You shall not k. 19.18
come, let us k. him and have his 21.38
of whom you will k. and crucify, 23.34
arrest Jesus by stealth and k. him. 26.04
to do harm, to save life or to k.?" Mk 3.04
against him, and wanted to k. him. 6.19
hands of men, and they will k. him; 9.31
'Do not k., Do not commit adultery, 10.19
him, and scourge him, and k. him; 10.34
come, let us k. him, and the inheritance 12.07
arrest him by stealth, and k. him; 14.01
of whom they will k. and persecute, Lk 11.49
do not fear those who k. the body, 12.04
here, for Herod wants to k. you." 13.31
and bring the fatted calf and k. it, 15.23
Do not k., Do not steal, Do not bear 18.20
they will scourge him and k. him, 18.33
let us k. him, that the inheritance 20.14

KILL (cont.)
Jews sought all the more to k. him, Jn 5.18
because the Jews sought to k. him. 7.01
the law. Why do you seek to k. me?" 7.19
a demon! Who is seeking to k. you?" 7.20
this the man whom they seek to k.? 7.25
"Will he k. himself, since he says, 8.22
yet you seek to k. me, because my 8.37
but now you seek to k. me, a man who 8.40
only to steal and k. and destroy; 10.10
were enraged and wanted to k. them. Ac 5.33
Do you want to k. me as you killed 7.28
passed, the Jews plotted to k. him, 9.23
the gates day and night, to k. him; 9.24
but they were seeking to k. him. 9.29
to him. "Rise, Peter; k. and eat." 10.13
to me, 'Rise, Peter; k. and eat.' 11.07
sword and was about to k. himself, 16.27
And as they were trying to k. him, 21.31
we are ready to k. him before he 23.15
an ambush to k. him on the way. 25.03
in the temple and tried to k. me. 26.21
plan was to k. the prisoners, 27.42
You shall not k., You shall not Rom 13.09
adultery," said also, "Do not k." Jas 2.11
do not commit adultery but do k., 2.11
desire and do not have; so you k. 4.02
to k. with sword and with famine Rev 6.08
but not to k. them, and their 9.05
the year, to k. a third of mankind. 9.15
them and conquer them and k. them, 11.07

KILLED
his brother Abel, and k. him. Gen 4.08
unawares, and k. all the males. 34.25
and k. a goat, and dipped the robe 37.31
no one he k. the Egyptian and hid Ex 2.12
to kill me as you k. the Egyptian?" 2.14
bull shall be k. before the LORD. Lev 4.15
offering is k. shall the sin 6.25
sin offering be k. before the LORD; 6.25
And Moses k. it, and took the blood, 8.15
And Moses k. it, and threw the blood 8.19
And Moses k. it, and took some of 8.23
and k. the calf of the sin offering, 9.08
And he k. the burnt offering; 9.12
and k. it, and offered it for sin, 9.15
He k. the ox also and the ram, the 9.18
bird that was k. over the running 14.06
blood of the bird that was k. and in 14.51
"You have k. the people of the LORD." Num 16.41
whoever of you has k. any person, 31.19
and it is not known who k. him, Deu 21.01
and the men of Ai k. about thirty-six Jos 7.05
men of Israel k. with the sword. 10.11
of Israel k. with the sword among 13.22
because he k. his neighbor unwittingly, 20.05
any one who k. a person without 20.09
And they k. at that time about ten Ju 3.29
who k. six hundred of the Philistines 3.31
they k. Oreb at the rock of Oreb, 7.25
and Zeeb they k. at the wine press 7.25
and k. the people that were in it; 9.45
men say of me, 'A woman k. him.'" 9.54
to Ashkelon and k. thirty men of 14.19
his armor-bearer k. them after him; 1Sa 14.13
beard, and smote him and k. him. 17.35
Your servant has k. both lions and 17.36
struck the Philistine, and k. him; 17.50
and k. him, and cut off his head 17.51
and k. two hundred of the Philistines 18.27
tonight, tomorrow you will be k." 19.11
whom you k. in the valley of Elah, 21.09
and he k. on that day eighty-five 22.18
that Saul had k. the priests of 22.21
that I have k. for my shearers, and 25.11
the house, and she quickly k. it, 28.24
they k. no one, but carried them off, 30.02
because he had k. their brother 2Sa 3.30
and they k. them, and cut off their 4.12
Who k. Abimelech the son of Jerubbesheth? 11.21
that they have k. all the young 13.32
one struck the other and k. him. 14.06
Absalom and struck him, and k. him. 18.15
the Philistines k. Saul on Gilboa; 21.12
attacked the Philistine and k. him. 21.17
up, and struck him down and k. him; 1Ki 2.34
met him on the road and k. him. 13.24
So Baasha k. him in the third year 15.28
he k. all the house of Jeroboam; 15.29
in and struck him down and k. him, 16.10
he k. all the house of Baasha; 16.11
conspired, and he has k. the king"; 16.16
when Jezebel k. the prophets of 18.13
brook Kishon, and k. them there. 18.40
And each k. his man; the Syrians fled 20.20
and k. the Syrians with a great 20.21
him, a lion met him and k. him. 20.36
"Have you k., and also taken 21.19
in his hand he k. his servants who 2Ki 14.05
He k. ten thousand Edomites in the 14.07
and k. him, and reigned in his stead. 15.10
captive to Kir, and he k. Rezin. 16.09
among them, which k. some of them. 17.25
and k. the king in his house. 21.23
attacked and k. Gedaliah and the 25.25
and k. also Shophach the commander 1Ch 19.18
And Ahab k. an abundance of sheep 2Ch 18.02
and also you have k. your brothers, 21.13
attended Ahaziah, and he k. them. 22.08
had shown him, but k. his son. 24.22
in his hand he k. his servants who 25.03
and k. three thousand people in 25.13
So they k. the bulls, and the 29.22
and they k. the rams and their 29.22
and they k. the lambs and their 29.22
and the priests k. them and made a 29.24
And they k. the passover lamb on 30.15
against him and k. him in his 33.24
and they k. the passover lamb on 35.01
And they k. the passover lamb, and 35.11
So they k. the passover lamb for Ez 6.20
their back and k. thy prophets, Neh 9.26
For the simple are k. by their Pro 1.32
and k. him, whom the king of Babylon Jer 41.02
and he sent and k. all the male Mt 2.16
and be k., and on the third day be 16.21
k. another, and stoned another, 21.35
out of the vineyard, and k. him. 21.39
my oxen and my fat calves are k., 22.04
them shamefully, and k. them. 22.06
and be k., and after three days Mk 8.31
and when he is k., after three days 9.31
And he sent another, and him they k.; 12.05
some they beat and some they k. 12.05
And they took him and k. him, 12.08
and be k., and on the third day be Lk 9.22
the prophets whom your fathers k. 11.47
for they k. them, and you build 11.48
after he has k., has power to cast 12.05
tower in Siloam fell and k. them, 13.04
your father has k. the fatted calf, 15.27
you k. for him the fatted calf!' 15.30
him out of the vineyard and k. him. 20.15
crucified and k. by the hands of Ac 2.23
and k. the Author of life, whom God 3.15
Jesus whom you k. by hanging him 5.30
kill me as you k. the Egyptian 7.28
And they k. those who announced 7.52
He k. James the brother of John 12.02
they asked Pilate to have him k. 13.28
the garments of those who k. him.' 22.20
nor drink till they had k. Paul. 23.12
taste no food till we have k. Paul. 23.14
nor drink till they have k. him; 23.21
and was about to be k. by them, 23.27

KILLED (cont.)
deceived me and by it k. me. Rom 7.11
we are being k. all the day long; 8.36
they have k. thy prophets, they have 11.03
as punished, and yet not k.; 2Co 6.09
who k. both the Lord Jesus and the 1Th 2.15
two, they were k. with the sword; Heb 11.37
you have k. the righteous man; Jas 5.06
instinct, born to be caught and k., 2Pe 2.12
who was k. among you, where Satan Rev 2.13
who were to be k. as they themselves 6.11
plagues a third of mankind was k., 9.18
who were not k. by these plagues, 9.20
them, thus he is doomed to be k. 11.05
people were k. in the earthquake, 11.13

KILLING
offering and k. it before the tent Lev 3.08
his father in k. his seventy Ju 9.56
blood by k. David without cause? 1Sa 19.05
they are k. them, because they do 2Ki 17.26
gladness, slaying oxen and k. sheep, Is 22.13
k., stealing, and committing adultery; Hos 4.02
k. the prophets and stoning those Mt 23.37
k. the prophets and stoning those Lk 13.34

KILLS
and it k. a man or a woman, the ox Ex 21.29
and k. it or sells it, he shall pay 22.01
house of Israel k. an ox or a lamb Lev 17.03
or k. it outside the camp, 17.03
He who k. a man shall be put to 24.17
He who k. a beast shall make it 24.18
He who k. a beast shall make it 24.21
and he who k. a man shall be put to 24.21
manslayer who k. any person Num 35.11
any one who k. any person without 35.15
If any one k. a person, the murderer 35.30
who k. his neighbor unintentionally, Deu 4.42
If any one k. his neighbor unintentionally 19.04
manslayer who k. any person without Jos 20.03
The LORD k. and brings to life; 1Sa 2.06
and the man who k. him, the king 17.25
for the man who k. this Philistine, 17.26
it be done to the man who k. him. 17.27
Surely vexation k. the fool, and Job 5.02
of the sluggard k. him for his Pro 21.25
an ox is like him who k. a man; Is 66.03
and whoever k. shall be liable to Mt 5.21
when whoever k. you will think he Jn 16.02
for the written code k., but the Spirit 2Co 3.06

KILN
"Take handfuls of ashes from the k., Ex 9.08
So they took ashes from the k., 9.10
it went up like the smoke of a k., 19.18

KIN
any one near of k. to him to Lev 18.06
is to make naked one's near k.; 20.19
except for his nearest of k., 21.02
his next of k. shall come and 25.25
of ours, one of our nearest k. Ru 2.20
maidservant, for you are next of k. 3.09
of the next of k. for you, well; 3.13
the part of the next of k. for you, 3.13
the part of the next of k. for you. 3.13
the next of k., of whom Boaz had 4.01
Then he said to the next of k., 4.03
Then the next of k. said, "I cannot 4.06
So when the next of k. said to Boaz, 4.08
you this day without next of k.; 4.14
the king is near of k. to us. 2Sa 19.42
own country, and among his own k., Mk 6.04

KINAH
K., Dimonah, Adadah, Jos 15.22

KIND
seed, each according to its k., Gen 1.11
seed, each according to its k. 1.12
winged bird according to its k. 1.21
the ground according to its k. 1.25
of the ground according to its k., 6.20
to keep their k. alive upon the 7.03
every beast according to its k., 7.14
on the earth according to its k., 7.14
and every bird according to its k., 7.14
or for any k. of lost thing, of Ex 22.09
the falcon according to its k., Lev 11.14
every raven according to its k., 11.15
the hawk according to its k., 11.16
the heron according to its k., 11.19
the locust according to its k., 11.22
bald locust according to its k., 11.22
the cricket according to its k., 11.22
grasshopper according to its k. 11.22
great lizard according to its k., 11.29
cattle breed with a different k.; 19.19
every raven after its k.; Deu 14.14
between one k. of homicide and 17.08
one k. of legal right and another, 17.08
or one k. of assault and another, 17.08
he who lies with any k. of beast. 27.21
"What k. of cities are these which 1Ki 9.13
"What k. of man was he who came to 2Ki 1.07
has skill for any k. of service; 1Ch 28.21
"If you will be k. to this people 2Ch 10.07
did work in every k. of service; 34.13
they loathed any k. of food, Ps 107.18
his ways, and k. in all his doings. 145.17
A man who is k. benefits himself, Pro 11.17
happy is he who is k. to the poor. 14.21
but he who is k. to the needy 14.31
He who is k. to the poor lends to 19.17
it for him who is k. to the poor. 28.08
of your great wealth of every k.; Eze 27.12
of your great wealth of every k.; 27.18
summon every k. of terror against 38.21
and every k. of music, you are to Dan 3.05
and every k. of music, all the 3.07
and every k. of music, shall fall 3.10
and every k. of music, to fall down 3.15
and no k. of hurt was found upon 6.23
or any k. of food, does it become Hag 2.12
sea and gathered fish of every k.; Mt 13.47
But this k. never comes out except * 17.21
"This k. cannot be driven out by Mk 9.29
for he is k. to the ungrateful and Lk 6.35
you have been k. enough to come. Ac 10.33
and of a k. that is not found even 1Co 5.01
one of one k. and one of another. 7.07
Love is patient and k.; love is not 13.04
With what k. of body do they come?" 15.35
and to each k. of seed its own body. 15.38
alike, but there is one k. for men, 15.39
practice every k. of uncleanness. Eph 4.19
and be k. to one another, tenderhearted, 4.32
Yet it was k. of you to share my Php 4.14
You know what k. of men we proved 1Th 1.05
k., and submissive to their husbands, Tit 2.05
we should be a k. of first fruits Jas 1.18
For every k. of beast and bird of 3.07
not only to the k. and gentle but 1Pe 2.18

KINDLE
you shall k. no fire in all your Ex 35.03
all you who k. a fire, who set Is 50.11
the fathers k. fire, and the women Jer 7.18
then I will k. a fire in its gates, 17.27
I will k. a fire in her forest, and 21.14
He shall k. a fire in the temples 43.12
And I will k. a fire in the wall of 49.27
and I will k. a fire in his cities, 50.32
I will k. a fire in you, and it Eze 20.47
k. the fire, boil well the flesh, and 24.10

KINDLE (cont.)
So I will k. a fire in the wall of Amo 1.14
you might not k. fire upon my Mal 1.10

KINDLED
Jacob's anger was k. against Rachel, Gen 30.02
treated me," his anger was k. 39.19
of the LORD was k. against Moses Ex 4.14
he that k. the fire shall make full 22.06
the burning which the LORD has k. Lev 10.06
his anger was k., and the fire of Num 11.01
of the LORD was k. against the 11.33
of the LORD was k. against them, 12.09
But God's anger was k. because he 22.22
and Balaam's anger was k., 22.27
anger was k. against Balaam, 24.10
of the LORD was k. against Israel; 25.03
LORD's anger was k. on that day, 32.10
lord's anger was k. against Israel, 32.13
LORD your God be k. against you, Deu 6.15
the LORD would be k. against you, 7.04
of the LORD be k. against you, 11.17
of the LORD was k. against this 29.27
anger will be k. against them in 31.17
For a fire is k. by my anger, and it 32.22
of the LORD will be k. against you, Jos 23.16
of the LORD was k. against Israel, Ju 2.14
of the LORD was k. against Israel; 2.20
of the LORD was k. against Israel, 3.08
the son of Ebed, his anger was k. 9.30
of the LORD was k. against Israel, 10.07
and his anger was greatly k. 1Sa 11.06
Eliab's anger was k. against David, 17.28
anger was k. against Jonathan, and 20.30
of the LORD was k. against Uzzah; 2Sa 6.07
was greatly k. against the man; 12.05
of the LORD was k. against Israel, 24.01
of the LORD was k. against Israel, 2Ki 13.03
of the LORD that is k. against us, 22.13
wrath will be k. against this 22.17
his anger was k. against Judah, 23.26
of the LORD was k. against Uzzah; 1Ch 13.10
He has k. his wrath against me, and Job 19.11
"My wrath is k. against you and 42.07
for his wrath is quickly k. Ps 2.12
a fire was k. against Jacob, his 78.21
of the LORD was k. against his 106.40
when their anger was k. against us; 124.03
of the LORD was k. against his Is 5.25
his glory a burning will be k., 10.16
by the brands which you have k.! 50.11
anger a fire is k. which shall Jer 15.14
anger a fire is k. which shall 17.04
forth and k. in the cities of 44.06
and he k. a fire in Zion, which Lam 4.11
see that I the LORD have k. it; Eze 20.48
and would that it were already k.! Lk 12.49
and when they had k. a fire in the 22.55
for they k. a fire and welcomed us Ac 28.02
heavens will be k. and dissolved, 2Pe 3.12

KINDLES
His breath k. coals, and a flame Job 41.21
it k. the thickets of the forest, Is 9.18
like a stream of brimstone, k. it. 30.33
he k. a fire and bakes bread; 44.15
as when fire k. brushwood and the 64.02

KINDLING
is a quarrelsome man for k. strife. Pro 26.21

KINDLY
that as I have dealt k. with you, Jos 2.12
also will deal k. with my father's 2.12
we will deal k. and faithfully 2.14
city, and we will deal k. with you. Ju 1.24
to speak k. to her and bring her 19.03
May the LORD deal k. with you, Ru 1.08
me and spoken k. to your maidservant, 2.13
Therefore deal k. with your servant, 1Sa 20.08
out and speak k. to your servants; 2Sa 19.07
and he spoke k. to him, and gave him 2Ki 25.28
and he spoke k. to him, and gave him Jer 52.32
and Julius treated Paul k., Ac 27.03
remember us k. and long to see us, 1Th 3.06
be quarrelsome but k. to every one, 2Ti 2.24

KINDNESS
shown me great k. in saving my Gen 19.19
'This is the k. you must do me: at 20.13
and do me the k., I pray you, to 40.14
did not show k. to the family of Ju 8.35
whose k. has not forsaken the Ru 2.20
made this last k. greater than the 3.10
for you showed k. to all the people 1Sa 15.06
I may show him k. for Jonathan's 2Sa 9.01
I may show the k. of God to him?" 9.03
I will show you k. for the sake of 9.07
not remember the k. which Jehoiada, 2Ch 24.22
"He who withholds k. from a friend Job 6.14
Let there be none to extend k. to him, Ps 109.12
For he did not remember to show k., 109.16
good man strike or rebuke me in k., 141.05
righteousness and k. will find life Pro 21.21
the teaching of k. is on her 31.26
that I am the LORD who practice k., Jer 9.24
There is no faithfulness or k., Hos 4.01
and to love k., and to walk humbly Mic 6.08
show k. and mercy each to his Zec 7.09
beg you in your k. to hear us Ac 24.04
And the natives showed us unusual k., 28.02
riches of his k. and forbearance Rom 2.04
know that God's k. is meant to 2.04
Note then the k. and the severity 11.22
but God's k. to you, provided you 11.22
provided you continue in his k.; 11.22
k., the Holy Spirit, genuine love, 2Co 6.06
k., goodness, faithfulness, Gal 5.22
of his grace in k. toward us in Eph 2.07
k., lowliness, meekness, and patience, Col 3.12
and loving k. of God our Savior Tit 3.04
you have tasted the k. of the Lord. 1Pe 2.03

KINDRED
and your k. and your father's house Gen 12.01
will go to my country and to my k., 24.04
to my father's house and to my k., 24.38
my son from my k. and from my 24.40
my oath, when you come to my k.; 24.41
died, and was gathered to his k. 25.17
of your fathers and to your k., 31.03
to your country and to your k., 32.09
carefully about ourselves and our k., 43.07
depart to my own land and to my k. Num 10.30
and they brought all her k., Jos 6.23
not made known her people or k., Est 2.10
made known her k. or her people, 2.20
to see the destruction of my k.?" 8.06
"None of your k. is called by this Lk 1.61
and from your k. and go into the Ac 7.03
Jacob his father and all his k., 7.14

KINDS
seed according to their own k., Gen 1.12
swarm, according to their k., 1.21
creatures according to their k.: 1.24
of the earth according to their k. 1.24
to their k. and the cattle according 1.25
the cattle according to their k., 1.25
Of the birds according to their k., 6.20
the animals according to their k., 6.20
the cattle according to their k., 7.14
and in all k. of work in the field; Ex 1.14
sow your field with two k. of seed; Lev 19.19
of cloth made of two k. of stuff. 19.19
and plant all k. of trees for food, 19.23

KINDS (cont.)
the buzzard, the kite, after their k.; Deu 14.13
sea gull, the hawk, after their k.; 14.15
the stork, the heron, after their k.; 14.18
your vineyard with two k. of seed, 22.09
have in your bag two k. of weights, 25.13
in your house two k. of measures, 25.14
all k. of goods of Damascus, forty 2Ki 8.09
and all k. of craftsmen without 1Ch 22.15
with various k. of spices prepared 2Ch 16.14
and for all k. of costly vessels; 32.27
and stalls for all k. of cattle, 32.28
and all k. of burdens, which they Neh 13.15
in fish and all k. of wares and 13.16
sellers of all k. of wares lodged 13.20
goblets, goblets of different k., Est 1.07
with all k. of wealth. The princess Ps 45.13
in them all k. of fruit trees. Ecc 2.05
over them four k. of destroyers, Jer 15.03
were all k. of creeping things, and Eze 8.10
it will dwell all k. of beasts; 17.23
wares the best of all k. of spices, 27.22
mighty men and all k. of warriors, 39.20
of all the first fruits of all k., 44.30
offering of all k. from all your 44.30
its fish will be of very many k., 47.10
will grow all k. of trees for food 47.12
and utter all k. of evil against Mt 5.11
In it were all k. of animals and Ac 10.12
in me all k. of covetousness. Rom 7.08
to another various k. of tongues, 1Co 12.10
speakers in various k. of tongues. 12.28
all k. of scented wood, all articles Rev 18.12
life with its twelve k. of fruit, 22.02

KING
In the days of Amraphel k. of Shinar, Gen 14.01
Arioch k. of Ellasar, Chedorlaomer 14.01
Chedorlaomer k. of Elam, and Tidal k. of 14.01
made war with Bera k. of Sodom, 14.02
Birsha k. of Gomorrah, Shinab k. of Admah, 14.02
Shemeber k. of Zeboiim, and the 14.02
and the k. of Bela (that is, Zoar). 14.02
the k. of Sodom, the k. of Gomorrah, 14.08
the k. of Admah, the k. of Zeboiim, 14.08
and the k. of Bela (that is, Zoar) 14.08
with Chedorlaomer k. of Elam, 14.09
Tidal k. of Goiim, Amraphel k. of Shinai, 14.09
and Arioch k. of Ellasar, four kings 14.09
the k. of Sodom went out to meet 14.17
And Melchizedek k. of Salem brought 14.18
And the k. of Sodom said to Abram, 14.21
But Abram said to the k. of Sodom, 14.22
And Abimelech k. of Gerar sent and 20.02
to Abimelech k. of the Philistines. 26.01
Abimelech k. of the Philistines 26.08
before any k. reigned over the 36.31
butler of the k. of Egypt and his 40.01
offended their lord the k. of Egypt. 40.01
and the baker of the k. of Egypt, 40.05
the service of Pharaoh k. of Egypt. 41.46
Now there arose a new k. over Egypt, Ex 1.08
Then the k. of Egypt said to the 1.15
not do as the k. of Egypt commanded 1.17
So the k. of Egypt called the 1.18
many days the k. of Egypt died. 2.23
shall go to the k. of Egypt and 3.18
I know that the k. of Egypt will 3.19
But the k. of Egypt said to them, 5.04
tell Pharaoh k. of Egypt to let the 6.11
and to Pharaoh k. of Egypt to 6.13
to Pharaoh k. of Egypt about 6.27
tell Pharaoh k. of Egypt all that I 6.29
When the k. of Egypt was told that 14.05
of Pharaoh k. of Egypt and he 14.08
from Kadesh to the k. of Edom, Num 20.14
the k. of Arad, who dwelt in the 21.01
to Sihon k. of the Amorites, saying, 21.21
of Sihon the k. of the Amorites, 21.26
the former k. of Moab and taken 21.26
captives, to an Amorite k., Sihon. 21.29
and Og the k. of Bashan came out 21.33
did to Sihon k. of the Amorites, 21.34
who was k. of Moab at that time, 22.04
k. of Moab, has sent to me, saying, 22.10
the k. of Moab from the eastern 23.07
the shout of a k. is among them. 23.21
his k. shall be higher than Agag, 24.07
of Sihon k. of the Amorites and 32.33
and the kingdom of Og k. of Bashan, 32.33
the k. of Arad, who dwelt in the 33.40
Sihon the k. of the Amorites, who Deu 1.04
and Og the k. of Bashan, who lived 1.04
k. of Heshbon, and his land; 2.24
Kedemoth to Sihon the k. of Heshbon, 2.26
But Sihon the k. of Heshbon would 2.30
and Og the k. of Bashan came out 3.01
to Sihon the k. of the Amorites, 3.02
the k. of Bashan, and all his people 3.03
we did to Sihon the k. of Heshbon, 3.06
(For only Og the k. of Bashan was 3.11
of Sihon the k. of the Amorites, 4.46
the land of Og the k. of Bashan, 4.47
the hand of Pharaoh k. of Egypt. 7.08
to Pharaoh the k. of Egypt and to 11.03
'I will set a k. over me, like all 17.14
indeed set as k. over you him whom 17.15
you shall set as k. over you; 17.15
and your k. whom you set over you, 28.36
Sihon the k. of Heshbon and Og the 29.07
and Og the k. of Bashan came out 29.07
Thus the LORD became k. in Jeshurun, 33.05
And it was told the k. of Jericho, Jos 2.02
Then the k. of Jericho sent to 2.03
with its k. and mighty men of valor 6.02
given into your hand the k. of Ai, 8.01
to Ai and its k. as you did to 8.02
as you did to Jericho and its k.; 8.02
And when the k. of Ai saw this he 8.14
But the k. of Ai they took alive, 8.23
And he hanged the k. of Ai on a 8.29
Sihon the k. of Heshbon, and Og k. of 9.10
When Adonizedek k. of Jerusalem 10.01
to Ai and its k. as he had done to 10.01
he had done to Jericho and its k., 10.01
So Adonizedek k. of Jerusalem sent 10.03
Jerusalem sent to Hoham k. of Hebron, 10.03
to Piram k. of Jarmuth, to Japhia k. of 10.03
and to Debir k. of Eglon, saying, 10.03
the k. of Jerusalem, the k. of Hebron, 10.05
the k. of Jarmuth, the k. of Lachish, 10.05
and the k. of Eglon, gathered their 10.05
the k. of Jerusalem, the k. of Hebron, 10.23
the k. of Jarmuth, the k. of Lachish, 10.23
of Lachish, and the k. of Eglon. 10.23
it and its k. with the edge of the 10.28
he did to the k. of Makkedah as he 10.28
he had done to the k. of Jericho. 10.28
it also and its k. into the hand 10.30
to its k. as he had done to the k. of 10.30
Then Horam k. of Gezer came up to 10.33
and its k. and its towns, and every 10.37
it with its k. and all its towns; 10.39
to Hebron and to Libnah and its k., 10.39
so he did to Debir and to its k. 10.39
When Jabin k. of Hazor heard of 11.01
this, he sent to Jobab k. of Madon, 11.01
the k. of Shimron, and to the k. of 11.01
and smote its k. with the sword; 11.10
Sihon k. of the Amorites who dwelt 12.02
and Og k. of Bashan, one of the 12.04
boundary of Sihon k. of Heshbon. 12.05
the k. of Jericho, one; the k. of Ai, 12.09
the k. of Jerusalem, one; the k. of Hebron, 12.10
the k. of Jarmuth, one; the k. of Lachish, 12.11
the k. of Eglon, one; the k. of Gezer, 12.12

KING (cont.)

the k. of Debir, one; the k. of Geder, Jos 12.13
the k. of Hormah, one; the k. of Arad, 12.14
the k. of Libnah, one; the k. of Adullam, 12.15
the k. of Makkedah, one; the k. of Bethel, 12.16
the k. of Tappuah, one; the k. of Hepher, 12.17
the k. of Aphek, one; the k. of Lasharon, 12.18
the k. of Madon, one; the k. of Hazor, 12.19
the k. of Shimronmeron, one; 12.20
the k. of Achshaph, one; 12.20
the k. of Taanach, one; the k. of Megiddo, 12.21
the k. of Kedesh, one; the k. of Jokneam 12.22
the k. of Dor in Naphathdor, one; 12.23
the k. of Goiim in Galilee, one; 12.23
the k. of Tirzah, one: in all, thirty-one 12.24
cities of Sihon k. of the Amorites, 13.10
of Sihon k. of the Amorites, who 13.21
the kingdom of Sihon k. of Heshbon, 13.27
whole kingdom of Og k. of Bashan, 13.30
k. of Moab, arose and fought against 24.09
Cushanrishathaim k. of Mesopotamia; Ju 3.08
Cushanrishathaim k. of Mesopotamia 3.10
Eglon the k. of Moab against 3.12
Eglon the k. of Moab eighteen 3.14
by him to Eglon the k. of Moab. 3.15
the tribute to Eglon k. of Moab. 3.17
a secret message for you, O k." 3.19
the hand of Jabin k. of Canaan, 4.02
Jabin the k. of Hazor and the 4.17
Jabin the k. of Canaan before the 4.23
harder on Jabin the k. of Canaan, 4.24
they destroyed Jabin k. of Canaan. 4.24
they resembled the sons of a k. 8.18
they went and made Abimelech k., 9.06
forth to anoint a k. over them; 9.08
you are anointing me k. over you, 9.15
honor when you made Abimelech k., 9.16
k. over the citizens of Shechem, 9.18
messengers to the k. of the Ammonites 11.12
And the k. of the Ammonites answered 11.13
again to the k. of the Ammonites 11.14
sent messengers to the k. of Edom, 11.17
but the k. of Edom would not listen 11.17
they sent also to the k. of Moab, 11.17
to Sihon k. of the Amorites, 11.19
k. of Heshbon; and Israel said to 11.19
the son of Zippor, k. of Moab? 11.25
But the k. of the Ammonites did not 11.28
days there was no k. in Israel; 17.06
days there was no k. in Israel. 18.01
when there was no k. in Israel, 19.01
days there was no k. in Israel; 21.25
he will give strength to his k., 1Sa 2.10
for us a k. to govern us like all 8.05
said, "Give us a k. to govern us." 8.06
rejected me from being k. over them. 8.07
the ways of the k. who shall reign 8.09
who were asking a k. from him. 8.10
the ways of the k. who will reign 8.11
will cry out because of your k., 8.18
but we will have a k. over us, 8.19
and that our k. may govern us and 8.20
to their voice, and make them a k. 8.22
said, 'No! but set a k. over us.' 10.19
people shouted, "Long live the k.!" 10.24
they made Saul k. before the LORD 11.15
to me, and have made a k. over you. 12.01
behold, the k. walks before you; 12.02
of the army of Jabin k. of Hazor, 12.09
into the hand of the k. of Moab; 12.09
that Nahash the k. of the Ammonites 12.12
but a k. shall reign over us,' when 12.12
when the LORD your God was your k. 12.12
And now behold the k. whom you have 12.13
the LORD has set a k. over you. 12.13
you and the k. who reigns over you 12.14
will be against you and your k. 12.15
in asking for yourselves a k." 12.17

evil, to ask for ourselves a k." 12.19
swept away, both you and your k." 12.25
to anoint you k. over his people 15.01
took Agag the k. of the Amalekites 15.08
"I repent that I have made Saul k.; 15.11
LORD anointed you k. over Israel. 15.17
have brought Agag the k. of Amalek, 15.20
also rejected you from being k." 15.23
you from being k. over Israel." 15.26
to me Agag the k. of the Amalekites." 15.32
he had made Saul k. over Israel. 15.35
him from being k. over Israel? 16.01
for myself a k. among his sons." 16.01
the k. will enrich with great 17.25
soul lives, O k., I cannot tell." 17.55
And the k. said, "Inquire whose son 17.56
to meet K. Saul, with timbrels, with 18.06
I should be son-in-law to the k.?" 18.18
the k. has delight in you, and all 18.22
'The k. desires no marriage present 18.25
given in full number to the k., 18.27
"Let not the k. sin against his 19.04
fail to sit at table with the k.; 20.05
came, the k. sat down to eat food. 20.24
The k. sat upon the seat, as at 20.25
"The k. has charged me with a 21.02
and went to Achish the k. of Gath. 21.10
not this David the k. of the land? 21.11
afraid of Achish the k. of Gath. 21.12
and he said to the k. of Moab, 22.03
And he left them with the k. of Moab, 22.04
Then the k. sent to summon Ahimelech 22.11
and all of them came to the k. 22.11
Then Ahimelech answered the k., 22.14
Let not the k. impute anything to 22.15
And the k. said, "You shall surely 22.16
And the k. said to the guard who 22.17
servants of the k. would not put 22.17
Then the k. said to Doeg, "You turn 22.18
you shall be k. over Israel, and I 23.17
O k., according to all your heart's 23.20
called after Saul, "My lord the k.!" 24.08
After whom has the k. of Israel 24.14
I know that you shall surely be k., 24.20
his house, like the feast of a k. 25.36
"Who are you that calls to the k.?" 26.14
kept watch over your lord the k.? 26.15
in to destroy the k. your lord. 26.15
"It is my voice, my lord, O k." 26.17
let my lord the k. hear the words 26.19
for the k. of Israel has come out 26.20
answer, "Here is the spear, O k.! 26.22
the son of Maoch, k. of Gath. 27.02
The k. said to her, "Have no fear; 28.13
k. of Israel, who has been with me 29.03
the enemies of my lord the k.?" 29.08
anointed David k. over the house 2Sa 2.04
Judah has anointed me k. over them." 2.07
and he made him k. over Gilead and 2.09
that David was k. in Hebron over 2.11
daughter of Talmai k. of Geshur; 3.03
been seeking David as k. over you. 3.17
all Israel to my lord the k., 3.21
the son of Ner came to the k., 3.23
Then Joab went to the k. and said, 3.24
And K. David followed the bier. 3.31
and the k. lifted up his voice and 3.32
And the k. lamented for Abner, 3.33
that the k. did pleased all the 3.36
And the k. said to his servants, "Do 3.38
this day weak, though anointed k.; 3.39
And they said to the k., "Here is the 4.08
my lord the k. this day on Saul 4.08
when Saul was k. over us, it was you 5.02
of Israel came to the k. at Hebron; 5.03
and K. David made a covenant with 5.03
they anointed David k. over Israel. 5.03
And the k. and his men went to 5.06

KING (cont.)

And Hiram k. of Tyre sent messengers 2Sa 5.11
had established him k. over Israel, 5.12
had been anointed k. over Israel, 5.17
And it was told K. David, "The LORD 6.12
and saw K. David leaping and dancing 6.16
"How the k. of Israel honored 6.20
Now when the k. dwelt in his house, 7.01
the k. said to Nathan the prophet, 7.02
And Nathan said to the k., "Go, do all 7.03
Then K. David went in and sat 7.18
k. of Zobah, as he went to restore 8.03
came to help Hadadezer k. of Zobah, 8.05
K. David took very much bronze. 8.08
When Tou k. of Hamath heard that 8.09
Tou sent his son Joram to K. David, 8.10
these also K. David dedicated to 8.11
the son of Rehob, k. of Zobah. 8.12
and the k. said to him, "Are you 9.02
And the k. said, "Is there not still 9.03
Ziba said to the k, "There is still 9.03
The k. said to him, "Where is he?" 9.04
And Ziba said to the k., "He is in 9.04
Then K. David sent and brought him 9.05
Then the k. called Ziba, Saul's 9.09
Then Ziba said to the k., "According 9.11
that my lord the k. commands his 9.11
After this the k. of the Ammonites 10.01
And the k. said, "Remain at Jericho 10.05
and the k. of Maacah with a thousand 10.06
followed him a present from the k. 11.08
news about the fighting to the k., 11.19
'I anointed you k. over Israel, 12.07
crown of their k. from his head; 12.30
"O son of the k., why are you so 13.04
and when the k. came to see him, 13.06
to see him, Amnon said to the k., 13.06
I pray you, speak to the k.; 13.13
daughters of the k. clad of old. 13.18
When K. David heard of all these 13.21
And Absalom came to the k., 13.24
pray let the k. and his servants go 13.24
But the k. said to Absalom, "No, my 13.25
And the k. said to him, "Why should 13.26
Then the k. arose, and rent his 13.31
not my lord the k. so take it to 13.33
And Jonadab said to the k., 13.35
and the k. also and all his servants 13.36
the son of Ammihud, k. of Geshur. 13.37
spirit of the k. longed to go 13.39
and go to the k., and speak thus to 14.03
When the woman of Tekoa came to the k., 14.04
obeisance, and said, "Help, O k." 14.04
And the k. said to her, "What is 14.05
Then the k. said to the woman, "Go 14.08
And the woman of Tekoa said to the k., 14.09
my lord the k., and on my father's 14.09
let the k. and his throne be guiltless." 14.09
The k. said, "If any one says 14.10
"Pray let the k. invoke the LORD 14.11
speak a word to my lord the k." 14.12
decision the k. convicts himself, 14.13
inasmuch as the k. does not bring 14.13
to my lord the k. because the 14.15
thought, 'I will speak to the k.; 14.15
may be that the k. will perform 14.15
For the k. will hear, and deliver 14.16
of my lord the k. will set me at 14.17
for my lord the k. is like the 14.17
Then the k. answered the woman, "Do 14.18
said, "Let my lord the k. speak." 14.18
The k. said, "Is the hand of Joab 14.19
my lord the k., one cannot turn to 14.19
that my lord the k. has said. 14.19
Then the k. said to Joab, "Behold 14.21
did obeisance, and blessed the k.; 14.22
my lord the k., in that the k. has 14.22
And the k. said, "Let him dwell 14.24
for Joab, to send him to the k.; 14.29
that I may send you to the k., 14.32
me go into the presence of the k.; 14.32
Then Joab went to the k., and told him; 14.33
So he came to the k., and bowed 14.33
the k.; and the k. kissed Absalom. 14.33
to come before the k. for judgment, 15.02
man deputed by the k. to hear you. 15.03
who came to the k. for judgment; 15.06
four years Absalom said to the k., 15.07
The k. said to him, "Go in peace." 15.09
then say, 'Absalom is k. at Hebron!'" 15.10
the king's servants said to the k., 15.15
do whatever my lord the k. decides. 15.15
So the k. went forth, and all his 15.16
And the k. left ten concubines to 15.16
And the k. went forth, and all the 15.17
from Gath, passed on before the k. 15.18
Then the k. said to Ittai the 15.19
Go back, and stay with the k.; 15.19
But Ittai answered the k., "As the 15.21
the k. lives, wherever my lord the k. 15.21
and the k. crossed the brook Kidron, 15.23
Then the k. said to Zadok, "Carry 15.25
The k. also said to Zadok the 15.27
'I will be your servant, O k.; 15.34
And the k. said to Ziba, "Why have 16.02
And the k. said, "And where is your 16.03
Ziba said to the k., "Behold, he 16.03
Then the k. said to Ziba, "Behold, 16.04
in your sight, my lord the k." 16.04
When K. David came to Bahurim, there 16.05
at all the servants of K. David; 16.06
the son of Zeruiah said to the k., 16.09
this dead dog curse my lord the k.? 16.09
But the k. said, "What have I to do 16.10
And the k., and all the people who 16.14
"Long live the k.! Long live the k.!" 16.16
I will strike down the k. only, 17.02
lest the k. and all the people who 17.16
they would go and tell K. David; 17.17
well, and went and told K. David. 17.21
And the k. said to the men, "I 18.02
The k. said to them, "Whatever seems 18.04
So the k. stood at the side of the 18.04
And the k. ordered Joab and Abishai 18.05
heard when the k. gave orders to 18.05
our hearing the k. commanded you 18.12
is nothing hidden from the k.), 18.13
tidings to the k. that the LORD 18.19
tell the k. what you have seen. 18.21
watchman called out and told the k. 18.25
And the k. said, "If he is alone, 18.25
The k. said, "He also brings tidings 18.26
And the k. said, "He is a good man, 18.27
cried out to the k., "All is well." 18.28
before the k. with his face to the 18.28
their hand against my lord the k." 18.28
And the k. said, "Is it well with 18.29
And the k. said, "Turn aside, and 18.30
"Good tidings for my lord the k.! 18.31
The k. said to the Cushite, "Is it 18.32
"May the enemies of my lord the k., 18.32
And the k. was deeply moved, and 18.33
the k. is weeping and mourning for 19.01
"The k. is grieving for his son." 19.02
The k. covered his face, and the 19.04
and the k. cried with a loud voice, 19.04
Joab came into the house to the k., 19.05
Then the k. arose, and took his seat 19.08
the k. is sitting in the gate"; and 19.08
all the people came before the k. 19.08
"The k. delivered us from the hand 19.09
nothing about bringing the k. back?" 19.10
And K. David sent this message to 19.11
to bring the k. back to his house, 19.11
of all Israel has come to the k.? 19.11
be the last to bring back the k.?" 19.12

KING (cont.)
so that they sent word to the k., 2Sa 19.14
So the k. came back to the Jordan; 19.15
to meet the k. and to bring the 19.15
to bring the k. over the Jordan. 19.15
the men of Judah to meet K. David; 19.16
down to the Jordan before the k., 19.17
of Gera fell down before the k., 19.18
and said to the k., "Let not my 19.19
day my lord the k. left Jerusalem; 19.19
let not the k. bear it in mind. 19.19
come down to meet my lord the k." 19.20
that I am this day k. over Israel?" 19.22
And the k. said to Shimei, "You 19.23
And the k. gave him his oath. 19.23
of Saul came down to meet the k.; 19.24
the day the k. departed until the 19.24
came from Jerusalem to meet the k., 19.25
the k. said to him, "Why did you not 19.25
O k., my servant deceived me; 19.26
ride upon it and go with the k.' 19.26
your servant to my lord the k. 19.27
But my lord the k. is like the 19.27
to death before my lord the k.; 19.28
have I, then, to cry to the k.?" 19.28
And the k. said to him, "Why speak 19.29
And Mephibosheth said to the k., 19.30
my lord the k. has come safely 19.30
went on with the k. to the Jordan, 19.31
provided the k. with food while he 19.32
And the k. said to Barzillai, "Come 19.33
But Barzillai said to the k., 19.34
go up with the k. to Jerusalem? 19.34
an added burden to my lord the k.? 19.35
way over the Jordan with the k. 19.36
Why should the k. recompense me 19.36
him go over with my lord the k.; 19.37
And the k. answered, "Chimham shall 19.38
the Jordan, and the k. went over; 19.39
and the k. kissed Barzillai and 19.39
The k. went on to Gilgal, and 19.40
Israel, brought the k. on his way. 19.40
the men of Israel came to the k., 19.41
and said to the k., "Why have our 19.41
and brought the k. and his household 19.41
"Because the k. is near of kin to 19.42
"We have ten shares in the k., 19.43
to speak of bringing back our k.?" 19.43
followed their k. steadfastly from 20.02
and the k. took the ten concubines 20.03
Then the k. said to Amasa, "Call the 20.04
up his hand against K. David; 20.21
returned to Jerusalem to the k. 20.22
So the k. called the Gibeonites. 21.02
They said to the k., "The man who 21.05
And the k. said, "I will give them." 21.06
But the k. spared Mephibosheth, the 21.07
The k. took the two sons of Rizpah 21.08
they did all that the k. commanded. 21.14
Great triumphs he gives to his k., 22.51
So the k. said to Joab and the 24.02
But Joab said to the k., "May the 24.03
of my lord the k. still see it; 24.03
my lord the k. delight in this 24.03
presence of the k. to number the 24.04
numbering of the people to the k.: 24.09
he saw the k. and his servants 24.20
obeisance to the k. with his face 24.20
has my lord the k. come to his 24.21
"Let my lord the k. take and offer 24.22
All this, O k., Araunah gives to the k." 24.23
And Araunah said to the k., "The Lord 24.23
But the k. said to Araunah, "No, but 24.24
Now K. David was old and advanced 1Ki 1.01
maiden be sought for my lord the k., 1.02
and let her wait upon the k., and be 1.02
that my lord the k. may be warm." 1.02
Shunammite, and brought her to the k. 1.03
to him; but the k. knew her not. 1.04
himself, saying, "I will be k."; 1.05
has become k. and David our lord 1.11
Go in at once to K. David, and say 1.13
my lord the k., swear to your 1.13
Why then is Adonijah k.?' 1.13
you are still speaking with the k., 1.14
went to the k. into his chamber 1.15
chamber (now the k. was very old, 1.15
Shunammite was ministering to the k.). 1.15
Bathsheba bowed and did obeisance to the k., 1.16
and the k. said, "What do you desire?" 1.16
Adonijah is k., although you, my 1.18
my lord the k., do not know it. 1.18
has invited all the sons of the k., 1.19
my lord the k., the eyes of all 1.20
throne of my lord the k. after him. 1.20
my lord the k. sleeps with his 1.21
she was still speaking with the k., 1.22
And they told the k., "Here is Nathan 1.23
And when he came in before the k., 1.23
he bowed before the k., with his 1.23
"My lord the k., have you said, 1.24
and saying, 'Long live K. Adonijah!' 1.25
by my lord the k. and you have not 1.27
throne of my lord the k. after him?" 1.27
Then K. David answered, "Call 1.28
presence, and stood before the k. 1.28
And the k. swore, saying, "As the 1.29
and did obeisance to the k., 1.31
"May my lord K. David live for ever!" 1.31
K. David said, "Call to me Zadok the 1.32
Jehoiada." So they came before the k. 1.32
And the k. said to them, "Take with 1.33
there anoint him k. over Israel; 1.34
and say, 'Long live K. Solomon!' 1.34
for he shall be k. in my stead; 1.35
of Jehoiada answered the k., "Amen! 1.36
the God of my lord the k., say so. 1.36
Lord has been with my lord the k., 1.37
the throne of my lord K. David." 1.37
Solomon to ride on K. David's mule, 1.38
people said, "Long live K. Solomon!" 1.39
for our lord K. David has made 1.43
King David has made Solomon k.; 1.43
and the k. has sent with him Zadok 1.44
have anointed him k. at Gihon; 1.45
to congratulate our lord K. David, 1.47
And the k. bowed himself upon the 1.47
And the k. also said, 'Blessed be 1.48
"Behold, Adonijah fears K. Solomon; 1.51
'Let K. Solomon swear to me first 1.51
So K. Solomon sent, and they brought 1.53
and did obeisance to K. Solomon; 1.53
"Pray ask K. Solomon—he will not 2.17
I will speak for you to the k." 2.18
So Bathsheba went to K. Solomon, 2.19
And the k. rose to meet her, and 2.19
And the k. said to her, "Make your 2.20
K. Solomon answered his mother, "And 2.22
Then K. Solomon swore by the Lord, 2.23
So K. Solomon sent Benaiah the son 2.25
to Abiathar the priest the k. said, 2.26
And when it was told K. Solomon, 2.29
"The k. commands, 'Come forth.'" 2.30
Benaiah brought the k. word again, 2.30
The k. replied to him, "Do as he has 2.31
The k. put Benaiah the son of 2.35
and the k. put Zadok the priest in 2.35
Then the k. sent and summoned 2.36
And Shimei said to the k., "What you 2.38
as my lord the k. has said, so will 2.38
Achish, son of Maacah, k. of Gath. 2.39
the k. sent and summoned Shimei, and 2.42
The k. also said to Shimei, "You 2.44
But K. Solomon shall be blessed, and 2.45
Then the k. commanded Benaiah the 2.46
alliance with Pharaoh k. of Egypt; 3.01

KING (cont.)
And the k. went to Gibeon to 1Ki 3.04
thy servant k. in place of David 3.07
that no other k. shall compare 3.13
Then two harlots came to the k., 3.16
Thus they spoke before the k. 3.22
Then the k. said, "The one says, 3.23
And the k. said, "Bring me a sword." 3.24
a sword was brought before the k. 3.24
And the k. said, "Divide the living 3.25
whose son was alive said to the k., 3.26
Then the k. answered and said, "Give 3.27
judgment which the k. had rendered; 3.28
and they stood in awe of the k., 3.28
K. Solomon was k. over all Israel, 4.01
food for the k. and his household; 4.07
of Sihon k. of the Amorites and of Og k. 4.19
supplied provisions for K. Solomon, 4.27
all who came to K. Solomon's table, 4.27
Now Hiram k. of Tyre sent his 5.01
anointed him k. in place of his 5.01
K. Solomon raised a levy of forced 5.13
The house which K. Solomon built 6.02
And K. Solomon sent and brought 7.13
He came to K. Solomon, and did all 7.14
that he did for K. Solomon on the 7.40
which Hiram made for K. Solomon, 7.45
of the Jordan the k. cast them, 7.46
the work that K. Solomon did on 7.51
before K. Solomon in Jerusalem, to 8.01
assembled to K. Solomon at the 8.02
And K. Solomon and all the congregation 8.05
Then the k. faced about, and blessed 8.14
Then the k., and all Israel with 8.62
So the k. and all the people of 8.63
The same day the k. consecrated the 8.64
and they blessed the k., and went to 8.66
and Hiram k. of Tyre had supplied 9.11
K. Solomon gave to Hiram twenty 9.11
Hiram had sent to the k. one 9.14
labor which K. Solomon levied to 9.15
(Pharaoh k. of Egypt had gone up 9.16
K. Solomon built a fleet of ships 9.26
and they brought it to K. Solomon. 9.28
hidden from the k. which he could 10.03
And she said to the k., "The report was 10.06
for ever, he has made you k., 10.09
Then she gave the k. a hundred and 10.10
queen of Sheba gave to K. Solomon. 10.10
And the k. made of the almug wood 10.12
And K. Solomon gave to the queen of 10.13
her by the bounty of K. Solomon. 10.13
K. Solomon made two hundred large 10.16
and the k. put them in the House of 10.17
The k. also made a great ivory 10.18
All K. Solomon's drinking vessels 10.21
For the k. had a fleet of ships of 10.22
Thus K. Solomon excelled all the 10.23
and with the k. in Jerusalem. 10.26
And the k. made silver as common in 10.27
Now K. Solomon loved many foreign 11.01
to Pharaoh k. of Egypt. who gave him 11.18
his master Hadadezer k. of Zobah. 11.23
there, and made him k. in Damascus. 11.24
lifted up his hand against the k. 11.26
lifted up his hand against the k. 11.27
and you shall be k. over Israel. 11.37
to Shishak k. of Egypt, and was in 11.40
had come to Shechem to make him k. 12.01
he had fled from K. Solomon), 12.02
Then K. Rehoboam took counsel with 12.06
as the k. said, "Come to me again 12.12
And the k. answered the people 12.13
So the k. did not hearken to the 12.15
saw that the k. did not hearken to 12.16
them, the people answered the k., 12.16
Then K. Rehoboam sent Adoram, who 12.18
And K. Rehoboam made haste to mount 12.18
and made him k. over all Israel. 12.20
k. of Judah, and to all the house of 12.23
to Rehoboam k. of Judah, and they 12.27
and return to Rehoboam k. of Judah. 12.27
So the k. took counsel, and made two 12.28
And when the k. heard the saying of 13.04
And the k. said to the man of God, 13.06
And the k. said to the man of God, 13.07
And the man of God said to the k., 13.08
also which he had spoken to the k., 13.11
I should be k. over this people. 14.02
up for himself a k. over Israel. 14.14
In the fifth year of K. Rehoboam, 14.25
Shishak k. of Egypt came up against 14.25
and K. Rehoboam made in their stead 14.27
And as often as the k. went into 14.28
eighteenth year of K. Jeroboam the 15.01
of Jeroboam k. of Israel Asa began 15.09
Asa and Baasha k. of Israel all 15.16
Baasha k. of Israel went up against 15.17
out or come in to Asa k. of Judah. 15.17
and K. Asa sent them to Benhadad 15.18
k. of Syria, who dwelt in Damascus, 15.18
league with Baasha k. of Israel, 15.19
And Benhadad hearkened to K. Asa, 15.20
Then K. Asa made a proclamation to 15.22
and with them K. Asa built Geba of 15.22
the second year of Asa k. of Judah; 15.25
the third year of Asa k. of Judah, 15.28
And as soon as he was k., he killed 15.29
Asa and Baasha k. of Israel all 15.32
In the third year of Asa k. of Judah, 15.33
twenty-sixth year of Asa k. of Judah, 16.08
twenty-seventh year of Asa k. of Judah, 16.10
year of Asa k. of Judah Zimri 16.15
conspired, and he has killed the k."; 16.16
k. over Israel that day in the camp 16.16
to make him k., and half followed 16.21
so Tibni died, and Omri became k. 16.22
thirty-first year of Asa k. of Judah, 16.23
thirty-eighth year of Asa k. of Judah, 16.29
of Ethbaal k. of the Sidonians, and 16.31
anoint Hazael to be k. over Syria; 19.15
shall anoint to be k. over Israel; 19.16
Benhadad the k. of Syria gathered 20.01
into the city to Ahab k. of Israel, 20.02
And the k. of Israel answered, "As 20.04
O k., I am yours, and all that I 20.04
Then the k. of Israel called all 20.07
of Benhadad, "Tell my lord the k., 20.09
And the k. of Israel answered, "Tell 20.11
near to Ahab k. of Israel and said, 20.13
but Benhadad k. of Syria escaped on 20.20
And the k. of Israel went out, and 20.21
came near to the k. of Israel, 20.22
the spring the k. of Syria will 20.22
servants of the k. of Syria said 20.23
near and said to the k. of Israel, 20.28
and go out to the k. of Israel; 20.31
and went to the k. of Israel and 20.32
and waited for the k. by the way, 20.38
as the k. passed, he cried to the k. 20.39
The k. of Israel said to him, "So 20.40
and the k. of Israel recognized him 20.41
And the k. of Israel went to his 20.43
the palace of Ahab k. of Samaria. 21.01
'You have cursed God and the k.' 21.10
"Naboth cursed God and the k." 21.13
"Arise, go down to meet Ahab k. of Israel, 21.18
Jehoshaphat the k. of Judah came 22.02
came down to the k. of Israel. 22.02
And the k. of Israel said to his 22.03
out of the hand of the k. of Syria?" 22.03
Jehoshaphat said to the k. of Israel, 22.04
Jehoshaphat said to the k. of Israel, 22.05
Then the k. of Israel gathered the 22.06
give it into the hand of the k." 22.06
And the k. of Israel said to 22.08

KING (cont.)

said, "Let not the k. say so." 1Ki 22.08
Then the k. of Israel summoned an 22.09
Now the k. of Israel and Jehoshaphat 22.10
Jehoshaphat the k. of Judah were 22.10
give it into the hand of the k." 22.12
one accord are favorable to the k.; 22.13
And when he had come to the k., 22.15
the k. said to him, "Micaiah, shall 22.15
give it into the hand of the k." 22.15
But the k. said to him, "How many 22.16
And the k. of Israel said to 22.18
And the k. of Israel said, "Seize 22.26
and say, 'Thus says the k., 22.27
So the k. of Israel and Jehoshaphat 22.29
Jehoshaphat the k. of Judah went 22.29
And the k. of Israel said to 22.30
And the k. of Israel disguised 22.30
Now the k. of Syria had commanded 22.31
but only with the k. of Israel." 22.31
"It is surely the k. of Israel." 22.32
that it was not the k. of Israel, 22.33
and struck the k. of Israel 22.34
and the k. was propped up in his 22.35
So the k. died, and was brought to 22.37
and they buried the k. in Samaria. 22.37
fourth year of Ahab k. of Israel. 22.41
made peace with the k. of Israel. 22.44
was no k. in Edom; a deputy was k. 22.47
year of Jehoshaphat k. of Judah, 22.51
messengers of the k. of Samaria, 2Ki 1.03
The messengers returned to the k., 1.05
'Go back to the k. who sent you, 1.06
Then the k. sent to him a captain 1.09
of God, the k. says, 'Come down.'" 1.09
Again the k. sent to him another 1.11
Again the k. sent the captain of a 1.13
and went down with him to the k., 1.15
became k. in his stead in the 1.17
k. of Judah, because Ahaziah had no 1.17
year of Jehoshaphat k. of Judah, 3.01
of Ahab became k. over Israel in 3.01
Now Mesha k. of Moab was a sheep 3.04
annually to the k. of Israel a 3.04
the k. of Moab rebelled against the 3.05
rebelled against the k. of Israel. 3.05
So K. Jehoram marched out of 3.06
word to Jehoshaphat k. of Judah, 3.07
"The k. of Moab has rebelled 3.07
So the k. of Israel went with the 3.09
the k. of Judah and the k. of Edom. 3.09
Then the k. of Israel said, "Alas! 3.10
Then one of the k. of Israel's 3.11
So the k. of Israel and Jehoshaphat 3.12
Jehoshaphat and the k. of Edom went 3.12
And Elisha said to the k. of Israel, 3.13
But the k. of Israel said to him, 3.13
for Jehoshaphat the k. of Judah, 3.14
When the k. of Moab saw that the 3.26
through, opposite the k. of Edom; 3.26
behalf to the k. or to the commander 4.13
of the army of the k. of Syria, 5.01
And the k. of Syria said, "Go now, 5.05
send a letter to the k. of Israel." 5.05
the letter to the k. of Israel, 5.06
And when the k. of Israel read the 5.07
heard that the k. of Israel had 5.08
his clothes, he sent to the k., 5.08
Once when the k. of Syria was 6.08
God sent word to the k. of Israel, 6.09
And the k. of Israel sent to the 6.10
And the mind of the k. of Syria was 6.11
who of us is for the k. of Israel?" 6.11
servants said, "None, my lord, O k.; 6.12
tells the k. of Israel the words 6.12
When the k. of Israel saw them he 6.21
Afterward Benhadad k. of Syria 6.24
Now as the k. of Israel was passing 6.26
him, saying, "Help, my lord, O k.!" 6.26
And the k. asked her, "What is your 6.28
When the k. heard the words of the 6.30
Now the k. had dispatched a man 6.32
the k. came down to him and said, 6.33
whose hand the k. leaned said to 7.02
the k. of Israel has hired against 7.06
And the k. rose in the night, and 7.12
and the k. sent them after the army 7.14
messengers returned, and told the k. 7.15
Now the k. had appointed the 7.17
said when the k. came down to him. 7.17
the man of God had said to the k., 7.18
appeal to the k. for her house and 8.03
Now the k. was talking with Gehazi 8.04
was telling the k. how Elisha had 8.05
appealed to the k. for her house 8.05
O k., here is the woman, and here is 8.05
And when the k. asked the woman, she 8.06
So the k. appointed an official for 8.06
Benhadad the k. of Syria was sick; 8.07
the k. said to Hazael, "Take a 8.08
son Benhadad k. of Syria has sent 8.09
that you are to be k. over Syria. 8.13
and Hazael became k. in his stead. 8.15
k. of Israel, Jehoram the son of 8.16
k. of Judah, began to reign. 8.16
years old when he became k., 8.17
and set up a k. of their own. 8.20
k. of Israel, Ahaziah the son of 8.25
k. of Judah, began to reign. 8.25
granddaughter of Omri k. of Israel. 8.26
against Hazael k. of Syria at 8.28
And K. Joram returned to be healed 8.29
fought against Hazael k. of Syria. 8.29
son of Jehoram k. of Judah went 8.29
LORD, I anoint you k. over Israel.' 9.03
I anoint you k. over the people of 9.06
LORD, I anoint you k. over Israel.'" 9.12
trumpet, and proclaimed, "Jehu is k." 9.13
Ramothgilead against Hazael k. of Syria; 9.14
but K. Joram had returned to be 9.15
he fought with Hazael k. of Syria. 9.15
And Ahaziah k. of Judah had come 9.16
"Thus says the k., 'Is it peace?'" 9.18
"Thus the k. has said, 'Is it peace?'" 9.19
Joram k. of Israel and Ahaziah k. of Judah 9.21
When Ahaziah the k. of Judah saw 9.27
We will not make any one k.; 10.05
the kinsmen of Ahaziah k. of Judah, 10.13
Jehosheba, the daughter of K. Joram, 11.02
shall surround the k., each with his 11.08
Be with the k. when he goes out and 11.08
shields that had been K. David's, 11.10
and they proclaimed him k., 11.12
hands, and said, "Long live the k.!" 11.12
there was the k. standing by the 11.14
and the trumpeters beside the k., 11.14
the LORD and the k. and people, 11.17
also between the k. and the people. 11.17
brought the k. down from the house 11.19
twenty-third year of K. Jehoash the 12.06
Therefore K. Jehoash summoned 12.07
time Hazael k. of Syria went up 12.17
Jehoash k. of Judah took all the 12.18
sent these to Hazael k. of Syria. 12.18
k. of Judah, Jehoahaz the son of 13.01
hand of Hazael k. of Syria and 13.03
how the k. of Syria oppressed them. 13.04
for the k. of Syria had destroyed 13.07
year of Joash k. of Judah Jehoash 13.10
fought against Amaziah k. of Judah, 13.12
Joash k. of Israel went down to him, 13.14
Then he said to the k. of Israel, 13.16
And he said to the k. of Israel, 13.18
Now Hazael k. of Syria oppressed 13.22
When Hazael k. of Syria died, 13.24
his son became k. in his stead. 13.24

KING (cont.)

k. of Israel, Amaziah the son of	2Ki 14.01
k. of Judah, began to reign.	14.01
who had slain the k. his father.	14.05
k. of Israel, saying, "Come, let us	14.08
And Jehoash k. of Israel sent word	14.09
sent word to Amaziah k. of Judah,	14.09
So Jehoash k. of Israel went up, and	14.11
he and Amaziah k. of Judah faced	14.11
And Jehoash k. of Israel captured	14.13
captured Amaziah k. of Judah,	14.13
he fought with Amaziah k. of Judah,	14.15
k. of Judah, lived fifteen years	14.17
son of Jehoahaz, k. of Israel.	14.17
and made him k. instead of his	14.21
after the k. slept with his fathers	14.22
k. of Judah, Jeroboam the son of	14.23
k. of Israel, began to reign in	14.23
of Jeroboam k. of Israel Azariah	15.01
k. of Judah, began to reign.	15.01
And the LORD smote the k., so that	15.05
year of Azariah k. of Judah	15.08
thirty-ninth year of Uzziah k. of Judah,	15.13
year of Azariah k. of Judah	15.17
Pul the k. of Assyria came against	15.19
man, to give to the k. of Assyria.	15.20
So the k. of Assyria turned back,	15.20
year of Azariah k. of Judah	15.23
year of Azariah k. of Judah Pekah	15.27
days of Pekah k. of Israel Tiglathpileser	15.29
Tiglathpileser k. of Assyria came	15.29
k. of Israel, Jotham the son of	15.32
k. of Judah, began to reign.	15.32
send Rezin the k. of Syria and	15.37
k. of Judah, began to reign.	16.01
Then Rezin k. of Syria and Pekah	16.05
k. of Israel, came up to wage war on	16.05
At that time the k. of Edom recovered	16.06
to Tiglathpileser k. of Assyria,	16.07
the hand of the k. of Syria and	16.07
from the hand of the k. of Israel,	16.07
a present to the k. of Assyria.	16.08
And the k. of Assyria hearkened to	16.09
the k. of Assyria marched up	16.09
When K. Ahaz went to Damascus to	16.10
meet Tiglathpileser k. of Assyria,	16.10
And K. Ahaz sent to Urijah the	16.10
with all that K. Ahaz had sent	16.11
before K. Ahaz arrived from Damascus	16.11
And when the k. came from Damascus,	16.12
the k. viewed the altar.	16.12
Then the k. drew near to the altar.	16.12
And K. Ahaz commanded Urijah the	16.15
did all this, as K. Ahaz commanded.	16.16
And K. Ahaz cut off the frames of	16.17
entrance for the k. he removed from	16.18
LORD, because of the k. of Assyria.	16.18
year of Ahaz k. of Judah Hoshea	17.01
came up Shalmaneser k. of Assyria;	17.03
But the k. of Assyria found treachery	17.04
k. of Egypt, and offered no tribute	17.04
no tribute to the k. of Assyria,	17.04
therefore the k. of Assyria shut	17.04
Then the k. of Assyria invaded all	17.05
of Hoshea the k. of Assyria	17.06
the hand of Pharaoh k. of Egypt,	17.07
made Jeroboam the son of Nebat k.	17.21
And the k. of Assyria brought	17.24
So the k. of Assyria was told, "The	17.26
Then the k. of Assyria commanded,	17.27
k. of Israel, Hezekiah the son of	18.01
k. of Judah, began to reign.	18.01
rebelled against the k. of Assyria,	18.07
In the fourth year of K. Hezekiah,	18.09
k. of Israel, Shalmaneser k. of Assyria	18.09
ninth year of Hoshea k. of Israel,	18.10
The k. of Assyria carried the	18.11
fourteenth year of K. Hezekiah	18.13
Sennacherib k. of Assyria came up	18.13
Hezekiah k. of Judah sent to the k. of	18.14
And the k. of Assyria required of	18.14
of Hezekiah k. of Judah three	18.14
which Hezekiah k. of Judah had	18.16
and gave it to the k. of Assyria.	18.16
And the k. of Assyria sent the	18.17
from Lachish to K. Hezekiah at	18.17
And when they called for the k.,	18.18
'Thus says the great k., the k. of Assyria:	18.19
Such is Pharaoh k. of Egypt to all	18.21
with my master the k. of Assyria:	18.23
word of the great k., the k. of Assyria!	18.28
Thus says the k.: 'Do not let	18.29
into the hand of the k. of Assyria.'	18.30
for thus says the k. of Assyria:	18.31
of the hand of the k. of Assyria?	18.33
When K. Hezekiah heard it, he rent	19.01
his master the k. of Assyria has	19.04
When the servants of K. Hezekiah	19.05
servants of the k. of Assyria have	19.06
and found the k. of Assyria fighting	19.08
heard that the k. had left Lachish.	19.08
k. heard concerning Tirhakah k. of Ethiopia,	19.09
you speak to Hezekiah k. of Judah:	19.10
into the hand of the k. of Assyria.	19.10
is the k. of Hamath, the k. of Arpad,	19.13
the k. of the city of Sepharvaim,	19.13
the k. of Hena, or the k. of Ivvah?	19.13
Sennacherib k. of Assyria I have	19.20
LORD concerning the k. of Assyria,	19.32
Then Sennacherib k. of Assyria	19.36
of the hand of the k. of Assyria,	20.06
k. of Babylon, sent envoys with	20.12
the prophet came to K. Hezekiah,	20.14
in the palace of the k. of Babylon.	20.18
as Ahab k. of Israel had done, and	21.03
"Because Manasseh k. of Judah has	21.11
and killed the k. in his house.	21.23
who had conspired against K. Amon,	21.24
Josiah his son k. in his stead.	21.24
In the eighteenth year of K. Josiah,	22.03
the k. sent Shaphan the son of	22.03
the secretary came to the k.,	22.09
and reported to the k., "Your	22.09
Then Shaphan the secretary told the k.,	22.10
And Shaphan read it before the k.	22.10
And when the k. heard the words of	22.11
And the k. commanded Hilkiah the	22.12
book which the k. of Judah has	22.16
But as to the k. of Judah, who sent	22.18
they brought back word to the k.	22.20
Then the k. sent, and all the elders	23.01
And the k. went up to the house of	23.02
And the k. stood by the pillar and	23.03
And the k. commanded Hilkiah, the	23.04
And the k. defiled the high places	23.13
Solomon the k. of Israel had built	23.13
And the k. commanded all the people,	23.21
eighteenth year of K. Josiah this	23.23
Before him there was no k. like him,	23.25
Pharaoh Neco k. of Egypt went up	23.29
went up to the k. of Assyria to	23.29
K. Josiah went to meet him;	23.29
and made him k. in his father's	23.30
son of Josiah k. in the place of	23.34
Nebuchadnezzar k. of Babylon came	24.01
And the k. of Egypt did not come	24.07
for the k. of Babylon had taken all	24.07
belonged to the k. of Egypt from	24.07
years old when he became k.,	24.08
Nebuchadnezzar k. of Babylon came	24.10
And Nebuchadnezzar k. of Babylon	24.11
and Jehoiachin the k. of Judah gave	24.12
himself up to the k. of Babylon,	24.12
The k. of Babylon took him prisoner	24.12
which Solomon k. of Israel had made,	24.13
And the k. of Babylon brought	24.16

KING (cont.)

And the k. of Babylon made Mattaniah, 2Ki 24.17
k. in his stead, and changed his 24.17
years old when he became k., 24.18
rebelled against the k. of Babylon. 24.20
Nebuchadnezzar k. of Babylon came 25.01
the eleventh year of K. Zedekiah. 25.02
the k. with all the men of war 25.04
of the Chaldeans pursued the k., 25.05
Then they captured the k., 25.06
him up to the k. of Babylon at 25.06
nineteenth year of K. Nebuchadnezzar, 25.08
k. of Babylon—Nebuzaradan, the 25.08
a servant of the k. of Babylon, 25.08
had deserted to the k. of Babylon, 25.11
them to the k. of Babylon at 25.20
And the k. of Babylon smote them, 25.21
Nebuchadnezzar k. of Babylon had 25.22
heard that the k. of Babylon had 25.23
and serve the k. of Babylon, and it 25.24
exile of Jehoiachin k. of Judah, 25.27
Evilmerodach k. of Babylon, in the 25.27
Jehoiachin k. of Judah from prison; 25.27
allowance was given him by the k., 25.30
Edom before any k. reigned over 1Ch 1.43
daughter of Talmai, k. of Geshur; 3.02
there with the k. for his work. 4.23
k. of Judah, and destroyed their 4.41
Tilgathpilneser k. of Assyria 5.06
in the days of Jotham k. of Judah, 5.17
the days of Jeroboam k. of Israel. 5.17
up the spirit of Pul k. of Assyria, 5.26
of Tilgathpilneser k. of Assyria, 5.26
In times past, even when Saul was k., 11.02
of Israel came to the k. at Hebron; 11.03
they anointed David k. over Israel, 11.03
to make him k., according to the 11.10
named to come and make David k. 12.31
to make David k. over all Israel; 12.38
of a single mind to make David k. 12.38
And Hiram k. of Tyre sent messengers 14.01
had established him k. over Israel, 14.02
been anointed k. over all Israel, 14.08
and saw K. David dancing and making 15.29
Then K. David went in and sat 17.16
defeated Hadadezer k. of Zobah, 18.03
came to help Hadadezer k. of Zobah, 18.05
When Tou k. of Hamath heard that 18.09
army of Hadadezer, k. of Zobah, 18.09
he sent his son Hadoram to K. David, 18.10
these also K. David dedicated to 18.11
officials in the service of the k. 18.17
this Nahash the k. of the Ammonites 19.01
And the k. said, "Remain at Jericho 19.05
chariots and the k. of Maacah with 19.07
crown of their k. from his head; 20.02
my lord the k., all of them my 21.03
let my lord the k. do what seems 21.23
But K. David said to Ornan, "No, but 21.24
Solomon his son k. over Israel. 23.01
them in the presence of the k., 24.06
Aaron, in the presence of K. David, 24.31
under the direction of the k. 25.02
were under the order of the k. 25.06
dedicated gifts which David the k., 26.26
LORD and for the service of the k. 26.30
K. David appointed him and his 26.32
God and for the affairs of the k. 26.32
who served the k. in all matters 27.01
in the chronicles of K. David. 27.24
stewards of K. David's property. 27.31
the divisions that served the k., 28.01
and cattle of the k. and his sons, 28.01
Then K. David rose to his feet and 28.02
house to be k. over Israel for 28.04
me to make me k. over all Israel. 28.04
And David the k. said to all the 29.01
David the k. also rejoiced 29.09
LORD, and did obeisance to the k. 29.20
son of David k. the second time, 29.22
of the LORD as k. instead of David 29.23
and also all the sons of K. David, 29.24
their allegiance to K. Solomon. 29.24
not been on any k. before him in 29.25
Now the acts of K. David, from first 29.29
and hast made me k. in his stead. 2Ch 1.08
hast made me k. over a people as 1.09
over whom I have made you k., 1.11
and with the k. in Jerusalem. 1.14
And the k. made silver and gold as 1.15
sent word to Huram the k. of Tyre: 2.03
Then Huram the k. of Tyre answered 2.11
he has made you k. over them." 2.11
who has given K. David a wise son, 2.12
that he did for K. Solomon on the 4.11
bronze for K. Solomon for the 4.16
of the Jordan the k. cast them, 4.17
before the k. at the feast which 5.03
And K. Solomon and all the congregation 5.06
Then the k. faced about, and blessed 6.03
Then the k. and all the people 7.04
K. Solomon offered as a sacrifice 7.05
So the k. and all the people 7.05
the LORD which K. David had made 7.06
the chief officers of K. Solomon, 8.10
in the house of David k. of Israel, 8.11
from what the k. had commanded the 8.15
gold and brought it to K. Solomon. 8.18
And she said to the k., "The report 9.05
his throne as k. for the LORD your 9.08
ever, he has made you k. over them, 9.08
Then she gave the k. a hundred and 9.09
queen of Sheba gave to K. Solomon. 9.09
And the k. made of the algum wood 9.11
And K. Solomon gave to the queen of 9.12
what she had brought to the k. 9.12
K. Solomon made two hundred large 9.15
and the k. put them in the House 9.16
The k. also made a great ivory 9.17
All K. Solomon's drinking vessels 9.20
Thus K. Solomon excelled all the 9.22
and with the k. in Jerusalem. 9.25
And the k. made silver as common in 9.27
had come to Shechem to make him k. 10.01
he had fled from K. Solomon), 10.02
Then K. Rehoboam took counsel with 10.06
as the k. said, "Come to me again 10.12
And the k. answered them harshly, 10.13
K. Rehoboam spoke to them according 10.14
So the k. did not hearken to the 10.15
saw that the k. did not hearken to 10.16
them, the people answered the k., 10.16
Then K. Rehoboam sent Hadoram, who 10.18
And K. Rehoboam made haste to mount 10.18
the son of Solomon k. of Judah, 11.03
for he intended to make him k. 11.22
In the fifth year of K. Rehoboam, 12.02
Shishak k. of Egypt came up against 12.02
Israel and the k. humbled themselves 12.06
So Shishak k. of Egypt came up 12.09
and K. Rehoboam made in their stead 12.10
And as often as the k. went into 12.11
So K. Rehoboam established himself 12.13
eighteenth year of K. Jeroboam 13.01
K. Asa removed from being queen 15.16
Baasha k. of Israel went up against 16.01
out or come in to Asa k. of Judah. 16.01
sent them to Benhadad k. of Syria, 16.02
league with Baasha k. of Israel, 16.03
And Benhadad hearkened to K. Asa, 16.04
Then K. Asa took all Judah, and they 16.06
the seer came to Asa k. of Judah, 16.07
you relied on the k. of Syria, 16.07
the army of the k. of Syria has 16.07
These were in the service of the k., 17.19
those whom the k. had placed in 17.19

KING (cont.)

k. of Israel said to Jehoshaphat k. of Judah. 2Ch 18.03
Jehoshaphat said to the k. of Israel, 18.04
Then the k. of Israel gathered the 18.05
give it into the hand of the k. 18.05
And the k. of Israel said to 18.07
said, "Let not the k. say so." 18.07
Then the k. of Israel summoned an 18.08
Now the k. of Israel and Jehoshaphat 18.09
Jehoshaphat the k. of Judah were 18.09
give it into the hand of the k. 18.11
one accord are favorable to the k.; 18.12
And when he had come to the k., 18.14
the k. said to him, "Micaiah, shall 18.14
But the k. said to him, "How many 18.15
And the k. of Israel said to 18.17
will entice Ahab the k. of Israel, 18.19
And the k. of Israel said, "Seize 18.25
and say, 'Thus says the k., 18.26
k. of Israel and Jehoshaphat the k. of Judah 18.28
And the k. of Israel said to 18.29
And the k. of Israel disguised 18.29
Now the k. of Syria had commanded 18.30
but only with the k. of Israel. 18.30
they said, "It is the k. of Israel." 18.31
that it was not the k. of Israel, 18.32
and struck the k. of Israel 18.33
and the k. of Israel propped 18.34
Jehoshaphat the k. of Judah returned 19.01
and said to K. Jehoshaphat, "Should 19.02
and K. Jehoshaphat: Thus says the 20.15
Jehoshaphat k. of Judah joined 20.35
joined with Ahaziah k. of Israel, 20.35
sons of Jehoshaphat k. of Judah. 21.02
years old when he became k., 21.05
and set up a k. of their own. 21.08
or in the ways of Asa k. of Judah, 21.12
his youngest son k. in his stead; 22.01
son of Jehoram k. of Judah reigned. 22.01
the son of Ahab k. of Israel to 22.05
against Hazael k. of Syria at 22.05
fought against Hazael k. of Syria. 22.06
son of Jehoram k. of Judah went 22.06
Jehoshabeath, the daughter of the k., 22.11
the daughter of K. Jehoram and 22.11
with the k. in the house of God. 23.03
The Levites shall surround the k., 23.07
Be with the k. when he comes in, and 23.07
shields that had been K. David's, 23.09
the people as a guard for the k., 23.10
and they proclaimed him k., 23.11
and they said, "Long live the k." 23.11
people running and praising the k., 23.12
there was the k. standing by his 23.13
and the trumpeters beside the k., 23.13
people and the k. that they should 23.16
brought the k. down from the house 23.20
they set the k. upon the royal 23.20
So the k. summoned Jehoiada the 24.06
So the k. commanded, and they made a 24.08
And the k. and Jehoiada gave it to 24.12
money before the k. and Jehoiada, 24.14
came and did obeisance to the k.; 24.17
then the k. hearkened to them. 24.17
command of the k. they stoned him 24.21
Thus Joash the k. did not remember 24.22
their spoil to the k. of Damascus. 24.23
who had slain the k. his father. 25.03
"O k., do not let the army of 25.07
he was speaking the k. said to him, 25.16
Then Amaziah k. of Judah took 25.17
k. of Israel, saying, "Come, let us 25.17
And Joash the k. of Israel sent 25.18
sent word to Amaziah k. of Judah, 25.18
So Joash k. of Israel went up; 25.21
he and Amaziah k. of Judah faced 25.21
k. of Israel captured Amaziah k. of 25.23
son of Joash k. of Judah lived 25.25
the son of Jehoahaz, k. of Israel. 25.25
and made him k. instead of his 26.01
after the k. slept with his fathers. 26.02
to help the k. against the enemy. 26.13
and they withstood K. Uzziah, 26.18
And K. Uzziah was a leper to the 26.21
He fought with the k. of the 27.05
into the hand of the k. of Syria, 28.05
into the hand of the k. of Israel, 28.05
the next in authority to the k. 28.07
K. Ahaz sent to the k. of Assyria 28.16
low because of Ahaz k. of Israel, 28.19
So Tilgathpilneser k. of Assyria 28.20
house of the k. and of the princes, 28.21
gave tribute to the k. of Assyria; 28.21
to the LORD—this same K. Ahaz. 28.22
went in as the k. had commanded, 29.15
in to Hezekiah the k. and said, 29.18
utensils which K. Ahaz discarded 29.19
Then Hezekiah the k. rose early and 29.20
brought to the k. and the assembly, 29.23
For the k. commanded that the burnt 29.24
instruments of David k. of Israel. 29.27
the k. and all who were present 29.29
And Hezekiah the k. and the princes 29.30
For the k. and his princes and all 30.02
right to the k. and all the 30.04
from the k. and his princes, as the 30.06
as the k. had commanded, saying, "O 30.06
to do what the k. and the princes 30.12
For Hezekiah k. of Judah gave the 30.24
son of David k. of Israel there 30.26
contribution of the k. from his own 31.03
of Hezekiah the k. and Azariah the 31.13
Sennacherib k. of Assyria came and 32.01
before the k. of Assyria and all 32.07
the words of Hezekiah k. of Judah. 32.08
After this Sennacherib k. of Assyria, 32.09
to Hezekiah k. of Judah and to all 32.09
"Thus says Sennacherib k. of Assyria, 32.10
the hand of the k. of Assyria"? 32.11
Then Hezekiah the k. and Isaiah the 32.20
in the camp of the k. of Assyria. 32.21
of Sennacherib k. of Assyria and 32.22
things to Hezekiah k. of Judah, 32.23
of the army of the k. of Assyria, 33.11
who had conspired against K. Amon; 33.25
Josiah his son k. in his stead. 33.25
Shaphan brought the book to the k., 34.16
and further reported to the k., 34.16
Then Shaphan the secretary told the k., 34.18
And Shaphan read it before the k. 34.18
When the k. heard the words of the 34.19
And the k. commanded Hilkiah, Ahikam 34.20
those whom the k. had sent went to 34.22
was read before the k. of Judah. 34.24
But to the k. of Judah, who sent you 34.26
they brought back word to the k. 34.28
Then the k. sent and gathered 34.29
And the k. went up to the house of 34.30
And the k. stood in his place and 34.31
son of David, k. of Israel, built; 35.03
of David k. of Israel and the 35.04
to the command of K. Josiah. 35.16
Neco k. of Egypt went up to fight 35.20
to do with each other, k. of Judah? 35.21
And the archers shot K. Josiah; 35.23
and the k. said to his servants, 35.23
and made him k. in his father's 36.01
Then the k. of Egypt deposed him in 36.03
And the k. of Egypt made Eliakim 36.04
his brother k. over Judah and 36.04
up Nebuchadnezzar k. of Babylon, 36.06
of the year K. Nebuchadnezzar sent 36.10
Zedekiah k. over Judah and Jerusalem. 36.10
rebelled against K. Nebuchadnezzar, 36.13
them the k. of the Chaldeans, who 36.17
treasures of the k. and of his 36.18

KING (cont.)

first year of Cyrus k. of Persia,	2Ch 36.22
spirit of Cyrus k. of Persia so	36.22
"Thus says Cyrus k. of Persia,	36.23
first year of Cyrus k. of Persia,	Ez 1.01
spirit of Cyrus k. of Persia so	1.01
"Thus says Cyrus k. of Persia:	1.02
Cyrus the k. also brought out the	1.07
Cyrus k. of Persia brought these	1.08
Nebuchadnezzar the k. of Babylon	2.01
they had from Cyrus k. of Persia.	3.07
directions of David k. of Israel;	3.10
of Esarhaddon k. of Assyria who	4.02
as K. Cyrus the k. of Persia has	4.03
all the days of Cyrus k. of Persia,	4.05
the reign of Darius k. of Persia.	4.05
wrote to Artaxerxes k. of Persia;	4.07
to Artaxerxes the k. as follows—	4.08
they sent—"To Artaxerxes the k.:	4.11
it known to the k. that the Jews	4.12
Now be it known to the k. that,	4.13
therefore we send and inform the k.,	4.14
We make known to the k. that,	4.16
The k. sent an answer: "To Rehum the	4.17
damage grow to the hurt of the k.?"	4.22
the copy of K. Artaxerxes' letter	4.23
the reign of Darius k. of Persia.	4.24
the River sent to Darius the k.;	5.06
"To Darius the k., all peace.	5.07
Be it known to the k. that we went	5.08
which a great k. of Israel built	5.11
of Nebuchadnezzar k. of Babylon,	5.12
first year of Cyrus k. of Babylon,	5.13
Cyrus the k. made a decree that	5.13
these Cyrus the k. took out of the	5.14
Therefore, if it seem good to the k.,	5.17
by Cyrus the k. for the rebuilding	5.17
And let the k. send us his pleasure	5.17
Then Darius the k. made a decree,	6.01
In the first year of Cyrus the k.,	6.03
Cyrus the k. issued a decree:	6.03
the life of the k. and his sons.	6.10
overthrow any k. or people that	6.12
to the word sent by Darius the k.,	6.13
what Darius the k. had ordered.	6.13
Darius and Artaxerxes k. of Persia;	6.14
year of the reign of Darius the k.	6.15
heart of the k. of Assyria to them,	6.22
reign of Artaxerxes k. of Persia,	7.01
and the k. granted him all that	7.06
seventh year of Artaxerxes the k.,	7.07
was in the seventh year of the k.;	7.08
letter which K. Artaxerxes gave to	7.11
"Artaxerxes, k. of kings, to Ezra the	7.12
are sent by the k. and his seven	7.14
gold which the k. and his counselors	7.15
"And I, Artaxerxes the k., make a	7.21
the realm of the k. and his sons.	7.23
of your God and the law of the k.,	7.26
as this into the heart of the k.,	7.27
love before the k. and his counselors,	7.28
in the reign of Artaxerxes the k.:	8.01
to ask the k. for a band of soldiers	8.22
since we had told the k., "The hand of	8.22
God which the k. and his counselors	8.25
Now I was cupbearer to the k.	Neh 1.11
twentieth year of K. Artaxerxes,	2.01
up the wine and gave it to the k.	2.01
And the k. said to me, "Why is your	2.02
to the k., "Let the k. live for ever!	2.03
Then the k. said to me, "For what do	2.04
said to the k., "If it pleases the k.,	2.05
And the k. said to me (the queen	2.06
So it pleased the k. to send me;	2.06
said to the k., "If it pleases the k.,	2.07
And the k. granted me what I	2.08
Now the k. had sent with me officers	2.09
words which the k. had spoken to	2.18
Are you rebelling against the k.?"	2.19
house of the k. at the court of	3.25
thirty-second year of Artaxerxes the k.,	5.14
and you wish to become their k.,	6.06
Jerusalem, 'There is a k. in Judah.'	6.07
reported to the k. according to	6.07
Nebuchadnezzar the k. of Babylon	7.06
land of Sihon k. of Heshbon and	9.22
and the land of Og k. of Bashan.	9.22
from the k. concerning them, and a	11.23
k. of Babylon I went to the k.	13.06
some time I asked leave of the k.	13.06
Did not Solomon k. of Israel sin on	13.26
nations there was no k. like him,	13.26
God made him k. over all Israel;	13.26
in those days when K. Ahasuerus sat	Est 1.02
the k. gave for all the people	1.05
according to the bounty of the k.	1.07
for the k. had given orders to all	1.08
which belonged to K. Ahasuerus.	1.09
heart of the k. was merry with	1.10
who served K. Ahasuerus as chamberlains,	1.10
before the k. with her royal crown,	1.11
At this the k. was enraged, and his	1.12
Then the k. said to the wise men	1.13
performed the command of K. Ahasuerus	1.15
presence of the k. and the princes,	1.16
"Not only to the k. has Queen	1.16
all the provinces of K. Ahasuerus.	1.16
'K. Ahasuerus commanded Queen	1.17
If it please the k., let a royal	1.19
come no more before K. Ahasuerus;	1.19
and let the k. give her royal	1.19
made by the k. is proclaimed	1.20
pleased the k. and the princes, and	1.21
and the k. did as Memucan proposed;	1.21
the anger of K. Ahasuerus had	2.01
virgins be sought out for the k.	2.02
And let the k. appoint officers in	2.03
who pleases the k. be queen instead	2.04
This pleased the k., and he did so.	2.04
away with Jeconiah k. of Judah,	2.06
Nebuchadnezzar k. of Babylon had	2.06
maiden to go in to K. Ahasuerus,	2.12
went in to the k. in this way she	2.13
he did not go in to the k. again,	2.14
unless the k. delighted in her and	2.14
own daughter, to go in to the k.,	2.15
was taken to K. Ahasuerus into his	2.16
the k. loved Esther more than all	2.17
Then the k. gave a great banquet to	2.18
to lay hands on K. Ahasuerus.	2.21
Esther told the k. in the name of	2.22
Chronicles in the presence of the k.	2.23
After these things K. Ahasuerus	3.01
for the k. had so commanded concerning	3.02
the twelfth year of K. Ahasuerus,	3.07
Then Haman said to K. Ahasuerus,	3.08
If it please the k., let it be decreed	3.09
So the k. took his signet ring from	3.10
And the k. said to Haman, "The money	3.11
in the name of K. Ahasuerus and	3.12
went in haste by order of the k.,	3.15
And the k. and Haman sat down to	3.15
to go to the k. to make supplication	4.08
goes to the k. inside the inner	4.11
one to whom the k. holds out the	4.11
come in to the k. these thirty	4.11
Then I will go to the k., though it	4.16
The k. was sitting on his royal	5.01
and when the k. saw Queen Esther	5.02
And the k. said to her, "What is it,	5.03
And Esther said, "If it please the k.,	5.04
let the k. and Haman come this day	5.04
that I have prepared for the k."	5.04
Then said the k., "Bring Haman	5.05
So the k. and Haman came to the	5.05
the k. said to Esther, "What is your	5.06

KING (cont.)
found favor in the sight of the k., Est 5.08
it please the k. to grant my 5.08
let the k. and Haman come tomorrow 5.08
I will do as the k. has said." 5.08
with which the k. had honored him. 5.11
princes and the servants of the k. 5.11
come with the k. to the banquet 5.12
by her together with the k. 5.12
tell the k. to have Mordecai 5.14
merrily with the k. to the dinner." 5.14
On that night the k. could not 6.01
and they were read before the k. 6.01
to lay hands upon K. Ahasuerus. 6.02
And the k. said, "What honor or 6.03
And the k. said, "Who is in the 6.04
to speak to the k. about having 6.04
And the k. said, "Let him come in." 6.05
and the k. said to him, "What shall 6.06
man whom the k. delights to honor?" 6.06
"Whom would the k. delight to honor 6.06
And Haman said to the k., "For the 6.07
man whom the k. delights to honor, 6.07
which the k. has worn, and the horse 6.08
the horse which the k. has ridden, 6.08
man whom the k. delights to honor, 6.09
man whom the k. delights to honor.'" 6.09
Then the k. said to Haman, "Make 6.10
man whom the k. delights to honor." 6.11
So the k. and Haman went in to 7.01
the k. again said to Esther, "What 7.02
O k., and if it please the k., let my 7.03
compared with the loss to the k." 7.04
Then K. Ahasuerus said to Queen 7.05
terror before the k. and the queen. 7.06
And the k. rose from the feast in 7.07
determined against him by the k. 7.07
And the k. returned from the palace 7.08
and the k. said, "Will he even 7.08
the words left the mouth of the k., 7.08
eunuchs in attendance on the k., 7.09
Mordecai. whose word saved the k., 7.09
And the k. said, "Hang him on that." 7.10
Then the anger of the k. abated. 7.10
On that day K. Ahasuerus gave to 8.01
And Mordecai came before the k., 8.01
and the k. took off his signet ring, 8.02
Then Esther spoke again to the k.; 8.03
And the k. held out the golden 8.04
rose and stood before the k. 8.05
and she said, "If it please the k., 8.05
the thing seem right before the k., 8.05
are in all the provinces of the k. 8.05
Then K. Ahasuerus said to Queen 8.07
to the Jews, in the name of the k., 8.08
the name of the k. and sealed with 8.08
in the name of K. Ahasuerus and 8.10
By these the k. allowed the Jews 8.11
all the provinces of K. Ahasuerus, 8.12
presence of the k. in royal robes 8.15
provinces of K. Ahasuerus to lay 9.02
the capital was reported to the k. 9.11
And the k. said to Queen Esther, "In 9.12
And Esther said, "If it please the k., 9.13
So the k. commanded this to be done; 9.14
all the provinces of K. Ahasuerus, 9.20
but when Esther came before the k., 9.25
K. Ahasuerus laid tribute on the 10.01
to which the k. advanced him, are 10.02
was next in rank to K. Ahasuerus, 10.03
like a k. prepared for battle. Job 15.24
is brought to the k. of terrors. 18.14
I dwelt like a k. among his troops, 29.25
who says to a k., 'Worthless one,' 34.18
he is k. over all the sons of pride." 41.34
"I have set my k. on Zion, my holy Ps 2.06
my K. and my God, for to thee do I 5.02
The LORD Is k. for ever and ever; 10.16
Great triumphs he gives to his k., 18.50
Give victory to the k., O LORD; 20.09
In thy strength the k. rejoices, 21.01
For the k. trusts in the LORD; 21.07
that the K. of glory may come in. 24.07
Who is the K. of glory? 24.08
that the K. of glory may come in! 24.09
Who is this K. of glory? 24.10
of hosts, he is the K. of glory! 24.10
LORD sits enthroned as k. for ever. 29.10
A k. is not saved by his great army; 33.16
Thou art my K. and my God, who 44.04
I address my verses to the k.; 45.01
and the k. will desire your beauty. 45.11
many-colored robes she is led to the k., 45.14
as they enter the palace of the k. 45.15
a great k. over all the earth. 47.02
praises to our K., sing praises! 47.06
For God is the k. of all the earth; 47.07
north, the city of the great K. 48.02
Prolong the life of the k.; 61.06
But the k. shall rejoice in God; 63.11
of my God, my K., into the sanctuary— 68.24
Give the k. thy justice, O God, and 72.01
Yet God my K. is from of old, 74.12
O LORD of hosts, my k. and my God. 84.03
our k. to the Holy One of Israel. 89.18
God, and a great K. above all gods. 95.03
noise before the K., the LORD! 98.06
Mighty K., lover of justice, thou 99.04
The k. sent and released him, the 105.20
Sihon, k. of the Amorites, and Og, 135.11
k. of Bashan, and all the kingdoms 135.11
Sihon, k. of the Amorites, for his 136.19
and Og, k. of Bashan, for his steadfast 136.20
my God and K., and bless thy name 145.01
sons of Zion rejoice in their K.! 149.02
son of David, k. of Israel: Pro 1.01
of people is the glory of a k., 14.28
Inspired decisions are on the lips of a k.; 16.10
Righteous lips are the delight of a k., 16.13
wrath of a k. is like the growling 20.02
A k. who sits on the throne of 20.08
A wise k. winnows the wicked, and 20.26
Loyalty and faithfulness preserve the k., 20.28
will have the k. as his friend. 22.11
My son, fear the LORD And the k., 24.21
men of Hezekiah k. of Judah copied. 25.01
wicked from the presence of the k., 25.05
By justice a k. gives stability to 29.04
If a k. judges the poor with equity 29.14
a slave when he becomes k., 30.22
the locusts have no k., yet all of 30.27
and a k. striding before his people. 30.31
k. of Massa, which his mother taught 31.01
the son of David, k. in Jerusalem. Ecc 1.01
have been k. over Israel in 1.12
the man do who comes after the k.? 2.12
youth than an old and foolish k., 4.13
But in all, a k. is an advantage to 5.09
For the word of the k. is supreme, 8.04
and a great k. came against it and 9.14
when your k. is a child, and your 10.16
when your k. is the son of free men, 10.17
your thought, do not curse the k., 10.20
The k. has brought me into his Sol 1.04
While the k. was on his couch, my 1.12
K. Solomon made himself a palanquin 3.09
and behold K. Solomon, with the 3.11
a k. is held captive in the tresses 7.05
In the year that K. Uzziah died I Is 6.01
for my eyes have seen the K., 6.05
k. of Judah, Rezin the k. of Syria 7.01
of Remaliah the k. of Israel came 7.01
of Tabeel as k. in the midst of it, 7.06
from Judah—the k. of Assyria." 7.17
with the k. of Assyria—the head 7.20
away before the k. of Assyria." 8.04

KING (cont.)

the k. of Assyria and all his glory;	Is 8.07
will curse their k. and their God,	8.21
boasting of the k. of Assyria and	10.12
taunt against the k. of Babylon:	14.04
In the year that K. Ahaz died came	14.28
and a fierce k. will rule over them,	19.04
sent by Sargon the k. of Assyria,	20.01
so shall the k. of Assyria lead	20.04
delivered from the k. of Assyria!	20.06
years, like the days of one k.	23.15
yea, for the k. it is made ready, its	30.33
Behold, a k. will reign in righteousness,	32.01
eyes will see the k. in his beauty;	33.17
is our ruler, the LORD is our k.;	33.22
the fourteenth year of K. Hezekiah,	36.01
Sennacherib k. of Assyria came up	36.01
And the k. of Assyria sent the	36.02
from Lachish to K. Hezekiah at	36.02
'Thus says the great k., the k. of Assyria:	36.04
Such is Pharaoh k. of Egypt to all	36.06
with my master the k. of Assyria:	36.08
the great king, the k. of Assyria!	36.13
Thus says the k.: 'Do not let	36.14
into the hand of the k. of Assyria.	36.15
for thus says the k. of Assyria:	36.16
of the hand of the k. of Assyria?	36.18
When K. Hezekiah heard it, he rent	37.01
his master the k. of Assyria has	37.04
When the servants of K. Hezekiah	37.05
servants of the k. of Assyria have	37.06
and found the k. of Assyria fighting	37.08
heard that the k. had left Lachish.	37.08
k. heard concerning Tirhakah k. of Ethiopia,	37.09
you speak to Hezekiah k. of Judah:	37.10
into the hand of the k. of Assyria.	37.10
are the k. of Hamath, the k. of Arpad,	37.13
the k. of the city of Sepharvaim,	37.13
the k. of Hena, or the k. of Ivvah?'"	37.13
concerning Sennacherib k. of Assyria,	37.21
LORD concerning the k. of Assyria:	37.33
Then Sennacherib k. of Assyria	37.37
of the hand of the k. of Assyria,	38.06
A writing of Hezekiah k. of Judah,	38.09
k. of Babylon, sent envoys with	39.01
the prophet came to K. Hezekiah,	39.03
in the palace of the k. of Babylon.	39.07
your proofs, says the K. of Jacob.	41.21
the Creator of Israel, your K."	43.15
the K. of Israel and his Redeemer,	44.06
k. of Judah, in the thirteenth year	Jer 1.02
k. of Judah, and until the end of	1.03
k. of Judah, until the captivity of	1.03
to me in the days of K. Josiah:	3.06
shall fail both k. and princes;	4.09
not in Zion? Is her K. not in her?"	8.19
not fear thee, O K. of the nations?	10.07
living God and the everlasting K.	10.10
Say to the k. and the queen mother:	13.18
k. of Judah, did in Jerusalem.	15.04
into the hand of the k. of Babylon;	20.04
when K. Zedekiah sent to him	21.01
Nebuchadrezzar k. of Babylon is	21.02
against the k. of Babylon and	21.04
will deliver Zedekiah k. of Judah,	21.07
Nebuchadrezzar k. of Babylon and	21.07
into the hand of the k. of Babylon,	21.10
the house of the k. of Judah say,	21.11
to the house of the k. of Judah,	22.01
O K. of Judah, who sit on the throne	22.02
the house of the k. of Judah:	22.06
k. of Judah, who reigned instead of	22.11
think you are a k. because you	22.15
k. of Judah: "They shall not lament	22.18
k. of Judah, were the signet ring on	22.24
Nebuchadrezzar k. of Babylon and	22.25
shall reign as k. and deal wisely,	23.05
After Nebuchadrezzar k. of Babylon	24.01
k. of Judah, together with the	24.01
I treat Zedekiah the k. of Judah,	24.08
k. of Judah (that was the first	25.01
of Nebuchadrezzar k. of Babylon),	25.01
k. of Judah, to this day, the word of	25.03
Nebuchadrezzar the k. of Babylon,	25.09
shall serve the k. of Babylon	25.11
will punish the k. of Babylon and	25.12
Pharaoh k. of Egypt, his servants,	25.19
after them the k. of Babylon shall	25.26
k. of Judah, this word came from the	26.01
the days of Hezekiah k. of Judah,	26.18
Did Hezekiah k. of Judah and all	26.19
And when K. Jehoiakim, with all his	26.21
the k. sought to put him to death;	26.21
Then K. Jehoiakim sent to Egypt	26.22
and brought him to K. Jehoiakim,	26.23
k. of Judah, this word came to	27.01
Send word to the k. of Edom,	27.03
k. of Moab, the k. of the sons of Ammon,	27.03
the k. of Tyre, and the k. of Sidon	27.03
Jerusalem to Zedekiah k. of Judah.	27.03
the k. of Babylon, my servant, and I	27.06
this Nebuchadnezzar k. of Babylon,	27.08
the yoke of the k. of Babylon,	27.08
shall not serve the k. of Babylon.	27.09
the yoke of the k. of Babylon and	27.11
To Zedekiah k. of Judah I spoke in	27.12
the yoke of the k. of Babylon,	27.12
will not serve the k. of Babylon?	27.13
shall not serve the k. of Babylon,'	27.14
serve the k. of Babylon and live.	27.17
in the house of the k. of Judah,	27.18
which Nebuchadnezzar k. of Babylon	27.20
k. of Judah, and all the nobles of	27.20
in the house of the k. of Judah,	27.21
the reign of Zedekiah k. of Judah,	28.01
the yoke of the k. of Babylon.	28.02
Nebuchadnezzar k. of Babylon took	28.03
k. of Judah, and all the exiles from	28.04
the yoke of the k. of Babylon.	28.04
Nebuchadnezzar k. of Babylon from	28.11
to Nebuchadnezzar k. of Babylon,	28.14
This was after K. Jeconiah, and the	29.02
whom Zedekiah k. of Judah sent to	29.03
to Nebuchadnezzar k. of Babylon.	29.03
concerning the k. who sits on the	29.16
of Nebuchadrezzar k. of Babylon,	29.21
whom the k. of Babylon roasted in	29.22
LORD their God and David their k.,	30.09
tenth year of Zedekiah k. of Judah,	32.01
the army of the k. of Babylon was	32.02
in the palace of the k. of Judah.	32.02
For Zedekiah k. of Judah had	32.03
into the hand of the k. of Babylon,	32.03
Zedekiah k. of Judah shall not	32.04
into the hand of the k. of Babylon,	32.04
of Nebuchadrezzar k. of Babylon,	32.28
the hand of the k. of Babylon by	32.36
Nebuchadrezzar k. of Babylon and	34.01
to Zedekiah k. of Judah and say to	34.02
into the hand of the k. of Babylon,	34.02
shall see the k. of Babylon eye to	34.03
the LORD, O Zedekiah k. of Judah!	34.04
words to Zedekiah k. of Judah,	34.06
when the army of the k. of Babylon	34.07
after K. Zedekiah had made a	34.08
And Zedekiah k. of Judah, and his	34.21
the army of the k. of Babylon	34.21
the son of Josiah, k. of Judah:	35.01
Nebuchadrezzar k. of Babylon came	35.11
k. of Judah, this word came to	36.01
k. of Judah, in the ninth month, all	36.09
report all these words to the k.	36.16
they went into the court to the k.,	36.20
reported all the words to the k.	36.20
Then the k. sent Jehudi to get the	36.21
read it to the k. and all the	36.21

KING (cont.)

princes who stood beside the k. Jer 36.21
and the k. was sitting in the 36.22
the k. would cut them off with a 36.23
Yet neither the k., nor any of his 36.24
urged the k. not to burn the 36.25
And the k. commanded Jerahmeel the 36.26
Now, after the k. had burned the 36.27
Jehoiakim the k. of Judah has 36.28
Jehoiakim k. of Judah you shall 36.29
in it that the k. of Babylon will 36.29
concerning Jehoiakim k. of Judah, 36.30
which Jehoiakim k. of Judah had 36.32
Nebuchadrezzar k. of Babylon made 37.01
of Babylon made k. in the land of 37.01
K. Zedekiah sent Jehucal the son of 37.03
you say to the k. of Judah who 37.07
K. Zedekiah sent for him, and 37.17
The k. questioned him secretly in 37.17
into the hand of the k. of Babylon. 37.17
Jeremiah also said to K. Zedekiah, 37.18
'The k. of Babylon will not come 37.19
O my Lord the k.: let my humble plea 37.20
So K. Zedekiah gave orders, and they 37.21
the army of the k. of Babylon and 38.03
Then the princes said to the k., 38.04
K. Zedekiah said, "Behold, he is in 38.05
for the k. can do nothing against 38.05
the k. was sitting in the Benjamin 38.07
king's house and said to the k., 38.08
"My lord the k., these men have 38.09
Then the k. commanded Ebedmelech, 38.10
and went to the house of the k., 38.11
K. Zedekiah sent for Jeremiah the 38.14
The k. said to Jeremiah, "I will ask 38.14
Then K. Zedekiah swore secretly to 38.16
the princes of the k. of Babylon, 38.17
the princes of the k. of Babylon, 38.18
K. Zedekiah said to Jeremiah, "I am 38.19
house of the k. of Judah were 38.22
princes of the k. of Babylon and 38.22
be seized by the k. of Babylon; 38.23
said to the k. and what the k. said 38.25
plea to the k. that he would not 38.26
them as the k. had instructed him. 38.27
ninth year of Zedekiah k. of Judah, 39.01
Nebuchadrezzar k. of Babylon and 39.01
princes of the k. of Babylon came 39.03
the offices of the k. of Babylon. 39.03
When Zedekiah k. of Judah and all 39.04
up to Nebuchadrezzar k. of Babylon, 39.05
The k. of Babylon slew the sons of 39.06
and the k. of Babylon slew all the 39.06
Nebuchadrezzar k. of Babylon gave 39.11
officers of the k. of Babylon 39.13
whom the k. of Babylon appointed 40.05
heard that the k. of Babylon had 40.07
and serve the k. of Babylon, and it 40.09
heard that the k. of Babylon had 40.11
that Baal is the k. of the Ammonites 40.14
of the chief officers of the k., 41.01
whom the k. of Babylon had appointed 41.02
cistern which K. Asa had made for 41.09
against Baasha k. of Israel; 41.09
whom the k. of Babylon had made 41.18
Do not fear the k. of Babylon, 42.11
Nebuchadrezzar the k. of Babylon, 43.10
Pharaoh Hophra k. of Egypt into 44.30
I gave Zedekiah k. of Judah into 44.30
of Nebuchadrezzar k. of Babylon, 44.30
the son of Josiah, k. of Judah: 45.01
k. of Egypt, which was by the river 46.02
Nebuchadrezzar k. of Babylon 46.02
the son of Josiah, k. of Judah: 46.02
Nebuchadrezzar k. of Babylon to 46.13
k. of Egypt, 'Noisy one who lets the 46.17
says the K., whose name is the LORD 46.18
Nebuchadrezzar k. of Babylon and 46.26
says the K., whose name is the LORD 48.15
Nebuchadrezzar k. of Babylon smote 49.28
Nebuchadrezzar k. of Babylon has 49.30
the reign of Zedekiah k. of Judah. 49.34
and destroy their k. and princes, 49.38
First the k. of Assyria devoured 50.17
Nebuchadrezzar k. of Babylon has 50.17
punishment on the k. of Babylon and 50.18
as I punished the k. of Assyria. 50.18
"The k. of Babylon heard the report 50.43
to tell the k. of Babylon that his 51.31
"Nebuchadrezzar the k. of Babylon 51.34
says the K., whose name is the LORD 51.57
with Zedekiah k. of Judah to 51.59
years old when he became k.; 52.01
rebelled against the k. of Babylon. 52.03
Nebuchadrezzar k. of Babylon came 52.04
the eleventh year of K. Zedekiah. 52.05
of the Chaldeans pursued the k., 52.08
Then they captured the k., and 52.09
him up to the k. of Babylon at 52.09
The k. of Babylon slew the sons of 52.10
and the k. of Babylon took him to 52.11
nineteenth year of K. Nebuchadrezzar, 52.12
k. of Babylon—Nebuzaradan the 52.12
who served the k. of Babylon, 52.12
had deserted to the k. of Babylon, 52.15
Solomon the k. had made for the 52.20
them to the k. of Babylon at 52.26
And the k. of Babylon smote them, 52.27
captivity of Jehoiachin k. of Judah, 52.31
Evilmerodach k. of Babylon, in the 52.31
in the year that he became k., 52.31
of Jehoiachin k. of Judah and 52.31
him by the k. according to his 52.34
indignation has spurned k. and priest. Lam 2.06
her k. and princes are among the 2.09
of the exile of K. Jehoiachin), Eze 1.02
The k. mourns, the prince is wrapped 7.27
the k. of Babylon came to Jerusalem, 17.12
and took her k. and her princes and 17.12
where the k. dwells who made him k., 17.16
brought him to the k. of Babylon; 19.09
poured out, I will be k. over you. 20.33
sword of the k. of Babylon to come 21.19
For the k. of Babylon stands at the 21.21
The k. of Babylon has laid siege to 24.02
north Nebuchadrezzar k. of Babylon, 26.07
k. of kings, with horses and chariots, 26.07
a lamentation over the k. of Tyre, 28.12
face against Pharaoh k. of Egypt, 29.02
Pharaoh k. of Egypt, the great 29.03
Nebuchadrezzar k. of Babylon made 29.18
to Nebuchadrezzar k. of Babylon; 29.19
of Nebuchadrezzar k. of Babylon. 30.10
the arm of Pharaoh k. of Egypt; 30.21
I am against Pharaoh k. of Egypt, 30.22
the arms of the k. of Babylon, 30.24
the arms of the k. of Babylon, 30.25
into the hand of the k. of Babylon, 30.25
say to Pharaoh k. of Egypt and to 31.02
lamentation over Pharaoh k. of Egypt, 32.02
sword of the k. of Babylon shall 32.11
and one k. shall be k. over them all; 37.22
David shall be k. over them; 37.24
the reign of Jehoiakim k. of Judah, Dan 1.01
Nebuchadnezzar k. of Babylon came 1.01
gave Jehoiakim k. of Judah into 1.02
Then the k. commanded Ashpenaz, his 1.03
The k. assigned them a daily 1.05
of the rich food which the k. ate, 1.05
they were to stand before the k. 1.05
Daniel "I fear lest my lord the k., 1.10
would endanger my head with the k." 1.10
when the k. had commanded that they 1.18
And the k. spoke with them, and 1.19
therefore they stood before the k. 1.19
which the k. inquired of them, he 1.20

KING (cont.)
until the first year of K. Cyrus. Dan 1.21
Then the k. commanded that the 2.02
summoned, to tell the k. his dreams. 2.02
came in and stood before the k. 2.02
And the k. said to them, "I had a 2.03
Chaldeans said to the k., "O k., live for ever! 2.04
The k. answered the Chaldeans, "The 2.05
"Let the k. tell his servants the 2.07
The k. answered, "I know with 2.08
The Chaldeans answered the k., 2.10
and powerful k. has asked such a 2.10
The thing that the k. asks is 2.11
show it to the k. except the gods, 2.11
Because of this the k. was angry 2.12
is the decree of the k. so severe?" 2.15
besought the k. to appoint him a 2.16
show to the k. the interpretation. 2.16
whom the k. had appointed to destroy 2.24
bring me in before the k., and I will 2.24
I will show the k. the interpretation." 2.24
in Daniel before the k. in haste, 2.25
known to the k. the interpretation." 2.25
The k. said to Daniel, whose name 2.26
Daniel answered the k., "No wise men, 2.27
the k. the mystery which the k. has asked, 2.27
made known to K. Nebuchadnezzar 2.28
To you, O k., as you lay in bed came 2.29
may be made known to the k., 2.30
"You saw, O k., and behold, a great 2.31
will tell the k. its interpretation. 2.36
You, O k., the k. of kings, to whom the 2.37
known to the k. what shall be 2.45
Then K. Nebuchadnezzar fell upon 2.46
The k. said to Daniel, "Truly, your 2.47
Then the k. gave Daniel high honors 2.48
Daniel made request of the k., 2.49
K. Nebuchadnezzar made an image of 3.01
Then K. Nebuchadnezzar sent to 3.02
the image which K. Nebuchadnezzar 3.02
the image the K. Nebuchadnezzar 3.03
image that K. Nebuchadnezzar has 3.05
image which K. Nebuchadnezzar had 3.07
They said to K. Nebuchadnezzar, "O 3.09
Nebuchadnezzer, "O k., live for ever! 3.09
You, O k., have made a decree, that 3.10
These men, O k., pay no heed to you; 3.12
brought these men before the k. 3.13
and Abednego answered the k., 3.16
deliver us out of your hand, O k. 3.17
O k., that we will not serve your 3.18
Then K. Nebuchadnezzar was astonished 3.24
They answered the k., "True, O k." 3.24
Then the k. promoted Shadrach, 3.30
K. Nebuchadnezzar to all peoples, 4.01
This dream I, K. Nebuchadnezzar, saw. 4.18
The k. said, "Belteshazzar, let not 4.19
it is you, O k., who have grown and 4.22
And whereas the k. saw a watcher, 4.23
O k.: It is a decree of the Most 4.24
has come upon my lord the k., 4.24
Therefore, O k., let my counsel be 4.27
All this came upon K. Nebuchadnezzar. 4.28
and the k. said, "Is not this great 4.30
"O K. Nebuchadnezzar, to you it is 4.31
extol and honor the K. of heaven; 4.37
K. Belshazzar made a great feast 5.01
that the k. and his lords, his wives, 5.02
and the k. and his lords, his wives, 5.03
and the k. saw the hand as it wrote. 5.05
The k. cried aloud to bring in the 5.07
The k. said to the wise men of 5.07
known to the k. the interpretation. 5.08
Then K. Belshazzar was greatly 5.09
the words of the k. and his lords, 5.10
queen said, "O k., live for ever! 5.10
and K. Nebuchadnezzar, your father, 5.11
whom the k. named Belteshazzar. 5.12
was brought in before the k. 5.13
The k. said to Daniel, "You are that 5.13
whom the k. my father brought from 5.13
Then Daniel answered before the k., 5.17
writing to the k. and make known 5.17
O k., the Most High God gave 5.18
Belshazzar the Chaldean k. was slain. 5.30
so that the k. might suffer no loss. 6.02
and the k. planned to set him over 6.03
agreement to the k. and said to him, 6.06
"O K. Darius, live for ever! 6.06
agreed that the k. should establish 6.07
O k., shall be cast into the den of 6.07
Now, O k., establish the interdict 6.08
Therefore K. Darius signed the 6.09
came near and said before the k., 6.12
concerning the interdict, "O k.! Did 6.12
O k., shall be cast into the den of 6.12
The k. answered, "The thing stands 6.12
Then they answered before the k., 6.13
O k., or the interdict you have 6.13
Then the k., when he heard these 6.14
these men came by agreement to the k., 6.15
and said to the k., "Know, O k., that 6.15
which the k. establishes can be 6.15
Then the k. commanded, and Daniel 6.16
The k. said to Daniel, "May your God, 6.16
and the k. sealed it with his own 6.17
Then the k. went to his palace, and 6.18
the k. arose and went in haste to 6.19
Then Daniel said to the k., "O k., live 6.21
you, O k., I have done no wrong." 6.22
Then the k. was exceedingly glad, 6.23
And the k. commanded, and those men 6.24
Then K. Darius wrote to all the 6.25
year of Belshazzar k. of Babylon, 7.01
of the reign of K. Belshazzar a 8.01
And the he-goat is the k. of Greece; 8.21
horn between his eyes is the first k. 8.21
a k. of bold countenance, one who 8.23
who became k. over the realm of the 9.01
year of Cyrus k. of Persia a word 10.01
Then a mighty k. shall arise, who 11.03
"Then the k. of the south shall be 11.05
daughter of the k. of the south 11.06
come to the k. of the north to 11.06
fortress of the k. of the north, 11.07
attacking the k. of the north. 11.08
realm of the k. of the south but 11.09
Then the k. of the south, moved with 11.11
and fight with the k. of the north; 11.11
For the k. of the north shall again 11.13
rise against the k. of the south; 11.14
Then the k. of the north shall come 11.15
against the k. of the south with a 11.25
and the k. of the south shall wage 11.25
"And the k. shall do according to 11.36
of the end the k. of the south 11.40
but the k. of the north shall rush 11.40
the son of Joash, k. of Israel. Hos 1.01
many days without k. or prince, 3.04
Lord their God, and David their k.; 3.05
Hearken, O house of the k.! For the 5.01
Assyria, and sent to the great k. 5.13
wickedness they make the k. glad, 7.03
On the day of our k. the princes 7.05
from anointing k. and princes. 8.10
"We have no k., for we fear not the 10.03
and a k., what could he do for us?" 10.03
Assyria, as tribute to the great k. 10.06
Samaria's k. shall perish, like a 10.07
the storm the k. of Israel shall 10.15
and Assyria shall be their k., 11.05
Where now is your k., to save you; 13.10
said, "Give me a k. and princes"? 13.10
days of Uzziah k. of Judah and in Amo 1.01
k. of Israel, two years before the 1.01
and their k. shall go into exile, he 1.15

KING (cont.)
lime the bones of the k. of Edom. Amo 2.01
You shall take up Sakkuth your k., 5.26
sent to Jeroboam k. of Israel, 7.10
Then tidings reached the k. of Nineveh, Jon 3.06
decree of the k. and his nobles: 3.07
Their k. will pass on before them, Mic 2.13
Is there no k. in you? Has your 4.09
what Balak k. of Moab devised, and 6.05
are asleep, O k. of Assyria; Nah 3.18
the son of Amon, k. of Judah. Zep 1.01
The K. of Israel, the Lord, is in 3.15
In the second year of Darius the k., Hag 1.01
In the second year of Darius the k., 2.01
In the fourth year of K. Darius, Zec 7.01
The k. shall perish from Gaza; 9.05
Lo, your k. comes to you; 9.09
and each into the hand of his k.; 11.06
in the days of Uzziah k. of Judah. 14.05
will become k. over all the earth; 14.09
year after year to worship the K., 14.16
up to Jerusalem to worship the K., 14.17
for I am a great K., says the Lord of Mal 1.14
and Jesse the father of David the k. Mt 1.06
Judea in the days of Herod the k., 2.01
who has been born k. of the Jews? 2.02
When Herod the k. heard this, he was 2.03
had heard the k. they went their 2.09
for it is the city of the great K. 5.35
And the k. was sorry; but because 14.09
compared to a k. who wished to 18.23
your k. is coming to you, humble, and 21.05
compared to a k. who gave a marriage 22.02
The k. was angry, and he sent his 22.07
"But when the k. came in to look at 22.11
Then the k. said to the attendants, 22.13
Then the K. will say to those at 25.34
And the K. will answer them, 'Truly, 25.40
him, "Are you the K. of the Jews?" 27.11
him, saying, "Hail, K. of the Jews!" 27.29
"This is Jesus the K. of the Jews." 27.37
He is the K of Israel; let him come 27.42
K. Herod heard of it; for Jesus' name Mk 6.14
and the k. said to the girl, "Ask me 6.22
immediately with haste to the k., 6.25
And the k. was exceedingly sorry; 6.26
And immediately the k. sent a 6.27
him, "Are you the K. of the Jews?" 15.02
release for you the K. of the Jews?" 15.09
whom you call the K. of the Jews?" 15.12
salute him, "Hail, K. of the Jews!" 15.18
him read, "The K. of the Jews." 15.26
the K. of Israel, come down now from 15.32
k. of Judea, there was a priest Lk 1.05
what k., going to encounter another k. 14.31
saying, "Blessed be the K. who comes 19.38
that he himself is Christ a k." 23.02
him, "Are you the K. of the Jews?" 23.03
"If you are the K. of the Jews, 23.37
him, "This is the K. of the Jews." 23.38
You are the K. of Israel!" Jn 1.49
take him by force to make him k., 6.15
of the Lord, even the K. of Israel!" 12.13
behold, your k. is coming, sitting on 12.15
to him, "Are you the K. of the Jews?" 18.33
Pilate said to him, "So you are a k.?" 18.37
answered, "You say that I am a k. 18.37
release for you the K. of the Jews?" 18.39
him, saying, "Hail K. of the Jews!" 19.03
makes himself a k. sets himself 19.12
said to the Jews, "Here is your K!" 19.14
to them, "Shall I crucify your K.?" 19.15
answered, "We have no k. but Caesar." 19.15
of Nazareth, the K. of the Jews." 19.19
'The K. of the Jews,' but, 'This man 19.21
'This man said, I am K. of the Jews.'" 19.21
k. of Egypt, who made him governor Ac 7.10
Egypt another k. who had not known 7.18
time Herod the k. laid violent 12.01
Then they asked for a k.; and God 13.21
he raised up David to be their k.; 13.22
that there is another k., Jesus. 17.07
Agrippa the k. and Bernice arrived 25.13
laid Paul's case before the k., 25.14
"K. Agrippa and all who are present 25.24
K. Agrippa, that, after we have 25.26
K. Agrippa, I am to make my defense 26.02
hope I am accused by Jews, O k.! 26.07
At midday, O k., I saw on the way a 26.13
"Wherefore, O K. Agrippa, I was not 26.19
For the k. knows about these things, 26.26
K. Agrippa, do you believe the 26.27
Then the k. rose, and the governor 26.30
governor under K. Aretas guarded 2Co 11.32
To the K. of ages, immortal, invisible, 1Ti 1.17
the K. of kings and Lord of lords, 6.15
k. of Salem, priest of the Most High Heb 7.01
k. of righteousness, and then he is 7.02
is also k. of Salem, that is, k. of peace. 7.02
afraid of the anger of the k.; 11.27
They have as k. over them the angel Rev 9.11
are thy ways, O K. of the ages! 15.03
is Lord of lords and K. of kings, 17.14
K. of kings and Lord of lords. 19.16

KINGDOM
The beginning of his k. was Babel, Gen 10.10
on me and my k. a great sin? 20.09
be to me a k. of priests and a Ex 19.06
and his k. shall be exalted. Num 24.07
the k. of Sihon king of the Amorites 32.33
Amorites and the k. of Og king of 32.33
the k. of Og in Bashan. Deu 3.04
cities of the k. of Og in Bashan. 3.10
the k. of Og, that is, all the region 3.13
he sits on the throne of his k., 17.18
he may continue long in his k., 17.20
all the k. of Og in Bashan, who Jos 13.12
and all the k. of Sihon king of the 13.21
the rest of the k. of Sihon king 13.27
the whole k. of Og king of Bashan, 13.30
cities of the k. of Og in Bashan; 13.31
But about the matter of the k., 1Sa 10.16
to Gilgal and there renew the k. 11.14
established your k. over Israel for 13.13
But now your k. shall not continue; 13.14
has torn the k. of Israel from you 15.28
what more can he have but the k.?" 18.08
you nor your k. shall be established. 20.31
and that the k. of Israel shall be 24.20
has torn the k. out of your hand, 28.17
to transfer the k. from the house 2Sa 3.10
"I and my k. are for ever guiltless 3.28
had exalted his k. for the sake of 5.12
body, and I will establish his k. 7.12
the throne of his k. for ever. 7.13
house and your k. shall be made 7.16
give me back the k. of my father.'" 16.03
has given the k. into the hand of 16.08
and his k. was firmly established. 1Ki 2.12
"You know that the k. was mine, 2.15
however the k. has turned about and 2.15
Ask for him the k. also; for he is 2.22
So the k. was established in the 2.46
of it was never made in any k. 10.20
surely tear the k. from you and 11.11
However I will not tear away all the k.; 11.13
to tear the k. from the hand of 11.31
take the whole k. out of his hand; 11.34
but I will take the k. out of his 11.35
to restore the k. to Rehoboam the 12.21
"Now the k. will turn back to the 12.26
and tore the k. away from the house 14.08
is no nation or k. whither my lord 18.10
take an oath of the k. or nation, 18.10
and turned the k. over to David 1Ch 10.14

KINGDOM (cont.)

gave him strong support in his k.,	1Ch 11.10
to turn the k. of Saul over to him,	12.23
and that his k. was highly exalted	14.02
nation, from one k. to another people,	16.20
sons, and I will establish his k.	17.11
house and in my k. for ever and	17.14
throne of the k. of the LORD over	28.05
establish his k. for ever if he	28.07
thine is the k., O LORD, and thou	29.11
established himself in his k.,	2Ch 1.01
of it was never made in any k.	9.19
to restore the k. to Rehoboam.	11.01
They strengthened the k. of Judah,	11.17
withstand the k. of the LORD in	13.08
And the k. had rest under him.	14.05
established the k. in his hand;	17.05
but he gave the k. to Jehoram,	21.03
had no one able to rule the k.	22.09
offering for the k. and for the	29.21
any nation or k. has been able to	32.15
him again to Jerusalem into his k.	33.13
establishment of the k. of Persia,	36.20
throughout all his k. and also put	36.22
throughout all his k. and also put	Ez 1.01
their priests or Levites in my k.,	7.13
They did not serve thee in their k.,	Neh 9.35
face. and sat first in the k.—:	Est 1.14
proclaimed throughout all his k.,	1.20
provinces of his k. to gather all	2.03
throughout the whole k. of Ahasuerus.	3.06
in all the provinces of your k.;	3.08
not come to the k. for such a time	4.14
you, even to the half of my k."	5.03
Even to the half of my k., it shall	5.06
Even to the half of my k., it shall	7.02
provinces of the k. of Ahasuerus,	9.30
heavens, and his k. rules over all.	Ps 103.19
from one k. to another people,	105.13
shall speak of the glory of thy k.,	145.11
the glorious splendor of thy k.	145.12
Thy k. is an everlasting k.,	145.13
or in his own k. had been born	Ecc 4.14
and over his k., to establish it,	Is 9.07
Ephraim, and the k. from Damascus;	17.03
city against city, k. against k;	19.02
They shall name it No K. There,	34.12
For the nation and k. that will not	60.12
concerning a nation or a k.,	Jer 18.07
a nation or a k. that I will build	18.09
any nation or k. will not serve	27.08
in dishonor the k. and its rulers.	Lam 2.02
that the k. might be humble and not	Eze 17.14
and there they shall be a lowly k.	29.14
enchanters that were in all his k.	Dan 1.20
the God of heaven has given the k.,	2.37
arise another k. inferior to you,	2.39
you, and yet a third k. of bronze,	2.39
And there shall be a fourth k.,	2.40
of iron, it shall be a divided k.;	2.41
so the k. shall be partly strong	2.42
will set up a k. which shall never	2.44
His k. is an everlasting k., and his	4.03
the Most High rules the k. of men,	4.17
wise men of my k. are not able to	4.18
the Most High rules the k. of men,	4.25
your k. shall be sure for you from	4.26
The k. has departed from you,	4.31
High rules the k. of men and gives	4.32
and his k. endures from generation	4.34
and for the glory of my k.,	4.36
me, and I was established in my k.,	4.36
shall be the third ruler in the k.	5.07
There is in your k. a man in whom	5.11
shall be the third ruler in the k.	5.16
Most High God rules the k. of men,	5.21
days of your k. and brought it to	5.26
PERES, your k. is divided and given	5.28

be the third ruler in the k.	5.29
And Darius the Mede received the k.,	5.31
to set over the k. a hundred and	6.01
to be throughout the whole k.;	6.01
to set him over the whole k.	6.03
Daniel with regard to the k.;	6.04
All the presidents of the k.,	6.07
his k. shall never be destroyed, and	6.26
given dominion and glory and k.,	7.14
and his k. one that shall not be	7.14
the Most High shall receive the k.,	7.18
and possess the k. for ever,	7.18
when the saints received the k.	7.22
shall be a fourth k. on earth,	7.23
out of this k. ten kings shall	7.24
And the k. and the dominion and the	7.27
their k. shall be an everlasting k.,	7.27
The prince of the k. of Persia	10.13
up all against the k. of Greece.	11.02
his k. shall be broken and divided	11.04
for his k. shall be plucked up and	11.04
with the strength of his whole k.,	11.17
daughter of women to destroy the k.;	11.17
through the glory of the k.;	11.20
and obtain the k. by flatteries.	11.21
an end to the k. of the house of	Hos 1.04
and it is a temple of the k.	Amo 7.13
Lord GOD are upon the sinful k.,	9.08
and the k. shall be the LORD'S.	Ob 1.21
the k. of the daughter of Jerusalem.	Mic 4.08
for the k. of heaven is at hand."	Mt 3.02
for the k. of heaven is at hand."	4.17
gospel of the k. and healing every	4.23
for theirs is the k. of heaven.	5.03
for theirs is the k. of heaven.	5.10
called least in the k. of heaven;	5.19
called great in the k. of heaven.	5.19
will never enter the k. of heaven.	5.20
Thy k. come, Thy will be done, On	6.10
For thine is the k. and the power	* 6.13
But seek first his k. and his	6.33
shall enter the k. of heaven,	7.21
and Jacob in the k. of heaven,	8.11
while the sons of the k. will be	8.12
and preaching the gospel of the k.,	9.35
'The k. of heaven is at hand.'	10.07
is least in the k. of heaven is	11.11
until now the k. of heaven has	11.12
"Every k. divided against itself is	12.25
how then will his k. stand?	12.26
then the k. of God has come upon	12.28
the secrets of the k. of heaven,	13.11
the word of the k. and does not	13.19
"The k. of heaven may be compared	13.24
"The k. of heaven is like a grain	13.31
"The k. of heaven is like leaven	13.33
good seed means the sons of the k.;	13.38
out of his k. all causes of sin	13.41
the sun in the k. of their Father.	13.43
"The k. of heaven is like treasure	13.44
"Again, the k. of heaven is like a	13.45
"Again. the k. of heaven is like a	13.47
trained for the k. of heaven is	13.52
you the keys of the k. of heaven,	16.19
the Son of man coming in his k."	16.28
the greatest in the k. of heaven?"	18.01
will never enter the k. of heaven.	18.03
the greatest in the k. of heaven.	18.04
"Therefore the k. of heaven may be	18.23
for the sake of the k. of heaven.	19.12
to such belongs the k. of heaven."	19.14
rich man to enter the k. of heaven.	19.23
a rich man to enter the k. of God."	19.24
"For the k. of heaven is like a	20.01
and one at your left, in your k."	20.21
go into the k. of God before you.	21.31
the k. of God will be taken away	21.43
"The k. of heaven may be compared	22.02

KINGDOM (cont.)

you shut the k. of heaven against	Mt 23.13
against nation, and k. against k.,	24.07
gospel of the k. will be preached	24.14
"Then the k. of heaven shall be	25.01
inherit the k. prepared for you	25.34
it new with you in my Father's k."	26.29
and the k. of God is at hand;	Mk 1.15
If a k. is divided against itself,	3.24
itself, that k. cannot stand.	3.24
given the secret of the k. of God,	4.11
"The k. of God is as if a man	4.26
what can we compare the k. of God,	4.30
will give you, even half of my k."	6.23
they see the k. of God come with	9.01
to enter the k. of God with one	9.47
or to such belongs the k. of God.	10.14
not receive the k. of God like a	10.15
have riches to enter the k. of God!"	10.23
hard it is to enter the k. of God!	10.24
a rich man to enter the k. of God."	10.25
Blessed be the k. of our father	11.10
"You are not far from the k. of God."	12.34
against nation, and k. against k.;	13.08
I drink it new in the k. of God.	14.25
himself looking for the k. of God,	15.43
and of his k. there will be no end."	Lk 1.33
news of the k. of God to the other	4.43
poor, for yours is the k. of God.	6.20
is least in the k. of God is	7.28
the good news of the k. of God.	8.01
know the secrets of the k. of God;	8.10
to preach the k. of God and to	9.02
and spoke to them of the k. of God,	9.11
before they see the k. of God."	9.27
you, go and proclaim the k. of God."	9.60
looks back is fit for the k. of God."	9.62
'The k. of God has come near to you.'	10.09
that the k. of God has come near.'	10.11
hallowed be thy name. Thy k. come.	11.02
"Every k. divided against itself is	11.17
himself, how will his k. stand?	11.18
then the k. of God has come upon	11.20
seek his k., and these things shall	12.31
good pleasure to give you the k.	12.32
therefore, "What is the k. of God like?	13.18
what shall I compare the k. of God?	13.20
prophets in the k. of God and you	13.28
and sit at table in the k. of God.	13.29
shall eat bread in the k. of God!	14.15
news of the k. of God is preached,	16.16
when the k. of God was coming, he	17.20
"The k. of God is not coming with	17.20
the k. of God is in the midst of	17.21
or to such belongs the k. of God.	18.16
not receive the k. of God like a	18.17
have riches to enter the k. of God!	18.24
a rich man to enter the k. of God.	18.25
for the sake of the k. of God,	18.29
that the k. of God was to appear	19.11
against nation, and k. against k.;	21.10
know that the k. of God is near.	21.31
it is fulfilled in the k. of God.	22.16
the vine until the k. of God comes.	22.18
as my Father appointed a k. for me,	22.29
eat and drink at my table in my k.,	22.30
he was looking for the k. of God.	23.51
anew, he cannot see the k. of God.	Jn 3.03
he cannot enter the k. of God.	3.05
and speaking of the k. of God.	Ac 1.03
this time restore the k. to Israel?	1.06
news about the k. of God and the	8.12
we must enter the k. of God.	14.22
and pleading about the k. of God;	19.08
preaching the k. will see my face	20.25
testifying to the k. of God and	28.23
preaching the k. of God and teaching	28.31
For the k. of God does not mean	Rom 14.17
For the k. of God does not consist	1Co 4.20
will not inherit the k. of God?	6.09
robbers will inherit the k. of God.	6.10
he delivers the k. to God the	15.24
blood cannot inherit the k. of God,	15.50
shall not inherit the k. of God.	Gal 5.21
inheritance in the k. of Christ and	Eph 5.05
us to the k. of his beloved Son,	Col 1.13
fellow workers for the k. of God,	4.11
you into his own k. and glory.	1Th 2.12
be made worthy of the k. of God,	2Th 1.05
and by his appearing and his k.:	2Ti 4.01
and save me for his heavenly k.	4.18
scepter is the scepter of thy k.	Heb 1.08
for receiving a k. that cannot be	12.28
heirs of the k. which he has	Jas 2.05
the eternal k. of our Lord and	2Pe 1.11
and made us a k., priests to his	Rev 1.06
tribulation and the k. and the	1.09
made them a k. and priests to our	5.10
"The k. of the world has become the k. of	11.15
power and the k. of our God and	12.10
and its k. was in darkness; men gnawed	16.10

KINGDOMS

do to all the k. into which you	Deu 3.21
horror to all the k. of the earth.	28.25
formerly was the head of all those k.	Jos 11.10
hand of all the k. that were	1Sa 10.18
over all the k. from the Euphrates	1Ki 4.21
alone, of all the k. of the earth;	2Ki 19.15
that all the k. of the earth may	19.19
upon all the k. of the countries.	1Ch 29.30
service of the k. of the countries."	2Ch 12.08
upon all the k. of the lands that	17.10
over all the k. of the nations?	20.06
came on all the k. of the countries	20.29
given me all the k. of the earth.	36.23
given me all the k. of the earth,	Ez 1.02
didst give them k. and peoples,	Neh 9.22
The nations rage, the k. totter;	Ps 46.06
Sing to God, O k. of the earth;	68.32
and on the k. that do not call on	79.06
together, and k., to worship the LORD.	102.22
Bashan, and all the k. of Canaan,	135.11
reached to the k. of the idols	Is 10.10
an uproar of k., of nations gathering	13.04
the glory of k., the splendor and	13.19
the earth tremble, who shook k.,	14.16
over the sea, he has shaken the k.;	23.11
with all the k. of the world upon	23.17
alone, of all the k. of the earth;	37.16
that all the k. of the earth may	37.20
more be called the mistress of k.	47.05
this day over nations and over k.,	Jer 1.10
the tribes of the k. of the north,	1.15
in all their k. there is none like	10.07
to all the k. of the earth because	15.04
horror to all the k. of the earth,	24.09
and all the k. of the world which	25.26
against many countries and great k.	28.08
horror to all the k. of the earth,	29.18
and all the k. of the earth under	34.01
horror to all the k. of the earth.	34.17
Concerning Kedar and the k. of	49.28
in pieces; with you I destroy k.;	51.20
her, summon against her the k.,	51.27
It shall be the most lowly of the k.,	Eze 29.15
and no longer divided into two k.	37.22
all these k. and bring them to an	Dan 2.44
shall be different from all the k.,	7.23
greatness of the k. under the whole	7.27
four k. shall arise from his nation,	8.22
Are they better than these K.?	Amo 6.02
nakedness and k. on your shame.	Nah 3.05
to assemble k., to pour out upon	Zep 3.08
and to overthrow the throne of k.;	Hag 2.22
strength of the k. of the nations,	2.22

KINGDOMS (cont.)
him all the k. of the world and Mt 4.08
him all the k. of the world in a Lk 4.05
who through faith conquered k., Heb 11.33

KINGLY
he was deposed from his k. throne, Dan 5.20
to receive k. power and then Lk 19.12
having received the k. power, 19.15
me when you come in your k. power." 23.42

KING'S
of Shaveh (that is, the K. Valley). Gen 14.17
place where the k. prisoners were 39.20
we will go along the K. Highway, Num 20.17
we will go by the K. Highway, 21.22
now then become the k. son-in-law. 1Sa 18.22
thing to become the k. son-in-law, 18.23
may be avenged of the k. enemies. 18.25
David well to be the k. son-in-law. 18.26
he might become the k. son-in-law. 18.27
he has not come to the k. table. 20.29
because the k. business required 21.08
who is the k. son-in-law, and 22.14
to surrender him into the k. hand. 23.20
and now see where the k. spear is, 26.16
not been the k. will to slay Abner 2Sa 3.37
table, like one of the k. sons. 9.11
or he ate always at the k. table. 9.13
upon the roof of the k. house, 11.02
And Uriah went out of the k. house, 11.08
the door of the k. house with all 11.09
then, if the k. anger rises, and if 11.20
some of the k. servants are dead; 11.24
Absalom invited all the k. sons. 13.23
and all the k. sons go with him. 13.27
Then all the k. sons arose, and each 13.29
"Absalom has slain all the k. sons, 13.30
all the young men the k. sons, 13.32
that all the k. sons are dead; 13.33
"Behold, the k. sons have come; 13.35
the k. sons came, and lifted up 13.36
that the k. heart went out to 14.01
did not come into the k. presence. 14.24
hundred shekels by the k. weight. 14.26
coming into the k. presence. 14.28
And the k. servants said to the 15.15
whatever you hear from the k. house, 15.35
are for the k. household to ride 16.02
forth my hand against the k. son; 18.12
pillar which is in the K. Valley, 18.18
tidings, because the k. son is dead." 18.20
to bring over the k. household, 19.18
we eaten at all at the k. expense? 19.42
But the k. word prevailed against 24.04
she became the k. nurse and 1Ki 1.04
the k. sons, and all the royal 1.09
and has invited all the k. sons, 1.25
so she came into the k. presence, 1.28
caused him to ride on the k. mule; 1.44
Moreover the k. servants came to 1.47
a seat brought for the k. mother; 2.19
of Nathan was priest and k. friend; 4.05
At the k. command, they quarried out 5.17
LORD and the k. house and all that 9.01
of the LORD and the k. house, 9.10
and for the k. house, lyres also and 10.12
and the k. traders received them 10.28
so through the k. traders they 10.29
and the k. hand was restored to him, 13.06
and the treasures of the k. house; 14.26
who kept the door of the k. house. 14.27
and the treasures of the k. house, 15.18
into the citadel of the k. house, 16.18
and burned the k. house over him 16.18
the city and to Joash the k. son; 22.26
this is the k. order, 'Come down 2Ki 1.11
us go and tell the k. household. 7.09
was told within the k. household. 7.11
bury her; for she is a k. daughter." 9.34
Now the k. sons, seventy persons, 10.06
they took the k. sons, and slew them, 10.07
brought the heads of the k. sons, 10.08
from among the k. sons who were 11.02
and he showed them the k. son. 11.04
the sabbath and guard the k. house 11.05
Then he brought out the k. son, 11.12
horses' entrance to the k. house, 11.16
gate of the guards to the k. house. 11.19
with the sword at the k. house. 11.20
the k. secretary and the high 12.10
of the LORD and of the k. house, 12.18
laid his hands upon the k. hands. 13.16
in the treasuries of the k. house, 14.14
And Jotham the k. son was over the 15.05
in the citadel of the k. house; 15.25
in the treasures of the k. house, 16.08
and the k. burnt offering, and his 16.15
in the treasuries of the k. house. 18.15
for the k. command was, "Do not 18.36
secretary, and Asaiah the k. servant, 22.12
and the treasures of the k. house, 24.13
the k. mother, the k. wives, his 24.15
by the k. garden, though the Chaldeans 25.04
and the k. house and all the houses 25.09
five men of the k. council who 25.19
he dined regularly at the k. table; 25.29
stationed hitherto in the k. gate 1Ch 9.18
But the k. word prevailed against 21.04
for the k. command was abhorrent to 21.06
were the sons of Heman the k. seer, 25.05
Over the k. treasuries was Azmaveth 27.25
of Hachmoni attended the k. sons. 27.32
Ahithophel was the k. counselor, 27.33
the Archite was the k. friend. 27.33
Joab was commander of the k. army. 27.34
and the officers over the k. work. 29.06
and the k. traders received them 2Ch 1.16
house of the LORD and the k. house; 7.11
of the LORD and for the k. house, 9.11
For the k. ships went to Tarshish 9.21
and the treasures of the k. house; 12.09
who kept the door of the k. house. 12.10
house of the LORD and the k. house, 16.02
the city and to Joash the k. son; 18.25
of Judah, in all the k. matters; 19.11
that belonged to the k. house, 21.17
from among the k. sons who were 22.11
said to them, "Behold, the k. son! 23.03
shall be at the k. house and one 23.05
Then he brought out the k. son, 23.11
of the horse gate of the k. house, 23.15
the upper gate to the k. house. 23.20
brought to the k. officers by the 24.11
the k. secretary and the officer of 24.11
the treasuries of the k. house, 25.24
Hananiah, one of the k. commanders. 26.11
his son was over the k. household, 26.21
Maaseiah the k. son and Azrikam 28.07
and of Gad the k. seer and of 29.25
secretary, and Asaiah the k. servant, 34.20
these were from the k. possessions. 35.07
according to the k. command. 35.10
Heman, and Jeduthun the k. seer; 35.15
for us to witness the k. dishonor, Ez 4.14
provide it out of the k. treasury. 7.20
before it all the k. mighty officers. 7.28
the k. commissions to the k. satraps 8.36
Asaph, the keeper of the k. forest, Neh 2.08
and gave them the k. letters. 2.09
Fountain Gate and to the K. Pool; 2.14
Pool of Shelah of the k. garden, 3.15
money for the k. tax upon our 5.04
was at the k. hand in all matters 11.24
of the garden of the k. palace. Est 1.05
to come at the k. command conveyed 1.12

KING'S (cont.)
this was the k. procedure toward Est 1.13
who saw the k. face, and sat first 1.14
telling it to all the k. princes, 1.18
Then the k. servants who attended 2.02
of Hegai the k. eunuch who is in 2.03
So when the k. order and his edict 2.08
taken into the k. palace and put 2.08
chosen maids from the k. palace, 2.09
from the harem to the k. palace. 2.13
Shaashgaz the k. eunuch who was in 2.14
except what Hegai the k. eunuch, 2.15
Mordecai was sitting at the k. gate. 2.19
Mordecai was sitting at the k. gate, 2.21
two of the k. eunuchs, who guarded 2.21
And all the k. servants who were at 3.02
who were at the k. gate bowed down 3.02
Then the k. servants who were at 3.03
who were at the k. gate said to 3.03
do you transgress the k. command?" 3.03
and they do not keep the k. laws, 3.08
is not for the k. profit to 3.08
who have charge of the k. business, 3.09
may put in into the k. treasuries." 3.09
Then the k. secretaries were 3.12
written to the k. satraps and to 3.12
and sealed with the k. ring. 3.12
couriers to all the k. provinces, 3.13
up to the entrance of the k. gate, 4.02
might enter the k. gate clothed 4.02
wherever the k. command and his 4.03
one of the k. eunuchs, who had been 4.05
the city in front of the k. gate, 4.06
to pay into the k. treasuries for 4.07
k. servants and the people of the k. provinces 4.11
not that in the k. palace you will 4.13
the inner court of the k. palace, 5.01
palace, opposite the k. hall. 5.01
Haman saw Mordecai in the k. gate, 5.09
the Jew sitting at the k. gate." 5.13
two of the k. eunuchs, who guarded 6.02
The k. servants who attended him 6.03
court of the k. palace to speak to 6.04
So the k. servants told him, "Haman 6.05
to one of the k. most noble 6.09
the Jew who sits at the k. gate. 6.10
Then Mordecai returned to the k. gate. 6.12
the k. eunuchs arrived and brought 6.14
king, and seal it with the k. ring; 8.08
sealed with the k. ring cannot be 8.08
The k. secretaries were summoned at 8.09
and sealed with the k. ring, 8.10
that were used in the k. service, 8.10
that were used in the k. service, 8.14
in haste, urged by the k. command; 8.14
wherever the k. command and his 8.17
when the k. command and edict were 9.01
Mordecai was great in the k. house, 9.04
in the rest of the k. provinces! 9.12
who were in the k. provinces also 9.16
in the heart of the k. enemies; Ps 45.05
who deals wisely has the k. favor, Pro 14.35
A k. wrath is a messenger of death, 16.14
In the light of a k. face there is 16.15
A k. wrath is like the growling of 19.12
The k. heart is a stream of water 21.01
forward in the k. presence or 25.06
Keep the k. command, and because of Ecc 8.02
for the k. command was, "Do not Is 36.21
up from the k. house to the house Jer 26.10
he went down to the k. house, 36.12
Jerahmeel the k. son and Seraiah 36.26
the k. son, which was in the court 38.06
a eunuch, who was in the k. house, 38.07
Ebedmelech went from the k. house 38.08
by way of the k. garden through 39.04
burned the k. house and the house 39.08
the k. daughters and all the people 41.10
by the k. garden, while the Chaldeans 52.07
and the k. house and all the houses 52.13
and seven men of the k. council, 52.25
he dined regularly at the k. table; 52.33
competent to serve in the k. palace, Dan 1.04
himself with the k. rich food, 1.08
who eat the k. rich food be 1.13
youths who ate the k. rich food. 1.15
earth who can meet the k. demand; 2.10
the captain of the k. guard, 2.14
the k. captain. "Why is the decree 2.15
made known to us the k. matter." 2.23
Daniel remained at the k. court. 2.49
Because the k. order was strict and 3.22
and the k. counselors gathered 3.27
and set at nought the k. command, 3.28
words were still in the k. mouth, 4.31
of the wall of the k. palace, 5.05
Then the k. color changed, and his 5.06
Then all the k. wise men came in, 5.08
and went about the k. business; 8.27
latter growth after the k. mowings. Amo 7.01
for it is the k. sanctuary, and it 7.13
officials and the k. sons and all Zep 1.08
of Hananel to the k. wine presses. Zec 14.10
the k. chamberlain, they asked for Ac 12.20
depended on the k. country for 12.20
were not afraid of the k. edict. Heb 11.23

KINGS
these k. made war with Bera king of Gen 14.02
Chedorlaomer and the k. who were 14.05
of Ellasar, four k. against five. 14.09
and as the k. of Sodom and Gomorrah 14.10
Chedorlaomer and the k. who were 14.17
and k. shall come forth from you. 17.06
k. of peoples shall come from her." 17.16
and k. shall spring from you. 35.11
These are the k. who reigned in the 36.31
They slew the k. of Midian with the Num 31.08
and Reba, the five k. of Midian; 31.08
hand of the two k. of the Amorites Deu 3.08
your God has done to these two k.; 3.21
the two k. of the Amorites, who 4.47
will give their k. into your hand, 7.24
the k. of the Amorites, and to their 31.04
did to the two k. of the Amorites Jos 2.10
When all the k. of the Amorites 5.01
and all the k. of the Canaanites 5.01
When all the k. who were beyond the 9.01
did to the two k. of the Amorites 9.10
Then the five k. of the Amorites, 10.05
for all the k. of the Amorites that 10.06
These five k. fled, and hid themselves 10.16
"The five k. have been found, hidden 10.17
those five k. out to me from the 10.22
those five k. out to him from the 10.23
brought those k. out to Joshua, 10.24
feet upon the necks of these k. 10.24
and the slopes, and all their k.; 10.40
took all these k. and their land 10.42
and to the k. who were in the 11.02
And all these k. joined their 11.05
And all the cities of those k., 11.12
and all their k., Joshua took, and 11.12
And he took all their k., and smote 11.17
war a long time with all those k. 11.18
Now these are the k. of the land, 12.01
And these are the k. of the land 12.07
Tirzah, one: in all, thirty-one k. 12.24
the two k. of the Amorites; it was not 24.12
"Seventy k. with their thumbs and Ju 1.07
"Hear, O k.; give ear, O princes; 5.03
"The k. came, they fought; 5.19
then fought the k. of Canaan, 5.19
and Zalmunna, the k. of Midian, 8.05
them and took the two k. of Midian, 8.12
garments worn by the k. of Midian, 8.26

KINGS (cont.)
against the k. of Zobah, and against 1Sa 14.47
belonged to the k. of Judah to 27.06
And when all the k. who were servants 2Sa 10.19
the time when k. go forth to battle. 11.01
over all the k. west of the Euphrates 1Ki 4.24
and from all the k. of the earth, 4.34
from all the k. of Arabia and from 10.15
excelled all the k. of the earth in 10.23
to all the k. of the Hittites and 10.29
the Hittites and the k. of Syria. 10.29
the Chronicles of the K. of Israel. 14.19
the Chronicles of the K. of Judah? 14.29
the Chronicles of the K. of Judah? 15.07
the Chronicles of the K. of Judah? 15.23
the Chronicles of the K. of Israel? 15.31
the Chronicles of the K. of Israel? 16.05
the Chronicles of the K. of Israel? 16.14
the Chronicles of the K. of Israel? 16.20
the Chronicles of the K. of Israel? 16.27
than all the k. of Israel who were 16.33
thirty-two k. were with him, and 20.01
drinking with the k. in the booths, 20.12
the thirty-two k. who helped him. 20.16
remove the k., each from his post, 20.24
heard that the k. of the house of 20.31
house of Israel are merciful k.; 20.31
the Chronicles of the K. of Israel? 22.39
the Chronicles of the K. of Judah? 22.45
the Chronicles of the K. of Israel? 2Ki 1.18
these three k. to give them into 3.10
these three k. to give them into 3.13
heard that the k. had come up to 3.21
the k. have surely fought together, 3.23
k. of the Hittites and the k. of Egypt 7.06
in the way of the k. of Israel, 8.18
the Chronicles of the K. of Judah? 8.23
the two k. could not stand before 10.04
the Chronicles of the K. of Israel? 10.34
his seat on the throne of the k. 11.19
the k. of Judah, had dedicated, and 12.18
the Chronicles of the K. of Judah? 12.19
the Chronicles of the K. of Israel? 13.08
the Chronicles of the K. of Israel? 13.12
in Samaria with the k. of Israel. 13.13
the Chronicles of the K. of Israel? 14.15
in Samaria with the k. of Israel; 14.16
the Chronicles of the K. of Judah? 14.18
the Chronicles of the K. of Israel? 14.28
the k. of Israel, and Zechariah his 14.29
the Chronicles of the K. of Judah? 15.06
the Chronicles of the K. of Israel. 15.11
the Chronicles of the K. of Israel. 15.15
the Chronicles of the K. of Israel? 15.21
the Chronicles of the K. of Israel. 15.26
the Chronicles of the K. of Israel. 15.31
the Chronicles of the K. of Judah? 15.36
in the way of the k. of Israel. 16.03
the Chronicles of the K. of Judah? 16.19
yet not as the k. of Israel who 17.02
which the k. of Israel had introduced 17.08
among all the k. of Judah after 18.05
heard what the k. of Assyria have 19.11
the k. of Assyria have laid waste 19.17
the Chronicles of the K. of Judah? 20.20
the Chronicles of the K. of Judah? 21.17
the Chronicles of the K. of Judah? 21.25
whom the k. of Judah had ordained 23.05
horses that the k. of Judah had 23.11
which the k. of Judah had made, and 23.12
which k. of Israel had made, provoking 23.19
days of the k. of Israel or of the k. of 23.22
the Chronicles of the K. of Judah? 23.28
the Chronicles of the K. of Judah? 24.05
seats of the k. who were with him 25.28
These are the k. who reigned in the 1Ch 1.43
in the Book of the K. of Israel. 9.01
he rebuked k. on their account, 16.21
and the k. who had come were by 19.09
the time when k. go forth to battle, 20.01
as none of the k. had who were 2Ch 1.12
k. of the Hittites and the k. of Syria. 1.17
and all the k. of Arabia and the 9.14
excelled all the k. of the earth in 9.22
And all the k. of the earth sought 9.23
over all the k. from the Euphrates 9.26
the Book of the K. of Judah and 16.11
in the Book of the K. of Israel. 20.34
in the way of the k. of Israel, 21.06
in the way of the k. of Israel, 21.13
but not in the tombs of the k. 21.20
in the city of David among the k., 24.16
bury him in the tombs of the k. 24.25
Commentary on the Book of the K. 24.27
the Book of the K. of Judah and 25.26
field which belonged to the k., 26.23
the Book of the K. of Israel and 27.07
in the ways of the k. of Israel. 28.02
the gods of the k. of Syria helped 28.23
the Book of the K. of Judah and 28.26
into the tombs of the k. of Israel. 28.27
from the hand of the k. of Assyria. 30.06
"Why should the k. of Assyria come 32.04
the Book of the K. of Judah and 32.32
the Chronicles of the K. of Israel. 33.18
which the k. of Judah had let go 34.11
none of the k. of Israel had kept 35.18
the Book of the K. of Israel and 35.27
the Book of the K. of Israel and 36.08
hurtful to k. and provinces, and Ez 4.15
from of old has risen against k., 4.19
And mighty k. have been over 4.20
king of k., to Ezra the priest, the 7.12
our k., and our priests have been 9.07
the hand of the k. of the lands, 9.07
love before the k. of Persia, 9.09
with their k. and the peoples of Neh 9.24
upon our k., our princes, our 9.32
the time of the k. of Assyria 9.32
our k., our princes, our priests, and 9.34
goes to the k. whom thou hast set 9.37
Chronicles of the K. of Media and Est 10.02
with k. and counselors of the earth Job 3.14
He looses the bonds of k., and binds 12.18
but with k. upon the throne he sets 36.07
The k. of the earth set themselves. Ps 2.02
Now therefore, O k., be wise; be warned, 2.10
daughters of k. are among your ladies 45.09
For lo, the k. assembled, they came 48.04
"The k. of the armies, they flee, 68.12
When the Almighty scattered k. there, 68.14
at Jerusalem k. bear gifts to thee. 68.29
May the k. of Tarshish and of the 72.10
may the k. of Sheba and Seba bring 72.10
May all k. fall down before him, all 72.11
is terrible to the k. of the earth. 76.12
the highest of the k. of the earth. 89.27
and all the k. of the earth thy 102.15
he rebuked k. on their account, 105.14
even in the chambers of their k. 105.30
he will shatter k. on the day of 110.05
speak of thy testimonies before k., 119.46
many nations and slew mighty k., 135.10
to him who smote great k., 136.17
and slew famous k., for his steadfast 136.18
All the k. of the earth shall 138.04
who givest victory to k, who rescuest 144.10
K. of the earth and all peoples, 148.11
to bind their k. with chains and 149.08
By me k. reign, and rulers decree Pro 8.15
is an abomination to k. to do evil, 16.12
he will stand before k.; he will not 22.29
the glory of k. is to search 25.02
so the mind of k. is unsearchable. 25.03
your ways to those who destroy k. 31.03
It is not for k., O Lemuel, it is 31.04

KINGS (cont.)

it is not for k. to drink wine, or Pro 31.04
the treasure of k. and provinces; Ecc 2.08
Ahaz, and Hezekiah, k. of Judah. Is 1.01
whose two k. you are in dread will 7.16
says: "Are not my commanders all k.? 10.08
all who were k. of the nations. 14.09
All the k. of the nations lie in 14.18
of the wise, a son of ancient k."? 19.11
and the k. of the earth, on the 24.21
heard what the k. of Assyria have 37.11
the k. of Assyria have laid waste 37.18
so that he tramples k. under foot; 41.02
him and ungird the loins of k., 45.01
"K. shall see and arise; princes, and 49.07
K. shall be your foster fathers, and 49.23
k. shall shut their mouths because 52.15
and k. to the brightness of your 60.03
and their k. shall minister to you; 60.10
with their k. led in procession. 60.11
you shall suck the breast of k.; 60.16
vindication, and all the k. your glory; 62.02
against the k. of Judah, its princes, Jer 1.18
their k., their princes, their 2.26
LORD, the bones of the k. of Judah, 8.01
the k. who sit on David's throne, the 13.13
by which the k. of Judah enter and 17.19
you k. of Judah, and all Judah, and 17.20
of this city k. who sit on the 17.25
O k. of Judah and inhabitants of 19.03
fathers nor the k. of Judah have 19.04
and the houses of the k. of Judah— 19.13
treasures of the k. of Judah into 20.05
of this house k. who sit on the 22.04
and great k. shall make slaves 25.14
its k. and princes, to make them a 25.18
k. of the land of Uz and all the k. of the 25.20
all the k. of Tyre, all the k. of Sidon, 25.22
and the k. of the coastland across 25.22
all the k. of Arabia and all the 25.24
and all the k. of the mixed tribes 25.24
all the k. of Zimri, all the k. of Elam, 25.25
and all the k. of Media; 25.25
all the k. of the north, far and 25.26
and great k. shall make him their 27.07
their k. and their princes, their 32.32
houses of the k. of Judah which 33.04
the former k. who were before you, 34.05
the wickedness of the k. of Judah, 44.09
our k. and our princes, in the 44.17
your k. and your princes, and the 44.21
and Egypt and her gods and her k., 46.25
nation and many k. are stirring 50.41
the spirit of the k. of the Medes, 51.11
the k. of the Medes, with their 51.28
seats of the k. who were with him 52.32
The k. of the earth did not believe, Lam 4.12
king of k., with horses and chariots, Eze 26.07
you enriched the k. of the earth. 27.33
and their k. are horribly afraid, 27.35
I exposed you before k., to feast 28.17
and their k. shall shudder because 32.10
her k. and all her princes, who for 32.29
nor their k., by their harlotry, and 43.07
by the dead bodies of their k., 43.07
bodies of their k. far from me, 43.09
he removes k. and sets up k.; Dan 2.21
the king of k., to whom the God of 2.37
days of those k. the God of heaven 2.44
God is God of gods and Lord of k., 2.47
beasts are four k. who shall arise 7.17
of this kingdom ten k. shall arise, 7.24
ones, and shall put down three k. 7.24
these are the k. of Media and 8.20
who spoke in thy name to our k., 9.06
to our k., to our princes, and to 9.08
three more k. shall arise in Persia; 11.02
And as for the two k., their minds 11.27
k. of Judah, and in the days of Hos 1.01
All their k. have fallen; and none 7.07
They made k., but not through me. 8.04
I have given you k. in my anger, 13.11
k. of Judah, which he saw concerning Mic 1.01
deceitful thing to the k. of Israel. 1.14
At k. they scoff, and of rulers they Hab 1.10
governors and k. for my sake, Mt 10.18
From whom do k. of the earth take 17.25
governors and k. for my sake, Mk 13.09
prophets and k. desired to see Lk 10.24
brought before k. and governors 21.12
"The k. of the Gentiles exercise 22.25
The k. of the earth set themselves Ac 4.26
Gentiles and k. and the sons of 9.15
Without us you have become k.! 1Co 4.08
for k. and all who are in high 1Ti 2.02
the King of k. and Lord of lords, 6.15
slaughter of the k. and blessed him; Heb 7.01
dead, and the ruler of k. on earth. Rev 1.05
Then the k. of the earth and the 6.15
and nations and tongues and k. 10.11
the way for the k. from the east. 16.12
abroad to the k. of the whole 16.14
with whom the k. of the earth have 17.02
they are also seven k., five of 17.10
you saw are ten k. who have not 17.12
authority as k. for one hour, 17.12
he is Lord of lords and King of k., 17.14
dominion over the k. of the earth. 17.18
and the k. of the earth have 18.03
And the k. of the earth, who committed 18.09
King of k. and Lord of lords. 19.16
to eat the flesh of k., the flesh of 19.18
beast and the k. of the earth with 19.19
and the k. of the earth shall bring 21.24

KINGS'

hands, yet it is in k. palaces. Pro 30.28
wear soft raiment are in k. houses. Mt 11.08
live in luxury are in k. courts. Lk 7.25

KINGSHIP

the rights and duties of the k.; 1Sa 10.25
When Saul had taken the k. over Israel, 14.47
Israel gave the k. over Israel for 2Ch 13.05
your father k. and greatness and Dan 5.18
"My k. is not of this world; Jn 18.36
if my k. were of this world, my 18.36
but my k. is not from the world." 18.36

KINSFOLK

Saul, "Who am I, and who are my k., 1Sa 18.18
two hundred thousand of their k., 2Ch 28.08
from your k. whom you have taken, 28.11
them to their k. at Jericho, 28.15
My k. and my close friends have Job 19.14
neighbors and k. heard that the Lk 1.58
him among their k. and acquaintances, 2.44

KINSMAN

heard that his k. had been taken Gen 14.14
back his k. Lot with his goods, and 14.16
of my master's k. for his son. 24.48
Rachel that he was her father's k., 29.12
to Jacob, "Because you are my k., 29.15
or a near k. belonging to his Lev 25.49
the man has no k. to whom restitution Num 5.08
inheritance to his k. that is next 27.11
Shechem, because he is your k.— Ju 9.18
Now Naomi had a k. of her husband's, Ru 2.01
Now is not Boaz our k., 3.02
now it is true that I am a near k., 3.12
yet there is a k. nearer than I. 3.12
which belonged to our k. Elimelech. 4.03
And when a man's k., he who burns Amo 6.10
a k. of the man whose ear Peter had Jn 18.26
Greet my k. Herodion. Greet those Rom 16.11

KINSMEN

my herdsmen; for we are k. Gen 13.08
dwell over against all his k. 16.12
way to the house of my master's k." 24.27
he took his k. with him and pursued 31.23
Laban with his k. encamped in the 31.25
presence of our k. point out what 31.32
here before my k. and your k., 31.37
And Jacob said to his k., "Gather stones," 31.46
and called his k. to eat bread; 31.54
to my k. in Egypt and see whether Ex 4.18
you, Benjamin, with your k.; Ju 5.14
to his mother's k. and said to 9.01
And his mother's k. spoke all these 9.03
moved into Shechem with his k.; 9.26
of Ebed and his k. have come to 9.31
Zebul drove out Gaal and his k., 9.41
among the daughters of your k., 14.03
You are my k., you are my bone and 2Sa 19.12
against your k. the people of 1Ki 12.24
male of his k. or his friends. 16.11
Jehu met the k. of Ahaziah king of 2Ki 10.13
"We are the k. of Ahaziah, and we 10.13
And his k. by their families, when 1Ch 5.07
And their k. according to their 5.13
Their k. belonging to all the 7.05
opposite their k. in Jerusalem, with their k. 8.32
sons of Zerah: Jeuel and their k., 9.06
and their k. according to their 9.09
besides their k., heads of their 9.13
and their k. (Shallum being the 9.17
and his k. of his fathers' house, 9.19
and their k. who were in their 9.25
Also some of their k. of the 9.32
opposite their k. in Jerusalem, with their k. 9.38
they were Benjaminites, Saul's k. 12.02
the k. of Saul, three thousand, of 12.29
and all their k. under their 12.32
their k., the sons of Kish, 23.22
and Jeduthun, their sons and k., 2Ch 5.12
the son of Shealtiel with his k., Ez 3.02
And Jeshua with his sons and his k., 3.09
and the Levites, their sons and k. 3.09
with his sons and k., eighteen; 8.18
with his k. and their sons, twenty; 8.19
and ten of their k. with them. 8.24
and his k., Shemaiah, Azarel, Milalai, Neh 12.36
plague, and my k. stand afar off. Ps 38.11
sight, as I cast out all your k., Jer 7.15
your k. who did not go out with you 29.16
to me and to my k. be upon Babylon, 51.35
brothers or your k. or rich neighbors, Lk 14.12
and brothers and k. and friends, 21.16
together his k. and close friends. Ac 10.24
sake of my brethren, my k. by race. Rom 9.03
my k. and my fellow prisoners; 16.07
and Jason and Sosipater, my k. 16.21

KINSWOMAN

she is your father's near k. Lev 18.12
for she is your mother's near k. 18.13
your k. Elizabeth in her old age Lk 1.36

KINSWOMEN

they are your near k.; it is wickedness. Lev 18.17

KIR

carrying its people captive to K., 2Ki 16.09
because K. is laid waste in a night Is 15.01
and K. uncovered the shield. 22.06
of Syria shall go into exile to K., Amo 1.05
Caphtor and the Syrians from K.? 9.07

KIRHARESETH

only its stones were left in K., 2Ki 3.25
stricken, for the raisin-cakes of K. Is 16.07

KIRHERES

lyre for Moab, and my heart for K. Is 16.11
for the men of K. I mourn. Jer 48.13
like a flute for the men of K.; 48.36

KIRIATHAIM

Reuben built Heshbon, Elealah, K., Num 32.39
and K., and Sibmah, and Zerethshahar Jos 13.19
and K. with its pasture lands. 1Ch 6.76
K. is put to shame, it is taken; Jer 48.01
and K., and Bethgamul, and Bethmeon, 48.23
Bethjeshimoth, Baalmeon, and K. Eze 25.09

KIRIATHARBA

And Sarah died at K. (that is, Gen 23.02
or K. (that is, Hebron), where 35.27
the name of Hebron formerly was K.; Jos 14.15
K., that is, Hebron (Arba was the 15.13
Humtah, K. (that is, Hebron), and Zior: 15.54
and K. (that is, Hebron) in the hill 20.07
They gave them K., Arba being the 21.11
name of Hebron was formerly K.); Ju 1.10
Judah lived in K. and its villages, Neh 11.25

KIRIATHARIM

The sons of K., Chephirah, and Ex 2.25

KIRIATHBAAL

K. (that is, Kiriathjearim), and Jos 15.60
Bethhoron, and it ends at K. (that is, 18.14

KIRIATHHUZOTH

with Balak, and they came to K. Num 22.39

KIRIATHJEARIM

Gibeon, Chephirah, Beeroth, and K. Jos 9.17
bends round to Baalah (that is K.); 15.09
K.), and Rabbah: two cities with 15.60
K.), a city belonging to the tribe 18.14
side begins at the outskirts of K.; 18.15
Gibeah and K.—fourteen cities with 18.28
up and encamped at K. in Judah. Ju 18.12
behold, it is west of K. 18.12
messengers to the inhabitants of K., 1Sa 6.21
And the men of K. came and took up 7.01
day that the ark was lodged at K., 7.02
Ephrathah: Shobal the father of K., 1Ch 2.50
Shobal the father of K. had other sons: 2.52
And the families of K.: the Ithrites, 2.53
to bring the ark of God from K. 13.05
to K. which belongs to Judah, to 13.06
ark of God from K. to the place 2Ch 1.04
The men of K., Chephirah, and Neh 7.29
Uriah the son of Shemaiah from K. Jer 26.20

KIRIATHSANNAH

Dannah, K. (that is, Debir), Jos 15.49

KIRIATHSEPHER

the name of Debir formerly was K. Jos 15.15
And Caleb said, "Whoever smites K., 15.16
the name of Debir was formerly K. Ju 1.11
"He who attacks K. and takes it, 1.12

KISH

man of Benjamin whose name was K., 1Sa 9.01
Now the asses of K., Saul's father, 9.03
So K. said to Saul his son, "Take 9.03
"What has come over the son of K.? 10.11
Saul the son of K. was taken by 10.21
K. was the father of Saul, and Ner 14.51
Zela, in the tomb of K. his father; 2Sa 21.14
Abdon, then Zur, K., Baal, Nadab, 1Ch 8.30
Ner was the father of K., 8.33
K. of Saul, Saul of Jonathan, Malchishua, 8.33
K., Baal, Ner, Nadab, 9.36
Ner was the father of K., 9.39
K. of Saul, Saul of Jonathan, Malchishua, 9.39
because of Saul the son of K.; 12.01

KISH (cont.)
the sons of Mahli: Eleazar and K. 1Ch 23.21
the sons of K., married them. 23.22
Of K., the sons of Kish: Jerahmeel. 24.29
Of Kish, the sons of K.: Jerahmeel. 24.29
the seer, and Saul the son of K., 26.28
K. the son of Abdi, and Azariah the 2Ch 29.12
son of K., a Benjaminite, Est 2.05
God gave them Saul the son of K., Ac 13.21

KISHI
of Merari: Ethan the son of K., 1Ch 6.44

KISHION
Rabbith, K., Ebez, Jos 19.20
K. with its pasture lands, Daberath 21.28

KISHON
by the river K. with his chariots Ju 4.07
Haroshethhagoiim to the river K. 4.13
The torrent K. swept them away, the 5.21
onrushing torrent, the torrent K. 5.21
brought them down to the brook K., 1Ki 18.40
Sisera and Jabin at the river K., Ps 83.09

KISS
him, "Come near and k. me, my son." Gen 27.26
permit me to k. my sons and my 31.28
and take hold of him, and k. him. 2Sa 15.05
with his right hand to k. him. 20.09
"Let me k. my father and my mother, 1Ki 19.20
k. his feet, lest he be angry, and Ps 2.12
and peace will k. each other. 85.10
O that you would k. me with the Sol 1.02
I would k. you, and none would 8.01
these, they say, Men k. calves! Hos 13.02
"The one I shall k. is the man; Mt 26.48
"The one I shall k. is the man; Mk 14.44
You gave me no k., but from the Lk 7.45
she has not ceased to k. my feet. 7.45
He drew near to Jesus to k. him; 22.47
betray the Son of man with a k.?" 22.48
Greet one another with a holy k. Rom 16.16
Greet one another with a holy k. 1Co 16.20
Greet one another with a holy k. 2Co 13.12
Greet all the brethren with a holy k. 1Th 5.26
Greet one another with the k. of love. 1Pe 5.14

KISSED
So he came near and k. him; Gen 27.27
Then Jacob k. Rachel, and wept aloud. 29.11
him, and embraced him and k. him, 29.13
and k. his grandchildren and his 31.55
and fell on his neck and k. him, 33.04
And he k. all his brothers and wept 45.15
and he k. them and embraced them. 48.10
and wept over him, and k. him. 50.01
at the mountain of God and k. him. Ex 4.27
and did obeisance and k. him; 18.07
Then she k. them, and they lifted up Ru 1.09
and Orpah k. her mother-in-law, but 1.14
and k. him and said, "Has not the 1Sa 10.01
and they k. one another, and wept 20.41
the king; and the king k. Absalom. 2Sa 14.33
and the king k. Barzillai and 19.39
every mouth that has not k. him. 1Ki 19.18
and my mouth has k. my hand; Job 31.27
"Hail Master!" And he k. him. Mt 26.49
said, "Master!" And he k. him. Mk 14.45
and k. his feet, and anointed them Lk 7.38
ran and embraced him and k. him. 15.20
wept and embraced Paul and k. him. Ac 20.37

KISSES
She seizes him and k. him, Pro 7.13
gives a right answer k. the lips. 24.26
profuse are the k. of an enemy. 27.06
kiss me with the k. of your mouth! Sol 1.02
and your k. like the best wine that 7.09

KITCHENS
"These are the k. where those who Eze 46.24

KITE
the k., the falcon according to its Lev 11.14
buzzard, the k., after their kinds; Deu 14.13

KITES
there shall the k. be gathered, Is 34.15

KITRON
drive out the inhabitants of K., Ju 1.30

KITTIM
Elishah, Tarshish, K., and Dodanim. Gen 10.04
shall come from K. and shall Num 24.24
Elishah, Tarshish, K., and Rodanim. 1Ch 1.07
For ships of K. shall come against Dan 11.30

KNAVE
nor the k. said to be honorable. Is 32.05
The knaveries of the k. are evil; 32.07

KNAVERIES
The k. of the knave are evil; Is 32.07

KNEAD
fine meal, k. it, and make cakes." Gen 18.06
and the women k. dough, to make Jer 7.18

KNEADED
and k. it and baked unleavened 1Sa 28.24
and k. it, and made cakes in his 2Sa 13.08

KNEADING
into your ovens and your k. bowls; Ex 8.03
their k. bowls being bound up in 12.34
from the k. of the dough until it Hos 7.04

KNEADING-TROUGH
Blessed shall be your basket and your k. Deu 28.05
Cursed shall be your basket and your k. 28.17

KNEE
they cried before him, "Bow the k.!" Gen 41.43
'To me every k. shall bow, every Is 45.23
who have not bowed the k. to Baal. Rom 11.04
every k. shall bow to me, and every 14.11
name of Jesus every k. should bow, Php 2.10

KNEE-DEEP
and it was k. Again he measured Eze 47.04

KNEEL
made the camels k. down outside Gen 24.11
let us k. before the LORD, our Maker! Ps 95.06

KNEELING
up to him and k. before him said, Mt 17.14
and k. before him she asked him for 20.20
And k. before him they mocked him, 27.29
and k. said to him, "If you will, you Mk 1.40
and k. down on the beach we prayed Ac 21.05

KNEELS
every one that k. down to drink. Ju 7.05

KNEES
her, that she may bear upon my k., Gen 30.03
Then Joseph removed them from his k., 48.12
Manasseh were born upon Joseph's k. 50.23
you on the k. and on the legs with Deu 28.35
She made him sleep upon her k.; Ju 16.19
and put his face between his k. 1Ki 18.42
all the k. that have not bowed to 19.18
and fell on his k. before Elijah, 2Ki 1.13
knelt upon his k. in the presence 2Ch 6.13
fell upon my k. and spread out my Ez 9.05
Why did the k. receive me? Or why Job 3.12
you have made firm the feeble k. 4.04

KNEES (cont.)
My k. are weak through fasting; Ps 109.24
hands, and make firm the feeble k. Is 35.03
her hip, and dandled upon her k. 66.12
feeble, and all k. weak as water. Eze 7.17
faint and all k. will be weak as 21.07
and his k. knocked together. Dan 5.06
down upon his k. three times a day 6.10
me trembling on my hands and k. 10.10
Hearts faint and k. tremble, Nah 2.10
So the servant fell on his k., Mt 18.26
saw it, he fell down at Jesus' k., Lk 5.08
reason I bow my k. before the Eph 3.14
hands and strengthen your weak k., Heb 12.12

KNELT
of the people k. down to drink Ju 7.06
where he had k. with hands outstretched 1Ki 8.54
Then he k. upon his knees in the 2Ch 6.13
came to him and k. before him, Mt 8.02
a ruler came in and k. before him, 9.18
But she came and k. before him, 15.25
a man ran up and k. before him, Mk 10.17
and they k. down in homage to him. 15.19
throw, and k. down and prayed, Lk 22.41
And he k. down and cried with a Ac 7.60
all outside and k. down and prayed; 9.40
he k. down and prayed with them all. 20.36

KNEW
and they k. that they were naked; Gen 3.07
Now Adam k. Eve his wife, and she 4.01
Cain k. his wife, and she conceived 4.17
And Adam k. his wife again, and she 4.25
so Noah k. that the waters had 8.11
his wine and k. what his youngest 9.24
But Onan k. that the offspring 38.09
and k. them, but he treated them 42.07
Thus Joseph k. his brothers, but 42.08
and God k. their condition. Ex 2.25
which you k., will he inflict upon Deu 7.15
LORD from the day that I k. you. 9.24
whom the LORD k. face to face, 34.10
Then Manoah k. that he was the Ju 13.21
and they k. her, and abused her all 19.25
And Elkanah k. Hannah his wife, and 1Sa 1.19
ever, for the iniquity which he k., 3.13
to Beersheba k. that Samuel was 3.20
And when all who k. him before saw 10.11
Saul saw and k. that the LORD was 18.28
If I k. that it was determined by 20.09
so Jonathan k. that his father was 20.33
But the lad k. nothing; only 20.39
Jonathan and David k. the matter. 20.39
and they k. that he fled, and did 22.17
"I k. on that day, when Doeg the 22.22
David k. that Saul was plotting 23.09
or k. it, nor did any awake; 26.12
And Saul k. that it was Samuel, and 28.14
place where he k. there were 2Sa 11.16
their simplicity, and k. nothing. 15.11
to him; but the king k. her not. 1Ki 1.04
Then Manasseh k. that the LORD was 2Ch 33.13
to the wise men who k. the times— Est 1.13
"Because his greed k. no rest, Job 20.20
Oh, that I k. where I might find him. 23.03
cripples whom I k. not slandered me Ps 35.15
you should say, 'Behold, I k. them.' Is 48.07
For I k. that you would deal very 48.08
nations that k. you not shall run 55.05
"Before I formed you in the womb I k. you, Jer 1.05
The LORD made it known to me and I k.; 11.18
Then I k. that this was the word of 32.08
Gedaliah, before any one k. of it, 41.04
serve other gods that they k. not, 44.03
Then all the men who k. that their 44.15
and I k. that they were cherubim. Eze 10.20
until he k. that the Most High God Dan 5.21
heart, though you k. all this, 5.22
When Daniel k. that the document 6.10
It was I who k. you in the wilderness, Hos 13.05
For the men k. that he was fleeing Jon 1.10
for I k. that thou art a gracious 4.02
k. that it was the word of the LORD. Zec 11.11
but k. her not until she had borne Mt 1.25
I declare to them, 'I never k. you; 7.23
I k. you to be a hard man, reaping 25.24
You k. that I reap where I have not 25.26
For he k. that it was out of envy 27.18
to speak, because they k. him. Mk 1.34
and k. them, and they ran there on 6.33
because they k. that he was the Lk 4.41
But he k. their thoughts, and he 6.08
servant who k. his master's will, 12.47
You k. that I was a severe man, 19.22
even today you k. the things that 19.42
him, yet the world k. him not. Jn 1.10
who had drawn the water k.), 2.09
because he k. all men and needed no 2.25
for he himself k. what was in man. 2.25
Now when the Lord k. that the 4.01
"If you k. the gift of God, and who 4.10
The father k. that was the hour 4.53
saw him and k. that he had been 5.06
for he himself k. what he would do. 6.06
For Jesus k. from the first who 6.64
if you k. me, you would know my 8.19
I k. that thou hearest me always, 11.42
that if any one k. where he was, 11.57
when Jesus k. that his hour had 13.01
For he k. who was to betray him; 13.11
at the table k. why he said this 13.28
Jesus k. that they wanted to ask 16.19
betrayed him, also k. the place; 18.02
They k. it was the Lord. 21.12
And when the brethren k. it, Ac 9.30
for they all k. that his father was 16.03
though he k. only the baptism of 18.25
for although they k. God they did Rom 1.21
made him to be sin who k. no sin, 2Co 5.21
since you k. that you yourselves Heb 10.34

KNEWEST
for thou k. that they acted insolently Neh 9.10

KNIFE
in his hand the fire and the k. Gen 22.06
and took the k. to slay his son. 22.10
he took a k., and laying hold of Ju 19.29
and put a k. to your throat if you Pro 23.02

KNIT
of Jonathan was k. to the soul of 1Sa 18.01
me, my heart will be k. to you; 1Ch 12.17
and k. me together with bones and Job 10.11
of his thighs are k. together. 40.17
thou didst k. me together in my Ps 139.13
Joined and k. together by every Eph 4.16
as they are k. together in love, to Col 2.02
nourished and k. together through 2.19

KNIVES
"Make flint k. and circumcise the Jos 5.02
So Joshua made flint k., and 5.03
are swords, whose teeth are k., Pro 30.14

KNOCK
k., and it will be opened to you. Mt 7.07
k., and it will be opened to you. Lk 11.09
outside and to k. at the door, 13.25
Behold, I stand at the door and k.; Rev 3.20

KNOCKED
way, and his knees k. together. Dan 5.06
And when he k. at the door of the Ac 12.13

KNOCKING

my beloved is k. "Open to me, Sol 5.02
But Peter continued k.; and when Ac 12.16

KNOCKS

If he k. out the tooth of his slave, Ex 21.27
and to him who k. it will be Mt 7.08
and to him who k. it will be Lk 11.10
him at once when he comes and k. 12.36

KNOW

He said, "I do not k., am I my Gen 4.09
"I k. that you are a woman beautiful 12.11
how am I to k. that I shall possess 15.08
"K. of a surety that your descendants 15.13
come to me; and if not, I will k." 18.21
out to us, that we may k. them." 19.05
he did not k. when she lay down or 19.33
and he did not k. when she lay down 19.35
I k. that you have done this in the 20.06
k. that you shall surely die, you, 20.07
"I do not k. who has done this 21.26
for now I k. that you fear God, 22.12
By this I shall k. that thou hast 24.14
I do not k. the day of my death. 27.02
to k. whether you are really my son 27.21
this place; and I did not k. it." 28.16
"Do you k. Laban the son of Nahor?" 29.05
They said, "We k. him." 29.05
for you k. the service which I have 30.26
"You yourself k. how I have served 30.29
You k. that I have served your 31.06
Jacob did not k. that Rachel had 31.32
for he did not k. that she was his 38.16
brothers, but they did not k. him. 42.08
They did not k. that Joseph understood 42.23
'By this I shall k. that you are 42.33
then I shall k. that you are not 42.34
we in any way k. that he would say, 43.07
We do not k. who put our money in 43.22
Do you not k. that such a man as I 44.15
'You k. that my wife bore me two 44.27
your face and k. that you are 46.30
and if you k. any able men among 47.06
"I k., my son, I k.; he also 48.19
over Egypt, who did not k. Joseph. Ex 1.08
to k. what would be done to him. 2.04
taskmasters; I k. their sufferings, 3.07
I k. that the king of Egypt will 3.19
I k. that he can speak well; 4.14
I do not k. the LORD, and moreover I 5.02
and you shall k. that I am the LORD 6.07
Egyptians shall k. that I am the 7.05
this you shall k. that I am the 7.17
that you may k. that there is no 8.10
that you may k. that I am the LORD 8.22
that you may k. that there is none 9.14
that you may k. that the earth is 9.29
I k. that you do not yet fear the 9.30
that you may k. that I am the LORD." 10.02
and we do not k. with what we must 10.26
that you may k. that the LORD makes 11.07
Egyptians shall k. that I am the 14.04
Egyptians shall k. that I am the 14.18
you shall k. that it was the LORD 16.06
then you shall k. that I am the 16.12
For they did not k. what it was. 16.15
Now I k. that the LORD is greater 18.11
and I make them k. the statutes of 18.16
and make them k. the way in which 18.20
you k. the heart of a stranger, for 23.09
And they shall k. that I am the 29.46
that you may k. that I, the LORD, 31.13
we do not k. what has become of him." 32.01
you k. the people, that they are set 32.22
we do not k. what has become of him.' 32.23
that I may k. what to do with you.'" 33.05
hast not let me k. whom thou wilt 33.12
'I k. you by name, and you have also 33.12
that I may k. thee and find favor 33.13
in my sight, and I k. you by name." 33.17
Moses did not k. that the skin of 34.29
intelligence to k. how to do any 36.01
has seen or come to k. the matter, Lev 5.01
he comes to k. it he shall be 5.03
he comes to k. it he shall in any 5.04
be done, though he does not k. it, 5.17
generations may k. that I made the 23.43
for you k. how we are to encamp in Num 10.31
whom you k. to be the elders of the 11.16
and they shall k. the land which 14.31
and you shall k. my displeasure.' 14.34
you shall k. that the LORD has 16.28
then you shall k. that these men 16.30
You k. all the adversity that has 20.14
for I k. that he whom you bless is 22.06
that I may k. what more the LORD 22.19
for I did not k. that thou didst 22.34
I will let you k. what this people 24.14
your cattle (I k. that you have Deu 3.19
that you might k. that the LORD is 4.35
k. therefore this day, and lay it to 4.39
K. therefore that the LORD your God 7.09
testing you to k. what was in your 8.02
with manna, which you did not k., 8.03
not know, nor did your fathers k.; 8.03
might make you k. that man does 8.03
K. then in your heart that, as a man 8.05
which your fathers did not k., 8.16
whom you k., and of whom you have 9.02
K. therefore this day that he who 9.03
"K. therefore, that the LORD your 9.06
to k. whether you love the LORD 13.03
'How may we k. the word which the 18.21
trees which you k. are not trees 20.20
near you, or if you do not k. him, 22.02
that you may k. that I am the LORD 29.06
"You k. how we dwelt in the land of 29.16
for I k. the purposes which they 31.21
For I k. how rebellious and stubborn 31.27
For I k. that after my death you 31.29
but I did not k. where they came Jos 2.04
where the men went I do not k.; 2.05
"I k. that the LORD has given you 2.09
that you may k. the way you shall 3.04
that they may k. that, as I was with 3.07
you shall k. that the living God 3.10
then you shall let your children k., 4.22
the earth may k. that the hand of 4.24
but he did not k. that there was an 8.14
"You k. what the LORD said to Moses 14.06
knows, and lets Israel itself k.! 22.22
"Today we k. that the LORD is in 22.31
k. assuredly that the LORD your God 23.13
and you k. in your hearts and souls, 23.14
who did not k. the LORD or the work Ju 2.10
the people of Israel might k. war, 3.02
to k. whether Israel would obey the 3.04
then I shall k. that thou wilt 6.37
Manoah did not k. that he was the 13.16
mother did not k. that it was from 14.04
"Do you not k. that the Philistines 15.11
And he did not k. that the LORD had 16.20
"Now I k. that the LORD will 17.13
that we may k. whether the journey 18.05
"Do you k. that in these houses 18.14
your house, that we may k. him. 19.22
Benjaminites did not k. that 20.34
people that you did not k. before. Ru 2.11
fellow townsmen k. that you are a 3.11
that I may k., for there is no one 4.04
Now Samuel did not yet k. the LORD, 1Sa 3.07
then we shall k. that it is not his 6.09
and you shall k. and see that your 12.17
people did not k. that Jonathan 14.03
and k. and see how this sin has 14.38

KNOW (cont.)

I k. your presumption, and the evil 1Sa 17.28
the earth may k. that there is a 17.46
assembly may k. that the LORD 17.47
thinks, 'Let not Jonathan k. this, 20.03
then k. that evil is determined by 20.07
do I not k. that you have chosen 20.30
'Let no one k. anything of the 21.02
till I k. what God will do for me." 22.03
k. and see the place where his 23.22
you may k. and see that there is no 24.11
I k. that you shall surely be king, 24.20
who come from I do not k. where?" 25.11
Now therefore k. this and consider 25.17
you shall k. what your servant can 28.02
"Surely you k. what Saul has done, 28.09
"I k. that you are as blameless in 29.09
"How do you k. that Saul and his 2Sa 1.05
Do you not k. that the end will be 2.26
You k. that Abner the son of Ner 3.25
and to k. your going out and your 3.25
and to k. all that you are doing." 3.25
but David did not k. about it. 3.26
"Do you not k. that a prince and a 3.38
greatness, to make thy servant k. it. 7.21
Did you not k. that they would 11.20
angel of God to k. all things that 14.20
us, seeing I go I k. not where? 15.20
"You k. that your father and his 17.08
but I do not k. what it was." 18.29
For do I not k. that I am this day 19.22
that I may k. the number of the 24.02
and David our lord does not k. it? 1Ki 1.11
my lord the king, do not k. it. 1.18
"Moreover you k. also what Joab the 2.05
you will k. what you ought to do to 2.09
He said, "You k. that the kingdom 2.15
k. for certain that you shall die; 2.37
'K. for certain that on the day you 2.42
"You k. in your own heart all the 2.44
I do not k. how to go out or come 3.07
"You k. that David my father could 5.03
for you k. that there is no one 5.06
the earth may k. thy name and fear 8.43
that they may k. that this house 8.43
the earth may k. that the LORD is 8.60
"Now I k. that you are a man of God, 17.24
will carry you whither I k. not; 18.12
that this people may k. that thou, 18.37
and you shall k. that I am the LORD." 20.13
and you shall k. that I am the LORD.'" 20.28
"Do you k. that Ramothgilead 22.03
"Do you k. that today the LORD will 2Ki 2.03
And he said, "Yes, I k. it; 2.03
"Do you k. that today the LORD will 2.05
And he answered, "Yes, I k. it; 2.05
and you k. that your servant feared 4.01
k. that I have sent to you Naaman 5.06
that he may k. that there is a 5.08
I k. that there is no God in all 5.15
They k. that we are hungry; 7.12
"Because I k. the evil that you 8.12
"You k. the fellow and his talk." 9.11
K. then that there shall fall to 10.10
Samaria do not k. the law of the 17.26
they do not k. the law of the god 17.26
of the earth may k. that thou, 19.19
"But I k. your sitting down and 19.27
to k. what Israel ought to do, two 1Ch 12.32
report, that I may k. their number." 21.02
k. the God of your father, and serve 28.09
I k., my God, that thou triest the 29.17
for I k. that your servants k. how to 2Ch 2.08
the earth may k. thy name and fear 6.33
that they may k. that this house 6.33
that they may k. my service and the 12.08
Ought you not to k. that the LORD 13.05

We do not k. what to do, but our 20.12
"I k. that God has determined to 25.16
Do you not k. what I and my fathers 32.13
try him and to k. all that was in 32.31
all such as k. the laws of your God; Ez 7.25
and those who do not k. them, 7.25
officials did not k. where I had Neh 2.16
"They will not k. or see till we 4.11
provinces k. that if any man or Est 4.11
You shall k. that your tent is safe, Job 5.24
You shall k. also that your descendants 5.25
Hear, and k. it for your good." 5.27
nor does his place k. him any more. 7.10
and k. nothing, for our days on 8.09
"Truly I k. that it is so: But how 9.02
and they k. it not, when he overturns 9.05
for I k. thou wilt not hold me 9.28
let me k. why thou dost contend 10.02
I k. that this was thy purpose. 10.13
K. then that God exacts of you less 11.06
Deeper than Sheol—what can you k.? 11.08
Who does not k. such things as 12.03
these does not k. that the hand of 12.09
What you k., I also k.; I am not 13.02
I k. that I shall be vindicated. 13.18
Make me k. my transgression and my 13.23
to honor, and he does not k. it; 14.21
What do you k. that we do not k.? 15.09
k. then that God has put me in the 19.06
For I k. that my Redeemer lives, and 19.25
that you may k. there is a judgment." 19.29
Do you not k. this from of old, 20.04
to themselves, that they may k. it. 21.19
"Behold, I k. your thoughts, and your 21.27
Therefore you say, 'What does God k.? 22.13
do those who k. him never see his 24.01
themselves up; they do not k. the light. 24.16
Man does not k. the way to it, and 28.13
the cause of him whom I did not k. 29.16
Yea, I k. that thou wilt bring me to 30.23
and let God k. my integrity! 31.06
For I do not k. how to flatter, else 32.22
what my lips k. they speak sincerely. 33.03
and give ear to me, you who k.; 34.02
therefore declare what you k. 34.33
Behold, God is great, and we k. him not; 36.26
man, that all men may k. his work. 37.07
Do you k. how God lays his command 37.15
Do you k. the balancings of the 37.16
its measurements—surely you k.! 38.05
caused the dawn to k. its place, 38.12
Declare, if you k. all this. 38.18
You k., for you were born then, and 38.21
Do you k. the ordinances of the 38.33
"Do you k. when the mountain goats 39.01
and do you k. the time when they 39.02
"I k. that thou canst do all things, 42.02
wonderful for me, which I did not k. 42.03
But k. that the LORD has set apart Ps 4.03
And those who k. thy name put their 9.10
Let the nations k. that they are 9.20
Now I k. that the LORD will help 20.06
Make me to k. thy ways, O LORD; 25.04
ask me of things that I k. not. 35.11
steadfast love to those who k. thee, 36.10
"LORD, let me k. my end, and what is 39.04
let me k. how fleeting my life is! 39.04
that I may k. gladness, before I 39.13
By this I k. that thou art pleased 41.11
"Be still, and k. that I am God. 46.10
I k. all the birds of the air, and 50.11
For I k. my transgressions, and my 51.03
This I k., that God is for me. 56.09
that men may k. that God rules over 59.13
And they say, "How can God k.? 73.11
that the next generation might k. them, 78.06
on the nations that do not k. thee, 79.06
Let them k. that thou alone, whose 83.18

KNOW (cont.)
Among those who k. me I mention Ps 87.04
the people who k. the festal shout, 89.15
The dull man cannot k., the stupid 92.06
K. that the LORD is God! It is he 100 03
far from me; I will k. nothing of evil. 101.04
Let them k. that this is thy hand; 109.27
I k., O LORD, that thy judgments are 119.75
that they may k. thy testimonies. 119.79
that I may k. thy testimonies! 119.125
For I k. that the LORD is great, and 135.05
Search me, O God, and k. my heart! 139.23
Try me and k. my thoughts! 139.23
I k. that the LORD maintains the 140.12
they do not k. his ordinances. 147.20
That men may k. wisdom and instruction, Pro 1.02
they do not k. over what they 4.19
wander, and she does not k. it. 5.06
he does not k. that it will cost 7.23
But he does not k. that the dead 9.18
the righteous k. what is acceptable, 10.32
we did not k. this," does not he who 24.12
keeps watch over your soul k. it, 24.12
K. that wisdom is such to your soul; 24.14
for you do not k. what a day may 27.01
K. well the condition of your 27.23
and does not k. that want will come 28.22
his son's name? Surely you k.! 30.04
to k. wisdom and to k. madness Ecc 1.17
I k. that there is nothing better 3.12
I k. that whatever God does endures 3.14
for they do not k. that they are 5.01
my mind to k. and to search out 7.25
and to k. the wickedness of folly 7.25
a wise man will k. the time and 8.05
For he does not k. what is to be, 8.07
yet I k. that it will be well with 8.12
When I applied my mind to k. wisdom, 8.16
though a wise man claims to k., 8.17
it is love or hate man does not k. 9.01
For the living k. that they will 9.05
but the dead k. nothing, and they 9.05
For man does not k. his time. 9.12
he does not k. the way to the city. 10.15
for you k. not what evil may happen 11.02
As you do not k. how the spirit 11.05
so you do not k. the work of God 11.05
for you do not k. which will 11.06
But k. that for all these things 11.09
If you do not k., O fairest among Sol 1.08
but Israel does not k., my people Is 1.03
and let it come, that we may k. it!" 5.19
and all the people will k., Ephraim 9.09
Egyptians will k. the LORD in that 19.21
the earth may k. that thou alone 37.20
'I k. your sitting down and your 37.28
that men may see and k., may consider 41.20
them, that we may k. their outcome; 41.22
that we may k. that you are gods; 41.23
that we might k., and beforetime, 41.26
blind in a way that they k. not, 42.16
that you may k. and believe me and 43.10
is no rock; I k. not any." 44.08
their witnesses neither see nor k., 44.09
They k. not, nor do they discern; 44.18
that you may k. that it is I, the 45.03
you, though you do not k. me. 45.04
gird you, though you do not k. me, 45.05
that men may k., from the rising of 45.06
as a widow or k. the loss of 47.08
suddenly, of which you k. nothing. 47.11
Because I k. that you are obstinate, 48.04
Then you will k. that I am the LORD; 49.23
all flesh shall k. that I am the 49.26
that I may k. how to sustain with a 50.04
and I k. that I shall not be put to 50.07
you who k. righteousness, the people 51.07
Therefore my people shall k. my name; 52.06
day they shall k. that it is I who 52.06
shall call nations that you k. not, 55.05
daily, and delight to k. my ways, 58.02
The way of peace they k. not, 59.08
and we k. our iniquities: 59.12
and you shall k. that I, the LORD, am 60.16
does not k. us and Israel does not 63.16
"For I k. their works and their 66.18
I do not k. how to speak, for I am Jer 1.06
who handle the law did not k. me; 2.08
K. and see that it is evil and 2.19
k. what you have done—a restive 2.23
people are foolish, they k. me not; 4.22
but how to do good they k. not. 4.22
for they do not k. the way of the 5.04
for they k. the way of the LORD, the 5.05
whose language you do not k., 5.15
They k. no bounds in deeds of 5.28
they did not k. how to blush. 6.15
and k., O congregation, what will 6.18
that you may k. and assay their 6.27
but my people k. not the ordinance 8.07
they did not k. how to blush. 8.12
to evil, and they do not k. me, 9.03
upon deceit, they refuse to k. me, 9.06
I k., O LORD, that the way of man is 10.23
upon the nations that k. thee not, 10.25
I did not k. it was against me they 11.19
we not indeed k. that every jar 13.12
in a land which you do not k., 15.14
k. that for thy sake I bear reproach 15.15
"Therefore, behold, I will make them k., 16.21
will make them k. my power and my 16.21
and they shall k. that my name is 16.21
in a land which you do not k., 17.04
Is not this to k. me? says the LORD. 22.16
into a land which they do not k.? 22.28
them a heart to k. that I am the 24.07
Only k. for certain that if you put 26.15
For I k. the plans I have for you, 29.11
'K. the LORD,' for they shall all k. me, 31.34
and let no one k. where you are." 36.19
"Let no one k. of these words and 38.24
"Do you k. that Baal is the king of 40.14
Nethaniah, and no one will k. it. 40.15
K. for a certainty that I have 42.19
Now therefore k. for a certainty 42.22
shall k. whose word will stand, mine 44.28
that you may k. that my words will 44.29
about him, and all who k. his name; 48.17
I k. his insolence, says the LORD; 48.30
O Babylon, and you did not k. it; 50.24
they will k. that there has been a Eze 2.05
and they shall k. that I, the LORD, 5.13
and you shall k. that I am the LORD. 6.07
And they shall k. that I am the 6.10
And you shall k. that I am the LORD, 6.13
Then they will k. that I am the 6.14
Then you will k. that I am the LORD. 7.04
Then you will k. that I am the LORD, 7.09
and they shall k. that I am the 7.27
for I k. the things that come into 11.05
and you shall k. that I am the LORD. 11.10
and you shall k. that I am the LORD; 11.12
And they shall k. that I am the 12.15
and may k. that I am the LORD. 12.16
and you shall k. that I am the LORD." 12.20
and you shall k. that I am the Lord 13.09
and you shall k. that I am the LORD, 13.14
and you shall k. that I am the LORD. 13.21
Then you will k. that I am the LORD." 13.23
and you shall k. that I am the LORD. 14.08
and you shall k. that I have not 14.23
and you will k. that I am the LORD, 15.07
and you shall k. that I am the LORD, 16.62
Do you not k. what these things 17.12
and you shall k. that I, the LORD, 17.21
the field shall k. that I the LORD 17.24

KNOW (cont.)
Then let them k. the abominations Eze 20.04
that they might k. that I the LORD 20.12
that you may k. that I the LORD am 20.20
that they might k. that I am the 20.26
Then you will k. that I am the LORD. 20.38
And you shall k. that I am the LORD, 20.42
And you shall k. that I am the LORD, 20.44
and all flesh shall k. that I the 21.05
and you shall k. that I am the LORD." 22.16
and you shall k. that I the LORD 22.22
and you shall k. that I am the Lord 23.49
then you will k. that I am the Lord 24.24
and they will k. that I am the LORD." 24.27
Then you will k. that I am the LORD. 25.05
Then you will k. that I am the LORD. 25.07
Then they will k. that I am the 25.11
and they shall k. my vengeance, 25.14
Then they will k. that I am the 25.17
Then they will k. that I am the 26.06
All who k. you among the peoples 28.19
And they shall k. that I am the 28.22
Then they will k. that I am the 28.23
Then they will k. that I am the 28.24
Then they will k. that I am the 28.26
of Egypt shall k. that I am the 29.06
Then they will k. that I am the 29.09
Then they will k. that I am the 29.16
Then they will k. that I am the 29.21
Then they will k. that I am the 30.08
Then they will k. that I am the 30.19
and they shall k. that I am the 30.25
Then they will k. that I am the 30.26
then they will k. that I am the 32.15
Then they will k. that I am the 33.29
then they will k. that a prophet 33.33
and they shall k. that I am the 34.27
And they shall k. that I, the LORD 34.30
and you shall k. that I am the LORD. 35.04
Then you will k. that I am the LORD. 35.09
And you shall k. that I, the LORD, 35.12
Then they will k. that I am the 35.15
Then you will k. that I am the LORD. 36.11
nations will k. that I am the LORD, 36.23
round about you shall k. that I, 36.36
Then they will k. that I am the 36.38
and you shall k. that I am the LORD." 37.06
And you shall k. that I am the LORD, 37.13
then you shall k. that I, the LORD, 37.14
nations will k. that I the LORD 37.28
land, that the nations may k. me, 38.16
Then they will k. that I am the 38.23
and they shall k. that I am the 39.06
nations shall k. that I am the 39.07
of Israel shall k. that I am the 39.22
nations shall k. that the house of 39.23
Then they shall k. that I am the 39.28
spirit is troubled to k. the dream." Dan 2.03
"I k. with certainty that you are 2.08
and I shall k. that you can show me 2.09
that you may k. the thoughts of 2.30
because I k. that the spirit of the 4.09
the living may k. that the Most 4.17
till you k. that the Most High 4.25
time that you k. that Heaven rules 4.26
which do not see or hear or k., 5.23
"K., O king, that it is a law of the 6.15
"Then I desired to k. the truth 7.19
K. therefore and understand that 9.25
"Do you k. why I have come to you? 10.20
the people who k. their God shall 11.32
fathers did not k. he shall honor 11.38
And she did not k. that it was I Hos 2.08
and you shall k. the LORD. 2.20
I k. Ephraim, and Israel is not hid 5.03
them, and they k. not the LORD. 5.04
Let us k., let us press on to k. the LORD; 6.03
cry, My God, we Israel k. thee. 8.02
Israel shall k. it. The prophet is 9.07
they did not k. that I healed them. 11.03
you k. no God but me, and besides me 13.04
is discerning, let him k. them; 14.09
You shall k. that I am in the midst Joe 2.27
"So you shall k. that I am the LORD 3.17
"They do not k. how to do right," Amo 3.10
For I k. how many are your transgressions, 5.12
that we may k. on whose account Jon 1.07
for I k. it is because of me that 1.12
who do not k. their right hand 4.11
Is it not for you to k. justice? Mic 3.01
But they do not k. the thoughts of 4.12
that you may k. the saving acts of 6.05
Then you will k. that the LORD of Zec 2.09
and you shall k. that the LORD of 2.12
me, "Do you not k. what these are?" 4.05
Then you will k. that the LORD of 4.09
me, "Do you not k. what these are?" 4.13
and you shall k. that the LORD of 6.15
So shall you k. that I have sent Mal 2.04
your left hand k. what your right Mt 6.03
k. how to give good gifts to your 7.11
You will k. them by their fruits. 7.16
Thus you will k. them by their 7.20
But that you may k. that the Son of 9.06
been given to k. the secrets of 13.11
"Do you k. that the Pharisees were 15.12
You k. how to interpret the 16.03
come, and they did not k. him, 17.12
"You do not k. what you are asking. 20.22
"You k. that the rulers of the 20.25
So they answered Jesus, "We do not k." 21.27
we k. that you are true, and teach 22.16
because you k. neither the scriptures 22.29
its leaves, you k. that summer is near. 24.32
you k. that he is near, at the very 24.33
and they did not k. until the flood 24.39
for you do not k. on what day your 24.42
But k. this, that if the householder 24.43
him and at an hour he does not k., 24.50
I say to you, I do not k. you." 25.12
for you k. neither the day nor the 25.13
"You k. that after two days the 26.02
saying, "I do not k. what you mean." 26.70
with an oath, "I do not k. the man." 26.72
and to swear, "I do not k. the man." 26.74
for I k. that you seek Jesus who 28.05
I k. who you are, the Holy One of Mk 1.24
But that you may k. that the Son of 2.10
them that no one should k. this, 5.43
and would not have any one k. it; 7.24
For he did not k. what to say, for 9.06
he would not have any one k. it; 9.30
You k. the commandments: 'Do not 10.19
"You do not k. what you are asking. 10.38
"You k. that those who are supposed 10.42
So they answered Jesus, "We do not k." 11.33
we k. that you are true, and care 12.14
that you k. neither the scriptures 12.24
its leaves, you k. that summer is near. 13.28
you k. that he is near, at the very 13.29
for you do not k. when the time 13.33
for you do not k. when the master 13.35
they did not k. what to answer him 14.40
"I neither k. nor understand what 14.68
"I do not k. this man of whom you 14.71
that you may k. the truth concerning Lk 1.04
to the angel, "How shall I k. this? 1.18
His parents did not k. it, 2.43
Did you not k. that I must be in my 2.49
I k. who you are, the Holy One of 4.34
But that you may k. that the Son of 5.24
been given to k. the secrets of 8.10
"You do not k. what manner of spirit * 9.55
nevertheless k. this, that the 10.11
k. how to give good gifts to your 11.13

KNOW (cont.)

But k. this, that if the householder Lk 12.39
him and at an hour he does not k., 12.46
But he who did not k., and did what 12.48
You k. how to interpret the appearance 12.56
why do you not k. how to interpret 12.56
'I do not k. where you come from.' 13.25
I do not k. where you come from; 13.27
You k. the commandments: 'Do not 18.20
that he might k. what they had 19.15
you did not k. the time of your 19.44
that they did not k. whence it was. 20.07
we k. that you speak and teach 20.21
then k. that its desolation has 21.20
yourselves and k. that the summer 21.30
you k. that the kingdom of God is 21.31
three times deny that you k. me. 22.34
it, saying, "Woman, I do not k. him." 22.57
I do not k. what you are saying." 22.60
for they k. not what they do." 23.34
who does not k. the things that 24.18
you stands one whom you do not k., Jn 1.26
I myself did not k. him; but for this I 1.31
I myself did not k. him; but he who 1.33
Nathanael said to him, "How do you k. me?" 1.48
and did not k. where it came from 2.09
we k. that you are a teacher come 3.02
but you do not k. whence it comes 3.08
say to you, we speak of what we k., 3.11
You worship what you do not k.; 4.22
we worship what we k., for salvation 4.22
"I k. that Messiah is coming (he 4.25
food to eat of which you do not k." 4.32
and we k. that this is indeed the 4.42
been healed did not k. who it was, 5.13
and I k. that the testimony which 5.32
But I k. that you have not the love 5.42
whose father and mother we k.? 6.42
have believed, and have come to k., 6.69
he shall k. whether the teaching is 7.17
authorities really k. that this is 7.26
Yet we k. where this man comes from 7.27
no one will k. where he comes from. 7.27
"You k. me, and you k. where I come 7.28
me is true, and him you do not k. 7.28
I k. him, for I come from him, and he 7.29
who do not k. the law, are accursed. 7.49
for I k. whence I have come and 8.14
but you do not k. whence I come or 8.14
"You k. neither me nor my Father; 8.19
me, you would k. my Father also." 8.19
then you will k. that I am he, and 8.28
and you will k. the truth, and the 8.32
I k. that you are descendants of 8.37
"Now we k. that you have a demon. 8.52
I k. him. If I said 8.55
I do not k. him, I should be a liar 8.55
but I do k. him and I keep his word. 8.55
"Where is he?" He said, "I do not k." 9.12
"We k. that this is our son, and 9.20
but how he now sees we do not k., 9.21
nor do we k. who opened his eyes. 9.21
we k. that this man is a sinner." 9.24
he is a sinner, I do not k.; 9.25
one thing I k., that though I was 9.25
We k. that God has spoken to Moses, 9.29
we do not k. where he comes from." 9.29
You do not k. where he comes from, 9.30
We k. that God does not listen to 9.31
follow him, for they k. his voice. 10.04
for they do not k. the voice of 10.05
I k. my own and my own k. me, 10.14
knows me and I k. the Father; 10.15
and I k. them, and they follow me; 10.27
that you may k. and understand that 10.38
And even now I k. that whatever you 11.22
"I k. that he will rise again in 11.24
to them, "You k. nothing at all; 11.49
he was, he should let them k., 11.57
darkness does not k. where he goes. 12.35
And I k. that his commandment is 12.50
"What I am doing you do not k. now, 13.07
"Do you k. what I have done to you? 13.12
If you k. these things, blessed are 13.17
I k. whom I have chosen; it is that 13.18
all men will k. that you are my 13.35
And you k. the way where I am going." 14.04
we do not k. where you are going; 14.05
how can we k. the way?" 14.05
henceforth you k. him and have seen 14.07
and yet you do not k. me, Philip? 14.09
you k. him, for he dwells with you, 14.17
day you will k. that I am in my 14.20
the world may k. that I love the 14.31
does not k. what his master is 15.15
k. that it has hated me before it 15.18
they do not k. him who sent me. 15.21
We do not k. what he means." 16.18
Now we k. that you k. all things, 16.30
that they k. thee the only true God, 17.03
Now they k. that everything that 17.07
them and k. in truth that I came 17.08
the world may k. that thou hast 17.23
and these k. that thou hast sent me. 17.25
to them; they k. what I said." 18.21
that you may k. that I find no 19.04
Do you not k. that I have power to 19.10
and we do not k. where they have 20.02
yet they did not k. the scripture, 20.09
and I do not k. where they have 20.13
but she did not k. that it was 20.14
disciples did not k. that it was 21.04
you k. that I love you." He said 21.15
you k. that I love you." He said 21.16
to him, "Lord, you k. everything; 21.17
you k. that I love you." 21.17
and we k. that his testimony is 21.24
not for you to k. times or seasons Ac 1.07
your midst, as you yourselves k.— 2.22
therefore k. assuredly that God 2.36
man strong whom you see and k.; 3.16
I k. that you acted in ignorance, as 3.17
we do not k. what has become of him.' 7.40
"You yourselves k. how unlawful it 10.28
You k. the word which he sent to 10.36
he did not k. that what was done by 12.09
you k. that in the early days God 15.07
"May we k. what this new teaching 17.19
we wish to k. therefore what these 17.20
"Jesus I k., and Paul I k.; but who 19.15
you k. that from this business we 19.25
of them did not k. why they had 19.32
who does not k. that the city of 19.35
"You yourselves k. how I lived 20.18
I k. that all you among whom I have 20.25
I k. that after my departure fierce 20.29
You yourselves k. that these hands 20.34
Thus all will k. that there is 21.24
And he said, "Do you k. Greek? 21.37
appointed you to k. his will, 22.14
they themselves k. that in every 22.19
desiring to k. the real reason why 22.30
"I did not k., brethren, that he was 23.05
And desiring to k. the charge on 23.28
done no wrong, as you k. very well. 25.10
the prophets? I k. that you believe." 26.27
to this sect we k. that everywhere 28.22
I want you to k., brethren, that I Rom 1.13
Though they k. God's decree that 1.32
We k. that the judgment of God 2.02
Do you not k. that God's kindness is 2.04
and k. his will and approve what is 2.18
and the way of peace they do not k. 3.17
Now we k. that whatever the law 3.19
Do you not k. that all of us who 6.03

KNOW (cont.)

We k. that our old self was crucified Rom 6.06
For we k. that Christ being raised 6.09
Do you not k. that if you yield 6.16
Do you not k., brethren—for I am 7.01
speaking to those who k. the law— 7.01
We k. that the law is spiritual; 7.14
For I k. that nothing good dwells 7.18
We k. that the whole creation has 8.22
for we do not k. how to pray as we 8.26
We k. that in everything God works 8.28
Do you not k. what the scripture 11.02
Besides this you k. what hour it is, 13.11
I k. and am persuaded in the Lord 14.14
and I k. that when I come to you I 15.29
I do not k. whether I baptized any 1Co 1.16
world did not k. God through 1.21
For I decided to k. nothing among 2.02
Do you not k. that you are God's 3.16
Do you not k. that a little leaven 5.06
Do you not k. that the saints will 6.02
Do you not k. that we are to judge 6.03
Do you not k. that the unrighteous 6.09
Do you not k. that your bodies are 6.15
Do you not k. that he who joins 6.16
Do you not k. that your body is a 6.19
k. whether you will save your husband? 7.16
k. whether you will save your wife? 7.16
we k. that "all of us possess 8.01
he does not yet k. as he ought to k. 8.02
we k. that "an idol has no real 8.04
Do you not k. that those who are 9.13
Do you not k. that in a race all 9.24
I want you to k., brethren, that our 10.01
You k. that when you were heathen, 12.02
Now I k. in part; then I shall 13.12
how will any one k. what is played? 14.07
how will any one k. what is said? 14.09
but if I do not k. the meaning of 14.11
he does not k. what you are saying? 14.16
is anything they desire to k., 14.35
you k. that the household of 16.15
for we k. that as you share in our 2Co 1.07
but to let you k. the abundant 2.04
test you and k. whether you are 2.09
For we k. that if the earthly tent 5.01
we k. that while we are at home in 5.06
We want you to k., brethren, about 8.01
For you k. the grace of our Lord 8.09
for I k. your readiness, of which I 9.02
I k. a man in Christ who fourteen 12.02
of the body I do not k., God knows. 12.02
And I k. that this man was caught 12.03
the body I do not k., God knows— 12.03
For I would have you k., brethren, that Gal 1.11
yet who k. that a man is not 2.16
Formerly, when you did not k. God, 4.08
but now that you have come to k. God, 4.09
you k. it was because of a bodily 4.13
that you may k. what is the hope to Eph 1.18
and to k. the love of Christ which 3.19
you also may k. how I am and what 6.21
that you may k. how we are, and that 6.22
I want you to k., brethren, that Php 1.12
For I k. that through your prayers 1.19
I k. that I shall remain and 1.25
But Timothy's worth you k., 2.22
that I may k. him and the power of 3.10
Let all men k. your forbearance. 4.05
I k. how to be abased, and I k. how to 4.12
yourselves k. that in the beginning 4.15
For I want you to k. how greatly I Col 2.01
so that you may k. how you ought 4.06
that you may k. how we are and that 4.08
For we k., brethren beloved by God, 1Th 1.04
You k. what kind of men we proved 1.05
For you yourselves k., brethren, that 2.01
as you k., we had courage in our 2.02
as you k., or a cloak for greed, as 2.05
for you k. how, like a father with 2.11
You yourselves k. that this is to 3.03
it has come to pass, and as you k. 3.04
I sent that I might k. your faith, 3.05
For you k. what instructions we 4.02
that each one of you k. how to take 4.04
like heathen who do not k. God; 4.05
For you yourselves k. well that the 5.02
who do not k. God and upon those 2Th 1.08
And you k. what is restraining him 2.06
For you yourselves k. how you ought 3.07
Now we k. that the law is good, if 1Ti 1.08
a man does not k. how to manage 3.05
you may k. how one ought to behave 3.15
those who believe and k. the truth. 4.03
for I k. whom I have believed and I 2Ti 1.12
and you well k. all the service he 1.18
you k. that they breed quarrels. 2.23
repent and come to k. the truth, 2.25
They profess to k. God, but they deny Tit 1.16
'K. the Lord,' for all shall k. me, Heb 8.11
For we k. him who said, "Vengeance 10.30
For you k. that afterward, when he 12.17
for you k. that the testing of your Jas 1.03
K. this, my beloved brethren. 1.19
for you k. that we who teach shall 3.01
Do you not k. that friendship with 4.04
whereas you do not k. about tomorrow. 4.14
let him k. that whoever brings back 5.20
You k. that you were ransomed from 1Pe 1.18
though you k. them and are established 2Pe 1.12
since I k. that the putting off of 1.14
this we may be sure that we k. him, 1Jn 2.03
He who says "I k. him" but disobeys 2.04
and does not k. where he is going, 2.11
because you k. him who is from the 2.13
children, because you k. the Father. 2.13
because you k. him who is from the 2.14
therefore we k. that it is the last 2.18
by the Holy One, and you all k. 2.20
because you do not k. the truth, 2.21
the truth, but because you k. it, 2.21
and k. that no lie is of the truth. 2.21
If you k. that he is righteous, you 2.29
world does not k. us is that it 3.01
know us is that it did not k. him. 3.01
but we k. that when he appears we 3.02
You k. that he appeared to take 3.05
We k. that we have passed out of 3.14
and you k. that no murderer has 3.15
By this we k. love, that he laid 3.16
By this we shall k. that we are of 3.19
And by this we k. that he abides in 3.24
By this you k. the Spirit of God: 4.02
By this we k. the spirit of truth 4.06
He who does not love does not k. God; 4.08
By this we k. that we abide in him 4.13
So we k. and believe the love God 4.16
By this we k. that we love the 5.02
that you may k. that you have 5.13
And if we k. that he hears us in 5.15
we k. that we have obtained the 5.15
We k. that any one born of God does 5.18
We k. that we are of God, and the 5.19
And we k. that the Son of God has 5.20
understanding, to k. him who is true; 5.20
I but also all who k. the truth, 2Jn 1.01
I k. that it is well with your soul 3Jn 1.02
and you k. my testimony is true. 1.12
that they k. by instinct as irrational Jud 1.10
" 'I k. your works, your toil and Rev 2.02
I k. you are enduring patiently and 2.03
" 'I k. your tribulation and your 2.09
" 'I k. where you dwell, where Satan's 2.13
" 'I k. your works, your love and 2.19
churches shall k. that I am he who 2.23
" 'I k. your works; you have the 3.01

KNOW (cont.)
you will not k. at what hour I Rev 3.03
" 'I k. your works. Behold, I have 3.08
I k. that you have but little power, 3.08
" 'I k. your works: you are neither 3.15
I said to him, "Sir, you k." 7.14

KNOWEST
For thou k. thy servant, O Lord GOD! 2Sa 7.20
render to each whose heart thou k., 1Ki 8.39
k. the hearts of all the children 8.39
thy servant? For thou k. thy servant. 1Ch 17.18
render to each whose heart thou k., 2Ch 6.30
k. the hearts of the children of 6.30
although thou k. that I am not Job 10.07
my lips, as thou k., O LORD. Ps 40.09
O God, thou k. my folly; the wrongs I 69.05
Thou k. my reproach, and my shame 69.19
Thou k. when I sit down and when I 139.02
lo, O LORD, thou k. it altogether. 139.04
are thy works! Thou k. me right well; 139.14
my spirit is faint, thou k. my way! 142.03
But thou, O LORD, k. me; thou seest me, Jer 12.03
O LORD, thou k.; remember me 15.15
the day of disaster, thou k.; 17.16
k. all their plotting to slay me. 18.23
I answered, "O Lord GOD, thou k." Eze 37.03
who k. the hearts of all men, show Ac 1.24

KNOWING
will be like God, k. good and evil." Gen 3.05
like one of us, k. good and evil; 3.22
each k. the affliction of his own 1Ki 8.38
of pottage, not k. what they were. 2Ki 4.39
each k. his own affliction, and his 2Ch 6.29
Thus, k. their works, he overturns Job 34.25
But Jesus, k. their thoughts, said, Mt 9.04
K. their thoughts, he said to them, 12.25
But the woman, k. what had been done Mk 5.33
k. that he was a righteous and holy 6.20
But k. their hypocrisy, he said to 12.15
laughed at him, k. that she was dead. Lk 8.53
one for Elijah"—not k. what he said. 9.33
But he, k. their thoughts, said to 11.17
men walk over them without k. it. 11.44
But Jesus, k. in himself that his Jn 6.61
Jesus, k. that the Father had given 13.03
Then Jesus, k. all that was to 18.04
k. that all was now finished, said 19.28
and k. that God had sworn with an Ac 2.30
wife came in, not k. what had happened. 5.07
not k. what shall befall me there; 20.22
k. that suffering produces endurance, Rom 5.03
k. that in the Lord your labor is 1Co 15.58
k. that he who raised the Lord 2Co 4.14
Therefore, k. the fear of the Lord, 5.11
k. that whatever good any one does, Eph 6.08
k. that he who is both their Master 6.09
k. that I am put here for the defense Php 1.16
worth of k. Christ Jesus my Lord. 3.08
k. that from the Lord you will Col 3.24
k. that you also have a Master in 4.01
believed, k. from whom you learned it 2Ti 3.14
k. that such a person is perverted Tit 3.11
k. that you will do even more than Phm 1.21
went out, not k. where he was to go. Heb 11.08
k. that the same experience of 1Pe 5.09
than after k. it to turn back from 2Pe 2.21
k. this beforehand, beware lest you 3.17
not k. that you are wretched, Rev 3.17

KNOWLEDGE
the tree of the k. of good and Gen 2.09
the tree of the k. of good and 2.17
with k. and all craftsmanship, Ex 31.03
with k., and with all craftsmanship, 35.31
without the k. of the congregation, Num 15.24
and knows the k. of the Most High, 24.16
day have no k. of good or evil, Deu 1.39
for the LORD is a God of k., 1Sa 2.03
without the k. of my father David, 1Ki 2.32
now wisdom and k. to go out and 2Ch 1.10
wisdom and k. for yourself that 1.11
wisdom and k. are cranted to you. 1.12
all who have k. and understanding, Neh 10.28
And this came to the k. of Mordecai, Est 2.22
"Should a wise man answer with windy k., Job 15.02
do not desire the k. of thy ways. 21.14
Will any teach God k., seeing that 21.22
and plentifully declared sound k.! 26.03
'Job speaks without k., his words are 34.35
he multiplies words without k. 35.16
I will fetch my k. from afar, 36.03
who is perfect in k. is with you. 36.04
by the sword, and die without k. 36.12
works of him who is perfect in k., 37.16
counsel by words without k.? 38.02
this that hides counsel without k.? 42.03
Have they no k., all the evildoers Ps 14.04
and night to night declares k. 19.02
for their number is past my k. 71.15
Is there k. in the Most High?" 73.11
They have neither k. nor understanding, 82.05
not chastise? He who teaches men k., 94.10
Teach me good judgment and k., 119.66
Such k. is too wonderful for me; 139.06
k. and discretion to the youth— Pro 1.04
of the LORD is the beginning of k.; 1.07
their scoffing and fools hate k.? 1.22
Because they hated k. and did not 1.29
of the LORD and find the k. of God. 2.05
his mouth come k. and understanding; 2.06
and k. will be pleasant to your 2.10
by his k. the deeps broke forth, and 3.20
discretion, and your lips may guard k. 5.02
and right to those who find k. 8.09
and k. rather than choice gold; 8.10
and I find k. and discretion. 8.12
and the k. of the Holy One is 9.10
Wise men lay up k., but the babbling 10.14
but by k. the righteous are delivered. 11.09
Whoever loves discipline loves k., 12.01
A prudent man conceals his k., 12.23
everything a prudent man acts with k., 13.16
but k. is easy for a man of understanding. 14.06
there you do not meet words of k. 14.07
the prudent are crowned with k. 14.18
The tongue of the wise dispenses k., 15.02
The lips of the wise spread k.; 15.07
him who has understanding seeks k., 15.14
He who restrains his words has k., 17.27
An intelligent mind acquires k., 18.15
and the ear of the wise seeks k. 18.15
good for a man to be without k., 19.02
understanding, and he will gain k. 19.25
only to stray from the words of k. 19.27
but the lips of k. are a precious 20.15
man is instructed, he gains k. 21.11
of the LORD keep watch over k., 22.12
wise, and apply your mind to my k.; 22.17
sayings of admonition and k., 22.20
instruction and your ear to words of k. 23.12
by k. the rooms are filled with all 24.04
and a man of k. than he who has 24.05
understanding and k. its stability 28.02
man does not understand such k. 29.07
nor have I k. of the Holy One. 30.03
great experience of wisdom and k. Ecc 1.16
who increases k. increases sorrow. 1.18
with wisdom and k. and skill must 2.21
God gives wisdom and k. and joy; 2.26
advantage of k. is that wisdom 7.12
or thought or k. or wisdom in 9.10
Preacher also taught the people k., 12.09
go into exile for want of k.; Is 5.13

KNOWLEDGE (cont.)

the spirit of k. and the fear of Ecc 11.02
be full of the k. of the LORD as 11.09
"Whom will he teach k., and to whom 28.09
of salvation, wisdom, and k.; 33.06
path of justice, and taught him k., 40.14
nor is there k. or discernment to 44.19
back, and makes their k. foolish; 44.25
They have no k. who carry about 45.20
wisdom and your k. led you astray, 47.10
by his k. shall the righteous one, 53.11
are blind, they are all without k.; 56.10
and thou takest no k. of it? 58.03
feed you with k. and understanding Jer 3.15
Every man is stupid and without k.; 10.14
through the land, and have no k. 14.18
Every man is stupid and without k.; 51.17
endowed with k., understanding Dan 1.04
to the wise and k. to those who 2.21
k., and understanding to interpret 5.12
to and fro, and k. shall increase. 12.04
and no k. of God in the land; Hos 4.01
are destroyed for lack of k.; 4.06
because you have rejected k., 4.06
the k. of God, rather than burnt 6.06
set up princes, but without my k. 8.04
filled with the k. of the glory of Hab 2.14
lips of a priest should guard k., Mal 2.07
to give k. of salvation to his Lk 1.77
you have taken away the key of k.; 11.52
and with his wife's k. he kept back Ac 5.02
a rather accurate k. of the Way, 24.22
the embodiment of k. and truth— Rom 2.20
through the law comes k. of sin. 3.20
riches and wisdom and k. of God! 11.33
of goodness, filled with all k., 15.14
him with all speech and all k.— 1Co 1.05
we know that "all of us possess k." 8.01
"K." puffs up, but love builds up. 8.01
However, not all possess this k. 8.07
a man of k., at table in an idol's 8.10
And so by your k. this weak man is 8.11
utterance of k. according to the 12.08
understand all mysteries and all k., 13.02
as for k., it will pass away. 13.08
For our k. is imperfect and our 13.09
revelation or k. or prophecy or 14.06
For some have no k. of God. 15.34
fragrance of the k. of him everywhere. 2Co 2.14
light of the k. of the glory of 4.06
by purity, k., forbearance, kindness, 6.06
in k., in all earnestness, and in 8.07
proud obstacle to the k. of God, 10.05
in speaking, I am not in k.; 11.06
of revelation in the k. of him, Eph 1.17
love of Christ which surpasses k., 3.19
and of the k. of the Son of God, to 4.13
with k. and all discernment, Php 1.09
filled with the k. of his will in Col 1.09
and increasing in the k. of God. 1.10
understanding and the k. of God's 2.02
all the treasures of wisdom and k. 2.03
renewed in k. after the image of 3.10
and to come to the k. of the truth. 1Th 2.04
of what is falsely called k., 6.20
never arrive at a k. of the truth. 2Ti 3.07
elect and their k. of the truth Tit 1.01
may promote the k. of all the good Phm 1.06
receiving the k. of the truth, Heb 10.26
to you in the k. of God and of 2Pe 1.02
through the k. of him who called us 1.03
with virtue, and virtue with k., 1.05
and k. with self-control, and 1.06
unfruitful in the k. of our Lord 1.08
through the k. of our Lord and 2.20
the grace and k. of our Lord and 3.18

KNOWN

two daughters who have not k. man; Gen 19.08
upon, a virgin, whom no man had k. 24.16
one would have k. that they had 41.21
made himself k. to his brothers. 45.01
thought, "Surely the thing is k." Ex 2.14
I did not make myself k. to them. 6.03
Or if it is k. that the ox has been 21.36
For how shall it be k. that I have 33.16
they have committed becomes k., Lev 4.14
he has committed is made k. to him, 4.23
committed is made k. to him he 4.28
make myself k. to him in a vision, Num. 12.06
woman who has k. man by lying with 31.17
who have not k. man by lying with 31.18
who had not k. man by lying with 31.35
Anakim they are also k. as Rephaim, Deu 2.11
(That also is k. as a land of 2.20
make them k. to your children and 4.09
who have not k. or seen it), 11.02
other gods which you have not k. 11.28
other gods,' which you have not k., 13.02
you nor your fathers have k., 13.06
gods,' which you have not k., 13.13
and it is not k. who killed him, 21.01
you have not k. shall eat up the 28.33
you nor your fathers have k.; 28.36
you nor your fathers have k., 28.64
they had not k. and whom he had 29.26
who have not k. it, may hear and 31.13
no gods, to gods they had never k., 32.17
Joshua and had k. all the work Jos 24.31
at least as had not k. it before. Ju 3.02
She had never k. a man. And it became 11.39
secret of his strength was not k. 16.09
who had not k. man by lying with 21.12
make yourself k. to the man until Ru 3.03
"Let it not be k. that the woman 3.14
and it will be k. to you why his 1Sa 6.03
that I may make k. to you the word 9.27
servant has k. nothing of all this, 22.15
upon it; and nothing was k. of it. 2Sa 17.19
people whom I had not k. served me. 22.44
that it be not k. that you are the 1Ki 14.02
let it be k. this day that thou art 18.36
make k. his deeds among the peoples! 1Ch 16.08
in making k. all these great things. 17.19
And now be it k. to the king that Ez 4.12
Now be it k. to the king that, if 4.13
We make k. to the king that, if this 4.16
Be it k. to the king that we went 5.08
that it was k. to us and that God Neh 4.15
and thou didst make k. to them thy 9.14
queen will be made k. to all women, Est 1.17
Esther had not made k. her people 2.10
had charged her not to make it k. 2.10
had not made k. her kindred or her 2.20
they had made k. to him the people 3.06
and all who had k. him before, Job 42.11
The LORD has made himself k., Ps 9.16
people whom I had not k. served me. 18.43
and he makes k. to them his covenant. 25.14
Lord, all my longing is k. to thee, 38.09
that thy way may be k. upon earth, 67.02
my dishonor; my foes are all k. to thee. 69.19
In Judah God is k., his name is 76.01
things that we have heard and k., 78.03
thy servants be k. among the 79.10
I hear a voice I had not k.: 81.05
Are thy wonders k. in the darkness, 88.12
The LORD has made k. his victory, 98.02
He made k. his ways to Moses, his 103.07
make k. his deeds among the peoples! 105.01
he might make k. his mighty power. 106.08
Long have I k. from thy testimonies 119.152
thou hast searched me and k. me! 139.01
to make k. to the sons of men thy 145.12
I will make my words k. to you. Pro 1.23

KNOWN (cont.)

The vexation of a fool is k. at once, Pro 12.16
but it is not k. in the heart of 14.33
child makes himself k. by his acts, 20.11
I have made them k. to you today, 22.19
Her husband is k. in the gates, when 31.23
not seen the sun or k. anything; Ecc 6.05
and it is k. what man is, and that 6.10
make k. his deeds among the nations, Is 12.04
let this be k. in all the earth. 12.05
you and make k. what the LORD of 19.12
make himself k. to the Egyptians; 19.21
father makes k. to the children 38.19
Have you not k.? Have you not 40.21
Have you not k.? Have you not 40.28
they have not k. I will guide them. 42.16
from my mouth and I made them k.; 48.03
things which you have not k. 48.06
never heard, you have never k., 48.08
shall be k. among the nations, and 61.09
make thy name k. to thy adversaries, 64.02
and it shall be k. that the hand of 66.14
other gods that you have not k., Jer 7.09
they nor their fathers have k.; 9.16
The LORD made it k. to me and I 11.18
you nor your fathers have k., 16.13
nor the kings of Judah have k.; 19.04
then it will be k. that the LORD 28.09
things which you have not k. 33.03
make k. to Jerusalem her abominations, Eze 16.02
making myself k. to them in the 20.05
I made myself k. to them in 20.09
countries which you have not k. 32.09
I will make myself k. among you, 35.11
let that be k. to you. Be ashamed 36.32
and make myself k. in the eyes of 38.23
I will make k. in the midst of my 39.07
and make k. to them all its ordinances 43.11
you do not make k. to me the dream Dan 2.05
you do not make the dream k. to me, 2.09
made the matter k. to Daniel. 2.15
and made the matter k. to Hananiah. 2.17
hast now made k. to me what we 2.23
thou hast made k. to us the king's 2.23
who can make k. to the king the 2.25
able to make k. to me the dream 2.26
and he has made k. to King Nebuchadnezzar 2.28
mysteries made k. to you what is 2.29
interpretation may be made k. to the king, 2.30
God has made k. to the king what 2.45
be it k. to you, O king, that we will 3.18
they might make k. to me the 4.06
could not make k. to me its 4.07
able to make k. to me the interpretation, 4.18
writing or make k. to the king the 5.08
and make k. to me its interpretation; 5.15
and make k. to me its interpretation, 5.16
king and make k. to him the 5.17
and made k. to me the interpretation 7.16
I will make k. to you what shall be 8.19
but Judah is still k. by God, Hos 11.12
"You only have I k. of all the Amo 3.02
the midst of the years make it k.; Hab 3.02
the nations which they had not k. Zec 7.14
continuous day (it is k. to the LORD), 14.07
or hidden that will not be k. Mt 10.26
And if you had k. what this means, 12.07
and ordered them not to make him k. 12.16
for the tree is k. by its fruit. 12.33
householder had k. in what part of 24.43
ordered them not to make him k. Mk 3.12
for Jesus' name had become k. 6.14
which the Lord has made k. to us. Lk 2.15
it they made k. the saying which 2.17
for each tree is k. by its own 6.44
he would have k. who and what sort 7.39
shall not be k. and come to light. 8.17
or hidden that will not be k. 12.02
householder had k. at what hour 12.39
and how he was k. to them in the 24.35
of the Father, he has made him k. Jn 1.18
secret if he seeks to be k. openly. 7.04
But you have not k. him; I know him. 8.55
k. me, you would have k. my Father 14.07
my Father I have made k. to you. 15.15
they have not k. the Father, 16.03
Father, the world has not k. thee, 17.25
not known thee, but I have k. thee; 17.25
I made k. to them thy name, and I 17.26
thy name, and I will make it k., 17.26
disciple was k. to the high priest, 18.15
who was k. to the high priest, went 18.16
And it became k. to all the inhabitants Ac 1.19
let this be k. to you, and give ear 2.14
Thou hast made k. to me the ways of 2.28
be it k. to you all, and to all the 4.10
made himself k. to his brothers, 7.13
family became k. to Pharaoh. 7.13
another king who had not k. Joseph. 7.18
but their plot became k. to Saul. 9.24
And it became k. throughout all 9.42
of what was k. as the Italian 10.01
Let it be k. to you therefore, 13.38
made these things k. from of old. 15.18
And this became k. to all residents 19.17
at Jerusalem, is k. by all the Jews. 26.04
They have k. for a long time, if 26.05
Let it be k. to you then that this 28.28
For what can be k. about God is Rom 1.19
the law, I should not have k. sin. 7.07
should not have k. what it is to 7.07
his wrath and to make k. his power, 9.22
in order to make k. the riches of 9.23
"For who has k. the mind of the 11.34
For while your obedience is k. to all, 16.19
writings is made k. to all nations, 16.26
"For who has k. the mind of the 1Co 2.16
if one loves God, one is k. by him. 8.03
to be k. and read by all men; 2Co 3.02
but what we are is k. to God, 5.11
I hope it is k. also to your 5.11
as unknown, and yet well k.; 6.09
And I was still not k. by sight to Gal 1.22
God, or rather to be k. by God, 4.09
For he has made k. to us in all Eph 1.09
was made k. to me by revelation, as 3.03
which was not made k. to the sons 3.05
now be made k. to the principalities 3.10
it has become k. throughout the Php 1.13
your requests be made k. to God. 4.06
and has made k. to us your love in Col 1.08
to make the word of God fully k., 1.25
chose to make k. how great among 1.27
in their hearts; they have not k. my ways.' Heb 3.10
when we made k. to you the power 2Pe 1.16
never to have k. the way of 2.21
sins has either seen him or k. him. 1Jn 3.06
and he made it k. by sending his Rev 1.01

KNOWS

For God k. that when you eat of it Gen 3.05
"My lord k. that the children are 33.13
and k. the knowledge of the Most Num 24.16
he k. your going through this great Deu 2.07
but no man k. the place of his 34.06
He k., and lets Israel itself know! Jos 22.22
"Your father k. well that I have 1Sa 20.03
next to you; Saul my father also k. this." 23.17
'Who k. whether the LORD will be 2Sa 12.22
your servant k. that I have found 14.22
for all Israel k. that your father 17.10
For your servant k. that I have 19.20
among us who k. how to cut timber 1Ki 5.06
And who k. whether you have not Est 4.14
For he k. worthless men; when he sees Job 11.11
He k. that a day of darkness is 15.23

KNOWS (cont.)
is the place of him who k. not God. Job 18.21
But he k. the way that I take; 23.10
"That path no bird of prey k., 28.07
the way to it, and he k. its place. 28.23
for the LORD k. the way of the Ps 1.06
The LORD k. the days of the blameless, 37.18
heaps up, and k. not who will gather! 39.06
For he k. the secrets of the heart. 44.21
is none among us who k. how long. 74.09
protect him, because he k. my name. 91.14
the LORD, k. the thoughts of man, 94.11
For he k. our frame; he remembers 103.14
gone, and its place k. it no more. 103.16
the sun k. its time for setting. 104.19
but the haughty he k. from afar. 138.06
she is wanton and k. no shame. Pro 9.13
The heart k. its own bitterness, and 14.10
and who k. the ruin that will come 24.22
A righteous man k. the rights of 29.07
and who k. whether he will be a Ecc 2.19
Who k. whether the spirit of man 3.21
man have who k. how to conduct 6.08
For who k. what is good for man 6.12
your heart k. that many times you 7.22
And who k. the interpretation of a 8.01
though no man k. what is to be, and 10.14
The ox k. its owner, and the ass its Is 1.03
honey when he k. how to refuse the 7.15
the child k. how to refuse the 7.16
the child k. how to cry 'My father' 8.04
"Who sees us? Who k. us?" 29.15
no one who goes in them k. peace. 59.08
stork in the heavens k. her times; Jer 8.07
that he understands and k. me, 9.24
I am the one who k., and I am 29.23
he k. what is in the darkness, and Dan 2.22
his strength, and he k. it not; Hos 7.09
sprinkled upon him, and he k. it not. 7.09
Who k. whether he will not turn and Joe 2.14
Who k., God may yet repent and turn Jon 3.09
he k. those who take refuge in him. Nah 1.07
no one k. where they are. 3.17
but the unjust k. no shame. Zep 3.05
for your Father k. what you need Mt 6.08
heavenly Father k. that you need 6.32
them, "See that no one k. it." 9.30
and no one k. the Son except the 11.27
and no one k. the Father except the 11.27
"But of that day and hour no one k., 24.36
sprout and grow, he k. not how. Mk 4.27
of that day or that hour no one k., 13.32
and no one k. who the Son is except Lk 10.22
and your Father k. that you need 12.30
before men, but God k. your hearts; 16.15
as the Father k. me and I know the Jn 10.15
it neither sees him nor k. him; 14.17
and he k. that he tells the truth— 19.35
And God who k. the heart bore Ac 15.08
For the kinng k. about these things, 26.26
hearts of men k. what is the mind Rom 8.27
For what person k. a man's thoughts 1Co 2.11
"The Lord k. that the thoughts of 3.20
one imagines that he k. something, 8.02
do not love you? God k. I do! 2Co 11.11
blessed for ever, k. that I do not lie. 11.31
of the body I do not know, God k. 12.02
the body I do not know, God k.— 12.03
up with conceit, he k. nothing; 1Ti 6.04
"The Lord k. those who are his," and, 2Ti 2.19
Whoever k. what is right to do and Jas 4.17
then the Lord k. how to rescue the 2Pe 2.09
our hearts, and he k. everything. 1Jn 3.20
Whoever k. God listens to us, and he 4.06
loves is born of God and k. God. 4.07
which no one k. except him who Rev 2.17
because he k. that his time is 12.12
which no one k. but himself. 19.12

KOA
Chaldeans, Pekod and Shoa and K., Eze 23.23

KOHATH
of Levi: Gershon, K., and Merari. Gen 46.11
K., and Merari, the years of the Ex 6.16
The sons of K.: Amram, Izhar, Hebron 6.18
of the life of K. being a hundred 6.18
names: Gershon and K. and Merari. Num 3.17
And the sons of K. by their families: 3.19
Of K. were the family of the 3.27
of the sons of K. were to encamp 3.29
of the sons of K. from among the 4.02
of the sons of K. in the tent of 4.04
the sons of K. shall come to carry 4.15
which the sons of K. are to carry. 4.15
But to the sons of K. he gave none, 7.09
son of K., son of Levi, and Dathan 16.01
of K., the family of the Kohathites 26.57
And K. was the father of Amram. 26.58
of Levi: Gershom, K., and Merari. 1Ch 6.01
The sons of K.: Amram, Izhar, Hebron, 6.02
of Levi: Gershom, K., and Merari. 6.16
The sons of K.: Amram, Izhar, Hebron, 6.18
The sons of K.: Amminadab his son, 6.22
son of K., son of Levi, son of 6.38
of the sons of K. had cities of 6.66
of the sons of K., Uriel the chief, 15.05
of Levi: Gershom, K., and Merari. 23.06
The sons of K.: Amram, Izhar, Hebron, 23.12

KOHATHITE
belonging to the K. families of the Jos 21.20

KOHATHITES
these are the families of the K. Num 3.27
house of the families of the K. 3.30
families of the K. be destroyed 4.18
numbered the sons of the K., 4.34
number of the families of the K., 4.37
Then the K. set out, carrying the 10.21
of Kohath, the family of the K.; 26.57
out for the families of the K. Jos 21.04
And the rest of the K. received by 21.05
families of the K. who belonged to 21.10
the rest of the K. belonging to 21.20
the rest of the K. were ten in all 21.26
Of the sons of the K.: Heman the 1Ch 6.33
of Aaron of the families of K., 6.54
To the rest of the K. were given by 6.61
the rest of the families of the K. 6.70
kinsmen of the K. had charge of 9.32
of the K. and the Korahites, stood 2Ch 20.19
of Azaraih, of the sons of the K.; 29.12
Meshullam, of the sons of the K., 34.12

KOLAIAH
son of K., son of Maaseiah, son of Neh 11.07
Ahab the son of K. and Zedekiah Jer 29.21

KORAH
Oholibamah bore Jeush, Jalam, and K. Gen 36.05
bore to Esau Jeush, Jalam, and K. 36.14
K., Gatam, and Amalek; 36.16
the chiefs Jeush, Jalam, and K.; 36.18
K., Nepheg, and Zichri. Ex 6.21
The sons of K.: Assir, Elkanah, and 6.24
Now K. the son of Izhar, son of Num 16.01
and he said to K. and all his 16.05
K. and all his company; 16.06
And Moses said to K., 16.08
And Moses said to K., 16.16
Then K. assembled all the congregation. 16.19
away from about the dwelling of K., 16.24
away from about the dwelling of K., 16.27
belonged to K. and all their goods 16.32
he become as K. and as his company 16.40
those who died in the affair of K. 16.49

KORAH (cont.)
and Aaron in the company of K., Num 26.09
swallowed them up together with K., 26.10
Notwithstanding, the sons of K. did not die. 26.11
the LORD in the company of K., 27.03
Reuel, Jeush, Jalam, and K. 1Ch 1.35
K., Tappuah, Rekem, and Shema. 2.43
K. his son, Assir his son, 6.22
Assir, son of Ebiasaph, son of K., 6.37
son of K., and his kinsmen of his 9.19

KORAHITE
the first-born of Shallum the K., 1Ch 9.31

KORAHITES
these are the families of the K. Ex 6.24
the Mushites, the family of the K. Num 26.58
the K., were in charge of the work 1Ch 9.19
Joezer, and Jashobeam, the K.; 12.06
of the K., Meshelemiah the son of 26.01
among the K. and the sons of 26.19
of the Kohathites and the K., 2Ch 20.19

KORAH'S
error, and perish in K. rebellion. Jud 1.11

KORE
Shallum the son of K., son of 1Ch 9.19
Korahites, Meshelemiah the son of K., 26.01
And K. the son of Imnah the Levite, 2Ch 31.14

KOZ
K. was the father of Anub, Zobebah, 1Ch 4.08

KUE
of horses was from Egypt and K., 1Ki 10.28
received them from K. at a price. 10.28
of horses was from Egypt and k., 2Ch 1.16
received them from K. for a price. 1.16

KUSHAIAH
brethren, Ethan the son of K.; 1Ch 15.17

L

LAADAH
L. the father of Mareshah, and the 1Ch 4.21

LABAN
Rebekah had a brother whose name was L.; Gen 24.29
and L. ran out to the man, to the 24.29
and L. ungirded the camels, and gave 24.32
Then L. and Bethuel answered, "The 24.50
the sister of L. the Aramean. 25.20
flee to L. my brother in Haran, 27.43
daughters of L. your mother's 28.02
and he went to Paddanaram to L., 28.05
Do you know L. the son of Nahor?" 29.05
the daughter of L. his mother's 29.10
the sheep of L. his mother's 29.10
the flock of L. his mother's 29.10
When L. heard the tidings of Jacob 29.13
Jacob told L. all these things, 29.13
and L. said to him, "Surely you are 29.14
Then L. said to Jacob, "Because you 29.15
Now L. had two daughters; 29.16
L. said, "It is better than I give 29.19
Then Jacob said to L., "Give me my 29.21
So L. gathered together all the men 29.22
(L. gave his maid Zilpah to his 29.24
and Jacob said to L., "What is this 29.25
L. said, "It is not so done in our 29.26
then L. gave him his daughter 29.28
(L. gave his maid Bilhah to his 29.29
and served L. for another seven 29.30
Jacob said to L., "Send me away, 30.25
But L. said to him, "If you will 30.27
L. said, "Good! Let it be 30.34
But that day L. removed the he-goats 30.35
all the black in the flock of L.; 30.40
that the sons of L. were saying, 31.01
And Jacob saw that L. did not 31.02
seen all that L. is doing to you. 31.12
L. had gone to shear his sheep, and 31.19
And Jacob outwitted L. the Aramean, 31.20
When it was told L. on the third 31.22
But God came to L. the Aramean in a 31.24
And L. overtook Jacob. Now Jacob had 31.25
and L. with his kinsmen encamped in 31.25
And L. said to Jacob, "What have you 31.26
Jacob answered L., "Because I was 31.31
So L. went into Jacob's tent, and 31.33
L. felt all about the tent, but did 31.34
became angry, and upbraided L.; 31.36
Jacob said to L., "What is my 31.36
Then L. answered and said to Jacob, 31.43
L. called it Jegarsahadutha: but 31.47
L. said, "This heap is a witness 31.48
Then L. said to Jacob, "See this 31.51
Early in the morning L. arose, 31.55
Jacob, 'I have sojourned with L., 32.04
whom L. gave to Leah his daughter, 46.18
whom L. gave to Rachel his daughter, 46.25
L., Hazeroth, and Dizahab. Deu 1.01

LABAN'S
and Jacob fed the rest of L. flock. Gen 30.36
and did not put them with L. flock. 30.40
so the feebler were L., and the stronger 30.42

LABOR
affliction and the l. of my hands, Gen 31.42
travailed, and she had hard l. 35.16
And when she was in her hard l., 35.17
And when she was in l., one put out 38.28
and became a slave at forced l. 49.15
that they may l. at it and pay no Ex 5.09
Six days you shall l., and do all 20.09
of the first fruits of your l., 23.16
the field the fruit of your l. 23.16
Six days you shall l., and do all Deu 5.13
shall do forced l. for you and 20.11
have become slaves to do forced l. Jos 16.10
put the Canaanites to forced l., 17.13
put the Canaanites to forced l., Ju 1.28
and became subject to forced l. 1.30
subject to forced l. for them. 1.33
they became subject to forced l. 1.35
and set them to l. with saws and 2Sa 12.31
was in charge of the forced l.; 20.24
was in charge of the forced l. 1Ki 4.06
levy of forced l. out of all 5.13
of the forced l. which King 9.15
all the forced l. of the house of 11.28
was taskmaster over the forced l., 12.18
and set them to l. with saws and 1Ch 20.03
was taskmaster over the forced l., 2Ch 10.18
for us by night and may l. by day." Neh 4.22
and from his l. who does not 5.13
why then do I l. in vain? Job 9.29
and will you leave to him your l.? 39.11
though her l. be in vain, yet she 39.16
fruit of their l. to the locust. Ps 78.46
work and to his l. until the 104.23
were bowed down with hard l.; 107.12
those who build it l. in vain. 127.01
the fruit of the l. of your hands; 128.02
slothful will be put to forced l. Pro 12.24
him for his hands refuse to l. 21.25
do not l. to comfort me for the Is 22.04
men shall be put to forced l. 31.08

LABOR (cont.)
and your l. for that which does not Is 55.02
They shall not l. in vain, or bear 65.23
Before she was in l. she gave birth; 66.07
as Zion was in l. she brought 66.08
on his loins like a woman in l.? Jer 30.06
The peoples l. for nought, and the 51.58
take away all the fruit of your l., Eze 23.29
made his army l. hard against Tyre; 29.18
to pay for the l. that he had 29.18
plant, for which you did not l., Jon 4.10
that peoples l. only for fire, Hab 2.13
all who l. and are heavy-laden, and Mt 11.28
reap that for which you did not l.; Jn 4.38
and you have entered into their l." 4.38
Do not l. for the food which 6.27
his wages according to his l. 1Co 3.08
and we l., working with our own 4.12
in the Lord your l. is not in vain. 15.58
steal, but rather let him l., Eph 4.28
that means fruitful l. for me. Php 1.22
did not run in vain or l. in vain. 2.16
of faith and l. of love and 1Th 1.03
For you remember our l. and toil, 2.09
and that our l. would be in vain. 3.05
those who l. among you and are 5.12
with toil and l. we worked night 2Th 3.08
those who l. in preaching and 1Ti 5.17

LABORED
you a land on which you had not l., Jos 24.13
who were engaged in the work l., 2Ch 24.13
with one hand l. on the work and Neh 4.17
So we l. at the work, and half of 4.21
which you have l. from your youth; Is 47.12
are those with whom you have l., 47.15
I have l. in vain, I have spent my 49.04
your wine for which you have l.; 62.08
all for which our fathers l. Jer 3.24
as his recompense for which he l., Eze 29.20
and he l. till the sun went down to Dan 6.14
others have l., and you have Jn 4.38
afraid I have l. over you in vain. Gal 4.11
for they have l. side by side with Php 4.03

LABORER
Sweet is the sleep of a l., Ecc 5.12
for the l. deserves his food. Mt 10.10
for the l. deserves his wages; Lk 10.07
and to every fellow worker and l. 1Co 16.16
"The l. deserves his wages." 1Ti 5.18

LABORERS
is plentiful, but the l. are few; Mt 9.37
to send out l. into his harvest." 9.38
morning to hire l. for his vineyard 20.01
with the l. for a denarius a day, 20.02
Call the l. and pay them their 20.08
is plentiful, but the l. are few; Lk 10.02
to send out l. into his harvest. 10.02
wages of the l. who mowed your Jas 5.04

LABORIOUS
you shall do no l. work. Lev 23.07
you shall do no l. work." 23.08
you shall do no l. work: it is a 23.21
You shall do no l. work; and you 23.25
you shall do no l. work. 23.35
you shall do no l. work. 23.36
convocation: you shall do no l. work, Num 28.18
you shall do no l. work. 28.25
you shall do no l. work, 28.26
you shall do no l. work. It is a day 29.01
you shall do no l. work, and you shall 29.12
assembly: you shall do no l. work, 29.35

LABORS
of your ground and of all your l.; Deu 28.33
and your l. go to the house of an Pro 5.10
and toil of my l. under the sun, Ecc 2.20
and cattle, and upon all their l. Hag 1.11
tumults, l., watching, hunger; 2Co 6.05
beyond limit, in other men's l.; 10.15
like a madman—with far greater l., 11.23
ceases from his l. as God did from Heb 4.10
that they may rest from their l., Rev 14.13

LACE
of the ephod with a l. of blue, Ex 28.28
it on the turban by a l. of blue; 28.37
of the ephod with a l. of blue, 39.21
And they tied to it a l. of blue, 39.31

LACHISH
of Jarmuth, to Japhia king of L., Jos 10.03
the king of L., and the king of 10.05
the king of L., and the king of 10.23
to L., and laid siege to it, and 10.31
and the LORD gave L. into the hand 10.32
king of Gezer came up to help L.; 10.33
with all Israel from L. to Eglon; 10.34
that day, as he had done to L. 10.35
Jarmuth, one; the king of L., one; 12.11
L., Bozkath, Eglon, 15.39
in Jerusalem, and he fled to L. 2Ki 14.19
But they sent after him to L., 14.19
sent to the king of Assyria at L., 18.14
great army from L. to King Hezekiah 18.17
he heard that the king had left L. 19.08
Adoraim, L., Azekah, 2Ch 11.09
in Jerusalem, and he fled to L. 25.27
But they sent after him to L., 25.27
was besieging L. with all his 32.09
L. and its fields, and Azekah and Neh 11.30
Rabshakeh from L. to King Hezekiah Is 36.02
heard that the king had left L. 37.08
that were left, L. and Azekah; Jer 34.07
to the chariots, inhabitants of L.; Mic 1.13

LACK
the whole city for l. of five?" Gen 18.28
he that gathered little had no l.; Ex 16.18
in which you will l. nothing, Deu 8.09
there is no l. of anything that is Ju 18.10
there is no l. of anything." 19.19
Do I l. madmen, that you have 1Sa 21.15
lion perishes for l. of prey, Job 4.11
any one perish for l. of clothing, 31.19
and wander about for l. of food? 38.41
who seek the LORD l. no good thing. Ps 34.10
He dies for l. of discipline, and Pro 5.23
but fools die for l. of sense. 10.21
For l. of wood the fire goes out; 26.20
and he will have no l. of gain. 31.11
in the streets for l. of wine; Is 24.11
their fish stink for l. of water, 50.02
shall never l. a man to sit on the Jer 33.17
shall never l. a man in my presence 33.18
shall never l. a man to stand 35.19
that they may l. bread and water, Eze 4.17
are destroyed for l. of knowledge; Hos 4.06
and l. of bread in all your places, Amo 4.06
observed; what do I still l.?" Mt 19.20
and said to him, "You l. one thing; Mk 10.21
to him, "One thing you still l. Lk 18.22
or sandals, did you l. anything?" 22.35
you through l. of self-control. 1Co 7.05
he who gathered little had no l. 2Co 8.15
on their way; see that they l. nothing. Tit 3.13
ill-clad and in l. of daily food, Jas 2.15

LACKED
been with you; you have l. nothing." Deu 2.07
What have you l. with me that you 1Ki 11.22
wilderness, and they l. nothing; Neh 9.21
we have l. everything and have been Jer 44.18

LACKING
five of the fifty righteous are l.? Gen 18.28
your God be l. from your cereal Lev 2.13
l. nothing that is in the earth, and Ju 18.07
be today one tribe l. in Israel?" 21.03
in his month; they let nothing be l. 1Ki 4.27
are many, transgression is not l., Pro 10.19
and what is l. cannot be numbered. Ecc 1.15
let not oil be l. on your head. 9.08
Truth is l., and he who departs Is 59.15
you are not l. in any spiritual 1Co 1.07
complete what is l. in Christ's Col 1.24
supply what is l. in your faith? 1Th 3.10
and complete, l. in nothing. Jas 1.04

LACKS
by the sword, or who l. bread!" 2Sa 3.29
for the back of him who l. sense. Pro 10.13
belittles his neighbor l. sense, 11.12
plays the great man but l. bread. 12.09
A ruler who l. understanding is a 28.16
so that he l. nothing of all that Ecc 6.02
he l. sense, and he says to every 10.03
bowl that never l. mixed wine. Sol 7.02
If any of you l. wisdom, let him ask Jas 1.05
For whoever l. these things is 2Pe 1.09

LAD
because of the l. and because of Gen 21.12
And God heard the voice of the l.; 21.17
the voice of the l. where he is. 21.17
lift up the l., and hold him fast 21.18
water, and gave the l. a drink. 21.19
And God was with the l., and he grew up; 21.20
I and the l. will go yonder and 22.05
hand on the l. or do anything to 22.12
he was a l. with the sons of Bilhah 37.02
brothers, and said, "The l. is gone; 37.30
tell you not to sin against the l.? 42.22
"Send the l. with me, and we will 43.08
'The l. cannot leave his father, for 44.22
and the l. is not with us, then, as 44.30
he sees that the l. is not with us, 44.31
surety for the l. to my father, 44.32
instead of the l. as a slave to my 44.33
and let the l. go back with his 44.33
my father if the l. is not with me? 44.34
said to the l. who held him by the Ju 16.26
And behold, I will send the l., 1Sa 20.21
If I say to the l., 'Look, the 20.21
David, and with him a little l. 20.35
And he said to his l., "Run and 20.36
As the l. ran, he shot an arrow 20.36
And when the l. came to the place 20.37
called after the l. and said, 20.37
And Jonathan called after the l., 20.38
So Jonathan's l. gathered up the 20.38
But the l. knew nothing; only Jonathan 20.39
Jonathan gave his weapons to his l., 20.40
And as soon as the l. had gone, 20.41
But a l. saw them, and told Absalom; 2Sa 17.18
"There is a l. here who has five Jn 6.09
And they took the l. away alive, Ac 20.12

LADAN
L. his son, Ammihud his son, Elishama 1Ch 7.26
sons of Gershom were L. and Shimei. 23.07
The sons of L.: Jehiel the chief, and 23.08
heads of the fathers' houses of L. 23.09
The sons of L., the sons of the 26.21
of the Gershonites belonging to L., 26.21
belonging to L. the Gershonite: 26.21

LADDER
there was a l. set up on the earth, Gen 28.12

LADEN
And Jesse took an ass l. with bread, 1Sa 16.20
burdens were l. in such a way that Neh 4.17
a people l. with iniquity, offspring Is 1.04
and heavily l. in the heart of the Eze 27.25
to me, all who labor and are heavy l., Mt 11.28

LADIES
Her wisest l. make answer, nay, she Ju 5.29
This very day the l. of Persia and Est 1.18
kings are among your l. of honor; Ps 45.09

LAD'S
life is bound up in the l. life, Gen 44.30

LADS
me from all evil, bless the l.; Gen 48.16

LADY
to the elect l. and her children, 2Jn 1.01
l., not as though I were writing 1.05

LAEL
the son of L. as head of the Num 3.24

LAGGED
at your rear all who l. behind you; Deu 25.18

LAHAD
was the father of Ahumai and L. 1Ch 4.02

LAHMAM
Cabbon, L., Chitlish, Jos 15.40

LAHMI
of Jair slew L. the brother of 1Ch 20.05

LAID
l. it upon both their shoulders, and Gen 9.23
and l. each half over against the 15.10
and l. it on Isaac his son; 22.06
and l. the wood in order, and bound 22.09
and l. him on the altar, upon the 22.09
breeding Jacob l. the rods in the 30.41
Then she l. up his garment by her 39.16
right hand and l. it upon the head 48.14
that his father l. his right hand 48.17
Let heavier work be l. upon the men Ex 5.09
So they l. it by till the morning, 16.24
If a ransom is l. on him, then he 21.30
his life whatever is l. upon him. 21.30
he l. its bases, and set up its 40.18
and his sons l. their hands upon Lev 8.14
and his sons l. their hands on the 8.18
and his sons l. their hands on the 8.22
and l. incense on it, and offered 10.01
in them and l. incense upon them, Num 16.18
and we l. waste until fire spread 21.30
and he l. his hands upon him, and 27.23
and l. upon us hard bondage. Deu 26.06
Is not this l. up in store with me, 32.34
for Moses had l. his hands upon him; 34.09
which she had l. in order on the Jos 2.06
if a hand is l. upon any one who 2.19
they lodged, and l. them down there. 4.08
Joshua l. an oath upon them at that 6.26
and they l. them down before the 7.23
and l. siege to it, and assaulted it: 10.31
and they l. siege to it, and assaulted 10.34
here, with stones l. in due order; Ju 6.26
their blood be l. upon Abimelech 9.24
and l. wait against Shechem in four 9.34
and l. wait in the fields; and he looked 9.43
took it up and l. it on his shoulder. 9.48
of barley, and l. it upon her; Ru 3.15
the child and l. him in her bosom, 4.16
in a book and l. it up before the 1Sa 10.25
for Saul l. an oath on the people, 14.24
Saul l. hold upon the skirt of his 15.27
an image and l. it on the bed and 19.13
of figs, and l. them on asses. 25.18
and she l. her hand on her head, and 2Sa 13.19

LAID (cont.)

foundations of the world were l. bare, 2Sa 22.16
he has l. hold of the horns of the 1Ki 1.51
and l. it in her bosom, and laid her 3.20
and l. her dead son in my bosom. 3.20
of the house of the LORD was l., 6.37
and l. hold on other gods, and 9.09
Then Ahijah l. hold of the new 11.30
my father l. upon you a heavy yoke, 12.11
man of God and l. it upon the ass, 13.29
And he l. the body in his own grave 13.30
he l. its foundation at the cost of 16.34
and l. him upon his own bed. 17.19
in pieces and l. it on the wood. 18.33
And she went up and l. him on the 2Ki 4.21
on ahead and l. the staff upon the 4.31
and l. them upon two of his servants 5.23
So they l. hands on her; and she went 11.16
And Elisha l. his hands upon the 13.16
of Assyria have l. waste the 19.17
and l. upon the land a tribute of a 23.33
Jerusalem, and l. siege to it; 25.01
and l. hold on other gods, and 2Ch 7.22
of the LORD was l. until it was 8.16
my father l. upon you a heavy yoke, 10.11
They l. him on a bier which had 16.14
So they l. hands on her; and she went 23.15
servant of God l. upon Israel in 24.09
and they l. their hands upon them, 29.23
their God, and l. them in heaps. 31.06
Jerusalem and l. upon the land a 36.03
temple of the LORD was not yet l. Ez 3.06
the builders l. the foundation of 3.10
of the house of the LORD was l. 3.11
foundation of this house being l., 3.12
was why this city was l. waste. 4.15
and timber is l. in the walls; 5.08
came and l. the foundations of the 5.16
they l. its beams and set its doors, Neh 3.03
they l. its beams and set its doors, 3.06
were before me l. heavy burdens 5.15
but they l. no hand on the plunder. Est 9.10
but they l. no hands on the plunder 9.15
but they l. no hands on the plunder 9.16
and as they had l. down for themselves 9.31
King Ahasuerus l. tribute on the 10.01
all my calamity l. in the balances! Job 6.02
But man dies, and is l. low; 14.10
years that are l. up for the 15.20
and have l. my strength in the dust. 16.15
Utter darkness is l. up for his 20.26
and l. their hand on their mouth; 29.09
earth and who l. on him the whole 34.13
Where were you when I l. the 38.04
or who l. its cornerstone, 38.06
he is l. low even at the sight of 41.09
foundations of the world were l. bare, Ps 18.15
which thou hast l. up for those 31.19
and l. low the picked men of Israel 78.31
they have l. Jerusalem in ruins. 79.01
and l. waste his habitation. 79.07
thou hast l. his strongholds in 89.40
who hast l. the beams of thy 104.03
the pangs of Sheol l. hold on me; 116.03
I have l. up thy word in my heart, 119.11
The wicked have l. a snare for me, 119.110
the trap which they have l. for me, 141.09
for many a victim has she l. low; Pro 7.26
wealth is l. up for the righteous. 13.22
But all this I l. to heart, examining Ecc 9.01
which I have l. up for you, O my Sol 7.13
saying, 'Since you were l. low, Is 14.08
you who l. the nations low! 14.12
Because Ar is l. waste in a night 15.01
because Kir is l. waste in a night 15.01
what they have l. up they carry 15.07
for Tyre is l. waste, without house 23.01
for your stronghold is l. waste. 23.14
be utterly l. waste and utterly 24.03
the city will be utterly l. low. 32.19
of Assyria have l. waste all the 37.18
Your foundation shall be l.'" 44.28
My hand l. the foundation of the 48.13
and those who l. you waste go forth 49.17
the heavens and l. the foundations 51.13
the LORD has l. on him the iniquity 53.06
nations shall be utterly l. waste. 60.12
disaster, the whole land is l. waste. Jer 4.20
its cities were l. in ruins before 4.26
they are l. waste so that no one 9.10
land ruined and l. waste like a 9.12
and have l. waste his habitation. 10.25
and l. snares for my feet. 18.22
and all the people l. hold of him, 26.08
Woe to Nebo, for it is l. waste! 48.01
the Arnon, that Moab is l. waste! 48.20
Wail, O Heshbon, for Ai is l. waste! 49.03
and they l. siege to it and built 52.04
l. in ruins its strongholds; Lam 2.05
l. in ruins the place of his 2.06
silence when he has l. it on him; 3.28
a moment, no hand being l. on it. 4.06
whom you have l. in the midst of Eze 11.07
inhabited cities shall be l. waste, 12.20
its foundation will be l. bare; 13.14
your shame was l. bare and your 16.36
and l. waste their cities; 19.07
to be l. on the necks of the 21.29
of Babylon has l. siege to Jerusalem 24.02
replenished, now that she is l. waste,' 26.02
When I make you a city l. waste, 26.19
among cities that are l. waste. 29.12
midst of cities that are l. waste. 30.07
and be l. with the uncircumcised.' 32.19
swords were l. under their heads, 32.27
their might are l. with those who 32.29
he shall be l. among the uncircumcised, 32.32
They are l. desolate, they are 35.12
my hand which I have l. on them. 39.21
were to be l. with which the burnt 40.42
flesh of the offering was to be l. 40.43
your houses shall be l. in ruins. Dan 2.05
limb, and their houses l. in ruins; 3.29
was brought and l. upon the mouth 6.17
It has l. waste my vines, and Joe 1.07
The fields are l. waste, the ground 1.10
I l. waste your gardens and your Amo 4.09
of Israel shall be l. waste, 7.09
siege is l. against us; with a rod Mic 5.01
the earth is l. waste before him, Nah 1.05
plundered, and their houses l. waste. Zep 1.13
for her cedar work will be l. bare. 2.14
I have l. waste their streets so 3.06
LORD's temple was l., consider: Hag 2.18
Zerubbabel have l. the foundation Zec 4.09
house of the LORD of hosts was l., 8.09
pride of Assyria shall be l. low, 10.11
jungle of the Jordan is l. waste! 11.03
I have l. waste his hill country Mal 1.03
Even now the axe is l. to the root Mt 3.10
divided against itself is l. waste, 12.25
And he l. his hands on them and 19.15
came up and l. hands on Jesus and 26.50
and l. it in his own new tomb, which 27.60
except that he l. his hands upon a Mk 6.05
took his body, and l. it in a tomb. 6.29
they l. the sick in the market 6.56
on his eyes and l. his hands upon 8.23
Then again he l. his hands upon his 8.25
And they l. hands on him and seized 14.46
and l. him in a tomb which had been 15.46
of Joses saw where he was l. 15.47
see the place where they l. him. 16.06
who heard them l. them up in their Lk 1.66
and l. him in a manger, because 2.07
Even now the ax is l. to the root 3.09

LAID (cont.)

and he l. his hands on every one of Lk 4.40
and l. the foundation upon rock; 6.48
divided against itself is l. waste, 11.17
ample goods l. up for many years; 12.19
And he l. his hands upon her, and 13.13
when he has l. a foundation, and is 14.29
which I kept l. away in a napkin; 19.20
and l. on him the cross, to carry it 23.26
and l. him in a rock-hewn tomb, 23.53
where no one had ever yet been l. 23.53
the tomb, and how his body was l.; 23.55
but no one l. hands on him, because Jn 7.30
him, but no one l. hands on him. 7.44
and he said, "Where have you l. him?" 11.34
l. aside his garments, and girded 13.04
tomb where no one had ever been l. 19.41
close at hand, they l. Jesus there. 19.42
do not know where they have l. him." 20.02
do not know where they have l. him." 20.13
tell me where you have l. him, 20.15
whom they l. daily at that gate of Ac 3.02
and l. it at the apostles' feet; 4.35
the money and l. it at the apostles' 4.37
only a part and l. it at the 5.02
and l. them on beds and pallets, 5.15
they prayed and l. their hands 6.06
to Shechem and l. in the tomb that 7.16
the witnesses l. down their 7.58
But Saul l. waste the church, and 8.03
Then they l. their hands on them 8.17
they l. her in an upper room. 9.37
Herod the king l. violent hands 12.01
praying they l. their hands on 13.03
the tree, and l. him in a tomb. 13.29
and was l. with his fathers, and saw 13.36
And when Paul had l. his hands upon 19.06
the crowd, and l. hands on him, 21.27
They l. before the governor their 24.01
everything l. down by the law or 24.14
Festus l. Paul's case before the 25.14
concerning the charge l. against him. 25.16
master builder I l. a foundation, 1Co 3.10
any one lay than that which is l., 3.11
For necessity is l. upon me. 9.16
and I l. before them (but privately Gal 2.02
because of the hope l. up for you Col 1.05
the law is not l. down for the 1Ti 1.09
when the elders l. their hands 4.14
Henceforth there is l. up for me 2Ti 4.08
are open and l. bare to the eyes Heb 4.13
You have l. up treasure for the Jas 5.03
that he l. down his life for us; 1Jn 3.16
But he l. his right hand upon me, Rev 1.17
all this wealth has been l. waste." 18.17
in one hour she has been l. waste. 18.19

LAIN

easily have l. with your wife, Gen 26.10
saying, 'If no man has l. with you, Num 5.19
than your husband has l. with you, 5.20
woman that has l. with a male you Ju 21.11
I should have l. down and been Job 3.13
and I have l. in wait at my neighbor's 31.09
Where have you not been l. with? Jer 3.02
youth men had l. with her and Eze 23.08
part of the ship and had l. down, Jon 1.05
where the body of Jesus had l., Jn 20.12
who had l. close to his breast at 21.20

LAIR

a heap of ruins, a l. of jackals; Jer 9.11
a desolation, a l. of jackals. 10.22
a l. for wild beasts! Every one Zep 2.15

LAIRS

Then the beasts go into their l., Job 37.08

LAISH

and came to L., and saw the people Ju 18.07
gone to spy out the country of L., 18.14
to him, the Danites came to L., 18.27
of the city was L. at the first. 18.29
wife, to Palti the son of L., 1Sa 25.44
her husband Paltiel the son of L. 2Sa 3.15

LAISHAH

Hearken, O L.! Answer her, Is 10.30

LAKE

LORD, possess the l. and the south." Deu 33.23
As waters fail from a l., Job 14.11
standing by the l. of Gennesaret. Lk 5.01
And he saw two boats by the l.; 5.02
across to the other side of the l. 8.22
storm of wind came down on the l., 8.23
bank into the l. and were drowned. 8.33
alive into the l. of fire that Rev 19.20
thrown into the l. of fire and 20.10
were thrown into the l. of fire. 20.14
the second death, the l. of fire; 20.14
he was thrown into the l. of fire. 20.15
shall be in the l. that burns with 21.08

LAKKUM

Adaminekeb, and Jabneel, as far as L.; Jos 19.33

LAMA

voice, "Eli, Eli, l. sabachthani?" Mt 27.46
voice, "Eloi, Eloi, l. sabachthani?" Mk 15.34

LAMB

where is the l. for a burnt Gen 22.07
himself the l. for a burnt offering, 22.08
spotted sheep and every black l., 30.32
and every l. that was black, and put 30.35
every man a l. according to their Ex 12.03
houses, a l. for a household; 12.03
household is too small for a l., 12.04
shall make your count for the l. 12.04
Your l. shall be without blemish, a 12.05
families, and kill the passover l. 12.21
an ass you shall redeem with a l., 13.13
One l. you shall offer in the 29.39
and the other l. you shall offer in 29.39
and with the first l. a tenth 29.40
And the other l. you shall offer in 29.41
an ass you shall redeem with a l., 34.20
If he offers a l. for his offering, Lev 3.07
If he brings a l. as his offering 4.32
the fat of the l. is removed from 4.35
a l. or a goat, for a sin offering; 5.06
But if he cannot afford a l., 5.07
sin offering, and a calf and a l., 9.03
of meeting a l. a year old for a 12.06
And if she cannot afford a l., 12.08
and one ewe l. a year old without 14.10
shall kill the l. in the place 14.13
take one male l. for a guilt offering 14.21
shall take the l. of the guilt 14.24
shall kill the l. of the guilt 14.25
an ox or a l. or a goat in the 17.03
A bull or a l. which has a part too 22.23
offer a male l. a year old without 23.12
bring a male l. a year old for a Num 6.12
one male l. a year old without 6.14
and one ewe l. a year old without 6.14
one male l. a year old, for a burnt 7.15
one male l. a year old, for a burnt 7.21
one male l. a year old, for a burnt 7.27
one male l. a year old, for a burnt 7.33
one male l. a year old, for a burnt 7.39
one male l. a year old, for a burnt 7.45
one male l. a year old, for a burnt 7.51
one male l. a year old, for a burnt 7.57
one male l. a year old, for a burnt 7.63

LAMB (cont.)

one male l. a year old, for a burnt Num 7.69
one male l. a year old, for a burnt 7.75
one male l. a year old, for a burnt 7.81
or for the sacrifice, for each l. 15.05
The one l. you shall offer in the 28.04
and the other l. you shall offer in 28.04
be a fourth of a hin for each l.; 28.07
The other l. you shall offer in the 28.08
as a cereal offering for every l.; 28.13
and a fourth of a hin for a l.; 28.14
took a sucking l. and offered it 1Sa 7.09
and took a l. from the flock, 17.34
had nothing but one little ewe l., 2Sa 12.03
him, but he took the poor man's l., 12.04
and he shall restore the l. fourfold, 12.06
the passover l. on the fourteenth 2Ch 30.15
the passover l. for every one who 30.17
the passover l. on the fourteenth 35.01
And they killed the passover l., 35.11
the passover l. with fire according 35.13
the passover l. for all the returned Ez 6.20
The wolf shall dwell with the l., Is 11.06
like a l. that is led to the slaughter, 53.07
The wolf and the l. shall feed 65.25
he who sacrifices a l., like him 66.03
like a gentle l. led to the slaughter. Jer 11.19
He shall provide a l. a year old Eze 46.13
Thus the l. and the meal offering 46.15
them like a l. in a broad pasture? Hos 4.16
they sacrificed the passover l., Mk 14.12
the passover l. had to be sacrificed. Lk 22.07
the L. of God, who takes away the Jn 1.29
and said, "Behold, the L. of God!" 1.36
slaughter or a l. before its shearer Ac 8.32
our paschal l., has been sacrificed. 1Co 5.07
like that of a l. without blemish 1Pe 1.19
I saw a L. standing, as though it Rev 5.06
elders fell down before the L., 5.08
"Worthy is the L. who was slain, 5.12
and to the L. be blessing and 5.13
Now I saw when the L. opened one of 6.01
and from the wrath of the L.; 6.16
the throne and before the L., 7.09
upon the throne, and to the L.!" 7.10
them white in the blood of the L. 7.14
For the L. in the midst of the 7.17
When the L. opened the seventh seal, 8.01
blood of the L. and by the word of 12.11
of life of the L. that was slain. 13.08
horns like a l. and it spoke like 13.11
and lo, on Mount Zion stood the L., 14.01
who follow the L. wherever he goes; 14.04
first fruits for God and the L., 14.04
and in the presence of the L. 14.10
of God, and the song of the L., 15.03
they will make war on the L., 17.14
and the L. will conquer them, for he 17.14
the marriage of the L. has come, 19.07
to the marriage supper of the L." 19.09
you the Bride, the wife of the L." 21.09
of the twelve apostles of the L. 21.14
Lord God the Almighty and the L. 21.22
its light, and its lamp is the L. 21.23
the throne of God and of the L. 22.01
God and of the L. shall be in it, 22.03

LAMB'S

are written in the L. book of life. Rev 21.27

LAMBS

Abraham set seven ewe l. of the Gen 21.28
these seven ewe l. which you have 21.29
"These seven ewe l. you will take 21.30
the goats and black among the l., 30.33
And Jacob separated the l., and set 30.40
shall kill their l. in the evening. Ex 12.06
Select l. for yourselves according 12.21
two l. a year old day by day 29.38
take two male l. without blemish, Lev 14.10
shall take one of the male l., 14.12
the bread seven l. a year old 23.18
and two male l. a year old as a 23.19
before the LORD, with the two l.; 23.20
goats, and five male l. a year old. Num 7.17
goats, and five male l. a year old. 7.23
goats, and five male l. a year old. 7.29
goats, and five male l. a year old. 7.35
goats, and five male l. a year old. 7.41
goats, and five male l. a year old. 7.47
goats, and five male l. a year old. 7.53
goats, and five male l. a year old. 7.59
goats, and five male l. a year old. 7.65
goats, and five male l. a year old. 7.71
goats, and five male l. a year old. 7.77
goats, and five male l. a year old. 7.83
twelve male l. a year old, with 7.87
the male l. a year old sixty. 7.88
each of the male l. or the kids. 15.11
two male l. a year old without 28.03
day two male l. a year old without 28.09
seven male l. a year old without 28.11
ram, and seven male l. a year old; 28.19
you offer for each of the seven l.; 28.21
one ram, seven male l. a year old; 28.27
a tenth for each of the seven l.; 28.29
seven male l. a year old without 29.02
one tenth for each of the seven l.; 29.04
one ram, seven male l. a year old; 29.08
a tenth for each of the seven l.: 29.10
rams, fourteen male l. a year old; 29.13
tenth for each of the fourteen l.; 29.15
fourteen male l. a year old without 29.17
and for the l. by number according 29.18
fourteen male l. a year old without 29.20
and for the l. by number according 29.21
fourteen male l. a year old without 29.23
and for the l. by number according 29.24
fourteen male l. a year old without 29.26
and for the l. by number according 29.27
fourteen male l. a year old without 29.29
and for the l. by number according 29.30
fourteen male l. a year old without 29.32
and for the l. by their number 29.33
seven male l. a year old without 29.36
and for the l. by their number 29.37
with fat of l. and rams, herds of Deu 32.14
and the l., and all that was good, 1Sa 15.09
of Israel a hundred thousand l., 2Ki 3.04
a thousand rams, and a thousand l., 1Ch 29.21
seven l., and seven he-goats for a 2Ch 29.21
they killed the l. and their blood 29.22
a hundred rams, and two hundred l.; 29.32
l. and kids from the flock to the 35.07
six hundred l. and kids and three 35.08
five thousand l. and kids and five 35.09
four hnudred l., and as a sin Ez 6.17
and l., with their cereal offerings 7.17
seventy-seven l., and as a sin 8.35
skipped like rams, the hills like l. Ps 114.04
skip like rams? O hills, like l.? 114.06
the l. will provide your clothing, Pro 27.26
blood of bulls, or of l., or of he-goats. Is 1.11
Then shall the l. graze as in their 5.17
They have sent l. to the ruler of 16.01
with the blood of l. and goats, 34.06
he will gather the l. in his arms, 40.11
them down like l. to the slaughter, Jer 51.40
were your favored dealers in l., Eze 27.21
of l., and of goats, of bulls, all of 39.18
shall be six l. without blemish 46.04
with the l. shall be as much as he 46.05
and six l. and a ram, which shall be 46.06
and with the l. as much as he is 46.07
and with the l. as much as one is 46.11
and eat l. from the flock, and Amo 6.04

LAMBS (cont.)
send you out as l. in the midst of Lk 10.03
He said to him, "Feed my l." Jn 21.15

LAME
shall draw near, a man blind or l., Lev 21.18
if it is l. or blind, or has any Deu 15.21
her haste, he fell, and became l. 2Sa 4.04
blind and the l. will ward you off"— 5.06
to attack the l. and the blind, 5.08
The blind and the l. shall not come 5.08
Now he was l. in both his feet. 9.13
with the king.' For your servant is l. 19.26
to the blind, and feet to the l. Job 29.15
Like a l. man's legs, which hang Pro 26.07
even the l. will take the prey. Is 33.23
then shall the l. man leap like a 35.06
among them the blind and the l., Jer 31.08
assemble the l. and gather those Mic 4.06
and the l. I will make the remnant; 4.07
I will save the l. and gather the Zep 3.19
offer those that are l. or sick, Mal 1.08
taken by violence or is l. or sick, 1.13
their sight and the l. walk, Mt 11.05
to him, bringing with them the l., 15.30
the l. walking, and the blind seeing 15.31
life maimed or l. than with two 18.08
blind and the l. came to him in 21.14
to enter life l. than with two Mk 9.45
the l. walk, lepers are cleansed, and Lk 7.22
the maimed, the l., the blind, 14.13
poor and maimed and blind and l.' 14.21
of invalids, blind, l., paralyzed. Jn 5.03
And a man l. from birth was being Ac 3.02
were paralyzed or l. were healed. 8.07
so that what is l. may not be put Heb 12.13

LAMECH
and Methushael the father of L. Gen 4.18
And L. took two wives; the name of 4.19
L. said to his wives: "Adah and 4.23
you wives of L., hearken to what I 4.23
sevenfold, truly L. seventy-sevenfold." 4.24
years, he became the father of L. 5.25
the birth of L. seven hundred and 5.26
When L. had lived a hundred and 5.28
L. lived after the birth of Noah 5.30
Thus all the days of L. were seven 5.31
Enoch, Methuselah, L.; 1Ch 1.03
the son of Noah, the son of L., Lk 3.36

LAMENT
year by year to l. the daughter of Ju 11.40
Jeremiah also uttered a l. for Josiah; 2Ch 35.25
And her gates shall l. and mourn; Is 3.26
The fishermen will mourn and l., 19.08
you with sackcloth, l. and wail; Jer 4.08
teach to your daughters a l., 9.20
her people l. on the ground, and the 14.02
mourning, or go to l., or bemoan them; 16.05
no one shall l. for them or cut 16.06
Judah: "They shall not l. for him, 22.18
They shall not l. for him, saying, 22.18
burn spices for you and l. for you, 34.05
l., and run to and fro among the 49.03
he caused rampart and wall to l., Lam 2.08
and l. over you: "Who was ever Eze 27.32
L. like a virgin girded with sackcloth Joe 1.08
Gird on sackcloth and l., O priests, 1.13
For this I will l. and wail; Mic 1.08
I say to you, you will weep and l., Jn 16.20

LAMENTATION
with a very great and sorrowful l.; Gen 50.10
with this l. over Saul and Jonathan 2Sa 1.17
was dead, she made l. for her husband. 11.26
buries, and their widows make no l. Job 27.15
sword, and their widows made no l. Ps 78.64
and there shall be moaning and l., Is 29.02
as for an only son, most bitter l.; Jer 6.26
raise a l. on the bare heights, for 7.29
and a l. for the pastures of the 9.10
heard in Ramah, l. and bitter weeping. 31.15
squares there is nothing but l.; 48.38
daughter of Judah mourning and l. Lam 2.05
on it words of l. and mourning and Eze 2.10
take up a l. for the princes of 19.01
This is a l., and has become a l. 19.14
And they will raise a l. over you, 26.17
son of man, raise a l. over Tyre, 27.02
wailing they raise a l. for you, 27.32
raise a l. over the king of Tyre, 28.12
raise a l. over Pharaoh king of 32.02
This is a l. which shall be chanted 32.16
which I take up over you in l., Amo 5.01
wailing those who are skilled in l., 5.16
mourning, and all your songs into l.; 8.10
I will make l. like the jackals, and Mic 1.08
against you, and wail with bitter l., 2.04
heard in Ramah, wailing and loud l., Mt 2.18
Stephen, and made great l. over him. Ac 8.02

LAMENTATIONS
the Chaldeans will be turned to l. Is 43.14

LAMENTED
they l. there with a very great and Gen 50.10
house of Israel l. after the LORD. 1Sa 7.02
And David l. with this lamentation 2Sa 1.17
And the king l. for Abner, saying, 3.33
They shall not be l., nor shall they Jer 16.04
They shall not be l., or gathered, or 25.33
of women who bewailed and l. him. Lk 23.27

LAMENTING
with fasting and weeping and l., Est 4.03
regard to their fasts and their l. 9.31
her maidens l., moaning like doves, Nah 2.07

LAMENTS
of Josiah in their l. to this day. 2Ch 35.25
behold, they are written in the L. 35.25
about as one who l. his mother, Ps 35.14

LAMP
that a l. may be set up to burn Ex 27.20
oil from beaten olives for the l., Lev 24.02
the l. of God had not yet gone out, 1Sa 3.03
lest you quench the l. of Israel." 2Sa 21.17
thou art my l., O LORD, and my God 22.29
always have a l. before me in 1Ki 11.36
his God gave him a l. in Jerusalem, 15.04
and a l., so that whenever he comes 2Ki 4.10
to give a l. to him and to his 8.19
to give a l. to him and to his 2Ch 21.07
and his l. above him in put out. Job 18.06
is it that the l. of the wicked is 21.17
when his l. shone upon my head, and 29.03
Yea, thou dost light my l.; the LORD Ps 18.28
Thy word is a l. to my feet and a 119.105
have prepared a l. for my anointed 132.17
commandment is a l. and the teaching Pro 6.23
but the l. of the wicked will be 13.09
his l. will be put out in utter 20.20
of man is the l. of the LORD, 20.27
the l. of the wicked, are sin. 21.04
the l. of the wicked will be put 24.20
Her l. does not go out at night. 31.18
millstones and the light of the l. Jer 25.10
Nor do men light a l. and put it Mt 5.15
"The eye is the l. of the body. 6.22
Is a l. brought in to be put under Mk 4.21
lighting a l. covers it with a Lk 8.16
lighting a l. puts it in a cellar 11.33
Your eye is the l. of your body; 11.34
as when a l. with its rays gives 11.36

LAMP (cont.)
not light a l. and sweep the house Lk 15.08
He was a burning and shining l., Jn 5.35
to this as to a l. shining in a 2Pe 1.19
and the light of a l. shall shine Rev 18.23
its light, and its l. is the Lamb. 21.23
they need no light of l. or sun, 22.05

LAMPS
oil for the l., spices for the Ex 25.06
you shall make the seven l. for it; 25.37
and the l. shall be set up so as to 25.37
he dresses the l. he shall burn it, 30.07
sets up the l. in the evening, 30.08
with its utensils and its l., 35.14
made its seven l. and its snuffers 37.23
gold and its l. with the l. set and 39.37
the lampstand, and set up its l. 40.04
and set up the l. before the LORD; 40.25
He shall keep the l. in order upon Lev 24.04
with its l., its snuffers, its trays, Num 4.09
Say to Aaron, When you set up the l., 8.02
the seven l. shall give light in 8.02
he set up its l. to give light in 8.03
the l., and the tongs, of gold; 1Ki 7.49
the golden lampstands and their l., 1Ch 28.15
gold for each lampstand and its l., 28.15
silver for a lampstand and its l., 28.15
and their l. of pure gold to burn 2Ch 4.20
the l., and the tongs, of purest 4.21
that its l. may burn every evening 13.11
the vestibule and put out the l., 29.07
I will search Jerusalem with l., Zep 1.12
and seven l. on it, with seven lips Zec 4.02
on each of the l. which are on the 4.02
who took their l. and went to meet Mt 25.01
For when the foolish took their l., 25.03
took flasks of oil with their l. 25.04
maidens rose and trimmed their l. 25.07
your oil, for our l. are going out. 25.08
be girded and your l. burning, Lk 12.35

LAMPSTAND
"And you shall make a l. of pure gold. Ex 25.31
shaft of the l. shall be made of 25.31
branches of the l. out of one side 25.32
branches of the l. out of the 25.32
six branches going out of the l.; 25.33
and on the l. itself four cups made 25.34
six branches going out from the l. 25.35
and the l. on the south side of the 26.35
and the l. and its utensils, and the 30.27
and the pure l with all its utensils, 31.08
the l. also for the light, with its 35.14
He also made the l. of pure gold. 37.17
and the shaft of the l. were made of 37.17
branches of the l. out of one side 37.18
branches of the l. out of the 37.18
six branches going out of the l. 37.19
And on the l. itself were four cups 37.20
the l. of pure gold and its lamps 39.27
and you shall bring in the l., 40.04
And he put the l. in the tent of 40.24
order upon the l. of pure gold Lev 24.04
the l., the altars, the vessels of Num 3.31
and cover the l. for the light. with 4.09
give light in front of the l." 8.02
to give light in front of the l., 8.03
this was the workmanship of the l., 8.04
had shown Moses, so he made the l. 8.04
of gold for each l. and its lamps, 1Ch 28.15
of silver for a l. and its lamps, 28.15
the use of each l. in the service, 28.15
for the golden l. that its lamps 2Ch 13.11
the king's palace. opposite the l.; Dan 5.05
a l. all of gold, with a bowl on the Zec 4.02
the right and the left of the l.?" 4.11

which were the l. and the table Heb 9.02
and remove your l. from its place, Rev 2.05

LAMPSTANDS
the l. of pure gold, five on the 1Ki 7.49
of the golden l. and their lamps, 1Ch 28.15
made ten golden l. as prescribed, 2Ch 4.07
the l. and their lamps of pure gold 4.20
and the l., and the dishes for Jer 52.19
on turning I saw seven golden l., Rev 1.12
midst of the l. one like a son of 1.13
hand, and the seven golden l., 1.20
and the seven l. are the seven 1.20
walks among the seven golden l. 2.01
and the two l. which stand before 11.04

LANCES
their custom with swords and l., 1Ki 18.28

LAND
place, and let the dry l. appear." Gen 1.09
God called the dry l. Earth, 1.10
around the whole l. of Havilah, 2.11
and the gold of that l. is good; 2.12
flows around the whole l. of Cush. 2.13
LORD, and dwelt in the l. of Nod, 4.16
everything on the dry l. in whose 7.22
all of them in the l. of Shinar. 10.10
From that l. he went into Assyria, 10.11
a plain in the l. of Shinar and 11.02
Terah in the l. of his birth, 11.28
to go into the l. of Canaan; 11.31
house to the l. that I will show 12.01
forth to go to the l. of Canaan. 12.05
they had come to the l. of Canaan, 12.05
through the l. to the place at 12.06
time the Canaanites were in the l. 12.06
descendants I will give this l." 12.07
Now there was a famine in the l. 12.10
the famine was severe in the l. 12.10
so that the l. could not support 13.06
and the Perizzites dwelt in the l. 13.07
Is not the whole l. before you? 13.09
like the l. of Egypt in the direction 13.10
Abram dwelt in the l. of Canaan, 13.12
for all the l. which you see I will 13.15
length and the breadth of the l., 13.17
to give you this l. to possess." 15.07
sojourners in a l. that is not 15.13
To your descendants I give this l., 15.18
the l. of the Kenites, the Kenizzites, 15.19
ten years in the l. of Canaan, 16.03
the l. of your sojournings, all the 17.08
all the l. of Canaan, for an everlasting 17.08
toward all the l. of the valley, 19.28
smoke of the l. went up like the 19.28
said, "Behold, my l. is before you; 20.15
wife for him from the l. of Egypt. 21.21
me and with the l. where you have 21.23
returned to the l. of the Philistines. 21.32
days in the l. of the Philistines. 21.34
and go to the l. of Moriah, and 22.02
is, Hebron) in the l. of Canaan; 23.02
the Hittites, the people of the l. 23.07
down before the people of the l. 23.12
hearing of the people of the l., 23.13
a piece of l. worth four hundred 23.15
is, Hebron) in the l. of Canaan. 23.19
be willing to follow me to this l.; 24.05
son back to the l. from which you 24.05
house and from the l. of my birth, 24.07
descendants I will give this l.,' 24.07
Canaanites, in whose l. I dwell; 24.37
Now there was a famine in the l., 26.01
dwell in the l. of which I shall 26.02
Sojourn in this l., and I will be 26.03
And Isaac sowed in that l., and 26.12
and we shall be fruitful in the l." 26.22

LAND (cont.)
these, one of the women of the l., Gen 27.46
possession of the l. of your 28.04
the l. on which you lie I will give 28.13
and will bring you back to this l.; 28.15
and came to the l. of the people 29.01
Return to the l. of your fathers 31.03
Now arise, go forth from this l., 31.13
and return to the l. of your birth.' " 31.13
to go to the l. of Canaan to his 31.18
Esau his brother in the l. of Seir, 32.03
which is in the l. of Canaan, 33.18
the piece of l. on which he had 33.19
out to visit the women of the l.; 34.01
the Hivite, the prince of the l., 34.02
and the l. shall be open to you; 34.10
dwell in the l. and trade in it, 34.21
the l. is large enough for them; 34.21
to the inhabitants of the l., 34.30
which is in the l. of Canaan, 35.06
The l. which I gave to Abraham and 35.12
I will give the l. to your descendants 35.12
dwelt in that l. Reuben went and 35.22
born to him in the l. of Canaan. 36.05
had acquired in the l. of Canaan; 36.06
he went into a l. away from his 36.06
the l. of their sojournings could 36.07
of Eliphaz in the l. of Edom; 36.16
chiefs of Reuel in the l. of Edom; 36.17
Horite, the inhabitants of the l.: 36.20
the sons of Seir in the l. of Edom. 36.21
to their clans in the l. of Seir. 36.30
who reigned in the l. of Edom, 36.31
Husham of the l. of the Temanites 36.34
places in the l. of their possession. 36.43
Jacob dwelt in the l. of his 37.01
sojournings, in the l. of Canaan. 37.01
out of the l. of the Hebrews; 40.15
never seen in all the l. of Egypt. 41.19
throughout all the l. of Egypt, 41.29
be forgotten in the l. of Egypt; 41.30
the famine will consume the l., 41.30
unknown in the l. by reason of 41.31
and set him over the l. of Egypt. 41.33
to appoint overseers over the l., 41.34
produce of the l. of Egypt during 41.34
reserve for the l. against the 41.36
are to befall the l. of Egypt, 41.36
so that the l. may not perish 41.36
set you over all the l. of Egypt." 41.41
set him over all the l. of Egypt. 41.43
or foot in all the l. of Egypt." 41.44
went out over the l. of Egypt. 41.45
went through all the l. of Egypt. 41.46
was plenty in the l. of Egypt, 41.48
fruitful in the l. of my affliction 41.52
prevailed in the l. of Egypt came 41.53
but in all the l. of Egypt there 41.54
When all the l. of Egypt was 41.55
famine had spread over all the l., 41.56
was severe in the l. of Egypt. 41.56
the famine was in the l. of Canaan. 42.05
Now Joseph was governor over the l.; 42.06
sold to all the people of the l. 42.06
"From the l. of Canaan, to buy food." 42.07
come to see the weakness of the l." 42.09
weakness of the l. that you have 42.12
of one man in the l. of Canaan; 42.13
their father in the l. of Canaan, 42.29
"The man, the lord of the l.; 42.30
and took us to be spies of the l. 42.30
our father in the l. of Canaan.' 42.32
Then the man, the lord of the l., 42.33
and you shall trade in the l.' " 42.34
Now the famine was severe in the l. 43.01
fruits of the l. in your bags, 43.11
back to you from the l. of Canaan; 44.08
has been in the l. these two years 45.06
and ruler over all the l. of Egypt. 45.08
you shall dwell in the l. of Goshen, 45.10
and go back to the l. of Canaan; 45.17
you the best of the l. of Egypt, 45.18
you shall eat the fat of the l.' 45.18
wagons from the l. of Egypt for 45.19
best of all the l. of Egypt is 45.20
and came to the l. of Canaan to 45.25
is ruler over all the l. of Egypt." 45.26
had gained in the l. of Canaan, 46.06
and Onan died in the l. of Canaan); 46.12
Joseph in the l. of Egypt were 46.20
they came into the l. of Goshen. 46.28
who were in the l. of Canaan, 46.31
you may dwell in the l. of Goshen; 46.34
have come from the l. of Canaan; 47.01
they are now in the l. of Goshen." 47.01
We have come to sojourn in the l.; 47.04
is severe in the l. of Canaan; 47.04
servants dwell in the l. of Goshen." 47.04
The l. of Egypt is before you; 47.06
brothers in the best of the l.; 47.06
let them dwell in the l. of Goshen; 47.06
a possession in the l. of Egypt, 47.11
of Egypt, in the best of the l., 47.11
in the l. of Rameses, as Pharaoh had 47.11
Now there was no food in all the l.; 47.13
so that the l. of Egypt and the 47.13
Egypt and the l. of Canaan languished 47.13
found in the l. of Egypt and in 47.14
of Egypt and in the l. of Canaan, 47.14
spent in the l. of Egypt and in 47.15
of Egypt and in the l. of Canaan, 47.15
your eyes, both we and our l.? 47.19
Buy us and our l. for food, and 47.19
and we with our l. will be slaves 47.19
and that the l. may not be desolate." 47.19
bought all the l. of Egypt for 47.20
upon them. The l. became Pharaoh's; 47.20
Only the l. of the priests he did 47.22
therefore they did not sell their l. 47.22
bought you and your l. for Pharaoh. 47.23
for you, and you shall sow the l. 47.23
statute concerning the l. of Egypt, 47.26
the l. of the priests alone did not 47.26
Thus Israel dwelt in the l. of Egypt, 47.27
in the l. of Goshen; and they gained 47.27
lived in the l. of Egypt seventeen 47.28
at Luz in the l. of Canaan and 48.03
will give this l. to your descendants 48.04
to you in the l. of Egypt before I 48.05
died in the l. of Canaan on the 48.07
again to the l. of your fathers. 48.21
good, and that the l. was pleasant; 49.15
in the l. of Canaan, which Abraham 49.30
out for myself in the l. of Canaan, 50.05
all the elders of the l. of Egypt, 50.07
were left in the l. of Goshen. 50.08
When the inhabitants of the l., 50.11
carried him to the l. of Canaan, 50.13
of this l. to the l. which he swore to 50.24
so that the l. was filled with them. Ex 1.07
against us and escape from the l." 1.10
and stayed in the l. of Midian; 2.15
been a sojourner in a foreign l." 2.22
out of that l. to a good and broad l., 3.08
a l. flowing with milk and honey, to 3.08
to the l. of the Canaanites, the 3.17
a l. flowing with milk and honey." ' 3.17
and went back to the l. of Egypt; 4.20
people of the l. are now many and 5.05
throughout all the l. of Egypt, 5.12
he will drive them out of his l." 6.01
to give them the l. of Canaan, 6.04
the l. in which they dwelt as 6.04
you into the l. which I swore to 6.08
people of Israel go out of his l." 6.11
of Israel out of the l. of Egypt. 6.13

LAND (cont.)
Israel from the l. of Egypt by Ex 6.26
spoke to Moses in the l. of Egypt, 6.28
people of Israel go out of his l. 7.02
and wonders in the l. of Egypt, 7.03
out of the l. of Egypt by great 7.04
throughout all the l. of Egypt, 7.19
throughout all the l. of Egypt. 7.21
frogs to come upon the l. of Egypt!'" 8.05
up and covered the l. of Egypt. 8.06
brought frogs upon the l. of Egypt. 8.07
together in heaps, and the l. stank. 8.14
throughout all the l. of Egypt.'" 8.16
throughout all the l. of Egypt. 8.17
I will set apart the l. of Goshen, 8.22
and in all the l. of Egypt the 8.24
of Egypt the l. was ruined by 8.24
sacrifice to your God within the l." 8.25
LORD will do this thing in the l." 9.05
fine dust over all the l. of Egypt, 9.09
throughout all the l. of Egypt." 9.09
may be hail in all the l. of Egypt, 9.22
field, throughout the l. of Egypt." 9.22
rained hail upon the l. of Egypt; 9.23
been in all the l. of Egypt since 9.24
throughout all the l. of Egypt, 9.25
Only in the l. of Goshen, where the 9.26
shall cover the face of the l., 10.05
so that no one can see the l.; 10.05
hand over the l. of Egypt for the 10.12
they may come upon the l. of Egypt, 10.12
and eat every plant in the l., 10.12
forth his rod over the l. of Egypt, 10.13
wind upon the l. all that day and 10.13
came up over all the l. of Egypt, 10.14
covered the face of the whole l., 10.15
so that the l. was darkened, and 10.15
plants in the l. and all the fruit 10.15
field, through all the l. of Egypt. 10.15
be darkness over the l. of Egypt, 10.21
in all the l. of Egypt three days; 10.22
was very great in the l. of Egypt, 11.03
first-born in the l. of Egypt shall 11.05
cry throughout all the l. of Egypt, 11.06
be multiplied in the l. of Egypt." 11.09
people of Israel go out of his l. 11.10
and Aaron in the l. of Egypt, 12.01
through the l. of Egypt that night, 12.12
the first-born in the l. of Egypt, 12.12
you, when I smite the l. of Egypt. 12.13
your hosts out of the l. of Egypt: 12.17
a sojourner or a native of the l. 12.19
you come to the l. which the LORD 12.25
the first-born in the l. of Egypt, 12.29
send them out of the l. in haste; 12.33
LORD went out from the l. of Egypt. 12.41
bring them out of the l. of Egypt; 12.42
he shall be as a native of the l. 12.48
out of the l. of Egypt by their 12.51
you into the l. of the Canaanites, 13.05
a l. flowing with milk and honey, 13.05
you into the l. of the Canaanites, 13.11
the first-born in the l. of Egypt, 13.15
by way of the l. of the Philistines, 13.17
up out of the l. of Egypt equipped 13.18
'They are entangled in the l.; 14.03
all night, and made the sea dry l., 14.21
had departed from the l. of Egypt. 16.01
of the LORD in the l. of Egypt, 16.03
brought you out of the l. of Egypt, 16.06
brought you out of the l. of Egypt.'" 16.32
till they came to a habitable l.; 16.35
to the border of the l. of Canaan. 16.35
been a sojourner in a foreign l."), 18.03
gone forth out of the l. of Egypt, 19.01
brought you out of the l. of Egypt, 20.02
be long in the l. which the LORD 20.12
were strangers in the l. of Egypt. 22.21
were strangers in the l. of Egypt. 23.09
shall sow your l. and gather in 23.10
her young or be barren in your l.; 23.26
lest the l. become desolate and the 23.29
are increased and possess the l. 23.30
inhabitants of the l. into your hand, 23.31
They shall not dwell in your l., 23.33
out of the l. of Egypt that I 29.46
us up out of the l. of Egypt, 32.01
you up out of the l. of Egypt!" 32.04
brought up out of the l. of Egypt, 32.07
you up out of the l. of Egypt!'" 32.08
out of the l. of Egypt with great 32.11
and all this l. that I have promised 32.13
us up out of the l. of Egypt, 32.23
brought up out of the l. of Egypt, 33.01
to the l. of which I swore to 33.01
Go up to a l. flowing with milk and 33.03
inhabitants of the l. whither you go, 34.12
with the inhabitants of the l., 34.15
shall any man desire your l., 34.24
the gecko, the l. crocodile, the Lev 11.30
you up out of the l. of Egypt, 11.45
"When you come into the l. of Canaan, 14.34
a house in the l. of your possession, 14.34
iniquities upon him to a solitary l.; 16.22
do as they do in the l. of Egypt, 18.03
do as they do in the l. of Canaan, 18.03
and the l. became defiled, so that I 18.25
and the l. vomited out its inhabitants 18.25
abominations the men of the l. did, 18.27
so that the l. became defiled); 18.27
lest the l. vomit you out, when you 18.28
"When you reap the harvest of your l., 19.09
come into the l. and plant all 19.23
lest the l. fall into harlotry and 19.29
harlotry and the l. become full of 19.29
sojourns with you in your l., 19.33
were strangers in the l. of Egypt: 19.34
brought you out of the l. of Egypt. 19.36
people of the l. shall stone him 20.02
people of the l. do at all hide 20.04
that the l. where I am bringing you 20.22
you, 'You shall inherit their l., 20.24
a l. flowing with milk and honey.' 20.24
LORD or sacrifice within your l.; 22.24
you out of the l. of Egypt to be 22.33
come into the l. which I give you 23.10
you reap the harvest of your l., 23.22
gathered in the produce of the l., 23.39
them out of the l. of Egypt: 23.43
come into the l. which I give you, 25.02
the l. shall keep a sabbath to the 25.02
sabbath of solemn rest for the l., 25.04
a year of solemn rest for the l. 25.05
The sabbath of the l. shall provide 25.06
are in your l. all its yield shall 25.07
the trumpet throughout all your l. 25.09
throughout the l. to all its 25.10
you will dwell in the l. securely. 25.18
The l. will yield its fruit, and you 25.19
The l. shall not be sold in perpetuity, 25.23
in perpetuity, for the l. is mine; 25.23
shall grant a redemption of the l. 25.24
of common l. belonging to their 25.34
out of the l. of Egypt to give you 25.38
Egypt to give you the l. of Canaan, 25.38
forth out of the l. of Egypt; 25.42
you, who have been born in your l.; 25.45
forth out of the l. of Egypt: 25.55
set up a figured stone in your l., 26.01
and the l. shall yield its increase, 26.04
and dwell in your l. securely. 26.05
And I will give peace in the l., 26.06
remove evil beasts from the l., 26.06
sword shall not go through your l. 26.06
you forth out of the l. of Egypt, 26.13
for your l. shall not yield its 26.20

LAND (cont.)

trees of the l. shall not yield Lev 26.20
And I will devastate the l., 26.32
and your l. shall be a desolation, 26.33
"Then the l. shall enjoy its 26.34
while you are in your enemies' l.; 26.34
then the l. shall rest, and enjoy 26.34
and the l. of your enemies shall 26.38
them into the l. of their enemies; 26.41
Abraham, and I will remember the l. 26.42
But the l. shall be left by them, 26.43
they are in the l. of their 26.44
out of the l. of Egypt in the 26.45
part of the l. which is his by 27.16
to whom the l. belongs as a possession 27.24
"All the tithe of the l., whether of 27.30
the seed of the l. or of the fruit 27.30
had come out of the l. of Egypt, Num 1.01
the first-born in the l. of Egypt, 3.13
first-born in the l. of Egypt I 8.17
had come out of the l. of Egypt, 9.01
to war in your l. against the 10.09
to my own l. and to my kindred." 10.30
to the l. which thou didst swear to 11.12
Send men to spy out the l. of Canaan, 13.02
whom Moses sent to spy out the l. 13.16
them to spy out the l. of Canaan, 13.17
and see what the l. is, and whether 13.18
and whether the l. that they dwell 13.19
and whether the l. is rich or poor, 13.20
bring some of the fruit of the l." 13.20
spied out the l. from the wilderness 13.21
returned from spying out the l. 13.25
showed them the fruit of the l. 13.26
"We came to the l. to which you 13.27
who dwell in the l. are strong, 13.28
dwell in the l. of the Negeb; 13.29
report of the l. which they had 13.32
"The l., through which we have gone, 13.32
is a l. that devours its inhabitants 13.32
we had died in the l. of Egypt! 14.02
the LORD bring us into this l., 14.03
those who had spied out the l., 14.06
"The l., which we passed through to 14.07
it out, is an exceedingly good l. 14.07
us into this l. and give it to us, 14.08
a l. which flows with milk and 14.08
do not fear the people of the l., 14.09
tell the inhabitants of this l. 14.14
people into the l. which he swore 14.16
shall see the l. which I swore to 14.23
bring into the l. into which he 14.24
come into the l. where I swore 14.30
shall know the l. which you have 14.31
days in which you spied out the l., 14.34
whom Moses sent to spy out the l., 14.36
up an evil report against the l., 14.36
up an evil report of the l., 14.37
men who went to spy out the l. 14.38
come into the l. you are to 15.02
come into the l. to which I bring 15.18
when you eat of the food of the l., 15.19
brought you out of the l. of Egypt, 15.41
us up out of a l. flowing with 16.13
us into a l. flowing with milk and 16.14
fruits of all that is in their l., 18.13
have no inheritance in their l., 18.20
into the l. which I have given 20.12
Now let us pass through your l. 20.17
on the border of the l. of Edom, 20.23
not enter the l. which I have 20.24
Sea, to go around the l. of Edom; 21.04
"Let me pass through your l.; 21.22
possession of his l. from the Arnon 21.24
taken all his l. out of his hand, 21.26
dwelt in the l. of the Amorites. 21.31
and all his people, and his l.; 21.34
and they possessed his l. 21.35

in the l. of Amaw to call him, 22.05
them and drive them from the l.; 22.06
of Balak, "Go to your own l.; 22.13
came forth out of the l. of Egypt, 26.04
and Onan died in the l. of Canaan. 26.19
"To these the l. shall be divided 26.53
But the l. shall be divided by lot; 26.55
and see the l. which I have given 27.12
saw the l. of Jazer the l. of Gilead, 32.01
the l. which the LORD smote before 32.04
of Israel, is a l. for cattle; 32.04
let this l. be given to your 32.05
over into the l. which the LORD 32.07
from Kadeshbarnea to see the l. 32.08
and saw the l., they discouraged 32.09
going into the l. which the LORD 32.09
shall see the l. which I swore to 32.11
of the inhabitants of the l. 32.17
and the l. is subdued before the 32.22
and this l. shall be your possession 32.22
Jordan and the l. shall be subdued 32.29
give them the l. of Gilead for a 32.29
among you in the l. of Canaan." 32.30
the LORD into the l. of Canaan, 32.32
the l. and its cities with their 32.33
cities of the l. throughout the 32.33
out of the l. of Egypt by their 33.01
Hor, on the edge of the l. of Edom. 33.37
had come out of the l. of Egypt, 33.38
in the Negeb in the l. of Canaan, 33.40
the Jordan into the l. of Canaan, 33.51
inhabitants of the l. from before 33.52
possession of the l. and settle in 33.53
have given the l. to you to possess 33.53
inherit the l. by lot according to 33.54
inhabitants of the l. from before 33.55
you in the l. where you dwell. 33.55
you enter the l. of Canaan (this 34.02
(this is the l. that shall fall to 34.02
the l. of Canaan in its full extent). 34.02
shall be your l. with its boundaries 34.12
This is the l. which you shall 34.13
divide the l. to you for inheritance: 34.17
to divide the l. for inheritance. 34.18
of Israel in the l. of Canaan." 34.29
them as pasture l. for their 35.05
the Jordan into the l. of Canaan, 35.10
three cities in the l. of Canaan, 35.14
return to the l. of his possession. 35.28
to dwell in the l. before the 35.32
pollute the l. in which you live; 35.33
for blood pollutes the l., 35.33
expiation can be made for the l., 35.33
not defile the l. in which you 35.34
to give the l. for inheritance by 36.02
in the l. of Moab, Moses undertook Deu 1.05
the l. of the Canaanites, and 1.07
Behold, I have set the l. before you; 1.08
possession of the l. which the LORD 1.08
your God has set the l. before you; 1.21
they may explore the l. for us, 1.22
fruit of the l. and brought it 1.25
'It is a good l. which the LORD our 1.25
us forth out of the l. of Egypt, 1.27
see the good l. which I swore to 1.35
I will give the l. upon which he 1.36
will not give you any of their l., 2.05
any of their l. for a possession, 2.09
did to the l. of their possession, 2.12
you any of the l. of the sons of 2.19
(That also is known as a l. of Rephaim; 2.20
king of Heshbon, and his l.; 2.24
'Let me pass through your l.; 2.27
Jordan into the l. which the LORD 2.29
give Sihon and his l. over to you; 2.31
possession, that you may occupy his l.' 2.31
Only to the l. of the sons of Ammon 2.37
people and his l. into your hand; 3.02

LAND (cont.)

So we took the l. at that time out Deu 3.08
possession of this l. at that time, 3.12
Bashan is called the l. of Rephaim. 3.13
has given you this l. to possess; 3.18
also occupy the l. which the LORD 3.20
see the good l. beyond the Jordan, 3.25
possession of the l. which you 3.28
possession of the l. which the LORD, 4.01
do them in the l. which you are 4.05
do them in the l. which you are 4.14
enter the good l. which the LORD 4.21
For I must die in this l., I must 4.22
take possession of that good l. 4.22
and have grown old in the l., 4.25
perish from the l. which you are 4.26
give you their l. for an inheritance, 4.38
days in the l. which the LORD your 4.40
in the l. of Sihon the king of the 4.46
possession of his l. and the l. of Og 4.47
brought you out of the l. of Egypt, 5.06
were a servant in the l. of Egypt, 5.15
in the l. which the LORD your God 5.16
do them in the l. which I give 5.31
long in the l. which you shall 5.33
do them in the l. to which you are 6.01
in a l. flowing with milk and honey. 6.03
you into the l. which he swore to 6.10
brought you out of the l. of Egypt, 6.12
of the good l. which the LORD 6.18
and give us the l. which he swore 6.23
you into the l. which you are 7.01
in the l. which he swore to your 7.13
and possess the l. which the LORD 8.01
God is bringing you into a good l., 8.07
a l. of brooks of water, of fountains 8.07
a l. of wheat and barley, of vines 8.08
a l. of olive trees and honey, 8.08
a l. in which you will eat bread 8.09
a l. whose stones are iron, and out 8.09
for the good l. he has given you. 8.10
brought you out of the l. of Egypt, 8.14
brought me in to possess this l.'; 9.04
you going in to possess their l.; 9.05
giving you this good l. to possess 9.06
you came out of the l. of Egypt, 9.07
possession of the l. which I have 9.23
lest the l. from which thou didst 9.28
them into the l. which he promised 9.28
a l. with brooks of water. 10.07
they may go in and possess the l., 10.11
were sojourners in the l. of Egypt. 10.19
king of Egypt and to all his l.; 11.03
possession of the l. which you are 11.08
long in the l. which the LORD 11.09
a l. flowing with milk and honey. 11.09
For the l. which you are entering 11.10
of it is not like the l. of Egypt, 11.10
but the l. which you are going over 11.11
to possess is a l. of hills and 11.11
a l. which the LORD your God cares 11.12
the rain for your l. in its season, 11.14
and the l. yield no fruit, and you 11.17
off the good l. which the LORD 11.17
multiplied in the l. which the LORD 11.21
upon all the l. that you shall 11.25
you into the l. which you are 11.29
in the l. of the Canaanites who 11.30
possession of the l. which the LORD 11.31
to do in the l. which the LORD, 12.01
and live in the l. which the LORD 12.10
as long as you live in your l. 12.19
them and dwell in their l., 12.29
you out of the l. of Egypt and 13.05
brought you out of the l. of Egypt, 13.10
you in the l. which the LORD your 15.04
within your l. which the LORD your 15.07
will never cease out of the l.; 15.11
needy and to the poor, in the l. 15.11
were a slave in the l. of Egypt, 15.15
came out of the l. of Egypt in 16.03
you came out of the l. of Egypt. 16.03
and inherit the l. which the LORD 16.20
"When you come to the l. which the 17.14
come into the l. which the LORD 18.09
nations whose l. the LORD your God 19.01
for you in the l. which the LORD 19.02
the area of the l. which the LORD 19.03
you all the l. which he promised 19.08
be shed in your l. which the LORD 19.10
hold in the l. that the LORD your 19.14
you up out of the l. of Egypt. 20.01
"If in the l. which the LORD your 21.01
not defile your l. which the LORD 21.23
you were a sojourner in his l. 23.07
undertake in the l. which you are 23.20
guilt upon the l. which the LORD 24.04
who are in your l. within your 24.14
were a slave in the l. of Egypt; 24.22
prolonged in the l. which the LORD 25.15
in the l. which the LORD your God 25.19
come into the l. which the LORD 26.01
from your l. that the LORD your 26.02
come into the l. which the LORD 26.03
this place and gave us this l., 26.09
a l. flowing with milk and honey. 26.09
a l. flowing with milk and honey.' 26.15
Jordan to the l. which the LORD 27.02
to enter the l. which the LORD 27.03
a l. flowing with milk and honey, as 27.03
you in the l. which the LORD your 28.08
within the l. which the LORD swore 28.11
rain of your l. in its season and 28.12
you off the l. which you are 28.21
rain of your l. powder and dust; 28.24
come down throughout all your l.; 28.52
your towns throughout all your l., 28.52
plucked off the l. which you are 28.63
people of Israel in the l. of Moab, 29.01
your eyes in the l. of Egypt, 29.02
his servants and to all his l., 29.02
we took their l., and gave it for 29.08
how we dwelt in the l. of Egypt, 29.16
foreigner who comes from a far l., 29.22
afflictions of that l. and the 29.22
the whole l. brimstone and salt, and 29.23
has the LORD done thus to this l.? 29.24
them out of the l. of Egypt, 29.25
LORD was kindled against this l., 29.27
them from their l. in anger and 29.28
and cast them into another l., 29.28
you into the l. which your fathers 30.05
you in the l. which you are 30.16
long in the l. which you are going 30.18
dwell in the l. which the LORD 30.20
and to their l., when he destroyed 31.04
people into the l. which the LORD 31.07
you live in the l. which you are 31.13
after the strange gods of the l., 31.16
them into the l. flowing with milk 31.20
them into the l. that I swore to 31.21
Israel into the l. which I swore 31.23
"He found him in a desert l., 32.10
expiation for the l. of his people. 32.43
long in the l. which you are going 32.47
Nebo, which is in the l. of Moab, 32.49
and view the l. of Canaan, which I 32.49
For you shall see the l. before you; 32.52
into the l. which I give to the 32.52
"Blessed by the LORD be his l., 33.13
the best of the l. for himself, 33.21
in a l. of grain and wine; yea, his 33.28
And the LORD showed him all the l., 34.01
the l. of Ephraim and Manasseh, all 34.02
all the l. of Judah as far as the 34.02
"This is the l. of which I swore to 34.04

LAND (cont.)
LORD died there in the l. of Moab, Deu 34.05
valley in the l. of Moab opposite 34.06
sent him to do in the l. of Egypt, 34.11
his servants and to all his l., 34.11
into the l. which I am giving to Jos 1.02
all the l. of the Hittites to the 1.04
to inherit the l. which I swore to 1.06
possession of the l. which the LORD 1.11
of rest, and will give you this l.' 1.13
remain in the l. which Moses gave 1.14
possession of the l. which the LORD 1.15
return to the l. of your possession, 1.15
the l. which Moses the servant of 1.15
view the l., especially Jericho." 2.01
here tonight to search out the l." 2.02
have come to search out all the l." 2.03
that the LORD has given you the l., 2.09
inhabitants of the l. melt away 2.09
you when the LORD gives us the l." 2.14
Behold, when we come into the l., 2.18
given all the l. into our hands; 2.24
inhabitants of the l. are fainthearted 2.24
them see the l. which the LORD had 5.06
a l. flowing with milk and honey. 5.06
they ate of the produce of the l., 5.11
they ate of the produce of the l.; 5.12
fruit of the l. of Canaan that 5.12
two men who had spied out the l., 6.22
and his fame was in all the l. 6.27
to them, "Go up and spy out the l." 7.02
inhabitants of the l. will hear of 7.09
his people, his city, and his l.; 8.01
Moses to give you all the l., 9.24
inhabitants of the l. from before 9.24
So Joshua defeated the whole l., 10.40
kings and their l. at one time, 10.42
under Hermon in the l. of Mizpah. 11.03
So Joshua took all that l., 11.16
and all the l. of Goshen and the 11.16
left in the l. of the people of 11.22
So Joshua took the whole l., 11.23
And the l. had rest from war. 11.23
Now these are the kings of the l., 12.01
of their l. beyond the Jordan 12.01
LORD gave their l. for a possession 12.06
kings of the l. whom Joshua and 12.07
gave their l. to the tribes of 12.07
the l. of the Hittites, the Amorites, 12.08
yet very much l. to be possessed. 13.01
This is the l. that yet remains: all 13.02
all the l. of the Canaanites, and 13.04
and the l. of the Gebalites, and all 13.05
only allot the l. to Israel for an 13.06
divide this l. for an inheritance 13.07
of Sihon, who dwelt in the l. 13.21
and half the l. of the Ammonites, to 13.25
received in the l. of Canaan, 14.01
was given to the Levites in the l., 14.04
commanded Moses; they allotted the l. 14.05
Kadeshbarnea to spy out the l.; 14.07
'Surely the l. on which your foot 14.09
And the l. had rest from war. 14.15
have set me in the l. of the Negeb, 15.19
besides the l. of Gilead and Bashan, 17.05
The l. of Gilead was allotted to 17.06
The l. of Tappuah belonged to 17.08
the l. to the south being Ephraim's 17.10
persisted in dwelling in that l. 17.12
yourselves in the l. of the Perizzites 17.15
the l. lay subdued before them. 18.01
in and take possession of the l., 18.03
set out and go up and down the l., 18.04
describe the l. in seven divisions 18.06
to write the description of the l., 18.08
and write a description of the l., 18.08
and down in the l. and set down in 18.09
apportioned the l. to the people 18.10
territories of the l. as inheritances, 19.49
So they finished dividing the l. 19.51
them at Shiloh in the l. of Canaan, 21.02
Israel all the l. which he swore 21.43
home in the l. where your possession 22.04
brethren in the l. west of the 22.07
which is in the l. of Canaan, 22.09
to go to the l. of Gilead, their own 22.09
their own l. of which they had 22.09
that lies in the l. of Canaan, 22.10
the frontier of the l. of Canaan, 22.11
in the l. of Gilead, Phinehas the 22.13
in the l. of Gilead, and they said 22.15
if your l. is unclean, pass over 22.19
into the LORD's l. where the LORD' 22.19
the l. of Gilead to the l. of Canaan, 22.32
to destroy the l. where the 22.33
and you shall possess their l., 23.05
off this good l. which the LORD 23.13
off this good l. which the LORD 23.15
off the good l. which he has given 23.16
him through all the l. of Canaan, 24.03
you to the l. of the Amorites, who 24.08
you took possession of their l., 24.08
I gave you a l. on which you had 24.13
the Amorites in whose l. you dwell; 24.15
fathers up from the l. of Egypt, 24.17
the Amorites who lived in the l.; 24.18
I have given the l. into his hand." Ju 1.02
have set me in the l. of the Negeb, 1.15
man went to the l. of the Hittites 1.26
persisted in dwelling in that l. 1.27
Canaanites, the inhabitants of the l.; 1.32
Canaanites, the inhabitants of the l.; 1.33
you into the l. which I swore to 2.01
with the inhabitants of this l.; 2.02
to take possession of the l. 2.06
them out of the l. of Egypt; 2.12
So the l. had rest forty years. 3.11
And the l. had rest for eighty 3.30
And the l. had rest for forty years 5.31
and destroy the produce of the l., 6.04
they wasted the l. as they came in 6.05
before you, and gave you their l.; 6.09
Amorites, in whose l. you dwell.' 6.10
And the l. had rest forty years in 8.28
down from the center of the l., 9.37
day, which are in the l. of Gilead. 10.04
Jordan in the l. of the Amorites, 10.08
brothers, and dwelt in the l. of Tob; 11.03
bring Jephthah from the l. of Tob; 11.05
come to me to fight against my l.?" 11.12
coming from Egypt took away my l., 11.13
take away the l. of Moab or the 11.15
of Moab or the l. of the Ammonites, 11.15
us pass, we pray, through your l.'; 11.17
the l. of Edom and the l. of Moab, 11.18
on the east side of the l. of Moab, 11.18
through your l. to our country.' 11.19
of all the l. of the Amorites, who 11.21
at Aijalon in the l. of Zebulun. 12.12
at Pirathon in the l. of Ephraim, 12.15
to spy out the l. and to explore 18.02
to them, "Go and explore the l." 18.02
for we have seen the l., and behold, 18.09
and enter in and possess the l. 18.09
The l. is broad; yea, God has given 18.10
had gone to spy out the l. went up, 18.17
the day of the captivity of the l. 18.30
up out of the l. of Egypt until 19.30
including the l. of Gilead, and the 20.01
which is in the l. of Canaan. 21.12
and go to the l. of Benjamin. 21.21
ruled there was a famine in the l., Ru 1.01
way to return to the l. of Judah. 1.07
and your native l. and came to a 2.11
the parcel of l. which belonged to 4.03
of your mice that ravage the l., 1Sa 6.05

LAND (cont.)

off you and your gods and your l. 1Sa 6.05
goes up on the way to its own l., 6.09
passed through the l. of Shalisha, 9.04
passed through the l. of Shaalim, 9.04
passed through the l. of Benjamin, 9.04
When they came to the l. of Zuph, 9.05
you a man from the l. of Benjamin, 9.16
fathers up out of the l. of Egypt. 12.06
the trumpet throughout all the l., 13.03
Jordan to the l. of Gad and Gilead. 13.07
toward Ophrah, to the l. of Shual, 13.17
throughout all the l. of Israel; 13.19
a furrow's length in an acre of l. 14.14
"My father has troubled the l.; 14.29
not this David the king of the l.? 21.11
depart, and go into the l. of Judah." 22.05
and if he is in the l., I will search 23.23
have made a raid upon the l." 23.27
escape to the l. of the Philistines; 27.01
inhabitants of the l. from of old, 27.08
as far as Shur, to the l. of Egypt. 27.08
And David smote the l., and left 27.09
and the wizards out of the l. 28.03
mediums and the wizards from the l. 28.09
return to the l. of the Philistines. 29.11
were spread abroad over all the l., 30.16
taken from the l. of the Philistines 30.16
Philistines and from the l. of Judah. 30.16
throughout the l. of the Philistines, 31.09
saying, "To whom does the l. belong? 2Sa 3.12
Jebusites, the inhabitants of the l., 5.06
to you all the l. of Saul your 9.07
servants shall till the l. for him, 9.10
came into the l. of the Ammonites. 10.02
"Oh that I were judge in the l.! 15.04
encamped in the l. of Gilead. 17.26
fled out of the l. from Absalom. 19.09
you and Ziba shall divide the l." 19.29
Jonathan in the l. of Benjamin in 21.14
heeded supplications for the l. 21.14
Kadesh in the l. of the Hittites; 24.06
they had gone through all the l., 24.08
of famine come to you in your l.? 24.13
three days' pestilence in your l.? 24.13
heeded supplications for the l., 24.25
Soco and all the l. of Hepher); 1Ki 4.10
in the l. of Gilead, the country of 4.19
was one officer in the l. of Judah. 4.19
Euphrates to the l. of the Philistines 4.21
Israel came out of the l. of Egypt, 6.01
they came out of the l. of Egypt. 8.09
them out of the l. of Egypt." 8.21
again to the l. which thou gavest 8.34
and grant rain upon they l., which thou 8.36
"If there is famine in the l., 8.37
live in the l. which thou gavest 8.40
captive to the l. of the enemy, 8.46
to heart in the l. to which they 8.47
to thee in the l. of their captors, 8.47
heart in the l. of their enemies, 8.48
and pray to thee toward their l., 8.48
Israel from the l. which I have 9.07
thus to this l. and to this house 9.08
fathers out of the l. of Egypt, 9.09
twenty cities in the l. of Galilee. 9.11
are called the l. of Cabul to this 9.13
wilderness, in the l. of Judah, 9.18
and in all the l. of his dominion. 9.19
who were left after them in the l., 9.21
of the Red Sea, in the l. of Edom. 9.26
heard in my own l. of your affairs 10.06
turned and went back to her own l., 10.13
and from the governors of the l. 10.15
allowance of food, and gave him l. 11.18
you up out of the l. of Egypt." 12.28
of this good l. which he gave to 14.15
male cult prostitutes in the l. 14.24
cult prostitutes out of the l., 15.12
with all the l. of Naphtali. 15.20
because there was no rain in the l. 17.07
"Go through the l. to all the 18.05
divided the l. between them to 18.06
called all the elders of the l., 20.07
Asa, he exterminated from the l. 22.46
is bad, and the l. is unfruitful." 2Ki 2.19
every good piece of l. with stones." 3.19
good piece of l. every man threw a 3.25
him and returned to their own l. 3.27
when there was a famine in the l. 4.38
little maid from the l. of Israel, 5.02
the maiden from the l. of Israel." 5.04
on raids into the l. of Israel. 6.23
come upon the l. for seven years. 8.01
sojourned in the l. of the Philistines 8.02
from the l. of the Philistines, she 8.03
the king for her house and her l. 8.03
the king for her house and her l. 8.05
day that she left the l. until now." 8.06
all the l. of Gilead, the Gadites, 10.33
while Athaliah reigned over the l. 11.03
people of the l. rejoicing and 11.14
people of the l. went to the house 11.18
and all the people of the l.; 11.19
So all the people of the l. rejoiced; 11.20
to invade the l. in the spring of 13.20
governing the people of the l. 15.05
of Assyria came against the l.; 15.19
and did not stay there in the l. 15.20
Galilee, all the l. of Naphtali; 15.29
of all the people of the l., 16.15
invaded all the l. and came to 17.05
up out of the l. of Egypt from 17.07
from their own l. to Assyria until 17.23
know the law of the god of the l.; 17.26
know the law of the god of the l." 17.26
them the law of the god of the l." 17.27
you out of the l. of Egypt with 17.36
said to me, Go up against this l., 18.25
you away to a l. like your own l., 18.32
a l. of grain and wine, a 18.32
a l. of bread and vineyards, a 18.32
a l. of olive trees and honey, that 18.32
delivered his l. out of the hand 18.33
a rumor and return to his own l.; 19.07
to fall by the sword in his own l.'" 19.07
and escaped into the l. of Ararat. 19.37
more out of the l. which I gave to 21.08
people of the l. slew all those 21.24
people of the l. made Josiah his 21.24
seen in the l. of Judah and in 23.24
people of the l. took Jehoahaz the 23.30
at Riblah in the l. of Hamath, 23.33
laid upon the l. a tribute of a 23.33
he taxed the l. to give the money 23.35
the gold of the people of the l., 23.35
did not come again out of his l., 24.07
the poorest people of the l. 24.14
and the chief men of the l., 24.15
no food for the people of the l. 25.03
poorest of the l. to be vinedressers 25.12
who mustered the people of the l.; 25.19
people of the l. who were found in 25.19
at Riblah in the l. of Hamath. 25.21
was taken into exile out of its l. 25.21
who remained in the l. of Judah, 25.22
dwell in the l., and serve the 25.24
reigned in the l. of Edom before 1Ch 1.43
Husham of the l. of the Temanites 1.45
twenty-three cities in the l. of Gilead. 2.22
and the l. was very broad, quiet, and 4.40
had multiplied in the l. of Gilead. 5.09
them in the l. of Bashan as far as 5.11
of Manasseh dwelt in the l.; 5.23
the gods of the peoples of the l., 5.25
Hebron in the l. of Judah and its 6.55

LAND (cont.)
Gath who were born in the l. slew, 1Ch 7.21
throughout the l. of the Philistines, 10.09
were, the inhabitants of the l. 11.04
who remain in all the l. of Israel, 13.02
you I will give the l. of Canaan, 16.18
to Hanun in the l. of the Ammonites, 19.02
to overthrow and to spy out the l.?" 19.03
the LORD, pestilence upon the l., 21.12
who were in the l. of Israel, 22.02
inhabitants of the l. into my hand; 22.18
and the l. is subdued before the 22.18
that you may possess this good l., 28.08
who were in the l. of Israel, 2Ch 2.17
my people out of the l. of Egypt, 6.05
again to the l. which thou gavest 6.25
and grant rain upon thy l., which 6.27
"If there is famine in the l., 6.28
live in the l. which thou gavest 6.31
away captive to a l. far or near; 6.36
to heart in the l. to which they 6.37
to thee in the l. of their captivity, 6.37
heart in the l. of their captivity, 6.38
captive, and pray toward their l., 6.38
the locust to devour the l., 7.13
their sin and heal their l. 7.14
you up from the l. which I have 7.20
thus to this l. and to this house?' 7.21
them out of the l. of Egypt, 7.22
and in all the l. of his dominion. 8.06
who were left after them in the l., 8.08
of the sea, in the l. of Edom. 8.17
heard in my own l. of your affairs 9.05
of them before in the l. of Judah. 9.11
turned and went back to her own l., 9.12
governors of the l. brought gold 9.14
Euphrates to the l. of the Philistines, 9.26
In his days the l. had rest for ten 14.01
in Judah, for the l. had rest. 14.06
the l. is still ours, because we 14.07
from all the l. of Judah and 15.08
set garrisons in the l. of Judah, 17.02
destroyed the Asherahs out of the l., 19.03
judges in the l. in all the 19.05
inhabitants of this l. before thy 20.07
they came from the l. of Egypt, 20.10
while Athaliah reigned over the l. 22.12
people of the l. rejoicing and 23.13
and all the people of the l.; 23.20
So all the people of the l. rejoiced; 23.21
governing the people of the l. 26.21
captors, and return to this l. 30.09
who came out of the l. of Israel, 30.25
of common l. belonging to their 31.19
brook that flowed through the l., 32.04
with shame of face to his own l. 32.21
sign that had been done in the l., 32.31
Israel from the l. which I appointed 33.08
people of the l. slew all those 33.25
people of the l. made Josiah his 33.25
throughout all the l. of Israel. 34.07
he had purged the l. and the house, 34.08
The people of the l. took Jehoahaz 36.01
laid upon the l. a tribute of a 36.03
until the l. had enjoyed its 36.21
people of the l. discouraged the Ez 4.04
peoples of the l. to worship the 6.21
'The l. which you are entering, to 9.11
is a l. unclean with the pollutions 9.11
strong, and eat the good of the l., 9.12
peoples of the l. and from the 10.11
plundered in a l. where they are Neh 4.04
their governor in the l. of Judah, 5.14
on this wall, and acquired no l.; 5.16
descendants the l. of the Canaanite, 9.08
and all the people of his l., 9.10
the midst of the sea on dry l.; 9.11
to possess the l. which thou hadst 9.15
possession of the l. of Sihon king 9.22
Heshbon and the l. of Og king of 9.22
them into the l. which thou hadst 9.23
went in and possessed the l., 9.24
them the inhabitants of the l., 9.24
kings and the peoples of the l., 9.24
fortified cities and a rich l., 9.25
large and rich l. which thou didst 9.35
in the l. that thou gavest to our 9.36
peoples of the l. or take their 10.30
peoples of the l. bring in wares 10.31
tribute on the l. and on the Est 10.01
There was a man in the l. of Uz, Job 1.01
possessions have increased in the l. 1.10
to the l. of gloom and deep darkness, 10.21
the l. of gloom and chaos, where 10.22
them out, they overwhelm the l. 12.15
to whom alone the l. was given, 15.19
The man with power possessed the l., 22.08
their portion is cursed in the l.; 24.18
not found in the l. of the living. 28.13
have been whipped out of the l. 30.08
"If my l. has cried out against me, 31.38
or for his l., or for love, he 37.13
to bring rain on a l. where no man 38.26
to satisfy the waste and desolate l., 38.27
and the salt l. for his dwelling 39.06
And in all the l. there were no 42.15
nations shall perish from his l. Ps 10.16
As for the saints in the l., 16.03
his children shall possess the l. 25.13
the LORD in the l. of the living! 27.13
quiet in the l. they conceive 35.20
so you will dwell in the l., 37.03
for the LORD shall possess the l. 37.09
But the meek shall possess the l., 37.11
by the LORD shall possess the l., 37.22
The righteous shall possess the l., 37.29
will exalt you to possess the l.; 37.34
he is called blessed in the l.; 41.02
thee from the l. of Jordan and of 42.06
own sword did they win the l., 44.03
you from the l. of the living. 52.05
Thou hast made the l. to quake, 60.02
a dry and weary l. where no water 63.01
He turned the sea into dry l.; 66.06
rebellious dwell in a parched l. 68.06
be abundance of grain in the l.; 72.16
meeting places of God in the l. 74.08
places of the l. are full of the 74.20
wrought marvels in the l. of Egypt, 78.12
And he brought them to his holy l., 78.54
took deep root and filled the l. 80.09
he went out over the l. of Egypt. 81.05
you up out of the l. of Egypt. 81.10
LORD, thou wast favorable to thy l.; 85.01
that glory may dwell in our l. 85.09
and our l. will yield its increase. 85.12
help in the l. of forgetfulness? 88.12
have dwelt in the l. of silence. 94.17
for his hands formed the dry l. 95.05
favor on the faithful in the l., 101.06
destroy all the wicked in the l., 101.08
I will give the l. of Canaan as 105.11
When he summoned a famine on the l., 105.16
Jacob sojourned in the l. of Ham. 105.23
and miracles in the l. of Ham. 105.27
darkness, and made the l. dark; 105.28
Their l. swarmed with frogs, even in 105.30
that flashed through their l. 105.32
all the vegetation in their l., 105.35
all the first-born in their l., 105.36
wondrous works in the l. of Ham, 106.22
Then they despised the pleasant l., 106.24
and the l. was polluted with blood. 106.38
a fruitful l. into a salty waste, 107.34
a parched l. into springs of water. 107.35
descendants will be mighty in the l.; 112.02

LAND (cont.)

the LORD in the l. of the living. Ps 116.09
rest upon the l. allotted to the 125.03
and gave their l. as a heritage, a 135.12
and gave their l. as a heritage, for 136.21
the LORD's song in a foreign l.? 137.04
slanderer be established in the l.; 140.11
one cleaves and shatters on the l., 141.07
my portion in the l. of the living. 142.05
thirsts for thee like a parched l. 143.06
For the upright will inhabit the l., Pro 2.21
wicked will be cut off from the l., 2.22
wicked will not dwell in the l. 10.30
He who tills his l. will have 12.11
in a desert l. than with a contentious 21.19
When a l. transgresses it has many 28.02
He who tills his l. will have 28.19
a king gives stability to the l., 29.04
he sits among the elders of the l. 31.23
advantage to a l. with cultivated Ecc 5.09
Woe to you, O l., when your king is 10.16
O l., when your king is the son of 10.17
the turtledove is heard in our l. Sol 2.12
presence aliens devour your l.; Is 1.07
you shall eat the good of the l.; 1.19
Their l. is filled with silver and 2.07
their l. is filled with horses, and 2.07
Their l. is filled with idols; 2.08
fruit of the l. shall be the pride 4.02
dwell alone in the midst of the l. 5.08
And if one look to the l., behold, 5.30
and the l. is utterly desolate, 6.11
are many in the midst of the l. 6.12
the l. before whose two kings you 7.16
bee which is in the l. of Assyria. 7.18
is left in the l. will eat curds 7.22
for all the l. will be briers and 7.24
the breadth of your l., O Immanuel." 8.08
They will pass through the l., 8.21
contempt the l. of Zebulun and the 9.01
of Zebulun and the l. of Naphtali, 9.01
the l. beyond the Jordan, Galilee of 9.01
who dwelt in a l. of deep darkness, 9.02
the LORD of hosts the l. is burned, 9.19
of his fruitful l. the LORD will 10.18
they came up from the l. of Egypt. 11.16
They come from a distant l., 13.05
every man will flee to his own l. 13.14
and will set them in their own l., 14.01
in the LORD's l. as male and 14.02
because you have destroyed your l., 14.20
I will break the Assyrian in my l., 14.25
cry has gone round the l. of Moab; 15.08
escape, for the remnant of the l. 15.09
sent lambs to the ruler of the l., 16.01
foot has vanished from the l., 16.04
Ah, l. of whirring wings which is 18.01
conquering, whose l. the rivers divide. 18.02
whose l. the rivers divide, to Mount 18.07
pillars of the l. will be crushed, 19.10
And the l. of Judah will become a 19.17
cities in the l. of Egypt which 19.18
in the midst of the l. of Egypt, 19.19
LORD of hosts in the l. of Egypt; 19.20
the desert, from a terrible l. 21.01
O inhabitants of the l. of Tema. 21.14
you like a ball into a wide l.; 22.18
From the l. of Cyprus it is revealed 23.01
Overflow your l. like the Nile, O 23.10
Behold the l. of the Chaldeans! 23.13
will be sung in the l. of Judah: 26.01
in the l. of uprightness he deals 26.10
enlarged all the borders of the l. 26.15
and on the l. of the shades thou 26.19
lost in the l. of Assyria and 27.13
out to the l. of Egypt will come 27.13
GOD of hosts upon the whole l. 28.22
Through a l. of trouble and anguish, 30.06
of a great rock in a weary l. 32.02
The l. mourns and languishes; 33.09
will behold a l. that stretches 33.17
great slaughter in the l. of Edom. 34.06
Their l. shall be soaked with blood, 34.07
her l. shall become burning pitch. 34.09
and the dry l. shall be glad, 35.01
up against this l. to destroy it?' " 36.10
said to me, Go up against this l., 36.10
you away to a l. like your own l., 36.17
a l. of grain and wine, a 36.17
a l. of bread and vineyards. 36.17
delivered his l. out of the hand 36.18
a rumor, and return to his own l.; 37.07
fall by the sword in his own l.' " 37.07
and escaped into the l. of Ararat. 37.38
the LORD in the l. of the living; 38.11
and the dry l. springs of water. 41.18
will pour water on the thirsty l., 44.03
in secret, in a l. of darkness; 45.19
to the people, to establish the l., 49.08
and these from the l. of Syene." 49.12
places and your devastated l.— 49.19
off out of the l. of the living, 53.08
refuge in me shall possess the l., 57.13
Violence shall no more be heard in your l., 60.18
they shall possess the l. for ever, 60.21
therefore in your l. you shall 61.07
and your l. shall no more be termed 62.04
is in her, and your l. Married; 62.04
and your l. shall be married. 62.04
himself in the l. shall bless 65.16
an oath in the l. shall swear by 65.16
Shall a l. be born in one day? 66.08
in Anathoth in the l. of Benjamin, Jer 1.01
upon all the inhabitants of the l. 1.14
bronze walls, against the whole l., 1.18
priests, and the people of the l. 1.18
the wilderness, in a l. not sown. 2.02
brought us up from the l. of Egypt, 2.06
in a l. of deserts and pits, in a 2.06
in a l. of drought and deep darkness, 2.06
in a l. that none passes through, 2.06
a plentiful l. to enjoy its fruits 2.07
when you came in you defiled my l., 2.07
They have made his l. a waste; 2.15
or a l. of thick darkness? 2.31
Would not that l. be greatly 3.01
polluted the l. with your vile 3.02
light to her, she polluted the l., 3.09
multiplied and increased in the l., 3.16
come from the l. of the north to 3.18
north to the l. that I gave your 3.18
sons, and give you a pleasant l., 3.19
"Blow the trumpet through the l.; 4.05
his place to make your l. a waste; 4.07
"Besiegers come from a distant l.; 4.16
disaster, the whole l. is laid waste. 4.20
the fruitful l. was a desert, and 4.26
The whole l. shall be a desolation 4.27
and served foreign gods in your l., 5.19
strangers in a l. that is not 5.19
thing has happened in the l.: 5.30
a desolation, an uninhabited l." 6.08
against the inhabitants of the l. 6.12
or sweet cane from a distant l.? 6.20
in the l. that I gave of old to 7.07
them out of the l. of Egypt, 7.22
came out of the l. of Egypt to 7.25
for the l. shall become a waste. 7.34
stallions the whole l. quakes. 8.16
and devour the l. and all that 8.16
the length and breadth of the l.: 8.19
truth has grown strong in the l.; 9.03
Why is the l. ruined and laid waste 9.12
because we have left the l., 9.19
inhabitants of the l. at this time, 10.18
them out of the l. of Egypt, 11.04

LAND (cont.)
to give them a l. flowing with Jer 11.05
them up out of the l. of Egypt, 11.07
him off from the l. of the living, 11.19
How long will the l. mourn, 12.04
and if in a safe l. you fall down, 12.05
The whole l. is made desolate, but 12.11
one end of the l. to the other; 12.12
I will pluck them up from their l., 12.14
to his heritage and each to his l. 12.15
all the inhabitants of this l.: 13.13
since there is no rain on the l., 14.04
thou be like a stranger in the l., 14.08
famines shall not come on this l.': 14.15
ply their trade through the l., 14.18
fork in the gates of the l.; 15.07
and contention to the whole l.! 15.10
enemies in a l. which you do not 15.14
fathers who begot them in this l.: 16.03
and small shall die in this l.; 16.06
you out of this l. into a l. which 16.13
of Israel out of the l. of Egypt,' 16.14
to their own l. which I gave to 16.15
polluted my l. with the carcasses 16.18
enemies in a l. which you do not 17.04
wilderness, in an uninhabited salt l. 17.06
from the l. of Benjamin, from the 17.26
making their l. a horror, a thing to 18.16
no more to see his native l. 22.10
he shall never see this l. again." 22.12
But to the l. to which they will 22.27
and cast into a l. which they do 22.28
O l., l., l., hear the word of the LORD! 22.29
and righteousness in the l. 23.05
of Israel out of the l. of Egypt,' 23.07
they shall dwell in their own l." 23.08
For the l. is full of adulterers; 23.10
because of the curse the l. mourns, 23.10
has gone forth into all the l." 23.15
place to the l. of the Chaldeans. 24.05
I will bring them back to this l. 24.06
of Jerusalem who remain in this l., 24.08
those who dwell in the l. of Egypt. 24.08
from the l. which I gave to them 24.10
dwell upon the l. which the LORD 25.05
against this l. and its inhabitants, 25.09
This whole l. shall become a ruin 25.11
the l. of the Chaldeans, for their 25.12
making the l. an everlasting waste. 25.12
bring upon that l. all the words 25.13
kings of the l. of Uz and all the 25.20
kings of the l. of the Philistines 25.20
for their l. has become a waste 25.38
elders of the l. arose and spoke 26.17
against this l. in words like 26.20
until the time of his own l. comes; 27.07
will be removed far from your l., 27.10
him, I will leave on its own l., 27.11
back to the l. which I gave to 30.03
from the l. of their captivity. 30.10
come back from the l. of the enemy. 31.16
words in the l. of Judah and in 31.23
bring them out of the l. of Egypt, 31.32
at Anathoth in the l. of Benjamin, 32.08
shall again be bought in this l." 32.15
and wonders in the l. of Egypt, 32.20
out of the l. of Egypt with signs 32.21
and thou gavest them this l., 32.22
a l. flowing with milk and honey; 32.22
them in this l. in faithfulness, 32.41
bought in this l. of which you are 32.43
in the l. of Benjamin, in the places 32.44
the fortunes of the l. as at first; 33.11
in the l. of Benjamin, the places 33.13
and righteousness in the l. 33.15
them out of the l. of Egypt, 34.13
people of the l. who passed 34.19
days in the l. where you sojourn.' 35.07
of Babylon came up against the l., 35.11
dwell in the l. which I gave to 35.15
certainly come and destroy this l., 36.29
made king in the l. of Judah, 37.01
people of the l. listened to the 37.02
to return to Egypt, to its own l. 37.07
to go to the l. of Benjamin to 37.12
against you and against this l.'? 37.19
at Riblah, in the l. of Hamath; 39.05
left in the l. of Judah some of the 39.10
See, the whole l. is before you; 40.04
the people who were left in the l. 40.06
son of Ahikam governor in the l., 40.07
poorest of the l. who had not been 40.07
Dwell in the l., and serve the king 40.09
driven and came to the l. of Judah, 40.12
had appointed governor in the l. 41.02
had made governor over the l. 41.18
If you will remain in this l., 42.10
and let you remain in your own l. 42.12
'We will not remain in this l., 42.13
'No, we will go to the l. of Egypt, 42.14
you there in the l. of Egypt; 42.16
LORD, to remain in the l. of Judah. 43.04
to live in the l. of Judah from 43.05
And they came into the l. of Egypt, 43.07
come and smite the l. of Egypt, 43.11
and he shall clean the l. of Egypt, 43.12
which is in the l. of Egypt; 43.13
Jews that dwelt in the l. of Egypt, 44.01
Memphis, and in the l. of Pathros, 44.01
gods in the l. of Egypt where you 44.08
committed in the l. of Judah and in 44.09
to come to the l. of Egypt to live, 44.12
in the l. of Egypt they shall fall; 44.12
those who dwell in the l. of Egypt, 44.13
to live in the l. of Egypt shall 44.14
or return to the l. of Judah, 44.14
in Pathros in the l. of Egypt, 44.15
princes, and the people of the l., 44.21
therefore your l. has become a 44.22
Judah who are in the l. of Egypt, 44.24
Judah who dwell in the l. of Egypt: 44.26
of Judah in all the l. of Egypt, 44.26
who are in the l. of Egypt shall 44.27
from the l. of Egypt to the l. of Judah, 44.28
who came to the l. of Egypt to 44.28
plucking up—that is, the whole l. 45.04
Babylon to smite the l. of Egypt: 46.13
people and to the l. of our birth, 46.16
from the l. of their captivity. 46.27
overflow the l. and all that fills 47.02
inhabitant of the l. shall wail. 47.02
all the cities of the l. of Moab, 48.24
away from the fruitful l. of Moab; 48.33
concerning the l. of the Chaldeans, 50.01
shall make her l. a desolation, 50.03
go out of the l. of the Chaldeans, 50.08
every one shall flee to his own l. 50.16
on the king of Babylon and his l., 50.18
"Go up against the l. of Merathaim, 50.21
The noise of battle is in the l., 50.22
to do in the l. of the Chaldeans. 50.25
and escape from the l. of Babylon, 50.28
For it is a l. of images, and they 50.38
against the l. of the Chaldeans: 50.45
her, and they shall empty her l., 51.02
slain in the l. of the Chaldeans, 51.04
but the l. of the Chaldeans is full 51.05
and every l. under their dominion. 51.28
The l. trembles and writhes in pain, 51.29
to make the l. of Babylon a desolation, 51.29
a l. of drought and a desert, a 51.43
a l. in which no one dwells, and 51.43
at the report heard in the l., 51.46
year, and violence is in the l., 51.46
her whole l. shall be put to shame, 51.47
through all her l. the wounded 51.52

LAND (cont.)

from the l. of the Chaldeans!	Jer 51.54
no food for the people of the l.	52.06
at Riblah in the l. of Hamath,	52.09
poorest of the l. to be vinedressers	52.16
who mustered the people of the l.;	52.25
sixty men of the people of the l.,	52.25
at Riblah in the l. of Hamath.	52.27
was carried captive out of its l.	52.27
of Edom, dweller in the l. of Uz;	Lam 4.21
in the l. of the Chaldeans by the	Eze 1.03
and make the l. desolate and waste,	6.14
the Lord GOD to the l. of Israel:	7.02
upon the four corners of the l.	7.02
to you, O inhabitant of the l.;	7.07
Because the l. is full of bloody	7.23
people of the l. are palsied by	7.27
us, the LORD has forsaken the l.'"	8.12
should fill the l. with violence,	8.17
the l. is full of blood, and the	9.09
say, 'The LORD has forsaken the l.,	9.09
to us this l. is given for a	11.15
I will give you the l. of Israel.'	11.17
face, that you may not see the l.;	12.06
may not see the l. with his eyes.	12.12
Babylon in the l. of the Chaldeans,	12.13
and say of the people of the l.,	12.19
of Jerusalem in the l. of Israel:	12.19
because their l. will be stripped	12.19
and the l. shall become a desolation;	12.20
you have about the l. of Israel,	12.22
shall they enter the l. of Israel;	13.09
when a l. sins against me by acting	14.13
wild beasts to pass through the l.,	14.15
but the l. would be desolate.	14.16
Or if I bring a sword upon that l.,	14.17
say, Let a sword go through the l.;	14.17
I send a pestilence into that l.,	14.19
And I will make the l. desolate,	15.08
are of the l. of the Canaanites;	16.03
with the trading l. of Chaldea;	16.29
and carried it to a l. of trade,	17.04
the seed of the l. and planted it	17.05
men of the l. he had taken away,	17.13
concerning the l. of Israel,	18.02
him with hooks to the l. of Egypt.	19.04
and the l. was appalled and all who	19.07
wilderness, in a dry and thirsty l.	19.13
known to them in the l. of Egypt,	20.05
them out of the l. of Egypt into a	20.06
of Egypt into a l. that I had	20.06
a l. flowing with milk and honey,	20.06
in the midst of the l. of Egypt.	20.08
them out of the l. of Egypt.	20.09
them out of the l. of Egypt and	20.10
them into the l. which I had given	20.15
a l. flowing with milk and honey,	20.15
them into the l. which I swore to	20.28
the wilderness of the l. of Egypt,	20.36
them out of the l. where they	20.38
shall not enter the l. of Israel.	20.38
of them, shall serve me in the l.;	20.40
I bring you into the l. of Israel,	20.42
against the forest l. in the Negeb;	20.46
prophesy against the l. of Israel	21.02
and say to the l. of Israel, Thus	21.03
shall come forth from the same l.	21.19
in the l. of your origin, I will	21.30
shall be in the midst of the l.;	21.32
You are a l. that is not cleansed,	22.24
The people of the l. have practiced	22.29
in the breach before me for the l.,	22.30
whose native l. was Chaldea.	23.15
the harlot in the l. of Egypt	23.19
brought from the l. of Egypt;	23.27
I put an end to lewdness in the l.,	23.48
and over the l. of Israel when it	25.03
you against the l. of Israel,	25.06
a place in the l. of the living.	26.20
Judah and the l. of Israel traded	27.17
in their own l. which I gave to my	28.25
and the l. of Egypt shall be a	29.09
I will make the l. of Egypt an	29.10
And I will make the l. of Egypt a	29.12
them back to the l. of Pathros,	29.14
the l. of their origin; and there	29.14
I will give the l. of Egypt to	29.19
given him the l. of Egypt as his	29.20
people of the l. that is in league,	30.05
be brought in to destroy the l.;	30.11
and fill the l. with the slain.	30.11
will sell the l. into the hand of	30.12
upon the l. and everything in it,	30.12
be a prince in the l. of Egypt;	30.13
I will put fear in the l. of Egypt.	30.13
it out against the l. of Egypt;	30.25
in all the watercourses of the l.;	31.12
I will drench the l. even to the	32.06
you, and put darkness upon your l.,	32.08
When I make the l. of Egypt desolate	32.15
and when the l. is stripped of all	32.15
terror in the l. of the living.	32.23
terror in the l. of the living,	32.24
was spread in the l. of the living,	32.25
terror in the l. of the living.	32.26
men was in the l. of the living.	32.27
terror in the l. of the living;	32.32
If I bring the sword upon a l.,	33.02
people of the l. take a man from	33.02
coming upon the l. and blows the	33.03
places in the l. of Israel keep	33.24
yet he got possession of the l.;	33.24
the l. is surely given us to	33.24
shall you then possess the l.?	33.25
shall you then possess the l.?	33.26
And I will make the l. a desolation	33.28
I have made the l. a desolation	33.29
will bring them into their own l.;	34.13
shall lie down in good grazing l.,	34.14
and banish wild beasts from the l.,	34.25
they shall be secure in their l.;	34.27
the beasts of the l. devour them;	34.28
be consumed with hunger in the l.,	34.29
who gave my l. to themselves as a	36.05
concerning the l. of Israel,	36.06
of Israel dwelt in their own l.,	36.17
which they had shed in the l.,	36.18
yet they had to go out of his l.'	36.20
and bring you into your own l.	36.24
dwell in the l. which I gave to	36.28
And the l. that was desolate shall	36.34
'This l. that was desolate has	36.35
you home into the l. of Israel.	37.12
I will place you in your own l.;	37.14
and bring them to their own l.;	37.21
make them one nation in the l.,	37.22
dwell in the l. where your fathers	37.25
of the l. of Magog, the chief prince	38.02
go against the l. that is restored	38.08
the l. where people were gathered	38.08
be like a cloud covering the l.,	38.09
up against the l. of unwalled	38.11
like a cloud covering the l.	38.16
I will bring you against my l.,	38.16
come against the l. of Israel,	38.18
great shaking in the l. of Israel;	38.19
them, in order to cleanse the l.	39.12
people of the l. will bury them;	39.13
through the l. continually and	39.14
remaining upon the face of the l.,	39.14
through the l. and any one sees a	39.15
Thus shall they cleanse the l.	39.16
in their l. with none to make them	39.26
gathered them into their own l.	39.28
of God into the l. of Israel,	40.02
"When you allot the l. as a possession,	45.01

LAND (cont.)

portion of the l. as a holy Eze 45.01
be the holy portion of the l.; 45.04
belong the l. on both sides of the 45.07
to the eastern boundary of the l. 45.07
Israel have the l. according to 45.08
people of the l. shall give this 45.16
people of the l. a young bull for 45.22
The people of the l. shall worship 46.03
people of the l. come before the 46.09
divide the l. for inheritance 47.13
and this l. shall fall to you as 47.14
"This shall be the boundary of the l.: 47.15
Gilead and the l. of Israel; 47.18
divide this l. among you according 47.21
from the holy portion of the l., 48.12
this choice portion of the l., 48.14
And the city shall have open l.: 48.17
This is the l. which you shall 48.29
brought them to the l. of Shinar, Dan 1.02
east, and toward the glorious l. 8.09
and to all the people of the l. 9.06
out of the l. of Egypt with a 9.15
but shall return into his own l. 11.09
he shall stand in the glorious l., 11.16
the fortresses of his own l.; 11.19
return to his l. with great 11.28
his will, and return to his own l. 11.28
shall divide the l. for a price. 11.39
He shall come into the glorious l. 11.41
and the l. of Egypt shall not 11.42
for the l. commits great harlotry Hos 1.02
and they shall go up from the l., 1.11
and set her like a parched l., 2.03
she came out of the l. of Egypt. 2.15
the sword, and war from the l.; 2.18
will sow him for myself in the l. 2.23
with the inhabitants of the l. 4.01
and no knowledge of God in the l.; 4.01
Therefore the l. mourns, and all who 4.03
their derision in the l. of Egypt. 7.16
not remain in the l. of the LORD; 9.03
They shall return to the l. of Egypt, 11.05
like doves from the l. of Assyria; 11.11
LORD your God from the l. of Egypt; 12.09
(Jacob fled to the l. of Aram, 12.12
LORD your God from the l. of Egypt; 13.04
wilderness, in the l. of drought; 13.05
ear, all inhabitants of the l.! Joe 1.02
a nation has come up against my l., 1.06
inhabitants of the l. to the house 1.14
the inhabitants of the l. tremble, 2.01
The l. is like the garden of Eden 2.03
the LORD became jealous for his l., 2.18
him into a parched and desolate l., 2.20
Fear not, O l.; be glad and rejoice, 2.21
nations, and have divided up my l., 3.02
shed innocent blood in their l. 3.19
you up out of the l. of Egypt, Amo 2.10
to possess the l. of the Amorite. 2.10
brought up out of the l. of Egypt: 3.01
the strongholds in the l. of Egypt, 3.09
"An adversary shall surround the l., 3.11
forsaken on her l., with none to raise 5.02
finished eating the grass of the l., 7.02
deep and was eating up the l. 7.04
the l. is not able to bear all his 7.10
go into exile away from his l.'" 7.11
go, flee away to the l. of Judah, 7.12
and your l. shall be parceled out 7.17
yourself shall die in an unclean l., 7.17
go into exile away from its l." 7.17
the poor of the l. to an end, 8.04
Shall not the l. tremble on this 8.08
I will send a famine on the l.; 8.11
up Israel from the l. of Egypt, 9.07
I will plant them upon their l., 9.15
up out of the l. which I have 9.15
Shephelah the l. of the Philistines; Ob 1.19
possess the l. of Ephraim and the 1.19
Ephraim and the l. of Samaria and 1.19
who made the sea and the dry l." Jon 1.09
hard to bring the ship back to l., 1.13
down to the l. whose bars closed 2.06
vomited out Jonah upon the dry l. 2.10
comes into our l. and treads upon Mic 5.05
they shall rule the l. of Assyria 5.06
and the l. of Nimrod with the drawn 5.06
comes into our l. and treads 5.06
cities of your l. and throw down 5.11
you up from the l. of Egypt, 6.04
forest in the midst of a garden l.; 7.14
came out of the l. of Egypt I will 7.15
gates of your l. are wide open to Nah 3.13
curtains of the l. of Midian did Hab 3.07
the LORD, all you humble of the l., Zep 2.03
O Canaan, l. of the Philistines; 2.05
a l. possessed by nettles and salt 2.09
drought upon the l. and the hills, Hag 1.11
people of the l., says the LORD; 2.04
earth and the sea and the dry l.; 2.06
against the l. of Judah to scatter Zec 1.21
Flee from the l. of the north, says 2.06
as his portion in the holy l., 2.12
guilt of this l. in a single day. 3.09
out over the face of the whole l.; 5.03
"This is the iniquity in all the l." 5.06
"To the l. of Shinar, to build a 5.11
people of the l. and the priests, 7.05
Thus the l. they left was desolate, 7.14
the pleasant l. was made desolate." 7.14
is against the l. of Hadrach and 9.01
a crown they shall shine on his l. 9.16
them home from the l. of Egypt, 10.10
them to the l. of Gilead and to 10.10
inhabitants of this l., says the LORD. 11.06
up in the l. a shepherd who does 11.16
The l. shall mourn, each family by 12.12
the names of the idols from the l., 13.02
remove from the l. the prophets 13.02
for the l. has been my possession 13.05
In the whole l., says the LORD, two 13.08
The whole l. shall be turned into a 14.10
for you will be a l. of delight, Mal 3.12
come and smite the l. with a curse." 4.06
in the l. of Judah, are by no means Mt 2.06
and go to the l. of Israel, for 2.20
and went to the l. of Israel. 2.21
l. of Zebulun and the l. of Naphtali, 4.15
judgment for the l. of Sodom and 10.15
judgment for the l. of Sodom than 11.24
many furlongs distant from the l., 14.24
they came to l. at Gennesaret. 14.34
traverse sea and l. to make a 23.15
over all the l. until the ninth 27.45
crowd was beside the sea on the l. Mk 4.01
sea, and he was alone on the l. 6.47
they came to l. at Gennesaret, and 6.53
over the whole l. until the ninth 15.33
a great famine over all the l.; Lk 4.25
in the l. of Sidon, to a woman who 4.26
to put out a little from the l. 5.03
they had brought their boats to l., 5.11
And as he stepped out on l., 8.27
"The l. of a rich man brought forth 12.16
neither for the l. nor for the 14.35
over the whole l. until the ninth 23.44
disciples went into the l. of Judea; Jn 3.22
boat was at the l. to which they 6.21
for they were not far from the l., 21.08
When they got out on l., 21.09
part of the proceeds of the l.? Ac 5.03
you sold the l. for so much." 5.08
from your l. and from your kindred 7.03
and go into the l. which I will 7.03
from the l. of the Chaldeans, and 7.04

LAND (cont.)
there into this l. in which you Ac 7.04
be aliens in a l. belonging to 7.06
an exile in the l. of Midian, 7.29
led us out from the l. of Egypt, 7.40
their stay in the l. of Egypt, 13.17
seven nations in the l. of Canaan, 13.19
gave them their l. as an inheritance, 13.19
intending himself to go by l. 20.13
northeaster, struck down from the l.; 27.14
suspected that they were nearing l. 27.27
day, they did not recognize the l., 27.39
overboard first and make for the l., 27.43
so it was that all escaped to l. 27.44
For l. which has drunk the rain Heb 6.07
lead them out of the l. of Egypt; 8.09
he sojourned in the l. of promise, 11.09
of promise, as in a foreign l., 11.09
thinking of that l. from which they 11.15
the Red Sea as if on dry l.; 11.29
a people out of the l. of Egypt, Jud 1.05
sea, and his left foot on the l., Rev 10.02
on sea and l. lifted up his right 10.05
standing on the sea and on the l." 10.08

LANDED
As he l. he saw a great throng, and Mk 6.34
When he had l. at Caesarea, he went Ac 18.22
we sailed to Syria, and l. at Tyre; 21.03

LANDINGS
the sea, settling down by his l. Ju 5.17

LANDMARK
not remove your neighbor's l., Deu 19.14
he who removes his neighbor's l.' 27.17
Remove not the ancient l. which Pro 22.28
an ancient l. or enter the fields 23.10
like those who remove the l.; Hos 5.10

LANDMARKS
Men remove l.; they seize flocks and Job 24.02

LANDS
the sons of Japheth in their l., Gen 10.05
languages, their l., and their nations. 10.20
languages, their l., and their nations. 10.31
descendants I will give all these l., 26.03
to your descendants all these l.; 26.04
There was famine in all l.; 41.54
my lord but our bodies and our l. 47.18
hearts in the l. of their enemies; Lev 26.36
your enemies' l. because of their 26.39
Levites pasture l. round about the Num 35.02
their pasture l. shall be for 35.03
The pasture l. of the cities, which 35.04
forty-eight, with their pasture l. 35.07
their pasture l. for their cattle Jos 14.04
their pasture l. for our cattle." 21.02
and pasture l. out of their 21.03
their pasture l. the people of 21.08
with the pasture l. round about it. 21.11
the slayer, with its pasture l., 21.13
Libnah with its pasture l., 21.13
Jattir with its pasture l., 21.14
Eshtemoa with its pasture l., 21.14
Holon with its pasture l., 21.15
Debir with its pasture l., 21.15
Ain with its pasture l., 21.16
Juttah with its pasture l., 21.16
Bethshemesh with its pasture l.— 21.16
Benjamin, Gibeon with its pasture l., 21.17
Geba with its pasture l., 21.17
Anathoth with its pasture l., 21.18
Almon with its pasture l.—four 21.18
cities with their pasture l. 21.19
its pasture l. in the hill country 21.21
Ephraim, Gezer with its pasture l., 21.21
Kibzaim with its pasture l., 21.22
Bethhoron with its pasture l.—four 21.22
of Dan, Elteke with its pasture l., 21.23
Gibbethon with its pasture l., 21.23
Aijalon with its pasture l., 21.24
Gathrimmon with its pasture l.—four 21.24
Taanach with its pasture l., 21.25
Gathrimmon with its pasture l.—two 21.25
ten in all with their pasture l. 21.26
in Bashan with its pasture l., 21.27
Beeshterah with its pasture l.—two 21.27
Kishion with its pasture l., 21.28
Daberath with its pasture l., 21.28
Jarmuth with its pasture l., 21.29
Engannim with its pasture l.—four 21.29
Asher, Mishal with its pasture l., 21.30
lands, Abdon with its pasture l., 21.30
Helkath with its pasture l., 21.31
Rehob with its pasture l.—four 21.31
in Galilee with its pasture l., 21.32
Hammothdor with its pasture l., 21.32
Kartan with its pasture l.—three 21.32
cities with their pasture l. 21.33
Jokneam with its pasture l., 21.34
Kartah with its pasture l., 21.34
Dimnah with its pasture l., 21.35
Nahalal with its pasture l.—four 21.35
Reuben, Bezer with its pasture l., 21.36
Jahaz with its pasture l., 21.36
Kedemoth with its pasture l., 21.37
Mephaath with its pasture l.—four 21.37
in Gilead with its pasture l., 21.38
Mahanaim with its pasture l., 21.38
Heshbon with its pasture l., 21.39
Jazer with its pasture l.—four 21.39
cities with their pasture l. 21.41
each its pasture l. round about it; 21.42
of Assyria have done to all l., 2Ki 9.11
waste the nations and their l., 19.17
all the pasture l. of Sharon to 1Ch 5.16
and its surrounding pasture l., 6.55
Hebron, Libnah with its pasture l., 6.57
Eshtemoa with its pasture l., 6.57
Hilen with its pasture l., 6.58
Debir with its pasture l., 6.58
Ashan with its pasture l., 6.59
Bethshemesh with its pasture l.; 6.59
Benjamin, Geba with its pasture l., 6.60
Alemeth, with its pasture l., 6.60
and Anathoth with its pasture l. 6.60
the cities with their pasture l. 6.64
its pasture l. in the hill country 6.67
Ephraim, Gezer with its pasture l., 6.67
Jokmeam with its pasture l., 6.68
Bethhoron with its pasture l., 6.68
Aijalon with its pasture l., 6.69
Gathrimmon with its pasture l., 6.69
Manasseh, Aner with its pasture l., 6.70
and Bileam with its pasture l., 6.70
Golan in Bashan with its pasture l. and 6.71
and Ashtaroth with its pasture l.; 6.71
Issachar: Kedesh with its pasture l., 6.72
Daberath with its pasture l., 6.72
Ramoth with its pasture l., 6.73
and Anem with its pasture l.; 6.73
Asher: Mashal with its pasture l., 6.74
Abdon with its pasture l., 6.74
Hukok with its pasture l., 6.75
and Rehob with its pasture l.; 6.75
in Galilee with its pasture l., 6.76
Hammon with its pasture l., 6.76
and Kiriathaim with its pasture l. 6.76
Rimmono with its pasture l., 6.77
Tabor with its pasture l., 6.77
in the steppe with its pasture l., 6.78
Jahzah with its pasture l., 6.78
Kedemoth with its pasture l., 6.79
and Mephaath with its pasture l.; 6.79

LANDS (cont.)
in Gilead with its pasture l., 1Ch 6.80
Mahanaim with its pasture l., 6.80
Heshbon with its pasture l., 6.81
and Jazer with its pasture l. 6.81
in the cities that have pasture l., 13.02
fame of David went out into all l., 14.17
fame and glory throughout all l.; 22.05
Solomon from Egypt and from all l. 2Ch 9.28
their common l. and their holdings 11.14
like the peoples of other l.? 13.09
all the inhabitants of the l. 15.05
kingdoms of the l. that were round 17.10
in the hills and in the fertile l., 26.10
to all the peoples of other l.? 32.13
of those l. at all able to deliver 32.13
to deliver their l. out of my hand? 32.13
nations of the l. who have not 32.17
because of the peoples of the l., Ez 3.03
peoples of the l. with their 9.01
itself with the peoples of the l. 9.02
the hand of the kings of the l., 9.07
pollutions of the peoples of the l., 9.11
women from the peoples of the l., 10.02
the hand of the peoples of the l. Neh 9.30
peoples of the l. to the law of 10.28
though they named l. their own. Ps 49.11
noise to the LORD, all the l.! 100.01
he gave them the l. of the nations; 105.44
scattering them over the l. 106.27
and gathered in from the l., 107.03
of Assyria have done to all l., Is 37.11
all the nations and their l., 37.18
given all these l. into the hand Jer 27.06
and in other l. heard that the 40.11
honey, the most glorious of all l. Eze 20.06
the most glorious of all l., 20.15
desperse them throughout the l. 30.23
them from their enemies' l., 39.27
in all the l. to which thou hast Dan 9.07
place, all the l. of the nations. Zep 2.11
father or mother or children or l., Mt 19.29
mother or father or children or l., Mk 10.29
and mothers and children and l., 10.30
possessors of l. or houses sold Ac 4.34
that place were l. belonging to 28.07
preach the gospel in l. beyond you, 2Co 10.16

LANES
to the streets and l. of the city, Lk 14.21

LANGUAGE
their lands, each with his own l., Gen 10.05
earth had one l. and few words. 11.01
people, and they have all one l.; 11.06
down, and there confuse their l., 11.07
confused the l. of all the earth; 11.09
a nation whose l. you do not Deu 28.49
to your servants in the Aramaic l., 2Ki 18.26
to us in the l. of Judah within 18.26
in a loud voice in the l. of Judah: 18.28
voice in the l. of Judah to the 2Ch 32.18
children spoke the l. of Ashdod, Neh 13.24
could not speak the l. of Judah, 13.24
Judah, but the l. of each people. 13.24
and to every people in its own l., Est 1.22
according to the l. of his people. 1.22
and every people in its own l.; 3.12
and to every people in its own l., 8.09
Jews in their script and their l. 8.09
Jacob from a people of strange l., Ps 114.01
which speak the l. of Canaan and Is 19.18
to us in the l. of Judah within 36.11
in a loud voice in the l. of Judah: 36.13
a nation whose l. you do not know, Jer 5.15
of foreign speech and a hard l., Eze 3.05
of foreign speech and a hard l., 3.06
the letters and l. of the Chaldeans. Dan 1.04
or l. that speaks anything against 3.29
was called in their l. Akeldama, Ac 1.19
heard them speaking in his own l. 2.06
each of us in his own native l.? 2.08
to them in the Hebrew l., saying: 21.40
he addressed them in the Hebrew l., 22.02
saying to me in the Hebrew l., 26.14
do not know the meaning of the l., 1Co 14.11

LANGUAGES
their l., their lands, and their Gen 10.20
their l., their lands, and their 10.31
O peoples, nations, and l., Dan 3.04
and l. fell down and worshiped the 3.07
and l., that dwell in all the earth: 4.01
and l. trembled and feared before 5.19
and l. that dwell in all the earth: 6.25
nations, and l. should serve him; 7.14
many different l. in the world, 1Co 14.10

LANGUISH
For the fields of Heshbon l., Is 16.08
and they will l. who spread nets 19.08
the heavens l. together with the 24.04
"Judah mourns and her gates l.; Jer 14.02
garden, and they shall l. no more. 31.12
wall to lament, they l. together. Lam 2.08
mourns, and all who dwell in it l., Hos 4.03

LANGUISHED
land of Canaan l. by reason of the Gen 47.13
restore thy heritage as it l.; Ps 68.09
She who bore seven has l.; Jer 15.09

LANGUISHES
My soul l. for thy salvation; Ps 119.81
withers, the world l. and withers; Is 24.04
the vine l., all the merry-hearted 24.07
The land mourns and l.; Lebanon is 33.09
destroyed, the wine fails, the oil l. Joe 1.10
The vine withers, the fig tree l. 1.12

LANGUISHING
and failing eyes, and a l. soul; Deu 28.65
gracious to me, O LORD, for I am l.; Ps 6.02
and every l. soul I will replenish." Jer 31.25

LANTERNS
went there with l. and torches and Jn 18.03

LAODICEA
for you, and for those at L., Col 2.01
for those in L. and in Hierapolis. 4.13
my greetings to the brethren at L., 4.15
you read also the letter from L. 4.16
and to Philadelphia and to L. Rev 1.11
angel of the church in L. write: 3.14

LAODICEANS
read also in the church of the L.; Col 4.16

LAP
the child sat on her l. till noon, 2Ki 4.20
from it his l. full of wild gourds, 4.39
I also shook out my l. and said, Neh 5.13
The lot is cast into the l., Pro 16.33
over, will be put into your l. Lk 6.38

LAPPED
And the number of those that l., Ju 7.06
men that l. I will deliver you, and 7.07

LAPPIDOTH
the wife of L., was judging Israel Ju 4.04

LAPS
"Every one that l. the water with Ju 7.05
as a dog l., you shall set by 7.05

LARGE
stone on the well's mouth was l., Gen 29.02
and had l. flocks, maidservants and 30.43
the land is l. enough for them; 34.21
cities are fortified and very l.; Num 13.28
To a l. tribe you shall give a 26.54
you shall give a l. inheritance, 26.54
to a l. tribe you shall give a 33.54
you shall give a l. inheritance, 33.54
kinds of weights, a l. and a small. Deu 25.13
of measures, a l. and a small. 25.14
you, you shall set up l. stones, 27.02
tribe of Judah was too l. for them, Jos 19.09
two hundred l. shields of beaten 1Ki 10.16
two hundred l. shields of beaten 2Ch 9.15
spears and the l. and small 23.09
for he had l. herds, both in the 26.10
The city was wide and l., but the Neh 7.04
and in the l. and rich land which 9.35
prepared for Tobiah a l. chamber 13.05
l. and beautiful houses, without Is 5.09
"Take a l. tablet and write upon it 8.01
cattle will graze in l. pastures; 30.23
slain was the l. cistern which Jer 41.09
"Take in your hands l. stones. 43.09
give him horses and a l. army. Eze 17.15
sister's cup which is deep and l.; 23.32
its boughs grew l. and its branches 31.05
and l. crowds followed him, and he Mt 19.02
might have been sold for a l. sum, 26.09
And a very l. crowd gathered about Mk 4.01
shrubs, and puts forth l. branches, 4.32
Many rich people put in l. sums. 12.41
will show you a l. upper room 14.15
rolled back; for it was very l. 16.04
and there was a l. company of tax Lk 5.29
and a l. crowd from the city was 7.12
Now a l. herd of swine was feeding 8.32
will show you a l. upper room 22.12
full of l. fish, a hundred and fifty Jn 21.11
And a l. company was added to the Ac 11.24
and taught a l. company of people; 11.26
this citizenship for a l. sum." 22.28
See with what l. letters I am Gal 6.11

LARGENESS
and l. of mind like the sand on the 1Ki 4.29

LARGER
lot between the l. and the smaller Num 26.56
from the l. tribes you shall take 35.08
and an army l. than your own, Deu 20.01
the smaller ledge to the l. ledge, Eze 43.14
down my barns, and build l. ones; Lk 12.18

LASEA
near which was the city of L. Ac 27.08

LASHA
Admah, and Zeboiim, as far as L. Gen 10.19

LASHARON
of Aphek, one; the king of L., one; Jos 12.18

LASHES
of the Jews the forty l. less one. 2Co 11.24

LAST
"This at l. is bone of my bones and Gen 2.23
old, all the people to the l. man, 19.04
I lay l. night with my father; 19.34
Abraham breathed his l. and died in 25.08
he breathed his l. and died, 25.17
your father spoke to me l. night, 31.29
my hands, and rebuked you l. night." 31.42
and Rachel and Joseph l. of all. 33.02
and l. Joseph and Rachel drew near, 33.07
And Isaac breathed his l.; 35.29
into the bed, and breathed his l., 49.33
threshing shall l. to the time of Lev 26.05
vintage shall l. to the time for 26.05
They shall set out l., standard by Num 2.31
until the l. of your dead bodies 14.33
and to the l. of the children who Deu 28.54
to the very l. had fallen by the Jos 8.24
have made this l. kindness greater Ru 3.10
and they halted at the l. house. 2Sa 15.17
you be the l. to bring the king 19.11
you be the l. to bring back the 19.12
Now these are the l. words of David: 23.01
for by the l. words of David these 1Ch 23.27
from first to l., are written in 29.29
from first to l., are they not 2Ch 9.29
from first to l., are they not 12.15
from first to l., are written in 16.11
from first to l., are written in 20.34
from first to l., are they not 25.26
from first to l., Isaiah the 26.22
from first to l., behold, they are 28.26
first and l., behold, they are 35.27
from the first day to the l. day, Neh 8.18
their hope is to breathe their l." Job 11.20
man breathes his l., and where is he? 14.10
and at l. he will stand upon the 19.25
the minstrels l., between them Ps 68.25
and their fate would l. for ever. 81.15
At the l. it bites like a serpent, Pro 23.32
for riches do not l. for ever; 27.24
LORD, the first, and with the l.; Is 41.04
"I am the first and I am the l.; 44.06
I am the first, and I am the l. 48.12
that they may l. for a long time. Jer 32.14
she shall be the l. of the nations, 50.12
and now at l. Nebuchadrezzar king 50.17
At l. Daniel came in before me—he Dan 4.08
and the higher one came up l. 8.03
even the l. of you with fishhooks. Amo 4.02
till you have paid the l. penny. Mt 5.26
and the l. state of that man 12.45
But many that are first will be l., 19.30
will be last, and the l. first. 19.30
their wages, beginning with the l., 20.08
saying, 'These l. worked only one 20.12
to give to this l. as I give to 20.14
So the l. will be first, and the 20.16
will be first, and the first l." 20.16
came forward. At l. two came forward 26.60
and the l. fraud will be worse than 27.64
he must be l. of all and servant of Mk 9.35
are first will be l., and the l. first." 10.31
L. of all the woman also died. 12.22
a loud cry, and breathed his l. 15.37
saw that he thus breathed his l., 15.39
and the l. state of that man Lk 11.26
you have paid the very l. copper. 12.59
some are l. who will be first, and 13.30
and some are first who will be l." 13.30
said this he breathed his l. 23.46
me, but raise it up at the l. day. Jn 6.39
I will raise him up at the l. day. 6.40
I will raise him up at the l. day. 6.44
I will raise him up at the l. day. 6.54
On the l. day of the feast, the 7.37
in the resurrection at the l. day." 11.24
will be his judge on the l. day. 12.48
'And in the l. days it shall be, God Ac 2.17
being saved was at l. abandoned. 27.20
I may now at l. succeed in coming Rom 1.10
exhibited us apostles as l. of all, 1Co 4.09
L. of all, as to one untimely born, 15.08
The l. enemy to be destroyed is 15.26
the l. Adam became a life-giving 15.45
of an eye, at the l. trumpet. 15.52
has been ready since l. year; 2Co 9.02
wrath has come upon them at l.! 1Th 2.16
that in the l. days there will come 2Ti 3.01

LAST (cont.)
but in these l. days he has spoken Heb 1.02
laid up treasure for the l. days. Jas 5.03
to be revealed in the l. time. 1Pe 1.05
the l. state has become worse for 2Pe 2.20
come in the l. days with scoffing, 3.03
Children, it is the l. hour; 1Jn 2.18
we know that it is the l. hour. 2.18
"In the l. time there will be Jud 1.18
not, I am the first and the l., Rev 1.17
'The words of the first and the l., 2.08
which are the l., for with them the 15.01
bowls full of the seven l. plagues, 21.09
the Omega, the first and the l., 22.13

LASTED
the seven days that their feast l.; Ju 14.17

LASTING
afflictions, afflictions severe and l., Deu 28.59
and sicknesses grievous and l. 28.59
a banquet l. for seven days, in the Est 1.05
For here we have no l. city, Heb 13.14

LATCH
My beloved put his hand to the l., Sol 5.04

LATE
for they are l. in coming up.) Ex 9.32
to new gods that had come in of l., Deu 32.17
It happened, l. one afternoon, when 2Sa 11.02
to go l. to rest, eating the bread Ps 127.02
who tarry l. into the evening till Is 5.11
And when it grew l., his disciples Mk 6.35
place, and the hour is now l.; 6.35
everything, as it was already l., 11.11
receives the early and the l. rain. Jas 5.07
fruitless trees in l. autumn, Jud 1.12

LATELY
l. come from Italy with his wife Ac 18.02

LATER
So my honesty will answer for me l., Gen 30.33
About three months l. Judah was told, 38.24
And about ten days l. the LORD 1Sa 25.38
of Adonikam, those who came l., Ez 8.13
remembrance of l. things yet to Ecc 1.11
those who come l. will not rejoice 4.16
Not many days l., the younger son Lk 15.13
And a little l. some one else saw 22.58
Eight days l., his disciples were Jn 20.26
says that in l. times some will 1Ti 4.01
but the sins of others appear l. 5.24
things that were to be spoken l., Heb 3.05
would not speak l. of another day. 4.08
which came l. than the law, appoints 7.28
l. it yields the peaceful fruit of 12.11

LATIN
in Hebrew, in L., and in Greek. Jn 19.20

LATRINE
Baal, and made it a l. to this day. 2Ki 10.27

LATTER
sign, they may believe the l. sign. Ex 4.08
do to your people in the l. days." Num 24.14
come upon you in the l. days, Deu 4.30
the early rain and the l. rain, 11.14
and the l. husband dislikes her and 24.03
or if the l. husband dies, who took 24.03
they would discern their l. end! 32.29
your l. days will be very great. Job 8.07
blessed the l. days of Job more 42.12
to pass in the l. days that the Is 2.02
but in the l. time he will make 9.01
said, "He will not see our l. end." Jer 12.04
In the l. days you will understand 23.20
In the l. days you will understand 30.24
fortunes of Moab in the l. days, 48.47
"But in the l. days I will restore 49.39
in the l. years you will go against Eze 38.08
In the l. days I will bring you 38.16
what will be in the l. days. Dan 2.28
shall be at the l. end of the 8.19
And at the l. end of their rule, 8.23
befall your people in the l. days. 10.14
Then the l. shall come into the 11.09
and to his goodness in the l. days. Hos 3.05
rain, the early and the l. rain, Joe 2.23
the shooting up of the l. growth; Amo 7.01
it was the l. growth after the 7.01
to pass in the l. days that the Mic 4.01
The l. splendor of this house shall Hag 2.09
The l. do it out of love, knowing Php 1.16
and that your l. works exceed the Rev 2.19

LATTICE
of Sisera gazed through the l.: Ju 5.28
through the l. in his upper 2Ki 1.02
I have looked out through my l., Pro 7.06
windows, looking through the l. Sol 2.09

LAUD
generation shall l. thy works to Ps 145.04

LAUGH
said to Abraham, "Why did Sarah l., Gen 18.13
denied, saying, "I did not l."; 18.15
He said, "No, but you did l." 18.15
one who hears will l. over me." 21.06
destruction and famine you shall l., Job 5.22
the innocent l. them to scorn, 22.19
and shall l. at him, saying, Ps 52.06
But thou, O LORD, dost l. at them; 59.08
and our enemies l. among themselves. 80.06
I also will l. at your calamity; Pro 1.26
a time to weep, and a time to l.; Ecc 3.04
They l. at every fortress, for they Hab 1.10
that weep now, for you shall l. Lk 6.21
Woe to you that l. now, 6.25

LAUGHED
Then Abraham fell on his face and l., Gen 17.17
So Sarah l. to herself, saying, 18.12
as her own, lest we be l. at; 38.23
but they l. them to scorn, and 2Ch 30.10
you shall be l. at and held in Eze 23.32
but sleeping." And they l. at him. Mt 9.24
And they l. at him. But he put them Mk 5.40
And they l. at him, knowing that she Lk 8.53

LAUGHINGSTOCK
I am a l. to my friends; I, who called Job 12.04
a just and blameless man, am a l. 12.04
the nations, a l. among the peoples. Ps 44.14
I have become a l. all the day; Jer 20.07
I have become the l. of all peoples, Lam 3.14

LAUGHS
she l. at the horse and his rider. Job 39.18
He l. at fear, and is not dismayed; 39.22
he l. at the rattle of javelins. 41.29
He who sits in the heavens l.; Ps 2.04
but the LORD l. at the wicked, for 37.13
a fool, the fool only rages and l., Pro 29.09
and she l. at the time to come. 31.25

LAUGHTER
Sarah said, "God has made l. for me; Gen 21.06
He will yet fill your mouth with l., Job 8.21
Then our mouth was filled with l., Ps 126.02
Even in l. the heart is sad, and the Pro 14.13
I said of l., "It is mad," and of Ecc 2.02
Sorrow is better than l., for by 7.03
a pot, so is the l. of the fools; 7.06

LAUGHTER (cont.)
Bread is made for l., and wine Ecc 10.19
Let your l. be turned to mourning Jas 4.09

LAVER
"You shall also make a l. of bronze, Ex 30.18
utensils and the l. and its base; 30.28
utensils, and the l. and its base, 31.09
its utensils, the l. and its base; 35.16
And he made the l. of bronze and 38.08
its utensils; the l. and its base; 39.39
and place the l. between the tent 40.07
also anoint the l. and its base, 40.11
And he set the l. between the tent 40.30
and the l. and its base, to consecrate Lev 8.11
corners were supports for a l. 1Ki 7.30
of bronze; each l. held forty baths, 7.38
each l. measured four cubits, and 7.38
and there was a l. for each of the 7.38
and removed the l. from them, 2Ki 16.17

LAVERS
And he made ten l. of bronze; 1Ki 7.38
and the ten l. upon the stands; 7.43
He also made ten l. in which to 2Ch 4.06
and the l. upon the stands, 4.14

LAVISH
Those who l. gold from the purse, Is 46.06

LAVISHED
royal wine was l. according to the Est 1.07
and l. your harlotries on any Eze 16.15
and who l. upon her silver and gold Hos 2.08
which he l. upon us. Eph 1.08

LAW
There shall be one l. for the Ex 12.49
that the l. of the LORD may be in 13.09
they will walk in my l. or not. 16.04
with the l. and the commandment, 24.12
This is the l. of the burnt offering Lev 6.09
"And this is the l. of the cereal 6.14
This is the l. of the sin offering. 6.25
"This is the l. of the guilt 7.01
offering, there is one l. for them; 7.07
And this is the l. of the sacrifice 7.11
This is the l. of the burnt offering, 7.37
This is the l. pertaining to beast 11.46
This is the l. for her who bears a 12.07
This is the l. for a leprous 13.59
"This shall be the l. of the leper 14.02
This is the l. for him in whom is a 14.32
This is the l. for any leprous 14.54
is clean. This is the l. for leprosy. 14.57
And this is the l. of his uncleanness 15.03
This is the l. for him who has a 15.32
You shall have one l. for the 24.22
"This is the l. in cases of jealousy, Num 5.29
shall execute upon her all this l. 5.30
"And this is the l. for the Nazirite, 6.13
"This is the l. for the Nazirite 6.21
according to the l. for his separation 6.21
One l. and one ordinance shall be 15.16
You shall have one l. for him who 15.29
statute of the l. which the LORD 19.02
"This is the l. when a man dies in 19.14
statute of the l. which the LORD 31.21
to explain this l., saying, Deu 1.05
as all this l. which I set before 4.08
This is the l. which Moses set 4.44
in a book a copy of this l., 17.18
words of this l. and these statutes, 17.19
upon them all the words of this l., 27.03
the words of this l. very plainly." 27.08
the words of this l. by doing them.' 27.26
words of this l. which are written 28.58
recorded in the book of this l., 28.61
written in this book of the l. 29.21
we may do all the words of this l. 29.29
are written in this book of the l., 30.10
And Moses wrote this l., 31.09
shall read this l. before all 31.11
to do all the words of this l., 31.12
the words of this l. in a book, 31.24
"Take this book of the l., 31.26
to do all the words of this l. 32.46
when Moses commanded us a l., 33.04
thy ordinances, and Israel thy l.; 33.10
to all the l. which Moses my Jos 1.07
This book of the l. shall not 1.08
in the book of the l. of Moses, 8.31
stones a copy of the l. of Moses, 8.32
he read all the words of the l., 8.34
is written in the book of the l. 8.34
commandment and the l. which Moses 22.05
in the book of the l. of Moses, 23.06
words in the book of the l. of God; 24.26
it is written in the l. of Moses, 1Ki 2.03
to walk in the l. of the LORD the 2Ki 10.31
in the book of the l. of Moses, 14.06
with all the l. which I commanded 17.13
do not know the l. of the god of 17.26
do not know the l. of the god of 17.26
teach them the l. of the god of 17.27
ordinances or the l. or the commandment 17.34
ordinances and the l. and the 17.37
to all the l. that my servant 21.08
the book of the l. in the house of 22.08
the words of the book of the l., 22.11
words of the l. which were written 23.24
according to all the l. of Moses; 23.25
written in the l. of the LORD 1Ch 16.40
may keep the l. of the LORD your 22.12
to walk in my l. as you have walked 2Ch 6.16
he forsook the l. of the LORD, 12.01
and to keep the l. and the commandment 14.04
a teaching priest, and without l.; 15.03
the book of the l. of the LORD 17.09
l. or commandment, statutes or 19.10
it is written in the l. of Moses, 23.18
to what is written in the l., 25.04
according to the l. of Moses the 30.16
is written in the l. of the LORD. 31.03
themselves to the l. of the LORD. 31.04
with the l. and the commandments, 31.21
all the l., the statutes, and the 33.08
the book of the l. of the LORD 34.14
the book of the l. in the house of 34.15
words of the l. he rent his 34.19
is written in the l. of the LORD, 35.26
written in the l. of Moses the man Ez 3.02
skilled in the l. of Moses which 7.06
heart to study the l. of the LORD, 7.10
scribe of the l. of the God of 7.12
according to the l. of your God, 7.14
scribe of the l. of the God of 7.21
not obey the l. of your God and 7.26
of your God and the l. of the king, 7.26
let it be done according to the l. 10.03
the book of the l. of Moses which Neh 8.01
brought the l. before the assembly, 8.02
attentive to the book of the l. 8.03
the people to understand the l., 8.07
from the l. of God, clearly; 8.08
they heard the words of the l. 8.09
order to study the words of the l. 8.13
written in the l. that the LORD 8.14
from the book of the l. of God. 8.18
the book of the l. of the LORD 9.03
statutes and a l. by Moses thy 9.14
and cast thy l. behind their back 9.26
order to turn them back to thy l. 9.29
not kept thy l. or heeded thy 9.34
of the lands to the l. of God, 10.28
walk in God's l. which was given 10.29

LAW (cont.)
God, as it is written in the l. Neh 10.34
cattle, as it is written in the l., 10.36
required by the l. for the priests 12.44
When the people heard the l., 13.03
And drinking was according to the l., Est 1.08
were versed in l. and judgment, 1.13
"According to the l., what is to be 1.15
being called, there is but one l.; 4.11
king, though it is against the l.; 4.16
delight is in the l. of the LORD, Ps 1.02
and on his l. he meditates day and 1.02
The l. of the LORD is perfect, 19.07
The l. of his God is in his heart; 37.31
my God; thy l. is within my heart." 40.08
because they keep no l., and do not 55.19
Jacob, and appointed a l. in Israel, 78.05
refused to walk according to his l. 78.10
forsake my l. and do not walk 89.30
thou dost teach out of thy l. 94.12
who walk in the l. of the LORD! 119.01
wondrous things out of thy l. 119.18
and graciously teach me thy l.! 119.29
I may keep thy l. and observe it 119.34
I will keep thy l. continually, 119.44
but I do not turn away from thy l. 119.51
of the wicked, who forsake thy l. 119.53
the night, O LORD, and keep thy l. 119.55
ensnare me, I do not forget thy l. 119.61
like fat, but I delight in thy l. 119.70
The l. of thy mouth is better to me 119.72
may live; for thy l. is my delight. 119.77
men who do not conform to thy l. 119.85
If thy l. had not been my delight, I 119.92
Oh, how I love thy l.! It is my 119.97
continually, but I do not forget thy l. 119.109
double-minded men, but I love thy l. 119.113
for thy l. has been broken. 119.126
because men do not keep thy l. 119.136
for ever, and thy l. is true. 119.142
purpose; they are far from thy l. 119.150
me, for I do not forget thy l. 119.153
abhor falsehood, but I love thy l. 119.163
Great peace have those who love thy l.; 119.165
O LORD, and thy l. is my delight. 119.174
Those who forsake the l. praise the Pro 28.04
who keep the l. strive against 28.04
He who keeps the l. is a wise son, 28.07
away his ear from hearing the l., 28.09
but blessed is he who keeps the l. 29.18
out of Zion shall go forth the l., Is 2.03
rejected the l. of the LORD of 5.24
and the coastlands wait for his l. 42.04
to magnify his l. and make it 42.21
and whose l. they would not obey? 42.24
for a l. will go forth from me, and 51.04
the people in whose heart is my l.; 51.07
justly, no one goes to l. honestly; 59.04
who handle the l. did not know me; Jer 2.08
of the LORD, the l. of their God. 5.04
of the LORD, the l. of their God." 5.05
and as for my l., they have rejected 6.19
and the l. of the LORD is with us'? 8.08
forsaken my l. which I set before 9.13
me and have not kept my l., 16.11
for the l. shall not perish from 18.18
to walk in my l. which I have set 26.04
I will put my l. within them, and I 31.33
obey thy voice or walk in thy l.; 32.23
walked in my l. and my statutes 44.10
or walk in his l. and in his 44.23
the l. is no more, and her prophets Lam 2.09
but the l. perishes from the priest, Eze 7.26
violence to my l. and have profaned 22.26
This is the l. of the temple: the 43.12
this is the l. of the temple. 43.12
connection with the l. of his God." Dan 6.05
according to the l. of the Medes 6.08
according to the l. of the Medes 6.12
that it is a l. of the Medes and 6.15
to change the times and the l.; 7.25
transgressed thy l. and turned 9.11
written in the l. of Moses the 9.11
As it is written in the l. of Moses, 9.13
have forgotten the l. of your God, Hos 4.06
covenant, and transgressed my l. 8.01
have rejected the l. of the LORD, Amo 2.04
out of Zion shall go forth the l., Mic 4.02
So the l. is slacked and justice Hab 1.04
sacred, they do violence to the l. Zep 3.04
should hear the l. and the words Zec 7.12
"Remember the l. of my servant Mal 4.04
to abolish the l. and the prophets Mt 5.17
pass from the l. until all is 5.18
for this is the l. and the prophets 7.12
prophets and the l. prophesied 11.13
not read in the l. how on the 12.05
is the great commandment in the l.?" 22.36
depend all the l. and the prophets 22.40
the weightier matters of the l., 23.23
according to the l. of Moses, Lk 2.22
is written in the l. of the Lord, 2.23
what is said in the l. of the LORD, 2.24
according to the custom of the l., 2.27
according to the l. of the Lord, 2.39
and teachers of the l. sitting by, 5.17
to him, "What is written in the l.? 10.26
The l. and the prophets were until 16.16
one dot of the l. to become void. 16.17
about me in the l. of Moses and 24.44
For the l. was given through Moses; Jn 1.17
Moses in the l. and also the 1.45
Did not Moses give you the l.? 7.19
Yet none of you keeps the l. 7.19
so that the l. of Moses may not be 7.23
do not know the l., are accursed." 7.49
"Does our l. judge a man without 7.51
Now in the l. Moses commanded us *8.05
In your l. it is written that the 8.17
them, "Is it not written in your l., 10.34
heard from the l. that the Christ 12.34
word that is written in their l., 15.25
and judge him by your own l." 18.31
"We have a l., and by that l. he 19.07
and by that l. he ought to die, 19.07
Gamaliel a teacher of the l., Ac 5.34
against this holy place and the l.; 6.13
received the l. as delivered by 7.53
reading of the l. and the prophets, 13.15
not be freed by the l. of Moses. 13.39
them to keep the l. of Moses. 15.05
to worship God contrary to the l." 18.13
words and names and your own l., 18.15
they are all zealous for the l., 21.20
live in observance of the l. 21.24
people and the l. and this place; 21.28
manner of the l. of our fathers, 22.03
a devout man according to the l., 22.12
to judge me according to the l., 23.03
contrary to the l. you order me to 23.03
about questions of their l., 23.29
have judged him according to our l. * 24.06
down by the l. or written in the 24.14
"Neither against the l. of the Jews, 25.08
both from the l. of Moses and from 28.23
sinned without the l. will also Rom 2.12
will also perish without the l., 2.12
under the l. will be judged by the l. 2.12
hearers of the l. who are righteous 2.13
doers of the l. who will be 2.13
have not the l. do by nature what 2.14
do by nature what the l. requires, 2.14
they are a l. to themselves, even 2.14
though they do not have the l. 2.14
that what the l. requires is 2.15
rely upon the l. and boast of your 2.17

LAW (cont.)

you are instructed in the l., Rom 2.18
having in the l. the embodiment of 2.20
You who boast in the l., do you 2.23
dishonor God by breaking the l.? 2.23
is of value if you obey the l.; 2.25
but if you break the l., your 2.25
keeps the precepts of the l., 2.26
but keep the l. will condemn you 2.27
and circumcision but break the l. 2.27
whatever the l. says it speaks to 3.19
to those who are under the l., 3.19
by works of the l. since through 3.20
through the l. comes knowledge of 3.20
has been manifested apart from l., 3.21
although the l. and the prophets 3.21
by faith apart from works of l. 3.28
overthrow the l. by this faith? 3.31
on the contrary, we uphold the l. 3.31
through the l. but through the 4.13
adherents of the l. who are to be 4.14
For the l. brings wrath, but where 4.15
there is no l. there is no transgression. 4.15
adherents of the l. but also to 4.16
the world before the l. was given, 5.13
not counted where there is no l. 5.13
L. came in, to increase the trespass; 5.20
are not under l. but under grace. 6.14
are not under l. but under grace? 6.15
speaking to those who know the l.— 7.01
that the l. is binding on a person 7.01
is bound by l. to her husband as 7.02
from the l. concerning the husband. 7.02
dies she is free from that l., 7.03
died to the l. through the body of 7.04
sinful passions, aroused by the l. 7.05
But now we are discharged from the l., 7.06
That the l. is sin? By no means! 7.07
Yet, if it had not been for the l., 7.07
is to covet if the l. had not said, 7.07
Apart from the l. sin lies dead. 7.08
I was once alive apart from the l., 7.09
So the l. is holy, and the commandment 7.12
We know that the l. is spiritual; 7.14
want, I agree that the l. is good. 7.16
find it to be a l. that when I 7.21
For I delight in the l. of God, 7.22
members another l. at war with the 7.23
at war with the l. of my mind and 7.23
captive to the l. of sin which 7.23
serve the l. of God with my mind, 7.25
my flesh I serve the l. of sin. 7.25
For the l. of the Spirit of life in 8.02
free from the l. of sin and death. 8.02
For God has done what the l., 8.03
requirement of the l. might be 8.04
it does not submit to God's l., 8.07
covenants, the giving of the l., 9.04
is based on l. did not succeed in 9.31
not succeed in fulfilling that l. 9.31
For Christ is the end of the l., 10.04
is based on the l. shall live by 10.05
his neighbor has fulfilled the l. 13.08
love is the fulfilling of the l. 13.10
he dare go to l. before the 1Co 6.01
but brother goes to l. against 6.06
Does not the l. say the same? 9.08
For it is written in the l. of Moses, 9.09
those under the l. I became as one 9.20
I became as one under the l.—though 9.20
not being myself under the l.—that 9.20
I might win those under the l. 9.20
outside the l. I became as one 9.21
I became as one outside the l.— 9.21
being without l. toward God but 9.21
God but under the l. of Christ— 9.21
I might win those outside the l. 9.21
In the l. it is written, "By men of 14.21
subordinate, as even the l. says. 14.34
and the power of sin is the l. 15.56
by works of the l. but through Gal 2.16
Christ, and not by works of the l., 2.16
by works of the l. shall no one be 2.16
For I through the l. died to the l., 2.19
justification were through the l., 2.21
the Spirit by works of the l., 3.02
among you do so by works of the l., 3.05
on works of the l. are under a 3.10
in the book of the l., and do them. 3.10
is justified before God by the l.; 3.11
but the l. does not rest on faith, 3.12
us from the curse of the l., 3.13
the l., which came four hundred and 3.17
For if the inheritance is by the l., 3.18
Why then the l.? It was added 3.19
Is the l. then against the promises 3.21
for if a l. had been given which 3.21
righteousness would indeed be by the l. 3.21
we were confined under the l., 3.23
So that the l. was our custodian 3.24
born of woman, born under the l., 4.04
redeem those who were under the l., 4.05
Tell me, you who desire to be under l., 4.21
do you not hear the l.? 4.21
he is bound to keep the whole l. 5.03
who would be justified by the l.; 5.04
For the whole l. is fulfilled in 5.14
Spirit you are not under the l. 5.18
against such there is no l. 5.23
and so fulfil the l. of Christ. 6.02
do not themselves keep the l., 6.13
his flesh the l. of commandments Eph 2.15
Hebrews; as to the l. a Pharisee, Php 3.05
righteousness under the l. blameless. 3.06
based on l., but that which is 3.09
desiring to be teachers of the l., 1Ti 1.07
Now we know that the l. is good, 1.08
that the l. is not laid down for 1.09
dissensions, and quarrels over the l., Tit 3.09
commandment in the l. to take Heb 7.05
it the people received the l.), 7.11
necessarily a change in the l. as well. 7.12
(for the l. made nothing perfect); 7.19
Indeed, the l. appoints men in their 7.28
oath, which came later than the l., 7.28
offer gifts according to the l. 8.04
commandment of the l. had been 9.19
under the l. almost everything is 9.22
For since the l. has but a shadow 10.01
are offered according to the l.), 10.08
violated the l. of Moses dies 10.28
But he who looks into the perfect l., Jas 1.25
the l. of liberty, and perseveres, 1.25
If you really fulfil the royal l., 2.08
convicted by the l. as transgressors. 2.09
keeps the whole l. but fails in 2.10
become a transgressor of the l. 2.11
be judged under the l. of liberty. 2.12
evil against the l. and judges the l. 4.11
But if you judge the l., you are 4.11
not a doer of the l. but a judge. 4.11

LAWFUL

it shall not be l. to impose Ez 7.24
and does what is l. and right— Eze 18.05
son has done what is l. and right, 18.19
and does what is l. and right, 18.21
and does what is l. and right, 18.27
sin and does what is l. and right, 33.14
he has done what is l. and right, 33.16
and does what is l. and right, 33.19
what is not l. to do on the Mt 12.02
it was not l. for him to eat nor 12.04
"Is it l. to heal on the sabbath?" 12.10

LAWFUL (cont.)
So it is l. to do good on the Mt 12.12
"It is not l. for you to have her." 14.04
"Is it l. to divorce one's wife for 19.03
Is it l. to pay taxes to Caesar, or 22.17
"It is not l. to put them into the 27.06
what is not l. on the sabbath?" Mk 2.24
which it is not l. for any but the 2.26
"Is it l. on the sabbath to do good 3.04
"It is not l. for you to have your 6.18
"Is it l. for a man to divorce his 10.02
Is it l. to pay taxes to Caesar, or 12.14
what is not l. to do on the Lk 6.02
which it is not l. for any but the 6.04
is it l. on the sabbath to do good 6.09
"Is it l. to heal on the sabbath, or 14.03
Is it l. for us to give tribute to 20.22
it is not l. for you to carry your Jn 5.10
"It is not l. for us to put any man 18.31
which it is not l. for us Romans Ac 16.21
"Is it l. for you to scourge a man 22.25
"All things are l. for me," but not 1Co 6.12
"All things are l. for me," but I will 6.12
"All things are l.," but not all things are 10.23
"All things are l.," but not all things build 10.23

LAWFULLY
is good, if any one uses it l., 1Ti 1.08

LAWGIVER
There is one l. and judge, he who is Jas 4.12

LAWLESS
and killed by the hands of l. men. Ac 2.23
And then the l. one will be revealed, 2Th 2.08
The coming of the l. one by the 2.09
but for the l. and disobedient, for 1Ti 1.09
revels, carousing, and l. idolatry. 1Pe 4.03
after day with their l. deeds), 2Pe 2.08
the error of l. men and lose your 3.17

LAWLESSNESS
tree of life, but l. takes away lives. Pro 11.30
and the man of l. is revealed, 2Th 2.03
For the mystery of l. is already at 2.07
loved righteousness and hated l.; Heb 1.09
commits sin is guilty of l.; sin is l. 1Jn 3.04

LAWS
commandments, my statutes, and my l." Gen 26.05
to keep my commandments and my l.? Ex 16.28
ordinances and l. which the LORD Lev 26.46
such as know the l. of your God; Ez 7.25
them right ordinances and true l., Neh 9.13
among the l. of the Persians and Est 1.19
their l. are different from those 3.08
and they do not keep the king's l., 3.08
his statutes, and observe his l. Ps 105.45
or they have transgressed the l., Is 24.05
all its ordinances and all its l.; Eze 43.11
perform all its l. and all its 43.11
temple of the LORD and all its l., 44.05
shall keep my l. and my statutes 44.24
LORD our God by following his l., Dan 9.10
for him my l. by ten thousands, Hos 8.12
I will put my l. into their minds, Heb 8.10
I will put my l. on their hearts, 10.16

LAWSUITS
To have l. at all with one another 1Co 6.07

LAWYER
a l., asked him a question, to test Mt 22.35
And behold, a l. stood up to put him Lk 10.25
speed Zenas the l. and Apollos on Tit 3.13

LAWYERS
Pharisees and the l. rejected the Lk 7.30
One of the l. answered him, "Teacher, 11.45
And he said, "Woe to you l. also! 11.46
Woe to you l.! for you have taken 11.52
spoke to the l. and Pharisees, 14.03

LAY
and l. uncovered in his tent. Gen 9.21
But before they l. down, the men of 19.04
went in, and l. with her father; 19.33
know when she l. down or when she 19.33
I l. last night with my father; 19.34
the younger arose, and l. with him; 19.35
know when she l. down or when she 19.35
"Do not l. your hand on the lad or 22.12
his head and l. down in that place 28.11
So he l. with her that night. 30.16
the flock he did not l. them there; 30.42
seized her and l. with her and 34.02
Reuben went and l. with Bilhah his 35.22
but l. no hand upon him"—that he 37.22
and l. up grain under the authority 41.35
heretofore you shall l. upon them, Ex 5.08
then I will l. my hand upon Egypt 7.04
and he did not l. even this to 7.23
the morning dew l. round about the 16.13
is left over l. by to be kept till 16.23
woman's husband shall l. upon him; 21.22
And he did not l. his hand on the 24.11
his sons shall l. their hands upon 29.10
his sons shall l. their hands upon 29.15
his sons shall l .their hands upon 29.19
he shall l. his hand upon the head Lev 1.04
and l. wood in order upon the fire; 1.07
the priests shall l. the pieces, 1.08
priest shall l. them in order upon 1.12
oil upon it, and l. frankincense on it; 2.15
And he shall l. his hand upon the 3.02
and l. his hand upon its head, and 3.13
and l. his hand on the head of the 4.04
congregation shall l. their hands 4.15
and shall l. his hand upon the head 4.24
And he shall l. his hand on the 4.29
and l. his hand upon the head of 4.33
and he shall l. the burnt offering 6.12
and Aaron shall l. both his hands 16.21
who heard him l. their hands upon 24.14
And I will l. your cities waste, and 26.31
of Israel shall l. their hands Num 8.10
Levites shall l. their hands upon 8.12
that thou dost l. the burden of 11.11
and l. incense on it, and carry it 16.46
the LORD, she l. down under Balaam; 22.27
He couched, he l. down like a lion, 24.09
spirit, and l. your hand upon him; 27.18
and l. it to your heart, that the Deu 4.39
but he will l. them upon all who 7.15
Then I l. prostrate before the LORD 9.18
"So I l. prostrate before the LORD 9.18
"You shall therefore l. up these 11.18
your God will l. the fear of you 11.25
and l. it up within your towns; 14.28
the man who l. with the woman, and 22.22
the man who l. with her shall die. 22.25
then the man who l. with her shall 22.29
"L. to heart all the words which I 32.46
Before they l. down, she came up to Jos 2.08
and l. them down in the place where 4.03
first-born shall he l. its foundation, 6.26
l. an ambush against the city, 8.02
and l. between Bethel and Ai, to the 8.09
the land l. subdued before them. 18.01
and there l. their lord dead on the Ju 3.25
and there l. Sisera dead, with the 4.22
he fell, he l. still at her feet; 5.27
of the East l. along the valley 7.12
down, so that the tent l. flat. 7.13
the place and l. in wait for him 16.02
But Samson l. till midnight, and at 16.03
uncovered his feet, and l. down. Ru 3.07

LAY (cont.)
and behold, a woman l. at his feet! Ru 3.08
So she l. at his feet until the 3.14
and how they l. with the women who 1Sa 2.22
down again." So he went and l. down. 3.05
Samuel went and l. down in his 3.09
Samuel l. until morning; then he 3.15
the roof, and he l. down to sleep. 9.25
and l. in wait in the valley. 15.05
and l. naked all that day and all 19.24
David saw the place where Saul l., 26.05
and there l. Saul sleeping within 26.07
Abner and the army l. around him 26.07
as he l. on his bed in his bedchamber, 2Sa 4.07
came to him, and he l. with her. 11.04
and went in and l. all night upon 12.16
went in to her, and l. with her; 12.24
So Amnon l. down, and pretended to 13.06
he forced her, and l. with her. 13.14
his garments, and l. on the earth; 13.31
And Amasa l. wallowing in his blood 20.12
in the night, because she l. on it. 1Ki 3.19
in order to l. the foundation of 5.17
yet if they l. it to heart in the 8.47
the altar, saying, "L. hold of him." 13.04
l. my bones beside his bones. 13.31
it in pieces and l. it on the wood, 18.23
other bull and l. it on the wood, 18.23
And he l. down and slept under a 19.05
ate and drank, and l. down again. 19.06
and l. hands on whatever pleases 20.06
And he l. down on his bed, and 21.04
and fasted and l. in sackcloth, 21.27
chamber in Samaria, and l. sick; 2Ki 1.02
and l. my staff upon the face of 4.29
Then he went up and l. upon the child, 4.34
to Jezreel, for Joram l. there. 9.16
"L. them in two heaps at the 10.08
them take and l. it on the boil, 20.07
for upon them l. the duty of 1Ch 9.27
yet if they l. it to heart in the 2Ch 6.37
of your brethren the l. people, 35.05
contributed to the l. people, 35.07
fathers' houses of the l. people, 35.12
them quickly to all the l. people. 35.13
days that it l. desolate it kept 36.21
We also l. upon ourselves the Neh 10.32
do so again I will l. hands on you." 13.21
and sought to l. hands on King Est 2.21
But he disdained to l. hands on 3.06
most of them l. in sackcloth and 4.03
had sought to l. hands upon King 6.02
he would l. hands on the Jews. 8.07
Ahasuerus to l. hands on such as 9.02
who might l. his hand upon us both. Job 9.33
"L. down a pledge for me with 17.03
and l. your hand upon your mouth. 21.05
and l. up his words in your heart. 22.22
if you l. gold in the dust, and gold 22.24
I would l. my case before him and 23.04
thee? I l. my hand on my mouth. 40.04
L. hands on him; think of the battle; 41.08
the ground, and l. my soul in the dust. Ps 7.05
thou dost l. me in the dust of 22.15
Those who seek my life l. their snares, 38.12
and l. the charge before you. 50.21
thou didst l. affliction on our 66.11
both rider and horse l. stunned. 76.06
They l. crafty plans against thy 83.03
where she may l. her young, at thy 84.03
Of old thou didst l. the foundation 102.25
life to those who l. hold of her; Pro 3.18
Wise men l. up knowledge, but the 10.14
and how to l. hold on folly, till I Ecc 2.03
and the living will l. it to heart. 7.02
palm tree and l. hold of its Sol 7.08
the LORD will l. bare their secret Is 3.17
and l. low the haughtiness of the 13.11
Go up, O Elam, l. siege, O Media; 21.02
the LORD will l. waste the earth 24.01
the LORD will l. low his pride 25.11
l. low, and cast to the ground, even 25.12
Or let them l. hold of my protection, 27.05
and l. a snare for him who reproves 29.21
owl nest and l. and hatch and 34.15
I will l. waste mountains and hills, 42.15
you did not l. these things to 47.07
and l. your foundations with 54.11
I will l. before this people Jer 6.21
They l. hold on bow and spear, they 6.23
They l. hold of bow and spear; 50.42
determined to l. in ruins the wall Lam 2.08
they l. in wait for us in the 4.19
and I l. a stumbling block before Eze 3.20
take a brick and l. it before you, 4.01
and I will l. the punishment of the 4.04
And I will l. the dead bodies of 6.05
that I may l. hold of the hearts of 14.05
therefore I will l. open the flank 25.09
And I will l. my vengeance upon 25.14
when I l. my vengeance upon them." 25.17
I will l. your cities waste, and you 35.04
it abundant and l. no famine upon 36.29
And I will l. sinews upon you, and 37.06
and l. them in the holy chambers; 44.19
head as you l. in bed are these: Dan 2.28
as you l. in bed came thoughts of 2.29
as I l. in bed the fancies and the 4.05
of my head as I l. in bed were 4.10
visions of my head as I l. in bed, 4.13
of his head as he l. in his bed. 7.01
overcome and l. sick for some days; 8.27
And I will l. waste her vines and Hos 2.12
they l. themselves down beside Amo 2.08
and l. not on us innocent blood; Jon 1.14
and all her idols I will l. waste; Mic 1.07
they shall l. their hands on their 7.16
that each will l. hold on the hand Zec 14.13
if you will not l. it to heart to Mal 2.02
because you do not l. it to heart. 2.02
"Do not l. up for yourselves Mt 6.19
but l. up for yourselves treasures 6.20
of man has nowhere to l. his head." 8.20
but come and l. your hand on her, 9.18
will not l. hold of it and lift it 12.11
that he might l. his hands on them 19.13
and l. them on men's shoulders; 23.04
Come, see the place where he l. 28.06
mother-in-law l. sick with a fever, Mk 1.30
pallet on which the paralytic l. 2.04
Come and l. your hands on her, so 5.23
besought him to l. his hand upon 7.32
they will l. their hands on the sick; * 16.18
him in and l. him before Jesus; Lk 5.18
and took up that on which he l., 5.25
of man has nowhere to l. his head." 9.58
And at his gate l. a poor man named 16.20
take up what you did not l. down, 19.21
what I did not l. down and reaping 19.22
tried to l. hands on him at that 20.19
this they will l. their hands on 21.12
temple, you did not l. hands on me. 22.53
In these l. a multitude of invalids, Jn 5.03
and I l. down my life for the sheep. 10.15
because I l. down my life, that I 10.17
but I l. it down of my own accord. 10.18
I have power to l. it down, 10.18
was a cave, and a stone l. upon it. 11.38
I will l. down my life for you." 13.37
"Will you l. down your life for me? 13.38
that a man l. down his life for his 15.13
one on whom I l. my hands may Ac 8.19
come in and l. his hands on him so 9.12
and to us to l. upon you no 15.28
day, and no small tempest l. on us, 27.20
of Publius l. sick with fever and 28.08

LAY (cont.)
can any one l. than that which is 1Co 3.11
why do you l. them before those who 6.04
not to l. any restraint upon you, 7.35
ought not to l. up for their 2Co 12.14
let us also l. aside every weight, Heb 12.01
and we ought to l. down our lives 1Jn 3.16
I do not l. upon you any other Rev 2.24

LAYEST
and before; and l. thy hand upon me. Ps 139.05

LAYING
l. his hand upon the head of his Lev 3.08
behold, I am l. a fleece of wool on Ju 6.37
and l. hold of his concubine he 19.29
then are you l. a snare for my 1Sa 28.09
all Israel were l. seige to 1Ki 15.27
they talk of l. snares secretly, Ps 64.05
I am l. in Zion for a foundation a Is 28.16
the heavens and l. the foundations of 51.16
For the LORD is l. Babylon waste, Jer 51.55
court without l. there the garments Eze 42.14
l. him bare from thigh to neck Hab 3.13
blessed them, l. his hands upon them. Mk 10.16
through the l. on of the apostles' Ac 8.18
And l. his hands on him he said, 9.17
pretense of l. out anchors from 27.30
"Behold I am l. in Zion a stone Rom 9.33
not be hasty in the l. on of hands, 1Ti 5.22
thus l. up for themselves a good 6.19
you through the l. on of my hands; 2Ti 1.06
not l. again a foundation of Heb 6.01
the l. on of hands, the resurrection 6.02
I am l. in Zion a stone, a cornerstone 1Pe 2.06

LAYS
he l. hold of it, but it does not Job 8.15
the heel, a snare l. hold of him. 18.09
know how God l. his command upon 37.15
The fear of man l. a snare, Pro 29.25
He l. it low, l. it low to the ground, Is 26.05
which the LORD l. upon them will 30.32
perishes, and no one l. it to heart; 57.01
desolate, but no man l. it to heart. Jer 12.11
So is he who l. up treasure for Lk 12.21
he l. it on his shoulders, rejoicing 15.05
good shepherd l. down his life for Jn 10.11

LAZARUS
his gate lay a poor man named L., Lk 16.20
far off and L. in his bosom. 16.23
and send L. to dip the end of his 16.24
and L. in like manner evil things; 16.25
L. of Bethany, the village of Mary Jn 11.01
her hair, whose brother L. was ill. 11.02
loved Martha and her sister and L. 11.05
"Our friend L. has fallen asleep, 11.11
told them plainly, "L. is dead; 11.14
he found that L. had already been 11.17
with a loud voice, "L., come out." 11.43
where L. was, whom Jesus had raised 12.01
but L. was one of those at table 12.02
of Jesus but also to see L., 12.09
planned to put L. also to death, 12.10
when he called L. out of the tomb 12.17

LAZY
liars, evil beasts, l. gluttons. Tit 1.12

LEAD
and I will l. on slowly, according Gen 33.14
God did not l. them by way of the Ex 13.17
of cloud to l. them along the way, 13.21
they sank as l. in the mighty 15.10
But now go, l. the people to the 32.34
who shall l. them out and bring Num 27.17
the iron, the tin, and the l., 31.22
where the LORD will l. you away. Deu 28.37
This would l. to the sweeping 29.19
the LORD alone did l. him, 32.12
going will not l. to your glory, Ju 4.09
"That the leaders took the l. in Israel, 5.02
Arise, Barak, l. away your captives, O 5.12
each man may l. away his wife and 1Sa 30.22
and l. him to an inner chamber. 2Ki 9.02
Azaziah were to l. with lyres 1Ch 15.21
thou didst l. them in the day, and Neh 9.12
an iron pen and l. they were Job 19.24
Can you l. forth the Mazzaroth in 38.32
L. me, O LORD, in thy righteousness Ps 5.08
L. me in thy truth, and teach me, for 25.05
and l. me on a level path because 27.11
thy name's sake l. me and guide me, 31.03
let them l. me, let them bring me to 43.03
Who will l. me to Edom? 60.09
L. thou me to the rock that is 61.02
In the l., the princes of Judah in 68.27
Thou didst l. thy people like a 77.20
Who will l. me to Edom? 108.10
on the day you l. your host upon 110.03
L. me in the path of thy commandments, 119.35
the LORD will l. away with evildoers! 125.05
even there thy hand shall l. me, 139.10
and l. me in the way everlasting! 139.24
thy good spirit l. me on a level 143.10
When you walk, they will l. you; Pro 6.22
of the diligent l. surely to 21.05
Let not your mouth l. you into sin, Ecc 5.06
I would l. you and bring you into Sol 8.02
who l. this people l. them astray, Is 9.16
and a little child shall l. them. 11.06
king of Assyria l. away the 20.04
and gently l. those that are with 40.11
And I will l. the blind in a way 42.16
who has pity on them will l. them, 49.10
I will l. him and requite him with 57.18
So thou didst l. thy people, to make 63.14
the l. is consumed by the fire; Jer 6.29
tell them and l. my people astray 23.32
consolations I will l. them back, 31.09
survivors to l. out sons and Eze 14.22
tin and iron and l. in the furnace, 22.18
and iron and l. and tin into a 22.20
and l. they exchanged for your 27.12
and l. you against the mountains of 39.02
Ephraim must l. forth his sons to Hos 9.13
prophets who l. my people astray, Mic 3.05
And l. us not into temptation, But Mt 6.13
and they will l. many astray. 24.05
will arise and l. many astray. 24.11
so as to l. astray, if possible, even 24.24
and they will l. many astray. Mk 13.06
to l. astray, if possible, the elect. 13.22
seize him and l. him away safely." 14.44
"Can a blind man l. a blind man? Lk 6.39
and l. us not into temptation." 11.04
and l. it away to water it? 13.15
people to l. him by the hand. Ac 13.11
is meant to l. you to repentance? Rom 2.04
let every one l. the life which the 1Co 7.17
beg you to l. a life worthy of the Eph 4.01
to l. a life worthy of the Lord, Col 1.10
to l. a life worthy of God, who 1Th 2.12
that we may l. a quiet and peaceable 1Ti 2.02
for it will l. people into more and 2Ti 2.16
by the hand to l. them out of the Heb 8.09

LEADEN
the l. cover was lifted, and there Zec 5.07
thrust down the l. weight upon its 5.08

LEADER
the l. of the people of Judah being Num 2.03
the l. of the people of Issachar 2.05
the l. of the people of Zebulun 2.07
the l. of the people of Reuben 2.10

LEADER (cont.)

the l. of the people of Simeon Num 2.12
the l. of the people of Gad being 2.14
the l. of the people of Ephraim 2.18
the l. of the people of Manasseh 2.20
the l. of the people of Benjamin 2.22
the l. of the people of Dan being 2.25
the l. of the people of Asher being 2.27
the l. of the people of Naphtali 2.29
one l. each day, for the dedication 7.11
the l. of Issachar, made an offering 7.18
the l. of the men of Zebulun: 7.24
the l. of the men of Reuben: 7.30
the l. of the men of Simeon: 7.36
Derrel, the l. of the men of Gad: 7.42
the l. of the men of Ephraim: 7.48
the l. of the men of Manasseh: 7.54
the l. of the men of Benjamin: 7.60
the l. of the men of Dan: 7.66
the l. of the men of Asher: 7.72
the l. of the men of Naphtali: 7.78
a man, every one a l. among them. 13.02
one for each l., according to their 17.06
You shall take one l. of every tribe, 34.18
Of the tribe of the sons of Dan a l., 34.22
tribe of the sons of Manasseh a l., 34.23
tribe of the sons of Ephraim a l., 34.24
tribe of the sons of Zebulun a l., 34.25
tribe of the sons of Issachar a l., 34.26
tribe of the sons of Asher a l., 34.27
tribe of the sons of Naphtali a l., 34.28
to Jephtahah, "Come and be our l., Ju 11.06
made him head and l. over them; 11.11
him and became l. of a marauding 1Ki 11.24
and made you l. over my people 14.07
and made you l. over my people 16.02
a l. of the Reubenites, and thirty 1Ch 11.42
thirty and a l. over the thirty; 12.04
and of hundreds, with every l. 13.01
Chenaniah, l. of the Levites in 15.22
Chenaniah the l. of the music of 15.27
for he chose Judah as l., and in the 28.04
and appointed a l. to return to Neh 9.17
who was the l. to begin the thanksgiving 11.17
sang with Jezrahiah as their l. 12.42
you shall be our l., and this heap Is 3.06
shall not make me l. of the people." 3.07
a l. and commander for the peoples. 55.04
and the l. as one who serves. Lk 22.26
at his right hand as L. and Savior, Ac 5.31

LEADERS

the l. of Moab, trembling seizes Ex 15.15
when all the l. of the congregation 16.22
and all the l. of the congregation 34.31
And the l. brought onyx stones and 35.27
the l. of their ancestral tribes, Num 1.16
with the help of the l. of Israel, 1.44
chief over the l. of the Levites, 3.32
Aaron and the l. of the congregation 4.34
Aaron and the l. of Israel numbered, 4.46
the l. of Israel, heads of their 7.02
the l. of the tribes, who were over 7.02
a wagon for every two of the l., 7.03
And the l. offered offerings for 7.10
and the l. offered their offering 7.10
from the l. of Israel: twelve silver 7.84
then the l., the heads of the 10.04
and fifty l. of the congregation, 16.02
from all their l. according to 17.02
and all their l. gave him rods, one 17.06
and before the l. and all the 27.02
and all the l. of the congregation, 31.13
and to the l. of the congregation, 32.02
before Moses and before the l., 36.01
and the l. of the congregation Jos 9.15
because the l. of the congregation 9.18
congregation murmured against the l. 9.18
But all the l. said to all the 9.19
And the l. said to them, "Let them 9.21
as the l. had said of them. 9.21
defeated with the l. of Midian, 13.21
Joshua the son of Nun and the l., 17.04
"That the l. took the lead in Ju 5.02
the l. of Gilead, said one to 10.18
hither, all you l. of the people; 1Sa 14.38
the l. of the fathers' houses of 1K 8.01
Seir, having as their l. Pelatiah, 1Ch 4.42
l., who lived in Jerusalem. 9.34
commanded all the l. of Israel to 22.17
assembled all the l. of Israel and 23.02
These were the l. of the tribes of 27.22
as did also the l. of the tribes, 29.06
All the l. and the mighty men, and 29.24
and to all the l. in all Israel, 2Ch 1.02
the l. of the fathers' houses of 5.02
and the l. stood behind all the Neh 4.16
Now the l. of the people lived in 11.01
your l. mislead you, and confuse the Is 3.12
you, all who were l. of the earth; 14.09
and all the l. of the forces in Jer 40.13
and all the l. of the forces with 41.11
and all the l. of the forces with 41.13
and all the l. of the forces with 41.16
shepherds, and I will punish the l.; Zec 10.03
together the local l. of the Jews; Ac 28.17
Remember your l., those who spoke Heb 13.07
Obey your l. and submit to them; 13.17
Greet all your l. and all the 13.24

LEADERSHIP

hosts under the l. of Moses and Num 33.01
left Egypt under the l. of Moses? Heb 3.16

LEADEST

thou who l. Joseph like a flock! Ps 80.01

LEADING

instruments l. in the celebration. 2Ch 23.13
All the l. priests and the people 36.14
and I gathered l. men from Israel Ez 7.28
l. men, and for Joiarib and Elnathan, 8.16
the l. man at the place Casiphia, 8.17
set apart twelve of the l. priests: 8.24
and made the l. priests and 10.05
l. captives in thy train, and Ps 68.18
there were seven steps l. up to it, Eze 40.26
officers and the l. men of Galilee. Mk 6.21
one of the twelve, was l. them. Lk 22.47
"No, he is l. the people astray." Jn 7.12
to the iron gate l. into the city. Ac 12.10
standing and the l. men of the city, 13.50
and Silas, l. men among the brethren, 15.22
which is the l. city of the district 16.12
and not a few of the l. women. 17.04
l. you to fall away from the living Heb 3.12

LEADS

He l. counselors away stripped, and Job 12.17
He l. priests away stripped, and 12.19
enlarges nations, and l. them away. 12.23
He l. me beside still waters; Ps 23.02
He l. me in paths of righteousness 23.03
He l. the humble in what is right, 25.09
he l. out the prisoners to prosperity; 68.06
The wage of the righteous l. to life, Pro 10.16
way of the wicked l. them astray. 12.26
but the way of error l. to death. 12.28
The wise man's path l. upward to life, 15.24
neighbor and l. him in a way that 16.29
The fear of the LORD l. to life; 19.23
peoples a bridle that l. astray. Is 30.28
who l. you in the way you should go. 48.17
that l. to destruction, and those Mt 7.13
that l. to life, and those who find 7.14
and if a blind man l. a blind man, 15.14

LEADS (cont.)

heed that no one l. you astray. Mt 24.04
heed that no one l. you astray. Mk 13.05
own sheep by name and l. them out. Jn 10.03
righteousness l. to acquittal and Rom 5.18
which l. to death, or of obedience, 6.16
which l. to righteousness? 6.16
in Christ always l. us in triumph, 2Co 2.14
repentance that l. to salvation 7.10

LEAF

mouth a freshly plucked olive l.; Gen 8.11
And gold l. was hammered out and Ex 39.03
of a driven l. shall put them to Lev 26.36
a driven l. and pursue dry chaff? Job 13.25
and its l. does not wither. In all that he Ps 1.03
will flourish like a green l. Pro 11.28
be like an oak whose l. withers, Is 1.30
We all fade like a l., and our iniquities 64.06
in the distance a fig tree in l., Mk 11.13
as soon as they come out in l., Lk 21.30

LEAFY

and boughs of l. trees, and willows Lev 23.40
and other l. trees to make booths, Neh 8.15
green tree, and under every l. oak, Eze 6.13
saw any high hill or any l. tree, 20.28
others spread l. branches which Mk 11.08

LEAGUE

my son makes a l. with the son of 1Sa 22.08
"Let there be a l. between me and 1Ki 15.19
break your l. with Baasha king of 15.19
"Let there be a l. between me and 2Ch 16.03
break your l. with Baasha king of 16.03
For you shall be in l. with the Job 5.23
"Syria is in l. with Ephraim," his Is 7.02
and who make a l., but not of my 30.01
people of the land that is in l., Eze 30.05

LEAH

the name of the older was L., Gen 29.16
his daughter L. and brought her to 29.23
to his daughter L. to be her maid.) 29.24
And in the morning, behold, it was L.; 29.25
and he loved Rachel more than L., 29.30
When the LORD saw that L. was hated, 29.31
And L. conceived and bore a son, and 29.32
When L. saw that she had ceased 30.09
And L. said, "Good fortune!" 30.11
And L. said, "Happy am I! For the women 30.13
and brought them to his mother L. 30.14
Then Rachel said to L., "Give me, I pray, 30.14
L. went out to meet him, and said, 30.16
And God hearkened to L., and she 30.17
L. said, "God has given me my hire 30.18
And L. conceived again, and she bore 30.19
Then L. said, "God has endowed me 30.20
Rachel and L. into the field where 31.04
Then Rachel and L. answered him, 31.14
children among L. and Rachel and 33.01
then L. with her children, and 33.02
L. likewise and her children drew 33.07
Now Dinah the daughter of L., 34.01
The sons of L.: Reuben (Jacob's 35.23
(these are the sons of L., 46.15
whom Laban gave to L. his daughter; 46.18
his wife; and there I buried L.— 49.31
your house, like Rachel and L., Ru 4.11

LEAH'S

L. eyes were weak, but Rachel was Gen 29.17
Then L. maid Zilpah bore Jacob a 30.10
L. maid Zilpah bore Jacob a second 30.12
and into L. tent, and into the tent 31.33
And he went out of L. tent, 31.33
L. maid: Gad and Asher. These were the 35.26

LEAKS

and through indolence the house l. Ecc 10.18

LEAN

The seven l. and gaunt cows that Gen 41.27
rests, that I may l. against them." Ju 16.26
will no more l. upon him that Is 10.20
but will l. upon the LORD, the Holy 10.20
the fat of his flesh will grow l. 17.04
the fat sheep and the l. sheep. Eze 34.20
yet they l. upon the LORD and say, Mic 3.11

LEANED

and he l. his weight upon them, his Ju 16.29
hand the king l. said to the man 2Ki 7.02
whose hand he l. to have charge of 7.17
Upon thee I have l. from my birth; Ps 71.06
and when they l. upon you, you broke, Eze 29.07
the house and l. with his hand Amo 5.19

LEANING

there was Saul l. upon his spear; 2Sa 1.06
l. on my arm, and I bow myself in 2Ki 5.18
like a l. wall, a tottering fence? Ps 62.03
l. upon her beloved? Under the apple tree Sol 8.05

LEANNESS

and my l. has risen up against me, Job 16.08

LEANS

and l. to the border of Moab. Num 21.15
the hand of any man who l. on it. 2Ki 18.21
He l. against his house, but it does Job 8.15
the hand of any man who l. on it. Is 36.06

LEAP

the goats that l. upon the flock Gen 31.12
with which to l. on the earth. Lev 11.21
and by my God I can l. over a wall. 2Sa 22.30
Do you make him l. like the locust? Job 39.20
flaming torches; sparks of fire l. forth. 41.19
and by my God I can l. over a wall. Ps 18.29
as locusts l., men l. upon it Is 33.04
then shall the lame man l. like a hart, 35.06
they l. on the tops of the mountains, Joe 2.05
They l. upon the city, they run upon 2.09
and l. for joy, for behold, your Lk 6.23

LEAPED

he-goats which l. upon the flock Gen 31.10
of Mary, the babe l. in her womb; Lk 1.41
the babe in my womb l. for joy. 1.44
the evil spirit was l. on them, Ac 19.16

LEAPING

saw King David l. and dancing 2Sa 6.16
l. upon the mountains, bounding over Sol 2.08
shall go forth l. like calves from Mal 4.02
And l. up he stood and walked and Ac 3.08
walking and l. and praising God. 3.08

LEAPS

lion's whelp, that l. forth from Bashan." Deu 33.22
trembles, and l. out of its place. Job 37.01
every one who l. over the threshold, Zep 1.09

LEARN

in silence to l. whether the LORD Gen 24.21
that they may l. to fear me all Deu 4.10
and you shall l. them and be 5.01
that you may l. to fear the LORD 14.23
that he may l. to fear the LORD his 17.19
you shall not l. to follow the 18.09
may hear and l. to fear the LORD 31.12
may hear and l. to fear the LORD 31.13
until you l. how the matter turns Ru 3.18
and if I l. anything I will tell 1Sa 19.03
the records and l. that this city Ez 4.15
to l. how Esther was and how she Est 2.11

LEARN (cont.)

to Mordecai to l. what this was Est 4.05
I would l. what he would answer me, Job 23.05
when I l. thy righteous ordinances. Ps 119.07
that I might l. thy statutes. 119.71
that I may l. thy commandments. 119.73
then they shall l. that the word 141.06
O simple ones, l. prudence; Pro 8.05
and the simple will l. prudence; 19.25
lest you l. his ways and entangle 22.25
l. to do good; seek justice, Is 1.17
neither shall they l. war any more. 2.04
of the world l. righteousness. 26.09
he does not l. righteousness; 26.10
"L. not the way of the nations, nor Jer 10.02
will diligently l. the ways of my 12.16
neither shall they l. war any more; Mic 4.03
Go and l. what this means, 'I desire Mt 9.13
Take my yoke upon you, and l. from me; 11.29
"From the fig tree l. its lesson: 24.32
"From the fig tree l. its lesson: Mk 13.28
as he could not l. the facts Ac 21.34
will be able to l. from him about 24.08
that you may l. by us to live 1Co 4.06
so that all may l. and all be 14.31
You did not so l. Christ! Eph 4.20
and try to l. what is pleasing to 5.10
that they may l. not to blaspheme. 1Ti 1.20
Let a woman l. in silence with all 2.11
let them first l. their religious 5.04
they l. to be idlers, gadding about 5.13
And let our people l. to apply Tit 3.14
and l. that I have loved you. Rev 3.09
No one could l. that song except 14.03

LEARNED

I have l. by divination that the Gen 30.27
When Jacob l. that there was grain 42.01
And when they l. that the ark of 1Sa 4.06
and l. of a certainty that Saul had 26.04
l. in matters of the commandments Ez 7.11
When Mordecai l. all that had been Est 4.01
the nations and l. to do as they Ps 106.35
I have not l. wisdom, nor have I Pro 30.03
is a commandment of men l. by rote; Is 29.13
lion, and he l. to catch prey; Eze 19.03
lion, and he l. to catch prey; 19.06
until you have l. that the Most Dan 4.32
And when he l. from the centurion Mk 15.45
when she l. that he was sitting at Lk 7.37
When the crowds l. it, they followed 9.11
And when he l. that he belonged to 23.07
has heard and l. from the Father Jn 6.45
of the Jews l. that he was there, 12.09
they l. of it and fled to Lystra Ac 14.06
of Thessalonica l. that the word 17.13
having l. that he was a Roman 23.27
When he l. that he was from Cilicia 23.34
we then l. that the island was 28.01
What you have l. and received and Php 4.09
for I have l., in whatever state I 4.11
circumstances I have l. the secret 4.12
as you l. it from Epaphras our Col 1.07
that as you l. from us how you 1Th 4.01
what you have l. and have firmly 2Ti 3.14
knowing from whom you l. it 3.14
he l. obedience through what he Heb 5.08
who have not l. what some call the Rev 2.24

LEARNING

also may hear and increase in l., Pro 1.05
man and he will increase in l. 9.09
understanding l., and competent to Dan 1.04
God gave them l. and skill in all 1.17
"How is it that this man has l., Jn 7.15
him a hearing and l. what he does?" 7.51
your great l. is turning you mad." Ac 26.24

LEASH

you put him on l. for your maidens? Job 41.05

LEAST

with us a while, at l. ten days; Gen 24.55
worthy of the l. of all the 32.10
will not be lessened in the l.'" Ex 5.11
he who gathered l. gathered ten Num 11.32
war to such at l. as had not known Ju 3.02
and I am the l. in my family." 6.15
from the l. of the tribes of Israel? 1Sa 9.21
among the l. of my master's servants, 2Ki 18.24
the l. of them in the lead, the Ps 68.27
among the l. of my master's servants, Is 36.09
The l. one shall become a clan, and 60.22
"For from the l. to the greatest of Jer 6.13
from the l. to the greatest every 8.10
from the l. of them to the greatest, 31.34
people from the l. to the greatest, 42.01
people from the l. to the greatest, 42.08
from the l. to the greatest, they 44.12
greatest of them to the l. of them. Jon 3.05
are by no means l. among the Mt 2.06
one of the l. of these commandments 5.19
shall be called l. in the kingdom 5.19
yet he who is l. in the kingdom of 11.11
to one of the l. of these my 25.40
it not to one of the l. of these, 25.45
yet he who is l. in the kingdom of Lk 7.28
for he who is l. among you all is 9.48
came by at l. his shadow might Ac 5.15
from the l. to the greatest, saying, 8.10
those who are l. esteemed by the 1Co 6.04
not an apostle, at l. I am to you; 9.02
For I am the l. of the apostles, 15.09
I am not in the l. inferior to 2Co 11.05
I am the very l. of all the saints, Eph 3.08
from the l. of them to the greatest. Heb 8.11

LEATHER

a girdle of l. about his loins." 2Ki 1.08
embroidered cloth and shod you with l., Eze 16.10
and a l. girdle around his waist; Mt 3.04
and had a l. girdle around his Mk 1.06

LEAVE

for I will not l. you until I have Gen 28.15
"Let me l. with you some of the men 33.15
l. one of your brothers with me, and 42.33
'The lad cannot l. his father, 44.22
for if he should l. his father, 44.22
"Let no man l. any of it till the Ex 16.19
and what they l. the wild beasts 23.11
he shall not l. any of it until the Lev 7.15
place, and shall l. them there; 16.23
you shall l. them for the poor and 19.10
you shall l. none of it until 22.30
you shall l. them for the poor and 23.22
They shall l. none of it until the Num 9.12
"Do not l. us, I pray you, for you 10.31
to make you l. the way in which the Deu 13.05
who also shall not l. you grain, 28.51
they did not l. any that breathed. Jos 11.14
and l. no sustenance in Israel, and Ju 6.04
'Shall I l. my fatness, by which 9.09
'Shall I l. my sweetness and my 9.11
'Shall I l. my wine which cheers 9.13
then my strength will l. me, 16.17
me not to l. you or to return from Ru 1.16
in another field or l. this one, 2.08
and l. it for her to glean, and do 2.16
When he turned his back to l. Samuel, 1Sa 10.09
let us not l. a man of them." 14.36
earnestly asked l. of me to run to 20.06
earnestly asked l. of me to go to 20.28
if by morning I l. so much as one 25.22
and l. to my husband neither name 2Sa 14.07
may he not l. us or forsake us; 1Ki 8.57

LEAVE (cont.)
he did not l. him a single male of 1Ki 16.11
Yet I will l. seven thousand in 19.18
yourself live, I will not l. you." 2Ki 2.02
yourself live, I will not l. you." 2.04
yourself live, I will not l. you." 2.06
yourself live, I will not l. you." 4.30
and l. it for inheritance to your 1Ch 28.08
to l. us a remnant, and to give us a Ez 9.08
and l. it for an inheritance to 9.12
Let us l. off this interest. Neh 5.10
stop while I l. it and come down 6.03
some time I asked l. of the king 13.06
L. out nothing that you have Est 6.10
and will you l. to him your labor? Job 39.11
may they l. something over to their Ps 17.14
must perish and l. their wealth to 49.10
do not l. me to my oppressors. 119.121
seek refuge; l. me not defenseless! 141.08
L. simpleness, and live, and walk in Pro 9.06
L. the presence of a fool, for there 14.07
that I must l. it to the man who Ecc 2.18
and skill must l. all to be 2.21
do not l. your place, for deference 10.04
and where will you l. your wealth? Is 10.03
l. the way, turn aside from the path, 30.11
to l. the craving of the hungry 32.06
You shall l. your name to my chosen 65.15
that I might l. my people and go Jer 9.02
by thy name; l. us not." 14.09
midst of his days they will l. him, 17.11
snow of Lebanon l. the crags of 18.14
I will l. on its own land, to till 27.11
will by no means l. you unpunished. 30.11
will by no means l. you unpunished." 46.28
"L. the cities, and dwell in the 48.28
you, would they not l. gleanings? 49.09
L. your fatherless children, I will 49.11
those whom I l. as a remnant. 50.20
"Yet I will l. some of you alive. Eze 6.08
fair jewels, and l. you naked and bare. 16.39
and l. you naked and bare, and the 23.29
nations, will cut it down and l. it. 31.12
will go from its shadow and l. it. 31.12
I will l. none of them remaining 39.28
But l. the stump of its roots in Dan 4.15
but l. the stump of its roots in 4.23
commanded to l. the stump of the 4.26
his LORD will l. his bloodguilt Hos 12.14
and l. a blessing behind him, a Joe 2.14
Let the bridegroom l. his room, 2.16
you, would they not l. gleanings? Ob 1.05
wolves that l. nothing till the Zep 3.03
For I will l. in the midst of you a 3.12
so that it will l. them neither Mal 4.01
l. your gift there before the altar Mt 5.24
and l. the dead to bury their own 8.22
begged him to l. their neighborhood. 8.34
feet as you l. that house or town. 10.14
does he not l. the ninety-nine on 18.12
a man shall l. his father and 19.05
So he gave them l. And the unclean Mk 5.13
stay there until you l. the place. 6.10
when you l., shake off the dust 6.11
And after he had taken l. of them, 6.46
You l. the commandment of God, and 7.08
a man shall l. his father and 10.07
enter there. So he gave them l. Lk 8.32
when you l. that town shake off the 9.05
him, and will hardly l. him. 9.39
"L. the dead to bury their own dead; 9.60
does not l. the ninety-nine in the 15.04
they will not l. one stone upon 19.44
"L. here and go to Judea, that your Jn 7.03
"I will not l. you desolate; I will come 14.18
Peace I l. with you; my peace I 14.27
to his home, and will l. me alone; 16.32
of Jesus, and Pilate gave him l. 19.38
God and asked l. to find a habitation Ac 7.46
yet he did not l. himself without 14.17
out and asked them to l. the city. 16.39
commanded all the Jews to l. Rome. 18.02
and then took l. of the brethren 18.18
but on taking l. of them he said, "I 18.21
them took l. of them and departed 20.01
And when he had given him l., 21.40
and gave him l. to go to his 27.03
but l. it to the wrath of God; Rom 12.19
So I took l. of them and went on to 2Co 2.13
about this, that it should l. me; 12.08
a man shall l. his father and Eph 5.31
Therefore let us l. the elementary Heb 6.01
l. that out, for it is given over to Rev 11.02

LEAVEN
shall put away l. out of your Ex 12.15
For seven days no l. shall be found 12.19
and no l. shall be seen with you in 13.07
the blood of my sacrifice with l.; 34.25
to the LORD shall be made with l.; Lev 2.11
shall burn no l. nor any honey as 2.11
It shall not be baked with l. 6.17
flour, they shall be baked with l., 23.17
No l. shall be seen with you in all Deu 16.04
heaven is like l. which a woman Mt 13.33
beware of the l. of the Pharisees 16.06
Beware of the l. of the Pharisees 16.11
them to beware of the l. of bread, 16.12
beware of the l. of the Pharisees Mk 8.15
the Pharisees and the l. of Herod." 8.15
"Beware of the l. of the Pharisees, Lk 12.01
It is like l. which a woman took 13.21
that a little l. ferments the 1Co 5.06
Cleanse out the old l. that you may 5.07
the festival, not with the old l., 5.08
the l. of malice and evil, but with 5.08

LEAVENED
for if any one eats what is l., Ex 12.15
for if any one eats what is l., 12.19
You shall eat nothing l.; in all your 12.20
took their dough before it was l., 12.34
out of Egypt, for it was not l., 12.39
this place; no l. bread shall be eaten. 13.03
no l. bread shall be seen with you, 13.07
of my sacrifice with l. bread, 23.18
offering with cakes of l. bread. Lev 7.13
You shall eat no l. bread with it; Deu 16.03
the kneading of the dough until it is l. Hos 7.04
thanksgiving of that which is l., Amo 4.05
measures of meal, till it was all l." Mt 13.33
measures of meal, till it was all l." Lk 13.21

LEAVENS
A little yeast l. the whole lump. Gal 5.09

LEAVES
Therefore a man l. his father and Gen 2.24
they sewed fig l. together and 3.07
"When a man l. a pit open, or when a Ex 21.33
the two l. of the one door were 1Ki 6.34
and the two l. of the other door 6.34
if I forbear, how much of it l. me? Job 16.06
they pick mallow and the l. of bushes, 30.04
For she l. her eggs to the earth, 39.14
Behind him he l. a shining wake; 41.32
A good man l. an inheritance to his Pro 13.22
is a beating rain that l. no food. 28.03
and Carmel shake off their l. Is 33.09
as l. fall from the vine, like 34.04
like l. falling from the fig tree. 34.04
as a faithless wife l. her husband, Jer 3.20
even the l. are withered, and what I 8.13
for its l. remain green, and is not 17.08
all its fresh sprouting l. wither? Eze 17.09

LEAVES (cont.)
The doors had two l. apiece, Eze 41.24
two swinging l. for each door. 41.24
Their l. will not wither nor their 47.12
for food, and their l. for healing." 47.12
Its l. were fair and its fruit Dan 4.12
strip off its l. and scatter its 4.14
whose l. were fair and its fruit 4.21
found nothing on it but l. only. Mt 21.19
tender and puts forth its l., 24.32
to it, he found nothing but l., Mk 11.13
a man's brother dies and l. a wife, 12.19
but l. no child, the man must take 12.19
tender and puts forth its l. 13.28
when he l. home and puts his 13.34
wolf coming and l. the sheep and Jn 10.12
and the l. of the tree were for the Rev 22.02

LEAVING
shall refrain from l. him with it, Ex 23.05
time from our l. Kadeshbarnea Deu 2.14
l. the camp as it was, and fled for 2Ki 7.07
l. him severely wounded, his servants 2Ch 24.25
like a bridegroom l. his chamber, Ps 19.05
midst of Judah, l. you no remnant? Jer 44.07
and l. Nazareth he went and dwelt Mt 4.13
And l. them, he went out of the city 21.17
So, l. them again, he went away and 26.44
And l. the crowd, they took him with Mk 4.36
and as he was l. Jericho with his 10.46
took her, and died, l. no children; 12.21
would have kept him from l. them; Lk 4.42
and departed, l. him half dead. 10.30
again, I am l. the world and going Jn 16.28
l. it on the left we sailed to Ac 21.03
l. the horsemen to go on with him. 23.32
l. you an example, that you should 1Pe 2.21

LEBANA
the sons of L., the sons of Hagaba, Neh 7.48

LEBANAH
the sons of L., the sons of Hagabah, Ez 2.45

LEBANON
and L., as far as the great river, Deu 1.07
that goodly hill country, and L. 3.25
wilderness to L. and from the 11.24
and this L. as far as the great Jos 1.04
coast of the Great Sea toward L., 9.01
the valley of L. below Mount Hermon. 11.17
in the valley of L. to Mount Halak, 12.07
and all L., toward the sunrising, 13.05
country from L. to Misrephothmaim, 13.06
the Hivites who dwelt on Mount L., Ju 3.03
bramble and devour the cedars of L.' 9.15
that is in L. to the hyssop that 1Ki 4.33
that cedars of L. be cut for me; 5.06
bring it down to the sea from L.; 5.09
And he sent them to L., ten thousand 5.14
be a month in l. and two months at 5.14
the House of the Forest of L.; 7.02
in L., and in all the land of his 9.19
in the House of the Forest of L. 10.17
the Forest of L. were of pure gold; 10.21
"A thistle on L. sent to a cedar on L., 2Ki 14.09
a wild beast of L. passed by and 14.09
mountains, to the far recesses of L.; 19.23
cypress, and algum timber from L., 2Ch 2.08
know how to cut timber in L. 2.08
whatever timber you need from L., 2.16
in L., and in all the land of his 8.06
in the House of the Forest of L. 9.16
the Forest of L. were of pure gold; 9.20
"A thistle on L. sent to a cedar on L., 25.18
a wild beast of L. passed by and 25.18
cedar trees from L. to the sea, Ez 3.07
the LORD breaks the cedars of L. Ps 29.05
He makes L. to skip like a calf, and 29.06
and towering like a cedar of L. 37.35
may its fruit be like L.; and may men 72.16
tree, and grow like a cedar in L. 92.12
the cedars of L. which he planted. 104.16
a palanquin from the wood of L. Sol 3.09
Come with me from L., my bride; 4.08
from L. Depart from the 4.08
garments is like the scent of L. 4.11
water, and flowing streams from L. 4.15
His appearance is like L., choice as 5.15
Your nose is like a tower of L., 7.04
against all the cedars of L., Is 2.13
and L. with its majestic trees will 10.34
the cedars of L., saying, 'Since you 14.08
while until L. shall be turned 29.17
L. is confounded and withers away; 33.09
The glory of L. shall be given to 35.02
mountains, to the far recesses of L.; 37.24
L. would not suffice for fuel, nor 40.16
The glory of L. shall come to you, 60.13
Does the snow of L. leave the crags Jer 18.14
Gilead to me, as the summit of L., 22.06
"Go up to L., and cry out, and lift 22.20
O inhabitant of L., nested among 22.23
came to L. and took the top of the Eze 17.03
a cedar from L. to make a mast for 27.05
Behold, I will liken you to a cedar in L., 31.03
I will clothe L. in gloom for it, 31.15
of Eden the choice and best of L., 31.16
olive, and his fragrance like L. Hos 14.06
shall be like the wine of L. 14.07
wither, the bloom of L. fades. Nah 1.04
violence done to L. will overwhelm Hab 2.17
to the land of Gilead and to L., Zec 10.10
O L., that the fire may devour your 11.01

LABAOTH
L., Shilhim, Ain, and Rimmon: in all, Jos 15.32

LEBONAH
Bethel to Shechem, and south of L. Ju 21.19

LECAH
son of Judah: Er the father of L., 1Ch 4.21

LED
he l. forth his trained men, born in Gen 14.14
the LORD has l. me in the way to 24.27
who had l. me by the right way to 24.48
the God who has l. me all my life 48.15
and he l. his flock to the west Ex 3.01
But God l. the people round by the 13.18
"Thou hast l. in thy steadfast love 15.13
Then Moses l. Israel onward from 15.22
your God has l. you these forty Deu 8.02
who l. you through the great and 8.15
I have l. you forty years in the 29.05
the River and l. him through all Jos 24.03
I l. you up from Egypt, and brought Ju 6.08
it was you that l. out and brought 2Sa 5.02
And he l. them to Samaria. 2Ki 6.19
it was you that l. out and brought 1Ch 11.02
since the day I l. up Israel to 17.05
Joab l. out the army, and ravaged 20.01
and l. the inhabitants of Jerusalem 2Ch 21.11
and have l. Judah and the inhabitants 21.13
house of Ahab l. Israel into 21.13
and l. out his people, and went to 25.11
of cloud which l. them in the way Neh 9.19
and l. them in procession to the Ps 42.04
robes she is l. to the kings, 45.14
they are l. along as they enter 45.15
In the daytime he l. them with a 78.14
by his power he l. out the south 78.26
Then he l. forth his people like 78.52
He l. them in safety, so that they 78.53
Then he l. forth Israel with silver 105.37

LED (cont.)
So he l. forth his people with joy, Ps 105.43
and he l. them through the deep as 106.09
he l. them by a straight way, till 107.07
to him who l. his people through 136.16
I have l. you in the paths of Pro 4.11
and whoever is l. astray by it is 20.01
those who are l. by them are Is 9.16
of her tribes have l. Egypt astray. 19.13
a deluded mind has l. him astray, 44.20
and your knowledge l. you astray, 47.10
not when he l. them through the 48.21
a lamb that is l. to the slaughter, 53.07
in joy, and be l. forth in peace; 55.12
with their kings l. in procession. 60.11
who l. them through the depths? 63.13
who l. us in the wilderness, in a Jer 2.06
God, when he l. you in the way? 2.17
a gentle lamb l. to the slaughter. 11.19
brought up and l. the descendants 23.08
by Baal and l. my people Israel 23.13
were being l. out to the princes 38.22
sons shall be l. out to the 38.23
shepherds have l. them astray, 50.06
he l. me off my way and tore me to Lam 3.11
So I l. them out of the land of Eze 20.10
And he l. me round among them; 37.02
and seven steps l. up to it; 40.22
And he l. me toward the south, and 40.24
and ten steps l. up to it; 40.49
of the temple a stairway l. upward, 41.07
Then he l. me out into the inner 42.01
he l. me out by the gate which 42.15
and l. me to the four corners of 46.21
and l. me round on the outside to 47.02
and then l. me through the water; 47.03
and l. me through the water; 47.04
a thousand, and l. me through the water; 47.04
Then he l. me back along the bank 47.06
of harlotry has l. them astray, Hos 4.12
I l. them with cords of compassion, 11.04
but their lies have l. them astray, Amo 2.04
and l. you forty years in the 2.10
Then Jesus was l. up by the Spirit Mt 4.01
and l. them up a high mountain 17.01
seized Jesus l. him to Caiaphas 26.57
bound him and l. him away and 27.02
and l. him away to crucify him. 27.31
and l. him out of the village; Mk 8.23
and l. them up a high mountain 9.02
And they l. Jesus to the high 14.53
bound Jesus and l. him away and 15.01
And the soldiers l. him away inside 15.16
And they l. him out to crucify him. 15.20
Jordan, and was l. by the Spirit Lk 4.01
and l. him to the brow of the hill 4.29
heed that you are not l. astray; 21.08
and be l. captive among all nations; 21.24
Then they seized him and l. him away, 22.54
and they l. him away to their 22.66
And as they l. him away, they seized 23.26
were l. away to be put to death 23.32
Then he l. them out as far as 24.50
"Are you l. astray, you also? Jn 7.47
First they l. him to Annas; 18.13
Then they l. Jesus from the house 18.28
He l. them out, having performed Ac 7.36
this Moses who l. us out from the 7.40
"As a sheep l. to the slaughter or 8.32
so they l. him by the hand and 9.08
uplifted arm he l. them out of it. 13.17
up a revolt and l. the four 21.38
I was l. by the hand by those who 22.11
man's trespass l. to condemnation Rom 5.18
For all who are l. by the Spirit of 8.14
you were l. astray to dumb idols, 1Co 12.02
thoughts will be l. astray from a 2Co 11.03
But if you are l. by the Spirit you Gal 5.18
on high he l. a host of captives, Eph 4.08
l. astray, slaves to various passions Tit 3.03
Do not be l. away by diverse and Heb 13.09

LEDGE
it under the l. of the altar so Ex 27.05
under its l., extending halfway 38.04
base on the ground to the lower l., Eze 43.14
the smaller l. to the larger l., 43.14
The l. also shall be square, fourteen 43.17
and on the four corners of the l., 43.20
corners of the l. of the altar, 45.19

LEE
we sailed under the l. of Cyprus, Ac 27.04
under the l. of Crete off Salmone. 27.07
under the l. of a small island 27.16

LEECH
The l. has two daughters; "Give, give," Pro 30.15

LEEKS
the l., the onions, and the garlic; Num 11.05

LEES
things, a feast of wine on the l., Is 25.06
marrow, of wine on the l. well refined. 25.06
youth and has settled on his l.; Jer 48.11
who are thickening upon their l., Zep 1.12

LEFT
Only Noah was l., and those that Gen 7.23
and they l. off building the city. 11.08
If you take the l. hand, 13.09
hand, then I will go to the l." 13.09
to the right hand or to the l." 24.49
Jacob l. Beersheba, and went toward 28.10
or inheritance l. to us in our 31.14
company which is l. will escape." 32.08
And Jacob was l. alone; and a man 32.24
So he l. all that he had in Joseph's 39.06
But he l. his garment in her hand, 39.12
saw that he had l. his garment in 39.13
he l. his garment with me, and fled 39.15
he l. his garment with me, and fled 39.18
brother is dead, and he only is l. 42.38
and he alone is l. of his mother's 44.20
one l. me, and I said, Surely he has 44.28
is nothing l. in the sight of my 47.18
right hand toward Israel's l. hand, 48.13
Manasseh in his l. hand toward 48.13
and his l. hand upon the head of 48.14
herds were l. in the land of 50.08
Why have you l. the man? Call him, Ex 2.20
houses and be l. only in the Nile." 8.09
they shall be l. only in the Nile. 8.11
of the LORD l. his slaves and his 9.21
eat what is l. to you after the 10.05
the land, all that the hail has l." 10.12
of the trees which the hail had l.; 10.15
locust was l. in all the country 10.19
not a hoof shall be l. behind, 10.26
their right hand and on their l. 14.22
their right hand and on their l. 14.29
some l. part of it till the morning, 16.20
and all that is l. over lay by to 16.23
the passover be l. until the 34.25
And what is l. of the cereal Lev 2.03
And what is l. of the cereal 2.10
and Ithamar, his sons who were l., 10.12
sons of Aaron who were l., saying, 10.16
into the palm of his own l. hand, 14.15
in the oil that is in his l. hand, 14.16
into the palm of his own l. hand; 14.26
that is in his l. hand seven times 14.27
and anything l. over until the 19.06
And as for those of you that are l., 26.36

LEFT (cont.)

of you that are l. shall pine away Lev 26.39
But the land shall be l. by them, 26.43
to the right hand or to the l., Num 20.17
was not one survivor l. to him; 21.35
either to the right or to the l. 22.26
he rose and l. the congregation, and 25.07
There was not l. a man of them, 26.65
neither to the right nor to the l. Deu 2.27
and children; we l. none remaining; 2.34
until no survivor was l. to him. 3.03
of Bashan was l. of the remnant of 3.11
and you will be l. few in number 4.27
to the right hand or to the l. 5.32
those who are l. and hide themselves 7.20
to the right hand or to the l. 17.11
to the right hand or to the l.; 17.20
to the right hand or to the l., 28.14
because he has nothing l. him, 28.55
you shall be l. few in number; 28.62
it to the right hand or to the l., Jos 1.07
there was no courage l. in any man, 2.11
There was not a man l. in Ai or 8.17
they l. the city open, and pursued 8.17
until there was l. none that 8.22
person in it, he l. none remaining; 10.28
he l. none remaining in it; 10.30
people, until he l. none remaining. 10.33
he l. none remaining, as he had done 10.37
he l. none remaining; as he had done 10.39
he l. none remaining, but utterly 10.40
them, until they l. none remaining. 11.08
there was none l. that breathed, 11.11
he l. nothing undone of all that 11.15
of the Anakim l. in the land of 11.22
(he alone was l. of the remnant of 13.12
to the right hand nor to the l., 23.06
these nations l. here among you, 23.07
of these nations l. here among you, 23.12
that Joshua l. when he died, Ju 2.21
So the LORD l. those nations, not 2.23
are the nations which the LORD l., 3.01
And Ehud reached with his l. hand, 3.21
of the sword; not a man was l. 4.16
in their l. hands the torches, and 7.20
all who were l. of all the army of 8.10
youngest son of Jerubbaal was l., 9.05
him, and his strength l. him. 16.19
not know that the LORD had l. him. 16.20
the one and his l. hand on the 16.29
and go away, and what have I l.? 18.24
do for wives for those who are l., 21.07
do for wives for those who are l., 21.16
and she was l. with her two sons. Ru 1.03
and how you l. your father and 2.11
satisfied, and she had some l. over. 2.14
food she had l. over after being 2.18
who has not l. you this day without 4.14
one who is l. in your house shall 1Sa 2.36
the trunk of Dagon was l. to him. 5.04
neither to the right nor to the l., 6.12
no two of them were l. together. 11.11
and l. the sheep with a keeper, and 17.20
And David l. the things in charge 17.22
whom have you l. those few sheep 17.28
And he l. them with the king of 22.04
And Saul rose up and l. the cave, 24.07
had not been l. to Nabal so much 25.34
and l. neither man nor woman alive, 27.09
those stayed who were l. behind. 30.09
and my master l. me behind because 30.13
who had been l. at the brook Besor; 30.21
hand nor to the l. from following 2Sa 2.19
to your right hand or to your l., 2.21
And the Philistines l. their idols 5.21
but l. enough for a hundred chariots. 8.04
still any one l. of the house of 9.01
sons, and not one of them is l." 13.30
would quench my coal which is l., 14.07
hand or to the l. from anything 14.19
And the king l. ten concubines to 15.16
on his right hand and on his l. 16.06
whom he has l. to keep the house; 16.21
men with him not one will be l. 17.12
not one was l. who had not crossed 17.22
and he was l. hanging between 18.09
day my lord the king l. Jerusalem; 19.19
whom he had l. to care for the 20.03
And Solomon l. all the vessels 1Ki 7.47
people who were l. of the Amorites, 9.20
who were l. after them in the land, 9.21
gold that were l. in the treasures 15.18
he l. to the house of Jeroboam not 15.29
that there was no breath l. in him. 17.17
am l. a prophet of the LORD; 18.22
and l. his servant there. 19.03
and I, even I only, am l.; 19.10
and I, even I only, am l.; 19.14
And he l. the oxen, and ran after 19.20
twenty-seven thousand men that were l. 20.30
on his right hand and on his l.; 22.19
its stones were l. in Kirhareseth, 2Ki 3.25
'They shall eat and have some l.' " 4.43
and had some l., according to the 4.44
those who are l. here will fare 7.13
day that she l. the land until now 8.06
until he l. him none remaining. 10.11
was not a man l. who did not come. 10.21
For there was not l. to Jehoahaz an 13.07
very bitter, for there was none l., 14.26
none was l. but the tribe of 17.18
prayer for the remnant that is l." 19.04
heard that the king had l. Lachish. 19.08
nothing shall be l., says the LORD. 20.17
to the right hand or to the l. 22.02
were on one's l. at the gate of 23.08
people who were l. in the city and 25.11
of the guard l. some of the 25.12
Nebuchadnezzar king of Babylon had l., 25.22
On the l. hand were their brethren 1Ch 6.44
either the right or the l. hand; 12.02
And they l. their gods there, and 14.12
So David l. Asaph and his brethren 16.37
And he l. Zadok the priest and his 16.39
but l. enough for a hundred chariots. 18.04
people who were l. of the Hittites, 2Ch 8.07
who were l. after them in the land, 8.08
For the Levites l. their common 11.14
on his right hand and on his l.; 18.18
that no son was l. to him except 21.17
So the armed men l. the captives 28.14
and had enough and have plenty l.; 31.10
that we have this great store l." 31.10
God l. him to himself, in order to 32.31
aside to the right or to the l. 34.02
those who are l. in Israel and in 34.21
for we are l. a remnant that has Ez 9.15
was no breach l. in it (although Neh 6.01
and Meshullam on his l. hand. 8.04
who gave thanks went to the l., 12.38
As the words l. the mouth of the Est 7.08
There was nothing l. after he had Job 20.21
what is l. in his tent will be 20.26
is nothing l. of your answers but 21.34
and what they l. the fire has 22.20
on the l. hand I seek him, but I 23.09
adversaries; not one of them was l. Ps 106.11
in her l. hand are riches and honor. Pro 3.16
swerve to the right or to the l.; 4.27
broken into and l. without walls. 25.28
but a child l. to himself brings 29.15
rights of all who are l. desolate. 31.08
but a fool's heart toward the l. Ecc 10.02
O that his l. hand were under my Sol 2.06

LEFT (cont.)

O that his l. hand were under my Sol 8.03
of Zion is l. like a booth in a Is 1.08
hosts had not l. us a few survivors, 1.09
And he who is l. in Zion and 4.03
one that is l. in the land will 7.22
hungry, and they devour on the l., 9.20
remnant which is l. of his people, 11.11
remnant which is l. of his people, 11.16
Gleanings will be l. in it, 17.06
all of them be l. to the birds of 18.06
are scorched, and few men are l. 24.06
Desolation is l. in the city, the 24.12
till you are l. like a flagstaff on 30.17
right or when you turn to the l. 30.21
prayer for the remnant that is l.'" 37.04
heard that the king had l. Lachish. 37.08
nothing shall be l., says the LORD. 39.06
Behold, I was l. alone; whence then 49.21
abroad to the right and to the l., 54.03
because we have l. the land, Jer 9.19
and none of them shall be l. 11.23
Like a lion he has l. his covert, 25.38
which are l. in the house of the 27.18
vessels which are l. in this city, 27.19
which are l. in the house of the 27.21
the cities of Judah that were l., 34.07
soldiers who are l. in this city, 38.04
there is no bread l. in the city." 38.09
all the women l. in the house of 38.22
So they l. off speaking with him, 38.27
the people who were l. in the city, 39.09
l. in the land of Judah some of the 39.10
the people who were l. in the land. 40.06
of Babylon had l. a remnant in 40.11
the people who were l. at Mizpah, 41.10
(for we are l. but a few of many, as 42.02
the guard had l. with Gedaliah the 43.06
But since we l. off burning incense 44.18
let nothing be l. of her. 50.26
people who were l. in the city and 52.15
of the guard l. some of the 52.16
he has l. me stunned, faint all the Lam 1.13
the face of an ox on the l. side, Eze 1.10
"Then lie upon your l. side, 4.04
and he that is l. and is preserved 6.12
and I was l. alone, I fell upon my 9.08
there should be l. in it any 14.22
to right and l. where your edge is 21.16
whom you l. behind shall fall by 24.21
that are l. round about you shall 36.36
strike your bow from your l. hand, 39.03
which was l. free was five cubits. 41.09
of the platform that was l. free, 41.11
part that was l. free was five 41.11
they are to be l. for salt. 47.11
was troubled, and his sleep l. him. Dan 2.01
sovereignty be l. to another 2.44
So I was l. alone and saw this 10.08
and no strength was l. in me; 10.08
so I l. him there with the prince 10.13
in me, and no breath is l. in me." 10.17
hand and his l. hand toward heaven; 12.07
and they have l. their God to play Hos 4.12
will bereave them till none is l. 9.12
What the cutting locust l., Joe 1.04
What the swarming locust l., 1.04
and what the hopping locust l., 1.04
a thousand shall have a hundred l., Amo 5.03
shall have ten l. to the house of 5.03
and what are l. of them I will slay 9.01
their right hand from their l., Jon 4.11
you till no inhabitant is l. Zep 2.05
those who are l. in Israel; 3.13
'Who is l. among you that saw this Hag 2.03
the bowl and the other on its l." Zec 4.03
right and the l. of the lampstand?" 4.11
Thus the land they l. was desolate, 7.14
those that are l. devour the flesh 11.09
and to the l. all the peoples 12.06
and all the families that are l., 12.14
and one third shall be l. alive. 13.08
country and l. his heritage to Mal 1.03
Then the devil l. him, and behold, Mt 4.11
Immediately they l. their nets and 4.20
Immediately they l. the boat and 4.22
do not let your l. hand know what 6.03
and the fever l. her, and she rose 8.15
Then he l. the crowds and went into 13.36
full of the broken pieces l. over. 14.20
full of the broken pieces l. over. 15.37
So he l. them and departed. 16.04
we have l. everything and followed 19.27
one who has l. houses or brothers 19.29
your right hand and one at your l., 20.21
hand and at my l. is not mine to 20.23
and they l. him and went away. 22.22
no children l. his wife to his 22.25
Jesus l. the temple and was going 24.01
will not be l. here one stone upon 24.02
the field; one is taken and one is l. 24.40
the mill; one is taken and one is l. 24.41
hand, but the goats at the l. 25.33
will say to those at his l. hand, 25.41
one on the right and one on the l. 27.38
immediately they l. their nets and Mk 1.18
and they l. their father Zebedee in 1.20
And immediately he l. the synagogue, 1.29
her up, and the fever l. her; 1.31
And immediately the leprosy l. him. 1.42
and l. the people, his disciples 7.17
the demon has l. your daughter." 7.29
took up the broken pieces l. over, 8.08
And he l. them, and getting into the 8.13
And he l. there and went to the 10.01
we have l. everything and followed 10.28
no one who has l. house or brothers 10.29
and one at your l., in your glory." 10.37
hand or at my l. is not mine to 10.40
so they l. him and went away. 12.12
and when he died l. no children; 12.20
and the seven l. no children. 12.22
will not be l. here one stone upon 13.02
but he l. the linen cloth and ran 14.52
one on his right and one on his l. 15.27
And he arose and l. the synagogue, Lk 4.38
rebuked the fever, and it l. her; 4.39
they l. everything and followed him. 5.11
And immediately the leprosy l. him. 5.13
And he l. everything, and rose and 5.28
and they took up what was l. over, 9.17
my sister has l. me to serve alone? 10.40
would not have l. his house to be 12.39
one will be taken and the other l. 17.34
one will be taken and the other l." 17.35
one will be taken and the other l." * 17.36
we have l. our homes and followed 18.28
no man who has l. house or wife or 18.29
all seven l. no children and died. 20.31
shall not be l. here one stone 21.06
one on the right and one on the l. 23.33
he l. Judea and departed again to Jn 4.03
So the woman l. her water jar, and 4.28
the seventh hour the fever l. him." 4.52
"Gather up the fragments l. over, 6.12
loaves, l. by those who had eaten. 6.13
Jesus was l. alone with the woman * 8.09
he has not l. me alone, for I always 8.29
Then they l. the presence of the Ac 5.41
and immediately the angel l. him. 12.10
And John l. them and returned to 13.13
After this he l. Athens and went to 18.01
And he l. there and went to the 18.07
to Ephesus, and he l. them there; 18.19

LEFT (cont.)
and diseases l. them and the evil Ac 19.12
it on the l. we sailed to Syria, 21.03
a favor, Felix l. Paul in prison. 24.27
"There is a man l. prisoner by 25.14
the anchors and l. them in the sea, 27.40
of hosts had not l. us children, Rom 9.29
thy altars, and I alone am l., 11.03
for the right hand and for the l.; 2Co 6.07
when I l. Macedonia, no church Php 4.15
willing to be l. behind at Athens 1Th 3.01
who are l. until the coming of the 4.15
who are l., shall be caught up 4.17
and is l. all alone, has set her 1Ti 5.05
cloak that I l. with Carpus at 2Ti 4.13
Trophimus I l. ill at Miletus. 4.20
This is why I l. you in Crete, that Tit 1.05
he l. nothing outside his control. Heb 2.08
all those who l. Egypt under the 3.16
By faith he l. Egypt, not being 11.27
If you are l. without discipline, in 12.08
position but l. their proper Jud 1.06
and his l. foot on the land, Rev 10.02

LEFT-HANDED
of Gera, the Benjaminite, a l. man. Ju 3.15
hundred picked men who were l.; 20.16

LEG
took up the l. and the upper 1Sa 9.24

LEGAL
one kind of l. right and another, or Deu 17.08
against us with its l. demands; Col 2.14
according to a l. requirement Heb 7.16

LEGION
He replied, "My name is L.; Mk 5.09
mind, the man who had had the l.; 5.15
And he said, "L."; for many demons Lk 8.30

LEGIONS
me more than twelve l. of angels? Mt 26.53

LEGS
head with its l. and its inner Ex 12.09
to the four corners at its four l. 25.26
and wash its entrails and its l., 29.17
to the four corners at its four l. 37.13
entrails and its l. he shall wash Lev 1.09
entrails and the l. he shall wash 1.13
its l., its entrails, and its dung, 4.11
entrails and the l. were washed 8.21
And he washed the entrails and the l., 9.14
which have l. above their feet, 11.21
and on the l. with grievous boils Deu 28.35
had greaves of bronze upon his l., 1Sa 17.06
his pleasure in the l. of a man; Ps 147.10
Like a lame man's l., which hang Pro 26.07
His l. are alabaster columns, set Sol 5.15
uncover your l., pass through the Is 47.02
Their l. were straight, and the Eze 1.07
its l. of iron, its feet partly of Dan 2.33
his arms and l. like the gleam of 10.06
from the mouth of the lion two l., Amo 3.12
that their l. might be broken. and Jn 19.31
came and broke the l. of the first, 19.32
dead, they did not break his l. 19.33
and his l. like pillars of fire. Rev 10.01

LEHABIM
of Ludim, Anamim, L., Naphtuhim, Gen 10.13
of Ludim, Anamim, L., Naphtuhim, 1Ch 1.11

LEHEM
and returned to L. (now the 1Ch 4.22

LEHI
in Judah, and made a raid on L. Ju 15.09
When he came to L., the Philistines 15.14
the hollow place that is at L., 15.19
it is at L. to this day. 15.19
Philistines gathered together at L., 2Sa 23.11

LEISURE
and they had no l. even to eat. Mk 6.31

LEMUEL
The words of L., king of Massa, Pro 31.01
O L., it is not for kings to drink 31.04

LEND
"If you l. money to any of my Ex 22.25
You shall not l. him your money at Lev 25.37
and you shall l. to many nations, Deu 15.06
and l. him sufficient for his need, 15.08
"You shall not l. upon interest to 23.19
foreigner you may l. upon interest, 23.20
you shall not l. upon interest; 23.20
and you shall l. to many nations, 28.12
He shall l. to you, and you shall not l. 28.44
does not l. at interest or take any Eze 18.08
And if you l. to those from whom Lk 6.34
Even sinners l. to sinners, to 6.34
and l., expecting nothing in return; 6.35
'Friend, l. me three loaves; 11.05

LENDER
borrower is the slave of the l. Pro 22.07
as with the l., so with the borrower; Is 24.02

LENDING
my servants are l. them money and Neh 5.10
He is ever giving liberally and l., Ps 37.26

LENDS
man who deals generously and l., Ps 112.05
is kind to the poor l. to the LORD, Pro 19.17
l. at interest, and takes increase; Eze 18.13

LENGTH
the l. of the ark three hundred Gen 6.15
through the l. and the breadth of 13.17
cubits and a half shall be its l., Ex 25.10
cubits and a half shall be its l., 25.17
two cubits shall be its l., 25.23
The l. of each curtain shall be 26.02
The l. of each curtain shall be 26.08
remains in the l. of the curtains 26.13
Ten cubits shall be the l. of a frame, 26.16
likewise for its l. on the north 27.11
The l. of the court shall be a 27.18
a span its l. and a span its 28.16
A cubit shall be its l., 30.02
The l. of each curtain was twenty-eight 36.09
The l. of each curtain was thirty 36.15
Ten cubits was the l. of a frame, 36.21
two cubits and a half was its l., 37.01
two cubits and a half was its l., 37.06
two cubits was its l., a cubit its 37.10
its l. was a cubit, and its breadth 37.25
five cubits was its l., and five 38.01
a span its l. and a span its 39.09
in measures of l. or weight or Lev 19.35
Nine cubits was its l., and four Deu 3.11
means life to you and l. of days, 30.20
with two edges, a cubit in l.; Ju 3.16
half a furrow's l. in an acre of 1Sa 14.14
at once full l. upon the ground, 28.20
Five cubits was the l. of one wing 1Ki 6.24
five cubits the l. of the other 6.24
its l. was a hundred cubits, and its 7.02
its l. was fifty cubits, and its 7.06
the l., in cubits of the old 2Ch 3.03
its l., corresponding to the 3.08

LENGTH (cont.)
and understanding in l. of days. Job 12.12
l. of days for ever and ever. Ps 21.04
for l. of days and years of life Pro 3.02
wearied with the l. of your way, Is 57.10
people from the l. and breadth of Jer 8.19
in the l. of its branches; Eze 31.07
and the l. of the measuring reed in 40.05
a cubit and a handbreadth in l.; 40.05
corresponding to the l. of the gates; 40.18
He measured its l. and its breadth. 40.20
its l. was fifty cubits, and its 40.21
its l. was fifty cubits, and its 40.25
its l. was fifty cubits, and its 40.29
its l. was fifty cubits, and its 40.33
its l. was fifty cubits, and its 40.36
The l. of the vestibule was twenty 40.49
he measured the l. of the nave 41.02
And he measured the l. of the room, 41.04
about, and its l. ninety cubits. 41.12
Then he measured the l. of the 41.15
The l. of the building which was on 42.02
of the same l. and breadth, with the 42.11
corresponding in l. to one of the 45.07
and in l. equal to one of the 48.08
twenty-five thousand cubits in l., 48.09
thousand in l. on the southern 48.10
cubits in l. and ten thousand in 48.13
The whole l. shall be twenty-five 48.13
and twenty-five thousand in l., 48.15
remainder of the l. alongside the 48.18
is its breadth and what is its l." Zec 2.02
its l. is twenty cubits, and its 5.02
So he questioned him at some l.; Lk 23.09
in it, not even a foot's l., Ac 7.05
the breadth and l. and height and Eph 3.18
that now at l. you have revived Php 4.10
its l. the same as its breadth; Rev 21.16
its l. and breadth and height are 21.16

LENGTHEN
walked, then I will l. your days." 1Ki 3.14
for the shadow to l. ten steps; 2Ki 20.10
l. your cords and strengthen your Is 54.02
for the shadows of evening l.!" Jer 6.04

LENGTHENING
perhaps be a l. of your tranquillity." Dan 4.27

LENT
what he has l. to his neighbor; Deu 15.02
anything that is l. for interest. 23.19
Therefore I have l. him to the LORD 1Sa 1.28
as he lives, he is l. to the LORD. 1.28
the loan which she l. to the LORD"; 2.20
I have not l., nor have I borrowed, Jer 15.10

LENTILS
gave Esau bread and pottage of l., Gen 25.34
meal, parched grain, beans and l., 2Sa 17.28
was a plot of ground full of l.; 23.11
beans and l., millet and spelt, and Eze 4.09

LEOPARD
and the l. shall lie down with the Is 11.06
A l. is watching against their Jer 5.06
his skin or the l. his spots? 13.23
like a l., with four wings of a Dan 7.06
like a l. I will lurk beside the Hos 13.07
the beast that I saw was like a l., Rev 13.02

LEOPARDS
of lions, from the mountains of l. Sol 4.08
Their horses are swifter than l., Hab 1.08

LEPER
"The l. who has the disease shall Lev 13.45
the law of the l. for the day of 14.02
disease is healed in the l., 14.03
Aaron who is a l. or suffers a 22.04
they put out of the camp every l., Num 5.02
man of valor, but he was a l. 2Ki 5.01
over the place, and cure the l. 5.11
he went out from his presence a l., 5.27
that he was a l. to the day of his 15.05
Uzziah was a l. to the day of his 2Ch 26.21
and being a l. dwelt in a separate 26.21
kings, for they said, "He is a l." 26.23
and behold, a l. came to him and Mt 8.02
in the house of Simon the l., 26.06
And a l. came to him beseeching him, Mk 1.40
in the house of Simon the l., 14.03

LEPERS
men who were l. at the entrance to 2Ki 7.03
And when these l. came to the edge 7.08
cleanse l., cast out demons. Mt 10.08
l. are cleansed and the deaf hear, 11.05
And there were many l. in Israel in Lk 4.27
l. are cleansed, and the deaf hear, 7.22
a village, he was met by ten l., 17.12

LEPROSY
him unclean; it is l. Lev 13.08
"When a man is afflicted with l., 13.09
it is a chronic l. in the skin of 13.11
And if the l. breaks out in the 13.12
so that the l. covers all the skin 13.12
and if the l. has covered all his 13.13
raw flesh is unclean, for it is l. 13.15
it is the disease of l., 13.20
than the skin, then it is l.; 13.25
a l. of the head or the beard. 13.30
it is l. breaking out on his bald 13.42
appearance of l. in the skin of 13.43
the disease is a malignant l.; 13.51
of skin, for it is a malignant l.; 13.52
him who is to be cleansed of l.; 14.07
it is a malignant l. in the house; 14.44
for l. in a garment or in a house, 14.55
it is clean. This is the law for l. 14.57
"Take heed, in an attack of l., Deu 24.08
He would cure him of his l." 2Ki 5.03
that you may cure him of his l." 5.06
word to me to cure a man of his l.? 5.07
Therefore the l. of Naaman shall 5.27
the priests l. broke out on his 2Ch 26.19
immediately his l. was cleansed. Mt 8.03
And immediately the l. left him, Mk 1.42
there came a man full of l.; Lk 5.12
And immediately the l. left him. 5.13

LEPROUS
his hand was l., as white as snow. Ex 4.06
it turns into a l. disease on the Lev 13.02
of his body, it is a l. disease; 13.03
him unclean; it is a l. disease. 13.25
him unclean; it is a l. disease. 13.27
he is a l. man, he is unclean; 13.44
"When there is a l. disease in a 13.47
it is a l. disease and shall be 13.49
whether the l. spot is on the back 13.55
the law for a l. disease in a 13.59
Then, if the l. disease is healed in 14.03
for him in whom is a l. disease, 14.32
and I put a l. disease in a house 14.34
This is the law for any l. disease: 14.54
Miriam was l., as white as snow. Num 12.10
Miriam, and behold, she was l. 12.10
or who is l., or who holds a 2Sa 3.29
he was l. in his forehead! 2Ch 26.20

LESHEM
went up and fought against L., Jos 19.47
calling L., Dan, after the name of 19.47

LESS
they gathered, some more, some l. Ex 16.17
and the poor shall not give l., 30.15
the LORD my God, to do l. or more. Num 22.18
how much l. this house which I have 1Ki 8.27
how much l. this house which I 2Ch 6.18
How much l. will your God deliver 32.15
punished us l. than our iniquities Ez 9.13
exacts of you l. than your guilt Job 11.06
how much l. one who is abominable 15.16
how much l. man, who is a maggot, and 25.06
How much l. when you say that you 35.14
hast made him little l. than God, Ps 8.05
still l. is false speech to a Pro 17.07
much l. for a slave to rule over 19.10
by him as l. than nothing and Is 40.17
shown herself l. guilty than false Jer 3.11
how much l., when the fire has Eze 15.05
not make it any l. a part of the 1Co 12.15
not make it any l. a part of the 12.16
which we think l. honorable we 12.23
the Jews the forty lashes l. one. 2Co 11.24
what were you l. favored than the 12.13
the more, am I to be loved the l.? 12.15
and that I may be l. anxious. Php 2.28
much l. shall we escape if we Heb 12.25

LESSEN
them, you shall by no means l. it; Ex 5.08
by no means l. your daily number 5.19

LESSENED
work will not be l. in the least.'" Ex 5.11

LESSER
and the l. light to rule the night; Gen 1.16
the l. over a hundred and the 1Ch 12.14

LESSON
"From the fig tree learn its l.: Mt 24.32
"From the fig tree learn its l.: Mk 13.28
a l., a revelation, a tongue, or an 1Co 14.26

LEST
shall you touch it, l. you die.'" Gen 3.03
and now, l. he put forth his hand 3.22
l. any who came upon him should 4.15
l. we be scattered abroad upon the 11.04
l. you should say, 'I have made 14.23
l. you be consumed in the punishment 19.15
to the hills, l. you be consumed." 19.17
l. the disaster overtake me, and I 19.19
"L. the men of the place should 26.07
'L. I die because of her.'" 26.09
l. he come and slay us all, the 32.11
l. he should give offspring to his 38.09
l. we be laughed at; you see, I 38.23
l. you and your household, and all 45.11
l. they multiply, and, if war befall Ex 1.10
l. he fall upon us with pestilence 5.03
"L. the people repent when they see 13.17
l. they break through to the LORD 19.21
l. the LORD break out upon them." 19.22
l. he break out against them." 19.24
let not God speak to us, l. we die." 20.19
l. the land become desolate and the 23.29
l. they make you sin against me; 23.33
and when he comes out, l. he die. 28.35
l. they bring guilt upon themselves 28.43
shall wash with water, l. they die. 30.20
l. they die: it shall be a statute 30.21
l. I consume you in the way, for you 33.03
l. you make a covenant with the 34.12
l. it become a snare in the midst 34.12
l. you make a covenant with the 34.15
the LORD has charged, l. you die; Lev 8.35
l. you die, and l. wrath come upon all 10.06
of the tent of meeting, l. you die; 10.07
the tent of meeting, l. you die; 10.09
with them, l. you become unclean. 11.43
l. all that is in the house be 14.36
l. they die in their uncleanness by 15.31
which is upon the ark, l. he die; 16.02
is upon the testimony, l. he die; 16.13
l. the land vomit you out, when you 18.28
l. you bear sin because of him. 19.17
l. the land fall into harlotry and 19.29
l. they bear sin for it and die 22.09
touch the holy things, l. they die. Num 4.15
even for a moment, l. they die." 4.20
Do not go up l. you be struck down 14.42
l. you be swept away with all their 16.26
"L. the earth swallow us up!" 16.34
l. he become as Korah and as his 16.40
murmurings against me, l. they die." 17.10
to the altar, l. they, and you, die. 18.03
of meeting, l. they bear sin and die. 18.22
the people of Israel, l. you die.'" 18.32
l. I come out with the sword 20.18
l. you be defeated before your Deu 1.42
l. you forget the things which your 4.09
and l. they depart from your heart 4.09
beware l. you act corruptly by 4.16
And beware l. you lift up your eyes 4.19
l. you forget the covenant of the 4.23
then take heed l. you forget the 6.12
l. the anger of the LORD your God 6.15
l. the wild beasts grow too numerous 7.22
l. you be ensnared by it; 7.25
"Take heed l. you forget the LORD 8.11
l., when you have eaten and are 8.12
Beware l. you say in your heart, 'My 8.17
l. the land from which thou didst 9.28
Take heed l. your heart be deceived, 11.16
Take heed l. there be a base 15.09
l. his heart turn away; nor shall he 17.17
this great fire any more, l. I die.' 18.16
l. the avenger of blood in hot 19.06
l. innocent blood be shed in your 19.10
l. he die in the battle and another 20.05
l. he die in the battle and another 20.06
l. he die in the battle and another 20.07
l. the heart of his fellows melt as 20.08
l. the whole yield be forfeited to 22.09
l. he cry against you to the LORD, 24.15
l., if one should go on to beat him 25.03
Beware l. there be among you a man 29.18
l. there be among you a root 29.18
l. their adversaries should judge 32.27
l. they should say, "Our hand is 32.27
l. the pursuers meet you; and hide Jos 2.16
l. when you have devoted them you 6.18
l. wrath be upon us, because of the 9.20
l. your children say to our children 22.27
l. you deal falsely with your God." 24.27
l. Israel vaunt themselves against Ju 7.02
l. men say of me, 'A woman killed 9.54
l. we burn you and your father's 14.15
l. angry fellows fall upon you, and 18.25
l. in another field you be molested." Ru 2.22
l. I impair my own inheritance. 4.06
l. you become slaves to the Hebrews 1Sa 4.09
l. my father cease to care about 9.05
"L. the Hebrews make themselves 13.19
l. I destroy you with them; 15.06
know this, l. he be grieved.' 20.03
"L. they should tell about us, and 27.11
l. in the battle he became an 29.04
l. these uncircumcised come and 31.04
l. the daughters of the Philistines 2Sa 1.20
l. the daughters of the uncircumcised 1.20
l. I take the city, and it be called 12.28
l. we be burdensome to you." He pressed 13.25
go in haste, l. he overtake us 15.14
l. the king and all the people who 17.16

LEST (cont.)

l. he get himself fortified cities, 2Sa 20.06
l. you quench the lamp of Israel." 21.17
go down, l. the rain stop you.'" 1Ki 18.44
l. these uncircumcised come and 1Ch 10.04
who is with me, l. he destroy you." 2Ch 35.21
l. his wrath be against the realm Ez 7.23
Beware l. you say, 'We have found Job 32.13
Beware l. wrath entice you into 36.18
kiss his feet, l. he be angry, and Ps 2.12
l. like a lion they rend me, dragging 7.02
l. I sleep the sleep of death; 13.03
l. my enemy say, "I have prevailed 13.04
l. my foes rejoice because I am 13.04
l., if thou be silent to me, I 28.01
l. I rend, and there be none to 50.22
Slay them not, l. my people forget; 59.11
l. you dash your foot against a 91.12
l. the righteous put forth their 125.03
l. I be like those who go down to 143.07
l. you give your honor to others Pro 5.09
l. strangers take their fill of 5.10
l. you come to poverty; open your 20.13
l. you learn his ways and entangle 22.25
l. the LORD see it, and be displeased, 24.18
l. he who hears you bring shame 25.10
l. you be sated with it and vomit 25.16
l. he become weary of you and hate 25.17
folly, l. you be like him yourself. 26.04
l. he be wise in his own eyes. 26.05
l. he rebuke you, and you be found a 30.06
l. I be full, and deny thee, and say, 30.09
or l. I be poor, and steal, and 30.09
l. he curse you, and you be held 30.10
l. they drink and forget what has 31.05
l. you hear your servant cursing Ecc 7.21
l. they see with their eyes, and Is 6.10
l. they rise and possess the earth, 14.21
L. any one harm it, I guard it night 27.03
l. your bonds be made strong; 28.22
l. they hold a bribe, who stops his 33.15
Beware l. Hezekiah mislead you by 36.18
l. you should say, 'My idol did them, 48.05
l. you should say, 'Behold, I knew 48.07
l. I dismay you before them. Jer 1.17
l. my wrath go forth like fire, and 4.04
l. I be alienated from you; 6.08
l. I make you a desolation, an 6.08
l. thou bring me to nothing. 10.24
l. my wrath go forth like fire, and 21.12
the secretary, l. I die there." 37.20
l. I be handed over to them and 38.19
l. iniquity be your ruin. Eze 18.30
l. they communicate holiness to the 44.19
"I fear l. my lord the king, who Dan 1.10
l. I strip her naked and make her Hos 2.03
l. he break out like fire in the Amo 5.06
like adamant l. they should hear Zec 7.12
l. I come and smite the land with a Mal 4.06
l. you strike your foot against a Mt 4.06
l. your accuser hand you over to 5.25
l. they trample them underfoot and 7.06
l. they should perceive with their 13.15
l. in gathering the weeds you root 13.29
l. they faint on the way." 15.32
l. there be a tumult among the 26.05
l. his disciples go and steal him 27.64
crowd, l. they should crush him; Mk 3.09
l. they should turn again, and be 4.12
l. he come suddenly and find you 13.36
l. there be a tumult of the people." 14.02
l. you strike your foot against a Lk 4.11
Therefore be careful l. the light 11.35
l. he drag you to the judge, and the 12.58
l. a more eminent man than you be 14.08
l. they also invite you in return, 14.12
l. they also come into this place 16.28
to yourselves l. your hearts be 21.34
l. his deeds should be exposed. Jn 3.20
l. the darkness overtake you; 12.35
l. they should see with their eyes 12.40
l. they should be put out of the 12.42
l. there come upon you what is said Ac 13.40
l. any should swim away and escape; 27.42
l. they should perceive with their 28.27
L. you be wise in your own conceits, Rom 11.25
l. I build on another man's foundation, 15.20
l. any one should say that you were 1Co 1.15
l. the cross of Christ be emptied 1.17
l. Satan tempt you through lack of 7.05
Only take care l. this liberty of 8.09
l. I cause my brother to fall. 8.13
l. after preaching to others I 9.27
he stands take heed l. he fall. 10.12
l. you come together to be condemned. 11.34
l. if some Macedonians come with me 2Co 9.04
l. somehow I should be running or Gal 2.02
yourself, l. you too be tempted. 6.01
of works, l. any man should boast. Eph 2.09
l. I should have sorrow upon sorrow. Php 2.27
l. they become discouraged. Col 3.21
l. we drift away from it. Heb 2.01
l. there be in any of you an evil, 3.12
let us fear l. any of you be judged 4.01
beware l. you be carried away with 2Pe 3.17
l. you take part in her sins, l. you share Rev 18.04
l. you share in her plagues; 18.04

LET

And God said, "L. there be light"; Gen 1.03
And God said, "L. there be a firmament 1.06
and l. it separate the waters from 1.06
And God said, "L. the waters under 1.09
and l. the dry land appear." 1.09
And God said, "L. the earth put 1.11
And God said, "L. there be lights in 1.14
and l. them be for signs and for 1.14
and l. them be lights in the 1.15
And God said, "L. the waters bring 1.20
and l. birds fly above the earth 1.20
and l. birds multiply on the earth." 1.22
And God said, "L. the earth bring 1.24
"L. us make man in our image, after 1.26
and l. them have dominion over the 1.26
"L. us go out to the field." 4.08
and l. Canaan be his slave." 9.26
and l. him dwell in the tents of 9.27
and l. Canaan be his slave." 9.27
l. us make bricks, and burn them 11.03
l. us build ourselves a city, and a 11.04
and l. us make a name for ourselves, 11.04
Come, l. us go down, and there 11.07
kill me, but they will l. you live. 12.12
"L. there be no strife between you 13.08
l. Aner, Eshcol, and Mamre take their 14.24
L. a little water be brought, and 18.04
"Oh l. not the LORD be angry, and I 18.30
"Oh l. not the LORD be angry, and I 18.32
l. me bring them out to you, and do 19.08
L. me escape there—is it not a 19.20
Come, l. us make our father drink 19.32
l. us make him drink wine tonight 19.34
therefore I did not l. you touch her. 20.06
"L. me not look upon the death of 21.16
the full price l. him give it to 23.09
L. the maiden to whom I shall say, 24.14
'Pray l. down your jar that I may 24.14
l. her be the one whom thou hast 24.14
and she quickly l. down her jar 24.18
l. the young woman who comes out to 24.43
l. her be the woman whom the 24.44
I said to her, 'Pray l. me drink.' 24.45
She quickly l. down her jar from 24.46
and l. her be the wife of your 24.51

LET (cont.)

"L. the maiden remain with us a Gen 24.55
l. me go that I may go to my master." 24.56
"L. me eat some of that red pottage, 25.30
so we say, l. there be an oath 26.28
and l. us make a covenant with you, 26.28
L. peoples serve you, and nations 27.29
"L. my father arise, and eat of his 27.31
I have served you, and l. me go; 30.26
l. me pass through all your flock 30.32
L. it be as you have said." 30.34
"L. not my lord be angry that I 31.35
Come now, l. us make a covenant, you 31.44
and l. it be a witness between you 31.44
Then he said, "L. me go, for the day 32.26
"I will not l. you go, unless you 32.26
"L. us journey on our way, and I 33.12
L. my lord pass on before his 33.14
So Esau said, "L. me leave with you 33.15
L. me find favor in the sight of my 33.15
"L. me find favor in your eyes, and 34.11
l. them dwell in the land and trade 34.21
l. us take their daughters in 34.21
and l. us give them our daughters. 34.21
Only l. us agree with them, and they 34.23
then l. us arise and go up to 35.03
'L. us go to Dothan.'" 37.17
Come now, l. us kill him and throw 37.20
"L. us not take his life." 37.21
Come, l. us sell him to the Ishmaelites, 37.27
and l. not our hand be upon him, for 37.27
l. me come in to you," for he did 38.16
"L. her keep the things as her own, 38.23
her out, and l. her be burned." 38.24
Now therefore l. Pharaoh select a 41.33
L. Pharaoh proceed to appoint 41.34
And l. them gather all the food of 41.35
in the cities, and l. them keep it. 41.35
and l. him bring your brother, while 42.16
l. one of your brothers remain 42.19
and l. the rest go and carry grain 42.19
then l. me bear the blame for ever; 43.09
himself he said, "L. food be served." 43.31
l. him die, and we also will be my 44.09
He said, "L. it be as you say: he 44.10
l. your servant, I pray you, speak a 44.18
and l. not your anger burn against 44.18
Now therefore, l. your servant, I 44.33
and l. the lad go back with his 44.33
"Now l. me die, since I have seen 46.30
l. your servants dwell in the land 47.04
l. them dwell in the land of Goshen; 47.06
but l. me lie with my fathers; 47.30
God has l. me see your children 48.11
and in them l. my name be perpetuated, 48.16
and l. them grow into a multitude 48.16
Naphtali is a hind l. loose, 49.21
Now therefore l. me go up, 50.05
Come, l. us deal shrewdly with them, Ex 1.10
but l. the male children live. 1.17
and l. the male children live?" 1.18
but you shall l. every daughter 1.22
l. us go a three days' journey into 3.18
Egypt will not l. you go unless 3.19
after that he will l. you go. 3.20
"L. me go back, I pray, to my kinsmen 4.18
that he will not l. the people go. 4.21
"L. my son go that he may serve me"; 4.23
if you refuse to l. him go, 4.23
So he l. him alone. Then it was 4.26
'L. my people go, that they may hold 5.01
heed his voice and l. Israel go? 5.02
moreover I will not l. Israel go." 5.02
l. us go, we pray, a three days' 5.03
l. them go and gather straw for 5.07
'L. us go and offer sacrifice to 5.08
L. heavier work be laid upon the 5.09
'L. us go and sacrifice to the LORD.' 5.17
of Egypt to l. the people of 6.11
tell Pharaoh to l. the people of 7.02
he refuses to l. the people go. 7.14
"L. my people go, that they may 7.16
"L. my people go, that they may 8.01
But if you refuse to l. them go, 8.02
and I will l. the people go to 8.08
"L. my people go, that they may 8.20
Else, if you will not l. my people go, 8.21
"I will l. you go, to sacrifice to 8.28
only l. not Pharaoh deal falsely 8.29
also, and did not l. the people go. 8.32
"L. my people go, that they may 9.01
you refuse to l. them go and still 9.02
and he did not l. the people go. 9.07
and l. Moses throw them toward 9.08
"L. my people go, that they may 9.13
this purpose have I l. you live, 9.16
my people, and will not l. them go. 9.17
I will l. you go, and you shall stay 9.28
and he did not l. the people of 9.35
L. my people go, that they may serve 10.03
For if you refuse to l. my people go, 10.04
L. the men go, that they may serve 10.07
if ever I l. you and your little 10.10
and he did not l. the children of 10.20
only l. your flocks and your herds 10.24
"You must also l. us have sacrifices 10.25
heart, and he would not l. them go. 10.27
afterwards he will l. you go hence; 11.01
and he did not l. the people of 11.10
And you shall l. none of it remain 12.10
so that they l. them have what they 12.36
l. all his males be circumcised, then 12.48
stubbornly refused to l. us go, 13.15
When Pharaoh l. the people go, God 13.17
that we have l. Israel go from 14.05
'L. us alone and let us serve the 14.12
us alone and l. us serve the 14.12
"L. us flee from before Israel; 14.25
"L. no man leave any of it till the 16.19
l. no man go out of his place on 16.29
'L. an omer of it be kept throughout 16.32
And l. them judge the people at all 18.22
Then Moses l. his father-in-law 18.27
and l. them wash their garments, 19.10
And also l. the priests who come 19.22
but do not l. the priests and the 19.24
but l. not God speak to us, lest we 20.19
then he shall l. her be redeemed; 21.08
but God l. him fall into his hand, 21.13
he shall l. the slave go free for 21.26
he shall l. the slave go free for 21.27
l. him bring it as evidence; 22.13
year you shall l. it rest and lie 23.11
nor l. such be heard out of your 23.13
or l. the fat of my feast remain 23.18
has a cause, l. him go to them." 24.14
And l. them make me a sanctuary, 25.08
now therefore l. me alone, that my 32.10
"L. not the anger of my lord burn 32.22
'L. any who have gold take it off'; 32.24
(for Aaron had l. them break loose, 32.25
thou hast not l. me know whom thou 33.12
and l. no man be seen throughout 34.03
l. no flocks or herds feed before 34.03
l. the LORD, I pray thee, go in the 34.09
l. him bring the LORD's offering: 35.05
"And l. every able man among you 35.10
"L. neither man nor woman do 36.06
you shall not l. the salt of the Lev 2.13
then l. him offer for the sin which 4.03
"Do not l. the hair of your heads 10.06
clothes and l. the hair of his 13.45
and shall l. the living bird go 14.07
and he shall l. the living bird go 14.53

LET (cont.)
and he shall l. the goat go in the Lev 16.22
You shall not l. your cattle breed 19.19
shall not l. the hair of his head 21.10
and l. all who heard him lay their 24.14
and l. all the congregation stone 24.14
l. him reckon the years since he 25.27
And I will l. loose the wild beasts 26.22
"L. not the tribe of the families Num 4.18
then' (l. the priest make the woman 5.21
he shall l. the locks of hair of 6.05
and l. them go with a razor over 8.07
Then l. them take a young bull and 8.08
"L. the people of Israel keep the 9.02
and l. thy enemies be scattered; 10.35
and l. them that hate thee flee 10.35
and l. them take their stand there 11.16
and l. them fall beside the camp, 11.31
L. her not be as one dead, of whom 12.12
L. her be shut up outside the camp 12.14
"L. us go up at once, and occupy it; 13.30
"L. us choose a captain, and go back 14.04
l. the power of the LORD be great 14.17
and l. every one of you take his 16.17
so l. them be made into hammered 16.38
Now l. us pass through your land. 20.17
l. me only pass through on foot, 20.19
"L. me pass through your land; 21.22
l. it be built, let the city of 21.27
l. the city of Sihon be established. 21.27
has refused to l. me go with you." 22.13
'L. nothing hinder you from coming 22.16
have slain you and l. her live." 22.33
L. me die the death of the righteous, 23.10
and l. my end be like his!" 23.10
come, I will l. you know what this 24.14
"L. the LORD, the God of the spirits 27.16
"Have you l. all the women live? 31.15
l. this land be given to your 32.05
them whom you l. remain shall be 33.55
'L. them marry whom they think best; 36.06
'L. us send men before us, that they Deu 1.22
'L. me pass through your land; 2.27
only l. me pass through on foot, 2.28
would not l. us pass by him; 2.30
L. me go over, I pray, and see the 3.25
said to me, 'L. it suffice you; 3.26
that I may l. them hear my words, so 4.10
Out of heaven he l. you hear his 4.36
and on earth he l. you see his 4.36
humbled you and l. you hunger and 8.03
l. me alone, that I may destroy them 9.14
'L. us go after other gods,' which 13.02
'and l. us serve them,' 13.02
'L. us go and serve other gods,' 13.06
'L. us go and serve other gods,' 13.13
year you shall l. him go free from 15.12
And when you l. him go free from 15.13
you shall not l. him go empty-handed; 15.13
when you l. him go free from you; 15.18
'L. me not hear again the voice of 18.16
l. not your heart faint; do not fear, 20.03
L. him go back to his house, lest he 20.05
L. him go back to his house, lest he 20.06
L. him go back to his house, lest he 20.07
L. him go back to his house, lest 20.08
but l. the guilt of blood be 21.08
you shall l. her go where she will; 21.14
you shall l. the mother go, but the 22.07
and l. the earth hear the words of 32.01
L. them rise up and help you, let 32.38
l. them be your protection! 32.38
"L. Reuben live, and not die; 33.06
nor l. his men be few." 33.06
L. these come upon the head of 33.16
l. him be the favorite of his 33.24
and l. him dip his foot in oil. 33.24
I have l. you see it with your 34.04
Then she l. them down by a rope Jos 2.15
through which you l. us down; 2.18
then you shall l. your children 4.22
he would not l. them see the land 5.06
and l. seven priests bear seven 6.06
and l. the armed men pass on before 6.07
not shout or l. your voice be 6.10
"L. not all the people go up, but 7.03
but l. about two or three thousand 7.03
covenant with them, to l. them live; 9.15
and l. them live, lest wrath be upon 9.20
leaders said to them, "L. them live." 9.21
and l. us smite Gibeon; for it has 10.04
do not l. them enter their cities; 10.19
'L. us now build an altar, not for 22.26
but they l. the man and all his Ju 1.25
l. him contend for himself, because 6.31
"L. Baal contend against him." 6.32
"L. not thy anger burn against me, 6.39
l. me speak but this once; 6.39
pray, l. me make trial only this 6.39
pray, l. it be dry only on the 6.39
on all the ground l. there be dew." 6.39
l. him return home.'" 7.03
and l. all the others go every man 7.07
"L. me make a request of you; 8.24
but if not, l. fire come out of the 9.15
and l. him also rejoice in you; 9.19
but if not, l. fire come out from 9.20
and l. fire come out from the 9.20
l. them deliver you in the time of 10.14
'L. us pass, we pray, through your 11.17
'L. us pass, we pray, through your 11.19
"L. this thing be done for me; 11.37
l. me alone two months, that I may 11.37
"L. me go over," the men of Gilead 12.05
l. the man of God whom thou didst 13.08
I said to the woman l. her beware. 13.13
neither l. her drink wine or strong 13.14
I commanded her l. her observe." 13.14
l. us detain you, and prepare a kid 13.15
"L. me now put a riddle to you; 14.12
he l. the foxes go into the standing 15.05
"L. us wait till the light of the 16.02
"L. me feel the pillars on which 16.26
"L. me die with the Philistines." 16.30
and l. us go up against them; 18.09
"Do not l. your voice be heard 18.25
and l. your heart be merry." 19.06
lodge here and l. your heart be 19.09
l. us turn aside to this city of 19.11
"Come and l. us draw near to one of 19.13
l. me bring them out now. 19.24
began to break, they l. her go. 19.25
to her, "Get up, l. us be going." 19.28
"L. us flee, and draw them away from 20.32
"L. me go to the field, and glean Ru 2.02
l. me clean and gather among the 2.07
L. your eyes be upon the field 2.09
"L. her glean even among the 2.15
l. him do it; but if he is 3.13
and he said, "L. it not be known 3.14
And she said, "L. your maidservant 1Sa 1.18
l. not arrogance come from your 2.03
"L. them burn the fat first, and 2.16
l. him do what seems good to him." 3.18
with him and l. none of his words 3.19
L. us bring the ark of the covenant 4.03
"L. the ark of the God of Israel be 5.08
and l. it return to its own place, 5.11
did not they l. the people go, and 6.06
send it off, and l. it go its way. 6.08
l. us go back, lest my father cease 9.05
L. us go there; perhaps he 9.06
l. us go the seer"; for he who is 9.09
come, l. us go." So they 9.10

LET (cont.)
morning I will l. you go and will 1Sa 9.19
l. us go to Gilgal and there renew 11.14
land, saying, "L. the Hebrews hear." 13.03
l. us go over to the Philistine 14.01
l. us go over to the garrison of 14.06
'L. every man bring his ox or his 14.34
"L. us go down after the Philistines 14.36
l. us not leave a man of them." 14.36
"L. us draw near hither to God." 14.36
L. our lord now command your 16.16
"L. David remain in my service, for 16.22
and l. him come down to me. 17.08
"L. no man's heart fail because of 17.32
and would not l. him return to his 18.02
"L. not my hand be upon him, but let 18.17
but l. the hand of the Philistines 18.17
Saul thought, "L. me give her to him, 18.21
"L. not the king sin against his 19.04
So Michal l. David down through the 19.12
and l. my enemy go, so that he has 19.17
Saul, "He said to me, 'L. me go; 19.17
'L. not Jonathan know this, lest he 20.03
but l. me go, that I may hide myself 20.05
l. us go out into the field." 20.11
l. not the name of Jonathan be cut 20.16
he said, 'L. me go; for our family 20.29
l. me get away, and see my brothers.' 20.29
'L. no one know anything of the 21.02
and l. his spittle run down his 21.13
"Pray l. my father and my mother 22.03
L. not the king impute anything to 22.15
will he l. him go away safe? 24.19
Therefore l. my young men find 25.08
pray l. your handmaid speak in your 25.24
L. not my lord regard this ill-natured 25.25
now then l. your enemies and those 25.26
And now l. this present which your 25.27
now therefore l. me pin him to the 26.08
and the jar of water, and l. us go." 26.11
Now therefore l. my lord the king 26.19
Now therefore, l. not my blood fall 26.20
L. one of the young men come over 26.22
l. a place be given me in one of 27.05
l. me set a morsel of bread before 28.22
l. there be no dew or rain upon you, 2Sa 1.21
Now therefore l. your hands be 2.07
"L. the young men arise and play 2.14
And Joab said, "L. them arise." 2.14
and he has l. him go, and he has 3.23
l. him get up the water shaft to 5.08
and l. us play the man for our 10.12
and tomorrow I will l. you depart." 11.12
'Do not l. this matter trouble you, 11.25
'L. my sister Tamar come and give 13.05
"Pray l. my sister Tamar come and 13.06
pray l. the king and his servants 13.24
l. us not all go, lest we be burdensome 13.25
pray l. my brother Amnon go with us." 13.26
him until he l. Amnon and all the 13.27
"L. not my lord suppose that they 13.32
Now therefore l. not my lord the 13.33
l. the king and his throne be 14.09
"Pray l. the king invoke the LORD 14.11
"Pray l. your handmaid speak a word 14.12
"L. my lord the king speak." 14.18
"L. him dwell apart in his own 14.24
Now therefore l. me go into the 14.32
is guilt in me, l. him kill me.'" 14.32
"Pray l. me go and pay my vow, which 15.07
Jerusalem, "Arise, and l. us flee; 15.14
me back and l. me see both it and 15.25
l. him do to me what seems good to 15.26
l. me ever find favor in your sight, 16.04
L. me go over and take off his head 16.09
L. him alone, and l. him curse; 16.11
"L. me choose twelve thousand men, 17.01
and l. us hear what he has to say." 17.05
"L. me run, and carry tidings to the 18.19
l. me also run after the Cushite." 18.22
"L. not my lord hold me guilty or 19.19
l. not the king bear it in mind. 19.19
l. him take it all, since my lord 19.30
Pray l. your servant return, that I 19.37
l. him go over with my lord the 19.37
l. him follow Joab." 20.11
'L. them but ask counsel at Abel'; 20.18
l. seven of his sons be given to us, 21.06
l. us fall into the hand of the 24.14
but l. me not fall into the hand of 24.14
L. thy hand, I pray thee, be against 24.17
"L. my lord the king take and offer 24.22
"L. a young maiden be sought for my 1Ki 1.02
and l. her wait upon the king, and 1.02
l. her lie in your bosom, that my 1.02
l. me give you counsel, that you may 1.12
and l. Zadok the priest and Nathan 1.34
'L. King Solomon swear to me first 1.51
but do not l. his head go down to 2.06
and l. them be among those who eat 2.07
She said, "L. Abishag the Shunammite 2.21
they l. nothing be lacking. 4.27
l. thy word be confirmed, which thou 8.26
L. thy eyes be open to the supplication 8.52
L. these words of mine, wherewith I 8.59
L. your heart therefore be wholly 8.61
"L. me depart, that I may go to my 11.21
And he said to him, "Only l. me go." 11.22
"L. there be a league between me 15.19
l. this child's soul come into him 17.21
L. two bulls be given to us; 18.23
and l. them choose one bull for 18.23
l. it be known this day that thou 18.36
l. not one of them escape." 18.40
"L. me kiss my father and my mother, 19.20
'L. not him that girds on his armor 20.11
but l. us fight against them in the 20.23
l. us put sackcloth on our loins 20.31
Benhadad says, 'Pray, l. me live.'" 20.32
"I will l. you go on these terms." 20.34
a covenant with him and l. him go. 20.34
you have l. go out of your hand 20.42
and l. your heart be cheerful; 21.07
and l. them bring a charge against 21.10
"L. not the king say so." 22.08
l. your word be like the word of 22.13
l. each return to his home in peace.'" 22.17
"L. my servants go with your 22.49
l. fire come down from heaven and 2Ki 1.10
l. fire come down from heaven and 1.12
l. my life, and the life of these 1.13
but now l. my life be precious in 1.14
l. me inherit a double share of 2.09
pray, l. them go, and seek your 2.16
L. us make a small roof chamber 4.10
"L. her alone, for she is in bitter 4.27
L. him come now to me, that he may 5.08
l. there be given to your servant 5.17
L. us go to the Jordan and each of 6.02
and l. us make a place for us to 6.02
If we say, 'L. us enter the city,' 7.04
So now come, l. us go over to the 7.04
l. us go and tell the king's household." 7.09
"L. some men take five of the 7.13
perished; l. us send and see." 7.13
then l. no one slip out of the city 9.15
and l. him say, 'Is it peace?' 9.17
l. none be missing, for I have a 10.19
l. not a man escape." So when they 10.25
"L. her not be slain in the house 11.15
l. the priests take, each from his 12.05
and l. them repair the house 12.05
l. us look one another in the face," 14.08

LET (cont.)

and l. him go and dwell there, and 2Ki 17.27
'Do not l. Hezekiah deceive you, for 18.29
Do not l. Hezekiah make you to rely 18.30
'Do not l. your God on whom you 19.10
And l. them take and lay it on the 20.07
rather l. the shadow go back ten 20.10
and l. it be given into the hand of 22.05
and l. them give it to the 22.05
And he said, "L. him be;" 23.18
l. no man move his bones." 23.18
So they l. his bones alone, with 23.18
l. us send abroad to our brethren 1Ch 13.02
Then l. us bring again the ark of 13.03
l. the hearts of those who seek 16.10
L. the heavens be glad, and let the 16.31
and l. the earth rejoice, and let 16.31
and l. them say among the nations, 16.31
L. the sea roar, and all that fills 16.32
l. the field exult, and everything 16.32
l. the word which thou hast spoken 17.23
and l. us play the man for our 19.13
l. me fall into the hand of the 21.13
but l. me not fall into the hand 21.13
L. thy hand, I pray thee, O LORD my 21.17
but l. not the plague be upon thy 21.17
and l. my lord the king do what 21.23
O LORD God, l. thy promise to David 2Ch 1.09
l. him send to his servants; 2.15
l. thy word be confirmed, which thou 6.17
Now, O my God, l. thy eyes be open 6.40
L. thy priests, O LORD God, be 6.41
and l. thy saints rejoice in thy 6.41
"L. us build these cities, and 14.07
l. not man prevail against thee." 14.11
Do not l. your hands be weak, for 15.07
"L. there be a league between me 16.03
Ramah, and l. his work cease. 16.05
"L. not the king say so." 18.07
l. your word be like the word of 18.12
l. each return to his home in 18.16
Now then, l. the fear of the LORD be 19.07
wouldest not l. Israel invade when 20.10
L. him reign, as the LORD spoke 23.03
L. no one enter the house of the 23.06
do not l. the army of Israel go 25.07
l. us look one another in the face." 25.17
therefore do not l. Hezekiah 32.15
kings of Judah had l. go to ruin. 34.11
and l. there be for each a part of 35.05
be with him. L. him go up.'" 36.23
and l. him go up to Jerusalem, which Ez 1.03
and l. each survivor, in whatever 1.04
"L. us build with you; for we worship 4.02
and l. the house of God be rebuilt 5.15
l. search be made in the royal 5.17
And l. the king send us his pleasure 5.17
l. the house be rebuilt, the place 6.03
l. the cost be paid from the 6.04
And also l. the gold and silver 6.05
l. the work on this house of God 6.07
l. the governor of the Jews and 6.07
l. that be given to them day by day 6.09
l. it be done with all diligence." 6.12
l. it be done in full for the house 7.23
l. judgment be strictly executed 7.26
Therefore l. us make a covenant 10.03
and l. it be done according to the 10.03
L. our officials stand for the 10.14
l. all in our cities who have taken 10.14
l. thy ear be attentive, and thy Neh 1.06
O Lord, l. thy ear be attentive to 1.11
"L. the king live for ever! 2.03
l. letters be given me to the 2.07
that they may l. me pass through 2.07
Come, l. us build the wall of 2.17
"L. us rise up and build." 2.18
and l. not their sin be blotted out 4.05
"L. every man and his servant pass 4.22
l. us get grain, that we may eat and 5.02
L. us leave off this interest. 5.10
"Come and l. us meet together in 6.02
and l. us take counsel together." 6.07
"L. us meet together in the house 6.10
and l. us close the doors of the 6.10
"L. not the gates of Jerusalem be 7.03
standing guard l. them shut and 7.03
l. not all the hardship seem little 9.32
l. a royal order go forth from him, Est 1.19
and l. it be written among the laws 1.19
and l. the king give her royal 1.19
"L. beautiful young virgins be 2.02
And l. the king appoint officers in 2.03
l. their ointments be given them. 2.03
And l. the maiden who pleases the 2.04
l. it be decreed that they be 3.09
l. the king and Haman come this day 5.04
l. the king and Haman come tomorrow 5.08
Queen Esther l. no one come with 5.12
"L. a gallows fifty cubits high be 5.14
And the king said, "L. him come in." 6.05
l. royal robes be brought, which the 6.08
and l. the robes and the horse be 6.09
l. him array the man whom the king 6.09
and l. him conduct the man on 6.09
l. my life be given me at my 7.03
l. an order be written to revoke 8.05
l. the Jews who are in Susa be 9.13
And l. the ten sons of Haman be 9.13
"L. the day perish wherein I was Job 3.03
L. that day be darkness! 3.04
L. gloom and deep darkness claim it. 3.05
L. clouds dwell upon it; 3.05
l. the blackness of the day terrify 3.05
That night—l. thick darkness seize 3.06
l. it not rejoice among the days of 3.06
l. it not come into the number of 3.06
Yea, l. that night be barren; 3.07
l. no joyful cry be heard in it. 3.07
L. those curse it who curse the day, 3.08
L. the stars of its dawn be dark; 3.09
l. it hope for light, but have none, 3.09
t hathe would l. loose his hand and 6.09
Turn, I pray, l. no wrong be done. 6.29
L me alone, for my days are a 7.16
nor l. me alone till I swallow my 7.19
he will not l. me get my breath, but 9.18
L. him take his rod away from me, 9.34
and l. not dread of him terrify me. 9.34
l. me know why thou dost contend 10.02
L. me alone, that I may find a 10.20
and l. not wickedness dwell in your 11.14
"L. me have silence, and I will 13.13
and l. come on me what may. 13.13
and l. my declaration be in your 13.17
and l. not dread of thee terrify me 13.21
or l. me speak, and do thou reply to 13.22
and l. such words go out of your 15.13
L. him not trust in emptiness, 15.31
and l. my cry find no resting place 16.18
thou wilt not l. them triumph. 17.04
though he is loath to l. it go, 20.13
and l. this be your consolation. 21.02
L. him recompense it to themselves, 21.19
L. their own eyes see their destruction, 21.20
and l. them drink of the wrath of 21.20
righteousness, and will not l. it go; 27.06
"L. my enemy be as the wicked, and 27.07
and l. him that rises up against me 27.07
(L. me be weighed in a just balance, 31.06
and l. God know my integrity!) 31.06
then l. me sow, and another eat; 31.08
and l. what grows for me be rooted 31.08
then l. my wife grind for another, 31.10

LET (cont.)

and l. others bow down upon her. Job 31.10
then l. my shoulder blade fall from 31.22
and l. my arm be broken from its 31.22
(I have not l. my mouth sin by 31.30
l. the Almighty answer me!) 31.35
l. thorns grow instead of wheat, and 31.40
I said, 'L. days speak, and many 32.07
l. me also declare my opinion.' 32.10
l. his flesh become fresh with 33.25
l. him return to the days of his 33.25
L. us choose what is right; 34.04
l. us determine among ourselves 34.04
and l. not the greatness of the 36.18
"Who has l. the wild ass go free? 39.05
argues with God, l. him answer it. 40.02
l. him who made him bring near his 40.19
"L. us burst their bonds asunder, Ps 2.03
l. them fall by their own counsels; 5.10
But l. all who take refuge in thee 5.11
l. them ever sing for joy; 5.11
l. the enemy pursue me and overtake 7.05
and l. him trample my life to the 7.05
L. the assembly of the peoples be 7.07
O l. the evil of the wicked come to 7.09
O LORD! L. not man prevail; 9.19
l. the nations be judged before 9.19
L. the nations know that they are 9.20
l. them be caught in the schemes 10.02
or l. thy godly one see the Pit. 16.10
From thee l. my vindication come! 17.02
L. thy eyes see the right! 17.02
l. them not have dominion over me! 19.13
L. the words of my mouth and the 19.14
l. him deliver him, let him rescue 22.08
l. him rescue him, for he delights 22.08
l. me not be put to shame; 25.02
l. not my enemies exult over me. 25.02
Yea, l. none that wait for thee be 25.03
l. them be ashamed who are wantonly 25.03
l. me not be put to shame, for I 25.20
and l. your heart take courage; 27.14
and hast not l. my foes rejoice 30.01
l. me never be put to shame; 31.01
L. thy face shine on thy servant; 31.16
L. me not be put to shame, O LORD, 31.17
l. the wicked be put to shame, let 31.17
l. them go dumbfounded to Sheol. 31.17
L. the lying lips be dumb, which 31.18
strong, and l. your heart take courage, 31.24
Therefore l. every one who is godly 32.06
L. all the earth fear the LORD, let 33.08
l. all the inhabitants of the world 33.08
L. thy steadfast love, O LORD, be 33.22
l. the afflicted hear and be glad. 34.02
and l. us exalt his name together! 34.03
L. them be put to shame and dishonor 35.04
L. them be turned back and confounded 35.04
L. them be like chaff before the 35.05
L. their way be dark and slippery, 35.06
L. ruin come upon them unawares! 35.08
And l. the net which they hid 35.08
l. them fall therein to ruin! 35.08
L. not those rejoice over me who 35.19
and l. not those wink the eye who 35.19
and l. them not rejoice over me! 35.24
L. them not say to themselves, "Aha, 35.25
L. them not say, "We have swallowed 35.25
L. them be put to shame and confusion 35.26
L. them be clothed with shame and 35.26
L. those who desire my vindication 35.27
L. not the foot of arrogance come 36.11
or l. him be condemned when he is 37.33
"Only l. them not rejoice over me, 38.16
"LORD, l. me know my end, and what is 39.04
l. me know how fleeting my life is! 39.04
l. thy steadfast love and thy 40.11
L. them be put to shame and confusion 40.14
l. them be turned back and brought 40.14
L. them be appalled because of 40.15
l. them lead me, let them bring me 43.03
l. them bring me to thy holy hill 43.03
l. your right hand teach you dread 45.04
l. Mount Zion be glad! 48.11
L. the daughters of Judah rejoice 48.11
l. the bones which thou hast broken 51.08
L. death come upon them; 55.15
l. them go down to Sheol alive; 55.15
l. them go away in terror into 55.15
L. thy glory be over all the earth! 57.05
L. thy glory be over all the earth! 57.11
L. them vanish like water that runs 58.07
like grass l. them be trodden down 58.07
L. them be like the snail which 58.08
my God will l. me look in triumph 59.10
l. them be trapped in their pride. 59.12
L. me dwell in thy tent for ever! 61.04
L. the righteous rejoice in the 64.10
L. all the upright in heart glory! 64.10
l. not the rebellious exalt themselves. 66.07
l. the sound of his praise be heard, 66.08
and has not l. our feet slip. 66.09
thou didst l. men ride over our 66.12
L. the peoples praise thee, O God; 67.03
l. all the peoples praise thee! 67.03
L. the nations be glad and sing for 67.04
L. the peoples praise thee, O God; 67.05
l. all the peoples praise thee! 67.05
l. all the ends of the earth fear 67.07
L. God arise, l. his enemies be 68.01
l. those who hate him flee before 68.01
l. the wicked perish before God! 68.02
But l. the righteous be joyful; 68.03
l. them exult before God; 68.03
l. them be jubilant with joy! 68.03
L. bronze be brought from Egypt; 68.31
l. Ethiopia hasten to stretch out 68.31
L. not those who hope in thee be 69.06
l. not those who seek thee be 69.06
l. me be delivered from my enemies 69.14
L. not the flood sweep over me, or 69.15
L. their own table before them 69.22
l. their sacrificial feasts be a 69.22
L. their eyes be darkened, so that 69.23
and l. thy burning anger overtake 69.24
l. no one dwell in their tents. 69.25
L. them be blotted out of the book 69.28
l. them not be enrolled among the 69.28
l. thy salvation, O God, set me on 69.29
L. the oppressed see it and be glad; 69.32
seek God, l. your hearts revive. 69.32
L. heaven and earth praise him, the 69.34
L. them be put to shame and confusion 70.02
L. them be turned back and brought 70.02
L. them be appalled because of 70.03
l. me never be put to shame! 71.01
L. the mountains bear prosperity 72.03
L. not the downtrodden be put to 74.21
l. the poor and needy praise thy 74.21
l. all around him bring gifts to 76.11
the sea and l. them pass through 78.13
he l. them fall in the midst of 78.28
He l. loose on them his fierce 78.49
l. thy compassion come speedily to 79.08
L. the avenging of the outpoured 79.10
L. the groans of the prisoners come 79.11
l. thy face shine, that we may be 80.03
l. thy face shine, that we may be 80.07
But l. thy hand be upon the man of 80.17
l. thy face shine, that we may be 80.19
l. us wipe them out as a nation; 83.04
l. the name of Israel be remembered 83.04
who said, "L. us take possession for 83.12
L. them be put to shame and dismayed 83.17

LET (cont.)

l. them perish in disgrace. Ps 83.17
L. them know that thou alone, whose 83.18
L. me hear what God the LORD will 85.08
L. my prayer come before thee, 88.02
L. the heavens praise thy wonders, O 89.05
L. thy work be manifest to thy 90.16
L. the favor of the Lord our God be 90.17
O come, l. us sing to the LORD; 95.01
l. us make a joyful noise to the 95.01
L. us come into his presence with 95.02
l. us make a joyful noise to him 95.02
O come, l. us worship and bow down, 95.06
l. us kneel before the LORD, our 95.06
L. the heavens be glad, and let the 96.11
and l. the earth rejoice; 96.11
l. the sea roar, and all that fills 96.11
l. the field exult, and everything 96.12
reigns; l. the earth rejoice; 97.01
l. the many coastlands be glad! 97.01
L. the sea roar, and all that fills 98.07
L. the floods clap their hands; 98.08
l. the hills sing for joy together 98.08
reigns; l. the peoples tremble! 99.01
cherubim; l. the earth quake! 99.01
L. them praise thy great and 99.03
l. my cry come to thee! 102.01
L. this be recorded for a generation 102.18
L. sinners be consumed from the 104.35
and l. the wicked be no more! 104.35
l. the hearts of those who seek the 105.03
And l. all the people say, "Amen!" 106.48
L. the redeemed of the LORD say so, 107.02
L. them thank the LORD for his 107.08
L. them thank the LORD for his 107.15
L. them thank the LORD for his 107.21
And l. them offer sacrifices of 107.22
L. them thank the LORD for his 107.31
L. them extol him in the congregation 107.32
and he does not l. their cattle 107.38
l. him give heed to these things; 107.43
l. men consider the steadfast love 107.43
L. thy glory be over all the earth! 108.05
l. an accuser bring him to trial. 109.06
l. him come forth guilty; 109.07
l. his prayer be counted as sin! 109.07
L. there be none to extend kindness 109.12
and l. not the sin of his mother be 109.14
L. them be before the LORD continually; 109.15
l. curses come on him! He did not 109.17
L. them know that this is thy hand; 109.27
L. them curse, but do thou bless! 109.28
L. my assailants be put to shame; 109.28
L. Israel say, "His steadfast love 118.02
L. the house of Aaron say, "His 118.03
L. those who fear the LORD say, "His 118.04
l. us rejoice and be glad in it. 118.24
l. me not wander from thy commandments! 119.10
l. me not be put to shame! 119.31
L. thy steadfast love come to me, O 119.41
L. thy steadfast love be ready to 119.76
L. thy mercy come to me, that I may 119.77
L. the godless be put to shame, 119.78
L. those who fear thee turn to me, 119.79
and l. me not be put to shame in my 119.116
l. not the godless oppress me. 119.122
and l. no iniquity get dominion 119.133
L. my cry come before thee, O LORD; 119.169
L. my supplication come before thee 119.170
L. thy hand be ready to help me, for 119.173
L. me live, that I may praise thee, 119.175
and l. thy ordinances help me. 119.175
He will not l. your foot be moved, 121.03
"L. us go to the house of the LORD!" 122.01
our side, l. Israel now say— 124.01
my youth," l. Israel now say— 129.01
L. them be like the grass on the 129.06
L. thy ears be attentive to the 130.02
"L. us go to his dwelling place; 132.07
l. us worship at his footstool!" 132.07
L. thy priests be clothed with 132.09
and l. thy saints shout for joy. 132.09
O Jerusalem, l. my right hand wither! 137.05
L. my tongue cleave to the roof of 137.06
If I say, "L. only darkness cover me, 139.11
l. the mischief of their lips 140.09
L. burning coals fall upon them! 140.10
L. them be cast into pits, no more 140.10
L. not the slanderer be established 140.11
l. evil hunt down the violent man 140.11
L. my prayer be counted as incense 141.02
and l. me not eat of their dainties 141.04
L. a good man strike or rebuke me 141.05
but l. the oil of the wicked never 141.05
L. the wicked together fall into 141.10
L. me hear in the morning of thy 143.08
L. thy good spirit lead me on a 143.10
and l. all flesh bless his holy 145.21
L. them praise the name of the LORD! 148.05
L. them praise the name of the LORD, 148.13
L. Israel be glad in his Maker, 149.02
l. the sons of Zion rejoice in 149.02
L. them praise his name with 149.03
L. the faithful exult in glory; 149.05
l. them sing for joy on their 149.05
L. the high praises of God be in 149.06
L. everything that breathes praise 150.06
l. us lie in wait for blood, Pro 1.11
l. us wantonly ambush the innocent; 1.11
like Sheol l. us swallow them alive 1.12
but l. your heart keep my commandments; 3.01
L. not loyalty and faithfulness 3.03
l. them not escape from your sight, 3.21
"L. your heart hold fast my words; 4.04
Keep hold of instruction, do not l. go; 4.13
L. them not escape from your sight; 4.21
L. your eyes look directly forward, 4.25
L. them be for yourself alone, and 5.17
L. your fountain be blessed, and 5.18
L. her affection fill you at all 5.19
and do not l. her capture you with 6.25
Come, l. us take our fill of love 7.18
l. us delight ourselves with love. 7.18
L. not your heart turn aside to her 7.25
"Whoever is simple, l. him turn in here!" 9.04
"Whoever is simple, l. him turn in here!" 9.16
The LORD does not l. the righteous 10.03
L. a man meet a she-bear robbed of 17.12
L. not your heart envy sinners, but 23.17
L. your father and mother be glad, 23.25
l. her who bore you rejoice. 23.25
and l. your eyes observe my ways. 23.26
and l. not your heart be glad when 24.17
L. your foot be seldom in your 25.17
L. another praise you, and not your 27.02
l. him be a fugitive until death; 28.17
l. no one help him. 28.17
l. them drink and forget their 31.07
and l. her works praise her in the 31.31
nor l. your heart be hasty to utter Ecc 5.02
therefore l. your words be few. 5.02
L. not your mouth lead you into sin, 5.06
of the rich will not l. him sleep. 5.12
L. your garments be always white; 9.08
l. not oil be lacking on your head. 9.08
l. him rejoice in them all; 11.08
but l. him remember that the days 11.08
and l. your heart cheer you in the 11.09
Draw me after you, l. us make haste. Sol 1.04
l. me see your face, l. me hear 2.14
and would not l. him go until I had 3.04
l. its fragrance be wafted abroad. 4.16
L. my beloved come to his garden, 4.16
l. us go forth into the fields, and 7.11

LET (cont.)
l. us go out early to the vineyards, Sol 7.12
he l. out the vineyard to keepers; 8.11
your voice; l. me hear it. 8.13
"Come now, l. us reason together, Is 1.18
l. us go up to the mountain of the 2.03
l. us walk in the light of the LORD. 2.05
only l. us be called by your name; 4.01
L. me sing for my beloved a love 5.01
who say: "L. him make haste, l. him 5.19
l. him speed his work that we may 5.19
l. the purpose of the Holy One of 5.19
and l. it come, that we may know it!" 5.19
and do not l. your heart be faint 7.04
"L. us go up against Judah and 7.06
and l. us conquer it for ourselves, 7.06
l. it be deep as Sheol or high as 7.11
cattle are l. loose and where 7.25
l. him be your fear, and l. him be 8.13
and l. him be your dread. 8.13
l. this be known in all the earth. 12.05
who did not l. his prisoners go 14.17
l. the outcasts of Moab sojourn 16.04
Therefore l. Moab wail, 16.07
l. every one wail for Moab. 16.07
L. them tell you and make known 19.12
l. him announce what he sees. 21.06
l. him listen diligently, very 21.07
l. me weep bitter tears; 22.04
"L. us eat and drink, for tomorrow 22.13
l. us be glad and rejoice in his 25.09
L. them see thy zeal for thy poeple, 26.11
L. the fire for thy adversaries 26.11
of the shades thou wilt l. it fall. 26.19
Or l. them lay hold of my protection, 27.05
l. them make peace with me, l. them 27.05
l. the feasts run their round. 29.01
l. us hear no more of the Holy One 30.11
who l. the feet of the ox and the 32.20
L. the earth listen, and all that 34.01
'Do not l. Hezekiah deceive you, for 36.14
Do not l. Hezekiah make you rely on 36.15
'Do not l. your God on whom you 37.10
"L. them take a cake of figs, and 38.21
l. the peoples renew their strength; 41.01
l. them approach, then l. them speak; 41.01
l. us together draw near for 41.01
L. them bring them, and tell us what 41.22
L. the sea roar and all that fills 42.10
L. the desert and its cities lift 42.11
l. the inhabitants of Sela sing for 42.11
l. them shout from the top of the 42.11
L. them give glory to the LORD, and 42.12
L. all the nations gather together, 43.09
and l. the peoples assemble. 43.09
L. them bring their witnesses to 43.09
and l. them hear and say, It is true. 43.09
l. us argue together; set forth your 43.26
L. him proclaim it, l. him declare and 44.07
L. them tell us what is yet to be. 44.07
l. them all assemble, l. them stand forth, 44.11
and l. the skies rain down righteousness; 45.08
l. the earth open, that salvation 45.08
and l. it cause righteousness to 45.08
l. them take counsel together! 45.21
l. them stand forth and save you, 47.13
L. us stand up together. 50.08
L. him come near to me. 50.08
and l. the curtains of your habitations 54.02
l. the wicked forsake his way, and 55.07
l. him return to the LORD, that he 55.07
L. not the foreigner who has joined 56.03
and l. not the eunuch say, "Behold, I 56.03
"l. us get wine, l. us fill ourselves 56.12
l. your collection of idols deliver 57.13
to l. the oppressed go free, and to 58.06
'L. the LORD be glorified, that we 66.05
L. them arise, if they can save you, Jer 2.28
L. us lie down in our shame, 3.25
and l. our dishonor cover us; 3.25
and l. us go into the fortified 4.05
'L. us fear the LORD our God, who 5.24
up, and l. us attack at noon!" 6.04
"Up, and l. us attack by night, and 6.05
and I will l. you dwell in this 7.03
then I will l. you dwell in this 7.07
l. us go into the fortified cities 8.14
L. every one beware of his neighbor, 9.04
l. them make haste and raise a 9.18
and l. your ear receive the word of 9.20
"L. not the wise man glory in his 9.23
l. not the mighty man glory in his 9.23
l. not the rich man glory in his 9.23
but l. him who glories glory in 9.24
"L. us destroy the tree with its 11.19
l. us cut him off from the land of 11.19
l. me see thy vengeance upon them, 11.20
'L. my eyes run down with tears 14.17
and l. them not cease, for the 14.17
out of my sight, and l. them go! 15.01
So l. it be, O LORD, if I have not 15.11
of the LORD? L. it come!" 17.15
L. those be put to shame who 17.18
but l. me not be put to shame; 17.18
l. them be dismayed, but l. me not 17.18
there I will l. you hear my words." 18.02
l. us make plots against Jeremiah, 18.18
Come, l. us smite him with the 18.18
and l. us not heed any of his words." 18.18
l. their wives become childless and 18.21
L. them be overthrown before thee; 18.23
L. us denounce him!" say all my 20.10
l. me see thy vengeance upon them, 20.12
bore me, l. it not be blessed! 20.14
L. that man be like the cities 20.16
l. him hear a cry in the morning 20.16
L. the prophet who has a dream tell 23.28
but l. him who has my word speak my 23.28
then l. them intercede with the 27.18
Do not l. your prophets and your 29.08
and l. us go up to Zion, to the LORD 31.06
and l. us go to Jerusalem for fear 35.11
and l. no one know where you are." 36.19
l. my humble plea come before you, 37.20
"L. this man be put to death, for he 38.04
which he l. down to Jeremiah in the 38.11
"L. no one know of these words and 38.24
the guard had l. him go from Ramah, 40.01
food and a present, and l. him go. 40.05
"L. me go and slay Ishmael the son 40.15
"L. our supplication come before 42.02
on you and l. you remain in your 42.12
L. the warriors go forth: men of 46.09
and l. us go back to our own people 46.16
l. us cut her off from being a 48.02
and l. your widows trust in me." 49.11
l. us join ourselves to the LORD in 50.05
l. nothing be left of her. 50.26
l. them go down to the slaughter. 50.27
l. no one escape. Requite her 50.29
fast, they refuse to l. them go. 50.33
L. not the archer bend his bow, and 51.03
and l. him not stand up in his coat 51.03
l. every man save his life! 51.06
and l. us go each to his own 51.09
come, l. us declare in Zion the work 51.10
l. the inhabitant of Zion say. 51.35
of Chaldea," l. Jerusalem say. 51.35
L. every man save his life from the 51.45
L. not your heart faint, and be not 51.46
and l. Jerusalem come into your 51.50
announced, and l. them be as I am. Lam 1.21
"L. all their evil doing come 1.22
L. tears stream down like a torrent 2.18

LET (cont.)

L. him sit alone in silence when he Lam 3.28
l. him put his mouth in the dust— 3.29
l. him give his cheek to the smiter, 3.30
L. us test and examine our ways, and 3.40
L. us lift up our hearts and hands 3.41
stood still, they l. down their wings. Eze 1.24
stood still, they l. down their wings. 1.25
he that will hear, l. him hear; 3.27
will refuse to hear, l. him refuse; 3.27
and l. it be in a state of siege, 4.03
I will l. you have cow's dung 4.15
and I will l. loose my anger upon 7.03
L. not the buyer rejoice, nor the 7.12
But I will l. a few of them escape 12.16
and I will l. the souls that you 13.20
should I l. myself be inquired of 14.03
L. a sword go through the land; 14.17
Then l. them know the abominations 20.04
'L. us be like the nations, like the 20.32
and I will l. you go in by number. 20.37
your hands and l. the sword come 21.14
and l. the bones be burned up. 24.10
Yea, I will l. men walk upon you, 36.12
and I will not l. you hear any more 36.15
l. that be known to you. 36.32
also I will l. the house of Israel 36.37
and I will not l. my holy name be 39.07
Now l. them put away their idolatry 43.09
l. there be an end to all your 44.06
their heads or l. their locks grow 44.20
but they shall l. the house of 45.08
l. us be given vegetables to eat Dan 1.12
Then l. our appearance and the 1.13
"L. the king tell his servants the 2.07
l. the beasts flee from under it 4.14
L. him be wet with the dew of 4.15
l. his lot be with the beasts in 4.15
l. his mind be changed from a man's, 4.16
and l. a beast's mind be given to 4.16
and l. seven times pass over him. 4.16
l. not the dream or the interpretation 4.19
and l. him be wet with the dew of 4.23
and l. his lot be with the beasts 4.23
l. my counsel be acceptable to you; 4.27
L. not your thoughts alarm you or 5.10
Now l. Daniel be called, and he will 5.12
"L. your gifts be for yourself, and 5.17
l. thy anger and thy wrath turn 9.16
"L. my lord speak, for you have 10.19
Yet l. no one contend, and l. none accuse, Hos 4.04
l. not Judah become guilty. 4.15
Ephraim is joined to idols, l. him alone. 4.17
"Come, l. us return to the LORD; 6.01
L. us know, l. us press on to know 6.03
l. him understand these things; 14.09
is discerning, l. him know them; 14.09
and l. your children tell their Joe 1.03
L. all the inhabitants of the land 2.01
L. the bridegroom leave his room, 2.16
and the altar l. the priests, 2.17
L. all the men of war draw near, 3.09
l. them come up. 3.09
l. the weak say, "I am a warrior." 3.10
L. the nations bestir themselves, 3.12
but l. justice roll down like Amo 5.24
l. us rise against her for battle!" Ob 1.01
l. us cast lots, that we may know on Jon 1.07
l. us not perish for this man's life, 1.14
L. neither man nor beast, herd nor 3.07
l. them not feed, or drink water, 3.07
but l. man and beast be covered 3.08
and l. them cry mightily to God; 3.08
yea, l. every one turn from his evil 3.08
and l. the Lord GOD be a witness Mic 1.02
l. us go up to the mountain of the 4.02
"L. her be profaned, and l. our eyes gaze 4.11
and l. the hills hear your voice. 6.01
l. them feed in Bashan and Gilead 7.14
and I will l. nations look on your Nah 3.05
l. all the earth keep silence Hab 2.20
l. not your hands grow weak. Zep 3.16
And I said, "L. them put a clean Zec 3.05
and l. none of you devise evil 7.10
"L. your hands be strong, you who in 8.09
Fear not, but l. your hands be 8.13
'L. us go at once to entreat the 8.21
'L. us go with you, for we have 8.23
What is to die, l. it die; 11.09
be destroyed, l. it be destroyed; 11.09
and l. those that are left devour 11.09
L. his arm be wholly withered, his 11.17
and l. none be faithless to the Mal 2.15
answered him, "L. it be so now; Mt 3.15
L. your light so shine before men, 5.16
l. him give her a certificate of 5.31
L. what you say be simply 'Yes' or 5.37
l. him have your cloak as well; 5.40
do not l. your left hand know what 6.03
L. the day's own trouble be sufficient 6.34
'L. me take the speck out of your 7.04
l. me first go and bury my father." 8.21
l. your peace come upon it; 10.13
l. your peace return to you. 10.13
He who has ears to hear, l. him hear. 11.15
He who has ears, l. him hear." 13.09
L. both grow together until the 13.30
He who has ears, l. him hear. 13.43
or mother, l. him surely die.' 15.04
L. them alone; they are blind 15.14
l. him deny himself and take up his 16.24
l. him be to you as a Gentile and a 18.17
together, l. no man put asunder." 19.06
to receive this, l. him receive it." 19.12
"L. the children come to me, and do 19.14
to him, "Lord, let our eyes be opened." 20.33
and l. it out to tenants, and went 21.33
come, l. us kill him and have his 21.38
and l. out the vineyard to other 21.41
the holy place (l. the reader 24.15
then l. those who are in Judea flee 24.16
l. him who is on the housetop not 24.17
and l. him who is in the field not 24.18
would not have l. his house be 24.43
l. this cup pass from me; nevertheless, 26.39
Rise, l. us be going; see, my 26.46
all said "L. him be crucified." 27.22
the more, "L. him be crucified." 27.23
l. him come down now from the cross, 27.42
l. God deliver him now, if he 27.43
l. us see whether Elijah will come 27.49
"L. us go on to the next towns, that Mk 1.38
they l. down the pallet on which 2.04
who has ears to hear, l. him hear." 4.09
man has ears to hear, l. him hear." 4.23
"L. us go across to the other side." 4.35
us to the swine, l. us enter them." 5.12
or mother, l. him surely die'; 7.10
man has ears to hear, l. him hear." * 7.16
"L. the children first be fed, for 7.27
l. him deny himself and take up his 8.34
l. us make three booths, one for you 9.05
together, l. no man put asunder." 10.09
"L. the children come to me, do not 10.14
"Master, l. me receive my sight." 10.51
had said; and they l. them go. 11.06
and l. it out to tenants, and went 12.01
come, l. us kill him, and the inheritance 12.07
me a coin, and l. me look at it." 12.15
not to be (l. the reader understand), 13.14
then l. those who are in Judea flee 13.14
l. him who is on the housetop not 13.15
and l. him who is in the field not 13.16
But Jesus said, "L. her alone; 14.06

LET (cont.)
Rise, l. us be going; see my betrayer Mk 14.42
But l. the scriptures be fulfilled." 14.49
L. the Christ, the King of Israel, 15.32
l. us see whether Elijah will come 15.36
l. it be to me according to your Lk 1.38
"L. us go over to Bethlehem and see 2.15
l. him share with him who has none; 3.11
has food, l. him do likewise." 3.11
the deep and l. down your nets for 5.04
your word I will l. down the nets." 5.05
on the roof and l. him down with 5.19
l. me take out the speck that is in 6.42
and l. my servant be healed. 7.07
who has ears to hear, l. him hear." 8.08
"L. us go across to the other side 8.22
begged him to l. them enter these. 8.32
l. him deny himself and take up his 9.23
l. us make three booths, one for you 9.33
"L. these words sink into your ears; 9.44
l. me first go and bury my father." 9.59
but l. me first say farewell to 9.61
"L. your loins be girded and your 12.35
'L. it alone, sir, this year also, 13.08
him and healed him, and l. him go. 14.04
who has ears to hear, l. him hear." 14.35
and l. us eat and make merry; 15.23
and the prophets; l. them hear them.' 16.29
On that day, l. him who is on the 17.31
and likewise l. him who is in the 17.31
"L. the children come to me, and do 18.16
"Lord, l. me receive my sight." 18.41
and l. it out to tenants, and went 20.09
l. us kill him, that the inheritance 20.14
Then l. those who are in Judea flee 21.21
and l. those who are inside the 21.21
and l. not those who are out in the 21.21
rather l. the greatest among you 22.26
l. him who has a purse take it, and 22.36
And l. him who has no sword sell 22.36
l. him save himself, if he is the 23.35
L. us have an answer for those who Jn 1.22
l. him come to me and drink. 7.37
"L. him who is without sin among 8.07
"L. us go into Judea again." 11.07
may believe, But l. us go to him." 11.15
"L. us also go, that we may die with 11.16
to them, "Unbind him, and l. him go." 11.44
If we l. him go on thus, every one 11.48
he should l. them know, so that they 11.57
Jesus said, "L. her alone, l. her 12.07
l. her keep it for the day of my 12.07
"L. not your hearts be troubled; 14.01
L. not your hearts be troubled, 14.27
troubled, neither l. them be afraid. 14.27
the Father. Rise, l. us go hence. 14.31
if you seek me, l. these men go." 18.08
"L. us not tear it, but cast lots 19.24
'l. his habitation become desolate, Ac 1.20
and l. there be no one to live in 1.20
and 'His office l. another take.' 1.20
l. this be known to you, and give 2.14
nor l. thy Holy One see corruption. 2.27
L. all the house of Israel therefore 2.36
l. us warn them to speak no more to 4.17
they l. them go, finding no way to 4.21
from these men and l. them alone; 5.38
the name of Jesus, and l. them go. 5.40
by night and l. him down over the 9.25
l. down by four corners upon the 10.11
l. down from heaven by four corners; 11.05
'Thou wilt not l. thy Holy One see 13.35
L. it be known to you therefore, 13.38
l. us return and visit the brethren 15.36
police, saying, "L. those men go." 16.35
magistrates have sent to l. you go; 16.36
l. them come themselves and take us 16.37
and the rest, they l. them go. 17.09
but the disciples would not l. him; 19.30
l. them bring charges against one 19.38
I beg you, l. me speak to the people." 21.39
Or else l. these men themselves say 24.20
"l. the men of authority among you 25.05
about the man, l. them accuse him." 25.05
they l. out four anchors from the 27.29
ropes of the boat, and l. it go. 27.32
L. it be known to you then that 28.28
L. God be true though every man be Rom 3.04
L. not sin therefore reign in your 6.12
"L. their feast become a snare and 11.09
l. their eyes be darkened so that 11.10
l. us use them: if prophecy, in 12.06
L. love be genuine; hate what is 12.09
L. every person be subject to the 13.01
L. us then cast off the works of 13.12
l. us conduct ourselves becomingly 13.13
L. not him who eats despise him who 14.03
and l. not him who abstains pass 14.03
L. every one be fully convinced in 14.05
Then l. us no more pass judgment on 14.13
Do not l. what you eat cause the 14.15
So do not l. what is good to you be 14.16
L. us then pursue what makes for 14.19
l. each of us please his neighbor 15.02
and l. all the peoples praise him"; 15.11
"L. him who boasts, boast of the 1Co 1.31
L. each man take care how he builds 3.10
L. no one deceive himself. 3.18
l. him become a fool that he may 3.18
So l. no one boast of men. 3.21
L. him who has done this be removed 5.02
L. us, therefore, celebrate the 5.08
l. her remain single or else be 7.11
desires to separate, l. it be so; 7.15
Only, l. every one lead the life 7.17
L. him not seek to remove the marks 7.18
L. him not seek circumcision. 7.18
there l. him remain with God. 7.24
from now on, l. those who have wives 7.29
l. him do as he wishes: let them 7.36
l. them marry—it is no sin. 7.36
Therefore l. any one who thinks 10.12
and he will not l. you be tempted 10.13
L. no one seek his own good, but the 10.24
or shaven, l. her wear a veil. 11.06
L. a man examine himself, and so eat 11.28
l. him eat at home—lest you come 11.34
L. all things be done for edification. 14.26
l. there be only two or at most 14.27
each in turn; and l. one interpret. 14.27
l. each of them keep silence in 14.28
L. two or three prophets speak, and 14.29
and l. the others weigh what is 14.29
sitting by, l. the first be silent. 14.30
l. them ask their husbands at home. 14.35
"L. us eat and drink, for tomorrow 15.32
So l. no one despise him. 16.11
L. all that you do be done in love. 16.14
l. him be accursed. Our Lord, come! 16.22
you pain but to l. you know the 2Co 2.04
"L. light shine out of darkness," 4.06
l. us cleanse ourselves from every 7.01
l. him remind himself that as he is 10.07
L. such people understand that what 10.11
"L. him who boasts, boast of the 10.17
I repeat, l. no one think me foolish 11.16
but I was l. down in a basket 11.33
preached to you, l. him be accursed. Gal 1.08
you received, l. him be accursed. 1.09
L. me ask you only this: Did you 3.02
l. us also walk by the Spirit. 5.25
L. us have no self-conceit, no 5.26
But l. each one test his own work, 6.04
L. him who is taught the word share 6.06

LET (cont.)
And l. us not grow weary in well-doing, Gal 6.09
l. us do good to all men, and 6.10
Henceforth l. no man trouble me; 6.17
l. every one speak the truth with Eph 4.25
do not l. the sun go down on your 4.26
L. the thief no longer steal, but 4.28
but rather l. him labor, doing 4.28
L. no evil talk come out of your 4.29
L. all bitterness and wrath and 4.31
L. there be no filthiness, nor silly 5.04
but instead l. there be thanksgiving 5.04
L. no one deceive you with empty 5.06
so l. wives also be subject in 5.24
however, l. each one of you love his 5.33
and l. the wife see that she 5.33
Only l. your manner of life be Php 1.27
L. each of you look not only to his 2.04
L. those of us who are mature be 3.15
Only l. us hold true to what we 3.16
L. all men know your forbearance. 4.05
thanksgiving l. your requests be 4.06
Therefore l. no one pass judgment Col 2.16
L. no one disqualify you, insisting 2.18
And l. the peace of Christ rule in 3.15
L. the word of Christ dwell in you 3.16
L. your speech always be gracious, 4.06
So then l. us not sleep, as others 1Th 5.06
but l. us keep awake and be sober. 5.06
l. us be sober, and put on the 5.08
L. no one deceive you in any way; 2Th 2.03
one will not work, l. him not eat. 3.10
L. a woman learn in silence with 1Ti 2.11
And l. them also be tested first; 3.10
blameless l. them serve as deacons. 3.10
L. deacons be married only once, and 3.12
and l. them manage their children 3.12
L. no one despise your youth, but 4.12
l. them first learn their religious 5.04
L. no one be enrolled as a widow 5.09
who are widows, l. her assist them; 5.16
l. the church not be burdened, so 5.16
L. the elders who rule well be 5.17
L. all who are under the yoke of 6.01
"L. every one who names the name of 2Ti 2.19
all authority. L. no one disregard you. Tit 2.15
And l. our people learn to apply 3.14
"L. all God's angels worship him." Heb 1.06
l. us fear lest any of you be 4.01
L. us therefore strive to enter 4.11
l. us hold fast our confession. 4.14
under that name l. him glorify God. 4.16
Therefore l. us leave the elementary 6.01
l. us draw near with a true heart 10.22
L. us hold fast the confession of 10.23
and l. us consider how to stir up 10.24
l. us also lay aside every weight, 12.01
and l. us run with perseverance the 12.01
Therefore l. us be grateful for 12.28
and thus l. us offer to God acceptable 12.28
L. brotherly love continue. 13.01
L. marriage be held in honor among 13.04
and l. the marriage bed be undefiled 13.04
Therefore l. us go forth to him 13.13
Through him then l. us continually 13.15
L. them do this joyfully, and not 13.17
And l. steadfastness have its full Jas 1.04
l. him ask God who gives to all men 1.05
But l. him ask in faith, with no 1.06
L. the lowly brother boast in his 1.09
L. no one say when he is tempted, "I 1.13
L. every man be quick to hear, slow 1.19
L. not many of you become teachers, 3.01
his good life l. him show his 3.13
L. your laughter be turned to 4.09
but l. your yes be yes and your no 5.12
you suffering? L. him pray. 5.13
any cheerful? L. him sing praise. 5.13
L. him call for the elders of the 5.14
and l. them pray over him, anointing 5.14
l. him know that whoever brings 5.20
L. not yours be the outward adorning 1Pe 3.03
but l. it be the hidden person of 3.04
do right and l. nothing terrify 3.06
l. him keep his tongue from evil 3.10
l. him turn away from evil and do 3.11
l. him seek peace and pursue it. 3.11
L. the time that is past suffice 4.03
But l. none of you suffer as a 4.15
l. him not be ashamed, but under 4.16
under that name l. him glorify God. 4.16
Therefore l. those who suffer 4.19
L. what you heard from the beginning 1Jn 2.24
l. no one deceive you. 3.07
l. us not love in word or speech 3.18
Beloved, l. us love one another; 4.07
l. him hear what the Spirit says to Rev 2.07
l. him hear what the Spirit says to 2.11
l. him hear what the Spirit says to 2.17
l. him hear what the Spirit says to 2.29
l. him hear what the Spirit says to 3.06
l. him hear what the Spirit says to 3.13
l. him hear what the Spirit says to 3.22
and refuse to l. them be placed in 11.09
If any one has an ear, l. him hear: 13.09
l. him who has understanding reckon 13.18
L. us rejoice and exult and give 19.07
L. the evildoer still do evil, and 22.11
And l. him who hears say, "Come." 22.17
And l. him who is thirsty come, 22.17
l. him who desires take the water 22.17

LETHECH
and a homer and a l. of barley. Hos 3.02

LETS
when he l. you go, he will drive you Ex 11.01
or l. his beast loose and it feeds 22.05
And he who l. the goat go to Azazel Lev 16.26
He knows, and l. Israel itself know! Jos 22.22
Under the whole heaven he l. it go, Job 37.03
and l. them be warmed on the ground, 39.14
And there he l. the hungry dwell, Ps 107.36
or an oak and l. it grow strong Is 44.14
'Noisy one who l. the hour go by.' Jer 46.17

LETTER
morning David wrote a l. to Joab, 2Sa 11.14
In the l. he wrote, "Set Uriah in 11.15
I will send a l. to the king of 2Ki 5.05
And he brought the l. to the king 5.06
"When this l. reaches you, know that 5.06
the king of Israel read the l., 5.07
as soon as this l. comes to you, 10.02
Then he wrote to them a second l., 10.06
And when the l. came to them, they 10.07
Hezekiah received the l. from the 19.14
answered in a l. which he sent to 2Ch 2.11
And a l. came to him from Elijah 21.12
the l. was written in Aramaic and Ez 4.07
scribe wrote a l. against Jerusalem 4.08
a copy of the l. that they sent—"To 4.11
the l. which you sent to us has 4.18
Artaxerxes' l. was read before 4.23
be returned by l. concerning it. 5.05
The copy of the l. which Tattenai 5.06
a copy of the l. which King 7.11
and a l. to Asaph, the keeper of the Neh 2.08
to me with an open l. in his hand. 6.05
of all that was written in this l., Est 9.26
confirming this second l. about Purim. 9.29
Hezekiah received the l. from the Is 37.14
words of the l. which Jeremiah the Jer 29.01
The l. was sent by the hand of 29.03
read this l. in the hearing of 29.29
with the following l.: "The brethren Ac 15.23

LETTER (cont.)
together, they delivered the l. Ac 15.30
we have sent a l. with our judgment 21.25
And he wrote a l. to this effect: 23.25
delivered the l. to the governor, 23.33
On reading the l., he asked to what 23.34
I Tertius, the writer of this l., Rom 16.22
to you in my l. not to associate 1Co 5.09
you accredit by l. to carry your 16.03
yourselves are our l. of recommendation, 2Co 3.02
that you are a l. from Christ 3.03
if I made you sorry with my l., 7.08
for I see that that l. grieved you, 7.08
that what we say by l. when absent, 10.11
And when this l. has been read Col 4.16
you read also the l. from Laodicea. 4.16
Lord that this l. be read to all 1Th 5.27
or by l. purporting to be from us, 2Th 2.02
either by word of mouth or by l. 2.15
to obey what we say in this l., 3.14
is the mark in every l. of mine; 3.17
now the second l. that I have 2Pe 3.01

LETTERS
So she wrote l. in Ahab's name and 1Ki 21.08
she sent the l. to the elders and 21.08
And she wrote in the l., "Proclaim 21.09
written in the l. which she had 21.11
So Jehu wrote l., and sent them to 2Ki 10.01
envoys with l. and a present to 20.12
and wrote l. also to Ephraim and 2Ch 30.01
and Judah with l. from the king 30.06
And he wrote l. to cast contempt on 32.17
let l. be given me to the governors Neh 2.07
River, and gave them the king's l. 2.09
of Judah sent many l. to Tobiah, 6.17
and Tobiah's l. came to them. 6.17
And Tobiah sent l. to make me 6.19
he sent l. to all the royal provinces, Est 1.22
L. were sent by couriers to all the 3.13
to revoke the l. devised by Haman 8.05
and l. were sent by mounted couriers 8.10
and sent l. to all the Jews who 9.20
L. were sent to all the Jews, to the 9.30
envoys with l. and a present to Is 39.01
You have sent l. in your name to Jer 29.25
teach them the l. and language of Dan 1.04
and skill in all l. and wisdom; 1.17
and asked him for l. to the synagogues Ac 9.02
them I received l. to the brethren, 22.05
received no l. from Judea about 28.21
l. of recomemndation to you, or from 2Co 3.01
carved in l. on stone, came with 3.07
seem to be frightening you with l. 10.09
"His l. are weighty and strong, but 10.10
See with what large l. I am writing Gal 6.11
speaking of this as he does in all his l. 2Pe 3.16

LETTEST
"Lord, now l. thou thy servant Lk 2.29

LETTING
again by not l. the people go to Ex 8.29
without l. go with him to battle, 2Ch 25.13
of strife is like l. out water; Pro 17.14
l. Jeremiah down by ropes. Jer 38.06

LETUSHIM
were Asshurim, L., and Leummim. Gen 25.03

LEUMMIM
were Asshurim, Letushim, and L. Gen 25.03

LEVEL
My foot stands on l. ground; in the great Ps 26.12
lead me on a l. path because of my 27.11
good spirit lead me on a l. path! 143.10
of the upright is a l. highway. Pro 15.19
The way of the righteous is l.; Is 26.07
the uneven ground shall become l., 40.04
the rough places into l. ground. 42.16
go before you and l. the mountains, 45.02
with them and stood on a l. place, Lk 6.17

LEVELED
When he has l. its surface, does he Is 28.25
shall be l. to the ground and her Jer 51.58

LEVI
therefore his name called L. Gen 29.34
Simeon and L., Dinah's brothers, took 34.25
Then Jacob said to Simeon and L., 34.30
L., Judah, Issachar, and Zebulun. 35.23
The sons of L.: Gershon, Kohath, and 46.11
Simeon and L. are brothers; 49.05
Reuben, Simeon, L., and Judah, Ex 1.02
the house of L. went and took to 2.01
and took to wife a daughter of L. 2.01
of the sons of L. according to 6.16
of the life of L. being a hundred 6.16
all the sons of L. gathered 32.26
And the sons of L. did according to 32.28
"Only the tribe of L. you shall not Num 1.49
"Bring the tribe of L. near, 3.06
"Number the sons of L., by fathers' 3.15
were the sons of L. by their names: 3.17
Kohath from among the sons of L., 4.02
son of L., and Dathan and Abiram 16.01
you have gone too far, sons of L.!" 16.07
Korah, "Hear now, you sons of L.: 16.08
brethren the sons of L. with you? 16.10
Aaron's name upon the rod of L. 17.03
the house of L. had sprouted and 17.08
the tribe of L., the tribe of your 18.02
These are the families of L.: 26.58
was Jochebed the daughter of L., 26.59
who was born to L. in Egypt; 26.59
the tribe of L. to carry the ark Deu 10.08
Therefore L. has no portion or 10.09
that is, all the tribe of L., 18.01
the sons of L. shall come forward, 21.05
L., Judah, Issachar, Joseph, and 27.12
it to the priests the sons of L., 31.09
of L. he said, "Give to L. thy Thummim, 33.08
To the tribe of L. alone Moses gave Jos 13.14
But to the tribe of L. Moses gave 13.33
L., Judah, Issachar, Zebulun, 1Ch 2.01
The sons of L.: Gershom, Kohath, and 6.01
The sons of L.: Gershom, Kohath, and 6.16
Kohath, son of L., son of Israel; 6.38
Jahath, son of Gershom, son of L. 6.43
of Mushi, son of Merari, son of L.; 6.47
did not include L. and Benjamin in 21.06
corresponding to the sons of L.: 23.06
were named among the tribe of L. 23.14
the sons of L. by their fathers' 23.24
And of the rest of the sons of L.: 24.20
for L., Hashabiah the son of Kemuel; 27.17
found there none of the sons of L. Ez 8.15
of the sons of Mahli the son of L., 8.18
and the sons of L. shall bring the Neh 10.39
The sons of L., heads of fathers' 12.23
O house of L., bless the LORD! Ps 135.20
the sons of L. may come near to Eze 40.46
gate of Judah, and the gate of L., 48.31
of the house of L. by itself, Zec 12.13
that my covenant with L. may hold, Mal 2.04
have corrupted the covenant of L., 2.08
the sons of L. and refine them 3.03
he saw L. the son of Alphaeus Mk 2.14
the son of L., the son of Melchi, Lk 3.24
the son of Matthat, the son of L., 3.29
named L., sitting at the tax office; 5.27
And L. made him a great feast in 5.29
descendants of L. who receive the Heb 7.05

LEVI (cont.)
One might even say that L. himself, Heb 7.09
twelve thousand of the tribe of L., Rev 7.07

LEVIATHAN
who are skilled to rouse up L. Job 3.08
"Can you draw out L. with a fishhook, 41.01
Thou didst crush the heads of L., Ps 74.14
and L. which thou didst form to 104.26
will punish L. the fleeing serpent, Is 27.01
L. the twisting serpent, and he will 27.01

LEVIED
King Solomon l. to build the house 1Ki 9.15
and Jerusalem the tax l. by Moses, 2Ch 24.06

LEVITE
not Aaron, your brother, the L.? Ex 4.14
and the L. that is within your Deu 12.12
and the L. who is within your towns; 12.18
not forsake the L. as long as you 12.19
not forsake the L. who is within 14.27
and the L., because he has no 14.29
the L. who is within your towns, the 16.11
the L., the sojourner, the fatherless, 16.14
"And if a L. comes from any of your 18.06
and the L., and the sojourner who 26.11
of tithing, giving it to the L., 26.12
moreover I have given it to the L., 26.13
the family of Judah, who was a L.; Ju 17.07
"I am a L. of Bethlehem in Judah, 17.09
And the L. was content to dwell 17.11
And Micah installed the L., 17.12
me, because I have a L. as priest." 17.13
recognized the voice of the young L.; 18.03
came to the house of the young L., 18.15
a certain L. was sojourning in the 19.01
And the L., the husband of the 20.04
a L., recorded them in the presence 1Ch 24.06
a L. of the sons of Asaph, in the 2Ch 20.14
charge of them was Conaniah the L., 31.12
And Kore the son of Imnah the L., 31.14
Shabbethai the L. supported them. Ez 10.15
So likewise a L., when he came to Lk 10.32
a L., a native of Cyprus, Ac 4.36

LEVITES
families of the L. according to Ex 6.19
houses of the L. by their families. 6.25
the work of the L. under the 38.21
Nevertheless the cities of the L., Lev 25.32
the L. may redeem at any time. 25.32
And if one of the L. does not 25.33
cities of the L. are their possession 25.33
But the L. were not numbered by Num 1.47
but appoint the L. over the tabernacle 1.50
the L. shall take it down; 1.51
the L. shall set it up. And if any one 1.51
but the L. shall encamp around the 1.53
and the L. shall keep charge of the 1.53
the camp of the L. in the midst of 2.17
But the L. were not numbered among 2.33
shall give the L. to Aaron and his 3.09
have taken the L. from among the 3.12
of Israel. The L. shall be mine, 3.12
These are the families of the L., 3.20
chief over the leaders of the L., 3.32
All who were numbered of the L., 3.39
And you shall take the L. for me— 3.41
cattle of the L. instead of all 3.41
"Take the L. instead of all the 3.45
cattle of the L. instead of their 3.45
and the L. shall be mine: I am the 3.45
above the number of the male L., 3.46
and above those redeemed by the L.; 3.49
be destroyed from among the L.; 4.18
All those who were numbered of the L., 4.46
meeting, and give them to the L., 7.05
the oxen, and gave them to the L. 7.06
"Take the L. from among the people 8.06
present the L. before the tent of 8.09
When you present the L. before the 8.10
shall lay their hands upon the L., 8.10
shall offer the L. before the LORD 8.11
Then the L. shall lay their hands 8.12
LORD, to make atonement for the L. 8.12
shall cause the L. to attend Aaron 8.13
separate the L. from among the 8.14
Israel, and the L. shall be mine. 8.14
And after that the L. shall go in 8.15
have taken the L. instead of all 8.18
have given the L. as a gift to 8.19
of the people of Israel to the L.; 8.20
commanded Moses concerning the L., 8.20
And the L. purified themselves from 8.21
And after that the L. went in to do 8.22
commanded Moses concerning the L., 8.22
"This is what pertains to the L.: 8.24
you do to the L. in assigning 8.26
brethren the L. from among the 18.06
"To the L. I have given every tithe 18.21
But the L. shall do the service of 18.23
given to the L. for an inheritance; 18.24
"Moreover you shall say to the L., 18.26
reckoned to the L. as produce of 18.30
These are the L. as numbered 26.57
them to the L. who have charge of 31.30
them to the L. who had charge of 31.47
Israel, that they give to the L., 35.02
give to the L. pasture lands round 35.02
which you shall give to the L., 35.04
you give to the L. shall be the 35.06
which you give to the L. shall be 35.07
shall give of its cities to the L." 35.08
like all his fellow L. who stand to Deu 18.07
And the L. shall declare to all the 27.14
Moses commanded the L. who carried 31.25
but to the L. he gave no inheritance Jos 14.03
was given to the L. in the land, 14.04
The L. have no portion among you, 18.07
houses of the L. came to Eleazar 21.01
gave to the L. the following 21.03
So those L. who were descendants of 21.04
of Israel gave by lot to the L., 21.08
Kohathites who belonged to the L.; 21.10
the Kohathite families of the L., 21.20
one of the families of the L., 21.27
And to the rest of the L., 21.34
remainder of the families of the L., 21.40
The cities of the L. in the midst 21.41
And the L. took down the ark of the 1Sa 6.15
with all the L., bearing the ark of 2Sa 15.24
priests and the L. brought them up 1Ki 8.04
the people, who were not of the L. 12.31
families of the L. according to 1Ch 6.19
brethren the L. were appointed for 6.48
Israel gave the L. the cities with 6.64
the L., and the temple servants. 9.02
Of the L.: Shemaiah the son of 9.14
gatekeepers of the camp of the L. 9.18
who were L., were in charge of the 9.26
one of the L., the first-born of 9.31
heads of fathers' houses of the L., 9.33
heads of fathers' houses of the L., 9.34
Of the L. four thousand six hundred. 12.26
the priests and L. in the cities 13.02
"No one but the L. may carry the 15.02
the sons of Aaron and the L.: 15.04
and the L. Uriel, Asaiah, Joel, 15.11
of the fathers' houses of the L.; 15.12
priests and the L. sanctified 15.14
And the L. carried the ark of God 15.15
chiefs of the L. to appoint their 15.16
So the L. appointed Heman the son 15.17
leader of the L. in music, should 15.22
God helped the L. who were carrying 15.26
were all the L. who were carrying 15.27

LEVITES (cont.)

certain of the L. as ministers 1Ch 16.04
Israel and the priests and the L. 23.02
The L., thirty years old and upward, 23.03
And so the L. no longer need to 23.26
number of the L. from twenty years 23.27
of the priests and of the L.; 24.06
the sons of the L. according to 24.30
of the priests and of the L. 24.31
And of the L., Ahijah had charge of 26.20
of the priests and of the L., 28.13
priests and the L. for all the 28.21
and the L. took up the ark. 2Ch 5.04
priests and the L. brought them up 5.05
the L. also, with the instruments 7.06
and the L. for their offices of 8.14
the priests and L. concerning any 8.15
priests and the L. that were in 11.13
For the L. left their common lands 11.14
and the L., and made priests for 13.09
Aaron, and L. for their service. 13.10
and with them the L., Shemaiah, 17.08
and with these L., the priests 17.08
appointed certain L. and priests 19.08
and the L. will serve you as 19.11
And the L., of the Kohathites and 20.19
gathered the L. from all the 23.02
you priests and L. who come off 23.04
the priests and ministering L.; 23.06
The L. shall surround the king, each 23.07
The L. and all Judah did according 23.08
priests and the L. whom David had 23.18
he gathered the priests and the L., 24.05
But the L. did not hasten it. 24.05
required the L. to bring in from 24.06
to the king's officers by the L., 24.11
He brought in the priests and the L., 29.04
and said to them, "Hear me, L.! 29.05
Then the L. arose, Mahath the son of 29.12
and the L. took it and carried it 29.16
stationed the L. in the house of 29.25
The L. stood with the instruments 29.26
commanded the L. to sing praises 29.30
their brethren the L. helped them, 29.34
for the L. were more upright in 29.34
priests and the L. were put to 30.15
received from the hand of the L. 30.16
therefore the L. had to kill the 30.17
and the L. and the priests 30.21
to all the L. who showed good 30.22
Judah, and the priests and the L., 30.25
priests and the L. arose and 30.27
of the priests and of the L., 31.02
service, the priests and the L., 31.02
due to the priests and the L., 31.04
priests and the L. about the heaps 31.09
that of the L. from twenty years 31.17
one among the L. who was enrolled. 31.19
which the L., the keepers of the 34.09
were set Jahath and Obadiah the L., 34.12
The L., all who were skilful with 34.12
and some of the L. were scribes, 34.13
Jerusalem and the priests and the L., 34.30
And he said to the L. who taught 35.03
part of a father's house of the L. 35.05
to the priests, and to the L. 35.08
and Jozabad, the chiefs of the L., 35.09
gave to the L. for the passover 35.09
and the L. in their divisions 35.10
them while the L. flayed the 35.11
so the L. prepared for themselves 35.14
brethren the L. prepared for them. 35.15
Josiah, and the priests and the L., 35.18
Benjamin, and the priests and the L., Ez 1.05
The L.: the sons of Jeshua and 2.40
the L., and some of the people 2.70
priests and the L. and all who had 3.08
They appointed the L., from twenty 3.08
the sons of Henadad and the L., 3.09
and the L., the sons of Asaph, with 3.10
the priests and L. and heads of 3.12
of Israel, the priests and the L., 6.16
divisions and the L. in their 6.18
priests and the L. had purified 6.20
and some of the priests and L., 7.07
their priests or L. in my kingdom, 7.13
the L., the singers, the doorkeepers, 7.24
had set apart to attend the L. 8.20
priests and the L. and the heads 8.29
priests and the L. took over the 8.30
Phinehas, and with them were the L., 8.33
priests and the L. have not 9.01
priests and L. and all Israel take 10.05
of the L.: Jozabad, Shimei, Kelaiah 10.23
After him the L. repaired: Rehum the Neh 3.17
and the L. had been appointed, 7.01
The L.: the sons of Jeshua, namely of 7.43
the L., the gatekeepers, the singers, 7.73
the L., helped the people to 8.07
and the L. who taught the people 8.09
So the L. stilled all the people, 8.11
with the priests and the L., 8.13
Upon the stairs of the L. stood Jeshua, 9.04
Then the L., Jeshua, Kadmiel, Bani, 9.05
our L., and our priests set their 9.38
And the L.: Jeshua the son of 10.09
the L., the gatekeepers, the singers, 10.28
the L., and the people, for the wood 10.34
to bring to the L. the tithes from 10.37
for it is the L. who collect the 10.37
be with the L. when the L. receive 10.38
and the L. shall bring up the tithe 10.38
the L., the temple servants, and the 11.03
And of the L.: Shemaiah the son of 11.15
Jozabad, of the chiefs of the L., 11.16
All the L. in the holy city were 11.18
and of the priests and the L., 11.20
The overseer of the L. in Jerusalem 11.22
divisions of the L. in Judah were 11.36
priests and the L. who came up 12.01
And the L.: Jeshua, Binnui, Kadmiel, 12.08
As for the L., in the days of 12.22
And the chiefs of the L.: Hashabiah, 12.24
they sought the L. in all their 12.27
priests and the L. purified 12.30
and for the L. according to the 12.44
priests and the L. who ministered. 12.44
apart that which was for the L.; 12.47
and the L. set apart that which was 12.47
given by commandment to the L., 13.05
portions of the L. had not been 13.10
so that the L. and the singers, who 13.10
the scribe, and Pedaiah of the L., 13.13
And I commanded the L. that they 13.22
of the priesthood and the L. 13.29
the duties of the priests and L., 13.30
priests and for L., says the LORD. Is 66.21
But the L. who went far from me, Eze 44.10
be for the L. who minister at the 45.05
Israel went astray, as the L. did. 48.11
adjoining the territory of the L. 48.12
the L. shall have an allotment 48.13
priests and L. from Jerusalem to Jn 1.19

LEVITICAL

and coming to the L. priests, and to Deu 17.09
is in charge of the L. priests; 17.18
"The L. priests, that is, all the 18.01
to all that the L. priests shall 24.08
And Moses and the L. priests said 27.09
being carried by the L. priests, Jos 3.03
ark before the L. priests who 8.33
and all the L. singers, Asaph, Heman, 2Ch 5.12
direction of the L. priests and the 23.18
and the L. priests shall never lack Jer 33.18
with the L. priests my ministers. 33.21

LEVITICAL (cont.)
and the L. priests who minister to Jer 33.22
give to the L. priests of the Eze 43.19
"But the L. priests, the sons of 44.15
through the L. priesthood (for Heb 7.11

LEVITY
talk, nor l., which are not fitting; Eph 5.04

LEVY
And l. for the LORD a tribute from Num 31.28
raised a l. of forced labor out of 1Ki 5.13
and the l. numbered thirty thousand 5.13
Adoniram was in charge of the l. 5.14
Solomon made a forced l. of slaves, 9.21
made a forced l. and so they are 2Ch 8.08

LEWD
your l. harlotries, on the hills in Jer 13.27
were ashamed of your l. behavior. Eze 16.27

LEWDLY
another l. defiles his daughter-in-law; Eze 22.11

LEWDNESS
not committed l. in addition to Eze 16.43
bear the penalty of your l. and your 16.58
men commit l. in your midst. 22.09
longed for the l. of your youth, 23.21
an end to your l. and your harlotry 23.27
Your l. and your harlotry shall be 23.29
consequences of your l. and harlotry." 23.35
and to Oholibah to commit l. 23.44
I put an end to l. in the land, 23.48
and not commit l. as you have done 23.48
And your l. shall be requited upon 23.49
Its rust is your filthy l. Because 24.13
uncover her l. in the sight of her Hos 2.10

LIABLE
kills shall be l. to judgment.' Mt 5.21
brother shall be l. to judgment; 5.22
brother shall be l. to the council, 5.22
shall be l. to the hell of fire. 5.22

LIAR
is not so, who will prove me a l., Job 24.25
of my right I am counted a l.; 34.06
and a l. gives heed to a mischievous Pro 17.04
and a poor man is better than a l. 19.22
rebuke you, and you be found a l. 30.06
for he is a l. and the father of Jn 8.44
him, I should be a l. like you; 8.55
we make him a l., and his word is 1Jn 1.10
disobeys his commandments is a l., 2.04
Who is the l. but he who denies 2.22
and hates his brother, he is a l.; 4.20
not believe God, has made him a l., 5.10

LIARS
the mouths of l. will be stopped. Ps 63.11
who frustrates the omens of l., Is 44.25
l., perjurers, and whatever else is 1Ti 1.10
pretensions of l. whose consciences 4.02
own, said, "Cretans are always l., Tit 1.12
and all l., their lot shall be in Rev 21.08

LIBATION
a fourth of a hin of wine for a l. Ex 29.40
it a cereal offering and its l., 29.41
and you shall pour no l. thereon. 30.09
for incense, and the bowls for l. Jer 52.19
be poured as a l. upon the sacrificial Php 2.17

LIBATIONS
and bowls with which to pour l.; Ex 25.29
and flagons with which to pour l. 37.16
there were the l. for the burnt 2Ch 29.35
their l. of blood I will not pour Ps 16.04

of heaven and pour out l. to her, Jer 44.17
heaven and pouring out l. to her, 44.18
of heaven and poured out l. to her, 44.19
her image and poured out l. to her?" 44.19
heaven and to pour out l. to her.' 44.25
They shall not pour l. of wine to Hos 9.04

LIBERAL
A l. man will be enriched, and one Pro 11.25
us about this l. gift which we are 2Co 8.20
in good deeds, l. and generous, 1Ti 6.18

LIBERALITY
and gave gifts with royal l. Est 2.18
he who contributes, in l.; Rom 12.08
in a wealth of l. on their part. 2Co 8.02

LIBERALLY
furnish him l. out of your flock, Deu 15.14
He is ever giving l. and lending, Ps 37.26
gave alms l. to the people, and Ac 10.02

LIBERTY
and proclaim l. throughout the land Lev 25.10
and I shall walk at l., for I have Ps 119.45
to proclaim l. to the captives, and Is 61.01
make a proclamation of l. to them, Jer 34.08
right in my eyes by proclaiming l., 34.15
not obeyed me by proclaiming l., 34.17
I proclaim to you l. to the sword, 34.17
it shall be his to the year of l.; Eze 46.17
to set at l. those who are oppressed, Lk 4.18
in custody but should have some l., Ac 24.23
me, they wished to set me at l., 28.18
the glorious l. of the children of Rom 8.21
care lest this l. of yours somehow 1Co 8.09
why should my l. be determined by 10.29
the law of l., and perseveres, being Jas 1.25
to be judged under the law of l. 2.12

LIBNAH
Rimmonperez, and encamped at L. Num 33.20
And they set out from L., and 33.21
to L., and fought against L.; Jos 10.29
And Joshua passed on from L., 10.31
person in it, as he had done to L. 10.32
to Hebron and to L. and its king, 10.39
the king of L., one; the king of 12.15
L., Ether, Ashan, 15.42
L. with its pasture lands, 21.13
Then L. revolted at the same time. 2Ki 8.22
of Assyria fighting against L.; 19.08
the daughter of Jeremiah of L. 23.31
the daughter of Jeremiah of L. 24.18
L. with its pasture lands, Jattir, 1Ch 6.57
At that time L. also revolted from 2Ch 21.10
of Assyria fighting against L.; Is 37.08
the daughter of Jeremiah of L. Jer 52.01

LIBNI
L. and Shimei, by their families. Ex 6.17
by their families: L. and Shimei. Num 3.18
the sons of Gershom: L. and Shimei. 1Ch 6.17
Of Gershom: L. his son, Jahath his 6.20
L. his son, Shimei his son, Uzzah his 6.29

LIBNITES
family of the L. and the family of Num 3.21
of Levi: the family of the L., 26.58

LIBYA
and L., and the people of the land Eze 30.05
the parts of L. belonging to Ac 2.10

LIBYANS
L., Sukkiim, and Ethiopians. 2Ch 12.03
Ethiopians and the L. a huge army 16.08
and the L. and the Ethiopians shall Dan 11.43
Put and the L. were here helpers. Nah 3.9

LICENTIOUS
entice with l. passions of the flesh 2Pe 2.18

LICENTIOUSNESS
l., envy, slander, pride, foolishness. Mk 7.22
drunkenness, not in debauchery and l., Rom 13.13
and l. which they have practiced. 2Co 12.21
plain: immorality, impurity, l., Gal 5.19
and have given themselves up to l., Eph 4.19
living in l., passions, drunkenness, 1Pe 4.03
And many will follow their l., 2Pe 2.02
distressed by the l. of the wicked 2.07
of our God into l. and deny our Jud 1.04

LICK
horde will now l. up all that is Num 22.04
shall dogs l. your own blood."'" 1Ki 21.19
him, and his enemies l. the dust! Ps 72.09
and l. the dust of your feet. Is 49.23
they shall l. the dust like a Mic 7.17

LICKED
and l. up the water that was in the 1Ki 18.38
where dogs l. up the blood of 21.19
and the dogs l. up his blood, and 22.38
the dogs came and l. his sores. Lk 16.21

LICKS
as the ox l. up the grass of the Num 22.04

LID
and bored a hole in the l. of it, 2Ki 12.09

LIE
and we will l. with him, that we may Gen 19.32
then you go in and l. with him, 19.34
on which you l. I will give to you 28.13
"Then he may l. with you tonight 30.15
and he did not l. with her again. 38.26
upon Joseph, and said, "L. with me." 39.07
to l. with her or to be with her. 39.10
by his garment, saying, "L. with me." 39.12
he came in to me to l. with me, 39.14
but let me l. with my fathers; 47.30
But if he did not l. in wait for Ex 21.13
shall let it rest and l. fallow, 23.11
Close to the frame the rings shall l., 25.27
that it may l. upon the skilfully 28.28
that it should l. upon the skilfully 39.21
And you shall not l. carnally with Lev 18.20
You shall not l. with a male as 18.22
And you shall not l. with any beast 18.23
herself to a beast to l. with it: 18.23
falsely, nor l. to one another. 19.11
and you shall l. down, and none 26.06
God is not man, that he should l., Num 23.19
it does not l. down till it devours 23.24
and when you l. down, and when you Deu 6.07
and when you l. down, and when you 11.19
cause him to l. down and be beaten 25.02
and another man shall l. with her; 28.30
you shall l. in ambush against the Jos 8.04
and l. in wait in the fields. Ju 9.32
"Go and l. in wait in the vineyards, 21.20
and uncover his feet and l. down; Ru 3.04
he went to l. down at the end of 3.07
you. L. down until the morning." 3.13
"I did not call; l. down again." 1Sa 3.05
call, my son; l. down again." 3.06
Therefore Eli said to Samuel, "Go, l. down; 3.09
of Israel will not l. or repent; 15.29
to l. in wait, as at this day." 22.08
to l. in wait, as at this day?" 22.13
fulfilled and you l. down with your 2Sa 7.12
making them l. down on the ground; 8.02
to drink, and to l. with my wife? 11.11
he went out to l. on his couch 11.13
and l. in his bosom, and it was like 12.03
and he shall l. with your wives in 12.11
"L. down on your bed, and pretend to 13.05
to her, "Come, l. with me, my sister." 13.11
let her l. in your bosom, that my 1Ki 1.02
do not l. to your maidservant." 2Ki 4.16
for I will not l. to your face. Job 6.28
When I l. down I say, 'When shall I 7.04
For now I shall l. in the earth; 7.21
You will l. down, and none will make 11.19
but it will l. down with him in the 20.11
They l. down alike in the dust, and 21.26
They l. all night naked, without 24.07
or l. in wait in their covert? 38.40
I l. down and sleep; I wake again, Ps 3.05
I will both l. down and sleep; 4.08
he makes me l. down in green 23.02
There the evildoers l. prostrate, 36.12
I l. in the midst of lions that 57.04
For, lo, they l. in wait for my life; 59.03
the slain that l. in the grave, 88.05
holiness; I will not l. to David. 89.35
I l. awake, I am like a lonely bird 102.07
them away and l. down in their 104.22
The wicked l. in wait to destroy me; 119.95
let us l. in wait for blood, let us Pro 1.11
but these men l. in wait for their 1.18
when you l. down, your sleep will be 3.24
How long will you l. there, 6.09
when you l. down, they will watch 6.22
of the wicked l. in wait for blood, 12.06
A faithful witness does not l., 14.05
Sheol and Abaddon l. upon before 15.11
L. not in wait as a wicked man 24.15
Again, if two l. together, they are Ecc 4.11
the tree falls, there it will l. 11.03
where you make it l. down at noon; Sol 1.07
"Until cities l. waste without Is 6.11
leopard shall l. down with the kid, 11.06
their young shall l. down together; 11.07
make their flocks l. down there. 13.20
But wild beasts will l. down there, 13.21
kings of the nations l. in glory, 14.18
and the needy l. down in safety; 14.30
which will l. down, and none will 17.02
The highways l. waste, the wayfaring 33.08
to generation it shall l. waste; 34.10
they l. down, they cannot rise, they 43.17
"Is there not a l. in my right hand?" 44.20
hand: you shall l. down in torment. 50.11
they l. at the head of every street 51.20
Achor a place for herds to l. down, 65.10
Let us l. down in our shame, and let Jer 3.25
the scribes has made it into a l. 8.08
For it is a l. which they are 27.10
for it is a l. which they are 27.14
for it is a l. which they are 27.16
made this people trust in a l. 28.15
for it is a l. which they are 29.09
prophesying a l. to you in my name: 29.21
and has made you trust in a l., 29.31
to Jeremiah, "You are telling a l. 43.02
of the streets l. the young and Lam 2.21
The holy stones l. scattered at the 4.01
up in purple l. on ash heaps. 4.05
"Then l. upon your left side, and I Eze 4.04
of the days that you l. upon it, 4.04
you shall l. down a second time, but 4.06
of days that you l. upon your side, 4.09
their slain l. among their idols 6.13
spoken falsehood and divined a l.; 13.06
its boughs will l. broken in all 31.12
you shall l. among the uncircumcised, 31.18
with her shall l. all her multitudes 32.20
they l. still, the uncircumcised, 32.21
And they do not l. with the fallen 32.27
be broken and l. among the uncircumcised, 32.28
they l. with the uncircumcised, with 32.29
they l. uncircumcised with those 32.30

LIE (cont.)
they shall l. down in good grazing Eze 34.14
and I will make them l. down, 34.15
prince shall l. between the 48.22
I will make you l. down in safety. Hos 2.18
As robbers l. in wait for a man, so 6.09
Woe to those who l. upon beds of Amo 6.04
they all l. in wait for blood, and Mic 7.02
hastens to the end—it will not l. Hab 2.03
they shall l. down at evening. Zep 2.07
Herds shall l. down in the midst of 2.14
For they shall pasture and l. down, 3.13
your heart to l. to the Holy Ac 5.03
of their men l. in ambush for him, 23.21
about God for a l. and worshiped Rom 1.25
for ever, knows that I do not l. 2Co 11.31
to you, before God, I do not l.!) Gal 1.20
Do not l. to one another, seeing Col 3.09
we l. and do not live according to 1Jn 1.06
know that no l. is of the truth. 2.21
and is no l., just as it has taught 2.27
but l.—behold, I will make them Rev 3.09
bodies will l. in the street of 11.08
and in their mouth no l. was found, 14.05

LIED
what was lost and l. about it, Lev 6.03
and l., and put them among their Jos 7.11
drink water.'" But he l. to him. 1Ki 13.18
they l. to him with their tongues. Ps 78.36
so that you l., and did not remember Is 57.11
You have not l. to men but to God." Ac 5.04

LIES
it l. between Kadesh and Bered. Gen 16.14
and l. with her, he shall give the Ex 22.16
"Whoever l. with a beast shall be 22.19
and he who l. down in the house Lev 14.47
the discharge l. shall be unclean; 15.04
If a man l. with a woman and has an 15.18
upon which she l. during her 15.20
And if any man l. with her, and her 15.24
bed on which he l. shall be 15.24
Every bed on which she l., 15.26
for the man who l. with a woman 15.33
"If a man l. carnally with a woman 19.20
The man who l. with his father's 20.11
If a man l. with his daughter-in-law, 20.12
If a man l. with a male as with a 20.13
If a man l. with a beast, he shall 20.15
approaches any beast and l. with it, 20.16
If a man l. with a woman having her 20.18
If a man l. with his uncle's wife, he 20.20
sabbaths as long as it l. desolate, 26.34
As long as it l. desolate it shall 26.35
while it l. desolate without them; 26.43
if a man l. with her carnally, and Num 5.13
dead bodies l. in the wilderness. 14.33
and l. in wait for him, and attacks Deu 19.11
her in the city and l. with her, 22.23
the man seizes her and l. with her, 22.25
and seizes her and l. with her, 22.28
be he who l. with his father's wife, 27.20
be he who l. with any kind of 27.21
be he who l. with his sister, 27.22
be he who l. with his mother-in-law." 27.23
mountain that l. over against the Jos 15.08
mountain that l. south of Lower 18.13
the mountain that l. to the south, 18.14
the land where your possession l., 22.04
that l. in the land of Canaan, the 22.10
which l. in the Negeb near Arad; Ju 1.16
see wherein his great strength l., 16.05
me wherein your great strength l. 16.06
you have mocked me, and told me l.; 16.10
you have mocked me, and told me l.; 16.13
me wherein your great strength l." 16.15
But when he l. down, observe the Ru 3.04
place where he l.; then, go and 3.04
"Jonathan l. slain upon thy high 2Sa 1.25
which l. before Giah on the way to 2.24
l. waste, and its gates have been Neh 2.03
how Jerusalem l. in ruins with its 2.17
As for you, you whitewash with l.; Job 13.04
So man l. down and rises not again; 14.12
Under the lotus plants he l., 40.21
love vain words, and seek after l.? Ps 4.02
Thou destroyest those who speak l.; 5.06
with mischief, and brings forth l. 7.14
Every one utters l. to his neighbor; 12.02
not rise again from where he l." 41.08
err from their birth, speaking l. 58.03
the cursing and l. which they 59.12
me, those who attack me with l. 69.04
Thy wrath l. heavy upon me, and thou 88.07
man who utters l. shall continue 101.07
The godless besmear me with l., 119.69
whose mouths speak l., and whose 144.08
of aliens, whose mouths speak l., 144.11
a false witness who breathes out l., Pro 6.19
and at every corner she l. in wait. 7.12
a false witness breathes out l. 14.05
one who utters l. is a betrayer. 14.25
he who utters l. will not escape. 19.05
and he who utters l. will perish. 19.09
She l. in wait like a robber and 23.28
be like one who l. down in the 23.34
like one who l. on the top of a 23.34
and it l. heavy upon men: Ecc 6.01
man's trouble l. heavy upon him. 8.06
that l. between my breasts. Sol 1.13
Your country l. desolate, your Is 1.07
prophet who teaches l. is the tail; 9.15
The earth l. polluted under its 24.05
its transgression l. heavy upon it, 24.20
there he l. down, and strips its 27.10
for we have made l. our refuge, 28.15
will sweep away the refuge of l., 28.17
your lips have spoken l., your tongue 59.03
pleas, they speak l., they conceive 59.04
taught their tongue to speak l.; Jer 9.05
forgotten me and trusted in l. 13.25
are prophesying l. in my name; 14.14
have inherited nought but l., 16.19
commit adultery and walk in l.; 23.14
said who prophesy l. in my name, 23.25
shall there be l. in the heart of 23.26
of the prophets who prophesy l., 23.26
astray by their l. and their 23.32
for Mount Zion which l. desolate; Lam 5.18
have uttered delusions and seen l., Eze 13.08
by your l. to my people, who listen 13.19
to my people. who listen to l. 13.19
while they divine l. for you— 21.29
visions and divining l. for them. 22.28
dragon that l. in the midst of his 29.03
Berothah, Sibraim (which l. on the 47.16
shall speak l. at the same table, Dan 11.27
them, but they speak l. against me. Hos 7.13
you have eaten the fruit of l. 10.13
Ephraim has encompassed me with l., 11.12
but their l. have led them astray, Amo 2.04
go about and utter wind and l., Mic 2.11
your inhabitants speak l., 6.12
from her who l. in your bosom; 7.05
all full of l. and booty—no end Nah 3.01
it, a metal image, a teacher of l.? Hab 2.18
shall do no wrong and utter no l., Zep 3.13
while this house l. in ruins? Hag 1.04
of my house that l. in ruins, 1.09
nonsense, and the diviners see l.; Zec 10.02
for you speak l. in the name of the 13.03
of Olives which l. before Jerusalem 14.04
When he l., he speaks according to Jn 8.44
he is a liar and the father of l. 8.44
Apart from the law sin l. dead. Rom 7.08

LIES (cont.)
to do right, evil l. close at hand. Rom 7.21
is read a veil l. over their minds; 2Co 3.15
forgetting what l. behind and Php 3.13
straining forward to what l. ahead, 3.13
who never l., promised ages ago Tit 1.02
for five months l. in their tails. Rev 9.10
The city l. foursquare, its length 21.16

LIFE
everything that has the breath of l., Gen 1.30
into his nostrils the breath of l.; 2.07
the tree of l. also in the midst of 2.09
shall eat all the days of your l. 3.14
eat of it all the days of your l.; 3.17
and take also of the tree of l., 3.22
to guard the way to the tree of l. 3.24
the breath of l. from under heaven; 6.17
six hundredth year of Noah's l., 7.11
which there was the breath of l. 7.15
nostrils was the breath of l. died. 7.22
shall not eat flesh with its l., 9.04
I will require the l. of man. 9.05
and that my l. may be spared on 12.13
forth, they said, "Flee for your l.; 19.17
me great kindness in saving my l.; 19.19
little one?—and my l. will be saved!" 19.20
were the years of the l. of Sarah. 23.01
days of the years of Abraham's l., 25.07
are the years of the l. of Ishmael, 25.17
and they made l. bitter for Isaac 26.35
am weary of my l. because of the 27.46
what good will my l. be to me?" 27.46
face, and yet my l. is preserved." 32.30
saying, "Let us not take his l." 37.21
by the l. of Pharaoh, you shall not 42.15
by the l. of Pharaoh, surely you are 42.16
as his l. is bound up in the lad's l., 44.30
life is bound up in the lad's l., 44.30
the sight of my father all my l.' 44.32
sent me before you to preserve l. 45.05
the days of the years of your l.?" 47.08
the days of the years of my l., 47.09
years of the l. of my fathers in 47.09
days of Jacob, the years of his l., 47.28
led me all my l. long to this day, 48.15
who were seeking your l. are dead." Ex 4.19
years of the l. of Levi being a 6.16
years of the l. of Kohath being a 6.18
years of the l. of Amram being one 6.20
and he shall serve him for l. 21.06
then you shall give l. for life, 21.23
then you shall give life for l., 21.23
redemption of his l. whatever is 21.30
For the l. of the flesh is in the Lev 17.11
atonement, by reason of the l. 17.11
"For the l. of every creature is 17.14
for the l. of every creature is its 17.14
against the l. of your neighbor: I 19.16
beast shall make it good, l. for l. 24.18
the eyes and cause l. to pine away. 26.16
ridden all your l. long to this Num 22.30
ransom for the l. of a murderer 35.31
your heart all the days of your l.; Deu 4.09
these cities he might save his l.: 4.42
you, all the days of your l.; 6.02
for the blood is the l., and you 12.23
not eat the l. with the flesh. 12.23
days of your l. you may remember 16.03
read in it all the days of his l., 17.19
by fleeing there may save his l. 19.04
of these cities and save his l.; 19.05
it shall be l. for l., eye for eye, 19.21
he would be taking a l. in pledge. 24.06
your l. shall hang in doubt before 28.66
and have no assurance of your l. 28.66
before you this day l. and good, 30.15
I have set before you l. and death, 30.19
therefore choose l.; that you and 30.19
for that means l. to you and length 30.20
trifle for you, but it is your l., 32.47
before you all the days of your l.; Jos 1.05
men said to her, "Our l. for yours! 2.14
of Moses, all the days of his l. 4.14
fought for you, and risked his l., Ju 9.17
I took my l. in my hand, and crossed 12.03
is to be the boy's manner of l., 13.12
whom he had slain during his l. 16.30
you lose your l. with the lives of 18.25
a restorer of l. and a nourisher Ru 4.15
to the LORD all the days of his l.; 1Sa 1.11
The LORD kills and brings to l.; 2.06
Israel all the days of his l. 7.15
for he took his l. in his hand and 19.05
"If you do not save your l. tonight, 19.11
your father, that he seeks me l.?" 20.01
that seeks my l. seeks your l.; with 22.23
Saul had come out to seek his l. 23.15
though you hunt my l. to take it. 24.11
to pursue you and to seek your l., 25.29
the l. of my lord shall be bound in 25.29
Israel has come out to seek my l., 26.20
because my l. was precious in your 26.21
as your l. was precious this day in 26.24
so may my l. be precious in the 26.24
will make you my bodyguard for l." 28.02
a snare for my l. to bring about 28.09
I have taken my l. in my hand, 28.21
me, and yet my l. still lingers." 2Sa 1.09
In l. and in death they were not 1.23
your enemy, who sought your l.; 4.08
has redeemed my l. out of every 4.09
him for the l. of his brother whom 14.07
take away the l. of him who 14.14
be, whether for death or for l., 15.21
"Behold, my own son seeks my l.; 16.11
You seek the l. of only one man, and 17.03
against his l. (and there is 18.13
who have this day saved your l., 19.05
your own l. and the l. of your son 1Ki 1.12
word does not cost Adonijah his l.! 2.23
yourself long l. or riches or the 3.11
riches or the l. of your enemies, 3.11
Solomon all the days of his l. 4.21
him ruler all the days of his l., 11.34
commanded him all the days of his l., 15.05
Jeroboam all the days of his l. 15.06
not make your l. as the l. of one of 19.02
and he arose and went for his l., 19.03
now, O LORD, take away my l.; 19.04
and they seek my l., to take it away." 19.10
and they seek my l., to take it away." 19.14
perhaps he will spare your l." 20.31
your l. shall be for his l., or else 20.39
therefore your l. shall go for his l., 20.42
my l., and the l. of these fifty servants 2Ki 1.13
but now let my l. be precious in 1.14
there was no sound or sign of l. 4.31
whose son he had restored to l., 8.01
Elisha had restored the dead to l., 8.05
had restored to l. appealed to the 8.05
her son whom Elisha restored to l." 8.05
to escape shall forfeit his l." 10.24
will add fifteen years to your l. 20.06
day of his l. he dined regularly 25.29
or the l. of those who hate you, and 2Ch 1.11
and have not even asked long l., 1.11
pray for the l. of the king and Ez 6.10
let my l. be given me at my petition, Est 7.03
to beg his l. from Queen Esther, 7.07
a man has he will give for his l. Job 2.04
in your power; only spare his l." 2.06
and l. to the bitter in soul, 3.20
"Remember that my l. is a breath; 7.07
I loathe my l.; I would not live 7.16
regard not myself; I loathe my l. 9.21

LIFE (cont.)

"I loathe my l.; I will give free	Job 10.01
Thou hast granted me l. and steadfast	10.12
Are not the days of my l. few?	10.20
And your l. will be brighter than	11.17
In his hand is the l. of every	12.10
my teeth, and put my l. in my hand.	13.14
prolongs the l. of the mighty by	24.22
rise up when they despair of l.	24.22
off, when God takes away his l.?	27.08
by asking for his l. with a curse);	31.30
breath of the Almighty gives me l.	33.04
his l. from perishing by the sword.	33.18
so that his l. loathes bread, and	33.20
and his l. to those who bring death	33.22
and my l. shall see the light."	33.28
that he may see the light of l.	33.30
youth, and their l. ends in shame.	36.14
Turn, O LORD, save my l.; deliver me	Ps 6.04
him trample my l. to the gound,	7.05
Thou dost show me the path of l.;	16.11
Deliver my l. from the wicked by	17.13
portion in l. is of the world.	17.14
He asked l. of thee; thou gavest it	21.04
my l. from the power of the dog!	22.20
follow me all the days of my l.;	23.06
Oh guard my l., and deliver me;	25.20
nor my l. with bloodthirsty men,	26.09
LORD is the stronghold of my l.;	27.01
of the LORD all the days of my l.,	27.04
restored me to l. from among those	30.03
For my l. is spent with sorrow, and	31.10
me, as they plot to take my l.	31.13
What man is there who desires l.,	34.12
redeems the l. of his servants;	34.22
and dishonor who seek after my l.!	35.04
cause they dug a pit for my l.	35.07
ravages, my l. from the lions!	35.17
For with thee is the fountain of l.;	36.09
Those who seek my l. lay their	38.12
let me know how fleeting my l. is!	39.04
who seek to snatch away my l.;	40.14
me, a prayer to the God of my l.	42.08
give to God the price of his l.,	49.07
for the ransom of his l. is costly,	49.08
me, ruthless men seek my l.;	54.03
the Lord is the upholder of my l.	54.04
As they have waited for my l.,	56.06
walk before God in the light of l.	56.13
For, lo, they lie in wait for my l.;	59.03
Prolong the l. of the king;	61.06
steadfast love is better than l.,	63.03
to destroy my l. shall go down	63.09
preserve my l. from dread of the	64.01
shame and confusion who seek my l.!	70.02
watch for my l. consult together,	71.10
and violence he redeems their l.;	72.14
not forget the l. of thy poor for	74.19
give us l., and we will call on thy	80.18
Preserve my l., for I am godly;	86.02
band of ruthless men seek my l.,	86.14
and my l. draws near to Sheol.	88.03
Remember, O Lord, what the measure of l. is,	89.47
The years of our l. are threescore	90.10
With long l. I will satisfy him, and	91.16
against the l. of the righteous,	94.21
who redeems your l. from the Pit,	103.04
those who speak evil against my l.!	109.20
LORD, I beseech thee, save my l.!"	116.04
and give me l. in thy ways.	119.37
in thy righteousness give me l.!	119.40
that thy promise gives me l.	119.50
In thy steadfast love spare my l.,	119.88
or by them thou hast given me l.	119.93
give me l., O LORD, according to thy	119.107
I hold my l. in my hand continually,	119.109
in thy justice preserve my l.	119.149
give me l. accordiig to thy promise!	119.154
give me l. according to thy justice.	119.156
Preserve my l. according to thy	119.159
from all evil; he will keep your l.	121.07
Jerusalem all the days of your l.!	128.05
the blessing, l. for evermore.	133.03
trouble, thou dost preserve my l.;	138.07
he has crushed my l. to the ground;	143.03
sake, O LORD, preserve my l.!	143.11
takes away the l. of its possessors.	Pro 1.19
nor do they regain the paths of l.	2.19
and years of l. and abundant	3.02
Long l. is in her right hand;	3.16
She is a tree of l. to those who	3.18
and they will be l. for your soul	3.22
the years of your l. may be many.	4.10
guard her, for she is your l.	4.13
For they are l. to him who finds	4.22
for from it flow the springs of l.	4.23
not take heed to the path of l.;	5.06
and at the end of your l. you groan,	5.11
of discipline are the way of l.,	6.23
adulteress stalks a man's very l.	6.26
know that it will cost him his l.	7.23
finds me finds l. and obtains	8.35
and years will be added to your l.	9.11
the righteous is a fountain of l.,	10.11
The wage of the righteous leads to l.,	10.16
instruction is on the path to l.;	10.17
The fear of the LORD prolongs l.,	10.27
of the righteous is a tree of l.,	11.30
has regard for the l. of his beast,	12.10
In the path of righteousness is l.,	12.28
guards his mouth preserves his l.;	13.03
ransom of a man's l. is his wealth,	13.08
a desire fulfilled is a tree of l.	13.12
of the wise is a fountain of l.,	13.14
of the LORD is a fountain of l.,	14.27
tranquil mind gives l. to the flesh,	14.30
A gentle tongue is a tree of l.,	15.04
wise man's path leads upward to l.,	15.24
light of a king's face there is l.,	16.15
guards his way preserves his l.	16.17
a fountain of l. to him who has it,	16.22
it is gained in a righteous l.	16.31
Death and l. are in the power of	18.21
keeps the commandment keeps his l.;	19.16
The fear of the LORD leads to l.;	19.23
him to anger forfeits his l.	20.02
kindness will find l. and honor.	21.21
LORD is riches and honor and l.	22.04
and despoil of l. those who despoil	22.23
you will save his l. from Sheol.	23.14
blameless, and the wicked seek his l.	29.10
of a thief hates his own l.;	29.24
not harm, all the days of her l.	31.12
during the few days of their l.	Ecc 2.03
So I hated l., because what is done	2.17
few days of his l. which God has	5.18
the days of his l. because God	5.20
lives the few days of his vain l.,	6.12
preserves the l. of him who has it.	7.12
In my vain l. I have seen everything;	7.15
prolongs his l. in his evil-doing.	7.15
hundred times and prolongs his l.,	8.12
the days of l. which God gives him	8.15
Enjoy l. with the wife whom you	9.09
of your vain l. which he has given	9.09
your portion in l. and in your	9.09
for laughter, and wine gladdens l.,	10.19
and the dawn of l. are vanity.	11.10
been recorded for l. in Jerusalem,	Is 4.03
will add fifteen years to your l.	38.05
a weaver I have rolled up my l.;	38.12
all these is the l. of my spirit.	38.16
held back my l. from the pit of	38.17
instruments all the days of our l.,	38.20
peoples in exchange for your l.	43.04
you found new l. for your strength,	57.10

LIFE (cont.)
and I have made the breath of l. Is 57.16
sword has reached their very l." Jer 4.10
lovers despise you; they seek your l. 4.30
be preferred to l. by all the 8.03
who seek your l., and say, "Do not 11.21
yet they have dug a pit for my l. 18.20
hand of those who seek their l. 19.07
who seek their l. afflict them.' 19.09
delivered the l. of the needy from 20.13
you the way of l. and the way of 21.08
shall have his l. as a prize of 21.09
the hand of those who seek your l., 22.25
their l. shall be like a watered 31.12
shall have his l. as a prize of 38.02
hand of these men who seek your l." 38.16
then your l. shall be spared, and 38.17
and your l. shall be spared. 38.20
shall have your l. as a prize of 39.18
son of Nethaniah to take your l.?" 40.14
Why should he take your l., 40.15
the hand of those who seek his l., 44.30
was his enemy and sought his l." 44.30
give you your l. as a prize of war 45.05
hand of those who seek their l., 46.26
and before those who seek their l.; 49.37
Babylon, let every man save his l.! 51.06
come, the thread of your l. is cut. 51.13
man save his l. from the fierce 51.45
day of his l. he dined regularly 52.33
as their l. is poured out on their Lam 2.12
O Lord, thou hast redeemed my l. 3.58
way, in order to save his l., Eze 3.18
but you will have saved your l. 3.19
and you will have saved your l." 3.21
iniquity, none can maintain his l. 7.13
from his wicked way to save his l.; 13.22
and right, he shall save his l. 18.27
by which they could not have l.; 20.25
moment, every one for his own l., 32.10
warning, he would have saved his l. 33.05
but you will have saved your l. 33.09
and walks in the statutes of l., 33.15
awake, some to everlasting l., Dan 12.02
nor shall the mighty save his l.; Amo 2.14
he who rides the horse save his l.; 2.15
us not perish for this man's l., Jon 1.14
didst bring up my l. from the Pit, 2.06
take my l. from me, I beseech thee, 4.03
you have forfeited your l. Hab 2.10
him was a covenant of l. and peace, Mal 2.05
sustained for us the spirit of l.? 2.15
who sought the child's l. are dead." Mt 2.20
do not be anxious about your l., 6.25
Is not l. more than food, and the 6.25
add one cubit to his span of l.? 6.27
that leads to l., and those who 7.14
He who finds his l. will lose it, 10.39
who loses his l. for my sake will 10.39
would save his l. will lose it, 16.25
loses his l. for my sake will find 16.25
whole world and forfeits his l.? 16.26
a man give in return for his l.? 16.26
you to enter l. maimed or lame 18.08
you to enter l. with one eye than 18.09
deed must I do, to have eternal l.?" 19.16
If you would enter l., keep the 19.17
hundredfold, and inherit eternal l. 19.29
and to give his l. as a ransom for 20.28
but the righteous into eternal l." 25.46
to do harm, to save l. or to kill?" Mk 3.04
would save his l. will lose it; 8.35
loses his l. for my sake and the 8.35
the whole world and forfeit his l.? 8.36
a man give in return for his l.? 8.37
you to enter l. maimed than with 9.43
you to enter l. lame than with two 9.45
must I do to inherit eternal l.?" 10.17
and in the age to come eternal l. 10.30
and to give his l. as a ransom for 10.45
before him all the days of our l. Lk 1.75
to save l. or to destroy it?" 6.09
and riches and pleasures of l., 8.14
would save his l. will lose it; 9.24
whoever loses his l. for my sake, 9.24
shall I do to inherit eternal l.?" 10.25
for a man's l. does not consist in 12.15
do not be anxious about your l., 12.22
For l. is more than food, and the 12.23
can add a cubit to his span of l.? 12.25
sisters, yes, and even his own l., 14.26
Whoever seeks to gain his l. will lose it, 17.33
loses his l. will preserve it. 17.33
shall I do to inherit eternal l.?" 18.18
and in the age to come eternal l." 18.30
drunkenness and cares of this l., 21.34
was l., and the l. was the light of men. Jn 1.04
believes in him may have eternal l." 3.15
not perish but have eternal l. 3.16
believes in the Son has eternal l.; 3.36
not obey the Son shall not see l., 3.36
of water welling up to eternal l." 4.14
and gathers fruit for eternal l., 4.36
raises the dead and gives them l., 5.21
the Son gives l. to whom he will. 5.21
him who sent me, has eternal l.; 5.24
but has passed from death to l. 5.24
For as the Father has l. in himself, 5.26
Son also to have l. in himself, 5.26
good, to the resurrection of l., 5.29
that in them you have eternal l.; 5.39
to come to me that you may have l. 5.40
food which endures to eternal l., 6.27
heaven, and gives l. to the world." 6.33
said to them, "I am the bread of l.; 6.35
in him should have eternal l.; 6.40
he who believes has eternal l. 6.47
I am the bread of l. 6.48
give for the l. of the world is my 6.51
his blood, you have no l. in you; 6.53
and drinks my blood has eternal l., 6.54
It is the spirit that gives l., 6.63
spoken to you are spirit and l. 6.63
You have the words of eternal l.; 6.68
but will have the light of l." 8.12
I came that they may have l., 10.10
lays down his l. for the sheep. 10.11
and I lay down my l. for the sheep. 10.15
loves me because I lay down my l., 10.17
and I give them eternal l., 10.28
"I am the resurrection and the l.; 11.25
He who loves his l. loses it, 12.25
who hates his l. in this world 12.25
world will keep it for eternal l. 12.25
that his commandment is eternal l. 12.50
I will lay down my l. for you." 13.37
"Will you lay down your l. for me? 13.38
the way, and the truth, and the l.; 14.06
lay down his l. for his friends. 15.13
to give eternal l. to all whom 17.02
And this is eternal l., that they know 17.03
you may have l. in his name. 20.31
made known to me the ways of l.; Ac 2.28
and killed the Author of l., 3.15
people all the words of this L." 5.20
For his l. is taken up from the 8.33
God has granted repentance unto l." 11.18
yourselves unworthy of eternal l., 13.46
ordained to eternal l. believed. 13.48
to all men l. and breath and 17.25
be alarmed, for his l. is in him." 20.10
not account my l. of any value nor 20.24
"My manner of l. from my youth, 26.04
will be no loss of l. among you, 27.22
immortality, he will give eternal l.; Rom 2.07
who gives l. to the dead and calls 4.17

LIFE (cont.)

shall we be saved by his l. Rom 5.10
reign in l. through the one man 5.17
to acquittal and l. for all men. 5.18
to eternal l. through Jesus Christ 5.21
we too might walk in newness of l. 6.04
but the l. he lives he lives to God. 6.10
have been brought from death to l., 6.13
sanctification and its end, eternal l. 6.22
God is eternal l. in Christ Jesus 6.23
on a person only during his l.? 7.01
but in the new l. of the Spirit. 7.06
which promised l. proved to be 7.10
the Spirit of l. in Christ Jesus 8.02
mind on the Spirit is l. and peace. 8.06
dead will give l. to your mortal 8.11
nor l., nor angels, nor principalities, 8.38
alone am left, and they seek my l." 11.03
acceptance mean but l. from the dead? 11.15
who risked their necks for my l., 16.04
source of your l. in Christ Jesus, 1Co 1.30
or the world or l. or death or the 3.22
matters pertaining to this l.! 6.03
one lead the l. which the Lord has 7.17
If in this l. we who are in Christ 15.19
does not come to l. unless it dies. 15.36
that we despaired of l. itself. 2Co 1.08
the other a fragrance from l. to l. 2.16
kills, but the Spirit gives l. 3.06
so that the l. of Jesus may also be 4.10
so that the l. of Jesus may be 4.11
is at work in us, but l. in you. 4.12
mortal may be swallowed up by l. 5.04
heard of my former l. in Judaism, Gal 1.13
and the l. I now live in the flesh 2.20
from the Spirit reap eternal l. 6.08
you to lead a l. worthy of the Eph 4.01
from the l. of God because of the 4.18
former manner of l. and is corrupt 4.22
my body, whether by l. or by death. Php 1.20
If it is to be l. in the flesh, that 1.22
your manner of l. be worthy of the 1.27
holding fast the word of l., 2.16
risking his l. to complete your 2.30
whose names are in the book of l. 4.03
to lead a l. worthy of the Lord, Col 1.10
have come to fulness of l. in him, 2.10
and your l. is hid with Christ in 3.03
When Christ who is our l. appears, 3.04
to lead a l. worthy of God, who 1Th 2.12
to believe in him for eternal l. 1Ti 1.16
may lead a quiet and peaceable l., 2.02
present l. and also for the l. to come. 4.08
of the eternal l. to which you 6.12
of God who gives l. to all things, 6.13
hold of the l. which is l. indeed. 6.19
promise of the l. which is in 2Ti 1.01
and brought l. and immortality to 1.10
my aim in l., my faith, my patience, 3.10
to live a godly l. in Christ Jesus 3.12
in hope of eternal l. which God, Tit 1.02
become heirs in hope of eternal l. 3.07
beginning of days nor end of l., Heb 7.03
the power of an indestructible l. 7.16
faith Joseph, at the end of his l., 11.22
might rise again to a better l. 11.35
Keep your l. free from love of 13.05
consider the outcome of their l., 13.07
the crown of l. which God has Jas 1.12
By his good l. let him show his 3.13
What is your l.? For you are a 4.14
are joint heirs of the grace of l., 1Pe 3.07
that would love l. and see good 3.10
that pertain to l. and godliness, 2Pe 1.03
hands, concerning the word of l.— 1Jn 1.01
the l. was made manifest, and we saw 1.02
you the eternal l. which was with 1.02
of the eyes and the pride of l., 2.16
he has promised us, eternal l. 2.25
have passed out of death into l., 3.14
has eternal l. abiding in him. 3.15
that he laid down his l. for us; 3.16
testimony, that God gave us eternal l., 5.11
and this l. is in his Son. 5.11
He who has the Son has l.; 5.12
he who has not the Son has not l. 5.12
may know that you have eternal l. 5.13
will give him l. for those whose 5.16
is the true God and eternal l. 5.20
testified to the truth of your l., 3Jn 1.03
Lord Jesus Christ unto eternal l. Jud 1.21
grant to eat of the tree of l., Rev 2.07
the last, who died and came to l. 2.08
I will give you the crown of l. 2.10
his name out of the book of l.; 3.05
a breath of l. from God entered 11.11
in the book of l. of the Lamb that 13.08
in the book of l. from the foundation 17.08
They came to l. again, and reigned 20.04
did not come to l. again until the 20.05
opened, which is the book of l. 20.12
found written in the book of l., 20.15
the fountain of the water of l. 21.06
written in the Lamb's book of l. 21.27
me the river of the water of l., 22.01
the tree of l. with its twelve 22.02
to the tree of l. and that they 22.14
take the water of l. without price. 22.17
in the tree of l. and in the holy 22.19

LIFEBLOOD

For your l. I will surely require a Gen 9.05
shall I drink the l. of these men? 1Ch 11.19
their l. is sprinkled upon my Is 63.03
I poured out their l. on the earth." 63.06
is found the l. of guiltless poor; Jer 2.34

LIVE-GIVING

the last Adam became a l. spirit. 1Co 15.45

LIFELESS

If even l. instruments, such as the 1Co 14.07

LIFELONG

death were subject to l. bondage. Heb 2.15

LIFETIME

priests in the l. of Aaron their Num 3.04
Now Absalom in his l. had taken and 2Sa 18.18
moment, and his favor is for a l. Ps 30.05
and my l. is as nothing in thy 39.05
you in your l. received your good Lk 16.25

LIFE'S

he does not enjoy l. good things, Ecc 6.03

LIFT

"L. up your eyes, and look from the Gen 13.14
Arise, l. up the lad, and hold him 21.18
And he said, 'L. up your eyes and 31.12
Pharaoh will l. up your head and 40.13
days Pharaoh will l. up your head— 40.19
no man shall l. up hand or foot in 41.44
L. up your rod, and stretch out your Ex 14.16
it, you shall help him to l. it up. 23.05
The Lord l. up his countenance upon Num 6.26
and l. up your eyes westward and Deu 3.27
And beware lest you l. up your eyes 4.19
shall help him to l. them up again. 22.04
you shall l. up no iron tool upon 27.05
For I l. up my hand to heaven, and 32.40
then could I l. up my face to your 2Sa 2.22
therefore l. up your prayer for 2Ki 19.04
and blush to l. my face to thee, my Ez 9.06
I cannot l. up my head, for I am Job 10.15
And if I l. myself up, thou dost 10.16
Surely then you will l. up your 11.15

LIFT (cont.)
and l. up your face to God. Job 22.26
"Can you l. up your voice to the 38.34
L. up the light of thy countenance Ps 4.06
l. thyself up against the fury of 7.06
O God, l. up thy hand; forget not 10.12
who does not l. up his soul to what 24.04
L. up your heads, O gates! and be 24.07
L. up your heads, O gates! and be 24.09
To thee, O LORD, I l. up my soul. 25.01
as I l. up my hands toward thy most 28.02
I will l. up my hands and call on 63.04
l. up a song to him who rides upon 68.04
the wicked, "Do not l. up your horn; 75.04
do not l. up your horn on high, or 75.05
thee, O Lord, do I l. up my soul. 86.04
the floods l. up their roaring. 93.03
therefore he will l. up his head. 110.07
I will l. up the cup of salvation 116.13
I l. up my eyes to the hills. 121.01
To thee I l. up my eyes, O thou who 123.01
L. up your hands to the holy place, 134.02
who l. themselves up against thee 139.20
Those who surround me l. up their head, 140.09
go, for to thee I l. up my soul. 143.08
eyes, how high their eyelids l.! Pro 30.13
fall, one will l. up his fellow; Ecc 4.10
and has not another to l. him up. 4.10
shall not l. up sword against Is 2.04
a staff should l. him who is not 10.15
the rod and l. up their staff 10.24
and he will l. it as he did in 10.26
They l. up their voices, they sing 24.14
the LORD, "now I will l. myself up; 33.10
therefore l. up your prayer for the 37.04
l. up your voice with strength, O 40.09
l. it up, fear not; say to the cities 40.09
L. up your eyes on high and see: who 40.26
He will not cry or l. up his voice, 42.02
and its cities l. up their voice, 42.11
They l. it upon their shoulders, 46.07
L. up your eyes round about and see 49.18
I will l. up my hand to the nations, 49.22
L. up your eyes to the heavens, and 51.06
your watchmen l. up their voice, 52.08
l. up your voice like a trumpet; 58.01
L. up your eyes round about, and see 60.04
l. up an ensign over the peoples. 62.10
L. up your eyes to the bare heights, Jer 3.02
or l. up cry or prayer for them, and 7.16
or l. up a cry or prayer on their 11.14
"L. up your eyes and see those who 13.20
I myself will l. up your skirts 13.26
and l. up your voice in Bashan; 22.20
I will surely l. you up and cast 23.39
and l. Jeremiah the prophet out of 38.10
L. your hands to him for the lives Lam 2.19
Let us l. up our hearts and hands 3.41
l. up your eyes now in the direction Eze 8.05
sight you shall l. the baggage 12.06
them shall l. his baggage upon his 12.12
be humble and not l. itself up, 17.14
mountains or l. up his eyes to the 18.06
mountains or l. up his eyes to the 18.15
to l. up the voice with shouting, to 21.22
you shall not l. up your eyes to 23.27
and l. up your eyes to your idols, 33.25
people shall l. themselves up in Dan 11.14
shall not l. up sword against Mic 4.03
and will l. up your skirts over Nah 3.05
"L. your eyes, and see what this is Zec 5.05
all who l. it shall grievously hurt 12.03
not lay hold of it and l. it out? Mt 12.11
would not even l. up his eyes to Lk 18.13
I tell you, l. up your eyes, and see Jn 4.35
Therefore l. your drooping hands Heb 12.12

LIFTED
And Lot l. up his eyes, and saw that Gen 13.10
He l. up his eyes and looked, and 18.02
the child l. up his voice and wept. 21.16
day Abraham l. up his eyes and saw 22.04
And Abraham l. up his eyes and 22.13
and he l. up his eyes and looked, 24.63
And Rebekah l. up her eyes, and when 24.64
And Esau l. up his voice and wept. 27.38
of the flock I l. up my eyes, 31.10
And Jacob l. up his eyes and looked, 33.01
Joseph up and l. him out of the 37.28
he heard that I l. up my voice and 39.15
but as soon as I l. up my voice and 39.18
and l. up the head of the chief 40.20
And he l. up his eyes, and saw his 43.29
he l. up the rod and struck the Ex 7.20
which l. the locusts and drove them 10.19
people of Israel l. up their eyes, 14.10
Then Aaron l. up his hands toward Lev 9.22
And Moses l. up his hand and struck Num 20.11
And Balaam l. up his eyes, and saw 24.02
then your heart be l. up, Deu 8.14
may not be l. up above his brethren, 17.20
feet were l. up on dry ground, the Jos 4.18
he l. up his eyes and looked, and 5.13
which no man has l. an iron tool"; 8.31
the people l. up their voices and Ju 2.04
and they l. up their heads no more. 8.28
And he l. up his eyes, and saw the 19.17
and they l. up their voices and 21.02
and they l. up their voices and Ru 1.09
Then they l. up their voices and 1.14
and when they l. up their eyes and 1Sa 6.13
And Saul l. up his voice and wept. 24.16
and the king l. up his voice and 2Sa 3.32
who kept the watch l. up his eyes, 13.34
and l. up their voice and wept; 13.36
and when he l. up his eyes and 18.24
has l. up his hand against King 20.21
also l. up his hand against the 1Ki 11.26
reason why he l. up his hand 11.27
And when he had l. him, and brought 2Ki 4.20
And he l. up his face to the window, 9.32
Edom, and your heart has l. you up. 14.10
voice and haughtily l. your eyes? 19.22
And David l. his eyes and saw the 1Ch 21.16
your heart has l. you up in 2Ch 25.19
those who mourn are l. to safety. Job 5.11
and be l. up, O ancient doors! Ps 24.07
and be l. up, O ancient doors! 24.09
head shall be l. up above my 27.06
bread, has l. his heel against me. 41.09
The floods have l. up, O LORD, the 93.03
the floods have l. up their voice, 93.03
which l. up the waves of the sea. 107.25
O LORD, my heart is not l. up, 131.01
against all that is l. up and high; Is 2.12
cedars of Lebanon, lofty and l. up; 2.13
upon a throne, high and l. up; 6.01
thy hand is l. up, but they see it 26.11
voice and haughtily l. your eyes? 37.23
Every valley shall be l. up, 40.04
he shall be exalted and l. up, 52.13
he l. them up and carried them all 63.09
she has l. up her voice against me; Jer 12.08
iniquity that your skirts are l. up, 13.22
with ropes and l. him out of the 38.13
and has been l. up even to the 51.09
l. up the head of Jehoiachin king 52.31
Then the Spirit l. me up, and as Eze 3.12
The Spirit l. me up and took me 3.14
and the Spirit l. me up between 8.03
So I l. up my eyes toward the 8.05
the cherubim l. up their wings to 10.16
And the cherubim l. up their wings 10.19
The Spirit l. me up, and brought me 11.01
Then the cherubim l. up their wings, 11.22

LIFTED (cont.)

And the Spirit l. me up and brought Eze 11.24
the Spirit l. me up, and brought me 43.05
l. my eyes to heaven, and my reason Dan 4.34
his heart was l. up and his spirit 5.20
but you have l. up yourself against 5.23
and it was l. up from the ground 7.04
I l. up my eyes and looked, and 10.05
filled, and their heart was l. up; Hos 13.06
Your hand shall be l. up over your Mic 5.09
its voice, it l. its hands on high. Hab 3.10
And I l. my eyes and saw, and behold, Zec 1.18
the nations who l. up their horns 1.21
And I l. my eyes and saw, and behold, 2.01
Again I l. my eyes and saw, and 5.01
And behold, the leaden cover was l., 5.07
Then I l. my eyes and saw, and 5.09
and they l. up the ephah between 5.09
And again I l. my eyes and saw, and 6.01
And when they l. up their eyes, they Mt 17.08
took her by the hand and l. her up, Mk 1.31
took him by the hand and l. him up, 9.27
And he l. up his eyes on his Lk 6.20
he l. up his eyes, and saw Abraham 16.23
and l. up their voices and said, 17.13
And as Moses l. up the serpent in Jn 3.14
so must the Son of man be l. up, 3.14
"When you have l. up the Son of man, 8.28
And Jesus l. up his eyes and said, 11.41
when I am l. up from the earth, will 12.32
that the Son of man must be l. up? 12.34
my bread has l. his heel against 13.18
he l. up his eyes to heaven and 17.01
he was l. up, and a cloud took him Ac 1.09
l. up his voice and addressed them, 2.14
they l. their voices together to 4.24
he gave her his hand and l. her up. 9.41
But Peter l. him up, saying, "Stand 10.26
they l. up their voices, saying in 14.11
then they l. up their voices and 22.22
on sea and land l. up his right Rev 10.05

LIFTER

me, my glory, and the l. of my head. Ps 3.03

LIFTEST

Thou l. me up on the wind, thou Job 30.22
O thou who l. me up from the gates Ps 9.13

LIFTING

"Amen, Amen," l. up their hands; Neh 8.06
from the wilderness comes l. up; Ps 75.06
putting down one and l. up another. 75.07
and the l. up of my hands as an 141.02
at the l. up of thyself nations are Is 33.03
and l. up his hands he blessed them. Lk 24.50
L. up his eyes, then, and seeing that Jn 6.05
l. holy hands without anger or 1Ti 2.08

LIFTS

up and as a lion it l. itself; Num 23.24
he l. the needy from the ash heap, 1Sa 2.08
The east wind l. him up and he is Job 27.21
and l. the needy from the ash heap, Ps 113.07
The LORD l. up those who are bowed 146.08
The LORD l. up the downtrodden, he 147.06
a rod should wield him who l. it, Is 10.15
l. up his eyes to the idols, commits Eze 18.12

LIGAMENTS

together through its joints and l., Col 2.19

LIGHT

"Let there be l."; and there was l. Gen 1.03
And God saw that the L. was good; 1.04
separated the l. from the darkness. 1.04
God called the l. Day, and the 1.05
heavens to give l. upon the earth. 1.15
the greater l. to rule the day, and 1.16
and the lesser l. to rule the night; 1.16
heavens to give l. upon the earth, 1.17
to separate the l. from the 1.18
As soon as the morning was l., 44.03
of Israel had l. where they dwelt. Ex 10.23
a pillar of fire to give them l., 13.21
so as to give l. upon the space in 25.37
pure beaten olive oil for the l., 27.20
oil for the l., spices for the 35.08
the lampstand also for the l., 35.14
its lamps, and the oil for the l.; 35.14
and spices and oil for the l., 35.28
utensils, and the oil for the l.; 39.37
that a l. may be kept burning Lev 24.02
and cover the lampstand for the l., Num 4.09
have charge of the oil for the l., 4.16
shall give l. in front of the 8.02
lamps to give l. in front of the 8.03
us wait till the l. of the morning; Ju 16.02
her master was, till it was l. 19.26
despoil them until the morning l.; 1Sa 14.36
at all until the morning l. 25.36
and depart as soon as you have l." 29.10
and we shall l. upon him as the dew 2Sa 17.12
he dawns on them like the morning l., 23.04
it had been a l. thing for him to 1Ki 16.31
This is a l. thing in the sight of 2Ki 3.18
and wait until the morning l., 7.09
in the night to l. for them the Neh 9.12
The Jews had l. and gladness and Est 8.16
not seek it, nor l. shine upon it. Job 3.04
let it hope for l., but have none, 3.09
as infants that never see the l.? 3.16
"Why is l. given to him that is in 3.20
Why is l. given to a man whose way 3.23
and chaos, where l. is as darkness." 10.22
and brings deep darkness to l. 12.22
They grope in the dark without l.; 12.25
'The l.,' they say, 'is near to the 17.12
"Yea, the l. of the wicked is put 18.05
The l. is dark in his tent, and his 18.06
He is thrust from l. into darkness, 18.18
your l. is darkened, so that you 22.11
and l. will shine on your ways. 22.28
are those who rebel against the l., 24.13
themselves up; they do not know the l. 24.16
Upon whom does his l. not arise? 25.03
boundary between l. and darkness. 26.10
that is hid he brings forth to l. 28.11
and by his l. I walked through 29.03
and the l. of my countenance they 29.24
I waited for l., darkness came. 30.26
Pit, and my life shall see the l." 33.28
that he may see the l. of life. 33.30
look on the l. when it is bright 37.21
From the wicked their l. is withheld, 38.15
"Where is the way to the dwelling of l., 38.19
place where the l. is distributed, 38.24
His sneezings flash forth l., 41.18
Lift up the l. of thy countenance Ps 4.06
Yea, thou dost l. my lamp; the LORD 18.28
The LORD is my l. and my salvation; 27.01
of life; in thy l. do we see l. 36.09
forth your vindication as the l., 37.06
and the l. of my eyes—it also has 38.10
Oh send out thy l. and thy truth; 43.03
and the l. of thy countenance; 44.03
who will never more see the l. 49.19
walk before God in the l. of life. 56.13
and all the night with a fiery l. 78.14
in the l. of thy countenance, 89.15
sins in the l. of thy countenance. 90.08
L. dawns for the righteous, and joy 97.11
thyself with l. as with a garment, 104.02
and fire to give l. by night. 105.39
L. rises in the darkness for the 112.04
is God, and he has given us l. 118.27

LIGHT (cont.)
to my feet and a l. to my path. Ps 119.105
The unfolding of thy words gives l.; 119.130
and the l. about me be night," 139.11
for darkness is as l. with thee. 139.12
righteous is like the l. of dawn, Pro 4.18
is a lamp and the teaching a l., 6.23
The l. of the righteous rejoices, 13.09
The l. of the eyes rejoices the 15.30
In the l. of a king's face there is 16.15
When your eyes l. upon it, it is 23.05
the LORD gives l. to the eyes of 29.13
excels folly as l. excels darkness. Ecc 2.13
L. is sweet, and it is pleasant for 11.07
before the sun and the l., 12.02
let us walk in the l. of the LORD. Is 2.05
darkness for l. and l. for darkness, 5.20
and the l. is darkened by its 5.30
in darkness have seen a great l.; 9.02
darkness, on them has l. shined. 9.02
Jacob, and it will l. upon Israel; 9.08
The l. of Israel will become a fire, 10.17
constellations will not give their l.; 13.10
and the moon will not shed its l. 13.10
For thy dew is a dew of l., 26.19
Moreover the l. of the moon will be 30.26
moon will be as the l. of the sun, 30.26
and the l. of the sun will be 30.26
as the l. of seven days, in the day 30.26
to the people, a l. to the nations, 42.06
the darkness before them into l., 42.16
I form l. and create darkness, I 45.07
"It is too l. a thing that you 49.06
give you as a l. to the nations, 49.06
walks in darkness and has no l., 50.10
Walk by the l. of your fire, and by 50.11
my justice for a l. to the peoples. 51.04
Then shall your l. break forth like 58.08
then shall your l. rise in the 58.10
we look for l., and behold, darkness, 59.09
for your l. has come, and the glory 60.01
And nations shall come to your l., 60.03
shall be no more your l. by day, 60.19
the moon give l. to you by night; 60.19
LORD will be your everlasting l., 60.19
LORD will be your everlasting l., 60.20
Because harlotry was so l. to her, Jer 3.09
to the heavens, and they had no l. 4.23
you look for l. he turns it into 13.16
millstones and the l. of the lamp. 25.10
the sun for l. by day and the 31.35
moon and stars for l. by night, 31.35
me into darkness without any l.; Lam 3.02
and the moon shall not give its l. Eze 32.07
and the l. dwells with him. Dan 2.22
of your father l. and understanding 5.11
and that l. and understanding and 5.14
my judgment goes forth as the l. Hos 6.05
It is darkness, and not l.; Amo 5.18
and not l., and gloom with no 5.20
the LORD will be a l. to me. Mic 7.08
He will bring me forth to the l.; 7.09
His brightness was like the l., Hab 3.04
habitation at the l. of thine 3.11
at evening time there shall be l. Zec 14.07
in darkness have seen a great l., Mt 4.16
and shadow of death l. has dawned." 4.16
"You are the l. of the world. 5.14
Nor do men l. a lamp and put it 5.15
and it gives l. to all in the house. 5.15
Let your l. so shine before men, 5.16
your whole body will be full of l.; 6.22
If then the l. in you is darkness, 6.23
you in the dark, utter in the l.; 10.27
yoke is easy, and my burden is l." 11.30
his garments became white as l. 17.02
But they made l. of it and went off, 22.05
and the moon will not give its l., 24.29
secret, except to come to l. Mk 4.22
and the moon will not give its l., 13.24
to give l. to those who sit in Lk 1.79
a l. for revelation to the Gentiles, 2.32
those who enter may see the l. 8.16
shall not be known and come to l. 8.17
those who enter may see the l. 11.33
your whole body is full of l.; 11.34
lest the l. in you be darkness. 11.35
then your whole body is full of l., 11.36
a lamp with its rays gives you l." 11.36
the dark shall be heard in the l., 12.03
beating, shall receive a l. beating. 12.48
does not l. a lamp and sweep the 15.08
own generation than the sons of l. 16.08
he sat in the l. and gazing at him, 22.56
while the sun's l. failed; and the 23.45
and the life was the l. of men. Jn 1.04
The l. shines in the darkness, and 1.05
testimony, to bear witness to the l., 1.07
He was not the l., but came to bear 1.08
but came to bear witness to the l. 1.08
The true l. that enlightens every 1.09
that the l. has come into the world, 3.19
men loved darkness rather than l., 3.19
one who does evil hates the l., 3.20
and does not come to the l., 3.20
does what is true comes to the l., 3.21
to rejoice for a while in his l. 5.35
saying, "I am the l. of the world; 8.12
but will have the l. of life." 8.12
world, I am the l. of the world." 9.05
he sees the l. of this world. 11.09
because the l. is not in him." 11.10
"The l. is with you for a little 12.35
Walk while you have the l., 12.35
While you have the l., believe in the l., 12.36
that you may become sons of l." 12.36
I have come as l. into the world, 12.46
and suddenly a l. from heaven Ac 9.03
and a l. shone in the cell; 12.07
set you to be a l. for the Gentiles, 13.47
noon a great l. from heaven 22.06
with me saw the l. but did not 22.09
of the brightness of that l., 22.11
I saw on the way a l. from heaven, 26.13
darkness to l. and from the power 26.18
would proclaim l. both to the 26.23
a l. to those who are in darkness, Rom 2.19
darkness and put on the armor of l.; 13.12
will bring to l. the things now 1Co 4.05
from seeing the l. of the gospel 2Co 4.04
"Let l. shine out of darkness," who 4.06
to give the l. of the knowledge of 4.06
what fellowship has l. with darkness? 6.14
disguises himself as an angel of l. 11.14
but now you are l. in the Lord; Eph 5.08
in the LORD; walk as children of l. 5.08
(for the fruit of l. is found in 5.09
exposed by the l. it becomes visible, 5.13
anything that becomes visible is l. 5.13
dead, and Christ shall give you l." 5.14
inheritance of the saints in l. Col 1.12
are all sons of l. and sons of the 1Th 5.05
and dwells in unapproachable l., 1Ti 6.16
immortality to l. through the 2Ti 1.10
of darkness into his marvelous l. 1Pe 2.09
that God is l. and in him is no 1Jn 1.05
if we walk in the l., as he is in the l., 1.07
and the true l. is already shining 2.08
he is in the l. and hates his 2.09
loves his brother abides in the l., 2.10
a third of their l. was darkened; Rev 8.12
and the l. of a lamp shall shine in 18.23
it, for the glory of God is its l., 21.23
By its l. shall the nations walk; 21.24
they need no l. of lamp or sun, for 22.05
for the Lord God will be their l., 22.05

LIGHTED
by night which l. for them the way Neh 9.19
thy lightnings l. up the world; Ps 77.18

LIGHTEN
perhaps he will l. his hand from 1Sa 6.05
Now therefore l. the hard service 1Ki 12.04
'L. the yoke that your father put 12.09
heavy, but do you l. it for us'; 12.10
Now therefore l. the hard service 2Ch 10.04
'L. the yoke that your father put 10.09
heavy, but do you l. it for us'; 10.10
l. my eyes, lest I sleep the sleep Ps 13.03
His lightnings l. the world; 97.04
into the sea, to l. it for them. Jon 1.05

LIGHTENED
they l. the ship, throwing out the Ac 27.38

LIGHTENS
O LORD, and my God l. my darkness. 2Sa 22.29
the LORD my God l. my darkness. Ps 18.28

LIGHTER
they are together l. than a breath. Ps 62.09

LIGHTING
"No one after l. a lamp covers it Lk 8.16
"No one after l. a lamp puts it in 11.33

LIGHTLY
despise me shall be l. esteemed. 1Sa 2.30
How l. you gad about, changing your Jer 2.36
healed the wound of my people l., 6.14
healed the wound of my people l., 8.11
do not regard l. the discipline of Heb 12.05

LIGHTNING
scattered them; l., and routed them. 2Sa 22.15
a way for the l. of the thunder; Job 28.26
Behold, he scatters his l. about him, 36.30
He covers his hands with the l., 36.32
and his l. to the corners of the 37.03
moisture; the clouds scatter his l. 37.11
and causes the l. of his cloud to 37.15
and l. that flashed through their Ps 105.32
Flash forth the l. and scatter them, 144.06
and out of the fire went forth l. Eze 1.13
to and fro, like a flash of l. 1.14
slaughter, polished to flash like l.! 21.10
it is made like l., it is polished 21.15
to glitter and to flash like l.— 21.28
his face like the appearance of l., Dan 10.06
like torches, they dart like l. Nah 2.04
and his arrow go forth like l.; Zec 9.14
For as the l. comes from the east Mt 24.27
His appearance was like l., 28.03
saw Satan fall like l. from heaven. Lk 10.18
For as the l. flashes and lights up 17.24
From the throne issue flashes of l., Rev 4.05
flashes of l., and an earthquake. 8.05
and there were flashes of l., loud noises, 11.19
And there were flashes of l., loud noises, 16.18

LIGHTNINGS
day there were thunders and l., Ex 19.16
thunderings and the l. and the 20.18
restrain the l. when his voice is Job 37.04
Can you send forth l., that they may 38.35
he flashed forth l., and routed them. Ps 18.14
thy l. lighted up the world; the earth 77.18
His l. lighten the world; the earth sees 97.04
who makes l. for the rain and brings 135.07
He makes l. for the rain, and he Jer 10.13
He makes l. for the rain, and he 51.16

LIGHTS
"Let there be l. in the firmament Gen 1.14
and let them be l. in the firmament 1.15
And God made the two great l., 1.16
to him who made the great l., Ps 136.07
All the bright l. of heaven will I Eze 32.08
flashes and l. up the sky from one Lk 17.24
And he called for l. and rushed in, Ac 16.29
There were many l. in the upper 20.08
whom you shine as l. in the world, Php 2.15
the Father of l. with whom there Jas 1.17

LIKEN
To whom then will you l. God, Is 40.18
"To whom will you l. me and make me 46.05
What can I l. to you, that I may Lam 2.13
Behold, I will l. you to a cedar in Eze 31.03

LIKENESS
man in our image, after our l.; Gen 1.26
man, he made him in the l. of God. 5.01
the father of a son in his own l., 5.03
or any l. of anything that is in Ex 20.04
figure, the l. of male or female, Deu 4.16
the l. of any beast that is on the 4.17
the l. of any winged bird that 4.17
the l. of anything that creeps on 4.18
the l. of any fish that is in the 4.18
or any l. of anything that is in 5.08
or what l. compare with him? Is 40.18
of it came the l. of four living Eze 1.05
As for the l. of their faces, each 1.10
and the four had the same l., 1.16
there was the l. of a firmament, 1.22
heads there was the l. of a throne, 1.26
above the l. of a throne was a 1.26
a throne was a l. as it were of a 1.26
appearance of the l. of the glory 1.28
appearance, the four had the same l., 10.10
And as for the l. of their faces, 10.22
one in the l. of the sons of men Dan 10.16
"Whose l. and inscription is this?" Mt 22.20
"Whose l. and inscription is this?" Mk 12.16
Whose l. and inscription has it?" Lk 20.24
come down to us in the l. of men!" Ac 14.11
own Son in the l. of sinful flesh Rom 8.03
into his l. from one degree of 2Co 3.18
of Christ, who is the l. of God. 4.04
after the l. of God in true Eph 4.24
being born in the l. of men. Php 2.07
arises in the l. of Melchizedek, Heb 7.15
men, who are made in the l. of God. Jas 3.09

LIKENESSES
room and the nave were carved l. Eze 41.17

LIKES
who l. to put himself first, does 3Jn 1.09

LIKEWISE
He l. instructed the second and the Gen 32.19
and l. everything that he had. 32.23
Leah l. and her children drew near 33.07
You shall do l. with your oxen and Ex 22.30
You shall do l. with your vineyard, 23.11
and l. you shall make loops on the 26.04
And l. for its length on the north 27.11
l. he made them on the edge of the 36.11
their gods?—that I also may do l.' Deu 12.30
to your bondwoman you shall do l. 15.17
and I l. will go with you into the Ju 1.03
l. every one that kneels down to 7.05
to them, "Look at me, and do l.; 7.17
L., when all the men of Israel who 1Sa 14.22
they l. fled before Abishai, and 2Sa 10.14
L. he made pomegranates; in two rows 1Ki 7.18
"L. when a foreigner, who is not of 8.41
their children l., and their children's 2Ki 17.41
l. all the rest of Israel were of 1Ch 12.38
they l. fled before Abishai, Joab's 19.15
the LORD, and l. at evening, 23.30

LIKEWISE (cont.)
l. through them these were 2Ch 1.17
"L. when a foreigner, who is not of 6.32
He l. provided cities for himself, 32.29
and the people l. were exceedingly 36.14
fowls l. were prepared for me, and Neh 5.18
We have l. cast lots, the priests, 10.34
L., when all the Jews who were in Jer 40.11
and fears, and does not do l., Eze 18.14
and l. the vestibule had windows 40.16
no children; and the third l.; Mk 12.21
and he who has food, let him do l." Lk 3.11
So l. a Levite, when he came to the 10.32
Jesus said to him, "Go and do l." 10.37
you repent you will all l. perish. 13.03
you repent you will all l. perish." 13.05
L. as it was in the days of Lot— 17.28
and l. let him who is in the field 17.31
and l. all seven left no children 20.31
l. the cup after supper, saying * 22.20
has a purse take it, and l. a bag. 22.36
he does, that the Son does l. Jn 5.19
and the men l. gave up natural Rom 1.27
and l. the father of the circumcised 4.12
L., my brethren, you have died to 7.04
L. the Spirit helps us in our 8.26
and l. the wife to her husband. 1Co 7.03
l. the husband does not rule over 7.04
L. he who was free when called is a 7.22
L. you also should be glad and Php 2.18
Deacons l. must be serious, not 1Ti 3.08
The women l. must be serious, no 3.11
Bid the older women l. to be Tit 2.03
L. urge the younger men to control 2.06
he himself l. partook of the same Heb 2.14
L. you wives, be submissive to your 1Pe 3.01
L. you husbands, live considerately 3.07
L. you that are younger be subject 5.05
who is l. chosen, sends you greetings; 5.13
which l. acted immorally and Jud 1.07
shining, and l. a third of the night. Rev 8.12

LIKHI
were Ahian, Shechem, L., and Aniam. 1Ch 7.19

LIKINGS
themselves teachers to suit their own l., 2Ti 4.03

LILIES
he pastures his flock among the l. Sol 2.16
a gazelle, that feed among the l. 4.05
His lips are l., distilling liquid myrrh. 5.13
in the gardens, and to gather l. 6.02
he pastures his flock among the l. 6.03
a heap of wheat, encircled with l. 7.02
Consider the l. of the field, how Mt 6.28
Consider the l., how they grow; Lk 12.27

LILY
of a cup, like the flower of a l.; 1Ki 7.26
of a cup, like the flower of a l.; 2Ch 4.05
of Sharon, a l. of the valleys. Sol 2.01
As a l. among brambles, so is my 2.02
he shall blossom as the l., he shall Hos 14.05

LILY-WORK
vestibule were of l., four cubits. 1Ki 7.19
the tops of the pillars was l. 7.22

LIMB
a mutilated face or a l. too long, Lev 21.18
l. by l., into twelve pieces, and sent Ju 19.29
you shall be torn l. from l., and your Dan 2.05
Abednego shall be torn l. from l., and 3.29

LIMBS
first-born of death consumes his l. Job 18.13
of bronze, his l. like bars of iron. 40.18
not keep silence concerning his l., 41.12
his l. gave way, and his knees Dan 5.06

LIME
peoples will be as if burned to l., Is 33.12
he burned to l. the bones of the Amo 2.01

LIMIT
find out the l. of the Almighty? Job 11.07
And do you l. wisdom to yourself? 15.08
I have seen a l. to all perfection, Ps 119.96
when he assigned to the sea its l., Pro 8.29
Egypt too, and that without l.; Nah 3.09
But we will not boast beyond l., 2Co 10.13
We do not boast beyond l., in other 10.15

LIMITATIONS
terms, because of your natural l. Rom 6.19

LIMITS
pasture lands of Sharon to their l. 1Ch 5.16
keep to the l. God has apportioned 2Co 10.13

LIMPED
And they l. about the altar which 1Ki 18.26

LIMPING
Penuel, l. because of his thigh. Gen 32.31
will you go l. with two different 1Ki 18.21

LINE
None of the l. of Aaron who is a Lev 22.04
mark out your l. to Mount Hor; Num 34.07
up the battle l. against them at Ju 20.20
the battle l. in the same place 20.22
drew up in l. against Israel, 1Sa 4.02
of Benjamin ran from the battle l., 4.12
and drew up in l. of battle 17.02
was going forth to the battle l., 17.20
the battle l. to meet the Philistine. 17.48
Moab, and measured them with a l., 2Sa 8.02
and one full l. to be spared. 8.02
and a l. of twelve cubits measured 1Ki 7.15
and a l. of thirty cubits measured 7.23
the measuring l. of Samaria, 2Ki 21.13
and a l. of thirty cubits measured 2Ch 4.02
drew up his l. of battle against 13.03
Or who stretched the l. upon it? Job 38.05
establish his l. for ever and his Ps 89.29
His l. shall endure for ever, his 89.36
l. upon l., l. upon l., here a little, Is 28.10
l. upon l., l. upon l., here a little, 28.13
and I will make justice the l., 28.17
stretch the l. of confusion over 34.11
portioned it out to them with the l.; 34.17
The carpenter stretches a l., 44.13
And the measuring l. shall go out Jer 31.39
he marked it off by the l.; Lam 2.08
with a l. of flax and a measuring Eze 40.03
Going on eastward with a l. in his hand, 47.03
a wall built with a plumb l., Amo 7.07
with a plumb l. in his hand. 7.07
And I said, "A plumb l." Then the 7.08
setting a plumb l. in the midst of 7.08
land shall be parceled out by l.; 7.17
to cast the l. by lot in the Mic 2.05
the measuring l. shall be stretched Zec 1.16
with a measuring l. in his hand! 2.01

LINEAGE
was of the house and l. of David, Lk 2.04

LINED
He l. the walls of the house on the 1Ki 6.15
The nave he l. with cypress, and 2Ch 3.05
So he l. the house with gold—its 3.07

LINEN

arrayed him in garments of fine l., Gen 41.42
and fine twined l., goats' hair, Ex 25.04
of fine twined l. and blue and 26.01
scarlet stuff and fine twined l.; 26.31
scarlet stuff and fine twined l., 26.36
of fine twined l. a hundred cubits 27.09
scarlet stuff and fine twined l., 27.16
of fine twined l. and bases of 27.18
scarlet stuff, and fine twined l. 28.05
stuff, and of fine twined l., 28.06
scarlet stuff, and fine twined l. 28.08
and fine twined l. shall you make 28.15
coat in checker work of fine l., 28.39
you shall make a turban of fine l., 28.39
make for them l. breeches to cover 28.42
scarlet stuff and fine twined l.; 35.06
stuff or fine l. or goats' hair or 35.23
scarlet stuff and fine twined l.; 35.25
scarlet stuff and fine twined l., 35.35
of fine twined l. and blue and 36.08
scarlet stuff and fine twined l.; 36.35
scarlet stuff and fine twined l., 36.37
the court were of fine twined l., 38.09
the court were of fine twined l. 38.16
scarlet stuff and fine twined l.; 38.18
scarlet stuff and fine twined l. 38.23
scarlet stuff, and fine twined l. 39.02
stuff, and into the fine twined l., 39.03
scarlet stuff, and fine twined l.; 39.05
scarlet stuff, and fine twined l. 39.08
scarlet stuff and fine twined l. 39.24
woven of fine l., for Aaron and his 39.27
turban of fine l., and the caps of fine l., 39.28
and the l. breeches of fine twined l., 39.28
of fine twined l. and of blue and 39.29
priest shall put on his l. garment, Lev 6.10
and put his l. breeches upon his 6.10
whether a woolen or a l. garment, 13.47
in warp or woof of l. or wool, 13.48
woolen or l., or anything or skin. 13.52
disease in a garment of wool or l., 13.59
He shall put on the holy l. coat, 16.04
shall have the l. breeches on his 16.04
body, be girded with the l. girdle, 16.04
girdle, and wear the l. turban; 16.04
put off the l. garments which he 16.23
wearing the holy l. garments; 16.32
stuff, wool and l. together. Deu 22.11
give you thirty l. garments and Ju 14.12
give me thirty l. garments and 14.13
LORD, a boy girded with a l. ephod. 1Sa 2.18
persons who wore the l. ephod. 22.18
David was girded with a l. ephod. 2Sa 6.14
of the house of l. workers at 1Ch 4.21
was clothed with a robe of fine l., 15.27
and David wore a l. ephod. 15.27
and crimson fabrics and fine l., 2Ch 2.14
and crimson fabrics and fine l., 3.14
and kinsmen, arrayed in fine l., 5.12
cords of fine l. and purple to Est 1.06
and a mantle of fine l. and purple, 8.15
colored spreads of Egyptian l.; Pro 7.16
her clothing is fine l. and purple. 31.22
She makes l. garments and sells 31.24
the l. garments, the turbans, and the Is 3.23
"Go and buy a l. waistcloth, and put Jer 13.01
with them was a man clothed in l., Eze 9.02
he called to the man clothed in l., 9.03
And lo, the man clothed in l., 9.11
And he said to the man clothed in l., 10.02
he commanded the man clothed in l., 10.06
the hands of the man clothed in l., 10.07
you in fine l. and covered you 16.10
and your raiment was of fine l., 16.13
embroidered l. from Egypt was your 27.07
work, fine l., coral, and agate. 27.16
court, they shall wear l. garments; 44.17
They shall have l. turbans upon 44.18
and l. breeches upon their loins; 44.18
and behold, a man clothed in l., Dan 10.05
And I said to the man clothed in l., 12.06
The man clothed in l., who was above 12.07
wrapped it in a clean l. shroud, Mt 27.59
nothing but a l. cloth about his Mk 14.51
but he left the l. cloth and ran 14.52
And he bought a l. shroud, and 15.46
down, wrapped him in the l. shroud, 15.46
purple and fine l. and who feasted Lk 16.19
down and wrapped it in a l. shroud, 23.53
he saw the l. cloths by themselves; * 24.12
and bound it in l. cloths with the Jn 19.40
he saw the l. cloths lying there, 20.05
tomb; he saw the l. cloths lying, 20.06
lying with the l. cloths but rolled 20.07
plagues, robed in pure bright l., Rev 15.06
fine l., purple, silk and scarlet, 18.12
city that was clothed in fine l., 18.16
her to be clothed with fine l., 19.08
for the fine l. is the righteous 19.08
of heaven, arrayed in fine l., 19.14

LINES

two l. he measured to be put to 2Sa 8.02
drew up their l. of battle in the 2Ch 14.10
The l. have fallen for me in Ps 16.06

LINGERED

But he l.; so the men seized him and Gen 19.16

LINGERS

has seized me, and yet my life still l.' 2Sa 1.09

LINTEL

doorposts and the l. of the houses Ex 12.07
and touch the l. and the two 12.22
blood on the l. and on the two 12.23
the l. and the doorposts formed a 1Ki 6.31

LINUS

do Pudens and L. and Claudia and 2Ti 4.21

LION

stooped down, he couched as a l., Gen 49.09
up and as a l. it lifts itself; Num 23.24
He couched, he lay down like a l., 24.09
Gad couches like a l., he tears the Deu 33.20
a young l. roared against him; Ju 14.05
and he tore the l. asunder as one 14.06
aside to see the carcass of the l., 14.08
in the body of the l., and honey. 14.08
honey from the carcass of the l. 14.09
What is stronger than a l.?" 14.18
and when there came a l., or a bear, 1Sa 17.34
the paw of the l. and from the paw 17.37
heart is like the heart of a l., 2Sa 17.10
down and slew a l. in a pit on a 23.20
he went away a l. met him on the 1Ki 13.24
the l. also stood beside the body. 13.24
and the l. standing by the body. 13.25
the LORD has given him to the l., 13.26
the ass and the l. standing beside 13.28
The l. had not eaten the body or 13.28
gone from me, a l. shall kill you. 20.36
a l. met him and killed him. 20.36
down and slew a l. in a pit on a 1Ch 11.22
roar of the l., the voice of the fierce l., Job 4.10
The strong l. perishes for lack of 4.11
up, thou dost hunt me like a l., 10.16
the l. has not passed over it. 28.08
"Can you hunt the prey for the l., 38.39
lest like a l. they rend me, dragging Ps 7.02
in secret like a l. in his covert; 10.09
They are like a l. eager to tear, 17.12
as a young l. lurking in ambush. 17.12

LION (cont.)
me, like a ravening and roaring l. Ps 22.13
Save me from the mouth of the l., 22.21
will tread on the l. and the adder, 91.13
the young l. and the serpent you 91.13
wrath is like the growling of a l., Pro 19.12
king is like the growling of a l.; 20.02
says, "There is a l. outside! I shall 22.13
says, "There is a l. in the road! 26.13
There is a l. in the streets!" 26.13
but the righteous are bold as a l. 28.01
Like a roaring l. or a charging 28.15
the l., which is mightiest among 30.30
dog is better than a dead l. Ecc 9.04
Their roaring is like a l., Is 5.29
calf and the l. and the fatling 11.06
and the l. shall eat straw like the 11.07
a l. for those of Moab who escape, 15.09
where come the lioness and the l., 30.06
As a l. or a young l. growls over his 31.04
No l. shall be there, nor shall any 35.09
like a l. he breaks all my bones; 38.13
the l. shall eat straw like the ox; 65.25
your prophets like a ravening l. Jer 2.30
A l. has gone up from his thicket, a 4.07
Therefore a l. from the forest 5.06
to me like a l. in the forest, 12.08
Like a l. he has left his covert, 25.38
Behold, like a l. coming up from the 49.19
like a l. coming up from the jungle 50.44
lying in wait, like a l. in hiding; Lam 3.10
the face of a l. on the right side, Eze 1.10
and the third the face of a l., 10.14
he became a young l., and he learned 19.03
her whelps and made him a young l. 19.05
he became a young l., and he learned 19.06
like a roaring l. tearing the prey; 22.25
Yourself a l. among the nations, 32.02
face of a young l. toward the palm 41.19
was like a l. and had eagles' Dan 7.04
For I will be like a l. to Ephraim, Hos 5.14
like a young l. to the house of 5.14
the LORD, he will roar like a l.; 11.10
So I will be to them like a l., 13.07
there I will devour them like a l., 13.08
Does a l. roar in the forest, when Amo 3.04
Does a young l. cry out from his 3.04
The l. has roared; who will not 3.08
from the mouth of the l. two legs, 3.12
as if a man fled from a l., 5.19
like a l. among the beasts of the Mic 5.08
like a young l. among the flocks of 5.08
where the l. brought his prey, where Nah 2.11
The l. tore enough for his whelps 2.12
prowls around like a roaring l., 1Pe 5.08
the first living creature like a l., Rev 4.07
lo, the L. of the tribe of Judah, the 5.05
a loud voice, like a l. roaring; 10.03

LION'S
Judah is a l. whelp; from the prey Gen 49.09
"Dan is a l. whelp, that leaps forth Deu 33.22
So I was rescued from the l. mouth. 2Ti 4.17
and its mouth was like a l. mouth. Rev 13.02

LIONESS
he couched as a lion, and as a l.; Gen 49.09
As a l. it rises up and as a lion Num 23.24
down like a lion, and like a l.; 24.09
the whelps of the l. are scattered. Job 4.11
where come the l. and the lion, Is 30.06
What a l. was your mother among Eze 19.02
and it has the fangs of a l. Joe 1.06

LIONESSES
and strangled prey for his l.; Nah 2.12

LIONS
has killed both l. and bears; 1Sa 17.36
eagles, they were stronger than l. 2Sa 1.23
were set in the frames were l., 1Ki 7.29
above and below the l. and oxen, 7.29
l., and palm trees, according to the 7.36
rests and two l. standing beside 10.19
while twelve l. stood there, one on 10.20
the LORD sent l. among them, 2Ki 17.25
therefore he has sent l. among them, 17.26
faces were like the faces of l., 1Ch 12.08
rests and two l. standing beside 2Ch 9.18
while twelve l. stood there, one on 9.19
teeth of the young l., are broken. Job 4.10
the appetite of the young l., 38.39
The young l. suffer want and hunger; Ps 34.10
their ravages, my life from the l.! 35.17
in the midst of l. that greedily 57.04
the fangs of the young l., O LORD! 58.06
The young l. roar for their prey, 104.21
and Hermon, from the dens of l., Sol 4.08
a lion, like young l. they roar; Is 5.29
The l. have roared against him, they Jer 2.15
a hunted sheep driven away by l. 50.17
"They shall roar together like l.; 51.38
a lioness was your mother among l.! Eze 19.02
couched in the midst of young l., 19.02
he prowled among the l.; he became 19.06
shall be cast into the den of l. Dan 6.07
shall be cast into the den of l.?" 6.12
brought and cast into the den of l. 6.16
and went in haste to the den of l. 6.19
able to deliver you from the l.?" 6.20
and cast into the den of l.— 6.24
of the den the l. overpowered them 6.24
Daniel from the power of the l." 6.27
den, the cave of the young l., Nah 2.11
sword shall devour your young l.; 2.13
officials within her are roaring l.; Zep 3.03
Hark, the roar of the l., for the Zec 11.03
promises, stopped the mouths of l., Heb 11.33

LIONS'
they shall growl like l. whelps. Jer 51.38
his angel and shut the l. mouths, Dan 6.22
its teeth are l. teeth, and it has Joe 1.06
Where is the l. den, the cave of the Nah 2.11
and their teeth like l. teeth; Rev 9.08
of the horses were like l. heads, 9.17

LIP
shall cover his upper l. and cry, Lev 13.45

LIPS
who am a man of uncircumcised l.?" Ex 6.12
"Behold, I am of uncircumcised l.; 6.30
utters with his l. a rash oath to Lev 5.04
utterance of her l. by which she Num 30.06
thoughtless utterance of her l., 30.08
out of her l. concerning her vows, 30.12
to perform what has passed your l., Deu 23.23
only her l. moved, and her voice was 1Sa 1.13
this Job did not sin with his l. Job 2.10
laughter, and your l. with shouting. 8.21
speak, and open his l. to you, 11.05
listen to the pleadings of my l. 13.06
your own l. testify against you. 15.06
solace of my l. would assuage your 16.05
from the commandment of his l.; 23.12
my l. will not speak falsehood, and 27.04
I must open my l. and answer. 32.20
and what my l. know they speak 33.03
with flattering l. and a double Ps 12.02
the LORD cut off all flattering l., 12.03
will prevail, our l. are with us; 12.04
out or take their names upon my l. 16.04
my prayer from l. free of deceit! 17.01
the word of thy l. I have avoided 17.04

LIPS (cont.)

not withheld the request of his l. Ps 21.02
Let the lying l. be dumb, which 31.18
and your l. from speaking deceit. 34.13
lo, I have not restrained my l., 40.09
grace is poured upon your l.; 45.02
or take my covenant on your l.? 50.16
open thou my l., and my mouth shall 51.15
and snarling with their l.— 59.07
mouths, the words of their l., 59.12
than life, my l. will praise thee. 63.03
mouth praises thee with joyful l., 63.05
that which my l. uttered and my 66.14
My l. will shout for joy, when I 71.23
word that went forth from my l. 89.34
With my l. I declare all the 119.13
My l. will pour forth praise that 119.171
from lying l., from a deceitful 120.02
and under their l. is the poison 140.03
mischief of their l. overwhelm them! 140.09
keep watch over the door of my l.! 141.03
and your l. may guard knowledge. Pro 5.02
For the l. of a loose woman drip 5.03
snared in the utterance of your l., 6.02
and from my l. will come what is 8.06
wickedness is an abomination to my l. 8.07
On the l. of him who has understanding 10.13
He who conceals hatred has lying l., 10.18
he who restrains his l. is prudent. 10.19
The l. of the righteous feed many, 10.21
The l. of the righteous know what 10.32
by the transgression of his l., 12.13
Truthful l. endure for ever, but a 12.19
Lying l. are an abomination to the 12.22
opens wide his l. comes to ruin. 13.03
but the l. of the wise will preserve 14.03
The l. of the wise spread knowledge; 15.07
Inspired decisions are on the l. of a king; 16.10
Righteous l. are the delight of a 16.13
and adds persuasiveness to his l. 16.23
compresses his l. brings evil to 16.30
An evildoer listens to wicked l.; 17.04
when he closes his l., he is deemed 17.28
a fool's l. bring strife, and his 18.06
and his l. are a snare to himself. 18.07
satisfied by the yield of his l. 18.20
but the l. of knowledge are a 20.15
all of them are ready on your l. 22.18
when your l. speak what is right. 23.16
and their l. talk of mischief. 24.02
gives a right answer kisses the l. 24.26
and do not deceive with your l. 24.28
are smooth l. with an evil heart. 26.23
with his l. and harbors deceit in 26.24
a stranger, and not your own l. 27.02
but the l. of a fool consume him. Ecc 10.12
Your l. are like a scarlet thread, Sol 4.03
Your l. distil nectar, my bride; 4.11
His l. are lilies, distilling liquid myrrh. 5.13
smoothly, gliding over l. and teeth. 7.09
for I am a man of unclean l., Is 6.05
midst of a people of unclean l.; 6.05
"Behold, this has touched your l.; 6.07
breath of his l. he shall slay the 11.04
men of strange l. and with an 28.11
mouth and honor me with their l., 29.13
his l. are full of indignation, and 30.27
his mourners the fruit of the l. 57.18
your l. have spoken lies, your 59.03
it is cut off from their l. Jer 7.28
came out of my l. was before thy 17.16
The l. and thoughts of my assailants Lam 3.62
do not cover your l., nor eat the Eze 24.17
you shall not cover your l., nor 24.22
and I will open your l. among them. 29.21
for with their l. they show much 33.31
of the sons of men touched my l.; Dan 10.16
Set the trumpet to your l., for a Hos 8.01
we will render the fruit of our l. 14.02
they shall all cover their l., Mic 3.07
my l. quiver at the sound; rottenness Hab 3.16
with seven l. on each of the lamps Zec 4.02
and no wrong was found on his l. Mal 2.06
For the l. of a priest should guard 2.07
'This people honors me with their l., Mt 15.08
people honors me with their l., Mk 7.06
heard it ourselves from his own l." Lk 22.71
venom of asps is under their l." Rom 3.13
on your l. and in your heart (that 10.08
with your l. that Jesus is Lord 10.09
confesses with his l. and so is saved. 10.10
and by the l. of foreigners will I 1Co 14.21
the fruit of l. that acknowledge Heb 13.15
sin; no guile was found on his l. 1Pe 2.22
from evil and his l. from speaking 3.10

LIQUID

of l. myrrh five hundred shekels, Ex 30.23
myrrh, my fingers with l. myrrh, Sol 5.05
lips are lilies, distilling l. myrrh. 5.13

LIST

The l. of those who did the work 1Ch 25.01
This is the l. of the people of 27.01

LISTEN

"My lord, l. to me; a piece of land Gen 23.15
But if you will not l. to us and be 34.17
he would not l. to her, to lie with 39.10
he besought us and we would not l.; 42.21
But you would not l. So now there 42.22
not believe me or l. to my voice, Ex 4.01
but they did not l. to Moses, 6.09
how then shall Pharaoh l. to me, 6.12
how then shall Pharaoh l. to me?" 6.30
Pharaoh will not l. to you; then I will 7.04
and he would not l. to them; as the 7.13
hardened, and he would not l. to them; 7.22
heart, and would not l. to them; as 8.15
and he would not l. to them; as the 8.19
Pharaoh, and he did not l. to them; 9.12
Moses, "Pharaoh will not l. to you; 11.09
But they did not l. to Moses; 16.20
L. now to my voice; I will give 18.19
you shall not l. to the words of Deu 13.03
not yield to him or l. to him, 13.08
but I would not l. to Balaam; Jos 24.10
they did not l. to their judges; Ju 2.17
"L. to me, you men of Shechem, that 9.07
of Shechem, that God may l. to you. 9.07
But the king of Edom would not l. 11.17
But the men would not l. to him. 19.25
would not l. to the voice of their 20.13
l., my daughter, do not go to glean Ru 2.08
they would not l. to the voice of 1Sa 2.25
refused to l. to the voice of 8.19
"Why do you l. to the words of men 24.09
Who would l. to you in this matter? 30.24
to him, and he did not l. to us; 2Sa 12.18
But he would not l. to her; and 13.14
But he would not l. to her. 13.16
Can I still l. to the voice of 19.35
"L. to the words of your maidservant." 20.17
But Amaziah would not l. So Jehoash 2Ki 14.11
But they would not l., but they were 17.14
However they would not l., but they did 17.40
Do not l. to Hezekiah; for thus says 18.31
And do not l. to Hezekiah when he 18.32
But they did not l., and Manasseh 21.09
But Amaziah would not l.; for it was 2Ch 25.20
He did not l. to the words of Neco 35.22
Shall we then l. to you and do all Neh 13.27
day and he would not l. to them, Est 3.04
and l. to the pleadings of my lips. Job 13.06
L. carefully to my words, and let my 13.17
"L. carefully to my words, and let 21.02

LISTEN (cont.)

Therefore I say, 'L. to me; Job 32.10
speech, O Job, and l. to all my words. 33.01
Give heed, O Job, l. to me; be 33.31
If not, l. to me; be silent and I will 33.33
understanding, hear this; l. to what I say. 34.16
Come, O sons, l. to me, I will teach Ps 34.11
Hear my cry, O God, l. to my prayer; 61.01
Israel, if you would but l. to me! 81.08
"But my people did not l. to my voice; 81.11
O that my people would l. to me, 81.13
have called and you refused to l., Pro 1.24
l. to me, and do not depart from the 5.07
I did not l. to the voice of my 5.13
l. to me, and be attentive to the 7.24
l. to me: happy are those who keep 8.32
a scoffer does not l. to rebuke. 13.01
L. to advice and accept instruction, 19.20
to draw near to l. is better than Ecc 5.01
make many prayers, I will not l.; Is 1.15
let him l. diligently, very diligently." 21.07
Let the earth l., and all that 34.01
Do not l. to Hezekiah; for thus says the 36.16
L. to me in silence, O coastlands; 41.01
will attend and l. for the time to 42.23
L. to me, O coastlands, and hearken, 49.01
"L. to me, my people, and give ear to 51.04
you did not l., but you did what 65.12
when I spoke they did not l.; 66.04
ears are closed, they cannot l.; Jer 6.10
to you persistently you did not l. 7.13
yet they did not l. to me, or incline 7.26
them, but they will not l. to you. 7.27
L. to my voice, and do all that I 11.04
cry to me, I will not l. to them. 11.11
for I will not l. when they call 11.14
But if any nation will not l., 12.17
and a glory, but they would not l. 13.11
But if you will not l., my soul will 13.17
evil will, refusing to l. to me; 16.12
Yet they did not l. or incline 17.23
" 'But if you l. to me, says the LORD, 17.24
But if you do not l. to me, to keep 17.27
but you said, 'I will not l.' This 22.21
"Do not l. to the words of the 23.16
It may be they will l., and every one 26.03
the LORD: If you will not l. to me, 26.04
So do not l. to your prophets, your 27.09
Do not l. to the words of the prophets 27.14
Do not l. to the words of your prophets 27.16
Do not l. to them; serve the king of 27.17
"L., Hananiah, the LORD has not sent 28.15
and do not l. to the dreams which 29.08
you would not l., says the LORD.'— 29.19
fathers did not l. to me or incline 34.14
instruction and l. to my words? says 35.13
not incline your ear or l. to me. 35.15
scroll, he would not l. to them. 36.25
But Irijah would not l. to him, 37.14
you counsel, you will not l. to me." 38.15
But they did not l. or incline 44.05
of the LORD, we will not l. to you. 44.16
you to such, they would l. to you. Eze 3.06
house of Israel will not l. to you; 3.07
they are not willing to l. to me; 3.07
lies to my people, who l. to lies. 13.19
against me and would not l. to me; 20.08
hereafter, if you will not l. to me; 20.39
melody of your harps I will not l. Amo 5.23
If you will not l., if you will not Mal 2.02
receive you or l. to your words, Mt 10.14
whom I am well pleased; l. to him." 17.05
But if he does not l., take one or 18.16
If he refuses to l. to them, tell it to 18.17
he refuses to l. even to the church, 18.17
"L.! A sower went out to sow. Mk 4.03
"This is my beloved Son; l. to him!" 9.07
is my Son, my Chosen; l. to him!" Lk 9.35
is a hard saying; who can l. to it?" Jn 6.60
you already, and you would not l. 9.27
that God does not l. to sinners, 9.31
demon, and he is mad; why l. to him?" 10.20
You shall l. to him in whatever he Ac 3.22
that does not l. to that prophet 3.23
sight of God to l. to your rather 4.19
Israel, and you that fear God, l. 13.16
James replied, "Brethren, l. to me. 15.13
I beg you to l. to me patiently. 26.03
sent to the Gentiles; they will l." 28.28
even then they will not l. to me, 1Co 14.21
who will l. to anybody and can 2Ti 3.07
L., my beloved brethren. Has not God Jas 2.05
is not of God does not l. to us. 1Jn 4.06

LISTENED

you have l. to the voice of your Gen 3.17
people of Israel have not l. to me; Ex 6.12
And God l. to the voice of Manoah, Ju 13.09
commanded; they neither l. nor obeyed. 2Ki 18.12
this and have not l. to my counsel." 2Ch 25.16
for this, and he l. to our entreaty. Ez 8.23
Have you l. in the council of God? Job 15.08
"Men l. to me, and waited, and kept 29.21
I l. for your wise sayings, while 32.11
heart, the Lord would not have l. Ps 66.18
But truly God has l.; he has given 66.19
I have given heed and l., but they Jer 8.06
has given heed to his word and l.? 23.18
to you, but you have not l. 25.03
You have neither l. nor inclined 25.04
Yet you have not l. to me, says the 25.07
they have not l. to receive instruction. 32.33
persistently, but you have not l. to me. 35.14
to them and they have not l., 35.17
of the land l. to the words of the 37.02
we have not l. to thy servants the Dan 9.06
Lord's feet and l. to his teaching Lk 10.39
He l. to Paul speaking; and Paul, Ac 14.09
and they l. to Barnabas and Paul as 15.12
Up to this word they l. to him; 22.22
"Men, you should have l. to me, 27.21
acceptable time I have l. to you, 2Co 6.02

LISTENING

And Sarah was l. at the tent door Gen 18.10
Now Rebekah was l. when Isaac spoke 27.05
And he answered, "I am l." 2Sa 20.17
believe that he was l. to my voice. Job 9.16
is a wise reprover to a l. ear. Pro 25.12
companions are l. for your voice; Sol 8.13
not l. to my voice, then I will Jer 18.10
l. to them and asking them questions; Lk 2.46
and the prisoners were l. to them, Ac 16.25
turn away from l. to the truth and 2Ti 4.04

LISTENS

but he who l. to me will dwell Pro 1.33
Happy is the man who l. to me, 8.34
eyes, but a wise man l. to advice. 12.15
An evildoer l. to wicked lips; 17.04
If a ruler l. to falsehood, all his 29.12
She l. to no voice, she accepts no Zep 3.02
If he l. to you, you have gained Mt 18.15
and does his will, God l. to him. Jn 9.31
world, and the world l. to them. 1Jn 4.05
Whoever knows God l. to us, and he 4.06

LITERAL

of the heart, spiritual and not l. Rom 2.29

LITTER

Behold, it is the l. of Solomon! Sol 3.07

LITTERED

all the way was l. with garments 2Ki 7.15

LITTERS
and in l., and upon mules, and upon Is 66.20

LITTLE
Let a l. water be brought, and wash Gen 18.04
to flee to, and it is a l. one. 19.20
me escape there—is it not a l. one? 19.20
"Pray give me a l. water to drink 24.17
"Pray give me a l. water from your 24.43
For you had l. before I came, and it 30.30
all their l. ones and their wives, 34.29
them, "Go again, buy us a l. food." 43.02
we and you and also our l. ones. 43.08
a l. balm and a l. honey, gum, myrrh, 43.11
'Go again, buy us a l. food,' 44.25
Egypt for your l. ones and for 45.19
their l. ones, and their wives, in 46.05
and as food for your l. ones." 47.24
provide for you and your l. ones." 50.21
ever I let you and your l. ones go! Ex 10.10
he that gathered l. had no lack; 16.18
L. by l. I will drive them out from 23.30
wives and our l. ones will become Num 14.03
But your l. ones, who you said would 14.31
their sons, and their l. ones. 16.27
women of Midian and their l. ones; 31.09
kill every male among the l. ones, 31.17
and cities for our l. ones, 32.16
and our l. ones shall live in the 32.17
Build cities for your l. ones, 32.24
Our l. ones, our wives, our flocks, 32.26
Moreover your l. ones, who you said Deu 1.39
your l. ones, and your cattle (I know 3.19
nations before you l. by l.; you may 7.22
the l. owl and the great owl, the 14.16
but the women and the l. ones, 20.14
the field, and shall gather l. in; 28.38
your l. ones, your wives, and the 29.11
and l. ones. and the sojourner 31.12
your l. ones, and your cattle shall Jos 1.14
and the l. ones, and the sojourners 8.35
"Pray, give me a l. water to drink; Ju 4.19
putting the l. ones and the cattle 18.21
also the women and the l. ones. 21.10
make for him a l. robe and take it 1Sa 2.19
I tasted a l. of this honey. 14.29
"I tasted a l. honey with the tip 14.43
"Though you are l. in your own eyes, 15.17
seem to you a l. thing to become 18.23
with David, and with him a l. lad. 20.35
nothing of all this, much or l. 22.15
had nothing but one l. ewe lamb, 2Sa 12.03
and if this were too l., I would add 12.08
men and all the l. ones who were 15.22
had passed a l. beyond the summit, 16.01
will go a l. way over the Jordan 19.36
although I am but a l. child; 1Ki 3.07
servants, Hadad being yet a l. child. 11.17
'My l. finger is thicker than my 12.10
"Bring me a l. water in a vessel, 17.10
in a jar, and a l. oil in a cruse; 17.12
first make me a l. cake of it and 17.13
a l. cloud like a man's hand is 18.44
And in a l. while the heavens grew 18.45
them like two l. flocks of goats, 20.27
carried off a l. maid from the 2Ki 5.02
like the flesh of a l. child, 5.14
and dash in pieces their l. ones. 8.12
to them, "Ahab served Baal a l.; 10.18
and of l. account, and sojourners in 1Ch 16.19
'My l. finger is thicker than my 2Ch 10.10
with their l. ones, their wives, and 20.13
enrolled with all their l. children, 31.18
and grant us a l. reviving in our Ez 9.08
hardship seem l. to thee that has Neh 9.32
that I may find a l. comfort Job 10.20
forth their l. ones like a flock, 21.11
They are exalted a l. while, 24.24
"Bear with me a l., and I will show 36.02
hast made him l. less than God, Ps 8.05
Yet a l. while, and the wicked will 37.10
Better is a l. that the righteous 37.16
of l. account, and sojourners in it, 105.12
who takes your l. ones and dashes 137.09
A l. sleep, a l. slumber, a Pro 6.10
a l. folding of the hands to rest, 6.10
mind of the wicked is of l. worth. 10.20
who gathers l. by l. will increase it. 13.11
Better is a l. with the fear of the 15.16
Better is a l. with righteousness 16.08
"A l. sleep, a l. slumber, a 24.33
a l. folding of the hands to rest," 24.33
laborer, whether he eats l. or much; Ecc 5.12
There was a l. city with few men in 9.14
so a l. folly outweighs wisdom and 10.01
the l. foxes, that spoil the vineyards, Sol 2.15
We have a l. sister, and she has no 8.08
Is it too l. for you to weary men, Is 7.13
For in a very l. while my indignation 10.25
and a l. child shall lead them. 11.06
yourselves for a l. while until the 26.20
upon line, here a l. there a l." 28.10
upon line, here a l., there a l.; 28.13
not yet a very l. while until 29.17
In l. more than a year you will 32.10
possessed thy sanctuary a l. while; 63.18
Even the l. ones of the flock shall Jer 49.20
Surely the l. ones of their flock 50.45
yet a l. while and the time of her 51.33
l. children and women, but touch no Eze 9.06
within a very l. time you were more 16.47
a l. one, before which three of the Dan 7.08
one of them came forth a l. horn, 8.09
fall, they shall receive a l. help,. 11.34
for yet a l. while, and I will Hos 1.04
cease for a l. while from anointing 8.10
their l. ones shall be dashed in 13.16
fragments, and the l. house into bits. Amo 6.11
who are l. to be among the clans of Mic 5.02
her l. ones were dashed in pieces Nah 3.10
You have sown much, and harvested l.; Hag 1.06
for much, and, lo, it came to l.; 1.09
in a l. while, I will shake the 2.06
was angry but a l. they furthered Zec 1.15
turn my hand against the l. ones. 13.07
more clothe you, O men of l. faith? Mt 6.30
are you afraid, O men of l. faith?" 8.26
to one of these l. ones even a cup 10.42
"O man of l. faith, why did you 14.31
"O men of l. faith, why do you discuss 16.08
to them, "Because of your l. faith. 17.20
one of these l. ones who believe 18.06
not despise one of these l. ones; 18.10
one of these l. ones should perish. 18.14
you have been faithful over a l., 25.21
you have been faithful over a l., 25.23
And going a l. farther he fell on 26.39
After a l. while the bystanders 26.73
And going on a l. farther, he saw Mk 1.19
"My l. daughter is at the point of 5.23
which means, "L. girl, I say to you, 5.41
whose l. daughter was possessed by 7.25
one of these l. ones who believe 9.42
And going a l. farther, he fell on 14.35
And after a l. while again the 14.70
him to put out a l. from the land. Lk 5.03
but he who is forgiven l., loves l." 7.47
he clothe you, O men of l. faith? 12.28
"Fear not, l. flock, for it is your 12.32
in a very l. is faithful also in 16.10
in a very l. is dishonest also in 16.10
cause one of these l. ones to sin. 17.02
have been faithful in a very l., 19.17
And a l. later some one else saw 22.58
bread for each of them to get a l." Jn 6.07
"I shall be with you a l. longer, 7.33

LITTLE (cont.)

light is with you for a l. longer. Jn 12.35
L. children, yet a l. while I am with you. 13.33
Yet a l. while, and the world will 14.19
"A l. while, and you will see me no 16.16
again a l. while, and you will see 16.16
'A l. while, and you will not see me, 16.17
and again a l. while, and you will 16.17
"What does he mean by 'a l. while'? 16.18
'A l. while, and you will not see me, 16.19
and again a l. while, and you will 16.19
remained no l. time with the Ac 14.28
there arose no l. stir concerning 19.23
brought no l. business to the 19.24
alive, and were not a l. comforted. 20.12
a l. farther on they sounded again 27.28
have enjoyed your company for a l. Rom 15.24
not know that a l. leaven ferments 1Co 5.06
and he who gathered l. had no lack." 2Co 8.15
if I boast a l. too much of our 10.08
bear with me in a l. foolishness. 11.01
fool, so that I too may boast a l. 11.16
My l. children, with whom I am again Gal 4.19
A l. yeast leavens the whole lump. 5.09
but use a l. wine for the sake of 1Ti 5.23
make him for a l. while lower than Heb 2.07
who for a l. while was made lower 2.09
"For yet a l. while, and the coming 10.37
So the tongue is a l. member and Jas 3.05
appears for a l. time and then 4.14
now for a l. while you may have to 1Pe 1.06
after you have suffered a l. while, 5.10
My l. children, I am writing this to 1Jn 2.01
l. children, because your sins are 2.12
And now, l. children, abide in him, so 2.28
L. children, let no one deceive you. 3.07
L. children, let us not love in word 3.18
L. children, you are of God, and have 4.04
L. children, keep yourselves from 5.21
I know that you have but l. power, Rev 3.08
robe and told to rest a l. longer, 6.11
He had a l. scroll open in his hand. 10.02
told him to give me the l. scroll; 10.09
And I took the l. scroll from the 10.10
he must remain only a l. while. 17.10
he must be loosed for a l. while. 20.03

LIVE

tree of life, and eat, and l. for ever"— Gen 3.22
kill me, but they will let you l. 12.12
that Ishmael might l. in thy sight!" 17.18
pray for you, and you shall l. 20.07
said, "If it is thus, why do I l.?" 25.22
By your sword you shall l., and you 27.40
you find your gods shall not l. 31.32
there, that we may l., and not die." 42.02
to them, "Do this and you will l., 42.18
that we may l. and not die, both we 43.08
that we may l., and not die, and 47.19
if it is a daughter, she shall l." Ex 1.16
them, but let the male children l. 1.17
this, and let the male children l.?" 1.18
you shall let every daughter l." 1.22
for this purpose have I let you l., 9.16
beast or man, he shall not l.' 19.13
shall sell the l. ox and divide 21.35
shall not permit a sorceress to l. 22.18
for man shall not see me and l." 33.20
he shall present the l. goat; Lev 16.20
hands upon the head of the l. goat, 16.21
a man shall l.: I am the LORD. 18.05
a sojourner he shall l. with you. 25.35
your brother may l. beside you. 25.36
that they may l. and not die when Num 4.19
as I l., and as all the earth shall 14.21
'As I l.,' says the LORD, 'what you 14.28
bitten, when he sees it, shall l." 21.08
look at the bronze serpent and l. 21.09
would have slain you and let her l." 22.33
who shall l. when God does this 24.23
"Have you let all the women l.? 31.15
ones shall l. in the fortified 32.17
and he shall l. in it until the 35.25
pollute the land in which you l.; 35.33
defile the land in which you l., 35.34
the sons of Esau, who l. in Seir; Deu 2.04
the sons of Esau who l. in Seir, 2.08
who l. in Seir, when he destroyed 2.22
of Esau who l. in Seir and the 2.29
Moabites who l. in Ar did for me, 2.29
that you may l., and go in and take 4.01
days that they l. upon the earth, 4.10
you will not l. long upon it, but 4.26
as you have heard, and still l.? 4.33
speak with man and man still l. 5.24
that you may l., and that it may go 5.33
that you may l. long in the land 5.33
that you may l. and multiply, and go 8.01
man does not l. by bread alone, 8.03
goodly houses and l. in them, 8.12
and that you may l. long in the 11.09
Canaaanites who l. in the Arabah, 11.30
when you possess it and l. in it, 11.31
days that you l. upon the earth. 12.01
and l. in the land which the LORD 12.10
about, so that you l. in safety, 12.10
as long as you l. in your land. 12.19
that you may l. and inherit the 16.20
with you, and that you may l. long. 22.07
possession of it, and l. in it, 26.01
all your soul, that you may l. 30.06
then you shall l. and multiply, 30.16
you shall not l. long in the land 30.18
you and your descendants may l., 30.19
as long as you l. in the land 31.13
(for it will l. unforgotten in the 31.21
and swear, As I l. for ever, 32.40
you shall l. long in the land 32.47
"Let Reuben l., and not die; 33.06
are with her in her house shall l., Jos 6.17
Hivites, "Perhaps you l. among us; 9.07
covenant with them, to let them l.; 9.15
and let them l., lest wrath be upon 9.20
leaders said to them, "Let them l." 9.21
they could not l. on at Shechem. Ju 9.41
to l. where he could find a place; 17.08
As you l., my lord, I am the woman 1Sa 1.26
people shouted, "Long l. the king!" 10.24
be found in you so long as you l. 25.28
he could not l. after he had 2Sa 1.10
As you l., and as your soul lives, I will 11.11
to me, that the child may l.?' 12.22
and said, "As surely as you l., 14.19
"Long l. the king! Long l. the king!" 16.16
"How many years have I still to l., 19.34
and saying, 'Long l. King Adonijah!' 1Ki 1.25
"May my lord King David l. for ever!" 1.31
and say, 'Long l. King Solomon!' 1.34
people said, "Long l. King Solomon!" 1.39
days that they l. in the land 8.40
Benhadad says, 'Pray, let me l.' " 20.32
And he said, "Does he still l.? 20.32
LORD lives, and as you yourself l., 2Ki 2.02
LORD lives, and as you yourself l., 2.04
LORD lives, and as you yourself l., 2.06
and your sons can l. on the rest." 4.07
LORD lives, and as you yourself l., 4.30
they spare our lives we shall l., 7.04
whoever is missing shall not l." 10.19
hands, and said, "Long l. the king!" 11.12
that you may l., and not die. 18.32
days that they l. in the land 2Ch 6.31
wife shall not l. in the house of 8.11
brethren who l. in their cities, 19.10
and they said, "Long l. the king." 23.11
associates who l. in Samaria and Ez 4.17

LIVE (cont.)
the king, "Let the king l. for ever! Neh 2.03
where they l. they will come up 4.12
I could go into the temple and l.? 6.11
observance of which a man shall l., 9.29
out of ten to l. in Jerusalem the 11.01
willingly offered to l. in Jerusalem. 11.02
the golden scepter that he may l. Est 4.11
who l. in the open towns, hold the 9.19
my life; I would not l. for ever. Job 7.16
If a man die, shall he l. again? 14.14
no survivor where he used to l. 18.19
Why do the wicked l., reach old age, 21.07
in a valley away from where men l.; 28.04
May your hearts l. for ever! Ps 22.26
should continue to l. on for ever, 49.09
shall not l. out half their days. 55.23
So I will bless thee as long as I l.; 63.04
May he l. while the sun endures, and 72.05
Long may he l., may gold of Sheba 72.15
What man can l. and never see death? 89.48
as long as you l. so that your 103.05
sing to the LORD as long as I l.; 104.33
and they establish a city to l. in; 107.36
I will call on him as long as I l. 116.02
but I shall l., and recount the 118.17
that I may l. and observe thy word. 119.17
mercy come to me, that I may l.; 119.77
that I may l., and let me not be 119.116
me understanding that I may l. 119.144
Let me l., that I may praise thee, 119.175
praise the LORD as long as I l.; 146.02
keep my commandments, and l.; Pro 4.04
keep my commandments and l., keep my 7.02
and l., and walk in the way of 9.06
steadfast in righteousness will l. 11.19
but he who hates bribes will l. 15.27
fitting for a fool to l. in luxury, 19.10
It is better to l. in a corner of 21.09
It is better to l. in a desert land 21.19
It is better to l. in a corner of 25.24
themselves as long as they l.; Ecc 3.12
he should l. a thousand years 6.06
is in their hearts while they l., 9.03
They are dead, they will not l.; Is 26.14
Thy dead shall l., their bodies 26.19
O Lord, by these things men l., 38.16
me to health and make me l.! 38.16
As I l., says the LORD, you shall 49.18
hear, that your soul may l.; 55.03
you shall l. and shall have his Jer 21.09
"As I l., says the LORD, though 22.24
serve him and his people, and l. 27.12
serve the king of Babylon and l. 27.17
Build houses and l. in them; plant 29.05
build houses and l. in them, and 29.28
but you shall l. in tents all your 35.07
that you may l. many days in the 35.07
goes out to the Chaldeans shall l.; 38.02
his life as a prize of war, and l. 38.02
and you and our house shall l. 38.17
to enter Egypt and go to l. there, 42.15
go to Egypt to l. there shall die 42.17
place where you desire to go to l." 42.22
'Do not go to Egypt to l. there'; 43.02
had returned to l. in the land of 43.05
of Egypt where you have come to l., 44.08
to come to the land of Egypt to l., 44.12
have come to l. in the land of 44.14
came to the land of Egypt to l., 44.28
"As I l., says the King, whose name 46.18
you who l. in the clefts of the 49.16
shadow we shall l. among the nations." Lam 4.20
does not sin, he shall surely l., Eze 3.21
as I l., says the Lord GOD, surely, 5.11
to what he has sold, while they l. 7.13
alive persons who should not l., 13.19
as I l., says the Lord GOD, they 14.16
as I l., says the LORD God, they 14.18
as I l.. says the Lord GOD, they 14.20
I said to you in your blood, 'L., 16.06
As I l., says the Lord GOD, your 16.48
As I l., says the Lord GOD, surely 17.16
As I l., surely my oath which he 17.19
As I l., says the Lord GOD, this 18.03
is righteous, he shall surely l., 18.09
shall he then l.? He shall not l. 18.13
father's iniquity; he shall surely l. 18.17
my statutes, he shall surely l. 18.19
and right, he shall surely l.; 18.21
which he has done he shall l. 18.22
he should turn from his way and l.? 18.23
the wicked man does, shall he l.? 18.24
had committed, he shall surely l., 18.28
says the Lord GOD; so turn, and l." 18.32
As I l., says the Lord GOD, I will 20.03
by whose observance man shall l. 20.11
by whose observance man shall l.; 20.13
by whose observance man shall l.; 20.21
As I l., says the Lord GOD, I will 20.31
"As I l., says the Lord GOD, surely 20.33
because of them; how then can we l.?' 33.10
As I l., says the Lord GOD. I have 33.11
wicked turn from his way and l.; 33.11
not be able to l. by his righteousness 33.12
righteous that he shall surely l., 33.13
he shall surely l., he shall not die. 33.15
lawful and right, he shall surely l. 33.16
lawful and right, he shall l. by it. 33.19
As I l., surely those who are in 33.27
As I l., says the LORD God, because 34.08
as I l., says the LORD God, I will 35.06
as I l., says the Lord GOD, I will 35.11
me, "Son of man, can these bones l.?" 37.03
to enter you, and you shall l. 37.05
breath in you, and you shall l.; 37.06
upon these slain, that they may l." 37.09
and you shall l., and I will place 37.14
possession for cities to l. in. 45.05
living creature which swarms will l. 47.09
everything will l. where the river 47.09
to the king, "O king, l. for ever! Dan 2.04
Nebuchadnezzar, "O king, l. for ever! 3.09
queen said, "O king, l. for ever! 5.10
to him, "O King Darius, l. for ever! 6.06
to the king, "O king, L. for ever! 6.21
us up, that we may l. before him. Hos 6.02
house of Israel: "'Seek me and l.; Amo 5.04
Seek the LORD and l., lest he break 5.06
and not evil that you may l.; 5.14
you who l. in the clefts of the Ob 1.03
is better for me to die than to l." Jon 4.03
is better for me to die than to l." 4.08
righteous shall l. by his faith. Hab 2.04
as I l.," says the LORD of hosts, Zep 2.09
the prophets, do they l. for ever? Zec 1.05
children they shall l. and return. 10.09
will say to him, 'You shall not l., 13.03
'Man shall not l. by bread alone, Mt 4.04
your hand on her, and she will l." 9.18
that she may be made well, and l." Mk 5.23
disciples not l. according to the 7.05
'Man shall not l. by bread alone.'" Lk 4.04
appareled and l. in luxury are in 7.25
right; do this, and you will l." 10.28
but of the living; for all l. to him." 20.38
said to him, "Go; your son will l." Jn 4.50
had said to him, "Your son will l."; 4.53
of God, and those who hear will l. 5.25
of this bread, he will l. for ever; 6.51
and I l. because of the Father, so 6.57
who eats me will l. because of me. 6.57
eats this bread will l. for ever. 6.58
though he die, yet shall he l., 11.25
me; because I l., you will l. also. 14.19
let there be no one to l. in it'; Ac 1.20

LIVE (cont.)
For those who l. in Jerusalem and Ac 13.27
does not l. in shrines made by man, 17.24
of men to l. on all the face of 17.26
for 'In him we l. and move and have 17.28
you yourself l. in observance of 21.24
the earth! For he ought not to l." 22.22
that he ought not to l. any longer. 25.24
justice has not allowed him to l." 28.04
through faith is righteous shall l." Rom 1.17
we who died to sin still l. in it? 6.02
that we shall also l. with him. 6.08
For those who l. according to the 8.05
but those who l. according to the 8.05
to l. according to the flesh— 8.12
for if you l. according to the 8.13
the deeds of the body you will l. 8.13
is based on the law shall l. by it. 10.05
L. in harmony with one another; 12.16
upon you, l. peaceably with all. 12.18
If we l., we l. to the Lord, and if 14.08
whether we l. or whether we die, we 14.08
"As I l., says the Lord, every knee 14.11
grant you to l. in such harmony 15.05
learn by us to l. according to 1Co 4.06
and she consents to l. with him, 7.12
and he consents to l. with her, 7.13
who have wives l. as though they 7.29
For while we l. we are always being 2Co 4.11
earthly tent we l. in is destroyed, 5.01
that those who l. might l. no longer 5.15
as dying, and behold we l.; 6.09
"I will l. in them and move among 6.16
to die together and to l. together. 7.03
For though we l. in the world we 10.03
you we shall l. with him by the 13.04
l. in peace, and the God of love and 13.11
l. like a Gentile and not like a Gal 2.14
the Gentiles to l. like Jews?" 2.14
to the law, that I might l. to God. 2.19
it is no longer I who l., but Christ 2.20
the life I now l. in the flesh I 2.20
I l. by faith in the Son of God, 2.20
faith is righteous shall l."; 3.11
"He who does them shall l. by them." 3.12
If we l. by the Spirit, let us also 5.25
appointed to l. for the praise of Eph 1.12
must no longer l. as the Gentiles 4.17
that you may l. long on the earth." 6.03
For to me to l. is Christ, and to Php 1.21
those who so l. as you have an 3.17
l. as enemies of the cross of 3.18
Jesus the Lord, so l. in him, Col 2.06
why do you l. as if you still 2.20
for now we l., if you stand fast in 1Th 3.08
you ought to l. and to please God, 4.01
to aspire to l. quietly, to mind 4.11
wake or sleep we might l. with him. 5.10
him, we shall also l. with him; 2Ti 2.11
who desire to l. a godly life in 3.12
and to l. sober, upright, and godly Tit 2.12
my righteous one shall l. by faith, Heb 10.38
to the Father of spirits and l.? 12.09
we shall l. and we shall do this or Jas 4.15
L. as free men, yet without using 1Pe 2.16
for evil; but l. as servants of God. 2.16
die to sin and l. to righteousness. 2.24
l. considerately with your wives, 3.07
so as to l. for the rest of the 4.02
they might l. in the spirit like 4.06
escaped from those who l. in error. 2Pe 2.18
lie and do not l. according to the 1Jn 1.06
so that we might l. through him. 4.09

LIVED
When Adam had l. a hundred and Gen 5.03
days that Adam l. were nine hundred 5.05
When Seth had l. a hundred and five 5.06
Seth l. after the birth of Enosh 5.07
When Enosh had l. ninety years, he 5.09
Enosh l. after the birth of Kenan 5.10
When Kenan had l. seventy years, he 5.12
Kenan l. after the birth of Mahalalel 5.13
When Mahalalel had l. sixty-five 5.15
Mahalalel l. after the birth of 5.16
When Jared had l. a hundred and 5.18
Jared l. after the birth of Enoch 5.19
When Enoch had l. sixty-five years, 5.21
When Methuselah had l. a hundred 5.25
Methuselah l. after the birth of 5.26
When Lamech had l. a hundred and 5.28
Lamech l. after the birth of Noah 5.30
After the flood Noah l. three 9.28
in which they l. extended from 10.30
and Shem l. after the birth of 11.11
When Arpachshad had l. thirty-five 11.12
and Arpachshad l. after the birth 11.13
When Shelah had l. thirty years, 11.14
and Shelah l. after the birth of 11.15
When Eber had l. thirty-four years, 11.16
and Eber l. after the birth of 11.17
When Peleg had l. thirty years, he 11.18
and Peleg l. after the birth of Reu 11.19
When Reu had l. thirty-two years, he 11.20
and Reu l. after the birth of Serug 11.21
When Serug had l. thirty years, he 11.22
and Serug l. after the birth of 11.23
When Nahor had l. twenty-nine years, 11.24
and Nahor l. after the birth of 11.25
When Terah had l. seventy years, he 11.26
he l. in the wilderness and became 21.20
He l. in the wilderness of Paran; 21.21
Sarah l. a hundred and twenty-seven 23.01
and l. on the allowance which 47.22
And Jacob l. in the land of Egypt 47.28
and Joseph l. a hundred and ten 50.22
who l. in Heshbon, and Og the king Deu 1.04
who l. in Ashtaroth and in Edrei. 1.04
Amorites who l. in that hill 1.44
(The Emim formerly l. there, a people 2.10
The Horites also l. in Seir formerly, 2.12
Rephaim formerly l. there, but the 2.20
who l. in villages as far as Gaza, 2.23
who l. at Heshbon, whom Moses and 4.46
who l. to the east beyond the 4.47
fire, as we have, and has still l.? 5.26
the sojourners who l. among them. Jos 8.35
'Your fathers l. of old beyond the 24.02
and you l. in the wilderness a long 24.07
who l. on the other side of the 24.08
the Amorites who l. in the land; 24.18
and he l. at Shamir in the hill Ju 10.01
They l. there about ten years; Ru 1.04
and she l. with her mother-in-law. 2.23
Shunem, where a wealthy woman l., 2Ki 4.08
l. fifteen years after the death of 14.17
day a portion, as long as he l. 25.30
leaders, who l. in Jerusalem. 1Ch 9.34
him from all places where they l. 2Ch 11.13
king of Judah l. fifteen years 25.25
the people who l. in Jerusalem to 31.04
and Judah who l. in the cities of 31.06
of the people l. in Jerusalem and Ez 2.70
temple servants l. in their towns, 2.70
When the Jews who l. by them came Neh 4.12
and all Israel, l. in their towns. 7.73
of the people l. in Jerusalem; 11.01
the province who l. in Jerusalem; 11.03
Judah every one l. on his property 11.03
And in Jerusalem l. certain of the 11.04
of Perez who l. in Jerusalem were 11.06
But the temple servants l. on Ophel; 11.21
people of Judah l. in Kiriatharba 11.25
Benjamin also l. from Geba onward, 11.31
who l. in the city, brought in fish 13.16
and has l. in desolate cities, in Job 15.28

LIVED (cont.)

And after this Job l. a hundred and Job 42.16
but we have l. in tents, and have Jer 35.10
day of his death as long as he l. 52.34
who l. with her daughters to the Eze 16.46
who l. to the south of you, is Sodom 16.46
and they l., and stood upon their 37.10
'If we had l. in the days of our Mt 23.30
who l. among the tombs; and no one Mk 5.03
having l. with her husband seven Lk 2.36
and he l. not in a house but among 8.27
Mesopotamia, before he l. in Haran, Ac 7.02
of the Chaldeans, and l. in Haran. 7.04
the Jews who l. in Damascus by 9.22
to the saints that l. at Lydda. 9.32
to the brethren who l. in Judea; 11.29
foreigners who l. there spent their 17.21
know how I l. among you all the 20.18
of by all the Jews who l. there, 22.12
I have l. before God in all good 23.01
religion I have l. as a Pharisee. 26.05
And he l. there two whole years at 28.30
this end Christ died and l. again, Rom 14.09
we all once l. in the passions of Eph 2.03
once walked, when you l. in them. Col 3.07
You have l. on the earth in luxury Jas 5.05
saw and heard as he l. among them, 2Pe 2.08
wounded by the sword and yet l.; Rev 13.14

LIVER

and the appendage of the l., and the Ex 29.13
and the appendage of the l., and the 29.22
appendage of the l. which he shall Lev 3.04
appendage of the l. which he shall 3.10
appendage of the l. which he shall 3.15
appendage of the l. which he shall 4.09
appendage of the l. which he shall 7.04
and the appendage of the l., 8.16
and the appendage of the l., 8.25
appendage of the l. from the sin 9.10
and the appendage of the l.; 9.19
the teraphim, he looks at the l. Eze 21.21

LIVES

thing that l. shall be food for Gen 9.03
And they said, "You have saved our l.; 47.25
and made their l. bitter with hard Ex 1.14
and the sojourner who l. with you; Lev 25.06
sinned at the cost of their l.; Num 16.38
but that man l. by everything that Deu 8.03
where he l.—and he may come when 18.06
the gate of the place where he l., 21.19
and deliver our l. from death." Jos 2.13
greatly for our l. because of you, 9.24
jeoparded their l. to the death; Ju 5.18
as the LORD l., if you had saved 8.19
life with the l. of your household." 18.25
as the LORD l., I will do the part Ru 3.13
as long as he l., he is lent to the 1Sa 1.28
For as the LORD l. who saves Israel, 14.39
As the LORD l., there shall not one 14.45
"As your soul l., O king, I cannot 17.55
"As the LORD l., he shall not be 19.06
as the LORD l. and as your soul l., 20.03
as the LORD l., it is safe for you 20.21
the son of Jesse l. upon the earth, 20.31
as the LORD l., and as your soul l., 25.26
and the l. of your enemies he shall 25.29
as the LORD the God of Israel l., 25.34
"As the LORD l., the LORD will 26.10
As the LORD l., you deserve to die, 26.16
"As the LORD l., no punishment 28.10
"As the LORD l., you have been 29.06
"As God l., if you had not spoken, 2Sa 2.27
"As the LORD l., who has redeemed 4.09
As you live, and as your soul l., 11.11
"As the LORD l., the man who has 12.05
"As the LORD l., not one hair of 14.11
"As the LORD l., and as my lord the king, l. 15.21
and the l. of your sons and your 19.05
and the l. of your wives and your 19.05
"The LORD l.; and blessed be 22.47
who went at the risk of their l.?" 23.17
"As the LORD l., who has redeemed 1Ki 1.29
Now therefore as the LORD l., 2.24
"As the LORD the God of Israel l., 17.01
And she said, "As the LORD your God l., 17.12
and Elijah said, "See, your son l." 17.23
As the LORD your God l., there is no 18.10
said, "As the LORD of hosts l., 18.15
"As the LORD l., what the LORD says 22.14
"as the LORD l., and as you yourself 2Ki 2.02
"As the LORD l., and as you youself 2.04
"As the LORD l., and as you yourself 2.06
said, "As the LORD of hosts l., 3.14
"As the LORD l., and as you yourself 4.30
"As the LORD l., whom I serve, I 5.16
As the LORD l., I will run after 5.20
if they spare our l. we shall live, 7.04
as it was, and fled for their l. 7.07
risk of their l. they brought it. 1Ch 11.19
"As the LORD l., what my God says, 2Ch 18.13
city to gather and defend their l., Est 8.11
also gathered to defend their l., 9.16
stoneheap; he l. among the rocks. Job 8.17
For I know that my Redeemer l., 19.25
"As God l., who has taken away my 27.02
The LORD l.; and blessed be Ps 18.46
while he l., he counts himself 49.18
and saves the l. of the needy. 72.13
but gave their l. over to the 78.50
he preserves the l. of his saints; 97.10
set an ambush for their own l. Pro 1.18
but lawlessness takes away l. 11.30
A truthful witness saves l., 14.25
and l. many years, so that the days Ecc 6.03
man while he l. the few days of 6.12
For if a man l. many years, let him 11.08
an infant that l. but a few days, Is 65.20
'As the LORD l.,' in truth, in justice, Jer 4.02
"As the LORD l.," yet they swear 5.02
'as the LORD l.,' even as they 12.16
'As the LORD l. who brought up the 16.14
but 'As the LORD l. who brought up 16.15
Take heed for the sake of your l., 17.21
hand of those who seek their l. 21.07
'As the LORD l. who brought up the 23.07
but 'As the LORD l. who brought up 23.08
hand of those who seek their l. 34.20
hand of those who seek their l., 34.21
"As the LORD l., who made our souls, 38.16
gone astray at the cost of your l. 42.20
Egypt, saying, 'As the Lord GOD l.' 44.26
to him for the l. of your children, Lam 2.19
our bread at the peril of our l., 5.09
but their own l. by their righteousness, Eze 14.14
but their own l. by their righteousness. 14.20
walls built to cut off many l. 17.17
they have devoured human l.; they have 22.25
destroying l. to get dishonest gain. 22.27
and honored him who l. for ever; Dan 4.34
but their l. were prolonged for a 7.12
by him who l. for ever that it 12.07
and swear not, "As the LORD l." Hos 4.15
'As thy god l., O Dan,' and, 'As the Amo 8.14
and, 'As the way of Beersheba l.,' 8.14
for by them he l. in luxury, Hab 1.16
not to destroy men's l. but to save *Lk 9.55
endurance you will gain your l. 21.19
and whoever l. and believes in me Jn 11.26
risked their l. for the sake of Ac 15.26
and the ship, but also of our l." 27.10
but the life he l. he l. to God. Rom 6.10
to her husband as long as he l.; 7.02
adulteress if she l. with another 7.03
None of us l. to himself, and none 14.07

LIVES (cont.)
to her husband as long as he l. 1Co 7.39
but l. by the power of God. For we are 2Co 13.04
who live, but Christ who l. in me; Gal 2.20
self-indulgent is dead even while she l. 1Ti 5.06
and godly l. in this world, Tit 2.12
for every one who l. on milk is Heb 5.13
of whom it is testified that he l. 7.08
since he always l. to make intercession 7.25
you to be in l. of holiness and 2Pe 3.11
to lay down our l. for the brethren. 1Jn 3.16
on the throne, who l. for ever and ever, Rev 4.09
worship him who l. for ever and 4.10
by him who l. for ever and ever, 10.06
loved not their l. even unto death. 12.11
of God who l. for ever and ever; 15.07

LIVESTOCK
all his l. which he had gained, the Gen 31.18
and for their l. and for all their Num 35.03
They carried off their l.: fifty thousand 1Ch 5.21

LIVING
bring forth swarms of l. creatures, Gen 1.20
bring forth l. creatures according 1.24
and over every l. thing that moves 1.28
of life; and man became a l. being. 2.07
the man called every l. creature, 2.19
she was the mother of all l. 3.20
And of every l. thing of all flesh, 6.19
and every l. thing that I have made 7.04
out every l. thing that was upon 7.23
with you every l. thing that is 8.17
destroy every l. creature as I 8.21
and with every l. creature that is 9.10
you and every l. creature that is 9.12
you and every l. creature of all 9.15
God and every l. creature of all 9.16
who was l. by the oaks of Mamre the 14.13
he was still l. he sent them away 25.06
These are the l. things which you Lev 11.02
and of the l. creatures that are 11.10
bird and every l. creature that 11.46
and between the l. creature that 11.47
eaten and the l. creature that may 11.47
be cleansed two l. clean birds and 14.04
He shall take the l. bird with the 14.06
them and the l. bird in the blood 14.06
shall let the l. bird go into the 14.07
stuff, along with the l. bird, 14.51
and with the l. bird, and with the 14.52
shall let the l. bird go out of 14.53
stood between the dead and the l.; Num 16.48
voice of the l. God speaking out Deu 5.26
and every l. thing that followed 11.06
know that the l. God is among you, Jos 3.10
and a suit of apparel, and your l." Ju 17.10
not forsaken the l. or the dead!" Ru 2.20
defy the armies of the l. God?" 1Sa 17.26
defied the armies of the l. God." 17.36
bundle of the l. in the care of 25.29
of their death, l. as if in widowhood. 2Sa 20.03
the l. child is mine, and the dead 1Ki 3.22
is yours, and the l. child is mine." 3.22
is dead, and my son is the l. one.'" 3.23
"Divide the l. child in two, and 3.25
give her the l. child, and by no 3.26
"Give the l. child to the first 3.27
has sent to mock the l. God, 2Ki 19.04
he has sent to mock the l. God. 19.16
temple servants l. on Ophel Neh 3.26
life of every l. thing and the Job 12.10
is not found in the land of the l. 28.13
It is hid from the eyes of all l., 28.21
to the house appointed for all l. 30.23
of the LORD in the land of the l.! Ps 27.13
thirsts for God, for the l. God. 42.02
uproot you from the land of the l. 52.05
who has kept us among the l., 66.09
blotted out of the book of the l.; 69.28
flesh sing for joy to the l. God. 84.02
l. things both small and great. 104.25
the LORD in the land of the l. 116.09
my portion in the land of the l. 142.05
for no man l. is righteous before 143.02
the desire of every l. thing. 145.16
than the l. who are still alive; Ecc 4.02
I saw all the l. who move about 4.15
to conduct himself before the l.? 6.08
and the l. will lay it to heart. 7.02
is joined with all the l. has hope, 9.04
for a l. dog is better than a dead 9.04
For the l. know that they will die, 9.05
a well of l. water, and flowing Sol 4.15
the dead on behalf of the l.? Is 8.19
has sent to mock the l. God, 37.04
he has sent to mock the l. God. 37.17
see the LORD in the land of the l.; 38.11
The l., the living, he thanks thee, 38.19
the l., he thanks thee, as I do this 38.19
cut off out of the land of the l., 53.08
me, the fountain of l. waters, Jer 2.13
he is the l. God and the everlasting 10.10
him off from the land of the l., 11.19
the LORD, the fountain of l. water. 17.13
pervert the words of the l. God, 23.36
have any one l. among this people 29.32
the Syrians?' So we are l. in Jerusalem." 35.11
Why should a l. man complain, a man, Lam 3.39
the likeness of four l. creatures. Eze 1.05
midst of the l. creatures there 1.13
to and fro among the l. creatures; 1.13
And the l. creatures darted to and 1.14
Now as I looked at the l. creatures, 1.15
the earth beside the l. creatures, 1.15
And when the l. creatures went, the 1.19
and when the l. creatures rose from 1.19
spirit of the l. creatures was in 1.20
spirit of the l. creatures was in 1.21
heads of the l. creatures there 1.22
wings of the l. creatures as they 3.13
These were the l. creatures that I 10.15
spirit of the l. creatures was in 10.17
These were the l. creatures that I 10.20
have a place in the land of the l. 26.20
who spread terror in the land of the l. 32.23
terror in the land of the l., and they bear 32.24
was spread in the land of the l., 32.25
spread terror in the land of the l. 32.26
mighty men was in the land of the l. 32.27
terror in the land of the l.; therefore 32.32
goes every l. creature which swarms 47.09
than all the l. has this mystery Dan 2.30
end that the l. may know that the 4.17
"O Daniel, servant of the l. God, 6.20
for he is the l. God, enduring for 6.26
said to them, "Sons of the l. God. Hos 1.10
On that day l. waters shall flow Zec 14.08
the Christ, the Son of the l. God." Mt 16.16
not God of the dead, but of the l." 22.32
to him, "I adjure you by the l. God, 26.63
not God of the dead, but of the l.; Mk 12.27
everything she had, her whole l. 12.44
And he divided his l. between them. Lk 15.12
squandered his property in loose l. 15.13
has devoured your l. with harlots, 15.30
not God of the dead, but of the l.; 20.38
put in all the l. that she had. 21.04
do you seek the l. among the dead? 24.05
he would have given you l. water." Jn 4.10
where do you get that l. water? 4.11
and told him that his son was l. 4.51
I am the l. bread which came down 6.51
As the l. Father sent me, and I live 6.57
shall flow rivers of l. water.'" 7.38
this land in which you are now l.; Ac 7.04

LIVING (cont.)
and he received l. oracles to give Ac 7.38
to be judge of the l. and the dead. 10.42
things to a l. God who made the 14.15
While we were l. in the flesh, our Rom 7.05
will be called 'sons of the l. God.'" 9.26
your bodies as a l. sacrifice, 12.01
both of the dead and of the l. 14.09
for a man is l. with his father's 1Co 5.01
to refrain from working for a l.? 9.06
should get their l. by the gospel. 9.14
first man Adam became a l. being"; 15.45
but with the Spirit of the l. God, 2Co 3.03
we are the temple of the l. God; 6.16
idols, to serve a l. and true God, 1Th 1.09
brother who is l. in idleness and 2Th 3.06
some of you are l. in idleness, 3.11
quietness and to earn their own l. 3.12
which is the church of the l. God, 1Ti 3.15
we have our hope set on the l. God, 4.10
is to judge the l. and the dead, 2Ti 4.01
you to fall away from the l. God. Heb 3.12
For the word of God is l. and active, 4.12
dead works to serve the l. God. 9.14
by the new and l. way which he 10.20
fall into the hands of the l. God. 10.31
l. in tents with Isaac and Jacob, 11.09
Zion and to the city of the l. God, 12.22
born anew to a l. hope through the 1Pe 1.03
through the l. and abiding word of 1.23
to that l. stone, rejected by men 2.04
and like l. stones be yourselves 2.05
l. in licentiousness, passions, 4.03
ready to judge the l. and the dead. 4.05
and the l. one; I died, and behold Rev 1.18
are four l. creatures, full of eyes 4.06
the first l. creature like a lion, 4.07
the second l. creature like an ox, 4.07
the third l. creature with the face 4.07
and the fourth l. creature like a 4.07
And the four l. creatures, each of 4.08
And whenever the l. creatures give 4.09
and the four l. creatures and 5.06
the four l. creatures and the 5.08
throne and the l. creatures and 5.11
And the four l. creatures said, 5.14
one of the four l. creatures say, 6.01
I heard the second l. creature say, 6.03
I heard the third l. creature say, 6.05
of the four l. creatures saying, "A 6.06
of the fourth l. creature say, 6.07
sun, with the seal of the l. God, 7.02
elders and the four l. creatures, 7.11
guide them to springs of l. water; 7.17
a third of the l. creatures in the 8.09
before the four l. creatures and 14.03
And one of the four l. creatures 15.07
and every l. thing died that was in 16.03
and the four l. creatures fell 19.04

LIZARD
the great l. according to its kind, Lev 11.29
the l., the sand lizard, and the 11.30
the sand l., and the chameleon. 11.30
the l. you can take in your hands, Pro 30.28

LO
and l., in her mouth a freshly Gen 8.11
and l., a dread and great darkness 15.12
and l., the smoke of the land went 19.28
and l., three flocks of sheep lying 29.02
and l., my sheaf arose and stood 37.07
"L., having me my master has no 39.08
and l., God has let me see your 48.11
and l., the babe was crying. Ex 2.06
and l., the bush was burning, yet it 3.02
"L., your father-in-law Jethro is 18.06
"L., I am coming to you in a thick 19.09
"L., I have come to you! Have I now 22.38
and l., he and all the princes of 23.06
l., a people dwelling alone, and not 23.09
l., he was standing beside his 23.17
and l., he has made shameful Deu 22.17
and now, l., I am this day eighty-five Jos 14.10
and l., a cake of barley bread Ju 7.13
for l., you shall conceive and bear 13.05
"L., you see the man is mad; 1Sa 21.14
L., this day your eyes have seen 24.10
and, l., he was holding a feast in 25.36
and l., the chariots and the 2Sa 1.06
and l., Zadok came also, with all 15.24
"L., I have sinned, and I have done 24.17
for, l., he has laid hold of the 1Ki 1.51
L., fire came down from heaven, and 2Ki 1.14
and l., they were in the midst of 6.20
and, l., all the way was littered 7.15
l., a marauding band was seen and 13.21
For l., our fathers have fallen by 2Ch 29.09
L., this we have searched out; Job 5.27
L., he passes by me, and I see him 9.11
"L., my eye has seen all this, my 13.01
L., these are but the outskirts of 26.14
for l., the wicked bend the bow, Ps 11.02
l., he was no more; though I sought 37.36
Then I said, "L., I come; in the roll 40.07
l., I have not restrained my lips, 40.09
For l., the kings assembled, they 48.04
For, l., they lie in wait for my 59.03
l., he sends forth his voice, his 68.33
For l., those who are far from thee 73.27
For l., thy enemies are in tumult; 83.02
For, l., thy enemies, O LORD, for, lo, 92.09
l., thy enemies shall perish; 92.09
L., sons are a heritage from the 127.03
L., thus shall the man be blessed 128.04
L., we heard of it in Ephrathah, we 132.06
l., O LORD, thou knowest it altogether. 139.04
And l., a woman meets him, dressed Pro 7.10
and l., it was all overgrown with 24.31
for l., the winter is past, the rain Sol 2.11
and l., swiftly, speedily it comes! Is 5.26
"L., this is our God; we have waited 25.09
L., it was for my welfare that I 38.17
L., these shall come from afar, and 49.12
and l., these from the north and 49.12
For, l., I am calling all the tribes Jer 1.15
and l., it was waste and void; 4.23
and l., they were quaking, and all 4.24
I looked, and l., there was no man, 4.25
I looked, and l., the fruitful land 4.26
l., they have rejected the word of 8.09
for l., I will save you from afar, 30.10
for l., I will save you from afar, 46.27
L., she shall be the last of the 50.12
l., a written scroll was in it; Eze 2.09
and, l., the glory of the LORD stood 3.23
l., a form that had the appearance 8.02
the wall, l., there was a door. 8.08
L., they put the branch to their 8.17
And l., six men came from the 9.02
And l., the man clothed in linen, 9.11
L., it is given the fire for fuel; 15.04
And l., this is what they did in my 23.39
was sent, and l., they came. 23.40
Egypt's doom; for l., it comes! 30.09
and l., it has not been bound up, to 30.21
And, l., you are to them like one 33.32
and l., they were very dry. 37.02
and l., another, like a leopard, with Dan 7.06
l., the prince of Greece will come. 10.20
For l., he who forms the mountains, Amo 4.13
and l., it was the latter growth 7.01
"For l., I will command, and shake 9.09
For l., I am rousing the Chaldeans, Hab 1.06
l., it came to little; and when you Hag 1.09
for l., I come and I will dwell in Zec 2.10

LO (cont.)
But l., the Lord will strip her of Zec 9.04
L., your king comes to you; triumphant 9.09
L., I will cause men to fall each 11.06
For l., I am raising up in the land 11.16
"L. I am about to make Jerusalem a 12.02
and l., the star which they had Mt 2.09
and l., a voice from heaven, saying, 3.17
when l., a bright cloud overshadowed 17.05
"L., we have left everything and 19.27
'L., here is the Christ!' or 'There he is!' 24.23
L., I have told you beforehand. 24.25
'L., he is in the wilderness.' do 24.26
if they say, 'L., he is in the inner 24.26
will see him. L., I have told you." 28.07
and l., I am with you always, to the 28.20
"L., we have left everything and Mk 10.28
'L., these three years I have come Lk 13.07
'L., these many years I have served 15.29
nor will they say, 'L., here it is!' 17.21
And they will say to you, 'L., there!' 17.23
or 'L., here!' Do not go, 17.23
"L., we have left our homes and 18.28
and l., God has granted you all Ac 27.24
L.! I tell you a mystery. 1Co 15.51
Then I said, 'L., I have come to do Heb 10.07
"L., I have come to do thy will." 10.09
and l., in heaven an open door! Rev 4.01
and l., a throne stood in heaven, 4.02
l., the Lion of the tribe of Judah, 5.05
and l., on Mount Zion stood the 14.01
and l., a white cloud, and seated on 14.14
("L., I am coming like a thief! 16.15

LOAD
l. your beasts and go back to the Gen 45.17
for you l. men with burdens hard to Lk 11.46
man will have to bear his own l. Gal 6.05

LOADED
Then they l. their asses with their Gen 42.26
and every man l. his ass, and they 44.13
ten asses l. with the good things 45.23
and ten she-asses l. with grain, 45.23
you carry are l. as burdens on Is 46.01

LOADING
of grain and l. them on asses; Neh 13.15

LOADS
goods of Damascus, forty camel l. 2Ki 8.09
He l. the thick cloud with moisture; Job 37.11
and boys stagger under l. of wood. Lam 5.13
and l. himself with pledges!" Hab 2.06

LOAF
and one l. of bread, and one cake of Ex 29.23
a piece of silver or a l. of bread, 1Sa 2.36
to each a l. of bread, a portion of 1Ch 16.03
may be hired for a l. of bread, Pro 6.26
and a l. of bread was given him Jer 37.21
you, if his son asks him for a l., Mt 7.09
had only one l. with them in the Mk 8.14
Because there is one l., we who are 1Co 10.17
for we all partake of the same l. 10.17

LOAN
your neighbor a l. of any sort, Deu 24.10
you make the l. shall bring the 24.11
woman for the l. which she lent to 1Sa 2.20

LOATH
though he is l. to let it go, and Job 20.13

LOATHE
Egyptians will l. to drink water Ex 7.18
and we l. this worthless food." Num 21.05
I l. my life; I would not live Job 7.16
regard not myself; I l. my life. 9.21
"I l. my life; I will give 10.01
And do I not l. them that rise up Ps 139.21
Does thy soul l. Zion? Jer 14.19
and you shall l. yourselves for all Eze 20.43
and you will l. yourselves for your 36.31

LOATHED
For forty years I l. that generation Ps 95.10
they l. any kind of food, and they 107.18
like a l. untimely birth, clothed Is 14.19
you loved and all those you l.; Eze 16.37
who l. her husband and her children; 16.45
who l. their husbands and their 16.45

LOATHES
so that his life l. bread, and his Job 33.20
He who is sated l. honey, but to one Pro 27.07

LOATHSOME
nostrils and becomes l. to you, Num 11.20
Job with l. sores from the sole of Job 2.07
they are as food that is l. to me. 6.07
l. to the sons of my own mother. 19.17
they will be l. in their own sight Eze 6.09
and l. beasts, and all the idols of 8.10

LOAVES
dwellings two l. of bread to be Lev 23.17
give l. of bread to the people who Ju 8.05
another carrying three l. of bread, 1Sa 10.03
you and give you two l. of bread, 10.04
and these ten l., and carry them 17.17
Give me five l. of bread, or whatever 21.03
haste, and took two hundred l., 25.18
bearing two hundred l. of bread, 2Sa 16.01
Take with you ten l., some cakes, 1Ki 14.03
twenty l. of barley, and fresh ears 2Ki 4.42
these stones to become l. of bread." Mt 4.03
have only five l. here and two 14.17
taking the five l. and the two 14.19
and gave the l. to the disciples, 14.19
said to them, "How many l. have you?" 15.34
he took the seven l. and the fish, 15.36
the five l. of the five thousand, 16.09
Or the seven l. of the four thousand, 16.10
said to them, "How many l. have you? Mk 6.38
And taking the five l. and the two 6.41
and broke the l., and gave them to 6.41
who ate the l. were five thousand 6.44
did not understand about the l., 6.52
asked them, "How many l. have you?" 8.05
and he took the seven l., and having 8.06
broke the five l. for the five 8.19
no more than five l. and two fish— Lk 9.13
And taking the five l. and the two 9.16
to him, 'Friend, lend me three l.; 11.05
has five barley l. and two fish; Jn 6.09
Jesus then took the l., and when he 6.11
fragments from the five barley l., 6.13
you ate your fill of the l. 6.26

LOCAL
together the l. leaders of the Ac 28.17

LOCK
and took me by a l. of my head; Eze 8.03

LOCKED
roof chamber upon him, and l. them. Ju 3.23
doors of the roof chamber were l., 3.24
A garden l. is my sister, my bride, a Sol 4.12
a garden l., a fountain sealed. 4.12
prison securely l. and the sentries Ac 5.23

LOCKS
shall let the l. of hair of his Num 6.05
weave the seven l. of my head with Ju 16.13
took the seven l. of his head and 16.14
shave off the seven l. of his head. 16.19

LOCKS (cont.)
my l. with the drops of the night. Sol 5.02
his l. are wavy, black as a raven. 5.11
your flowing l. are like purple; 7.05
heads or let their l. grow long; Eze 44.20

LOCUST
not a single l. was left in all the Ex 10.19
the l. according to its kind, the Lev 11.22
the bald l. according to its kind, 11.22
for the l. shall consume it. Deu 28.38
your ground the l. shall possess. 28.42
or mildew or l. or caterpillar; 1Ki 8.37
or mildew or l. or caterpillar; 2Ch 6.28
or command the l. to devour the 7.13
Do you make him leap like the l.? Job 39.20
the fruit of their labor to the l. Ps 78.46
at evening; I am shaken off like a l. 109.23
What the cutting l. left, Joe 1.04
left, the swarming l. has eaten. 1.04
What the swarming l. left, 1.04
the hopping l. has eaten, and what 1.04
and what the hopping l. left, 1.04
left, the destroying l. has eaten. 1.04
which the swarming l. has eaten, 2.25
your olive trees the l. devoured; Amo 4.09
It will devour you like the l. Nah 3.15
Multiply yourselves like the l., 3.15
The l. spreads its wings and flies 3.16

LOCUSTS
I will bring l. into your country, Ex 10.04
over the land of Egypt for the l., 10.12
the east wind had brought the l. 10.13
And the l. came up over all the 10.14
dense swarm of l. as had never 10.14
lifted the l. and drove them into 10.19
tents, coming like l. for number; Ju 6.05
the valley like l. for multitude; 7.12
l. came, and young l. without number; Ps 105.34
the l. have no king, yet all of them Pro 30.27
as l. leap, men leap upon it. Is 33.04
they are more numerous than l.; Jer 46.23
as many as l., and they shall raise 51.14
bring up horses like bristling l. 51.27
he was forming l. in the beginning Amo 7.01
like clouds of l. settling on the Nah 3.17
and his food was l. and wild honey. Mt 3.04
waist, and ate l. and wild honey. Mk 1.06
the smoke came l. on the earth, Rev 9.03
In appearance the l. were like 9.07

LOD
built Ono and L. with its towns, 1Ch 8.12
The sons of L., Hadid, and Ono, seven Ez 2.33
The sons of L., Hadid, and Ono, seven Neh 7.37
L., and Ono, the valley of craftsmen. 11.35
the L., the God of Israel, who call Is 45.03

LODEBAR
of Machir the son of Ammiel, at L. 2Sa 9.04
of Machir the son of Ammiel, at L. 9.05
Machir the son of Ammiel from L., 17.27
you who rejoice in L., who say, Amo 6.13

LODGE
father's house for us to l. in?" Gen 24.23
provender enough, and room to l. in." 24.25
"L. here this night, and I will Num 22.08
in the place where you l. tonight.'" Jos 4.03
l. here and let your heart be merry; Ju 19.09
go, and where you l. I will l.; Ru 1.16
'Do not l. tonight at the fords of 2Sa 17.16
"Why do you l. before the wall? Neh 13.21
I would l. in the wilderness, Ps 55.07
the fields, and l. in the villages; Sol 7.11
like a l. in a cucumber field, like Is 1.08
at Geba they l. for the night; 10.29
the thickets in Arabia you will l., 21.13
your evil thoughts l. within you? Jer 4.14
hedgehog shall l. in her capitals; Zep 2.14
to l. and get provisions; for we are Lk 9.12
disciple, with whom we should l. Ac 21.16

LODGED
So he l. there that night, and took Gen 32.13
and he himself l. that night in the 32.21
whose name was Rahab, and l. there. Jos 2.01
and l. there before they passed 3.01
them to the place where they l. 4.08
the house of Micah, and l. there. Ju 18.02
they ate and drank, and l. there. 19.04
urged him, till he l. there again. 19.07
the ark was l. at Kiriathjearim, a 1Sa 7.02
where he l., and laid him upon his 1Ki 17.19
he came to a cave and l. there; 19.09
And they l. round about the house 1Ch 9.27
kinds of wares l. outside Jerusalem Neh 13.20
sojourner has not l. in the street; Job 31.32
Righteousness l. in her, but now Is 1.21
the city to Bethany and l. there. Mt 21.17
he went out and l. on the mount Lk 21.37

LODGES
for anger l. in the bosom of fools. Ecc 7.09

LODGING
his ass provender at the l. place, Gen 42.27
we came to the l. place we opened 43.21
At a l. place on the way the LORD Ex 4.24
the desert a wayfarers' l. place, Jer 9.02
he is l. with Simon, a tanner, whose Ac 10.06
who was called Peter was l. there. 10.18
he is l. in the house of Simon, a 10.32
to him at his l. in great numbers. 28.23

LOFTILY
l. they threaten oppression. Ps 73.08

LOFTINESS
of his l., his pride, and his Jer 48.29

LOFTY
the highest stars, how l. they are! Job 22.12
From thy l. abode thou waterest the Ps 104.13
how l. are their eyes, how high Pro 30.13
against all that is proud and l., Is 2.12
of Lebanon, l. and lifted up; 2.13
and against all the l. hills; 2.14
and the l. will be brought low. 10.33
inhabitants of the height, the l. city. 26.05
And upon every l. mountain and 30.25
Upon a high and l. mountain you 57.07
the high and l. One who inhabits 57.15
made yourself a l. place in every Eze 16.24
you built your l. place and 16.25
and making your l. place in every 16.31
and break down your l. places; 16.39
sprig from the l. top of the cedar, 17.22
it upon a high and l. mountain; 17.22
may grow to l. height or set their 31.14
and against the l. battlements. Zep 1.16
of God in l. words or wisdom. 1Co 2.01

LOG
mixed with oil, and one l. of oil. Lev 14.10
offering, along with the l. of oil, 14.12
shall take some of the l. of oil, 14.15
a cereal offering, and a l. of oil; 14.21
and the l. of oil, and the priest 14.24
and each of us get there a l., 2Ki 6.02
But as one was felling a l., 6.05
not notice the l. that is in your Mt 7.03
there is the l. in your own eye? 7.04
first take the l. out of your own 7.05
not notice the l. that is in your Lk 6.41

LOG (cont.)
do not see the l. that is in your Lk 6.42
first take the l. out of your own 6.42

LOGS
he who splits l. is endangered by Ecc 10.09
of the flock, pile the l. under it; Eze 24.05
Heap on the l., kindle the fire, 24.10

LOINS
and put sackcloth upon his l., Gen 37.34
your l. girded, your sandals on your Ex 12.11
from the l. to the thighs they 28.42
the fat that is on them at the l., Lev 3.04
the fat that is on them at the l., 3.10
the fat that is on them at the l., 3.15
the fat that is on them at the l., 4.09
he fat that is on them at the l., 7.04
crush the l. of his adversaries, of Deu 33.11
in its sheath fastened upon his l., 2Sa 20.08
blood upon the girdle about my l., 1Ki 2.05
is thicker than my father's l. 12.10
girded up his l. and ran before 18.46
sackcloth on our l. and ropes upon 20.31
So they girded sackcloth on their l., 20.32
a girdle of leather about his l. 2Ki 1.08
"Gird up your l., and take my staff 4.29
"Gird up your l., and take this 9.01
is thicker than my father's l. 2Ch 10.10
and binds a waistcloth on their l. Job 12.18
fat, and gathered fat upon his l., 15.27
if his l. have not blessed me, and 31.20
Gird up your l. like a man, I will 38.03
"Gird up your l. like a man; 40.07
Behold, his strength in his l., 40.16
For my l. are filled with burning, Ps 38.07
didst lay affliction on our l.; 66.11
and make their l. tremble continually. 69.23
She girds her l. with strength and Pro 31.17
faithfulness the girdle of his l. Is 11.05
from your l. and take off your 20.02
Therefore my l. are filled with 21.03
and gird sackcloth upon your l. 32.11
him and ungird the l. of kings, 45.01
came forth from the l. of Judah; 48.01
But you, gird up your l.; Jer 1.17
waistcloth, and put it on your l., 13.01
of the LORD, and put it on my l. 13.02
have bought, which is upon your l., 13.04
waistcloth clings to the l. of a man, 13.11
hands on his l. like a woman in 30.06
gashes, and on the l. is sackcloth. 48.37
of his l. I saw as it were gleaming Eze 1.27
of his l. I saw as it were the 1.27
appeared to be his l. it was fire, 8.02
and above his l. it was like the 8.02
girded with belts on their l., 23.15
and made all their l. to shake; 29.07
and linen breeches upon their l.; 44.18
the water; and it was up to the l. 47.04
whose l. were girded with gold of Dan 10.05
I will bring sackcloth upon all l., Amo 8.10
Gird your l.; collect all your Nah 2.01
tremble, anguish is on all l., 2.10
"Let your l. be girded and your Lk 12.35
having girded your l. with truth, Eph 6.14
still in the l. of his ancestor Heb 7.10

LOIS
grandmother L. and your mother 2Ti 1.05

LONELY
for I am l. and afflicted. Ps 25.16
I am like a l. bird on the housetop. 102.07
How l. sits the city that was full Lam 1.01
in a boat to a l. place apart. Mt 14.13
"This is a l. place and the day is 14.15
he rose and went out to a l. place, Mk 1.35
away by yourselves to a l. place, 6.31
the boat to a l. place by themselves. 6.32
"This is a l. place, and the hour is 6.35
departed and went into a l. place. Lk 4.42
for we are here in a l. place." 9.12

LONG
When he had been there a l. time, Gen 26.08
he made him a l. robe with sleeves. 37.03
the l. robe with sleeves that he 37.23
and they sent the l. robe with 37.32
led me all my life l. to this day, 48.15
'How l. will you refuse to humble Ex 10.03
"How l. shall this man be a snare 10.07
"How l. do you refuse to keep my 16.28
When the trumpet sounds a l. blast, 19.13
days may be l. in the land which 20.12
five cubits l. and five cubits 27.01
a hundred cubits l. for one side; 27.09
be hangings a hundred cubits l., 27.11
shall be a screen twenty cubits l., 27.16
twenty cubits l. and five cubits 38.18
unclean as l. as he has the Lev 13.46
a multilated face or limb too l., 21.18
has a part too l. or too short you 22.23
And you shall eat old store l. kept, 26.10
its sabbaths as l. as it lies 26.34
As l. as it lies desolate it shall 26.35
locks of hair of his head grow l. Num 6.05
as l. as the cloud rested over the 9.18
"How l. will this people despise me? 14.11
And how l. will they not believe in 14.11
"How l. shall this wicked congregation 14.27
and we dwelt in Egypt a l. time; 20.15
all your life l. to this day? 22.30
How l. shall Asshur take you away 24.22
'You have stayed l. enough at this Deu 1.06
this mountain country l. enough; 2.03
you will not live l. upon it, 4.26
you may live l. in the land which 5.33
you may live l. in the land which 11.09
as l. as the heavens are above the 11.21
the Levite as l. as you live in 12.19
And if the way is too l. for you, 14.24
he may continue l. in his kingdom, 17.20
overtake him, because the way is l., 19.06
"When you besiege a city for a l. time, 20.19
with you, and that you may live l. 22.07
shall not live l. in the land 30.18
as l. as you live in the land which 31.13
you shall live l. in the land 32.47
he encompasses him all the day l., 33.12
they make a l. blast with the ram's Jos 6.05
worn out from the very l. journey. 9.13
Joshua made war a l. time with all 11.18
"How l. will you be slack to go in 18.03
A l. time afterward, when the LORD 23.01
lived in the wilderness a l. time. 24.07
Why is his chariot so l. in coming? Ju 5.28
as l. as the house of God was at 18.31
"How l. will you be drunken? Put away 1Sa 1.14
as l. as he lives, he is lent to the 1.28
a l. time passed, some twenty years, 7.02
people shouted, "L. live the king!" 10.24
"How l. will you grieve over Saul, 16.01
For as l. as the son of Jesse lives 20.31
fields, as l. as we went with them; 25.15
be found in you so l. as you live. 25.28
How l. will it be before you bid 2Sa 2.26
there was a l. war between the 3.01
was wearing a l. robe with sleeves; 13.18
"L. live the king! L. live the king!" 16.16
and saying 'L. live King Adonijah!' 1Ki 1.25
and say, 'L. live King Solomon!' 1.34
people said "L. live King Solomon!" 1.39
for yourself l. life or riches or 3.11
for the LORD was sixty cubits l., 6.02
of the house was twenty cubits l., 6.03

LONG (cont.)

sanctuary, was forty cubits l. 1Ki 6.17
sanctuary was twenty cubits l., 6.20
each stand was four cubits l., 7.27
poles were so l. that the ends of 8.08
gone up to Jerusalem l. enough. 12.28
"How l. will you go limping with 18.21
so l. as the harlotries and the 2Ki 9.22
hands, and said, "L. live the king!" 11.12
heard that I determined it l. ago? 19.25
day a portion, as l. as he lived. 25.30
and have not even asked l. life, 2Ch 1.11
of the house was twenty cubits l., 3.04
twenty cubits l., and twenty cubits 4.01
poles were so l. that the ends of 5.09
a bronze platform five cubits l., 6.13
For a l. time Israel was without 15.03
and they said, "L. live the king." 23.11
and as l. as he sought the LORD, 26.05
"How l. will you be gone, and when Neh 2.06
so l. as I see Mordecai the Jew Est 5.13
who l. for death, but it comes not, Job 3.21
But the night is l., and I am 7.04
How l. wilt thou not look away from 7.19
"How l. will you say these things, 8.02
thou wouldest l. for the work of 14.15
"How l. will you hunt for words? 18.02
"How l. will you torment me, and 19.02
as l. as my breath is in me, and the 27.03
Do not l. for the night, when 36.20
O men, how l. shall my honor suffer Ps 4.02
How l. will you love vain words, and 4.02
troubled. But thou, O LORD—how l.? 6.03
How l., O Lord? Wilt thou forget 13.01
How l. wilt thou hide thy face from 13.01
How l. must I bear pain in my soul, 13.02
How l. shall my enemy be exalted 13.02
for thee I wait all the day l. 25.05
through my groaning all day l. 32.03
How l., O LORD, wilt thou look on? 35.17
and of thy praise all the day l. 35.28
meditate treachery all the day l. 38.12
so l. as the wicked are in my 39.01
All day l. my disgrace is before me, 44.15
sake we are slain all the day l., 44.22
all day l. foremen oppress me; 56.01
enemies trample upon me all day l., 56.02
All day l. they seek to injure my 56.05
How l. will you set upon a man to 62.03
So I will bless thee as l. as I live; 63.04
thy righteous help all the day l., 71.24
and as l. as the moon, throughout 72.05
L. may he live, may gold of Sheba be 72.15
his fame continue as l. as the sun! 72.17
For all the day l. I have been 73.14
is none among us who knows how l. 74.09
How l., O God, is the foe to scoff? 74.10
old, I remember the years l. ago. 77.05
How l., O LORD? Wilt thou be angry 79.05
how l. wilt thou be angry with thy 80.04
"How l. will you judge unjustly and 82.02
surround me like a flood all day l.; 88.17
his throne as l. as the sun before 89.36
How l., O LORD? Wilt thou hide 89.46
How l. will thy wrath burn like 89.46
How l.? Have pity on thy 90.13
With l. life I will satisfy him, and 91.16
O LORD, how l. shall the wicked, 94.03
how l. shall the wicked exult? 94.03
with good as l. as you live so 103.05
sing to the LORD as l. as I live; 104.33
I will call on him as l. as I live. 116.02
Behold, I l. for thy precepts; 119.40
How l. must thy servant endure? 119.84
because I l. for thy commandments. 119.131
L. have I known from thy testimonies 119.152
I l. for thy salvation, O LORD, and 119.174
Too l. have I had my dwelling among 120.06
Too l. our soul has been sated with 123.04
they made l. their furrows. 129.03
sit in darkness like those l. dead. 143.03
praise the LORD as l. as I live; 146.02
"How l., O simple ones, will you Pro 1.22
How l. will scoffers delight in 1.22
L. life is in her right hand; 3.16
How l. will you lie there, O sluggard? 6.09
he has gone on a l. journey; 7.19
All day l. the wicked covets, but 21.26
Those who tarry l. over wine, 23.30
its stability will l. continue, 28.02
all will have been l. forgotten. Ecc 2.16
themselves as l. as they live; 3.12
Then I said, "How l., O Lord?" Is 6.11
for him who planned it l. ago. 22.11
burning place has l. been prepared; 30.33
heard that I determined it l. ago? 37.26
For a l. time I have held my peace, 42.14
Who told this l. ago? Who declared 45.21
They are created now, not l. ago; 48.07
of old, the generations of l. ago. 51.09
even for a l. time, and so you do 57.11
in our sins we have been a l. time, 64.05
my chosen shall l. enjoy the work 65.22
"For l. ago you broke your yoke and Jer 2.20
How l. shall your evil thoughts 4.14
How l. must I see the standard, and 4.21
How l. will the land mourn, and the 12.04
How l. will it be before you are 13.27
a reproach and derision all day l. 20.08
to which they will l. to return, 22.27
How l. shall there be lies in the 23.26
saying, "Your exile will be l.; 29.28
How l. will you waver, O faithless 31.22
that they may last for a l. time. 32.14
how l. will you gash yourselves? 47.05
How l. till you are quiet? Put yourself 47.06
day of his death as l. as he lived. 52.34
me stunned, faint all the day l. Lam 1.13
as he ordained l. ago, he has demolished 2.17
again and again the whole day l. 3.03
darkness like the dead of l. ago. 3.06
burden of their songs all day l. 3.14
are against me all the day l. 3.62
why dost thou so l. forsake us? 5.20
so l. shall you bear the punishment Eze 4.05
Israel, saying, 'The days grow l., 12.22
with great wings and l. pinions, 17.03
grew large and its branches l., 31.05
the man's hand was six l. cubits, 40.05
one reed l., and one reed broad; 40.07
twenty-five cubits l. and five 40.30
offering, a cubit and a half l., 40.42
a handbreadth l., were fastened 40.43
the court, a hundred cubits l., 40.47
a full reed of six l. cubits. 41.08
the temple, a hundred cubits l.; 41.13
its walls, a hundred cubits l.; 41.13
two cubits l., and two cubits broad; 41.22
wide and hundred cubits l., 42.04
the chambers, fifty cubits l. 42.07
outer court were fifty cubits l., 42.08
temple were a hundred cubits l. 42.08
hundred cubits l. and five hundred 42.20
twelve cubits l. by twelve broad. 43.16
fourteen cubits l. by fourteen 43.17
heads or let their locks grow l.; 44.20
thousand cubits l. and twenty 45.01
thousand cubits l. and ten thousand 45.03
thousand cubits l. and ten thousand 45.05
and twenty-five thousand cubits l.; 45.06
forty cubits l. and thirty broad; 46.22
Belteshazzar, was dismayed for a l. time, Dan 4.19
hair grew as l. as eagles' feathers, 4.33
"For how l. is the vision concerning 8.13
"How l. shall it be till the end of 12.06
How l. will it be till they are Hos 8.05

LONG (cont.)
pursues the east wind all day l.; Hos 12.01
O LORD, how l. shall I cry for help Hab 1.02
up what is not his own—for how l.?— 2.06
how l. wilt thou have no mercy on Zec 1.12
guests mourn as l. as the bridegroom Mt 9.15
have repented l. ago in sackcloth 11.21
how l. am I to be with you? How l. am I 17.17
phylacteries broad and their fringes l., 23.05
for a pretense you make l. prayers; * 23.14
Now after a l. time the master of 25.19
As l. as they have the bridegroom Mk 2.19
some of them have come a l. way." 8.03
how l. am I to be with you? 9.19
How l. am I to bear with you? 9.19
"How l. has he had this?" And he said, 9.21
who like to go about in l. robes, 12.38
and for a pretense make l. prayers. 12.40
for a l. time he had worn no Lk 8.27
how l. am I to be with you and bear 9.41
they would have repented l. ago, 10.13
Will he delay l. over them? 18.07
another country for a l. while. 20.09
who like to go about in l. robes, 20.46
and for a pretense make l. prayers. 20.47
for he had l. desired to see him, 23.08
he had been lying there a l. time, Jn 5.06
As l. as I am in the world, I am the 9.05
"How l. will you keep us in suspense? 10.24
to him, "Have I been with you so l., 14.09
because for a l. time he had amazed Ac 8.11
So they remained for a l. time, 14.03
he coversed with them a l. while, 20.11
They have known for a l. time, 26.05
And Paul said, "Whether short or l., 26.29
As they had been l. without food, 27.21
had waited a l. time and saw no 28.06
For I l. to see you, that I may Rom 1.11
to her husband as l. as he lives; 7.02
we are being killed all the day l.; 8.36
"All day l. I have held out my 10.21
which was kept secret for l. ages 16.25
to her husband as l. as he lives. 1Co 7.39
a man to wear l. hair is degrading 11.14
but if a woman has l. hair, 11.15
and l. to put on our heavenly 2Co 5.02
while they l. for you and pray for 9.14
as l. as he is a child, is no better Gal 4.01
that you may live l. on the earth. Eph 6.03
brethren, whom I love and l. for, Php 4.01
remember us kindly and l. to see us, 1Th 3.06
to see us, as we l. to see you— 3.06
I l. night and day to see you, that 2Ti 1.04
as l. as it is called "today," that Heb 3.13
through David so l. afterward, 4.07
yet opened as l. as the outer tent 9.08
not in force as l. as the one who 9.17
into which angels l. to look. 1Pe 1.12
l. for the pure spiritual milk, that 2.20
as l. as I am in this body, to 2Pe 1.13
word of God heavens existed l. ago, 3.05
by some who l. ago were designated Jud 1.04
clothed with a l. robe and with a Rev 1.13
how l. before thou wilt judge and 6.10
they will l. to die, and death flies 9.06

LONGED
because you l. greatly for your Gen 31.30
of the king l. to go forth to 2Sa 13.39
the twilight I l. for has been Is 21.04
Ah, this is the day we l. for; Lam 2.16
Thus you l. for the lewdness of Eze 23.21
righteous men l. to see what you Mt 13.17
since I have l. for many years to Rom 15.23
which thy soul l. has gone from Rev 18.14

LONGER
it shall no l. yield to you its Gen 4.12
No l. shall your name be Abram, but 17.05
no l. shall your name be called 35.10
hide him no l. she took for him a Ex 2.03
"You shall no l. give the people 5.07
you go, and you shall stay no l." 9.28
and the rain no l. poured upon the 9.33
or a l. time, that the cloud continued Num 9.22
your heart, and be no l. stubborn. Deu 10.16
I am no l. able to go out and come 31.02
they are no l. his children because 32.05
there was no l. any spirit in them, Jos 5.01
they could no l. withstand their Ju 2.14
and her countenance was no l. sad. 1Sa 1.18
seeking me any l. within the 27.01
should I wait for the LORD any l.?" 2Ki 6.33
the Levites no l. need to carry 1Ch 23.26
you need no l. carry it upon your 2Ch 35.03
that we may no l. suffer disgrace." Neh 2.17
Its measure is l. than the earth, Job 11.09
their name is no l. remembered; 24.20
for there is no l. any that is Ps 12.01
there is no l. any prophet, and 74.09
king, who will no l. take advice, Ecc 4.13
so that it will no l. be a people.) Is 7.08
LORD, when it shall no l. be said, Jer 16.14
the LORD, when men shall no l. say, 23.07
In those days they shall no l. say: 31.29
And no l. shall each man teach his 31.34
they are no l. a nation in their 33.24
The LORD could no l. bear your evil 44.22
be destroyed and be no l. a people, 48.42
nations shall no l. flow to him; 51.44
"They shall stay with us no l." Lam 4.15
he will keep you in exile no l.; 4.22
It will no l. be delayed, but in Eze 12.25
of my words will be delayed any l., 12.28
you shall speak and be no l. dumb. 24.27
there shall no l. be a prince in 30.13
was opened, and I was no l. dumb. 33.22
no l. shall the shepherds feed 34.10
flock, they shall no l. be a prey; 34.22
and no l. suffer the reproach of 34.29
you shall no l. bereave them of 36.12
therefore you shall no l. devour 36.14
men and no l. bereave your nation 36.14
you shall no l. bear the disgrace 36.15
peoples and no l. cause your 36.15
they shall be no l. two nations, 37.22
and no l. divided into two kingdoms. 37.22
and no l. will you call me, 'My Hos 2.16
you shall no l. be haughty in my Zep 3.11
For I will no l. have pity on the Zec 11.06
there shall no l. be a trader in 14.21
because he no l. regards the Mal 2.13
It is no l. good for anything Mt 5.13
So they are no l. two but one. 19.06
Jesus could no l. openly enter a Mk 1.45
that there was no l. room for them, 2.02
then you no l. permit him to do 7.12
around they no l. saw any one with 9.08
So they are no l. two but one. 10.08
I am no l. worthy to be called your Lk 15.19
I am no l. worthy to be called your 15.21
for you can no l. be steward.' 16.02
For they no l. dared to ask him any 20.40
"It is no l. because of your words Jn 4.42
back and no l. went about with him. 6.66
"I shall be with you a little l., 7.33
stayed two days l. in the place 11.06
Jesus therefore no l. went about 11.54
light is with you for a little l. 12.35
I will no l. talk much with you, for 14.30
No l. do I call you servants, for 15.15
she no l. remembers the anguish, for 16.21
when I shall no l. speak to you in 16.25
After this Paul stayed many days l., Ac 18.18
asked him to stay for a l. period, 18.20

LONGER (cont.)
deep sleep as Paul talked still l.; Ac 20.09
that he ought not to live any l. 25.24
and we might no l. be enslaved to Rom 6.06
death no l. has dominion over him. 6.09
So then it is no l. I that do it, 7.17
it is no l. I that do it, but sin 7.20
it is no l. on the basis of works; 11.06
otherwise grace would no l. be grace. 11.06
you are no l. walking in love. 14.15
since I no l. have any room for 15.23
might live no l. for themselves 2Co 5.15
of view, we regard him thus no l. 5.16
it is no l. I who live, but Christ Gal 2.20
by the law, it is no l. by promise; 3.18
we are no l. under a custodian; 3.25
God you are no l. a slave but a 4.07
So then you are no l. strangers and Eph 2.19
so that we may no l. be children, 4.14
you must no l. live as the Gentiles 4.17
Let the thief no l. steal, but rather 4.28
Therefore when we could bear it no l., 1Th 3.01
reason, when I could bear it no l., 3.05
No l. drink only water, but use a 1Ti 5.23
no l. as a slave but more than a Phm 1.16
they would no l. have any consciousness Heb 10.02
there is no l. any offering for sin. 10.18
there no l. remains a sacrifice for 10.26
in the flesh no l. by human passions 1Pe 4.02
robe and told to rest a little l., Rev 6.11
there was no l. any place for them 12.08

LONG-HAIRED
from the l. heads of the enemy. Deu 32.42

LONGING
and fail with l. for them all the Deu 28.32
Lord, all my l. is known to thee, my Ps 38.09
consumed with l. for thy ordinances 119.20
with eager l. for the revealing of Rom 8.19
in you, as he told us of your l., 2Co 7.07
what l., what zeal, what punishment! 7.11
for he has been l. for you all, Php 2.26

LONGINGLY
And David said l., "O that some one 2Sa 23.15
And David said l., "O that some one 1Ch 11.17

LONGS
my son Shechem l. for your daughter; Gen 34.08
Like a slave who l. for the shadow, Job 7.02
him in the safety for which he l. Ps 12.05
As a hart l. for flowing streams, so 42.01
so l. my soul for thee, O God. 42.01
My soul l., yea, faints for the 84.02

LONG-SLEEVED
and rent the l. robe which she wore; 2Sa 13.19

LOOK
I will l. upon it and remember the Gen 9.16
and l. from the place where you are, 13.14
"L. toward heaven, and number the 15.05
do not l. back or stop anywhere in 19.17
"Let me not l. upon the death of 21.16
The maiden was very fair to l. upon, 24.16
because she was fair to l. upon. 26.07
you come to l. into my wages with 30.33
sons, "Why do you l. at one another?" 42.01
for he was afraid to l. at God. Ex 3.06
"The LORD l. upon you and judge, 5.21
L., you have some evil purpose in 10.10
again on the seventh day, and l.; Lev 14.39
then the priest shall go and l.; 14.44
not go in to l. upon the holy Num 4.20
at all but this manna to l. at." 11.06
you a tassel to l. upon and 15.39
he would l. at the bronze serpent 21.09
L. down from thy holy habitation, Deu 26.15
while your eyes l. on and fail 28.32
"L. at me, and do likewise; Ju 7.17
"L., men are coming down from the 9.36
"L., men are coming down from the 9.37
wilt indeed l. on the affliction 1Sa 1.11
Why then l. with greedy eye at my 2.29
you will l. with envious eye on 2.32
and arise, go and l. for the asses." 9.03
"L., Hebrews are coming out of the 14.11
"Do not l. on his appearance or on 16.07
'L., the arrows are on this side of 20.21
'L., the arrows are beyond you,' 20.22
that you should l. upon a dead dog 2Sa 9.08
"L., go back to the city in peace, 15.27
the LORD will l. upon my affliction, 16.12
L. now to your own house, David." 1Ki 12.16
"Go up now, l. toward the sea." 18.43
Judah, I would neither l. at you, 2Ki 3.14
"L., yonder is the Shunammite, 4.25
L., when the messenger comes, shut 6.32
l. there for Jehu the son of 9.02
let us l. one another in the face." 14.08
L. now to your own house, David." 2Ch 10.16
let us l. one another in the face." 25.17
causing them to l. with contempt Est 1.17
The caravans of Tema l., the travelers Job 6.19
"But now, be pleased to l. at me; 6.28
long wilt thou not l. away from me, 7.19
disgrace and l. upon my affliction. 10.15
l. away from him, and desist, that he 14.06
If I l. for Sheol as my house, if I 17.13
He will not l. upon the rivers, the 20.17
L. at me, and be appalled, and lay 21.05
how then could I l. upon a virgin? 31.01
L. at the heavens, and see; 35.05
"And now men cannot l. on the light 37.21
and l. on every one that is proud, 40.11
L. on every one that is proud, and 40.12
When I l. at thy heavens, the work Ps 8.03
L. to him, and be radiant; so your 34.05
How long, O LORD, wilt thou l. on? 35.17
though you l. well at his place, he 37.10
you will l. on the destruction of 37.34
L. away from me, that I may know 39.13
God will let me l. in triumph on 59.10
Why l. you with envy, O many-peaked 68.16
L. down from heaven, and see; 80.14
l. upon the face of thine anointed! 84.09
righteousness will l. down from the 85.11
You will only l. with your eyes and 91.08
I will l. with favor on the faithful 101.06
These all l. to thee, to give them 104.27
I shall l. in triumph on those who 118.07
L. on my affliction and deliver me, 119.153
I l. at the faithless with disgust, 119.158
of servants l. to the hand of 123.02
so our eyes l. to the LORD our God, 123.02
I l. to the right and watch, but 142.04
The eyes of all l. to thee, 145.15
Let your eyes l. directly forward, Pro 4.25
Do not l. at wine when it is red, 23.31
righteous will l. upon their 29.16
and those that l. through the Ecc 12.03
to l. at the blossoms of the valley, Sol 6.11
return, that we may l. upon you. 6.13
Why should you l. upon the Shulammite, 6.13
And if one l. to the land, behold, Is 5.30
and they will l. to the earth, but 8.22
They will l. aghast at one another; 13.08
their eyes will l. to the Holy One 17.07
they will not l. to what their own 17.08
is raised on the mountains, l.! 18.03
"I will quietly l. from my dwelling 18.04
"L. away from me, let me weep bitter 22.04

LOOK (cont.)
But you did not l. to him who did Is 22.11
but do not l. to the Holy One of 31.01
L. upon Zion, the city of our 33.20
I shall l. upon man no more among 38.11
But when I l. there is no one; 41.28
and l., you blind, that you may see! 42.18
l. to the rock from which you were 51.01
L. to Abraham your father and to 51.02
and l. at the earth beneath; for the heavens 51.06
comeliness that we should l. at him, 53.02
we l. for light, and behold, darkness, 59.09
we l. for justice, but there is none; 59.11
L. down from heaven and see, from 63.15
this is the man to whom I will l., 66.02
go forth and l. on the dead bodies 66.24
L. at your way in the valley; know what Jer 2.23
I will not l. on you in anger, for I 3.12
of Jerusalem, l. and take note! 5.01
Lord, do not thy eyes l. for truth? 5.03
and l., and ask for the ancient 6.16
and while you l. for light he turns 13.16
of their enemies while you l. on. 20.04
"Take him, l. after him well and do 39.12
come, and I will l. after you well; 40.04
they l. not back—terror on every 46.05
the fathers l. not back to their 47.03
"L., O Lord, and behold, for I am Lam 1.11
L. and see if there is any sorrow 1.12
L., O Lord, and see! With whom 2.20
and l. at one another in dismay, and Eze 4.17
l. with your eyes, and hear with 40.04
is I who answer and l. after you. Hos 14.08
fatted beasts I will not l. upon. Amo 5.22
shall I again l. upon thy holy Jon 2.04
I will l. to the Lord, I will wait Mic 7.07
let nations l. on your nakedness Nah 3.05
And all who l. on you will shrink 3.07
me see wrongs and l. upon trouble? Hab 1.03
L. among the nations, and see; 1.05
evil and canst not l. on wrong, 1.13
why dost thou l. on faithless men, 1.13
and l. forth to see what he will 2.01
when they l. on him whom they have Zec 12.10
do not l. dismal, like the hypocrites, Mt 6.16
L. at the birds of the air: they 6.26
come, or shall we l. for another?" 11.03
"L., your disciples are doing what 12.02
king came in to l. at the guests, 22.11
"L., why are they doing what is not Mk 2.24
but they l. like trees, walking." 8.24
and said to him, "Master, l.! 11.21
me a coin, and let me l. at it." 12.15
"L., Teacher, what wonderful stones 13.01
'L., here is the Christ!' or 'L., there he is!' 13.21
come, or shall we l. for another?" Lk 7.19
come, or shall we l. for another?" 7.20
I beg you to l. upon my son, for he 9.38
l. up and raise your heads, because 21.28
"L. at the fig tree, and all the 21.29
"L., Lord, here are two swords." 22.38
l., the world has gone after him." Jn 12.19
"They shall l. on him whom they 19.37
and stooping to l. in, he saw the 20.05
she stooped to l. into the tomb; 20.11
him, with John, and said, "L. at us." Ac 3.04
And now, Lord, l. upon their threats, 4.29
and as he drew near to l., the voice 7.31
trembled and did not dare to l. 7.32
went to Tarsus to l. for Saul; 11.25
could not l. at Moses' face 2Co 3.07
because we l. not to the things 4.18
L. at what is before your eyes. 10.07
L. to yourself, lest you too be Gal 6.01
L. carefully then how you walk, not Eph 5.15
Let each of you l. not only to his Php 2.04
They all l. after their own interests, 2.21
L. out for the dogs, look out for 3.02
l. out for the evil-workers, look 3.02
l. out for those who mutilate the 3.02
Do not l. on him as an enemy, but 2Th 3.15
L. at the ships also; though they Jas 3.04
into which angels long to l. 1Pe 1.12
L. to yourselves, that you may not 2Jn 1.08
open the scroll or to l. into it, Rev 5.03
open the scroll or to l. into it. 5.04

LOOKED
and l., and behold, the face of the Gen 8.13
she l. with contempt on her mistress. 16.04
she l. on me with contempt. May the Lord 16.05
He lifted up his eyes and l., and behold, 18.02
there, and they l. toward Sodom; 18.16
But Lot's wife behind him l. back, 19.26
and he l. down toward Sodom and 19.28
And Abraham lifted up his eyes and l., 22.13
and he lifted up his eyes and l., 24.63
the Philistines l. out of a window 26.08
As he l., he saw a well in the 29.02
the Lord has l. upon my affliction; 29.32
And Jacob lifted up his eyes and l., 33.01
and the men l. at one another in 43.33
his people and l. on their burdens; Ex 2.11
He l. this way and that, and seeing 2.12
and he l., and lo, the bush was 3.02
and of cloud l. down upon the host 14.24
they l. toward the wilderness, and 16.10
and l. after Moses, until he had 33.08
and they l., and each man took his Num 17.09
Then he l. on Amalek, and took up 24.20
And he l. on the Kenite, and took up 24.21
And I l., and behold, you had sinned Deu 9.16
he lifted up his eyes and l., Jos 5.13
So when the men of Ai l. back, 8.20
and he l. and saw the men coming Ju 9.43
while Manoah and his wife l. on; 13.20
who l. on while Samson made sport. 16.27
the Benjaminites l. behind them; 20.40
because they l. into the ark of the 1Sa 6.19
of Saul in Gibeah of Benjamin l.; 14.16
he l. on Eliab and thought, "Surely 16.06
And when the Philistine l., and saw 17.42
And when Saul l. behind him, David 24.08
And when he l. behind him, he saw me, 2Sa 1.07
Then Abner l. behind him and said, 2.20
daughter of Saul l. out of the 6.16
and l., and behold, many people were 13.34
when he lifted up his eyes and l., 18.24
They l., but there was none to save 22.42
And when Araunah l. down, he saw 24.20
but when I l. at it closely in the 1Ki 3.21
And he went up and l., and said, 18.43
And he l., and behold, there was at 19.06
and the people l., and behold, he 2Ki 6.30
her head, and l. out of the window. 9.30
Two or three eunuchs l. out at him. 9.32
and when she l., there was the king 11.14
daughter of Saul l. out of the 1Ch 15.29
Ornan l. and saw David and went 21.21
And when Judah l., behold, the 2Ch 13.14
they l. toward the multitude; 20.24
and when she l., there was the king 23.13
l. at him, and behold, he was leprous 26.20
And I l., and arose, and said to the Neh 4.14
But when I l. for good, evil came; Job 30.26
if I have l. at the sun when it 31.26
All men have l. on it; man beholds 36.25
and my eye has l. in triumph on my Ps 54.07
So I have l. upon thee in the 63.02
I l. for pity, but there was none; 69.20
that he l. down from his holy 102.19
heaven the Lord l. at the earth, 102.19
The sea l. and fled, Jordan turned 114.03
my house I have l. out through my Pro 7.06

LOOKED (cont.)
I l. and received instruction. Pro 24.32
and he l. for it to yield grapes, Is 5.02
When I l. for it to yield grapes, 5.04
and he l. for justice, but behold, 5.07
In that day you l. to the weapons 22.08
bed, you have l. on nakedness. 57.08
I l., but there was no one to help; 63.05
terrible things which we l. not for, 64.03
I l. on the earth, and lo, it was Jer 4.23
I l. on the mountains, and lo, they 4.24
I l., and lo, there was no man, and 4.25
I l., and lo, the fruitful land was 4.26
We l. for peace, but no good came, 8.15
We l. for peace, but no good came; 14.19
Thereupon I awoke and l., and my sleep 31.26
As I l., behold, a stormy wind came Eze 1.04
something that l. like burning 1.13
Now as I l. at the living creatures, 1.15
And when I l., behold, a hand was 2.09
and when I l., behold, there was a 8.07
Then I l., and behold, on the 10.01
And I l., and behold, there were 10.09
by you again and l. upon you, 16.08
And as I l., there were sinews on 37.08
and I l., and behold, the glory of 44.04
As you l., a stone was cut out by Dan 2.34
Then as I l. its wings were plucked 7.04
After this I l., and lo, another, 7.06
As I l., thrones were placed and 7.09
I l. then because of the sound of 7.11
And as I l., the beast was slain, 7.11
As I l., this horn made war with 7.21
I lifted up my eyes and l., 10.05
Then I Daniel l., and behold, two 12.05
he l. and shook the nations; Hab 3.06
You have l. for much, and, lo, it came Hag 1.09
the two fish he l. up to heaven, Mt 14.19
But Jesus l. at them and said to 19.26
And he l. around at them with anger, Mk 3.05
And he l. around to see who had 5.32
the two fish he l. up to heaven, 6.41
And he l. up and said, "I see men; 8.24
and he l. intently and was restored, 8.25
And Jesus l. around and said to his 10.23
Jesus l. at them and said, "With men 10.27
and when he had l. round at everything, 11.11
she l. at him, and said, "You also 14.67
to me in the days when he l. on me, Lk 1.25
And he l. around on them all, and 6.10
the two fish he l. up to heaven, 9.16
he l. up and said to him, "Zacchaeus, 19.05
But he l. at them and said, "What 20.17
He l. up and saw the rich putting 21.01
And the Lord turned and l. at Peter. 22.61
and he l. at Jesus as he walked, and Jn 1.36
Jesus l. at him, and said, "So you 1.42
Jesus l. up and said to her, "Woman, * 8.10
The disciples l. at one another, 13.22
the Holy Spirit, l. intently at him Ac 13.09
For he l. forward to the city which Heb 11.10
of Egypt, for he l. to the reward. 11.26
which we have l. upon and touched 1Jn 1.01
After this I l., and lo, in heaven Rev 4.01
a rainbow that l. like an emerald. 4.03
Then I l., and I heard around the 5.11
I l., and behold, there was a great 6.12
After this I l., and behold, a great 7.09
Then I l., and I heard an eagle 8.13
heads were what l. like crowns of 9.07
Then I l., and lo, on Mount Zion 14.01
Then I l., and lo, a white cloud, and 14.14
After this I l., and the temple of 15.05

LOOKING
and l. up they saw a caravan of Gen 37.25
Turn my eyes from l. at vanities; Ps 119.37
the windows, l. through the lattice. Sol 2.09
shuts his eyes from l. upon evil. Is 33.15
My eyes are weary with l. upward. 38.14
all of them l. like officers, a Eze 23.15
l. on from afar, who had followed Mt 27.55
And l. around on those who sat Mk 3.34
and l. up to heaven, he sighed, and 7.34
And suddenly l. around they no 9.08
And Jesus l. upon him loved him, and 10.21
There were also women l. on from afar, 15.40
also himself l. for the kingdom of 15.43
And l. up, they saw that the stone 16.04
l. for the consolation of Israel, Lk 2.25
to all who were l. for the redemption 2.38
and I have been l. for you anxiously." 2.48
Jesus l. at him said, "How hard it 18.24
and he was l. for the kingdom of 23.51
stooping and l. in, he saw the linen * 24.12
And they stood still, l. sad. 24.17
The Jews were l. for him at the Jn 7.11
They were l. for Jesus and saying 11.56
as they were l. on, he was lifted up, Ac 1.09
why do you stand l. into heaven? 1.11
"Behold, three men are l. for you. 10.19
said, "I am the one you are l. for; 10.21
L. at it closely I observed animals 11.06
and Paul, l. intently at him and 14.09
And Paul, l. intently at the council, 23.01
l. northeast and southeast, and 27.12
l. to Jesus the pioneer and perfecter Heb 12.02
l. after themselves; waterless clouds, Jud 1.12

LOOKS
of Pisgah which l. down upon the Num 21.20
the border that l. down upon the 1Sa 13.18
man l. on the outward appearance, 16.07
but the LORD l. on the heart." 16.07
a hireling who l. for his wages, Job 7.02
For he l. to the ends of the earth, 28.24
The LORD l. down from heaven upon Ps 14.02
The LORD l. down from heaven, he 33.13
enthroned he l. forth on all the 33.14
God l. down from heaven upon the 53.02
man of haughty l. and arrogant 101.05
who l. on the earth and it trembles, 104.32
who l. far down upon the heavens 113.06
but the prudent l. where he is Pro 14.15
and a backbiting tongue, angry l. 25.23
She l. well to the ways of her 31.27
"Who is this that l. forth like the Sol 6.10
The haughty l. of man shall be Is 2.11
LORD from heaven l. down and sees; Lam 3.50
words, nor be dismayed at their l., Eze 2.06
not, nor be dismayed at their l., 3.09
the teraphim, he l. at the liver. 21.21
every one who l. at a woman Mt 5.28
to the plow and l. back is fit for Lk 9.62
But he who l. into the perfect law, Jas 1.25

LOOM
away the pin, the l., and the web. Ju 16.14
he cuts me off from the l.; Is 38.12

LOOMS
for evil l. out of the north, and Jer 6.01

LOOPS
And you shall make l. of blue on Ex 26.04
you shall make l. on the edge of 26.04
Fifty l. you shall make on the one 26.05
and fifty l. you shall make on the 26.05
the l. shall be opposite one 26.05
make fifty l. on the edge of the 26.10
and fifty l. on the edge of the curtain 26.10
and put the clasps into the l., 26.11
And he made l. of blue on the edge 36.11
he made fifty l. on the one curtain, 36.12

LOOPS (cont.)
he made fifty l. on the edge of Ex 36.12
the l. were opposite one another. 36.12
And he made fifty l. on the edge of 36.17
and fifty l. on the edge of the other 36.17

LOOSE
when you break l. you shall break Gen 27.40
Naphtali is a hind let l., that bears 49.21
lets his beast l. and it feeds in Ex 22.05
shall not come l. from the ephod. 28.28
saw that the people had broken l. 32.25
(for Aaron had let them break l., 32.25
should not come l. from the ephod; 39.21
let the hair of your heads hang l., Lev 10.06
let the hair of his head hang l., 13.45
let the hair of his head hang l., 21.10
And I will let l. the wild beasts 26.22
he would let l. his hand and cut Job 6.09
Pleiades, or l. the cords of Orion? 38.31
He let l. on them his fierce anger, Ps 78.49
You will be saved from the l. woman, Pro 2.16
For the lips of a l. woman drip 5.03
with a l. woman and embrace the 5.20
to preserve you from the l. woman, 7.05
The mouth of a l. woman is a deep 22.14
or sleeps, not a waistcloth is l., Is 5.27
cattle are let l. and where sheep 7.25
and l. the sackcloth from your 20.02
Your tackle hangs l.; it cannot hold 33.23
l. the bonds from your neck, O 52.02
to l. the bonds of wickedness, to 58.06
when I l. against you my deadly Eze 5.16
which I will l. to destroy you, and 5.16
and I will let l. my anger upon 7.03
He answered, "But I see four men l., Dan 3.25
whatever you l. on earth shall be Mt 16.19
whatever you l. on earth shall be 18.18
squandered his property in l. living. Lk 15.13

LOOSED
Because God has l. my cord and Job 30.11
Who has l. the bonds of the swift 39.05
thou hast l. my sackcloth and Ps 30.11
handmaid. Thou hast l. my bonds. 116.16
on earth shall be l. in heaven." Mt 16.19
on earth shall be l. in heaven. 18.18
mouth was opened and his tongue l., Lk 1.64
be l. from this bond on the 13.16
having l. the pangs of death, Ac 2.24
that he must be l. for a little Rev 20.03
Satan will be l. from his prison 20.07

LOOSEN
You shall l. your hand from your Jer 17.04

LOOSENING
the same time l. the ropes that Ac 27.40

LOOSES
He l. the bonds of kings, and binds Job 12.18
and l. the belt of the strong. 12.21

LOOTED
should not have l. his goods in Ob 1.13

LOP
of hosts will l. the boughs with Is 10.33

LOR
And the L. spoke to the fish, and it Jon 2.10

LORD
day that the L. God made the earth Gen 2.04
for the L. God had not caused it to 2.05
then the L. God formed man of dust 2.07
And the L. God planted a garden in 2.08
the ground the L. God made to grow 2.09
The L. God took the man and put him 2.15
And the L. God commanded the man, 2.16
Then the L. God said, "It is not 2.18
the ground the L. God formed every 2.19
So the L. God caused a deep sleep 2.21
rib which the L. God had taken 2.22
creature that the L. God had made. 3.01
sound of the L. God walking in the 3.08
presence of the L. God among the 3.08
But the L. God called to the man, 3.09
Then the L. God said to the woman, 3.13
The L. God said to the serpent, 3.14
And the L. God made for Adam and 3.21
Then the L. God said, "Behold, the 3.22
therefore the L. God sent him forth 3.23
a man with the help of the L." 4.01
brought to the L. an offering of 4.03
And the L. had regard for Abel and 4.04
The L. said to Cain, "Why are you 4.06
Then the L. said to Cain, "Where is 4.09
And the L. said, "What have you done? 4.10
Cain said to the L., "My punishment 4.13
Then the L. said to him, "Not so! 4.15
And the L. put a mark on Cain, lest 4.15
away from the presence of the L., 4.16
to call upon the name of the L. 4.26
which the L. has cursed this one 5.29
Then the L. said, "My spirit shall 6.03
The L. saw that the wickedness of 6.05
And the L. was sorry that he had 6.06
So the L. said, "I will blot out man 6.07
found favor in the eyes of the L. 6.08
Then the L. said to Noah, "Go into 7.01
all that the L. had commanded him. 7.05
commanded him; and the L. shut him in. 7.16
Then Noah built an altar to the L., 8.20
And when the L. smelled the pleasing 8.21
the L. said in his heart, "I will 8.21
"Blessed by the L. my God be Shem; 9.26
He was a mighty hunter before the L.; 10.09
a mighty hunter before the L." 10.09
And the L. came down to see the 11.05
And the L. said, "Behold, they are 11.06
So the L. scattered them abroad 11.08
there the L. confused the language 11.09
from there the L. scattered them 11.09
Now the L. said to Abram, "Go from 12.01
Abram went, as the L. had told him; 12.04
Then the L. appeared to Abram, and 12.07
he built there an altar to the L., 12.07
an altar to the L. and called on 12.08
and called on the name of the L. 12.08
But the L. afflicted Pharaoh and 12.17
Abram called on the name of the L. 13.04
everywhere like the garden of the L., 13.10
was before the L. destroyed Sodom 13.10
great sinners against the L. 13.13
The L. said to Abram, after Lot had 13.14
there he built an altar to the L. 13.18
have sworn to the L. God Most High, 14.22
the word of the L. came to Abram 15.01
"O L. GOD, what wilt thou give me, 15.02
the word of the L. came to him, 15.04
And he believed the L.; and he reckoned 15.06
"I am the L. who brought you from 15.07
"O L. GOD, how am I to know that I 15.08
Then the L. said to Abram, "Know of 15.13
On that day the L. made a covenant 15.18
the L. has prevented me from 16.02
May the L. judge between you and me!" 16.05
The angel of the L. found her by a 16.07
The angel of the L. said to her, 16.09
The angel of the L. also said to 16.10
And the angel of the L. said to her, 16.11
because the L. has given heed to 16.11
the name of the L. who spoke to 16.13
years old the L. appeared to Abram, 17.01

LORD (cont.)

And the L. appeared to him by the Gen 18.01
and said, "My l., if I have found 18.03
The L. said to Abraham, "Why did 18.13
Is anything too hard for the L.? 18.14
The L. said, "Shall I hide from 18.17
the way of the L. by doing righteousness 18.19
so that the L. may bring to Abraham 18.19
Then the L. said, "Because the 18.20
Abraham still stood before the L. 18.22
And the L. said, "If I find at Sodom 18.26
upon myself to speak to the L., 18.27
said, "Oh let not the L. be angry, 18.30
upon myself to speak to the L. 18.31
said, "Oh let not the L. be angry, 18.32
And the L. went his way, when he had 18.33
has become great before the L., 19.13
and the L. has sent us to destroy 19.13
for the L. is about to destroy the 19.14
the L. being merciful to him, and 19.16
Then the L. rained on Sodom and 19.24
and fire from the L. out of heaven; 19.24
where he had stood before the L.; 19.27
so he said, "L., wilt thou slay an 20.04
For the L. had closed all the wombs 20.18
The L. visited Sarah as he had said, 21.01
and the L. did to Sarah as he had 21.01
called there on the name of the L., 21.33
angel of the L. called to him from 22.11
of that place The L. will provide; 22.14
mount of the L. it shall be provided." 22.14
angel of the L. called to Abraham 22.15
says the L., because you have done 22.16
"Hear us, my l.; you are a 23.06
"No, my l., hear me; I give you 23.11
"My l., listen to me; a piece of 23.15
and the L. had blessed Abraham in 24.01
and I will make you swear by the L., 24.03
The L., the God of heaven, who took 24.07
"O L., God of my master Abraham, 24.12
She said, "Drink, my l."; and she 24.18
whether the L. had prospered his 24.21
bowed his head and worshiped the L., 24.26
and said, "Blessed be the L., the God 24.27
the L. has led me in the way to the 24.27
said, "Come in, O blessed of the L.; 24.31
The L. has greatly blessed my 24.35
'The L., before whom I walk, will 24.40
'O L., the God of my master Abraham, 24.42
woman whom the L. has appointed 24.44
bowed my head and worshiped the L., 24.48
the LORD, and blessed the L., 24.48
"The thing comes from the L.; 24.50
master's son, as the L. has spoken." 24.51
himself to the earth before the L. 24.52
since the L. has prospered my way; 24.56
prayed to the L. for his wife, 25.21
and the L. granted his prayer, and 25.21
so she went to inquire of the L. 25.22
And the L. said to her, "Two nations 25.23
And the L. appeared to him, and said, 26.02
hundredfold. The L. blessed him, 26.12
"For now the L. has made room for 26.22
And the L. appeared to him the same 26.24
and called upon the name of the L., 26.25
plainly that the L. is with you; 26.28
you are now the blessed of the L." 26.29
you before the L. before I die.' 27.07
"Because the L. your God granted me 27.20
a field which the L. has blessed! 27.27
Be l. over your brothers, and may 27.29
"Behold, I have made him your l., 27.37
the L. stood above it and said, "I 28.13
"I am the L., the God of Abraham 28.13
"Surely the L. is in this place; 28.16
then the L. shall be my God, 28.21
When the L. saw that Leah was hated, 29.31
"Because the L. has looked upon my 29.32
"Because the L. has heard that I am 29.33
"This time I will praise the L."; 29.35
"May the L. add to me another son!" 30.24
that the L. has blessed me because 30.27
and the L. has blessed you wherever 30.30
Then the L. said to Jacob, "Return 31.03
"Let not my l. be angry that I 31.35
"The L. watch between you and me, 31.49
"Thus you shall say to my l. Esau: 32.04
and I have sent to tell my l., 32.05
O L. who didst say to me, 'Return to 32.09
are a present sent to my l. Esau; 32.18
find favor in the sight of my l." 33.08
"My l. knows that the children are 33.13
Let my l. pass on before his 33.14
until I come to my l. in Seir." 33.14
find favor in the sight of my l." 33.15
was wicked in the sight of the L.; 38.07
and the L. slew him. 38.07
displeasing in the sight of the L., 38.10
The L. was with Joseph, and he 39.02
saw that the L. was with him, 39.03
and that the L. caused all that he 39.03
that he had the L. blessed the 39.05
blessing of the L. was upon all 39.05
But the L. was with Joseph and 39.21
care, because the L. was with him; 39.23
he did, the L. made it prosper. 39.23
offended their l. the king of 40.01
my l., but to buy food have your 42.10
"The man, the l. of the land, spoke 42.30
the l. of the land, said to us, 'By 42.33
my l., we came down the first time 43.20
it not from this that my l. drinks, 44.05
"Why does my l. speak such words as 44.07
said, "What shall we say to my l.? 44.16
"O my l., let your servant, I pray 44.18
My l. asked his servants, saying, 44.19
And we said to my l., 'We have a 44.20
We said to my l., 'The lad cannot 44.22
we told him the words of my l. 44.24
of the lad as a slave to my l.; 44.33
and l. of all his house and ruler 45.08
God has made me l. of all Egypt; 45.09
hide from my l. that our money is 47.18
the sight of my l. but our bodies 47.18
may it please my l., we will be 47.25
I wait for thy salvation, O L. 49.18
angel of the L. appeared to him in Ex 3.02
When the L. saw that he turned 3.04
Then the L. said, "I have seen the 3.07
'The L., the God of your fathers, 3.15
'The L., the God of your fathers, 3.16
'The L., the God of the Hebrews, has 3.18
we may sacrifice to the L. our God.' 3.18
'The L. did not appear to you.' 4.01
The L. said to him, "What is that in 4.02
But the L. said to Moses, "Put out 4.04
"that they may believe that the L., 4.05
Again, the L. said to him, "Put your 4.06
But Moses said to the L., "Oh, my 4.10
my L., I am not eloquent, either 4.10
Then the L. said to him, "Who has 4.11
or seeing, or blind? Is it not I, the L.? 4.11
my L., send, I pray, some other 4.13
anger of the L. was kindled 4.14
And the L. said to Moses in Midian, 4.19
And the L. said to Moses, "When you 4.21
say to Pharaoh, 'Thus says the L., 4.22
on the way the L. met him and 4.24
The L. said to Aaron, "Go into the 4.27
words of the L. with which he had 4.28
words which the L. had spoken to 4.30
heard that the L. had visited the 4.31
Pharaoh and said, "Thus says the L., 5.01
"Who is the L., that I should heed 5.02

LORD (cont.)
I do not know the L., and moreover Ex 5.02
and sacrifice to the L. our God, 5.03
'Let us go and sacrifice to the L.' 5.17
"The L. look upon you and judge, 5.21
turned again to the L. and said, 5.22
"O L., why hast thou done evil to 5.22
But the L. said to Moses, "Now you 6.01
And God said to Moses, "I am the L. 6.02
by my name the L. I did not make 6.03
'I am the L., and I will bring you 6.06
know that I am the L. your God, 6.07
a possession. I am the L.'" 6.08
And the L. said to Moses, 6.10
But Moses said to the L., "Behold, 6.12
But the L. spoke to Moses and Aaron, 6.13
and Moses to whom the L. said: 6.26
day when the L. spoke to Moses in 6.28
the L. said to Moses, "I am the L.; 6.29
But Moses said to the L., 6.30
And the L. said to Moses, "See, I 7.01
shall know that I am the L., 7.05
they did as the L. commanded them. 7.06
And the L. said to Moses and Aaron, 7.08
and did as the L. commanded; 7.10
to them; as the L. had said. 7.13
Then the L. said to Moses, "Pharaoh's 7.14
'The L., the God of the Hebrews, 7.16
Thus says the L., "By this you 7.17
you shall know that I am the L.: 7.17
And the L. said to Moses, "Say to 7.19
Moses and Aaron did as the L. commanded; 7.20
listen to them; as the L. had said. 7.22
after the L. had struck the Nile. 7.25
Then the L. said to Moses, "Go in to 8.01
and say to him, 'Thus says the L., 8.01
And the L. said to Moses, "Say to 8.05
"Entreat the L. to take away the 8.08
people go to sacrifice to the L." 8.08
is no one like the L. our God. 8.10
cried to the L. concerning the 8.12
And the L. did according to the 8.13
listen to them; as the L. had said. 8.15
Then the L. said to Moses, "Say to 8.16
listen to them; as the L. had said. 8.19
Then the L. said to Moses, "Rise up 8.20
and say to him, 'Thus says the L., 8.20
that I am the L. in the midst of 8.22
And the L. did so; there came 8.24
sacrifice to the L. our God offerings 8.26
sacrifice to the L. our God as he 8.27
sacrifice to the L. your God in the 8.28
pray to the L. that the swarms of 8.29
people go to sacrifice to the L." 8.29
from Pharaoh and prayed to the L. 8.30
And the L. did as Moses asked, and 8.31
Then the L. said to Moses, "Go in to 9.01
and say to him, 'Thus says the L., 9.01
behold, the hand of the L. will fall 9.03
But the L. will make a distinction 9.04
And the L. set a time, saying, 9.05
"Tomorrow the L. will do this thing 9.05
the morrow the L. did this thing; 9.06
And the L. said to Moses and Aaron, 9.08
But the L. hardened the heart of 9.12
as the L. had spoken to Moses. 9.12
Then the L. said to Moses, "Rise up 9.13
and say to him, 'Thus says the L., 9.13
the word of the L. among the 9.20
the word of the L. left his slaves 9.21
And the L. said to Moses, "Stretch 9.22
and the L. sent thunder and hail, 9.23
And the L. rained hail upon the 9.23
the L. is in the right, and I and my 9.27
Entreat the L.; for there has 9.28
stretch out my hands to the L.; 9.29
you do not yet fear the L. God." 9.30
stretched out his hands to the L.; 9.33
as the L. had spoken through Moses. 9.35
Then the L. said to Moses, "Go in to 10.01
that you may know that I am the L." 10.02
and said to him, "Thus says the L., 10.03
they may serve the L. their God; 10.07
to them, "Go, serve the L. your God; 10.08
for we must hold a feast to the L." 10.09
"The L. be with you, if ever I let 10.10
and serve the L., for that is what 10.11
Then the L. said to Moses, "Stretch 10.12
and the L. brought an east wind 10.13
sinned against the L. your God, 10.16
and entreat the L. your God only 10.17
from Pharaoh, and entreated the L. 10.18
And the L. turned a very strong 10.19
But the L. hardened Pharaoh's heart, 10.20
Then the L. said to Moses, "Stretch 10.21
Moses, and said, "Go, serve the L.; 10.24
we may sacrifice to the L. our God. 10.25
of them to serve the L. our God, 10.26
must serve the L. until we arrive 10.26
But the L. hardened Pharaoh's heart, 10.27
The L. said to Moses, "Yet one 11.01
And the L. gave the people favor in 11.03
And Moses said, "Thus says the L.: 11.04
know that the L. makes a distinction 11.07
Then the L. said to Moses, "Pharaoh 11.09
and the L. hardened Pharaoh's heart, 11.10
The L. said to Moses and Aaron in 12.01
execute judgments: I am the L. 12.12
shall keep it as a feast to the L.; 12.14
For the L. will pass through to 12.23
the L. will pass over the door, and 12.23
land which the L. will give you, 12.25
as the L. had commanded Moses and 12.28
At midnight the L. smote all the 12.29
serve the L., as you have said. 12.31
and the L. had given the people 12.36
hosts of the L. went out from the 12.41
It was a night of watching by the L., 12.42
kept to the L. by all the people 12.42
And the L. said to Moses and Aaron, 12.43
would keep the passover to the L., 12.48
as the L. commanded Moses and Aaron, 12.50
very day the L. brought the people 12.51
The L. said to Moses, 13.01
of hand the L. brought you out 13.03
And when the L. brings you into the 13.05
there shall be a feast to the L. 13.06
of what the L. did for me when I 13.08
the law of the L. may be in your 13.09
strong hand the L. has brought you 13.09
"And when the L. brings you into 13.11
apart to the L. all that first 13.12
of hand the L. brought us out of 13.14
the L. slew all the first-born in 13.15
sacrifice to the L. all the males 13.15
strong hand the L. brought us out 13.16
And the L. went before them by day 13.21
Then the L. said to Moses, 14.01
shall know that I am the L." 14.04
And the L. hardened the heart of 14.08
of Israel cried out to the L.; 14.10
and see the salvation of the L., 14.13
The L. will fight for you, and you 14.14
The L. said to Moses, "Why do you 14.15
shall know that I am the L., 14.18
and the L. drove the sea back by a 14.21
watch the L. in the pillar of fire 14.24
for the L. fights for them against 14.25
Then the L. said to Moses, "Stretch 14.26
and the L. routed the Egyptians in 14.27
Thus the L. saved Israel that day 14.30
work which the L. did against the 14.31
and the people feared the L.; 14.31
believed in the L. and in his 14.31

LORD (cont.)

of Israel sang this song to the L.,	Ex 15.01
saying, "I will sing to the L.,	15.01
The L. is my strength and my song,	15.02
The L. is a man of war;	15.03
the L. is his name.	15.03
O L., glorious in power, thy right	15.06
O L., shatters the enemy.	15.06
O L., among the gods?	15.11
O L., pass by, till the people pass	15.16
O L., which thou hast made for thy	15.17
O L., which thy hands have established.	15.17
The L. will reign for ever and ever."	15.18
the L. brought back the waters of	15.19
"Sing to the L., for he has triumphed	15.21
And he cried to the L.;	15.25
and the L. showed him a tree, and he	15.25
There the L. made for them a	15.25
to the voice of the L. your God,	15.26
for I am the L., your healer."	15.26
the hand of the L. in the land of	16.03
Then the L. said to Moses, "Behold, I	16.04
that it was the L. who brought you	16.06
you shall see the glory of the L.,	16.07
your murmurings against the L.	16.07
"When the L. gives you in the	16.08
because the L. has heard your	16.08
not against us but against the L."	16.08
Israel, 'Come near before the L.,	16.09
glory of the L. appeared in the	16.10
And the L. said to Moses,	16.11
know that I am the L. your God.'"	16.12
bread which the L. has given you	16.15
This is what the L. has commanded:	16.16
"This is what the L. has commanded:	16.23
rest, a holy sabbath to the L.;	16.23
for today is a sabbath to the L.;	16.25
And the L. said to Moses, "How long	16.28
The L. has given you the sabbath,	16.29
"This is what the L. has commanded:	16.32
in it, and place it before the L.,	16.33
As the L. commanded Moses, so Aaron	16.34
to the commandment of the L.,	17.01
Why do you put the L. to the proof?"	17.02
So Moses cried to the L., "What shall I	17.04
And the L. said to Moses, "Pass on	17.05
they put the L. to the proof by	17.07
"Is the L. among us or not?"	17.07
And the L. said to Moses, "Write	17.14
name of it, The L. is my banner,	17.15
saying, "A hand upon the banner of the L.!	17.16
The L. will have war with Amalek	17.16
how the L. had brought Israel out	18.01
all that the L. had done to	18.08
and how the L. had delivered them.	18.08
good which the L. had done to	18.09
And Jethro said, "Blessed be the L.,	18.10
Now I know that the L. is greater	18.11
and the L. called him out of the	19.03
words which the L. had commanded	19.07
"All that the L. has spoken we will	19.08
the words of the people to the L.	19.08
And the L. said to Moses, "Lo, I am	19.09
the words of the people to the L.	19.09
And the L. said to Moses, "Go to the	19.10
third day the L. will come down	19.11
because the L. descended upon it in	19.18
And the L. came down upon Mount	19.20
and the L. called Moses to the top	19.20
And the L. said to Moses, "Go down	19.21
through to the L. to gaze and many	19.21
near to the L. consecrate themselves,	19.22
lest the L. break out upon them."	19.22
And Moses said to the L.,	19.23
And the L. said to him, "Go down, and	19.24
break through to come up to the L.,	19.24
"I am the L. your God, who brought	20.02
for I the L. your God am a jealous	20.05
the name of the L. your God in	20.07
for the L. will not hold him	20.07
is a sabbath to the L. your God;	20.10
for in six days the L. made heaven	20.11
therefore the L. blessed the	20.11
land which the L. your God gives	20.12
And the L. said to Moses, "Thus you	20.22
an oath by the L. shall be between	22.11
save to the L. only, shall be	22.20
males appear before the L. God.	23.17
into the house of the L. your God.	23.19
You shall serve the L. your God,	23.25
said to Moses, "Come up to the L.,	24.01
Moses alone shall come near to the L.;	24.02
words of the L. and all the ordinances;	24.03
words which the L. has spoken we	24.03
wrote all the words of the L.	24.04
peace offerings of oxen to the L.	24.05
"All that the L. has spoken we will	24.07
which the L. has made with you in	24.08
The L. said to Moses, "Come up to me	24.12
The glory of the L. settled on	24.16
glory of the L. was like a devouring	24.17
The L. said to Moses,	25.01
evening to morning before the L.	27.21
before the L. upon his two shoulders	28.12
continual remembrance before the L.	28.29
when he goes in before the L.;	28.30
heart before the L. continually.	28.30
into the holy place before the L.,	28.35
of a signet, 'Holy to the L.'	28.36
they may be accepted before the L.	28.38
shall kill the bull before the L.,	29.11
it is a burnt offering to the L.;	29.18
an offering by fire to the L.	29.18
bread that is before the L.;	29.23
for a wave offering before the L.	29.24
as a pleasing odor before the L.;	29.25
is an offering by fire to the L.	29.25
for a wave offering before the L.;	29.26
it is their offering to the L.	29.28
an offering by fire to the L.	29.41
the tent of meeting before the L.,	29.42
know that I am the L. their God,	29.46
among them; I am the L. their God.	29.46
before the L. throughout your	30.08
it is most holy to the L."	30.10
The L. said to Moses,	30.11
himself to the L. when you number	30.12
a shekel as an offering to the L.	30.13
to remembrance before the L.,	30.16
The L. said to Moses,	30.17
burn an offering by fire to the L.,	30.20
Moreover, the L. said to Moses,	30.22
And the L. said to Moses, "Take	30.34
it shall be for you holy to the L.	30.37
The L. said to Moses,	31.01
And the L. said to Moses	31.12
know that I, the L., sanctify you.	31.13
of solemn rest, holy to the L.;	31.15
in six days the L. made heaven and	31.17
"Tomorrow shall be a feast to the L."	32.05
And the L. said to Moses, "Go down;	32.07
And the L. said to Moses, "I have	32.09
But Moses besought the L. his God,	32.11
"O L., why does thy wrath burn hot	32.11
And the L. repented of the evil	32.14
not the anger of my l. burn hot;	32.22
"Thus says the L. God of Israel,	32.27
yourselves for the service of the L.,	32.29
And now I will go up to the L.;	32.30
So Moses returned to the L. and said,	32.31
But the L. said to Moses, "Whoever	32.33
And the L. sent a plague upon the	32.35
The L. said to Moses, "Depart, go up	33.01
For the L. had said to Moses, "Say	33.05

LORD (cont.)

who sought the L. would go out to Ex 33.07
and the L. would speak with Moses. 33.09
Thus the L. used to speak to Moses 33.11
Moses said to the L., "See, thou 33.12
And the L. said to Moses, "This very 33.17
before you my name 'The L.'; 33.19
And the L. said, "Behold, there is a 33.21
The L. said to Moses, "Cut two 34.01
as the L. had commanded him, and 34.04
And the L. descended in the cloud 34.05
and proclaimed the name of the L. 34.05
The L. passed before him, and 34.06
"The L., the LORD, a God merciful 34.06
the L., a God merciful and gracious, 34.06
O L., let the LORD, I pray thee, go 34.09
let the L., I pray thee, go in the 34.09
are shall see the work of the L.; 34.10
for the L., whose name is Jealous, 34.14
males appear before the L. God, 34.23
before the L. your God three times 34.24
to the house of the L. your God. 34.26
And the L. said to Moses, "Write 34.27
there with the L. forty days and 34.28
all that the L. had spoken with 34.32
in before the L. to speak with him, 34.34
which the L. has commanded you to 35.01
sabbath of solemn rest to the L.; 35.02
thing which the L. has commanded. 35.04
among you an offering to the L.; 35.05
make all that the L. has commanded: 35.10
an offering of gold to the L. 35.22
work which the L. had commanded by 35.29
their freewill offering to the L. 35.29
the L. has called by name Bezalel 35.30
man in whom the L. has put ability 36.01
with all that the L. has commanded." 36.01
whose mind the L. had put ability, 36.02
work which the L. has commanded us 36.05
all that the L. commanded Moses; 38.22
for Aaron; as the L. had commanded Moses. 39.01
linen; as the L. had commanded Moses. 39.05
of Israel; as the L. had commanded Moses. 39.07
the ephod; as the L. had commanded Moses. 39.21
ministering; as the L. had commanded Moses. 39.26
needlework; as the L. had commanded Moses. 39.29
of a signet, "Holy to the L." 39.30
above; as the L. had commanded Moses. 39.31
to all that the L. had commanded 39.32
According to all that the L. had 39.42
as the L. had commanded, so had they 39.43
The L. said to Moses, 40.01
to all that the L. commanded him, 40.16
over it, as the L. had commanded Moses. 40.19
testimony; as the L. had commanded Moses. 40.21
bread in order on it before the L.; 40.23
as the L. had commanded Moses. 40.23
and set up the lamps before the L.; 40.25
as the L. had commanded Moses. 40.25
upon it; as the L. had commanded Moses. 40.27
offering; as the L. had commanded Moses. 40.29
washed; as the L. commanded Moses. 40.32
glory of the L. filled the tabernacle. 40.34
glory of the L. filled the tabernacle. 40.35
cloud of the L. was upon the 40.38
The L. called Moses, and spoke to Lev 1.01
you brings an offering to the L., 1.02
he may be accepted before the L.; 1.03
shall kill the bull before the L.; 1.05
by fire, a pleasing odor to the L. 1.09
side of the altar before the L., 1.11
by fire, a pleasing odor to the L. 1.13
offering to the L. is a burnt 1.14
by fire, a pleasing odor to the L. 1.17
offering as an offering to the L., 2.01
by fire, a pleasing odor to the L. 2.02
of the offerings by fire to the L. 2.03
is made of these things to the L.; 2.08
by fire, a pleasing odor to the L. 2.09
of the offerings by fire to the L. 2.10
bring to the L. shall be made with 2.11
as an offering by fire to the L. 2.11
you may bring them to the L., 2.12
offering of first fruits to the L., 2.14
is an offering by fire to the L. 2.16
it without blemish before the L. 3.01
as an offering by fire to the L., 3.03
by fire, a pleasing odor to the L. 3.05
offering to the L. is an animal 3.06
he shall offer it before the L., 3.07
by fire to the L. he shall offer 3.09
as food offered by fire to the L. 3.11
he shall offer it before the L., 3.12
for an offering by fire to the L., 3.14
And the L. said to Moses, 4.01
which the L. has commanded not to 4.02
blemish to the L. for a sin 4.03
the tent of meeting before the L., 4.04
and kill the bull before the L. 4.04
before the L. in front of the veil 4.06
before the L. which is in the tent 4.07
which the L. has commanded not to 4.13
the head of the bull before the L., 4.15
bull shall be killed before the L. 4.15
before the L. in front of the veil 4.17
the tent of meeting before the L.; 4.18
which the L. his God has commanded 4.22
the burnt offering before the L.; 4.24
which the L. has commanded not to 4.27
for a pleasing odor to the L.; 4.31
the offerings by fire to the L.; 4.35
offering to the L. for the sin 5.06
offering to the L. for the sin 5.07
the offerings by fire to the L.; 5.12
The L. said to Moses, 5.14
any of the holy things of the L., 5.15
as his guilt offering to the L., 5.15
which the L. has commanded not to 5.17
offering; he is guilty before the L." 5.19
The L. said to Moses, 6.01
against the L. by deceiving his 6.02
his guilt offering to the L., 6.06
atonement for him before the L., 6.07
The L. said to Moses, 6.08
Aaron shall offer it before the L., 6.14
altar, a pleasing odor to the L. 6.15
The L. said to Moses, 6.19
offer to the L. in the day when he 6.20
it for a pleasing odor to the L. 6.21
offer it to the L. as decreed for 6.22
The L. said to Moses, 6.24
offering be killed before the L.; 6.25
as an offering by fire to the L.; 7.05
which one may offer to the L. 7.11
offering, as an offering to the L.; 7.14
The L. said to Moses, 7.22
is made to the L. shall be cut off 7.25
The L. said to Moses, 7.28
offerings to the L. shall bring his 7.29
shall bring his offering to the L.; 7.29
the offerings by fire to the L.; 7.30
as a wave offering before the L. 7.30
offerings made by fire to the L., 7.35
to serve as priests of the L.; 7.35
the L. commanded this to be given 7.36
which the L. commanded Moses on 7.38
to bring their offerings to the L., 7.38
The L. said to Moses, 8.01
And Moses did as the L. commanded him; 8.04
thing which the L. has commanded 8.05
crown, as the L. commanded Moses. 8.09
on them, as the L. commanded Moses. 8.13
camp, as the L. commanded Moses. 8.17
an offering by fire to the L., 8.21

LORD (cont.)

as the L. commanded Moses. Lev 8.21
was before the L. he took one 8.26
as a wave offering before the L. 8.27
an offering by fire to the L. 8.28
for a wave offering before the L.; 8.29
ordination, as the L. commanded Moses. 8.29
the L. has commanded to be done to 8.34
performing what the L. has charged, 8.35
which the L. commanded by Moses. 8.36
and offer them before the L. 9.02
offerings, to sacrifice before the L., 9.04
for today the L. will appear to you.'" 9.04
drew near and stood before the L. 9.05
thing which the L. commanded you 9.06
glory of the L. will appear to you." 9.06
for them; as the L. has commanded." 9.07
the altar, as the L. commanded Moses. 9.10
for a wave offering before the L.; 9.21
glory of the L. appeared to all 9.23
from before the L. and consumed 9.24
offered unholy fire before the L., 10.01
presence of the L. and devoured 10.02
them, and they died before the L. 10.02
"This is what the L. has said, 10.03
burning which the L. has kindled. 10.06
anointing oil of the L. is upon you." 10.07
And the L. spoke to Aaron, saying, 10.08
which the L. has spoken to them by 10.11
of the offerings by fire to the L., 10.12
the offerings by fire to the L.; 10.13
for a wave offering before the L., 10.15
for ever; as the L. has commanded." 10.15
atonement for them before the L.? 10.17
their burnt offering before the L.; 10.19
acceptable in the sight of the L.?" 10.19
And the L. said to Moses and Aaron, 11.01
For I am the L. your God; consecrate 11.44
For I am the L. who brought you up 11.45
The L. said to Moses, 12.01
and he shall offer it before the L., 12.07
The L. said to Moses and Aaron, 13.01
The L. said to Moses, 14.01
and these things before the L., 14.11
for a wave offering before the L.; 14.12
finger seven times before the L., 14.16
atonement for him before the L. 14.18
the tent of meeting, before the L.; 14.23
for a wave offering before the L., 14.24
hand seven times before the L.; 14.27
atonement for him before the L. 14.29
before the L. for him who is being 14.31
The L. said to Moses and Aaron, 14.33
The L. said to Moses and Aaron, 15.01
come before the L. to the door of 15.14
him before the L. for his discharge 15.15
her before the L. for her unclean 15.30
The L. spoke to Moses, after the 16.01
drew near before the L. and died; 16.01
and the L. said to Moses, "Tell 16.02
them before the L. at the door of 16.07
one lot for the L. and the other 16.08
on which the lot fell for the L., 16.09
before the L. to make atonement 16.10
fire from the altar before the L., 16.12
incense on the fire before the L., 16.13
is before the L. and make atonement 16.18
you shall be clean before the L. 16.30
Moses did as the L. commanded him. 16.34
And the L. said to Moses, 17.01
thing which the L. has commanded. 17.02
a gift to the L. before the 17.04
before the tabernacle of the L., 17.04
that they may bring them to the L., 17.05
of peace offerings to the L.; 17.05
altar of the L. at the door of the 17.06
fat for a pleasing odor to the L. 17.06
meeting, to sacrifice it to the L.; 17.09
And the L. said to Moses, 18.01
of Israel, I am the L. your God. 18.02
in them, I am the L. your God. 18.04
a man shall live: I am the L. 18.05
uncover nakedness. I am the L. 18.06
the name of your God: I am the L. 18.21
by them: I am the L. your God." 18.30
And the L. said to Moses, 19.01
for I the L. your God am holy. 19.02
my sabbaths: I am the L. your God. 19.03
molten gods: I am the L. your God. 19.04
of peace offerings to the L., 19.05
profaned a holy thing of the L.; 19.08
sojourner: I am the L. your God. 19.10
the name of your God: I am the L. 19.12
shall fear your God: I am the L. 19.14
life of your neighbor: I am the L. 19.16
neighbor as yourself: I am the L. 19.18
offering for himself to the L., 19.21
before the L. for his sin which he 19.22
an offering of praise to the L. 19.24
for you: I am the L. your God. 19.25
any marks upon you: I am the L. 19.28
reverence my sanctuary: I am the L. 19.30
by them: I am the L. your God. 19.31
shall fear your God: I am the L. 19.32
of Egypt: I am the L. your God. 19.34
I am the L. your God, who brought 19.36
ordinances, and do them: I am the L. 19.37
The L. said to Moses, 20.01
be holy; for I am the L. your God. 20.07
do them; I am the L. who sanctify you. 20.08
'I am the L. your God, who have 20.24
for I the L. am holy, and have 20.26
And the L. said to Moses, "Speak to 21.01
the offerings by fire to the L., 21.06
for I the L., who sanctify you, am 21.08
his God is upon him: I am the L. 21.12
for I am the L. who sanctify him." 21.15
And the L. said to Moses, 21.16
for I am the L. who sanctify them. 21.23
And the L. said to Moses, 22.01
holy name; I am the L. 22.02
of Israel dedicate to the L., 22.03
off from my presence: I am the L. 22.03
defiling himself by it: I am the L.' 22.08
I am the L. who sanctify them. 22.09
which they offer to the L., 22.15
for I am the L. who sanctify them." 22.16
And the L. said to Moses, 22.17
offered to the L. as a burnt 22.18
of peace offerings to the L., 22.21
offer to the L. or make of them an 22.22
by fire upon the altar to the L. 22.22
offer to the L. or sacrifice 22.24
And the L. said to Moses, 22.26
as an offering by fire to the L. 22.27
sacrifice of thanksgiving to the L., 22.29
of it until morning: I am the L. 22.30
commandments and do them: I am the L. 22.31
I am the L. who sanctify you, 22.32
Egypt to be your God: I am the L." 22.33
The L. said to Moses, 23.01
feasts of the L. which you shall 23.02
sabbath to the L. in all your 23.03
are the appointed feasts of the L., 23.04
of unleavened bread to the L.; 23.06
by fire to the L. seven days; 23.08
And the L. said to Moses, 23.09
shall wave the sheaf before the L., 23.11
as a burnt offering to the L. 23.12
to be offered by fire to the L., 23.13
offering of new grain to the L. 23.16
leaven, as first fruits to the L. 23.17
be a burnt offering to the L., 23.18
by fire, a pleasing odor to the L. 23.18

LORD (cont.)
as a wave offering before the L., Lev 23.20
be holy to the L. for the priest. 23.20
the stranger: I am the L. your God." 23.22
And the L. said to Moses, 23.23
an offering by fire to the L. 23.25
And the L. said to Moses, 23.26
an offering by fire to the L. 23.27
for you before the L. your God. 23.28
And the L. said to Moses, 23.33
is the feast of booths to the L. 23.34
offerings by fire to the L.; 23.36
an offering by fire to the L.; 23.36
are the appointed feasts of the L., 23.37
presenting to the L. offerings by 23.37
besides the sabbaths of the L., 23.38
offerings, which you give to the L. 23.38
the feast of the L. seven days; 23.39
before the L. your God seven days, 23.40
a feast to the L. seven days in 23.41
of Egypt: I am the L. your God." 23.43
the appointed feasts of the L. 23.44
The L. said to Moses, 24.01
morning before the L. continually; 24.03
gold before the L. continually. 24.04
to be offered by fire to the L. 24.07
before the L. continually on 24.08
of the offerings by fire to the L., 24.09
the will of the L. should be 24.12
And the L. said to Moses, 24.13
the name of the L. shall be put to 24.16
the native; for I am the L. your God." 24.22
did as the L. commanded Moses. 24.23
The L. said to Moses on Mount Sinai, 25.01
shall keep a sabbath to the L. 25.02
for the land, a sabbath to the L.; 25.04
for I am the L. your God. 25.17
I am the L. your God, who brought 25.38
of Egypt: I am the L. your God. 25.55
to them; for I am the L. your God. 26.01
reverence my sanctuary: I am the L. 26.02
I am the L. your God, who brought 26.13
for I am the L. their God; 26.44
I might be their God: I am the L." 26.45
laws which the L. made between him 26.46
The L. said to Moses, 27.01
persons to the L. at your valuation, 27.02
men offer as an offering to the L., 27.09
any man gives to the L. is holy. 27.09
offered as an offering to the L., 27.11
his house to be holy to the L., 27.14
dedicates to the L. part of the 27.16
jubilee, shall be holy to the L., 27.21
dedicates to the L. a field which 27.22
that day as a holy thing to the L. 27.23
as a firstling belongs to the L., 27.26
thing that a man devotes to the L., 27.28
thing is most holy to the L. 27.78
it is holy to the L. 27.30
staff, shall be holy to the L. 27.32
which the L. commanded Moses for 27.34
The L. spoke to Moses in the Num 1.01
as the L. commanded Moses. So he 1.19
For the L. said to Moses, 1.48
to all that the L. commanded Moses 1.54
The L. said to Moses and Aaron, 2.01
of Israel, as the L. commanded Moses. 2.33
to all that the L. commanded Moses, 2.34
time when the L. spoke with Moses 3.01
died before the L. when they 3.04
fire before the L. in the wilderness 3.04
And the L. said to Moses, 3.05
And the L. said to Moses, 3.11
they shall be mine: I am the L." 3.13
And the L. said to Moses in the 3.14
according to the word of the L., 3.16
at the commandment of the L., 3.39
And the L. said to Moses, "Number 3.40
I am the L.—instead of all the 3.41
of Israel, as the L. commanded him. 3.42
And the L. said to Moses, 3.44
Levites shall be mine: I am the L. 3.45
according to the word of the L., 3.51
as the L. commanded Moses. 3.51
The L. said to Moses and Aaron, 4.01
The L. said to Moses and Aaron, 4.17
The L. said to Moses, 4.21
the commandment of the L. by Moses. 4.37
to the commandment of the L. 4.41
the commandment of the L. by Moses. 4.45
commandment of the L. through Moses 4.49
by him, as the L. commanded Moses. 4.49
The L. said to Moses, 5.01
as the L. said to Moses, so the 5.04
And the L. said to Moses, 5.05
by breaking faith with the L., 5.06
shall go to the L. for the priest, 5.08
And the L. said to Moses, 5.11
near, and set her before the L.; 5.16
shall set the woman before the L., 5.18
the woman) 'the L. make you an 5.21
when the L. makes your thigh fall 5.21
before the L. and bring it to the 5.25
shall set the woman before the L., 5.30
And the L. said to Moses, 6.01
to separate himself to the L., 6.02
he separates himself to the L., 6.05
himself to the L. he shall not go 6.06
separation he is holy to the L. 6.08
himself to the L. for the days of 6.12
and he shall offer his gift to the L., 6.14
them before the L. and offer his 6.16
of peace offering to the L., 6.17
for a wave offering before the L.; 6.20
offering to the L. shall be 6.21
The L. said to Moses, 6.22
The L. bless you and keep you: 6.24
The L. make his face to shine upon 6.25
The L. lift up his countenance upon 6.26
their offerings before the L., 7.03
Then the L. said to Moses, 7.04
And the L. said to Moses, "They 7.11
of meeting to speak with the L., 7.89
Now the L. said to Moses, 8.01
lampstand, as the L. commanded Moses. 8.03
which the L. had shown Moses, so he 8.04
And the L. said to Moses, 8.05
present the Levites before the L., 8.10
before the L. as a wave offering 8.11
theirs to do the service of the L. 8.11
for a burnt offering to the L., 8.12
them as a wave offering to the L. 8.13
to all that the L. commanded Moses 8.20
as a wave offering before the L., 8.21
as the L. had commanded Moses 8.22
And the L. said to Moses, 8.23
And the L. spoke to Moses in the 9.01
to all that the L. commanded Moses, 9.05
hear what the L. will command 9.08
The L. said to Moses, 9.09
still keep the passover to the L. 9.10
will keep the passover to the L., 9.14
command of the L. the people of 9.18
command of the L. they encamped; 9.18
Israel kept the charge of the L., 9.19
command of the L. they remained in 9.20
the command of the L. they set out. 9.20
command of the L. they encamped, 9.23
the command of the L. they set out; 9.23
they kept the charge of the L., 9.23
at the command of the L. by Moses. 9.23
The L. said to Moses, 10.01
remembered before the L. your God, 10.09
your God: I am the L. your God." 10.10

LORD (cont.)

at the command of the L. by Moses.	Num 10.13
for the place of which the L. said,	10.29
for the L. has promised good to	10.29
whatever good the L. will do to us,	10.32
mount of the L. three days' journey;	10.33
covenant of the L. went before	10.33
cloud of the L. was over them by	10.34
O L., and let thy enemies be	10.35
O L., to the ten thousand thousands	10.36
hearing of the L. about their	11.01
and when the L. heard it, his anger	11.01
the fire of the L. burned among	11.01
and Moses prayed to the L.,	11.02
the fire of the L. burned among	11.03
the anger of the L. blazed hotly,	11.10
Moses said to the L., "Why hast	11.11
And the L. said to Moses, "Gather	11.16
have wept in the hearing of the L.,	11.18
Therefore the L. will give you meat,	11.18
rejected the L. who is among you,	11.20
And the L. said to Moses, "Is the	11.23
the people the words of the L.;	11.24
Then the L. came down in the cloud	11.25
"My l. Moses, forbid them."	11.28
that the L. would put his spirit	11.29
went forth a wind from the L.,	11.31
anger of the L. was kindled	11.33
and the L. smote the people with a	11.33
"Has the L. indeed spoken only	12.02
us also?" And the L. heard it.	12.02
And suddenly the L. said to Moses	12.04
And the L. came down in a pillar of	12.05
I the L. make myself known to him	12.06
and he beholds the form of the L.	12.08
anger of the L. was kindled	12.09
my l., do not punish us because we	12.11
And Moses cried to the L.,	12.13
But the L. said to Moses, "If her	12.14
The L. said to Moses,	13.01
according to the command of the L.,	13.03
Why does the L. bring us into this	14.03
If the L. delights in us, he will	14.08
Only, do not rebel against the L.;	14.09
from them, and the L. is with us;	14.09
glory of the L. appeared at the	14.10
And the L. said to Moses, "How long	14.11
But Moses said to the L.,	14.13
O L., art in the midst of this	14.14
for thou, O L., art seen face to	14.14
'Because the L. was not able to	14.16
power of the L. be great as thou	14.17
'The L. is slow to anger, and	14.18
Then the L. said, "I have pardoned,	14.20
filled with the glory of the L.,	14.21
And the L. said to Moses and to	14.26
says the L., 'what you have said	14.28
I, the L., have spoken; surely this	14.35
land, died by plague before the L.	14.37
place which the L. has promised;	14.40
transgressing the command of the L.,	14.41
for the L. is not among you.	14.42
turned back from following the L.,	14.43
the L. will not be with you."	14.43
the ark of the covenant of the L.,	14.44
The L. said to Moses,	15.01
offer to the L. from the herd or	15.03
to make a pleasing odor to the L.,	15.03
offer to the L. a cereal offering	15.04
of wine, a pleasing odor to the L.	15.07
or for peace offerings to the L.,	15.08
by fire, a pleasing odor to the L.	15.10
by fire, a pleasing odor to the L.	15.13
by fire, a pleasing odor to the L.,	15.14
the sojourner be before the L.	15.15
The L. said to Moses,	15.17
present an offering to the L.	15.19
give to the L. an offering throughout	15.21
which the L. has spoken to Moses,	15.22
all that the L. has commanded you	15.23
day that the L. gave commandment,	15.23
offering, a pleasing odor to the L.,	15.24
an offering by fire to the L.,	15.25
their sin offering before the L.,	15.25
before the L. for the person who	15.28
reviles the L., and that person	15.30
he has despised the word of the L.,	15.31
And the L. said to Moses, "The man	15.35
with stones, as the L. commanded Moses.	15.36
The L. said to Moses,	15.37
all the commandments of the L.,	15.39
I am the L. your God, who brought	15.41
be your God: I am the L. your God."	15.41
of them, and the L. is among them;	16.03
above the assembly of the L.?"	16.03
the morning the L. will show who	16.05
upon them before the L. tomorrow,	16.07
man whom the L. chooses shall be	16.07
in the tabernacle of the L.,	16.09
is against the L. that you and all	16.11
was very angry, and said to the L.,	16.15
before the L., you and they, and	16.16
you bring before the L. his censer,	16.17
glory of the L. appeared to all	16.19
And the L. said to Moses and to	16.20
And the L. said to Moses,	16.23
know that the L. has sent me to do	16.28
then the L. has not sent me.	16.29
But if the L. creates something new,	16.30
these men have despised the L."	16.30
And fire came forth from the L.,	16.35
Then the L. said to Moses,	16.36
they offered them before the L.;	16.38
near to burn incense before the L.,	16.40
as the L. said to Eleazar through	16.40
have killed the people of the L."	16.41
and the glory of the L. appeared.	16.42
and the L. said to Moses,	16.44
wrath has gone forth from the L.,	16.46
The L. said to Moses,	17.01
rods before the L. in the tent of	17.07
from before the L. to all the	17.09
And the L. said to Moses, "Put back	17.10
as the L. commanded him, so he did.	17.11
tabernacle of the L., shall die.	17.13
So the L. said to Aaron, "You and	18.01
given to the L., to do the service	18.06
Then the L. said to Aaron, "And	18.08
they give to the L., I give to you.	18.12
land, which they bring to the L.,	18.13
beast, which they offer to the L.,	18.15
by fire, a pleasing odor to the L.;	18.17
present to the L. I give to you,	18.19
ever before the L. for you and for	18.19
And the L. said to Aaron, "You shall	18.20
present as an offering to the L.,	18.24
And the L. said to Moses,	18.25
an offering from it to the L.,	18.26
offering to the L. from all your	18.28
every offering due to the L.,	18.29
Now the L. said to Moses and to	19.01
the law which the L. has commanded:	19.02
defiles the tabernacle of the L.,	19.13
defiled the sanctuary of the L.;	19.20
our brethren died before the L.!	20.03
assembly of the L. into this	20.04
glory of the L. appeared to them,	20.06
and the L. said to Moses,	20.07
took the rod from before the L.,	20.09
And the L. said to Moses and Aaron,	20.12
of Irael contended with the L.,	20.13
and when we cried to the L.,	20.16
And the L. said to Moses and Aaron	20.23
Moses did as the L. commanded;	20.27

LORD (cont.)

And Israel vowed a vow to the L., Num 21.02
And the L. hearkened to the voice 21.03
Then the L. sent fiery serpents 21.06
against the L. and against you; 21.07
pray to the L., that he take away 21.07
And the L. said to Moses, "Make a 21.08
in the Book of the Wars of the L., 21.14
well of which the L. said to Moses, 21.16
But the L. said to Moses, "Do not 21.34
to you, as the L. speaks to me"; 22.08
for the L. has refused to let me go 22.13
the command of the L. my God, 22.18
what more the L. will say to me." 22.19
angel of the L. took his stand in 22.22
angel of the L. standing in the 22.23
angel of the L. stood in a narrow 22.24
the ass saw the angel of the L., 22.25
Then the angel of the L. went ahead, 22.26
When the ass saw the angel of the L., 22.27
Then the L. opened the mouth of the 22.28
Then the L. opened the eyes of 22.31
angel of the L. standing in the 22.31
And the angel of the L. said to him, 22.32
Balaam said to the angel of the L., 22.34
the angel of the L. said to Balaam, 22.35
perhaps the L. will come to meet me; 23.03
And the L. put a word in Balaam's 23.05
whom the L. has not denounced? 23.08
speak what the L. puts in my mouth?" 23.12
offering, while I meet the L. yonder." 23.15
And the L. met Balaam, and put a 23.16
to him, "What has the L. spoken?" 23.17
The L. their God is with them, and 23.21
'All that the L. says, that I must 23.26
it pleased the L. to bless Israel, 24.01
like aloes that the L. has planted, 24.06
but the L. has held you back 24.11
to go beyond the word of the L., 24.13
what the L. speaks, that will I 24.13
anger of the L. was kindled 25.03
and the L. said to Moses, "Take all 25.04
hang them in the sun before the L., 25.04
anger of the L. may turn away from 25.04
And the L. said to Moses, 25.10
And the L. said to Moses, 25.16
After the plague the L. said to 26.01
upward." as the L. commanded Moses. 26.04
they contended against the L., 26.09
The L. said to Moses: 26.52
offered unholy fire before the L. 26.61
For the L. had said of them, "They 26.65
against the L. in the company of 27.03
Moses brought their case before the L. 27.05
And the L. said to Moses, 27.06
as the L. commanded Moses. 27.11
The L. said to Moses, "Go up into 27.12
Moses said to the L., 27.15
"Let the L., the God of the spirits 27.16
congregation of the L. may not be 27.17
And the L. said to Moses, "Take 27.18
judgment of the Urim before the L.; 27.21
And Moses did as the L. commanded him; 27.22
him as the L. directed through 27.23
The L. said to Moses, 28.01
which you shall offer to the L.: 28.03
an offering by fire to the L. 28.06
offering of strong drink to the L. 28.07
by fire, a pleasing odor to the L. 28.08
offer a burnt offering to the L.: 28.11
an offering by fire to the L. 28.13
goat for a sin offering to the L.; 28.15
fire, a burnt offering to the L.: 28.19
by fire, a pleasing odor to the L.; 28.24
grain to the L. at your feast of 28.26
offering, a pleasing odor to the L.: 28.27
offering, a pleasing odor to the L.: 29.02
an offering by fire to the L. 29.06
offer a burnt offering to the L., 29.08
keep a feast to the L. seven days; 29.12
by fire, a pleasing odor to the L. 29.13
by fire, a pleasing odor to the L.: 29.36
offer to the L. at your appointed 29.39
just as the L. had commanded Moses. 29.40
"This is what the L. has commanded. 30.01
When a man vows a vow to the L., 30.02
Or when a woman vows a vow to the L., 30.03
and the L. will forgive her, because 30.05
herself; and L. will forgive her. 30.08
them void, and the L. will forgive her. 30.12
which the L. commanded Moses, as 30.16
The L. said to Moses, 31.01
as the L. commanded Moses, and slew 31.07
against the L. in the matter of 31.16
among the congregation of the L. 31.16
law which the L. has commanded 31.21
The L. said to Moses, 31.25
And levy for the L. a tribute from 31.28
priest as an offering to the L. 31.29
charge of the tabernacle of the L." 31.30
did as the L. commanded Moses. 31.31
which was the offering for the L., 31.41
as the L. commanded Moses. 31.41
charge of the tabernacle of the L.; 31.47
as the L. commanded Moses. 31.47
for ourselves before the L." 31.50
that they offered to the L., 31.52
the people of Israel before the L. 31.54
the land which the L. smote before 32.04
land which the L. has given them? 32.07
land which the L. had given them. 32.09
they have wholly followed the L.' 32.12
the sight of the L. was consumed. 32.13
anger of the L. against Israel! 32.14
to go before the L. for the war, 32.20
pass over the Jordan before the L., 32.21
and the land is subdued before the L.; 32.22
obligation to the L. and to Israel; 32.22
be your possession before the L. 32.22
you have sinned against the L.; 32.23
servants will do as my l. commands. 32.25
before the L. to battle, as my l. orders." 32.27
is armed to battle before the L., 32.29
"As the L. has said to your servants, 32.31
before the L. into the land of 32.32
by stage, by command of the L.; 33.02
whom the L. had struck down among 33.04
gods also the L. executed judgments 33.04
Mount Hor at the command of the L., 33.38
And the L. said to Moses in the 33.50
The L. said to Moses, 34.01
which the L. has commanded to give 34.13
The L. said to Moses, 34.16
men whom the L. commanded to 34.29
The L. said to Moses in the plains 35.01
And the L. said to Moses, 35.09
for I the L. dwell in the midst of 35.34
"The L. commanded my l. to give 36.02
and my l. was commanded by the L. 36.02
according to the word of the L., 36.05
This is what the L. commands concerning 36.06
did as the L. commanded Moses; 36.10
which the L. commanded by Moses to 36.13
to all that the L. had given him Deu 1.03
"The L. our God said to us in Horeb, 1.06
land which the L. swore to your 1.08
the L. your God has multiplied you, 1.10
May the L., the God of your fathers, 1.11
as the L. our God commanded us; 1.19
which the L. our God gives us. 1.20
Behold, the L. your God has set the 1.21
as the L., the God of your fathers, 1.21
land which the L. our God gives us.' 1.25
the command of the L. your God; 1.26

LORD (cont.)
'Because the L. hated us he has Deu 1.27
The L. your God who goes before you 1.30
seen how the L. your God bore you, 1.31
did not believe the L. your God, 1.32
"And the L. heard your words, and 1.34
he has wholly followed the L.!' 1.36
The L. was angry with me also on 1.37
me, 'We have sinned against the L.; 1.41
just as the L. our God commanded us.' 1.41
And the L. said to me, 'Say to them, 1.42
against the command of the L., 1.43
returned and wept before the L.; 1.45
but the L. did not hearken to your 1.45
of the Red Sea, as the L. told me; 2.01
Then the L. said to me, 2.02
For the L. your God has blessed you 2.07
forty years the L. your God has 2.07
And the L. said to me, 'Do not 2.09
possession, which the L. gave to them.) 2.12
as the L. had sworn to them. 2.14
the hand of the L. was against 2.15
the L. said to me, 2.17
but the L. destroyed them before 2.21
land which the L. our God gives to 2.29
for the L. your God hardened his 2.30
And the L. said to me, 'Behold, I 2.31
And the L. our God gave him over to 2.33
the L. our God gave all into our 2.36
wherever the L. our God forbade us 2.37
But the L. said to me, 'Do not fear 3.02
So the L. our God gave into our 3.03
'The L. your God has given you this 3.18
until the L. gives rest to your 3.20
land which the L. your God gives 3.20
all that the L. your God has done 3.21
so will the L. do to all the 3.21
for it is the L. your God who 3.22
"And I besought the L. at that time, 3.23
'O L. GOD, thou hast only begun to 3.24
But the L. was angry with me on 3.26
and the L. said to me, 'Let it 3.26
possession of the land which the L., 4.01
commandments of the L. your God 4.02
seen what the L. did at Baalpeor; 4.03
for the L. your God destroyed from 4.03
fast to the L. your God are all 4.04
as the L. my God commanded me, that 4.05
to it as the L. our God is to us, 4.07
before the L. your God at Horeb, 4.10
the L. said to me, 'Gather the 4.10
Then the L. spoke to you out of the 4.12
And the L. commanded me at that 4.14
day that the L. spoke to you at 4.15
which the L. your God has allotted 4.19
But the L. has taken you, and 4.20
Furthermore the L. was angry with 4.21
land which the L. your God gives 4.21
the covenant of the L. your God, 4.23
which the L. your God has forbidden 4.23
For the L. your God is a devouring 4.24
in the sight of the L. your God, 4.25
And the L. will scatter you among 4.27
where the L. will drive you. 4.27
you will seek the L. your God, 4.29
return to the L. your God and obey 4.30
for the L. your God is a merciful 4.31
to all that the L. your God did 4.34
you might know that the L. is God; 4.35
that the L. is God in heaven above 4.39
land which the L. your God gives 4.40
The L. our God made a covenant with 5.02
fathers did the L. make this 5.03
The L. spoke with you face to face 5.04
between the L. and you at that 5.05
declare to you the word of the L.; 5.05
"'I am the L. your God, who brought 5.06
for I the L. your God am a jealous 5.09
the name of the L. your God in 5.11
for the L. will not hold him 5.11
as the L. your God commanded you. 5.12
is a sabbath to the L. your God; 5.14
and the L. your God brought you out 5.15
therefore the L. your God commanded 5.15
as the L. your God commanded you; 5.16
land which the L. your God gives 5.16
"These words the L. spoke to all 5.22
the L. our God has shown us his 5.24
voice of the L. our God any more, 5.25
all that the L. our God will say; 5.27
us all that the L. our God will 5.27
"And the L. heard your words, when 5.28
and the L. said to me, 'I have heard 5.28
therefore as the L. your God has 5.32
way which the L. your God has 5.33
which the L. your God commanded me 6.01
that you may fear the L. your God, 6.02
as the L., the God of your fathers, 6.03
The L. our God is one LORD; 6.04
Israel: The LORD our God is one L.; 6.04
shall love the L. your God with 6.05
"And when the L. your God brings 6.10
then take heed lest you forget the L., 6.12
You shall fear the L. your God; 6.13
for the L. your God in the midst of 6.15
anger of the L. your God be 6.15
not put the L. your God to the 6.16
commandments of the L. your God, 6.17
and good in the sight of the L., 6.18
land which the L. swore to give to 6.18
before you, as the L. has promised. 6.19
which the L. our God has commanded 6.20
and the L. brought us out of Egypt 6.21
and the L. showed signs and wonders, 6.22
And the L. commanded us to do all 6.24
to fear the L. our God, for our good 6.24
commandment before the L. our God, 6.25
"When the L. your God brings you 7.01
and when the L. your God gives them 7.02
anger of the L. would be kindled 7.04
a people holy to the L. your God; 7.06
the L. your God has chosen you to 7.06
people that the L. set his love 7.07
but it is because the L. loves you, 7.08
that the L. has brought you out 7.08
that the L. your God is God, the 7.09
the L. your God will keep with you 7.12
And the L. will take away from you 7.15
that the L. your God will give 7.16
what the L. your God did to 7.18
by which the L. your God brought 7.19
so will the L. your God do to all 7.19
Moreover the L. your God will send 7.20
for the L. your God is in the midst 7.21
The L. your God will clear away 7.22
But the L. your God will give them 7.23
an abomination to the L. your God. 7.25
land which the L. swore to give to 8.01
way which the L. your God has led 8.02
proceeds out of the mouth of the L. 8.03
the L. your God disciplines you. 8.05
commandments of the L. your God, 8.06
For the L. your God is bringing you 8.07
shall bless the L. your God for 8.10
lest you forget the L. your God, 8.11
up, and you forget the L. your God, 8.14
You shall remember the L. your God, 8.18
you forget the L. your God and go 8.19
that the L. makes to perish before 8.20
obey the voice of the L. your God. 8.20
devouring fire is the L. your God; 9.03
as the L. has promised you. 9.03
after the L. your God has thrust 9.04
that the L. has brought me in to 9.04

LORD (cont.)
that the L. is driving them out Deu 9.04
nations the L. your God is driving 9.05
word which the L. swore to your 9.05
that the L. your God is not giving 9.06
provoked the L. your God to wrath 9.07
been rebellious against the L. 9.07
Horeb you provoked the L. to wrath, 9.08
and the L. was so angry with you 9.08
covenant which the L. made with you, 9.09
And the L. gave me the two tables 9.10
words which the L. had spoken with 9.10
nights the L. gave me the two 9.11
Then the L. said to me, 'Arise, go 9.12
"Furthermore the L. said to me, 9.13
had sinned against the L. your God; 9.16
way which the L. had commanded you. 9.16
prostrate before the L. as before, 9.18
was evil in the sight of the L., 9.18
which the L. bore against you, so 9.19
But the L. hearkened to me that 9.19
And the L. was so angry with Aaron 9.20
you provoked the L. to wrath. 9.22
And when the L. sent you from 9.23
the commandment of the L. your God, 9.23
against the L. from the day that I 9.24
before the L. for these forty days 9.25
because the L. had said he would 9.25
And I prayed to the L., 9.26
'O L. God, destroy not thy people 9.26
"Because the L. was not able to 9.28
"At that time the L. said to me, 10.01
which the L. had spoken to you on 10.04
and the L. gave them to me. 10.04
they are, as the L. commanded me. 10.05
At that time the L. set apart the 10.08
the ark of the covenant of the L., 10.08
before the L. to minister to him 10.08
the L. is his inheritance, as the 10.09
as the L. your God said to him.) 10.09
and the L. hearkened to me that 10.10
the L. was unwilling to destroy you. 10.10
And the L. said to me, 'Arise, go on 10.11
what does the L. your God require 10.12
you, but to fear the L. your God, 10.12
to serve the L. your God with all 10.12
commandments and statutes of the L., 10.13
Behold, to the L. your God belong 10.14
yet the L. set his heart in love 10.15
For the L. your God is God of gods 10.17
God is God of gods and L. of lords, 10.17
You shall fear the L. your God; 10.20
and now the L. your God has made 10.22
therefore love the L. your God, 11.01
the discipline of the L. your God, 11.02
and how the L. has destroyed them 11.04
great work of the L. which he did. 11.07
land which the L. swore to your 11.09
a land which the L. your God cares 11.12
the eyes of the L. your God are 11.12
to love the L. your God, and to 11.13
anger of the L. be kindled against 11.17
good land which the L. gives you. 11.17
land which the L. swore to your 11.21
loving the L. your God, walking in 11.22
then the L. will drive out all 11.23
the L. your God will lay the fear 11.25
commandments of the L. your God, 11.27
commandments of the L. your God, 11.28
And when the L. your God brings you 11.29
land which the L. your God gives 11.31
to do in the land which the L., 12.01
shall not do so to the L. your God. 12.04
place which the L. your God will 12.05
shall eat before the L. your God, 12.07
in which the L. your God has 12.07
which the L. your God gives you. 12.09
land which the L. your God gives 12.10
place which the L. your God will 12.11
offerings which you vow to the L. 12.11
rejoice before the L. your God, 12.12
place which the L. will choose in 12.14
blessing of the L. your God which 12.15
them before the L. your God in the 12.18
place which the L. your God will 12.18
before the L. your God in all that 12.18
"When the L. your God enlarges your 12.20
place which the L. your God will 12.21
which the L. has given you, as I 12.21
is right in the sight of the L. 12.25
place which the L. will choose, 12.26
on the altar of the L. your God; 12.27
on the altar of the L. your God, 12.27
in the sight of the L. your God. 12.28
"When the L. your God cuts off 12.29
shall not do so to the L. your God; 12.31
thing which the L. hates they have 12.31
for the L. your God is testing you, 13.03
you love the L. your God with all 13.03
walk after the L. your God and 13.04
rebellion against the L. your God, 13.05
in which the L. your God commanded 13.05
draw you away from the L. your God, 13.10
which the L. your God gives you to 13.12
burnt offering to the L. your God; 13.16
that the L. may turn from the 13.17
obey the voice of the L. your God, 13.18
in the sight of the L. your God. 13.18
"You are the sons of the L. your God; 14.01
a people holy to the L. your God, 14.02
and the L. has chosen you to be a 14.02
a people holy to the L. your God. 14.21
And before the L. your God, in the 14.23
to fear the L. your God always. 14.23
when the L. your God blesses you, 14.24
which the L. your God chooses, to 14.24
place which the L. your God 14.25
before the L. your God and rejoice, 14.26
that the L. your God may bless you 14.29
you (for the L. will bless you in 15.04
land which the L. your God gives 15.04
obey the voice of the L. your God, 15.05
For the L. your God will bless you, 15.06
land which the L. your God gives 15.07
and he cry to the L. against you, 15.09
for this the L. your God will 15.10
as the L. your God has blessed you, 15.14
and the L. your God redeemed you; 15.15
So the L. your God will bless you 15.18
consecrate to the L. your God; 15.19
before the L. your God year by year 15.20
the place which the L. will choose. 15.20
sacrifice it to the L. your God. 15.21
the passover to the L. your God; 16.01
of Abib the L. your God brought 16.01
sacrifice to the L. your God, 16.02
the place which the L. will choose, 16.02
towns which the L. your God gives 16.05
place which the L. your God will 16.06
place which the L. your God will 16.07
solemn assembly to the L. your God; 16.08
of weeks to the L. your God with 16.10
give as the L. your God blesses 16.10
rejoice before the L. your God, 16.11
place which the L. your God will 16.11
place which the L. your God at the 16.15
the place which the L. will choose; 16.15
because the L. your God will bless 16.15
before the L. your God at the 16.16
appear before the L. empty-handed; 16.16
blessing of the L. your God which 16.17
towns which the L. your God gives 16.18
land which the L. your God gives 16.18
land which the L. your God gives 16.20

LORD (cont.)

altar of the L. your God which you Deu 16.21
which the L. your God hates. 16.22
sacrifice to the L. your God an ox 17.01
an abomination to the L. your God. 17.01
towns which the L. your God gives 17.02
in the sight of the L. your God, 17.02
place which the L. your God will 17.08
place which the L. will choose; 17.10
there before the L. your God, 17.12
land which the L. your God gives 17.14
him whom the L. your God will 17.15
since the L. has said to you, 'You 17.16
may learn to fear the L. his God, 17.19
the offerings by fire to the L., 18.01
the L. is their inheritance, as he 18.02
For the L. your God has chosen him 18.05
and minister in the name of the L., 18.05
place which the L. will choose, 18.06
in the name of the L. his God, 18.07
to minister there before the L. 18.07
land which the L. your God gives 18.09
things is an abomination to the L.; 18.12
practices the L. your God is 18.12
blameless before the L. your God. 18.13
the L. your God has not allowed you 18.14
"The L. your God will raise up for 18.15
desired of the L. your God at 18.16
again the voice of the L. my God, 18.16
And the L. said to me, 'They have 18.17
word which the L. has not spoken?'— 18.21
speaks in the name of the L., 18.22
a word which the L. has not spoken; 18.22
"When the L. your God cuts off the 19.01
whose land the L. your God gives 19.01
land which the L. your God gives 19.02
land which the L. your God gives 19.03
And if the L. your God enlarges 19.08
by loving the L. your God and by 19.09
land which the L. your God gives 19.10
land that the L. your God gives 19.14
dispute shall appear before the L., 19.17
for the L. your God is with you, who 20.01
for the L. your God is he that goes 20.04
and when the L. your God gives it 20.13
which the L. your God has given you. 20.14
that the L. your God gives you for 20.16
as the L. your God has commanded; 20.17
so to sin against the L. your God. 20.18
land which the L. your God gives 21.01
for the L. your God has chosen them 21.05
and to bless in the name of the L., 21.05
Forgive, O L., thy people Israel, 21.08
is right in the sight of the L. 21.09
and the L. your God gives them into 21.10
land which the L. your God gives 21.23
an abomination to the L. your God. 22.05
not enter the assembly of the L. 23.01
shall enter the assembly of the L.; 23.02
shall enter the assembly of the L. 23.02
shall enter the assembly of the L.; 23.03
the assembly of the L. for ever; 23.03
Nevertheless the L. your God would 23.05
but the L. your God turned the 23.05
because the L. your God loved you. 23.05
May enter the assembly of the L. 23.08
Because the L. your God walks in 23.14
house of the L. your God in 23.18
an abomination to the L. your God. 23.18
that the L. your God may bless you 23.20
"When you make a vow to the L. your God, 23.21
for the L. your God will surely 23.21
vowed to the L. your God what you 23.23
is an abomination before the L., 24.04
land which the L. your God gives 24.04
Remember what the L. your God did 24.09
to you before the L. your God. 24.13

lest he cry against you to the L., 24.15
Egypt and the L. your God redeemed 24.18
that the L. your God may bless you 24.19
land which the L. your God gives 25.15
an abomination to the L. your God. 25.16
Therefore when the L. your God has 25.19
land which the L. your God gives 25.19
land which the L. your God gives 26.01
land that the L. your God gives 26.02
place which the L. your God will 26.02
this day to the L. your God that I 26.03
land which the L. swore to our 26.03
the altar of the L. your God. 26.04
response before the L. your God, 26.05
Then we cried to the L. the God of 26.07
and the L. heard our voice, and saw 26.07
and the L. brought us out of Egypt 26.08
which thou, O L., hast given me.' 26.10
set it down before the L. your God, 26.10
and worship before the L. your God; 26.10
good which the L. your God has 26.11
shall say before the L. your God, 26.13
obeyed the voice of the L. my God, 26.14
"This day the L. your God commands 26.16
concerning the L. that he is your 26.17
and the L. has declared this day 26.18
a people holy to the L. your God, 26.19
land which the L. your God gives 27.02
land which the L. your God gives 27.03
as the L., the God of your fathers, 27.03
build an altar to the L. your God, 27.05
an altar to the L. your God of 27.06
offerings on it to the L. your God; 27.06
rejoice before the L. your God. 27.07
the people of the L. your God. 27.09
obey the voice of the L. your God, 27.10
image, an abomination to the L., 27.15
obey the voice of the L. your God, 28.01
the L. your God will set you high 28.01
obey the voice of the L. your God. 28.02
"The L. will cause your enemies who 28.07
The L. will command the blessing 28.08
land which the L. your God gives 28.08
The L. will establish you as a 28.09
commandments of the L. your God, 28.09
are called by the name of the L.; 28.10
And the L. will make you abound in 28.11
land which the L. swore to your 28.11
The L. will open to you his good 28.12
And the L. will make you the head, 28.13
commandments of the L. your God, 28.13
voice of the L. your God or be 28.15
"The L. will send upon you curses, 28.20
The L. will make the pestilence 28.21
The L. will smite you with consumption, 28.22
The L. will make the rain of your 28.24
"The L. will cause you to be 28.25
The L. will smite you with the 28.27
The L. will smite you with madness 28.28
The L. will smite you on the knees 28.35
"The L. will bring you, and your 28.36
where the L. will lead you away, 28.37
obey the voice of the L. your God, 28.45
not serve the L. your God with 28.47
whom the L. will send against you, 28.48
The L. will bring a nation against 28.49
which the L. your God has given you. 28.52
whom the L. your God has given you, 28.53
and awful name, the L. your God, 28.58
then the L. will bring on you and 28.59
the L. will bring upon you, until 28.61
obey the voice of the L. your God. 28.62
And as the L. took delight in doing 28.63
so the L. will take delight in 28.63
And the L. will scatter you among 28.64
but the L. will give you there a 28.65
And the L. will bring you back in 28.68

LORD (cont.)

which the L. commanded Moses to Deu 29.01
all that the L. did before your 29.02
but to this day the L. has not 29.04
may know that I am the L. your God. 29.06
all of you before the L. your God; 29.10
sworn covenant of the L. your God, 29.12
which the L. your God makes with 29.12
us this day before the L. our God. 29.15
day from the L. our God to go and 29.18
The L. would not pardon him, but 29.20
anger of the L. and his jealousy 29.20
and the L. would blot out his name 29.20
And the L. would single him out 29.21
with which the L. has made it sick— 29.22
which the L. overthrew in his anger 29.23
'Why has the L. done thus to this 29.24
forsook the covenant of the L., 29.25
anger of the L. was kindled 29.27
and the L. uprooted them from their 29.28
things belong to the L. our God; 29.29
where the L. your God has driven 30.01
and return to the L. your God, 30.02
then the L. your God will restore 30.03
where the L. your God has scattered 30.03
from there the L. your God will 30.04
and the L. your God will bring you 30.05
And the L. your God will circumcise 30.06
will love the L. your God with all 30.06
And the L. your God will put all 30.07
again obey the voice of the L., 30.08
The L. your God will make you 30.09
for the L. will again take delight 30.09
obey the voice of the L. your God, 30.10
you turn to the L. your God with 30.10
commandments of the L. your God 30.16
by loving the L. your God, by 30.16
and the L. your God will bless you 30.16
loving the L. your God, obeying his 30.20
land which the L. swore to your 30.20
The L. has said to me, 'You shall 31.02
The L. your God himself will go 31.03
at your head, as the L. has spoken. 31.03
And the L. will do to them as he 31.04
And the L. will give them over to 31.05
for it is the L. your God who goes 31.06
land which the L. has sworn to 31.07
It is the L. who goes before you; 31.08
the ark of the covenant of the L., 31.09
before the L. your God at the 31.11
and learn to fear the L. your God, 31.12
and learn to fear the L. your God, 31.13
And the L. said to Moses, "Behold, 31.14
And the L. appeared in the tent in 31.15
And the L. said to Moses, "Behold, 31.16
And the L. commissioned Joshua the 31.23
the ark of the covenant of the L., 31.25
of the covenant of the L. your God, 31.26
been rebellious against the L.; 31.27
is evil in the sight of the L., 31.29
I will proclaim the name of the L. 32.03
Do you thus requite the L., 32.06
the L. alone did lead him, and there 32.12
"The L. saw it, and spurned them, 32.19
the L. has not wrought all this."' 32.27
and the L. had given them up? 32.30
For the L. will vindicate his 32.36
And the L. said to Moses that very 32.48
He said, "The L. came from Sinai, and 33.02
Thus the L. became king in Jeshurun, 33.05
O L., the voice of Judah, and bring 33.07
Bless, O L., his substance, and 33.11
he said, "The beloved of the L., 33.12
"Blessed by the L. be his land, 33.13
commands and just decrees of the L." 33.21
and full of the blessing of the L., 33.23
like you, a people saved by the L., 33.29
And the L. showed him all the land, 34.01
And the L. said to him, "This is the 34.04
servant of the L. died there in 34.05
according to the word of the L., 34.05
and did as the L. had commanded 34.09
whom the L. knew face to face, 34.10
which the L. sent him to do in the 34.11
of Moses the servant of the L., Jos 1.01
the L. said to Joshua the son of 1.01
for the L. your God is with you 1.09
land which the L. your God gives 1.11
servant of the L. commanded you, 1.13
'The L. your God is providing you a 1.13
until the L. gives rest to your 1.15
land which the L. your God is 1.15
servant of the L. gave you beyond 1.15
only may the L. your God be with 1.17
"I know that the L. has given you 2.09
heard how the L. dried up the 2.10
for the L. your God is he who is 2.11
to me by the L. that as I have 2.12
you when the L. gives us the land." 2.14
"Truly the L. has given all the 2.24
covenant of the L. your God being 3.03
tomorrow the L. will do wonders 3.05
And the L. said to Joshua, "This day 3.07
hear the words of the L. your God." 3.09
covenant of the L. of all the 3.11
priests who bear the ark of the L., 3.13
the L. of all the earth, shall rest 3.13
covenant of the L. stood on dry 3.17
the Jordan, the L. said to Joshua, 4.01
the ark of the L. your God into 4.05
the ark of the covenant of the L.; 4.07
of Israel, as the L. told Joshua; 4.08
that the L. commanded Joshua to 4.10
the ark of the L. and the priests 4.11
over before the L. for battle, 4.13
On that day the L. exalted Joshua 4.14
And the L. said to Joshua, 4.15
covenant of the L. came up from 4.18
For the L. your God dried up the 4.23
as the L. your God did to the Red 4.23
that the hand of the L. is mighty; 4.24
may fear the L. your God for ever." 4.24
heard that the L. had dried up the 5.01
At that time the L. said to Joshua, 5.02
not hearken to the voice of the L.; 5.06
to them the L. swore that he would 5.06
land which the L. had sworn to 5.06
And the L. said to Joshua, "This day 5.09
the army of the L. I have now come 5.14
"What does my l. bid his servant?" 5.14
And the L. said to Joshua, "See, I 6.02
horns before the ark of the L." 6.06
pass on before the ark of the L." 6.07
horns before the L. went forward, 6.08
covenant of the L. following them. 6.08
the ark of the L. to compass the 6.11
priests took up the ark of the L. 6.12
before the ark of the L. passed on, 6.13
guard came after the ark of the L., 6.13
for the L. has given you the city. 6.16
devoted to the L. for destruction; 6.17
and iron, are sacred to the L.; 6.19
go into the treasury of the L." 6.19
treasury of the house of the L. 6.24
before the L. be the man that 6.26
So the L. was with Joshua; 6.27
anger of the L. burned against the 7.01
the ark of the L. until the 7.06
O L. God, why hast thou brought this 7.07
O L., what can I say, when Israel 7.08
The L. said to Joshua, "Arise, why 7.10
for thus says the L., 7.13
tribe which the L. takes shall come near 7.14
family which the L. takes shall come near 7.14

LORD (cont.)
household which the L. takes shall come near Jos 7.14
transgressed the covenant of the L., 7.15
give glory to the L. God of Israel, 7.19
against the L. God of Israel, 7.20
they laid them down before the L. 7.23
The L. brings trouble on you today." 7.25
then the L. turned from his burning 7.26
And the L. said to Joshua, "Do not 8.01
for the L. your God will give it 8.07
fire, doing as the L. has bidden; 8.08
Then the L. said to Joshua, "Stretch 8.18
word of the L. which he commanded 8.27
an altar in Mount Ebal to the L., 8.30
servant of the L. had commanded 8.31
on it burnt offerings to the L., 8.31
the ark of the covenant of the L., 8.33
servant of the L. had commanded at 8.33
of the name of the L. your God; 9.09
did not ask direction from the L. 9.14
had sworn to them by the L., 9.18
had sworn to them by the L., 9.19
that the L. your God had commanded 9.24
and for the altar of the L., 9.27
And the L. said to Joshua, "Do not 10.08
And the L. threw them into a panic 10.10
the L. threw down great stones from 10.11
Joshua to the L. in the day when 10.12
day when the L. gave the Amorites 10.12
when the L. hearkened to the voice 10.14
for the L. fought for Israel. 10.14
for the L. your God has given them 10.19
for thus the L. will do to all your 10.25
and the L. gave it also and its 10.30
and the L. gave Lachish into the 10.32
as the L. God of Israel commanded. 10.40
because the L. God of Israel fought 10.42
And the L. said to Joshua, "Do not 11.06
And the L. gave them into the hand 11.08
did to them as the L. bade him; 11.09
servant of the L. had commanded. 11.12
As the L. had commanded Moses his 11.15
of all that the L. had commanded 11.15
as the L. commanded Moses. 11.20
to all that the L. had spoken to 11.23
Moses, the servant of the L., 12.06
servant of the L. gave their land 12.06
and the L. said to him, "You are old 13.01
the servant of the L. gave them: 13.08
by fire to the L. God of Israel 13.14
the L. God of Israel is their 13.33
as the L. had commanded Moses for 14.02
did as the L. commanded Moses; 14.05
know what the L. said to Moses the 14.06
servant of the L. sent me from 14.07
I wholly followed the L. my God. 14.08
have wholly followed the L. my God.' 14.09
the L. has kept me alive, as he said, 14.10
time that the L. spoke this word 14.10
of which the L. spoke on that day; 14.12
may be that the L. will be with me, 14.12
drive them out as the L. said. 14.12
because he wholly followed the L., 14.14
commandment of the L. to Joshua, 15.13
"The L. commanded Moses to give us 17.04
commandment of the L. he gave them 17.04
hitherto the L. has blessed me?" 17.14
which the L., the God of your 18.03
for you here before the L. our God. 18.06
priesthood of the L. is their 18.07
the servant of the L. gave them. 18.07
you here before the L. in Shiloh." 18.08
for them in Shiloh before the L.; 18.10
By command of the L. they gave him 19.50
by lot at Shiloh before the L., 19.51
Then the L. said to Joshua, 20.01
"The L. commanded through Moses 21.02
command of the L. the people of 21.03
as the L. had commanded through 21.08
Thus the L. gave to Israel all the 21.43
And the L. gave them rest on every 21.44
for the L. had given all their 21.44
which the L. had made to the house 21.45
servant of the L. commanded you, 22.02
keep the charge of the L. your God. 22.03
And now the L. your God has given 22.04
servant of the L. gave you on the 22.04
servant of the L. commanded you, 22.05
to love the L. your God, and to walk 22.05
by command of the L. through Moses. 22.09
the whole congregation of the L., 22.16
this day from following the L., 22.16
day in rebellion against the L.? 22.16
upon the congregation of the L., 22.17
this day from following the L.? 22.18
rebel against the L. today he will 22.18
only do not rebel against the L., 22.19
than the altar of the L. our God. 22.19
the L.! The Mighty One, God, the L.! 22.22
in breach of faith toward the L., 22.22
to turn away from following the L.; 22.23
may the L. himself take vengeance. 22.23
'What have you to do with the L., 22.24
For the L. has made the Jordan a 22.25
you have no portion in the L.' 22.25
children cease to worship the L. 22.25
service of the L. in his presence 22.27
"You have no portion in the L."' 22.27
the copy of the altar of the L., 22.28
we should rebel against the L., 22.29
following the L. by building an 22.29
altar of the L. our God that 22.29
know that the L is in the midst 22.31
this treachery against the L.; 22.31
of Israel from the hand of the L." 22.31
between us that the L. is God." 22.34
when the L. had given rest to 23.01
all that the L. your God has done 23.03
for it is the L. your God had done 23.03
for it is the L. your God who has 23.03
The L. your God will push them back 23.05
as the L. your God promised you. 23.05
but cleave to the L. your God as 23.08
For the L. has driven out before 23.09
since it is the L. your God who 23.10
therefore, to love the L. your God. 23.11
that the L. your God will not 23.13
land which the L. your God has 23.13
which the L. your God promised 23.14
which the L. your God promised 23.15
so the L. will bring upon you all 23.15
land which the L. your God has 23.15
the covenant of the L. your God, 23.16
anger of the L. will be kindled 23.16
all the people, "Thus says the L., 24.02
And when they cried to the L., 24.07
"Now therefore fear the L., 24.14
and in Egypt, and serve the L. 24.14
you be unwilling to serve the L., 24.15
and my house, we will serve the L." 24.15
us that we should forsake the L., 24.16
for it is the L. our God who 24.17
and the L. drove out before us all 24.18
therefore we also will serve the L., 24.18
people, "You cannot serve the L.; 24.19
If you forsake the L. and serve 24.20
"Nay; but we will serve the L." 24.21
have chosen the L., to serve him." 24.22
and incline your heart to the L., 24.23
"The L. our God we will serve, and 24.24
the oak in the sanctuary of the L. 24.26
words of the L. which he spoke to 24.27
son of Nun, the servant of the L., 24.29
served the L. all the days of 24.31

LORD (cont.)
work which the L. did for Israel. Jos 24.31
of Israel inquired of the L., Ju 1.01
The L. said, "Judah shall go up; 1.02
went up and the L. gave the 1.04
And the L. was with Judah, and he 1.19
and the L. was with them. 1.22
angel of the L. went up from 2.01
angel of the L. spoke these words 2.04
they sacrificed there to the L. 2.05
served the L. all the days of 2.07
work which the L. had done for 2.07
son of Nun, the servant of the L., 2.08
not know the L. or the work which 2.10
sight of the L. and served the 2.11
and they forsook the L., the God 2.12
and they provoked the L. to anger. 2.12
They forsook the L., and served the 2.13
anger of the L. was kindled 2.14
the hand of the L. was against 2.15
as the L. had warned, and as the 2.15
and as the L. had sworn to them; 2.15
Then the L. raised up judges, who 2.16
obeyed the commandments of the L., 2.17
Whenever the L. raised up judges 2.18
the L. was with the judge, and he 2.18
for the L. was moved to pity by 2.18
anger of the L. was kindled 2.20
the way of the L. as their fathers 2.22
So the L. left those nations, not 2.23
are the nations which the L. left, 3.01
obey the commandments of the L., 3.04
was evil in the sight of the L., 3.07
forgetting the L. their God, and 3.07
anger of the L. was kindled 3.08
people of Israel cried to the L., 3.09
the L. raised up a deliverer for 3.09
The Spirit of the L. came upon him, 3.10
and the L. gave Cushanrishathaim 3.10
was evil in the sight of the L.; 3.12
and the L. strengthened Eglon the 3.12
was evil in the sight of the L. 3.12
people of Israel cried to the L., 3.15
the L. raised up for them a deliverer, 3.15
there lay their l. dead on the 3.25
for the L. has given your enemies 3.28
was evil in the sight of the L., 4.01
And the L. sold them into the hand 4.02
of Israel cried to the L. for help; 4.03
"Does not the L., the God of Israel, 4.06
for the L. will sell Sisera into 4.09
in which the L. has given Sisera 4.14
Does not the L. go out before you?" 4.14
And the L. routed Sisera and all 4.15
"Turn aside, my l., turn aside to me; 4.18
themselves willingly, bless the L.! 5.02
to the L. I will sing, I will make 5.03
make melody to the L., the God of 5.03
"L., when thou didst go forth from 5.04
The mountains quaked before the L., 5.05
the LORD, yon Sinai before the L., 5.05
among the people. Bless the L. 5.09
they repeat the triumphs of the L., 5.11
gates marched the people of the L. 5.11
people of the L. marched down for 5.13
"Curse Meroz, says the angel of the L., 5.23
came not to the help of the L., 5.23
the help of the L. against the 5.23
"So perish all thine enemies, O L.! 5.31
was evil in the sight of the L.; 6.01
and the L. gave them into the hand 6.01
of Israel cried for help to the L. 6.06
cried to the L. on account of the 6.07
the L. sent a prophet to the people 6.08
he said to them, "Thus says the L., 6.08
said to you, 'I am the L. your God; 6.10
angel of the L. came and sat under 6.11
angel of the L. appeared to him 6.12
"The L. is with you, you mighty man 6.12
if the L. is with us, why then has 6.13
'Did not the L. bring us up from 6.13
But now the L. has cast us off, and 6.13
And the L. turned to him and said, 6.14
L., how can I deliver Israel? 6.15
And the L. said to him, "But I will 6.16
angel of the L. reached out the 6.21
angel of the L. vanished from his 6.21
that he was the angel of the L.; 6.22
and Gideon said, "Alas, O L. GOD! 6.22
the angel of the L. face to face." 6.22
But the L. said to him, "Peace be to 6.23
built an altar there to the L., 6.24
and called it, The L. is peace. 6.24
That night the L. said to him, "Take 6.25
an altar to the L. your God on the 6.26
and did as the L. had told him; 6.27
Spirit of the L. took possession 6.34
The L. said to Gideon, "The people 7.02
And the L. said to Gideon, "The 7.04
and the L. said to Gideon, "Every 7.05
And the L. said to Gideon, "With the 7.07
That same night the L. said to him, 7.09
for the L. has given the host of 7.15
shout, 'For the L. and for Gideon.'" 7.18
"A sword for the L. and for Gideon!" 7.20
the L. set every man's sword against 7.22
when the L. has given Zebah and 8.07
as the L. lives, if you had saved 8.19
the L. will rule over you." 8.23
did not remember the L. their God, 8.34
was evil in the sight of the L., 10.06
and they forsook the L., and did not 10.06
anger of the L. was kindled 10.07
people of Israel cried to the L., 10.10
And the L. said to the people of 10.11
people of Israel said to the L., 10.15
from among them and served the L.; 10.16
and the L. gives them over to me, I 11.09
"The L. will be witness between us; 11.10
his words before the L. at Mizpah. 11.11
And the L., the God of Israel, gave 11.21
So then the L., the God of Israel, 11.23
all that the L. our God has 11.24
the L., the Judge, decide this day 11.27
Spirit of the L. came upon Jephthah, 11.29
And Jephthah made a vow to the L., 11.30
and the L. gave them into his hand. 11.32
I have opened my mouth to the L., 11.35
have opened your mouth to the L., 11.36
now that the L. has avenged you on 11.36
and the L. gave them into my hand; 12.03
was evil in the sight of the L.; 13.01
and the L. gave them into the hand 13.01
angel of the L. appeared to the 13.03
Then Manoah entreated the L., 13.08
L., I pray thee, let the man of God 13.08
the angel of the L. said to Manoah, 13.13
Manoah said to the angel of the L., 13.15
the angel of the L. said to Manoah, 13.16
offering, then offer it to the L." 13.16
that he was the angel of the L. 13.16
Manoah said to the angel of the L., 13.17
And the angel of the L. said to him, 13.18
offered it upon the rock to the L., 13.19
angel of the L. ascended in the 13.20
The angel of the L. appeared no 13.21
that he was the angel of the L. 13.21
"If the L. had meant to kill us, he 13.23
boy grew, and the L. blessed him. 13.24
Spirit of the L. began to stir him 13.25
not know that it was from the L.; 14.04
Spirit of the L. came mightily 14.06
Spirit of the L. came mightily 14.19
Spirit of the L. came mightily 15.14

LORD (cont.)

and he called on the L. and said, Ju 15.18
not know that the L. had left him. 16.20
Then Samson called to the L. and said, 16.28
"O L. God, remember me, I pray thee, 16.28
said, "Blessed be my son by the L." 17.02
silver to the L. from my hand for 17.03
I know that the L. will prosper me, 17.13
you go is under the eye of the L." 18.06
as one man to the L. at Mizpah. 20.01
And the L. said, "Judah shall go up 20.18
wept before the L. until the 20.23
and they inquired of the L., 20.23
And the L. said, "Go up against them." 20.23
they sat there before the L., 20.26
and peace offerings before the L. 20.26
inquired of the L. (for the ark of 20.27
And the L. said, "Go up; 20.28
And the L. defeated Benjamin before 20.35
"O L., the God of Israel, why has 21.03
come up in the assembly to the L.?" 21.05
not come up to the L. to Mizpah, 21.05
sworn by the L. that we will not 21.07
not come up to the L. to Mizpah?" 21.08
because the L. had made a breach 21.15
yearly feast of the L. at Shiloh, 21.19
Moab that the L. had visited his Ru 1.06
May the L. deal kindly with you, as 1.08
The L. grant that you may find a 1.09
the hand of the L. has gone forth 1.13
May the L. do so to me and more 1.17
and the L. has brought me back 1.21
when the L. has afflicted me and 1.21
to the reapers, "The L. be with you!" 2.04
they answered, "The L. bless you." 2.04
The L. recompense you for what you 2.12
full reward be given you by the L., 2.12
my l., for you have comforted me 2.13
daughter-in-law, "Blessed be he by the L., 2.20
be blessed by the L., my daughter; 3.10
as the L. lives, I will do the part 3.13
May the L. make the woman, who is 4.11
that the L. will give you by this 4.12
and the L. gave her conception, and 4.13
said to Naomi, "Blessed be the L., 4.14
sacrifice to the L. of hosts at 1Sa 1.03
Phinehas, were priests of the L. 1.03
because the L. had closed her womb. 1.05
because the L. had closed her womb. 1.06
she went up to the house of the L., 1.07
doorpost of the temple of the L. 1.09
distressed and prayed to the L., 1.10
"O L. of hosts, if thou wilt indeed 1.11
give him to the L. all the days of 1.11
continued praying before the L., 1.12
my l., I am a woman sorely troubled; 1.15
pouring out my soul before the L. 1.15
and worshiped before the L.; 1.19
wife, and the L. remembered her; 1.19
said, "I have asked him of the L." 1.20
to offer to the L. the yearly 1.21
appear in the presence of the L., 1.22
only, may the L. establish his word." 1.23
to the house of the L. at Shiloh; 1.24
And she said, "Oh, my l.! As you 1.26
my l., I am the woman who was 1.26
your presence, praying to the L. 1.26
and the L. has granted me my 1.27
Therefore I have lent him to the L.; 1.28
as he lives, he is lent to the L." 1.28
And they worshiped the L. there. 1.28
said, "My heart exults in the L.; 2.01
my strength is exalted in the L. 2.01
"There is none holy like the L., 2.02
for the L. is a God of knowledge, 2.03
The L. kills and brings to life; 2.06
The L. makes poor and makes rich; 2.07
adversaries of the L. shall be 2.10
The L. will judge the ends of the 2.10
And the boy ministered to the L., 2.11
they had no regard for the L. 2.12
very great in the sight of the L.; 2.17
offering of the L. with contempt. 2.17
Samuel was ministering before the L., 2.18
"The L. give you children by this 2.20
the loan which she lent to the L."; 2.20
And the L. visited Hannah, and she 2.21
grew in the presence of the L. 2.21
people of the L. spreading abroad. 2.24
but if a man sins against the L., 2.25
the will of the L. to slay them. 2.25
in favor with the L. and with men. 2.26
"Thus the L. has said, 'I revealed 2.27
Therefore the L. the God of Israel 2.30
but now the L. declares: 'Far be it 2.30
ministering to the L. under Eli. 3.01
the word of the L. was rare in 3.01
down within the temple of the L., 3.03
Then the L. called, "Samuel! Samuel!" 3.04
And the L. called again, "Samuel!" 3.06
Now Samuel did not yet know the L., 3.07
the word of the L. had not yet 3.07
And the L. called Samuel again the 3.08
that the L. was calling the boy. 3.08
'Speak, L., for thy servant hears.'" 3.09
And the L. came and stood forth, 3.10
Then the L. said to Samuel, "Behold, 3.11
the doors of the house of the L. 3.15
And he said, "It is the L.; let him 3.18
and the L. was with him and let 3.19
established as a prophet of the L. 3.20
And the L. appeared again at Shiloh, 3.21
for the L. revealed himself to 3.21
at Shiloh by the word of the L. 3.21
"Why has the L. put us to rout 4.03
covenant of the L. here from 4.03
of the covenant of the L. of hosts, 4.04
covenant of the L. came into the 4.05
the ark of the L. had come to the 4.06
ground before the ark of the L. 5.03
ground before the ark of the L., 5.04
The hand of the L. was heavy upon 5.06
the hand of the L. was against the 5.09
The ark of the L was in the 6.01
shall we do with the ark of the L.? 6.02
the ark of the L. and place it on 6.08
put the ark of the L. on the cart, 6.11
cows as a burnt offering to the L. 6.14
the ark of the L. and the box that 6.15
sacrifices on that day to the L. 6.15
as a guilt offering to the L.: 6.17
they set down the ark of the L., 6.18
they looked into the ark of the L.; 6.19
because the L. had made a great 6.19
stand before the L., this Holy God? 6.20
have returned the ark of the L. 6.21
came and took up the ark of the L., 7.01
have charge of the ark of the L. 7.01
of Israel lamented after the L. 7.02
returning to the L. with all your 7.03
and direct your heart to the L., 7.03
and they served the L. only. 7.04
and I will pray to the L. for you." 7.05
and poured it out before the L., 7.06
"We have sinned against the L." 7.06
to cry to the L. our God for us, 7.08
a whole burnt offering to the L.; 7.09
Samuel cried to the L. for Israel, 7.09
Israel, and the L. answered him. 7.09
but the L. thundered with a mighty 7.10
"Hitherto the L. has helped us." 7.12
the hand of the L. was against the 7.13
he built there an altar to the L. 7.17
And Samuel prayed to the L. 8.06

LORD (cont.)
And the L. said to Samuel, "Hearken 1Sa 8.07
words of the L. to the people who 8.10
but the L. will not answer you in 8.18
repeated them in the ears of the L. 8.21
And the L. said to Samuel, "Hearken 8.22
the L. had revealed to Samuel: 9.15
the L. told him, "Here is the man of 9.17
"Has not the L. anointed you to be 10.01
people of the L. and you will save 10.01
to you that the L. has anointed 10.01
spirit of the L. will come mightily 10.06
together to the L. at Mizpah; 10.17
people of Israel, "Thus says the L., 10.18
before the L. by your tribes and 10.19
So they inquired again of the L., 10.22
and the L. said, "Behold, he has 10.22
you see him whom the L. has chosen? 10.24
book and laid it up before the L. 10.25
dread of the L. fell upon the 11.07
for today the L. has wrought 11.13
Saul king before the L. in Gilgal. 11.15
peace offerings before the L., 11.15
me before the L. and before his 12.03
"The L. is witness against you, and 12.05
"The L. is witness, who appointed 12.06
you before the L. concerning all 12.07
deeds of the L. which he performed 12.07
your fathers cried to the L. and 12.08
and the L. sent Moses and Aaron, 12.08
But they forgot the L. their God; 12.09
And they cried to the L., 12.10
because we have forsaken the L., 12.10
And the L. sent Jerubbaal and Barak, 12.11
when the L. your God was your 12.12
behold, the L. has set a king over 12.13
will fear the L. and serve him and 12.14
against the commandment of the L., 12.14
you will follow the L. your God, 12.14
not hearken to the voice of the L., 12.15
against the commandment of the L., 12.15
the hand of the L. will be against 12.15
which the L. will do before your 12.16
I will call upon the L., that he 12.17
have done in the sight of the L., 12.17
So Samuel called upon the L., 12.18
and the L. sent thunder and rain 12.18
greatly feared the L. and Samuel. 12.18
your servants to the L. your God, 12.19
turn aside from following the L., 12.20
but serve the L. with all your 12.20
For the L. will not cast away his 12.22
has pleased the L. to make you a 12.22
sin against the L. by ceasing to 12.23
Only fear the L., and serve him 12.24
not entreated the favor of the L.'; 13.12
the commandment of the L. your God, 13.13
for now the L. would have established 13.13
the L. has sought out a man after 13.14
and the L. has appointed him to be 13.14
not kept what the L. commanded you." 13.14
the priest of the L in Shiloh, 14.03
may be that the L. will work for 14.06
can hinder the L. from saving by 14.06
for the L. has given them into our 14.10
for the L. has given them into the 14.12
So the L. delivered Israel that day 14.23
people are sinning against the L., 14.33
sin against the L. by eating with 14.34
And Saul built an altar to the L.; 14.35
altar that he built to the L. 14.35
For as the L. lives who saves 14.39
"O L. God of Israel, why hast thou 14.41
O L., God of Israel, give Urim; 14.41
As the L. lives, there shall not one 14.45
"The L. sent me to anoint you king 15.01
hearken to the words of the L. 15.01
Thus says the L. of hosts, 'I will 15.02
The word of the L. came to Samuel: 15.10
and he cried to the L. all night. 15.11
to him, "Blessed be you to the L.; 15.13
performed the commandment of the L." 15.13
to sacrifice to the L. your God; 15.15
you what the L. said to me this 15.16
The L. anointed you king over 15.17
And the L. sent you on a mission, 15.18
you not obey the voice of the L.? 15.19
was evil in the sight of the L.?" 15.19
"I have obeyed the voice of the L., 15.20
mission on which the L. sent me, 15.20
sacrifice to the L. your God in 15.21
"Has the L. as great delight in 15.22
as in obeying the voice of the L.? 15.22
have rejected the word of the L., 15.23
commandment of the L. and your words, 15.24
with me, that I may worship the L." 15.25
have rejected the word of the L., 15.26
and the L. has rejected you from 15.26
"The L. has torn the kingdom of 15.28
that I may worship the L. your God." 15.30
and Saul worshiped the L. 15.31
in pieces before the L. in Gilgal. 15.33
And the L. repented that he had 15.35
The L. said to Samuel, "How long 16.01
And the L. said, "Take a heifer with 16.02
'I have come to sacrifice to the L.' 16.02
Samuel did what the L. commanded, 16.04
I have come to sacrifice to the L.; 16.05
But the L. said to Samuel, "Do not 16.07
for the L. sees not as man sees; 16.07
but the L. looks on the heart." 16.07
"Neither has the L. chosen this one 16.08
"Neither has the L. chosen this one 16.09
"The L. has not chosen these." 16.10
And the L. said, "Arise, anoint him; 16.12
Spirit of the L. came mightily 16.13
Spirit of the L. departed from 16.14
spirit from the L. tormented him. 16.14
Let our l. now command your servants, 16.16
presence; and the L. is with him." 16.18
"The L. who delivered me from the 17.37
David, "Go, and the L. be with you!" 17.37
you in the name of the L. of hosts, 17.45
This day the L. will deliver you 17.46
know that the L. saves not with 17.47
because the L. was with him but had 18.12
for the L. was with him. 18.14
knew that the L. was with David, 18.28
and the L. wrought a great victory 19.05
"As the L. lives, he shall not be 19.06
spirit from the L. came upon Saul, 19.09
as the L. lives and as your soul 20.03
"The L., the God of Israel, be 20.12
the L. do so to Jonathan, and more 20.13
May the L. be with you, as he has 20.13
show me the loyal love of the L., 20.14
When the L. cuts off every one of 20.15
And may the L. take vengeance on 20.16
as the L. lives, it is safe for you 20.21
for the L. has sent you away. 20.22
the L. is between you and me for 20.23
both of us in the name of the L., 20.42
'The L. shall be between me and you, 20.42
is removed from before the L., 21.06
that day, detained before the L.; 21.07
and he inquired of the L. for him, 22.10
And he answered, "Here I am, my l." 22.12
and kill the priests of the L.; 22.17
to fall upon the priests of the L. 22.17
had killed the priests of the L. 22.21
Therefore David inquired of the L., 23.02
And the L. said to David, "Go and 23.02
Then David inquired of the L. again. 23.04
And the L. answered him, "Arise, go 23.04

LORD (cont.)
“O L., the God of Israel, thy 1Sa 23.10
O L., the God of Israel, I beseech 23.11
And the L. said, “He will come down.” 23.11
And the L. said, “They will surrender 23.12
them made a covenant before the L.; 23.18
said, “May you be blessed by the L.; 23.21
day of which the L. said to you, 24.04
“The L. forbid that I should do 24.06
I should do this thing to my l., 24.06
called after Saul, “My l. the king!” 24.08
seen how the L. gave you today 24.10
put forth my hand against my l.; 24.10
May the L. judge between me and you, 24.12
may the L. avenge me upon you; 24.12
May the L. therefore be judge, and 24.15
me when the L. put me into your 24.18
So may the L. reward you with good 24.19
therefore by the L. that you will 24.21
“Upon me alone, my l., be the guilt; 25.24
Let not my l. regard this ill-natured 25.25
young men of my l., whom you sent. 25.25
Now then, my l., as the L. lives, and 25.26
seeing the L. has restrained you 25.26
to do evil to my l. be as Nabal. 25.26
brought to my l. be given to the 25.27
to the young men who follow my l. 25.27
for the L. will certainly make my 25.28
certainly make my l. a sure house, 25.28
because my l. is fighting the 25.28
is fighting the battles of the L.; 25.28
the life of my l. shall be bound 25.29
in the care of the L. your God; 25.29
the L. has done to my l. according 25.30
my l. shall have no cause of grief, 25.31
cause or for my l. taking vengeance 25.31
when the L. has dealt well with my l., 25.31
said to Abigail, “Blessed be the L., 25.32
surely as the L. the God of Israel 25.34
ten days later the L. smote Nabal; 25.38
“Blessed be the L. who has avenged 25.39
the L. has returned the evil-doing 25.39
the feet of the servants of my l.” 25.41
“As the L. lives, the L. will smite 26.10
The L. forbid that I should put 26.11
sleep from the L. had fallen upon 26.12
kept watch over your l. the king? 26.15
in to destroy the king your l. 26.15
As the L. lives, you deserve to die, 26.16
have not kept watch over your l., 26.16
“It is my voice, my l., O king.” 26.17
“Why does my l. pursue after his 26.18
therefore let my l. the king hear 26.19
If it is the L. who has stirred you 26.19
may they be cursed before the L., 26.19
no share in the heritage of the L., 26.19
away from the presence of the L.; 26.20
The L. rewards every man for his 26.23
for the L. gave you into my hand 26.23
be precious in the sight of the L., 26.24
And when Saul inquired of the L., 28.06
the L. did not answer him, either by 28.06
But Saul swore to her by the L., 28.10
“As the L. lives, no punishment 28.10
since the L. has turned from you 28.16
The L. has done to you as he spoke 28.17
for the L. has torn the kingdom out 28.17
did not obey the voice of the L., 28.18
therefore the L. has done this 28.18
there the L. has done this 28.18
Moreover the L. will give Israel 28.19
the L. will give the army of Israel 28.19
fellow reconcile himself to his l.? 29.04
“As the L. lives, you have been 29.06
the enemies of my l. the king?” 29.08
servants of your l. who came with 29.10
strengthened himself in the L. his God. 30.06
And David inquired of the L., 30.08
with what the L. has given us; 30.23
spoil of the enemies of the L.”; 30.26
I have brought them here to my l.” 2Sa 1.10
people of the L. and for the house 1.12
After this David inquired of the L., 2.01
And the L. said to him, “Go up.” 2.01
them, “May you be blessed by the L., 2.05
this loyalty to Saul your L., 2.05
Now may the L. show steadfast love 2.06
for Saul your l. is dead, and the 2.07
David what the L. has sworn to him, 3.09
for the L. has promised David, 3.18
all Israel to my l. the king, 3.21
before the L. for the blood of 3.28
The L. requite the evildoer according 3.39
the L. has avenged my l. the king this 4.08
“As the L. lives, who has redeemed 4.09
and the L. said to you, ‘You shall 5.02
with them at Hebron before the L., 5.03
for the L., the God of hosts, was 5.10
that the L. had established him 5.12
And David inquired of the L., 5.19
And the L. said to David, “Go up; 5.19
“The L. has broken through my 5.20
And when David inquired of the L., 5.23
for then the L. has gone out before 5.24
And David did as the L. commanded him, 5.25
the name of the L. of hosts who 6.02
before the L. with all their might, 6.05
anger of the L. was kindled 6.07
because the L. had broken forth 6.08
was afraid of the L. that day; 6.09
can the ark of the L. come to me?” 6.09
the ark of the L. into the city of 6.10
And the ark of the L. remained in 6.11
and the L. blessed Obededom and all 6.11
“The L. has blessed the household 6.12
the ark of the L. had gone six 6.13
before the L. with all his might; 6.14
up the ark of the L. with shouting, 6.15
As the ark of the L. came into the 6.16
leaping and dancing before the L.; 6.16
And the brought in the ark of the L., 6.17
and peace offerings before the L. 6.17
in the name of the L. of hosts, 6.18
to Michal, “It was before the L., 6.21
over Israel, the people of the L.— 6.21
I will make merry before the L. 6.21
and the L. had given him rest from 7.01
heart; for the L. is with you.” 7.03
the word of the L. came to Nathan, 7.04
servant David, ‘Thus says the L.: 7.05
David, ‘Thus says the L. of hosts, 7.08
Moreover the L. declares to you 7.11
to you that the L. will make you a 7.11
went in and sat before the L., 7.18
O L. GOD, and what is my house, that 7.18
small thing in thy eyes, O L. GOD; 7.19
me future generations, O L. GOD! 7.19
thou knowest thy servant, O L. GOD! 7.20
Therefore thou art great, O L. God; 7.22
and thou, O L., didst become their 7.24
And now, O L. God, confirm for ever 7.25
‘The L. of hosts is God over Israel, 7.26
For thou, O L. of hosts, the God of 7.27
And now, O L. GOD, thou art God, and 7.28
for thou, O L. GOD, hast spoken, and 7.29
And the L. gave victory to David 8.06
King David dedicated to the L., 8.11
And the L. gave victory to David 8.14
to all that my l. the king commands 9.11
Ammonites said to Hanun their l., 10.03
and may the L. do what seems good 10.12
with all the servants of his l., 11.09
and my l. Joab and the servants of 11.11
servants of my l. are camping in 11.11

LORD (cont.)
couch with the servants of his l., 2Sa 11.13
David had done displeased the L. 11.27
And the L. sent Nathan to David. 12.01
"As the L. lives, the man who has 12.05
Thus says the L., the God of Israel, 12.07
you despise the word of the L. 12.09
Thus says the L., 'Behold, I will 12.11
"I have sinned against the L." 12.13
"The L. also has put away your sin; 12.13
you have utterly scorned the L., 12.14
And the L. struck the child that 12.15
the house of the L., and worshiped; 12.20
whether the L. will be gracious to 12.22
Solomon. And the L. loved him, 12.24
name Jedidiah, because of the L. 12.25
"Let not my l. suppose that they 13.32
let not my l. the king so take it 13.33
my l. the king, and on my father's 14.09
the king invoke the L. your God, 14.11
"As the L. lives, not one hair of 14.11
speak a word to my l. the king." 14.12
say this to my l. the king because 14.15
'The word of my l. the king will 14.17
for my l. the king is like the 14.17
evil. The L. your God be with you!" 14.17
said, "Let my l. the king speak." 14.18
my l. the king, one cannot turn to 14.19
anything that my l. the king has 14.19
But my l. has wisdom like the 14.20
my l. the king, in that the king has 14.22
I have vowed to the L., in Hebron. 15.07
'If the L. will indeed bring me 15.08
I will offer worship to the L.'" 15.08
do whatever my l. the king decides." 15.15
and may the L. show steadfast love 15.20
L. lives, and as my l. the king lives, 15.21
wherever my l. the king shall be, 15.21
I find favor in the eyes of the L., 15.25
"O L., I pray thee, turn the counsel 15.31
in your sight, my l. the king." 16.04
The L. has avenged upon you all the 16.08
and the L. has given the kingdom 16.08
this dead dog curse my l. the king? 16.09
because the L. has said to him, 16.10
for the L. has bidden him. 16.11
It may be that the L. will look 16.12
and that the L. will repay me with 16.12
for whom the L. and this people and 16.18
For the L. had ordained to defeat 17.14
so that the L. might bring evil 17.14
king that the L. has delivered him 18.19
said, "Blessed be the L. your God, 18.28
their hand against my l. the king." 18.28
"Good tidings for my l. the king! 18.31
For the L. has delivered you this 18.31
"May the enemies of my l. the king, 18.32
for I swear by the L., if you do 19.07
"Let not my l. hold me guilty or 19.19
on the day my l. the king left 19.19
come down to meet my l. the king." 19.20
"My l., O king, my servant deceived 19.26
your servant to my l. the king. 19.27
But my l. the king is like the 19.27
to death before my l. the king; 19.28
since my l. the king has come 19.30
an added burden to my l. the king? 19.35
him go over with my l. the king; 19.37
swallow up the heritage of the L.?" 20.19
David sought the face of the L. 21.01
And the L. said, "There is blood 21.01
may bless the heritage of the L.?" 21.03
up before the L. at Gibeon on the 21.06
Gibeon on the mountain of the L." 21.06
the oath of the L. which was 21.07
them on the mountain before the L., 21.09
spoke to the L. the words of this 22.01
day when the L. delivered him from 22.01
He said, "The L. is my rock, and my 22.02
I call upon the L., who is worthy 22.04
"In my distress I called upon the L.; 22.07
The L. thundered from heaven, and 22.14
laid bare, at the rebuke of the L., 22.16
calamity; but the L. was my stay. 22.19
"The L. rewarded me according to my 22.21
For I have kept the ways of the L., 22.22
Therefore the L. has recompensed me 22.25
O L., and my God lightens my 22.29
the promise of the L. proves true; 22.31
"For who is God, but the L.? And 22.32
they cried to the L., but he did 22.42
"The L. lives; and blessed be my 22.47
O L., among the nations, and sing 22.50
"The Spirit of the L. speaks by me, 23.02
and the L. wrought a great victory 23.10
and the L. wrought a great victory. 23.12
of it; he poured it out to the L., 23.16
O L., that I should do this. Shall 23.17
anger of the L. was kindled 24.01
"May the L. your God add to the 24.03
the eyes of my l. the king still 24.03
but why does my l. the king delight 24.03
people. And David said to the L., 24.10
But now, O L., I pray thee, take away 24.10
the word of the L. came to the 24.11
say to David, 'Thus says the L., 24.12
us fall into the hand of the L., 24.14
So the L. sent a pestilence upon 24.15
the L. repented of the evil, and 24.16
angel of the L. was by the threshing 24.16
spoke to the L. when he saw the 24.17
an altar to the L. on the threshing 24.18
at Gad's word, as the L. commanded. 24.19
"Why has my l. the king come to his 24.21
order to build an altar to the L., 24.21
"Let my l. the king take and offer 24.22
"The L. your God accept you." 24.23
offerings to the L. my God which 24.24
built there an altar to the L., 24.25
So the L. heeded supplications for 24.25
be sought for my l. the king, 1Ki 1.02
that my l. the king may be warm." 1.02
and David our l. does not know it? 1.11
my l. the king, swear to your 1.13
"My l., you swore to your maidservant 1.17
by the L. your God, saying, 1.17
my l. the king, do not know it. 1.18
And now, my l. the king, the eyes of 1.20
throne of my l. the king after him. 1.20
when my l. the king sleeps with his 1.21
"My l. the king, have you said, 1.24
about by my l. the king and you 1.27
throne of my l. the king after him?" 1.27
"As the L. lives, who has redeemed 1.29
as I swore to you by the L., 1.30
"May my l. King David live for ever!" 1.31
with you the servants of your l., 1.33
May the L., the God of my l. the king, 1.36
As the L. has been with my l. the king, 1.37
the throne of my l. King David." 1.37
for our l. king David has made 1.43
to congratulate our l. King David, 1.47
king also said, 'Blessed be the L., 1.48
keep the charge of the L. your God, 2.03
that the L. may establish his word 2.04
Jordan, I swore to him by the L., 2.08
brother's, for it was his from the L. 2.15
Then King Solomon swore by the L., 2.23
Now therefore as the L. lives, 2.24
the ark of the L. God before David 2.26
from being priest to the L., 2.27
the word of the L. which he had 2.27
the tent of the L. and caught hold 2.28
has fled to the tent of the L., 2.29

LORD (cont.)
Benaiah came to the tent of the L., 1Ki 2.30
The L. will bring back his bloody 2.32
be peace from the L. for evermore." 2.33
as my l. the king has said, so will 2.38
"Did I not make you swear by the L., 2.42
oath to the L. and the commandment 2.43
so the L. will bring back your evil 2.44
established before the L. for ever. 2.45
house of the L. and the wall 3.01
been built for the name of the L. 3.02
Solomon loved the L., walking in the 3.03
At Gibeon the L. appeared to 3.05
And now, O L. my God, thou hast made 3.07
It pleased the L. that Solomon had 3.10
the ark of the covenant of the L., 3.15
my l., this woman and I dwell in 3.17
my l., give her the living child, 3.26
the name of the L. his God because 5.03
until the L. put them under the 5.03
But now the L. my God has given me 5.04
for the name of the L. my God, 5.05
as the L. said to David my father, 5.05
said, "Blessed be the L. this day, 5.07
And the L. gave Solomon wisdom, as 5.12
began to build the house of the L. 6.01
built for the L. was sixty cubits 6.02
Now the word of the L. came to 6.11
the ark of the covenant of the L. 6.19
of the house of the L. was laid, 6.37
house of the L. to the great court 7.09
inner court of the house of the L., 7.12
Solomon on the house of the L.: 7.40
vessels in the house of the L., 7.45
that were in the house of the L.: 7.48
the house of the L. was finished. 7.51
treasuries of the house of the L. 7.51
covenant of the L. out of the city 8.01
And they brought up the ark of the L., 8.04
covenant of the L. to its place, 8.06
where the L. made a covenant with 8.09
cloud filled the house of the L., 8.10
glory of the L. filled the house of the L. 8.11
"The L. has set the sun in the 8.12
And he said, "Blessed be the L., 8.15
a house for the name of the L., 8.17
But the L. said to David my father, 8.18
Now the L. has fulfilled his 8.20
as the L. promised, and I have built 8.20
the house for the name of the L., 8.20
covenant of the L. which he made 8.21
altar of the L. in the presence of 8.22
and said, "O L., God of Israel, there 8.23
O L., God of Israel, keep with thy 8.25
O L. my God, hearkening to the cry 8.28
pray to the L. toward the city 8.44
our fathers out of Egypt, O L. GOD." 8.53
prayer and supplication to the L., 8.54
from before the altar of the L., 8.54
"Blessed be the L. who has given 8.56
The L. our God be with us, as he was 8.57
made supplication before the L., 8.59
be near to the L. our God day and 8.59
earth may know that the L. is God; 8.60
be wholly true to the L. our God, 8.61
offered sacrifice before the L. 8.62
offerings to the L. twenty-two 8.63
dedicated the house of the L. 8.63
was before the house of the L.; 8.64
was before the L. was too small to 8.64
before the L. our God, seven days. 8.65
that the L. had shown to David his 8.66
house of the L. and the king's 9.01
the L. appeared to Solomon a second 9.02
And the L. said to him, "I have 9.03
'Why has the L. done thus to this 9.08
forsook the L. their God who 9.09
therefore the L. has brought all 9.09
house of the L. and the king's house. 9.10
house of the L. and his own house 9.15
the altar which he built to the L., 9.25
burning incense before the L. 9.25
concerning the name of the L., 10.01
he offered at the house of the L., 10.05
Blessed be the L. your God, who has 10.09
Because the L. loved Israel for 10.09
supports for the house of the L., 10.12
which the L. had said to the 11.02
not wholly true to the L. his God, 11.04
was evil in the sight of the L., 11.06
and did not wholly follow the L., 11.06
And the L. was angry with Solomon, 11.09
heart had turned away from the L., 11.09
did not keep what the L. commanded. 11.10
Therefore the L. said to Solomon, 11.11
And the L. raised up an adversary 11.14
for thus says the L., the God of 11.31
about by the L. that he might 12.15
which the L. spoke by Ahijah the 12.15
'Thus says the L., You shall not go 12.24
hearkened to the word of the L., 12.24
according to the word of the L. 12.24
the house of the L. at Jerusalem, 12.27
people will turn again to their l., 12.27
by the word of the L. to Bethel. 13.01
the altar by the word of the L., 13.02
thus says the L.: 'Behold, a son 13.02
is the sign that the L. has spoken: 13.03
had given by the word of the L. 13.05
now the favor of the L. your God, 13.06
the man of God entreated the L.; 13.06
commanded me by the word of the L., 13.09
said to me by the word of the L., 13.17
spoke to me by the word of the L., 13.18
the word of the L. came to the 13.20
came from Judah, "Thus says the L., 13.21
have disobeyed the word of the L., 13.21
which the L. your God commanded 13.21
who disobeyed the word of the L.; 13.26
therefore the L. has given him to 13.26
the word which the L. spoke to him." 13.26
the word of the L. against the 13.32
And the L. said to Ahijah, "Behold, 14.05
Go, tell Jeroboam, 'Thus says the L., 14.07
eat; for the L. has spoken it."' 14.11
found something pleasing to the L., 14.13
Moreover the L. will raise up for 14.14
the L. will smite Israel, as a reed 14.15
Asherim, provoking the L. to anger. 14.15
according to the word of the L., 14.18
city which the L. had chosen out 14.21
was evil in the sight of the L., 14.22
which the L. drove out before the 14.24
house of the L. and the treasures 14.26
king went into the house of the L., 14.28
not wholly true to the L. his God, 15.03
sake the L. his God gave him a 15.04
was right in the eyes of the L., 15.05
was right in the eyes of the L., 15.11
wholly to the L. all his days. 15.14
house of the L. the votive gifts 15.15
house of the L. and the treasures 15.18
was evil in the sight of the L., 15.26
the word of the L. which he spoke 15.29
anger to which he provoked the L., 15.30
was evil in the sight of the L., 15.34
And the word of the L. came to Jehu 16.01
Moreover the word of the L. came by 16.07
that he did in the sight of the L., 16.07
according to the word of the L., 16.12
provoking the L. God of Israel to 16.13
doing evil in the sight of the L., 16.19
was evil in the sight of the L., 16.25
provoking the L., the God of Israel, 16.26

LORD (cont.)

sight of the L. more than all that 1Ki 16.30
Ahab did more to provoke the L., 16.33
according to the word of the L., 16.34
"As the L. the God of Israel lives, 17.01
And the word of the L. came to him, 17.02
according to the word of the L.; 17.05
Then the word of the L. came to him, 17.08
"As the L. your God lives, I have 17.12
For thus says the L. the God of 17.14
day that the L. sends rain upon 17.14
the word of the L. which he spoke 17.16
And he cried to the L., "O L. my God, 17.20
three times, and cried to the L., 17.21
"O L. my God, let this child's soul 17.21
And the L. hearkened to the voice 17.22
the word of the L. in your mouth 17.24
the word of the L. came to Elijah, 18.01
(Now Obadiah revered the L. greatly; 18.03
cut off the prophets of the L., 18.04
and said, "Is it you, my l. Elijah?" 18.07
Go, tell your l., 'Behold, Elijah is 18.08
As the L. your God lives, there is 18.10
whither my l. has not sent to seek 18.10
tell your l., "Behold, Elijah is 18.11
Spirit of the L. will carry you 18.12
have revered the L. from my youth. 18.12
been told my l. what I did when 18.13
killed the prophets of the L., 18.13
tell your l., "Behold, Elijah is 18.14
"As the L. of hosts lives, before 18.15
commandments of the L. and followed 18.18
If the L. is God, follow him; 18.21
only, am left a prophet of the L.; 18.22
I will call on the name of the L.; 18.24
altar of the L. that had been 18.30
to whom the word of the L. came, 18.31
an altar in the name of the L. 18.32
"O L., God of Abraham, Isaac, and 18.36
Answer me, O L., answer me, that this 18.37
O L., art God, and that thou hast 18.37
Then the fire of the L. fell, 18.38
"The L., he is God; the L., he is God." 18.39
And the hand of the L. was on Elijah; 18.46
now, O L., take away my life; 19.04
angel of the L. came again a 19.07
the word of the L. came to him, 19.09
have been very jealous for the L., 19.10
stand upon the mount before the L." 19.11
the L. passed by, and a great and 19.11
in pieces the rocks before the L., 19.11
but the L. was not in the wind; 19.11
but the L. was not in the earthquake; 19.11
but the L. was not in the fire; 19.12
have been very jealous for the L., 19.14
And the L. said to him, "Go, return 19.15
my l., O king, I am yours, and all 20.04
"Tell my l. the king, 'All that you 20.09
Israel and said, "Thus says the L., 20.13
you shall know that I am the L." 20.13
He said, "Thus says the L., By the 20.14
king of Israel, "Thus says the L., 20.28
"The L. is a god of the hills but 20.28
you shall know that I am the L.'" 20.28
fellow at the command of the L., 20.35
not obeyed the voice of the L., 20.36
"Thus says the L., 'Because you 20.42
"The L. forbid that I should give 21.03
Then the word of the L. came to 21.17
say to him, 'Thus says the L., "Have 21.19
say to him, 'Thus says the L.: "In 21.19
is evil in the sight of the L. 21.20
And of Jezebel the L. also said, 21.23
in the sight of the L. like Ahab, 21.25
whom the L. cast out before the 21.26
And the word of the L. came to 21.28
first for the word of the L." 22.05
for the L. will give it into the 22.06
prophet of the L. of whom we may 22.07
by whom we may inquire of the L., 22.08
iron, and said, "Thus says the L., 22.11
the L. will give it into the hand 22.12
"As the L. lives, what the L. says to 22.14
the L. will give it into the hand 22.15
the truth in the name of the L.?" 22.16
and the L. said, 'These have no 22.17
"Therefore hear the word of the L.: 22.19
I saw the L. sitting on his throne, 22.19
and the L. said, 'Who will entice 22.20
forward and stood before the L., 22.21
And the L. said to him, 'By what 22.22
the L. has put a lying spirit in 22.23
the L. has spoken evil concerning 22.23
Spirit of the L. go from me to 22.24
the L. has not spoken by me." 22.28
the word of the L. which he had 22.38
was right in the sight of the L.; 22.43
was evil in the sight of the L., 22.52
worshiped him, and provoked the L., 22.53
angel of the L. said to Elijah the 2Ki 1.03
Now therefore thus says the L., 1.04
Thus says the L., Is it because 1.06
the angel of the L. said to Elijah, 1.15
and said to him, "Thus says the L., 1.16
the word of the L. which Elijah 1.17
Now when the L. was about to take 2.01
for the L. has sent me as far as 2.02
"As the L. lives, and as you yourself 2.02
that today the L. will take away 2.03
for the L. has sent me to Jericho." 2.04
"As the L. lives, and as you yourself 2.04
that today the L. will take away 2.05
for the L. has sent me to the 2.06
"As the L. lives, and as you yourself 2.06
"Where is the L., the God of Elijah?" 2.14
Spirit of the L. has caught him up 2.16
city is pleasant, as my l. sees; 2.19
in it, and said, "Thus says the L., 2.21
cursed them in the name of the L. 2.24
was evil in the sight of the L., 3.02
The L. has called these three kings 3.10
"Is there no prophet of the L. here, 3.11
whom we may inquire of the L.?" 3.11
"The word of the L. is with him." 3.12
it is the L. who has called these 3.13
"As the L. of hosts lives, whom I 3.14
the power of the L. came upon him. 3.15
And he said, "Thus says the L., 3.16
For thus says the L., 'I will make 3.17
light thing in the sight of the L.; 3.18
that your servant feared the L., 4.01
she said, "No, my l., O man of God; 4.16
and the L. has hidden it from me, 4.27
said, "Did I ask my l. for a son? 4.28
"As the L. lives, and as you yourself 4.30
two of them, and prayed to the L. 4.33
they may eat, for thus says the L., 4.43
according to the word of the L. 4.44
by him the L. had given victory to 5.01
"Would that my l. were with the 5.03
So Naaman went in and told his l., 5.04
call on the name of the L. his God, 5.11
"As the L. lives, whom I serve, I 5.16
or sacrifice to any god but the L. 5.17
matter may the L. pardon your 5.18
the L. pardon your servant in this 5.18
As the L. lives, I will run after 5.20
servants said, "None, my l., O king; 6.12
"O L., I pray thee, open his eyes 6.17
So the L. opened the eyes of the 6.17
him, Elisha prayed to the L., 6.18
"O L., open the eyes of these men, 6.20
So the L. opened their eyes, and 6.20
him, saying, "Help, my l., O king!" 6.26

LORD (cont.)

"If the L. will not help you, whence 2Ki 6.27
said, "This trouble is from the L.! 6.33
I wait for the L. any longer?" 6.33
said, "Hear the word of the L.: 7.01
thus says the L., Tomorrow about 7.01
"If the L. himself should make 7.02
For the L. has made the army of the 7.06
according to the word of the L. 7.16
"If the L. himself should make 7.19
for the L. has called for a famine, 8.01
"My l., O king, here is the woman, 8.05
and inquire of the L. through him, 8.08
but the L. has shown me that he 8.10
And Hazael said, "Why does my l. weep?" 8.12
"The L. has shown me that you are 8.13
was evil in the sight of the L. 8.18
Yet the L. would not destroy Judah, 8.19
was evil in the sight of the L., 8.27
head, and say, 'Thus says the L., 9.03
"Thus says the L. the God of Israel, 9.06
the people of the L., over Israel. 9.06
of all the servants of the L. 9.07
to me, saying, 'Thus says the L., 9.12
how the L. uttered this oracle 9.25
says the L.—I will requite you on 9.26
accordance with the word of the L." 9.26
said, "This is the word of the L., 9.36
nothing of the word of the L., 10.10
which the L. spoke concerning the 10.10
for the L. has done what he said by 10.10
me, and see my zeal for the L." 10.16
the word of the L. which he spoke 10.17
servant of the L. here among you, 10.23
And the L. said to Jehu, "Because 10.30
the law of the L. the God of 10.31
In those days the L. began to cut 10.32
years, hid in the house of the L., 11.03
come to him in the house of the L.; 11.04
under oath in the house of the L., 11.04
and guard the house of the L., 11.07
which were in the house of the L.; 11.10
the house of the L. to the people; 11.13
be slain in the house of the L." 11.15
between the L. and the king and 11.17
watchmen over the house of the L. 11.18
king down from the house of the L., 11.19
in the eyes of the L. all his days, 12.02
brought into the house of the L., 12.04
to bring into the house of the L., 12.04
as one entered the house of the L.; 12.09
brought into the house of the L. 12.09
was found in the house of the L. 12.10
oversight of the house of the L.; 12.11
worked upon the house of the L., 12.11
repairs on the house of the L., 12.12
house of the L. basins of silver, 12.13
brought into the house of the L., 12.13
the house of the L. with it. 12.14
brought into the house of the L.; 12.16
house of the L. and of the king's 12.18
was evil in the sight of the L., 13.02
anger of the L. was kindled 13.03
Then Jehoahaz besought the L., 13.04
and the L. hearkened to him; 13.04
(Therefore the L. gave Israel a 13.05
was evil in the sight of the L.; 13.11
But the L. was gracious to them and 13.23
was right in the eyes of the L., 14.03
where the L. commanded, "The fathers 14.06
house of the L. and in the treasuries 14.14
was evil in the sight of the L.; 14.24
according to the word of the L., 14.25
For the L. saw that the affliction 14.26
But the L. had not said that he 14.27
was right in the eyes of the L., 15.03
And the L. smote the king, so that 15.05
was evil in the sight of the L., 15.09
promise of the L. which he gave to 15.12
was evil in the sight of the L.; 15.18
was evil in the sight of the L.; 15.24
was evil in the sight of the L.; 15.28
was right in the eyes of the L., 15.34
upper gate of the house of the L. 15.35
In those days the L. began to send 15.37
in the eyes of the L. his God, 16.02
whom the L. drove out before the 16.03
house of the L. and in the treasures 16.08
was before the L. he removed from 16.14
his altar and the house of the L., 16.14
removed from the house of the L., 16.18
was evil in the sight of the L., 17.02
sinned against the L. their God, 17.07
whom the L. drove out before the 17.08
against the L. their God things 17.09
did whom the L. carried away 17.11
things, provoking the L. to anger, 17.11
of which the L. had said to them, 17.12
Yet the L. warned Israel and Judah 17.13
not believe in the L. their God. 17.14
whom the L. had commanded them 17.15
commandments of the L. their God, 17.16
to do evil in the sight of the L., 17.17
Therefore the L. was very angry 17.18
commandments of the L. their God, 17.19
And the L. rejected all the descendants 17.20
following the L. and made them 17.21
until the L. removed Israel out of 17.23
there, they did not fear the L.; 17.25
therefore the L. sent lions among 17.25
them how they should fear the L. 17.28
They also feared the L., and 17.32
So they feared the L. but also 17.33
They do not fear the L., and they 17.34
which the L. commanded the children 17.34
The L. made a covenant with them, 17.35
but you shall fear the L., who 17.36
but you shall fear the L. your God, 17.39
So these nations feared the L., 17.41
was right in the eyes of the L., 18.03
He trusted in the L. the God of 18.05
For he held fast to the L.; 18.06
which the L. commanded Moses. 18.06
And the L. was with him; wherever 18.07
voice of the L. their God but 18.12
the servant of the L. commanded; 18.12
was found in the house of the L., 18.15
the doors of the temple of the L., 18.16
to me, "We rely on the L. our God, 18.22
it without the L. that I have come 18.25
The L. said to me, Go up against 18.25
you to rely on the L. by saying, 18.30
The L. will surely deliver us, and 18.30
by saying, The L. will deliver us. 18.32
that the L. should deliver Jerusalem 18.35
and went into the house of the L. 19.01
It may be that the L. your God 19.04
words which the L. your God has 19.04
to your master, 'Thus says the L.: 19.06
went up to the house of the L., 19.14
and spread it before the L. 19.14
And Hezekiah prayed before the L., 19.15
"O L. the God of Israel, who art 19.15
Incline thy ear, O L., and hear; 19.16
open thy eyes, O L., and see; 19.16
Of a truth, O L., the kings of 19.17
So now, O L. our God, save us, I 19.19
that thou, O L., art God alone. 19.19
Hezekiah, saying, "Thus says the L., 19.20
word that the L. has spoken 19.21
messengers you have mocked the L., 19.23
The zeal of the L. will do this. 19.31
"Therefore thus says the L. concerning 19.32
come into this city, says the L. 19.33

LORD (cont.)

the angel of the L. went forth, 2Ki 19.35
and said to him, "Thus says the L., 20.01
and prayed to the L., saying, 20.02
O L., I beseech thee, how I have 20.03
the word of the L. came to him: 20.04
Thus says the L., the God of David 20.05
shall go up to the house of the L. 20.05
the sign that the L. will heal me, 20.08
house of the L. on the third day?" 20.08
is the sign to you from the L., 20.09
that the L. will do the thing that 20.09
Isaiah the prophet cried to the L.; 20.11
Hezekiah, "Hear the word of the L.: 20.16
nothing shall be left, says the L. 20.17
"The word of the L. which you have 20.19
was evil in the sight of the L., 21.02
whom the L. drove out before the 21.02
altars in the house of the L., 21.04
of which the L. had said, "In 21.04
two courts of the house of the L. 21.05
much evil in the sight of the L., 21.06
of which the L. said to David and 21.07
done whom the L. destroyed before 21.09
And the L. said by his servants the 21.10
therefore thus says the L., 21.12
was evil in the sight of the L. 21.16
was evil in the sight of the L., 21.20
he forsook the L., the God of his 21.22
did not walk in the way of the L. 21.22
was right in the eyes of the L., 22.02
to the house of the L., saying, 22.03
brought into the house of the L., 22.04
oversight of the house of the L.; 22.05
who are at the house of the L., 22.05
of the law in the house of the L." 22.08
oversight of the house of the L." 22.09
"Go, inquire of the L. for me, 22.13
wrath of the L. that is kindled 22.13
she said to them, "Thus says the L., 22.15
Thus says the L., Behold, I will 22.16
who sent you to inquire of the L., 22.18
Thus says the L., the God of Israel 22.18
you humbled yourself before the L., 22.19
I also have heard you, says the L. 22.19
went up to the house of the L., 23.02
been found in the house of the L. 23.02
and made a covenant before the L., 23.03
walk after the L. and to keep his 23.03
temple of the L. all the vessels 23.04
Asherah from the house of the L., 23.06
which were in the house of the L., 23.07
the altar of the L. in Jerusalem, 23.09
entrance to the house of the L., 23.11
two courts of the house of the L., 23.12
the word of the L. which the man 23.16
provoking the L. to anger, Josiah 23.19
the passover to the L. your God, 23.21
was kept to the L. in Jerusalem. 23.23
found in the house of the L. 23.24
turned to the L. with all his 23.25
Still the L. did not turn from the 23.26
And the L. said, "I will remove 23.27
was evil in the sight of the L., 23.32
was evil in the sight of the L., 23.37
And the L. sent against him bands 24.02
the word of the L. which he spoke 24.02
Judah at the command of the L., 24.03
and the L. would not pardon. 24.04
was evil in the sight of the L., 24.09
treasures of the house of the L., 24.13
of gold in the temple of the L., 24.13
had made, as the L. had foretold. 24.13
was evil in the sight of the L., 24.19
anger of the L. it came to the 24.20
And he burned the house of the L., 25.09
that were in the house of the L., 25.13
had made for the house of the L., 25.16
was wicked in the sight of the L., 1Ch 2.03
exile when the L. sent Judah and 6.15
of song in the house of the L., 6.31
the house of the L. in Jerusalem; 6.32
in charge of the camp of the L., 9.19
in time past; the L. was with him. 9.20
the gates of the house of the L., 9.23
unfaithful to the L. in that he did 10.13
did not keep the command of the L. 10.13
and did not seek guidance from the L. 10.14
Therefore the L. slew him, and 10.14
and the L. your God said to you, 11.02
with them at Hebron before the L., 11.03
to the word of the L. by Samuel. 11.03
for the L. of hosts was with him. 11.09
the word of the L. concerning 11.10
and the L. saved them by a great 11.14
he poured it out to the L., 11.18
according to the word of the L. 12.23
it is the will of the L. our God, 13.02
the name of the L. who sits 13.06
anger of the L. was kindled 13.10
because the L. had broken forth 13.11
and the L. blessed the household 13.14
that the L. had established him 14.02
And the L. said to him, "Go up, and 14.10
and the L. brought the fear of him 14.17
for the L. chose them to carry the 15.02
the ark of the L. and to minister 15.02
up the ark of the L. to its place, 15.03
you may bring up the ark of the L., 15.12
the L. our God broke forth upon us, 15.13
to bring up the ark of the L., 15.14
according to the word of the L. 15.15
covenant of the L. from the house 15.25
the ark of the covenant of the L., 15.26
covenant of the L. with shouting, 15.28
covenant of the L. came to the 15.29
the people in the name of the L., 16.02
ministers before the ark of the L., 16.04
to thank, and to praise the L., 16.04
be sung to the L. by Asaph and his 16.07
O give thanks to the L., call on his 16.08
of those who seek the L. rejoice! 16.10
Seek the L. and his strength, seek 16.11
He is the L. our God; his judgments 16.14
Sing to the L., all the earth! 16.23
For great is the L., and greatly 16.25
but the L. made the heavens. 16.26
Ascribe to the L., O families of 16.28
ascribe to the L. glory and 16.28
Ascribe to the L. the glory due his 16.29
Worship the L. in holy array; 16.29
among the nations, "The L. reigns!" 16.31
wood sing for joy before the L., 16.33
O give thanks to the L., for he is 16.34
Blessed be the L., the God of Israel, 16.36
said "Amen!" and praised the L. 16.36
covenant of the L. to minister 16.37
tabernacle of the L. in the high 16.39
offerings to the L. upon the altar 16.40
the law of the L. which he commanded 16.40
named to give thanks to the L., 16.41
covenant of the L. is under a tent 17.01
the word of the L. came to Nathan, 17.03
servant David, 'Thus says the L.: 17.04
David, 'Thus says the L. of hosts, 17.07
to you that the L. will build you 17.10
went in and sat before the L., 17.16
O L. God, and what is my house, that 17.16
me future generations, O L. God! 17.17
O L., and according to thy own 17.19
O L., and there is no God besides 17.20
and thou, O L., didst become their 17.22
And now, O L., let the word which 17.23
'The L. of hosts, the God of Israel, 17.24

LORD (cont.)
And now, O L., thou art God, and thou 1Ch 17.26
O L., hast blessed is blessed for 17.27
And the L. gave victory to David 18.06
King David dedicated to the L., 18.11
And the L. gave victory to David 18.13
and may the L. do what seems good 19.13
"May the L. add to his people a 21.03
my l. the king, all of them my lord's 21.03
Why then should my l. require this? 21.03
And the L. spoke to Gad, David's seer, 21.09
say to David, 'Thus says the L., 21.10
and said to him, "Thus says the L., 21.11
three days of the sword of the L., 21.12
angel of the L. destroying throughout 21.12
me fall into the hand of the L., 21.13
So the L. sent a pestilence upon 21.14
the L. saw, and he repented of the 21.15
angel of the L. was standing by 21.15
angel of the L. standing between 21.16
O L. my God, be against me and 21.17
angel of the L. commanded Gad to 21.18
an altar to the L. on the threshing 21.18
had spoken in the name of the L. 21.19
build on it an altar to the L.— 21.22
and let my l. the king do what 21.23
not take for the L. what is yours, 21.24
an altar to the L. and presented 21.26
offerings, and called upon the L., 21.26
Then the L. commanded the angel; 21.27
saw that the L. had answered him 21.28
For the tabernacle of the L., 21.29
the sword of the angel of the L. 21.30
house of the L. God and here the 22.01
built for the L. must be exceedingly 22.05
him to build a house for the L., 22.06
house to the name of the L. my God. 22.07
But the word of the L. came to me, 22.08
the L. be with you, so that you may 22.11
the house of the L. your God, 22.11
Only, may the L. grant you discretion 22.12
keep the law of the L. your God. 22.12
which the L. commanded Moses for 22.13
house of the L. a hundred thousand 22.14
be doing! The L. be with you!" 22.16
"Is not the L. your God with you? 22.18
before the L. and his people. 22.18
and heart to seek the L. your God. 22.19
build the sanctuary of the L. God, 22.19
covenant of the L. and the holy 22.19
house built for the name of the L." 22.19
of the work in the house of the L., 23.04
praises to the L. with the instruments 23.05
should burn incense before the L., 23.13
the service of the house of the L. 23.24
"The L., the God of Israel, has 23.25
the service of the house of the L., 23.28
thanking and praising the L., 23.30
are offered to the L. on sabbaths, 23.31
of them, continually before the L. 23.31
the service of the house of the L." 23.32
house of the L. according to the 24.19
as the L. God of Israel had commanded 24.19
thanksgiving and praise to the L. 25.03
the house of the L. with cymbals, 25.06
were trained in singing to the L., 25.07
ministering in the house of the L.; 26.12
treasuries of the house of the L. 26.22
maintenance of the house of the L. 26.27
the work of the L. and for the 26.30
for the L. had promised to make 27.23
the ark of the covenant of the L., 28.02
Yet the L. God of Israel chose me 28.04
my sons (for the L. has given me 28.05
the kingdom of the L. over Israel. 28.05
all Israel, the assembly of the L., 28.08
commandments of the L. your God; 28.08
for the L. searches all hearts, 28.09
for the L. has chosen you to build 28.10
the courts of the house of the L., 28.12
the service in the house of the L.; 28.13
service in the house of the L., 28.13
the ark of the covenant of the L. 28.18
the hand of the L. concerning it, 28.19
for the L. God, even my God, is 28.20
of the house of the L. is finished. 28.20
not be for man but for the L. God. 29.01
consecrating himself today to the L.?" 29.05
treasury of the house of the L., 29.08
they had offered freely to the L.; 29.09
blessed the L. in the presence of 29.10
O L., the God of Israel our father, 29.10
Thine, O L., is the greatness, and 29.11
O L., and thou art exalted as head 29.11
O L. our God, all this abundance 29.16
O L., the God of Abraham, Isaac, and 29.18
assembly, "Bless the L. your God." 29.20
all the assembly blessed the L., 29.20
their heads, and worshiped the L., 29.20
performed sacrifices to the L., 29.21
offered burnt offerings to the L., 29.21
before the L. on that day with 29.22
anointed him as prince for the L., 29.22
throne of the L. as king instead 29.23
And the L. gave Solomon great 29.25
and the L. his God was with him and 2Ch 1.01
servant of the L. had made in the 1.03
before the tabernacle of the L. 1.05
and the assembly sought the L. 1.05
to the bronze altar before the L., 1.06
O L. God, let thy promise to David 1.09
a temple for the name of the L., 2.01
the name of the L. my God and 2.04
appointed feasts of the L. our God, 2.04
"Because the L. loves his people he 2.11
"Blessed be the L. God of Israel, 2.12
who will build a temple for the L., 2.12
craftsmen, the craftsmen of my l., 2.14
of which my l. has spoken, let him 2.15
house of the L. in Jerusalem on 3.01
where the L. had appeared to David 3.01
Solomon for the house of the L. 4.16
the house of the L. was finished. 5.01
covenant of the L. out of the city 5.02
covenant of the L. to its place, 5.07
where the L. made a covenant with 5.10
praise and thanksgiving to the L.), 5.13
instruments, in praise to the L., 5.13
the house, the house of the L., 5.13
glory of the L. filled the house 5.14
"The L. has said that he would 6.01
And he said, "Blessed be the L., 6.04
a house for the name of the L., 6.07
But the L. said to David my father, 6.08
Now the L. has fulfilled his 6.10
as the L. promised, and I have built 6.10
the house for the name of the L., 6.10
covenant of the L. which he made 6.11
altar of the L. in the presence of 6.12
and said, "O L., God of Israel, there 6.14
O L., God of Israel, keep with thy 6.16
O L., God of Israel, let thy word be 6.17
O L. my God, hearkening to the cry 6.19
O L. God, and go to thy resting 6.41
O L. God, be clothed with salvation, 6.41
O L. God, do not turn away the face 6.42
glory of the L. filled the temple. 7.01
not enter the house of the L., 7.02
glory of the L. filled the LORD's 7.02
glory of the L. upon the temple, 7.03
worshiped and gave thanks to the L., 7.03
offered sacrifice before the L. 7.04
music to the L. which King David 7.06
made for giving thanks to the L.— 7.06

LORD (cont.)
was before the house of the L.; 2Ch 7.07
that the L. had shown to David and 7.10
house of the L. and the king's 7.11
house of the L. and in his own 7.11
Then the L. appeared to Solomon in 7.12
'Why has the L. done thus to this 7.21
forsook the L. the God of their 7.22
house of the L. and his own house, 8.01
the ark of the L. has come are 8.11
offerings to the L. upon the altar of the L. 8.12
house of the L. was laid until it 8.16
the house of the L. was completed. 8.16
he offered at the house of the L., 9.04
Blessed be the L. your God, who has 9.08
throne as king for the L. your God! 9.08
house of the L. and for the king's 9.11
by God that the L. might fulfil 10.15
But the word of the L. came to 11.02
'Thus says the L., You shall not go 11.04
hearkened to the word of the L., 11.04
from serving as priests of the L., 11.14
to seek the L. God of Israel came 11.16
Jerusalem to sacrifice to the L., 11.16
he forsook the law of the L., 12.01
they had been unfaithful to the L., 12.02
and said to them, "Thus says the L., 12.05
and said, "The L. is righteous." 12.06
When the L. saw that they humbled 12.07
the word of the L. came to Shemaiah: 12.07
house of the L. and the treasures 12.09
king went into the house of the L., 12.11
wrath of the L. turned from him, so 12.12
city which the L. had chosen out 12.13
not set his heart to seek the L. 12.14
know that the L. God of Israel 13.05
up and rebelled against his l.; 13.06
kingdom of the L. in the hand of 13.08
driven out the priests of the L., 13.09
the L is our God, and we have not 13.10
ministering to the L. who are sons 13.10
They offer to the L. every morning 13.11
keep the charge of the L. our God, 13.11
do not fight against the L., 13.12
and they cried to the L., and the 13.14
because they relied upon the L., 13.18
and the L. smote him, and he died. 13.20
in the eyes of the L. his God. 14.02
and commanded Judah to seek the L., 14.04
years, for the L. gave him peace. 14.06
we have sought the L. our God; 14.07
And Asa cried to the L. his God, 14.11
"O L., there is none like thee to 14.11
Help us, O L. our God, for we rely on 14.11
O L., thou art our God; let not man 14.11
So the L. defeated the Ethiopians 14.12
broken before the L. and his army. 14.13
the fear of the L. was upon them. 14.14
The L. is with you, while you are 15.02
distress they turned to the L., 15.04
altar of the L. that was in front 15.08
vestibule of the house of the L. 15.08
saw that the L. his God was with 15.09
They sacrificed to the L. on that day, 15.11
into a covenant to seek the L., 15.12
that whoever would not seek the L., 15.13
oath to the L. with a loud voice, 15.14
and the L. gave them rest round 15.15
house of the L. and the king's 16.02
did not rely on the L. your God, 16.07
Yet because you relied on the L., 16.08
For the eyes of the L. run to and 16.09
his disease he did not seek the L., 16.12
The L. was with Jehoshaphat, because 17.03
Therefore the L. established the 17.05
courageous in the ways of the L.; 17.06
of the law of the L. with them; 17.09
And the fear of the L. fell upon 17.10
volunteer for the service of the L., 17.16
first for the word of the L." 18.04
prophet of the L. of whom we may 18.06
by whom we may inquire of the L., 18.07
iron, and said, "Thus says the L., 18.10
the L. will give it into the hand 18.11
"As the L. lives, what my God says, 18.13
the truth in the name of the L.?" 18.15
and the L. said, 'These have no 18.16
"Therefore hear the word of the L.: 18.18
I saw the L. sitting on his throne, 18.18
and the L. said, 'Who will entice 18.19
forward and stood before the L., 18.20
And the L. said to him, 'By what 18.20
the L. has put a lying spirit in 18.22
the L. has spoken evil concerning 18.22
Spirit of the L. go from me to 18.23
the L. has not spoken by me." 18.27
cried out, and the L. helped him. 18.31
and love those who hate the L.? 19.02
gone out against you from the L. 19.02
and brought them back to the L., 19.04
judge not for man but for the L.; 19.06
let the fear of the L. be upon you; 19.07
of justice with the L. our God, 19.07
judgment for the L. and to decide 19.08
you shall do in the fear of the L., 19.09
before the L. and wrath may not 19.10
over you in all matters of the L.; 19.11
and may the L. be with the upright!" 19.11
and set himself to seek the L., 20.03
assembled to seek help from the L.; 20.04
of Judah they came to seek the L. 20.04
Jerusalem, in the house of the L., 20.05
and said, "O L., God of our fathers, 20.06
men of Judah stood before the L., 20.13
Spirit of the L. came upon Jahaziel 20.14
Thus says the L. to you, 'Fear not, 20.15
victory of the L. on your behalf, 20.17
and the L. will be with you." 20.17
before the L., worshiping the L. 20.18
Korahites, stood up to praise the L., 20.19
Believe in the L. your God, and you 20.20
to sing to the L. and praise him 20.21
and say, "Give thanks to the L. 20.21
the L. set an ambush against the 20.22
for there they blessed the L.; 20.26
for the L. had made them rejoice 20.27
trumpets, to the house of the L. 20.28
heard that the L. had fought 20.29
was right in the sight of the L. 20.32
the L. will destroy what you have 20.37
was evil in the sight of the L. 21.06
Yet the L. would not destroy the 21.07
because he had forsaken the L., 21.10
prophet, saying, "Thus says the L., 21.12
behold, the L. will bring a great 21.14
And the L. stirred up against 21.16
all this the L. smote him in his 21.18
was evil in the sight of the L., 22.04
whom the L. had anointed to destroy 22.07
who sought the L. with all his 22.09
as the L. spoke concerning the sons 23.03
the courts of the house of the L. 23.05
house of the L. except the priests 23.06
shall keep the charge of the L. 23.06
the house of the L. to the people; 23.12
slay her in the house of the L." 23.14
house of the L. under the direction 23.18
in charge of the house of the L., 23.18
to offer burnt offerings to the L., 23.18
house of the L. so that no one 23.19
king down from the house of the L., 23.20
the eyes of the L. all the days of 24.02
to restore the house of the L. 24.04
by Moses, the servant of the L., 24.06

LORD (cont.)

the house of the L. for the Baals. 2Ch 24.07
the gate of the house of the L. 24.08
in for the L. the tax that Moses 24.09
of the work of the house of the L., 24.12
to restore the house of the L., 24.12
to repair the house of the L. 24.12
utensils for the house of the L., 24.14
house of the L. continually all 24.14
And they forsook the house of the L., 24.18
them to bring them back to the L.; 24.19
transgress the commandments of the L., 24.20
Because you have forsaken the L., 24.20
the court of the house of the L. 24.21
he said, "May the L. see and avenge!" 24.22
the L. delivered into their hand a 24.24
because they had forsaken the L., 24.24
was right in the eyes of the L., 25.02
where the L. commanded, "The fathers 25.04
for the L. is not with Israel, with 25.07
"The L. is able to give you much 25.09
Therefore the L. was angry with 25.15
away from the L. they made a 25.27
was right in the eyes of the L., 26.04
and as long as he sought the L., 26.05
For he was false to the L. his God, 26.16
temple of the L. to burn incense. 26.16
priests of the L. who were men of 26.17
Uzziah, to burn incense to the L., 26.18
bring you no honor from the L. God. 26.18
the priests in the house of the L., 26.19
because the L. had smitten him. 26.20
excluded from the house of the L. 26.21
the eyes of the L. according to 27.02
not invade the temple of the L. 27.02
upper gate of the house of the L., 27.03
his ways before the L. his God. 27.06
was right in the eyes of the L., 28.01
whom the L. drove out before the 28.03
Therefore the L. his God gave him 28.05
because they had forsaken the L., 28.06
But a prophet of the L. was there, 28.09
because the L., the God of your 28.09
your own against the L. your God? 28.10
fierce wrath of the L. is upon you." 28.11
against the L. in addition to our 28.13
For the L. brought Judah low 28.19
and had been faithless to the L. 28.19
house of the L. and the house of 28.21
yet more faithless to the L.— 28.22
the doors of the house of the L.; 28.24
gods, provoking to anger the L., 28.25
was right in the eyes of the L., 29.02
the doors of the house of the L., 29.03
and sanctify the house of the L., 29.05
in the sight of the L. our God; 29.06
from the habitation of the L., 29.06
wrath of the L. came on Judah and 29.08
to make a covenant with the L., 29.10
for the L. has chosen you to stand 29.11
commanded, by the words of the L., 29.15
to cleanse the house of the L. 29.15
the house of the L. to cleanse it, 29.16
temple of the L. into the court of 29.16
the court of the house of the L.; 29.16
came to the vestibule of the L.; 29.17
sanctified the house of the L., 29.17
cleansed all the house of the L., 29.18
are before the altar of the L. 29.19
and went up to the house of the L. 29.20
offer them on the altar of the L. 29.21
the house of the L. with cymbals, 29.25
was from the L. through his 29.25
the song to the L. began also, 29.27
praises to the L. with the words 29.30
consecrated yourselves to the L.; 29.31
offerings to the house of the L." 29.31
for a burnt offering to the L. 29.32
the house of the L. was restored. 29.35
the house of the L. at Jerusalem, 30.01
passover to the L. the God of 30.01
passover to the L. the God of 30.05
return to the L., the God of 30.06
faithless to the L. God of their 30.07
but yield yourselves to the L., 30.08
and serve the L. your God, that his 30.08
For if you return to the L., 30.09
For the L. your God is gracious and 30.09
commanded by the word of the L. 30.12
offerings into the house of the L. 30.15
clean, to make it holy to the L. 30.17
"The good L. pardon every one 30.18
the L. the God of his fathers, even 30.19
And the L. heard Hezekiah, and 30.20
priests praised the L. day by day, 30.21
with all their might to the L. 30.21
skill in the service of the L. 30.22
thanks to the L. the God of their 30.22
the camp of the L. and to give 31.02
it is written in the law of the L. 31.03
themselves to the law of the L. 31.04
consecrated to the L. their God, 31.06
blessed the L. and his people 31.08
house of the L. we have eaten and 31.10
for the L. has blessed his people, 31.10
chambers in the house of the L.; 31.11
reserved for the L. and the most 31.14
house of the L. as the duty of 31.16
and faithful before the L. his God. 31.20
but with us is the L. our God, 32.08
"The L. our God will deliver us 32.11
against the L. God and against his 32.16
contempt on the L. the God of 32.17
And the L. sent an angel, who cut 32.21
So the L. saved Hezekiah and the 32.22
gifts to the L. to Jerusalem and 32.23
of death, and he prayed to the L.; 32.24
wrath of the L. did not come upon 32.26
was evil in the sight of the L., 33.02
whom the L. drove out before the 33.02
altars in the house of the L., 33.04
of which the L. had said, "In 33.04
two courts of the house of the L. 33.05
much evil in the sight of the L., 33.06
whom the L. destroyed before the 33.09
The L. spoke to Manasseh and to his 33.10
Therefore the L. brought upon them 33.11
favor of the L. his God and 33.12
Manasseh knew that the L. was God. 33.13
the idol from the house of the L., 33.15
house of the L. and in Jerusalem, 33.15
altar of the L. and offered upon 33.16
to serve the L. the God of Israel. 33.16
but only to the L. their God. 33.17
the name of the L. the God of 33.18
was evil in the sight of the L., 33.22
not humble himself before the L., 33.23
was right in the eyes of the L., 34.02
repair the house of the L. his God. 34.08
oversight of the house of the L.; 34.10
house of the L. gave it for 34.10
brought into the house of the L., 34.14
the law of the L. given through 34.14
of the law in the house of the L."; 34.15
house of the L. and have delivered 34.17
"Go, inquire of the L. for me and 34.21
wrath of the L. that is poured out 34.21
have not kept the word of the L., 34.21
she said to them, "Thus says the L., 34.23
Thus says the L., Behold, I will 34.24
who sent you to inquire of the L., 34.26
Thus says the L., the God of Israel: 34.26
I also have heard you, says the L. 34.27
went up to the house of the L., 34.30

LORD (cont.)
been found in the house of the L. 2Ch 34.30
and made a covenant before the L., 34.31
walk after the L. and to keep his 34.31
in Israel serve the L. their God. 34.33
following the L. the God of their 34.33
a passover to the L. in Jerusalem; 35.01
the service of the house of the L. 35.02
Israel and who were holy to the L., 35.03
Now serve the L. your God and his 35.03
to the word of the L. by Moses. 35.06
the lay people, to offer to the L., 35.12
service of the L. was prepared 35.16
offerings on the altar of the L., 35.16
is written in the law of the L., 35.26
in the sight of the L. his God. 36.05
house of the L. to Babylon and put 36.07
was evil in the sight of the L. 36.09
vessels of the house of the L., 36.10
in the sight of the L. his God. 36.12
who spoke from the mouth of the L. 36.12
heart against turning to the L., 36.13
house of the L. which he had 36.14
The L., the God of their fathers, 36.15
wrath of the L. rose against his 36.16
treasures of the house of the L., 36.18
the word of the L. by the mouth of 36.21
the word of the L. by the mouth of 36.22
the L. stirred up the spirit of 36.22
'The L., the God of heaven, has 36.23
may the L. his God be with him. 36.23
the word of the L. by the mouth of Ez 1.01
the L. stirred up the spirit of 1.01
The L., the God of heaven, has given 1.02
and rebuild the house of the L., 1.03
house of the L. which is in 1.05
house of the L. which Nebuchadnezzar 1.07
house of the L. which is in 2.68
burnt offerings upon it to the L., 3.03
all the appointed feasts of the L., 3.05
made a freewill offering to the L. 3.05
to offer burnt offerings to the L. 3.06
temple of the L. was not yet laid. 3.06
of the work of the house of the L. 3.08
foundation of the temple of the L., 3.10
to praise the L., according to the 3.10
and giving thanks to the L., 3.11
shout, when they praised the L., 3.11
of the house of the L. was laid. 3.11
were building a temple to the L., 4.01
but we alone will build to the L., 4.03
of the land to worship the L., 6.21
for the L. had made them joyful, 6.22
Moses which the L. the God of 7.06
the hand of the L. his God was 7.06
heart to study the law of the L., 7.10
commandments of the L. and his 7.11
Blessed be the L., the God of our 7.27
house of the L. which is in 7.27
the hand of the L. my God was upon 7.28
to them, "You are holy to the L., 8.28
are a freewill offering to the L., 8.28
chambers of the house of the L." 8.29
was a burnt offering to the L. 8.35
out my hands to the L. my God, 9.05
has been shown by the L. our God, 9.08
O L. the God of Israel, thou art 9.15
counsel of my l. and of those who 10.03
confession to the L. the God of 10.11
And I said, "O L. God of heaven, the Neh 1.05
O L., let thy ear be attentive to 1.11
necks to the work of their L. 3.05
Remember the L., who is great and 4.14
said "Amen" and praised the L. 5.13
Moses which the L. had given to 8.01
Ezra blessed the L., the great God; 8.06
worshiped the L. with their faces 8.06
day is holy to the L. your God; 8.09
for this day is holy to our L.; 8.10
the joy of the L. is your strength. 8.10
law that the L. had commanded by 8.14
the law of the L. their God for a 9.03
and worshiped the L. their God. 9.03
a loud voice to the L. their God. 9.04
and bless the L. your God from 9.05
said: "Thou art the L., thou alone; 9.06
Thou art the L., the God who didst 9.07
commandments of the L. our L. and his 10.29
upon the altar of the L. our God, 10.34
by year, to the house of the L.; 10.35
every man be l. in his own house Est 1.22
present themselves before the L., Job 1.06
The L. said to Satan, "Whence have 1.07
Satan answered the L., "From going 1.07
And the L. said to Satan, "Have you 1.08
Then Satan answered the L., "Does 1.09
And the L. said to Satan, "Behold, 1.12
forth from the presence of the L. 1.12
the L. gave, and the L. has taken away; 1.21
blessed be the name of the L." 1.21
present themselves before the L., 2.01
to present himself before the L. 2.01
And the L. said to Satan, "Whence 2.02
Satan answered the L., "From going 2.02
And the L. said to Satan, "Have you 2.03
Then Satan answered the L., "Skin 2.04
And the L. said to Satan, "Behold, he 2.06
forth from the presence of the L., 2.07
the hand of the L. has done this? 12.09
man, 'Behold, the fear of the L., 28.28
Then the L. answered Job out of the 38.01
And the L. said to Job: 40.01
Then Job answered the L.: 40.03
Then the L. answered Job out of the 40.06
Then Job answered the L.: 42.01
After the L. had spoken these words 42.07
the L. said to Eliphaz the Temanite: 42.07
and did what the L. had told them; 42.09
and the L. accepted Job's prayer. 42.09
And the L. restored the fortunes of 42.10
and the L. gave Job twice as much 42.10
evil that the L. had brought upon 42.11
And the L. blessed the latter days 42.12
delight is in the law of the L., Ps 1.02
for the L. knows the way of the 1.06
against the L. and his anointed, 2.02
laughs; the L. has them in derision. 2.04
I will tell of the decree of the L.: 2.07
Serve the L. with fear, with trembling 2.11
O L., how many are my foes! Many are 3.01
But thou, O L., art a shield about 3.03
I cry aloud to the L., and he 3.04
wake again, for the L. sustains me. 3.05
Arise, O L.! Deliver me, O my God! 3.07
Deliverance belongs to the L.; 3.08
But know that the L. has set apart 4.03
the L. hears when I call to him. 4.03
and put your trust in the L. 4.05
of thy countenance upon us, O L.!" 4.06
O L., makest me dwell in safety. 4.08
Give ear to my words, O L.; give 5.01
O L., in the morning thou dost hear 5.03
the L. abhors bloodthirsty and 5.06
Lead me, O L., in thy righteousness 5.08
dost bless the righteous, O L.; 5.12
O L., rebuke me not in thy anger, 6.01
to me, O L., for I am languishing; 6.02
O L., heal me, for my bones are 6.02
troubled. But thou, O L.—how long? 6.03
Turn, O L., save my life; deliver me 6.04
for the L. has heard the sound of 6.08
The L. has heard my supplication; 6.09
the L. accepts my prayer. 6.09
O L. my God, in thee do I take 7.01

LORD (cont.)

O L. my God, if I have done this, if Ps 7.03
Arise, O L., in thy anger, lift 7.06
The L. judges the peoples; 7.08
judge me, O L., according to my 7.08
give to the L. the thanks due to 7.17
the name of the L., the Most High. 7.17
O L., our L., how majestic is thy name 8.01
O L., our L., how majestic is thy name 8.09
thanks to the L. with my whole 9.01
But the L. sits enthroned for ever, 9.07
The L. is a stronghold for the 9.09
O L., hast not forsaken those who 9.10
Sing praises to the L., who dwells 9.11
be gracious to me, O L.! Behold 9.13
The L. has made himself known, he 9.16
Arise, O L.! Let not man prevail; 9.19
Put them in fear, O L.! Let the 9.20
Why dost thou stand afar off, O L.? 10.01
gain curses and renounces the L. 10.03
Arise, O L.; O God, lift up thy 10.12
The L. is king for ever and ever; 10.16
O L., thou wilt hear the desire of 10.17
In the L. I take refuge; how can you 11.01
The L. is in his holy temple, the 11.04
The L. tests the righteous and the 11.05
For the L. is righteous, he loves 11.07
Help, L.; for there is no longer 12.01
May the L. cut off all flattering 12.03
I will now arise," says the L.; 12.05
The promises of the L. are promises 12.06
Do thou, O L., protect us, guard us 12.07
How long, O L.? Wilt thou forget me 13.01
Consider and answer me, O L. my God; 13.03
I will sing to the L., because he has 13.06
The L. looks down from heaven upon 14.02
bread, and do not call upon the L.? 14.04
the poor, but the L. is his refuge. 14.06
When the L. restores the fortunes 14.07
O L., who shall sojourn in thy tent? 15.01
who honors those who fear the L.; 15.04
I say to the L., "Thou art my L.; 16.02
The L. is my chosen portion and my 16.05
I bless the L. who gives me counsel; 16.07
I keep the L. always before me; 16.08
Hear a just cause, O L.; attend to 17.01
Arise, O L.! confront them, overthrow 17.13
O L., from men whose portion in 17.14
I love thee, O L., my strength. 18.01
The L. is my rock, and my fortress, 18.02
I call upon the L., who is worthy to 18.03
In my distress I called upon the L.; 18.06
The L. also thundered in the heavens, 18.13
O L., at the blast of the breath of 18.15
my calamity; but the L. was my stay. 18.18
The L. rewarded me according to my 18.20
for I have kept the ways of the L., 18.21
Therefore the L. has recompensed me 18.24
the L. my God lightens my darkness. 18.28
the promise of the L. proves true; 18.30
For who is God, but the L.? And who 18.31
none to save, they cried to the L., 18.41
The L. lives; and blessed be my 18.46
O L., among the nations, and sing 18.49
The law of the L. is perfect, 19.07
the testimony of the L. is sure, 19.07
the precepts of the L. are right, 19.08
the commandment of the L. is pure, 19.08
the fear of the L. is clean, 19.09
the ordinances of the L. are true, 19.09
O L., my rock and my redeemer. 19.14
The L. answer you in the day of 20.01
May the L. fulfil all your petitions! 20.05
Now I know that the L. will help 20.06
of the name of the L. our God. 20.07
Give victory to the king, O L.; 20.09
strength the king rejoices, O L.; 21.01
For the king trusts in the L.; 21.07
The L. will swallow them up in his 21.09
Be exalted, O L., in thy strength! 21.13
"He committed his cause to the L.; 22.08
But thou, O L., be not far off! 22.19
you who fear the L., praise him! 22.23
who seek him shall praise the L.! 22.26
shall remember and turn to the L.; 22.27
For dominion belongs to the L., 22.28
tell of the L. to the coming 22.30
The L. is my shepherd, I shall not 23.01
in the house of the L. for ever. 23.06
Who shall ascend the hill of the L.? 24.03
He will receive blessing from the L., 24.05
The L., strong and mighty, the 24.08
The L., mighty in battle! 24.08
The L. of hosts, he is the King of 24.10
To thee, O L., I lift up my soul. 25.01
Make me to know thy ways, O L.; 25.04
O L., and of thy steadfast love, for 25.06
me, for thy goodness' sake, O L.! 25.07
Good and upright is the L.; 25.08
paths of the L. are steadfast love 25.10
O L., pardon my guilt, for it is 25.11
Who is the man that fears the L.? 25.12
friendship of the L. is for those 25.14
My eyes are ever toward the L., 25.15
O L., for I have walked in my 26.01
trusted in the L. without wavering. 26.01
Prove me, O L., and try me; 26.02
and go about thy altar, O L., 26.06
O L., I love the habitation of thy 26.08
congregation I will bless the L. 26.12
The L. is my light and my salvation; 27.01
The L. is the stronghold of my life; 27.01
One thing have I asked of the L., 27.04
house of the L. all the days of my 27.04
to behold the beauty of the L., 27.04
sing and make melody to the L. 27.06
Hear, O L., when I cry aloud, be 27.07
to thee, "Thy face, L., do I seek." 27.08
but the L. will take me up. 27.10
Teach me thy way, O L.; and lead me 27.11
goodness of the L. in the land of 27.13
Wait for the L.; be strong, and let 27.14
take courage; yea, wait for the L.! 27.14
To thee, O L., I call; my rock, be 28.01
do not regard the works of the L., 28.05
Blessed be the L.! for he has heard 28.06
The L. is my strength and my shield; 28.07
The L. is the strength of his people, 28.08
Ascribe to the L., O heavenly beings, 29.01
ascribe to the L. glory and strength. 29.01
Ascribe to the L. the glory of his 29.02
name; worship the L. in holy array. 29.02
The voice of the L. is upon the 29.03
thunders, the L., upon many waters. 29.03
The voice of the L. is powerful, 29.04
voice of the L. is full of majesty. 29.04
The voice of the L. breaks the 29.05
the L. breaks the cedars of Lebanon. 29.05
The voice of the L. flashes forth 29.07
The voice of the L. shakes the 29.08
the L. shakes the wilderness of 29.08
The voice of the L. makes the oaks 29.09
The L. sits enthroned over the 29.10
The L. sits enthroned as king for 29.10
May the L. give strength to his 29.11
May the L. bless his people with 29.11
O L., for thou hast drawn me up, and 30.01
O L. my God, I cried to thee for 30.02
O L., thou hast brought up my soul 30.03
Sing praises to the L., O you his 30.04
O L., thou hadst established me as 30.07
To thee, O L., I cried; 30.08
and to the L. I made supplication: 30.08
Hear, O L., and be gracious to me! 30.10

LORD (cont.)
O L., be thou my helper!" Ps 30.10
O L. my God, I will give thanks to 30.12
In thee, O L., do I seek refuge; 31.01
redeemed me, O L., faithful God. 31.05
vain idols; but I trust in the L. 31.06
to me, O L., for I am in distress; 31.09
O L., I say, "Thou art my God." 31.14
shame, O L., for I call on thee; 31.17
Blessed be the L., for he has 31.21
Love the L., all you his saints! 31.23
The L. preserves the faithful, but 31.23
courage, all you who wait for the L.! 31.24
man to whom the L. imputes no 32.02
my transgressions to the L."; 32.05
surrounds him who trusts in the L. 32.10
Be glad in the L., and rejoice, O 32.11
Rejoice in the L., O you righteous! 33.01
Praise the L. with the lyre, make 33.02
For the word of the L. is upright; 33.04
of the steadfast love of the L. 33.05
By the word of the L. the heavens 33.06
Let all the earth fear the L., 33.08
The L. brings the counsel of the 33.10
The counsel of the L. stands for 33.11
Blessed is the nation whose God is the L., 33.12
The L. looks down from heaven, he 33.13
Behold, the eye of the L. is on 33.18
Our soul waits for the L.; he is our 33.20
O L., be upon us, even as we hope in 33.22
I will bless the L. at all times; 34.01
My soul makes its boast in the L.; 34.02
O magnify the L. with me, and let us 34.03
I sought the L., and he answered me, 34.04
and the L. heard him, and saved him 34.06
The angel of the L. encamps around 34.07
O taste and see that the L. is good! 34.08
O fear the L., you his saints, for 34.09
who seek the L. lack no good thing. 34.10
will teach you the fear of the L. 34.11
The eyes of the L. are toward the 34.15
The face of the L. is against 34.16
the L. hears, and delivers them out 34.17
The L. is near to the brokenhearted, 34.18
but the L. delivers him out of them 34.19
The L. redeems the life of his 34.22
Contend, O L., with those who 35.01
angel of the L. driving them on! 35.05
the angel of the L. pursuing them! 35.06
Then my soul shall rejoice in the L., 35.09
"O L., who is like thee, thou who 35.10
How long, O L., wilt thou look on? 35.17
Thou hast seen, O L.; be not silent! 35.22
O L., be not far from me! 35.22
for my cause, my God and my L.! 35.23
O L., my God, according to thy 35.24
"Great is the L., who delights in 35.27
O L., extends to the heavens, thy 36.05
man and beast thou savest, O L. 36.06
Trust in the L., and do good; 37.03
Take delight in the L., and he will 37.04
Commit your way to the L.; trust in 37.05
Be still before the L., and wait 37.07
wait for the L. shall possess the 37.09
but the L. laughs at the wicked, for 37.13
but the L. upholds the righteous. 37.17
The L. knows the days of the 37.18
enemies of the L. are like the 37.20
blessed by the L. shall possess 37.22
The steps of a man are from the L., 37.23
for the L. is the stay of his hand. 37.24
For the L. loves justice; he will not 37.28
The L. will not abandon him to his 37.33
Wait for the L., and keep to his 37.34
of the righteous is from the L.; 37.39
The L. helps them and delivers them; 37.40
O L., rebuke me not in thy anger, 38.01
L., all my longing is known to thee, 38.09
But for thee, O L., do I wait; 38.15
It is thou, O L. my God, who wilt 38.15
Do not forsake me, O L.! O my God, 38.21
to help me, O L., my salvation! 38.22
"L., let me know my end, and what is 39.04
"And now, L., for what do I wait? 39.07
O L., and give ear to my cry; 39.12
I waited patiently for the L.; 40.01
and put their trust in the L. 40.03
the man who makes the L. his trust, 40.04
O L. my God, thy wondrous deeds and 40.05
my lips., as thou knowest, O L. 40.09
Do not thou, O L., withhold thy 40.11
Be pleased, O L., to deliver me! 40.13
O L., make haste to help me! 40.13
say continually, "Great is the L.!" 40.16
but the L. takes thought for me. 40.17
The L. delivers him in the day of 41.01
the L. protects him and keeps him 41.02
The L. sustains him on his sickbed; 41.03
"O L., be gracious to me; heal me, 41.04
But do thou, O L., be gracious to me, 41.10
Blessed be the L., the God of 41.13
By day the L. commands his steadfast 42.08
Why sleepest thou, O L.? Awake! Do 44.23
Since he is your l., bow to him; 45.11
The L. of hosts is with us; the 46.07
Come, behold the works of the L., 46.08
The L. of hosts is with us; 46.11
For the L., the Most High, is 47.02
the L. with the sound of a trumpet. 47.05
Great is the L. and greatly to be 48.01
in the city of the L. of hosts, 48.08
God the L., speaks and summons the 50.01
O L., open thou my lips, and my 51.15
the L. is the upholder of my life. 54.04
to thy name, O L., for it is good. 54.06
plans, O L., confuse their tongues; 55.09
upon God; and the L. will save me. 55.16
Cast your burden on the L., and he 55.22
in the L., whose word I praise, 56.10
to thee, O L., among the peoples; 57.09
the fangs of the young lions, O L.! 58.06
transgression or sin of mine, O L., 59.03
Thou, L. God of hosts, art God of 59.05
But thou, O L., dost laugh at them; 59.08
bring them down, O L., our shield! 59.11
to thee, O L., belongs steadfast love. 62.12
Let the righteous rejoice in the L., 64.10
the L. would not have listened. 66.18
his name is the L., exult before him! 68.04
The L. gives the command; great is 68.11
where the L. will dwell for ever? 68.16
the L. came from Sinai into the 68.17
that the L. God may dwell there. 68.18
Blessed be the L., who daily bears 68.19
the L., belongs escape from death. 68.20
The L. said, "I will bring them back 68.22
the L., O you who are of Israel's 68.26
the earth; sing praises to the L., 68.32
through me, O L. GOD of hosts; 69.06
for me, my prayer is to thee, O L. 69.13
Answer me, O L., for thy steadfast 69.16
This will please the L. more than 69.31
For the L. hears the needy, and does 69.33
O L., make haste to help me! 70.01
my deliverer; O L., do not tarry! 70.05
In thee, O L., do I take refuge; 71.01
For thou, O L., art my hope, my trust, 71.05
my trust, O L., from my youth. 71.05
deeds of the L. GOD I will come, I 71.16
Blessed be the L., the God of 72.18
I have made the L. GOD my refuge, 73.28
O L., how the enemy scoffs, and an 74.18
the hand of the L. there is a cup, 75.08
Make your vows to the L. your God, 76.11

LORD (cont.)
day of my trouble I seek the L.; Ps 77.02
"Will the L. spurn for ever, and 77.07
call to mind the deeds of the L.; 77.11
the glorious deeds of the L., 78.04
when the L. heard, he was full of 78.21
Then the L. awoke as from sleep, 78.65
How long, O L.? Wilt thou be angry 79.05
which they have taunted thee, O L.! 79.12
O L. God of hosts, how long wilt 80.04
Restore us, O L. God of hosts! 80.19
I am the L. your God, who brought 81.10
Those who hate the L. would cringe 81.15
that they may seek thy name, O L. 83.16
thou alone, whose name is the L., 83.18
thy dwelling place, O L. of hosts! 84.01
faints for the courts of the L.; 84.02
O L. of hosts, my king and my God. 84.03
O L. God of hosts, hear my prayer; 84.08
For the L. God is a sun and shield; 84.11
thing does the L. withhold from 84.11
O L. of hosts, blessed is the man 84.12
L., thou wast favorable to thy land; 85.01
O L., and grant us thy salvation. 85.07
me hear what God the L. will speak, 85.08
Yea, the L. will give what is good, 85.12
O L., and answer me, for I am poor 86.01
O L., for to thee do I cry all the 86.03
for to thee, O L., do I lift up my soul. 86.04
For thou, O L., art good and forgiving, 86.05
Give ear, O L., to my prayer; 86.06
O L., nor are there any works like 86.08
O L., and shall glorify thy name. 86.09
O L., that I may walk in thy truth; 86.11
O L. my God, with my whole heart, and 86.12
But thou, O L., art a God merciful 86.15
L., hast helped me and comforted me. 86.17
The L. loves the gates of Zion more 87.02
The L. records as he registers the 87.06
O L., my God, I call for help by day; 88.01
Every day I call upon thee, O L.; 88.09
But I, O L., cry to thee; in the 88.13
O L., why dost thou cast me off? 88.14
thy steadfast love, O L., for ever; 89.01
O L., thy faithfulness in the 89.05
skies can be compared to the L.? 89.06
heavenly beings is like the L., 89.06
O L. God of hosts, who is mighty as 89.08
O L., with thy faithfulness round 89.08
O L., in the light of thy countenance, 89.15
For our shield belongs to the L., 89.18
How long, O L.? Wilt thou hide 89.46
Remember, O L., what the measure of 89.47
L., where is thy steadfast love of 89.49
Remember, O L., how thy servant is 89.50
O L., with which they mock the 89.51
Blessed be the L. for ever! 89.52
L., thou hast been our dwelling 90.01
Return, O L.! How long? Have 90.13
favor of the L. our God be upon us, 90.17
will say to the L., "My refuge and 91.02
Because you have made the L. your refuge, 91.09
It is good to give thanks to the L., 92.01
For thou, O L., hast made me glad by 92.04
How great are thy works, O L.! 92.05
but thou, O L., art on high for ever. 92.08
O L., for, lo, thy enemies shall 92.09
are planted in the house of the L., 92.13
to show that the L. is upright; 92.15
The L. reigns; he is robed in majesty; 93.01
the L. is robed, he is girded with 93.01
O L., the floods have lifted up 93.03
of the sea, the L. on high is mighty! 93.04
thy house, O L., for evermore. 93.05
O L., thou God of vengeance, thou 94.01
O L., how long shall the wicked, how 94.03
O L., and afflict thy heritage. 94.05
and they say, "The L. does not see; 94.07
the L., knows the thoughts of man, 94.11
O L., and whom thou dost teach out 94.12
For the L. will not forsake his 94.14
If the L. had not been my help, my 94.17
steadfast love, O L., held me up. 94.18
But the L. has become my stronghold, 94.22
the L. our God will wipe them out. 94.23
O come, let us sing to the L.; 95.01
For the L. is a great God, and a 95.03
us kneel before the L., our Maker! 95.06
O sing to the L. a new song; 96.01
sing to the L., all the earth! 96.01
Sing to the L., bless his name; 96.02
For great is the L., and greatly 96.04
but the L. made the heavens. 96.05
Ascribe to the L., O families of 96.07
ascribe to the L. glory and 96.07
Ascribe to the L. the glory due his 96.08
Worship the L. in holy array; 96.09
Say among the nations, "The L. reigns! 96.10
before the L., for he comes, for he 96.13
The L. reigns; let the earth rejoice; 97.01
mountains melt like wax before the L., 97.05
before the L. of all the earth. 97.05
For thou, O L., art most high over 97.09
The L. loves those who hate evil; 97.10
Rejoice in the L., O you righteous, 97.12
O sing to the L. a new song, for he 98.01
The L. has made known his victory, 98.02
noise to the L., all the earth; 98.04
Sing prasies to the L. with the lyre, 98.05
noise before the King, the L.! 98.06
before the L., for he comes to rule 98.09
The L. reigns; let the peoples tremble! 99.01
The L. is great in Zion; he is exalted 99.02
Extol the L. our God; worship at his 99.05
They cried to the L., and he answered 99.06
O L. our God, thou didst answer them; 99.08
Extol the L. our God, and worship at 99.09
for the L. our God is holy! 99.09
noise to the L., all the lands! 100.01
Serve the L. with gladness! Come into 100.02
Know that the L. is God! It is he that 100.03
For the L. is good; his steadfast love 100.05
justice; to thee, O L., I will sing. 101.01
evildoers from the city of the L. 101.08
Hear my prayer, O L.; let my cry 102.01
But thou, O L., art enthroned for 102.12
will fear the name of the L., 102.15
For the L. will build up Zion, he 102.16
yet unborn may praise the L.: 102.18
from heaven the L. looked at the 102.19
declare in Zion the name of the L., 102.21
and kingdoms, to worship the L. 102.22
Bless the L., O my soul; and all 103.01
Bless the L., O my soul, and forget 103.02
The L. works vindication and 103.06
The L. is merciful and gracious, 103.08
so the L. pities those who fear him. 103.13
love of the L. is from everlasting 103.17
The L. has established his throne 103.19
Bless the L., O you his angels, you 103.20
Bless the L., all his hosts, his 103.21
Bless the L., all his works, in all 103.22
Bless the L., O my soul! 103.22
Bless the L., O my soul! O L. my God, 104.01
The trees of the L. are watered 104.16
O L., how manifold are thy works! 104.24
glory of the L. endure for ever, 104.31
may the L. rejoice in his works, 104.31
sing to the L. as long as I live; 104.33
to him, for I rejoice in the L. 104.34
Bless the L., O my soul! Praise the L.! 104.35
O give thanks to the L., 105.01
of those who seek the L. rejoice! 105.03
Seek the L. and his strength, seek 105.04

LORD (cont.)
He is the L. our God; his judgments Ps 105.07
pass the word of the L. tested him. 105.19
he made him l. of his house, and 105.21
And the L. made his people very 105.24
observe his laws. Praise the L.! 105.45
Praise the L.! O give thanks to the L., 106.01
utter the mighty doings of the L., 106.02
Remember me, O L., when thou showest 106.04
and Aaron, the holy one of the L., 106.16
did not obey the voice of the L. 106.25
they provoked the L. to anger with 106.29
peoples, as the L. commanded them, 106.34
anger of the L. was kindled against 106.40
Save us, O L. our God, and gather us 106.47
Blessed be the L., the God of 106.48
people say, "Amen!" Praise the L.! 106.48
O give thanks to the L., for he is 107.01
Let the redeemed of the L. say so, 107.02
cried to the L. in their trouble, 107.06
Let them thank the L. for his 107.08
cried to the L. in their trouble, 107.13
Let them thank the L. for his 107.15
cried to the L. in their trouble, 107.19
Let them thank the L. for his 107.21
they saw the deeds of the L., 107.24
cried to the L. in their trouble, 107.28
Let them thank the L. for his 107.31
the steadfast love of the L. 107.43
O L., among the peoples, I will sing 108.03
be remembered before the L., 109.14
Let them be before the L. continually; 109.15
reward of my accusers from the L., 109.20
O GOD my L., deal on my behalf for 109.21
Help me, O L. my God! Save me 109.26
thy hand; thou, O L., hast done it! 109.27
I will give great thanks to the L.; 109.30
The L. says to my l.: "Sit at my 110.01
The L. sends forth from Zion your 110.02
The L. has sworn and will not 110.04
The L. is at your right hand; 110.05
Praise the L. I will give 111.01
thanks to the L. with my whole 111.01
Great are the works of the L., 111.02
the L. is gracious and merciful. 111.04
The fear of the L. is the beginning 111.10
Praise the L. Blessed is the man 112.01
is the man who fears the L., 112.01
the L. is gracious, merciful, and 112.04
heart is firm, trusting in the L. 112.07
Praise the L.! Praise, O servants of the L., 113.01
praise the name of the L.! 113.01
the name of the L. from this time 113.02
the name of the L. is to be 113.03
The L. is high above all nations, 113.04
Who is like the L. our God, 113.05
mother of children. Praise the L.! 113.09
O earth, at the presence of the L. 114.07
Not to us, O L., not to us, but to 115.01
O Israel, trust in the L.! 115.09
of Aaron, put your trust in the L.! 115.10
You who fear the L., trust in the L.! 115.11
The L. has been mindful of us; 115.12
he will bless those who fear the L., 115.13
May the L. give you increase, you 115.14
May you be blessed by the L., 115.15
The dead do not praise the L., 115.17
will bless the L. from this time 115.18
for evermore. Praise the L.! 115.18
I love the L., because he has heard 116.01
Then I called on the name of the L.: 116.04
"O L., I beseech thee, save my life!" 116.04
Gracious is the L., and righteous; 116.05
The L. preserves the simple; 116.06
for the L. has dealt bountifully 116.07
I walk before the L. in the land of 116.09
I render to the L. for all his 116.12
and call on the name of the L., 116.13
my vows to the L. in the presence 116.14
sight of the L. is the death of 116.15
O L., I am thy servant; I am thy 116.16
and call on the name of the L. 116.17
my vows to the L. in the presence 116.18
in the courts of the house of the L., 116.19
O Jerusalem. Praise the L.! 116.19
Praise the L., all nations! Extol 117.01
of the L. endures for ever. Praise the L.! 117.02
O give thanks to the L., for he is 118.01
Let those who fear the L. say, 118.04
Out of my distress I called on the L.; 118.05
the L. answered me and set me free. 118.05
With the L. on my side I do not 118.06
The L. is on my side to help me; 118.07
take refuge in the L. than to put 118.08
take refuge in the L. than to put 118.09
the name of the L. I cut them off! 118.10
the name of the L. I cut them off! 118.11
the name of the L. I cut them off! 118.12
was falling, but the L. helped me. 118.13
The L. is my strength and my song; 118.14
hand of the L. does valiantly, 118.15
the right hand of the L. is exalted, 118.16
hand of the L. does valiantly! 118.16
and recount the deeds of the L. 118.17
The L. has chastened me sorely, but 118.18
them and give thanks to the L. 118.19
This is the gate of the L.; 118.20
This is the day which the L. has made; 118.24
we beseech thee, O L.! O L., we beseech 118.25
who enters in the name of the L.! 118.26
bless you from the house of the L. 118.26
The L. is God, and he has given us 118.27
O give thanks to the L., for he is 118.29
who walk in the law of the L.! 119.01
Blessed be thou, O L.; teach me thy 119.12
I cleave to thy testimonies, O L.; 119.31
Teach me, O L., the way of thy 119.33
O L., thy salvation according to 119.41
from of old, I take comfort, O L. 119.52
the night, O L., and keep thy law. 119.55
The L. is my portion; I promise to 119.57
The earth, O L., is full of thy 119.64
O L. according to thy word. 119.65
I know, O L., that thy judgments are 119.75
For ever, O L., thy word is firmly 119.89
O L., according to thy word! 119.107
O L., and teach me thy ordinances. 119.108
It is time for the L. to act, 119.126
O L., and right are thy judgments. 119.137
heart I cry; answer me, O L.! 119.145
O L., in thy justice preserve my 119.149
O L., and all thy commandments are 119.151
Great is thy mercy, O L.; give me 119.156
O L., and I do thy commandments. 119.166
Let my cry come before thee, O L.; 119.169
O L., and thy law is my delight. 119.174
In my distress I cry to the L., 120.01
"Deliver me, O L., from lying lips, 120.02
My help comes from the L., who 121.02
The L. is your keeper; 121.05
the L. is your shade on your right 121.05
The L. will keep you from all evil; 121.07
The L. will keep your going out and 121.08
"Let us go to the house of the L.!" 122.01
tribes go up, the tribes of the L., 122.04
give thanks to the name of the L. 122.04
of the house of the L. our God, 122.09
so our eyes look to the L. our God, 123.02
O L., have mercy upon us, for we 123.03
not been the L. who was on our 124.01
not been the L. who was on our 124.02
Blessed be the L., who has not 124.06
Our help is in the name of the L., 124.08
trust in the L. are like Mount 125.01

LORD (cont.)

so the L. is round about his people, Ps 125.02
Do good, O L., to those who are good, 125.04
ways the L. will lead away with 125.05
When the L. restored the fortunes 126.01
"The L. has done great things for 126.02
The L. had done great things for us; 126.03
O L., like the water-courses in the 126.04
Unless the L. builds the house, 127.01
Unless the L. watches over the city, 127.01
Lo, sons are a heritage from the L., 127.03
Blessed is every one who fears the L., 128.01
man be blessed who fears the L. 128.04
The L. bless you from Zion! May you 128.05
The L. is righteous; he has cut the 129.04
"The blessing of the L. be upon you! 129.08
We bless you in the name of the L.!" 129.08
Out of the depths I cry to thee, O L.! 130.01
L., hear my voice! Let thy ears be 130.02
If thou, O L., shouldst mark iniquities, 130.03
iniquities, L., who could stand? 130.03
I wait for the L., my soul waits, 130.05
waits for the L. more than watchmen 130.06
O Israel, hope in the L.! For with 130.07
with the L. there is steadfast love, 130.07
O L., my heart is not lifted up, my 131.01
hope in the L. from this time forth 131.03
Remember, O L., in David's favor, all 132.01
how he swore to the L. and vowed to 132.02
until I find a place for the L., 132.05
Arise, O L., and go to thy resting 132.08
The L. swore to David a sure oath 132.11
For the L. has chosen Zion; he has 132.13
For there the L. has commanded the 133.03
bless the L., all you servants of the L., 134.01
by night in the house of the L.! 134.01
the holy place, and bless the L.! 134.02
May the L. bless you from Zion, he 134.03
Praise the L. Praise the name of the L., 135.01
give praise, O servants of the L., 135.02
you that stand in the house of the L., 135.02
Praise the L., for the L. is good; 135.03
For the L. has chosen Jacob for 135.04
For I know that the L. is great, 135.05
and that our L. is above all gods. 135.05
Whatever the L. pleases he does, in 135.06
Thy name, O L., endures for ever, thy 135.13
renown, O L., throughout all ages. 135.13
For the L. will vindicate his 135.14
O house of Israel, bless the L.! 135.19
O house of Aaron, bless the L.! 135.19
O house of Levi, bless the L.! 135.20
You that fear the L., bless the L.! 135.20
Blessed be the L. from Zion, he who 135.21
in Jerusalem! Praise the L.! 135.21
O give thanks to the L., for he is 136.01
O give thanks to the L. of lords, 136.03
Remember, O L., against the Edomites 137.07
O L., with my whole heart; 138.01
O L., for they have heard the words 138.04
shall sing of the ways of the L., 138.05
for great is the glory of the L. 138.05
For though the L. is high, he 138.06
The L. will fulfil his purpose for 138.08
steadfast love, O L., endures for ever. 138.08
O L., thou hast searched me and 139.01
O L., thou knowest it altogether. 139.04
not hate them that hate thee, O L.? 139.21
Deliver me, O L., from evil men; 140.01
Guard me, O L., from the hands of 140.04
I say to the L., Thou art my God; 140.06
voice of my supplications, O L.! 140.06
O L., my L., my strong deliverer, thou 140.07
Grant not, O L., the desires of the 140.08
I know that the L. maintains the 140.12
I call upon thee, O L.; make haste 141.01
O L., keep watch over the door of 141.03
that the word of the L. is true. 141.06
But my eyes are toward thee, O L. God; 141.08
I cry with my voice to the L., 142.01
I make supplication to the L., 142.01
I cry to thee, O L.; I say, Thou art 142.05
Hear my prayer, O L.; give ear to my 143.01
Make haste to answer me, O L.! 143.07
Deliver me, O L., from my enemies! 143.09
name's sake, O L., preserve my life! 143.11
Blessed be the L., my rock, who 144.01
O L., what is man that thou dost 144.03
Bow thy heavens, O L., and come down! 144.05
the people whose God is the L.! 144.15
Great is the L., and greatly to be 145.03
The L. is gracious and merciful, 145.08
The L. is good to all, and his 145.09
O L., and all thy saints shall 145.10
The L. is faithful in all his words, 145.13
The L. upholds all who are falling, 145.14
The L. is just in all his ways, and 145.17
The L. is near to all who call upon 145.18
The L. preserves all who love him; 145.20
will speak the praise of the L., 145.21
Praise the L.! Praise the L., O my soul! 146.01
I will praise the L. as long as I 146.02
whose hope is in the L. his God, 146.05
The L. sets the prisoners free; 146.07
the L. opens the eyes of the blind. 146.08
The L. lifts up those who are bowed 146.08
the L. loves the righteous. 146.08
The L. watches over the sojourners, 146.09
The L. will reign for ever, thy God, 146.10
to all generations. Praise the L.! 146.10
Praise the L.! For it is good to sing 147.01
The L. builds up Jerusalem; 147.02
Great is our L., and abundant in 147.05
The L. lifts up the downtrodden, he 147.06
Sing to the L. with thanksgiving; 147.07
but the L. takes pleasures in those 147.11
Praise the L., O Jerusalem! 147.12
know his ordinances. Praise the L.! 147.20
Praise the L.! Praise the L. from the 148.01
Let them praise the name of the L.! 148.05
Praise the L. from the earth, you 148.07
Let them praise the name of the L., 148.13
are near to him. Praise the L.! 148.14
Praise the L.! Sing to the L. a new song, 149.01
For the L. takes pleasure in his 149.04
all his faithful ones. Praise the L.! 149.09
Praise the L.! Praise God in his 150.01
breathes praise the L.! Praise the L.! 150.06
The fear of the L. is the beginning Pro 1.07
did not choose the fear of the L., 1.29
the fear of the L. and find the 2.05
For the L. gives wisdom; 2.06
Trust in the L. with all your heart, 3.05
fear the L., and turn away from 3.07
Honor the L. with your substance 3.09
for the L. reproves him whom he 3.12
The L. by wisdom founded the earth; 3.19
for the L. will be your confidence 3.26
man is an abomination to the L., 3.32
ways are before the eyes of the L. 5.21
There are six things which the L. hates, 6.16
The fear of the L. is hatred of 8.13
The L. created me at the beginning 8.22
life and obtains favor from the L.; 8.35
The fear of the L. is the beginning 9.10
The L. does not let the righteous 10.03
The blessing of the L. makes rich, 10.22
The fear of the L. prolongs life, 10.27
The L. is a stronghold to him whose 10.29
balance is an abomination to the L., 11.01
mind are an abomination to the L., 11.20
good man obtains favor from the L., 12.02
Lying lips are an abominaton to the L., 12.22
walks in uprightness fears the L., 14.02

LORD (cont.)
In the fear of the L. one has Pro 14.26
The fear of the L. is a fountain of 14.27
The eyes of the L. are in every 15.03
wicked is an abomination to the L., 15.08
wicked is an abomination to the L., 15.09
and Abaddon lie open before the L., 15.11
the fear of the L. than great 15.16
The L. tears down the house of the 15.25
wicked are an abomination to the L., 15.26
The L. is far from the wicked, but 15.29
The fear of the L. is instruction 15.33
answer of the tongue is from the L. 16.01
eyes, but the L. weighs the spirit. 16.02
Commit your work to the L., and your 16.03
The L. has made everything for its 16.04
arrogant is an abomination to the L.; 16.05
the fear of the L. a man avoids 16.06
When a man's ways please the L., 16.07
way, but the L. directs his steps. 16.09
happy is he who trusts in the L. 16.20
the decision is wholly from the L. 16.33
for gold, and the L. tries hearts. 17.03
both alike an abomination to the L. 17.15
The name of the L. is a strong tower; 18.10
and obtains favor from the L. 18.22
his heart rages against the L. 19.03
but a prudent wife is from the L. 19.14
kind to the poor lends to the L., 19.17
purpose of the L. that will be 19.21
The fear of the L. leads to life; 19.23
alike an abomination to the L. 20.10
eye, the L. has made them both. 20.12
wait for the L., and he will help 20.22
are an abomination to the L., 20.23
A man's steps are ordered by the L.; 20.24
of man is the lamp of the L., 20.27
of water in the hand of the L.; 21.01
eyes, but the L. weighs the heart. 21.02
acceptable to the L. than sacrifice. 21.30
counsel, can avail against the L. 21.30
but the victory belongs to the L. 21.31
the L. is the maker of them all. 22.02
and fear of the L. is riches and 22.04
The eyes of the L. keep watch over 22.12
with whom the L. is angry will 22.14
That your trust may be in the L., 22.19
for the L. will plead their cause 22.23
in the fear of the L. all the day. 23.17
lest the L. see it, and be displeased, 24.18
fear the L. and the king, and do not 24.21
his head, and the L. will reward you. 25.22
those who seek the L. understand it 28.05
is the man who fears the L. always; 28.14
trusts in the L. will be enriched. 28.25
the L. gives light to the eyes of 29.13
he who trusts in the L. is safe. 29.25
but from the L. a man gets justice. 29.26
deny thee, and say, "Who is the L.?" 30.09
who fears the L. is to be praised. 31.30
for the L. has spoken: "Sons have I Is 1.02
They have forsaken the L., they have 1.04
If the L. of hosts had not left us 1.09
Hear the word of the L., you rulers 1.10
of your sacrifices? says the L.; 1.11
says the L.: though your sins are 1.18
for the mouth of the L. has spoken. 1.20
the L. says, the L. of hosts, 1.24
who forsake the L. shall be 1.28
house of the L. shall be established 2.02
us go up to the mountain of the L., 2.03
the word of the L. from Jerusalem. 2.03
let us walk in the light of the L. 2.05
from before the terror of the L., 2.10
and the L. alone will be exalted in 2.11
For the L. of hosts has a day 2.12
and the L. alone will be exalted in 2.17
from before the terror of the L., 2.19
from before the terror of the L., 2.21
the L., the L. of hosts, is taking away 3.01
and their deeds are against the L., 3.08
The L. has taken his place to contend, 3.13
The L. enters into judgment with 3.14
the poor?" says the L. GOD of hosts. 3.15
The L. said: Because the daughters 3.16
the L. will smite with a scab the 3.17
and the L. will lay bare their 3.17
In that day the L. will take away 3.18
branch of the L. shall be beautiful 4.02
when the L. shall have washed away 4.04
Then the L. will create over the 4.05
vineyard of the L. of hosts is the 5.07
The L. of hosts has sworn in my 5.09
do not regard the deeds of the L., 5.12
But the L. of hosts is exalted in 5.16
rejected the law of the L. of hosts, 5.24
anger of the L. was kindled against 5.25
died I saw the L. sitting upon a 6.01
holy, holy is the L. of hosts; 6.03
seen the King, the L. of hosts! 6.05
I heard the voice of the L. saying, 6.08
Then I said, "How long, O L.?" And 6.11
and the L. removes men far away, and 6.12
And the L. said to Isaiah, "Go forth 7.03
thus says the L. GOD: It shall not 7.07
Again the L. spoke to Ahaz, 7.10
"Ask a sign of the L. your God; 7.11
I will not put the L. to the test." 7.12
Therefore the L. himself will give 7.14
The L. will bring upon you and upon 7.17
In that day the L. will whistle for 7.18
In that day the L. will shave with 7.20
Then the L. said to me, "Take a 8.01
Then the L. said to me, "Call his 8.03
The L. spoke to me again: 8.05
the L. is bringing up against them 8.07
For the L. spoke thus to me with 8.11
But the L. of hosts, him you shall 8.13
I will wait for the L., who is hiding 8.17
whom the L. has given me are signs 8.18
in Israel from the L. of hosts, 8.18
The zeal of the L. of hosts will do 9.07
The L. has sent a word against 9.08
So the L. raises adversaries against 9.11
them, nor seek the L. of hosts. 9.13
So the L. cut off from Israel head 9.14
Therefore the L. does not rejoice 9.17
wrath of the L. of hosts the land 9.19
When the L. has finished all his 10.12
Therefore the L., the L. of hosts, will 10.16
fruitful land the L. will destroy, 10.18
them, but will lean upon the L., 10.20
For the L., the L. of hosts, will 10.23
Therefore thus says the L., 10.24
the L. of hosts: "O my people, who 10.24
And the L. of hosts will wield 10.26
Behold, the L., the L. of hosts will 10.33
Spirit of the L. shall rest upon 11.02
knowledge and the fear of the L. 11.02
shall be in the fear of the L. 11.03
knowledge of the L. as the waters 11.09
In that day the L. will extend his 11.11
And the L. will utterly destroy the 11.15
O L., for though thou wast angry 12.01
for the L. GOD is my strength and 12.02
in that day: "Give thanks to the L., 12.04
"Sing praises to the L., for he has 12.05
The L. of hosts is mustering a host 13.04
the L. and the weapons of his 13.05
Wail, for the day of the L. is near; 13.06
Behold, the day of the L. comes, 13.09
wrath of the L. of hosts in the 13.13
The L. will have compassion on 14.01
When the L. has given you rest from 14.03

LORD (cont.)

The L. has broken the staff of the Is 14.05
says the L. of hosts, "and will cut 14.22
offspring and posterity, says the L. 14.22
destruction, says the L. of hosts." 14.23
The L. of hosts has sworn: "As I 14.24
For the L. of hosts has purposed, 14.27
"The L. has founded Zion, and in her 14.32
word which the L. spoke concerning 16.13
But now the L. says, "In three years, 16.14
of Israel, says the L. of hosts. 17.03
tree, says the L. God of Israel. 17.06
For thus the L. said to me: "I will 18.04
brought to the L. of hosts from a 18.07
of the name of the L. of hosts. 18.07
Behold, the L. is riding on a swift 19.01
them, says the L., the L. of hosts. 19.04
known what the L. of hosts has 19.12
The L. has mingled within her a 19.14
hand which the L. of hosts shakes 19.16
which the L. of hosts has purposed 19.17
swear allegiance to the L. of hosts. 19.18
an altar to the L. in the midst of 19.19
a pillar to the L. at its border. 19.19
witness to the L. of hosts in the 19.20
when they cry to the L. because of 19.20
And the L. will make himself known 19.21
will know the L. in that day and 19.21
vows to the L. and perform them. 19.21
And the L. will smite Egypt, smiting 19.22
and they will return to the L., 19.22
whom the L. of hosts has blessed, 19.25
at that time the L. had spoken by 20.02
the L. said, "As my servant Isaiah 20.03
For thus the L. said to me: "Go, set 21.06
O L., continually by day, and at my 21.08
I have heard from the L. of hosts, 21.10
For thus the L. said to me, "Within 21.16
for the L., the God of Israel, has 21.17
For the L. God of hosts has a day 22.05
In that day the L. God of hosts, 22.12
The L. of hosts has revealed 22.14
you die," says the L. God of hosts. 22.14
Thus says the L. God of hosts, "Come, 22.15
Behold, the L. will hurl you away 22.17
says the L. of hosts, the peg that 22.25
be cut off, for the L. has spoken. 22.25
The L. of hosts has purposed it, to 23.09
the L. has given command concerning 23.11
the L. will visit Tyre, and she will 23.17
hire will be dedicated to the L.; 23.18
for those who dwell before the L. 23.18
Behold, the L. will lay waste the 24.01
for the L. has spoken this word. 24.03
majesty of the L. they shout from 24.14
Therefore in the east give glory to the L.; 24.15
of the sea, to the name of the L., 24.15
On that day the L. will punish the 24.21
for the L. of hosts will reign on 24.23
O L., thou art my God; I will exalt 25.01
mountain the L. of hosts will make 25.06
and the L. God will wipe away tears 25.08
the earth; for the L. has spoken. 25.08
This is the L.; we have waited 25.09
For the hand of the L. will rest on 25.10
but the L. will lay low his pride 25.11
trust in the L. for ever, for the 26.04
for the L. God is an everlasting 26.04
O L., we wait for thee; thy memorial 26.08
does not see the majesty of the L. 26.10
O L., thy hand is lifted up, but 26.11
O L., thou wilt ordain peace for us, 26.12
O L. our God, other lords besides 26.13
O L., thou hast increased the 26.15
O L., in distress they sought thee, 26.16
so were we because of thee, O L.; 26.17
the L. is coming forth out of his 26.21
In that day the L. with his hard 27.01
I, the L., am its keeper; every 27.03
of Egypt the L. will thresh out 27.12
and worship the L. on the holy 27.13
Behold, the L. has one who is mighty 28.02
In that day the L. of hosts will be 28.05
tongue the L. will speak to this 28.11
Therefore the word of the L. will 28.13
Therefore hear the word of the L., 28.14
therefore thus says the L. God, 28.16
For the L. will rise up as on Mount 28.21
from the L. God of hosts upon the 28.22
This also comes from the L. of hosts; 28.29
visited by the L. of hosts with 29.06
For the L. has poured out upon you 29.10
And the L. said: "Because this 29.13
deep from the L. their counsel, 29.15
shall obtain fresh joy in the L., 29.19
Therefore thus says the L., who 29.22
rebellious children," says the L., 30.01
not hear the instruction of the L.; 30.09
For thus said the L. God, the Holy 30.15
Therefore the L. waits to be 30.18
For the L. is a God of justice; 30.18
And though the L. give you the 30.20
day when the L. binds up the hurt 30.26
Behold, the name of the L. comes from far, 30.27
to go to the mountain of the L., 30.29
And the L. will cause his majestic 30.30
terror-stricken at the voice of the L., 30.31
which the L. lays upon them will 30.32
the breath of the L., like a stream 30.33
Holy One of Israel or consult the L.! 31.01
When the L. stretches out his hand, 31.03
For thus the L. said to me, As a 31.04
so the L. of hosts will come down 31.04
so the L. of hosts will protect 31.05
says the L., whose fire is in Zion; 31.09
to utter error concerning the L., 32.06
O L., be gracious to us; we wait for 33.02
The L. is exalted, for he dwells on 33.05
the fear of the L. is his treasure. 33.06
says the L., "now I will lift 33.10
But there the L. in majesty will be 33.21
For the L. is our judge, the L. is 33.22
the L. is our ruler, the L. is our king; 33.22
For the L. is enraged against all 34.02
The L. has a sword; it is sated 34.06
For the L. has a sacrifice in 34.06
For the L. has a day of vengeance, a 34.08
Seek and read from the book of the L.: 34.16
the mouth of the L. has commanded, 34.16
They shall see the glory of the L., 35.02
ransomed of the L. shall return, 35.10
to me, "We rely on the L. our God," 36.07
it without the L. that I have come 36.10
The L. said to me, Go up against 36.10
make you rely on the L. by saying, 36.15
"The L. will surely deliver us; 36.15
"The L. will deliver us." Has any of 36.18
that the L. should deliver Jerusalem 36.20
and went into the house of the L. 37.01
It may be that the L. your God 37.04
words which the L. your God has 37.04
to your master, 'Thus says the L.: 37.06
went up to the house of the L., 37.14
and spread it before the L. 37.14
And Hezekiah prayed to the L.: 37.15
"O L. of hosts, God of Israel, who 37.16
Incline thy ear, O L., and hear; 37.17
open thy eyes, O L., and see; 37.17
Of a truth, O L., the kings of 37.18
So now, O L. our God, save us from 37.20
know that thou alone art the L." 37.20
Hezekiah, saying, "Thus says the L., 37.21
word that the L. has spoken concerning 37.22
servants you have mocked the L., 37.24

LORD (cont.)
The zeal of the L. of hosts will Is 37.32
"Therefore thus says the L. concerning 37.33
come into this city, says the L. 37.34
And the angel of the L. went forth, 37.36
and said to him, "Thus says the L.: 38.01
to the wall, and prayed to the L., 38.02
O L., I beseech thee, how I have 38.03
Then the word of the L. came to Isaiah: 38.04
Thus says the L., the God of David 38.05
"This is the sign to you from the L., 38.07
that the L. will do this thing that 38.07
not see the L. in the land of the 38.11
O L., I am oppressed; be thou my 38.14
O L., by these things men live, and 38.16
The L. will save me, and we will 38.20
our life, at the house of the L. 38.20
shall go up to the house of the L.? 38.22
"Hear the word of the L. of hosts: 39.05
nothing shall be left, says the L. 39.06
"The word of the L. which you have 39.08
wilderness prepare the way of the L., 40.03
glory of the L. shall be revealed, 40.05
for the mouth of the L. has spoken. 40.05
the breath of the L. blows upon it; 40.07
Behold, the L. GOD comes with might, 40.10
Who has directed the Spirit of the L., 40.13
Israel "My way is hid from the L., 40.27
The L. is the everlasting God, the 40.28
wait for the L. shall renew their 40.31
I, the L., the first, and with the 41.04
For I., the L. your God, hold your 41.13
I will help you, says the L.; your redeemer 41.14
And you shall rejoice in the L.; 41.16
I the L. will answer them, I the God 41.17
the hand of the L. has done this, 41.20
Set forth your case, says the L.; 41.21
the L., who created the heavens and 42.05
"I am the L., I have called you in 42.06
I am the L., that is my name; my glory 42.08
Sing to the L. a new song, his praise 42.10
Let them give glory to the L., 42.12
The L. goes forth like a mighty man, 42.13
or blind as the servant of the L.? 42.19
The L. was pleased, for his righteousness' 42.21
Was it not the L., against whom we 42.24
But now thus says the L., he who 43.01
For I am the L. your God, the Holy 43.03
says the L., "and my servant whom 43.10
I, I am the L., and besides me there 43.11
you are my witnesses," says the L. 43.12
Thus says the L., your Redeemer, the 43.14
I am the L., your Holy One, the 43.15
Thus says the L., who makes a way 43.16
Thus says the L. who made you, who 44.02
Thus says the L., the King of 44.06
the L. of hosts: "I am the first and 44.06
Sing, O heavens, for the L. has done it; 44.23
For the L. has redeemed Jacob, and 44.23
Thus says the L., your Redeemer, who 44.24
"I am the L., who made all things, 44.24
Thus says the L. to his anointed, to 45.01
I am the L., and there is no other, 45.05
I am the L., and there is no other. 45.06
I am the L., who do all these 45.07
spring up also; I the L. have created it. 45.08
Thus says the L., the Holy One of 45.11
or reward," says the L. of hosts. 45.13
Thus says the L.: "The wealth of 45.14
is saved by the L. with everlasting 45.17
For thus says the L., who created 45.18
"I am the L., and there is no 45.18
I the L. speak the truth, I 45.19
Was it not I., the L.? And there is no 45.21
"Only in the L., it shall be said 45.24
In the L. all the offspring of 45.25
the L. of hosts is his name—is the 47.04
who swear by the name of the L., 48.01
of Israel; the L. of hosts is his name. 48.02
the L. loves him; he shall perform 48.14
And now the L. GOD has sent me 48.16
Thus says the L., your Redeemer, the 48.17
"I am the L. your God, who teaches 48.17
say, "The L. has redeemed his 48.20
says the L., "for the wicked." 48.22
The L. called me from the womb, from 49.01
yet surely my right is with the L., 49.04
And now the L. says, who formed me 49.05
I am honored in the eyes of the L., 49.05
Thus says the L., the Redeemer of 49.07
because of the L., who is faithful, 49.07
Thus says the L.: "In a time of 49.08
For the L. has comforted his people, 49.13
"The L. has forsaken me, my L. has 49.14
says the L., you shall put them all 49.18
Thus says the L. GOD: "Behold, I will 49.22
you will know that I am the L.; 49.23
thus says the L.: "Even the captives 49.25
know that I am the L. your Savior, 49.26
Thus says the L.: "Where is your 50.01
The L. GOD has given me the tongue 50.04
The L. GOD has opened my ear, and I 50.05
For the L. GOD helps me; therefore 50.07
Behold, the L. GOD helps me; 50.09
you fears the L. and obeys the 50.10
the name of the L. and relies upon 50.10
deliverance, you who seek the L.; 51.01
For the L. will comfort Zion; 51.03
desert like the garden of the L.; 51.03
put on strength, O arm of the L.; 51.09
ransomed of the L. shall return, 51.11
and have forgotten the L., your Maker, 51.13
For I am the L. your God, who stirs 51.15
the L. of hosts is his name. 51.15
the hand of the L. the cup of his 51.17
are full of the wrath of the L., 51.20
Thus says your L., the L., your God 51.22
For thus says the L.: "You were sold 52.03
For thus says the L. GOD: My people 52.04
says the L., seeing that my people 52.05
says the L., and continually all 52.05
see the return of the L. to Zion. 52.08
for the L. has comforted his people, 52.09
The L. has bared his holy arm 52.10
you who bear the vessels of the L. 52.11
for the L. will go before you, and 52.12
the arm of the L. been revealed? 53.01
and the L. has laid on him the 53.06
the will of the L. to bruise him; 53.10
the will of the L. shall prosper in 53.10
her that is married, says the L. 54.01
the L. of hosts is his name; 54.05
For the L. has called you like a 54.06
on you, says the L., your Redeemer. 54.08
says the L., who has compassion on 54.10
sons shall be taught by the L., 54.13
servants of the L. and their 54.17
vindication from me, says the L. 54.17
to you, because of the L. your God, 55.05
"Seek the L. while he may be found, 55.06
let him return to the L., that he may 55.07
are your ways my ways, says the L. 55.08
shall be to the L. for a memorial, 55.13
Thus says the L.: "Keep justice, and 56.01
has joined himself to the L. say, 56.03
"The L. will surely separate me 56.03
For thus says the L.: "To the eunuchs 56.04
who join themselves to the L., 56.06
to him, to love the name of the L., 56.06
Thus says the L. GOD, who gathers 56.08
far and to the near, says the L.; 57.19
and a day acceptable to the L.? 58.05
glory of the L. shall be your rear 58.08
shall call, and the L. will answer; 58.09

LORD (cont.)
And the L. will guide you continually, Is 58.11
the holy day of the L. honorable; 58.13
then you shall take delight in the L., 58.14
for the mouth of the L. has spoken." 58.14
transgressing, and denying the L., 59.13
The L. saw it, and it displeased him 59.15
the name of the L. from the west, 59.19
which the wind of the L. drives. 59.19
from transgression, says the L. 59.20
says the L.: my spirit which is upon 59.21
says the L., from this time forth 59.21
glory of the L. has risen upon you 60.01
but the L. will arise upon you, and 60.02
proclaim the praise of the L. 60.06
for the name of the L. your God, 60.09
shall call you the City of the L., 60.14
the L., am your Savior and your 60.16
but the L. will be your everlasting 60.19
for the L. will be your everlasting 60.20
I am the L.; in its time I 60.22
The Spirit of the L. God is upon me, 61.01
because the L. has anointed me to 61.01
righteousness, the planting of the L., 61.03
be called the priests of the L., 61.06
For I the L. love justice, I hate 61.08
a people whom the L. has blessed. 61.09
I will greatly rejoice in the L., 61.10
so the L. God will cause righteousness 61.11
the mouth of the L. will give. 62.02
of beauty in the hand of the L., 62.03
for the L. delights in you, and your 62.04
you who put the L. in remembrance, 62.06
The L. has sworn by his right hand 62.08
it shall eat it and praise the L., 62.09
Behold, the L. has proclaimed to the 62.11
people, The redeemed of the L.; 62.12
the steadfast love of the L., 63.07
of the Lord, the praises of the L., 63.07
to all that the L. has granted us, 63.07
Spirit of the L. gave them rest. 63.14
thou, O L., art our Father, our 63.16
O L., why dost thou make us err 63.17
Yet, O L., thou art our Father; 64.08
O L., and remember not iniquity for 64.09
thyself at these things, O L.? 64.12
iniquities together, says the L.; 65.07
Thus says the L.: "As the wine is 65.08
But you who forsake the L., 65.11
Therefore thus says the L. God: 65.13
and the L. God will slay you; 65.15
offspring of the blessed of the L., 65.23
all my holy mountain, says the L. 65.25
Thus says the L.: "Heaven is my 66.01
these things are mine, says the L. 66.02
Hear the word of the L., you who 66.05
'Let the L. be glorified, that we 66.05
The voice of the L., rendering 66.06
says the L.; shall I, who 66.09
For thus says the L.: "Behold, I 66.12
the hand of the L. is with his 66.14
the L. will come in fire, and his 66.15
fire will the L. execute judgment, 66.16
slain by the L. shall be many. 66.16
to an end together, says the L. 66.17
nations as an offering to the L., 66.20
says the L., just as the Israelites 66.20
vessel to the house of the L. 66.20
and for Levites, says the L. 66.21
remain before me, says the L.; 66.22
to worship before me, says the L. 66.23
the word of the L. came in the Jer 1.02
Now the word of the L. came to me 1.04
Then I said, "Ah, L. God! Behold, 1.06
But the L. said to me, "Do not say, 1.07
you to deliver you, says the L." 1.08
Then the L. put forth his hand and 1.09
and the L. said to me, "Behold, I 1.09
And the word of the L. came to me, 1.11
Then the L. said to me, "You have 1.12
The word of the L. came to me a 1.13
Then the L. said to me, "Out of the 1.14
kingdoms of the north, says the L.; 1.15
says the L., to deliver you. 1.19
The word of the L. came to me, 2.01
Thus says the L., I remember the 2.02
Israel was holy to the L., 2.03
evil came upon them, says the L." 2.03
Hear the word of the L., 2.04
Thus says the L.: "What wrong did 2.05
'Where is the L. who brought us up 2.06
did not say, 'Where is the L.?' 2.08
says the L., and with your children's 2.09
be utterly desolate, says the L., 2.12
by forsaking the L. your God, 2.17
for you to forsake the L. your God; 2.19
in you, says the L. God of hosts. 2.19
is still before me, says the L. God 2.22
rebelled against me, says the L. 2.29
generation, heed the word of the L. 2.31
for the L. has rejected those in 2.37
return to me? says the L. 3.01
The L. said to me in the days of 3.06
but in pretence, says the L." 3.10
And the L. said to me, "Faithless 3.11
faithless Israel, says the L. 3.12
for I am merciful, says the L.; 3.12
against the L. your God and 3.13
not obeyed my voice, says the L. 3.13
Return, O faithless children, says the L.; 3.14
says the L., they shall no more say, 3.16
"The ark of the covenant of the L." 3.16
be called the throne of the L., 3.17
presence of the L. in Jerusalem, 3.17
me, O house of Israel, says the L. 3.20
have forgotten the L. their God. 3.21
for thou art the L. our God. 3.22
Truly in the L. our God is the 3.23
have sinned against the L. our God, 3.25
obeyed the voice of the L. our God." 3.25
says the L., to me you should 4.01
'As the L. lives,' in truth, in 4.02
For thus says the L. to the men of 4.03
Circumcise yourselves to the L., 4.04
anger of the L. has not turned 4.08
says the L., courage shall fail 4.09
L. God, surely thou hast utterly 4.10
rebelled against me, says the L. 4.17
were laid in ruins before the L., 4.26
For thus says the L., "The whole land 4.27
"As the L. lives," yet they swear 5.02
O L., do not thy eyes look for 5.03
they do not know the way of the L., 5.04
for they know the way of the L., 5.05
says the L.; and shall I not 5.09
faithless to me, says the L. 5.11
They have spoken falsely of the L., 5.12
Therefore thus says the L., 5.14
O house of Israel, says the L. 5.15
says the L., I will not make a full 5.18
'Why has the L. our God done all 5.19
says the L.; Do you not 5.22
'Let us fear the L. our God, 5.24
says the L., and shall I not avenge 5.29
For thus says the L. of hosts: 6.06
Thus says the L. of hosts: "Glean 6.09
the word of the L. is to them an 6.10
Therefore I am full of the wrath of the L.; 6.11
inhabitants of the land," says the L. 6.12
shall be overthrown," says the L. 6.15
Thus says the L.: "Stand by the 6.16
Therefore thus says the L.: 6.21
Thus says the L.: "Behold, a people 6.22
for the L. has rejected them." 6.30

LORD (cont.)

that came to Jeremiah from the L.: Jer 7.01
and say, Hear the word of the L., 7.02
these gates to worship the L. 7.02
Thus says the L. of hosts, the God 7.03
'This is the temple of the L.,' 7.04
I myself have seen it, says the L. 7.11
says the L., and when I spoke to 7.13
says the L. Is it not 7.19
Therefore thus says the L. GOD: 7.20
Thus says the L. of hosts, the God 7.21
obey the voice of the L. their God, 7.28
for the L. has rejected and forsaken 7.29
done evil in my sight, says the L.; 7.30
says the L., when it will no more 7.32
says the L., the bones of the kings 8.01
driven them, says the L. of hosts. 8.03
Thus says the L.: When men fall, do 8.04
know not the ordinance of the L. 8.07
and the law of the L. is with us'? 8.08
have rejected the word of the L., 8.09
shall be overthrown, says the L. 8.12
says the L., there are no grapes on 8.13
for the L. our God has doomed us to 8.14
we have sinned against the L. 8.14
they shall bite you," says the L. 8.17
of the land: "Is the L. not in Zion? 8.19
they do not know me, says the L. 9.03
refuse to know me, says the L. 9.06
Therefore thus says the L. of hosts: 9.07
says the L.; and shall I not 9.09
has the mouth of the L. spoken, 9.12
And the L. says: "Because they have 9.13
Therefore thus says the L. of hosts, 9.15
Thus says the L. of hosts: "Consider, 9.17
Hear, O women, the word of the L., 9.20
Speak, "Thus says the L.: 9.22
Thus says the L.: "Let not the wise 9.23
that I am the L. who practice 9.24
things I delight, says the L." 9.24
says the L., when I will punish all 9.25
word which the L. speaks to you, 10.01
Thus says the L.: "Learn not the way 10.02
There is none like thee, O L.; 10.06
But the L. is the true God; 10.10
the L. of hosts is his name. 10.16
For thus says the L.: "Behold, I am 10.18
do not inquire of the L.; 10.21
I know, O L., that the way of man is 10.23
Correct me, O L., but in just 10.24
that came to Jeremiah from the L.: 11.01
Thus says the L., the God of Israel: 11.03
Then I answered, "So be it, L." 11.05
And the L. said to me, "Proclaim all 11.06
Again the L. said to me, "There is 11.09
thus says the L., Behold, I am 11.11
The L. once called you, 'A green 11.16
The L. of hosts, who planted you, has 11.17
The L. made it known to me and I 11.18
But, O L. of hosts, who judgest 11.20
Therefore thus says the L. concerning 11.21
not prophesy in the name of the L., 11.21
therefore thus says the L. of hosts: 11.22
O L., when I complain to thee; 12.01
But thou, O L., knowest me; 12.03
sword of the L. devours from one 12.12
of the fierce anger of the L. 12.13
Thus says the L. concerning all my 12.14
'As the L. lives,' even as they 12.16
it up and destroy it, says the L. 12.17
Thus said the L. to me, "Go and buy 13.01
according to the word of the L., 13.02
And the word of the L. came to me a 13.03
Euphrates, as the L. commanded me. 13.05
And after many days the L. said to me, 13.06
Then the word of the L. came to me: 13.08
"Thus says the L.: Even so will I 13.09
says the L., that they might be for 13.11
them this word: 'Thus says the L., 13.12
say to them, 'Thus says the L.: 13.13
and sons together, says the L. 13.14
not proud, for the L. has spoken. 13.15
Give glory to the L. your God 13.16
says the L., because you have 13.25
The word of the L. which came to 14.01
O L., for thy name's sake; 14.07
Yet thou, O L., art in the midst of 14.09
Thus says the L. concerning this 14.10
therefore the L. does not accept 14.10
The L. said to me: "Do not pray for 14.11
L. GOD, behold, the prophets say to 14.13
And the L. said to me: "The prophets 14.14
Therefore thus says the L. concerning 14.15
O L., and the iniquity of our 14.20
Art thou not he, O L. our God? 14.22
Then the L. said to me, "Though 15.01
say to them, 'Thus says the L.: 15.02
says the L.: the sword to slay, the 15.03
says the L., you keep going backward; 15.06
before their enemies, says the L. 15.09
O L., if I have not entreated thee 15.11
O L., thou knowest; remember me 15.15
by thy name, O L., God of hosts. 15.16
Therefore thus says the L.: 15.19
you and deliver you, says the L. 15.20
The word of the L. came to me: 16.01
For thus says the L. concerning the 16.03
"For thus says the L.: Do not enter 16.05
says the L., my steadfast love and 16.05
For thus says the L. of hosts, 16.09
'Why has the L. pronounced all this 16.10
committed against the L. our God?' 16.10
says the L., and have gone after 16.11
says the L., when it shall no 16.14
'As the L. lives who brought up the 16.14
but 'As the L. lives who brought up 16.15
says the L., and they shall catch 16.16
O L., my strength and my stronghold, 16.19
shall know that my name is the L." 16.21
Thus says the L.: "Cursed is the man 17.05
whose heart turns away from the L. 17.05
"Blessed is the man who trusts in the L., 17.07
in the LORD, whose trust is the L. 17.07
"I the L. search the mind and try 17.10
O L., the hope of Israel, all who 17.13
for they have forsaken the L., 17.13
Heal me, O L., and I shall be healed 17.14
to me, "Where is the word of the L.? 17.15
Thus said the L. to me: "Go and 17.19
and say: 'Hear the word of the L., 17.20
Thus says the L.: Take heed for the 17.21
says the L., and bring in no burden 17.24
offerings to the house of the L. 17.26
that came to Jeremiah from the L.: 18.01
Then the word of the L. came to me: 18.05
says the L. Behold, like the 18.06
of Jerusalem: 'Thus says the L., 18.11
"Therefore thus says the L.: 18.13
O L., and hearken to my plea. 18.19
Yet, thou, O L., knowest all their 18.23
Thus said the L., "Go, buy a potter's 19.01
say, 'Hear the word of the L., 19.03
Thus says the L. of hosts, the God 19.03
says the L., when this place shall 19.06
them, 'Thus says the L. of hosts: 19.11
says the L., and to its inhabitants, 19.12
where the L. had sent him to 19.14
"Thus says the L. of hosts, the God 19.15
officer in the house of the L., 20.01
Gate of the house of the L. 20.02
"The L. does not call your name 20.03
For thus says the L.: Behold, I will 20.04
O L., thou hast deceived me, and I 20.07
the word of the L. has become for 20.08

LORD (cont.)
But the L. is with me as a dread Jer 20.11
O L. of hosts, who triest the 20.12
Sing to the L; praise the L.! 20.13
which the L. overthrew without 20.16
which came to Jeremiah from the L., 21.01
"Inquire of the L. for us, 21.02
perhaps the L. will deal with us 21.02
say to Zedekiah, 'Thus says the L., 21.04
says the L., I will deliver Zedekiah 21.07
you shall say: 'Thus says the L.: 21.08
says the L.: it shall be given into 21.10
say, 'Hear the word of the L., 21.11
Thus says the L.: " 'Execute justice 21.12
O rock of the plain, says the L.; 21.13
fruit of your doings, says the L.; 21.14
Thus says the L.: "Go down to the 22.01
and say, 'Hear the word of the L., 22.02
Thus says the L.: Do justice and 22.03
says the L., that this house shall 22.05
For thus says the L. concerning the 22.06
"Why has the L. dealt thus with 22.08
the covenant of the L. their God, 22.09
For thus says the L. concerning 22.11
to know me? says the L. 22.16
Therefore thus says the L. concerning 22.18
not lament for him, saying, 'Ah l.!' 22.18
says the L., though Coniah the son 22.24
land, hear the word of the L.! 22.29
Thus says the L.: "Write this man 22.30
of my pasture!" says the L. 23.01
Therefore thus says the L., 23.02
for your evil doings, says the L. 23.02
shall any be missing, says the L. 23.04
says the L., when I will raise up 23.05
'The L. is our righteousness.' 23.06
says the L., when men shall no 23.07
'As the L. lives who brought up the 23.07
but 'As the L. lives who brought up 23.08
because of the L. and because of 23.09
their wickedness, says the L. 23.11
of their punishment, says the L. 23.12
Therefore thus says the L. of hosts 23.15
Thus says the L. of hosts: "Do not 23.16
not from the mouth of the L. 23.16
who despise the word of the L., 23.17
council of the L. to perceive and 23.18
Behold, the storm of the L.! 23.19
The anger of the L. will not turn 23.20
says the L., and not a God afar off? 23.23
says the L. Do I not fill 23.24
and earth? says the L. 23.24
with wheat? says the L. 23.28
says the L., and like a hammer 23.29
says the L., who steal my words 23.30
says the L., who use their tongues 23.31
tongues and say, 'Says the L.' 23.31
says the L., and who tell them and 23.32
this people at all, says the L. 23.32
you, 'What is the burden of the L.?' 23.33
I will cast you off, says the L.' 23.33
who says, 'The burden of the L.,' 23.34
brother, 'What has the L. answered?' 23.35
or 'What has the L. spoken?' 23.35
burden of the L.' you shall mention 23.36
living God, the L. of hosts, our God. 23.36
'What has the L. answered you?' 23.37
or 'What has the L. spoken?' 23.37
'The burden of the L.,' thus says the L. 23.38
these words, "The burden of the L.," 23.38
not say, 'The burden of the L.,' " 23.38
the L. showed me this vision: Behold, 24.01
placed before the temple of the L. 24.01
And the L. said to me, "What do you 24.03
Then the word of the L. came to me: 24.04
"Thus says the L., the God of 24.05
a heart to know that I am the L.; 24.07
"But thus says the L.: Like the bad 24.08
the word of the L. has come to me, 25.03
although the L. persistently sent 25.04
land which the L. has given to you 25.05
says the L., that you might provoke 25.07
"Therefore thus says the L. of hosts: 25.08
says the L., and for Nebuchadrezzar 25.09
says the L., making the land an 25.12
Thus the L., the God of Israel, said 25.15
to whom the L. sent me drink it: 25.17
them, 'Thus says the L. of hosts, 25.27
them, 'Thus says the L. of hosts: 25.28
of the earth, says the L. of hosts.' 25.29
'The L. will roar from on high, and 25.30
for the L. has an indictment 25.31
will put to the sword, says the L. 25.31
"Thus says the L. of hosts: Behold, 25.32
slain by the L. on that day shall 25.33
For the L. is despoiling their 25.36
of the fierce anger of the L. 25.37
because of the sword of the L., 25.38
Judah, this word came from the L., 26.01
"Thus says the L.: Stand in the 26.02
house of the L. all the words that 26.02
say to them, 'Thus says the L.: 26.04
these words in the house of the L. 26.07
all that the L. had commanded him 26.08
prophesied in the name of the L., 26.09
Jeremiah in the house of the L. 26.09
house of the L. and took their 26.10
New Gate of the house of the L. 26.10
"The L. sent me to prophesy against 26.12
obey the voice of the L. your God, 26.13
and the L. will repent of the evil 26.13
in truth the L. sent me to you to 26.15
us in the name of the L. our God." 26.16
Judah: 'Thus says the L. of hosts, 26.18
the L. and entreat the favor of the L., 26.19
and did not the L. repent of the 26.19
prophesied in the name of the L., 26.20
word came to Jeremiah from the L. 27.01
Thus the L. said to me: "Make 27.02
masters: 'Thus says the L. of hosts, 27.04
says the L., until I have consumed 27.08
it and dwell there, says the L." ' " 27.11
as the L. has spoken concerning any 27.13
says the L., but they are prophesying 27.15
people, saying, "Thus says the L.: 27.16
if the word of the L. is with them, 27.18
intercede with the L. of hosts, 27.18
are left in the house of the L., 27.18
For thus says the L. of hosts 27.19
thus says the L. of hosts, the God 27.21
are left in the house of the L., 27.21
attention to them, says the L. 27.22
spoke to me in the house of the L., 28.01
"Thus says the L. of hosts, the God 28.02
says the L., for I will break the 28.04
standing in the house of the L.; 28.05
May the L. do so; may the L. 28.06
the vessels of the house of the L., 28.06
known that the L. has truly sent 28.09
people, saying, "Thus says the L.: 28.11
the word of the L. came to Jeremiah: 28.12
"Go, tell Hananiah, 'Thus says the L.: 28.13
For thus says the L. of hosts, 28.14
the L. has not sent you, and you 28.15
Therefore thus says the L.: 28.16
uttered rebellion against the L.' " 28.16
"Thus says the L. of hosts, the God 29.04
and pray to the L. on its behalf, 29.07
For thus says the L. of hosts, 29.08
I did not send them, says the L. 29.09
"For thus says the L.: when seventy 29.10
says the L., plans for welfare and 29.11
says the L., and I will restore 29.14
says the L., and I will bring you 29.14

LORD (cont.)

'The L. has raised up prophets for	Jer 29.15
Thus says the L. concerning the	29.16
'Thus says the L. of hosts, Behold,	29.17
says the L., which I persistently	29.19
you would not listen, says the L.	29.19
Hear the word of the L. all you exiles	29.20
'Thus says the L. of hosts, the God	29.21
"The L. make you like Zedekiah and	29.22
and I am witness, says the L.' "	29.23
"Thus says the L. of hosts, the God	29.25
'The L. has made you priest instead	29.26
house of the L. over every madman	29.26
Then the word of the L. came to	29.30
'Thus says the L. concerning	29.31
therefore thus says the L.:	29.32
the L., for he has talked rebellion against the L.' "	29.32
that came to Jeremiah from the L.:	30.01
"Thus says the L. the God of	30.02
says the L. when I will restore	30.03
says the L., and I will bring them	30.03
words which the L. spoke concerning	30.04
"Thus says the L.: We have heard a	30.05
says the L. of hosts, that I will	30.08
shall serve the L. their God and	30.09
says the L., nor be dismayed, O	30.10
with you to save you, says the L.;	30.11
"For thus says the L.: Your hurt is	30.12
says the L., because they have	30.17
"Thus says the L.: Behold, I will	30.18
to approach me? says the L.	30.21
Behold the storm of the L.!	30.23
anger of the L. will not turn back	30.24
says the L., I will be the God of	31.01
Thus says the L.: "The people who	31.02
the L. appeared to him from afar.	31.03
go up to Zion, to the L. our God.	31.06
For thus says the L.: "Sing aloud	31.07
'The L. has saved his people, the	31.07
"Hear the word of the L., O nations,	31.10
For the L. has ransomed Jacob, and	31.11
over the goodness of the L.,	31.12
with my goodness, says the L."	31.14
Thus says the L.: "A voice is heard	31.15
Thus says the L.: "Keep your voice	31.16
says the L., and they shall come	31.16
says the L., and your children	31.17
restored, for thou art the L. my God.	31.18
have mercy on him, says the L.	31.20
For the L. has created a new thing	31.22
Thus says the L. of hosts, the God	31.23
'The L. bless you, O habitation of	31.23
says the L., when I will sow the	31.27
to build and to plant, says the L.	31.28
says the L., when I will make a new	31.31
I was their husband, says the L.	31.32
says the L.: I will put my law	31.33
'Know the L.,' for they shall all	31.34
them to the greatest, says the L.;	31.34
Thus says the L., who gives the sun	31.35
the L. of hosts is his name:	31.35
says the L., then shall the descendants	31.36
Thus says the L.: "If the heavens	31.37
that they have done, says the L."	31.37
says the L., when the city shall be	31.38
rebuilt for the L. from the tower	31.38
east, shall be sacred to the L.	31.40
from the L. in the tenth year of	32.01
prophesy and say, 'Thus says the L.:	32.03
until I visit him, says the L.;	32.05
"The word of the L. came to me:	32.06
accordance with the word of the L.,	32.08
that this was the word of the L.'	32.08
'Thus says the L. of hosts, the God	32.14
For thus says the L. of hosts,	32.15
I prayed to the L., saying:	32.16
'Ah L. GOD! It is thou	32.17
God whose name is the L. of hosts,	32.18
Yet thou, O L. GOD, hast said to me,	32.25
The word of the L. came to Jeremiah:	32.26
I am the L., the God of all flesh;	32.27
thus says the L.: Behold, I am giving	32.28
work of their hands, says the L.	32.30
"Now therefore thus says the L.,	32.36
"For thus says the L.: Just as I	32.42
their fortunes, says the L.	32.44
The word of the L. came to Jeremiah	33.01
"Thus says the L. who made the	33.02
the L. who formed it to establish	33.02
to establish it—the L. is his name:	33.02
For thus says the L., the God of	33.04
"Thus says the L.: In this place of	33.10
offerings to the house of the L.:	33.11
'Give thanks to the L. of hosts,	33.11
for the L. is good, for his steadfast	33.11
the land as at first, says the L.	33.11
"Thus says the L. of hosts: In this	33.12
one who counts them, says the L.	33.13
says the L., when I will fulfil the	33.14
'The L. is our righteousness.'	33.16
"For thus says the L.: David shall	33.17
The word of the L. came to Jeremiah:	33.19
"Thus says the L.: If you can break	33.20
The word of the L. came to Jeremiah:	33.23
'The L. has rejected the two	33.24
Thus says the L.: If I have not	33.25
which came to Jeremiah from the L.,	34.01
"Thus says the L., the God of	34.02
and say to him, 'Thus says the L.:	34.02
Yet hear the word of the L.,	34.04
Thus says the L. concerning you:	34.04
lament for you, saying, "Alas, l.!' "	34.05
have spoken the word, says the L."	34.05
which came to Jeremiah from the L.,	34.08
The word of the L. came to Jeremiah	34.12
LORD came to Jeremiah from the L.:	34.12
"Thus says the L., the God of	34.13
thus says the L.: You have not	34.17
pestilence, and to famine, says the L.	34.17
says the L., and will bring them	34.22
from the L. in the days of Jehoiakim	35.01
bring them to the house of the L.,	35.02
house of the L. into the chamber	35.04
Then the word of the L. came to	35.12
"Thus says the L. of hosts, the God	35.13
to my words? says the L.	35.13
thus says the L., the God of hosts,	35.17
said, "Thus says the L. of hosts,	35.18
therefore thus says the L. of hosts,	35.19
word came to Jeremiah from the L.:	36.01
words of the L. which he had	36.04
from going to the house of the L.;	36.05
words of the L. from the scroll	36.06
supplication will come before the L.,	36.07
wrath that the L. has pronounced	36.07
words of the L. in the LORD's house	36.08
proclaimed a fast before the L.	36.09
the scroll, in the house of the L.,	36.10
words of the L. from the scroll,	36.11
the prophet, but the L. hid them.	36.26
the word of the L. came to Jeremiah:	36.27
you shall say, 'Thus says the L.,	36.29
Therefore thus says the L. concerning	36.30
words of the L. which he spoke	37.02
"Pray for us to the L. our God."	37.03
Then the word of the L. came to	37.06
"Thus says the L., God of Israel:	37.07
Thus says the L., Do not deceive	37.09
"Is there any word from the L."	37.17
O my l. the king: let my humble plea	37.20
"Thus says the L., He who stays in	38.02
Thus says the L., This city shall	38.03
"My l. the king, these men have done	38.09
entrance of the temple of the L.	38.14

LORD (cont.)

"As the L. lives, who made our souls, Jer 38.16
said to Zedekiah, "Thus says the L., 38.17
voice of the L. in what I say to 38.20
which the L. has shown to me: 38.21
The word of the L. came to Jeremiah 39.15
Ethiopian, 'Thus says the L. of hosts, 39.16
says the L., and you shall not be 39.17
put your trust in me, says the L.'" 39.18
from the L. after Nebuzaradan the 40.01
"The L. your God pronounced this 40.02
the L. has brought it about, and has 40.03
because you sinned against the L., 40.03
to present at the temple of the L. 41.05
and pray to the L. your God for us, 42.02
that the L. your God may show us 42.03
pray to the L. your God according 42.04
whatever the L. answers you I will 42.04
"May the L. be a true and faithful 42.05
with which the L. your God sends 42.05
voice of the L. our God to whom we 42.06
obey the voice of the L. our God." 42.06
the word of the L. came to Jeremiah. 42.07
and said to them, "Thus says the L., 42.09
says the L., for I am with you, to 42.11
the voice of the L. your God 42.13
then hear the word of the L., 42.15
Thus says the L. of hosts, the God 42.15
"For thus says the L. of hosts, 42.18
The L. has said to you, O remnant of 42.19
For you sent me to the L. your God, 42.20
'Pray for us to the L. our God, 42.20
whatever the L. our God says 42.20
voice of the L. your God in 42.21
these words of the L. their God, 43.01
with which the L. their God had 43.01
The L. our God did not send you to 43.02
did not obey the voice of the L., 43.04
did not obey the voice of the L. 43.07
Then the word of the L. came to 43.08
them, 'Thus says the L. of hosts, 43.10
"Thus says the L. of hosts, the God 44.02
And now thus says the L. God of hosts, 44.07
"Therefore thus says the L. of hosts, 44.11
spoken to us in the name of the L., 44.16
land, did not the L. remember it? 44.21
The L. could no longer bear your 44.22
against the L. and did not obey 44.23
voice of the L. or walk in his law 44.23
the women, "Hear the word of the L., 44.24
Thus says the L. of hosts, the God 44.25
Therefore hear the word of the L., 44.26
says the L., that my name shall no 44.26
saying, 'As the L. God lives.' 44.26
says the L., that I will punish you 44.29
Thus says the L., Behold I will 44.30
"Thus says the L., the God of 45.02
for the L. has added sorrow to my 45.03
Thus says the L.: Behold, what I have 45.04
evil upon all flesh, says the L.; 45.05
The word of the L. which came to 46.01
on every side! says the L. 46.05
is the day of the L. God of hosts, 46.10
For the L. God of hosts holds a 46.10
The word which the L. spoke to 46.13
Because the L. thrust him down. 46.15
whose name is the L. of hosts, 46.18
says the L., though it is impenetrable, 46.23
The L. of hosts, the God of Israel, 46.25
as in the days of old, says the L. 46.26
says the L., for I am with you. 46.28
The word of the L. that came to 47.01
"Thus says the L.: Behold, waters are 47.02
For the L. is destroying the 47.04
Ah, sword of the L.! How long 47.06
when the L. has given it a charge? 47.07
Thus says the L. of hosts, the God 48.01

be destroyed, as the L. has spoken. 48.08
the work of the L. with slackness; 48.10
says the L., when I shall send to 48.12
whose name is the L. of hosts. 48.15
and his arm is broken, says the L. 48.25
magnified himself against the L.; 48.26
I know his insolence, says the L.; 48.30
says the L., him who offers sacrifice 48.35
which no one cares, says the L. 48.38
For thus says the L.: 48.40
magnified himself against the L. 48.42
inhabitant of Moab: says the L. 48.43
of their punishment, says the L. 48.44
in the latter days, says the L." 48.47
Thus says the L.: "Has Israel no 49.01
says the L., when I will cause the 49.02
who dispossessed him, says the L. 49.02
says the L. God of hosts, from all 49.05
of the Ammonites, says the L. 49.06
Thus says the L. of hosts: "Is 49.07
For thus says the L.: "If those who 49.12
says the L., that Bozrah shall 49.13
I have heard tidings from the L., 49.14
you down from there, says the L. 49.16
says the L., no man shall dwell 49.18
plan which the L. has made against 49.20
in that day, says the L. of hosts. 49.26
Thus says the L.: "Rise up, advance 49.28
of Hazor! says the L. 49.30
says the L., that has no gates or 49.31
every side of them, says the L. 49.32
The word of the L. that came to 49.34
Thus says the L. of hosts: "Behold, I 49.35
them, my fierce anger, says the L. 49.37
king and princes, says the L. 49.38
the fortunes of Elam, says the L." 49.39
The word which the L. spoke concerning 50.01
says the L., the people of Israel 50.04
they shall seek the L. their God. 50.04
ourselves to the L. in an everlasting 50.05
they have sinned against the L., 50.07
the L. the hope of their fathers. 50.07
her shall be sated, says the L. 50.10
wrath of the L. she shall not be 50.13
for she has sinned against the L. 50.14
this is the vengeance of the L.: 50.15
thus says the L. of hosts, the God 50.18
says the L., iniquity shall be 50.20
says the L., and do all that I have 50.21
because you strove against the L. 50.24
The L. has opened his armory, and 50.25
for the L. God of hosts has a work 50.25
the vengeance of the L. our God, 50.28
for she has proudly defiled the L., 50.29
destroyed on that day, says the L. 50.30
one, says the L. God of hosts; 50.31
"Thus says the L. of hosts: The 50.33
the L. of hosts is his name. 50.34
says the L., and upon the inhabitants 50.35
says the L., so no man shall dwell 50.40
plan which the L. has made against 50.45
Thus says the L.: "Behold, I will 51.01
by their God, the L. of hosts; 51.05
The L. has brought forth our 51.10
in Zion the work of the L. our God. 51.10
The L. has stirred up the spirit of 51.11
that is the vengeance of the L., 51.11
for the L. has both planned and 51.12
The L. of hosts has sworn by 51.14
the L. of hosts is his name. 51.19
have done in Zion, says the L. 51.24
says the L., which destroys the 51.25
be a perpetual waste, says the L. 51.26
For thus says the L. of hosts, 51.33
Therefore thus says the L.: 51.36
sleep and not wake, says the L. 51.39
from the fierce anger of the L.! 51.45

LORD (cont.)
them out of the north, says the L. Jer 51.48
Remember the L. from afar, and let 51.50
says the L., when I will execute 51.52
come from me upon her, says the L. 51.53
For the L. is laying Babylon waste, 51.55
for the L. is a God of recompense, 51.56
whose name is the L. of hosts. 51.57
"Thus says the L. of hosts: The 51.58
and say, 'O L., thou hast said 51.62
was evil in the sight of the L., 52.02
anger of the L. things came to 52.03
And he burned the house of the L., 52.13
that were in the house of the L., 52.17
had made for the house of the L., 52.20
because the L. has made her suffer Lam 1.05
"O L., behold my affliction, for the 1.09
"Look, O L., and behold, for I am 1.11
which the L. inflicted on the day 1.12
the L. gave me into the hands of 1.14
"The L. flouted all my mighty men 1.15
the L. has trodden as in a wine 1.15
the L. has commanded against Jacob 1.17
"The L. is in the right, for I have 1.18
"Behold, O L., for I am in distress, 1.20
How the L. in his anger has set the 2.01
The L. has destroyed without mercy 2.02
The L. has become like an enemy, he 2.05
the L. has brought to an end in 2.06
The L. has scorned his altar, 2.07
house of the L. as on the day of 2.07
The L. determined to lay in ruins 2.08
obtain no vision from the L. 2.09
The L. has done what he purposed, 2.17
Cry aloud to the L.! 2.18
before the presence of the L.! 2.19
Look, O L., and see! With whom hast thou 2.20
slain in the sanctuary of the L.? 2.20
anger of the L. none escaped or 2.22
and my expectation from the L. 3.18
love of the L. never ceases, 3.22
"The L. is my portion," says my soul, 3.24
The L. is good to those who wait 3.25
for the salvation of the L. 3.26
For the L. will not cast off for 3.31
the L. does not approve. 3.36
unless the L. has ordained it? 3.37
our ways, and return to the L.! 3.40
until the L. from heaven looks down 3.50
O L., from the depths of the pit; 3.55
O L., thou hast redeemed my life. 3.58
seen the wrong done to me, O L.; 3.59
O L., all their devices against me. 3.61
O L., according to the work of 3.64
them from under thy heavens, O L. 3.66
The L. gave full vent to his wrath, 4.11
The L. himself has scattered them, 4.16
Remember, O L., what has befallen us; 5.01
But thou, O L., dost reign for ever; 5.19
O L., that we may be restored! 5.21
the word of the L. came to Ezekiel Eze 1.03
the hand of the L. was upon him 1.03
likeness of the glory of the L. 1.28
say to them, 'Thus says the L. GOD.' 2.04
to them, 'Thus says the L. GOD'; 3.11
glory of the L. arose from its 3.12
the hand of the L. being strong 3.14
the word of the L. came to me: 3.16
And the hand of the L. was there 3.22
the glory of the L. stood there, 3.23
to them, 'Thus says the L. God'; 3.27
And the L. said, "Thus shall the 4.13
Then I said, "Ah L. GOD! 4.14
Thus says the L. GOD: This is 5.05
Therefore thus says the L. GOD: 5.07
therefore thus says the L. GOD: 5.08
says the L. GOD, surely, because you 5.11
the L., have spoken in my jealousy, 5.13
chastisements—I, the L., have spoken— 5.15
upon you. I., the L., have spoken." 5.17
The word of the L. came to me: 6.01
hear the word of the L. GOD! 6.03
Thus says the L. GOD to the mountains 6.03
you shall know that I am the L. 6.07
And they shall know that I am the L.; 6.10
Thus says the L. GOD: "Clap your 6.11
And you shall know that I am the L. 6.13
they will know that I am the L." 6.14
The word of the L. came to me: 7.01
thus says the L. GOD to the land of 7.02
you will know that I am the L. 7.04
"Thus says the L. GOD: Disaster 7.05
know that I am the L., who smite. 7.09
in the day of the wrath of the L.; 7.19
they shall know that I am the L." 7.27
the hand of the L. GOD fell there 8.01
'The L. does not see us, the LORD 8.12
the L. has forsaken the land.'" 8.12
north gate of the house of the L.; 8.14
inner court of the house of the L.; 8.16
the door of the temple of the L., 8.16
backs to the temple of the L., 8.16
And the L. said to him, "Go through 9.04
upon my face, and cried, "Ah L. GOD! 9.08
'The L. has forsaken the land, and 9.09
the land, and the L. does not see.' 9.09
glory of the L. went up from the 10.04
brightness of the glory of the L. 10.04
glory of the L. went forth from 10.18
east gate of the house of the L.; 10.19
east gate of the house of the L., 11.01
And the Spirit of the L. fell upon me, 11.05
Thus says the L.: So you think, O 11.05
Therefore thus says the L. GOD: 11.07
sword upon you says the L. GOD. 11.08
you shall know that I am the L. 11.10
and you shall know that I am the L.; 11.12
a loud voice, and said, "Ah L. GOD! 11.13
And the word of the L. came to me: 11.14
'They have gone far from the L.; 11.15
Therefore say, 'Thus says the L. GOD: 11.16
Therefore say, 'Thus says the L.: 11.17
their own heads, says the L. GOD." 11.21
glory of the L. went up from the 11.23
things that the L. had showed me. 11.25
The word of the L. came to me: 12.01
the word of the L. came to me: 12.08
Say to them, 'Thus says the L. GOD: 12.10
And they shall know that I am the L., 12.15
go, and may know that I am the L. 12.16
Moreover the word of the L. came to me: 12.17
Thus says the L. GOD concerning the 12.19
you shall know that I am the L. 12.20
And the word of the L. came to me: 12.21
therefore, 'Thus says the L. GOD: 12.23
But I the L. will speak the word 12.25
and perform it, says the L. GOD." 12.25
Again the word of the L. came to me: 12.26
Thus says the L. GOD: None of my 12.28
will be performed, says the L. GOD." 12.28
The word of the L. came to me: 13.01
minds: 'Hear the word of the L.!' 13.02
Thus says the L. GOD, Woe to the 13.03
in battle in the day of the L. 13.05
'Says the L.,' when the L. has not sent 13.06
'Says the L.,' although I have not 13.07
Therefore thus says the L. GOD: 13.08
I am against you, says the L. GOD. 13.08
shall know that I am the L. GOD. 13.09
Therefore thus says the L. GOD: 13.13
you shall know that I am the L. 13.14
was no peace, says the L. GOD. 13.16
Thus says the L. GOD: Woe to the 13.18
"Wherefore thus says the L. GOD: 13.20

LORD (cont.)

you shall know that I am the L.	Eze 13.21
you will know that I am the L."	13.23
And the word of the L. came to me:	14.02
Thus says the L. God: Any man of the	14.04
I the L. will answer him myself	14.04
Thus says the L. God: Repent and	14.06
I the L. will answer him myself;	14.07
you shall know that I am the L.	14.08
the L., have deceived that prophet,	14.09
may be their God, says the L. God.	14.11
And the word of the L. came to me:	14.12
righteousness, says the L. God.	14.14
says the L. God, they would deliver	14.16
says the L. God, they would deliver	14.18
says the L. God, they would deliver	14.20
"For thus says the L. God:	14.21
I have done in it, says the L. God."	14.23
And the word of the L. came to me:	15.01
Therefore thus says the L. God:	15.06
and you will know that I am the L.,	15.07
acted faithlessly, says the L. God."	15.08
Again the word of the L. came to me:	16.01
Thus says the L. God to Jerusalem:	16.03
says the L. God, and you became mine.	16.08
bestowed upon you, says the L. God.	16.14
a pleasing odor, says the L. God.	16.19
woe to you! says the L. God),	16.23
says the L. God, seeing you did all	16.30
O harlot, hear the word of the L.:	16.35
Thus says the L. God, Because your	16.36
upon your head, says the L. God.	16.43
says the L. God, your sister Sodom	16.48
and your abominations, says the L.	16.58
thus says the L. God: I will deal	16.59
you shall know that I am the L.,	16.62
you have done, says the L. God."	16.63
The word of the L. came to me:	17.01
Thus says the L. God: A great eagle	17.03
Thus says the L. God: Will it thrive?	17.09
Then the word of the L. came to me:	17.11
says the L. God, surely in the place	17.16
Therefore thus says the L. God:	17.19
know that I, the L., have spoken.	17.21
Thus says the L. God: "I myself will	17.22
know that I the L. bring low the	17.24
I the L. have spoken, and I will do	17.24
The word of the L. came to me again:	18.01
says the L. God, this proverb shall	18.03
shall surely live, says the L. God.	18.09
says the L. God, and not rather that	18.23
'The way of L. is not just.'	18.25
'The way of the L. is not just.	18.29
to his ways, says the L. God.	18.30
death of any one, says the L. God;	18.32
Israel came to inquire of the L.,	20.01
And the word of the L. came to me:	20.02
Thus says the L. God, Is it to	20.03
says the L. God, I will not be	20.03
Thus says the L. God: On the day	20.05
them, saying, I am the L. your God.	20.05
idols of Egypt; I am the L. your God.	20.07
know that I the L. sanctify them.	20.12
I the L. am your God; walk in my	20.19
may know that I the L. am your God.	20.20
they might know that I am the L.	20.26
Thus says the L. God: In this again	20.27
Thus says the L. God: Will you	20.30
says the L. God, I will not be	20.31
says the L. God, surely with a	20.33
judgment with you, says the L. God.	20.36
you will know that I am the L.	20.38
thus says the L. God: Go serve every	20.39
says the L. God, there all the house	20.40
And you shall know that I am the L.,	20.42
And you shall know that I am the L.,	20.44
O house of Israel, says the L. God."	20.44

And the word of the L. came to me:	20.45
the Negeb, Hear the word of the L.:	20.47
Thus says the L. God, Behold, I will	20.47
see that I the L. have kindled it;	20.48
Then I said, "Ah L. God!	20.49
The word of the L. came to me:	21.01
Thus says the L.: Behold, I am	21.03
know that I the L. have drawn my	21.05
be fulfilled,' " says the L. God.	21.07
And the word of the L. came to me;	21.08
Thus says the L., Say: A sword, a	21.09
despise the rod?" says the L. God.	21.23
my fury; I the L. have spoken."	21.17
The word of the L. came to me again:	21.18
"Therefore thus says the L. God:	21.24
thus says the L. God: Remove the	21.26
Thus says the L. God concerning the	21.28
remembered; for I the L. have spoken."	21.32
Moreover the word of the L. came to me,	22.01
Thus says the L. God: A city that	22.03
have forgotten me, says the L. God.	22.12
I the L. have spoken, and I will do	22.14
you shall know that I am the L."	22.16
And the word of the L. came to me:	22.17
Therefore thus says the L. God:	22.19
know that I the L. have poured out	22.22
And the word of the L. came to me:	22.23
saying, 'Thus says the L. God,'	22.28
God,' when the L. has not spoken.	22.28
upon their heads, says the L. God."	22.31
The word of the L. came to me:	23.01
thus says the L. God: "Behold, I will	23.22
For thus says the L. God: Behold, I will	23.28
Thus says the L. God: "You shall	23.32
for I have spoken, says the L. God.	23.34
Therefore thus says the L. God:	23.35
The L. said to me: "Son of man, will	23.36
For thus says the L. God: "Bring up	23.46
shall know that I am the L. God.	23.49
the word of the L. came to me:	24.01
Thus says the L. God: Set on the pot,	24.03
"Therefore thus says the L. God:	24.06
Therefore thus says the L. God:	24.09
I the L. have spoken; it shall come	24.14
I will judge you, says the L. God."	24.14
Also the word of the L. came to me:	24.15
"The word of the L. came to me:	24.20
Thus says the L. God: Behold, I will	24.21
you will know that I am the L. God.	24.24
they will know that I am the L.	24.27
The word of the L. came to me:	25.01
Hear the word of the L. God:	25.03
Thus says the L. God, Because you	25.03
you will know that I am the L.	25.05
For thus says the L. God:	25.06
you will know that I am the L.	25.07
"Thus says the L. God: Because Moab	25.08
they will know that I am the L.	25.11
"Thus says the L. God: Because Edom	25.12
therefore thus says the L. God,	25.13
know my vengeance, says the L. God.	25.14
"Thus says the L. God: Because the	25.15
therefore thus says the L. God,	25.16
they will know that I am the L.,	25.17
the word of the L. came to me:	26.01
therefore thus says the L. God:	26.03
for I have spoken, says the L. God;	26.05
they will know that I am the L.	26.06
"For thus says the L. God: Behold,	26.07
for I the L. have spoken, says the L. God.	26.14
"Thus says the L. God to Tyre: Will	26.15
"For thus says the L. God: When	26.19
be found again, says the L. God.	26.21
The word of the L. came to me:	27.01
thus says the L. God: "O Tyre, you	27.03
The word of the L. came to me:	28.01
Thus says the L. God: "Because your	28.02

LORD (cont.)
therefore thus says the L. GOD: Eze 28.06
for I have spoken, says the L. GOD." 28.10
Moreover the word of the L. came to me: 28.11
Thus says the L. GOD: "You were the 28.12
The word of the L. came to me: 28.20
Thus says the L. GOD: "Behold, I am 28.22
that I am L. when I execute 28.22
they will know that I am the L. 28.23
will know that I am the L. GOD. 28.24
"Thus says the L. GOD: When I gather 28.25
know that I am the L. their God. 28.26
the word of the L. came to me: 29.01
Thus says the L. GOD: "Behold, I am 29.03
Egypt shall know that I am the L. 29.06
therefore thus says the L. GOD: 29.08
they will know that I am the L. 29.09
"For thus says the L. GOD: At the end 29.13
will know that I am the L. GOD. 29.16
the word of the L. came to me: 29.17
Therefore thus says the L. GOD: 29.19
worked for me, says the L GOD. 29.20
they will know that I am the L." 29.21
The word of the L. came to me: 30.01
Thus says the L. GOD: "Wail, 'Alas 30.02
is near, the day of the L. is near; 30.03
"Thus says the L.: Those who support 30.06
her by the sword, says the L. GOD. 30.06
Then they will know that I am the L., 30.08
"Thus says the L. GOD: I will put an 30.10
of foreigners; I, the L., have spoken. 30.12
"Thus says the L. GOD: I will 30.13
they will know that I am the L. 30.19
the word of the L. came to me: 30.20
Therefore thus says the L. GOD: 30.22
they shall know that I am the L. 30.25
they will know that I am the L." 30.26
the word of the L. came to me: 31.01
"Therefore thus says the L. GOD: 31.10
"Thus says the L. GOD: When it goes 31.15
all his multitude, says the L. GOD." 31.18
the word of the L. came to me: 32.01
Thus says the L. GOD: I will throw 32.03
upon your land, says the L. GOD. 32.08
For thus says the L. GOD: The sword 32.11
to run like oil, says the L. GOD. 32.14
they will know that I am the L. 32.15
they chant it, says the L. GOD." 32.16
the word of the L. came to me: 32.17
by the sword, says the L. GOD. 32.31
all his multitude, says the L. GOD." 32.32
The word of the L. came to me: 33.01
says the L. GOD, I have no pleasure 33.11
'The way of the L. is not just'; 33.17
'The way of the L. is not just.' 33.20
Now the hand of the L. had been 33.22
The word of the L. came to me: 33.23
Thus says the L. GOD: You eat flesh 33.25
Thus says the L. GOD: As I live, 33.27
Then they will know that I am the L., 33.29
is that comes forth from the L. 33.30
The word of the L. came to me: 34.01
Thus says the L. GOD: Ho, shepherds 34.02
shepherds, hear the word of the L.: 34.07
says the L. GOD, because my sheep 34.08
shepherds, hear the word of the L.: 34.09
Thus says the L. GOD, Behold, I am 34.10
"For thus says the L. GOD: Behold, 34.11
them lie down, says the L. GOD. 34.15
thus says the L. GOD: Behold, I judge 34.17
thus says the L. GOD to them: Behold, 34.20
And I, the L., will be their God, and 34.24
among them; I, the L., have spoken. 34.24
they shall know that I am the L., 34.27
the L. their God, am with them, and 34.30
are my people, says the L. GOD. 34.30
and I am your God, says the L. GOD." 34.31
The word of the L. came to me: 35.01
Thus says the L. GOD: Behold, I am 35.03
you shall know that I am the L. 35.04
says the L. GOD, I will prepare you 35.06
you will know that I am the L. 35.09
them,'—although the L. was there— 35.10
says the L. GOD, I will deal with 35.11
the L, have heard all the revilings 35.12
Thus says the L. GOD: For the 35.14
they will know that I am the L. 35.15
of Israel, hear the word of the L. 36.01
Thus says the L. GOD: Because the 36.02
Thus says the L. GOD: Because, yea, 36.03
hear the word of the L. GOD: 36.04
Thus says the L. GOD to the mountains 36.04
therefore thus says the L. GOD: 36.05
Thus says the L. GOD: Behold, I speak 36.06
therefore thus says the L. GOD: 36.07
you will know that I am the L. 36.11
Thus says the L. GOD: Because men 36.13
of children, says the L. GOD; 36.14
nation to stumble, says the L. GOD." 36.15
The word of the L. came to me: 36.16
'These are the people of the L., 36.20
Thus says the L. GOD: It is not for 36.22
nations will know that I am the L., 36.23
says the L. GOD, when through you I 36.23
that I will act, says the L. GOD; 36.32
"Thus says the L. GOD: On the day 36.33
the L., have rebuilt the ruined 36.36
I, the L., have spoken, and I will do 36.36
"Thus says the L. GOD: This also I 36.37
they will know that I am the L. 36.38
The hand of the L. was upon me, 37.01
me out by the Spirit of the L., 37.01
I answered, "O L. GOD, thou knowest." 37.03
dry bones, hear the word of the L. 37.04
Thus says the L. GOD to these bones: 37.05
you shall know that I am the L. 37.06
Thus says the L. GOD: Come from the 37.09
Thus says the L. GOD: "Behold, I will 37.12
And you shall know that I am the L., 37.13
L., have spoken, and I have done it, says the L." 37.14
The word of the L. came to me: 37.15
Thus says the L. GOD: Behold, I am 37.19
Thus says the L. GOD: Behold, I will 37.21
know that I the L. sanctify Israel, 37.28
The word of the L. came to me: 38.01
Thus says the L. GOD: Behold, I am 38.03
"Thus says the L. GOD: On that day 38.10
Thus says the L. GOD: On that day 38.14
"Thus says the L. GOD: Are you he of 38.17
says the L. GOD, my wrath will be 38.18
against Gog, says the L. GOD; 38.21
they will know that I am the L. 38.23
Thus says the L. GOD: Behold, I am 39.01
for I have spoken, says the L. GOD. 39.05
they shall know that I am the L. 39.06
shall know that I am the L., 39.07
be brought about, says the L. GOD. 39.08
plundered them, says the L. GOD. 39.10
I show my glory, says the L. GOD. 39.13
thus says the L. GOD: Speak to the 39.17
of warriors,' says the L. GOD. 39.20
know that I am the L. their God, 39.22
"Therefore thus says the L. GOD: 39.25
that I am the L. their God because 39.28
house of Israel, says the L. GOD." 39.29
the hand of the L. was upon me, 40.01
near to the L. to minister to him. 40.46
the table which is before the L. 41.22
approach the L. shall eat the most 42.13
glory of the L. entered the temple 43.04
glory of the L. filled the temple. 43.05
thus says the L. GOD: These are the 43.18
says the L. GOD, a bull for a sin 43.19
You shall present them before the L., 43.24

LORD (cont.)

up as a burnt offering to the L. Eze 43.24
I will accept you, says the L. GOD. 43.27
for the L., the God of Israel, has 44.02
in it to eat bread before the L.; 44.03
of the L. filled the temple of the L.; 44.04
And the L. said to me, "Son of man, 44.05
temple of the L. and all its laws; 44.05
thus says the L. GOD: O house of 44.06
"Therefore thus says the L. GOD: 44.09
says the L. GOD, that they shall 44.12
fat and the blood, says the L. GOD; 44.15
his sin offering, says the L. GOD. 44.27
apart for the L. a portion of the 45.01
approach the L. to minister to him; 45.04
"Thus says the L. GOD: Enough, O 45.09
of my people, says the L. GOD. 45.09
atonement for them, says the L. GOD. 45.15
"Thus says the L. GOD: In the first 45.18
offering to the L. seven young 45.23
"Thus says the L GOD: The gate of 46.01
gate before the L. on the sabbaths 46.03
offers to the L. on the sabbath 46.04
as a freewill offering to the L., 46.12
a burnt offering to the L. daily; 46.13
as a cereal offering to the L.; 46.14
"Thus says the L. GOD: If the prince 46.16
Thus says the L. GOD: "These are the 47.13
his inheritance, says the L. GOD. 47.23
apart for the L. shall be twenty-five 48.09
sanctuary of the L. in the midst of 48.10
the land, for it is holy to the L. 48.14
several portions, says the L. GOD. 48.29
henceforth shall be, The L. is there." 48.35
And the L. gave Jehoiakim king of Dan 1.02
Daniel, "I fear lest my l. the king, 1.10
God is God of gods and L. of kings, 2.47
"My l., may the dream be for those 4.19
has come upon my l. the king, 4.24
yourself against the L. of heaven; 5.23
the word of the L. to Jeremiah the 9.02
Then I turned my face to the L. God, 9.03
I prayed to the L. my God and made 9.04
"O L., the great and terrible God, 9.04
To thee, O L., belongs righteousness, 9.07
To us, O L., belongs confusion of 9.08
To the L. our God belong mercy and 9.09
voice of the L. our God by following 9.10
the favor of the L. our God, 9.13
Therefore the L. has kept ready the 9.14
for the L. our God is righteous in 9.14
And now, O L. our God, who didst 9.15
O L., according to all thy righteous 9.16
O L., cause thy face to shine upon 9.17
O L., hear; O L., forgive; 9.19
O L., give heed and act; 9.19
before the L. my God for the holy 9.20
"O my l., by reason of the vision 10.16
my lord's servant talk with my l.? 10.17
"Let my l. speak, for you have 10.19
"O my l., what shall be the issue 12.08
The word of the L. that came to Hos 1.01
When the L. first spoke through 1.02
the L. said to Hosea, "Go, take to 1.02
great harlotry by forsaking the L. 1.02
And the L. said to him, "Call his 1.04
And the L. said to him, "Call her 1.06
deliver them by the L. their God; 1.07
And the L. said, "Call his name Not 1.09
lovers, and forgot me, says the L. 2.13
says the L., you will call me, 'My 2.16
faithfulness; and you shall know the L. 2.20
says the L., I will answer the 2.21
And the L. said to me, "Go again, 3.01
even as the L. loves the people of 3.01
return and seek the L. their God, 3.05
in fear of the L. and to his 3.05
Hear the word of the L., O people 4.01
for the L. has a controversy with 4.01
forsaken the L. to cherish harlotry. 4.10
and swear not, "As the L. lives." 4.15
can the L. now feed them like a 4.16
them, and they know not the L. 5.04
herds they shall go to seek the L., 5.06
have dealt faithlessly with the L.; 5.07
"Come, let us return to the L.; 6.01
let us press on to know the L.; 6.03
do not return to the L. their God, 7.10
is over the house of the L., 8.01
but the L. has no delight in them. 8.13
not remain in the land of the L.; 9.03
pour libations of wine to the L.; 9.04
not come to the house of the L. 9.04
on the day of the feast of the L.? 9.05
Give them, O L.—what wilt thou 9.14
The L. will break down their altars, 10.02
no king, for we fear not the L., 10.03
for it is the time to seek the L., 10.12
They shall go after the L., 11.10
them to their homes, says the L. 11.11
The L. has an indictment against 12.02
the L. the God of hosts, the L. is 12.05
I am the L. your God from the land 12.09
By a prophet the L. brought Israel 12.13
so his L. will leave his bloodguilt 12.14
I am the L. your God from the land 13.04
the east wind, the wind of the L., 13.15
to the L. your God, for you have 14.01
you words and return to the L.; 14.02
for the ways of the L. are right, 14.09
The word of the L. that came to Joe 1.01
cut off from the house of the L. 1.09
mourn, the ministers of the L. 1.09
to the house of the L. your God; 1.14
and cry to the L. 1.14
For the day of the L. is near, 1.15
Unto thee, O L., I cry. 1.19
for the day of the L. is coming, 2.01
The L. utters his voice before his 2.11
the day of the L. is great and 2.11
says the L., "return to me with 2.12
Return to the L., your God, 2.13
offering for the L., your God? 2.14
priests, the ministers of the L., 2.17
O L., and make not thy heritage a 2.17
Then the L. became jealous for his 2.18
The L. answered and said to his 2.19
for the L. has done great things! 2.21
and rejoice in the L., your God; 2.23
praise the name of the L. your God, 2.26
the L., am your God and there is 2.27
and terrible day of the L. comes. 2.31
the name of the L. shall be 2.32
as the L. has said, and among the 2.32
shall be those whom the L. calls. 2.32
far off; for the L. has spoken." 3.08
Bring down thy warriors, O L. 3.11
the day of the L. is near in the 3.14
And the L. roars from Zion, and 3.16
But the L. is a refuge to his 3.16
know that I am the L. your God, 3.17
house of the L. and water the 3.18
guilty, for the L. dwells in Zion." 3.21
"The L. roars from Zion, and utters Amo 1.02
Thus says the L.: "For three transgressions 1.03
go into exile to Kir," says the L. 1.05
Thus says the L.: "For three transgressions 1.06
shall perish," says the L. GOD. 1.08
Thus says the L.: "For three transgressions 1.09
Thus says the L.: "For three transgressions 1.11
Thus says the L.: "For three transgressions 1.13
his princes together," says the L. 1.15
Thus says the L.: "For three transgressions 2.01
its princes with him," says the L. 2.03

LORD (cont.)

Thus says the L.: "For three transgressions Amo 2.04
have rejected the law of the L., 2.04
Thus says the L.: "For three transgressions 2.06
People of Israel?" says the L. 2.11
naked in that day," says the L. 2.16
word that the L. has spoken 3.01
a city, unless the L. has done it? 3.06
Surely the L. GOD does nothing, 3.07
The L. GOD has spoken; who can 3.08
says the L., "those who store up 3.10
Therefore thus says the L. GOD: 3.11
Thus says the L.: "As the shepherd 3.12
says the L. GOD, the God of hosts, 3.13
shall come to an end," says the L. 3.15
The L. GOD has sworn by his holiness 4.02
forth into Harmon," says the L. 4.03
people of Israel!" says the L. GOD. 4.05
did not return to me," says the L. 4.06
did not return to me," says the L. 4.08
did not return to me," says the L. 4.09
did not return to me," says the L. 4.10
did not return to me," says the L. 4.11
the L., the God of hosts, is his 4.13
For thus says the L. GOD: 5.03
For thus says the L. to the house 5.04
Seek the L. and live, lest he break 5.06
of the earth, the L. is his name, 5.08
and so the L., the God of hosts, 5.14
it may be that the L., the God of 5.15
Therefore thus says the L., 5.16
the L.: "In all the squares there 5.16
the midst of you," says the L. 5.17
you who deserve the day of the L.! 5.18
would you have the day of the L.? 5.18
Is not the day of the L. darkness, 5.20
says the L., whose name is the 5.27
L. GOD has sworn by himself (says the L., 6.08
not mention the name of the L. 6.10
the L. commands, and the great house 6.11
says the L., the God of hosts; 6.14
Thus the L. GOD showed me: behold, he 7.01
"O L. GOD, forgive, I beseech thee! 7.02
The L. repented concerning this; 7.03
"It shall not be," said the L. 7.03
Thus the L. GOD showed me: behold, 7.04
the L. GOD was calling for a 7.04
"O L. GOD, cease, I beseech thee! 7.05
The L. repented concerning this; 7.06
shall not be," said the L. GOD. 7.06
the L. was standing beside a wall 7.07
And the L. said to me, "Amos, what do 7.08
Then the L. said, "Behold, I am 7.08
and the L. took me from following 7.15
and the L. said to me, "Go, prophesy 7.15
"Now therefore hear the word of the L. 7.16
Therefore thus says the L.: 7.17
Thus the L. GOD showed me: behold, a 8.01
Then the L. said to me, "The end 8.02
in that day," says the L. GOD; 8.03
The L. has sworn by the pride of 8.07
says the L. GOD, "I will make the 8.09
says the L. GOD, "when I will send 8.11
but of hearing the words of the L. 8.11
fro, to seek the word of the L., 8.12
I saw the L. standing beside the 9.01
The L., GOD of hosts, he who touches 9.05
of the earth—the L. is his name. 9.06
says the L. "Did I not 9.07
Behold, the eyes of the L. GOD are 9.08
the house of Jacob," says the L. 9.08
name," says the L. who does this. 9.12
says the L., "when the plowman 9.13
given them," says the L. your God. 9.15
Thus says the L. GOD concerning Ob 1.01
We have heard tidings from the L., 1.01
I will bring you down, says the L. 1.04
says the L., destroy the wise men 1.08
For the day of the L. is near upon 1.15
house of Esau; for the L. has spoken. 1.18
Now the word of the L. came to Jon 1.01
to Tarshish from the presence of the L. 1.03
away from the presence of the L. 1.03
But the L. hurled a great wind upon 1.04
and I fear the L., the God of 1.09
from the presence of the L., 1.10
cried to the L., "We beseech thee, O L., 1.14
for thou, O L., hast done as it 1.14
Then the men feared the L. exceedingly, 1.16
sacrifice to the L. and made vows. 1.16
And the L. appointed a great fish 1.17
prayed to the L. his God from the 2.01
saying, "I called to the L., 2.02
my life from the Pit, O L. my God. 2.06
within me, I remembered the L.; 2.07
Deliverance belongs to the L.! 2.09
Then the word of the L. came to 3.01
according to the word of the L. 3.03
And he prayed to the L. and said, 4.02
L., is not this what I said when I 4.02
O L., take my life from me, I 4.03
And the L. said, "Do you do well to 4.04
And the L. God appointed a plant, 4.06
And the L. said, "You pity the plant, 4.10
The word of the L. that came to Mic 1.01
and let the L. GOD be a witness 1.02
the L. from his holy temple. 1.02
the L. is coming forth out of his 1.03
down from the L. to the gate of 1.12
Therefore thus says the L.: 2.03
by lot in the assembly of the L. 2.05
is the Spirit of the L. impatient? 2.07
before them, the L. at their head. 2.13
Then they will cry to the L., 3.04
Thus says the L. concerning the 3.05
power, with the Spirit of the L., 3.08
yet they lean upon the L. and say, 3.11
"Is not the L. in the midst of us? 3.11
house of the L. shall be established 4.01
us go up to the mountain of the L., 4.02
the word of the L. from Jerusalem. 4.02
mouth of the L. of hosts has spoken. 4.04
the name of the L. our God for 4.05
says the L., I will assemble the 4.06
and the L. will reign over them in 4.07
there the L. will redeem you from 4.10
do not know the thoughts of the L., 4.12
shall devote their gain to the L., 4.13
wealth to the L. of the whole 4.13
flock in the strength of the L., 5.04
of the name of the L. his God. 5.04
many peoples like dew from the L., 5.07
says the L., I will cut off your 5.10
Hear what the L. says: Arise, plead 6.01
mountains, the controversy of the L., 6.02
for the L. has a controversy with 6.02
may know the saving acts of the L. 6.05
"With what shall I come before the L., 6.06
Will the L. be pleased with thousands 6.07
what does the L. require of you 6.08
The voice of the L. cries to the 6.09
But as for me, I will look to the L., 7.07
the L. will be a light to me. 7.08
indignation of the L. because I 7.09
to me, "Where is the L. your God?" 7.10
turn in dread to the L. our God, 7.17
The L. is a jealous God and avenging, Nah 1.02
the L. is avenging and wrathful; 1.02
the L. takes vengeance on his adversaries 1.02
The L. is slow to anger and of 1.03
and the L. will by no means clear 1.03
The L. is good, a stronghold in the 1.07
What do you plot against the L.? 1.09
who plotted evil against the L., 1.11

LORD (cont.)
Thus says the L., "Though they be Nah 1.12
The L. has given commandment about 1.14
(For the L. is restoring the 2.02
says the L. of hosts, and I will 2.13
says the L. of hosts, and will lift 3.05
O L., how long shall I cry for help, Hab 1.02
O L. my God, my Holy One? We shall not 1.12
O L., thou hast ordained them as a 1.12
And the L. answered me: "Write the 2.02
it not from the L. of hosts that 2.13
knowledge of the glory of the L., 2.14
But the L. is in his holy temple; 2.20
O L., I have heard the report of 3.02
and thy work, O L., do I fear. 3.02
thy wrath against the rivers, O L.? 3.08
yet I will rejoice in the L., 3.18
God, the L., is my strength; 3.19
The word of the L. which came to Zep 1.01
face of the earth," says the L. 1.02
face of the earth," says the L. 1.03
swear to the L. and yet swear by 1.05
turned back from following the L., 1.06
do not seek the L. or inquire of 1.06
Be silent before the L. God! 1.07
For the day of the L. is at hand; 1.07
the L. has prepared a sacrifice and 1.07
says the L., "a cry will be heard 1.10
'The L. will not do good, nor will 1.12
The great day of the L. is near, 1.14
of the day of the L. is bitter, 1.14
they have sinned against the L.; 1.17
on the day of the wrath of the L., 1.18
you the fierce anger of the L., 2.02
you the day of the wrath of the L. 2.02
Seek the L., all you humble of the 2.03
on the day of the wrath of the L. 2.03
the word of the L. is against you, 2.05
For the L. their God will be 2.07
says the L. of hosts, the God of 2.09
the people of the L. of hosts. 2.10
The L. will be terrible against 2.11
She does not trust in the L., 3.02
The L. within her is righteous, he 3.05
says the L., "for the day when I 3.08
the name of the L. and serve him 3.09
seek refuge in the name of the L., 3.12
The L. has taken away the judgments 3.15
the L., is in your midst; 3.15
The L., your God, is in your midst, a 3.17
before your eyes," says the L. 3.20
the word of the L. came by Haggai Hag 1.01
"Thus says the L. of hosts: This 1.02
to rebuild the house of the L. 1.02
Then the word of the L. came by 1.03
therefore thus says the L. of hosts: 1.05
"Thus says the L. of hosts: Consider 1.07
appear in my glory, says the L. 1.08
says the L. of hosts. 1.09
the voice of the L. their God, 1.12
as the L. their God had sent him; 1.12
the people feared before the L. 1.12
Then Haggai, the messenger of the L., 1.13
message, "I am with you, says the L." 1.13
And the L. stirred up the spirit of 1.14
on the house of the L. of hosts, 1.14
the word of the L. came by Haggai! 2.01
courage, O Zerubbabel, says the L.; 2.04
people of the land, says the L.; 2.04
am with you, says the L. of hosts, 2.04
For thus says the L. of hosts: 2.06
splendor, says the L. of hosts. 2.07
gold is mine, says the L. of hosts. 2.08
the former, says the L. of hosts; 2.09
prosperity, says the L. of hosts.' " 2.09
the word of the L. came by Haggai 2.10
"Thus says the L. of hosts; Ask the 2.11
this nation before me, says the L.; 2.14
a stone in the temple of the L., 2.15
did not return to me, says the L. 2.17
The word of the L. came a second 2.20
says the L. of hosts, I will take 2.23
says the L., and make you like a 2.23
chosen you, says the L.of hosts. 2.23
the word of the L. came to Zechariah Zec 1.01
"The L. was very angry with your 1.02
Thus says the L. of hosts: Return to 1.03
says the L. of hosts, and I will 1.03
to you, says the L. of hosts. 1.03
out, 'Thus says the L. of hosts, 1.04
not hear or heed me, says the L. 1.04
As the L. of hosts purposed to deal 1.06
the word of the L. came to Zechariah 1.07
Then I said, 'What are these, my l.?" 1.09
they whom the L. has sent to 1.10
angel of the L. who was standing 1.11
Then the angel of the L. said, 1.12
'O L. of hosts, how long wilt thou 1.12
And the L. answered gracious and 1.13
Thus says the L. of hosts: I am 1.14
thus says the L., I have returned 1.16
says the L. of hosts, and the 1.16
Thus says the L. of hosts: My cities 1.17
and the L. will again comfort Zion 1.17
Then the L. showed me four smiths. 1.20
says the L., and I will be the 2.05
the land of the north, says the L.; 2.06
winds of the heavens, says the L. 2.06
For thus said the L. of hosts, 2.08
know that the L. of hosts has sent 2.09
in the midst of you, says the L. 2.10
themselves to the L. in that day, 2.11
know that the L. of hosts has sent 2.12
And the L. will inherit Judah as 2.12
Be silent, all flesh, before the L.; 2.13
standing before the angel of the L., 3.01
And the L. said to Satan, "The Lord 3.02
"The L. rebuke you, O Satan! 3.02
The L. who has chosen Jerusalem 3.02
angel of the L. was standing by. 3.05
angel of the L. enjoined Joshua, 3.06
"Thus says the L. of hosts: If you 3.07
says the L. of hosts, and I will 3.09
says the L. of hosts, every one of 3.10
with me, "What are these, my l.?" 4.04
these are?" I said, "No, my l." 4.05
the word of the L. to Zerubbabel: 4.06
by my Spirit, says the L. of hosts. 4.06
Moreover the word of the L. came to me, 4.08
know that the L. of hosts has sent 4.09
"These seven are the eyes of the L., 4.10
These are?" I said, "No, my l." 4.13
stand by the L. of the whole earth." 4.14
says the L. of hosts, and it shall 5.04
with me, "What are these, my l.?" 6.04
before the L. of all the earth. 6.05
And the word of the L. came to me: 6.09
to him, 'Thus says the L. of hosts, 6.12
shall build the temple of the L. 6.12
shall build the temple of the L., 6.13
temple of the L. as a reminder to 6.14
help to build the temple of the L.; 6.15
know that the L. of hosts has sent 6.15
obey the voice of the L. your God." 6.15
the word of the L. came to Zechariah 7.01
to entreat the favor of the L., 7.02
house of the L. of hosts and the 7.03
Then the word of the L. of hosts 7.04
words which the L. proclaimed by 7.07
And the word of the L. came to 7.08
"Thus says the L. of hosts, Render 7.09
words which the L. of hosts had 7.12
wrath came from the L. of hosts. 7.12
not hear," says the L. of hosts, 7.13

LORD (cont.)
And the word of the L. of hosts Zec 8.01
"Thus says the L. of hosts: I am 8.02
Thus says the L.: I will return to 8.03
the mountain of the L. of hosts, 8.03
Thus says the L. of hosts: Old men 8.04
Thus says the L. of hosts: If it is 8.06
in my sight, says the L. of hosts? 8.06
Thus says the L. of hosts: Behold, I 8.07
Thus says the L. of hosts: "Let your 8.09
house of the L. of hosts was laid, 8.09
former days, says the L. of hosts. 8.11
For thus says the L. of hosts: 8.14
not relent, says the L. of hosts, 8.14
these things I hate, says the L." 8.17
And the word of the L. of hosts 8.18
"Thus says the L. of hosts: The fast 8.19
"Thus says the L. of hosts: Peoples 8.20
to entreat the favor of the L., 8.21
and to seek the L. of hosts; 8.21
to seek the L. of hosts in Jerusalem, 8.22
and to entreat the favor of the L. 8.22
Thus says the L. of hosts: In those 8.23
The word of the L. is against the 9.01
For to the L. belong the cities of 9.01
But lo, the L. will strip her of her 9.04
Then the L. will appear over them, 9.14
the L. God will sound the trumpet, 9.14
The L. of hosts will protect them, 9.15
On that day the L. their God will 9.16
Ask rain from the L. in the season 10.01
from the L. who makes the storm 10.01
for the L. of hosts cares for his 10.03
fight because the L. is with them, 10.05
for I am the L. their God and I 10.06
their hearts shall exult in the L. 10.07
strong in the L. and they shall 10.12
glory in his name," says the L. 10.12
Thus said the L. my God: "Become 11.04
sell them say, 'Blessed be the L., 11.05
inhabitants of this land, says the L. 11.06
that it was the word of the L. 11.11
Then the L. said to me, "Cast it 11.13
treasury in the house of the L. 11.13
Then the L. said to me, "Take once 11.15
The word of the L. concerning 12.01
Thus says the L., who stretched out 12.01
says the L., I will strike every 12.04
strength through the L. of hosts, 12.05
"And the L. will give victory to 12.07
On that day the L. will put a 12.08
the angel of the L., at their head. 12.08
says the L. of hosts, I will cut off 13.02
speak lies in the name of the L.'; 13.03
next to me," says the L. of hosts. 13.07
says the L., two thirds shall be 13.08
they will say, 'The L. is my God.'" 13.09
a day of the L. is coming, when the 14.01
Then the L. will go forth and fight 14.03
Then the L. your God will come, and 14.05
continuous day (it is known to the L.), 14.07
And the L. will become king over 14.09
on that day the L. will be one and 14.09
with which the L. will smite all 14.12
panic from the L. shall fall on 14.13
the L. of hosts, and to keep the 14.16
the L. of hosts, there will be no 14.17
with which the L. afflicts the 14.18
of the horses, "Holy to the L." 14.20
house of the L. shall be as the 14.20
shall be sacred to the L. of hosts, 14.21
house of the L. of hosts on that 14.21
the word of the L. to Israel by Mal 1.01
"I have loved you," says the L. 1.02
says the L. "Yet I have loved 1.02
the L. of hosts says, "They may 1.04
with whom the L. is angry for ever." 1.04
"Great is the L., beyond the border 1.05
says the L. of hosts to you, O priests, 1.06
you favor? says the L. of hosts. 1.08
any of you? says the L. of hosts. 1.09
says the L. of hosts, and I will not 1.10
the nations, says the L. of hosts. 1.11
sniff at me, says the L. of hosts. 1.13
says the L. You bring 1.13
sacrifices to the L. what is 1.14
says the L. of hosts, and my name is 1.14
says the L. of hosts, then I will 2.02
may hold, says the L. of hosts. 2.04
the messenger of the L. of hosts. 2.07
of Levi, says the L. of hosts, 2.08
profaned the sanctuary of the L., 2.11
May the L. cut off from the tents 2.12
an offering to the L. of hosts! 2.12
Because the L. was witness to the 2.14
says the L. the God of Israel, and 2.16
violence, says the L. of hosts. 2.16
wearied the L. with your words. 2.17
is good in the sight of the L., 2.17
and the L. whom you seek will 3.01
he is coming, says the L. of hosts. 3.01
present right offerings to the L. 3.03
pleasing to the L. as in the days 3.04
not fear me, says the L. of hosts. 3.05
"For I the L. do not change; 3.06
to you, says the L. of hosts. 3.07
says the L. of hosts, if I will not 3.10
fail to bear, says the L. of hosts. 3.11
of delight, says the L. of hosts. 3.12
been stout against me, says the L. 3.13
in mourning before the L. of hosts? 3.14
who feared the L. spoke with one 3.16
the L. heeded and heard them, and a 3.16
who feared the L. and thought on 3.16
says the L. of hosts, my special 3.17
says the L. of hosts, so that it 4.01
when I act, says the L. of hosts. 4.03
and terrible day of the L. comes. 4.05
an angel of the L. appeared to him Mt 1.20
fulfil what the L. had spoken by 1.22
the angel of the L. commanded him; 1.24
an angel of the L. appeared to 2.13
fulfil what the L. had spoken by 2.15
an angel of the L. appeared in a 2.19
wilderness: Prepare the way of the L., 3.03
shall not tempt the L. your God.'" 4.07
worship the L. your God and him 4.10
perform to the L. what you have 5.33
'L., L.' shall enter the kingdom 7.21
'L., L., did we not prophesy in 7.22
"L., if you will, you can make me 8.02
and saying, "L., my servant is lying 8.06
"L., I am not worthy to have you 8.08
"L., let me first go and bury my 8.21
and woke him, saying, "Save, L.; 8.25
They said to him, "Yes, L." 9.28
pray therefore the L. of the 9.38
L. of heaven and earth, that thou 11.25
Son of man is l. of the sabbath. 12.08
"L., if it is you, bid me come to 14.28
to sink he cried out, "L., save me." 14.30
mercy on me, O L., Son of David; 15.22
before him, saying, "L., help me." 15.25
L., yet even the dogs eat the 15.27
rebuke him, saying, "God forbid, L.! 16.22
"L., it is well that we are here; 17.04
"L., have mercy on my son, for he is 17.15
"L., how often shall my brother sin 18.21
his l. ordered him to be sold, with 18.25
'L., have patience with me, and I 18.26
for him the l. of that servant 18.27
to their l. all that had taken 18.31
Then his l. summoned him and said 18.32
And in anger his l. delivered him 18.34

LORD (cont.)
of the Gentiles l. it over them, Mt 20.25
"L., have mercy on us, Son of David!" 20.31
"L., let our eyes be opened." 20.33
'The L. has need of them,' and he 21.03
he who comes in the name of the L.! 21.09
shall love the L. your God with 22.37
the Spirit, calls him L., saying, 22.43
'The L. said to my L., Sit at my 22.44
If David thus calls him L., 22.45
he who comes in the name of the L. 23.39
know on what day your L. is coming. 24.42
saying 'L., l., open to us.' 25.11
'L., when did we see thee hungry 25.37
'L., when did we see thee hungry or 25.44
him one after another, "Is it I, L.?" 26.22
field, as the L. directed me." 27.10
an angel of the L. descended from 28.02
wilderness: Prepare the way of the L. Mk 1.03
Son of man is l. even of the 2.28
how much the L. has done for you, 5.19
But she answered him, "Yes, L.; 7.28
over the Gentiles l. it over them, 10.42
say, 'The L. has need of it and 11.03
he who comes in the name of the L.! 11.09
The L. our God, the L. is one; 12.29
shall love the L. your God with 12.30
'The L. said to my L., Sit at my 12.36
David himself calls him L.; 12.37
And if the L. had not shortened the 13.20
the L. Jesus, after he had spoken to them, * 16.19
while the L. worked with them and * 16.20
and ordinances of the L. blameless. Lk 1.06
temple of the L. and burn incense. 1.09
an angel of the L. standing on the 1.11
for he will be great before the L., 1.15
of Israel to the L. their God, 1.16
ready for the L. a people prepared." 1.17
"Thus the L. has done to me in the 1.28
O favored one, the L. is with you!" 1.28
and the L. God will give to him the 1.32
"Behold I am the handmaid of the L.; 1.38
mother of my L. should come to me? 1.43
what was spoken to her from the L." 1.45
said, "My soul magnifies the L., 1.46
heard that the L. had shown great 1.58
the hand of the L. was with him. 1.66
"Blessed be the L. God of Israel, 1.68
go before the L. to prepare his 1.76
And an angel of the L. appeared to 2.09
glory of the L. shone around them, 2.09
a Savior, who is Christ the L. 2.11
which the L. has made known to us." 2.15
Jerusalem to present him to the L. 2.22
it is written in the law of the L., 2.23
shall be called holy to the L.") 2.23
what is said in the law of the L., 2.24
"L., now lettest thou thy servant 2.29
according to the law of the L., 2.39
wilderness: Prepare the way of the L., 3.04
'You shall worship the L. your God, 4.08
shall not tempt the L. your God.'" 4.12
"The Spirit of the L. is upon me, 4.18
the acceptable year of the L." 4.19
me, for I am a sinful man, O L." 5.08
"L., if you will, you can make me 5.12
power of the L. was with him to 5.17
Son of man is l. of the sabbath." 6.05
"Why do you call me 'L., L.,' 6.46
"L., do not trouble yourself, for I 7.06
And when the L. saw her, he had 7.13
his disciples, sent them to the L., 7.19
"L., do you want us to bid fire 9.54
"L., let me first go and bury my 9.59
Another said, "I will follow you, L.; 9.61
After this the L. appointed seventy 10.01
therefore the L. of the harvest to 10.02
"L., even the demons are subject to 10.17
L. of heaven and earth, that thou 10.21
shall love the L. your God with 10.27
"L., do you not care that my sister 10.40
But the L. answered her, "Martha, 10.41
"L., teach us to pray, as John 11.01
And the L. said to him, "Now you 11.39
Peter said, "L., are you telling 12.41
And the L. said, "Who then is the 12.42
Then the L. answered him, "You 13.15
"L., will those who are saved be 13.23
the door, saying, 'L., open to us.' 13.25
he who comes in the name of the L.!'" 13.35
The apostles said to the L., 17.05
And the L. said, "If you had faith 17.06
And they said to him, "Where, L.?" 17.37
And the L. said, "Hear what the 18.06
He said, "L., let me receive my 18.41
Zacchaeus stood and said to the L., 19.08
L., the half of my goods I give to 19.08
'L., your pound has made ten pounds 19.16
'L., your pound has made five 19.18
'L., here is your pound, which I 19.20
'L., he has ten pounds!') 19.25
say this, 'The L. has need of it.'" 19.31
And they said, "The L. has need of it." 19.34
who comes in the name of the L.! 19.38
he calls the L. the God of Abraham 20.37
'The L. said to my L., Sit at my 20.42
David thus calls him L.; 20.44
"L., I am ready to go with you to 22.33
L., here are two swords." 22.38
"L., shall we strike with the sword?" 22.49
And the L. turned and looked at 22.61
remembered the word of the L., 22.61
who said, "The L. has risen indeed, 24.34
'Make straight the way of the L.,' Jn 1.23
Now when the L. knew that the 4.01
angel of the L. went down at certain * 5.04
bread after the L. had given 6.23
"L., give us this bread always." 6.34
"L., to whom shall we go 6.68
She said, "No one, L." * 8.11
He said, "L. I believe"; and he 9.38
anointed the L. with ointment and 11.02
"L., he whom you love is ill." 11.03
"L., if he has fallen asleep, he 11.12
"L., if you had been here, my 11.21
She said to him, "Yes, L.; 11.27
"L., if you had been here, my 11.32
They said to him, "L., come and see." 11.34
"L., by this time there will be an 11.39
he who comes in the name of the L., 12.13
"L., who has believed our report, 12.38
the arm of the L. been revealed? 12.38
"L., do you wash my feet?" 13.06
"L., not my feet only but also my 13.09
You call me Teacher and L.; 13.13
your L. and Teacher, have washed 13.14
he said to him, "L., who is it?" 13.25
"L., where are you going?" 13.36
"L., why cannot I follow you now? 13.37
"L., we do not know where you are 14.05
"L., show us the Father, and we 14.08
"L., how is it that you will 14.22
have taken the L. out of the tomb, 20.02
"Because they have taken away my L., 20.13
the disciples, "I have seen the L."; 20.18
were glad when they saw the L. 20.20
told him, "We have seen the L." 20.25
Thomas answered him, "My L. and my God!" 20.28
loved said to Peter, "It is the L.!" 21.07
Peter heard that it was the L., 21.07
are you?" They knew it was the L. 21.12
He said to him, "Yes, L.; you know 21.15
He said to him, "Yes, L.; you know 21.16
"L., you know everything; you know 21.17

LORD (cont.)

“L., who is it that is going to Jn 21.20
“L., what about this man?” 21.21
“L., will you at this time restore Ac 1.06
time that the L. Jesus went in and 1.21
“L., who knowest the hearts of all 1.24
before the day of the L. comes, 2.20
the name of the L. shall be saved.’ 2.21
‘I saw the L. always before me, for 2.25
‘The L. said to my L., Sit at my 2.34
has made him both L. and Christ, 2.36
one whom the L. our God calls to 2.39
And the L. added to their number 2.47
come from the presence of the L., 3.19
‘The L. God will raise up for ycu a 3.22
“Sovereign L., who didst make the 4.24
against the L. and against his 4.26
And now, L., look upon their threats, 4.29
the resurrection of the L. Jesus, 4.33
to tempt the Spirit of the L.? 5.09
believers were added to the L., 5.14
an angel of the L. opened the 5.19
to look, the voice of the L. came, 7.31
And the L. said to him, ‘Take off 7.33
says the L., or what is the place 7.49
“L. Jesus, receive my spirit.” 7.59
“L., do not hold this sin against 7.60
in the name of the L. Jesus. 8.16
of yours, and pray to the L. that, 8.22
answered, “Pray for me to the L., 8.24
and spoken the word of the L., 8.25
But an angel of the L. said to Philip, 8.26
Spirit of the L. caught up Philip; 8.39
against the diciples of the L., 9.01
And he said, “Who are you, L.?” 9.05
The L. said to him in a vision, 9.10
And he said, “Here I am, L.” 9.10
And the L. said to him, “Rise and go 9.11
“L., I have heard from many about 9.13
But the L. said to him, “Go, for he 9.15
the L. Jesus who appeared to you on 9.17
how on the road he had seen the L., 9.27
preaching boldly in the name of the L. 9.29
the fear of the L. and in the 9.31
saw him, and they turned to the L. 9.35
Joppa, and many believed in the L. 9.42
terror, and said, “What is it, L.?” 10.04
But Peter said, “No, L.; for I have 10.14
you have been commanded by the L.” 10.33
by Jesus Christ (he is L. of all), 10.36
L.: for nothing common or unclean 11.08
And I remembered the word of the L., 11.16
we believed in the L. Jesus Christ, 11.17
also, preaching the L. Jesus. 11.20
And the hand of the L. was with them, 11.21
that believed turned to the L. 11.21
faithful to the L. with steadfast 11.23
large company was added to the L. 11.24
an angel of the L. appeared. 12.07
sure that the L. has sent his 12.11
to them how the L. had brought him 12.17
Immediately an angel of the L. smote him, 12.23
were worshiping the L. and fasting, 13.02
the straight paths of the L.? 13.10
the hand of the L. is upon you, 13.11
astonished at the teaching of the L. 13.12
For so the L. has commanded us, 13.47
And the word of the L. spread 13.49
time, speaking boldly for the L., 14.03
them to the L. in whom they 14.23
through the grace of the L. Jesus, 15.11
that the rest of men may seek the L., 15.17
says the L., who has made these 15.18
the sake of our L. Jesus Christ. 15.26
and preaching the word of the L., 15.35
we proclaimed the word of the L., 15.36
brethren to the grace of the L. 15.40
The L. opened her heart to give 16.14
judged me to be faithful to the L., 16.15
they said, “Believe in the L. Jesus, 16.31
the word of the L. to him and to 16.32
being L. of heaven and earth, does 17.24
the synagogue, believed in the L., 18.08
And the L. said to Paul one night 18.09
instructed in the way of the L.; 18.25
in the name of the L. Jesus. 19.05
of Asia heard the word of the L., 19.10
the name of the L. Jesus over 19.13
the name of the L. Jesus was 19.17
So the word of the L. grew and 19.20
serving the L. with all humility 20.19
of faith in our L. Jesus Christ. 20.21
which I received from the L. Jesus, 20.24
church of the L. which he obtained 20.28
remembering the words of the L. Jesus, 20.35
for the name of the L. Jesus. 21.13
said, “The will of the L. be done.” 21.14
And I answered, ‘Who are you, L.?’ 22.08
And I said, ‘What shall I do, L?’ 22.10
And the L. said to me, ‘Rise, and 22.10
And I said, ‘L., they themselves 22.19
night the L. stood by him and said, 23.11
to write to my l. about him. Therefore 25.26
And I said, ‘Who are you, L.?’ 26.15
And the L. said, ‘I am Jesus whom 26.15
about the L. Jesus Christ quite 28.31
the dead, Jesus Christ our L., Rom 1.04
our Father and the L. Jesus Christ. 1.07
whom the L. will not reckon his 4.08
raised from the dead Jesus our L., 4.24
God through our L. Jesus Christ. 5.01
in God through our L. Jesus Christ, 5.11
life through Jesus Christ our L. 5.21
life in Christ Jesus our L. 6.23
to God through Jesus Christ our L.! 7.25
love of God in Christ Jesus our L. 8.39
for the L. will execute his sentence 9.28
“If the L. of hosts had not left us 9.29
that Jesus is L. and believe in 10.09
the same L. is L. of all and 10.12
the name of the L. will be saved. 10.13
“L., who has believed what he has 10.16
“L., they have killed thy prophets, 11.03
“For who has known the mind of the L., 11.34
with the Spirit, serve the L. 12.11
is mine, I will repay, says the L.” 12.19
But put on the L. Jesus Christ, and 13.14
observes it in honor of the L. 14.06
who eats, eats in honor of the L., 14.06
in honor of the L. and gives 14.06
If we live, we live to the L., 14.08
and if we die, we die to the L.; 14.08
he might be L. both of the dead 14.09
says the L., every knee shall bow 14.11
persuaded in the L. Jesus that 14.14
and Father of our L. Jesus Christ. 15.06
“Praise the L., all Gentiles, and 15.11
by our L. Jesus Christ and by the 15.30
her in the L. as befits the saints, 16.02
Greet Ampliatus, my beloved in the L. 16.08
those in the L. who belong to the 16.11
Greet those workers in the L., 16.12
who has worked hard in the L. 16.12
Greet Rufus, eminent in the L., 16.13
persons do not serve our L. Christ, 16.18
grace of our L. Jesus Christ be 16.20
this letter, greet you in the L. 16.22
The grace of our L. Jesus Christ * 16.24
on the name of our L. Jesus Christ, 1Co 1.02
Christ, both their L. and ours: 1.02
our Father and the L. Jesus Christ. 1.03
revealing of our L. Jesus Christ; 1.07
in the day of our L. Jesus Christ. 1.08
of his Son, Jesus Christ our L. 1.09

LORD (cont.)

by the name of our L. Jesus Christ, 1Co 1.10
him who boasts, boast of the L. 1.31
not have crucified the L. of glory. 2.08
the mind of the L. so as to 2.16
as the L. assigned to each. 3.05
"The L. knows that the thoughts of 3.20
It is the L. who judges me. 4.04
before the L. comes, who will bring 4.05
and faithful child in the L., 4.17
if the L. wills, and I will find out 4.19
in the name of the L. Jesus on the 5.04
with the power of our L. Jesus, 5.04
saved in the day of the L. Jesus. 5.05
the name of the L. Jesus Christ 6.11
but for the L., and the L. for 6.13
And God raised the L. and will also 6.14
united to the L. becomes one 6.17
not I but the L., that the wife 7.10
not the L., that if any brother has 7.12
life which the L. has assigned to 7.17
the L. as a slave is a freedman of the L. 7.22
I have no command of the L., 7.25
about the affairs of the L., 7.32
of the Lord, how to please the L.; 7.32
about the affairs of the L., 7.34
your undivided devotion to the L. 7.35
to whom she wishes, only in the L. 7.39
and one L., Jesus Christ, through 8.06
Have I not seen Jesus our L.? 9.01
not you my workmanship in the L.? 9.01
seal of my apostleship in the L. 9.02
the brothers of the L. and Cephas? 9.05
the L. commanded that those who 9.14
We must not put the L. to the test, 10.09
the cup of the L. and the cup of 10.21
table of the L. and the table of 10.21
Shall we provoke the L. to jealousy? 10.22
in the L. woman is not independent 11.11
from the L. what I also delivered 11.23
that the L. Jesus on the night when 11.23
the cup of the L. in an unworthy 11.27
the body and blood of the L. 11.27
But when we are judged by the L., 11.32
say "Jesus is L." except by the 12.03
of service, but the same L.; 12.05
will not listen to me, says the L." 14.21
to you is a command of the L. 14.37
I have in Christ Jesus our L., 15.31
through our L. Jesus Christ. 15.57
abounding in the work of the L., 15.58
that in the L. your labor is not 15.58
time with you, if the L. permits. 16.07
doing the work of the L., as I am. 16.10
you hearty greetings in the L. 16.19
If any one has no love for the L., 16.22
be accursed. Our L., come! 16.22
The grace of the L. Jesus be with 16.23
our Father and the L. Jesus Christ. 2Co 1.02
and Father of our L. Jesus Christ, 1.03
of you, on the day of the L. Jesus. 1.14
Not that we l. it over your faith; 1.24
a door was opened for me in the L.; 2.12
turns to the L. the veil is 3.16
Now the L. is the Spirit, and where 3.17
and where the Spirit of the L. is, 3.17
beholding the glory of the L., 3.18
comes from the L. who is the 3.18
ourselves, but Jesus Christ as L., 4.05
who raised the L. Jesus will raise 4.14
the body we are away from the L., 5.06
the body and at home with the L. 5.08
Therefore, knowing the fear of the L., 5.11
says the L., and touch nothing 6.17
daughters, says the L. Almighty. 6.18
themselves to the L. and to us by 8.05
the grace of our L. Jesus Christ, 8.09
glory of the L. and to show our 8.19
which the L. gave for building you 10.08
"Let him who boasts, boast of the L." 10.17
but the man whom the L. commends. 10.18
The God and Father of the L. Jesus, 11.31
visions and revelations of the L. 12.01
times I besought the L. about this, 12.08
which the L. has given me for 13.10
The grace of the L. Jesus Christ 13.14
Father and our L. Jesus Christ, Gal 1.03
confidence in the L. that you will 5.10
the cross of our L. Jesus Christ, 6.14
The grace of our L. Jesus Christ be 6.18
our Father and the L. Jesus Christ. Eph 1.02
and Father of our L. Jesus Christ, 1.03
faith in the L. Jesus and your 1.15
that the God of our L. Jesus Christ, 1.17
grows into a holy temple in the L.; 2.21
realized in Christ Jesus our L., 3.11
I therefore, a prisoner for the L., 4.01
one L., one faith, one baptism, 4.05
I affirm and testify in the L., 4.17
but now you are light in the L.; 5.08
learn what is pleasing to the L. 5.10
understand what the will of the L. is. 5.17
melody to the L. with all your 5.19
the name of our L. Jesus Christ to 5.20
to your husbands, as to the L. 5.22
Children, obey your parents in the L., 6.01
discipline and instruction of the L. 6.04
will as to the L. and not to men, 6.07
receive the same again from the L., 6.08
strong in the L. and in the 6.10
minister in the L. will tell you 6.21
the Father and the L. Jesus Christ. 6.23
who love our L. Jesus Christ. 6.24
our Father and the L. Jesus Christ. Php 1.02
confident in the L. because of my 1.14
confess that Jesus Christ is L., 2.11
I hope in the L. Jesus to send 2.19
and I trust in the L. that shortly 2.24
receive him in the L. with all joy; 2.29
Finally, my brethren, rejoice in the L. 3.01
of knowing Christ Jesus my L. 3.08
a Savior, the L. Jesus Christ, 3.20
firm thus in the L., my beloved. 4.01
Syntyche to agree in the L. 4.02
Rejoice in the L. always; again I will 4.04
forbearance. The L. is at hand. 4.05
I rejoice in the L. greatly that 4.10
The grace of the L. Jesus Christ be 4.23
the Father of our L. Jesus Christ, Col 1.03
to lead a life worthy of the L., 1.10
you received Christ Jesus the L., 2.06
as the L. has forgiven you, so you 3.13
in the name of the L. Jesus, 3.17
husbands, as is fitting in the L. 3.18
everything, for this pleases the L. 3.20
singleness of heart, fearing the L. 3.22
as serving the L. and not men, 3.23
knowing that from the L. you will 3.24
you are serving the L. Christ. 3.24
and fellow servant in the L. 4.07
which you have received in the L. 4.17
the Father and the L. Jesus Christ: 1Th 1.01
of hope in our L. Jesus Christ. 1.03
imitators of us and of the L., 1.06
the word of the L. sounded forth 1.08
who killed both the L. Jesus and 2.15
before our L. Jesus at his coming? 2.19
live, if you stand fast in the L. 3.08
and our L. Jesus, direct our way to 3.11
and may the L. make you increase 3.12
coming of our L. Jesus with all 3.13
and exhort you in the L. Jesus, 4.01
we gave you through the L. Jesus. 4.02
because the L. is an avenger in all 4.06

LORD (cont.)

to you by the word of the L. 1Th 4.15
left until the coming of the L., 4.15
For the L. himself will descend 4.16
clouds to meet the L. in the air; 4.17
so we shall always be with the L. 4.17
the day of the L. will come like a 5.02
through our L. Jesus Christ, 5.09
over you in the L. and admonish 5.12
the coming of our L. Jesus Christ. 5.23
you by the L. that this letter be 5.27
The grace of our L. Jesus Christ be 5.28
Father and the L. Jesus Christ: 2Th 1.01
the Father and the L. Jesus Christ. 1.02
when the L. Jesus is revealed from 1.07
obey the gospel of our L. Jesus. 1.08
presence of the L. and from the 1.09
the name of our L. Jesus may be 1.12
of our God and the L. Jesus Christ. 1.12
coming of our L. Jesus Christ and 2.01
that the day of the L. has come. 2.02
and the L. Jesus will slay him with 2.08
you, brethren beloved by the L., 2.13
the glory of our L. Jesus Christ. 2.14
Now may our L. Jesus Christ himself, 2.16
the word of the L. may speed on 3.01
But the L. is faithful; he will 3.03
confidence in the L. about you, 3.04
May the L. direct your hearts to 3.05
in the name of our L. Jesus Christ, 3.06
exhort in the L. Jesus Christ to 3.12
Now may the L. of peace himself 3.16
in all ways. The L. be with you all. 3.16
The grace of our L. Jesus Christ be 3.18
the Father and Christ Jesus our L. 1Ti 1.02
for this, Christ Jesus our L., 1.12
grace of our L. overflowed for me 1.14
words of our L. Jesus Christ and 6.03
appearing of our L. Jesus Christ; 6.14
the King of kings and L. of lords, 6.15
the Father and Christ Jesus our L. 2Ti 1.02
then of testifying to our L., 1.08
May the L. grant mercy to the 1.16
may the L. grant him to find mercy 1.18
mercy from the L. on that Day— 1.18
for the L. will grant you understanding 2.07
them before the L. to avoid 2.14
"The L. knows those who are his," 2.19
the name of the L. depart from 2.19
call upon the L. from a pure heart. 2.22
from them all the L. rescued me. 3.11
which the L., the righteous judge, 4.08
the L. will requite him for his 4.14
But the L. stood by me and gave me 4.17
The L. will rescue me from every 4.18
The L. be with your spirit. 4.22
our Father and the L. Jesus Christ. Phm 1.03
have toward the L. Jesus and all 1.05
both in the flesh and in the L. 1.16
some benefit from you in the L. 1.20
The grace of the L. Jesus Christ be 1.25
And, "Thou, L., didst found the earth Heb 1.10
It was declared at first by the L., 2.03
that our L. was descended from 7.14
"The L. has sworn and will not 7.21
is set up not by man but by the L. 8.02
says the L., when I will establish 8.08
paid no heed to them, says the L. 8.09
says the L.: I will put my laws into 8.10
'Know the L.,' for all shall know 8.11
says the L.: I will put my laws on 10.16
"The L. will judge his people." 10.30
lightly the discipline of the L., 12.05
For the L. disciplines him whom he 12.06
which no one will see the L. 12.14
"The L. is my helper, I will not be 13.06
again from the dead our L. Jesus, 13.20
of God and of the L. Jesus Christ, Jas 1.01
will receive anything from the L. 1.07
the faith of our L. Jesus Christ, 2.01
Lord Jesus Christ, the L. of glory. 2.01
With it we bless the L. and Father, 3.09
before the L. and he will exalt 4.10
"If the L. wills, we shall live and 4.15
the ears of the L. of hosts. 5.04
brethren, until the coming of the L. 5.07
the coming of the L. is at hand. 5.08
who spoke in the name of the L. 5.10
have seen the purpose of the L., 5.11
how the L. is compassionate and 5.11
him with oil in the name of the L. 5.14
and the L. will raise him up; 5.15
and Father and our L. Jesus Christ! 1Pe 1.03
but the word of the L. abides for 1.25
have tasted the kindness of the L. 2.03
obeyed Abraham, calling him l. 3.06
For the eyes of the L. are upon the 3.12
the face of the L. is against 3.12
your hearts reverence Christ as L. 3.15
knowledge of God and of Jesus our L. 2Pe 1.02
knowledge of our L. Jesus Christ. 1.08
kingdom of our L. and Savior Jesus 1.11
as our L. Jesus Christ showed me. 1.14
and coming of our L. Jesus Christ, 1.16
then the L. knows how to rescue the 2.09
judgment upon them before the L. 2.11
knowledge of our L. and Savior 2.20
commandment of the L. and Savior 3.02
that with the L. one day is as a 3.08
The L. is not slow about his 3.09
But the day of the L. will come 3.10
forbearance of our L. as salvation. 3.15
knowledge of our L. and Savior 3.18
only Master and L., Jesus Christ. Jud 1.04
him, but said, "The L. rebuke you." 1.09
the L. came with his holy myriads, 1.14
apostles of our L. Jesus Christ; 1.17
mercy of our L. Jesus Christ unto 1.21
Savior through Jesus Christ our L., 1.25
says the L. God, who is and who Rev 1.08
is the L. God Almighty, who was and 4.08
our L. and God, to receive glory and 4.11
"O Sovereign L., holy and true, how 6.10
stand before the L. of the earth. 11.04
where their L. was crucified. 11.08
kingdom of our L. and of his 11.15
L. God almighty, who art and who 11.17
dead who die in the L. henceforth. 14.13
O L. God the Almighty! Just and true 15.03
fear and glorify thy name, O L.? 15.04
L. God the Almighty, true and just 16.07
for he is L. of lords and King of 17.14
mighty is the L. God who judges 18.08
For the L. our God the Almighty 19.06
King and kings and L. of lords. 19.16
temple is the L. God the Almighty 21.22
for the L. God will be their light, 22.05
And the L., the God of the spirits 22.06
soon." Amen. Come, L. Jesus! 22.20
The grace of the L. Jesus be with 22.21

LORDED

their servants l. it over the Neh 5.15

LORDLY

she brought him curds in a l. bowl. Ju 5.25
the l. price at which I was paid Zec 11.13

LORD'S

silver or gold from your l. house? Gen 44.08
and we also will be my l. slaves. 44.09
we are my l. slaves, both we and he 44.16
you, speak a word in my l. ears, 44.18
and the herds of cattle are my l.; 47.18
may know that the earth is the L. Ex 9.29

LORD'S (cont.)
it in haste. It is the L. passover. Ex 12.11
the sacrifice of the L. passover, 12.27
that are males shall be the L. 13.12
upward, shall give the L. offering. 30.14
you give the L. offering to make 30.15
and said, "Who is on the L. side? 32.26
let him bring the L. offering: 35.05
and brought the L. offering to be 35.21
brought it as the L. offering; 35.24
pleasing odor. All fat is the L. Lev 3.16
from the L. offerings by fire; 6.18
sacrifice of the L. peace offerings 7.20
sacrifice of the L. peace offerings, 7.21
to offer the L. offerings by fire; 21.21
in the evening, is the L. passover. 23.05
whether ox or sheep, it is the L. 27.26
the fruit of the trees, is the L.; 27.30
offering the L. offering at its Num 9.07
not offer the L. offering at its 9.13
to Moses, "Is the L. hand shortened? 11.23
that all the L. people were 11.29
shall give the L. offering to 18.28
the first month is the L. passover. 28.16
to execute the L. vengeance on 31.03
and the L. tribute of sheep was six 31.37
of which the L. tribute was seventy-two 31.38
of which the L. tribute was sixty-one 31.39
of which the L. tribute was thirty-two 31.40
And we have brought the L. offering, 31.50
And the L. anger was kindled on 32.10
And the L. anger was kindled 32.13
because the L. release has been Deu 15.02
For the L. portion is his people, 32.09
commander of the L. army said to Jos 5.15
For it was the L. doing to harden 11.20
over into the L. land where the 22.19
land where the L. tabernacle 22.19
shall be the L., and I will offer Ju 11.31
pillars of the earth are the L., 1Sa 2.08
"Surely the L. anointed is before 16.06
battle is the L. and he will give 17.47
for me and fight the L. battles. 18.17
the L. anointed, and put forth my 24.06
him, seeing he is the L. anointed." 24.06
for he is the L. anointed.' 24.10
his hand against the L. anointed, 26.09
my hand against the L. anointed; 26.11
over your lord, the L. anointed. 26.16
my hand against the L. anointed. 26.23
hand to destroy the L. anointed?" 2Sa 1.14
'I have slain the L. anointed.'" 1.16
because he cursed the L. anointed?" 19.21
take your l. servants and pursue 20.06
men of the L. prophets by fifties 1Ki 18.13
that they should be the L. people; 2Ki 11.17
"The L. arrow of victory, the arrow 13.17
king, all of them my l. servants? 1Ch 21.03
of the LORD filled the L. house. 2Ch 7.02
that they should be the L. people. 23.16
the L. throne is in heaven; Ps 11.04
The earth is the L. and the fulness 24.01
The heavens are the L. heavens, 115.16
This is the L. doing; it is 118.23
we sing the L. song in a foreign 137.04
not despise the L. discipline or Pro 3.11
The L. curse is on the house of the 3.33
just balance and scales are the L.; 16.11
them in the L. land as male and Is 14.02
from the L. hand double for all 40.02
'I am the L.,' another will call 44.05
'The L.,' and surname himself by 44.05
Behold, the L. hand is not shortened, 59.01
to proclaim the year of the L. favor, 61.02
branches, for they are not the L. Jer 5.10
"Stand in the gate of the L. house, 7.02
because the L. flock has been taken 13.17
stood in the court of the L. house, 19.14
So I took the cup from the L. hand, 25.17
Stand in the court of the L. house, 26.02
vessels of the L. house will now 27.16
all the vessels of the L. house, 28.03
people of the L. house you shall 36.06
words of the LORD in the L. house. 36.08
of the New Gate of the L. house. 36.10
is the time of the L. vengeance, 51.06
Babylon was a golden cup in the L. hand, 51.07
for the L. purposes against Babylon 51.29
the holy places of the L. house.' 51.51
the L. anointed, was taken in their Lam 4.20
How can my l. servant talk with my Dan 10.17
and the kingdom shall be the L. Ob 1.21
The cup in the L. right hand will Hab 2.16
And on the day of the L. sacrifice— Zep 1.08
to the people with the L. message, Hag 1.13
foundation of the L. temple was 2.18
that the L. table may be despised. Mal 1.07
say that the L. table is polluted, 1.12
You cover the L. altar with tears, 2.13
this was the L. doing, and it is Mt 21.42
this was the L. doing, and it is Mk 12.11
before he had seen the L. Christ. Lk 2.26
who sat at the L. feet and listened 10.39
or whether we die, we are the L. Rom 14.08
one who by the L. mercy is trustworthy. 1Co 7.25
For "the earth is the L., and everything 10.26
it is not the L. supper that you 11.20
proclaim the L. death until he 11.26
not only in the L. sight but also 2Co 8.21
not with the L. authority but as a 11.17
except James the L. brother. Gal 1.19
And the L. servant must not be 2Ti 2.24
Be subject for the L. sake to every 1Pe 2.13
I was in the Spirit on the L. day, Rev 1.10

LORDS
and said, "My l., turn aside, I pray Gen 19.02
And Lot said to them, "Oh, no, my l.; 19.18
the l. of the heights of the Arnon. Num 21.28
God is God of gods and Lord of l., Deu 10.17
the five l. of the Philistines, and Ju 3.03
And the l. of the Philistines came 16.05
Then the l. of the Philistines 16.08
and called the l. of the Philistines, 16.18
Then the l. of the Philistines came 16.18
Now the l. of the Philistines 16.23
all the l. of the Philistines were 16.27
fell upon the l. and upon all the 16.30
together all the l. of the Philistines, 1Sa 5.08
together all the l. of the Philistines, 5.11
number of the l. of the Philistines, 6.04
upon all of you and upon your l. 6.04
and the l. of the Philistines went 6.12
And when the five l. of the Philistines 6.16
Philistines belonging to the five l., 6.18
the l. of the Philistines went up 7.07
As the l. of the Philistines were 29.02
Nevertheless the l. do not approve 29.06
displease the l. of the Philistines." 29.07
counselors and his l. and all Ez 8.25
O give thanks to the Lord of l., Ps 136.03
while man l. it over man to his Ecc 8.09
the l. of the nations have struck Is 16.08
other l. besides thee have ruled 26.13
you l. of the flock, for the days of Jer 25.34
nor escape for the l. of the flock. 25.35
the wail of the l. of the flock! 25.36
counselors and my l. sought me, Dan 4.36
feast for a thousand of his l., 5.01
brought, that the king and his l., 5.02
and the king and his l., 5.03
and his l. were perplexed. 5.09
the words of the king and his l., 5.10
and you and your l., 5.23

LORDS (cont.)
and with the signet of his l., Dan 6.17
are many "gods" and many "l."— 1Co 8.05
the King of kings and Lord of l., 1Ti 6.15
he is Lord of l. and King of kings, Rev 17.14
King of kings and Lord of l. 19.16

LORDSHIP
the Gentiles exercise l. over them; Lk 22.25

LOSE
and you l. your life with the lives Ju 18.25
and not l. some of the animals. 1Ki 18.05
a time to seek, and a time to l.; Ecc 3.06
she will not l. sight of all that I Zep 3.07
better that you l. one of your Mt 5.29
better that you l. one of your 5.30
He who finds his life will l. it, 10.39
to you, he shall not l. his reward." 10.42
would save his life will l. it, 16.25
would save his life will l. it; Mk 8.35
will by no means l. his reward. 9.41
would save his life will l. it; Lk 9.24
Whoever seeks to gain his life will l. it, 17.33
always to pray and not l. heart. 18.01
that I should l. nothing of all Jn 6.39
mercy of God, we do not l. heart. 2Co 4.01
So we do not l. heart. Though our 4.16
shall reap, if we do not l. heart. Gal 6.09
ask you not to l. heart over what Eph 3.13
nor l. courage when you are punished Heb 12.05
lawless men and l. your own 2Pe 3.17
you may not l. what you have 2Jn 1.08

LOSES
brother's, which he l. and you find; Deu 22.03
and he who l. his life for my sake Mt 10.39
and whoever l. his life for my sake 16.25
and whoever l. his life for my sake Mk 8.35
and whoever l. his life for my sake, Lk 9.24
whole world and l. or forfeits 9.25
if she l. one coin, does not light a 15.08
but whoever l. his life will 17.33
He who loves his life l. it, Jn 12.25

LOSS
I bore the l. of it myself; Gen 31.39
shall pay for the l. of his time, Ex 21.19
till they were utterly at a l.; Ju 3.25
compared with the l. to the king. Est 7.04
widow or know the l. of children"; Is 47.08
the l. of children and widowhood 47.09
that the king might suffer no l. Dan 6.02
Being at a l. how to investigate Ac 25.20
will be with injury and much l., 27.10
and incurred this injury and l. 27.21
will be no l. of life among you, 27.22
is burned up, he will suffer l., 1Co 3.15
that you suffered no l. through us. 2Co 7.09
I counted as l. for the sake of Php 3.07
everything as l. because of the 3.08
have suffered the l. of all things, 3.08

LOST
or for any kind of l. thing. Ex 22.09
found what was l. and lied about Lev 6.03
or the l. thing which he found, 6.04
do with any l. thing of your Deu 22.03
of the Danites was l. to them, Jos 19.47
of Kish, Saul's father, were l. 1Sa 9.03
asses that were l. three days ago, 9.20
Foreigners l. heart, and came 2Sa 22.46
like the army that you have l., 1Ki 20.25
way of escape will be l. to them, Job 11.20
Foreigners l. heart, and came Ps 18.45
I have gone astray like a l. sheep; 119.176
of his great folly he is l. Pro 5.23
riches were l. in a bad venture; Ecc 5.14
but the memory of them is l. 9.05
For I am l.; for I am a man Is 6.05
those who were l. in the land of 27.13
"My people have been l. sheep; Jer 50.06
over my head; I said, 'I am l.' Lam 3.54
was baffled, that her hope was l., Eze 19.05
the l. you have not sought, and with 34.04
I will seek the l., and I will bring 34.16
are dried up, and our hope is l.; 37.11
but if salt has l. its taste, Mt 5.13
rather to the l. sheep of the 10.06
only to the l. sheep of the house 15.24
Son of man came to save the l. * 18.11
the skins, and the wine is l., Mk 2.22
if the salt has l. its saltness, 9.50
but if salt has l. its taste, Lk 14.34
if he has l. one of them, does not 15.04
and go after the one which is l., 15.04
I have found my sheep which was l.' 15.06
have found the coin which I had l.' 15.09
he was l., and is found.' And they began 15.24
and is alive; he was l., and is found.'" 15.32
came to seek and to save the l. 19.10
left over, that nothing may be l. Jn 6.12
none of them is l. but the son of 17.12
whom thou gavest me I l. not one." 18.09
As much time had been l., Ac 27.09
and thy splendor are l. to thee, Rev 18.14

LOT
and Haran was the father of L. Gen 11.27
his son and L. the son of Haran, 11.31
and L. went with him. Abram was 12.04
and L. his brother's son, and all 12.05
and L. with him, into the Negeb. 13.01
And L., who went with Abram, also 13.05
Then Abram said to L., "Let there be 13.08
And L. lifted up his eyes, and saw 13.10
So L. chose for himself all the 13.11
valley, and L. journeyed east; 13.11
while L. dwelt among the cities of 13.12
after L. had separated from him, 13.14
they also took L., the son of 14.12
back his kinsman L. with his goods, 14.16
and L. was sitting in the gate of 19.01
When L. saw them, he rose to meet 19.01
and they called to L., "Where are the 19.05
L. went out of the door to the men, 19.06
pressed hard against the man L., 19.09
and brought L. into the house to 19.10
Then the men said to L., "Have you 19.12
So L. went out and said to his 19.14
dawned, the angels urged L., 19.15
And L. said to them, "Oh, no, my lords, 19.18
on the earth when L. came to Zoar. 19.23
and sent L. out of the midst of the 19.29
the cities in which L. dwelt. 19.29
Now L. went out of Zoar, and 19.30
daughters of L. were with child by 19.36
one l. for the LORD and the other Lev 16.08
LORD and the other l. for Azazel. 16.08
on which the l. fell for the LORD, 16.09
on which the l. fell for Azazel 16.10
But the land shall be divided by l.; Num 26.55
according to l. between the larger 26.56
the land by l. according to your 33.54
wherever the l. falls to any man, 33.54
land which you shall inherit by l., 34.13
inheritance by l. to the people of 36.02
away from the l. of our inheritance. 36.03
to the sons of L. for a possession.' Deu 2.09
to the sons of L. for a possession.' 2.19
Their inheritance was by l., Jos 14.02
The l. for the tribe of the people 15.01
me but one l. and one portion as 17.14
you shall not have one l. only, 17.17
The l. of the tribe of Benjamin 18.11
The second l. came our for Simeon, 19.01
The third l. came up for the tribe 19.10

LOT (cont.)
The fourth l. came our for Issachar, Jos 19.17
The fifth l. came out for the tribe 19.24
The sixth l. came out for the tribe 19.32
The seventh l. came out for the 19.40
distributed by l. at Shiloh before 19.51
The l. came out for the families of 21.04
received by l. from the tribes of 21.04
received by l. from the families 21.05
received by l. from the families 21.06
Israel gave by l. to the Levites, 21.08
since the l. fell to them first. 21.10
we will go up against it by l., Ju 20.09
tribe of Benjamin was taken by l. 1Sa 10.20
of the Matrites was taken by l.; 10.21
the son of Kish was taken by l. 10.21
"Cast the l. between me and my son 14.42
Kohathites, for theirs was the l., 1Ch 6.54
were given by l. out of the family 6.61
gave them by l. out of the tribes 6.65
They organized them by l., all alike, 24.05
The first l. fell to Jehoiarib, the 24.07
The first l. fell for Asaph to 25.09
The l. for the east fell to Shelemiah 26.14
and his l. came out for the north. 26.14
that is the l., before Haman day Est 3.07
that is the l., to crush and 9.24
and my cup; thou holdest my l. Ps 16.05
strong arm of the children of L. 83.08
throw in your l. among us, we will Pro 1.14
The l. is cast into the lap, but the 16.33
The l. puts an end to disputes and 18.18
enjoy his work, for that is his l.; Ecc 3.22
has given him, for this is his l. 5.18
to accept his l. and find enjoyment 5.19
and the l. of those who plunder us. Is 17.14
He has cast the l. for them, 34.17
they, they, are your l.; to them 57.06
you shall rejoice in your l.; 61.07
This is your l., the portion I have Jer 13.25
hand comes the l. for Jerusalem, Eze 21.22
let his l. be with the beasts in Dan 4.15
and let his l. be with the beasts 4.23
and the l. fell upon Jonah. Jon 1.07
the line by l. in the assembly of Mic 2.05
This shall be their l. in return Zep 2.10
fell to him by l. to enter the Lk 1.09
Likewise as it was in the days of L.— 17.28
but on the day when L. went out 17.29
and the l. fell on Matthias; Ac 1.26
neither part nor l. in this matter, 8.21
know that this is to be our l. 1Th 3.03
and if he rescued righteous L., 2Pe 2.07
their l. shall be in the lake that Rev 21.08

LOTAN
L., Shobal, Zibeon, Anah, Gen 36.20
The sons of L. were Jori and Heman; 36.22
the chiefs of L., Shobal, Zibeon, Anah, 36.29
L., Shobal, Zibeon, Anah, Dishon, Ezer, 1Ch 1.38
The sons of L.: Hori and Homam; 1.39

LOTAN'S
and L. sister was Timna. Gen 36.22
and L. sister was Timna. 1Ch 1.39

LOT'S
and the herdsmen of L. cattle. Gen 13.07
But L. wife behind him looked back, 19.26
Remember L. wife. Lk 17.32

LOTS
shall cast l. upon the two goats, Lev 16.08
and I will cast l. for you here Jos 18.06
and I will cast l. for you here 18.08
and Joshua cast l. for them in 18.10
cast l., just as their brethren the 1Ch 24.31
And they cast l. for their duties, 25.08
and they cast l. by fathers' houses, 26.13
They cast l. also for his son 26.14
We have likewise cast l., Neh 10.34
the people cast l. to bring one 11.01
You would even cast l. over the Job 6.27
and for my raiment they cast l. Ps 22.18
and have cast l. for my people, and Joe 3.03
gates and cast l. for Jerusalem, Ob 1.11
let us cast l., that we may know on Jon 1.07
So they cast l., and the lot fell 1.07
for her honored men l. were cast, Nah 3.10
garments among them by casting l.; Mt 27.35
casting l. for them, to decide what Mk 15.24
And they cast l. to divide his Lk 23.34
but cast l. for it to see whose it Jn 19.24
and for my clothing they cast l. 19.24
And they cast l. for them, and Ac 1.26

LOTUS
Under the l. plants he lies, in the Job 40.21
For his shade the l. trees cover 40.22

LOUD
and I cried out with a l. voice; Gen 39.14
and a very l. trumpet blast, so that Ex 19.16
send abroad the l. trumpet on the Lev 25.09
the congregation raised a l. cry; Num 14.01
the deep gloom, with a l. voice; Deu 5.22
the men of Israel with a l. voice: 27.14
"Then l. beat the horses' hoofs Ju 5.22
she cried out with a l. voice; 1Sa 28.12
and the king cried with a l. voice, 2Sa 19.04
of Israel with a l. voice, saying, 1Ki 8.55
called out in a l. voice in the 2Ki 18.28
and made l. music on harps and 1Ch 15.28
oath to the LORD with a l. voice, 2Ch 15.14
of Israel, with a very l. voice. 20.19
it with a l. voice in the language 32.18
wept with a l. voice when they saw Ez 3.12
assembly answered with a l. voice, 10.12
cried with a l. voice to the LORD Neh 9.04
wailing with a l. and bitter cry; Est 4.01
on the strings, with l. shouts. Ps 33.03
shout to God with l. songs of joy! 47.01
Because of my l. groaning my bones 102.05
praise him with l. clashing cymbals 150.05
She is l. and wayward, her feet do Pro 7.11
his neighbor with a l. voice, 27.14
called out in a l. voice in the Is 36.13
cry in my ears with a l. voice, Eze 8.18
cried in my ears with a l. voice, 9.01
my face, and cried with a l. voice, 11.13
a l. crash from the hills. Zep 1.10
exult over you with l. singing 3.17
wailing and l. lamentation, Rachel Mt 2.18
his angels with a l. trumpet call, 24.31
hour Jesus cried with a l. voice, 27.46
again with a l. voice and yielded 27.50
him and crying with a l. voice, Mk 1.26
and crying out with a l. voice, 5.07
hour Jesus cried with a l. voice, 15.34
And Jesus uttered a l. cry, 15.37
and she exclaimed with a l. cry, Lk 1.42
and he cried out with a l. voice, 4.33
him, and said with a l. voice, 8.28
back, praising God with a l. voice; 17.15
God with a l. voice for all the 19.37
demanding with l. cries that he 23.23
crying with a l. voice, said, "Father, 23.46
this, he cried with a l. voice, Jn 11.43
out with a l. voice and stopped Ac 7.57
down and cried with a l. voice, 7.60
possessed, crying with a l. voice; 8.07
said in a l. voice, 'Stand upright 14.10
But Paul cried with a l. voice, 16.28
Festus said with a l. voice, 26.24
with l. cries and tears, to him who Heb 5.07
For, uttering l. boats of folly, 2Pe 2.18

LOUD (cont.)
will pass away with a l. noise, 2Pe 3.10
behind me a l. voice like a Rev 1.10
angel proclaiming with a l. voice, 5.02
saying with a l. voice, "Worthy is 5.12
they cried out with a l. voice, 6.10
called with a l. voice to the four 7.02
and crying out with a l. voice, 7.10
l. noises, flashes of lightning, and 8.05
an eagle crying with a l. voice, 8.13
and called out with a l. voice, 10.03
Then they heard a l. voice from 11.12
and there were l. voices in heaven, 11.15
l. noises, peals of thunder, an 11.19
And I heard a l. voice in heaven, 12.10
and like the sound of l. thunder; 14.02
and he said with a l. voice, 14.07
saying with a l. voice, "If any one 14.09
calling with a l. voice to him who 14.15
called with a l. voice to him who 14.18
Then I heard a l. voice from the 16.01
l. noises, peals of thunder, and a 16.18
and with a l. voice he called to 19.17

LOUDER
of the trumpet grew l. and l., Ex 19.19

LOUDLY
who should play l. on musical 1Ch 15.16
against him, they have roared l. Jer 2.15
and people weeping and wailing l. Mk 5.38

LOUD-MOUTHED
l. boasters, flattering people to Jud 1.16

LOVE
whom you l., and go to the land of Gen 22.02
show steadfast l. to my master 24.12
shown steadfast l. to my master." 24.14
his steadfast l. and his faithfulness 24.27
such as I l., and bring it to me 27.04
because of the l. he had for her. 29.20
surely now my husband will l. me." 29.32
the steadfast l. and all the 32.10
Joseph and showed him steadfast l., 39.21
thy steadfast l. the people whom Ex 15.13
steadfast l. to thousands of those 20.06
of those who l. me and keep my 20.06
'I l. my master, my wife, and my 21.05
in steadfast l. and faithfulness, 34.06
keeping steadfast l. for thousands, 34.07
but you shall l. your neighbor as Lev 19.18
and you shall l. him as yourself; 19.34
and abounding in steadfast l., Num 14.18
the greatness of thy steadfast l., 14.19
steadfast l. to thousands of those Deu 5.10
of those who l. me and keep my 5.10
and you shall l. the LORD your God 6.05
LORD set his l. upon you and chose 7.07
and steadfast l. with those who 7.09
with those who l. him and keep his 7.09
the steadfast l. which he swore to 7.12
he will l. you, bless you, and 7.13
to l. him, to serve the LORD your 10.12
his heart in l. upon your fathers 10.15
L. the sojourner therefore; 10.19
"You shall therefore l. the LORD 11.01
to l. the LORD your God, and to 11.13
whether you l. the LORD your God 13.03
that you will l. the LORD your God 30.06
to l. the LORD your God, and to walk Jos 22.05
therefore, to l. the LORD your God. 23.11
"You only hate me, you do not l. me; Ju 14.16
'I l. you,' when your heart is not 16.15
you, and all his servants l. you; 1Sa 18.22
show me the loyal l. of the LORD, 20.14
swear again by his l. for him; 20.17
your l. to me was wonderful, passing 2Sa 1.26
wonderful, passing the l. of women. 1.26
show steadfast l. and faithfulness 2.06
not take my steadfast l. from him, 7.15
"I l. Tamar, my brother Absalom's 13.04
than the l. with which he had 13.15
show steadfast l. and faithfulness 15.20
because you l. those who hate you 19.06
hate you and hate those who l. you. 19.06
shows steadfast l. to his anointed, 22.51
and steadfast l. to thy servant 1Ki 3.06
him this great and steadfast l., 3.06
steadfast l. to thy servants who 8.23
Solomon clung to these in l. 11.02
his steadfast l. endures for ever! 1Ch 16.34
his steadfast l. endures for ever. 16.41
not take my steadfast l. from him, 17.13
and steadfast l. to David my 2Ch 1.08
his steadfast l. endures for ever," 5.13
steadfast l. to thy servants who 6.14
thy steadfast l. for David thy 6.42
his steadfast l. endures for ever." 7.03
his steadfast l. endures for ever— 7.06
the wicked and l. those who hate 19.02
his steadfast l. endures for ever." 20.21
his steadfast l. endures for ever Ez 3.11
his steadfast l. before the king 7.28
his steadfast l. before the kings 9.09
and steadfast l. with those who Neh 1.05
with those who l. him and keep his 1.05
and abounding in steadfast l., 9.17
keepest covenant and steadfast l., 9.32
the greatness of thy steadfast l. 13.22
granted me life and steadfast l.; Job 10.12
or for l., he causes it to happen. 37.13
they the pinions and plumage of l.? 39.13
How long will you l. vain words, Ps 4.02
thy steadfast l. will enter thy 5.07
that those who l. thy name may 5.11
for the sake of thy steadfast l. 6.04
I have trusted in thy steadfast l.; 13.05
Wondrously show thy steadfast l., 17.07
I l. thee, O LORD, my strength. 18.01
shows steadfast l. to his anointed, 18.50
the steadfast l. of the Most High 21.07
O LORD, and of thy steadfast l., 25.06
to thy steadfast l. remember me, 25.07
are steadfast l. and faithfulness, 25.10
For thy steadfast l. is before my 26.03
O LORD, I l. the habitation of thy 26.08
and be glad for thy steadfast l., 31.07
save me in thy steadfast l.! 31.16
his steadfast l. to me when I was 31.21
L. the LORD, all you his saints! The 31.23
but steadfast l. surrounds him who 32.10
of the steadfast l. of the LORD. 33.05
who hope in his steadfast l., 33.18
Let thy steadfast l., O LORD, 33.22
Thy steadfast l., O LORD, extends to 36.05
precious is thy steadfast l., O God! 36.07
thy steadfast l. to those who know 36.10
thy steadfast l. and thy faithfulness 40.10
thy steadfast l. and thy faithfulness 40.11
may those who l. thy salvation say 40.16
the LORD commands his steadfast l.; 42.08
for the sake of thy steadfast l.! 44.26
you l. righteousness and hate 45.07
We have thought of thy steadfast l., 48.09
God, according to thy steadfast l.; 51.01
You l. evil more than good, and 52.03
You l. all words that devour, O 52.04
the steadfast l. of God for ever 52.08
his steadfast l. and his faithfulness! 57.03
For thy steadfast l. is great to 57.10
in his steadfast l. will meet me; 59.10
of thy steadfast l. in the morning. 59.16
the God who shows me steadfast l. 59.17
bid steadfast l. and faithfulness 61.07

LOVE (cont.)
thee, O Lord, belongs steadfast l. Ps 62.12
Because thy steadfast l. is better 63.03
removed his steadfast l. from me! 66.20
of thy steadfast l. answer me. 69.13
LORD, for thy steadfast l. is good; 69.16
and those who l. his name shall 69.36
May those who l. thy salvation say 70.04
Has his steadfast l. for ever 77.08
Show us thy steadfast l., 85.07
Steadfast l. and faithfulness will 85.10
in steadfast l. to all who call on 86.05
is thy steadfast l. toward me; 86.13
in steadfast l. and faithfulness. 86.15
Is thy steadfast l. declared in the 88.11
I will sing of thy steadfast l., 89.01
For thy steadfast l. was established 89.02
steadfast l. and faithfulness go 89.14
my steadfast l. shall be with him, 89.24
My steadfast l. I will keep for him 89.28
remove from him my steadfast l., 89.33
Lord, where is thy steadfast l. of old, 89.49
the morning with thy steadfast l., 90.14
Because he cleaves to me in l., 91.14
thy steadfast l. in the morning, 92.02
"My foot slips," thy steadfast l., 94.18
his steadfast l. and faithfulness 98.03
his steadfast l. endures for ever, 100.05
you with steadfast l. and mercy, 103.04
and abounding in steadfast l. 103.08
his steadfast l. toward those who 103.11
But the steadfast l. of the LORD is 103.17
his steadfast l. endures for ever! 106.01
the abundance of thy steadfast l., 106.07
the abundance of his steadfast l. 106.45
his steadfast l. endures for ever! 107.01
the LORD for his steadfast l., 107.08
the LORD for his steadfast l., 107.15
the LORD for his steadfast l., 107.21
the LORD for his steadfast l., 107.31
the steadfast l. of the LORD. 107.43
For thy steadfast l. is great above 108.04
In return for my l. they accuse me, 109.04
for good, and hatred for my l. 109.05
because thy steadfast l. is good, 109.21
me according to thy steadfast l.! 109.26
thy steadfast l. and thy faithfulness 115.01
I l. the LORD, because he has heard 116.01
is his steadfast l. toward us; 117.02
his steadfast l. endures for ever! 118.01
"His steadfast l. endures for ever." 118.02
"His steadfast l. endures for ever." 118.03
"His steadfast l. endures for ever." 118.04
his steadfast l. endures for ever! 118.29
Let thy steadfast l. come to me, 119.41
in thy commandments, which I l. 119.47
which I l., and I will meditate on 119.48
LORD, is full of thy steadfast l.; 119.64
Let thy steadfast l. be ready to 119.76
In thy steadfast l. spare my life, 119.88
Oh, how I l. thy law! It is my 119.97
double-minded men, but I l. thy law. 119.113
therefore I l. thy testimonies. 119.119
according to thy steadfast l., 119.124
Therefore I l. thy commandments 119.127
wont toward those who l. thy name. 119.132
Hear my voice in thy steadfast l.; 119.149
Consider how I l. thy precepts! 119.159
life according to thy steadfast l. 119.159
abhor falsehood, but I l. thy law. 119.163
Great peace have those who l. thy law; 119.165
testimonies; I l. them exceedingly. 119.167
"May they prosper who l. you! 122.06
the LORD there is steadfast l., 130.07
his steadfast l. endures for ever. 136.01
his steadfast l. endures for ever. 136.02
his steadfast l. endures for ever; 136.03
his steadfast l. endures for ever; 136.04
his steadfast l. endures for ever; 136.05
his steadfast l. endures for ever; 136.06
his steadfast l. endures for ever; 136.07
his steadfast l. endures for ever; 136.08
his steadfast l. endures for ever; 136.09
his steadfast l. endures for ever; 136.10
his steadfast l. endures for ever; 136.11
his steadfast l. endures for ever; 136.12
his steadfast l. endures for ever; 136.13
his steadfast l. endures for ever; 136.14
his steadfast l. endures for ever; 136.15
his steadfast l. endures for ever; 136.16
his steadfast l. endures for ever; 136.17
his steadfast l. endures for ever; 136.18
his steadfast l. endures for ever; 136.19
his steadfast l. endures for ever; 136.20
his steadfast l. endures for ever; 136.21
his steadfast l. endures for ever. 136.22
his steadfast l. endures for ever; 136.23
his steadfast l. endures for ever; 136.24
his steadfast l. endures for ever. 136.25
his steadfast l. endures for ever. 136.26
thy steadfast l. and thy faithfulness 138.02
thy steadfast l., O LORD, endures 138.08
in the morning of thy steadfast l., 143.08
thy steadfast l. cut off my 143.12
and abounding in steadfast l. 145.08
The LORD preserves all who l. him; 145.20
those who hope in his steadfast l. 147.11
ones, will you l. being simple? Pro 1.22
l. her, and she will guard you. 4.06
be infatuated always with her l. 5.19
take our fill of l. till morning; 7.18
let us delight ourselves with l. 7.18
I l. those who l. me, and those who 8.17
endowing with wealth those who l. me, 8.21
all who hate me l. death." 8.36
a wise man, and he will l. you. 9.08
but l. covers all offenses. 10.12
of herbs where l. is than a fatted 15.17
He who forgives an offense seeks l., 17.09
and those who l. it will eat its 18.21
L. not sleep, lest you come to 20.13
Better is open rebuke than hidden l. 27.05
a time to l., and a time to hate; Ecc 3.08
whether it is l. or hate man does 9.01
Their l. and their hate and their 9.06
Enjoy life with the wife whom you l., 9.09
For your l. is better than wine, Sol 1.02
out; therefore the maidens l. you. 1.03
will extol your l. more than wine; 1.04
wine; rightly do they l. you. 1.04
my l., to a mare of Pharaoh's 1.09
Behold, you are beautiful, my l.; 1.15
brambles, so is my l. among maidens. 2.02
and his banner over me was l. 2.04
with apples; for I am sick with l. 2.05
up nor awaken l. until it please. 2.07
my l., my fair one, and come away; 2.10
Arise, my l., my fair one, and come 2.13
up nor awaken l. until it please. 3.05
my l., behold. you are beautiful! 4.01
You are all fair, my l.; there is 4.07
How sweet is your l., my sister, 4.10
much better is your l. than wine, 4.10
my l., my dove, my perfect one; 5.02
you tell him I am sick with l. 5.08
my l., comely as Jerusalem, terrible 6.04
bloom. There I will give you my l. 7.12
up nor awaken l. until it please. 8.04
for l. is strong as death, jealousy 8.06
Many waters cannot quench l., 8.07
man offered for l. all the wealth 8.07
my beloved a l. song concerning Is 5.01
in steadfast l. and on it will sit 16.05
and I l. you, I give men in return 43.04

LOVE (cont.)

everlasting l. I will have compassion Is 54.08
my steadfast l. shall not depart 54.10
my steadfast, sure l. for David. 55.03
to l. the name of the LORD, and to 56.06
For I the LORD l. justice, I hate 61.08
the steadfast l. of the LORD, 63.07
the abundance of his steadfast l. 63.07
in his l. and in his pity he 63.09
glad for her, all you who l. her; 66.10
your l. as a bride, how you followed Jer 2.02
my people l. to have it so, but what 5.31
LORD, my steadfast l. and mercy. 16.05
loved you with an everlasting l.; 31.03
who showest steadfast l. to thousands, 32.18
his steadfast l. endures for ever!' 33.11
The steadfast l. of the LORD never Lam 3.22
the abundance of his steadfast l.; 3.32
behold, you were at the age for l.; Eze 16.08
came to her into the bed of l., 23.17
with their lips they show much l., 33.31
one who sings l. songs with a 33.32
and steadfast l. with those who Dan 9.04
with those who l. him and keep his 9.04
in steadfast l., and in mercy. Hos 2.19
l. a woman who is beloved of a 3.01
other gods and l. cakes of raisins." 3.01
they l. shame more than their glory. 4.18
Your l. is like a morning cloud, 6.04
steadfast l. and not sacrifice, the 6.06
They l. sacrifice; they sacrifice 8.13
I will l. them no more; all their 9.15
reap the fruit of steadfast l.; 10.12
compassion, with the bands of l., 11.04
hold fast to l. and justice, and 12.06
I will l. them freely, for my anger 14.04
and abounding in steadfast l., Joe 2.13
for so you l. to do, O people of Amo 4.05
Hate evil, and l. good, and establish 5.15
and abounding in steadfast l., Jon 4.02
You who hate the good and l. the evil, Mic 3.02
and to l. kindness, and to walk 6.08
he delights in steadfast l. 7.18
Jacob and steadfast l. to Abraham, 7.20
he will renew you in his l.; Zep 3.17
and l. no false oath, for all these Zec 8.17
therefore l. truth and peace. 8.19
You shall l. your neighbor and Mt 5.43
L. your enemies and pray for those 5.44
For if you l. those who l. you, what 5.46
for they l. to stand and pray in 6.05
will hate the one and l. the other, 6.24
You shall l. your neighbor as 19.19
"You shall l. the Lord your God 22.37
You shall l. your neighbor as 22.39
and they l. the place of honor at 23.06
most men's l. will grow cold 24.12
and you shall l. the Lord your God Mk 12.30
'You shall l. your neighbor as 12.31
and to l. him with all the heart, 12.33
and to l. one's neighbor as oneself, 12.33
L. your enemies, do good to those Lk 6.27
"if you l. those who l. you, what 6.32
even sinners l. those who l. them. 6.32
But l. your enemies, and do good, and 6.35
Now which of them will l. him more?" 7.42
"You shall l. the Lord your God 10.27
neglect justice and the l. of God; 11.42
for you l. the best seat in the 11.43
will hate the one and l. the other, 16.13
and l. salutations in the market 20.46
have not the l. of God within you. Jn 5.42
you would l. me, for I proceeded and 8.42
"Lord, he whom you l. is ill." 11.03
to you, that you l. one another; 13.34
you, that you also l. one another. 13.34
if you have l. for one another." 13.35
"If you l. me, you will keep my 14.15
and I will l. him and manifest 14.21
my word, and my Father will l. him 14.23
He who does not l. me does not keep 14.24
may know that I l. the Father. 14.31
I loved you; abide in my l. 15.09
commandments, you will abide in my l., 15.10
commandments and abide in his l. 15.10
that you l. one another as I have 15.12
Greater l. has no man than this, 15.13
This I command you, to l. one another. 15.17
world, the world would l. its own; 15.19
given me in thy l. for me before 17.24
that the l. with which thou hast 17.26
do you l. me more than these?" 21.15
"Yes, Lord; you know that I l. you." 21.15
"Simon, son of John, do you l. me?" 21.16
"Yes, Lord; you know that I l. you." 21.16
"Simon, son of John, do you l. me?" 21.17
him the third time, "Do you l. me?" 21.17
everything; you know that I l. you." 21.17
because God's l. has been poured Rom 5.05
But God shows his l. for us in that 5.08
for good with those who l. him, 8.28
separate us from the l. of Christ? 8.35
us from the l. of God in Christ 8.39
Let l. be genuine; hate what is 12.09
l. one another with brotherly 12.10
anything, except to l. one another; 13.08
"You shall l. your neighbor as 13.09
L. does no wrong to a neighbor; 13.10
therefore l. is the fulfilling of 13.10
you are no longer walking in l. 14.15
Christ and by the l. of the Spirit, 15.30
prepared for those who l. him," 1Co 2.09
or with l. in a spirit of gentleness? 4.21
"Knowledge" puffs up, but l. builds up. 8.01
but have not l., I am a noisy gong 13.01
but have not l., I am nothing. 13.02
but have not l., I gain nothing. 13.03
L. is patient and kind; 13.04
l. is not jealous or boastful; 13.04
L. does not insist on its own way; 13.05
L. bears all things, believes all 13.07
L. never ends; as for prophecy, it 13.08
faith, hope, l. abide, these three; 13.13
but the greatest of these is l. 13.13
Make l. your aim, and earnestly 14.01
Let all that you do be done in l. 16.14
If any one has no l. for the Lord, 16.22
My l. be with you all in Christ 16.24
the abundant l. that I have for 2Co 2.04
you to reaffirm your l. for him. 2.08
For the l. of Christ controls us, 5.14
the Holy Spirit, genuine l., 6.06
and in your l. for us—see that you 8.07
that your l. also is genuine. 8.08
of your l. and of our boasting 8.24
Because I do not l. you? God knows 11.11
If I l. you the more, am I to be 12.15
and the God of l. and peace will 13.11
Christ and the l. of God and the 13.14
but faith working through l. Gal 5.06
but through l. be servants of one 5.13
"You shall l. your neighbor as 5.14
But the fruit of the Spirit is l., 5.22
He destined us in l. to be his sons Eph 1.05
Jesus and your l. toward all the 1.15
of the great l. with which he 2.04
being rooted and grounded in l., 3.17
and to know the l. of Christ which 3.19
forbearing one another in l., 4.02
Rather, speaking the truth in l., 4.15
growth and upbuilds itself in l. 4.16
And walk in l., as Christ loved us 5.02
Husbands, l. your wives, as Christ 5.25
husbands should l. their wives as 5.28

LOVE (cont.)

each one of you l. his wife as Eph 5.33
and l. with faith, from God the 6.23
Grace be with all who l. our Lord 6.24
Lord Jesus Christ with l. undying. 6.24
that your l. may abound more and Php 1.09
The latter do it out of l., 1.16
in Christ, any incentive of l., 2.01
the same mind, having the same l., 2.02
whom I l. and long for, my joy and 4.01
and of the l. which you have for Col 1.04
known to us your l. in Spirit. 1.08
as they are knit together in l., 2.02
And above all these put on l., 3.14
Husbands, l. your wives, and do not 3.19
and labor of l. and steadfastness 1Th 1.03
your faith and l. and reported 3.06
and abound in l. to one another 3.12
But concerning l. of the brethren 4.09
taught by God to l. one another; 4.09
and indeed you do l. all the 4.10
on the breastplate of faith and l., 5.08
very highly in l. because of their 5.13
and the l. of every one of you for 2Th 1.03
they refused to l. the truth and 2.10
hearts to the l. of God and to the 3.05
our charge is l. that issues from 1Ti 1.05
the faith and l. that are in 1.14
in faith and l. and holiness, 2.15
in l., in faith, in purity. 4.12
For the l. of money is the root of 6.10
l., steadfastness, gentleness. 6.11
of power and l. and self-control. 2Ti 1.07
the faith and l. which are in 1.13
l., and peace, along with those who 2.22
patience, my l., my steadfastness, 3.10
For Demas, in l. with this present 4.10
in l., and in steadfastness. Tit 2.02
young women to l. their husbands 2.04
Greet those who l. us in the faith. 3.15
because I hear of your l. and of Phm 1.05
much joy and comfort from your l., 1.07
work and the l. which you showed Heb 6.10
one another to l. and good works, 10.24
Let brotherly l. continue. 13.01
Keep your life free from l. of money, 13.05
has promised to those who l. him. Jas 1.12
has promised to those who l. him? 2.05
"You shall l. your neighbor as 2.08
Without having seen him you l. him; 1Pe 1.08
for a sincere l. of the brethren, 1.22
l. one another earnestly from the 1.22
L. the brotherhood. Fear God. Honor 2.17
l. of the brethren, a tender heart 3.08
For "He that would l. life and see 3.10
that we should l. one another, 3.11
unfailing your l. for one another, 4.08
since l. covers a multitude of sins. 4.08
Greet one another with the kiss of l. 5.14
and brotherly affection with l. 2Pe 1.07
in him truly l. for God is perfected 1Jn 2.05
Do not l. the world or the things 2.15
l. for the Father is not in him. 2.15
See what l. the Father has given us, 3.01
nor he who does not l. his brother. 3.10
that we should love one another, 3.11
life, because we l. the brethren. 3.14
He who does not l. remains in death. 3.14
By this we know l., that he laid 3.16
how does God's l. abide in him? 3.17
let us not l. in word or speech but 3.18
Jesus Christ and l. one another, 3.23
Beloved, let us l. one another; 4.07
for l. is of God, and he who loves 4.07
He who does not l. does not know 4.08
know God; for God is l. 4.08
In this the l. of God was made 4.09
In this is l., not that we loved 4.10
we also ought to l. one another. 4.11
if we l. one another, God abides in 4.12
in us and his l. is perfected in 4.12
and believe the l. God has for us. 4.16
God is l., and he who abides in l. abides 4.16
In this is l. perfected with us, 4.17
There is no fear in l., but 4.18
but perfect l. casts out fear. 4.18
who fears is not perfected in l. 4.18
We l. because he first loved us. 4.19
"I l. God," and hates his brother, he 4.20
he who does not l. his brother 4.20
cannot l. God whom he has not seen. 4.20
God should l. his brother also. 4.21
we know that we l. the children of 5.02
when we l. God and obey his commandments. 5.02
For this is the l. of God, that we 5.03
whom I l. in the truth, and not only 2Jn 1.01
the Father's Son, in truth and l. 1.03
beginning, that we l. one another. 1.05
And this is l., that we follow his 1.06
the beginning, that you follow l. 1.06
Gaius, whom I l. in the truth. 3Jn 1.01
testified to your l. before the 1.06
and l. be multiplied to you. Jud 1.02
These are blemishes on your l. feasts, 1.12
keep yourselves in the l. of God; 1.21
abandoned the l. you had at first. Rev 2.04
your l. and faith and service and 2.19
Those whom I l., I reprove and 3.19

LOVED

became his wife; and he l. her. Gen 24.67
Isaac l. Esau, because he ate of his 25.28
of his game; but Rebekah l. Jacob. 25.28
savory food, such as his father l. 27.14
Jacob l. Rachel; and he said, "I will 29.18
and he l. Rachel more than Leah, and 29.30
he l. the maiden and spoke tenderly 34.03
Now Israel l. Joseph more than any 37.03
their father l. him more than all 37.04
And because he l. your fathers and Deu 4.37
the one l. and the other disliked, 21.15
both the l. and the disliked, and if 21.15
the son of the l. as the first-born 21.16
because the LORD your God l. you. 23.05
Yea, he l. his people; all those 33.03
After this he l. a woman in the Ju 16.04
although he l. Hannah, he would give 1Sa 1.05
And Saul l. him greatly, and he 16.21
and Jonathan l. him as his own soul. 18.01
because he l. him as his own soul. 18.03
But all Israel and Judah l. David; 18.16
Now Saul's daughter Michal l. David; 18.20
David, and that all Israel l. him, 18.28
for he l. him as he l. his own soul. 20.17
Solomon. And the LORD l. him, 2Sa 12.24
a time Amnon, David's son, l. her. 13.01
the love with which he had l. her. 13.15
Solomon l. the LORD, walking in the 1Ki 3.03
father; for Hiram always l. David. 5.01
the LORD l. Israel for ever, he has 10.09
Now King Solomon l. many foreign 11.01
your God l. Israel and would 2Ch 9.08
Rehoboam l. Maacah the daughter of 11.21
fertile lands, for he l. the soil. 26.10
the king l. Esther more than all Est 2.17
those whom I l. have turned Job 19.19
He l. to curse; let curses come Ps 109.17
O l. one, delectable maiden! Sol 7.06
you have l. their bed, you have Is 57.08
for I have l. strangers, and after Jer 2.25
which they have l. and served, 8.02
"They have l. to wander thus, they 14.10
I have l. you with an everlasting 31.03
all those you l. and those you Eze 16.37
You have l. a harlot's hire upon all Hos 9.01

LOVED (cont.)
detestable like the thing they l. Hos 9.10
a trained heifer that l. to thresh, 10.11
I l. him, and out of Egypt I called 11.01
"I have l. you," says the LORD. Mal 1.02
But you say, "How hast thou l. us?" 1.02
says the LORD. "Yet I have l. Jacob 1.02
And Jesus looking upon him l. him, Mk 10.21
are forgiven, for she l. much; Lk 7.47
For God so l. the world that he Jn 3.16
and men l. darkness rather than 3.19
Now Jesus l. Martha and her sister 11.05
So the Jews said, "See how he l. him!" 11.36
for they l. the praise of men more 12.43
having l. his own who were in the 13.01
world, he l. them to the end. 13.01
whom Jesus l., was lying close to 13.23
even as I have l. you, that you also 13.34
loves me will be l. by my Father, 14.21
If you l. me, you would have 14.28
As the Father has l. me, so have I l. you; 15.09
love one another as I have l. you. 15.12
you have l. me and have believed 16.27
l. them even as thou hast l. me. 17.23
which thou hast l. me may be in 17.26
disciple whom he l. standing near, 19.26
disciple, the one whom Jesus l., 20.02
whom Jesus l. said to Peter, 21.07
them the disciple whom Jesus l., 21.20
conquerors through him who l. us. Rom 8.37
"Jacob I l., but Esau I hated." 9.13
the more, am I to be l. the less? 2Co 12.15
who l. me and gave himself for me. Gal 2.20
great love with which he l. us, Eph 2.04
as Christ l. us and gave himself up 5.02
as Christ l. the church and gave 5.25
who l. us and gave us eternal 2Th 2.16
to all who have l. his appearing. 2Ti 4.08
Thou hast l. righteousness and Heb 1.09
who l. gain from wrongdoing, 2Pe 2.15
not that we l. God but that he 1Jn 4.10
God but that he l. us and sent his 4.10
if God so l. us, we also ought to 4.11
We love, because he first l. us. 4.19
feet, and learn that I have l. you. Rev 3.09
for they l. not their lives even 12.11

LOVELY
but Rachel was beautiful and l. Gen 29.17
"Saul and Jonathan, beloved and l.! 2Sa 1.23
the maiden was beautiful and l., Est 2.07
How l. is thy dwelling place, O LORD Ps 84.01
a l. hind, a graceful doe. Pro 5.19
a l. hind, my beloved, truly l. Sol 1.16
thread, and your mouth is l. 4.03
whatever is l., whatever is gracious, Php 4.08

LOVER
Thou hast caused l. and friend to Ps 88.18
Mighty King, l. of justice, thou hast 99.04
you l. of pleasures, who sit securely, Is 47.08
quarrelsome, and no l. of money. 1Ti 3.03
a l. of goodness, master of himself, Tit 1.08

LOVERS
and drink: drink deeply, O l.! Sol 5.01
you direct your course to seek l.! Jer 2.33
played the harlot with many l.; 3.01
sat awaiting l. like an Arab in 3.02
Your l. despise you; they seek your 4.30
for all your l. are destroyed. 22.20
and your l. shall go into captivity; 22.22
All your l. have forgotten you; 30.14
among all her l. she has none to Lam 1.02
"I called to my l. but they deceived 1.19
you gave your gifts to all your l., Eze 16.33
in your harlotries with your l., 16.36
therefore, behold, I will gather all your l., 16.37
give you into the hand of your l., 16.39
she doted on her l. the Assyrians, 23.05
her into the hands of her l., 23.09
you your l. from whom you turned 23.22
she said, I will go after my l., Hos 2.05
She shall pursue her l., 2.07
lewdness in the sight of her l., 2.10
my hire, which my l. have given me.' 2.12
and jewelry, and went after her l., 2.13
alone; Ephraim has hired l. 8.09
who were l. of money, heard all this, Lk 16.14
For men will be l. of self, 2Ti 3.02
l. of money, proud, arrogant, abusive, 3.02
l. of pleasure rather than l. of God, 3.04

LOVE'S
yet for l. sake I prefer to appeal Phm 1.09

LOVES
for your father, such as he l.; Gen 27.09
children; and his father l. him.' 44.20
but it is because the LORD l. you Deu 7.08
and l. the sojourner, giving him 10.18
because he l. you and your 15.16
your daughter-in-law who l. you, Ru 4.15
the LORD l. his people he has made 2Ch 2.11
soul hates him that l. violence. Ps 11.05
he l. righteous deeds; the upright 11.07
He l. righteousness and justice; 33.05
For the LORD l. justice; he will 37.28
us, the pride of Jacob whom he l. 47.04
of Judah, Mount Zion, which he l. 78.68
the LORD l. the gates of Zion more 87.02
The LORD l. those who hate evil; 97.10
well tried, and thy servant l. it. 119.140
bowed down; the LORD l. the righteous. 146.08
for the LORD reproves him whom he l., Pro 3.12
Whoever l. discipline l. knowledge, but 12.01
but he who l. him is diligent to 13.24
but he l. him who pursues righteousness. 15.09
and he l. him who speaks what is 16.13
a friend l. at all times, and a 17.17
He who l. transgression l. strife; he 17.19
He who gets wisdom l. himself; 19.08
He who l. pleasure will be a poor 21.17
He who l. wine and oil will not be 21.17
He who l. purity of heart, and whose 22.11
He who l. wisdom makes his father 29.03
He who l. money will not be satisfied Ecc 5.10
nor he who l. wealth, with gain: this 5.10
Tell me, you whom my soul l., Sol 1.07
night I sought him whom my soul l.; 3.01
I will seek him whom my soul l. 3.02
"Have you seen him whom my soul l.?" 3.03
when I found him whom my soul l. 3.04
Every one l. a bribe and runs after Is 1.23
The LORD l. him; he shall perform 48.14
as the LORD l. the people of Hos 3.01
false balances, he l. to oppress. 12.07
which he l., and has married the Mal 2.11
He who l. father or mother more Mt 10.37
and he who l. son or daughter more 10.37
for he l. our nation, and he built Lk 7.05
who is forgiven little, l. little." 7.47
the Father l. the Son, and has given Jn 3.35
For the Father l. the Son, and shows 5.20
For this reason the Father l. me, 10.17
He who l. his life loses it, and he 12.25
and keeps them, he it is who l. me; 14.21
and he who l. me will be loved by 14.21
"If a man l. me, he will keep my 14.23
for the Father himself l. you, 16.27
for he who l. his neighbor has Rom 13.08
But if one l. God, one is known by 1Co 8.03
for God l. a cheerful giver. 2Co 9.07
He who l. his wife l. himself. Eph 5.28

LOVES (cont.)
Lord disciplines him whom he l. Heb 12.06
He who l. his brother abides in the 1Jn 2.10
If anyone l. the world, love for 2.15
and he who l. is born of God and 4.07
that he who l. God should love his 4.21
one who l. the parent l. the child. 5.01
To him who l. us and has freed us Rev 1.05
every one who l. and practices 22.15

LOVESICK
"How l. is your heart, says the Lord Eze 16.30

LOVING
l. the LORD your God, walking in all Deu 11.22
by l. the LORD your God and by 19.09
by l. the LORD your God, by walking 30.16
l. the LORD your God, obeying his 30.20
dreaming, lying down, l. to slumber, Is 56.10
goodness and l. kindness of God Tit 3.04

LOVINGLY
it was l. wrought within by the Sol 3.10

LOW
brought very l. because of Midian; Ju 6.06
you have brought me very l., 11.35
he brings l., he also exalts. 1Sa 2.07
brought Judah l. because of Ahaz 2Ch 28.19
to their husbands, high and l." Est 1.20
or the ox l. over his fodder? Job 6.05
But man dies, and is laid l.; 14.10
they are brought l., and he 14.21
that is proud, and bring him l.; 40.12
he is laid l. even at the sight of 41.09
both l. and high, rich and poor Ps 49.02
Men of l. estate are but a breath, 62.09
and laid l. the picked men of 78.31
us, for we are brought very l. 79.08
were brought l. through their 106.43
and brought l. through oppression, 107.39
when I was brought l., he saved me. 116.06
who remembered us in our l. estate, 136.23
for I am brought very l.! 142.06
for many a victim has she laid l.; Pro 7.26
A man's pride will bring him l., 29.23
and the rich sit in a l. place. Ecc 10.06
the sound of the grinding is l., 12.04
daughters of song are brought l.; 12.04
humbled, and men are brought l.— Is 2.09
looks of man shall be brought l., 2.11
pride of men shall be brought l.; 2.17
bowed down, and men are brought l., 5.15
and the lofty will be brought l., 10.33
and lay l. the haughtiness of the 13.11
saying, 'Since you were laid l., 14.08
you who laid the nations l.! 14.12
glory of Jacob will be brought l., 17.04
LORD will lay l. his pride together 25.11
lay l., and cast to the ground, even 25.12
For he has brought l. the inhabitants 26.05
lays it l., lays l. to the ground, 26.05
from l. in the dust your words 29.04
the city will be utterly laid l. 32.19
every mountain and hill be made l.; 40.04
you shall come bending l. to you; 60.14
and became a l. spreading vine, Eze 17.06
I the LORD bring l. the high tree, 17.24
tree, and make high the l. tree, 17.24
exalt that which is l., 21.26
the everlasting hills sank l. Hab 3.06
pride of Assyria shall be laid l., Zec 10.11
regarded the l. estate of his Lk 1.48
and exalted those of l. degree; 1.52
and hill shall be brought l., 3.05
God chose what is l. and despised 1Co 1.28

LOWER
make it with l., second, and third Gen 6.16
in front to the l. part of the two Ex 28.27
in front of the l. part of the two 39.20
you shall come down l. and l. Deu 28.43
to the l. end of the Sea of Chinnereth, Jos 13.27
upper springs and the l. springs. 15.19
as the territory of l. Bethhoron, 16.03
that lies south of L. Bethhoron. 18.13
upper springs and the l. springs. Ju 1.15
Gezer) and Bethhoron the l. 1Ki 9.17
who built both l. and upper 1Ch 7.24
Upper Bethhoron and L. Bethhoron, 2Ch 8.05
than to be put l. in the presence Pro 25.07
collected the waters of the l. pool, Is 22.09
gates; this was the l. pavement. Eze 40.18
front of the l. gate to the outer 40.19
than from the l. and middle 42.05
more than the l. and the middle 42.06
base on the ground to the l. ledge, 43.14
into the l. parts of the earth? Eph 4.09
a little while l. than the angels, Heb 2.07
while was made l. than the angels, 2.09

LOWERED
man quickly l. his sack to the Gen 44.11
and whenever he l. his hand, Ex 17.11
they l. the gear, and so were driven Ac 27.17
and had l. the boat into the sea, 27.30

LOWERING
down over the wall, l. him in a basket. Ac 9.25

LOWEST
The l. story was five cubits broad, 1Ki 6.06
entrance for the l. story was on 6.08
So in the l. parts of the space Neh 4.13
cast them down into the l pit; Ps 55.23
up from the l. story to the top Eze 41.07
with shame to take the l. place. Lk 14.09
invited, go and sit in the l. place, 14.10

LOWING
along one highway, l. as they went; 1Sa 6.12
and the l. of the oxen which I hear?" 15.14
and the l. of cattle is not heard; Jer 9.10

LOWLAND
in the hill country and in the l., Deu 1.07
and in the l. all along the coast Jos 9.01
Negeb and the l. and the slopes, 10.40
and in the l., and in Naphothdor on 11.02
Goshen and the l. and the Arabah 11.16
country of Israel and its l. 11.16
in the l., in the Arabah, in the 12.08
And in the l., Eshtaol, Zorah, Ashnah, 15.33
in the Negeb, and in the l. Ju 1.09
South and the l. were inhabited, Zec 7.07

LOWLIEST
and sets over it the l. of men.' Dan 4.17

LOWLINESS
with all l. and meekness, with Eph 4.02
kindness, l., meekness, and patience, Col 3.12

LOWLY
he sets on high those who are l., Job 5.11
the proud, but he saves the l. 22.29
LORD is high, he regards the l.; Ps 38.06
to be of a l. spirit with the poor Pro 16.19
but he who is l. in spirit will 29.23
"Take a l. seat, for your beautiful Jer 13.18
there they shall be a l. kingdom. Eze 29.14
be the most l. of the kingdoms, and 29.15
of you a people humble and l. Zep 3.12
for I am gentle and l. in heart, Mt 11.29
haughty, but associate with the l.; Rom 12.16

LOWLY (cont.)
who will change our l. body to be Php 3.21
Let the l. brother boast in his Jas 1.09

LOYAL
show me the l. love of the LORD, 1Sa 20.14
"With the l. thou dost show thyself l.; 2Sa 22.26
With the l. thou dost show thyself l.; Ps 18.25
it is a l. thing you do when you 3Jn 1.05

LOYALLY
but as I have dealt l. with you, Gen 21.23
you will deal l. and truly with my 24.49
promise to deal l. and truly with 47.29
"I will deal l. with Hanun the son 2Sa 10.02
as his father dealt l. with me." 10.02
But deal l. with the sons of 1Ki 2.07
"I will deal l. with Hanun the son 1Ch 19.02
for his father dealt l. with me." 19.02

LOYALTY
cut off your l. from my house for 1Sa 20.15
you showed this l. to Saul your 2Sa 2.05
I keep showing l. to the house of 3.08
"Is this your l. to your friend? 16.17
for with such l. they met me when I 1Ki 2.07
I will sing of l. and of justice; Ps 101.01
Let not l. and faithfulness forsake Pro 3.03
good meet l. and faithfulness. 14.22
By l. and faithfulness iniquity is 16.06
What is desired in a man is l., 19.22
Many a man proclaims his own l., 20.06
L. and faithfulness preserve the 20.28
vain idols forsake their true l. Jon 2.08

LUCIUS
L. of Cyrene, Manaen a member of the Ac 13.01
so do L. and Jason and Sosipater, my Rom 16.21

LUD
Asshur, Arpachshad, L., and Aram. Gen 10.22
L., Aram, Uz, Hul, Gether, and Meshech. 1Ch 1.17
and L., who draw the bow, to Tubal Is 66.19
men of L., skilled in handling the Jer 46.09
"Persia and L. and Put were in your Eze 27.10
and L., and all Arabia, and Libya, 30.05

LUDIM
Egypt became the father of L., Gen 10.13
Egypt was the father of L., Anamim, 1Ch 1.11

LUHITH
the ascent of L. they go up weeping; Is 15.05
the ascent of L. they go up weeping; Jer 48.05

LUKE
L. the beloved physician and Demas Col 4.14
L. alone is with me. Get Mark and 2Ti 4.11
Demas, and L., my fellow workers. Phm 1.24

LUKEWARM
So, because you are l., and neither Rev 3.16

LUMINARIES
established the l. and the sun. Ps 74.16

LUMP
out of the same l. one vessel for Rom 9.21
fruits is holy, so is the whole l.; 11.16
ferments the whole l. of dough? 1Co 5.06
A little yeast leavens the whole l. Gal 5.09

LURED
when he is l. and enticed by his Jas 1.14

LURK
they l., they watch my steps. Ps 56.06
they l. like fowlers lying in wait. Jer 5.26
a leopard I will l. beside the way. Hos 13.07

LURKING
note of all the l. places where he 1Sa 23.23
tear, as a young lion l. in ambush. Ps 17.12

LURKS
he l. in secret like a lion in his Ps 10.09
he l. that he may seize the poor, he 10.09

LUST
foot those who l. after tribute; Ps 68.30
are taken captive by their l. Pro 11.06
you who burn with l. among the oaks, Is 57.05
Who can restrain her l.? Jer 2.24
and poured out their l. upon her. Eze 23.08
and they defiled her with their l.; 23.17
the passion of l. like heathen who 1Th 4.05
indulge in the l. of defiling 2Pe 2.10
l. of the flesh and the l. of the eyes 1Jn 2.16
passes away, and the l. of it; 2.17
and indulged in unnatural l., Jud 1.07

LUSTER
himself his crown will shed its l. Ps 132.18

LUSTFUL
your l. neighbors, multiplying your Eze 16.26

LUSTFULLY
at a woman l. has already committed Mt 5.28

LUSTS
them up in the l. of their hearts Rom 1.24
is corrupt through deceitful l., Eph 4.22

LUSTY
They were well-fed l. stallions, Jer 5.08

LUTE
to the music of the l. and the harp, Ps 92.03
sound; praise him with l. and harp! 150.03

LUXURIANT
Israel is a l. vine that yields its Hos 10.01

LUXURY
fitting for a fool to live in l., Pro 19.10
for by them he lives in l., Hab 1.16
and live in l. are in kings' Lk 7.25
on the earth in l. and in pleasure; Jas 5.05

LUZ
of the city was L. at the first. Gen 28.19
And Jacob came to L. (that is, 35.06
to me at L. in the land of Canaan 48.03
then going from Bethel to L., Jos 16.02
southward in the direction of L., 18.13
the shoulder of L. (the same is 18.13
name of the city was formerly L. Ju 1.23
a city, and called its name L.; 1.26

LYCAONIA
cities of L., and to the surrounding Ac 14.06

LYCAONIAN
saying in L., "The gods have come Ac 14.11

LYCIA
Pamphylia, we came to Myra in L. Ac 27.05

LYDDA
to the saints that lived at L. Ac 9.32
residents of L. and Sharon saw him, 9.35
Since L. was near Joppa, the disciples, 9.38

LYDIA
One who heard us was a woman named L., Ac 16.14
out of the prison, and visited L.; 16.40

LYE
and cleanse my hands with l., Job 9.30

LYE (cont.)
dross as with l. and remove all Is 1.25
yourself with l. and use much soap, Jer 2.22

LYING
three flocks of sheep l. beside it; Gen 29.02
in Israel by l. with Jacob's 34.07
it and pay no regard to l. words." Ex 5.09
who hates you l. under its burden, 23.05
to the valley l. in the region of Num 21.20
who has known man by l. with him. 31.17
have not known man by l. with him, 31.18
had not known man by l. with him. 31.35
l. in wait, so that he died, 35.20
anything on him without l. in wait, 35.22
l. in the open country, and it is Deu 21.01
"If a man is found l. with the wife 22.22
and he was l. fast asleep from Ju 4.21
Now she had men l. in wait in an 16.09
And the man l. in wait were in an 16.12
his concubine l. at the door of 19.27
had not known man by l. with him; 21.12
was l. down in his own place; 1Sa 3.02
and Samuel was l. down within the 3.03
his hands were l. cut off upon the 5.04
Saul was l. within the encampment, 26.05
house, where he was l. down. 2Sa 13.08
and will be a l. spirit in the 1Ki 22.22
LORD has put a l. spirit in the 22.23
saw the child l. dead on his bed. 2Ki 4.32
and will be a l. spirit in the 2Ch 18.21
LORD has put a l. spirit in the 18.22
were dead bodies l. on the ground; 20.24
Let the l. lips be dumb, which speak Ps 31.18
and l. more than speaking the truth. 52.03
speaking against me with l. tongues 109.02
from l. lips, from a deceitful 120.02
searchest out my path and my l. down, 139.03
a l. tongue, and hands that shed Pro 6.17
He who conceals hatred has l. lips, 10.18
but a l. tongue is but for a moment 12.19
L. lips are an abomination to the 12.22
treasures by a l. tongue is a 21.06
A l. tongue hates its victims, and a 26.28
Remove far from me falsehood and l.; 30.08
l. sons, sons who will not hear the Is 30.09
to ruin the poor with l. words, 32.07
dreaming, l. down, loving to slumber. 56.10
uttering from the heart l. words. 59.13
they lurk like fowlers l. in wait. Jer 5.26
are prophesying to you a l. vision, 14.14
those who prophesy l. dreams, 23.32
in my name l. words which I did 29.23
He is to me like a bear l. in wait, Lam 3.10
and uttered a l. divination, whenever Eze 13.07
and who give l. divinations; 13.09
agreed to speak l. and corrupt Dan 2.09
l., killing, stealing, and committing Hos 4.02
my servant is l. paralyzed at home, Mt 8.06
mother-in-law l. sick with a fever; 8.14
to him a paralytic, l. on his bed; 9.02
and found the child l. in bed, Mk 7.30
swaddling clothes and l. in a manger. Lk 2.12
and the babe l. in a manger. 2.16
l. in wait for him, to catch at 11.54
he had been l. there a long time, Jn 5.06
was l. close to the breast of Jesus; 13.23
So l. thus, close to the breast of 13.25
he saw the linen cloths l. there, 20.05
he saw the linen cloths l., 20.06
not l. with the linen cloths but 20.07
with fish l. on it, and bread. 21.09
the truth in Christ, I am not l.; Rom 9.01
I am not l.), a teacher of the 1Ti 2.07

LYRE
all those who play the l. and pipe. Gen 4.21
and songs, with tambourine and l.? 31.27
and l. before them, prophesying. 1Sa 10.05
who is skilful in playing the l.; 16.16
David took the l. and played it 16.23
while David was playing the l., 18.10
and David was playing the l. 19.09
with the l. in thanksgiving and 1Ch 25.03
They sing to the tambourine and the l., Job 21.12
My l. is turned to mourning, and my 30.31
Praise the LORD with the l., Ps 33.02
thee with the l., O God, my God. 43.04
my riddle to the music of the l. 49.04
Awake, O harp and l.! 57.08
sing praises to thee with the l., 71.22
timbrel, the sweet l. with the harp. 81.02
the harp, to the melody of the l. 92.03
Sing praises to the LORD with the l., 98.05
with the l. and the sound of melody! 98.05
Awake, O harp and l.! 108.02
make melody to our God upon the l.! 147.07
melody to him with timbrel and l.! 149.03
They have l. and harp, timbrel and Is 5.12
Therefore my soul moans like a l. for Moab, 16.11
the mirth of the l. is stilled. 24.08
l., trigon, harp, bagpipe, and every Dan 3.05
l., trigon, harp, bagpipe, and every 3.07
l., trigon, harp, bagpipe, and every 3.10
l., trigon, harp, bagpipe, and every 3.15

LYRES
with songs and l. and harps and 2Sa 6.05
l. also and harps for the singers; 1Ki 10.12
with song and l. and harps and 1Ch 13.08
on harps and l. and cymbals, to 15.16
to lead with l. according to the 15.21
made loud music on harps and l. 15.28
who were to play harps and l.; 16.05
who should prophesy with l., 25.01
and l. for the service of the house 25.06
and l., stood east of the altar 2Ch 5.12
l. also and harps for the singers; 9.11
with harps and l. and trumpets, 20.28
and l., according to the commandment 29.25
with cymbals, harps and l. Neh 12.27
willows there we hung up our l. Ps 137.02
be to the sound of timbrels and l.; Is 30.32
sound of your l. shall be heard no Eze 26.13

LYSANIAS
Trachonitis, and L. tetrarch of Abilene, Lk 3.01

LYSIAS
"Claudius L. to his Excellency the Ac 23.26
But the chief captain L. came and *24.07
"When L. the tribune comes down, I 24.22

LYSTRA
of it and fled to L. and Derbe, Ac 14.06
Not at L. there was a man sitting, 14.08
returned to L. and to Iconium and 14.21
And he came also to Derbe and to L. 16.01
by the brethren at L. and Iconium. 16.02
and at L., what persecutions I 2Ti 3.11

MAACAH
bore Tebah, Gaham, Tahash, and M. Gen 22.24
the son of M. the daughter of 2Sa 3.03
and the king of M. with a thousand 10.06
Rehob, and the men of Tob and M., 10.08
Eliphelet the son of Ahasbai of M., 23.34
to Achish, son of M., king of Gath. 1Ki 2.39
name was M. the daughter of 15.02
name was M. the daughter of 15.10
He also removed M. his mother from 15.13
M., Caleb's concubine, bore Sheber 1Ch 2.48
third Absalom, whose mother was M., 3.02
The name of his sister was M. 7.15
And M. the wife of Machir bore a 7.16
and the name of his wife was M. 8.29
and the name of his wife was M., 9.35
Hanan the son of M., 11.43
and the king of M. with his army, 19.07
Simeonites, Shephatiah the son of M.; 27.16
After her he took M. the daughter 2Ch 11.20
Rehoboam loved M. the daughter of 11.21
the son of M. as chief prince 11.22
Even M., his mother, King Asa 15.16

MAACATH
but Geshur and M. dwell in the Jos 13.13

MAACATHITE
and Jaazaniah the son of the M. 2Ki 25.23
the Garmite and Eshtemoa the M. 1Ch 4.19
Netophathite, Jezaniah the son of the M., Jer 40.08

MAACATHITES
of the Geshurites and the M., Deu 3.14
of the Geshurites and the M., Jos 12.05
region of the Geshurites and M., 13.11
drive out the Geshurites or the M.; 13.13

MAADAI
Of the sons of Bani: M., Amram, Uel, Ez 10.34

MAADIAH
Mijamin, M., Bilgah, Neh 12.05

MAAI
M., Nethanel, Judah, and Hanani, with Neh 12.36

MAARATH
M., Bethanoth, and Eltekon: six Jos 15.59

MAASAI
and M. the son of Adiel, son of 1Ch 9.12

MAASEIAH
M., Mattithiah, Eliphelehu, and 1Ch 15.18
M., and Benaiah were to play harps 15.20
M. the son of Adaiah, and Elishaphat 2Ch 23.01
the secretary and M. the officer, 26.11
slew M. the king's son and Azrikam 28.07
and M. the governor of the city, and 34.08
foreign women were found M., Ez 10.18
M., Elijah, Shemaiah, Jehiel, and 10.21
M., Ishmael, Nethanel, Jozabad, and 10.22
M., Mattaniah, Bezalel, Binnui, and 10.30
After them Azariah the son of M., Neh 3.23
and M. on his right hand; 8.04
M., Kelita, Azariah, Jozabad, Hanan, 8.07
Rehum, Hashabnah, M., 10.25
and M. the son of Baruch, son of 11.05
son of M., son of Ithiel, son of 11.07
M., Miniamin, Micaiah, Elioenai, 12.41
and M., Shemaiah, Eleazar, Uzzi, 12.42
the priest, the son of M., saying, Jer 21.01
Kolaiah and Zedekiah the son of M., 29.21
Zephaniah the son of M. the priest, 29.25
the chamber of M. the son of 35.04
the son of M., to Jeremiah the 37.03

MAATH
the son of M., the son of Mattathias, Lk 3.26

MAAZ
M., Jamin, and Eker. 1Ch 2.27

MAAZIAH
Delaiah, the twenty-fourth to M. 1Ch 24.18
M., Bilgai, Shemaiah; Neh 10.08

MACEDONIA
a man of M. was standing beseeching Ac 16.09
"Come over to M. and help us." 16.09
immediately we sought to go on into M., 16.10
leading city of the district of M., 16.12
When Silas and Timothy arrived from M., 18.05
to pass through M. and Achaia and 19.21
sent into M. two of his helpers, 19.22
leave of them and departed for M. 20.01
he determined to return through M. 20.03
For M. and Achaia have been pleased Rom 15.26
visit you after passing through M., 1Co 16.05
for I intend to pass through M., 16.05
to visit you on my way to M., 2Co 1.16
to you from M. and have you send 1.16
leave of them and went on to M. 2.13
For even when we came into M., 7.05
been shown in the churches of M., 8.01
about you to the people of M., 9.02
by the brethren who came from M. 11.09
when I left M., no church entered Php 4.15
the believers in M. and in Achaia. 1Th 1.07
forth from you in M. and Achaia, 1.08
all the brethren throughout M. 4.10
I urged you when I was going to M., 1Ti 1.03

MACEDONIAN
Aristarchus, a M. from Thessalonica. Ac 27.02

MACEDONIANS
M. who were Paul's companions in Ac 19.29
lest if some M. come with me and 2Co 9.04

MACHBANNAI
Jeremiah tenth, M. eleventh. 1Ch 12.13

MACHBENAH
the father of M. and the father of 1Ch 2.49

MACHI
tribe of Gad, Geuel the son of M. Num 13.15

MACHIR
children also of M. the son of Gen 50.23
of M., the family of the Machirites; Num 26.29
and M. was the father of Gilead; 26.29
son of M., son of Manasseh, from the 27.01
And the sons of M. the son of 32.39
gave Gilead to M. the son of 32.40
the sons of Gilead the son of M., 36.01
To M. I gave Gilead, Deu 3.15
the people of M. the son of Jos 13.31
To M. the first-born of Manasseh, 17.01
son of M., son of Manasseh, had no 17.03
from M. marched down the commanders, Ju 5.14
in the house of M. the son of 2Sa 9.04
the house of M. the son of Ammiel, 9.05
and M. the son of Ammiel from 17.27
the daughter of M. the father of 1Ch 2.21
All these were descendants of M., 2.23
she bore M. the father of Gilead. 7.14
And M. took a wife for Huppim and 7.15
And Maacah the wife of M. bore a son, 7.16
the sons of Gilead the son of M., 7.17

MACHIRITES
of Machir, the family of the M.; Num 26.29
the half of the M. according to Jos 13.31

MACHNADEBAI
M., Shashai, Sharai, Ez 10.40

MACHPELAH
me the cave of M., which he owns; Gen 23.09
So the field of Ephron in M., 23.17
of the field of M. east of Mamre 23.19
sons buried him in the cave of M., 25.09
cave that is in the field at M., 49.30
him in the cave of the field at M., 50.13

MAD
shall be driven m. by the sight Deu 28.34
feigned himself m. in their hands, 1Sa 21.13
servants, "Lo, you see the man is m.; 21.14
Why did this m. fellow come to you?" 2Ki 9.11
"It is m.," and of pleasure, "What Ecc 2.02
images, and they are m. over idols. Jer 50.38
therefore the nations went m. 51.07
fool, the man of the spirit is m., Hos 9.07
said, "He has a demon, and he is m.; Jn 10.20
They said to her, "You are m." Ac 12.15
a loud voice, "Paul, you are m.; 26.24
great learning is turning you m." 26.24
"I am not m., most excellent Festus, 26.25
will they not say that you are m.? 1Co 14.23

MADAI
M., Javan, Tubal, Meshech, and Tiras. Gen 10.02
M., Javan, Tubal, Meshech, and Tiras. 1Ch 1.05

MADE
And God m. the firmament and Gen 1.07
And God m. the two great lights, the 1.16
the night; he m. the stars also. 1.16
And God m. the beasts of the earth 1.25
And God saw everything that he had m., 1.31
the LORD God m. the earth and the 2.04
the LORD God m. to grow every tree 2.09
from the man he m. into a woman 2.22
creature that the LORD God had m. 3.01
together and m. themselves aprons. 3.07
And the LORD God m. for Adam and 3.21
he m. him in the likeness of God. 5.01
that he had m. man on the earth, 6.06
for I am sorry that I have m. them." 6.07
that I have m. I will blot out 7.04
And God m. a wind blow over the 8.01
window of the ark which he had m., 8.06
for God m. man in his own image. 9.06
where he had m. an altar at the 13.04
these kings m. war with Bera king 14.02
should say, 'I have m. Abram rich.' 14.23
day the LORD m. a covenant with 15.18
for I have m. you the father of a 17.05
and he m. them a feast, and baked 19.03
So they m. their father drink wine 19.33
So they m. their father drink wine 19.35
"God has m. laughter for me; 21.06
and Abraham m. a great feast on the 21.08
and the two men m. a covenant. 21.27
So they m. a covenant at Beersheba. 21.32
its whole area, was m. over 23.17
is in it were m. over to Abraham 23.20
And he m. the camels kneel down 24.11
My master m. me swear, saying, 'You 24.37
now the LORD has m. room for us, 26.22
So he m. them a feast, and they are 26.30
and they m. life bitter for Isaac 26.35
I have m. him your lord, and all his 27.37
Then Jacob m. a vow, saying, "If God 28.20
men of the place and m. a feast. 29.22
a pillar and m. a vow to me. 31.13
they took stones, and m. a heap; 31.46
and m. booths for his cattle; 33.17
they captured and m. their prey. 34.29
and he m. him a long robe with 37.03
a breach you have m. for yourself!" 38.29
and he m. him overseer of his house 39.04
time that he m. him overseer in 39.05
he did, the LORD m. it prosper. 39.23
he m. a feast for all his servants, 40.20
and he m. him to ride in his second 41.43
"God has m. me forget all my 41.51
"For God has m. me fruitful in the 41.52
they m. ready the present for 43.25
bowed their heads and m. obeisance. 43.28
Then Joseph m. haste, for his heart 43.30
him when Joseph m. himself known 45.01
and he has m. me a father to 45.08
God has m. me lord of all Egypt; 45.09
Then Joseph m. ready his chariot 46.29
he m. slaves of them from one end 47.21
So Joseph m. it a statute concerning 47.26
his arms were m. agile by the hands 49.24
My father m. me swear, saying 'I am 50.05
your father, as he m. you swear." 50.06
and he m. a mourning for his father 50.10
So they m. the people of Israel Ex 1.13
and m. their lives bitter with hard 1.14
their work they m. them serve with 1.14
for him a basket m. of bulrushes, 2.03
"Who m. you a prince and a judge 2.14
to him, "Who has m. man's mouth? 4.11
which they m. heretofore you shall 5.08
you have m. us offensive in the 5.21
of Pharaoh m. his slaves and his 9.20
son how I have m. sport of the 10.02
So he m. ready his chariot and took 14.06
and m. the sea dry land, and the 14.21
which thou hast m. for thy abode, 15.17
There the LORD m. for them a 15.25
it was like wafers m. with honey. 16.31
and m. them heads over the people, 18.25
days the LORD m. heaven and earth, 20.11
the LORD has m. with you in 24.08
shall be m. of hammered work; 25.31
three cups m. like almonds, each 25.33
and three cups m. like almonds, 25.33
itself four cups m. like almonds, 25.34
talent of pure gold shall it be m., 25.39
work shall it be m., with cherubim; 26.31
on the mountain, so shall it be m. 27.08
things with which atonement was m., 29.33
days the LORD m. heaven and earth, 31.17
when he had m. an end of speaking 31.18
graving tool, and m. a molten calf; 32.04
and Aaron m. proclamation and said, 32.05
they have m. for themselves a 32.08
he took the calf which they had m., 32.20
and m. the people of Israel drink 32.20
they have m. for themselves gods of 32.31
they m. the calf which Aaron m. 32.35
And Moses m. haste to bow his head 34.08
words I have m. a covenant with 34.27
the workmen m. the tabernacle with 36.08
they were m. of fine twined linen 36.08
And he m. loops of blue on the edge 36.11
likewise he m. them on the edge of 36.11
he m. fifty loops on the one 36.12
and he m. fifty loops on the edge 36.12
And he m. fifty clasps of gold, and 36.13
He also m. curtains of goats' hair 36.14
tabernacle; he m. eleven curtains. 36.14
And he m. fifty loops on the edge 36.17
And he m. fifty clasps of bronze to 36.18
And he m. for the tent a covering 36.19
Then he m. the upright frames for 36.20
for the tabernacle he m. thus: 36.23
and he m. forty vases of silver 36.24
north side, he m. twenty frames 36.25
tabernacle westward he m. six frames. 36.27
And he m. two frames for corners of 36.28
he m. two of them thus, for the two 36.29
And he m. bars of acacia wood, five 36.31
And he m. the middle bar to pass 36.33

MADE (cont.)
and m. their rings of gold for Ex 36.34
And he m. the veil of blue and 36.35
cherubim skilfully worked he m. it. 36.35
And for it he m. four pillars of 36.36
He also m. a screen for the door of 36.37
Bezalel m. the ark of acacia wood; 37.01
and m. a molding of gold around it. 37.02
And he m. poles of acacia wood, and 37.04
And he m. a mercy seat of pure gold; 37.06
And he m. two cherubim of hammered 37.07
ends of the mercy seat he m. them, 37.07
mercy seat he m. the cherubim on 37.08
He also m. the table of acacia wood; 37.10
and m. a molding of gold around it. 37.11
And he m. around it a frame a 37.12
and m. a molding of gold around the 37.12
He m. the poles of acacia wood to 37.15
And he m. the vessels of pure gold 37.16
He also m. the lampstand of pure 37.17
lampstand were m. of hammered work; 37.17
three cups m. like almonds, each 37.19
and three cups m. like almonds, 37.19
were four cups m. like almonds, 37.20
And he m. its seven lamps and its 37.23
He m. it and all its utensils of a 37.24
He m. the altar of incense of 37.25
and he m. a molding of gold round 37.26
and m. two rings of gold on it 37.27
And he m. the poles of acacia wood, 37.28
He m. the holy anointing oil also, 37.29
He m. the altar of burnt offering 38.01
He m. horns for it on its four 38.02
And he m. all the utensils of the 38.03
all its utensils he m. of bronze. 38.03
And he m. for the altar a grating, a 38.04
he m. the poles of acacia wood, and 38.06
he m. it hollow, with boards. 38.07
And he m. the laver of bronze and 38.08
And he m. the court; for the 38.09
m. all that the LORD commanded 38.22
shekels he m. hooks for the 38.28
capitals and m. fillets for them. 38.28
with it he m. the bases for the 38.30
stuff they m. finely wrought 39.01
they m. the holy garments for Aaron; 39.01
And he m. the ephod of gold, blue 39.02
They m. for the ephod shoulder-pieces, 39.04
He m. the breastpiece, in skilled 39.08
the breastpiece was m. double, 39.09
And they m. on the breastpiece 39.15
and they m. two settings of gold 39.16
Then they m. two rings of gold, and 39.19
And they m. two rings of gold, and 39.20
He also m. the robe of the ephod 39.22
the robe they m. pomegranates of 39.24
They also m. bells of pure gold, and 39.25
They also m. the coats, woven of 39.27
And they m. the plate of the holy 39.30
it shall be m. of fine flour with Lev 2.07
offering that is m. of these things 2.08
the LORD shall be m. with leaven; 2.11
has committed is m. known to him, 4.23
committed is m. known to him he 4.28
It shall be m. with oil on a 6.21
by fire is m. to the LORD shall be 7.25
the offerings m. by fire to the 7.35
a skin or in anything m. of skin, 13.48
in skin or in anything m. of skin, 13.49
out and has m. atonement for 16.17
"And when he has m. an end of 16.20
day shall atonement be m. for you, 16.30
atonement may be m. for the people 16.34
of cloth m. of two kinds of stuff. 19.19
he has m. naked her fountain, and 20.18
which he may be m. unclean or a 22.05
m. of two tenths of an ephah; 23.17

may know that I m. the people of 23.43
city shall be m. sure in perpetuity 25.30
of your yoke and m. you walk erect. 26.13
which the LORD m. between him and 26.46
shall be m. from your valuation. 27.18
restitution may be m. for the wrong, Num 5.08
with which atonement is m. for him. 5.08
And when he had m. her drink the 5.27
no vinegar m. from wine or strong 6.03
leader of Issachar, m. an offering; 7.18
Moses, so he m. the lampstand. 8.04
and Aaron m. atonement for them to 8.21
it in pots, and m. cakes of it; 11.08
returned and m. all the congregation 14.36
it had not been m. plain what 15.34
so let them be m. into hammered 16.38
and m. atonement for the people. 16.47
is kept of the offerings m. to me, 18.08
And why have you m. us come up out 20.05
So Moses m. a bronze serpent, and 21.09
He has m. his sons fugitives, and 21.29
"Because you have m. sport of me. 22.29
and m. atonement for the people of 25.13
her husband has m. them void, 30.12
and he m. them wander in the 32.13
expiation can be m. for the land, 35.33
brethren have m. our hearts melt, Deu 1.28
his spirit and m. his heart 2.30
which he m. with you, and make a 4.23
The LORD our God m. a covenant with 5.02
covenant which the LORD m. with you, 9.09
they have m. themselves a molten 9.12
you had m. yourselves a molten calf; 9.16
thing, the calf which you had m., 9.21
So I m. an ark of acacia wood, and 10.03
tables in the ark which I had m.; 10.05
your God has m. you as the stars Deu 10.22
how he m. the water of the Red Sea 11.04
officers have m. an end of speaking 20.09
and lo, he has m. shameful charges 22.17
above all nations that he has m., 26.19
a thing m. by the hands of a 27.15
which he had m. with them at Horeb. 29.01
which the LORD has m. it sick— 29.22
which he m. with them when he 29.25
covenant which I have m. with them. 31.16
who m. you and established you? 32.06
He m. him ride on the high places 32.13
and he m. him suck honey out of the 32.13
then he forsook God who m. him, 32.15
yours which you have m. us swear. Jos 2.17
oath which you have m. us swear." 2.20
pursuers had m. search all along 2.22
So Joshua m. flint knives, and 5.03
m. haste and went out early to the 8.14
and all Israel m. a pretence of 8.15
and they m. haste to set the city 8.19
and m. it for ever a heap of ruins, 8.28
and went and m. ready provisions, 9.04
And Joshua m. peace with them, and 9.15
and m. a covenant with them, to let 9.15
after they had m. a covenant with 9.16
But Joshua m. them that day hewers 9.27
of Gibeon had m. peace with Israel 10.01
for it has m. peace with Joshua and 10.04
Gibeon, and m. war against it. 10.05
Joshua m. war a long time with all 11.18
not a city that m. peace with the 11.19
went up with me m. the heart of 14.08
Then allotment was m. to the tribe 17.01
And allotments were m. to the rest 17.02
the LORD had m. to the house of 21.45
For the LORD has m. the Jordan a 22.25
of the LORD, which our fathers m., 22.28
and m. his offspring many. 24.03
and m. the sea come upon them and 24.07
So Joshua m. a covenant with the 24.25
and m. statutes and ordinances for 24.25

MADE (cont.)
And Ehud m. for himself a sword Ju 3.16
of Israel m. for themselves the 6.02
after they had m. search and 6.29
And Gideon m. an ephod of it and 8.27
and m. Baalberith their god. 8.33
they went and m. Abimelech king, 9.06
honor when you m. Abimelech king, 9.16
and have m. Abimelech, the son of 9.18
And God also m. all the wickedness 9.57
the Ammonites m. war against 11.04
the Ammonites m. war against 11.05
and the people m. him head and 11.11
And Jephthah m. a vow to the LORD, 11.30
according to his vow which he had m. 11.39
woman, and Samson m. a feast there; 14.10
in Judah, and m. a raid on Lehi. 15.09
And she m. them tight with the pin, 16.14
She m. him sleep upon her knees; 16.19
and he m. sport before them. 16.25
They m. him stand between the 16.25
looked on while Samson m. sport. 16.27
who m. it into a graven image and a 17.04
and he m. an ephod and teraphim, and 17.05
said, "You take my gods which I m., 18.24
And taking what Micah had m., 18.27
Micah's graven image which he m., 18.31
m. him stay, and he remained with 19.04
men in ambush m. haste and rushed 20.37
that when they m. a great cloud of 20.38
the LORD had m. a breach in the 21.15
you have m. this last kindness Ru 3.10
petition which you have m. to him." 1Sa 1.17
me my petition which I m. to him. 1.27
After he had m. sport of them, did 6.06
the LORD had m. a great slaughter 6.19
he m. his sons judges over Israel. 8.01
and there they m. Saul king before 11.15
and have m. a king over you. 12.01
and m. them dwell in this place. 12.08
Jonathan and his armor-bearer m., 14.14
"I repent that I have m. Saul king; 15.11
your sword has m. women childless, 15.33
that he had m. Saul king over 15.35
and m. him pass before Samuel. 16.08
And Jesse m. Shammah pass by. 16.09
And Jesse m. seven of his sons pass 16.10
Then Jonathan m. a covenant with 18.03
to one another as they m. merry, 18.07
and m. him a commander of a thousand; 18.13
and m. a great slaughter among them, 19.08
And Jonathan m. David swear again 20.17
I have m. an appointment with the 21.02
and m. marks on the doors of the 21.13
and m. a great slaughter among them 23.05
And the two of them m. a covenant 23.18
Philistines have m. a raid upon the 23.27
Then Abigail m. haste, and took two 25.18
she m. haste, and alighted from the 25.23
unless you had m. haste and come 25.34
And Abigail m. haste and rose and 25.42
And David m. answer, "Here is the 26.22
and m. raids upon the Geshurites, 27.08
whom have you m. a raid today?" 27.10
"He has m. himself utterly abhorred 27.12
And Achish m. answer to David, "I 29.09
Amalekites had m. a raid upon the 30.01
We had m. a raid upon the Negeb of 30.14
day forward he m. it a statute and 30.25
and he m. him king over Gilead and 2Sa 2.09
David m. a feast for Abner and the 3.20
and King David m. a covenant with 5.03
shall be m. sure for ever before 7.16
hast m. this revelation to thy 7.27
they m. peace with Israel, and 10.19
and drank, so that he m. him drunk; 11.13
she m. lamentation for her husband. 11.26
and m. them toil at the brickkilns; 12.31
tormented that he m. himself ill 13.02
and m. cakes in his sight, and baked 13.08
Tamar took the cakes she had m., 13.10
the people have m. me afraid; 14.15
that you have m. yourself odious 16.21
For you have m. it clear today that 19.06
m. haste to come down with the men 19.16
He m. darkness around him his 22.12
refuge, and has m. my way safe. 22.33
He m. my feet like hinds' feet, and 22.34
salvation, and thy help m. me great. 22.36
For he has m. with me an everlasting 23.05
King David has m. Solomon king; 1Ki 1.43
and who has m. me a house, as he 2.24
Solomon m. a marriage alliance with 3.01
thou hast m. thy servant king in 3.07
and m. a feast for all his servants. 3.15
and the two of them m. a treaty. 5.12
And he m. for the house windows 6.04
and he m. side chambers all around. 6.05
of the house he m. offsets on the 6.06
and he m. the ceiling of the house 6.09
He also m. an altar of cedar. 6.20
sanctuary he m. two cherubim of 6.23
sanctuary he m. doors of olivewood; 6.31
So also he m. for the entrance to 6.33
And he m. the Hall of Pillars; 7.06
And he m. the Hall of the Throne 7.07
Solomon also m. a house like this 7.08
All these were m. of costly stones, 7.09
He also m. two capitals of molten 7.16
Then he m. two nets of checker work 7.17
Likewise he m. pomegranates; 7.18
Then he m. the molten sea; 7.23
its brim was m. like the brim of a 7.26
He also m. the ten stands of bronze 7.27
was round, as a pedestal is m., 7.31
The wheels were m. like a chariot 7.33
After this manner he m. the ten stands; 7.37
And he m. ten lavers of bronze; 7.38
Hiram also m. the pots, the shovels, 7.40
which Hiram m. for King Solomon, 7.45
So Solomon m. all the vessels that 7.48
the cherubim m. a covering above 8.07
where the LORD m. a covenant with 8.09
fulfilled his promise which he m.; 8.20
LORD which he m. with our fathers, 8.21
neighbor and is m. to take an oath, 8.31
supplication is m. by any man or 8.38
wherewith I have m. supplication 8.59
which you have m. before me; 9.03
these Solomon m. a forced levy of 9.21
of Israel Solomon m. no slaves; 9.22
he has m. you king, that you may 10.09
And the king m. of the almug wood 10.12
King Solomon m. two hundred large 10.16
And he m. three hundred shields of 10.17
The king also m. a great ivory 10.18
of it was never m. in any kingdom. 10.20
And the king m. silver as common in 10.27
and he m. cedar as plentiful as the 10.27
and m. him king in Damascus. 11.24
"Your father m. your yoke heavy. 12.04
'Your father m. our yoke heavy, but 12.10
"My father m. your yoke heavy, but I 12.14
King Rehoboam m. haste to mount 12.18
assembly and m. him king over all 12.20
and m. two calves of gold. 12.28
He also m. houses on high places, 12.31
to the calves that he had m. 12.32
of the high places that he had m. 12.32
which he had m. in Bethel on the 12.33
but m. priests for the high places 13.33
and m. you leader over my people 14.07
have gone and m. for yourself 14.09
because they have m. their Asherim, 14.15
and which he m. Israel to sin. 14.16
of gold which Solomon had m.; 14.26

MADE (cont.)
and King Rehoboam m. in their stead 1Ki 14.27
the idols that his fathers had m. 15.12
an abominable image m. for Asherah; 15.13
Then King Asa m. a proclamation to 15.22
his sin which he m. Israel to sin. 15.26
and which he m. Israel to sin, 15.30
his sin which he m. Israel to sin. 15.34
of the dust and m. you leader over 16.02
and have m. my people Israel to sin, 16.02
and which they m. Israel to sin, 16.13
therefore all Israel m. Omri, 16.16
and the conspiracy which he m., 16.20
the sins which he m. Israel to sin, 16.26
And Ahab m. an Asherah. 16.33
about the altar which they had m. 18.26
And he m. a trench about the altar, 18.32
So he m. a covenant with him and 20.34
Then he m. haste to take the 20.41
because you have m. Israel to sin. 21.22
of Chenaanah m. for himself horns 22.11
Jehoshaphat also m. peace with the 22.44
Jehoshaphat m. ships of Tarshish to 22.48
son of Nebat, who m. Israel to sin. 22.52
I have m. this water wholesome; 2Ki 2.21
of Baal which his father had m. 3.02
Nebat, which he m. Israel to sin; 3.03
when they had m. a circuitous 3.09
it in there, and m. the iron float. 6.06
For the Lord has m. the army of the 7.06
And they m. ready his chariot. 9.21
soon as he had m. an end of 10.25
and m. it a latrine to this day. 10.27
which he m. Israel to sin, the 10.29
Jeroboam, which he m. Israel to sin. 10.31
and he m. a covenant with them and 11.04
And Jehoiada m. a covenant between 11.17
the priests had m. no repairs on 12.06
But there were not m. for the house 12.13
servants arose and m. a conspiracy, 12.20
Nebat, which he m. Israel to sin; 13.02
which he m. Israel to sin, but 13.06
them and m. them like the dust at 13.07
which he m. Israel to sin, but he 13.11
until you have m. an end of them." 13.17
until you had m. an end of it, 13.19
And they m. a conspiracy against 14.19
and m. him king instead of his 14.21
Nebat, which he m. Israel to sin. 14.24
Nebat, which he m. Israel to sin. 15.09
and the conspiracy which he m., 15.15
Nebat, which he m. Israel to sin. 15.18
Nebat, which he m. Israel to sin. 15.24
Nebat, which he m. Israel to sin. 15.28
the son of Elah m. a conspiracy 15.30
Damascus, so Urijah the priest m. it, 16.11
covenant that he m. with their 17.15
and m. for themselves molten images 17.16
and they m. an Asherah, and 17.16
of David they m. Jeroboam the son 17.21
the LORD and m. them commit great 17.21
nation still m. gods of its own, 17.29
places which the Samaritans had m., 17.29
the men of Babylon m. Succothbenoth, 17.30
Succothbenoth, the men of Cuth m. Nergal, 17.30
the men of Hamath m. Ashima, 17.30
and the Avvites m. Nibhaz and 17.31
The LORD m. a covenant with them, 17.35
covenant that I have m. with you. 17.38
bronze serpent that Moses had m., 18.04
thou hast m. heaven and earth. 19.15
and how he m. the pool and the 20.20
and m. an Asherah, as Ahab king of 21.03
that he had m. he set in the house 21.07
and has m. Judah also to sin with 21.11
sin which he m. Judah to sin so 21.16
of the land m. Josiah his son king 21.24
the pillar and m. a covenant 23.03
LORD all the vessels m. for Baal, 23.04
which the kings of Judah had m., 23.12
Manasseh had m. in the two courts 23.12
who m. Israel to sin, that altar 23.15
which kings of Israel had m., 23.19
and m. him king in his father's 23.30
And Pharaoh Neco m. Eliakim the son 23.34
Solomon king of Israel had m., 24.13
And the king of Babylon m. Mattaniah, 24.17
Then a breach was m. in the city; 25.04
Solomon had m. for the house of 25.16
of Saul they m. war on the Hagrites, 1Ch 5.10
They m. war upon the Hagrites, Jetur, 5.19
and his sons m. offerings upon the 6.49
and David m. a covenant with them 11.03
and m. them officers of his troops. 12.18
brethren had m. preparation for 12.39
had come and m. a raid in the 14.09
yet again m. a raid in the valley. 14.13
and m. loud music on harps and 15.28
the covenant which he m. with Abraham, 16.16
but the LORD m. the heavens. 16.26
with it Solomon m. the bronze sea 18.08
that they had m. themselves odious 19.06
they m. peace wth David, and became 19.19
he m. his sacrifices there. 21.28
which Moses had m. in the wilderness, 21.29
he m. Solomon his son king over 23.01
instruments which I have m. for praise." 23.05
first-born, his father m. him chief), 26.10
search was m. and men of great 26.31
and I m. preparations for building 28.02
of incense m. of refined gold, and 28.18
All this he m. clear by the writing 28.19
fathers' houses m. their freewill 29.06
for which I have m. provision." 29.19
And they m. Solomon the son of 29.22
with him and m. him exceedingly 2Ch 1.01
of the LORD had m. in the wilderness, 1.03
had m., was there before the 1.05
and hast m. me king in his stead. 1.08
for thou hast m. me king over a 1.09
over whom I have m. you king, 1.11
And the king m. silver and gold as 1.15
and he m. cedar as plentiful as the 1.15
people he has m. you king over 2.11
who m. heaven and earth, who has 2.12
and m. palms and chains on it. 3.05
And he m. the most holy place; 3.08
holy place he m. two cherubim of 3.10
And he m. the veil of blue and 3.14
of the house he m. two pillars 3.15
He m. chains like a necklace and 3.16
and he m. a hundred pomegranates, 3.16
He m. an altar of bronze, twenty 4.01
Then he m. the molten sea; 4.02
its brim was m. like the brim of a 4.05
He also m. ten lavers in which to 4.06
And he m. ten golden lampstands as 4.07
He also m. ten tables, and placed 4.08
And he m. a hundred basins of gold. 4.08
He m. the court of the priests, and 4.09
Huram also m. the pots, the shovels, 4.11
He m. the stands also, and the 4.14
these Huramabi m. of burnished 4.16
Solomon m. all these things in 4.18
So Solomon m. all the things that 4.19
the cherubim m. a covering above 5.08
where the LORD m. a covenant with 5.10
fulfilled his promise which he m.; 6.10
LORD which he m. with the people 6.11
Solomon had m. a bronze platform 6.13
neighbor and is m. to take an oath, 6.22
supplication is m. by any man or 6.29
King David had m. for giving 7.06
Solomon had m. could not hold the 7.07
prayer that is m. in this place. 7.15
these Solomon m. a forced levy and 8.08

MADE (cont.)
Israel Solomon m. no slaves for 2Ch 8.09
he has m. you king over them, that 9.08
And the king m. of the algum wood 9.11
King Solomon m. two hundred large 9.15
And he m. three hundred shields of 9.16
The king also m. a great ivory 9.17
of it was never m. in any kingdom. 9.19
And the king m. silver as common in 9.27
"Your father m. our yoke heavy. 10.04
'Your father m. our yoke heavy, but 10.10
"My father m. your yoke heavy, but I 10.14
King Rehoboam m. haste to mount 10.18
He m. the fortresses strong, and put 11.11
and m. them very strong. 11.12
and for the calves which he had m. 11.15
years they m. Rehoboam the son of 11.17
of gold which Solomon had m.; 12.09
and King Rehoboam m. in their stead 12.10
which Jeroboam m. you for gods. 13.08
and m. priests for yourselves like 13.09
because she had m. an abominable 15.16
and they m. a very great fire in 16.14
and they m. no war against Jehoshaphat. 17.10
and he m. a marriage alliance 18.01
of Chenaanah m. for himself horns 18.10
when they had m. an end of the 20.23
the LORD had m. them rejoice over 20.27
LORD will destroy what you have m." 20.37
covenant which he had m. with David, 21.07
Moreover he m. high places in the 21.11
and m. Judah go astray. 21.11
His people m. no fire in his honor, 21.19
like the fires m. for his fathers. 21.19
of Jerusalem m. Ahaziah his 22.01
the assembly m. a covenant with 23.03
And Jehoiada m. a covenant between 23.16
and they m. a chest, and set it 24.08
proclamation was m. throughout 24.09
with it were m. utensils for the 24.14
"Have we m. you a royal counselor? 25.16
the LORD they m. a conspiracy 25.27
and m. him king instead of his 26.01
the LORD, God m. him prosper. 26.05
He went out and m. war against the 26.06
in the muster m. by Jeiel the 26.11
In Jerusalem he m. engines, 26.15
He even m. molten images for the 28.02
Philistines had m. raids on the 28.18
and he m. himself altars in every 28.24
of Judah he m. high places to burn 28.25
and he has m. them an object of 29.08
we have m. ready and sanctified; 29.19
killed them and m. a sin offering 29.24
should be m. for all Israel. 29.24
so that he m. them a desolation, as 30.07
He also m. weapons and shields in 32.05
and he m. for himself treasuries 32.27
and m. Asherahs, and worshiped all 33.03
which he had m. he set in the 33.07
that Manasseh his father had m., 33.22
of the land m. Josiah his son king 33.25
and he m. dust of them and strewed 34.04
his place and m. a covenant before 34.31
Then he m. all who were present in 34.32
and m. all who were in Israel serve 34.33
They m. these an ordinance in 35.25
of Josiah and m. him king in his 36.01
king of Egypt m. Eliakim his 36.04
and m. his brother Zedekiah king 36.10
who had m. him swear by God; 36.13
so that he m. a proclamation 36.22
so that he m. a proclamation Ez 1.01
m. freewill offerings for the house 2.68
every one who m. a freewill 3.05
the son of Jozadak m. a beginning, 3.08
and m. them afraid to build, 4.04
search may be m. in the book of 4.15
And I m. a decree, and search has 4.19
a decree, and search has been m., 4.19
and sedition have been m. in it. 4.19
that these men be m. to cease, 4.21
rebuilt, until a decreee is m. by me. 4.21
by force and power m. them cease. 4.23
Cyrus the king m. a decree that 5.13
Sheshbazzar, whom he had m. governor; 5.14
let search be m. in the royal 5.17
Then Darius the king m. a decree, 6.01
and search was m. in Babylonia, 6.01
his house shall be m. a dunghill. 6.11
for the LORD had m. them joyful, 6.22
While Ezra prayed and m. confession, 10.01
Then Ezra arose and m. the leading 10.05
proclamation was m. throughout 10.07
which they had m. for the purpose; Neh 8.04
them and m. booths for themselves, 8.16
the captivity m. booths and dwelt 8.17
of it they m. confession and 9.03
thou hast m. heaven, the heaven of 9.06
Even when they had m. for themselves 9.18
their enemies, who m. them suffer; 9.27
for God had m. them rejoice with 12.43
and I m. them take oath in the name 13.25
and God m. him king over all Israel; 13.26
foreign women m. even him to sin. 13.26
queen will be m. known to all Est 1.17
So when the decree m. by the king 1.20
Esther had not m. known her people 2.10
on her head and m. her queen 2.17
Now Esther had not m. known her 2.20
as they had m. known to him the 3.06
a gallows fifty cubits high be m., 5.14
Haman, and he had the gallows m. 5.14
Mordecai and m. him ride through 6.11
they rested and m. that a day of 9.17
and m. a raid upon the camels and Job 1.17
They m. an appointment together to 2.11
and you have m. firm the feeble 4.04
which m. all my bones shake. 4.14
Why hast thou m. me thy mark? 7.20
who m. the Bear and Orion, the 9.09
Thy hands fashioned and m. me; 10.08
Remember that thou hast m. me of clay; 10.09
he has m. desolate all my company. 16.07
"He has m. me a byword of the 17.06
God has m. my heart faint; 23.16
By his wind the heavens were m. fair; 26.13
Almighty, who has m. my soul bitter; 27.02
shall be m. of coral or of crystal; 28.18
when he m. a decree for the rain, 28.26
and m. him drop his prey from his 29.17
"I have m. a covenant with my eyes; 31.01
Did not he who m. me in the womb 31.15
"If I have m. gold my trust, or 31.24
The spirit of God has m. me, 33.04
when I m. clouds its garment, and 38.09
because God has m. her forget 39.17
Behemoth, which I m. as I m. you; 40.15
let him who m. him bring near his 40.19
His back is m. of rows of shields, 41.15
into the hole which he has m. Ps 7.15
Yet thou hast m. him little less 8.05
have sunk in the pit which they m.; 9.15
The LORD has m. himself known, he 9.16
He m. darkness his covering around 18.11
with strength, and m. my way safe. 18.32
He m. my feet like hinds' feet, and 18.33
me, and thy help m. me great. 18.35
and to the LORD I m. supplication: 30.08
of the LORD the heavens were m., 33.06
thou hast m. my days a few handbreadths, 39.05
Thou hast m. us turn back from the 44.10
Thou hast m. us like sheep for 44.11
Thou hast m. us the taunt of our 44.13
Thou hast m. us a byword among the 44.14
who m. a covenant with me by 50.05

MADE (cont.)
Thou hast m. the land to quake, thou Ps 60.02
Thou hast m. thy people suffer hard 60.03
us wine to drink that m. us reel. 60.03
When I m. sackscoth my clothing, I 69.11
Thou who hast m. me see many sore 71.20
May prayer be m. for him continually, 72.15
I have m. the Lord GOD my refuge, 73.28
thou hast m. summer and winter. 74.17
and m. the waters stand like a heap 78.13
He m. streams come out of the rock, 78.16
So he m. their days vanish like a 78.33
He m. a path for his anger; 78.50
and their widows m. no lamentation. 78.64
whom thou hast m. strong for 80.17
He m. it a decree in Joseph, when he 81.05
thou hast m. shall come and bow 86.09
thou hast m. me a thing of horror 88.08
"I have m. a covenant with my 89.03
thou hast m. all his enemies 89.42
thou hast not m. him stand in 89.43
Because you have m. the LORD your 91.09
hast m. me glad by thy work; 92.04
The sea is his, for he m. it; 95.05
but the LORD m. the heavens. 96.05
The LORD has m. known his victory, 98.02
It is he that m. us, and we are his; 100.03
He m. known his ways to Moses, his 103.07
Thou hast m. the moon to mark the 104.19
In wisdom hast thou m. them all; 104.24
the covenant which he m. with Abraham, 105.09
he m. him lord of his house, and 105.21
And the LORD m. his people very 105.24
and m. them stronger than their 105.24
darkness, and m. the land dark; 105.28
They m. a calf in Horeb and worshiped 106.19
for they m. his spirit bitter, and 106.33
he m. the storm be still, and the 107.29
who m. heaven and earth! 115.15
This is the day which the LORD has m.; 118.24
in which thou hast m. me hope. 119.49
Thy hands have m. and fashioned me; 119.73
They have almost m. an end of me on 119.87
who m. heaven and earth. 121.02
who m. heaven and earth. 124.08
they m. long their furrows. 129.03
he who m. heaven and earth! 134.03
by understanding m. the heavens, 136.05
to him who m. the great lights, for 136.07
and m. Israel pass through the 136.14
when I was being m. in secret, 139.15
he has m. me sit in darkness like 143.03
compassion is over all that he has m. 145.09
who m. heaven and earth, the sea, and 146.06
they have m. some one stumble. Pro 4.16
before he had m. the earth with its 8.26
when he m. firm the skies above, 8.28
The LORD has m. everything for its 16.04
Who can say, "I have m. my heart clean; 20.09
eye, the LORD has m. them both. 20.12
The horse is m. ready for the day 21.31
I have m. them known to you today, 22.19
What is crooked cannot be m. straight, Ecc 1.15
I m. great works; I built houses 2.04
I m. myself gardens and parks, and 2.05
I m. myself pools from which to 2.06
He has m. everything beautiful in 3.11
God has m. it so, in order that men 3.14
countenance the heart is m. glad. 7.03
straight what he has m. crooked? 7.13
God has m. the one as well as the 7.14
that God m. man upright, but they 7.29
Bread is m. for laughter, and wine 10.19
they m. me keeper of the vineyeards; Sol 1.06
King Solomon m. himself a palanquin 3.09
He m. its posts of silver, its back 3.10
to what their own fingers have m. Is 2.08
which they m. for themselves to 2.20
and you are m. to dwell alone in 5.08
with which you were m. to serve, 14.03
the man who m. the earth tremble, 14.16
who m. the world like a desert and 14.17
to what their own fingers have m., 17.08
and they have m. Egypt stagger in 19.14
You m. a reservoir between the two 22.11
her palaces, they m. her a ruin. 23.13
For thou hast m. the city a heap, 25.02
therefore he who m. them will not 27.11
"We have m. a covenant with death, 28.15
for we have m. lies our refuge, and 28.15
lest your bonds be m. strong; 28.22
that the thing m. should say of its 29.16
yea, for the king it is m. ready, 30.33
its pyre m. deep and wide, with fire 30.33
hands have sinfully m. for you. 31.07
when you have m. an end of dealing 33.01
and their soil m. rich with fat. 34.07
thou hast m. heaven and earth. 37.16
every mountain and hill be m. low; 40.04
my glory, whom I formed and m.," 43.07
Thus says the LORD who m. you, 44.02
who m. all things, who stretched out 44.24
I m. the earth, and created man upon 45.12
the earth and m. it (he established 45.18
I have m., and I will bear; 46.04
on the aged you m. your yoke 47.06
from my mouth and I m. them known; 48.03
he m. water flow for them from the 48.21
He m. my mouth like a sharp sword, 49.02
he m. me a polished arrow, in his 49.02
and I blessed him and m. him many. 51.02
son of man who is m. like grass, 51.12
and you have m. your back like the 51.23
the chastisement that m. us whole, 53.05
And they m. his grave with the 53.09
and m. intercession for the transgressors. 53.12
Behold, I m. him a witness to the 55.04
gone up to it, you have m. it wide; 57.08
and you have m. a bargain for 57.08
and I have m. the breath of life. 57.16
iniquities have m. a separation 59.02
they have m. their roads crooked, no 59.08
I m. them drunk in my wrath, and I 63.06
All these things my hand has m., 66.02
and m. my heritage an abomination. Jer 2.07
They have m. his land a waste; 2.15
your gods that you m. for yourself? 2.28
it shall not be m. again. 3.16
They have m. their faces harder 5.03
"I have m. you an assayer and 6.27
where I m. my name dwell at first, 7.12
the scribes has m. it into a lie. 8.08
It is he who m. the earth by his 10.12
covenant which I m. with their 11.10
The LORD m. it known to me and I 11.18
they have m. my pleasant portion a 12.10
They have m. it a desolation; 12.11
The whole land is m. desolate, 12.11
so I m. the whole house of Israel 13.11
will it be before you are m. clean?" 13.27
I have m. their widows more in 15.08
I have m. anguish and terror fall 15.08
and m. all the nations to whom the 25.17
outstretched arm have m. the earth, 27.05
and you have m. this people trust 28.15
'The LORD has m. you priest instead 29.26
and has m. you trust in a lie, 29.31
covenant which I m. with their 31.32
thou who hast m. the heavens and 32.17
and hast m. thee a name, as at this 32.20
thou hast m. all this evil come 32.23
"Thus says the LORD who m. the earth, 33.02
the promise I m. to the house of 33.14
Zedekiah had m. a covenant with 34.08
I m. a covenant with your fathers 34.13
and you m. a covenant before me in 34.15

MADE (cont.)

covenant which they m. before me, Jer 34.18
king of Babylon m. king in the 37.01
for it had been m. a prison. 37.15
who m. our souls, I will not put you 38.16
'I m. a humble plea to the king 38.26
month, a breach was m. in the city. 39.02
King Asa had m. for defense 41.09
of Babylon had m. governor over 41.18
approval that we m. cakes for her 44.19
perform our vows that we have m., 44.25
I have m. the wine cease from the 48.33
the LORD has m. against Edom and 49.20
of Babylon has m. a plan against 49.30
the LORD has m. against Babylon, 50.45
"It is he who m. the earth by his 51.15
he has m. me an empty vessel, he has 51.34
Then a breach was m. in the city; 52.07
the king had m. for the house of 52.20
the LORD has m. her suffer for the Lam 1.05
into my bones he m. it descend; 1.13
he has m. the enemy rejoice over 2.17
He has m. my flesh and my skin 3.04
he has m. me dwell in darkness like 3.06
he has m. my paths crooked. 3.09
he has m. me desolate; 3.11
He has m. my teeth grind on gravel, 3.16
and m. me cower in ashes; 3.16
Thou hast m. us offscouring and 3.45
Behold, I have m. your face hard Eze 3.08
than flint have I m. your forehead; 3.09
I have m. you a watchman for the 3.17
blown the trumpet and m. all ready; 7.14
and they m. their abominable images 7.20
for I have m. you a sign for the 12.06
and it be m. desolate, so that no 14.15
and m. for youself gaily decked 16.16
and m. for yourself images of men, 16.17
and m. yourself a lofty place in 16.24
and have m. your sisters appear 16.51
for you have m. judgment favorable 16.52
for you have m. your sisters appear 16.52
seed royal and m. a covenant with 17.13
the king dwells who m. him king, 17.16
her whelps and m. him a young lion. 19.05
whose sight I m. myself known to 20.09
it is m. like lightning, it is 21.15
you have m. your guilt to be 21.24
by the idols which you have m.; 22.04
Therefore I have m. you a reproach 22.04
dishonest gain which you have m., 22.13
they have m. many widows in the 22.25
they have m. no distinction between 22.26
of Israel when it was m. desolate, 25.03
slaughter is m. in the midst of 26.15
your builders m. perfect your 27.04
They m. all your planks of fir 27.05
Of oaks of Bashan they m. your oars; 27.06
they m. your deck of pines from the 27.06
they m. perfect your beauty. 27.11
bound with cords and m. secure; 27.24
'My Nile is my own; I m. it.' 29.03
and m. all their loins to shake; 29.07
'The Nile is mine, and I m. it,' 29.09
king of Babylon m. his army labor 29.18
every head was m. bald and every 29.18
the deep m. it grow tall, making its 31.04
of the air m. their nests in its 31.06
I m. it beautiful in the mass of 31.09
They have m. her a bed among the 32.25
I have m. a watchman for the house 33.07
when I have m. the land of desolation 33.29
because they m. you desolate, and 36.03
with hearths m. at the bottom 46.23
Then Arioch m. the matter known Dan 2.15
his house and m. the matter known 2.17
and hast now m. known to me what we 2.23
for thou hast m. known to us the 2.23
and he has m. known to King Nebuchadnezzar 2.28
mysteries m. known to you what is 2.29
interpretation may be m. known to 2.30
A great God has m. known to the 2.45
and m. him ruler over the whole 2.48
Daniel m. request of the king, and 2.49
King Nebuchadnezzar m. an image of 3.01
have m. a decree, that every man who 3.10
which I have m., well and good; 3.15
I had a dream which m. me afraid; 4.05
Therefore I m. a decree that all 4.06
you shall be m. to eat grass like 4.25
you shall be m. to eat grass like 4.32
King Belshazzar m. a great feast 5.01
m. him chief of the magicians, 5.11
his mind was m. like that of a 5.21
proclamation was m. concerning him, 5.29
the ground and m. to stand upon 7.04
and m. known to me the interpretation 7.16
this horn m. war with the saints, 7.21
the LORD my God and m. confession, 9.04
and hast m. thee a name, as at this 9.15
an alliance is m. with him he 11.23
And they have m. deep the pit of Hos 5.02
They m. kings, but not through me. 8.04
and gold they m. idols for their 8.04
A workman m. it; it is not God. 8.06
idols skillfully m. of their silver, 13.02
their branches are m. white. Joe 1.07
"But you m. the Nazirites drink Amo 2.12
unless they have m. an appointment? 3.03
and I m. the stench of your camp go 4.10
He who m. the Pleiades and Orion, 5.08
which you m. for yourselves; 5.26
of Isaac shall be m. desolate, 7.09
who m. the sea and the dry land. Jon 1.09
sacrifice to the LORD and m. vows. 1.16
And he m. proclamation and published 3.07
That is why I m. haste to flee to 4.02
and m. a booth for himself there. 4.05
and m. it come up over Jonah, that 4.06
they have m. their deeds evil. Mic 3.04
my people and m. boasts against Zep 2.08
their cities have been m. desolate, 3.06
promise that I m. you when you Hag 2.05
They m. their hearts like adamant Zec 7.12
the pleasant land was m. desolate. 7.14
I have m. Ephraim its arrow. 9.13
which I had m. with all the 11.10
Has not the one God m. and sustained Mal 2.15
garment, and a worse tear is m. Mt 9.16
his garment, I shall be m. well." 9.21
your faith has m. you well." 9.22
instantly the woman was m. well. 9.22
Then he m. the disciples get into 14.22
as many as touched it were m. well. 14.36
you have m. void the word of God. 15.06
that he had, and payment to be m. 18.25
that he who m. them from the 19.04
the beginning m. them male and 19.04
who have been m. eunuchs by men, 19.12
who have m. themselves eunuchs for 19.12
and you have m. them equal to us 20.12
I have m. ready my dinner, my oxen 22.04
But they m. light of it and went 22.05
temple that has m. the gold sacred? 23.17
and he m. five talents more. 25.16
the two talents m. two talents 25.17
here I have m. five talents more.' 25.20
here I have m. two talents more.' 25.22
and elders, he m. no answer. 27.12
sepulchre to be m. secure until 27.64
So they went and m. the sepulchre 27.66
left him, and he was m. clean. Mk 1.42
and when they had m. an opening, 2.04
the old, and a worse tear is m. 2.21
and as they m. their way his 2.23
them, "The sabbath was m. for man, 2.27

MADE (cont.)
hid, except to be m. manifest; Mk 4.22
that she may be m. well, and live." 5.23
his garments, I shall be m. well." 5.28
"Daughter, your faith has m. you well; 5.34
Immediately he m. his disciples get 6.45
as many as touched it were m. well. 6.56
'God m. them male and female.' 10.06
your faith has m. you well." 10.52
But you have m. it a den of robbers." 11.17
this temple that is m. with hands, 14.58
build another, not m. with hands.'" 14.58
But he was silent and m. no answer. 14.61
But Jesus m. no further answer, so 15.05
and he m. signs to them and remained Lk 1.22
And they m. signs to his father, 1.62
which the Lord has m. known to us." 2.15
saw it they m. known the saying 2.17
the crooked shall be m. straight, 3.05
the rough ways shall be m. smooth; 3.05
And Levi m. him a great feast in 5.29
hid that shall not be m. manifest, 8.17
"Daughter, your faith has m. you well; 8.48
and m. them all sit down. 9.15
Did not he who m. the outside make 11.40
who m. me a judge or divider over 12.14
immediately she was m. straight, 13.13
of the air m. nests in its branches." 13.19
your faith has m. you well." 17.19
your faith has m. you well." 18.42
So he m. haste and came down, and 19.06
your pound has m. ten pounds more.' 19.16
your pound has m. five pounds.' 19.18
but you have m. it a den of robbers." 19.46
some length; but he m. no answer. 23.09
all things were m. through him, Jn 1.03
was not anything m. that was m. 1.03
and the world was m. through him, 1.10
of the Father, he has m. him known. 1.18
where he had m. the water wine. 4.46
the sabbath I m. a man's whole body 7.23
you say, 'You will be m. free'?" 8.33
of God might be m. manifest in him. 9.03
the ground and m. clay of the 9.06
called Jesus m. clay and anointed 9.11
day when Jesus m. the clay and 9.14
There they m. him a supper; 12.02
You are already m. clean by the 15.03
my Father I have m. known to you. 15.15
with thee before the world was m. 17.05
I m. known to them thy name, and I 17.26
officers had m. a charcoal fire, 18.18
because he has m. himself the Son 19.07
his garments and m. four parts, 19.23
Thou hast m. known to me the ways Ac 2.28
that God has m. him both Lord and 2.36
his feet and ankles were m. strong. 3.07
power or piety we had m. him walk? 3.12
has m. this man strong whom you see 3.16
distribution was m. to each as any 4.35
who m. him governor over Egypt and 7.10
visit Joseph m. himself known to 7.13
'Who m. you a ruler and a judge 7.27
'Who m. you a ruler and a judge?' 7.35
And they m. a calf in those days, 7.41
figures which you m. to worship; 7.43
not dwell in houses m. with hands; 7.48
and m. great lamentation over him. 8.02
the man who m. havoc in Jerusalem 9.21
which Dorcas m. while she was with 9.39
having m. inquiry for Simon's house, 10.17
the third day and m. him manifest; 10.40
for him was m. to God by the 12.05
and m. an oration to them. 12.21
our fathers and m. the people 13.17
When an attempt was m. by both 14.05
that he had faith to be m. well, 14.09
living God who m. the heaven and 14.15
city and had m. many disciples, 14.21
early days God m. choice among you, 15.07
and he m. no distinction between us 15.09
who has m. these things known from 15.18
we m. a direct voyage to Samothrace, 16.11
The God who m. the world and 17.24
not live in shrines m. by man, 17.24
And he m. from one every nation of 17.26
the Jews m. a united attack upon 18.12
who m. silver shrines of Artemis, 19.24
that gods m. with hands are not 19.26
when a plot was m. against him by 20.03
Holy Spirit has m. you guardians, 20.28
After these days we m. ready and 21.15
"As I m. my journey and drew near 22.06
the Jews m. a plot and bound 23.12
than forty who m. this conspiracy. 23.13
I m. no delay, but on the next day 25.17
out his hand and m. his defense: 26.01
in the promise m. by God to our 26.06
And as he thus m. his defense, 26.24
to the wind they m. for the beach. 27.40
And from there we m. a circuit and 28.13
after Paul had m. one statement: 28.25
in the things that have been m. Rom 1.20
"I have m. you the father of many 4.17
No distrust m. him waver concerning 4.20
disobedience many were m. sinners, 5.19
obedience many will be m. righteous. 5.19
molder, "Why have you m. me thus?" 9.20
of wrath m. for destruction, 9.22
Sodom and been m. like Gomorrah. 9.29
writings is m. known to all 16.26
Has not God m. foolish the wisdom 1Co 1.20
whom God m. our wisdom, our righteousness 1.30
we have not m. use of this right, 9.12
But I have m. no use of any of 9.15
I have m. myself a slave to all, 9.19
(For man was not m. from woman, 11.08
for as woman was m. from man, 11.12
and all were m. to drink of one 12.13
If a revelation is m. to another 14.30
in Christ shall all be m. alive. 15.22
contributions need not be m. when I come. 16.02
they have m. up for your absence; 16.17
For I m. up my mind not to make you 2Co 2.01
who should have m. me rejoice, 2.03
a house not m. with hands, eternal 5.01
For our sake he m. him to be sin 5.21
For even if I m. you sorry with my 7.08
as he had already m. a beginning, 8.06
must do as he has m. up his mind, 9.07
way we have m. this plain to you 11.06
Who is m. to fall, and I am not 11.29
for my power is m. perfect in 12.09
promises were m. to Abraham and to Gal 3.16
to whom the promise had been m.; 3.19
it is always good to be m. much of, 4.18
For he has m. known to us in all Eph 1.09
the dead and m. him sit at his 1.20
feet and has m. him the head over 1.22
And you he m. alive, when you were 2.01
m. us alive together with Christ 2.05
and m. us sit with him in the 2.06
which is m. in the flesh by hands— 2.11
who has m. us both one, and has 2.14
how the mystery was m. known to me 3.03
which was not m. known to the sons 3.05
gospel I was m. a minister according 3.07
might now be m. known to the 3.10
have been m. confident in the Lord Php 1.14
Christ Jesus has m. me his own. 3.12
consider that I have m. it my own; 3.13
your requests be m. known to God. 4.06
and has m. known to us your love in Col 1.08
generations but now m. manifest to 1.26
a circumcision m. without hands, 2.11
God m. alive together with him, 2.13

MADE (cont.)
and powers and m. a public example Col 2.15
uncleanness, nor is it m. with guile; 1Th 2.03
we might have m. demands as 2.06
that you may be m. worthy of the 2Th 1.05
persons have m. shipwreck of their 1Ti 1.19
thanksgiving be m. for all men, 2.01
called when you m. the good 6.12
Pontius Pilate m. the good confession, 6.13
and this will be m. manifest at the 6.15
When he had m. purification for Heb 1.03
while was m. lower than the angels, 2.09
Therefore he had to be m. like his 2.17
himself to be m. a high priest, 5.05
and being m. perfect he became the 5.09
For when God m. a promise to 6.13
(for the law m. nothing perfect); on 7.19
who has been m. perfect for ever. 7.28
covenant that I m. with their 8.09
These preparations having thus been m., 9.06
perfect tent (not m. with hands, 9.11
of the one who m. it must be 9.16
long as the one who m. it is alive. 9.17
not into a sanctuary m. with hands, 9.24
should be m. a stool for his feet. 10.13
is seen was m. out of things which 11.03
m. mention of the exodus of the 11.22
us they should not be m. perfect. 11.40
whose words m. the hearers entreat 12.19
spirits of just men m. perfect, 12.23
is shaken, as of what has been m., 12.27
have you not m. distinctions among Jas 2.04
who are m. in the likeness of God. 3.09
which he has m. to dwell in us"? 4.05
world but was m. manifest at the 1Pe 1.20
the flesh but m. alive in the 3.18
myths when we m. known to you the 2Pe 1.16
the prophetic word m. more sure. 1.19
extinction and m. them an example 2.06
the life was m. manifest, and we saw 1Jn 1.02
Father and was m. manifest to us— 1.02
love of God was m. manifest among 4.09
has m. him a liar, because he has 5.10
obtained the requests m. of him. 5.15
and he m. it known by sending his Rev 1.01
and m. us a kingdom, priests to his 1.06
and hast m. them a kingdom and 5.10
their robes and m. them white in 7.14
seven trumpets m. ready to blow 8.06
water, because it was m. bitter. 8.11
eaten it my stomach was m. bitter. 10.10
worship him who m. heaven and 14.07
she who m. all nations drink the 14.08
the earth was m. bright with his 18.01
and his Bride has m. herself ready; 19.07
of the gates m. of a single pearl, 21.21

MADMAN
to play the m. in my presence? 1Sa 21.15
Like a m. who throws firebrands, Pro 26.18
LORD over every m. who prophesies, Jer 29.26
better one—I am talking like a m.— 2Co 11.23

MADMANNAH
Ziklag, M. Sansannah, Jos 15.31
She also bore Shaaph the father of M., 1Ch 2.49

MADMEN
Do I lack m., that you have brought 1Sa 21.15
You also, O M., shall be brought Jer 48.02

MADMENAH
M. is in flight, the inhabitants of Is 10.31

MADNESS
smite you with m. and blindness Deu 28.28
wisdom and to know m. and folly. Ecc 1.17
consider wisdom and m. and folly; 2.12
and the foolishness which is m. 7.25
and m. is in their hearts while 9.03
the end of his talk is wicked m. 10.13
with panic, and its rider with m. Zec 12.04
and restrained the prophet's m. 2Pe 2.16

MADON
this, he sent to Joab king of M., Jos 11.01
the king of M., one; the king of 12.19

MAGADAN
boat and went to the region on M. Mt 15.39

MAGBISH
The sons of M., one hundred and Ez 2.30

MAGDALENE
among whom were Mary M., Mt 27.56
Mary M. and the other Mary were 27.61
Mary M. and the other Mary went to 28.01
from afar, among whom were Mary M., Mk 15.40
Mary M. and Mary the mother of 15.47
Mary M., and Mary the mother of 16.01
he appeared first to Mary M., from whom * 16.09
called M., from whom seven demons Lk 8.02
Now it was Mary M. and Joanna and 24.10
the wife of Clopas, and Mary M. Jn 19.25
the week Mary M. came to the tomb 20.01
Mary M. went and said to the 20.18

MAGDIEL
M., and Iram; these are the chiefs of Gen 36.43
M., and Iram; these are the chiefs of 1Ch 1.54

MAGGOT
who is a m., and the son of man, who Job 25.06

MAGGOTS
m. are the bed beneath you, and Is 14.11

MAGIC
A bribe is like a m. stone in the Pro 17.08
women who sew m. bands upon all Eze 13.18
am against your m. bands with 13.20
practiced m. in the city and Ac 8.09
he had amazed them with his m. 8.11
who practiced m. arts brought 19.19

MAGICIAN
and the skilful m. and the expert Is 3.03
a thing of any m. or enchanter or Dan 2.10
they came upon a certain m., Ac 13.06
But Elymas the m. (for that is the 13.08

MAGICIANS
for all the m. of Egypt and all Gen 41.08
And I told it to the m., 41.24
the m. of Egypt, did the same by Ex 7.11
But the m. of Egypt did the same by 7.22
But the m. did the same by their 8.07
The m. tried by their secret arts 8.18
And the m. said to Pharaoh, "This is 8.19
And the m. could not stand before 9.11
were upon the m. and upon all the 9.11
than all the m. and enchanters Dan 1.20
Then the king commanded that the m., 2.02
m., or astrologers can show to the 2.27
Then the m., the enchanters, the 4.07
chief of the m., because I know 4.09
father, made him chief of the m., 5.11

MAGISTRATE
go with your accuser before the m., Lk 12.58

MAGISTRATES
appoint m. and judges who may judge Ez 7.25
the m., and all the officials of Dan 3.02
the m., and all the officials of 3.03
brought them to the m. they said, Ac 16.20
and the m. tore the garments off 16.22

MAGISTRATES (cont.)
the m. sent the police, saying, "Let Ac 16.35
"The m. have sent to let you go; 16.36
reported these words to the m., 16.38

MAGNIFICENCE
may even be deposed from her m., Ac 19.27

MAGNIFICENT
the LORD must be exceedingly m., 1Ch 22.05

MAGNIFIED
and thy name will be m. for ever, 2Sa 7.26
be established and m. for ever, 1Ch 17.24
because he m. himself against the Jer 48.26
because he m. himself against the 48.42
And you m. yourselves against me Eze 35.13
did as he pleased and m. himself. Dan 8.04
Then the he-goat m. himself exceedingly; 8.08
It m. itself, even up to the Prince 8.11

MAGNIFIES
And Mary said, "My soul m. the Lord, Lk 1.46

MAGNIFY
If indeed you m. yourselves against Job 19.05
O m. the LORD with me, and let us Ps 34.03
dishonor who m. themselves against 35.26
I will m. him with thanksgiving. 69.30
or the saw m. itself against him Is 10.15
to m. his law and make it glorious. 42.21
his own mind he shall m. himself. Dan 8.25
himself and m. himself above every 11.36
for he shall m. himself above all. 11.37
acknowledge him he shall m. with honor. 11.39
to the Gentiles, I m. my ministry Rom 11.13

MAGOG
M., Madai, Javan, Tubal, Meshech, and Gen 10.02
M., Madai, Javan, Tubal, Meshech, and 1Ch 1.05
face toward Gog, of the land of M., Eze 38.02
send fire on M. and on those who 39.06
Gog and M., to gather them for Rev 20.08

MAGPIASH
M., Meshullam, Hezir, Neh 10.20

MAHALAB
it ends at the sea; M., Achzib, Jos 19.29

MAHALALEEL
the son of M., the son of Cainan, Lk 3.37

MAHALALEL
years, he became the father of M. Gen 5.12
the birth of M. eight hundred and 5.13
When M. had lived sixty-five years, 5.15
M. lived after the birth of Jared 5.16
Thus all the days of M. were eight 5.17
Kenan, M., Jared; 1Ch 1.02
son of M., of the sons of Perez; Neh 11.04

MAHALATH
M. the daughter of Ishmael Abraham's Gen 28.09
Rehoboam took as wife M. the 2Ch 11.18

MAHANAIM
called the name of that place M. Gen 32.02
and from M. to the territory of Jos 13.26
Their region extended from M., 13.30
M. with its pasture lands, 21.38
Saul, and brought him over to M.; 2Sa 2.08
Saul, went out from M. to Gibeon. 2.12
the whole forenoon they came to M. 2.29
Then David came to M. And Absalom 17.24
When David came to M., Shobi the 17.27
with food while he stayed at M.; 19.32
curse on the day when I went to M.; 1Ki 2.08
Ahinadab the son of Iddo, in M.; 4.14
M. with its pasture lands, 1Ch 6.80

MAHANEHDAN
the LORD began to stir him in M., Ju 13.25
place is called M. to this day; 18.12

MAHARAI
Zalmon the Ahohite, M. of Netophah, 2Sa 23.28
M. of Netophah, Heled the son of 1Ch 11.30
was M. of Netophah, of the Zerahites; 27.13

MAHATH
of Elkanah, son of M., son of Amasai, 1Ch 6.35
M. the son of Amasai, and Joel the 2Ch 29.12
M., and Benaiah were overseers 31.13

MAHAVITE
Eliel the M., and Jeribai, and 1Ch 11.46

MAHAZIOTH
Joshbekashah, Mallothi, Hothir, M. 1Ch 25.04
to M., his sons and his brethren, 25.30

MAHERSHALALHASHBAZ
characters, 'Belonging to M.'" Is 8.01
LORD said to me, "Call his name M.; 8.03

MAHLAH
daughters of Zelophehad were M., Num 26.33
M., Noah, Hoglah, Milcah, and Tirzah. 27.01
for M., Tirzah, Hoglah, Milcah, and 36.11
M., Noah, Hoglah, Milcah, and Tirzah. Jos 17.03
bore Ishod, Abiezer, and M. 1Ch 7.18

MAHLI
The sons of Merari: M. and Mushi. Ex 6.19
by their families: M. and Mushi. Num 3.20
The sons of Merari: M. and Mushi. 1Ch 6.19
M., Libni his son, Shimei his son, 6.29
son of M., son of Mushi, son of 6.47
The sons of Merari: M. and Mushi. 23.21
The sons of M.: Eleazar and Kish. 23.21
M., Eder, and Jeremoth, three. 23.23
The sons of Merari: M. and Mushi. 24.26
Of M.: Eleazar, who had no sons. 24.28
M., Eder, and Jerimoth. 24.30
of the sons of M. the son of Levi, Ez 8.18

MAHLITES
family of the M. and the family of Num 3.33
Hebronites, the family of the M., 26.58

MAHLON
his two sons were M. and Chilion; Ru 1.02
and both M. and Chilion died, so 1.05
that belonged to Chilion and to M. 4.09
the widow of M., I have bought to 4.10

MAHOL
Calcol, and Darda, the sons of M.; 1Ki 4.31

MAHSEIAH
Baruch the son of Neriah son of M., Jer 32.12
son of M., when he went with 51.59

MAID
had an Egyptian m. whose name was Gen 16.01
go in to my m.; it may be that 16.02
took Hagar the Egyptian her m., 16.03
I gave my m. to your embrace, and 16.05
your m. is in your power; 16.06
m. of Sarai, where have you come 16.08
Sarah's m., bore to Abraham. 25.12
(Laban gave his m. Zilpah to his 29.24
to his daughter Leah to be her m.) 29.24
(Laban gave his m. Bilhah to his 29.29
his daughter Rachel to be her m.) 29.29
Then she said, "Here is my m. Bilhah; 30.03
gave him her m. Bilhah as a wife; 30.04

MAID (cont.)

Rachel's m. Bilhah conceived again Gen 30.07
she took her m. Zilpah and gave her 30.09
Then Leah's m. Zilpah bore Jacob a 30.10
Leah's m. Zilpah bore Jacob a second 30.12
I gave my m. to my husband"; 30.18
Rachel's m.: Dan and Naphtali. 35.25
Zilpah, Leah's m.: Gad and Asher. 35.26
reeds and sent her m. to fetch it. Ex 2.05
off a little m. from the land of 2Ki 5.02
the eyes of a m. to the hand of Ps 123.02
and a m. when she succeeds her Pro 30.23
as with the m., so with her mistress; Is 24.02
And a m. came up to him, and said, Mt 26.69
another m. saw him, and she said to 26.71
And the m. saw him, and began again Mk 14.69
Then a m., seeing him as he sat in Lk 22.56
spoke to the m. who kept the door, Jn 18.16
The m. who kept the door said to 18.17
a m. named Rhoda came to answer. Ac 12.13

MAIDEN

Let the m. to whom I shall say, Gen 24.14
The m. was very fair to look upon, a 24.16
Then the m. ran and told her 24.28
"Let the m. remain with us a while, 24.55
"We will call the m., and ask her." 24.57
he loved the m. and spoke tenderly 34.03
saying, "Get me this m. for my wife." 34.04
only give me the m. to be my wife." 34.12
A m. or two for every man; Ju 5.30
of the reapers, "Whose m. is this?" Ru 2.05
answered, "It is the Moabite m., 2.06
"Let a young m. be sought for my 1Ki 1.02
for a beautiful m. throughout all 1.03
The m. was very beautiful; 1.04
so spoke the m. from the land of 2Ki 5.04
And let the m. who pleases the king Est 2.04
the m. was beautiful and lovely, and 2.07
And the m. pleased him and won his 2.09
came for each m. to go in to King 2.12
when the m. went in to the king in 2.13
and the way of a man with a m. Pro 30.19
your feet in sandals, O queenly m.! Sol 7.01
are, O loved one, delectable m.! 7.06
Can a m. forget her ornaments, or a Jer 2.32
in pieces the young man and the m.; 51.22
his father go in to the same m., Amo 2.07

MAIDENHOOD

became tall and arrived at full m.; Eze 16.07

MAIDENS

and her m. walked beside the river; Ex 2.05
this one, but keep close to my m. Ru 2.08
that you go out with his m., 2.22
So she kept close to the m. of Boaz, 2.23
kinsman, with whose m. you were? 3.02
they met young m. coming out to 1Sa 9.11
ass, and her five m. attended her; 25.42
and when many m. were gathered in Est 2.08
you put him on leash for your m.? Job 41.05
between them m. playing timbrels: Ps 68.25
and their m. had no marriage song. 78.63
Young men and m. together, old men 148.12
and maintenance for your m. Pro 27.27
her household and tasks for her m. 31.15
therefore the m. love you. Sol 1.03
brambles, so is my love among m. 2.02
concubines, and m. without number. 6.08
The m. saw her and called her happy; 6.09
Then shall the m. rejoice in the Jer 31.13
her m. have been dragged away, and Lam 1.04
my m. and my young men have gone 1.18
the m. of Jerusalem have bowed 2.10
my m. and my young men have fallen 2.21
the fate of all the m. of my city. 3.51
young men and m., little children Eze 9.06
her m. lamenting, moaning like doves, Nah 2.07
men flourish, and new wine the m. Zec 9.17
compared to ten m. who took their Mt 25.01
Then all those m. rose and trimmed 25.07
Afterward the other m. came also, 25.11

MAIDS

Then Rebekah and her m. arose, Gen 24.61
his two m., and his eleven children, 32.22
Leah and Rachel and the two m. 33.01
And he put the m. with their 33.02
Then the m. drew near, they and 33.06
the eyes of his servants' m., 2Sa 6.20
but by the m. of whom you have 6.22
seven chosen m. from the king's Est 2.09
her and her m. to the best place 2.09
When Esther's m. and her eunuchs 4.04
I and my m. will also fast as you 4.16
sent out her m. to call from the Pro 9.03
one of the m. of the high priest Mk 14.66

MAIDSERVANT

first-born of the m. who is behind Ex 11.05
or your m., or your cattle, or the 20.10
or his m., or his ox, or his ass, or 20.17
or your m., or your ox, or your ass, Deu 5.14
and your m. may rest as well as 5.14
or his m., his ox, or his ass, or 5.21
your manservant and your m., and the 12.18
your manservant and your m., the 16.11
your manservant and your m., the 16.14
made Abimelech, the son of his m., Ju 9.18
for me and your m. and the young 19.19
me and spoken kindly to your m. Ru 2.13
she answered, "I am Ruth, your m.; 3.09
spread your skirt over your m., 3.09
look on the affliction of thy m., 1Sa 1.11
remember me, and not forget thy m., 1.11
but wilt give to thy m. a son, 1.11
Do not regard your m. as a base 1.16
"Let your m. find favor in your 1.18
a m. used to go and tell them, and 2Sa 17.17
"Listen to the words of your m." 20.17
swear to your m., saying, "Solomon 1Ki 1.13
swore to your m. by the LORD your 1.17
while your m. slept, and laid it in 3.20
"Your m. has nothing in the house, 2Ki 4.02
man of God; do not lie to your m." 4.16
cause of my manservant or my m., Job 31.13

MAIDSERVANTS

menservants, m., she-asses, and camels. Gen 12.16
and gold, menservants and m., 24.35
m. and menservants, and camels and 30.43
and into the tent of the two m., 31.33
asses, flocks, menservants, and m.; 32.05
your menservants and your m., Deu 12.12
though I am not one of your m. Ru 2.13
He will take your menservants and m., 1Sa 8.16
sheep and oxen, menservants and m.? 2Ki 5.26
besides their menservants and m., Ez 2.65
besides their menservants and m., Neh 7.67
my m. count me as a stranger; Job 19.15
menservants and m. in those days, Joe 2.29
to beat the menservants and the m., Lk 12.45
menservants and my m. in those days Ac 2.18

MAIL

and he was armed with a coat of m., 1Sa 17.05
and clothed him with a coat of m. 17.38
coats of m., bows, and stones for 2Ch 26.14
shields, bows, and coats of m.; Neh 4.16
penetrate his double coat of m.? Job 41.13
spears, put on your coats of m.! Jer 46.04
him not stand up in his coat of m. 51.03

MAIMED

or heal the m., or nourish the Zec 11.16
the m., the blind, the dumb, and many Mt 15.30

MAIMED (cont.)

the m. whole, the lame walking, and Mt 15.31
to enter life m. or lame than with 18.08
to enter life m. than with two Mk 9.43
the m., the lame, the blind, Lk 14.13
in the poor and m. and blind and 14.21

MAIN

to m. encampment which was north Jos 8.13
Moab and the m. part of the Dan 11.41

MAINLAND

daughters on the m. shall be slain Eze 26.06
the sword your daughters on the m.; 26.08
imposed your terror on all the m.! 26.17

MAINSTAY

bow of Elam, the m. of their might; Jer 49.35

MAINTAIN

and cannot m. himself with you, you Lev 25.35
himself with you, you shall m. him; 25.35
supplication, and m. their cause. 1Ki 8.45
supplication, and m. their cause 8.49
and may he m. the cause of his 8.59
supplication, and m. their cause. 2Ch 6.35
and m. their cause and forgive thy 6.39
that he would m. the right of a man Job 16.21
m. the right of the afflicted and Ps 82.03
m. the rights of the poor and needy Pro 31.09
his iniquity, none can m. his life. Eze 7.13
everything and m. the traditions 1Co 11.02
eager to m. the unity of the Spirit Eph 4.03
M. good conduct among the Gentiles, 1Pe 2.12

MAINTAINED

For thou hast m. my just cause; Ps 9.04

MAINTAINS

that the LORD m. the cause of the Ps 140.12
but m. the widow's boundaries. Pro 15.25

MAINTENANCE

gifts for the m. of the house of 1Ch 26.27
household and m. for your maidens. Pro 27.27

MAJESTIC

m. in holiness, terrible in glorious Ex 15.11
with his m. voice and he does not Job 37.04
His m. snorting is terrible. 39.20
how m. is thy name in all the earth! Ps 8.01
how m. is thy name in all the earth! 8.09
more m. than the everlasting 76.04
with its m. trees will fall. Is 10.34
will cause his m. voice to be 30.30
I will make you m. for ever, 60.15
and the daughters of m. nations, Eze 32.18
was borne to him by the M. Glory, 2Pe 1.17

MAJESTY

greatness of thy m. thou overthrowest Ex 15.07
His firstling bull has m., Deu 33.17
and in his m. through the skies. 33.26
Honor and m. are before him; 1Ch 16.27
glory, and the victory, and the m.; 29.11
him such royal m. as had not been 29.25
and pomp of his m. for many days, Est 1.04
Will not his m. terrify you, and the Job 13.11
and I could not have faced his m. 31.23
God is clothed with terrible m. 37.22
"Deck yourself with m. and dignity; 40.10
splendor and m. thou dost bestow Ps 21.05
voice of the LORD is full of m. 29.04
O mighty one, in your glory and m.! 45.03
In your m. ride forth victoriously 45.04
whose m. is over Israel, and his 68.34
LORD reigns; he is robed in m.; 93.01
Honor and m. are before him; 96.06
art clothed with honor and m., 104.01
Full of honor and m. is his work, 111.03
Of the glorious splendor of thy m., 145.05
LORD, and from the glory of his m., Is 2.10
LORD, and from the glory of his m., 2.19
LORD, and from the glory of his m., 2.21
over the m. of the LORD they shout 24.14
does not see the m. of the LORD. 26.10
the LORD in m. will be for us a 33.21
the m. of Carmel and Sharon. 35.02
of the LORD, the m. of our God. 35.02
'Ah lord!' or 'Ah his m.!' Jer 22.18
of Zion has departed all her m. Lam 1.06
residence and for the glory of my m.?" Dan 4.30
my m. and splendor returned to me. 4.36
and greatness and glory and m.; 5.18
to whom royal m. has not been 11.21
in the m. of the name of the LORD Mic 5.04
restoring the m. of Jacob as the Nah 2.02
of Jacob as the m. of Israel, 2.02
were astonished at the m. of God. Lk 9.43
the right hand of the M. on high, Heb 1.03
of the throne of the M. in heaven, 8.01
but we were eyewitnesses of his m. 2Pe 1.16
m., dominion, and authority, before Jud 1.25

MAJORITY

of whom the m. had hitherto kept 1Ch 12.29
the m. advised to put to sea from Ac 27.12
punishment by the m. is enough; 2Co 2.06

MAKAZ

Bendeker, in M., Shaalbim, Bethshemesh, 1Ki 4.09

MAKE

"Let us m. man in our image, after Gen 1.26
I will m. him a helper fit for him." 2.18
was to be desired to m. one wise, 3.06
determined to m. an end of all 6.13
M. yourself an ark of gopher wood; 6.14
m. rooms in the ark, and cover it 6.14
This is how you are to m. it: 6.15
M. a roof for the ark, and finish it 6.16
m. it with lower, second, and third 6.16
covenant which I m. between me and 9.12
let us m. bricks, and burn them 11.03
and let us m. a name for ourselves, 11.04
And I will m. of you a great nation, 12.02
and m. your name great, so that you 12.02
I will m. your descendants as the 13.16
And I will m. my covenant between 17.02
I will m. you exceedingly fruitful; 17.06
and I will m. nations of you, and 17.06
bless him and m. him fruitful and 17.20
and I will m. him a great nation. 17.20
"M. ready quickly three measures of 18.06
fine meal, knead it, and m. cakes." 18.06
M. haste, escape there; for I can 19.22
Come, let us m. our father drink 19.32
let us m. him drink wine tonight 19.34
And I will m. a nation of the son 21.13
for I will m. him a great nation." 21.18
and I will m. you swear by the LORD, 24.03
and let us m. a covenant with you, 26.28
bless you and m. you fruitful and 28.03
let us m. a covenant, you and I; 31.44
and m. your descendants as the sand 32.12
M. marriages with us; give your 34.09
and m. there an altar to the God 35.01
that I may m. there an altar to the 35.03
to m. mention of me to Pharaoh, and 40.14
on the journey that you are to m., 42.38
slaughter an animal and m. ready, 43.16
to m. slaves of us and seize our 43.18
"M. every one go out from me." 45.01
M. haste and go up to my father and 45.09
M. haste and bring my father down 45.13
I will there m. of you a great 46.03
me, 'Behold I will m. you fruitful, 48.04

MAKE (cont.)

and I will m. of you a company of Gen 48.04
'God m. you as Ephraim and as 48.20
many and you m. them rest from Ex 5.05
give the people straw to m. bricks, 5.07
yet they say to us, 'M. bricks!' 5.16
LORD I did not m. myself known to 6.03
I m. you as God to Pharaoh; 7.01
very far away. M. entreaty for me." 8.28
But the LORD will m. a distinction 9.04
eat you shall m. your count for 12.04
and I m. them know the statutes of 18.16
and m. them know the way in which 18.20
"You shall not m. yourself a graven 20.04
You shall not m. gods of silver to 20.23
nor shall you m. for yourselves 20.23
earth you shall m. for me and 20.24
And if you m. me an altar of stone, 20.25
the owner of the pit shall m. it good; 21.34
He shall m. restitution; if he has 22.01
he shall m. restitution from the 22.05
the fire shall m. full restitution. 22.06
and he shall not m. restitution. 22.11
he shall m. restitution to its 22.12
he shall not m. restitution for 22.13
he shall m. full restitution. 22.14
it, he shall not m. restitution; 22.15
for her, and m. her his wife. 22.16
ad m. no mention of the names of 23.13
and I will m. all your enemies turn 23.27
You shall m. no covenant with them 23.32
lest they m. you sin against me; 23.33
And let them m. me a sanctuary, that 25.08
its furniture, so you shall m. it. 25.09
"They shall m. an ark of acacia 25.10
and you shall m. upon it a molding 25.11
You shall m. poles of acacia wood, 25.13
Then you shall m. a mercy seat of 25.17
And you shall m. two cherubim of 25.18
of hammered work shall you m. them, 25.18
M. one cherub on the one end, and 25.19
seat shall you m. the cherubim on 25.19
"And you shall m. a table of acacia 25.23
and m. a molding of gold around it. 25.24
And you shall m. around it a frame 25.25
And you shall m. for it four rings 25.26
You shall m. the poles of acacia 25.28
And you shall m. its plates and 25.29
of pure gold you shall m. them. 25.29
"And you shall m. a lampstand of 25.31
And you shall m. the seven lamps 25.37
And see that you m. them after the 25.40
"Moreover you shall m. the tabernacle 26.01
skilfully worked shall you m. them. 26.01
And you shall m. loops of blue on 26.04
you shall m. loops on the edge of 26.04
Fifty loops you shall m. on the one 26.05
loops you shall m. on the edge of 26.05
And you shall m. fifty clasps of 26.06
"You shall also m. curtains of 26.07
eleven curtains shall you m. 26.07
And you shall m. fifty loops on the 26.10
"And you shall m. fifty clasps of 26.11
And you shall m. for the tent a 26.14
"And you shall m. upright frames 26.15
You shall m. the frames for the 26.18
you shall m. under the twenty 26.19
westward you shall m. six frames. 26.22
And you shall m. two frames for 26.23
"And you shall m. bars of acacia 26.26
and shall m. their rings of gold 26.29
"And you shall m. a veil of blue 26.31
"And you shall m. a screen for the 26.36
And you shall m. for the screen 26.37
"You shall m. the altar of acacia 27.01
And you shall m. horns for it on 27.02
You shall m. pots for it to receive 27.03
utensils you shall m. of bronze. 27.03
You shall also m. for it a grating, 27.04
net you shall m. four bronze rings 27.04
And you shall m. poles for the 27.06
You shall m. it hollow, with boards; 27.08
"You shall m. the court of the 27.09
And you shall m. holy garments for 28.02
that they m. Aaron's garments to 28.03
the garments which they shall m.: 28.04
they shall m. holy garments for 28.04
And they shall m. the ephod of gold, 28.06
And you shall m. settings of gold 28.13
"And you shall m. a breastpiece of 28.15
work of the ephod you shall m. it; 28.15
fine twined linen shall you m. it. 28.15
And you shall m. for the breastpiece 28.22
and you shall m. for the breastpiece 28.23
And you shall m. two rings of gold, 28.26
And you shall m. two rings of gold, 28.27
"And you shall m. the robe of the 28.31
you shall m. pomegranates of blue 28.33
"And you shall m. a plate of pure 28.36
and you shall m. a turban of fine 28.39
and you shall m. a girdle embroidered 28.39
sons you shall m. coats and 28.40
you shall m. them for glory and 28.40
And you shall m. for them linen 28.42
You shall m. them of fine wheat 29.02
when you m. atonement for it, and 29.36
Seven days you shall m. atonement 29.37
"You shall m. an altar to burn 30.01
of acacia wood shall you m. it. 30.01
and you shall m. for it a molding 30.03
golden rings shall you m. for it; 30.04
sides of it shall you m. them, 30.04
You shall m. the poles of acacia 30.05
Aaron shall m. atonement upon its 30.10
he shall m. atonement for it once 30.10
offering to m. atonement for 30.15
so as to m. atonement for yourselves." 30.16
"You shall also m. a laver of 30.18
and you shall m. of these a sacred 30.25
and you shall m. no other like it 30.32
and m. an incense blended as by the 30.35
which you shall m. according to 30.37
you shall not m. for yourselves; 30.37
that they may m. all that I have 31.06
m. us gods, who shall go before us; 32.01
of you I will m. a great nation." 32.10
'M. us gods, who shall go before us; 32.23
perhaps I can m. atonement for your 32.30
"I will m. all my goodness pass 33.19
And he said, "Behold, I m. a covenant. 34.10
lest you m. a covenant with the 34.12
lest you m. a covenant with the 34.15
their gods and m. your sons play 34.16
"You shall m. for yourself no 34.17
you come and m. all that the LORD 35.10
Every one who could m. an offering 35.24
for him to m. atonement for him. Lev 1.04
priest shall m. atonement for them, 4.20
priest shall m. atonement for him 4.26
priest shall m. atonement for him, 4.31
priest shall m. atonement for him 4.35
priest shall m. atonement for him 5.06
priest shall m. atonement for him 5.10
priest shall m. atonement for him 5.13
He shall also m. restitution for 5.16
priest shall m. atonement for him 5.16
priest shall m. atonement for him 5.18
priest shall m. atonement for him 6.07
of meeting to m. atonement in the 6.30
it, to m. atonement for it. 8.15
to be done to m. atonement for you. 8.34
and m. atonement for yourself and 9.07
and m. atonement for them; 9.07
to m. atonement for them before 10.17
You shall not m. yourselves abominable 11.43
to m. a distinction between the 11.47

MAKE (cont.)
the LORD, and m. atonement for her; Lev 12.07
priest shall m. atonement for her, 12.08
the priest shall m. an examination, 13.08
the priest shall m. an examination, 13.10
the priest shall m. an examination, 13.13
the priest shall m. an examination, 13.20
the priest shall m. an examination, 13.39
the priest shall m. an examination. 14.03
priest shall m. atonement for him 14.18
to m. atonement for him who is to 14.19
priest shall m. atonement for him, 14.20
to m. atonement for him, and a tenth 14.21
to m. atonement for him before the 14.29
priest shall m. atonement before 14.31
so he shall m. atonement for the 14.53
priest shall m. atonement for him 15.15
priest shall m. atonement for her 15.30
and shall m. atonement for himself 16.06
the LORD to m. atonement over it, 16.10
and shall m. atonement for himself 16.11
thus he shall m. atonement for the 16.16
he enters to m. atonement in the 16.17
the LORD and m. atonement for it, 16.18
and m. atonement for himself and 16.24
brought in to m. atonement in the 16.27
father's place shall m. atonement, 16.32
he shall m. atonement for the 16.33
and he shall m. atonement for the 16.33
and he shall m. atonement for the 16.33
the altar to m. atonement for your 17.11
to idols or m. for yourselves 19.04
priest shall m. atonement for him 19.22
You shall not m. any cuttings in 19.28
for that is to m. naked one's near 20.19
You shall therefore m. a distinction 20.25
you shall not m. yourselves abominable 20.25
They shall not m. tonsures upon 21.05
nor m. any cuttings in their flesh. 21.05
to the LORD or m. of them an 22.22
And you shall m. proclamation on 23.21
to m. atonement for you before the 23.28
who kills a beast shall m. it good, 24.18
who kills a beast shall m. it good; 24.21
you shall not m. him serve as a 25.39
you may m. slaves of them, but over 25.46
he shall m. a reckoning with him; 25.52
"You shall m. for yourselves no 26.01
down, and none shall m. you afraid; 26.06
for you and m. you fruitful and 26.09
out the old to m. way for the new. 26.10
And I will m. my abode among you, 26.11
and I will m. your heavens like 26.19
and m. you few in number, so that 26.22
and will m. your sanctuaries 26.31
and they m. amends for their 26.41
and they shall m. amends for their 26.43
twenty gerahs shall m. a shekel. 27.25
and he shall m. full restitution Num 5.07
priest shall m. her take an oath, 5.19
then' (let the priest m. the woman 5.21
'the LORD m. you an execration and 5.21
your bowels and m. your body swell 5.22
and he shall m. the woman drink the 5.24
afterward shall m. the woman drink 5.26
shall he m. himself unclean; 6.07
and m. atonement for him, because he 6.11
The LORD m. his face to shine upon 6.25
to m. atonement for the Levites. 8.12
and to m. atonement for the people 8.19
"M. two silver trumpets; 10.02
of hammered work you shall m. them; 10.02
I the LORD m. myself known to him 12.06
and I will m. of you a nation 14.12
I swore that I would m. you dwell, 14.30
to m. a pleasing odor to the LORD, 15.03
priest shall m. atonement for all 15.25
priest shall m. atonement before 15.28
to m. atonement for him: and he 15.28
and bid them to m. tassels on the 15.38
you must also m. yourself a prince 16.13
and m. atonement for them; for 16.46
thus I will m. to cease from me the 17.05
that you may m. an end of their 17.10
"M. a fiery serpent, and set it on a 21.08
sin offering, to m. atonement for you. 28.22
male goat, to m. atonement for you. 28.30
sin offering, to m. atonement for you; 29.05
then he shall m. void her vow which 30.08
establish, or her husband may m. void. 30.13
to m. atonement for ourselves 31.50
m. you a thousand times as many as Deu 1.11
m. them known to your children and 4.09
and m. a graven image in the form 4.23
did the LORD m. this covenant, 5.03
"'You shall not m. for yourself a 5.08
you shall m. no covenant with them, 7.02
You shall not m. marriages with 7.03
you may not m. an end of them at 7.22
and you shall m. their name perish 7.24
that he might m. you know that man 8.03
and m. them perish quickly, as the 9.03
and I will m. of you a nation 9.14
mountain, and m. an ark of wood. 10.01
his name and m. his habitation 12.05
to m. his name dwell there, thither 12.11
to m. you leave the way in which 13.05
inquire and m. search and ask 13.14
yourselves or m. any baldness on 14.01
to m. his name dwell there, you 14.23
to m. his name dwell there. 16.02
to m. his name dwell in it, there 16.06
to m. his name dwell there. 16.11
when you m. your ingathering from 16.13
LORD your God which you shall m. 16.21
you shall m. a parapet for your 22.08
"You shall m. yourself tassels on 22.12
"When you m. a vow to the LORD your 23.21
"When you m. your neighbor a loan 24.10
man to whom you m. the loan shall 24.11
to m. his name to dwell there. 26.02
"And you shall m. response before 26.05
And the LORD will m. you abound in 28.11
And the LORD will m. you the head, 28.13
The LORD will m. the pestilence 28.21
The LORD will m. the rain of your 28.24
that you should never m. again; 28.68
Moses to m. with the people of 29.01
you only that I m. this sworn 29.14
and he will m. you more prosperous 30.05
your God will m. you abundantly 30.09
I will m. the remembrance of them 32.26
I kill and I m. alive; I wound 32.39
I will m. my arrows drunk with 32.42
then you shall m. your way prosperous, Jos 1.08
"M. flint knives and circumcise the 5.02
And when they m. a long blast with 6.05
things and m. the camp of Israel a 6.18
do not m. the whole people toil up 7.03
so now m. a covenant with us. 9.06
then how can we m. a covenant with 9.07
come now, m. a covenant with us. 9.11
at Shiloh, to m. war against them. 22.12
or m. us as rebels by building 22.19
children might m. our children 22.25
or m. mention of the names of their 23.07
and m. marriages with them, so that 23.12
and you shall m. no covenant with Ju 2.02
I will m. melody to the LORD, the 5.03
Her wisest ladies m. answer, 5.29
pray, let me m. trial only this once 6.39
"Let me m. a request of you; 8.24
m. haste to do, as I have done." 9.48
but if you m. ready a burnt offering, 13.16
the web and m. it tight with the 16.13
that he may m. sport for us." 16.25

MAKE (cont.)
to m. a graven image and a molten Ju 17.03
but do not m. yourself known to the Ru 3.03
May the LORD m. the woman, who is 4.11
to m. them sit with princes and 1Sa 2.08
mother used to m. for him a little 2.19
So you must m. images of your 6.05
and to m. his implements of war and 8.12
to their voice, and m. them a king. 8.22
M. haste; he has come just now 9.12
that I may m. known to you the word 9.27
"M. a treaty with us, and we will 11.01
condition I will m. a treaty with 11.02
the LORD to m. you a people for 12.22
the Hebrews m. themselves swords 13.19
and m. his father's house free in 17.25
Saul thought to m. David fall by 18.25
"Hurry, m. haste, stay not." 20.38
will he m. you all commanders of 22.07
Go, m. yet more sure; know and 23.22
to Saul, saying, "M. haste and come; 23.27
will certainly m. my lord a sure 25.28
wooed Abigail, to m. her his wife. 25.39
I will m. you my bodyguard for life." 28.02
me through, and m. sport of me." 31.04
M. your covenant with me, and behold, 2Sa 3.12
I will m. a covenant with you; 3.13
that they may m. a covenant with 3.21
and I will m. merry before the LORD. 6.21
I will m. myself yet more contemptible 6.22
and I will m. for you a great name, 7.09
that the LORD will m. you a house. 7.11
greatness, to m. thy servant know it. 7.21
Tamar come and m. a couple of 13.06
shall I today m. you wander about 15.20
And how shall I m. expiation, 21.03
thou didst m. my assailants sink 22.40
Thou didst m. my enemies turn their 22.41
and m. his throne greater than the 1Ki 1.37
'Your God m. the name of Solomon 1.47
and m. his throne greater than your 1.47
I have one request to m. of you; 2.16
one small request to m. of you; 2.20
"M. your request, my mother; 2.20
"Did I not m. you swear by the LORD, 2.42
each man had to m. provision for 4.07
and I will m. it into rafts to go 5.09
and pray and m. supplication to 8.33
and m. supplication to thee in the 8.47
but I will m. him ruler all the 11.34
had come to Shechem to m. him king. 12.01
and I will m. your house like the 16.03
to m. him king, and half followed 16.21
but first m. me a little cake of it 17.13
and afterward m. for yourself and 17.13
if I do not m. your life as the 19.02
and I will m. your house like the 21.22
'I will m. this dry stream-bed full 2Ki 3.16
Let us m. a small roof chamber with 4.10
"Am I God, to kill and to m. alive, 5.07
and let us m. a place for us to 6.02
himself should m. windows in 7.02
himself should m. windows in 7.19
son of Ahab to m. war against 8.28
And I will m. the house of Ahab 9.09
Joram said, "M. ready." And they 9.21
We will not m. any one king; 10.05
Come now, m. a wager with my master 18.23
let Hezekiah m. you to rely on the 18.30
'M. your peace with me and come out 18.31
and to m. atonement for Israel, 1Ch 6.49
uncircumcised come and m. sport of me." 10.04
to m. him king, according to the 11.10
named to come and m. David king. 12.31
full intent to m. David king over 12.38
of a single mind to m. David king. 12.38
m. known his deeds among the 16.08
and I will m. for you a name, like 17.08
And thou didst m. thy people Israel 17.22
will therefore m. preparation for 22.05
had promised to m. Israel as many 27.23
in me to m. me king over all 28.04
hand it is to m. great and to give 29.12
as overseers to m. the people work 2Ch 2.18
and singers to m. themselves heard 5.13
and pray and m. supplication to 6.24
and m. supplication to thee in the 6.37
and will m. it a proverb and a 7.20
had come to Shechem to m. him king. 10.01
for he intended to m. him king. 11.22
so as not to m. a complete destruction; 12.12
of Israel to m. war against Hazael 22.05
who could m. war with mighty power, 26.13
in my heart to m. a covenant with 29.10
to m. atonement for all Israel. 29.24
So they decreed to m. a proclamation 30.05
to m. it holy to the LORD. 30.17
Hezekiah did not m. return according 32.25
God has commanded me to m. haste. 35.21
We m. known to the king that, if Ez 4.16
Therefore m. a decree that these 4.21
Moreover I m. a decree regarding 6.08
Also I m. a decree that if any one 6.11
I Darius m. a decree; let it be 6.12
I m. a decree that any one of the 7.13
counselors to m. inquiries about 7.14
m. a decree to all the treasurers 7.21
Therefore let us m. a covenant with 10.03
Now then m. confession to the LORD 10.11
to m. my name dwell there. Neh 1.09
to me, "For what do you m. request?" 2.04
me timber to m. beams for the 2.08
God of heaven will m. us prosper, 2.20
prophets who wanted to m. me afraid. 6.14
sent letters to m. me afraid. 6.19
portions and to m. great rejoicing, 8.12
and other leafy trees to m. booths. 8.15
and didst m. with him the covenant 9.08
and thou didst m. known to them thy 9.14
thou didst not m. an end of them 9.31
Because of all this we m. a firm 9.38
offerings to m. atonement for 10.33
had charged her not to m. it known. Est 2.10
to the king to m. supplication to 4.08
"M. haste, take the robes and the 6.10
no one could m. a stand against 9.02
they should m. them days of 9.22
Have I said, 'M. me a gift'? Or, 'From Job 6.22
m. me understand how I have erred. 6.24
that thou dost m. so much of him, 7.17
seek God and m. supplication to 8.05
down, and none will m. you afraid; 11.19
M. me know my transgression and my 13.23
They m. night into day; 'The light,' 17.12
and m. my humiliation an argument 19.05
to him if you m. your ways blameless? 22.03
You will m. your prayer to him, and 22.27
rows of the wicked they m. oil; 24.11
and their widows m. no lamentation. 27.15
"But now they m. sport of me, men 30.01
he who made me in the womb m. him? 31.15
his ways he will m. it befall him. 34.11
Will he then m. requital to suit 34.33
and to m. the ground put forth 38.27
Do you m. him leap like the locust? 39.20
Will he m. many supplications to 41.03
Will he m. a covenant with you to 41.04
The arrow cannot m. him flee; 41.28
and I will m. the nations your Ps 2.08
m. thy way straight before me. 5.08
M. them bear their guilt, O God; 5.10
thou didst m. my assailants sink 18.39
Thou didst m. my enemies turn their 18.40
thou didst m. me the head of the 18.43
Yea, thou dost m. him most blessed 21.06
thou dost m. him glad with the joy 21.06

MAKE (cont.)
You will m. them as a blazing oven Ps 21.09
they m. mouths at me, they wag their 22.07
M. me to know thy ways, O LORD; 25.04
I will sing and m. melody to the 27.06
m. melody to him with the harp of 33.02
M. haste to help me, O Lord, my 38.22
M. me not the scorn of the fool! 39.08
O LORD, m. haste to help me! 40.13
stringed instruments m. you glad; 45.08
you will m. them princes in all the 45.16
whose streams m. glad the city of 46.04
who would not m. God his refuge, 52.07
I will sing and m. melody! 57.07
of mine, they run and m. ready. 59.04
m. them totter by thy power, and 59.11
M. a joyful noise to God, all the 66.01
I will m. an offering of bulls and 66.15
bless us and m. his face to shine 67.01
the drunkards m. songs about me. 69.12
in distress, m. haste to answer me. 69.17
and m. their loins tremble continually. 69.23
O LORD, m. haste to help me! 70.01
O my God, m. haste to help me! 71.12
thou dost m. them fall to ruin. 73.18
M. your vows to the LORD your God, 76.11
Thou dost m. us the scorn of our 80.06
against thee they m. a covenant— 83.05
M. their nobles like Oreb and Zeeb, 83.11
O my God, m. them like whirling dust, 83.13
of Baca they m. it a place of 84.06
and m. his footsteps a way. 85.13
And I will m. him the first-born, 89.27
M. us glad as many days as thou 90.15
let us m. a joyful noise to the 95.01
let us m. a joyful noise to him 95.02
who m. their boast in worthless 97.07
M. a joyful noise to the LORD, all 98.04
of the horn m. a joyful noise 98.06
M. a joyful noise to the LORD, all 100.01
oil to m. his face shine, and bread 104.15
m. known his deeds among the 105.01
that he might m. known his mighty 106.08
that he would m. them fall in the 106.26
even as I m. prayer for them. 109.04
till I m. your enemies your footstool." 110.01
to m. them sit with princes, with 113.08
and they do not m. a sound in their 115.07
Those who m. them are like them; 115.08
M. me understand the way of thy 119.27
M. thy face shine upon thy servant, 119.135
nothing can m. them stumble. 119.165
There I will m. a horn to sprout 132.17
Like them be those who m. them! 135.18
If I m. my bed in Sheol, thou art 139.08
They m. their tongue sharp as a 140.03
m. haste to me! Give ear to my 141.01
with my voice I m. supplication to 142.01
M. haste to answer me, O LORD! 143.07
to m. known to the sons of men thy 145.12
m. melody to our God upon the lyre! 147.07
and they m. haste to shed blood. Pro 1.16
I will m. my words known to you. 1.23
and he will m. straight your paths. 3.06
feet that m. haste to run to evil, 6.18
By insolence the heedless m. strife, 13.10
To m. an apt answer is a joy to a 15.23
strokes m. clean the innermost 20.30
M. no friendship with a man given 22.24
Oil and perfume m. the heart glad, 27.09
and m. my heart glad, that I may 27.11
yet they m. their homes in the 30.26
I will m. a test of pleasure; Ecc 2.01
who can m. straight what he has 7.13
and do not m. yourself overwise; 7.16
Dead flies m. the perfumer's ointment 10.01
deference will m. amends for great 10.04
Draw me after you, let us m. haste. Sol 1.04
where you m. it lie down at noon; 1.07
We will m. you ornaments of gold, 1.11
M. haste, my beloved, and be like a 8.14
even though you m. many prayers, Is 1.15
yourselves; m. yourselves clean; 1.16
And I will m. boys their princes, 3.04
you shall not m. me leader of the 3.07
I will m. it a waste; 5.06
"Let him m. haste, let him speed his 5.19
M. the heart of this people fat, and 6.10
time he will m. glorious the way 9.01
that they may m. the fatherless 10.02
will m. a full end, as decreed, in 10.23
m. known his deeds among the 12.04
to m. the earth a desolation and to 13.09
I will m. men more rare than fine 13.12
Therefore I will m. the heavens 13.13
shepherds will m. their flocks lie 13.20
I will m. myself like the Most High 14.14
And I will m. it a possession of 14.23
m. your shade like night at the 16.03
down, and none will m. them afraid. 17.02
though you m. them grow on the day 17.11
and m. them blossom in the morning 17.11
tell you and m. known what the 19.12
And the LORD will m. himself known 19.21
and they will m. vows to the LORD 19.21
M. sweet melody, sing many songs, 23.16
waste the earth and m. it desolate, 24.01
of hosts will m. for all peoples a 25.06
thou dost m. smooth the path of the 26.07
let them m. peace with me, let them 27.05
with me, let them m. peace with me. 27.05
women come and m. a fire of them. 27.11
And I will m. justice the line, and 28.17
of its maker, "He did not m. me"; 29.16
who by a word m. a man out to be an 29.21
and who m. a league, but not of my 30.01
strip, and m. yourselves bare, and 32.11
and m. firm the feeble knees. 35.03
Come now, m. a wager with my master 36.08
let Hezekiah m. you rely on the 36.15
M. your peace with me and come out 36.16
and I will m. him fall by the sword 37.07
that you should m. fortified cities 37.26
Behold, I will m. the shadow cast by 38.08
me to health and m. me live! 38.16
m. straight in the desert a highway 40.03
Behold, I will m. of you a threshing 41.15
and you shall m. the hills like 41.15
I will m. the wilderness a pool of 41.18
or m. it heard in the street; 42.02
magnify his law and m. it glorious. 42.21
I will m. a way in the wilderness 43.19
All who m. idols are nothing, and 44.09
and shall I m. the residue of it an 44.19
I m. weal and create woe, I am the 45.07
and I will m. straight all his ways; 45.13
They will m. supplication to you, 45.14
will you liken me and m. me equal, 46.05
time forth I m. you hear new 48.06
And I will m. all my mountains a 49.11
m. room for me to dwell in.' 49.20
I will m. your oppressors eat their 49.26
I m. the rivers a desert; their fish 50.02
and m. sackcloth their covering." 50.03
and will m. her wilderness like 51.03
that didst m. the depths of the sea 51.10
m. many to be accounted righteous; 53.11
I will m. your pinnacles of agate, 54.12
and I will m. with you an everlasting 55.03
and m. them joyful in my house of 56.07
day will not m. your voice to be 58.04
and m. your bones strong; and you shall 58.11
and I will m. you ride upon the 58.14
cover themselves with what they m. 59.06
and they m. haste to shed innocent 59.07
and I will m. the place of my feet 60.13

MAKE (cont.)

I will m. you majestic for ever, a Is 60.15
I will m. your overseers peace and 60.17
and I will m. an everlasting covenant 61.08
before them to m. for himself an 63.12
to m. for thyself a glorious name. 63.14
why dost thou m. us err from thy 63.17
to m. thy name known to thy adversaries, 64.02
which I will m. shall remain before me, 66.22
I m. you this day a fortified city, Jer 1.18
his place to m. your land a waste; 4.07
yet I will not m. a full end. 4.27
and destroy, but m. not a full end; 5.10
I will not m. a full end of you. 5.18
to m. it prosper, and they do not 5.28
lest I m. you a desolation, an 6.08
m. mourning as for an only son, most 6.26
to m. cakes for the queen of heaven; 7.18
And I will m. to cease from the 7.34
I will m. Jerusalem a heap of ruins, 9.11
and I will m. the cities of Judah a 9.11
let them m. haste and raise a 9.18
who did not m. the heavens and the 10.11
country to m. the cities of Judah 10.22
And I will m. them a horror to all 15.04
I will m. you serve your enemies in 15.14
And I will m. you to this people a 15.20
cut himself or m. himself bald for 16.06
I will m. to cease from this place, 16.09
Can man m. for himself gods? 16.20
I will m. them know, this once I 16.21
I will m. them know my power and 16.21
and I will m. you serve your 17.04
let us m. plots against Jeremiah, 18.18
place I will m. void the plans of 19.07
And I will m. this city a horror, a 19.08
And I will m. them eat the flesh of 19.09
I will m. you a terror to yourself 20.04
and will m. him withdraw from us." 21.02
yet surely I will m. you a desert, 22.06
who think to m. my people forget my 23.27
I will m. them a horror to all the 24.09
and m. them a horror, a hissing, and 25.09
kings shall m. slaves even of them 25.14
and m. all the nations to whom I 25.15
to m. them a desolation and a waste, 25.18
then I will m. this house like 26.06
and I will m. this city a curse for 26.06
"M. yourself thongs and yoke-bars, 27.02
kings shall m. him their slave. 27.07
may the LORD m. the words which you 28.06
but I will m. in their place bars 28.13
and I will m. them like vile figs 29.17
and will m. them a horror to all 29.18
"The LORD m. you like Zedekiah and 29.22
shall no more m. servants of them. 30.08
ease, and none shall m. him afraid. 30.10
I will m. a full end of all the 30.11
of you I will not m. a full end. 30.11
who prey on you I will m. a prey. 30.16
the voices of those who m. merry. 30.19
I will m. them honored, and they 30.19
I will m. him draw near, and he 30.21
I will m. them walk by brooks of 31.09
m. yourself guideposts; consider 31.21
when I will m. a new covenant with 31.31
which I will m. with the house of 31.33
and I will m. them dwell in safety. 32.37
I will m. with them an everlasting 32.40
torn down to m. a defense against 33.04
offerings, and to m. sacrifices for ever." 33.18
in Jerusalem to m. a proclamation 34.08
I will m. you a horror to all the 34.17
I will m. like the calf which they 34.18
I will m. the cities of Judah a 34.22
ease, and none shall m. him afraid. 46.27
I will m. a full end of all the 46.28
of you I will not m. a full end. 46.28
"M. him drunk, because he magnified 48.26
I will m. you small among the 49.15
Though you m. your nest as high as 49.16
I will suddenly m. them run away 49.19
which shall m. her land a desolation, 50.03
I will suddenly m. them run away 50.44
m. the watch strong; set up 51.12
and m. you a burnt mountain. 51.25
to m. the land of Babylon a desolation, 51.29
up her sea and m. her fountain dry 51.36
them a feast and m. them drunk, 51.39
I will m. drunk her princes and her 51.57
and I will m. your tongue cleave to Eze 3.26
vessel, and m. bread of them. 4.09
Moreover I will m. you a desolation 5.14
and m. the land desolate and waste, 6.14
therefore I will m. it an unclean 7.20
and m. a desolation. "Because the 7.23
wilt thou m. a full end of the 11.13
I will m. a stormy wind break out 13.13
and m. veils for the heads of 13.18
I will m. him a sign and a byword 14.08
Is wood taken from it to m. anything? 15.03
And I will m. the land desolate, 15.08
"Son of man, m. known to Jerusalem 16.02
I will m. you stop playing the 16.41
and m. high the low tree, dry up the 17.24
and m. the dry tree flourish. 17.24
wilderness, to m. a full end of them. 20.13
destroy them or m. a full end of 20.17
I will m. you pass under the rod, 20.37
Or do we m. mirth? You have 21.10
And m. a signpost, m. it at the head 21.19
A ruin, ruin, ruin I will m. it; 21.27
increase and m. gain of your 22.12
and m. them an object of terror and 23.46
I also will m. the pile great. 24.09
m. no mourning for the dead. 24.17
among you and m. their dwellings 25.04
I will m. Rabbah a pasture for 25.05
and will m. you perish out of the 25.07
and I will m. it desolate; from Teman 25.13
soil from her, and m. her a bare rock. 26.04
They will m. a spoil of your riches 26.12
I will m. you a bare rock; you shall be 26.14
When I m. you a city laid waste, 26.19
and I will m. you to dwell in the 26.20
from Lebanon to m. a mast for you. 27.05
they m. themselves bald for you, and 27.31
and m. the fish of your streams 29.04
and I will m. the land of Egypt an 29.10
And I will m. the land of Egypt a 29.12
and I will m. them so small that 29.15
I will m. Pathros a desolation, and 30.14
and I will m. the sword fall from 30.22
to Sheol I will m. the deep mourn 31.15
I will m. the nations quake at the 31.16
and m. their stars dark; I will cover 32.07
of heaven will I m. dark over you, 32.08
I will m. many peoples appalled at 32.10
Then I will m. their waters clear, 32.14
When I m. the land of Egypt desolate 32.15
among them, and m. him their watchman; 33.02
And I will m. the land a desolation 33.28
and I will m. them lie down, says 34.15
"I will m. with them a covenant of 34.25
And I will m. them and the places 34.26
and none shall m. them afraid. 34.28
and I will m. you a desolation and 35.03
I will m. Mount Seir a waste and a 35.07
I will m. you a perpetual desolation, 35.09
and I will m. myself known among 35.11
whole earth I will m. you desolate. 35.14
the grain and m. it abundant and 36.29
I will m. the fruit of the tree and 36.30
and m. them one stick, that they may 37.19
and I will m. them one nation in 37.22
I will m. a covenant of peace with 37.26

MAKE (cont.)
my holiness and m. myself known in Eze 38.23
and will m. your arrows drop out of 39.03
name I will m. known in the midst 39 07
go forth and m. fires of the weapons 39.09
and they will m. fires of them for 39.09
for they will m. their fires of the 39.10
months they will m. their search. 39.14
land with none to m. them afraid, 39.26
to m. a separation between the holy 42.20
and m. known to them all its ordinances 43.11
the altar and m. atonement for it. 43.20
Seven days shall they m. atonement 43.26
is the offering which you shall m.: 45.13
to m. atonement for them, says the 45.15
to m. atonement for the house of 45.17
so you shall m. atonement for the 45.20
he shall m. the same provision for 45.25
if you do not m. known to me the Dan 2.05
that if you do not m. the dream 2.09
a man who can m. known to the king 2.25
"Are you able to m. known to me the 2.26
Therefore I m. a decree: Any people, 3.29
that they might m. known to me the 4.06
they could not m. known to me its 4.07
are not able to m. known to me the 4.18
the writing or m. known to the 5.08
writing and m. known to me its 5.15
the writing and m. known to me its 5.16
to the king and m. known to him 5.17
I m. a decree, that in all my royal 6.26
m. this man understand the vision." 8.16
I will m. known to you what shall 8.19
he shall m. deceit prosper under 8.25
And he shall m. a strong covenant 9.27
and came to m. you understand what 10.14
years they shall m. an alliance, 11.06
the king of the north to m. peace; 11.06
are wise shall m. many understand, 11.33
cleanse them and to m. them white, 11.35
He shall m. them rulers over many 11.39
and m. themselves white, and be 12.10
her naked and m. her as in the day Hos 2.03
and m. her like a wilderness, and 2.03
I will m. them a forest, and the 2.12
and m. the Valley of Achor a door 2.15
And I will m. for you a covenant on 2.18
and I will m. you lie down in 2.18
and m. offerings upon the hills, 4.13
wickedness they m. the king glad, 7.03
with empty oaths they m. covenants; 10.04
How can I m. you like Admah! How can I 11.08
they m. a bargain with Assyria, and 12.01
I will again m. you dwell in tents, 12.09
and m. for themselves molten images, 13.02
and m. not thy heritage a reproach, Joe 2.17
I will no more m. you a reproach 2.19
that we may m. the ephah small and Amo 8.05
"I will m. the sun go down at noon, 8.09
I will m. it like the mourning for 8.10
and they shall m. gardens and eat 9.14
Behold, I will m. you small among Ob 1.02
nor did you m. it grow, which came Jon 4.10
Therefore I will m. Samaria a heap Mic 1.06
I will m. lamentation like the 1.08
M. yourselves bald and cut off your 1.16
m. yourselves as bald as the eagle, 1.16
and none shall m. them afraid; 4.04
and the lame I will m. the remnant; 4.07
for I will m. your horn iron and 4.13
that I may m. you a desolation, and 6.16
flood he will m. a full end of his Nah 1.08
He will m. a full end; he will not 1.09
I will m. your grave, for you are 1.14
contempt, and m. you a gazingstock. 3.06
Why dost thou m. me see wrongs and Hab 1.03
scoff, and of rulers they m. sport. 1.10
m. it plain upon tablets, so he may 2.02
awake who will m. you tremble? 2.07
the midst of the years m. it known; 3.02
end he will m. of all the inhabitants Zep 1.18
and he will m. Nineveh a desolation, 2.13
were eager to m. all their deeds 3.07
and none shall m. them afraid." 3.13
yea, I will m. you renowned and 3.20
and m. you like a signet ring; Hag 2.23
and m. a crown, and set it upon the Zec 6.11
that are true and m. for peace, 8.16
and I will m. an end of the pride 9.06
Grain shall m. the young men 9.17
and will m. them like his proud 10.03
I will m. them strong in the LORD 10.12
"Lo I am about to m. Jerusalem a 12.02
On that day I will m. Jerusalem a 12 03
"On that day I will m. the clans of 12.06
and so I m. you despised and abased Mal 2.09
the Lord, m. his paths straight." Mt 3.03
and I will m. you fishers of men." 4.19
M. friends quickly with your 5.25
for you cannot m. one hair white 5.36
if you will, you can m. me clean." 8.02
and ordered them not to m. him known. 12.16
"Either m. the tree good, and its 12.33
or m. the tree bad, and its fruit 12.33
air come and m. nests in its 13.32
I will m. three booths here, one for 17.04
but you m. it a den of robbers." 21.13
for they m. their phylacteries 23 05
for a pretense you m. long prayers; *23.14
sea and land to m. a single 23.15
you m. him twice as much a child of 23.15
and said, "Have you no answer to m.? 26.62
go, m. it as secure as you can." 27.65
Go therefore and m. disciples of 28.19
the Lord, m. his paths straight—" Mk 1.03
me and I will m. you become 1.17
"If you will, you can m. me clean." 1.40
ordered them not to m. him known. 3.12
of the air can m. nests in its 4.32
"Why do you m. a tumult and weep? 5.39
let us m. three booths, one for you 9.05
and for a pretense m. long prayers. 12.40
two copper coins, which m. a penny. 12.42
Jesus, "Have you no answer to m.? 14.60
him, "Have you no answer to m.? 15.04
to m. ready for the Lord a people Lk 1.17
the Lord, m. his paths straight. 3.04
if you will, you can m. me clean." 5.12
and m. an offering for your cleansing, 5.14
"Can you m. wedding guests fast 5.34
"M. them sit down in companies, 9.14
let us m. three booths, one for you 9.33
Samaritans, and m. ready for him; 9.52
the outside m. the inside also? 11.40
but did not m. ready or act according 12.47
m. an effort to settle with him on 12.58
they all alike began to m. excuses. 14.18
it, and let us eat and m. merry; 15.23
is found.' And they began to m. merry. 15.24
that I might m. merry with my 15.29
It was fitting to m. merry and be 15.32
m. friends for yourselves by means 16.09
m. haste and come down; for I must 19.05
knew the things that m. for peace! 19.42
till I m. thy enemies a stool for 20.43
and for a pretense m. long prayers. 20.47
furnished; there m. ready." 22.12
'M. straight the way of the Lord.' Jn 1.23
you shall not m. my Father's house a 2.16
Jesus said, "M. the people sit down." 6.10
take him by force to m. him king, 6.15
and the truth will m. you free." 8.32
you, being a man, m. yourself God." 10.33
come to him and m. our home with 14.23
and I will m. it known, that the 17.26
thou wilt m. me full of gladness Ac 2.28

MAKE (cont.)
till I m. thy enemies a stool for Ac 2.35
who didst m. the heaven and the 4.24
'M. for us gods to go before us; 7.40
to Moses directed him to m. it, 7.44
Did not my hand m. all these things?' 7.50
rise and m. your bed." And immediately 9.34
why do you m. trial of God by 15.10
wishing to m. a defense to the 19.33
defense which I now m. before you." 22.01
'M. haste and get quickly out of 22.18
nation, I cheerfully m. my defense. 24.10
before you and to m. an accusation, 24.19
opportunity to m. his defense 25.16
I am to m. my defense today against 26.02
and tried to m. them blaspheme; 26.11
you think to m. me a Christian!" 26.28
overboard first and m. for the land, 27.43
purpose was to m. him the father Rom 4.11
to m. you obey their passions. 6.12
to m. out of the same lump one 9.21
wrath and to m. known his power, 9.22
in order to m. known the riches of 9.23
a stone that will m. men stumble, 9.33
a rock that will m. them fall; 9.33
"I will m. you jealous of those who 10.19
foolish nation I will m. you angry." 10.19
Gentiles, so as to m. Israel jealous. 11.11
in order to m. my fellow Jews 11.14
and m. no provision for the flesh, 13.14
the Master is able to m. him stand. 14.04
for any one to m. others fall by 14.20
been pleased to m. some contribution 15.26
not write this to m. you ashamed, 1Co 4.14
of Christ and m. them members of a 6.15
preaching I may m. the gospel free 9.18
that would not m. it any less a 12.15
that would not m. it any less a 12.16
M. love your aim, and earnestly 14.01
but that was to m. us rely not on 2Co 1.09
Do I m. my plans like a worldly man, 1.17
my mind not to m. you another 2.01
who is there to m. me glad but the 2.02
we m. it our aim to please him. 5.09
and m. holiness perfect in the fear 7.01
so as to m. the promise void. Gal 3.17
been given which could m. alive, 3.21
They m. much of you, but for no good 4.17
out, that you may m. much of them. 4.17
who want to m. a good showing in 6.12
and to m. all men see what is the Eph 3.09
but I press on to m. it my own, Php 3.12
to m. the word of God fully known, Col 1.25
God chose to m. known how great 1.27
that I may m. it clear, as I ought 4.04
and may the Lord m. you increase 1Th 3.12
our God may m. you worthy of his 2Th 1.11
to m. them believe what is false, 2.11
about which they m. assertions. 1Ti 1.07
own family and m. some return to 5.04
are those who m. their way into 2Ti 3.06
till I m. thy enemies a stool for Heb 1.13
Thou didst m. him for a little 2.07
should m. the pioneer of their 2.10
to m. expiation for the sins of the 2.17
always lives to m. intercession 7.25
"See that you m. everything according 8.05
that I will m. with the house of 8.10
m. perfect those who draw near. 10.01
that I will m. with them after 10.16
who speak thus m. it clear that 11.14
and m. straight paths for your feet, 12.13
For we all m. many mistakes, and if Jas 3.02
in peace by those who m. peace. 3.18
and "A stone that will m. men stumble, 1Pe 2.08
a rock that will m. them fall"; 2.08
be prepared to m. a defense to any 3.15
very reason m. every effort to 2Pe 1.05
we m. him a liar, and his word is 1Jn 1.10
Behold, I will m. those of the Rev 3.09
I will m. them come and bow down 3.09
I will m. him a pillar in the 3.12
pit will m. war upon them and 11.07
over them and m. merry and exchange 11.10
and went off to m. war on the rest 12.17
was allowed to m. war on the 13.07
bidding them m. an image for the 13.14
to m. her drain the cup of the fury 16.19
they will m. war on the Lamb, and 17.14
they will m. her desolate and naked, 17.16
gathered to m. war against him who 19.19
said, "Behold, I m. all things new." 21.05

MAKER
Most High, m. of heaven and earth; Gen 14.19
Most High, m. of heaven and earth, 14.22
Can a man be pure before his M.? Job 4.17
else would my M. soon put an end to 32.22
But none says, 'Where is God my M., 35.10
and ascribe righteousness to my M. 36.03
us kneel before the LORD, our M.! Ps 95.06
Let Israel be glad in his M., 149.02
oppresses a poor man insults his M., Pro 14.31
He who mocks the poor insults his M.; 17.05
the LORD is the m. of them all. 22.02
In that day men will regard their M., Is 17.07
thing made should say of its m., 29.16
"Woe to him who strives with his M., 45.09
and his M.: "Will you question me 45.11
your M., who stretched out the 51.13
For your M. is your husband, the 54.05
me, 'Is he not a m. of allegories?'" Eze 20.49
For Israel has forgotten his M., Hos 8.14
an idol when its m. has shaped it, Hab 2.18
whose builder and m. is God. Heb 11.10

MAKERS
the m. of idols go in confusion Is 45.16

MAKES
Who m. him dumb, or deaf, or seeing, Ex 4.11
that the LORD m. a distinction 11.07
man whose heart m. him willing you 25.02
Whoever m. any like it to use as 30.38
the priest who m. atonement with it Lev 7.07
priest comes and m. an examination, 14.48
it is the blood that m. atonement, 17.11
When a man m. a special vow of 27.02
and if he m. any exchange of beast 27.10
when the LORD m. your thigh fall Num 5.21
a man or a woman m. a special vow, 6.02
But if her husband m. them null and 30.12
But if he m. them null and void 30.15
that the LORD m. to perish before Deu 8.20
But if it m. no peace with you, but 20.12
but m. war against you, then you 20.12
the city that m. war with you, 20.20
be the man who m. a graven or 27.15
LORD your God m. with you this day; 29.12
and m. expiation for the land of 32.43
and m. his dwelling between his 33.12
The LORD m. poor and m. rich; 1Sa 2.07
me when my son m. a league with 22.08
like rain that m. grass to sprout 2Sa 23.04
stripped, and judges he m. fools. Job 12.17
He m. nations great, and he destroys 12.23
and m. them wander in a pathless 12.24
and he m. them stagger like a 12.25
he m. peace in his high heaven. 25.02
like a booth which a watchman m. 27.18
When he m. inquiry, what shall I 31.14
Almighty, that m. him understand. 32.08
and m. us wiser than the birds of 35.11
mounts up and m. his nest on high? 39.27
he dwells and m. his home in the 39.28
He m. his tail stiff like a cedar: 40.17

MAKES (cont.)
He m. the deep boil like a pot; Job 41.31
he m. the sea like a pot of ointment. 41.31
He m. a pit, digging it out, and Ps 7.15
the tongue that m. great boasts, 12.03
he m. me lie down in green pastures. 23.02
and he m. known to them his covenant. 25.14
He m. Lebanon to skip like a calf, 29.06
of the LORD m. the oaks to whirl, 29.09
My soul m. its boast in the LORD; 34.02
Blessed is the man who m. the LORD 40.04
He m. wars cease to the end of the 46.09
princes and m. them wander in 107.40
and m. their families like flocks. 107.41
Thy commandment m. me wiser than my 119.98
He it is who m. the clouds rise at 135.07
who m. lightnings for the rain and 135.07
he m. grass grow upon the hills. 147.08
He m. peace in your borders; 147.14
he m. his wind blow, and the waters 147.18
For jealousy m. a man furious, and Pro 6.34
A wise son m. a glad father, but a 10.01
the hand of the diligent m. rich. 10.04
he who boldly reproves m. peace. 10.10
The blessing of the LORD m. rich, 10.22
down, but a good word m. him glad. 12.25
Hope deferred m. the heart sick, but 13.12
but passion m. the bones rot. 14.30
A glad heart m. a cheerful countenance, 15.13
A wise son m. a glad father, but a 15.20
for unjust gain m. trouble for his 15.27
he m. even his enemies to be at 16.07
of the wise m. his speech judicious, 16.23
he who m. his door high seeks 17.19
A man's gift m. room for him and 18.16
and he who m. haste with his feet 19.02
Good sense m. a man slow to anger, 19.11
Even a child m. himself known by 20.11
loves wisdom m. his father glad, 29.03
strength and m. her arms strong. 31.17
She m. herself coverings; her clothing 31.22
She m. linen garments and sells 31.24
Surely oppression m. the wise man Ecc 7.07
A man's wisdom m. his face shine, 8.01
the work of God who m. everything. 11.05
when he m. all the stones of the Is 27.09
the father m. known to the children 38.19
and m. the rulers of the earth as 40.23
he m. them like dust with his sword, 41.02
who m. a way in the sea, a path in 43.16
also he m. a god and worships it, he 44.15
he m. it a graven image and falls 44.15
And the rest of it he m. into a god, 44.17
and m. fools of diviners; who turns 44.25
and m. their knowledge foolish; 44.25
goldsmith, and he m. it into a god; 46.06
when he m. himself an offering for 53.10
from evil m. himself a prey. 59.15
Jerusalem and m. it a praise in 62.07
he who m. a memorial offering of 66.03
and he m. the mist rise from the Jer 10.13
He m. lightnings for the rain, and 10.13
into gloom and m. it deep darkness. 13.16
trusts in man and m. flesh his arm, 17.05
who m. his neighbor serve him for 22.13
"She m. a sound like a serpent 46.22
and he m. the mist rise from the 51.16
He m. lightnings for the rain, and 51.16
and that m. idols to defile herself! Eze 22.03
If the prince m. a gift to any of 46.16
But if he m. a gift out of his 46.17
that whoever m. petition to any god Dan 6.07
any man who m. petition to any god 6.12
but m. his petition three times a 6.13
the transgression that m. desolate, 8.13
shall come one who m. desolate, 9.27
the abomination that m. desolate. 11.31
abomination that m. desolate is set 12.11
who m. the morning darkness, and Amo 4.13
who m. destruction flash forth 5.09
He rebukes the sea and m. it dry, Nah 1.04
Woe to him who m. his neighbors Hab 2.15
and m. them drunk, to gaze on their 2.15
own creation whn he m. dumb idols! 2.18
he m. my feet like hinds' feet, he 3.19
he m. me tread upon my high places. 3.19
the LORD who m. the storm clouds, Zec 10.01
m. her an adulteress; and whoever Mt 5.32
for he m. his sun rise on the evil 5.45
m. her commit adultery * 19.09
the altar that m. the gift sacred? 23.19
he even m. the deaf hear and the Mk 7.37
So if the Son m. you free, you will Jn 8.36
every one who m. himself a king 19.12
pursue what m. for peace and for Rom 14.19
anything that m. your brother 14.21
bear it if a man m. slaves of you, 2Co 11.20
(what they were m. no difference to Gal 2.06
m. bodily growth and upbuilds Eph 4.16
it that no one m. a prey of you by Col 2.08
"Who m. his angels winds, and his Heb 1.07
This m. Jesus the surety of a 7.22
and if any one m. no mistakes in Jas 3.02
of the world m. himself an enemy 4.04
and m. the earth and its inhabitants Rev 13.12
righteousness he judges and m. war. 19.11

MAKEST
and m. me inherit the iniquities of Job 13.26
thou m. me ride on it, and thou 30.22
O LORD, m. me dwell in safety. Ps 4.08
thou m. the outgoings of the 65.08
who m. the clouds thy chariot, who 104.03
who m. the winds thy messengers, 104.04
Thou m. springs gush forth in the 104.10
Thou m. darkness, and it is night, 104.20
For thou m. men like the fish of Hab 1.14

MAKHELOTH
from Haradah, and encamped at M. Num 33.25
And they set out from M., 33.26

MAKING
on me by m. me odious to the Gen 34.30
all your task of m. bricks today, Ex 5.14
your daughter by m. her a harlot, Lev 19.29
corruptly by m. a graven image for Deu 4.16
corruptly by m. a graven image in 4.25
m. war against it in order to take 20.19
no more of m. war against them, to Jos 22.33
you do me wrong by m. war on me; Ju 11.27
As they were m. their hearts merry, 19.22
and David was m. haste to get away 1Sa 23.26
Abner was m. himself strong in the 2Sa 3.06
of Israel were m. merry before the 6.05
m. himself a name, and doing for 7.23
m. them lie down on the ground; 8.02
for m. any work in bronze. 1Ki 7.14
he committed, m. Israel to sin. 16.19
stone for m. repairs on the house 2Ki 12.12
was in charge of m. the flat cakes. 1Ch 9.31
all Israel were m. merry before 13.08
King David dancing and m. merry; 15.29
in m. known all these great things. 17.19
m. for thyself a name for great and 17.21
worshiped them, m. offerings to them. 2Ch 25.14
m. that a day of feasting and Est 9.18
m. his arrows fiery shafts. Ps 7.13
LORD is sure, m. wise the simple; 19.07
upon a rock, m. my steps secure. 40.02
m. her the joyous mother of children. 113.09
m. melody to him with timbrel and 149.03
m. your ear attentive to wisdom and Pro 2.02
to reflect only after m. his vows. 20.25
Of m. many books there is no end, Ecc 12.12
who fashions it, 'What are you m.'? Is 45.09

MAKING (cont.)
m. it bring forth and sprout, giving Is 55.10
Of whom are you m. sport? Against whom 57.04
I am m. my words in your mouth a Jer 5.14
vessel he was m. of clay was 18.04
m. their land a horror, a thing to 18.16
inhabitants, m. this city like Topheth. 19.12
is born to you," m. him very glad. 20.15
of Babylon is m. war against us; 21.02
m. the land an everlasting waste. 25.12
m. all the earth drunken; the nations 51.07
and m. your lofty place in every Eze 16.31
m. myself known to them in the land 20.05
very gifts in m. them offer by 20.26
after piece, without m. any choice. 24.06
m. its rivers flow round the place 31.04
m. you rule over them all—you are Dan 2.38
found Daniel m. petition and 6.11
m. you desolate because of your Mic 6.13
players, and the crowd m. a tumult, Mt 9.23
thus m. void the word of God Mk 7.13
And m. a whip of cords, he drove Jn 2.15
that Jesus was m. and baptizing 4.01
m. himself equal with God. 5.18
you not stop m. crooked the Ac 13.10
of my mind and m. me captive to Rom 7.23
thus m. it my ambition to preach 15.20
not m. full use of my right in the 1Co 9.18
God m. his appeal through us. 2Co 5.20
as poor, yet m. many rich; 6.10
in place of the two, so m. peace, Eph 2.15
m. the most of the time, because the 5.16
singing and m. melody to the Lord 5.19
m. supplication for all the saints, 6.18
for you all m. my prayer with joy, Php 1.04
m. peace by the blood of his cross. Col 1.20
outsiders, m. the most of the time. 4.05
even m. fire come down from heaven Rev 13.13

MAKKEDAH
smote them as far as Azekah and M. Jos 10.10
hid themselves in the cave at M. 10.16
found, hidden in the cave at M. 10.17
safe to Joshua in the camp at M.; 10.21
And Joshua took M. on that day, 10.28
to the king of M. as he had done 10.28
Then Joshua passed on from M., 10.29
the king of M.. one; the king of 12.16
Gederoth, Bethdagon, Naamah, and M.; 15.41

MALACHI
word of the LORD to Israel by M. Mal 1.01

MALCAM
his wife: Jobab, Zibia, Mesha, M., 1Ch 8.09

MALCHIAH
the son of M. and Zephaniah the Jer 21.01
the son of M. heard the words that 38.01
cast him into the cistern of M., 38.06

MALCHIEL
sons of Beriah: Heber and M. Gen 46.17
of M., the family of the Malchielites. Num 26.45
Heber and M., who was the father of 1Ch 7.31

MALCHIELITES
of Malchiel, the family of the M. Num 26.45

MALCHIJAH
son of Baaseiah, son of M., 1Ch 6.40
son of M., and Maasai the son of 9.12
the fifth to M., the sixth to 24.09
M., Mijamin, Eleazar, Hashabiah, and Ez 10.25
M., Shemaiah, Shimeon, 10.31
M. the son of Harim and Hasshub the Neh 3.11
M. the son of Rechab, ruler of the 3.14
After him M., one of the goldsmiths, 3.31
M., Hashum, Hashbaddanah, Zechariah, 8.04
Pashhur, Amariah, M., 10.03
Zechariah, son of Pashhur, son of M., 11.12
M., Elam, and Ezer. And the singers 12.42

MALCHIRAM
M., Pedaiah, Shenazzar, Jekamiah, 1Ch 3.18

MALCHISHUA
Saul were Jonathan, Ishvi, and M.; 1Sa 14.49
slew Jonathan and Abinadab and M., 31.02
M., Abinadab, and Eshbaal; 1Ch 8.33
M., Abinadab, and Eshbaal; 9.39
slew Jonathan and Abinadab and M., 10.02

MALCHUS
The slave's name was M. Jn 18.10

MALCONTENTS
m., following their own passions, Jud 1.16

MALE
m. and female he created them. Gen 1.27
M. and female he created them, and 5.02
they shall be m. and female. 6.19
clean animals, the m. and his mate; 7.02
are not clean, the m. and his mate; 7.02
m. and female, to keep their kind 7.03
two and two, m. and female, went into 7.09
m. and female of all flesh, went in 7.16
Every m. among you shall be circumcised. 17.10
every m. throughout your generations, 17.12
Any uncircumcised m. who is not 17.14
every m. among the men of Abraham's 17.23
and m. and female slaves, and gave 20.14
are and every m. of you be circumcised. 34.15
that every m. among us be circumcised 34.22
and every m. was circumcised, all 34.24
them, but let the m. children live. Ex 1.17
this, and let the m. children live?" 1.18
without blemish, a m. a year old; 12.05
not go out as the m. slaves do. 21.07
m. or female, with a rod and the 21.20
m. or female, and destroys it, he 21.26
m. or female, he shall let the slave 21.27
m. or female, the owner shall give 21.32
all your m. cattle, the firstlings 34.19
shall offer a m. without blemish; Lev 1.03
shall offer a m. without blemish; 1.10
m. or female, he shall offer it 3.01
m. or female, he shall offer it 3.06
a goat, a m. without blemish, 4.23
Every m. among the children of 6.18
every m. among the priests may eat 6.29
Every m. among the priests may eat 7.06
'Take a m. goat for a sin offering, 9.03
and bears a m. child, then she shall 12.02
bears a child, either m. or female. 12.07
shall take two m. lambs without 14.10
shall take one of the m. lambs, 14.12
shall take one m. lamb for a guilt 14.21
m. or female, who has a discharge, 15.33
of Israel two m. goats for a sin 16.05
not lie with a m. as with a woman; 18.22
man lies with a m. as with a woman, 20.13
shall offer a m. without blemish, 22.19
shall offer a m. lamb a year old 23.12
shall offer one m. goat for a sin 23.19
and two m. lambs a year old as a 23.19
and for your m. and female slaves 25.06
As for your m. and female slaves 25.44
you may buy m. and female slaves 25.44
valuation of a m. from twenty 27.03
shall be for a m. twenty shekels, 27.05
shall be for a m. five shekels of 27.06
valuation for a m. shall be 27.07
of names, every m., head by head; Num 1.02
every m. from twenty years old and 1.20

MALE (cont.)

every m. from twenty years old and Num 1.22
every m. from a month old and 3.15
the number of the m. Levites, 3.46
you shall put out both m. and female, 5.03
and bring a m. lamb a year old for 6.12
one m. lamb a year old without 6.14
one m. lamb a year old, for a burnt 7.15
one m. goat for a sin offering; 7.16
five m. goats, and five m. lambs a year 7.17
one m. lamb a year old, for a burnt 7.21
one m. goat for a sin offering; 7.22
five m. goats, and five m. lambs a year 7.23
one m. lamb a year old, for a burnt 7.27
one m. goat for a sin offering; 7.28
five m. goats, and five m. lambs a year 7.29
one m. lamb a year old, for a burnt 7.33
one m. goat for a sin offering; 7.34
five m. goats, and five m. lambs a year 7.35
one m. lamb a year old, for a burnt 7.39
one m. goat for a sin offering; 7.40
five m. goats, and five m. lambs a year 7.41
one m. lamb a year old, for a burnt 7.45
one m. goat for a sin offering; 7.46
five m. goats, and five m. lambs a year 7.47
one m. lamb a year old, for a burnt 7.51
one m. goat for a sin offering; 7.52
five m. goats, and five m. lambs a 7.53
one m. lamb a year old, for a burnt 7.57
one m. goat for a sin offering; 7.58
five m. goats, and five m. lambs a 7.59
one m. lamb a year old, for a burnt 7.63
one m. goat for a sin offering; 7.64
five m. goats, and five m. lambs a 7.65
one m. lamb a year old, for a burnt 7.69
one m. goat for a sin offering; 7.70
five m. goats, and five m. lambs a 7.71
one m. lamb a year old, for a burnt 7.75
one m. goat for a sin offering; 7.76
five m. goats, and five m. lambs a 7.77
one m. lamb a year old, for a burnt 7.81
one m. goat for a sin offering; 7.82
five m. goats, and five m. lambs a 7.83
twelve m. lambs a year old, with 7.87
and twelve m. goats for a sin 7.87
the m. goats sixty, the m. lambs a 7.88
for each of the m. lambs or the 15.11
and one m. goat for a sin offering. 15.24
every m. may eat of it; 18.10
every m. from a month old and 26.62
two m. lambs a year old without 28.03
sabbath day two m. lambs a year 28.09
seven m. lambs a year old without 28.11
Also one m. goat for a sin offering 28.15
and seven m. lambs a year old; 28.19
also one m. goat for a sin offering, 28.22
seven m. lambs a year old; 28.27
with one m. goat, to make atonement 28.30
seven m. lambs a year old without 29.02
with one m. goat for a sin offering, 29.05
seven m. lambs a year old; 29.08
also one m. goat for a sin offering, 29.11
fourteen m. lambs a year old; 29.13
also one m. goat for a sin offering, 29.16
fourteen m. lambs a year old 29.17
also one m. goat for a sin offering, 29.19
fourteen m. lambs a year old 29.20
also one m. goat for a sin offering, 29.22
fourteen m. lambs a year old 29.23
also one m. goat for a sin offering, 29.25
fourteen m. lambs a year old 29.26
also one m. goat for a sin offering; 29.28
fourteen m. lambs a year old 29.29
also one m. goat for a sin offering; 29.31
fourteen m. lambs a year old 29.32
also one m. goat for a sin offering; 29.34
seven m. lambs a year old without 29.36
also one m. goat for a sin offering; 29.38
commanded Moses, and slew every m. 31.07
kill every m. among the little ones, 31.17
the likeness of m. or female, Deu 4.16
shall not be m. or female barren 7.14
or whose m. member is cut off 23.01
your enemies as m. and female 28.68
these were the m. descendants of Jos 17.02
every m. and every woman that has Ju 21.11
has lain with a m. you shall 21.11
so much as one m. of all who 1Sa 25.22
left to Nabal so much as one m." 25.34
slain, he slew every m. in Edom 1Ki 11.15
he had cut off every m. in Edom); 11.16
cut off from Jeroboam every m., 14.10
and there were also m. cult prostitutes 14.24
He put away the m. cult prostitutes 15.12
him a single m. of his kinsmen or 16.11
will cut off from Ahab every m., 21.21
remnant of the m. cult prostitutes 22.46
I will cut off from Ahab every m., 2Ki 9.08
m. and female, as your slaves. 2Ch 28.10
to every m. among the priests and 31.19
had two hundred m. and female Ez 2.65
forty-five singers, m. and female. Neh 7.67
I bought m. and female slaves, and Ecc 2.07
LORD's land as m. and female Is 14.02
m. and female, so that no one should Jer 34.09
m. or female, so that they would not 34.10
took back the m. and female slaves 34.11
took back his m. and female slaves, 34.16
cheat who has a m. in his flock, Mal 1.14
killed all the m. children in Mt 2.16
beginning made them m. and female, 19.04
'God made them m. and female.' Mk 10.06
"Every m. that opens the womb shall Lk 2.23
there is neither m. nor female; Gal 3.28
she brought forth a m. child, Rev 12.05
woman who had borne the m. child. 12.13

MALES

unawares, and killed all the m. Gen 34.25
let all his m. be circumcised, then Ex 12.48
cattle that are m. shall be the 13.12
LORD all the m. that first open 13.15
shall all your m. appear before 23.17
shall all your m. appear before 34.23
of all the m. from a month old and Num 3.22
According to the number of all the m., 3.28
of all the m. from a month old and 3.34
all the m. from a month old and 3.39
the first-born m. of the people of 3.40
And all the first-born m., 3.43
"All the firstling m. that are born Deu 15.19
a year all your m. shall appear 16.16
shall put all its m. to the sword, 20.13
all the m. of the people who came Jos 5.04
m. from three years old and upwards, 2Ch 31.16

MALICE

My enemies say of me in m.: Ps 41.05
They scoff and speak with m.; 73.08
with all the m. within you against Eze 25.06
vengeance with m. of heart to 25.15
But Jesus, aware of their m., Mt 22.18
wickedness, evil, covetousness, m. Rom 1.29
the leaven of m. and evil, but with 1Co 5.08
be put away from you, with all m., Eph 4.31
m., slander, and foul talk from Col 3.08
passing our days in m. and envy, Tit 3.03
So put away all m. and all guile 1Pe 2.01

MALICIOUS

a wicked man, to be a m. witness. Ex 23.01
If a m. witness rises against any Deu 19.16
M. witnesses rise up; they ask me Ps 35.11

MALICIOUSLY

men who m. defy thee, who lift Ps 139.20
forward and m. accused the Jews. Dan 3.08

MALIGN
more will they m. those of his Mt 10.25

MALIGNANT
skin, the disease is a m. leprosy; Lev 13.51
of skin, for it is a m. leprosy; 13.52
it is a m. leprosy in the house; 14.44

MALIGNITY
deceit, m., they are gossips, Rom 1.29

MALLET
her right hand to the workmen's m.; Ju 5.26

MALLOTHI
Joshbekashah, M., Hothir, Mahazioth. 1Ch 25.04
to M., his sons and his brethren, 25.26

MALLOW
they wither and fade like the m.; Job 24.24
they pick m. and the leaves of 30.04

MALLUCH
of Kishi, son of Abdi, son of M., 1Ch 6.44
M., Adaiah, Jashub, Sheal, and Jeremoth Ez 10.29
Benjamin, M., and Shemariah. 10.32
Hattush, Shebaniah, M., Neh 10.04
M., Harim, Baanah. 10.27
Amariah, M., Hattush, 12.02

MALLUCHI
of M., Jonathan; of Shebaniah, Neh 12.14

MALTA
that the island was called M. Ac 28.01

MAMMON
You cannot serve God and m. Mt 6.24
yourselves by means of unrighteous m., Lk 16.09
faithful in the unrighteous m., 16.11
You cannot serve God and m." 16.13

MAMRE
came and dwelt by the oaks of M., Gen 13.18
by the oaks of M. the Amorite, 14.13
Aner, Eshcol, and M. take their share." 14.24
appeared to him by the oaks of M., 18.01
which was to the east of M., 23.17
of Machpelah east of M. (that is, 23.19
of Zohar the Hittite, east of M., 25.09
came to his father Isaac at M., 35.27
at Machpelah, to the east of M., 49.30
at Machpelah, to the east of M., 50.13

MAN
"Let us make m. in our image, after Gen 1.26
So God created m. in his own image, 1.27
there was no m. to till the ground 2.05
LORD God formed m. of dust from 2.07
of life; and m. became a living being. 2.07
he put the m. whom he had formed. 2.08
God took the m. and put him in the 2.15
And the LORD God commanded the m., 2.16
good that the m. should be alone; 2.18
them to the m. to see what he 2.19
whatever the m. called every 2.19
The m. gave names to all cattle, and 2.20
but for the m. there was not found 2.20
a deep sleep to fall upon the m., 2.21
taken from the m. he made into a 2.22
a woman and brought her to the m. 2.22
Then the m. said, "This at last is 2.23
because she was taken out of M." 2.23
Therefore a m. leaves his father 2.24
And the m. and his wife were both 2.25
and the m. and his wife hid themselves 3.08
But the LORD God called to the m., 3.09
The m. said, "The woman whom thou 3.12
The m. called his wife's name Eve, 3.20
the m. has become like one of us, 3.22
He drove out the m.; and at the 3.24
"I have gotten a m. with the help 4.01
I have slain a m. for wounding me, 4.23
a young m. for striking me. 4.23
When God created m., he made him 5.01
and named them M. when they were 5.02
shall not abide in m. for ever, 6.03
wickedness of m. was great in the 6.05
that he had made m. on the earth, 6.06
"I will blot out m. whom I have 6.07
m. and beast and creeping things 6.07
Noah was a righteous m., blameless 6.09
swarm upon the earth, and every m.; 7.21
m. and animals and creeping things 7.23
curse the ground because of m., 8.21
beast I will require it and of m.; 9.05
I will require the life of m. 9.05
Whoever sheds the blood of m., 9.06
by m. shall his blood be shed; 9.06
for God made m. in his own image. 9.06
first on earth to be a mighty m. 10.08
"This m. shall not be your heir; 15.04
He shall be a wild ass of a m., 16.12
against every m. and every man's 16.12
be born to a m. who is a hundred years 17.17
old, all the people to the last m., 19.04
daughters who have not known m.; 19.08
pressed hard against the m. Lot, 19.09
there is not a m. on earth to come 19.31
to him, "Behold, you are a dead m., 20.03
a virgin, whom no m. had known. 24.16
The m. gazed at her in silence to 24.21
the m. took a gold ring weighing a 24.22
The m. bowed his head and worshiped 24.26
ran out to the m., to spring. 24.29
"Thus the m. spoke to me," he went to the m.; 24.30
So the m. came into the house; 24.32
to her, "Will you go with this m.?" 24.58
the camels and followed the m.; 24.61
"Who is the m. yonder, walking in 24.65
an old m. and full of years, and was 25.08
a m. of the field, while Jacob was a quiet m., 25.27
touches this m. or his wife shall 26.11
and the m. became rich, and gained 26.13
Esau is a hairy m., and I am a smooth m. 27.11
I should give her to any other m.; 29.19
Thus the m. grew exceedingly rich, 30.43
although no m. is with us, remember, 31.50
and a m. wrestled with him until 32.24
When the m. saw that he did not 32.25
And the young m. did not delay to 34.19
And a m. found him wandering in the 37.15
and the m. asked him, "What are you 37.15
And the m. said, "They have gone 37.17
"By the m. to whom these belong, I 38.25
and he became a successful m.; 39.02
interpretation to each m. according 41.12
select a m. discreet and wise, and 41.33
"Can we find such a m. as this, 41.38
your consent no m. shall lift up 41.44
We are all sons of one m., 42.11
the sons of one m. in the land of 42.13
"The m., the lord of the land, spoke 42.30
Then the m., the lord of the land, 42.33
"The m. solemnly warned us, saying, 43.03
for the m. said to us, 'You shall 43.05
as to tell the m. that you had 43.06
"The m. questioned us carefully 43.07
and carry down to the m. a present, 43.11
and arise, go again to the m.; 43.13
grant you mercy before the m., 43.14
The m. did as Joseph bade him, and 43.17
And when the m. had brought the men 43.24
the old m. of whom you spoke? 43.27
Then every m. quickly lowered his 44.11
and every m. opened his sack. 44.11
and every m. loaded his ass, and 44.13

MAN (cont.)
that such a m. as I can indeed Gen 44.15
Only the m. in whose hand the cup 44.17
an old m., and a young brother, the 44.20
Now a m. from the house of Levi Ex 2.01
he said to the m. that did the 2.13
Why have you left the m.? Call him, 2.20
was content to dwell with the m., 2.21
who am a m. of uncircumcised lips?" 6.12
For every m. cast down his rod, and 7.12
there came gnats on m. and beast; 8.17
there were gnats on m. and beast. 8.18
out in sores on m. and beast 9.09
out in sores on m. and beast. 9.10
down upon every m. and beast that 9.19
upon m. and beast and every plant 9.22
land of Egypt, both m. and beast; 9.25
long shall this m. be a snare to 10.07
every m. of his neighbor and every 11.02
Moreover, the m. Moses was very 11.03
either m. or beast, not a dog shall 11.07
take every m. a lamb according to 12.03
then a m. and his neighbor next to 12.04
land of Egypt, both m. and beast; 12.12
both of m. and of beast, is mine. 13.02
first-born of m. among your sons 13.13
first-born of m. and the first-born 13.15
The LORD is a m. of war; the LORD 15.03
every m. of you, as much as he can 16.16
"Let no m. leave any of it till the 16.19
remain every m. of you in his place, 16.29
let no m. go out of his place on 16.29
between a m. and his neighbor, and 18.16
whether beast or m., he shall not 19.13
"When a m. sells his daughter as a 21.07
"Whoever strikes a m. so that he 21.12
But if a m. willfully attacks 21.14
"Whoever steals a m., whether 21.16
fist and the m. does not die but 21.18
then if the m. rises again and 21.19
"When a m. strikes his slave, male 21.20
"When a m. strikes the eye of his 21.26
"When an ox gores a m. or a woman 21.28
in, and it kills a m. or a woman, 21.29
"When a m. leaves a pit open, or 21.33
or when a m. digs a pit and does 21.33
"If a m. steals an ox or a sheep, 22.01
"When a m. causes a field or 22.05
"If a m. delivers to his neighbor 22.07
"If a m. delivers to his neighbor 22.10
"If a m. borrows anything of his 22.14
"If a m. seduces a virgin who is 22.16
not join hands with a wicked m., 23.01
partial to a poor m. in his suit. 23.03
from every m. whose heart makes him 25.02
the m. who brought us up out of the 32.01
the m. who brought us up out of the 32.23
'Put every m. his sword on his side, 32.27
and slay every m. his brother, 32.27
and every m. his companion, and every m. 32.27
and no m. put on his ornaments. 33.04
and every m. stood at his tent door, 33.08
every m. at his tent door. 33.10
as a m. speaks to his friend. 33.11
a young m., did not depart from the 33.11
for m. shall not see me and live." 33.20
No m. shall come up with you, and 34.03
and let no m. be seen throughout 34.03
shall any m. desire your land, when 34.24
"And let every able m. among you 35.10
every m. dedicating an offering of 35.22
And every m. with whom was found 35.23
and every m. with whom was found 35.24
and every able m. in whom the LORD 36.01
and every able m. in whose mind 36.02
"Let neither m. nor woman do 36.06
When any m. of you brings an Lev 1.02
When a m. is guilty in any of these, 5.05
uncleanness of m. or an unclean 7.21
"When a m. has on the skin of his 13.02
"When a m. is afflicted with leprosy, 13.09
"When a m. or woman has a disease 13.29
"When a m. or a woman has spots on 13.38
he is a leprous m., he is unclean; 13.44
shall set the m. who is to be 14.11
When any m. has a discharge from 15.02
"And if a m. has an emission of 15.16
If a m. lies with a woman and has 15.18
And if any m. lies with her, and her 15.24
and for the m. who lies with a 15.33
There shall be no m. in the tent of 16.17
the hand of a m. who is in readiness 16.21
If any m. of the house of Israel 17.03
shall be imputed to that m.; 17.04
and that m. shall be cut off from 17.04
Any m. of the house of Israel, or of 17.08
that m. shall be cut off from his 17.09
"If any m. of the house of Israel 17.10
Any m. also of the people of Israel, 17.13
by doing which a m. shall live: 18.05
"If a m. lies carnally with a woman 19.20
to another m. and not yet ransomed 19.20
and honor the face of an old m., 19.32
Any m. of the people of Israel, or 20.02
will set my face against that m., 20.03
all hide their eyes from that m., 20.04
against that m. and against his 20.05
"If a m. commits adultery with the 20.10
The m. who lies with his father's 20.11
If a m. lies with his daughter-in-law, 20.12
If a m. lies with a male as with a 20.13
If a m. takes a wife and her mother 20.14
If a m. lies with a beast, he shall 20.15
"If a m. takes his sister, a daughter 20.17
If a m. lies with a woman having 20.18
If a m. lies with his uncle's wife, 20.20
If a m. takes his brother's wife, it 20.21
"A m. or a woman who is a medium or 20.27
a m. blind or lame, or one who has a 21.18
or a m. who has an injured foot or 21.19
or a m. with a defect in his sight 21.20
no m. of the descendants of Aaron 21.21
the dead or a m. who has had an 22.04
unclean or a m. from whom he may 22.05
And if a m. eats of a holy thing 22.14
son and a m. of Israel quarreled 24.10
He who kills a m. shall be put to 24.17
When a m. causes a disfigurement in 24.19
as he has disfigured a m., he shall be 24.20
he who kills a m. shall be put to 24.21
If a m. has no one to redeem it, and 25.26
overpayment to the m. to whom he 25.27
"If a m. sells a dwelling house in 25.29
When a m. makes a special vow of 27.02
And if a m. is too poor to pay your 27.08
such that any m. gives to the LORD 27.09
then the m. shall bring the animal 27.11
"When a m. dedicates his house to 27.14
"If a m. dedicates to the LORD part 27.16
has sold the field to another m., 27.20
and the m. shall give the amount of 27.23
to the LORD, no m. may dedicate; 27.26
thing that a m. devotes to the 27.28
whether of m. or beast, or of his 27.28
If a m. wishes to redeem any of his 27.31
A m. shall not inquire whether it 27.33
be with you a m. from each tribe, Num 1.04
each m. being the head of the house 1.04
every m. able to go forth to war: 1.26
every m. able to go forth to war: 1.28
every m. able to go forth to war: 1.30
every m. able to go forth to war: 1.32
every m. able to go forth to war: 1.34
every m. able to go forth to war: 1.36
every m. able to go forth to war: 1.38
every m. able to go forth to war: 1.40

MAN (cont.)
every m. able to go forth to war: Num 1.42
every m. able to go forth to war in 1.45
every m. by his own camp and every m. 1.52
in Israel, both of m. and of beast; 3.13
When a m. or woman commits any of 5.06
But if the m. has no kinsman to 5.08
whatever any m. gives to the priest 5.10
if a m. lies with her carnally, and 5.13
then the m. shall bring his wife to 5.15
'If no m. has lain with you, and if 5.19
and some m. other than your husband 5.20
comes upon a m. and he is jealous 5.30
The m. shall be free from iniquity, 5.31
When either a m. or a woman makes a 6.02
"And if any m. dies very suddenly 6.09
to each m. according to his service." 7.05
are mine, both of m. and of beast; 8.17
touching the dead body of a m., 9.06
touching the dead body of a m.; 9.07
If any m. of you or of your descendants 9.10
But the m. who is clean and is not 9.13
that m. shall bear his sin. 9.13
every m. at the door of his tent; 11.10
And a young m. ran and told Moses, 11.27
Now the m. Moses was very meek, more 12.03
their fathers shall you send a m., 13.02
dost kill this people as one m., 14.15
they found a m. gathering sticks on 15.32
"The m. shall be put to death; 15.35
and the m. whom the LORD chooses 16.07
So every m. took his censer, and 16.18
shall one m. sin, and wilt thou be 16.22
And the rod of the m. whom I choose 17.05
looked, and each m. took his rod. 17.09
whether m. or beast, which they 18.15
first-born of m. you shall redeem, 18.15
And a m. who is clean shall gather 19.09
the body of any m. who has died, 19.13
the law when a m. dies in a tent: 19.14
or a dead body, or a bone of a m., 19.16
"But the m. who is unclean and does 19.20
and if a serpent bit any m., 21.09
God is not m., that he should lie, 23.19
or a son of m., that he should 23.19
oracle of the m. whose eye is 24.03
oracle of the m. whose eye is 24.15
and went after the m. of Israel 25.08
the m. of Israel and the woman, 25.08
The name of the slain m. of Israel, 25.14
there was not a m. of those 26.64
There was not left a m. of them, 26.65
'If a m. dies, and has no son, then 27.08
appoint a m. over the congregation, 27.16
a m. in whom is the spirit, and lay 27.18
When a m. vows a vow to the LORD, or 30.02
as between a m. and his wife, and 30.16
the booty, both of m. and of beast. 31.11
who has known m. by lying with him. 31.17
have not known m. by lying with 31.18
both of m. and of beast, you and 31.26
had not known m. by lying with him. 31.35
there is not a m. missing from us. 31.49
what each m. found, articles of gold, 31.50
taken booty, every m. for himself. 31.53
and every armed m. of you will pass 32.21
every m. who is armed for war, 32.27
every m. who is armed to battle 32.29
wherever the lot falls to any m., 33.54
by which a m. may die, and he died, 35.17
by which a m. may die, and he died, 35.18
by which a m. may die, and without 35.23
For the m. must remain in his city 35.28
between a m. and his brother or Deu 1.16
not be afraid of the face of m., 1.17
men of you, one m. for each tribe; 1.23
as a m. bears his son, in all the 1.31
And every m. of you girded on his 1.41
return every m. to his possession 3.20
that God created m. upon the earth, 4.32
God speak with m. and m. still live. 5.24
not a m. shall be able to stand 7.24
you know that m. does not live by 8.03
but that m. lives by everything 8.03
as a m. disciplines his son, the 8.05
No m. shall be able to stand 11.25
every m. doing whatever is right in 12.08
"If there is among you a poor m., 15.07
a Hebrew m., or a Hebrew woman, is 15.12
every m. shall give as he is able, 16.17
a m. or woman who does what is evil 17.02
your gates that m. or woman who 17.05
stone that m. or woman to death 17.05
The m. who acts presumptuously, by 17.12
or the judge, that m. shall die; 17.12
as when a m. goes into the forest 19.05
though the m. did not deserve to 19.06
"But if any m. hates his neighbor, 19.11
and the m. flees into one of these 19.11
against a m. for any crime or for 19.15
against any m. to accuse him of 19.16
'What m. is there that has built a 20.05
battle and another m. dedicate it. 20.05
And what m. is there that has 20.06
and another m. enjoy its fruit. 20.06
And what m. is there that has 20.07
the battle and another m. take her.' 20.07
'What m. is there that is fearful 20.08
to the slain m. shall take a 21.03
to the slain m. shall wash their 21.06
"If a m. has two wives, the one 21.15
"If a m. has a stubborn and rebellious 21.18
"And if a m. has committed a crime 21.22
for a hanged m. is accursed by God; 21.23
anything that pertains to a m., 22.05
nor shall a m. put on a woman's 22.05
"If any m. takes a wife, and goes in 22.13
my daughter to this m. to wife, 22.16
shall take the m. and whip him; 22.18
"If a m. is found lying with the 22.22
lying with the wife of another m., 22.22
the m. who lay with the woman, and 22.22
and a m. meets her in the city and 22.23
and the m. because he violated his 22.24
open country a m. meets a young 22.25
and the m. seizes her and lies with 22.25
then only the m. who lay with her 22.25
like that of a m. attacking and 22.26
"If a m. meets a virgin who is not 22.28
then the m. who lay with her shall 22.29
"A m. shall not take his father's 22.30
among you any m. who is not clean 23.10
"When a m. takes a wife and marries 24.01
"When a m. is newly married, he 24.05
"No m. shall take a mill or an 24.06
"If a m. is found stealing one of 24.07
and the m. to whom you make the 24.11
And if he is a poor m., you shall not 24.12
every m. shall be put to death for 24.16
then if the guilty m. deserves to 25.02
And if the m. does not wish to take 25.07
be done to the m. who does not 25.09
" 'Cursed be the m. who makes a 27.15
misleads a blind m. on the road. 27.18
and another m. shall lie with her; 28.30
The m. who is the most tender and 28.54
slaves, but no m. will buy you." 28.68
be among you a m. or woman or 29.18
would smoke against that m., 29.20
destroying both young m. and virgin, 32.25
child with the m. of gray hairs. 32.25
which Moses the m. of God blessed 33.01
but no m. knows the place of his 34.06
No m. shall be able to stand before Jos 1.05
was no courage left in any m., 2.11
of Israel, from each tribe a m. 3.12

MAN (cont.)

the people, from each tribe a m., Jos 4.02
appointed, a m. from each tribe; 4.04
a m. stood before him with his 5.13
go up every m. straight before him 6.05
every m. straight before him, and 6.20
the LORD be the m. that rises up 6.26
takes shall come near m. by m. 7.14
family of the Zerahites m. by m., 7.17
near his household m. by m., 7.18
There was not a m. left in Ai or 8.17
upon which no m. has lifted an iron 8.31
shall not a m. of them stand 10.08
hearkened to the voice of a m.; 10.14
not a m. moved his tongue against 10.21
but every m. they smote with the 11.14
to Moses the m. of God in Kadeshbarnea 14.06
the greatest m. among the Anakim. 14.15
Bashan, because he was a m. of war. 17.01
no m. has been able to withstand 23.09
One m. of you puts to flight a 23.10
every m. to his inheritance. 24.28
And the spies saw a m. coming out Ju 1.24
they let the m. and all his family 1.25
And the m. went to the land of the 1.26
the Benjaminite, a left-handed m. 3.15
Now Eglon was a very fat m. 3.17
and allowed not a m. to pass over. 3.28
able-bodied men; not a m. escaped. 3.29
of the sword; not a m. was left. 4.16
and if any m. comes and asks you, 4.20
show you the m. whom you are 4.22
A maiden or two for every m.; 5.30
with you, you mighty m. of valor." 6.12
smite the Midianites as one m." 6.16
'This m. shall go with you,' shall 7.04
'This m. shall not go with you,' 7.04
the others go every m. to his home." 7.07
of Israel every m. to his tent, 7.08
behold a m. was telling a dream to 7.13
the son of Joash, a m. of Israel; 7.14
They stood every m. in his place 7.21
And he caught a young m. of Succoth, 8.14
for as the m. is, so is his strength 8.21
give me every m. of you the earrings 8.24
and every m. cast in it the earrings 8.25
to the young m. his armor-bearer, 9.54
And his young m. thrust him through, 9.54
they departed every m. to his home. 9.55
son of Dodo, a m. of Issachar; 10.01
"Who is the m. that will begin to 10.18
She had never known a m. And it became 11.39
And there was a certain m. of Zorah, 13.02
"A m. of God came to me, and his 13.06
let the m. of God whom thou didst 13.08
the m. who came to me the other day 13.10
and came to the m. and said to him, 13.11
"Are you the m. who spoke to this 13.11
companion, who had been his best m. 14.20
weak, and be like any other m." 16.07
weak, and be like any other m." 16.11
weak, and be like any other m." 16.13
weak, and be like any other m." 16.17
and she called a m., and had him 16.19
There was a m. of the hill country 17.01
And the m. Micah had a shrine, and 17.05
every m. did what was right in his 17.06
was a young m. of Bethlehem in 17.07
And the m. departed from the town 17.08
was content to dwell with the m.; 17.11
and the young m. became to him like 17.11
and the young m. became his priest, 17.12
be priest to the house of one m., 18.19
the girl's father said to the m., 19.06
And when the m. rose up to go, his 19.07
And when the m. and his concubine 19.09
But the m. would not spend the 19.10
for no m. took them into his house 19.15
an old m. was coming from his work 19.16
the m. was from the hill country of 19.16
and the old m. said, "Where are you 19.17
and the young m. with your servants; 19.19
And the old m. said, "Peace be to 19.20
and they said to the old m., 19.22
"Bring out the m. who came into 19.22
And the m., the master of the house, 19.23
that this m. has come into my 19.23
against this m. do not do so vile 19.24
So the m. seized his concubine, and 19.25
and the m. rose up and went away to 19.28
assembled as one m. to the LORD at 20.01
And all the people arose as one m., 20.08
against the city, united as one m. 20.11
had not known m. by lying with him; 21.12
and seize each m. his wife from 21.21
take for each m. of them his wife 21.22
every m. to his tribe and family, 21.24
there every m. to his inheritance. 21.24
every m. did what was right in his 21.25
and a certain m. of Bethlehem in Ru 1.01
The name of the m. was Elimelech 1.02
a m. of wealth, of the family of 2.01
Blessed be the m. who took notice 2.19
"The m. is a relative of ours, one 2.20
known to the m. until he has 3.03
At midnight the m. was startled, 3.08
all that the m. had done for her, 3.16
for the m. will not rest, but will 3.18
There was a certain m. of Ramathaimzophim 1Sa 1.01
Now this m. used to go up year by 1.03
And the m. Elkanah and all his 1.21
not by might shall a m. prevail. 2.09
that when any m. offered sacrifice, 2.13
and say to the m. who was sacrificing, 2.15
And if the m. said to him, "Let them 2.16
If a m. sins against a m., God will 2.25
but if a m. sins against the LORD, 2.25
And there came a m. of God to Eli, 2.27
not be an old m. in your house. 2.31
not be an old m. in your house for 2.32
The m. of you whom I shall not cut 2.33
they fled, every m. to his home; 4.10
A m. of Benjamin ran from the 4.12
And when the m. came into the city 4.13
Then the m. hastened and came and 4.14
And the m. said to Eli, "I am he who 4.16
for he was an old m., and heavy. 4.18
of Israel, "Go every m. to his city." 8.22
There was a m. of Benjamin whose 9.01
a Benjaminite, a m. of wealth; 9.01
name was Saul, a handsome young m. 9.02
There was not a m. among the people 9.02
there is a m. of God in this city, 9.06
and he is a m. that is held in 9.06
if we go, what can we bring the m.? 9.07
present to bring to the m. of God. 9.07
I will give it to the m. of God, 9.08
when a m. went to inquire of God, he 9.09
the city where the m. of God was. 9.10
send to you a m. from the land of 9.16
"Here is the m. of whom I spoke to 9.17
them and be turned into another m. 10.06
And a m. of the place answered, "And 10.12
of the Matrites near m. by m., 10.21
the LORD, "Did the m. come hither?" 10.22
said, "How can this m. save us?" 10.27
and they came out as one m. 11.07
"Not a m. shall be put to death 11.13
he sent home, every m. to his tent. 13.02
sought out a m. after his own 13.14
to the young m. who bore his armor, 14.01
to the young m. who bore his armor, 14.06
"Cursed be the m. who eats food 14.24
but no m. put his hand to his mouth; 14.26
'Cursed be the m. who eats food 14.28
'Let every m. bring his ox or his 14.34

MAN (cont.)
let us not leave a m. of them." 1Sa 14.36
there was not a m. among all the 14.39
saw any strong m., or any valiant m., 14.52
but kill both m. and woman, infant 15.03
for he is not a m., that he should 15.29
for the LORD sees not as m. sees; 16.07
m. looks on the outward appearance, 16.07
to seek out a m. who is skilful in 16.16
for me a m. who can play well, and 16.17
a m. of valor, a m. of war, prudent in speech, 16.18
and a m. of good presence; 16.18
Choose a m. for yourselves, and let 17.08
give me a m., that we may fight 17.10
of Saul the m. was already old and 17.12
of Israel, when they saw the m., 17.24
you seen this m. who has come up? 17.25
and the m. who kills him, the king 17.25
be done for the m. who kills this 17.26
it be done to the m. who kills him." 17.27
he has been a m. of war from his 17.33
him, "Whose son are you, young m.?" 17.58
I am a poor m. and of no repute?" 18.23
Now a certain m. of the servants of 21.07
servants, "Lo, you see the m. is mad; 21.14
For if a m. finds his enemy, will he 24.19
And there was a m. in Maon, 25.02
The m. was very rich; he had 25.02
Now the name of the m. was Nabal, 25.03
but the m. was churlish and ill-behaved; 25.03
"Every m. gird on his sword!" 25.13
And every m. of them girded on his 25.13
No m. saw it, or knew it, nor did any 26.12
said to Abner, "Are you not a m.? 26.15
rewards every m. for his righteousness 26.23
every m. with his household, and 27.03
left neither m. nor woman alive, 27.09
saved neither m. nor woman alive, 27.11
she said, "An old m. is coming up; 28.14
"Send the m. back, that he may 29.04
"I am a young m. of Egypt, servant 30.13
and not a m. of them escaped, except 30.17
that each m. may lead away his 30.22
a m. came from Saul's camp, with his 2Sa 1.02
said to the young m. who told him, 1.05
And the young m. who told him said, 1.06
said to the young m. who told him, 1.13
and a great m. has fallen this day 3.38
of Rimmon a m. of Benjamin from 4.02
a righteous m. in his own house 4.11
let us play the m. for our people, 10.12
The rich m. had very many flocks 12.02
but the poor m. had nothing but one 12.03
came a traveler to the rich m., 12.04
it for the m. who had come to him." 12.04
was greatly kindled against the m.; 12.05
the m. who has done this deserves 12.05
Nathan said to David, "You are the m. 12.07
and Jonadab was a very crafty m. 13.03
the young m. who served him and 13.17
And the young m. who kept the watch 13.34
'Give up the m. who struck his 14.07
the hand of the m. who would 14.16
bring back the young m. Absalom." 14.21
and when any m. had a suit to come 15.02
but there is no m. deputed by the 15.03
Then every m. with a suit or cause 15.04
And whenever a m. came near to do 15.05
came out a m. of the family of the 16.05
you m. of blood, you worthless 16.07
is on you; for you are a m. of blood." 16.08
You seek the life of only one m., 17.03
Then even the valiant m., whose heart 17.10
that your father is a mighty m., 17.10
to the house of a m. at Bahurim, 17.18
the son of a m. named Ithra the 17.25
my sake with the young m. Absalom." 18.05
And a certain m. saw it, and told 18.10
Joab said to the m. who told him, 18.11
But the m. said to Joab, "Even if I 18.12
sake protect the young m. Absalom.' 18.12
looked, he saw a m. running alone. 18.24
watchman saw another m. running; 18.26
"See, another m. running alone!" 18.26
"He is a good m., and comes with 18.27
it well with the young m. Absalom?" 18.29
it well with the young m. Absalom?" 18.32
for evil, be like that young m. 18.32
not a m. will stay with you this 19.07
had fled every m. to his own home. 19.08
of all the men of Judah as one m.; 19.14
Barzillai was a very aged m., 19.32
for he was a very wealthy m. 19.32
every m. to his tents, O Israel!" 20.01
and when the m. saw that all the 20.12
But the m. of the hill country of 20.21
the city, every m. to his home. 20.22
us to put any m. to death in 21.04
"The m. who consumed us and planned 21.05
there was a m. of great stature, 21.20
the blameless m. thou dost show 22.26
oracle of the m. who was raised on 23.01
but the m. who touches them arms 23.07
was a valiant m. of Kabzeel, 23.20
he slew an Egyptian, a handsome m. 23.21
me not fall into the hand of m. 24.14
He was also a very handsome m.; 1Ki 1.06
are a worthy m. and bring good 1.42
"If he prove to be a worthy m., 1.52
Be strong, and show yourself a m., 2.02
not fail you a m. on the throne of 2.04
guiltless, for you are a wise m.; 2.09
each m. had to make provision for 4.07
every m. under his vine and under 4.25
and his father was a m. of Tyre, 7.14
fail you a m. before me to sit 8.25
"If a m. sins against his neighbor 8.31
is made by any m. or by all thy 8.38
thee—for there is no m. who does not 8.46
not fail you a m. upon the throne 9.05
The m. Jeroboam was very able, and 11.28
that the young m. was industrious 11.28
came to Shemaiah the m. of God: 12.22
Return every m. to his home, for 12.24
And behold, a m. of God came out of 13.01
And the m. cried against the altar 13.02
heard the saying of the m. of God, 13.04
sign which the m. of God had given 13.05
And the king said to the m. of God, 13.06
And the m. of God entreated the 13.06
And the king said to the m. of God, 13.07
And the m. of God said to the king, 13.08
all that the m. of God had done 13.11
way which the m. of God who came 13.12
And he went after the m. of God, 13.14
"Are you the m. of God who came 13.14
and he cried to the m. of God who 13.21
"It is the m. of God, who disobeyed 13.26
the body of the m. of God and laid 13.29
in which the m. of God is buried; 13.31
as a m. burns up dung until it is 14.10
have you against me, O m. of God? 17.18
I know that you are a m. of God, 17.24
see how this m. is seeking trouble; 20.07
And each killed his m.; the Syrians 20.20
And a m. of God came near and said 20.28
And a certain m. of the sons of the 20.35
But the m. refused to strike him. 20.35
Then he found another m., and said, 20.37
And the m. struck him, smiting and 20.37
turned and brought a m. to me, 20.39
and said, 'Keep this m.; 20.39
your hand the m. whom I had 20.42
is yet one m. by whom we may 22.08
But a certain m. drew his bow at a 22.34

MAN (cont.)

"Every m. to his city, and every 1Ki 22.36
city, and every m. to his country! 22.36
"There came a m. to meet us, and 2Ki 1.06
"What kind of m. was he who came to 1.07
"O m. of God, the king says, 'Come 1.09
"If I am a m. of God, let fire come 1.10
"O m. of God, this is the king's 1.11
"If I am a m. of God, let fire come 1.12
"O m. of God, I pray you, let my life, 1.13
of land every m. threw a stone, 3.25
She came and told the m. of God, 4.07
that this is a holy m. of God, 4.09
she said, "No, my lord, O m. of God; 4.16
him on the bed of the m. of God, 4.21
I may quickly go to the m. of God, 4.22
and came to the m. of God at Mount 4.25
When the m. of God saw her coming, 4.25
to the mountain to the m. of God, 4.27
But the m. of God said, "Let her 4.27
"O m. of God, there is death in the 4.40
A m. came from Baalshalishah, 4.42
bringing the m. of God bread of the 4.42
was a great m. with his master and 5.01
He was a mighty m. of valor, 5.01
that this m. sends word to me to 5.07
to me to cure a m. of his leprosy? 5.07
But when Elisha the m. of God heard 5.08
to the word of the m. of God; 5.14
Then he returned to the m. of God, 5.15
servant of Elisha the m. of God, 5.20
spirit when the m. turned from his 5.26
Then the m. of God said, "Where did 6.06
But the m. of God sent word to the 6.09
of which the m. of God told him. 6.10
servant of the m. of God rose 6.15
eyes of the young m., and he saw; 6.17
bring you to the m. whom you seek." 6.19
dispatched a m. from his presence; 6.32
king leaned said to the m. of God, 7.02
as the m. of God had said when the 7.17
For when the m. of God had said to 7.18
captain had answered the m. of God, 7.19
to the word of the m. of God; 8.02
the servant of the m. of God, 8.04
"The m. of God has come here," 8.07
you and go to meet the m. of God, 8.08
was ashamed. And the m. of God wept. 8.11
So the young m., the prophet, went 9.04
and the young m. poured the oil on 9.06
Then in haste every m. of them took 9.13
So a m. on horseback went to meet 9.18
there was not a m. left who did 10.21
"The m. who allows any of those 10.24
let not a m. escape." So when they 10.25
every m. with his weapons in his 11.11
for which each m. is assessed— 12.04
Then the m. of God was angry with 13.19
And as a m. was being buried, lo, a 13.21
seen and the m. was cast into the 13.21
as soon as the m. touched the 13.21
but every m. shall die for his 14.06
and every m. fled to his home. 14.12
shekels of silver from every m., 15.20
the hand of any m. who leans on it 18.21
'Tell the m. who sent you to me, 22.15
LORD which the m. of God proclaimed, 23.16
the tomb of the m. of God who came 23.17
let no m. move his bones." So they let 23.18
was a valiant m. of Kabzeel, 1Ch 11.22
a m. of great stature, five cubits 11.23
a mighty m. among the thirty and a 12.04
Zadok, a young m. mighty in valor, 12.28
let us play the m. for our people, 19.13
there was a m. of great stature, 20.06
me not fall into the hand of m." 21.13
he shall be a m. of peace. I will give 22.09
of Moses the m. of God were named 23.14
was a mighty m. of the thirty and 27.06
being a m. of understanding and a 27.32
every willing m. who has skill for 28.21
will not be for m. but for the 29.01
So now send me a m. skilled to work 2Ch 2.07
"Now I have sent a skilled m., 2.13
and his father was a m. of Tyre. 2.14
and I chose no m. as prince over 6.05
fail you a m. before me to sit 6.16
dwell indeed with m. on the earth? 6.18
"If a m. sins against his neighbor 6.22
is made by any m. or by all thy 6.29
for there is no m. who does not 6.36
not fail you a m. to rule Israel.' 7.18
so David the m. of God had commanded 8.14
came to Shemaiah the m. of God: 11.02
Return every m. to his home, for 11.04
let not m. prevail against thee." 14.11
whether young or old, m. or woman. 15.13
a mighty m. of valor, with two 17.17
is yet one m. by whom we may 18.07
But a certain m. drew his bow at a 18.33
judge not for m. but for the LORD; 19.06
every m. of Judah and Jerusalem, and 20.27
every m. with his weapon in his 23.10
but every m. shall die for his 25.04
But a m. of God came to him and 25.07
And Amaziah said to the m. of God, 25.09
The m. of God answered, "The LORD 25.09
and every m. fled to his home. 25.22
a mighty m. of Ephraim, slew Maaseiah 28.07
to the law of Moses the m. of God; 30.16
every m. to his possession. 31.01
'Tell the m. who sent you to me, 34.23
young m. or virgin, old m. or aged; 36.17
gathered as one m. to Jerusalem. Ez 3.01
in the law of Moses the m. of God. 3.02
the leading m. at the place Casiphia, 8.17
they brought us a m. of discretion, 8.18
him mercy in the sight of this m. Neh 1.11
The m. who sounded the trumpet was 4.18
"Let every m. and his servant pass 4.22
shake out every m. from his house 5.13
I said, "Should such a m. as I flee? 6.11
And what m. such as I could go into 6.11
and God-fearing m. than many. 7.02
gathered as one m. into the square 8.01
observance of which a m. shall live, 9.29
commandment of David the m. of God, 12.24
instruments of David the m. of God; 12.36
palace to do as every m. desired. Est 1.08
that every m. be lord in his own 1.22
that if any m. or woman goes to 4.11
be done to the m. whom the king 6.06
"For the m. whom the king delights 6.07
him array the m. whom the king 6.09
him conduct the m. on horseback 6.09
be done to the m. whom the king 6.09
be done to the m. whom the king 6.11
for the m. Mordecai grew more and 9.04
There was a m. in the land of Uz, Job 1.01
and that m. was blameless and 1.01
so that this m. was the greatest of 1.03
earth, a blameless and upright m., 1.08
earth, a blameless and upright m., 2.03
All that a m. has he will give for 2.04
given to a m. whose way is hid, 3.23
'Can mortal m. be righteous before 4.17
Can a m. be pure before his Maker? 4.17
but m. is born to trouble as the 5.07
happy is the m. whom God reproves; 5.17
speech of a despairing m. is wind? 6.26
"Has not m. a hard service upon 7.01
What is m., that thou dost make so 7.17
of the godless m. shall perish. 8.13
God will not reject a blameless m., 8.20
But how can a m. be just before God? 9.02
For he is not a m., as I am, 9.32

MAN (cont.)
of flesh? Dost thou see as m. sees? Job 10.04
Are thy days as the days of m., 10.05
and a m. full of talk be vindicated? 11.02
But a stupid m. will get understanding, 11.12
a wild ass's colt is born a m. 11.12
me, a just and blameless m., am a 12.04
if he shuts a m. in, none can open. 12.14
them stagger like a drunken m. 12.25
deceive him, as one deceives a m.? 13.09
that a godless m. shall not come 13.16
M. wastes away like a rotten thing, 13.28
"M. that is born of a woman is of 14.01
But m. dies, and is laid low; 14.10
m. breathes his last, and where is 14.10
So m. lies down and rises not again 14.12
If a m. die, shall he live again? 14.14
so thou destroyest the hope of m. 14.19
"Should a wise m. answer with windy 15.02
"Are you the first m. that was born? 15.07
What is m., that he can be clean? 15.14
a m. who drinks iniquity like water 15.16
The wicked m. writhes in pain all 15.20
houses which no m. should inhabit, 15.28
maintain the right of a m. with God, 16.21
like that of a m. with his neighbor 16.21
shall not find a wise m. among you. 17.10
since m. was placed upon earth, 20.04
for me, is my complaint against m.? 21.04
that the wicked m. is spared in the 21.30
"Can a m. be profitable to God? 22.02
The m. with power possessed the 22.08
and the favored m. dwelt in it. 22.08
He delivers the innocent m.; 22.30
There an upright m. could reason 23.07
the vineyard of the wicked m. 24.06
How then can m. be righteous before 25.04
how much less m., who is a maggot, 25.06
and the son of m., who is a worm! 25.06
portion of a wicked m. with God, 27.13
"M. puts his hand to the flinty 28.09
M. does not know the way to it, and 28.13
And he said to m., 'Behold, the fear 28.28
or a poor m. without covering; 31.19
But it is the spirit in a m., 32.08
God may vanquish him, not m. 32.13
or use flattery toward any m. 32.21
answer you. God is greater than m. 33.12
though m. does not perceive it. 33.14
that he may turn m. aside from his 33.17
deed, and cut off pride from m.; 33.17
"M. is also chastened with pain 33.19
to declare to m. what is right for 33.23
Then m. prays to God, and he accepts 33.26
twice, three times, with a m., 33.29
What m. is like Job, who drinks up 34.07
'It profits a m. nothing that he 34.09
the work of a m. he will requite 34.11
and m. would return to dust. 34.15
one,' and to nobles, 'Wicked m.'; 34.18
his eyes are upon the ways of a m., 34.21
a time for any m. to go before God 34.23
whether it be a nation or a m.? 34.29
that a godless m. should not reign, 34.30
and the wise m. who hears me will 34.34
concerns a m. like yourself, 35.08
and your righteousness a son of m. 35.08
looked on it; m. beholds it from afar. 36.25
down, and drop upon m. abundantly. 36.28
He seals up the hand of every m., 37.07
Did a m. ever wish that he would be 37.20
Gird up your loins like a m., 38.03
rain on a land where no m. is, 38.26
the desert in which there is no m.; 38.26
"Gird up your loins like a m.; 40.07
the hope of a m. is disappointed; 41.09
an old m., and full of days. 42.17
Blessed is the m. who walks not in Ps 1.01
If a m. does not repent, God will 7.12
the wicked m. conceives evil, and is 7.14
what is m. that thou are mindful of 8.04
and the son of m. that thou dost 8.04
Let not m. prevail; let the nations 9.19
and the m. greedy for gain curses 10.03
so that m. who is of the earth may 10.18
the blameless m. thou dost show 18.25
like a strong m. runs its course 19.05
But I am a worm, and no m.; 22.06
Who is the m. that fears the LORD? 25.12
Blessed is the m. to whom the LORD 32.02
This poor m. cried, and the LORD 34.06
Happy is the m. who takes refuge in 34.08
What m. is there who desires life, 34.12
m. and beast thou savest, O LORD. 36.06
over the m. who carries out evil 37.07
The steps of a m. are from the LORD, 37.23
I have seen a wicked m. overbearing, 37.35
Mark the blameless m., and behold 37.37
is posterity for the m. of peace. 37.37
But I am like a deaf m., I do not 38.13
like a dumb m. who does not open 38.13
I am like a m. who does not hear, 38.14
Surely every m. stands as a mere 39.05
Surely m. goes about as a shadow! 39.06
m. heaps up, and knows not who will 39.06
dost chasten m. with rebukes for 39.11
surely every m. is a mere breath! 39.11
Blessed is the m. who makes the 40.04
Truly no m. can ransom himself, or 49.07
M. cannot abide in his pomp, he is 49.12
and though a m. gets praise when he 49.18
M. cannot abide in his pomp, he is 49.20
O mighty m., of mischief done 52.01
"See the m. who would not make God 52.07
without a fear. What can m. do to me? 56.11
foe, for vain is the help of m.! 60.11
you set upon a m. to shatter him, 62.03
dost requite a m. according to his 62.12
mind and heart of a m. are deep! 64.06
grasp of the unjust and cruel m. 71.04
M. ate of the bread of the angels; 78.25
like a strong m. shouting because 78.65
be upon the m. of thy right hand, 80.17
the son of m. whom thou hast made 80.17
blessed is the m. who trusts in 84.12
I am a m. who has no strength, 88.04
What m. can live and never see 89.48
Thou turnest m. back to the dust, 90.03
The dull m. cannot know, the stupid 92.06
the LORD, knows the thoughts of m., 94.11
Blessed is the m. whom thou dost 94.12
The m. of haughty looks and arrogant 101.05
No m. who practices deceit shall 101.07
no m. who utters lies shall continue 101.07
As for m., his days are like grass; 103.15
and plants for m. to cultivate, 104.14
and wine to gladden the heart of m., 104.15
M. goes forth to his work and to 104.23
he had set a m. ahead of them, 105.17
foe, for vain is the help of m.! 108.12
Appoint a wicked m. against him; 109.06
Blessed is the m. who fears the 112.01
well with the m. who deals generously 112.05
The wicked m. sees it and is angry; 112.10
of the wicked m. comes to nought. 112.10
do not fear. What can m. do to me? 118.06
LORD than to put confidence in m. 118.08
How can a young m. keep his way 119.09
Happy is the m. who has his quiver 127.05
Lo, thus shall the m. be blessed who 128.04
of Egypt, both of m. and of beast; 135.08
hunt down the violent m. speedily! 140.11
Let a good m. strike or rebuke me 141.05
remains to me, no m. cares for me. 142.04
for no m. living is righteous 143.02
what is m. that thou dost regard 144.03

MAN (cont.)
or the son of m. that thou dost Ps 144.03
M. is like a breath, his days are 144.04
in a son of m., in whom there is no 146.03
his pleasure in the legs of a m.; 147.10
the wise m. also may hear and Pro 1.05
and the m. of understanding acquire 1.05
repute in the sight of God and m. 3.04
Happy is the m. who finds wisdom, 3.13
and the m. who gets understanding, 3.13
contend with a m. for no reason, 3.30
Do not envy a m. of violence and do 3.31
for the perverse m. is an abomination 3.32
vagabond, and want like an armed m. 6.11
a wicked m., goes about with 6.12
and a m. who sows discord among 6.19
Can a m. carry fire in his bosom 6.27
For jealousy makes a m. furious, 6.34
youths, a young m. without sense, 7.07
Happy is the m. who listens to me, 8.34
reproves a wicked m. incurs injury. 9.07
reprove a wise m., and he will 9.08
Give instruction to a wise m., 9.09
a righteous m. and he will increase 9.09
pleasure to a m. of understanding. 10.23
the godless m. would destroy his 11.09
but a m. of understanding remains 11.12
A m. who is kind benefits himself, 11.17
but a cruel m. hurts himself. 11.17
A wicked m. earns deceptive wages, 11.18
an evil m. will not go unpunished, 11.21
One m. gives freely, yet grows all 11.24
A liberal m. will be enriched, and 11.25
A good m. obtains favor from the 12.02
but a m. of evil devices he condemns. 12.02
A m. is not established by wickedness, 12.03
A m. is commended according to his 12.08
Better is a m. of humble standing 12.09
plays the great m. but lacks bread. 12.09
A righteous m. has regard for the 12.10
An evil m. is ensnared by the 12.13
of his words a m. is satisfied 12.14
but a wise m. listens to advice. 12.15
but the prudent m. ignores an 12.16
A prudent m. conceals his knowledge, 12.23
A righteous m. turns away from evil, 12.26
A slothful m. will not catch his 12.27
the diligent m. will get precious 12.27
of his mouth a good m. eats good, 13.02
A righteous m. hates falsehood, but 13.05
but a wicked m. acts shamefully and 13.05
One m. pretends to be rich, yet has 13.07
but a poor m. has no means of 13.08
a prudent m. acts with knowledge, 13.16
A good m. leaves an inheritance to 13.22
is easy for a m. of understanding. 14.06
of a prudent m. is to discern his 14.08
is a way which seems right to a m., 14.12
A perverse m. will be filled with 14.14
and a good m. with the fruit of his 14.14
A wise m. is cautious and turns 14.16
A m. of quick temper acts foolishly, 14.17
but a m. of discretion is patient. 14.17
oppresses a poor m. insults his 14.31
the mind of a m. of understanding, 14.33
A hot-tempered m. stirs up strife, 15.18
but a foolish m. despises his 15.20
but a m. of understanding walks 15.21
an apt answer is a joy to a m., 15.23
The plans of the mind belong to m., 16.01
All the ways of a m. are pure in 16.02
fear of the LORD a m. avoids evil. 16.06
and a wise m. will appease it. 16.14
is called a m. of discernment, 16.21
is a way which seems right to a m., 16.25
A worthless m. plots evil, and his 16.27
A perverse m. spreads strife, and a 16.28
A m. of violence entices his 16.29
deeper into a m. of understanding 17.10
An evil m. seeks only rebellion, and 17.11
Let a m. meet a she-bear robbed of 17.12
If a m. returns evil for good, evil 17.13
A m. without sense gives a pledge, 17.18
A m. of crooked mind does not 17.20
A wicked m. accepts a bribe from 17.23
A m. of understanding sets his face 17.24
fine on a righteous m. is not good; 17.26
spirit is a m. of understanding. 17.27
good to be partial to a wicked m., 18.05
deprive a righteous m. of justice. 18.05
the righteous m. runs into it and 18.10
of his mouth a m. is satisfied; 18.20
Better is a poor m. who walks in 19.01
integrity than a m. who is perverse 19.01
not good for a m. to be without 19.02
but a poor m. is deserted by his 19.04
May seek the favor of a generous m., 19.06
a friend to a m. who gives gifts. 19.06
Good sense makes a m. slow to anger, 19.11
A m. of great wrath will pay the 19.19
Many are the plans in the mind of a m., 19.21
What is desired in a m. is loyalty, 19.22
and a poor m. is better than a liar. 19.22
reprove a m. of understanding, and 19.25
an honor for a m. to keep aloof 20.03
but a m. of understanding will draw 20.05
Many a m. proclaims his own loyalty, 20.06
but a faithful m. who can find? 20.06
A righteous m. who walks in his 20.07
Bread gained by deceit is sweet to a m., 20.17
how then can m. understand his way? 20.24
It is a snare for a m. to say rashly, 20.25
The spirit of m. is the lamp of the 20.27
Every way of a m. is right in his 21.02
when a wise m. is instructed, he 21.11
A m. who wanders from the way of 21.16
loves pleasure will be a poor m.; 21.17
man's dwelling, but a foolish m. devours it. 21.20
A wise m. scales the city of the 21.22
haughty m. who acts with arrogant 21.24
the word of a m. who hears will 21.28
A wicked m. puts on a bold face, but 21.29
but an upright m. considers his 21.29
A prudent m. sees danger and hides 22.03
friendship with a m. given to anger, 22.24
anger, nor go with a wrathful m., 22.24
Do you see a m. skilful in his work? 22.29
if you are a m. given to appetite. 23.02
the bread of a m. who is stingy; 23.06
drowsiness will clothe a m. with rags. 23.21
A wise m. is mightier than a strong m., 24.05
and a m. of knowledge than he who 24.05
he not requite m. according to his 24.12
as a wicked m. against the dwelling 24.15
for a righteous m. falls seven 24.16
for the evil m. has no future; 24.20
I will pay the m. back for what he 24.29
the vineyard of a m. without sense; 24.30
robber, and want like an armed m. 24.34
rain is a m. who boasts of a gift 25.14
A m. who bears false witness 25.18
Trust in a faithless m. in time of 25.19
is a righteous m. who gives way 25.26
A m. without self-control is like a 25.28
Do you see a m. who is wise in his 26.12
is the m. who deceives his neighbor 26.19
a quarrelsome m. for kindling 26.21
is a m. who strays from his home. 27.08
A prudent m. sees danger and hides 27.12
and one m. sharpens another. 27.17
so the mind of m. reflects the m. 27.19
never satisfied are the eyes of m. 27.20
and a m. is judged by his praise. 27.21
A poor m. who oppresses the poor is 28.03
Better is a poor m. who walks in 28.06
than a rich m. who is perverse in 28.06

MAN (cont.)

A rich m. is wise in his own eyes,	Pro 28.11
but a poor m. who has understanding	28.11
Blessed is the m. who fears the	28.14
If a m. is burdened with the blood	28.17
A faithful m. will abound with	28.20
piece of bread a m. will do wrong.	28.21
A miserly m. hastens after wealth,	28.22
He who rebukes a m. will afterward	28.23
the companion of a m. who destroys.	28.24
A greedy m. stirs up strife, but he	28.25
A m. who flatters his neighbor spreads	29.05
An evil m. is ensnared in his transgression,	29.06
but a righteous m. sings and rejoices.	29.06
A righteous m. knows the rights of	29.07
a wicked m. does not understand	29.07
If a wise m. has an argument with a	29.09
but a wise m. quietly holds it back	29.11
The poor m. and the oppressor meet	29.13
Do you see a m. who is hasty in his	29.20
A m. of wrath stirs up strife, and a	29.22
and a m. given to anger causes much	29.22
The fear of m. lays a snare, but he	29.25
from the LORD a m. gets justice.	29.26
An unjust m. is an abomination to	29.27
The m. says to Ithiel, to Ithiel and	30.01
Surely I am too stupid to be a m.	30.02
have not the understanding of a m.	30.02
and the way of a m. with a maiden.	30.19
What does m. gain by all the toil	Ecc 1.03
a m. cannot utter it; the eye is not	1.08
what can the m. do who comes after	2.12
The wise m. has his eyes in his	2.14
For of the wise m. as of the fool	2.16
How the wise m. dies just like the	2.16
leave it to the m. who will come	2.18
he will be a wise m. or a fool?	2.19
because sometimes a m. who has	2.21
be enjoyed by a m. who did not	2.21
What has a m. from all the toil and	2.22
better for a m. than that he	2.24
For to the m. who pleases him God	2.26
God's gift to m. that every one	3.13
and m. has no advantage over the	3.19
the spirit of m. goes upward and	3.21
than that a m. should enjoy his	3.22
And though a m. might prevail	4.12
Every m. also to whom God has given	5.19
a m. to whom God gives wealth,	6.02
If a m. begets a hundred children,	6.03
All the toil of m. is for his mouth,	6.07
has the wise m. over the fool?	6.08
does the poor m. have who knows	6.08
named, and it is known what m. is,	6.10
vanity, and what is m. the better?	6.11
is good for m. while he lives the	6.12
who can tell m. what will be after	6.12
It is better for a m. to hear the	7.05
oppression makes the wise m. foolish,	7.07
so that m. may not find out anything	7.14
is a righteous m. who perishes in	7.15
is a wicked m. who prolongs his	7.15
to the wise m. more than ten rulers	7.19
not a righteous m. on earth who	7.20
One m. among a thousand I found, but	7.28
that God made m. upright, but they	7.29
Who is like the wise m.? And who knows	8.01
mind of a wise m. will know the	8.05
No m. has power to retain the	8.08
while m. lords it over m. to his hurt.	8.09
for m. has no good thing under the	8.15
that m. cannot find out the work	8.17
However much m. may toil in seeking,	8.17
though a wise m. claims to know,	8.17
is love or hate m. does not know.	9.01
As is the good m., so is the sinner;	9.02
For m. does not know his time.	9.12
was found in it a poor wise m.,	9.15
Yet no one remembered that poor m.	9.15
though no m. knows what is to be,	10.14
For if a m. lives many years, let	11.08
O young m., in your youth, and let	11.09
because m. goes to his eternal home,	12.05
for this is the whole duty of m.	12.13
If a m. offered for love all the	Sol 8.07
So m. is humbled, and men are	Is 2.09
looks of m. shall be brought low,	2.11
haughtiness of m. shall be humbled,	2.17
Turn away from m. in whose nostrils	2.22
the mighty m. and the soldier, the	3.02
of fifty and the m. of rank,	3.03
every m. his fellow and every man	3.05
fellow and every m. his neighbor;	3.05
When a m. takes hold of his brother	3.06
take hold of one m. in that day,	4.01
M. is bowed down, and men are	5.15
for I am a m. of unclean lips, and I	6.05
In that day a m. will keep alive a	7.21
the elder and honored m. is the head,	9.15
for the fire; no m. spares his brother.	9.19
be as when a sick m. wastes away.	10.18
every m. will turn to his own	13.14
and every m. will flee to his own	13.14
'Is this the m. who made the earth	14.16
every m. against his brother and	19.02
and every m. against his neighbor,	19.02
as a drunken m. staggers in his	19.14
away violently, O you strong m.	22.17
The earth staggers like a drunken m.,	24.20
when a m. sees it, he eats it up as	28.04
As when a hungry m. dreams he is	29.08
when a thirsty m. dreams he is	29.08
a word make a m. out to be an	29.21
shall fall by a sword, not of m.;	31.08
not of m., shall devour him;	31.08
lie waste, the wayfaring m. ceases.	33.08
despised, there is no regard for m.	33.08
then shall the lame m. leap like a	35.06
the hand of any m. who leans on it.	36.06
shall look upon m. no more among	38.11
The LORD goes forth like a mighty m.,	42.13
like a m. of war he stirs up his	42.13
figure of a m., with the beauty of a m.,	44.13
Then it becomes fuel for a m.;	44.15
the earth, and created m. upon it;	45.12
the m. of my counsel from a far	46.11
vengeance, and I will spare no m.	47.03
Why, when I came, was there no m.?	50.02
that you are afraid of m. who dies,	51.12
of the son of m. who is made like	51.12
a m. of sorrows, and acquainted with	53.03
and with a rich m. in his death,	53.09
the unrighteous m. his thoughts;	55.07
Blessed is the m. who does this, and	56.02
and the son of m. who holds it	56.02
The righteous m. perishes, and no	57.01
the righteous m. is taken away	57.01
a day for a m. to humble himself?	58.05
He saw that there was no m.,	59.16
For as a young m. marries a virgin,	62.05
or an old m. who does not fill out	65.20
But this is the m. to whom I will	66.02
an ox is like him who kills a m.;	66.03
passes through, where no m. dwells?	Jer 2.06
"If a m. divorces his wife and she	3.01
there was no m., and all the birds	4.25
foresaken, and no m. dwells in them.	4.29
to see if you can find a m.,	5.01
set in array as a m. for battle,	6.23
upon m. and beast, upon the trees of	7.20
no m. repents of his wickedness,	8.06
Who is the m. so wise that he can	9.12
not the wise m. glory in his wisdom,	9.23
not the mighty m. glory in his	9.23
not the rich m. glory in his riches;	9.23
Every m. is stupid and without	10.14

MAN (cont.)

that the way of m. is not in Jer 10.23
it is not in m. who walks to 10.23
Cursed be the m. who does not heed 11.03
but no m. lays it to heart. 12.11
clings to the loins of a m., 13.11
shouldst thou be like a m. confused, 14.09
like a mighty m. who cannot save? 14.09
a m. of strife and contention to 15.10
Can m. make for himself gods? 16.20
"Cursed is the m. who trusts in m. 17.05
"Blessed is the m. who trusts in 17.07
give to every m. according to his 17.10
Cursed be the m. who brought the 20.15
Let that m. be like the cities 20.16
of this city, both m. and beast; 21.06
and every m. will say to his 22.08
Is this m. Coniah a despised, broken 22.28
"Write this m. down as childless, a m. 22.30
drunken m., like a m. overcome by wine, 23.09
Can a m. hide himself in secret 23.24
punish that m. and his household. 23.34
"This m. deserves the sentence of 26.11
"This m. does not deserve the 26.16
There was another m. who prophesied 26.20
and see, can a m. bear a child? 30.06
do I see every m. with his hands 30.06
the earth: a woman protects a m." 31.22
the seed of m. and the seed of 31.27
each m. who eats sour grapes, his 31.30
shall each m. teach his neighbor 31.34
rewarding every m. according to 32.19
a desolation, without m. or beast; 32.43
'It is a waste without m. or beast,' 33.10
without m. or inhabitant or beast, 33.10
without m. or beast, and in all of 33.12
never lack a m. to sit on the 33.17
never lack a m. in my presence to 33.18
the m. of God, which was near the 35.04
never lack a m. to stand before me 35.19
will cut off from it m. and beast?" 36.29
every m. in his tent, they would 37.10
"Let this m. be put to death, for he 38.04
For this m. is not seeking the 38.04
to cut off from you m. and woman, 44.07
mouth of any m. of Judah in all 44.26
every m. straight before him, with 49.05
no m. shall dwell there, no m. shall 49.18
no m. shall dwell there, no m. shall 49.33
both m. and beast shall flee away. 50.03
no m. shall dwell there, and no son of m. 50.40
arrayed as a m. for battle against 50.42
Babylon, let every m. save his life! 51.06
Every m. is stupid and without 51.17
you I break in pieces m. and woman; 51.22
in pieces the old m. and the youth; 51.22
pieces the young m. and the maiden; 51.22
through which no son of m. passes. 51.43
Let every m. save his life from the 51.45
I am the m. who has seen affliction Lam 3.01
It is good for a m. that he bear 3.27
the right of a m. in the presence 3.35
to subvert a m. in his cause, the 3.36
Why should a living m. complain, a m., 3.39
each had the face of a m. in front; Eze 1.10
"Son of m., stand upon your feet, 2.01
"Son of m., I send you to the 2.03
son of m., be not afraid of them, 2.06
son of m., hear what I say to you; 2.08
"Son of m., eat what is offered to 3.01
"Son of m., eat this scroll that I 3.03
"Son of m., go, get you to the house 3.04
"Son of m., all my words that I 3.10
"Son of m., I have made you a 3.17
that wicked m. shall die in his 3.18
Again, if a righteous m. turns from 3.20
warn the righteous m. not to sin, 3.21
O son of m., behold, cords will be 3.25
O son of m., take a brick and lay 4.01
"Son of m., behold, I will break the 4.16
O son of m., take a sharp sword; 5.01
"Son of m., set your face toward 6.02
O son of m., thus says the Lord God 7.02
that had the appearance of a m.; 8.02
"Son of m., lift up your eyes now 8.05
"Son of m., do you see what they 8.06
"Son of m., dig in the wall"; and 8.08
"Son of m., have you seen what the 8.12
every m. in his room of pictures? 8.12
"Have you seen this, O son of m.? 8.15
"Have you seen this, O son of m.? 8.17
every m. with his weapon for 9.02
with them was a m. clothed in 9.02
called to the m. clothed in linen, 9.03
And lo, the m. clothed in line, with 9.11
And he said to the m. clothed in 10.02
of the house, when the m. went in; 10.03
commanded the m. clothed in linen, 10.06
hands of the m. clothed in linen, 10.07
second face was the face of a m., 10.14
"Son of m., these are the men who 11.02
them, prophesy, O son of m." 11.04
"Son of m., your brethren, even your 11.15
"Son of m., you dwell in the midst 12.02
son of m., prepare for yourself an 12.03
"Son of m., has not the house of 12.09
"Son of m., eat your bread with 12.18
"Son of m., what is this proverb 12.22
"Son of m., behold, they of the 12.27
"Son of m., prophesy against the 13.02
son of m., set your face against 13.17
"Son of m., these men have taken 14.03
Any m. of the house of Israel who 14.04
I will set my face against that m., 14.08
"Son of m., when a land sins 14.13
and cut off from it m. and beast, 14.13
so that no m. may pass through 14.15
and I cut off from it m. and beast; 14.17
to cut off from it m. and beast; 14.19
to cut off from it m. and beast! 14.21
"Son of m., how does the wood of 15.02
"Son of m., make known to Jerusalem 16.02
"Son of m., propound a riddle, and 17.02
Can a m. escape who does such 17.15
"If a m. is righteous and does what 18.05
true justice between m. and m., 18.08
"But if this m. begets a son who 18.14
"But if a wicked m. turns away from 18.21
a righteous m. turns away from his 18.24
things that the wicked m. does, 18.24
When a righteous m. turns away from 18.26
when a wicked m. turns away from 18.27
"Son of m., speak to the elders of 20.03
son of m., will you judge them? 20.04
did not every m. cast away the 20.08
by whose observance m. shall live. 20.11
by whose observance m. shall live; 20.13
by whose observance m. shall live; 20.21
son of m., speak to the house of 20.27
"Son of m., set your face toward 20.46
"Son of m., set your face toward 21.02
Sigh therefore, son of m.; sigh with 21.06
"Son of m., prophesy and say, Thus 21.09
son of m., for it is against my 21.12
"Prophesy therefore, son of m.; 21.14
"Son of m., mark two ways for the 21.19
son of m., prophesy, and say, Thus 21.28
son of m., will you judge, will you 22.02
"Son of m., the house of Israel has 22.18
"Son of m., say to her, You are a 22.24
And I sought for a m. among them 22.30
"Son of m., there were two women, 23.02
"Son of m., will you judge Oholah 23.36
"Son of m., write down the name of 24.02
"Son of m., behold, I am about to 24.16
son of m., on the day when I take 24.25

MAN (cont.)
"Son of m., set your face toward Eze 25.02
and cut off from it m. and beast; 25.13
"Son of m., because Tyre said 26.02
son of m., raise a lamentation over 27.02
"Son of m., say to the prince of 28.02
of the seas,' yet you are but a m., 28.02
slay you, though you are but a m., 28.09
"Son of m., raise a lamentation 28.12
"Son of m., set your face toward 28.21
"Son of m., set your face against 29.02
will cut off from you m. and beast; 29.08
No foot of m. shall pass through it, 29.11
"Son of m., Nebuchadrezzar king of 29.18
"Son of m., prophesy, and say, Thus 30.02
"Son of m., I have broken the arm 30.21
him like a m. mortally wounded. 30.24
"Son of m., say to Pharaoh king of 31.02
"Son of m., raise a lamentation 32.02
and no foot of m. shall trouble 32.13
"Son of m., wail over the multitude 32.18
"Son of m., speak of your people 33.02
the land take a m. from among them, 33.02
that m. is taken away in his 33.06
son of m., I have made a watchman 33.07
O wicked m., you shall surely die, 33.08
that wicked m. shall die in his 33.08
son of m., say to the house of 33.10
son of m., say to your people, The 33.12
a m. who had escaped from Jerusalem 33.21
by the time the m. came to me in 33.22
"Son of m., the inhabitants of 33.24
saying, 'Abraham was only one m., 33.24
son of m., your people who talk 33.30
"Son of m., prophesy against the 34.02
"Son of m., set your face against 35.02
son of m., prophesy to the mountains 36.01
multiply upon you m. and beast; 36.11
"Son of m., when the house of 36.17
"Son of m., can these bones live?" 37.03
son of m., and say to the breath, 37.09
"Son of m., these bones are the 37.11
"Son of m., take a stick and write 37.16
"Son of m., set your face toward 38.02
son of m., prophesy, and say to Gog, 38.14
son of m., prophesy against Gog, and 39.01
son of m., thus says the Lord GOD: 39.17
there was a m., whose appearance 40.03
And the m. said to me, "Son of m., 40.04
the face of a m. toward the palm 41.19
While the m. was standing beside me, 43.06
"Son of m., this is the place of my 43.07
son of m., describe to the house of 43.10
"Son of m., thus says the Lord GOD: 43.18
"Son of m., mark well, see with your 44.05
the m. measured a thousand cubits, 47.03
"Son of m., have you seen this?" 47.06
"There is not a m. on earth who can Dan 2.10
from Judah a m. who can make known 2.25
that every m. who hears the sound 3.10
your kingdom a m. in whom is the 5.11
to any god or m. for thirty days, 6.07
that any m. who makes petition to 6.12
to any god or m. within thirty 6.12
to stand upon two feet like a m.; 7.04
the mind of a m. was given to it. 7.04
were eyes like the eyes of a m., 7.08
there came one like a son of m., 7.13
one having the appearance of a m. 8.15
make this m. understand the vision." 8.16
O son of m., that the vision is for 8.17
the m. Gabriel, whom I had seen in 9.21
a m. clothed in linen, whose loins 10.05
m. greatly beloved, give heed to the 10.11
appearance of a m. touched me and 10.18
"O m. greatly beloved, fear not, 10.19
And I said to the m. clothed in 12.06
The m. clothed in linen, who was 12.07

harlot, or belong to another m.; Hos 3.03
As robbers lie in wait for a m., 6.09
the m. of the spirit is mad, because 9.07
for I am God and not m., the Holy One 11.09
a m. and his father go into the Amo 2.07
and declares to m. what is his 4.13
as if a m. fled from a lion, and a 5.19
so that every m. from Mount Esau Ob 1.09
Let neither m. nor beast, herd nor Jon 3.07
but let m. and beast be covered 3.08
they oppress a m. and his house, Mic 2.02
a m. and his inheritance. 2.02
If a m. should go about and utter 2.11
shall sit every m. under his vine 4.04
has showed you, O m., what is good; 6.08
Shall I acquit the m. with wicked 6.11
The godly m. has perished from the 7.02
and the great m. utters the evil 7.03
M. the ramparts; watch the road; Nah 2.01
swallows up the m. more righteous Hab 1.13
the arrogant m. shall not abide. 2.05
"I will sweep away m. and beast; Zep 1.03
the mighty m. cries aloud there. 1.14
without a m., without an inhabitant 3.06
a m. riding upon a red horse! Zec 1.08
So the m. who was standing among 1.10
so that no m. raised his head; 1.21
a m. with a measuring line in his 2.01
to him, "Run, say to that young m., 2.04
like a m. that is wakened out of 4.01
the m. whose name is the Branch: for 6.12
was no wage for m. or any wage for 8.10
for I set every m. against his 8.10
the spirit of m. within him: 12.01
against the m. who stands next to 13.07
for the m. who does this, any to Mal 2.12
Will m. rob God? Yet you are 3.08
spare them as a m. spares his son 3.17
being a just m. and unwilling to Mt 1.19
'M. shall not live by bread alone, 4.04
Or what m. of you, if his son asks 7.09
be like a wise m. who built his 7.24
like a foolish m. who built his 7.26
For I am a m. under authority, with 8.09
but the Son of m. has nowhere to 8.20
"What sort of m. is this, that even 8.27
themselves, "This m. is blaspheming." 9.03
that the Son of m. has authority 9.06
he saw a m. called Matthew sitting 9.09
been cast out, the dumb m. spoke; 9.33
Israel, before the Son of m. comes. 10.23
come to set a m. against his 10.35
a righteous m. because he is a 10.41
is a righteous m. shall receive a 10.41
To see a m. clothed in soft raiment? 11.08
the Son of m. came eating and 11.19
For the Son of m. is lord of the 12.08
there was a m. with a withered hand. 12.10
"What m. of you, if he has one sheep 12.11
more value is a m. than a sheep! 12.12
Then he said to the m., "Stretch out 12.13
And the m. stretched it out, and 12.13
so that the dumb m. spoke and saw. 12.22
that this m. casts out demons." 12.24
he first binds the strong m.? 12.29
the Son of m. will be forgiven; 12.32
The good m. out of his good treasure 12.35
and the evil m. out of his evil 12.35
will the Son of m. be three days 12.40
spirit has gone out of a m., 12.43
state of that m. becomes worse 12.45
But he replied to the m. who told him, 12.48
compared to a m. who sowed good 13.24
seed which a m. took and sowed in 13.31
the good seed is the Son of m.; 13.37
The Son of m. will send his angels, 13.41
which a m. found and covered up; 13.44
"Where did this m. get this wisdom 13.54

MAN (cont.)

then did this m. get all this?" Mt 13.56
"O m. of little faith, why did you 14.31
goes into the mouth defiles a m., 15.11
out of the mouth, this defiles a m." 15.11
And if a blind m. leads a blind m., 15.14
the heart, and this defiles a m. 15.18
These are what defile a m.; 15.20
unwashed hands does not defile a m." 15.20
do men say that the Son of m. is?" 16.13
"If any m. would come after me, let 16.24
For what will it profit a m., 16.26
Or what shall a m. give in return 16.26
For the Son of m. is to come with 16.27
repay every m. for what he has 16.27
see the Son of m. coming in his 16.28
the Son of m. is raised from the 17.09
also the Son of m. will suffer at 17.12
a m. came up to him and kneeling 17.14
"The Son of m. is to be delivered 17.22
but woe to the m. by whom the 18.07
For the Son of m. came to save the * 18.11
If a m. has a hundred sheep, and one 18.12
this reason a m. shall leave his 19.05
together, let no m. put asunder." 19.06
is the case of a m. with his wife, 19.10
The young m. said to him, "All these 19.20
When the young m. heard this he 19.22
hard for a rich m. to enter the 19.23
than for a rich m. to enter the 19.24
when the Son of m. shall sit on 19.28
and the Son of m. will be delivered 20.18
even as the Son of m. came not to 20.28
A m. had two sons; and he went 21.28
he saw there a m. who had no 22.11
God truthfully, and care for no m.; 22.16
'If a m. dies, having no children, 22.24
And call no m. your father on earth, 23.09
be the coming of the Son of m. 24.27
sign of the Son of m. in heaven, 24.30
see the Son of m. coming on the 24.30
be the coming of the Son of m. 24.37
be the coming of the Son of m. 24.39
for the Son of m. is coming at an 24.44
be as when a m. going on a journey 25.14
Master, I knew you to be a hard m., 25.24
"When the Son of m. comes in his 25.31
and the Son of m. will be delivered 26.02
The Son of m. goes as it is written 26.24
m. by whom the Son of m. is betrayed! 26.24
better for that m. if he had not 26.24
and the Son of m. is betrayed into 26.45
"The one I shall kiss is the m.; 26.48
see the Son of m. seated at the 26.64
"This m. was with Jesus of Nazareth." 26.71
with an oath, "I do not know the m." 26.72
and to swear, "I do not know the m." 26.74
to do with that righteous m., for I 27.19
out, they came upon a m. of Cyrene, 27.32
this m. they compelled to carry his 27.32
"This m. is calling Elijah." 27.47
came a rich m. from Arimathea, 27.57
synagogue a m. with an unclean Mk 1.23
"Why does this m. speak thus? 2.07
that the Son of m. has authority 2.10
was made for m., not m. for the sabbath; 2.27
so the Son of m. is lord even of 2.28
and a m. was there who had a 3.01
And he said to the m. who had the 3.03
of heart, and said to the m., 3.05
he first binds the strong m.; 3.27
If any m. has ears to hear, let him 4.23
God is as if a m. should scatter 4.26
of the tombs a m. with an unclean 5.02
said to him, "Come out of the m., 5.08
the m. who had had the legion; 5.15
the m. who had been possessed with 5.18
"Where did this m. get all this? 6.02
he was a righteous and holy m., 6.20
'If a m. tells his father or his 7.11
outside a m. which by going into 7.15
come out of a m. are what defile 7.15
"If any m. has ears to hear, * 7.16
goes into a m. from outside cannot 7.18
comes out of a m. is what defiles a m., 7.20
within, out of the heart of m., 7.21
from within, and they defile a m." 7.23
to him a m. who was deaf and had 7.32
people brought to him a blind m., 8.22
And he took the blind m. by the hand, 8.23
that the Son of m. must suffer 8.31
"If any m. would come after me, let 8.34
For what does it profit a m., 8.36
For what can a m. give in return 8.37
will the Son of m. also be ashamed, 8.38
the Son of m. should have risen 9.09
how is it written of the Son of m., 9.12
"The Son of m. will be delivered 9.31
we saw a m. casting out demons in 9.38
it lawful for a m. to divorce his 10.02
"Moses allowed a m. to write a 10.04
'For this reason a m. shall leave 10.07
together, let not m. put asunder." 10.09
a m. ran up and knelt before him, 10.17
than for a rich m. to enter the 10.25
and the Son of m. will be delivered 10.33
For the Son of m. also came not to 10.45
And they called the blind m., 10.49
And the blind m. said to him, 10.51
"A m. planted a vineyard, and set a 12.01
you are true, and care for no m.; 12.14
the m. must take the wife, and raise 12.19
see the Son of m. coming in clouds 13.26
It is like a m. going on a journey, 13.34
and a m. carrying a jar of water 14.13
For the Son of m. goes as it is 14.21
m. by whom the Son of m. is betrayed! 14.21
better for that m. if he had not 14.21
the Son of m. is betrayed into the 14.41
"The one I shall kiss is the m.; 14.44
And a young m. followed him, with 14.51
see the Son of m. sitting at the 14.62
bystanders, "This m. is one of them." 14.69
not know this m. of whom you speak 14.71
there was a m. called Barabbas. 15.07
I do with the m. whom you call the 15.12
"Truly this m. was a son of God!" 15.39
saw a young m. sitting on the 16.05
For I am an old m., and my wife Lk 1.18
betrothed to a m. whose name was 1.27
Now there was a m. in Jerusalem, 2.25
and this m. was righteous and 2.25
and in favor with God and m. 2.52
'M. shall not live by bread alone.'" 4.04
there was a m. who had the spirit 4.33
me, for I am a sinful m., O Lord. 5.08
there came a m. full of leprosy; 5.12
on a bed a m. who was paralyzed, 5.18
"M., your sins are forgiven you." 5.20
that the Son of m. has authority 5.24
he said to the m. who was paralyzed— 5.24
"The Son of m. is lord of the 6.05
a m. was there whose right hand was 6.06
he said to the m. who had the 6.08
evil, on account of the Son of m.! 6.22
"Can a blind m. lead a blind m.? 6.39
The good m. out of the good treasure 6.45
and the evil m. out of his evil 6.45
he is like a m. building a house, 6.48
them is like a m. who built a 6.49
For I am a m. set under authority, 7.08
a m. who had died was being carried 7.12
"Young m., I say to you, arise." 7.14
And the dead m. sat up, and began to 7.15
A m. clothed in soft raiment? 7.25
The Son of m. has come eating and 7.34

MAN (cont.)

“If this m. were a prophet, he would	Lk 7.39
there met him a m. from the city	8.27
spirit to come out of the m.	8.29
came out of the m. and entered the	8.33
and found the m. from whom the	8.35
The m. from whom the demons had	8.38
And there came a m. named Jairus,	8.41
a m. from the ruler's house came and	8.49
“The Son of m. must suffer many	9.22
“If any m. would come after me, let	9.23
if profit a m. if he gains the	9.25
will the Son of m. be ashamed when	9.26
And behold, a m. from the crowd	9.38
for the Son of m. is to be delivered	9.44
we saw a m. casting out demons in	9.49
Son of m. came not to destroy men's	* 9.55
a m. said to him, “I will follow you	9.57
but the Son of m. has nowhere to	9.58
“A m. was going down from Jerusalem	10.30
neighbor to the m. who fell among	10.36
the dumb m. spoke, and the people	11.14
When a strong m., fully armed,	11.21
spirit has gone out of a m.,	11.24
state of that m. becomes worse	11.26
will the Son of m. be to this	11.30
the Son of m. also will acknowledge	12.08
the Son of m. will be forgiven;	12.10
“M., who made me a judge or divider	12.14
land of a rich m. brought forth	12.16
for the Son of m. is coming at an	12.40
“A m. had a fig tree planted in his	13.06
seed which a m. took and sowed in	13.19
there was a m. before him who had	14.02
a more eminent m. than you be	14.08
say to you, ‘Give place to this m.,	14.09
also to the m. who had invited him,	14.12
“A m. once gave a great banquet, and	14.16
saying, ‘This m. began to build, and	14.30
“This m. receives sinners and eats	15.02
“What m. of you, having a hundred	15.04
“There was a m. who had two sons;	15.11
was a rich m. who had a steward,	16.01
him that this m. was wasting his	16.01
“There was a rich m., who was	16.19
gate lay a poor m. named Lazarus,	16.20
The poor m. died and was carried by	16.22
The rich m. also died and was	16.22
one of the days of the Son of m.,	17.22
will the Son of m. be in his day.	17.24
it be in the days of the Son of m.	17.26
day when the Son of m. is revealed.	17.30
neither feared God nor regarded m.;	18.02
I neither fear God nor regard m.,	18.04
Nevertheless, when the Son of m. comes,	18.08
this m. went down to his house	18.14
than for a rich m. to enter the	18.25
there is no m. who has left house	18.29
of the Son of m. by the prophets	18.31
a blind m. was sitting by the	18.35
And there was a m. named Zacchaeus;	19.02
the guest of a m. who is a sinner.	19.07
For the Son of m. came to seek and	19.10
not want this m. to reign over us.’	19.14
you, because you are a severe m.;	19.21
You knew that I was a severe m.,	19.22
“A m. planted a vineyard, and let it	20.09
the m. must take the wife and raise	20.28
see the Son of m. coming in a	21.27
and to stand before the Son of m.	21.36
a m. carrying a jar of water will	22.10
For the Son of m. goes as it has	22.22
but woe to that m. by whom he is	22.22
and the m. called Judas, one of the	22.47
betray the Son of m. with a kiss?	22.48
“This m. also was with him.”	22.56
But Peter said, “M., I am not.”	22.58
“Certainly this m. also was with	22.59
“M., I do not know what you are	22.60
on the Son of m. shall be seated	22.69
“We found this m. perverting our	23.02
multitudes, “I find no crime in this m.”	23.04
whether the m. was a Galilean.	23.06
brought me this m. as one who was	23.14
not find this m. guilty of any of	23.14
obliged to release one m. to them	* 23.17
out together, “Away with this m.,	23.18
a m. who had been thrown into	23.19
He released the m. who had been	23.25
but this m. has done nothing wrong.”	23.41
“Certainly this m. was innocent!”	23.47
Now there was a m. named Joseph	23.50
council, a good and righteous m.,	23.50
This m. went to Pilate and asked	23.52
that the Son of m. must be delivered	24.07
There was a m. sent from God, whose	Jn 1.06
enlightens every m. was coming into	1.09
nor of the will of m., but of God.	1.13
me comes a m. who ranks before me,	1.30
and descending upon the Son of m.”	1.51
“Every m. serves the good wine	2.10
no one to bear witness of m.;	2.25
for he himself knew what was in m.	2.25
Now there was a m. of the Pharisees,	3.01
This m. came to Jesus by night and	3.02
“How can a m. be born when he is	3.04
descended from heaven, the Son of m.	3.13
must the Son of m. be lifted up,	3.14
“Come, see a m. who told me all that	4.29
“The m. believed the word that	4.50
One m. was there, who had been ill	5.05
The sick m. answered him, “Sir, I	5.07
I have no m. to put me into the	5.07
And at once the m. was healed,	5.09
Jews said to the m. who was cured,	5.10
“The m. who healed me said to me,	5.11
“Who is the m. who said to you,	5.12
Now the m. who had been healed did	5.13
The m. went away and told the Jews	5.15
because he is the Son of m.	5.27
testimony which I receive is from m.;	5.34
the Son of m. will give to you;	6.27
that a m. may eat of it and not die.	6.50
“How can this m. give us his flesh	6.52
of the Son of m. and drink his	6.53
see the Son of m. ascending where	6.62
For no m. works in secret if he	7.04
“He is a good m.,” others said, “No,	7.12
is it that this m. has learning,	7.15
circumcise a m. upon the sabbath.	7.22
the sabbath a m. receives circumcision,	7.23
“Is not this the m. whom they seek	7.25
Yet we know where this m. comes from;	7.27
more signs that this m. has done?”	7.31
“Where does this m. intend to go	7.35
“No m. ever spoke like this m.!”	7.46
“Does our law judge a m. without	7.51
you have lifted up the Son of m.,	8.28
a m. who has told you the truth	8.40
he saw a m. blind from his birth.	9.01
this m. or his parents, that he was	9.02
“It was not that this m. sinned,	9.03
“Is not this the m. who used to sit	9.08
He said, “I am the m.”	9.09
“The m. called Jesus made clay and	9.11
Pharisees the m. who had formerly	9.13
“This m. is not from God, for he	9.16
“How can a m. who is a sinner do	9.16
So they again said to the blind m.,	9.17
parents of the m. who had received	9.18
they called the m. who had been	9.24
we know that this m. is a sinner.”	9.24
to Moses, but as for this m.,	9.29
The m. answered, “Why, this is a	9.30
opened the eyes of a m. born blind.	9.32
If this m. were not from God, he	9.33

MAN (cont.)

"Do you believe in the Son of m.?" Jn 9.35
that m. is a thief and a robber; 10.01
being a m., make yourself God." 10.33
John said about this m. was true." 10.41
Now a certain m. was ill, Lazarus of 11.01
blind m. have kept this m. from dying?" 11.37
Martha, the sister of the dead m., 11.39
The dead m. came out, his hands and 11.44
For this m. performs many signs. 11.47
you that one m. should die for the 11.50
for the Son of m. to be glorified. 12.23
that the Son of m. must be lifted 12.34
up? Who is this Son of m.?" 12.34
"Now is the Son of m. glorified, 13.31
"If a m. loves me, he will keep my 14.23
If a m. does not abide in me, he is 15.06
Greater love has no m. than this, 15.13
that a m. lay down his life for his 15.13
every m. to his home, and will leave 16.32
that one m. should die for the 18.14
kinsman of the m. whose ear Peter 18.26
do you bring against this m.?" 18.29
"If this m. were not an evildoer, we 18.30
for us to put any m. to death." 18.31
release one m. for you at the 18.39
again, "Not this m., but Barabbas!" 18.40
said to them, "Here is the m.!" 19.05
cried out, "If you release this m., 19.12
'This m. said, I am King of the Jews.'" 19.21
to Jesus, "Lord, what about this m.?" 21.21
(Now this m. bought a field with Ac 1.18
a m. attested to you by God with 2.22
And a m. lame from birth was being 3.02
has made this m. strong whom you 3.16
has given the m. this perfect 3.16
what means this m. has been healed, 4.09
by him this m. is standing before 4.10
But seeing the m. that had been 4.14
For the m. on whom this sign of 4.22
But a m. named Ananias with his 5.01
a m. full of faith and of the Holy 6.05
"This m. never ceases to speak 6.13
the oppressed m. and avenged him 7.24
But the m. who was wronging his 7.27
and the Son of m. standing at the 7.56
the feet of a young m. named Saul. 7.58
But there was a m. named Simon who 8.09
"This m. is that power of God which 8.10
of Judas for a m. of Tarsus named 9.11
and he has seen a m. named Ananias 9.12
have heard from many about this m., 9.13
"Is not this the m. who made havoc 9.21
There he found a m. named Aeneas, 9.33
there was a m. named Cornelius, a 10.01
a devout m. who feared God with all 10.02
an upright and God-fearing m., 10.22
"Stand up; I too am a m." 10.26
not call any m. common or unclean. 10.28
and behold, a m. stood before me in 10.30
for he was a good m., full of the 11.24
"The voice of a god, and not of m.!" 12.22
a m. of intelligence, who summoned 13.07
a m. of the tribe of Benjamin, for 13.21
son of Jesse a m. after my heart, 13.22
through this m. forgiveness of 13.38
Now at Lystra there was a m. sitting, 14.08
a m. of Macedonia was standing 16.09
not live in shrines made by m., 17.24
by the art and imagination of m. 17.29
righteousness by a m. whom he has 17.31
the house of a m. named Titius 18.07
and no m. shall attack you to harm 18.10
saying, "This m. is persuading men 18.13
He was an eloquent m., well versed 18.24
And the m. in whom the evil spirit 19.16
For a m. named Demetrius, a silversmith, 19.24
what m. is there who does not know 19.35
And a young m. named Eutychus was 20.09
bind the m. who owns this girdle 21.11
This is the m. who is teaching men 21.28
a devout m. according to the law, 22.12
to scourge a m. who is a Roman 22.25
For this m. is a Roman citizen." 22.26
"We find nothing wrong in this m. 23.09
"Bring this young m. to the tribune; 23.17
me to bring this young m. to you, 23.18
the tribune dismissed the young m., 23.22
This m. was seized by the Jews, and 23.27
would be a plot against the m., 23.30
have found this m. a pestilent 24.05
to have the m. sent to Jerusalem, 25.03
is anything wrong about the m., 25.05
"There is a m. left prisoner by 25.14
and ordered the m. to be brought 25.17
should like to hear the m. myself. 25.22
you see this m. about whom the 25.24
"This m. is doing nothing to 26.31
"This m. could have been set free 26.32
"No doubt this m. is a murderer. 28.04
to the chief m. of the island, 28.07
resembling mortal m. or birds or Rom 1.23
O m., whoever you are, when you 2.01
O m., that when you judge those who 2.03
render to every m. according to 2.06
So, if a m. who is uncircumcised 2.26
be true though every m. be false, 3.04
For we hold that a m. is justified 3.28
upon the m. to whom God reckons 4.06
blessed is the m. against whom the 4.08
hardly die for a righteous m.— 5.07
for a good m. one will dare even 5.07
through one m. and death through 5.12
of that one m. Jesus Christ 5.15
death reigned through that one m., 5.17
through the one m. Jesus Christ. 5.17
with another m. while her husband 7.03
marries another m. she is not an 7.03
Wretched m. that I am! 7.24
had conceived children by one m., 9.10
a m., to answer back to God? 9.20
Moses writes that the m. who 10.05
For m. believes with his heart and 10.10
As for the m. who is weak in faith, 14.01
while the weak m. eats only 14.02
One m. esteems one day as better 14.05
while another m. esteems all days 14.05
Where is the wise m.? Where is the 1Co 1.20
nor the heart of m. conceived, 2.09
spirit of the m. which is in him? 2.11
The unspiritual m. does not receive 2.14
The spiritual m. judges all things, 2.15
and another m. is building upon it. 3.10
Let each m. take care how he builds 3.10
work which any m. has built on the 3.14
Then every m. will receive his 4.05
for a m. is living with his father's 5.01
Jesus on the m. who has done such 5.04
to deliver this m. to Satan for 5.05
there is no m. among you wise 6.05
sin which a m. commits is outside 6.18
but the immoral m. sins against his 6.18
is well for a m. not to touch a 7.01
each m. should have his own wife 7.02
The unmarried m. is anxious about 7.32
but the married m. is anxious about 7.33
a m. of knowledge, at table in an 8.10
knowledge this weak m. is destroyed, 8.11
you that is not common to m. 10.13
consideration for the m. who 10.28
the head of every m. is Christ, 11.03
Any m. who prays or prophesies with 11.04
For a m. ought not to cover his 11.07
but woman is the glory of m. 11.07
(For m. was not made from woman, but 11.08
made from woman, but woman from m. 11.08

MAN (cont.)
Neither was m. created for woman, 1Co 11.09
for woman, but woman for m.) 11.09
independent of m. nor m. of woman 11.11
for as woman was made from m., 11.12
so m. is now born of woman. 11.12
you that for a m. to wear long 11.14
Let a m. examine himself, and so eat 11.28
when I became a m., I gave up 13.11
but the other m. is not edified. 14.17
For as by a m. came death, by a 15.21
by a m. has come also the resurrection 15.21
You foolish m.! What you sow 15.36
"The first m. Adam became a living 15.45
m. was from the earth, a m. of dust; 15.47
the second m. is from heaven. 15.47
As was the m. of dust, so are those 15.48
and as is the m. of heaven, so are 15.48
borne the image of the m. of dust, 15.49
bear the image of the m. of heaven. 15.49
I make my plans like a worldly m., 2Co 1.17
but when a m. turns to the Lord the 3.16
acceptable according to what a m. has, 8.12
For it is not the m. who commends 10.18
but the m. whom the Lord commends. 10.18
bear it if a m. makes slaves of 11.20
I know a m. in Christ who fourteen 12.02
know that this m. was caught up 12.03
be told, which m. may not utter. 12.04
On behalf of this m. I will boast, 12.05
apostle—not from men nor through m., Gal 1.01
For I did not receive it from m., 1.12
yet who know that a m. is not 2.16
evident that no m. is justified 3.11
again to every m. who receives 5.03
Brethren, if a m. is overtaken in 6.01
For each m. will have to bear his 6.05
not mocked, for whatever a m. sows, 6.07
Henceforth let no m. trouble me; 6.17
of works, lest any m. should boast. Eph 2.09
himself one new m. in place of the 2.15
his Spirit in the inner m., 3.16
this, that no immoral or impure m., 5.05
For no m. ever hates his own flesh, 5.29
"For this reason a m. shall leave 5.31
If any other m. thinks he has Php 3.04
warning every m. and teaching every Col 1.28
teaching every m. in all wisdom, 1.28
present every m. mature in Christ. 1.28
free m., but Christ is all, and in 3.11
that no m. transgress, and wrong his 1Th 4.06
this, disregards not m. but God, 4.08
and the m. of lawlessness is 2Th 2.03
note that m., and have nothing to 3.14
God and men, the m. Christ Jesus, 1Ti 2.05
for if a m. does not know how to 3.05
rebuke an older m. but exhort him 5.01
m. of God, shun all this; aim at 6.11
whom no m. has ever seen or can see 6.16
that the m. of God may be complete, 2Ti 3.17
As for a m. who is factious, after Tit 3.10
"What is m. that thou art mindful Heb 2.06
or the son of m., that thou carest 2.06
everything in subjection to m., 2.08
But this m. who has not their 7.06
set up not by m. but by the Lord. 8.02
A m. who has violated the law of 10.28
deserved by the m. who has spurned 10.29
Therefore from one m., and him as 11.12
not be afraid; what can m. do to me?" 13.06
suppose that a double minded m., Jas 1.07
will the rich m. fade away in the 1.11
Blessed is the m. who endures trial, 1.12
Let every m. be quick to hear, slow 1.19
for the anger of m. does not work 1.20
he is like a m. who observes his 1.23
For if a m. with gold rings and in 2.02
and a poor m. in shabby clothing 2.02
while you say to the poor m., 2.03
But you have dishonored the poor m. 2.06
if a m. says he has faith but has 2.14
You see that a m. is justified by 2.24
in what he says he is a perfect m., 3.02
you have killed the righteous m.; 5.06
of faith will save the sick m., 5.15
of a righteous m. has great power 5.16
Elijah was a m. of like nature with 5.17
the righteous m. is scarcely saved, 1Pe 4.18
ever came by the impulse of m., 2Pe 1.21
that righteous m. saw and heard as 2.08
for whatever overcomes a m., 2.19
No m. has ever seen God; 1Jn 4.12
lampstands one like a son of m., Rev 1.13
creature with the face of a m., 4.07
multitude which no m. could number, 7.09
of a scorpion, when it stings a m. 9.05
on the cloud one like a son of m., 14.14
became like the blood of a dead m., 16.03

MANAEN
M. a member of the court of Herod Ac 13.01

MANAGE
He must m. his own household well, 1Ti 3.04
not know how to m. his own household, 3.05
and let them m. their children and 3.12

MANAGED
we m. with difficulty to secure the Ac 27.16

MANAHATH
M., Ebal, Shepho, and Onam. Gen 36.23
M., Ebal, Shephi, and Onam. 1Ch 1.40
were carried into exile to M.): 8.06

MANAHATHITES
and half of the M., the Zorites. 1Ch 2.54

MANASSEH
the name of the first-born M., Gen 41.51
of Egypt were born M. and Ephraim, 46.20
him his two sons, M. and Ephraim. 48.01
Ephraim and M. shall be mine, as 48.05
and M. in his left hand toward 48.13
his left hand upon the head of M., 48.14
for M. was the first-born. 48.14
make you as Ephraim and as M.' "; 48.20
and thus he put Ephraim before M. 48.20
the son of M. were born upon 50.23
and from M., Gamaliel the son of Num 1.10
Of the people of M., their generations, 1.34
of the tribe of M. was thirty-two 1.35
to him shall be the tribe of M., 2.20
the people of M. being Gamaliel 2.20
the leader of the men of M.: 7.54
of the men of M. was Gamaliel the 10.23
(that is from the tribe of M.), 13.11
to their families: M. and Ephraim. 26.28
The sons of M.: of Machir, the family 26.29
These are the families of M.; 26.34
son of M., from the families of 27.01
the families of M. the son of 27.01
half-tribe of M. the son of Joseph, 32.33
the son of M. went to Gilead and 32.39
Gilead to Machir the son of M., 32.40
And Jair the son of M. went and 32.41
and also the half-tribe of M.; 34.14
tribe of the sons of M. a leader, 34.23
son of M., of the fathers' houses 36.01
of the sons of M. the son of 36.12
I gave to the half-tribe of M. Deu 3.13
and such are the thousands of M." 33.17
Naphtali, the land of Ephraim and M., 34.02
the half-tribe of M. Joshua said, Jos 1.12
half tribe of M. passed over armed 4.12
Gadites and the half-tribe of M. 12.06

MANASSEH (cont.)
tribes and half the tribe of M." Jos 13.07
of the tribe of M. the Reubenites 13.08
inheritance to the half-tribe of M.; 13.29
the son of M. for the half of the 13.31
were two tribes, M. and Ephraim; 14.04
M. and Ephraim, received their 16.04
was made to the tribe of M., 17.01
To Machir the first-born of M., 17.01
to the rest of the tribe of M., 17.02
descendants of M. the son of 17.02
son of M., had no sons, but only 17.03
Thus there fell to M. ten portions, 17.05
daughters of M. received an 17.06
The territory of M. reached from 17.07
The land of Tappuah belonged to M., 17.08
the boundary of M. belonged to the 17.08
the brook, among the cities of M., 17.09
the boundary of M. goes on the 17.09
and in Asher M. had Bethshean and 17.11
Yet the sons of M. could not take 17.12
house of Joseph, to Ephraim and M., 17.17
the tribe of M. have received 18.07
in Bashan, from the tribe of M. 20.08
the half-tribe of M., ten cities. 21.05
the half-tribe of M. in Bashan, 21.06
and out of the half-tribe of M., 21.25
given out of the half-tribe of M., 21.27
Gadites, and the half-tribe of M., 22.01
of the tribe of M. Moses had given 22.07
the half-tribe of M. returned home, 22.09
half-tribe of M. built there an 22.10
half-tribe of M. have built an 22.11
Gadites and the half-tribe of M., 22.13
Gadites, and the half-tribe of M., 22.15
half-tribe of M. said in answer to 22.21
M. did not drive out the inhabitants Ju 1.27
my clan is the weakest in M., 6.15
sent messengers throughout all M.; 6.35
and from Asher and from all M., 7.23
he passed through Gilead and M., 11.29
in the midst of Ephraim and M." 12.04
the villages of Jair the son of M., 1Ki 4.13
and M. his son reigned in his 2Ki 20.21
M. was twelve years old when he 21.01
and M. seduced them to do more evil 21.09
"Because M. king of Judah has 21.11
Moreover M. shed very much innocent 21.16
Now the rest of the acts of M., 21.17
And M. slept with his fathers, and 21.18
as M. his father had done. 21.20
altars which M. had made in the 23.12
with which M. had provoked him. 23.26
of his sight, for the sins of M., 24.03
son, Hezekiah his son, M. his son, 1Ch 3.13
half-tribe of M. had valiant men, 5.18
half-tribe of M. dwelt in the land 5.23
Gadites, and the half-tribe of M., 5.26
half-tribe, the half of M., ten cities. 6.61
Asher, Naphtali, and M. in Bashan. 6.62
and out of the half-tribe of M., 6.70
given out of the half-tribe of M.: 6.71
The sons of M.: Asriel, whom his 7.14
the son of Machir, son of M. 7.17
and M. dwelt in Jerusalem: 9.03
Some of the men of M. deserted to 12.19
these men of M. deserted to him: 12.20
Zillethai, chiefs of thousands in M. 12.20
half-tribe of M. eighteen thousand, 12.31
half-tribe of M. from beyond the 12.37
for the half tribe of M., 27.20
for the half tribe of M. in Gilead, 27.21
M., and Simeon who were sojourning 2Ch 15.09
letters also to Ephraim and M., 30.01
the country of Ephraim and M., 30.10
of M., and of Zebulun humbled 30.11
M., Issachar, and Zebulun, had not 30.18
Benjamin, and in Ephraim and M., 31.01
And M. his son reigned in his stead. 32.33
M. was twelve years old when he 33.01
M. seduced Judah and the inhabitants 33.09
The LORD spoke to M. and to his 33.10
who took M. with hooks and bound 33.11
Then M. knew that the LORD was God. 33.13
Now the rest of the acts of M., 33.18
So M. slept with his fathers, and 33.20
as M. his father had done. 33.22
the images that M. his father had 33.22
as M. his father had humbled 33.23
And in the cities of M., 34.06
collected from M. and Ephraim and 34.09
Mattaniah, Bezalel, Binnui, and M. Ez 10.30
Eliphelet, Jeremai, M., and Shimei. 10.33
M. is mine; Ephraim is my helmet; Ps 60.07
before Ephraim and Benjamin and M.! 80.02
M. is mine; Ephraim is my helmet; 108.08
M. Ephraim, and Ephraim M., and Is 9.21
because of what M. the son of Jer 15.04
side to the west, M., one portion. Eze 48.04
Adjoining the territory of M., 48.05
and Hezekiah the father of M., Mt 1.10
and M. the father of Amos, and Amos 1.10
thousand of the tribe of M., Rev 7.06

MANASSEH'S
it from Ephraim's head to M. head. Gen 48.17
and that to the north being M., Jos 17.10

MANASSITE
Jair the M. took all the region of Deu 3.14

MANASSITES
and Golan in Bashan for the M. Deu 4.43
and the half-tribe of the M. 29.08
half-tribe of the M. according to Jos 13.29
within the inheritance of the M., 16.09
was allotted to the rest of the M. 17.06
and the Gadites and the M. spoke, 22.30
Reubenites and the Gadites and the M., 22.31
and the M., from Aroer, which is by 2Ki 10.33
also along the borders of the M., 1Ch 7.29
half-tribe of the M. for everything 26.32

MAN-CHILD
which said, 'A m. is conceived.' Job 3.03

MANDRAKES
went and found m. in the field, Gen 30.14
me, I pray, some of your son's m." 30.14
you take away my son's m. also?" 30.15
with you tonight for your son's m." 30.15
I have hired you with my son's m." 30.16
The m. give forth fragrance, and Sol 7.13

MANGER
cloths, and laid him in a m., Lk 2.07
swaddling cloths and lying in a m." 2.12
Joseph, and the babe lying in a m. 2.16
his ox or his ass from the m., 13.15

MANHOOD
and in his m. he strove with god. Hos 12.03
to mature m., to the measure of the Eph 4.13

MANIFEST
Let thy work be m. to thy servants, Ps 90.16
his elders he will m. his glory. Is 24.23
and I will m. my holiness among you Eze 20.41
and I will m. my glory in the midst 28.22
and m. my holiness in her; 28.22
and m. my holiness in them in the 28.25
nothing hid, except to be made m.; Mk 4.22
is hid that shall not be made m., Lk 8.17
of God might be made m. in him. Jn 9.03
will love him and m. myself to him." 14.21
it that you will m. yourself to us, 14.22
Lord comes, the great and m. day. Ac 2.20

MANIFEST (cont.)
through them is m. to all the Ac 4.16
on the third day and made him m.; 10.40
each man's work will become m.; 1Co 3.13
but now made m. to his saints. Col 1.26
will be made m. at the proper time 1Ti 6.15
but was made m. at the end of the 1Pe 1.20
the life was made m., 1Jn 1.02
the Father and was made m. to us— 1.02
love of God was made m. among us, 4.09

MANIFESTATION
till the day of his m. to Israel. Lk 1.80
is given the m. of the Spirit for 1Co 12.07

MANIFESTATIONS
you are eager for m. of the Spirit, 1Co 14.12

MANIFESTED
who hast m. thy might among the Ps 77.14
Cana in Galilee, and m. his glory; Jn 2.11
"I have m. thy name to the men whom 17.06
of God has been m. apart from law, Rom 3.21
Jesus may also be m. in our bodies. 2Co 4.10
of Jesus may be m. in our mortal 4.11
He was m. in the flesh, vindicated 1Ti 3.16
and now has m. through the appearing 2Ti 1.10
the proper time m. in his word Tit 1.03
Shepherd is m. you will obtain the 1Pe 5.04

MANIFOLD
For he is m. in understanding. Job 11.06
O LORD, how m. are thy works! Ps 104.24
not receive m. more in this time, Lk 18.30
the church the m. wisdom of God Eph 3.10

MANKIND
thing and the breath of all m. Job 12.10
and m. than the gold of Ophir. Is 13.12
day in Israel and among all m., Jer 32.20
I will cut off m. from the face of Zep 1.03
of wrath, like the rest of m. Eph 2.03
only those of m. who have not the Rev 9.04
the year, to kill a third of m. 9.15
plagues a third of m. was killed, 9.18
The rest of m., who were not killed 9.20
redeemed from m. as first fruits 14.04

MANNA
house of Israel called its name m.; Ex 16.31
a jar, and put an omer of m. in it, 16.33
of Israel ate the m. forty years, 16.35
they ate the m., till they came to 16.35
at all but this m. to look at. Num 11.06
Now the m. was like coriander seed, 11.07
in the night, the m. fell with it. 11.09
let you hunger and fed you with m., Deu 8.03
wilderness with m. which your 8.16
And the m. ceased on the morrow, Jos 5.12
people of Israel had m. no more, 5.12
withhold thy m. from their mouth, Neh 9.20
he rained down upon them m. to eat, Ps 78.24
Our fathers ate the m. in the Jn 6.31
Your fathers ate the m. in the 6.49
a golden urn holding the m., Heb 9.04
I will give some of the hidden m., Rev 2.17

MANNER
with Sarah after the m. of women. Gen 18.11
to us after the m. of all the 19.31
In this m. you shall eat it: your Ex 12.11
And this is the m. of the release: Deu 15.02
city in the same m. seven times: Jos 6.15
what is to be the boy's m. of life, Ju 13.12
after the m. of the Sidonians, quiet 18.07
this was the m. of attesting in Ru 4.07
After this m. he made the ten 1Ki 7.37
after the m. of the nations from 2Ki 17.33
they do according to the former m. 17.34
did according to their former m. 17.40
and I answered them in the same m. Neh 6.04
be full, providing all m. of store; Ps 144.13
king of Judah I spoke in like m.: Jer 27.12
after the m. of your fathers and Eze 20.30
a pestilence after the m. of Egypt; Amo 4.10
And these in like m. are the ones Mk 4.16
do not know what m. of spirit you *Lk 9.55
and Lazarus in like m. evil things; 16.25
to the strict m. of the law of our Ac 22.03
"My m. of life from my youth, spent 26.04
filled with all m. of wickedness, Rom 1.29
in an unworthy m. will be guilty 1Co 11.27
to your former m. of life and is Eph 4.22
Only let your m. of life be worthy Php 1.27
Yet in like m. these men in their Jud 1.08

MANOAH
of the Danites, whose name was M.; Ju 13.02
Then M. entreated the LORD, and said, 13.08
And God listened to the voice of M., 13.09
but M. her husband was not with her. 13.09
And M. arose and went after his 13.11
And M. said, "Now when your words 13.12
And the angel of the LORD said to M., 13.13
M. said to the angel of the LORD, 13.15
And the angel of the LORD said to M., 13.16
(For M. did not know that he was 13.16
And M. said to the angel of the 13.17
So M. took the kid with the cereal 13.19
the altar while M. and his wife 13.20
no more to M. and to his wife. 13.21
Then M. knew that he was the angel 13.21
And M. said to his wife, "We shall 13.22
in the tomb of M. his father. 16.31

MAN'S
imagination of m. heart is evil Gen 8.21
of every m. brother I will require 9.05
man and every m. hand against him; 16.12
have taken; for she is a m. wife." 20.03
Now then restore the m. wife; 20.07
replace every m. money in his sack, 42.25
every m. bundle of money was in his 42.35
there was every m. money in the 43.21
and put each m. money in the mouth 44.01
cannot see the m. face unless our 44.26
said to him, "Who has made m. mouth? Ex 4.11
If it gores a m. son or daughter, he 21.31
"When one m. ox hurts another's, so 21.35
and it feeds in another m. field, 22.05
it is stolen out of the m. house, 22.07
"If a m. offering is a sacrifice of Lev 3.01
who offers any m. burnt offering 7.08
"If a m. hair has fallen from his 13.40
And if a m. hair has fallen from 13.41
and every m. holy things shall be Num 5.10
If any m. wife goes astray and acts 5.12
Write each m. name upon his rod, 17.02
goes and becomes another m. wife, Deu 24.02
LORD set every m. sword against Ju 7.22
the door of the m. house where her 19.26
"The m. name with whom I worked Ru 2.19
or taken anything from any m. hand." 1Sa 12.04
every m. sword was against his 14.20
"Let no m. heart fail because of 17.32
him, but he took the poor m. lamb 2Sa 12.04
cloud like a m. hand is rising out 1Ki 18.44
money which a m. heart prompts him 2Ki 12.04
of man, or thy years as m. years, Job 10.05
This is the wicked m. portion from 20.29
and bread to strengthen m. heart. Ps 104.15
Redeem me from m. oppression, that I 119.134
For a m. ways are before the eyes Pro 5.21
adulteress stalks a m. very life. 6.26
A rich m. wealth is his strong city 10.15

MAN'S (cont.)
the work of a m. hand comes back Pro 12.14
Anxiety in a m. heart weighs him 12.25
The ransom of a m. life is his 13.08
The wise m. path leads upward to 15.24
When a m. ways please the LORD, he 16.07
A m. mind plans his way, but the 16.09
The words of a m. mouth are deep 18.04
A rich m. wealth is his strong city, 18.11
Before destruction a m. heart is 18.12
A m. spirit will endure sickness; 18.14
A m. gift makes room for him and 18.16
When a m. folly brings his way to 19.03
All a poor m. brothers hate him; 19.07
The purpose in a m. mind is like 20.05
Take a m. garment when he has given 20.16
A m. steps are ordered by the LORD; 20.24
remains in a wise m. dwelling, 21.20
Like a lame m. legs, which hang 26.07
Take a m. garment when he has given 27.13
A m. pride will bring him low, but 29.23
and many concubines, m. delight. Ecc 2.08
he has put eternity into m. mind, 3.11
come from a m. envy of his neighbor. 4.04
A m. wisdom makes his face shine, 8.01
although m. trouble lies heavy upon 8.06
though the poor m. wisdom is 9.16
A wise m. heart inclines him toward 10.02
The words of a wise m. mouth win 10.12
and every m. heart will melt, Is 13.07
him and becomes another m. wife, Jer 3.01
the burden is every m. own word, 23.36
every m. sword will be against his Eze 38.21
land and any one sees a m. bone, 39.15
reed in the m. hand was six long 40.05
let his mind be changed from a m., Dan 4.16
fingers of a m. hand appeared and 5.05
And I heard a m. voice between the 8.16
And when a m. kinsman, he who burns Amo 6.10
let us not perish for this m. life, Jon 1.14
a m. enemies are the men of his own Mic 7.06
and a m. foes will be those of his Mt 10.36
receive a righteous m. reward. 10.41
enter a strong m. house and 12.29
"I am innocent of this m. blood; 27.24
enter a strong m. house and Mk 3.27
us that if a m. brother dies and 12.19
for a m. life does not consist in Lk 12.15
what fell from the rich m. table; 16.21
for us that if a m. brother dies, 20.28
if any m. will is to do his will, he Jn 7.17
I made a m. whole body well? 7.23
anointed the m. eyes with the clay, 9.06
you also one of this m. disciples? 18.17
to bring this m. blood upon us. Ac 5.28
me, and we entered the m. house. 11.12
Of this m. posterity God has 13.23
many died through one m. trespass, Rom 5.15
like the effect of that one m. sin. 5.16
If, because of one m. trespass, 5.17
Then as one m. trespass led to 5.18
so one m. act of righteousness 5.18
For as by one m. disobedience many 5.19
so by one m. obedience many will be 5.19
not upon m. will or exertion, but 9.16
I build on another m. foundation, 15.20
person knows a m. thoughts except 1Co 2.11
each m. work will become manifest; 3.13
If any m. work is burned up, he will 3.15
determined by another m. scruples? 10.29
to every m. conscience in the 2Co 4.02
themselves on a m. position and 5.12
preached by me is not m. gospel. Gal 1.11
no one annuls even a m. will, 3.15
nor participate in another m. sins; 1Ti 5.22
his heart, this m. religion is vain. Jas 1.26
forty-four cubits by a m. measure, Rev 21.17

MANSERVANT
your m., or your maidservant, or Ex 20.10
or his m., or his maidservant, or 20.17
or your m., or your maidservant, or Deu 5.14
that your m. and your maidservant 5.14
or his m., or his maidservant, his 5.21
your m. and your maidservant, and 12.18
your m. and your maidservant, the 16.11
your m. and your maidservant, the 16.14
the cause of my m. or my maidservant, Job 31.13

MANSLAYER
you shall permit the m. to flee, Num 35.06
that the m. who kills any person 35.11
that the m. may not die until he 35.12
between the m. and the avenger of 35.24
rescue the m. from the hand of the 35.25
But if the m. shall at any time go 35.26
the avenger of blood slays the m., 35.27
high priest the m. may return to 35.28
that the m. might flee there, who Deu 4.42
so that any m. can flee to them. 19.03
"This is the provision for the m., 19.04
pursue the m. and overtake him, 19.06
that the m. who kills any person Jos 20.03

MANSLAYERS
and murderers of mothers, for m., 1Ti 1.09

MANTELET
to the wall, the m. is set up. Nah 2.05

MANTLE
red, all his body like a hairy m.; Gen 25.25
covering, it is his m. for his body; Ex 22.27
spoil a beautiful m. from Shinar, Jos 7.21
silver and the m. and the bar of 7.24
"Bring the m. you are wearing and Ru 3.15
his face in his m. and went out 1Ki 19.13
by him and cast his m. upon him. 19.19
Then Elijah took his m., 2Ki 2.08
And he took up the m. of Elijah 2.13
Then he took the m. of Elijah that 2.14
this, I rent my garments and my m., Ez 9.03
with my garments and my m. rent, 9.05
crown and a m. of fine linen and Est 8.15
in their own shame as in a m.! Ps 109.29
wounded me, they took away my m., Sol 5.07
his father, saying: "You have a m.; Is 3.06
there is neither bread nor m.; 3.07
wrapped himself in fury as a m. 59.17
the m. of praise instead of a faint 61.03
put on a hairy m. in order to Zec 13.04
field not turn back to take his m. Mt 24.18
throwing off his m. he sprang up Mk 10.50
field not turn back to take his m. 13.16
And the high priest tore his m., 14.63
no sword sell his m. and buy one. Lk 22.36
"Wrap your m. around you and follow Ac 12.08
like a m. thou wilt roll them up, Heb 1.12

MANTLES
up in their m. on their shoulders. Ex 12.34
the m., the cloaks, and the handbags; Is 3.22
Then these men were bound in their m., Dan 3.21
their m. were not harmed, and no 3.27

MANURE
till I dig about it and put on m. Lk 13.08

MANY
as m. as came out of the ark. Gen 9.10
sojourned m. days in the land of 21.34
and mourned for his son m. days. 37.34
to keep alive for you m. survivors. 45.07
"How m. are the days of the years 47.08
for so m. are required for embalming. 50.03
it about that m. people should be 50.20
Israel are too m. and too mighty Ex 1.09

MANY (cont.)

course of those m. days the king Ex 2.23
land are now m. and you make them 5.05
and very m. cattle, both flocks and 12.38
LORD to gaze and m. of them perish. 19.21
all fours, or whatever has m. feet, Lev 11.42
a discharge of blood for m. days, 15.25
If the years are m. you shall 25.16
If there are still m. years, 25.51
you, sevenfold as m. as your sins. 26.21
over the tabernacle m. days, Num 9.19
weak, whether they are few or m., 13.18
came out against them with m. men, 20.20
so that m. people of Israel died. 21.06
the people, because they were m.; 22.03
and his seed shall be in m. waters, 24.07
larger tribes you shall take m., 35.08
a thousand times as m. as you are, Deu 1.11
So you remained at Kadesh m. days, 1.46
and for m. days we went about Mount 2.01
lived there, a people great and m., 2.10
a people great and m., and tall 2.21
besides very m. unwalled villages. 3.05
that you have m. cattle) shall 3.19
and clears away m. nations before 7.01
and you shall lend to m. nations, 15.06
and you shall rule over m. nations, 15.06
as m. as you wish, but you shall not 23.24
and you shall lend to m. nations, 28.12
and m. evils and troubles will come 31.17
And when m. evils and troubles have 31.21
the years of m. generations; 32.07
with very m. horses and chariots. Jos 11.04
your brethren these m. days, 22.03
and with very m. cattle, with silver, 22.08
Canaan, and made his offspring m. 24.03
you are too m. for me to give the Ju 7.02
"The people are still too m.; 7.04
own offspring, for he had m. wives. 8.30
and m. fell wounded, up to the 9.40
country, who has slain m. of us. 16.24
but she who has m. children is 1Sa 2.05
LORD from saving by m. or by few. 14.06
There are m. servants nowadays who 25.10
You will do m. things and will 26.25
and m. of the people also have 2Sa 1.04
man had very m. flocks and herds; 12.02
m. people were coming from the 13.34
been mourning m. days for the dead; 14.02
"How m. years have I still to live, 19.34
me, he drew me out of m. waters. 22.17
a hundred times as m. as they are, 24.03
Shimei dwelt in Jerusalem m. days. 1Ki 2.38
Israel were as m. as the sand by 4.20
because there were so m. of them; 7.47
sacrificing so m. sheep and oxen 8.05
Solomon loved m. foreign women: 11.01
and her household ate for m. days. 17.15
After m. days the word of the LORD 18.01
prepare it first, for you are m.; 18.25
"How m. times shall I adjure you 22.16
of your mother Jezebel are so m.?" 2Ki 9.22
'With my m. chariots I have gone up 19.23
his brothers had not m. children, 1Ch 4.27
For m. fell slain, because the war 5.22
for they had m. wives and sons. 7.04
their father mourned m. days, 7.22
having m sons and grandsons, one 8.40
a hundred times as m. as they are! 21.03
Jeush and Beriah had not m. sons, 23.11
the sons of Rehabiah were very m. 23.17
make Israel as m. as the stars of 27.23
has given me m. sons) he has chosen 28.05
a people as m. as the dust of the 2Ch 1.09
sacrificing so m. sheep and oxen 5.06
exceedingly m. chariots and 16.08
"How m. times shall I adjure you 18.15
and of the m. oracles against him, 24.27
and hewed out m. cisterns, for he 26.10
And m. people came together in 30.13
For there were m. in the assembly 30.17
m. of them from Ephraim, Manasseh, 30.18
A great m. people were gathered, and 32.04
And m. brought gifts to the LORD to 32.23
But m. of the priests and Levites Ez 3.12
though m. shouted aloud for joy; 3.12
house that was built m. years ago, 5.11
But the people are m., and it is a 10.13
sons and our daughters, we are m.; Neh 5.02
of Judah sent m. letters to Tobiah, 6.17
For m. in Judah were bound by oath 6.18
and God-fearing man than m. 7.02
and m. times thou didst deliver 9.28
M. years thou didst bear with them, 9.30
Among the m. nations there was no 13.26
pomp of his majesty for m. days, Est 1.04
and when m. maidens were gathered 2.08
And m. from the peoples of the 8.17
she-asses, and very m. servants; Job 1.03
Behold, you have instructed m., 4.03
that your descendants shall be m., 5.25
m. will entreat your favor. 11.19
How m. are my iniquities and my 13.23
"I have heard m. such things; 16.02
and m. such things are in his mind. 23.14
and m. years teach wisdom. 32.07
Will he make m. supplications to 41.03
O LORD, how m. are my foes! Ps 3.01
M. are rising against me; 3.01
m. are saying of me, there is no 3.02
There are m. who say, "O that we 4.06
of their m. transgressions cast 5.10
me, he drew me out of m. waters. 18.16
M. bulls encompass me, strong bulls 22.12
Consider how m. are my foes, and 25.19
thunders, the LORD, upon m. waters. 29.03
Yea, I hear the whispering of m.— 31.13
M. are the pangs of the wicked; 32.10
and covets m. days, that he may 34.12
M. are the afflictions of the 34.19
than the abundance of m. wicked. 37.16
and m. are those who hate me 38.19
M. will see and fear, and put their 40.03
for m. are arrayed against me. 55.18
for m. fight against me proudly. 56.02
I have been as a portent to m.; 71.07
made me see m. sore troubles wilt 71.20
Make us glad as m. days as thou 90.15
and as m. years as we have seen 90.15
Mightier than the thunders of m. waters, 93.04
When the cares of my heart are m., 94.19
let the m. coastlands be glad! 97.01
M. times he delivered them, but they 106.43
M. are my persecutors and my 119.157
who smote m. nations and slew 135.10
and deliver me from the m. waters, 144.07
the years of your life may be m. Pro 4.10
for m. a victim has she laid low; 7.26
When words are m., transgression is 10.19
The lips of the righteous feed m., 10.21
but the rich has m. friends. 14.20
but with m. advisers they succeed. 15.22
Wealth brings m. new friends, but a 19.04
M. seek the favor of a generous man, 19.06
M. are the plans in the mind of a 19.21
M. a man proclaims his own loyalty, 20.06
land transgresses it has m. rulers; 28.02
hides his eyes will get m. a curse. 28.27
M. seek the favor of a ruler, but 29.26
"M. women have done excellently, but 31.29
and m. concubines, man's delight. Ecc 2.08
and a fool's voice with m. words. 5.03
increase, empty words grow m.: 5.07
and lives m. years, so that the days 6.03
that the days of his years are m., 6.03
knows that m. times you have 7.22

MANY (cont.)

they have sought out m. devices. Ecc 7.29
folly is set in m. high places, 10.06
for you will find it after m. days. 11.01
For if a man lives m. years, 11.08
the days of darkness will be m. 11.08
Of making m. books there is no end, 12.12
M. waters cannot quench love, Sol 8.07
even though you make m. prayers, Is 1.15
and m. peoples shall come, and say: 2.03
and shall decide for m. peoples; 2.04
"Surely m. houses shall be desolate, 5.09
places are m. in the midst of the 6.12
mighty and m., the king of Assyria 8.07
And m. shall stumble thereon; 8.15
Ah, the thunder of m. peoples, 17.12
roar like the roaring of m. waters, 17.13
of the city of David were m., 22.09
over the sea and were on m. waters; 23.02
sing m. songs, that you may be 23.16
and after m. days they will be 24.22
they are m. and in horsemen 31.01
With my m. chariots I have gone up 37.24
He sees m. things, but does not 42.20
spite of your m. sorceries and the 47.09
enchantments and your m. sorceries, 47.12
You are wearied with your m. counsels; 47.13
and I blessed him and made him m. 51.02
As m. were astonished at him—his 52.14
so shall he startle m. nations; 52.15
make m. to be accounted righteous; 53.11
yet he bore the sin of m., 53.12
the foundations of m. generations; 58.12
the devastations of m. generations. 61.04
slain by the LORD shall be m. 66.16
for as m. as your cities are your Jer 2.28
played the harlot with m. lovers; 3.01
their transgressions are m., 5.06
have become as m. as your cities, 11.13
and as m. as the streets of Jerusalem 11.13
M. shepherds have destroyed my 12.10
And after m. days the LORD said to 13.06
for our backslidings are m., 14.07
"Behold, I am sending for m. fishers, 16.16
afterwards I will send for m. hunters, 16.16
For I hear m. whispering. Terror is 20.10
" 'And m. nations will pass by this 22.08
For m. nations and great kings 25.14
then m. nations and great kings 27.07
pestilence against m. countries and 28.08
you may live m. days in the land 35.07
and m. similar words were added to 36.32
cells, and remained there m. days, 37.16
(for we are left but a few of m., 42.02
In vain you have used m. medicines; 46.11
nation and m. kings are stirring 50.41
O you who dwell by m. waters, 51.13
as m. as locusts, and they shall 51.14
Their waves roar like m. waters, 51.55
my groans are m. and my heart is Lam 1.22
wings like the sound of m. waters, Eze 1.24
not to m. peoples of foreign speech 3.06
that he sees is for m. days hence, 12.27
upon you in the sight of m. women; 16.41
rich in plumage of m. colors, 17.03
a strong arm or m. people to pull 17.09
walls built to cut off m. lives. 17.17
and m. fall at all their gates. 21.15
they have made m. widows in the 22.25
will bring up m. nations against 26.03
horsemen and a host of m. soldiers. 26.07
will be so m. that their dust will 26.10
of the peoples on m. coastlands, 27.03
m. coastlands were your own special 27.15
the seas, you satisfied m. peoples; 27.33
and m. waters shall be stopped; 31.15
over you with a host of m. peoples; 32.03
trouble the hearts of m. peoples, 32.09
I will make m. peoples appalled at 32.10
its beasts from beside m. waters; 32.13
but we are m.; the land is surely 33.24
there were very m. upon the valley; 37.02
hordes—m. peoples are with you. 38.06
After m. days you will be mustered; 38.08
gathered from m. nations upon the 38.08
hordes, and m. peoples with you. 38.09
you and m. peoples with you, all of 38.15
hordes and the m. peoples that are 38.22
known in the eyes of m. nations. 38.23
holiness in the sight of m. nations. 39.27
was like the sound of m. waters; 43.02
the river very m. trees on the one 47.07
and there will be very m. fish; 47.09
its fish will be of very m. kinds, 47.10
high honors and m. great gifts, Dan 2.48
warning he shall destroy m.; 8.25
for it pertains to m. days hence." 8.26
covenant with m. for one week; 9.27
"In those times m. shall rise 11.14
coastlands, and shall take m. of them; 11.18
and m. shall fall down slain. 11.26
are wise shall make m. understand, 11.33
And m. shall join themselves to 11.34
rulers over m. and shall divide 11.39
and horsemen, and with m. ships; 11.40
exterminate and utterly destroy m. 11.44
And m. of those who sleep in the 12.02
those who turn m. to righteousness, 12.03
M. shall run to and fro, and knowledge 12.04
M. shall purify themselves, and make 12.10
"You must dwell as mine for m. days; Hos 3.03
shall dwell m. days without king 3.04
For I know how m. are your transgressions, Amo 5.12
"the dead bodies shall be m.; in 8.03
and m. nations shall come, and say: Mic 4.02
He shall judge between m. peoples, 4.03
Now m. nations are assembled 4.11
shall beat in pieces m. peoples, 4.13
in the midst of m. peoples like 5.07
nations, in the midst of m. peoples, 5.08
LORD, "Though they be strong and m., Nah 1.12
Because you have plundered m. nations, Hab 2.08
house by cutting off m. peoples; 2.10
And m. nations shall join themselves Zec 2.11
as I have done for so m. years?" 7.03
even the inhabitants of m. cities; 8.20
M. peoples and strong nations shall 8.22
and they shall be as m. as of old. 10.08
and he turned m. from iniquity. Mal 2.06
you have caused m. to stumble by 2.08
But when he saw m. of the Pharisees Mt 3.07
will be heard for their m. words. 6.07
and those who enter by it are m. 7.13
On that day m. will say to me, 'Lord, 7.22
and do m. mighty works in your name?' 7.22
I tell you, m. will come from east 8.11
brought to him m. who were possessed 8.16
Now a herd of m. swine was feeding 8.30
m. tax collectors and sinners came 9.10
are of more value than m. sparrows. 10.31
And m. followed him, and he healed 12.15
And he told them m. things in 13.03
m. prophets and righteous men 13.17
And he did not do m. mighty works 13.58
this time was m. furlongs distant 14.24
and as m. as touched it were made 14.36
and m. others, and they put them at 15.30
"How m. loaves have you?" 15.34
and how m. baskets you gathered? 16.09
and how m. baskets you gathered? 16.10
and suffer m. things from the 16.21
forgive him? As m. as seven times?" 18.21
But m. that are first will be last, 19.30
give his life as a ransom for m." 20.28
marriage feast as m. as you find.' 22.09
For m. are called, but few are 22.14

MANY (cont.)

For m. will come in my name, saying,	Mt 24.05
and they will lead m. astray.	24.05
And then m. will fall away, and	24.10
And m. false prophets will arise	24.11
will arise and lead m. astray.	24.11
poured out for m. for the forgiveness	26.28
though m. false witnesses came	26.60
not hear how m. things they	27.13
and m. bodies of the saints who had	27.52
the holy city and appeared to m.	27.53
There were also m. women there,	27.55
And he healed m. who were sick with	Mk 1.34
diseases, and cast out m. demons;	1.34
And m. were gathered together, so	2.02
m. tax collectors and sinners were	2.15
for there were m. who followed him.	2.15
for he had healed m., so that all	3.10
And he taught them m. things in	4.02
With m. such parables he spoke the	4.33
"My name is Legion; for we are m."	5.09
suffered much under m. physicians,	5.26
and m. who heard him were astonished,	6.02
And they cast out m. demons,	6.13
with oil m. that were sick and	6.13
For m. were coming and going, and	6.31
Now m. saw them going, and knew them,	6.33
he began to teach them m. things.	6.34
"How m. loaves have you? Go and	6.38
and as m. as touched it were made	6.56
and there are m. other traditions	7.04
And m. such things you do."	7.13
them, "How m. loaves have you?"	8.05
how m. baskets full of broken	8.19
how m. baskets full of broken	8.20
Son of man must suffer m. things,	8.31
should suffer m. things and be	9.12
But m. that are first will be last,	10.31
give his life as a ransom for m."	10.45
And m. rebuked him, telling him to	10.48
And m. spread their garments on the	11.08
and so with m. others, some they	12.05
M. rich people put in large sums.	12.41
M. will come in my name, saying, 'I	13.06
and they will lead m. astray.	13.06
covenant, which is poured out for m.	14.24
For m. bore false witness against	14.56
priests accused him of m. things.	15.03
See how m. charges they bring	15.04
and also m. other women who came up	15.41
Inasmuch as m. have undertaken to	Lk 1.01
and m. will rejoice at his birth;	1.14
And he will turn m. of the sons of	1.16
fall and rising of m. in Israel,	2.34
thoughts out of m. hearts may be	2.35
So, with m. other exhortations, he	3.18
there were m. widows in Israel in	4.25
And there were m. lepers in Israel	4.27
And demons also came out of m.,	4.41
hour he cured m. of diseases and	7.21
and on m. that were blind he	7.21
which are m., are forgiven, for she	7.47
and m. others, who provided for them	8.03
(For m. a time it had seized him;	8.29
for m. demons had entered him.	8.30
Son of man must suffer m. things,	9.22
For I tell you that m. prophets and	10.24
and troubled about m. things;	10.41
provoke him to speak of m. things,	11.53
when so m. thousands of the multitude	12.01
are of more value than m. sparrows.	12.07
ample goods laid up for m. years;	12.19
for m., I tell you, will seek to	13.24
a great banquet, and invited m.;	14.16
Not m. days later, the younger son	15.13
'how m. of my father's hired servants	15.17
these m. years I have served you,	15.29
he must suffer m. things and be	17.25
for m. will come in my name, saying,	21.08
And they spoke m. other words	22.65
m. believed in his name when they	Jn 2.23
M. Samaritans from that city	4.39
And m. more believed because of his	4.41
but what are they among so m.?"	6.09
M. of his disciples, when they heard	6.60
After this m. of his disciples drew	6.66
Yet m. of the people believed in	7.31
he spoke thus, m. believed in him.	8.30
M. of them said, "He has a demon, and	10.20
have shown you m. good works from	10.32
And m. came to him; and they said,	10.41
And m. believed in him there.	10.42
and m. of the Jews had come to	11.19
M. of the Jews therefore, who had	11.45
For this man performs m. signs.	11.47
and m. went up from the country to	11.55
account of him m. of the Jews were	12.11
Though he had done so m. signs	12.37
Nevertheless m. even of the authorities	12.42
In my Father's house are m. rooms;	14.02
"I have yet m. things to say to you,	16.12
M. of the Jews read this title, for	19.20
Now Jesus did m. other signs in the	20.30
and although there were so m.,	21.11
But there are also m. other things	21.25
after his passion by m. proofs,	Ac 1.03
but before m. days you shall be	1.05
testified with m. other words and	2.40
and m. wonders and signs were done	2.43
But m. of those who heard the word	4.04
for as m. as were possessors of	4.34
Now m. signs and wonders were done	5.12
and a great m. of the priests were	6.07
came out of m. who were possessed,	8.07
and m. who were paralyzed or lame	8.07
the gospel to m. villages of the	8.25
have heard from m. about this man,	9.13
When m. days had passed, the Jews	9.23
and m. believed in the Lord.	9.42
in Joppa for m. days with one	9.43
in and found m. persons gathered;	10.27
where m. were gathered together and	12.12
and for m. days he appeared to	13.31
m. Jews and devout converts to	13.43
and as m. as were ordained to	13.48
city and had made m. disciples,	14.21
that through m. tribulations we	14.22
brethren with m. words and strengthened	15.32
of the Lord, with m. others also.	15.35
And this she did for m. days.	16.18
had inflicted m. blows upon them,	16.23
as did a great m. of the devout	17.04
M. of them therefore believed, with	17.12
and m. of the Corinthians hearing	18.08
for I have m. people in this city."	18.10
After this Paul stayed m. days longer,	18.18
M. also of those who were now	19.18
There were m. lights in the upper	20.08
how m. thousands there are among	21.20
that for m. years you have been	24.10
against him m. serious charges	25.07
And as they stayed there m. days,	25.14
I ought to do m. things in opposing	26.09
only shut up m. of the saints in	26.10
nor stars appeared for m. a day,	27.20
They presented m. gifts to us;	28.10
you the father of m. nations"—	Rom 4.17
become the father of m. nations;	4.18
For if m. died through one man's	5.15
man Jesus Christ abounded for m.	5.15
gift following m. trespasses	5.16
disobedience m. were made sinners,	5.19
man's obedience m. will be made	5.19
the first-born among m. brethren.	8.29
For as in one body we have m. members,	12.04
so we, though m., are one body in	12.05

MANY (cont.)
have longed for m. years to come Rom 15.23
a helper of m. and of myself as 16.02
not m. of you were wise according 1Co 1.26
not m. were powerful, not m. were of 1.26
Christ, you do not have m. fathers. 4.15
there are m. "gods" and m. "lords"— 8.05
we who are m. are one body, for we 10.17
but that of m., that they may be 10.33
That is why m. of you are weak and 11.30
the body is one and has m. members, 12.12
though m., are one body, so it is 12.12
consist of one member but of m. 12.14
there are m. parts, yet one body. 12.20
There are doubtless m. different 14.10
me, and there are m. adversaries. 16.09
so that m. will give thanks on our 2Co 1.11
granted us in answer to m. prayers. 1.11
anguish of heart and with m. tears, 2.04
like so m., peddlers of God's word; 2.17
as poor, yet making m. rich; 6.10
and found earnest in m. matters, 8.22
overflows in m. thanksgivings to 9.12
since m. boast of worldly things, I 11.18
through m. a sleepless night, in 11.27
to mourn over m. of those who 12.21
Judaism beyond m. of my own age Gal 1.14
experience so m. things in vain? 3.04
to offsprings," referring to m.; 3.16
For as m. of you as were baptized 3.27
For m., of whom I have often told Php 3.18
into m. senseless and hurtful 1Ti 6.09
pierced their hearts with m. pangs. 6.10
in the presence of m. witnesses. 6.12
from me before m. witnesses 2Ti 2.02
For there are m. insubordinate men, Tit 1.10
In m. and various ways God spoke of Heb 1.01
in bringing m. sons to glory, should 2.10
The former priests were m. in number, 7.23
once to bear the sins of m., 9.28
descendants as m. as the stars of 11.12
and by it the m. become defiled; 12.15
Let not m. of you become teachers, Jas 3.01
For we all make m. mistakes, 3.02
And m. will follow their licentiousness, 2Pe 2.02
so now m. antichrists have come; 1Jn 2.18
for m. false prophets have gone out 4.01
For m. deceivers have gone out into 2Jn 1.07
was like the sound of m. waters; Rev 1.15
the elders the voice of m. angels, 5.11
and m. men died of the water, 8.11
the noise of m. chariots with 9.09
prophesy about m. peoples and 10.11
the sound of m. waters and like 14.02
who is seated upon m. waters, 17.01
the sound of m. waters and like 19.06
and on his head are m. diadems; 19.12

MANY-COLORED
in m. robes she is led to the king, Ps 45.14

MANY-PEAKED
O m. mountain, mountain of Bashan! Ps 68.15
O m. mountain, at the mount which 68.16

MAOCH
Achish the son of M., king of Gath. 1Sa 27.02

MAON
M., Carmel, Ziph, Juttah, Jos 15.55
men were in the wilderness of M., 1Sa 23.24
which is in the wilderness of M. 23.25
David in the wilderness of M. 23.25
And there was a man in M., 25.02
The son of Shammai: M.; 1Ch 2.45
and M. was the father of Bethzur. 2.45

MAONITES
Amalekites, and the M., oppressed you; Ju 10.12

MAR
your temples or m. the edges of Lev 19.27

MARA
call me M., for the Almighty has Ru 1.20

MARAH
When they came to M., they could Ex 15.23
drink the water of M. because it was 15.23
bitter, therefore it was named M. 15.23
of Etham, and encamped at M. Num 33.08
And they set out from M., and came 33.09

MARAUDER
bringest the m. suddenly upon them! Jer 18.22

MARAUDING
him and became leader of a m. band, 1Ki 11.24
a m. band was seen and the man was 2Ki 13.21

MARBLE
sorts of precious stones, and m. 1Ch 29.02
to silver rings and m. pillars, Est 1.06
m., mother-of-pearl and precious 1.06
costly wood, bronze, iron and m., Rev 18.12

MARCH
They shall set out first on the m. Num 2.09
They shall set out third on the m. 2.24
the order of m. of the people of 10.28
set out on the m. till Miriam was 12.15
You shall m. around the city, all Jos 6.03
day you shall m. around the city 6.04
m. around the city, and let the 6.07
when thou didst m. from the region Ju 5.04
M. on, my soul, with might! 5.21
that you should m. out and in with 1Sa 29.06
Then he said, "By which way shall we m.?" 2Ki 3.08
made a circuitous m. of seven days, 3.09
when thou didst m. through the Ps 68.07
king, yet all of them m. in rank; Pro 30.27
for her enemies m. in force, Jer 46.22
They m. each on his way, they do not Joe 2.07
who m. through the breadth of the Hab 1.06
so that none shall m. to and fro; Zec 9.08
and m. forth in the whirlwinds of 9.14

MARCHED
second day they m. around the city Jos 6.14
and m. around the city in the same 6.15
day that they m. around the city 6.15
having m. up all night from Gilgal. 10.09
Whenever they m. out, the hand of Ju 2.15
to the gates m. the people of the 5.11
Then down m. the remnant of the 5.13
of the LORD m. down for him 5.13
from Machir m. down the commanders, 5.14
and Joab and his men m. all night, 2Sa 2.32
all the army m. out of hundreds 18.04
So King Jehoram m. out of Samaria 2Ki 3.06
king of Assyria m. up against 16.09
And they m. up over the broad earth Rev 20.09

MARCHES
one another, each m. in his path; Joe 2.08

MARCHING
the Egyptians were m. after them; Ex 14.10
and m. the whole forenoon they came 2Sa 2.29
the sound of m. in the tops of the 5.24
m. through the gate of the guards 2Ki 11.19
the sound of m. in the tops of the 1Ch 14.15
m. through the upper gate to the 2Ch 23.20
m. in the greatness of his strength? Is 63.01
As they were m. out, they came upon Mt 27.32

MARE
to a m. of Pharaoh's chariots. Sol 1.09

MAREAL
and on to M., and touches Dabbesheth, Jos 19.11

MARESHAH
and M.: nine cities with their Jos 15.44
M. his first-born, who was the 1Ch 2.42
The sons of M.: Hebron. 2.42
of Lecah, Laadah the father of M., 4.21
Gath, M., Ziph, 2Ch 11.08
chariots, and came as far as M. 14.09
in the valley of Zephathah at M. 14.10
of Dodavahu of M. prophesied 20.37
upon you, inhabitants of M.; Mic 1.15

MARINERS
the sea with their m. were in you, Eze 27.09
your m. and your pilots, your 27.27
The m. and all the pilots of the 27.29
Then the m. were afraid, and each Jon 1.05

MARITAL
food, her clothing, or her m. rights. Ex 21.10

MARK
And the LORD put a m. on Cain, Gen 4.15
"M., I pray you, whose these are, the 38.25
It shall be as a m. on your hand or Ex 13.16
Sea you shall m. out your line to Num 34.07
Hor you shall m. it out to the 34.08
"You shall m. out your eastern 34.10
of it, as though I shot at a m. 1Sa 20.20
"M. when Amnon's heart is merry with 2Sa 13.28
"M., now, and see how this man is 1Ki 20.07
Why hast thou made me thy m.? Job 7.20
thou dost m. me, and dost not acquit 10.14
and commands it to strike the m. 36.32
M. the blameless man, and behold the Ps 37.37
"M. this, then, you who forget God, 50.22
made the moon to m. the seasons; 104.19
shouldst m. iniquities, Lord, who 130.03
and set me as a m. for his arrow. Lam 3.12
and put a m. upon the foreheads of Eze 9.04
touch no one upon whom is the m. 9.06
"Son of man, m. two ways for the 21.19
m. a way for the sword to come to 21.20
m. well, see with your eyes, and hear 44.05
and m. well those who may be 44.05
my finger in the m. of the nails, Jn 20.25
of John whose other name was M., Ac 12.12
them John whose other name was M. 12.25
to take with them John called M. 15.37
Barnabas took M. with him and 15.39
and m. those who so live as you Php 3.17
and M. the cousin of Barnabas Col 4.10
This is the m. in every letter of 2Th 3.17
have missed the m. as regards the 1Ti 6.21
Get M. and bring him with you; 2Ti 4.11
and so do M., Aristarchus, Demas, and Phm 1.24
and so does my son M. 1Pe 5.13
buy or sell unless he has the m., Rev 13.17
and receives a m. on his forehead 14.09
receives the m. of its name. 14.11
who bore the m of the beast and 16.02
received the m. of the beast and 19.20
received its m. on their foreheads 20.04

MARKED
when he m. out the foundations of Pro 8.29
of his hand and m. off the heavens Is 40.12
he m. it off by the line; Lam 2.08
when he m. how they chose the Lk 14.07
to be m. on the right hand or the Rev 13.16

MARKET
do not depart from its m. place. Ps 55.11
now in the m., and at every corner Pro 7.12
sitting in the m. places and Mt 11.16
standing idle in the m. place; 20.03
and salutations in the m. places, 23.07
laid the sick in the m. places, Mk 6.56
and when they come from the m. place, 7.04
have salutations in the m. places 12.38
sitting in the m. place and Lk 7.32
and salutations in the m. places. 11.43
salutations in the m. places and 20.46
them into the m. place before the Ac 16.19
and in the m. place every day with 17.17
in the meat m. without raising any 1Co 10.25

MARKETS
in the m. she raises her voice; Pro 1.20
coastlands were your own special m., Eze 27.15

MARKS
the dead or tattoo any m. upon you: Lev 19.28
and made m. on the doors of the 1Sa 21.13
a line, he m. it out with a pencil; Is 44.13
planes, and m. it with a compass; 44.13
to remove the m. of circumcision. 1Co 7.18
I bear on my body the m. of Jesus. Gal 6.17

MAROTH
inhabitants of M. wait anxiously Mic 1.12

MARRED
at him—his appearance was so m., Is 52.14

MARRIAGE
I pray you, give her to him in m. Gen 34.08
ever so much as m. present and 34.12
let us take their daughters in m., 34.21
had not been given to him in m. 38.14
and he gave him in m. Asenath, 41.45
shall give the m. present for her, Ex 22.16
equivalent to the m. present for 22.17
he gave in m. outside his clan, and Ju 12.09
his daughter in m. to Benjamin. 21.01
king desires no m. present except 1Sa 18.25
Solomon made a m. alliance with 1Ki 3.01
daughter whom he had taken in m. 7.08
shall not enter into m. with them, 11.02
he gave him in m. the sister of 11.19
his daughter in m. to Jarha his 1Ch 2.35
and he made a m. alliance with 2Ch 18.01
and their maidens had no m. song. Ps 78.63
and give your daughters in m., Jer 29.06
will mix with one another in m., Dan 2.43
king who gave a m. feast for his Mt 22.02
who were invited to the m. feast; 22.03
is ready; come to the m. feast.' 22.04
invite to the m. feast as many as 22.09
neither marry nor are given in m., 22.30
drinking, marrying and giving in m., 24.38
went in with him to the m. feast; 25.10
neither marry nor are given in m., Mk 12.25
to come home from the m. feast, Lk 12.36
invited by any one to a m. feast, 14.08
married, they were given in m., 17.27
this age marry and are given in m.; 20.34
neither marry nor are given in m., 20.35
day there was a m. at Cana in Jn 2.01
Jesus also was invited to the m., 2.02
free from a wife? Do not seek m. 1Co 7.27
refrains from m. will do better. 7.38
who forbid m. and enjoin abstinence 1Ti 4.03
Let m. be held in honor among all, Heb 13.04
and let the m. bed be undefiled; 13.04
for the m. of the Lamb has come, and Rev 19.07
invited to the m. supper of the 19.09

MARRIAGES
Make m. with us; give your daughters Gen 34.09
You shall not make m. with them, Deu 7.03
and make m. with them, so that you Jos 23.12

MARRIED

Shua; he m. her and went in to her, Gen 38.02
if he comes in m., then his wife Ex 21.03
daughter is m. to an outsider she Lev 22.12
the Cushite woman whom he had m., Num 12.01
for he had m. a Cushite woman; 12.01
And if she is m. to a husband, while 30.06
But if they are m. to any of the 36.03
were m. to sons of their father's 36.11
They were m. into the families of 36.12
"When a man is newly m., he shall Deu 24.05
shall not be m. outside the family 25.05
who had m. Abigal the daughter of 2Sa 17.25
Caleb m. Ephrath, who bore him Hur. 1Ch 2.19
whom he m. when he was sixty years 2.21
daughter of Pharaoh, whom Mered m.; 4.17
kinsmen, the sons of Kish, m. them. 23.22
God and have m. foreign women from Ez 10.02
trespassed and m. foreign women, 10.10
the men who had m. foreign women. 10.17
priests who had m. foreign women 10.18
All these had m. foreign women, and 10.44
Jews who had m. women of Ashdod, Neh 13.23
of her that is m., says the LORD. Is 54.01
is in her, and your land M.; 62.04
in you, and your land shall be m. 62.04
and has m. the daughter of a Mal 2.11
the first m., and died, and having Mt 22.25
Philip's wife; because he had m. her. Mk 6.17
'I have m. a wife, and therefore I Lk 14.20
they m., they were given in marriage, 17.27
Thus a m. woman is bound by law to Rom 7.02
To the m. I give charge, not I but 1Co 7.10
but the m. man is anxious about 7.33
but the m. woman is anxious about 7.34
is free to be m. to whom she 7.39
m. only once, temperate, sensible, 1Ti 3.02
Let deacons be m. only once, and let 3.12
age, or has been m. more than once; 5.09
m. only once, whose children are Tit 1.06

MARRIES

If Jacob m. one of the Hittite Gen 27.46
"When a man takes a wife and m. her, Deu 24.01
For as a young man m. a virgin, Is 62.05
and whoever m. a divorced woman Mt 5.32
and m. another, commits adultery. 19.09
he who m. a divorced woman commits * 19.09
divorces his wife and m. another, Mk 10.11
divorces her husband and m. another, 10.12
his wife and m. another commits Lk 16.18
and he who m. a woman divorced from 16.18
and if she m. another man she is Rom 7.03
and if a girl m. she does not sin. 1Co 7.28
So that he who m. his betrothed 7.38

MARROW

of fat and the m. of his bones Job 21.24
soul is feasted as with m. and fat, Ps 63.05
the lees, of fat things full of m., Is 25.06
of joints and m., and discerning Heb 4.12

MARRY

who were to m. his daughters, "Up, Gen 19.14
"You shall not m. one of the 28.01
"You shall not m. one of the 28.06
They shall not m. a harlot or a Lev 21.07
shall they m. a woman divorced 21.07
or a harlot, these he shall not m.; 21.14
'Let them m. whom they think best; Num 36.06
they shall m. within the family of 36.06
so that you m. their women and they Jos 23.12
virgin, so shall your sons m. you, Is 62.05
They shall not m. a widow, or a Eze 44.22
wife, it is not expedient to m." Mt 19.10
his brother must m. the widow, 22.24
they neither m. nor are given in 22.30
they neither m. nor are given in Mk 12.25
of this age m. and are given in Lk 20.34
dead neither m. nor are given in 20.35
self-control, they should m. 1Co 7.09
it is better to m. than to be 7.09
But if you m., you do not sin, and 7.28
Yet those who m. will have worldly 7.28
he wishes: let them m.—it is no sin. 7.36
against Christ they desire to m., 1Ti 5.11
So I would have younger widows m., 5.14

MARRYING

you therefore refrain from m.? Ru 1.13
our God by m. foreign women?" Neh 13.27
m. and giving in marriage, until the Mt 24.38

MARSENA

M., and Memucan, the seven princes Est 1.14

MARSH

"Can papyrus grow where there is no m.? Job 8.11
covert of the reeds and in the m. 40.21

MARSHAL

appoint a m. against her, bring up Jer 51.27

MARSHAL'S

Zebulun those who bear the m. staff; Ju 5.14

MARSHES

But its swamps and m. will not become Eze 47.11

MARTHA

a woman named M. received him into Lk 10.38
But M. was distracted with much 10.40
"M., M., you are anxious and troubled 10.41
village of Mary and her sister M. Jn 11.01
Now Jesus loved M. and her sister 11.05
had come to M. and Mary to console 11.19
When M. heard that Jesus was coming, 11.20
M. said to Jesus, "Lord, if you had 11.21
M. said to him, "I know that he will 11.24
in the place where M. had met him. 11.30
M., the sister of the dead man, 11.39
M. served, but Lazarus was one of 12.02

MARTYRS

and the blood of the m. of Jesus. Rev 17.06

MARVEL

Do not m. that I said to you, 'You Jn 3.07
will he show him, that you may m. 5.20
Do not m. at this; for the hour is 5.28
did one deed, and you all m. at it. 7.21
The man answered, "Why, this is a m.! 9.30
But the angel said to me, "Why m.? Rev 17.07
will m. to behold the beast, because 17.08

MARVELED

he m., and said to those who Mt 8.10
And the men m., saying, "What sort 8.27
and the crowds m., saying, "Never 9.33
When the disciples saw it they m., 21.20
When they heard it, they m.; 22.22
had done for him; and all men m. Mk 5.20
And he m. because of their unbelief. 6.06
"His name is John." And they all m. Lk 1.63
and his mother m. at what was said 2.33
When Jesus heard this he m. at him, 7.09
and they m., saying to one another, 8.25
dumb man spoke, and the people m. 11.14
They m. that he was talking with a Jn 4.27
The Jews m. at it, saying, "How is it 7.15
and to be m. at in all who have 2Th 1.10
When I saw her I m. greatly. Rev 17.06

MARVELING

they were all m. at everything he Lk 9.43
but m. at his answer they were 20.26

MARVELOUS
his m. works among all the peoples! 1Ch 16.24
unsearchable, m. things without number: Job 5.09
and m. things without number. 9.10
his m. works among all the peoples! Ps 96.03
song, for he has done m. things! 98.01
LORD's doing; it is m. in our eyes. 118.23
things too great and too m. for me. 131.01
I will again do m. things with Is 29.14
with this people, wonderful and m.; 29.14
Egypt I will show them m. things. Mic 7.15
If it is m. in the sight of the Zec 8.06
should it also be m. in my sight, 8.06
doing, and it is m. in our eyes'! Mt 21.42
doing, and it is m. in our eyes'? Mk 12.11
out of darkness into his m. light. 1Pe 2.09

MARVELOUSLY
for he was m. helped, till he was 2Ch 26.15

MARVELS
all your people I will do m., Ex 34.10
he wrought m. in the land of Egypt, Ps 78.12

MARY
father of Joseph the husband of M., Mt 1.16
When his mother M. had been betrothed 1.18
do not fear to take M. your wife, 1.20
saw the child with M. his mother, 2.11
Is not his mother called M.? And 13.55
among whom were M. Magdalene, 27.56
and M. the mother of James and 27.56
M. Magdalene and the other M. were 27.61
M. Magdalene and the other M. went 28.01
the son of M. and brother of James Mk 6.03
afar, among whom were M. Magdalene, 15.40
and M. the mother of James the 15.40
M. Magdalene and M. the mother of 15.47
M. Magdalene, and M. the mother of 16.01
he appeared first to M. Magdalene, from * 16.09
and the virgin's name was M. Lk 1.27
M., for you have found favor with 1.30
And M. said to the angel, "How can 1.34
And M. said, "Behold I am the 1.38
In those days M. arose and went 1.39
Elizabeth heard the greeting of M., 1.41
And M. said, "My soul magnifies the 1.46
And M. remained with her about 1.56
to be enrolled with M., his 2.05
and found M. and Joseph, and the 2.16
But M. kept all these things, 2.19
them and said to M. his mother, 2.34
M., called Magdalene, from whom 8.02
And she had a sister called M., 10.39
M. has chosen the good portion, 10.42
Now it was M. Magdalene and Joanna 24.10
and M. the mother of James and 24.10
the village of M. and her sister Jn 11.01
It was M. who anointed the Lord 11.02
to Martha and M. to console them 11.19
while M. sat in the house. 11.20
she went and called her sister M., 11.28
saw M. rise quickly and go out, they 11.31
Then M., when she came where Jesus 11.32
had come with M. and had seen what 11.45
M. took a pound of costly ointment 12.03
M. the wife of Clopas, and M. Magdalene. 19.25
day of the week M. Magdalene came 20.01
But M. stood weeping outside the 20.11
Jesus said to her, "M." She turned 20.16
M. Magdalene went and said to the 20.18
the women and M. the mother of Ac 1.14
this, he went to the house of M., 12.12
Greet M., who has worked hard among Rom 16.06

MASH
of Aram: Uz, Hul, Gether, and M. Gen 10.23

MASHAL
M. with its pasture lands, Abdon 1Ch 6.74

MASONRY
of the four courts was a row of m., Eze 46.23

MASONS
carpenters and m. who built David 2Sa 5.11
and to the m. and the stonecutters, 2Ki 12.12
and to the m., as well as for 22.06
also m. and carpenters to build a 1Ch 14.01
m., carpenters, and all kinds of 22.15
and they hired m. and carpenters 2Ch 24.12
money to the m. and the carpenters, Ez 3.07

MASREKAH
and Samlah of M. reigned in his Gen 36.36
Samlah of M. reigned in his stead. 1Ch 1.47

MASS
they m. themselves together against Job 16.10
runs into a m. and the clods 38.38
height with the m. of its branches Eze 19.11
beautiful in the m. of its branches, 31.09

MASSA
Mishma, Dumah, M., Gen 25.14
Mishma, Dumah, M., Hadad, Tema, 1Ch 1.30
The words of Agur son of Jakeh of M. Pro 30.01
king of M., which his mother taught 31.01

MASSAH
name of the place M. and Meribah, Ex 17.07
the test, as you tested him at M. Deu 6.16
and at M., and at Kibrothhattaavah, 9.22
one, whom thou didst test at M., 33.08
on the day at M. in the wilderness, Ps 95.08

MAST
one who lies on the top of a m. Pro 23.34
cannot hold the m. firm in its Is 33.23
from Lebanon to make a m. for you. Eze 27.05

MASTER
is for you, but you must m. it." Gen 4.07
under the thigh of Abraham his m., 24.09
sorts of choice gifts from his m.; 24.10
God of my m. Abraham, grant me 24.12
steadfast love to my m. Abraham. 24.12
hast shown steadfast love to my m." 24.14
the God of my m. Abraham, who has 24.27
and his faithfulness toward my m. 24.27
The LORD has greatly blessed my m., 24.35
a son to my m. when she was old; 24.36
My m. made me swear, saying, 'You 24.37
I said to my m., 'perhaps the woman 24.39
the God of my m. Abraham, if now 24.42
the God of my m. Abraham, who had 24.48
and truly with my m., tell me; 24.49
he said, "Send me back to my m." 24.54
let me go that I may go to my m." 24.56
The servant said, "It is my m." 24.65
the house of his m. the Egyptian, 39.02
and his m. saw that the LORD was 39.03
having me my m. has no concern 39.08
by her until his m. came home, 39.16
When his m. heard the words which 39.19
And Joseph's m. took him and put him 39.20
If his m. gives him a wife and she Ex 21.04
'I love my m., my wife, and my 21.05
then his m. shall bring him to God, 21.06
and his m. shall bore his ear 21.06
If she does not please her m., 21.08
give to their m. thirty shekels of 21.32
give up to his m. a slave who has Deu 23.15
who has escaped from his m. to you; 23.15
and the servant said to his m., Ju 19.11
And his m. said to him, "We will not 19.12
the m. of the house, "Bring out the 19.22

MASTER (cont.)
the m. of the house, went out to Ju 19.23
the man's house where her m. was, 19.26
And her m. rose up in the morning, 19.27
up the arrows, and came to his m. 1Sa 20.38
of the wilderness to salute our m.; 25.14
against our m. and against all his 25.17
and my m. left me behind because I 30.13
deliver me into the hands of my m., 30.15
fled from his m. Hadadezer king of 1Ki 11.23
the LORD said, 'These have no m.; 22.17
take away your m. from over you?" 2Ki 2.03
take away your m. from over you?" 2.05
let them go, and seek your m.; 2.16
man with his m. and in high favor, 5.01
when my m. goes into the house of 5.18
my m. has spared this Naaman the 5.20
My m. has sent me to say, 'There 5.22
He went in, and stood before his m., 5.25
and he cried out, "Alas, my m.! It 6.05
And the servant said, "Alas, my m.! 6.15
eat and drink and go to their m." 6.22
away, and they went to their m. 6.23
from Elisha, and came to his m., 8.14
down the house of Ahab your m., 9.07
came out to the servants of his m., 9.11
you Zimri, murderer of your m.?" 9.31
against my m., and slew him; 10.09
a wager with my m. the king of 18.23
"Has my m. sent me to speak these 18.27
these words to your m. and to you, 18.27
whom his m. the king of Assyria has 19.04
"Say to your m., 'Thus says the 19.06
he will desert to his m. Saul.") 1Ch 12.19
the LORD said, 'These have no m.; 2Ch 18.16
and the slave is free from his m. Job 3.19
lips are with us; who is our m.?" Ps 12.04
look to the hand of their m., 123.02
was beside him, like a m. workman; Pro 8.30
who guards his m. will be honored. 27.18
Do not slander a servant to his m., 30.10
Yet he will be m. of all for which Ecc 2.19
like jewels, the work of a m. hand. Sol 7.01
Egyptians into the hand of a hard m.; Is 19.04
as with the slave, so with his m.; 24.02
a wager with my m. the king of 36.08
"Has my m. sent me to speak these 36.12
these words to your m. and to you, 36.12
whom his m. the king of Assyria has 37.04
"Say to your m., 'Thus says the 37.06
says the LORD; for I am your m.; Jer 3.14
his father, and a servant his m. Mal 1.06
And if I am a m., where is my fear? 1.06
teacher, nor a servant above his m.; Mt 10.24
and the servant like his m. 10.25
have called the m. of the house 10.25
for you have one m., the Christ. 23.10
whom his m. has set over his 24.45
whom his m. when he comes will 24.46
to himself, 'My m. is delayed,' 24.48
the m. of that servant will come on 24.50
a long time the m. of those 25.19
'M., you delivered to me five 25.20
His m. said to him, 'Well done, good 25.21
enter into the joy of your m.' 25.21
'M., you delivered to me two 25.22
His m. said to him, 'Well done, good 25.23
enter into the joy of your m.' 25.23
'M., I knew you to be a hard man, 25.24
But his m. answered him, 'You wicked 25.26
betrayed him, said, "Is it I, M.?" 26.25
to Jesus at once and said, "Hail M.!" 26.49
"M., it is well that we are here; Mk 9.05
"M., let me receive my sight." 10.51
remembered and said to him, "M., look! 11.21
know when the m. of the house will 13.35
up to him at once, and said, "M.!" 14.45
"M., we toiled all night and took Lk 5.05
"M., M., we are perishing!" And 8.24
"M., the multitudes surround you 8.45
"M., it is well that we are here; 9.33
"M., we saw a man casting out 9.49
for their m. to come home from the 12.36
whom the m. finds awake when he 12.37
whom his m. will set over his 12.42
whom his m. when he comes will 12.43
'My m. is delayed in coming,' and 12.45
the m. of that servant will come on 12.46
came and reported this to his m. 14.21
And the m. said to the servant, 'Go 14.23
since my m. is taking the stewardship 16.03
first, 'How much do you owe my m.?' 16.05
The m. commended the dishonest 16.08
"Jesus, M., have mercy on us." 17.13
servant is not greater than his m.; Jn 13.16
does not know what his m. is doing; 15.15
servant is not greater than his m.' 15.20
before his own m. that he stands Rom 14.04
for the M. is able to make him 14.04
like a skilled m. builder I laid a 1Co 3.10
is both their M. and yours is in Eph 6.09
that you also have a M. in heaven. Col 4.01
and useful to the m. of the house, 2Ti 2.21
m. of himself, upright, holy, and self Tit 1.08
denying the M. who bought them, 1Pe 2.01
and deny our only M. and Lord, Jud 1.04

MASTERED
m. all of them, and overpowered them, Ac 19.16

MASTER'S
took ten of his m. camels and Gen 24.10
way to the house of my m. kinsmen." 24.27
And Sarah my m. wife bore a son to 24.36
LORD has appointed for my m. son.' 24.44
daughter of my m. kinsman for his 24.48
let her be the wife of your m. son, 24.51
a time his m. wife cast her eyes 39.07
he refused and said to his m. wife, 39.08
him in custody in his m. house, 40.07
shall be her m. and he shall go Ex 21.04
house I have given to your m. son. 2Sa 9.09
that your m. son may have bread to 9.10
Mephibosheth your m. son shall 9.10
and I gave you your m. house, 12.08
and your m. wives into your bosom, 12.08
said, "And where is your m. son?" 16.03
sound of his m. feet behind him?" 2Ki 6.32
seeing your m. sons are with you, 10.02
fittest of your m. sons and set 10.03
and fight for your m. house." 10.03
me, take the heads of your m. sons, 10.06
among the least of my m. servants, 18.24
its owner, and the ass its m. crib; Is 1.03
chariots, you shame of your m. house. 22.18
among the least of my m. servants, 36.09
who fill their m. house with Zep 1.09
that fall from their m. table." Mt 15.27
in the ground and hid his m. money. 25.18
And that servant who knew his m. will, Lk 12.47
summoning his m. debtors one by one, 16.05

MASTERS
are breaking away from their m. 1Sa 25.10
he refreshes the spirit of his m. Pro 25.13
Give them this charge for their m.: Jer 27.04
is what you shall say to your m.: 27.04
"No one can serve two m.; for either Mt 6.24
Neither be called m., for you have 23.10
No servant can serve two m.; Lk 16.13
to those who are your earthly m., Eph 6.05
M., do the same to them, and forbear 6.09
those who are your earthly m., Col 3.22
M., treat your slaves justly and 4.01
regard their m. as worthy of all 1Ti 6.01
have believing m. must not be 6.02

MASTERS (cont.)
to their m. and to give satisfaction Tit 2.09
submissive to your m. with all 1Pe 2.18

MASTERY
Jews hoped to get the m. over them, Est 9.01
should get the m. over their foes, 9.01

MATCH
from the new will not m. the old. Lk 5.36

MATCHED
it may be m. by your completing it 2Co 8.11

MATE
clean animals, the male and his m.; Gen 7.02
are not clean, the male and his m.; 7.02
be gathered, each one with her m. Is 34.15
none shall be without her m. 34.16

MATERIAL
and the smith has m. for a vessel; Pro 25.04
of service to them in m. blessings. Rom 15.27
much if we reap your m. benefits? 1Co 9.11

MATERIALS
be of the same workmanship and m., Ex 28.08
was of the same m. and workmanship, 39.05
David provided m. in great quantity 1Ch 22.05

MATING
In the m. season of the flock I Gen 31.10

MATRED
was Mehetabel, the daughter of M., Gen 36.39
name Mehetabel the daughter of M., 1Ch 1.50

MATRITES
family of the M. was taken by lot; 1Sa 10.21
family of the M. near man by man, 10.21

MATTAN
and they slew M. the priest of Baal 2Ki 11.18
and they slew M. the priest of Baal 2Ch 23.17
Now Shephatiah the son of M., Jer 38.01

MATTANAH
the wilderness they went on to M., Num 21.18
and from M. to Nahaliel, and from 21.19

MATTANIAH
And the king of Babylon made M., 2Ki 24.17
and M. the son of Mica, son of 1Ch 9.15
M., Uzziel, Shebuel, and Jerimoth, 25.04
the ninth to M., his sons and his 25.16
son of M., a Levite of the sons of 2Ch 20.14
sons of Asaph, Zechariah and M.; 29.13
M., Zechariah, Jehiel, Abdi, Jeremoth, Ez 10.26
M., Jeremoth, Zabad, and Aziza. 10.27
M., Bezalel, Binnui, and Manasseh. 10.30
M., Mattenai, Jaasu. 10.37
and M. the son of Mica, son of Zabdi, Neh 11.17
son of M., son of Mica, of the sons 11.22
and M., who with his brethren was 12.08
M., Bakbukiah, Obadiah, Meshullam, 12.25
son of M., son of Micaiah, son of 12.35
son of M., for they were counted 13.13

MATTATHA
the son of M., the son of Nathan, Lk 3.31

MATTATHIAS
the son of M., the son of Amos, the Lk 3.25
the son of M., the son of Semein, 3.26

MATTATTAH
M., Zabad, Eliphelet, Jeremai, Manasseh, Ez 10.33

MATTENAI
M., Mattattah, Zabad, Eliphelet, Ez 10.33
Mattaniah, M., Jaasu. 10.37
of Joiarib, M.; of Jedaiah, Uzzi; Neh 12.19

MATTER
swore to him concerning this m. Gen 24.09
"Is it a small m. that you have 30.15
every great m. they shall bring to Ex 18.22
but any small m. they shall decide 18.22
but any small m. they decided 18.26
he has seen or come to know the m., Lev 5.01
neighbor in a m. of deposit or 6.02
beguiled you in the m. of Peor, Num 25.18
and in the m. of Cozbi, the daughter 25.18
against the LORD in the m. of Peor, 31.16
speak no more to me of this m. Deu 3.26
faith in the m. of the devoted Jos 22.20
you learn how the m. turns out, Ru 3.18
rest, but will settle the m. today." 3.18
But about the m. of the kingdom, 1Sa 10.16
reported the m. in the ears of the 11.04
yourself when the m. was in hand, 20.19
And as for the m. of which you and 20.23
Jonathan and David knew the m. 20.39
"The king has charged me with a m., 21.02
anything of the m. about which I 21.02
Who would listen to you in this m.? 30.24
'Do not let this m. trouble you, 2Sa 11.25
then are you angry over this m.? 19.42
and so they settled a m. 20.18
"It is not a m. of silver or gold 21.04
desire in the m. of cedar and 1Ki 5.08
except in the m. of Uriah the 15.05
In this m. may the LORD pardon your 2Ki 5.18
pardon your servant in this m." 5.18
transgressed in the m. of the 1Ch 2.07
concerning any m. and concerning 2Ch 8.15
and see that you hasten the m." 24.05
And so in the m. of the envoys of 32.31
care not to be slack in this m.; Ez 4.22
send us his pleasure in this m. 5.17
because of this m. and because of 10.09
greatly transgressed in this m. 10.13
God over this m. be averted from 10.14
they sat down to examine the m.; 10.16
of what they had faced in this m., Est 9.26
If it is a m. of justice, who can Job 9.19
'The root of the m. is found in him'; 19.28
You will decide on a m., and it will 22.28
who repeats a m. alienates a Pro 17.09
a time for every m. under heaven: Ecc 3.01
has appointed a time for every m., 3.17
away, do not be amazed at the m.; 5.08
delay when the m. is unpleasant, 8.03
For every m. has its time and way, 8.06
some winged creature tell the m. 10.20
The end of the m.; all has been 12.13
Were your harlotries so small a m. Eze 16.20
So he hearkened to them in this m., Dan 1.14
And in every m. of wisdom and 1.20
Arioch made the m. known to Daniel. 2.15
and made the m. known to Hananiah, 2.17
made known to us the king's m." 2.23
no need to answer you in this m. 3.16
show the interpretation of the m. 5.15
This is the interpretation of the m.: 5.26
dream, and told the sum of the m. 7.01
"Here is the end of the m. As 7.28
but I kept the m. in my mind." 7.28
So they kept the m. to themselves, Mk 9.10
asked him again about this m. 10.10
neither part nor lot in this m., Ac 8.21
together to consider this m. 15.06
"If it were a m. of wrongdoing or 18.14
but since it is a m. of questions 18.15
expounded the m. to them from 28.23
circumcision is a m. of the heart, Rom 2.29

MATTER (cont.)
yourselves guiltless in the m. 2Co 7.11
And in this m. I give my advice: it 8.10
but that as a m. of equality your 8.14
and wrong his brother in this m., 1Th 4.06
scripture is a m. of one's own 2Pe 1.20

MATTERS
the king in all m. concerning the 1Ch 27.01
is over you in all m. of the LORD; 2Ch 19.11
of Judah, in all the king's m.; 19.11
learned in m. of the commandments Ez 7.11
hand in all m. concerning the Neh 11.24
the weightier m. of the law, Mt 23.23
m. pertaining to this life! 1Co 6.03
Now concerning the m. about which 7.01
and found earnest in many m., 2Co 8.22
reviling in m. of which they are 2Pe 2.12

MATTHAN
Eleazar, and Eleazar the father of M., Mt 1.15
and M. the father of Jacob, 1.15

MATTHAT
the son of M., the son of Levi, the Lk 3.24
the son of M., the son of Levi, 3.29

MATTHEW
a man called M. sitting at the tax Mt 9.09
Thomas and M. the tax collector; 10.03
and M., and Thomas, and James the Mk 3.18
and M., and Thomas, and James the Lk 6.15
and Thomas, Bartholomew and M., Ac 1.13

MATTHIAS
who was surnamed Justus, and M. Ac 1.23
for them, and the lot fell on M.; 1.26

MATTITHIAH
and M., one of the Levites, the 1Ch 9.31
M., Eliphelehu, and Mikneiah, and the 15.18
but M., Eliphelehu, Mikneiah, Obededom, 15.21
M., Eliab, Benaiah, Obededom, and 16.05
and M., six, under the direction of 25.03
M., his sons and his brethren, 25.21
M., Zabad, Zebina, Jaddai, Joel, and Ez 10.43
and beside him stood M., Neh 8.04

MATTOCK
his m., his axe, or his sickle; 1Sa 13.20

MATTOCKS
for the plowshares and for the m., 1Sa 13.21

MATURE
life, and their fruit does not m. Lk 8.14
Yet among the m. we do impart 1Co 2.06
in evil, but in thinking be m. 14.20
to m. manhood, to the measure of the Eph 4.13
of us who are m. be thus minded; Php 3.15
may present every man m. in Christ. Col 1.28
you may stand m. and fully assured 4.12
But solid food is for the m., Heb 5.14

MATURITY
doctrines of Christ and go on to m., Heb 6.01

MAXIMS
Your m. are proverbs of ashes, your Job 13.12

MAZZAROTH
lead forth the M. in their season, Job 38.32

MEADOWS
the m. clothe themselves with Ps 65.13
m. for shepherds and folds for Zep 2.06

MEAL
quickly three measures of fine m., Gen 18.06
a tenth of an ephah of barley m.; Num 5.15
of your coarse m. you shall 15.20
of your coarse m. you shall give 15.21
the son of Jesse come to the m., 1Sa 20.27
m., parched grain, beans and lentils, 2Sa 17.28
flour, and sixty measures of m., 1Ki 4.22
only a handful of m. in a jar, 17.12
'The jar of m. shall not be spent, 17.14
The jar of m. was not spent, neither 17.16
He said, "Then bring m." And he 2Ki 4.41
measure of fine m. shall be sold 7.01
measure of fine m. was sold for a 7.16
a measure of fine m. for a shekel, 7.18
on oxen, abundant provisions of m., 1Ch 12.40
bring the first of our coarse m., Neh 10.37
Take the millstones and grind m., Is 47.02
the first of your coarse m., Eze 44.30
lamb and the m. offering and the 46.15
has no heads, it shall yield no m.; Hos 8.07
and hid in three measures of m., Mt 13.33
and hid in three measures of m., Lk 13.21
one goes ahead with his own m., 1Co 11.21
his birthright for a single m. Heb 12.16

MEALTIME
And at m. Boaz said to her, "Come Ru 2.14

MEAN
"What do you m. by all this company Gen 33.08
Do you m. to kill me as you killed Ex 2.14
'What do you m. by this service?' 12.26
son asks you, 'What does this m.?' 13.14
'What do those stones m. to you?' Jos 4.06
to come, 'What do these stones m.?' 4.21
in the camp of the Hebrews m.?" 1Sa 4.06
does this uproar in the city m.?" 1Ki 1.41
What do you m. by crushing my Is 3.15
What do you m. that you have gone 22.01
what do you m. that you dress in Jer 4.30
you not know what these things m.? Eze 17.12
"What do you m. by repeating this 18.02
us what these things m. for us, 24.19
not show us what you m. by these?' 37.18
him, "What do you m., you sleeper? Jon 1.06
saying, "I do not know what you m." Mt 26.70
know nor understand what you m." Mk 14.68
What does he m. by saying, 'You will Jn 7.36
"What does he m. by 'a little while'? 16.18
to one another, "What does this m.?" Ac 2.12
vision which he had seen might m., 10.17
therefore what these things m. 17.20
Cilicia, a citizen of no m. city; 21.39
more will their full inclusion m.! Rom 11.12
acceptance m. but life from the 11.15
of God does not m. food and drink 14.17
What I m. is that each one of you 1Co 1.12
I m., brethren, the appointed time 7.29
I m. his conscience, not yours—do 10.29
Otherwise, what do people m. by 15.29
I do not m. that others should be 2Co 8.13
This is what I m.: the law, which Gal 3.17
I m. that the heir, as long as he is 4.01
what does it m. but that he had Eph 4.09
I take it to m. Christ and the 5.32

MEANING
"What is the m. of these seven ewe Gen 21.29
and each dream with its own m. 40.05
having a dream with its own m. 41.11
'What is the m. of the testimonies Deu 6.20
(for that is the m. of his name) Ac 13.08
not at all m. the immoral of this 1Co 5.10
the world, and none is without m.; 14.10
do not know the m. of the language, 14.11

MEANS
Pharaoh's dream m. that the thing Gen 41.32
them, you shall by no m. lessen it; Ex 5.08
"You shall by no m. lessen your 5.19

MEANS (cont.)

who will by no m. clear the guilty, Ex 34.07
finds sufficient m. to redeem it, Lev 25.26
not sufficient m. to get it back 25.28
And if he is not redeemed by these m., 25.54
he will by no m. clear the guilty, Num 14.18
What m. the heat of this great Deu 29.24
for that m. life to you and length 30.20
and by what m. we may overpower him, Ju 16.05
but by all m. return him a guilt 1Sa 6.03
him who devises m. not to keep his 2Sa 14.14
wilderness, but by all m. pass over; 17.16
living child, and by no m. slay it. 1Ki 3.26
first woman, and by no m. slay it; 3.27
if by any m. he be missing, your 20.39
And the LORD said to him, 'By what m.?' 22.22
the LORD said to him, 'By what m.?' 2Ch 18.20
a poor man has no m. of redemption. Pro 13.08
I will by no m. leave you unpunished Jer 30.11
I will by no m. leave you unpunished 46.28
LORD will by no m. clear the Nah 1.03
Emmanuel" (which m., God with us). Mt 1.23
are by no m. least among the rulers 2.06
Go and learn what this m., 9.13
And if you had known what this m., 12.07
the good seed m. the sons of the 13.38
Golgotha (which m. the place of a 27.33
which m., "Little girl, I say to you, Mk 5.41
will by no m. lose his reward. 9.41
Golgotha (which m. the place of a 15.22
which m., "My God, my God, why hast 15.34
Jesus himself sent out by m. of them, * 16.08
provided for them out of their m. Lk 8.03
yourselves by m. of unrighteous 16.09
"Rabbi (which m. Teacher), where are Jn 1.38
the Messiah" (which m. Christ). 1.41
be called Cephas" (which m. Peter). 1.42
the pool of Siloam" (which m. Sent). 9.07
God may be glorified by m. of it. 11.04
We do not know what he m." 16.18
"Rabboni!" (which m. Teacher). 20.16
by what m. this man has been healed, Ac 4.09
by the apostles Barnabas (which m., 4.36
which m. Dorcas or Gazelle. 9.36
By no m.! Let God be true though Rom 3.04
By no m.! For then how could God 3.06
By no m.! On the contrary, we uphold 3.31
By no m.! How can we who died in 6.02
law but under grace? By no m.! 6.15
By no m.! Yet, if it had not been for 7.07
By no m.! It was sin, working death 7.13
This m. that it is not the children 9.08
injustice on God's part? By no m.! 9.14
By no m.! I myself am an Israelite, 11.01
By no m.! But through their trespass 11.11
their trespass m. riches for the 11.12
their failure m. riches for the 11.12
their rejection m. the reconciliation 11.15
that I might by all m. save some. 1Co 9.22
For they gave according to their m., 2Co 8.03
I can testify, and beyond their m., 8.03
that m. fruitful labor for me. Php 1.22
that godliness is a m. of gain. 1Ti 6.05
out of water and by m. of water, 2Pe 3.05
and by m. of them they wound. Rev 9.19

MEANT

As for you, you m. evil against me; Gen 50.20
but God m. it for good, to bring it 50.20
him as he had m. to do to his Deu 19.19
him, "If the LORD had m. to kill us, Ju 13.23
they m. to kill me, and they ravished 20.05
on the sea. He m. to pass by them, Mk 6.48
what the rising from the dead m. 9.10
asked him what this parable m., Lk 8.09
servants and asked what this m. 15.26
going by, he inquired what this m. 18.36
thought that he m. taking rest in Jn 11.13
what I m. by saying, 'A little while, 16.19
kindness is m. to lead you to Rom 2.04
"Food is m. for the stomach and the 1Co 6.13
the body is not m. for immorality, 6.13

MEANTIME

In the m., when so many thousands Lk 12.01

MEANWHILE

M. the Midianites had sold him in Gen 37.36
M. all the men of Judah stood 2Ch 20.13
M. the disciples besought him, Jn 4.31

MEARAH

and M. which belongs to the Sidonians, Jos 13.04

MEASURE

the sea, until he ceased to m. it, Gen 41.49
all the curtains shall have one m. Ex 26.02
curtains shall have the same m. 26.08
lamb a tenth m. of fine flour 29.40
all the curtains had the same m. 36.09
eleven curtains had the same m. 36.15
And you shall m., outside the city, Num 35.05
and they shall m. the distance to Deu 21.02
a full and just m. you shall have; 25.15
wisdom and understanding beyond m., 1Ki 4.29
had the same m. and the same form. 6.25
stones, hewn according to m., 7.09
of the same m. and the same form. 7.37
this time a m. of fine meal shall 2Ki 7.01
So a m. of fine meal was sold for a 7.16
and a m. of fine meal for a shekel, 7.18
Its m. is longer than the earth, and Job 11.09
and meted out the waters by m.; 28.25
end, and what is the m. of my days; Ps 39.04
them tears to drink in full m. 80.05
what the m. of life is, for what 89.47
his understanding is beyond m. 147.05
and opened its mouth beyond m., Is 5.14
M. by m., by exile thou didst contend 27.08
the earth in a m. and weighed the 40.12
shall come upon you in full m., 47.09
be like this day, great beyond m. 56.12
I will m. into their bosom payment 65.07
Correct me, O LORD, but in just m.; Jer 10.24
I will chasten you in just m., 30.11
I will chasten you in just m., 46.28
And water you shall drink by m., Eze 4.11
drink water by m. and in dismay. 4.16
you shall m. off a section twenty-five 45.03
the bath shall be of the same m., 45.11
the homer shall be the standard m. 45.11
thousand five hundred cubits by m., 48.30
thousand five hundred cubits by m., 48.33
transgressors have reached their full m., Dan 8.23
and the scant m. that is accursed? Mic 6.10
"To m. Jerusalem, to see what is its Zec 2.02
the m. you give will be the m. you get. Mt 7.02
up, then, the m. of your fathers. 23.32
the m. you give will be the m. you get, Mk 4.24
And they were astonished beyond m., 7.37
good m., pressed down, shaken Lk 6.38
m. you give will be the m. you get back. 6.38
it is not by m. that he gives the Jn 3.34
might become sinful beyond m. Rom 7.13
according to the m. of faith which 12.03
but in some m.—not to put it too 2Co 2.05
But when they m. themselves by one 10.12
according to the m. of Christ's gift Eph 4.07
to the m. of the stature of the 4.13
to fill up the m. of their sins. 1Th 2.16
"Rise and m. the temple of God and Rev 11.01
but do not m. the court outside the 11.02
give her a like m. of torment and 18.07
rod of gold to m. the city and its 21.15
forty-four cubits by a man's m., 21.17

MEASURED

measure it, for it could not be m. Gen 41.49
But when they m. it with an omer, he Ex 16.18
and he m. out six measures of Ru 3.15
and m. them with a line, making them 2Sa 8.02
two lines he m. to be put to death, 8.02
The other cherub also m. ten cubits; 1Ki 6.25
twelve cubits m. its circumference 7.15
thirty cubits m. its circumference 7.23
each laver m. four cubits, and there 7.38
thirty cubits m. its circumference 2Ch 4.02
Who has m. the waters in the hollow Is 40.12
the portion I have m. out to you, Jer 13.25
"If the heavens above can be m., 31.37
the sands of the sea cannot be m., 33.22
so he m. the thickness of the wall, Eze 40.05
and m. the threshold of the gate, 40.06
Then he m. the vestibule of the 40.08
Then he m. the breadth of the 40.11
Then he m. the gate from the back 40.13
He m. also the vestibule, twenty 40.14
Then he m. the distance from the 40.19
He m. its length and its breadth. 40.20
and he m. from gate to gate, a 40.23
and he m. its jambs and its vestibule 40.24
and he m. from gate to gate toward 40.27
gate, and he m. the south gate; 40.28
the east side, and he m. the gate; 40.32
me to the north gate, and he m. it; 40.35
And he m. the court, a hundred 40.47
the temple and m. the jambs of the 40.48
me to the nave, and m. the jambs; 41.01
and he m. the length of the nave 41.02
inner room and m. the jambs of the 41.03
And he m. the length of the room, 41.04
Then he m. the wall of the temple, 41.05
side chambers m. a full reed of 41.08
Then he m. the temple, a hundred 41.13
Then he m. the length of the 41.15
and m. the temple area round about. 42.15
He m. the east side with the 42.16
Then he turned and m. the north side, 42.17
Then he turned and m. the south side, 42.18
Then he turned to the west side and m., 42.19
He m. it on the four sides. 42.20
the man m. a thousand cubits, and 47.03
Again he m. a thousand, and led me 47.04
Again he m. a thousand, and led me 47.04
Again he m. a thousand, and it was a 47.05
can be neither m. nor numbered; Hos 1.10
He stood and m. the earth; Hab 3.06
and he m. the city with his rod, Rev 21.16
He also m. its wall, a hundred and 21.17

MEASUREMENT

hewn according to m., and cedar. 1Ki 7.11

MEASUREMENTS

These are Solomon's m. for building 2Ch 3.03
Who determined its m.—surely you Job 38.05

MEASURES

quickly three m. of fine meal, Gen 18.06
in m. of length or weight or Lev 19.35
have in your house two kinds of m., Deu 25.14
he measured out six m. of barley, Ru 3.15
"These six m. of barley he gave to 3.17
and five m. of parched grain, and a 1Sa 25.18
m. of fine flour, and sixty m. of meal, 1Ki 4.22
as would contain two m. of seed. 18.32
and two m. of barley for a shekel, 2 Ki 7.01
and two m. of barley for a shekel, 7.16
"Two m. of barley shall be sold for 7.18
and all m. of quantity or size. 1Ch 23.29
a hundred m. of wheat, a hundred Ez 7.22
and diverse m. are both alike an Pro 20.10
When one came to a heap of twenty m., Hag 2.16
to the winevat to draw fifty m., 2.16
took and hid in three m. of meal, Mt 13.33
took and hid in three m. of meal, Lk 13.21
He said, 'A hundred m. of oil.' 16.06
He said, 'A hundred m. of wheat.' 16.07
they took m. to undergird the ship; Ac 27.17

MEASURING

Jerusalem the m. line of Samaria, 2Ki 21.13
And the m. line shall go out Jer 31.39
of flax and a m. reed in his hand; Eze 40.03
length of the m. reed in the man's 40.05
he had finished m. the interior of 42.15
the east side with the m. reed, 42.16
five hundred cubits by the m. reed. 42.16
five hundred cubits by the m. reed. 42.17
five hundred cubits by the m. reed. 42.18
five hundred cubits by the m. reed. 42.19
an allotment m. twenty-five 48.10
and the m. line shall be stretched Zec 1.16
a man with a m. line in his hand! 2.01
Then I was given a m. rod like a Rev 11.01
to me had a m. rod of gold to 21.15

MEAT

and said, "O that we had m. to eat! Num 11.04
Where am I to get m. to give to all 11.13
'Give us m., that we may eat.' 11.13
for tomorrow, and you shall eat m.; 11.18
saying, "Who will give us m. to eat? 11.18
Therefore the LORD will give you m., 11.18
hast said, 'I will give them m., 11.21
While the m. was yet between their 11.33
the m. he put in a basket, and the Ju 6.19
"Take the m. and the unleavened 6.20
and touched the m. and the unleavened 6.21
while the m. was boiling, with a 1Sa 2.13
"Give m. for the priest to roast; 2.15
will not accept boiled m. from you, 2.15
my water and my m. that I have 25.11
a portion of m., and a cake of 2Sa 6.19
him bread and m. in the morning, 1Ki 17.06
and bread and m. in the evening; 17.06
a portion of m., and a cake of 1Ch 16.03
has not been filled with his m.? Job 31.31
or provide m. for his people? Ps 78.20
or among gluttonous eaters of m.; Pro 23.20
he roasts m. and is satisfied; Is 44.16
no m. or wine entered my mouth, nor Dan 10.03
chop them up like m. in a kettle, Mic 3.03
not to eat m. or drink wine or do Rom 14.21
falling, I will never eat m., 1Co 8.13
is sold in the m. market without 10.25

MEBUNNAI

of Anathoth, M. the Hushathite, 2Sa 23.27

MECHERATHITE

Hepher the M., Ahijah the Pelonite, 1Ch 11.36

MECONAH

in Ziklag, in M. and its villages, Neh 11.28

MEDAD

Eldad, and the other named M., Num 11.26
"Eldad and M. are prophesying in 11.27

MEDAN

M., Midian, Ishbak, and Shuah. Gen 25.02
M., Midian, Ishbak, and Shuah. 1Ch 1.32

MEDDLES

He who m. in a quarrel not his own Pro 26.17

MEDE

And Darius the M. received the Dan 5.31
by birth a M., who became king over 9.01
in the first year of Darius the M., 11.01

MEDEBA
laid waste until fire spread to M. Num 21.30
tableland of M. as far as Dibon: Jos 13.09
and all the tableland by M.; 13.16
who came and encamped before M. 1Ch 19.07
over Nebo and over M. Moab wails. Is 15.02

MEDES
Gozan, and in the cities of the M. 2Ki 17.06
and in the cities of the M., 18.11
Persians and the M. so that it may Est 1.19
am stirring up the M. against them, Is 13.17
the spirit of the kings of the M., Jer 51.11
against her, the kings of the M., 51.28
and given to the M. and Persians. Dan 5.28
the law of the M. and the Persians, 6.08
to the law of the M. and Persians, 6.12
is a law of the M. and Persians 6.15
Parthians and M. and Elamites and Ac 2.09

MEDIA
which is in the province of M., Ez 6.02
of Persia and M. and the nobles Est 1.03
the seven princes of Persia and M., 1.14
of Persia and M. who have heard of 1.18
of the Kings of M. and Persia? 10.02
Go up, O Elam, lay siege, O M.; Is 21.02
of Elam, and all the kings of M.; Jer 25.25
are the kings of M. and Persia. Dan 8.20

MEDIATE
against a man, God will m. for him; 1Sa 2.25

MEDIATES
as the covenant he m. is better, Heb 8.06

MEDIATOR
a m., one of the thousand, to Job 33.23
there is one m. between God and 1Ti 2.05
Therefore he is the m. of a new Heb 9.15
the m. of a new covenant, and to the 12.24

MEDIATORS
and your m. transgressed against me. Is 43.27

MEDICINE
A cheerful heart is good m., but a Pro 17.22
no m. for your wound, no healing for Jer 30.13

MEDICINES
In vain you have used many m.; there Jer 46.11

MEDITATE
went out to m. in the field in the Gen 24.63
but you shall m. on it day and Jos 1.08
and m. treachery all the day long. Ps 38.12
and m. on thee in the watches of 63.06
moan; I m., and my spirit faints. 77.03
night; I m. and search my spirit: 77.06
I will m. on all thy work, and muse 77.12
I will m. on thy precepts, and fix 119.15
servant will m. on thy statutes. 119.23
and I will m. on thy wondrous works 119.27
and I will m. on thy statutes. 119.48
for me, I will m. on thy precepts. 119.78
that I may m. upon thy promise. 119.148
I m. on all that thou hast done; 143.05
of thy wondrous works, I will m. 145.05
not to m. beforehand how to answer; Lk 21.14

MEDITATES
and on his law he m. day and night. Ps 1.02

MEDITATION
God, and hindering m. before God, Job 15.04
mouth and the m. of my heart be Ps 19.14
the m. of my heart shall be understanding 49.03
May my m. be pleasing to him, for I 104.34
thy law! It is my m. all the day. 119.97
teachers, for thy testimonies are my m. 119.99

MEDIUM
woman who is a m. or a wizard Lev 20.27
or a m., or a wizard, or a necromancer. Deu 18.11
out for me a woman who is a m., 1Sa 28.07
"Behold, there is a m. at Endor." 28.07
the LORD, and also consulted a m., 1Ch 10.12

MEDIUMS
"Do not turn to m. or wizards; Lev 19.31
"If a person turns to m. and wizards, 20.06
had put the m. and the wizards out 1Sa 28.03
has cut off the m. and the wizards 28.09
and dealt with m. and with wizards 2Ki 21.06
put away the m. and the wizards 23.24
and dealt with m. and with wizards 2Ch 33.06
"Consult the m. and the wizards who Is 8.19
and the m. and the wizards; 19.03

MEEK
Now the man Moses was very m., Num 12.03
wilt hear the desire of the m.; Ps 10.17
But the m. shall possess the land, 37.11
equity for the m. of the earth; Is 11.04
The m. shall obtain fresh joy in 29.19
"Blessed are the m., for they shall Mt 5.05

MEEKNESS
by the m. and gentleness of Christ— 2Co 10.01
with all lowliness and m., with Eph 4.02
lowliness, m., and patience, Col 3.12
receive with m. the implanted word, Jas 1.21
show his works in the m. of wisdom. 3.13

MEET
went out to m. him at the Valley Gen 14.17
ran from the tent door to m. them, 18.02
he rose to m. them, and bowed 19.01
Then the servant ran to m. her, 24.17
walking in the field to m. us?" 24.65
he ran to m. him, and embraced him 29.13
evening, Leah went out to m. him, 30.16
Esau, and he is coming to m. you, 32.06
thing to Esau when you m. him, 32.19
But Esau ran to m. him, and 33.04
and went up to m. Israel his 46.29
behold, he is coming out to m. you, Ex 4.14
"Go into the wilderness to m. Moses." 4.27
Moses went out to m. his father-in-law, 18.07
people out of the camp to m. God; 19.17
"If you m. your enemy's ox or his 23.04
There I will m. with you, and from 25.22
where I will m. with you, to speak 29.42
There I will m. with the people of 29.43
testimony, where I will m. with you. 30.06
meeting where I shall m. with you; 30.36
the testimony, where I m. with you. Num 17.04
he went out to m. him at the city 22.36
the LORD will come to m. me; 23.03
while I m. the LORD yonder. 23.15
to m. with omens, but set his face 24.01
went forth to m. them outside the 31.13
because they did not m. you with Deu 23.04
hills, lest the pursuers m. you; Jos 2.16
the Arabah to m. Israel in battle; 8.14
and go to m. them, and say to them, 9.11
to m. you by the river Kishon with Ju 4.07
And Jael came out to m. Sisera, 4.18
Sisera, Jael went out to m. him, 4.22
and they went up to m. them. 6.35
the doors of my house to m. me, 11.31
came out to m. him with timbrels 11.34
Philistines came shouting to m. him; 15.14
him, he came with joy to m. him. 19.03
for you will m. him immediately. 1Sa 9.13
today you will m. two men by 10.02
to God at Bethel will m. you there, 10.03

MEET (cont.)
you will m. a band of prophets 1Sa 10.05
Now when these signs m. you, 10.07
went out to m. him and salute him. 13.10
rose early to m. Saul in the 15.12
the city came to m. him trembling, 16.04
and came and drew near to m. David, 17.48
battle line to m. the Philistine. 17.48
to m. King Saul, with timbrels, with 18.06
Ahimelech came to m. David trembling, 21.01
who sent you this day to m. me! 25.32
had made haste and come to m. me, 25.34
to m. David and to m. the people who 30.21
of Saul came out to m. David, 2Sa 6.20
he sent to m. them, for the men were 10.05
Archite came to m. him with his 15.32
chanced to m. the servants of 18.09
to Gilgal to m. the king and to 19.15
the men of Judah to m. King David; 19.16
to come down to m. my lord the 19.20
of Saul came down to m. the king; 19.24
came from Jerusalem to m. the king, 19.25
in Gibeon, Amasa came to m. them. 20.08
he came down to m. me at the 1Ki 2.08
And the king rose to m. her, 2.19
and you shall m. my wishes by 5.09
So Obadiah went to m. Ahab, 18.16
and Ahab went to m. Elijah. 18.16
go down to m. Ahab king of Israel, 21.18
go up to m. the messengers of the 2Ki 1.03
to him, "There came a man to m. us, 1.06
he who came to m. you and told you 1.07
And they came to m. him, 2.15
run at once to m. her, and say to 4.26
If you m. any one, do not salute him 4.29
Therefore he returned to m. him, 4.31
alighted from the chariot to m. him, 5.21
turned from his chariot to m. you? 5.26
you and go to m. the man of God, 8.08
So Hazael went to m. him, 8.09
and sent to m. them, and let him say, 9.17
So a man on horseback went to m. him, 9.18
and went to m. Jehu, and met him at 9.21
the son of Rechab coming to m. him; 10.15
to Damascus to m. Tiglathpileser 16.10
King Josiah went to m. him; 23.29
David went out to m. them and said 1Ch 12.17
he sent to m. them, for the men were 19.05
And Asa went out to m. him, 2Ch 14.10
and he went out to m. Asa, 15.02
Hanani the seer went out to m. him, 19.02
with Jehoram to m. Jehu the son of 22.07
he went out to m. the army that 28.09
"Come and let us m. together in one Neh 6.02
"Let us m. together in the house of 6.10
for they did not m. the children of 13.02
They m. with darkness in the Job 5.14
days of affliction come to m. me. 30.27
he goes out to m. the weapons. 39.21
generations I shall not m. adversity. Ps 10.06
For thou dost m. him with goodly 21.03
in his steadfast love will m. me; 59.10
compassion come speedily to m. us, 79.08
Steadfast love and faithfulness will m.; 85.10
so now I have come out to m. you, Pro 7.15
you do not m. words of knowledge. 14.07
who devise good m. loyalty and 14.22
Let a man m. a she-bear robbed of 17.12
The rich and the poor m. together; 22.02
man and the oppressor m. together; 29.13
obeys a command will m. no harm, Ecc 8.05
"Go forth to m. Ahaz, you and Is 7.03
stirred up to m. you when you come, 14.09
m. the fugitive with bread, O 21.14
And wild beasts shall m. with hyenas, 34.14
May their men m. death by pestilence, Jer 18.21
came out from Mizpah to m. them, 41.06
One runner runs to m. another, 51.31
and one messenger to m. another, 51.31
earth who can m. the king's demand; Dan 2.10
prepare to m. your God, O Israel!" Amo 4.12
'Evil shall not overtake or m. us.' 9.10
angel came forward to m. him, Zec 2.03
all the city came out to m. Jesus; Mt 8.34
and went to m. the bridegroom. 25.01
the bridegroom! Come out to m. him.' 25.06
carrying a jar of water will m. you; Mk 14.13
ten thousand to m. him who comes Lk 14.31
carrying a jar of water will m. you; 22.10
palm trees and went out to m. him, Jn 12.13
crowd went to m. him was that they 12.18
priests and all the council to m., Ac 22.30
Appius and Three Taverns to m. us. 28.15
When you m. together, it is not the 1Co 11.20
indeed you fail to m. the test! 2Co 13.05
the clouds to m. the Lord in the 1Th 4.17
and our assembling to m. him, 2Th 2.01
it did not m. with faith in the Heb 4.02
not neglecting to m. together, 10.25
when you m. various trials, Jas 1.02

MEETEST
Thou m. him that joyfully works Is 64.05

MEETING
In the tent of m., outside the veil Ex 27.21
when they go into the tent of m., 28.43
sons to the door of the tent of m., 29.04
the bull before the tent of m. 29.10
at the door of the tent of m., 29.11
the tent of m. to minister in the 29.30
at the door of the tent of m. 29.32
of the tent of m. before the LORD, 29.42
the tent of m. and the altar; 29.44
for the service of the tent of m.; 30.16
the tent of m. and the altar, 30.18
When they go into the tent of m., 30.20
it the tent of m. and the ark of 30.26
in the tent of m. where I shall 30.36
the tent of m., and the ark of 31.07
and he called it the tent of m. 33.07
would go out to the tent of m., 33.07
to be used for the tent of m., 35.21
at the door of the tent of m. 38.08
for the door of the tent of m., 38.30
of the tent of m. was finished; 39.32
the tabernacle, for the tent of m.; 39.40
the tabernacle of the tent of m. 40.02
the tabernacle of the tent of m., 40.06
the tent of m. and the altar, 40.07
sons to the door of the tent of m., 40.12
he put the table in the tent of m., 40.22
the lampstand in the tent of m., 40.24
in the tent of m. before the veil, 40.26
the tabernacle of the tent of m., 40.29
the tent of m. and the altar, 40.30
when they went into the tent of m., 40.32
Then the cloud covered the tent of m., 40.34
not able to enter the tent of m., 40.35
him from the tent of m., saying, Lev 1.01
it at the door of the tent of m., 1.03
is at the door of the tent of m. 1.05
it at the door of the tent of m.; 3.02
killing it before the tent of m.; 3.08
and kill it before the tent of m.; 3.13
of the tent of m. before the LORD, 4.04
and bring it to the tent of m.; 4.05
LORD which is in the tent of m., 4.07
is at the door of the tent of m. 4.07
and bring it before the tent of m.; 4.14
of the bull to the tent of m., 4.16
in the tent of m. before the LORD; 4.18
is at the door of the tent of m. 4.18
of the tent of m. they shall eat 6.16
in the court of the tent of m. 6.26
the tent of m. to make atonement 6.30

MEETING (cont.)

at the door of the tent of m. Lev 8.03
at the door of the tent of m. 8.04
at the door of the tent of m., 8.31
of the tent of m. for seven days, 8.33
of the tent of m. you shall remain 8.35
commanded before the tent of m.; 9.05
and Aaron went into the tent of m.; 9.23
of the tent of m., lest you die; 10.07
into the tent of m., lest you die; 10.09
of the tent of m. a lamb a year 12.06
at the door of the tent of m. 14.11
to the door of the tent of m., 14.23
LORD to the door of the tent of m., 15.14
to the door of the tent of m. 15.29
LORD at the door of the tent of m.; 16.07
so he shall do for the tent of m., 16.16
in the tent of m. when he enters 16.17
and the tent of m. and the altar, 16.20
shall come into the tent of m., 16.23
for the tent of m. and for the 16.33
it to the door of the tent of m., 17.04
at the door of the tent of m., 17.05
LORD at the door of the tent of m., 17.06
it to the door of the tent of m., 17.09
to the door of the tent of m., 19.21
the testimony, in the tent of m., 24.03
of Sinai, in the tent of m., Num 1.01
the tent of m. on every side. 2.02
"Then the tent of m. shall set out, 2.17
congregation before the tent of m., 3.07
the furnishings of the tent of m., 3.08
in the tent of m. was to be the 3.25
for the door of the tent of m., 3.25
the tent of m. toward the sunrise, 3.38
to do the work in the tent of m. 4.03
sons of Kohath in the tent of m.: 4.04
of the tent of m. which the sons 4.15
to do the work in the tent of m. 4.23
and the tent of m. with its 4.25
for the door of the tent of m., 4.25
the Gershonites in the tent of m., 4.28
to do the work of the tent of m. 4.30
of their service in the tent of m.: 4.31
of their service in the tent of m., 4.33
service, for work in the tent of m.; 4.35
all who served in the tent of m., 4.37
for work in the tent of m.— 4.39
all who served in the tent of m., 4.41
for work in the tent of m.— 4.43
bearing burdens in the tent of m., 4.47
to the door of the tent of m., 6.10
to the door of the tent of m., 6.13
head at the door of the tent of m., 6.18
the service of the tent of m., 7.05
the tent of m. to speak with the 7.89
the Levites before the tent of m., 8.09
in to do service at the tent of m., 8.15
people of Israel at the tent of m., 8.19
in the tent of m. in attendance 8.22
in the service of the tent of m.; 8.24
their brethren in the tent of m., 8.26
at the entrance of the tent of m. 10.03
and bring them to the tent of m., 11.16
out, you three, to the tent of m. 12.04
at the tent of m. to all the 14.10
of the tent of m. with Moses and 16.18
at the entrance of the tent of m. 16.19
they turned toward the tent of m.; 16.42
to the front of the tent of m., 16.43
at the entrance of the tent of m., 16.50
in the tent of m. before the 17.04
you, and attend to the tent of m., 18.04
do the service of the tent of m. 18.06
their service in the tent of m. 18.21
shall not come near the tent of m., 18.22
do the service of the tent of m., 18.23
for your service in the tent of m. 18.31
of the tent of m. seven times. 19.04
to the door of the tent of m., 20.06
at the door of the tent of m. 25.06
door of the tent of m., saying, 27.02
and brought it into the tent of m., 31.54
yourselves in the tent of m., Deu 31.14
themselves in the tent of m. 31.14
and set up the tent of m. there; Jos 18.01
at the door of the tent of m. 19.51
at the entrance of the tent of m. 1Sa 2.22
the tent of m., and all the holy 1Ki 8.04
the tabernacle of the tent of m., 1Ch 6.32
at the entrance of the tent of m. 9.21
of the tent of m. and the sanctuary, 23.32
for the tent of m. of God, 2Ch 1.03
LORD, which was at the tent of m., 1.06
the tent of m., to Jerusalem. 1.13
the tent of m., and all the holy 5.05
burned all the m. places of God in Ps 74.08
And when the m. of the synagogue Ac 13.43

MEETS

"When Esau my brother m. you, Gen 32.17
when he m. him, he shall put him to Num 35.19
murderer to death, when he m. him. 35.21
and a man m. her in the city and Deu 22.23
country a man m. a young woman who 22.25
"If a man m. a virgin who is not 22.28
a woman m. him, dressed as a harlot, Pro 7.10
east whom victory m. at every step? Is 41.02

MEGIDDO

Taanach, one; the king of M., one; Jos 12.21
inhabitants of M. and its villages 17.11
inhabitants of M. and its villages Ju 1.27
at Taanach, by the waters of M.; 5.19
M., and all Bethshean which is 1Ki 4.12
Jerusalem and Hazor and M. and Gezer 9.15
And he fled to M., and died there. 2Ki 9.27
and Pharaoh Neco slew him at M., 23.29
him dead in a chariot from M., 23.30
M. and its towns, Dor and its towns. 1Ch 7.29
joined battle in the plain of M. 2Ch 35.22
for Hadadrimmon in the plain of M. Zec 12.11

MEHETABEL

his wife's name was M., the daughter Gen 36.39
his wife's name M. the daughter of 1Ch 1.50
son of M., who was shut up, he said, Neh 6.10

MEHIDA

the sons of M., the sons of Harsha, Ez 2.52
the sons of M., the sons of Harsha, Neh 7.54

MEHIR

of Shuhah, was the father of M., 1Ch 4.11

MEHOLATHITE

given to Adriel the M. for a wife. 1Sa 18.19
Adriel the son of Barzillai the M.; 2Sa 21.08

MEHUJAEL

and Irad was the father of M., Gen 4.18
and M. the father of Methushael, and 4.18

MEHUMAN

he commanded M., Biztha, Harbona, Est 1.10

MEJARKON

and M. and Rakkon with the territory Jos 19.46

MELATIAH

them repaired M. the Gibeonite and Neh 3.07

MELCHI

the son of M., the son of Jannai, Lk 3.24
the son of M., the son of Addi, the 3.28

MELCHIZEDEK

And M. king of Salem brought out	Gen 14.18
for ever after the order of M.	Ps 110.04
for ever, after the order of M.	Heb 5.06
high priest after the order of M.	5.10
for ever after the order of M.	6.20
For this M., king of Salem, priest	7.01
of his ancestor when M. met him.	7.10
to arise after the order of M.,	7.11
arises in the likeness of M.,	7.15
for ever, after the order of M.	7.17

MELEA

the son of M., the son of Menna, the	Lk 3.31

MELECH

of Micah: Pithon, M., Tarea, and Ahaz.	1Ch 8.35
of Micah: Pithon, M., Tahrea, and Ahaz;	9.41

MELODY

I will make m. to the LORD, the God	Ju 5.03
will sing and make m. to the LORD.	Ps 27.06
make m. to him with the harp of ten	33.02
steadfast! I will sing and make m.!	57.07
the harp, to the m. of the lyre.	92.03
with the lyre and the sound of m.!	98.05
make m. to our God upon the lyre!	147.07
making m. to him with timbrel and	149.03
Make sweet m., sing many songs, that	Is 23.16
to the m. of your harps I will not	Amo 5.23
and making m. to the Lord with all	Eph 5.19

MELONS

the m., the leeks, the onions, and	Num 11.05

MELT

brethren have made our hearts m.,	Deu 1.28
of his fellows m. as his heart.	20.08
of the land m. away before you.	Jos 2.09
me made the heart of the people m.;	14.08
a lion, will utterly m. with fear;	2Sa 17.10
The mountains m. like wax before	Ps 97.05
and m. in fear before Rezin and the	Is 8.06
and every man's heart will m.,	13.07
m. in fear, O Philistia, all of you!	14.31
the Egyptians will m. within them.	19.01
they m. in fear, they are troubled	Jer 49.23
heart will m. and all hands will	Eze 21.07
that their hearts may m., and many	21.15
the fire upon it in order to m. it;	22.20
and I will put you in and m. you.	22.20
mountains will m. under him and	Mic 1.04
quake before him, the hills m.;	Nah 1.05
and the elements will m. with fire!	2Pe 3.12

MELTED

inhabitants of Canaan have m. away.	Ex 15.15
but when the sun grew hot, it m.	16.21
our hearts m., and there was no	Jos 2.11
their heart m., and there was no	5.01
And the hearts of the people m.,	7.05
and his bonds m. off his hands.	Ju 15.14
it is m. within my breast;	Ps 22.14
their courage m. away in their evil	107.26
you shall be m. in the midst of it	Eze 22.21
As silver is m. in a furnace, so you	22.22
so you shall be m. in the midst of	22.22
its filthiness may be m. in it,	24.11

MELTS

he utters his voice, the earth m.	Ps 46.06
as wax m. before fire, let the	68.02
he gnashes his teeth and m. away;	112.10
My soul m. away for sorrow;	119.28
He sends forth his word, and m. them;	147.18
every one wails and m. in tears.	Is 15.03
he who touches the earth and it m.,	Amo 9.05

MEMBER

or to a m. of the stranger's family,	Lev 25.47
or whose male m. is cut off shall	Deu 23.01
a respected m. of the council, who	Mk 15.43
He was a m. of the council, a good	Lk 23.50
Manaen a m. of the court of Herod	Ac 13.01
a m. of the tribe of Benjamin.	Rom 11.01
not consist of one m. but of many.	1Co 12.14
If one m. suffers, all suffer	12.26
if one m. is honored, all rejoice	12.26
is a little m. and boasts of great	Jas 3.05

MEMBERS

and all the m. of his household, his	Gen 36.06
The m. of the half-tribe of Manasseh	1Ch 5.23
and all my m. are like a shadow.	Job 17.07
whose m. were like those of asses,	Eze 23.20
one of your m. than that your	Mt 5.29
one of your m. than that your	5.30
Do not yield your m. to sin as	Rom 6.13
and your m. to God as instruments	6.13
yielded your m. to impurity and to	6.19
now yield your m. to righteousness	6.19
at work in our m. to bear fruit	7.05
but I see in my m. another law at	7.23
law of sin which dwells in my m.	7.23
For as in one body we have many m.,	12.04
and all the m. do not have the same	12.04
and individually m. one of another.	12.05
decide between m. of the brotherhood,	1Co 6.05
that your bodies are m. of Christ?	6.15
take the m. of Christ and make	6.15
and make them m. of a prostitute?	6.15
as the body is one and has many m.,	12.12
and all the m. of the body, though	12.12
but that the m. may have the same	12.25
Christ and individually m. of it.	12.27
the saints and m. of the household	Eph 2.19
m. of the same body, and partakers	3.06
for we are m. one of another.	4.25
because we are m. of his body.	5.30
an unrighteous world among our m.,	Jas 3.06
passions that are at war in your m.?	4.01

MEMORABLE

orders to bring the book of m. deeds,	Est 6.01

MEMORIAL

"This day shall be for you a m. day,	Ex 12.14
hand and as a m. between your eyes,	13.09
"Write this as a m. in a book and	17.14
this as its m. portion upon the	Lev 2.02
offering its m. portion and burn	2.09
burn as its m. portion part of the	2.16
of it as its m. portion and burn	5.12
this as its m. portion on the	6.15
a m. proclaimed with blast of	23.24
the bread as a m. portion to be	24.07
as its m. portion, and burn it upon	Num 5.26
as a m. for the people of Israel	31.54
the people of Israel a m. for ever.	Jos 4.07
or right or m. in Jerusalem.	Neh 2.20
thy m. name is the desire of our	Is 26.08
it shall be to the LORD for a m.,	55.13
he who makes a m. offering of	66.03
have ascended as a m. before God.	Ac 10.04

MEMORY

His m. perishes from the earth, and	Job 18.17
the very m. of them has perished.	Ps 9.06
and may his m. be cut off from the	109.15
The m. of the righteous is a	Pro 10.07
reward; but the m. of them is lost.	Ecc 9.05
has done will be told in m. of her.	Mt 26.13
has done will be told in m. of her.	Mk 14.09

MEMPHIS

and the princes of M. are deluded;	Is 19.13
the men of M. and Tahpanhes have	Jer 2.16

MEMPHIS (cont.)

at M., and in the land of Pathros, Jer 44.01
proclaim in M. and Tahpanhes; 46.14
For M. shall become a waste, a ruin, 46.19
put an end to the images, in M.; Eze 30.13
M. shall bury them. Nettles shall Hos 9.06

MEMUCAN

and M., the seven princes of Persia Est 1.14
Then M. said in presence of the 1.16
and the king did as M. proposed; 1.21

MEN

At that time m. began to call upon Gen 4.26
When m. began to multiply on the 6.01
that the daughters of m. were fair; 6.02
God came in to the daughters of m., 6.04
were the mighty m. that were of 6.04
that were of old, the m. of renown. 6.04
And as m. migrated in the east, they 11.02
which the sons of m. had built. 11.05
And Pharaoh gave m. orders concerning 12.20
Now the m. of Sodom were wicked, 13.13
he led forth his trained m., 14.14
but what the young m. have eaten, 14.24
share of the m. who went with me; 14.24
male among the m. of Abraham's 17.23
and all the m. of his house, those 17.27
three m. stood in front of him. 18.02
Then the m. set out from there, and 18.16
So the m. turned from there, and 18.22
the m. of the city, the m. of Sodom, 19.04
"Where are the m. who came to you 19.05
Lot went out of the door of the m., 19.06
only do nothing to these m., 19.08
But the m. put forth their hands 19.10
blindness the m. who were at the 19.11
Then the m. said to Lot, "Have you 19.12
so the m. seized him and his wife 19.16
and the m. were very much afraid. 20.08
and the two m. made a covenant. 21.27
took two of his young m. with him, 22.03
Then Abraham said to his young m., 22.05
So Abraham returned to his young m., 22.19
daughters of the m. of the city are 24.13
the feet of the m. who were with 24.32
And he and the m. who were with him 24.54
and Abraham's servant and his m. 24.59
When the m. of the place asked him 26.07
"Lest the m. of the place should 26.07
together all the m. of the place 29.22
you, and four hundred m. with him. 32.06
have striven with God and with m., 32.28
and four hundred m. with him. 33.01
you some of the m. who are with me 33.15
and the m. were indignant and very 34.07
and spoke to the m. of their city, 34.20
"These m. are friendly with us; 34.21
will the m. agree to dwell with us, 34.22
And he asked the m. of the place, 38.21
and also the m. of the place said, 38.22
and none of the m. of the house 39.11
she called to the m. of her household 39.14
of Egypt and all its wise m.; 41.08
we are honest m., your servants are 42.11
if you are honest m., let one of 42.19
But we said to him, 'We are honest m., 42.31
shall know that you are honest m.: 42.33
you are not spies but honest m., 42.34
So the m. took the present, and they 43.15
"Bring the m. into the house, and 43.16
for the m. are to dine with me at 43.16
and brought the m. to Joseph's 43.17
And the m. were afraid because they 43.18
had brought the m. into Joseph's 43.24
and the m. looked at one another in 43.33
the m. were sent away with their 44.03
steward, "Up, follow after the m.; 44.04
and the m. are shepherds, for they 46.32
he took five m. and presented them 47.02
if you know any able m. among them, 47.06
for in their anger they slay m., 49.06
for all the m. who were seeking Ex 4.19
laid upon the m. that they may 5.09
the wise m. and the sorcerers; 7.11
Let the m. go, that they may serve 10.07
Go, the m. among you, and serve the 10.11
or they said, "We are all dead m." 12.33
six hundred thousand m. on foot, 12.37
said to Joshua, "Choose for us m., 17.09
Moreover choose able m. from all 18.21
m. who are trustworthy and who hate 18.21
and place such m. over the people 18.21
Moses chose able m. out of all 18.25
"When m. quarrel and one strikes 21.18
"When m. strive together, and hurt a 21.22
"You shall be m. consecrated to me; 22.31
And he sent young m. of the people 24.05
on the chief m. of the people of 24.11
upon the bodies of ordinary m., 30.32
have given to all able m. ability, 31.06
that day about three thousand m. 32.28
So they came, both m. and women; 35.22
All the m. and women, the people of 35.29
all the able m. who were doing 36.04
And all the able m. among the 36.08
thousand, five hundred and fifty m. 38.26
sort of rash oath that m. swear, Lev 5.04
things which m. do and sin therein, 6.03
abominations the m. of the land did, 18.27
animal such as m. offer as an 27.09
be utterly destroyed from among m., 27.29
names of the m. who shall attend Num 1.05
took these m. who have been named, 1.17
twelve m., each representing his 1.44
the sins that m. commit by breaking 5.06
the leader of the m. of Zebulun: 7.24
the leader of the m. of Reuben: 7.30
the leader of the m. of Simeon: 7.36
the leader of the m. of Gad: 7.42
the leader of the m. of Ephraim: 7.48
the leader of the m. of Manasseh: 7.54
the leader of the m. of Benjamin: 7.60
the leader of the m. of Dan: 7.66
the leader of the m. of Asher: 7.72
the leader of the m. of Naphtali: 7.78
were certain m. who were unclean 9.06
and those m. said to him, "We are 9.07
the camp of the m. of Judah set 10.14
tribe of the m. of Issachar was 10.15
tribe of the m. of Zebulun was 10.16
tribe of the m. of Simeon was 10.19
tribe of the m. of Gad was Eliasaph 10.20
the camp of the m. of Ephraim set 10.22
tribe of the m. of Manasseh was 10.23
tribe of the m. of Benjamin was 10.24
of the camp of the m. of Dan, 10.25
tribe of the m. of Asher was 10.26
tribe of the m. of Naphtali was 10.27
for me seventy m. of the elders of 11.16
gathered seventy m. of the elders 11.24
Now two m. remained in the camp, one 11.26
of Moses, one of his chosen m., 11.28
more than all m. that were on the 12.03
"Send m. to spy out the land of 13.02
all of them m. who were heads of 13.03
names of the m. whom Moses sent to 13.16
which the m. of Israel cut down 13.24
Then the m. who had gone up with 13.31
saw in it are m. of great stature. 13.32
none of the m. who have seen my 14.22
And the m. whom Moses sent to spy 14.36
the m. who brought up an evil 14.37
of those m. who went to spy out the 14.38
took m.; and they rode up before 16.02
from the assembly, well-known m.; 16.02

MEN (cont.)

you put out the eyes of these m.? Num 16.14
from the tents of these wicked m., 16.26
m. die the common death of all m., 16.29
are visited by the fate of all m., 16.29
know that these m. have despised 16.30
and all the m. that belonged to 16.32
and fifty m. offering the incense. 16.35
of these m. who have sinned at the 16.38
came out against them with many m., 20.20
He gathered all his m. together, 21.23
said, "Who are these m. with you?" 22.09
"If the m. have come to call you, 22.20
said to Balaam, "Go with the m.; 22.35
of you slay his m. who have yoked 25.05
devoured two hundred and fifty m.; 26.10
"Arm m. from among you for the war, 31.03
said to the m. of war who had gone 31.21
from the m. of war who went out to 31.28
spoil that the m. of war took was: 31.32
that of the m. who had gone to war 31.42
counted the m. of war who are 31.49
(The m. of war had taken booty, 31.53
'Surely none of the m. who came up 32.11
stead, a brood of sinful m., 32.14
names of the m. who shall divide 34.17
These are the names of the m.: 34.19
These are the m. whom the LORD 34.29
understanding, and experienced m., Deu 1.13
tribes, wise and experienced m., 1.15
'Let us send m. before us, that they 1.22
to me, and I took twelve m. of you, 1.23
'Not one of these m. of this evil 1.35
the m. of war, had perished from the 2.14
"So when all the m. of war had 2.16
city, m., women, and children; 2.34
city, m., women, and children. 3.06
all your m. of valor shall pass 3.18
you all the m. who followed the 4.03
which the m. of old have set. 19.14
in the field m. that they should 20.19
Then all the m. of the city shall 21.21
and the m. of her city shall stone 22.21
"If there is a dispute between m., 25.01
"When m. fight with one another, and 25.11
to all the m. of Israel with a 27.14
officers, all the m. of Israel, 29.10
Then m. would say, 'It is because 29.25
m., women, and little ones, and the 31.12
when he separated the sons of m., 32.08
of them cease from among m.," 32.26
not die, nor let his m. be few." 33.06
but all the m. of valor among you Jos 1.14
of Nun sent two m. secretly from 2.01
certain m. of Israel have come here 2.02
"Bring forth the m. that have come 2.03
taken the two m. and hidden them; 2.04
m. came to me, but I did not know 2.04
closed, at dark, the m. went out; 2.05
where the m. went I do not know; 2.05
So the m. pursued after them on the 2.07
and said to the m., "I know that 2.09
And the m. said to her, "Our life 2.14
The m. said to her, "We will be 2.17
Then the two m. came down again 2.23
take twelve m. from the tribes of 3.12
"Take twelve m. from the people, 4.02
the twelve m. from the people of 4.04
And the m. of Israel did as Joshua 4.08
all the m. of war, had died on the 5.04
the m. of war that came forth out 5.06
its king and mighty m. of valor. 6.02
all the m. of war going around the 6.03
let the armed m. pass on before 6.07
And the armed m. went before the 6.09
and the armed m. went before them, 6.13
both m. and women, young and old, 6.21
said to the two m. who had spied 6.22
So the young m. who had been spies 6.23
Joshua sent m. from Jericho to Ai, 7.02
And the m. went up and spied out Ai. 7.02
three thousand m. go up and attack 7.03
and they fled before the m. of Ai, 7.04
m. of Ai killed about thirty-six m. 7.05
take all the fighting m. with you, 8.01
arose, and all the fighting m., 8.03
thirty thousand mighty m. of valor, 8.03
the fighting m. who were with him 8.11
And he took about five thousand m., 8.12
the m. of the city, made haste and 8.14
So when the m. of Ai looked back, 8.20
turned back and smote the m. of Ai. 8.21
both m. and women, were twelve 8.25
to him and to the m. of Israel, 9.06
But the m. of Israel said to the 9.07
So the m. partook of their provisions, 9.14
Ai, and all its m. were mighty. 10.02
And the m. of Gibeon sent to Joshua 10.06
and all the mighty m. of valor. 10.07
than the m. of Israel killed with 10.11
Amorites over the m. of Israel; 10.12
and set m. by it to guard them; 10.18
When Joshua and the m. of Israel 10.20
summoned all the m. of Israel, 10.24
chiefs of the m. of war who had 10.24
Provide three m. from each tribe, 18.04
So the m. started on their way; 18.08
So the m. went and passed up and 18.09
and the m. of Jericho fought 24.11
And the m. of Judah fought against Ju 1.08
And afterward the m. of Judah went 1.09
Moabites, all strong, able-bodied m.; 3.29
gather your m. at Mount Tabor, 4.06
ten thousand m. went up at his 4.10
and all the m. who were with him, 4.13
with ten thousand m. following him. 4.14
So Gideon took ten m. of his 6.27
family and the m. of the town to 6.27
When the m. of the town rose early 6.28
Then the m. of the town said to 6.30
their mouths, was three hundred m.; 7.06
three hundred m. that lapped I 7.07
but retained the three hundred m.; 7.08
of the armed m. that were in the 7.11
three hundred m. into three 7.16
and the hundred m. who were with 7.19
And the m. of Israel were called 7.23
So all the m. of Ephraim were 7.24
And the m. of Ephraim said to him, 8.01
three hundred m. who were with him, 8.04
So he said to the m. of Succoth, 8.05
and the m. of Penuel answered him 8.08
him as the m. of Succoth had 8.08
And he said to the m. of Penuel, 8.09
army, about fifteen thousand m., 8.10
twenty thousand m. who drew the 8.10
of Succoth, seventy-seven m. 8.14
And he came to the m. of Succoth, 8.15
bread to your m. who are faint?'" 8.15
with them taught the m. of Succoth. 8.16
and slew the m. of the city. 8.17
"Where are the m. whom you slew at 8.18
Then the m. of Israel said to 8.22
the ears of all the m. of Shechem; 9.03
seventy m., upon one stone; 9.05
you m. of Shechem, that God may 9.07
by which gods and m. are honored, 9.09
my wine which cheers gods and m., 9.13
seventy m. on one stone, and have 9.18
Abimelech and the m. of Shechem; 9.23
and the m. of Shechem dealt treacherously 9.23
and upon the m. of Shechem, who 9.24
m. of Sechem put m. in ambush 9.25
and the m. of Shechem put confidence 9.26

MEN (cont.)

serve the m. of Hamor the father Ju 9.28
you and the m. that are with you, 9.32
when he and the m. that are with 9.33
and all the m. that were with him 9.34
Abimelech and the m. that were with 9.35
And when Gaal saw the m., he said to 9.36
m. are coming down from the mountain 9.36
the mountains as if they were m." 9.36
m. are coming down from the center 9.37
not these the m. whom you despised? 9.38
at the head of the m. of Shechem, 9.39
following day the m. went out into 9.42
He took his m. and divided them 9.43
and saw the m. coming out of the 9.43
he and all the m. that were with 9.48
he said to the m. that were with 9.48
about a thousand m. and women. 9.49
all the m. and women, and shut 9.51
lest m. say of me, 'A woman killed 9.54
And when the m. of Israel saw that 9.55
wickedness of the m. of Shechem 9.57
The m. of Ephraim were called to 12.01
gathered all the m. of Gilead and 12.04
and the m. of Gilead smote Ephraim, 12.04
the m. of Gilead said to him, 12.05
for so the young m. used to do. 14.10
And the m. of the city said to him 14.18
and killed thirty m. of the town, 14.19
And the m. of Judah said, "Why have 15.10
Then three thousand m. of Judah 15.11
and with it he slew a thousand m. 15.15
an ass have I slain a thousand m. 15.16
Now she had m. lying in wait in an 16.09
And the m. lying in wait were in an 16.12
the house was full of m. and women; 16.27
about three thousand m. and women, 16.27
sent five able m. from the whole 18.02
Then the five m. departed, and came 18.07
And six hundred m. of the tribe of 18.11
Then the five m. who had gone to 18.14
Now the six hundred m. of the Danites, 18.16
and the five m. who had gone to spy 18.17
the six hundred m. armed with 18.17
the m. who were in the houses near 18.22
So the two m. sat and ate and drank 19.06
the m. of the place were Benjaminites 19.16
the m. of the city, base fellows, 19.22
But the m. would not listen to him. 19.25
thousand m. on foot that drew the 20.02
And the m. of Gibeah rose against 20.05
will take ten m. of a hundred 20.10
So all the m. of Israel gathered 20.11
of Israel sent m. through all the 20.12
Now therefore give up the m., 20.13
thousand m. that drew the sword, 20.15
mustered seven hundred picked m. 20.15
hundred picked m. who were left-handed; 20.16
And the m. of Israel, apart from 20.17
thousand m. that drew sword; 20.17
all these were m. of war. 20.17
And the m. of Israel went out to 20.20
and the m. of Israel drew up the 20.20
thousand m. of the Israelites. 20.21
the m. of Israel, took courage, and 20.22
thousand m. of the people of 20.25
all these were m. who drew the 20.25
So Israel set m. in ambush round 20.29
country, about thirty m. of Israel. 20.31
But the m. of Israel said, "Let us 20.32
And all the m. of Israel rose up 20.33
and the m. of Israel who were in 20.33
thousand picked m. out of all 20.34
and the m. of Israel destroyed 20.35
one hundred m. of Benjamin that 20.35
all these were m. who drew the 20.35
The m. of Israel gave ground to 20.36
trusted to the m. in ambush whom 20.36
And the m. in ambush made haste and 20.37
the m. in ambush moved out and 20.37
m. of Israel and the m. in ambush was 20.38
the m. of Israel should turn in 20.39
and kill about thirty m. of Israel; 20.39
Then the m. of Israel turned, and 20.41
and the m. of Benjamin were dismayed, 20.41
before the m. of Israel in the 20.42
Eighteen thousand m. of Benjamin 20.44
fell, all of them m. of valor. 20.44
five thousand m. of them were cut 20.45
two thousand m. of them were slain. 20.45
thousand m. that drew the sword, 20.46
the sword, all of them m. of valor. 20.46
But six hundred m. turned and fled 20.47
And the m. of Israel turned back 20.48
m. and beasts and all that they 20.48
Now the m. of Israel had sworn at 21.01
thousand of their bravest m., 21.10
the young m. not to molest you? Ru 2.09
drink what the young m. have drawn." 2.09
Boaz instructed his young m., 2.15
you have not gone after young m., 3.10
And he took ten m. of the elders of 4.02
Now the sons of Eli were worthless m.; 1Sa 2.12
of the young m. was very great in 2.17
for the m. treated the offering of 2.17
in favor with the LORD and with m. 2.26
house shall die by the sword of m. 2.33
four thousand m. on the field of 4.02
and acquit yourselves like m., 4.09
acquit yourselves like m. and fight." 4.09
And when the m. of Ashdod saw how 5.07
he afflicted the m. of the city, 5.09
the m. who did not die were stricken 5.12
The m. did so, and took two milch 6.10
and the m. of Bethshemesh offered 6.15
slew some of the m. of Bethshemesh, 6.19
he slew seventy m. of them, 6.19
Then the m. of Bethshemesh said, 6.20
And the m. of Kiriathjearim came 7.01
And the m. of Israel went out of 7.11
then said to the m. of Israel, 8.22
will meet two m. by Rachel's tomb 10.02
three m. going up to God at Bethel 10.03
with him went m. of valor whose 10.26
and all the m. of Jabesh said to 11.01
the tidings of the m. of Jabesh. 11.05
the m. of Israel were three hundred 11.08
and the m. of Judah thirty thousand. 11.08
you say to the m. of Jabeshgilead: 11.09
came and told the m. of Jabesh, 11.09
Therefore the m. of Jabesh said, 11.10
Bring the m., that we may put them 11.12
and all the m. of Israel rejoiced 11.15
Saul chose three thousand m. of Israel; 13.02
When the m. of Israel saw that they 13.06
with him, about six hundred m. 13.15
him were about six hundred m., 14.02
we will cross over to the m., 14.08
And the m. of the garrison hailed 14.12
of about twenty m. within as it 14.14
when all the m. of Israel who had 14.22
And the m. of Israel were distressed 14.24
two hundred thousand m. on foot, 15.04
foot, and ten thousand m. of Judah. 15.04
One of the young m. answered, 16.18
And Saul and the m. of Israel were 17.02
and all the m. of Israel, were in 17.19
All the m. of Israel, when they saw 17.24
And the m. of Israel said, "Have you 17.25
said to the m. who stood by him, 17.26
heard when he spoke to the m.; 17.28
And the m. of Israel and Judah rose 17.52
Saul set him over the m. of war. 18.05
David arose and went, along with his m., 18.27

MEN (cont.)
with the young m. for such and 1Sa 21.02
only the young m. have kept 21.04
vessels of the young m. are holy, 21.05
with him about four hundred m. 22.02
and the m. who were with him. 22.06
both m. and women, children and 22.19
But David's m. said to him, "Behold, 23.03
And David and his m. went to Keilah, 23.05
to besiege David and his m. 23.08
Will the m. of Keilah surrender me 23.11
"Will the m. of Keilah surrender me 23.12
me and my m. into the hand of Saul?" 23.12
Then David and his m., who were 23.13
David and his m. were in the 23.24
And Saul and his m. went to seek 23.25
David and his m. on the other side 23.26
as Saul and his m. were closing in 23.26
David and his m. to capture them, 23.26
thousand chosen m. out of all 24.02
David and his m. in front of the 24.02
David and his m. were sitting in 24.03
And the m. of David said to him, 24.04
He said to his m., "The LORD forbid 24.06
persuaded his m. with these words, 24.07
listen to the words of m. who say, 24.09
David and his m. went up to the 24.22
So David sent ten young m.; 25.05
and David said to the young m., 25.05
Ask your young m., and they will 25.08
let my young m. find favor in your 25.08
When David's young m. came, 25.09
and give it to m. who come from I 25.11
So David's young m. turned away, 25.12
And David said to his m., 25.13
four hundred m. went up after 25.13
But one of the young m. told Abigail, 25.14
Yet the m. were very good to us, and 25.15
And she said to her young m., 25.19
David and his m. came down toward 25.20
not see the young m. of my lord, 25.25
to the young m. who follow my lord 25.27
If m. rise up to pursue you and to 25.29
three thousand chosen m. of Israel, 26.02
but if it is m., may they be cursed 26.19
of the young m. come over and 26.22
the six hundred m. who were with 27.02
he and his m., every man with his 27.03
Now David and his m. went up, 27.08
you and your m. are to go out with 28.01
and went, he and two m. with him; 28.08
David and his m. were passing on 29.02
be with the heads of the m. here? 29.04
out with his m. early in the 29.11
David and his m. came to Ziklag on 30.01
David and his m. came to the city, 30.03
the six hundred m. who were with 30.09
pursuit, he and four hundred m.; 30.10
except four hundred young m., 30.17
Then David came to the two hundred m., 30.21
among the m. who had gone with 30.22
where David and his m. had roamed. 30.31
and the m. of Israel fled before 31.01
and all his m., on the same day 31.06
And when the m. of Israel who were 31.07
saw that the m. of Israel had fled 31.07
all the valiant m. arose, and went 31.12
so did all the m. who were with 2Sa 1.11
one of the young m. and said, 1.15
brought up his m. who were with 2.03
And the m. of Judah came, and there 2.04
"It was the m. of Jabeshgilead who 2.04
messengers to the m. of Jabeshgilead, 2.05
"Let the young m. arise and play 2.14
Abner and the m. of Israel were 2.17
and seize one of the young m., 2.21
surely the m. would have given up 2.27
and all the m. stopped, and pursued 2.28
And Abner and his m. went all that 2.29
servants nineteen m. besides Asahel. 2.30
hundred and sixty of Abner's m. 2.31
Joab and his m. marched all night, 2.32
with twenty m. to David at Hebron, 3.20
Abner and the m. who were with him 3.20
these m. the sons of Zeruiah are 3.39
son had two m. who were captains 4.02
when wicked m. have slain a righteous 4.11
And David commanded his young m., 4.12
king and his m. went to Jerusalem 5.06
David and his m. carried them away 5.21
all the chosen m. of Israel, 6.01
both m. and women, to each a cake of 6.19
and violent m. shall afflict them 7.10
chasten him with the rod of m., 7.14
with the stripes of the sons of m.; 7.14
twenty-two thousand m. of the Syrians. 8.05
for the m. were greatly ashamed. 10.05
king of Maacah with a thousand m., 10.06
and the m. of Tob, twelve thousand m. 10.06
and all the host of the mighty m. 10.07
and the m. of Tob and Maacah, were 10.08
some of the picked m. of Israel, 10.09
the rest of his m. he put in the 10.10
the Syrians the m. of seven 10.18
he knew there were valiant m. 11.16
And the m. of the city came out and 11.17
"The m. gained an advantage over us, 11.23
"There were two m. in a certain 12.01
all the young m. the king's sons, 13.32
and fifty m. to run before him. 15.01
the hearts of the m. of Israel. 15.06
two hundred m. from Jerusalem who 15.11
hearts of the m. of Israel have 15.13
with all his m. and all the little 15.22
fruit for the young m. to eat, 16.02
all the mighty m. were on his 16.06
So David and his m. went on the 16.13
the m. of Israel, came to Jerusalem, 16.15
and all the m. of Israel have 16.18
"Let me choose twelve thousand m., 17.01
your father and his m. are mighty m., 17.08
who are with him are valiant m. 17.10
him and all the m. with him not 17.12
and all the m. of Israel said, 17.14
the m. came up out of the well, and 17.21
Jordan with all the m. of Israel. 17.24
mustered the m. who were with him, 18.01
And the king said to the m., 18.02
But the m. said, "You shall not go 18.03
And the m. of Israel were defeated 18.07
on that day, twenty thousand m. 18.07
And ten young m., Joab's armor-bearers, 18.15
delivered up the m. who raised 18.28
of all the m. of Judah as one man; 19.14
down with the m. of Judah to meet 19.16
were a thousand m. from Benjamin. 19.17
house were but m. doomed to death 19.28
of singing m. and singing women 19.35
Then all the m. of Israel came to 19.41
brethren the m. of Judah stolen 19.41
and all David's m. with him?" 19.41
m. of Judah answered the m. of Israel, 19.42
m. of Israel answered the m. of Judah, 19.43
words of the m. of Judah were 19.43
than the words of the m. of Israel. 19.43
So all the m. of Israel withdrew 20.02
but the m. of Judah followed their 20.02
"Call the m. of Judah together to 20.04
Pelethites, and all the mighty m.; 20.07
And one of Joab's m. took his stand 20.11
And all the m. who were with Joab 20.15
from the m. of Jabeshgilead, who 21.12
Then David's m. adjured him, "You 21.17
deliver me from m. of violence. 22.49

MEN (cont.)

justly over m. ruling in the fear	2Sa 23.03
But godless m. are all like thorns	23.06
of the mighty m. whom David had:	23.08
three mighty m. was Eleazar the	23.09
and the m. of Israel withdrew.	23.09
and the m. returned after him only	23.10
and the m. fled from the Philistines	23.11
of the thirty chief m. went down,	23.13
three mighty m. broke through the	23.16
blood of the m. who went at the	23.17
things did the three mighty m.	23.17
three hundred m. and slew them,	23.18
a name beside the three mighty m.	23.22
thousand valiant m. who drew the	24.09
and the m. of Judah were five	24.09
to Beersheba seventy thousand m.	24.15
and fifty m. to run before him.	1Ki 1.05
David's mighty m. were not with	1.08
or the mighty m. or Solomon his	1.10
the sword two m. more righteous	2.32
For he was wiser than all other m.,	4.31
And m. came from all peoples to	4.34
levy numbered thirty thousand m.	5.13
builders and the m. of Gebal did	5.18
And all the m. of Israel assembled	8.02
hearts of all the children of m.);	8.39
and took m. with them from Paran	11.18
And he gathered m. about him and	11.24
took counsel with the old m.,	12.06
counsel which the old m. gave him,	12.08
with the young m. who had grown up	12.08
And the young m. who had grown up	12.10
which the old m. had given him,	12.13
to the counsel of the young m.,	12.14
And behold, m. passed by, and saw the	13.25
I hid a hundred m. of the LORD's	18.13
are four hundred and fifty m.	18.22
in the booths, he said to his m.,	20.12
"M. are coming out from Samaria."	20.17
twenty-seven thousand m. that were left.	20.30
Now the m. were watching for an	20.33
And the m. of his city, the elders	21.11
together, about four hundred m.,	22.06
captain of fifty m. with his fifty.	2Ki 1.09
captain of fifty m. with his fifty.	1.11
of fifty m. with their fifties;	1.14
Fifty m. of the sons of the prophets	2.07
with your servants fifty strong m.;	2.16
They sent therefore fifty m.;	2.17
Now the m. of the city said to	2.19
And they poured out for the m. to eat.	4.40
pot, and said, "Pour out for the m.,	4.41
"Give to the m., that they may eat."	4.42
I to set this before a hundred m.?"	4.43
he repeated, "Give them to the m.,	4.43
two young m. of the sons of the	5.22
and he sent the m. away,	5.24
"O LORD, open the eyes of these m.,	6.20
Now there were four m. who were	7.03
"Let some m. take five of the	7.13
So they took two mounted m.,	7.14
slay their young m. with the sword,	8.12
were with the great m. of the city,	10.06
all his great m., and his familiar	10.11
had stationed eighty m. outside,	10.24
brought his m. who were to go off	11.09
from the m. into whose hand they	12.15
that is, from all the wealthy m.,	15.20
him with fifty m. of the Gileadites,	15.25
and drove the m. of Judah from	16.06
the m. of Babylon made Succothbenoth,	17.30
the m. of Cuth made Nergal, the men	17.30
the m. of Hamath made Ashima,	17.30
and not to the m. sitting on the	18.27
and when m. arose early in the	19.35
said to him, "What did these m. say?	20.14
him all the m. of Judah and all	23.02
their places with the bones of m.	23.14
And the m. of the city told him,	23.17
burned the bones of m. upon them.	23.20
and all the mighty m. of valor,	24.14
and the chief m. of the land, he	24.15
to Babylon all the m. of valor,	24.16
with all the m. of war fled by	25.04
been in command of the m. of war,	25.19
and five m. of the king's council	25.19
and sixty m. of the people of the	25.19
and their m. heard that the king	25.23
came with their m. to Gedaliah at	25.23
Gedaliah swore to them and their m.,	25.24
came with ten m., and attacked and	25.25
Irnahash. These are the m. of Recah.	1Ch 4.12
and the m. of Cozeba, and Joash, and	4.22
multiply like the m. of Judah.	4.27
five hundred m. of the Simeonites,	4.42
half-tribe of Manasseh had valiant m.,	5.18
and a hundred thousand m. alive.	5.21
famous m., heads of their fathers'	5.24
These are the m. whom David put in	6.31
These are the m. who served and	6.33
Isshiah, five, all of them chief m.;	7.03
whom the m. of Gath who were born	7.21
All of these were m. of Asher,	7.40
in war, was twenty-six thousand m.	7.40
to their generations, chief m.	8.28
of Ulam were m. who were mighty	8.40
very able m. for the work of the	9.13
and the m. of Israel fled before	10.01
And when all the m. of Israel who	10.07
all the valiant m. arose, and took	10.12
the chiefs of David's mighty m.,	11.10
is an account of David's mighty m.:	11.11
three mighty m. was Eleazar the	11.12
and the m. fled from the Philistines	11.13
thirty chief m. went down to the	11.15
three mighty m. broke through the	11.18
I drink the lifeblood of these m.?	11.19
things did the three mighty m.	11.19
three hundred m. and slew them,	11.20
a name beside the three mighty m.	11.24
The mighty m. of the armies were	11.26
Now these are the m. who came to	12.01
the mighty m. who helped him in	12.01
These are the m. who crossed the	12.15
And some of the m. of Benjamin and	12.16
Some of the m. of Manasseh deserted	12.19
to Ziklag these m. of Manasseh	12.20
they were all mighty m. of valor,	12.21
For from day to day m. kept coming	12.22
The m. of Judah bearing shield and	12.24
mighty m. of valor for war, seven	12.25
mighty m. of valor, famous men in	12.30
famous m. in their fathers' houses.	12.30
Of Issachar m. who had understanding	12.32
thousand m. armed with shield and	12.34
six hundred m. equipped for battle	12.35
twenty thousand m. armed with all	12.37
All these, m. of war, arrayed in	12.38
both m. and women, to each a loaf of	16.03
and violent m. shall waste them	17.09
twenty-two thousand m. of the Syrians.	18.05
When David was told concerning the m.,	19.05
for the m. were greatly ashamed.	19.05
and all the army of the mighty m.	19.08
some of the picked m. of Israel,	19.10
the rest of his m. he put in the	19.11
the Syrians the m. of seven	19.18
thousand m. who drew the sword, and	21.05
fell seventy thousand m. of Israel.	21.14
total was thirty-eight thousand m.	23.03
Since more chief m. were found	24.04
for they were m. of great ability.	26.06
whose brethren were able m.,	26.07

MEN (cont.)

able m. qualified for the service; 1Ch 26.08
and brethren, able m., eighteen. 26.09
corresponding to their chief m., 26.12
seven hundred m. of ability, 26.30
was made and m. of great ability 26.31
seven hundred m. of ability, 26.32
the mighty m., and all the seasoned 28.01
All the leaders and the mighty m., 29.24
thousand m. to bear burdens and 2Ch 2.02
And all the m. of Israel assembled 5.03
the hearts of the children of m.); 6.30
took counsel with the old m., 10.06
counsel which the old m. gave him, 10.08
with the young m. who had grown up 10.08
And the young m. who had grown up 10.10
forsaking the counsel of the old m., 10.13
to the counsel of the young m., 10.14
an army of valiant m. of war, 13.03
four hundred thousand picked m.; 13.03
Then the m. of Judah raised the 13.15
And when the m. of Judah shouted, 13.15
The m. of Israel fled before Judah, 13.16
five hundred thousand picked m. 13.17
Thus the m. of Israel were subdued 13.18
and the m. of Judah prevailed, 13.18
eighty thousand m. from Benjamin, 14.08
all these were mighty m. of valor. 14.08
of a million m. and three hundred 14.09
The m. of Judah carried away very 14.13
mighty m. of valor, in Jerusalem. 17.13
thousand mighty m. of valor, 17.14
thousand mighty m. of valor. 17.16
thousand m. armed with bow and 17.17
four hundred m., and said to them, 18.05
Some m. came and told Jehoshaphat, 20.02
the m. of Ammon and Moab and Mount 20.10
Meanwhile all the m. of Judah stood 20.13
an ambush against the m. of Ammon, 20.22
For the m. of Ammon and Moab rose 20.23
for the band of m. that came with 22.01
They each brought his m., who were 23.08
the Syrians had come with few m., 24.24
Then Amaziah assembled the m. of Judah, 25.05
three hundred thousand picked m., 25.05
thousand mighty m. of valor from 25.06
and smote ten thousand m. of Seir. 25.11
The m. of Judah captured another 25.12
But the m. of the army whom Amaziah 25.13
brought the gods of the m. of Seir, 25.14
of mighty m. of valor was two 26.12
engines, invented by skilful m., 26.15
of the LORD who were m. of valor; 26.17
all of them m. of valor, because 28.06
The m. of Israel took captive two 28.08
Certain chiefs also of the m. of Ephraim, 28.12
So the armed m. left the captives 28.14
And the m. who have been mentioned 28.15
Only a few m. of Asher, of Manasseh, 30.11
there were m. in the several cities 31.19
and his mighty m. to stop the 32.03
And the m. did the work faithfully. 34.12
with all the m. of Judah and the 34.30
all the singing m. and singing 35.25
their young m. with the sword in 36.17
assisted by the m. of his place Ez 1.04
number of the m. of the people of 2.02
The m. of Netophah, fifty-six. 2.22
The m. of Anathoth, one hundred and 2.23
The m. of Michmas, one hundred and 2.27
The m. of Bethel and Ai, two hundred 2.28
old m. who had seen the first house, 3.12
the m. of Erech, the Babylonians, the 4.09
the m. of Susa, that is, the Elamites, 4.09
the m. of the province Beyond the 4.11
that these m. be made to cease, and 4.21
names of the m. who are building 5.04
the names of the m. at their head. 5.10
paid to these m. in full and 6.08
gathered leading m. from Israel to 7.28
registered one hundred and fifty m. 8.03
and with him two hundred m. 8.04
and with him three hundred m. 8.05
of Jonathan, and with him fifty m. 8.06
Athaliah, and with him seventy m. 8.07
of Michael, and with him eighty m. 8.08
him two hundred and eighteen m. 8.09
with him a hundred and sixty m. 8.10
and with him twenty-eight m. 8.11
and with him a hundred and ten m. 8.12
Shemaiah, and with them sixty m. 8.13
Zakkur, and with them seventy m. 8.14
leading m., and for Joiarib and 8.16
Elnathan, who were m. of insight, 8.16
and chief m. has been foremost. 9.02
God, a very great assembly of m., 10.01
Then all the m. of Judah and 10.09
Ezra the priest selected m., 10.16
end of all the m. who had married 10.17
came with certain m. out of Judah; Neh 1.02
the night, I and a few m. with me; 2.12
And next to him the m. of Jericho 3.02
the m. of Gibeon and of Mizpah, who 3.07
and to the house of the mighty m. 3.16
the m. of the Plain, repaired. 3.22
servants nor the m. of the guard 4.23
for other m. have our fields and 5.05
at my table a hundred and fifty m., 5.17
number of the m. of the people of 7.07
The m. of Bethlehem and Netophah, a 7.26
The m. of Anathoth, a hundred and 7.27
The m. of Bethazmaveth, forty-two. 7.28
The m. of Kiriathjearim, Chephirah, 7.29
The m. of Ramah and Geba, six 7.30
The m. of Michmas, a hundred and 7.31
The m. of Bethel and Ai, a hundred 7.32
The m. of the other Nebo, fifty-two. 7.33
both m. and women and all who could 8.02
presence of the m. and the women 8.03
blessed all the m. who willingly 11.02
hundred and sixty-eight valiant m. 11.06
mighty m. of valor, a hundred and 11.14
On that day m. were appointed over 12.44
I saw in Judah m. treading wine 13.15
M. of Tyre also, who lived in the 13.16
to the wise m. who knew the times— Est 1.13
the m. next to him being Carshena, 1.14
the m. were both hanged on the 2.23
Then his wise m. and his wife 6.13
m. and women, I would have held my 7.04
and destroyed five hundred m., 9.06
five hundred m. and also the ten 9.12
they slew three hundred m. in Susa; 9.15
when deep sleep falls on m., Job 4.13
I do to thee, thou watcher of m.? 7.20
Should your babble silence m., 11.03
For he knows worthless m.; when he sees 11.11
(what wise m. have told, and their 15.18
M. have gaped at me with their 16.10
and I am one before whom m. spit. 17.06
Upright m. are appalled at this, and 17.08
all m. follow after him, and those 21.33
old way which wicked m. have trod? 22.15
M. remove landmarks; they seize 24.02
M. put an end to darkness, and 28.03
a valley away from there m. live; 28.04
travelers, they hang afar from m., 28.04
the young m. saw me and withdrew, 29.08
"M. listened to me, and waited, and 29.21
m. who are younger than I, whose 30.01
of their hands, m. whose vigor is gone? 30.02
They are driven out from among m.; 30.05
if the m. of my tent have not said, 31.31
concealed my transgressions from m., 31.33

MEN (cont.)

So these three m. ceased to answer Job 32.01
in the mouth of these three m., 32.05
when deep sleep falls upon m., 33.15
then he opens the ears of m., 33.16
He recounts to m. his salvation, 33.26
and he sings before m., and says: 33.27
you wise m., and give ear to me, you 34.02
evildoers and walks with wicked m.? 34.08
you m. of understanding, far be it 34.10
wickedness in the sight of m., 34.26
M. of understanding will say to me, 34.34
because he answers like wicked m. 34.36
because of the pride of evil m. 35.12
his work, of which m. have sung. 36.24
All m. have looked on it; man holds 36.25
that all m. may know his work. 37.07
"And now m. cannot look on the 37.21
Therefore m. fear him; he does not 37.24
O m., how long shall my honor Ps 4.02
bloodthirsty and deceitful m. 5.06
nations know that they are but m.! 9.20
eyelids test, the children of m. 11.04
vanished from among the sons of m. 12.01
is exalted among the sons of m. 12.08
heaven upon the children of m., 14.02
With regard to the works of m., 17.04
from m. by thy hand, O Lord, from 17.14
from m. whose portion in life is of 17.14
deliver me from m. of violence. 18.48
children from among the sons of m. 21.10
scorned by m., and despised by the 22.06
m. shall tell of the Lord to the 22.30
I do not sit with false m., 26.04
nor my life with bloodthirsty m., 26.09
m. in whose hands are evil devices, 26.10
in the sight of the sons of m.! 31.19
hidest them from the plots of m.; 31.20
heaven, he sees all the sons of m.; 33.13
The children of m. take refuge in 36.07
while m. say to me continually, 42.03
deceitful and unjust m. deliver me! 43.01
You are the fairest of the sons of m.; 45.02
m. who trust in their wealth and 49.06
the sons of m. to see if there are 53.02
For insolent m. have risen against 54.03
me, ruthless m. seek my life; 54.03
m. of blood and treachery shall not 55.23
for m. trample upon me; all day long 56.01
greedily devour the sons of m.; 57.04
you judge the sons of m. uprightly? 58.01
M. will say, "Surely there is a 58.11
and save me from bloodthirsty m. 59.02
fierce m. band themselves against 59.03
that m. may know that God rules 59.13
M. of low estate are but a breath, 62.09
m. of high estate are a delusion; 62.09
Then all m. will fear; they tell 64.09
is terrible in his deeds among m. 66.05
m. passed through the river on foot 66.06
thou didst let m. ride over our 66.12
and receiving gifts among m., 68.18
and may m. blossom forth from the 72.16
May m. bless themselves by him, all 72.17
are not in trouble as other m. are; 73.05
are not stricken like other m. 73.05
all the m. of war were unable to 76.05
Surely the wrath of m. shall paise 76.10
laid low the picked m. of Israel. 78.31
the tent where he dwelt among m., 78.60
Fire devoured their young m., 78.63
nevertheless, you shall die like m., 82.07
Blessed are the m. whose strength 84.05
insolent m. have risen up against 86.14
a band of ruthless m. seek my life, 86.14
hast created all the sons of m.! 89.47
"Turn back, O children of m.!" 90.03
Thou dost sweep m. away; they are like 90.05
chastise? He who teaches m. knowledge, 94.10
that m. may declare in Zion the 102.21
When m. in the camp were jealous of 106.16
wonderful works to the sons of m.! 107.08
wonderful works to the sons of m.! 107.15
wonderful works to the sons of m.! 107.21
and staggered like drunken m., 107.27
wonderful works to the sons of m.! 107.31
let m. consider the steadfast love 107.43
he has given to the sons of m. 115.16
"M. are all a vain hope." 116.11
Godless m. utterly deride me, but I 119.51
Godless m. have dug pitfalls for me, 119.85
m. who do not conform to thy law. 119.85
I hate double-minded m., but I love 119.113
because m. do not keep thy law. 119.136
on our side, when m. rose up against us, 124.02
and that m. of blood would depart 139.19
m. who maliciously defy thee, who 139.20
Deliver me, O Lord, from evil m.; 140.01
preserve me from violent m., 140.01
preserve me from violent m., who have 140.04
Arrogant m. have hidden a trap for 140.05
in company with m. who work 141.04
M. shall proclaim the might of thy 145.06
to the sons of m. thy mighty deeds, 145.12
Young m. and maidens together, old m. and 148.12
That m. may know wisdom and instruction, Pro 1.02
but these m. lie in wait for their 1.18
of evil, from m. of perverted speech, 2.12
m. whose paths are crooked, and who 2.15
the way of good m. and keep to the 2.20
and m. of integrity will remain in 2.21
do not walk in the way of evil m. 4.14
Do not m. despise a thief if he 6.30
"To you, O m., I call, and my cry is 8.04
and my cry is to the sons of m. 8.04
O foolish m., pay attention. 8.05
and delighting in the sons of m. 8.31
Wise m. lay up knowledge, but the 10.14
honor, and violent m. get riches. 11.16
M. of perverse mind are an abomination 11.20
mouth of the upright delivers m. 12.06
messenger plunges m. into trouble, 13.17
walks with wise m. becomes wise, 13.20
how much more the hearts of m.! 15.11
not good; to flog noble m. is wrong. 17.26
him and brings him before great m. 18.16
The glory of young m. is their 20.29
beauty of old m. is their gray 20.29
will not stand before obscure m. 22.29
increases the faithless among m. 23.28
Be not envious of evil m., nor desire 24.01
scoffer is an abomination to m. 24.09
which the m. of Hezekiah king of 25.01
eyes than seven m. who can answer 26.16
but with m. of understanding and 28.02
Evil m. do not understand justice, 28.05
wicked rise, m. hide themselves. 28.12
m. hide themselves, but when they 28.28
but wise m. turn away wrath. 29.08
Bloodthirsty m. hate one who is 29.10
the earth, the needy from among m. 30.14
to the sons of m. to be busy with. Ecc 1.13
for the sons of m. to do under 2.03
both m. and women, and many concubines, 2.08
to the sons of m. to be busy with. 3.10
in order that m. should fear before 3.14
to the sons of m. that God is 3.18
of the sons of m. and the fate of 3.19
sun, and it lies heavy upon m.: 6.01
for this is the end of all m., 7.02
heed to all the things that m. say, 7.21
of the sons of m. is fully set to 8.11
are righteous m. to whom it 8.14
are wicked m. to whom it happens 8.14

MEN (cont.)

the hearts of m. are full of evil, Ecc 9.03
nor favor to the m. of skill; 9.11
so the sons of m. are snared at an 9.12
a little city with few m. in it; 9.14
your king is the son of free m., 10.17
tremble, and the strong m. are bent, 12.03
so is my beloved among young m. Sol 2.03
mighty m. of the mighty m. of Israel, 3.07
and m. are brought low—forgive Is 2.09
the pride of m. shall be humbled; 2.11
the pride of m. shall be brought 2.17
And m. shall enter the caves of the 2.19
In that day m. will cast forth 2.20
Your m. shall fall by the sword and 3.25
sword and your mighty m. in battle. 3.25
of Jerusalem and m. of Judah, 5.03
and the m. of Judah are his pleasant 5.07
their honored m. are dying of 5.13
and m. are brought low, and the eyes 5.15
and valiant m. in mixing strong 5.22
inhabitant, and houses without m., 6.11
and the LORD removes m. far away, 6.12
it too little for you to weary m., 7.13
With bow and arrows m. will come 7.24
as m. rejoice when they divide the 9.03
not rejoice over their young m., 9.17
and as m. gather eggs that have 10.14
channels that m. may cross dryshod. 11.15
my mighty m. to execute my anger, 13.03
I will make m. more rare than fine 13.12
Their bows will slaughter the young m.; 13.18
the armed m. of Moab cry aloud; 15.04
In that day m. will regard their 17.07
Where then are your wise m.? 19.12
of the mighty m. of the sons of 21.17
reared young m. nor brought up 23.04
are scorched, and few m. are left. 24.06
Nay, but by m. of strange lips and 28.11
When m. give it to one who can read, 29.11
commandment of m. learned by rote; 29.13
of their wise m. shall perish, 29.14
their discerning m. shall be hid. 29.14
the poor among m. shall exult in 29.19
The Egyptians are m., and not God; 31.03
and his young m. shall be put to 31.08
as locusts leap, m. leap upon it. 33.04
and not to the m. sitting on the 36.12
and when m. arose early in the 37.36
O Lord, by these things m. live, 38.16
said to him, "What did these m. say? 39.03
and young m. shall fall exhausted; 40.30
you worm Jacob, you m. of Israel! 41.14
that m. may see and know, may 41.20
I give m. in return for you, peoples 43.04
and the craftsmen are but m.; 44.11
who turns wise m. back, and makes their 44.25
that m. may know, from the rising of 45.06
m. of stature, shall come over to 45.14
fear not the reproach of m., and be not 51.07
beyond that of the sons of m.— 52.14
He was despised and rejected by m.; 53.03
one from whom m. hide their faces 53.03
devout m. are taken away, while no 57.01
m. will not cover themselves with 59.06
in full vigor we are like dead m. 59.10
that m. may bring to you the wealth 60.11
m. shall speak of you as the 61.06
bodies of the m. that have rebelled 66.24
Moreover, the m. of Memphis and Jer 2.16
the LORD to the m. of Judah and to 4.03
O m. of Judah and inhabitants of 4.04
open tomb, they are all mighty m. 5.16
For wicked m. are found among my 5.26
They set a trap; they catch m. 5.26
the gatherings of young m., also; 6.11
all you m. of Judah who enter these 7.02

When m. fall, do they not rise again? 8.04
The wise m. shall be put to shame, 8.09
a company of treacherous m. 9.02
and the young m. from the squares. 9.21
dead bodies of m. shall fall like 9.22
M. deck it with silver and gold; 10.04
are all the work of skilled m. 10.09
speak to the m. of Judah and the 11.02
among the m. of Judah and the 11.09
LORD concerning the m. of Anathoth, 11.21
the young m. shall die by the sword 11.22
bring evil upon the m. of Anathoth, 11.23
because m. said, "He will not see 12.04
"If you have raced with m. on foot, 12.05
of young m. a destroyer at noonday 15.08
the m. of Judah and the inhabitants 17.25
say to the m. of Judah and the 18.11
May their m. meet death by pestilence, 18.21
sight of the m. who go with you, 19.10
M. shall bury in Topheth because 19.11
when m. shall no longer say, 'As the 23.07
Jehoiakim sent to Egypt certain m., 26.22
with the m. and animals that are on 27.05
and the young m. and the old shall 31.13
are open to all the ways of m., 32.19
the m. of Judah and the inhabitants 32.32
dead bodies of m. whom I shall 33.05
so m. shall burn spices for you and 34.05
And the m. who transgressed my 34.18
and say to the m. of Judah and the 35.13
of all the m. of Judah who come 36.06
and upon the m. of Judah, all the 36.31
remained of them only wounded m., 37.10
these m. have done evil in all that 38.09
"Take three m. with you from here, 38.10
took the m. with him and went to 38.11
hand of these m. who seek your 38.16
the hand of the m. of whom you are 39.17
and their m. heard that the king 40.07
land, and had committed to him m., 40.07
the Maacathite, they and their m. 40.08
Shaphan, swore to them and their m., 40.09
came with ten m. to Gedaliah the 41.01
and the ten m. with him rose up 41.02
eighty m. arrived from Shechem and 41.05
Nethaniah and the m. with him slew 41.07
But there were ten m. among them 41.08
bodies of the m. whom he had slain 41.09
they took all their m. and went to 41.12
escaped from Johanan with eight m., 41.15
All the m. who set their faces to 42.17
the insolent m. said to Jeremiah, 43.02
the m., the women, the children, the 43.06
in the sight of the m. of Judah, 43.09
Then all the m. who knew that their 44.15
m. and women, all the people who had 44.20
all the m. of Judah who are in the 44.27
m. of Ethiopia and Put who handle 46.09
m. of Lud, skilled in handling the 46.09
M. shall cry out, and every inhabitant 47.02
are heroes and mighty m. of war"? 48.14
of his young m. have gone down to 48.15
for the m. of Kirheres I mourn. 48.31
a flute for the m. of Kirheres; 48.36
the nations despised among m. 49.15
Therefore her young m. shall fall 49.26
and m. shall cry to them: 'Terror on 49.29
Therefore her young m. shall fall 50.30
upon her princes and her wise m.! 50.35
Spare not her young m.; utterly destroy 51.03
Surely I will fill you with m., 51.14
drunk her princes and her wise m., 51.57
neither m. nor beast, and it shall 51.62
and all the m. of war fled and went 52.07
been in command of the m. of war, 52.25
and seven m. of the king's council, 52.25
and sixty m. of the people of the 52.25

MEN (cont.)
all my mighty m. in the midst of Lam 1.15
against me to crush my young m.; 1.15
and my young m. have gone into 1.18
like wounded m. in the streets of 2.12
and my young m. have fallen by the 2.21
afflict or grieve the sons of m. 3.33
m. cried at them; "Away! Away! 4.15
m. said among the nations, "They 4.15
M. dogged our steps so that we 4.18
Young m. are compelled to grind at 5.13
The old m. have quit the city gate, 5.14
gate, the young m. their music. 5.14
appearance: they had the form of m., Eze 1.05
stood seventy m. of the elders of 8.11
altar, were about twenty-five m., 8.16
And lo, six m. came from the direction 9.02
foreheads of the m. who sigh and 9.04
slay old m. outright, young m. and 9.06
gateway there were twenty-five m.; 11.01
these are the m. who devise iniquity 11.02
as m. do who must go into exile. 12.04
these m. have taken their idols 14.03
even if these three m., Noah, Daniel, 14.14
even if these three m. were in it, 14.16
though these three m. were in it, 14.18
Do m. take a peg from it to hang 15.03
and made for yourself images of m., 16.17
M. give gifts to all harlots: 16.33
(The chief m. of the land he had 17.13
to catch prey; he devoured m. 19.03
to catch prey; he devoured m. 19.06
you into the hands of brutal m., 21.31
There are m. in you who slander to 22.09
and m. in you who eat upon the 22.09
m. commit lewdness in your midst. 22.09
In you m. uncover their fathers' 22.10
In you m. take bribes to shed blood 22.12
As m. gather silver and bronze and 22.20
all of them desirable young m., 23.06
the choicest m. of Assyria all of 23.07
in her youth m. had lain with her 23.08
all of them desirable young m. 23.12
she saw m. portrayed upon the wall, 23.14
with them, desirable young m., 23.23
They even sent for m. to come from 23.40
and with m. of the common sort 23.42
Do not m. now commit adultery when 23.43
as m. go in to a harlot. Thus they went 23.44
But righteous m. shall pass judgment 23.45
skilled m. of Zemer were in you, 27.08
and her skilled m. were in you, 27.09
in your army as your m. of war; 27.10
The m. of Arvad and Helech were 27.11
and m. of Gamad were in your towers; 27.11
the persons of m. and vessels of 27.13
The m. of Rhodes traded with you; 27.15
and all your m. of war who are in 27.27
the land into the hand of evil m.; 30.12
The young m. of On and of Pibeseth 30.17
the nether world among mortal m., 31.14
fallen mighty m. of old who went 32.27
of the mighty m. was in the land 32.27
and I will multiply m. upon you, 36.10
I will let m. walk upon you, even my 36.12
Because m. say to you, 'You devour m., 36.13
longer devour m. and no longer 36.14
in that m. said of them, 'These are 36.20
to increase their m. like a flock. 36.37
cities be filled with flocks of m. 36.38
and all the m. that are upon the 38.20
They will set apart m. to pass 39.14
with mighty m. and all kinds of 39.20
all the wise m. of Babylon be Dan 2.12
that the wise m. were to be slain, 2.13
out to slay the wise m. of Babylon; 2.14
the rest of the wise m. of Babylon. 2.18
to destroy the wise m. of Babylon; 2.24
not destroy the wise m. of Babylon; 2.24
"No wise m., enchanters, magicians, 2.27
the sons of m., the beasts of the 2.38
over all the wise m. of Babylon. 2.48
These m., O king, pay no need to you; 3.12
brought these m. before the king. 3.13
certain mighty m. of his army to 3.20
Then these m. were bound in their 3.21
fire slew those m. who took up 3.22
And these three m., Shadrach, Meshach, 3.23
not cast three m. bound into the 3.24
He answered, "But I see four m. loose, 3.25
power over the bodies of those m.; 3.27
all the wise m. of Babylon should 4.06
Most High rules the kingdom of m., 4.17
sets over it the lowliest of m.' 4.17
all the wise m. of my kingdom are 4.18
that you shall be driven from among m., 4.25
Most High rules the kingdom of m., 4.25
and you shall be driven from among m., 4.32
the kingdom of m. and gives it to 4.32
He was driven from among m., 4.33
said to the wise m. of Babylon, 5.07
Then all the king's wise m. came in, 5.08
Now the wise m., the enchanters, 5.15
he was driven from among m., 5.21
High God rules the kingdom of m., 5.21
Then these m. said, "We shall not 6.05
Then these m. came by agreement and 6.11
Then these m. came by agreement to 6.15
and those m. who had accused Daniel 6.24
royal dominion m. tremble and fear 6.26
destroy mighty m. and the people 8.24
to the m. of Judah, to the inhabitants 9.07
for the m. who were with me did not 10.07
of the sons of m. touched my lips; 10.16
and the m. of violence among your 11.14
for the m. themselves go aside with Hos 4.14
When Ephraim spoke, m. trembled; 13.01
these, they say. M. kiss calves! 13.02
you aged m., give ear, all inhabitants Joe 1.02
gladness fails from the sons of m. 1.12
your old m. shall dream dreams, and 2.28
and your young m. shall see 2.28
Prepare war, stir up the mighty m. 3.09
Let all the m. of war draw near, let 3.09
of your young m. for Nazirites. Amo 2.11
slew your young m. with the sword; 4.10
the notable m. of the first of the 6.01
And if ten m. remain in one house, 6.09
and the young m. shall faint for 8.13
destroy the wise m. out of Edom, Ob 1.08
And your mighty m. shall be dismayed, 1.09
Then the m. were exceedingly afraid, Jon 1.10
For the m. knew that he was 1.10
Nevertheless the m. rowed hard to 1.13
Then the m. feared the LORD exceedingly, 1.16
pasture, a noisy multitude of m. Mic 2.12
shepherds and eight princes of m.; 5.05
tarry not for m. nor wait for the sons of m. 5.07
Your rich m. are full of violence; 6.12
and there is none upright among m.; 7.02
enemies are the m. of his own 7.06
The shield of his mighty m. is red, Nah 2.03
or her honored m. lots were cast, 3.10
all her great m. were bound in 3.10
guilty m., whose own might is their Hab 1.11
why dost thou look on faithless m., 1.13
For thou makest m. like the fish of 1.14
the blood of m. and violence to 2.08
the blood of m. and violence to 2.17
will punish the m. who are thickening Zep 1.12
I will bring distress on m., 1.17
Her prophets are wanton, faithless m.; 3.04
upon m. and cattle, and upon all Hag 1.11
multitude of m. and cattle in it. Zec 2.04

MEN (cont.)

for they are m. of good omen: behold, Zec 3.08
and Regemmelech and their m., 7.02
Old m. and old women shall again 8.04
those days ten m. from the nations 8.23
shall make the young m. flourish, 9.17
who gives m. showers of rain, to 10.01
shall be like mighty m. in battle, 10.05
I will cause m. to fall each into 11.06
and m. should seek instruction from Mal 2.07
wise m. from the East came to Mt 2.01
the wise m. secretly and ascertained 2.07
he had been tricked by the wise m., 2.16
had ascertained from the wise m. 2.16
and I will make you fishers of m." 4.19
"Blessed are you when m. revile you 5.11
for so m. persecuted the prophets 5.12
out and trodden under foot by m. 5.13
Nor do m. light a lamp and put it 5.15
Let your light so shine before m., 5.16
commandments and teaches m. so, 5.19
that it was said to the m. of old, 5.21
that it was said to the m. of old, 5.33
piety before m. in order to be 6.01
that they may be praised by m. 6.02
that they may be seen by m. 6.05
For if you forgive m. their trespasses, 6.14
do not forgive m. their trespasses, 6.15
their fasting may be seen by m. 6.16
not be seen by m. but by your 6.18
clothe you, O m. of little faith? 6.30
you wish that m. would do to you, 7.12
there m. will weep and gnash their 8.12
O m. of little faith?" Then he rose 8.26
And the m. marveled, saying, "What 8.27
who had given such authority to m. 9.08
two blind m. followed him, crying 9.27
house, the blind m. came to him; 9.28
Beware of m.; for they will 10.17
one who acknowledges me before m., 10.32
but whoever denies me before m., 10.33
and m. of violence take it by force. 11.12
and blasphemy will be forgiven m., 12.31
day of judgment m. will render 12.36
The m. of Nineveh will arise at the 12.41
and righteous m. longed to see 13.17
but while m. were sleeping, his 13.25
there m. will weep and gnash their 13.42
m. drew it ashore and sat down and 13.48
there m. will weep and gnash their 13.50
ate were about five thousand m., 14.21
And when the m. of that place 14.35
as doctrines the precepts of m.'" 15.09
Those who ate were four thousand m., 15.38
"O m. of little faith, why do you 16.08
"Who do m. say that the Son of man 16.13
not on the side of God, but of m." 16.23
be delivered into the hands of m., 17.22
"Not all m. can receive this 19.11
who have been made eunuchs by m., 19.12
"With m. this is impossible, but 19.26
and their great m. exercise 20.25
two blind m. sitting by the roadside, 20.30
From heaven or from m.?" And they 21.25
'From m.,' we are afraid of the 21.26
there m. will weep and gnash their 22.13
do not regard the position of m. 22.16
all their deeds to be seen by m.; 23.05
and being called rabbi by m. 23.07
the kingdom of heaven against m.; 23.13
You blind m.! For which is 23.19
outwardly appear righteous to m., 23.28
prophets and wise m. and scribes, 23.34
Then two m. will be in the field; 24.40
there m. will weep and gnash their 24.51
there m. will weep and gnash their 25.30
it that these m. testify against 26.62

trembled and became like dead m. 28.04
will make you become fishers of m." Mk 1.17
him a paralytic carried by four m. 2.03
will be forgiven the sons of m., 3.28
done for him; and all m. marveled. 5.20
and preached that m. should repent. 6.12
and the leading m. of Galilee. 6.21
the loaves were five thousand m. 6.44
as doctrines the precepts of m.' 7.07
and hold fast the tradition of m." 7.08
one feed these m. with bread here 8.04
And he looked up and said, "I see m.; 8.24
disciples, "Who do m. say that I am?" 8.27
not on the side of God, but of m." 8.33
be delivered into the hands of m., 9.31
"With m. it is impossible, but not 10.27
and their great m. exercise authority 10.42
of John from heaven or from m.? 11.30
But shall we say, 'From m.'?" 11.32
do not regard the position of m., 12.14
it that these m. testify against 14.60
to take away my reproach among m." Lk 1.25
peace among m. with whom he is 2.14
and all m. questioned in their 3.15
henceforth you will be catching m." 5.10
And behold, m. were bringing on a 5.18
"Blessed are you when m. hate you, 6.22
when all m. speak well of you, for 6.26
you wish that m. would do to you, 6.31
And when the m. had come to him, 7.20
I compare the m. of this generation, 7.31
For there were about five thousand m. 9.14
two m. talked with him, Moses and 9.30
and the two m. who stood with him. 9.32
And as the m. were parting from him, 9.33
be delivered into the hands of m." 9.44
became a sign to the m. of Nineveh, 11.30
with the m. of this generation and 11.31
The m. of Nineveh will arise at the 11.32
and m. walk over them without 11.44
for you load m. with burdens hard 11.46
one who acknowledges me before m., 12.08
me before m. will be denied before 12.09
clothe you, O m. of little faith? 12.28
and be like m. who are waiting for 12.36
of him to whom m. commit much they 12.48
And m. will come from east and west, 13.29
none of those m. who were invited 14.24
m. throw it away. He who has 14.35
who justify yourselves before m., 16.15
exalted among m. is an abomination 16.15
there will be two m. in one bed; 17.34
"Two m. will be in the field; * 17.36
"Two m. went up into the temple to 18.10
thee that I am not like other m., 18.11
impossible with m. is possible 18.27
the principal m. of the people 19.47
of John from heaven or from m.?" 20.04
'From m.,' all the people will 20.06
m. fainting with fear and with 21.26
Now the m. who were holding Jesus 22.63
two m. stood by them in dazzling 24.04
the m. said to them, "Why do you 24.05
into the hands of sinful m., 24.07
"O foolish m., and slow of heart to 24.25
and the life was the light of m. Jn 1.04
and when m. have drunk freely, then 2.10
because he knew all m. and needed 2.25
and m. loved darkness rather than 3.19
the place where m. ought to 4.20
I do not receive glory from m. 5.41
so the m. sat down, in number about 6.10
the testimony of two m. is true; 8.17
earth, will draw all m. to myself." 12.32
the praise of m. more than the 12.43
By this all m. will know that you 13.35
thy name to the m. whom thou 17.06

MEN (cont.)
if you seek me, let these m. go." Jn 18.08
two m. stood by them in white robes, Ac 1.10
and said, "M. of Galilee, why do you 1.11
So one of the m. who have accompanied 1.21
one of these m. must become with us 1.22
who knowest the hearts of all m., 1.24
devout m. from every nation under 2.05
"M. of Judea and all who dwell in 2.14
For these m. are not drunk, as you 2.15
and your young m. shall see 2.17
and your old m. shall dream dreams; 2.17
"M. of Israel, hear these words: 2.22
killed by the hands of lawless m. 2.23
"M. of Israel, why do you wonder at 3.12
number of the m. came to about 4.04
given among m. by which we must be 4.12
uneducated, common m., they wondered; 4.13
saying, "What shall we do with these m.? 4.16
for all m. praised God for what had 4.21
You have not lied to m. but to God." 5.04
The young m. rose and wrapped him 5.06
When the young m. came in they 5.10
multitudes both of m. and women, 5.14
"The m. whom you put in prison are 5.25
"We must obey God rather than m. 5.29
and ordered the m. to be put 5.34
"M. of Israel, take care what you do 5.35
care what you do with these m. 5.35
to be somebody, and a number of m., 5.36
away from these m. and let them 5.38
undertaking is of m., it will fail; 5.38
among you seven m. of good repute, 6.03
Then they secretly instigated m., 6.11
'M., you are brethren, why do you 7.26
Devout m. buried Stephen, and made 8.02
he dragged off m. and women and 8.03
were baptized, both m. and women. 8.12
m. or women, he might bring them 9.02
The m. who were traveling with him 9.07
sent two m. to him entreating him, 9.38
And now send m. to Joppa, and bring 10.05
the m. that were sent by Cornelius, 10.17
three m. are looking for you. 10.19
Peter went down to the m. and said, 10.21
uncircumcised m. and eat with them?" 11.03
moment three m. arrived at the 11.11
m. of Cyprus and Cyrene, who on 11.20
"M. of Israel, and you that fear God, 13.16
and the leading m. of the city, 13.50
down to us in the likeness of m.!" 14.11
"M., why are you doing this? 14.15
We also are m., of like nature with 14.15
But some m. came down from Judea 15.01
that the rest of m. may seek the 15.17
to choose m. from among them and 15.22
leading m. among the brethren, 15.22
to choose m. and send them to you 15.25
m. who have risked their lives for 15.26
"These m. are servants of the Most 16.17
"These m. are Jews and they are 16.20
"M., what must I do to be saved?" 16.30
police, saying, "Let those m. go." 16.35
m. who are Roman citizens, and have 16.37
"These m. who have turned the world 17.06
of high standing as well as m. 17.12
M. of Athens, I perceive that in 17.22
gives to all m. life and breath 17.25
every nation of m. to live on all 17.26
he commands all m. everywhere to 17.30
assurance to all m. by raising him 17.31
But some m. joined him and believed, 17.34
is persuading m. to worship God 18.13
"M., you know that from this 19.25
"M. of Ephesus, what man is there 19.35
brought these m. here who are 19.37
will arise m. speaking perverse 20.30
We have four m. who are under a vow 21.23
take these m. and purify yourself 21.24
Then Paul took the m., and the next 21.26
crying out, "M. of Israel, help! 21.28
who is teaching m. everywhere 21.28
four thousand m. of the Assassins 21.38
to prison both m. and women, 22.04
for him to all m. of what you have 22.15
forty of their m. lie in ambush 23.21
conscience toward God and toward m. 24.16
Or else let these m. themselves say 24.20
the principal m. of the Jews 25.02
"let the m. of authority among you 25.05
and the prominent m. of the city. 25.23
"M., you should have listened to me, 27.21
So take heart, m., for I have faith 27.25
"Unless these m. stay in the ship, 27.31
wickedness of m. who by their Rom 1.18
and the m. likewise gave up natural 1.27
m. committing shameless acts with m. 1.27
the secrets of m. by Christ Jesus. 2.16
praise is not from m. but from God. 2.29
I have already charged that all m., 3.09
spread to all m. because all m. sinned— 5.12
led to condemnation for all m., 5.18
to acquittal and life for all m. 5.18
to God as m. who have been brought 6.13
the hearts of m. knows what is the 8.27
a stone that will make m. stumble, 9.33
But how are m. to call upon him in 10.14
And how can m. preach unless they 10.15
seven thousand m. who have not 11.04
consigned all m. to disobedience, 11.32
acceptable to God and approved by m. 14.18
they are m. of note among the 16.07
foolishness of God is wiser than m., 1Co 1.25
weakness of God is stronger than m. 1.25
the wisdom of m. but in the power 2.05
not address you as spiritual m., 3.01
but as m. of the flesh, as babes in 3.01
and behaving like ordinary m.? 3.03
to Apollos," are you not merely m.? 3.04
So let no one boast of m. 3.21
like m. sentenced to death; 4.09
to the world, to angels and to m. 4.09
not to associate with immoral m.; 5.09
do not become slaves of m. 7.23
For though I am free from all m., 9.19
I have become all things to all m., 9.22
I speak as to sensible m.; 10.15
to please all m. in everything I 10.33
in the tongues of m. and of angels, 13.01
tongue speaks not to m. but to God; 14.02
speaks to m. for their upbuilding 14.03
"By m. of strange tongues and by 14.21
we are of all m. most to be pitied. 15.19
but there is one kind for m., 15.39
subject to such m. and to every 16.16
Give recognition to such m. 16.18
but as m. of sincerity, as commissioned 2Co 2.17
to be known and read by all m.; 3.02
fear of the Lord, we persuade m.; 5.11
sight but also in the sight of m. 8.21
our boasting about you to these m. 8.24
For such m. are false apostles, 11.13
not from m. nor through man, but Gal 1.01
seeking the favor of m., or of God? 1.10
Or am I trying to please m.? 1.10
If I were still pleasing m., 1.10
For before certain m. came from 2.12
see that it is m. of faith who are 3.07
those who are m. of faith are 3.09
opportunity, let us do good to all m., 6.10
to the sons of m. in other generations Eph 3.05
and to make all m. see what is the 3.09
captives, and he gave gifts to m. 4.08
of doctrine, by the cunning of m., 4.14

MEN (cont.)
not as unwise m. but as wise, Eph 5.15
will as to the Lord and not to m., 6.07
being born in the likeness of m. Php 2.07
with all joy; and honor such m., 2.29
Let all m. know your forbearance. 4.05
as serving the Lord and not m., Col 3.23
are the only m. of the circumcision 4.11
what kind of m. we proved to be 1Th 1.05
not to please m., but to please God 2.04
nor did we seek glory from m., 2.06
as the word of m. but as what it 2.13
displease God and oppose all m. 2.15
love to one another and to all m., 3.12
delivered from wicked and evil m.; 2Th 3.02
thanksgivings be made for all m., 1Ti 2.01
who desires all m. to be saved and 2.04
is one mediator between God and m., 2.05
in every place the m. should pray, 2.08
teach or to have authority over m.; 2.12
God, who is the Savior of all m., 4.10
treat younger m. like brothers, 5.01
The sins of some m. are conspicuous, 5.24
and wrangling among m. who are 6.05
that plunge m. into ruin and 6.09
to faithful m. who will be able to 2Ti 2.02
For m. will be lovers of self, 3.02
so these m. also oppose the truth, 3.08
m. of corrupt mind and counterfeit 3.08
all, as was that of those two m. 3.09
while evil m. and impostors will go 3.13
m. who are blameless, married only Tit 1.06
For there are many insubordinate m., 1.10
to commands of m. who reject the 1.14
Bid the older m. be temperate, 2.02
the younger m. to control themselves 2.06
for the salvation of all m., 2.11
perfect courtesy toward all m. 3.02
hated by m. and hating one another; 3.03
are excellent and profitable to m. 3.08
from among m. is appointed to act Heb 5.01
on behalf of m. in relation to God, 5.01
M. indeed swear by a greater than 6.16
Here tithes are received by mortal m.; 7.08
law appoints m. in their weakness 7.28
it is appointed for m. to die once, 9.27
For by it the m. of old received 11.02
able to raise m. even from the 11.19
Strive for peace with all m., 12.14
spirits of just m. made perfect, 12.23
as m. who will have to give account 13.17
gives to all m. generously and Jas 1.05
Father, and with it we curse m., 3.09
your hearts, you m. of double mind. 4.08
rejected by m. but in God's sight 1Pe 2.04
and "A stone that will make m. stumble, 2.08
the ignorance of foolish m. 2.15
Live as free m., yet without using 2.16
Honor all m. Love the brotherhood. 2.17
though judged in the flesh like m., 4.06
but m. moved by the Holy Spirit 2Pe 1.21
of the flesh m. who have barely 2.18
and destruction of ungodly m. 3.07
of lawless m. and lose your own 3.17
young m., because you have overcome 1Jn 2.13
young m., because you are strong, 2.14
If we receive the testimony of m., 5.09
m. who will not acknowledge the 2Jn 1.07
So we ought to support such m., 3Jn 1.08
manner these m. in their dreamings Jud 1.08
But these m. revile whatever they 1.10
bear evil m. but have tested those Rev 2.02
didst ransom m. for God from every 5.09
so that m. should slay one another; 6.04
and the great m. and the generals 6.15
and many m. died of the water, 8.11
And in those days m. will seek 9.06
of hurting m. for five months lies 9.10
days and a half m. from the 11.09
M. worshiped the dragon, for he had 13.04
heaven to earth in the sight of m.; 13.13
came upon the m. who bore the mark 16.02
For m. have shed the blood of 16.06
was allowed to scorch m. with fire; 16.08
m. were scorched by the fierce heat, 16.09
m. gnawed their tongues in anguish 16.10
been since m. were on the earth, so 16.18
dropped on m. from heaven, till 16.21
till m. cursed God for the plague 16.21
all shipmasters and seafaring m., 18.17
were the great m. of the earth, 18.23
captains, the flesh of mighty m., 19.18
riders, and the flesh of all m., 19.18
the dwelling of God is with m. 21.03

MENAHEM
Then M. the son of Gadi came up 2Ki 15.14
At that time M. sacked Tappuah and 15.16
king of Judah M. the son of Gadi 15.17
and M. gave Pul a thousand 15.19
M. exacted the money from Israel, 15.20
Now the rest of the deeds of M., 15.21
And M. slept with his fathers, and 15.22
the son of M. began to reign over 15.23

MEND
them the hour when he began to m., Jn 4.52
M. your ways, heed my appeal, agree 2Co 13.11

MENDED
wineskins, worn-out and torn and m., Jos 9.04
vessel, so that it can never be m. Jer 19.11

MENDING
m. their nets, and he called them. Mt 4.21
who were in their boat m. the nets. Mk 1.19

MENE
M., M., TEKEL, and PARSIN. Dan 5.25
M., God has numbered the days of 5.26

MENIAL
for beauty and another for m. use? Rom 9.21

MENNA
the son of M., the son of Mattatha, Lk 3.31

MEN-PLEASERS
as m., but as servants of Christ, Eph 6.06
as m., but in singleness of heart, Col 3.22

MEN'S
"Fill the m. sacks with food, as Gen 44.01
the work of m. hands, that neither Deu 4.28
and m. bones shall be burned upon 1Ki 13.02
no gods, but the work of m. hands, 2Ki 19.18
which are the work of m. hands. 2Ch 32.19
and gold, the work of m. hands. Ps 115.04
and gold, the work of m. hands. 135.15
no gods, but the work of m. hands, Is 37.19
bear, and lay them on m. shoulders; Mt 23.04
full of dead m. bones and all 23.27
multiplied, most m. love will grow cold. 24.12
not to destroy m. lives but to save *Lk 9.55
beyond limit, in other m. labors; 2Co 10.15

MENSERVANTS
m., maidservants, she-asses, and Gen 12.16
m. and maidservants, camels and 24.35
large flocks, maidservants and m., 30.43
m., and maidservants; and I have 32.05
your m. and your maidservants, and Deu 12.12
He will take your m. and maidservants, 1Sa 8.16
sheep and oxen, m. and maidservants? 2Ki 5.26
besides their m. and maidservants, Ez 2.65
besides their m. and maidservants, Neh 7.67

MENSERVANTS (cont.)
Even upon the m. and maidservants Joe 2.29
to beat the m. and the maidservants, Lk 12.45
yea, and on my m. and my maidservants Ac 2.18

MENSTRUAL
while she is in her m. uncleanness. Lev 18.19

MENSTRUATION
as at the time of her m., she shall be Lev 12.02
be unclean two weeks, as in her m.; 12.05

MENTION
to make m. of me to Pharaoh, and so Gen 40.14
and make no m. of the names of Ex 23.13
or make m. of the names of their Jos 23.07
No m. shall be made of coral or of Job 28.18
who know me I m. Rahab and Babylon; Ps 87.04
"I will not m. him, or speak any Jer 20.09
of the LORD' you shall m. no more, 23.36
We must not m. the name of the LORD." Amo 6.10
ceasing I m. you always in my Rom 1.09
made m. of the exodus of the Heb 11.22

MENTIONED
the following cities m. by name, Jos 21.09
When he m. the ark of God, Eli fell 1Sa 4.18
these m. by name were princes in 1Ch 4.38
these cities which are m. by name. 6.65
who have been m. by name rose and 2Ch 28.15
Levites. These were all m. by name. Ez 8.20
Leave out nothing that you have m. Est 6.10
to whom it is m. will fear because Is 19.17
they shall be m. by name no more. Hos 2.17

MENTIONING
constantly m. you in our prayers, 1Th 1.02

MENUHOTH
other sons: Haroeh, half of the M. 1Ch 2.52

MEONOTHAI
sons of Othniel: Hathath and M. 1Ch 4.13
M. was the father of Ophrah; 4.14

MEPHAATH
and Jahaz, and Kedemoth, and M., Jos 13.18
and M. with its pasture lands—four cities 21.37
and M. with its pasture lands; 1Ch 6.79
upon Holon, and Jahzah, and M., Jer 48.21

MEPHIBOSHETH
became lame. And his name was M. 2Sa 4.04
And M. the son of Jonathan, son of 9.06
And David said, "M.!" And he answered, 9.06
but M. your master's son shall 9.10
So M. ate at David's table, like one 9.11
And M. had a young son, whose name 9.12
So M. dwelt in Jerusalem; 9.13
Ziba the servant of M. met him, 16.01
that belonged to M. is now yours. 16.04
And M. the son of Saul came down to 19.24
"Why did you not go with me, M.?" 19.25
And M. said to the king, "Oh, let him 19.30
But the king spared M., the son of 21.07
she bore to Saul, Armoni and M.; 21.08

MEPHIBOSHETH'S
in Ziba's house became M. servants. 2Sa 9.12

MERAB
the name of the first-born was M., 1Sa 14.49
"Here is my elder daughter M.; I will 18.17
But at the time when M., Saul's daughter 18.19

MERAIAH
of fathers' houses: of Seraiah, M.; Neh 12.12

MERAIOTH
Uzzi of Zerahiah, Zerahiah of M., 1Ch 6.06
M. of Amariah, Amariah of Ahitub, 6.07
M. his son, Amariah his son, Ahitub 6.52
son of M., son of Ahitub, the chief 9.11
Amariah, son of Azariah, son of M., Ez 7.03
son of M., son of Ahitub, ruler of Neh 11.11
of Harim, Adna; of M., Helkai; 12.15

MERARI
of Levi: Gershon, Kohath, and M. Gen 46.11
and M., the years of the life of Ex 6.16
The sons of M.: Mahli and Mushi. 6.19
names: Gershon and Kohath and M. Num 3.17
And the sons of M. by their families: 3.20
Of M. were the family of the 3.33
these are the families of M. 3.33
the families of M. was Zuriel the 3.35
of the sons of M. was to be the 3.36
"As for the sons of M., you shall 4.29
of the families of the sons of M., 4.33
of the families of the sons of M., 4.42
of the families of the sons of M., 4.45
oxen he gave to the sons of M., 7.08
sons of Gershon and the sons of M., 10.17
of M., the family of the Merarites. 26.57
of Levi: Gershom, Kohath, and M. 1Ch 6.01
of Levi: Gershom, Kohath, and M. 6.16
The sons of M.: Mahli and Mushi. 6.19
The sons of M.: Mahli, Libni his son, 6.29
were their brethren the sons of M.: 6.44
of Mushi, son of M., son of Levi; 6.47
of Hashabiah, of the sons of M.; 9.14
of the sons of M., Asaiah the chief, 15.06
and of the sons of M., their brethren 15.07
of Levi: Gershom, Kohath, and M. 23.06
The sons of M.: Mahli and Mushi. 23.21
The sons of M.: Mahli and Mushi. 24.26
The sons of M.: of Jaaziah, Beno, 24.27
And Hosah, of the sons of M., 26.10
the Korahites and the sons of M. 26.19
and of the sons of M., Kish the son 2Ch 29.12
the Levites, of the sons of M., 34.12
him Jeshaiah of the sons of M., Ez 8.19

MERARITE
the M. families, were given out of Jos 21.34
cities of the several M. families, 21.40

MERARITES
of Merari, the family of the M. Num 26.57
The M. according to their families Jos 21.07
To the M. according to their 1Ch 6.63
To the rest of the M. were allotted 6.77

MERATHAIM
"Go up against the land of M., Jer 50.21

MERCHANDISE
perceives that her m. is profitable. Pro 31.18
Her m. and her hire will be dedicated Is 23.18
but her m. will supply abundant food and 23.18
of Egypt and the m. of Ethiopia, 45.14
your riches and a prey of your m.; Eze 26.12
and vessels of bronze for your m. 27.13
they exchanged for your m. wheat, 27.17
calamus were bartered for your m. 27.19
traveled for you with your m. 27.25
your m., your mariners and your 27.27
your caulkers, your dealers in m., 27.27
wealth and m. you enriched the 27.33
your m. and all your crew have sunk 27.34

MERCHANT
She is like the ships of the m., Pro 31.14
she delivers girdles to the m. 31.24
all the fragrant powders of the m.? Sol 3.06
you were the m. of the nations. Is 23.03

MERCHANT (cont.)
m. of the peoples of many coastlands, Eze 27.03
is like a m. in search of fine Mt 13.45

MERCHANTS
the weights current among the m. Gen 23.16
and from the traffic of the m., 1Ki 10.15
which the traders and m. brought; 2Ch 9.14
the temple servants and of the m., Neh 3.31
the goldsmiths and the m. repaired. 3.32
Then the m. and sellers of all 13.20
they divide him up among the m.? Job 41.06
O m. of Sidon, your messengers Is 23.02
whose m. were princes, whose traders 23.08
trade, and set it in a city of m. Eze 17.04
The m. among the peoples hiss at 27.36
Dedan and the m. of Tarshish and 38.13
You increased your m. more than the Nah 3.16
and the m. of the earth have grown Rev 18.03
And the m. of the earth weep and 18.11
The m. of these wares, who gained 18.15
for thy m. were the great men of 18.23

MERCIES
thou in thy great m. didst not Neh 9.19
to thy great m. thou didst give 9.27
deliver them according to thy m. 9.28
Nevertheless in thy great m. thou 9.31
his m. never come to an end; Lam 3.22
by the m. of God, to present your Rom 12.01
the Father of m. and God of all 2Co 1.03

MERCIFUL
the hand, the LORD being m. to him, Gen 19.16
a God m. and gracious, slow to anger, Ex 34.06
for the LORD your God is a m. God; Deu 4.31
the house of Israel are m. kings; 1Ki 20.31
LORD your God is gracious and m., 2Ch 30.09
gracious and m., slow to anger and Neh 9.17
for thou art a gracious and m. God. 9.31
Be m. to me, O God, be m. to me, Ps 57.01
art a God m. and gracious, slow to 86.15
The LORD is m. and gracious, slow to 103.08
the LORD is gracious and m. 111.04
is gracious, m., and righteous. 112.04
and righteous; our God is m. 116.05
The LORD is gracious and m., 145.08
anger, for I am m., says the LORD; Jer 3.12
God, for he is gracious and m., Joe 2.13
thou art a gracious God and m., Jon 4.02
"Blessed are the m., for they Mt 5.07
Be m., even as your Father is m. Lk 6.36
saying, 'God, be m. to me a sinner!' 18.13
might become a m. and faithful Heb 2.17
For I will be m. toward their 8.12
the LORD is compassionate and m. Jas 5.11

MERCILESS
to others and your years to the m.; Pro 5.09
enemy, the punishment of a m. foe, Jer 30.14

MERCILESSLY
and m. slaying nations for ever? Hab 1.17

MERCY
grant you m. before the man, Gen 43.14
shall make a m. seat of pure gold; Ex 25.17
on the two ends of the m. seat. 25.18
piece with the m. seat shall you 25.19
overshadowing the m. seat with 25.20
toward the m. seat shall the faces 25.20
shall put the m. seat on the top 25.21
you, and from above the m. seat, 25.22
You shall put the m. seat upon the 26.34
before the m. seat that is over the 30.06
and the m. seat that is thereon, and 31.07
and will show m. on whom I will show m. 33.19
the m. seat, and the veil of the 35.12
And he made a m. seat of pure gold; 37.06
two ends of the m. seat he made 37.07
piece with the m. seat he made the 37.08
overshadowing the m. seat with 37.09
toward the m. seat were the faces 37.09
with its poles and the m. seat; 39.35
and set the m. seat above on the 40.20
before the m. seat which is upon Lev 16.02
in the cloud upon the m. seat. 16.02
may cover the m. seat which is 16.13
finger on the front of the m. seat, 16.14
and before the m. seat he shall 16.14
m. seat and before the m. seat; 16.15
from above the m. seat that was Num 7.89
with them, and show no m. to them. Deu 7.02
and show you m., and have compassion 13.17
receive no m. but be exterminated, Jos 11.20
of the LORD, for his m. is great; 2Sa 24.14
the LORD, for his m. is very great; 1Ch 21.13
and of the room for the m. seat; 28.11
and grant him m. in the sight of Neh 1.11
I must appeal for m. to my accuser. Job 9.15
Surely goodness and m. shall follow Ps 23.06
Be mindful of thy m., O LORD; 25.06
withhold thy m. from me, let thy 40.11
Have m. on me, O God, according to 51.01
to thy abundant m. blot out my 51.01
to thy abundant m., turn to me. 69.16
you with steadfast love and m., 103.04
Let thy m. come to me, that I may 119.77
Great is thy m., O LORD; give me life 119.156
our God, till he have m. upon us. 123.02
Have m. upon us, O LORD, have m. 123.03
but the m. of the wicked is cruel. Pro 12.10
neighbor finds no m. in his eyes. 21.10
and forsakes them will obtain m. 28.13
will have no m. on the fruit of Is 13.18
exalts himself to show m. to you. 30.18
your hand, you showed them no m.; 47.06
LORD, that he may have m. on him, 55.07
in my favor I have had m. on you. 60.10
granted them according to his m., 63.07
they are cruel and have no m., Jer 6.23
the LORD, my steadfast love and m. 16.05
I will surely have m. on him, 31.20
fortunes, and will have m. upon them. 33.26
I will grant you m., that he may have m. 42.12
they are cruel, and have no m. 50.42
destroyed without m. all the Lam 2.02
them, slaughtering without m. 2.21
and have m. upon the whole house of Eze 39.25
them to seek m. of the God of Dan 2.18
by showing m. to the oppressed, 4.27
our God belong m. and forgiveness; 9.09
but on the ground of thy great m. 9.18
in steadfast love, and in m. Hos 2.19
our hands. In thee the orphan finds m. 14.03
it known; in wrath remember m. Hab 3.02
thou have no m. on Jerusalem and Zec 1.12
kindness and m. each to his 7.09
merciful, for they shall obtain m. Mt 5.07
'I desire m., and not sacrifice.' 9.13
"Have m. on us, Son of David." 9.27
'I desire m., and not sacrifice,' 12.07
"Have m. on me, O Lord, Son of David; 15.22
"Lord, have m. on my son, for he is 17.15
you have had m. on your fellow 18.33
fellow servant, as I had m. on you?' 18.33
"Have m. on us, Son of David!" 20.30
have m. on us, Son of David!" 20.31
the law, justice and m. and faith; 23.23
you, and how he has m. on you. Mk 5.19
"Jesus, Son of David, have m. on me!" 10.47
more, "Son of David, have m. on me!" 10.48
And his m. is on those who fear him Lk 1.50
Israel, in remembrance of his m., 1.54
the Lord had shown great m. to her, 1.58

MERCY (cont.)

to perform the m. promised to our Lk 1.72
through the tender m. of our God, 1.78
said, "The one who showed m. on him." 10.37
have m. upon me, and send Lazarus to 16.24
said, "Jesus, Master, have m. on us." 17.13
"Jesus, Son of David, have m. on me!" 18.38
more, "Son of David, have m. on me!" 18.39
"I will have m. on whom I have m., Rom 9.15
or exertion, but upon God's m. 9.16
So then he has m. upon whomever he 9.18
of his glory for the vessels of m., 9.23
have received m. because of their 11.30
that by the m. shown to you they 11.31
to you they also may receive m. 11.31
that he may have m. upon all. 11.32
he who does acts of m., 12.08
might glorify God for his m. 15.09
by the Lord's m. is trustworthy. 1Co 7.25
this ministry by the m. of God, 2Co 4.01
Peace and m. be upon all who walk Gal 6.16
But God, who is rich in m., Eph 2.04
But God had m. on him, and not only Php 2.27
m., and peace from God the Father 1Ti 1.02
but I received m. because I had 1.13
but I received m. for this reason, 1.16
m., and peace from God the Father 2Ti 1.02
May the Lord grant m. to the 1.16
him to find m. from the Lord on 1.18
but in virture of his own m., Tit 3.05
we may receive m. and find grace Heb 4.16
of glory overshadowing the m. seat. 9.05
dies without m. at the testimony 10.28
without m. to one who has shown no m.; Jas 2.13
yet m. triumphs over judgment. 2.13
full of m. and good fruits, without 3.17
By his great m. we have been born 1Pe 1.03
m. but now you have received m. 2.10
Grace, m., and peace will be with us, 2Jn 1.03
May m., peace, and love be multiplied Jud 1.02
wait for the m. of our Lord Jesus 1.21
on some have m. with fear, hating 1.23

MERE

You think that m. words are counsel 2Ki 18.20
every man stands as a m. breath! Ps 39.05
surely every man is a m. breath! 39.11
but m. talk tends only to want. Pro 14.23
By m. words a servant is not 29.19
Do you think that m. words are Is 36.05
They utter m. words; with empty Hos 10.04
m. busybodies, not doing any work. 2Th 3.11

MERED

M., Epher, and Jalon. 1Ch 4.17
of Pharaoh, whom M. married; 4.17

MERELY

If we had been sold m. as slaves, Est 7.04
who are not m. circumcised but Rom 4.12
to Apollos," are you not m. men? 1Co 3.04

MEREMOTH

into the hands of M. the priest, Ez 8.33
Vaniah, M., Eliashib, 10.36
And next to them M. the son of Neh 3.04
After him M. the son of Uriah, son 3.21
Harim, M., Obadiah, 10.05
Shecaniah, Rehum, M., 12.03

MERES

M., Marsena, and Memucan, the seven Est 1.14

MERIBAH

name of the place Massah and M., Ex 17.07
These are the waters of M., Num 20.13
my command at the waters of M. 20.24
the waters of M. of Kadesh in the 27.14
didst strive at the waters of M.; Deu 33.08
I tested you at the waters of M. Ps 81.07
as at M., as on the day at Massah 95.08
They angered him at the waters of M., 106.32

MERIBATHKADESH

of Israel at the waters of M., Deu 32.51
Tamar as far as the waters of M., Eze 47.19
run from Tamar to the waters of M., 48.28

MERIBBAAL

and the son of Jonathan was M.; 1Ch 8.34
and M. was the father of Micah. 8.34
and the son of Jonathan was M.; 9.40
and M. was the father of Micah. 9.40

MEROB

five sons of M. the daughter of 2Sa 21.08

MERODACH

is put to shame, M. is dismayed. Jer 50.02

MERODACHBALADAN

At that time M. the son of Baladan, 2Ki 20.12
At that time M. the son of Baladan, Is 39.01

MEROM

together at the waters of M., Jos 11.05
people of war, by the waters of M., 11.07

MERONOTHITE

the she-asses was Jehdeiah the M. 1Ch 27.30
the Gibeonite and Jadon the M., Neh 3.07

MEROZ

"Curse M., says the angel of the Ju 5.23

MERRILY

then go m. with the king to the Est 5.14

MERRY

So they drank and were m. with him. Gen 43.34
And when their hearts were m., Ju 16.25
night, and let your heart be m. 19.06
here and let your heart be m.; 19.09
As they were making their hearts m., 19.22
and drunk, and his heart was m., Ru 3.07
to one another as they made m., 1Sa 18.07
Nabal's heart was m. within him, 25.36
were making m. before the LORD 2Sa 6.05
and I will make m. before the LORD 6.21
when Amnon's heart is m. with wine, 13.28
were making m. before God with all 1Ch 13.08
King David dancing and making m.; 15.29
heart of the king was m. with wine, Est 1.10
drink your wine with a m. heart; Ecc 9.07
the voices of those who make m. Jer 30.19
young men and the old shall be m. 31.13
take your ease, eat, drink, be m.' Lk 12.19
it, and let us eat and make m.; 15.23
And they began to make m. 15.24
I might make m. with my friends. 15.29
was fitting to make m. and be glad, 15.32
them and make m. and exchange Rev 11.10

MERRY-HEARTED

vine languishes, all the m. sigh. Is 24.07

MERRYMAKERS

I did not sit in the company of m., Jer 15.17
go forth in the dance of the m. 31.04

MESHA

extended from M. in the direction Gen 10.30
Now M. king of Moab was a sheep 2Ki 3.04
wife: Jobab, Zibia, M., Malcam, 1Ch 8.09

MESHACH

Shadrach, Mishael he called M., Dan 1.07
m., and Abednego over the affairs 2.49

MESHACH (cont.)

Babylon: Shadrach, M., and Abednego. Dan 3.12
M., and Abednego be brought. 3.13
M., and Abednego, that you do not 3.14
Shadrach, M., and Abednego answered 3.16
against Shadrach, M., and Abednego. 3.19
M., and Abednego, and to cast them 3.20
took up Shadrach, M., and Abednego. 3.22
M., and Abednego, fell bound into 3.23
M., and Abednego, servants of the 3.26
M., and Abednego came out from the 3.26
M., and Abednego, who has sent his 3.28
M., and Abednego shall be torn limb 3.29
M., and Abednego in the province of 3.30

MESHECH

Madai, Javan, Tubal, M., and Tiras. Gen 10.02
Madai, Javan, Tubal, M., and Tiras. 1Ch 1.05
Lud, Aram, Uz, Hul, Gether, and M. 1.17
Woe is me, that I sojourn in M., Ps 120.05
and M. traded with you; Eze 27.13
"M. and Tubal are there, and all 32.26
the chief prince of M. and Tubal, 38.02
Gog, chief prince of M. and Tubal; 38.03
Gog, chief prince of M. and Tubal; 39.01

MESHELEMIAH

Zechariah the son of M. was gatekeeper 1Ch 9.21
M. the son of Kore, of the sons of 26.01
And M. had sons: Zechariah the first 26.02
And M. had sons and brethren, able 26.09

MESHEZABEL

of Berechiah, son of M. repaired. Neh 3.04
M., Zadok, Jaddua, 10.21
And Pethahiah the son of M., 11.24

MESHILLEMITH

Meshullam, son of M., son of Immer; 1Ch 9.12

MESHILLEMOTH

Johanan, Berechiah the son of M., 2Ch 28.12
of Ahzai, son of M., son of Immer, Neh 11.13

MESHOBAB

M., Jamlech, Joshah the son of 1Ch 4.34

MESHULLAM

son of M., the secretary, to the 2Ki 22.03
M. and Hananiah, and Shelomith was 1Ch 3.19
M., Sheba, Jorai, Jacan, Zia, and Eber, 5.13
Zebadiah, M., Hizki, Heber, 8.17
Benjaminites: Sallu the son of M., 9.07
and M. the son of Shephatiah, son of 9.08
son of M., son of Zadok, son of 9.11
son of M., son of Meshillemith, son 9.12
of Merari, and Zechariah and M., 2Ch 34.12
and M., leading men, and for Joiarib Ez 8.16
and M. and Shabbethai the Levite 10.15
Of the sons of Bani were M., 10.29
next to them M. the son of Berechiah, Neh 3.04
of Paseah and M. the son of 3.06
After him M. the son of Berechiah 3.30
the daughter of M. the son of 6.18
Zechariah, and M. on his left hand. 8.04
M., Abijah, Mijamin, 10.07
Magpiash, M., Hezir, 10.20
of Benjamin: Sallu the son of M., 11.07
son of M., son of Zadok, son of 11.11
of Ezra, M.; of Amariah, 12.13
Zechariah, of Ginnethon, M.; 12.16
M., Talmon, and Akkub were gatekeepers 12.25
and Azariah, Ezra, M., 12.33

MESHULLEMETH

name was M. the daughter of Haruz 2Ki 21.19

MESOPOTAMIA

and went to M., to the city of Gen 24.10
from Pethor of M., to curse you. Deu 23.04
of Cushanrishathaim king of M.; Ju 3.08
Cushanrishathaim king of M. into his hand; 3.10
hire chariots and horsemen from M., 1Ch 19.06
and Elamites and residents of M., Ac 2.09
father Abraham, when he was in M., 7.02

MESSAGE

So they sent a m. to Joseph, saying, Gen 50.16
to Balaam, and gave him Balak's m. Num 22.07
said, "I have a secret m. for you, Ju 3.19
"I have a m. from God for you." 3.20
not heed the m. of Jephthah which 11.28
and sent a m. by Nathan the prophet 2Sa 12.25
David sent this m. to Zadok and 19.11
have heard the m. which you have 1Ki 5.08
heard this m. as he was drinking 20.12
and gave him a m. for Mordecai, Est 4.10
He who sends a m. by the hand of a Pro 26.06
and to whom will he explain the m.? Is 28.09
sheer terror to understand the m. 28.19
to it the m. that I tell you. Jon 3.02
to the people with the LORD's m., Hag 1.13
them and confirmed the m. by the signs *Mk 16.20
to you a m. by which you will be Ac 11.14
been sent the m. of this salvation 13.26
speech and my m. were not in 1Co 2.04
to us the m. of reconciliation. 2Co 5.19
for he strongly opposed our m. 2Ti 4.15
For if the m. declared by angels Heb 2.02
but the m. which they heard did not 4.02
This is the m. we have heard from 1Jn 1.05
For this is the m. which you have 3.11

MESSAGES

that no further m. be spoken to Heb 12.19

MESSENGER

when a m. came to Saul, saying, "Make 1Sa 23.27
and he instructed the m., 2Sa 11.19
So the m. went, and came and told 11.22
The m. said to David, "The men 11.23
David said to the m., "Thus shall you 11.25
And a m. came to David, saying, "The 15.13
Then Jezebel sent a m. to Elijah, 1Ki 19.02
And the m. who went to summon 22.13
And Elisha sent a m. to him, 2Ki 5.10
but before the m. arrived Elisha 6.32
when the m. comes, shut the door, and 6.32
"The m. reached them, but he is not 9.18
When the m. came and told him, "They 10.08
And the m. who went to summon 2Ch 18.12
and there came a m. to Job, Job 1.14
A bad m. plunges men into trouble, Pro 13.17
A king's wrath is a m. of death, 16.14
and a cruel m. will be sent against 17.11
is a faithful m. to those who send 25.13
say before the m. that it was a Ecc 5.06
or deaf as my m. whom I send? Is 42.19
and a m. has been sent among the Jer 49.14
and one m. to meet another, to tell 51.31
to whom a m. was sent, and lo, they Eze 23.40
and a m. has been sent among the Ob 1.01
the m. of the LORD, spoke to the Hag 1.13
for he is the m. of the LORD of Mal 2.07
I send my m. to prepare the way 3.01
the m. of the covenant in whom you 3.01
I send my m. before thy face, who Mt 11.10
I send my m. before thy face, who Mk 1.02
I send my m. before thy face, who Lk 7.27
a m. of Satan, to harass me, to keep 2Co 12.07
and your m. and minister to my need, Php 2.25

MESSENGERS

And Jacob sent m. before him to Gen 32.03
And the m. returned to Jacob, saying, 32.06

MESSENGERS (cont.)

Moses sent m. from Kadesh to the Num 20.14
Then Israel sent m. to Sihon king 21.21
sent m. to Balaam the son of Beor 22.05
I not tell your m. whom you sent 24.12
"So I sent m. from the wilderness Deu 2.26
she hid the m. that we sent. Jos 6.17
she hid the m. whom Joshua sent to 6.25
So Joshua sent m., and they ran to 7.22
And he sent m. throughout all Ju 6.35
And he sent m. to Asher, Zebulun, and 6.35
And Gideon sent m. throughout all 7.24
And he sent m. to Abimelech at 9.31
Then Jephthah sent m. to the king 11.12
answered the m. of Jephthah, 11.13
And Jephthah sent m. again to the 11.14
Israel then sent m. to the king of 11.17
Israel then sent m. to Sihon king 11.19
So they sent m. to the inhabitants 1Sa 6.21
we may send m. through all the 11.03
When the m. came to Gibeah of Saul, 11.04
of Israel by the hand of m., 11.07
And they said to the m. who had come, 11.09
When the m. came and told the men 11.09
Therefore Saul sent m. to Jesse, 16.19
That night Saul sent m. to David's 19.11
And when Saul sent m. to take David, 19.14
Then Saul sent the m. to see David, 19.15
And when the m. came in, behold, the 19.16
Then Saul sent m. to take David; 19.20
of God came upon the m. of Saul, 19.20
he sent other m., and they also 19.21
And Saul sent m. again the third 19.21
David sent m. out of the wilderness 25.14
she went after the m. of David, 25.42
and sent m. throughout the land of 31.09
David sent m. to the men of Jabeshgilead, 2Sa 2.05
And Abner sent m. to David at 3.12
Then David sent m. to Ishbosheth 3.14
he sent m. after Abner, and they 3.26
king of Tyre sent m. to David, 5.11
So David sent m., and took her; 11.04
And Joab sent m. to David, and said, 12.27
sent secret m. throughout all the 15.10
And he sent m. into the city to 1Ki 20.02
The m. came again, and said, "Thus 20.05
So he said to the m. of Benhadad, 20.09
And the m. departed and brought him 20.09
so he sent m., telling them, "Go, 2Ki 1.02
up to meet the m. of the king of 1.03
The m. returned to the king, and he 1.05
you have sent m. to inquire of 1.16
And the m. returned, and told the 7.15
Then Amaziah sent m. to Jehoash the 14.08
So Ahaz sent m. to Tiglathpileser 16.07
for he had sent m. to So, king 17.04
he sent m. again to Hezekiah, 19.09
the hand of the m., and read it; 19.14
By your m. you have mocked the Lord, 19.23
and sent m. throughout the land of 1Ch 10.09
king of Tyre sent m. to David, 14.01
So David sent m. to console him 19.02
they sent m. and brought out the 19.16
persistently to them by his m., 2Ch 36.15
but they kept mocking the m. of God, 36.16
And I sent m. to them, saying, "I am Neh 6.03
who makest the winds thy m., Ps 104.04
one answer the m. of the nation? Is 14.32
Go, you swift m., to a nation, tall 18.02
your m. passed over the sea and 23.02
he sent m. to Hezekiah, saying, 37.09
the hand of the m., and read it; 37.14
and performs the counsel of his m.; 44.26
and sent m. to them in Chaldea. Eze 23.16
"On that day swift m. shall go 30.09
voice of your m. shall no more be Nah 2.13
When the m. of John had gone, he Lk 7.24
And he sent m. ahead of him, 9.51
they are m. of the churches, the 2Co 8.23
received the m. and sent them out Jas 2.25

MESSIAH

have found the M." (which means Jn 1.41
"I know that M. is coming (he who 4.25

MET

way and the angels of God m. him; Gen 32.01
by all this company which I m.? 33.08
God of the Hebrews, has m. with us; Ex 3.18
way the LORD m. him and sought to 4.24
and m. him at the mountain of God 4.27
God of the Hebrews has m. with us; 5.03
They m. Moses and Aaron, who were 5.20
And God m. Balaam; and Balaam Num 23.04
And the LORD m. Balaam, and put a 23.16
they m. young maidens coming out to 1Sa 9.11
behold, a band of prophets m. him; 10.10
down toward her; and she m. them. 25.20
went out and m. them at the pool of 2Sa 2.13
the servant of Mephibosheth m. him, 16.01
loyalty they m. me when I fled 1Ki 2.07
away a lion m. him on the road and 13.24
on the way, behold, Elijah m. him; 18.07
a lion m. him and killed him. 20.36
and m. him at the property of 2Ki 9.21
Jehu m. the kinsmen of Ahaziah king 10.13
he m. Jehonadab the son of Rechab 10.15
he m. the princes of Judah and the 2Ch 22.08
If I m. you outside, I would kiss Sol 8.01
As he m. them, he said to them, "Come Jer 41.06
He m. God at Bethel, and there God Hos 12.04
from a lion, and a bear m. him; Amo 5.19
two demoniacs m. him, coming out of Mt 8.28
Jesus m. them and said, "Hail!" 28.09
there m. him out of the tombs a man Mk 5.02
there m. him a man from the city Lk 8.27
the mountain, a great crowd m. him. 9.37
he was m. by ten lepers, who stood 17.12
his servants m. him and told him Jn 4.51
she went and m. him, while Mary sat 11.20
the place where Martha had m. him. 11.30
for Jesus often m. there with his 18.02
Cornelius m. him and fell down at Ac 10.25
whole year they m. with the church, 11.26
we were m. by a slave girl who had 16.16
and Stoic philosophers m. him. 17.18
And when he m. us at Assos, we took 20.14
the accused m. the accusers face 25.16
we may appear to have m. the test, 2Co 13.07
m. Abraham returning from the Heb 7.01
ancestor when Melchizedek m. him. 7.10

METAL

a m. image, a teacher of lies? Hab 2.18

METED

and m. out the waters by measure; Job 28.25

METHEGHAMMAH

and David took M. out of the hand 2Sa 8.01

METHUSELAH

years, he became the father of M. Gen 5.21
the birth of M. three hundred 5.22
When M. had lived a hundred and 5.25
M. lived after the birth of Lamech 5.26
Thus all the days of M. were nine 5.27
Enoch, M., Lamech; 1Ch 1.03
the son of M., the son of Enoch, the Lk 3.37

METHUSHAEL

and Mehujael the father of M., Gen 4.18
and M. the father of Lamech. 4.18

MEUNIM

tents and the M. who were found 1Ch 4.41

MEUNIM (cont.)
the sons of M., the sons of Nephisim, Ez 2.50
the sons of M., the sons of Nephushesim, Neh 7.52

MEUNITES
and with them some of the M., 2Ch 20.01
in Gurbaal, and against the M. 26.07

MEZAHAB
daughter of Matred, daughter of M. Gen 36.39
of Matred, the daughter of M. 1Ch 1.50

MEZOBAITE
Eliel, and Obed, and Jaasiel the M. 1Ch 11.47

MIBHAR
of Nathan, M. the son of Hagri, 1Ch 11.38

MIBSAM
of Ishmael, and Kedar, Adbeel, M., Gen 25.13
Nebaioth; and Kedar, Adbeel, M., 1Ch 1.29
M. his son, Mishma his son. 4.25

MIBZAR
Kenaz, Teman, M., Gen 36.42
Kenaz, Teman, M., 1Ch 1.53

MICA
had a young son, whose name was M. 2Sa 9.12
Galal, and Mattaniah the son of M., 1Ch 9.15
M., Rehob, Hashabiah, Neh 10.11
and Mattaniah the son of M., 11.17
son of M., of the sons of Asaph, the 11.22

MICAH
of Ephraim, whose name was M. Ju 17.01
and it was in the house of M. 17.04
And the man M. had a shrine, and he 17.05
of Ephraim to the house of M. 17.08
And M. said to him, "From where do 17.09
And M. said to him, "Stay with me, 17.10
And M. installed the Levite, and the 17.12
priest, and was in the house of M. 17.12
Then M. said, "Now I know that the 17.13
of Ephraim, to the house of M., 18.02
When they were by the house of M., 18.03
"Thus and thus has M. dealt with me: 18.04
and came to the house of M. 18.13
young Levite, at the home of M., 18.15
a good way from the home of M., 18.22
who turned round and said to M., 18.23
and when M. saw that they were too 18.26
And taking what M. had made, 18.27
M. his son, Reaiah his son, Baal his 1Ch 5.05
and Meribbaal was the father of M. 8.34
The sons of M.: Pithon, Melech, Tarea, 8.35
and Meribbaal was the father of M. 9.40
The sons of M.: Pithon, Melech, Tahrea, 9.41
M. the chief and Isshiah the second 23.20
The sons of Uzziel, M.; of the sons of M., 24.24
The brother of M., Isshiah; 24.25
of Shaphan, Abdon the son of M., 2Ch 34.20
"M. of Moresheth prophesied in the Jer 26.18
that came to M. of Moresheth in Mic 1.01

MICAH'S
these went into M. house and took Ju 18.18
the houses near M. house were 18.22
So they set up M. graven image 18.31

MICAIAH
M. the son of Imlah; but I hate 1Ki 22.08
"Bring quickly M. the son of Imlah." 22.09
who went to summon M. said to him, 22.13
But M. said, "As the LORD lives, what 22.14
"M., shall we go to Ramothgilead to 22.15
And M. said, "Therefore hear the 22.19
near and struck M. on the cheek, 22.24
And M. said, "Behold, you shall see 22.25
"Seize M., and take him back to 22.26
And M. said, "If you return in peace, 22.28
Shaphan, and Achbor the son of M., 2Ki 22.12
name was M. the daughter of Uriel 2Ch 13.02
and M., to teach in the cities of 17.07
M. the son of Imlah; but I hate 18.07
"Bring quickly M. the son of Imlah." 18.08
who went to summon M. said to him, 18.12
But M. said, "As the LORD lives, what 18.13
"M., shall we go to Ramothgilead to 18.14
And M. said, "Therefore hear the 18.18
near and struck M. on the cheek, 18.23
And M. said, "Behold, you shall see 18.24
"Seize M., and take him back to 18.25
And M. said, "If you return in peace, 18.27
son of M., son of Zaccur, son of Neh 12.35
M., Elioenai, Zechariah, and Hananiah, 12.41
When M. the son of Gemariah, son of Jer 36.11
And M. told them all the words that 36.13

MICE
golden tumors and five golden m., 1Sa 6.04
images of your m. that ravage the 6.05
with the golden m. and the images 6.11
also the golden m., according to the 6.18
flesh and the abomination and m., Is 66.17

MICHAEL
of Asher, Sethur the son of M.; Num 13.13
M., Meshullam, Sheba, Jorai, Jacan, Zia, 1Ch 5.13
son of M., son of Jeshishai, son of 5.14
son of M., son of Baaseiah, son of 6.40
M., Obadiah, Joel, and Isshiah, five, 7.03
M., Ishpah, and Joha were sons of 8.16
M., Jozabad, Elihu, and Zillethai, 12.20
for Issachar, Omri the son of M.; 27.18
M., and Shephatiah; all these were 2Ch 21.02
Shephatiah, Zebadiah the son of M., Ez 8.08
but M., one of the chief princes, Dan 10.13
these except M., your prince. 10.21
"At that time shall arise M., 12.01
But when the archangel M., contending Jud 1.09
M. and his angels fighting against Rev 12.07

MICHAL
and the name of the younger M.; 1Sa 14.49
Now Saul's daughter M. loved David; 18.20
him his daughter M. for a wife. 18.27
But M., David's wife, told him, "If 19.11
So M. let David down through the 19.12
M. took an image and laid it on the 19.13
Saul said to M., "Why have you 19.17
And M. answered Saul, "He said to me, 19.17
Saul had given M. his daughter, 25.44
my face, unless you first bring M., 2Sa 3.13
son, saying, "Give me my wife M., 3.14
M. the daughter of Saul looked out 6.16
But M. the daughter of Saul came 6.20
And David said to M., "It was before 6.21
And M. the daughter of Saul had no 6.23
M. the daughter of Saul looked out 1Ch 15.29

MICHMAS
The men of M., one hundred and Ez 2.27
The men of M., a hundred and twenty Neh 7.31

MICHMASH
with Saul in M. and the hill 1Sa 13.02
they came up and encamped in M., 13.05
Philistines had mustered at M., 13.11
but the Philistines encamped in M. 13.16
Philistines went out to the pass of M. 13.23
rose on the north in front of M., 14.05
that day from M. to Aijalon. 14.31
at M., Aija, Bethel and its villages, Neh 11.31
at M. he stores his baggage; Is 10.28

MICHMETHATH
on the north is M.; then on the Jos 16.06
Manasseh reached from Asher to M., 17.07

MICHRI
son of M., and Meshullam the son of 1Ch 9.08

MID-COURSE
He has broken my strength in m.; Ps 102.23

MIDDAY
And as m. passed, they raved on 1Ki 18.29
Gate from early morning until m., Neh 8.03
At m., O king, I saw on the way a Ac 26.13

MIDDIN
wilderness, Betharabah, M., Secacah, Jos 15.61

MIDDLE
The m. bar, halfway up the frames, Ex 26.28
And he made the m. bar to pass 36.33
cubits, the city being in the m.; Num 35.05
with the m. of the valley as a Deu 3.16
and from the m. of the valley as Jos 12.02
that is in the m. of the valley, 13.09
that is in the m. of the valley, 13.16
at the beginning of the m. watch, Ju 7.19
grasped the two m. pillars upon 16.29
cut off their garments in the m., 2Sa 10.04
that is in the m. of the valley, 24.05
the m. one was six cubits broad, 1Ki 6.06
went up by stairs to the m. story, 6.08
and from the m. story to the third. 6.08
each other in the m. of the house. 6.27
consecrated the m. of the court 8.64
had gone out of the m. court, 2Ki 20.04
cut off their garments in the m., 1Ch 19.04
consecrated the m. of the court 2Ch 7.07
came and sat in the m. gate: Jer 39.03
and the m. of it is charred, is it Eze 15.04
the top story through the m. story. 41.07
the lower and m. chambers in the 42.05
than the lower and the m. ones. 42.06
a fire in the m. of the courtyard Lk 22.55
About the m. of the feast Jesus Jn 7.14
open in the m. and all his bowels Ac 1.18
standing in the m. of the Areopagus, 17.22
through the m. of the street of the Rev 22.02

MIDHEAVEN
as it flew in m., "Woe, woe, woe to Rev 8.13
Then I saw another angel flying in m., 14.06
to all the birds that fly in m., 19.17

MIDIAN
Medan, M., Ishbak, and Shuah. Gen 25.02
The sons of M. were Ephah, Epher, 25.04
who defeated M. in the country of 36.35
and stayed in the land of M.; Ex 2.15
Now the priest of M. had seven 2.16
father-in-law, Jethro, the priest of M.; 3.01
And the LORD said to Moses in M., 4.19
the priest of M., Moses' father-in-law, 18.01
And Moab said to the elders of M., Num 22.04
the elders of M. departed with the 22.07
people of a fathers' house in M. 25.15
the daughter of the prince of M., 25.18
war, that they may go against M., 31.03
execute the LORD's vengeance on M. 31.03
They warred against M., 31.07
the kings of M. with the rest of 31.08
and Reba, the five kings of M.; 31.08
the women of M. and their little 31.09
defeated with the leaders of M., Jos 13.21
into the hand of M. seven years. Ju 6.01
And the hand of M. prevailed over 6.02
and because of M. the people of 6.02
was brought very low because of M.; 6.06
and given us into the hand of M. 6.13
deliver Israel from the hand of M.; 6.14
and the camp of M. was north of 7.01
and the camp of M. was below him in 7.08
bread tumbled into the camp of M., 7.13
God has given M. and all the host." 7.14
the host of M. into your hand." 7.15
Manasseh, and they pursued after M. 7.23
two princes of M., Oreb and Zeeb; 7.25
press of Zeeb, as they pursued M.; 7.25
us when you went to fight with M.? 8.01
the princes of M., Oreb and Zeeb; 8.03
and Zalmunna, the kings of M. 8.05
them and took the two kings of M., 8.12
delivered us out of the hand of M. 8.22
garments worn by the kings of M., 8.26
So M. was subdued before the people 8.28
rescued you from the hand of M.; 9.17
They set out from M. and came to 1Ki 11.18
Medan, M., Ishbak, and Shuah. 1Ch 1.32
The sons of M.: Ephah, Epher, Hanoch, 1.33
who defeated M. in the country of 1.46
Do to them as thou didst to M., Ps 83.09
hast broken as on the day of M. Is 9.04
when he smote M. at the rock of 10.26
the young camels of M. and Ephah; 60.06
of the land of M. did tremble. Hab 3.07
became an exile in the land of M., Ac 7.29

MIDIANITE
Then M. traders passed by; Gen 37.28
to Hobab the son of Reuel the M., Num 10.29
and brought a M. woman to his 25.06
who was slain with the M. woman, 25.14
And the name of the M. woman who 25.15

MIDIANITES
Meanwhile the M. had sold him in Gen 37.36
"Harass the M., and smite them; Num 25.17
"Avenge the people of Israel on the M.; 31.02
put in seed the M. and the Amalekites Ju 6.03
to the LORD on account of the M., 6.07
wine press, to hide it from the M. 6.11
you shall smite the M. as one man. 6.16
Then all the M. and the Amalekites 6.33
me to give the M. into their hand, 7.02
and give the M. into your hand; 7.07
And the M. and the Amalekites and 7.12
against the M. and seize the 7.24

MIDNIGHT
About m. I will go forth in the Ex 11.04
At m. the LORD smote all the 12.29
But Samson lay till m., and at m. Ju 16.03
At m. the man was startled, and Ru 3.08
And she arose at m., and took my 1Ki 3.20
at m. the people are shaken and Job 34.20
At m. I rise to praise thee, because Ps 119.62
But at m. there was a cry, 'Behold, Mt 25.06
or at m., or at corkcrow, or in the Mk 13.35
go to him at m. and say to him, Lk 11.05
But about m. Paul and Silas were Ac 16.25
he prolonged his speech until m. 20.07
about m. the sailors suspected that 27.27

MIDST
firmament in the m. of the waters, Gen 1.06
life also in the m. of the garden, 2.09
which is in the m. of the garden, 3.03
Lot out of the m. of the overthrow, 19.29
a multitude in the m. of the earth." 48.16
of fire out of the m. of a bush; Ex 3.02
am the LORD in the m. of the earth. 8.22
continually in the m. of the hail, 9.24
I will go forth in the m. of Egypt; 11.04
went into the m. of the sea on dry 14.22
after them into the m. of the sea, 14.23
the Egyptians in the m. of the sea. 14.27

MIDST (cont.)
on dry ground in the m. of the sea. Ex 15.19
sickness away from the m. of you. 23.25
Moses out of the m. of the cloud. 24.16
that I may dwell in their m. 25.08
go in the m. of us, although it is a 34.09
it become a snare in the m. of you. 34.12
my tabernacle that is in their m." Lev 15.31
them in the m. of their uncleannesses. 16.16
the Levites in the m. of the camps; Num 2.17
in the m. of which I dwell." 5.03
LORD, art in the m. of this people; 14.14
from the m. of the assembly. 16.33
"Get away from the m. of this 16.45
ran into the m. of the assembly; 16.47
them into the m. of the burning of 19.06
off from the m. of the assembly, 19.20
through the m. of the sea into the 33.08
in the m. of which I dwell; 35.34
dwell in the m. of the people of 35.34
for I am not in the m. of you; Deu 1.42
to you out of the m. of the fire; 4.12
Horeb out of the m. of the fire, 4.15
speaking out of the m. of the fire, 4.33
from the m. of another nation, by 4.34
words out of the m. of the fire. 4.36
mountain, out of the m. of the fire, 5.04
mountain out of the m. of the fire, 5.22
out of the m. of the darkness, 5.23
voice out of the m. of the fire; 5.24
God speaking out of the m. of fire, 5.26
your God in the m. of you is a 6.15
LORD your God is in the m. of you, 7.21
out of the m. of the fire on the 9.10
out of the m. of the fire on the 10.04
them, in the m. of all Israel; 11.06
purge the evil from the m. of you. 13.05
spoil into the m. of its open 13.16
purge the evil from the m. of you. 17.07
purge the evil from the m. of you. 19.19
blood in the m. of thy people 21.08
of innocent blood from your m., 21.09
shall purge the evil from your m.; 21.21
purge the evil from the m. of you. 22.21
purge the evil from the m. of you. 22.24
God walks in the m. of your camp, 23.14
in your m., in the place which he 23.16
purge the evil from the m. of you. 24.07
through the m. of the nations 29.16
with me in the m. of the people of 32.51
as holy in the m. of the people of 32.51
dry ground in the m. of the Jordan, Jos 3.17
here out of the m. of the Jordan, 4.03
your God into the m. of the Jordan, 4.05
stones out of the m. of the Jordan, 4.08
stones in the m. of the Jordan, 4.09
ark stood in the m. of the Jordan, 4.10
came up from the m. of the Jordan, 4.18
devoted things in the m. of you, 7.13
so they were in the m. of Israel, 8.22
The sun stayed in the m. of heaven, 10.13
dwell in the m. of Israel to this 13.13
dwelt in the m. of Ephraim to this 16.10
was in the m. of the inheritance 19.01
inheritance in the m. of their 19.09
Levites in the m. of the possession 21.41
that the LORD is in the m. of us, 22.31
with what I did in the m. of it; 24.05
in the m. of Ephraim and Manasseh. Ju 12.04
and went in the m. of the people. 18.20
destroyed them in the m. of them. 20.42
came into the m. of the camp in 1Sa 11.11
him in the m. of his brothers; 16.13
fallen in the m. of the battle! 2Sa 1.25
aside into the m. of the gate to 3.27
his stand in the m. of the plot, 23.12
is in the m. of thy people whom 1Ki 3.08
from the m. of the iron furnace). 8.51
went out into the m. of the battle; 20.39
lo, they were in the m. of Samaria. 2Ki 6.20
his stand in the m. of the plot, 1Ch 11.14
in the m. of the assembly. 2Ch 20.14
come into the m. of them and kill Neh 4.11
through the m. of the sea on dry 9.11
went out into the m. of the city, Est 4.01
in the m. of the congregation I Ps 22.22
God is in the m. of her, she shall 46.05
O God, in the m. of thy temple. 48.09
ruin is in its m.; oppression and 55.11
I lie in the m. of lions that 57.04
roared in the m. of thy holy place 74.04
salvation in the m. of the earth. 74.12
them fall in the m. of their camp, 78.28
in the m. of the gods he holds 82.01
me not hence in the m. of my days, 102.24
praise him in the m. of the throng. 109.30
Rule in the m. of your foes! 110.02
the LORD, in your m., O Jerusalem. 116.19
who in thy m., O Egypt, sent signs 135.09
Israel pass through the m. of it, 136.14
Though I walk in the m. of trouble, 138.07
who lies down in the m. of the sea, Pro 23.34
from its m. by a spirit of judgment Is 4.04
built a watchtower in the m. of it, 5.02
dwell alone in the m. of the land. 5.08
as refuse in the m. of the streets. 5.25
I dwell in the m. of a people of 6.05
are many in the m. of the land. 6.12
Tabeel as king in the m. of it," 7.06
in the m. of all the earth. 10.23
great in your m. is the Holy One 12.06
the LORD in the m. of the land of 19.19
a blessing in the m. of the earth, 19.24
shall be in the m. of the earth 24.13
hands in the m. of it as a swimmer 25.11
in his m., they will sanctify my 29.23
fountains in the m. of the valleys; 41.18
go out from the m. of her, 52.11
away from the m. of you the yoke, 58.09
offspring in the m. of the peoples; 61.09
who put in the m. of them his holy 63.11
gardens, following one in the m., 66.17
Benjamin, from the m. of Jerusalem! Jer 6.01
be built up in the m. of my people. 12.16
art in the m. of us, and we are 14.09
in the m. of his days they will 17.11
together into the m. of this city. 21.04
shall come forth from their m.; 30.21
from the m. of Judah, leaving you no 44.07
soldiers in her m. are like fatted 46.21
"Flee from the m. of Babylon, and go 50.08
all the foreign troops in her m., 50.37
"Flee from the m. of Babylon, let 51.06
"Go out of the m. of her, my people! 51.45
slain shall fall in the m. of her. 51.47
it into the m. of the Euphrates, 51.63
were found in the m. of the city. 52.25
her in the m. of her distress. Lam 1.03
all my mighty men in the m. of me; 1.15
who shed in the m. of her the 4.13
and in the m. of the fire, as it Eze 1.04
And from the m. of it came the 1.05
In the m. of the living creatures 1.13
in the fire in the m. of the city, 5.02
judgments in the m. of you in the 5.08
eat their sons in the m. of you, 5.10
with famine in the m. of you; 5.12
slain shall fall in the m. of you, 6.07
your abominations are in your m. 7.04
your abominations are in your m. 7.09
whom you have laid in the m. of it, 11.07
brought forth out of the m. of it. 11.07
you forth out of the m. of it, 11.09
you be the flesh in the m. of it; 11.11
went up from the m. of the city, 11.23

MIDST (cont.)
dwell in the m. of a rebellious Eze 12.02
you shall perish in the m. of it; 13.14
him off from the m. of my people; 14.08
him from the m. of my people 14.09
own fortunes in the m. of them, 16.53
couched in the m. of young lions, 19.02
them in the m. of the land of 20.08
shall be in the m. of the land; 21.32
that sheds blood in the m. of her, 22.03
suffers extortion in your m.; 22.07
men commit lewdness in your m. 22.09
which has been in the m. of you. 22.13
you into the m. of Jerusalem. 22.19
shall be melted in the m. of it. 22.21
shall be melted in the m. of it; 22.22
Her princes in the m. of her are 22.25
made many widows in the m. of her. 22.25
Her princes in the m. of her are 22.27
has shed is still in the m. of her; 24.07
make their dwellings in your m.; 25.04
She shall be in the m. of the sea a 26.05
cast into the m. of the waters. 26.12
slaughter is made in the m. of you? 26.15
your company that is in your m., 27.27
like Tyre in the m. of the sea? 27.32
in the m. of the stones of fire you 28.14
out from the m. of the stones of 28.16
forth fire from the m. of you; 28.18
manifest my glory in the m. of you. 28.22
slain shall fall in the m. of her, 28.23
that lies in the m. of his streams, 29.03
up out of the m. of your streams, 29.04
desolation in the m. of desolated 29.12
desolated in the m. of desolated 30.07
shall be in the m. of cities that 30.07
out of the m. of Sheol: 'They have 32.21
me down in the m. of the valley; 37.01
sanctuary in the m. of them for 37.26
is in the m. of them for evermore." 37.28
known in the m. of my people 39.07
dwell in the m. of the people of 43.07
I will dwell in their m. for ever. 43.09
with the sanctuary in the m. of it. 48.08
of the LORD in the m. of it. 48.10
In the m. of it shall be the city; 48.15
sanctuary of the temple in its m., 48.21
shall be in the m. of that which 48.22
walking in the m. of the fire, Dan 3.25
a tree in the m. of the earth; 4.10
not man, the Holy One in your m., Hos 11.09
know that I am in the m. of Israel, Joe 2.27
will cut off the ruler from its m., Amo 2.03
her, and the oppressions in her m. 3.09
I will pass through the m. of you, 5.17
calves from the m. of the stall; 6.04
line in the m. of my people Israel; 7.08
you in the m. of the house of 7.10
"Is not the LORD in the m. of us? Mic 3.11
shall be in the m. of many peoples 5.07
in the m. of many peoples, like a 5.08
a forest in the m. of a garden 7.14
Behold your troops are women in your m. Nah 3.13
In the m. of the years renew it; Hab 3.02
in the m. of the years make it 3.02
Herds shall lie down in the m. of her, Zep 2.14
from your m. your proudly exultant 3.11
leave in the m. of you a people 3.12
of Israel, the LORD, is in your m.; 3.15
is in your m., a warrior who gives 3.17
and I will dwell in the m. of you, Zec 2.10
and I will dwell in the m. of you, 2.11
will dwell in the m. of Jerusalem, 8.03
to dwell in the m. of Jerusalem; 8.08
a blazing pot in the m. of wood, 12.06
will be divided in the m. of you. 14.01
out as sheep in the m. of wolves; Mt 10.16
he put him in the m. of them, 18.02
name, there am I in the m. of them." 18.20
and put him in the m. of them; Mk 9.36
the high priest stood up in the m., 14.60
through the m. of them he went Lk 4.30
had thrown him down in the m., 4.35
the tiles into the m. before Jesus. 5.19
out as lambs in the m. of wolves. 10.03
kingdom of God is in the m. of you." 17.21
adultery, and placing her in the m. *Jn 8.03
God did through him in your m., Ac 2.22
And when they had set them in the m., 4.07
blemish in the m. of a crooked and Php 2.15
in the m. of the congregation I Heb 2.12
away in the m. of his pursuits. Jas 1.11
and in the m. of the lampstands one Rev 1.13
a voice in the m. of the four 6.06
For the Lamb in the m. of the 7.17

MIDWIFE
the m. said to her, "Fear not; Gen 35.17
and the m. took and bound on his 38.28
"When you serve as m. to the Hebrew Ex 1.16
before the m. comes to them. 1.19

MIDWIVES
of Egypt said to the Hebrew m., Ex 1.15
But the m. feared God, and did not 1.17
So the king of Egypt called the m., 1.18
The m. said to Pharaoh, "Because the 1.19
So God dealt well with the m.; 1.20
And because the m. feared God he 1.21

MIGDALEL
Yiron, M., Horem, Bethanath, and Jos 19.38

MIGDALGAD
Zenan, Hadashah, M., Jos 15.37

MIGDOL
between M. and the sea, in front of Ex 14.02
and they encamped before M. Num 33.07
at M., at Tahpanhes, at Memphis, and Jer 44.01
"Declare in Egypt, and proclaim in M.; 46.14
from M. to Syene, as far as the Eze 29.10
from M. to Syene they shall fall 30.06

MIGHT
"Oh that Ishmael m. live in thy Gen 17.18
of the people m. easily have lain 26.10
that they m. breed among the rods, 30.41
so that I m. have sent you away 31.27
that he m. rescue him out of their 37.22
he feared that harm m. befall him. 42.04
the Egyptians m. not eat bread 43.32
my m., and the first fruits of my 49.03
that they m. travel by day and by Ex 13.21
of Egypt that I m. dwell among 29.46
together that it m. be one whole. 36.18
opening, that it m. not be torn. 39.23
that I m. be their God: I am the Lev 26.45
people in thy m. from among them, Num 14.13
that he m. give him into your hand, Deu 2.30
that you m. do them in the land 4.14
that you m. know that the LORD is 4.35
voice, that he m. discipline you; 4.36
that the manslayer m. flee there, 4.42
these cities he m. save his life: 4.42
that it m. go well with them and 5.29
your soul, and with all your m. 6.05
that he m. bring us in and give us 6.23
that he m. preserve us alive, as at 6.24
that he m. humble you, testing you 8.02
that he m. make you know that man 8.03
that he m. humble you and test you, 8.16
power and the m. of my hand have 8.17
so that he m. not die by the hand Jos 20.09
your children m. say to our 22.24
your children m. make our children 22.25

MIGHT (cont.)

the people of Israel m. know war, Ju 3.02
that he m. teach war to such at 3.02
March on, my soul, with m.! 5.21
like the sun as he rises in his m." 5.31
"Go in this m. of yours and deliver 6.14
of Jerubbaal m. come and their 9.24
and how you m. be bound, that one 16.06
please tell me how you m. be bound." 16.10
tell me how you m. be bound." 16.13
Then he bowed with all his m.; 16.30
for not by m. shall a man prevail. 1Sa 2.09
that you m. eat with the guests." 9.24
that he m. become the king's son-in-law. 18.27
that he m. kill him in the morning. 19.11
before the LORD with all their m., 2Sa 6.05
before the LORD with all his m.; 6.14
with a suit or cause m. come to me, 15.04
that the LORD m. bring evil upon 17.14
a house, that my name m. be there; 1Ki 8.16
LORD that he m. fulfil his word, 12.15
that he m. permit no one to go out 15.17
all his m., and all that he did, and 15.23
and his m., are they not written in 16.05
and the m. that he showed, are they 16.27
and he asked that he m. die, 19.04
and his m. that he showed, and how 22.45
and all his m., are they not 2Ki 10.34
and his m., are they not written in 13.08
and the m. with which he fought 13.12
and his m., and how he fought with 14.15
and his m., how he fought, and how 14.28
that he m. help him to confirm his 15.19
and all his m., and how he made the 20.20
that they m. provoke me to anger 22.17
that no one m. burn his son or his 23.10
that he m. establish the words of 23.24
all his soul and with all his m.; 23.25
that he m. not reign in Jerusalem, 23.33
and that thy hand m. be with me, 1Ch 4.10
harm so that it m. not hurt me!" 4.10
merry before God with all their m., 13.08
In thy hand are power and m.; 29.12
rule and his m. and of the circumstances 29.30
that my name m. be there, and I 2Ch 6.05
place, thou and the ark of thy m. 6.41
that the LORD m. fulfil his word, 10.15
that he m. permit no one to go out 16.01
to show his m. in behalf of those 16.09
In thy hand are power and m., 20.06
order that he m. give them into 25.20
with all their m. to the LORD. 30.21
that they m. give themselves to the 31.04
order that they m. take the city. 32.18
that they m. provoke me to anger 34.25
that they m. distribute them 35.12
of Jeremiah m. be accomplished, the 36.22
of Jeremiah m. be accomplished, the Ez 1.01
that we m. write down the names of 5.10
that we m. humble ourselves before 8.21
that they m. do with them as they Neh 9.24
that no burden m. be brought in on 13.19
for no one m. enter the king's gate Est 4.02
so that he m. take off his sackcloth, 4.04
that he m. show it to Esther and 4.08
or province that m. attack them, 8.11
And all the acts of his power and m., 10.02
"O that I m. have my request, and Job 6.08
that I m. answer him, that we should 9.32
who m. lay his hand upon us both. 9.33
"With God are wisdom and m.; 12.13
Oh, that I knew where I m. find him, 23.03
that I m. come even to his seat! 23.03
with the m. of thy hand thou dost 30.21
that it m. take hold of the skirts 38.13
"Do you give the horse his m.? 39.19
say, "O that we m. see some good! Ps 4.06
sinks down, and falls by his m. 10.10
and by its great m. it cannot save. 33.17
name, and vindicate me by thy m. 54.01
But I will sing of thy m.; 59.16
mountains, being girded with m.; 65.06
who rules by his m. for ever, 66.07
Summon thy m., O God; 68.28
I proclaim thy m. to all the 71.18
Thou didst divide the sea by thy m.; 74.13
manifested thy m. among the 77.14
and his m., and the wonders which 78.04
that the next generation m. know them, 78.06
Stir up thy m., and come to save us 80.02
so that they m. not again cover the 104.09
that he m. make known his mighty 106.08
that I m. not sin against thee. 119.11
that I m. learn thy statutes. 119.71
place, thou and the ark of thy m. 132.08
proclaim the m. of thy terrible 145.06
that the waters m. not transgress Pro 8.29
till I m. see what was good for the Ecc 2.03
And though a man m. prevail against 4.12
finds to do, do it with your m.; 9.10
say that wisdom is better than m., 9.16
the spirit of counsel and m., Is 11.02
waited for him, that he m. save us. 25.09
who are near, acknowledge my m. 33.13
Behold, the Lord GOD comes with m., 40.10
by the greatness of his m., 40.26
him who has no m. he increases 40.29
that we m. know, and beforetime, that 41.26
that we m. say, "He is right"? There 41.26
of his anger and the m. of battle; 42.25
that they m. declare my praise. 43.21
and that Israel m. be gathered to 49.05
my hands, that I m. be glorified. 60.21
Where are thy zeal and thy m.? 63.15
the mountains m. quake at thy 64.01
the nations m. tremble at thy 64.02
that I m. weep day and night for Jer 9.01
that I m. leave my people and go 9.02
not the mighty man glory in his m., 9.23
great, and thy name is great in m. 10.06
that they m. be for me a people, a 13.11
make them know my power and my m., 16.21
that they m. not hear and receive 17.23
is evil, and their m. is not right. 23.10
that you m. provoke me to anger 25.07
of Elam, the mainstay of their m.; 49.35
fierce anger all the m. of Israel; Lam 2.03
and exalted the m. of your foes. 2.17
will put an end to their proud m., Eze 7.24
that it m. stand in battle in the 13.05
toward him that he m. water it. 17.07
that it m. bring forth branches, and 17.08
that the kingdom m. be humble and 17.14
keeping his covenant it m. stand. 17.14
that they m. give him horses and a 17.15
that they m. know that I the LORD 20.12
first-born, that I m. horrify them; 20.26
it that they m. know that I am the 20.26
and her proud m. shall come down; 30.06
and her proud m. shall come to an 30.18
for all their m. are laid with 32.29
which they caused by their m.; 32.30
and her proud m. shall come to an 33.28
that they m. possess it and plunder 36.05
in order that I m. show it to you; 40.04
that he m. show to the king the Dan 2.16
his companions m. not perish with 2.18
ever, to whom belong wisdom and m. 2.20
and the m., and the glory, 2.37
that they m. make known to me the 4.06
his concubines m. drink from them. 5.02
so that the king m. suffer no loss. 6.02
that nothing m. be changed concerning 6.17
that they m. enlarge their border. Amo 1.13
that it m. be a shade over his head, Jon 4.06
and he asked that he m. die, 4.08

MIGHT (cont.)

the Lord, and with justice and m., Mic 3.08
see and be ashamed of all their m.; 7.16
is slow to anger and of great m., Nah 1.03
men, whose own m. is their god! Hab 1.11
Not by m., nor by power, but by my Zec 4.06
their ears that they m. not hear. 7.11
laid, that the temple m. be built. 8.09
that you m. not kindle fire upon my Mal 1.10
gave them to him, that he m. fear; 2.05
by the prophets m. be fulfilled, Mt 2.23
prophet Isaiah m. be fulfilled: 4.14
sabbath?" so that they m. accuse him. 12.10
to give her whatever she m. ask. 14.07
him that they m. only touch the 14.36
to him that he m. lay his hands on 19.13
For this ointment m. have been sold 26.09
of the prophets m. be fulfilled. 26.56
Jesus that they m. put him to death, 26.59
sabbath, so that they m. accuse him. Mk 3.02
begged him that he m. be with him. 5.18
him that they m. touch even the 6.56
to him, that he m. touch them; 10.13
For this ointment m. have been sold 14.05
possible, the hour m. pass from him. 14.35
so that they m. go and anoint him. 16.01
what sort of greeting this m. be. Lk 1.29
m. serve him without fear, 1.74
that they m. throw him down headlong. 4.29
so that they m. find an accusation 6.07
another what they m. do to Jesus. 6.11
gone begged that he m. be with him; 8.38
to catch at something he m. say. 11.54
that I m. make merry with my 15.29
to him that he m. touch them; 18.15
that he m. know what they had 19.15
that they m. take hold of what he 20.20
captains how he m. betray him to 22.04
that he m. sift you like wheat, 22.31
that all m. believe through him. Jn 1.07
that he m. be revealed to Israel. 1.31
that the world m. be saved through 3.17
that they m. have some charge to * 8.06
works of God m. be made manifest 9.03
know, so that they m. arrest him. 11.57
the prophet Isaiah m. be fulfilled: 12.38
that the scripture m. be fulfilled. 17.12
so that they m. not be defiled, but 18.28
but m. eat the passover. 18.28
that I m. not be handed over to the 18.36
that their legs m. be broken, 19.31
and that they m. be taken away. 19.31
that the scripture m. be fulfilled, 19.36
Pilate that he m. take away the 19.38
his shadow m. fall on some of them. Ac 5.15
You m. even be found opposing God!" 5.39
that they m. not be kept alive. 7.19
them that they m. receive the Holy 8.15
he m. bring them bound to Jerusalem. 9.02
him so that he m. regain his sight." 9.12
vision which he had seen m. mean, 10.17
these things m. be told them the 13.42
hope that they m. feel after him 17.27
so that he m. not have to spend 20.16
me this day m. become such as I am— 26.29
And fearing that we m. run on the 27.29
grace also m. reign through righteousness Rom 5.21
we too m. walk in newness of life. 6.04
the sinful body m. be destroyed, 6.06
and we m. no longer be enslaved to 6.06
order that sin m. be shown to be 7.13
the commandment m. become sinful 7.13
of the law m. be fulfilled in us, 8.04
order that he m. be the first-born 8.29
purpose of election m. continue, 9.11
off so that I m. be grafted in." 11.19
a gift to him that he m. be repaid?" 11.35
that he m. be Lord both of the dead 14.09
of the scriptures we m. have hope. 15.04
the Gentiles m. glorify God for 15.09
no human being m. boast in the 1Co 1.29
that your faith m. not rest in the 2.05
that we m. understand the gifts 2.12
so that we m. share the rule with 4.08
m. he not be encouraged, if his 8.10
to all, that I m. win the more. 9.19
that I m. win those under the law. 9.20
that I m. win those outside the law. 9.21
weak, that I m. win the weak. 9.22
that I m. by all means save some. 9.22
so that you m. have a double 2Co 1.15
when I came I m. not be pained by 2.03
that I m. test you and know whether 2.09
the Israelites m. not see the end 3.13
those who live m. live no longer 5.15
that in him we m. become the 5.21
zeal for us m. be revealed to you 7.12
by his poverty you m. become rich. 8.09
myself so that you m. be exalted, 11.07
in order that I m. preach him Gal 1.16
that they m. bring us into bondage— 2.04
of the gospel m. be preserved for 2.05
to the law, that I m. live to God. 2.19
of Abraham m. come upon the 3.14
that we m. receive the promise of 3.14
in Jesus Christ m. be given to 3.22
that we m. be justified by faith. 3.24
so that we m. receive adoption as 4.05
to the working of his great m. Eph 1.19
coming ages he m. show the immeasurable 2.07
that he m. create in himself one 2.15
and m. reconcile us both to God in 2.16
wisdom of God m. now be made known 3.10
strengthened with m. through his 3.16
that he m. fill all things. 4.10
that he m. sanctify her, having 5.26
that the church m. be presented 5.27
that she m. be holy and without 5.27
Lord and in the strength of his m. 6.10
according to his glorious m., Col 1.11
in everything he m. be pre-eminent. 1.18
though we m. have made demands as 1Th 2.06
that we m. not burden any of you, 2.09
I sent that I m. know your faith, 3.05
wake or sleep we m. live with him. 5.10
Lord and from the glory of his m., 2Th 1.09
that we m. not burden any of you. 3.08
Jesus Christ m. display his perfect 1Ti 1.16
that all the Gentiles m. hear it. 2Ti 4.17
that you m. amend what was defective, Tit 1.05
so that we m. be justified by his 3.07
order that he m. serve me on your Phm 1.13
your goodness m. not be by compulsion 1.14
that you m. have him back for ever, 1.15
grace of God he m. taste death for Heb 2.09
death he m. destroy him who has 2.14
so that he m. become a merciful and 2.17
fled for refuge m. have strong 6.18
One m. even say that Levi himself, 7.09
the first-born m. not touch them. 11.28
that they m. rise again to a better 11.35
fervently that it m. not rain, Jas 5.17
that we m. die to sin and live to 1Pe 2.24
that he m. bring us to God, being 3.18
they m. live in the spirit like God. 4.06
though greater in m. and power, 2Pe 2.11
that it m. be plain that they all 1Jn 2.19
so that we m. live through him. 4.09
that they m. eat food sacrificed to Rev 2.14
and wisdom and m. and honor and 5.12
and glory and m. for ever and ever!" 5.13
that no wind m. blow on earth or 7.01
and power and m. be to our God for 7.12
that he m. devour her child when 12.04
eagle that she m. fly from the 12.14

MIGHTIER
for you are much m. than we. Gen 26.16
a nation greater and m. than they. Num 14.12
greater and m. than yourselves, to Deu 4.38
greater and m. than yourselves, 7.01
greater and m. than yourselves, 9.01
of you a nation m. and greater 9.14
greater and m. than yourselves. 11.23
M. than the thunders of many waters, Ps 93.04
m. than the waves of the sea, the 93.04
A wise man is m. than a strong man, Pro 24.05
is coming after me is m. than I, Mt 3.11
"After me comes he who is m. than I, Mk 1.07
but he who is m. than I is coming, Lk 3.16

MIGHTIEST
which is m. among beasts and does Pro 30.30

MIGHTILY
prevailed so m. upon the earth Gen 7.19
of the LORD came m. upon him, Ju 14.06
of the LORD came m. upon him, 14.19
of the LORD came m. upon him, 15.14
of the LORD will come m. upon you, 1Sa 10.06
the spirit of God came m. upon him, 10.10
of God came m. upon Saul when he 11.06
the LORD came m. upon David from 16.13
he will roar m. against his fold, Jer 25.30
sackcloth, and let them cry m. to God; Jon 3.08
of the Lord grew and prevailed m. Ac 19.20
energy which he m. inspires within Col 1.29

MIGHTY
These were the m. men that were of Gen 6.04
the first on earth to be a m. man. 10.08
He was a m. hunter before the LORD; 10.09
"Like Nimrod a m. hunter before the 10.09
shall become a great and m. nation, 18.18
you are a m. prince among us. 23.06
"With m. wrestlings I have wrestled 30.08
hands of the M. One of Jacob (by 49.24
your father are m. beyond the 49.26
are too many and too m. for us. Ex 1.09
go unless compelled by a m. hand. 3.19
they sank as lead in the m. waters. 15.10
great power and with a m. hand? 32.11
me, since they are too m. for me; Num 22.06
thy greatness and thy m. hand; Deu 3.24
do such works and m. acts as thine? 3.24
by a m. hand and an outstretched 4.34
thence with a m. hand and an 5.15
us out of Egypt with a m. hand; 6.21
has brought you out with a m. hand, 7.08
the m. hand, and the outstretched 7.19
out of Egypt with a m. hand. 9.26
the m., and the terrible God, who is 10.17
his m. hand and his outstretched 11.02
a nation, great, m., and populous. 26.05
of Egypt with a m. hand and an 26.08
and for all the m. power and all 34.12
that the hand of the LORD is m.; Jos 4.24
with its king and m. men of valor. 6.02
thirty thousand m. men of valor, 8.03
than Ai, and all its men were m. 10.02
him, and all the m. men of valor. 10.07
"The M. One, God, the LORD! 22.22
down for him against the m. Ju 5.13
help of the LORD against the m. 5.23
is with you, you m. man of valor." 6.12
the Gileadite was a m. warrior, 11.01
The bows of the m. are broken, 1Sa 2.04
camp, all Israel gave a m. shout, 4.05
us from the power of these m. gods? 4.08
thundered with a m. voice that day 7.10
thy high places! How are the m. fallen! 2Sa 1.19
the shield of the m. was defiled, 1.21
the slain, from the fat of the m., 1.22
"How are the m. fallen in the midst 1.25
"How are the m. fallen, and the 1.27
and all the host of the m. men. 10.07
and all the m. men were on his 16.06
your father and his men are m. men, 17.08
knows that your father is a m. man, 17.10
the Pelethites, and all the m. men; 20.07
for they were too m. for me. 22.18
names of the m. men whom David had: 23.08
among the three m. men was Eleazar 23.09
Then the three m. men broke through 23.16
these things did the three m. men. 23.17
won a name beside the three m. men. 23.22
and David's m. men were not with 1Ki 1.08
Benaiah or the m. men or Solomon 1.10
and thy m. hand, and of thy outstretched 8.42
He was a m. man of valor, but he was 2Ki 5.01
and all the m. men of valor, ten 24.14
began to be a m. one in the earth. 1Ch 1.10
m. warriors, famous men, heads of 5.24
m. warriors of their generations, 7.02
eighty-seven thousand m. warriors, 7.05
of fathers' houses, m. warriors; 7.07
m. warriors, was twenty thousand two 7.09
m. warriors, seventeen thousand and 7.11
m. warriors, chief of the princes. 7.40
Ulam were men who were m. warriors, 8.40
are the chiefs of David's m. men, 11.10
This is an account of David's m. men: 11.11
among the three m. men was Eleazar 11.12
Then the three m. men broke through 11.18
these things did the three m. men. 11.19
won a name beside the three m. men. 11.24
The m. men of the armies were 11.26
were among the m. men who helped 12.01
a m. man among the thirty and a 12.04
the wilderness m. and experienced 12.08
or they were all m. men of valor, 12.21
m. men of valor for war, seven 12.25
a young man m. in valor, and twenty-two 12.28
m. men of valor, famous men in their 12.30
and all the army of the m. men. 19.08
who was a m. man of the thirty and 27.06
the m. men, and all the seasoned 28.01
All the leaders and the m. men, 29.24
and thy m. hand, and thy outstretched 2Ch 6.32
thousand picked m. warriors. 13.03
But Abijah grew m. And he took 13.21
all these were m. men of valor. 14.08
help, between the m. and the weak. 14.11
m. men of valor, in Jerusalem. 17.13
hundred thousand m. men of valor, 17.14
hundred thousand m. men of valor. 17.16
a m. man of valor, with two hundred 17.17
thousand m. men of valor from 25.06
houses of m. men of valor was two 26.12
who could make war with m. power, 26.13
So Jotham became m., because he 27.06
And Zichri, a m. man of Ephraim, slew 28.07
officers and his m. men to stop the 32.03
cut off all the m. warriors and 32.21
And m. kings have been over Jerusalem, Ez 4.20
before all the king's m. officers. 7.28
and to the house of the m. men. Neh 3.16
depths, as a stone into m. waters. 9.11
the great and m. and terrible God, 9.32
m. men of valor, a hundred and 11.14
the needy from the hand of the m. Job 5.15
and m. in strength—who has hardened 9.04
stripped, and overthrows the m. 12.19
old age, and grow m. in power? 21.07
the life of the m. by his power; 24.22
him who is righteous and m., 34.17
and the m. are taken away by no 34.20
He shatters the m. without investigation, 34.24
help because of the arm of the m. 35.09
God is m., and does not despise any 36.05
he is m. in strength of understanding 36.05
or his m. strength, or his goodly 41.12

MIGHTY (cont.)

himself up the m. are afraid; Job 41.25
for they were too m. for me. Ps 18.17
heaven with m. victories by his 20.06
strong and m., the LORD, m. in battle! 24.08
in the m. throng I will praise thee 35.18
are my foes without cause are m., 38.19
O m. one, in your glory and majesty! 45.03
The M. One, God the LORD, speaks and 50.01
fire, round about him a m. tempest. 50.03
O m. man, of mischief done against 52.01
my m. rock, my refuge is God. 62.07
O m. mountain, mountain of Bashan; 68.15
With m. chariotry, twice ten thousand, 68.17
forth his voice, his m. voice. 68.33
m. are those who would destroy me, 69.04
With the m. deeds of the Lord GOD I 71.16
thy work, and muse on thy m. deeds. 77.12
the m. cedars with its branches; 80.10
who is m. as thou art, O LORD, with 89.08
thy enemies with thy m. arm. 89.10
Thou hast a m. arm; strong is thy 89.13
set the crown upon one who is m., 89.19
of the sea, the LORD on high is m.! 93.04
M. King, lover of justice, thou hast 99.04
you m. ones who do his word, hearkening 103.20
Who can utter the m. doings of the 106.02
he might make known his m. power. 106.08
forth from Zion your m. scepter. 110.02
descendants will be m. in the land; 112.02
and vowed to the M. One of Jacob, 132.02
place for the M. One of Jacob. 132.05
many nations and slew m. kings, 135.10
and shall declare thy m. acts. 145.04
to the sons of men thy m. deeds, 145.12
praise him in his m. firmament! 150.01
Praise him for his m. deeds; 150.02
yea, all her slain are a m. host. Pro 7.26
to anger is better than the m., 16.32
the city of the m. and brings down 21.22
The badgers are a people not m., 30.26
sixty m. men of the m. men of Israel, Sol 3.07
the M. One of Israel: "Ah, I will Is 1.24
the m. man and the soldier, the 3.02
sword and your m. men in battle. 3.25
m. and many, the king of Assyria and 8.07
M. God, Everlasting Father, Prince of 9.06
remnant of Jacob, to the m. God. 10.21
summoned my m. men to execute my 13.03
roar like the roaring of m. waters! 17.12
a nation m. and conquering, whose 18.02
a nation m. and conquering, whose 18.07
archers of the m. men of the sons 21.17
Lord has one who is m. and strong; 28.02
tempest, like a storm of m., 28.02
and young steers with the m. bulls. 34.07
The LORD goes forth like a m. man, 42.13
shows himself m. against his foes. 42.13
the sea, a path in the m. waters, 43.16
Can the prey be taken from the m., 49.24
captives of the m. shall be taken, 49.25
your Redeemer, the M. One of Jacob." 49.26
The dogs have a m. appetite; they 56.11
your Redeemer, the M. One of Jacob. 60.16
and the smallest one a m. nation; 60.22
his right hand and by his m. arm: 62.08
announcing vindication, m. to save. 63.01
an open tomb, they are all m. men. Jer 5.16
let not the m. man glory in his 9.23
like a m. man who cannot save? 14.09
O great and m. God whose name is 32.18
great in counsel and m. in deed; 32.19
'We are heroes and m. men of war'? 48.14
say, 'How the m. scepter is broken, 48.17
a m. nation and many kings are 50.41
waste, and stilling her m. voice. 51.55
flouted all my m. men in the midst Lam 1.15
Pharaoh with his m. army and great Eze 17.17
surely with a m. hand and an 20.33
with a m. hand and an outstretched 20.34
and your m. pillars will fall to 26.11
that was m. on the sea, you and your 26.17
the hand of a m. one of the 31.11
to fall by the swords of m. ones, 32.12
The m. chiefs shall speak of them, 32.21
with the fallen m. men of old who 32.27
terror of the m. men was in the 32.27
on horses, a great host, a m. army; 38.15
You shall eat the flesh of the m., 39.18
with m. men and all kinds of 39.20
This image, m. and of exceeding Dan 2.31
ordered certain m. men of his army 3.20
are his signs, how m. his wonders! 4.03
built by my m. power as a royal 4.30
and he ran at him in his m. wrath. 8.06
and destroy m. men and the people 8.24
the land of Egypt with a m. hand, 9.15
Then a m. king shall arise, who 11.03
an exceedingly great and m. army; 11.25
Prepare war, stir up the m. men. Joe 3.09
nor shall the m. save his life; Amo 2.14
heart among the m. shall flee away 2.16
And your m. men shall be dismayed, O Ob 1.09
and there was a m. tempest on the Jon 1.04
The shield of his m. men is red, Nah 2.03
horses, the surging of m. waters. Hab 3.15
the m. man cries aloud there. Zep 1.14
shall be like m. men in battle, Zec 10.05
shall become like a m. warrior, 10.07
and do many m. works in your name?' Mt 7.22
most of his m. works had been done, 11.20
for if the m. works done in you had 11.21
For if the m. works done in you had 11.23
get this wisdom and these m. works? 13.54
And he did not do many m. works there, 13.58
What m. works are wrought by his Mk 6.02
And he could do no m. work there, 6.05
one who does a m. work in my name 9.39
for he who is m. has done great Lk 1.49
put down the m. from their thrones, 1.52
for if the m. works done in you had 10.13
for all the m. works that they had 19.37
was a prophet m. in deed and word 24.19
heaven like the rush of a m. wind, Ac 2.02
own tongues the m. works of God. 2.11
you by God with m. works and 2.22
and he was m. in his words and 7.22
signs and wonders and m. works. 2Co 12.12
heaven with his m. angels in 2Th 1.07
became m. in war, put foreign armies Heb 11.34
therefore under the m. hand of God, 1Pe 5.06
Then I saw another m. angel coming Rev 10.01
And he called out with a m. voice, 18.02
for m. is the Lord God who judges 18.08
great city, thou m. city, Babylon! 18.10
Then a m. angel took up a stone 18.21
to be the m. voice of a great 19.01
like the sound of m. thunderpeals, 19.06
the flesh of m. men, the flesh of 19.18

MIGRATED

And as men m. in the east, they Gen 11.02

MIGRON

pomegranate tree which is at M.; 1Sa 14.02
he has passed through M., at Michmash Is 10.28

MIJAMIN

to Malchijah, the sixth to M., 1Ch 24.09
M., Eleazar, Hashabiah, and Benaiah. Ez 10.25
Meshullam, Abijah, M., Neh 10.07
M., Maadiah, Bilgah, 12.05

MIKLOTH

and M. (he was the father of 1Ch 8.32
Gedor, Ahio, Zechariah, and M.; 9.37
and M. was the father of Shimeam; 9.38

MIKNEIAH
and M., and the gatekeepers Obededom 1Ch 15.18
M., Obededom, Jeiel, and Azaziah were 15.21

MILALAI
M., Gilalai, Maai, Nethanel, Judah, and Neh 12.36

MILCAH
M., the daughter of Haran the Gen 11.29
Haran the father of M. and Iscah. 11.29
M. also has borne children to your 22.20
These eight M. bore to Nahor, 22.23
was born to Bethuel the son of M., 24.15
daughter of Bethuel the son of M., 24.24
Nahor's son, whom M. bore to him. 24.47
Noah, Hoglah, M., and Tirzah. Num 26.33
Noah, Hoglah, M., and Tirzah. 27.01
M., and Noah, the daughters of 36.11
Noah, Hoglah, M., and Tirzah. Jos 17.03

MILCH
thirty m. camels and their colts, Gen 32.15
cart and two m. cows upon which 1Sa 6.07
and took two m. cows and yoked them 6.10

MILCOM
and after M. the abomination of the 1Ki 11.05
and M. the god of the Ammonites, and 11.33
and for M. the abomination of the 2Ki 23.13
Why then has M. dispossessed Gad, Jer 49.01
For M. shall go into exile, with his 49.03
to the LORD and yet swear by M.; Zep 1.05

MILDEW
and with blasting, and with m.; Deu 28.22
or blight or m. or locust or 1Ki 8.37
or blight or m. or locust or 2Ch 6.28
"I smote you with blight and m.; Amo 4.09
toil with blight and m. and hail; Hag 2.17

MILE
if any one forces you to go one m., Mt 5.41

MILES
to go one mile, go with him two m. Mt 5.41
about seven m. from Jerusalem, Lk 24.13
had rowed about three or four m., Jn 6.19
near Jerusalem, about two m. off, 11.18

MILETUS
the day after that we came to M. Ac 20.15
And from M. he sent to Ephesus and 20.17
Trophimus I left ill at M. 2Ti 4.20

MILITARY
hall with the m. tribunes and the Ac 25.23

MILK
and m., and the calf which he had Gen 18.08
wine, and his teeth white with m. 49.12
a land flowing with m. and honey, Ex 3.08
a land flowing with m. and honey. 3.17
a land flowing with m. and honey, 13.05
not boil a kid in its mother's m. 23.19
a land flowing with m. and honey; 33.03
not boil a kid in its mother's m. 34.26
a land flowing with m. and honey. Lev 20.24
it flows with m. and honey, and this Num 13.27
land which flows with m. and honey. 14.08
a land flowing with m. and honey, 16.13
a land flowing with m. and honey, 16.14
a land flowing with m. and honey. Deu 6.03
a land flowing with m. and honey. 11.09
not boil a kid in its mother's m. 14.21
a land flowing with m. and honey. 26.09
a land flowing with m. and honey. 26.15
a land flowing with m. and honey, 27.03
the land flowing with m. and honey, 31.20
and m. from the flock, with fat of 32.14
a land flowing with m. and honey. Jos 5.06
a skin of m. and gave him a drink Ju 4.19
He asked water and she gave him m., 5.25
me out like m. and curdle me like Job 10.10
when my steps were washed with m., 29.06
be enough goats' m. for your food, Pro 27.27
For pressing m. produces curds, 30.33
honey and m. are under your tongue; Sol 4.11
honey, I drink my wine with my m. 5.01
of water, bathed in m., fitly set. 5.12
abundance of m. which they give, he Is 7.22
Those who are weaned from the m., 28.09
buy wine and m. without money and 55.01
You shall suck the m. of nations, 60.16
a land flowing with m. and honey, Jer 11.05
a land flowing with m. and honey; 32.22
purer than snow, whiter than m.; Lam 4.07
a land flowing with m. and honey, Eze 20.06
a land flowing with m. and honey, 20.15
and they shall drink your m. 25.04
and the hills shall flow with m., Joe 3.18
I fed you with m., not solid food; 1Co 3.02
without getting some of the m.? 9.07
You need m., not solid food; Heb 5.12
who lives on m. is unskilled in 5.13
long for the pure spiritual m., 1Pe 2.02

MILL
maidservant who is behind the m.; Ex 11.05
shall take a m. or an upper Deu 24.06
he ground at the m. in the prison. Ju 16.21
are compelled to grind at the m.; Lam 5.13
Two women will be grinding at the m.; Mt 24.41

MILLET
m. and spelt, and put them into a Eze 4.09

MILLION
there were one m. one hundred 1Ch 21.05
a m. talents of silver, and bronze 22.14
an army of a m. men and three 2Ch 14.09

MILLO
round about from the M. inward. 2Sa 5.09
house and the M. and the wall of 1Ki 9.15
built for her; then he built the M. 9.24
Solomon built the M., and closed up 11.27
and slew Joash in the house of M., 2Ki 12.20
about from the M. in complete 1Ch 11.08
strengthened the M. in the city of 2Ch 32.05

MILLS
ground it in m. or beat it in Num 11.08

MILLSTONE
a mill or an upper m. in pledge; Deu 24.06
threw an upper m. upon Abimelech's Ju 9.53
cast an upper m. upon him from the 2Sa 11.21
as a stone, hard as the nether m. Job 41.24
to have a great m. fastened round Mt 18.06
him if a great m. were hung round Mk 9.42
for him if a m. were hung round Lk 17.02
like a great m. and threw it into Rev 18.21
sound of the m. shall be heard in 18.22

MILLSTONES
Take the m. and grind meal, put off Is 47.02
grinding of the m. and the light Jer 25.10

MINA
and your m. shall be fifty shekels. Eze 45.12

MINAS
three m. of gold went into each 1Ki 10.17
five thousand m. of silver, and one Ez 2.69
thousand two hundred m. of silver. Neh 7.71
two thousand m. of silver, and sixty 7.72

MINCING
m. along as they go, tinkling with Is 3.16

MIND

his father kept the saying in m. Gen 37.11
you have some evil purpose in m. Ex 10.10
the m. of Pharaoh and his servants 14.05
I have endowed with an able m., 28.03
man in whose m. the LORD had put 36.02
they had such a m. as this always, Deu 5.29
and blindness and confusion of m.; 28.28
not given you a m. to understand, 29.04
call them to m. among all the 30.01
And he told her all his m., Ju 16.17
that he had told her all his m., 16.18
for he has told me all his m." 16.18
what is in my heart and in my m.; 1Sa 2.35
tell you all that is on your m. 9.19
ago, do not set your m. on them, 9.20
"Do all that your m. inclines to; 14.07
with you, as is your m. so is mine." 14.07
let not the king bear it in m. 2Sa 19.19
understanding m. to govern thy 1Ki 3.09
give you a wise and discerning m., 3.12
largeness of m. like the sand on 4.29
with all their m. and with all 8.48
told him all that was on her m. 10.02
which God had put into his m. 10.24
has been your m. and you have not 11.11
And the m. of the king of Syria was 2Ki 6.11
so Jehu said, "If this is your m., 9.15
of a single m. to make David king. 1Ch 12.38
Now set your m. and heart to seek 22.19
whole heart and with a willing m.; 28.09
that he had in m. for the courts 28.12
with all their m. and with all 2Ch 6.38
told him all that was on her m. 9.01
which God had put into his m. 9.23
For the people had a m. to work. Neh 4.06
inventing them out of your own m." 6.08
put it into my m. to assemble the 7.05
thou dost set thy m. upon him, Job 7.17
and many such things are in his m. 23.14
test my heart and my m. Ps 26.02
passed out of m. like one who is 31.12
For the inward m. and heart of a 64.06
I will call to m. the deeds of the 77.11
They did not keep in m. his power, 78.42
sworn and will not change his m., 110.04
the m. of the wicked is of little Pro 10.20
Men of perverse m. are an abomination 11.20
but one of perverse m. is despised. 12.08
A tranquil m. gives life to the 14.30
Wisdom abides in the m. of a man of 14.33
The m. of him who has understanding 15.14
The m. of the righteous ponders how 15.28
The plans of the m. belong to man, 16.01
A man's m. plans his way, but the 16.09
The m. of the wise makes his speech 16.23
to buy wisdom, when he has no m.? 17.16
A man of crooked m. does not 17.20
An intelligent m. acquires knowledge, 18.15
Many are the plans in the m. of a man, 19.21
in a man's m. is like deep water, 20.05
and apply your m. to my knowledge; 22.17
Apply your m. to instruction and 23.12
and direct your m. in the way. 23.19
and your m. utter perverse things. 23.33
so the m. of kings is unsearchable. 25.03
so the m. of man reflects the man. 27.19
who trusts in his own m. is a fool; 28.26
And I applied my m. to seek and to Ecc 1.13
and my m. has had great experience 1.16
And I applied my m. to know wisdom 1.17
searched with my m. how to cheer my 2.03
my m. still guiding me with wisdom— 2.03
in the night his m. does not rest. 2.23
he has put eternity into man's m., 3.11
and a bribe corrupts the m. 7.07
I turned my m. to know and to 7.25
which my m. has sought repeatedly, 7.28
and the m. of a wise man will know 8.05
applying my m. to all that is done 8.09
When I applied my m. to know wisdom, 8.16
Remove vexation from your m., 11.10
and his m. does not so think; Is 10.07
but it is in his m. to destroy, 10.07
My m. reels, horror has appalled me; 21.04
whose m. is stayed on thee, because 26.03
The m. of the rash will have good 32.04
and his m. plots iniquity: to 32.06
Your m. will muse on the terror: 33.18
a deluded m. has led him astray, and 44.20
recall it to m., you transgressors, 46.08
not be remembered or come into m. 65.17
It shall not come to m., or be remembered, Jer 3.16
command, nor did it come into my m. 7.31
who triest the heart and the m., 11.20
me, and triest my m. toward thee. 12.03
LORD search the m. and try the 17.10
decree, nor did it come into my m.; 19.05
who seest the heart and the m., 20.12
accomplished the intents of his m. 23.20
accomplished the intents of his m. 30.24
them, nor did it enter into my m., 32.35
Did it not come into his m.? 44.21
let Jerusalem come into your m.: 51.50
But this I call to m., and therefore Lam 3.21
the things that come into your m. Eze 11.05
"What is in your m. shall never 20.32
thoughts will come into your m., 38.10
and set your m. upon all that I 40.04
may know the thoughts of your m. Dan 2.30
let his m. be changed from a man's, 4.16
let a beast's m. be given to him; 4.16
and his m. was made like that of a 5.21
and set his m. to deliver Daniel; 6.14
and the m. of a man was given to it 7.04
but I kept the matter in my m." 7.28
and in his own m. he shall magnify 8.25
you set your m. to understand and 10.12
your soul, and with all your m. Mt 22.37
there, clothed and in his right m., Mk 5.15
your soul, and with all your m., 12.30
considered in her m. what sort of Lk 1.29
Jesus, clothed and in his right m.; 8.35
strength, and with all your m.; 10.27
are to drink, nor be of anxious m. 12.29
up to a base m. and to improper Rom 1.28
the law of my m. and making me 7.23
serve the law of God with my m., 7.25
To set the m. on the flesh is death, 8.06
but to set the m. on the Spirit is 8.06
For the m. that is set on the flesh 8.07
knows what is the m. of the Spirit, 8.27
"For who has known the m. of the Lord, 11.34
transformed by the renewal of your m.. 12.02
be fully convinced in his own m. 14.05
in the same m. and the same 1Co 1.10
has known the m. of the Lord so as 2.16
But we have the m. of Christ. 2.16
Never m. But if you can 7.21
prays but my m. is unfruitful. 14.14
and I will pray with the m. also; 14.15
and I will sing with the m. also. 14.15
rather speak five words with my m., 14.19
Come to your right m., and sin no 15.34
For I made up my m. not to make you 2Co 2.01
but my m. could not rest because I 2.13
are in our right m., it is for you. 5.13
because his m. has been set at rest 7.13
must do as he has made up his m., 9.07
following the desires of body and m., Eph 2.03
with one m. striving side by side Php 1.27
complete my joy by being of the same m., 2.02
being in full accord and of one m. 2.02
Have this m. among yourselves, which 2.05
were estranged and hostile in m., Col 1.21
without reason by his sensuous m., 2.18

MIND (cont.)
to m. your own affairs, and to work 1Th 4.11
be quickly shaken in m. or excited, 2Th 2.02
are depraved in m. and bereft of 1Ti 6.05
men of corrupt m. and counterfeit 2Ti 3.08
sworn and will not change his m., Heb 7.21
your hearts, you men of double m. Jas 4.08
a tender heart and a humble m. 1Pe 3.08
your sincere m. by way of reminder 2Pe 3.01
I am he who searches m. and heart, Rev 2.23
This calls for a m. with wisdom: 17.09
These are of one m. and give over 17.13
by being of one m. and giving over 17.17

MINDED
of us who are mature be thus m.; Php 3.15
in anything you are otherwise m., 3.15
not suppose that a double m. man, Jas 1.07

MINDFUL
He is m. of his covenant for ever, 1Ch 16.15
and were not m. of the wonders Neh 9.17
what is man that thou art m. of him, Ps 8.04
he who avenges blood is m. of them; 9.12
Be m. of thy mercy, O LORD, and of 25.06
He is m. of his covenant for ever, 105.08
he is ever m. of his covenant. 111.05
The LORD has been m. of us; 115.12
God will be m. of them and restore Zep 2.07
is man that thou art m. of him, Heb 2.06
m. of God, he endures pain while 1Pe 2.19

MINDS
closed their m. to understanding, Job 17.04
thou who triest the m. and hearts, Ps 7.09
knowledge; not so the m. of fools. Pro 15.07
for their m. devise violence, and 24.02
and their m., so that they cannot Is 44.18
and the deceit of their own m. Jer 14.14
they speak visions of their own m., 23.16
who prophesy out of their own m.: Eze 13.02
who prophesy out of their own m.; 13.17
their m. shall be bent on mischief; Dan 11.27
Settle it therefore in your m., Lk 21.14
Then he opened their m. to understand 24.45
poisoned their m. against the brethren. Ac 14.02
you with words, unsettling your m., 15.24
changed their m. and said that he 28.06
their senseless m. were darkened. Rom 1.21
flesh set their m. on the things 8.05
the Spirit set their m. on the things of 8.05
But their m. were hardened; for to this 2Co 3.14
is read a veil lies over their m.; 3.15
has blinded the m. of the unbelievers, 4.04
do, in the futility of their m.; Eph 4.17
renewed in the spirit of your m., 4.23
with m. set on earthly things. Php 3.19
hearts and your m. in Christ Jesus 4.07
Set your m. on things that are Col 3.02
their very m. and consciences are Tit 1.15
I will put my laws into their m., Heb 8.10
their hearts, and write them on their m.," 10.16
Therefore gird up your m., be sober, 1Pe 1.13

MINGLE
and m. tears with my drink, Ps 102.09
much incense to m. with the Rev 8.03

MINGLED
of fine flour m. with a fourth of Ex 29.40
You shall not wear a m. stuff, Deu 22.11
but they m. with the nations and Ps 106.35
The LORD has m. within her a spirit Is 19.14
him wine to drink, m. with gall; Mt 27.34
offered him wine m. with myrrh; Mk 15.23
Pilate had m. with their sacrifices Lk 13.01
to be a sea of glass m. with fire, Rev 15.02

MINIAMIN
Eden, M., Jeshua, Shemaiah, Amariah, 2Ch 31.15
of M., of Moadiah, Piltai; Neh 12.17
M., Micaiah, Elioenai, Zechariah, and 12.41

MINISTER
the altar to m. in the holy place; Ex 28.43
of meeting to m. in the holy place. 29.30
they come near the altar to m., 30.20
he ordained to m. in the priest's Num 3.03
priest, that they may m. to him. 3.06
as they m. at the tabernacle; 3.07
Israel as they m. at the tabernacle. 3.08
sanctuary with which the priests m., 3.31
but m. to their brethren in the 8.26
the m. of Moses, one of his chosen 11.28
the congregation to m. to them; 16.09
and m. to you while you and your 18.02
the LORD to m. to him and to bless Deu 10.08
who stands to m. there before the 17.12
to stand and m. in the name of the 18.05
then he may m. in the name of the 18.07
who stand to m. there before the 18.07
chosen them to m. to him and to 21.05
Joshua the son of Nun, Moses' m., Jos 1.01
not stand to m. because of the 1Ki 8.11
the LORD and to m. to him for ever." 1Ch 15.02
of the LORD to m. continually 16.37
and m. to him and pronounce blessings 23.13
not stand to m. because of the 2Ch 5.14
to m. to him, and to be his ministers 29.11
to m. in the gates of the camp of 31.02
the priests who m. in the house of Neh 10.36
sanctuary, and the priests that m., 10.39
that is blameless shall m. to me. Ps 101.06
to m. to him, to love the name of Is 56.06
rams of Nebaioth shall m. to you; 60.07
and their kings shall m. to you; 60.10
the Levitical priests who m. to me." Jer 33.22
come near to the LORD to m. to him. Eze 40.46
the garments in which they m., 42.14
who draw near to me to m. to me, 43.19
shall come near to me to m. to me; 44.15
to m. to me, and they shall keep my 44.16
while they m. at the gates of the 44.17
to m. in the holy place, he shall 44.27
who m. in the sanctuary and approach 45.04
and approach the LORD to m. to him; 45.04
the Levites who m. at the temple, 45.05
where those who m. at the temple 46.24
in prison, and did not m. to thee?' Mt 25.44
a m. of Candace the queen of the Ac 8.27
to be a m. of Christ Jesus to the Rom 15.16
I was made a m. according to the Eph 3.07
and faithful m. in the Lord will 6.21
your messenger and m. to my need, Php 2.25
is a faithful m. of Christ on our Col 1.07
and of which I, Paul, became a m. 1.23
I became a m. according to the 1.25
and faithful m. and fellow servant 4.07
will be a good m. of Christ Jesus, 1Ti 4.06
a m. in the sanctuary and the true Heb 8.02

MINISTERED
women who m. at the door of the Ex 38.08
his son Eleazar m. as priest in Deu 10.06
m. before it in those days), saying, Ju 20.28
And the boy m. to the LORD, in the 1Sa 2.11
the king's nurse and m. to him; 1Ki 1.04
went after Elijah, and m. to him. 19.21
They m. with song before the 1Ch 6.32
the priests and the Levites who m. Neh 12.44
Because they m. to them before Eze 44.12
behold, angels came and m. to him. Mt 4.11
and the angels m. to him. Mk 1.13
followed him, and m. to him; 15.41
these hands m. to my necessities, Ac 20.34

MINISTERING
garments for m. in the holy place, Ex 35.19
from the mirrors of the m. women who 38.08
garments, for m. in the holy place; 39.01
upon the skirts of the robe for m.; 39.26
garments for m. in the holy place, 39.41
Samuel was m. before the LORD, a boy 1Sa 2.18
boy Samuel was m. to the LORD 3.01
the Shunammite was m. to the king). 1Ki 1.15
m. in the house of the LORD; 1Ch 26.12
We have priests m. to the LORD who 2Ch 13.10
except the priests and m. Levites; 23.06
garments in which they have been m., Eze 44.19
Jesus from Galilee, m. to him; Mt 27.55
Are they not all m. spirits sent Heb 1.14

MINISTERS
And it shall be upon Aaron when he m., Ex 28.35
the Levites as m. before the ark 1Ch 16.04
and to be his m. and burn incense 2Ch 29.11
to send us m. for the house of our Ez 8.17
his m. that do his will! Ps 103.21
messengers, fire and flame thy m. 104.04
speak of you as the m. of our God; Is 61.06
with the Levitical priests my m. Jer 33.21
They shall be m. in my sanctuary, Eze 44.11
priests mourn, the m. of the LORD. Joe 1.09
O priests, wail, O m. of the altar. 1.13
night in sackcloth, O m. of my God! 1.13
the m. of the LORD, weep and say, 2.17
eyewitnesses and m. of the word, Lk 1.02
for the authorities are m. of God, Rom 13.06
us to be m. of a new covenant, not 2Co 3.06

MINISTRY
David offered praises by their m.; 2Ch 7.06
of praise and m. before the 8.14
Jesus, when he began his m., Lk 3.23
was allotted his share in this m. Ac 1.17
place in this m. and apostleship 1.25
prayer and to the m. of the word. 6.04
course and the m. which I received 20.24
among the Gentiles through his m. 21.19
Gentiles, I magnify my m. Rom 11.13
having this m. by the mercy of God, 2Co 4.01
and gave us the m. of reconciliation 5.18
no fault may be found with our m., 6.03
of the saints, for the work of m., Eph 4.12
you fulfil the m. which you have Col 4.17
of an evangelist, fulfil your m. 2Ti 4.05
has obtained a m. which is as much Heb 8.06

MINNI
kingdoms, Ararat, M., and Ashkenaz; Jer 51.27

MINNITH
Aroer to the neighborhood of M., Ju 11.33

MINSTREL
But now bring me a m." And when 2Ki 3.15
the m. played, the power of the LORD 3.15

MINSTRELS
the m. last, between them maidens Ps 68.25
and the sound of harpers and m., Rev 18.22

MINT
for you tithe m. and dill and Mt 23.23
for you tithe m. and rue and every Lk 11.42

MIRACLE
'Prove yourselves by working a m.,' Ex 7.09

MIRACLES
Pharaoh all the m. which I have Ex 4.21
and the m. that he had shown them. Ps 78.11
and his m. in the fields of Zoan. 78.43
his m., and the judgments he 105.05
and m. in the land of Ham. 105.27
signs and great m. performed, Ac 8.13
extraordinary m. by the hands of 19.11
to another the working of m., 1Co 12.10
third teachers, then workers of m., 12.28
Are all teachers? Do all work m.? 12.29
you and works m. among you do so Gal 3.05
and various m. and by gifts of the Heb 2.04

MIRE
down like the m. of the streets. 2Sa 22.43
God has cast me into the m., Job 30.19
like a threshing sledge on the m. 41.30
out like the m. of the streets. Ps 18.42
I sink in deep m., where there is 69.02
rescue me from sinking in the m.; 69.14
down like the m. of the streets. Is 10.06
and its waters toss up m. and dirt. 57.20
only m., and Jeremiah sank in the m. Jer 38.06
that your feet are sunk in the m., 38.22
down like the m. of the streets. Mic 7.10
is washed only to wallow in the m. 2Pe 2.22

MIRIAM
Then M., the prophetess, the sister Ex 15.20
And M. sang to them: "Sing to the 15.21
M. and Aaron spoke against Moses Num 12.01
said to Moses and to Aaron and M., 12.04
the tent, and called Aaron and M.; 12.05
M. was leprous, as white as snow. 12.10
And Aaron turned towards M., 12.10
So M. was shut up outside the camp 12.15
the march till M. was brought in 12.15
and M. died there, and was buried 20.01
and Moses and M. their sister. 26.59
your God did to M. on the way as Deu 24.09
and she conceived and bore M., 1Ch 4.17
of Amram: Aaron, Moses, and M. 6.03
before you Moses, Aaron, and M. Mic 6.04

MIRMAH
Jeuz, Sachia, and M. These were his 1Ch 8.10

MIRROR
out the skies, hard as a molten m.? Job 37.18
For now we see in a m. dimly, 1Co 13.12
observes his natural face in a m.; Jas 1.23

MIRRORS
from the m. of the ministering Ex 38.08

MIRTH
sent you away with m. and songs, Gen 31.27
m., saying, "Sing us one of the Ps 137.03
of fools is in the house of m. Ecc 7.04
The m. of the timbrels is stilled, Is 24.08
the m. of the lyre is stilled. 24.08
the voice of m. and the voice of Jer 7.34
the voice of m. and the voice of 16.09
the voice of m. and the voice of 25.10
the voice of m. and the voice of 33.11
Or do we make m.? You have despised Eze 21.10
And I will put an end to all her m., Hos 2.11

MIRY
out of the m. bog, and set my feet Ps 40.02
saw iron mixed with the m. clay. Dan 2.41
saw the iron mixed with m. clay, 2.43

MISCARRIAGE
with child, so that there is a m., Ex 21.22
death nor m. shall come from it. 2Ki 2.21

MISCARRIED
and your she-goats have not m., Gen 31.38

MISCARRYING
Give them a m. womb and dry breasts Hos 9.14

MISCHANCE
suffering no m. or failure in bearings Ps 144.14

MISCHIEF
the Philistines, when I do them m." Ju 15.03
of Solomon, doing m. as Hadad did; 1Ki 11.25
They conceive m. and bring forth Job 15.35
evil, and is pregnant with m., Ps 7.14
His m. returns upon his own head, 7.16
his tongue are m. and iniquity. 10.07
against you, if they devise m., 21.11
while m. is in their hearts. 28.03
of his mouth are m. and deceit; 36.03
He plots m. while on his bed; 36.04
words, while his heart gathers m.; 41.06
of m. done against the godly? 52.01
and m. and trouble are within it, 55.10
with thee, who frame m. by statute? 94.20
let the m. of their lips overwhelm 140.09
violence, and their lips talk of m. Pro 24.02
they conceive m. and bring forth Is 59.04
their minds shall be bent on m.; Dan 11.27

MISCHIEF-MAKER
to do evil will be called a m. Pro 24.08
a thief, or a wrongdoer, or a m.; 1Pe 4.15

MISCHIEVOUS
a liar gives heed to a m. tongue. Pro 17.04

MISDEEDS
their sins and their m. no more. Heb 10.17

MISERABLE
things; m. comforters are you all. Job 16.02
put those wretches to a m. death, Mt 21.41

MISERIES
howl for the m. that are coming Jas 5.01

MISERLY
A m. man hastens after wealth, and Pro 28.22

MISERY
indignant over the m. of Israel. Ju 10.16
light given to him that is in m., Job 3.20
and nights of m. are apportioned to 7.03
You will forget your m.; 11.16
the force of m. will come upon him 20.22
my strength fails because of my m., Ps 31.10
and remember their m. no more. Pro 31.07
in their paths are ruin and m., Rom 3.16

MISFORTUNE
He has not beheld m. in Jacob; Num 23.21
here is neither adversary nor m. 1Ki 5.04
at ease there is contempt for m.; Job 12.05
M. pursues sinners, but prosperity Pro 13.21
your brother in the day of his m.; Ob 1.12
time and saw no m. come to him, Ac 28.06

MISFORTUNES
hearing of the Lord about their m.; Num 11.01

MISHAEL
M., Elzaphan, and Sithri. Ex 6.22
And Moses called M. and Elzaphan, Lev 10.04
and Pedaiah, M., Malchijah, Hashum, Neh 8.04
M., and Azariah of the tribe of Dan 1.06
M. he called Meshach, and Azariah he 1.07
Daniel, Hananiah, M., and Azariah; 1.11
Daniel, Hananiah, M., and Azariah; 1.19
M., and Azariah, his companions, 2.17

MISHAL
Allammelech, Amad, and M.; Jos 19.26
M. with its pasture lands, Abdon 21.30

MISHAM
M., and Shemed, who built Ono and 1Ch 8.12

MISHMA
M., Dumah, Massa, Gen 25.14
M., Dumah, Massa, Hadad, Tema, 1Ch 1.30
son, Mibsam his son, M. his son. 4.25
The sons of M.: Hammuel his son, 4.26

MISHMANNAH
M. fourth, Jeremiah fifth, 1Ch 12.10

MISHRAITES
the Shumathites, and the M.; 1Ch 2.53

MISLEAD
deceive you or m. you in this 2Ch 32.15
your leaders m. you, and confuse the Is 3.12
Beware lest Hezekiah m. you by saying, 36.18

MISLEADING
Is not Hezekiah m. you, that he 2Ch 32.11
seen for you oracles false and m. Lam 2.14

MISLEADS
be he who m. a blind man on the Deu 27.18
Hezekiah when he m. you by saying, 2Ki 18.32
He who m. the upright into an evil Pro 28.10

MISLED
because they have m. my people, Eze 13.10

MISMATED
Do not be m. with unbelievers. 2Co 6.14

MISPAR
M., Bigvai, Rehum, and Baanah. Ez 2.02

MISPERETH
M., Bigvai, Nehum, Baanah. Neh 7.07

MISREPHOTHMAIM
them as far as Great Sidon and M., Jos 11.08
hill country from Lebanon to M., 13.06

MISREPRESENTING
We are even found to be m. God, 1Co 15.15

MISS
a stone at a hair, and not m. Ju 20.16
and we did not m. anything when we 1Sa 25.15
inspect your fold and m. nothing. Job 5.24

MISSED
and you will be m., because your 1Sa 20.18
third day you will be greatly m.; 20.19
and they m. nothing, all the time 25.07
nothing was m. of all that belonged 25.21
to mind, or be remembered, or m.; Jer 3.16
it some have m. the mark as 1Ti 6.21

MISSES
If your father m. me at all, then 1Sa 20.06
but he who m. me injures himself; Pro 8.36
haste with his feet m. his way. 19.02

MISSING
and there is not a man m. from us. Num 31.49
Nothing was m., whether small or 1Sa 30.19
there were m. of David's servants 2Sa 2.30
if by any means he be m., 1Ki 20.39
let none be m., for I have a great 2Ki 10.19
whoever is m. shall not live. 10.19
Lord: Not one of these shall be m.; Is 34.16
is strong in power not one is m. 40.26
shall any be m., says the Lord. Jer 23.04

MISSION
And the Lord sent you on a m., 1Sa 15.18
gone on the m. on which the Lord 15.20
when they had fulfilled their m., Ac 12.25
their boasted m. they work on the 2Co 11.12
Peter for the m. to the circumcised Gal 2.08

MIST
but a m. went up from the earth and Gen 2.06
water, he distils his m. in rain Job 36.27
a cloud, and your sins like m.; Is 44.22
he makes the m. rise from the ends Jer 10.13
he makes the m. rise from the ends 51.16
the morning m. or like the dew Hos 13.03
Immediately m. and darkness fell Ac 13.11
For you are a m. that appears for a Jas 4.14

MISTAKE
the messenger that it was a m.; Ecc 5.06

MISTAKES
For we all make many m., and if Jas 3.02
one makes no m. in what he says he 3.02

MISTRESS
she looked with contempt on her m. Gen 16.04
"I am fleeing from my m. Sarai." 16.08
said to her, "Return to your m., 16.09
the m. of the house, became ill; 1Ki 17.17
She said to her m., "Would that 2Ki 5.03
of a maid to the hand of her m., Ps 123.02
a maid when she succeeds her m. Pro 30.23
as with the maid, so with her m.; Is 24.02
more be called the m. of kingdoms. 47.05
"I shall be m. for ever," so that 47.07
its m. is stripped, she is carried Nah 2.07

MISTS
or given understanding to the m.? Job 38.36
springs and m. driven by a storm; 2Pe 2.17

MITHKAH
out from Terah, and encamped at M. Num 33.28
And they set out from m., and 33.29

MITHNITE
of Maacah, and Joshaphat the M., 1Ch 11.43

MITHREDATH
out in charge of M. the treasurer, Ez 1.08
Bishlam and M. and Tabeel and the 4.07

MITYLENE
took him on board and came to M. Ac 20.14

MIX
so they will m. with one another in Dan 2.43
just as iron does not m. with clay. 2.43
m. a double draught for her in the Rev 18.06

MIXED
A m. multitude also went up with Ex 12.38
unleavened cakes m. with oil, 29.02
cakes of fine flour m. with oil, Lev 2.04
fine flour unleavened, m. with oil; 2.05
you shall bring it well m., in 6.21
m. with oil or dry, shall be for all 7.10
unleavened cakes m. with oil, 7.12
of fine flour well m. with oil. 7.12
and a cereal offering m. with oil; 9.04
an ephah of fine flour m. with oil, 14.10
of fine flour m. with oil for a 14.21
an ephah of fine flour m. with oil, 23.13
cakes of fine flour m. with oil, Num 6.15
of fine flour m. with oil for a 7.13
of fine flour m. with oil for a 7.19
of fine flour m. with oil for a 7.25
of fine flour m. with oil for a 7.31
of fine flour m. with oil for a 7.37
of fine flour m. with oil for a 7.43
of fine flour m. with oil for a 7.49
of fine flour m. with oil for a 7.55
of fine flour m. with oil for a 7.61
of fine flour m. with oil for a 7.67
of fine flour m. with oil for a 7.73
of fine flour m. with oil for a 7.79
offering of fine flour m. with oil, 8.08
m. with a fourth of a hin of oil; 15.04
of fine flour m. with a third of a 15.06
m. with half a hin of oil, 15.09
m. with a fourth of a hin of beaten 28.05
m. with oil, and its drink offering: 28.09
m. with oil, for each bull; 28.12
m. with oil, for the one ram; 28.12
of fine flour m. with oil as a 28.13
offering of fine flour m. with oil; 28.20
offering of fine flour m. with oil, 28.28
offering of fine flour m. with oil, 29.03
offering of fine flour m. with oil, 29.09
offering of fine flour m. with oil, 29.14
that you may not be m. with these Jos 23.07
the offering m. with oil, and all 1Ch 23.29
holy race has m. itself with the Ez 9.02
a cup, with foaming wine, well m.; Ps 75.08
she has m. her wine, she has also Pro 9.02
and drink of the wine I have m. 9.05
wine, those who go to try m. wine. 23.30
bowl that never lacks m. wine. Sol 7.02
dross, your wine m. with water. Is 1.22
fill cups of m. wine for Destiny; 65.11
kings of the m. tribes that dwell Jer 25.24
as you saw iron m. with the miry Dan 2.41
you saw the iron m. with miry clay, 2.43
m. with blood, which fell on the Rev 8.07
draught for her in the cup she m. 18.06

MIXES
Ephraim m. himself with the peoples Hos 7.08

MIXING
prepared the m. of the spices, 1Ch 9.30
valiant men in m. strong drink, Is 5.22

MIXTURE
came bringing a m. of myrrh and Jn 19.39

MIZAR
Jordan and of Hermon, from Mount M. Ps 42.06

MIZPAH
and the pillar M., for he said, "The Gen 31.49
under Hermon in the land of M. Jos 11.03
together, and they encamped at M. Ju 10.17
his words before the LORD at M. 11.11
and passed on to M. of Gilead, 11.29
and from M. of Gilead he passed on 11.29
Then Jephthah came to his home at M.; 11.34
as one man to the LORD at M. 20.01
people of Israel had gone up to M. 20.03
Now the men of Israel had sworn at M., 21.01
did not come up to the LORD to M., 21.05
did not come up to the LORD to M.?" 21.08
said, "Gather all Israel at M., 1Sa 7.05
So they gathered at M., and drew 7.06
judged the people of Israel at M. 7.06
of Israel had gathered at M., 7.07
went out of M. and pursued the 7.11
set it up between M. and Jeshanah, 7.12
by year to Bethel, Gilgal, and M.; 7.16
people together to the LORD at M.; 10.17
Asa built Geba of Benjamin and M. 1Ki 15.22
with their men to Gedaliah at M., 2Ki 25.23
Chaldeans who were with him at M. 25.25
and with them he built Geba and M. 2Ch 16.06
the men of Gibeon and of M., Neh 3.07
ruler of the district of M., 3.15
ruler of M., repaired another 3.19
at M., and dwelt with him among the Jer 40.06
they went to Gedaliah at M.— 40.08
As for me, I will dwell at M., 40.10
land of Judah, to Gedaliah at M.; 40.12
country came to Gedaliah at Mizpah 40.13
spoke secretly to Gedaliah at M., 40.15
Gedaliah the son of Ahikam, at M. 41.01

MIZPAH (cont.)
ate bread together there at M., Jer 41.01
Jews who were with Gedaliah at M., 41.03
came out from M. to meet them, 41.06
rest of the people who were in M., 41.10
all the people who were left at M., 41.10
captive from M. turned about and 41.14
captive from M. after he had slain 41.16
for you have been a snare at M., Hos 5.01

MIZPEH
eastward as far as the valley of M.; Jos 11.08
Dilean, M., Joktheel, 15.38
M., Chephirah, Mozah, 18.26
went from there to M. of Moab; 1Sa 22.03

MIZZAH
Nahath, Zerah, Shammah, and M. Gen 36.13
Nahath, Zerah, Shammah, and M.; 36.17
Nahath, Zerah, Shammah, and M. 1Ch 1.37

MNASON
us to the house of M. of Cyprus, Ac 21.16

MOAB
bore a son, and called his name M.; Gen 19.37
Midian in the country of M., reigned 36.35
the leaders of M., trembling seizes Ex 15.15
wilderness which is opposite M., Num 21.11
the Arnon is the boundary of M., 21.13
between M. and the Amorites. 21.13
Ar, and leans to the border of M. 21.15
the region of M. by the top of 21.20
former king of M. and taken all 21.26
It devoured Ar of M., the lords of 21.28
Woe to you, O M.! You are undone, 21.29
the plains of M. beyond the Jordan 22.01
And M. was in great dread of the 22.03
M. was overcome with fear of the 22.03
And M. said to the elders of Midian, 22.04
who was king of M. at that time, 22.04
So the elders of M. and the elders 22.07
the princes of M. stayed with 22.08
king of M., has sent to me, saying, 22.10
So the princes of M. rose and went 22.14
and went with the princes of M. 22.21
out to meet him at the city of M., 22.36
the princes of M. were standing 23.06
the king of M. from the eastern 23.07
and the princes of M. with him. 23.17
it shall crush the forehead of M., 24.17
harlot with the daughters of M. 25.01
the plains of M. by the Jordan at 26.03
the plains of M. by the Jordan at 26.63
the plains of M. by the Jordan at 31.12
Iyeabarim, in the territory of M. 33.44
the plains of M. by the Jordan at 33.48
as Abelshittim in the plains of M. 33.49
the plains of M. by the Jordan at 33.50
the plains of M. by the Jordan at 35.01
the plains of M. by the Jordan at 36.13
Beyond the Jordan, in the land of M., Deu 1.05
direction of the wilderness of M. 2.08
'Do not harass M. or contend with 2.09
pass over the boundary of M. at Ar; 2.18
people of Israel in the land of M., 29.01
Nebo, which is in the land of M., 32.49
the plains of M. to Mount Nebo, 34.01
LORD died there in the land of M., 34.05
in the land of M. opposite Bethpeor; 34.06
in the plains of M. thirty days; 34.08
distributed in the plains of M., Jos 13.32
king of M., arose and fought 24.09
the king of M. against Israel, Ju 3.12
the king of M. eighteen years. 3.14
by him to Eglon the king of M. 3.15
the tribute to Eglon king of M. 3.17
So M. was subdued that day under 3.30
the gods of M., the gods of the 10.06
the land of M. or the land of the Ammonites, 11.15
they sent also to the king of M., 11.17
land of Edom and the land of M., 11.18
on the east side of the land of M., 11.18
did not enter the territory of M., 11.18
the Arnon was the boundary of M. 11.18
the son of Zippor, king of M.? 11.25
to sojourn in the country of M., Ru 1.01
the country of M. and remained 1.02
to return from the country of M., 1.06
the country of M. that the LORD 1.06
returned from the country of M. 1.22
with Naomi from the country of M. 2.06
come back from the country of M., 4.03
into the hand of the king of M.; 1Sa 12.09
against M., against the Ammonites, 14.47
went from there to Mizpeh of M.; 22.03
and he said to the king of M., 22.03
And he left them with the king of M., 22.04
And he defeated M., and measured 2Sa 8.02
from Edom, M., the Ammonites, the 8.12
great deeds; he smote two ariels of M. 23.20
for Chemosh the abomination of M., 1Ki 11.07
Sidonians, Chemosh the god of M., 11.33
M. rebelled against Israel. 2Ki 1.01
Now Mesha king of M. was a sheep 3.04
the king of M. rebelled against the 3.05
"The king of M. has rebelled 3.07
go with me to battle against M.?" 3.07
to give them into the hand of M." 3.10
to give them into the hand of M." 3.13
Now then, M., to the spoil!" 3.23
When the king of M. saw that the 3.26
for Chemosh the abomination of M., 23.13
Midian in the country of M., 1Ch 1.46
who ruled in M. and returned to 4.22
the country of M. after he had 8.08
he smote two ariels of M. 11.22
And he defeated M., and the 18.02
M., the Ammonites, the Philistines, 18.11
men of Ammon and M. and Mount Seir, 2Ch 20.10
M., and Mount Seir, who had come 20.22
of Ammon and M. rose against the 20.23
women of Ashdod, Ammon, and M.; Neh 13.23
M. is my washbasin; upon Edom Ps 60.08
Ishmaelites, M. and the Hagrites, 83.06
M. is my washbasin; upon Edom 108.09
their hand against Edom and M., Is 11.14
An oracle concerning M. Because Ar 15.01
is laid waste in a night M. is undone; 15.01
because Kir is laid waste in a night M. 15.01
over Nebo and over Medeba M. wails. 15.02
the armed men of M. cry aloud; 15.04
My heart cries out for M.; 15.05
cry has gone round the land of M.; 15.08
a lion for those of M. who escape, 15.09
daughters of M. at the fords of 16.02
let the outcasts of M. sojourn 16.04
We have heard of the pride of M., 16.06
let M. wail, let every one wail for M. 16.07
Therefore my soul moans like a lyre for M., 16.11
And when M. presents himself, when 16.12
spoke concerning M. in the past. 16.13
the glory of M. will be brought 16.14
and M. shall be trodden down in his 25.10
M., and all who dwell in the desert Jer 9.26
Edom, M., and the sons of Ammon; 25.21
the king of M., the king of the 27.03
who were in M. and among the 40.11
Concerning M. Thus says the LORD 48.01
the renown of M. is no more. In 48.02
M. is destroyed; a cry is heard as 48.04
"Give wings to M., for she would 48.09
"M. has been at ease from his youth 48.11
Then M. shall be ashamed of Chemosh, 48.13
The destroyer of M. and his cities 48.15
The calamity of M. is near at hand 48.16

MOAB (cont.)
destroyer of M. has come up against Jer 48.18
M. is put to shame, for it is broken 48.20
the Arnon, that M. is laid waste. 48.20
of the land of M., far and near. 48.24
The horn of M. is cut off, and his 48.25
so that M. shall wallow in his 48.26
in the rock, O inhabitants of M.! 48.28
We have heard of the pride of M.— 48.29
I wail for M.; I cry out for all M.; 48.31
away from the fruitful land of M.; 48.33
And I will bring to an end in M., 48.35
my heart moans for M. like a flute, 48.36
housetops of M. and in the squares 48.38
I have broken M. like a vessel for 48.38
How M. has turned his back in shame 48.39
So M. has become a derision and a 48.39
and spread his wings against M.; 48.40
the warriors of M. shall be in 48.41
M. shall be destroyed and be no 48.42
are before you, O inhabitant of M.! 48.43
things upon M. in the year of 48.44
has destroyed the forehead of M., 48.45
Woe to you, O M.! The people of 48.46
the fortunes of M. in the latter 48.47
Thus far is the judgment on M. 48.47
Because M. said, Behold, the house of Eze 25.08
the flank of M. from the cities on 25.09
and I will execute judgments upon M. 25.11
Edom and M. and the main part of Dan 11.41
"For three transgressions of M., Amo 2.01
So I will send a fire upon M., 2.02
and M. shall die amid uproar, amid 2.02
what Balak king of M. devised, Mic 6.05
the taunts of M. and the revilings Zep 2.08
"M. shall become like Sodom, and the 2.09

MOABITE
"No Ammonite or M. shall enter the Deu 23.03
These took M. wives; the name of Ru 1.04
"It is the M. maiden, who came back 2.06
and M., Ammonite, Edomite, Sidonian, 1Ki 11.01
sons of Elnaam, and Ithmah the M., 1Ch 11.46
no Ammonite or M. should ever Neh 13.01

MOABITES
the father of the M. to this day. Gen 19.37
Rephaim, but the M. call them Emim. Deu 2.11
in Seir and the M. who live in Ar 2.29
your enemies the M. into your hand. Ju 3.28
fords of the Jordan against the M., 3.28
time about ten thousand of the M., 3.29
And the M. became servants to David 2Sa 8.02
also give the M. into your hand, 2Ki 3.18
When all the M. heard that the 3.21
the M. saw the water opposite them 3.22
Israelites rose and attacked the M., 3.24
slaughtering the M. as they went. 3.24
Now bands of M. used to invade the 13.20
the Syrians, and bands of the M., 24.02
and the M. became servants to David 1Ch 18.02
After this the M. and Ammonites, and 2Ch 20.01
the M., the Egyptians, and the Ez 9.01

MOABITESS
and Ruth the M. her daughter-in-law Ru 1.22
And Ruth the M. said to Naomi, "Let 2.02
And Ruth the M. said, "Besides, he 2.21
you are also buying Ruth the M., 4.05
Also Ruth the M., the widow of 4.10
Jehozabad the son of Shimrith the M. 2Ch 24.26

MOADIAH
of Miniamin, of M., Piltai; Neh 12.17

MOAN
noon I utter my complaint and m., Ps 55.17
I think of God, and I m.; 77.03
a crane I clamor, I m. like a dove. Is 38.14
like bears, we m. and m. like doves; 59.11

MOANING
I am weary with my m.; every night Ps 6.06
there shall be m. and lamentation, Is 29.02
all of them m., every one over his Eze 7.16
m. like doves, and beating their Nah 2.07

MOANS
Therefore my soul m. like a lyre Is 16.11
Therefore my heart m. for Moab like Jer 48.36
and my heart m. like a flute for 48.36

MOAT
be built again with squares and m., Dan 9.25

MOB
for the m. of the people followed, Ac 21.36

MOCK
has sent to m. the living God, 2Ki 19.04
he has sent to m. the living God. 19.16
and when you m., shall no one shame Job 11.03
and after I have spoken, m. on. 21.03
All who see me m. at me, they make Ps 22.07
with which they m. the footsteps 89.51
I will m. when panic strikes you, Pro 1.26
has sent to m. the living God, Is 37.04
he has sent to m. the living God. 37.17
who are far from you will m. you, Eze 22.05
and they will m. him, and spit upon Mk 10.34
all who see it begin to m. him, Lk 14.29

MOCKED
you have m. me, and told me lies; Ju 16.10
Samson, "Until now you have m. me, 16.13
You have m. me these three times, 16.15
And at noon Elijah m. then saying, 1Ki 18.27
"Whom have you m. and reviled? 2Ki 19.22
messengers you have m. the Lord, 19.23
laughed them to scorn, and m. them. 2Ch 30.10
they impiously m. more and more, Ps 35.16
m. and derided by those round about 79.04
'Whom have you m. and reviled? Is 37.23
your servants you have m. the Lord, 37.24
Gentiles to be m. and scourged and Mt 20.19
kneeling before him they m. him, 27.29
And when they had m. him, 27.31
and elders, m. him, saying, 27.41
And when they had m. him, Mk 15.20
chief priests m. him to one 15.31
and will be m. and shamefully Lk 18.32
holding Jesus m. him and beat him; 22.63
him with contempt and m. him; 23.11
The soldiers also m. him, 23.36
resurrection of the dead, some m.; Ac 17.32
God is not m., for whatever a man Gal 6.07

MOCKER
Wine is a m., strong drink a brawler; Pro 20.01

MOCKERS
Surely there are m. about me, Job 17.02
he stretched out his hand with m. Hos 7.05

MOCKING
me, and I shall seem to be m. him, Gen 27.12
but they kept m. the messengers of 2Ch 36.16
gloated over her, m. at her downfall. Lam 1.07
and a m. to all the countries. Eze 22.04
But others m. said, "They are filled Ac 2.13
Others suffered m. and scourging, Heb 11.36

MOCKS
he m. at the calamity of the Job 9.23
He who m. the poor insults his Pro 17.05
A worthless witness m. at justice, 19.28
The eye that m. a father and scorns 30.17
all the day; every one m. me. Jer 20.07

MODEL
the priest a m. of the altar, 2Ki 16.10
in all respects a m. of good deeds, Tit 2.07

MODESTLY
themselves m. and sensibly in seemly 1Ti 2.09

MODESTY
parts are treated with greater m., 1Co 12.23
and love and holiness, with m. 1Ti 2.15

MOIST
sweeping away of m. and dry alike. Deu 29.19
fat and the marrow of his bones m. Job 21.24

MOISTEN
of a hin of oil to m. the flour, Eze 46.14

MOISTURE
He loads the thick cloud with m.; Job 37.11
withered away, because it had no m. Lk 8.06

MOLADAH
Amam, Shema, M., Jos 15.26
inheritance Beersheba, Sheba, M., 19.02
in Beersheba, M., Hazarshual, 1Ch 4.28
in Jeshua and in M. and Bethpelet, Neh 11.26

MOLD
mortar, take hold of the brick m.! Nah 3.14

MOLDED
Will what is molded say to its m., Rom 9.20

MOLDER
Will what is molded say to its m., Rom 9.20

MOLDING
make upon it a m. of gold round Ex 25.11
and make a m. of gold around it. 25.24
and a m. of gold around the frame. 25.25
make for it a m. of gold round 30.03
under its m. on two opposite sides 30.04
and made a m. of gold around it. 37.02
and made a m. of gold around it. 37.11
and made a m. of gold around the 37.12
and he made a m. of gold round 37.26
rings of gold on it under its m., 37.27

MOLDY
their provisions were dry and m. Jos 9.05
but now, behold, it is dry and m.; 9.12

MOLECH
to devote them by fire to M., Lev 18.21
his children to M. shall be put to 20.02
given one of his children to M., 20.03
he gives one of his children to M., 20.04
him in playing the harlot after M. 20.05
and for M. the abomination of the 1Ki 11.07
his daughter as an offering to M. 2Ki 23.10
You journeyed to M. with oil and Is 57.09
up their sons and daughters to M., Jer 32.35

MOLES
worship, to the m. and to the bats, Is 2.20

MOLEST
charged the young men not to m. you? Ru 2.09
rulers, to m. them and to stone them, Ac 14.05

MOLESTED
lest in another field you be m." Ru 2.22

MOLID
and she bore him Ahban and M. 1Ch 2.29

MOLOCH
And you took up the tent of M., Ac 7.43

MOLTEN
a graving tool, and made a m. calf; Ex 32.04
have made for themselves a m. calf, 32.08
shall make for yourself no m. gods. 34.17
or make for yourselves m. gods: Lev 19.04
and destroy all their m. images, Num 33.52
have made themselves a m. image. Deu 9.12
you had made yourselves a m. calf; 9.16
man who makes a graven or m. image, 27.15
make a graven image and a m. image; Ju 17.03
into a graven image and a m. image; 17.04
a graven image, and a m. image? 18.14
and the m. image, while the priest 18.17
and the m. image, the priest said to 18.18
made two capitals of m. bronze, 1Ki 7.16
Then he made the m. sea; 7.23
and m. images, provoking me to anger, 14.09
for themselves m. images of two 2Ki 17.16
Then he made the m. sea; 2Ch 4.02
He even made m. images for the 28.02
and the graven and the m. images. 34.03
and the graven and the m. images, 34.04
for themselves a m. calf and said, Neh 9.18
out the skies, hard as a m. mirror? Job 37.18
in Horeb and worshiped a m. image. Ps 106.19
and your gold-plated m. images. Is 30.22
their m. images are empty wind. 41.29
who say to m. images, "You are our 42.17
image and my m. image commanded 48.05
gods with their m. images and with Dan 11.08
and make for themselves m. images, Hos 13.02
the graven image and the m. image. Nah 1.14

MOMENT
if for a single m. I should go up Ex 33.05
even for a m., lest they die. Num 4.20
that I may consume them in a m. 16.21
that I may consume them in a m. 16.45
now, without resting even for a m. Ru 2.07
But now for a brief m. favor has Ez 9.08
morning, and test him every m.? Job 7.18
joy of the godless but for a m.? 20.05
In a m. they die; at midnight 34.20
back, and be put to shame in a m. Ps 6.10
For his anger is but for a m., 30.05
How they are destroyed in a m., 73.19
in a m. he will be broken beyond Pro 6.15
but a lying tongue is but for a m. 12.19
am its keeper; every m. I water it. Is 27.03
come to you in a m., in one day; 47.09
For a brief m. I forsook you, but 54.07
wrath for a m. I hid my face from 54.08
nation be brought forth in one m.? 66.08
are destroyed, my curtains in a m. Jer 4.20
which was overthrown in a m., Lam 4.06
the ground and tremble every m., Eze 26.16
they shall tremble every m., 32.10
servant was healed at that very m. Mt 8.13
And from that m. he sought an 26.16
of the world in a m. of time, Lk 4.05
At that very m. three men arrived Ac 11.11
in a m., in the twinkling of an eye, 1Co 15.52
not yield submission even for a m., Gal 2.05
For the m. all discipline seems Heb 12.11

MOMENTARY
For this slight m. affliction is 2Co 4.17

MONEY
with your m. from any foreigner Gen 17.12
and he that is bought with your m., 17.13
in his house or bought with his m., 17.23
bought with m. from a foreigner, 17.27
been using up the m. given for us. 31.15
pieces of m. the piece of land on 33.19
replace every man's m. in his sack, 42.25
he saw his m. in the mouth of his 42.27
"My m. has been put back; 42.28

MONEY (cont.)
man's bundle of m. was in his sack; Gen 42.35
father saw their bundles of m., 42.35
Take double the m. with you; 43.12
with you the m. that was returned 43.12
they took double the m. with them, 43.15
they said, "It is because of the m., 43.18
was every man's m. in the mouth of 43.21
of his sack, our m. in full weight; 43.21
brought other m. down in our hand 43.22
know who put our m. in our sacks." 43.22
sacks for you; I received your m." 43.23
put each man's m. in the mouth of 44.01
youngest, with his m. for the grain." 44.02
Behold, the m. which we found in the 44.08
up all the m. that was found in 47.14
brought the m. into Pharaoh's house 47.14
And when the m. was all spent in 47.15
your eyes? For our m. is gone." 47.15
your cattle, if your m. is gone." 47.16
my lord that our m. is all spent; 47.18
is bought for m. may eat of it Ex 12.44
for nothing, without payment of m. 21.11
for the slave is his m. 21.21
he shall give m. to its owner, and 21.34
to his neighbor m. or goods to 22.07
he shall pay m. equivalent to the 22.17
"If you lend m. to any of my people 22.25
the atonement m. from the people 30.16
a slave as his property for m., Lev 22.11
not lend him your m. at interest, 25.37
refund the m. for his redemption. 25.52
fifth of the valuation in m. to it, 27.15
fifth of the valuation in m. to it, 27.19
and give the m. by which the excess Num 3.48
the redemption m. from those who 3.49
people of Israel he took the m., 3.50
the redemption m. to Aaron and his 3.51
purchase food from them for m., Deu 2.06
also buy water of them for m., 2.06
You shall sell me food for m., 2.28
may eat, and give me water for m., 2.28
then you shall turn it into m., 14.25
and bind up the m. in your hand, 14.25
and spend the m. for whatever you 14.26
but you shall not sell her for m., 21.14
interest on m., interest on victuals, 23.19
Shechem for a hundred pieces of m.; Jos 24.32
and brought the m. in their hands. Ju 16.18
he restored the m. to his mother, 17.04
I will give you its value in m." 1Ki 21.02
him, 'Give me your vineyard for m.; 21.06
he refused to give you for m.; 21.15
a time to accept m. and garments, 2Ki 5.26
"All the m. of the holy things 12.04
the m. for which each man is 12.04
the m. from the assessment of 12.04
and the m. which a man's heart 12.04
take no more m. from your acquaintances, 12.07
take no more m. from the people, 12.08
in it all the m. that was brought 12.09
there was much m. in the chest, 12.10
up in bags the m. that was found 12.10
would give the m. that was weighed 12.11
from the m. that was brought into 12.13
delivered the m. to pay out to the 12.15
The m. from the guilt offerings and 12.16
offerings and the m. from the sin 12.16
Menahem exacted the m. from Israel, 15.20
amount of the m. which has been 22.04
them for the m. which is delivered 22.07
emptied out the m. that was found 22.09
to give the m. according to the 23.35
from all Israel m. to repair the 2Ch 24.05
saw that there was much m. in it, 24.11
day, and collected m. in abundance. 24.11
the rest of the m. before the king 24.14
delivered the m. that had been 34.09
bringing out the m. that had been 34.14
emptied out the m. that was found 34.17
So they gave m. to the masons and Ez 3.07
With this m., then, you shall with 7.17
have borrowed m. for the king's tax Neh 5.04
are lending them m. and grain. 5.10
houses and the hundredth of m., 5.11
"The m. is given to you, the people Est 3.11
exact sum of m. that Haman had 4.07
him a piece of m. and a ring of Job 42.11
not put out his m. at interest, Ps 15.05
he took a bag of m. with him; Pro 7.20
loves m. will not be satisfied with m.; Ecc 5.10
is like the protection of m.; 7.12
and m. answers everything. 10.19
not bought me sweet cane with m., Is 43.24
you shall be redeemed without m. 52.03
and he who has no m., come, buy 55.01
milk without m. and without price. 55.01
you spend your m. for that which 55.02
and weighed out the m. to him, Jer 32.09
and weighed the m. on scales. 32.10
the field for m. and get witnesses"— 32.25
Fields shall be bought for m., 32.44
hire, its prophets divine for m.; Mic 3.11
Show me the m. for the tax. Mt 22.19
the ground and hid his master's m. 25.18
invested my m. with the bankers, 25.27
treasury, since they are blood m. 27.06
gave a sum of m. to the soldiers 28.12
So they took the m. and did as they 28.15
no bag, no m. in their belts; Mk 6.08
multitude putting m. into the 12.41
glad, and promised to give him m. 14.11
staff, nor bag, nor bread, nor m.; Lk 9.03
The Pharisees, who were lovers of m., 16.14
to whom he had given the m., 19.15
you not put my m. into the bank, 19.23
glad, and engaged to give him m. 22.05
as he had the m. box he used to Jn 12.06
that, because Judas had the m. box, 13.29
and brought the m. and laid it at Ac 4.37
apostles' hands, he offered them m., 8.18
obtain the gift of God with m.! 8.20
he hoped that m. would be given 24.26
quarrelsome, and no lover of m. 1Ti 3.03
For the love of m. is the root of 6.10
lovers of m., proud, arrogant, 2Ti 3.02
Keep your life free from love of m., Heb 13.05

MONEY-CHANGERS
tables of the m. and the seats of Mt 21.12
tables of the m. and the seats of Mk 11.15
and the m. at their business. Jn 2.14
coins of the m. and overturned 2.15

MONEY-VALUE
compute the m. for it according to Lev 27.18

MONGREL
a m. people shall dwell in Ashdod; Zec 9.06

MONSTER
or a sea m., that thou settest a Job 7.12
he has swallowed me like a m.; Jer 51.34

MONSTERS
the earth, you sea m. and all deeps, Ps 148.07

MONTH
in the second m., on the seventeenth Gen 7.11
on the seventeenth day of the m., 7.11
and in the seventh m., on the 8.04
on the seventeenth day of the m., 8.04
to abate until the tenth m.; 8.05
tenth m., on the first day of the m., 8.05
the first m., the first day of the m., 8.13
the second m., on the twenty-seventh 8.14
the twenty-seventh day of the m., 8.14

MONTH (cont.)
And he stayed with him a m. Gen 29.14
"This m. shall be for you the Ex 12.02
be the first m. of the year for 12.02
day of this m. they shall take 12.03
the fourteenth day of this m., 12.06
first m., on the fourteenth day of the m. 12.18
twenty-first day of the m. at evening. 12.18
are to go forth, in the m. of Abib. 13.04
shall keep this service in this m. 13.05
of the second m. after they had 16.01
appointed time in the m. of Abib, 23.15
the time appointed in the m. Abib; 34.18
for in the m. Abib you came out 34.18
of the first m. you shall erect 40.02
And in the first m. in the second 40.17
year, on the first day of the m., 40.17
for ever that in the seventh m., Lev 16.29
on the tenth day of the m., you 16.29
In the first m., on the fourteenth 23.05
day of the m. in the evening, 23.05
day of the same m. is the feast of 23.06
seventh m., on the first day of the m., 23.24
of this seventh m. is the day of 23.27
day of the m. beginning at evening, 23.32
of this seventh m. and for seven 23.34
fifteenth day of the seventh m., 23.39
shall keep it in the seventh m. 23.41
on the tenth day of the seventh m.; 25.09
is from a m. old up to five years 27.06
on the first day of the second m., Num 1.01
and on the first day of the second m., 1.18
male from a m. old and upward you 3.15
males from a m. old and upward was 3.22
from a m. old and upward, there were 3.28
males from a m. old and upward was 3.34
the males from a m. old and upward, 3.39
from a m. old and upward, taking 3.40
from a m. old and upward as numbered 3.43
in the first m. of the second year 9.01
On the fourteenth day of this m., 9.03
kept the passover in the first m., 9.05
on the fourteenth day of the m., 9.05
In the second m. on the fourteenth 9.11
or a m., or a longer time, that the 9.22
in the second m., on the twentieth 10.11
on the twentieth day of the m., 10.11
but a whole m., until it comes out 11.20
meat, that they may eat a whole m.!' 11.21
price (at a m. old you shall redeem 18.16
wilderness of Zin in the first m., 20.01
male from a m. old and upward; 26.62
offering of each m. throughout the 28.14
of the first m. is the LORD's 28.16
fifteenth day of this m. is a feast; 28.17
of the seventh m. you shall have a 29.01
of this seventh m. you shall have 29.07
of the seventh m. you shall have a 29.12
out from Rameses in the first m., 33.03
the fifteenth day of the first m.; 33.03
on the first day of the fifth m. 33.38
the first day of the eleventh m., Deu 1.03
"Observe the m. of Abib, and keep 16.01
for in the m. of Abib the LORD your 16.01
father and her mother a full m.; 21.13
on the tenth day of the first m., Jos 4.19
day of the m. at evening in the 5.10
no food the second day of the m., 1Sa 20.34
provision for one m. in the year. 1Ki 4.07
Solomon's table, each one in his m.; 4.27
ten thousand a m. in relays; 5.14
they would be a m. in Lebanon and 5.14
m. of Ziv, which is the second m., 6.01
LORD was laid, in the m. of Ziv. 6.37
m. of Bul, which is the eighth m., 6.38
m. Ethanim, which is the seventh m. 8.02
of the eighth m. like the feast 12.32
the fifteenth day in the eighth m., 12.33
in the m. which he had devised of 12.33
and he reigned one m. in Samaria. 2Ki 15.13
tenth m., on the tenth day of the m., 25.01
of the fourth m. the famine was so 25.03
fifth m., on the seventh day of the m.— 25.08
But in the seventh m., Ishmael the 25.25
king of Judah, in the twelfth m., 25.27
the twenty-seventh day of the m., 25.27
crossed the Jordan in the first m., 1Ch 12.15
m. after m. throughout the year, 27.01
the first division in the first m.; 27.02
of the army for the first m. 27.03
of the division of the second m.; 27.04
for the third m., was Benaiah, the 27.05
Joab was fourth, for the fourth m., 27.07
for the fifth m., was Shamhuth, the 27.08
for the sixth m., was Ira, the son 27.09
Seventh, for the seventh m., was 27.10
Eighth, for the eighth m., was 27.11
for the ninth m., was Abiezer of 27.12
for the tenth m., was Maharai of 27.13
Eleventh, for the eleventh m., 27.14
Twelfth, for the twelfth m., was 27.15
in the second m. of the fourth 2Ch 3.02
feast which is in the seventh m. 5.03
of the seventh m. he sent the 7.10
in the third m. of the fifteenth 15.10
in the first m., he opened the 29.03
on the first day of the first m., 29.17
day of the m. they came to the 29.17
day of the first m. they finished. 29.17
the passover in the second m.— 30.02
unleavened bread in the second m., 30.13
fourteenth day of the second m. 30.15
In the third m. they began to pile 31.07
finished them in the seventh m. 31.07
the fourteenth day of the first m. 35.01
When the seventh m. came, and the Ez 3.01
of the seventh m. they began to 3.06
in the second m., Zerubbabel the 3.08
on the third day of the m. of Adar, 6.15
of the first m. the returned 6.19
came to Jerusalem in the fifth m., 7.08
of the first m. he began to go up 7.09
of the fifth m. he came to Jerusalem, 7.09
on the twelfth day of the first m., 8.31
ninth m., on the twentieth day of the m. 10.09
of the tenth m. they sat down to 10.16
of the first m. they had come to 10.17
it happened in the m. of Chislev, Neh 1.01
In the m. of Nisan, in the twentieth 2.01
twenty-fifth day of the m. Elul, 6.15
And when the seventh m. had come, 7.73
on the first day of the seventh m. 8.02
the feast of the seventh m., 8.14
day of this m. the people of 9.01
tenth m., which is the m. of Tebeth, Est 2.16
first m., which is the m. of Nisan, 3.07
they cast it m. after m. till the 3.07
twelfth m., which is the m. of Adar. 3.07
the thirteenth day of the first m., 3.12
twelfth m., which is the m. of Adar, 3.13
third m., which is the m. of Sivan, on 8.09
twelfth m., which is the m. of Adar. 8.12
twelfth m., which is the m. of Adar, 9.01
day of the m. of Adar and they 9.15
thirteenth day of the m. of Adar, 9.17
day of the m. of Adar as a day for 9.19
day of the m. Adar and also the 9.21
and as the m. that had been turned 9.22
of Jerusalem in the fifth m. Jer 1.03
in her m. they will find her. 2.24
in the fifth m. of the fourth year, 28.01
In that same year, in the seventh m., 28.17
in the ninth m., all the people in 36.09
It was the ninth m., and the king 36.22
in the tenth m., Nebuchadrezzar 39.01
fourth m., on the ninth day of the m., 39.02

MONTH (cont.)
In the seventh m., Ishmael the son Jer 41.01
tenth m., on the tenth day of the m., 52.04
of the fourth m. the famine was so 52.06
fifth m., on the tenth day of the m.— 52.12
king of Judah, in the twelfth m., 52.31
on the twenty-fifth day of the m., 52.31
fourth m., on the fifth day of the m., Eze 1.01
day of the m. (it was the fifth 1.02
sixth m., on the fifth day of the m., 8.01
fifth m., on the tenth day of the m., 20.01
tenth m., on the tenth day of the m., 24.01
year, on the first day of the m., 26.01
tenth m., on the twelfth day of the m., 29.01
first m., on the first day of the m., 29.17
first m., on the seventh day of the m., 30.20
third m., on the first day of the m., 31.01
twelfth m., on the first day of the m., 32.01
first m., on the fifteenth day of the m., 32.17
tenth m., on the fifth day of the m., 33.21
year, on the tenth day of the m., 40.01
first m., on the first day of the m., 45.18
day of the m. for any one who has 45.20
first m., on the fourteenth day of the m., 45.21
seventh m., on the fifteenth day of the m. 45.25
will bear fresh fruit every m., 47.12
twenty-fourth day of the first m., Dan 10.04
sixth m., on the first day of the m., Hag 1.01
day of the m., in the sixth m. 1.15
Darius the king, in the seventh m., 2.01
on the twenty-first day of the m., 2.01
twenty-fourth day of the ninth m., 2.10
twenty-fourth day of the ninth m. 2.18
the twenty-fourth day of the m., 2.20
In the eighth m., in the second Zec 1.01
eleventh m. which is the m. of Shebat, 1.07
in the fourth day of the ninth m., 7.01
I mourn and fast in the fifth m., 7.03
in the fifth m. and in the seventh, 7.05
hosts: The fast of the fourth m., 8.19
In one m. I destroyed the three 11.08
In the sixth m. the angel Gabriel Lk 1.26
is the sixth m. with her who was 1.36
the m., and the year, to kill a Rev 9.15
fruit, yielding its fruit each m.; 22.02

MONTHS
About three m. later Judah was told, Gen 38.24
goodly child, she hid him three m. Ex 2.02
be for you the beginning of m.; 12.02
and at the beginnings of your m., Num 10.10
beginnings of your m. you shall 28.11
throughout the m. of the year. 28.14
sun, and the rich yield of the m., Deu 33.14
let me alone two m., that I may Ju 11.37
And he sent her away for two m.; 11.38
And at the end of two m., she 11.39
Judah, and was there some four m. 19.02
at the rock of Rimmon four m. 20.47
of the Philistines seven m. 1Sa 6.01
Philistines was a year and four m. 27.07
Judah was seven years and six m. 2Sa 2.11
over Judah seven years and six m.; 5.05
of Obededom the Gittite three m.; 6.11
the end of nine m. and twenty days. 24.08
you flee three m. before your foes 24.13
in Lebanon and two m. at home; 1Ki 5.14
all Israel remained there six m., 11.16
over Israel in Samaria six m. 2Ki 15.08
he reigned three m. in Jerusalem. 23.31
he reigned three m. in Jerusalem. 24.08
reigned for seven years and six m. 1Ch 3.04
of Obededom in his house three m.; 13.14
or three m. of devastation by 21.12
he reigned three m. in Jerusalem. 2Ch 36.02
reigned three m. and ten days in 36.09
being twelve m. under the regulations Est 2.12
six m. with oil of myrrh and six 2.12
six m. with spices and ointments 2.12
not come into the number of the m. Job 3.06
so I am allotted m. of emptiness, 7.03
the number of his m. is with thee, 14.05
the number of their m. is cut off? 21.21
"Oh, that I were as in the m. of old, 29.02
Can you number the m. that they 39.02
For seven m. the house of Israel Eze 39.12
end of seven m. they will make 39.14
end of twelve m. he was walking on Dan 4.29
were yet three m. to the harvest; Amo 4.07
and for five m. she hid herself, Lk 1.24
remained with her about three m., 1.56
was shut up three years and six m., 4.25
not say, 'There are yet four m., Jn 4.35
up for three m. in his father's Ac 7.20
And he stayed a year and six m., 18.11
and for three m. spoke boldly, 19.08
There he spent three m., and 20.03
After three m. we set sail in a 28.11
and m., and seasons, and years! Gal 4.10
hid for three m. by his parents, Heb 11.23
years and six m. it did not rain Jas 5.17
to torture them for five m., Rev 9.05
men for five m. lies in their 9.10
the holy city for forty-two m. 11.02
exercise authority for forty-two m.; 13.05

MONUMENT
he set up a m. for himself and 1Sa 15.12
is called Absalom's m. to this day. 2Sa 18.18
said, "What is yonder m. that I see?" 2Ki 23.17
to set up his m. at the river 1Ch 18.03
my walls a m. and a name better Is 56.05

MONUMENTS
and adorn the m. of the righteous, Mt 23.29

MOON
the m., and eleven stars were Gen 37.09
On the third new m. after the Ex 19.01
besides the burnt offering of the new m., Num 29.06
the sun and the m. and the stars, Deu 4.19
the sun or the m. or any of the 17.03
and thou M. in the valley of Jos 10.12
and the m. stayed, until the nation 10.13
"Behold, tomorrow is the new m., 1Sa 20.05
to him, "Tomorrow is the new m.; 20.18
and when the new m. came, 20.24
day, the morrow after the new m., 20.27
It is neither new m. nor sabbath. 2Ki 4.23
and the m., and the constellations, 23.05
at the new m. and at all the Ez 3.05
even the m. is not bright and the Job 25.05
He covers the face of the m., 26.09
or the m. moving in splendor, 31.26
the m. and the stars which thou Ps 8.03
sun endures, and as long as the m., 72.05
abound, till the m. be no more! 72.07
Blow the trumpet at the new m., 81.03
at the full m., on our feast day. 81.03
Like the m. it shall be established 89.37
Thou hast made the m. to mark the 104.19
you by day, nor the m. by night. 121.06
the m. and stars to rule over the 136.09
sun and m., praise him, all you 148.03
at full m. he will come home. Pro 7.20
and the m., and the stars are Ecc 12.02
fair as the m., bright as the sun, Sol 6.10
New m. and sabbath and the calling Is 1.13
rising and the m. will not shed 13.10
Then the m. will be confounded, and 24.23
light of the m. will be as the 30.26
shall the m. give light to you by 60.19
nor your m. withdraw itself; 60.20
From new m. to new m., and from 66.23
the sun and the m. and all the Jer 8.02
order of the m. and the stars for 31.35

MOON (cont.)
and the m. shall not give its light Eze 32.07
day of the new m. it shall be 46.01
day of the new m. he shall offer a 46.06
Now the new m. shall devour them Hos 5.07
The sun and the m. are darkened, Joe 2.10
and the m. to blood, before the 2.31
The sun and the m. are darkened, 3.15
saying, "When will the new m. be over, Amo 8.05
The sun and m. stood still in their Hab 3.11
and the m. will not give its light, Mt 24.29
and the m. will not give its light, Mk 13.24
be signs in sun and m. and stars, Lk 21.25
darkness and the m. into blood, Ac 2.20
sun, and another glory of the m., 1Co 15.41
festival or a new m. or a sabbath. Col 2.16
the full m. became like blood, Rev 6.12
was struck, and a third of the m., 8.12
with the m. under her feet, and on 12.01
need of sun or m. to shine upon it, 21.23

MOONS
new m., and feast days, according to 1Ch 23.31
and the new m. and the appointed 2Ch 2.04
the new m., and the three annual 8.13
the new m., and the appointed 31.03
the new m., the appointed feasts, Neh 10.33
Your new m. and your appointed Is 1.14
who at the new m. predict what 47.13
the new m., and the sabbaths, all Eze 45.17
on the sabbaths and on the new m. 46.03
her new m., her sabbaths, and all Hos 2.11

MOORED
at Gennesaret, and m. to the shore. Mk 6.53

MORALS
deceived: "Bad company ruins good m." 1Co 15.33

MORBID
he has a m. craving for controversy 1Ti 6.04

MORDECAI
M., Bilshan, Mispar, Bigvai, Rehum, and Ez 2.02
M., Bilshan, Mispereth, Bigvai, Nehum, Neh 7.07
Susa the capital whose name was M., Est 2.05
M. adopted her as his own daughter. 2.07
for M. had charged her not to make 2.10
And every day M. walked in front of 2.11
daughter of Abihail the uncle of M., 2.15
M. was sitting at the king's gate. 2.19
as M. had charged her; 2.20
Esther obeyed M. just as when she 2.20
as M. was sitting at the king's gate, 2.21
And this came to the knowledge of M., 2.22
told the king in the name of M. 2.22
But M. did not bow down or do 3.02
were at the king's gate said to M., 3.03
Haman saw that M. did not bow down 3.05
disdained to lay hands on M. alone. 3.06
made known to him the people of M., 3.06
the people of M., throughout the 3.06
When M. learned all that had been 4.01
M. rent his clothes and put on 4.01
she sent garments to clothe M., 4.04
him to go to M. to learn what this 4.05
Hathach went out to M. in the open 4.06
and M. told him all that had 4.07
M. also gave him a copy of the 4.08
and told Esther what M. had said. 4.09
gave him a message for M., saying, 4.10
And they told M. what Esther had 4.12
Then M. told them to return answer 4.13
Then Esther told them to reply to M., 4.15
M. then went away and did everything 4.17
when Haman saw M. in the king's 5.09
was filled with wrath against M. 5.09
long as I see M. the Jew sitting 5.13
the king to have M. hanged upon it; 5.14
written how M. had told about 6.02
has been bestowed on M. for this?" 6.03
about having M. hanged on the 6.04
and do so to M. the Jew who sits at 6.10
and he arrayed M. and made him 6.11
Then M. returned to the king's gate. 6.12
"If M., before whom you have begun 6.13
which Haman has prepared for M., 7.09
which he had prepared for M. 7.10
And M. came before the king, for 8.01
from Haman, and gave it to M. 8.02
And Esther set M. over the house of 8.02
to Queen Esther and to M. the Jew, 8.07
to all that M. commanded concerning 8.09
Then M. went out from the presence 8.15
for the fear of M. had fallen upon 9.03
For M. was great in the king's house, 9.04
for the man M. grew more and more 9.04
And M. recorded these things, and 9.20
and as M. had written to them. 9.23
and M. the Jew gave full written 9.29
as M. the Jew and Queen Esther 9.31
account of the high honor of M., 10.02
For M. the Jew was next in rank to 10.03

MORDECAI'S
to see whether M. words would Est 3.04

MORE
Now the serpent was m. subtle than Gen 3.01
she did not return to him any m. 8.12
and gained m. and m. until he became 26.13
and he loved Rachel m. than Leah, 29.30
name shall no m. be called Jacob, 32.28
loved Joseph m. than any other of 37.03
loved him m. than all his brothers, 37.04
brothers they only hated him the m. 37.05
hated him yet m. for his dreams 37.08
"She is m. righteous than I, inasmuch 38.26
with our father, and one is no m." 42.13
one is no m., and the youngest is 42.32
Joseph is no m., and Simeon is no m., 42.36
you, you shall see my face no m.' 44.23
But the m. they were oppressed, the Ex 1.12
the m. they multiplied and the m. they 1.12
and there will be no m. hail, 9.29
"Yet one plague m. I will bring 11.01
they gathered, some m., some less. 16.17
The rich shall not give m., 30.15
bring much m. than enough for 36.05
do anything m. for the offering 36.06
sufficient to do all the work, and m. 36.07
shall shut him up seven days m.; Lev 13.05
itching disease for seven days m.; 13.33
he shall shut it up seven days m.; 13.54
So they shall no m. slay their 17.07
they may yield m. richly for you: 19.25
I will bring m. plagues upon you, 26.21
it shall not be redeemed any m.; 27.20
of the service and serve no m., Num 8.25
But they did so no m. 11.25
m. than all men that were on the 12.03
be wrath no m. upon the people of 18.05
pass through on foot, nothing m. 20.19
m. in number and m. honorable than 22.15
the LORD my God, to do less or m. 22.18
I may know what m. the LORD will 22.19
increase still m. the fierce anger 32.14
speak no m. to me of this matter. Deu 3.26
a loud voice; and he added no m. 5.22
LORD our God any m., we shall die. 5.25
you were m. in number than any 7.07
this great fire any m., lest I die. 18.16
may be given him, but not m.; 25.03
beat him with m. stripes than 25.03
will make you m. prosperous and 30.05
how much m. after my death! 31.27

MORE (cont.)

people of Israel had manna no m., Jos 5.12
I will be with you no m., 7.12
there were m. who died because of 10.11
and spoke no m. of making war 22.33
they lifted up their heads no m. Ju 8.28
therefore I will deliver you no m. 10.13
appeared no m. to Manoah and to 13.21
his death were m. than those whom 16.30
do so to me and m. also if even Ru 1.17
to go with her, she said no m. 1.18
who is m. to you than seven sons, 4.15
Am I not m. to you than ten sons?" 1Sa 1.08
Talk no m. so very proudly, let not 2.03
May God do so to you and m. also, 3.17
of Israel m. handsome than he; 9.02
of the Philistines increased m. and m.; 14.19
said, "God do so to me and m. also; 14.44
and what m. can he have but the 18.08
Saul was still m. afraid of David. 18.29
out David had m. success than all 18.30
and m. also, if I do not disclose it 20.13
how much m. today will their 21.05
how much m. than if we go to Keilah 23.03
Go, make yet m. sure; know and 23.22
"You are m. righteous than I; 24.17
God do so to David and m. also, 25.22
for I will no m. do you harm, 26.21
to Gath, he sought for him no m. 27.04
away from me and answers me no m., 28.15
they had no m. strength to weep. 30.04
stopped, and pursued Israel no m., 2Sa 2.28
nor did they fight any m. 2.28
and m. also, if I do not accomplish 3.09
"God do so to me and m. also, 3.35
How much m., when wicked men have 4.11
And David took m. concubines and 5.13
and m. sons and daughters were born 5.13
make myself yet m. contemptible 6.22
own place, and be disturbed no m.; 7.10
afflict them no m., as formerly, 7.10
And what m. can David say to thee? 7.20
to help the Ammonites any m. 10.19
I would add to you as much m. 12.08
the avenger of blood slay no m., 14.11
how much m. now may this Benjaminite 16.11
forest devoured m. people that day 18.08
and m. also, if you are not commander 19.13
"Why speak any m. of your affairs? 19.29
in David also we have m. than you. 19.43
will do us m. harm than Absalom; 20.06
"You shall no m. go out with us to 21.17
name of Solomon m. famous than 1Ki 1.47
do so to me and m. also if this 2.23
sword two men m. righteous and 2.32
there was no m. spirit in her. 10.05
m. than all that their fathers had 14.22
and did m. evil than all who were 16.25
of the LORD m. than all that were 16.30
Ahab did m. to provoke the LORD, the 16.33
and m. also, if I do not make your 19.02
and m. also, if the dust of Samaria 20.10
horsemen!" And he saw him no m. 2Ki 2.12
himself there m. than once or 6.10
are with us are m. than those who 6.16
Syrians came no m. on raids into 6.23
and m. also, if the head of Elisha 6.31
they found no m. of her than the 9.35
therefore take no m. money from 12.07
should take no m. money from the 12.08
an army of m. than fifty horsemen 13.07
to wander any m. out of the land 21.08
them to do m. evil than the 21.09
has done things m. wicked than all 21.11
Jabez was m. honorable than his 1Ch 4.09
And David took m. wives in Jerusalem, 14.03
and David begot m. sons and 14.03
own place, and be disturbed no m.; 17.09
waste them no m., as formerly, 17.09
And what m. can David say to thee 17.18
to help the Ammonites any m. 19.19
Since m. chief men were found among 24.04
there was no m. spirit in her. 2Ch 9.04
And there was no m. war until the 15.19
until they could carry no m. 20.25
able to give you much m. than this." 25.09
he became yet m. faithless to the 28.22
Levites were m. upright in heart 29.34
said still m. against the Lord God 32.16
and I will no m. remove the foot of 33.08
that they did m. evil than the 33.09
Amon incurred guilt m. and m. 33.23
for he was a m. faithful and God-fearing Neh 7.02
Yet you bring m. wrath upon Israel 13.18
is to come no m. before King Est 1.19
loved Esther m. than all the women, 2.17
in his sight m. than all the 2.17
will escape any m. than all the 4.13
king delight to honor m. than me?" 6.06
Mordecai grew m. and m. powerful. 9.04
and dig for it m. than for hid Job 3.21
how much m. those who dwell in 4.19
who sees me will behold me no m.; 7.08
he returns no m. to his house, nor 7.10
nor does his place know him any m. 7.10
tent of the wicked will be no m. 8.22
heavens are no m. he will not 14.12
which saw him will see him no m., 20.09
will his place any m. behold him. 20.09
to bed rich, but will do so no m.; 27.19
are discomfited, they answer no m.; 32.15
they stand there, and answer no m.? 32.16
regards the rich m. than the poor, 34.19
I will not offend any m.; 34.31
done iniquity, I will do it no m.'? 34.32
who teaches us m. than the beasts 35.11
days of Job m. than his beginnings; 42.12
Thou hast put m. joy in my heart Ps 4.07
the earth may strike terror no m. 10.18
their children have m. than enough; 17.14
M. to be desired are they than gold, 19.10
them down and build them up no m. 28.05
they impiously mocked m. and m., 35.16
and the wicked will be no m.; 37.10
I passed by, and, lo, he was no m.; 37.36
before I depart and be no m.! 39.13
they would be m. than can be 40.05
they are m. than the hairs of my 40.12
who will never m. see the light. 49.19
You love evil m. than good, and 52.03
and lying m. than speaking the 52.03
consume them till they are no m., 59.13
M. in number than the hairs of my 69.04
wounded, they afflict still m. 69.26
please the LORD m. than an ox or a 69.31
will praise thee yet m. and m. 71.14
abound, till the moon be m.! 72.07
m. majestic than the everlasting 76.04
Yet they sinned still m. against him, 78.17
name of Israel be remembered no m.! 83.04
gates of Zion m. than all the 87.02
whom thou dost remember no m., 88.05
gone, and its place knows it no m. 103.16
earth, and let the wicked be no m.! 104.35
I have m. understanding than all my 119.99
I understand m. than the aged, for I 119.100
And what m. shall be done to you, 120.03
for we have had m. than enough of 123.03
m. than watchmen for the morning, 130.06
them, they are m. than the sand. 139.18
be cast into pits, no m. to rise! 140.10
She is m. precious than jewels, and Pro 3.15
passes, the wicked is no m., 10.25
how much m. the wicked and the 11.31
are overthrown and are no m., 12.07
how much m. the hearts of men! 15.11

MORE (cont.)
how much m. do his friends go far Pro 19.07
and justice is m. acceptable to 21.03
how much m. when he brings it with 21.27
There is m. hope for a fool than 26.12
afterward find m. favor than he 28.23
There is m. hope for a fool than 29.20
and remember their misery no m. 31.07
She is far m. precious than jewels. 31.10
m. than any who had been before me Ecc 2.07
already dead m. fortunate than the 4.02
The m. words, the m. vanity, and what 6.11
to the wise man m. than ten rulers 7.19
And I found m. bitter than death 7.26
nothing, and they have no m. reward; 9.05
they have no m. for ever any share 9.06
he must put forth m. strength; 10.10
will extol your love m. than wine; Sol 1.04
What is your beloved m. than 5.09
beloved m. than another beloved, 5.09
Bring no m. vain offerings; Is 1.13
shall they learn war any m. 2.04
What m. was there to do for my 5.04
field, until there is no m. room, 5.08
Jacob will no m. lean upon him 10.20
I will make men m. rare than fine 13.12
growth fails, the verdure is no m. 15.06
I will bring upon Dibon even m., 15.09
When the oppressor is no m., 16.04
Before morning, they are no m.! 17.14
up, be driven away, and be no m. 19.07
there is no restraint any m. 23.10
"You will no m. exult O oppressed 23.12
No m. do they drink wine with 24.09
palace of aliens is a city no m., 25.02
and will no m. cover her slain. 26.21
"Jacob shall no m. be ashamed, 29.22
no m. shall his face grow pale. 29.22
let us hear no m. of the Holy One 30.11
Jerusalem; you shall weep no m. 30.19
will not hide himself any m., 30.20
The fool will no m. be called noble, 32.05
In little m. than a year you will 32.10
You will see no m. the insolent 33.19
upon man no m. among the inhabitants 38.11
you shall no m. be called tender 47.01
you shall no m. be called the 47.05
of my wrath you shall drink no m.; 51.22
there shall no m. come into you 52.01
one will be m. than the children 54.01
widowhood you will remember no m. 54.04
Noah should no m. go over the 54.09
Violence shall no m. be heard in 60.18
The sun shall be no m. your light 60.19
Your sun shall no m. go down, 60.20
You shall no m. be termed Forsaken, 62.04
land shall no m. be termed Desolate; 62.04
no m. shall be heard in it the 65.19
No m. shall there be in it an 65.20
free, we will come no m. to thee"? Jer 2.31
they shall no m. say, "The ark of 3.16
they shall no m. stubbornly follow 3.17
when it will no m. be called 7.32
that his name be remembered no m." 11.19
their widows m. in number than the 15.08
place shall no m. be called 19.06
him, or speak any m. in his name," 20.09
shall return no m. to see his 22.10
place: "He shall return here no m., 22.11
them, and they shall fear no m., 23.04
the LORD' you shall mention no m., 23.36
and vomit, fall and rise no m., 25.27
shall no m. make servants of them. 30.08
and they shall languish no m. 31.12
"Once m. they shall use these words 31.23
I will remember their sin no m." 31.34
or overthrown any m. for ever." 31.40
You shall see this place no m. 42.18
name shall no m. be invoked by the 44.26
they are m. numerous than locusts; 46.23
the renown of Moab is no m. 48.02
M. than for Jazer I weep for you, O 48.32
of hosts: "Is wisdom no m. in Teman? 49.07
and his neighbors; and he is no m. 49.10
shall be peopled no m. for ever, 50.39
to rise no m., because of the evil 51.64
the law is no m., and her prophets Lam 2.09
bodies were m. ruddy than coral, 4.07
them, he will regard them no m.; 4.16
Our fathers sinned, and are no m.; 5.07
my ordinances m. than the nations, Eze 5.06
my statutes m. than the countries 5.06
Because you are m. turbulent than 5.07
I bring m. and m. famine upon you, 5.16
they shall no m. use it as a 12.23
shall be no m. any false vision or 12.24
will say to you, The wall is no m., 13.15
shall be no m. in your hand as 13.21
therefore you shall no m. see 13.23
Israel may go no m. astray from me, 14.11
themselves any m. with all their 14.11
How much m. when I send upon 14.21
and you shall also give hire no m. 16.41
be calm, and will no m. be angry. 16.42
time you were m. corrupt than they 16.47
have committed m. abominations 16.51
which you acted m. abominably than 16.52
they are m. in the right than you. 16.52
shall no m. be used by you in 18.03
voice should no m. be heard upon 19.09
you shall no m. profane with your 20.39
you shall be no m. remembered; 21.32
yet she was m. corrupt than she in 23.11
Egyptians or remember them any m. 23.27
be cleansed any m. till I have 24.13
remembered no m. among the nations, 25.10
of your lyres shall be heard no m. 26.13
end, and you shall be no m.; 26.21
end and shall be no m. for ever.'" 27.36
end and shall be no m. for ever." 28.19
shall be no m. a brier to prick or 28.24
of man shall trouble them any m., 32.13
They shall no m. be a prey to the 34.28
they shall no m. be consumed with 34.29
and will do m. good to you than 36.11
you hear any m. the reproach of 36.15
themselves any m. with their idols 37.23
my holy name be profaned any m.; 39.07
remaining among the nations any m.; 39.28
not hide my face any m. from them, 39.29
galleries took m. away from them 42.05
from the ground m. than the lower 42.06
Israel shall no m. defile my holy 43.07
shall no m. oppress my people; 45.08
that I have m. than all the living Dan 2.30
seven times m. than it was wont to 3.19
and still m. greatness was added to 4.36
Behold, three m. kings shall arise 11.02
for I will no m. have pity on the Hos 1.06
shall be mentioned by name no m. 2.17
m. they increased, the m. they sinned 4.07
they love shame m. than their glory 4.18
I will love them no m.; 9.15
The m. his fruit increased the m. altars 10.01
The m. I called them, the m. they went 11.02
And now they sin m. and m., and make 13.02
and we will say no m., 'Our God,' 14.03
and I will no m. make you a reproach Joe 2.19
"Fallen, no m. to rise, is the virgin Amo 5.02
the sea grew m. and m. tempestuous. Jon 1.11
the sea grew m. and m. tempestuous 1.13
which there are m. than a hundred 4.11
shall they learn war any m.; Mic 4.03
you shall have no m. soothsayers; 5.12
bow down no m. to the work of your 5.13
you, I will afflict you no m. Nah 1.12

MORE (cont.)
"No m. shall your name be perpetuated Nah 1.14
messengers shall no m. be heard. 2.13
your merchants m. than the stars 3.16
m. fierce than the evening wolves; Hab 1.08
up the man m. righteous than he? 1.13
For all the traders are no m.; Zep 1.11
But all the m. they were eager to 3.07
you shall fear evil no m. 3.15
"Take once m. the implements of a Zec 11.15
they shall be remembered no m.; 13.02
for there shall be no m. curse; 14.11
Then once m. you shall distinguish Mal 3.18
consoled, because they were no m. Mt 2.18
anything m. than this comes from 5.37
what m. are you doing than others? 5.47
Is not life m. than food, and the 6.25
and the body m. than clothing? 6.25
Are you not of m. value than they? 6.26
will he not much m. clothe you, 6.30
how much m. will your Father who is 7.11
it shall be m. tolerable on the day 10.15
how much m. will they malign those 10.25
you are of m. value than many 10.31
or mother m. than me is not worthy 10.37
son or daughter m. than me is not 10.37
I tell you, and m. than a prophet. 11.09
it shall be m. tolerable on the day 11.22
it shall be m. tolerable on the 11.24
Of how much m. value is a man than 12.12
other spirits m. evil than himself, 12.45
For to him who has will m. be given, 13.12
rejoices over it m. than over the 18.13
they thought they would receive m.; 20.10
but they cried out the m., 20.31
other servants, m. than the first; 21.36
dare to ask him any m. questions. 22.46
and he made five talents m. 25.16
two talents made two talents m. 25.17
forward, bringing five talents m., 25.20
here I have made five talents m.' 25.20
here I have made two talents m.' 25.22
every one who has will m. be given, 25.29
at once send me m. than twelve 26.53
But they shouted all the m., 27.23
and still m. will be given you. Mk 4.24
For to him who has will m. be given; 4.25
and no one could bind him any m., 5.03
but the m. he charged them, the 7.36
the m. zealously they proclaimed it 7.36
but he cried out all the m., 10.48
is much m. than all whole burnt 12.33
has put in m. than all those who 12.43
been sold for m. than three 14.05
shouted all the m., "Crucify him." 15.14
"Collect no m. than is appointed Lk 3.13
But so much the m. the report went 5.15
I tell you, and m. than a prophet. 7.26
Now which of them will love him m.?" 7.42
I suppose, to whom he forgave m." 7.43
to him who has will m. be given, 8.18
do not trouble the Teacher any m." 8.49
"We have no m. than five loaves and 9.13
it shall be m. tolerable on that 10.12
But it shall be m. tolerable in the 10.14
and whatever m. you spend, I will 10.35
how much m. will the heavenly 11.13
other spirits m. evil than himself, 11.26
that have no m. that they can do. 12.04
you are of m. value than many 12.07
For life is m. than food, and the 12.23
and the body m. than clothing. 12.23
Of how much m. value are you than 12.24
how much m. will he clothe you, O 12.28
much they will demand the m. 12.48
lest a m. eminent man than you be 14.08
there will be m. joy in heaven over 15.07
receive manifold m. in this time, 18.30
but he cried out all the m., 18.39
your pound has made ten pounds m.' 19.16
every one who has will m. be given; 19.26
for they cannot die any m., 20.36
has put in m. than all of them; 21.03
in an agony he prayed m. earnestly; 22.44
But Jesus said, "No m. of this!" 22.51
Pilate addressed them once m., 23.20
and baptizing m. disciples than Jn 4.01
And many m. believed because of his 4.41
Sin no m., that nothing worse 5.14
Jews sought all the m. to kill him, 5.18
will he do m. signs than this man 7.31
And once m. he bent down and wrote * 8.08
praise of men m. than the praise 12.43
and the world will see me no m., 14.19
prunes, that it may bear m. fruit. 15.02
Father, and you will see me no m.; 16.10
while, and you will see me no m.; 16.16
And now I am no m. in the world, 17.11
these words, he was the m. afraid; 19.08
John, do you love me m. than these?" 21.15
to speak no m. to any one in this Ac 4.17
performed was m. than forty years 4.22
And m. than ever believers were 5.14
and the eunuch saw him no m., 8.39
increased all the m. in strength, 9.22
no m. to return to corruption, he 13.34
Now these Jews were m. noble than 17.11
him the way of God m. accurately. 18.26
the kingdom will see my face no m. 20.25
'It is m. blessed to give than to 20.35
they should see his face no m. 20.38
language, they were the m. quiet. 22.02
There were m. than forty who made 23.13
to determine his case m. exactly. 23.15
somewhat m. closely about him. 23.20
for m. than forty of their men lie 23.21
it is not m. than twelve days since 24.11
among them not m. than eight or 25.06
centurion paid m. attention to the 27.11
M. than that, we rejoice in our Rom 5.03
much m. shall we be saved by him 5.09
much m., now that we are reconciled, 5.10
much m. have the grace of God and 5.15
much m. will those who receive the 5.17
increased, grace abounded all the m., 5.20
things we are m. than conquerors 8.37
how much m. will their full inclusion 11.12
how much m. will these natural 11.24
of himself m. highly than he ought 12.03
Then let us no m. pass judgment on 14.13
How much m., matters pertaining to 1Co 6.03
claim upon you, do not we still m.? 9.12
to all, that I might win the m. 9.19
which our m. presentable parts do 12.24
show you a still m. excellent way. 12.31
tongues, but even m. to prophesy. 14.05
I speak in tongues m. than you all; 14.18
Then he appeared to m. than five 15.06
Come to your right mind, and sin no m. 15.34
and still m. toward you, with 2Co 1.12
permanent must have much m. splendor. 3.11
extends to m. and m. people it may 4.15
me, so that I rejoiced still m. 7.07
rejoiced still m. at the joy of 7.13
heart goes out all the m. to you, 7.15
but who is now m. earnest than 8.22
far m. imprisonments, with countless 11.23
one may think m. of me than he 12.06
I will all the m. gladly boast of 12.09
If I love you the m., am I to be 12.15
intermediary implies m. than one; Gal 3.20
slaves you want to be once m.? 4.09
desolate hath m. children than she 4.27
able to do far m. abundantly than Eph 3.20
your love may abound m. and m., Php 1.09
and are much m. bold to speak the 1.14

MORE (cont.)
in the flesh is m. necessary on Php 1.24
presence but much m. in my absence, 2.12
I am the m. eager to send him, 2.28
confidence in the flesh, I have m.: 3.04
have received full payment, and m.; 4.18
endeavored the m. eagerly and with 1Th 2.17
you are doing, you do so m. and m. 4.01
you, brethren, to do so m. and m., 4.10
or has been married m. than once; 1Ti 5.09
people into m. and m. ungodliness, 2Ti 2.16
have nothing m. to do with him, Tit 3.10
as a slave but m. than a slave, Phm 1.16
to me but how much m. to you, 1.16
you will do even m. than I say. 1.21
has obtained is m. excellent than Heb 1.04
of as much m. glory than Moses as 3.03
of a house has m. honor than the 3.03
desired to show m. convincingly to 6.17
This becomes even m. evident when 7.15
is as much m. excellent than the 8.06
I will remember their sins no m." 8.12
the greater and m. perfect tent 9.11
how much m. shall the blood of 9.14
sins and their misdeeds no m." 10.17
and all the m. as you see the Day 10.25
to God a m. acceptable sacrifice 11.04
And what m. shall I say? For time 11.32
we not much m. be subject to the 12.09
that speaks m. graciously than the 12.24
"Yet once m. I will shake not only 12.26
"Yet once m.," indicates the 12.27
I urge you the m. earnestly to do 13.19
No m. can salt water yield fresh. Jas 3.12
But he gives m. grace; therefore it 4.06
m. precious than gold which though 1Pe 1.07
be the m. zealous to confirm your 2Pe 1.10
the prophetic word made m. sure. 1.19
hunger no m., neither thirst any m.; Rev 7.16
that there should be no m. delay, 10.06
no one buys their cargo any m., 18.11
violence, and shall be found no m.; 18.21
shall be heard in thee no m.; 18.22
craft shall be found in thee no m.; 18.22
shall be heard in thee no m.; 18.22
a lamp shall shine in thee no m.; 18.23
bride shall be heard in thee no m.; 18.23
Once m. they cried, "Hallelujah! 19.03
should deceive the nations no m., 20.03
passed away, and the sea was no m. 21.01
eyes, and death shall be no m., 21.04
mourning nor crying nor pain any m., 21.04
There shall be no m. be anything 22.03
And night shall be no m.; 22.05

MOREH
place at Shechem, to the oak of M. Gen 12.06
Gilgal, beside the oak of M.? Deu 11.30
by the hill of M., in the valley. Ju 7.01

MOREOVER
and m. I will give you a son by her; Gen 17.16
M., his concubine, whose name was 22.24
and m. he is behind us.'" 32.18
'M. your servant Jacob is behind us.'" 32.20
and m. she is with child by harlotry." 38.24
M. Pharaoh said to Joseph, "I am 41.44
M., all the earth came to Egypt to 41.57
M. I have given to you rather than 48.22
and m. I will not let Israel go." Ex 5.02
M. I have heard the groaning of the 6.05
M., the man Moses was very great in 11.03
M. choose able men from all the 18.21
"M. you shall make the tabernacle 26.01
M., the LORD said to Moses, 30.22
M. you shall eat no blood whatever, Lev 7.26
M. he who enters the house while it 14.46
M. you have not brought us into a Num 16.14
"M. you shall say to the Levites, 18.26
M. you shall accept no ransom for 35.31
and m. we have seen the sons of the Deu 1.28
M. your little ones, who you said 1.39
M. the LORD your God will send 7.20
and m. I have given it to the 26.13
and m. all the inhabitants of the Jos 2.24
M., before the fat was burned, the 1Sa 2.15
M. as for me, far be it from me that 12.23
M. the LORD will give Israel also 28.19
M. the LORD declares to you that 2Sa 7.11
m., I have taken the city of waters. 12.27
Absalom said m., "Oh that I were 15.04
M. Ahithophel said to Absalom, "Let 17.01
Hushai said m., "You know that your 17.08
M. the king's servants came to 1Ki 1.47
"M. you know also what Joab the son 2.05
M. each stand had four bronze 7.30
M. the fleet of Hiram, which brought 10.11
M. the LORD will raise up for 14.14
M. the word of the LORD came by the 16.07
M., is it without the LORD that I 2Ki 18.25
M. Manasseh shed very much innocent 21.16
M. the altar at Bethel, the high 23.15
M. Josiah put away the mediums and 23.24
M. he appointed certain of the 1Ch 16.04
M. I declare to you that the LORD 17.10
M., in addition to all that I have 29.03
M. the bronze altar that Bezalel 2Ch 1.05
M. the servants of Huram and the 9.10
m., conditions were good in Judah. 12.12
M. in Jerusalem Jehoshaphat appointed 19.08
M. he made high places in the hill 21.11
M. Uzziah built towers in Jerusalem 26.09
M. Uzziah had an army of soldiers, 26.11
M. he built cities in the hill 27.04
M. I make a decree regarding what Ez 6.08
M. I and my brethren and my servants Neh 5.10
M. from the time that I was appointed 5.14
M. there were at my table a hundred 5.17
M. in those days the nobles of 6.17
"M., the gallows which Haman has Est 7.09
M. by them is thy servant warned; Ps 19.11
M. I saw under the sun that in the Ecc 3.16
m. it has not seen the sun or known 6.05
M. the light of the moon will be as Is 30.26
M., is it without the LORD that I 36.10
M., the men of Memphis and Tahpanhes Jer 2.16
M., I will give all the wealth of 20.05
M., I will banish from them the 25.10
M. he said to me, "Son of man, all my Eze 3.10
M. he said to me, "Son of man, behold, 4.16
M. I will make you a desolation and 5.14
M. the word of the LORD came to me: 12.17
M. I gave them my sabbaths, as a 20.12
M. I swore to them in the wilderness 20.15
M. I swore to them in the wilderness 20.23
M. I gave them statutes that were 20.25
M. the word of the LORD came to me, 22.01
M. this they have done to me: they 23.38
M. the word of the LORD came to me: 28.11
M., wine is treacherous; the arrogant Hab 2.05
M. the word of the LORD came to me, Zec 4.08
m. the dogs came and licked his Lk 16.21
M., some women of our company 24.22
m. my flesh will dwell in hope. Ac 2.26
m. he also brought Greeks into the 21.28
M. it is required of stewards that 1Co 4.02
m. he must be well thought of by 1Ti 3.07

MORESHETH
"Micah of M. prophesied in the days Jer 26.18
to Micah of M. in the days of Mic 1.01

MORESHETHGATH
you shall give parting gifts to M.; Mic 1.14

MORIAH

you love, and go to the land of M., Gen 22.02
the LORD in Jerusalem on Mount M., 2Ch 3.01

MORNING

evening and there was m., one day. Gen 1.05
and there was m., a second day. 1.08
and there was m., a third day. 1.13
and there was m., a fourth day. 1.19
and there was m., a fifth day. 1.23
and there was m., a sixth day. 1.31
When m. dawned, the angels urged Lot, 19.15
early in the m. to the place where 19.27
So Abimelech rose early in the m., 20.08
So Abraham rose early in the m., 21.14
So Abraham rose early in the m., 22.03
When they arose in the m., 24.54
In the m. they rose early and took 26.31
So Jacob rose early in the m., 28.18
And in the m., behold, it was Leah; 29.25
Early in the m. Laban arose, and 31.55
to them in the m. and saw them, 40.06
So in the m. his spirit was troubled 41.08
As soon as the m. was light, the men 44.03
in the m. devouring the prey, and at 49.27
Go to Pharaoh in the m., Ex 7.15
up early in the m. and wait for 8.20
up early in the m. and stand 9.13
and when it was m. the east wind 10.13
let none of it remain until the m., 12.10
until the m. you shall burn. 12.10
the door of his house until the m. 12.22
And in the m. watch the LORD in the 14.24
wonted flow when the m. appeared; 14.27
and in the m. you shall see the 16.07
eat and in the m. bread to the 16.08
and in the m. you shall be filled 16.12
and in the m. dew lay round about 16.13
no man leave any of it till the m. 16.19
some left part of it till the m., 16.20
M. by m. they gathered it, each as 16.21
over lay by to be kept till the m.' " 16.23
So they laid it by till the m., 16.24
about Moses from m. till evening. 18.13
about you from m. till evening?" 18.14
On the m. of the third day there 19.16
of my feast remain until the m. 23.18
And he rose early in the m., 24.04
from evening to m. before the LORD 27.21
of the bread, remain until the m., 29.34
One lamb you shall offer in the m., 29.39
as in the m., for a pleasing odor, 29.41
every m. when he dresses the lamps 30.07
m., and come up in the m. to Mount Sinai, 34.02
early in the m. and went up on 34.04
the passover be left until the m. 34.25
him freewill offerings every m. 36.03
the altar all night until the m., Lev 6.09
shall burn wood on it every m., 6.12
of it in the m. and half in the 6.20
not leave any of it until the m. 7.15
the burnt offering of the m. 9.17
with you all night until the m. 19.13
none of it until m.: I am the LORD. 22.30
from evening to m. before the LORD 24.03
leave none of it until the m., Num 9.12
the appearance of fire until m. 9.15
remained from evening until m.; 9.21
the cloud was taken up in the m., 9.21
And they rose early in the m., 14.40
"In the m. the LORD will show who 16.05
So Balaam rose in the m., 22.13
So Balaam rose in the m., 22.21
one lamb you shall offer in the m., 28.04
like the cereal offering of the m., 28.08
the burnt offering of the m., 28.23
day remain all night until m. Deu 16.04
and in the m. you shall turn and go 16.07
In the m. you shall say, 'Would it 28.67
you shall say, 'Would it were m.!' 28.67
Early in the m. Joshua rose and set Jos 3.01
Then Joshua rose early in the m., 6.12
In the m. therefore you shall be 7.14
So Joshua rose early in the m., 7.16
early in the m. and mustered the 8.10
of the town rose early in the m., Ju 6.28
him shall be put to death by m. 6.31
rose early next m. and squeezed 6.38
Then in the m., as soon as the sun 9.33
us wait till the light of the m.; 16.02
day they arose early in the m., 19.05
he arose early in the m. to depart; 19.08
early in the m. for your journey, 19.09
abused her all night until the m. 19.25
And as m. appeared, the woman came 19.26
And her master rose up in the m., 19.27
people of Israel rose in the m., 20.19
continued from early m. until now, Ru 2.07
and in the m., if he will do the 3.13
for you. Lie down until the m." 3.13
So she lay at his feet until the m., 3.14
early in the m. and worshiped 1Sa 1.19
Samuel lay until m.; then he opened 3.15
they rose early on the next m., 5.04
and in the m. I will let you go and 9.19
midst of the camp in the m. watch, 11.11
despoil them until the m. light; 14.36
rose early to meet Saul in the m.; 15.12
and took his stand, m. and evening. 17.16
And David rose early in the m., 17.20
take heed to yourself in the m., 19.02
that he might kill him in the m. 19.11
In the m. Jonathan went out into 20.35
if by m. I leave so much as one 25.22
truly by m. there had not been left 25.34
nothing at all until the m. light. 25.36
And in the m., when the wine had 25.37
early in the m. with the servants 29.10
and start early in the m., and 29.10
out with his men early in the m., 29.11
of their brethren in the m. 2Sa 2.27
In the m. David wrote a letter to 11.14
why are you so haggard m. after m.? 13.04
he dawns on them like the m. light, 23.04
shining forth upon a cloudless m., 23.04
And when David arose in the m., 24.11
Israel from the m. until the 24.15
When I rose in the m. to nurse my 1Ki 3.21
I looked at it closely in the m., 3.21
him bread and meat in the m., 17.06
name of Baal from m. until noon, 18.26
The next m., about the time of 2Ki 3.20
And when they rose early in the m., 3.22
rose early in the m. and went out, 6.15
silent and wait until the m. light, 7.09
entrance of the gate until the m. 10.08
Then in the m., when he went out, he 10.09
altar burn the m. burnt offering, 16.15
and when men arose early in the m., 19.35
had charge of opening it every m. 1Ch 9.27
offering continually m. and evening, 16.40
And they shall stand every m., 23.30
for burnt offerings m. and evening, 2Ch 2.04
the LORD every m. and every 13.11
early in the m. and went out into 20.20
burnt offerings of m. and evening, 31.03
burnt offerings m. and evening. Ez 3.03
Gate from early m. until midday, Neh 8.03
and in the m. she came back to the Est 2.14
and in the m. tell the king to have 5.14
early in the m. and offer burnt Job 1.05
nor see the eyelids of the m.; 3.09
Between m. and evening they are 4.20
dost visit him every m., and test 7.18
its darkness will be like the m. 11.17
deep darkness is m. to all of them; 24.17

MORNING (cont.)
when the m. stars sang together, and Job 38.07
commanded the m. since your days 38.12
O LORD, in the m. thou dost hear my Ps 5.03
in the m. I prepare a sacrifice for 5.03
night, but joy comes with the m. 30.05
Evening and m. and at noon I utter 55.17
of thy steadfast love in the m. 59.16
outgoings of the m. and the evening 65.08
stricken, and chastened every m. 73.14
in the m. my prayer comes before 88.13
grass which is renewed in the m.: 90.05
in the m. it flourishes and is 90.06
Satisfy us in the m. with thy 90.14
thy steadfast love in the m., 92.02
M. by m. I will destroy all the 101.08
the womb of the m. like dew your 110.03
LORD more than watchmen for the m., 130.06
wings of the m. and dwell in the 139.09
Let me hear in the m. of thy 143.08
us take our fill of love till m.; Pro 7.18
loud voice, rising early in the m., 27.14
and your princes feast in the m.! Ecc 10.16
In the m. sow your seed, and at 11.06
Woe to those who rise early in the m., Is 5.11
blossom in the m. that you sow; 17.11
Before m., they are no more! This 17.14
"M. comes, and also the night. 21.12
for m. by m. it will pass through 28.19
Be our arm every m., our salvation 33.02
and when men arose early in the m., 37.36
I cry for help until m.; like a 38.13
m. by m. he wakens, he wakens my 50.04
a cry in the m. and an alarm at Jer 20.16
LORD: " 'Execute justice in the m., 21.12
they are new every m.; great is thy Lam 3.23
In the m. the word of the LORD came Eze 12.08
So I spoke to the people in the m., 24.18
And on the next m. I did as I was 24.18
time the man came to me in the m.; 33.22
m. by m. he shall provide it. 46.13
cereal offering with it m. by m., 46.14
provided, m. by m., for a continual burnt 46.15
Your love is like a m. cloud, Hos 6.04
in the m. it blazes like a flaming 7.06
be like the m. mist or like the 13.03
bring your sacrifices every m., Amo 4.04
who makes the m. darkness, and 4.13
turns deep darkness into the m., 5.08
When the m. dawns, they perform it, Mic 2.01
that leave nothing till the m. Zep 3.03
every m. he shows forth his justice, 3.05
And in the m., 'It will be stormy Mt 16.03
early in the m. to hire laborers 20.01
In the m., as he was returning to 21.18
When m. came, all the chief priests 27.01
And in the m., a great while before Mk 1.35
As they passed by in the m., 11.20
or at cockcrow, or in the m.— 13.35
soon as it was m. the chief 15.01
And early in the m. all the people Lk 21.38
were at the tomb early in the m. 24.22
Early in the m. he came again to *Jn 8.02
to them from m. till evening, Ac 28.23
dawns and the m. star rises in 2Pe 1.19
and I will give him the m. star. Rev 2.28
of David, the bright m. star. 22.16

MORNINGS
and three hundred evenings and m.; Dan 8.14
evenings and the m. which has been 8.26

MORROW
And on the m. the LORD did this Ex 9.06
On the m. Moses sat to judge the 18.13
And they rose up early on the m., 32.06
On the m. Moses said to the people, 32.30
and on the m. what remains of it Lev 7.16
day you offer it, or on the m.; 19.06
on the m. after the sabbath the 23.11
count from the m. after the 23.15
days to the m. after the seventh 23.16
But on the m. all the congregation Num 16.41
And on the m. Moses went into the 17.08
And on the m. Balak took Balaam and 22.41
And on the m. after the passover, on Jos 5.11
And the manna ceased on the m., 5.12
And on the m. the people rose early, Ju 21.04
And on the m. Saul put the people 1Sa 11.11
And on the m. an evil spirit from 18.10
the m. after the new moon, David's 20.27
On the m., when the Philistines 31.08
But on the m. he took the coverlet 2Ki 8.15
On the m., when the Philistines 1Ch 10.08
On the m., when Pashhur released Jer 20.03
put them in custody until the m., Ac 4.03
On the m. their rulers and elders 4.05
intending to depart on the m.; 20.07
On the m. we departed and came to 21.08
But on the m., desiring to know the 22.30
And on the m. they returned to the 23.32
So on the m. Agrippa and Bernice 25.23

MORSEL
while I fetch a m. of bread, that you Gen 18.05
your heart with a m. of bread, Ju 19.05
bread, and dip your m. in the wine." Ru 2.14
that I may eat a m. of bread." ' " 1Sa 2.36
let me set a m. of bread before you; 28.22
it used to eat of his m., 2Sa 12.03
"Bring me a m. of bread in your 1Ki 17.11
or have eaten my m. alone, Job 31.17
Better is a dry m. with quiet than Pro 17.01
shall give this m. when I have Jn 13.26
So when he had dipped the m., 13.26
Then after the m., Satan entered 13.27
So, after receiving the m., 13.30

MORSELS
He casts forth his ice like m.; Ps 147.17
a whisperer are like delicious m.; Pro 18.08
vomit up the m. which you have 23.08
a whisperer are like delicious m.; 26.22

MORTAL
'Can m. man be righteous before God? Job 4.17
to the nether world among m. men, Eze 31.14
resembling m. man or birds or Rom 1.23
therefore reign in your m. bodies, 6.12
life to your m. bodies also 8.11
and this m. nature must put on 1Co 15.53
and the m. puts on immortality, then 15.54
may be manifested in our m. flesh. 2Co 4.11
so that what is m. may be swallowed 5.04
Here tithes are received by m. men; Heb 7.08
committing what is not a m. sin, 1Jn 5.16
life for those whose sin is not m. 5.16
There is sin which is m.; 5.16
but there is sin which is not m. 5.17
heads seemed to have a m. wound, Rev 13.03
but its m. wound was healed, and the 13.03
whose m. wound was healed. 13.12

MORTALLY
and wound him m., though the man Deu 19.06
and wounds him m. so that he dies, 19.11
before him like a man m. wounded. Eze 30.24

MORTAR
for stone, and bitumen for m. Gen 11.03
in m. and brick, and in all kinds of Ex 1.14
Crush a fool in a m. with a pestle Pro 27.22
shall trample on rulers as on m., Is 41.25
them in the m. in the pavement Jer 43.09
tread the m., take hold of the Nah 3.14
Wail, O inhabitants of the M.! Zep 1.11

MORTARS
ground it in mills or beat it in m., Num 11.08

MORTGAGING
"We are m. our fields, our vineyards, Neh 5.03

MOSAIC
and silver on a m. pavement of Est 1.06

MOSERAH
from Beeroth Benejaakan to M. Deu 10.06

MOSEROTH
from Hashmonah, and encamped at M. Num 33.30
And they set out from M., and encamped 33.31

MOSES
and she named him M., for she said, Ex 2.10
One day, when M. had grown up, he 2.11
Then M. was afraid, and thought, 2.14
to kill M. But M. fled from Pharaoh, 2.15
but M. stood up and helped them, and 2.17
And M. was content to dwell with 2.21
and he gave M. his daughter Zipporah 2.21
Now M. was keeping the flock of his 3.01
And M. said, "I will turn aside and 3.03
to him out of the bush, "M., M.!" 3.04
And M. hid his face, for he was 3.06
But M. said to God, "Who am I that I 3.11
Then M. said to God, "If I come to 3.13
God said to M., "I AM WHO I AM." 3.14
God also said to M., "Say this to 3.15
Then M. answered, "But behold, they 4.01
a serpent; and M. fled from it. 4.03
But the LORD said to M., "Put out 4.04
But M. said to the LORD, "Oh, my Lord, 4.10
was kindled against M. and he said, 4.14
M. went back to Jethro his father-in-law 4.18
And Jethro said to M., "Go in peace." 4.18
And the LORD said to M. in Midian, 4.19
So M. took his wife and his sons 4.20
and in his hand M. took the rod of 4.20
And the LORD said to M., "When you 4.21
"Go into the wilderness to meet M." 4.27
And M. told Aaron all the words of 4.28
Then M. and Aaron went and gathered 4.29
which the LORD had spoken to M., 4.30
Afterward M. and Aaron went to 5.01
"M. and Aaron, why do you take the 5.04
They met M. and Aaron, who were 5.20
Then M. turned again to the LORD 5.22
But the LORD said to M., "Now you 6.01
And God said to M., "I am the LORD. 6.02
M. spoke thus to the people of 6.09
but they did not listen to M., 6.09
And the LORD said to M., 6.10
But M. said to the LORD, "Behold, the 6.12
But the LORD spoke to M. and Aaron, 6.13
and she bore him Aaron and M., 6.20
the Aaron and M. to whom the LORD 6.26
from Egypt, this M. and this Aaron. 6.27
LORD spoke to M. in the land of 6.28
the LORD said to M., "I am the LORD; 6.29
But M. said to the LORD, "Behold, I 6.30
And the LORD said to M., "See, I make 7.01
And M. and Aaron did so; they did as 7.06
Now M. was eighty years old, and 7.07
And the LORD said to M. and Aaron, 7.08
So M. and Aaron went to Pharaoh and 7.10
Then the LORD said to M., "Pharaoh's 7.14
And the LORD said to M., "Say to 7.19
M. and Aaron did as the LORD 7.20
Then the LORD said to M., "Go in to 8.01
And the LORD said to M., "Say to 8.05
Then Pharaoh called M. and Aaron, 8.08
M. said to Pharaoh, "Be pleased to 8.09
M. said, "Be it as you say, that you 8.10
So M. and Aaron went out from 8.12
and M. cried to the LORD concerning 8.12
did according to the word of M.; 8.13
Then the LORD said to M., "Say to 8.16
Then the LORD said to M., "Rise 8.20
Then Pharaoh called M. and Aaron, 8.25
But M. said, "It would not be right 8.26
Then M. said, "Behold, I am going out 8.29
So M. went out from Pharaoh and 8.30
And the LORD did as M. asked, 8.31
Then the LORD said to M., "Go in to 9.01
And the LORD said to M. and Aaron, 9.08
and let M. throw them toward heaven 9.08
and M. threw them toward heaven, and 9.10
stand before M. because of the 9.11
as the LORD had spoken to M. 9.12
Then the LORD said to M., "Rise up 9.13
And the LORD said to M., "Stretch 9.22
Then M. stretched forth his rod 9.23
and called M. and Aaron, and said to 9.27
M. said to him, "As soon as I have 9.29
So M. went out of the city from 9.33
as the LORD had spoken through M. 9.35
Then the LORD said to M., "Go in to 10.01
So M. and Aaron went in to Pharaoh, 10.03
So M. and Aaron were brought back 10.08
And M. said, "We will go with our 10.09
Then the LORD said to M., "Stretch 10.12
So M. stretched forth his rod over 10.13
Then Pharaoh called M. and Aaron in 10.16
Then the LORD said to M., "Stretch 10.21
So M. stretched out his hand toward 10.22
Then Pharaoh called M., and said, 10.24
But M. said, "You must also let us 10.25
M. said, "As you say! I will not see 10.29
The LORD said to M., "Yet one plague 11.01
the man M. was very great in the 11.03
And M. said, "Thus says the LORD: 11.04
Then the LORD said to M., "Pharaoh 11.09
M. and Aaron did all these wonders 11.10
The LORD said to M. and Aaron in 12.01
Then M. called all the elders of 12.21
LORD had commanded M. and Aaron, 12.28
And he summoned M. and Aaron by 12.31
had also done as M. told them, 12.35
And the LORD said to M. and Aaron, 12.43
as the LORD commanded M. and Aaron, 12.50
The LORD said to M., 13.01
And M. said to the people, "Remember 13.03
And M. took the bones of Joseph 13.19
Then the LORD said to M., 14.01
and they said to M., "Is it because 14.11
And M. said to the people, "Fear not, 14.13
The LORD said to M., "Why do you 14.15
Then M. stretched out his hand over 14.21
Then the LORD said to M., "Stretch 14.26
So M. stretched forth his hand over 14.27
in the LORD and in his servant M. 14.31
Then M. and the people of Israel 15.01
Then M. led Israel onward from the 15.22
And the people murmured against M., 15.24
murmured against M. and Aaron in 16.02
Then the LORD said to M., "Behold 16.04
So M. and Aaron said to all the 16.06
And M. said, "When the LORD gives 16.08
And M. said to Aaron, "Say to the 16.09
And the LORD said to M., 16.11
And M. said to them, "It is the 16.15
And M. said to them, "Let no man 16.19
But they did not listen to M.; 16.20
and M. was angry with them. 16.20
the congregation came and told M., 16.22
till the morning, as M. bade them; 16.24
M. said, "Eat it today, for today is 16.25
And the LORD said to M., "How long 16.28
And M. said, "This is what the LORD 16.32
And M. said to Aaron, "Take a jar, 16.33
As the LORD commanded M., so Aaron 16.34
Therefore the people found fault with M., 17.02

MOSES (cont.)

And M. said to them, "Why do you Ex 17.02
and the people murmured against M., 17.03
So M. cried to the LORD, "What shall 17.04
And the LORD said to M., "Pass on 17.05
And M. did so, in the sight of the 17.06
And M. said to Joshua, "Choose for 17.09
So Joshua did as M. told him, 17.10
and M., Aaron, and Hur went up to 17.10
Whenever M. held up his hand, Israel 17.11
And the LORD said to M., "Write 17.14
And M. built an altar and called 17.15
had done for M. and for Israel his 18.01
and his wife to M. in the wilderness 18.05
And when one told M., "Lo, your 18.06
M. went out to meet his father-in-law, 18.07
Then M. told his father-in-law all 18.08
On the morrow M. sat to judge the 18.13
stood about M. from morning till 18.13
And M. said to his father-in-law, 18.15
So M. gave heed to the voice of his 18.24
M. chose able men out of all Israel, 18.25
hard cases they brought to M., 18.26
Then M. let his father-in-law 18.27
And M. went up to God, and the LORD 19.03
So M. came and called the elders of 19.07
And M. reported the words of the 19.08
And the LORD said to M., "Lo, I am 19.09
Then M. told the words of the 19.09
And the LORD said to M., "Go to the 19.10
So M. went down from the mountain 19.14
Then M. brought the people out of 19.17
M. spoke, and God answered him in 19.19
the LORD called M. to the top of 19.20
of the mountain, and M. went up. 19.20
And the LORD said to M., "Go down 19.21
And M. said to the LORD, "The people 19.23
So M. went down to the people and 19.25
and said to M., "You speak to us, 20.19
And M. said to the people, "Do not 20.20
while M. drew near to the thick 20.21
And the LORD said to M., "Thus you 20.22
And he said to M., "Come up to the 24.01
M. alone shall come near to the 24.02
M. came and told the people all the 24.03
And M. wrote all the words of the 24.04
And M. took half of the blood and 24.06
And M. took the blood and threw it 24.08
Then M. and Aaron, Nadab, and Abihu, 24.09
The LORD said to M., "Come up to 24.12
So M. rose with his servant Joshua, 24.13
and M. went up into the mountain of 24.13
Then M. went up on the mountain, and 24.15
he called to M. out of the midst 24.16
And M. entered the cloud, and went 24.18
And M. was on the mountain forty 24.18
The LORD said to M., 25.01
The LORD said to M., 30.11
The LORD said to M., 30.17
Moreover, the LORD said to M., 30.22
And the LORD said to M., "Take 30.34
The LORD said to M., 31.01
And the LORD said to M., 31.12
And he gave to M., when he had made 31.18
people saw that M. delayed to come 32.01
as for this M., the man who brought 32.01
And the LORD said to M., "Go down; 32.07
And the LORD said to M., "I have seen 32.09
But M. besought the LORD his God, 32.11
And M. turned, and went down from 32.15
he said to M., "There is a noise of 32.17
And M. said to Aaron, "What did this 32.21
as for this M., the man who brought 32.23
And when M. saw that the people had 32.25
then M. stood in the gate of the 32.26
did according to the word of M.; 32.28
And M. said, "Today you have ordained 32.29
On the morrow M. said to the people, 32.30

So M. returned to the LORD and said, 32.31
But the LORD said to M., "Whoever 32.33
The LORD said to M., "Depart, go 33.01
For the LORD had said to M., 33.05
Now M. used to take the tent and 33.07
Whenever M. went out to the tent, 33.08
his tent door, and looked after M., 33.08
When M. entered the tent, the pillar 33.09
and the LORD would speak with M. 33.09
used to speak to M. face to face, 33.11
When M. turned again into the camp, 33.11
M. said to the LORD, "See, thou 33.12
And the LORD said to M., "This 33.17
M. said, "I pray thee, show me thy 33.18
The LORD said to M., "Cut two 34.01
So M. cut two tables of stone like 34.04
And M. made haste to bow his head 34.08
And the LORD said to M., "Write 34.27
When M. came down from Mount Sinai, 34.29
M. did not know that the skin of 34.29
all the people of Israel saw M., 34.30
But M. called to them; and Aaron 34.31
to him, and M. talked with them. 34.31
And when M. had finished speaking 34.33
but whenever M. went in before the 34.34
of Israel saw the face of M., 34.35
and M. would put the veil upon his 34.35
M. assembled all the congregation 35.01
M. said to all the congregation of 35.04
departed from the presence of M. 35.20
had commanded by M. to be done, 35.29
And M. said to the people of Israel, 35.30
And M. called Bezalel and Oholiab 36.02
received from M. all the freewill 36.03
and said to M., "The people bring 36.05
So M. gave command, and word was 36.06
counted at the commandment of M., 38.21
all that the LORD commanded M.; 38.22
as the LORD had commanded M. 39.01
as the LORD had commanded M. 39.05
as the LORD had commanded M. 39.07
as the LORD had commanded M. 39.21
as the LORD had commanded M. 39.26
as the LORD had commanded M. 39.29
as the LORD had commanded M. 39.31
all that the LORD had commanded M.; 39.32
And they brought the tabernacle to M., 39.33
all that the LORD had commanded M., 39.42
And M. saw all the work, and behold, 39.43
they done it. And M. blessed them. 39.43
The LORD said to M., 40.01
Thus did M.; according to all that 40.16
M. erected the tabernacle; 40.18
it, as the LORD had commanded M. 40.19
as the LORD had commanded M. 40.21
as the LORD had commanded M. 40.23
as the LORD had commanded M. 40.25
as the LORD had commanded M. 40.27
as the LORD had commanded M. 40.29
with which M. and Aaron and his 40.31
as the LORD commanded M. 40.32
court. So M. finished the work. 40.33
And M. was not able to enter the 40.35
The LORD called M., and spoke Lev 1.01
And the LORD said to M., 4.01
The LORD said to M., 5.14
The LORD said to M., 6.01
The LORD said to M., 6.08
The LORD said to M., 6.19
The LORD said to M., 6.24
The LORD said to M., 7.22
The LORD said to M., 7.28
LORD commanded M. on Mount Sinai, 7.38
The LORD said to M., 8.01
And M. did as the LORD commanded 8.04
And M. said to the congregation, 8.05
And M. brought Aaron and his sons, 8.06
crown, as the LORD commanded M. 8.09

MOSES (cont.)

Then M. took the anointing oil, and Lev 8.10
And M. brought Aaron's sons, and 8.13
on them, as the LORD commanded M. 8.13
And M. killed it, and took the blood, 8.15
and M. burned them on the altar. 8.16
the camp, as the LORD commanded M. 8.17
And M. killed it, and threw the 8.19
M. burned the head and the pieces 8.20
M. burned the whole ram on the 8.21
the LORD, as the LORD commanded M. 8.21
And M. killed it, and took some of 8.23
and M. put some of the blood on the 8.24
and M. threw the blood upon the 8.24
Then M. took them from their hands, 8.28
And M. took the breast, and waved it 8.29
ordination, as the LORD commanded M. 8.29
Then M. took some of the anointing 8.30
And M. said to Aaron and his sons, 8.31
which the LORD commanded by M. 8.36
On the eighth day M. called Aaron 9.01
brought what M. commanded before 9.05
And M. said, "This is the thing 9.06
Then M. said to Aaron, "Draw near to 9.07
altar, as the LORD commanded M. 9.10
before the LORD; as M. commanded. 9.21
And M. and Aaron went into the tent 9.23
Then M. said to Aaron, "This is what 10.03
And M. called Mishael and Elzaphan, 10.04
out of the camp, as M. had said. 10.05
And M. said to Aaron and to Eleazar 10.06
did according to the word of M. 10.07
the LORD has spoken to them by M. 10.11
And M. said to Aaron and to Eleazar 10.12
Now M. diligently inquired about 10.16
And Aaron said to M., "Behold, 10.19
And when M. heard that, he was 10.20
And the LORD said to M. and Aaron, 11.01
The LORD said to M., 12.01
The LORD said to M. and Aaron, 13.01
The LORD said to M., 14.01
The LORD said to M. and Aaron, 14.33
The LORD said to M. and Aaron, 15.01
The LORD spoke to M., after the death 16.01
and the LORD said to M., "Tell Aaron 16.02
And M. did as the LORD commanded him. 16.34
And the LORD said to M., 17.01
And the LORD said to M., 18.01
And the LORD said to M., 19.01
The LORD said to M., 20.01
And the LORD said to M., 21.01
And the LORD said to M., 21.16
So M. spoke to Aaron and to his 21.24
And the LORD said to M., 22.01
And the LORD said to M., 22.17
And the LORD said to M., 22.26
The LORD said to M., 23.01
And the LORD said to M., 23.09
And the LORD said to M., 23.23
And the LORD said to M., 23.26
And the LORD said to M., 23.33
Thus M. declared to the people of 23.44
The LORD said to M., 24.01
And they brought him to M. His 24.11
And the LORD said to M., 24.13
So M. spoke to the people of Israel 24.23
Israel did as the LORD commanded M. 24.23
The LORD said to M. on Mount Sinai, 25.01
of Israel on Mount Sinai by M. 26.46
The LORD said to M., 27.01
LORD commanded M. for the people 27.34
The LORD spoke to M. in the wilderness Num 1.01
M. and Aaron took these men who 1.17
as the LORD commanded M. So he 1.19
whom M. and Aaron numbered with the 1.44
For the LORD said to M., 1.48
to all that the LORD commanded M. 1.54
The LORD said to M. and Aaron, 2.01
Israel, as the LORD commanded M. 2.33
to all that the LORD commanded M., 2.34
of Aaron and M. at the time when 3.01
LORD spoke with M. on Mount Sinai. 3.01
And the LORD said to M., 3.05
And the LORD said to M., 3.11
LORD said to M. in the wilderness 3.14
So M. numbered them according to 3.16
were M. and Aaron and his sons, 3.38
whom M. and Aaron numbered at the 3.39
And the LORD said to M., 3.40
So M. numbered all the first-born 3.42
And the LORD said to M., 3.44
So M. took the redemption money 3.49
and M. gave the redemption money to 3.51
the LORD, as the LORD commanded M. 3.51
The LORD said to M. and Aaron, 4.01
The LORD said to M. and Aaron, 4.17
The LORD said to M., 4.21
And M. and Aaron and the leaders of 4.34
whom M. and Aaron numbered according 4.37
the commandment of the LORD by M. 4.37
whom M. and Aaron numbered according 4.41
whom M. and Aaron numbered according 4.45
the commandment of the LORD by M. 4.45
whom M. and Aaron and the leaders 4.46
LORD through M. they were appointed, 4.49
by him, as the LORD commanded M. 4.49
The LORD said to M., 5.01
as the LORD said to M., so the people 5.04
And the LORD said to M., 5.05
And the LORD said to M., 5.11
And the LORD said to M., 6.01
The LORD said to M., 6.22
On the day when M. had finished 7.01
Then the LORD said to M., 7.04
So M. took the wagons and the oxen, 7.06
And the LORD said to M., "They shall 7.11
And when M. went into the tent of 7.89
Now the LORD said to M., 8.01
lampstand, as the LORD commanded M. 8.03
which the LORD had shown M., so he 8.04
And the LORD said to M., 8.05
Thus did M. and Aaron and all the 8.20
LORD commanded M. concerning the 8.20
had commanded M. concerning the 8.22
And the LORD said to M., 8.23
LORD spoke to M. in the wilderness 9.01
So M. told the people of Israel 9.04
to all that the LORD commanded M., 9.05
came before M. and Aaron on that 9.06
And M. said to them, "Wait, that I 9.08
The LORD said to M., 9.09
at the command of the LORD by M. 9.23
The LORD said to M., 10.01
at the command of the LORD by M. 10.13
And M. said to Hobab the son of 10.29
M. said, "Arise, O LORD, and let thy 10.35
Then the people cried to M.; 11.02
and M. prayed to the LORD, and the 11.02
M. heard the people weeping throughout 11.10
hotly, and M. was displeased. 11.10
M. said to the LORD, "Why hast thou 11.11
And the LORD said to M., "Gather 11.16
But M. said, "The people among whom 11.21
And the LORD said to M., "Is the 11.23
So M. went out and told the people 11.24
And a young man ran and told M., 11.27
the son of Nun, the minister of M., 11.28
men, said, "My lord M., forbid them." 11.28
But M. said to him, "Are you jealous 11.29
And M. and the elders of Israel 11.30
spoke against M. because of the 12.01
LORD indeed spoken only through M.? 12.02
Now the man M. was very meek, more 12.03
LORD said to M. and to Aaron and 12.04
Not so with my servant M.; 12.07
to speak against my servant M.?" 12.08

MOSES (cont.)
And Aaron said to M., "Oh, my Num 12.11
And M. cried to the LORD, "Heal her, 12.13
But the LORD said to M., "If her 12.14
The LORD said to M., 13.01
So M. sent them from the wilderness 13.03
of the men whom M. sent to spy out 13.16
And M. called Hoshea the son of Nun 13.16
M. sent them to spy out the land of 13.17
And they came to M. and Aaron and 13.26
Caleb quieted the people before M., 13.30
murmured against M. and Aaron; 14.02
Then M. and Aaron fell on their 14.05
And the LORD said to M., "How long 14.11
But M. said to the LORD, "Then the 14.13
And the LORD said to M. and to Aaron, 14.26
And the men whom M. sent to spy out 14.36
And M. told these words to all the 14.39
But M. said, "Why now are you 14.41
nor M., departed out of the camp. 14.44
The LORD said to M., 15.01
The LORD said to M., 15.17
which the LORD has spoken to M., 15.22
the LORD has commanded you by M., 15.23
sticks brought him to M. and Aaron, 15.33
And the LORD said to M., "The man 15.35
stones, as the LORD commanded M. 15.36
The LORD said to M., 15.37
and they rose up before M., 16.02
together against M. and against 16.03
When M. heard it, he fell on his 16.04
And M. said to Korah, "Hear now, you 16.08
And M. sent to call Dathan and 16.12
And M. was very angry, and said to 16.15
And M. said to Korah, "Be present, 16.16
tent of meeting with M. and Aaron. 16.18
And the LORD said to M. and to Aaron, 16.20
And the LORD said to M., 16.23
Then M. rose and went to Dathan and 16.25
And M. said, "Hereby you shall know 16.28
Then the LORD said to M., 16.36
LORD said to Eleazar through M. 16.40
murmured against M. and against 16.41
assembled against M. and against 16.42
And M. and Aaron came to the front 16.43
and the LORD said to M., 16.44
And M. said to Aaron, "Take your 16.46
So Aaron took it as M. said, 16.47
returned to M. at the entrance of 16.50
The LORD said to M., 17.01
M. spoke to the people of Israel; 17.06
And M. deposited the rods before 17.07
And on the morrow M. went into the 17.08
Then M. brought out all the rods 17.09
And the LORD said to M., "Put 17.10
Thus did M.; as the LORD commanded 17.11
And the people of Israel said to M., 17.12
And the LORD said to M., 18.25
Now the LORD said to M. and to Aaron, 19.01
together against M. and against 20.02
And the people contended with M., 20.03
Then M. and Aaron went from the 20.06
and the LORD said to M., 20.07
And M. took the rod from before the 20.09
And M. and Aaron gathered the 20.10
And M. lifted up his hand and 20.11
And the LORD said to M. and Aaron, 20.12
M. sent messengers from Kadesh to 20.14
LORD said to M. and Aaron at Mount 20.23
M. did as the LORD commanded; 20.27
And M. stripped Aaron of his 20.28
Then M. and Eleazar came down from 20.28
spoke against God and against M., 21.05
And the people came to M., 21.07
So M. prayed for the people. 21.07
And the LORD said to M., "Make a 21.08
So M. made a bronze serpent, and set 21.09
well of which the LORD said to M., 21.16
And M. sent to spy out Jazer; 21.32
But the LORD said to M., "Do not 21.34
and the LORD said to M., "Take 25.04
And M. said to the judges of Israel, 25.05
in the sight of M. and in the 25.06
And the LORD said to M., 25.10
And the LORD said to M., 25.16
LORD said to M. and to Eleazar the 26.01
And M. and Eleazar the priest spoke 26.03
upward," as the LORD commanded M. 26.04
contended against M. and Aaron in 26.09
The LORD said to M.: 26.52
Amram Aaron and M. and Miriam 26.59
numbered by M. and Eleazar the 26.63
numbered by M. and Aaron the 26.64
And they stood before M., and 27.02
M. brought their case before the 27.05
And the LORD said to M., 27.06
ordinance, as the LORD commanded M. 27.11
The LORD said to M., "Go up into this 27.12
M. said to the LORD, 27.15
And the LORD said to M., "Take 27.18
And M. did as the LORD commanded 27.22
as the LORD directed through M. 27.23
The LORD said to M., 28.01
And M. told the people of Israel 29.40
just as the LORD had commanded M. 29.40
M. said to the heads of the tribes 30.01
which the LORD commanded M., 30.16
The LORD said to M., 31.01
And M. said to the people, "Arm men 31.03
And M. sent them to the war, a 31.06
Midian, as the LORD commanded M., 31.07
and the booty and the spoil to M., 31.12
M., and Eleazar the priest, and all 31.13
And M. was angry with the officers 31.14
M. said to them, "Have you let all 31.15
which the LORD has commanded M.: 31.21
The LORD said to M., 31.25
And M. and Eleazar the priest did 31.31
did as the LORD commanded M. 31.31
And M. gave the tribute, which was 31.41
priest, as the LORD commanded M. 31.41
which M. separated from that of the 31.42
Israel's half M. took one of every 31.47
the LORD; as the LORD commanded M. 31.47
of hundreds, came near to M., 31.48
and said to M., "Your servants have 31.49
And M. and Eleazar the priest 31.51
And M. and Eleazar the priest 31.54
and said to M. and to Eleazar the 32.02
But M. said to the sons of Gad and 32.06
So M. said to them, "If you will do 32.20
and the sons of Reuben said to M., 32.25
So M. gave command concerning them 32.28
And M. said to them, "If the sons of 32.29
And M. gave to them, to the sons of 32.33
And M. gave Gilead to Machir the 32.40
the leadership of M. and Aaron. 33.01
M. wrote down their starting places, 33.02
LORD said to M. in the plains of 33.50
The LORD said to M., 34.01
M. commanded the people of Israel, 34.13
The LORD said to M., 34.16
The LORD said to M. in the plains 35.01
And the LORD said to M., 35.09
spoke before M. and before the 36.01
And M. commanded the people of 36.05
did as the LORD commanded M.; 36.10
commanded by M. to the people of 36.13
the words that M. spoke to all Deu 1.01
M. spoke to the people of Israel 1.03
M. undertook to explain this law, 1.05
Then M. set apart three cities in 4.41
the law which M. set before the 4.44
which M. spoke to the children of 4.45
whom M. and the children of Israel 4.46
And M. summoned all Israel, and said 5.01

MOSES (cont.)

Now M. and the elders of Israel Deu 27.01
And M. and the Levitical priests 27.09
And M. charged the people the same 27.11
LORD commanded M. to make with the 29.01
And M. summoned all Israel and said 29.02
So M. continued to speak these 31.01
Then M. summoned Joshua, and said to 31.07
And M. wrote this law, and gave it 31.09
And M. commanded them, "At the end 31.10
And the LORD said to M., 31.14
And M. and Joshua went and presented 31.14
And the LORD said to M., "Behold, you 31.16
So M. wrote this song the same day, 31.22
When M. had finished writing the 31.24
M. commanded the Levites who 31.25
Then M. spoke the words of this 31.30
M. came and recited all the words 32.44
And when M. had finished speaking 32.45
the LORD said to M. that very day, 32.48
with which M. the man of God 33.01
when M. commanded us a law, as a 33.04
And M. went up from the plains of 34.01
So M. the servant of the LORD died 34.05
M. was a hundred and twenty years 34.07
Israel wept for M. in the plains 34.08
and mourning for M. were ended. 34.08
for M. had laid his hands upon him; 34.09
did as the LORD had commanded M. 34.09
a prophet since in Israel like M., 34.10
deeds which M. wrought in the 34.12
After the death of M. the servant Jos 1.01
"M. my servant is dead; now therefore 1.02
given to you, as I promised to M. 1.03
as I was with M., so I will be with 1.05
the law which M. my servant 1.07
"Remember the word which M. the 1.13
the land which M. gave you beyond 1.14
the land which M. the servant of 1.15
Just as we obeyed M. in all things, 1.17
God be with you, as he was with M.! 1.17
as I was with M., so I will be with 3.07
to all that M. had commanded Joshua. 4.10
of Israel, as M. had bidden them; 4.12
as they had stood in awe of M., 4.14
as M. the servant of the LORD had 8.31
in the book of the law of M., 8.31
the stones a copy of the law of M., 8.32
as M. the servant of the LORD had 8.33
of all that M. commanded which 8.35
his servant M. to give you all the 9.24
as M. the servant of the LORD had 11.12
LORD had commanded M. his servant, 11.15
so M. commanded Joshua, and so 11.15
all that the LORD had commanded M. 11.15
exterminated, as the LORD commanded M. 11.20
all that the LORD had spoken to M.; 11.23
M., the servant of the LORD, and the 12.06
and M. the servant of the LORD gave 12.06
which M. gave them, beyond the 13.08
as M. the servant of the LORD gave 13.08
these M. had defeated and driven 13.12
of Levi alone M. gave no inheritance 13.14
And M. gave an inheritance to the 13.15
whom M. defeated with the leaders 13.21
And M. gave an inheritance also to 13.24
And M. gave an inheritance to the 13.29
inheritances which M. distributed 13.32
tribe of Levi M. gave no inheritance 13.33
had commanded M. for the nine and 14.02
For M. had given an inheritance to 14.03
did as the LORD commanded M.; 14.05
LORD said to M. the man of God in 14.06
years old when M. the servant of 14.07
And M. swore on that day, saying, 14.09
the LORD spoke this word to M., 14.10
I was in the day that M sent me; 14.11
LORD commanded M. to give us an 17.04
which M. the servant of the LORD 18.07
which I spoke to you through M., 20.02
commanded through M. that we be 21.02
the LORD had commanded through M. 21.08
kept all that M. the servant of 22.02
which M. the servant of the LORD 22.04
the law which M. the servant of 22.05
of Manasseh M. had given a possession 22.07
by command of the LORD through M. 22.09
in the book of the law of M., 23.06
And I sent M. and Aaron, and I 24.05
was given to Caleb, as M. had said; Ju 1.20
he commanded their fathers by M. 3.04
of Hobab the father-in-law of M., 4.11
son of M., and his sons were 18.30
who appointed M. and Aaron and 1Sa 12.06
and the LORD sent M. and Aaron, 12.08
as it is written in the law of M., 1Ki 2.03
of stone which M. put there at 8.09
as thou didst declare through M., 8.53
which he uttered by M. his servant. 8.56
in the book of the law of M., 2Ki 14.06
bronze serpent that M. had made, 18.04
which the LORD commanded M. 18.06
even all that M. the servant of the 18.12
that my servant M. commanded them. 21.08
according to all the law of M.; 23.25
of Amram: Aaron, M., and Miriam. 1Ch 6.03
to all that M. the servant of God 6.49
as M. had commanded according to 15.15
which M. had made in the wilderness, 21.29
the LORD commanded M. for Israel. 22.13
The sons of Amram: Aaron and M. 23.13
But the sons of M. the man of God 23.14
The sons of M.: Gershom and Eliezer. 23.15
son of M., was chief officer in 26.24
which M. the servant of the LORD 2Ch 1.03
tables which M. put there at Horeb, 5.10
commandment of M. for the sabbaths, 8.13
as it is written in the law of M., 23.18
and Jerusalem the tax levied by M., 24.06
the tax that M. the servant of God 24.09
in the law, in the book of M., 25.04
to the law of M. the man of God; 30.16
the ordinances given through M. 33.08
law of the LORD given through M. 34.14
to the word of the LORD by M. 35.06
as it is written in the book of M. 35.12
in the law of M. the man of God. Ez 3.02
as it is written in the book of M. 6.18
in the law of M. which the LORD 7.06
thou didst command thy servant M. Neh 1.07
thou didst command thy servant M., 1.08
of the law of M. which the LORD 8.01
commanded by M. that the people of 8.14
and a law by M. thy servant. 9.14
was given by M. the servant of God, 10.29
the book of M. in the hearing of 13.01
flock by the hand of M. and Aaron. Ps 77.20
M. and Aaron were among his priests, 99.06
He made known his ways to M., 103.07
He sent M. his servant, and Aaron 105.26
camp were jealous of M. and Aaron, 106.16
had not M., his chosen one, stood in 106.23
went ill with M. on their account; 106.32
the days of old, of M. his servant. Is 63.11
arm to go at the right hand of M., 63.12
"Though M. and Samuel stood before Jer 15.01
in the law of M. the servant of Dan 9.11
As it is written in the law of M., 9.13
and I sent before you M., Aaron, Mic 6.04
"Remember the law of my servant M., Mal 4.04
offer the gift that M. commanded, Mt 8.04
appeared to them M. and Elijah, 17.03
you and one for M. and one for 17.04
"Why then did M. command one to 19.07
of heart M. allowed you to divorce 19.08
M. said, 'If a man dies, having no 22.24

MOSES (cont.)

your cleansing what M. commanded, Mk 1.44
For M. said, 'Honor your father and 7.10
appeared to them Elijah with M.; 9.04
you and one for M. and one for 9.05
them, "What did M. command you?" 10.03
They said, "M. allowed a man to 10.04
"Teacher, M. wrote for us that if a 12.19
you not read in the book of M., 12.26
purification according to the law of M., Lk 2.22
as M. commanded, for a proof to the 5.14
talked with him, M. and Elijah, 9.30
you and one for M. and one for 9.33
'They have M. and the prophets; 16.29
do not hear M. and the prophets, 16.31
M. wrote for us that if a man's 20.28
even M. showed, in the passage about 20.37
And beginning with M. and all the 24.27
in the law of M. and the prophets 24.44
For the law was given through M.; Jn 1.17
him of whom M. in the law and also 1.45
And as M. lifted up the serpent in 3.14
it is M. who accuses you, on whom 5.45
If you believed M., you would 5.46
it was not M. who gave you the 6.32
Did not M. give you the law? 7.19
M. gave you circumcision (not that 7.22
it is from M., but from the fathers), 7.22
that the law of M. may not be 7.23
Now in the law M. commanded us to * 8.05
disciple, but we are disciples of M. 9.28
We know that God has spoken to M., 9.29
M. said, 'The Lord God will raise up Ac 3.22
blasphemous words against M. and God. 6.11
customs which M. delivered to us. 6.14
At this time M. was born, and was 7.20
And M. was instructed in all the 7.22
At this retort M. fled, and became 7.29
When M. saw it he wondered at the 7.31
And M. trembled and did not dare 7.32
"This M. whom they refused, saying, 7.35
This is the M. who said to the 7.37
as for this M. who led us out from 7.40
he who spoke to M. directed him to 7.44
not be freed by the law of M. 13.39
according to the custom of M., 15.01
charge them to keep the law of M. 15.05
generations M. has had in every 15.21
among the Gentiles to forsake M., 21.21
prophets and M. said would come to 26.22
from the law of M. and from the 28.23
Yet death reigned from Adam to M., Rom 5.14
For he says to M., "I will have 9.15
M. writes that the man who practices 10.05
First M. says, "I will make you 10.19
For it is written in the law of M., 1Co 9.09
baptized into M. in the cloud and 10.02
not like M., who put a veil over 2Co 3.13
day whenever M. is read a veil 3.15
As Jannes and Jambres opposed M., 2Ti 3.08
just as M. also was faithful in Heb 3.02
more glory than M. as the builder 3.03
Now M. was faithful in all God's 3.05
Egypt under the leadership of M.? 3.16
with that tribe M. said nothing 7.14
for when M. was about to erect the 8.05
declared by M. to all the people, 9.19
the law of M. dies without mercy 10.28
By faith M., when he was born, was 11.23
By faith M., when he was grown up, 11.24
terrifying was the sight that M. said, 12.21
disputed about the body of M., Jud 1.09
And they sing the song of M., Rev 15.03

MOSES'

and touched M. feet with it, and Ex 4.25
But M. hands grew weary; 17.12
M. father-in-law, heard of all that 18.01
Now Jethro, M. father-in-law, had 18.02
M. wife, after he had sent her away, 18.02
And Jethro, M. father-in-law, came 18.05
And Jethro, M. father-in-law, offered 18.12
eat bread with M. father-in-law 18.12
When M. father-in-law saw all that 18.14
M. father-in-law said to him, "What 18.17
M. anger burned hot, and he threw 32.19
that the skin of M. face shone; 34.35
it was M. portion of the ram of Lev 8.29
M. father-in-law, "We are setting Num 10.29
the son of Nun, M. minister, Jos 1.01
M. father-in-law, went up with the Ju 1.16
and the Pharisees sit on M. seat; Mt 23.02
not look at M. face because of its 2Co 3.07

MOST

he was priest of God M. High. Gen 14.18
"Blessed be Abram by God M. High, 14.19
and blessed be God M. High, 14.20
have sworn to the LORD God M. High, 14.22
Now he was the m. honored of all 34.19
the holy place from the m. holy. Ex 26.33
the testimony in the m. holy place. 26.34
it, and the altar shall be m. holy; 29.37
it is m. holy to the LORD. 30.10
them, that they may be m. holy; 30.29
it shall be for you m. holy. 30.36
and the altar shall be m. holy. 40.10
it is a m. holy part of the offerings Lev 2.03
it is a m. holy part of the offerings 2.10
it is a thing m. holy, like the sin 6.17
before the LORD; it is m. holy. 6.25
priests may eat of it; it is m. holy. 6.29
the guilt offering. It is m. holy; 7.01
eaten in a holy place; it is m. holy. 7.06
the altar, for it is m. holy; 10.12
it is a thing m. holy and has been 10.17
belongs to the high priest; it is m. holy. 14.13
both of the m. holy and of the holy 21.22
it is for him a m. holy portion 24.09
thing is m. holy to the LORD. 27.28
of meeting: the m. holy things. Num 4.04
come near to the m. holy things: 4.19
be yours of the m. holy things, 18.09
shall be m. holy to you and to your 18.09
In a m. holy place shall you eat of 18.10
knows the knowledge of the M. High, 24.16
The man who is the m. tender and Deu 28.54
The m. tender and delicately bred 28.56
When the M. High gave to the 32.08
"M. blessed of women be Jael, the Ju 5.24
of tent-dwelling women m. blessed. 5.24
"You are m. gracious to me, my lord, Ru 2.13
and the M. High uttered his voice. 2Sa 22.14
He was the m. renowned of the 23.19
sanctuary, as the m. holy place. 1Ki 6.16
the m. holy place, and for the doors 7.50
in the m. holy place, underneath the 8.06
all the work of the m. holy place, 1Ch 6.49
He was the m. renowned of the 11.21
to consecrate the m. holy things, 23.13
And he made the m. holy place; 2Ch 3.08
In the m. holy place he made two 3.10
doors to the m. holy place and for 4.22
in the m. holy place, underneath the 5.07
the LORD and the m. holy offerings. 31.14
not to partake of the m. holy food, Ez 2.63
not to partake of the m. holy food, Neh 7.65
and m. of them lay in sackcloth and Est 4.03
one of the king's m. noble princes; 6.09
the name of the LORD, the M. High. Ps 7.17
sing praise to thy name. O M. High. 9.02
and the M. High uttered his voice, 18.13
dost make him m. blessed for ever; 21.06
love of the M. High he shall not 21.07
hands toward thy m. holy sanctuary. 28.02
the holy habitation of the M. High. 46.04

MOST (cont.)
the M. High, is terrible, a great Ps 47.02
and pay your vows to the M. High; 50.14
I cry to God M. High, to God who 57.02
is there knowledge in the M. High? 73.11
hand of the M. High has changed. 77.10
against the M. High in the desert. 78.17
the M. High God their redeemer. 78.35
rebelled against the M. High God, 78.56
sons of the M. High, all of you; 82.06
art the M. High over all the earth. 83.18
for the M. High himself will 87.05
in the shelter of the M. High, 91.01
the M. High your habitation, 91.09
praises to thy name, O M. High; 92.01
art m. high over all the earth; 97.09
against the M. High at the Red Sea. 106.07
spurned the counsel of the M. High. 107.11
His speech is m. sweet, and he is Sol 5.16
of fire, a m. vehement flame. 8.06
will make myself like the M. High.' Is 14.14
a heritage m. beauteous of all Jer 3.19
m. bitter lamentation; for suddenly 6.26
in the presence of the M. High, Lam 3.35
mouth of the M. High that good and 3.38
the m. glorious of all lands. Eze 20.06
the m. glorious of all lands, 20.15
the m. terrible of the nations; 28.07
It shall be the m. lowly of the 29.15
the m. terrible of the nations, 30.11
the m. terrible of the nations, will 31.12
all of them m. terrible among the 32.12
to me, This is the m. holy place. 41.04
shall eat the m. holy offerings; 42.13
shall put the m. holy offerings— 42.13
of the mountain shall be m. holy. 43.12
and the things that are m. sacred; 44.13
the sanctuary, the m. holy place. 45.03
a m. holy place, adjoining the 48.12
servants of the M. High God, Dan 3.26
that the M. High God has wrought 4.02
know that the M. High rules the 4.17
It is a decree of the M. High, 4.24
know that the M. High rules the 4.25
that the M. High rules the kingdom 4.32
to me, and I blessed the M. High, 4.34
O king, the M. High God gave Nebuchadnezzar 5.18
knew that the M. High God rules 5.21
saints of the M. High shall 7.18
for the saints of the M. High, 7.22
speak words against the M. High, 7.25
wear out the saints of the M. High, 7.25
of the saints of the M. High; 7.27
and to anoint a m. holy place. 9.24
the m. upright of them a thorn Mic 7.04
cities where m. of his mighty Mt 11.20
M. of the crowd spread their 21.08
m. men's love will grow cold. 24.12
me, Jesus, Son of the M. High God? Mk 5.07
so that m. of them said, "He is dead 9.26
account for you, m. excellent Theophilus, Lk 1.03
be called the Son of the M. High; 1.32
power of the M. High will overshadow 1.35
called the prophet of the M. High; 1.76
you will be sons of the M. High; 6.35
me, Jesus, Son of the M. High God? 8.28
Yet the M. High does not dwell in Ac 7.48
are servants of the M. High God, 16.17
and m. of them did not know why 19.32
sorrowing m. of all because of the 20.38
m. excellent Felix, reforms are 24.02
m. excellent Festus, but I am 26.25
Nevertheless with m. of them God 1Co 10.05
there be only two or at m. three, 14.27
m. of whom are still alive, though 15.06
we are of all men m. to be pitied. 15.19
zeal has stirred up m. of them. 2Co 9.02
I will m. gladly spend and be spent 12.15
making the m. of the time, because Eph 5.16
and m. of the brethren have been Php 1.14
outsiders, making the m. of the time. Col 4.05
priest of the m. high God, met Heb 7.01
yourselves up on your m. holy faith; Jud 1.20
its radiance like a m. rare jewel, Rev 21.11

MOTH
who are crushed before the m. Job 4.19
consume like a m. what is dear to Ps 39.11
the m. will eat them up. Is 50.09
For the m. will eat them up like a 51.08
Therefore I am like a m. to Ephraim, Hos 5.12
where m. and rust consume and where Mt 6.19
where neither m. nor rust consumes 6.20
approaches and no m. destroys. Lk 12.33

MOTH-EATEN
thing, like a garment that is m. Job 13.28
rotted and your garments are m. Jas 5.02

MOTHER
father and his m. and cleaves to Gen 2.24
she was the m. of all living. 3.20
and she shall be a m. of nations; 17.16
but not the daughter of my m.; 20.12
and his m. took a wife for him from 21.21
and to her m. costly ornaments. 24.53
Her brother and her m. said, 24.55
be the m. of thousands of ten 24.60
But Jacob said to Rebekah his m., 27.11
His m. said to him, "Upon me be your 27.13
them and brought them to his m.; 27.14
and his m. prepared savory food, 27.14
of Rebekah, Jacob's and Esau's m. 28.05
father and his m. and gone to 28.07
and brought them to his m. Leah. 30.14
I and your m. and your brothers 37.10
went and called the child's m. Ex 2.08
"Honor your father and your m., 20.12
father or his m. shall be put to 21.15
father or his m. shall be put to 21.17
which is the nakedness of your m.; Lev 18.07
she is your m., you shall not 18.07
father or the daughter of your m., 18.09
shall revere his m. and his father, 19.03
father or his m. shall be put to 20.09
he has cursed his father or his m., 20.09
a man takes a wife and her m. also, 20.14
his father or a daughter of his m., 20.17
his m., his father, his son, his 21.02
even for his father or for his m.; 21.11
remain seven days with its m.; and from the 22.27
And whether the m. is a cow or a 22.28
Neither for his father nor for his m., Num 6.07
"'Honor your father and your m., Deu 5.16
"If your brother, the son of your m., 13.06
her father and her m. a full month; 21.13
his father or the voice of his m., 21.18
father and his m. shall take hold 21.19
or eggs and the m. sitting upon 22.06
not take the m. with the young; 22.06
you shall let the m. go, but the young 22.07
woman and her m. shall take and 22.15
who dishonors his father or his m. 27.16
father or the daughter of his m. 27.22
who said of his father and m., 33.09
and save alive my father and m., Jos 2.13
into your house your father and m., 2.18
her father and m. and brothers and 6.23
Deborah, arose as a m. in Israel. Ju 5.07
the m. of Sisera gazed through the 5.28
my brothers, the sons of my m.; 8.19
up, and told his father and m., 14.02
But his father and m. said to him, 14.03
His father and m. did not know that 14.04
with his father and m. to Timnah, 14.05
father or his m. what he had done. 14.06

MOTHER (cont.)

and he came to his father and m., Ju 14.09
have not told my father nor my m., 14.16
And he said to his m., "The eleven hundred 17.02
And his m. said, "Blessed be my son 17.02
hundred pieces of silver to his m.; 17.03
and his m. said, "I consecrate the 17.03
he restored the money to his m., 17.04
his m. took two hundred pieces of 17.04
your father and m. and your native Ru 2.11
And his m. used to make for him a 1Sa 2.19
so shall your m. be childless among 15.33
my father and my m. stay with you, 22.03
of Nahash, sister of Zeruiah, Joab's m. 2Sa 17.25
the grave of my father and my m. 19.37
a city which is a m. in Israel; 20.19
to Bathsheba the m. of Solomon, 1Ki 1.11
to Bathsheba the m. of Solomon. 2.13
a seat brought for the king's m.; 2.19
to her, "Make your request, my m.; 2.20
King Solomon answered his m., 2.22
means slay it; she is its m." 3.27
Maacah his m. from being queen m. 15.13
house, and delivered him to his m.; 17.23
"Let me kiss my father and my m., 19.20
father, and in the way of his m., 22.52
though not like his father and m., 2Ki 3.02
father and the prophets of your m." 3.13
his servant, "Carry him to his m." 4.19
him, and brought him to his m., 4.20
Then the m. of the child said, "As 4.30
sorceries of your m. Jezebel are so 9.22
and the sons of the queen m." 10.13
Athaliah the m. of Ahaziah saw 11.01
and his m., and his servants, and 24.12
the king's m., the king's wives, his 24.15
was Atarah; she was the m. of Onam. 1Ch 2.26
whose m. was Maacah, the daughter of 3.02
Adonijah, whose m. was Haggith; 3.02
and his m. called his name Jabez, 4.09
his m., King Asa removed from being 2Ch 15.16
being queen m. because she had 15.16
for his m. was his counselor in 22.03
Athaliah the m. of Ahaziah saw 22.10
for she had neither father nor m.; Est 2.07
when her father and her m. died, 2.07
to the worm, 'My m.,' or 'My sister,' Job 17.14
loathsome to the sons of my own m. 19.17
and since my m. bore me thou hast Ps 22.10
father and my m. have forsaken me, 27.10
about as one who laments his m., 35.14
and in sin did my m. conceive me. 51.05
the sin of his m. be blotted out! 109.14
her the joyous m. of children. 113.09
only one in the sight of my m., Pro 4.03
foolish son is a sorrow to his m. 10.01
but a foolish man despises his m. 15.20
chases away his m. is a son who 19.26
If one curses his father or his m., 20.20
despise your m. when she is old. 23.22
Let your father and m. be glad, 23.25
robs his father or his m. and says, 28.24
to himself brings shame to his m. 29.15
to obey a m. will be picked out by 30.17
of Massa, which his m. taught him: 31.01
with which his m. crowned him on Sol 3.11
is only one, the darling of her m., 6.09
bring you into the house of my m., 8.02
There your m. was in travail with 8.05
how to cry 'My father' or 'My m.,' Is 8.04
the body of my m. he named my name 49.01
transgressions your m. was put away. 50.01
As one whom his m. comforts, 66.13
Say to the king and the queen m.: Jer 13.18
Woe is me, my m., that you bore me, a 15.10
to drink for his father or his m. 16.07
The day when my m. bore me, let it not be 20.14
so my m. would have been my grave, 20.17
you and the m. who bore you into 22.26
and the queen m., the eunuchs, the 29.02
your m. shall be utterly shamed, and 50.12
an Amorite, and your m. a Hittite. Eze 16.03
about you. 'Like m., like daughter.' 16.44
You are the daughter of your m., 16.45
Your m. was a Hittite and your 16.45
a lioness was your m. among lions! 19.02
Your m. was like a vine in a 19.10
Father and m. are treated with 22.07
two women, the daughters of one m.; 23.02
for father or m., for son or 44.25
"Plead with your m., plead— Hos 2.02
For their m. has played the harlot; 2.05
and I will destroy your m. 4.05
daughter rises up against her m., Mic 7.06
father and m. who bore him will say Zec 13.03
m. who bore him shall pierce him 13.03
When his m. Mary had been betrothed Mt 1.18
saw the child with Mary his m., 2.11
"Rise, take the child and his m., 2.13
took the child and his m. by night, 2.14
"Rise, take the child and his m., 2.20
rose and took the child and his m., 2.21
and a daughter against her m., 10.35
loves father or m. more than me is 10.37
his m. and his brothers stood outside, 12.46
"Your m. and your brothers are standing * 12.47
"Who is my m., and who are my brothers?" 12.48
"Here are my m. and my brothers! 12.49
is my brother, and sister, and m." 12.50
Is not his m. called Mary? And are not 13.55
Prompted by her m., she said, "Give 14.08
girl, and she brought it to her m. 14.11
'Honor your father and your m.,' 15.04
He who speaks evil of father or m., 15.04
any one tells his father or his m., 15.05
his father and m. and be joined to 19.05
Honor your father and m., 19.19
or father or m. or children or 19.29
Then the m. of the sons of Zebedee 20.20
and Mary the m. of James and Joseph, 27.56
and the m. of the sons of Zebedee. 27.56
And his m. and his brothers came; Mk 3.31
"Your m. and your brothers are 3.32
"Who are my m. and my brothers?" 3.33
"Here are my m. and my brothers! 3.34
is my brother, and sister, and m." 3.35
father and m. and those who were 5.40
And she went out, and said to her m., 6.24
and the girl gave it to her m. 6.28
'Honor your father and your m.'; 7.10
He who speaks evil of father or m., 7.10
a man tells his father or his m., 7.11
do anything for his father or m., 7.12
his father and m. and be joined to 10.07
defraud, Honor your father and m.'" 10.19
or sisters or m. or father or 10.29
and Mary the m. of James the 15.40
and Mary the m. of Joses saw where 15.47
and Mary the m. of James, and Salome, 16.01
that the m. of my Lord should come Lk 1.43
but his m. said, "Not so; 1.60
father and his m. marveled at what 2.33
them and said to Mary his m., 2.34
and his m. said to him, "Son, why 2.48
and his m. kept all these things in 2.51
out, the only son of his m., and she was 7.12
began to speak. And he gave him to his m. 7.15
Then his m. and his brothers came 8.19
"Your m. and your brothers are 8.20
"My m. and my brothers are those 8.21
and the father and m. of the child. 8.51
m. against daughter and daughter 12.53
and daughter against her m., 12.53
own father and m. and wife and 14.26
witness, Honor your father and m.'" 18.20
and Mary the m. of James and the 24.10

MOTHER (cont.)
and the m. of Jesus was there; Jn 2.01
the m. of Jesus said to him, "They 2.03
His m. said to the servants, "Do 2.05
with his m. and his brothers and 2.12
whose father and m. we know? 6.42
by the cross of Jesus were his m., 19.25
When Jesus saw his m., and the disciple 19.26
standing near, he said to his m., 19.26
to the disciple, "Behold your m.!" 19.27
the women and Mary the m. of Jesus, Ac 1.14
the m. of John whose other name was 12.12
in the Lord, also his m. and mine. Rom 16.13
above is free, and she is our m. Gal 4.26
his father and m. and be joined to Eph 5.31
"Honor your father and m." (this is 6.02
Lois and your m. Eunice and now, 2Ti 1.05
without father or m. or genealogy, Heb 7.03
m. of harlots and of earth's abominations." Rev 17.05

MOTHER-IN-LAW
" 'Cursed be he who lies with his m., Deu 27.23
and Orpah kissed her m., Ru 1.14
done for your m. since the death 2.11
she showed her m. what she had 2.18
And her m. said to her, "Where did 2.19
So she told her m. with whom she 2.19
wheat harvests; and she lived with her m. 2.23
Then Naomi her m. said to her, "My 3.01
did just as her m. had told her. 3.06
And when she came to her m., 3.16
go back empty-handed to your m.' " 3.17
the daughter-in-law against her m.; Mic 7.06
he saw his m. lying sick with a Mt 8.14
a daughter-in-law against her m.; 10.35
Now Simon's m. lay sick with a fever, Mk 1.30
Now Simon's m. was ill with a high Lk 4.38
m. against her daughter-in-law and 12.53
and daughter-in-law against her m." 12.53

MOTHER-OF-PEARL
porphyry, marble, m. and precious stones. Est 1.06

MOTHER'S
and told her m. household about Gen 24.28
was comforted after his m. death. 24.67
and may your m. sons bow down to 27.29
house of Bethuel your m. father; 28.02
daughters of Laban your m. brother. 28.02
daughter of Laban his m. brother, 29.10
the sheep of Laban his m. brother, 29.10
the flock of Laban his m. brother. 29.10
his m. son, and said, "Is this your 43.29
alone is left of his m. children; 44.20
not boil a kid in its m. milk. Ex 23.19
not boil a kid in its m. milk. 34.26
the nakedness of your m. sister, Lev 18.13
for she is your m. near kinswoman. 18.13
nakedness of your m. sister or of 20.19
His m. name was Shelomith, the 24.11
when he comes out of his m. womb." Num 12.12
not boil a kid in its m. milk. Deu 14.21
Shechem to his m. kinsmen and said Ju 9.01
the whole clan of his m. family, 9.01
And his m. kinsmen spoke all these 9.03
a Nazarite to God from my m. womb. 16.17
return each of you to her m. house. Ru 1.08
to the shame of your m. nakedness? 1Sa 20.30
whose m. name was Zeruah, a widow, 1Ki 11.26
His m. name was Naamah the Ammonitess. 14.21
His m. name was Naamah the Ammonitess. 14.31
His m. name was Maacah the daughter 15.02
His m. name was Maacah the daughter 15.10
His m. name was Azubah the daughter 22.42
His m. name was Athaliah; she was a 2Ki 8.26
His m. name was Zibiah of Beersheba. 12.01
His m. name was Jehoaddin of 14.02
His m. name was Jecoliah of Jerusalem. 15.02
His m. name was Jerusha the daughter 15.33
His m. name was Abi the daughter of 18.02
in Jerusalem. His m. name was Hephzibah. 21.01
His m. name was Meshullemeth the 21.19
His m. name was Jedidah the daughter 22.01
His m. name was Hamutal the daughter 23.31
His m. name was Zebidah the daughter 23.36
His m. name was Nehushta the daughter 24.08
His m. name was Hamutal the daughter 24.18
His m. name was Naamah the Ammonitess. 2Ch 12.13
His m. name was Micaiah the daughter 13.02
His m. name was Azubah the daughter 20.31
His m. name was Athaliah, the granddaughter 22.02
his m. name was Zibiah of Beersheba. 24.01
His m. name was Jehoaddan of Jerusalem. 25.01
His m. name was Jecoliah of Jerusalem. 26.03
His m. name was Jerushah the daughter 27.01
His m. name was Abijah the daughter 29.01
said, "Naked I came from my m. womb, Job 1.21
not shut the doors of my m. womb, 3.10
and from his m. womb I guided him); 31.18
keep me safe upon my m. breasts. Ps 22.09
you slander your own m. son. 50.20
brethren, an alien to my m. sons. 69.08
art he who took me from my m. womb. 71.06
a child quieted at its m. breast; 131.02
knit me together in my m. womb. 139.13
and reject not your m. teaching; Pro 1.08
and forsake not your m. teaching. 6.20
came from his m. womb he shall go Ecc 5.15
My m. sons were angry with me, they Sol 1.06
I had brought him into my m. house, 3.04
to me, that nursed at my m. breast! 8.01
"Where is your m. bill of divorce, Is 50.01
His m. name was Hamutal the daughter Jer 52.01
Holy Spirit, even from his m. womb. Lk 1.15
time into his m. womb and be born?" Jn 3.04
and his m. sister, Mary the wife of 19.25

MOTHERS
slay us all, the m. with the children. Gen 32.11
fathers and do not bless their m. Pro 30.11
and their queens your nursing m. Is 49.23
against the m. of young men a Jer 15.08
concerning the m. who bore them 16.03
They cry to their m., "Where is bread Lam 2.12
fatherless; our m. are like widows. 5.03
m. were dashed in pieces with their Hos 10.14
and sisters and m. and children Mk 10.30
of fathers and murderers of m., 1Ti 1.09
older women like m., younger women 5.02

MOTHERS'
is poured out on their m. bosom. Lam 2.12

MOTIONED
And Alexander m. with his hand, Ac 19.33
m. with his hand to the people; 21.40
governor had m. to him to speak, 24.10

MOTIONING
But m. to them with his hand to be Ac 12.17
and m. with his hand said: "Men of 13.16

MOTTLED
were striped, spotted, and m. Gen 31.10
flock are striped, spotted, and m.; 31.12

MOUND
they cast up a m. against the city, 2Sa 20.15
shield or cast up a m. against it. 2Ki 19.32
or cast up a siege m. against it. Is 37.33
cast up a siege m. against Jerusalem Jer 6.06
city shall be rebuilt upon its m., 30.18
it shall become a desolate m., 49.02
it, and cast up a m. against it; Eze 4.02
you, and throw up a m. against you, 26.08

MOUNDS

that stood on m. did Israel burn,	Jos 11.13
the siege m. have come up to the	Jer 32.24
the siege m. and before the sword:	33.04
when m. are cast up and siege walls	Eze 17.17
to cast up m., to build siege	21.22

MOUNT

in their M. Seir as far as Elparan	Gen 14.06
"On the m. of the LORD it shall be	22.14
come down upon M. Sinai in the	Ex 19.11
And M. Sinai was wrapped in smoke,	19.18
And the LORD came down upon M. Sinai,	19.20
people cannot come up to M. Sinai;	19.23
of the LORD settled on M. Sinai,	24.16
of speaking with him upon M. Sinai,	31.18
ornaments, from M. Horeb onward.	33.06
come up in the morning to M. Sinai,	34.02
morning and went up on M. Sinai,	34.04
When Moses came down from M. Sinai,	34.29
had spoken with him in M. Sinai.	34.32
LORD commanded Moses on M. Sinai,	Lev 7.38
The LORD said to Moses on M. Sinai,	25.01
of Israel on M. Sinai by Moses.	26.46
the people of Israel on M. Sinai.	27.34
LORD spoke with Moses on M. Sinai.	Num 3.01
out from the m. of the LORD three	10.33
whole congregation, came to M. Hor.	20.22
said to Moses and Aaron at M. Hor,	20.23
son, and bring them up to M. Hor;	20.25
they went up M. Hor in the sight	20.27
From M. Hor they set out by the way	21.04
was ordained at M. Sinai for a	28.06
Kehelathah, and encamped at M. Shepher.	33.23
And they set out from M. Shepher,	33.24
Kadesh, and encamped at M. Hor,	33.37
priest went up M. Hor at the	33.38
years old when he died on M. Hor.	33.39
And they set out from M. Hor,	33.41
shall mark out your line to M. Hor;	34.07
from M. Hor you shall mark it out	34.08
by the way of M. Seir to Kadeshbarnea.	Deu 1.02
many days we went about M. Seir.	2.01
I have given M. Seir to Esau as a	2.05
valley of the Arnon to M. Hermon	3.08
as far as M. Sirion (that is, Hermon)	4.48
the blessing on M. Gerizim and the	11.29
Gerizim and the curse on M. Ebal.	11.29
on M. Ebal, and you shall plaster	27.04
stand upon M. Gerizim to bless the	27.12
stand upon M. Ebal for the curse:	27.13
among you shall m. above you	28.43
M. Nebo, which is in the land of	32.49
brother died in M. Hor and was	32.50
he shone forth from M. Paran,	33.02
from the plains of Moab to M. Nebo,	34.01
an altar in M. Ebal to the LORD,	Jos 8.30
in front of M. Gerizim and half of	8.33
half of them in front of M. Ebal,	8.33
from M. Halak, that rises toward	11.17
valley of Lebanon below M. Hermon.	11.17
valley of the Arnon to M. Hermon,	12.01
and ruled over M. Hermon and	12.05
the valley of Lebanon to M. Halak,	12.07
Baalgad below M. Hermon to the	13.05
and all M. Hermon, and all Bashan to	13.11
there to the cities of M. Ephron;	15.09
circles west of Baalah to M. Seir,	15.10
shoulder of M. Jearim (that is	15.10
and passes along to M. Baalah,	15.11
of Ephraim, north of M. Gaash.	Ju 2.09
Hivites who dwelt on M. Lebanon,	3.03
from M. Baalhermon as far as the	3.03
'Go, gather your men at M. Tabor,	4.06
Abinoam had gone up to M. Tabor,	4.12
went down from M. Tabor with ten	4.14
and stood on the top of M. Gerizim,	9.07
And Abimelech went up to M. Zalmon,	9.48
and fell slain on M. Gilboa.	1Sa 31.01
his three sons fallen on M. Gilboa.	31.08
I happened to be on M. Gilboa;	2Sa 1.06
up the ascent of the M. of Olives,	15.30
made haste to m. his chariot,	1Ki 12.18
all Israel to me at M. Carmel,	18.19
the prophets together at M. Carmel.	18.20
nights to Horeb the m. of God.	19.08
stand upon the m. before the LORD.	19.11
From there he went on to M. Carmel,	2Ki 2.25
to the man of God at M. Carmel.	4.25
and out of M. Zion a band of	19.31
the south of the m. of corruption,	23.13
he saw the tombs there on the m.;	23.16
went to M. Seir, having as their	1Ch 4.42
Baalhermon, Senir, and M. Hermon.	5.23
and fell slain on M. Gilboa.	10.01
and his sons fallen on M. Gilboa.	10.08
the LORD in Jerusalem on M. Moriah,	2Ch 3.01
made haste to m. his chariot,	10.18
stood up on M. Zemaraim which is	13.04
men of Ammon and Moab and M. Seir,	20.10
and M. Seir, who had come against	20.22
against the inhabitants of M. Seir,	20.23
Thou didst come down upon M. Sinai,	Neh 9.13
Though his height m. up to the	Job 20.06
and of Hermon, from M. Mizar.	Ps 42.06
M. Zion, in the far north, the city	48.02
let M. Zion be glad! Let the daughters	48.11
at the m. which God desired for his	68.16
Thou didst ascend the high m.,	68.18
Remember M. Zion, where thou hast	74.02
of Judah, M. Zion, which he loves.	78.68
On the holy m. stands the city he	87.01
trust in the LORD are like M. Zion,	125.01
whole site of M. Zion and over her	Is 4.05
of hosts, who dwells on M. Zion.	8.18
all his work on M. Zion and on	10.12
his fist at the m. of the daughter	10.32
will sit on the m. of assembly in	14.13
to the m. of the daughter of Zion.	16.01
to M. Zion, the place of the name of	18.07
will reign on M. Zion and in	24.23
LORD will rise up as on M. Perazim,	28.21
be that fight against M. Zion.	29.08
to fight upon M. Zion and upon its	31.04
and out of M. Zion a band of	37.32
they shall m. up with wings like	40.31
and proclaims evil from M. Ephraim.	Jer 4.15
m., O horsemen! Take your stations	46.04
one shall m. up and fly swiftly	49.22
Though Babylon should m. up to heaven,	51.53
for M. Zion which lies desolate;	Lam 5.18
their wings to m. up from the	Eze 10.16
man, set your face against M. Seir,	35.02
M. Seir, and I will stretch out my	35.03
I will make M. Seir a waste and a	35.07
M. Seir, and all Edom, all of it.	35.15
for in M. Zion and in Jerusalem	Joe 2.32
and understanding out of M. Esau?	Ob 1.08
every man from M. Esau will be cut	1.09
But in M. Zion there shall be those	1.17
of the Negeb shall possess M. Esau,	1.19
go up to M. Zion to rule M. Esau;	1.21
over them in M. Zion from this	Mic 4.07
and the Holy One from M. Paran.	Hab 3.03
stand on the M. of Olives which	Zec 14.04
and the M. of Olives shall be split	14.04
one half of the M. shall withdraw	14.04
to the M. of Olives, then Jesus sent	Mt 21.01
As he sat on the M. of Olives,	24.03
they went out to the M. of Olives.	26.30
at the M. of Olives, he sent two of	Mk 11.01
he sat on the M. of Olives opposite	13.03
they went out to the M. of Olives.	14.26
at the m. that is called Olivet, he	Lk 19.29
at the descent of the M. of Olives,	19.37
and lodged on the m. called Olivet.	21.37

MOUNT (cont.)

his custom, to the M. of Olives; Lk 22.39
but Jesus went to the M. of Olives. *Jn 8.01
Jerusalem from the m. called Olivet, Ac 1.12
him in the wilderness of M. Sinai, 7.30
angel who spoke to him at M. Sinai, 7.38
One is from M. Sinai, bearing Gal 4.24
Now Hagar is M. Sinai in Arabia; 4.25
have come to M. Zion and to the Heb 12.22
on M. Zion stood the Lamb, and with Rev 14.01

MOUNTAIN

removed to the m. on the east of Gen 12.08
them, and the rest fled to the m. 14.10
sacrifice on the m. and called his 31.54
and tarried all night on the m. 31.54
brothers one m. slope which I took 48.22
and came to Horeb, the m. of God. Ex 3.01
you shall serve God upon this m." 3.12
met him at the m. of God and 4.27
in, and plant them on thy own m., 15.17
he was encamped at the m. of God. 18.05
Israel encamped before the m. 19.02
the LORD called him out of the m., 19.03
go up into the m. or touch the 19.12
touches the m. shall be put to 19.12
they shall come up to the m. 19.13
down from the m. to the people, 19.14
and a thick cloud upon the m., 19.16
their stand at the foot of the m. 19.17
and the whole m. quaked greatly. 19.18
Mount Sinai, to the top of the m.; 19.20
called Moses to the top of the m., 19.20
saying, 'Set bounds about the m., 19.23
of the trumpet and the m. smoking, 20.18
an altar at the foot of the m., 24.04
to Moses, "Come up to me on the m., 24.12
Moses went up into the m. of God. 24.13
Then Moses went up on the m., 24.15
and the cloud covered the m. 24.15
the top of the m. in the sight of 24.17
the cloud, and went up on the m. 24.18
was on the m. forty days and forty 24.18
which is being shown you on the m. 25.40
which has been shown you on the m. 26.30
as it has been shown you on the m., 27.08
delayed to come down from the m., 32.01
down from the m. with the two 32.15
broke them at the foot of the m. 32.19
there to me on the top of the m. 34.02
man be seen throughout all the m.; 34.03
or herds feed before that m. 34.03
hand as he came down from the m., 34.29
died there on the top of the m. Num 20.28
and Eleazar came down from the m. 20.28
"Go up into this m. of Abarim, 27.12
have stayed long enough at this m.; Deu 1.06
about this m. country long enough; 2.03
and stood at the foot of the m., 4.11
while the m. burned with fire to 4.11
with you face to face at the m., 5.04
and you did not go up into the m. 5.05
assembly at the m. out of the 5.22
while the m. was burning with fire, 5.23
When I went up the m. to receive 9.09
remained on the m. forty days and 9.09
with you on the m. out of the 9.10
I turned and came down from the m., 9.15
and the m. was burning with fire; 9.15
brook that descended out of the m. 9.21
first, and come up to me on the m., 10.01
and went up the m. with the two 10.03
to you on the m. out of the midst 10.04
I turned and came down from the m., 10.05
"I stayed on the m., as at the first 10.10
"Ascend this m. of the Abarim, Mount 32.49
and die on the m. which you ascend, 32.50
They shall call peoples to their m.; 33.19
the top of the m. that lies over Jos 15.08
the top of the m. to the spring of 15.09
upon the m. that lies south of 18.13
from the m. that lies to the south, 18.14
border of the m. that overlooks 18.16
Ephraim, north of the m. of Gaash. 24.30
ambush against him on the m. tops, Ju 9.25
are coming down from the m. tops!" 9.36
stood on the m. on the one side, 1Sa 17.03
stood on the m. on the other side, 17.03
Saul went on one side of the m., 23.26
men on the other side of the m.; 23.26
came down under cover of the m., 25.20
afar off on the top of the m., 26.13
Horonaim road by the side of the m. 2Sa 13.34
at Gibeon on the m. of the LORD. 21.06
them on the m. before the LORD, and 21.09
on the m. east of Jerusalem. 1Ki 11.07
him upon some m. or into some 2Ki 2.16
she came to the m. to the man; 4.27
the m. was full of horses and 6.17
built on the m. of the house of 2Ch 33.15
"But the m. falls and crumbles away, Job 14.18
know when the m. goats bring forth? 39.01
established me as a strong m.; Ps 30.07
His holy m., beautiful in elevation, 48.02
O mighty m., m. of Bashan; 68.15
O many-peaked m., m. of Bashan! 68.15
O many-peaked m., at the mount 68.16
to the m. which his right hand had 78.54
God, and worship at his holy m.; 99.09
hie me to the m. of myrrh and the Sol 4.06
days that the m. of the house of Is 2.02
let us go up to the m. of the LORD, 2.03
hurt or destroy in all my holy m.; 11.09
On this m. the LORD of hosts will 25.06
destroy on this m. the covering 25.07
of the LORD will rest on this m., 25.10
LORD on the holy m. at Jerusalem. 27.13
a flagstaff on the top of a m., 30.17
every lofty m. and every high hill 30.25
flute to go to the m. of the LORD, 30.29
and every m. and hill be made low; 40.04
Get you up to a high m., O Zion, 40.09
these I will bring to my holy m., 56.07
high and lofty m. you have set 57.07
land, and shall inherit my holy m. 57.13
the LORD, who forget my holy m., 65.11
in all my holy m., says the LORD. 65.25
to my holy m. Jerusalem, says the 66.20
them from every m. and every hill, Jer 16.16
Do the m. waters run dry, the cold 18.14
and the m. of the house a wooded 26.18
from m. to hill they have gone, they 50.06
O destroying m., says the LORD, 51.25
the crags, and make you a burnt m. 51.25
stood upon the m. which is on the Eze 11.23
plant it upon a high and lofty m.; 17.22
on the m. height of Israel will I 17.23
my holy m., the m. height of Israel, 20.40
you were on the holy m. of God; 28.14
a profane thing from the m. of God, 28.16
and upon the m. heights of Israel 34.14
set me down upon a very high m., 40.02
the top of the m. shall be most 43.12
became a great m. and filled the Dan 2.35
was cut from a m. by no human hand, 2.45
the sea and the glorious holy m.; 11.45
sound the alarm on my holy m.! Joe 2.01
God, who dwell in Zion, my holy m. 3.17
who are in the m. of Samaria, Amo 4.01
feel secure on the m. of Samaria, 6.01
For as you have drunk upon my holy m., Ob 1.16
and the m. of the house a wooded Mic 3.12
days that the m. of the house of 4.01
let us go up to the m. of the LORD, 4.02
from sea to sea and from m. to m. 7.12
no longer be haughty in my holy m. Zep 3.11

MOUNTAIN (cont.)
What are you, O great m.? Before Zec 4.07
m. of the LORD of hosts, the holy m. 8.03
devil took him to a very high m., Mt 4.08
Seeing the crowds, he went up on the m., 5.01
When he came down from the m., 8.01
and led them up a high m. apart. 17.01
And as they were coming down the m., 17.09
seed, you will say to this m., 17.20
but even if you say to this m., 21.21
to the m. to which Jesus had 28.16
them up a high m. apart by themselves; Mk 9.02
And as they were coming down the m., 9.09
to you, whoever says to this m., 11.23
and every m. and hill shall be Lk 3.05
and went up on the m. to pray. 9.28
they had come down from the m., 9.37
Our fathers worshiped on this m.; Jn 4.20
neither on this m. nor in Jerusalem 4.21
which was shown you on the m. Heb 8.05
"If even a beast touches the m., 12.20
we were with him on the holy m. 2Pe 1.18
and every m. and island was removed Rev 6.14
and something like a great m., 8.08
high m., and showed me the holy 21.10

MOUNTAINS
all the high m. under the whole Gen 7.19
the waters prevailed above the m., 7.20
came to rest upon the m. of Ararat. 8.04
the month, the tops of the m. were seen. 8.05
upon one of the m. of which I shall tell you." 22.02
the blessings of the eternal m., 49.26
them forth, to slay them in the m., Ex 32.12
king of Moab from the eastern m.: Num 23.07
For from the top of the m. I see him, 23.09
and encamped in the m. of Abarim, 33.47
they set out from the m. of Abarim, 33.48
upon the high m. and upon the hills Deu 12.02
on fire the foundations of the m. 32.22
finest produce of the ancient m., 33.15
The m. quaked before the LORD, yon Ju 5.05
the dens which are in the m., 6.02
shadow of the m. as if they were 9.36
that I may go and wander on the m., 11.37
bewailed her virginity upon the m. 11.38
who hunts a partridge in the m. 1Sa 26.20
"Ye m. of Gilboa, let there be no 2Sa 1.21
great and strong wind rent the m., 1Ki 19.11
all Israel scattered upon the m., 22.17
have gone up the heights of the m., 2Ki 19.23
swift as gazelles upon the m.: 1Ch 12.08
all Israel scattered upon the m., 2Ch 18.16
he who removes m., and they know it Job 9.05
They are wet with the rain of the m., 24.08
and overturns m. by the roots. 28.09
He ranges the m. as his pasture, and 39.08
For the m. yield food for him where 40.20
to me, "Flee like a bird to the m.; Ps 11.01
also of the m. trembled and quaked, 18.07
righteousness is like the m. of God, 36.06
though the m. shake in the heart of 46.02
though the m. tremble with its tumult. 46.03
strength hast established the m., 65.06
Let the m. bear prosperity for the 72.03
in the tops of the m. may it wave; 72.16
majestic than the everlasting m. 76.04
The m. were covered with its shade, 80.10
as the flame sets the m. ablaze, 83.14
Before the m. were brought forth, or 90.02
the heights of the m. are his also. 95.04
The m. melt like wax before the 97.05
the waters stood above the m. 104.06
The m. rose, the valleys sank down 104.08
lofty abode thou waterest the m.; 104.13
The high m. are for the wild goats; 104.18
who touches the m. and they smoke! 104.32
lead your host upon the holy m. 110.03
The m. skipped like rams, the hills 114.04
O m., that you skip like rams? 114.06
As the m. are round about Jerusalem, 125.02
which falls on the m. of Zion! 133.03
Touch the m. that they smoke! 144.05
M. and all hills, fruit trees and 148.09
Before the m. had been shaped, Pro 8.25
the herbage of the m. is gathered, 27.25
he comes, leaping upon the m., Sol 2.08
or a young stag upon rugged m. 2.17
of lions, from the m. of leopards. 4.08
a young stag upon the m. of spices. 8.14
established as the highest of the m., Is 2.02
against all the high m., and against 2.14
and smote them, and the m. quaked; 5.25
Hark, a tumult on the m. as of a 13.04
and upon my m. trample him under 14.25
chaff on the m. before the wind 17.13
a signal is raised on the m., look! 18.03
of prey of the m. and to the beasts 18.06
of walls and a shouting to the m. 22.05
the m. shall flow with their blood. 34.03
have gone up the heights of the m., 37.24
and weighed the m. in scales and 40.12
shall thresh the m. and crush them, 41.15
them shout from the top of the m. 42.11
I will lay waste m. and hills, 42.15
O m., O forest, and every tree in it 44.23
go before you and level the m., 45.02
And I will make all my m. a way, 49.11
break forth, O m., into singing! 49.13
upon the m. are the feet of him 52.07
For the m. may depart and the hills 54.10
the m. and the hills before you 55.12
that the m. might quake at thy 64.01
the m. quaked at thy presence. 64.03
upon the m. and reviled me upon 65.07
and from Judah inheritors of my m.; 65.09
a delusion, the orgies on the m. Jer 3.23
I looked on the m., and lo, they 4.24
"Take up weeping and wailing for the m., 9.10
feet stumble on the twilight m., 13.16
on the m. in the open country. 17.03
vineyards upon the m. of Samaria; 31.05
of hosts, like Tabor among the m., 46.18
turning them away on the m.; 50.06
they chased us on the m., Lam 4.19
your face toward the m. of Israel, Eze 6.02
and say, You m. of Israel, hear the 6.03
Lord GOD to the m. and the hills, 6.03
not of joyful shouting upon the m. 7.07
escape, they will be on the m., 7.16
eat upon the m. or lift up his 18.06
but eats upon the m., defiles his 18.11
eat upon the m. or lift up his 18.15
be heard upon the m. of Israel. 19.09
and men in you who eat upon the m.; 22.09
On the m. and in all the valleys 31.12
I will strew your flesh upon the m., 32.05
even to the m. with your flowing 32.06
and the m. of Israel shall be so 33.28
over all the m. and on every high 34.06
will feed them on the m. of Israel, 34.13
shall feed on the m. of Israel. 34.14
I will fill your m. with the slain; 35.08
uttered against the m. of Israel, 35.12
man, prophesy to the m. of Israel, 36.01
O m. of Israel, hear the word of the 36.01
therefore, O m. of Israel, hear the 36.04
Lord GOD to the m. and the hills, 36.04
and say to the m. and hills, 36.06
"But you, O m. of Israel, shall shoot 36.08
in the land, upon the m. of Israel; 37.22
many nations upon the m. of Israel, 38.08
and the m. shall be thrown down, and 38.20
lead you against the m. of Israel; 39.02
You shall fall upon the m. of Israel, 39.04
feast upon the m. of Israel, 39.17

MOUNTAINS (cont.)

They sacrifice on the tops of the m., Hos 4.13
and they shall say to the m., 10.08
spread upon the m. a great and Joe 2.02
they leap on the tops of the m., 2.05
"And in that day the m. shall drip 3.18
yourselves upon the m. of Samaria, Amo 3.09
For lo, he who forms the m., 4.13
the m. shall drip sweet wine, and 9.13
at the roots of the m. I went down Jon 2.06
And the m. will melt under him and Mic 1.04
established as the highest of the m., 4.01
plead your case before the m., 6.01
Hear, you m., the controversy of the 6.02
The m. quake before him, the hills Nah 1.05
Behold, on the m. the feet of him 1.15
scattered on the m. with none to 3.18
then the eternal m. were scattered, Hab 3.06
The m. saw thee, and writhed; 3.10
came out from between two m.; Zec 6.01
and the m. were m. of bronze. 6.01
valley of my m. shall be stopped 14.05
valley of the m. shall touch the 14.05
who are in Judea flee to the m.; Mt 24.16
and on the m. he was always crying Mk 5.05
who are in Judea flee to the m.; 13.14
who are in Judea flee to the m., Lk 21.21
to say to the m., 'Fall on us'; 23.30
have all faith, so as to remove m., 1Co 13.02
worthy—wandering over deserts and m., Heb 11.38
and among the rocks of the m., Rev 6.15
calling to the m. and rocks, "Fall 6.16
and no m. were to be found; 16.20

MOUNTAIN-SHEEP

the ibex, the antelope, and the m. Deu 14.05

MOUNTAINTOPS

on all the m., under every green Eze 6.13

MOUNTED

haste and rose and m. on an ass, 1Sa 25.42
young men, who m. camels and fled. 30.17
and each m. his mule and fled. 2Sa 13.29
the ass for him and he m. it. 1Ki 13.13
So they took two m. men, and the king 2Ki 7.14
Then Jehu m. his chariot, and went 9.16
our guilt has m. up to the heavens Ez 9.06
were sent by m. couriers riding on Est 8.10
m. on their swift horses that were 8.14
Jacob, his anger m. against Israel; Ps 78.21
They m. up to heaven, they went down 107.26
And the cherubim m. up. These were Eze 10.15
and when they m. up, these m. up 10.17
their wings and m. up from the 10.19
and m. on an ass, and on a colt, the Mt 21.05

MOUNTS

that the eagle m. up and makes his Job 39.27
Also provide m. for Paul to ride, Ac 23.24

MOURN

went in to m. for Sarah and to Gen 23.02
on sackcloth, and m. before Abner. 2Sa 3.31
to the city, to m. and to bury him. 1Ki 13.29
And all Israel shall m. for him, 14.13
LORD your God; do not m. or weep." Neh 8.09
and those who m. are lifted to Job 5.11
a time to m., and a time to dance; Ecc 3.04
And her gates shall lament and m.; Is 3.26
M., utterly stricken, for the raisin 16.07
The fishermen will m. and lament, 19.08
of our God, to comfort all who m.; 61.02
to grant to those who m. in Zion— 61.03
in joy, all you who m. over her; 66.10
For this the earth shall m., Jer 4.28
I m., and dismay has taken hold on 8.21
How long will the land m., 12.04
for the men of Kirheres I m. 48.31
The roads of Zion m., Lam 1.04
buyer rejoice, nor the seller m., Eze 7.12
you shall not m. or weep nor shall 24.16
you shall not m. or weep, but you 24.23
I will make the deep m. for it, 31.15
Its people shall m. for it, Hos 10.05
The priests m., the ministers of Joe 1.09
the pastures of the shepherds m., Amo 1.02
and every one m. who dwells in it, 8.08
melts, and all who dwell in it m., 9.05
"Should I m. and fast in the fifth Zec 7.03
they shall m. for him, as one mourns 12.10
The land shall m., each family by 12.12
"Blessed are those who m., for they shall Mt 5.04
wedding guests m. as long as the 9.15
we wailed, and you did not m.' 11.17
the tribes of the earth will m., 24.30
now, for you shall m. and weep. Lk 6.25
Ought you not rather to m.? 1Co 5.02
and those who m. as though they 7.30
I may have to m. over many of 2Co 12.21
Be wretched and m. and weep. Jas 4.09
of the earth weep and m. for her, Rev 18.11

MOURNED

and m. for his son many days. Gen 37.34
heard these evil tidings, they m.; Ex 33.04
Israel, and the people m. greatly. Num 14.39
and the people m. because the LORD 1Sa 6.19
Israel assembled and m. for him, 25.01
all Israel had m. for him and 28.03
and they m. and wept and fasted 2Sa 1.12
And David m. for his son day after 13.37
and they m. over him, saying, "Alas, 1Ki 13.30
Israel buried him and m. for him, 14.18
And Ephraim their father m. many days, 1Ch 7.22
Judah and Jerusalem m. for Josiah. 2Ch 35.24
sat down and wept, and m. for days; Neh 1.04
you fasted and m. in the fifth Zec 7.05
had been with him, as they m. and wept. *Mk 16.10
their heads, as they wept and m., Rev 18.19

MOURNER

said to her, "Pretend to be a m., 2Sa 14.02
No one shall break bread for the m., Jer 16.07

MOURNERS

troops, like one who comforts m. Job 29.25
and the m. go about the streets; Ecc 12.05
creating for his m. the fruit of Is 57.18
your lips, nor eat the bread of m. Eze 24.17
your lips, nor eat the bread of m. 24.22

MOURNERS'

Their bread shall be like m. bread; Hos 9.04

MOURNING

"The days of m. for my father are Gen 27.41
go down to Sheol to my son, m." 37.35
and he made a m. for his father 50.10
saw the m. on the threshing floor 50.11
is a grievous m. to the Egyptians." 50.11
eaten of the tithe while I was m., Deu 26.14
of weeping and m. for Moses were 34.08
And when the m. was over, David sent 2Sa 11.27
a mourner, and put on m. garments; 14.02
who has been m. many days for the 14.02
king is weeping and m. for Absalom. 19.01
was turned into m. for all the 19.02
for he was m. over the faithlessness Ez 10.06
there was great m. among the Jews, Est 4.03
m. and with his head covered. 6.12
gladness and from m. into a holiday; 9.22
My lyre is turned to m., Job 30.31
turned for me my m. into dancing; Ps 30.11
his mother, bowed down and in m. 35.14
and prostrate; all the day I go about m. 38.06
Why go I m. because of the oppression 42.09

MOURNING (cont.)

Why go I m. because of the oppression Ps 43.02
to the house of m. than to go to Ecc 7.02
of the wise is in the house of m.; 7.04
of hosts, called to weeping and m., Is 22.12
and your days of m. shall be ended. 60.20
the oil of gladness instead of m., 61.03
make m. as for an only son, most Jer 6.26
and call for the m. women to come; 9.17
LORD: Do not enter the house of m., 16.05
I will turn their m. into joy, I will 31.13
daughter of Judah m. and lamentation. Lam 2.05
our dancing has been turned to m. 5.15
of lamentation and m. and woe. Eze 2.10
make no m. for the dead. Bind on your 24.17
bitterness of soul, with bitter m. 27.31
I, Daniel, was m. for three weeks. Dan 10.02
fasting, with weeping, and with m.; Joe 2.12
the farmers to m. and to wailing Amo 5.16
I will turn your feasts into m., 8.10
it like the m. for an only son, and 8.10
the jackals, and m. like the ostriches. Mic 1.08
On that day the m. in Jerusalem Zec 12.11
as great as the m. for Hadadrimmon 12.11
walking as in m. before the LORD Mal 3.14
mourn as though they were not m., 1Co 7.30
your m., your zeal for me, so that I 2Co 7.07
be turned to m. and your joy to Jas 4.09
a like measure of torment and m. Rev 18.07
no widow, m. I shall never see,' 18.07
day, pestilence and m. and famine, 18.08
her torment, weeping and m. aloud, 18.15
shall there be m. nor crying nor 21.04

MOURNS

and he m. only for himself. Job 14.22
The earth m. and withers, the world Is 24.04
The wine m., the vine languishes, 24.07
The land m. and languishes; 33.09
desolate, it m. to me. The whole Jer 12.11
"Judah m. and her gates languish; 14.02
because of the curse the land m., 23.10
The king m., the prince is wrapped Eze 7.27
Therefore the land m., and all who Hos 4.03
are laid waste, the ground m.; Joe 1.10
as one m. for an only child, and Zec 12.10

MOUSE

the m., the great lizard according Lev 11.29

MOUTH

has opened its m. to receive your Gen 4.11
in her m. a freshly plucked olive 8.11
stone on the well's m. was large, 29.02
the stone from the m. of the well, 29.03
its place upon the m. of the well. 29.03
is rolled from the m. of the well; 29.08
the stone from the well's m., 29.10
his money in the m. of his sack; 42.27
here it is in the m. of my sack!" 42.28
returned in the m. of your sacks; 43.12
man's money in the m. of his sack, 43.21
man's money in the m. of his sack, 44.01
in the m. of the sack of the 44.02
we found in the m. of our sacks, 44.08
that it is my m. that speaks to you 45.12
said to him, "Who has made man's m.? Ex 4.11
be with your m. and teach you what 4.12
to him and put the words in his m.; 4.15
be with your m. and with his m., 4.15
and he shall be a m. for you, 4.16
law of the LORD may be in your m.; 13.09
let such be heard out of your m. 23.13
With him I speak m. to m., clearly, Num 12.08
new, and the ground opens its m., 16.30
opened its m. and swallowed them 16.32
Then the LORD opened the m. of the ass, 22.28
The word that God puts in my m., 22.38
the LORD put a word in Balaam's m., 23.05
speak what the LORD puts in my m.?" 23.12
Balaam, and put a word in his m., 23.16
opened its m. and swallowed them 26.10
to all that proceeds out of his m. 30.02
proceeds out of the m. of the LORD. Deu 8.03
opened its m. and swallowed them 11.06
and I will put my words in his m., 18.18
you have promised with your m. 23.23
it is in your m. and in your heart, 30.14
the earth hear the words of my m. 32.01
shall not depart out of your m., Jos 1.08
shall any word go out of your m., 6.10
stones against the m. of the cave, 10.18
"Open the m. of the cave, and bring 10.22
stones against the m. of the cave, 10.27
Salt Sea, to the m. of the Jordan. 15.05
of the sea at the m. of the Jordan; 15.05
said to him, "Where is your m. now, Ju 9.38
I have opened my m. to the LORD, 11.35
have opened your m. to the LORD, 11.36
what have gone forth from your m., 11.36
quiet, put your hand upon your m., 18.19
the LORD, Eli observed her m. 1Sa 1.12
My m. derides my enemies, because I 2.01
not arrogance come from your m.; 2.03
but no man put his hand to his m.; 14.26
honeycomb, and put his hand to his m.; 14.27
him and delivered it out of his m.; 17.35
for your own m. has testified 2Sa 1.16
So Joab put the words in her m. 14.03
words in the m. of your handmaid. 14.19
a covering over the well's m., 17.19
alone, there are tidings in his m. 18.25
and devouring fire from his m.; 22.09
with his m. to David my father, 1Ki 8.15
yea, thou didst speak with thy m., 8.24
of the LORD in your m. is truth." 17.24
and every m. that has not kissed 19.18
spirit in the m. of all his 22.22
spirit in the m. of all these your 22.23
putting his m. upon his m., his eyes 2Ki 4.34
in your nose and my bit in your m., 19.28
with his m. to David my father, 2Ch 6.04
yea, thou didst speak with thy m., 6.15
spirit in the m. of all his 18.21
spirit in the m. of these your 18.22
words of Neco from the m. of God, 35.22
who spoke from the m. of the LORD. 36.12
of the LORD by the m. of Jeremiah, 36.21
the LORD by the m. of Jeremiah 36.22
the LORD by the m. of Jeremiah Ez 1.01
withhold thy manna from their m., Neh 9.20
the words left the m. of the king, Est 7.08
Job opened his m. and cursed the Job 3.01
saves the fatherless from their m., 5.15
hope, and injustice shuts her m. 5.16
"Therefore I will not restrain my m.; 7.11
words of your m. be a great wind? 8.02
yet fill your m. with laughter, 8.21
my own m. would condemn me; 9.20
For your iniquity teaches your m., 15.05
Your own m. condemns you, and not I; 15.06
let such words go out of your m.? 15.13
I could strengthen you with my m., 16.05
Men have gaped at me with their m., 16.10
I must beseech him with my m. 19.16
"Though wickedness is sweet in his m., 20.12
let it go, and holds it in his m., 20.13
and lay your hand upon your m. 21.05
Receive instruction from his m., 22.22
him and fill my m. with arguments. 23.04
in my bosom the words of his m. 23.12
and laid their hand on their m.; 29.09
cleaved to the roof of their m. 29.10
and my m. has kissed my hand; 31.27
(I have not let my m. sin by asking 31.30
answer in the m. of these three 32.05

MOUTH (cont.)
Behold, I open my m.; Job 33.02
the tongue in my m. speaks. 33.02
Job opens his m. in empty talk, he 35.16
rumbling that comes from his m. 37.02
answer thee? I lay my hand on my m. 40.04
Jordan rushes against his m. 40.23
Out of his m. go flaming torches; 41.19
a flame comes forth from his m. 41.21
For there is no truth in their m.; Ps 5.09
by the m. of babes and infants, thou 8.02
His m. is filled with cursing and 10.07
my m. does not transgress. 17.03
and devouring fire from his m.; 18.08
Let the words of my m. and the 19.14
Save me from the m. of the lion, 22.21
their host by the breath of his m. 33.06
shall continually be in my m. 34.01
The words of his m. are mischief 36.03
The m. of the righteous utters 37.30
dumb man who does not open his m. 38.13
and in whose m. are no rebukes. 38.14
I will bridle my m., so long as 39.01
I am dumb, I do not open my m.; 39.09
He put a new song in my m., 40.03
My m. shall speak wisdom; the meditation 49.03
"You give your m. free rein for 50.19
and my m. shall show forth thy 51.15
give ear to the words of my m. 54.02
and my m. praises thee with joyful 63.05
uttered and my m. promised when I 66.14
or the pit close its m. over me. 69.15
My m. is filled with thy praise, and 71.08
My m. will tell of thy righteous 71.15
your ears to the words of my m.! 78.01
I will open my m. in a parable; 78.02
Open your m. wide, and I will fill 81.10
with my m. I will proclaim thy 89.01
and all wickedness stops its m. 107.42
With my m. I will give great thanks 109.30
all the ordinances of thy m. 119.13
word of truth utterly out of my m., 119.43
The law of thy m. is better to me 119.72
may keep the testimonies of thy m. 119.88
taste, sweeter than honey to my m.! 119.103
With open m. I pant, because I long 119.131
Then our m. was filled with laughter, 126.02
tongue cleave to the roof of my m., 137.06
have heard the words of thy m.; 138.04
Set a guard over my m., O LORD, 141.03
bones be strewn at the m. of Sheol. 141.07
My m. will speak the praise of the 145.21
from his m. come knowledge and Pro 2.06
turn away from the words of my m. 4.05
not depart from the words of my m. 5.07
caught in the words of your m.; 6.02
be attentive to the words of my m. 7.24
for my m. will utter truth; 8.07
All the words of my m. are righteous; 8.08
but the m. of the wicked conceals 10.06
The m. of the righteous is a 10.11
but the m. of the wicked conceals 10.11
The m. of the righteous brings 10.31
but the m. of the wicked, what is 10.32
With his m. the godless man would 11.09
overthrown by the m. of the wicked. 11.11
but the m. of the upright delivers 12.06
fruit of his m. a good man eats 13.02
He who guards his m. preserves his 13.03
but the m. of the wicked pours out 15.28
his m. does not sin in judgment. 16.10
for him; his m. urges him on. 16.26
of a man's m. are deep waters; 18.04
and his m. invites a flogging. 18.06
A fool's m. is his ruin, and his lips 18.07
fruit of his m. a man is satisfied 18.20
not even bring it back to his m. 19.24
and the m. of the wicked devours 19.28
afterward his m. will be full of 20.17
He who keeps his m. and his tongue 21.23
The m. of a loose woman is a deep 22.14
the gate he does not open his m. 24.07
is a proverb in the m. of fools. 26.07
is a proverb in the m. of fools. 26.09
him out to bring it back to his m. 26.15
and a flattering m. works ruin. 26.28
praise you, and not your own m.; 27.02
and wipes her m., and says "I have 30.20
evil, put your hand on your m. 30.32
Open your m. for the dumb, for the 31.08
Open your m., judge righteously, 31.09
She opens her m. with wisdom, and 31.26
Be not rash with your m., Ecc 5.02
Let not your m. lead you into sin, 5.06
All the toil of man is for his m., 6.07
of a wise man's m. win him favor, 10.12
the words of his m. is foolishness, 10.13
kiss me with the kisses of your m.! Sol 1.02
thread, and your m. is lovely. 4.03
for the m. of the LORD has spoken. Is 1.20
and opened its m. beyond measure, 5.14
And he touched my m., and said, 6.07
west devour Israel with open m. 9.12
evildoer, and every m. speaks folly. 9.17
wing, or opened the m., or chirped. 10.14
the earth with the rod of his m., 11.04
near with their m. and honor me 29.13
For the m. of the LORD has commanded, 34.16
in your nose and my bit in your m., 37.29
for the m. of the LORD has spoken. 40.05
from my m. has gone forth in 45.23
forth from my m. and I made them 48.03
He made my m. like a sharp sword, in 49.02
And I have put my words in your m., 51.16
afflicted, yet he opened not his m.; 53.07
is dumb, so he opened not his m. 53.07
and there was no deceit in his m. 53.09
word be that goes forth from my m.; 55.11
you open your m. wide and put out 57.04
for the m. of the LORD has spoken. 58.14
words which I have put in your m., 59.21
shall not depart out of your m., 59.21
or out of the m. of your children, 59.21
or out of the m. of your children's 59.21
name which the m. of the LORD will 62.02
forth his hand and touched my m.; Jer 1.09
I have put my words in your m. 1.09
making my words in your m. a fire, 5.14
with his m. each speaks peaceably 9.08
To whom has the m. of the LORD 9.12
ear receive the word of his m.; 9.20
near in their m. and far from 12.02
worthless, you shall be as my m. 15.19
minds, not from the m. of the LORD. 23.16
invoked by the m. of any man of 44.26
in the sides of the m. of a gorge. 48.28
take out of his m. what he has 51.44
let him put his m. in the dust— Lam 3.29
Is it not from the m. of the Most 3.38
to the roof of its m. for thirst; 4.04
open your m., and eat what I give Eze 2.08
So I opened my m., and he gave me 3.02
it was in my m. as sweet as honey. 3.03
whenever you hear a word from my m., 3.17
cleave to the roof of your m., 3.26
with you, I will open your m., 3.27
nor has foul flesh come into my m. 4.14
byword in your m. in the day of 16.56
never open your m. again because 16.63
to open the m. with a cry, to lift 21.22
On that day your m. will be opened 24.27
whenever you hear a word from my m., 33.07
had opened my m. by the time the 33.22
so my m. was opened, and I was no 33.22
yourselves against me with your m., 35.13
words were still in the king's m., Dan 4.31

MOUTH (cont.)
and laid upon the m. of the den, Dan 6.17
ribs in its m. between its teeth; 7.05
and a m. speaking great things. 7.08
had eyes and a m. that spoke great 7.20
no meat or wine entered my m., 10.03
then I opened my m. and spoke. 10.16
the names of the Baals from her m., Hos 2.17
slain them by the words of my m., 6.05
himself at the m. of the womb. 13.13
for it is cut off from your m. Joe 1.05
from the m. of the lion two legs, Amo 3.12
for the m. of the LORD of hosts has Mic 4.04
tongue is deceitful in their m. 6.12
doors of your m. from her who lies 7.05
they fall into the m. of the eater. Nah 3.12
found in their m. a deceitful Zep 3.13
down the leaden weight upon its m. Zec 5.08
words from the m. of the prophets, 8.09
take away its blood from its m., 9.07
True instruction was in his m., Mal 2.06
seek instruction from his m., 2.07
that proceeds from the m. of God. Mt 4.04
And he opened his m. and taught 5.02
abundance of the heart the m. speaks. 12.34
"I will open my m. in parables, 13.35
goes into the m. defiles a man, 15.11
man, but what comes out of the m., 15.11
goes into the m. passes into the 15.17
out of the m. proceeds from the 15.18
you open its m. you will find a 17.27
'Out of the m. of babes and sucklings 21.16
rolled about, foaming at the m. Mk 9.20
And immediately his m. was opened Lk 1.64
as he spoke by the m. of his holy 1.70
which proceeded out of his m.; 4.22
abundance of the heart his m. speaks. 6.45
condemn you out of your own m., 19.22
for I will give you a m. and wisdom, 21.15
on hyssop and held it to his m. Jn 19.29
beforehand by the m. of David, Ac 1.16
foretold by the m. of all the 3.18
spoke by the m. of his holy 3.21
who by the m. of our father David, 4.25
is dumb, so he opens not his m. 8.32
Then Philip opened his m., 8.35
And Peter opened his m. and said: 10.34
or unclean has ever entered my m.' 11.08
that by my m. the Gentiles should 15.07
you the same things by word of m. 15.27
when Paul was about to open his m., 18.14
and to hear a voice from his m.; 22.14
by him to strike him on the m. 23.02
"Their m. is full of curses and Rom 3.14
so that every m. may be stopped, and 3.19
Our m. is open to you, Corinthians; 2Co 6.11
in opening my m. boldly to proclaim Eph 6.19
slander, and foul talk from your m. Col 3.08
breath of his m. and destroy him 2Th 2.08
either by word of m. or by letter. 2.15
I was rescued from the lion's m. 2Ti 4.17
From the same m. come blessing and Jas 3.10
from his m. issued a sharp two-edged Rev 1.16
them with the sword of my m. 2.16
hot, I will spew you out of my m. 3.16
but sweet as honey in your m. 10.09
it was sweet as honey in my m., 10.10
from their m. and consumes their 11.05
out of his m. after the woman, to 12.15
opened its m. and swallowed the 12.16
the dragon had poured from his m. 12.16
and its m. was like a lion's m. 13.02
was given a m. uttering haughty 13.05
it opened its m. to utter blasphemies 13.06
and in their m. no lie was found, 14.05
from the m. of the dragon and from 16.13
and from the m. of the false 16.13
From his m. issues a sharp sword 19.15
the sword that issues from his m.; 19.21

MOUTHS
put it in their m., that this song Deu 31.19
unforgotten in the m. of their 31.21
putting their hands to their m., Ju 7.06
opened their m. as for the spring Job 29.23
with their m. they speak arrogantly Ps 17.10
they make m. at me, they wag their 22.07
they open wide their m. at me, 22.13
They open wide their m. against me; 35.21
O God, break the teeth in their m.; 58.06
There they are, bellowing with their m., 59.07
For the sin of their m., the words 59.12
They bless with their m., but inwardly 62.04
for the m. of liars will be stopped. 63.11
They set their m. against the 73.09
the food was still in their m., 78.30
But they flattered him with their m.; 78.36
and deceitful m. are opened 109.02
They have m., but do not speak; 115.05
They have m., but they speak not, 135.16
is there any breath in their m. 135.17
whose m. speak lies, and whose right 144.08
whose m. speak lies, and whose right 144.11
but the m. of fools pour out folly. Pro 15.02
but the m. of fools feed on folly. 15.14
shall shut their m. because of him; Is 52.15
wives have declared with your m., Jer 44.25
will rescue my sheep from their m., Eze 34.10
his angel and shut the lions' m., Dan 6.22
him who puts nothing into their m. Mic 3.05
shall lay their hands on their m.; 7.16
tongues shall rot in their m. Zec 14.12
Let no evil talk come out of your m., Eph 4.29
promises, stopped the m. of lions, Heb 11.33
bits into the m. of horses that Jas 3.03
and sulphur issued from their m. Rev 9.17
and sulphur issuing from their m. 9.18
is in their m. and in their tails; 9.19

MOVE
let no man m. his bones." So they let 2Ki 23.18
he could not m. about freely 1Ch 12.01
and all that m. in the field feed Ps 80.13
the living who m. about under the Ecc 4.15
set up an image that will not m. Is 40.20
it cannot m. from its place. If one cries 46.07
and nails so that it cannot m. Jer 10.04
'M. hence to yonder place,' and it Mt 17.20
to yonder place,' and it will m.; 17.20
will not m. them with their finger 23.04
him we live and m. and have our Ac 17.28
live in them and m. among them, 2Co 6.16

MOVED
flesh died that m. upon the earth, Gen 7.21
the valley and m. his tent as far 13.12
So Abram m. his tent, and came and 13.18
And he m. from there and dug 26.22
And they m. on from Succoth, and Ex 13.20
host of Israel m. and went behind 14.19
pillar of cloud m. from before 14.19
of Israel m. on from the wilderness 17.01
and every one whose spirit m. him, 35.21
hearts were m. with ability spun 35.26
whose heart m. them to bring 35.29
not a man m. his tongue against any Jos 10.21
the LORD was m. to pity by their Ju 2.18
the son of Ebed m. into Shechem 9.26
men in ambush m. out and smote all 20.37
only her lips m., and her voice was 1Sa 1.13
where I have m. with all the 2Sa 7.07
And the king was deeply m., 18.33
world stands firm, never to be m. 1Ch 16.30
where I have m. with all Israel, 17.06
although you m. me against him, to Job 2.03

MOVED (cont.)

in his heart, "I shall not be m.; Ps 10.06
these things shall never be m. 15.05
my right hand, I shall not be m. 16.08
the Most High he shall not be m. 21.07
my prosperity, "I shall never be m. 30.06
midst of her, she shall not be m.; 46.05
permit the righteous to be m. 55.22
I shall not be greatly m. 62.02
they m. him to jealousy with their 78.58
established; it shall never be m.; 93.01
established, it shall never be m., 96.10
For the righteous will never be m.; 112.06
He will not let your foot be m., 121.03
Mount Zion, which cannot be m., 125.01
of the righteous will never be m. Pro 12.03
and there was none that m. a wing, Is 10.14
with nails so that it cannot be m. 41.07
and all the hills m. to and fro. Jer 4.24
m. with anger, shall come out and Dan 11.11
M. with pity, he stretched out his Mk 1.41
he was deeply m. in spirit and Jn 11.33
deeply m. again, came to the tomb; 11.38
however you may have been m. 1Co 12.02
that no one be m. by these afflictions 1Th 3.03
but men m. by the Holy Spirit spoke 2Pe 1.21

MOVES

and every living creature that m., Gen 1.21
thing that m. upon the earth." 1.28
everything that m. upon the earth, 8.19
creature that m. through the Lev 11.46
he m. on, but I do not perceive him. Job 9.11
and all that m. in the field is Ps 50.11
and everything that m. therein. 69.34

MOVING

of God was m. over the face of the Gen 1.02
Every m. thing that lives shall be 9.03
but I have been m. about in a tent 2Sa 7.06
shone, or the moon m. in splendor, Job 31.26
m. down the slopes of Gilead. Sol 4.01
m. down the slopes of Gilead. 6.05
like torches m. to and fro among Eze 1.13
waiting for the m. of the water *Jn 5.03

MOWED

And Joshua m. down Amalek and his Ex 17.13
of the laborers who m. your fields, Jas 5.04

MOWINGS

latter growth after the king's m. Amo 7.01

MOWN

rain that falls on the m. grass, Ps 72.06

MOZA

concubine, bore Haran, M., and Gazez; 1Ch 2.46
Zimri was the father of M. 8.36
M. was the father of Binea; 8.37
and Zimri was the father of M. 9.42
M. was the father of Binea; 9.43

MOZAH

Mizpeh, Chephirah, M., Jos 18.26

MUCH

and the men were very m. afraid. Gen 20.08
for you are m. mightier than we." 26.16
Ask of me ever so m. as marriage 34.12
five times as m. as any of theirs. 43.34
as m. as they can carry, and put 44.01
not so m. as one of them remained. Ex 14.28
be twice as m. as they gather 16.05
man of you, as m. as he can eat; 16.16
that gathered m. had nothing over, 16.18
each as m. as he could eat; 16.21
they gathered twice as m. bread, 16.22
sweet-smelling cinnamon half as m., 30.23
people bring m. more than enough 36.05
he is poor and cannot afford so m., Lev 14.21
not so m. as for the sole of the Deu 2.05
as m. as you desire, according to 12.15
you may eat as m. flesh as you 12.20
your towns as m. as you desire. 12.21
You shall carry m. seed into the 28.38
how m. more after my death! 31.27
yet very m. land to be possessed. Jos 13.01
back to your homes with m. wealth, 22.08
and iron, and with m. clothing; 22.08
and then take as m. as you wish, 1Sa 2.16
How m. better if the people had 14.30
fled from him, and were m. afraid. 17.24
Saul's son, delighted m. in David. 19.01
how m. more today will their 21.05
and was m. afraid of Achish the 21.12
nothing of all this, m. or little." 22.15
how m. more then if we go to Keilah 23.03
I leave so m. as one male of all 25.22
left to Nabal so m. as one male." 25.34
bringing m. spoil with them. 2Sa 3.22
How m. more, when wicked men have 4.11
King David took very m. bronze. 8.08
I would add to you as m. more. 12.08
was no one so m. to be praised for 14.25
how m. more now may this Benjaminite 16.11
how m. less this house which I have 1Ki 8.27
as m. as he desired, King Solomon 9.11
and very m. gold, and precious 10.02
and mules, so m. year by year. 10.25
How m. rather, then, when he says to 2Ki 5.13
a little; but Jehu will serve him m. 10.18
that there was m. money in the 12.10
He did m. evil in the sight of the 21.06
shed very m. innocent blood, 21.16
Hadadezer, David took very m. bronze; 1Ch 18.08
'You have shed m. blood and have 22.08
have shed so m. blood before me 22.08
weighing, for there is so m. of it; 22.14
how m. less this house which I 2Ch 6.18
spices and very m. gold and 9.01
and mules, so m. year by year. 9.24
Judah carried away very m. booty. 14.13
for there was m. plunder in them. 14.14
in taking the spoil, it was so m. 20.25
saw that there was m. money in it, 24.11
able to give you m. more than this. 25.09
people in them, and took m. spoil. 25.13
and did m. building on the wall of 27.03
they also took m. spoil from them 28.08
of Assyria come and find m. water?" 32.04
How m. less will your God deliver 32.15
He did m. evil in the sight of the 33.06
salt without prescribing how m. Ez 7.22
the heart." Then I was very m. afraid. Neh 2.02
failing, and there is m. rubbish; 4.10
how m. more those who dwell in Job 4.19
that thou dost make so m. of him, 7.17
how m. less one who is abominable 15.16
I forbear, how m. of it leaves me? 16.06
how m. less man, who is a maggot, and 25.06
or because my hand had gotten m.; 31.25
How m. less when you say that you 35.14
Job twice as m. as he had before. 42.10
they than gold, even m. fine gold; Ps 19.10
I delight as m. as in all riches. 119.14
With m. seductive speech she Pro 7.21
how m. more the wicked and the 11.31
ground of the poor yields m. food, 13.23
the righteous there is m. treasure, 15.06
how m. more the hearts of men! 15.11
how m. more do his friends go far 19.07
m. less for a slave to rule over 19.10
how m. more when he brings it with 21.27
It is not good to eat m. honey, 25.27
to anger causes m. transgression. 29.22

MUCH (cont.)
For in m. wisdom is m. vexation, Ecc 1.18
For a dream comes with m. business, 5.03
whether he eats little or m.; 5.12
in m. vexation and sickness and 5.17
For he will not m. remember the 5.20
However m. man may toil in seeking, 8.17
but one sinner destroys m. good. 9.18
and m. study is a weariness of the 12.12
how m. better is your love than Sol 4.10
yourself with lye and use m. soap, Jer 2.22
How m. more when I send upon Eze 14.21
how m. less, when the fire has 15.05
with great wings and m. plumage; 17.07
in derision, for it contains m.; 23.32
with their lips they show m. love, 33.31
lambs shall be as m. as he is able, 46.05
with the lambs as m. as he is able, 46.07
the lambs as m. as one is able to 46.11
was m. distressed, and set his mind Dan 6.14
was told, 'Arise, devour m. flesh.' 7.05
their left, and also m. cattle?" Jon 4.11
You have sown m., and harvested Hag 1.06
You have looked for m., and lo, it came 1.09
will he not m. more clothe you, O Mt 6.30
how m. more will your Father who is 7.11
how m. more will they malign those 10.25
Of how m. more value is a man than 12.12
ground, where they had not m. soil, 13.05
him twice as m. a child of hell as 23.15
a little, I will set you over m.; 25.21
a little, I will set you over m.; 25.23
I have suffered m. over him today 27.19
ground, where it had not m. soil, Mk 4.05
tell them how m. the Lord has done 5.19
Decapolis how m. Jesus had done 5.20
had suffered m. under many physicians, 5.26
he heard him, he was m. perplexed; 6.20
is m. more than all whole burnt 12.33
But so m. the more the report went Lk 5.15
to sinners, to receive as m. again. 6.34
are forgiven, for she loved m.; 7.47
and declare how m. God has done 8.39
whole city how m. Jesus had done 8.39
was distracted with m. serving; 10.40
how m. more will the heavenly 11.13
Of how m. more value are you than 12.24
how m. more will he clothe you, O 12.28
Every one to whom m. is given, 12.48
given, of him will m. be required; 12.48
whom men commit m. they will 12.48
'How m. do you owe my master?' 16.05
to another, 'And how m. do you owe?' 16.07
very little is faithful also in m.; 16.10
little is dishonest also in m. 16.10
because there was m. water there; Jn 3.23
Now there was m. grass in the 6.10
the fish, as m. as they wanted. 6.11
And there was m. muttering about 7.12
m. to say about you and m. to judge; 8.26
but if it dies, it bears m. fruit. 12.24
I will no longer talk m. with you, 14.30
him, he it is that bears m. fruit, 15.05
that you bear m. fruit, and so prove 15.08
you sold the land for so m." Ac 5.08
And she said, "Yes, for so m." 5.08
they were m. perplexed about them, 5.24
So there was m. joy in that city. 8.08
how m. evil he has done to thy 9.13
show him how m. he must suffer for 9.16
And after there had been m. debate, 15.07
her owners m. gain by soothsaying. 16.16
had given them m. encouragement, 20.02
through you we enjoy m. peace, 24.02
As m. time had been lost, and the 27.09
will be with injury and m. loss, 27.10
holding m. dispute among themselves. * 28.29
M. in every way. To begin with Rom 3.02
m. more shall we be saved by him 5.09
m. more, now that we are reconciled, 5.10
m. more have the grace of God and 5.15
m. more will those who receive the 5.17
endured with m. patience the 9.22
how m. more will their full inclusion 11.12
how m. more will these natural 11.24
weakness and in m. fear and 1Co 2.03
How m. more, matters pertaining to 6.03
is it too m. if we reap your 9.11
you out of m. affliction and 2Co 2.04
permanent must have m. more splendor. 3.11
"He who gathered m. had nothing 8.15
a little too m. of our authority, 10.08
They make m. of you, but for no good Gal 4.17
out, that you may make m. of them. 4.17
it is always good to be made m. of, 4.18
and are m. more bold to speak the Php 1.14
my presence but m. more in my 2.12
received the word in m. affliction, 1Th 1.06
double-tongued, not addicted to m. wine, 1Ti 3.08
For I have derived m. joy and comfort Phm 1.07
to me but how m. more to you, both in 1.16
having become as m. superior to Heb 1.04
worthy of as m. more glory than 3.03
About this we have m. to say which 5.11
which is as m. more excellent than 8.06
how m. more shall the blood of 9.14
How m. worse punishment do you 10.29
Shall we not m. more be subject to 12.09
m. less shall we escape if we 12.25
Though I have m. to write to you, I 2Jn 1.12
I had m. to write to you, but I 3Jn 1.13
and I wept m. that no one was found Rev 5.04
he was given m. incense to mingle 8.03

MUD
the foe in the m. of the streets; Zec 10.05

MUDDIED
Like a m. spring or a polluted Pro 25.26

MULE
and each mounted his m. and fled. 2Sa 13.29
Absalom was riding upon his m., 18.09
and the m. went under the thick 18.09
while the m. that was under him 18.09
my son to ride on my own m., 1Ki 1.33
Solomon to ride on King David's m., 1.38
him to ride on the king's m.; 1.44
Be not like a horse or a m., Ps 32.09

MULES
and m., so much year by year. 1Ki 10.25
and save the horses and m. alive, 18.05
on camels and on m. and on oxen, 1Ch 12.40
and m., so much year by year. 2Ch 9.24
their m. were two hundred and forty Ez 2.66
their m. two hundred and forty-five, Neh 7.68
and upon m., and upon dromedaries, Is 66.20
wares horses, war horses, and m. Eze 27.14
the m., the camels, the asses, and Zec 14.15

MULES'
servant two m. burden of earth; 2Ki 5.17

MULTIPLIED
were fruitful and m. exceedingly. Gen 47.27
they m. and grew exceedingly strong; Ex 1.07
the more they m. and the more they 1.12
and the people m. and grew very 1.20
wonders may be m. in the land of 11.09
the LORD your God has m. you. Deu 1.10
and your silver and gold is m., 8.13
and all that you have is m., 8.13
children may be m. in the land 11.21
cattle had m. in the land of 1Ch 5.09

MULTIPLIED (cont.)
If his children are m., it is for the Job 27.14
and if your transgressions are m., 35.06
Thou hast m., O LORD my God, thy Ps 40.05
For by me your days will be m., Pro 9.11
Thou hast m. the nation, thou hast Is 9.03
with oil and m. your perfumes; 57.09
transgressions are m. before thee, 59.12
And when you have m. and increased Jer 3.16
and he has m. in the daughter of Lam 2.05
You have m. your slain in this city, Eze 11.06
You m. your harlotry also with the 16.29
and m. your words against me; 35.13
all the earth: Peace be m. to you! Dan 4.01
all the earth: "Peace be m. to you. 6.25
Because Ephraim has m. altars for Hos 8.11
and Judah has m. fortified cities; 8.14
it was I who m. visions, and through 12.10
And because wickedness is m., Mt 24.12
the disciples m. greatly in Ac 6.07
the people grew and m. in Egypt 7.17
of the Holy Spirit it was m. 9.31
But the word of God grew and m. 12.24
May grace and peace be m. to you. 1Pe 1.02
and peace be m. to you in the 2Pe 1.02
peace, and love be m. to you. Jud 1.02

MULTIPLIES
and m. my wounds without cause; Job 9.17
and m. his words against God. 34.37
he m. words without knowledge. 35.16
A fool m. words, though no man knows Ecc 10.14

MULTIPLY
"Be fruitful and m. and fill the Gen 1.22
and let birds m. on the earth. 1.22
said to them, "Be fruitful and m., 1.28
"I will greatly m. your pain in 3.16
When men began to m. on the face of 6.01
be fruitful and m. upon the earth." 8.17
said to them, "Be fruitful and m., 9.01
And you, be fruitful and m., 9.07
abundantly on the earth and m. in it." 9.07
will so greatly m. your descendants 16.10
and will m. you exceedingly." 17.02
fruitful and m. him exceedingly; 17.20
and I will m. your descendants as 22.17
I will m. your descendants as the 26.04
bless you and m. your descendants 26.24
and make you fruitful and m. you, 28.03
God Almighty: be fruitful and m.; 35.11
and m. you, and I will make of you a 48.04
lest they m., and, if war befall us, Ex 1.10
and though I m. my signs and 7.03
and the wild beasts m. against you. 23.29
'I will m. your descendants as the 32.13
and make you fruitful and m. you, Lev 26.09
you, and that you may m. greatly, Deu 6.03
love you, bless you, and m. you; 7.13
to do, that you may live and m., 8.01
and when your herds and flocks m., 8.13
and m. you, as he swore to your 13.17
Only he must not m. horses for 17.16
to Egypt in order to m. horses, 17.16
And he shall not m. wives for 17.17
he greatly m. for himself silver 17.17
ordinances, then you shall live and m., 30.16
their family m. like the men of 1Ch 4.27
Thou didst m. their descendants as Neh 9.23
and I shall m. my days as the sand, Job 29.18
another god m. their sorrows; Ps 16.04
By his blessing they m. greatly; 107.38
be appeased though you m. gifts. Pro 6.35
and they shall be fruitful and m. Jer 23.03
m. there, and do not decrease. 29.06
I will m. them, and they shall not 30.19
so I will m. the descendants of 33.22
and I will m. men upon you, the Eze 36.10
and I will m. upon you man and 36.11
and I will bless them and m. them, 37.26
shall play the harlot, but not m.; Hos 4.10
they m. falsehood and violence; 12.01
to Gilgal, and m. transgression; Amo 4.04
M. yourselves like the locust, Nah 3.15
m. like the grasshopper! 3.15
will supply and m. your resources 2Co 9.10
"Surely I will bless you and m. you." Heb 6.14

MULTIPLYING
in doing you good and m. you, Deu 28.63
passer-by, and m. your harlotry. Eze 16.25
m. your harlotry, to provoke me to 16.26

MULTITUDE
they cannot be numbered for m. Gen 16.10
be the father of a m. of nations. 17.04
you the father of a m. of nations. 17.05
which cannot be numbered for m. 32.12
grow into a m. in the midst of the 48.16
shall become a m. of nations. 48.19
A mixed m. also went up with them, Ex 12.38
You shall not follow a m. to do evil; 23.02
a suit, turning aside after a m., 23.02
Gad had a very great m. of cattle; Num 32.01
day as the stars of heaven for m. Deu 1.10
you as the stars of heaven for m. 10.22
were as the stars of heaven for m., 28.62
the valley like locusts for m.; Ju 7.12
which is upon the seashore for m. 7.12
the sand on the seashore in m.; 1Sa 13.05
the m. was surging hither and 14.16
the whole m. of Israel, both men and 2Sa 6.19
as the sand by the sea for m., 17.11
be numbered or counted for m. 1Ki 3.08
Have you seen all this great m.? 20.13
all this great m. into your hand, 20.28
like the whole m. of Israel that 2Ki 7.13
together with the rest of the m., 25.11
you are a great m. and have with 2Ch 13.08
name we have come against this m. 14.11
"A great m. is coming against you 20.02
this great m. that is coming 20.12
be not dismayed at this great m.; 20.15
wilderness, they looked toward the m.; 20.24
For a m. of the people, many of them 30.18
and their daughters, the whole m.; 31.18
with the m. of his brethren, for he Est 10.03
"Should a m. of words go unanswered, Job 11.02
because I stood in great fear of the m., 31.34
"Because of the m. of oppressions 35.09
of thanksgiving, a m. keeping festival. Ps 42.04
In a m. of people is the glory of a Pro 14.28
"What to me is the m. of your Is 1.11
and their m. is parched with thirst 5.13
of Jerusalem and her m. go down, 5.14
on the mountains as of a great m.! 13.04
in spite of all his great m., 16.14
But the m. of your foes shall be 29.05
and the m. of the ruthless like 29.05
And the m. of all the nations that 29.07
so shall the m. of all the nations 29.08
A m. of camels shall cover you, the 60.06
Your m. stumbled and fell, and they Jer 46.16
suffer for the m. of her transgressions; Lam 1.05
for wrath is upon all their m. Eze 7.12
For wrath is upon all their m.; 7.13
for my wrath is upon all their m. 7.14
because of the m. of his idols, 14.04
of a carefree m. was with her; 23.42
By the m. of your iniquities, in the 28.18
and cut off the m. of Thebes. 30.15
king of Egypt and to his m.: 31.02
"This is Pharaoh and all his m., 31.18
I will cause your m. to fall by the 32.12
Egypt, and all its m. shall perish. 32.12
over Egypt, and over all her m., 32.16

MULTITUDE (cont.)
wail over the m. of Egypt, and send Eze 32.18
and all her m. about her grave; 32.24
among the slain with all her m., 32.25
and all their m., their graves 32.26
comfort himself for all his m., 32.31
the sword, Pharaoh and all his m., 32.32
Gog and all his m. will be buried; 39.11
his words like the noise of a m. Dan 10.06
and assemble a m. of great forces, 11.10
and he shall raise a great m., 11.11
And when the m. is taken, his heart 11.12
the north shall again raise a m., 11.13
and in the m. of your warriors, Hos 10.13
in its pasture, a noisy m. of men. Mic 2.12
because of the m. of men and Zec 2.04
From men,' we are afraid of the m.; Mt 21.26
and a great m. from Galilee followed Mk 3.07
about Tyre and Sidon a great m., 3.08
him aside from the m. privately, 7.33
to him the m. with his disciples, 8.34
with his disciples and a great m., 10.46
because all the m. was astonished 11.18
to arrest him, but feared the m., 12.12
and watched the m. putting money 12.41
And the whole m. of the people were Lk 1.10
the angel a m. of the heavenly 2.13
and a great m. of people from all 6.17
and said to the m. that followed 7.09
thousands of the m. had gathered 12.01
One of the m. said to him, "Teacher, 12.13
and hearing a m. going by, he 18.36
the whole m. of the disciples began 19.37
Pharisees in the m. said to him, 19.39
to them in the absence of the m. 22.06
him a great m. of the people, 23.27
In these lay a m. of invalids, blind, Jn 5.03
And a m. followed him, because they 6.02
seeing that a m. was coming to him, 6.05
at this sound the m. came together, Ac 2.06
they said pleased the whole m., 6.05
rushed out among the m., crying, 14.14
death and will cover a m. of sins. Jas 5.20
since love covers a m. of sins. 1Pe 4.08
a great m. which no man could Rev 7.09
voice of a great m. in heaven, 19.01
to be the voice of a great m., 19.06

MULTITUDES
and with her shall lie all her m. Eze 32.20
M., m. in the valley of Joe 3.14
to arrest him, they feared the m., Mt 21.46
therefore to the m. that came out Lk 3.07
And the m. asked him, "What then 3.10
and great m. gathered to hear and 5.15
the m. surround you and press upon 8.45
He also said to the m., "When you see 12.54
Now great m. accompanied him; 14.25
to the chief priests and the m., 23.04
And all the m. who assembled to see 23.48
to the Lord, m. both of men and women, Ac 5.14
And the m. with one accord gave 8.06
But when the Jews saw the m., 13.45
are peoples and m. and nations and Rev 17.15

MUPPIM
Ehi, Rosh, M., Huppim, and Ard Gen 46.21

MURDER
sojourner, and m. the fatherless; Ps 94.06
m., commit adultery, swear falsely, Jer 7.09
On the day after the m. of Gedaliah, 41.04
all bounds and m. follows m. Hos 4.02
they m. on the way to Shechem, yea, 6.09
m., adultery, fornication, theft, Mt 15.19
fornication, theft, m., adultery, Mk 7.21
had committed m. in the insurrection, 15.07
started in the city, and for m. Lk 23.19
prison for insurrection and m., 23.25
threats and m. against the disciples Ac 9.01
Full of envy, m., strife, deceit, Rom 1.29
And why did he m. him? Because his 1Jn 3.12

MURDERED
husband of the woman who was m., Ju 20.04
whom he m., avenging in time of 1Ki 2.05
sons of those who m. the prophets. Mt 23.31
whom you m. between the sanctuary 23.35
whom you have now betrayed and m., Ac 7.52
of the evil one and m. his brother. 1Jn 3.12

MURDERER
iron, so that he died, he is a m.; Num 35.16
the m. shall be put to death. 35.16
may die, and he died, he is a m.; 35.17
the m. shall be put to death. 35.17
may die, and he died, he is a m.; 35.18
the m. shall be put to death. 35.18
shall himself put the m. to death; 35.19
he is a m.; the avenger of 35.21
of blood shall put the m. to death, 35.21
the m. shall be put to death on the 35.30
the life of a m. who is guilty of 35.31
see how this m. has sent to take 2Ki 6.32
you Zimri, m. of your master? 9.31
The m. rises in the dark, that he Job 24.14
He was a m. from the beginning, and Jn 8.44
and asked for a m. to be granted Ac 3.14
another, "No doubt this man is a m. 28.04
But let none of you suffer as a m., 1Pe 4.15
Any one who hates his brother is a m., 1Jn 3.15
know that no m. has eternal life 3.15

MURDERERS
to death the children of the m.; 2Ki 14.06
Righteousness lodged in her, but now m. Is 1.21
"Woe is me! I am fainting before m." Jer 4.31
destroyed those m. and burned Mt 22.07
m. of fathers and m. of mothers, 1Ti 1.09
as for m., fornicators, sorcerers, Rev 21.08
fornicators and m. and idolaters, 22.15

MURDERING
man attacking and m. his neighbor; Deu 22.26

MURDERS
hiding places he m. the innocent. Ps 10.08
repent of their m. or their Rev 9.21

MURMUR
are we, that you m. against us?" Ex 16.07
murmurings which you m. against him— 16.08
wicked congregation m. against me? Num 14.27
Israel, which they m. against me. 14.27
congregation to m. against him by 14.36
is Aaron that you m. against him?" 16.11
Israel, which they m. against you." 17.05
and those who m. will accept Is 29.24
"Do not m. among yourselves. Jn 6.43

MURMURED
And the people m. against Moses, Ex 15.24
of Israel m. against Moses and 16.02
and the people m. against Moses, 17.03
of Israel m. against Moses and Num 14.02
upward, who have m. against me, 14.29
of Israel m. against Moses and 16.41
and you m. in your tents, and said, Deu 1.27
congregation m. against the Jos 9.18
They m. in their tents, and did not Ps 106.25
their scribes m. against his Lk 5.30
And the Pharisees and the scribes m., 15.02
And when they saw it they all m., 19.07
The Jews then m. at him, because he Jn 6.41
that his disciples m. at it, 6.61
the Hellenists m. against the Ac 6.01

MURMURINGS
has heard your m. against the LORD. Ex 16.07
has heard your m. which you murmur 16.08
Your m. are not against us but 16.08
the LORD, for he has heard your m.'" 16.09
"I have heard the m. of the people 16.12
have heard the m. of the people of Num 14.27
from me the m. of the people of 17.05
make an end of their m. against me, 17.10

MUSCLES
his power in the m. of his belly. Job 40.16

MUSE
thy work, and m. on thy mighty deeds. Ps 77.12
I m. on what thy hands have wrought. 143.05
Your mind will m. on the terror: Is 33.18

MUSED
As I m., the fire burned; then I spoke Ps 39.03

MUSHI
The sons of Merari: Mahli and M. Ex 6.19
by their families: Mahli and M. Num 3.20
The sons of Merari: Mahli and M. 1Ch 6.19
son of M., son of Merari, son of 6.47
The sons of Merari: Mahli and M. 23.21
The sons of M.: Mahli, Eder, and 23.23
The sons of Merari: Mahli and M. 24.26
The sons of M.: Mahli, Eder, and 24.30

MUSHITES
Mahlites and the family of the M.: Num 3.33
the Mahlites, the family of the M., 26.58

MUSIC
of joy, and with instruments of m. 1Sa 18.06
in m., should direct the m., for he 1Ch 15.22
leader of the m. of the singers; 15.27
and made loud m. on harps and lyres. 15.28
cymbals for the m. and instruments 16.42
father in the m. in the house of 25.06
instruments for m. to the LORD 2Ch 7.06
skilful with instruments of m. 34.12
my riddle to the m. of the lyre. Ps 49.04
to the m. of the lute and the harp, 92.03
city gate, the young men their m. Lam 5.14
And I will stop the m. of your songs, Eze 26.13
bagpipe, and every kind of m., Dan 3.05
bagpipe, and every kind of m., 3.07
bagpipe, and every kind of m., 3.10
bagpipe, and every kind of m., 3.15
for themselves instruments of m.; Amo 6.05
the house, he heard m. and dancing. Lk 15.25

MUSICAL
play loudly on m. instruments, 1Ch 15.16
cymbals and other m. instruments, 2Ch 5.13
with their m. instruments leading 23.13
with the m. instruments of David Neh 12.36

MUSICIANS
To the sound of m. at the watering Ju 5.11

MUSING
either he is m., or he has gone 1Ki 18.27

MUST
is for you, but you m. master it." Gen 4.07
'This is the kindness you m. do me: 20.13
m. I then take your son back to the 24.05
only you m. not take my son back 24.08
and said, "You m. come in to me; 30.16
"If it m. be so, then do this: take 43.11
of your father m. have put treasure 43.23
You m. tell my father of all my 45.13
time drew near that Israel m. die, 47.29
We m. go three days' journey into Ex 8.27
for we m. hold a feast to the LORD. 10.09
"You m. also let us have sacrifices 10.25
Our cattle also m. go with us; 10.26
for we m. take of them to serve the 10.26
with what we m. serve the LORD 10.26
but what every one m. eat, that only may 12.16
then you m. carry my bones with you 13.19
they m. walk and what they m. do. 18.20
it m. be put into water, and it Lev 11.32
the priest m. pronounce him unclean; 13.44
forbidden to you, it m. not be eaten. 19.23
to be accepted it m. be perfect; 22.21
but they m. not touch the holy Num 4.15
that you m. also make yourself a 16.13
puts in my mouth, that m. I speak." 22.38
"M. I not take heed to speak what 23.12
that the LORD says, that I m. do'?" 23.26
You m. wash your clothes on the 31.24
For the man m. remain in his city 35.28
way by which we m. go up and the Deu 1.22
For I m. die in this land, I m. not 4.22
then you m. utterly destroy them; 7.02
Only he m. not multiply horses for 17.16
therefore your camp m. be holy, 23.14
the days approach when you m. die; 31.14
that you m. turn away this day from Jos 22.18
that you m. go to take a wife from Ju 14.03
"There m. be an inheritance for the 21.17
'You m. not go back empty-handed to Ru 3.17
would say, "No, you m. give it now; 1Sa 2.16
God of Israel m. not remain with 5.07
So you m. make images of your 6.05
since he m. bless the sacrifice; 9.13
We m. all die, we are like water 2Sa 14.14
for they m. not be seen entering 17.17
he is asleep and m. be awakened." 1Ki 18.27
for the LORD m. be exceedingly 1Ch 22.05
I have provided. To these you m. add. 22.14
we m. do as you have said. Ez 10.12
I m. appeal for mercy to my accuser. Job 9.15
I m. beseech him with my mouth. 19.16
of the torrents they m. dwell, 30.06
I m. speak, that I may find relief; 32.20
I m. open my lips and answer. 32.20
For you m. choose, and not I; 34.33
How long m. I bear pain in my soul, Ps 13.02
which m. be curbed with bit and 32.09
stupid alike m. perish and leave 49.10
My vows to thee I m. perform, O God; 56.12
I did not steal m. I now restore? 69.04
How long m. thy servant endure? 119.84
seeing that I m. leave it to the Ecc 2.18
and skill m. leave all to be 2.21
he m. put forth more strength; 10.10
noontide of my days I m. depart; Is 38.10
How long m. I see the standard, and Jer 4.21
is the city which m. be punished; 6.06
is an affliction, and I m. bear it. 10.19
the LORD of hosts: You m. drink! 25.28
each of you m. set free the fellow 34.14
you m. set him free from your 34.14
"We m. report all these words to 36.16
to drink the cup m. drink it, 49.12
go unpunished, but you m. drink. 49.12
Babylon m. fall for the slain of 51.49
We m. pay for the water we drink, Lam 5.04
the wood we get m. be bought. 5.04
as men do who m. go into exile. Eze 12.04
that you m. tread down with your 34.18
that you m. foul the rest with your 34.18
And m. my sheep eat what you have 34.19
m. pass before the end of the Dan 9.02
"You m. dwell as mine for many days Hos 3.03
Ephraim m. lead forth his sons to 9.13
now they m. bear their guilt. 10.02
Judah m. plow, Jacob m. harrow for 10.11
We m. not mention the name of the Amo 6.10
and Israel m. go into exile away 7.11
m. be perfect, as your heavenly Mt 5.48

MUST (cont.)
you m. not be like the hypocrites; Mt 6.05
disciples that he m. go to Jerusalem 16.21
say that first Elijah m. come?" 17.10
"Teacher, what good deed m. I do, 19.16
great among you m. be your servant, 20.26
first among you m. be your slave; 20.27
his brother m. marry the widow, and 22.24
for this m. take place, but the end 24.06
Therefore you also m. be ready; 24.44
"Even if I m. die with you, I will 26.35
be fulfilled, that it m. be so?" 26.54
the Son of man m. suffer many Mk 8.31
say that first Elijah m. come?" 9.11
he m. be last of all and servant of 9.35
what m. I do to inherit eternal 10.17
great among you m. be your servant, 10.43
first among you m. be slave of all 10.44
the man m. take the wife, and raise 12.19
this m. take place, but the end is 13.07
And the gospel m. first be preached 13.10
"If I m. die with you, I will not 14.31
not know that I m. be in my Lk 2.49
"I m. preach the good news of the 4.43
But new wine m. be put into fresh 5.38
saying, "The Son of man m. suffer 9.22
You also m. be ready; 12.40
Nevertheless I m. go on my way 13.33
and I m. go out and see it; 14.18
'I repent,' you m. forgive him." 17.04
But first he m. suffer many things 17.25
for I m. stay at your house today." 19.05
the man m. take the wife and raise 20.28
for this m. first take place, but 21.09
this scripture m. be fulfilled in 22.37
that the Son of man m. be delivered 24.07
and the psalms m. be fulfilled." 24.44
said to you, 'You m. be born anew.' Jn 3.07
so m. the Son of man be lifted up, 3.14
He m. increase, but I m. decrease." 3.30
who worship him m. worship in spirit 4.24
"What m. we do, to be doing the work 6.28
We m. work the works of him who 9.04
I m. bring them also, and they will 10.16
any one serves me, he m. follow me; 12.26
the Son of man m. be lifted up? 12.34
that he m. rise from the dead. 20.09
of these men m. become with us a Ac 1.22
whom heaven m. receive until the 3.21
among men by which we m. be saved." 4.12
rather than to God, you m. judge; 4.19
"We m. obey God rather than men. 5.29
him how much he m. suffer for the 9.16
has cleansed, you m. not call common." 10.15
cleansed you m. not call common.' 11.09
tribulations we m. enter the 14.22
"Men, what m. I do to be saved?" 16.30
been there, I m. also see Rome." 19.21
by so toiling one m. help the weak, 20.35
so you m. bear witness also at Rome." 23.11
that the Christ m. suffer, and that, by 26.23
you m. stand before Caesar; and lo, God 27.24
say that one m. not commit adultery, Rom 2.22
So you also m. consider yourselves 6.11
Therefore one m. be subject, not 13.05
We m. not indulge in immorality as 1Co 10.08
We m. not put the Lord to the test, 10.09
for there m. be factions among you 11.19
For he m. reign until he has put 15.25
perishable nature m. put on the 15.53
mortal nature m. put on immortality. 15.53
You also m. help us by prayer, so 2Co 1.11
righteousness m. far exceed it in 3.09
is permanent m. have much more 3.11
For we m. all appear before the 5.10
Each one m. do as he has made up 9.07
To my shame, I m. say, we were too 11.21
If I m. boast, I will boast of the 11.30
I m. boast; there is nothing 12.01
Any charge m. be sustained by the 13.01
that you m. no longer live as the Eph 4.17
or covetousness m. not even be 5.03
you, so you also m. forgive. Col 3.13
Now a bishop m. be above reproach, 1Ti 3.02
He m. manage his own household well, 3.04
He m. not be a recent convert, or he 3.06
moreover he m. be well thought of 3.07
Deacons likewise m. be serious, 3.08
they m. hold the mystery of the 3.09
The women likewise m. be serious, 3.11
and she m. be well attested for her 5.10
believing masters m. not be disrespectful 6.02
rather they m. serve all the better 6.02
Lord's servant m. not be quarrelsome 2Ti 2.24
as God's steward, m. be blameless; Tit 1.07
he m. not be arrogant or quick-tempered 1.07
he m. hold firm to the sure word as 1.09
they m. be silenced, since they are 1.11
Therefore we m. pay the closer Heb 2.01
one who made it m. be established. 9.16
near to God m. believe that he 11.06
For that person m. not suppose that Jas 1.07
First of all you m. understand this, 2Pe 1.20
First of all you m. understand this, 3.03
But you m. remember, beloved, the Jud 1.17
servants what m. soon take place; Rev 1.01
show you what m. take place after 4.01
"You m. again prophesy about many 10.11
with the sword m. he be slain. 13.10
he comes he m. remain only a 17.10
he said to me, "You m. not do that! 19.10
After that he m. be loosed for a 20.03
servants what m. soon take place. 22.06
but he said to me, "You m. not do that! 22.09

MUSTARD
like a grain of m. seed which a Mt 13.31
have faith as a grain of m. seed, 17.20
It is like a grain of m. seed, Mk 4.31
like a grain of m. seed which a Lk 13.19
had faith as a grain of m. seed, 17.06

MUSTER
and m. an army like the army that 1Ki 20.25
This was the m. of them by fathers' 2Ch 17.14
numbers in the m. made by Jeiel 26.11
opposite the M. Gate, and to the Neh 3.31

MUSTERED
in the morning and m. the people, Jos 8.10
Benjaminites m. out of their Ju 20.15
who m. seven hundred picked men. 20.15
m. four hundred thousand men that 20.17
For when the people were m., 21.09
When he m. them at Bezek, the men of 1Sa 11.08
And the Philistines m. to fight 13.05
Philistines had m. at Michmash, 13.11
Then David m. the men who were with 2Sa 18.01
Then he m. the servants of the 1Ki 20.15
after them he m. all the people of 20.15
the spring Benhadad m. the Syrians, 20.26
And the people of Israel were m., 20.27
at that time and m. all Israel. 2Ki 3.06
king of Syria m. his entire army, 6.24
of the army who m. the people of 25.19
Ammonites were m. from their 1Ch 19.07
He m. those twenty years old and 2Ch 25.05
of the army who m. the people of Jer 52.25
After many days you will be m.; Eze 38.08
flash like flame when m. in array; Nah 2.03

MUSTERING
of hosts is m. a host for battle. Is 13.04

MUTILATE
unsettle you would m. themselves! Gal 5.12
out for those who m. the flesh. Php 3.02

MUTILATED
one who has a m. face or a limb Lev 21.18
or disabled or m. or having a discharge 22.22

MUTILATION
in them, because of their m., they will not Lev 22.25

MUTTER
and the wizards who chirp and m., Is 8.19

MUTTERING
And there was much m. about him Jn 7.12
heard the crowd thus m. about him, 7.32

MUTTERS
lies, your tongue m. wickedness. Is 59.03

MUTUAL
for peace and for m. upbuilding. Rom 14.19

MUTUALLY
that we may be m. encouraged by Rom 1.12

MUZZLE
"You shall not m. an ox when it Deu 25.04
"You shall not m. an ox when it is 1Co 9.09
"You shall not m. an ox when it is 1Ti 5.18

MYRA
Pamphylia, we came to M. in Lycia. Ac 27.05

MYRIADS
the Lord came with his holy m., Jud 1.14
numbering m. of myriads and thousands Rev 5.11
myriads of m. and thousands of 5.11

MYRRH
and m., on their way to carry it Gen 37.25
m., pistachio nuts, and almonds. 43.11
of liquid m. five hundred shekels, Ex 30.23
m., spices, horses, and mules, so much 1Ki 10.25
m., spices, horses, and mules, so much 2Ch 9.24
with oil of m. and six months with Est 2.12
fragrant with m. and aloes and Ps 45.08
I have perfumed my bed with m., Pro 7.17
My beloved is to me a bag of m., Sol 1.13
perfumed with m. and frankincense, 3.06
the mountain of m. and the hill of 4.06
m. and aloes, with all chief spices 4.14
I gather my m. with my spice, I eat 5.01
with m., my fingers with liquid m., 5.05
lips are lilies, distilling liquid m. 5.13
gold and frankincense and m. Mt 2.11
offered him wine mingled with m.; Mk 15.23
bringing a mixture of m. and aloes, Jn 19.39
m., frankincense, wine, oil, fine Rev 18.13

MYRTLE
m., palm, and other leafy trees to Neh 8.15
the acacia, the m., and the olive; Is 41.19
of the brier shall come up the m.; 55.13
among the m. trees in the glen; Zec 1.08
among the m. trees answered, 1.10
was standing among the m. trees, 1.11

MYSELF
I was naked and I hid m." Gen 3.10
have taken upon m. to speak to the 18.27
have taken upon m. to speak to the 18.31
and said, "By m. I have sworn, says 22.16
a curse upon m. and not a blessing." 27.12
I bore the loss of it m.; of my hand 31.39
I hewed out for m. in the land of 50.05
I did not make m. known to them. Ex 6.03
wings and brought you to m. 19.04
'I will show m. holy among those Lev 10.03
I m. will set my face against that 20.03
and I m. will smite you sevenfold 26.24
chastise you m. sevenfold for your 26.28
Israel, I have taken them for m. Num 8.16
Egypt I consecrated them for m. 8.17
I the LORD make m. known to him in 12.06
in my name, I m. will require it of him. Deu 18.19
I will m. drive them out from Jos 13.06
at other times, and shake m. free." Ju 16.20
said, "I cannot redeem it for m., Ru 4.06
'I revealed m. to the house of your 1Sa 2.27
raise up for m. a faithful priest, 2.35
so I forced m., and offered the 13.12
provided for m. a king among his 16.01
that I may hide m. in the field 20.05
from avenging m. with my own hand! 25.33
I will make m. yet more contemptible 2Sa 6.22
"I m. will also go out with you." 18.02
him, and I kept m. from guilt. 22.24
and prepare it for m. and my son, 1Ki 17.12
I will surely show m. to him today." 18.15
"I will disguise m. and go into 22.30
and I bow m. in the house of Rimmon, 2Ki 5.18
when I bow m. in the house of 5.18
this place for m. as a house of 2Ch 7.12
"I will disguise m. and go into 18.29
I took counsel with m., and I brought Neh 5.07
to the banquet she prepared but m. Est 5.12
I regard not m.; I loathe my life. Job 9.21
If I wash m. with snow, and cleanse 9.30
fear of him, for I am not so in m. 9.35
And if I lift m. up, thou dost hunt 10.16
I will not hide m. from thy face: 13.20
erred, my error remains with m. 19.04
therefore I despise m., and I repent 42.06
him, and I kept m. from guilt. Ps 18.23
I afflicted m. with fasting. 35.13
I do not occupy m. with things too 131.01
to busy m. with wicked deeds in 141.04
I said to m., "I have acquired Ecc 1.16
I said to m., "Come now, I will make 2.01
and planted vineyards for m.; 2.04
I made m. gardens and parks, and 2.05
I made m. pools from which to water 2.06
gathered for m. silver and gold 2.08
Then I said to m., "What befalls 2.15
And I said to m. that this also 2.15
and depriving m. of pleasure? 4.08
My vineyard, my very own, is for m.; Sol 8.12
enemies, and avenge m. on my foes. Is 1.24
I m. have commanded my consecrated 13.03
I will make m. like the Most High.' 14.14
the LORD, "now I will lift m. up; now I will 33.10
have kept still and restrained m.; 42.14
I formed for m. that they might 43.21
By m. I have sworn, from my mouth 45.23
I not avenge m. on a nation such Jer 5.09
I not avenge m. on a nation such 5.29
Behold, I m. have seen it, says the 7.11
I not avenge m. on a nation such 9.09
I m. will lift up your skirts over 13.26
I m. will fight against you with 21.05
I swear by m., says the LORD, that 22.05
'I will build m. a great house with 22.14
For I have sworn by m., says the LORD, 49.13
behold, I have never defiled m.; Eze 4.14
my fury upon them and satisfy m.; 5.13
should I let m. be inquired of at 14.03
will answer him m. because of the 14.04
me, I the LORD will answer him m.; 14.07
"I m. will take a sprig from the 17.22
and I m. will plant it upon a high 17.22
making m. known to them in the land 20.05
sight I made m. known to them in 20.09
In vain I have wearied m.; its thick rust 24.12
I m. will search for my sheep, and 34.11
I m. will be the shepherd of my 34.15
I m. will judge between the fat 34.20
and I will make m. known among you, 35.11
and make m. known in the eyes of 38.23
mouth, nor did I anoint m. at all, Dan 10.03

MYSELF (cont.)
and I will sow him for m. in the land. Hos 2.23
rich, I have gained wealth for m."; 12.08
and bow m. before God on high? Mic 6.06
and station m. on the tower, and Hab 2.01
hands and my feet, that it is I m.; Lk 24.39
I m. did not know him; but for this Jn 1.31
I m. did not know him; but he who 1.33
If I bear witness to m., my testimony 5.31
"Even if I do bear witness to m., 8.14
I bear witness to m., and the Father 8.18
"If I glorify m., my glory is 8.54
the earth, will draw all men to m." 12.32
come again and will take you to m., 14.03
love him and manifest m. to him." 14.21
And for their sake I consecrate m., 17.19
of any value nor as precious to m., Ac 20.24
"I should like to hear the man m." 25.22
"I think m. fortunate that it is 26.02
"I m. was convinced that I ought to 26.09
So then, I of m. serve the law of Rom 7.25
wish that I m. were accursed and 9.03
I have shown m. to those who did 10.20
I m. am an Israelite, a descendant 11.01
"I have kept for m. seven thousand 11.04
I m. am satisfied about you, my 15.14
a helper of many and of m. as well. 16.02
human court. I do not even judge m. 1Co 4.03
not aware of anything against m., 4.04
all this to m. and Apollos for 4.06
I wish that all were as I m. am. 7.07
I have made m. a slave to all, that 9.19
though not being m. under the law— 9.20
to others I m. should be disqualified. 9.27
I, Paul, m. entreat you, by the 2Co 10.01
sin in abasing m. so that you 11.07
except that I m. did not burden you? 12.13
But granting that I m. did not 12.16
then I prove m. a transgressor. Gal 2.18
that shortly I m. shall come also. Php 2.24
Though I m. have reason for confidence 3.04
even as I m. have received power Rev 2.27
as I m. conquered and sat down with 3.21

MYSIA
And when they had come opposite M., Ac 16.07
so, passing by M., they went down to 16.08

MYSTERIES
is a God in heaven who reveals m., Dan 2.28
he who reveals m. made known to 2.29
of kings, and a revealer of m., 2.47
and stewards of the m. of God. 1Co 4.01
understand all m. and all knowledge, 13.02
but he utters m. in the Spirit. 14.02

MYSTERIOUS
he reveals deep and m. things; Dan 2.22

MYSTERY
God of heaven concerning this m., Dan 2.18
Then the m. was revealed to Daniel 2.19
to the king the m. which the king 2.27
living has this m. been revealed 2.30
have been able to reveal this m." 2.47
you and that no m. is difficult 4.09
I want you to understand this m., Rom 11.25
revelation of the m. which was kept 16.25
I tell you a m. We shall not all 1Co 15.51
and insight the m. of his will, Eph 1.09
how the m. was made known to me by 3.03
my insight into the m. of Christ, 3.04
the plan of the m. hidden for ages 3.09
This is a great m., and I take it to 5.32
to proclaim the m. of the gospel, 6.19
the m. hidden for ages and generations Col 1.26
the riches of the glory of this m., 1.27
knowledge of God's m., of Christ, 2.02
word, to declare the m. of Christ, 4.03
For the m. of lawlessness is 2Th 2.07
they must hold the m. of the faith 1Ti 3.09
is the m. of our religion: He was 3.16
As for the m. of the seven stars Rev 1.20
the m. of God, as he announced to 10.07
forehead was written a name of m.: 17.05
will tell you the m. of the woman, 17.07

MYTHS
themselves with m. and endless 1Ti 1.04
to do with godless and silly m. 4.07
to the truth and wander into m. 2Ti 4.04
heed to Jewish m. or to commands Tit 1.14
cleverly devised m. when we made 2Pe 1.16

N

NAAM
of Jephunneh: Iru, Elah, and N.; 1Ch 4.15

NAAMAH
The sister of Tubalcain was N. Gen 4.22
Gederoth, Bethdagon, N., and Makkedah; Jos 15.41
mother's name was N. the Ammonitess. 1Ki 14.21
mother's name was N. the Ammonitess. 14.31
mother's name was N. the Ammonitess. 2Ch 12.13

NAAMAN
N., Ehi, Rosh, Muppim, Huppim, and Ard Gen 46.21
And the sons of Bela were Ard and N.: Num 26.40
of N., the family of the Naamites. 26.40
N., commander of the army of the 2Ki 5.01
So N. went in and told his lord, 5.04
I have sent to you N. my servant, 5.06
So N. came with his horses and 5.09
But N. was angry, and went away, 5.11
Then N. said, "If not, I pray you, let 5.17
"But when N. had gone from him a 5.19
has spared this N. the Syrian, 5.20
So Gehazi followed N. And when N. saw 5.21
And N. said, "Be pleased to accept 5.23
Therefore the leprosy of N. shall 5.27
Abishua, N., Ahoah, 1Ch 8.04
N., Ahijah, and Gera, that is, Heglam, 8.07
cleansed, but only N. the Syrian. Lk 4.27

NAAMAN'S
Israel, and she waited on N. wife. 2Ki 5.02

NAAMATHITE
the Shuhite, and Zophar the N. Job 2.11
Then Zophar the N. answered: 11.01
Then Zophar the N. answered: 20.01
and Zophar the N. went and did 42.09

NAAMITES
of Naaman, the family of the N. Num 26.40

NAARAH
from Janoah to Ataroth and to N., Jos 16.07
Tekoa, had two wives, Helah and N.; 1Ch 4.05
N. bore him Ahuzzam, Hepher, Temeni, 4.06
These were the sons of N. 4.06

NAARAI
of Carmel, N. the son of Ezbai, 1Ch 11.37

NAARAN
and eastward N., and westward Gezer 1Ch 7.28

NABAL

Now the name of the man was N., 1Sa 25.03
wilderness that N. was shearing 25.04
and go to N., and greet him in my 25.05
all this to N. in the name of 25.09
And N. answered David's servants, 25.10
she did not tell her husband N. 25.19
regard this ill-natured fellow, N.; 25.25
N. is his name, and folly is with 25.25
to do evil to my lord be as N. 25.26
been left to N. so much as one 25.34
And Abigail came to N.; and lo, he was 25.36
when the wine had gone out of N., 25.37
ten days later the LORD smote N.; 25.38
When David heard that N. was dead, 25.39
I received at the hand of N., 25.39
evil-doing of N. upon his own head." 25.39
Abigail the widow of N. of Carmel. 30.05
Abigail the widow of N. of Carmel. 2Sa 2.02
Abigail the widow of N. of Carmel; 3.03

NABAL'S

N. wife, "Behold, David sent messengers 1Sa 25.14
And N. heart was merry within him, 25.36
and Abigail of Carmel, N. widow. 27.03

NABOTH

Now N. the Jezreelite had a vineyard 1Ki 21.01
And after this Ahab said to N., 21.02
But N. said to Ahab, "The LORD 21.03
because of what N. the Jezreelite 21.04
I spoke to N. the Jezreelite, 21.06
the vineyard of N. the Jezreelite." 21.07
who dwelt with N. in his city. 21.08
and set N. on high among the people; 21.09
and set N. on high among the people. 21.12
brought a charge against N., 21.13
"N. cursed God and the king." 21.13
"N. has been stoned; he is dead." 21.14
heard that N. had been stoned and 21.15
the vineyard of N. the Jezreelite, 21.15
for N. is not alive, but dead." 21.15
as Ahab heard that N. was dead, 21.16
the vineyard of N. the Jezreelite, 21.16
he is in the vineyard of N., 21.18
up the blood of N. shall dogs lick 21.19
the property of N. the Jezreelite. 2Ki 9.21
belonging to N. the Jezreelite; 9.25
the blood of N. and the blood of 9.26

NACON

came to the threshing floor of N., 2Sa 6.06

NADAB

and she bore him N., Abihu, Ex 6.23
N., and Abihu, and seventy of the 24.01
N., and Abihu, and seventy of the 24.09
N. and Abihu, Eleazar and Ithamar. 28.01
Now N. and Abihu, the sons of Aaron, Lev 10.01
N. the first-born, and Abihu, Eleazar, Num 3.02
But N. and Abihu died before the 3.04
And to Aaron were born N., 26.60
But N. and Abihu died when they 26.61
and N. his son reigned in his stead. 1Ki 14.20
N. the son of Jeroboam began to 15.25
for N. and all Israel were laying 15.27
Now the rest of the acts of N., 15.31
sons of Shammai: N. and Abishur. 1Ch 2.28
The sons of N.: Seled and Appaim; 2.30
N., Abihu, Eleazar, and Ithamar. 6.03
Abdon, then Zur, Kish, Baal, N., 8.30
then Zur, Kish, Baal, Ner, N., 9.36
N., Abihu, Eleazar, and Ithamar. 24.01
But N. and Abihu died before their 24.02

NAGGAI

the son of Esli, the son of N., Lk 3.25

NAHALAL

and Kattath, N., Shimron, Idalah, and Jos 19.15
N. with its pasture lands—four 21.35

NAHALIEL

from Mattanah to N., and from N. to Num 21.19

NAHALOL

Kitron, or the inhabitants of N.; Ju 1.30

NAHAM

the sister of N., were the fathers 1Ch 4.19

NAHAMANI

N., Mordecai, Bilshan, Mispereth, Neh 7.07

NAHARAI

N. of Beeroth, the armor-bearer of 2Sa 23.37
N. of Beeroth, the armor-bearer of 1Ch 11.39

NAHASH

Then N. the Ammonite went up and 1Sa 11.01
all the men of Jabesh said to N., 11.01
But N. the Ammonite said to them, 11.02
you saw that N. the king of the 12.12
loyally with Hanun the son of N., 2Sa 10.02
married Abigal the daughter of N., 17.25
the son of N. from Rabbah of the 17.27
Now after this N. the king of the 1Ch 19.01
loyally with Hanun the son of N., 19.02

NAHATH

N., Zerah, Shammah, and Mizzah. Gen 36.13
the chiefs N., Zerah, Shammah, and 36.17
N., Zerah, Shammah, and Mizzah. 1Ch 1.37
son, Zophai his son, N. his son, 6.26
N., Asahel, Jerimoth, Jozabad, Eliel, 2Ch 31.13

NAHBI

of Naphtali, N. the son of Vophsi; Num 13.14

NAHOR

years, he became the father of N.; Gen 11.22
the birth of N. two hundred years, 11.23
When N. had lived twenty-nine years, 11.24
and N. lived after the birth of 11.25
the father of Abram, N., and Haran. 11.26
the father of Abram, N., and Haran; 11.27
And Abram and N. took wives; 11.29
borne children to your brother N.: 22.20
These eight Milcah bore to N., 22.23
to Mesopotamia, to the city of N. 24.10
the wife of N., Abraham's brother, 24.15
son of Milcah, whom she bore to N. 24.24
"Do you know Laban the son of N.?" 29.05
The God of Abraham and the God of N., 31.53
the father of Abraham and of N.; Jos 24.02
Serug, N., Terah; 1Ch 1.26
the son of Terah, the son of N., Lk 3.34

NAHOR'S

was Sarai, and the name of N. wife, Gen 11.29
N. son, whom Milcah bore to him. 24.47

NAHSHON

of Amminadab and the sister of N.; Ex 6.23
from Judah, N. the son of Amminadab; Num 1.07
of Judah being N. the son of 2.03
first day was N. the son of 7.12
the offering of N. the son of 7.17
their host was N. the son of 10.14
Amminadab of N., N. of Salmon, Ru 4.20
and Amminadab was the father of N., 1Ch 2.10
N. was the father of Salma, Salma of 2.11
and Amminadab the father of N., Mt 1.04
and N. the father of Salmon, 1.04
the son of Sala, the son of N., Lk 3.32

NAHUM
book of the vision of N. of Elkosh. Nah 1.01
the son of N., the son of Esli, the Lk 3.25

NAILING
he set aside, n. it to the cross. Col 2.14

NAILS
shave her head and pare her n. Deu 21.12
of iron for n. for the doors of 1Ch 22.03
The weight of the n. was one shekel 2Ch 3.09
and like n. firmly fixed are the Ecc 12.11
fasten it with n. so that it Is 41.07
with hammer and n. so that it Jer 10.04
and his n. were like birds' claws. Dan 4.33
in his hands the print of the n., Jn 20.25
my finger in the mark of the n., 20.25

NAIN
he went to a city called N., Lk 7.11

NAIOTH
he and Samuel went and dwelt at N. 1Sa 19.18
"Behold, David is at N. in Ramah." 19.19
"Behold, they are at N. in Ramah." 19.22
And he went from there to N. in Ramah; 19.23
until he came to N. in Ramah. 19.23
Then David fled from N. in Ramah, 20.01

NAKED
And the man and his wife were both n., Gen 2.25
and they knew that they were n.; 3.07
and I was afraid, because I was n.; 3.10
"Who told you that you were n.? 3.11
breeches to cover their n. flesh; Ex 28.42
he has made n. her fountain, and she Lev 20.18
that is to make n. one's near kin; 20.19
and lay n. all that day and all 1Sa 19.24
all that were n. among them; 2Ch 28.15
And he said, "N. I came from my Job 1.21
womb, and n. shall I return; 1.21
stripped the n. of their clothing. 22.06
They lie all night n., without 24.07
They go about n., without clothing; 24.10
Sheol is n. before God, and Abaddon 26.06
n. as he came, and shall take Ecc 5.15
done so, walking n. and barefoot— Is 20.02
has walked n. and barefoot for 20.03
n. and barefoot, with buttocks 20.04
when you see the n., to cover him, 58.07
yet you were n. and bare. Eze 16.07
when you were n. and bare, weltering 16.22
jewels, and leave you n. and bare. 16.39
and covers the n. with a garment, 18.07
and covers the n. with a garment, 18.16
and leave you n. and bare, and the 23.29
lest I strip her n. and make her as Hos 2.03
shall flee away n. in that day, Amo 2.16
I will go stripped and n.; Mic 1.08
I was n. and you clothed me, I was Mt 25.36
welcome thee, or n. and clothe thee? 25.38
n. and you did not clothe me, sick 25.43
a stranger or n. or sick or in 25.44
the linen cloth and ran away n. Mk 14.52
out of that house n. and wounded. Ac 19.16
it on we may not be found n. 2Co 5.03
pitiable, poor, blind, and n. Rev 3.17
he may not go n. and be seen 16.15
they will make her desolate and n., 17.16

NAKEDNESS
saw the n. of his father, and told Gen 9.22
and covered the n. of their father 9.23
they did not see their father's n. 9.23
that your n. be not exposed on it.' Ex 20.26
near of kin to him to uncover n. Lev 18.06
not uncover the n. of your father, 18.07
which is the n. of your mother; 18.07
you shall not uncover her n. 18.07
not uncover the n. of your father's 18.08
it is your father's n. 18.08
not uncover the n. of your sister, 18.09
not uncover the n. of your son's 18.10
for their n. is your own n. 18.10
not uncover the n. of your father's 18.11
not uncover the n. of your father's 18.12
not uncover the n. of your mother's 18.13
not uncover the n. of your father's 18.14
not uncover the n. of your daughter-in-law; 18.15
wife, you shall not uncover her n. 18.15
not uncover the n. of your brother's 18.16
she is your brother's n. 18.16
not uncover the n. of a woman and 18.17
daughter's daughter to uncover her n.; 18.17
uncovering her n. while her sister 18.18
to uncover her n. while she is in 18.19
wife has uncovered his father's n.; 20.11
and sees her n., and she sees his n., 20.17
he has uncovered his sister's n., 20.17
her sickness, and uncovers her n., 20.18
not uncover the n. of your mother's 20.19
he has uncovered his uncle's n.; 20.20
he has uncovered his brother's n., 20.21
in n., and in want of all things; Deu 28.48
to the shame of your mother's n.? 1Sa 20.30
Your n. shall be uncovered, and your Is 47.03
their bed, you have looked on n. 57.08
her, for they have seen her n.; Lam 1.08
over you, and covered your n.: Eze 16.08
bare and your n. uncovered in your 16.36
and will uncover your n. to them, 16.37
that they may see all your n. 16.37
In you men uncover their fathers' n.; 22.10
These uncovered her n.; 23.10
so openly and flaunted her n., 23.18
and the n. of your harlotry shall 23.29
flax, which were to cover her n. Hos 2.09
of Shaphir, in n. and shame; Mic 1.11
look on your n. and kingdoms on Nah 3.05
or n., or peril, or sword? Rom 8.35
shame of your n. from being seen, Rev 3.18

NAME
The n. of the first is Pishon; Gen 2.11
The n. of the second river is Gihon; 2.13
And the n. of the third river is 2.14
living creature, that was its n. 2.19
The man called his wife's n. Eve, 3.20
n. of the city after the n. of his son, 4.17
the n. of the one was Adah, and the 4.19
and the n. of the other Zillah. 4.19
His brother's n. was Jubal; 4.21
bore a son and called his n. Seth, 4.25
born, and he called his n. Enosh. 4.26
to call upon the n. of the LORD. 4.26
and called his n. Noah, saying, "Out 5.29
the n. of the one was Peleg, for in 10.25
and his brother's n. was Joktan. 10.25
and let us make a n. for ourselves, 11.04
Therefore its n. was called Babel, 11.09
the n. of Abram's wife was Sarai, and 11.29
and the n. of Nahor's wife, Milcah, 11.29
and make your n. great, so that you 12.02
and called on the n. of the LORD. 12.08
Abram called on the n. of the LORD. 13.04
Egyptian maid whose n. was Hagar; 16.01
you shall call his n. Ishmael; 16.11
So she called the n. of the LORD 16.13
and Abram called the n. of his son, 16.15
No longer shall your n. be Abram, 17.05
but your n. shall be Abraham; 17.05
n. Sarai, but Sarah shall be her n. 17.15
and you shall call his n. Isaac. 17.19
Therefore the n. of the city was 19.22
bore a son, and called his n. Moab; 19.37
a son, and called his n. Benammi; 19.38

NAME (cont.)

Abraham called the n. of his son Gen 21.03
called there on the n. of the LORD, 21.33
called the n. of that place The 22.14
whose n. was Reumah, bore Tebah, 22.24
Rebekah had a brother whose n. was Laban; 24.29
another wife, whose n. was Keturah. 25.01
so they called his n. Esau. 25.25
so his n. was called Jacob. 25.26
(Therefore his n. was called Edom. 25.30
he called the n. of the well Esek, 26.20
so he called its n. Sitnah. 26.21
so he called its n. Rehoboth, 26.22
and called upon the n. of the LORD, 26.25
therefore the n. of the city is 26.33
He called the n. of that place 28.19
but the n. of the city was Luz at 28.19
the n. of the older was Leah, and 29.16
and the n. of the younger was 29.16
son, and she called his n. Reuben; 29.32
and she called his n. Simeon. 29.33
therefore his n. was called Levi. 29.34
therefore she called his n. Judah; 29.35
therefore she called his n. Dan. 30.06
so she called his n. Naphtali. 30.08
so she called his n. Gad. 30.11
so she called his n. Asher. 30.13
so she called his n. Issachar. 30.18
so she called his n. Zebulun. 30.20
daughter, and called her n. Dinah. 30.21
and she called his n. Joseph, 30.24
n. your wages, and I will give it." 30.28
he called the n. of that place 32.02
And he said to him, "What is your n.?" 32.27
"Your n. shall no more be called 32.28
him, "Tell me, I pray, your n." 32.29
said, "Why is it that you ask my n.?" 32.29
called the n. of the place Peniel, 32.30
therefore the n. of the place is 33.17
so the n. of it was called Allonbacuth. 35.08
And God said to him, "Your n. is Jacob; 35.10
shall your n. be called Jacob, but 35.10
Jacob, but Israel shall be your n." 35.10
So his n. was called Israel. 35.10
called the n. of the place where 35.15
died), she called his n. Benoni; 35.18
his father called his n. Benjamin. 35.18
the n. of his city being Dinhabah. 36.32
the n. of his city being Avith. 36.35
the n. of his city being Pau; 36.39
his wife's n. was Mehetabel, the 36.39
Adullamite, whose n. was Hirah. 38.01
Canaanite whose n. was Shua; 38.02
a son, and he called his n. Er. 38.03
a son, and she called his n. Onan. 38.04
son, and she called his n. Shelah. 38.05
first-born, and her n. was Tamar. 38.06
Therefore his n. was called Perez, 38.29
and his n. was called Zerah. 38.30
called Joseph's n. Zaphenathpaneah; 41.45
Joseph called the n. of the first-born 41.51
The n. of the second he called 41.52
called by the n. of their brothers 48.06
in them let my n. be perpetuated, 48.16
and the n. of my fathers Abraham 48.16
of Jacob (by the n. of the Shepherd, 49.24
son, and he called his n. Gershom; Ex 2.22
and they ask me, 'What is his n.?' 3.13
this is my n. for ever, and thus I 3.15
came to Pharaoh to speak in thy n., 5.23
but by my n. the LORD I did not 6.03
so that my n. may be declared 9.16
man of war; the LORD is his n. 15.03
of Israel called its n. manna; 16.31
And he called the n. of the place 17.07
an altar and called the n. of it, 17.15
of whom the n. of the one was 18.03
and the n. of the other, Eliezer 18.04
not take the n. of the LORD your 20.07
guiltless who takes his n. in vain. 20.07
I cause my n. to be remembered I 20.24
transgression; for my n. is in him. 23.21
signets, each engraved with its n., 28.21
have called by n. Bezalel the son 31.02
thou hast said, 'I know you by n., 33.12
in my sight, and I know you by n." 33.17
before you my n. 'The LORD'; 33.19
and proclaimed the n. of the LORD. 34.05
whose n. is Jealous, is a jealous 34.14
has called by n. Bezalel the son 35.30
signets, each engraved with its n., 39.14
and so profane the n. of your God: Lev 18.21
shall not swear by my n. falsely, 19.12
and so profane the n. of your God: 19.12
sanctuary and profaning my holy n. 20.03
not profane the n. of their God; 21.06
they may not profane my holy n.; 22.02
And you shall not profane my holy n., 22.32
son blasphemed the N., and cursed. 24.11
His mother's n. was Shelomith, the 24.11
blasphemes the n. of the LORD 24.16
native, when he blasphemes the N., 24.16
shall assign by n. the objects Num 4.32
they put my n. upon the people of 6.27
So the n. of that place was called 11.03
Therefore the n. of that place was 11.34
write each man's n. upon his rod, 17.02
and write Aaron's n. upon the rod of 17.03
so the n. of the place was called 21.03
The n. of the slain man of Israel, 25.14
And the n. of the Midianite woman 25.15
And the n. of the daughter of Asher 26.46
The n. of Amram's wife was Jochebed 26.59
Why should the n. of our father be 27.04
called it Nobah, after his own n. 32.42
the villages after his own n., Deu 3.14
not take the n. of the LORD your 5.11
guiltless who takes his n. in vain. 5.11
serve him, and swear by his n. 6.13
make their n. perish from under 7.24
blot out their n. from under 9.14
to bless in his n., to this day. 10.08
and by his n. you shall swear. 10.20
destroy their n. out of that place 12.03
to put his n. and make his habitation 12.05
to make his n. dwell there, thither 12.11
to put his n. there is too far 12.21
to make his n. dwell there, you 14.23
God chooses, to set his n. there, 14.24
choose, to make his n. dwell there. 16.02
to make his n. dwell in it, there 16.06
choose, to make his n. dwell there. 16.11
and minister in the n. of the LORD, 18.05
minister in the n. of the LORD his 18.07
which he shall speak in my n., 18.19
a word in my n. which I have not 18.20
who speaks in the n. of other gods, 18.20
speaks in the n. of the LORD, 18.22
and to bless in the n. of the LORD, 21.05
and brings an evil n. upon her, 22.14
brought an evil n. upon a virgin 22.19
succeed to the n. of his brother 25.06
that his n. may not be blotted out 25.06
perpetuate his brother's n. in Israel; 25.07
And the n. of his house shall be 25.10
to make his n. to dwell there. 26.02
are called by the n. of the LORD; 28.10
fear this glorious and awful n., 28.58
blot out his n. from under heaven. 29.20
I will proclaim the n. of the LORD. 32.03
of a harlot whose n. was Rahab, Jos 2.01
And so the n. of that place is 5.09
and cut off our n. from the earth; 7.09
what wilt thou do for thy great n.?" 7.09

NAME (cont.)
to this day the n. of that place Jos 7.26
because of the n. of the LORD your 9.09
Now the n. of Hebron formerly was 14.15
now the n. of Debir formerly was 15.15
after the n. of Dan their ancestor. 19.47
following cities mentioned by n., 21.09
Hebron (now the n. of Hebron was Ju 1.10
The n. of Debir was formerly 1.11
So the n. of the city was called 1.17
(Now the n. of the city was formerly 1.23
a city, and called its n. Luz; 1.26
that is its n. to this day. 1.26
And they called the n. of that 2.05
and he called his n. Abimelech. 8.31
the Danites, whose n. was Manoah; 13.02
was, and he did not tell me his n.; 13.06
"What is your n., so that, when your 13.17
said to him, "Why do you ask my n., 13.18
a son, and called his n. Samson; 13.24
Therefore the n. of it was called 15.19
of Sorek, whose n. was Delilah. 16.04
of Ephraim, whose n. was Micah. 17.01
after the n. of Dan their ancestor, 18.29
but the n. of the city was Laish at 18.29
The n. of the man was Elimelech and Ru 1.02
and the n. of his wife Naomi, and 1.02
the n. of the one was Orpah and the 1.04
Orpah and the n. of the other Ruth. 1.04
of Elimelech, whose n. was Boaz. 2.01
"The man's n. with whom I worked 2.19
to restore the n. of the dead to 4.05
perpetuate the n. of the dead in 4.10
that the n. of the dead may not be 4.10
and may his n. be renowned in 4.14
of the neighborhood gave him a n., 4.17
whose n. was Elkanah the son of 1Sa 1.01
the n. of the one was Hannah, and 1.02
and the n. of the other Peninnah. 1.02
son, and she called his n. Samuel, 1.20
Jeshanah, and called its n. Ebenezer; 7.12
The n. of his first-born son was 8.02
and the n. of his second, Abijah; 8.02
man of Benjamin whose n. was Kish, 9.01
and he had a son whose n. was Saul, 9.02
the n. of the one was Bozez, and the 14.04
and the n. of the other Seneh. 14.04
the n. of the first-born was Merab, 14.49
and the n. of the younger Michal; 14.49
and the n. of Saul's wife was 14.50
And the n. of the commander of his 14.50
anoint for me him whom I n. to you. 16.03
Goliath by n., came up out of the 17.23
to you in the n. of the LORD of 17.45
so that his n. was highly esteemed. 18.30
let not the n. of Jonathan be cut 20.16
both of us in the n. of the LORD, 20.42
his n. was Doeg the Edomite, the 21.07
not destroy my n. out of my 24.21
Now the n. of the man was Nabal, and 25.03
and the n. of his wife Abigail. 25.03
to Nabal, and greet him in my n. 25.05
this to Nabal in the n. of David; 25.09
for as his n. is, so is he; 25.25
Nabal is his n., and folly is with 25.25
for me whomever I shall n. to you." 28.08
whose n. was Rizpah, the daughter of 2Sa 3.07
the n. of the one was Baanah, and 4.02
and the n. of the other Rechab, sons 4.02
And his n. was Mephibosheth. 4.04
Therefore the n. of that place is 5.20
called by the n. of the LORD of 6.02
people in the n. of the LORD of 6.18
and I will make for you a great n., 7.09
like the n. of the great ones of 7.09
He shall build a house for my n., 7.13
be his people, making himself a n., 7.23
and thy n. will be magnified for 7.26
And David won a n. for himself. 8.13
house of Saul whose n. was Ziba, 9.02
had a young son, whose n. was Mica. 9.12
son, and called his n. Solomon. 12.24
so he called his n. Jedidiah, 12.25
city, and it be called by my n. 12.28
beautiful sister, whose n. was Tamar; 13.01
whose n. was Jonadab, the son of 13.03
husband neither n. nor remnant 14.07
one daughter whose n. was Tamar; 14.27
whose n. was Shimei, the son of Gera; 16.05
son to keep my n. in remembrance"; 18.18
called the pillar after his own n., 18.18
whose n. was Sheba, the son of 20.01
nations, and sing praises to thy n. 22.50
and won a n. beside the three. 23.18
and won a n. beside the three 23.22
God make the n. of Solomon more 1Ki 1.47
been built for the n. of the LORD. 3.02
a house for the n. of the LORD his 5.03
a house for the n. of the LORD my 5.05
shall build the house for my n.' 5.05
the south and called its n. Jachin; 7.21
the north and called its n. Boaz. 7.21
a house, that my n. might be there; 8.16
a house for the n. of the LORD, 8.17
heart to build a house for my n., 8.18
shall build the house for my n.' 8.19
the house for the n. of the LORD, 8.20
'My n. shall be there,' that thou 8.29
to thee, and acknowledge thy n., 8.33
this place, and acknowledge thy n., 8.35
(for they shall hear of thy great n., 8.42
may know thy n. and fear thee, 8.43
I have built is called by thy n. 8.43
which I have built for thy n., 8.44
which I have built for thy n.; 8.48
and put my n. there for ever; 9.03
consecrated for my n. I will cast 9.07
concerning the n. of the LORD, 10.01
whose mother's n. was Zeruah, 11.26
where I have chosen to put my n. 11.36
the house of David, Josiah by n.; 13.02
of Israel, to put his n. there. 14.21
His mother's n. was Naamah the 14.21
His mother's n. was Naamah the 14.31
His mother's n. was Maacah the 15.02
His mother's n. was Maacah the 15.10
and called the n. of the city 16.24
after the n. of Shemer, the owner of 16.24
And you call on the n. of your god 18.24
I will call on the n. of the LORD; 18.24
and call on the n. of your god, 18.25
called on the n. of Baal from 18.26
saying, "Israel shall be your n."; 18.31
an altar in the n. of the LORD. 18.32
in Ahab's n. and sealed them with 21.08
the truth in the n. of the LORD?" 22.16
His mother's n. was Azubah the 22.42
cursed them in the n. of the LORD. 2Ki 2.24
and call on the n. of the LORD his 5.11
His mother's n. was Athaliah; 8.26
His mother's n. was Zibiah of 12.01
His mother's n. was Jehoaddin of 14.02
which is its n. to this day. 14.07
blot out the n. of Israel from 14.27
His mother's n. was Jecoliah of 15.02
His mother's n. was Jerusha the 15.33
His mother's n. was Abi the daughter 18.02
His mother's n. was Hephzibah. 21.01
"In Jerusalem will I put my n." 21.04
Israel, I will put my n. for ever; 21.07
His mother's n. was Meshullemeth the 21.19
His mother's n. was Jedidah the 22.01
which I said, My n. shall be there." 23.27
His mother's n. was Hamutal the 23.31

NAME (cont.)
and changed his n. to Jehoiakim. 2Ki 23.34
His mother's n. was Zebidah the 23.36
His mother's n. was Nehushta the 24.08
and changed his n. to Zedekiah. 24.17
His mother's n. was Hamutal the 24.18
the n. of the one was Peleg (for in 1Ch 1.19
and the n. of his brother Joktan. 1.19
the n. of whose city was Dinhabah. 1.43
and the n. of his city was Avith. 1.46
and the n. of his city was Pai, 1.50
and his wife's n. Mehetabel the 1.50
another wife, whose n. was Atarah; 2.26
The n. of Abishur's wife was Abihail, 2.29
Egyptian slave, whose n. was Jarha. 2.34
and the n. of their sister was 4.03
and his mother called his n. Jabez, 4.09
these mentioned by n. were princes 4.38
registered by n., came in the days 4.41
cities which are mentioned by n. 6.65
The n. of his sister was Maacah. 7.15
And the n. of the second was 7.15
son, and she called his n. Peresh; 7.16
and the n. of his brother was 7.16
and he called his n. Beriah, 7.23
and the n. of his wife was Maacah. 8.29
and the n. of his wife was Maacah, 9.35
and won a n. beside the three. 11.20
and won a n. beside the three 11.24
called by the n. of the LORD who 13.06
Therefore the n. of that place is 14.11
the people in the n. of the LORD, 16.02
call on his n., make known his 16.08
Glory in his holy n.; let the hearts 16.10
Ascribe to the LORD the glory due his n.; 16.29
we may give thanks to thy holy n., 16.35
and I will make for you a n., 17.08
like the n. of the great ones of 17.08
for thyself a n. for great and 17.21
and thy n. will be established and 17.24
had spoken in the n. of the LORD. 21.19
a house to the n. of the LORD my 22.07
shall not build a house to my n., 22.08
for his n. shall be Solomon, and I 22.09
He shall build a house for my n. 22.10
house built for the n. of the LORD." 22.19
blessings in his n. for ever. 23.13
may not build a house for my n., 28.03
God, and praise thy glorious n. 29.13
for thy holy n. comes from thy 29.16
a temple for the n. of the LORD, 2Ch 2.01
a house for the n. of the LORD my 2.04
that my n. might be there, and I 6.05
Jerusalem that my n. may be there 6.06
a house for the n. of the LORD, 6.07
heart to build a house for my n., 6.08
shall build the house for my n. 6.09
the house for the n. of the LORD, 6.10
thou hast promised to set thy n., 6.20
turn again and acknowledge thy n., 6.24
this place, and acknowledge thy n., 6.26
for the sake of thy great n., 6.32
may know thy n. and fear thee, 6.33
I have built is called by thy n. 6.33
which I have built for thy n., 6.34
which I have built for thy n., 6.38
called by my n. humble themselves, 7.14
house that my n. may be there for 7.16
which I have consecrated for my n., 7.20
of Israel to put his n. there. 12.13
His mother's n. was Naamah the 12.13
His mother's n. was Micaiah the 13.02
and in thy n. we have come against 14.11
the truth in the n. of the LORD?" 18.15
it a sanctuary for thy n., saying, 20.08
for thy n. is in this house, and cry 20.09
therefore the n. of that place 20.26
His mother's n. was Azubah the 20.31
His mother's n. was Athaliah, the 22.02
his mother's n. was Zibiah of 24.01
His mother's n. was Jehoaddan of 25.01
His mother's n. was Jecoliah of 26.03
His mother's n. was Jerushah the 27.01
LORD was there, whose n. was Oded; 28.09
mentioned by n. rose and took the 28.15
His mother's n. was Abijah the 29.01
designated by n. to distribute 31.19
Jerusalem shall my n. be for ever." 33.04
Israel, I will put my n. for ever; 33.07
to him in the n. of the LORD the 33.18
and changed his n. to Jehoiakim. 36.04
and was called by their n.). Ez 2.61
in the n. of the God of Israel who 5.01
to one whose n. was Sheshbazzar, 5.14
has caused his n. to dwell there 6.12
These were all mentioned by n. 8.20
each of them designated by n. 10.16
chosen, to make my n. dwell there. Neh 1.09
servants who delight to fear thy n.; 1.11
so they could give me an evil n., 6.13
and was called by their n.). 7.63
by thy glorious n. which is 9.05
and give him the n. Abraham; 9.07
and thou didst get thee a n., 9.10
them take oath in the n. of God, 13.25
the capital whose n. was Mordecai, Est 2.05
in her and she was summoned by n. 2.14
the king in the n. of Mordecai. 2.22
written in the n. of King Ahasuerus 3.12
in the n. of the king, and seal it 8.08
written in the n. of the king and 8.08
was in the n. of King Ahasuerus 8.10
the land of Uz, whose n. was Job; Job 1.01
blessed be the n. of the LORD. 1.21
and he has no n. in the street. 18.17
their n. is no longer remembered; 24.20
he called the n. of the first Jemimah; 42.14
and the n. of the second Keziah; 42.14
and the n. of the third Kerenhappuch. 42.14
who love thy n. may exult in thee. Ps 5.11
sing praise to the n. of the LORD, 7.17
majestic is thy n. in all the 8.01
majestic is thy n. in all the 8.09
sing praise to thy n., O Most High. 9.02
out their n. for ever and ever. 9.05
who know thy n. put their trust in 9.10
nations, and sing praises to thy n. 18.49
The n. of the God of Jacob protect 20.01
and in the n. of our God set up our 20.05
we boast of the n. of the LORD our 20.07
will tell of thy n. to my brethren; 22.22
Ascribe to the LORD the glory of his n.; 29.02
and give thanks to his holy n. 30.04
because we trust in his holy n. 33.21
and let us exalt his n. together! 34.03
will he die, and his n. perish? 41.05
through thy n. we tread down our 44.05
give thanks to thy n. for ever. 44.08
we had forgotten the n. of our God, 44.20
I will cause your n. to be celebrated 45.17
As thy n., O God, so thy praise 48.10
I will proclaim thy n., 52.09
by thy n., and vindicate me by thy 54.01
I will give thanks to thy n., 54.06
heritage of those who fear thy n. 61.05
will I ever sing praises to thy n., 61.08
up my hands and call on thy n. 63.04
sing the glory of his n.; give to him 66.02
to thee, sing praises to thy n. 66.04
Sing to God, sing praises to his n.; 68.04
his n. is the LORD, exult before him 68.04
I will praise the n. of God with a 69.30
who love his n. shall dwell in it. 69.36
May his n. endure for ever, his fame 72.17

NAME (cont.)

Blessed be his glorious n. for ever; Ps 72.19
the dwelling place of thy n. 74.07
enemy to revile thy n. for ever? 74.10
an impious people reviles thy n. 74.18
the poor and needy praise thy n. 74.21
we call on thy n. and recount thy 75.01
his n. is great in Israel. 76.01
kingdoms that do not call on thy n.! 79.06
salvation, for the glory of thy n.; 79.09
life, and we will call on thy n.! 80.18
let the n. of Israel be remembered 83.04
that they may seek thy n., O LORD. 83.16
whose n. is the LORD, art the Most 83.18
O Lord, and shall glorify thy n. 86.09
unite my heart to fear thy n. 86.11
and I will glorify thy n. for ever. 86.12
and Hermon joyously praise thy n. 89.12
who exult in thy n. all the day, 89.16
and in my n. shall his horn be 89.24
him, because he knows my n. 91.14
praises to thy n., O Most High; 92.01
Sing to the LORD, bless his n.; 96.02
Ascribe to the LORD the glory due his n.; 96.08
and give thanks to his holy n.! 97.12
praise thy great and terrible n.! 99.03
among those who called on his n. 99.06
Give thanks to him, bless his n.! 100.04
deride me use my n. for a curse. 102.08
thy n. endures to all generations. 102.12
will fear the n. of the LORD, 102.15
declare in Zion the n. of the LORD, 102.21
is within me, bless his holy n.! 103.01
call on his n., make known his 105.01
Glory in his holy n.; let the hearts 105.03
to thy holy n. and glory in thy 106.47
may his n. be blotted out in the 109.13
Holy and terrible is his n.! 111.09
LORD, praise the n. of the LORD! 113.01
Blessed be the n. of the LORD from 113.02
its setting the n. of the LORD is 113.03
but to thy n. give glory, for the 115.01
Then I called on the n. of the LORD: 116.04
and call on the n. of the LORD, 116.13
and call on the n. of the LORD. 116.17
in the n. of the LORD I cut them 118.10
in the n. of the LORD I cut them 118.11
in the n. of the LORD I cut them 118.12
who enters in the n. of the lord! 118.26
I remember thy n. in the night, O 119.55
wont toward those who love thy n. 119.132
give thanks to the n. of the LORD. 122.04
Our help is in the n. of the LORD, 124.08
We bless you in the n. of the LORD! 129.08
Praise the n. of the LORD, give 135.01
sing to his n., for he is gracious! 135.03
Thy n., O LORD, endures for ever, thy 135.13
thanks to thy n. for thy steadfast 138.02
everything thy n. and thy word. 138.02
shall give thanks to thy n.; 140.13
that I may give thanks to thy n.! 142.07
and bless thy n. for ever and ever. 145.01
and praise thy n. for ever and 145.02
bless his holy n. for ever and 145.21
Let them praise the n. of the LORD! 148.05
Let them praise the n. of the LORD, 148.13
for his n. alone is exalted; 148.13
Let them praise his n. with dancing, 149.03
but the n. of the wicked will rot. Pro 10.07
The n. of the LORD is a strong 18.10
"Scoffer" is the n. of the proud, 21.24
A good n. is to be chosen rather 22.01
What is his n., and what is his son's n.? 30.04
and profane the n. of my God. 30.09
and in darkness its n. is covered; Ecc 6.04
A good n. is better than precious 7.01
your n. is oil poured out; Sol 1.03

only let us be called by your n.; Is 4.01
and shall call his n. Immanuel. 7.14
"Call his n. Mahershalalhashbaz; 8.03
and his n. will be called "Wonderful 9.06
to the LORD, call upon his n.; 12.04
proclaim that his n. is exalted. 12.04
off from Babylon n. and remnant, 14.22
place of the n. of the LORD of 18.07
to the n. of the LORD, the God of 24.15
exalt thee, I will praise thy n.; 25.01
thy memorial n. is the desire of 26.08
but thy n. alone we acknowledge. 26.13
midst, they will sanctify my n.; 29.23
Behold, the n. of the LORD comes 30.27
They shall n. it No Kingdom There, 34.12
by number, calling them all by n.; 40.26
sun, and he shall call on my n.; 41.25
I am the LORD, that is my n.; 42.08
called you by n., you are mine. 43.01
every one who is called by my n., 43.07
call himself by the n. of Jacob, 44.05
himself by the n. of Israel. 44.05
of Israel, who call you by your n. 45.03
my chosen, I call you by your n., 45.04
the LORD of hosts is his n.— 47.04
who are called by the n. of Israel, 48.01
who swear by the n. of the LORD, 48.01
the LORD of hosts is his n. 48.02
for how should my n. be profaned? 48.11
their n. would never be cut off or 48.19
body of my mother he named my n. 49.01
trusts in the n. of the LORD and 50.10
roar—the LORD of hosts is his n. 51.15
all the day my n. is despised. 52.05
Therefore my people shall know my n.; 52.06
the LORD of hosts is his n.; 54.05
monument and a n. better than sons 56.05
an everlasting n. which shall not 56.05
to love the n. of the LORD, and to 56.06
whose n. is Holy: "I dwell in the 57.15
shall fear the n. of the LORD from 59.19
for the n. of the LORD your God, and 60.09
called by a new n. which the mouth 62.02
for himself an everlasting n., 63.12
to make for thyself a glorious n. 63.14
our Redeemer from of old is thy n. 63.16
those who are not called by thy n. 63.19
to make thy n. known to thy adversaries, 64.02
There is no one that calls upon thy n., 64.07
nation that did not call on my n. 65.01
leave your n. to my chosen for a 65.15
he will call by a different n. 65.15
descendants and your n. remain. 66.22
house, which is called by my n., Jer 7.10
house, which is called by my n., 7.11
where I made my n. dwell at first, 7.12
the house which is called by my n., 7.14
is called by my n., to defile it. 7.30
and thy n. is great in might. 10.06
the LORD of hosts is his n. 10.16
peoples that call not on thy n.; 10.25
that his n. be remembered no more." 11.19
not prophesy in the n. of the LORD, 11.21
of my people, to swear by my n., 12.16
a n., a praise, and a glory, but they 13.11
of us, and we are called by thy n.; 14.09
are prophesying lies in my n.; 14.14
prophesy in my n. although I did 14.15
for I am called by thy n., 15.16
shall know that my n. is the LORD." 16.21
LORD does not call your n. Pashhur, 20.03
him, or speak any more in his n." 20.09
And this is the n. by which he will 23.06
said who prophesy lies in my n., 23.25
forget my n. by their dreams which 23.27
fathers forgot my n. for Baal? 23.27
the city which is called by my n., 25.29

NAME (cont.)
prophesied in the n. of the LORD, Jer 26.09
to us in the n. of the LORD our 26.16
prophesied in the n. of the LORD, 26.20
are prophesying falsely in my n., 27.15
are prophesying to you in my n.; 29.09
prophesying a lie to you in my n.: 29.21
spoken in my n. lying words which 29.23
letters in your n. to all the 29.25
the LORD of hosts is his n.: 31.35
God whose n. is the LORD of hosts, 32.18
mankind, and hast made thee a n., 32.20
is called by my n., to defile it. 32.34
to establish it—the LORD is his n.: 33.02
city shall be to me a n. of joy, 33.09
And this is the n. by which it will 33.16
the house which is called by my n.; 34.15
and profaned my n. when each of 34.16
spoken to us in the n. of the LORD, 44.16
I have sworn by my great n., 44.26
that my n. shall no more be invoked 44.26
Call the n. of Pharaoh, king of 46.17
whose n. is the LORD of hosts, like 46.18
whose n. is the LORD of hosts. 48.15
about him, and all who know his n.; 48.17
the LORD of hosts is his n. 50.34
the LORD of hosts is his n. 51.19
whose n. is the LORD of hosts. 51.57
His mother's n. was Hamutal the 52.01
"I called on thy n., O LORD, from Lam 3.55
But I acted for the sake of my n., Eze 20.09
But I acted for the sake of my n., 20.14
and acted for the sake of my n., 20.22
So its n. is called Bamah to this 20.29
but my holy n. you shall no more 20.39
Oholah was the n. of the elder and 23.04
and Oholibah the n. of her sister. 23.04
man, write down the n. of this day, 24.02
came, they profaned my holy n., 36.20
But I had concern for my holy n., 36.21
but for the sake of my holy n., 36.22
the holiness of my great n., 36.23
"And my holy n. I will make known 39.07
not let my holy n. be profaned any 39.07
I will be jealous for my holy n. 39.25
shall no more defile my holy n., 43.07
defiled my holy n. by their 43.08
And the n. of the city henceforth 48.35
"Blessed be the n. of God for ever Dan 2.20
whose n. was Belteshazzar, "Are you 2.26
Belteshazzar after the n. of my god, 4.08
whose n. was Belteshazzar, was 4.19
who spoke in thy n. to our kings, 9.06
hand, and hast made thee a n., 9.15
the city which is called by thy n.; 9.18
thy people are called by thy n." 9.19
every one whose n. shall be found 12.01
said to him, "Call his n. Jezreel; Hos 1.04
"Call her n. Not pitied, for I will 1.06
"Call his n. Not my people, for you 1.09
shall be mentioned by n. no more. 2.17
God of hosts, the LORD is his n.: 12.05
and praise the n. of the LORD your Joe 2.26
call upon the n. of the LORD shall 2.32
so that my holy n. is profaned; Amo 2.07
LORD, the God of hosts, is his n.! 4.13
of the earth, the LORD is his n., 5.08
whose n. is the God of hosts. 5.27
not mention the n. of the LORD." 6.10
of the earth—the LORD is his n. 9.06
nations who are called by my n., 9.12
walk each in the n. of its god, Mic 4.05
walk in the n. of the LORD our God 4.05
majesty of the n. of the LORD his 5.04
it is sound wisdom to fear thy n.: 6.09
more shall your n. be perpetuated; Nah 1.14
of Baal and the n. of the idolatrous Zep 1.04

may call on the n. of the LORD and 3.09
seek refuge in the n. of the LORD, 3.12
of him who swears falsely by my n.; Zec 5.04
the man whose n. is the Branch: for 6.12
and they shall glory in his n., 10.12
speak lies in the n. of the LORD'; 13.03
They will call on my n., and I will 13.09
LORD will be one and his n. one. 14.09
you, O priests, who despise my n. Mal 1.06
say, 'How have we despised thy n.?' 1.06
its setting my n. is great among 1.11
place incense is offered to my n., 1.11
for my n. is great among the 1.11
and my n. is feared among the 1.14
it to heart to give glory to my n., 2.02
me, he stood in awe of my n. 2.05
the LORD and thought on his n. 3.16
you who fear my n. the sun of 4.02
and you shall call his n. Jesus, Mt 1.21
and his n. shall be called Emmanuel" 1.23
a son; and he called his n. Jesus. 1.25
art in heaven, Hallowed be thy n. 6.09
did we not prophesy in your n., 7.22
and cast out demons in your n., 7.22
do many mighty works in your n.?' 7.22
and in his n. will the Gentiles 12.21
such child in my n. receives me; 18.05
two or three are gathered in my n., 18.20
he who comes in the n. of the Lord! 21.09
he who comes in the n. of the LORD.'" 23.39
For many will come in my n., 24.05
upon a man of Cyrene, Simon by n.; 27.32
them in the n. of the Father and 28.19
And Jesus asked him, "What is your n.?" Mk 5.09
He replied, "My n. is Legion; for 5.09
of the synagogue, Jairus by n.; 5.22
for Jesus' n. had become known. 6.14
such child in my n. receives me; 9.37
man casting out demons in your n., 9.38
work in my n. will be able soon 9.39
because you bear the n. of Christ, 9.41
he who comes in the n. of the Lord! 11.09
Many will come in my n., saying, 13.06
in my n. they will cast out demons; * 16.17
of Aaron, and her n. was Elizabeth. Lk 1.05
and you shall call his n. John. 1.13
to a man whose n. was Joseph, 1.27
and the virgin's n. was Mary. 1.27
and you shall call his n. Jesus. 1.31
things for me, and holy is his n. 1.49
your kindred is called by this n." 1.61
tablet, and wrote, "His n. is John." 1.63
the n. given by the angel before he 2.21
whose n. was Simeon, and this man 2.25
you, and cast out your n. as evil, 6.22
Jesus then asked him, "What is your n.?" 8.30
this child in my n. receives me, 9.48
man casting out demons in your n., 9.49
are subject to us in your n.!" 10.17
say: "Father, hallowed be thy n. 11.02
he who comes in the n. of the Lord!'" 13.35
who comes in the n. of the Lord! 19.38
for many will come in my n., 21.08
preached in his n. to all nations, 24.47
sent from God, whose n. was John. Jn 1.06
him, who believed in his n., 1.12
believed in his n. when they saw 2.23
believed in the n. of the only Son 3.18
I have come in my Father's n., 5.43
if another comes in his own n., 5.43
own sheep by n. and leads them out 10.03
works that I do in my Father's n., 10.25
he who comes in the n. of the Lord, 12.13
Father, glorify thy n." Then a voice 12.28
Whatever you ask in my n., I will 14.13
anything in my n., I will do it. 14.14
whom the Father will send in my n., 14.26

NAME (cont.)

you ask the Father in my n., Jn 15.16
he will give it to you in my n. 16.23
Hitherto you have asked nothing in my n.; 16.24
In that day you will ask in my n.; 16.26
manifested thy n. to the men whom 17.06
them in thy n. which thou hast 17.11
them in thy n. which thou hast 17.12
I made known to them thy n., 17.26
The slave's n. was Malchus. 18.10
you may have life in his n. 20.31
calls on the n. of the Lord shall Ac 2.21
of you in the n. of Jesus Christ 2.38
in the n. of Jesus Christ of 3.06
And his n., by faith in his name, 3.16
And his name, by faith in his n., 3.16
or by what n. did you do this?" 4.07
that by the n. of Jesus Christ of 4.10
is no other n. under heaven given 4.12
no more to any one in this n. 4.17
or teach at all in the n. of Jesus. 4.18
through the n. of thy holy servant 4.30
you not to teach in this n., 5.28
not to speak in the n. of Jesus, 5.40
to suffer dishonor for the n. 5.41
of God and the n. of Jesus Christ, 8.12
baptized in the n. of the Lord 8.16
to bind all who call upon thy n." 9.14
to carry my n. before the Gentiles 9.15
must suffer for the sake of my n. 9.16
of those who called on this n.? 9.21
preached boldly in the n. of Jesus. 9.27
preaching boldly in the n. of the Lord. 9.29
forgiveness of sins through his n. 10.43
baptized in the n. of Jesus Christ 10.48
of John whose other n. was Mark, 12.12
them John whose other n. was Mark. 12.25
meaning of his n.) withstood them, 13.08
out of them a people for his n. 15.14
Gentiles who are called by my n., 15.17
you in the n. of Jesus Christ to 16.18
baptized in the n. of the Lord 19.05
pronounce the n. of the Lord Jesus 19.13
and the n. of the Lord Jesus was 19.17
Jerusalem for the n. of the Lord 21.13
away your sins, calling on his n.' 22.16
in opposing the n. of Jesus of 26.09
the sake of his n. among all the Rom 1.05
"The n. of God is blasphemed among 2.24
so that my n. may be proclaimed in 9.17
calls upon the n. of the Lord will 10.13
the Gentiles, and sing to thy n."; 15.09
call on the n. of our Lord Jesus 1Co 1.02
by the n. of our Lord Jesus Christ, 1.10
you baptized in the n. of Paul? 1.13
that you were baptized in my n. 1.15
in the n. of the Lord Jesus on the 5.04
who bears the n. of brother if he 5.11
justified in the n. of the Lord 6.11
and above every n. that is named, Eph 1.21
thanks in the n. of our Lord Jesus 5.20
on him the n. which is above every n., Php 2.09
that at the n. of Jesus every knee 2.10
everything in the n. of the Lord Col 3.17
so that the n. of our Lord Jesus 2Th 1.12
in the n. of our Lord Jesus Christ, 3.06
so that the n. of God and the 1Ti 6.01
who names the n. of the Lord 2Ti 2.19
angels as the n. he has obtained Heb 1.04
proclaim thy n. to my brethren, 2.12
is first, by translation of his n., 7.02
of lips that acknowledge his n. 13.15
that honorable n. by which you are Jas 2.07
who spoke in the n. of the Lord. 5.10
him with oil in the n. of the Lord; 5.14
reproached for the n. of Christ, 1Pe 4.14
but under that n. let him glorify 4.16
believe in the n. of his Son Jesus 1Jn 3.23
believe in the n. of the Son of 5.13
hold fast my n. and you did not Rev 2.13
with a new n. written on the stone 2.17
you have the n. of being alive, and 3.01
not blot his n. out of the book of 3.05
confess his n. before my Father 3.05
my word and have not denied my n. 3.08
will write on him the n. of my God, 3.12
and the n. of the city of my God, 3.12
out of heaven, and my own new n. 3.12
and its rider's n. was Death, 6.08
The n. of the star is Wormwood. 8.11
his n. in Hebrew is Abaddon, and in 9.11
saints, and those who fear thy n., 11.18
a blasphemous n. upon its heads. 13.01
blaspheming his n. and his dwelling, 13.06
every one whose n. has not been 13.08
n. of the beast or the number of its n. 13.17
who had his n. and his Father's 14.01
his Father's n. written on their 14.01
receives the mark of its n. 14.11
its image and the number of its n., 15.02
fear and glorify thy n., O LORD? 15.04
they cursed the n. of God who had 16.09
was written a n. of mystery: 17.05
and he has a n. inscribed which no 19.12
and the n. by which he is called is 19.13
on his thigh he has a n. inscribed, 19.16
and if any one's n. was not found 20.15
and his n. shall be on their 22.04

NAMED

them and n. them Man when they Gen 5.02
after his image, and n. him Seth. 5.03
Isaac shall your descendants be n. 21.12
which he had n. in the hearing of 23.16
n. in the order of their birth: 25.13
Esau said, "Is he not rightly n. Jacob? 27.36
Therefore he n. it Galeed, 31.48
the place was n. Abelmizraim; 50.11
one of whom was n. Shiphrah and Ex 1.15
and she n. him Moses, for she said, 2.10
bitter; therefore it was n. Marah. 15.23
took these men who have been n., Num 1.17
one n. Eldad, and the other n. Medad, 11.26
And they n. the city Dan, after the Ju 18.29
They n. him Obed; he was the Ru 4.17
And she n. the child Ichabod, saying, 1Sa 4.21
Philistines a champion n. Goliath, 17.04
n. Jesse, who had eight sons. 17.12
n. Abiathar, escaped and fled after 22.20
son of a man n. Ithra the Ishmaelite, 2Sa 17.25
of Jacob, whom he n. Israel. 2Ki 17.34
were expressly n. to come and make 1Ch 12.31
and expressly n. to give thanks to 16.41
man of God were n. among the tribe 23.14
though they n. lands their own. Ps 49.11
has come to be has already been n., Ecc 6.10
of evildoers nevermore be n.! Is 14.20
body of my mother he n. my name. 49.01
a sentry there n. Irijah the son Jer 37.13
the city being n. after the tribes Eze 48.31
he who was n. Belteshazzar after Dan 4.08
whom the king n. Belteshazzar. 5.12
to Daniel, who was n. Belteshazzar. 10.01
one I n. Grace, the other I n. Union. Zec 11.07
n. Joseph, who also was a disciple Mt 27.57
there was a priest n. Zechariah, Lk 1.05
to a city of Galilee n. Nazareth, 1.26
they would have n. him Zechariah 1.59
n. Levi, sitting at the tax office; 5.27
them twelve, whom he n. apostles; 6.13
Simon, whom he n. Peter, and Andrew 6.14
And there came a man n. Jairus, 8.41
and a woman n. Martha received him 10.38
his gate lay a poor man n. Lazarus, 16.20
And there was a man n. Zacchaeus; 19.02

NAMED (cont.)

Now there was a man n. Joseph from Lk 23.50
were going to a village n. Emmaus, 24.13
n. Cleopas, answered him, "Are you 24.18
n. Nicodemus, a ruler of the Jews. Jn 3.01
But a man n. Ananias with his wife Ac 5.01
Pharisee in the council n. Gamaliel, 5.34
at the feet of a young man n. Saul. 7.58
But there was a man n. Simon who 8.09
a disciple at Damascus n. Ananias. 9.10
Judas for a man of Tarsus n. Saul; 9.11
has seen a man n. Ananias come in 9.12
There he found a man n. Aeneas, 9.33
was at Joppa a disciple n. Tabitha, 9.36
there was a man n. Cornelius, 10.01
And one of them n. Agabus stood up 11.28
a maid n. Rhoda came to answer. 12.13
Jewish false prophet, n. Bar-Jesus. 13.06
n. Timothy, the son of a Jewish 16.01
One who heard us and was a woman n. Lydia, 16.14
and a woman n. Damaris and others 17.34
And he found a Jew n. Aquila, 18.02
house of a man n. Titius Justus, 18.07
Now a Jew n. Apollos, a native of 18.24
high priest n. Sceva were doing 19.14
For a man n. Demetrius, a silversmith, 19.24
And a young man n. Eutychus was 20.09
a prophet n. Agabus came down from 21.10
of the Augustan Cohort, n. Julius. 27.01
n. Publius, who received us and 28.07
Isaac shall your descendants be n. Rom 9.07
where Christ has already been n., 15.20
and above every name that is n., Eph 1.21
in heaven and on earth is n., 3.15
must not even be n. among you, 5.03
rather than one n. after the order Heb 7.11
Isaac shall your descendants be n. 11.18

NAMELY

n., of the people of Ephraim, their Num 1.32
n., Ishmael the son of Nethaniah, 2Ki 25.23
n., the Reubenites, the Gadites, and 1Ch 5.26
n., Asaph the son of Berechiah, son 6.39
n. of Tola, mighty warriors of their 7.02
n. the sons of Jeshua and Joab, two Ez 2.06
n. of Hezekiah, ninety-eight. 2.16
n., to send us ministers for the 8.17
n. Sherebiah with his sons and 8.18
n. the sons of Jeshua and Joab, two Neh 7.11
n. of Hezekiah, ninety-eight. 7.21
n. the house of Jeshua, nine hundred 7.39
n. of Kadmiel of the sons of 7.43
of Jerusalem, n., seventy years. Dan 9.02
n., his eternal power and deity, has Rom 1.20

NAME'S

for his great n. sake, because it 1Sa 12.22
from a far country for thy n. sake 1Ki 8.41
of righteousness for his n. sake. Ps 23.03
For thy n. sake, O LORD, pardon my 25.11
for thy n. sake lead me and guide 31.03
forgive our sins, for thy n. sake! 79.09
Yet he saved them for his n. sake, 106.08
deal on my behalf for thy n. sake; 109.21
For thy n. sake, O LORD, preserve my 143.11
"For my n. sake I defer my anger, Is 48.09
you out for my n. sake have said, 66.05
us, act, O LORD, for thy n. sake; Jer 14.07
Do not spurn us, for thy n. sake; 14.21
I deal with you for my n. sake, Eze 20.44
be hated by all for my n. sake. Mt 10.22
for my n. sake, will receive a 19.29
by all nations for my n. sake. 24.09
be hated by all for my n. sake. Mk 13.13
kings and governors for my n. sake. Lk 21.12
be hated by all for my n. sake. 21.17
and bearing up for my n. sake, Rev 2.03

NAMES

The man gave n. to all cattle, and Gen 2.20
These are the n. of the sons of 25.13
of Ishmael and these are their n., 25.16
gave them the n. which his father 26.18
These are the n. of Esau's sons: 36.10
These are the n. of the chiefs of 36.40
by their n.: the chiefs Timna, Alvah, 36.40
Now these are the n. of the descendants 46.08
These are the n. of the sons of Ex 1.01
These are the n. of the sons of 6.16
no mention of the n. of other gods, 23.13
on them the n. of the sons of 28.09
six of their n. on the one stone, 28.10
and the n. of the remaining six on 28.10
stones with the n. of the sons of 28.11
bear their n. before the LORD upon 28.12
n. according to the n. of the sons 28.21
shall bear the n. of the sons of 28.29
according to the n. of the sons of 39.06
n. according to the n. of the sons 39.14
according to the number of n., Num 1.02
And these are the n. of the men who 1.05
the number of n. from twenty years 1.18
according to the number of n., 1.20
according to the number of n., 1.22
according to the number of the n., 1.24
according to the number of n., 1.26
according to the number of n., 1.28
according to the number of n., 1.30
according to the number of n., 1.32
according to the number of n., 1.34
according to the number of n., 1.36
according to the number of n., 1.38
according to the number of n., 1.40
according to the number of n., 1.42
These are the n. of the sons of 3.02
these are the n. of the sons of 3.03
were the sons of Levi by their n.: 3.17
And these are the n. of the sons of 3.18
upward, taking their number by n. 3.40
according to the number of n., 3.43
And these were their n.: 13.04
These were the n. of the men whom 13.16
and the n. of the daughters of 26.33
according to the number of n. 26.53
according to the n. of the tribes 26.55
The n. of his daughters were: Mahlah, 27.01
Baalmeon (their n. to be changed), 32.38
they gave other n. to the cities 32.38
"These are the n. of the men who 34.17
These are the n. of the men: Of the 34.19
these are the n. of his daughters: Jos 17.03
mention of the n. of their gods, 23.07
and the n. of his two sons were Ru 1.02
and the n. of his two daughters 1Sa 14.49
and the n. of his three sons who 17.13
And these are the n. of those who 2Sa 5.14
These are the n. of the mighty men 23.08
These were their n.: Benhur, in the 1Ki 4.08
And these are the n. of the sons of 1Ch 6.17
six sons, and these are their n. 8.38
six sons and these are their n.: 9.44
These are the n. of the children 14.04
number of the n. of the individuals 23.24
"What are the n. of the men who are Ez 5.04
We also asked them their n., 5.10
write down the n. of the men at the 5.10
their n. being Eliphelet, Jeuel, and 8.13
out or take their n. upon my lips. Ps 16.04
he gives to all of them their n. 147.04
As for their n., Oholah is Samaria, Eze 23.04
"These are the n. of the tribes: 48.01
chief of the eunuchs gave them n.: Dan 1.07
will remove the n. of the Baals Hos 2.17
cut off the n. of the idols from Zec 13.02
The n. of the twelve apostles are Mt 10.02

NAMES (cont.)
that your n. are written in heaven." Lk 10.20
about words and n. and your own Ac 18.15
whose n. are in the book of life. Php 4.03
every one who n. the name of the 2Ti 2.19
Yet you have still a few n. in Sardis, Rev 3.04
which was full of blasphemous n., 17.03
on earth whose n. have not been 17.08
the gates the n. of the twelve 21.12
them the twelve n. of the twelve 21.14

NAOMI
and the name of his wife N., Ru 1.02
But Elimelech, the husband of N., 1.03
But N. said to her two daughters-in-law, 1.08
But N. said, "Turn back, my daughters, 1.11
And when N. saw that she was 1.18
and the women said, "Is this N.?" 1.19
She said to them, "Do not call me N., 1.20
Why call me N., when the LORD has 1.21
So N. returned, and Ruth the Moabitess 1.22
Now N. had a kinsman of her husband's, 2.01
And Ruth the Moabitess said to N., 2.02
came back with N. from the country 2.06
And N. said to her daughter-in-law, 2.20
N. also said to her, "The man is a 2.20
And N. said to Ruth, her daughter-in-law, 2.22
Then N. her mother-in-law said to 3.01
"N., who has come back from the 4.03
buy the field from the hand of N., 4.05
the hand of N. all that belonged 4.09
Then the women said to N., 4.14
Then N. took the child and laid him 4.16
saying, "A son has been born to N." 4.17

NAPHATH
Megiddo and its villages; the third is N. Jos 17.11

NAPHATHDOR
the king of Dor in N., one; Jos 12.23
in all N. (he had Taphath the 1Ki 4.11

NAPHISH
Hadad, Tema, Jetur, N., and Kedemah. Gen 25.15
Jetur, N., and Kedemah. 1Ch 1.31
the Hagrites, Jetur, N., and Nodab; 5.19

NAPHOTHDOR
lowland, and in N. on the west, Jos 11.02

NAPHTALI
so she called his name N. Gen 30.08
Bilhah, Rachel's maid: Dan and N. 35.25
The sons of N.: Jahzeel, Guni, Jezer, 46.24
N. is a hind let loose, that bears 49.21
Dan and N., Gad and Asher. Ex 1.04
from N., Ahira the son of Enan. Num 1.15
Of the people of N., their generations, 1.42
of the tribe of N. was fifty-three 1.43
Then the tribe of N., the leader 2.29
the people of N. being Ahira the 2.29
Enan, the leader of the men of N.: 7.78
of the men of N. was Ahira the son 10.27
from the tribe of N., Nahbi the 13.14
The sons of N. according to their 26.48
the families of N. according to 26.50
tribe of the sons of N. a leader, 34.28
Gad, Asher, Zebulun, Dan, and N. Deu 27.13
And of N. he said, "O N., satisfied 33.23
all N., the land of Ephraim and 34.02
lot came out for the tribe of N., Jos 19.32
for the tribe of N., according to 19.32
the inheritance of the tribe of N. 19.39
Galilee in the hill country of N., 20.07
of Asher, from the tribe of N., 21.06
and out of the tribe of N., 21.32
N. did not drive out the inhabitants Ju 1.33
son of Abinoam from Kedesh in N., 4.06
the tribe of N. and the tribe of 4.06
summoned Zebulun and N. to Kedesh; 4.10
N. too, on the heights of the field. 5.18
messengers to Asher, Zebulun, and N.; 6.35
called out from N. and from Asher 7.23
Ahimaaz, in N. (he had taken Basemath 1Ki 4.15
son of a widow of the tribe of N., 7.14
Chinneroth, with all the land of N. 15.20
and Galilee, all the land of N.; 2Ki 15.29
Joseph, Benjamin, N., Gad, and Asher. 1Ch 2.02
N., and Manasseh in Bashan. 6.62
and out of the tribe of N.: 6.76
The sons of N.: Jahziel, Guni, Jezer, 7.13
Of N. a thousand commanders with 12.34
far as Issachar and Zebulun and N., 12.40
for N., Jeremoth the son of 27.19
and all the store-cities of N. 2Ch 16.04
and as far as N., in their ruins 34.06
of Zebulun, the princes of N. Ps 68.27
land of Zebulun and the land of N., Is 9.01
side to the west, N., one portion. Eze 48.03
Adjoining the territory of N., 48.04
gate of Asher, and the gate of N. 48.34
the territory of Zebulun and N., Mt 4.13
land of Zebulun and the land of N., 4.15
twelve thousand of the tribe of N., Rev 7.06

NAPHTUHIM
father of Ludim, Anamim, Lehabim, N., Gen 10.13
father of Ludim, Anamim, Lehabim, N., 1Ch 1.11

NAPKIN
which I kept laid away in a n.; Lk 19.20
and the n., which had been on his Jn 20.07

NARCISSUS
Lord who belong to the family of N. Rom 16.11

NARD
my n. gave forth its fragrance. Sol 1.12
choicest fruits, henna with n., 4.13
n. and saffron, calamus and cinnamon, 4.14
alabaster jar of ointment of pure n., Mk 14.03
ointment of pure n. and anointed Jn 12.03

NARRATIVE
to compile a n. of the things which Lk 1.01

NARROW
LORD stood in a n. path between Num 22.24
ahead, and stood in a n. place, 22.26
of Ephraim is too n. for you. Jos 17.15
pit; an adventuress is a n. well. Pro 23.27
covering too n. to wrap oneself in Is 28.20
you will be too n. for your 49.19
ears: 'The place is too n. for me; 49.20
"Enter by the n. gate; for the Mt 7.13
For the gate is n. and the way is 7.14
"Strive to enter by the n. door; Lk 13.24

NARROWER
Now the upper chambers were n., Eze 42.05

NARROWING
n. inward into their jambs in the Eze 40.16

NATHAN
Shammua, Shobab, N., Solomon, 2Sa 5.14
the king said to N. the prophet, 7.02
And N. said to the king, "Go, do all 7.03
the word of the LORD came to N., 7.04
all this vision, N. spoke to David. 7.17
And the LORD sent N. to David. 12.01
and he said to N., "As the LORD 12.05
N. said to David, "You are the man. 12.07
David said to N., "I have sinned 12.13
And N. said to David, "The LORD also 12.13
Then N. went to his house. And the 12.15
and sent a message by N. the prophet; 12.25

NATHAN (cont.)
Igal the son of N. of Zobah, Bani 2Sa 23.36
and N. the prophet, and Shimei, and 1Ki 1.08
did not invite N. the prophet or 1.10
Then N. said to Bathsheba the 1.11
the king, N. the prophet came in. 1.22
the king, "Here is N. the prophet." 1.23
And N. said, "My lord the king, have 1.24
N. the prophet, and Benaiah the son 1.32
the priest and N. the prophet 1.34
N. the prophet, and Benaiah the son 1.38
N. the prophet, and Benaiah the son 1.44
the priest and N. the prophet have 1.45
Azariah the son of N. was over the 4.05
the son of N. was priest and king's 4.05
the father of N. and N. of Zabad, 1Ch 2.36
N., and Solomon, four by Bathshua, 3.05
Joel the brother of N., Mibhar the 11.38
Shammua, Shobab, N., Solomon, 14.04
David said to N. the prophet, 17.01
And N. said to David, "Do all that 17.02
the word of the LORD came to N., 17.03
all this vision, N. spoke to David. 17.15
the Chronicles of N. the prophet, 29.29
in the history of N. the prophet, 2Ch 9.29
king's seer and of N. the prophet; 29.25
N., Zechariah, and Meshullam, leading Ez 8.16
Shelemiah, N., Adaiah, 10.39
of the house of N. by itself, Zec 12.12
the son of N., the son of David, Lk 3.31

NATHANAEL
Philip found N., and said to him, Jn 1.45
N. said to him, "Can anything good 1.46
Jesus saw N. coming to him, and said 1.47
N. said to him, "How do you know me?" 1.48
N. answered him, "Rabbi, you are the 1.49
N. of Cana in Galilee, the sons of 21.02

NATHANMELECH
the chamber of N. the chamberlain, 2Ki 23.11

NATION
And I will make of you a great n., Gen 12.02
judgment on the n. which they 15.14
and I will make him a great n. 17.20
shall become a great and mighty n., 18.18
And I will make a n. of the son of 21.13
for I will make him a great n." 21.18
a n. and a company of nations shall 35.11
will there make of you a great n. 46.03
land of Egypt since it became a n. Ex 9.24
a kingdom of priests and a holy n. 19.06
but of you I will make a great n." 32.10
too that this n. is thy people." 33.13
in all the earth or in any n.; 34.10
vomited out the n. that was before Lev 18.28
customs of the n. which I am 20.23
make of you a n. greater and Num 14.12
this great n. is a wise and Deu 4.06
For what great n. is there that has 4.07
And what great n. is there that has 4.08
go and take a n. for himself from 4.34
from the midst of another n., 4.34
make of you a n. mightier and 9.14
and there he became a n., 26.05
A n. which you have not known shall 28.33
to a n. that neither you nor your 28.36
will bring a n. against you from 28.49
a n. whose language you do not 28.49
a n. of stern countenance, who shall 28.50
provoke them with a foolish n. 32.21
"For they are a n. void of counsel, 32.28
until all the n. finished passing Jos 3.17
When all the n. had finished 4.01
till all the n., the men of war 5.06
circumcising of all the n. was done, 5.08
until the n. took vengeance on 10.13
What other n. on earth is like thy 2Sa 7.23
his people a n. and its gods? 7.23
there is no n. or kingdom whither 1Ki 18.10
take an oath of the kingdom or n., 18.10
But every n. still made gods of its 2Ki 17.29
every n. in the cities in which 17.29
wandering from n. to n., from one 1Ch 16.20
What other n. on earth is like thy 17.21
n. against n. and city against city, 2Ch 15.06
no god of any n. or kingdom has 32.15
him, whether it be a n. or a man?— Job 34.29
Blessed is the n. whose God is the Ps 33.12
"Come, let us wipe them out as a n.; 83.04
wandering from n. to n., from one 105.13
rejoice in the gladness of thy n., 106.05
not dealt thus with any other n.; 147.20
Righteousness exalts a n., Pro 14.34
Ah, sinful n., a people laden with Is 1.04
n. shall not lift up sword against n., 2.04
raise a signal for a n. afar off, 5.26
Thou hast multiplied the n., 9.03
Against a godless n. I send him, 10.06
answer the messengers of the n.? 14.32
to a n., tall and smooth, to a 18.02
a n. mighty and conquering, whose 18.02
a n. mighty and conquering, whose 18.07
the righteous n. which keeps faith 26.02
But thou hast increased the n., 26.15
O LORD, thou hast increased the n.; 26.15
people, and give ear to me, my n.; 51.04
if they were a n. that did righteousness 58.02
For the n. and kingdom that will 60.12
and the smallest one a mighty n.; 60.22
to a n. that did not call on my 65.01
Shall a n. be brought forth in one 66.08
Has a n. changed its gods, even Jer 2.11
avenge myself on a n. such as this?" 5.29
bringing upon you a n. from afar, 5.15
an enduring n., it is an ancient n., 5.15
a n. whose language you do not know, 5.15
avenge myself on a n. such as this?" 5.29
a great n. is stirring from the 6.22
'This is the n. that did not obey 7.28
avenge myself on a n. such as this? 9.09
But if any n. will not listen, then 12.17
concerning a n. or a kingdom, 18.07
and if that n., concerning which I 18.08
concerning a n. or a kingdom that 18.09
the king of Babylon and that n., 25.12
evil is going forth from n. to n., 25.32
" 'But if any n. or kingdom will 27.08
will punish that n. with the sword, 27.08
But any n. which will bring its 27.11
concerning any n. which will not 27.13
from being a n. before me for ever 31.36
are no longer a n. in their sight. 33.24
let us cut her off from being a n.' 48.02
"Rise up, advance against a n. at ease, 49.31
shall be no n. to which those 49.36
of the north a n. has come up 50.03
a mighty n. and many kings are 50.41
watched for a n. which could not Lam 4.17
to a n. of rebels, who have rebelled Eze 2.03
you bereave your n. of children,' 36.13
longer bereave your n. of children, 36.14
no longer cause your n. to stumble, 36.15
will make them one n. in the land, 37.22
n., or language that speaks anything Dan 3.29
kingdoms shall arise from his n., 8.22
there was a n. till that time; 12.01
For a n. has come up against my Joe 1.06
to the Sabeans, to a n. far off; 3.08
I will raise up against you a n., Amo 6.14
n. shall not lift up sword against n.; Mic 4.03
who were cast off, a strong n.; 4.07
Chaldeans, that bitter and hasty n., Hab 1.06
and hold assembly, O shameless n., Zep 2.01

NATION (cont.)
seacoast, you n. of the Cherethites! Zep 2.05
survivors of my n. shall possess 2.09
and with this n. before me, says the Hag 2.14
robbing me; the whole n. of you. Mal 3.09
and given to a n. producing the Mt 21.43
For n. will rise against n., and 24.07
For n. will rise against n., and Mk 13.08
for he loves our n., and he built Lk 7.05
them, "N. will rise against n., and 21.10
found this man perverting our n., 23.02
both our holy place and our n. Jn 11.48
that the whole n. should not 11.50
that Jesus should die for the n., 11.51
and not for the n. only, but to 11.52
Your own n. and the chief priests 18.35
men from every n. under heaven. Ac 2.05
will judge the n. which they serve, 7.07
city and amazed the n. of Samaria, 8.09
spoken of by the whole Jewish n., 10.22
or to visit any one of another n.; 10.28
but in every n. any one who fears 10.35
from one every n. of men to live 17.26
introduced on behalf of this n., 24.02
you have been judge over this n., 24.10
to bring to my n. alms and offerings 24.17
among my own n. and at Jerusalem, 26.04
no charge to bring against my n. 28.19
jealous of those who are not a n.; Rom 10.19
with a foolish n. I will make you 10.19
a holy n., God's own people, that you 1Pe 2.09
and tongue and people and n., Rev 5.09
from every n., from all tribes and 7.09
and people and tongue and n., 13.07
to every n. and tribe and tongue 14.06

NATIONS
by their families, in their n. Gen 10.05
languages, their lands, and their n. 10.20
languages, their lands, and their n. 10.31
to their genealogies, in their n.; 10.32
from these the n. spread abroad on 10.32
be the father of a multitude of n. 17.04
the father of a multitude of n. 17.05
and I will make n. of you, and kings 17.06
and she shall be a mother of n.; 17.16
and all the n. of the earth shall 18.18
shall all the n. of the earth 22.18
"Two n. are in your womb, and two 25.23
descendants all the n. of the earth 26.04
serve you, and n. bow down to you. 27.29
a company of n. shall come from 35.11
shall become a multitude of n. 48.19
For I will cast out n. before you, Ex 34.24
all these the n. I am casting out Lev 18.24
from among the n. that are round 25.44
And I will scatter you among the n., 26.33
And you shall perish among the n., 26.38
of Egypt in the sight of the n., 26.45
then the n. who have heard thy fame Num 14.15
not reckoning itself among the n.! 23.09
eat up the n. his adversaries, and 24.08
"Amalek was the first of the n., 24.20
among the n. where the LORD will Deu 4.27
driving out before you n. greater 4.38
and clears away many n. before you, 7.01
seven n. greater and mightier than 7.01
'These n. are greater than I; 7.17
away these n. before you little by 7.22
Like the n. that the LORD makes to 8.20
to dispossess n. greater and 9.01
of these n. that the LORD is 9.04
of these n. the LORD your God is 9.05
drive out all these n. before you, 11.23
will dispossess n. greater and 11.23
where the n. whom you shall 12.02
before you the n. whom you go in 12.29
'How did these n. serve their gods?— 12.30
you, and you shall lend to many n., 15.06
and you shall rule over many n., 15.06
like all the n. that are round 17.14
abominable practices of those n. 18.09
For these n., which you are about 18.14
cuts off the n. whose land the 19.01
are not cities of the n. here. 20.15
high above all n. that he has made, 26.19
high above all the n. of the earth. 28.01
and you shall lend to many n., 28.12
And among these n. you shall find 28.65
midst of the n. through which you 29.16
go and serve the gods of those n.; 29.18
yea, all the n. would say, 'Why has 29.24
among all the n. where the LORD 30.01
will destroy these n. before you, 31.03
gave to the n. their inheritance, 32.08
"Praise his people, O you n.; 32.43
done to all these n. for your sake, Jos 23.03
your tribes those n. that remain, 23.04
with all the n. that I have 23.04
with these n. left here among you, 23.07
out before you great and strong n.; 23.09
of these n. left here among you, 23.12
to drive out these n. before you; 23.13
them any of the n. that Joshua Ju 2.21
So the LORD left those n., not 2.23
Now these are the n. which the LORD 3.01
These are the n.: the five lords of 3.03
king to govern us like all the n. 1Sa 8.05
that we also may be like all the n., 8.20
from all the n. he subdued, 2Sa 8.11
keep me as the head of the n.; 22.44
among the n., and sing praises to 22.50
fame was in all the n. round about. 1Ki 4.31
from the n. concerning which the 11.02
abominations of the n. which the 14.24
practices of the n. whom the LORD 2Ki 16.03
customs of the n. whom the LORD 17.08
as the n. did whom the LORD carried 17.11
followed the n. that were round 17.15
"The n. which you have carried away 17.26
manner of the n. from among whom 17.33
So these n. feared the LORD, and 17.41
the gods of the n. ever delivered 18.33
Have the gods of the n. delivered them, 19.12
the n. which my fathers destroyed, 19.12
laid waste the n. and their lands, 19.17
practices of the n. whom the LORD 21.02
evil than the n. had done whom the 21.09
the fear of him upon all n. 1Ch 14.17
Declare his glory among the n., 16.24
and let them say among the n., 16.31
and save us from among the n., 16.35
in driving out n. before thy 17.21
he had carried off from all the n., 18.11
over all the kingdoms of the n.? 2Ch 20.06
practices of the n. whom the LORD 28.03
the gods of the n. of those lands 32.13
gods of those n. which my fathers 32.14
the gods of the n. of the lands 32.17
sight of all n. from that time 32.23
practices of the n. whom the LORD 33.02
evil than the n. whom the LORD 33.09
all the abominations of the n.; 36.14
and the rest of the n. whom the Ez 4.10
who have been sold to the n.; Neh 5.08
the taunts of the n. our enemies? 5.09
to us from the n. which were about 5.17
"It is reported among the n., 6.06
all the n. round about us were 6.16
Among the many n. there was no king 13.26
He makes n. great, and he destroys Job 12.23
he enlarges n., and leads them away. 12.23
Why do the n. conspire, and the Ps 2.01
I will make the n. your heritage, 2.08

NATIONS (cont.)

Thou hast rebuked the n., Ps 9.05
The n. have sunk in the pit which 9.15
all the n. that forget God. 9.17
let the n. be judged before thee! 9.19
Let the n. know that they are but 9.20
the n. shall perish from his land. 10.16
didst make me the head of the n.; 18.43
among the n., and sing praises to 18.49
families of the n. shall worship 22.27
the LORD, and he rules over the n. 22.28
the counsel of the n. to nought; 33.10
own hand didst drive out the n., 44.02
and hast scattered us among the n. 44.11
hast made us a byword among the n., 44.14
The n. rage, the kingdoms totter; 46.06
I am exalted among the n., 46.10
under us, and n. under our feet. 47.03
God reigns over the n.; 47.08
sing praises to thee among the n. 57.09
Awake to punish all the n.; 59.05
dost hold all the n. in derision. 59.08
whose eyes keep watch on the n.— 66.07
thy saving power among all n. 67.02
Let the n. be glad and sing for joy, 67.04
equity and guide the n. upon earth. 67.04
down before him, all n. serve him! 72.11
by him, all n. call him blessed! 72.17
He drove out n. before them; 78.55
anger on the n. that do not know 79.06
Why should the n. say, "Where is 79.10
known among the n. before our eyes! 79.10
drive out the n. and plant it. 80.08
for to thee belong all the n.! 82.08
All the n. thou hast made shall 86.09
He who chastens the n., does he 94.10
Declare his glory among the n., 96.03
Say among the n., "The LORD reigns! 96.10
vindication in the sight of the n. 98.02
The n. will fear the name of the 102.15
And he gave them the lands of the n.; 105.44
their descendants among the n., 106.27
with the n. and learned to do as 106.35
he gave them into the hand of the n., 106.41
and gather us from among the n., 106.47
sing praises to thee among the n. 108.03
will execute judgment among the n., 110.06
giving them the heritage of the n. 111.06
The LORD is high above all n., 113.04
Why should the n. say, "where is 115.02
Praise the LORD, all n.! Extol him, 117.01
All n. surrounded me; in the name of 118.10
then they said among the n., 126.02
who smote many n. and slew mighty 135.10
The idols of the n. are silver and 135.15
vengeance on the n. and chastisement 149.07
cursed by peoples, abhorred by n.; Pro 24.24
and all the n. shall flow to it, Is 2.02
He shall judge between the n., 2.04
the Jordan, Galilee of the n. 9.01
and to cut off n. not a few; 10.07
him shall the n. seek, and his 11.10
He will raise an ensign for the n., 11.12
make known his deeds among the n., 12.04
of kingdoms, of n. gathering together! 13.04
that ruled the n. in anger with 14.06
all who were kings of the n. 14.09
ground, you who laid the n. low! 14.12
All the kings of the n. lie in glory, 14.18
is stretched out over all the n. 14.26
lords of the n. have struck down 16.08
the roar of n., they roar like the 17.12
The n. roar like the roaring of 17.13
you were the merchant of the n. 23.03
midst of the earth among the n., 24.13
of ruthless n. will fear thee. 25.03
veil that is spread over all n. 25.07
of all the n. that fight against 29.07
of all the n. be that fight 29.08
to sift the n. with the sieve of 30.28
up of thyself n. are scattered; 33.03
Draw near, O n., to hear, and hearken, 34.01
LORD is enraged against all the n., 34.02
the gods of the n. delivered is 36.18
Have the gods of the n. delivered them, 37.12
the n. which my fathers destroyed, 37.12
waste all the n. and their lands, 37.18
Behold, the n. are like a drop from 40.15
All the n. are as nothing before 40.17
He gives up n. before him, so that 41.02
will bring forth justice to the n. 42.01
to the people, a light to the n., 42.06
Let all the n. gather together, and 43.09
to subdue n. before him and ungird 45.01
together, you survivors of the n.! 45.20
will give you as a light to the n., 49.06
despised, abhorred by the n., 49.07
I will lift up my hand to the n., 49.22
arm before the eyes of all the n.; 52.10
so shall he startle many n.; 52.15
possess the n. and will people the 54.03
Behold, you shall call n. that you 55.05
and n. that knew you not shall run 55.05
And n. shall come to your light, and 60.03
wealth of the n. shall come to you 60.05
bring to you the wealth of the n., 60.11
those n. shall be utterly laid 60.12
You shall suck the milk of n., 60.16
you shall eat the wealth of the n., 61.06
shall be known among the n., 61.09
to spring forth before all the n. 61.11
The n. shall see your vindication, 62.02
and that the n. might tremble at 64.02
wealth of the n. like an overflowing 66.12
to gather all n. and tongues; 66.18
I will send survivors to the n., 66.19
declare my glory among the n. 66.19
from all the n. as an offering to 66.20
appointed you a prophet to the n. Jer 1.05
this day over n. and over kingdoms, 1.10
and all n. shall gather to it, to 3.17
heritage most beauteous of all n. 3.19
then n. shall bless themselves in 4.02
a destroyer of n. has set out; 4.07
Warn the n. that he is coming; 4.16
O n., and know, O congregation, what 6.18
them among the n. whom neither 9.16
for all these n. are uncircumcised, 9.26
LORD: "Learn not the way of the n., 10.02
because the n. are dismayed at 10.02
not fear thee, O King of the n.? 10.07
ones of the n. and in all their 10.07
and the n. cannot endure his 10.10
wrath upon the n. that know thee 10.25
gods of the n. that can bring rain? 14.22
thee shall the n. come from the 16.19
Ask among the n., who has heard the 18.13
" 'And many n. will pass by this 22.08
against all these n. round about; 25.09
and these n. shall serve the king 25.11
prophesied against all the n. 25.13
For many n. and great kings shall 25.14
make all the n. to whom I send you 25.15
made all the n. to whom the Lord 25.17
has an indictment against the n.; 25.31
curse for all the n. of the earth. 26.06
All the n. shall serve him and his 27.07
then many n. and great kings shall 27.07
neck of all the n. within two 28.11
of all these n. an iron yoke of 28.14
from all the n. and all the places 29.14
among all the n. where I have 29.18
end of all the n. among whom I 30.11
shouts for the chief of the n.; 31.07

NATIONS (cont.)

O n., and declare it in the coastlands Jer 31.10
before all the n. of the earth who 33.09
Israel and Judah and all the n., 36.02
from all the n. to which they had 43.05
among all the n. of the earth? 44.08
the prophet concerning the n. 46.01
The n. have heard of your shame, and 46.12
end of all the n. to which I have 46.28
messenger has been sent among the n.: 49.14
small among the n. despised among 49.15
"Declare among the n. and proclaim, 50.02
Babylon a company of great n., 50.09
she shall be the last of the n., 50.12
has become a horror among the n.! 50.23
cry shall be heard among the n. 50.46
n. drank of her wine, therefore the n. 51.07
war: with you I break n. in pieces; 51.20
blow the trumpet among the n.; 51.27
prepare the n. for war against her, 51.27
Prepare the n. for war against her, 51.28
has become a horror among the n.! 51.41
The n. shall no longer flow to him; 51.44
and the n. weary themselves only 51.58
she that was great among the n.! Lam 1.01
she dwells now among the n., 1.03
has seen the n. invade her sanctuary, 1.10
king and princes are among the n.; 2.09
wanderers; men said among the n., 4.15
shadow we shall live among the n." 4.20
among the n. whither I will drive Eze 4.13
set her in the center of the n., 5.05
my ordinances more than the n., 5.06
than the n. that are round about 5.07
ordinances of the n. that are round 5.07
of you in the sight of the n. 5.08
among the n. round about you and 5.14
to the n. round about you, when I 5.15
have among the n. some who escape 6.08
me among the n. where thy are 6.09
worst of the n. to take possession 7.24
ordinances of the n. that are round 11.12
removed them far off among the n., 11.16
them among the n. and scatter them 12.15
abominations among the n. where they go, 12.16
forth among the n. because of your 16.14
The n. sounded an alarm against him 19.04
Then the n. set against him snares 19.08
sight of the n. among whom they 20.09
be profaned in the sight of the n., 20.14
be profaned in the sight of the n., 20.22
them among the n. and disperse 20.23
thought, 'Let us be like the n., 20.32
among you in the sight of the n. 20.41
have made you a reproach to the n., 22.04
you among the n. and disperse you 22.15
through you in the sight of the n.; 22.16
you played the harlot with the n., 23.30
hand you over as spoil to the n.; 25.07
of Judah is like all the other n., 25.08
remembered no more among the n., 25.10
will bring up many n. against you, 26.03
she shall become a spoil to the n.; 26.05
you, the most terrible of the n.; 28.07
in them in the sight of the n., 28.25
scatter the Egyptians among the n., 29.12
again exalt itself above the n.; 29.15
will never again rule over the n. 29.15
clouds, a time of doom for the n. 30.03
him, the most terrible of the n., 30.11
scatter the Egyptians among the n., 30.23
among the n. and disperse them 30.26
its shadow dwelt all great n. 31.06
the hand of a mighty one of the n.; 31.11
Foreigners, the most terrible of the n., 31.12
I will make the n. quake at the 31.16
shadow among the n. shall perish. 31.17
yourself a lion among the n., 32.02
I carry you captive among the n., 32.09
of them most terrible among the n. 32.12
daughters of the n. shall chant it; 32.16
and the daughters of majestic n., 32.18
They shall no more be a prey to the n., 34.28
suffer the reproach of the n. 34.29
'These two n. and these two countries 35.10
possession of the rest of the n., 36.03
to the rest of the n. round about; 36.04
jealousy against the rest of the n., 36.05
suffered the reproach of the n.; 36.06
swear that the n. that are round 36.07
any more the reproach of the n., 36.15
I scattered them among the n., 36.19
But when they came to the n., 36.20
among the n. to which they came. 36.21
among the n. to which you came. 36.22
has been profaned among the n., 36.23
and the n. will know that I am the 36.23
For I will take you from the n., 36.24
disgrace of famine among the n. 36.30
Then the n. that are left round 36.36
Israel from the n. among which 37.21
and they shall be no longer two n., 37.22
Then the n. will know that I the 37.28
from many n. upon the mountains of 38.08
out from the n. and now dwell 38.08
who were gathered from the n., 38.12
that the n. may know me, when 38.16
known in the eyes of many n. 38.23
and the n. shall know that I am the 39.07
"And I will set my glory among the n.; 39.21
and all the n. shall see my judgment 39.21
And the n. shall know that the 39.23
holiness in the sight of many n. 39.27
sent them into exile among the n., 39.28
remaining among the n. any more; 39.28
O peoples, n., and languages, Dan 3.04
n., and languages fell down and 3.07
n., and languages, that dwell in all 4.01
n., and languages trembled and 5.19
n., and languages that dwell in all 6.25
n., and languages should serve him; 7.14
are among the n. as a useless Hos 8.08
Though they hire allies among the n., 8.10
shall be wanderers among the n. 9.17
and n. shall be gathered against 10.10
a reproach, a byword among the n. Joe 2.17
make you a reproach among the n. 2.19
gather all the n. and bring them 3.02
have scattered them among the n., 3.02
Proclaim this among the n.: 3.09
all you n. round about, gather 3.11
Let the n. bestir themselves, and 3.12
to judge all the n. round about. 3.12
notable men of the first of the n., Amo 6.01
among all the n. as one shakes 9.09
and all the n. who are called by 9.12
been sent among the n.: "Rise up! Ob 1.01
I will make you small among the n., 1.02
the LORD is near upon all the n. 1.15
all the n. round about shall drink; 1.16
and many n. shall come, and say: Mic 4.02
decide for strong n. afar off; 4.03
Now many n. are assembled against 4.11
of Jacob shall be among the n., 5.08
upon the n. that did not obey. 5.15
The n. shall see and be ashamed of 7.16
who betrays n. with her harlotries, Nah 3.04
and I will let n. look on your 3.05
Look among the n., and see; Hab 1.05
mercilessly slaying n. for ever? 1.17
He gathers for himself all n., 2.05
Because you have plundered many n., 2.08
and n. weary themselves for naught? 2.13
he looked and shook the n.; 3.06

NATIONS (cont.)
thou didst trample the n. in anger. Hab 3.12
its place, all the lands of the n. Zep 2.11
"I have cut off n.; their battlements 3.06
For my decision is to gather n., 3.08
and I will shake all n., so that Hag 2.07
treasures of all n. shall come in, 2.07
strength of the kingdoms of the n., 2.22
angry with the n. that are at ease Zec 1.15
horns of the n. who lifted up 1.21
sent me to the n. who plundered 2.08
And many n. shall join themselves 2.11
among all the n. which they had 7.14
a byword of cursing among the n., 8.13
and strong n. shall come to seek 8.22
men from the n. of every tongue 8.23
he shall command peace to the n.; 9.10
Though I scattered them among the n., 10.09
And all the n. of the earth will 12.03
destroy all the n. that come 12.09
gather all the n. against Jerusalem 14.02
against those n. as when he fights 14.03
of all the n. round about shall be 14.14
of all the n. that have come 14.16
afflicts the n. that do not go up 14.18
to all the n. that do not go up to 14.19
my name is great among the n., Mal 1.11
for my name is great among the n., 1.11
and my name is feared among the n. 1.14
Then all n. will call you blessed, 3.12
be hated by all n. for my name's Mt 24.09
world, as a testimony to all n.; 24.14
Before him will be gathered all the n., 25.32
and make disciples of all n., 28.19
a house of prayer for all the n.'? Mk 11.17
must first be preached to all n. 13.10
For all the n. of the world seek Lk 12.30
and be led captive among all n.; 21.24
distress of n. in perplexity at 21.25
be preached in his name to all n., 24.47
dispossessed the n. which God Ac 7.45
destroyed seven n. in the land of 13.19
allowed all the n. to walk in 14.16
sake of his name among all the n., Rom 1.05
made you the father of many n."— 4.17
become the father of many n.; 4.18
writings is made known to all n., 16.26
thee shall all the n. be blessed. Gal 3.08
by angels, preached among the n., 1Ti 3.16
I will give him power over the n., Rev 2.26
peoples and n. and tongues and 10.11
for it is given over to the n., 11.02
and tongues and n. gaze at their 11.09
The n. raged, but thy wrath came, and 11.18
to rule all the n. with a rod of 12.05
who made all n. drink the wine of 14.08
All n. shall come and worship thee, 15.04
and the cities of the n. fell, 16.19
and multitudes and n. and tongues. 17.15
for all n. have drunk the wine of 18.03
and all n. were deceived by thy 18.23
sword with which to smite the n., 19.15
he should deceive the n. no more, 20.03
to deceive the n. which are at the 20.08
By its light shall the n. walk; 21.24
the glory and the honor of the n. 21.26
were for the healing of the n. 22.02

NATIVE
is a sojourner or a n. of the land. Ex 12.19
he shall be as a n. of the land. 12.48
one law for the n. and for the 12.49
either the n. or the stranger who Lev 16.29
whether he is a n. or a sojourner, 17.15
either the n. or the stranger who 18.26
be to you as the n. among you, 19.34
all that are n. in Israel shall 23.42
the sojourner as well as the n., 24.16
for the sojourner and for the n.; 24.22
for the sojourner and for the n. Num 9.14
All who are n. shall do these 15.13
for him who is n. among the people 15.29
whether he is n. or a sojourner, 15.30
mother and your n. land and came Ru 2.11
and from the gate of his n. place; 4.10
return no more to see his n. land. Jer 22.10
Babylonians whose n. land was Eze 23.15
each of us in his own n. language? Ac 2.08
encouragement), a Levite, a n. of Cyprus, 4.36
a n. of Pontus, lately come from 18.02
a n. of Alexandria, came to Ephesus. 18.24

NATIVE-BORN
be to you as n. sons of Israel; Eze 47.22

NATIVES
And the n. showed us unusual kindness, Ac 28.02
When the n. saw the creature hanging 28.04

NATURAL
not dim, nor his n. force abated. Deu 34.07
exchanged n. relations for unnatural, Rom 1.26
likewise gave up n. relations with 1.27
because of your n. limitations. 6.19
God did not spare the n. branches, 11.21
more will these n. branches be 11.24
observes his n. face in a mirror; Jas 1.23

NATURE
he speaks according to his own n., Jn 8.44
of like n. with you, and bring you Ac 14.15
of the world his invisible n., Rom 1.20
the law do by n. what the law 2.14
from what is by n. a wild olive 11.24
contrary to n., into a cultivated 11.24
Does not n. itself teach you that 1Co 11.14
For this perishable n. must put on 15.53
and this mortal n. must put on 15.53
our outer n. is wasting away, our 2Co 4.16
our inner n. is being renewed every 4.16
to beings that by n. are no gods; Gal 4.08
so we were by n. children of wrath, Eph 2.03
Put off your old n. which belongs 4.22
and put on the new n., created after 4.24
you have put off the old n. with its Col 3.09
and have put on the new n., which 3.10
and bears the very stamp of his n., Heb 1.03
likewise partook of the same n., 2.14
setting on fire the cycle of n., Jas 3.06
a man of like n. with ourselves 5.17
become partakers of the divine n. 2Pe 1.04
for God's n. abides in him, and he 1Jn 3.09

NAUGHT
and every vision comes to n.'? Eze 12.22
nations weary themselves for n.? Hab 2.13

NAVE
in front of the n. of the house 1Ki 6.03
both the n. and the inner sanctuary 6.05
the n. in front of the inner 6.17
entrance to the n. doorposts of 6.33
the doors of the n. of the temple. 7.50
in front of the n. of the house 2Ch 3.04
The n. he lined with cypress, and 3.05
stood on their feet, facing the n. 3.13
doors of the n. of the temple were 4.22
Then he brought me to the n., Eze 41.01
the length of the n. forty cubits, 41.02
twenty cubits, beyond the n. 41.04
The n. of the temple and the inner 41.15
room and the n. were carved 41.17
The doorposts of the n. were squared; 41.21
The n. and the holy place had each 41.23
doors of the n. were carved 41.25

NAVEL

Your n. is a rounded bowl that Sol 7.02
were born your n. string was not Eze 16.04

NAY

N., but we did it from fear that in Jos 22.24
And the people said to Joshua, "N.; 24.21
n., she gives answer to herself, Ju 5.29
N., for thy sake we are slain all Ps 44.22
N., in your hearts you devise 58.02
N., but by men of strange lips and Is 28.11

NAZARENE

fulfilled, "He shall be called a N." Mt 2.23
"You also were with the N., Jesus." Mk 14.67

NAZARENES

a ringleader of the sect of the N. Ac 24.05

NAZARETH

went and dwelt in a city called N., Mt 2.23
and leaving N. he went and dwelt in 4.13
prophet Jesus from N. of Galilee. 21.11
"This man was with Jesus of N." 26.71
Jesus came from N. of Galilee and Mk 1.09
you to do with us, Jesus of N.? 1.24
he heard that it was Jesus of N., 10.47
you seek Jesus of N., who was 16.06
God to a city of Galilee named N., Lk 1.26
from Galilee, from the city of N., 2.04
Galilee, to their own city, N. 2.39
went down with them and came to N., 2.51
And he came to N., where he had 4.16
you to do with us, Jesus of N.? 4.34
him, "Jesus of N. is passing by." 18.37
to him, "Concerning Jesus of N., 24.19
Jesus of N., the son of Joseph." Jn 1.45
"Can anything good come out of N?" 1.46
They answered him, "Jesus of N." 18.05
And they said, "Jesus of N." 18.07
"Jesus of N., the King of the Jews." 19.19
Jesus of N., a man attested to you Ac 2.22
name of Jesus Christ of N., walk." 3.06
by the name of Jesus Christ of N., 4.10
this Jesus of N. will destroy this 6.14
Jesus of N. with the Holy Spirit 10.38
'I am Jesus of N. whom you are 22.08
opposing the name of Jesus of N. 26.09

NAZIRITE

the vow of a N., to separate Num 6.02
"And this is the law for the N., 6.13
And the N. shall shave his consecrated 6.18
put them upon the hands of the N., 6.19
after that the N. may drink wine. 6.20
the law for the N. who takes a vow 6.21
be according to his vow as a N., 6.21
the law for his separation as a N. 6.21
boy shall be a N. to God from Ju 13.05
boy shall be a N. to God from 13.07
I have been a N. to God from my 16.17

NAZIRITES

and some of your young men for N. Amo 2.11
"But you made the N. drink wine, 2.12

NEAH

on to Rimmon it bends toward N.; Jos 19.13

NEAPOLIS

Samothrace, and the following day to N., Ac 16.11

NEAR

Then Abraham drew n., and said, Gen 18.23
and drew n. to break the door. 19.09
Behold, yonder city is n. enough to 19.20
"Come n., that I may feel you, my 27.21
So Jacob went n. to Isaac his 27.22
"Come n. and kiss me, my son." 27.26
So he came n. and kissed him; 27.27
until he came n. to his brother. 33.03
Then the maids drew n., they and 33.06
children drew n. and bowed down; 33.07
and last Joseph and Rachel drew n., 33.07
under the oak which was n. Shechem. 35.04
their father's flock n. Shechem. 37.12
before he came n. to them they 37.18
"Come n. to me, I pray you." 45.04
And they came n. And he said, 45.04
of Goshen, and you shall be n. me, 45.10
the time drew n. that Israel must 47.29
So Joseph brought them n. him; 48.10
hand, and brought them n. him. 48.13
Then he said, "Do not come n.; Ex 3.05
then he may come n. and keep it; 12.48
Philistines, although that was n.; 13.17
When Pharaoh drew n., the people 14.10
one coming n. the other all night. 14.20
'Come n. before the LORD, for he has 16.09
third day; do not go n. a woman." 19.15
who come n. to the LORD consecrate 19.22
Moses drew n. to the thick cloud 20.21
of the house shall come n. to God, 22.08
Moses alone shall come n. to the LORD; 24.02
but the others shall not come n., 24.02
"Then bring n. to you Aaron your 28.01
when they come n. the altar to 28.43
when they come n. the altar to 30.20
soon as he came n. the camp and 32.19
they were afraid to come n. him. 34.30
all the people of Israel came n., 34.32
congregation drew n. and stood Lev 9.05
"Draw n. to the altar, and offer 9.07
So Aaron drew n. to the altar, and 9.08
holy among those who are n. me, 10.03
"Draw n., carry your brethren from 10.04
So they drew n., and carried them 10.05
when they drew n. before the LORD 16.01
approach any one n. of kin to him 18.06
he is your father's n. kinswoman. 18.12
she is your mother's n. kinswoman. 18.13
they are your n. kinswomen; 18.17
that is to make naked one's n. kin; 20.19
sister (who is n. to him because 21.03
who has a blemish shall draw n., 21.18
shall come n. to offer the LORD's 21.21
shall not come n. to offer the 21.21
shall not come n. the veil or 21.23
or a n. kinsman belonging to his 25.49
And if any one else comes n., Num 1.51
"Bring the tribe of Levi n., 3.06
but if any one else comes n., 3.10
else who came n. was to be put to 3.38
when they come n. to the most holy 4.19
"And the priest shall bring her n., 5.16
he shall not go n. a dead body. 6.06
should come n. the sanctuary. 8.19
n. the entrance of Hamath. 13.21
will cause him to come n. to him; 16.05
he will cause to come n. to him. 16.05
to bring you n. to himself, to do 16.09
and that he has brought you n. him, 16.10
should draw n. to burn incense 16.40
Every one who comes n., 17.13
who comes n. to the tabernacle of 17.13
shall not come n. to the vessels 18.03
and no one else shall come n. you. 18.04
else who comes n. shall be put to 18.07
shall not come n. the tent of 18.22
which is n. the River, in the land 22.05
Then drew n. the daughters of 27.01
of hundreds, came n. to Moses, 31.48
Then they came n. to him, and said, 32.16
came n. and spoke before Moses and 36.01
Then all of you came n. me, Deu 1.22

NEAR (cont.)
sons of Ammon you did not draw n., Deu 2.37
has a god so n. to it as the LORD 4.07
And you came n. and stood at the 4.11
you came n. to me, all the heads of 5.23
Go n., and hear all that the LORD 5.27
whether n. you or far off from you, 13.07
year, the year of release is n., 15.09
And when you draw n. to the battle, 20.02
you draw n. this day to battle 20.03
"When you draw n. to a city to 20.10
And if he is not n. you, 22.02
this woman, and when I came n. her, 22.14
the one draws n. to rescue her 25.11
But the word is very n. you; 30.14
thousand cubits; do not come n. it." Jos 3.04
which is n. Bethaven, east of Bethel, 7.02
shall be brought n. by your tribes; 7.14
takes shall come n. by families; 7.14
takes shall come n. by households; 7.14
takes shall come n. man by man. 7.14
brought Israel n. tribe by tribe, 7.16
and he brought n. the families of 7.17
and he brought n. the family of the 7.17
and he brought n. his household man 7.18
and drew n. before the city, and 8.11
"Come n., put your feet upon the 10.24
Then they came n., and put their 10.24
which lies in the Negeb n. Arad; Ju 1.16
at the sculptured stones n. Gilgal, 3.19
in Zaanannim, which is n. Kedesh. 4.11
and drew n. to the door of the 9.52
in the houses n. Micah's house were 18.22
When they were n. Jebus, the day was 19.11
and let us draw n. to one of these 19.13
sun went down on them n. Gibeah, 19.14
we again draw n. to battle against 20.23
of Israel came n. against the 20.24
it is true that I am a n. kinsman, Ru 3.12
Philistines drew n. to attack 1Sa 7.10
all the tribes of Israel n., 10.20
of Benjamin n. by its families, and 10.21
of the Matrites n. man by man, 10.21
said, "Let us draw n. hither to God." 14.36
and he drew n. to the Philistine. 17.40
came on and drew n. to David, 17.41
and came and drew n. to meet David, 17.48
when David drew n. to the people 30.21
with him drew n. to battle against 2Sa 10.13
did you go so n. the city to fight 11.20
Why did you go so n. the wall?' 11.21
she brought them n. him to eat, 13.11
which is n. Ephraim, and Absalom 13.23
a man came n. to do obeisance to 15.05
And he came apace, and drew n. 18.25
n. the grave of my father and my 19.37
the king is n. of kin to us. 19.42
And he came n. her; and the woman 20.17
When David's time to die drew n., 1Ki 2.01
land of the enemy, far off or n.; 8.46
be n. to the LORD our God day and 8.59
which is n. Eloth on the shore of 9.26
And Elijah came n. to all the 18.21
to all the people, "Come n. to me"; 18.30
and all the people came n. to him. 18.30
the prophet came n. and said, 18.36
a prophet came n. to Ahab king of 20.13
prophet came n. to the king of 20.22
man of God came n. and said to the 20.28
garden, because it is n. my house; 21.02
Chenaanah came n. and struck 22.24
were at Jericho drew n. to Elisha, 2Ki 2.05
servants came n. and said to him, 5.13
Then the king drew n. to the altar, 16.12
with him drew n. before the 1Ch 19.14
away captive to a land far or n.; 2Ch 6.36
Chenaanah came n. and struck 18.23
Arabs who are n. the Ethiopians; 21.16
come n., bring sacrifices and 29.31
King Ahasuerus, both n. and far, Est 9.20
they say, 'is n. to the darkness.' Job 17.12
His soul draws n. the Pit, and his 33.22
who made him bring n. his sword! 40.19
One is so n. to another that no air 41.16
for trouble is n. and there is Ps 22.11
The LORD is n. to the brokenhearted, 34.18
whom thou dost choose and bring n., 65.04
Draw n. to me, redeem me, set me free 69.18
But for me it is good to be n. God; 73.28
and my life draws n. to Sheol. 88.03
but it will not come n. you. 91.07
you, no scourge come n. your tent. 91.10
and they drew n. to the gates of 107.18
They draw n. who persecute me with 119.150
But thou art n., O LORD, and all thy 119.151
The LORD is n. to all who call upon 145.18
people of Israel who are n. to him. 148.14
and do not go n. the door of her Pro 5.08
passing along the street n. her corner, 7.08
babbling of a fool brings ruin n. 10.14
neighbor who is n. than a brother 27.10
to draw n. to listen is better than Ecc 5.01
of the Holy One of Israel draw n., Is 5.19
Wail, for the day of the LORD is n.; 13.06
to a people feared n. and far, 18.02
from a people feared n. and far, 18.07
when she is n. her time, so were we 26.17
people draw n. with their mouth 29.13
and you who are n., acknowledge 33.13
Draw n., O nations, to hear, and 34.01
us together draw n. for judgment. 41.01
they have drawn n. and come. 41.05
draw n. together, you survivors of 45.20
I bring n. my deliverance, it is not 46.13
Draw n. to me, hear this: from the 48.16
he who vindicates me is n. Who will 50.08
my adversary? Let him come n. to me. 50.08
My deliverance draws n. speedily, 51.05
for it shall not come n. you. 54.14
call upon him while he is n.; 55.06
But you, draw n. hither, sons of the 57.03
far and to the n., says the LORD; 57.19
they delight to draw n. to God. 58.02
do not come n. me, for I am set 65.05
thou art n. in their mouth and far Jer 12.02
far and n., one after another, and 25.26
I will make him draw n., and he 30.21
which was n. the chamber of the 35.04
at Geruth Chimham n. Bethlehem, 41.17
least to the greatest, came n. 42.01
of Moab is n. at hand and his 48.16
of the land of Moab, far and n. 48.24
Thou didst come n. when I called on Lam 3.57
our end drew n.; our days were 4.18
and he that is n. shall fall by the Eze 6.12
the day is n., a day of tumult, and 7.07
The time has come, the day draws n. 7.12
"Draw n., you executioners of the 9.01
'The time is not n. to build houses 11.03
and you have brought your day n., 22.04
Those who are n. and those who are 22.05
day is n., the day of the LORD is n.; 30.03
Levi may come n. to the LORD to 40.46
before they go n. to that which is 42.14
who draw n. to me to minister to me, 43.19
They shall not come n. to me, 44.13
nor come n. any of my sacred things 44.13
shall come n. to me to minister to 44.15
by going n. to a dead person; 44.25
Nebuchadnezzar came n. to the door Dan 3.26
Then they came n. and said before 6.12
When he came n. to the den where 6.20
So he came n. where I stood; 8.17
those that are n. and those that 9.07

NEAR (cont.)

For the day of the LORD is n., Joe 1.15
of the LORD is coming, it is n., 2.01
Let all the men of war draw n., 3.09
of the LORD is n. in the valley of 3.14
and bring n. the seat of violence? Amo 6.03
of the LORD is n. upon all the Ob 1.15
great day of the LORD is n., n. and Zep 1.14
she does not draw n. to her God. 3.02
"Then I will draw n. to you for Mal 3.05
And when they drew n. to Jerusalem Mt 21.01
When the season of fruit drew n., 21.34
leaves, you know that summer is n. 24.32
things, you know that he is n., 24.33
could not get n. him because of Mk 2.04
And when they drew n. to Jerusalem, 11.01
leaves, you know that summer is n. 13.28
place, you know that he is n., 13.29
As he drew n. to the gate of the Lk 7.12
When the days drew n. for him to be 9.51
kingdom of God has come n. to you. 10.09
the kingdom of God has come n.' 10.11
were all drawing n. to hear him. 15.01
he came and drew n. to the house, 15.25
As he drew n. to Jericho, a blind 18.35
and when he came n., he asked him, 18.40
because he was n. to Jerusalem, 19.11
When he drew n. to Bethphage and 19.29
As he was now drawing n., at the 19.37
And when he drew n. and saw the 19.41
that its desolation has come n. 21.20
your redemption is drawing n." 21.28
know that the summer is already n. 21.30
know that the kingdom of God is n. 21.31
feast of Unleavened Bread drew n., 22.01
He drew n. to Jesus to kiss him; 22.47
himself drew n. and went with them. 24.15
So they drew n. to the village to 24.28
was baptizing at Aenon n. Salim, Jn 3.23
n. the field that Jacob gave to his 4.05
the sea and drawing n. to the boat. 6.19
Tiberias came n. the place where 6.23
of the Pharisees n. him heard this, 9.40
Bethany was n. Jerusalem, about two 11.18
to the country n. the wilderness, 11.54
was crucified was n. the city; 19.20
disciple whom he loved standing n., 19.26
which is n. Jerusalem, a sabbath Ac 1.12
as the time of the promise drew n., 7.17
and as he drew n. to look, the 7.31
Since Lydda was n. Joppa, the 9.38
journey and coming n. the city, 10.09
my journey and drew n. to Damascus, 22.06
to kill him before he comes n. 23.15
n. which was the city of Lasea. 27.08
The word is n. you, on your lips and Rom 10.08
beatings, and often n. death. 2Co 11.23
been brought n. in the blood of Eph 2.13
off and peace to those who were n.; 2.17
Indeed he was ill, n. to death. Php 2.27
confidence draw n. to the throne Heb 4.16
worthless and n. to being cursed; 6.08
through which we draw n. to God. 7.19
those who draw n. to God through 7.25
make perfect those who draw n. 10.01
let us draw n. with a true heart in 10.22
more as you see the Day drawing n. 10.25
would draw n. to God must believe 11.06
Draw n. to God and he will draw n. Jas 4.08
written therein; for the time is n. Rev 1.03
of this book, for the time is n. 22.10

NEARER

yet there is a kinsman n. than I. Ru 3.12
salvation is n. to us now than Rom 13.11

NEAREST

except for his n. of kin, his mother, Lev 21.02
there he saw the n. of the people. Num 22.41
you shall see only the n. of them, 23.13
city which is n. to the slain man Deu 21.03
of that city n. to the slain man 21.06
relative of ours, one of our n. kin." Ru 2.20

NEARIAH

Igal, Bariah, N., and Shaphat, six. 1Ch 3.22
The sons of N.: Elioenai, Hizkiah, and 3.23
N., Rephaiah, and Uzziel, the sons of 4.42

NEARING

suspected that they were n. land. Ac 27.27

NEARLY

for he n. died for the work of Php 2.30

NEBAI

Hariph, Anathoth, N., Neh 10.19

NEBAIOTH

N., the first-born of Ishmael; Gen 25.13
Abraham's son, the sister of N. 28.09
Ishmael's daughter, the sister of N. 36.03
the first-born of Ismael, N.; 1Ch 1.29
the rams of N. shall minister to Is 60.07

NEBALLAT

Hadid, Zeboim, N., Neh 11.34

NEBAT

Jeroboam the son of N., 1Ki 11.26
the son of N. heard of it (for he 12.02
Shilonite to Jeroboam the son of N. 12.15
of King Jeroboam the son of N., 15.01
house of Jeroboam the son of N., 16.03
the way of Jeroboam the son of N., 16.26
the sins of Jeroboam the son of N., 16.31
house of Jeroboam the son of N., 21.22
the way of Jeroboam the son of N., 22.52
the sin of Jeroboam the son of N., 2Ki 3.03
house of Jeroboam the son of N., 9.09
the sins of Jeroboam the son of N., 10.29
the sins of Jeroboam the son of N., 13.02
the sins of Jeroboam the son of N., 13.11
the sins of Jeroboam the son of N., 14.24
the sins of Jeroboam the son of N., 15.09
the sins of Jeroboam the son of N., 15.18
the sins of Jeroboam the son of N., 15.24
the sins of Jeroboam the son of N., 15.28
made Jeroboam the son of N. king. 17.21
erected by Jeroboam the son of N., 23.15
concerning Jeroboam the son of N.? 2Ch 9.29
the son of N. heard of it (for he 10.02
Shilonite to Jeroboam the son of N. 10.15
Yet Jeroboam the son of N., 13.06

NEBO

Elealeah, Sebam, N., and Beon, Num 32.03
N., and Baalmeon (their names to be 32.38
the mountains of Abarim, before N. 33.47
Mount N., which is in the land of Deu 32.49
the plains of Moab to Mount N., 34.01
Aroer, as far as N. and Baalmeon. 1Ch 5.08
The sons of N., fifty-two. Ez 2.29
Of the sons of N.: Jeiel, Mattithiah, 10.43
The men of the other N., fifty-two. Neh 7.33
over N. and over Medeba Moab wails. Is 15.02
Bel bows down, N. stoops, their idols 46.01
"Woe to N., for it is laid waste! Jer 48.01
and Dibon, and N., and Bethdiblathaim, 48.22

NEBUCHADNEZZAR

In his days N. king of Babylon came 2Ki 24.01
the servants of N. king of Babylon 24.10
And N. king of Babylon came to the 24.11

NEBUCHADNEZZAR (cont.)

N. king of Babylon came with all 2Ki 25.01
was the nineteenth year of King N., 25.08
whom N. king of Babylon had left, he 25.22
into exile by the hand of N. 1Ch 6.15
Against him came up N. king of 2Ch 36.06
N. also carried part of the vessels 36.07
the year King N. sent and brought 36.10
He also rebelled against King N., 36.13
the LORD which N. had carried away Ez 1.07
exiles whom N. the king of Babylon 2.01
the hand of N. king of Babylon, the 5.12
which N. had taken out of the 5.14
which N. took out of the temple 6.05
exiles whom N. the king of Babylon Neh 7.06
whom N. king of Babylon had carried Est 2.06
these lands into the hand of N., Jer 27.06
not serve this N. king of Babylon, 27.08
which N. king of Babylon did not 27.20
which N. king of Babylon took away 28.03
the yoke of N. king of Babylon 28.11
of servitude to N. king of Babylon, 28.14
whom N. had taken into exile from 29.01
to Babylon to N. king of Babylon. 29.03
N. king of Babylon came to Jerusalem Dan 1.01
eunuchs brought them in before N. 1.18
the second year of the reign of N., 2.01
N. had dreams; and his spirit was 2.01
known to King N. what will be in 2.28
Then King N. fell upon his face, and 2.46
King N. made an image of gold, whose 3.01
Then King N. sent to assemble the 3.02
the image which King N. had set up. 3.02
the image the King N. had set up; 3.03
the image that N. had set up. 3.03
image that King N. has set up; 3.05
image which King N. had set up. 3.07
They said to King N., "O king, live 3.09
Then N. in furious rage commanded 3.13
N. said to them, "Is it true, O 3.14
"O N., we have no need to answer 3.16
Then N. was full of fury, and the 3.19
Then King N. was astonished and 3.24
Then N. came near to the door of 3.26
N. said, "Blessed be the God of 3.28
King N. to all peoples, nations, and 4.01
I, N., was at ease in my house and 4.04
This dream I, King N., saw. And 4.18
All this came upon King N. 4.28
"O King N., to you it is spoken: The 4.31
Immediately the word was fulfilled upon N. 4.33
N., lifted my eyes to heaven, and my 4.34
Now I, N., praise and extol and 4.37
of silver which N. his father had 5.02
and King N., your father, made him 5.11
High God gave N. your father 5.18

NEBUCHADREZZAR

for N. king of Babylon is making Jer 21.02
the hand of N. king of Babylon and 21.07
the hand of N. king of Babylon and 22.25
After N. king of Babylon had taken 24.01
first year of N. king of Babylon), 25.01
and for N. the king of Babylon, my 25.09
the hand of N. king of Babylon, and 29.21
was the eighteenth year of N. 32.01
the hand of N. king of Babylon, and 32.28
when N. king of Babylon and all his 34.01
But when N. king of Babylon came up 35.11
whom N. king of Babylon made king 37.01
N. king of Babylon and all his army 39.01
him up to N. king of Babylon, at 39.05
N. king of Babylon gave command 39.11
send and take N. the king of 43.10
the hand of N. king of Babylon, who 44.30
and which N. king of Babylon 46.02
the coming of N. king of Babylon 46.13
the hand of N. king of Babylon and 46.26
of Hazor which N. king of Babylon 49.28
For N. king of Babylon has made a 49.30
and now at last N. king of Babylon 50.17
"N. the king of Babylon has devoured 51.34
N. king of Babylon came with all 52.04
was the nineteenth year of King N., 52.12
the people whom N. carried away 52.28
eighteenth year of N. he carried 52.29
in the twenty-third year of N., 52.30
from the north N. king of Babylon, Eze 26.07
"Son of man, N. king of Babylon made 29.18
of Egypt to N. king of Babylon; 29.19
by the hand of N. king of Babylon. 30.10

NEBUSHAZBAN

N. the Rabsaris, Nergalsharezer the Jer 39.13

NEBUZARADAN

N., the captain of the bodyguard, 2Ki 25.08
N. the captain of the guard carried 25.11
And N. the captain of the guard 25.20
Then N., the captain of the guard, Jer 39.09
N., the captain of the guard, left 39.10
concerning Jeremiah through N., 39.11
So N. the captain of the guard, 39.13
the LORD after N. the captain of 40.01
whom N., the captain of the guard, 41.10
person whom N. the captain of the 43.06
N. the captain of the bodyguard 52.12
And N. the captain of the guard 52.15
But N. the captain of the guard 52.16
And N. the captain of the guard 52.26
N. the captain of the guard carried 52.30

NECESSARILY

there is n. a change in the law as Heb 7.12

NECESSARY

For it is n. that temptations come, Mt 18.07
Was it not n. that the Christ Lk 24.26
"It was n. that the word of God Ac 13.46
"It is n. to circumcise them, and to 15.05
burden than these n. things: 15.28
that it was n. for the Christ to 17.03
So I thought it n. to urge the 2Co 9.05
flesh is more n. on your account. Php 1.24
I have thought it n. to send to you 2.25
hence it is n. for this priest also Heb 8.03
Thus it was n. for the copies of 9.23
I found it n. to write appealing to Jud 1.03

NECESSITIES

these hands ministered to my n., Ac 20.34

NECESSITY

being under no n. but having his 1Co 7.37
For n. is laid upon me. Woe to me 9.16

NECK

and upon the smooth part of his n.; Gen 27.16
shall break his yoke from your n." 27.40
and fell on his n. and kissed him, 33.04
and put a gold chain about his n.; 41.42
his brother Benjamin's n. and wept; 45.14
and Benjamin wept upon his n. 45.14
himself to him, and fell on his n., 46.29
and wept on his n. a good while. 46.29
shall be on the n. of your enemies 49.08
redeem it you shall break its n. Ex 13.13
redeem it you shall break its n. 34.20
shall wring its head from its n., Lev 5.08
the heifer's n. there in the Deu 21.04
heifer whose n. was broken in the 21.06
put a yoke of iron upon your n., 28.48
embroidered for my n. as spoil?' Ju 5.30
and his n. was broken and he died, 1Sa 4.18
stiffened his n. and hardened his 2Ch 36.13

NECK (cont.)

stiffened their n. and did not Neh 9.16
stiffened their n. and appointed a 9.17
stiffened their n. and would not 9.29
me by the n. and dashed me to Job 16.12
Do you clothe his n. with strength? 39.19
In his n. abides strength, and 41.22
the waters have come up to my n. Ps 69.01
on high, or speak with insolent n. 75.05
his n. was put in a collar of iron; 105.18
head, and pendants for your n. Pro 1.09
bind them about your n., write them 3.03
soul and adornment for your n. 3.22
always; tie them about your n. 6.21
stiffens his n. will suddenly be 29.01
your n. with strings of jewels. Sol 1.10
Your n. is like the tower of David, 4.04
Your n. is like an ivory tower. 7.04
pass on, reaching even to the n.; Is 8.08
will be destroyed from your n. 10.27
stream that reaches up to the n.; 30.28
and your n. is an iron sinew and 48.04
loose the bonds from your n., 52.02
like him who breaks a dog's n.; 66.03
their ear, but stiffened their n. Jer 7.26
their ear, but stiffened their n., 17.23
they have stiffened their n., 19.15
yoke-bars, and put them on your n. 27.02
and put its n. under the yoke of 27.08
will bring its n. under the yoke 27.11
from the n. of Jeremiah the 28.10
from the n. of all the nations 28.11
from off the n. of Jeremiah the 28.12
put upon the n. of all these 28.14
break the yoke from off their n., 30.08
together; they were set upon my n.; Lam 1.14
your arms, and a chain on your n. Eze 16.11
have a chain of gold about his n., Dan 5.07
have a chain of gold about your n., 5.16
chain of gold was put about his n., 5.29
thresh, and I spared her fair n.; Hos 10.11
laying him bare from thigh to n. Hab 3.13
round his n. and to be drowned in Mt 18.06
hung round his n. and he were Mk 9.42
hung round his n. and he were cast Lk 17.02
a yoke upon the n. of the disciples Ac 15.10

NECKLACE

chains like a n. and put them on 2Ch 3.16
Therefore pride is their n.; Ps 73.06
eyes, with one jewel of your n. Sol 4.09

NECKS

feet upon the n. of these kings. Jos 10.24
and put their feet on their n. 10.24
were on the n. of their camels. Ju 8.21
were about the n. of their camels. 8.26
not put their n. to the work of Neh 3.05
and walk with outstretched n., Is 3.16
"Bring your n. under the yoke of Jer 27.12
With a yoke on our n. we are hard Lam 5.05
be laid on the n. of the unhallowed Eze 21.29
which you cannot remove your n.; Mic 2.03
who risked their n. for my life, Rom 16.04

NECO

days Pharaoh N. king of Egypt went 2Ki 23.29
and Pharaoh N. slew him at 23.29
And Pharaoh N. put him in bonds at 23.33
And Pharaoh N. made Eliakim the son 23.34
assessment, to give it to Pharaoh N. 23.35
N. king of Egypt went up to fight 2Ch 35.20
to the words of N. from the mouth 35.22
but N. took Jehoahaz his brother 36.04
concerning the army of Pharaoh N., Jer 46.02

NECROMANCER

or a medium, or a wizard, or a n. Deu 18.11

NECTAR

Your lips distil n., my bride; honey Sol 4.11

NEDABIAH

Shenazzar, Jekamiah, Hoshama, and N.; 1Ch 3.18

NEED

But he said, "What n. is there? Gen 33.15
the priest n. not seek for the Lev 13.36
and lend him sufficient for his n., Deu 15.08
you n. not be afraid of him. 18.22
wherever any n. of repairs is 2Ki 12.05
no longer n. to carry the tabernacle 1Ch 23.26
whatever timber you n. from Lebanon, 2Ch 2.16
You will not n. to fight in this 20.17
you n. no longer carry it upon 35.03
they did not n. to depart from 35.15
Behold, no fear of me n. terrify you; Job 33.07
who seek her n. weary themselves; Jer 2.24
the king according to his daily n., 52.34
they will not n. to take wood out Eze 39.10
we have no n. to answer you in this Dan 3.16
"I n. to be baptized by you, and do Mt 3.14
knows what you n. before you ask 6.08
Father knows that you n. them all. 6.32
are well have no n. of a physician, 9.12
Jesus said, "They n. not go away; 14.16
he n. not honor his father.' 15.05
'The Lord has n. of them,' and he 21.03
Why do we still n. witnesses? You 26.65
are well have no n. of a physician, Mk 2.17
when he was in n. and was hungry, 2.25
'The Lord has n. of it and will 11.03
said, "Why do we still n. witnesses? 14.63
are well have no n. of a physician, Lk 5.31
cured those who had n. of healing. 9.11
your Father knows that you n. them. 12.30
persons who n. no repentance. 15.07
say this, 'The Lord has n. of it.'" 19.31
And they said, "The Lord has n. of it." 19.34
"What further testimony do we n.? 22.71
who has bathed does not n. to wash, Jn 13.10
him, "Buy what we n. for the feast"; 13.29
and n. none to question you; 16.30
distributed them to all, as any had n. Ac 2.45
was made to each as any had n. 4.35
then you would n. to go out of the 1Co 5.10
"I have no n. of you," nor again the 12.21
to the feet, "I have no n. of you." 12.21
contributions n. not be made when 16.02
Or do we n., as some do, letters of 2Co 3.01
may be able to give to those in n. Eph 4.28
messenger and minister to my n., Php 2.25
supply every n. of yours according 4.19
so that we n. not say anything. 1Th 1.08
you have no n. to have any one 4.09
you have no n. to have anything 5.01
who has no n. to be ashamed, 2Ti 2.15
so as to help cases of urgent n., Tit 3.14
find grace to help in time of n. Heb 4.16
you n. some one to teach you again 5.12
You n. milk, not solid food; 5.12
what further n. would there have 7.11
He has no n., like those high 7.27
For you have n. of endurance, so 10.36
and you have no n. that any one 1Jn 2.27
goods and sees his brother in n., 3.17
I have prospered, and I n. nothing; Rev 3.17
And the city has no n. of sun or 21.23
they n. no light of lamp or sun, for 22.05

NEEDED

And whatever is n.—young bulls, Ez 6.09
all men and n. no one to bear Jn 2.25
as though he n. anything, since he Ac 17.25
they put on board whatever we n. 28.10
them the things n. for the body, Jas 2.16

NEEDFUL
with the food that is n. for me, Pro 30.08
one thing is n. Mary has chosen Lk 10.42

NEEDLE
the eye of a n. than for a rich Mt 19.24
the eye of a n. than for a rich Mk 10.25
the eye of a n. than for a rich Lk 18.25

NEEDLEWORK
twined linen, embroidered with n. Ex 26.36
twined linen, embroidered with n.; 27.16
make a girdle embroidered with n. 28.39
twined linen, embroidered with n.; 36.37
embroidered with n. in blue and 38.18
scarlet stuff, embroidered with n.; 39.29

NEEDS
do all that n. to be done with Num 4.26
rise and give him whatever he n. Lk 11.08
prevented from attending to his n. Ac 24.23
Contribute to the n. of the saints, Rom 12.13
for my n. were supplied by the 2Co 11.09

NEEDY
to the n. and to the poor, in the Deu 15.11
a hired servant who is poor and n., 24.14
he lifts the n. from the ash heap, 1Sa 2.08
the n. from the hand of the mighty. Job 5.15
that he may kill the poor and n.; 24.14
For the n. shall not always be Ps 9.18
because the n. groan, I will now 12.05
the weak and n. from him who 35.10
to bring down the poor and n., 37.14
As for me, I am poor and n.; 40.17
God, thou didst provide for the n. 68.10
For the LORD hears the n., 69.33
But I am poor and n.; hasten to 70.05
people, give deliverance to the n., 72.04
For he delivers the n. when he calls, 72.12
He has pity on the weak and the n., 72.13
and saves the lives of the n. 72.13
the poor and n. praise thy name. 74.21
Rescue the weak and the n.; 82.04
answer me, for I am poor and n. 86.01
raises up the n. out of affliction, 107.41
the poor and n. and the brokenhearted 109.16
For I am poor and n., and my 109.22
stands at the right hand of the n., 109.31
and lifts the n. from the ash heap, 113.07
and executes justice for the n. 140.12
who is kind to the n. honors him. Pro 14.31
the earth, the n. from among men. 30.14
the rights of the poor and n. 31.09
reaches out her hands to the n. 31.20
to turn aside the n. from justice Is 10.02
and the n. lie down in safety; 14.30
stronghold to the n. in his distress, 25.04
of the poor, the steps of the n. 26.06
when the plea of the n. is right. 32.07
When the poor and n. seek water, 41.17
do not defend the rights of the n. Jer 5.28
the life of the n. from the hand 20.13
the cause of the poor and n.; 22.16
but did not aid the poor and n. Eze 16.49
oppresses the poor and n., 18.12
have oppressed the poor and n., 22.29
and the n. for a pair of shoes— Amo 2.06
who crush the n., who say to their 4.01
and turn aside the n. in the gate. 5.12
Hear this, you who trample upon the n., 8.04
silver and the n. for a pair of 8.06
There was not a n. person among Ac 4.34

NEGEB
on, still going toward the N. Gen 12.09
had, and Lot with him, into the N. 13.01
on from the N. as far as Bethel, to 13.03
toward the territory of the N., 20.01
Beerlahairoi, and was dwelling in the N. 24.62
to them, "Go up into the N. yonder, Num 13.17
They went up into the N., 13.22
dwell in the land of the N.; 13.29
king of Arad, who dwelt in the N., 21.01
dwelt in the N. in the land of 33.40
and in the N., and by the seacoast, Deu 1.07
the N., and the Plain, that is, the 34.03
country and the N. and the lowland Jos 10.40
and all the N. and all the land of 11.16
and in the N., the land of the 12.08
have set me in the land of the N., 15.19
as Baalathbeer, Ramah of the N. 19.08
in the N., and in the lowland. Ju 1.09
have set me in the land of the N., 1.15
which lies in the N. near Arad; 1.16
"Against the N. of Judah," or 1Sa 27.10
or "Against the N. of the Jerahmeelites," 27.10
or, "Against the N. of the Kenites." 27.10
a raid upon the N. and upon Ziklag. 30.01
a raid upon the N. of the Cherethites 30.14
to Judah and upon the N. of Caleb; 30.14
in Ramoth of the N., in Jattir, 30.27
went out to the N. of Judah at 2Sa 24.07
the Shephelah and the N. of Judah, 2Ch 28.18
like the water-courses in the N.! Ps 126.04
As whirlwinds in the N. sweep on, Is 21.01
An oracle on the beasts of the N. 30.06
The cities of the N. are shut up, Jer 13.19
and from the N., bringing burnt 17.26
and in the cities of the N.; 32.44
and in the cities of the N., 33.13
against the forest land in the N.; Eze 20.46
say to the forest of the N., 20.47
Those of the N. shall possess Mount Ob 1.19
shall possess the cities of the N. 1.20

NEGLECT
We will not n. the house of our God. Neh 10.39
and be wise, and do not n. it. Pro 8.33
and n. justice and the love of God; Lk 11.42
Do not n. the gift you have, which 1Ti 4.14
we escape if we n. such a great Heb 2.03
Do not n. to show hospitality to 13.02
Do not n. to do good and to share 13.16

NEGLECTED
for we n. it in the days of Saul. 1Ch 13.03
and have n. the weightier matters Mt 23.23
their widows were n. in the daily Ac 6.01

NEGLECTING
have done, without n. the others. Mt 23.23
have done, without n. the others. Lk 11.42
not n. to meet together, as is the Heb 10.25

NEGLIGENT
do not now be n., for the LORD has 2Ch 29.11

NEHELAM
To Shemaiah of N. you shall say: Jer 29.24
the LORD concerning Shemaiah of N.: 29.31
Shemaiah of N. and his descendants 29.32

NEHEMIAH
N., Seraiah, Reelaiah, Mordecai, Ez 2.02
The words of N. the son of Hacaliah Neh 1.01
After him N. the son of Azbuk, ruler 3.16
N., Azariah, Raamiah, Nahamani, 7.07
And N., who was the governor, and 8.09
set their seal are N. the governor, 10.01
in the days of N. the governor and 12.26
in the days of N. gave the daily 12.47

NEHUM
Mispereth, Bigvai, N., Baanah. Neh 7.07

NEHUSHTA
mother's name was N. the daughter of 2Ki 24.08

NEHUSHTAN
burned incense to it; it was called N. 2Ki 18.04

NEIEL
northward to Bethemek and N.; then Jos 19.27

NEIGH
heifer at grass, and n. like stallions, Jer 50.11

NEIGHBOR
but each woman shall ask of her n., Ex 3.22
man of his n. and every woman of her n., 11.02
a man and his n. next to his house 12.04
I decide between a man and his n., 18.16
bear false witness against your n. 20.16
delivers to his n. money or goods 22.07
condemn shall pay double to his n. 22.09
delivers to his n. an ass or an ox 22.10
"If a man borrows anything of his n., 22.14
companion, and every man his n. 32.27
deceiving his n. in a matter of Lev 6.02
if he has oppressed his n. 6.02
not oppress your n. or rob him. 19.13
righteousness shall you judge your n. 19.15
the life of your n.: I am the LORD. 19.16
but you shall reason with your n., 19.17
you shall love your n. as yourself: 19.18
adultery with the wife of his n., 20.10
causes a disfigurement in his n., 24.19
sell to your n. or buy from your n., 25.14
jubilee, you shall buy from your n., 25.15
who kills his n. unintentionally, Deu 4.42
bear false witness against your n. 5.20
release what he has lent to his n.; 15.02
he shall not exact it of his n., 15.02
one kills his n. unintentionally 19.04
the forest with his n. to cut wood, 19.05
and strikes his n. so that he dies 19.05
at enmity with his n. in time past. 19.06
"But if any man hates his n., 19.11
man attacking and murdering his n.; 22.26
"When you make your n. a loan of 24.10
be he who slays his n. in secret. 27.24
he killed his n. unwittingly, Jos 20.05
and has given it to a n. of yours, 1Sa 15.28
and given it to your n., David. 28.17
eyes, and give them to your n., 2Sa 12.11
against his n. and is made to take 1Ki 8.31
against his n. and is made to take 2Ch 6.22
like that of a man with his n. Job 16.21
Every one utters lies to his n.; Ps 12.02
takes up a reproach against his n.; 15.03
slanders his n. secretly I will 101.05
Do not say to your n., "Go, and Pro 3.28
against your n. who dwells trustingly 3.29
you have become surety for your n., 6.01
go, hasten, and importune your n. 6.03
godless man would destroy his n., 11.09
He who belittles his n. lacks sense, 11.12
The poor is disliked even by his n., 14.20
He who despises his n. is a sinner, 14.21
entices his n. and leads him in a 16.29
surety in the presence of his n. 17.18
his n. finds no mercy in his eyes. 21.10
against your n. without cause, 24.28
when your n. puts you to shame? 25.08
Argue your case with your n. himself, 25.09
against his n. is like a war club, 25.18
man who deceives his n. and says, 26.19
Better is a n. who is near than a 27.10
He who blesses his n. with a loud 27.14
flatters his n. spreads a net for 29.05
come from a man's envy of his n. Ecc 4.04
his fellow and every man his n.; Is 3.05
and every man against his n., 19.02
Every one helps his n., and says 41.06
n. and friend shall perish. Jer 6.21
Let every one beware of his n., 9.04
and every n. goes about as a 9.04
Every one deceives his n., 9.05
each speaks peaceably to his n., 9.08
lament, and each to her n. a dirge. 9.20
flesh of his n. in the seige and 19.09
and every man will say to his n., 22.08
who makes his n. serve him for 22.13
one to his n. and every one to his 23.35
man teach his n. and each his 31.34
each to his n., and you made a 34.15
one to his brother and to his n.; 34.17
and their n. cities were overthrown, 49.18
and Gomorrah and their n. cities, 50.40
Put no trust in a n., have no Mic 7.05
will invite his n. under his vine Zec 3.10
shall love your n. and hate your Mt 5.43
You shall love your n. as yourself." 19.19
You shall love your n. as yourself. 22.39
'You shall love your n. as yourself.' Mk 12.31
and to love one's n. as oneself, 12.33
your mind; and your n. as yourself." Lk 10.27
said to Jesus, "And who is my n.?" 10.29
proved n. to the man who fell among 10.36
wronging his n. thrust him aside, Ac 7.27
who loves his n. has fulfilled the Rom 13.08
"You shall love your n. as yourself." 13.09
Love does no wrong to a n.; 13.10
of us please his n. for his good, 15.02
own good, but the good of his n. 1Co 10.24
"You shall love your n. as yourself." Gal 5.14
in himself alone and not in his n. 6.04
one speak the truth with his n., Eph 4.25
"You shall love your n. as yourself," Jas 2.08
who are you that you judge your n.? 4.12

NEIGHBORHOOD
as far as the n. of Gaza, and leave Ju 6.04
from Aroer to the n. of Minnith, 11.33
women of the n. gave him a name, Ru 4.17
they begged him to leave their n. Mt 8.34
beg Jesus to depart from their n. Mk 5.17
about the whole n. and began to 6.55
Now in the n. of that place were Ac 28.07

NEIGHBOR'S
"You shall not covet your n. house; Ex 20.17
you shall not covet your n. wife, 20.17
ass, or anything that is your n." 20.17
has put his hand to his n. goods. 22.08
put his hand to his n. property; 22.11
you take your n. garment in pledge, 22.26
not lie carnally with your n. wife, Lev 18.20
shall you covet your n. wife; Deu 5.21
you shall not desire your n. house, 5.21
ass, or anything that is your n." 5.21
shall not remove your n. landmark, 19.14
because he violated his n. wife; 22.24
"When you go into your n. vineyard, 23.24
you go into your n. standing grain, 23.25
a sickle to your n. standing grain. 23.25
be he who removes his n. landmark.' 27.17
I have lain in wait at my n. door; Job 31.09
you have come into your n. power: Pro 6.03
So is he who goes in to his n. wife; 6.29
foot be seldom in your n. house, 25.17
each devours his n. flesh, Is 9.20
each neighing for his n. wife. Jer 5.08
not defile his n. wife or approach Eze 18.06
mountains, defiles his n. wife, 18.11
does not defile his n. wife, 18.15
abomination with his n. wife; 22.11
each of you defiles his n. wife; 33.26

NEIGHBORS
and to all their n. in Arabah, Deu 1.07
they heard that they were their n., Jos 9.16
borrow vessels of all your n., 2Ki 4.03
And also their n., from as far as 1Ch 12.40
who speak peace with their n., Ps 28.03
my adversaries, a horror to my n., 31.11
Thou hast made us the taunt of our n., 44.13
We have become a taunt to our n., 79.04
bosom of our n. the taunts with 79.12
Thou dost make us the scorn of our n.; 80.06
he has become the scorn of his n. 89.41
all my evil n. who touch the Jer 12.14
and his brothers, and his n.; 49.10
Jacob that his n. should be his Lam 1.17
your lustful n., multiplying your Eze 16.26
daughters of Edom and all her n., 16.57
make gain of your n. by extortion; 22.12
among all their n. who have 28.24
upon all their n. who have treated 28.26
who makes his n. drink of the cup Hab 2.15
And her n. and kinsfolk heard that Lk 1.58
And fear came on all their n. 1.65
brothers or your kinsmen or rich n., 14.12
together his friends and his n., 15.06
calls together her friends and n., 15.09
The n. and those who had seen him Jn 9.08

NEIGHBORS'
adultery with their n. wives, Jer 29.23

NEIGHING
each n. for his neighbor's wife. Jer 5.08
sound of the n. of their stallions 8.16

NEIGHINGS
abominations, your adulteries and n., Jer 13.27

NEITHER
n. shall you touch it, lest you die.' " Gen 3.03
n. will I ever again destroy every 8.21
you speak to Jacob n. good nor bad.' 31.29
there will be n. plowing nor 45.06
as n. your fathers nor your grandfathers Ex 10.06
n. tree nor plant of the field, 10.15
n. had they prepared for themselves 12.39
n. shall any man desire your land, 34.24
n. shall the sacrifice of the feast 34.25
he n. ate bread nor drank water. 34.28
"Let n. man nor woman do anything 36.06
that you eat n. fat nor blood." Lev 3.17
n. shall it be credited to him; 7.18
n. shall any stranger who sojourns 17.12
n. shall any woman give herself to 18.23
n. shall you gather the gleanings 19.09
n. shall you gather the fallen 19.10
n. shall they marry a woman divorced 21.07
n. shall he go out of the sanctuary, 21.12
n. shall you offer as the bread of 22.25
And you shall eat n. bread nor 23.14
in it you shall n. sow, nor reap 25.11
n. will I abhor them so as to 26.44
good or bad; n. shall he exchange it; 27.33
N. for his father nor for his Num 6.07
although n. the ark of the covenant 14.44
n. shall you have any portion among 18.20
n. will we drink water from a well; 20.17
"N. curse them at all, nor bless 23.25
will turn aside n. to the right Deu 2.27
that n. see, nor hear, nor eat, nor 4.28
" 'N. shall you commit adultery. 5.18
" 'N. shall you steal. 5.19
" 'N. shall you bear false witness 5.20
" 'N. shall you covet your neighbor's 5.21
n. shall you serve their gods, for 7.16
I n. ate bread nor drank water. 9.09
I n. ate bread nor drank water, 9.18
which n. you nor your fathers have 13.06
which is n. plowed nor sown, and 21.04
blood, n. did our eyes see it shed. 21.07
n. shall there be a cult prostitute 23.17
commandments, n. have I forgotten them; 26.13
a nation that n. you nor your 28.36
but you shall n. drink of the wine 28.39
which n. you nor your fathers have 28.64
too hard for you, n. is it far off. 30.11
N. is it beyond the sea, that you 30.13
be not frightened, n. be dismayed; Jos 1.09
n. shall any word go out of your 6.10
aside from it n. to the right hand 23.06
her he had n. son nor daughter. Ju 11.34
n. let her drink wine or strong 13.14
n. did you give them to them, else 21.22
I have drunk n. wine nor strong 1Sa 1.15
they turned n. to the right nor to 6.12
there was n. sword nor spear found 13.22
And he said, "N. has the LORD chosen 16.08
And he said, "N. has the LORD chosen 16.09
n. you nor your kingdom shall be 20.31
I have brought n. my sword nor my 21.08
and left n. man nor woman alive, but 27.09
And David saved n. man nor woman 27.11
went he turned n. to the right 2Sa 2.19
spoke to Amnon n. good nor bad; 13.22
to my husband n. name nor remnant 14.07
he had n. dressed his feet, nor 19.24
n. is it for us to put any man to 21.04
"It shall be n. mine nor yours; 1Ki 3.26
there is n. adversary nor misfortune 5.04
so that n. hammer nor axe nor any 6.07
n. shall they with you, for surely 11.02
'You shall n. eat bread, nor drink 13.09
n. will I eat bread nor drink water 13.16
'You shall n. eat bread nor drink 13.17
there shall be n. dew nor rain 17.01
n. did the curse of oil fail, 17.16
"Fight with n. small nor great, but 22.31
henceforth n. death nor miscarriage 2Ki 2.21
I would n. look at you, nor see you. 3.14
It is n. new moon nor sabbath." 4.23
they n. listened nor obeyed. 18.12
"Fight with n. small nor great, but 2Ch 18.30
n. take their daughters for your Ez 9.12
n. eating bread nor drinking water; 10.06
So n. I nor my brethren nor my Neh 4.23
n. I nor my brethren ate the food 5.14
for she had n. father nor mother; Est 2.07
and n. eat nor drink for three days, 4.16
that he n. rose nor trembled before 5.09
They have n. knowledge nor understanding, Ps 82.05
Israel will n. slumber nor sleep. 121.04
give me n. poverty nor riches; Pro 30.08
Be not wicked overmuch, n. be a fool; Ecc 7.17
n. will he prolong his days like a 8.13
how n. day nor night one's eyes see 8.16
quench love, n. can floods drown it. Sol 8.07
n. shall they learn war any more. Is 2.04
house there is n. bread nor mantle 3.07
"I have n. travailed nor given 23.04
I have n. reared young men nor 23.04
that brings n. help nor profit, but 30.05
their witnesses n. see nor know, 44.09
n. scorching wind nor sun shall 49.10
the Pit, n. shall his bread fail. 51.14
n. are your ways my ways, says the 55.08
nations whom n. they nor their Jer 9.16
n. is it in them to do good. 10.05
a land which n. you nor your 16.13
other gods whom n. they nor their 19.04
n. shall any be missing, says the 23.04
You have n. listened nor inclined 25.04
n. you nor your sons for ever; 35.06
Yet n. the king, nor any of his 36.24
But n. he nor his servants nor the 37.02
n. they, nor you, nor your fathers. 44.03

NEITHER (cont.)

n. men nor beast, and it shall be Jer 51.62
n. shall there be pre-eminence Eze 7.11
would deliver n. sons nor daughters 14.16
would deliver n. sons nor daughters, 14.18
would deliver n. son nor daughter; 14.20
n. have they taught the difference 22.26
yet n. he nor his army got anything 29.18
n. they, nor their kings, by their 43.07
broken, n. in anger nor in battle. Dan 11.20
shall do what n. his fathers nor 11.24
which can be n. measured nor Hos 1.10
Let n. man nor beast, herd nor flock, Jon 3.07
n. shall they learn war any more; Mic 4.03
N. their silver nor their gold Zep 1.18
n. was there any safety from the Zec 8.10
there shall be n. cold nor frost. 14.06
will leave them n. root nor branch Mal 4.01
n. will your Father forgive your Mt 6.15
where n. moth nor rust consumes and 6.20
they n. sow nor reap nor gather 6.26
they grow; they n. toil nor spin; 6.28
N. is new wine put into old wineskins 9.17
For John came n. eating nor drinking, 11.18
"N. will I tell you by what authority 21.27
you know n. the scriptures nor the 22.29
resurrection they n. marry nor are 22.30
N. be called masters, for you have 23.10
for you n. enter yourselves, nor 23.13
for you know n. the day nor the 25.13
if you do not forgive, n. will your * Mk 11.26
"N. will I tell you by what authority 11.33
that you know n. the scriptures nor 12.24
they n. marry nor are given in 12.25
"I n. know nor understand what you 14.68
they n. sow nor reap, they have Lk 12.24
they have n. storehouse nor barn, 12.24
they grow; they n. toil nor spin; 12.27
It is fit n. for the land nor for 14.35
n. will they be convinced if some 16.31
was a judge who n. feared God nor 18.02
'Though I n. fear God nor regard 18.04
"N. will I tell you by what authority 20.08
from the dead n. marry nor are 20.35
n. did Herod, for he sent him back 23.15
if you are n. the Christ, nor Elijah, Jn 1.25
is coming when n. on this mountain 4.21
"N. do I condemn you; go, and do * 8.11
"You know n. me nor my Father; 8.19
because it n. sees him nor knows 14.17
be troubled; n. let them be afraid. 14.27
n. can you, unless you abide in me. 15.04
You have n. part nor lot in this Ac 8.21
sight, and n. ate nor drank. 9.09
disciples which n. our fathers nor 15.10
here who are n. sacrilegious nor 19.37
by an oath n. to eat nor drink 23.12
by an oath n. to eat nor drink 23.21
N. can they prove to you what they 24.13
"N. against the law of the Jews, nor 25.08
And when n. sun nor stars appeared 27.20
For I am sure that n. death, Rom 8.38
natural branches, n. will he spare you. 11.21
So n. he who plants nor he who 1Co 3.07
n. the immoral, nor idolaters, nor 6.09
For n. circumcision counts for 7.19
N. was man created for woman, but 11.09
There is n. Jew nor Greek, there is Gal 3.28
there is n. slave nor free, there is n. 3.28
For in Christ Jesus n. circumcision 5.06
For n. circumcision counts for 6.15
and has n. beginning of days nor Heb 7.03
"Thou hast n. desired nor taken 10.08
works: you are n. cold nor hot. Rev 3.15
and n. cold nor hot, I will spew you 3.16
hunger no more, n. thirst any more; 7.16
n. shall there be mourning nor 21.04

NEKODA

the sons of N., the sons of Gazzam, Ez 2.48
sons of Tobiah, and the sons of N., 2.60
the sons of Rezin, the sons of N., Neh 7.50
the sons of N., six hundred and 7.62

NEMUEL

sons of Eliab: N., Dathan, and Abiram. Num 26.09
of N., the family of the Nemuelites 26.12
N., Jamin, Jarib, Zerah, Shaul; 1Ch 4.24

NEMUELITES

of Nemuel, the family of the N.; Num 26.12

NEPHEG

of Izhar: Korah, U., and Zichri. Ex 6.21
Ibhar, Elishua, N., Japhia, 2Sa 5.15
Nogah, N., Japhia, 1Ch 3.07
Nogah, N., Japhia, 14.06

NEPHILIM

The N. were on the earth in those Gen 6.04
we saw the N. (the sons of Anak, Num 13.33
of Anak, who come from the N.); 13.33

NEPHISIM

sons of Meunim, the sons of N., Ez 2.50

NEPHTOAH

to the spring of the Waters of N., Jos 15.09
to the spring of the Waters of N.; 18.15

NEPHUSHESIM

sons of Meunim, the sons of N., Neh 7.52

NER

Abner the son of N., Saul's uncle; 1Sa 14.50
and N. the father of Abner was the 14.51
Saul lay, with Abner the son of N., 26.05
army, and to Abner the son of N., 26.14
Now Abner the son of N., commander 2Sa 2.08
Abner the son of N., and the servants 2.12
the son of N. came to the king, and 3.23
the son of N. came to deceive you, 3.25
the blood of Abner the son of N. 3.28
will to slay Abner the son of N. 3.37
of Israel, Abner the son of N., 1Ki 2.05
than himself, Abner the son of N., 2.32
N. was the father of Kish, Kish of 1Ch 8.33
then Zur, Kish, Baal, N., Nadab, 9.36
N. was the father of Kish, Kish of 9.39
of Kish, and Abner the son of N., 26.28

NEREUS

N. and his sister, and Olympas, and Rom 16.15

NERGAL

Succothbenoth, the men of Cuth made N., 2Ki 17.30

NERGALSHAREZER

N., Samgarnebo, Sarsechim the Jer 39.03
N. the Rabmag, with all the rest of 39.03
N. the Rabmag, and all the chief 39.13

NERI

son of Shealtiel, the son of N., Lk 3.27

NERIAH

the son of N. son of Mahseiah, in Jer 32.12
purchase to Baruch the son of N., 32.16
called Baruch the son of N., 36.04
the son of N. did all that Jeremiah 36.08
the son of N. took the scroll in 36.14
the son of N., who wrote on it at 36.32
the son of N. has set you against 43.03
prophet and Baruch the son of N. 43.06
spoke to Baruch the son of N., 45.01
commanded Seraiah the son of N., 51.59

NEST

and your n. is set in the rock; Num 24.21
chance to come upon a bird's n., Deu 22.06
Like an eagle that stirs up its n., 32.11
Then I thought, 'I shall die in my n., Job 29.18
mounts up and makes his n. on high? 39.27
and the swallow a n. for herself, Ps 84.03
Like a bird that strays from its n., Pro 27.08
found like a n. the wealth of the Is 10.14
There shall the owl n. and lay and 34.15
you make your n. as high as the Jer 49.16
birds of every sort will n. Eze 17.23
though your n. is set among the Ob 1.04
to set his n. on high, to be safe Hab 2.09

NESTED

n. among the cedars, how you will Jer 22.23

NESTLINGS

fluttering birds, like scattered n., Is 16.02

NESTS

In them the birds build their n.; Ps 104.17
the dove that n. in the sides of Jer 48.28
air made their n. in its boughs; Eze 31.06
and birds of the air have n.; Mt 8.20
come and make n. in its branches. 13.32
the air can make n. in its shade. Mk 4.32
and birds of the air have n.; Lk 9.58
of the air made n. in its branches 13.19

NET

and upon the n. you shall make four Ex 27.04
so that the n. shall extend half 27.05
a n. for the one capital, and a n. for 1Ki 7.17
is cast into a n. by his own feet, Job 18.08
wrong, and closed his n. about me. 19.06
in the n. which they hid has their Ps 9.15
poor when he draws him into his n. 10.09
will pluck my feet out of the n. 25.15
take me out of the n. which is 31.04
cause they hid their n. for me; 35.07
And let the n. which they hid 35.08
They set a n. for my steps; 57.06
Thou didst bring us into the n.; 66.11
with cords they have spread a n., 140.05
For in vain is a n. spread in the Pro 1.17
neighbor spreads a n. for his feet. 29.05
fish which are taken in an evil n., Ecc 9.12
street like an antelope in a n.; Is 51.20
he spread a n. for my feet; Lam 1.13
And I will spread my n. over him, Eze 12.13
I will spread my n. over him, 17.20
they spread their n. over him; 19.08
I will throw my n. over you with a 32.03
and a n. spread upon Tabor. Hos 5.01
go, I will spread over them my n.; 7.12
each hunts his brother with a n. Mic 7.02
he drags them out with his n., Hab 1.15
sacrifices to his n. and burns 1.16
he then to keep on emptying his n., 1.17
brother, casting a n. into the sea; Mt 4.18
is like a n. which was thrown into 13.47
of Simon casting a n. in the sea; Mk 1.16
"Cast the n. on the right side of Jn 21.06
dragging the n. full of fish, for 21.08
aboard and hauled the n. ashore, 21.11
were so many, the n. was not torn. 21.11

NETAIM

and inhabitants of N. and Gederah; 1Ch 4.23

NETHANEL

from Issachar, N. the son of Zuar; Num 1.08
Issachar being N. the son of Zuar, 2.05
On the second day N. the son of 7.18
the offering of N. the son of Zuar 7.23
of Issachar was N. the son of Zuar 10.15
N. the fourth, Raddai the fifth, 1Ch 2.14
N., Amasai, Zechariah, Benaiah, and 15.24
And the scribe Shemaiah the son of N., 24.06
Sachar the fourth, N. the fifth, 26.04
N., and Micaiah, to teach in the 2Ch 17.07
and Shemaiah and N. his brothers, 35.09
N., Jozabad, and Elasah. Ez 10.22
of Hilkiah, Hashabiah; of Jedaiah, N. Neh 12.21
N., Judah, and Hanani, with the 12.36

NETHANIAH

namely, Ishmael the son of N., 2Ki 25.23
month, Ishmael the son of N., 25.25
N., and Asharelah, sons of Asaph, 1Ch 25.02
the fifth to N., his sons and his 25.12
N., Zebadiah, Asahel, Shemiramoth, 2Ch 17.08
princes sent Jehudi the son of N., Jer 36.14
at Mizpah—Ishmael the son of N., 40.08
the son of N. to take your life?" 40.14
go and slay Ishmael the son of N., 40.15
month, Ishmael the son of N., 41.01
Ishmael the son of N. and the ten 41.02
the son of N. came out from Mizpah 41.06
the son of N. and the men with him 41.07
the son of N. filled it with the 41.09
the son of N. took them captive 41.10
Ishmael the son of N. had done, 41.11
against Ishmael the son of N. 41.12
the son of N. escaped from Johanan 41.15
the son of N. had carried away 41.16
the son of N. had slain Gedaliah 41.18

NETHER

a stone, hard as the n. millstone. Job 41.24
make you to dwell in the n. world, Eze 26.20
to the n. world among mortal men, 31.14
will be comforted in the n. world. 31.16
the trees of Eden to the n. world; 31.18
to the n. world, to those who have 32.18
uncircumcised into the n. world, 32.24
them to pits of n. gloom to be 2Pe 2.04
for them the n. gloom of darkness 2.17
chains in the n. gloom until the Jud 1.06
for whom the n. gloom of darkness 1.13

NETOPHAH

Zalmon the Ahohite, Maharai of N., 2Sa 23.28
Heleb the son of Baanah of N., 23.29
N., Heled the son of Baanah of N., 1Ch 11.30
the tenth month, was Maharai of N., 27.13
The men of N., fifty-six. Ez 2.22
The men of Bethlehem and N., Neh 7.26

NETOPHATHITE

Seraiah the son of Tanhumeth the N., 2Ki 25.23
was Heldai the N., of Othniel; 1Ch 27.15
Tanhumeth, the sons of Ephai the N., Jer 40.08

NETOPHATHITES

the N., Atrothbethjoab, and half of 1Ch 2.54
dwelt in the villages of the N. 9.16
and from the villages of the N.; Neh 12.28

NETS

Then he made two n. of checker work 1Ki 7.17
together fall into their own n., Ps 141.10
woman whose heart is snares and n., Ecc 7.26
who spread n. upon the water. Is 19.08
a place for the spreading of n.; Eze 26.05
be a place for the spreading of n.; 26.14
be a place for the spreading of n.; 47.10
Immediately they left their n. and Mt 4.20
mending their n., and he called 4.21
they left their n. and followed Mk 1.18
were in their boat mending the n. 1.19
of them and were washing their n. Lk 5.02
and let down your n. for a catch." 5.04
your word I will let down the n." 5.05
and as their n. were breaking, 5.06

NETTLES
under the n. they huddle together. Job 30.07
the ground was covered with n., Pro 24.31
n. and thistles in its fortresses. Is 34.13
N. shall possess their precious Hos 9.06
land possessed by n. and salt pits, Zep 2.09

NETWORK
for it a grating, a n. of bronze; Ex 27.04
a n. of bronze, under its ledge, 38.04
rows round about upon the one n., 1Ki 7.18
projection which was beside the n.; 7.20
rows of pomegranates for each n., 7.42
a n. and pomegranates, all of 2Ki 25.17
pillar had the like, with the n. 25.17
rows of pomegranates for each n., 2Ch 4.13
a n. and pomegranates, all of bronze, Jer 52.22
a hundred upon the n. round about. 52.23

NETWORKS
and the two n. to cover the two 1Ki 7.41
pomegranates for the two n., 7.42
and the two n. to cover the two 2Ch 4.12
pomegranates for the two n., 4.13

NEVER
"I will n. again curse the ground Gen 8.21
that n. again shall all flesh be 9.11
and n. again shall there be a flood 9.11
waters shall n. again become a 9.15
such as I had n. seen in all the 41.19
and I have n. seen him since. 44.28
such as n. has been in Egypt from Ex 9.18
such as had n. been in all the land 9.24
of locusts as had n. been before, 10.14
n. see my face again; for in the 10.28
Egypt, such as there has n. been, 11.06
see today, you shall n. see again. 14.13
So keep my charge n. to practice Lev 18.30
and n. to defile yourselves by them: 18.30
and upon which a yoke has n. come. Num 19.02
and n. again do any such wickedness Deu 13.11
For the poor will n. cease out of 15.11
'You shall n. return that way again 17.16
and shall n. again commit any such 19.20
which has n. been worked and which 21.03
that you should n. make again; 28.68
no gods, to gods they had n. known, 32.17
whom your fathers had n. dreaded. 32.17
'I will n. break my covenant with Ju 2.01
She had n. known a man. And it 11.39
"A razor has n. come upon my head; 16.17
a thing has n. happened or been 19.30
which there has n. come a yoke, 1Sa 6.07
house of Joab n. be without one 2Sa 3.29
the sword shall n. depart from 12.10
and he shall n. touch you again." 14.10
His father had n. at any time 1Ki 1.06
'There shall n. fail you a man 8.25
n. again came such an abundance of 10.10
like of it was n. made in any 10.20
for he n. prophesies good concerning 22.08
world stands firm, n. to be moved. 1Ch 16.30
'There shall n. fail you a man 2Ch 6.16
there n. was seen the like of 9.11
like of it was n. made in any 9.19
for he n. prophesies good concerning 18.07
and n. seek their peace or prosperity, Ez 9.12
of Purim should n. fall into Est 9.28
as infants that n. see the light? Job 3.16
my eye will n. again see good. 7.07
him, saying, 'I have n. seen you.' 8.18
of soul, n. having tasted of good. 21.25
those who know him n. see his days? 24.01
is in turmoil, and is n. still; 30.27
hidden his face, he will n. see it. Ps 10.11
these things shall n. be moved. 15.05
my prosperity, "I shall n. be moved." 30.06
let me n. be put to shame; 31.01
so your faces shall n. be ashamed. 34.05
is costly, and can n. suffice, 49.08
on for ever, and n. see the Pit. 49.09
who will n. more see the light. 49.19
he will n. permit the righteous to 55.22
untimely birth that n. sees the sun. 58.08
let me n. be put to shame! 71.01
and n. again be favorable? 77.07
Then we will n. turn back from thee 80.18
What man can live and n. see death? 89.48
established; it shall n. be moved; 93.01
established, it shall n. be moved; 96.10
so that it should n. be shaken. 104.05
For the righteous will n. be moved; 112.06
I will n. forget thy precepts; 119.93
of the wicked n. anoint my head; 141.05
The righteous will n. be removed, Pro 10.30
of the righteous will n. be moved. 12.03
Sheol and Abaddon are n. satisfied, 27.20
and n. satisfied are the eyes of 27.20
Three things are n. satisfied; four n. 30.15
and the fire which n. says, "Enough." 30.16
his eyes are n. satisfied with Ecc 4.08
so that he n. asks, "For whom am I 4.08
on earth who does good and n. sins. 7.20
bowl that n. lacks mixed wine. Sol 7.02
It will n. be inhabited or dwelt in Is 13.20
no more, it will n. be rebuilt. 25.02
whose stakes will n. be plucked up, 33.20
today you have n. heard of them, 48.07
You have n. heard, you have n. known, 48.08
name would n. be cut off or 48.19
my deliverance will n. be ended. 51.06
appetite; they n. have enough. 56.11
the night they shall n. be silent. 62.06
those over whom thou hast n. ruled, 63.19
so that it can n. be mended. Jer 19.11
dishonor will n. be forgotten. 20.11
and he shall n. see this land again 22.12
David shall n. lack a man to sit on 33.17
priests shall n. lack a man in my 33.18
of Rechab shall n. lack a man to 35.19
covenant which will n. be forgotten. 50.05
steadfast love of the LORD n. ceases, Lam 3.22
his mercies n. come to an end; 3.22
behold, I have n. defiled myself; Eze 4.14
till now I have n. eaten what died 4.14
with you what I have n. yet done, 5.09
like of which I will n. do again. 5.09
the like has n. been, nor ever shall 16.16
and n. open your mouth again 16.63
"What is in your mind shall n. happen— 20.32
you shall n. be rebuilt; for I the 26.14
you will n. be found again, says the 26.21
and n. again exalt itself above the 29.15
that they will n. again rule over 29.15
And it shall n. again be the 29.16
that you may n. again suffer the 36.30
which shall n. be destroyed, Dan 2.44
his kingdom shall n. be destroyed, 6.26
such as n. has been since there was 12.01
his riches can n. offset the guilt Hos 12.08
their like has n. been from of old, Joe 2.02
my people shall n. again be put to 2.26
my people shall n. again be put to 2.27
strangers shall n. again pass 3.17
I will n. again pass by them; Amo 7.08
but n. again prophesy at Bethel, for 7.13
I will n. again pass by them. 8.02
"Surely I will n. forget any of 8.07
they shall fall, and n. rise again." 8.14
and they shall n. again be plucked 9.15
for n. again shall the wicked come Nah 1.15
slacked and justice n. goes forth. Hab 1.04
like death he has n. enough. 2.05
you eat, but you n. have enough; Hag 1.06

NEVER (cont.)
drink, but you n. have your fill; Hag 1.06
you will n. enter the kingdom of Mt 5.20
you will n. get out till you have 5.26
I declare to them, 'I n. knew you; 7.23
"N. was anything like this seen in 9.33
indeed hear but n. understand, 13.14
shall indeed see but n. perceive. 13.14
This shall n. happen to you." 16.22
"But this kind n. comes out except *17.21
you will n. enter the kingdom of 18.03
ninety-nine that n. went astray. 18.13
have you n. read, 'Out of the mouth 21.16
if you have faith and n. doubt, 21.21
"Have you n. read in the scriptures: 21.42
until now, no, and n. will be. 24.21
of you, I will n. fall away." 26.33
"We n. saw anything like this!" Mk 2.12
"Have you n. read what David did, 2.25
the Holy Spirit n. has forgiveness, 3.29
of him, and n. enter him again." 9.25
created until now, and n. will be. 13.19
you will n. get out till you have Lk 12.59
and I n. disobeyed your command; 15.29
yet you n. gave me a kid, that I 15.29
barren, and the wombs that n. bore, 23.29
and the breasts that n. gave suck!' 23.29
I shall give him will n. thirst; Jn 4.14
n. heard, his form you have n. seen; 5.37
who believes in me shall n. thirst. 6.35
learning, when he has n. studied?" 7.15
and have n. been in bondage to any 8.33
my word, he will n. see death." 8.51
my word, he will n. taste death.' 8.52
N. since the world began has it 9.32
life, and they shall n. perish, 10.28
and believes in me shall n. die. 11.26
to him, "You shall n. wash my feet." 13.08
"This man n. ceases to speak words Ac 6.13
for I have n. eaten anything that 10.14
days, a deed you will n. believe, 13.41
from birth, who had n. walked. 14.08
we have n. even heard that there is 19.02
indeed hear but n. understand, 28.26
shall indeed see but n. perceive. 28.26
from the dead will n. die again; Rom 6.09
in him of whom they have n. heard? 10.14
N. flag in zeal, be aglow with the 12.11
with the lowly; n. be conceited. 12.16
Beloved, n. avenge yourselves, but 12.19
rather decide n. to put a stumbling 14.13
see who have n. been told of him, 15.21
understand who have n. heard of him." 15.21
them members of a prostitute? N.! 1Co 6.15
N. mind. But if you can gain your 7.21
I will n. eat meat, lest I cause my 8.13
Love n. ends; as for prophecy, it 13.08
For we n. used either words of 1Th 2.05
N. admit any charge against an 1Ti 5.19
anybody and can n. arrive at a 2Ti 3.07
who n. lies, promised ages ago Tit 1.02
same, and thy years will n. end. Heb 1.12
'They shall n. enter my rest.'" 3.11
that they should n. enter his rest, 3.18
'They shall n. enter my rest,'" 4.03
said, "They shall n. enter my rest." 4.05
it can n., by the same sacrifices 10.01
which can n. take away sins. 10.11
"I will n. fail you nor forsake you 13.05
if you do this you will n. fall; 2Pe 1.10
better for them n. to have known 2.21
n. shall he go out of it, and I will Rev 3.12
and night they n. cease to sing, 4.08
such as had n. been since men were 16.18
widow, mourning I shall n. see,' 18.07
to thee, n. to be found again!" 18.14
and its gates shall n. be shut by 21.25

NEVER-ENDING
of heart to destroy in n. enmity; Eze 25.15

NEVERMORE
descendants of evildoers n. be named! Is 14.20

NEVERTHELESS
n. his younger brother shall be Gen 48.19
N., in the day when I visit, I will Ex 32.34
N. among those that chew the cud or Lev 11.04
N. a spring or a cistern holding 11.36
N. the cities of the Levites, the 25.32
n. the first-born of man you shall Num 18.15
n. Kain shall be wasted. How long 24.22
N. those that died by the plague 25.09
N. it shall also be purified with 31.23
N. the LORD your God would not Deu 23.05
n. the inhabitants of Bethshemesh Ju 1.33
n., the road on which you are going 4.09
N. the lords do not approve of you. 1Sa 29.06
n. the commanders of the Philistines 29.09
N. David took the stronghold of 2Sa 5.07
N., because by this deed you have 12.14
n. you shall not build the house, 1Ki 8.19
N. I will not take the whole 11.34
N. the high places were not taken 15.04
N. the heart of Asa was wholly true 15.14
n. I will send my servants to you 20.06
N. he clung to the sin of Jeroboam 2Ki 3.03
N. the high places were not taken 12.03
N. they did not depart from the 13.06
N. the high places were not taken 15.04
N. the high places were not removed 15.35
N. David took the stronghold of 1Ch 11.05
n. you shall not build the house, 2Ch 6.09
N. they shall be servants to him, 12.08
N. the heart of Asa was blameless 15.17
N. some good is found in you, for 19.03
N. the people still sacrificed at 33.17
N. Josiah would not turn away from 35.22
"N. they were disobedient and Neh 9.26
N. in thy great mercies thou didst 9.31
n. foreign women made even him to 13.26
N. Haman restrained himself, and Est 5.10
N. I am continually with thee; Ps 73.23
n., you shall die like men, and fall 82.07
N. he regarded their distress, when 106.44
N. if you warn the righteous man Eze 3.21
N. my eye spared them, and I did not 20.17
n. I will read the writing to the Dan 5.17
N. the men rowed hard to bring the Jon 1.13
n., not as I will, but as thou wilt." Mt 26.39
n. know this, that the kingdom of Lk 10.11
N. do not rejoice in this, that the 10.20
N. I must go on my way today and 13.33
N., when the Son of man comes, will 18.08
n. not my will, but thine, be done." 22.42
N. many even of the authorities Jn 12.42
N. I tell you the truth: it is to 16.07
N., we have not made use of this 1Co 9.12
N. with most of them God was not 10.05
(N., in the Lord woman is not 11.11
n., in church I would rather speak 14.19

NEW
Now there arose a n. king over Ex 1.08
On the third n. moon after the 19.01
fruits crushed n. grain from fresh Lev 2.14
offering of n. grain to the LORD. 23.16
out the old to make way for the n. 26.10
But if the LORD creates something n., Num 16.30
offering of n. grain to the LORD 28.26
besides the burnt offering of the n. moon, 29.06
has built a n. house and has not Deu 20.05
"When you build a n. house, 22.08
to n. gods that had come in of late, 32.17
these wineskins were n. when we Jos 9.13
When n. gods were chosen, then war Ju 5.08

NEW (cont.)

they bound him with two n. ropes, Ju 15.13
bind me with n. ropes that have 16.11
So Delilah took n. ropes and bound 16.12
and prepare a n. cart and two 1Sa 6.07
"Behold, tomorrow is the n. moon, 20.05
to him, "Tomorrow is the n. moon; 20.18
and when the n. moon came, the king 20.24
day, the morrow after the n. moon, 20.27
the ark of God upon a n. cart, 2Sa 6.03
Abinadab, were driving the n. cart 6.03
and who was girded with a n. sword, 21.16
had clad himself with a n. garment; 1Ki 11.29
hold of the n. garment that was on 11.30
"Bring me a n. bowl, and put salt in 2Ki 2.20
It is neither n. moon nor sabbath. 4.23
the ark of God upon a n. cart, 1Ch 13.07
n. moons, and feast days, according 23.31
sabbaths and the n. moons and the 2Ch 2.04
the n. moons, and the three annual 8.13
of the LORD, before the n. court, 20.05
the n. moons, and the appointed 31.03
offerings at the n. moon and at all Ez 3.05
the n. moons, the appointed feasts, Neh 10.33
me, and my bow ever n. in my hand. Job 29.20
like n. wineskins, it is ready to 32.19
Sing to him a n. song, play skilfully Ps 33.03
He put a n. song in my mouth, a song 40.03
and put a n. and right spirit 51.10
Blow the trumpet at the n. moon, 81.03
O sing to the LORD a n. song; 96.01
O sing to the LORD a n. song, 98.01
I will sing a n. song to thee, O God 144.09
Sing to the LORD a n. song, 149.01
Wealth brings many n. friends, Pro 19.04
and the n. growth appears, and the 27.25
there is nothing n. under the sun. Ecc 1.09
which it is said, "See, this is n."? 1.10
n. as well as old, which I have laid Sol 7.13
N. moon and sabbath and the calling Is 1.13
Your n. moons and your appointed 1.14
the n. growth fails, the verdure is 15.06
n., sharp, and having teeth; you shall 41.15
and n. things I now declare; before they 42.09
Sing to the LORD a n. song, 42.10
Behold, I am doing a n. thing; 43.19
who at the n. moons predict what 47.13
forth I make you hear n. things, 48.06
you found n. life for your strength, 57.10
be called by a n. name which the 62.02
I create n. heavens and a n. earth; 65.17
"For as the n. heaven and the n. earth 66.22
From n. moon to n. moon, and from 66.23
entry of the N. Gate of the house Jer 26.10
has created a n. thing on the 31.22
I will make a n. covenant with the 31.31
entry of the N. Gate of the LORD's 36.10
they are n. every morning; Lam 3.23
and put a n. spirit within them; Eze 11.19
yourselves a n. heart and a n. spirit! 18.31
A n. heart I will give you, and a n. spirit 36.26
the n. moons, and the sabbaths, all 45.17
the day of the n. moon it shall be 46.01
the sabbaths and on the n. moons. 46.03
On the day of the n. moon he shall 46.06
her n. moons, her sabbaths, and all Hos 2.11
Wine and n. wine take away the 4.11
Now the n. moon shall devour them 5.07
and the n. wine shall fail them. 9.02
saying, "When will the n. moon be over, Amo 8.05
the n. wine, the oil, upon what the Hag 1.11
flourish, and n. wine the maidens. Zec 9.17
Neither is n. wine put into old Mt 9.17
but n. wine is put into fresh 9.17
treasure what is n. and what is old." 13.52
in the n. world, when the Son of man 19.28
when I drink it n. with you in my 26.29
and laid it in his own n. tomb, 27.60
A n. teaching! With authority Mk 1.27
the n. from the old, and a worse 2.21
And no one puts n. wine into old 2.22
but n. wine is for fresh skins." 2.22
when I drink it n. in the kingdom 14.25
demons; they will speak in n. tongues; * 16.17
a piece from a n. garment and puts Lk 5.36
if he does, he will tear the n., 5.36
piece from the n. will not match 5.36
And no one puts n. wine into old 5.37
the n. wine will burst the skins 5.37
But n. wine must be put into fresh 5.38
after drinking old wine desires n.; 5.39
is the n. covenant in my blood * 22.20
A n. commandment I give to you, that Jn 13.34
in the garden a n. tomb where no 19.41
said, "They are filled with n. wine." Ac 2.13
know what this n. teaching is 17.19
telling or hearing something n. 17.21
code but in the n. life of the Rom 7.06
"This cup is the n. covenant in my 1Co 11.25
to be ministers of a n. covenant, 2Co 3.06
is in Christ, he is a n. creation; 5.17
away, behold, the n. has come. 5.17
uncircumcision, but a n. creation. Gal 6.15
in himself one n. man in place of Eph 2.15
and put on the n. nature, created 4.24
a festival or a n. moon or a Col 2.16
and have put on the n. nature, 3.10
establish a n. covenant with the Heb 8.08
In speaking of a n. covenant he 8.13
is the mediator of a n. covenant, 9.15
by the n. and living way which he 10.20
the mediator of a n. covenant, 12.24
we wait for n. heavens and a n. earth 2Pe 3.13
I am writing you no n. commandment, 1Jn 2.07
Yet I am writing you a n. commandment, 2.08
were writing you a n. commandment, 2Jn 1.05
with a n. name written on the stone Rev 2.17
the N. Jerusalem which comes down 3.12
out of heaven, and my own n. name. 3.12
and they sang a n. song, saying, "Worthy 5.09
and they sing a n. song before the 14.03
Then I saw a n. heaven and a n. earth; 21.01
n. Jerusalem, coming down out of 21.02
said, "Behold, I make all things n. 21.05

NEWBORN

forsakes her n. calf because there Jer 14.05
Like n. babes, long for the pure 1Pe 2.02

NEWLY

"When a man is n. married, he shall Deu 24.05

NEWNESS

we too might walk in n. of life. Rom 6.04

NEWS

came into the city and told the n., 1Sa 4.13
carry the good n. to their idols 31.09
old when the n. about Saul and 2Sa 4.04
thought he was bringing good n., 4.10
the reward I gave him for his n. 4.10
David all the n. about the fighting 11.18
telling all the n. about the 11.19
are a worthy man and bring good n." 1Ki 1.42
When the n. came to Joab—for Joab 2.28
This day is a day of good n.; 2Ki 7.09
to go and tell the n. in Jezreel." 9.15
carry the good n. to their idols 1Ch 10.09
told the glad n. of deliverance in Ps 40.09
and good n. refreshes the bones. Pro 15.30
so is good n. from a far country. 25.25
who brought the n. to my father, Jer 20.15
besieging Jerusalem heard n. of them, 37.05
to you to report to you the n. Eze 24.26
who hear the n. of you clap their Nah 3.19

NEWS (cont.)
poor have good n. preached to them. Mt 11.05
about it, and to spread the n., Mk 1.45
you, and to bring you this good n. Lk 1.19
bring you good n. of a great joy 2.10
he preached good n. to the people. 3.18
me to preach good n. to the poor. 4.18
preach the good n. of the kingdom 4.43
poor have good n. preached to them. 7.22
the good n. of the kingdom of God. 8.01
then the good n. of the kingdom of 16.16
preached good n. about the kingdom Ac 8.12
he told him the good n. of Jesus. 8.35
preaching good n. of peace by 10.36
N. of this came to the ears of the 11.22
you the good n. that what God 13.32
with you, and bring you good n., 14.15
feet of those who preach good n.! Rom 10.15
that I may be cheered by n. of you. Php 2.19
us the good n. of your faith and 1Th 3.06
For good n. came to us just as to Heb 4.02
the good n. failed to enter 4.06
the good n. to you through the 1Pe 1.12
is the good n. which was preached 1.25

NEXT
bear to you at this season n. year." Gen 17.21
And on the n. day, the first-born 19.34
When he went out the n. day, Ex 2.13
his neighbor n. to his house shall 12.04
on its inside edge n. to the ephod. 28.26
on its inside edge n. to the ephod. 39.19
then his n. of kin shall come and Lev 25.25
Those to encamp n. to him shall be Num 2.05
And those to encamp n. to him shall 2.12
And n. to him shall be the tribe of 2.20
And those to encamp n. to him shall 2.27
and all the n. day, and gathered the 11.32
kinsman that is n. to him of his 27.11
he rose early n. morning and Ju 6.38
maidservant, for you are n. of kin. Ru 3.09
the part of the n. of kin for you, well; 3.13
the part of the n. of kin for you, then, 3.13
the part of the n. of kin for you. Lie down 3.13
the n. of kin, of whom Boaz had 4.01
Then he said to the n. of kin, 4.03
Then the n. of kin said, "I cannot 4.06
So when the n. of kin said to Boaz, 4.08
you this day without n. of kin; 4.14
of Ashdod rose early the n. day, 1Sa 5.03
they rose early on the n. morning, 5.04
and n. to him Abinadab, and the 17.13
Israel, and I shall be n. to you; 23.17
until the evening of the n. day; 30.17
in Jerusalem that day, and the n. 2Sa 11.12
"See, Joab's field is n. to mine, 14.30
And n. to him among the three 23.09
And n. to him was Shammah, the son 23.11
and he was born n. after Absalom. 1Ki 1.06
The n. morning, about the time of 2Ki 3.20
And on the n. day I said to her, 6.29
And n. to him among the three 1Ch 11.12
and on the n. day offered burnt 29.21
and n. to him Jehohanan the commander, 2Ch 17.15
and n. to him Amasiah the son of 17.16
and n. to him Jehozabad with a 17.18
and Elkanah the n. in authority to 28.07
And n. to him the men of Jericho Neh 3.02
And n. to them Zaccur the son of 3.02
And n. to them Meremoth the son of 3.04
And n. to them Meshullam the son of 3.04
And n. to them Zadok the son of 3.04
And n. to them the Tekoites repaired 3.05
And n. to them repaired Melatiah 3.07
N. to them Uzziel the son of 3.08
N. to him Hananiah, one of the 3.08
N. to them Rephaiah the son of Hur, 3.09
N. to them Jedaiah the son of 3.10
and n. to him Hattush the son of 3.10
N. to him Shallum the son of 3.12
n. to him Hashabiah, ruler of half 3.17
n. to him Ezer the son of Jeshua, 3.19
the men n. to him being Carshena, Est 1.14
the Jew was n. in rank to King 10.03
you may tell the n. generation Ps 48.13
that the n. generation might know 78.06
And on the n. morning I did as I Eze 24.18
But when dawn came up the n. day, Jon 4.07
the man who stands n. to me, Zec 13.07
you in one town, flee to the n.; Mt 10.23
N. day, that is, after the day of 27.62
them, "Let us go on to the n. towns, Mk 1.38
On the n. day, when they had come Lk 9.37
And the n. day he took out two 10.35
And if it bears fruit n. year, 13.09
The n. day he saw Jesus coming Jn 1.29
The n. day again John was standing 1.35
The n. day Jesus decided to go to 1.43
On the n. day the people who 6.22
The n. day a great crowd who had 12.12
The n. day, as they were on their Ac 10.09
The n. day he rose and went off 10.23
might be told them the n. sabbath. 13.42
The n. sabbath almost the whole 13.44
and on the n. day he went on with 14.20
his house was n. door to the 18.07
the n. day we touched at Samos; 20.15
and the n. day to Rhodes, and from 21.01
and the n. day he purified himself 21.26
and the n. day he took his seat on 25.06
but on the n. day took my seat on 25.17
The n. day we put in at Sidon; 27.03
they began n. day to throw the 27.18

NEZIAH
the sons of N., and the sons of Ez 2.54
the sons of N., the sons of Hatipha. Neh 7.56

NEZIB
Iphtah, Ashnah, N., Jos 15.43

NIBHAZ
and the Avvites made N. and Tartak; 2Ki 17.31

NIBSHAN
N., the City of Salt, and Engedi: six Jos 15.62

NICANOR
and N., and Timon, and Parmenas, and Ac 6.05

NICODEMUS
named N., a ruler of the Jews. Jn 3.01
N. said to him, "How can a man be 3.04
N. said to him, "How can this be?" 3.09
N., who had gone to him before, and 7.50
N. also, who had at first come to 19.39

NICOLAITANS
have, you hate the works of the N., Rev 2.06
who hold the teaching of the N. 2.15

NICOLAUS
and N., a proselyte of Antioch. Ac 6.05

NICOPOLIS
do your best to come to me at N., Tit 3.12

NIGER
Barnabas, Symeon who was called N., Ac 13.01

NIGH
but not n.: a star shall come forth Num 24.17
my steps had well n. slipped. Ps 73.02
days come, and the years draw n., Ecc 12.01

NIGHT

Day, and the darkness he called N. Gen 1.05
to separate the day from the n.; 1.14
the lesser light to rule the n.; 1.16
to rule over the day and over the n., 1.18
day and n., shall not cease. 8.22
his forces against them by n., 14.15
servant's house and spend the n., 19.02
we will spend the n. in the street." 19.02
their father drink wine that n.; 19.33
I lay last n. with my father; 19.34
father drink wine that n. also; 19.35
came to Abimelech in a dream by n., 20.03
drank, and they spent the n. there. 24.54
to him the same n. and said, 26.24
place, and stayed there that n., 28.11
mandrakes." So he lay with her that n. 30.16
Laban the Aramean in a dream by n., 31.24
of your father spoke to me last n., 31.29
stolen by day or stolen by n. 31.39
consumed me, and the cold by n., 31.40
my hands, and rebuked you last n." 31.42
and tarried all n. on the mountain 31.54
So he lodged there that n., and took 32.13
himself lodged that n. in the camp. 32.21
The same n. he arose and took his 32.22
And one n. they both dreamed—the 40.05
we dreamed on the same n., he and I, each 41.11
to Israel in visions of the n., 46.02
land all that day and all that n.; Ex 10.13
eat the flesh that n., roasted; 12.08
through the land of Egypt that n., 12.12
And Pharaoh rose up in the n., 12.30
And he summoned Moses and Aaron by n., 12.31
It was a n. of watching by the Lord, 12.42
so this same n. is a n. of watching 12.42
and by n. in a pillar of fire to 13.21
they might travel by day and by n.; 13.21
of fire by n. did not depart from 13.22
and the n. passed without one 14.20
one coming near the other all n. 14.20
back by a strong east wind all n., 14.21
by day, and fire was in it by n., 40.38
the altar all n. until the morning, Lev 6.09
remain day and n. for seven days, 8.35
with you all n. until the morning. 19.13
and the appearance of fire by n. Num 9.16
if it continued for a day and a n., 9.21
dew fell upon the camp in the n., 11.09
and all n., and all the next day, 11.32
and the people wept that n. 14.01
day and in a pillar of fire by n. 14.14
said to them, "Lodge here this n., 22.08
Pray, now, tarry here this n. also, 22.19
to Balaam at n. and said to him, 22.20
in fire by n., to show you by what Deu 1.33
God brought you out of Egypt by n. 16.01
day remain all n. until morning. 16.04
not remain all n. upon the tree, 21.23
of what chances to him by n., 23.10
n. and day you shall be in dread, 28.66
shall meditate on it day and n., Jos 1.08
camp, and spent the n. in the camp. 6.11
valor, and sent them forth by n. 8.03
spent that n. among the people. 8.09
Joshua spent that n. in the valley. 8.13
marched up all n. from Gilgal. 10.09
That n. the Lord said to him, "Take Ju 6.25
to do it by day, he did it by n. 6.27
And God did so that n.; 6.40
That same n. the Lord said to him, 7.09
go by n., you and the men that are 9.32
that were with him rose up by n., 9.34
for him all n. at the gate of the 16.02
They kept quiet all n., 16.02
man, "Be pleased to spend the n., 19.06
pray tarry all n. Behold, the day 19.09
But the man would not spend the n.; 19.10
Jebusites, and spend the n. in it. 19.11
and spend the n. at Gibeah or at 19.13
go in and spend the n. at Gibeah, 19.15
into his house to spend the n. 19.15
do not spend the n. in the square. 19.20
abused her all n. until the 19.25
and my concubine, to spend the n. 20.04
the house round about me by n.; 20.05
a husband this n. and should bear Ru 1.12
Remain this n., and in the morning, 3.13
brought his ox with him that n., 1Sa 14.34
Philistines by n. and despoil them 14.36
and he cried to the Lord all n. 15.11
what the Lord said to me this n. 15.16
That n. Saul sent messengers to 19.11
naked all that day and all that n. 19.24
a wall to us both by n. and by day, 25.16
and Abishai went to the army by n.; 26.07
and they came to the woman by n. 28.08
eaten nothing all day and all n. 28.20
they rose and went away that n. 28.25
and went all n., and took the body 31.12
went all that n. through the 2Sa 2.29
Joab and his men marched all n., 2.32
by the way of the Arabah all n., 4.07
But that same n. the word of the 7.04
in and lay all n. upon the ground. 12.16
not spend the n. with the people. 17.08
a man will stay with you this n.; 19.07
or the beasts of the field by n. 21.10
to Solomon in a dream by n.; 1Ki 3.05
And this woman's son died in the n., 3.19
may be open n. and day toward this 8.29
to the Lord our God day and n., 8.59
and they came by n., and surrounded 2Ki 6.14
And the king rose in the n., 7.12
and rose by n., and he and his 8.21
And that n. the angel of the Lord 19.35
of war fled by n. by the way of 25.04
for they were on duty day and n. 1Ch 9.33
But that same n. the word of the 17.03
In that n. God appeared to Solomon, 2Ch 1.07
be open day and n. toward this 6.20
Solomon in the n. and said to him: 7.12
and he rose by n. and smote the 21.09
offerings and the fat parts until n.; 35.14
of Eliashib, where he spent the n., Ez 10.06
thee day and n. for the people of Neh 1.06
Then I arose in the n., I and a few men 2.12
I went out by n. by the Valley Gate 2.13
went up in the n. by the valley 2.15
protection against them day and n. 4.09
pass the n. within Jerusalem, that 4.22
guard for us by n. and may labor 4.22
at n. they are coming to kill you." 6.10
of fire in the n. to light for 9.12
of fire by n. which lighted for 9.19
drink for three days, n. or day. Est 4.16
On that n. the king could not sleep 6.01
and the n. which said, 'A man-child Job 3.03
That n.—let thick darkness seize 3.06
Yea, let that n. be barren; 3.07
Amid thoughts from visions of the n., 4.13
and grope at noonday as in the n. 5.14
'But the n. is long, and I am full 7.04
They make n. into day; 'The light,' they 17.12
away like a vision of the n. 20.08
They lie all n. naked, without 24.07
and in the n. he is as a thief. 24.14
in the n. a whirlwind carries him 27.20
with the dew all n. on my branches, 29.19
The n. racks my bones, and the pain 30.17
In a dream, in a vision of the n., 33.15
works, he overturns them in the n., 34.25
Maker, who gives songs in the n., 35.10
Do not long for the n., when peoples 36.20

NIGHT (cont.)

will he spend the n. at your crib? Job 39.09
on his law he meditates day and n. Ps 1.02
every n. I flood my bed with tears; 6.06
in the n. also my heart instructs 16.07
heart, if thou visitest me by n., 17.03
and n. to n. declares knowledge. 19.02
and by n., but find no rest. 22.02
Weeping may tarry for the n., 30.05
For day and n. thy hand was heavy 32.04
tears have been my food day and n., 42.03
and at n. his song is with me, a 42.08
Day and n. they go around it on its 55.10
on thee in the watches of the n.; 63.06
Thine is the day, thine also the n.; 74.16
in the n. my hand is stretched out 77.02
I commune with my heart in the n.; 77.06
and all the n. with a fiery light. 78.14
I cry out in the n. before thee. 88.01
is past, or as a watch in the n. 90.04
will not fear the terror of the n., 91.05
and thy faithfulness by n., 92.02
and it is n., when all the beasts 104.20
a covering, and fire to give light by n. 105.39
I remember thy name in the n., 119.55
awake before the watches of the n., 119.148
you by day, nor the moon by n. 121.06
who stand by n. in the house of the 134.01
moon and stars to rule over the n., 136.09
me, and the light about me be n.," 139.11
the n. is bright as the day; 139.12
at the time of n. and darkness. Pro 7.09
while it is yet n. and provides 31.15
Her lamp does not go out at n. 31.18
even in the n. his mind does not Ecc 2.23
neither day nor n. one's eyes see 8.16
Upon my bed by n. I sought him whom Sol 3.01
at his thigh, against alarms by n. 3.08
my locks with the drops of the n. 5.02
shining of a flaming fire by n.; Is 4.05
at Geba they lodge for the n.; 10.29
laid waste in a n. Moab is undone; 15.01
Kir is laid waste in a n. Moab is undone. 15.01
your shade like n. at the height 16.03
Seir, "Watchman, what of the n.? 21.11
"Morning comes, and also the n. 21.12
My soul yearns for thee in the n., 26.09
one harm it, I guard it n. and day; 27.03
pass through, by day and by n.; 28.19
like a dream, a vision of the n. 29.07
song as in the n. when a holy 30.29
N. and day it shall not be quenched 34.10
yea, there shall the n. hag alight, 34.14
from day to n. thou dost bring me 38.12
from day to n. thou dost bring me 38.13
day and n. they shall not be shut; 60.11
the moon give light to you by n.; 60.19
day and all the n. they shall 62.06
and spend the n. in secret places; 65.04
"Up, and let us attack by n., and destroy Jer 6.05
weep day and n. for the slain of 9.01
who turns aside to tarry for a n.? 14.08
run down with tears n. and day, 14.17
shall serve other gods day and n., 16.13
moon and the stars for light by n., 31.35
day and my covenant with the n., 33.20
so that day and n. will not come 33.20
with day and n. and the ordinances 33.25
heat by day and the frost by n. 36.30
of the city at n. by way of the 39.04
If thieves came by n., would they not 49.09
the city by n. by the way of a 52.07
She weeps bitterly in the n., Lam 1.02
down like a torrent day and n.! 2.18
Arise, cry out in the n., 2.19
to Daniel in a vision of the n. Dan 2.19
That very n. Belshazzar the Chaldean 5.30
palace, and spent the n. fasting; 6.18
Daniel said, "I saw in my vision by n., 7.02
After this I saw in the n. visions, 7.07
I saw in the n. visions, and behold, 7.13
also shall stumble with you by n.; Hos 4.05
all n. their anger smolders; 7.06
pass the n. in sackcloth, O ministers Joe 1.13
and darkens the day into n., Amo 5.08
came to you, if plunderers by n.— Ob 1.05
being in a n., and perished in a n. Jon 4.10
Therefore it shall be n. to you, Mic 3.06
"I saw in the n., and behold, a man Zec 1.08
to the LORD), not day and not n., 14.07
the child and his mother by n., Mt 2.14
watch of the n. he came to them, 14.25
part of the n. the thief was 24.43
fall away because of me this n.; 26.31
this very n., before the cock crows, 26.34
disciples came by n. and stole him 28.13
and should sleep and rise n. and day, Mk 4.27
N. and day among the tombs and on 5.05
watch of the n. he came to them, 6.48
this very n., before the cock crows 14.30
watch over their flock by n. Lk 2.08
with fasting and prayer n. and day. 2.37
we toiled all n. and took nothing! 5.05
and all n. he continued in prayer 6.12
This n. your soul is required of 12.20
in that n. there will be two men in 17.34
elect, who cry to him day and n.? 18.07
but at n. he went out and lodged on 21.37
to Jesus by n. and said to him, Jn 3.02
n. comes, when no one can work. 9.04
But if any one walks in the n., 11.10
immediately went out; and it was n. 13.30
who had at first come to him by n., 19.39
but that n. they caught nothing. 21.03
But at n. an angel of the Lord Ac 5.19
the gates day and n., to kill him; 9.24
took him by n. and let him down 9.25
The very n. when Herod was about to 12.06
vision appeared to Paul in the n.: 16.09
took them the same hour of the n., 16.33
and Silas away by n. to Beroea; 17.10
said to Paul one n. in a vision, 18.09
I did not cease n. or day to 20.31
The following n. the Lord stood by 23.11
hour of the n. get ready two 23.23
brought him by n. to Antipatris. 23.31
they earnestly worship n. and day. 26.07
For this very n. there stood by me 27.23
When the fourteenth n. had come, 27.27
the n. is far gone, the day is at Rom 13.12
Jesus on the n. when he was 1Co 11.23
a n. and a day I have been adrift 2Co 11.25
through many a sleepless n., 11.27
we worked n. and day, that we might 1Th 2.09
praying earnestly n. and day that 3.10
will come like a thief in the n. 5.02
are not of the n. or of darkness. 5.05
For those who sleep sleep at n., 5.07
who get drunk are drunk at n. 5.07
and labor we worked n. and day, 2Th 3.08
supplications and prayers n. and day; 1Ti 5.05
I long n. and day to see you, that I 2Ti 1.04
and day and n. they never cease to Rev 4.08
him day and n. within his temple; 7.15
and likewise a third of the n. 8.12
them day and n. before our God. 12.10
day or n., these worshipers of the 14.11
tormented day and n. for ever and 20.10
day—and there shall be no n. there; 21.25
And n. shall be no more; they need no 22.05

NIGHTHAWK

the n., the sea gull, the hawk Lev 11.16
the n., the sea gull, the hawk, after Deu 14.15

NIGHTS
the earth forty days and forty n.; Gen 7.04
the earth forty days and forty n. 7.12
mountain forty days and forty n. Ex 24.18
the LORD forty days and forty n.; 34.28
mountain forty days and forty n.; Deu 9.09
days and forty n. the LORD gave me 9.11
as before, forty days and forty n.; 9.18
for these forty days and forty n., 9.25
time, forty days and forty n., 10.10
water for three days and three n. 1Sa 30.12
days and forty n. to Horeb the 1Ki 19.08
the ground seven days and seven n., Job 2.13
and n. of misery are apportioned to 7.03
at my post I am stationed whole n. Is 21.08
the fish three days and three n. Jon 1.17
And he fasted forty days and forty n., Mt 4.02
days and three n. in the belly of 12.40
days and three n. in the heart of 12.40

NILE
that he was standing by the N., Gen 41.01
up out of the N. seven cows sleek 41.02
came up out of the N. after them, 41.03
other cows on the bank of the N. 41.03
standing on the banks of the N.; 41.17
up out of the N. and fed in the 41.18
Hebrews you shall cast into the N., Ex 1.22
water from the N. and pour it upon 4.09
take from the N. will become blood 4.09
that is in the N. with the rod 7.17
and the fish in the N. shall die, 7.18
and the N. shall become foul, and 7.18
loathe to drink water from the N. 7.18
the water that was in the N., 7.20
that was in the N. turned to blood 7.20
And the fish in the N. died; 7.21
and the N. became foul, so that the 7.21
could not drink water from the N.; 7.21
round about the N. for water to 7.24
not drink the water of the N. 7.24
after the LORD had struck the N. 7.25
the N. shall swarm with frogs which 8.03
houses and be left only in the N. 8.09
they shall be left only in the N. 8.11
which you struck the N., and go. 17.05
which sends ambassadors by the N., Is 18.02
waters of the N. will be dried up, 19.05
of Egypt's N. will diminish and 19.06
by the N., on the brink of the N., 19.07
that is sown by the N. will dry up, 19.07
all who cast hook in the N.; 19.08
of Shihor, the harvest of the N.; 23.03
Overflow your land like the N., 23.10
to drink the waters of the N.? Jer 2.18
"Who is this, rising like the N., 46.07
Egypt rises like the N., like rivers 46.08
that says, 'My N. is my own; Eze 29.03
'The N. is mine, and I made it,' 29.09
And I will dry up the N., 30.12
it, and all of it rise like the N., Amo 8.08
sink again, like the N. of Egypt? 8.08
and all of it rises like the N., 9.05
sinks again, like the N. of Egypt; 9.05
than Thebes that sat by the N., Nah 3.08
all the depths of the N. dried up. Zec 10.11

NIMRAH
N., Heshbon, Elealeh, Sebam, Nebo, and Num 32.03

NIMRIM
the waters of N. are a desolation; Is 15.06
the waters of N. also have become Jer 48.34

NIMROD
Cush became the father of N.; Gen 10.08
"Like N. a mighty hunter before the 10.09
Cush was the father of N.; he began to be 1Ch 1.10
and the land of N. with the drawn Mic 5.06

NIMSHI
and Jehu the son of N. you shall 1Ki 19.16
the son of Jehoshaphat, son of N.; 2Ki 9.02
the son of N. conspired against 9.14
the driving of Jehu the son of N.; 9.20
Jehoram to meet Jehu the son of N., 2Ch 22.07

NINE
Adam lived were n. hundred and Gen 5.05
of Seth were n. hundred and twelve 5.08
of Enosh were n. hundred and five 5.11
of Kenan were n. hundred and ten 5.14
of Jared were n. hundred and sixty 5.20
Methuselah were n. hundred and 5.27
of Noah were n. hundred and fifty 9.29
of Reu two hundred and n. years, 11.19
"On the fifth day n. bulls, Num 29.26
to give to the n. tribes and to 34.13
N. cubits was its length, and four Deu 3.11
inheritance to the n. tribes and Jos 13.07
Moses for the n. and one-half tribes, 14.02
n. cities with their villages. 15.44
n. cities with their villages. 15.54
n. cities out of these two tribes; 21.16
for he had n. hundred chariots of Ju 4.03
n. hundred chariots of iron, and all 4.13
at the end of n. months and twenty 2Sa 24.08
Israel, and he reigned n. years. 2Ki 17.01
Elishama, Eliada, and Eliphelet, n. 1Ch 3.08
n. hundred and fifty-six. All these were 9.09
of Zattu, n. hundred and forty-five. Ez 2.08
of Jeshua, n. hundred and seventy-three. 2.36
three thousand n. hundred and thirty. Neh 7.38
of Jeshua, n. hundred and seventy-three. 7.39
while n. tenths remained in the 11.01
Sallai, n. hundred and twenty-eight. 11.08
ten cleansed? Where are the n.? Lk 17.17

NINETEEN
of Terah a hundred and n. years, Gen 11.25
n. cities with their villages. Jos 19.38
servants n. men besides Asahel. 2Sa 2.30

NINETEENTH
which was the n. year of King 2Ki 25.08
the n. to Pethahiah, the twentieth 1Ch 24.16
to the n., to Mallothi, his sons and 25.26
which was the n. year of King Jer 52.12

NINETY
When Enosh had lived n. years, Gen 5.09
who is n. years old, bear a child?" 17.17
their kinsmen, six hundred and n. 1Ch 9.06
of days, three hundred and n. days, Eze 4.05
side, three hundred and n. days, 4.09
about, and its length n. cubits. 41.12
a thousand two hundred and n. days. Dan 12.11

NINETY-EIGHT
Now Eli was n. years old and his 1Sa 4.15
of Ater, namely of Hezekiah, n. Ez 2.16
of Ater, namely of Hezekiah, n. Neh 7.21

NINETY-FIVE
were eight hundred and n. years; Gen 5.17
of Noah five hundred and n. years, 5.30
The sons of Gibbar, n. Ez 2.20
The sons of Gibeon, n. Neh 7.25

NINETY-NINE
When Abram was n. years old the Gen 17.01
Abraham was n. years old when he 17.24
not leave the n. on the hills and Mt 18.12
than over the n. that never went 18.13
not leave the n. in the wilderness, Lk 15.04
than over n. righteous persons who 15.07

NINETY-SIX
n. rams, seventy-seven lambs, and as Ez 8.35
There were n. pomegranates on the Jer 52.23

NINETY-TWO
servants were three hundred and n. Ez 2.58
servants were three hundred and n. Neh 7.60

NINEVEH
and built N., Rehoboth-Ir, Calah, and Gen 10.11
Resen between N. and Calah; 10.12
and went home, and dwelt at N. 2Ki 19.36
and went home and dwelt at N. Is 37.37
"Arise, go to N., that great city, Jon 1.02
"Arise, go to N., that great city, 3.02
So Jonah arose and went to N., 3.03
Now N. was an exceedingly great 3.03
and N. shall be overthrown! 3.04
And the people of N. believed God; 3.05
Then tidings reached the king of N., 3.06
proclamation and published through N., 3.07
And should not I pity N., that great 4.11
An oracle concerning N. The book of Nah 1.01
N. is like a pool whose waters run 2.08
from you and say, Wasted is N.; 3.07
and he will make N. a desolation, Zep 2.13
The men of N. will arise at the Mt 12.41
became a sign to the men of N., Lk 11.30
The men of N. will arise at the 11.32

NINTH
on the n. day of the month beginning Lev 23.32
until the n. year, when its produce 25.22
On the n. day Abidan the son of Num 7.60
In the n. year of Hoshea the king 2Ki 17.06
which was the n. year of Hoshea 18.10
And in the n. year of his reign, in 25.01
On the n. day of the fourth month 25.03
Johanan eight, Elzabad n., 1Ch 12.12
the n. to Jeshua, the tenth to 24.11
the n. to Mattaniah, his sons and 25.16
N., for the n. month, was Abiezer 27.12
it was the n. month, on the twentieth Ez 10.09
in the n. month, all the people in Jer 36.09
It was the n. month, and the king 36.22
In the n. year of Zedekiah king of 39.01
on the n. day of the month, a breach 39.02
And in the n. year of his reign, in 52.04
On the n. day of the fourth month 52.06
In the n. year, in the tenth month, Eze 24.01
twenty-fourth day of the n. month, Hag 2.10
twenty-fourth day of the n. month, 2.18
in the fourth day of the n. month, Zec 7.01
the sixth hour and the n. hour, Mt 20.05
all the land until the n. hour. 27.45
And about the n. hour Jesus cried 27.46
the whole land until the n. hour. Mk 15.33
And at the n. hour Jesus cried with 15.34
the whole land until the n. hour, Lk 23.44
at the hour of prayer, the n. hour. Ac 3.01
About the n. hour of the day he saw 10.03
was keeping the n. hour of prayer 10.30
the n. topaz, the tenth chrysoprase, Rev 21.20

NISAN
In the month of N., in the twentieth Neh 2.01
month, which is the month of N., Est 3.07

NISROCH
worshiping in the house of N. his god, 2Ki 19.37
worshiping in the house of N. his god, Is 37.38

NOADIAH
of Jeshua and N. the son of Binnui Ez 8.33
the prophetess N. and the rest of Neh 6.14

NOAH
and called his name N., saying, "Out of Gen 5.29
the birth of N. five hundred and 5.30
After N. was five hundred years old, 5.32
N. became the father of Shem, Ham, 5.32
But N. found favor in the eyes of 6.08
These are the generations of N. 6.09
N. was a righteous man, blameless in 6.09
generation; N. walked with God. 6.09
And N. had three sons, Shem, Ham, and 6.10
And God said to N., "I have 6.13
N. did this; he did all that God 6.22
Then the LORD said to N., 7.01
And N. did all that the LORD had 7.05
N. was six hundred years old when 7.06
And N. and his sons and his wife 7.07
ark with N., as God had commanded N. 7.09
On the very same day N. and his sons, 7.13
They went into the ark with N., 7.15
Only N. was left, and those that 7.23
But God remembered N. and all the 8.01
of forty days N. opened the window 8.06
so N. knew that the waters had 8.11
and N. removed the covering of the 8.13
Then God said to N., 8.15
So N. went forth, and his sons and 8.18
Then N. built an altar to the LORD, 8.20
And God blessed N. and his sons, 9.01
Then God said to N. and to his sons 9.08
God said to N., "This is the sign 9.17
The sons of N. who went forth from 9.18
These three were the sons of N.; 9.19
N. was the first tiller of the soil 9.20
When N. awoke from his wine and 9.24
After the flood N. lived three 9.28
All the days of N. were nine 9.29
the generations of the sons of N., 10.01
are the families of the sons of N., 10.32
N., Hoglah, Milcah, and Tirzah. Num 26.33
N., Hoglah, Milcah, and Tirzah. 27.01
and N., the daughters of Zelophehad, 36.11
N., Hoglah, Milcah, and Tirzah. Jos 17.03
N., Shem, Ham, and Japheth. 1Ch 1.04
"For this is like the days of N. to me: Is 54.09
the waters of N. should no more go 54.09
N., Daniel, and Job, were in it, they Eze 14.14
even if N., Daniel, and Job were in 14.20
As were the days of N., so will be Mt 24.37
the day when N. entered the ark, 24.38
the son of N., the son of Lamech, Lk 3.36
As it was in the days of N., 17.26
the day when N. entered the ark, 17.27
By faith N., being warned by God Heb 11.07
patience waited in the days of N., 1Pe 3.20
but preserved N., a herald of 2Pe 2.05

NOAH'S
In the six hundredth year of N. life, Gen 7.11
and N. wife and the three wives of 7.13

NOB
Then came David to N. to Ahimelech 1Sa 21.01
saw the son of Jesse coming to N., 22.09
house, the priests who were at N.; 22.11
And N., the city of the priests, he 22.19
Anathoth, N., Ananiah, Neh 11.32
This very day he will halt at N., Is 10.32

NOBAH
And N. went and took Kenath and its Num 32.42
and called it N., after his own 32.42
route east of N. and Jogbehah, Ju 8.11

NOBILITY
and the n. of Jerusalem and her Is 5.14
of the royal family and of the n., Dan 1.03

NOBLE
down marched the remnant of the n.; Ju 5.13
the great and n. Osnappar deported Ez 4.10
one of the king's most n. princes; Est 6.09
they are the n., in whom is all my Ps 16.03
Hear, for I will speak n. things, Pro 8.06
not good; to flog n. men is wrong. 17.26
The fool will no more be called n., Is 32.05
But he who is n. devises n. things, 32.08
and by n. things he stands. 32.08
bear fruit, and become a n. vine. Eze 17.08
bear fruit, and become a n. cedar; 17.23
adorned with n. stones and offerings, Lk 21.05
Jews were more n. than those in Ac 17.11
for what is n. in the sight of all Rom 12.17
powerful, not many were of n. birth; 1Co 1.26
of bishop, he desires a n. task. 1Ti 3.01
and some for n. use, some for 2Ti 2.20
he will be a vessel for n. use, 2.21

NOBLEMAN
"A n. went into a far country to Lk 19.12

NOBLES
which the n. of the people delved, Num 21.18
elders and the n. who dwelt with 1Ki 21.08
elders and the n. who dwelt in his 21.11
the n., the governors of the people, 2Ch 23.20
the n., the officials, and the rest Neh 2.16
but their n. did not put their 3.05
and said to the n. and to the 4.14
And I said to the n. and to the 4.19
against the n. and the officials. 5.07
those days the n. of Judah sent 6.17
to assemble the n. and the officials 7.05
their n., and enter into a curse 10.29
with the n. of Judah and said to 13.17
Media and the n. and governors of Est 1.03
the voice of the n. was hushed, Job 29.10
one,' and to n., 'Wicked man'; 34.18
Make their n. like Oreb and Zeeb, Ps 83.11
and their n. with fetters of iron, 149.08
princes rule, and n. govern the earth. Pro 8.16
them to enter the gates of the n. Is 13.02
the plummet of chaos over its n. 34.11
Her n. send their servants for Jer 14.03
and all the n. of Judah and Jerusalem 27.20
Babylon slew all the n. of Judah. 39.06
the decree of the king and his n.: Jon 3.07
your n. slumber. Your people Nah 3.18

NOBODY
and n. takes me into his house. Ju 19.18
outsiders, and be dependent on n. 1Th 4.12

NOD
in the land of N., east of Eden. Gen 4.16

NODAB
Hagrites, Jetur, Naphish, and N.; 1Ch 5.19

NOGAH
N., Nepheg, Japhia, 1Ch 3.07
N., Nepheg, Japhia, 14.06

NOHAH
them down from N. as far as Ju 20.43
N. the fourth, and Rapha the fifth. 1Ch 8.02

NOISE
heard the n. of the people as they Ex 32.17
"There is a n. of war in the camp." 32.17
heard the n. of the shouting, they 1Sa 4.06
the earth was split by their n. 1Ki 1.40
This is the n. that you have heard. 1.45
heard the n. of the guard and of 2Ki 11.13
heard the n. of the people running 2Ch 23.12
distraught by the n. of the enemy, Ps 55.03
Make a joyful n. to God, all the 66.01
make a joyful n. to the rock of 95.01
make a joyful n. to him with songs 95.02
Make a joyful n. to the LORD, all 98.04
make a joyful n. before the King, 98.06
Make a joyful n. to the LORD, all 100.01
the n. of the jubilant has ceased, Is 24.08
dost subdue the n. of the aliens; 25.05
and with earthquake and great n., 29.06
shouting or daunted at their n., 31.04
At the thunderous n. peoples flee, 33.03
At the n. of horseman and archer Jer 4.29
At the n. of the stamping of the 47.03
The n. of battle is in the land, and 50.22
The n. of great destruction from 51.54
the n. of their voice is raised; 51.55
shake at the n. of the horsemen Eze 26.10
there was a n., and behold, a 37.07
words like the n. of a multitude. Dan 10.06
Take away from me the n. of your songs; Amo 5.23
will pass away with a loud n., 2Pe 3.10
and the n. of their wings was like Rev 9.09
was like the n. of many chariots 9.09

NOISES
loud n., flashes of lightning, and Rev 8.05
loud n., peals of thunder, an 11.19
loud n., peals of thunder, and a 16.18

NOISY
A foolish woman is n.; she is wanton Pro 9.13
'N. one who lets the hour go by.' Jer 46.17
its pasture, a n. multitude of men. Mic 2.12
I am a n. gong or a clanging cymbal 1Co 13.01

NONE
n. of us will withhold from you his Gen 23.06
This is n. other than the house of 28.17
do his work and n. of the men of 39.11
but there was n. who could interpret 41.08
there is n. so discreet and wise as 41.39
that there is n. like me in all Ex 9.14
And you shall let n. of it remain 12.10
and n. of you shall go out of the 12.22
I will put n. of the diseases upon 15.26
is a sabbath, there will be n. 16.26
out to gather, and they found n. 16.27
N. shall appear before me empty-handed. 23.15
N. shall cast her young or be 23.26
And n. shall appear before me empty. 34.20
"N. of you shall approach any one Lev 18.06
ordinances and do n. of these 18.26
to them that n. of them shall 21.01
"Say to Aaron, N. of your descendants 21.17
N. of the line of Aaron who is a 22.04
you shall leave n. of it until 22.30
and n. shall make you afraid; 26.06
you shall flee when n. pursues you. 26.17
they shall fall when n. pursues. 26.36
escape a sword, though n. pursues; 26.37
But to the sons of Kohath he gave n., Num 7.09
They shall leave n. of it until the 9.12
n. of the men who have seen my 14.22
and n. of those who despised me 14.23
'Surely n. of the men who came up 32.11
n. except Caleb the son of Jephunneh 32.12
and children, we left n. remaining; Deu 2.34
and n. of the evil diseases of 7.15
N. of the devoted things shall 13.17
generation n. of his descendants 23.02
generation n. belonging to them 23.03
there shall be n. to frighten them 28.26
and there shall be n. to help you. 28.29
and there shall be n. to help you. 28.31
and there is n. remaining, bond or 32.36
and there is n. that can deliver 32.39
"There is n. like God, O Jeshurun, 33.26
n. like him for all the signs and 34.11

NONE (cont.)
n. went out, and n. came in. Jos 6.01
there was left n. that survived or 8.22
person in it, he left n. remaining; 10.28
he left n. remaining in it; 10.30
people, until he left n. remaining. 10.33
he left n. remaining, as he had done 10.37
he left n. remaining; as he had 10.39
he left n. remaining, but utterly 10.40
them, until they left n. remaining. 11.08
there was n. left that breathed, and 11.11
But n. of the cities that stood on 11.13
There was n. of the Anakim left in 11.22
and n. of us will return to his Ju 20.08
"There is n. holy like the LORD, 1Sa 2.02
there is n. besides thee; there is no 2.02
him and let n. of his words fall 3.19
There is n. like him among all the 10.24
So n. of the people tasted food. 14.24
it, for there is n. but that here. 21.09
David said, "There is n. like that; give it 21.09
n. of you is sorry for me or 22.08
for there is n. like thee, and there 2Sa 7.22
They looked, but there was n. to save; 22.42
so that n. like you has been before 1Ki 3.12
before you and n. like you shall 3.12
n. were of silver, it was not 10.21
There was n. that followed the 12.20
n. was exempt, and they carried away 15.22
There was n. who sold himself to do 21.25
whom I serve, I will receive n. 2Ki 5.16
"N., my lord, O king; but Elisha, 6.12
of Jezreel, and n. shall bury her. 9.10
until he left him n. remaining. 10.11
persons, and he spared n. of them. 10.14
let n. be missing, for I have a 10.19
for there was n. left, bond or free, 14.26
and there was n. to help Israel. 14.26
n. was left but the tribe of 17.18
that there was n. like him among 18.05
n. remained, except the poorest 24.14
There is n. like thee, O LORD, and 1Ch 17.20
such as n. of the kings had who 2Ch 1.12
and n. after you shall have the 1.12
there is n. like thee to help, 14.11
fell until n. remained alive; 14.13
so that n. is able to withstand 20.06
on the ground; n. had escaped. 20.24
n. of the kings of Israel had 35.18
I found there n. of the sons of Ez 8.15
for n. can stand before thee 9.15
n. of us took off our clothes; Neh 4.23
that there is n. like him on the Job 1.08
that there is n. like him on the 2.03
but have n., nor see the eyelids of 3.09
and there is n. to deliver out of 10.07
and n. will make you afraid; 11.19
If he tears down, n. can rebuild; 12.14
if he shuts a man in, n. can open. 12.14
dwells that which is n. of his; 18.15
fatherless who had n. to help him. 29.12
there was n. that confuted Job, or 32.12
'He will answer n. of my words'? 33.13
But n. says, 'Where is God my Maker, 35.10
dragging me away, with n. to rescue. Ps 7.02
his wickedness till thou find n. 10.15
deeds, there is n. that does good. 14.01
there is n. that does good, no, not 14.03
but there was n. to save, they cried 18.41
is near and there is n. to help. 22.11
Yea, let n. that wait for thee be 25.03
n. of those who take refuge in him 34.22
n. can compare with thee! Were I to 40.05
I rend, and there be n. to deliver! 50.22
iniquity; there is n. that does good. 53.01
there is n. that does good, no, not 53.03
spare n. of those who treacherously 59.05
looked for pity, but there was n.; 69.20
and for comforters, but I found n. 69.20
for there is n. to deliver him. 71.11
and there is n. among us who knows 74.09
and there was n. to bury them. 79.03
Israel would have n. of me. 81.11
There is n. like thee among the 86.08
and there was n. among his tribes 105.37
they fell down, with n. to help. 107.12
Let there be n. to extend kindness 109.12
when as yet there was n. of them. 139.16
but there is n. who takes notice of 142.04
and would have n. of my reproof, Pro 1.25
would have n. of my counsel, and 1.30
n. who go to her come back nor do 2.19
n. who touches her will go unpunished. 6.29
kiss you, and n. would despise me. Sol 8.01
together, with n. to quench them. Is 1.31
N. is weary, n. stumbles, n. slumbers or 5.27
carry it off, and n. can rescue. 5.29
and there was n. that moved a wing, 10.14
like sheep with n. to gather them, 13.14
and n. will make them afraid. 17.02
he shall open, and n. shall shut; 22.22
he shall shut, and n. shall open. 22.22
is shut up so that n. can enter. 24.10
with whom n. has dealt treacherously! 33.01
n. shall pass through it for ever 34.10
n. shall be without her mate. 34.16
and there is n., and their tongue 41.17
There was n. who declared it, 41.26
n. who proclaimed, n. who heard your words. 41.26
become a prey with n. to rescue, 42.22
a spoil with n. to say, "Restore!" 42.22
there is n. who can deliver from my 43.13
west, that there is n. besides me; 45.06
there is n. besides me. 45.21
I am God, and there is n. like me, 46.09
There is n. to guide her among all 51.18
there is n. to take her by the hand 51.18
look for justice, but there is n.; 59.11
in a land that n. passes through, Jer 2.06
N. who seek her need weary themselves; 2.24
and burn with n. to quench it, 4.04
and n. will frighten them away. 7.33
and n. shall gather them. 9.22
There is n. like thee, O LORD; 10.06
kingdoms there is n. like thee. 10.07
and n. of them shall be left. 11.23
are shut up, with n. to open them; 13.19
with n. to bury them—them, their 14.16
and burn with n. to quench it, 21.12
for n. of his offspring shall 22.30
is so great there is n. like it; 30.07
and n. shall make him afraid. 30.10
There is n. to uphold your cause, no 30.13
and they drink n. to this day, 35.14
He shall have n. to sit upon the 36.30
so that n. of the remnant of Judah 44.14
and n. shall make him afraid. 46.27
with n. to gather the fugitives. 49.05
and n. shall dwell in it; 50.03
in Israel, and there shall be n.; 50.20
in Judah, and n. shall be found; 50.20
with n. to raise him up, and I will 50.32
lovers she has n. to comfort her; Lam 1.02
for n. come to the appointed feasts 1.04
and there was n. to help her, the 1.07
but there is n. to comfort her; 1.17
there is n. to comfort me. 1.21
of the LORD n. escaped or survived 2.22
with blood that n. could touch 4.14
there is n. to deliver us from 5.08
n. of them shall remain, nor their Eze 7.11
n. can maintain his life. 7.13
but n. goes to battle, for my wrath 7.14
seek peace, but there shall be n. 7.25

NONE (cont.)

N. of my words will be delayed any Eze 12.28
n. solicited you to play the harlot 16.34
who does n. of these duties, 18.10
N. of the transgressions which he 18.22
N. of the righteous deeds which he 18.24
not destroy it; but I found n. 22.30
n. of his righteous deeds shall be 33.13
N. of the sins that he has committed 33.16
desolate that n. will pass through 33.28
with n. to search or seek for them. 34.06
and n. shall make them afraid. 34.28
their land with n. to make them 39.26
I will leave n. of them remaining 39.28
so that n. of my people shall be 46.18
among them all n. was found like Dan 1.19
and n. can show it to the king 2.11
and n. can stay his hand or say to 4.35
there is n. who contends by my side 10.21
and n. shall stand before him; 11.16
to his end, with n. to help him. 11.45
and n. of the wicked shall understand 12.10
and let n. accuse, for with you is Hos 4.04
carry off, and n. shall rescue. 5.14
and n. of them calls upon me. 7.07
will bereave them till n. is left. 9.12
to the yoke, and n. shall remove it. 11.07
am your God and there is n. else. Joe 2.27
on her land, with n. to raise her up." Amo 5.02
with n. to quench it for Bethel, 5.06
Therefore you will have n. to cast Mic 2.05
and n. shall make them afraid; 4.04
pieces, and there is n. to deliver. 5.08
and there is n. upright among men; 7.02
they cry; but n. turns back. Nah 2.08
his cubs were, with n. to disturb? 2.11
mountains with n. to gather them. 3.18
herself, "I am and there is n. else. Zep 2.15
streets so that n. walks in them; 3.06
and n. shall make them afraid. 3.13
and let n. of you devise evil Zec 7.10
so that n. shall march to and fro; 9.08
I will deliver n. from their hand. 11.06
and let n. be faithless to the wife Mal 2.15
seeking rest, but he finds n. Mt 12.43
but they found n., though many 26.60
him to death; but they found n. Mk 14.55
"N. of your kindred is called by Lk 1.61
let him share with him who has n.; 3.11
was sent to n. of them but only to 4.26
and n. of them was cleansed, but 4.27
born of women n. is greater than 7.28
and finding n. he says, 'I will 11.24
seeking fruit on it and found n. 13.06
on this fig tree, and I find n. 13.07
n. of those men who were invited 14.24
and n. may cross from there to us.' 16.26
But they understood n. of these 18.34
which n. of your adversaries will 21.15
but n. said, "What do you wish?" Jn 4.27
Yet n. of you keeps the law. 7.19
yet n. of you asks me, 'Where are 16.05
and need n. to question you; 16.30
and n. of them is lost but the son 17.12
"Now n. of the disciples dared ask 21.12
N. of the rest dared join them, but Ac 5.13
speaking the word to n. except Jews. 11.19
and that n. of his friends should 24.23
persuaded that n. of these things 26.26
and n. of the brethren coming here 28.21
"N. is righteous, no, not one; Rom 3.10
N. of us lives to himself, and 14.07
and n. of us dies to himself. 14.07
that I baptized n. of you except 1Co 1.14
N. of the rulers of this age 2.08
that n. of you may be puffed up in 4.06
wives live as though they had n.; 7.29
in the world, and n. is without meaning; 14.10
But I saw n. of the other apostles Gal 1.19
See that n. of you repays evil for 1Th 5.15
that n. of you may be hardened by Heb 3.13
But let n. of you suffer as a 1Pe 4.15

NONSENSE

For the teraphim utter n., Zec 10.02

NOON

the men are to dine with me at n." Gen 43.16
present for Joseph's coming at n., 43.25
name of Baal from morning until n., 1Ki 18.26
And at n. Elijah mocked them saying, 18.27
And they went out at n., while Benhadad 20.16
the child sat on her lap till n., 2Ki 4.20
morning and at n. I utter my Ps 55.17
where you make it lie down at n.; Sol 1.07
like night at the height of n.; Is 16.03
we stumble at n. as in the twilight, 59.10
up, and let us attack at n.!" Jer 6.04
in the morning and an alarm at n., 20.16
"I will make the sun go down at n., Amo 8.09
people shall be driven out at n., Zep 2.04
about n. a great light from heaven Ac 22.06

NOONDAY

and you shall grope at n., Deu 28.29
as he was taking his n. rest. 2Sa 4.05
and grope at n. as in the night. Job 5.14
life will be brighter than the n.; 11.17
light, and your right as the n. Ps 37.06
the destruction that wastes at n. 91.06
and your gloom be as the n. Is 58.10
of young men a destroyer at n.; Jer 15.08

NOONTIDE

I said, In the n. of my days I must Is 38.10

NOR

speak to Jacob neither good n. bad.' Gen 31.29
n. has he kept back anything from 39.09
will be neither plowing n. harvest. 45.06
n. the ruler's staff from between 49.10
your fathers n. your grandfathers Ex 10.06
been before, n. ever shall be again. 10.14
neither tree n. plant of the field, 10.15
n. did any rise from his place for 10.23
never been, n. ever shall be again. 11.06
n. shall you make for yourselves 20.23
n. curse a ruler of your people. 22.28
n. shall you bear witness in a suit, 23.02
n. shall you be partial to a poor 23.03
n. let such be heard out of your 23.13
n. serve them, n. do according to 23.24
n. burnt offering, n. cereal offering; 30.09
neither ate bread n. drank water. 34.28
"Let neither man n. woman do 36.06
burn no leaven n. any honey as an Lev 2.11
that you eat neither fat n. blood. 3.17
no wine n. strong drink, you n. your 10.09
n. come into the sanctuary, until 12.04
n. deal falsely, n. lie to one another. 19.11
n. shall there come upon you a 19.19
n. shave off the edges of their 21.05
n. make any cuttings in their flesh. 21.05
hang loose, n. rend his clothes; 21.10
n. defile himself, even for his 21.11
n. profane the sanctuary of his God; 21.12
neither bread n. grain parched or 23.14
n. shall you gather the gleanings 23.22
n. reap what grows of itself, n. gather 25.11
n. give him your food for profit. 25.37
Neither for his father n. for his mother, Num 6.07
n. for brother or sister, if they 6.07
n. break a bone of it; according to 9.12
n. Moses, departed out of the camp. 14.44
n. given us inheritance of fields 16.14

NOR (cont.)
n. has he seen trouble in Israel. Num 23.21
them at all, n. bless them at all." 23.25
to the right n. to the left. Deu 2.27
I command you, n. take from it; 4.02
n. hear, n. eat, n. smell. 4.28
n. did your fathers know; that he might 8.03
I neither ate bread n. drank water. 9.09
I neither ate bread n. drank water, 9.18
neither you n. your fathers have 13.06
n. shall your eye pity him, 13.08
n. shall you spare him, n. shall 13.08
n. shear the firstling of your 15.19
n. shall any of the flesh which you 16.04
n. shall he greatly multiply for 17.17
which is neither plowed n. sown, 21.04
n. shall a man put on a woman's 22.05
n. shall he uncover her who is his 22.30
n. shall the children be put to 24.16
neither you n. your fathers have 28.36
of the wine n. gather the grapes; 28.39
neither you n. your fathers have 28.64
N. is it with you only that I make 29.14
not die, n. let his men be few." 33.06
n. his natural force abated. 34.07
burnt offering, n. for sacrifice, Jos 22.26
n. for sacrifice, but to be a 22.28
to the right hand n. to the left, 23.06
her he had neither son n. daughter. Ju 11.34
not told my father n. my mother, 14.16
drunk neither wine n. strong drink, 1Sa 1.15
to the right n. to the left, 6.12
neither sword n. spear found in 13.22
neither you n. your kingdom shall 20.31
my sword n. my weapons with me, 21.08
it, or knew it, n. did any awake; 26.12
left neither man n. woman alive, 27.09
saved neither man n. woman alive, 27.11
n. upsurging of the deep! For there the 2Sa 1.21
the right hand n. to the left from 2.19
Israel no more, n. did they fight any more. 2.28
he would not, n. did he eat food with them. 12.17
spoke to Amnon neither good n. bad; 13.22
neither name n. remnant upon the 14.07
n. trimmed his beard, n. washed his 19.24
"It shall be neither mine n. yours; 1Ki 3.26
is neither adversary n. misfortune. 5.04
neither hammer n. axe n. any tool of 6.07
n. drink water, n. return by the way 13.09
I eat bread n. drink water with 13.16
eat bread n. drink water there, 13.17
n. return by the way that you came. 13.17
be neither dew n. rain these years, 17.01
"Fight with neither small n. great, 22.31
neither death n. miscarriage shall 2Ki 2.21
neither look at you, n. see you. 3.14
it is neither new moon n. sabbath. 4.23
n. has he cast them from his 13.23
n. among those who were before him. 18.05
they neither listened n. obeyed. 18.12
n. did any like him arise after 23.25
n. did all their family multiply 1Ch 4.27
n. offer burnt offerings which cost 21.24
"Fight with neither small n. great, 2Ch 18.30
n. had the people assembled in 30.03
be no remnant, n. any to escape? Ez 9.14
eating bread n. drinking water; 10.06
N. is this a work for one day or 10.13
So neither I n. my brethren Neh 4.23
n. my brethren n. my servants n. the 4.23
neither I n. my brethren ate the 5.14
fathers' houses n. their descent, 7.61
n. the pillar of fire by night 9.19
she had neither father n. mother; Est 2.07
and neither eat n. drink for three 4.16
he neither rose n. trembled before 5.09
n. should the commemoration of 9.28
not seek it, n. light shine upon it. Job 3.04
n. see the eyelids of the morning; 3.09
n. hide trouble from my eyes. 3.10
I am not at ease, n. am I quiet; 3.26
n. does trouble sprout from the 5.06
n. does his place know him any more 7.10
n. let me alone till I swallow my 7.19
n. take the hand of evildoers. 8.20
n. will he strike root in the earth 15.29
n. will his place any more behold 20.09
n. can it be exchanged for jewels 28.17
n. can it be valued in pure gold. 28.19
n. the aged that understand what is 32.09
n. regards the rich more than the 34.19
n. does the Almighty regard it. 35.13
n. the spear, the dart, or the 41.26
n. stands in the way of sinners, Ps 1.01
n. sits in the seat of scoffers; 1.01
n. sinners in the congregation of 1.05
n. chasten me in thy wrath. 6.01
n. takes up a reproach against his 15.03
n. are there words; their voice 19.03
n. do I consort with dissemblers; 26.04
n. my life with bloodthirsty men, 26.09
n. the hand of the wicked drive me 36.11
thy anger, n. chasten me in thy wrath! 38.01
n. did their own arm give them 44.03
n. can my sword save me. 44.06
n. have our steps departed from thy 44.18
n. he-goat from your folds. 50.09
neither knowledge n. understanding, 82.05
n. are there any works like thine. 86.08
n. the arrow that flies by day, 91.05
n. the pestilence that stalks in 91.06
n. the destruction that wastes at 91.06
n. will he keep his anger for ever. 103.09
n. requite us according to our 103.10
n. any to pity his fatherless 109.12
n. do any that go down into silence 115.17
will neither slumber n. sleep. 121.04
you by day, n. the moon by night. 121.06
n. is there any breath in their 135.17
n. his pleasure in the legs of a 147.10
her come back n. do they regain Pro 2.19
n. be appeased though you multiply 6.35
n. go with a wrathful man, 22.24
n. desire to be with them; 24.01
n. have I knowledge of the Holy One 30.03
give me neither poverty n. riches; 30.08
n. the ear filled with hearing. Ecc 1.08
n. will there be any remembrance of 1.11
n. anything taken from it; 3.14
n. let your heart be hasty to utter 5.02
n. he who loves wealth, with gain: 5.10
n. will wickedness deliver those 8.08
how neither day n. night one's eyes 8.16
n. the battle to the strong, 9.11
n. bread to the wise, n. riches to 9.11
n. favor to the men of skill; 9.11
n. in your bedchamber curse the 10.20
you stir not up n. awaken love Sol 2.07
you stir not up n. awaken love 3.05
you stir not up n. awaken love 8.04
there is neither bread n. mantle; Is 3.07
what they fear, n. be in dread. 8.12
n. seek the LORD of hosts. 9.13
neither travailed n. given birth, 23.04
young men n. brought up virgins. 23.04
n. is a cart wheel rolled over 28.27
that brings neither help n. profit, 30.05
n. the knave said to be honorable. 32.05
n. will any of its cords be broken. 33.20
oars can go, n. stately ship can pass. 33.21
n. shall any ravenous beast come up 35.09
n. are its beasts enough for a 40.16
n. my praise to graven images. 42.08
n. shall there be any after me. 43.10

NOR (cont.)
n. consider the things of old. Is 43.18
Fear not, n. be afraid; 44.08
witnesses neither see n. know, 44.09
They know not, n. do they discern; 44.18
n. is there knowledge or discernment 44.19
scorching wind n. sun shall smite 49.10
n. will I always be angry; for from me 57.16
n. for brightness shall the moon 60.19
n. your moon withdraw itself; 60.20
not relented n. will I turn back. Jer 4.28
n. shall we see sword or famine. 5.12
n. can you understand what they say 5.15
n. your sacrifices pleasing to me. 6.20
n. walk on the road; for the enemy 6.25
n. did it come into my mind. 7.31
n. figs on the fig tree; even the leaves 8.13
neither they n. their fathers have 9.16
n. be dismayed at the signs of the 10.02
n. shall you have famine, but I will 14.13
n. did I command them or speak to 14.14
n. have I borrowed, yet all of them 15.10
of merrymakers, n. did I rejoice; 15.17
n. shall you have sons or daughters 16.02
n. shall they be buried; they shall be 16.04
n. shall any one give him the cup 16.07
neither you n. your fathers have 16.13
n. is their iniquity concealed from 16.17
n. have I desired the day of 17.16
n. counsel from the wise, nor the 18.18
n. the word from the prophet. 18.18
n. blot out their sin from thy 18.23
they n. their fathers n. the kings 19.04
n. did it come into my mind; 19.05
n. shed innocent blood in this 22.03
for him who is dead, n. bemoan him; 22.10
n. be dismayed, neither shall any be 23.04
listened n. inclined your ears to 25.04
n. escape for the lords of the 25.35
n. be dismayed, O Israel; for lo, I will 30.10
n. did it enter into my mind, that 32.35
neither you n. your sons for ever; 35.06
n. any of his servants who heard 36.24
n. did they rend their garments. 36.24
neither he n. his servants n. the people 37.02
n. you, n. your fathers. 44.03
n. have they feared, n. walked in my 44.10
n. the warrior escape; in the north 46.06
n. be dismayed, O Israel; for lo, I will 46.27
n. has he gone into exile; so his taste 48.11
n. inhabited for all generations. 50.39
neither men n. beast, and it shall 51.62
n. be afraid of their words, though Eze 2.06
n. be dismayed at their looks, for 2.06
n. be dismayed at their looks, for 3.09
n. speak to warn the wicked from 3.18
n. has foul flesh come into my 4.14
n. will I have pity; but I will 7.04
n. will I have pity; I will punish 7.09
n. their abundance, n. their wealth 7.11
n. the seller mourn, for wrath is 7.12
n. will I have pity; and though they 8.18
n. will I have pity, but I will 9.10
n. shall you be the flesh in the 11.11
n. executed my ordinances, but have 11.12
n. be enrolled in the register of 13.09
n. shall they enter the land of 13.09
wall is no more, n. those who daubed it, 13.15
delusive visions n. practice 13.23
n. defile themselves any more with 14.11
deliver neither sons n. daughters; 14.16
deliver neither sons n. daughters, 14.18
deliver neither son n. daughter; 14.20
n. were you washed with water to 16.04
n. rubbed with salt, n. swathed with bands. 16.04
has never been, n. ever shall be. 16.16
n. the father suffer for the 18.20
n. did they forsake the idols of 20.08
n. observe their ordinances, n. defile 20.18
n. according to your corrupt doings, 20.44
mourn or weep n. shall your tears 24.16
n. eat the bread of mourners. 24.17
n. eat the bread of mourners. 24.22
yet neither he n. his army got 29.18
n. the fir trees equal its boughs; 31.08
n. shall the hoofs of beasts 32.13
n. shall the beasts of the land 34.28
n. their kings, by their harlotry, 43.07
n. come near any of my sacred 44.13
will not wither n. their fruit 47.12
n. shall its sovereignty be left to Dan 2.44
n. did I anoint myself at all, for 10.03
n. according to the dominion with 11.04
neither in anger n. in battle. 11.20
his fathers n. his fathers' fathers 11.24
them by bow, n. by sword, n. by war, Hos 1.07
n. by horses, n. by horsemen." 1.07
by neither measured n. numbered; 1.10
n. your brides when they commit 4.14
n. go up to Bethaven, and swear not, 4.15
their God, n. seek him, for all this. 7.10
n. will be again after them through Joe 2.02
n. shall the mighty save his life; Amo 2.14
n. shall he who rides the horse 2.15
n. a prophet's son; but I am 7.14
n. a thirst for water, but of 8.11
nobles: Let neither man n. beast, Jon 3.07
herd n. flock, taste anything; 3.07
n. did you make it grow, which came 4.10
not for men n. wait for the sons Mic 5.07
n. fruit be on the vines, the Hab 3.17
not do good, n. will he do ill. Zep 1.12
Neither their silver n. their gold 1.18
n. shall there be found in their 3.13
n. by power, but by my Spirit, says Zec 4.06
shall be neither cold n. frost. 14.06
leave them neither root n. branch. Mal 4.01
N. do men light a lamp and put it Mt 5.15
neither moth n. rust consumes and 6.20
n. about your body, what you shall 6.25
neither sow n. reap n. gather into 6.26
they neither toil n. spin; 6.28
n. can a bad tree bear good fruit. 7.18
Take no gold, n. silver, n. copper 10.09
n. two tunics, n. sandals, n. a staff; 10.10
n. a servant above his master; 10.24
came neither eating n. drinking, 11.18
for him to eat n. for those who 12.04
n. will any one hear his voice in 12.19
do not hear, n. do they understand. 13.13
the scriptures n. the power of God. 22.29
neither marry n. are given in 22.30
n. from that day did any one dare 22.46
n. allow those who would enter to 23.13
n. the Son, but the Father only. 24.36
know neither the day n. the hour. 25.13
n. is anything secret, except to Mk 4.22
the scriptures n. the power of God? 12.24
neither marry n. are given in 12.25
n. enter his house, to take anything 13.15
n. the Son, but only the Father. 13.32
"I neither know n. understand what 14.68
drink no wine n. strong drink, Lk 1.15
n. again does a bad tree bear good 6.43
n. are grapes picked from a bramble 6.44
n. anything secret that shall not 8.17
n. bag, n. bread, n. money; 9.03
n. about your body, what you shall 12.22
ravens: they neither sow n. reap, 12.24
have neither storehouse n. barn, 12.24
they neither toil n. spin; 12.27
to drink, n. be of anxious mind. 12.29
for the land n. for the dunghill; 14.35
n. will they say, 'Lo, here it is!' 17.21

NOR (cont.)

neither feared God n. regarded man; Lk 18.02
I neither fear God n. regard man, 18.04
neither marry n. are given in 20.35
not of blood n. of the will of the Jn 1.13
of the flesh n. of the will of man, 1.13
Christ, n. Elijah, n. the prophet?" 1.25
not thirst, n. come here to draw." 4.15
this mountain n. in Jerusalem will 4.21
n. his disciples, they themselves 6.24
"You know neither me n. my Father; 8.19
n. do we know who opened his eyes. 9.21
n. is he who is sent greater than 13.16
it neither sees him n. knows him; 14.17
have not known the Father, n. me. 16.03
n. let thy Holy One see corruption. Ac 2.27
n. did his flesh see corruption. 2.31
neither part n. lot in this matter, 8.21
sight, and neither ate n. drank. 9.09
recognize him n. understand the 13.27
our fathers n. we have been able 15.10
n. is he served by human hands, as 17.25
sacrilegious n. blasphemers of our 19.37
of any value n. as precious to 20.24
resurrection, n. angel, n. spirit; 23.08
neither to eat n. drink till they 23.12
neither to eat n. drink till they 23.21
n. against the temple, n. against Caesar 25.08
neither sun n. stars appeared for 27.20
n. is true circumcision something Rom 2.28
neither death, n. life, n. angels, 8.28
n. principalities, n. things present, 8.38
n. things to come, n. powers, 8.38
n. height, n. depth, n. anything else 8.39
n. ear heard, n. the heart of man conceived, 1Co 2.09
he who plants n. he who waters is 3.07
n. idolaters, n. adulterers, n. homosexuals, 6.09
n. thieves, n. the greedy, n. drunkards, 6.10
n. revilers, n. robbers will inherit 6.10
for anything n. uncircumcision, 7.19
n. am I writing this to secure any 9.15
n. grumble, as some of them did and 10.10
independent of man n. man of woman; 11.11
practice, n. do the churches of God. 11.16
n. again the head to the feet, 12.21
n. does the perishable inherit the 15.50
n. on account of the one who 2Co 7.12
not from men n. through man, but Gal 1.01
n. was I taught it, but it came 1.12
n. did I go up to Jerusalem to 1.17
There is neither Jew n. Greek, 3.28
there is neither slave n. free, 3.28
there is neither male n. female; 3.28
circumcision n. uncircumcision is 5.06
n. uncircumcision, but a new creation 6.15
n. silly talk, n. levity, which are Eph 5.04
n. is it made with guile; 1Th 2.03
n. did we seek glory from men, 2.06
n. to occupy themselves with myths 1Ti 1.04
n. participate in another man's sins 5.22
n. to set their hopes on uncertain 6.17
n. of me his prisoner, but take your 2Ti 1.08
n. to pilfer, but to show entire and Tit 2.10
beginning of days n. end of life, Heb 7.03
N. was it to offer himself repeatedly, 9.25
neither desired n. taken pleasure 10.08
n. lose courage when you are 12.05
will never fail you n. forsake you. 13.05
no fear of them, n. be troubled, 1Pe 3.14
n. he who does not love his brother 1Jn 3.10
works: you are neither cold n. hot. Rev 3.15
lukewarm, and neither cold n. hot, 3.16
strike them, n. any scorching heat. 7.16
of their hands n. give up worshiping 9.20
n. did they repent of their murders 9.21
be mourning n. crying n. pain any more, 21.04
n. any one who practices abomination 21.27

NORTH

them to Hobah, n. of Damascus. Gen 14.15
east and to the n. and to the 28.14
on the n. side twenty frames, Ex 26.20
shall put the table on the n. side. 26.35
length on the n. side there shall 27.11
on the n. side, he made twenty 36.25
And for the n. side a hundred 38.11
on the n. side of the tabernacle, 40.22
kill it on the n. side of the Lev 1.11
"On the n. side shall be the Num 2.25
encamp on the n. side of the 3.35
and for the n. side two thousand 35.05
and encamped on the n. side of Ai, Jos 8.11
which was n. of the city and its 8.13
boundary on the n. side runs from 15.05
and passes along n. of Betharabah; 15.06
shoulder of the hill n. of Ekron, 15.11
on the n. is Michmethath; then on the 16.06
goes on the n. side of the brook 17.09
and that to the n. being Manasseh's, 17.10
on the n. Asher is reached, and on 17.10
in their territory on the n. 18.05
On the n. side their boundary began 18.12
up to the shoulder n. of Jericho, 18.12
which is at the n. end of the 18.16
on to the n. of the shoulder of 18.18
on to the n. of the shoulder of 18.19
then on the n. the boundary turns 19.14
it continues in the n. to Cabul, 19.27
n. of the mountain of Gaash. 24.30
of Ephraim, n. of Mount Gaash. Ju 2.09
the camp of Midian was n. of them, 7.01
which is n. of Bethel, on the east 21.19
rose on the n. in front of Michmash, 1Sa 14.05
pillar on the n. and called its 1Ki 7.21
three facing n., three facing west, 7.25
and five on the n. side of the 7.39
the south side and five on the n., 7.49
house to the n. side of the house, 2Ki 11.11
put it on the n. side of his altar 16.14
sides, east, west, n., and south; 1Ch 9.24
and his lot came out for the n. 26.14
on the n. four each day, on the 26.17
on the south, the other on the n.; 2Ch 3.17
Jachin, and that on the n. Boaz. 3.17
three facing n., three facing west, 4.04
side, and five on the n. side. 4.06
the south side and five on the n. 4.07
the south side and five on the n. 4.08
house to the n. side of the house, 23.10
stretches out the n. over the void, Job 26.07
Out of the n. comes golden splendor 37.22
in the far n., the city of the Ps 48.02
The n. and the south, thou hast 89.12
from the n. and from the south. 107.03
The n. wind brings forth rain; Pro 25.23
south, and goes round to the n.; Ecc 1.06
falls to the south or to the n., 11.03
Awake, O n. wind, and come, O south Sol 4.16
mount of assembly in the far n.; Is 14.13
For smoke comes out of the n., 14.31
I stirred up one from the n., 41.25
I will say to the n., Give up, 43.06
these from the n. and from the 49.12
pot, facing away from the n. Jer 1.13
"Out of the n. evil shall break 1.14
kingdoms of the n., says the LORD; 1.15
proclaim these words toward the n., 3.12
the land of the n. to the land 3.18
not, for I bring evil from the n., 4.06
for evil looms out of the n., 6.01
is coming from the n. country, 6.22
out of the n. country to make the 10.22
and see those who come from the n. 13.20
iron, iron from the n., and bronze? 15.12
out of the n. country and out of 16.15

NORTH (cont.)
out of the n. country and out of Jer 23.08
send for all the tribes of the n., 25.09
all the kings of the n., far and near, 25.26
bring them from the n. country, 31.08
in the n. by the river Euphrates 46.06
sacrifice in the n. country by the 46.10
gadfly from the n. has come upon 46.20
the hand of a people from the n. 46.24
waters are rising out of the n., 47.02
"For out of the n. a nation has 50.03
great nations, from the n. country; 50.09
"Behold, a people comes from the n.; 50.41
them out of the n., says the LORD. 51.48
a stormy wind came out of the n., Eze 1.04
of the inner court that faces n., 8.03
now in the direction of the n." 8.05
I lifted up my eyes toward the n., 8.05
n. of the altar gate, in the entrance, 8.05
entrance of the n. gate of the 8.14
which faces n., every man with his 9.02
her daughters to the n. of you; 16.46
from south to n. shall be scorched 20.47
against all flesh from south to n.; 21.04
you from the n. with chariots and 23.24
Tyre from the n. Nebuchadrezzar 26.07
"The princes of the n. are there, 32.30
parts of the n. with all his 38.06
of the uttermost parts of the n., 38.15
from the uttermost parts of the n., 39.02
Then he went before me to the n., 40.20
a gate which faced toward the n., 40.20
And opposite the gate on the n., 40.23
Then he brought me to the n. gate, 40.35
entrance of the n. gate were two 40.40
the side of the n. gate facing 40.44
side of the south gate facing n. 40.44
which faces n. is for the priests 40.46
left free, one door toward the n., 41.11
toward the n., and he brought me to 42.01
opposite the building on the n. 42.01
was on the n. side was a hundred 42.02
and their doors were on the n. 42.04
similar to the chambers on the n., 42.11
"The n. chambers and the south 42.13
he turned and measured the n. side, 42.17
by way of the n. gate to the front 44.04
enters by the n. gate to worship 46.09
gate shall go out by the n. gate: 46.09
to the n. row of the holy chambers 46.19
me out by way of the n. gate, 47.02
On the n. side, from the Great Sea 47.15
the border of Hamath to the n. 47.17
This shall be the n. side. 47.17
the n. side four thousand five 48.16
on the n. two hundred and fifty 48.17
On the n. side, which is to be four 48.30
the king of the n. to make peace; Dan 11.06
the fortress of the king of the n., 11.07
from attacking the king of the n. 11.08
and fight with the king of the n.; 11.11
For the king of the n. shall again 11.13
Then the king of the n. shall come 11.15
the king of the n. shall rush upon 11.40
east and the n. shall alarm him, 11.44
sea to sea, and from n. to east; Amo 8.12
out his hand against the n., Zep 2.13
the land of the n., says the LORD; Zec 2.06
horses goes toward the n. country, 6.06
go toward the n. country have set 6.08
Spirit at rest in the n. country. 6.08
and from n. and south, and sit at Lk 13.29
on the n. three gates, on the south Rev 21.13

NORTHEAST
looking n. and southeast, and winter Ac 27.12

NORTHEASTER
called the n., struck down from the Ac 27.14

NORTHERLY
then it bends in a n. direction Jos 18.17

NORTHERN
"This shall be your n. boundary: Num 34.07
this shall be your n. boundary. 34.09
who were in the n. hill country, Jos 11.02
at the n. end of the valley of 15.08
along to the n. shoulder of Mount 15.10
ends at the n. bay of the Salt Sea, 18.19
which is on the n. border of Eze 47.17
tribes: Beginning at the n. border, 48.01
(which is on the n. border of 48.01
thousand cubits on the n. side, 48.10

NORTHERNER
"I will remove the n. far from you, Joe 2.20

NORTHWARD
n. and southward and eastward and Gen 13.14
country long enough; turn n. Deu 2.03
westward and n. and southward and 3.27
n. to the boundary of Ekron, it is Jos 13.03
and so n., turning toward Gilgal, 15.07
of Iphtahel n. to Bethemek and 19.27
westward and n. and southward; Dan 8.04
of the Mount shall withdraw n., Zec 14.04

NOSE
So I put the ring on her n., Gen 24.47
my hook in your n. and my bit in 2Ki 19.28
or pierce his n. with a snare? Job 40.24
Can you put a rope in his n., 41.02
pressing the n. produces blood, and Pro 30.33
Your n. is like a tower of Lebanon, Sol 7.04
the signet rings and n. rings; Is 3.21
my hook in your n. and my bit in 37.29
they put the branch to their n. Eze 8.17
And I put a ring on your n., 16.12
cut off your n. and your ears, 23.25

NOSES
do not hear; n., but do not smell. Ps 115.06

NOSTRILS
into his n. the breath of life; Gen 2.07
land in whose n. was the breath of 7.22
blast of thy n. the waters piled Ex 15.08
out at your n. and becomes loathsome Num 11.20
Smoke went up from his n., and devouring 2Sa 22.09
the blast of the breath of his n. 22.16
and the spirit of God is in my n.; Job 27.03
Out of his n. comes forth smoke, as 41.20
Smoke went up from his n., and devouring Ps 18.08
the blast of the breath of thy n. 18.15
from man in whose n. is breath, Is 2.22
These are a smoke in my n., 65.05
The breath of our n., the LORD's Lam 4.20
of your camp go up into your n.; Amo 4.10

NOTABLE
the n. men of the first of the Amo 6.01
For that a n. sign has been performed Ac 4.16

NOTE
and take n. of all the lurking 1Sa 23.23
thou dost n. trouble and vexation, Ps 10.14
of Jerusalem, look and take n.! Jer 5.01
N. then the kindness and the Rom 11.22
they are men of n. among the 16.07
to take n. of those who create 16.17
n. that man, and have nothing to do 2Th 3.14

NOTES
the harp, do not give distinct n., 1Co 14.07

NOTHING

and n. that they propose to do will Gen 11.06
I will take n. but what the young 14.24
only do n. to these men, for they 19.08
for I can do n. till you arrive 19.22
done to you n. but good and have 26.29
you therefore serve me for n.? 29.15
I have done n. that they should 40.15
there is n. left in the sight of my 47.18
so that n. shall die of all that Ex 9.04
You shall eat n. leavened; in all your 12.20
he that gathered much had n. over, 16.18
he shall go out free, for n. 21.02
for her, she shall go out for n., 21.11
if he has n., then he shall be sold 22.01
he shall eat n. that is produced Num 6.04
the fish we ate in Egypt for n., 11.05
and there is n. at all but this 11.06
and touch n. of theirs, lest you be 16.26
only pass through on foot, n. more." 20.19
'Let n. hinder you from coming to 22.16
you have done n. but bless them." 23.11
bound herself, and says n. to her; 30.04
and says n. to her on the day that 30.07
and said n. to her, and did not 30.11
husband says n. to her from day to 30.14
because he said n. to her on the 30.14
with you; you have lacked n.' Deu 2.07
scarcity, in which you will lack n., 8.09
poor brother, and you give him n., 15.09
shall save alive n. that breathes, 20.16
to the young woman you shall do n.; 22.26
eating, because he has n. left him, 28.55
and growing n., where no grass can 29.23
all along the way and found n. Jos 2.22
he left n. undone of all that the 11.15
strong drink, and eat n. unclean, Ju 13.04
and eat n. unclean, for the boy 13.07
and he had n. in his hand. But he did 14.06
lacking n. that is in the earth, and 18.07
And will you do n.? Do not be slow 18.09
him everything and hid n. from him. 1Sa 3.18
For n. like this has happened 4.07
for n. can hinder the LORD from 14.06
my father does n. either great or 20.02
But the lad knew n.; only Jonathan 20.39
servant has known n. of all this, 22.15
them no harm, and they missed n., 25.07
so that n. was missed of all that 25.21
so she told him n. at all until the 25.36
there is n. better for me than that 27.01
he had eaten n. all day and all 28.20
I have found n. wrong in you from 29.06
N. was missing, whether small or 30.19
poor man had n. but one little ewe 2Sa 12.03
in their simplicity, and knew n. 15.11
grain upon it; and n. was known of it. 17.19
(and there is n. hidden from the 18.13
commanders and servants are n. to you; 19.06
why do you say n. about bringing 19.10
the LORD my God which cost me n." 24.24
in his month; they let n. be lacking. 1Ki 4.27
There was n. in the ark except the 8.09
there was n. hidden from the king 10.03
I have n. baked, only a handful of 17.12
and looked, and said, "There is n." And 18.43
you speak to me n. but the truth 22.16
maidservant has n. in the house, 2Ki 4.02
n. but the horses tied, and the 7.10
to the earth n. of the word of the 10.10
there was n. in his house or in 20.13
there is n. in my storehouses 20.15
n. shall be left, says the LORD. 20.17
burnt offerings which cost me n. 1Ch 21.24
There was n. in the ark except the 2Ch 5.10
there was n. hidden from Solomon 9.02
you speak to me n. but the truth 18.15

there had been n. like this in 30.26
"You have n. to do with us in Ez 4.03
This is n. else but sadness of the Neh 2.02
these and require n. from them. 5.12
to him for whom n. is prepared; 8.10
the wilderness, and they lacked n.; 9.21
she asked for n. except what Hegai Est 2.15
him said, "N. has been done for him." 6.03
Leave out n. that you have mentioned 6.10
inspect your fold and miss n. Job 5.24
and know n., for our days on earth 8.09
There was n. left after he had 20.21
There is n. left of your answers 21.34
pledges of your brothers for n., 22.06
that there is n. in what I say? 24.25
void, and hangs the earth upon n. 26.07
profits a man n. that he should 34.09
and there is n. hid from its heat. Ps 19.06
my lifetime is as n. in thy sight. 39.05
when he dies he will carry n. away; 49.17
And there is n. upon earth that I 73.25
far from me; I will know n. of evil. 101.04
love thy law; n. can make them stumble. 119.165
and n. you desire can compare with Pro 3.15
there is n. twisted or crooked in 8.08
and gets n., while the soul of the 13.04
pretends to be rich, yet has n.; 13.07
will seek at harvest and have n. 20.04
If you have n. with which to pay, 22.27
hears the curse, but discloses n. 29.24
and there is n. new under the sun. Ecc 1.09
and there was n. to be gained under 2.11
There is n. better for a man than 2.24
that there is n. better for them 3.12
n. can be added to it, nor anything 3.14
that there is n. better than that 3.22
a son, but he has n. in his hand. 5.14
and shall take n. for his toil, 5.15
that he lacks n. of all that he 6.02
will die, but the dead know n., 9.05
N. remains but to crouch among the Is 10.04
And there will be n. for Egypt 19.15
and all its princes shall be n. 34.12
There was n. in his house or in all 39.02
there is n. in my storehouses that 39.04
n. shall be left, says the LORD. 39.06
All the nations are as n. before him, 40.17
him as less than n. and emptiness. 40.17
the rulers of the earth as n. 40.23
you shall be as n. and shall 41.11
against you shall be as n. at all. 41.12
you are n., and your work is nought 41.24
their works are n.; their molten 41.29
All who make idols are n., and the things 44.09
image, that is profitable for n.? 44.10
you suddenly, of which you know n. 47.11
my strength for n. and vanity; 49.04
the LORD: "You were sold for n., 52.03
the Assyrian oppressed them for n. 52.04
my people are taken away for n.? 52.05
and have said, 'He will do n.; Jer 5.12
there is n. but oppression within 6.06
anger, lest thou bring me to n. 10.24
tired themselves out but profit n. 12.13
was spoiled; it was good for n. 13.07
waistcloth, which is good for n. 13.10
his neighbor serve him for n., 22.13
they care n. for you; for I have 30.14
outstretched arm! N. is too hard for thee, 32.17
they did n. of all thou didst 32.23
Judah have done n. but evil in my 32.30
have done n. but provoke me to 32.30
for the king can do n. against you. 38.05
you a question; hide n. from me." 38.14
hide n. from us and we will not put 38.25
of the poor people who owned n., 39.10
I will keep n. back from you. 42.04

NOTHING (cont.)

there is n. but lamentation; Jer 48.38
her utterly; let n. be left of her. 50.26
so that n. shall dwell in it, 51.62
"Is it n. to you, all you who pass Lam 1.12
their own spirit, and have seen n.! Eze 13.03
it was whole, it was used for n.; 15.05
trees were as n. compared with its 31.08
they shall have n. of wool on them, 44.17
of the earth are accounted as n.; Dan 4.35
that n. might be changed concerning 6.17
be cut off, and shall have n.; 9.26
wilderness, and n. escapes them. Joe 2.03
from his den, if he has taken n.? Amo 3.04
the ground, when it has taken n.? 3.05
Surely the Lord GOD does n., 3.07
him who puts n. into their mouths. Mic 3.05
that leave n. till the morning. Zep 3.03
Is it not in your sight as n.? Hag 2.03
and the olive tree still yield n.? 2.19
"See that you say n. to any one; Mt 8.04
for n. is covered that will not be 10.26
indeed he said n. to them without a 13.34
now three days, and have n. to eat; 15.32
and n. will be impossible to you." 17.20
and found n. on it but leaves only. 21.19
one swears by the temple, it is n.; 23.16
one swears by the altar, it is n.; 23.18
"Have n. to do with that righteous 27.19
Pilate saw that he was gaining n., 27.24
"See that you say n. to any one; Mk 1.44
For there is n. hid, except to be 4.22
them to take n. for their journey 6.08
there is n. outside a man which by 7.15
and they had n. to eat, he called 8.01
now three days, and have n. to eat; 8.02
he found n. but leaves, for it was 11.13
with n. but a linen cloth about his 14.51
and they said n. to any one, for 16.08
For with God n. will be impossible." Lk 1.37
And he ate n. in those days; 4.02
we toiled all night and took n.! 5.05
and lend, expecting n. in return; 6.35
For n. is hid that shall not be 8.17
"Take n. for your journey, no staff, 9.03
of the enemy; and n. shall hurt you. 10.19
and I have n. to set before him'; 11.06
N. is covered up that will not be 12.02
lack anything?" They said, "N." 22.35
Behold, n. deserving death has been 23.15
but this man has done n. wrong." 23.41
you have n. to draw with, and the Jn 4.11
sin no more, that n. worse befall you." 5.14
the Son can do n. of his own 5.19
"I can do n. on my own authority; 5.30
left over, that n. may be lost. 6.12
I should lose n. of all that he 6.39
openly, and they say n. to him! 7.26
and that I do n. on my own authority 8.28
and has n. to do with the truth, 8.44
I glorify myself, my glory is n.; 8.54
were not from God, he could do n." 9.33
hireling and cares n. for the sheep. 10.13
said to them, "You know n. at all; 11.49
another, "You see that you can do n.; 12.19
for apart from me you can do n. 15.05
Hitherto you have asked n. in my name; 16.24
come together; I have said n. secretly. 18.20
but that night they caught n. 21.03
they had n. to say in opposition. Ac 4.14
him were dispersed and came to n. 5.36
that n. of what you have said may 8.24
eyes were opened, he could see n.; 9.08
for n. common or unclean has ever 11.08
charge him with n. deserving death, 13.28
their time in n. except telling or 17.21
goddess Artemis may count for n., 19.27
ought to be quiet and do n. rash. 19.36
that there is n. in what they have 21.24
"We find n. wrong in this man. 23.09
charged with n. deserving death or 23.29
but if there is n. in their charges 25.11
he had done n. deserving death; 25.25
But I have n. definite to write to 25.26
saying n. but what the prophets and 26.22
man is doing n. to deserve death 26.31
and without food, having taken n. 27.33
I had done n. against the people 28.17
For I know that n. good dwells Rom 7.18
and had done n. either good or bad, 9.11
Lord Jesus that n. is unclean in 14.14
to bring to n. things that are, 1Co 1.28
decided to know n. among you 2.02
and humiliate those who have n.? 11.22
mountains, but have not love, I am n. 13.02
but have not love, I gain n. 13.03
For we write you n. but what you 2Co 1.13
as having n., and yet possessing 6.10
the Lord, and touch n. unclean; 6.17
"He who gathered much had n. over, 8.15
to say n. of you—for being so 9.04
there is n. to be gained by it, but 12.01
apostles, even though I am n. 12.11
who were of repute added n. to me; Gal 2.06
when he is n., he deceives himself. 6.03
Do n. from selfishness or conceit, Php 2.03
and have n. to do with him, that he 2Th 3.14
and n. is to be rejected if it is 1Ti 4.04
Have n. to do with godless and 4.07
without favor, doing n. from partiality. 5.21
up with conceit, he knows n.; 6.04
for we brought n. into the world, 6.07
Have n. to do with stupid, senseless 2Ti 2.23
corrupt and unbelieving n. is pure; Tit 1.15
having n. evil to say of us. 2.08
have n. more to do with him, 3.10
on their way; see that they lack n. 3.13
preferred to do n. without your Phm 1.14
to say n. of your owing me even 1.19
he left n. outside his control. Heb 2.08
tribe Moses said n. about priests. 7.14
(for the law made n. perfect); 7.19
and complete, lacking in n. Jas 1.04
do right and let n. terrify you. 1Pe 3.06
have accepted n. from the heathen. 3Jn 1.07
I have prospered, and I need n.; Rev 3.17
But n. unclean shall enter it, nor 21.27

NOTHINGS

will you comfort me with empty n.? Job 21.34

NOTICE

that you should take n. of me, Ru 2.10
be the man who took n. of you." 2.19
And all the people took n. of it, 2Sa 3.36
there is none who takes n. of me; Ps 142.04
but do not n. the log that is in Mt 7.03
but do not n. the log that is in Lk 6.41
to give n. when the days of purification Ac 21.26
give n. now to the tribune to bring 23.15
of these things has escaped his n., 26.26

NOTICED

but they n. a bay with a beach, on Ac 27.39

NOTIFY

We also n. you that it shall not be Ez 7.24

NOTORIOUS

And they had then a n. prisoner, Mt 27.16

NOTWITHSTANDING

N., the sons of Korah did not die. Num 26.11

NOUGHT
the LORD, "Does Job fear God for n.? Job 1.09
the counsel of the nations to n.; Ps 33.10
Surely for n. are they in turmoil; 39.06
of the wicked man comes to n. 112.10
expectation of the wicked comes to n. Pro 10.28
expectation of the godless comes to n. 11.07
together, but it will come to n.; Is 8.10
shall come to n. and the scoffer 29.20
who brings princes to n., 40.23
are nothing, and your work is n.; 41.24
fathers have inherited n. but lies, Jer 16.19
The peoples labor for n., 51.58
shall bring to n. the pride of Eze 32.12
and set at n. the king's command, and Dan 3.28
they shall surely come to n.; Hos 12.11
exile, and Bethel shall come to n. Amo 5.05

NOURISH
or n. the sound, but devours the Zec 11.16

NOURISHED
The waters n. it, the deep made it Eze 31.04
n. and knit together through its Col 2.19
n. on the words of the faith and of 1Ti 4.06
in which to be n. for one thousand Rev 12.06
where she is to be n. for a time, 12.14

NOURISHER
of life and a n. of your old age; Ru 4.15

NOURISHES
plants a cedar and the rain n. it. Is 44.14
but n. and cherishes it, as Christ Eph 5.29

NOWADAYS
many servants n. who are breaking 1Sa 25.10

NOWHERE
And he said, "Your servant went n." 2Ki 5.25
Son of man has n. to lay his head." Mt 8.20
"Go n. among the Gentiles, and enter 10.05
Son of man has n. to lay his head." Lk 9.58
for I have n. to store my crops?' 12.17

NULL
makes them n. and void on the day Num 30.12
he makes them n. and void after he 30.15
faith is n. and the promise is void Rom 4.14

NULLIFY
faithlessness n. the faithfulness Rom 3.03
I do not n. the grace of God; Gal 2.21

NUMBER
n. the stars, if you are able to n. them." Gen 15.05
according to the n. of their 47.12
But the n. of bricks which they Ex 5.08
deliver the same n. of bricks." 5.18
lessen your daily n. of bricks." 5.19
according to the n. of persons; 12.04
according to the n. of the persons 16.16
I will fulfil the n. of your days. 23.26
to the LORD when you n. them, 30.12
plague among them when you n. them. 30.12
According to the n. of years after Lev 25.15
according to the n. of years for crops 25.15
for it is the n. of the crops that 25.16
be according to the n. of years; 25.50
cattle, and make you few in n., 26.22
according to the n. of names, Num 1.02
war, you and Aaron shall n. them, 1.03
according to the n. of names from 1.18
according to the n. of names, 1.20
the n. of the tribe of Reuben was 1.21
according to the n. of names, 1.22
the n. of the tribe of Simeon was 1.23
according to the n. of the names, 1.24
the n. of the tribe of Gad was 1.25
according to the n. of names, 1.26
the n. of the tribe of Judah was 1.27
according to the n. of names, 1.28
the n. of the tribe of Issachar was 1.29
according to the n. of names, 1.30
the n. of the tribe of Zebulun was 1.31
according to the n. of names, 1.32
the n. of the tribe of Ephraim was 1.33
according to the n. of names, 1.34
the n. of the tribe of Manasseh was 1.35
according to the n. of names, 1.36
the n. of the tribe of Benjamin was 1.37
according to the n. of names, 1.38
the n. of the tribe of Dan was 1.39
according to the n. of names, 1.40
the n. of the tribe of Asher was 1.41
according to the n. of names, 1.42
the n. of the tribe of Naphtali was 1.43
So the whole n. of the people of 1.45
their whole n. was six hundred and 1.46
the tribe of Levi you shall not n., 1.49
The whole n. of the camp of Judah, 2.09
The whole n. of the camp of Reuben, 2.16
The whole n. of the camp of Ephraim, 2.24
The whole n. of the camp of Dan is 2.31
"N. the sons of Levi, by fathers' 3.15
month old and upward you shall n." 3.15
Their n. according to the n. of all 3.22
According to the n. of all the 3.28
Their n. according to the n. of all 3.34
"N. all the first-born males of the 3.40
upward, taking their n. by names. 3.40
according to the n. of names, from a 3.43
and above the n. of the male 3.46
the excess n. of them is redeemed 3.48
you shall n. them, all who can enter 4.23
you shall n. them by their families 4.29
you shall n. them, every one that 4.30
and their n. by families was two 4.36
This was the n. of the families of 4.37
The n. of the sons of Gershon, by 4.38
their n. by their families and 4.40
This was the n. of the families of 4.41
The n. of the families of the sons 4.42
their n. by families was three 4.44
among whom I am n. six hundred 11.21
wilderness; and of all your n., 14.29
According to the n. of the days in 14.34
According to the n. that you 15.12
every one according to their n. 15.12
with a n. of the people of Israel, 16.02
more in n. and more honorable than 22.15
or n. the fourth part of Israel? 23.10
and their n. was forty-three 26.07
sons of Gad according to their n., 26.18
of Judah according to their n., 26.22
of Issachar according to their n., 26.25
Zebulunites according to their n., 26.27
and their n. was fifty-two thousand 26.34
of Ephraim according to their n., 26.37
and their n. was forty-five thousand 26.41
Shuhamites, according to their n., 26.43
of Asher according to their n., 26.47
and their n. was forty-five thousand 26.50
This was the n. of the people of 26.51
according to the n. of names. 26.53
the lambs by n. according to the 29.18
the lambs by n. according to the 29.21
the lambs by n. according to the 29.24
the lambs by n. according to the 29.27
the lambs by n. according to the 29.30
lambs by their n. according to the 29.33
lambs by their n. according to the 29.37
was in n. three hundred and thirty-seven 31.36
be left few in n. among the Deu 4.27
were more in n. than any other 7.07

NUMBER (cont.)
presence with a n. of stripes in Deu 25.02
and sojourned there, few in n.; 26.05
you shall be left few in n.; 28.62
according to the n. of the sons of 32.08
according to the n. of the tribes Jos 4.05
according to the n. of the tribes 4.08
in n. like the sand that is upon 11.04
tents, coming like locusts for n.; Ju 6.05
And the n. of those that lapped, 7.06
and their camels were without n., 7.12
from the whole n. of their tribe, 18.02
their wives, according to their n., 21.23
according to the n. of the lords of 1Sa 6.04
according to the n. of all the 6.18
"N. and see who has gone from us." 14.17
were given in full n. to the king, 18.27
And the n. of the days that David 27.07
Then they arose and passed over by n., 2Sa 2.15
on each foot, twenty-four in n.; 21.20
"Go, n. Israel and Judah." 24.01
and n. the people, that I may know 24.02
I may know the n. of the people." 24.02
of the king to n. the people of 24.04
according to the n. of the tribes 1Ki 18.31
their n. in the days of David being 1Ch 7.02
Their n. enrolled by genealogies, 7.40
When they were few in n., and of little 16.19
on each foot, twenty-four in n.; 20.06
and incited David to n. Israel. 21.01
n. Israel, from Beersheba to Dan, and 21.02
a report, that I may know their n." 21.02
who gave command to n. the people? 21.17
and cedar timbers without n.; 22.04
all kinds of craftsmen without n., 22.15
according to the n. of the names of 23.24
these were the n. of the Levites 23.27
according to the n. required of 23.31
The n. of them along with their 25.07
David did not n. those below twenty 27.23
Joab the son of Zeruiah began to n., 27.24
and the n. was not entered in the 27.24
were without n. who came with him 2Ch 12.03
The whole n. of the heads of 26.12
captive a great n. of his people 28.05
The n. of the burnt offerings which 29.32
Besides the great n. of burnt 29.35
themselves in sufficient n., 30.03
flock to the n. of thirty thousand, 35.07
And this was the n. of them: Ez 1.09
The n. of the men of the people of 2.02
offerings by n. according to the 3.04
according to the n. of the tribes 6.17
The n. of the men of the people of Neh 7.07
the n. of his sons, all the promotions Est 5.11
That very day the n. of those slain 9.11
according to the n. of them all; Job 1.05
not come into the n. of the months. 3.06
marvelous things without n.: 5.09
and marvelous things without n. 9.10
and the n. of his months is with 14.05
For then thou wouldest n. my steps, 14.16
when the n. of their months is cut 21.21
Is there any n. to his armies? 25.03
see my ways, and n. all my steps? 31.04
the n. of his years is unsearchable 36.26
and the n. of your days is great! 38.21
Who can n. the clouds by wisdom? 38.37
Can you n. the months that they 39.02
have encompassed me without n.; Ps 40.12
go round about her, n. her towers, 48.12
More in n. than the hairs of my 69.04
for their n. is past my knowledge. 71.15
So teach us to n. our days that we 90.12
When they were few in n., of little 105.12
came, and young locusts without n.; 105.34
He determines the n. of the stars, 147.04
concubines, and maidens without n. Sol 6.08
He who brings out their host by n., Is 40.26
have forgotten me days without n. Jer 2.32
widows more in n. than the sand of 15.08
to the land of Judah, few in n.; 44.28
than locusts; they are without n. 46.23
This is the n. of the people whom 52.28
for the n. of the days that you lie Eze 4.04
For I assign to you a n. of days, 4.05
equal to the n. of the years of 4.05
During the n. of days that you lie 4.09
shall take from these a small n., 5.03
and I will let you go in by n. 20.37
in the books the n. of years which, Dan 9.02
Yet the n. of the people of Israel Hos 1.10
my land, powerful and without n.; Joe 1.06
who was of the n. of the twelve; Lk 22.03
set down, in n. about five thousand. Jn 6.10
added to their n. day by day those Ac 2.47
and the n. of the men came to about 4.04
and a n. of men, about four hundred 5.36
disciples were increasing in n., 6.01
and the n. of the disciples multiplied 6.07
and a great n. that believed turned 11.21
And a n. of those who practiced 19.19
We sailed slowly for a n. of days, 27.07
"Though the n. of the sons of Rom 9.27
until the full n. of the Gentiles 11.25
The former priests were many in n., Heb 7.23
until the n. of their fellow Rev 6.11
And I heard the n. of the sealed, 7.04
multitude which no man could n., 7.09
The n. of the troops of cavalry was 9.16
ten thousand; I heard their n. 9.16
of the beast or the n. of its name. 13.17
understanding reckon the n. of the beast, 13.18
of the beast, for it is a human n., 13.18
its n. is six hundred and sixty-six. 13.18
its image and the n. of its name, 15.02
their n. is like the sand of the 20.08

NUMBERED
they cannot be n. for multitude. Gen 16.10
which cannot be n. for multitude. 32.12
and his daughters n. thirty-three). 46.15
Each who is n. in the census shall Ex 30.13
Every one who is n. in the census, 30.14
who were n. was a hundred talents 38.25
every one who was n. in the census, 38.26
So he n. them in the wilderness of Num 1.19
houses, those of them that were n., 1.22
These are those who were n., 1.44
Moses and Aaron n. with the help 1.44
were not n. by their ancestral 1.47
his host as n. being seventy-four 2.04
his host as n. being fifty-four 2.06
his host as n. being fifty-seven 2.08
his host as n. being forty-six 2.11
his host as n. being fifty-nine 2.13
his host as n. being forty-five 2.15
his host as n. being forty thousand 2.19
his host as n. being thirty-two 2.21
his host as n. being thirty-five 2.23
his host as n. being sixty-two 2.26
his host as n. being forty-one 2.28
his host as n. being fifty-three 2.30
of Israel as n. by their fathers' 2.32
camps who were n. by their companies 2.32
were not n. among the people of 2.33
So Moses n. them according to the 3.16
All who were n. of the Levites, whom 3.39
Moses and Aaron n. at the commandment 3.39
So Moses n. all the first-born 3.42
and upward as n. were twenty-two 3.43
congregation n. the sons of the 4.34
Moses and Aaron n. according to 4.37
Moses and Aaron n. according to 4.41

NUMBERED (cont.)
those who were n. of the families Num 4.45
Moses and Aaron n. according to 4.45
All those who were n. of the Levites, 4.46
Aaron and the leaders of Israel n., 4.46
those who were n. of them were 4.48
thus they were n. by him, as the LORD 4.49
who were over those who were n., 7.02
n. from twenty years old and upward, 14.29
the Levites as n. according to 26.57
And those n. of them were twenty-three 26.62
they were not n. among the people 26.62
These were those n. by Moses and 26.63
who n. the people of Israel in the 26.63
a man of those n. by Moses and 26.64
who had n. the people of Israel in 26.64
And Saul n. the people who were 1Sa 13.15
And when they had n., behold, Jonathan 14.17
and n. them in Telaim, two hundred 15.04
him after he had n. the people. 2Sa 24.10
that cannot be n. or counted for 1Ki 3.08
and the levy n. thirty thousand men. 5.13
they could not be counted or n. 8.05
were n., and the total was thirty-eight 1Ch 23.03
they could not be counted or n. 2Ch 5.06
they would be more than can be n. Ps 40.05
and what is lacking cannot be n. Ecc 1.15
and was n. with the transgressors; Is 53.12
cannot be n. and the sands of the Jer 33.22
our days were n.; for our end Lam 4.18
God has n. the days of your kingdom Dan 5.26
can be neither measured nor n.; Hos 1.10
the hairs of your head are all n. Mt 10.30
the hairs of your head are all n. Lk 12.07
For he was n. among us, and was Ac 1.17

NUMBERING
the sum of the n. of the people to 2Sa 24.09
the sum of the n. of the people to 1Ch 21.05
Levi and Benjamin in the n., 21.06
each division n. twenty-four 27.01
and the herd, n. about two thousand, Mk 5.13
n. myriads of myriads and thousands Rev 5.11

NUMBERS
my n. are few, and if they gather Gen 34.30
inheritance according to its n. Num 26.54
These are the n. of the divisions 1Ch 12.23
for great n. had deserted to him 2Ch 15.09
they found cattle in great n., 20.25
according to the n. in the muster 26.11
kept it in great n. as prescribed. 30.05
sanctified themselves in great n. 30.24
and they increased in n. daily. Ac 16.05
to him at his lodging in great n. 28.23

NUMEROUS
wild beasts grow too n. for you. Deu 7.22
prosperous and n. than your fathers. 30.05
inheritance, although I am a n. people, Jos 17.14
"If you are a n. people, go up to 17.15
"You are a n. people, and have great 17.17
they were very n. from Bashan to 1Ch 5.23
they are more n. than locusts; Jer 46.23

NUN
his servant Joshua the son of N., Ex 33.11
And Joshua the son of N., the minister Num 11.28
of Ephraim, Hoshea the son of N.; 13.08
called Hoshea the son of N. Joshua. 13.16
the son of N. and Caleb the son of 14.06
Jephunneh and Joshua the son of N. 14.30
the son of N. and Caleb the son of 14.38
Jephunneh and Joshua the son of N. 26.65
Moses, "Take Joshua the son of N., 27.18
Kenizzite and Joshua the son of N., 32.12
and to Joshua the son of N., 32.28
priest and Joshua the son of N. 34.17
Joshua the son of N., who stands Deu 1.38
Joshua the son of N. and said, 31.23
he and Joshua the son of N. 32.44
the son of N. was full of the 34.09
LORD said to Joshua the son of N., Jos 1.01
the son of N. sent two men secretly 2.01
and came to Joshua the son of N.; 2.23
the son of N. called the priests 6.06
priest, and Joshua the son of N., 14.01
the son of N. and the leaders, and 17.04
among them to Joshua the son of N. 19.49
the son of N. and the heads of the 19.51
the son of N. and to the heads of 21.01
After these things Joshua the son of N., 24.29
And Joshua the son of N., the servant Ju 2.08
he spoke by Joshua the son of N. 1Ki 16.34
N. his son, Joshua his son. 1Ch 7.27
the son of N. to that day the Neh 8.17

NURSE
Rebekah their sister and her n., Gen 24.59
Rebekah's n., died, and she was 35.08
and call you a n. from the Hebrew Ex 2.07
Hebrew women to n. the child for 2.07
and n. him for me, and I will give 2.09
as a n. carries the sucking child, Num 11.12
in her bosom, and became his n. Ru 4.16
and his n. took him up, and fled; 2Sa 4.04
wait upon the king, and be his n.; 1Ki 1.02
the king's n. and ministered to 1.04
rose in the morning to n. my child, 3.21
put him and his n. in a bedchamber 2Ki 11.02
put him and his n. in a bedchamber 2Ch 22.11
like a n. taking care of her 1Th 2.07

NURSED
woman took the child and n. him. Ex 2.09
the woman remained and n. her son, 1Sa 1.23
that n. at my mother's breast! Sol 8.01

NURSING
and their queens your n. mothers. Is 49.23
the children, even n. infants. Joe 2.16

NURSING
The tongue of the n. cleaves to the Lam 4.04

NUT
I went down to the n. orchard, Sol 6.11

NUTS
myrrh, pistachio n., and almonds. Gen 43.11

NYMPHA
and to N. and the church in her Col 4.15

O

OAK
at Shechem, to the o. of Moreh. Gen 12.06
them under the o. which was near 35.04
buried under an o. below Bethel; 35.08
Gilgal, beside the o. of Moreh? Deu 11.30
from the o. in Zaanannim, and Jos 19.33
there under the o. in the sanctuary 24.26
as far away as the o. in Zaanannim, Ju 4.11
and sat under the o. at Ophrah, 6.11
him under the o. and presented 6.19
by the o. of the pillar at Shechem. 9.06
the direction of the Diviners' O. 9.37
and come to the o. of Tabor; 1Sa 10.03
the thick branches of a great o., 2Sa 18.09
and his head caught fast in the o., 18.09
I saw Absalom hanging in an o." 18.10

OAK (cont.)
while he was still alive in the o. 2Sa 18.14
and found him sitting under an o.; 1Ki 13.14
their bones under the o. in Jabesh, 1Ch 10.12
be like an o. whose leaf withers, Is 1.30
again, like a terebinth or an o., 6.13
holm tree or an o. and lets it 44.14
tree, and under every leafy o., Eze 6.13
under o., poplar, and terebinth, Hos 4.13

OAKS
came and dwelt by the o. of Mamre, Gen 13.18
living by the o. of Mamre the 14.13
appeared to him by the o. of Mamre, 18.01
of the LORD makes the o. to whirl, Ps 29.09
ashamed of the o. in which you Is 1.29
and against all the o. of Bashan; 2.13
you who burn with lust among the o., 57.05
may be called o. of righteousness, 61.03
Of o. of Bashan they made your oars Eze 27.06
and who was as strong as the o.; Amo 2.09
Wail, o. of Bashan, for the thick Zec 11.02

OAR
ships come all that handle the o. Eze 27.29

OARS
where no galley with o. can go, Is 33.21
Of oaks of Bashan they made your o.; Eze 27.06

OATH
there both of them swore an o. Gen 21.31
will be free from this o. of mine; 24.08
then you will be free from my o., 24.41
you, you will be free from my o." 24.41
will fulfil the o. which I swore 26.03
let there be an o. between you and 26.28
early and took o. with one another; 26.31
Then Joseph took an o. of the sons 50.25
an o. by the LORD shall be between Ex 22.11
and the owner shall accept the o., 22.11
his lips a rash o. to do evil or Lev 5.04
any sort of rash o. that men swear, 5.04
priest shall make her take an o., Num 5.19
the woman take the o. of the curse, 5.21
execration and an o. among your 5.21
or swears an o. to bind himself by 30.02
herself by a pledge with an o., 30.10
and any binding o. to afflict 30.13
is keeping the o. which he swore Deu 7.08
respect to this o. of yours which Jos 2.17
respect to your o. which you have 2.20
Joshua laid an o. upon them at that 6.26
because of the o. which we swore 9.20
taken a great o. concerning him Ju 21.05
for Saul laid an o. on the people, 1Sa 14.24
for the people feared the o. 14.26
charge the people with the o.; 14.27
charged the people with an o., 14.28
And the king gave him his o. 2Sa 19.23
because of the o. of the LORD 21.07
not kept your o. to the LORD and 1Ki 2.43
neighbor and is made to take an o., 8.31
and swears his o. before thine 8.31
would take an o. of the kingdom or 18.10
put them under o. in the house of 2Ki 11.04
neighbor and is made to take an o., 2Ch 6.22
and swears his o. before thy altar 6.22
They took o. to the LORD with a 15.14
And all Judah rejoiced over the o.; 15.15
all Israel take o. that they would Ez 10.05
been said. So they took the o. 10.05
and took an o. of them to do as Neh 5.12
in Judah were bound by o. to him, 6.18
a curse and an o. to walk in God's 10.29
made them take o. in the name of 13.25
I have sworn an o. and confirmed it, Ps 119.106
to David a sure o. from which he 132.11
of your sacred o. be not dismayed; Ecc 8.02
swears is as he who shuns an o. 9.02
he who takes an o. in the land Is 65.16
may perform the o. which I swore Jer 11.05
despised the o. in breaking the Eze 16.59
with him, putting him under o. 17.13
whose o. he despised, and whose 17.16
Because he despised the o. and 17.18
surely my o. which he despised, and 17.19
the curse and o. which are written Dan 9.11
one another, and love no false o., Zec 8.17
promised with an o. to give her Mt 14.07
the temple, he is bound by his o.' 23.16
the altar, he is bound by his o.' 23.18
And again he denied it with an o., 26.72
the o. which he swore to our father Lk 1.73
sworn with an o. to him that he Ac 2.30
themselves by an o. neither to eat 23.12
ourselves by an o. to taste no 23.14
themselves by an o. neither to eat 23.21
disputes an o. is final for Heb 6.16
purpose, he interposed with an o., 6.17
And it was not without an o. 7.20
took their office without an o., 7.21
this one was addressed with an o., 7.21
priests, but the word of the o., 7.28
or by earth or with any other o., Jas 5.12

OATHS
they have sworn solemn o.; Eze 21.23
with empty o. they make covenants; Hos 10.04
because of his o. and his guests Mt 14.09
because of his o. and his guests Mk 6.26

OBADIAH
And Ahab called O., who was 1Ki 18.03
(Now O. revered the LORD greatly; 18.03
O. took a hundred prophets and hid 18.04
And Ahab said to O., "Go through 18.05
and O. went in another direction by 18.06
And as O. was on the way, behold, 18.07
and O. recognized him, and fell on 18.07
So O. went to meet Ahab, and told 18.16
his son O., his son Shecaniah. 1Ch 3.21
O., Joel, and Isshiah, five, all of 7.03
Ishmael, Sheariah, O., and Hanan. 8.38
and O. the son of Shemaiah, son of 9.16
Ishmael, Sheariah, O., and Hanan; 9.44
Ezer the chief, O. second, Eliab third, 12.09
for Zebulun, Ishmaiah the son of O.; 27.19
O., Zechariah, Nethanel, and Micaiah, 2Ch 17.07
were set Jahath and O. the Levites, 34.12
O. the son of Jehiel, and with him Ez 8.09
Harim, Meremoth, O., Neh 10.05
O., Meshullam, Talmon, and Akkub were 12.25
The vision of O. Thus says the Ob 1.01

OBAL
O., Abimael, Sheba, Gen 10.28

OBED
They named him O.; he was the father Ru 4.17
Salmon of Boaz, Boaz of O., 4.21
O. of Jesse, and Jesse of David. 4.22
Boaz of O., O. of Jesse. 1Ch 2.12
father of Ephlal, and Ephlal of O. 2.37
O. was the father of Jehu, and Jehu 2.38
Eliel, and O., and Jaasiel the 11.47
O., and Elzabad, whose brethren were 26.07
Jehohanan, Azariah the son of O., 2Ch 23.01
and Boaz the father of O. by Ruth, Mt 1.05
and O. the father of Jesse, 1.05
the son of O., the son of Boaz, the Lk 3.32

OBEDEDOM
to the house of O. the Gittite. 2Sa 6.10
in the house of O. the Gittite 6.11
LORD blessed O. and all his 6.11

OBEDEDOM (cont.)
household of O. and all that 2Sa 6.12
the house of O. to the city of 6.12
to the house of O. the Gittite. 1Ch 13.13
household of O. in his house three 13.14
household of O. and all that he 13.14
and the gatekeepers O. and Jeiel. 15.18
O., Jeiel, and Azaziah were to lead 15.21
O. and Jehiah also were to be 15.24
the house of O. with rejoicing. 15.25
O., and Jeiel, who were to play 16.05
and also O. and his sixty-eight 16.38
while O., the son of Jeduthun, and 16.38
And O. had sons: Shemaiah the first-born, 26.04
of the sons of O. with their sons 26.08
for the service; sixty-two of O. 26.08
the house of God, and O. with them; 2Ch 25.24

OBEDEDOM'S
O. came out for the south, and to 1Ch 26.15

OBEDIENCE
him shall be the o. of the peoples. Gen 49.10
to bring about o. to the faith for Rom 1.05
so by one man's o. many will be 5.19
or of o., which leads to righteousness? 6.16
me to win o. from the Gentiles, by 15.18
For while your o. is known to all, 16.19
to bring about o. to the faith— 16.26
as he remembers the o. of you all, 2Co 7.15
God by your o. in acknowledging 9.13
disobedience, when your o. is complete. 10.06
Confident of your o., I write to you, Phm 1.21
he learned o. through what he Heb 5.08
the Spirit for o. to Jesus Christ 1Pe 1.02
souls by your o. to the truth for 1.22

OBEDIENT
we will do, and we will be o. Ex 24.07
If you are willing and o., Is 1.19
to Nazareth, and was o. to them; Lk 2.51
the priests were o. to the faith. Ac 6.07
yourselves to any one as o. slaves, Rom 6.16
sin have become o. from the heart 6.17
whether you are o. in everything. 2Co 2.09
Slaves, be o. to those who are your Eph 6.05
himself and became o. unto death, Php 2.08
to be o., to be ready for any Tit 3.01
As o. children, do not be conformed 1Pe 1.14

OBEISANCE
they bowed their heads and made o. Gen 43.28
father-in-law, and did o. and kissed him; Ex 18.07
his face to the earth, and did o. 1Sa 24.08
his face to the ground, and did o. 28.14
he fell to the ground and did o. 2Sa 1.02
and fell on his face and did o. 9.06
And he did o., and said, "What is 9.08
and did o., and said, "Help, O king." 14.04
and did o., and blessed the king; 14.22
a man came near to do o. to him, 15.05
And Ziba said, "I do o.; 16.04
and did o. to the king with his 24.20
Bathsheba bowed and did o. to the king, 1Ki 1.16
and did o. to the king, and said, 1.31
he came and did o. to King Solomon; 1.53
and did o. to David with his face 1Ch 21.21
the LORD, and did o. to the king. 29.20
Judah came and did o. to the king; 2Ch 24.17
bowed down and did o. to Haman; Est 3.02
Mordecai did not bow down or do o. 3.02
did not bown down or do o. to him, 3.05

OBELISKS
He shall break the o. of Heliopolis Jer 43.13

OBEY
o. my word as I command you. Gen 27.08
only o. my word, and go, fetch them 27.13
Now therefore, my son, o. my voice; 27.43
if you will o. my voice and keep my Ex 19.05
of the people of Israel may o. Num 27.20
LORD your God and o. his voice, Deu 4.30
you would not o. the voice of the 8.20
not believe him or o. his voice. 9.23
"And if you will o. my commandments 11.13
if you o. the commandments of the 11.27
if you do not o. the commandments 11.28
his commandments and o. his voice, 13.04
if you o. the voice of the LORD 13.18
if only you will o. the voice of 15.05
who will not o. the voice of his 21.18
rebellious, he will not o. our voice; 21.20
ordinances, and will o. his voice; 26.17
You shall therefore o. the voice of 27.10
"And if you o. the voice of the 28.01
if you o. the voice of the LORD 28.02
if you o. the commandments of the 28.13
"But if you will not o. the voice 28.15
you did not o. the voice of the 28.45
you did not o. the voice of the 28.62
and o. his voice in all that I 30.02
And you shall again o. the voice of 30.08
if you o. the voice of the LORD 30.10
If you o. the commandments of the 30.16
in all things, so we will o. you; Jos 1.17
serve, and his voice we will o." 24.24
Israel would o. the commandments Ju 3.04
did you not o. the voice of the 1Sa 15.19
Behold, to o. is better than sacrifice, 15.22
Because you did not o. the voice of 28.18
'What you say is good; I o.' 1Ki 2.42
my statutes and o. my ordinances 6.12
and if you are ready to o. me, 2Ki 10.06
because they did not o. the voice 18.12
Whoever will not o. the law of your Ez 7.26
and did not o. thy commandments; Neh 9.16
they refused to o., and were not 9.17
and did not o. thy commandments, 9.29
their neck and would not o. 9.29
and did not o. the voice of the Ps 106.25
and scorns to o. a mother will be Pro 30.17
and the Ammonites shall o. them. Is 11.14
and whose law they would not o.? 42.24
'O. my voice, and I will be your God, Jer 7.23
But they did not o. or incline 7.24
that did not o. the voice of the 7.28
to this day, saying, O. my voice. 11.07
Yet they did not o. or incline 11.08
For if you will indeed o. this word, 22.04
and o. the voice of the LORD your 26.13
they did not o. thy voice or walk 32.23
O. now the voice of the LORD in 38.20
and did not o. his voice, this thing 40.03
we will o. the voice of the LORD 42.06
with us when we o. the voice of 42.06
people did not o. the voice of the 43.04
they did not o. the voice of the 43.07
and did not o. the voice of the 44.23
and keep my ordinances and o. them; Eze 11.20
dominions shall serve and o. them.' Dan 7.27
aside, refusing to o. thy voice. 9.11
upon the nations that did not o. Mic 5.15
will diligently o. the voice of Zec 6.15
that even winds and sea o. him?" Mt 8.27
unclean spirits, and they o. him." Mk 1.27
that even wind and sea o. him?" 4.41
wind and water, and they o. him?" Lk 8.25
in the sea,' and it would o. you. 17.06
he who does not o. the Son shall Jn 3.36
"We must o. God rather than men. Ac 5.29
God has given to those who o. him." 5.32
Our fathers refused to o. him, 7.39

OBEY (cont.)
factious and do not o. the truth, Rom 2.08
but o. wickedness, there will be 2.08
is of value if you o. the law; 2.25
to make you o. their passions. 6.12
are slaves of the one whom you o., 6.16
thought captive to o. Christ, 2Co 10.05
Children, o. your parents in the Eph 6.01
Children, o. your parents in everything, Col. 3.20
Slaves, o. in everything those who 3.22
who do not o. the gospel of our 2Th 1.08
one refuses to o. what we say in 3.14
salvation to all who o. him, Heb 5.09
O. your leaders and submit to them; 13.17
of horses that they may o. us, Jas 3.03
though they do not o. the word, 1Pe 3.01
who formerly did not o., when God's patience 3.20
who do not o. the gospel of God? 4.17
we love God and o. his commandments. 1Jn 5.02

OBEYED
because you have o. my voice." Gen 22.18
because Abraham o. my voice and 26.05
and that Jacob had o. his father 28.07
and behold, you have not yet o." Ex 7.16
I have o. the voice of the LORD my Deu 26.14
so the people of Israel o. him, 34.09
Just as we o. Moses in all things, Jos 1.17
and have o. my voice in all that I 22.02
But you have not o. my command. Ju 2.02
who had o. the commandments of the 2.17
fathers, and have not o. my voice, 2.20
"I have o. the voice of the LORD, I 1Sa 15.20
the people and o. their voice. 15.24
as they heard of me, they o. me. 2Sa 22.45
you have not o. the voice of the 1Ki 20.36
they neither listened nor o. 2Ki 18.12
have not o. the words of this book, 22.13
prospered, and all Israel o. him. 1Ch 29.23
for Esther o. Mordecai just as when Est 2.20
as they heard of me they o. me; Ps 18.44
and that you have not o. my voice, Jer 3.13
and we have not o. the voice of the 3.25
and we have not o. my voice, or walked 9.13
that you have not o. my voice. 22.21
Because you have not o. my words, 25.08
And they o., all the princes and 34.10
they o. and set them free. 34.10
You have not o. me by proclaiming 34.17
We have o. the voice of Jonadab the 35.08
and have o. and done all that 35.10
for they have o. their father's 35.14
but this people has not o. me. 35.16
you have o. the command of Jonadab 35.18
you have not o. the voice of the 42.21
and have not o. the voice of the Dan 9.10
done, and we have not o. his voice. 9.14
o. the voice of the LORD their God, Hag 1.12
Therefore, my beloved, as you have always o., Php 2.12
By faith Abraham o. when he was Heb 11.08
as Sarah o. Abraham, calling him 1Pe 3.06

OBEYING
by not o. the priest who stands to Deu 17.12
o. his voice, and cleaving to him; 30.20
as in o. the voice of the LORD? 1Sa 15.22
who hindered you from o. the truth? Gal 5.07

OBEYS
He who o. a command will meet no Ecc 8.05
the LORD and o. the voice of his Is 50.10

OBIL
Over the camels was O. the Ishmaelite; 1Ch 27.30

OBJECT
he has made them an o. of horror, 2Ch 29.08
an o. of dread to my acquaintances; Ps 31.11
I am an o. of scorn to my accusers; 109.25
the LORD is to them an o. of scorn, Jer 6.10
desolation and an o. of reproach Eze 5.14
like her an o. of reproach for the 16.57
make them an o. of terror and a 23.46
so-called god or o. of worship, 2Th 2.04

OBJECTED
But when the Jews o., I was compelled Ac 28.19

OBJECTION
I was sent for, I came without o. Ac 10.29

OBJECTS
and armlets, all sorts of gold o., Ex 35.22
by name the o. which they are Num 4.32
observed the o. of your worship, I Ac 17.23

OBLATION
the time of the offering of the o., 1Ki 18.29
the time of the offering of the o., 18.36

OBLIGATE
We o. ourselves to bring the first Neh 10.35

OBLIGATION
and be free of o. to the LORD and Num 32.22
ourselves the o. to charge ourselves Neh 10.32
I am under o. both to Greeks and to Rom 1.14

OBLIGED
villages were o. to come in every 1Ch 9.25
Now he was o. to release one man to *Lk 23.17

OBOTH
Israel set out, and encamped in O. Num 21.10
And they set out from O., 21.11
out from Punon, and encamped at O. 33.43
And they set out from O., and encamped 33.44

OBSCURE
he will not stand before o. men. Pro 22.29
people of an o. speech which you Is 33.19

OBSERVANCE
by the o. of which a man shall live, Neh 9.29
ordinances, by whose o. man shall live. Eze 20.11
ordinances, by whose o. man shall live; 20.13
ordinances, by whose o. man shall live; 20.21
to them for o. the decisions which Ac 16.04
you yourself live in o. of the law. 21.24

OBSERVE
you shall o. it as an ordinance Ex 12.14
And you shall o. the feast of 12.17
therefore you shall o. this day, 12.17
You shall o. this rite as an 12.24
"O. what I command you this day. 34.11
And you shall o. the feast of weeks, 34.22
And you shall o. all my statutes Lev 19.37
you shall o. a day of solemn rest, a 23.24
my statutes and o. my commandments 26.03
and do not o. all these commandments Num 15.22
" 'O. the sabbath day, to keep it Deu 5.12
"O. the month of Abib, and keep the 16.01
be careful to o. these statutes. 16.12
Take good care to o. the commandment Jos 22.05
that I commanded her let her o." Ju 13.14
o. the place where he lies; Ru 3.04
But Amasa did not o. the sword 2Sa 20.10
are careful to o. the statutes and 1Ch 22.13
o. and seek out all the commandments 28.08
and to o. and do all the commandments Neh 10.29
Do you o. the calving of the hinds? Job 39.01
and did not o. his testimonies, Ps 78.56
keep his statutes, and o. his laws. 105.45
Blessed are they who o. justice, 106.03
I will o. thy statutes; O forsake 119.08
that I may live and o. thy word. 119.17

OBSERVE (cont.)

thy law and o. it with my whole Ps 119.34
to o. thy righteous ordinances. 119.106
that I may o. thy testimonies. 119.146
o. carefully what is before you; Pro 23.01
and let your eyes o. my ways. 23.26
many things, but does not o. them; Is 42.20
is careful to o. my ordinances— Eze 18.09
been careful to o. all my statutes, 18.19
nor o. their ordinances, nor defile 20.18
be careful to o. my ordinances, 20.19
not careful to o. my ordinances, 20.21
and be careful to o. my ordinances. 36.27
and be careful to o. my statutes. 37.24
that they may o. and perform all 43.11
so practice and o. whatever they Mt 23.03
teaching them to o. all that I have 28.20
other traditions which they o., Mk 7.04
their children or o. the customs. Ac 21.21
You o. days, and months, and seasons, Gal 4.10

OBSERVED

"I have o. you and what has been Ex 3.16
for ever to be o. throughout their 27.21
For they o. thy word, and kept thy Deu 33.09
before the LORD, Eli o. her mouth. 1Sa 1.12
Purim should be o. at their Est 9.31
All this I o. while applying my Ecc 8.09
"Have you not o. what these people Jer 33.24
the king's rich food be o. by you Dan 1.13
said to him, "All these I have o.; Mt 19.20
all these I have o. from my youth." Mk 10.20
is not coming with signs to be o.; Lk 17.20
"All these I have o. from my youth." 18.21
Looking at it closely I o. animals Ac 11.06
and o. the objects of your worship, 17.23
Now you have o. my teaching, my 2Ti 3.10

OBSERVES

of them all, and o. all their deeds. Ps 33.15
The righteous o. the house of the Pro 21.12
He who o. the wind will not sow; Ecc 11.04
o. my ordinances, and walks in my Eze 18.17
He who o. the day, o. it in Rom 14.06
like a man who o. his natural face Jas 1.23
for he o. himself and goes away and 1.24

OBSERVING

o. the sabbath throughout their Ex 31.16
o. the tradition of the elders; Mk 7.03

OBSOLETE

covenant he treats the first as o. Heb 8.13
is becoming o. and growing old is 8.13

OBSTACLE

than put an o. in the way of the 1Co 9.12
We put no o. in any one's way, so 2Co 6.03
and every proud o. to the knowledge 10.05

OBSTINATE

his spirit and made his heart o., Deu 2.30
Because I know that you are o., Is 48.04

OBSTRUCTION

remove every o. from my people's way." Is 57.14

OBTAIN

be that I shall o. children by her." Gen 16.02
and forsakes them will o. mercy. Pro 28.13
is lowly in spirit will o. honor. 29.23
The meek shall o. fresh joy in the Is 29.19
they shall o. joy and gladness, and 35.10
they shall o. joy and gladness, and 51.11
her prophets o. no vision from the Lam 2.09
warning and o. the kingdom by Dan 11.21
merciful, for they shall o. mercy. Mt 5.07
you could o. the gift of God with Ac 8.20
to decay and o. the glorious Rom 8.21
Israel failed to o. what it sought. 11.07
So run that you may o. it. 1Co 9.24
but to o. salvation through our 1Th 5.09
so that you may o. the glory of 2Th 2.14
they also may o. the salvation 2Ti 2.10
of those who are to o. salvation? Heb 1.14
no one fail to o. the grace of God; 12.15
And you covet and cannot o.; Jas 4.02
your faith you o. the salvation of 1Pe 1.09
called, that you may o. a blessing. 3.09
you will o. the unfading crown of 5.04

OBTAINED

tribe of Simeon o. an inheritance Jos 19.09
to your sister, "She has o. pity." Hos 2.01
Lord which he o. with his own Ac 20.28
that they had o. their purpose, 27.13
Through him we have o. access to Rom 5.02
The elect o. it, but the rest were 11.07
I have already o. this or am Php 3.12
the name he has o. is more excellent Heb 1.04
patiently endured, o. the promise. 6.15
Christ has o. a ministry which is 8.06
those who have o. a faith of equal 2Pe 1.01
that we have o. the requests made 1Jn 5.15

OBTAINS

finds life and o. favor from the Pro 8.35
A good man o. favor from the LORD, 12.02
and o. favor from the LORD. 18.22

OCCASION

he may seek o. against us and fall Gen 43.18
you may do to them as o. offers." Ju 9.33
was seeking an o. against the 14.04
God, which you have o. to provide, Ez 7.20
as fits the o., that it may impart Eph 4.29
give the enemy no o. to revile us. 1Ti 5.14
would have been no o. for a second. Heb 8.07

OCCASIONED

I have o. the death of all the 1Sa 22.22

OCCASIONS

he finds o. against me, he counts me Job 33.10

OCCUPATION

you, and says, 'What is your o.' Gen 46.33
to his brothers, "What is your o.?" 47.03
What is your o.? And whence do Jon 1.08
with the workmen of like o., Ac 19.25

OCCUPIED

God keeps him o. with joy in his Ecc 5.20
Paul was o. with preaching, testifying Ac 18.05

OCCUPY

"Let us go up at once, and o. it; Num 13.30
possession, that you may o. his land.' Deu 2.31
and they also o. the land which the 3.20
and for the house which I shall o." Neh 2.08
I do not o. myself with things too Ps 131.01
nor to o. themselves with myths and 1Ti 1.04

OCCURRED

believed, when he saw what had o., Ac 13.12
a death has o. which redeems them Heb 9.15

OCHRAN

from Asher, Pagiel the son of O.; Num 1.13
Asher being Pagiel the son of O., 2.27
eleventh day Pagiel the son of O., 7.72
offering of Pagiel the son of O. 7.77
of Asher was Pagiel the son of O. 10.26

ODED

came upon Azariah the son of O., 2Ch 15.01
prophecy of Azariah the son of O., 15.08
LORD was there, whose name was O.; 28.09

ODIOUS
me by making me o. to the inhabitants Gen 34.30
had become o. to the Philistines. 1Sa 13.04
that they had become o. to David, 2Sa 10.06
made yourself o. to your father, 16.21
had made themselves o. to David, 1Ch 19.06

ODOR
the LORD smelled the pleasing o., Gen 8.21
it is a pleasing o., an offering by Ex 29.18
as a pleasing o. before the LORD; 29.25
in the morning, for a pleasing o., 29.41
by fire, a pleasing o. to the LORD. Lev 1.09
by fire, a pleasing o. to the LORD. 1.13
by fire, a pleasing o. to the LORD. 1.17
by fire, a pleasing o. to the LORD. 2.02
by fire, a pleasing o. to the LORD. 2.09
on the altar for a pleasing o. 2.12
by fire, a pleasing o. to the LORD. 3.05
offered by fire for a pleasing o. 3.16
for a pleasing o. to the LORD; 4.31
altar, a pleasing o. to the LORD. 6.15
it for a pleasing o. to the LORD. 6.21
a pleasing o., an offering by fire 8.21
a pleasing o., an offering by fire 8.28
fat for a pleasing o. to the LORD. 17.06
by fire to the LORD, a pleasing o.; 23.13
by fire, a pleasing o. to the LORD. 23.18
to make a pleasing o. to the LORD, Num 15.03
of wine, a pleasing o. to the LORD. 15.07
by fire, a pleasing o. to the LORD. 15.10
by fire, a pleasing o. to the LORD. 15.13
a pleasing o. to the LORD, he shall 15.14
a pleasing o. to the LORD, with its 15.24
by fire, a pleasing o. to the LORD; 18.17
my pleasing o., you shall take heed 28.02
at Mount Sinai for a pleasing o., 28.06
by fire, a pleasing o. to the LORD. 28.08
a burnt offering of pleasing o., 28.13
by fire, a pleasing o. to the LORD; 28.24
a pleasing o. to the LORD: two young 28.27
a pleasing o. to the LORD: one young 29.02
a pleasing o., an offering by fire 29.06
a pleasing o.: one young bull, one 29.08
a pleasing o. to the LORD, thirteen 29.13
a pleasing o. to the LORD: one bull, 29.36
ointment give off an evil o.; Ecc 10.01
pleasing o. to all their idols. Eze 6.13
set before them for a pleasing o., 16.19
As a pleasing o. I will accept you, 20.41
by this time there will be an o., Jn 11.39

ODORS
I will not smell your pleasing o., Lev 26.31
they sent up their soothing o., Eze 20.28

OFF
were dried from o. the earth; Gen 8.13
flesh be cut o. by the waters of a 9.11
and they left o. building the city. 11.08
shall be cut o. from his people; 17.14
over against him a good way o., 21.16
his eyes and saw the place afar o. 22.04
They saw him afar o., and before he 37.18
she put o. her widow's garments, and 38.14
and taking o. her veil she put on 38.19
put o. your shoes from your feet, Ex 3.05
a flint and cut o. her son's 4.25
have been cut o. from the earth; 9.15
person shall be cut o. from Israel. 12.15
shall be cut o. from the congregation 12.19
and trembled; and they stood afar o., 20.18
And the people stood afar o., 20.21
of Israel, and worship afar o. 24.01
shall be cut o. from his people.'" 30.33
shall be cut o. from his people." 30.38
shall be cut o. from among his 31.14
"Take o. the rings of gold which 32.02
the people took o. the rings of 32.03
'Let any who have gold take it o.'; 32.24
So now put o. your ornaments from 33.05
the camp, far o. from the camp; 33.07
with him, he took the veil o., 34.34
to the altar and wring o. its head, Lev 1.15
Then he shall put o. his garments, 6.11
shall be cut o. from his people. 7.20
shall be cut o. from his people." 7.21
shall be cut o. from his people. 7.25
shall be cut o. from his people." 7.27
and shave o. all his hair, and bathe 14.08
shave all his hair o. his head; 14.09
he shall shave o. his beard and his 14.09
they scrape o. they shall pour 14.41
and shall put o. the linen garments 16.23
shall be cut o. from among his 17.04
shall be cut o. from his people. 17.09
will cut him o. from among his 17.10
whoever eats it shall be cut o. 17.14
shall be cut o. from among their 18.29
shall be cut o. from his people. 19.08
You shall not round o. the hair on 19.27
will cut him o. from among his 20.03
will cut them o. from among their 20.05
will cut him o. from among his 20.06
shall be cut o. in the sight of 20.17
shall be cut o. from among their 20.18
nor shave o. the edges of their 21.05
shall be cut o. from my presence: I 22.03
shall be cut o. from his people. 23.29
and wash them o. into the water of Num 5.23
or is afar o. on a journey, he shall 9.10
shall be cut o. from his people, 9.13
shall be cut o. from among his 15.30
person shall be utterly cut o.; 15.31
put fire therein from o. the altar, 16.46
person shall be cut o. from Israel; 19.13
shall be cut o. from the midst of 19.20
you from o. the face of the earth. Deu 6.15
perish quickly o. the good land 11.17
your God cuts o. before you the 12.29
near you or far o. from you, 13.07
your God cuts o. the nations whose 19.01
And she shall put o. her captive's 21.13
member is cut o. shall not enter 23.01
and pull his sandal o. his foot, 25.09
him that had his sandal pulled o. 25.10
then you shall cut o. her hand; 25.12
and cut o. at your rear all who 25.18
consumed you o. the land which you 28.21
for your olives shall drop o. 28.40
be plucked o. the land which you 28.63
sandals have not worn o. your feet; 29.05
hard for you, neither is it far o. 30.11
stood and rose up in a heap far o., Jos 3.16
the Salt Sea, were wholly cut o.; 3.16
Jordan were cut o. before the ark 4.07
waters of the Jordan were cut o. 4.07
"Put o. your shoes from your feet; 5.15
and cut o. our name from the earth; 7.09
nations that I have already cut o., 23.04
you perish from o. this good land 23.13
you from o. this good land which 23.15
quickly from o. the good land 23.16
and cut o. his thumbs and his great Ju 1.06
great toes cut o. used to pick up 1.07
But now the LORD has cast us o., 6.13
for the army was o. its guard. 8.11
and his bonds melted o. his hands. 15.14
the ropes o. his arms like a 16.12
had him shave o. the seven locks 16.19
tribe is cut o. from Israel this 21.06
the dancers whom they carried o.; 21.23
the one drew o. his sandal and gave Ru 4.07
yourself," he drew o. his sandal. 4.08
may not be cut o. from among his 4.10
wicked shall be cut o. in darkness; 1Sa 2.09

OFF (cont.)
when I will cut o. your strength 1Sa 2.31
I shall not cut o. from my altar 2.33
were lying cut o. upon the threshold; 5.04
his hand from o. you and your gods 6.05
Then send it o., and let it go its 6.08
used to them." And David put them o. 17.39
you down, and cut o. your head; 17.46
and cut o. his head with it. 17.51
And he too stripped o. his clothes, 19.24
and do not cut o. your loyalty from 20.15
the LORD cuts o. every one of the 20.15
Jonathan be cut o. from the house 20.16
stealthily cut o. the skirt of 24.04
because he had cut o. Saul's skirt. 24.05
fact that I cut o. the skirt of 24.11
will not cut o. my descendants 24.21
and stood afar o. on the top of 26.13
how he has cut o. the mediums and 28.09
killed no one, but carried them o., 30.02
And they cut o. his head, and 31.09
and stripped o. his armor, and sent 31.09
and cut o. their hands and feet, and 2Sa 4.12
and the lame will ward you o."— 5.06
and have cut o. all your enemies 7.09
and shaved o. half the beard of 10.04
and cut o. their garments in the 10.04
me go over and take o. his head." 16.09
and went o. home to his own city. 17.23
And they cut o. the head of Sheba 20.22
land of the enemy, far o. or near; 1Ki 8.46
then I will cut o. Israel from the 9.07
he had cut o. every male in Edom); 11.16
so as to cut it o. and to destroy 13.34
and will cut o. from Jeroboam every 14.10
who shall cut o. the house of 14.14
Jezebel cut o. the prophets of the 18.04
himself as he that puts it o.'" 20.11
and will cut o. from Ahab every 21.21
had carried o. a little maid from 2Ki 5.02
he cut o. a stick, and threw it in 6.06
has sent to take o. my head? 6.32
they carried o. silver and gold 7.08
and carried o. things from it, and 7.08
and I will cut o. from Ahab every 9.08
began to cut o. parts of Israel. 10.32
those who come o. duty on the 11.05
who were to go o. duty on the 11.09
And King Ahaz cut o. the frames of 16.17
the sea from o. the bronze oxen 16.17
And I will cast o. the remnant of 21.14
and I will cast o. this city which 23.27
and carried o. all the treasures of 24.13
So Jehoiachin put o. his prison 25.29
They carried o. their livestock: 1Ch 5.21
and have cut o. all your enemies 17.08
he had carried o. from all the 18.11
and cut o. their garments in the 19.04
him, he will cast you o. for ever. 28.09
were to rinse o. what was used for 2Ch 4.06
who come o. duty on the sabbath, 23.04
who were to go o. duty on the 23.08
who cut o. all the mighty warriors 32.21
me, none of us took o. our clothes; Neh 4.23
Let us leave o. this interest. 5.10
joy of Jerusalem was heard afar o. 12.43
he might take o. his sackcloth; Est 4.04
and the king took o. his signet 8.02
Or where were the upright cut o.? Job 4.07
let loose his hand and cut me o.! 6.09
I will put o. my sad countenance, 9.27
He will shake o. his unripe grape, 15.33
and cast o. his blossom, like the 15.33
are past, my plans are broken o., 17.11
dragged o. in the day of God's wrath, 20.28
number of their months is cut o.? 21.21
'Surely our adversaries are cut o., 22.20
They thrust the poor o. the road; 24.04
they are cut o. like the heads of 24.24
the godless when God cuts him o., 27.08
night a whirlwind carries him o. 27.20
they have cast o. restraint in my 30.11
deed, and cut o. pride from man; 33.17
How am I better o. than if I had 35.03
peoples are cut o. in their place. 36.20
his eyes behold it afar o. 39.29
Who can strip o. his outer garment? 41.13
Why dost thou stand afar o., O LORD? Ps 10.01
May the LORD cut o. all flattering 12.03
But thou, O LORD, be not far o.! 22.19
Cast me not o., forsake me not, O God 27.09
Take me not o. with the wicked, with 28.03
to cut o. the remembrance of them 34.16
For the wicked shall be cut o.; 37.09
cursed by him shall be cut o. 37.22
of the wicked shall be cut o. 37.28
of the wicked shall be cut o. 37.38
and my kinsmen stand afar o. 38.11
why hast thou cast me o.? 43.02
thou hast cast us o. and abased us, 44.09
Do not cast us o. for ever! 44.23
Do not cast me o. in the time of 71.09
why dost thou cast us o. for ever? 74.01
horns of the wicked he will cut o., 75.10
who cuts o. the spirit of princes, 76.12
for they are cut o. from thy hand. 88.05
O LORD, why dost thou cast me o.? 88.14
now thou hast cast o. and rejected, 89.38
cutting o. all the evildoers from 101.08
May his posterity be cut o.; 109.13
memory be cut o. from the earth! 109.15
I am shaken o. like a locust. 109.23
the name of the LORD I cut them o.! 118.10
the name of the LORD I cut them o.! 118.11
the name of the LORD I cut them o.! 118.12
steadfast love cut o. my enemies, 143.12
will be cut o. from the land, Pro 2.22
the perverse tongue will be cut o. 10.31
a fool throws o. restraint and is 14.16
and your hope will not be cut o. 23.18
and your hope will not be cut o. 24.14
one who takes o. a garment on a 25.20
of a fool cuts o. his own feet and 26.06
the people cast o. restraint, 29.18
devour the poor from o. the earth, 30.14
untimely birth is better o. than he. Ecc 6.03
is far o., and deep, very deep; 7.24
ointment give o. an evil odor; 10.01
I had put o. my garment, how could I So. 5.03
a signal for a nation afar o., Is 5.26
they carry it o., and none can 5.29
So the LORD cut o. from Israel head 9.14
and to cut o. nations not a few; 10.07
who harass Judah shall be cut o.; 11.13
"and will cut o. from Babylon name 14.22
he will cut o. the shoots with 18.05
loins and take o. your shoes from 20.02
that was upon it will be cut o., 22.25
watch to do evil shall be cut o., 29.20
and Carmel shake o. their leaves. 33.09
Hear, you who are far o., 33.13
he cuts me o. from the loom; 38.12
hand and marked o. the heavens 40.12
carries them o. like stubble. 40.24
chosen you and not cast you o."; 41.09
it is not far o., and my salvation 46.13
put o. your veil, strip off your 47.02
strip o. your robe, uncover your 47.02
for you, that I may not cut you o. 48.09
never be cut o. or destroyed from 48.19
that he was cut o. out of the land 53.08
when she is cast o., says your God. 54.06
sign which shall not be cut o." 55.13
name which shall not be cut o. 56.05

OFF (cont.)

you sent your envoys far o., Is 57.09
The wind will carry them o., 57.13
and righteousness stands afar o.; 59.14
Javan, to the coastlands afar o., 66.19
it is cut o. from their lips. Jer 7.28
Cut o. your hair and cast it away; 7.29
cutting o. the children from the 9.21
let us cut him o. from the land of 11.19
hand, yet I would tear you o. 22.24
the LORD, and not a God afar o.? 23.23
I will cast you o., says the LORD.' 23.33
yoke-bars from o. the neck of 28.12
break the yoke from o. their neck, 30.08
it in the coastlands afar o.; 31.10
I will cast o. all the descendants 31.37
would cut them o. with a penknife 36.23
and will cut o. from it man and 36.29
So they left o. speaking with him, 38.27
to cut o. from you man and woman, 44.07
you may be cut o. and become a 44.08
you for evil, to cut o. all Judah. 44.11
But since we left o. burning 44.18
to cut o. from Tyre and Sidon every 47.04
let us cut her o. from being a 48.02
The horn of Moab is cut o., 48.25
is shaved and every beard cut o.; 48.37
Cut o. from Babylon the sower, and 50.16
Be not cut o. in her punishment, for 51.06
place that thou wilt cut it o., 51.62
So Jehoiachin put o. his prison 52.33
he marked it o. by the line; Lam 2.08
he led me o. my way and tore me to 3.11
Lord will not cast o. for ever, 3.31
He that is far o. shall die of Eze 6.12
them far o. among the nations, and 11.16
and he prophesies of times far o.' 12.27
Your veils also I will tear o., 13.21
and cut him o. from the midst of 14.08
and cut o. from it man and beast, 14.13
and I cut o. from it man and beast; 14.17
to cut o. from it man and beast; 14.19
to cut o. from it man and beast! 14.21
and washed o. your blood from you, 16.09
he broke o. the topmost of its 17.04
its roots and cut o. its branches, 17.09
walls built to cut o. many lives. 17.17
I will break o. from the topmost of 17.22
its fruit was stripped o., its strong 19.12
and will cut o. from you both 21.03
Because I will cut o. from you both 21.04
the turban, and take o. the crown; 21.26
They shall cut o. your nose and 23.25
I will cut you o. from the peoples 25.07
and cut o. from it man and beast; 25.13
and I will cut o. the Cherethites, 25.16
and strip o. their embroidered 26.16
and will cut o. from you man and 29.08
he shall carry o. its wealth and 29.19
and cut o. the multitude of Thebes. 30.15
and I will cut o. from it all who 35.07
hope is lost; we are clean cut o.' 37.11
to seize spoil and carry o. plunder; 38.12
your hosts to carry o. plunder, 38.13
they shall put o. the garments in 44.19
shall measure o. a section twenty-five 45.03
the tree and cut o. its branches, Dan 4.14
strip o. its leaves and scatter its 4.14
break o. your sins by practicing 4.27
I looked its wings were plucked o., 7.04
an anointed one shall be cut o., 9.26
also carry o. to Egypt their gods 11.08
I will carry o., and none shall Hos 5.14
My God will cast them o., 9.17
of Israel shall be utterly cut o. 10.15
for it is cut o. from your mouth. Joe 1.05
it has stripped o. their bark and 1.07
offering are cut o. from the house 1.09
the food cut o. before our eyes, 1.16
to the Sabeans, to a nation far o.; 3.08
and cut o. the inhabitants from the Amo 1.05
I will cut o. the inhabitants from 1.08
and cast o. all pity, and his anger 1.11
I will cut o. the ruler from its 2.03
shall be cut o. and fall to the 3.14
Esau will be cut o. by slaughter. Ob 1.09
and you shall be cut o. for ever. 1.10
strangers carried o. his wealth, 1.11
the ways to cut o. his fugitives; 1.14
yourselves bald and cut o. your hair, Mic 1.16
tear the skin from o. my people, 3.02
their flesh from o. their bones; 3.02
and flay their skin from o. them, 3.03
decide for strong nations afar o.; 4.03
and those who were cast o., 4.07
all your enemies shall be cut o. 5.09
I will cut o. your horses from 5.10
and I will cut o. the cities of 5.11
and I will cut o. sorceries from 5.12
and I will cut o. your images and 5.13
they will be cut o. and pass away. Nah 1.12
his yoke from o. you and will 1.13
gods I will cut o. the graven 1.14
against you, he is utterly cut o. 1.15
is stripped, she is carried o., 2.07
I will cut o. your prey from the 2.13
you, the sword will cut you o. 3.15
house by cutting o. many peoples; Hab 2.10
flock be cut o. from the fold and 3.17
I will cut o. mankind from the face Zep 1.03
and I will cut o. from this place 1.04
who weigh out silver are cut o. 1.11
"I have cut o. nations; 3.06
every one who steals shall be cut o. Zec 5.03
who swears falsely shall be cut o. 5.03
impatient to get o. and patrol the 6.07
who are far o. shall come and help 6.15
I will cut o. the chariot from 9.10
and the battle bow shall be cut o., 9.10
at which I was paid o. by them. 11.13
tearing o. even their hoofs. 11.16
I will cut o. the names of the 13.02
thirds shall be cut o. and perish, 13.08
shall not be cut o. from the city. 14.02
May the LORD cut o. from the tents Mal 2.12
cut it o. and throw it away; Mt 5.30
shake o. the dust from your feet as 10.14
cut it o. and throw it from you; 18.08
But they made light of it and went o., 22.05
high priests, and cut o. his ear. 26.51
shake o. the dust that is on your Mk 6.11
hand causes you to sin, cut it o.; 9.43
foot causes you to sin, cut it o.; 9.45
And throwing o. his mantle he 10.50
the high priest and cut o. his ear. 14.47
that town shake o. the dust from Lk 9.05
our feet, we wipe o. against you; 10.11
the other is yet a great way o., 14.32
saw Abraham far o. and Lazarus in 16.23
standing far o., would not even 18.13
priest and cut o. his right ear. 22.50
Jerusalem, about two miles o., Jn 11.18
slave and cut o. his right ear. 18.10
the man whose ear Peter had cut o., 18.26
land, but about a hundred yards o. 21.08
children and to all that are far o., Ac 2.39
'Take o. the shoes from your feet, 7.33
he dragged o. men and women and 8.03
Caesarea, and sent him o. to Tarsus. 9.30
day he rose and went o. with them, 10.23
and the chains fell o. his hands. 12.07
hands on them and sent them o. 13.03
But they shook o. the dust from 13.51
So when they were sent o., 15.30

OFF (cont.)
they were sent o. in peace by the Ac 15.33
the garments o. them and gave 16.22
sent Paul o. on his way to the sea, 17.14
put them o., saying, "When Lysias 24.22
sea which is o. Cilicia and 27.05
arrived with difficulty o. Cnidus, 27.07
under the lee of Crete o. Salmone. 27.07
So they cast o. the anchors and 27.40
shook o. the creature into the fire 28.05
Are we Jews any better o.? Rom 3.09
accursed and cut o. from Christ for 9.03
of the branches were broken o., 11.17
were broken o. so that I might be 11.19
were broken o. because of their 11.20
otherwise you too will be cut o. 11.22
us then cast o. the works of 13.12
We are no worse o. if we do not eat, 1Co 8.08
not eat, and no better o. if we do. 8.08
then she should cut o. her hair; 11.06
once were far o. have been brought Eph 2.13
who were far o. and peace to those 2.17
Put o. your old nature which 4.22
by putting o. the body of flesh in Col 2.11
you have put o. the old nature 3.09
the putting o. of my body will be 2Pe 1.14
and went o. to make war on the rest Rev 12.17
they will stand far o., in fear of 18.10
wealth from her, will stand far o., 18.15
trade is on the sea, stood far o. 18.17

OFFEND
chastisement; I will not o. any more; Job 34.31

OFFENDED
and his baker o. their lord the Gen 40.01
a word with you, will you be o.? Job 4.02
has grievously o. in taking Eze 25.12
Pharisees were o. when they heard Mt 15.12
against Caesar have I o. at all." Ac 25.08

OFFENDER
a word make a man out to be an o., Is 29.21

OFFENDERS
my son Solomon will be counted o." 1Ki 1.21
they were worse o. than all the Lk 13.04

OFFENSE
Jacob said to Laban, "What is my o.? Gen 31.36
with any o. that he has committed; Deu 19.15
there is no o. punishable by death, 22.26
of stripes in proportion to his o. 25.02
He who forgives an o. seeks love, Pro 17.09
it is his glory to overlook an o. 19.11
a sanctuary, and a stone of o., Is 8.14
blessed is he who takes no o. at me." Mt 11.06
And they took o. at him. But Jesus 13.57
not to give o. to them, go to the 17.27
with us?" And they took o. at him. Mk 6.03
blessed is he who takes no o. at me." Lk 7.23
to them, "Do you take o. at this? Jn 6.61
Give no o. to Jews or to Greeks or 1Co 10.32

OFFENSES
up strife, but love covers all o. Pro 10.12
deference will make amends for great o. Ecc 10.04

OFFENSIVE
have made us o. in the sight of Ex 5.21

OFFER
and o. him there as a burnt offering Gen 22.02
'Let us go and o. sacrifice to our Ex 5.08
not delay to o. from the fulness 22.29
"You shall not o. the blood of my 23.18
day you shall o. a bull as a sin 29.36
Also you shall o. a sin offering 29.36
what you shall o. upon the altar: 29.38
One lamb you shall o. in the morning, 29.39
lamb you shall o. in the evening; 29.39
lamb you shall o. in the evening, 29.41
and shall o. with it a cereal 29.41
You shall o. no unholy incense 30.09
"You shall not o. the blood of my 34.25
he shall o. a male without blemish; Lev 1.03
he shall o. it at the door of the 1.03
he shall o. a male without blemish; 1.10
and the priest shall o. the whole, 1.13
your offerings you shall o. salt. 2.13
"If you o. a cereal offering of 2.14
you shall o. for the cereal offering 2.14
he shall o. it without blemish 3.01
he shall o. the fat covering the 3.03
he shall o. it without blemish. 3.06
then he shall o. it before the LORD, 3.07
to the LORD he shall o. its fat, 3.09
then he shall o. it before the LORD, 3.12
Then he shall o. from it, as his 3.14
then let him o. for the sin which 4.03
assembly shall o. a young bull for 4.14
who shall o. first the one for the 5.08
Then he shall o. the second for a 5.10
of Aaron shall o. it before the 6.14
his sons shall o. to the LORD on 6.20
and o. it for a pleasing odor to 6.21
shall o. it to the LORD as decreed 6.22
which one may o. to the LORD. 7.11
then he shall o. with the thank 7.12
such he shall o. one cake from 7.14
and o. them before the LORD. 9.02
and o. your sin offering and your 9.07
and he shall o. it before the LORD, 12.07
and o. it for a guilt offering, 14.12
The priest shall o. the sin offering, 14.19
priest shall o. the burnt offering 14.20
And he shall o., of the turtledoves 14.30
and the priest shall o. them, 15.15
priest shall o. one for a sin 15.30
"And Aaron shall o. the bull as a 16.06
and o. it as a sin offering; 16.09
and o. his burnt offering and the 16.24
to o. it as a gift to the LORD 17.04
"When you o. a sacrifice of peace 19.05
you shall o. it so that you may be 19.05
be eaten the same day you o. it, 19.06
for they o. the offerings by fire 21.06
may approach to o. the bread of 21.17
come near to o. the LORD's offerings 21.21
come near to o. the bread of his 21.21
Israel, which they o. to the LORD, 22.15
you shall o. a male without 22.19
You shall not o. anything that has 22.20
you shall not o. to the LORD or 22.22
you shall not o. to the LORD or 22.24
neither shall you o. as the bread 22.25
you shall o. a male lamb a year old 23.12
And you shall o. one male goat for 23.19
such as men o. as an offering to 27.09
priest shall o. one for a sin Num 6.11
and he shall o. his gift to the 6.14
the LORD and o. his sin offering 6.16
and he shall o. the ram as a 6.17
priest shall o. also its cereal 6.17
"They shall o. their offerings, one 7.11
and Aaron shall o. the Levites 8.11
and you shall o. the one for a sin 8.12
and shall o. them as a wave offering 8.13
he did not o. the LORD's offering 9.13
and you o. to the LORD from the 15.03
offering shall o. to the LORD a 15.04
you shall o. a third of a hin of 15.07
then one shall o. with the bull a 15.09
and you shall o. for the drink 15.10
he wishes to o. an offering by 15.14

OFFER (cont.)
congregation shall o. one young Num 15.24
he shall o. a female goat a year 15.27
which they o. to the LORD, shall be 18.15
take heed to o. to me in its due 28.02
which you shall o. to the LORD: 28.03
lamb you shall o. in the morning, 28.04
lamb you shall o. in the evening; 28.04
lamb you shall o. in the evening; 28.08
you shall o. it as an offering by 28.08
you shall o. a burnt offering to 28.11
but o. an offering by fire, a burnt 28.19
an ephah shall you o. for a bull, 28.20
a tenth shall you o. for each of 28.21
You shall o. these besides the 28.23
In the same way you shall o. daily, 28.24
when you o. a cereal offering of 28.26
but o. a burnt offering, a pleasing 28.27
you shall o. them and their drink 28.31
and you shall o. a burnt offering, a 29.02
but you shall o. a burnt offering 29.08
and you shall o. a burnt offering, 29.13
but you shall o. a burnt offering, 29.36
"These you shall o. to the LORD at 29.39
that you do not o. your burnt Deu 12.13
there you shall o. your burnt 12.14
and o. your burnt offerings, the 12.27
And you shall o. the passover 16.02
You may not o. the passover sacrifice 16.05
there you shall o. the passover 16.06
against it, o. terms of peace to it. 20.10
and you shall o. burnt offerings on 27.06
there you shall o. yourselves for 28.68
there they o. right sacrifices; 33.19
if we did so to o. burnt offerings Jos 22.23
and o. it as a burnt offering with Ju 6.26
and I will o. him up for a burnt 11.31
offering, then o. it to the LORD." 13.16
gathered to o. a great sacrifice 16.23
went up to o. to the LORD the 1Sa 1.21
her husband to o. the yearly 2.19
to you to o. burnt offerings and 10.08
then I will o. worship to the LORD.'" 2Sa 15.08
the LORD, Three things I o. you; 24.12
king take and o. up what seems 24.22
I will not o. burnt offerings to 24.24
Solomon used to o. a thousand burnt 1Ki 3.04
Solomon used to o. up burnt 9.25
people go up to o. sacrifices in 12.27
will not o. burnt offering or 2Ki 5.17
a great sacrifice to o. to Baal; 10.19
Then he went in to o. sacrifices 10.24
to o. burnt offerings to the LORD 1Ch 16.40
the LORD, Three things I o. you; 21.10
nor o. burnt offerings which cost 21.24
thousand shall o. praises to the 23.05
Who then will o. willingly, consecrating 29.05
be able thus to o. willingly? 29.14
They o. to the LORD every morning 2Ch 13.11
to o. burnt offerings to the LORD, 23.18
of Aaron to o. them on the altar 29.21
to o. to the LORD, as it is written 35.12
passover and to o. burnt offerings 35.16
to o. burnt offerings upon it, as it Ez 3.02
they began to o. burnt offerings 3.06
that they may o. pleasing sacrifices 6.10
and you shall o. them upon the 7.17
the morning and o. burnt offerings Job 1.05
your wealth o. a bribe for me'? 6.22
and o. up for yourselves a burnt 42.08
O. right sacrifices, and put your Ps 4.05
and I will o. in his tent sacrifices 27.06
one who is godly o. prayer to thee; 32.06
O. to God a sacrifice of thanksgiving, 50.14
I will o. to thee burnt offerings 66.15
And let them o. sacrifices of 107.22
Your people will o. themselves 110.03
I will o. to thee the sacrifice of 116.17
"I had to o. sacrifices, and today I Pro 7.14
better than to o. the sacrifice of Ecc 5.01
you went up to o. sacrifice. Is 57.07
and though they o. burnt offering Jer 14.12
to o. up their sons and daughters 32.35
my presence to o. burnt offerings, 33.18
then o. them wine to drink." 35.02
in making them o. by fire all Eze 20.26
When you o. your gifts and sacrifice 20.31
day you shall o. a he-goat without 43.22
you shall o. a bull without blemish 43.23
upon them and o. them up as a 43.24
priests shall o. upon the altar 43.27
when you o. to me my food, the fat 44.07
attend on me to o. me the fat and 44.15
he shall o. his sin offering, says 44.27
priests shall o. his burnt offering 46.02
moon he shall o. a young bull 46.06
and he shall o. his burnt offering 46.12
o. a sacrifice of thanksgiving of Amo 4.05
Even though you o. me your burnt 5.22
that we may o. wheat for sale, that 8.05
and what they o. there is unclean. Hag 2.14
When you o. blind animals in Mal 1.08
And when you o. those that are lame 1.08
and then come and o. your gift. Mt 5.24
and o. the gift that Moses commanded, 8.04
and o. for your cleansing what Mk 1.44
and to o. a sacrifice according to Lk 2.24
of John fast often and o. prayers, 5.33
on the cheek, o. the other also; 6.29
'Did you o. to me slain beasts and Ac 7.42
and wanted to o. sacrifice with 14.13
sacrifice they o. to demons and 1Co 10.20
to o. gifts and sacrifices for sins Heb 5.01
he is bound to o. sacrifice for 5.03
to o. sacrifices daily, first for 7.27
is appointed to o. gifts and 8.03
also to have something to o. 8.03
are priests who o. gifts according 8.04
Nor was it to o. himself repeatedly, 9.25
was ready to o. up his only son, 11.17
and thus let us o. to God acceptable 12.28
us continually o. up a sacrifice 13.15
to o. spiritual sacrifices acceptable 1Pe 2.05

OFFERED
and o. burnt offerings on the altar. Gen 8.20
and o. it up as a burnt offering 22.13
and Jacob o. a sacrifice on the 31.54
and o. sacrifices to the God of his 46.01
o. a burnt offering and sacrifices Ex 18.12
who o. burnt offerings and sacrificed 24.05
and which is o. from the ram of 29.27
portion to be o. by the people of 29.28
and o. burnt offerings and brought 32.06
and o. upon it the burnt offering 40.29
shall not be o. on the altar for a Lev 2.12
altar as food o. by fire to the 3.11
altar as food o. by fire for a 3.16
And all its fat shall be o., 7.03
the burnt offering which he has o. 7.08
thigh that is o. I have taken from 7.34
and o. it for sin, like the first 9.15
and o. it according to the ordinance. 9.16
and o. unholy fire before the LORD, 10.01
thigh that is o. you shall eat in 10.14
The thigh that is o. and the breast 10.15
today they have o. their sin 10.19
which is o. to the LORD as a burnt 22.18
to be o. by fire to the LORD, a 23.13
portion to be o. by fire to the 24.07
such as is not o. as an offering 27.11
LORD when they o. unholy fire Num 3.04
is waved and the thigh that is o.; 6.20
o. and brought their offerings 7.03
they o. them before the tabernacle. 7.03

OFFERED (cont.)
And the leaders o. offerings for Num 7.10
and the leaders o. their offering 7.10
He who o. his offering the first 7.12
he o. for his offering one silver 7.19
them and o. them as a wave offering. 8.15
and Aaron o. them as a wave offering 8.21
for they o. them before the LORD; 16.38
which those who were burned had o.; 16.39
'When you have o. from it the best 18.30
when you have o. the best of it. 18.32
and Balaam o. on each altar a bull 23.02
and I have o. upon each altar a 23.04
and o. bull and a ram on each 23.14
and o. a bull and a ram on each 23.30
died when they o. unholy fire 26.61
it shall be o. besides the continual 28.15
it shall be o. besides the continual 28.24
offering that they o. to the LORD, 31.52
or o. any of it to the dead; Deu 26.14
and they o. on it burnt offerings Jos 8.31
that the people o. themselves Ju 5.02
of Israel who o. themselves 5.09
second bull was o. upon the altar 6.28
and o. it upon the rock to the LORD, 13.19
and o. burnt offerings and peace 20.26
and o. burnt offerings and peace 21.04
was that when any man o. sacrifice, 1Sa 2.13
of the cart and o. the cows as a 6.14
of Bethshemesh o. burnt offerings 6.15
lamb and o. it as a whole burnt 7.09
And he o. the burnt offering. 13.09
myself, and o. the burnt offering." 13.12
and David o. burnt offerings and 2Sa 6.17
and o. burnt offerings and peace 24.25
and o. up burnt offerings and peace 1Ki 3.15
o. sacrifice before the LORD. 8.62
Solomon o. as peace offerings to 8.63
for there he o. the burnt offering 8.64
which he o. at the house of the 10.05
and he o. sacrifices upon the altar 12.32
and o. him for a burnt offering 2Ki 3.27
and o. no tribute to the king of 17.04
and they o. burnt offerings and 1Ch 16.01
offerings are o. to the LORD on 23.31
heart they had o. freely to the 29.09
I have freely o. all these things, 29.17
on the next day o. burnt offerings 29.21
and o. a thousand burnt offerings 2Ch 1.06
all the people o. sacrifice before 7.04
King Solomon o. as a sacrifice 7.05
whenever David o. praises by their 7.06
for there he o. the burnt offering 7.07
Then Solomon o. up burnt offerings 8.12
which he o. at the house of the 9.04
And they o. burnt offerings in the 24.14
incense or o. burnt offerings in 29.07
burnt offering be o. on the altar. 29.27
of the LORD and o. upon it sacrifices 33.16
besides all that was freely o. Ez 1.06
and they o. burnt offerings upon it 3.03
and o. the daily burnt offerings by 3.04
sacrifices are o. and burnt 6.03
They o. at the dedication of this 6.17
have freely o. to the God of 7.15
all Israel there present had o.; 8.25
o. burnt offerings to the God of 8.35
who willingly o. to live in Neh 11.02
And they o. great sacrifices that 12.43
then bulls will be o. on thy altar. Ps 51.19
and ate sacrifices o. to the dead; 106.28
If a man o. for love all the wealth Sol 8.07
has been o. to Baal and drink Jer 32.29
their wives had o. incense to 44.15
"Son of man, eat what is o. to you; Eze 3.01
wherever they o. pleasing odor to 6.13
there they o. their sacrifices and 20.28
they have even o. up to them for 23.37
and incense be o. up to him. Dan 2.46
and they o. a sacrifice to the LORD Jon 1.16
place incense is o. to my name, Mal 1.11
they o. him gifts, gold and frankincense Mt 2.11
they o. him wine to drink, mingled 27.34
And they o. him wine mingled with Mk 15.23
and o. a sacrfice to the idol and Ac 7.41
apostles' hands, he o. them money, 8.18
If the dough o. as first fruits is Rom 11.16
Now concerning food o. to idols: 1Co 8.01
to the eating of food o. to idols, 8.04
eat food as really o. to an idol; 8.07
is weak, to eat food o. to idols? 8.10
That food o. to idols is anything, 10.19
you, "This has been o. in sacrifice, 10.28
Jesus o. up prayers and supplications, Heb 5.07
once for all when he o. up himself. 7.27
sacrifices are o. which cannot 9.09
eternal Spirit o. himself without 9.14
having been o. once to bear the 9.28
are continually o. year after year, 10.01
they not have ceased to be o.? 10.02
(these are o. according to the law), 10.08
But when Christ had o. for all time 10.12
By faith Able o. to God a more 11.04
o. up Isaac, and he who had received 11.17
when he o. his son Isaac upon the Jas 2.21

OFFERING
to the LORD an o. of the fruit of Gen 4.03
had regard for Abel and his o., 4.04
Cain and his o. he had no regard. 4.05
as a burnt o. upon one of the 22.02
he cut the wood for the burnt o., 22.03
took the wood of the burnt o., 22.06
where is the lamb for a burnt o." 22.07
the lamb for a burnt o., my son." 22.08
up as a burnt o. instead of his 22.13
and he poured out a drink o. on it, 35.14
offered a burnt o. and sacrifices Ex 18.12
that they take for me an o.; 25.02
you shall receive the o. for me. 25.02
And this is the o. which you shall 25.03
in the holy o. which the people of 28.38
fire outside the camp; it is a sin o. 29.14
it is a burnt o. to the LORD; 29.18
odor, an o. by fire to the LORD. 29.18
them for a wave o. before the LORD 29.24
altar in addition to the burnt o., 29.25
it is an o. by fire to the LORD. 29.25
it for a wave o. before the LORD; 29.26
consecrate the breast of the wave o., 29.27
it is their o. to the LORD. 29.28
a bull as a sin o. for atonement. 29.36
shall offer a sin o. for the altar, 29.36
it a cereal o. and its libation, as 29.41
odor, an o. by fire to the LORD. 29.41
continual burnt o. throughout your 29.42
nor burnt o., nor cereal offering; 30.09
nor burnt offering, nor cereal o.; 30.09
of the sin o. of atonement he 30.10
half a shekel as an o. to the LORD. 30.13
upward, shall give the LORD's o. 30.14
give the LORD's o. to make atonement 30.15
to burn an o. by fire to the LORD, 30.20
altar of burnt o. with all its 30.28
altar of burnt o. with all its 31.09
Take from among you an o. to the LORD; 35.05
heart, let him bring the LORD's o.: 35.05
the altar of burnt o., with its grating 35.16
the LORD's o. to be used for the 35.21
dedicating an o. of gold to the 35.22
could make an o. of silver or 35.24
bronze brought it as the LORD's o.; 35.24
as their freewill o. to the LORD. 35.29
the freewill o. which the people 36.03

OFFERING (cont.)

more for the o. for the sanctuary." Ex 36.06
altar of burnt o. also of acacia 38.01
sanctuary, the gold from the o., 38.24
altar of burnt o. before the door 40.06
altar of burnt o. and all its 40.10
altar of burnt o. at the door of 40.29
upon it the burnt o. and the cereal o.; 40.29
of you brings an o. to the Lord, Lev 1.02
bring your o. of cattle from the 1.02
"If his o. is a burnt o. from the herd, 1.03
hand upon the head of the burnt o. 1.04
flay the burnt o. and cut it into 1.06
as a burnt o., an o. by fire, a pleasing 1.09
for a burnt o. is from the flock, 1.10
it is a burnt o., an o. by fire, a 1.13
o. to the Lord is a burnt o. of birds, 1.14
shall bring his o. of turtledoves 1.14
it is a burnt o., an o. by fire, a 1.17
brings a cereal o. as an o. to the Lord, 2.01
his o. shall be of fine flour; 2.01
an o. by fire, a pleasing odor to 2.02
of the cereal o. shall be for 2.03
cereal o. baked in the oven as an o., 2.04
And if your o. is a cereal o. baked 2.05
pour oil on it; it is a cereal o. 2.06
And if your o. is a cereal o. cooked 2.07
the cereal o. that is made of 2.08
from the cereal o. its memorial 2.09
an o. by fire, a pleasing odor to 2.09
of the cereal o. shall be for 2.10
"No cereal o. which you bring to 2.11
any honey as an o. by fire to the 2.11
As an o. of first fruits you may 2.12
God be lacking from your cereal o.; 2.13
offer a cereal o. of first fruits 2.14
for the cereal o. of your first 2.14
frankincense on it; it is a cereal o. 2.15
it is an o. by fire to the Lord. 2.16
man's o. is a sacrifice of peace o., 3.01
the head of his o. and kill it at 3.02
from the sacrifice of the peace o., 3.03
as an o. by fire to the Lord, he 3.03
it on the altar upon the burnt o., 3.05
it is an o. by fire, a pleasing odor 3.05
"If his o. for a sacrifice of peace o. 3.06
If he offers a lamb for his o., 3.07
the head of his o. and killing it 3.08
of the peace o. as an o. by fire to 3.09
"If his o. is a goat, then he shall 3.12
as his o. for an o. by fire to the 3.14
blemish to the Lord for a sin o. 4.03
altar of burnt o. which is at the 4.07
bull of the sin o. he shall take 4.08
them upon the altar of burnt o. 4.10
bull for a sin o. and bring it 4.14
altar of burnt o. which is at the 4.18
he did with the bull of the sin o., 4.20
it is the sin o. for the assembly. 4.21
he shall bring as his o. a goat, 4.23
burnt o. before the Lord; it is a sin o. 4.24
of the sin o. with his finger and 4.25
the horns of the altar of burnt o., 4.25
the base of the altar of burnt o. 4.25
he shall bring for his o. a goat, 4.28
his hand on the head of the sin o., 4.29
kill the sin o. in the place of 4.29
offering in the place of burnt o. 4.29
the horns of the altar of burnt o., 4.30
brings a lamb as his o. for a sin o., 4.32
hand upon the head of the sin o., 4.33
and kill it for a sin o. in the place 4.33
where they kill the burnt o. 4.33
of the sin o. with his finger and 4.34
the horns of the altar of burnt o., 4.34
bring his guilt o. to the Lord for 5.06
a lamb or a goat, for a sin o.; 5.06
as his guilt o. to the Lord for the 5.07
one for a sin o. and the other for a burnt o. 5.07
offer first the one for the sin o.; 5.08
of the sin o. on the side of the 5.09
base of the altar; it is a sin o. 5.09
for a burnt o. according to the 5.10
as his o. for the sin which he has 5.11
ephah of fine flour for a sin o.; 5.11
frankincense on it, for it is a sin o. 5.11
by fire to the Lord; it is a sin o. 5.12
the priest, as in the cereal o. 5.13
as his guilt o. to the Lord, a ram 5.15
shekel of the sanctuary; it is a guilt o. 5.15
him with the ram of the guilt o., 5.16
by you at the price for a guilt o., 5.18
It is a guilt o.; he is guilty before 5.19
belongs, on the day of his guilt o. 6.05
priest his guilt o. to the Lord, 6.06
by you at the price for a guilt o.; 6.06
This is the law of the burnt o. 6.09
The burnt o. shall be on the hearth 6.09
consumed the burnt o. on the altar, 6.10
lay the burnt o. in order upon it, 6.12
"And this is the law of the cereal o. 6.14
of the cereal o. with its oil and 6.15
frankincense which is on the cereal o., 6.15
holy like the sin o. and the guilt o. 6.17
"This is the o. which Aaron and his 6.20
fine flour as a regular cereal o., 6.20
in baked pieces like a cereal o., 6.21
Every cereal o. of a priest shall 6.23
This is the law of the sin o. 6.25
where the burnt o. is killed shall 6.25
shall the sin o. be killed before 6.25
But no sin o. shall be eaten from 6.30
"This is the law of the guilt o. 7.01
kill the burnt o. they shall kill 7.02
they shall kill the guilt o., 7.02
the altar as an o. by fire to the 7.05
Lord; it is a guilt o. 7.05
The guilt o. is like the sin o., 7.07
any man's burnt o. shall have for 7.08
of the burnt o. which he has 7.08
And every cereal o. baked in the 7.09
And every cereal o., mixed with oil 7.10
with the thank o. unleavened cakes 7.12
shall bring his o. with cakes of 7.13
cake from each o., as an o. to the Lord; 7.14
be eaten on the day of his o.; 7.15
sacrifice of his o. is a votive o., 7.16
or a freewill o., it shall be eaten 7.16
of his peace o. is eaten on the 7.18
of which an o. by fire is made to 7.25
shall bring his o. to the Lord; 7.29
waved as a wave o. before the Lord. 7.30
priest as an o. from the sacrifice 7.32
This is the law of the burnt o., 7.37
of the cereal o., of the sin o., 7.37
of the guilt o., of the consecration, 7.37
oil, and the bull of the sin o., 8.02
Then he brought the bull of the sin o.; 8.14
the head of the bull of the sin o. 8.14
presented the ram of the burnt o.; 8.18
as a burnt o., a pleasing odor, an 8.21
an o. by fire to the Lord, as the 8.21
them as a wave o. before the Lord. 8.27
them on the altar with the burnt o., 8.28
ordination o., an o. by fire to the Lord. 8.28
it for a wave o. before the Lord; 8.29
"Take a bull calf for a sin o., 9.02
and a ram for a burnt o., both 9.02
'Take a male goat for a sin o., 9.03
without blemish, for a burnt o., 9.03
and a cereal o. mixed with oil; 9.04
offer your sin o. and your burnt o., 9.07
and bring the o. of the people, and 9.07
and killed the calf of the sin o., 9.08

OFFERING (cont.)

from the sin o. he burned upon the	Lev 9.10
And he killed the burnt o.;	9.12
they delivered the burnt o. to him,	9.13
with the burnt o. on the altar.	9.14
Then he presented the people's o.,	9.15
goat of the sin o. which was for	9.15
it for sin, like the first sin o.	9.15
And he presented the burnt o.,	9.16
And he presented the cereal o.,	9.17
besides the burnt o. of the morning.	9.17
for a wave o. before the LORD;	9.21
came down from o. the sin o. and the	9.22
and the burnt o. and the peace	9.22
the burnt o. and the fat upon the	9.24
"Take the cereal o. that remains of	10.12
wave for a wave o. before the LORD,	10.15
about the goat of the sin o.,	10.16
eaten the sin o. in the place of	10.17
their sin o. and their burnt o. before	10.19
If I had eaten the sin o. today,	10.19
a lamb a year old for a burnt o.,	12.06
or a turtledove for a sin o.,	12.06
a burnt o. and the other for a sin o.;	12.08
and a cereal o. of three tenths of	14.10
lambs, and offer it for a guilt o.,	14.12
them for a wave o. before the LORD;	14.12
kill the sin o. and the burnt o.,	14.13
for the guilt o., like the sin o.,	14.13
some of the blood of the guilt o.,	14.14
upon the blood of the guilt o.;	14.17
The priest shall offer the sin o.,	14.19
afterward he shall kill the burnt o.;	14.19
offer the burnt o. and the cereal o.	14.20
lamb for a guilt o. to be waved,	14.21
mixed with oil for a cereal o.,	14.21
be a sin o. and the other a burnt o.	14.22
take the lamb of the guilt o.,	14.24
them for a wave o. before the LORD.	14.24
kill the lamb of the guilt o.;	14.25
some of the blood of the guilt o.,	14.25
the blood of the guilt o. was put;	14.28
a sin o. and the other for a burnt o.,	14.31
along with a cereal o.; and the priest	14.31
a sin o. and the other for a burnt o.;	15.15
a sin o. and the other for a burnt o.;	15.30
bull for a sin o. and a ram for a burnt o.	16.03
Israel two male goats for a sin o.,	16.05
and one ram for a burnt o.	16.05
the bull as a sin o. for himself,	16.06
the LORD, and offer it as a sin o.;	16.09
shall present the bull as a sin o.	16.11
kill the bull as a sin o. for himself.	16.11
goat of the sin o. which is for	16.15
offer his burnt o. and the burnt	16.24
and the burnt o. of the people,	16.24
fat of the sin o. he shall burn	16.25
for the sin o. and the goat for the sin o.	16.27
offers a burnt o. or sacrifice,	17.08
bring a guilt o. for himself to	19.21
of meeting, a ram for a guilt o.	19.21
of the guilt o. before the LORD	19.22
an o. of praise to the LORD.	19.24
not eat of the o. of the holy	22.12
sojourners in Israel presents his o.,	22.18
as a freewill o. which is offered	22.18
offered to the LORD as a burnt o.,	22.18
fulfil a vow or as a freewill o.,	22.21
make of them an o. by fire upon	22.22
you may present for a freewill o.;	22.23
for a votive o. it cannot be	22.23
acceptable as an o. by fire to the	22.27
present an o. by fire to the LORD	23.08
blemish as a burnt o. to the LORD.	23.12
And the cereal o. with it shall be	23.13
and the drink o. with it shall be	23.13
have brought the o. of your God:	23.14

brought the sheaf of the wave o.;	23.15
a cereal o. of new grain to the	23.16
shall be a burnt o. to the LORD,	23.18
their cereal o. and their drink	23.18
an o. by fire, a pleasing odor to	23.18
offer one male goat for a sin o.,	23.19
as a wave o. before the LORD, with	23.20
present an o. by fire to the LORD.	23.25
and present an o. by fire to the	23.27
and present an o. by fire to the	23.36
as men offer as an o. to the LORD,	27.09
not offered as an o. to the LORD,	27.11
and the flagons for the drink o.;	Num 4.07
incense, the continual cereal o.,	4.16
And every o., all the holy things	5.09
and bring the o. required of her, a	5.15
for it is a cereal o. of jealousy,	5.15
a cereal o. of remembrance, bringing	5.15
hands the cereal o. of remembrance,	5.18
which is the cereal o. of jealousy.	5.18
take the cereal o. of jealousy out	5.25
wave the cereal o. before the LORD	5.25
take a handful of the cereal o.,	5.26
a sin o. and the other for a burnt o.,	6.11
lamb a year old for a guilt o.;	6.12
old without blemish for a burnt o.,	6.14
old without blemish as a sin o.,	6.14
ram without blemish as a peace o.,	6.14
their cereal o. and their drink	6.15
offer his sin o. and his burnt o.,	6.16
sacrifice of peace o. to the LORD,	6.17
also its cereal o. and its drink o.	6.17
the sacrifice of the peace o.	6.18
them for a wave o. before the LORD;	6.20
His o. to the LORD shall be according	6.21
offered their o. before the altar.	7.10
He who offered his o. the first day	7.12
and his o. was one silver plate	7.13
mixed with oil for a cereal o.;	7.13
lamb a year old, for a burnt o.;	7.15
one male goat for a sin o.;	7.16
This was the o. of Nahshon the son	7.17
the leader of Issachar, made an o.;	7.18
he offered for his o. one silver	7.19
mixed with oil for a cereal o.;	7.19
lamb a year old, for a burnt o.;	7.21
one male goat for a sin o.;	7.22
This was the o. of Nethanel the son	7.23
his o. was one silver plate, whose	7.25
mixed with oil for a cereal o.;	7.25
lamb a year old, for a burnt o.;	7.27
one male goat for a sin o.;	7.28
This was the o. of Eliab the son of	7.29
his o. was one silver plate whose	7.31
mixed with oil for a cereal o.;	7.31
lamb a year old, for a burnt o.;	7.33
one male goat for a sin o.;	7.34
This was the o. of Elizur the son	7.35
his o. was one silver plate, whose	7.37
mixed with oil for a cereal o.;	7.37
lamb a year old, for a burnt o.;	7.39
one male goat for a sin o.;	7.40
This was the o. of Shelumiel the	7.41
his o. was one silver plate, whose	7.43
mixed with oil for a cereal o.;	7.43
lamb a year old for a burnt o.;	7.45
one male goat for a sin o.;	7.46
This was the o. of Eliasaph the son	7.47
his o. was one silver plate, whose	7.49
mixed with oil for a cereal o.;	7.49
lamb a year old, for a burnt o.;	7.51
one male goat for a sin o.;	7.52
This was the o. of Elishama the son	7.53
his o. was one silver plate, whose	7.55
mixed with oil for a cereal o.;	7.55
lamb a year old, for a burnt o.;	7.57
one male goat for a sin o.;	7.58

OFFERING (cont.)
This was the o. of Gamaliel the son Num 7.59
his o. was one silver plate, whose 7.61
mixed with oil for a cereal o.; 7.61
lamb a year old, for a burnt o.; 7.63
one male goat for a sin o.; 7.64
This was the o. of Abidan the son 7.65
his o. was one silver plate, whose 7.67
mixed with oil for a cereal o.; 7.67
lamb a year old, for a burnt o.; 7.69
one male goat for a sin o.; 7.70
This was the o. of Ahiezer the son 7.71
his o. was one silver plate, whose 7.73
mixed with oil for a cereal o.; 7.73
lamb a year old, for a burnt o.; 7.75
one male goat for a sin o.; 7.76
This was the o. of Pagiel the son 7.77
his o. was one silver plate, whose 7.79
mixed with oil for a cereal o.; 7.79
lamb a year old, for a burnt o.; 7.81
one male goat for a sin o.; 7.82
This was the o. of Ahira the son of 7.83
the dedication o. for the altar, 7.84
for the burnt o. twelve bulls, 7.87
a year old, with their cereal o.; 7.87
and twelve male goats for a sin o.; 7.87
the dedication o. for the altar, 7.88
and its cereal o. of fine flour 8.08
another young bull for a sin o. 8.08
LORD as a wave o. from the people 8.11
one for a sin o. and the other for 8.12
other for a burnt o. to the LORD, 8.12
them as a wave o. to the LORD. 8.13
them and offered them as a wave o. 8.15
them as a wave o. before the LORD, 8.21
we kept from o. the LORD's o. at its 9.07
the LORD's o. at its appointed 9.13
the flock an o. by fire or a burnt o. 15.03
as a freewill o. or at your 15.03
who brings his o. shall offer to 15.04
LORD a cereal o. of a tenth of an 15.04
and wine for the drink o., 15.05
shall prepare with the burnt o., 15.05
for a cereal o. two tenths of an 15.06
and for the drink o. you shall 15.07
you prepare a bull for a burnt o., 15.08
bull a cereal o. of three tenths 15.09
for the drink o. half a hin of 15.10
as an o. by fire, a pleasing odor to 15.10
in this way, in o. an o. by fire, 15.13
he wishes to offer an o. by fire, 15.14
shall present an o. to the LORD. 15.19
you shall present a cake as an o.; 15.20
as an o. from the threshing floor, 15.20
to the LORD an o. throughout your 15.21
one young bull for a burnt o., 15.24
with its cereal o. and its drink o., 15.24
and one male goat for a sin o. 15.24
and they have brought their o., 15.25
an o. by fire to the LORD, and their 15.25
and their sin o. before the LORD, 15.25
goat a year old for a sin o. 15.27
the LORD, "Do not respect their o. 16.15
hundred and fifty men o. the incense. 16.35
every o. of theirs, every cereal o. 18.09
every sin o. of theirs and every guilt o. 18.09
the o. of their gift, all the wave 18.11
burn their fat as an o. by fire, 18.17
they present as an o. to the LORD, 18.24
present an o. from it to the LORD, 18.26
And your o. shall be reckoned to 18.27
also present an o. to the LORD 18.28
give the LORD's o. to Aaron the 18.28
present every o. due to the LORD, 18.29
some ashes of the burnt sin o., 19.17
your burnt o., and I will go; 23.03
were standing beside his burnt o. 23.06
"Stand here beside your burnt o., 23.15
was standing beside his burnt o., 23.17
'My o., my food for my offerings by 28.02
This is the o. by fire which you 28.03
day by day, as a continual o. 28.03
of fine flour for a cereal o., 28.05
It is a continual burnt o., which 28.06
pleasing odor, an o. by fire to the LORD. 28.06
Its drink o. shall be a fourth of a 28.07
out a drink o. of strong drink to 28.07
like the cereal o. of the morning, 28.08
the morning, and like its drink o., 28.08
shall offer it as an o. by fire, 28.08
of fine flour for a cereal o., 28.09
mixed with oil, and its drink o.: 28.09
this is the burnt o. of every sabbath, 28.10
continual burnt o. and its drink o. 28.10
shall offer a burnt o. to the LORD: 28.11
of fine flour for a cereal o., 28.12
oil as a cereal o. for every lamb; 28.13
for a burnt o. of pleasing odor, an 28.13
an o. by fire to the LORD. 28.13
is the burnt o. of each month 28.14
male goat for a sin o. to the LORD; 28.15
continual burnt o. and its drink o. 28.15
but offer an o. by fire, a burnt o. to 28.19
also their cereal o. of fine flour 28.20
also one male goat for a sin o., 28.22
besides the burnt o. of the morning, 28.23
which is for a continual burnt o. 28.23
days, the food of an o. by fire, 28.24
continual burnt o. and its drink o. 28.24
offer a cereal o. of new grain to 28.26
but offer a burnt o., a pleasing 28.27
also their cereal o. of fine flour 28.28
continual burnt o. and its cereal o., 28.31
offer them and their drink o. 28.31
and you shall offer a burnt o., 29.02
also their cereal o. of fine flour 29.03
with one male goat for a sin o., 29.05
burnt o. of the new moon, and its cereal o., 29.06
continual burnt o. and its cereal o., 29.06
and their drink o., according to 29.06
pleasing odor, an o. by fire to the LORD. 29.06
shall offer a burnt o. to the LORD, 29.08
and their cereal o. of fine flour 29.09
also one male goat for a sin o., 29.11
besides the sin o. of atonement, 29.11
continual burnt o. and its cereal o., 29.11
shall offer a burnt o., an o. by fire, 29.13
and their cereal o. of fine flour 29.14
also one male goat for a sin o., 29.16
besides the continual burnt o., 29.16
its cereal o. and its drink o. 29.16
with the cereal o. and the drink 29.18
also one male goat for a sin o., 29.19
continual burnt o. and its cereal o., 29.19
with the cereal o. and the drink 29.21
also one male goat for a sin o., 29.22
besides the continual burnt o. and 29.22
and its cereal o. and its drink o. 29.22
with the cereal o. and the drink 29.24
also one male goat for a sin o., 29.25
besides the continual burnt o., 29.25
its cereal o. and its drink o. 29.25
with the cereal o. and the drink 29.27
also one male goat for a sin o.; 29.28
and its cereal o. and its drink o. 29.28
with the cereal o. and the drink 29.30
also one male goat for a sin o.; 29.31
the continual burnt o., its cereal o., 29.31
with the cereal o. and the drink 29.33
also one male goat for a sin o.; 29.34
besides the continual burnt o., 29.34
its cereal o., and its drink o. 29.34
shall offer a burnt o., an o. by fire, 29.36
and the cereal o. and the drink 29.37

OFFERING (cont.)

also one male goat for a sin o.; Num 29.38
besides the continual burnt o. and 29.38
and its cereal o. and its drink o. 29.38
the priest as an o. to the LORD. 31.29
which was the o. for the LORD, to 31.41
And we have brought the LORD's o., 31.50
the gold of the o. that they 31.52
tithes and the o. that you present, Deu 12.06
tithes and the o. that you present, 12.11
or the o. that you present; 12.17
a whole burnt o. to the LORD your 13.16
of a freewill o. from your hand, 16.10
from those o. a sacrifice, whether 18.03
his son or his daughter as an o., 18.10
drank the wine of their drink o.? 32.38
and whole burnt o. upon thy altar. 33.10
not for burnt o., nor for sacrifice, Jos 22.26
by building an altar for burnt o., 22.29
cereal o., or sacrifice, other than 22.29
it as a burnt o. with the wood of Ju 6.26
I will offer him up for a burnt o." 11.31
but if you make ready a burnt o., 13.16
took the kid with the cereal o., 13.19
accepted a burnt o. and a cereal o. 13.23
men treated the o. of the LORD 1Sa 2.17
parts of every o. of my people 2.29
by sacrifice or o. for ever." 3.14
by all means return him a guilt o. 6.03
is the guilt o. that we shall 6.04
are returning to him as a guilt o. 6.08
the cows as a burnt o. to the LORD. 6.14
returned as a guilt o. to the LORD: 6.17
it as a whole burnt o. to the LORD; 7.09
As Samuel was o. up the burnt o., 7.10
"Bring the burnt o. here to me, 13.09
And he offered the burnt o. 13.09
he had finished o. the burnt o., 13.10
myself, and offered the burnt o. 13.12
up against me, may he accept an o.; 26.19
had finished o. the burnt offerings 2Sa 6.18
Abasalom was o. the sacrifices, 15.12
here are the oxen for the burnt o., 24.22
finished o. all this prayer and 1Ki 8.54
offered the burnt o. and the cereal o. 8.64
receive the burnt o. and the cereal o. 8.64
the time of the o. of the oblation, 18.29
water, and pour it on the burnt o., 18.33
the time of the o. of the oblation, 18.36
fell and consumed the burnt o., 18.38
about the time of o. the sacrifice, 2Ki 3.20
him for a burnt o. upon the wall. 3.27
not offer burnt o. or sacrifice to 5.17
had made an end of o. the burnt o., 10.25
He even burned his son as an o., 16.03
burned his burnt o. and his cereal o., 16.13
and poured his drink o., and threw 16.13
morning burnt o., and the evening cereal o., 16.15
the king's burnt o., and his cereal o., 16.15
with the burnt o. of all the people 16.15
their cereal o., and their drink o.; 16.15
it all the blood of the burnt o., 16.15
And he burned his son as an o., 21.06
or his daughter as an o. to Molech. 23.10
altar of burnt o. and upon the 1Ch 6.49
had finished o. the burnt offerings 16.02
bring an o., and come before him! 16.29
altar of burnt o. continually 16.40
and the wheat for a cereal o. 21.23
heaven upon the altar of burnt o. 21.26
altar of burnt o. were at that 21.29
the altar of burnt o. for Israel." 22.01
the flour for the cereal o., 23.29
the baked o., the o. mixed with oil, 23.29
o. freely and joyously to thee. 29.17
the continual o. of the showbread, 2Ch 2.04
off what was used for the burnt o., 4.06
the burnt o. and the sacrifices, 7.01
the burnt o. and the fat of the 7.07
hold the burnt o. and the cereal o. 7.07
o. according to the commandment of 8.13
and burned his sons as an o., 28.03
altar of burnt o. and all its 29.18
for a sin o. for the kingdom and 29.21
for the sin o. were brought to the 29.23
and made a sin o. with their blood 29.24
that the burnt o. and the sin 29.24
and the sin o. should be made for 29.24
that the burnt o. be offered on 29.27
And when the burnt o. began, 29.27
until the burnt o. was finished. 29.28
When the o. was finished, the king 29.29
were for a burnt o. to the LORD. 29.32
his sons as an o. in the valley of 33.06
were busied in o. the burnt 35.14
who made a freewill o. to the LORD. Ez 3.05
and as a sin o. for all Israel 6.17
the o. for the house of our God 8.25
gold are a freewill o. to the LORD, 8.28
and as a sin o. twelve he-goats; 8.35
this was a burnt o. to the LORD. 8.35
and their guilt o. was a ram of 10.19
showbread, the continual cereal o., Neh 10.33
the continual burnt o., the sabbaths, 10.33
for the wood o., to bring it into 10.34
had previously put the cereal o., 13.05
with the cereal o. and the frankincense. 13.09
and I provided for the wood o., 13.31
offer up for yourselves a burnt o.; Job 42.08
Sacrifice and o. thou dost not Ps 40.06
Burnt o. and sin o. thou hast not 40.06
were I to give a burnt o., thou 51.16
With a freewill o. I will sacrifice 54.06
I will make an o. of bulls and 66.15
bring an o., and come into his 96.08
with sacrifice and burnt o., and Is 19.21
its beasts enough for a burnt o. 40.16
chooses for an o. wood that will 40.20
he makes himself an o. for sin, 53.10
you have poured out a drink o., 57.06
you have brought a cereal o., 57.06
he who presents a cereal o., 66.03
a memorial o. of frankincense, like 66.03
the nations as an o. to the LORD, 66.20
their cereal o. in a clean vessel 66.20
offer burnt o. and cereal o., I will Jer 14.12
them up as an o. by fire to them? Eze 16.21
o. yourself to any passer-by, and 16.25
the provocation of their o.; 20.28
where the burnt o. was to be washed. 40.38
which the burnt o. and the sin o. 40.39
the guilt o. were to be slaughtered. 40.39
of hewn stone for the burnt o., 40.42
the flesh of the o. was to be laid. 40.43
the cereal o., the sin o., and the 42.13
and the guilt o., for the place is 42.13
is erected for o. burnt offerings 43.18
the Lord GOD, a bull for a sin o. 43.19
also take the bull of the sin o., 43.21
without blemish for a sin o.; 43.22
them up as a burnt o. to the LORD. 43.24
provide daily a goat for a sin o.; 43.25
slay the burnt o. and the sacrifice 44.11
place, he shall offer his sin o., 44.27
They shall eat the cereal o., the sin o. 44.29
and the guilt o.; and every devoted 44.29
and every o. of all kinds from all 44.30
"This is the o. which you shall 45.13
This is the o. for cereal offerings, 45.15
shall give this o. to the prince 45.16
of the sin o. and put it on the 45.19
the land a young bull for a sin o. 45.22
as a burnt o. to the LORD seven 45.23
and a he-goat daily for a sin o. 45.23

OFFERING (cont.)

as a cereal o. an ephah for each Eze 45.24
offer his burnt o. and his peace 46.02
The burnt o. that the prince offers 46.04
and the cereal o. with the ram 46.05
and the cereal o. with the lambs 46.05
as a cereal o. he shall provide an 46.07
the cereal o. with a young bull 46.11
When the prince provides a freewill o., 46.12
either a burnt o. or peace offerings 46.12
as a freewill o. to the LORD 46.12
offer his burnt o. or his peace 46.12
for a burnt o. to the LORD daily; 46.13
a cereal o. with it morning by 46.14
flour, as a cereal o. to the LORD; 46.14
ordinance for the continual burnt o. 46.14
and the meal o. and the oil shall 46.15
morning, for a continual burnt o. 46.15
boil the guilt o. and the sin o., 46.20
they shall bake the cereal o., 46.20
commanded that an o. and incense be Dan 2.46
continual burnt o. was taken away 8.11
continual burnt o. through transgression; 8.12
concerning the continual burnt o., 8.13
cause sacrifice and o. to cease; 9.27
take away the continual burnt o. 11.31
continual burnt o. is taken away, 12.11
The cereal o. and the drink o. are cut Joe 1.09
Because cereal o. and drink o. are 1.13
cereal o. and a drink o. for the LORD, 2.14
dispersed ones, shall bring my o. Zep 3.10
By o. polluted food upon my altar. Mal 1.07
not accept an o. from your hand. 1.10
offered to my name, and a pure o.; 1.11
and this you bring as your o.! 1.13
or to bring an o. to the LORD of 2.12
regards the o. or accepts it with 2.13
Then the o. of Judah and Jerusalem 3.04
So if you are o. your gift at the Mt 5.23
and make an o. for your cleansing, Lk 5.14
him, coming up and o. him vinegar, 23.36
will think he is o. service to God. Jn 16.02
the people from o. sacrifice to Ac 14.18
fulfilled and the o. presented for 21.26
so that the o. of the Gentiles may Rom 15.16
to you about the o. for the saints, 2Co 9.01
a fragrant o. and sacrifice to God. Eph 5.02
the sacrificial o. of your faith, Php 2.17
a fragrant o., a sacrifice acceptable 4.18
through the o. of the body of Heb 10.10
o. repeatedly the same sacrifices, 10.11
For by a single o. he has perfected 10.14
there is no longer any o. for sin. 10.18

OFFERINGS

and offered burnt o. on the altar. Gen 8.20
LORD our God o. abominable to the Ex 8.26
If we sacrifice o. abominable to 8.26
us have sacrifices and burnt o., 10.25
on it your burnt o. and your peace o., 20.24
offered burnt o. and sacrificed peace o. 24.05
of Israel from their peace o.; 29.28
offered burnt o. and brought peace o.; 32.06
him freewill o. every morning, 36.03
part of the o. by fire to the LORD. Lev 2.03
part of the o. by fire to the LORD. 2.10
all your cereal o. with salt; 2.13
with all your o. you shall offer 2.13
of the sacrifice of the peace o.), 4.10
fat of the sacrifice of peace o.; 4.26
fat is removed from the peace o., 4.31
from the sacrifice of peace o., 4.35
upon the o. by fire to the LORD; 4.35
upon the o. by fire to the LORD; 5.12
burn on it the fat of the peace o. 6.12
as their portion of my o. by fire; 6.17
generations, from the LORD's o. by fire; 6.18
of peace o. which one may offer to 7.11
of his peace o. for thanksgiving 7.13
throws the blood of the peace o. 7.14
of his peace o. for thanksgiving 7.15
LORD's peace o. while an uncleanness 7.20
sacrifice of the LORD's peace o. 7.21
of his peace o. to the LORD shall 7.29
from the sacrifice of his peace o. 7.29
own hands the o. by fire to the 7.30
the sacrifice of your peace o.; 7.32
of the peace o. and the fat shall 7.33
the sacrifices of their peace o., 7.34
sons from the o. made by fire to 7.35
consecration, and of the peace o., 7.37
to bring their o. to the LORD, 7.38
is in the basket of ordination o., 8.31
and an ox and a ram for peace o., 9.04
sacrifice of peace o. for the people; 9.18
burnt offering and the peace o. 9.22
remains of the o. by fire to the 10.12
from the o. by fire to the LORD; 10.13
of the peace o. by the people of 10.14
bring with the o. by fire of the 10.15
afford the o. for his cleansing." 14.32
sacrifices of peace o. to the LORD; 17.05
sacrifice of peace o. to the LORD, 19.05
they offer the o. by fire to the 21.06
to offer the LORD's o. by fire; 21.21
sacrifice of peace o. to the LORD, 22.21
cereal offering and their drink o., 23.18
old as a sacrifice of peace o. 23.19
shall present o. by fire to the 23.36
presenting to the LORD o. by fire, 23.37
burnt o. and cereal o., sacrifices 23.37
and drink o., each on its proper day; 23.37
and besides all your votive o., 23.38
and besides all your freewill o., 23.38
out of the o. by fire to the LORD, 24.09
cereal offering and their drink o. Num 6.15
brought their o. before the LORD, 7.03
leaders offered o. for the dedication 7.10
Moses, "They shall offer their o., 7.11
and for the sacrifice of peace o., 7.17
and for the sacrifice of peace o., 7.23
and for the sacrifice of peace o., 7.29
and for the sacrifice of peace o., 7.35
and for the sacrifice of peace o., 7.41
and for the sacrifice of peace o., 7.47
and for the sacrifice of peace o., 7.53
and for the sacrifice of peace o., 7.59
and for the sacrifice of peace o., 7.65
and for the sacrifice of peace o., 7.71
and for the sacrifice of peace o., 7.77
and for the sacrifice of peace o., 7.83
of peace o. twenty-four bulls, the 7.88
over your burnt o. and over the 10.10
the sacrifices of your peace o.; 10.10
vow, or for peace o. to the LORD, 15.08
is kept of the o. made to me, 18.08
all the wave o. of the people of 18.11
All the holy o. which the people of 18.19
offering, my food for my o. by fire, 28.02
Their drink o. shall be half a hin 28.14
offering, and their drink o. 29.11
and the drink o. for the bulls, 29.18
offering and their drink o. 29.19
and the drink o. for the bulls, 29.21
and the drink o. for the bulls, 29.24
and the drink o. for the bulls, 29.27
continual burnt o. and its cereal 29.28
and the drink o. for the bulls, 29.30
cereal offering, and its drink o. 29.31
and the drink o. for the bulls, 29.33
and the drink o. for the bull, 29.37
to your votive o. and your freewill o., 29.39
your burnt o., and for your cereal o. 29.39
for your drink o., and for your peace o. 29.39

OFFERINGS (cont.)
your burnt o. and your sacrifices, Deu 12.06
your votive o., your freewill o., 12.06
your burnt o. and your sacrifices, 12.11
all your votive o. which you vow 12.11
your burnt o. at every place that 12.13
you shall offer your burnt o., 12.14
of your votive o. which you vow, 12.17
or your freewill o., or the offering 12.17
due from you, and your votive o., 12.26
and offer your burnt o., the flesh 12.27
shall eat the o. by fire to the 18.01
offer burnt o. on it to the LORD 27.06
and you shall sacrifice peace o., 27.07
offered on it burnt o. to the LORD Jos 8.31
the LORD, and sacrificed peace o. 8.31
the o. by fire to the LORD God of 13.14
offer burnt o. or cereal o. or peace o. 22.23
burnt o. and sacrifices and peace o.; 22.27
not for burnt o., nor for sacrifice, 22.28
offered burnt o. and peace o. before Ju 20.26
altar, and offered burnt o. and peace o. 21.04
father all my o. by fire from the 1Sa 2.28
sacrifices and my o. which I 2.29
offered burnt o. and sacrificed 6.15
offer burnt o. and to sacrifice peace o. 10.08
sacrificed peace o. before the LORD, 11.15
here to me, and peace o." 13.09
delight in burnt o. and sacrifices, 15.22
offered burnt o. and peace o. before 2Sa 6.17
the burnt o. and the peace o., he 6.18
not offer burnt o. to the LORD my 24.24
LORD and offered burnt o. and peace o. 24.25
thousand burnt o. upon that altar. 1Ki 3.04
offered up burnt o. and peace o., 3.15
as peace o. to the LORD twenty-two 8.63
and the fat pieces of the peace o., 8.64
offer up burnt o. and peace o. upon 9.25
and his burnt o. which he offered 10.05
to offer sacrifices and burnt o. 2Ki 10.24
from the guilt o. and the money 12.16
from the sin o. was not brought 12.16
of his peace o. upon the altar. 16.13
sons and their daughters as o., 17.17
his sons made o. upon the altar of 1Ch 6.49
offered burnt o. and peace o. before 16.01
the burnt o. and the peace o., he blessed 16.02
to offer burnt o. to the LORD upon 16.40
see, I give the oxen for burnt o., 21.23
nor offer burnt o. which cost me 21.24
presented burnt o. and peace o., 21.26
and whenever burnt o. are offered 23.31
houses made their freewill o., 29.06
day offered burnt o. to the LORD, 29.21
thousand lambs, with their drink o., 29.21
a thousand burnt o. upon it. 2Ch 1.06
and for burnt o. morning and 2.04
and the fat of the peace o., 7.07
up burnt o. to the LORD upon the 8.12
and his burnt o. which he offered 9.04
evening burnt o. and incense of 13.11
to offer burnt o. to the LORD, 23.18
the service and for the burnt o., 24.14
offered burnt o. in the house of 24.14
worshiped them, making o. to them. 25.14
offered burnt o. in the holy place 29.07
and thank o. to the house of the 29.31
brought sacrifices and thank o.; 29.31
a willing heart brought burnt o. 29.31
of the burnt o. which the assembly 29.32
And the consecrated o. were six 29.33
could not flay all the burnt o., 29.34
number of burnt o. there was the 29.35
there was the fat of the peace o., 29.35
the libations for the burnt o. 29.35
brought burnt o. into the house of 30.15
sacrificing peace o. and giving 30.22
and seven thousand sheep for o., 30.24
for burnt o. and peace o., to minister 31.02
possessions was for the burnt o.: 31.03
the burnt o. of morning and evening, 31.03
and the burnt o. for the sabbaths, 31.03
was over the freewill o. to God, 31.14
for the LORD and the most holy o., 31.14
of peace o. and of thanksgiving; 33.16
as passover o. for all that were 35.07
the passover o. two thousand six 35.08
the passover o. five thousand 35.09
aside the burnt o. that they might 35.12
they boiled the holy o. in pots, 35.13
the burnt o. and the fat parts 35.14
to offer burnt o. on the altar of 35.16
freewill o. for the house of God Ez 1.04
made freewill o. for the house of 2.68
Israel, to offer burnt o. upon it, 3.02
offered burnt o. upon it to the 3.03
LORD, burnt o. morning and evening. 3.03
offered the daily burnt o. by number 3.04
and after that the continual burnt o., 3.05
the o. at the new moon and at all 3.05
and the o. of every one who made a 3.05
to offer burnt o. to the LORD. 3.06
offered and burnt o. are brought; 6.03
sheep for burnt o. to the God of 6.09
the freewill o. of the people and 7.16
their cereal o. and their drink o. 7.17
offered burnt o. to the God of 8.35
and the sin o. to make atonement Neh 10.33
and offer burnt o. according to Job 1.05
May he remember all your o., and Ps 20.03
your burnt o. are continually 50.08
in burnt o. and whole burnt o.; then 51.19
I will render thank o. to thee. 56.12
come into thy house with burnt o.; 66.13
offer to thee burnt o. of fatlings, 66.15
Accept my o. of praise, O LORD and 119.108
enough of burnt o. of rams and the Is 1.11
Bring no more vain o.; incense is 1.13
brought me your sheep for burnt o., 42.23
I have not burdened you with o., 43.23
their burnt o. and their sacrifices 56.07
Your burnt o. are not acceptable, Jer 6.20
pour out drink o. to other gods, 7.18
"Add your burnt o. to your sacrifices, 7.21
concerning burnt o. and sacrifices. 7.22
bringing burnt o. and sacrifices, 17.26
cereal o. and frankincense, and 17.26
bringing thank o. to the house of 17.26
in the fire as burnt o. to Baal, 19.05
and drink o. have been poured out 19.13
Baal and drink o. have been poured 32.29
bring thank o. to the house of the 33.11
to offer burnt o., to burn cereal o. 33.18
bringing cereal o. and incense to 41.05
they poured out their drink o. Eze 20.28
gifts, with all your sacred o. 20.40
which the burnt o. and the sacrifices 40.42
LORD shall eat the most holy o.; 42.13
they shall put the most holy o.— 42.13
offering burnt o. upon it and for 43.18
your burnt o. and your peace o.; 43.27
of all kinds from all your o., 44.30
This is the offering for cereal o., 45.15
burnt o., and peace o., to make 45.15
duty to furnish the burnt o., 45.17
cereal o., and drink o., at the 45.17
he shall provide the sin o., 45.17
cereal o., burnt o., and peace o., 45.17
make the same provision for sin o., 45.25
burnt o., and cereal o., and for the 45.25
burnt offering and his peace o., 46.02
or peace o. as a freewill offering 46.12
or his peace o. as he does on the 46.12
and make o. upon the hills, under Hos 4.13

OFFERINGS (cont.)
of God, rather than burnt o. Hos 6.06
proclaim freewill o., publish them; Amo 4.05
offer me your burnt o. and cereal o., 5.22
and the peace o. of your fatted 5.22
sacrifices and o. the forty years 5.25
I come before him with burnt o., Mic 6.06
your faces, the dung of your o., Mal 2.03
they present right o. to the LORD. 3.03
robbing thee?' In your tithes and o. 3.08
all whole burnt o. and sacrifices." Mk 12.33
with noble stones and o., he said, Lk 21.05
to bring to my nation alms and o. Ac 24.17
altar share in the sacrificial o.? 1Co 9.13
"Sacrifices and o. thou hast not Heb 10.05
in burnt o. and sin o. thou hast 10.06
sacrifices and o. and burnt o. and sin o." 10.08

OFFERS
if he o. an animal from the herd, Lev 3.01
If he o. a lamb for his offering, 3.07
The priest who o. it for sin shall 6.26
And the priest who o. any man's 7.08
belong to the priest who o. it. 7.09
If he o. it for a thanksgiving, then 7.12
the day that he o. his sacrifice, 7.16
he who o. it shall not be accepted, 7.18
He that o. the sacrifice of his 7.29
of Aaron who o. the blood of the 7.33
who o. a burnt offering or sacrifice, 17.08
for he o. the bread of your God; 21.08
And when any one o. a sacrifice of 22.21
you may do to them as occasion o." Ju 9.33
thy servant o. toward this place. 1Ki 8.29
thy servant o. toward this place. 2Ch 6.20
who freely o. to go to Jerusalem, Ez 7.13
like him who o. swine's blood; Is 66.03
him who o. sacrifice in the high Jer 48.35
that the prince o. to the LORD on Eze 46.04
blood which he o. for himself and Heb 9.07

OFFICE
head and restore you to your o.; Gen 40.13
I was restored to my o., and the 41.13
to minister in the priest's o. Num 3.03
judge who is in o. in those days, Deu 17.09
judges who are in o. in those days; 19.17
priest who is in o. at that time, 26.03
established them in their o. of trust. 1Ch 9.22
I will thrust you from your o., Is 22.19
Matthew sitting at the tax o.; Mt 9.09
of Alphaeus sitting at the tax o., Mk 2.14
named Levi, sitting at the tax o.; Lk 5.27
and 'His o. let another take.' Ac 1.20
to the divine o. which was given Col 1.25
one aspires to the o. of bishop, 1Ti 3.01
the priestly o. have a commandment Heb 7.05
took their o. without an oath, but 7.21
by death from continuing in o.; 7.23

OFFICER
an o. of Pharaoh, the captain of the Gen 37.36
an o. of Pharaoh, the captain of the 39.01
and Zebul his o. serve the men of Ju 9.28
there was one o. in the land of 1Ki 4.19
of Israel summoned an o. and said, 22.09
city he took an o. who had been in 2Ki 25.19
the chief o. the the house of God; 1Ch 9.11
was chief o. in charge of the 26.24
the son of Zichri was chief o.; 27.16
of Israel summoned an o. and said, 2Ch 18.08
secretary and the o. of the chief 24.11
the secretary and Maaseiah the o., 26.11
The chief o. in charge of them was 31.12
the chief o. of the house of God. 31.13
Without having any chief, o. or ruler, Pro 6.07
who was chief o. in the house of Jer 20.01
city he took an o. who had been in 52.25
the judge hand you over to the o., Lk 12.58
and the o. put you in prison. 12.58

OFFICERS
And Pharaoh was angry with his two o. Gen 40.02
asked Pharaoh's o. who were with 40.07
of Egypt with o. over all of them. Ex 14.07
and his picked o. are sunk in the 15.04
of the people and o. over them; Num 11.16
was angry with the o. of the army, 31.14
Then the o. who were over the 31.48
and o., throughout your tribes. Deu 1.15
judges and o. in all your towns 16.18
Then the o. shall speak to the 20.05
And the o. shall speak further to 20.08
And when the o. have made an end of 20.09
and your o., all the men of Israel, 29.10
and your o., that I may speak these 31.28
commanded the o. of the people, Jos 1.10
three days the o. went through the 3.02
elders and o. and their judges, 8.33
and heads, their judges and o., 23.02
the judges, and the o. of Israel; 24.01
give it to his o. and to his 1Sa 8.15
Azariah the son of Nathan was over the o.; 1Ki 4.05
Solomon had twelve o. over all 4.07
And those o. supplied provisions 4.27
hundred chief o. who were over the 5.16
These were the chief o. who were 9.23
the hands of the o. of the guard, 14.27
said to the guard and to the o., 2Ki 10.25
guard and the o. cast them out and 10.25
These Gadites were o. of the army, 1Ch 12.14
and made them o. of his troops. 12.18
thousand shall be o. and judges, 23.04
for there were o. of the sanctuary 24.05
sanctuary and o. of God among both 24.05
and the o. of the thousands and the 26.26
for Israel, as o. and judges. 26.29
and their o. who served the king in 27.01
the o. of the divisions that served 28.01
also the o. and all the people 28.21
and the o. over the king's work. 29.06
and his o., the commanders of his 2Ch 8.09
were the chief o. of King Solomon, 8.10
the hands of the o. of the guard, 12.10
the Levites will serve you as o. 19.11
to the king's o. by the Levites, 24.11
with his o. and his mighty men to 32.03
commanders and o. in the camp of 32.21
the chief o. of the house of God, 35.08
before all the king's mighty o. Ez 7.28
sent with me o. of the army and Neh 2.09
king appoint o. in all the provinces Est 2.03
and his o. desert the standard in Is 31.09
the rest of the o. of the king of Jer 39.03
all the chief o. of the king of 39.13
one of the chief o. of the king 41.01
Nebuchadrezzar king of Babylon and his o. 46.26
heads, all of them looking like o., Eze 23.15
o. and warriors, all of them riding 23.23
The o. are summoned, they stumble as Nah 2.05
courtiers and o. and the leading Mk 6.21
Pharisees sent o. to arrest him. Jn 7.32
The o. then went back to the chief 7.45
The o. answered, "No man ever spoke 7.46
and some o. from the chief priests 18.03
captain and the o. of the Jews 18.12
servants and o. had made a charcoal 18.18
one of the o. standing by struck 18.22
chief priests and the o. saw him, 19.06
But when the o. came, they did not Ac 5.22
with the o. went and brought them, 5.26
for their o. of praise and ministry 2Ch 8.14
service according to their o., 31.16
upwards was according to their o., 31.17
to their o. and encouraged them in 35.02

OFFICIAL
the king appointed an o. for her, 2Ki 8.06
for the high o. is watched by a Ecc 5.08
there was an o. whose son was ill. Jn 4.46
The o. said to him, "Sir, come down 4.49

OFFICIALS
bribe, for a bribe blinds the o., Ex 23.08
And the o. of Succoth said, "Are Ju 8.06
for him the o. and elders of 8.14
and all the royal o. of Judah, 1Ki 1.09
and these were his high o.: 4.02
they were his o., his commanders, 9.22
his table, the seating of his o., 10.05
and his princes, and his palace o. 2Ki 24.12
his o., and the chief men of the 24.15
afraid because of the Chaldean o.; 25.24
were the chief o. in the service 1Ch 18.17
at Jerusalem all the o. of Israel, 28.01
the o. of the tribes, the officers 28.01
sons, together with the palace o., 28.01
his table, the seating of his o., 2Ch 9.04
and gathered the o. of the city, 29.20
were scribes, and o., and gatekeepers. 34.13
the o., the Persians, the men of Ez 4.09
David and his o. had set apart to 8.20
the o. approached me and said, "The 9.01
the hand of the o. and chief men 9.02
by order of the o. and the elders 10.08
Let our o. stand for the whole 10.14
And the o. did not know where I had Neh 2.16
the o., and the rest that were to 2.16
and to the o. and to the rest of 4.14
and to the o. and to the rest of 4.19
against the nobles and the o. 5.07
Jews and o. besides those who came 5.17
nobles and the o. and the people 7.05
and I and half of the o. with me; 12.40
remonstrated with the o. and said, 13.11
to all the o. of his palace to do Est 1.08
and the royal o. also helped the 9.03
falsehood, all his o. will be wicked. Pro 29.12
For though his o. are at Zoan and Is 30.04
and all the o. of the provinces to Dan 3.02
and all the o. of the provinces, 3.03
will punish the o. and the king's Zep 1.08
Her o. within her are roaring lions 3.03

OFFSCOURING
Thou hast made us o. and refuse Lam 3.45
of the world the o. of all things. 1Co 4.13

OFFSET
enlargement of the o. from story to Eze 41.07
can never o. the guilt he has Hos 12.08

OFFSETS
house he made o. on the wall in 1Ki 6.06
There were o. all around the wall Eze 41.06

OFFSPRING
"Behold, thou hast given me no o.; Gen 15.03
foreigner who is not of your o., 17.12
we may preserve o. through our 19.32
we may preserve o. through our 19.34
woman also, because he is your o." 21.13
me or with my o. or with my 21.23
and raise up o. for your brother." 38.08
knew that the o. would not be his; 38.09
he should give o. to his brother. 38.09
Jacob and all his o. with him, 46.06
all his o. he brought with him into 46.07
into Egypt, who were his own o., 46.26
And the o. born to you after them 48.06
All the o. of Jacob were seventy Ex 1.05
for you and for your o. with you." Num 18.19
and shall eat the o. of your cattle Deu 28.51
shall eat the o. of your own body, 28.53
on you and your o. extraordinary 28.59
your heart and the heart of your o., 30.06
of Canaan, and made his o. many. Jos 24.03
his own o., for he had many wives. Ju 8.30
this day on Saul and on his o." 2Sa 4.08
one of my o. to sit on my throne 1Ki 1.48
and Shallum, the o. of Bilhah. 1Ch 7.13
O o. of Abraham his servant, sons of 16.13
I will raise up your o. after you 17.11
and your o. as the grass of the Job 5.25
He has no o. or descendant among 18.19
and their o. before their eyes. 21.08
and his o. have not enough to eat. 27.14
when they crouch, bring forth their o., 39.03
destroy their o. from the earth, Ps 21.10
O o. of Abraham his servant, sons of 105.06
o. of evildoers, sons who deal Is 1.04
o. and posterity, says the LORD. 14.22
the o. and issue, every small vessel, 22.24
the o. of Abraham, my friend; 41.08
I will bring your o. from the east, 43.05
descendants, and my blessing on your o. 44.03
I did not say to the o. of Jacob, 45.19
LORD all the o. of Israel shall 45.25
your o. would have been like the 48.19
for sin, he shall see his o., 53.10
o. of the adulterer and the harlot. 57.03
transgression, the o. of deceit, 57.04
and their o. in the midst of the 61.09
shall be the o. of the blessed of 65.23
kinsmen, all the o. of Ephraim. Jer 7.15
for none of his o. shall succeed in 22.30
and your o. from the land of their 30.10
him and his o. and his servants 36.31
and your o. from the land of their 46.27
Should women eat their o., Lam 2.20
and he and his o. shall not endure; Dan 11.06
Behold, I will rebuke your o., Mal 2.03
what does he desire? Godly o. 2.15
said, 'For we are indeed his o.' Ac 17.28
Being then God's o., we ought not 17.29
were made to Abraham and to his o. Gal 3.16
"And to your o.," which is Christ. 3.16
till the o. should come to whom the 3.19
Christ's then you are Abraham's o., 3.29
to make war on the rest of her o., Rev 12.17
I am the root and the o. of David, 22.16

OFFSPRINGS
"And to o.," referring to many; but, Gal 3.16

OFTEN
as o. as she went up to the house 1Sa 1.07
and as o. as they came out David 18.30
Hadadezer had o. been at war with 2Sa 8.10
And as o. as the king went into the 1Ki 14.28
Hadadezer had o. been at war with 1Ch 18.10
And as o. as the king went into the 2Ch 12.11
"How o. is it that the lamp of the Job 21.17
he restrained his anger o., and did Ps 78.38
How o. they rebelled against him in 78.40
He who is o. reproved, yet stiffens Pro 29.01
As o. as it passes through it will Is 28.19
For as o. as I speak against him, I Jer 31.20
for o. he falls into the fire, and Mt 17.15
the fire, and o. into the water. 17.15
how o. shall my brother sin against 18.21
How o. would I have gathered your 23.37
for he had o. been bound with Mk 5.04
And it has o. cast him into the 9.22
of John fast o. and offer prayers, Lk 5.33
How o. would I have gathered your 13.34
for Jesus o. met there with his Jn 18.02
he sent for him o. and conversed Ac 24.26
And I punished them o. in all the 26.11
that I have o. intended to come to Rom 1.13
why I have so o. been hindered 15.22
Do this, as o. as you drink it, in 1Co 11.25

OFTEN (cont.)
For as o. as you eat this bread and 1Co 11.26
whom we have o. tested and found 2Co 8.22
countless beatings, and o. near death. 11.23
o. without food, in cold and exposure. 11.27
of whom I have o. told you and now Php 3.18
Onesiphorus, for he o. refreshed me; 2Ti 1.16
the rain that o. falls upon it, Heb 6.07
every plague, as o. as they desire. Rev 11.06

OG
and O. the king of Bashan came out Num 21.33
the kingdom of O. king of Bashan, 32.33
and O. the king of Bashan, who lived Deu 1.04
and O. the king of Bashan came out 3.01
our God gave into our hand O. also, 3.03
Argob, the kingdom of O. in Bashan. 3.04
of the kingdom of O. in Bashan. 3.10
(For only O. the king of Bashan was 3.11
and all Bashan, the kingdom of O., 3.13
and the land of O. the king of 4.47
of Heshbon and O. the king of 29.07
to them as he did to Sihon and O., 31.04
to Sihon and O., whom you utterly Jos 2.10
and O. king of Bashan, who dwelt in 9.10
and O. king of Bashan, one of the 12.04
all the kingdom of O. in Bashan, 13.12
whole kingdom of O. king of Bashan, 13.30
of the kingdom of O. in Bashan; 13.31
Amorites and of O. king of Bashan. 1Ki 4.19
and the land of O. king of Bashan. Neh 9.22
and O., king of Bashan, and all the Ps 135.11
and O., king of Bashan, for his 136.20

OHAD
O., Jachin, Zohar, and Shaul, the son Gen 46.10
O., Jachin, Zohar, and Shaul, the son Ex 6.15

OHEL
and Hashubah, O., Berechiah, Hasadiah, 1Ch 3.20

OHOLAH
O. was the name of the elder and Eze 23.04
O. is Samaria, and Oholibah is 23.04
"O. played the harlot while she was 23.05
will you judge O. and Oholibah? 23.36
they went in to O. and to Oholibah 23.44

OHOLIAB
I have appointed with him O., Ex 31.06
both him and O. the son of Ahisamach 35.34
Bezalel and O. and every able man 36.01
Bezalel and O. and every able man 36.02
and with him was O. the son of 38.23

OHOLIBAH
the elder and O. the name of her Eze 23.04
is Samaria, and O. is Jerusalem. 23.04
"Her sister O. saw this, yet she was 23.11
Therefore, O O., thus says the Lord 23.22
man, will you judge Oholah and O.? 23.36
Oholah and to O. to commit lewdness. 23.44

OHOLIBAMAH
O. the daughter of Anah the son of Gen 36.02
and O. bore Jeush, Jalam, and Korah. 36.05
These are the sons of O. the daughter 36.14
These are the sons of O., Esau's wife: 36.18
chiefs born of O. the daughter of 36.18
Dishon and O. the daughter of Anah. 36.25
O., Elah, Pinon, 36.41
O., Elah, Pinon, 1Ch 1.52

OIL
and poured o. on the top of it. Gen 28.18
offering on it, and poured o. on it. 35.14
o. for the lamps, spices for the Ex 25.06
the anointing o. and for the 25.06
pure beaten olive o. for the light, 27.20
unleavened cakes mixed with o., 29.02
unleavened wafers spread with o. 29.02
And you shall take the anointing o., 29.07
the altar, and of the anointing o., 29.21
and one cake of bread with o., 29.23
a fourth of a hin of beaten o., 29.40
sanctuary, and of olive o. a hin; 30.24
anointing o. blended as by the 30.25
a holy anointing o. it shall be. 30.25
holy anointing o. throughout your 30.31
and the anointing o. and the 31.11
o. for the light, spices for the 35.08
the anointing o. and for the 35.08
lamps, and the o. for the light; 35.14
the anointing o. and the fragrant 35.15
and spices and o. for the light, and 35.28
light, and for the anointing o., 35.28
He made the holy anointing o. also, 37.29
utensils, and the o. for the light; 39.37
the anointing o. and the fragrant 39.38
Then you shall take the anointing o., 40.09
he shall pour o. upon it, and put Lev 2.01
a handful of the fine flour and o., 2.02
cakes of fine flour mixed with o., 2.04
unleavened wafers spread with o. 2.04
flour unleavened, mixed with o.; 2.05
it in pieces, and pour o. on it; 2.06
be made of fine flour with o. 2.07
And you shall put o. upon it, 2.15
and of the o. with all of its 2.16
he shall put no o. upon it, 5.11
with its o. and all the frankincense 6.15
shall be made with o. on a griddle; 6.21
mixed with o. or dry, shall be for 7.10
unleavened cakes mixed with o., 7.12
unleavened wafers spread with o., 7.12
of fine flour well mixed with o. 7.12
the garments, and the anointing o., 8.02
Then Moses took the anointing o., 8.10
the anointing o. on Aaron's head, 8.12
and one cake of bread with o., 8.26
the anointing o. and of the blood 8.30
a cereal offering mixed with o.; 9.04
the anointing o. of the LORD is 10.07
ephah of fine flour mixed with o., 14.10
mixed with oil, and one log of o. 14.10
offering, along with the log of o. 14.12
shall take some of the log of o., 14.15
finger in the o. that is in his 14.16
sprinkle some o. with his finger 14.16
And some of the o. that remains in 14.17
and the rest of the o. that is in 14.18
mixed with o. for a cereal offering, 14.21
a cereal offering, and a log of o.; 14.21
guilt offering, and the log of o., 14.24
some of the o. into the palm of 14.26
some of the o. that is in his left 14.27
put some of the o. that is in his 14.28
and the rest of the o. that is in 14.29
head the anointing o. is poured, 21.10
the anointing o. of his God is 21.12
ephah of fine flour mixed with o., 23.13
bring you pure o. from beaten 24.02
the vessels for o. with which it Num 4.09
charge of the o. for the light, 4.16
offering, and the anointing o., 4.16
shall pour no o. upon it and put 5.15
cakes of fine flour mixed with o., 6.15
unleavened wafers spread with o., 6.15
mixed with o. for a cereal offering; 7.13
mixed with o. for a cereal offering; 7.19
mixed with o. for a cereal offering; 7.25
mixed with o. for a cereal offering; 7.31
mixed with o. for a cereal offering; 7.37
mixed with o. for a cereal offering; 7.43
mixed with o. for a cereal offering; 7.49

OIL (cont.)

mixed with o. for a cereal offering; Num 7.55
mixed with o. for a cereal offering; 7.61
mixed with o. for a cereal offering; 7.67
mixed with o. for a cereal offering; 7.73
mixed with o. for a cereal offering; 7.79
of fine flour mixed with o., 8.08
the taste of cakes baked with o. 11.08
mixed with a fourth of a hin of o.; 15.04
mixed with a third of a hin of o.; 15.06
mixed with half a hin of o., 15.09
All the best of the o., and all the 18.12
a fourth of a hin of beaten o. 28.05
mixed with o., and its drink 28.09
mixed with o., for each bull; 28.12
mixed with o., for the one ram; 28.12
mixed with o. as a cereal offering 28.13
of fine flour mixed with o.; 28.20
of fine flour mixed with o., 28.28
of fine flour mixed with o., 29.03
of fine flour mixed with o., 29.09
of fine flour mixed with o., 29.14
who was anointed with the holy o. 35.25
grain and your wine and your o., Deu 7.13
grain and your wine and your o. 11.14
or of your wine or of your o., 12.17
and of your o., and the firstlings 14.23
grain, of your wine and of your o., 18.04
not anoint yourself with the o.; 28.40
or o., the increase of your cattle 28.51
and o. out of the flinty rock. 32.13
and let him dip his foot in o. 33.24
took a vial of o. and poured it on 1Sa 10.01
Fill your horn with o., and go; 16.01
Then Samuel took the horn of o., 16.13
of Saul, not anointed with o. 2Sa 1.21
do not anoint yourself with o., 14.02
took the horn of o. from the tent, 1Ki 1.39
twenty thousand cors of beaten o. 5.11
a jar, and a little o. in a cruse; 17.12
and the cruse of o. shall not fail, 17.14
neither did the cruse of o. fail, 17.16
in the house, except a jar of o." 2Ki 4.02
Then the o. stopped flowing. 4.06
sell the o. and pay your debts, and 4.07
take this flask of o. in your hand, 9.01
Then take the flask of o., 9.03
man poured the o. on his head, 9.06
the precious o., his armory, all 20.13
the o., the incense, and the spices. 1Ch 9.29
and wine and o., oxen and sheep, for 12.40
offering, the offering mixed with o., 23.29
over the stores of o. was Joash. 27.28
and twenty thousand baths of o. 2Ch 2.10
o. and wine, of which my lord has 2.15
and stores of food, o., and wine. 11.11
o., honey, and of all the produce of 31.05
the yield of grain, wine, and o.; 32.28
and o. to the Sidonians and the Ez 3.07
or o., as the priests at Jerusalem 6.09
of wine, a hundred baths of o., 7.22
and o. which you have been exacting Neh 5.11
of every tree, the wine and the o., 10.37
and o. to the chambers, where are 10.39
and o., which were given by commandment 13.05
grain, wine, and o. into the storehouses. 13.12
six months with o. of myrrh and Est 2.12
rows of the wicked they make o.; Job 24.11
poured out for me streams of o.! 29.06
thou anointest my head with o., Ps 23.05
you with the o. of gladness above 45.07
his words were softer than o., 55.21
with my holy o. I have anointed him; 89.20
thou hast poured over me fresh o. 92.10
o. to make his face shine, and bread 104.15
like water, like o. into his bones! 109.18
like the precious o. upon the head, 133.02
but let the o. of the wicked never 141.05
and her speech is smoother than o.; Pro 5.03
loves wine and o. will not be rich. 21.17
O. and perfume make the heart glad, 27.09
or to grasp o. in his right hand. 27.16
let not o. be lacking on your head. Ecc 9.08
fragrant, your name is o. poured out; Sol 1.03
or bound up, or softened with o. Is 1.06
Arise, O princes, o. the shield! 21.05
the precious o., his whole armory, 39.02
to Molech with o. and multiplied 57.09
the o. of gladness instead of 61.03
and the o., and over the young of Jer 31.12
wine and summer fruits and o., 40.10
o., and honey hidden in the fields." 41.08
from you, and anointed you with o. Eze 16.09
ate fine flour and honey and o. 16.13
and set my o. and my incense before 16.18
with fine flour and o. and honey— 16.19
had placed my incense and my o. 23.41
early figs, honey, o., and balm. 27.17
cause their rivers to run like o., 32.14
and as the fixed portion of o., 45.14
ram, and a hin of o. to each ephah. 45.24
cereal offerings, and for the o. 45.25
with a hin of o. to each ephah. 46.05
with a hin of o. to each ephah. 46.07
with a hin of o. to an ephah. 46.11
of a hin of o. to moisten the 46.14
offering and the o. shall be 46.15
and my flax, my o. and my drink.' Hos 2.05
and the o., and who lavished upon 2.08
and the o., and they shall answer 2.22
and o. is carried to Egypt. 12.01
the wine fails, the o. languishes. Joe 1.10
and o., and you will be satisfied; 2.19
shall overflow with wine and o. 2.24
with ten thousands of rivers of o.? Mic 6.07
but not anoint yourselves with o.; 6.15
the o., upon what the ground brings Hag 1.11
or o., or any kind of food, does it 2.12
from which the o. is poured out?" Zec 4.12
lamps, they took no o. with them; Mt 25.03
took flasks of o. with their lamps. 25.04
the wise, 'Give us some of your o., 25.08
anointed with o. many that were Mk 6.13
You did not anoint my head with o., Lk 7.46
his wounds, pouring on o. and wine; 10.34
He said, 'A hundred measures of o.' 16.06
thee with the o. of gladness Heb 1.09
him with o. in the name of the Jas 5.14
but do not harm o. and wine!" Rev 6.06
o., fine flour and wheat, cattle and 18.13

OILS

your anointing o. are fragrant, your Sol 1.03
fragrance of your o. than any spice! 4.10
themselves with the finest o., Amo 6.06

OINTMENT

He makes the sea like a pot of o. Job 41.31
name is better than precious o.; Ecc 7.01
the perfumer's o. give off an evil 10.01
alabaster jar of very expensive o., Mt 26.07
For this o. might have been sold 26.09
In pouring this o. on my body she 26.12
alabaster jar of o. of pure nard, Mk 14.03
indignantly, "Why was the o. thus wasted? 14.04
For this o. might have been sold 14.05
brought an alabaster flash of o., Lk 7.37
and anointed them with the o. 7.38
she has anointed my feet with o. 7.46
the Lord with o. and wiped his Jn 11.02
pound of costly o. of pure nard 12.03
with the fragrance of the o. 12.03
"Why was this o. not sold for three 12.05

OINTMENTS
let their o. be given them. Est 2.03
her with her o. and her portion of 2.09
with spices and o. for women— 2.12
returned, and prepared spices and o. Lk 23.56

OLD
After Noah was five hundred years o., Gen 5.32
the mighty men that were of o., 6.04
hundred years o. when the flood of 7.06
When Shem was a hundred years o., 11.10
seventy-five years o. when he 12.04
"Bring me a heifer three years o., 15.09
a she-goat three years o., a 15.09
a ram three years o., a turtledove, 15.09
shall be buried in a good o. age. 15.15
eighty-six years o. when Hagar bore 16.16
ninety-nine years o. the LORD 17.01
is eight days o. among you shall 17.12
to a man who is a hundred years o.? 17.17
is ninety years o., bear a child?" 17.17
ninety-nine years o. when he was 17.24
thirteen years o. when he was 17.25
Now Abraham and Sarah were o., 18.11
I have grown o., and my husband is o., 18.12
bear a child, now that I am o.?" 18.13
men of Sodom, both young and o., 19.04
to the younger "Our father is o., 19.31
a son in his o. age at the time of 21.02
Isaac when he was eight days o., 21.04
a hundred years o. when his son 21.05
have borne him a son in his o. age." 21.07
Now Abraham was o., well advanced in 24.01
a son to my master when she was o.; 24.36
his last and died in a good o. age, 25.08
an o. man and full of years, and was 25.08
was forty years o. when he took to 25.20
was sixty years o. when she bore 25.26
When Esau was forty years o., 26.34
When Isaac was o. and his eyes were 27.01
He said. "Behold, I am o., I do not 27.02
to his people, o. and full of days; 35.29
Joseph, being seventeen years o., 37.02
he was the son of his o. age; 37.03
thirty years o. when he entered 41.46
the o. man of whom you spoke? Is he 43.27
an o. man, and a young brother, the 44.20
brother, the child of his o. age; 44.20
being a hundred and ten years o.; 50.26
Now Moses was eighty years o., Ex 7.07
and Aaron eighty-three years o., 7.07
will go with our young and our o.; 10.09
without blemish, a male a year o.; 12.05
lambs a year o. day by day continually. 29.38
from twenty years o. and upward, 30.14
from twenty years o. and upward, 38.26
both a year o. without blemish, for Lev 9.03
a lamb a year o. for a burnt 12.06
ewe lamb a year o. without blemish, 14.10
and honor the face of an o. man, 19.32
lamb a year o. without blemish as 23.12
lambs a year o. without blemish, 23.18
lambs a year o. as a sacrifice of 23.19
you will be eating o. produce; 25.22
comes in, you shall eat the o. 25.22
And you shall eat o. store long 26.10
clear out the o. to make way for 26.10
twenty years o. up to sixty years o. 27.03
from five years o. up to twenty years o., 27.05
is from a month o. up to five years o., 27.06
is sixty years o. and upward, 27.07
from twenty years o. and upward, Num 1.03
from twenty years o. and upward, 1.18
from twenty years o. and upward, 1.20
from twenty years o. and upward, 1.22
from twenty years o. and upward, 1.24
from twenty years o. and upward, 1.26
from twenty years o. and upward, 1.28
from twenty years o. and upward, 1.30
from twenty years o. and upward, 1.32
from twenty years o. and upward, 1.34
from twenty years o. and upward, 1.36
from twenty years o. and upward, 1.38
from twenty years o. and upward, 1.40
from twenty years o. and upward, 1.42
from twenty years o. and upward, 1.45
from a month o. and upward you 3.15
from a month o. and upward was 3.22
from a month o. and upward, there 3.28
from a month o. and upward was six 3.34
males from a month o. and upward, 3.39
from a month o. and upward, taking 3.40
from a month o. and upward as 3.43
from thirty years o. up to fifty years o., 4.03
from thirty years o. up to fifty years o., 4.23
from thirty years o. up to fifty years o., 4.30
from thirty years o. up to fifty years o., 4.35
from thirty years o. up to fifty years o., 4.39
from thirty years o. up to fifty years o., 4.43
from thirty years o. up to fifty years o., 4.47
lamb a year o. for a guilt offering; 6.12
lamb a year o. without blemish for 6.14
ewe lamb a year o. without blemish 6.14
one ram, one male lamb a year o., 7.15
and five male lambs a year o. 7.17
one ram, one male lamb a year o., 7.21
and five male lambs a year o. 7.23
one ram, one male lamb a year o., 7.27
and five male lambs a year o. 7.29
one ram, one male lamb a year o., 7.33
and five male lambs a year o. 7.35
one ram, one male lamb a year o., 7.39
and five male lambs a year o. 7.41
one ram, one male lamb a year o., 7.45
and five male lambs a year o. 7.47
one ram, one male lamb a year o., 7.51
and five male lambs a year o. 7.53
one ram, one male lamb a year o., 7.57
and five male lambs a year o. 7.59
one ram, one male lamb a year o., 7.63
and five male lambs a year o. 7.65
one ram, one male lamb a year o., 7.69
and five male lambs a year o. 7.71
one ram, one male lamb a year o., 7.75
and five male lambs a year o. 7.77
one ram, one male lamb a year o., 7.81
and five male lambs a year o. 7.83
rams, twelve male lambs a year o., 7.87
the male lambs a year o. sixty. 7.88
twenty-five years o. and upward 8.24
from twenty years o. and upward, 14.29
goat a year o. for a sin offering. 15.27
(at a month o. you shall redeem 18.16
from twenty years o. and upward, 26.02
from twenty years o. and upward, 26.04
male from a month o. and upward; 26.62
lambs a year o. without blemish, 28.03
lambs a year o. without blemish, 28.09
lambs a year o. without blemish; 28.11
and seven male lambs a year o.; 28.19
ram, seven male lambs a year o.; 28.27
lambs a year o. without blemish; 29.02
ram, seven male lambs a year o.; 29.08
fourteen male lambs a year o.; 29.13
lambs a year o. without blemish, 29.17
lambs a year o. without blemish, 29.20
lambs a year o. without blemish, 29.23
lambs a year o. without blemish, 29.26
lambs a year o. without blemish, 29.29
lambs a year o. without blemish, 29.32
lambs a year o. without blemish, 29.36
from twenty years o. and upward, 32.11
twenty-three years o. when he died 33.39
and have grown o. in the land, Deu 4.25

OLD (cont.)
which the men of o. have set. Deu 19.14
person of the o. or show favor to 28.50
and twenty years o. this day; 31.02
Remember the days of o., consider 32.07
and twenty years o. when he died; 34.07
young and o., oxen, sheep, and asses, Jos 6.21
Now Joshua was o. and advanced in 13.01
"You are o. and advanced in years, 13.01
I was forty years o. when Moses the 14.07
I am this day eighty-five years o. 14.10
and Joshua was o. and well advanced 23.01
"I am now o. and well advanced in 23.02
lived of o. beyond the Euphrates, 24.02
being a hundred and ten years o. 24.29
the second bull seven years o., Ju 6.25
son of Joash died in a good o. age, 8.32
And behold, an o. man was coming 19.16
and the o. man said, "Where are you 19.17
And the o. man said, "Peace be to 19.20
and they said to the o. man, 19.22
for I am too o. to have a husband. Ru 1.12
and a nourisher of your o. age; 4.15
Now Eli was very o., and he heard 1Sa 2.22
will not be an o. man in your 2.31
shall not be an o. man in your 2.32
ninety-eight years o. and his eyes 4.15
for he was an o. man, and heavy. 4.18
men of the city, both young and o., 5.09
When Samuel became o., he made 8.01
you are o. and your sons do not 8.05
and I am o. and gray, and behold, my 12.02
years o. when he began to reign; 13.01
man was already o. and advanced in 17.12
inhabitants of the land from of o., 27.08
"An o. man is coming up; and he is 28.14
was forty years o. when he began 2Sa 2.10
was five years o. when the news 4.04
thirty years o. when he began to 5.04
daughters of the king clad of o. 13.18
a very aged man, eighty years o.; 19.32
I am this day eighty years o.; 19.35
"They were wont to say in o. time, 20.18
Now King David was o. and advanced 1Ki 1.01
chamber (now the king was very o., 1.15
Solomon was o. his wives turned 11.04
took counsel with the o. men, 12.06
counsel which the o. men gave him, 12.08
which the o. men had given him, 12.13
Now there dwelt an o. prophet in 13.11
city where the o. prophet dwelt. 13.25
forty-one years o. when he began 14.21
But in his o. age he was diseased 15.23
thirty-five years o. when he began 22.42
has no son; and her husband is o." 2Ki 4.14
thirty-two years o. when he became 8.17
twenty-two years o. when he began 8.26
Jehoash was seven years o. when he 11.21
twenty-five years o. when he began 14.02
Azariah, who was sixteen years o., 14.21
sixteen years o. when he began to 15.02
twenty-five years o. when he began 15.33
twenty years o. when he began to 16.02
twenty-five years o. when he began 18.02
from days of o. what now I bring 19.25
twelve years o. when he began to 21.01
twenty-two years o. when he began 21.19
Josiah was eight years o. when he 22.01
twenty-three years o. when he began 23.31
twenty-five years o. when he began 23.36
eighteen years o. when he became 24.08
twenty-one years o. when he became 24.18
married when he was sixty years o.; 1Ch 2.21
When David was o. and full of days, 23.01
thirty years o. and upward, were 23.03
twenty years o. and upward who 23.24
from twenty years o. and upward— 23.27
Then he died in a good o. age, 29.28
in cubits of the o. standard, 2Ch 3.03
took counsel with the o. men, 10.06
counsel which the o. men gave him, 10.08
forsaking the counsel of the o. men, 10.13
forty-one years o. when he began 12.13
whether young or o., man or woman. 15.13
thirty-five years o. when he began 20.31
thirty-two years o. when he became 21.05
thirty-two years o. when he began 21.20
forty-two years o. when he began 22.02
Joash was seven years o. when he 24.01
But Jehoiada grew o. and full of 24.15
and thirty years o. at his death. 24.15
twenty-five years o. when he began 25.01
those twenty years o. and upward, 25.05
Uzziah, who was sixteen years o., 26.01
sixteen years o. when he began to 26.03
twenty-five years o. when he began 27.01
twenty-five years o. when he began 27.08
twenty years o. when he began to 28.01
when he was twenty-five years o., 29.01
o. and young alike, by divisions, 31.15
from three years o. and upwards. 31.16
twenty years o. and upwards was 31.17
twelve years o. when he began to 33.01
twenty-two years o. when he began 33.21
Josiah was eight years o. when he 34.01
twenty-three years o. when he began 36.02
twenty-five years o. when he began 36.05
Jehoiachin was eight years o. when 36.09
twenty-one years o. when he began 36.11
man or virgin, o. man or aged; 36.17
from twenty years o. and upward, Ez 3.08
o. men who had seen the first house, 3.12
was stirred up in it from of o. 4.15
city from of o. has risen against 4.19
of Besodeiah repaired the O. Gate; Neh 3.06
and by the O. Gate, and by the Fish 12.39
and Asaph of o. there was a chief 12.46
young and o., women and children, in Est 3.13
come to your grave in ripe o. age, Job 5.26
Though its root grow o. in the earth, 14.08
Do you not know this from of o., 20.04
reach o. age, and grow mighty in 21.07
Will you keep to the o. way which 22.15
that I were as in the months of o., 29.02
It is not the o. that are wise, nor 32.09
an o. man, and full of days. 42.17
for they have been from of o. Ps 25.06
I have been young, and now am o.; 37.25
in their days, in the days of o.: 44.01
he who is enthroned from of o.; 55.19
cast me off in the time of o. age; 71.09
So even to o. age and gray hairs, O. 71.18
which thou hast gotten of o., 74.02
Yet God my King is from of o., 74.12
I consider the days of o., 77.05
I will remember thy wonders of o. 77.11
utter dark sayings from of o., 78.02
Of o. thou didst speak in a vision 89.19
Lord, where is thy steadfast love of o., 89.49
They still bring forth fruit in o. age, 92.14
thy throne is established from of o.; 93.02
Of o. thou didst lay the foundation 102.25
think of thy ordinances from of o., 119.52
I remember the days of o., I meditate 143.05
maidens together, o. men and children! 148.12
work, the first of his acts of o. Pro 8.22
the beauty of o. men is their gray 20.29
and when he is o. he will not 22.06
despise your mother when she is o. 23.22
youth than an o. and foolish king, Ecc 4.13
choice fruits, new as well as o., Sol 7.13
exiles, both the young and the o., Is 20.04
walls for the water of the o. pool. 22.11
whose origin is from days of o., 23.07

OLD (cont.)

wonderful things, plans formed of o., Is 25.01
from days of o. what now I bring 37.26
nor consider the things of o. 43.18
announced from of o. the things to 44.07
you from of o. and declared it? 44.08
Who declared it of o.? Was it not 45.21
even to your o. age I am He, and to 46.04
remember the former things of o.; 46.09
"The former things I declared of o., 48.03
I declared them to you from of o., 48.05
from of o. your ear has not been 48.08
as in days of o., the generations 51.09
carried them all the days of o. 63.09
Then he remembered the days of o., 63.11
Redeemer from of o. is thy name. 63.16
From of o. no one has heard or 64.04
or an o. man who does not fill out 65.20
child shall die a hundred years o., 65.20
sinner a hundred years o. shall be 65.20
the o. folk and the very aged. Jer 6.11
that I gave of o. to your fathers 7.07
fathers from of o. and for ever; 25.05
shall be as they were of o., 30.20
men and the o. shall be merry. 31.13
took from there o. rags and worn-out 38.11
in the days of o., says the LORD. 46.26
in pieces the o. man and the youth; 51.22
twenty-one years o. when he became 52.01
that were hers from days of o. Lam 1.07
streets lie the young and the o.; 2.21
The o. men have quit the city gate, 5.14
restored! Renew our days as of o.! 5.21
slay o. men outright, young men and Eze 9.06
into the Pit, to the people of o., 26.20
mighty men of o. who went down to 32.27
a lamb a year o. without blemish 46.13
being about sixty-two years o. Dan 5.31
like has never been from of o., Joe 2.02
your o. men shall dream dreams, and 2.28
rebuild it as in the days of o.; Amo 9.11
Israel, whose origin is from of o., Mic 5.02
offerings, with calves a year o.? 6.06
and Gilead as in the days of o. 7.14
to our fathers from the days of o. 7.20
sank low. His ways were as of o. Hab 3.06
O. men and o. women shall again Zec 8.04
and they shall be as many as of o. 10.08
in the days of o. and as in former Mal 3.04
who were two years o. or under, Mt 2.16
that it was said to the men of o., 5.21
that it was said to the men of o., 5.33
of unshrunk cloth on an o. garment, 9.16
Neither is new wine put into o. wineskins; 9.17
treasure what is new and what is o." 13.52
of unshrunk cloth on an o. garment; Mk 2.21
away from it, the new from the o., 2.21
puts new wine into o. wineskins; 2.22
for she was twelve years o. 5.42
like one of the prophets of o. 6.15
For I am an o. man, and my wife is Lk 1.18
Elizabeth in her o. age has also 1.36
of his holy prophets from of o., 1.70
And when he was twelve years o., 2.42
and puts it upon an o. garment; 5.36
from the new will not match the o. 5.36
puts new wine into o. wineskins; 5.37
after drinking o. wine desires new; 5.39
for he says, 'The o. is good.'" 5.39
that one of the o. prophets had 9.08
that one of the o. prophets has 9.19
with purses that do not grow o., 12.33
can a man be born when he is o.? Jn 3.04
"You are not yet fifty years o., 8.57
but when you are o., you will 21.18
and your o. men shall dream dreams; Ac 2.17
of his holy prophets from of o. 3.21
was more than forty years o. 4.22
"When he was forty years o., 7.23
made these things known from of o.' 15.18
he was about a hundred years o., Rom 4.19
We know that our o. self was 6.06
not under the o. written code but 7.06
Cleanse out the o. leaven that you 1Co 5.07
not with the o. leaven, the leaven 5.08
when they read the o. covenant, 2Co 3.14
the o. has passed away, behold, the 5.17
Put off your o. nature which Eph 4.22
put off the o. nature with its Col 3.09
God spoke of o. to our fathers by Heb 1.01
will all grow o. like a garment, 1.11
than the o. as the covenant he 8.06
and growing o. is ready to vanish 8.13
it the men of o. received divine 11.02
he was cleansed from his o. sins. 2Pe 1.09
from of o. their condemnation has 2.03
but an o. commandment which you had 1Jn 2.07
the o. commandment is the word 2.07

OLDER

not see, he called Esau his o. son, Gen 27.01
best garments of Esau her o. son, 27.15
of Esau her o. son were told to 27.42
the name of the o. was Leah, 29.16
the camp had slain all the o. sons. 2Ch 22.01
are among us, o. than your father. Job 15.10
Job because they were o. than he. 32.04
Do not rebuke an o. man but exhort 1Ti 5.01
o. women like mothers, younger women 5.02
Bid the o. men be temperate, serious, Tit 2.02
Bid the o. women like wise to be 2.03

OLDEST

the o. of his house, who had charge Gen 24.02
armor, from the youngest to the o., 2Ki 3.21

OLIVE

mouth a freshly plucked o. leaf; Gen 8.11
vineyard, and with your o. orchard. Ex 23.11
you pure beaten o. oil for the 27.20
the sanctuary, and of o. oil a hin; 30.24
hew, and vineyards and o. trees, Deu 6.11
a land of o. trees and honey, 8.08
When you beat your o. trees, 24.20
You shall have o. trees throughout 28.40
and they said to the o. tree, Ju 9.08
But the o. tree said to them, 'Shall 9.09
grain, as well as the o. orchards. 15.05
vineyards and o. orchards and give 1Sa 8.14
o. orchards and vineyards, sheep and 2Ki 5.26
a land of o. trees and honey, that 18.32
Over the o. and sycamore trees in 1Ch 27.28
their o. orchards, and their houses, Neh 5.11
the hills and bring branches of o., 8.15
wild o., myrtle, palm, and other 8.15
o. orchards and fruit trees in 9.25
off his blossom, like the o. tree. Job 15.33
among the o. rows of the wicked 24.11
am like a green o. tree in the Ps 52.08
will be like o. shoots around your 128.03
as when an o. tree is beaten—two Is 17.06
as when an o. tree is beaten, as at 24.13
the acacia, the myrtle, and the o.; 41.19
'A green o. tree, fair with goodly Jer 11.16
his beauty shall be like the o., Hos 14.06
trees and your o. trees the locust Amo 4.09
produce of the o. fail and the Hab 3.17
and the o. tree still yield nothing? Hag 2.19
And there are two o. trees by it, Zec 4.03
are these two o. trees on the 4.11
these two branches of the o. trees, 4.12
a wild o. shoot, were grafted in Rom 11.17
share the richness of the o. tree, 11.17
what is by nature a wild o. tree, 11.24
nature, into a cultivated o. tree, 11.24

OLIVE (cont.)
back into their own o. tree. Rom 11.24
These are the two o. trees and the Rev 11.04

OLIVES
oil from beaten o. for the lamp, Lev 24.02
oil; for your o. shall drop off. Deu 28.40
up the ascent of the Mount of O., 2Sa 15.30
o. and early figs, honey, oil, and Eze 27.17
you shall tread o., but not anoint Mic 6.15
on the Mount of O. which lies Zec 14.04
the Mount of O. shall be split in 14.04
to Bethphage, to the Mount of O., Mt 21.01
As he sat on the Mount of O., 24.03
they went out to the Mount of O. 26.30
and Bethany, at the Mount of O., Mk 11.01
on the Mount of O. opposite the 13.03
they went out to the Mount of O. 14.26
at the descent of the Mount of O., Lk 19.37
was his custom, to the Mount of O.; 22.39
but Jesus went to the Mount of O. *Jn 8.01
yield o., or a grapevine figs? Jas 3.12

OLIVET
at the mount that is called O., Lk 19.29
and lodged on the mount called O. 21.37
Jerusalem from the mount called O., Ac 1.12

OLIVEWOOD
sanctuary he made two cherubim of o., 1Ki 6.23
sanctuary he made doors of o.; 6.31
two doors of o. with carvings of 6.32
entrance to the nave doorposts of o., 6.33

OLIVEYARDS
vineyards and o. which you did not Jos 24.13

OLYMPAS
and O., and all the saints who are Rom 16.15

OMAR
O., Zepho, Gatam, and Kenaz. Gen 36.11
chiefs Teman, O., Zepho, Kenaz, 36.15
O., Zephi, Gatam, Kenaz, Timna, and 1Ch 1.36

OMEGA
"I am the Alpha and the O.," says the Rev 1.08
is done! I am the Alpha and the O., 21.06
I am the Alpha and the O., the first 22.13

OMEN
Now the men were watching for an o., 1Ki 20.33
you, for they are men of good o.: Zec 3.08
This is a clear o. to them of their Php 1.28

OMENS
to meet with o., but set his face Num 24.01
who frustrates the o. of liars, Is 44.25

OMER
you shall take an o. apiece, according Ex 16.16
But when they measured it with an o., 16.18
'Let an o. of it be kept throughout 16.32
and put an o. of manna in it, and 16.33
(An o. is the tenth part of an ephah.) 16.36

OMERS
twice as much bread, two o. apiece; Ex 16.22

OMRI
therefore all Israel made O., the 1Ki 16.16
So O. went up from Gibbethon, and 16.17
him king, and half followed O. 16.21
who followed O. overcame the people 16.22
so Tibni died, and O. became king. 16.22
O. began to reign over Israel, and 16.23
O. did what was evil in the sight 16.25
of the acts of O. which he did, 16.27
And O. slept with his fathers, and 16.28
Ahab the son of O. began to reign 16.29
Ahab the son of O. reigned over 16.29
And Ahab the son of O. did evil in 16.30
granddaughter of O. king of Israel. 2Ki 8.26
O., Jeremoth, Abijah, Anathoth, and 1Ch 7.08
son of O., son of Imri, son of Bani, 9.04
for Issachar, O. the son of 27.18
Athaliah, the granddaughter of O. 2Ch 22.02
For you have kept the statutes of O., Mic 6.16

ONAM
Alvan, Manahath, Ebal, Shepho, and O. Gen 36.23
Alian, Manahath, Ebal, Shephi, and O. 1Ch 1.40
was Atarah; she was the mother of O. 2.26
The sons of O.: Shammai and Jada. 2.28

ONAN
a son, and she called his name O. Gen 38.04
Then Judah said to O., "Go in to 38.08
But O. knew that the offspring 38.09
O., Shelah, Perez, and Zerah (but Er 46.12
(but Er and O. died in the land of 46.12
The sons of Judah were Er and O.; Num 26.19
and Er and O. died in the land of 26.19
The sons of Judah: Er, O., and Shelah; 1Ch 2.03

ONCE
and I will speak again but this o. Gen 18.32
O. when Jacob was boiling pottage, 25.29
only this o., and entreat the LORD Ex 10.17
atonement upon its horns o. a year; 30.10
atonement for it o. in the year 30.10
of Israel o. in the year because Lev 16.34
kill me at o., if I find favor in Num 11.15
"Let us go up at o., and occupy it; 13.30
O. again Balak sent princes, more in 22.15
may not make an end of them at o., Deu 7.22
of war going around the city o. Jos 6.03
the city, going about it o.; 6.11
they marched around the city o., 6.14
nations, not driving them out at o., Ju 2.23
me, let me speak but this o.; 6.39
trial only this o. with the fleece; 6.39
The trees o. went forth to anoint a 9.08
"Come up this o., for he has told 16.18
only this o., O God, that I may be 16.28
Then Saul fell at o. full length 1Sa 28.20
Go in at o. to King David, and say 1Ki 1.13
O. every three years the fleet of 10.22
run at o. to meet her, and say to 2Ki 4.26
and walked o. to and fro in the 4.35
O. when the king of Syria was 6.08
himself there more than o. or twice. 6.10
o. every three years the ships of 2Ch 9.21
outside Jerusalem o. or twice. Neh 13.20
not answer him o. in a thousand Job 9.03
I have spoken o., and I will not 40.05
O. God has spoken; twice have I Ps 62.11
thee when o. thy anger is roused? 76.07
O. for all I have sworn by my 89.35
All at o. he follows her, as an ox Pro 7.22
The vexation of a fool is known at o., 12.16
The LORD o. called you, 'A green Jer 11.16
this o. I will make them know my 16.21
"O. more they shall use these words 31.23
a day; o. a day you shall eat it. Eze 4.10
of a hin; o. a day you shall drink. 4.11
O. again, in a little while, I will Hag 2.06
'Let us go at o. to entreat the Zec 8.21
"Take o. more the implements of a 11.15
Then o. more you shall distinguish Mal 3.18
And the fig tree withered at o. Mt 21.19
"How did the fig tree wither at o.?" 21.20
talents went at o. and traded with 25.16
he came up to Jesus at o. and said, 26.49
and he will at o. send me more 26.53
And one of them at o. ran and took 27.48

ONCE (cont.)

And at o. his fame spread everywhere Mk 1.28
him, and sent him away at o., 1.43
at o. he puts in the sickle, because 4.29
to give me at o. the head of John 6.25
he came, he went up to him at o., 14.45
returned, and she got up at o.; Lk 8.55
open to him at o. when he comes 12.36
you say at o., 'A shower is coming'; 12.54
When o. the householder has risen 13.25
"A man o. gave a great banquet, and 14.16
'Come at o. and sit down at table'? 17.07
but the end will not be at o." 21.09
Pilate addressed them o. more, 23.20
And at o. the man was healed, and he Jn 5.09
And o. more he bent down and wrote * 8.08
in himself, and glorify him at o. 13.32
denied it; and at o. the cock crowed. 18.27
and at o. there came out blood and 19.34
thing was taken up at o. to heaven. Ac 10.16
So I sent to you at o., and you 10.33
wounds, and he was baptized at o., 16.33
and at o. the gates were shut. 21.30
He at o. took soldiers and centurions, 21.32
the man, I sent him to you at o., 23.30
o. for all, but the life he lives he Rom 6.10
you who were o. slaves of sin have 6.17
For just as you o. yielded your 6.19
I was o. alive apart from the law, 7.09
Just as you were o. disobedient to 11.30
o. I have enjoyed your company for 15.24
man, ready to say Yes and No at o.? 2Co 1.17
what o. had splendor has come to 3.10
even though we o. regarded Christ 5.16
beaten with rods; o. I was stoned. 11.25
"He who o. persecuted us is now Gal 1.23
the faith he o. tried to destroy." 1.23
adds to it, o. it has been ratified. 3.15
slaves you want to be o. more? 4.09
in which you o. walked, following Eph 2.02
Among these we all o. lived in the 2.03
Jesus you who o. were far off have 2.13
for o. you were darkness, but now 5.08
you sent me help o. and again. Php 4.16
And you, who o. were estranged and Co. 1.21
In these you o. walked, when you 3.07
married only o., temperate, sensible, 1Ti 3.02
Let deacons be married only o., 3.12
or has been married more than o.; 5.09
married only o., whose children are Tit 1.06
For we ourselves were o. foolish, 3.03
after admonishing him o. or twice, 3.10
those who have o. been enlightened, Heb 6.04
he did this o. for all when he 7.27
and he but o. a year, and not 9.07
he entered o. for all into the Holy 9.12
he has appeared o. for all at the 9.26
it is appointed for men to die o., 9.27
been offered o. to bear the sins 9.28
worshipers had o. been cleansed, 10.02
body of Jesus Christ o. for all. 10.10
"Yet o. more I will shake not only 12.26
"Yet o. more," indicates the removal 12.27
away and at o. forgets what he was Jas 1.24
O. you were no people but now you 1Pe 2.10
o. you had not received mercy but 2.10
So o. the holy women who hoped in 3.05
also died for sins o. for all, 3.18
faith which was o. for all delivered Jud 1.03
though you were o. for all fully 1.05
At o. I was in the Spirit, and lo, a Rev 4.02
O. more they cried, "Hallelujah! The 19.03

ONE-HALF

Moses for the nine and o. tribes. Jos 14.02
to the two and o. tribes beyond 14.03

ONE'S

in the skin of o. body a boil that Lev 13.18
that is to make naked o. near kin; 20.19
which were on o. left at the gate 2Ki 23.08
and he departed with no o. regret. 2Ch 21.20
a warrior are the sons of o. youth. Ps 127.04
day nor night o. eyes see sleep; Ecc 8.16
and covering o. garment with Mal 2.16
to divorce o. wife for any cause?" Mt 19.03
and to love o. neighbor as oneself, Mk 12.33
and every o. fetters were unfastened. Ac 16.26
I coveted no o. silver or gold or 20.33
We put no obstacle in any o. way, 2Co 6.03
we did not eat any o. bread without 2Th 3.08
is a matter of o. own interpretation, 2Pe 1.20
and if any o. name was not found Rev 20.15

ONES

their little o. and their wives, Gen 34.29
we and you and also our little o. 43.08
for your little o. and for your 45.19
their little o., and their wives, in 46.05
and as food for your little o." 47.24
provide for you and your little o." 50.21
I let you and your little o. go! Ex 10.10
These were the o. chosen from the Num 1.16
and our little o. will become a 14.03
But your little o., who you said 14.31
their sons, and their little o. 16.27
of Midian and their little o.; 31.09
every male among the little o., 31.17
and cities for our little o., 32.16
and our little o. shall live in the 32.17
Build cities for your little o., 32.24
Our little o., our wives, our flocks, 32.26
Moreover your little o., who you Deu 1.39
your little o., and your cattle (I 3.19
But these are the o. which you 14.12
but the women and the little o., 20.14
with young o. or eggs and the 22.06
your little o., your wives, and the 29.11
and little o., and the sojourner 31.12
from the ten thousands of holy o., 33.02
your little o., and your cattle Jos 1.14
and the women, and the little o., 8.35
the little o. and the cattle and Ju 18.21
also the women and the little o. 21.10
guard the feet of his faithful o.; 1Sa 2.09
name of the great o. of the earth. 2Sa 7.09
all the little o. who were with 15.22
and dash in pieces their little o., 2Ki 8.12
sons of Jacob, his chosen o.! 1Ch 16.13
saying, "Touch not my anointed o., 16.22
name of the great o. of the earth. 17.08
the LORD, with their little o., 2Ch 20.13
of rubbish, and burned o. at that?" Neh 4.02
which of the holy o. will you turn? Job 5.01
Behold, God puts no trust in his holy o., 15.15
forth their little o. like a flock, 21.11
prey, when its young o. cry to God, 38.41
Their young o. become strong, they 39.04
His young o. suck up blood; and where 39.30
"Gather to me my faithful o., who Ps 50.05
together against thy protected o. 83.03
in the assembly of the holy o.! 89.05
in the council of the holy o., 89.07
you mighty o. who do his word, 103.20
sons of Jacob, his chosen o.! 105.06
saying, "Touch not my anointed o., 105.15
joy, his chosen o. with singing. 105.43
the prosperity of thy chosen o., 106.05
accursed o., who wander from thy 119.21
your little o. and dashes them 137.09
is glory for all his faithful o. 149.09
O simple o., will you love being Pro 1.22
O simple o., learn prudence; 8.05
there are yet higher o. over them. Ecc 5.08

ONES (cont.)

have commanded my consecrated o., Is 13.03
my anger, my proudly exulting o. 13.03
ease, shudder, you complacent o.; 32.11
Behold the valiant o. cry without; 33.07
all the wise o. of the nations and Jer 10.07
Even the little o. of the flock 49.20
the little o. of their flock shall 50.45
to fall by the swords of mighty o., Eze 32.12
than the lower and the middle o. 42.06
decision by the word of the holy o., Dan 4.17
be different from the former o., 7.24
their little o. shall be dashed in Hos 13.16
her little o. were dashed in pieces Nah 3.10
the daughter of my dispersed o., Zep 3.10
midst your proudly exultant o., 3.11
the white o. go toward the west Zec 6.06
and the dappled o. go toward the 6.06
devours the flesh of the fat o., 11.16
turn my hand against the little o. 13.07
come, and all the holy o. with him. 14.05
of these little o. even a cup of Mt 10.42
of these little o. who believe in 18.06
not despise one of these little o.; 18.10
of these little o. should perish. 18.14
And these are the o. along the path, Mk 4.15
manner are the o. sown upon rocky 4.16
And others are the o. sown among 4.18
soil are the o. who hear the word 4.20
of these little o. who believe in 9.42
The o. along the path are those who Lk 8.12
And the o. on the rock are those 8.13
down my barns, and build larger o.; 12.18
one of these little o. to sin. 17.02
are you the only o. it has reached? 1Co 14.36
Put on then, as God's chosen o., Col 3.12
afraid to revile the glorious o., 2Pe 2.10
authority, and revile the glorious o. Jud 1.08

ONESELF

is too short to stretch o. on it, Is 28.20
too narrow to wrap o. in it. 28.20
No coal for warming o. is this, 47.14
and to love one's neighbor as o., Mk 12.33
and to keep o. unstained from the Jas 1.27

ONESIMUS

and with him O., the faithful and Col 4.09
O., whose father I have become in Phm 1.10

ONESIPHORUS

grant mercy to the household of O., 2Ti 1.16
Aquila, and the household of O. 4.19

ONIONS

melons, the leeks, the o., and the garlic; Num 11.05

ONLY

his heart was o. evil continually. Gen 6.05
O. Noah was left, and those that 7.23
O. you shall not eat flesh with its 9.04
and this is o. the beginning of 11.06
o. do nothing to these men, for they 19.08
your o. son Isaac, whom you love, and 22.02
your son, your o. son, from me." 22.12
withheld your son, your o. son, 22.16
o. you must not take my son back 24.08
o. obey my word, and go, fetch them 27.13
for with o. my staff I crossed this 32.10
o. give me the maiden to be my wife." 34.12
O. on this condition will we 34.15
O. on this condition will the men 34.22
O. let us agree with them, and they 34.23
brothers they o. hated him the 37.05
o. as regards the throne will I be 41.40
brother is dead, and he o. is left. 42.38
O. the man in whose hand the cup 44.17
O. the land of the priests he did 47.22
o. their children, their flocks, and 50.08
houses and be left o. in the Nile." Ex 8.09
they shall be left o. in the Nile." 8.11
o. you shall not go very far away. 8.28
o. let not Pharaoh deal falsely 8.29
O. in the land of Goshen, where the 9.26
o. this once, and entreat the LORD 10.17
LORD your God o. to remove this 10.17
o. let your flocks and your herds 10.24
that o. may be prepared by you. 12.16
you, and you have o. to be still." 14.14
o. he shall pay for the loss of his 21.19
to any god, save to the LORD o., 22.20
for that is his o. covering, 22.27
it is o. an eruption; and he shall Lev 13.06
"O. the tribe of Levi you shall not Num 1.49
But if they blow o. one, then the 10.04
indeed spoken o. through Moses? 12.02
O., do not rebel against the LORD; 14.09
let me o. pass through on foot, 20.19
but o. what I bid you, that shall 22.20
but o. the word which I bid you, 22.35
you shall see o. the nearest of 23.13
o. the gold, the silver, the bronze, 31.22
o., they shall marry within the 36.06
I will go o. by the road, I will Deu 2.27
o. let me pass through on foot, 2.28
o. the cattle we took as spoil for 2.35
O. to the land of the sons of Ammon 2.37
(For o. Og the king of Bashan was 3.11
thou hast o. begun to show thy 3.24
"O. take heed, and keep your soul 4.09
saw no form; there was o. a voice. 4.12
O. you shall not eat the blood; 12.16
O. be sure that you do not eat the 12.23
if o. you will obey the voice of 15.05
O. you shall not eat its blood; 15.23
Justice, and o. justice, you shall 16.20
O. he must not multiply horses for 17.16
o. on the evidence of two witnesses, 19.15
O. the trees which you know are not 20.20
then o. the man who lay with her 22.25
and you shall tend upward o., 28.13
you shall be o. oppressed and 28.29
you shall be o. oppressed and 28.33
Nor is it with you o. that I make 29.14
O. be strong and very courageous, Jos 1.07
o. may the LORD your God be with 1.17
O. be strong and of good courage." 1.18
it was o. on that day that they 6.15
o. Rahab the harlot and all who are 6.17
o. the silver and gold, and the 6.24
o. its spoil and its cattle you 8.02
O. the cattle and the spoil of that 8.27
did Israel burn, except Hazor o.; 11.13
o. in Gaza, in Gath, and in Ashdod, 11.22
o. allot the land to Israel for an 13.06
but o. cities to dwell in, with 14.04
had no sons, but o. daughters; 17.03
you shall not have one lot o., 17.17
o. do not rebel against the LORD, or 22.19
it was o. that the generations of Ju 3.02
"He is o. relieving himself in the 3.24
me make trial o. this once with 6.39
let it be dry o. on the fleece, and 6.39
for it was dry on the fleece o., 6.40
o. deliver us, we pray thee, this day." 10.15
she was his o. child; beside her he 11.34
"You o. hate me, you do not love me; 14.16
we will o. bind you and give you 15.13
o. this once, O God, that I may be 16.28
o., do not spend the night in the 19.20
would give Hannah o. one portion, 1Sa 1.05
o. her lips moved, and her voice was 1.13
o., may the LORD establish his word 1.23
o. the trunk of Dagon was left to 5.04
and serve him o., and he will 7.03
and they served the LORD o. 7.04

ONLY (cont.)

o., you shall solemnly warn them, 1Sa 8.09
O. fear the LORD, and serve him 12.24
o. be valiant for me and fight the 18.17
o. Jonathan and David knew the 20.39
if o. the young men have kept 21.04
You came o. yesterday, and shall I 2Sa 15.20
I will strike down the king o., 17.02
You seek the life of o. one man, 17.03
after him o. to strip the slain. 23.10
o., he sacrificed and burnt incense 1Ki 3.03
o. we two were in the house. 3.18
if o. your sons take heed to their 8.25
thou o., knowest the hearts of all 8.39
and he said to him, "O, let me go." 11.22
David, but the tribe of Judah o. 12.20
doing o. that which was right in my 14.08
for he o. of Jeroboam shall come to 14.13
o. a handful of meal in a jar, and a 17.12
even I o., am left a prophet of the 18.22
and I, even I o., am left; and they 19.10
and I, even I o., am left; and they 19.14
but o. with the king of Israel." 22.31
till o. its stones were left in 2Ki 3.25
O. consider, and see how he is 5.07
but o. the worshipers of Baal. 10.23
strike down Syria o. three times." 13.19
was left but the tribe of Judah o. 17.18
if o. they will be careful to do 21.08
Now Sheshan had no sons, o. daughters; 1Ch 2.34
O., may the LORD grant you discretion 22.12
having no sons, but o. daughters; 23.22
if o. your sons take heed to their 2Ch 6.16
thou o., knowest the hearts of the 6.30
but o. with the king of Israel. 18.30
o. he did not invade the temple of 27.02
O. a few men of Asher, of Manasseh, 30.11
if o. they will be careful to do 33.08
but o. to the LORD their God. 33.17
O. Jonathan the son of Asahel and Ez 10.15
"Not o. to the king has Queen Est 1.16
o. upon himself do not put forth Job 1.12
in your power; o. spare his life." 2.06
O. grant two things to me, then I 13.20
He feels o. the pain of his own 14.22
body, and he mourns o. for himself." 14.22
not yourself; it tends o. to evil. Ps 37.08
For I pray, "O. let them not rejoice 38.16
thee o., have I sinned, and done 51.04
He o. is my rock and my salvation, 62.02
They o. plan to thrust him down 62.04
He o. is my rock and my salvation, 62.06
You will o. look with your eyes and 91.08
If I say, "Let o. darkness cover me, 139.11
the o. one in the sight of my Pro 4.03
of the righteous ends o. in good; 11.23
should give, and o. suffers want. 11.24
but mere talk tends o. to want. 14.23
An evil man seeks o. rebellion, 17.11
but o. in expressing his opinion. 18.02
you will o. have to do it again. 19.19
instruction o. to stray from the 19.27
and to reflect o. after making his 20.25
one who is hasty comes o. to want. 21.05
to the rich, will o. come to want. 22.16
eat o. enough for you, lest you be 25.16
neighbor and says, "I am o. joking!" 26.19
the fool o. rages and laughs, and 29.09
O. what he has already done. Ecc 2.12
o. to give to one who pleases God. 2.26
is o. one, the darling of her mother, Sol 6.09
o. let us be called by your name; Is 4.01
o. a remnant of them will return. 10.22
you, saying: 'God is with you o., 45.14
"O. in the LORD, it shall be said of 45.24
you fast o. to quarrel and to fight 58.04
how to speak, for I am o. a youth." Jer 1.06
me, "Do not say, 'I am o. a youth'; 1.07
O. acknowledge your guilt, that you 3.13
"These are o. the poor, they have no 5.04
make mourning as for an o. son, 6.26
o. to go on doing all these 7.10
eyes and heart o. for your dishonest 22.17
O. know for certain that if you put 26.15
these were the o. fortified cities 34.07
remained of them o. wounded men, 37.10
but o. mire, and Jeremiah sank in 38.06
not destroy o. enough for themselves? 49.09
weary themselves o. for fire." 51.58
'Abraham was o. one man, yet he got Eze 33.24
with o. a wall between me and them. 43.08
O. the prince may sit in it to eat 44.03
they shall o. trim the hair of 44.20
but o. a virgin of the stock of the 44.22
o. his sons may keep a gift from 46.17
strongholds, but o. for a time. Dan 11.24
bread shall be for their hunger o.; Hos 9.04
"You o. have I known of all the Amo 3.02
it like the mourning for an o. son, 8.10
they not steal o. enough for Ob 1.05
that peoples labor o. for fire, Hab 2.13
him, as one mourns for an o. child, Zec 12.10
evildoers not o. prosper but when Mal 3.15
God and him o. shall you serve.'" Mt 4.10
And if you salute o. your brethren, 5.47
but o. say the word, and my servant 8.08
"If I o. touch his garment, I shall 9.21
were with him, but o. for the priests? 12.04
"It is o. by Beelzebul, the prince 12.24
"We have o. five loaves here and 14.17
that they might o. touch the 14.36
"I was sent o. to the lost sheep of 15.24
eyes, they saw no one but Jesus o. 17.08
but o. those to whom it is given. 19.11
saying, 'These last worked o. one hour, 20.12
found nothing on it but leaves o. 21.19
you will not o. do what has been 21.21
nor the Son, but the Father o. 24.36
synagogue, "Do not fear, o. believe." Mk 5.36
and they had o. one loaf with them 8.14
saw any one with them but Jesus o. 9.08
nor the Son, but o. the Father. 13.32
and him o. shall you serve.'" Lk 4.08
none of them but o. to Zarephath, 4.26
cleansed, but o. Naaman the Syrian." 4.27
Who can forgive sins but God o.?" 5.21
the o. son of his mother, and she 7.12
for he had an o. daughter, about 8.42
o. believe, and she shall be well." 8.50
upon my son, for he is my o. child; 9.38
we have o. done what was our duty.'" 17.10
"Are you the o. visitor to Jerusalem 24.18
glory as of the o. Son from the Jn 1.14
the o. Son, who is in the bosom of 1.18
the world that he gave his o. Son, 3.16
in the name of the o. Son of God. 3.18
did not baptize, but o. his disciples), 4.02
because he not o. broke the 5.18
but o. what he sees the Father 5.19
glory that comes from the o. God? 5.44
there had been o. one boat there, 6.22
The thief comes o. to steal and 10.10
and not for the nation o., 11.52
not o. on account of Jesus but also 12.09
not my feet o. but also my hands 13.09
they know thee the o. true God, 17.03
"I do not pray for these o., 17.20
since it is o. the third hour of Ac 2.15
and brought o. a part and laid it 5.02
but they had o. been baptized in 8.16
though he knew o. the baptism of 18.25
hear that not o. at Ephesus but 19.26
is danger not o. that this trade 19.27
if o. I may accomplish my course 20.24

ONLY (cont.)

I am ready not o. to be imprisoned Ac 21.13
I not o. shut up many of the saints 26.10
to God that not o. you but also 26.29
not o. of the cargo and the ship, 27.10
life among you, but o. of the ship. 27.22
they not o. do them but approve Rom 1.32
Or is God the God of Jews o.? 3.29
pronounced o. upon the circumcised, 4.09
not o. to the adherents of the law 4.16
Not o. so, but we also rejoice in 5.11
on a person o. during his life? 7.01
and not o. the creation, but we 8.23
And not o. so, but also when Rebecca 9.10
from the Jews o. but also from the 9.24
o. a remnant of them will be saved; 9.27
you stand fast o. through faith. 11.20
not o. to avoid God's wrath but also 13.05
the weak man eats o. vegetables. 14.02
to whom not o. I but also all the 16.04
to the o. wise God be glory for 16.27
but o. God who gives the growth. 1Co 3.07
will be saved, but o. as through fire. 3.15
O., let every one lead the life 7.17
to whom she wishes, o. in the Lord. 7.39
O. take care lest this liberty of 8.09
Or is it o. Barnabas and I who have 9.06
but o. one receives the prize? 9.24
let there be o. two or at most 14.27
or are you the o. ones it has 14.36
we who are in Christ have o. hope, 15.19
because o. through Christ is it 2Co 3.14
it is veiled o. to those who are 4.03
and not o. by his coming but also 7.07
grieved you though o. for a while. 7.08
you began not o. to do but to 8.10
For he not o. accepted our appeal, 8.17
and not o. that, but he has been 8.19
honorable not o. in the Lord's 8.21
service not o. supplies the wants 9.12
the truth, but o. for the truth. 13.08
they o. heard it said, "He who once Gal 1.23
o. they would have us remember the 2.10
Let me ask you o. this: Did you 3.02
and not o. when I am present with 4.18
o. do not use your freedom as an 5.13
and o. in order that they may not 6.12
not o. in this age but also in that Eph 1.21
but o. such as is good for edifying, 4.29
O. that in every way, whether in Php 1.18
O. let your manner of life be 1.27
you should not o. believe in him 1.29
of you look not o. to his own 2.04
not o. as in my presence but much 2.12
and not o. on him but on me also, 2.27
O. let us hold true to what we have 3.16
giving and receiving except you o.; 4.15
These are o. a shadow of what is to Col 2.17
These are the o. men of the circumcision 4.11
gospel came to you not o. in word, 1Th 1.05
For not o. has the word of the Lord 1.08
with you not o. the gospel of God 2.08
o. he who now restrains it will do 2Th 2.07
the o. God, be honor and glory for 1Ti 1.17
married o. once, temperate, sensible, 3.02
Let deacons be married o. once, 3.12
and not o. idlers but gossips and 5.13
No longer drink o. water, but use a 5.23
by the blessed and o. Sovereign, 6.15
does no good, but o. ruins the hearers. 2Ti 2.14
there are not o. vessels of gold 2.20
and not o. to me but also to all 4.08
married o. once, whose children are Tit 1.06
if o. we hold our first confidence Heb 3.14
but into the second o. the high 9.07
but deal o. with food and drink and 9.10
For a will takes effect o. at death, 9.17
was ready to offer up his o. son, 11.17
will shake not o. the earth but 12.26
of the word, and not hearers o., Jas 1.22
not o. to the kind and gentle but 1Pe 2.18
sow is washed o. to wallow in the 2Pe 2.22
not for ours o. but also for the 1Jn 2.02
God sent his o. Son into the world, 4.09
with the water o. but with the 5.06
and not o. I but also all who know 2Jn 1.01
and deny our o. Master and Lord, Jud 1.04
to the o. God, our Savior through 1.25
o. hold fast what you have, until I Rev 2.25
but o. those of mankind who have 9.04
he must remain o. a little while. 17.10
but o. those who are written in the 21.27

ONO

who built O. and Lod with its towns, 1Ch 8.12
and O., seven hundred and twenty-five, Ez 2.33
of the villages in the plain of O. Neh 6.02
and O., seven hundred and twenty-one. 7.37
Lod, and O., the valley of craftsmen. 11.35

ONRUSHING

the o. torrent, the torrent Kishon. Ju 5.21

ONWARD

led Israel o. from the Red Sea, and Ex 15.22
ornaments, from Mount Horeb o. 33.06
the people of Israel would go o.; 40.36
they did not go o. till the day 40.37
and o. throughout your generations, Num 15.23
of all nations from that time o. 2Ch 32.23
Benjamin also lived from Geba o., Neh 11.31
the eighth day o. the priests Eze 43.27
will come to pass from this day o. Hag 2.15
Consider from this day o., from the 2.18

ONYCHA

and o., and galbanum, sweet spices Ex 30.34

ONYX

bdellium and o. stone are there. Gen 2.12
o. stones, and stones for setting, Ex 25.07
And you shall take two o. stones, 28.09
row a beryl, an o., and a jasper; 28.20
and o. stones and stones for 35.09
leaders brought o. stones and 35.27
The o. stones were prepared, enclosed 39.06
row, a beryl, an o., and a jasper; 39.13
quantities of o. and stones for 1Ch 29.02
Ophir, in precious o. or sapphire. Job 28.16
and o., sapphire, carbuncle, and Eze 28.13
the fifth o., the sixth carnelian, Rev 21.20

OPEN

and the land shall be o. to you; Gen 34.10
is the first to o. the womb among Ex 13.02
the males that first o. the womb; 13.15
"When a man leaves a pit o., 21.33
living bird go into the o. field. Lev 14.07
out of the city into the o. field; 14.53
which they slay in the o. field, 17.05
instead of all that o. the womb, Num 8.16
And every o. vessel, which has no 19.15
Whoever in the o. field touches one 19.16
into the midst of its o. square, Deu 13.16
but you shall o. your hand to him, 15.08
You shall o. wide your hand to your 15.11
lying in the o. country, and it is 21.01
"But if in the o. country a man 22.25
he came upon her in the o. country, 22.27
The LORD will o. to you his good 28.12
In the o. the sword shall bereave, 32.25
they left the city o., Jos 8.17
of Ai in the o. wilderness where 8.24
"O. the mouth of the cave, and bring 10.22
still did not o. the doors of the Ju 3.25

OPEN (cont.)

And God split o. the hollow place Ju 15.19
sat down in the o. square of the 19.15
wayfarer in the o. square of the 19.17
and in the o. country, about thirty 20.31
an Egyptian in the o. country, 1Sa 30.11
by themselves in the o. country. 2Sa 10.08
lord are camping in the o. field; 11.11
the form of gourds and o. flowers; 1Ki 6.18
and palm trees and o. flowers, 6.29
cherubim, palm trees, and o. flowers; 6.32
and palm trees and o. flowers; 6.35
that thy eyes may be o. night and 8.29
Let thy eyes be o. to the supplication 8.52
them were alone in the o. country. 11.29
who dies in the o. country the 14.11
who dies in the o. country the 21.24
o. his eyes that he may see." 2Ki 6.17
o. the eyes of these men, that they 6.20
hide themselves in the o. country, 7.12
Then o. the door and flee; 9.03
And he said, "O. the window eastward"; 13.17
Because they did not o. it to him, 15.16
o. thy eyes, O LORD, and see; 19.16
forces in the o. country and their 25.23
by themselves in the o. country. 1Ch 19.09
that thy eyes may be o. day and 2Ch 6.20
let thy eyes be o. and thy ears 6.40
Now my eyes will be o. and my ears 7.15
sat in the o. square before the Ez 10.09
we cannot stand in the o. 10.13
and thy eyes o., to hear the prayer Neh 1.06
in o. places, I stationed the people 4.13
to me with an o. letter in his 6.05
Mordecai in the o. square of the Est 4.6
through the o. square of the city, 6.09
through the o. square of the city, 6.11
villages, who live in the o. towns, 9.19
would speak, and o. his lips to you, Job 11.05
if he shuts a man in, none can o. 12.14
And dost thou o. thy eyes upon such 14.03
He slashes o. my kidneys, and does 16.13
They o. shafts in a valley away 28.04
I must o. my lips and answer. 32.20
Behold, I o. my mouth; the tongue 33.02
strong, they grow up in the o.; 39.04
Who can o. the doors of his face? 41.14
their throat is an o. sepulchre, Ps 5.09
they o. wide their mouths at me, 22.13
They o. wide their mouths against 35.21
dumb man who does not o. his mouth. 38.13
I am dumb, I do not o. my mouth; 39.09
but thou hast given me an o. ear. 40.06
O Lord, o. thou my lips and my mouth 51.15
to quake, thou hast rent it o.; 60.02
Thou didst cleave o. springs and 74.15
I will o. my mouth in a parable; 78.02
O. your mouth wide, and I will fill 81.10
O. to me the gates of righteousness, 118.19
O. my eyes, that I may behold 119.18
With o. mouth I pant, because I long 119.131
Sheol and Abaddon lie o. before the Pro 15.11
o. your eyes, and you will have 20.13
the gate he does not o. his mouth. 24.07
Better is o. rebuke than hidden 27.05
O. your mouth for the dumb, for the 31.08
O. your mouth, judge righteously, 31.09
"O. to me, my sister, my love, my dove, Sol 5.02
I arose to o. to my beloved, and my 5.05
west devour Israel with o. mouth. Is 9.12
he shall o., and none shall shut; 22.22
he shall shut, and none shall o. 22.22
O. the gates, that the righteous 26.02
he continually o. and harrow his 28.24
o. thy eyes, O LORD, and see; 37.17
I will o. rivers on the bare 41.18
to o. the eyes that are blind, to 42.07
his ears are o., but he does not 42.20
to o. doors before him that gates 45.01
let the earth o., that salvation 45.08
whom do you o. your mouth wide and 57.04
Your gates shall be o. continually; 60.11
Their quiver is like an o. tomb, Jer 5.16
fall like dung upon the o. field, 9.22
are shut up, with none to o. them; 13.19
on the mountains in the o. country. 17.03
and conditions, and the o. copy; 32.11
deed of purchase and this o. deed, 32.14
whose eyes are o. to all the ways 32.19
forces in the o. country and their 40.07
forces in the o. country came to 40.13
o. her granaries; pile her up 50.26
o. your mouth, and eat what I give Eze 2.08
I will o. your mouth, and you shall 3.27
you were cast out on the o. field, 16.05
and never o. your mouth again 16.63
to o. the mouth with a cry, to lift 21.22
therefore I will lay o. the flank 25.09
is broken, it has swung o. to me; 26.02
you shall fall upon the o. field, 29.05
and I will o. your lips among them. 29.21
on the o. field I will fling you, 32.04
that is in the o. field I will 33.27
I will o. your graves, and raise you 37.12
when I o. your graves, and raise you 37.13
You shall fall in the o. field; 39.05
cubits for an o. space around it. 45.02
for dwellings and for o. country. 48.15
And the city shall have o. land: 48.17
upper chamber o. toward Jerusalem; Dan 6.10
o. thy eyes and behold our desolations, 9.18
I will tear o. their breast, and Hos 13.08
and their pregnant women ripped o. 13.16
Samaria a heap in the o. country, Mic 1.06
city and dwell in the o. country; 4.10
your land are wide o. to your foes; Nah 3.13
O. your doors, O Lebanon, that the Zec 11.01
house of Judah I will o. my eyes, 12.04
if I will not o. the windows of Mal 3.10
"I will o. my mouth in parables, I Mt 13.35
and when you o. its mouth you will 17.27
saying, 'Lord, lord, o. to us." 25.11
at the door out in the o. street; Mk 11.04
that they may o. to him at once Lk 12.36
the door, saying, 'Lord, o. to us." 13.25
do to you? How did he o. your eyes?" Jn 9.26
Can a demon o. the eyes of the 10.21
he burst o. in the middle and all Ac 1.18
joy she did not o. the gate but 12.14
saw that the prison doors were o., 16.27
Paul was about to o. his mouth, 18.14
against any one, the courts are o., 19.38
to open their eyes, that they may turn 26.18
"Their throat is an o. grave, Rom 3.13
but by the o. statement of the 2Co 4.02
Our mouth is o. to you, Corinthians; 6.11
O. your hearts to us; we have wronged 7.02
that God may o. to us a door for Col 4.03
believers and not o. to the charge Tit 1.06
but all are o. and laid bare to the Heb 4.13
o. to reason, full of mercy and good Jas 3.17
his ears are o. to their prayer. 1Pe 3.12
I have set before you an o. door, Rev 3.08
and lo, in heaven an o. door! 4.01
is worthy to o. the scroll and 5.02
was able to o. the scroll or to 5.03
found worthy to o. the scroll or 5.04
so that he can o. the scroll and 5.05
the scroll and to o. its seals, 5.09
had a little scroll o. in his hand. 10.02
scroll which is o. in the hand of 10.08

OPENED

you eat of it your eyes will be o., Gen 3.05
Then the eyes of both were o., 3.07

OPENED (cont.)

which has o. its mouth to receive Gen 4.11
the windows of the heavens were o. 7.11
forty days Noah o. the window of 8.06
Then God o. her eyes, and she saw a 21.19
Leah was hated, he o., her womb; 29.31
hearkened to her and o. her womb, 30.22
Joseph o. all the storehouses, and 41.56
And as one of them o. his sack to 42.27
the lodging place we o. our sacks, 43.21
ground, and every man o. his sack. 44.11
When she o. it she saw the child; Ex 2.06
and the earth o. its mouth and Num 16.32
Then the LORD o. the mouth of the 22.28
Then the LORD o. the eyes of Balaam, 22.31
oracle of the man whose eye is o., 24.03
oracle of the man whose eye is o., 24.15
and the earth o. its mouth and 26.10
how the earth o. its mouth and Deu 11.06
they took the key and o. them; Ju 3.25
So she o. a skin of milk and gave 4.19
for I have o. my mouth to the LORD, 11.35
if you have o. your mouth to the 11.36
and when he o. the doors of the 19.27
then he o. the doors of the house 1Sa 3.15
times, and the child o. his eyes. 2Ki 4.35
So the LORD o. the eyes of the 6.17
So the LORD o. their eyes, and 6.20
Then he o. the door, and fled. 9.10
and he o. it. Then Elisha said, 13.17
he o. the doors of the house of the 2Ch 29.03
of Jerusalem be o. until the sun Neh 7.03
And Ezra o. the book in the sight 8.05
and when he o. it all the people 8.05
should not be o. until after the 13.19
After this Job o. his mouth and Job 3.01
and they o. their mouths as for the 29.23
I have o. my doors to the wayfarer); 31.32
and o. the doors of heaven; Ps 78.23
He o. the rock, and water gushed 105.41
the earth o. and swallowed up 106.17
deceitful mouths are o. against me, 109.02
I o. to my beloved, but my beloved Sol 5.06
blossoms have o. and the pomegranates 7.12
appetite and o. its mouth beyond Is 5.14
or o. the mouth, or chirped." 10.14
For the windows of heaven are o., 24.18
Then the eyes of the blind shall be o., 35.05
of old your ear has not been o. 48.08
The Lord GOD has o. my ear, 50.05
afflicted, yet he o. not his mouth; 53.07
is dumb, so he o. not his mouth. 53.07
The LORD has o. his armory, and Jer 50.25
river Chebar, the heavens were o., Eze 1.01
So I o. my mouth, and he gave me the 3.02
mouth will be o. to the fugitive, 24.27
and he had o. my mouth by the time 33.22
so my mouth was o., and I was no longer 33.22
side chambers o. on the part of 41.11
it shall not be o., and no one 44.02
day it shall be o. and on the day 46.01
day of the new moon it shall be o. 46.01
facing east shall be o. for him; 46.12
in judgment, and the books were o. Dan 7.10
in judgment, and the books were o. Dan 7.10
then I o. my mouth and spoke. 10.16
The river gates are o., Nah 2.06
be a fountain o. for the house of Zec 13.01
heavens were o. and he saw the Mt 3.16
And he o. his mouth and taught them, 5.02
knock, and it will be o. to you. 7.07
to him who knocks it will be o. 7.08
And their eyes were o. And Jesus 9.30
to him, "Lord, let our eyes be o." 20.33
the tombs also were o., and many 27.52
saw the heavens o. and the Spirit Mk 1.10
to him, "Ephphatha," that is, "Be o." 7.34
And his ears were o., his tongue 7.35
his mouth was o. and his tongue Lk 1.64
was praying, the heaven was o., 3.21
He o. the book and found the place 4.17
knock, and it will be o. to you. 11.09
to him who knocks it will be o. 11.10
And their eyes were o. and they 24.31
while he o. to us the scriptures?" 24.32
Then he o. their minds to understand 24.45
say to you, you will see heaven o., Jn 1.51
to him, "Then how are your eyes o.?" 9.10
made the clay and o. his eyes. 9.14
him, since he has o. your eyes?" 9.17
nor do we know who o. his eyes. 9.21
comes from, and yet he o. my eyes. 9.30
that any one o. the eyes of a man 9.32
not he who o. the eyes of the 11.37
of the Lord o. the prison doors Ac 5.19
but when we o. it we found no one 5.23
said, "Behold, I see the heavens o., 7.56
Then Philip o. his mouth, and 8.35
and when his eyes were o., 9.08
And she o. her eyes and when she 9.40
and saw the heaven o., and something 10.11
And Peter o. his mouth and said: 10.34
It o. to them of its own accord, and 12.10
and when they o., they saw him and 12.16
and how he had o. a door of faith 14.27
The Lord o. her heart to give heed 16.14
the doors were o. and every one's 16.26
for effective work has o. to me, 1Co 16.09
a door was o. for me in the Lord; 2Co 2.12
is not yet o. as long as the outer Heb 9.08
way which he o. for us through the 10.20
when the Lamb o. one of the seven Rev 6.01
When he o. the second seal, I heard 6.03
When he o. the third seal, I heard 6.05
When he o. the fourth seal, I heard 6.07
When he o. the fifth seal, I saw 6.09
When he o. the sixth seal, I looked, 6.12
When the Lamb o. the seventh seal, 8.01
he o. the shaft of the bottomless 9.02
Then God's temple in heaven was o., 11.19
and the earth o. its mouth and 12.16
it o. its mouth to utter blasphemies 13.06
tent of witness in heaven was o., 15.05
Then I saw heaven o., and behold, 19.11
the throne, and books were o. 20.12
Also another book was o., 20.12

OPENEST

when thou o. thy hand, they are Ps 104.28
Thou o. thy hand, thou satisfiest 145.16

OPENING

have in it an o. for the head, Ex 28.32
with a woven binding around the o., 28.32
like the o. in a garment, that it 28.32
and the o. of the robe in it was 39.23
in it was like the o. in a garment, 39.23
with a binding around the o., 39.23
Its o. was within a crown which 1Ki 7.31
its o. was round, as a pedestal is 7.31
At its o. there were carvings; 7.31
had charge of o. it every morning. 1Ch 9.27
and the o. of the prison to those Is 61.01
breadth of the o. of the gateway, Eze 40.11
Then, o. their treasures, they Mt 2.11
and when they had made an o., Mk 2.04
be given me in o. my mouth boldly Eph 6.19
from the same o. fresh water and Jas 3.11

OPENLY

her harlotry so o. and flaunted Eze 23.18
could no longer o. enter a town, Mk 1.45
secret if he seeks to be known o. Jn 7.04
of the Jews no one spoke o. of him. 7.13
speaking o., and they say nothing 7.26

OPENLY (cont.)

went about o. among the Jews, Jn 11.54
him, "I have spoken o. to the world; 18.20
Christ quite o. and unhindered. Ac 28.31

OPENS

LORD all that first o. the womb. Ex 13.12
All that o. the womb is mine, all 34.19
first-born that o. the womb among Num 3.12
new, and the ground o. its mouth, 16.30
Everything that o. the womb of all 18.15
to you is peace and it o. to you, Deu 20.11
he o. his eyes, and his wealth is Job 27.19
then he o. the ears of men, and 33.16
Job o. his mouth in empty talk, he 35.16
He o. their ears to instruction, and 36.10
and o. their ear by adversity. 36.15
the LORD o. the eyes of the blind. Ps 146.08
he who o. wide his lips comes to Pro 13.03
She o. her hand to the poor, and 31.20
She o. her mouth with wisdom, and 31.26
He who o. the breach will go up Mic 2.13
"Every male that o. the womb shall Lk 2.23
To him the gatekeeper o.; the sheep Jn 10.03
is dumb, so he o. not his mouth. Ac 8.32
who o. and no one shall shut, who Rev 3.07
shut, who shuts and no one o. 3.07
one hears my voice and o. the door, 3.20

OPHEL

much building on the wall of O. 2Ch 27.03
Fish Gate, and carried it round O., 33.14
living on O. repaired to a point Neh 3.26
tower as far as the wall of O. 3.27
But the temple servants lived on O.; 11.21

OPHIR

O., Havilah, and Jobab; all these were Gen 10.29
and they went to O., and brought 1Ki 9.28
Hiram, which brought gold from O., 10.11
brought from O. a very great amount 10.11
of Tarshish to go to O. for gold; 22.48
O., Havilah, and Jobab; all these were 1Ch 1.23
talents of gold, of the gold of O., 29.04
they went to O. together with the 2Ch 8.18
Solomon, who brought gold from O., 9.10
and gold of O. among the stones of Job 22.24
cannot be valued in the gold of O., 28.16
stands the queen in gold of O. Ps 45.09
and mankind than the gold of O. Is 13.12

OPHNI

Chepharammoni, O., Geba—twelve Jos 18.24

OPHRAH

Avvim, Parah, O., Jos 18.23
came and sat under the oak at O., Ju 6.11
to this day it still stands at O., 6.24
it and put it in his city, in O.; 8.27
his father, at O. of the Abiezrites. 8.32
went to his father's house at O., 9.05
one company turned toward O., 1Sa 13.17
Meonothai was the father of O.; 1Ch 4.14

OPINION

and afraid to declare my o. to you. Job 32.06
let me also declare my o.' 32.10
I also will declare my o. 32.17
but only in expressing his o. Pro 18.02
but I give my o. as one who by the 1Co 7.25

OPINIONS

go limping with two different o.? 1Ki 18.21
him, but not for disputes over o. Rom 14.01

OPPONENT

And each caught his o. by the head, 2Sa 2.16
so that an o. may be put to shame, Tit 2.08

OPPONENT'S

thrust his sword in his o. side; 2Sa 2.16

OPPONENTS

frightened in anything by your o. Php 1.28
correcting his o. with gentleness. 2Ti 2.25

OPPORTUNE

departed from him until an o. time. Lk 4.13

OPPORTUNITY

he sought an o. to betray him. Mt 26.16
But an o. came when Herod on his Mk 6.21
and he sought an o. to betray him. 14.11
and sought an o. to betray him to Lk 22.06
when I have an o. I will summon you." Ac 24.25
and had o. to make his defense 25.16
finding o. in the commandment, Rom 7.08
finding o. in the commandment, 7.11
freedom, avail yourself of the o. 1Co 7.21
He will come when he has o. 16.12
freedom as an o. for the flesh, Gal 5.13
as we have o., let us do good to 6.10
and give no o. to the devil. Eph 4.27
concerned for me, but you had no o. Php 4.10
they would have had o. to return. Heb 11.15

OPPOSE

nothing to her, and did not o. her; Num 30.11
and displease God and o. all men 1Th 2.15
so these men also o. the truth, 2Ti 3.08

OPPOSED

her, because her father o. her. Num 30.05
Jahzeiah the son of Tikvah o. this, Ez 10.15
And when they o. and reviled him, he Ac 18.06
to Antioch I o. him to his face, Gal 2.11
for these are o. to each other, to 5.17
As Jannes and Jambres o. Moses, 2Ti 3.08
for he strongly o. our message. 4.15

OPPOSES

who o. and exalts himself against 2Th 2.04
"God o. the proud, but gives grace Jas 4.06
for "God o. the proud, but gives 1Pe 5.05

OPPOSING

to Israel in o. them on the way, 1Sa 15.02
Cease o. God, who is with me, lest he 2Ch 35.21
You might even be found o. God!" Ac 5.39
many things in o. the name of 26.09

OPPOSITE

which is o. Egypt in the direction Gen 25.18
the loops shall be o. one another. Ex 26.05
of the tabernacle o. the table; 26.35
molding on two o. sides of it 30.04
the loops were o. one another. 36.12
on two o. sides of it, as holders 37.27
o. the table on the south side of 40.24
in the wilderness which is o. Moab, Num 21.11
earth, and they are dwelling o. me. 22.05
remained in the valley o. Bethpeor. Deu 3.29
Jordan in the valley o. Bethpeor, 4.46
is in the land of Moab, o. Jericho; 32.49
top of Pisgah, which is o. Jericho. 34.01
in the land of Moab o. Bethpeor; 34.06
the people passed over o. Jericho. Jos 3.16
stood on o. sides of the ark before 8.33
which is o. the ascent of Adummim, 15.07
o. Bethhoron, and it ends at Kiriathbaal 18.14
which is o. the ascent of Adummim; 18.17
and arrived o. Jebus (that is, Ju 19.10
Nohah as far as o. Gibeah on the 20.43
Jonathan sat o., and Abner sat by 1Sa 20.25
come upon them o. the balsam trees. 2Sa 5.23
on the hillside o. him and cursed 16.13
and window o. window in three tiers. 1Ki 7.04

OPPOSITE (cont.)
and window was o. window in three 1Ki 7.05
And they encamped o. one another 20.29
and set two base fellows o. him, 21.10
fellows came in and sat o. him; 21.13
saw the water o. them as red as 2Ki 3.22
o. the king of Edom; 3.26
also dwelt o. their kinsmen in 1Ch 8.32
also dwelt o. their kinsmen in 9.38
come upon them o. the balsam trees. 14.14
o. them the priests sounded trumpets; 2Ch 7.06
of Harumaph repaired o. his house; Neh 3.10
to a point o. the sepulchres of 3.16
another section o. the ascent to 3.19
Hasshub repaired o. their house. 3.23
Uzai repaired o. the Angle and the 3.25
to a point o. the Water Gate on 3.26
another section o. the great 3.27
repaired, each one o. his own house. 3.28
of Immer repaired o. his own house. 3.29
Berechiah repaired o. his chamber. 3.30
o. the Muster Gate, and to the upper. 3.31
station and each o. his own house. 7.03
brethren stood o. them in the 12.09
king's palace, o. the king's hall. Est 5.01
the palace o. the entrance to the 5.01
was a structure like a city o. me. Eze 40.02
And o. the gate on the north, as on 40.23
which were o. the temple yard and 42.01
temple yard and o. the building on 42.01
o. the chambers, fifty cubits long. 42.07
while those o. the temple were a 42.08
o. the yard and o. the building, 42.10
and o. there was a dividing wall. 42.12
south chambers o. the yard are the 42.13
to a point o. the entrance of 47.20
king's palace, o. the lampstand; Dan 5.05
them, "Go into the village o. you, Mt 21.02
there, sitting o. the sepulchre. 27.61
them, "Go into the village o. you, Mk 11.02
And he sat down o. the treasury, 12.41
the Mount of Olives o. the temple, 13.03
the Gerasenes, which is o. Galilee. Lk 8.26
saying, "Go into the village o., 19.30
And when they had come o. Mysia, Ac 16.07
we came the following day o. Chios; 20.15

OPPOSITION
they had nothing to say in o. Ac 4.14
in o. to the doctrine which you Rom 16.17
of God in the face of great o. 1Th 2.02

OPPRESS
with which the Egyptians o. them. Ex 3.09
not wrong a stranger or o. him, 22.21
"You shall not o. a stranger; 23.09
"you shall not o. your neighbor or Lev 19.13
him best; you shall not o. him. Deu 23.16
"You shall not o. a hired servant 24.14
he allowed no one to o. them; 1Ch 16.21
Does it seem good to thee to o., Job 10.03
all day long foemen o. me; Ps 56.01
he allowed no one to o. them; 105.14
let not the godless o. me. 119.122
And the people will o. one another, Is 3.05
and o. all your workers. 58.03
if you do not o. the alien, the Jer 7.06
and I will punish all who o. them. 30.20
does not o. any one, but restores to Eze 18.07
princes shall no more o. my people; 45.08
are false balances, he loves to o. Hos 12.07
who o. the poor, who crush the needy, Amo 4.01
"and they shall o. you from the 6.14
they o. a man and his house, a man Mic 7.10
do not o. the widow, the fatherless, Zec 7.10
those who o. the hireling in his Mal 3.05
Is it not the rich who o. you, Jas 2.06

OPPRESSED
they will be o. for four hundred Gen 15.13
But the more they were o., Ex 1.12
or if he has o. his neighbor Lev 6.02
shall be only o. and robbed Deu 28.29
shall be only o. and crushed 28.33
of those who afflicted and o. them. Ju 2.18
and o. the people of Israel cruelly 4.03
from the hand of all who o. you, 6.09
crushed and o. the children of 10.08
years they o. all the people of 10.08
Amalekites, and the Maonites, o. you; 10.12
Whom have I o.? Or from whose 1Sa 12.03
defrauded us or o. us or taken 12.04
Egypt and the Egyptians o. them, 12.08
how the king of Syria o. them. 2Ki 13.04
king of Syria o. Israel all the 13.22
The LORD is a stronghold for the o., Ps 9.09
to the fatherless and the o., 10.18
Let the o. see it and be glad; 69.32
to save all the o. of the earth. 76.09
and justice for all who are o. 103.06
Their enemies o. them, and they were 106.42
who executes justice for the o.; 146.07
And behold, the tears of the o., Ecc 4.01
the poor o. and justice and right 5.08
and rule over those who o. them. Is 14.02
no more exult O. o. virgin daughter 23.12
O Lord, I am o.; be thou my 38.14
the Assyrian o. them for nothing. 52.04
He was o., and he was afflicted, yet 53.07
to let the o. go free, and to break 58.06
of those who o. you shall come 60.14
hosts: The people of Israel are o., Jer 50.33
they have o. the poor and needy, and Eze 22.29
iniquities by showing mercy to the o., Dan 4.27
Ephraim is o., crushed in judgment, Hos 5.11
to set at liberty those who are o., Lk 4.18
he defended the o. man and avenged Ac 7.24
all that were o. by the devil, 10.38

OPPRESSES
against the adversary who o. you, Num 10.09
He who o. a poor man insults his Pro 14.31
He who o. the poor to increase his 22.16
A poor man who o. the poor is a 28.03
o. the poor and needy, commits Eze 18.12

OPPRESSING
all the kingdoms that were o. you. 1Sa 10.18
rebellious and defiled, the o. city! Zep 3.01

OPPRESSION
I have seen the o. with which the Ex 3.09
by robbery, or what he got by o., Lev 6.04
affliction, our toil, and our o.; Deu 26.07
for he saw the o. of Israel, 2Ki 13.04
with cursing and deceit and o.; Ps 10.07
because of the o. of the enemy? 42.09
because of the o. of the enemy? 43.02
thou forget our affliction and o.? 44.24
because of the o. of the wicked. 55.03
o. and fraud do not depart from its 55.11
From o. and violence he redeems 72.14
speak with malice; loftily they threaten o. 73.08
diminished and brought low through o., 107.39
Redeem me from man's o., that I may 119.134
Surely o. makes the wise man Ecc 7.07
seek justice, correct o.; Is 1.17
the writers who keep writing o., 10.01
and trust in o. and perverseness, 30.12
By o. and judgment he was taken 53.08
you shall be far from o., 54.14
speaking o. and revolt, conceiving 59.13
there is nothing but o. within her. Jer 6.06
Heaping o. upon o., and deceit 9.06
and for practicing o. and violence." 22.17
Put away violence and o., Eze 45.09

OPPRESSIONS
the multitude of o. people cry out; Job 35.09
Again I saw all the o. that are Ecc 4.01
he who despises the gain of o., Is 33.15
her, and the o. in her midst." Amo 3.09

OPPRESSOR
to the needy, and crush the o.! Ps 72.04
lacks understanding is a cruel o.; Pro 28.16
The poor man and the o. meet together; 29.13
his shoulder, the rod of his o., Is 9.04
"How the o. has ceased, the insolent 14.04
When the o. is no more, and destruction 16.04
day because of the fury of the o., 51.13
And where is the fury of the o.? 51.13
the hand of the o. him who has Jer 21.12
the hand of the o. him who has 22.03
because of the sword of the o. 46.16
because of the sword of the o., 50.16
no o. shall again overrun them, for Zec 9.08

OPPRESSORS
Or, 'Ransom me from the hand of o.'? Job 6.23
heritage which o. receive from the 27.13
just and right; do not leave me to my o. Ps 119.121
side of their o. there was power, Ecc 4.01
My people—children are their o., Is 3.12
LORD because of o. he will send 19.20
I will make your o. eat their own 49.26
time I will deal with all your o. Zep 3.19

ORACLE
"The o. of Balaam the son of Beor, Num 24.03
the o. of the man whose eye is 24.03
the o. of him who hears the words 24.04
"The o. of Balaam the son of Beor, 24.15
the o. of the man whose eye is 24.15
the o. of him who hears the words 24.16
as if one consulted the o. of God; 2Sa 16.23
The o. of David, the son of Jesse, 23.01
the o. of the man who was raised on 23.01
LORD uttered this o. against him: 2Ki 9.25
The o. concerning Babylon which Is 13.01
that King Ahaz died came this o.: 14.28
An o. concerning Moab. Because Ar 15.01
An o. concerning Damascus. Behold, 17.01
An o. concerning Egypt. Behold, the 19.01
The o. concerning the wilderness of 21.01
The o. concerning Dumah. One is calling 21.11
The o. concerning Arabia. In the thickets 21.13
The o. concerning the valley of vision. 22.01
The o. concerning Tyre. Wail, O ships 23.01
An o. on the beasts of the Negeb. 30.06
This o. concerns the prince in Eze 12.10
An o. concerning Nineveh. Nah 1.01
The o. of God which Habakkuk the Hab 1.01
The o. of the word of the LORD to Mal 1.01

ORACLES
and of the many o. against him, 2Ch 24.27
seen for you o. false and misleading Lam 2.14
and their staff gives them o. Hos 4.12
received living o. to give to us. Ac 7.38
are entrusted with the o. of God. Rom 3.02
as one who utters o. of God; 1Pe 4.11

ORATION
the throne, and made an o. to them. Ac 12.21

ORCHARD
vineyard, and with your olive o. Ex 23.11
Your shoots are an o. of pomegranates Sol 4.13
I went down to the nut o., 6.11

ORCHARDS
grain, as well as the olive o. Ju 15.05
and olive o. and give them to his 1Sa 8.14
olive o. and vineyards, sheep and 2Ki 5.26
their olive o., and their houses, Neh 5.11
olive o. and fruit trees in abundance; 9.25

ORDAIN
anoint them and o. them and Ex 28.41
Thus you shall o. Aaron and his 29.09
to o. and consecrate them, but an 29.33
seven days shall you o. them, 29.35
it will take seven days to o. you. Lev 8.33
thou wilt o. peace for us, thou hast Is 26.12

ORDAINED
be anointed in them and o. in them. Ex 29.29
"Today you have o. yourselves for 32.29
whom he o. to minister in the Num 3 03
which was o. at Mount Sinai for a 28.06
the LORD had o. to defeat the good 2Sa 17.14
and he o. a feast for the people of 1Ki 12.33
of Judah had o. to burn incense in 2Ki 23.05
care for it in the way that is o. 1Ch 15.13
as o. for ever for Israel. 2Ch 2.04
But it was o. by God that the 22.07
the Jews o. and took it upon Est 9.27
as he o. long ago, he has demolished Lam 2.17
to pass, unless the Lord has o. it? 3.37
thou hast o. them as a judgment; Hab 1.12
he is the one o. by God to be Ac 10.42
as many as were o. to eternal life 13.48
and it was o. by angels through an Gal 3.19

ORDAINEST
who o. victories for Jacob. Ps 44.04

ORDEAL
at the fiery o. which comes upon 1Pe 4.12

ORDER
there, and laid the wood in o., Gen 22.09
named in the o. of their birth: 25.13
in o. that I may find favor in your 32.05
my people shall o. themselves as 41.40
in o. that you may dwell in the 46.34
stone, in the o. of their birth. Ex 28.10
and set its arrangements in o.; 40.04
the bread in o. on it before the 40.23
and lay wood in o. upon the fire; Lev 1.07
in o. upon the wood that is on the 1.08
lay them in o. upon the wood that 1.12
the burnt offering in o. upon it, 6.12
keep it in o. from evening to 24.03
the lamps in o. upon the lampstand 24.04
shall set it in o. before the LORD 24.08
This was the o. of march of the Num 10.28
to Egypt in o. to multiply horses, Deu 17.16
war against it in o. to take it, 20.19
she had laid in o. on the roof. Jos 2.06
in o. that they should be utterly 11.20
here, with stones laid in due o.; Ju 6.26
in o. to restore the name of the Ru 4.05
In o. to change the course of 2Sa 14.20
And he set his house in o., 17.23
in o. to build an altar to the LORD, 24.21
stones in o. to lay the foundation 1Ki 5.17
on the wall in o. that the supporting 6.06
in o. that all the peoples of the 8.43
And he put the wood in o., 18.33
man of God, this is the king's o., 2Ki 1.11
with cunning in o. to destroy the 10.19
the LORD, 'Set your house in o.; 20.01
and the priests of the second o., 23.04
performed their service in due o. 1Ch 6.32
men of war, arrayed in battle o., 12.38
their brethren of the second o., 15.18
were under the o. of the king. 25.06
in o. that all the peoples of the 2Ch 6.33
according to the o. of David. 23.18
in o. that he might give them into 25.20
in o. that they might take the city 32.18

ORDER (cont.)
in o. to try him and to know all 2Ch 32.31
himself in o. to fight with him. 35.22
in o. that search may be made in Ez 4.15
by o. of the officials and the 10.08
me an evil name, in o. to taunt me. Neh 6.13
the scribe in o. to study the 8.13
warned them in o. to turn them 9.26
warn them in o. to turn them back 9.29
in o. to show the peoples and the Est 1.11
let a royal o. go forth from him, 1.19
So when the king's o. and his edict 2.08
in o. to see whether Mordecai's 3.04
went in haste by o. of the king, 3.15
let an o. be written to revoke the • 8.05
set your words in o. before me; Job 33.05
ever after the o. of Melchizedek." Ps 110.04
evil way, in o. to keep thy word. 119.101
in o. that men should fear before Ecc 3.14
the LORD: Set your house in o.; Is 38.01
and the fixed o. of the moon and Jer 31.35
"If this fixed o. departs from 31.36
in o. that you may know that my 44.29
in o. to save his life, that wicked Eze 3.18
the fire upon it in o. to melt it; 22.20
All this is in o. that no trees by 31.14
burying them, in o. to cleanse the land. 39.12
brought here in o. that I might 40.04
in o. not to bring them out into 46.20
but in o. that the interpretation Dan 2.30
Because the king's o. was strict and 3.22
themselves up in o. to fulfil the 11.14
a hairy mantle in o. to deceive, Zec 13.04
before men in o. to be seen by Mt 6.01
it empty, swept, and put in o. 12.44
together in o. to arrest Jesus by 26.04
Therefore o. the sepulchre to be 27.64
in o. to keep your tradition! Mk 7.09
came up and in o. to test him 10.02
priests in o. to betray him to 14.10
he finds it swept and put in o. Lk 11.25
in o. that those who would pass 16.26
in o. to prevent the bodies from Jn 19.31
But in o. that it may spread no Ac 4.17
began and explained to them in o.: 11.04
to the law you o. me to be struck?" 23.03
in o. that I may reap some harvest Rom 1.13
in o. that the promise may rest on 4.16
the dead in o. that we may bear 7.04
in o. that sin might be shown to be 7.13
in o. that the just requirement of 8.04
with him in o. that we may also be 8.17
in o. that he might be the first-born 8.29
in o. that God's purpose of election 9.11
in o. to make known the riches of 9.23
in o. to make my fellow Jews 11.14
disobedient in o. that by the 11.31
in o. to confirm the promises given 15.08
and in o. that the Gentiles might 15.09
to promote good o. and to secure 1Co 7.35
became as a Jew, in o. to win Jews; 9.20
among you in o. that those who are 11.19
in o. to instruct others, than ten 14.19
should be done decently and in o. 14.40
But each in his own o.: Christ the first 15.23
but in o. that your zeal for us 2Co 7.12
from them in o. to serve you. 11.08
in o. to undermine the claim of 11.12
of Damascus in o. to seize me, 11.32
in o. that when I come I may not 13.10
in o. that I might preach him among Gal 1.16
in o. to be justified by faith in 2.16
and only in o. that they may not be 6.12
as refuse, in o. that I may gain Christ Php 3.08
in o. to present you holy and Col 1.22
I say this in o. that no one may 2.04
see your good o. and the firmness 2.05
in o. that he might serve me on Phm 1.13
your consent in o. that your 1.14
ever, after the o. of Melchizedek." Heb 5.06
priest after the o. of Melchizedek. 5.10
ever after the o. of Melchizedek. 6.20
arise after the o. of Melchizedek, 7.11
one named after the o. of Aaron? 7.11
ever, after the o. of Melchizedek." 7.17
the first in o. to establish the 10.09
not endure the o. that was given, 12.20
in o. that what cannot be shaken 12.27
the gate in o. to sanctify the 13.12
to do this in o. that I may be 13.19
in o. that your prayers may not be 1Pe 3.07
in o. that in everything God may be 4.11

ORDERED
And the king o. Joab and Abishai 2Sa 18.05
o. in all things and secure. 23.05
And Jehu o., "Sanctify a solemn 2Ki 10.20
because he o. his ways before the 2Ch 27.06
what Darius the king had o. Ez 6.13
and o. him to go to Mordecai to Est 4.05
everything as Esther had o. him. 4.17
A man's steps are o. by the LORD; Pro 20.24
And Jeremiah o. Baruch, saying, "I am Jer 36.05
the prophet o. him about reading 36.08
He o. the furnace heated seven Dan 3.19
And he o. certain mighty men of his 3.20
and o. them not to make him known. Mt 12.16
Then he o. the crowds to sit down 14.19
his lord o. him to be sold, with his 18.25
Then Pilate o. it to be given to 27.58
And he strictly o. them not to make Mk 3.12
stood up and o. the men to be put Ac 5.34
sentries and o. that they should 12.19
and o. him to be bound with two 21.33
he o. him to be brought into the 21.34
and o. him to be examined by 22.24
tribunal and o. Paul to be brought 25.06
tribunal and o. the man to be 25.17
He o. those who could swim to throw 27.43

ORDERING
o. his accusers also to state Ac 23.30

ORDERLY
to write an o. account for you, most Lk 1.03

ORDERS
Pharaoh gave men o. concerning him; Gen 12.20
And Joseph gave o. to fill their 42.25
the LORD to battle, as my lord o." Num 32.27
and I will give o. concerning you." 2Sa 14.08
the king gave o. to all the 18.05
Then I have o. and they cleansed Neh 13.09
shut and gave o. that they should 13.19
king had given o. to all the Est 1.08
and he gave o. to bring the book of 6.01
he gave o. in writing that his 9.25
to him who o. his way aright I will Ps 50.23
So King Zedekiah gave o., Jer 37.21
he gave o. to go over to the other Mt 8.18
guard and gave o. to bring his Mk 6.27
had given o. that if any one knew Jn 11.57
them and gave o. to beat them with Ac 16.22
Then he gave o. to the centurion 24.23

ORDINANCE
shall observe it as an o. for ever. Ex 12.14
generations, as an o. for ever. 12.17
this rite as an o. for you and for 12.24
"This is the o. of the passover: no 12.43
keep this o. at its appointed time 13.10
statute and an o. and there he 15.25
burnt offering according to the o.; Lev 5.10
and offered it according to the o. 9.16
passover and according to its o., Num 9.14

ORDINANCE (cont.)

One law and one o. shall be for you Num 15.16
offering, according to the o., 15.24
people of Israel a statute and o., 27.11
according to the o. for them, 29.06
by number according to the o.; 29.18
by number according to the o.; 29.21
by number according to the o.; 29.24
by number according to the o.; 29.27
by number according to the o.; 29.30
their number according to the o.; 29.33
their number according to the o.; 29.37
a statute and o. to you throughout 35.29
statute and an o. for Israel to 1Sa 30.25
According to the o. of David his 2Ch 8.14
lamb with fire according to the o.; 35.13
They made these an o. in Israel; 35.25
by number according to the o., Ez 3.04
assembly, according to the o. Neh 8.18
for Israel, an o. of the God of Jacob. Ps 81.04
did not forsake the o. of their God; Is 58.02
people know not the o. of the LORD. Jer 8.07
this is the o. for the continual Eze 46.14
establish an o. and enforce an Dan 6.07
no interdict or o. which the king 6.15

ORDINANCES

"Now these are the o. which you Ex 21.01
words of the LORD and all the o.; 24.03
You shall do my o. and keep my Lev 18.04
therefore keep my statutes and my o., 18.05
statutes and my o. and do none of 18.26
all my statutes and all my o., 19.37
statutes and all my o., and do them; 20.22
and keep my o. and perform them; 25.18
and if your soul abhors my o., 26.15
iniquity, because they spurned my o., 26.43
statutes and o. and laws which the 26.46
and all its o. you shall keep it." Num 9.03
blood, in accordance with these o.; 35.24
commandments and the o. which the 36.13
statutes and the o. which I teach Deu 4.01
Behold, I have taught you statutes and o., 4.05
statutes and o. so righteous as 4.08
time to teach you statutes and o., 4.14
and the o., which Moses spoke to 4.45
statutes and the o. which I speak 5.01
statutes and the o. which you shall 5.31
statutes and the o. which the LORD 6.01
statutes and the o. which the LORD 6.20
and the o., which I command you 7.11
"And because you hearken to these o., 7.12
commandments and his o. and his 8.11
his o., and his commandments always 11.01
statutes and the o. which I set 11.32
statutes and o. which you shall be 12.01
you to do these statutes and o.; 26.16
and his commandments and his o., 26.17
and his statutes and his o., 30.16
They shall teach Jacob thy o., 33.10
statutes and o. for them at Jos 24.25
For all his o. were before me, and 2Sa 22.23
his o., and his testimonies, as it 1Ki 2.03
and obey my o. and keep all my 6.12
and his o., which he commanded our 8.58
and keeping my statutes and my o., 9.04
and keeping my statutes and my o., 11.33
statutes or the o. or the law or 2Ki 17.34
statutes and the o. and the law and 17.37
statutes and the o. which the LORD 1Ch 22.13
keeping my commandments and my o., 28.07
and keeping my statutes and my o., 2Ch 7.17
statutes or o., then you shall 19.10
and the o. given through Moses." 33.08
his statutes and o. in Israel. Ez 7.10
and the o. which thou didst command Neh 1.07
give them right o. and true laws, 9.13
commandments, but sinned against thy o., 9.29
Lord and his o. and his statutes. 10.29
Do you know the o. of the heavens? Job 38.33
For all his o. were before me, and Ps 18.22
the o. of the LORD are true, and 19.09
do not walk according to my o., 89.30
heart, when I learn thy righteous o. 119.07
I declare all the o. of thy mouth. 119.13
longing for thy o. at all times. 119.20
faithfulness, I set thy o. before me. 119.30
which I dread; for thy o. are good. 119.39
my mouth, for my hope is in thy o. 119.43
When I think of thy o. from of old, 119.52
thee, because of thy righteous o. 119.62
I do not turn aside from thy o., 119.102
it, to observe thy righteous o. 119.106
O LORD, and teach me thy o. 119.108
thy righteous o. endures for ever. 119.160
I praise thee for thy righteous o. 119.164
thee, and let thy o. help me. 119.175
his statutes and o. to Israel. 147.19
they do not know his o. Praise the 147.20
night and the o. of heaven and Jer 33.25
against my o. more than the nations, Eze 5.06
by rejecting my o. and not walking 5.06
in my statutes or kept my o., 5.07
according to the o. of the nations 5.07
in my statutes, nor executed my o., 11.12
according to the o. of the nations 11.12
and keep my o. and obey them; 11.20
and is careful to observe my o.— 18.09
observes my o., and walks in my 18.17
my statutes and showed them my o., 20.11
in my statutes but rejected my o., 20.13
rejected my o. and did not walk in 20.16
your fathers, nor observe their o., 20.18
and be careful to observe my o., 20.19
were not careful to observe my o., 20.21
because they had not executed my o., 20.24
not good and o. by which they 20.25
and be careful to observe my o. 36.27
shall follow my o. and be careful 37.24
to them all its o. and all its laws; 43.11
all its laws and all its o. 43.11
These are the o. for the altar: On 43.18
concerning all the o. of the temple 44.05
aside from thy commandments and o.; Dan 9.05
statutes and o. that I commanded Mal 4.04
commandments and o. of the Lord Lk 1.06
the law of commandments and o., Eph 2.15

ORDINARY

poured upon the bodies of o. men, Ex 30.32
shall be for o. use for the city, Eze 48.15
flesh, and behaving like o. men? 1Co 3.03

ORDINATION

thigh (for it is a ram of o.), Ex 29.22
ram of Aaron's o. and wave it for 29.26
is offered from the ram of o., 29.27
"You shall take the ram of o., 29.31
And if any of the flesh for the o., 29.34
the other ram, the ram of o.; Lev 8.22
as an o. offering, a pleasing odor, 8.28
Moses' portion of the ram of o., 8.29
is in the basket of o. offerings, 8.31
the days of your o. are completed, 8.33

ORE

and copper is smelted from the o. Job 28.02
bound the o. in gloom and deep 28.03

OREB

two princes of Midian, O. and Zeeb; Ju 7.25
they killed O. at the rock of O., 7.25
the heads of O. and Zeeb to Gideon 7.25
the princes of Midian, O. and Zeeb; 8.03

OREB (cont.)
Make their nobles like O. and Zeeb, Ps 83.11
he smote Midian at the rock of O.; Is 10.26

OREN
first-born, Bunah, O., Ozem, and Ahijah. 1Ch 2.25

ORGAN
If all were a single o., where would 1Co 12.19

ORGANIZED
And David o. them in divisions 1Ch 23.06
David o. them according to the 24.03
they o. them under sixteen heads of 24.04
They o. them by lot, all alike, for 24.05
whom David had o. to be in charge 2Ch 23.18

ORGANS
God arranged the o. in the body, 1Co 12.18

ORGIES
the o. on the mountains. Truly in the Jer 3.23

ORIGIN
city whose o. is from days of old, Is 23.07
Your o. and your birth are of the Eze 16.03
created, in the land of your o., 21.30
of Pathros, the land of their o.; 29.14
whose o. is from of old, from Mic 5.02
who are sanctified have all one o. Heb 2.11

ORIGINATE
Did the word of God o. with you, 1Co 14.36

ORION
who made the Bear and O., the Pleiades Job 9.09
Pleiades, or loose the cords of O.? 38.31
He who made the Pleiades and O., Amo 5.08

ORNAMENT
gold ring or an o. of gold is a Pro 25.12
you shall put them all on as an o., Is 49.18
Their beautiful o. they used for Eze 7.20

ORNAMENTS
and to her mother costly o. Gen 24.53
they mourned; and no man put on his o. Ex 33.04
So now put off your o. from you, 33.05
stripped themselves of their o., 33.06
who put o. of gold upon your 2Sa 1.24
Your cheeks are comely with o., Sol 1.10
We will make you o. of gold, 1.11
Can a maiden forget her o., Jer 2.32
you deck yourself with o. of gold, 4.30
And I decked you with o., Eze 16.11
eyes, and decked yourself with o.; 23.40

ORNAN
threshing floor of O. the Jebusite. 1Ch 21.15
threshing floor of O. the Jebusite. 21.18
Now O. was threshing wheat; 21.20
As David came to O., O. looked and 21.21
And David said to O., "Give me the 21.22
Then O. said to David, "Take it; 21.23
But King David said to O., 21.24
So David paid O. six hundred shekels 21.25
threshing floor of O. the Jebusite, 21.28
threshing floor of O. the Jebusite. 2Ch 3.01

ORPAH
of the one was O. and the name of Ru 1.04
and O. kissed her mother-in-law, but 1.14

ORPHAN
You shall not afflict any widow or o. Ex 22.22
our hands. In thee the o. finds mercy." Hos 14.03
in his wages, the widow and the o., Mal 3.05

ORPHANS
We have become o., fatherless; Lam 5.03
to visit o. and widows in their Jas 1.27

OSNAPPAR
great and noble O. deported and Ez 4.10

OSPREY
the eagle, the ossifrage, the o., Lev 11.13
the eagle, the vulture, the o., Deu 14.12

OSSIFRAGE
the eagle, the o., the osprey, Lev 11.13

OSTRICH
the o., the nighthawk, the sea gull, Lev 11.16
the o., the nighthawk, the sea gull, Deu 14.15
"The wings of the o. wave proudly; Job 39.13

OSTRICHES
of jackals, and a companion of o. Job 30.29
there o. will dwell, and there Is 13.21
haunt of jackals, an abode for o. 34.13
honor me, the jackals and the o.; 43.20
and o. shall dwell in her; Jer 50.39
like the o. in the wilderness. Lam 4.03
jackals, and mourning like the o. Mic 1.08

OTHER
subtle than any o. wild creature Gen 3.01
and the name of the o. Zillah. 4.19
and he had o. sons and daughters. 5.04
and had o. sons and daughters. 5.07
and had o. sons and daughters. 5.10
and had o. sons and daughters. 5.13
and had o. sons and daughters. 5.16
and had o. sons and daughters. 5.19
and had o. sons and daughters. 5.22
and had o. sons and daughters. 5.26
and had o. sons and daughters. 5.30
and had o. sons and daughters. 11.11
and had o. sons and daughters. 11.13
and had o. sons and daughters. 11.15
and had o. sons and daughters. 11.17
and had o. sons and daughters. 11.19
and had o. sons and daughters. 11.21
and had o. sons and daughters. 11.23
and had o. sons and daughters. 11.25
thus they separated from each o. 13.11
laid each half over against the o.; 15.10
one shall be stronger than the o., 25.23
This is none o. than the house of 28.17
I should give her to any o. man; 29.19
give you the o. also in return for 29.27
when we are absent one from the o. 31.49
more than any o. of his children, 37.03
seven o. cows, gaunt and thin, came 41.03
stood by the o. cows on the bank 41.03
and seven o. cows came up after 41.19
send back your o. brother and 43.14
and we have brought o. money down 43.22
from one end of Egypt to the o. 47.21
named Shiphrah and the o. Puah, Ex 1.15
Lord, send, I pray, some o. person. 4.13
and all the o. chariots of Egypt 14.07
one coming near the o. all night. 14.20
and the o. on the o. side; 17.12
and the name of the o., Eliezer 18.04
they asked each o. of their welfare, 18.07
"You shall have no o. gods before me. 20.03
one strikes the o. with a stone or 21.18
no mention of the names of o. gods, 23.13
and two rings on the o. side of it. 25.12
end, and one cherub on the o. end; 25.19
lampstand out of the o. side of it; 25.32
on the o. branch—so for the six 25.33
and the o. five curtains shall be 26.03
one to the o. with the clasps, that 26.06

OTHER (cont.)
side, and the cubit on the o. side, Ex 26.13
frames of the o. side of the 26.27
On the o. side the hangings shall 27.15
the remaining six on the o. stone, 28.10
"You shall take the o. ram; and Aaron 29.19
and the o. lamb you shall offer in 29.39
And the o. lamb you shall offer in 29.41
shall make no o. like it in 30.32
side and on the o. were they 32.15
from all o. people that are upon 33.16
(for you shall worship no o. god, 34.14
and the o. five curtains he coupled 36.10
curtains one to the o. with clasps; 36.13
the edge of the o. connecting 36.17
frames of the o. side of the 36.32
side and two rings on its o. side. 37.03
end, and one cherub on the o. end; 37.08
lampstand out of the o. side of it; 37.18
on the o. branch—so for the six 37.19
And so for the o. side; on this hand 38.15
offering and the o. for a burnt Lev 5.07
and put on o. garments, and carry 6.11
beasts, may be put to any o. use, 7.24
Then he presented the o. ram, 8.22
But all o. winged insects which 11.23
offering and the o. for a sin 12.08
offering and the o. a burnt offering. 14.22
offering and the o. for a burnt offering, 14.31
then they shall take o. stones and 14.42
he shall take o. plaster and 14.42
offering and the o. for a burnt 15.15
offering and the o. for a burnt 15.30
the LORD and the o. lot for Azazel. 16.08
and some man o. than your husband Num 5.20
offering and the o. for a burnt 6.11
offering and the o. for a burnt 8.12
and the o. named Medad, and the 11.26
and a day's journey on the o. side, 11.31
encamped on the o. side of the 21.13
as at o. times, to meet with omens, 24.01
and the o. lamb you shall offer in 28.04
The o. lamb you shall offer in the 28.08
them on the o. side of the Jordan 32.19
and they gave o. names to the 32.38
the sons of the o. tribes of the 36.03
from one end of heaven to the o., Deu 4.32
there is no o. besides him. 4.35
the earth beneath; there is no o. 4.39
shall have no o. gods before me. 5.07
You shall not go after o. gods, 6.14
following me, to serve o. gods; 7.04
number than any o. people that the 7.07
and go after o. gods and serve 8.19
aside and serve o. gods and 11.16
to go after o. gods which you have 11.28
he says, 'Let us go after o. gods, 13.02
'Let us go and serve o. gods, 13.06
one end of the earth to the o., 13.07
'Let us go and serve o. gods, 13.13
gone and served o. gods and 17.03
who speaks in the name of o. gods, 18.20
shall add three o. cities to these 19.09
the one loved and the o. disliked, 21.15
to go after o. gods to serve them. 28.14
and there you shall serve o. gods, 28.36
one end of the earth to the o.; 28.64
and there you shall serve o. gods, 28.64
and went and served o. gods and 29.26
away to worship o. gods and serve 30.17
they have turned to o. gods. 31.18
will turn to o. gods and serve 31.20
With the o. half of the tribe of Jos 13.08
which is on the o. side of the 17.05
it goes in the o. direction 19.12
gave you on the o. side of the 22.04
but to the o. half Joshua had given 22.07
an altar o. than the altar of the 22.19
o. than the altar of the LORD our 22.29
go and serve o. gods and bow down 23.16
of Nahor; and they served o. gods. 24.02
lived on the o. side of the Jordan; 24.08
forsake the LORD, to serve o. gods; 24.16
they went after o. gods, from among the Ju 2.12
harlot after o. gods and bowed 2.17
going after o. gods, serving them 2.19
"This is no o. than the sword of 7.14
forsaken me and served o. gods; 10.13
camped on the o. side of the Arnon; 11.18
came to me the o. day has appeared 13.10
weak, and be like any o. man." 16.07
weak, and be like any o. man." 16.11
weak, and be like any o. man." 16.13
weak, and be like any o. man." 16.17
said, "I will go out as at o. times, 16.20
one and his left hand on the o. 16.29
against Gibeah, as at o. times. 20.30
and as at o. times they began to 20.31
up to Bethel and the o. to Gibeah, 20.31
Orpah and the name of the o. Ruth. Ru 1.04
his sandal and gave it to the o., 4.07
and the name of the o. Peninnah. 1Sa 1.02
calling as at o. times, "Samuel! 3.10
forsaking me and serving o. gods, 8.08
and a rocky crag on the o. side; 14.04
and the name of the o. Seneh. 14.04
and the o. on the south in front of 14.05
my son will be on the o. side." 14.40
on the mountain on the o. side, 17.03
he sent o. messengers, and they also 19.21
as at o. times, upon the seat by the 20.25
his men on the o. side of the 23.26
Then David went over to the o. side, 26.13
LORD, saying, 'Go, serve o. gods.' 26.19
himself and put on o. garments, 28.08
who were on the o. side of the 31.07
and the o. on the o. side of the pool. 2Sa 2.13
and the name of the o. Rechab, 4.02
What o. nation on earth is like thy 7.23
city, the one rich and the o. poor. 12.01
than the o. which you did to me." 13.16
one struck the o. and killed him. 14.06
of the pits, or in some o. place. 17.09
On the o. hand, if I had dealt 18.13
so that no o. king shall compare 1Ki 3.13
But the o. woman said, "No, the 3.22
and the o. says, 'No; 3.23
to the one, and half to the o." 3.25
But the o. said, "It shall be 3.26
as far as the o. side of Jokmeam; 4.12
For he was wiser than all o. men, 4.31
length of the o. wing of the 6.24
of one wing to the tip of the o. 6.24
The o. cherub also measured ten 6.25
and so was that of the o. cherub. 6.26
a wing of the o. cherub touched the o. 6.27
their o. wings touched each o. 6.27
leaves of the o. door were folding 6.34
in the o. court back of the hall, 7.08
height of the o. capital was five 7.16
and a net for the o. capital. 7.17
did the same with the o. capital. 7.18
and so with the o. capital. 7.20
LORD is God; there is no o. 8.60
go and serve o. gods and worship 9.06
of Egypt, and laid hold on o. gods, 9.09
away his heart after o. gods; 11.04
he should not go after o. gods; 11.10
Bethel, and the o. he put in Dan. 12.29
Bethel and to the o. as far as Dan. 12.30
gone and made for yourself o. gods, 14.09
prepare the o. bull and lay it on 18.23
to the one side and to the o., 2Ki 2.08
to the one side and to the o.; 2.14

OTHER (cont.)

was filled from one end to the o. 2Ki 10.21
priest and the o. priests and said 12.07
of Egypt, and had feared o. gods 17.07
shall not fear o. gods or bow 17.35
You shall not fear o. gods, 17.37
You shall not fear o. gods, 17.38
and have burned incense to o. gods, 22.17
of Kiriathjearim had o. sons: 1Ch 2.52
of the temple free from o. service, 9.33
What o. nation on earth is like thy 17.21
Eliezer had no o. sons, but the sons of 23.17
and its o. wing, of five cubits, 2Ch 3.11
touched the wing of the o. cherub; 3.11
and the o. wing, also of five cubits, 3.12
on the south, the o. on the north; 3.17
and cymbals and o. musical instruments, 5.13
go and serve o. gods and worship 7.19
of Egypt, and laid hold on o. gods, 7.22
like the peoples of o. lands? 13.09
places to burn incense to o. gods, 28.25
so until o. priests had sanctified 29.34
to all the peoples of o. lands? 32.13
and have burned incense to o. gods, 34.25
to do with each o., king of Judah? 35.21
silver, and a thousand o. vessels; Ez 1.10
The sons of the o. Elam, 2.31
or o. servants of this house of God. 7.24
and with the o. held his weapon. Neh 4.17
for o. men have our fields and our 5.05
The men of the o. Nebo, fifty-two. 7.33
The sons of the o. Elam, 7.34
and o. leafy trees to make booths, 8.15
nine tenths remained in the o. towns. 11.01
The o. company of those who gave 12.38
from those of every o. people, Est 3.08
any more than all the o. Jews. 4.13
Now the o. Jews who were in the 9.16
they wither before any o. plant. Job 8.12
they clasp each o. and cannot be 41.17
They are not in trouble as o. men are; Ps 73.05
they are not stricken like o. men. 73.05
and peace will kiss each o. 85.10
not dealt thus with any o. nation; 147.20
until the o. comes and examines him Pro 18.17
as one dies, so dies the o. Ecc 3.19
has made the one as well as the o., 7.14
o. lords besides thee have ruled Is 26.13
my glory I give to no o., 42.08
I am the LORD, and there is no o., 45.05
I am the LORD, and there is no o. 45.06
with you only, and there is no o., 45.14
"I am the LORD, and there is no o. 45.18
and there is no o. god besides me, 45.21
For I am God, and there is no o. 45.22
for I am God, and there is no o.; 46.09
have burned incense to o. gods, Jer 1.16
do not go after o. gods to your 7.06
and go after o. gods that you have 7.09
out drink offerings to o. gods, 7.18
have gone after o. gods to serve 11.10
from one end of the land to the o.; 12.12
have gone after o. gods to serve 13.10
have gone after o. gods and have 16.11
you shall serve o. gods day and 16.13
in it to o. gods whom neither they 19.04
have been poured out to o. gods— 19.13
and worshiped o. gods and served 22.09
but the o. basket had very bad figs, 24.02
do not go after o. gods to serve 25.06
one end of the earth to the o. 25.33
have been poured out to o. gods, 32.29
do not go after o. gods to serve 35.15
in Edom and in o. lands heard that 40.11
and serve o. gods that they knew 44.03
and burn no incense to o. gods. 44.05
incense to o. gods in the land of 44.08
had offered incense to o. gods, 44.15
turn from one side to the o., Eze 4.08
and keep o. souls alive for your 13.18
different from o. women in your 16.34
Judah is like all the o. nations, 25.08
side room to the back of the o., 40.13
and on the o. side of the vestibule 40.40
the o. at the side of the south 40.44
the palm tree on the o. side. 41.19
shall put on o. garments before 42.14
and they shall put on o. garments, 44.19
on the one side and on the o. 47.07
and their o. garments, and they were Dan 3.21
for there is no o. god who is able 3.29
above all the o. presidents and 6.03
and the o. horn which came up and 7.20
but one was higher than the o., 8.03
shall not give heed to any o. god, 11.37
they turn to o. gods and love Hos 3.01
of the bowl and the o. on its left. Zec 4.03
named Grace, the o. I named Union. 11.07
northward, and the o. half southward. 14.04
raised against the hand of the o.; 14.13
from there he saw two o. brothers, Mt 4.21
cheek turn to him the o. also; 5.39
will hate the one and love the o., 6.24
to the one and despise the o. 6.24
orders to go over to the o. side. 8.18
And when he came to the o. side, 8.28
it was restored, whole like the o. 12.13
with him seven o. spirits more 12.45
O. seeds fell on rocky ground, where 13.05
O. seeds fell upon thorns, and the 13.07
O. seeds fell on good soil and 13.08
and go before him to the o. side, 14.22
When the disciples reached the o. side, 16.05
Again he sent o. servants, more than 21.36
the vineyard to o. tenants who 21.41
Again he sent o. servants, saying, 22.04
from one end of heaven to the o. 24.31
Afterward the o. maidens came also, 25.11
Magdalene and the o. Mary were 27.61
Magdalene and the o. Mary went to 28.01
O. seed fell on rocky ground, where Mk 4.05
O. seed fell among thorns and the 4.07
And o. seeds fell into good soil 4.08
and the desire for o. things, 4.19
"Let us go across to the o. side." 4.35
And o. boats were with him. 4.36
They came to the o. side of the sea, 5.01
again in the boat to the o. side, 5.21
and go before him to the o. side, 6.45
there are many o. traditions which 7.04
again he departed to the o. side. 8.13
He had still one o., a beloved son; 12.06
There is no o. commandment greater 12.31
is one, and there is no o. but he; 12.32
and also many o. women who came up 15.41
So, with many o. exhortations, he Lk 3.18
of God to the o. cities also; 4.43
partners in the o. boat to come 5.07
on the cheek, offer the o. also; 6.29
hundred denarii, and the o. fifty. 7.41
across to the o. side of the lake. 8.22
him he passed by on the o. side. 10.31
saw him, passed by on the o. side. 10.32
brings seven o. spirits more evil 11.26
sinners than all the o. Galileans, 13.02
while the o. is yet a great way off, 14.32
will hate the one and love the o., 16.13
to the one and despise the o. 16.13
up the sky from one side to the o., 17.24
one will be taken and the o. left. 17.34
one will be taken and the o. left." 17.35
one will be taken and the o. left" * 17.36
Pharisee and the o. a tax collector. 18.10
thee that I am not like o. men, 18.11

OTHER (cont.)
house justified rather than the o.; Lk 18.14
And they spoke many o. words 22.65
friends with each o. that very day, 23.12
had been at enmity with each o. 23.12
But the o. rebuked him, saying, "Do 23.40
James and the o. women with them 24.10
with each o. about all these 24.14
holding with each o. as you walk?" 24.17
They said to each o., "Did not our 24.32
went to the o. side of the Sea of Jn 6.01
remained on the on. side of the sea 6.22
him on the o. side of the sea, they 6.25
And I have o. sheep, that are not of 10.16
So the o. disciple, who was known to 18.16
and of the o. who had been crucified 19.32
to Simon Peter and the o. disciple, 20.02
then came out with the o. disciple, 20.03
but the o. disciple outran Peter 20.04
Then the o. disciple, who reached 20.08
So the o. disciples told him, "We 20.25
Now Jesus did many o. signs in the 20.30
But the o. disciples came in the 21.08
are also many o. things which 21.25
and began to speak in o. tongues, Ac 2.04
with many o. words and exhorted 2.40
for there is no o. name under 4.12
brethren, why do you wrong each o.?' 7.26
of John whose o. name was Mark, 12.12
them John whose o. name was Mark. 12.25
that they separated from each o.; 15.39
Sadducees and the o. Pharisees, 23.06
Paul and some o. prisoners to a 27.01
and any o. commandment, are summed Rom 13.09
For no o. foundation can any one 1Co 3.11
will destroy both one and the o. 6.13
Every o. sin which a man commits is 6.18
as the o. apostles and the brothers 9.05
we recognize no o. practice, 11.16
About the o. things I will give 11.34
On the o. hand, he who prophesies 14.03
but the o. man is not edified. 14.17
of wheat or of some o. grain. 15.37
to visit you with the o. brethren, 16.12
to the o. a fragrance from life to 2Co 2.16
beyond limit, in o. men's labors; 10.15
I robbed o. churches by accepting 11.08
apart from o. things, there is the 11.28
saw none of the o. apostles except Gal 1.19
you will take no o. view than mine; 5.10
for these are opposed to each o., 5.17
sons of men in o. generations as Eph 3.05
If any o. man thinks he has reason Php 3.04
against another, forgiving each o.; Col 3.13
on the o. hand, a better hope is Heb 7.19
or by earth or with any o. oath, Jas 5.12
with seven o. persons, when he 2Pe 2.05
as they do the o. scriptures. 3.16
do not lay upon you any o. burden; Rev 2.24
blasts of the o. trumpets which 8.13
the o. has not yet come, and when he 17.10

OTHER'S
encouraged by each o. faith, Rom 1.12

OTHERS
came to buy among the o. who came, Gen 42.05
but the o. shall not come near, and Ex 24.02
And the o. came forth from the city Jos 8.22
and let all the o. go every man to Ju 7.07
O. of them were appointed over the 1Ch 9.29
O., of the sons of the priests, 9.30
out of the earth o. will spring. Job 8.19
and let o. bow down upon her. 31.10
investigation, and sets o. in their place. 34.24
and leave their wealth to o. Ps 49.10
your honor to o. and your years to Pro 5.09
times you have yourself cursed o. Ecc 7.22
will gather yet. to him besides Is 56.08
Their houses shall be turned over to o., Jer 6.12
their wives to o. and their fields 8.10
the son of Achbor and o. with him, 26.22
And to the o. he said in my hearing, Eze 9.05
wheel faced the o. followed 10.11
they had the same size as the o. 40.24
vestibule, like the windows of the o.; 40.25
it was of the same size as the o. 40.28
were of the same size as the o.; 40.29
it was of the same size as the o. 40.32
were of the same size as the o.; 40.33
it had the same size as the o. 40.35
were of the same size as the o.; 40.36
in place of which four o. arose, Dan 8.22
up and go to o. besides these. 11.04
two o. stood, one on this bank of 12.05
what more are you doing than o.? Mt 5.47
and many o., and they put them at 15.30
o. say Elijah, and others Jeremiah 16.14
and o. Jeremiah or one of the 16.14
From their sons or from o.?" 17.25
"From on," Jesus said to him, "Then 17.26
take one or two o. along with you, 18.16
hour he saw o. standing idle in 20.03
he went out and found o. standing; 20.06
and o. cut branches from the trees 21.08
done, without neglecting the o. 23.23
"He saved o.; he cannot save 27.42
But the o. said, "Wait, let us see 27.49
And o. are the ones sown among Mk 4.18
But o. said, "It is Elijah." 6.15
And o. said, "It is a prophet, like 6.15
the Baptist; and o. say, Elijah; 8.28
and o. one of the prophets." 8.28
and o. spread leafy branches which 11.08
and so with many o., some they beat 12.05
and give the vineyard to o. 12.09
the scribes, saying, "He saved o.; 15.31
collectors and o. sitting at table Lk 5.29
and many o., who provided for them 8.03
but for o. they are in parables, so 8.10
and by o. that one of the old 9.08
the Baptist; but o. say, Elijah; 9.19
and o., that one of the old prophets 9.19
this the LORD appointed seventy o., 10.01
while o., to test him, sought from 11.16
done, without neglecting the o. 11.42
than all the o. who dwelt in 13.04
were righteous and despised o.: 18.09
and give the vineyard to o." 20.16
Two o. also, who were criminals, were 23.32
at him, saying, "He saved o.; 23.35
o. have labored, and you have Jn 4.38
o. said, "No, he is leading the people astray." 7.12
O. said, "This is the Christ." 7.41
o. said "No, but he is like him." 9.09
But o. said, "How can a man who is 9.16
O. said, "These are not the sayings 10.21
O. said, "An angel has spoken to him 12.29
or did o. say it to you about me?" 18.34
crucified him, and with him two o., 19.18
and two o. of his disciples were 21.02
But o. mocking said, "They are Ac 2.13
aliens in a land belonging to o., 7.06
and some of the o. were appointed 15.02
of the LORD, with many o. also. 15.35
O. said, "He seems to be a preacher 17.18
but o. said, "We will hear you again 17.32
named Damaris and o. with them. 17.34
what he said, while o. disbelieved. 28.24
you then who teach o., will you not Rom 2.21
And even the o., if they do not 11.23
any one to make o. fall by what he 14.20
If to o. I am not an apostle, at 1Co 9.02
If o. share this rightful claim 9.12
preaching to o. I myself should be 9.27

OTHERS (cont.)
my mind, in order to instruct o., 1Co 14.19
and let the o. weigh what is said. 14.29
earnestness of o. that your love 2Co 8.08
not mean that o. should be eased 8.13
contribution for them and for all o.; 9.13
who sinned before and all the o., 13.02
and rivalry, but o. from good will. Php 1.15
humility count o. better than 2.03
but also to the interests of o. 2.04
men, whether from you or from o., 1Th 206
not grieve as o. do who have no 4.13
as o. do, but let us keep awake and 5.06
but the sins of o. appear later. 1Ti 5.24
who will be able to teach o. also. 2Ti 2.02
O. suffered mocking and scourging, Heb 11.36

OTHERWISE
O. it will come to pass, when my 1Ki 1.21
the passover o. than as prescribed. 2Ch 30.18
O., when he has laid a foundation, Lk 14.29
o. grace would no longer be grace. Rom 11.06
o. you too will be cut off. 11.22
O., your children would be unclean, 1Co 7.14
O., if you bless with the spirit, 14.16
O., what do people mean by being 15.29
if in anything you are o. minded, Php 3.15
If any one teaches o. and does not 1Ti 6.03
O., would they not have ceased to Heb 10.02

OTHNI
O., Rephael, Obed, and Elzabad, whose 1Ch 26.07

OTHNIEL
And O. the son of Kenaz, the brother Jos 15.17
And O. the son of Kenaz, Caleb's Ju 1.13
O. the son of Kenaz, Caleb's younger 3.09
Then O. the son of Kenaz died. 3.11
The sons of Kenaz: O. and Seraiah; 1Ch 4.13
and the sons of O.: Hathath and Meonothai. 4.13
was Heldai the Netophathite, of O.; 27.15

OUGHT
me things that o. not to be done. Gen 20.09
for such a thing o. not to be done. 34.07
You certainly o. to have eaten it Lev 10.18
will know what you o. to do to him, 1Ki 2.09
to know what Israel o. to do, 1Ch 12.32
O. you not to know that the LORD 2Ch 13.05
O. you not to walk in the fear of Neh 5.09
these you o. to have done, without Mt 23.23
Then you o. to have invested my 25.27
set up where it o. not to be (let Mk 13.14
these you o. to have done, without Lk 11.42
that very hour what you o. to say." 12.12
days on which work o. to be done; 13.14
And o. not this woman, a daughter of 13.16
that they o. always to pray and 18.01
the place where men o. to worship." Jn 4.20
you also o. to wash one another's 13.14
law, and by that law he o. to die, 19.07
we o. not to think that the Deity Ac 17.29
you o. to be quiet and do nothing 19.36
the earth! For he o. not to live." 22.22
they o. to be here before you and 24.19
tribunal, where I o. to be tried; 25.10
shouting that he o. not to live any 25.24
convinced that I o. to do many 26.09
do not know how to pray as we o., Rom 8.26
more highly than he o. to think, 12.03
We who are strong o. to bear with 15.01
they o. also to be of service to 15.27
O. you not rather to mourn? Let him 1Co 5.02
does not yet know as he o. to know. 8.02
For a man o. not to cover his head, 11.07
That is why a woman o. to have a 11.10
for I o. to have been commended by 2Co 12.11
for children o. not to lay up for 12.14
it boldly, as I o. to speak. Eph 6.20
make it clear, as I o. to speak. Col 4.04
know how you o. to answer every 4.06
from us how you o. to live and to 1Th 4.01
know how you o. to imitate us; 2Th 3.07
know how one o. to behave in the 1Ti 3.15
farmer who o. to have the first 2Ti 2.06
by this time you o. to be teachers, Heb 1.12
my brethren, this o. not to be so. Jas 3.10
Instead you o. to say, "If the Lord 4.15
sort of persons o. you to be in 2Pe 3.11
abides in him o. to walk in the 1Jn 2.06
and we o. to lay down our lives for 3.16
we also o. to love one another. 4.11
So we o. to support such men, that 3Jn 1.08

OURSELVES
let us build o. a city, and a tower Gen 11.04
and let us make a name for o., 11.04
we will take your daughters to o., 34.16
come to bow o. to the ground 37.10
carefully about o. and our kindred, 43.07
Or how can we clear o.? God has found 44.16
we seemed to o. like grasshoppers, Num 13.33
atonement for o. before the LORD." 31.50
the cattle we took as spoil for o., Deu 2.35
even yet we have not cleansed o., Jos 22.17
save us, we will give o. up to you." 1Sa 11.03
"Tomorrow we will give o. up to you, 11.10
this evil, to ask for o. a king." 12.19
men, and we will show o. to them. 14.08
we might humble o. before our God, Ez 8.21
from him a straight way for o., 8.21
We also lay upon o. the obligation Neh 10.32
to charge o. yearly with the third 10.32
We obligate o. to bring the first 10.35
us determine among o. what is good. Job 34.04
possession for o. of the pastures Ps 83.12
let us delight o. with love. Pro 7.18
it, and let us conquer it for o., Is 7.06
let us fill o. with stronk drink; 56.12
Why have we humbled o., and thou 58.03
about to bring great evil upon o." Jer 26.19
o., our wives, our sons, or our 35.08
let us join o. to the LORD in an 50.05
own strength taken Karnaim for o.?" Amo 6.13
for we o. forgive every one who is Lk 11.04
have heard it o. from his own lips." 22.71
believe, for we have heard for o., Jn 4.42
But we will devote o. to prayer and Ac 6.04
strictly bound o. by an oath to 23.14
but we o., who have the first Rom 8.23
let us conduct o. becomingly as in 13.13
of the weak, and not to please o.; 15.01
But if we judged o. truly, 1Co 11.31
with which we o. are comforted by 2Co 1.04
us rely not on o. but on God who 1.09
Are we beginning to commend o. again? 3.01
sufficient of o. to claim anything 3.05
would commend o. to every man's 4.02
For what we preach is not o., 4.05
with o. as your servants for Jesus' 4.05
not commending o. to you again but 5.12
if we are beside o., it is for God; 5.13
of God we commend o. in every way: 6.04
let us cleanse o. from every 7.01
or compare o. with some of those 10.12
For we are not overextending o., 10.14
have been defending o. before you? 12.19
We o., who are Jews by birth and Gal 2.15
we o. were found to be sinners, is 2.17
Therefore we o. boast of you in the 2Th 1.04
For we o. were once foolish, disobedient, Tit 3.03
nature with o. and he prayed Jas 5.17
we deceive o., and the truth is not 1Jn 1.08

OUTCAST
not to keep his banished one an o. 2Sa 14.14

OUTCAST (cont.)
because they have called you an o.: Jer 30.17
save the lame and gather the o., Zep 3.19

OUTCASTS
If your o. are in the uttermost Deu 30.04
he gathers the o. of Israel. Ps 147.02
and will assemble the o. of Israel, Is 11.12
hide the o., betray not the fugitive; 16.03
let the o. of Moab sojourn among 16.04
GOD, who gathers the o. of Israel, 56.08

OUTCOME
them, that we may know their o.; Is 41.22
consider the o. of their life, and Heb 13.07
As the o. of your faith you obtain 1Pe 1.09

OUTCRY
"Because the o. against Sodom and Gen 18.20
according to the o. which has come 18.21
because the o. against its people 19.13
When Eli heard the sound of the o., 1Sa 4.14
arose a great o. of the people and Neh 5.01
I heard their o. and these words. 5.06
There is an o. in the streets for Is 24.11

OUTDO
o. one another in showing honor. Rom 12.10

OUTER
flowers, in the inner and o. rooms. 1Ki 6.29
gold in the inner and o. rooms. 6.30
and the o. entrance for the king he 2Ki 16.18
Afterward he built an o. wall to 2Ch 33.14
entered the o. court of the king's Est 6.04
Who can strip off his o. garment? Job 41.13
was heard as far as the o. court, Eze 10.05
Then he brought me into the o. court; 40.17
gate to the o. front of the inner 40.19
north, belonging to the o. court. 40.20
Its vestibule faced the o. court, 40.31
Its vestibule faced the o. court, 40.34
Its vestibule faced the o. court, 40.37
thickness of the o. wall of the 41.09
inner room and the o. vestibule 41.15
which belonged to the o. court, 42.03
like the pillars of the o. court; 42.06
toward the o. court, opposite the 42.07
chambers on the o. court were 42.08
one enters them from the o. court, 42.09
of it into the o. court without 42.14
me back to the o. gate of the 44.01
go out into the o. court to the 44.19
out into the o. court and so 46.20
brought me forth to the o. court, 46.21
on the outside to the o. gate, 47.02
be thrown into the o. darkness; Mt 8.12
and cast him into the o. darkness; 22.13
servant into the o. darkness; 25.30
Though our o. nature is wasting 2Co 4.16
the o. one, in which were the Heb 9.02
go continually into the o. tent, 9.06
as long as the o. tent is still 9.08

OUTFIT
carrying my o. upon my shoulder in Eze 12.07

OUTFLOW
and from the o. of your presses. Ex 22.29

OUTGOINGS
thou makest the o. of the morning Ps 65.08

OUTLAY
and for any o. upon the repairs of 2Ki 12.12

OUTLET
the upper o. of the waters of 2Ch 32.30

OUTLIVED
the elders who o. Joshua and had Jos 24.31
days of the elders who o. Joshua, Ju 2.07

OUTLYING
consumed some o. parts of the camp. Num 11.01

OUTMOST
the edge of the o. curtain in the Ex 26.04
the curtain that is o. in one set, 26.10
which is o. in the second set. 26.10
the edge of the o. curtain of the 36.11
the edge of the o. curtain of the 36.17

OUTPOSTS
servant to the o. of the armed men Ju 7.11

OUTPOURED
avenging of the o. blood of thy Ps 79.10

OUTPOURING
Israel in the o. of thy wrath upon Eze 9.08

OUTRAGED
and o. the Spirit of grace? Heb 10.29

OUTRAN
of the plain, and o. the Cushite. 2Sa 18.23
other disciple o. Peter and Jn 20.04

OUTRIGHT
slay old men o., young men and Eze 9.06

OUTSIDE
and told his two brothers o. Gen 9.22
And he brought him o. and said, 15.05
him forth and set him o. the city. 19.16
kneel down o. the city by the well 24.11
why do you stand o.? For I have 24.31
any of the flesh o. the house; Ex 12.46
shall set the table o. the veil, 26.35
o. the veil which is before the 27.21
shall burn with fire o. the camp; 29.14
the tent and pitch it o. the camp, 33.07
of meeting, which was o. the camp. 33.07
of the tabernacle, o. the veil, 40.22
carry forth o. the camp to a clean Lev 4.12
carry forth the bull o. the camp, 4.21
forth the ashes o. the camp to a 6.11
he burned with fire o. the camp, 8.17
he burned with fire o. the camp. 9.11
alone in a habitation o. the camp. 13.46
but shall dwell o. his tent seven 14.08
into an unclean place o. the city; 14.40
into an unclean place o. the city; 14.41
shall be carried forth o. the camp; 16.27
the camp, or kills it o. the camp, 17.03
O. the veil of the testimony, in the 24.03
putting them o. the camp, that they Num 5.03
did so, and drove them o. the camp; 5.04
her be shut up o. the camp seven 12.14
was shut up o. the camp seven days 12.15
stone him with stones o. the camp." 15.35
congregation brought him o. the camp, 15.36
shall be taken o. the camp and 19.03
deposit them o. the camp in a 19.09
forth to meet them o. the camp. 31.13
Encamp o. the camp seven days; 31.19
o. the city, for the east side two 35.05
blood finds him o. the bounds of 35.27
then he shall go o. the camp, Deu 23.10
have a place o. the camp and you 23.12
and when you sit down o., you shall dig 23.13
You shall stand o., and the man 24.11
not be married o. the family to a 25.05
and set them o. the camp of Israel. Jos 6.23
he gave in marriage o. his clan, Ju 12.09
he brought in from o. for his sons. 12.09

OUTSIDE (cont.)
for around the o. of the house he 1Ki 6.06
but they could not be seen from o.; 8.08
So they took him o. the city, 21.13
"Go o., borrow vessels of all your 2Ki 4.03
Jehu had stationed eighty men o., 10.24
he burned them o. Jerusalem in the 23.04
o. Jerusalem, to the brook Kidron, 23.06
appointed to o. duties for Israel, 1Ch 26.29
but they could not be seen from o.; 2Ch 5.09
and set it o. the gate of the house 24.08
the springs that were o. the city; 32.03
and o. it he built another wall; 32.05
and he threw them o. of the city. 33.15
were over the o. work of the house Neh 11.16
of wares lodged o. Jerusalem once 13.20
The sluggard says, "There is a lion o.! Pro 22.13
Prepare your work o., get everything 24.27
If I met you o., I would kiss you, Sol 8.01
who are besieging you o. the walls; Jer 21.04
all around the o. of the temple Eze 40.05
And on the o. of the vestibule at 40.40
tables on the o. of the side of 40.41
to the inner room, and on the o. 41.17
wood in front of the vestibule o. 41.25
was a wall o. parallel to the 42.07
where the o. wall begins. On the south 42.10
to the temple, o. the sacred area. 43.21
me round on the o. to the outer 47.02
But when the crowd had been put o., Mt 9.25
mother and his brothers stood o., 12.46
and your brothers are standing o., * 12.47
you cleanse the o. of the cup and 23.25
that the o. also may be clean. 23.26
was sitting o. in the courtyard. 26.69
and standing o. they sent to him Mk 3.31
mother and your brothers are o., 3.32
but for those o. everything is in 4.11
But he put them all o., 5.40
there is nothing o. a man which by 7.15
into a man from o. cannot defile 7.18
were praying o. at the hour of Lk 1.10
and your brothers are standing o., 8.20
cleanse the o. of the cup and of 11.39
he who made the o. make the inside 11.40
begin to stand o. and to knock at 13.25
while Peter stood o. at the door. Jn 18.16
But Mary stood weeping o. the tomb, 20.11
the men to be put o. for a while. Ac 5.34
put them all o. and knelt down and 9.40
day we went o. the gate to the 16.13
our way till we were o. the city; 21.05
God judges those o. Drive out the 1Co 5.13
which a man commits is o. the body; 6.18
To those o. the law I became as one o. the law— 9.21
that I might win those o. the law. 9.21
he left nothing o. his control. Heb 2.08
for sin are burned o. the camp. 13.11
also suffered o. the gate in order 13.12
let us go forth to him o. the camp, 13.13
measure the court o. the temple; Rev 11.02
wine press was trodden o. the city, 14.20
O. are the dogs and sorcerers and 22.15

OUTSIDER
but an o. shall not eat of them, Ex 29.33
any of it on an o. shall be cut 30.33
"An o. shall not eat of a holy Lev 22.10
married to an o. she shall not eat 22.12
yet no o. shall eat of it. 22.13
position of an o. say the "Amen" to 1Co 14.16
and an unbeliever or o. enters, 14.24

OUTSIDERS
For what have I to do with judging o.? 1Co 5.12
and o. or unbelievers en er, will 14.23
Conduct yourselves wisely toward o., Col 4.05
you may command the respect of o., 1Th 4.12
moreover he must be well thought of by o., 1Ti 3.07

OUTSKIRTS
begins at the o. of Kiriathjearim; Jos 18.15
when I come to the o. of the camp, Ju 7.17
him came to the o. of the camp at 7.19
going down to the o. of the city, 1Sa 9.27
staying in the o. of Gibeah under 14.02
Lo, these are but the o. of his ways; Job 26.14

OUTSPREAD
and its o. wings will fill the Is 8.08

OUTSTRETCHED
you with an o. arm and with great Ex 6.06
by a mighty hand and an o. arm, Deu 4.34
with a mighty hand and an o. arm; 5.15
and the o. arm, by which the LORD 7.19
thy great power and by thy o. arm.' 9.29
his mighty hand and his o. arm, 11.02
with a mighty hand and an o. arm, 26.08
and of thy o. arm), when he comes 1Ki 8.42
knelt with hands o. toward heaven; 8.54
great power and with an o. arm; 2Ki 17.36
and thy o. arm, when he comes and 2Ch 6.32
with a strong hand and an o. arm, Ps 136.12
are haughty and walk with o. necks, Is 3.16
you with o. hands and strong arm, in Jer 21.05
power and my o. arm have made the 27.05
thy great power and by thy o. arm! 32.17
with a strong hand and o. arm, 32.21
with a mighty hand and an o. arm, Eze 20.33
with a mighty hand and an o. arm, 20.34

OUTSTRIP
Your builders o. your destroyers, Is 49.17

OUTWARD
of the city o. a thousand cubits Num 35.04
man looks on the o. appearance, 1Sa 16.07
yours be the o. adorning with 1Pe 3.03

OUTWARDLY
which o. appear beautiful, but Mt 23.27
So you also o. appear righteous to 23.28
he is not a real Jew who is one o., Rom 2.28

OUTWEIGHS
a little folly o. wisdom and honor. Ecc 10.01

OUTWIT
The enemy shall not o. him, the wicked Ps 89.22

OUTWITTED
And Jacob o. Laban the Aramean, in Gen 31.20

OVEN
baked in the o. as an offering, Lev 2.04
baked in the o. and all that is 7.09
whether o. or stove, it shall be 11.35
shall bake your bread in one o., 26.26
as a blazing o. when you appear. Ps 21.09
is hot as an o. with the burning Lam 5.10
they are like a heated o., whose baker Hos 7.04
For like an o. their hearts burn 7.06
All of them are hot as an o., 7.07
the day comes, burning like an o., Mal 4.01
and tomorrow is thrown into the o., Mt 6.30
and tomorrow is thrown into the o., Lk 12.28

OVENS
and into your o. and your kneading Ex 8.03
section and the Tower of the O. Neh 3.11

OVERBEARING
I have seen a wicked man o., Ps 37.35
kind and gentle but also to the o. 1Pe 2.18

OVERBOARD
next day to throw the cargo o.; Ac 27.18
themselves o. first and make for 27.43

OVERCAME
followed Omri o. the people who 1Ki 16.22

OVERCOME
for we are well able to o. it." Num 13.30
Moab was o. with fear of the people 22.03
They had o. Ziklag, and burned it 1Sa 30.01
and answer me; I am o. by my trouble. Ps 55.02
rich valley of those o. with wine! Is 28.01
then we can o. him, and take our Jer 20.10
will stumble, they will not o. me. 20.11
like a man o. by wine, because of 23.09
was o. and lay sick for some days; Dan 8.27
they were o. with amazement. Mk 5.42
and the darkness has not o. it. Jn 1.05
of good cheer, I have o. the world." 16.33
and being o. by sleep, he fell down Ac 20.09
Do not be o. by evil, but o. evil Rom 12.21
because you have o. the evil one. 1Jn 2.13
you, and you have o. the evil one. 2.14
you are of God, and have o. them; 4.04

OVERCOMES
than he assails him and o. him, Lk 11.22
for whatever o. a man, to that he is 2Pe 2.19
is born of God o. the world; 1Jn 5.04
is the victory that o. the world, 5.04
Who is it that o. the world but he 5.05

OVERDRIVEN
and if they are o. for one day, Gen 33.13

OVEREXTENDING
For we are not o. ourselves, as 2Co 10.14

OVERFLOW
of the Red Sea o. them as they Deu 11.04
their hearts o. with follies. Ps 73.07
it will o. and pass on, reaching Is 8.08
O. your land like the Nile, O daughter 23.10
they shall o. the land and all that Jer 47.02
come on and o. and pass through, Dan 11.10
and shall o. and pass through. 11.40
the vats shall o. with wine and Joe 2.24
The vats o., for their wickedness 3.13
shall again o. with prosperity, and Zec 1.17

OVERFLOWED
their place and o. all its banks, Jos 4.18
water gushed out and streams o. Ps 78.20
poverty have o. in a wealth of 2Co 8.02
of our Lord o. for me with the 1Ti 1.14

OVERFLOWING
when it was o. all its banks, and 1Ch 12.15
is decreed, o. with righteousness. Is 10.22
o. waters, he will cast down to the 28.02
is like an o. stream that reaches 30.28
In o. wrath for a moment I hid my 54.08
of the nations like an o. stream; 66.12
and shall become an o. torrent; Jer 47.02
But with an o. flood he will make a Nah 1.08
pour down for you an o. blessing. Mal 3.10

OVERFLOWINGS
Pour forth the o. of your anger, and Job 40.11

OVERFLOWS
(the Jordan o. all its banks Jos 3.15
my head with oil, my cup o. Ps 23.05
My heart o. with a goodly theme; 45.01
saints but also o. in many thanksgivings 2Co 9.12

OVERGROWN
of a sluggard is o. with thorns, Pro 15.19
and lo, it was all o. with thorns; 24.31

OVERHEARD
the conversation had not been o. Jer 38.27

OVERJOYED
With all our affliction, I am o. 2Co 7.04

OVERLAID
pillars of acacia o. with gold, Ex 26.32
And he o. the frames with gold, and 36.34
and o. the bars with gold. 36.34
of acacia, and o. them with gold; 36.36
He o. their capitals, and their 36.38
And he o. it with pure gold within 37.02
acacia wood, and o. them with gold, 37.04
and he o. it with pure gold, and 37.11
the table, and o. them with gold. 37.15
He o. it with pure gold, its top, and 37.26
acacia wood, and o. them with gold. 37.28
with it, and he o. it with bronze. 38.02
acacia wood, and o. them with bronze. 38.06
and o. their capitals and made 38.28
and he o. it with pure gold. 1Ki 6.20
And Solomon o. the inside of the 6.21
sanctuary, and o. it with gold. 6.21
And he o. the whole house with gold, 6.22
inner sanctuary he o. with gold. 6.22
And he o. the cherubim with gold. 6.28
of the house he o. with gold in 6.30
he o. them with gold, and spread 6.32
and he o. them with gold evenly 6.35
and o. it with the finest gold. 10.18
of Judah had o. and gave it to the 2Ki 18.16
He o. it on the inside with pure 2Ch 3.04
he o. it with six hundred talents 3.08
And he o. the upper chambers with 3.09
of wood and o. them with gold. 3.10
and o. their doors with bronze; 4.09
and o. it with pure gold. 9.17
Behold, it is o. with gold and Hab 2.19

OVERLAY
And you shall o. it with pure gold, Ex 25.11
within and without shall you o. it, 25.11
acacia wood, and o. them with gold. 25.13
You shall o. it with pure gold, and 25.24
and o. them with gold, and the table 25.28
You shall o. the frames with gold, 26.29
and you shall o. the bars with gold. 26.29
of acacia, and o. them with gold; 26.37
and you shall o. it with bronze. 27.02
acacia wood, and o. them with bronze; 27.06
And you shall o. it with pure gold, 30.03
acacia wood, and o. them with gold. 30.05

OVERLAYING
the o. of their capitals was also Ex 38.17
and the o. of their capitals and 38.19
for o. the walls of the house, 1Ch 29.04

OVERLAYS
and a goldsmith o. it with gold, Is 40.19

OVERLOOK
it is his glory to o. an offense. Pro 19.11
so unjust as to o. your work and Heb 6.10

OVERLOOKED
The times of ignorance God o., Ac 17.30

OVERLOOKING
a tower of Lebanon, o. Damascus. Sol 7.04

OVERLOOKS
top of Peor, that o. the desert. Num 23.28
mountain that o. the valley of the Jos 18.16

OVERMUCH
Be not righteous o., and do not make Ecc 7.16
Be not wicked o., neither be a fool; 7.17

OVERPAYMENT
pay back the o. to the man to whom Lev 25.27

OVERPOWER
and by what means we may o. him, Ju 16.05

OVERPOWERED
den the lions o. them and broke Dan 6.24
and o. them, so that they fled out Ac 19.16
are again entangled in them and o., 2Pe 2.20

OVERRUN
no oppressor shall again o. them, Zec 9.08

OVERSEE
thousand six hundred to o. them. 2Ch 2.02

OVERSEER
and he made him o. of his house Gen 39.04
he made him o. in his house and 39.05
Joel the son of Zichri was their o.; Neh 11.09
their o. was Zabdiel the son of 11.14
The o. of the Levites in Jerusalem 11.22

OVERSEERS
to appoint o. over the land, Gen 41.34
six hundred as o. to make the 2Ch 2.18
Benaiah were o. assisting Conaniah 31.13
the hand of the o. and the workmen." 34.17
will make your o. peace and your Is 60.17

OVERSHADOW
power of the Most High will o. you; Lk 1.35

OVERSHADOWED
when lo, a bright cloud o. them, Mt 17.05
And a cloud o. them, and a voice Mk 9.07
this, a cloud came and o. them; Lk 9.34

OVERSHADOWING
o. the mercy seat with their wings, Ex 25.20
o. the mercy seat with their wings, 37.09
cherubim of glory o. the mercy seat. Heb 9.05

OVERSIGHT
of your sacks; perhaps it was an o. Gen 43.12
and to have o. of those who had Num 3.32
with the o. of all the tabernacle 4.16
to be under the o. of Ithamar the 4.28
who had the o. of the house of the 2Ki 12.11
who have the o. of the house of 22.05
who have the o. of the house of 22.09
had the o. of Israel westward of 1Ch 26.30
to have the o. of the Reubenites, 26.32
who had the o. of the house of the 2Ch 34.10
sons of the Kohathites, to have o. 34.12
to have the o. of the work of the Ez 3.08
took the o. of the workmen in the 3.09
having o. at the gates of the Eze 44.11

OVERTAKE
lest the disaster o. me, and I die. Gen 19.19
and when you o. them, say to them, 44.04
I will o., I will divide the spoil, Ex 15.09
pursue the manslayer and o. him, Deu 19.06
shall come upon you and o. you, 28.02
shall come upon you and o. you. 28.15
upon you and pursue you and o. you, 28.45
them quickly, for you will o. them." Jos 2.05
Shall I o. them?" He answered him, 1Sa 30.08
shall surely o. and shall surely 30.08
lest he o. us quickly, and bring 2Sa 15.14
light, punishment will o. us; 2Ki 7.09
Terrors o. him like a flood; Job 27.20
let the enemy pursue me and o. me, Ps 7.05
and let thy burning anger o. them. 69.24
and righteousness does not o. us; Is 59.09
you fear shall o. you there in the Jer 42.16
pursue her lovers, but not o. them; Hos 2.07
Shall not war o. them in Gibeah? 10.09
say, 'Evil shall not o. or meet us.' Amo 9.10
plowman shall o. the reaper and 9.13
of such things; disgrace will not o. us." Mic 2.06
did they not o. your fathers? Zec 1.06
light, lest the darkness o. you; Jn 12.35

OVERTAKEN
my iniquities have o. me, till I cannot Ps 40.12
have all o. her in the midst of Lam 1.03
No temptation has o. you that is 1Co 10.13
if a man is o. in any trespass, you Gal 6.01

OVERTAKES
the sword of your enemies o. you; 1Ch 21.12

OVERTHREW
and he o. those cities, and all the Gen 19.25
when he o. the cities in which Lot 19.29
which the LORD o. in his anger and Deu 29.23
And they o. the cities, and on every 2Ki 3.25
And Joab smote Rabbah, and o. it. 1Ch 20.01
but o. Pharaoh and his host in the Ps 136.15
and Gomorrah when God o. them. Is 13.19
like a desert and o. its cities, 14.17
which the LORD o. without pity, Jer 20.16
As when God o. Sodom and Gomorrah 50.40
"I o. some of you, as when God Amo 4.11
as when God o. Sodom and Gomorrah, 4.11

OVERTHROW
that I will not o. the city of Gen 19.21
Lot out of the midst of the o., 19.29
shall utterly o. them and break Ex 23.24
an o. like that of Sodom and Deu 29.23
and to spy it out, and to o. it?" 2Sa 10.03
attack upon the city, and o. it.' 11.25
search and to o. and to spy out 1Ch 19.03
to dwell there o. any king or Ez 6.12
confront them, o. them! Deliver my Ps 17.13
break down, to destroy and to o., Jer 1.10
to o., destroy, and bring evil, so I 31.28
I will o. the wicked; I will cut off Zep 1.03
and to o. the throne of kingdoms; Hag 2.22
and o. the chariots and their 2.22
you will not be able to o. them. Ac 5.39
Do we then o. the law by this faith? Rom 3.31

OVERTHROWEST
majesty thou o. thy adversaries; Ex 15.07

OVERTHROWN
but it is o. by the mouth of the Pro 11.11
The wicked are o. and are no more, 12.07
The wicked is o. through his 14.32
but the wicked are o. by calamity. 24.16
it is desolate, as o. by aliens. Is 1.07
they shall be o.," says the LORD. Jer 6.15
they shall be o., says the LORD. 8.12
Let them be o. before thee; deal with 18.23
be uprooted or o. any more for 31.40
and their neighbor cities were o., 49.18
which was o. in a moment, no hand Lam 4.06
the place of his sanctuary was o. Dan 8.11
days, and Nineveh shall be o.!" Jon 3.04
for they were o. in the wilderness. 1Co 10.05

OVERTHROWS
away stripped, and o. the mighty. Job 12.19
is upright, but sin o. the wicked. Pro 13.06
but he o. the words of the faithless. 22.12

OVERTOOK
And Laban o. Jacob. Now Jacob had Gen 31.25
When he o. them, he spoke to them 44.06

OVERTOOK (cont.)

and o. them encamped at the sea, by Ex 14.09
out, and they o. the Danites. Ju 18.22
but the battle o. them, and those who 20.42
And the Philistines o. Saul and his 1Sa 31.02
and o. him in the plains of Jericho; 2Ki 25.05
And the Philistines o. Saul and his 1Ch 10.02
me, or exulted when evil o. him Job 31.29
I pursued my enemies and o. them; Ps 18.37
and o. Zedekiah in the plains of Jer 39.05
and o. Zedekiah in the plains of 52.08

OVERTURNED

and he o. the tables of the money-changers Mt 21.12
and he o. the tables of the money-changers Mk 11.15
money-changers and o. their tables. Jn 2.15

OVERTURNS

know it not, when he o. them in his anger; Job 9.05
flinty rock, and o. mountains by the roots. 28.09
he o. them in the night, and they 34.25

OVERWHELM

sends them out, they o. the land. Job 12.15
and thou dost o. me with all thy Ps 88.07
the mischief of their lips o. them! 140.09
and waters will o. the shelter." Is 28.17
the rivers, they shall not o. you; 43.02
done to Lebanon will o. you; Hab 2.17

OVERWHELMED

but the sea o. their enemies. Ps 78.53
by thy anger, by thy wrath we are o. 90.07
And I sat there o. among them seven Eze 3.15
or he may be o. by excessive sorrow. 2Co 2.07

OVERWHELMING

Wrath is cruel, anger is o.; but who can Pro 27.04
when the o. scourge passes through Is 28.15
when the o. scourge passes through 28.18

OVERWHELMS

you, and sudden terror o. you; Job 22.10
come upon me, and horror o. me. Ps 55.05

OVERWISE

and do not make yourself o.; Ecc 7.16

OWE

throat he said, 'Pay what you o.' Mt 18.28
'How much do you o. my master?' Lk 16.05
another, 'And how much do you o.?' 16.07
O. no one anything, except to love Rom 13.08

OWED

O. no one anything, except to love Rom 13.08
servants who o. him a hundred denarii; 18.28
one o. five hundred denarii, and the Lk 7.41

OWES

or o. you anything, charge that to Phm 1.18

OWING

nothing of your o. me even your Phm 1.19

OWL

the o., the cormorant, the ibis, Lev 11.17
the little o. and the great owl, the Deu 14.16
and the great o., the water hen 14.16
like an o. of the waste places; Ps 102.06
the o. and the raven shall dwell in Is 34.11
There shall the o. nest and lay and 34.15
the o. shall hoot in the window, the Zep 2.14

OWN

seed according to their o. kinds, Gen 1.12
So God created man in his o. image, 1.27
father of a son in his o. likeness, 5.03
for God made man in his o. image. 9.06
each with his o. language, by their 10.05
your o. son shall be your heir." 15.04
I may go to my o. home and country. 30.25
I provide for my o. household also?" 30.30
and he put his o. droves apart, 30.40
he is our brother, our o. flesh." 37.27
"Let her keep the things as her o., 38.23
in the prison—each his o. dream, 40.05
and each dream with its o. meaning. 40.05
having a dream with its o. meaning. 41.11
who were his o. offspring, not 46.26
and four fifths shall be your o., 47.24
but the fault is in your o. people." Ex 5.16
and plant them on thy o. mountain, 15.17
he went his way to his o. country. 18.27
you shall be my o. possession among all 19.05
his o. field and in his o. vineyard. 22.05
thou didst swear by thine o. self, 32.13
bring with his o. hands the Lev 7.30
into the palm of his o. left hand, 14.15
into the palm of his o. left hand; 14.26
nakedness is your o. nakedness. 18.10
against the sons of your o. people, 19.18
to wife a virgin of his o. people, 21.14
him, and go back to his o. family, 25.41
man by his o. camp and every man Num 1.52
and every man by his o. standard; 1.52
encamp each by his o. standard, 2.02
consecrated for my o. all the first 3.13
depart to my o. land and to my 10.30
after your o. heart and your o. eyes, 15.39
it has not been of my o. accord. 16.28
of Balak, "Go to your o. land; 22.13
either good or bad of my o. will; 24.13
of Korah, but died for his o. sin; 27.03
called it Nobah, after his o. name. 32.42
shall cleave to its o. inheritance.'" 36.09
the villages after his o. name, Deu 3.14
be a people of his o. possession, 4.20
out of Egypt with his o. presence, 4.37
be a people for his o. possession, 7.06
whatever is right in his o. eyes; 12.08
your friend who is as your o. soul, 13.06
be a people for his o. possession, 14.02
and an army larger than your o., 20.01
be put to death for his o. sin. 24.16
are a people for his o. possession, 26.18
eat the offspring of your o. body, 28.53
and put them among their o. stuff. Jos 7.11
again to his o. town and his o. home, 20.06
their o. land of which they had 22.09
him in his o. inheritance at 24.30
and their o. daughters they gave to Ju 3.06
'My o. hand has delivered me.' 7.02
went and dwelt in his o. house. 8.29
his o. offspring, for he had many 8.30
did what was right in his o. eyes. 17.06
did what was right in his o. eyes. 21.25
lest I impair my o. inheritance. Ru 4.06
was lying down in his o. place; 1Sa 3.02
and let it return to its o. place, 5.11
goes up on the way to its o. land, 6.09
out a man after his o. heart; 13.14
Philistines went to their o. place. 14.46
you are little in your o. eyes, 15.17
Jonathan loved him as his o. soul. 18.01
he loved him as his o. soul. 18.03
loved him as he loved his o. soul. 20.17
the son of Jesse to your o. shame, 20.30
taking vengeance with your o. hand, 25.26
avenging myself with my o. hand! 25.33
evil-doing of Nabal upon his o. head. 25.39
buried him in Ramah, his o. city. 28.03
Therefore Saul took his o. sword, 31.04

OWN (cont.)

for your o. mouth has testified 2Sa 1.16
man in his o. house upon his bed, 4.11
they may dwell in their o. place, 7.10
and according to thy o. heart, 7.21
take one of his o. flock or herd 12.04
against you out of your o. house; 12.11
he then went to his o. house; 12.20
"Let him dwell apart in his o. house; 14.24
Absalom dwelt apart in his o. house, 14.24
my o. son seeks my life; how much more 16.11
and went off home to his o. city. 17.23
fled every one to his o. home. 18.17
the pillar after his o. name, 18.18
had fled every man to his o. home. 19.08
that I may die in my o. city, 19.37
and he returned to his o. home. 19.39
and slew him with his o. spear. 23.21
may save your o. life and the life 1Ki 1.12
my son to ride on my o. mule, 1.33
this day, my o. eyes seeing it.' " 1.48
and rose, and each went his o. way. 1.49
his bloody deeds upon his o. head, 2.32
buried in his o. house in the 2.34
blood shall be upon your o. head." 2.37
know in your o. heart all the evil 2.44
back your evil upon your o. head; 2.44
building his o. house and the 3.01
building his o. house thirteen 7.01
His o. house where he was to dwell, 7.08
his conduct upon his o. head, 8.32
affliction of his o. heart and 8.38
Lord and his o. house and the 9.15
of David to her o. house which 9.24
I heard in my o. land of your 10.06
I came and my o. eyes had seen it; 10.07
and went back to her o. land, 10.13
marriage the sister of his o. wife, 11.19
that I may go to my o. country." 11.21
seeking to go to your o. country?" 11.22
Look now to your o. house, David." 12.16
he had devised of his o. heart; 12.33
And he laid the body in his o. grave; 13.30
his father and his o. votive gifts, 15.15
and laid him upon his o. bed. 17.19
shall dogs lick your o. blood." ' " 21.19
hold of his o. clothes and rent 2Ki 2.12
him and returned to their o. land. 3.27
answered, "I dwell among my o. people." 4.13
"You shall see it with your o. eyes, 7.02
"You shall see it with your o. eyes, 7.19
and set up a king of their o. 8.20
and his o. votive gifts, and all the 12.18
every man shall die for his o. sin." 14.06
from their o. land to Assyria until this 17.23
nation still made gods of its o., 17.29
Lord but also served their o. gods, 17.33
their o. dung and to drink their o. urine? 18.27
one of you will eat of his o. vine, 18.31
and every one of his o. fig tree, 18.31
drink the water of his o. cistern; 18.31
away to a land like your o. land, 18.32
a rumor and return to his o. land; 19.07
fall by the sword in his o. land.' " 19.07
for my o. sake and for the sake of 19.34
city for my o. sake and for my 20.06
And some of your o. sons, who are born 20.18
and buried him in his o. tomb. 23.30
Therefore Saul took his o. sword, 1Ch 10.04
and slew him with his o. spear. 11.23
commanders from his o. father's house. 12.28
they may dwell in their o. place, 17.09
one of your o. sons, and I will 17.11
and according to thy o. heart, 17.19
treasure of my o. of gold and 29.03
and of thy o. have we given thee. 29.14
from thy hand and is all thy o. 29.16
his conduct upon his o. head, 2Ch 6.23
each knowing his o. affliction, 6.29
and his o. sorrow and stretching 6.29
Lord and in his o. house he successfully 7.11
the house of the Lord and his o. house, 8.01
I heard in my o. land of your affairs 9.05
I came and my o. eyes had seen it; 9.06
and went back to her o. land, with her 9.12
Look now to your o. house, David." 10.16
appointed his o. priests for the 11.15
his father and his o. votive gifts, 15.18
and set up a king of their o. 21.08
every man shall die for his o. sin." 25.04
deliver their o. people from your 25.15
sins of your o. against the Lord 28.10
as you see with your o. eyes. 29.08
king from his o. possessions was 31.03
with shame of face to his o. land. 32.21
some of his o. sons struck him down 32.21
and Judah, each to his o. town. Ez 2.01
of Ananiah repaired beside his o. house. Neh 3.23
repaired, each one opposite his o. house. 3.28
repaired opposite his o. house. After him 3.29
their taunt upon their o. heads, and give 4.04
inventing them out of your o. mind." 6.08
fell greatly in their o. esteem; 6.16
and each opposite his o. house. 7.03
province in its o. script and to Est 1.22
to every people in its o. language, 1.22
be lord in his o. house and speak 1.22
adopted her as his o. daughter. 2.07
had adopted her as his o. daughter, 2.15
province in its o. script and 3.12
every people in its o. language; 3.12
in my presence, in my o. house?" 7.08
province in its o. script and to 8.09
to every people in its o. language, 8.09
Jews should come upon his o. head, 9.25
they came each from his o. place, Job 2.11
the wise in their o. craftiness; 5.13
my o. mouth would condemn me; 9.20
and my o. clothes will abhor me. 9.31
feels only the pain of his o. body, 14.22
Your o. mouth condemns you, and not 15.06
your o. lips testify against you. 15.06
shortened and his o. schemes throw 18.07
is cast into a net by his o. feet, 18.08
loathsome to the sons of my o. mother. 19.17
perish for ever like his o. dung; 20.07
Let their o. eyes see their destruction, 21.20
he was righteous in his o. eyes. 32.01
who are wise in their o. conceit. 37.24
that your o. right hand can give 40.14
with your o. hearts on your beds, Ps 4.04
let them fall by their o. counsels; 5.10
His mischief returns upon his o. head, 7.16
and on his o. pate his violence descends. 7.16
hid has their o. foot been caught. 9.15
snared in the work of their o. hands. 9.16
swears to his o. hurt and does not 15.04
himself in his o. eyes that his 36.02
their sword shall enter their o. heart, 37.15
thou with thy o. hand didst drive 44.02
for not by their o. sword did they 44.03
nor did their o. arm give them 44.03
though they named lands their o. 49.11
you slander your o. mother's son. 50.20
Let their o. table before them 69.22
not despise his o. that are in 69.33
set up their o. signs for signs. 74.04
hearts, to follow their o. counsels. 81.12
in their o. shame as in a mantle! 109.29
for himself, Israel as his o. possession. 135.04
together fall into their o. nets, 141.10
men lie in wait for their o. blood, Pro 1.18
set an ambush for their o. lives. 1.18
and be sated with their o. devices. 1.31

OWN (cont.)
and do not rely on your o. insight. Pro 3.05
Be not wise in your o. eyes; 3.07
Drink water from your o. cistern, 5.15
flowing water from your o. well. 5.15
wicked falls by his o. wickedness. 11.05
of a fool is right in his o. eyes, 12.15
folly with her o. hands tears it 14.01
The heart knows its o. bitterness, 14.10
of a man are pure in his o. eyes, 16.02
Many a man proclaims his o. loyalty, 20.06
of a man is right in his o. eyes, 21.02
the poor to increase his o. wealth, 22.16
lest he be wise in his o. eyes. 26.05
cuts off his o. feet and drinks 26.06
a man who is wise in his o. eyes? 26.12
is wiser in his o. eyes than seven 26.16
quarrel not his o. is like one who 26.17
praise you, and not your o. mouth; 27.02
a stranger, and not your o. lips. 27.02
evil way will fall into his o. pit; 28.10
A rich man is wise in his o. eyes, 28.11
trusts in his o. mind is a fool; 28.26
of a thief hates his o. life; 29.24
pure in their o. eyes but are not 30.12
his hands, and eats his o. flesh. Ecc 4.05
or in his o. kingdom had been born 4.14
but, my o. vineyard I have not kept! Sol 1.06
vineyard, my very o. is for myself; 8.12
to what their o. fingers have made. Is 2.08
our o. bread and wear our o. clothes, 4.01
who are wise in their o. eyes, 5.21
eyes, and shrewd in their o. sight! 5.21
man will turn to his o. people, 13.14
every man will flee to his o. land. 13.14
and will set them in their o. land, 14.01
lie in glory, each in his o. tomb; 14.18
to what their o. fingers have made, 17.08
eat their o. dung and drink their o. urine?" 36.12
one of you will eat of his o. vine, 36.16
and every one of his o. fig tree, 36.16
drink the water of his o. cistern; 36.16
away to a land like your o. land, 36.17
a rumor, and return to his o. land; 37.07
fall by the sword in his o. land.'" 37.07
for my o. sake and for the sake of 37.35
And some of your o. sons, who are 39.07
your transgressions for my o. sake, 43.25
about each in his o. direction; 47.15
For my o. sake, for my o. sake, I do it, 48.11
your oppressors eat their o. flesh, 49.26
with their o. blood as with wine. 49.26
turned every one to his o. way; 53.06
have all turned to their o. way, 56.11
each to his o. gain, one and all. 56.11
backsliding in the way of his o. heart. 57.17
fast you seek your o. pleasure, 58.03
hide yourself from your o. flesh? 58.07
honor it, not going your o. ways, 58.13
ways, or seeking your o. pleasure, 58.13
then his o. arm brought him victory, 59.16
so my o. arm brought me victory, and 63.05
good, following their o. devices; 65.02
These have chosen their o. ways, 66.03
worshiped the works of their o. hands. Jer 1.16
your o. sword devoured your prophets 2.30
you shepherds after my o. heart, 3.15
stubbornly follow their o. evil heart. 3.17
after other gods to your o. hurt, 7.06
themselves, to their o. confusion? 7.19
walked in their o. counsels and 7.24
every one turns to his o. course, 8.06
followed their o. hearts and have 9.14
follow their o. heart and have 13.10
and the deceit of their o. minds. 14.14
back to their o. land which I gave 16.15
We wil follow our o. plans, and will 18.12
they shall dwell in their o. land." 23.08
speak visions of their o. minds, 23.16
stubbornly follows his o. heart, 23.17
the deceit of their o. heart, 23.26
the burden is every man's o. word, 23.36
work of your hands to your o. harm. 25.07
you have heard with your o. ears." 26.11
the time of his o. land comes; 27.07
him, I will leave on its o. land, 27.11
come back to their o. country. 31.17
every one shall die for his o. sin; 31.30
for their o. good and the good of 32.39
to return to Egypt, to its o. land. 37.07
and let you remain in your o. land. 42.12
your o. wickedness, and the wickedness 44.09
go back to our o. people and to 46.16
one shall turn to his o. people, 50.16
one shall flee to his o. land. 50.16
let us go each to his o. country; 51.09
have boiled their o. children; Lam 4.10
in their o. sight for the evils Eze 6.09
to their o. judgments I will judge 7.27
their deeds upon their o. heads, 11.21
through the wall with my o. hands; 12.07
who prophesy out of their o. minds: 13.02
prophets who follow their o. spirit, 13.03
who prophesy out of their o. minds; 13.17
but their o. lives by their righteousness, 14.14
but their o. lives by their righteousness. 14.20
restore your o. fortunes in the 16.53
were your o. special markets, they 27.15
dwell in their o. land which I 28.25
that says, 'My Nile is my o.; I made 29.03
moment, every one for his o. life, 32.10
blood shall be upon his o. head. 33.04
it is their o. way that is not 33.17
will bring them into their o. land; 34.13
of Israel dwelt in their o. land, 36.17
and bring you into your o. land. 36.24
I will place you in your o. land; 37.14
and bring them to their o. land; 37.21
gathered them into their o. land. 39.28
inheritance out of his o. property, 46.18
the youths who are of your o. age. Dan 1.10
any god except their o. God. 3.28
it with his o. signet and with the 6.17
and in his o. mind he shall magnify 8.25
and for thy o. sake, O LORD, cause 9.17
for thy o. sake, O my God, because 9.19
but shall return into his o. land. 11.09
among your o. people shall lift 11.14
shall do according to his o. will, 11.16
the fortresses of his o. land; 11.19
will, and return to his o. land. 11.28
idols for their o. destruction. Hos 8.04
deed upon your o. head swiftly and Joe 3.04
them far from their o. border. 3.06
your deed upon your o. head. 3.07
we not by our o. strength taken Amo 6.13
deeds shall return on your o. head. Ob 1.15
shall possess their o. possessions. 1.17
are the men of his o. house. Mic 7.06
to seize habitations not their o. Hab 1.06
whose o. might is their god! 1.11
and collects as his o. all peoples." 2.05
up what is not his o.—for how long? 2.06
trusts in his o. creation when he 2.18
yourselves each with his o. house. Hag 1.09
for now I see with my o. eyes. Zec 9.08
and their o. shepherds have no pity 11.05
Your o. eyes shall see this, and you Mal 1.05
to their o. country by another way. Mt 2.12
Let the day's o. trouble be sufficient 6.34
the log that is in your o. eye? 7.03
there is the log in your o. eye? 7.04
take the log out of your o. eye, 7.05

OWN (cont.)
the dead to bury their o. dead." Mt 8.22
over and came to his o. city. 9.01
will be those of his o. household. 10.36
and coming to his o. country he 13.54
in his o. country and in his o. house." 13.57
what was my o. with interest. 25.27
and put his o. clothes on him, and 27.31
and laid it in his o. new tomb, 27.60
privately to his o. disciples he Mk 4.34
there and came to his o. country; 6.01
except in his o. country, and among 6.04
among his o. kin, and in his o. house." 6.04
and put his o. clothes on him. 15.20
be enrolled, each to his o. city. Lk 2.03
pierce through your o. soul also), 2.35
Galilee, to their o. city, Nazareth. 2.39
do here also in your o. country. 4.23
is acceptable in his o. country.'" 4.24
the log that is in your o. eye? 6.41
see the log that is in your o. eye? 6.42
take the log out of your o. eye, 6.42
each tree is known by its o. fruit. 6.44
the dead to bury their o. dead; 9.60
set him on his o. beast and 10.34
guards his o. palace, his goods are 11.21
not hate his o. father and mother 14.26
and even his o. life, he cannot be 14.26
not bear his o. cross and come 14.27
wiser in their o. generation than 16.08
give you that which is your o.? 16.12
condemn you out of your o. mouth, 19.22
it ourselves from his o. lips. 22.71
He came to his o. home, and his Jn 1.11
and his o. people received him not. 1.11
has no honor in his o. country. 4.44
can do nothing of his o. accord, 5.19
"I can do nothing on my o. authority; 5.30
I seek not my o. will but the will 5.30
if another comes in his o. name, 5.43
not to do my o. will, but the will 6.38
I am speaking on my o. authority. 7.17
on his o. authority seeks his o. glory; 7.18
I have not come of my o. accord; 7.28
They went each to his o. house, * 7.53
nothing on my o. authority but 8.28
I came not of my o. accord, but he 8.42
speaks according to his o. nature, 8.44
Yet I do not seek my o. glory; 8.50
he calls his o. sheep by name and 10.03
When he has brought out all his o., 10.04
whose o. the sheep are not, sees the 10.12
I know my o. and my o. know me, 10.14
but I lay it down of my o. accord. 10.18
He did not say this of his o. accord, 11.51
have not spoken on my o. authority; 12.49
loved his o. who were in the world, 13.01
I do not speak on my o. authority; 14.10
world, the world would love its o.; 15.19
will not speak on his o. authority, 16.13
thou me in thy o. presence with 17.05
and judge him by your o. law." 18.31
"Do you say this of your o. accord, 18.34
Your o. nation and the chief priests 18.35
bearing his o. cross, to the place 19.17
disciple took her to his o. home. 19.27
has fixed by his o. authority. Ac 1.07
aside, to go to his o. place. 1.25
them speaking in his o. language. 2.06
of us in his o. native language? 2.08
telling in our o. tongues the 2.11
though by our o. power or piety we 3.12
which he possessed was his o., 4.32
unsold, did it not remain your o.? 5.04
and brought him up as her o. son. 7.21
It opened to them of its o. accord, 12.10
of God in his o. generation, fell asleep, 13.36
nations to walk in their o. ways; 14.16
words and names and your o. law, 18.15
he obtained with his o. blood. 20.28
and from among your o. selves will 20.30
and bound his o. feet and hands, 21.11
him about their o. superstition 25.19
among my o. nation and at Jerusalem, 26.04
out with their o. hands the tackle 27.19
two whole years at his o. expense, 28.30
in their o. persons the due penalty Rom 1.27
when he considered his o. body, 4.19
I do not understand my o. actions. 7.15
sending his o. Son in the likeness 8.03
not of its o. will but by the will 8.20
not spare his o. Son but gave him 8.32
and seeking to establish their o., 10.03
back into their o. olive tree. 11.24
Lest you be wise in your o. conceits, 11.25
is before his o. master that he 14.04
be fully convinced in his o. mind. 14.05
but their o. appetites, and by fair 16.18
labor, working with our o. hands. 1Co 4.12
and that even your o. brethren. 6.08
man sins against his o. body. 6.18
have from God? You are not your o.; 6.19
should have his o. wife and each 7.02
wife and each woman her o. husband. 7.02
does not rule over her o. body, 7.04
does not rule over his o. body, 7.04
each has his o. special gift from 7.07
I say this for your o. benefit, 7.35
as a soldier at his o. expense? 9.07
For if I do this of my o. will, 9.17
but if not of my o. will, 9.17
Let no one seek his o. good, 10.24
I do, not seeking my o. advantage, 10.33
one goes ahead with his o. meal, 11.21
Love does not insist on its o. way; 13.05
But each in his o. order: Christ the 15.23
to each kind of seed its o. body. 15.38
this greeting with my o. hand. 16.21
restricted in your o. affections. 2Co 6.12
And besides our o. comfort we 7.13
means, of their o. free will, 8.03
is going to you of his o. accord. 8.17
robbers, danger from my o. people, 11.26
but on my o. behalf I will not 12.05
many of my o. age among my people, Gal 1.14
But let each one test his o. work, 6.04
man will have to bear his o. load. 6.05
who sows to his o. flesh will from 6.08
am writing to you with my o. hand. 6.11
and this is not your o. doing, Eph 2.08
their wives as their o. bodies. 5.28
For no man ever hates his o. flesh, 5.29
look not only to his o. interests, Php 2.04
work out your o. salvation with 2.12
They all look after their o. interests, 2.21
having a righteousness of my o., 3.09
but I press on to make it my o., 3.12
Christ Jesus has made me his o. 3.12
consider that I have made it my o.; 3.13
this greeting with my o. hand. Col 4.18
of God but also our o. selves, 1Th 2.08
you into his o. kingdom and glory. 2.12
from your o. countrymen as they 2.14
to mind your o. affairs, and to work 4.11
and to earn their o. living. 2Th 3.12
this greeting with my o. hand. 3.17
He must manage his o. household well, 1Ti 3.04
how to manage his o. household, 3.05
duty to their o. family and make 5.04
and especially for his o. family, 5.08
virtue of his o. purpose and the 2Ti 1.09
teachers to suit their o. likings, 4.03
themselves, a prophet of their o., Tit 1.12
a people of his o. who are zealous 2.14

OWN (cont.)

but in virtue of his o. mercy, Tit 3.05
compulsion but of your o. free will. Phm 1.14
I, Paul, write this with my o. hand, 1.19
of your owing me even your o. self. 1.19
distributed according to his o. will. Heb 2.04
sacrifice for his o. sins as well 5.03
of God on their o. account and 6.06
first for his o. sins and then for 7.27
goats and calves but his o. blood, 9.12
Place yearly with blood not his o.; 9.25
the people through his o. blood. 13.12
lured and enticed by his o. desire. Jas 1.14
Of his o. will he brought us forth 1.18
God's o. people, that you may declare 1Pe 2.09
us to his o. glory and excellence, 2Pe 1.03
matter of one's o. interpretation, 1.20
rebuked for his o. transgression; 2.16
The dog turns back to his o. vomit, 2.22
scoffing, following their o. passions 3.03
twist to their o. destruction, as they 3.16
men and lose your o. stability. 3.17
Because his o. deeds were evil and 1Jn 3.12
he has given us of his o. Spirit. 4.13
not keep their o. position but Jud 1.06
up the foam of their o. shame; 1.13
following their o. passions, 1.16
following their o. ungodly passions." 1.18
out of heaven, and my o. new name. Rev 3.12

OWNED

of the poor people who o. nothing, Jer 39.10

OWNER

but the o. of the ox shall be clear. Ex 21.28
and its o. has been warned but has 21.29
and its o. also shall be put to 21.29
the o. shall give to their master 21.32
the o. of the pit shall make it 21.34
he shall give money to its o., 21.34
and its o. has not kept it in, he 21.36
the o. of the house shall come near 22.08
and the o. shall accept the oath, 22.11
shall make restitution to its o. 22.12
the o. not being with it, he shall 22.14
If the o. was with it, he shall not 22.15
he was with his o. shall be rated Lev 25.50
name of Shemer, the o. of the hill. 1Ki 16.24
gain has their o. but to see them Ecc 5.11
were kept by their o. to his hurt, 5.13
The ox knows its o., and the ass Is 1.03
the o. of the vineyard said to his Mt 20.08
When therefore the o. of the 21.40
What will the o. of the vineyard do? Mk 12.09
Then the o. of the vineyard said, Lk 20.13
then will the o. of the vineyard 20.15
and to the o. of the ship than to Ac 27.11
he is the o. of all the estate; Gal 4.01

OWNERS

and caused the death of its o.; Job 31.39
its o. said to them, "Why are you Lk 19.33
and brought her o. much gain by Ac 16.16
But when her o. saw that their hope 16.19

OWNS

the cave of Machpelah, which he o.; Gen 23.09
then he who o. the house shall come Lev 14.35
the man who o. this girdle and Ac 21.11

OX

or his o., or his ass, or anything Ex 20.17
"When an o. gores a man or a woman 21.28
the o. shall be stoned, and its 21.28
the owner of the o. shall be clear. 21.28
But if the o. has been accustomed 21.29
the o. shall be stoned, and its 21.29
If the o. gores a slave, male or 21.32
and the o. shall be stoned. 21.32
and an o. or an ass falls into it, 21.33
"When one man's o. hurts another's, so 21.35
sell the live o. and divide the 21.35
known that the o. has been accustomed 21.36
he shall pay o. for o., and the dead 21.36
"If a man steals an o. or a sheep, 22.01
he shall pay five oxen for an o., 22.01
it is an o. or an ass or a sheep, 22.04
of trust, whether it is for o., 22.09
an ass or an o. or a sheep or any 22.10
your enemy's o. or his ass going 23.04
that your o. and your ass may have 23.12
taken from the o. of the sacrifice Lev 4.10
eat no fat of o., or sheep, or goat. 7.23
and an o. and a ram for peace 9.04
He killed the o. also and the ram, 9.18
and the fat of the o. and of the ram, 9.19
Israel kills an o. or a lamb or a 17.03
whether o. or sheep, it is the LORD's. 27.26
leaders, and for each one an o.; Num 7.03
as the o. licks up the grass of the 22.04
it were the horns of the wild o. 23.22
it were the horns of the wild o., 24.08
or your o., or your ass, or any of Deu 5.14
his o., or his ass, or anything that 5.21
may eat: the o., the sheep, the goat, 14.04
your God an o. or a sheep in which 17.01
whether it be o. or sheep: they 18.03
your brother's o. or his sheep go 22.01
ass or his o. fallen down by the 22.04
plow with an o. and an ass together. 22.10
not muzzle an o. when it treads 25.04
Your o. shall be slain before your 28.31
horns are the horns of a wild o.; 33.17
Israel, and no sheep or o. or ass. Ju 6.04
Whose o. have I taken? Or whose ass 1Sa 12.03
man bring his o. or his sheep, 14.34
brought his o. with him that night, 14.34
and suckling, o. and sheep, camel and ass. 15.03
he sacrificed an o. and a fatling. 2Sa 6.13
one day was one o. and six choice Neh 5.18
or the o. low over his fodder? Job 6.05
take the widow's o. for a pledge. 24.03
"Is the wild o. willing to serve 39.09
I made you; he eats grass like an o. 40.15
and Sirion like a young wild o. Ps 29.06
more than an o. or a bull with 69.31
my horn like that of the wild o.; 92.10
the image of an o. that eats grass. 106.20
as an o. goes to the slaughter, or Pro 7.22
come by the strength of the o. 14.04
than a fatted o. and hatred with 15.17
The o. knows its owner, and the ass Is 1.03
lion shall eat straw like the o. 11.07
the feet of the o. and the ass 32.20
lion shall eat straw like the o.; 65.25
slaughters an o. is like him who 66.03
the face of an o. on the left side, Eze 1.10
be made to eat grass like an o., Dan 4.25
be made to eat grass like an o.; 4.32
men, and ate grass like an o., 4.33
he was fed grass like an o., 5.21
untie his o. or his ass from the Lk 13.15
an ass or an o. that has fallen 14.05
not muzzle an o. when it is 1Co 9.09
not muzzle an o. when it is 1Ti 5.18
second living creature like an o., Rev 4.07

OXEN

o., he-asses, menservants, maidservants, Gen 12.16
Then Abimelech took sheep and o., 20.14
took sheep and o. and gave them to 21.27

OXEN (cont.)
and I have o., asses, flocks, menservants, Gen 32.05
their wantonness they hamstring o. 49.06
offerings, your sheep and your o.; Ex 20.24
it, he shall pay five o. for an ox, 22.01
with your o. and with your sheep: 22.30
peace offerings of o. to the LORD. 24.05
six covered wagons and twelve o., Num 7.03
So Moses took the wagons and the o., 7.06
Two wagons and four o. he gave to 7.07
and eight o. he gave to the sons 7.08
two o., five rams, five male goats, 7.17
two o., five rams, five male goats, 7.23
two o., five rams, five male goats, 7.29
two o., five rams, five male goats, 7.35
two o., five rams, five male goats, 7.41
two o., five rams, five male goats, 7.47
two o., five rams, five male goats, 7.53
two o., five rams, five male goats, 7.59
two o., five rams, five male goats, 7.65
two o., five rams, five male goats, 7.71
two o., five rams, five male goats, 7.77
two o., five rams, five male goats, 7.83
And Balak sacrificed o. and sheep, 22.40
and of the o. and of the asses and 31.28
of the o., of the asses, and of the 31.30
o., or sheep, or wine or strong Deu 14.26
o., sheep, and asses, with the edge Jos 6.21
and his o. and asses and sheep, and 7.24
from the field behind the o.; 1Sa 11.05
He took a yoke of o., and cut them 11.07
so shall it be done to his o.! 11.07
and took sheep and o. and calves, 14.32
and of the o. and of the fatlings, 15.09
the lowing of the o. which I hear? 15.14
best of the sheep and of the o., 15.15
sheep and o., the best of the 15.21
o., asses and sheep, he put to the 22.19
the o., the asses, the camels, and 27.09
hold of it, for the o. stumbled. 2Sa 6.06
here are the o. for the burnt 24.22
the yokes of the o. for the wood. 24.22
floor and the o. for fifty shekels 24.24
o., and fatlings by the serpent's 1Ki 1.09
He has sacrificed o., fatlings, and 1.19
this day, and has sacrificed o., 1.25
ten fat o., and twenty pasture-fed 4.23
It stood upon twelve o., three facing 7.25
were lions, o., and cherubim. 7.29
above and below the lions and o., 7.29
and the twelve o. underneath the 7.44
many sheep and o. that they could 8.05
twenty-two thousand o. and a hundred and 8.63
with twelve yoke of o. before him, 19.19
And he left the o., and ran after 19.20
him, and took the yoke of o., 19.21
flesh with the yokes of the o., 19.21
sheep and o., menservants and 2Ki 5.26
off the bronze o. that were under 16.17
on camels and on mules and on o., 1Ch 12.40
o. and sheep, for there was joy in 12.40
hold the ark, for the o. stumbled. 13.09
I give the o. for burnt offerings, 21.23
It stood upon twelve o., three facing 2Ch 4.04
and the twelve o. underneath it. 4.15
many sheep and o. that they could 5.06
thousand o. and a hundred and 7.05
seven hundred o. and seven thousand 15.11
of sheep and o. for him and for 18.02
camels, five hundred yoke of o., Job 1.03
"The o. were plowing and the asses 1.14
camels, a thousand yoke of o., 42.12
all sheep and o., and also the Ps 8.07
soul from the horns of the wild o.! 22.21
Where there are no o., there is no Pro 14.04
slaying o. and killing sheep, eating Is 22.13
and the o. and the asses that till 30.24
Wild o. shall fall with them, and 34.07
Does one plow the sea with o.? Amo 6.12
my o. and my fat calves are killed, Mt 22.04
'I have bought five yoke of o., Lk 14.19
were selling o. and sheep and Jn 2.14
them all, with the sheep and o., 2.15
brought o. and garlands to the Ac 14.13
Is it for o. that God is concerned? 1Co 9.09

OXGOAD
of the Philistines with an o.; Ju 3.31

OZEM
O. the sixth, David the seventh; 1Ch 2.15
Bunah, Oren, O., and Ahijah. 2.25

OZNI
of O., the family of the Oznites; Num 26.16

OZNITES
of Ozni, the family of the O.; Num 26.16

P

PAARAI
Hezro of Carmel, P. the Arbite, 2Sa 23.35

PACE
according to the p. of the cattle Gen 33.14
acording to the p. of the children, 33.14
not slacken the p. for me unless I 2Ki 4.24

PACES
ark of the LORD had gone six p., 2Sa 6.13

PADDAN
For when I came from P., Rachel to Gen 48.07

PADDAN-ARAM
of Bethuel the Aramean of P., Gen 25.20
Arise, go to P., to the house of Bethuel 28.02
and he went to P. to Laban, 28.05
him away to P. to take a wife from 28.06
and his mother and gone to P. 28.07
which he had acquired in P., to go to 31.18
land of Canaan, on his way from P.; 33.18
Jacob again, when he came from P., 35.09
Jacob who were born to him in P. 35.26
Leah, whom she bore to Jacob in P., 46.15

PADON
the sons of Siaha, the sons of P., Ez 2.44
the sons of Sia, the sons of P., Neh 7.47

PAGANS
that is not found even among p.; 1Co 5.01
imply that what p. sacrifice they 10.20

PAGIEL
from Asher, P. the son of Ochran; Num 1.13
of Asher being P. the son of 2.27
eleventh day P. the son of Ochran, 7.72
the offering of P. the son of 7.77
of Asher was P. the son of Ochran. 10.26

PAHATHMOAB
The sons of P., namely the sons of Ez 2.06
Of the sons of P., Eliehoenai the 8.04
Of the sons of P.: Adna, Chelal, 10.30
the son of P. repaired another Neh 3.11
The sons of P., namely the sons of 7.11
people: Parosh, P., Elam, Zattu, Bani, 10.14

PAI
and the name of his city was P., 1Ch 1.50

PAID

of the prison p. no heed to Gen 39.23
of the price p. for him the price Lev 25.51
and they p. it out to the carpenters 2Ki 12.11
his vassal, and p. him tribute. 17.03
So David p. Ornan six hundred 1Ch 21.25
The Ammonites p. tribute to Uzziah, 2Ch 26.08
The Ammonites p. him the same 27.05
tribute, custom, and toll were p. Ez 4.20
let the cost be p. from the royal 6.04
cost is to be p. to these men in 6.08
It will be p. in full before his Job 15.32
and today I have p. my vows; Pro 7.14
so he p. the fare, and went on board, Jon 1.03
at which I was p. off by them. Zec 11.13
till you have p. the last penny. Mt 5.26
And they p. him thirty pieces of 26.15
till you have p. the very last Lk 12.59
But Gallio p. no attention to this. Ac 18.17
But the centurion p. more attention 27.11
wrongdoer will be p. back for the Col 3.25
receives tithes, p. tithes through Abraham, Heb 7.09
and so I p. no heed to them, says 8.09

PAIN

multiply your p. in childbearing; Gen 3.16
in p. you shall bring forth children, 3.16
enter into her and cause bitter p. Num 5.24
enter into her and cause bitter p., 5.27
saying, "Because I bore him in p." 1Ch 4.09
I would even exult in p. unsparing; Job 6.10
He feels only the p. of his own 14.22
man writhes in p. all his days, 15.20
of my lips would assuage your p. 16.05
my p. is not assuaged, and if I 16.06
and the p. that gnaws me takes no 30.17
chastened with p. upon his bed, 33.19
How long must I bear p. in my soul, Ps 13.02
to fall, and my p. is ever with me. 38.17
But I am afflicted and in p.; 69.29
For all his days are full of p., Ecc 2.23
and put away p. from your body; 11.10
rest from your p. and turmoil and Is 14.03
in a day of grief and incurable p. 17.11
you shall cry out for p. of heart, 65.14
before her p. came upon her she was 66.07
I writhe in p.! Oh, the walls Jer 4.19
p. as of a woman in travail. 6.24
Why is my p. unceasing, my wound 15.18
p. as of a woman in travail! 22.23
Your p. is incurable. Because your 30.15
the LORD has added sorrow to my p.; 45.03
seized him, p. as of a woman in travail. 50.43
Take balm for her p.; 51.08
The land trembles and writhes in p., 51.29
For if I cause you p., who is there 2Co 2.02
to cause you p. but to let you 2.04
But if any one has caused p., 2.05
he endures p. while suffering 1Pe 2.19
of heaven for their p. and sores, Rev 16.11
mourning nor crying nor p. any more, 21.04

PAINED

me glad but the one whom I have p.? 2Co 2.02
I might not be p. by those who 2.03

PAINFUL

not to make you another p. visit. 2Co 2.01
discipline seems p. rather than Heb 12.11

PAINS

gave birth; for her p. came upon her. 1Sa 4.19
With great p. I have provided for 1Ch 22.14
God distributes p. in his anger? Job 21.17
of the vision p. have come upon me, Dan 10.16
with various diseases and p., Mt 4.24
So I always take p. to have a clear Ac 24.16

PAINT

that you enlarge your eyes with p.? Jer 4.30

PAINTED

and she p. her eyes, and adorned her 2Ki 9.30
p. your eyes, and decked yourself Eze 23.40

PAINTING

with cedar, and p. it with vermilion. Jer 22.14

PAIR

and a p. of the animals that are Gen 7.02
it under each p. of the six Ex 25.35
it under each p. of the six 37.21
a torch between each p. of tails. Ju 15.04
and the needy for a p. of shoes— Amo 2.06
and the needy for a p. of sandals, 8.06
"a p. of turtledoves, or two young Lk 2.24

PAIRS

Take with you seven p. of all clean Gen 7.02
and seven p. of the birds of the 7.03
horsemen in p., riders on asses, Is 21.07
here come riders, horsemen in p.!" 21.09

PALACE

Ahishar was in charge of the p.; 1Ki 4.06
beside the p. of Ahab king of 21.01
So he who was over the p., 2Ki 10.05
the guards), shall guard the p.; 11.06
which had been built inside the p., 16.18
eunuchs in the p. of the king of 20.18
his princes, and his p. officials. 24.12
together with the p. officials, 1Ch 28.01
for the p. will not be for man 29.01
may build the p. for which I have 29.19
LORD, and a royal p. for himself. 2Ch 2.01
LORD, and a royal p. for himself. 2.12
commander of the p. and Elkanah the 28.07
and put them in his p. in Babylon. 36.07
the salt of the p. and it is not Ez 4.14
of the garden of the king's p. Est 1.05
officials of his p. to do as every 1.08
women in the p. which belonged to 1.09
into the king's p. and put in 2.08
chosen maids from the king's p., 2.09
from the harem to the king's p. 2.13
into his royal p. in the tenth 2.16
in the king's p. you will escape 4.13
the inner court of the king's p., 5.01
the p. opposite the entrance to the p.; 5.01
of the king's p. to speak to the 6.04
wrath and went into the p. garden; 7.07
from the p. garden to the place 7.08
as they enter the p. of the king. Ps 45.15
cut for the structure of a p.; 144.12
the p. of aliens is a city no more, Is 25.02
For the p. will be forsaken, the 32.14
eunuchs in the p. of the king of 39.07
and the p. shall stand where it Jer 30.18
was in the p. of the king of Judah. 32.02
to Pharaoh's p. in Tahpanhes, 43.09
competent to serve in the king's p., Dan 1.04
my house and prospering in my p. 4.04
roof of the royal p. of Babylon, 4.29
of the wall of the king's p., 5.05
Then the king went to his p., 6.18
are opened, the p. is in dismay; Nah 2.06
gathered in the p. of the high Mt 26.03
led him away inside the p. (that is, Mk 15.16
fully armed, guards his own p., Lk 11.21

PALACES

and burned all its p. with fire, 2Ch 36.19
From ivory p. stringed instruments Ps 45.08
your hands, yet it is in kings' p. Pro 30.28
and jackals in the pleasant p.; Is 13.22

PALACES (cont.)
siege towers, they razed her p., Is 23.13
by night and destroy her p.!" Jer 6.05
our windows, it has entered our p., 9.21
devour the p. of Jerusalem and 17.27
it shall devour the p. of Benhadad." 49.27
he has destroyed all its p., Lam 2.05
of the enemy the walls of her p.; 2.07
forgotten his Maker, and built p.; Hos 8.14

PALAL
P. the son of Uzai repaired opposite Neh 3.25

PALANQUIN
made himself a p. from the wood of Sol 3.09

PALATE
try words as the p. tastes food? Job 12.11
tests words as the p. tastes food. 34.03

PALATIAL
shall pitch his p. tents between Dan 11.45

PALE
no more shall his face grow p. Is 29.22
Why has every face turned p.? Jer 30.06
are in anguish, all faces grow p. Joe 2.06
is on all loins, all faces grow p.! Nah 2.10
a p. horse, and its rider's name was Rev 6.08

PALLET
let down the p. on which the Mk 2.04
'Rise, take up your p. and walk'? 2.09
rise, take up your p. and go home." 2.11
took up the p. and went out before 2.12
"Rise, take up your p., and walk." Jn 5.08
and he took up his p. and walked. 5.09
lawful for you to carry your p." 5.10
to me, 'Take up your p., and walk.'" 5.11
you, 'Take up your p., and walk'?" 5.12

PALLETS
people on their p. to any place Mk 6.55
and laid them on beds and p., Ac 5.15

PALLU
Reuben: Hanoch, P., Hezron, and Carmi. Gen 46.09
P., Hezron and Carmi; these are the Ex 6.14
of P., the family of the Palluites; Num 26.05
And the sons of P.: Eliab. 26.08
Israel: Hanoch, P., Hezron, and Carmi. 1Ch 5.03

PALLUITES
of Pallu, the family of the P.; Num 26.05

PALM
of water and seventy p. trees; Ex 15.27
it into the p. of his own left Lev 14.15
oil into the p. of his own left 14.26
branches of p. trees, and boughs of 23.40
of water and seventy p. trees, Num 33.09
of Jericho the city of p. trees, Deu 34.03
sit under the p. of Deborah Ju 4.05
of cherubim and p. trees and open 1Ki 6.29
p. trees, and open flowers; he overlaid 6.32
the cherubim and upon the p. trees. 6.32
cherubim and p. trees and open 6.35
and p. trees, according to the space 7.36
at Jericho, the city of p. trees. 2Ch 28.15
p., and other leafy trees to make Neh 8.15
righteous flourish like the p. tree, Ps 92.12
You are stately as a p. tree, Sol 7.07
will climb the p. tree and lay 7.08
p. branch and reed in one day— Is 9.14
or tail, p. branch or reed, may do. 19.15
and on the jambs were p. trees. Eze 40.16
and its p. trees were of the same 40.22
and it had p. trees on its jambs, 40.26
and p. trees were on its jambs, and 40.31
and it had p. trees on its jambs, 40.34
and it had p. trees on its jambs, 40.37
of cherubim and p. trees, 41.18
a p. tree between cherub and cherub. 41.18
man toward the p. tree on the one 41.19
lion toward the p. tree on the 41.19
cherubim and p. trees were carved 41.20
were carved cherubim and p. trees, 41.25
windows and p. trees on either 41.26
Pomegranate, p., and apple, all the Joe 1.12
branches of p. trees and went out Jn 12.13
with p. branches in their hands, Rev 7.09

PALMS
the city of p. into the wilderness Ju 1.16
took possession of the city of p. 3.13
the feet and the p. of her hands. 2Ki 9.35
and made p. and chains on it. 2Ch 3.05
graven you on the p. of my hands; Is 49.16

PALSIED
of the land are p. by terror. According Eze 7.27

PALTI
of Benjamin, P. the son of Raphu; Num 13.09
to P. the son of Laish, who was of 1Sa 25.44

PALTIEL
a leader, P. the son of Azzan. Num 34.26
her husband P. the son of Laish. 2Sa 3.15

PALTITE
Helez the P., Ira the son of Ikkesh 2Sa 23.26

PAMPERS
He who p. his servant from childhood, Pro 29.21

PAMPHYLIA
Phrygia and P., Egypt and the parts Ac 2.10
Paphos, and came to Perga in P. 13.13
through Pisidia, and came to P. 14.24
who had withdrawn from them in P., 15.38
sea which is off Cilicia and P., 27.05

PAN
a cereal offering cooked in a p., Lev 2.07
prepared on a p. or a griddle 7.09
and he would thrust it into the p., 1Sa 2.14
And she took the p. and emptied it 2Sa 13.09

PANELED
were p. and round about all three Eze 41.16
the temple was p. with wood round 41.16
yourselves to dwell in your p. houses, Hag 1.04

PANELING
p. it with cedar, and painting it Jer 22.14

PANELS
they had p., and the p. were set 1Ki 7.28
and on the p. that were set in the 7.29
and its p. were square, not round. 7.31
four wheels were underneath the p.; 7.32
stays and its p. were of one piece 7.35
surfaces of its stays and on its p., 7.36

PANGS
p. have seized on the inhabitants Ex 15.14
or p. of conscience, for having shed 1Sa 25.31
Many are the p. of the wicked; Ps 32.10
For they have no p.; their bodies 73.04
the p. of Sheol laid hold on me; 116.03
P. and agony will seize them; Is 13.08
p. have seized me, like the p. of a woman 21.03
writhes and cries out in her p., 26.17
Will not p. take hold of you, like Jer 13.21
will groan when p. come upon you, 22.23
the heart of a woman in her p.; 48.41
the heart of a woman in her p. 49.22

PANGS (cont.)
The p. of childbirth come for him, Hos 13.13
that p. have seized you like a Mic 4.09
up, having loosed the p. of death, Ac 2.24
pierced their hearts with many p. 1Ti 6.10
she cried out in her p. of birth, Rev 12.02

PANIC
threw them into a p. before Israel, Jos 10.10
he threw all the army into a p. Ju 8.12
the city, causing a very great p., 1Sa 5.09
was a deathly p. throughout the 5.11
And there was a p. in the camp, 14.15
and it became a very great p. 14.15
discouraged, and throw him into a p.; 2Sa 17.02
they were in p., they took to Ps 48.05
I will mock when p. strikes you, Pro 1.26
when p. strikes you like a storm, 1.27
Do not be afraid of sudden p., 3.25
officers desert the standard in p., Is 31.09
LORD: We have heard a cry of p., Jer 30.05
turned to flee, and p. seized her; 49.24
fire, and the soldiers are in p. 51.32
p. and pitfall have come upon us, Lam 3.47
I will strike every horse with p., Zec 12.04
day a great p. from the LORD shall 14.13

PANS
and basins and forks and fire p.; Ex 27.03
and the fire p.: all its utensils he 38.03
and in p., and carried them quickly 2Ch 35.13

PANT
and the thirsty p. after his wealth Job 5.05
With open mouth I p., because I long Ps 119.131
in travail, I will gasp and p. Is 42.14
they p. for air like jackals; Jer 14.06

PAPER
I would rather not use p. and ink, 2Jn 1.12

PAPHOS
the whole island as far as P., Ac 13.06
and his company set sail from P., 13.13

PAPYRUS
"Can p. grow where there is no Job 8.11
in vessels of p. upon the waters! Is 18.02

PARABLE
I will open my mouth in a p.; Ps 78.02
"Hear then the p. of the sower. Mt 13.18
Another p. he put before them, 13.24
Another p. he put before them, 13.31
He told them another p. "The kingdom 13.33
said nothing to them without a p. 13.34
to us the p. of the weeds of the 13.36
said to him, "Explain the p. to us." 15.15
"Hear another p. There was a 21.33
"Do you not understand this p.? Mk 4.13
or what p. shall we use for it? 4.30
did not speak to them without a p., 4.34
disciples asked him about the p. 7.17
he had told the p. against them; 12.12
He told them a p. also: "No one Lk 5.36
He also told them a p.: "Can a blind 6.39
town came to him, he said in a p.: 8.04
asked him what this p. meant, 8.09
Now the p. is this: The seed is the 8.11
And he told them a p., saying, "The land 12.16
telling this p. for us or for all?" 12.41
And he told this p.: "A man had 13.06
Now he told a p. to those who were 14.07
So he told them this p.: 15.03
And he told them a p., to the effect 18.01
He also told this p. to some who 18.09
things, he proceeded to tell a p., 19.11
began to tell the people this p.: 20.09
he had told this p. against them. 20.19
And he told them a p.: "Look at the 21.29

PARABLES
and through the prophets gave p. Hos 12.10
And he told them many things in p., Mt 13.03
"Why do you speak to them in p.?" 13.10
This is why I speak to them in p., 13.13
Jesus said to the crowds in p.; 13.34
prophet: "I will open my mouth in p., 13.35
And when Jesus had finished these p., 13.53
and the Pharisees heard his p., 21.45
Jesus spoke to them in p., saying, 22.01
to him, and said to them in p., Mk 3.23
And he taught them many things in p., 4.02
twelve asked him concerning the p. 4.10
those outside everything is in p.; 4.11
will you understand all the p.? 4.13
With many such p. he spoke the word 4.33
And he began to speak to them in p. 12.01
but for others they are in p., Lk 8.10

PARADISE
today you will be with me in P." Lk 23.43
this man was caught up into P.— 2Co 12.03
of life, which is in the p. of God. Rev 2.07

PARAH
Avvim, P., Ophrah, Jos 18.23

PARALLEL
a wall outside p. to the chambers, Eze 42.07
p. to the tribal portions, it shall 48.21

PARALYTIC
And behold, they brought to him a p., Mt 9.02
saw their faith he said to the p., 9.02
he then said to the p.—"Rise, take up 9.06
to him a p. carried by four men. Mk 2.03
the pallet on which the p. lay. 2.04
saw their faith, he said to the p., 2.05
to say to the p., 'Your sins are 2.09
forgive sins"—he said to the p.— 2.10

PARALYTICS
and p., and he healed them. Mt 4.24

PARALYZED
my servant is lying p. at home, Mt 8.06
bringing on a bed a man who was p., Lk 5.18
he said to the man who was p.—"I say 5.24
of invalids, blind, lame, p. Jn 5.03
many who were p. or lame were Ac 8.07
bedridden for eight years and was p. 9.33

PARAMOUR
is beloved of a p. and is an Hos 3.01

PARAMOURS
and doted upon her p. there, Eze 23.20

PARAN
He lived in the wilderness of P.; Gen 21.21
down in the wilderness of P. Num 10.12
encamped in the wilderness of P. 12.16
them from the wilderness of P., 13.03
in the wilderness of P., at Kadesh; 13.26
between P. and Tophel, Laban, Hazeroth, Deu 1.01
he shone forth from Mount P., 33.02
went down to the wilderness of P. 1Sa 25.01
set out from Midian and came to P., 1Ki 11.18
with them from P. and came to 11.18
and the Holy One from Mount P. Hab 3.03

PARAPET
you shall make a p. for your roof, Deu 22.08

PARBAR
and for the p. on the west there 1Ch 26.18
four at the road and two at the p. 26.18

PARCEL
is selling the p. of land which Ru 4.03

PARCELED
your land shall be p. out by line; Amo 7.17

PARCHED
from fresh ears, p. with fire. Lev 2.14
bread nor grain p. or fresh until 23.14
unleavened cakes and p. grain. Jos 5.11
and he passed to her p. grain; Ru 2.14
brothers an ephah of this p. grain, 1Sa 17.17
and five measures of p. grain, 25.18
p. grain, beans and lentils, 2Sa 17.28
the rebellious dwell in a p. land. Ps 68.06
my throat is p. My eyes grow 69.03
a p. land into springs of water. 107.35
thirsts for thee like a p. land. 143.06
their multitude is p. with thirst. Is 5.13
and the river will be p. and dry; 19.05
and their tongue is p. with thirst. 41.17
dwell in the p. places of the Jer 17.06
glory, and sit on the p. ground, 48.18
wilderness, and set her like a p. land, Hos 2.03
dry up, his spring shall be p.; 13.15
him into a p. and desolate land, Joe 2.20

PARCHMENTS
the books, and above all the p. 2Ti 4.13

PARDON
for he will not p. your transgression; Ex 23.21
and p. our iniquity and our sin, and 34.09
P. the iniquity of this people, I Num 14.19
The LORD would not p. him, Deu 29.20
p. my sin, and return with me, that I 1Sa 15.25
may the LORD p. your servant: 2Ki 5.18
the LORD p. your servant in this 5.18
blood, and the LORD would not p. 24.04
saying, "The good LORD p. every one 2Ch 30.18
Why dost thou not p. my transgression Job 7.21
O LORD, p. my guilt, for it is great. Ps 25.11
people; thou didst p. all their sin. 85.02
our God, for he will abundantly p. Is 55.07
and seeks truth; that I may p. her. Jer 5.01
"How can I p. you? Your children 5.07
for I will p. those whom I leave as 50.20

PARDONED
"I have p., according to your word; Num 14.20
is ended, that her iniquity is p., Is 40.02

PARDONING
p. iniquity and passing over Mic 7.18

PARE
shave her head and p. her nails. Deu 21.12

PARENT
who loves the p. loves the child. 1Jn 5.01

PARENTS
rise against p. and have them put Mt 10.21
rise against p. and have them put Mk 13.12
and when the p. brought in the Lk 2.27
Now his p. went to Jerusalem every 2.41
in Jerusalem. His p. did not know it, 2.43
And her p. were amazed; but he charged 8.56
wife or brothers or p. or children, 18.29
up even by p. and brothers and 21.16
who sinned, this man or his p., Jn 9.02
or his p., but that the works of 9.03
they called the p. of the man who 9.18
His p. answered, "We know that this 9.20
His p. said this because they 9.22
Therefore his p. said, "He is of age, 9.23
of evil, disobedient to p., Rom 1.30
to lay up for their p., but p. 2Co 12.14
obey your p. in the Lord, for this Eph 6.01
obey your p. in everything, for this Col 3.20
and make some return to their p.; 1Ti 5.04
abusive, disobedient to their p., 2Ti 3.02
was hid for three months by his p., Heb 11.23

PARKS
I made myself gardens and p., Ecc 2.05

PARMASHTA
and P. and Arisai and Aridai and Est 9.09

PARMENAS
and P., and Nicolaus, a proselyte of Ac 6.05

PARNACH
a leader, Elizaphan the son of P. Num 34.25

PAROSH
the sons of P., two thousand one Ez 2.03
Of the sons of P., Zechariah, with 8.03
And of Israel: of the sons of P.: 10.25
After him Pedaiah the son of P. Neh 3.25
the sons of P., two thousand a 7.08
P., Pahathmoab, Elam, Zattu, Bani, 10.14

PARSHANDATHA
and also slew P. and Dalphon and Est 9.07

PARSIN
inscribed: MENE, MENE, TEKEL, and P. Dan 5.25

PART
and upon the smooth p. of his neck; Gen 27.16
take the fifth p. of the produce 41.34
some left p. of it till the morning, Ex 16.20
(An omer is the tenth p. of an ephah.) 16.36
And the p. that remains of the 26.12
lower p. of the two shoulder-pieces 28.27
and shall take p. of the blood of 29.12
and take p. of its blood and put it 29.20
Then you shall take p. of the blood 29.21
each shall there be an equal p.), 30.34
and put p. of it before the testimony 30.36
lower p. of the two shoulder-pieces 39.20
is a most holy p. of the offerings Lev 2.03
is a most holy p. of the offerings 2.10
memorial portion p. of the crushed 2.16
and sprinkle p. of the blood seven 4.06
into the inner p. of the sanctuary. 10.18
that chew the cud or p. the hoof, 11.04
the cud but does not p. the hoof, 11.04
the cud but does not p. the hoof, 11.05
the cud but does not p. the hoof. 11.06
carries any p. of their carcass 11.25
upon which any p. of their carcass 11.35
And if any p. of their carcass 11.37
seed and any p. of their carcass 11.38
which has a p. too long or too 22.23
and sells p. of his property, then 25.25
to the LORD p. of the land which 27.16
which is not a p. of his possession 27.22
giving the hallowed p. from them. Num 18.29
or numbered the fourth p. of Israel? 23.10
the cud but do not p. the hoof, Deu 14.07
they on their p. acted with cunning, Jos 9.04
Simeon formed p. of the territory 19.09
to come to the p. of the field Ru 2.03
he will do the p. of the next of 3.13
to do the p. of the next of kin 3.13
I will do the p. of the next of kin 3.13
me the fourth p. of a shekel of 1Sa 9.08
and our p. shall be to surrender 23.20
he sent p. of the spoil to his 30.26
there was no one to p. them, 2Sa 14.06
in the innermost p. of the house, 1Ki 6.19

PART (cont.)
in the innermost p. of the house; 1Ki 6.27
of the innermost p. of the house, 7.50
and the fourth p. of a kab of 2Ki 6.25
able on your p. to set riders upon 18.23
into the inner p. of the house of 2Ch 29.16
be for each a p. of a father's 35.05
Nebuchadnezzar also carried p. of 36.07
with the third p. of a shekel for Neh 10.32
able on your p. to set riders upon Is 36.08
he takes a p. of it and warms 44.15
by measure, the sixth p. of a hin; Eze 4.11
A third p. you shall burn in the 5.02
and a third p. you shall take and 5.02
and a third p. you shall scatter to 5.02
A third p. of you shall die of 5.12
a third p. shall fall by the sword 5.12
and a third p. I will scatter to 5.12
and the p. of the platform which 41.09
opened on the p. of the platform 41.11
breadth of the p. that was left 41.11
and the main p. of the Ammonites. Dan 11.41
corner of a couch and p. of a bed. Amo 3.12
into the inner p. of the ship and Jon 1.05
not have taken p. with them in Mt 23.30
known in what p. of the night the 24.43
having no p. dark, it will be wholly Lk 11.36
not wash you, you have no p. in me." Jn 13.08
brought only a p. and laid it at Ac 5.02
to keep back p. of the proceeds of 5.03
You have neither p. nor lot in this 8.21
that one p. were Sadducees and the 23.06
Is there injustice on God's p.? Rom 9.14
hardening has come upon p. of Israel, 11.25
make it any less a p. of the body. 1Co 12.15
make it any less a p. of the body. 12.16
greater honor to the inferior p., 12.24
Now I know in p.; then I shall 13.12
as you have understood in p., 2Co 1.14
a wealth of liberality on their p. 8.02
favor of taking p. in the relief 8.04
when each p. is working properly, Eph 4.16
Take no p. in the unfruitful works 5.11
my first defense no one took my p.; 2Ti 4.16
apportioned a tenth p. of everything. Heb 7.02
lest you take p. in her sins, lest Rev 18.04

PARTAKE
were not to p. of the most holy Ez 2.63
were not to p. of the most holy Neh 7.65
for we all p. of the same loaf. 1Co 10.17
You cannot p. of the table of the 10.21
If I p. with thankfulness, why am I 10.30

PARTAKER
as well as a p. in the glory that 1Pe 5.01

PARTAKERS
and p. of the promise in Christ Eph 3.06
for you are all p. with me of Php 1.07
and have become p. of the Holy Heb 6.04
and become p. of the divine nature. 2Pe 1.04

PARTED
the water was p. to the one side 2Ki 2.08
the water was p. to the one side 2.14
While he blessed them, he p. from them. Lk 21.51
"They p. my garments among them, and Jn 19.24
And when we had p. from them and Ac 21.01
is why he was p. from you for a Phm 1.15

PARTHIANS
P. and Medes and Elamites and Ac 2.09

PARTIAL
nor shall you be p. to a poor man Ex 23.03
shall not be p. to the poor or Lev 19.15
You shall not be p. in judgment; Deu 1.17
who is not p. and takes no bribe. 10.17
not good to be p. to a wicked man, Pro 18.05

PARTIALITY
you shall not show p.; and you shall Deu 16.19
our God, or p., or taking bribes." 2Ch 19.07
Will you show p. toward him, will Job 13.08
you if in secret you show p. 13.10
I will not show p. to any person or 32.21
who shows no p. to princes, nor 34.19
unjustly and show p. to the wicked? Ps 82.02
P. in judging is not good. Pro 24.23
To show p. is not good; but for a 28.21
Their p. witnesses against them; Is 3.09
but have shown p. in your instruction." Mal 2.09
and show no p., but truly teach the Lk 20.21
I perceive that God shows no p., Ac 10.34
For God shows no p. Rom 2.11
God shows no p.)—those, I say, who Gal 2.06
and that there is no p. with him. Eph 6.09
he has done, and there is no p. Col 3.25
favor, doing nothing from p. 1Ti 5.21
show no p. as you hold the faith of Jas 2.01
But if you show p., you commit 2.09

PARTICIPATE
nor p. in another man's sins; 1Ti 5.22

PARTICIPATED
discipline, in which all have p., Heb 12.08

PARTICIPATION
is it not a p. in the blood of 1Co 10.16
is it not a p. in the body of 10.16
any p. in the Spirit, any affection Php 2.01

PARTIES
case of both p. shall come before Ex 22.09
then both p. to the dispute shall Deu 19.17

PARTING
p. from the people of Israel at Jos 22.09
stands at the p. of the way, Eze 21.21
stood at the p. of the ways to cut Ob 1.14
Therefore you shall give p. gifts Mic 1.14
And as the men were p. from him, Lk 9.33

PARTISANSHIP
the former proclaim Christ out of p., Php 1.17

PARTLY
its feet p. of iron and p. of clay. Dan 2.33
p. of potter's clay and p. of iron, 2.41
of the feet were p. iron and p. clay, 2.42
shall be p. strong and p. brittle. 2.42
among you; and I p. believe it, 1Co 11.18

PARTNER
The p. of a thief hates his own Pro 29.24
the unbelieving p. desires to 1Co 7.15
he is my p. and fellow worker in 2Co 8.23
So if you consider me your p., Phm 1.17

PARTNERS
to their p. in the other boat to Lk 5.07
of Zebedee, who were p. with Simon. 5.10
eat the sacrifices p. in the altar? 1Co 10.18
not want you to be p. with demons. 10.20
sometimes being p. with those so Heb 10.33

PARTNERSHIP
For what p. have righteousness and 2Co 6.14
thankful for your p. in the gospel Php 1.05
entered into p. with me in giving 4.15

PARTOOK
So the men p. of their provisions, Jos 9.14
they p. of food with glad and Ac 2.46
likewise p. of the same nature, Heb 2.14

PARTRIDGE
one who hunts a p. in the mountains." 1Sa 26.20
Like the p. that gathers a brood Jer 17.11

PARTS
with its legs and its inner p. Ex 12.09
Whatever p. the hoof and is cloven-footed Lev 11.03
because it p. the hoof and is 11.07
Every animal which p. the hoof but 11.26
some outlying p. of the camp. Num 11.01
and divide the booty into two p., 31.27
Every animal that p. the hoof and Deu 14.06
because it p. the hoof but does not 14.08
into three p. the area of the land 19.03
and seizes him by the private p., 25.11
are in the uttermost p. of heaven, 30.04
in the remote p. of the hill Ju 19.01
to the remote p. of the hill 19.18
also if even death p. me from you." Ru 1.17
the choicest p. of every offering 1Sa 2.29
in the innermost p. of the cave. 24.03
house was finished in all its p., 1Ki 6.38
all their hinder p. were inward. 7.25
of Israel were divided into two p.; 16.21
LORD began to cut off p. of Israel. 2Ki 10.32
all their hinder p. were inward. 2Ch 4.04
offerings and the fat p. until night; 35.14
So in the lowest p. of the space Neh 4.13
in the uttermost p. of the sea, Ps 139.09
For thou didst form my inward p., 139.13
down into the inner p. of the body. Pro 18.08
searching all his innermost p. 20.27
strokes make clean the innermost p. 20.30
down into the inner p. of the body. 26.22
LORD will lay bare their secret p. Is 3.17
from the farthest p. of the earth. Jer 6.22
from the farthest p. of the earth! 25.32
from the farthest p. of the earth, 31.08
in two and passed between its p.— 34.18
passed between the p. of the calf; 34.19
from the farthest p. of the earth. 50.41
set in the uttermost p. of the Pit. Eze 32.23
the uttermost p. of the north with 38.06
of the utermost p. of the north, 38.15
from the uttermost p. of the north, 39.02
the richest p. of the province; Dan 11.24
in the innermost p. of the house., Amo 6.10
shall be hunger in your inward p.; Mic 6.14
took his garments and made four p., Jn 19.23
Egypt and the p. of Libya belonging Ac 2.10
to the uttermost p. of the earth. 13.47
through these p. and had given 20.02
there are many p., yet one body. 1Co 12.20
the p. of the body which seem to be 12.22
and those p. of the body which we 12.23
unpresentable p. are treated with 12.23
more presentable p. do not require. 12.24
into the lower p. of the earth? Eph 4.09
great city was split into three p., Rev 16.19

PARTY
the p. of the Sadducees, and filled Ac 5.17
the circumcision p. criticized him. 11.02
belonged to the p. of the Pharisees 15.05
the Pharisees' p. stood up and 23.09
the strictest p. of our religion 26.05
himself, fearing the circumcision p. Gal 2.12
selfishness, dissension, p. spirit, 5.20
especially the circumcision p.; Tit 1.10

PARUAH
Jehoshaphat the son of P. in Issachar; 1Ki 4.17

PARVAIM
precious stones. The gold was gold of P. 2Ch 3.06

PASACH
P., Bimhal, and Ashvath. These are the 1Ch 7.33

PASCHAL
our p. lamb, has been sacrificed. 1Co 5.07

PASDAMMIM
with David at P. when the Philistines 1Ch 11.13

PASEAH
P., and Tehinnah the father of 1Ch 4.12
the sons of P., the sons of Besai, Ez 2.49
the son of P. and Meshullam the Neh 3.06
the sons of Uzza, the sons of P., 7.51

PASHHUR
son of P., son of Malchijah, and 1Ch 9.12
The sons of P., one thousand two Ez 2.38
Of the sons of P.: Elioenai, Maaseiah. 10.22
The sons of P., a thousand two Neh 7.41
P., Amariah, Malchijah, 10.03
son of P., son of Malchijah, 11.12
Now P. the priest, the son of Immer, Jer 20.01
Then P. beat Jeremiah the prophet, 20.02
when P. released Jeremiah from the 20.03
LORD does not call your name P., 20.03
And you, P., and all who dwell in 20.06
sent to him P. the son of Malchiah 21.01
of Mattan, Gedaliah the son of P., 38.01
and P. the son of Malchiah heard 38.01

PASS
do not p. by your servant. Gen 18.03
and after that you may p. on— 18.05
let me p. through all your flock 30.32
that I will not p. over this heap 31.52
you will not p. over this heap and 31.52
"P. on before m, and put a space 32.16
Let my lord p. on before his 33.14
interpreted to us, so it came to p.; 41.13
God will shortly bring it to p. 41.32
For I will p. through the land of Ex 12.12
I will p. over you, and no plague 12.13
For the LORD will p. through to 12.23
the LORD will p. over the door, and 12.23
p. by, till the people p. by whom 15.16
"P. on before the people, taking 17.05
shall p. through from end to end. 26.28
make all my goodness p. before you, 33.19
middle bar to p. through from end 36.33
of all that p. under herdsman's Lev 27.32
the curse p. into your bowels and Num 5.22
Now let us p. through your land. 20.17
We will not p. through field or 20.17
to him, "You shall not p. through." 20.18
let me only p. through on foot, 20.19
But he said, "You shall not p. through." 20.20
"Let me p. through your land; 21.22
allow Israel to p. through his 21.23
of their father to p. to them. 27.07
inheritance to p. to his daughter. 27.08
you shall p. through the fire, and 31.23
you shall p. through the water. 31.23
man of you will p. over the Jordan 32.21
but your servants will p. over, 32.27
will p. with you over the Jordan 32.29
they will not p. over with you 32.30
We will p. over armed before the 32.32
When you p. over the Jordan into 33.51
Hazaraddar, and p. along to Azmon; 34.04
are about to p. through the Deu 2.04
'This day you are to p. over the 2.18
'Let me p. through your land; 2.27
only let me p. through on foot, 2.28
Heshbon would not let us p. by him; 2.30
of valor shall p. over armed 3.18
you are to p. over the Jordan this 9.01
For you are to p. over the Jordan 11.31
which he tells you comes to p., 13.02
does not come to p. or come true, 18.22
And on the day you p. over the 27.02

PASS (cont.)

when you p. over to enter the land Deu 27.03
"P. through the camp, and command Jos 1.11
days you are to p. over this 1.11
among you shall p. over armed 1.14
and p. on before the people. 3.06
the earth is to p. over before you 3.11
to p. over the Jordan with the 3.14
"P. on before the ark of the LORD 4.05
the armed men p. on before the ark 6.07
Israel had failed; all came to p. 21.45
p. over into the LORD's land where 22.19
all have come to p. for you, 23.14
and allowed not a man to p. over. Ju 3.28
'Let us p., we pray, through your 11.17
'Let us p., we pray, through your 11.19
trust Israel to p. through his 11.20
but we will p. on to Gibeah." 19.12
was this wickedness brought to p.?" 20.03
why has this come to p. in Israel, 21.03
the servant to p. on before us, 1Sa 9.27
these signs came to p. that day. 10.09
went out to the p. of Michmash. 13.23
In the p., by which Jonathan sought 14.04
and made him p. before Samuel. 16.08
Then Jesse made Shammah p. by. 16.09
seven of his sons p. before Samuel. 16.10
said to Ittai, "Go then, p. on." 2Sa 15.22
wilderness, but by all means p. over; 17.16
Otherwise it will come to p., 1Ki 1.21
Samaria, shall surely come to p." 13.32
land between them to p. through it; 18.06
that you do not p. this place, 2Ki 6.09
fourth generation." And so it came to p.) 15.12
days of old what now I bring to p., 19.25
they may let me p. through until I Neh 2.07
the beast that was under me to p. 2.14
and his servant p. the night within 4.22
torrent-bed, as freshets that p. away, Job 6.15
his bounds that he cannot p., 14.05
up my way, so that I cannot p., 19.08
the people are shaken and p. away, 34.20
the storms of destruction p. by. Ps 57.01
the sea and let them p. through it, 78.13
so that all who p. along the way 80.12
All that p. by despoil him; 89.41
For all our days p. away under thy 90.09
For my days p. away like smoke, and 102.03
like raiment, and they p. away; 102.26
a bound which they should not p., 104.09
said came to p. the word of the 105.19
while those who p. by do not say, 129.08
and made Israel p. through the 136.14
turn away from it and p. on. Pro 4.15
calling to those who p. by, 9.15
compresses his lips brings evil to p. 16.30
It shall come to p. in the latter Is 2.02
And the idols shall utterly p. away. 2.18
stand, and it shall not come to p. 7.07
Judah, it will overflow and p. on, 8.08
They will p. through the land, 8.21
they have crossed over the p., 10.29
P. over to Tarshish, wail, O inhabitants 23.06
arise, p. over to Cyprus, even there 23.12
by morning it will p. through, 28.19
His rock shall p. away in terror, 31.09
can go, nor stately ship can p. 33.21
none shall p. through it for ever 34.10
the unclean shall not p. over it, 35.08
days of old what now I bring to p., 37.26
Behold, the former things have come to p., 42.09
When you p. through the waters I 43.02
spoken, and I will bring it to p.; 46.11
your legs, p. through the rivers. 47.02
I did them and they came to p. 48.03
they came to p. I announced them 48.05
a way for the redeemed to p. over? 51.10
'Bow down, that we may p. over'; 51.23
the street for them to p. over." 51.23
perpetual barrier which it cannot p.; Jer 5.22
they roar, they cannot p. over it. 5.22
grape-gatherer p. your hand again 6.09
And it shall come to p., if they will 12.16
many nations will p. by this city, 22.08
word of that prophet comes to p., 28.09
"And it shall come to p. in that day, 30.08
shall come to p. that as I have 31.28
thou didst speak has come to p., 32.24
shall again p. under the hands of 33.13
came to such a p. in Jerusalem and 52.03
nothing to you, all you who p. by? Lam 1.12
All who p. along the way clap their 2.15
Who has commanded and it came to p., 3.37
so that no prayer can p. through. 3.44
but to you also the cup shall p.; 4.21
razor and p. it over your head and Eze 5.01
and in the sight of all that p. by. 5.14
and blood shall p. through you; 5.17
"P. through the city after him, and 9.05
And it came to p., while I was 11.13
wild beasts to p. through the land, 14.15
that no man may p. through because 14.15
I will make you p. under the rod, 20.37
men shall p. judgment on them with 23.45
it shall come to p., I will do it; 24.14
No foot of man shall p. through it, 29.11
foot of beast shall p. through it; 29.11
desolate that none will p. through. 33.28
apart men to p. through the land 39.14
And when these p. through the land 39.15
river that I could not p. through, 47.05
and let seven times p. over him. Dan 4.16
till seven times p. over him; 4.23
and seven times shall p. over you, 4.25
and seven times shall p. over you, 4.32
dominion, which shall not p. away, 7.14
must p. before the end of the 9.02
on and overflow and p. through, 11.10
and shall overflow and p. through. 11.40
Go in, p. the night in sackcloth, O Joe 1.13
"And it shall come to p. afterward, 2.28
shall come to p. that all who call 2.32
shall never again p. through it. 3.17
for I will p. through the midst of Amo 5.17
P. over to Calneh, and see; 6.02
stretch themselves shall p. away." 6.07
I will never again p. by them; 7.08
I will never again p. by them. 8.02
P. on your way, inhabitants of Mic 1.11
from those who p. by trustingly 2.08
will break through and p. the gate, 2.13
their king will p. on before them, 2.13
It shall come to p. in the latter 4.01
they will be cut off and p. away. Nah 1.12
will come to p. from this day Hag 2.15
And this shall come to p., if you will Zec 6.15
They shall p. through the sea of 10.11
you, till heaven and earth p. away, Mt 5.18
will p. from the law until all is 5.18
that no one could p. that way. 8.28
will not p. away till all these 24.34
Heaven and earth will p. away, 24.35
but my words will not p. away. 24.35
possible, let this cup p. from me; 26.39
if this cannot p. unless I drink 26.42
He meant to p. by them, Mk 6.48
that what he says will come to p., 11.23
will not p. away before all these 13.30
Heaven and earth will p. away, 13.31
but my words will not p. away. 13.31
possible, the hour might p. from him. 14.35
day that these things come to p., Lk 1.20
for heaven and earth to p. away, 16.17
those who would p. from here to 16.26
see him, for he was to p. that way. 19.04
will not p. away till all has 21.32

PASS (cont.)
Heaven and earth will p. away, Lk 21.33
but my words will not p. away. 21.33
He had to p. through Samaria. Jn 4.04
the Spirit to p. through Macedonia Ac 19.21
and Moses said would come to p.: 26.22
who abstains p. judgment on him Rom 14.03
Who are you to p. judgment on the 14.04
Why do you p. judgment on your 14.10
Then let us no more p. judgment on 14.13
age, who are doomed to p. away. 1Co 2.06
as for prophecy, it will p. away; 13.08
as for knowledge, it will p. away. 13.08
comes, the imperfect will p. away. 13.10
shall come to p. the saying that 15.54
for I intend to p. through Macedonia, 16.05
Therefore let no one p. judgment on Col 2.16
just as it has come to p., 1Th 3.04
of the grass he will p. away. Jas 1.10
heavens will p. away with a loud 2Pe 3.10

PASSAGE
to give Israel p. through his Num 20.21
the chambers was a p. inward, Eze 42.04
with a p. in front of them; 42.11
east side, where one enters the p., 42.12
in the p. about the bush, how God Mk 12.26
in the p. about the bush, where he Lk 20.37
Now the p. of the scripture which Ac 8.32

PASSED
Abram p. through the land to the Gen 12.06
a flaming torch p. between these 15.17
So the present p. on before him; 32.21
The sun rose upon him as he p. Penuel, 32.31
Then Midianite traders p. by; 37.28
Seven days p. after the LORD had Ex 7.25
for he p. over the houses of the 12.27
and the night p. without one coming 14.20
with my hand until I have p. by; 33.22
The LORD p. before him, and proclaimed, 34.06
which we p. through to spy it out, Num 14.07
until we have p. through your 20.17
until we have p. through your 21.22
and p. through the midst of the sea 33.08
to perform what has p. your lips, Deu 23.23
And when you have p. over the 27.04
"When you have p. over the Jordan, 27.12
the nations through which you p.; 29.16
and p. over and came to Joshua the Jos 2.23
lodged there before they p. over. 3.01
you have not p. this way before. 3.04
and the people p. over opposite 3.16
when it p. over the Jordan, the 4.07
The people p. over in haste; 4.10
and the priests p. over before the 4.11
of Manasseh p. over armed before 4.12
armed for war p. over before the 4.13
'Israel p. over this Jordan on dry 4.22
Jordan for you until you p. over, 4.23
dried up for us until we p. over, 4.23
before the ark of the LORD p. on, 6.13
Then Joshua p. on from Makkedah, and 10.29
And Joshua p. on from Libnah, and 10.31
And Joshua p. on with all Israel 10.34
men went and p. up and down in the 18.09
all the peoples through whom we p.; 24.17
and p. beyond the sculptured stones, Ju 3.26
came to the Jordan and p. over, 8.04
robbed all who p. by them along 9.25
and he p. through Gilead and 11.29
and p. on to Mizpah of Gilead, and 11.29
of Gilead he p. on to the Ammonites. 11.29
And they p. on from there to the 18.13
So they p. on and went their way; 19.14
and he p. to her parched grain; Ru 2.14
a long time p., some twenty years, 1Sa 7.02
And they p. through the hill 9.04
of Ephraim and p. through the land 9.04
Then they p. through the land of 9.04
and when he has p. on stop here 9.27
and the battle p. beyond Bethaven. 14.23
and p. on, and went down to Gilgal." 15.12
Then they arose and p. over by number, 2Sa 2.15
And all his servants p. by him; 15.18
from Gath, p. on before the king. 15.18
So Ittai the Gittite p. on, with all 15.22
wept aloud as all the people p. by, 15.23
all the people p. on toward the 15.23
people had all p. out of the city. 15.24
When David had p. a little beyond 16.01
And Sheba p. through all the tribes 20.14
men p. by, and saw the body thrown 1Ki 13.25
And as midday p., they raved on 18.29
the LORD p. by, and a great and 19.11
Elijah p. by him and cast his 19.19
And as the king p., he cried to the 20.39
So whenever he p. that way, 2Ki 4.08
Then Joram p. over to Zair with all 8.21
of Lebanon p. by and trampled down 14.09
who p. sentence upon him. 25.06
Then Jehoram p. over with his 2Ch 21.09
of Lebanon p. by and trampled down 25.18
it as waters that have p. away. Job 11.16
and no stranger p. among them). 15.19
the lion has not p. over it. 28.08
prosperity has p. away like a 30.15
the wind has p. and cleared them. 37.21
I have p. out of mind like one who Ps 31.12
Again I p. by, and, lo, he was no more, 37.36
men p. through the river on foot. 66.06
their bounds which cannot be p. 148.06
I p. by the field of a sluggard by Pro 24.30
Scarcely had I p. them, when I found Sol 3.04
he has p. through Migron, at Michmash Is 10.28
spread abroad and p. over the sea. 16.08
your messengers p. over the sea 23.02
I gave them has p. away from them." Jer 8.13
cut in two and p. between its 34.18
of the land who p. between the 34.19
and he p. sentence upon him. 39.05
Your branches p. over the sea, 48.32
and he p. sentence upon him. 52.09
"And when I p. by you, and saw you Eze 16.06
"When I p. by you again and looked 16.08
was in the sight of all who p. by. 36.34
river that could not be p. through. 47.05
waves and thy billows p. over me. Jon 2.03
As Jesus p. on from there, he saw a Mt 9.09
And as Jesus p. on from there, two 9.27
from there and p. along the Sea of 15.29
And those who p. by derided him, 27.39
And as he p. on, he saw Levi the son Mk 2.14
from there and p. through Gailiee, 9.30
As they p. by in the morning, they 11.20
And those who p. by derided him, 15.29
he saw him he p. by on the other Lk 10.31
and saw him, p. by on the other side. 10.32
but has p. from death to life. Jn 5.24
As he p. by, he saw a man blind from 9.01
"Now when forty years had p., Ac 7.30
When many days had p., the Jews plotted 9.23
When they had p. the first and the 12.10
went out and p. on through one 12.10
but they p. on from Perga and came 13.14
Then they p. through Pisidia, and 14.24
they p. through both Phonenica and 15.03
Now when they had p. through 17.01
For as I p. along, and observed the 17.23
Paul p. through the upper country 19.01
Now when some days had p., 25.13
forbearance he had p. over former Rom 3.25
and all p. through the sea, 1Co 10.01
the old has p. away, behold, the new 2Co 5.17
priest who has p. through the Heb 4.14
that we have p. out of death into 1Jn 3.14

PASSED cont.)
The first woe has p.; behold, two Rev 9.12
The second woe has p.; behold, the 11.14
and the first earth had p. away, 21.01
for the former things have p. away." 21.04

PASSER-BY
lavished your harlotries on any p. Eze 16.15
offering yourself to any p., 16.25
And they compelled a p., Simon of Cyrene, Mk 15.21

PASSES
and while my glory p. by I will put Ex 33.22
p. along to Zin, and goes up south Jos 15.03
p. along to Azmon, goes out by the 15.04
and p. along north of Betharabah; 15.06
the boundary p. along to the 15.07
p. along to the northern shoulder 15.10
to Bethshemesh, and p. along by Timnah; 15.10
and p. along to Mount Baalah, and 15.11
it p. along to Ataroth, the territory 16.02
and p. along beyond it on the east 16.06
the boundary p. along southward in 18.13
then the boundary p. on to the 18.19
from there it p. along on the east 19.13
Lo, he p. by me, and I see him not; Job 9.11
If he p. through, and imprisons, and 11.10
for ever against him, and he p.; 14.20
whatever p. along the paths of the Ps 8.08
a wind that p. and comes not again. 78.39
for the wind p. over it, and it is 103.16
When the tempest p., the wicked is Pro 10.25
life, which he p. like a shadow? Ecc 6.12
overwhelming scourge p. through it Is 28.15
overwhelming scourge p. through you 28.18
As often as it p. through it will 28.19
He pursues them and p. on safely, 41.03
in a land that none p. through, Jer 2.06
waste so that no one p. through, 9.10
wilderness, so that no one p. through? 9.12
Every one who p. by it is horrified 18.16
every one who p. by it will be 19.08
every one who p. by it will be 49.17
every one who p. by Babylon shall 50.13
and through which no son of man p. 51.43
Every one who p. by her hisses and Zep 2.15
he p. through waterless places Mt 12.43
p. into the stomach, and so p. on? 15.17
but his stomach, and so p. on?" Mk 7.19
he p. through waterless places Lk 11.24
which p. all understanding, will Php 4.07
And the world p. away, and the lust 1Jn 2.17

PASSING
all Israel were p. over on dry Jos 3.17
nation finished p. over the Jordan. 3.17
had finished p. over the Jordan, 4.01
the people had finished p. over, 4.11
and p. on to the north of the 18.18
"We are p. from Bethlehem in Judah Ju 19.18
Philistines were p. on by hundreds 1Sa 29.02
his men were p. on in the rear 29.02
wonderful, p. the love of women. 2Sa 1.26
every one p. by it will be astonished, 1Ki 9.08
God, who is continually p. our way. 2Ki 4.09
of Israel was p. by upon the wall, 6.26
now he was p. by upon the wall—and 6.30
every one p. by will be astonished, 2Ch 7.21
For I am thy p. guest, a sojourner, Ps 39.12
his days are like a p. shadow. 144.04
p. along the street near her corner, Pro 7.08
he who hires a p. fool or drunkard 26.10
one who takes a p. dog by the ears. 26.17
of the ruthless like p. chaff. Is 29.05
with no one p. through, I will make 60.15
in the sea are dismayed at your p.' Eze 26.18
iniquity and p. over transgression Mic 7.18
they heard that Jesus was p. by, Mt 20.30
And p. along by the Sea of Galilee, Mk 1.16
But p. through the midst of them he Lk 4.30
Jerusalem he was p. along between 17.11
him, "Jesus of Nazareth is p. by." 18.37
entered Jericho and was p. through. 19.01
and p. on he preached the gospel to Ac 8.40
so, p. by Mysia, they went down to 16.08
for in p. judgment upon him you Rom 2.01
to see you in p. as I go to Spain, 15.24
the form of this world is p. away. 1Co 7.31
visit you after p. through Macedonia, 16.05
not want to see you now just in p.; 16.07
p. our days in malice and envy, Tit 3.03
the darkness is p. away and the 1Jn 2.08

PASSION
but p. makes the bones rot. Pro 14.30
alive after his p. by many proofs, Ac 1.03
consumed with p. for one another, Rom 1.27
to marry than to be aflame with p. 1Co 7.09
p., evil desire, and covetousness, Col 3.05
not in the p. of lust like heathen 1Th 4.05
that is in the world because of p., 2Pe 1.04
of defiling p. and despise authority. 2.10
drink the wine of her impure p." Rev 14.08
drunk the wine of her impure p., 18.03

PASSIONS
gave them up to dishonorable p. Rom 1.26
bodies, to make you obey their p. 6.12
our sinful p., aroused by the law, 7.05
if his p. are strong, and it has to 1Co 7.36
the flesh with its p. and desires. Gal 5.24
once lived in the p. of our flesh, Eph 2.03
So shun youthful p. and aim at 2Ti 2.22
renounce irreligion and worldly p., Tit 2.12
slaves to various p. and pleasures, 3.03
Is it not your p. that are at war Jas 4.01
Wrongly, to spend it on your p. 4.03
conformed to the p. of your former 1Pe 1.14
from the p. of the flesh that wage 2.11
longer by human p. but by the will 4.02
p., drunkenness, revels, carousing, 4.03
with licentious p. of the flesh 2Pe 2.18
scoffing, followed their own p. 3.03
malcontents, following their own p., Jud 1.16
following their own ungodly p." 1.18

PASSOVER
it in haste. It is the LORD's p. Ex 12.11
families, and kill the p. lamb. 12.21
is the sacrifice of the LORD's p., 12.27
"This is the ordinance of the p.: 12.43
and would keep the p. to the LORD, 12.48
feast of the p. be left until the 34.25
in the evening, is the LORD's p. Lev 23.05
Israel keep the p. at its appointed Num 9.02
that they should keep the p. 9.04
And they kept the p. in the first 9.05
could not keep the p. on that day; 9.06
still keep the p. to the LORD. 9.10
statute for the p. they shall keep 9.12
yet refrains from keeping the p., 9.13
and will keep the p. to the LORD, 9.14
statute of the p. and according to 9.14
the first month is the LORD's p. 28.16
day after the p. the people of 33.03
and keep the p. to the LORD your Deu 16.01
shall offer the p. sacrifice to 16.02
not offer the p. sacrifice within 16.05
you shall offer the p. sacrifice, 16.06
they kept the p. on the fourteenth Jos 5.10
And on the morrow after the p., 5.11
"Keep the p. to the LORD your God, 2Ki 23.21
For no such p. had been kept since 23.22
Josiah this p. was kept to the 23.23
to keep the p. to the LORD the God 2Ch 30.01

PASSOVER (cont.)
to keep the p. in the second month 2Ch 30.02
and keep the p. to the LORD the 30.05
And they killed the p. lamb on the 30.15
had to kill the p. lamb for every 30.17
they ate the p. otherwise than as 30.18
Josiah kept a p. to the LORD in 35.01
they killed the p. lamb on the 35.01
And kill the p., and sanctify 35.06
as p. offerings for all that were 35.07
priests for the p. offerings two 35.08
Levites for the p. offerings five 35.09
And they killed the p. lamb, 35.11
roasted the p. lamb with fire 35.13
to keep the p. and to offer burnt 35.16
present kept the p. at that time, 35.17
No p. like it had been kept in 35.18
had kept such a p. as was kept by 35.18
reign of Josiah this p. was kept. 35.19
the returned exiles kept the p. Ez 6.19
they killed the p. lamb for all 6.20
celebrate the feast of the p., Eze 45.21
after two days the P. is coming, Mt 26.02
us prepare for you to eat the p.?" 26.17
I will keep the p. at your house 26.18
them, and they prepared the p. 26.19
days before the P. and the feast Mk 14.01
when they sacrificed the p. lamb, 14.12
and prepare for you to eat the p.?" 14.12
I am to eat the p. with my disciples?' 14.14
and they prepared the p. 14.16
every year at the feast of the P. Lk 2.41
drew near, which is called the P. 22.01
on which the p. lamb had to be 22.07
"Go and prepare the p. for us, 22.08
I am to eat the p. with my disciples?' 22.11
and they prepared the p. 22.13
to eat this p. with you before I 22.15
The P. of the Jews was at hand, and Jn 2.13
was in Jerusalem at the P. feast, 2.23
Now the P., the feast of the Jews, 6.04
Now the P. of the Jews was at hand, 11.55
country to Jerusalem before the P., 11.55
Six days before the P., Jesus came 12.01
Now before the feast of the P., 13.01
be defiled, but might eat the p. 18.28
release one man for you at the P.; 18.39
the day of Preparation for the P.; 19.14
after the P. to bring him out to Ac 12.04
he kept the P. and sprinkled the Heb 11.28

PAST
days of weeping for him were p., Gen 50.04
been accustomed to gore in the p., Ex 21.29
been accustomed to gore in the p., 21.36
"For ask now of the days that are p., Deu 4.32
at enmity with him in time p., 4.42
at enmity with him in time p.— 19.04
with his neighbor in time p. 19.06
no enmity against him in times p. Jos 20.05
the bitterness of death is p." 1Sa 15.32
"For some time p. you have been 2Sa 3.17
In times p., when Saul was king 5.02
your father's servant in time p., 15.34
was the ruler over them in time p.; 1Ch 9.20
In times p., even when Saul was 11.02
A spirit glided p. my face; Job 4.15
conceal me until thy wrath be p., 14.13
My days are p., my plans are broken 17.11
their number is p. my knowledge. Ps 71.15
are but as yesterday when it is p., 90.04
the winter is p., the rain is over Sol 2.11
spoke concerning Moab in the p. Is 16.13
little while until the wrath is p. 26.20
"The harvest is p., the summer is Jer 8.20
And when the sabbath was p., Mk 16.01
things closely for some time p., Lk 1.03
In p. generations he allowed all Ac 14.16
had decided to sail p. Ephesus, 20.16
the resurrection is p. already. 2Ti 2.18
even when she was p. the age, Heb 11.11
time that is p. suffice for doing 1Pe 4.03

PASTORS
evangelists, some p. and teachers, Eph 4.11

PASTURE
water the sheep, and go, p. them. Gen 29.07
brothers went to p. their father's 37.12
for there is no p. for your servants' 47.04
to the Levites p. lands round Num 35.02
and their p. lands shall be for 35.03
The p. lands of the cities, which 35.04
to them as p. land for their 35.05
forty-eight, with their p. lands. 35.07
with their p. lands for their Jos 14.04
with their p. lands for our cattle 21.02
cities and p. lands out of their 21.03
and their p. lands the people of 21.08
along with the p. lands round 21.11
with its p. lands, Libnah with its p. lands, 21.13
p. lands, Eshtemoa with its p. lands, 21.14
its p. lands, Debir with its p. lands, 21.15
its p. lands, Juttah with its p. lands, 21.16
Bethshemesh with its p. lands— 21.16
its p. lands, Geba with its p. lands, 21.17
p. lands, and Almon with its p. lands— 21.18
thirteen cities with their p. lands. 21.19
with its p. lands in the hill 21.21
Ephraim, Gezer with its p. lands, 21.21
p. lands, Bethhoron with its p. lands— 21.22
p. lands, Gibbethon with its p. lands, 21.23
p. lands, Gathrimmon with its p. lands— 21.24
Manasseh, Taanach with its p. lands, 21.25
and Gathrimmon with its p. lands— 21.25
ten in all with their p. lands. 21.26
Golan in Bashan with its p. lands, 21.27
and Beeshterah with its p. land— 21.27
p. lands, Daberath with its p. lands, 21.28
p. lands, Engannim with its p. lands— 21.29
its p. lands, Abdon with its p. lands, 21.30
its p. lands, and Rehob with its p. lands— 21.31
in Galilee with its p. lands, 21.32
p. lands, and Kartan with its p. lands— 21.32
thirteen cities with their p. lands. 21.33
its p. lands, Kartah with its p. lands, 21.34
p. lands, Nahalal with its p. lands— 21.35
its p. lands, Jahaz with its p. lands, 21.36
Kedemoth with its p. lands, 21.37
and Mephaath with its p. lands— 21.37
Ramoth in Gilead with its p. lands, 21.38
Mahanaim with its p. lands, 21.38
its p. lands, Jazer with its p. lands— 21.39
forty-eight cities with their p. lands, 21.41
had each its p. lands round about 21.42
of hosts, I took you from the p., 2Sa 7.08
to seek p. for their flocks, 1Ch 4.39
good p., and the land was very 4.40
there was p. there for their 4.41
and in all the p. lands of Sharon 5.16
and its surrounding p. lands, 6.55
Hebron, Libnah with its p. lands, 6.57
Eshtemoa with its p. lands, 6.57
its p. lands, Debir with its p. lands, 6.58
p. lands, and Bethshemesh with its p. lands; 6.59
Geba with its p. lands, Alemeth with its p. 6.60
and Anathoth with its p. lands. 6.60
the cities with their p. lands. 6.64
withits p. lands in the hill 6.67
Ephraim, Gezer with its p. lands, 6.67
its p. lands, Bethhoron with its p. lands, 6.68
p. lands, Gathrimmon with its p. lands, 6.69
its p. lands, and Bileam with its p. lands, 6.70
p. lands and Ashtaroth with its p. lands; 6.71
its p. lands, Daberath with its p. lands, 6.72
p. lands, and Anem with its p. lands; 6.73

PASTURE (cont.)
its p. lands, Abdon with its p. lands, 1Ch 6.74
its p. lands, and Rehob with its p. lands; 6.75
its p. lands, Hammon with its p. lands, 6.76
and Kiriathaim with its p. lands. 6.76
its p. lands, Tabor with its p. lands, 6.77
its p. lands, Jahzah with its p. lands, 6.78
p. lands, and Mephaath with its p. lands; 6.79
p. lands, Mahanain with its p. lands, 6.80
its p. lands, Jazer with its p. lands. 6.81
in the cities that have p. lands, 13.02
of hosts, I took you from the p., 17.07
they seize flocks and p. them. Job 24.02
He ranges the mountains as his p., 39.08
smoke against the sheep of thy p.? Ps 74.01
we thy people, the flock of thy p., 79.13
and we are the people of his p., 95.07
people, and the sheep of his p. 100.03
where you p. your flock, where you Sol 1.07
and p. your kids beside the shepherds' 1.08
to p. his flock in the gardens, and 6.02
the lambs graze as in their p., Is 5.17
joy of wild asses, a p. of flocks; 32.14
all bare heights shall be their p.; 49.09
Sharon shall become a p. for flocks, 65.10
they shall p., each in his place. Jer 6.03
and scatter the sheep of my p.!" 23.01
the Lord is despoiling their p., 25.36
I will restore Israel to his p., 50.19
become like harts that find no p.; Lam 1.06
make Rabbah a p. for camels and Eze 25.05
I will feed them with good p., 34.14
of Israel shall be their p.; 34.14
and on fat p. they shall feed on 34.14
for you to feed on the good p., 34.18
with your feet the rest of your p.; 34.18
are my sheep, the sheep of my p., 34.31
them like a lamb in a broad p.? Hos 4.16
because there is no p. for them; Joe 1.18
in a fold, like a flock in its p., Mic 2.12
of Judah, on which they shall p., Zep 2.07
For they shall p. and lie down, 3.13
and will go in and out and find p. Jn 10.09

PASTURED
as he p. the asses of Zibeon his Gen 36.24
Over the herds that p. in Sharon 1Ch 27.29

PASTURE-FED
and twenty p. cattle, a hundred 1Ki 4.23

PASTURES
he makes me lie down in green p. Ps 23.02
Lord are like the glory of the p., 37.20
The p. of the wilderness drip, the 65.12
for ourselves of the p. of God. 83.12
he p. his flock among the lilies. Sol 2.16
he p. his flock among the lilies. 6.03
the thornbushes, and on all the p. Is 7.19
your cattle will graze in large p.; 30.23
lamentation for the p. of the Jer 9.10
and the p. of the wilderness are 23.10
devoured the p. of the wilderness, Joe 1.19
devoured the p. of the wilderness. 1.20
for the p. of the wilderness are 2.22
the p. of the shepherds mourn, and Amo 1.02
shall be p., meadows for shepherds Zep 2.06

PASTURING
your brothers p. the flock at Gen 37.13
you, where they are p. the flock." 37.16

PATARA
to Rhodes, and from there to P. Ac 21.01

PATCH
for the p. tears away from the Mt 9.16
the p. tears away from it, the new Mk 2.21

PATCHED
with worn-out, p. sandals on their Jos 9.05

PATE
and on his own p. his violence Ps 7.16

PATH
in the way, a viper by the p., Gen 49.17
in a narrow p. between the vineyards, Num 22.24
ground, a trap for him in the p. Job 18.10
"That p. no bird of prey knows, and 28.07
They break up my p., they promote 30.13
Thou dost show me the p. of life; Ps 16.11
me on a level p. because of my 27.11
thy p. through the great waters; 77.19
He made a p. for his anger; 78.50
Lead me in the p. of thy commandments, 119.35
to my feet and a light to my p. 119.105
searchest out my p. and my lying 139.03
In the p. where I walk they have 142.03
good spirit lead me on a level p.! 143.10
justice and equity, every good p.; Pro 2.09
Do not enter the p. of the wicked, 4.14
But the p. of the righteous is like 4.18
Take heed to the p. of your feet, 4.26
her steps follow the p. to Sheol; 5.05
not take heed to the p. of life; 5.06
instruction is on the p. to life, 10.17
in the p. of righteousness is life, 12.28
but the p. of the upright is a 15.19
The wise man's p. leads upward to 15.24
make smooth the p. of the righteous. Is 26.07
In the p. of thy judgments, O Lord, 26.08
leave the way, turn aside from the p., 30.11
who taught him the p. of justice, 40.14
in the sea, a p. in the mighty waters, 43.16
in a straight p. in which they Jer 31.09
another, each marches in his p.; Joe 2.08
some seeds fell along the p., Mt 13.04
this is what was sown along the p. 13.19
sowed, some seed fell along the p., Mk 4.04
And these are the ones along the p., 4.15
he sowed, some fell along the p., Lk 8.05
The ones along the p. are those who 8.12

PATHLESS
makes them wander in a p. waste. Job 12.24

PATHROS
from P., from Ethiopia, from Elam, Is 11.11
at Memphis, and in the land of P., Jer 44.01
who dwelt in P. in the land of 44.15
bring them back to the land of P., Eze 29.14
I will make P. a desolation, and 30.14

PATHRUSIM
P., Casluhim (whence came the Gen 10.14
P., Casluhim (whence came the 1Ch 1.12

PATHS
Such are the p. of all who forget Job 8.13
the stocks, and watchest all my p.; 13.27
and he has set darkness upon my p. 19.08
ways, and do not stay in its p. 24.13
the stocks, and watches all my p.' 33.11
you may discern the p. to its home? 38.20
passes along the p. of the sea. Ps 8.08
My steps have held fast to thy p., 17.05
He leads me in p. of righteousness 23.03
O Lord; teach me thy p. 25.04
All the p. of the Lord are steadfast 25.10
hold back your foot from their p.; Pro 1.15
guarding the p. of justice and 2.08
who forsake the p. of uprightness 2.13
men whose p. are crooked, and who 2.15
to death, and her p. to the shades; 2.18
nor do they regain the p. of life. 2.19
and keep to the p. of the righteous. 2.20

PATHS (cont.)
and he will make straight your p. Pro 3.06
pleasantness, and all her p. are peace. 3.17
led you in the p. of uprightness. 4.11
LORD, and he watches all his p. 5.21
her ways, do not stray into her p.; 7.25
in the p. she takes her stand; 8.02
righteousness, in the p. of justice, 8.20
and that we may walk in his p." Is 2.03
and confuse the course of your p. 3.12
by p. his feet have not trod. 41.03
in p. that they have not known I 42.16
there is no justice in their p.; 59.08
look, and ask for the ancient p., Jer 6.16
like slippery p. in the darkness, 23.12
stones, he has made my p. crooked, Lam 3.09
so that she cannot find her p. Hos 2.06
they do not swerve from their p. Joe 2.07
his ways and we may walk in his p. Mic 4.02
of the Lord, make his p. straight." Mt 3.03
the LORD, make his p. straight—" Mk 1.03
the Lord, make his p. straight. Lk 3.04
the straight p. of the LORD? Ac 13.10
in their p. are ruin and misery, Rom 3.16
and make straight p. for your feet, Heb 12.13

PATIENCE
With p. a ruler may be persuaded, Pro 25.15
have p. with me, and I will pay you Mt 18.26
'Have p. with me, and I will pay you.' 18.29
and bring forth fruit with p. Lk 8.15
kindness and forbearance and p.? Rom 2.04
to those who by p. in well-doing 2.07
do not see, we wait for it with p. 8.25
with much p. the vessels of wrath 9.22
were performed among you in all p., 2Co 12.12
p., kindness, goodness, faithfulness, Gal 5.22
with p., forbearing one another in Eph 4.02
for all endurance and p. with joy, Col 1.11
lowliness, meekness, and p., 3.12
his perfect p. for an example to 1Ti 1.16
my p., my love, my steadfastness, 2Ti 3.10
be unfailing in p. and in teaching. 4.02
faith and p. inherit the promises, Heb 6.12
As an example of suffering and p., Jas 5.10
when God's p. waited in the days of 1Pe 3.20

PATIENT
is my end, that I should be p.? Job 6.11
but a man of discretion is p. Pro 14.17
and the p. in spirit is better than Ecc 7.08
be p. in tribulation, be constant in Rom 12.12
Love is p. and kind; love is not 1Co 13.04
help the weak, be p. with them all. 1Th 5.14
Be p., therefore, brethren, until the Jas 5.07
being p. over it until it receives 5.07
You also be p. Establish your 5.08
the kingdom and the p. endurance, Rev 1.09
your toil and your p. endurance, 2.02
faith and service and p. endurance, 2.19
have kept my word of p. endurance, 3.10

PATIENTLY
the LORD and wait p. for him; Ps 37.07
I waited p. for the LORD; 40.01
I beg you to listen to me p. Ac 26.03
when you p. endure the same 2Co 1.06
having p. endured, obtained the Heb 6.15
are beaten for it you take it p.? 1Pe 2.20
and suffer for it you take it p., 2.20
are enduring p. and bearing up for Rev 2.03

PATMOS
island called P. on account of the Rev 1.09

PATRIARCH
confidently of the p. David that he Ac 2.29
Abraham the p. gave him a tithe of Heb 7.04

PATRIARCHS
Jacob, and Jacob of the twelve p. Ac 7.08
"And the p., jealous of Joseph, sold 7.09
to them belong the p., and of their race, Rom 9.05
the promises given to the p., 15.08

PATRIMONY
receives from the sale of his p. Deu 18.08

PATROBAS
P., Hermas, and the brethren who are Rom 16.14

PATROL
the LORD has sent to p. the earth. Zec 1.10
to get off and p. the earth. 6.07
And he said, "Go, p. the earth." 6.07

PATROLLED
We have p. the earth, and behold, Zec 1.11
So they p. the earth. 6.07

PATTERN
concerning the p. of the tabernacle, Ex 25.09
make them after the p. for them, 25.40
according to the p. which the LORD Num 8.04
and its p., exact in all its 2Ki 16.10
according to the p. that he had Ac 7.44
Follow the p. of the sound words 2Ti 1.13
according to the p. which was shown Heb 8.05

PAU
the name of his city being P.; Gen 36.39

PAUL
But Saul, who is also called P., Ac 13.09
Now P. and his company set sail 13.13
So P. stood up, and motioning with 13.16
Judaism followed P. and Barnabas, 13.43
contradicted what was spoken by P., 13.45
And P. and Barnabas spoke out 13.46
persecution against P. and Barnabas, 13.50
He listened to P. speaking; 14.09
and P., looking intently at him and 14.09
the crowds saw what P. had done, 14.11
and P., because he was the chief 14.12
Barnabas and P. heard of it, 14.14
they stoned P. and dragged him out 14.19
And when P. and Barnabas had no 15.02
P. and Barnabas and some of the 15.02
to Barnabas and P. as they related 15.12
to Antioch with P. and Barnabas. 15.22
with our beloved Barnabas and P., 15.25
But P. and Barnabas remained in 15.35
And after some days P. said to 15.36
But P. thought best not to take 15.38
but P. chose Silas and departed, 15.40
P. wanted Timothy to accompany him; 16.03
vision appeared to P. in the night: 16.09
give heed to what was said by P. 16.14
She followed P. and us, crying, 16.17
But P. was annoyed, and turned and 16.18
they seized P. and Silas and 16.19
But about midnight P. and Silas 16.25
But P. cried with a loud voice, "Do 16.28
he fell down before P. and Silas, 16.29
jailer reported the words to P., 16.36
But P. said to them, "They have 16.37
And P. went in, as was his custom, 17.02
persuaded, and joined P. and Silas; 17.04
immediately sent P. and Silas away 17.10
proclaimed by P. at Beroea also, 17.13
immediately sent P. off on his way 17.14
Those who conducted P. brought him 17.15
Now while P. was waiting for them 17.16
So P., standing in the middle of 17.22
So P. went out from among them. 17.33
P. was occupied with preaching, 18.05
Corinthians hearing P. believed and 18.08
Lord said to P. one night in a 18.09

PAUL (cont.)
attack upon P. and brought him Ac 18.12
But when P. was about to open his 18.14
After this P. stayed many days 18.18
P. passed through the upper country 19.01
And P. said, "John baptized with the 19.04
And when P. had laid his hands upon 19.06
miracles by the hands of P., 19.11
you by the Jesus whom P. preaches." 19.13
them, "Jesus I know, and P. I know; 19.15
these events P. resolved in the 19.21
all Asia this P. has persuaded and 19.26
P. wished to go in among the crowd, 19.30
P. sent for the disciples and 20.01
P. talked with them, intending to 20.07
a deep sleep as P. talked still 20.09
But P. went down and bent over him, 20.10
And when P. had gone up and had 20.11
intending to take P. aboard there; 20.13
For P. had decided to sail past 20.16
and embraced P. and kissed him, 20.37
they told P. not to go on to 21.04
Then P. answered, "What are you 21.13
following day P. went in with us 21.18
Then P. took the men, and the next 21.26
supposed that P. had brought him 21.29
they seized P. and dragged him out 21.30
soldiers, they stopped beating P. 21.32
As P. was about to be brought into 21.37
P. replied, "I am a Jew, from Tarsus 21.39
P., standing on the steps, motioned 21.40
P. said to the centurion who was 22.25
P. said, "But I was born a citizen." 22.28
realized that P. was a Roman 22.29
and he brought P. down and set him 22.30
And P., looking intently at the 23.01
Then P. said to him, "God shall 23.03
And P. said, "I did not know, brethren, 23.05
But when P. perceived that one part 23.06
afraid that P. would be torn in 23.10
nor drink till they had killed P. 23.12
no food till we have killed P. 23.14
entered the barracks and told P. 23.16
And P. called one of the centurions 23.17
"P. the prisoner called me and 23.18
you to bring P. down to the 23.20
Also provide mounts for P. to ride, 23.24
took P. and brought him by night to 23.31
they presented P. also before him. 23.33
the governor their case against P.; 24.01
P. replied: "Realizing that for many 24.10
and he sent for P. and heard him 24.24
money would be given him by P. 24.26
a favor, Felix left P. in prison. 24.27
the Jews informed him against P.; 25.02
Festus replied that P. was being 25.04
and ordered P. to be brought. 25.06
P. said in his defense, "Neither 25.08
said to P., "Do you wish to go up 25.09
But P. said, "I am standing before 25.10
but whom P. asserted to be alive. 25.19
But when P. had appealed to be kept 25.21
of Festus P. was brought in. 25.23
Agrippa said to P., "You have 26.01
Then P. stretched out his hand 26.01
with a loud voice, "P., you are mad; 26.24
But P. said, "I am not mad, most 26.25
And Agrippa said to P., "In a short 26.28
And P. said, "Whether short or long, 26.29
they delivered P. and some other 27.01
and Julius treated P. kindly, 27.03
already gone by, P. advised them, 27.09
of the ship than to what P. said. 27.11
P. then came forward among them and 27.21
and he said, 'Do not be afraid, P.; 27.24
P. said to the centurion and the 27.31
P. urged them all to take some food, 27.33
but the centurion, wishing to save P., 27.43
P. had gathered a bundle of sticks 28.03
and P. visited him and prayed, and 28.08
On seeing them P. thanked God and 28.15
P. was allowed to stay by himself, 28.16
after P. had made one statement: 28.25
P., a servant of Jesus Christ, Rom 1.01
P., called by the will of God to be 1Co 1.01
"I belong to P.," or "I belong to 1.12
Was P. crucified for you? 1.13
you baptized in the name of P.? 1.13
"I belong to P.," and another, "I 3.04
What is P.? Servants through whom 3.05
whether P. or Apollos or Cephas or 3.22
I, P., write this greeting with my 16.21
P., an apostle of Christ Jesus by 2Co 1.01
I, P., myself entreat you, by the 10.01
P. an apostle—not from men nor Gal 1.01
Now I, P., say to you that if you 5.02
P., an apostle of Christ Jesus by Eph 1.01
P., a prisoner for Christ Jesus on 3.01
P. and Timothy, servants of Christ Php 1.01
P., an apostle of Christ Jesus by Col 1.01
of which I, P., became a minister. 1.23
I, P., write this greeting with my 4.18
P., Silvanus, and Timothy, To the 1Th 1.01
P., again and again—but Satan 2.18
P., Silvanus, and Timothy, To the 2Th 1.01
I, P., write this greeting with my 3.17
P., an apostle of Christ Jesus by 1Ti 1.01
P., an apostle of Christ Jesus by 2Ti 1.01
P., a servant of God and an apostle Tit 1.01
P., a prisoner for Christ Jesus, and Phm 1.01
P., an ambassador and now a prisoner 1.09
I, P., write this with my own hand, I 1.19
beloved brother P. wrote to you 2Pe 3.15

PAUL'S
who were P. companions in travel. Ac 19.29
to us he took P. gridle and bound 21.11
Now the son of P. sister head of 23.16
Festus laid P. case before the king, 25.14

PAULUS
Sergius P., a man of intelligence, Ac 13.07

PAVEMENT
as it were a p. of sapphire stone, Ex 24.10
their faces to the earth on the p., 2Ch 7.03
silver on a mosaic p. of porphyry, Est 1.06
mortar in the p. which is at the Jer 43.09
there were chambers and a p., Eze 40.17
thirty chambers fronted on the p. 40.17
And the p. ran along the side of 40.18
the gates; this was the lower p. 40.18
and facing the p. which belonged 42.03
seat at a place called The P., Jn 19.13

PAVILION
clouds, the thunderings of his p.? Job 36.29
there will be a canopy and a p. Is 4.05

PAW
me from the p. of the lion and 1Sa 17.37
lion and from the p. of the bear, 17.37

PAWS
And all that go on their p., Lev 11.27
He p. in the valley, and exults in Job 39.21

PAY
hate us and p. us back for all the Gen 50.15
labor at it and p. no regard to Ex 5.09
only he shall p. for the loss of 21.19
and he shall p. as the judges 21.22
he shall p. ox for ox, and the dead 21.36
he shall p. five oxen for an ox, and 22.01
ass or a sheep, he shall p. double. 22.04
thief is found, he shall p. double. 22.07
condemn shall p. double to his 22.09

PAY (cont.)
he shall p. money equivalent to the Ex 22.17
he sold it and p. back the overpayment Lev 25.27
is too poor to p. your valuation, 27.08
my cattle, then I will p. for it; Num 20.19
you shall not be slack to p. it; Deu 23.21
you shall not p. reverence to the Ju 6.10
sacrifice, and to p. his vow. 1Sa 1.21
king, "Pray let me go and p. my vow, 2Sa 15.07
and I will p. you for your servants 1Ki 5.06
else you shall p. a talent of 20.39
"Go, sell the oil and p. your debts, 2Ki 4.07
the money to p. out to the workmen, 12.15
they will not p. tribute, custom, or Ez 4.13
and I will p. ten thousand talents Est 3.09
had promised to p. into the king's 4.07
and you will p. your vows. Job 22.27
my vows I will p. before those who Ps 22.25
those who p. regard to vain idols; 31.06
and cannot p. back, but the righteous 37.21
and p. your vows to the Most High; 50.14
as I p. my vows day after day. 61.08
offerings; I will p. thee my vows, 66.13
I will p. my vows to the LORD in 116.14
I will p. my vows to the LORD in 116.18
he is caught, he will p. sevenfold; Pro 6.31
O foolish men, p. attention. 8.05
of great wrath will p. the penalty; 19.19
If you have nothing with which to p., 22.27
I will p. the man back for what he 24.29
in fools. P. what you vow. Ecc 5.04
that you should vow and not p. 5.05
We must p. for the water we drink, Lam 5.04
from Tyre to p. for the labor that Eze 29.18
men, O king, p. no heed to you; Dan 3.12
Those who p. regard to vain idols Jon 2.08
what I have vowed I will p. 2.09
received without p., give without p. Mt 10.08
"Does not your teacher p. the tax?" 17.24
and as he could not p., 18.25
me, and I will p. you everything.' 18.26
throat he said, 'P. what you owe.' 18.28
patience with me, and I will p. you.' 18.29
prison till he should p. the debt. 18.30
till he should p. all his debt. 18.34
laborers and p. them their wages, 20.08
Is it lawful to p. taxes to Caesar, 22.17
Is it lawful to p. taxes to Caesar, Mk 12.14
Should we p. them, or should we not?" 12.15
When they could not p., he forgave them Lk 7.42
with them and p. their expenses, Ac 21.24
For the same reason you also p. taxes, Rom 13.06
P. all of them their dues, taxes to 13.07
Therefore we must p. the closer Heb 2.01
and you p. attention to the one who Jas 2.03
will do well to p. attention to 2Pe 1.19

PAYING
have finished p. all the tithe of Deu 26.12
a vow to God, do not delay p. it; Ecc 5.04
Are you p. me back for something? Joe 3.04
If you are p. me back, I will 3.04
not eat any one's bread without p., 2Th 3.08

PAYMENT
for nothing, without p. of money. Ex 21.11
whether in p. of a vow or as a Lev 22.18
LORD your God in p. for any vow; Deu 23.18
if I have eaten its yield without p., Job 31.39
their bosom p. for their former Is 65.07
brought you in p. ivory tusks and Eze 27.15
all that he had, and p. to be made. Mt 18.25
I have received full p., and more; Php 4.18

PAYS
yet God p. no attention to their Job 24.12
p. no heed to you, O king, or the Dan 6.13

PEACE
you shall go to your fathers in p.; Gen 15.15
good and have sent you away in p. 26.29
and they departed from him in p. 26.31
again to my father's house in p., 28.21
Jacob held his p. until they came. 34.05
you, go up in p. to your father." 44.17
And Jethro said to Moses, "Go in p." Ex 4.18
also will go to their place in p." 18.23
offerings and your p. offerings, 20.24
and sacrificed p. offerings of 24.05
of Israel from their p. offerings; 29.28
offerings and brought p. offerings; 32.06
is a sacrifice of p. offering, Lev 3.01
the sacrifice of the p. offering, 3.03
a sacrifice of p. offering to the 3.06
sacrifice of the p. offering as an 3.09
the sacrifice of the p. offerings), 4.10
of the sacrifice of p. offerings; 4.26
is removed from the p. offerings, 4.31
from the sacrifice of p. offerings, 4.35
on it the fat of the p. offerings. 6.12
sacrifice of p. offerings which 7.11
sacrifice of his p. offerings for 7.13
the blood of the p. offerings. 7.14
sacrifice of his p. offerings for 7.15
sacrifice of his p. offering is 7.18
of the LORD's p. offerings while 7.20
sacrifice of the LORD's p. offerings, 7.21
sacrifice of his p. offerings to the 7.29
the sacrifice of his p. offerings 7.29
the sacrifice of your p. offerings; 7.32
blood of the p. offerings and the 7.33
sacrifices of their p. offerings, 7.34
consecration, and of the p. offerings, 7.37
and an ox and a ram for p. offerings, 9.04
sacrifice of p. offerings for the 9.18
offering and the p. offerings. 9.22
glorified.' " And Aaron held his p. 10.03
sacrifices of the p. offerings of 10.14
sacrifices of p. offerings to the 17.05
a sacrifice of p. offerings to the 19.05
a sacrifice of p. offerings to the 22.21
old as a sacrifice of p. offerings. 23.19
And I will give p. in the land, 23.96
without blemish as a p. offering, Num 6.14
a sacrifice of p. offering to the 6.17
the sacrifice of the p. offering. 6.18
countenance upon you, and give you p. 6.26
and for the sacrifice of p. offerings, 7.17
and for the sacrifice of p. offerings, 7.23
and for the sacrifice of p. offerings, 7.29
and for the sacrifice of p. offerings, 7.35
and for the sacrifice of p. offerings, 7.41
and for the sacrifice of p. offerings, 7.47
and for the sacrifice of p. offerings, 7.53
and for the sacrifice of p. offerings, 7.59
and for the sacrifice of p. offerings, 7.65
and for the sacrifice of p. offerings, 7.71
and for the sacrifice of p. offerings, 7.77
and for the sacrifice of p. offerings, 7.83
sacrifice of p. offerings twenty-four 7.88
sacrifices of your p. offerings; 10.10
or for p. offerings to the LORD, 15.08
I give to him my covenant of p.; 25.12
offerings, and for you p. offerings." 29.39
Heshbon, with words of p., saying, Deu 2.26
it, offer terms of p. to it. 20.10
to you is p. and it opens to you, 20.11
But if it makes no p. with you, 20.12
not seek their p. or their prosperity 23.06
and you shall sacrifice p. offerings, 27.07
LORD, and sacrificed p. offerings. Jos 8.31
And Joshua made p. with them, 9.15
Gibeon had made p. with Israel and 10.01
for it has made p. with Joshua and 10.04
city that made p. with the people 11.19
offerings or p. offerings on it, 22.23

PEACE (cont.)

and sacrifices and p. offerings;	Jos 22.27
for there was p. between Jabin the	Ju 4.17
the LORD said to him, "P. be to you;	6.23
and called it, The LORD is p.	6.24
of Penuel, "When I come again in p.,	8.09
"Go in p. The journey on which you	18.06
And the old man said, "P. be to you;	19.20
offerings and p. offerings before	20.26
burnt offerings and p. offerings.	21.04
Rimmon, and proclaimed p. to them.	21.13
"Go in p., and the God of Israel	1Sa 1.17
There was p. also between Israel	7.14
and to sacrifice p. offerings.	10.08
no present. But he held his p.	10.27
they sacrificed p. offerings	11.15
here to me, and the p. offerings."	13.09
"Go in p., forasmuch as we have	20.42
'P. be to you, and p. be to your house,	25.06
and p. be to all that you have.	25.06
to her, "Go up in p. to your house;	25.35
Abner away; and he went in p.	2Sa 3.21
him away, and he had gone in p.	3.22
let him go, and he has gone in p."	3.23
offerings and p. offerings before	6.17
offerings and the p. offerings,	6.18
they made p. with Israel, and became	10.19
Now hold your p., my sister;	13.20
The king said to him, "Go in p."	15.09
"Look, go back to the city in p.,	15.27
and all the people will be at p."	17.03
burnt offerings and p. offerings.	24.25
in time of p. blood which had been	1Ki 2.05
his head go down to Sheol in p.	2.06
there shall be p. from the LORD	2.33
burnt offerings and p. offerings,	3.15
and he had p. on all sides round	4.24
and there was p. between Hiram and	5.12
Solomon offered as p. offerings to	8.63
the fat pieces of the p. offerings,	8.64
offerings and p. offerings upon	9.25
said, "If they have come out for p.,	20.18
let each return to his home in p.'"	22.17
and water, until I come in p."'"	22.27
And Micaiah said, "If you return in p.,	22.28
Jehoshaphat also made p. with the	22.44
I know it; hold your p."	2Ki 2.03
I know it; hold your p."	2.05
He said to him, "Go in p."	5.19
them, and let him say, 'Is it p.?'"	9.17
"Thus says the king, 'Is it p.?'"	9.18
said, "What have you to do with p.?	9.18
"Thus the king has said, 'It is p.?'"	9.19
"What have you to do with p.?	9.19
saw Jehu, he said, "Is it p., Jehu?"	9.22
"What p. can there be, so long as	9.22
"Is it p., you Zimri, murderer of	9.31
blood of his p. offerings upon the	16.13
'Make your p. with me and come out	18.31
there will be p. and security in	20.19
be gathered to your grave in p.,	22.20
P., p. to you, and p. to your helpers!	1Ch 12.18
offerings and p. offerings before	16.01
offerings and the p. offerings,	16.02
they made p. with David, and became	19.19
burnt offerings and p. offerings,	21.26
he shall be a man of p.	22.09
I will give him p. from all his	22.09
and I will give p. and quiet to	22.09
he not given you p. on every side?	22.18
Israel, has given p. to his people;	23.25
and the fat of the p. offerings,	2Ch 7.07
years, for the LORD gave him p.	14.06
he has given us p. on every side."	14.07
there was no p. to him who went	15.05
let each return to his home in p.'"	18.16
and water, until I return in p.'"	18.26
And Micaiah said, "If you return in p.,	18.27
was the fat of the p. offerings,	29.35
sacrificing p. offerings and giving	30.22
burnt offerings and p. offerings,	31.02
sacrifices of p. offerings and of	33.16
be gathered to your grave in p.,	34.28
follows: "To Darius the king, all p.	Ez 5.07
never seek their p. or prosperity,	9.12
and women, I would have held my p.;	Est 7.04
Ahasuerus, in words of p. and truth,	9.30
and spoke p. to all his people.	10.03
the field shall be at p. with you.	Job 5.23
The tents of robbers are at p.,	12.06
and in p. they go down to Sheol.	21.13
"Agree with God, and be at p.;	22.21
he makes p. in his high heaven.	25.02
in p. I will both lie down and	Ps 4.08
who speak p. with their neighbors,	28.03
the LORD bless his people with p.!	29.11
do good; seek p., and pursue it.	34.14
for they do not speak p., but against	35.20
is posterity for the man of p.	37.37
silent, I held my p. to no avail;	39.02
hold not thy p. at my tears!	39.12
and p. abound, till the moon be no	72.07
do not hold thy p. or be still,	83.01
for he will speak p. to his people,	85.08
righteousness and p. will kiss each	85.10
great p. have those who love thy	119.165
dwelling among those who hate p.	120.06
I am for p.; but when I speak,	120.07
Pray for the p. of Jerusalem!	122.06
P. be within your walls, and security	122.07
sake I will say, "P. be within you!"	122.08
with evildoers! P. be in Israel!	125.05
children's children! P. be upon Israel!	128.06
He makes p. in your borders;	147.14
pleasantness, and all her paths are p.	Pro 3.17
he who boldly reproves makes p.	10.10
his enemies to be at p. with him.	16.07
time for war, and a time for p.	Ecc 3.08
in his eyes as one who brings p.	Sol 8.10
Everlasting Father, Prince of P.	Is 9.06
government and of p. there will be	9.07
Thou dost keep him in perfect p.,	26.03
O LORD, thou wilt ordain p. for us,	26.12
p. with me, let them make p. with me."	27.05
effect of righteousness will be p.,	32.17
the envoys of p. weep bitterly.	33.07
Make your p. with me and come out	36.16
"There will be p. and security in	39.08
For a long time I have held my p.,	42.14
Then your p. would have been like a	48.18
"There is no p.," says the LORD,	48.22
who publishes p., who brings good	52.07
my covenant of p. shall not be	54.10
out in joy, and be led forth in p.;	55.12
he enters into p.; they rest in	57.02
Have I not held my p., even for a long	57.11
P., p., to the far and to the	57.19
There is no p., says my God, for the	57.21
The way of p. they know not, and	59.08
no one who goes in them knows p.	59.08
your overseers p. and your taskmasters	60.17
'P., p.,' when there is no p.	Jer 6.14
'P., p.,' when there is no p.	8.11
We looked for p., but no good came,	8.15
the other; no flesh has p.	12.12
give you assured p. in this place.'"	14.13
We looked for p., but no good came;	14.19
taken away my p. from this people,	16.05
As for the prophet who prophesies p.,	28.09
cry of panic, of terror, and no p.	30.05
You shall die in p. And as spices	34.05
he shall go away from there in p.	43.12
my soul is bereft of p.,	Lam 3.17
When anguish comes, they will seek p.,	Eze 7.25
'P.,' when there is no p.;	13.10

PEACE (cont.)

and saw visions of p. for her,	Eze 13.16
when there was no p., says the	13.16
a covenant of p. and banish wild	34.25
make a covenant of p. with them;	37.26
offerings and your p. offerings;	43.27
and p. offerings, to make atonement	45.15
and p. offerings, to make atonement	45.17
offering and his p. offerings,	46.02
offering or p. offerings as a	46.12
offering or his p. offerings as he	46.12
P. be multiplied to you!	Dan 4.01
"P. be multiplied to you.	6.25
beloved, fear not, p. be with you;	10.19
the king of the north to make p.;	11.06
bring terms of p. and perform them.	11.17
and the p. offerings of your fatted	Amo 5.22
who cry "P." when they have something	Mic 3.05
And this shall be p., when the	5.05
good tidings, who proclaim p.!	Nah 1.15
be a sowing of p. and prosperity;	Zec 8.12
that are true and make for p.,	8.16
therefore love truth and p.	8.19
he shall command p. to the nations;	9.10
him was a covenant of life and p.,	Mal 2.05
with me in p. and uprightness, and	2.06
worthy, let your p. come upon it;	Mt 10.13
worthy, let your p. return to you.	10.13
I have come to bring p. on earth;	10.34
not come to bring p., but a sword.	10.34
the wind, and said to the sea, "P.!	Mk 4.39
go in p., and be healed of your	5.34
and be at p. with one another."	9.50
guide our feet into the way of p."	Lk 1.79
and on earth p. among men with whom	2.14
thou thy servant depart in p.,	2.29
has saved you; go in p."	7.50
make you well; go in p."	8.48
say, 'P. be to this house!'	10.05
And if a son of p. is there,	10.06
your p. shall rest upon him;	10.06
own palace, his goods are in p.;	11.21
I have come to give p. on earth?	12.51
an embassy and asks terms of p.	14.32
P. in heaven and glory in the	19.38
knew the things that make for p.!	19.42
P. I leave with you; my p. I give to	Jn 14.27
to you, that in me you may have p.	16.33
and said to them, "P. be with you."	20.19
"P. be with you. As the Father	20.21
them, and said, "P. be with you."	20.26
and Samaria had p. and was built	Ac 9.31
good news of p. by Jesus Christ	10.36
chamberlain, they asked for p.,	12.20
sent off in p. by the brethren to	15.33
therefore come out and go in p."	16.36
"Since through you we enjoy much p.,	24.02
to you and p. from God our Father	Rom 1.07
and honor and p. for every one who	2.10
and the way of p. they do not know.	3.17
we have p. with God through our	5.01
mind on the Spirit is life and p.	8.06
righteousness and p. and joy in the	14.17
what makes for p. and for mutual	14.19
with all joy and p. in believing,	15.13
The God of p. be with you all.	15.33
Then the God of p. will soon crush	16.20
Grace to you and p. from God our	1Co 1.03
For God has called us to p.	7.15
not a God of confusion but of p.	14.33
Speed him on his way in p.,	16.11
Grace to you and p. from God our	2Co 1.02
in p., and the God of love and p. will	13.11
Grace to you and p. from God the	Gal 1.03
p., patience, kindness, goodness,	5.22
P. and mercy be upon all who walk	6.16
Grace to you and p. from God our	Eph 1.02
For he is our p., who has made us	2.14
in place of the two, so making p.,	2.15
and preached p. to you who were	2.17
far off and p. to those who were	2.17
of the Spirit in the bond of p.	4.03
the equipment of the gospel of p.;	6.15
P. be to the brethren, and love with	6.23
Grace to you and p. from God our	Php 1.02
And the p. of God, which passes all	4.07
and the God of p. will be with you.	4.09
to you and p. from God our Father.	Col 1.02
making p. by the blood of his cross.	1.20
And let the p. of Christ rule in	3.15
Jesus Christ: Grace to you and p.	1Th 1.01
"There is p. and security," then	5.03
Be at p. among yourselves.	5.13
May the God of p. himself sanctify	5.23
Grace to you and p. from God the	2Th 1.02
Now may the Lord of p. himself give	3.16
give you p. at all times in all	3.16
and p. from God the Father and	1Ti 1.02
and p. from God the Father and	2Ti 1.02
and p., along with those who call	2.22
Grace and p. from God the Father	Tit 1.04
Grace to you and p. from God our	Phm 1.03
king of Salem, that is, king of p.	Heb 7.02
Strive for p. with all men, and for	12.14
Now may the God of p. who brought	13.20
"Go in p., be warmed and filled."	Jas 2.16
is sown in p. by those who make p.	3.18
May grace and p. be multiplied to	1Pe 1.02
let him seek p. and pursue it.	3.11
P. to all of you that are in Christ.	5.14
May grace and p. be multiplied to	2Pe 1.02
without spot or blemish, and at p.	3.14
and p. will be with us, from God the	2Jn 1.03
P. be to you. The friends greet	3Jn 1.15
May mercy, p., and love be multiplied	Jud 1.02
to you and p. from him who is and	Rev 1.04
permitted to take p. from the earth,	6.04

PEACEABLE

those who are p. and faithful in	2Sa 20.19
we may lead a quiet and p. life,	1Ti 2.02
then p., gentle, open to reason, full	Jas 3.17

PEACEABLY

him, and could not speak p. to him.	Gen 37.04
now therefore restore it p."	Ju 11.13
trembling, and said, "Do you come p.?"	1Sa 16.04
And he said, "P.; I have come	16.05
and go p., that you may not displease	29.07
said "Do you come p.?" He said, "P."	1Ki 2.13
each speaks p. to his neighbor, but	Jer 9.08
depends upon you, live p. with all.	Rom 12.18

PEACEFUL

land was very broad, quiet, and p.;	1Ch 4.40
will abide in a p. habitation,	Is 32.18
and the p. folds are devastated,	Jer 25.37
you strip the robe from the p.,	Mic 2.08
and p. understanding shall be	Zec 6.13
it yields the p. fruit of righteousness	Heb 12.11

PEACEMAKERS

"Blessed are the p.,	Mt 5.09

PEACOCKS

gold, silver, ivory, apes, and p.	1Ki 10.22
gold, silver, ivory, apes, and p.	2Ch 9.21

PEAK

Depart from the p. of Amana,	Sol 4.08
from the p. of Senir and Hermon,	4.08

PEALS

and voices and p. of thunder,	Rev 4.05
and there were p. of thunder,	8.05
p. of thunder, an earthquake, and	11.19
p. of thunder, and a great earthquake	16.18

PEARL
who, on finding one p. of great value, Mt 13.46
of the gates made of a single p., Rev 21.21

PEARLS
the price of wisdom is above p. Job 28.18
do not throw your p. before swine, Mt 7.06
a merchant in search of fine p., 13.45
hair or gold or p. or costly 1Ti 2.09
with gold and jewels and p., Rev 17.04
jewels and p., fine linen, purple, 18.12
gold, with jewels, and with p.! 18.16
And the twelve gates were twelve p., 21.21

PEASANTRY
The p. ceased in Israel, they ceased Ju 5.07
the triumphs of his p. in Israel. 5.11

PEBBLE
not even a p. is to be found there." 2Sa 17.13
but no p. shall fall upon the earth. Amo 9.09

PEDAHEL
a leader, P. the son of Ammihud. Num 34.28

PEDAHZUR
Manasseh, Gamaliel the son of P.; Num 1.10
being Gamaliel the son of P., 2.20
eighth day Gamaliel the son of P., 7.54
offering of Gamaliel the son of P. 7.59
Manasseh was Gamaliel the son of P. 10.23

PEDAIAH
the daughter of P. of Rumah. 2Ki 23.36
Malchiram, P., Shenazzar, Jekamiah, 1Ch 3.18
and the sons of P.: Zerubbabel and Shimei; 3.19
of Manasseh, Joel the son of P.; 27.20
After him P. the son of Parosh Neh 3.25
and P., Mishael, Malchijah, Hashum, 8.04
son of P., son of Kolaiah, son of 11.07
and p. of the Levites, and as their 13.13

PEDDLERS
like so many, p. of God's word; 2Co 2.17

PEDESTAL
as a p. is made, a cubit and a half 1Ki 7.31

PEDIMENT
it, and put it upon a p. of stone. 2Ki 16.17

PEELED
and p. white streaks in them, Gen 30.37
which he had p. in front of the 30.38

PEERED
"Out of the window she p., Ju 5.28

PEG
the wife of Heber took a tent p., Ju 4.21
and drove the p. into his temple, 4.21
with the tent p. in his temple. 4.22
to the tent p. and her right hand 5.26
him like a p. in a sure place, and Is 22.23
the p. that was fastened in a sure 22.25
Do men take a p. from it to hang Eze 15.03
cornerstone, out of them the tent p., Zec 10.04

PEGS
its p. and all the p. of the court, Ex 27.19
and p. of the tabernacle and the p. of 35.18
And all the p. for the tabernacle 38.20
all the p. of the tabernacle, and 38.31
all the p. round about the court. 38.31
the court, its cords, and its p.; 39.40
with their bases and p. and cords. Num 3.37
p., and cords, with all their 4.32

PEKAH
And P. the son of Remaliah, his 2Ki 15.25
king of Judah P. the son of 15.27
In the days of P. king of Israel 15.29
conspiracy against P. the son of 15.30
Now the rest of the acts of P., 15.31
second year of P. the son of 15.32
of Syria and P. the son of Remaliah 15.37
seventeenth year of P. the son of 16.01
of Syria and P. the son of Remaliah, 16.05
For P. the son of Remaliah slew a 2Ch 28.06
of Syria and P. the son of Remaliah Is 7.01

PEKAHIAH
and P. his son reigned in his stead. 2Ki 15.22
king of Judah P. the son of 15.23
Now the rest of the deeds of P., 15.26

PEKOD
and against the inhabitants of P. Jer 50.21
P. and Shoa and Koa, and all the Eze 23.23

PELAIAH
O., Akkub, Johanan, Delaiah, and Anani, 1Ch 3.24
P., the Levites, helped the people Neh 8.07
Shebaniah, Hodiah, Kelita, P., Hanan, 10.10
son of P., son of Amzi, son of 11.12

PELATIAH
P. and Jeshaiah, his son Rephaiah, 1Ch 3.21
Seir, having as their leaders P., 4.42
P., Hanan, Anaiah, Neh 10.22
and P. the son of Benaiah, princes Eze 11.01
that p. the son of Benaiah died. 11.13

PELEG
sons: the name of the one was P., Gen 10.25
years, he became the father of P.; 11.16
the birth of P. four hundred and 11.17
When P. had lived thirty years, he 11.18
and P. lived after the birth of Reu 11.19
of the one was P. (for in his days 1Ch 1.19
Eber, P., Reu; 1.25
the son of P., the son of Eber, the Lk 3.35

PELET
Jotham, Geshan, P., Ephah, and Shaaph. 1Ch 2.47
also Jeziel and P. the sons of 12.03

PELETH
of Eliab, and On the son of P., Num 16.01
The sons of Jonathan: P. and Zaza. 1Ch 2.33

PELETHITES
over the Cherethites and the P.; 2Sa 8.18
and all the P., and all the six 15.18
and the Cherethites and the P., 20.07
of the Cherethites and the P.; 20.23
and the Cherethites and the P., 1Ki 1.38
and the Cherethites and the P.; 1.44
over the Cherethites and the P.; 1Ch 18.17

PELICAN
the water hen, the p., the vulture, Lev 11.18
and the p., the carrion vulture and Deu 14.17

PELONITE
Shammoth of Harod, Helez the P., 1Ch 11.27
Hepher the Mecherathite, Ahijah the P., 11.36
was Helez the P., of the sons of 27.10

PELUSIUM
And I will pour my wrath upon P., Eze 30.15
P. shall be in great agony; 30.16

PEN
with an iron p. and lead they were Job 19.24
is like the p. of a ready scribe. Ps 45.01
the false p. of the scribes has Jer 8.08

PEN (cont.)
Judah is written with a p. of iron; Jer 17.01
rather not write with p. and ink; 3Jn 1.13

PENALTY
man of great wrath will pay the p.; Pro 19.19
You bear the p. of your lewdness Eze 16.58
shall bear the p. for your sinful 23.49
reason for the death p. in my case. Ac 28.18
persons the due p. for their error. Rom 1.27

PENCIL
a line, he marks it out with a p.; Is 44.13

PENDANTS
crescents and the p. and the purple Ju 8.26
your head, and p. for your neck. Pro 1.09
the p., the bracelets, and the Is 3.19

PENETRATE
Who can p. his double coat of mail? Job 41.13

PENIEL
called the name of the place P., Gen 32.30

PENINNAH
and the name of the other P. 1Sa 1.02
And P. had children, but Hannah had 1.02
portions to P. his wife and to all 1.04

PENITENT
because your heart was p., 2Ki 22.19
because your heart was p. and you 2Ch 34.27

PENKNIFE
them off with a p. and throw them Jer 36.23

PENNIES
Are not five sparrows sold for two p.? Lk 12.06

PENNY
out till you have paid the last p. Mt 5.26
Are not two sparrows sold for a p.? 10.29
two copper coins, which make a p. Mk 12.42

PENTAGON
and the doorposts formed a p. 1Ki 6.31

PENTECOST
When the day of P. had come, Ac 2.01
if possible, on the day of P. 20.16
But I will stay in Ephesus until P., 1Co 16.08

PENUEL
The sun rose upon him as he passed P., Gen 32.31
And from there he went up to P., Ju 8.08
and the men of P. answered him as 8.08
And he said to the men of P., 8.09
And he broke down the tower of P., 8.17
went out from there and built P. 1Ki 12.25
and P. was the father of Gedor, and 1Ch 4.04
Iphediah, and P. were the sons of 8.25

PEOPLE
they are one p., and they have all Gen 11.06
goods, and the women and the p. 14.16
shall be cut off from his p.; 17.14
all the p. to the last man, surrounded 19.04
against its p. has become great 19.13
wilt thou slay an innocent p.? 20.04
the Hittites, the p. of the land. 23.07
the sons of my p. I give it to you; 23.11
down before the p. of the land. 23.12
the hearing of the p. of the land, 23.13
years, and was gathered to his p. 25.08
he settled over against all his p. 25.18
One of the p. might easily have 26.10
So Abimelech warned all the p., 26.11
to the land of the p. of the east. 29.01
he divided the p. that were with 32.07
dwell with you and become one p. 34.16
to become one p.: that every male 34.22
he and all the p. who were with 35.06
he died and was gathered to his p., 35.29
and all my p. shall order themselves 41.40
the p. cried to Pharaoh for bread; 41.55
who sold to all the p. of the land. 42.06
and as for the p., he made slaves 47.21
Then Joseph said to the p., "Behold, 47.23
he also shall become a p., and he also 48.19
Dan shall judge his p. as one of 49.16
them, "I am to be gathered to my p.; 49.29
last, and was gathered to his p. 49.33
about that many p. should be kept 50.20
And he said to his p., "Behold, Ex 1.09
the p. of Israel are too many and 1.09
were in dread of the p. of Israel. 1.12
So they made the p. of Israel serve 1.13
and the p. multiplied and grew very 1.20
Then Pharaoh commanded all his p., 1.22
went out to his p. and looked on 2.11
beating a Hebrew, one of his p. 2.11
And the p. of Israel groaned under 2.23
And God saw the p. of Israel, 2.25
affliction of my p. who are in 3.07
the cry of the p. of Israel has 3.09
that you may bring forth my p., 3.10
brought forth the p. out of Egypt, 3.12
I come to the p. of Israel and say 3.13
said, "Say this to the p. of Israel, 3.14
"Say this to the p. of Israel, 3.15
will give this p. favor in the 3.21
He shall speak for you to the p.; 4.16
so that he will not let the p. go. 4.21
all the elders of the p. of Israel. 4.29
the signs in the sight of the p. 4.30
And the p. believed; and when they 4.31
had visited the p. of Israel and 4.31
'Let my p. go, that they may hold a 5.01
do you take the p. away from their 5.04
the p. of the land are now many and 5.05
taskmasters of the p. and their 5.06
longer give the p. straw to make 5.07
of the p. went out and said to the p., 5.10
So the p. were scattered abroad 5.12
And the foremen of the p. of Israel, 5.14
foremen of the p. of Israel came 5.15
but the fault is in your own p." 5.16
The foremen of the p. of Israel saw 5.19
why hast thou done evil to this p.? 5.22
name, he has done evil to this p., 5.23
hast not delivered thy p. at all." 5.23
groaning of the p. of Israel whom 6.05
Say therefore to the p. of Israel, 6.06
and I will take you for my p., 6.07
Moses spoke thus to the p. of Israel; 6.09
to let the p. of Israel go out of 6.11
the p. of Israel have not listened 6.12
a charge to the p. of Israel and 6.13
to bring the p. of Israel out of 6.13
"Bring out the p. of Israel from 6.26
bringing out the p. of Israel from 6.27
to let the p. of Israel go out of 7.02
my p. the sons of Israel, out of the 7.04
bring out the p. of Israel from 7.05
he refuses to let the p. go. 7.14
"Let my p. go, that they may serve 7.16
"Let my p. go, that they may serve 8.01
of your servants and of your p., 8.03
you and on your p. and on all your 8.04
the frogs from me and from my p.; 8.08
I will let the p. go to sacrifice 8.08
for your servants and for your p., 8.09
and your servants and your p.; 8.11
"Let my p. go, that they may serve 8.20
Else, if you will not let my p. go, 8.21
you and your servants and your p., 8.21

PEOPLE (cont.)

where my p. dwell, so that no swarms Ex 8.22
between my p. and your p. 8.23
servants, and from his p., tomorrow; 8.29
not letting the p. go to sacrifice 8.29
from his servants, and from his p.; 8.31
also, and did not let the p. go. 8.32
"Let my p. go, that they may serve 9.01
that belongs to the p. of Israel.'" 9.04
cattle of the p. of Israel not one 9.06
and he did not let the p. go. 9.07
"Let my p. go, that they may serve 9.13
and upon your servants and your p., 9.14
you and your p. with pestilence, 9.15
exalting yourself against my p., 9.17
where the p. of Israel were, there 9.26
and I and my p. are in the wrong. 9.27
he did not let the p. of Israel go; 9.35
Let my p. go, that they may serve me. 10.03
For if you refuse to let my p. go, 10.04
but all the p. of Israel had light 10.23
Speak now in the hearing of the p., 11.02
LORD gave the p. favor in the 11.03
servants and in the sight of the p. 11.03
But against any of the p. of Israel, 11.07
out, and all the p. who follow you.' 11.08
did not let the p. of Israel go 11.10
houses of the p. of Israel in 12.27
And the p. bowed their heads and 12.27
Then the p. of Israel went and did 12.28
"Rise up, go forth from among my p., 12.31
both you and the p. of Israel; 12.31
Egyptians were urgent with the p., 12.33
So the p. took their dough before 12.34
The p. of Israel had also done as 12.35
had given the p. favor in the 12.36
And the p. of Israel journeyed from 12.37
The time that the p. of Israel 12.40
LORD by all the p. of Israel 12.42
Thus did all the p. of Israel; 12.50
brought the p. of Israel out of 12.51
the womb among the p. of Israel, 13.02
And Moses said to the p., 13.03
When Pharaoh let the p. go, 13.17
"Lest the p. repent when they see 13.17
But God led the p. round by the way 13.18
And the p. of Israel went up out of 13.18
solemnly sworn the p. of Israel, 13.19
did not depart from before the p. 13.22
"Tell the p. of Israel to turn back 14.02
will say of the p. of Israel, 14.03
was told that the p. had fled, 14.05
servants was changed toward the p., 14.05
he pursued the p. of Israel as 14.08
the p. of Israel lifted up their 14.10
And the p. of Israel cried out to 14.10
And Moses said to the p., "Fear not, 14.13
Tell the p. of Israel to go forward. 14.15
that the p. of Israel may go on dry 14.16
And the p. of Israel went into the 14.22
But the p. of Israel walked on dry 14.29
and the p. feared the LORD; 14.31
Then Moses and the p. of Israel 15.01
love the p. whom thou hast redeemed, 15.13
till thy p., O LORD, pass by, till 15.16
till the p. pass by whom thou hast 15.16
but the p. of Israel walked on dry 15.19
And the p. murmured against Moses, 15.24
congregation of the p. of Israel 16.01
congregation of the p. of Israel 16.02
and the p. shall go out and gather 16.04
Aaron said to all the p. of Israel, 16.06
whole congregation of the p. of Israel, 16.09
congregation of the p. of Israel, 16.10
the murmurings of the p. of Israel; 16.12
When the p. of Israel saw it, they 16.15
And the p. of Israel did so; they gathered 16.17
day some of the p. went out to 16.27
So the p. rested on the seventh day. 16.30
And the p. of Israel ate the manna 16.35
congregation of the p. of Israel 17.01
was no water for the p. to drink. 17.01
Therefore the p. found fault with 17.02
But the p. thirsted there for water, 17.03
and the p. murmured against Moses, 17.03
LORD, "What shall I do with this p.? 17.04
to Moses, "Pass on before the p., 17.05
out of it, that the p. may drink." 17.06
Amalek and his p. with the edge of 17.13
for Moses and for Israel his p., 18.01
delivered the p. from under the 18.11
morrow Moses sat to judge the p., 18.13
and the p. stood about Moses from 18.13
all that he was doing for the p., 18.14
this that you are doing for the p.? 18.14
and all the p. stand about you from 18.14
"Because the p. come to me to 18.15
You and the p. with you will wear 18.18
shall represent the p. before God, 18.19
Moreover choose able men from all the p., 18.21
men over the p. as rulers of 18.21
let them judge the p. at all times; 18.22
and all this p. also will go to 18.23
and made them heads over the p., 18.25
And they judged the p. at all times; 18.26
moon after the p. of Israel; had 19.01
Jacob, and tell the p. of Israel: 19.03
and called the elders of the p., 19.07
And all the p. answered together 19.08
the words of the p. to the LORD. 19.08
that the p. may hear when I speak 19.09
the words of the p. to the LORD. 19.09
"Go to the p. and consecrate them 19.10
Sinai in the sight of all the p. 19.11
set bounds for the p. round about, 19.12
to the p., and consecrated the p.; 19.14
And he said to the p., "Be ready 19.15
so that all the p. who were in the 19.16
brought the p. out of the camp to 19.17
to Moses, "Go down and warn the p., 19.21
"The p. cannot come up to Mount 19.23
priests and the p. break through 19.24
went down to the p. and told them. 19.25
Now when all the p. perceived the 20.18
the p. were afraid and trembled; 20.18
And Moses said to the p., "Do not fear; 20.20
And the p. stood afar off, while 20.21
you shall say to the p. of Israel: 20.22
right to sell her to a foreign p., 21.08
to any of my p. with you who is 22.25
God, nor curse a ruler of your p. 22.28
that the poor of your p. may eat; 23.11
confusion all the p. against whom 23.27
and the p. shall not come up with 24.02
and told the p. all the words of 24.03
and all the p. answered with one 24.03
sent young men of the p. of Israel, 24.05
read it in the hearing of the p.; 24.07
the blood and threw it upon the p., 24.08
the chief men of the p. of Israel; 24.11
in the sight of the p. of Israel. 24.17
"Speak to the p. of Israel, that 25.02
commandment for the p. of Israel. 25.22
command the p. of Israel that they 27.20
generations by the p. of Israel. 27.21
him, from among the p. of Israel, 28.01
judgment of the p. of Israel upon 28.30
which the p. of Israel hallow as 28.38
perpetual due from the p. of Israel, 29.28
offered by the p. of Israel from 29.28
There I will meet with the p. of Israel, 29.43
will dwell among the p. of Israel, 29.45
the census of the p. of Israel, 30.12
money from the p. of Israel, and shall 30.16
may bring the p. of Israel to remembrance 30.16
And you shall say to the p. of Israel, 30.31

PEOPLE (cont.)
shall be cut off from his p.' " Ex 30.33
shall be cut off from his p." 30.38
"Say to the p. of Israel, 'You shall 31.13
shall be cut off from among his p. 31.14
Wherefore the p. of Israel shall 31.16
me and the p. of Israel that in 31.17
When the p. saw that Moses delayed 32.01
the p. gathered themselves together 32.01
So all the p. took off the rings of 32.03
and the p. sat down to eat and 32.06
for your p., whom you brought up 32.07
said to Moses, "I have seen this p., 32.09
behold, it is a stiff-necked p.; 32.09
thy wrath burn hot against thy p., 32.11
repent of this evil against thy p. 32.12
which he thought to do to his p. 32.14
noise of the p. as they shouted, he 32.17
and made the p. of Israel drink it. 32.20
"What did this p. do to you that 32.21
you know the p., that they are set 32.22
saw that the p. had broken loose, 32.25
fell of the p. that day about 32.28
On the morrow Moses said to the p., 32.30
this p. have sinned a great sin; 32.31
lead the p. to the place of which I 32.34
the LORD sent a plague upon the p., 32.35
you and the p. whom you have 33.01
way, for you are a stiff-necked p." 33.03
When the p. heard these evil 33.04
to the p. of Israel, 'You are a stiff-necked p.; 33.05
Therefore the p. of Israel stripped 33.06
all the p. rose up, and every man 33.08
And when all the p. saw the pillar 33.10
all the p. would rise up and 33.10
sayest to me, 'Bring up this p.'; 33.12
too that this nation is thy p." 33.13
favor in thy sight, I and thy p.? 33.16
I and thy p., from all other p. 33.16
although it is a stiff-necked p.; 34.09
Before all your p. I will do 34.10
and all the p. among whom you are 34.10
and all the p. of Israel saw Moses, 34.30
afterward all the p. of Israel came 34.32
and told the p. of Israel what he 34.34
the p. of Israel saw the face of 34.35
congregation of the p. of Israel, 35.01
congregation of the p. of Israel, 35.04
congregation of the p. of Israel 35.20
the p. of Israel. whose heart moved 35.29
And Moses said to the p. of Israel, 35.30
which the p. of Israel had brought 36.03
"The p. bring much more than enough 36.05
So the p. were restrained from 36.06
and the p. of Israel had done 39.32
so the p. of Israel had done all 39.42
the p. of Israel would go onward; 40.36
"Speak to the p. of Israel, and say Lev 1.02
"Say to the p. of Israel, If any one 4.02
thus bringing guilt on the p., 4.03
of the common p. sins unwittingly 4.27
shall be cut off from his p. 7.20
"Say to the p. of Israel, You shall 7.23
LORD shall be cut off from his p. 7.25
shall be cut off from his p." 7.27
person shall be cut off from his p." 7.21
"Say to the p. of Israel, He that 7.29
I have taken from the p. of Israel, 7.34
perpetual due from the p. of Israel. 7.34
be given them by the p. of Israel, 7.36
commanded the p. of Israel to 7.38
And say to the p. of Israel, 'Take a 9.03
for yourself and for the p.; 9.07
and bring the offering of the p., 9.07
sin offering which was for the p., 9.15
of peace offerings for the p.; 9.18
toward the p. and blessed them; 9.22
they came out they blessed the p., 9.23
of the LORD appeared to all the p. 9.23
and when all the p. saw it, 9.24
before all the p. I will be 10.03
to teach the p. of Israel all the 10.11
offerings of the p. of Israel. 10.14
"Say to the p. of Israel, these are 11.02
"Say to the p. of Israel, If a woman 12.02
"Say to the p. of Israel, When any 15.02
shall keep the p. of Israel 15.31
congregation of the p. of Israel 16.05
sin offering which is for the p., 16.15
uncleannesses of the p. of Israel, 16.16
uncleannesses of the p. of Israel. 16.19
the iniquities of the p. of Israel, 16.21
and the burnt offering of the p., 16.24
atonement for himself and for the p. 16.24
and for all the p. of the assembly. 16.33
be made for the p. of Israel once 16.34
sons, and to all the p. of Israel, 17.02
shall be cut off from among his p. 17.04
end that the p. of Israel may 17.05
man shall be cut off from his p. 17.09
will cut him off from among his p. 17.10
Therefore I have said to the p. of Israel, 17.12
Any man also of the p. of Israel, 17.13
I have said to the p. of Israel, 17.14
"Say to the p. of Israel, I am the 18.02
be cut off from among their p. 18.29
congregation of the p. of Israel, 19.02
shall be cut off from his p. 19.08
down as a slanderer among your p., 19.16
against the sons of your own p., 19.18
"Say to the p. of Israel, Any man of the p. 20.02
the p. of the land shall stone him 20.02
will cut him off from among his p., 20.03
And if the p. of the land do at all 20.04
cut them off from among their p., 20.05
will cut him off from among his p. 20.06
sight of the children of their p.; 20.17
be cut off from among their p. 20.18
himself for the dead among his p., 21.01
among his p. and so profane 21.04
to wife a virgin of his own p., 21.14
profane his children among his p.; 21.15
sons and to all the p. of Israel. 21.24
holy things of the p. of Israel, 22.02
which the p. of Israel dedicate to 22.03
holy things of the p. of Israel, 22.15
his sons and all the p. of Israel, 22.18
be hallowed among the p. of Israel; 22.32
"Say to the p. of Israel, The 23.02
"Say to the p. of Israel, When you 23.10
"Say to the p. of Israel, In the 23.24
day shall be cut off from his p. 23.29
I will destroy from among his p. 23.30
"Say to the p. of Israel, On the 23.34
that I made the p. of Israel dwell 23.43
declared to the p. of Israel the 23.44
"Command the p. of Israel to bring 24.02
behalf of the p. of Israel as a 24.08
went out among the p. of Israel; 24.10
And say to the p. of Israel, Whoever 24.15
So Moses spoke to the p. of Israel; 24.23
Thus the p. of Israel did as the 24.23
"Say to the p. of Israel, When you 25.02
possession among the p. of Israel. 25.33
brethren the p. of Israel you 25.46
For to me the p. of Israel are 25.55
your God, and you shall be my p. 26.12
him and the p. of Israel on Mount 26.46
"Say to the p. of Israel, When a man 27.02
Moses for the p. of Israel on 27.34
congregation of the p. of Israel, Num 1.02
The p. of Reuben, Israel's first-born, 1.20
Of the p. of Simeon, their generations, 1.22
Of the p. of Gad, their generations, 1.24
Of the p. of Judah, their generations, 1.26
Of the p. of Issachar, their generations, 1.28

PEOPLE (cont.)
Of the p. of Zebulun, their generations, Num 1.30
Of the p. of Joseph, namely, of the 1.32
Of the p. of Ephraim, their generations, 1.32
Of the p. of Manasseh, their generations, 1.34
Of the p. of Benjamin, their generations, 1.36
Of the p. of Dan, their generations, 1.38
Of the p. of Asher, their generations, 1.40
Of the p. of Naphtali, their generations, 1.42
whole number of the p. of Israel, 1.45
of them among the p. of Israel; 1.49
The p. of Israel shall pitch their 1.52
congregation of the p. of Israel; 1.53
Thus did the p. of Israel; 1.54
"The p. of Israel shall encamp each 2.02
leader of the p. of Judah being 2.03
leader of the p. of Issachar being 2.05
leader of the p. of Zebulun being 2.07
leader of the p. of Reuben being 2.10
leader of the p. of Simeon being 2.12
leader of the p. of Gad being 2.14
leader of the p. of Ephraim being 2.18
leader of the p. of Manasseh being 2.20
leader of the p. of Benjamin being 2.22
leader of the p. of Dan being 2.25
leader of the p. of Asher being 2.27
leader of the p. of Naphtali being 2.29
These are the p. of Israel as 2.32
numbered among the p. of Israel, 2.33
Thus did the p. of Israel. 2.34
duties for the p. of Israel as 3.08
to him from among the p. of Israel. 3.09
from among the p. of Israel 3.12
the womb among the p. of Israel. 3.12
to be done for the p. of Israel; 3.38
first-born males of the p. of Israel, 3.40
first-born among the p. of Israel, 3.41
the cattle of the p. of Israel." 3.41
first-born among the p. of Israel, 3.42
first born among the p. of Israel, 3.45
the first-born of the p. of Israel, 3.46
first-born of the p. of Israel he 3.50
"Command the p. of Israel that they 5.02
And the p. of Israel did so, and 5.04
to Moses, so the p. of Israel did. 5.04
"Say to the p. of Israel, When a man 5.06
holy things of the p. of Israel, 5.09
"Say to the p. of Israel, If any 5.12
execration and an oath among your p., 5.21
become an execration among her p. 5.27
"Say to the p. of Israel, When 6.02
you shall bless the p. of Israel: 6.23
put my name upon the p. of Israel, 6.27
from among the p. of Israel, 8.06
congregation of the p. of Israel. 8.09
the p. of Israel shall lay their 8.10
offering from the p. of Israel, 8.11
from among the p. of Israel, 8.14
to me from among the p. of Israel; 8.16
first-born of all the p. of Israel, 8.16
among the p. of Israel are mine, 8.17
first-born among the p. of Israel. 8.18
sons from among the p. of Israel, 8.19
service for the p. of Israel at 8.19
atonement for the p. of Israel, 8.19
among the p. of Israel in case the p. 8.19
congregation of the p. of Israel to 8.20
the p. of Israel did to them. 8.20
"Let the p. of Israel keep the 9.02
So Moses told the p. of Israel that 9.04
Moses, so the p. of Israel did. 9.05
time among the p. of Israel?" 9.07
"Say to the p. of Israel, If any man 9.10
shall be cut off from his p., 9.13
after that the p. of Israel set 9.17
there the p. of Israel encamped. 9.17
of the LORD the p. of Israel set 9.18
the p. of Israel kept the charge of 9.19
the p. of Israel remained in camp 9.22
and the p. of Israel set out by 10.12
of march of the p. of Israel 10.28
And the p. complained in the 11.01
Then the p. cried to Moses; and Moses 11.02
and the p. of Israel also wept 11.04
The p. went about and gathered it, 11.08
Moses heard the p. weeping throughout 11.10
the burden of all this p. upon me? 11.11
Did I conceive all this p.? 11.12
to get meat to give to all this p.? 11.13
able to carry all this p. alone, 11.14
elders of the p. and officers over 11.16
bear the burden of the p. with you, 11.17
And say to the p., 'Consecrate 11.18
"The p. among whom I am number six 11.21
and told the p. the words of the 11.24
men of the elders of the p., 11.24
all the LORD's p. were prophets, 11.29
And the p. rose all that day, and 11.32
LORD was kindled against the p., 11.33
LORD smote the p. with a very 11.33
they buried the p. who had the 11.34
Kibrothhattaavah the p. journeyed 11.35
and the p. did not set out on the 12.15
After that the p. set out from 12.16
which I gave to the p. of Israel; 13.02
who were heads of the p. of Israel. 13.03
and whether the p. who dwell in it 13.18
congregation of the p. of Israel in 13.26
Yet the p. who dwell in the land 13.28
But Caleb quieted the p. before Moses, 13.30
not able to go up against the p.; 13.31
brought to the p. of Israel an 13.32
and all the p. that we saw in it 13.32
a loud cry; and the p. wept that night. 14.01
And all the p. of Israel murmured 14.02
congregation of the p. of Israel. 14.05
congregation of the p. of Israel, 14.07
and do not fear the p. of the land, 14.09
of meeting to all the p. of Israel. 14.10
"How long will this p. despise me? 14.11
bring up this p. in thy might from 14.13
LORD, art in the midst of this p.; 14.14
thou dost kill this p. as one man, 14.15
to bring this p. into the land 14.16
Pardon the iniquity of this p., 14.19
as thou hast forgiven this p., 14.19
the murmurings of the p. of Israel, 14.27
words to all the p. of Israel, 14.39
and the p. mourned greatly. 14.39
"Say to the p. of Israel, When you 15.02
"Say to the p. of Israel, When you 15.18
congregation of the p. of Israel, 15.25
congregation of the p. of Israel 15.26
is native among the p. of Israel, 15.29
shall be cut off from among his p. 15.30
While the p. of Israel were in the 15.32
"Speak to the p. of Israel, and bid 15.38
with a number of the p. of Israel, 16.02
be a sign to the p. of Israel." 16.38
to be a reminder to the p. of Israel, 16.40
congregation of the p. of Israel 16.41
"You have killed the p. of the LORD." 16.41
had already begun among the p.; 16.47
and made atonement for the p. 16.47
"Speak to the p. of Israel, and get 17.02
the murmurings of the p. of Israel, 17.05
Moses spoke to the p. of Israel; 17.06
the LORD to all the p. of Israel; 17.09
And the p. of Israel said to Moses, 17.12
no more upon the p. of Israel. 18.05
from among the p. of Israel; 18.06
consecrated things of the p. of Israel; 18.08
wave offerings of the p. of Israel; 18.11
which the p. of Israel present to 18.19
inheritance among the p. of Israel. 18.20
And henceforth the p. of Israel 18.22

PEOPLE (cont.)

and among the p. of Israel they Num 18.23
For the tithe of the p. of Israel, 18.24
inheritance among the p. of Israel." 18.24
take from the p. of Israel the 18.26
you receive from the p. of Israel; 18.28
holy things of the p. of Israel, 18.32
Tell the p of Israel to bring you 19.02
congregation of the p. of Israel 19.09
this shall be to the p. of Israel, 19.10
And the p. of Israel, the whole 20.01
and the p. stayed in Kadesh; 20.01
And the p. contended with Moses, and 20.03
me in the eyes of the p. of Israel, 20.12
where the p. of Israel contended 20.13
And the p. of Israel said to him, 20.19
and the p. of Israel, the whole 20.22
"Aaron shall be gathered to his p.; 20.24
I have given to the p. of Israel, 20.24
Aaron shall be gathered to his p., 20.26
indeed give this p. into my hand, 21.02
and the p. became impatient on the 21.04
And the p. spoke against God and 21.05
among the p., and they bit the p., 21.06
so that many p. of Israel died. 21.06
And the p. came to Moses, and said, 21.07
from us." So Moses prayed for the p. 21.07
And the p. of Israel set out, and 21.10
"Gather the p. together, and I will 21.16
which the nobles of the p. delved, 21.18
You are undone, O p. of Chemosh! 21.29
against them, he and all his p., 21.33
hand, and all his p., and his land; 21.34
and all his p., until there was not 21.35
Then the p. of Israel set out, and 22.01
And Moab was in great dread of the p., 22.03
with fear of the p. of Israel. 22.03
a p. has come out of Egypt; they cover 22.05
curse this p. for me, since they are 22.06
'Behold, a p. has come out of Egypt, 22.11
you shall not curse the p., for they are 22.12
I will do; come, curse this p. for me.'" 22.17
there he saw the nearest of the p. 22.41
lo, a p. dwelling alone, and not 23.09
Behold, a p.! As a lioness 23.24
And now, behold, I am going to my p.; 24.14
know what this p. will do to your p. 24.14
in Shittim the p. began to play 25.01
These invited the p. to the sacrifices 25.02
and the p. ate, and bowed down to 25.02
"Take all the chiefs of the p., 25.04
one of the p. of Israel came and 25.06
congregation of the p. of Israel, 25.06
was stayed from the p. of Israel. 25.08
my wrath from the p. of Israel, 25.11
not consume the p. of Israel in my 25.11
atonement for the p. of Israel. 25.13
the head of the p. of a fathers' 25.15
congregation of the p. of Israel, 26.02
"Take a census of the p., from twenty years 26.04
The p. of Israel, who came forth out 26.04
was the number of the p. of Israel, 26.51
numbered among the p. of Israel, 26.62
to them among the p. of Israel. 26.62
numbered the p. of Israel in the 26.63
numbered the p. of Israel in the 26.64
And you shall say to the p. of Israel, 27.08
shall be to the p. of Israel a 27.11
I have given to the p. of Israel. 27.12
also shall be gathered to your p., 27.13
congregation of the p. of Israel 27.20
he and all the p. of Israel with 27.21
"Command the p. of Israel, and say 28.02
And Moses told the p. of Israel 29.40
of the tribes of the p. of Israel, 30.01
"Avenge the p. of Israel on the 31.02
you shall be gathered to your p." 31.02

And Moses said to the p., "Arm men 31.03
And the p. of Israel took captive 31.09
congregation of the p. of Israel, 31.12
Behold, these caused the p. of Israel, 31.16
And from the p. of Israel's half you 31.30
From the p. of Israel's half, which 31.42
from the p. of Israel's half Moses 31.47
memorial for the p. of Israel 31.54
heart of the p. of Israel from 32.07
heart of the p. of Israel from 32.09
and you will destroy all this p. 32.15
to go before the p. of Israel, 32.17
homes until the p. of Israel have 32.18
of the tribes of the p. of Israel. 32.28
are the stages of the p. of Israel, 33.01
passover the p. of Israel went out 33.03
So the p. of Israel set out from 33.05
was no water for the p. to drink. 33.14
year after the p. of Israel had 33.38
of the coming of the p. of Israel. 33.40
"Say to the p. of Israel, When you 33.51
"Command the p. of Israel, and say 34.02
Moses commanded the p. of Israel, 34.13
inheritance for the p. of Israel in 34.29
"Command the p. of Israel, that they 35.02
the possession of the p. of Israel, 35.08
"Say to the p. of Israel, When you 35.10
be for refuge for the p. of Israel, 35.15
the midst of the p. of Israel." 35.34
fathers' houses of the p. of Israel; 36.01
inheritance by lot to the p. of Israel; 36.02
tribes of the p. of Israel then 36.03
jubilee of the p. of Israel comes, 36.04
commanded the p. of Israel according 36.05
inheritance of the p. of Israel 36.07
one of the p. of Israel shall 36.07
in any tribe of the p. of Israel, 36.08
one of the p. of Israel may 36.08
tribes of the p. of Israel shall 36.09
by Moses to the p. of Israel in 36.13
spoke to the p. of Israel according Deu 1.03
"The p. are greater and taller than 1.28
And command the p., You are about 2.04
a p. great and many, and tall as the 2.10
and were dead from among the p., 2.16
a p. great and many, and tall as the 2.21
out against us, he and all his p., 2.32
him and his sons and all his p. 2.33
out against us, he and all his p., 3.01
him and all his p. and his land 3.02
the king of Bashan., and all his p.; 3.03
your brethren the p. of Israel. 3.18
go over at the head of this p., 3.28
is a wise and understanding p.' 4.06
'Gather the p. to me, that I may let 4.10
to be a p. of his own possession, as 4.20
Did any p. ever hear the voice of a 4.33
'I have heard the words of this p., 5.28
"For you are a p. holy to the LORD 7.06
you to be a p. for his own possession, 7.06
than any other p. that the LORD 7.07
a p. great and tall, the sons of the 9.02
righteousness; for you are a stubborn p. 9.06
for your p. whom you have brought 9.12
said to me, 'I have seen this p., 9.13
and behold, it is a stubborn p.; 9.13
destroy not thy p. and thy heritage, 9.26
regard the stubbornness of this p., 9.27
For they are thy p. and thy heritage, 9.29
(The p. of Israel journeyed from 10.06
your journey at the head of the p., 10.11
afterwards the hand of all the p. 13.09
For you are a p. holy to the LORD 14.02
you to be a p. for his own possession, 14.02
for you are a p. holy to the LORD 14.21
shall judge the p. with righteous 16.18
afterward the hand of all the p. 17.07
And all the p. shall hear, and fear, 17.13

PEOPLE (cont.)

or cause the p. to return to Egypt Deu 17.16
be the priests' due from the p., 18.03
come forward and speak to the p., 20.02
the officers shall speak to the p., 20.05
shall speak further to the p., 20.08
made an end of speaking to the p., 20.09
be appointed at the head of the p. 20.09
then all the p. who are found in it 20.11
thy p. Israel, whom thou hast 21.08
in the midst of thy p. Israel; 21.08
the p. of Israel, and if he treats 24.07
and bless thy p. Israel and the 26.15
that you are a p. for his own 26.18
you shall be a p. holy to the LORD 26.19
elders of Israel commanded the p., 27.01
have become the p. of the LORD 27.09
And Moses charged the p. the same day, 27.11
upon Mount Gerizim to bless the p.: 27.12
And all the p. shall answer and 27.15
And all the p. shall say, 'Amen.' 27.16
And all the p. shall say, 'Amen.' 27.17
And all the p. shall say, 'Amen.' 27.18
And all the p. shall say, 'Amen.' 27.19
And all the p. shall say, 'Amen.' 27.20
And all the p. shall say, 'Amen.' 27.21
And all the p. shall say, 'Amen.' 27.22
And all the p. shall say, 'Amen.' 27.23
And all the p. shall say, 'Amen.' 27.24
And all the p. shall say, 'Amen.' 27.25
And all the p. shall say, 'Amen.' 27.26
you as a p. holy to himself, as he 28.09
shall be given to another p., 28.32
make with the p. of Israel in the 29.01
establish you this day as his p., 29.13
go with this p. into the land 31.07
Assemble the p., men, women, and 31.12
then this p. will rise and play the 31.16
and teach it to the p. of Israel; 31.19
for me against the p. of Israel. 31.19
and taught it to the p. of Israel. 31.22
LORD, you foolish and senseless p.? 32.06
For the LORD's portion is his p., 32.09
jealousy with those who are no p.; 32.21
vindicate his p. and have compassion 32.36
"Praise his p., O you nations; 32.43
expiation for the land of his p. 32.43
this song in the hearing of the p., 32.44
I give to the p. of Israel for a 32.49
Ascend, and be gathered to your p., 32.50
Hor and was gathered to his p.; 32.50
midst of the p. of Israel at the 32.51
in the midst of the p. of Israel. 32.51
which I give to the p. of Israel. 32.52
Yea, he loved his p.; all those 33.03
the heads of the p. were gathered, 33.05
Judah, and bring him in to his p. 33.07
and he came to the heads of the p., 33.21
a p. saved by the LORD, the shield 33.29
And the p. of Israel wept for Moses 34.08
so the p. of Israel obeyed him, and 34.09
this Jordan, you and all this p., Jos 1.02
to them, to the p. of Israel. 1.02
cause this p. to inherit the land 1.06
commanded the officers of the p., 1.10
the camp, and command the p., 1.11
Shittim, with all the p. of Israel; 3.01
and commanded the p., "When you see 3.03
And Joshua said to the p., "Sanctify 3.05
covenant, and pass on before the p." 3.06
covenant, and went before the p. 3.06
And Joshua said to the p. of Israel, 3.09
So, when the p. set out from their 3.14
ark of the covenant before the p., 3.14
and the p. passed over oppposite 3.16
"Take twelve men from the p., 4.02
twelve men from the p. of Israel, 4.04
of the tribes of the p. of Israel, 4.05
shall be to the p. of Israel a 4.07
of the tribes of the p. of Israel, 4.08
commanded Joshua to tell the p., 4.10
The p. passed over in haste; 4.10
and when all the p. had finished 4.11
priests passed over before the p. 4.11
over armed before the p. of Israel, 4.12
The p. came up out of the Jordan on 4.19
And he said to the p. of Israel, 4.21
Jordan for the p. of Israel until 5.01
them, because of the p. of Israel. 5.01
circumcised the p. of Israel again 5.02
circumcised the p. of Israel at 5.03
males of the p. who came out of 5.04
Though all the p. who came out had 5.05
yet all the p. that were born on 5.05
For the p. of Israel walked forty 5.06
While the p. of Israel were encamped 5.10
and the p. of Israel had manna no 5.12
because of the p. of Israel; 6.01
then all the p. shall shout with a 6.05
and the p. shall go up every man 6.05
And he said to the p., "Go forward; 6.07
And as Joshua had commanded the p., 6.08
But Joshua commanded the p., 6.10
Joshua said to the p., "Shout; 6.16
So the p. shouted, and the trumpets 6.20
As soon as the p. heard the sound 6.20
the p. raised a great shout, and the 6.20
so that the p. went up into the 6.20
But the p. of Israel broke faith in 7.01
burned against the p. of Israel. 7.01
to him, "Let not all the p. go up, 7.03
make the whole p. toil up there, 7.03
thousand went up there from the p.; 7.04
And the hearts of the p. melted, 7.05
brought this p. over the Jordan at 7.07
Therefore the p. of Israel cannot 7.12
sanctify the p., and say, 'Sanctify 7.13
to Joshua and all the p. of Israel; 7.23
and his p., his city, and his land; 8.01
and all the p. who are with me, will 8.05
spent that night among the p. 8.09
in the morning and mustered the p., 8.10
of Israel, before the p. to Ai. 8.10
of Ai saw this he and all his p., 8.14
So all the p. who were in the city 8.16
for the p. that fled to the wilderness 8.20
twelve thousand, all the p. of Ai. 8.25
had commanded the p. of Israel, 8.31
the presence of the p. of Israel, 8.32
they should bless the p. of Israel. 8.33
And the p. of Israel set out and 9.17
But the p. of Israel did not kill 9.18
of the hand of the p. of Israel; 9.26
Joshua and with the p. of Israel.'" 10.04
he and all the p. of war with him, 10.07
all the p. returned safe to Joshua 10.21
against any of the p. of Israel. 10.21
and Joshua smote him and his p., 10.33
upon them with all his p. of war, 11.07
the p. of Israel took for their 11.14
made peace with the p. of Israel, 11.19
in the land of the p. of Israel; 11.22
whom the p. of Israel defeated, and 12.01
and the p. of Israel defeated them; 12.06
Joshua and the p. of Israel 12.07
out from before the p. of Israel; 13.06
Yet the p. of Israel did not drive 13.13
the p. of Israel killed with the 13.22
border of the p. of Reuben was the 13.23
allotted to the p. of Machir the 13.31
which the p. of Israel received in 14.01
tribes of the p. of Israel distributed 14.01
For the p. of Joseph were two 14.04
The p. of Israel did as the LORD 14.05
Then the p. of Judah came to Joshua 14.06
me made the heart of the p. melt; 14.08

PEOPLE (cont.)

tribe of the p. of Judah according Jos 15.01
round about the p. of Judah 15.12
a portion among the p. of Judah, 15.20
tribe of the p. of Judah according 15.20
tribe of the p. of Judah in the 15.21
the p. of Judah could not drive out; 15.63
dwell with the p. of Judah at 15.63
The p. of Joseph, Manasseh and 16.04
But when the p. of Israel grew 17.13
although I am a numerous p., 17.14
to them, "If you are a numerous p., 17.15
Manasseh, "You are a numerous p., 17.17
congregation of the p. of Israel 18.01
among the p. of Israel seven 18.02
So Joshua said to the p. of Israel, 18.03
the land to the p. of Israel, 18.10
the p. of Israel gave an inheritance 19.49
tribes of the p. of Israel distributed 19.51
"Say to the p. of Israel, 'Appoint 20.02
designated for all the p. of Israel, 20.09
of the tribes of the p. of Israel; 21.01
of the LORD the p. of Israel gave 21.03
lands the p. of Israel gave by lot 21.08
possession of the p. of Israel were 21.41
from the p. of Israel at Shiloh. 22.09
And the p. of Israel heard say, 22.11
that belongs to the p. of Israel. 22.11
And when the p. of Israel heard of 22.12
assembly of the p. of Israel 22.12
Then the p. of Israel sent to the 22.13
have saved the p. of Israel from 22.31
to the p. of Israel, and brought 22.32
report pleased the p. of Israel; 22.33
and the p. of Israel blessed God 22.33
And Joshua said to all the p., 24.02
Then the p. answered, "Far be it 24.16
But Joshua said to the p., 24.19
And the p. said to Joshua, "Nay; 24.21
Then Joshua said to the p., 24.22
and the p. said to Joshua, "The LORD 24.24
a covenant with the p. that they come. 24.25
And Joshua said to all of the p., 24.27
So Joshua sent the p. away, 24.28
which the p. of Israel brought up 24.32
of Joshua the p. of Israel inquired Ju 1.01
up with the p. of Judah from the 1.16
they went and settled with the p. 1.16
But the p. of Benjamin did not 1.21
dwelt with the p. of Benjamin in 1.21
words to all the p. of Israel, 2.04
the p. lifted up their voices and 2.04
When Joshua dismissed the p., 2.06
the p. of Israel went each to his 2.06
And the p. served the LORD all the 2.07
And the p. of Israel did what was 2.11
"Because this p. have transgressed 2.20
generations of the p. of Israel 3.02
So the p. of Israel dwelt among the 3.05
And the p. of Israel did what was 3.07
the p. of Israel served Cushanrishathaim 3.08
But when the p. of Israel cried to 3.09
a deliverer for the p. of Israel, 3.09
And the p. of Israel again did what 3.12
And the p. of Israel served Eglon 3.14
But when the p. of Israel cried to 3.15
The p. of Israel sent tribute by 3.15
sent away the p. that carried the 3.18
and the p. of Israel went down with 3.27
and the p. of Israel again did what 4.01
Then the p. of Israel cried to the 4.03
oppressed the p. of Israel cruelly 4.03
and the p. of Israel came up to her 4.05
of Canaan before the p. of Israel. 4.23
And the hand of the p. of Israel 4.24
that the p. offered themselves 5.02
themselves willingly among the p. 5.09
gates marched the p. of the LORD. 5.11
the p. of the LORD marched down for 5.13
Zebulun is a p. that jeoparded 5.18
The p. of Israel did what was evil 6.01
of Midian the p. of Israel made 6.02
Amalekites and the p. of the East 6.03
and the p. of Israel cried for help 6.06
When the p. of Israel cried to the 6.07
sent a prophet to the p. of Israel; 6.08
Amalekites and the p. of the East 6.33
and all the p. who were with him 7.01
"The p. with you are too many for 7.02
proclaim in the ears of the p., 7.03
"The p. are still too many; 7.04
So he brought the p. down to the 7.05
the rest of the p. knelt down to 7.06
the jars of the p. from their 7.08
and all the p. of the East lay 7.12
of bread to the p. who follow me; 8.05
all the army of the p. of the East; 8.10
subdued before the p. of Israel, 8.28
the p. of Israel turned again and 8.33
And the p. of Israel did not 8.34
Would that this p. were under my 9.29
and killed the p. that were in it; 9.45
When all the p. of the Tower of 9.46
that all the p. of the Tower of 9.47
one of the p. cut down his bundle 9.49
so that all the p. of the Tower of 9.49
and all the p. of the city fled to 9.51
And the p. of Israel again did what 10.06
oppressed all the p. of Israel that 10.08
And the p. of Israel cried to the 10.10
And the LORD said to the p. of Israel, 10.11
And the p. of Israel said to the 10.15
and the p. of Israel came together, 10.17
And the p., the leaders of Gilead, 10.18
and the p. made him head and leader 11.11
Sihon gathered all his p. together, 11.20
and all his p. into the hand of 11.21
Amorites from before his p. Israel; 11.23
day between the p. of Israel and 11.27
of Israel and the p. of Ammon. 11.27
subdued before the p. of Israel. 11.33
"I and my p. had a great feud with 12.02
And the p. of Israel again did what 13.01
your kinsmen, or among all our p., 14.03
And when the p. saw him, they 14.11
And when the p. saw him, they 16.24
upon all the p. that were in it. 16.30
and saw the p. who were there, how 18.07
will come to an unsuspecting p. 18.10
and went in the midst of the p. 18.20
to a p. quiet and unsuspecting, and 18.27
do not belong to the p. of Israel; 19.12
day that the p. of Israel came up 19.30
Then all the p. of Israel came out, 20.01
And the chiefs of all the p., 20.02
in the assembly of the p. of God, 20.02
heard that the p. of Israel had 20.03
And the p. of Israel said, "Tell us, 20.03
Behold, you p. of Israel, all of you, 20.07
And all the p. arose as one man, 20.08
to bring provisions for the p., 20.10
their brethren, the p. of Israel. 20.13
to battle against the p. of Israel. 20.14
The p. of Israel arose and went up 20.18
Then the p. of Israel rose in the 20.19
But the p., the men of Israel, took 20.22
And the p. of Israel went up and 20.23
So the p. of Israel came near 20.24
thousand men of the p. of Israel; 20.25
Then all the p. of Israel, the whole 20.26
And the p. of Israel inquired of 20.27
And the p. of Israel went up 20.30
Benjaminites went out against the p., 20.31
to smite and kill some of the p., 20.31
And the p. came to Bethel, and sat 21.02

PEOPLE (cont.)
And on the morrow the p. rose early, Ju 21.04
And the p. of Israel said, "Which of 21.05
And the p. of Israel had compassion 21.06
For when the p. were mustered, 21.09
And the p. had compassion on 21.15
For the p. of Israel had sworn, 21.18
And the p. of Israel departed from 21.24
had visited his p. and given them Ru 1.06
we will return with you to your p." 1.10
back to her p. and to her gods; 1.15
your p. shall be my p., and your 1.16
and came to a p. that you did not 2.11
presence of the elders of my p. 4.04
said to the elders and all the p., 4.09
Then all the p. who were at the 4.11
with the p. was that when any man 1Sa 2.13
your evil dealings from all the p. 2.23
that I hear the p. of the LORD 2.24
by fire from the p. of Israel. 2.28
of every offering of my p. Israel?' 2.29
So the p. sent to Shiloh, and 4.04
a great slaughter among the p.; 4.17
And when the p. of Ashdod rose 5.03
was heavy upon the p. of Ashdod, 5.06
the p. of Ekron cried out, "They 5.10
of Israel to slay us and our p." 5.10
that it may not slay us and our p." 5.11
them, did not they let the p. go, 6.06
Now the p. of Bethsehmesh were 6.13
and the p. mourned because the LORD 6.19
a great slaughter among the p. 6.19
judged the p. of Israel at Mizpah. 7.06
heard that the p. of Israel had 7.07
And when the p. of Israel heard of 7.07
And the p. of Israel said to Samuel, 7.08
voice of the p. in all that they 8.07
the LORD to the p. who were asking 8.10
But the p. refused to listen to the 8.19
had heard all the words of the p., 8.21
a man among the p. of Israel more 9.02
he was taller than any of the p. 9.02
because the p. have a sacrifice 9.12
for the p. will not eat till he 9.13
him to be prince over my p. Israel. 9.16
shall save my p. from the hand of 9.16
have seen the affliction of my p., 9.16
He it is who shall rule over my p. 9.17
to be prince over his p Israel? 10.01
reign over the p. of the LORD and 10.01
the p. said to one another, "What 10.11
called the p. together to the LORD 10.17
and he said to the p. of Israel, 10.18
and when he stood among the p., 10.23
taller than any of the p. from his 10.23
And Samuel said to all the p., 10.24
is none like him among all the p." 10.24
And all the p. shouted, "Long live 10.24
Then Samuel told the p. the rights 10.25
Then Samuel sent all the p. away, 10.25
the matter in the ears of the p.; 11.04
and all the p. wept aloud. 11.04
and Saul said, "What ails the p., 11.05
dread of the LORD fell upon the p., 11.07
Saul put the p. in three companies; 11.11
Then the p. said to Samuel, "Who is 11.12
Then Samuel said to the p., "Come 11.14
So all the p. went to Gilgal, and 11.15
And Samuel said to the p., "The 12.06
and all the p. greatly feared the 12.18
And all the p. said to Samuel, "Pray 12.19
And Samuel said to the p., "Fear not; 12.20
the LORD will not cast away his p., 12.22
LORD to make you a p. for himself. 12.22
the rest of the p. he sent home, 13.02
And the p. were called out to join 13.04
straits (for the p. were hard 13.06
the p. hid themselves in caves and 13.06
and all the p. followed him trembling. 13.07
and the p. were scattering from him. 13.08
I saw that the p. were scattering 13.11
him to be prince over his p., 13.14
numbered the p. who were present 13.15
and the p. who were present with 13.16
of any of the p. with Saul and 13.22
the p. who were with him were about 14.02
And the p. did not know that 14.03
in the field, and among all the p.; 14.15
said to the p. who were with him, 14.17
at that time with the p. of Israel. 14.18
and all the p. who were with him 14.20
for Saul laid an oath on the p., 14.24
So none of the p. tasted food. 14.24
And all the p. came into the forest; 14.25
And when the p. entered the forest., 14.26
mouth; for the p. feared the oath. 14.26
father charge the p. with the oath; 14.27
Then one of the p. said, "Your 14.28
charged the p. with an oath, saying, 14.28
food this day.' " And the p. were faint. 14.28
better if the p. had eaten freely 14.30
Aijalon. And the p. were very faint; 14.31
the p. flew upon the spoil, and took 14.32
and the p. ate them with the blood. 14.32
the p. are sinning aginst the LORD, 14.33
"Disperse yourselves among the p., 14.34
one of the p. brought his ox with 14.34
hither, all you leaders of the p.; 14.38
among all the p. that answered him. 14.39
And the p. said to Saul, "Do what 14.40
if this guilt is in thy p. Israel, 14.41
were taken, but the p. escaped. 14.41
Then the p. said to Saul, "Shall 14.45
So the p. ransomed Jonathan, that he 14.45
anoint you king over his p. Israel; 15.01
So Saul summoned the p., and 15.04
to all the p. of Israel when they 15.06
destroyed all the p. with the edge 15.08
But Saul and the p. spared Agag, 15.09
for the p. spared the best of the 15.15
But the p. took of the spoil, sheep 15.21
I feared the p. and obeyed their 15.24
elders of my p. and before Israel, 15.30
And the p. answered him in the same 17.27
and the p. answered him agains as 17.30
of all the p. and also in the 18.05
went out and came in before the p. 18.13
And Saul summoned all the p. to war, 23.08
For one of the p. came in to 26.15
utterly abhorred by his p. Israel; 27.12
Then David and the p. who were with 30.04
for the p. spoke of stoning him, 30.06
because all the p. were bitter in 30.06
and the p. drove those cattle 30.20
and to meet the p. who were with 30.21
near to the p. he saluted them. 30.21
news to their idols and to the p. 31.09
"The p. have fled from the battle, 2Sa 1.04
and many of the p. also have 1.04
son and for the p. of the LORD and 1.12
be taught to the p. of Judah; 1.18
you bid your p. turn from the 2.26
had gathered all the p. together, 2.30
I will save my p. Israel from the 3.18
and to all the p. who were with 3.31
grave of Abner; and all the p. wept. 3.32
And all the p. wept again over him. 3.34
Then all the p. came to persuade 3.35
And all the p. took notice of it, 3.36
the king did pleased all the p. 3.36
So all the p. and all Israel 3.37
shall be shepherd of my p. Israel, 5.02
for the sake of his p. Israel. 5.12
with all the p. who were with him 6.02
he blessed the p. in the name of 6.18
and distributed among all the p., 6.19

PEOPLE (cont.)

Then all the p. departed, each to 2Sa 6.19
the p. of the LORD—and I will make 6.21
brought up the p. of Israel from 7.06
moved with all the p. of Israel, 7.07
commanded to shepherd my p. Israel, 7.07
should be prince over my p. Israel; 7.08
appoint a place over my p. Israel, 7.10
appointed judges over my p. Israel; 7.11
on earth is like thy p. Israel. 7.23
God went to redeem to be his p., 7.23
out before his p. a nation and its 7.23
for thyself thy p. Israel to be 7.24
Israel to be thy p. for ever; 7.24
justice and equity to all his p. 8.15
and let us play the man for our p., 10.12
So Joab and the p. who were with 10.13
and how the p. fared, and how the 11.07
servants of David among the p. fell. 11.17
gather the rest of the p. together, 12.28
gathered all the p. together and 12.29
forth the p. who were in it, 12.31
and all the p. returned to Jerusalem. 12.31
many p. were coming from the 13.34
such a thing against the p. of God? 14.13
because the p. have made me afraid; 14.15
and the p. with Absalom kept 15.12
forth, and all the p. after him; 15.17
wept aloud as all the p. passed by, 15.23
and all the p. passed on toward the 15.23
until the p. had all passed out of 15.24
and all the p. who were with him 15.30
and all the p. and all the mighty 16.06
and all the p. who were with him, 16.14
Now Absalom and all the p., 16.15
LORD and this p. and all the men 16.18
and all the p. who are with him 17.02
bring all the p. back to you as a 17.03
and all the p. will be at peace." 17.03
not spend the night with the p. 17.08
some of the p. fall at the first 17.09
among the p. who follow Absalom.' 17.09
and all the p. who are with him be 17.16
and all the p. who were with him, 17.22
David and the p. with him to eat; 17.29
"The p. are hungry and weary and 17.29
And all the p. heard when the king 18.05
devoured more p. that day than the 18.08
into mourning for all the p.; 19.02
for the p. heard that day, "The king 19.02
And the p. stole into the city that 19.03
that day as p. steal in who are 19.03
And the p. were all told, "Behold, 19.08
and all the p. came before the king. 19.08
And all the p. were at strife 19.09
Then all the p. went over the 19.39
p. of Judah, and also half the p. of 19.40
man saw that all the p. stopped, 20.12
all the p. went on after Joab to 20.13
went to all the p. in her wisdom. 20.22
were not of the p. of Israel, 21.02
although the p. of Israel had sworn 21.02
zeal of the p. of Israel and 21.02
Thou dost deliver a humble p., 22.28
p. whom I had not known served me. 22.44
to Beersheba, and number the p., 24.02
I may know the number of the p." 24.02
God add to the p. a hundred times 24.03
king to number the p. of Israel. 24.04
numbering of the p. to the king: 24.09
him after he had numbered the p. 24.10
died of the p. from Dan to Beersheba 24.15
destruction among the p., "It is enough; 24.16
the angel who was smiting the p. 24.17
plague may be averted from the p." 24.21
and all the p. said, "Long live King 1Ki 1.39
And all the p. went up after him, 1.40
The p. were sacrificing at the high 3.02
midst of thy p. whom thou hast 3.08
a great p., that cannot be numbered 3.08
understanding mind to govern thy p., 3.09
able to govern this thy great p.?" 3.09
wisdom of all the p. of the east, 4.30
wise son to be over this great p." 5.07
charge of the p. who carried on 5.16
year after the p. of Israel came 6.01
and will not forsake my p. Israel." 6.13
fathers' houses of the p. of Israel, 8.01
a covenant with the p. of Israel, 8.09
I brought my p. Israel out of 8.16
David to be over my p. Israel.' 8.16
thy servant and of thy p. Israel, 8.30
"When thy p. Israel are defeated 8.33
forgive the sin of thy p. Israel, 8.34
thy p. Israel, when thou dost teach 8.36
given to thy p. as an inheritance. 8.36
by any man or by all thy p. Israel, 8.38
who is not of thy p. Israel, 8.41
as do thy p. Israel, and that they 8.43
"If thy p. go out to battle against 8.44
and forgive thy p. who have sinned 8.50
(for they are thy p., and thy 8.51
the supplication of thy p. Israel, 8.52
has given rest to his p. Israel, 8.56
and the cause of his p. Israel, 8.59
and all the p. of Israel dedicated 8.63
the eighth day he sent the p. away; 8.66
his servant and to Israel his p. 8.66
All the p. who were left of the 9.20
who were not of the p. of Israel— 9.20
whom the p. of Israel were unable 9.21
But of the p. of Israel Solomon 9.22
charge of the p. who carried on 9.23
LORD had said to the p. of Israel, 11.02
again to me." So the p. went away. 12.05
do you advise me to answer this p.?" 12.06
servant to this p. today and serve 12.07
we answer this p. who have said to 12.09
speak to this p. who said to you, 12.10
and all the p. came to Rehoboam 12.12
And the king answered the p. harshly, 12.13
the king did not hearken to the p.; 12.15
the p. answered the king, "What 12.16
over the p. of Israel who dwelt in 12.17
Benjamin, and to the rest of the p., 12.23
your kinsmen the p. of Israel. 12.24
if this p. go up to offer sacrifices 12.27
heart of this p. will turn again 12.27
And he said to the p., "You have 12.28
for the p. went to the one at 12.30
priests from among all the p., 12.31
a feast for the p. of Israel, 12.33
places again from among all the p.; 13.33
that I should be king over this p. 14.02
I exalted you from among the p., 14.07
made you leader over my p. Israel, 14.07
drove out before the p. of Israel. 14.24
made you leader over my p. Israel, 16.02
and have made my p. Israel to sin, 16.02
Then the p. of Israel were divided 16.21
half of the p. followed Tibni the 16.21
But the p. who followed Omri 16.22
overcame the p. who followed Tibni 16.22
So Ahab sent to all the p. of Israel, 18.20
And Elijah came near to all the p., 18.21
And the p. did not answer him a 18.21
Then Elijah said to the p., 18.22
And all the p. answered, "It is well 18.24
Then Elijah said to all the p., 18.30
and all the p. came near to him. 18.30
that this p. may know that thou, O 18.37
And when all the p. saw it, 18.39
for the p. of Israel have forsaken 19.10
for the p. of Israel have forsaken 19.14
gave it to the p., and they ate. 19.21
elders and all the p. said to him, 20.08

PEOPLE (cont.)
for all the p. who follow me." 1Ki 20.10
he mustered all the p. of Israel, 20.15
And the p. of Israel were mustered, 20.27
the p. of Israel encamped before 20.27
and the p. of Israel smote of the 20.29
life, and your p. for his p.' " 20.42
set Naboth on high among the p.; 21.09
set Naboth on high among the p. 21.12
Naboth, in the presence of the p., 21.13
cast out before the p. of Israel. 21.26
my p. as your p., my horses as your 22.04
and the p. still sacrificed and 22.43
my p. as your p., my horses as your 2Ki 3.07
answered, "I dwell among my own p." 4.13
"Strike this p., I pray thee, with 6.18
and the p. looked, and behold, he had 6.30
Then the p. went out, and plundered 7.16
and the p. trod upon him in the 7.17
for the p. trod upon him in the 7.20
you will do to the p. of Israel; 8.12
you king over the p. of the LORD, 9.06
he stood, and said to all the p., 10.09
Then Jehu assembled all the p., 10.18
noise of the guard and of the p., 11.13
the house of the LORD to the p.; 11.13
and all the p. of the land rejoicing 11.14
the LORD and the king and p., 11.17
that they should be the LORD's p.; 11.17
also between the king and the p. 11.17
Then all the p. of the land went to 11.18
guards, and all the p. of the land; 11.19
So all the p. of the land rejoiced; 11.20
the p. continued to sacrifice and 12.03
take no more money from the p., 12.08
and the p. of Israel dwelt in 13.05
the p. still sacrificed and burned 14.04
And all the p. of Judah took Azariah, 14.21
the p. still sacrificed and burned 15.04
household, governing the p. of the land. 15.05
he carried the p. captive to Assyria. 15.29
the p. still sacrificed and burned 15.35
drove out before the p. of Israel. 16.03
carrying its p. captive to Kir, and 16.09
offering of all the p. of the land, 16.15
because the p. of Israel had sinned 17.07
drove out before the p. of Israel, 17.08
And the p. of Israel did secretly 17.09
The p. of Israel walked in all the 17.22
of Assyria brought p. from Babylon, 17.24
instead of the p. of Israel; and 17.24
all sorts of p. as priests of the 17.32
those days the p. of Israel had 18.04
hearing of the p. who are on the 18.26
But the p. were silent and answered 18.36
and the p. of Eden who were in 19.12
to Hezekiah the prince of my p., 20.05
drove out before the p. of Israel. 21.02
destroyed before the p. of Israel. 21.09
But the p. of the land slew all 21.24
and the p. of the land made Josiah 21.24
threshold have collected from the p.; 22.04
and for the p., and for all Judah, 22.13
all the p., both small and great; 23.02
and all the p. joined in the covenant. 23.03
upon the graves of the common p. 23.06
And the king commanded all the p., 23.21
And the p. of the land took Jehoahaz 23.30
and the gold of the p. of the land, 23.35
except the poorest p. of the land. 24.14
was no food for the p. of the land. 25.03
And the rest of the p. who were 25.11
who mustered the p. of the land; 25.19
men of the p. of the land who were 25.19
And over the p. who remained in the 25.22
Then all the p., both small and 25.26
So the p. of Israel gave the 1Ch 6.64
And some of the p. of Judah, Benjamin, 9.03
news to their idols and to the p. 10.09
shall be shepherd of my p. Israel, 11.02
shall be prince over my p. Israel. 11.02
right in the eyes of all the p. 13.04
for the sake of his p. Israel. 14.02
he blessed the p. in the name of 16.02
from one kingdom to another p., 16.20
Then all the p. said "Amen!" and 16.36
Then all the p. departed each to 16.43
whom I commanded to shepherd my p., 17.06
should be prince over my p. Israel; 17.07
appoint a place for my p. Israel, 17.09
appointed judges over my p. Israel; 17.10
on earth is like thy p. Israel, 17.21
God went to redeem to be his p., 17.21
before thy p. whom thou didst 17.21
didst make thy p. Israel to be thy p. 17.22
justice and equity to all his p. 18.14
and let us play the man for our p., 19.13
So Joab and the p. who were with 19.14
forth the p. who were in it, 20.03
and all the p. returned to Jerusalem. 20.03
LORD add to his p. a hundred times 21.03
the numbering of the p. to David. 21.05
who gave command to number the p.? 21.17
let not the plague be upon thy p." 21.17
plague may be averted from the p." 21.22
subdued before the LORD and his p. 22.18
Israel, has given peace to his p.; 23.25
This is the list of the p. of Israel, 27.01
"Hear me, my brethren and my p. 28.02
and all the p. will be wholly at 28.21
Then the p. rejoiced because these 29.09
"But who am I, and what is my p., 29.14
things, and now I have seen thy p., 29.17
thoughts in the hearts of thy p., 29.18
me king over a p. as many as the 2Ch 1.09
go out and come in before this p., 1.10
for who can rule this thy p., 1.10
you may rule my p. over whom I 1.11
LORD loves his p. he has made you 2.11
as overseers to make the p. work. 2.18
fathers' houses of the p. of Israel, 5.02
a covenant with the p. of Israel, 5.10
I brought my p. out of the land of 6.05
no man as prince over my p. Israel; 6.05
David to be over my p. Israel. 6.06
he made with the p. of Israel. 6.11
thy servant and of thy p. Israel, 6.21
"If thy p. Israel are defeated 6.24
forgive the sin of thy p. Israel, 6.25
thy p. Israel, when thou dost teach 6.27
given to thy p. as an inheritance. 6.27
by any man or by all thy p. Israel, 6.29
who is not of thy p. Israel, 6.32
as do thy p. Israel, and that they 6.33
"If thy p. go out to battle against 6.34
and forgive thy p. who have sinned 6.39
and all the p. offered sacrifice 7.04
and all the p. dedicated the house 7.05
he sent the p. away to their homes, 7.10
to Solomon and to Israel his p. 7.10
or send pestilence among my p., 7.13
if my p. who are called by my name 7.14
and settled the p. of Israel in 8.02
All the p. who were left of the 8.07
whom the p. of Israel had not 8.08
But of the p. of Israel Solomon 8.09
exercised authority over the p. 8.10
three days." So the p. went away. 10.05
do you advise me to answer this p.?" 10.06
be kind to this p. and please them, 10.07
we answer this p. who have said to 10.09
speak to the p. who said to you, 10.10
and all the p. came to Rehoboam 10.12
the king did not hearken to the p.; 10.15
the p. answered the king, "What 10.16
over the p. of Israel who dwelt in 10.17

PEOPLE (cont.)
and the p. of Israel stoned him to 2Ch 10.18
And the p. were without number who 12.03
Abijah and his p. slew them with a 13.17
Asa and the p. that were with him 14.13
some of the p. at the same time. 16.10
of Judah and taught among the p. 17.09
him and for the p. who were with 18.02
as you are, my p. as your p. We will 18.03
and he went out again among the p., 19.04
of this land before thy p. Israel, 20.07
he had taken counsel with the p., 20.21
Jehoshaphat and his p. came to take 20.25
the p. had not yet set their 20.33
bring a great plague on your p., 21.14
His p. made no fire in his honor, 21.19
and all the p. shall be in the 23.05
but all the p. shall keep the 23.06
and he set all the p. as a guard 23.10
noise of the p. running and 23.12
the house of the LORD to the p.; 23.12
and all the p. of the land rejoicing 23.13
and all the p. and the king that 23.16
that they should be the LORD's p. 23.16
Then all the p. went to the house 23.17
the nobles, the governors of the p., 23.20
and all the p. of the land; and they 23.20
So all the p. of the land rejoiced; 23.21
princes and all the p. rejoiced and 24.10
and he stood above the p., and said 24.20
princes of the p. from among the p., 24.23
took courage, and led out his p., 25.11
killed three thousand p. in them, 25.13
you resorted to the gods of a p., 25.15
their own p. from your hand?" 25.15
And all the p. of Judah took Uzziah, 26.01
governing the p. of the land. 26.21
But the p. still followed corrupt 27.02
drove out before the p. of Israel. 28.03
number of his p. and brought them 28.05
subjugate the p. of Judah and 28.10
and all the p. rejoiced because of 29.36
of what God had done for the p.; 29.36
nor had the p. assembled in Jerusalem— 30.03
that the p. should come and keep 30.05
"O p. of Israel. return to the LORD, 30.06
And many p. came together in 30.13
For a multitude of the p., many of 30.18
heard Hezekiah, and healed the p. 30.20
And the p. of Israel that were 30.21
So the p. ate the food of the 30.22
Levites arose and blessed the p., 30.27
Then all the p. of Israel returned 31.01
commanded the p. who lived in 31.04
the p. of Israel gave in abundance 31.05
And the p. of Israel and Judah who 31.06
blessed the LORD and his p. Israel. 31.08
for the LORD has blessed his p., 31.10
A great many p. were gathered, and 32.04
set combat commanders over the p., 32.06
And the p. took confidence from 32.08
and to all the p. of Judah that 32.09
to deliver his p. from my hand, 32.14
to deliver his p. from my hand or 32.15
delivered their p. from my hands, 32.17
not deliver his p. from my hand." 32.17
of Judah to the p. of Jerusalem 32.18
drove out before the p. of Israel. 33.02
destroyed before the p. of Israel. 33.09
spoke to Manasseh and to his p., 33.10
Nevertheless the p. still sacrificed 33.17
But the p. of the land slew all 33.25
and the p. of the land made 33.25
all the p. both great and small; 34.30
that belonged to the p. of Israel, 34.33
LORD your God and his p. Israel. 35.03
houses of your brethren the lay p., 35.05
Then Josiah contributed to the lay p., 35.07
contributed willingly to the p., 35.08
the fathers' houses of the lay p., 35.12
them quickly to all the lay p. 35.13
And the p. of Israel who were 35.17
The p. of the land took Jehoahaz 36.01
priests and the p. likewise were 36.14
compassion on his p. and on his 36.15
of the LORD rose against his p., 36.16
Whoever is among you of all his p., 36.23
Whoever is among you of all his p., Ez 1.03
Now these were the p. of the 2.01
of the men of the p. of Israel: 2.02
and some of the p. lived in 2.70
the p. gathered as one man to 3.01
And all the p. shouted with a 3.11
so that the p. could not distinguish 3.13
for the p. shouted with a great 3.13
the p. of the land discouraged the p. 4.04
carried away the p. to Babylonia. 5.12
any king or p. that shall put 6.12
And the p. of Israel, the priests 6.16
eaten by the p. of Israel who had 6.21
some of the p. of Israel, and some 7.07
any one of the p. of Israel or 7.13
offerings of the p. and the priests, 7.16
judge all the p. in the province 7.25
I reviewed the p. and the priests, 8.15
they aided the p. and the house of 8.36
"The p. of Israel and the priests 9.01
of Israel; for the p. wept bitterly. 10.01
And all the p. sat in the open 10.09
But the p. are many, and it is a 10.13
night for the p. of Israel thy Neh 1.06
the sins of the p. of Israel. 1.06
They are thy servants and thy p., 1.10
For the p. had a mind to work. 4.06
I stationed the p. according to 4.13
officials and to the rest of the p., 4.14
officials and to the rest of the p., 4.19
I also said to the p. at that time, 4.22
outcry of the p. and of their 5.01
And the p. did as they had promised. 5.13
me laid heavy burdens upon the p., 5.15
servants lorded it over the p. 5.15
servitude was heavy upon this p. 5.18
all that I have done for this p. 5.19
but the p. within it were few and 7.04
officials and the p. to be enrolled 7.05
These were the p. of the province 7.06
of the men of the p. of Israel: 7.07
the rest of the p. gave was twenty 7.72
some of the p., the temple servants, 7.73
And all the p. gathered as one man 8.01
ears of all the p. were attentive 8.03
book in the sight of all the p., 8.05
for he was above all the p.; 8.05
when he opened it all the p. stood. 8.05
and all the p. answered, "Amen, Amen," 8.06
helped the p. to understand the law, 8.07
while the p. remained in their places. 8.07
so that the p. understood the reading. 8.08
who taught the p. said to all the p., 8.09
For all the p. wept when they 8.09
So the Levites stilled all the p., 8.11
And all the p. went their way to 8.12
of fathers' houses of all the p., 8.13
Moses that the p. of Israel should 8.14
So the p. went out and brought them 8.16
to that day the p. of Israel had 8.17
this month the p. of Israel were 9.01
servants and all the p. of his land, 9.10
and all thy p., since the time of 9.32
The chiefs of the p.: Parosh, Pahathmoab, 10.14
The rest of the p., the priests, the 10.28
and the p., for the wood offering, 10.34
For the p. of Israel and the sons 10.39
leaders of the p. lived in Jerusalem; 11.01
the rest of the p. cast lots to 11.01

PEOPLE (cont.)

And the p. blessed all the men who	Neh 11.02
in all matters concerning the p.	11.24
some of the p. of Judah lived in	11.25
The p. of Benjamin also lived from	11.31
purified the p. and the gates and	12.30
followed them with half of the p.,	12.38
of Moses in the hearing of the p.;	13.01
When the p. heard the law, they	13.03
on the sabbath to the p. of Judah,	13.16
Judah, but the language of each p.	13.24
for all the p. present in Susa the	Est 1.05
and to every p. in its own language,	1.22
according to the language of his p.	1.22
not made known her p. or kindred,	2.10
made known her kindred or her p.,	2.20
known to him the p. of Mordecai,	3.06
the p. of Mordecai, throughout the	3.06
is a certain p. scattered abroad	3.08
from those of every other p., and	3.08
the p. also, to do with them as it	3.11
and every p. in its own language;	3.12
to him and entreat him for her p.	4.08
servants and the p. of the king's	4.11
begun to fall, is of the Jewish p.,	6.13
petition, and my p. at my request.	7.03
I and my p., to be destroyed, to be	7.04
calamity that is coming to my p.?	8.06
and to every p. in its own language,	8.09
force of any p. or province that	8.11
he sought the welfare of his p.	10.03
and spoke peace to all his p.	10.03
greatest of all the p. of the east.	Job 1.03
and it fell upon the young p.,	1.19
"No doubt you are the p.,	12.02
the chiefs of the p. of the earth,	12.24
offspring or descendant among his p.,	18.19
at midnight the p. are shaken and	34.20
that he should not ensnare the p.	34.30
multitude of oppressions p. cry out;	35.09
thousands of p. who have set	Ps 3.06
thy blessing be upon thy p.!	3.08
who eat up my p. as they eat bread,	14.04
restores the fortunes of his p.,	14.07
For thou dost deliver a humble p.;	18.27
p. whom I had not known served me.	18.43
by men, and despised by the p.	22.06
his deliverance to a p. yet unborn,	22.31
The LORD is the strength of his p.,	28.08
O save thy p., and bless thy	28.09
May the LORD give strength to his p.!	29.11
the LORD bless his p. with peace!	29.11
the p. whom he has chosen as his	33.12
my cause against an ungodly p.;	43.01
Thou hast sold thy p. for a trifle,	44.12
forget your p. and your father's	45.10
the p. of Tyre will sue your favor	45.12
gifts, the richest of the p.	45.12
gather as the p. of the God of	47.09
earth, that he may judge his p.:	50.04
"Hear, O my p., and I will speak, O	50.07
who eat up my p. as they eat bread,	53.04
restores the fortunes of his p.,	53.06
Slay them not, lest my p. forget;	59.11
Thou hast made thy p. suffer hard	60.03
Trust in him at all times, O p.;	62.08
thou didst go forth before thy p.,	68.07
gives power and strength to his p.	68.35
May he judge thy p. with righteousness,	72.02
mountains bear prosperity for the p.,	72.03
the cause of the poor of the p.,	72.04
Therefore the p. turn and praise	73.10
and an impious p. reviles thy name.	74.18
Thou didst with thy arm redeem thy p.,	77.15
Thou didst lead thy p. like a flock	77.20
Give ear, O my p., to my teaching;	78.01
bread, or provide meat for his p.?"	78.20
Then he led forth his p. like sheep,	78.52
He gave his p. over to the sword,	78.62
to be the shepherd of Jacob his p.,	78.71
Then we thy p., the flock of thy	79.13
Hear, O my p., while I admonish you!	81.08
"But my p. did not listen to my	81.11
O that my p. would listen to me,	81.13
They lay crafty plans against thy p.;	83.03
forgive the iniquity of thy p.;	85.02
that thy p. may rejoice in thee?	85.06
for he will speak peace to his p.,	85.08
Blessed are the p. who know the	89.15
exalted one chosen from the p.	89.19
They crush thy p., O LORD, and	94.05
Understand, O dullest of the p.!	94.08
For the LORD will not forsake his p.;	94.14
and we are the p. of his pasture,	95.07
"They are a p. who err in heart, and	95.10
we are his p., and the sheep of his	100.03
so that a p. yet unborn may praise	102.18
his acts to the p. of Israel.	103.07
from one kingdom to another p.,	105.13
the LORD made his p. very fruitful,	105.24
turned their hearts to hate his p.,	105.25
So he led forth his p. with joy,	105.43
when thou showest favor to thy p.;	106.04
LORD was kindled against his p.,	106.40
And let all the p. say, "Amen!"	106.48
him in the congregation of the p.,	107.32
Your p. will offer themselves	110.03
He has shown his p. the power of	111.06
He sent redemption to his p.;	111.09
princes, with the princes of his p.	113.08
of Jacob from a p. of strange	114.01
LORD in the presence of all his p.	116.14
in the presence of all his p.,	116.18
so the LORD is round about his p.,	125.02
a heritage to his p. Israel.	135.12
For the LORD will vindicate his p.,	135.14
to him who led his p. through the	136.16
Happy the p. to whom such blessings	144.15
Happy the p. whose God is the LORD!	144.15
He has raised up a horn for his p.,	148.14
for the p. of Israel who are near	148.14
For the LORD takes pleasure in his p.;	149.04
Where there is no guidance, a p. falls;	Pro 11.14
the p. curse him who holds back	11.26
In a multitude of p. is the glory	14.28
but without a p. a prince is ruined.	14.28
but sin is a reproach to any p.	14.34
is a wicked ruler over a poor p.	28.15
are in authority, the p. rejoice;	29.02
when the wicked rule, the p. groan.	29.02
no prophecy the p. cast off	29.18
the ants are a p. not strong, yet	30.25
The badgers are a p. not mighty,	30.26
and a king striding before his p.	30.31
there was no end of all the p.;	Ecc 4.16
also taught the p. knowledge,	12.09
know, my p. does not understand."	Is 1.03
a p. laden with iniquity, offspring	1.04
of our God, you p. of Gomorrah!	1.10
For thou hast rejected thy p.,	2.06
And the p. will oppress one another,	3.05
shall not make me leader of the p."	3.07
My p.—children are their oppressors,	3.12
O my p., your leaders mislead you.	3.12
contend, he stands to judge his p.	3.13
the elders and princes of his p.:	3.14
What do you mean by crushing my p.,	3.15
Therefore my p. go into exile for	5.13
LORD was kindled against his p.,	5.25
the midst of a p. of unclean lips;	6.05
And he said, "Go, and say to this p.:	6.09
Make the heart of this p. fat,	6.10
heart of his p. shook as the trees	7.02
so that it will no longer be a p.)	7.08
and upon your p. and upon your	7.17
"Because this p. have refused the	8.06

PEOPLE (cont.)
in the way of this p., saying: Is 8.11
all that this p. call conspiracy, 8.12
should not a p. consult their God? 8.19
The p. who walked in darkness have 9.02
and all the p. will know, Ephraim 9.09
The p. did not turn to him who 9.13
who lead this p. lead them astray, 9.16
and the p. are like fuel for the 9.19
the poor of my p. of their right, 10.02
and against the p. of my wrath I 10.06
For though your p. Israel be as the 10.22
"O my p., who dwell in Zion, be not 10.24
remnant which is left of his p., 11.11
shall plunder the p. of the east. 11.14
remnant which is left of his p., 11.16
every man will turn to his own p., 13.14
your land, you have slain your p. 14.20
afflicted of his p. find refuge." 14.32
to a p. feared near and far, a 18.02
of hosts from a p. tall and smooth, 18.07
from a p. feared near and far, a 18.07
saying, "Blessed be Egypt my p., 19.25
destruction of the daughter of my p." 22.04
This is the p.; it was not Assyria. 23.13
as with the p., so with the priest; 24.02
reproach of his p. he will take 25.08
Let them see thy zeal for thy p., 26.11
Come, my p.. enter your chambers, and 26.20
For this is a p. without discernment; 27.11
gathered one by one, O p. of Israel. 27.12
beauty, to the remnant of his p.; 28.05
the LORD will speak to this p., 28.11
who rule this p. in Jerusalem! 28.14
"Because this p. draw near with 29.13
do marvelous things with this p., 29.14
shame through a p. that cannot 30.05
to a p. that cannot profit them. 30.06
For they are a rebellious p., 30.09
Yea, O p. in Zion who dwell at 30.19
LORD binds up the hurt of his p., 30.26
deeply revolted, O p. of Israel. 31.06
for the soil of my p. growing up in 32.13
My p. will abide in a peaceful 32.18
You will see no more the insolent p., 33.19
the p. of an obscure speech which 33.19
the p. who dwell there will be 33.24
Edom, upon the p. I have doomed. 34.05
hearing of the p. who are on the 36.11
and the p. of Eden who were in 37.12
Comfort, comfort my p., says your God. 40.01
upon it; surely the p. is grass. 40.07
gives breath to the p. upon it and 42.05
given you as a covenant to the p., 42.06
But this is a p. robbed and plundered, 42.22
Bring forth the p. who are blind, 43.08
to give drink to my chosen p., 43.20
the p. whom I formed for myself 43.21
I was angry with my p., I profaned 47.06
given you as a covenant to the p., 49.08
for the LORD has comforted his p., 49.13
my p., and give ear to me, my nation; 51.04
the p. in whose heart is my law; 51.07
and saying to Zion, 'You are my p.'" 51.16
God who pleads the cause of his p.: 51.22
My p. went down at the first into 52.04
seeing that my p. are taken away 52.05
Therefore my p. shall know my name; 52.06
or the LORD has comforted his p., 52.09
for the transgression of my p.? 53.08
and will p. the desolate cities. 54.03
surely separate me from his p."; 56.03
declare to my p. their transgression, 58.01
Your p. shall all be righteous; 60.21
that they are a p. whom the LORD 61.09
gates, prepare the way for the p.; 62.10
And they shall be called the holy p., 62.12
For he said, Surely they are my p., 63.08
So thou didst lead thy p., 63.14
Thy holy p. possessed thy sanctuary 63.18
consider, we are all thy p. 64.09
all the day to a rebellious p., 65.02
a p. who provoke me to my face 65.03
for my p. who have sought me. 65.10
a rejoicing, and her p. a joy. 65.18
in Jerusalem, and be glad in my p.; 65.19
a tree shall the days of my p. be, 65.22
priests, and the p. of the land. Jer 1.18
But my p. have changed their glory 2.11
for my p. have committed two evils: 2.13
Why then do my p. say, 'We are free, 2.31
Yet my p. have forgotten me days 2.32
deceived this p. and Jerusalem, 4.10
be said to this p. and to Jerusalem. 4.11
toward the daughter of my p., 4.11
"For my p. are foolish, they know me 4.22
and this p. wood, and the fire shall 5.14
And when your p. say, 'Why has the 5.19
"Hear this, O foolish and senseless p., 5.21
But this p. has a stubborn and 5.23
For wicked men are found among my p.; 5.26
my p. love to have it so, but what 5.31
O p. of Benjamin, from the midst of 6.01
healed the wound of my p. lightly, 6.14
I am bringing evil upon this p., 6.19
lay before this p. stumbling blocks 6.21
a p. is coming from the north 6.22
O daughter of my p., gird on sackcloth, 6.26
an assayer and tester among my p., 6.27
for the wickedness of my p. Israel. 7.12
"As for you, do not pray for this p., 7.16
your God, and you shall be my p.; 7.23
bodies of this p. will be food for 7.33
Why then has this p. turned away in 8.05
but my p. know not the ordinance of 8.07
healed the wound of my p. lightly, 8.11
daughter of my p. from the length 8.19
daughter of my p. is my heart 8.21
daughter of my p. not been restored? 8.22
the slain of the daughter of my p.! 9.01
might leave my p. and go away from 9.02
else can I do, because of my p.? 9.07
I will feed this p. with wormwood, 9.15
So shall you be my p., and I will 11.04
"Therefore do not pray for this p., 11.14
I have given my p. Israel to inherit: 12.14
diligently learn the ways of my p., 12.16
they taught my p. to swear by Baal, 12.16
be built up in the midst of my p. 12.16
This evil p., who refuse to hear my 13.10
that they might be for me a p., 13.11
her p. lament on the ground, and the 14.02
Thus says the LORD concerning this p.: 14.10
pray for the welfare of this p. 14.11
And the p. to whom they prophesy 14.16
daughter of my p. is smitten with 14.17
would not turn toward this p. 15.01
them, I have destroyed my p.; 15.07
you to this p. a fortified wall of 15.20
taken away my peace from this p., 16.05
you tell this p. all these words, 16.10
brought up the p. of Israel out of 16.14
brought up the p. of Israel out of 16.15
And p. shall come from the cities 17.26
But my p. have forgotten me, they 18.15
elders of the p. and some of the 19.01
Because the p. have forsaken me, and 19.04
cause their p. to fall by the sword 19.07
will I break this p. and this city, 19.11
house, and said to all the p.: 19.14
and the p. in this city who survive 21.07
"And to this p. you shall say: 'Thus 21.08
and your p. who enter these gates. 22.02
and their servants, and their p. 22.04
the shepherds who care for my p.: 23.02
brought up the p. of Israel out of 23.07

PEOPLE (cont.)

Baal and led my p. Israel astray. Jer 23.13
have proclaimed my words to my p., 23.22
to make my p. forget my name by 23.27
and lead my p. astray by their 23.32
they do not profit this p. at all, 23.32
"When one of this p., or a prophet, 23.33
or one of the p. who says, 'The 23.34
shall be my p. and I will be their 24.07
concerning all the p. of Judah, 25.01
to all the p. of Judah and all the 25.02
servants, his princes, all his p., 25.19
and all the p. heard Jeremiah 26.07
commanded him to speak to all the p., 26.08
and all the p. laid hold of him, 26.08
And all the p. gathered about Jeremiah 26.09
to the princes and to all the p., 26.11
to all the princes and all the p., 26.12
and all the p. said to the priests 26.16
to all the assembled p., saying, 26.17
and said to all the p. of Judah: 26.18
the burial place of the common p. 26.23
over to the p. to be put to death. 26.24
and serve him and his p., and live. 27.12
you and your p. die by the sword, 27.13
to the priests and to all this p., 27.16
priests and all the p., saying, 28.01
and all the p. who were standing 28.05
and in the hearing of all the p. 28.07
in the presence of all the p., 28.11
have made this p. trust in a lie. 28.15
and all the p., whom Nebuchadnezzar 29.01
concerning all the p. who dwell in 29.16
name to all the p. who are in 29.25
among this p. to see the good that 29.32
the good that I will do to my p., 29.32
will restore the fortunes of my p., 30.03
And you shall be my p., and I will 30.22
of Israel, and they shall be my p." 31.01
"The p. who survived the sword 31.02
say, 'The LORD has saved his p., 31.07
and my p. shall be satisfied with 31.14
their God, and they shall be my p. 31.33
Thou didst bring thy p. Israel out 32.21
And they shall be my p., and I will 32.38
all this great evil upon this p., 32.42
observed what these p. are saying, 33.24
despised my p. so that they are no 33.24
with all the p. in Jerusalem to 34.08
and all the p. who had entered 34.10
and all the p. of the land who 34.19
but this p. has not obeyed me. 35.16
of all the p. in the LORD's house 36.06
has pronounced against this p. 36.07
the p. in Jerusalem and all the p. who 36.09
Then, in the hearing of all the p., 36.10
scroll in the hearing of the p. 36.13
in the hearing of the p., and come." 36.14
servants nor the p. of the land 37.02
going in and out among the p., 37.04
his portion there among the p. 37.12
to you or your servants or this p., 37.18
Jeremiah was saying to all the p., 38.01
city, and the hands of all the p., 38.04
not seeking the welfare of this p., 38.04
house and the house of the p., 39.08
the rest of the p. who were left 39.09
to him, and the p. who remained. 39.09
of the poor p. who owned nothing, 39.10
home. So he dwelt among the p. 39.14
and dwell with him among the p.; 40.05
him among the p. who were left in 40.06
the rest of the p. who were in 41.10
and all the p. who were left at 41.10
And when all the p. who were with 41.13
So all the p. whom Ishmael had 41.14
the rest of the p. whom Ishmael 41.16
and all the p. from the least to 42.01
and all the p. from the least to 42.08
to all the p. all these words of 43.01
and all the p. did not obey the 43.04
all the p. who dwelt in Pathros in 44.15
Then Jeremiah said to all the p., 44.20
all the p. who had given him this 44.20
and the p. of the land, did not the 44.21
Jeremiah said to all the p. and all 44.24
back to our own p. and to the land 46.16
the hand of a p. from the north. 46.24
be destroyed and be no longer a p., 48.42
The p. of Chemosh is undone; 48.46
and his p. settled in its cities? 49.01
Destroy the p. of the east! 49.28
the p. of Israel and the p. of Judah 50.04
"My p. have been lost sheep; 50.06
every one shall turn to his own p., 50.16
The p. of Israel are oppressed, and 50.33
and the p. of Judah with them; 50.33
"Behold, a p. comes from the north; 50.41
"Go out of the midst of her, my p.! 51.45
was no food for the p. of the land. 52.06
poorest of the p. and the rest of the p. 52.15
who mustered the p. of the land; 52.25
sixty men of the p. of the land, 52.25
number of the p. whom Nebuchadrezzar 52.28
sits the city that was full of p.! Lam 1.01
When her p. fell into the hand of 1.07
All her p. groan as they search for 1.11
destruction of the daughter of my p., 2.11
destruction of the daughter of my p. 3.48
daughter of my p. has become cruel, 4.03
daughter of my p. has been greater 4.06
destruction of the daughter of my p. 4.10
I send you to the p. of Israel, Eze 2.03
The p. also are impudent and 2.04
not sent to a p. of foreign speech 3.05
to your p., and say to them, 'Thus 3.11
you cannot go out among the p.; 3.25
"Thus shall the p. of Israel eat 4.13
bodies of the p. of Israel before 6.05
hands of the p. of the land are 7.27
son of Benaiah, princes of the p. 11.01
and they shall be my p., and I will 11.20
and say of the p. of the land, Thus 12.19
not be in the council of my p., 13.09
because they have misled my p., 13.10
when the p. build a wall, these 13.10
against the daughters of your p., 13.17
hunt down souls belonging to my p., 13.18
me among my p. for handfuls of 13.19
not live, by your lies to my p., 13.19
and deliver my p. out of your hand, 13.21
will deliver my p. out of your 13.23
him off from the midst of my p.; 14.08
him from the midst of my p. Israel. 14.09
they may be my p. and I may be 14.11
arm or many p. to pull it from its 17.09
did what is not good among his p., 18.18
of man, for it is against my p.; 21.12
over to the sword with my p. 21.12
The p. of the land have practiced 22.29
So I spoke to the p. in the morning, 24.18
And the p. said to me, "Will you not 24.19
you over to the p. of the East for 25.04
Ammonites to the p. of the East as 25.10
Edom by the hand of my p. Israel; 25.14
will slay your p. with the sword; 26.11
to the p. of old, and I will make 26.20
and the p. of the land that is in 30.05
He and his p. with him, the most 30.11
speak to your p. and say to them, If 33.02
and the p. of the land take a man 33.02
blows the trumpet and warns the p.; 33.03
so that the p. are not warned, and 33.06
say to your p., The righteousness 33.12
"Yet your p. say, 'The way of the 33.17
your p. who talk together about you 33.30

PEOPLE (cont.)

And they come to you as p. come, Eze 33.31
and they sit before you as my p., 33.31
are my p., says the Lord GOD. 34.30
gave over the p. of Israel to the 35.05
the talk and evil gossip of the p.; 36.03
yield your fruit to my p. Israel; 36.08
walk upon you, even my p. Israel; 36.12
'These are the p. of the LORD, 36.20
and you shall be my p., and I will 36.28
you from your graves, O my p.; 37.12
you from your graves, O my p. 37.13
And when your p. say to you, 'Will 37.18
I will take the p. of Israel from 37.21
and they shall be my p., and I will 37.23
their God, and they shall be my p. 37.27
the land where p. were gathered 38.08
its p. were brought out from the 38.08
upon the quiet p. who dwell 38.11
and the p. who were gathered from 38.12
day when my p. Israel are dwelling 38.14
you will come up against my p. Israel, 38.16
known in the midst of my p. Israel; 39.07
All the p. of the land will bury 39.13
near to that which is for the p. 42.14
midst of the p. of Israel for ever. 43.07
who are among the p. of Israel, 44.09
and the sacrifice for the p., 44.11
attend on the p., to serve them. 44.11
when the p. of Israel went astray 44.15
out into the outer court to the p., 44.19
holiness to the p. with their 44.19
They shall teach my p. the difference 44.23
shall no more oppress my p.; 45.08
cease your evictions of my p., 45.09
All the p. of the land shall give 45.16
and all the p. of the land a young 45.22
The p. of the land shall worship at 46.03
"When the p. of the land come 46.09
any of the inheritance of the p., 46.18
that none of my p. shall be 46.18
so communicate holiness to the p." 46.20
boil the sacrifices of the p." 46.24
astray when the p. of Israel went 48.11
to bring some of the p. of Israel, Dan 1.03
sovereignty be left to another p. 2.44
Any p., nation, or language that 3.29
be given to the p. of the saints 7.27
men and the p. of the saints. 8.24
and to all the p. of the land. 9.06
didst bring thy p. out of the land 9.15
Jerusalem and thy p. have become a 9.16
city and thy p. are called by thy 9.19
my sin and the sin of my p. Israel, 9.20
concerning your p. and your holy 9.24
and the p. of the prince who is to 9.26
to befall your p. in the latter 10.14
among your own p. shall lift 11.14
become strong with a small p. 11.23
but the p. who know their God shall 11.32
And those among the p. who are wise 11.33
prince who has charge of your p. 12.01
that time your p. shall be delivered, 12.01
of the holy p. comes to an end all 12.07
LORD said, "Call his name Not my p., Hos 1.09
you are not my p. and I am not 1.09
number of the p. of Israel shall 1.10
said to them, "You are not my p.," 1.10
p. of Judah and the p. of Israel 1.11
"My p.," and to your sister, "She 2.01
will say to Not my p., 'You are my p.'; 2.23
as the LORD loves the p. of Israel, 3.01
word of the LORD, O p. of Israel; 4.01
My p. are destroyed for lack of 4.06
They feed on the sin of my p.; 4.08
And it shall be like p., like priest; 4.09
My p. inquire of a thing of wood, 4.12
and a p. without understanding 4.14
restore the fortunes of my p., 6.11
the p. of my God, yet a fowler's 9.08
Its p. shall mourn for it, and its 10.05
the wayward p. to chastise them; 10.10
of war shall arise among your p., 10.14
My p. are bent on turning away from 11.07
mountains a great and powerful p.; Joe 2.02
gather the p. Sanctify the congregation; 2.16
"Spare thy p., O LORD, and make not 2.17
his land, and had pity on his p. 2.18
The LORD answered and said to his p., 2.19
And my p. shall never again be put 2.26
And my p. shall never again be put 2.27
Account of my p. and my heritage 3.02
and have cast lots for my p., 3.03
You have sold the p. of Judah and 3.06
But the LORD is a refuge to his p., 3.16
a stronghold to the p. of Israel. 3.16
violence done to the p. of Judah, 3.19
and the p. of Syria shall go into Amo 1.05
exile a whole p. to deliver them 1.06
delivered up a whole p. to Edom. 1.09
it not indeed so, O p. of Israel?" 2.11
O p. of Israel, against the whole 3.01
a city, and the p. are not afraid? 3.06
so shall the p. of Israel who dwell 3.12
so you love to do, O p. of Israel!" 4.05
line in the midst of my p. Israel; 7.08
me, 'Go, prophesy to my p. Israel.' 7.15
"The end has come upon my p. Israel; 8.02
them on the heads of all the p.; 9.01
Ethiopians to me, O p. of Israel?" 9.07
sinners of my p. shall die by the 9.10
the fortunes of my p. Israel, 9.14
over the p. of Judah in the day of Ob 1.12
the gate of my p. in the day of 1.13
who are of the p. of Israel shall 1.20
country? And of what p. are you?" Jon 1.08
And the p. of Nineveh believed God; 3.05
to the gate of my p., to Jerusalem. Mic 1.09
he changes the portion of my p.; 2.04
you rise against my p. as an enemy; 2.08
The women of my p. you drive out 2.09
would be the preacher for this p.! 2.11
who tear the skin from off my p., 3.02
who eat the flesh of my p., 3.03
the prophets who lead my p. astray, 3.05
shall return to the p. of Israel. 5.03
LORD has a controversy with his p., 6.02
"O my p., what have I done to you? 6.03
O my p., remember what Balak king 6.05
Shepherd thy p. with thy staff, the 7.14
harlotries, and p. with her charms. Nah 3.04
Your p. are scattered on the 3.18
forth for the salvation of thy p., Hab 3.13
to come upon p. who invade us. 3.16
Ashdod's p. shall be driven out at Zep 2.04
have taunted my p. and made boasts 2.08
remnant of my p. shall plunder 2.09
against the p. of the LORD of 2.10
midst of you a p. humble and lowly 3.12
This p. say the time has not yet Hag 1.02
with all the remnant of the p., 1.12
and the p. feared before the LORD. 1.12
spoke to the p. with the LORD's 1.13
of all the remnant of the p.; 1.14
the remnant of the p., and say, 2.02
all you p. of the land, says the 2.04
Haggai said, "So is it with this p., 2.14
in that day, and shall be my p.; Zec 2.11
Now the p. of Bethel had sent 7.02
"Say to all the p. of the land and 7.05
remnant of this p. in these days, 8.06
I will save my p. from the east 8.07
shall be my p. and I will be their 8.08
remnant of this p. as in the 8.11
remnant of this p. to possess all 8.12
a mongrel p. shall dwell in Ashdod; 9.06

PEOPLE (cont.)
for they are the flock of his p.; Zec 9.16
Therefore the p. wander like sheep; 10.02
I will say, 'They are my p.'; 13.09
the rest of the p. shall not be 14.02
the p. with whom the LORD is angry Mal 1.04
and abased before all the p., 2.09
will save his p. from their sins." Mt 1.21
priests and scribes of the p., 2.04
ruler who will govern my p. Israel.'" 2.06
the p. who sat in darkness have 4.16
and every infirmity among the p. 4.23
commanded, for a proof to the p." 8.04
And all the p. were amazed, and said, 12.23
While he was still speaking to the p., 12.46
he feared the p., because they held 14.05
'This p. honors me with their lips, 15.08
And he called the p. to him and 15.10
The disciples rebuked the p.; 19.13
elders of the p. came up to him as 21.23
elders of the p. gathered in the 26.03
there be a tumult among the p." 26.05
priests and the elders of the p. 26.47
elders of the p. took counsel 27.01
persuaded the p. to ask for 27.20
And all the p. answered, "His blood 27.25
and tell the p., 'He has risen from 27.64
"Tell p., 'His disciples came by 28.13
Judea, and all the p. of Jerusalem; Mk 1.05
commanded, for a proof to the p." 1.44
and p. came to him from every 1.45
and p. came and said to him, "Why do 2.18
And p. came to see what it was that 5.14
and p. weeping and wailing loudly. 5.38
upon a few sick p. and healed them. 6.05
the disciples to set before the p.; 6.41
Immediately the p. recognized him, 6.54
to bring sick p. on their pallets 6.55
'This p. honors me with their lips, 7.06
And he called the p. to him again, 7.14
and left the p., his disciples 7.17
his disciples to set before the p.; 8.06
And there were about four thousand p. 8.09
And some p. brought to him a blind 8.22
were afraid of the p., for all held 11.32
Many rich p. put in large sums. 12.41
lest there be a tumult of the p." 14.02
multitude of the p. were praying Lk 1.10
ready for the Lord a p. prepared." 1.17
And the p. were waiting for Zechariah, 1.21
has visited and redeemed his p., 1.68
salvation to his p. in the forgiveness 1.77
joy which will come to all the p.; 2.10
and for glory to thy p. Israel. 2.32
As the p. were in expectation, and 3.15
he preached good news to the p. 3.18
Now when all the p. were baptized, 3.21
And the p. sought him and came to 4.42
While the p. pressed upon him to 5.01
and taught the p. from the boat. 5.03
commanded, for a proof to the p." 5.14
multitude of p. from all Judea and 6.17
hearing of the p. he entered 7.01
and "God has visited his p.!" 7.16
this all the p. and the tax 7.29
together and p. from town after 8.04
Then p. went out to see what had 8.35
Then all the p. of the surrounding 8.37
As he went, the p. pressed round him. 8.42
of all the p. why she had touched 8.47
go and buy food for all these p." 9.13
them, "Who do the p. say that I am?" 9.18
but the p. would not receive him, 9.53
man spoke, and the p. marveled. 11.14
said to the p., "There are six days 13.14
and all the p. rejoiced at all the 13.17
and compel p. to come in, that my 14.23
so that p. may receive me into 16.04
and all the p., when they saw it, 18.43
men of the p. sought to destroy 19.47
for all the p. hung upon his words. 19.48
teaching the p. in the temple and 20.01
men,' all the p. will stone us; 20.06
began to tell the p. this parable: 20.09
very hour, but they feared the p.; 20.19
presence of the p. to catch him by 20.26
of all the p. he said to his 20.45
the earth and wrath upon this p.; 21.23
morning all the p. came to him in 21.38
to death; for they feared the p. 22.02
elders of the p. gathered together, 22.66
urgent, saying, "He stirs up the p., 23.05
priests and the rulers and the p. 23.13
as one who was perverting the p.; 23.14
him a great multitude of the p., 23.27
And the p. stood by, watching; 23.35
word before God and all the p., 24.19
and his own p. received him not. Jn 1.11
and p. came and were baptized. 3.23
into the city, and said to the p., 4.28
bread, so that these p. may eat?" 6.05
Jesus said, "Make the p. sit down." 6.10
When the p. saw the sign which he 6.14
next day the p. who remained on 6.22
So when the p. saw that Jesus was 6.24
muttering about him among the p. 7.12
"No, he is leading the p. astray." 7.12
The p. answered, "You have a demon! 7.20
Some of the p. of Jerusalem therefore 7.25
Yet many of the p. believed in him; 7.31
some of the p. said, "This is really 7.40
a division among the p. over him. 7.43
all the p. came to him and he sat * 8.02
on account of the p. standing by, 11.42
that one man should die for the p., 11.50
that one man should die for the p. 18.14
and having favor with all the p. Ac 2.47
And all the p. saw him walking and 3.09
all the p. ran together to them in 3.11
Peter saw it he addressed the p., 3.12
shall be destroyed from the p.' 3.23
And as they were speaking to the p., 4.01
teaching the p. and proclaiming in 4.02
them, "Rulers of the p. and elders, 4.08
all, and to all the p. of Israel, 4.10
may spread no further among the p., 4.17
to punish them, because of the p.; 4.21
done among the p. by the hands of 5.12
but the p. held them in high honor. 5.13
The p. also gathered from the towns 5.16
speak to the p. all the words of 5.20
in the temple and teaching the p." 5.25
afraid of being stoned by the p. 5.26
law, held in honor by all the p., 5.34
drew away some of the p. after him; 5.37
wonders and signs among the p. 6.08
stirred up the p. and the elders 6.12
the p. grew and multiplied in Egypt 7.17
ill-treatment of my p. that are in 7.34
"You stiff-necked p., uncircumcised 7.51
gave alms liberally to the p., 10.02
not to all the p. but to us who 10.41
commanded us to preach to the p., 10.42
baptizing these p. who have 10.47
and taught a large company of p.; 11.26
Passover to bring him out to the p. 12.04
that the Jewish p. were expecting. 12.11
angry with the p. of Tyre and 12.20
And the p. shouted, "The voice of a 12.22
about seeking p. to lead him by 13.11
of exhortation for the p., say it." 13.15
The God of this p. Israel chose our 13.17
and made the p. great during their 13.17
repentance to all the p. of Israel. 13.24
are now his witnesses to the p. 13.31
the p. begged that these things 13.42

PEOPLE (cont.)

But the p. of the city were divided; Ac 14.04
to offer sacrifice with the p. 14.13
restrained the p. from offering 14.18
and having persuaded the p., they 14.19
take out of them a p. for his name. 15.14
to bring them out to the p. 17.05
And the p. and the city authorities 17.08
for I have many p. in this city. 18.10
telling the p. to believe in the 19.04
away a considerable company of p., 19.26
to make a defense to the p. 19.33
we and the p. there begged him not 21.12
against the p. and the law and 21.28
aroused, and the p. ran together; 21.30
for the mob of the p. followed, 21.36
I beg you, let me speak to the p." 21.39
motioned with his hand to the p.; 21.40
speak evil of a ruler of your p.'" 23.05
the whole Jewish p. petitioned me, 25.24
delivering you from the p. and from 26.17
both to the p. and to the Gentiles." 26.23
the rest of the p. on the island 28.09
against the p. or the customs of 28.17
'Go to this p., and say, You shall 28.26
as some p. slanderously charge us Rom 3.08
who were not my p. I will call 'my p.,' 9.25
said to them, 'You are not my p.,' 9.26
to a disobedient and contrary p." 10.21
ask, then, has God rejected his p.? 11.01
rejected his p. whom he foreknew. 11.02
"Rejoice, O Gentiles, with his p."; 15.10
me by Chloe's p. that there is 1Co 1.11
these arrogant p. but their power. 4.19
"The p. sat down to eat and drink 10.07
foreigners will I speak to this p., 14.21
what do p. mean by being baptized 15.29
why are p. baptized on their behalf? 15.29
more and more p. it may increase 2Co 4.15
their God, and they shall be my p. 6.16
about you to the p. of Macedonia, 9.02
Let such p. understand that what we 10.11
robbers, danger from my own p., 11.26
many of my own age among my p., Gal 1.14
of the p. of Israel, of the tribe of Php 3.05
When p. say, "There is peace and 1Th 5.03
it will lead p. into more and more 2Ti 2.16
the power of it. Avoid such p. 3.05
is coming when p. will not endure 4.03
for himself a p. of his own who Tit 2.14
And let our p. learn to apply 3.14
expiation for the sins of the p. Heb 2.17
a sabbath rest for the p. of God; 4.09
as well as for those of the p. 5.03
the law to take tithes from the p., 7.05
under it the p. received the law), 7.11
sins and then for those of the p.; 7.27
their God, and they shall be my p. 8.10
and for the errors of the p. 9.07
declared by Moses to all the p., 9.19
the book itself and all the p., 9.19
again, "The Lord will judge his p." 10.30
For p. who speak thus make it clear 11.14
with the p. of God than to enjoy 11.25
By faith the p. crossed the Red Sea 11.29
to sanctify the p. through his own 13.12
God's own p., that you may declare 1Pe 2.09
you were no p. but now you are God's p.; 2.10
prophets also arose among the p., 2Pe 2.01
he who saved a p. out of the land Jud 1.05
flattering p. to gain advantage. 1.16
worldly p., devoid of the Spirit. 1.19
p. who have not soiled their Rev 3.04
and tongue and p. and nation, 5.09
seven thousand p. were killed in 11.13
every tribe and p. and tongue and 13.07
nation and tribe and tongue and p.; 14.06
my p., lest you take part in her 18.04
them, and they shall be his p., 21.03

PEOPLED

from these the whole earth was p. Gen 9.19
she shall be p. no more for ever, Jer 50.39

PEOPLE'S

Then he presented the p. offering, Lev 9.15
from the sound of the p. weeping, Ez 3.13
thou be angry with thy p. prayers? Ps 80.04
every obstruction from my p. way." Is 57.14
For this p. heart has grown dull, Mt 13.15
For this p. heart has grown dull, Ac 28.27

PEOPLES

From these the coastland p. spread. Gen 10.05
kings of p. shall come from her. 17.16
and two p., born of you, shall be 25.23
Let p. serve you, and nations bow 27.29
you may become a company of p. 28.03
I will make of you a company of p., 48.04
shall be the obedience of the p. 49.10
The p. have heard, they tremble; Ex 15.14
be my own possession among all p.; 19.05
who have separated you from the p. Lev 20.24
and have separated you from the p., 20.26
of you upon the p. that are under Deu 2.25
understanding in the sight of the p., 4.06
to all the p. under the whole 4.19
LORD will scatter you among the p., 4.27
the gods of the p. who are round 6.14
out of all the p. that are on the 7.06
for you were the fewest of all p.; 7.07
You shall be blessed above all p.; 7.14
destroy all the p. that the LORD 7.16
do to all the p. of whom you are 7.19
you above all p., as at this day. 10.15
the gods of the p. that are round 13.07
out of all the p. that are on the 14.02
cities of these p. that the LORD 20.16
And all the p. of the earth shall 28.10
among all the p. where the LORD 28.37
LORD will scatter you among all p., 28.64
from all the p. where the LORD 30.03
bounds of the p. according to the 32.08
with them he shall push the p., 33.17
They shall call p. to their mountain, 33.19
so that all the p. of the earth may Jos 4.24
among all the p. through whom we 24.17
drove out before us all the p., 24.18
the gods of the p. who were round Ju 2.12
deliver me from strife with the p.; 2Sa 22.44
and brought down p. under me, 22.48
came from all p. to hear the 1Ki 4.34
that all the p. of the earth may 8.43
from among all the p. of the earth, 8.53
that all the p. of the earth may 8.60
proverb and a byword among all p. 9.07
And he said, "Hear, all you p.!" 22.28
the gods of the p. of the land, 1Ch 5.25
make known his deeds among the p.! 16.08
marvelous works among all the p.! 16.24
For all the gods of the p. are idols; 16.26
Ascribe to the LORD, O families of the p., 16.28
that all the p. of the earth may 2Ch 6.33
proverb and a byword among all p. 7.20
yourselves like the p. of other lands? 13.09
And he said, "Hear, all you p.!" 18.27
done to all the p. of other lands? 32.13
of the gods of the p. of the earth. 32.19
because of the p. of the lands, Ez 3.03
pollutions of the p. of the land to 6.21
from the p. of the lands with 9.01
itself with the p. of the lands. 9.02
pollutions of the p. of the lands, 9.11
with the p. who practice these 9.14
women from the p. of the lands, 10.02

PEOPLES (cont.)

from the p. of the land and from Ez 10.11
I will scatter you among the p.; Neh 1.08
didst give them kingdoms and p., 9.22
their kings and the p. of the land, 9.24
the hand of the p. of the lands. 9.30
from the p. of the lands to the 10.28
daughters to the p. of the land or 10.30
and if the p. of the land bring in 10.31
to show the p. and the princes her Est 1.11
and all the p. who are in all the 1.16
among the p. in all the provinces 3.08
and to the princes of all the p., 3.12
to all the p. to be ready for that 3.14
and by proclamation to all p., 8.13
many from the p. of the country 8.17
of them had fallen upon all p. 9.02
"He has made me a byword of the p., Job 17.06
when p. are cut off in their place. 36.20
For by these he judges p.; 36.31
conspire, and the p. plot in vain? Ps 2.01
assembly of the p. be gathered 7.07
The LORD judges the p.; judge me, 7.08
he judges the p. with equity. 9.08
Tell among the p. his deeds! 9.11
deliver me from strife with the p.; 18.43
vengeance and subdued p. under me; 18.47
he frustrates the plans of the p. 33.10
thou didst afflict the p., but them 44.02
nations, a laughingstock among the p. 44.14
king's enemies; the p. fall under you. 45.05
therefore the p. will praise you 45.17
Clap your hands, all p.! Shout to 47.01
He subdued p. under us, and nations 47.03
The princes of the p. gather as the 47.09
Hear this, all p.! Give ear, all 49.01
in wrath cast down the p., O God! 56.07
to thee, O Lord, among the p.; 57.09
their waves, the tumult of the p.; 65.07
O p., let the sound of his praise 66.08
Let the p. praise thee, O God; 67.03
let all the p. praise thee! 67.03
dost judge the p. with equity and 67.04
Let the p. praise thee, O God; 67.05
let all the p. praise thee! 67.05
of bulls with the calves of the p. 68.30
scatter the p. who delight in war. 68.30
manifested thy might among the p. 77.14
records as he registers the p., 87.06
in my bosom the insults of the p., 89.50
marvelous works among all the p.! 96.03
For all the gods of the p. are idols; 96.05
Ascribe to the LORD, O families of the p., 96.07
he will judge the p. with equity. 96.10
righteousness, and the p. with his truth. 96.13
and all the p. behold his glory. 97.06
righteousness, and the p. with equity. 98.09
the LORD reigns; let the p. tremble! 99.01
he is exalted over all the p. 99.02
when p. gather together, and kingdoms, 102.22
make known his deeds among the p.! 105.01
the ruler of the p. set him free; 105.20
They did not destroy the p., 106.34
among the p., I will sing praises 108.03
all nations! Extol him, all p.! 117.01
who subdues the p. under him. 144.02
Kings of the earth and all p., 148.11
nations and chastisement on the p., 149.07
innocent," will be cursed by p., Pro 24.24
and many p. shall come, and say: Is 2.03
and shall decide for many p.; 2.04
Be broken, you p., and be dismayed; 8.09
have removed the boundaries of p., 10.13
like a nest the wealth of the p.; 10.14
shall stand as an ensign to the p.; 11.10
And the p. will take them and bring 14.02
that smote the p. in wrath with 14.06
Ah, the thunder of many p., they 17.12
Therefore strong p. will glorify 25.03
make for all p. a feast of fat 25.06
covering that is cast over all p., 25.07
the jaws of the p. a bridle that 30.28
At the thunderous noise p. flee, 33.03
And the p. will be as if burned to 33.12
nations, to hear, and hearken, O p.! 34.01
let the p. renew their strength; 41.01
p. in exchange for you life. 43.04
together, and let the p. assemble. 43.09
and hearken, you p. from afar. 49.01
and raise my signal to the p.; 49.22
my justice for a light to the p. 51.04
and my arms will rule the p.; 51.05
Behold, I made him a witness to the p., 55.04
a leader and commander for the p. 55.04
a house of prayer for all p. 56.07
earth, and thick darkness the p.; 60.02
offspring in the midst of the p.; 61.09
lift up an ensign over the p. 62.10
and from the p. no one was with me; 63.03
I trod down the p. in my anger, Is 63.06
for the customs of the p. are false. Jer 10.03
and upon the p. that call not on 10.25
and all the p. were fighting 34.01
The p. labor for nought, and the 51.58
all you p., and behold my suffering, Lam 1.18
become the laughingstock of all p., 3.14
offscouring and refuse among the p. 3.45
not to many p. of foreign speech Eze 3.06
I will gather you from the p., 11.17
out from the p. and gather you out 20.34
you into the wilderness of the p., 20.35
when I bring you out from the p., 20.41
and wagons and a host of p.; 23.24
off from the p. and will make you 25.07
'Aha, the gate of the p. is broken, 26.02
merchant of the p. on many coastlands, 27.03
the seas, you satisfied many p.; 27.33
merchants among the p. hiss at you; 27.36
you among the p. are appalled at 28.19
Israel from the p. among whom they 28.25
from the p. among whom they were 29.13
and all the p. of the earth will go 31.12
over you with a host of many p.; 32.03
will trouble the hearts of many p., 32.09
I will make many p. appalled at you, 32.10
And I will bring them out from the p.. 34.13
disgrace of the p. and no longer 36.15
all his hordes—many p. are with you. 38.06
your hordes, and many p. with you. 38.09
you and many p. with you, all of 38.15
and the many p. that are with him, 38.22
hordes and the p. that are with 39.04
back from the p. and gathered them 39.27
O p., nations, and languages, Dan 3.04
soon as all the p. heard the sound 3.07
all the p., nations, and languages 3.07
King Nebuchadnezzar to all p., 4.01
all p., nations, and languages 5.19
Then King Darius wrote to all the p., 6.25
that all p., nations, and languages 7.14
Ephraim mixes himself with the p.; Hos 7.08
Exult not like the p.; for you have 9.01
Before them p. are in anguish, all Joe 2.06
Why should they say among the p., 2.17
Hear, you p., all of you; hearken, Mic 1.02
the hills; and p. shall flow to it, 4.01
He shall judge between many p., 4.03
For all the p. walk each in the 4.05
you shall beat in pieces many p., 4.13
midst of many p. like dew from the 5.07
nations, in the midst of many p., 5.08
you shall bear the scorn of the p." 6.16
and collects as his own all p." Hab 2.05
remnant of the p. shall plunder 2.08
your house by cutting off many p.; 2.10
of hosts that p. labor only for 2.13

PEOPLES (cont.)

speech of the p. to a pure speech, Zep 3.09
among all the p. of the earth, 3.20
P. shall yet come, even the inhabitants Zec 8.20
Many p. and strong nations shall 8.22
which I had made with all the p. 11.10
reeling to all the p. round about; 12.02
a heavy stone for all the p.; 12.03
horse of the p. with blindness. 12.04
to the left all the p. round about, 12.06
smite all the p. that wage war 14.12
prepared in the presence of all p., Lk 2.31
and the p. imagine vain things? Ac 4.25
the Gentiles and the p. of Israel, 4.27
and let all the p. praise him"; Rom 15.11
from all tribes and p. and tongues, Rev 7.09
about many p. and nations and 10.11
men from the p. and tribes and 11.09
are p. and multitudes and nations 17.15

PEOPLES'

possession of the fruit of the p. toil, Ps 105.44

PEOR

Balak took Balaam to the top of P., Num 23.28
Israel yoked himself to Baal of P. 25.03
yoked themselves to Baal of P. 25.05
beguiled you in the matter of P., 25.18
day of the plague on account of P. 25.18
the LORD in the matter of P., 31.16
men who followed the Baal of P.; Deu 4.03
of the sin at P. from which even Jos 22.17
themselves to the Baal of P., Ps 106.28

PERAZIM

LORD will rise up as on Mount P., Is 28.21

PERCEIVE

for today I p. that if Absalom were 2Sa 19.06
I p. that this is a holy man of God, 2Ki 4.09
he moves on, but I do not p. him. Job 9.11
and backward, but I cannot p. him; 23.08
in two, though man does not p. it. 33.14
the God of Jacob does not p. Ps 94.07
not he who weighs the heart p. it? Pro 24.12
see and see, but do not p.' Is 6.09
it springs forth, do you not p. it? 43.19
of the LORD to p. and to hear his Jer 23.18
you shall indeed see but never p. Mt 13.14
they should p. with their eyes, and 13.15
Do you not yet p.? Do you not 16.09
you fail to p. that I did not 16.11
they may indeed see but not p., Mk 4.12
Do you not yet p. or understand? 8.17
for I p. that power has gone forth Lk 8.46
them, that they should not p. it; 9.45
I p. that you are a prophet. Jn 4.19
their eyes and p. with their heart, 12.40
"Truly I p. that God shows no Ac 10.34
I p. that in every way you are very 17.22
I p. that the voyage will be with 27.10
you shall indeed see but never p. 28.26
they should p. with their eyes, and 28.27
this you can p. my insight into Eph 3.04

PERCEIVED

all the people p. the thunderings Ex 20.18
Then Gideon p. that he was the Ju 6.22
Then Eli p. that the LORD was 1Sa 3.08
And David p. that the LORD had 2Sa 5.12
David p. that the child was dead; 12.19
son of Zeruiah p. that the king's 14.01
because they p. that the wisdom of 1Ki 3.28
And David p. that the LORD had 1Ch 14.02
for they p. that this work had been Neh 6.16
sanctuary of God; then I p. their end. Ps 73.17
I have p. among the youths, a young Pro 7.07
I p. that this also is but a Ecc 1.17
and yet I p. that one fate comes to 2.14
no one has heard or p. by the ear, Is 64.04
p. in the books the number of years Dan 9.02
they p. that he was speaking about Mt 21.45
for they p. that he had told the Mk 12.12
For he p. that it was out of envy 15.10
and they p. that he had seen a Lk 1.22
When Jesus p. their questionings, he 5.22
But when Jesus p. the thought of 9.47
for they p. that he had told this 20.19
But he p. their craftiness, and said 20.23
and p. that they were uneducated, Ac 4.13
But when Paul p. that one part were 23.06
been clearly p. in the things that Rom 1.20
and when they p. the grace that was Gal 2.09

PERCEIVES

are brought low, and he p. it not. Job 14.21
She p. that her merchandise is Pro 31.18

PERCEIVING

p. in his spirit that they thus Mk 2.08
And Jesus, p. in himself that power 5.30
P. then that they were about to Jn 6.15

PERDITION

me, the torrents of p. assailed me; 2Sa 22.05
me, the torrents of p. assailed me; Ps 18.04
of them is lost but the son of p., Jn 17.12
is revealed, the son of p., 2Th 2.03
the bottomless pit and go to p.; Rev 17.08
to the seven, and it goes to p. 17.11

PERES

P., your kingdom is divided and Dan 5.28

PERESH

a son, and she called his name P.; 1Ch 7.16

PEREZ

therefore his name was called P. Gen 38.29
P., and Zerah (but Er and Onan died 46.12
and the sons of P. were Hezron and 46.12
of P., the family of the Perezites; Num 26.20
And the sons of P. were: of Hezron, 26.21
your house be like the house of P., Ru 4.12
Now these are the descendants of P.: 4.18
P. was the father of Hezron, 4.18
Tamar also bore him P. and Zerah. 1Ch 2.04
The sons of P.: Hezron and Hamul. 2.05
P., Hezron, Carmi, Hur, and Shobal. 4.01
the sons of P. the son of Judah. 9.04
He was a descendant of P., 27.03
of Mahalalel, of the sons of P.; Neh 11.04
All the sons of P. who lived in 11.06
the father of P. and Zerah by Mt 1.03
and P. the father of Hezron, and 1.03
the son of P., the son of Judah, Lk 3.33

PEREZITES

of Perez, the family of the P.; of Num 26.20

PEREZUZZA

that place is called P., to this day. 1Ch 13.11

PEREZUZZAH

place is called P., to this day. 2Sa 6.08

PERFECT

to be accepted it must be p.; there Lev 22.21
"The Rock, his work is p.; for all Deu 32.04
This God—his way is p.; the promise 2Sa 22.31
one who is p. in knowledge is with Job 36.04
of him who is p. in knowledge, 37.16
This God—his way is p.; the promise Ps 18.30
The law of the LORD is p., reviving 19.07
I hate them with p. hatred; I count 139.22
my love, my dove, my p. one; Sol 5.02
My dove, my p. one, is only one, the 6.09

PERFECT (cont.)
Thou dost keep him in p. peace, Is 26.03
for it was p. through the splendor Eze 16.14
you have said, 'I am p. in beauty.' 27.03
our builders made p. your beauty. 27.04
about; they made p. your beauty. 27.11
full of wisdom and p. in beauty. 28.12
be p., as your heavenly Father is p. Mt 5.48
Jesus said to him, "If you would be p., 19.21
thou hast brought p. praise'? 21.16
the man this p. health in the Ac 3.16
what is good and acceptable and p. Rom 12.02
but when the p. comes, the imperfect 1Co 13.10
make holiness p. in the fear of 2Co 7.01
because I have p. confidence in 7.16
my power is made p. in weakness." 12.09
obtained this or am already p.; Php 3.12
everything together in p. harmony. Col 3.14
display his p. patience for an 1Ti 1.16
and to show p. courtesy toward all Tit 3.02
their salvation p. through suffering. Heb 2.10
and being made p. he became the 5.09
(for the law made nothing p.); 7.19
Son who has been made p. for ever. 7.28
which cannot p. the conscience of 9.09
and more p. tent (not made with 9.11
make p. those who draw near. 10.01
from us they should not be made p. 11.40
the spirits of just men made p., 12.23
that you may be p. and complete, Jas 1.04
and every p. gift is from above, 1.17
But he who looks into the p. law, 1.25
in what he says he is a p. man, 3.02
but p. love casts out fear. 1Jn 4.18
your works p. in the sight of my Rev 3.02

PERFECTED
offering he has p. for all time Heb 10.14
in him truly love for God is p. 1Jn 2.05
in us and his love is p. in us. 4.12
In this is love p. with us, 4.17
and he who fears is not p. in love. 4.18

PERFECTER
the pioneer and p. of our faith, Heb 12.02

PERFECTION
the p. of beauty, God shines forth. Ps 50.02
I have seen a limit to all p., 119.96
which was called the p. of beauty, Lam 2.15
God: "You were the signet of p., Eze 28.12
Now if p. had been attainable Heb 7.11

PERFECTLY
in me, that they may become p. one, Jn 17.23

PERFORM
and p. the duty of a brother-in-law Gen 38.08
you are not able to p. it alone. Ex 18.18
and keep my ordinances and p. them; Lev 25.18
They shall p. duties for him and Num 3.07
shall go in to p. the work in the 8.24
which he commanded you to p., Deu 4.13
be careful to p. what has passed 23.23
and p. the duty of a husband's 25.05
he will not p. the duty of a 25.07
that we do p. the service of the Jos 22.27
the king will p. the request of 2Sa 14.15
to p. the words of this covenant 2Ki 23.03
to p. the words of the covenant 2Ch 34.31
labor who does not p. this promise. Neh 5.13
and didst p. signs and wonders 9.10
which thou didst p. among them; 9.17
deeds thou didst p. in their days. Ps 44.01
My vows to thee I must p., O God; 56.12
to the LORD your God, and p. them; 76.11
my heart to p. thy statutes for 119.112
make vows to the LORD and p. them. Is 19.21
he shall p. his purpose on Babylon, 48.14
am watching over my word to p. it. Jer 1.12
that I may p. the oath which I 11.05
'We will surely p. our vows that 44.25
confirm your vows and p. your vows! 44.25
I will speak the word and p. it, Eze 12.25
may observe and p. all its laws 43.11
bring terms of peace and p. them. Dan 11.17
they p. it, because it is in the Mic 2.01
but shall p. to the Lord what you Mt 5.33
to p. the mercy promised to our Lk 1.72
out demons and p. cures today and 13.32
believe you? What work do you p.? Jn 6.30
turn to God and p. deeds worthy of Ac 26.20

PERFORMED
LORD which he p. for you and for 1Sa 12.07
and has not p. my commandments. 15.11
I have p. the commandment of the 15.13
and they p. their service in due 1Ch 6.32
And they p. sacrifices to the LORD, 29.21
And they p. the service of their Neh 12.45
she has not p. the command of King Est 1.15
and to thee shall vows be p., Ps 65.01
to be p. with faithfulness and 111.08
Who has p. and done this, calling Is 41.04
I will speak, and it will be p. Eze 12.25
the word which I speak will be p., 12.28
labor that he had p. against it. 29.18
And when they had p. everything Lk 2.39
sign has been p. through them is Ac 4.16
of healing was p. was more than 4.22
and wonders are p. through the 4.30
having p. wonders and signs in 7.36
great miracles p., he was amazed. 8.13
apostle were p. among you in all 2Co 12.12

PERFORMING
p. what the LORD has charged, lest Lev 8.35
p. all, and that he may build the 1Ch 29.19
outer tent, p. their ritual duties; Heb 9.06
p. signs, who go abroad to the kings Rev 16.14

PERFORMS
and p. the counsel of his messengers; Is 44.26
to do? For this man p. many signs. Jn 11.47

PERFUME
it to use as p. shall be cut off Ex 30.38
Oil and p. make the heart glad, but Pro 27.09
the p. boxes, and the amulets; Is 3.20
Instead of p. there will be rottenness; 3.24

PERFUMED
I have p. my bed with myrrh, aloes, Pro 7.17
p. with myrrh and frankincense, with Sol 3.06

PERFUMER
anointing oil blended as by the p.; Ex 30.25
and incense blended as by the p., 30.35
incense, blended as by the p. 37.29

PERFUMER'S
of spices prepared by the p. art; 2Ch 16.14
Dead flies make the p. ointment Ecc 10.01

PERFUMERS
daughters to be p. and cooks and 1Sa 8.13
Hananiah, one of the p., repaired; Neh 3.08

PERFUMES
Molech with oil and multiplied your p.; Is 57.09

PERGA
from Paphos, and came to P. in Pamphylia. Ac 13.13
they passed on from P. and came to 13.14
when they had spoken the word in P., 14.25

PERGAMUM

Smyrna and to P. and to Thyatira and to — Rev 1.11
to the angel of the church in P. write: — 2.12

PERHAPS

"P. the woman may not be willing to — Gen 24.05
'P. the woman will not follow me.' — 24.39
P. my father will feel me, and I — 27.12
see his face; p. he will accept me." — 32.20
of your sacks; p. it was an oversight. — 43.12
p. I can make atonement for your — Ex 32.30
p. I shall be able to defeat them — Num 22.06
p. I shall be able to fight against — 22.11
p. the LORD will come to meet me; — 23.03
p. it will please God that you may — 23.27
"P. you live among us; then how — Jos 9.07
p. he will lighten his hand from — 1Sa 6.05
p. he can tell us about the journey — 9.06
p. we may find grass and save the — 1Ki 18.05
or p. he is asleep and must be — 18.27
p. he will spare your life." — 20.31
p. you may be able to succeed, — Is 47.12
p. you may inspire terror. — 47.12
"P. he will be deceived, then we can — Jer 20.10
p. the LORD will deal with us — 21.02
for her pain; p. she may be healed. — 51.08
P. they will understand, though they — Eze 12.03
that there may p. be a lengthening — Dan 4.27
P. the god will give a thought to — Jon 1.06
p. you may be hidden on the day of — Zep 2.03
'P. there will not be enough for us — Mt 25.09
whether p. he were the Christ, — Lk 3.15
thoughts accuse or p. excuse them — Rom 2.15
though p. for a good man one will — 5.07
another except p. by agreement for — 1Co 7.05
p. of wheat or of some other grain. — 15.37
and p. I will stay with you or even — 16.06
For I fear that p. I may come and — 2Co 12.20
that p. there may be quarreling, — 12.20
God may p. grant that they will — 2Ti 2.25
P. this is why he was parted from — Phm 1.15

PERIDA

sons of Sophereth, the sons of P., — Neh 7.57

PERIL

"At p. to our heads he will desert — 1Ch 12.19
our bread at the p. of our lives, — Lam 5.09
or nakedness, or p., or sword? — Rom 8.35
Why am I in p. every hour? — 1Co 15.30
he delivered us from so deadly a p.. — 2Co 1.10

PERIOD

was the regular p. of their — Est 2.12
stay for a longer p., he declined; — Ac 18.20

PERIODS

allotted p. and the boundaries of — Ac 17.26

PERISH

land may not p. through the famine — Gen 41.36
LORD to gaze and many of them p. — Ex 19.21
And you shall p. among the nations, — Lev 26.38
we p., we are undone, we are all — Num 17.12
shall die. Are we all to p." — 17.13
soon utterly p. from the land — Deu 4.26
make their name p. from under — 7.24
this day that you shall surely p. — 8.19
the LORD makes to p. before you, — 8.20
so shall you p., because you would — 8.20
and make them p. quickly, as the — 9.03
and you p. quickly off the good — 11.17
you are destroyed and p. quickly, — 28.20
they shall pursue you until you p. — 28.22
until they have caused you to p. — 28.51
to you this day, that you shall p.; — 30.18
And he did not p. alone for his — Jos 22.20
till you p. from off this good land — 23.13
and you shall p. quickly from off — 23.16
"So p. all thine enemies, O LORD! — Ju 5.31
shall go down into battle and p. — 1Sa 26.10
"I shall now p. one day by the hand — 27.01
For the whole house of Ahab shall p.; — 2Ki 9.08
and your father's house will p. — Est 4.14
against the law; and if I p., I p." — 4.16
"Let the day p. wherein I was born, — Job 3.03
By the breath of God they p., — 4.09
they p. for ever without any — 4.20
they go up into the waste, and p. — 6.18
hope of the godless man shall p. — 8.13
he will p. for ever like his own — 20.07
who was about to p. came upon me, — 29.13
seen any one p. for lack of — 31.19
all flesh would p. together, — 34.15
they p. by the sword, and die — 36.12
but the way of the wicked will p. — Ps 1.06
he be angry, and you p. in the way; — 2.12
of the poor shall not p. for ever. — 9.18
the nations shall p. from his land. — 10.16
But the wicked p.; the enemies — 37.20
"When will he die, and his name p.?" — 41.05
alike must p. and leave their — 49.10
he is like the beasts that p. — 49.12
he is like the beasts that p. — 49.20
fire, let the wicked p. before God! — 68.02
who are far from thee shall p.; — 73.27
may they p. at the rebuke of thy — 80.16
for ever; let them p. in disgrace. — 83.17
for, lo, thy enemies shall p.; — 92.09
They will p., but thou dost endure; — 102.26
on that very day his plans p. — 146.04
when the wicked p. there are — Pro 11.10
and he who utters lies will p. — 19.09
A false witness will p., but the — 21.28
but when they p., the righteous — 28.28
wisdom of their wise men shall p., — Is 29.14
and they will all p. together. — 31.03
shall be as nothing and shall p. — 41.11
that will not serve you shall p.; — 60.12
neighbor and friend shall p. — Jer 6.21
the fortified cities and p. there; — 8.14
LORD our God has doomed us to p., — 8.14
the earth shall p. from the earth — 10.11
of their punishment they shall p. — 10.15
They shall p. by the sword and by — 16.04
law shall not p. from the priest, — 18.18
drive you out, and you will p. — 27.10
will drive you out and you will p., — 27.15
and the remnant of Judah would p.?" — 40.15
the valley shall p., and the plain — 48.08
of their punishment they shall p. — 51.18
on dainties p. in the streets; — Lam 4.05
you shall p. in the midst of it; — Eze 13.14
will make you p. out of the — 25.07
shadow among the nations shall p. — 31.17
and all its multitude shall p. — 32.12
might not p. with the rest of the — Dan 2.18
Samaria's king shall p., like a — Hos 10.07
remnant of the Philistines shall p., — Amo 1.08
Flight shall p. from the swift, and — 2.14
and the houses of ivory shall p., — 3.15
a thought to us, that we do not p." — Jon 1.06
let us not p. for this man's life, — 1.14
fierce anger, so that we p. not?" — 3.09
The king shall p. from Gaza; — Zec 9.05
two thirds shall be cut off and p., — 13.08
one of these little ones should p. — Mt 18.14
the sword will p. by the sword. — 26.52
"Teacher, do you not care if we p.?" — Mk 4.38
repent you will all likewise p. — Lk 13.03
repent you will all likewise p." — 13.05
that a prophet should p. away from — 13.33
spare, but I p. here with hunger! — 15.17
But not a hair of your head will p. — 21.18
him should not p. but have eternal — Jn 3.16
life, and they shall never p., — 10.28

PERISH (cont.)
the whole nation should not p. Jn 11.50
"Your silver p. with you, because Ac 8.20
'Behold, you scoffers, and wonder, and p.; 13.41
a hair is to p. from the head of 27.34
law will also p. without the law, Rom 2.12
which all p. as they are used), Col 2.22
deception for those who are to p., 2Th 2.10
they will p., but thou remainest; Heb 1.11
harlot did not p. with those who 11.31
not wishing that any should p., 2Pe 3.09
error, and p. in Korah's rebellion. Jud 1.11

PERISHABLE
they do it to receive a p. wreath, 1Co 9.25
What is sown is p., what is raised 15.42
nor does the p. inherit the imperishable. 15.50
For this p. nature must put on the 15.53
When the p. puts on the imperishable, 15.54
which though p. is tested by fire, 1Pe 1.07
not with p. things such as silver 1.18
not of p. seed but of imperishable, 1.23

PERISHED
and they p. from the midst of the Num 16.33
So their posterity p. from Heshbon, 21.30
had p. from the camp, as the LORD Deu 2.14
from the camp, until they had p. 2.15
men of war had p. and were dead 2.16
p., because they did not hearken to Jos 5.06
fallen, and the weapons of war p.! 2Sa 1.27
and the seven of them p. together. 21.09
of Israel that have already p.; 2Ki 7.13
now, who that was innocent ever p.? Job 4.07
they stumbled and p. before thee. Ps 9.03
the very memory of them has p. 9.06
I should have p. in my affliction. 119.92
and their envy have already p., Ecc 9.06
truth has p.; it is cut off from Jer 7.28
come upon Gaza, Ashkelon has p. 47.05
the riches they gained have p. 48.36
Has counsel p. from the prudent? 49.07
priest and elders p. in the city, Lam 1.19
the harvest of the field has p. Joe 1.11
in a night, and p. in a night. Jon 4.10
Has your counselor p., that pangs Mic 4.09
The godly man has p. from the earth, 7.02
into the sea, and p. in the waters. Mt 8.32
who p. between the altar and the Lk 11.51
he also p., and all who followed Ac 5.37
fallen asleep in Christ have p. 1Co 15.18
was deluged with water and p. 2Pe 3.06

PERISHES
The strong lion p. for lack of prey, Job 4.11
His memory p. from the earth, and he 18.17
his hope p., and the expectation of Pro 11.07
righteous man who p. in his righteousness, Ecc 7.15
The righteous man p., and no one Is 57.01
but the law p. from the priest, and Eze 7.26
Do not labor for the food which p., Jn 6.27
flower falls, and its beauty p. Jas 1.11

PERISHING
Pit, his life from p. by the sword. Job 33.18
Give strong drink to him who is p., Pro 31.06
who does not care for the p., Zec 11.16
saying, "Save, Lord; we are p." Mt 8.25
saying, "Master, Master, we are p.!" Lk 8.24
cross is folly to those who are p., 1Co 1.18
saved and among those who are p., 2Co 2.15
is veiled only to those who are p. 4.03

PERIZZITE
Amorite, the p., the Jebusite, and the Neh 9.08

PERIZZITES
Canaanites and the P. dwelt in the Gen 13.07
the Hittites, the P., the Rephaim, 15.20
land, the Canaanites and the P.; 34.30
the P., the Hivites, and the Jebusites. Ex 3.08
the P., the Hivites, and the Jebusites, 3.17
and the P., and the Canaanites, the 23.23
the P., the Hivites, and the Jebusites. 33.02
the P., the Hivites, and the Jebusites. 34.11
the P., the Hivites, and the Jebusites, Deu 7.01
Amorites, the Canaanites and the p., 20.17
the P., the Girgashites, the Amorites, Jos 3.10
the P., the Hivites, and the Jebusites, 9.01
the P., and the Jebusites in the 11.03
the P., the Hivites, and the Jebusites): 12.08
the land of the P. and the Rephaim, 17.15
the P., the Canaanites, the Hittites, 24.11
Canaanites and the P. into their Ju 1.04
defeated the Canaanites and the P. 1.05
the P., the Hivites, and the Jebusites; 3.05
the P., the Hivites, and the Jebusites, 1Ki 9.20
the P., the Hivites, and the Jebusites, 2Ch 8.07
the P., the Jebusites, the Ammonites, Ez 9.01

PERJURERS
p., and whatever else is contrary 1Ti 1.10

PERMANENT
what is p. must have much more splendor. 2Co 3.11

PERMANENTLY
but he holds his priesthood p., Heb 7.24

PERMISSION
"You have p. to speak for yourself." Ac 26.01

PERMIT
but God did not p. him to harm me. Gen 31.07
And why did you not p. me to kiss 31.28
"You shall not p. a sorceress to Ex 22.18
where you shall p. the manslayer Num 35.06
and did not p. them to attack Saul. 1Sa 24.07
that he might p. no one to go out 1Ki 15.17
that he might p. no one to go out 2Ch 16.01
he will never p. the righteous to Ps 55.22
Their deeds do not p. them to Hos 5.04
he would not p. the demons to Mk 1.34
then you no longer p. him to do 7.12
I p. no woman to teach or to have 1Ti 2.12

PERMITS
some time with you, if the Lord p. 1Co 16.07
And this we will do if God p. Heb 6.03

PERMITTED
he p. no one to enter with him, Lk 8.51
For they are not p. to speak, 1Co 14.34
its rider was p. to take peace from Rev 6.04

PERPETUAL
This shall be a p. statute for him Ex 28.43
shall be theirs by a p. statute. 29.09
his sons as a p. due from the 29.28
a p. incense before the LORD 30.08
generations, as a p. covenant. 31.16
admit them to a p. priesthood 40.15
It shall be a p. statute throughout Lev 3.17
as a p. due from the people of 7.34
it is a p. due throughout their 7.36
by fire to the LORD, a p. due. 24.09
for that is their p. possession. 25.34
be to you for a p. statute throughout Num 10.08
a p. statute throughout your 15.15
and to your sons as a p. due. 18.08
daughters with you, as a p. due; 18.11
daughters with you, as a p. due; 18.19
it shall be a p. statute throughout 18.23
sojourns among them, a p. statute. 19.10
And it shall be a p. statute for 19.21
the covenant of a p. priesthood, 25.13
Direct thy steps to the p. ruins; Ps 74.03
a p. barrier which it cannot pass; Jer 5.22

PERPETUAL (cont.)

turned away in p. backsliding? Jer 8.05
everlasting reproach and p. shame, 23.40
all her cities shall be p. wastes. 49.13
but you shall be a p. waste, 51.26
and sleep a p. sleep and not wake, 51.39
shall sleep a p. sleep and not 51.57
Because you cherished p. enmity, Eze 35.05
I will make you a p. desolation. 35.09

PERPETUALLY

all pity, and his anger tore p., Amo 1.11

PERPETUATE

refuses to p. his brother's name in Deu 25.07
to p. the name of the dead in his Ru 4.10

PERPETUATED

and in them let my name be p., Gen 48.16
you: "No more shall your name be p.; Nah 1.14

PERPETUITY

The land shall not be sold in p., Lev 25.23
be made sure in p. to him who 25.30

PERPLEXED

to drink; but the city of Susa was p. Est 3.15
color changed; and his lords were p. Dan 5.09
of cattle are p. because there is Joe 1.18
when he heard him, he was much p.; Mk 6.20
and he was p., because it was said Lk 9.07
While they were p. about this, 24.04
And all were amazed and p., Ac 2.12
they were much p. about them, 5.24
was inwardly p. as to what the 10.17
p., but not driven to despair; 2Co 4.08
my tone, for I am p. about you. Gal 4.20

PERPLEXITY

of nations in p. at the roaring of Lk 21.25

PERSECUTE

might of thy hand thou dost p. me. Job 30.21
For they p. him whom thou hast Ps 69.26
wilt thou judge those who p. me? 119.84
they p. me with falsehood; 119.86
They draw near who p. me with evil 119.150
Princes p. me without cause, but my 119.161
Let those be put to shame who p. me, Jer 17.18
revile you and p. you and utter Mt 5.11
and pray for those who p. you, 5.44
When they p. you in one town, flee 10.23
synagogues and p. from town to 23.34
of whom they will kill and p.,' Lk 11.49
lay their hands on you and p. you, 21.12
persecuted me, they will p. you; Jn 15.20
prophets did not your fathers p.? Ac 7.52
him, "Saul, Saul, why do you p. me?" 9.04
me, 'Saul, Saul, why do you p. me?' 22.07
'Saul, Saul, why do you p. me? 26.14
Bless those who p. you; bless and Rom 12.14

PERSECUTED

your foes and enemies who p. you. Deu 30.07
those who are p. for righteousness' Mt 5.10
for so men p. the prophets who were 5.12
And this was why the Jews p. Jesus, Jn 5.16
If they p. me, they will persecute 15.20
I p. this Way to the death, binding Ac 22.04
I p. them even to foreign cities. 26.11
reviled, we bless; when p., we endure; 1Co 4.12
because I p. the church of God. 15.09
p., but not forsaken; struck down, 2Co 4.09
how I p. the church of God violently Gal 1.13
"He who once p. us is now preaching 1.23
to the flesh p. him who was born 4.29
circumcision, why am I still p.? 5.11
they may not be p. for the cross 6.12
blasphemed and p. and insulted him; 1Ti 1.13
life in Christ Jesus will be p., 2Ti 3.12

PERSECUTING

said, "I am Jesus, whom you are p.; Ac 9.05
Jesus of Nazareth whom you are p.' 22.08
said, 'I am Jesus whom you are p. 26.15

PERSECUTION

nations in anger with unrelenting p. Is 14.06
tribulation or p. arises on account Mt 13.21
tribulation or p. arises on account Mk 4.17
day a great p. arose against the Ac 8.01
because of the p. that arose over 11.19
and stirred up p. against Paul and 13.50
or p., or famine, or nakedness, or Rom 8.35

PERSECUTIONS

with p., and in the age to come Mk 10.30
insults, hardships, p., and calamities; 2Co 12.10
in all your p. and in the afflictions 2Th 1.04
my p., my sufferings, what befell me 2Ti 3.11
and at Lystra, what p. I endured; 3.11

PERSECUTOR

as to zeal a p. of the church, as to Php 3.06

PERSECUTORS

from the hand of my enemies and p.! Ps 31.15
iniquity of my p. surrounds me, 49.05
Many are my p. and my adversaries, 119.157
Deliver me from my p.; for they are 142.06
and take vengeance for me on my p. Jer 15.15
therefore my p. will stumble, they 20.11

PERSEVERANCE

To that end keep alert with all p., Eph 6.18
let us run with p. the race that Heb 12.01

PERSEVERES

and p., being no hearer that forgets Jas 1.25

PERSIA

establishment of the kingdom of P., 2Ch 36.20
the first year of Cyrus king of P., 36.22
Cyrus king of P. so that he made a 36.22
"Thus says Cyrus king of P., 36.23
the first year of Cyrus king of P., Ez 1.01
stirred up the spirit of Cyrus king of P. 1.01
"Thus says Cyrus king of P.: 1.02
Cyrus king of P. brought these out 1.08
they had from Cyrus king of P. 3.07
the king of P. has commanded us." 4.03
all the days of Cyrus king of P., 4.05
the reign of Darius king of P. 4.05
wrote to Artaxerxes king of P.; 4.07
of the reign of Darius king of P. 4.24
Darius and Artaxerxes king of P.; 6.14
the reign of Artaxerxes king of P., 7.01
love before the kings of P., 9.09
army chiefs of P. and Media and Est 1.03
the seven princes of P. and Media, 1.14
the ladies of P. and Media who 1.18
of the Kings of Media and P.? 10.02
"P. and Lud and Put were in your Eze 27.10
P., Cush, and Put are with them, all 38.05
are the kings of Media and P. Dan 8.20
Cyrus king of P. a word was 10.01
the kingdom of P. withstood me 10.13
prince of the kingdom of P. 10.13
to fight against the prince of P.; 10.20
three more kings shall arise in P.; 11.02

PERSIAN

until the reign of Darius the P. Neh 12.22
and the reign of Cyrus the P. Dan 6.28

PERSIANS

the P., the men of Erech, the Ez 4.09
the laws of the P. and the Medes Est 1.19

PERSIANS (cont.)
and given to the Medes and P. Dan 5.28
to the law of the Medes and the P., 6.08
to the law of the Medes and P., 6.12
the Medes and P. that no interdict 6.15

PERSIS
Greet the beloved P., who has worked Rom 16.12

PERSIST
if they do not p. in their unbelief, Rom 11.23
As for those who p. in sin, rebuke 1Ti 5.20

PERSISTED
the Canaanites p. in dwelling in Jos 17.12
the Canaanites p. in dwelling in Ju 1.27
the Amorites p. in dwelling in 1.35

PERSISTENTLY
sent p. to them by messengers, 2Ch 36.15
I spoke to you p. you did not Jer 7.13
I have p. sent all my servants the 7.25
warning them p., even to this day, 11.07
to me, and I have spoken p. to you, 25.03
the LORD p. sent to you all his 25.04
which I p. sent to you by my servants 29.19
taught them p. they have not listened 32.33
I have spoken to you p., but you have 35.14
sending them p., saying, 'Turn now 35.15
Yet I p. sent to you all my servants 44.04

PERSISTS
and if he p., saying, 'I do not wish Deu 25.08

PERSON
Lord, send, I pray, some other p. Ex 4.13
that p. shall be cut off from 12.15
that p. shall be cut off from the 12.19
uncircumcised p. shall eat of it. 12.48
but the p. who eats of the flesh of Lev 7.20
that p. shall be cut off from his 7.20
that p. shall be cut off from his 7.21
For every p. who eats of the fat of 7.25
that p. shall be cut off from his 7.27
up the diseased p. for seven days; 13.04
of the diseased p. from head to 13.12
pronounce the diseased p. clean; 13.17
shut up the p. with the itching 13.31
shut up the p. with the itching 13.33
against that p. who eats blood, 17.10
No p. among you shall eat blood, 17.12
And every p. that eats what dies of 17.15
and that p. shall be cut off from 19.08
"If a p. turns to mediums and 20.06
I will set my face against that p., 20.06
that p. shall be cut off from my 22.03
the p. who touches any such shall 22.06
that p. I will destroy from among 23.30
If the p. is a female, your valuation 27.04
If the p. is from five years old up 27.05
If the p. is from a month old up to 27.06
And if the p. is sixty years old 27.07
shall bring the p. before the 27.08
the LORD, and that p. is guilty, Num 5.06
that p. shall be cut off from his 9.13
"If one p. sins unwittingly, he 15.27
LORD for the p. who commits an 15.28
But the p. who does anything with a 15.30
and that p. shall be cut off from 15.30
that p. shall be utterly cut off; 15.31
body of any p. shall be unclean 19.11
Whoever touches a dead p., the 19.13
and that p. shall be cut off from 19.13
then a clean p. shall take hyssop, 19.18
and the clean p. shall sprinkle 19.19
that p. shall be cut off from the 19.20
the unclean p. touches shall be 19.22
whoever of you has killed any p., 31.19
who kills any p. without intent 35.11
who kills any p. without intent 35.15
If any one kills a p., the murderer 35.30
but no p. shall be put to death on 35.30
a p. shall not be put to death on Deu 17.06
a bribe to slay an innocent p. 27.25
not regard the p. of the old or 28.50
utterly destroyed every p. in it, Jos 10.28
of the sword, and every p. in it; 10.30
and every p. in it, as he had done 10.32
and every p. in it he utterly 10.35
and its towns, and every p. in it; 10.37
destroyed it with every p. in it. 10.37
utterly destroyed every p. in it; 10.39
who kills any p. without intent or 20.03
who killed a p. without intent 20.09
and that you go to battle in p. 2Sa 17.11
partiality to any p. or use flattery Job 32.21
A worthless p., a wicked man, goes Pro 6.12
and an idle p. will suffer hunger. 19.15
a p. who has no one, either son or Ecc 4.08
and every p. whom Nebuzaradan the Jer 43.06
themselves by going near to a dead p.; Eze 44.25
a contemptible p. to whom royal Dan 11.21
There was not a needy p. among them, Ac 4.34
is binding on a p. only during his Rom 7.01
Let every p. be subject to the 13.01
For what p. knows a man's thoughts 1Co 2.11
out the wicked p. from among you. 5.13
is well for a p. to remain as he 7.26
in p. not in heart, we endeavored 1Th 2.17
knowing that such a p. is perverted Tit 3.11
For that p. must not suppose that a Jas 1.07
but each p. is tempted when he is 1.14
they inquired what p. or time was 1Pe 1.11
be the hidden p. of the heart with 3.04

PERSONS
and the p. that they had gotten in Gen 12.05
"Give me the p., but take the goods 14.21
these she bore to Jacob—sixteen p.). 46.18
born to Jacob—fourteen p. in all). 46.22
she bore to Jacob—seven p. in all). 46.25
All the p. belonging to Jacob who 46.26
wives, were sixty-six p. in all; 46.26
all the p. of the house of Jacob, 46.27
offspring of Jacob were seventy p.; Ex 1.05
take according to the number of p.; 12.04
number of the p. whom each of you 16.16
the p. that do them shall be cut Lev 18.29
special vow of p. to the LORD at 27.02
and upon the p. who were there, and Num 19.18
of the p. and of the oxen and of 31.28
of the p., of the oxen, of the asses, 31.30
and thirty-two thousand p. in all, 31.35
The p. were sixteen thousand, of 31.40
LORD's tribute was thirty-two p. 31.40
and sixteen thousand p.— 31.46
both of p. and of beasts, and gave 31.47
went down to Egypt seventy p.; Deu 10.22
invited, who were about thirty p. 1Sa 9.22
day eighty-five p. who wore the 22.18
of all the p. of your father's 22.22
seventy p., were with the great men 2Ki 10.06
seventy p., and put their heads in 10.07
forty-two p., and he spared none of 10.14
money from the assessment of p.— 12.04
eighty hundred and thirty-two p.; Jer 52.29
seven hundred and forty-five p.; 52.30
all the p. were four thousand and 52.30
the heads of p. of every stature, Eze 13.18
to death p. who should not die and 13.19
keeping alive p. who should not 13.19
exchanged the p. of men and 27.13
twenty thousand p. who do not know Jon 4.11
righteous p. who need no repentance Lk 15.07
(the company of p. was in all about Ac 1.15
went in and found many p. gathered; 10.27
heard that some p. from us have 15.24

PERSONS (cont.)
with the Jews and the devout p., Ac 17.17
and seventy-six p. in the ship. 27.37
in their own p. the due penalty Rom 1.27
For such p. do not serve our Lord 16.18
Now such p. we command and exhort 2Th 3.12
charge certain p. not to teach any 1Ti 1.03
Certain p. by swerving from these 1.06
immoral p., sodomites, kidnapers, 1.10
certain p. have made shipwreck of 1.19
of defiled p. with the blood of Heb 9.13
eight p., were saved through water. 1Pe 3.20
righteousness, with seven other p., 2Pe 2.05
what sort of p. ought you to be in 3.11
ungodly p. who pervert the grace of Jud 1.04

PERSUADE
people came to p. David to eat 2Sa 3.35
the fear of the Lord, we p. men; 2Co 5.11

PERSUADED
So David p. his men with these 1Sa 24.07
With patience a ruler may be p., Pro 25.15
and the elders p. the people to Mt 27.20
and having p. Blastus, the king's Ac 12.20
and having p. the people, they 14.19
And some of them were p., and joined 17.04
every sabbath, and p. Jews and Greeks. 18.04
this Paul has p. and turned away a 19.26
And when he would not be p., 21.14
for I am p. that none of these 26.26
I know and am p. in the Lord Jesus Rom 14.14

PERSUADES
With much seductive speech she p. him; Pro 7.21

PERSUADING
"This man is p. men to worship God Ac 18.13

PERSUASION
This p. is not from him who called Gal 5.08

PERSUASIVENESS
and pleasant speech increases p. Pro 16.21
judicious, and adds p. to his lips. 16.23

PERTAIN
all things that p. to life and godliness, 2Pe 1.03

PERTAINING
This is the law p. to beast and Lev 11.46
cords; all the service p. to these. Num 3.26
screen; all the service p. to these. 3.31
all the service p. to these. 3.36
for everything p. to God and for 1Ch 26.32
much more, matters p. to this life! 1Co 6.03

PERTAINS
"This is what p. to the Levites: Num 8.24
not wear anything that p. to a man, Deu 22.05
for it p. to the appointed time of Dan 8.19
for it p. to many days hence." 8.26
For the judgment p. to you; for you Hos 5.01

PERUDA
of Hassophereth, the sons of P., Ez 2.55

PERVERSE
because your way is p. before me; Num 22.32
they are a p. and crooked generation. Deu 32.05
be, for they are a p. generation, 32.20
"You son of a p., rebellious woman, 1Sa 20.30
crooked thou dost show thyself p. 2Sa 22.27
am blameless, he would prove me p. Job 9.20
crooked thou dost show thyself p. Ps 18.26
for the p. man is an abomination to Pro 3.32
but the p. tongue will be cut off. 10.31
mouth of the wicked, what is p. 10.32
Men of p. mind are an abomination 11.20
but one of p. mind is despised. 12.08
A p. man will be filled with the 14.14
A p. man spreads strife, and a 16.28
who winks his eyes plans p. things, 16.30
and one with a p. tongue falls 17.20
than a man who is p. in speech, 19.01
snares are in the way of the p.; 22.05
and your mind utter p. things. 23.33
a rich man who is p. in his ways. 28.06
but he who is p. in his ways will 28.18
"O faithless and p. generation, Mt 17.17
"O faithless and p. generation, Lk 9.41
will arise men speaking p. things, Ac 20.30
of a crooked and p. generation, Php 2.15

PERVERSELY
and have acted p. and wickedly'; 1Ki 8.47
and have acted p. and wickedly'; 2Ch 6.37
he deals p. and does not see the Is 26.10

PERVERSENESS
P. of heart shall be far from me; Ps 101.04
evil and delight in the p. of evil; Pro 2.14
but p. in its breaks the spirit. 15.04
and trust in oppression and p., Is 30.12

PERVERSION
a beast to lie with it: it is p. Lev 18.23
for there is no p. of justice with 2Ch 19.07

PERVERT
a multitude, so as to p. justice; Ex 23.02
"You shall not p. the justice due 23.06
You shall not p. justice; you Deu 16.19
"You shall not p. the justice due 24.17
Does God p. justice? Or does the Job 8.03
or does the Almighty p. the right? 8.03
the Almighty will not be justice. 34.12
the bosom to p. the ways of Pro 17.23
and p. the rights of all the afflicted. 31.05
and you p. the words of the living Jer 23.36
abhor justice and p. all equity, Mic 3.09
you and want to p. the gospel of Gal 1.07
persons who p. the grace of our Jud 1.04

PERVERTED
they took bribes and p. justice. 1Sa 8.03
and p. what was right, and it was Job 33.27
of evil, from men of p. speech, Pro 2.12
with p. heart devises evil, continually 6.14
way of evil and p. speech I hate. 8.13
because they have p. their way, Jer 3.21
righteous, so justice goes forth p. Hab 1.04
such a person is p. and sinful; Tit 3.11

PERVERTING
"We found this man p. our nation, Lk 23.02
man as one who was p. the people; 23.14

PERVERTS
"Cursed be he who p. the justice due to Deu 27.19
he who p. his ways will be found out. Pro 10.09

PESTILENCE
upon us with p. or with the sword. Ex 5.03
struck you and your people with p., 9.15
cities I will send p. among you, Lev 26.25
them with the p. and disinherit Num 14.12
will make the p. cleave to you Deu 28.21
with burning heat and poisonous p.; 32.42
be three days' p. in your land? 2Sa 24.13
So the LORD sent a p. upon Israel 24.15
if there is p. or blight or mildew 1Ki 8.37
p. upon the land, and the angel of 1Ch 21.12
So the LORD sent a p. upon Israel; 21.14
if there is p. or blight or mildew 2Ch 6.28
or send p. among my people, 7.13
or p., or famine, we will stand 20.09
Those who survive him the p. buries, Job 27.15

PESTILENCE (cont.)
the fowler and from the deadly p.; Ps 91.03
nor the p. that stalks in darkness, 91.06
by the sword, by famine, and by p. Jer 14.12
LORD: 'Those who are for p., to p., 15.02
May their men meet death by p., 18.21
they shall die of a great p. 21.06
in this city who survive the p., 21.07
by the sword, by famine, and by p.; 21.09
and p. upon them, until they shall 24.10
and with p., says the LORD, until I 27.08
and by p., as the LORD has spoken 27.13
and p. against many countries and 28.08
and p., and I will make them like 29.17
and p., and will make them a horror 29.18
and famine and p. the city is 32.24
by sword, by famine, and by p.': 32.36
to p., and to famine, says the LORD. 34.17
by the sword, by famine, and by p.; 38.02
by the sword, by famine, and by p.; 42.17
and by p. in the place where you 42.22
giving to the p. those who are 43.11
those who are doomed to the p., 43.11
sword, with famine, and with p., 44.13
shall die of p. and be consumed Eze 5.12
p. and blood shall pass through you; 5.17
by the sword, by famine, and by p. 6.11
He that is far off shall die of p.; 6.12
p. and famine are within; he that 7.15
in the city famine and p. devour. 7.15
from the sword, from famine and p., 12.16
Or if I send a p. into that land, 14.19
and p., to cut off from it man and 14.21
for I will send p. into her, and 28.23
and in caves shall die by p. 33.27
With p. and bloodshed I will enter 38.22
among you a p. after the manner of Amo 4.10
Before him went p., and plague Hab 3.05
famine and with p. and by wild Rev 6.08
p. and mourning and famine, and she 18.08

PESTILENCES
in various places famines and p.; Lk 21.11

PESTILENT
we have found this man a p. fellow, Ac 24.05

PESTLE
Crush a fool in a mortar with a p. Pro 27.22

PETER
who is called P. and Andrew his Mt 4.18
who is called P., and Andrew his 10.02
And P. answered him, "Lord, if it is 14.28
So P. got out of the boat and 14.29
But P. said to him, "Explain the 15.15
Simon P. replied, "You are the Christ, 16.16
you are P., and on this rock I will 16.18
And P. took him and began to rebuke 16.22
But he turned and said to P., 16.23
took with him P. and James and 17.01
And P. said to Jesus, "Lord, it is 17.04
half-shekel tax went up to P. and said, 17.24
Then P came up and said to him, 18.21
Then P. said in reply, "Lo, we have 19.27
P. declared to him, "Though they all 26.33
P. said to him, "Even if I must die 26.35
And taking with him P. and the two 26.37
and he said to P., "So, could you 26.40
But P. followed him at a distance, 26.58
Now P. was sitting outside in the 26.69
bystanders came up and said to P., 26.73
And P. remembered the saying of 26.75
Simon whom he surnamed P.; Mk 3.16
him except P. and James and John 5.37
P. answered him, "You are the Christ." 8.29
And P. took him, and began to rebuke 8.32
he rebuked P., and said, "Get behind 8.33
took with him P. and James and 9.02
And P. said to Jesus, "Master, it is 9.05
P. began to say to him, "Lo, we have 10.28
And P. remembered and said to him, 11.21
P. and James and John and Andrew 13.03
P. said to him, "Even though they 14.29
took with him P. and James and 14.33
them sleeping, and he said to P., 14.37
And P. had followed him at a 14.54
And as P. was below in the courtyard, 14.66
and seeing P. warming himself, she 14.67
again the bystanders said to P., 14.70
And P. remembered how Jesus had 14.72
disciples and P. that he is going 16.07
they reported briefly to P. and those * 16.08
But when Simon P. saw it, he fell Lk 5.08
whom he named P., and Andrew his 6.14
P. said, "Master, the multitudes 8.45
except P. and John and James, and 8.51
And P. answered, "The Christ of 9.20
took with him P. and John and 9.28
Now P. and those who were with him 9.32
P. said to Jesus, "Master, it is well 9.33
P. said, "Lord, are you telling this 12.41
And P. said, "Lo, we have left our 18.28
So Jesus sent P. and John, saying, 22.08
P., the cock will not crow this day, 22.34
house. P. followed at a distance; 22.54
down together, P. sat among them. 22.55
But P. said, "Man, I am not." 22.58
But P. said, "Man, I do not know what 22.60
Lord turned and looked at P. And P. 22.61
But P. rose and ran to the tomb; * 24.12
be called Cephas" (which means P.). Jn 1.42
Bethsaida, the city of Andrew and P. 1.44
Simon P. answered him, "Lord, to whom 6.68
He came to Simon P.; and P. said to 13.06
P. said to him, "You shall never 13.08
Simon P. said to him, "Lord, not my 13.09
so Simon P. beckoned to him and 13.24
Simon P. said to him, "Lord, where 13.36
P. said to him, "Lord, why cannot I 13.37
Then Simon P., having a sword, drew 18.10
Jesus said to P., "Put your sword 18.11
Simon P. followed Jesus, and so did 18.15
while P. stood outside at the door. 18.16
kept the door, and brought P. in. 18.16
The maid who kept the door said to P., 18.17
P. also was with them, standing and 18.18
Now Simon P. was standing and 18.25
the man whose ear P. had cut off, 18.26
P. again denied it; and at once 18.27
went to Simon P. and the other 20.02
P. then came out with the other 20.03
disciple outran P. and reached the 20.04
Then Simon P. came, following him, 20.06
Simon P., Thomas called the Twin, 21.02
Simon P. said to them, "I am going 21.03
whom Jesus loved said to P., 21.07
When Simon P. heard that it was 21.07
So Simon P. went aboard and hauled 21.11
breakfast, Jesus said to Simon P., 21.15
P. was grieved because he said to 21.17
P. turned and saw following them 21.20
When P. saw him, he said to Jesus, 21.21
P. and John and James and Andrew, Ac 1.13
In those days P. stood up among the 1.15
But P., standing with the eleven, 2.14
and said to P. and the rest of the 2.37
And P. said to them, "Repent, and be 2.38
Now P. and John were going up to 3.01
Seeing P. and John about to go into 3.03
And P. directed his gaze at him, 3.04
But P. said, "I have no silver and 3.06
While he clung to P. and John, 3.11
And when P. saw it he addressed the 3.12
Then P., filled with the Holy Spirit, 4.08

PETER (cont.)
saw the boldness of P. and John, Ac 4.13
But P. and John answered them, 4.19
But P. said, "Ananias, why has Satan 5.03
And P. said to her, "Tell me whether 5.08
But P. said to her, "How is it that 5.09
that as P. came by at least his 5.15
But P. and the apostles answered, 5.29
they sent to them P. and John, 8.14
But P. said to him, "Your silver 8.20
Now as P. went here and there among 9.32
And P. said to him, "Aeneas, Jesus 9.34
hearing that P. was there, sent two 9.38
So P. rose and went with them. 9.39
But P. put them all outside and 9.40
and when she saw P. she sat up. 9.40
bring one Simon who is called P.; 10.05
P. went upon the housetop to pray, 10.09
came a voice to him, "Rise, P.; 10.13
But P. said, "No, Lord; for I have 10.14
Now while P. was inwardly perplexed 10.17
who was called P. was lodging 10.18
And while P. was pondering the 10.19
And P. went down to the men and 10.21
When P. entered, Cornelius met him 10.25
But P. lifted him up, saying, "Stand 10.26
and ask for Simon who is called P.; 10.32
And P. opened his mouth and said: 10.34
While P. was still saying this, the 10.44
who came with P. were amazed, 10.45
tongues and extolling God. Then P. declared, 10.46
So when P. went up to Jerusalem, the 11.02
But P. began and explained to them 11.04
a voice saying to me, 'Rise, P.; 11.07
to Joppa and bring Simon called P.; 11.13
he proceeded to arrest P. also. 12.03
So P. was kept in prison; but earnest 12.05
P. was sleeping between two soldiers, 12.06
and he struck P. on the side and 12.07
And P. came to himself, and said, 12.11
and told that P. was standing at 12.14
But P. continued knocking; and when 12.16
soldiers over what had become of P. 12.18
P. rose and said to them, "Brethren, 15.07
just as P. has been entrusted with Gal 2.07
worked through P. for the mission 2.08
P., an apostle of Jesus Christ, To 1Pe 1.01
Simon P., a servant and apostle of 2Pe 1.01

PETER'S
And when Jesus entered P. house, Mt 8.14
him, was Andrew, Simon P. brother. Jn 1.40
Simon P. brother, said to him, 6.08
Recognizing P. voice, in her joy she Ac 12.14

PETHAHIAH
the nineteenth to P., the twentieth 1Ch 24.16
Kelita), P., Judah, and Eliezer. Ez 10.23
and P., said, "Stand up and bless Neh 9.05
And P. the son of Meshezabel, of the 11.24

PETHOR
to Balaam the son of Beor at P., Num 22.05
son of Beor from P. of Mesopotamia, Deu 23.04

PETHUEL
that came to Joel, the son of P.: Joe 1.01

PETITION
grant your p. which you have made 1Sa 1.17
granted me my p. which I made to 1.27
voice, and I have granted your p. 25.35
said to Esther, "What is you p.? Est 5.06
said, "My p. and my request is: 5.07
to grant my p. and fulfil my request, 5.08
"What is your p., Queen Esther? It 7.02
let my life be given me at my p., 7.03
Now what is your p.? It shall be 9.12
whoever makes p. to any god or man Dan 6.07
Daniel making p. and supplication 6.11
man who makes p. to any god or man 6.12
but makes his p. three times a day. 6.13

PETITIONED
whom the whole Jewish people p. me, Ac 25.24

PETITIONS
May the LORD fulfil all your p.! Ps 20.05

PEULLETHAI
Issachar the seventh, P. the eighth; 1Ch 26.05

PHANTOMS
on awaking you despise their p. Ps 73.20

PHANUEL
prophetess, Anna, the daughter of P., Lk 2.36

PHARAOH
And when the princes of P. saw her, Gen 12.15
saw her, they praised her to P. 12.15
LORD afflicted P. and his house 12.17
So P. called Abram, and said, "What 12.18
And P. gave men orders concerning 12.20
an officer of P., the captain of 37.36
an officer of P., the captain of 39.01
And P. was angry with his two 40.02
within three days P. will lift up 40.13
you, to make mention of me to P., 40.14
all sorts of baked food for P., 40.17
within three days P. will lift up 40.19
P. dreamed that he was standing by 41.01
sleek and fat cows. And P. awoke. 41.04
And P. awoke, and behold, it was a 41.07
and P. told them his dream, but 41.08
none who could interpret it to P. 41.08
Then the chief butler said to P., 41.09
When P. was angry with his servants, 41.10
Then P. sent and called Joseph, and 41.14
his clothes, he came in before P. 41.14
And P. said to Joseph, "I have had a 41.15
Joseph answered P., "It is not in 41.16
God will give P. a favorable answer." 41.16
Then P. said to Joseph, "Behold, in 41.17
Joseph said to P., "The dream of P. 41.25
God has revealed to P. what he is 41.25
is as I told P., God has shown to P., 41.28
Now therefore let P. select a man 41.33
Let P. proceed to appoint overseers 41.34
authority of P. for food in the 41.35
seemed good to P. and to all his 41.37
And P. said to his servants, "Can we 41.38
So P. said to Joseph, "Since God has 41.39
And P. said to Joseph, "Behold, I 41.41
Then P. took his signet ring from 41.42
Moreover P. said to Joseph, "I am 41.44
"I am P., and without your consent 41.44
P. called Joseph's name Zaphenathpaneah; 41.45
the service of P. king of Egypt. 41.46
went out from the presence of P., 41.46
the people cried to P. for bread; 41.55
and P. said to all the Egyptians, 41.55
shall be tested: by the life of P., 42.15
or else, by the life of P., surely 42.16
servant; for you are like P. himself. 44.18
and the household of P. heard it. 45.02
and he has made me a father to P., 45.08
it pleased P. and his servants 45.16
And P. said to Joseph, "Say to your 45.17
according to the command of P., 45.21
wagons which P. had sent to carry 46.05
household, "I will go up and tell P., 46.31
When P. calls you, and says, 'What is 46.33
So Joseph went in and told P., 47.01
five men and presented them to P. 47.02
P. said to his brothers, "What is 47.03

PHARAOH (cont.)

And they said to P., "Your servants Gen 47.03
They said to P., "We have come to 47.04
Then P. said to Joseph, "Your father 47.05
set him before P., and Jacob blessed P. 47.07
And P. said to Jacob, "How many are 47.08
And Jacob said to P., "The days of 47.09
And Jacob blessed P., and went 47.10
went out from the presence of P. 47.10
of Rameses, as P. had commanded. 47.11
with our land will be slaves to P.; 47.19
all the land of Egypt for P.; 47.20
had a fixed allowance from P., 47.22
the allowance which P. gave them; 47.22
bought you and your land for P. 47.23
you shall give a fifth to P., 47.24
my lord, we will be slaves to P." 47.25
that P. should have the fifth; 47.26
spoke to the household of P., 50.04
you, in the ears of P., saying, 50.04
And P. answered, "Go up, and bury 50.06
him went up all the servants of P., 50.07
and they built for P. store-cities, Ex 1.11
The midwives said to P., "Because 1.19
Then P. commanded all his people, 1.22
Now the daughter of P. came down to 2.05
When P. heard of it, he sought to 2.15
But Moses fled from P., and stayed 2.15
send you to P. that you may bring 3.10
"Who am I that I should go to P., 3.11
you do before P. all the miracles 4.21
And you shall say to P., 'Thus says 4.22
and Aaron went to P. and said, 5.01
But P. said, "Who is the LORD, that I 5.02
And P. said, "Behold, the people of 5.05
The same day P. commanded the 5.06
"Thus says P., 'I will not give you 5.10
of Israel came and cried to P., 5.15
them, as they came forth from P.; 5.20
in the sight of P. and his servants, 5.21
For since I came to P. to speak in 5.23
you shall see what I will do to P.; 6.01
"Go in, tell P. king of Egypt to let 6.11
how then shall P. listen to me, 6.12
Israel and to P. king of Egypt to 6.13
who spoke to P. king of Egypt 6.27
tell P. king of Egypt all that I 6.29
how then shall P. listen to me?" 6.30
"See, I make you as God to P.; 7.01
shall tell P. to let the people of 7.02
P. will not listen to you; then 7.04
years old, when they spoke to P. 7.07
"When P. says to you, 'Prove yourselves 7.09
rod and cast it down before P., 7.09
Aaron went to P. and did as the 7.10
his rod before P. and his servants, 7.10
Then P. summoned the wise men and 7.11
Go to P. in the morning, as he is 7.15
in the sight of P. and in the sight 7.20
P. turned and went into his house, 7.23
"Go in to P. and say to him, 'Thus 8.01
Then P. called Moses and Aaron, and 8.08
Moses said to P., "Be pleased to 8.09
So Moses and Aaron went out from P.; 8.12
frogs, as he had agreed with P. 8.12
But when P. saw that there was a 8.15
And the Magicians said to P., 8.19
in the morning and wait for P., 8.20
the house of P. and into his 8.24
Then P. called Moses and Aaron, and 8.25
So P. said, "I will let you go, to 8.28
swarms of flies may depart from P., 8.29
only let not P. deal falsely again 8.29
went out from P. and prayed to the 8.30
the swarms of flies from P., 8.31
But P. hardened his heart this time 8.32
"Go in to P., and say to him, 'Thus 9.01
And P. sent, and behold, not one of 9.07
But the heart of P. was hardened, 9.07
toward heaven in the sight of P. 9.08
from the kiln, and stood before P., 9.10
But the LORD hardened the heart of P., 9.12
in the morning and stand before P., 9.13
the servants of P. made his slaves 9.20
Then P. sent, and called Moses and 9.27
Moses went out of the city from P., 9.33
But when P. saw that the rain and 9.34
So the heart of P. was hardened, 9.35
LORD said to Moses, "Go in to P.; 10.01
So Moses and Aaron went in to P., 10.03
he turned and went out from P. 10.06
and Aaron were brought back to P.; 10.08
Then P. called Moses and Aaron in 10.16
So he went out from P., and 10.18
Then P. called Moses, and said, "Go, 10.24
Then P. said to him, "Get away from 10.28
will bring upon P. and upon Egypt; 11.01
first-born of P. who sits upon his 11.05
he went out from P. in hot anger. 11.08
"P. will not listen to you; 11.09
did all these wonders before P.; 11.10
first-born of P. who sat on his 12.29
And P. rose up in the night, he, and 12.30
For when P. stubbornly refused to 13.15
When P. let the people go, God did 13.17
For P. will say of the people of 14.03
get glory over P. and all his host; 14.04
the mind of P. and his servants was 14.05
the heart of P. king of Egypt and 14.08
When P. drew near, the people of 14.10
get glory over P. and all his host, 14.17
when I have gotten glory over P., 14.18
all the host of P. that had 14.28
the horses of P. with his chariots 15.19
delivered me from the sword of P."). 18.04
had done to P. and to the Egyptians 18.08
Egyptians and out of the hand of P. 18.10
and against P. and all his household, Deu 6.22
from the hand of P. king of Egypt. 7.08
your God did to P. and to all Egypt, 7.18
did in Egypt to P. the king of 11.03
to P. and to all his servatns and 29.02
to P. and to all his servants and 34.11
Egypt subject to the house of P. 1Sa 2.27
Egyptians and P. hardened their 6.06
alliance with P. king of Egypt; 1Ki 3.01
(P. king of Egypt had gone up and 9.16
foreign women: the daughter of P., 11.01
to P. king of Egypt, who gave him a 11.18
great favor in the sight of P., 11.19
Pharaoh's house among the sons of P. 11.20
Hadad said to P., "Let me depart, 11.21
But P. said to him, "What have you 11.22
under the hand of P. king of Egypt, 2Ki 17.07
Such is P. king of Egypt to all who 18.21
In his days P. Neco king of Egypt 23.29
and P. Neco slew him at Megiddo, 23.39
And P. Neco put him in bonds at 23.33
And P. Neco made Eliakim the son of 23.34
gave the silver and the gold to P., 23.35
according to the command of P. 23.35
assessment, to give it to P. Neco. 23.35
of Bithiah, the daughter of P., 1Ch 4.17
wonders against P. and all his Neh 9.10
wonders against P. and all his Ps 135.09
but overthrew P. and his host in 136.15
counselors of P. give stupid Is 19.11
How can you say to P., 19.11
refuge in the protection of P., 30.02
protection of P. turn to your 30.03
Such is P. king of Egypt to all who 36.06
P. king of Egypt, his servants, his Jer 25.19
The army of P. had come out of 37.05
I will give P. Hophra king of 44.30

PHARAOH (cont.)

Concerning the army of P. Neco, Jer 46.02
Call the name of P., king of Egypt, 46.17
and P., and Egypt and her gods and 46.25
upon P. and those who trust in him. 46.25
Philistines, before P. smote Gaza. 47.01
P. with his mighty army and great Eze 17.17
your face against P. king of Egypt, 29.02
P. king of Egypt, the great dragon 29.03
broken the arm of P. king of Egypt, and 30.22
but I will break the arms of P., 30.24
but the arms of P. shall fall; 30.25
say to P. king of Egypt and to his 31.02
"This is P. and all his multitude, 31.18
lamentation over P. king of Egypt, 32.02
"When P. sees them, he will comfort 32.31
P. and all his army, slain by the 32.31
P. and all his multitude, says the 32.32
him favor and wisdom before P., Ac 7.10
Joseph's family became known to P. 7.13
For the scripture says to P., Rom 9.17

PHARAOH'S

the woman was taken into P. house. Gen 12.15
So he asked P. officers who were 40.07
P. cup was in my hand; and I took 40.11
and pressed them into P. cup, 40.11
cup, and placed the cup in P. hand." 40.11
you shall place P. cup in his hand 40.13
which was P. birthday, he made a 40.20
and he placed the cup in P. hand; 40.21
And the doubling of P. dream means 41.32
When the report was heard in P. house, 45.16
brought the money into P. house. 47.14
severe upon them. The land became P.; 47.20
priests alone did not become P. 47.26
Then his sister said to P. daughter, Ex 2.07
And P. daughter said to her, "Go." 2.08
And P. daughter said to her, "Take 2.09
and she brought him to P. daughter, 2.10
whom P. taskmasters had set over 5.14
But I will harden P. heart, 7.03
Still P. heart was hardened, and he 7.13
"P. heart is hardened, he refuses to 7.14
so P. heart remained hardened, and 7.22
But P. heart was hardened, and he 8.19
And P. servants said to him, "How 10.07
were driven out from P. presence. 10.11
But the LORD hardened P. heart, 10.20
But the LORD hardened P. heart, 10.27
in the sight of P. servants and in 11.03
and the LORD hardened P. heart, 11.10
And I will harden P. heart, 14.04
all P. horses and chariots and his 14.09
all P. horses, his chariots, and his 14.23
"P. chariots and his host he cast 15.04
'We were P. slaves in Egypt; Deu 6.21
he took P. daughter, and brought her 1Ki 3.01
this hall for P. daughter whom he 7.08
But P. daughter went up from the 9.24
whom Tahpenes weaned in P. house; 11.20
Genubath was in P. house among the 11.20
Solomon brought P. daughter up from 2Ch 8.11
my love, to a mare of P. chariots. Sol 1.09
P. army which came to help you is Jer 37.07
at the approach of P. army, 37.11
the entrance to P. palace in 43.09
P. daughter adopted him and brought Ac 7.21
be called the son of P. daughter, Heb 11.24

PHARISEE

You blind P.! first cleanse the inside Mt 23.26
Now when the P. who had invited him Lk 7.39
a P. asked him to dine with him; 11.37
The P. was astonished to see that 11.38
one a P. and the other a tax 18.10
The P. stood and prayed thus with 18.11
But a P. in the council named Ac 5.34
I am a P., a son of Pharisees; 23.06
our religion I have lived as a P. 26.05
born of Hebrews; as to the law a P., Php 3.05

PHARISEE'S

him, and he went into the P. house, Lk 7.36
sitting at table in the P. house, 7.37

PHARISEES

saw many of the P. and Sadducees Mt 3.07
exceeds that of the scribes and P., 5.20
And when the P. saw this, they said 9.11
saying, "Why do we and the P. fast, 9.14
But the P. said, "He casts out 9.34
But when P. saw it, they said to him, 12.02
But the P. went out and took 12.14
But when the P. heard it they said, 12.24
of the scribes and P. said to him, 12.38
Then P. and scribes came to Jesus 15.01
know that the P. were offended 15.12
And the P. and Sadducees came, and 16.01
the leaven of the P. and Sadducees. 16.06
the leaven of the P. and Sadducees. 16.11
teaching of the P. and Sadducees. 16.12
And P. came up to him and tested 19.03
priests and the P. heard his 21.45
Then the P. went and took counsel 22.15
But when the P. heard that he had 22.34
Now while the P. were gathered 22.41
"The scribes and the P. sit on 23.02
to you, scribes and P., hypocrites! 23.13
you, scribes and P., hypocrites! * 23.14
to you, scribes and P., hypocrites! 23.15
to you, scribes and P., hypocrites! 23.23
to you, scribes and P., hypocrites! 23.25
to you, scribes and P., hypocrites! 23.27
to you, scribes and P., hypocrites! 23.29
priests and the P. gathered before 27.62
And the scribes of the P., Mk 2.16
disciples and the P. were fasting; 2.18
and the disciples of the P. fast, 2.18
And the P. said to him, "Look, why 2.24
The P. went out, and immediately 3.06
Now when the P. gathered together 7.01
(For the P., and all the Jews, do 7.03
And the P. and the scribes asked 7.05
The P. came and began to argue with 8.11
leaven of the P. and the leaven of 8.15
And P. came up and in order to test 10.02
him some of the P. and some of the 12.13
there were P. and teachers of the Lk 5.17
scribes and the P. began to 5.21
And the P. and their scribes 5.30
and so do the disciples of the P., 5.33
But some of the P. said, 6.02
the scribes and the P. watched him, 6.07
but the P. and the lawyers rejected 7.30
One of the P. asked him to eat with 7.36
"Now you P. cleanse the outside of 11.39
"But woe to you P.! for you tithe 11.42
Woe to you P.! for you love the 11.43
scribes and the P. began to press 11.53
"Beware of the leaven of the P., 12.01
At that very hour some P. came, 13.31
of a ruler who belonged to the P., 14.01
And Jesus spoke to the lawyers and P., 14.03
And the P. and the scribes murmured, 15.02
The P., who were lovers of money, 16.14
Being asked by the P. when the 17.20
And some of the P. in the multitude 19.39
Now they had been sent from the P. Jn 1.24
Now there was a man of the P., 3.01
knew that the P. had heard that 4.01
The P. heard the crowd thus muttering 7.32
priests and P. sent officers to 7.32
back to the chief priests and P., 7.45
The P. answered them, "Are you led 7.47

PHARISEES (cont.)
or of the P. believed in him? Jn 7.48
The scribes and the P. brought a * 8.03
The P. then said to him, "You are 8.13
They brought to the P. the man who 9.13
The P. again asked him how he had 9.15
Some of the P. said, "This man is 9.16
Some of the P. near him heard this, 9.40
went to the P. and told them what 11.46
priests and the P. gathered the 11.47
priests and the P. had given 11.57
The P. then said to one another, 12.19
for fear of the P. they did not 12.42
from the chief priests and the P., 18.03
to the party of the P. rose up, Ac 15.05
were Sadducees and the other P., 23.06
I am a Pharisee, a son of P.; 23.06
between the P. and the Sadducees; 23.07
but the P. acknowledge them all. 23.08

PHARISEES'
scribes of the P. party stood up Ac 23.09

PHARPAR
Are not Abana and P., the rivers of 2Ki 5.12

PHICOL
Abimelech and P. the commander of Gen 21.22
Abimelech and P. the commander of 21.32
his adviser and P. the commander 26.26

PHILADELPHIA
Sardis and to P. and to Laodicea. Rev 1.11
angel of the church in P. write: 3.07

PHILEMON
To P. our beloved fellow worker Phm 1.01

PHILETUS
Among them are Hymenaeus and P., 2Ti 2.17

PHILIP
P. and Bartholomew; Thomas and Mt 10.03
Andrew, and P., and Bartholomew, and Mk 3.18
and his brother P. tetrarch of the Lk 3.01
and John, and P., and Bartholomew, 6.14
And he found P. and said to him, Jn 1.43
Now P. was from Bethsaida, the city 1.44
P. found Nathanael, and said to him, 1.45
P. said to him, "Come and see." 1.46
"Before P. called you, when you were 1.48
Jesus said to P., "How are we to 6.05
P. answered him, "Two hundred 6.07
So these came to P., who was from 12.21
P. went and told Andrew; Andrew 12.22
went with P. and they told Jesus. 12.22
P. said to him, "Lord, show us the 14.08
and yet you do not know me, P.? 14.09
P. and Thomas, Bartholomew and Ac 1.13
and P., and Prochorus, and Nicanor, 6.05
P. went down to a city of Samaria, 8.05
gave heed to what was said by P., 8.06
they believed P. as he preached 8.12
baptized he continued with P. 8.13
But an angel of the Lord said to P., 8.26
And the Spirit said to P., 8.29
So P. ran to him, and heard him 8.30
And he invited P. to come up and 8.31
And the eunuch said to P., 8.34
Then P. opened his mouth, and 8.35
And P. said, "If you believe with * 8.37
P. and the eunuch, and he baptized 8.38
Spirit of the Lord caught up P.; 8.39
But P. was found at Azotus, and 8.40
the house of P. the evangelist, 21.08

PHILIPPI
into the district of Caesarea P., Mt 16.13
to the villages of Caesarea P.; Mk 8.27
and from there to P., which is the Ac 16.12
away from P. after the days of 20.06
in Christ Jesus who are at P., Php 1.01
and been shamefully treated at P., 1Th 2.02

PHILIPPIANS
And you P. yourselves know that in Php 4.15

PHILIP'S
of Herodias, his brother P. wife; Mt 14.03
of Herodias, his brother P. wife; Mk 6.17

PHILISTIA
seized on the inhabitants of P. Ex 15.14
over P. I shout in triumph. Ps 60.08
P. with the inhabitants of Tyre; 83.07
behold, P. and Tyre, with Ethiopia— 87.04
over P. I shout in triumph. 108.09
O P., all of you, that the rod which Is 14.29
melt in fear, O P., all of you! 14.31
Sidon, and all the regions of P.? Joe 3.04
make an end of the pride of P. Zec 9.06

PHILISTINE
go over to the P. garrison on yonder 1Sa 14.01
sought to go over to the P. garrison, 14.04
Am I not a P., and are you not 17.08
And the P. said, "I defy the ranks 17.10
Israel heard these words of the P., 17.11
For forty days the P. came forward 17.16
the P. of Gath, Goliath by name, came 17.23
done for the man who kills this P., 17.26
For who is this uncircumcised P., 17.26
will go and fight with this P." 17.32
go against this P. to fight with 17.33
uncircumcised P. shall be one of 17.36
me from the hand of this P." 17.37
hand, and he drew near to the P. 17.40
And the P. came on and drew near to 17.41
And when the P. looked, and saw 17.42
And the P. said to David, "Am I a 17.43
and the P. cursed David by his gods. 17.43
The P. said to David. "Come to me, 17.44
Then David said to the P., 17.45
When the P. arose and came and drew 17.48
the battle line to meet the P. 17.48
and struck the P. on his forehead; 17.49
over the P. with a sling and with 17.50
with a stone, and struck the P., 17.50
Then David ran and stood over the P., 17.51
the head of the P. and brought it 17.54
saw David go forth against the P., 17.55
from the slaughter of the P., 17.57
the head of the P. in his hand. 17.57
David returned from slaying the P., 18.06
in his hand and he slew the P., 19.05
said, "The sword of Goliath the P., 21.09
him the sword of Goliath the P." 22.10
and attacked the P. and killed him. 2Sa 21.17
they smote the P. army from Gibeon 1Ch 14.16

PHILISTINES
Pathrusim, Casluhim (whence came the P.), Gen 10.14
and returned to the land of the P. 21.32
many days in the land of the P. 21.34
Gerar, to Abimelech king of the P. 26.01
king of the P. looked out of a 26.08
household, so that the P. envied him. 26.14
(Now the P. had stopped and filled 26.15
for the P. had stopped them after 26.18
them by way of the land of the P., Ex 13.17
the Red Sea to the sea of the P., 23.31
remains: all the regions of the P., Jos 13.02
there are five rulers of the P., 13.03
nations: The five lords of the P., Ju 3.03
hundred of the P. with an oxgoad; 3.31
Ammonites, and the gods of the P.; 10.06
the hand of the P. and into the 10.07

PHILISTINES (cont.)

from the Ammonites and from the P.? Ju 10.11
the hand of the P. for forty years 13.01
Israel from the hand of the P." 13.05
saw one of the daughters of the P. 14.01
the daughters of the P. at Timnah; 14.02
a wife from the uncircumcised P.?" 14.03
seeking an occasion against the P. 14.04
that time the P. had dominion over 14.04
be blameless in regard to the P., 15.03
into the standing grain of the P., 15.05
Then the P. said, "Who has done this?" 15.06
And the P. came up, and burned her 15.06
Then the P. came up and encamped in 15.09
know that the P. are rulers over 15.11
give you into the hands of the P." 15.12
the P. came shouting to meet him; 15.14
in the days of the P. twenty years. 15.20
lords of the P. came to her and 16.05
lords of the P. brought her seven 16.08
"The P. are upon you, Samson!" 16.09
"The P. are upon you, Samson!" 16.12
"The P. are upon you, Samson!" 16.14
and called the lords of the P., 16.18
the lords of the P. came up to her, 16.18
"The P. are upon you, Samson!" 16.20
And the P. seized him and gouged 16.21
lords of the P. gathered to offer 16.23
all the lords of the P. were there, 16.27
upon the P. for one of my two eyes." 16.28
said, "Let me die with the P." 16.30
went out to battle against the P.; 1Sa 4.01
and the P. encamped at Aphek. 4.01
The P. drew up in line against 4.02
Israel was fefeated by the P., 4.02
put us to rout today before the P.? 4.03
And when the P. heard the noise of 4.06
the P. were afraid; for they said, 4.07
O P., lest you become slaves to the 4.09
So the P. fought, and Israel was 4.10
"Israel has fled before the P., 4.17
When the P. captured the ark of God, 5.01
then the P. took the ark of God and 5.02
together all the lords of the P., 5.08
together all the lords of the P., 5.11
the country of the P. seven months. 6.01
And the P. called for the priests 6.02
the number of the lords of the P.; 6.04
lords of the P. went after them as 6.12
the five lords of the P. saw it, 6.16
which the P. returned as a guilt 6.17
cities of the P. belonging to the 6.18
"The P. have returned the ark of 6.21
you out of the hand of the P." 7.03
Now when the P. heard that the 7.07
lords of the P. went up against 7.07
of it they were afraid of the P. 7.07
save us from the hand of the P." 7.08
the P. drew near to attack Israel; 7.10
day against the P. and threw them 7.10
out of Mizpah and pursued the P., 7.11
So the P. were subdued and did not 7.13
was against the P. all the days of 7.13
which the P. had taken from Israel 7.14
territory from the hand of the P. 7.14
my people from the hand of the P.; 9.16
there is a garrison of the P.; 10.05
Hazor, and into the hand of the P., 12.09
garrison of the P. which was at 13.03
and the P. heard of it. And Saul 13.03
defeated the garrison of the P., 13.04
Israel had become odious to the P. 13.04
And the P. mustered to fight with 13.05
and that the P. had mustered at 13.11
'Now the P. will come down upon me 13.12
but the p. encamped in Michmash. 13.16
the camp of the P. in three 13.17
for the P. said, "Lest the Hebrews 13.19
down to the P. to sharpen his 13.20
garrison of the P. went out to the 13.23
themselves to the garrison of the P.; 14.11
and the P. said, "Look, Hebrews are 14.11
the camp of the P. increased more 14.19
been with the P. before that time 14.21
heard that the P. were fleeing, 14.22
among the P. has not been great." 14.30
They struck down the P. that day 14.31
down after the P. by night and 14.36
God, "Shall I go down after the P.? 14.37
Then Saul went up from pursuing the P.; 14.46
and the P. went to their own place. 14.46
kings of Zobah, and against the P.; 14.47
against the P. all the days of 14.52
Now the P. gathered their armies 17.01
in line of battle against the P. 17.02
And the P. stood on the mountain on 17.03
the camp of the P. a champion 17.04
of Elah, fighting with the P. 17.19
And Israel and the P. drew up for 17.21
came up out of the ranks of the P., 17.23
the host of the P. this day to the 17.46
When the P. saw that their champion 17.51
and pursued the P. as far as Gath 17.52
the wounded P. fell on the way 17.52
came back from chasing the P., 17.53
let the hand of the P. be upon him." 18.17
the hand of the P. may be against 18.21
a hundred foreskins of the P., 18.25
David fall by the hand of the P. 18.25
and killed two hundred of the P.; 18.27
princes of the P. came out to 18.30
went out and fought with the P., 19.08
the P. are fighting against Keilah, 23.01
"Shall I go and attack these P.?" 23.02
and attack the P. and save Keilah." 23.02
against the armies of the P.?" 23.03
I will give the P. into your hand." 23.04
to Keilah, and fought with the P. 23.05
for the P. have made a raid upon 23.27
David, and went against the P.; 23.28
returned from following the P., 24.01
escape to the land of the P.; 27.01
country of the P. was a year and 27.07
he dwelt in the country of the P. 27.11
In those days the P. gathered their 28.01
The P. assembled, and came and 28.04
When Saul saw the army of the P., 28.05
for the P. are warring against me, 28.15
with you into the hand of the P.; 28.19
also into the hand of the P." 28.19
Now the P. gathered all their 29.01
lords of the P. were passing on by 29.02
the commanders of the P. said, 29.03
said to the commanders of the P., 29.03
commanders of the P. were angry 29.04
commanders of the P. said to him, 29.04
not displease the lords of the P." 29.07
the commanders of the P. have said, 29.09
to return to the land of the P. 29.11
But the P. went up to Jezreel. 29.11
the land of the P. and from the 30.16
Now the P. fought against Israel; 31.01
men of Israel fled before the P., 31.01
And the P. overtook Saul and his 31.02
and the p. slew Johnathan and 31.02
and the P. came and dwelt in them. 31.07
when the P. came to strip the slain, 31.08
throughout the land of the P., 31.09
heard what the P. had done to Saul, 31.11
the daughters of the P. rejoice, 2Sa 1.20
of a hundred foreskins of the P." 3.14
Israel from the hand of the P., 3.18
When the P. heard that David had 5.17
all the P. went up in search of 5.17

PHILISTINES (cont.)

Now the P. had come and spread out 2Sa 5.18
LORD, "Shall I go up against the P.? 5.19
certainly give the P. into your hand." 5.19
And the P. left their idols there, 5.21
And the P. came up yet again, and 5.22
you to smite the army of the P." 5.24
and smote the P. from Geba to Gezer. 5.25
defeated the P. and subdued them, 8.01
Metheghammah out of the hand of the P. 8.01
the P., Amalek, and from the spoil 8.12
saved us from the hand of the P.; 19.09
where the P. had hanged them, on the 21.12
on the day the P. killed Saul on 21.12
The P. had war again with Israel, 21.15
and they fought against the P.; 21.15
was again war with the P. at Gob; 21.18
was again war with the P. at Gob; 21.19
they defied the P. who were 23.09
struck down the P. until his hand 23.10
The P. gathered together at Lehi, 23.11
and the men fled from the P. 23.11
and defended it, and slew the P.; 23.12
when a band of P. was encamped in 23.13
garrison of the P. was then at 23.14
broke through the camp of the P., 23.16
the land of the P. and to the 1Ki 4.21
Gibbethon, which belonged to the P.; 15.27
Gibbethon, which belonged to the P., 16.15
in the land of the P. seven years. 2Ki 8.02
returned from the land of the P., 8.03
He smote the P. as far as Gaza and 18.08
Pathrusim, Casluhim (whence came the P.), 1Ch 1.12
Now the P. fought against Israel; 10.01
men of Israel fled before the P., 10.01
And the P. overtook Saul and his 10.02
and the P. slew Jonathan and 10.02
and the P. came and dwelt in them 10.07
when the P. came to strip the slain, 10.08
throughout the land of the P., 10.09
all that the P. had done to Saul, 10.11
when the P. were gathered there 11.13
and the men fled from the P. 11.13
and defended it, and slew the P.; 11.14
the army of P. was encamped in the 11.15
garrison of the P. was then at 11.16
broke through the camp of the P., 11.18
came with the P. for the battle 12.19
rulers of the P. took counsel and 12.19
When the P. heard that David had 14.08
all the P. went up in search of 14.08
Now the P. had come and made a raid 14.09
God, "Shall I go up against the P.? 14.10
And the P. yet again made a raid in 14.13
you to smite the army of the P." 14.15
defeated the P. and subdued them, 18.01
villages out of the hand of the P. 18.01
the Ammonites, the P., and Amalek, 18.11
arose war with the P. at Gezer; 20.04
the giants; and the P. were subdued. 20.04
And there was again war with the P.; 20.05
Euphrates to the land of the P., 2Ch 9.26
Some of the P. brought Jehoshaphat 17.11
anger of the P. and of the Arabs 21.16
out and made war against the P., 26.06
Ashdod and elsewhere among the P. 26.06
God helped him against the P., 26.07
And the P. had made raids on the 28.18
and of soothsayers like the P., Is 2.06
east and the P. on the west devour 9.12
the shoulder of the P. in the west, 11.14
of the land of the P. (Ashkelon, Jer 25.20
the prophet concerning the P., 47.01
is coming to destroy all the P., 47.04
for the LORD is destroying the P., 47.04
enemies, the daughters of the P., Eze 16.27
and for the daughters of the P., 16.57
Because the P. acted revengefully 25.15
stretch out my hand against the P., 25.16
the remnant of the P. shall perish, Amo 1.08
then go down to Gath of the P. 6.02
and the P. from Caphtor and the 9.07
the Shephelah the land of the P.; Ob 1.19
you, O Canaan, land of the P.; Zep 2.05

PHILOLOGUS

Greet P., Julia, Nereus and his Rom 16.15

PHILOSOPHERS

the Epicurean and Stoic p. met him. Ac 17.18

PHILOSOPHY

prey of you by p. and empty deceit, Col 2.08

PHINEHAS

daughters of Putiel; and she bore him P. Ex 6.25
When P. the son of Eleazar, son of Num 25.07
"P. the son of Eleazar, son of Aaron 25.11
together with P. the son of Eleazar 31.06
P. the son of Eleazar the priest, Jos 22.13
When P. the priest and the chiefs 22.30
And P. the son of Eleazar the 22.31
Then P. the son of Eleazar the 22.32
the town of P. his son, which had 24.33
and P. the son of Eleazar, son of Ju 20.28
Hophni and P., were priests of the 1Sa 1.03
Hophni and P., shall be the sign to 2.34
Hophni and P., were there with the 4.04
of Eli, Hophni and P., were slain. 4.11
Hophni and P., are dead, and the ark 4.17
the wife of P., was with child, 4.19
son of P., son of Eli, the priest of 14.03
was the father of P., P. of Abishua, 1Ch 6.04
P. his son, Abishua his son, 6.50
And P. the son of Eleazar was the 9.20
son of P., son of Eleazar, son of Ez 7.05
Of the sons of P., Gershom. 8.02
with him was Eleazar the son of P., 8.33
Then P. stood up and interposed, and Ps 106.30

PHLEGON

P., Hermes, Patrobas, Hermas, and the Rom 16.14

PHOEBE

I commend to you our sister P., a Rom 16.01

PHOENICIA

shall possess P. as far as Zarephath Ob 1.20
as far as P. and Cyprus and Antioch, Ac 11.19
passed through both P. and Samaria, 15.03
having found a ship crossing to P., 21.02

PHOENIX

that somehow they could reach P., Ac 27.12

PHRASE

This P., "Yet once more," indicates Heb 12.27

PHRASES

heap up empty p. as the Gentiles Mt 6.07

PHRYGIA

P. and Pamphylia, Egypt and the Ac 2.10
the region of P. and Galatia, 16.06
the region of Galatia and P., 18.23

PHYGELUS

and among them P. and Hermogenes. 2Ti 1.15

PHYLACTERIES

they make their p. broad and their Mt 23.05

PHYSICAL

circumcision something external and p. Rom 2.28
It is sown a p. body, it is raised a 1Co 15.44

PHYSICAL (cont.)
If there is a p. body, there is also 1Co 15.44
spiritual which is first but the p., 15.46

PHYSICALLY
Then those who are p. uncircumcised Rom 2.27

PHYSICIAN
balm in Gilead? Is there no p. there? Jer 8.22
who are well have no need of a p., Mt 9.12
who are well have no need of a p., Mk 2.17
this proverb, 'P., heal yourself; Lk 4.23
who are well have no need of a p., 5.31
Luke the beloved p. and Demas greet Col 4.14

PHYSICIANS
servants the p. to embalm his Gen 50.02
So the p. embalmed Israel; 50.02
the LORD, but sought help from p. 2Ch 16.12
with lies; worthless p. are you all. Job 13.04
had suffered much under many p., Mk 5.26

PIBESETH
of On and of P. shall fall by the Eze 30.17

PICK
cut off used to p. up scraps under Ju 1.07
they p. mallow and the leaves of Job 30.04
And all the p. of his troops shall Eze 17.21
they will p. up serpents, and if they *Mk 16.18
p. out from among you seven men of Ac 6.03

PICKED
six hundred p. chariots and all Ex 14.07
and his p. officers are sunk in the 15.04
who mustered seven hundred p. men. Ju 20.15
seven hundred p. men who were 20.16
ten thousand p. men out of all 20.34
chose some of the p. men of Israel, 2Sa 10.09
chose some of the p. men of Israel, 1Ch 19.00
war, four hundred thousand p. men; 2Ch 13.03
thousand p. mighty warriors. 13.03
five hundred thousand p. men. 13.17
were three hundred thousand p. men, 25.05
and laid low the p. men of Israel. Ps 78.31
mother will be p. out by the Pro 30.17
or even his p. troops, for there Dan 11.15
nor are grapes p. from a bramble Lk 6.44

PICKS
saws and iron p. and iron axes, 2Sa 12.31
with saws and iron p. and axes; 1Ch 20.03

PICTURE
a p. of Babylonians whose native Eze 23.15

PICTURES
dark, every man in his room of p.? Eze 8.12

PIECE
a p. of land worth four hundred Gen 23.15
of money the p. of land on which 33.19
of one p. with the mercy seat shall Ex 25.19
flowers shall be of one p. with it; 25.31
capital of one p. with it under 25.35
branches shall be of one p. with it, 25.36
whole of it one p. of hammered 25.36
horns shall be of one p. with it, 27.02
horns shall be of one p. with it. 30.02
of one p. with the mercy seat he 37.08
its flowers were of one p. with it. 37.17
capital of one p. with it under 37.21
branches were of one p. with it; 37.22
of it was one p. of hammered work 37.22
its horns were of one p. with it. 37.25
its horns were of one p. with it, 38.02
offering to him, p. by p., and the head; Lev 9.13
him for a p. of silver or a loaf 1Sa 2.36
and they gave him a p. of a cake of 30.12
were of one p. with the stands; 1Ki 7.32
were of one p. with the stands. 7.34
its panels were of one p. with it. 7.35
ruin every good p. of land with 2Ki 3.19
on every good p. of land every man 3.25
I too was formed from a p. of clay. Job 33.06
them gave him a p. of money and a 42.11
but for a p. of bread a man will do Pro 28.21
Take out of it p. after p., without Eze 24.06
or a p. of an ear, so shall the Amo 3.12
And no one puts a p. of unshrunk Mt 9.16
No one sews a p. of unshrunk cloth Mk 2.21
"No one tears a p. from a new Lk 5.36
and the p. from the new will not 5.36
They gave him a p. of broiled fish, 24.42
Sapphira sold a p. of property, Ac 5.01

PIECES
flaming torch passed between these p. Gen 15.17
brother a thousand p. of silver; 20.16
for a hundred p. of money the 33.19
Joseph is without doubt torn to p." 37.33
Surely he has been torn to p.; 44.28
them and break their pillars in p. Ex 23.24
Then you shall cut the ram into p., 29.17
put them with its p. and its head, 29.17
burnt offering and cut it into p.; Lev 1.06
sons the priests shall lay the p., 1.08
And he shall cut it into p., with 1.12
you shall break it in p., and pour 2.06
in baked p. like a cereal offering, 6.21
And when the ram was cut into p., 8.20
the head and the p. and the fat. 8.20
or stove, it shall be broken in p.; 11.35
and shall break their bones in p., Num 24.08
and dash in p. their pillars, and Deu 7.05
and dash in p. their pillars, and 12.03
Shechem for a hundred p. of money; Jos 24.32
two p. of dyed work embroidered for Ju 5.30
him seventy p. of silver out of 9.04
you eleven hundred p. of silver. 16.05
eleven hundred p. of silver which 17.02
eleven hundred p. of silver to his 17.03
took two hundred p. of silver, 17.04
give you ten p. of silver a year, 17.10
into twelve p., and sent her 19.29
my concubine and cut her in p., 20.06
of the LORD shall be broken to p.; 1Sa 2.10
and cut them in p. and sent them 11.07
hewed Agag in p. before the LORD 15.33
to give you ten p. of silver and a 2Sa 18.11
weight of a thousand p. of silver, 18.12
and the fat p. of the peace offerings, 1Ki 8.64
and the cereal offering and the fat p. 8.64
on him, and tore it into twelve p. 11.30
Jeroboam, "Take for youself ten p.; 11.31
and cut it in p. and lay it on the 18.23
cut the bull in p. and laid it on 18.33
and broke in p. the rocks before 19.11
clothes and rent them in two p. 2Ki 2.12
and dash in p. their little ones, 8.12
and his images they broke in p., 11.18
And he broke in p. the bronze 18.04
he pulled down and broke in p., 23.12
And he broke in p. the pillars, 23.14
down and he broke in p. its stones, 23.15
and cut in p. all the vessels of 24.13
LORD, the Chaldeans broke in p., 25.13
They were broken in p., 2Ch 15.06
and his images they broke in p., 23.17
and they were all dashed to p. 25.12
God and cut in p. the vessels of 28.24
and broke in p. the pillars and 31.01
and he broke in p. the Asherim and 34.04
me by the neck and dashed me to p.; Job 16.12
me, and break me in p. with words? 19.02
dash them in p. like a potter's Ps 2.09
thousands of gold and silver p. 119.72

PIECES (cont.)

its fruit a thousand p. of silver. Sol 8.11
be broken to p. so that it will no Is 7.08
be dashed in p. before their eyes; 13.16
like chalkstones crushed to p., 27.09
I will break in p. the doors of 45.02
thou that didst cut Rahab in p., 51.09
out of them shall be torn in p.; Jer 5.06
hammer which breaks the rock in p.? 23.29
vessels, and break his jars in p. 48.12
with you I break nations in p.; 51.20
with you I break in p. the horse 51.21
you I break in p. the chariot and 51.21
with you I break in p. man and woman; 51.22
you I break in p. the old man and 51.22
you I break in p. the young man 51.22
with you I break in p. the shepherd 51.23
you I break in p. the farmer and 51.23
you I break in p. governors and 51.23
taken, their bows are broken in p.; 51.56
LORD, the Chaldeans broke in p., 52.17
me off my way and tore me to p.; Lam 3.11
of barley and for p. of bread, Eze 13.19
and cut you to p. with their 16.40
it the p. of flesh, all the good p., 24.04
boil its p., seethe also its bones 24.05
and clay, and broke them in p.; Dan 2.34
all together were broken in p., 2.35
iron breaks to p. and shatters all 2.40
shall break in p. all these 2.44
and that it broke in p. the iron, 2.45
and broke all their bones in p. 6.24
it devoured and broke in p., 7.07
and which devoured and broke in p., 7.19
it down, and break it to p. 7.23
of Samaria shall be broken to p. Hos 8.06
were dashed in p. with their 10.14
little ones shall be dashed in p., 13.16
All her images shall be beaten to p., Mic 1.07
them, and break their bones in p., 3.03
you shall beat in p. many peoples, 4.13
treads down and tears in p., 5.08
were dashed in p. at the head of Nah 3.10
full of the broken p. left over. Mt 14.20
full of the broken p. left over. 15.37
on this stone will be broken to p.; * 21.44
they paid him thirty p. of silver. 26.15
back the thirty p. of silver to 27.03
down the p. of silver in the 27.05
taking the p. of silver, said, "It is 27.06
they took the thirty p. of silver, 27.09
and the fetters he broke in p.; Mk 5.04
full of broken p. and of the fish. 6.43
took up the broken p. left over, 8.08
full of broken p. did you take up?" 8.19
full of broken p. did you take up?" 8.20
over, twelve baskets of broken p. Lk 9.17
on that stone will be broken to p.; 20.18
to fifty thousand p. of silver. Ac 19.19
Paul would be torn in p. by them, 23.10
on planks or on p. of the ship. 27.44
when earthen pots are broken in p., Rev 2.27

PIERCE

and p. them through with his arrows. Num 24.08
which will p. the hand of any man 2Ki 18.21
hooks, or p. his nose with a snare? Job 40.24
his nose, or p. his jaw with a hook? 41.02
which will p. the hand of any man Is 36.06
pieces, that didst p. the dragon? 51.09
Thou didst p. with thy shafts the Hab 3.14
bore him shall p. him through when Zec 13.03
(and a sword will p. through your Lk 2.35

PIERCED

and p. both of them, the man of Num 25.08
she shattered and p. his temple. Ju 5.26
so that the arrow p. his heart, 2Ki 9.24
his hand p. the fleeing serpent. Job 26.13
they have p. my hands and feet— Ps 22.16
those p. by the sword, who go down Is 14.19
they look on him whom they have p., Zec 12.10
another took a spear and p. his *Mt 27.49
of the soldiers p. his side with a Jn 19.34
look on him whom they have p. 19.37
the faith and p. their hearts with 1Ti 6.10
will see him, every one who p. him; Rev 1.07

PIERCES

till an arrow p. its entrails; Pro 7.23

PIERCING

p. to the division of soul and Heb 4.12

PIETY

practicing your p. before men in Mt 6.01
own power or p. we had made him Ac 3.12

PIGEON

old, a turtledove, and a young p. Gen 15.09
and a young p. or a turtledove for Lev 12.06

PIGEONS

of turtledoves or of young p. Lev 1.14
two turtledoves or two young p., 5.07
two turtledoves or two young p., 5.11
two turtledoves or two young p., 12.08
also two turtledoves or two young p., 14.22
or young p. such as he can afford, 14.30
two turtledoves or two young p., 15.14
two turtledoves or two young p., 15.29
or two young p. to the priest to Num 6.10
and the seats of those who sold p. Mt 21.12
and the seats of those who sold p.; Mk 11.15
of turtledoves, or two young p. Lk 2.24
were selling oxen and sheep and p., Jn 2.14
And he told those who sold the p., 2.16

PIHAHIROTH

back and encamp in front of P., Ex 14.02
by P., in front of Baalzephon. 14.09
from Etham, and turned back to P., Num 33.07

PILATE

delivered him to P. the governor. Mt 27.02
Then P. said to him, "Do you not 27.13
P. said to them, "Whom do you want 27.17
P. said to them, "Then what shall I 27.22
So when P. saw that he was gaining 27.24
He went to P. and asked for the 27.58
Then P. ordered it to be given to 27.58
Pharisees gathered before P. 27.62
P. said to them, "You have a guard 27.65
him away and delivered him to P. Mk 15.01
And P. asked him, "Are you the King 15.02
And P. again asked him, "Have you no 15.04
further answer, so that P. wondered. 15.05
began to ask P. to do as he was 15.08
And P. again said to them, "Then 15.12
And P. said to them, "Why, what evil 15.14
So P., wishing to satisfy the crowd, 15.15
God, took courage and went to P., 15.43
And P. wondered if he were already 15.44
Pontius P. being governor of Judea, Lk 3.01
whose blood P. had mingled with 13.01
arose, and brought him before P. 23.01
And P. asked him, "Are you the King 23.03
And P. said to the chief priests 23.04
When P. heard this, he asked whether 23.06
apparel, he sent him back to P. 23.11
And Herod and P. became friends 23.12
P. then called together the chief 23.13
P. addressed them once more, desiring 23.20
So P. gave sentence that their 23.24
This man went to P. and asked for 23.52

PILATE (cont.)
So P. went out to them and said, Jn 18.29
P. said to them, "Take him yourselves 18.31
P. entered the praetorium again and 18.33
P. answered, "Am I a Jew? Your own 18.35
P. said to him, "So you are a king?" 18.37
P. said to him, "What is truth?" 18.38
Then P. took Jesus and scourged him. 19.01
P. went out again, and said to them, 19.04
P. said to them, "Here is the man!" 19.05
P. said to them, "Take him yourselves 19.06
When P. heard these words, he was 19.08
P. therefore said to him, "You will 19.10
Upon this P. sought to release him, 19.12
When P. heard these words, he 19.13
P. said to them, "Shall I crucify 19.15
P. also wrote a title and put it on 19.19
of the Jews then said to P., 19.21
P. answered, "What I have written I 19.22
the Jews asked P. that their legs 19.31
asked P. that he might take away 19.38
of Jesus, and P. gave him leave. 19.38
and denied in the presence of P., Ac 3.13
anoint, both Herod and Pontius P., 4.27
yet they asked P. to have him 13.28
before Pontius P. made the good 1Ti 6.13

PILDASH
Chesed, Hazo, P., Jidlaph, and Bethuel Gen 22.22

PILE
month they began to p. up the heaps, 2Ch 31.07
dust, and p. up clothing like clay; Job 27.16
he may p. it up, but the just will 27.17
p. her up like heaps of grain, and Jer 50.26
p. the logs under it; boil its Eze 24.05
I also will make the p. great. 24.09

PILED
of thy nostrils the waters p. up, Ex 15.08

PILFER
nor to p., but to show entire and Tit 2.10

PILGRIMAGE
been my songs in the house of my p. Ps 119.54

PILHA
Hallohesh, P., Shobek, Neh 10.24

PILLAGED
How Esau has been p., his treasures Ob 1.06

PILLAR
back, and she became a p. of salt. Gen 19.26
set it up for a p. and poured oil 28.18
which I have set up for a p., 28.22
you anointed a p. and made a vow 31.13
a stone, and set it up as a p. 31.45
and the p. Mizpah, for he said, "The 31.49
to Jacob, "See this heap and the p., 31.51
and the p. is a witness, that I will 31.52
over this heap and this p. to me, 31.52
And Jacob set up a p. in the place 35.14
had spoken with him, a p. of stone; 35.14
and Jacob set up a p. upon her grave; 35.20
it is the p. of Rachel's tomb, which 35.20
by day in a p. of cloud to lead Ex 13.21
by night in a p. of fire to give 13.21
the p. of cloud by day and the p. of 13.22
and the p. of cloud moved from 14.19
the LORD in the p. of fire and of 14.24
the p. of cloud would descend and 33.09
people saw the p. of cloud standing 33.10
and erect no graven image or p., Lev 26.01
LORD came down in a p. of cloud, Num 12.05
in a p. of cloud by day and in a p. of 14.14
And you shall not set up a p., Deu 16.22
in a p. of cloud; and the p. 31.15
by the oak of the p. at Shechem. Ju 9.06
for himself the p. which is in the 2Sa 18.18
he called the p. after his own name, 18.18
cubits was the height of one p., 1Ki 7.15
the second p. was the same. 7.15
that was upon the top of the p.; 7.18
he set up the p. on the south and 7.21
he set up the p. on the north and 7.21
he put away the p. of Baal which 2Ki 3.02
brought out the p. that was in the 10.26
And they demolished the p. of Baal, 10.27
was the king standing by the p., 11.14
stood by the p. and made a covenant 23.03
of the one p. was eighteen cubits, 25.17
And the second p. had the like, 25.17
standing by his p. at the entrance, 2Ch 23.13
By a p. of cloud thou didst lead Neh 9.12
and by a p. of fire in the night to 9.12
the p. of cloud which led them in 9.19
nor the p. of fire by night which 9.19
He spoke to them in the p. of cloud; Ps 99.07
and a p. to the LORD at its border. Is 19.19
an iron p., and bronze walls, Jer 1.18
of the one p. was eighteen cubits, 52.21
And the second p. had the like, 52.22
or prince, without sacrifice or p., Hos 3.04
the p. and bulwark of the truth. 1Ti 3.15
will make him a p. in the temple Rev 3.12

PILLARS
them and break their p. in pieces. Ex 23.24
and twelve p., according to the 24.04
it upon four p. of acacia overlaid 26.32
for the screen five p. of acacia, 26.37
their p. shall be twenty and their 27.10
hooks of the p. and their fillets 27.10
their p. twenty and their bases 27.11
hooks of the p. and their fillets 27.11
cubits, with ten p. and ten bases. 27.12
with three p. and three bases. 27.14
with three p. and three bases. 27.15
shall have four p. and with them 27.16
All the p. around the court shall 27.17
their altars, and break their p., 34.13
its bars, its p., and its bases; 35.11
its p. and its bases, and the screen 35.17
And for it he made four p. of acacia, 36.36
and its five p. with their hooks. 36.38
their p. were twenty and their 38.10
hooks of the p. and their fillets 38.10
their p. twenty, their bases twenty, 38.11
hooks of the p. and their fillets 38.11
their p. ten, and their sockets ten; 38.12
hooks of the p. and their fillets 38.12
with three p. and three bases. 38.14
with three p. and three bases. 38.15
bases for the p. were of bronze, 38.17
hooks of the p. and their fillets 38.17
and all the p. of the court were 38.17
And their p. were four; their 38.19
shekels he made hooks for the p., 38.28
its bars, its p., and its bases; 39.33
its p., and its bases, and the 39.40
in its poles, and raised up its p.; 40.18
the p., the bases, and all their Num 3.36
Also the p. of the court round 3.37
with its bars, p., and bases, 4.31
and the p. of the court round about 4.32
and dash in pieces their p., Deu 7.05
and dash in pieces their p., 12.03
They made him stand between the p.; Ju 16.25
"Let me feel the p. on which the 16.26
the two middle p. upon which the 16.29
For the p. of the earth are the 1Sa 2.08
built upon three rows of cedar p., 1Ki 7.02
with cedar beams upon the p. 7.02

PILLARS (cont.)
that were upon the forty-five p., 1Ki 7.03
And he made the Hall of P.; 7.06
there was a porch in front with p., 7.06
He cast two p. of bronze. 7.15
to set upon the tops of the p.; 7.16
capitals upon the tops of the p.; 7.17
the tops of the p. in the vestibule 7.19
upon the two p. and also above the 7.20
He set up the p. at the vestibule 7.21
the tops of the p. was lily-work. 7.22
the work of the p. was finished. 7.22
the two p., the two bowls of the 7.41
tops of the p., and the two networks 7.41
that were on the tops of the p.; 7.41
the capitals that were upon the p.; 7.42
and p., and Asherim on every high 14.23
for themselves p. and Asherim on 2Ki 17.10
and broke the p., and cut down the 18.04
And he broke in pieces the p., 23.14
And the p. of bronze that were in 25.13
As for the two p., the one sea, and 25.16
sea and the p. and the vessels of 1Ch 18.08
he made two p. thirty-five cubits 2Ch 3.15
and put them on the tops of the p.; 3.16
He set up the p. in front of the 3.17
the two p., the bowls, and the two 4.12
two capitals on the top of the p.; 4.12
that were on the top of the p.; 4.12
the capitals that were upon the p. 4.13
broke down the p. and hewed down 14.03
in pieces the p. and hewed down 31.01
to silver rings and marble p., Est 1.06
of its place, and its p. tremble; Job 9.06
The p. of heaven tremble, and are 26.11
it is I who keep steady its p. Ps 75.03
like corner p. cut for the structure 144.12
house, she has set up her seven p. Pro 9.01
Those who are the p. of the land Is 19.10
LORD of hosts concerning the p., Jer 27.19
And the p. of bronze that were in 52.17
As for the two p., the one sea, the 52.20
As for the p., the height of the 52.21
and your mighty p. will fall to the Eze 26.11
and there were p. beside the jambs 40.49
and they had no p. like the p. of 42.06
improved he improved his p. Hos 10.01
their altars, and destroy their p. 10.02
images and your p. from among you, Mic 5.13
John, who were reputed to be p., Gal 2.09
sun, and his legs like p. of fire. Rev 10.01

PILLOW
bed and put a p. of goats' hair at 1Sa 19.13
with the p. of goats' hair at its 19.16

PILOT
wherever the will of the p. directs. Jas 3.04

PILOTS
were in you, they were your p. Eze 27.08
merchandise, your mariners and your p., 27.27
the cry of your p. the countryside 27.28
and all the p. of the sea stand on 27.29

PILTAI
Zichri; of Miniamin, of Moadiah, P.; Neh 12.17

PIM
charge was a p. for the plowshares 1Sa 13.21

PIN
web and make it tight with the p., Ju 16.13
she made them tight with the p., 16.14
his sleep, and pulled away the p., 16.14
"I will p. David to the wall." 1Sa 18.11
And Saul sought to p. David to the 19.10
therefore let me p. him to the 26.08

PINE
the eyes and cause life to p. away. Lev 26.16
are left shall p. away in your 26.39
they shall p. away like them. 26.39
are cedar, our rafters are p. Sol 1.17
But I say, "I p. away, I p. away. Woe Is 24.16
the plane and the p. together; 41.19
and the p., to beautify the place 60.13
but you shall p. away in your Eze 24.23

PINED
who p. away, stricken by want of the Lam 4.09

PINES
your deck of p. from the coasts of Eze 27.06

PINIONS
them, bearing them on its p., Deu 32.11
are they the p. and plumage of Job 39.13
with silver, its p. with green gold. Ps 68.13
he will cover you with his p., 91.04
eagle with great wings and long p., Eze 17.03

PINNNACLE
set him on the p. of the temple, Mt 4.05
set him on the p. of the temple, Lk 4.09

PINNACLES
I will make your p. of agate, your Is 54.12

PINON
Oholibamah, Elah, P., Gen 36.41
Oholibamah, Elah, P., 1Ch 1.52

PIONEER
should make the p. of their Heb 2.10
looking to Jesus the p. and perfecter 12.02

PIPE
all those who play the lyre and p. Gen 4.21
and rejoice to the sound of the p. Job 21.12
and my p. to the voice of those who 30.31
praise him with strings and p.! Ps 150.04
p., lyre, trigon, harp, bagpipe, and Dan 3.05
p., lyre, trigon, harp, bagpipe, and 3.07
p., lyre, trigon, harp, bagpipe, and 3.10
p., lyre, trigon, harp, bagpipe, and 3.15

PIPED
'We p. to you, and you did not dance; Mt 11.17
'We p. to you, and you did not dance; Lk 7.32

PIPES
playing on p., and rejoicing with 1Ki 1.40
the two golden p. from which the Zec 4.12

PIPING
to hear the p. for the flocks? Ju 5.16

PIRAM
to P. king of Jarmuth, to Japhia Jos 10.03

PIRATHON
was buried at P. in the land of Ju 12.15
Benaiah of P., Hiddai of the brooks 2Sa 23.30
the Benjaminites, Benaiah of P., 1Ch 11.31
eleventh month, was Benaiah of P., 27.14

PIRATHONITE
son of Hillel the P. judged Israel. Ju 12.13
the son of Hillel the P. died, 12.15

PISGAH
by the top of P. which looks down Num 21.20
to the top of P., and built seven 23.14
under the slopes of P. on the east. Deu 3.17
Go up to the top of P., and lift 3.27
the Arabah, under the slopes of P. 4.49
to the top of P., which is opposite 34.01

PISGAH (cont.)
to the foot of the slopes of P.; Jos 12.03
and Bethpeor, and the slopes of P., 13.20

PISHON
The name of the first is P.; it is the Gen 2.11

PISIDIA
from Perga and came to Antioch of P. Ac 13.14
Then they passed through P., and came 14.24

PISPA
of Jether: Jephunneh, P., and Ara. 1Ch 7.38

PISTACHIO
honey, gum, myrrh, p. nuts, and almonds. Gen 43.11

PIT
him into this p. here in the Gen 37.22
took him and cast him into a p. 37.24
The p. was empty, there was no water 37.24
up and lifted him out of the p., 37.28
returned to the p. and saw that 37.29
saw that Joseph was not in the p., 37.29
"When a man leaves a p. open, Ex 21.33
a man digs a p. and does not cover 21.33
the owner of the p. shall make it 21.34
him into a great p. in the forest, 2Sa 18.17
a lion in a p. on a day when snow 23.20
slew them at the p. of Betheked, 2Ki 10.14
a lion in a p. on a day when snow 1Ch 11.22
yet thou wilt plunge me into a p., Job 9.31
if I say to the p., "You are my 17.14
he keeps back his soul from the P., 33.18
His soul draws near the P., 33.22
him from going down into the P., 33.24
soul from going down into the P., 33.28
to bring back his soul from the P., 33.30
He makes a p., digging it out, and Ps 7.15
sunk in the p. which they made; 9.15
or let thy godly one see the P. 16.10
like those who go down to the P. 28.01
among those gone down to the P. 30.03
my death, if I go down to the P.? 30.09
cause they dug a p. for my life. 35.07
He drew me up from the desolate p., 40.02
on for ever, and never see the P. 49.09
cast them down into the lowest p.; 55.23
They dug a p. in my way, but they 57.06
or the p. close its mouth over me. 69.15
among those who go down to the P.; 88.04
put me in the depths of the P., 88.06
until a p. is dug for the wicked. 94.13
who redeems your life from the P., 103.04
like those who go down to the P. 143.07
like those who go down to the P.; Pro 1.12
of a loose woman is a deep p.; 22.14
For a harlot is a deep p.; 23.27
He who digs a p. will fall into it, 26.27
evil way will fall into his own p.; 28.10
in his way will fall into a p. 28.18
He who digs a p. will fall into it; Ecc 10.08
to Sheol, to the depths of the P. Is 14.15
go down to the stones of the P., 14.19
and the p., and the snare are upon 24.17
the terror shall fall into the p.; 24.18
out of the p. shall be caught in 24.18
together as prisoners in a p.; 24.22
my life from the p. of destruction, 38.17
go down to the p. cannot hope for 38.18
not die and go down to the P., 51.14
Yet they have dug a p. for my life. Jer 18.20
for they have dug a p. to take me, 18.22
Terror, p., and snare are before you, 48.43
the terror shall fall into the p., 48.44
out of the p. shall be caught in 48.44
alive into the p. and cast stones Lam 3.53
O LORD, from the depths of the p.; 3.55
he was taken in their p.; Eze 19.04
he was taken in their p. 19.08
with those who descend into the P., 26.20
with those who go down to the P., 26.20
They shall thrust you down into the P., 28.08
with those who go down to the P. 31.14
with those who go down to the P.; 31.16
who have gone down to the P.: 32.18
in the uttermost parts of the P., 32.23
with those who go down to the P. 32.24
with those who go down to the P.; 32.25
with those who go down to the P.; 32.29
with those who go down to the P. 32.30
have made deep the p. of Shittim; Hos 5.02
my life from the P., O LORD my God. Jon 2.06
captives free from the waterless p. Zec 9.11
it falls into a p. on the sabbath, Mt 12.11
man, both will fall into a p. 15.14
and dug a p. for the wine press, and Mk 12.01
will they not both fall into a p.? Lk 6.39
of the shaft of the bottomless p.; Rev 9.01
the shaft of the bottomless p., 9.02
the angel of the bottomless p.; 9.11
the bottomless p. will make war 11.07
the bottomless p. and go to 17.08
the bottomless p. and a great 20.01
and threw him into the p., 20.03

PITCH
cover it inside and out with p. Gen 6.14
and daubed it with bitumen and p.; Ex 2.03
the tent and p. it outside the 33.07
of Israel shall p. their tents by Num 1.52
you out a place to p. your tents, Deu 1.33
no Arab will p. his tent there, no Is 13.20
of Edom shall be turned into p., 34.09
her land shall become burning p. Is 34.09
they shall p. their tents around Jer 6.03
And he shall p. his palatial tents Dan 11.45

PITCHED
and p. his tent, with Bethel on the Gen 12.08
of the LORD, and p. his tent there. 26.25
Now Jacob had p. his tent in the 31.25
land on which he had p. his tent. 33.19
and p. his tent beyond the tower of 35.21
when the tabernacle is to be p., Num 1.51
and had p. his tent as far away as Ju 4.11
the tent which David had p. for it; 2Sa 6.17
So they p. a tent for Absalom upon 16.22
ark of God, and p. a tent for it. 1Ch 15.01
the tent which David had p. for it; 16.01
for he had p. a tent for it in 2Ch 1.04

PITCHER
or the p. is broken at the fountain, Ecc 12.06

PITCHERS
before the Rechabites p. full of wine, Jer 35.05

PITFALL
his own feet, and he walks on a p. Job 18.08
panic and p. have come upon us, Lam 3.47
a p. and a retribution for them; Rom 11.09

PITFALLS
Godless men have dug p. for me, men Ps 119.85

PITHOM
Pharaoh store cities, P. and Raamses. Ex 1.11

PITHON
of Micah: P., Melech, Tarea, and Ahaz. 1Ch 8.35
of Micah: P., Melech, Tahrea, and Ahaz; 9.41

PITIABLE
wretched, p., poor, blind, and naked. Rev 3.17

PITIED

them to be p. by all those who Ps 106.46
No eye p. you, to do any of these Eze 16.05
said to him, "Call her name Not p., Hos 1.06
When she had weaned Not p., she 1.08
And I will have pity on Not p., 2.23
we are of all men most to be p. 1Co 15.19

PITIES

As a father p. his children, so the Ps 103.13
so the LORD p. those who fear him. 103.13

PITS

of Siddim was full of bitumen p.; Gen 14.10
and throw him into one of the p.; 37.20
hidden himself in one of the p., 2Sa 17.09
Let them be cast into p., no more Ps 140.10
in a land of deserts and p., Jer 2.06
anointed, was taken in their p., Lam 4.20
possessed by nettles and salt p., Zep 2.09
committed them to p. of nether 2Pe 2.04

PITY

She took p. on him and said, "This Ex 2.06
to you, your eye shall not p. them; Deu 7.16
to him, nor shall your eye p. him, 13.08
Your eye shall not p. him, but you 19.13
Your eye shall not p.; it shall be 19.21
her hand; your eye shall have no p. 25.12
was moved to p. by their groaning Ju 2.18
thing, and because he had no p. 2Sa 12.06
Have p. on me, have p. on me, O you my Job 19.21
It hurls at him without p.; he 27.22
They close their hearts to p.; Ps 17.10
I looked for p., but there was none; 69.20
He has p. on the weak and the needy, 72.13
Turn to me and take p. on me; 86.16
How long? Have p. on thy servants! 90.13
Thou wilt arise and have p. on Zion; 102.13
dear, and have p. on her dust. 102.14
nor any to p. his fatherless 109.12
their eyes will not p. children. Is 13.18
for he who has p. on them will 49.10
love and in his p. he redeemed 63.09
I will not p. or spare or have Jer 13.14
"Who will have p. on you, O Jerusalem, 15.05
the LORD overthrew without p.; 20.16
he shall not p. them, or spare them, 21.07
ago, he has demolished without p.; Lam 2.17
and pursued us, slaying without p.; 3.43
not spare, and I will have no p. Eze 5.11
not spare you, nor will I have p.; 7.04
will not spare, nor will I have p.; 7.09
will not spare, nor will I have p.; 8.18
spare, and you shall show no p.; 9.05
will not spare, nor will I have p., 9.10
no more have p. on the house of Hos 1.06
But I will have p. on the house of 1.07
your sister, "She has obtained p." 2.01
children also I will have no p., 2.04
And I will have p. on Not pitied, 2.23
his land, and had p. on his people. Joe 2.18
the sword, and cast off all p., Amo 1.11
"You p. the plant, for which you did Jon 4.10
And should not I p. Nineveh, 4.11
own shepherds have no p. on them. Zec 11.05
no longer have p. on the inhabitants 11.06
And out of p. for him the lord of Mt 18.27
And Jesus in p. touched their eyes, 20.34
Moved with p., he stretched out his Mk 1.41
anything, have p. on us and help us." 9.22

PLACE

be gathered together into one p., Gen 1.09
and closed up its p. with flesh; 2.21
dove found no p. to set her foot, 8.09
the land to the p. at Shechem, 12.06
to the p. where his tent had been 13.03
to the p. where he had made an 13.04
and look from the p. where you are, 13.14
destroy the p. and not spare it 18.24
spare the whole p. for their sake. 18.26
and Abraham returned to his p. 18.33
the city, bring them out of the p.; 19.12
for we are about to destroy this p., 19.13
daughters, "Up, get out of this p.; 19.14
morning to the p. where he had 19.27
no fear of God at all in this p., 20.11
at every p. to which we come, say of 20.13
Therefore that p. was called 21.31
and went to the p. of which God 22.03
his eyes and saw the p. afar off. 22.04
came to the p. of which God had 22.09
name of that p. The LORD will 22.14
property among you for a burying p., 23.04
as a possession for a burying p. 23.09
for a burying p. by the Hittites. 23.20
the house and a p. for the camels. 24.31
When the men of the p. asked him 26.07
the men of the p. should kill me 26.07
And he came to a certain p., 28.11
Taking one of the stones of the p., 28.11
and lay down in that p. to sleep. 28.11
"Surely the LORD is in this p.; 28.16
and said, "How awesome is this p.! 28.17
He called the name of that p. Bethel; 28.19
back in its p. upon the mouth of 29.03
the men of the p. and made a feast. 29.22
"Am I in the p. of God, who has 30.02
the name of that p. Mahanaim. 32.02
called the name of the p. Peniel, 32.30
the name of the p. is called 33.17
altar, and called the p. Elbethel, 35.07
from him in the p. where he had 35.13
a pillar in the p. where he had 35.14
the name of the p. where God had 35.15
And he asked the men of the p., 38.21
and also the men of the p. said, 38.22
the p. where the king's prisoners 39.20
and you shall p. Pharaoh's cup in 40.13
go from this p. unless your 42.15
ass provender at the lodging p., 42.27
to the lodging p. we opened our 43.21
brother, and he sought a p. to weep. 43.30
and bury me in their burying p." 47.30
he saw that a resting p. was good, 49.15
Hittite to possess as a burying p. 49.30
Therefore the p. was named Abelmizraim 50.11
Hittite, to possess as a burying p. 50.13
not, for am I in the p. of God? 50.19
for the p. on which you are standing Ex 3.05
to the p. of the Canaanites, the 3.08
At a lodging p. on the way the LORD 4.24
rise from his p. for three days; 10.23
LORD brought you out from this p.; 13.03
the p., O LORD, which thou hast made 15.17
remain every man of you in his p., 16.29
go out of his p. on the seventh 16.29
and p. it before the LORD, to be 16.33
the name of the p. Massah and 17.07
and p. such men over the people as 18.21
also will go to their p. in peace. 18.23
in every p. where I cause my name 20.24
for you a p. to which he may flee. 21.13
you to the p. which I have prepared. 23.20
you the holy p. from the most holy 26.33
the testimony in the most holy p. 26.34
when he goes into the holy p., 28.29
into the holy p. before the LORD, 28.35
altar to minister in the holy p.; 28.43
priest in his p. shall wear them 29.30
meeting to minister in the holy p. 29.30
and boil its flesh in a holy p.; 29.31
fragrant incense for the holy p. 31.11

PLACE (cont.)

people to the p. of which I have Ex 32.34
there is a p. by me where you shall 33.21
for ministering in the holy p., 35.19
for ministering in the holy p.; 39.01
for ministering in the holy p., 39.41
and p. the laver between the tent 40.07
And he put in p. the screen for the 40.28
the east side, in the p. for ashes; Lev 1.16
outside the camp to a clean p., 4.12
kill it in the p. where they kill 4.24
offering in the p. of burnt 4.29
offering in the p. where they kill 4.33
outside the camp to a clean p. 6.11
be eaten unleavened in a holy p.; 6.16
In the p. were the burnt offering 6.25
in a holy p. it shall be eaten, in 6.26
it was a sprinkled in a holy p. 6.27
to make atonement in the holy p.; 6.30
in the p. where they kill the burnt 7.02
it shall be eaten in a holy p.; 7.06
you shall eat it in a holy p., 10.13
you shall eat in any clean p., 10.14
offering in the p. of the sanctuary, 10.17
and in the p. of the boil there 13.19
remains in one p. and does not 13.23
remains in one p. and does not 13.28
the lamb in the p. where they kill 14.13
the burnt offering, in the holy p.; 14.13
in the p. where the blood of the 14.28
into an unclean p. outside the 14.40
into an unclean p. outside the 14.41
put them in the p. of hose stones, 14.42
out of the city to an unclean p. 14.45
into the holy p. within the veil, 16.02
shall Aaron come into the holy p.: 16.03
make atonement for the holy p., 16.16
in the holy p. until he comes out 16.17
for the holy p. and the tent of 16.20
on when he went into the holy p., 16.23
his body in water in a holy p., 16.24
to make atonement in the holy p., 16.27
in his father's p. shall make 16.32
and they shall eat it in a holy p., 24.09
and p. in her hands the cereal Num 5.18
and in the p. where the cloud 9.17
out for the p. of which the LORD 10.29
to seek out a resting p. for them. 10.33
name of that p. was called Taberah, 11.03
name of that p. was called Kibrothhattaavah, 11.34
That p. was called the Valley of 13.24
go up to the p. which the LORD has 14.40
In a most holy p. shall you eat of 18.10
and you may eat it in any p., 18.31
outside the camp in a clean p.; 19.09
Egypt, to bring us to this evil p.? 20.05
It is no p. for grain, or figs, or 20.05
the name of the p. was called 21.03
ahead, and stood in a narrow p., 22.26
to him, "Come with me to another p., 23.13
now, I will take you to another p.; 23.27
Therefore now flee to your p.; 24.11
said, "Enduring is your dwelling p., 24.21
rose, and went back to his p.; 24.25
in the holy p. you shall pour out a 28.07
the p. was a place for cattle. 32.01
the place was a p. for cattle. 32.01
we have brought them to their p.; 32.17
you went until you came to this p.' Deu 1.31
seek you out a p. to pitch your 1.33
Egypt, until you came to this p., 9.07
wilderness, until you came to this p.; 11.05
Every p. on which the sole of your 11.24
destroy their name out of that p. 12.03
shall seek the p. which the LORD 12.05
then to the p. which the LORD your 12.11
offerings at every p. that you see; 12.13
but at the p. which the LORD will 12.14
your God in the p. which the LORD 12.18
If the p. which the LORD your God 12.21
shall go to the p. which the LORD 12.26
in the p. which he will choose, to 14.23
because the p. is too far from you, 14.24
and go to the p. which the LORD 14.25
by year at the p. which the LORD 15.20
at the p. which the LORD will 16.02
but at the p. which the LORD your 16.06
eat it at the p. which the LORD 16.07
at the p. which the LORD your God 16.11
your God at the p. which the LORD 16.15
your God at the p. which he will 16.16
go up to the p. which the LORD 17.08
you from that p. which the LORD 17.10
to the p. which the LORD will 18.06
the gate of the p. where he lives, 21.19
"You shall have a p. outside the 23.12
in the p. which he shall choose 23.16
shall go to the p. which the LORD 26.02
us into this p. and gave us this 26.09
And when you came to this p., 29.07
your God at the p. which he will 31.11
The eternal God is your dwelling p., 33.27
man knows the p. of his burial to 34.06
Every p. that the sole of your foot Jos 1.03
God is providing you a p. of rest, 1.13
out from your p. and follow it, 3.03
from the very p. where the priests' 4.03
down in the p. where you lodge 4.03
them to the p. where they lodged, 4.08
in the p. where the feet of the 4.09
to their p. and overflowed all its 4.18
name of that p. is called Gilgal. 5.09
for the p. where you stand is holy. 5.15
name of that p. is called the 7.26
and they went to the p. of ambush, 8.09
rose quickly out of their p., 8.19
in the p. which he should choose. 9.27
into the city, and give him a p., 20.04
called the name of that p. Bochim; Ju 2.05
man in his p. round about the camp, 7.21
and that p. was called Ramathlehi. 15.17
open the hollow p. that is at Lehi, 15.19
surrounded the p. and lay in wait 16.02
to live where he could find a p.; 17.08
to sojourn where I may find a p." 17.09
What are you doing in this p.? 18.03
a p. where there is no lack of 18.10
account that p. is called Mahanehdan 18.12
the men of the p. were Benjaminites. 19.16
this that has taken p. among you? 20.12
in the same p. where they had 20.22
of Israel rose up out of their p., 20.33
out of their p. west of Geba. 20.33
set out from the p. where she was, Ru 1.07
down, observe the p. where he lives; 3.04
and from the gate of his native p.; 4.10
see, was lying down in his own p.; 1Sa 3.02
Samuel went and lay down in his p. 3.09
Dagon and put him back in his p. 5.03
and let it return to its own p., 5.11
what we shall send it to its p." 6.02
of the LORD and p. it on the cart, 6.08
a sacrifice today on the high p. 9.12
he goes up to the high p. to eat; 9.13
them on his way up to the high p. 9.14
go up before me to the high p., 9.19
and gave them a p. at the head of 9.22
from the high p. into the city, 9.25
down from the high p. with harp, 10.05
And a man of the p. answered, 10.12
prophesying, he came to the high p. 10.13
and made them dwell in this p. 12.08
then we will stand still in our p., 14.09
Philistines went to their own p. 14.46

PLACE (cont.)
in a secret p. and hide yourself; 1Sa 19.02
then go to the p. where you hid 20.19
side, but David's p. was empty. 20.25
the new moon, David's p. was empty. 20.27
lad came to the p. of the arrow 20.37
young men for such and such a p. 21.02
and see the p. where his haunt is, 23.22
therefore that p. was called the 23.28
and came to the p. where Saul had 26.05
David saw the p. where Saul lay, 26.05
way, and Saul returned to his p. 26.25
let a p. be given me in one of the 27.05
return to the p. to which you have 29.04
Therefore that p. was called 2Sa 2.16
who came to the p. where Asahel 2.23
name of that p. is called Baalperazim. 5.20
and that p. is called Perezuzzah, to 6.08
of the LORD, and set it in its p., 6.17
will appoint a p. for my people 7.10
they may dwell in their own p., 7.10
Uriah to the p. where he knew 11.16
in whose p. you have reigned; 16.08
of the pits, or in some other p. 17.09
him in some p. where he is to be 17.12
my army henceforth in p. of Joab. 19.13
should have no p. in all the 21.05
He brought me forth into a broad p.; 22.20
give a wide p. for my steps under 22.37
over the army in p. of Joab, 1Ki 2.35
the priest in the p. of Abiathar. 2.35
from there to any p. whatever. 2.36
go forth and go to any p. whatever, 2.42
for that was the great high p.; 3.04
servant king in p. of David my 3.07
brought to the p. where it was 4.28
him king in p. of his father; 5.01
set upon your throne in your p., 5.05
to go by sea to the p. you direct, 5.09
sanctuary, as the most holy p. 6.16
the most holy p., and for the doors 7.50
the covenant of the LORD to its p., 8.06
of the house, in the most holy p., 8.06
their wings over the p. of the ark, 8.07
from the holy p. before the inner 8.08
priests came out of the holy p., 8.10
a p. for thee to dwell in for ever. 8.13
risen in the p. of David my father, 8.20
I have provided a p. for the ark, 8.21
the p. of which thou hast said, 'My 8.29
thy servant offers toward this p. 8.29
when they pray toward this p.; 8.30
thou in heaven thy dwelling p.; 8.30
thee, if they pray toward this p., 8.35
thou in heaven thy dwelling p., 8.39
hear thou in heaven thy dwelling p., 8.43
thy dwelling p. their prayer and 8.49
built a high p. for Chemosh the 11.07
bread or drink water in this p.; 13.08
drink water with you in this p.; 13.16
water n the p. of which he said 13.22
anoint to be prophet in your p. 19.16
"In the p. where dogs licked up the 21.19
God, and wave his hand over the p., 2Ki 5.11
the p. where we dwell under your 6.01
let us make a p. for us to dwell 6.02
When he showed him the p., 6.06
such and such a p. shall be my 6.08
that you do not pass this p., 6.09
sent to the p. of which the man of 6.10
from the p. between his altar and 16.14
up against this place to destroy it?'" 18.25
evil upon this p. and upon its 22.16
will be kindled against this p., 22.17
heard how I spoke against this p., 22.19
which I will bring upon this p.'" 22.20
the high p. erected by Jeroboam the 23.15
with the high p. he pulled down 23.15
king in the p. of Josiah his 23.34
this day, and settled in their p., 1Ch 4.41
dwelt in their p. until the exile. 5.22
all the work of the most holy p., 6.49
and that p. is called Perezuzza 13.11
name of that p. is called Baalperazim. 14.11
he prepared a p. for the ark of 15.01
up the ark of the LORD to its p., 15.03
to the p. that I have prepared for 15.12
strength and joy are in his p. 16.27
in the high p. that was at Gibeon, 16.39
will appoint a p. for my people 17.09
they may dwell in their own p., 17.09
that time in the high p. at Gibeon; 21.29
to the high p. that was at Gibeon; 2Ch 1.03
Kiriathjearim to the p. that David 1.04
came from the high p. at Gibeon, 1.13
except as a p. to burn incense 2.06
at the p. that David had appointed, 3.01
And he made the most holy p.; 3.08
In the most holy p. he made two 3.10
the most holy p. and for the doors 4.22
the covenant of the LORD to its p., 5.07
of the house, in the most holy p., 5.07
their wings over the p. of the ark, 5.08
from the holy p. before the inner 5.09
out of the holy p. (for all the 5.11
a p. for thee to dwell in for ever. 6.02
risen in the p. of David my father, 6.10
the p. where thou hast promised to 6.20
thy servant offers toward this p. 6.20
when they pray toward this p.; 6.21
thou from heaven thy dwelling p.; 6.21
thee, if they pray toward this p., 6.26
thou from heaven thy dwelling p., 6.30
hear thou from heaven thy dwelling p., 6.33
thy dwelling p. their prayer and 6.39
attentive to a prayer of this p. 6.40
LORD God, and go to thy resting p., 6.41
chosen this p. for myself as a 7.12
the prayer that is made in this p. 7.15
name of that p. has been called 20.26
take it and return it to its p. 24.11
out the filth from the holy p. 29.05
in the holy p. to the God of 29.07
evil upon this p. and upon its 34.24
out upon this p. and will not be 34.25
against this p. and its inhabitants, 34.27
bring upon this p. and its inhabitants.'" 34.28
stood in his p. and made a covenant 34.31
in the holy p. according to the 35.05
for, the priests stood in their p., 35.10
were in their p. according to the 35.15
his people and on his dwelling p.; 36.15
in whatever p. he sojourns, be Ez 1.04
the men of his p. with silver and 1.04
They set the altar in its p., 3.03
the p. where sacrifices are offered 6.03
is in Jerusalem, each to its p.; 6.05
the leading man at the p. Casiphia, 8.17
temple servants at the p. Casiphia, 8.17
a secure hold within his holy p., 9.08
them to the p. which I have chosen, Neh 1.09
the p. of my fathers' sepulchres, 2.03
there was no p. for the beast that 2.14
In the p. where you hear the sound 4.20
up in their p. and read from the 9.03
While this was taking p. I was not 13.06
maids to the best p. in the harem. Est 2.09
garden to the p. where they were 7.08
they came each from his own p., Job 2.11
is hot, they vanish from their p. 6.17
nor does his p. know him any more. 7.10
If he is destroyed from his p., 8.18
who shakes the earth out of its p., 9.06
the rock is removed from its p.; 14.18

PLACE (cont.)

as you do, if you were in my p.; Job 16.04
and let my cry find no resting p. 16.18
the rock be removed out of its p.? 18.04
such is the p. of him who knows not 18.21
nor will his p. any more behold him. 20.09
it sweeps him out of his p. 27.21
him, and hisses at him from its p. 27.23
and a p. for gold which they refine. 28.01
Its stones are the p. of sapphires, 28.06
where is the p. of understanding? 28.12
where is the p. of understanding? 28.20
the way to it, and he knows its p. 28.23
and sets others in their p. 34.24
into a broad p. where there was no 36.16
peoples are cut off in their p. 36.20
trembles, and leaps out of its p. 37.01
caused the dawn to know its p., 38.12
and where is the p. of darkness, 38.19
the way to the p. where the light 38.24
the salt land for his dwelling p.? 39.06
"I will p. him in the safety for Ps 12.05
He brought me forth into a broad p.; 18.19
give a wide p. for my steps under 18.36
And who shall stand in his holy p.? 24.03
and the p. where thy glory dwells. 26.08
hast set my feet in a broad p. 31.08
Thou art a hiding p. for me, 32.07
though you look well at his p., 37.10
broken us in the p. of jackals, 44.19
do not depart from its market p. 55.11
brought us forth to a spacious p. 66.12
came from Sinai into the holy p. 68.17
roared in the midst of thy holy p.; 74.04
the dwelling p. of thy name. 74.07
in Salem, his dwelling p. in Zion. 76.02
you in the secret p. of thunder; 81.07
God has taken his p. in the divine 82.10
How lovely is thy dwelling p., 84.01
Baca they make it a p. of springs; 84.06
our dwelling p. in all generations. 90.01
and its p. knows it no more. 103.16
down to the p. which thou didst 104.08
until I find a p. for the LORD, a 132.05
a dwelling p. for the Mighty One of 132.05
"Let us go to his dwelling p.; 132.07
Arise, O LORD, and go to thy resting p., 132.08
"This is my resting p. for ever; 132.14
Lift up your hands to the holy p., 134.02
She will p. on your head a fair Pro 4.09
The eyes of the LORD are in every p., 15.03
or stand in the p. of the great; 25.06
hastens to the p. where it rises. Ecc 1.05
to the p. where the streams flow, 1.07
the sun that in the p. of justice, 3.16
and in the p. of righteousness, even 3.16
All go to one p.; all are from the 3.20
youth, who was to stand in his p.; 4.15
no good—do not all go to the one p.? 6.06
to go in and out of the holy p., 8.10
a vanity which takes p. on earth, 8.14
against you, do not leave your p., 10.04
and the rich sit in a low p. 10.06
in the p. where the tree falls, 11.03
The LORD has taken his p. to contend, Is 3.13
In that day every p. where there 7.23
will become a p. where cattle are 7.25
but we will put cedars in their p. 9.10
earth will be shaken out of its p., 13.13
them and bring them to their p., 14.02
wearies himself upon the high p., 16.12
the p. of the name of the LORD of 18.07
And I will p. on his shoulder the 22.22
fasten him like a peg in a sure p., 22.23
fastened in a sure p. will give way; 22.25
like heat in a dry p. Thou dost 25.05
shall be trodden down in his p., 25.10
out of his p. to punish the 26.21
no p. is without filthiness. 28.08
rows and barley in its proper p., 28.25
and to p. on the jaws of the 30.28
For a burning p. has long been 30.33
like streams of water in a dry p., 32.02
his p. of defense will be the 33.16
be for us a p. of broad rivers and 44.12
hold the mast firm in its p., 33.23
and find for herself a resting p. 34.14
carry it, they set it in its p., 46.07
it cannot move from its p. 46.07
'The p. is too narrow for me; 49.20
Enlarge the p. of your tent, and let 54.02
"I dwell in the high and holy p., 57.15
to beautify the p. of my sanctuary; 60.13
I will make the p. of my feet 60.13
of Achor a p. for herds to lie 65.10
me, and what is the p. of my rest? 66.01
forth from his p. to make your Jer 4.07
they shall pasture, each in his p. 6.03
I will let you dwell in this p., 7.03
or shed innocent blood in this p., 7.06
then I will let you dwell in this p., 7.07
Go now to my p. that was in Shiloh, 7.12
and to the p. which I gave to you 7.14
will be poured out on this p., 7.20
have built the high p. of Topheth, 7.31
the desert a wayfarers' lodging p., 9.02
from the p. where I had hidden it. 13.07
give you assured peace in this p.'" 14.13
have sons or daughters in this p. 16.02
daughters who are born in this p., 16.03
I will make to cease from this p., 16.09
beginning is the p. of our sanctuary. 17.12
evil upon this p. that the ears of 19.03
profaned this p. by burning 19.04
filled this p. with the blood of 19.04
when this p. shall no more be 19.06
And in this p. I will make void the 19.07
there will be no p. else to bury. 19.11
Thus will I do to this p., says 19.12
be defiled like the p. of Topheth. 19.13
nor shed innocent blood in this p. 22.03
and who went away from this p.: 22.11
but in the p. where they have 22.12
away from this p. to the land of 24.05
into the burial p. of the common 26.23
back and restore them to this p. 27.22
back to this p. all the vessels of 28.03
away from this p. and carried to 28.03
back to this p. Jeconiah the son 28.04
back to this p. from Babylon the 28.06
will make in their p. bars of iron. 28.13
and bring you back to this p. 29.10
you back to the p. from which I 29.14
I will bring them back to this p., 32.37
In this p. of which you say, 'It is 33.10
In this p. which is waste, without 33.12
pronounced this evil against this p.; 40.02
You shall see this p. no more. 42.18
pestilence in the p. where you 42.22
that I will punish you in this p., 44.29
in the high p. and burns incense 48.35
concerning this p. that thou wilt 51.62
nations, but finds no resting p.; Lam 1.03
in ruins the p. of his appointed 2.06
of the LORD arose from its p., Eze 3.12
and p. it as an iron wall between 4.03
they may profane my precious p.; 7.22
exile from your p. to another p. 12.03
yourself a lofty p. in every square; 16.24
your lofty p. and prostituted your 16.25
your lofty p. in every square. 16.31
surely in the p. where the king 17.16
is the high p. to which you go? 20.29
In the p. where you were created, in 21.30

PLACE (cont.)

of the sea a p. for the spreading Eze 26.05
you shall be a p. for the spreading 26.14
or have a p. in the land of the 26.20
flow round the p. of its planting, 31.04
and I will p. you in your own land; 37.14
My dwelling p. shall be with them; 37.27
and come from your p. out of the 38.15
give to Gog a p. for burial in 39.11
to me, This is the most holy p. 41.04
of the holy p. was something 41.21
and the holy p. had each a double 41.23
guilt offering, for the p. is holy. 42.13
When the priests enter the holy p., 42.14
the p. of my throne and the p. of 43.07
the appointed p. belonging to the 43.21
day that he goes into the holy p., 44.27
court, to minister in the holy p.; 44.27
be the sanctuary, the most holy p. 45.03
a p. for their houses and a holy p. 45.04
there I saw a p. at the extreme 46.19
"This is the p. where the priests 46.20
it will be a p. for the spreading 47.10
a most holy p., adjoining the 48.12
and the p. of his sanctuary was Dan 8.11
in p. of which four others arose, 8.22
and to anoint a most holy p. 9.24
her roots shall arise in his p.; 11.07
arise in his p. one who shall send 11.20
In his p. shall arise a contemptible 11.21
your allotted p. at the end of the 12.13
and in the p. where it was said to Hos 1.10
I will return again to my p., 5.15
up from the p. to which you have Joe 3.07
"Behold, I will press you down in your p., Amo 2.13
in every p. they shall be cast out 8.03
LORD is coming forth out of his p., Mic 1.03
like waters poured down a steep p. 1.04
a p. for planting vineyards; 1.06
take away from you its standing p. 1.11
Arise and go, for this is no p. to rest; 2.10
off from this p. the remnant of Zep 1.04
each in its p., all the lands of 2.11
and in this p. I will give prosperity, Hag 2.09
for he shall grow up in his p., Zec 6.12
inhabited in its p., in Jerusalem. 12.06
Benjamin to the p. of the former 14.10
and in every p. incense is offered Mal 1.11
Jesus Christ took p. in this way, Mt 1.18
All this took p. to fulfil what the 1.22
rest over the p. where the child 2.09
over Judea in p. of his father 2.22
in a boat to a lonely p. apart. 14.13
him and said, "This is a lonely p., 14.15
the men of that p. recognized him, 14.35
mountain, 'Move hence to yonder p.,' 17.20
servants saw what had taken p., 18.31
their lord all that had taken p. 18.31
standing idle in the market p.; 20.03
This took p. to fulfil what was 21.04
and they love the p. of honor at 23.06
for this must take p., but the end 24.06
in the holy p. (let the reader 24.15
away till all these things take p. 24.34
and he will p. the sheep at his 25.33
with them to a p. called Gethsemane, 26.36
"Put your sword back into its p.; 26.52
But all this has taken p., 26.56
they came to a p. called Golgotha 27.33
(which means the p. of a skull), 27.33
the earthquakea nd what took p., 27.54
Come, see the p. where he lay. 28.06
priests all that had taken p. 28.11
rose and went out to a lonely p., Mk 1.35
stay there until you leave the p. 6.10
And if any p. will not receive you 6.11
away by yourselves to a lonely p., 6.31
boat to a lonely p. by themselves. 6.32
him and said, "This is a lonely p., 6.35
pallets to any p. where they heard 6.55
and when they come from the market p., 7.04
this must take p., but the end 13.07
you see these things taking p., 13.29
before all these things take p. 13.30
And they went to a p. which was 14.32
him to the p. called Golgotha 15.22
(which means the p. of a skull). 15.22
see the p. where they laid him. 16.06
there was no p. for them in the Lk 2.07
and found the p. where it was 4.17
out into every p. in the surrounding 4.37
departed and went into a lonely p. 4.42
with them and stood on a level p., 6.17
in the market p. and calling to 7.32
for we are here in a lonely p." 9.12
every town and p. where he himself 10.01
when he came to the p. and saw him, 10.32
He was praying in a certain p., 11.01
do not sit down in a p. of honor, 14.08
'Give p. to this man,' and then you 14.09
with shame to take the lowest p. 14.09
go and sit in the lowest p., 14.10
also come into this p. of torment. 16.28
And when Jesus came to the p., 19.05
sign when this is about to take p.?" 21.07
for this must first take p., 21.09
when these things begin to take p., 21.28
you see these things taking p., 21.31
pass away till all has taken p. 21.32
all these things that will take p., 21.36
he came to the p. he said to them, 22.40
from Galilee even to this p. 23.05
came to the p. which is called The 23.33
centurion saw what had taken p., 23.47
when they saw what had taken p., 23.48
This took p. in Bethany beyond the Jn 1.28
Jerusalem is the p. where men ought 4.02
as there was a crowd in the p. 5.13
Now there was much grass in the p.; 6.10
came near the p. where they ate 6.23
because my word finds no p. in you. 8.37
Jordan to the p. where John at 10.40
days longer in the p. where he was. 11.06
still in the p. where Martha had 11.30
both our holy p. and our nation. 11.48
his garments, and resumed his p., 13.12
you this now, before it takes p., 13.19
it does take p. you may believe 13.19
that I go to prepare a p. for you? 14.02
when I go and prepare a p. for you, 14.03
I have told you before it takes p., 14.29
so that when it does take p., 14.29
who betrayed him, also knew the p.; 18.02
seat at a p. called The Pavement, 19.13
to the p. called the p. of a skull, 19.17
for the p. where Jesus was crucified 19.20
things took p. that the scripture 19.36
Now in the p. where he was crucified 19.41
but rolled up in a p. by itself. 20.07
and p. my finger in the mark of the 20.25
and p. my hand in his side, I will 20.25
your hand, and p. it in my side; 20.27
to take the p. in this ministry and Ac 1.25
turned aside, to go to his own p. 1.25
they were all together in one p. 2.01
plan had predestined to take p. 4.28
the p. in which they were gathered 4.31
against this holy p. and the law; 6.13
of Nazareth will destroy this p., 6.14
come out and worship me in this p. 7.07
for the p. where you are standing 7.33
Lord, or what is the p. of my rest? 7.49
and this took p. in the days of 11.28
he departed and went to another p. 12.17

PLACE (cont.)

supposed there was a p. of prayer; Ac 16.13
As we were going to the p. of prayer, 16.16
into the market p. before the 16.19
in the market p. every day with 17.17
and went from p. to p. through the 18.23
the people and the law and this p.; 21.28
and he has defiled this holy p. 21.28
of sins and a p. among those who 26.18
we came to a p. called Fair Havens, 27.08
neighborhood of that p. were lands 28.07
And when this had taken p., 28.09
"And in the very p. where it was Rom 9.26
in their p. to share the richness 11.17
who in every p. call on the name 1Co 1.02
in the first p., when you assemble 11.18
one new man in p. of the two, Eph 2.15
for a dwelling p. of God in the 2.22
everything that has taken p. here. Col 4.09
that in every p. the men should 1Ti 2.08
And again in this p. he said, Heb 4.05
as he says also in another p., 5.06
it is called the Holy P. 9.02
once for all into the Holy P., 9.12
enters the Holy P. yearly with 9.25
to go out to a p. which he was to 11.08
as to a lamp shining in a dark p., 2Pe 1.19
servants what must soon take p.; Rev 1.01
and what is to take p. hereafter. 1.19
remove your lampstand from its p., 2.05
you what must take p. after this. 4.01
and island was removed from its p. 6.14
where she has a p. prepared by God, 12.06
no longer any p. for them in 12.08
to the p. where she is to be 12.14
them at the p. which is called in 16.16
has become a dwelling p. of demons, 18.02
and no p. was found for them. 20.11
servants what must soon take p. 22.06

PLACED

garden of Eden he p. the cherubim, Gen 3.24
and p. the cup in Pharaoh's hand. 40.11
and he p. the cup in Pharaoh's hand; 40.21
child in it and p. it among the Ex 2.03
so Aaron p. it before the Testimony, 16.34
And he p. the breastpiece on him, Lev 8.08
and p. them on the fat and on the 8.26
and p. them round about the tent. Num 11.24
and it was p. on David's head. 2Sa 12.30
and p. me on the throne of David my 1Ki 2.24
and he p. in Bethel the priests of 12.32
and p. them in Halah, and on the 2Ki 17.06
and p. them in the cities of 17.24
away and p. in the cities of 17.26
and it was p. on David's head. 1Ch 20.02
and p. them in the temple, five on 2Ch 4.08
He p. forces in all the fortified 17.02
the king and p. in the fortified 17.19
Jerusalem and p. in the house of Ez 1.07
old, since man was p. upon earth, Job 20.04
I p. the sand as the bound for the Jer 5.22
baskets of figs p. before the 24.01
cords will be p. upon you, and you Eze 3.25
he p. it beside abundant waters. 17.05
which you had p. my incense and my 23.41
anointed guardian cherub I p. you; 28.14
they are p. among the slain. 32.25
and p. the vessels in the treasury Dan 1.02
thrones were p. and one that was 7.09
a stone was p. upon a stone in the Hag 2.15
to let them be p. in a tomb, Rev 11.09

PLACES

families and their dwelling p., Gen 36.40
their dwelling p. in the land of 36.43
generations, in all your dwelling p., Lev 3.17
And I will destroy your high p., 26.30
cities in the p. where they dwelt, Num 31.10
Moses wrote down their starting p., 33.02
according to their starting p. 33.02
and demolish all their high p., 33.52
destroy all the p. where the Deu 12.02
ride on the high p. of the earth, 32.13
you shall tread upon their high p. 33.29
in their p. in the camp till they Jos 5.08
of musicians at the watering p., Ju 5.11
us draw near to one of these p., 19.13
you, in one of the priest's p., 1Sa 2.36
he judged Israel in all these p. 7.16
all the lurking p. where he hides, 23.23
for all the p. where David and his 30.31
Israel, is slain upon thy high p.! 2Sa 1.19
lies slain upon thy high p. 1.25
In all p. where I have moved with 7.07
were sacrificing at the high p., 1Ki 3.02
and burnt incense at the high p. 3.03
He also made houses on high p., 12.31
of the high p. that he had made. 12.32
of the high p. who burn incense 13.02
of the high p. which are in the 13.32
for the high p. again from among 13.33
to be priests of the high p. 13.33
also built for themselves high p., 14.23
But the high p. were not taken away. 15.14
and put commanders in their p.; 20.24
yet the high p. were not taken away, 22.43
and burned incense on the high p. 22.43
Nevertheless the high p. were not 2Ki 12.03
and burn incense on the high p. 12.03
But the high p. were not removed; 14.04
and burned incense on the high p. 14.04
Nevertheless the high p. were not 15.04
and burned incense on the high p., 15.35
and burned incense on the high p., 16.04
themselves high p. at all their 17.09
burned incense on all the high p., 17.11
of the high p. which the Samaritans 17.29
people as priests of the high p., 17.32
them in the shrines of the high p. 17.32
He removed the high p., 18.04
he whose high p. and altars 18.22
the high p. which Hezekiah his 21.03
in the high p. at the cities of 23.05
the high p. where the priests had 23.08
down the high p. of the gates that 23.08
of the high p. did not come up to 23.09
the high p. that were east of 23.13
filled their p. with the bones of 23.14
of the high p. that were in the 23.19
of the high p. who were there, 23.20
their dwelling p. according to 1Ch 6.54
In all p. where I have moved with 17.06
for the p. to which the ark of the 2Ch 8.11
to him from all p. where they 11.13
his own priests for the high p., 11.15
the foreign altars and the high p., 14.03
Judah the high p. and the incense 14.05
But the high p. were not taken out 15.17
took the high p. and the Asherim 17.06
The high p., however, were not taken 20.33
Moreover he made high p. in the 21.11
and burned incense on the high p., 28.04
he made high p. to burn incense to 28.25
down the high p. and the altars 31.01
away his high p. and his altars 32.12
the high p. which his father 33.03
still sacrificed at the high p., 33.17
he built high p. and set up the 33.19
Judah and Jerusalem of the high p., 34.03
"From all the p. where they live Neh 4.12
in open p., I stationed the people 4.13
the people remained in their p. 8.07
sought the Levites in all their p., 12.27

PLACES (cont.)
in hiding p. he murders the innocent Ps 10.08
have fallen for me in pleasant p.; 16.06
their dwelling p. to all generations, 49.11
Truly thou dost set them in slippery p.; 73.18
all the meeting p. of God in the 74.08
for the dark p. of the land are 74.20
him to anger with their high p.; 78.58
than all the dwelling p. of Jacob. 87.02
like an owl of the waste p.; 102.06
in all p. of his dominion. 103.22
from the highest p. in the town, Pro 9.03
a seat on the high p. of the town, 9.14
folly is set in many high p., Ecc 10.06
the forsaken p. are many in the Is 6.12
has gone up to the high p. to weep; 15.02
the deserted p. of the Hivites and 17.09
There will be bare p. by the Nile, 19.07
dwellings, and in quiet resting p. 32.18
he whose high p. and altars 36.07
level, and the rough p. a plain. 40.04
the rough p. into level ground. 42.16
and the hoards in secret p., 45.03
your desolate p. and your devastated 49.19
he will comfort all her waste p., 51.03
singing, you waste p. of Jerusalem; 52.09
our pleasant p. have become ruins. 64.11
and spend the night in secret p.; 65.04
in all the p. where I have driven Jer 8.03
in the parched p. of the wilderness, 17.06
Judah and the p. round about 17.26
built the high p. of Baal to burn 19.05
in secret p. so that I cannot see 23.24
in all the p. where I shall drive 24.09
and all the p. where I have driven 29.14
They built the high p. of Baal in 32.35
in the p. about Jerusalem, and in 32.44
the p. about Jerusalem, and in the 33.13
from all the p. to which they had 40.12
of war in all p. to which you may 45.05
I have uncovered his hiding p., 49.10
into the holy p. of the LORD's 51.51
and I will destroy your high p. Eze 6.03
be waste and your high p. ruined, 6.06
and their holy p. shall be profaned. 7.24
and break down your lofty p.; 16.39
of these waste p. in the land of 33.24
in the waste p. shall fall by the 33.27
them from all p. where they have 34.12
the inhabited p. of the country. 34.13
them and the p. round about my 34.26
inhabited and the waste p. rebuilt; 36.10
and the waste p. shall be rebuilt. 36.33
LORD, have rebuilt the ruined p., 36.36
the waste p. which are now inhabited, 38.12
The high p. of Aven, the sin of Hos 10.08
and lack of bread in all your p., Amo 4.06
the high p. of Isaac shall be made 7.09
upon the high p. of the earth. Mic 1.03
he makes me tread upon my high p. Hab 3.19
in the market p. and calling to Mt 11.16
through waterless p. seeking rest, 12.43
and salutations in the market p., 23.07
and earthquakes in various p.: 24.07
laid the sick in the market p., Mk 6.56
have salutations in the market p. 12.38
synagogues and the p. of honor at 12.39
will be earthquakes in various p., 13.08
through waterless p. seeking rest; Lk 11.24
and salutations in the market p. 11.43
how they chose the p. of honor, 14.07
in the market p. and the best 20.46
synagogues and the p. of honor at 20.46
and in various p. famines and 21.11
of the Jews that were in those p., Ac 16.03
blessing in the heavenly p., Eph 1.03
his right hand in the heavenly p., 1.20
in the heavenly p. in Christ Jesus, 2.06
and powers in the heavenly p. 3.10
of wickedness in the heavenly p. 6.12

PLACING
caught in adultery, and p. her in the *Jn 8.03

PLAGUE
I will p. all your country with Ex 8.02
a very severe p. upon your cattle 9.03
"Yet one p. more I will bring upon 11.01
and no p. shall fall upon you to 12.13
there be no p. among them when you 30.12
And the LORD sent a p. upon the 32.35
there may be no p. among the Num 8.19
the people with a very great p. 11.33
land, died by p. before the LORD. 14.37
from the LORD, the p. has begun. 16.46
the p. had already begun among the 16.47
the living; and the p. was stopped. 16.48
who died by the p. were fourteen 16.49
meeting, when the p. was stopped. 16.50
Thus the p. was stayed from the 25.08
died by the p. were twenty-four 25.09
the day of the p. on account of 25.18
After the p. the LORD said to Moses 26.01
and so the p. came among the 31.16
there came a p. upon the congregation Jos 22.17
every sort of p. in the wilderness. 1Sa 4.08
for the same p. was upon all of you 6.04
that the p. may be averted from the 2Sa 24.21
and the p. was averted from Israel. 24.25
whatever p., whatever sickness 1Ki 8.37
but let not the p. be upon thy 1Ch 21.17
that the p. may be averted from the 21.22
whatever p., whatever sickness 2Ch 6.28
bring a great p. on your people, 21.14
companions stand aloof from my p., Ps 38.11
gave their lives over to the p. 78.50
and a p. broke out among them. 106.29
interposed, and the p. was stayed. 106.30
and p. followed close behind. Hab 3.05
shall be the p. with which the Zec 14.12
And a p. like this plague shall 14.15
like this p. shall fall on the 14.15
shall come the p. with which the 14.18
to smite the earth with every p., Rev 11.06
cursed God for the p. of the hail, 16.21
the hail, so fearful was that p. 16.21

PLAGUED
and I p. Egypt with what I did in Jos 24.05

PLAGUES
with great p. because of Sarai, Gen 12.17
send all my p. upon your heart, and Ex 9.14
me, I will bring more p. upon you, Lev 26.21
O Death, where are your p.? O Sheol, Hos 13.14
of diseases and p. and evil spirits, Lk 7.21
By these three p. a third of mankind Rev 9.18
who were not killed by these p., 9.20
wonderful, seven angels with seven p., 15.01
the seven angels with the seven p., 15.06
until the seven p. of the seven 15.08
of God who had power over these p., 16.09
her sins, lest you share in her p.; 18.04
so shall her p. come in a single 18.08
bowls full of the seven last p., 21.09
add to him the p. described in 22.18

PLAIN
they found a p. in the land of Gen 11.02
not been made p. what should be Num 15.34
and the P., that is, the valley of Deu 34.03
dwell in the p. have chariots of Jos 17.16
out the inhabitants of the p., Ju 1.19
allow them to come down to the p.; 1.34
Ahimaaz ran by the way of the p., 2Sa 18.23

PLAIN (cont.)
In the p. of the Jordan the king 1Ki 7.46
us fight against them in the p., 20.23
will fight against them in the p., 20.25
In the p. of the Jordan the king 2Ch 4.17
in the Shephelah and in the p., 26.10
joined battle in the p. of Megiddo. 35.22
the men of the P., repaired. Neh 3.22
of the villages in the p. of Ono. 6.02
level, and the rough places a p. Is 40.04
O rock of the p., says the LORD; Jer 21.13
and the p. shall be destroyed, as 48.08
to me, "Arise, go forth into the p., Eze 3.22
I arose and went forth into the p.; 3.23
the vision that I saw in the p. 8.04
He set it up on the p. of Dura, Dan 3.01
make it p. upon tablets, so he may Hab 2.02
Zerubbabel you shall become a p.; Zec 4.07
Hadadrimmon in the p. of Megiddo. 12.11
turned into a p. from Geba to 14.10
be known about God is p. to them, Rom 1.19
it is p. that he is excepted who 1Co 15.27
have made this p. to you in all 2Co 11.06
Now the works of the flesh are p.: Gal 5.19
for their folly will be p. to all, 2Ti 3.09
it might be p. that they all are 1Jn 2.19

PLAINLY
"We see p. that the LORD is with Gen 26.28
But if the slave p. says, Ex 21.05
all the words of this law very p. Deu 27.08
"He told us p. that the asses had 1Sa 10.16
to us has been p. read before me. Ez 4.18
was released, and he spoke p. Mk 7.35
And he said this p. And Peter 8.32
If you are the Christ, tell us p." Jn 10.24
Then Jesus told them p., "Lazarus 11.14
but tell you p. of the Father. 16.25
said, "Ah, now you are speaking p., 16.29

PLAINS
encamped in the p. of Moab beyond Num 22.01
them in the p. of Moab by the 26.03
Israel in the p. of Moab by the 26.63
the camp on the p. of Moab by the 31.12
encamped in the p. of Moab by the 33.48
as Abelshittim in the p. of Moab. 33.49
to Moses in the p. of Moab by the 33.50
to Moses in the p. of Moab by the 35.01
Israel in the p. of Moab by the 36.13
up from the p. of Moab to Mount Deu 34.01
Moses in the p. of Moab thirty 34.08
for battle, to the p. of Jericho. Jos 4.13
at evening in the p. of Jericho. 5.10
distributed in the p. of Moab, 13.32
overtook him in the p. of Jericho; 2Ki 25.05
Zedekiah in the p. of Jericho; Jer 39.05
Zedekiah in the p. of Jericho; 52.08

PLAITED
And the soldiers p. a crown of thorns, Jn 19.02

PLAITING
and p. a crown of thorns they put Mt 27.29
and p. a crown of thorns they put Mk 15.17

PLAN
according to the p. for it which Ex 26.30
understands every p. and thought. 1Ch 28.09
his son the p. of the vestibule of 28.11
and the p. of all that he had in 28.12
also his p. for the golden 28.18
to be done according to the p. 28.19
and the p. seemed right to the king 2Ch 30.04
that God had frustrated their p. Neh 4.15
If they p. evil against you, if they Ps 21.11
They only p. to thrust him down 62.04
who p. evil things in their heart, 140.02
Do not p. evil against your neighbor Pro 3.29
but those who p. good have joy. 12.20
"who carry out a p., but not mine; Is 30.01
you and devising a p. against you. Jer 18.11
hear the p. which the LORD has 49.20
Babylon has made a p. against you, 49.30
Therefore hear the p. which the 50.45
temple and its appearance and p., Eze 43.10
they do not understand his p., Mic 4.12
to the definite p. and foreknowledge Ac 2.23
hand and thy p. had predestined to 4.28
for if this p. or this undertaking 5.38
The soldiers' p. was to kill the 27.42
as a p. for the fulness of time, to Eph 1.10
see what is the p. of the mystery 3.09

PLANE
rods of poplar and almond and p., Gen 30.37
the p. and the pine together; Is 41.19
the p., and the pine, to beautify 60.13
the p. trees were as nothing Eze 31.08

PLANES
he fashions it with p., and marks Is 44.13

PLANKS
the house of beams and p. of cedar. 1Ki 6.09
They made all your p. of fir trees Eze 27.05
and the rest on p. or on pieces of Ac 27.44

PLANNED
then have you p. such a thing 2Sa 14.13
consumed us and p. to destroy us, 21.05
I p. from days of old what now I 2Ki 19.25
Solomon had p. to do in the house 2Ch 7.11
he p. with his officers and his 32.02
who have p. to trip up my feet. Ps 140.04
"As I have p., so shall it be, and Is 14.24
regard for him who p. it long ago. 22.11
I p. from days of old what now I 37.26
In Heshbon they p. evil against her: Jer 48.02
LORD has both p. and done what he 51.12
and the king p. to set him over the Dan 6.03
chief priests p. to put Lazarus Jn 12.10
on which they p. if possible to Ac 27.39

PLANNING
comforts himself by p. to kill you. Gen 27.42
p. an ambush to kill him on the way Ac 25.03

PLANS
my p. are broken off, the desires of Job 17.11
You would confound the p. of the poor, Ps 14.06
desire, and fulfil all your p.! 20.04
frustrates the p. of the peoples. 33.10
Destroy their p., O Lord, confuse 55.09
They lay crafty p. against thy 83.03
on that very day his p. perish. 146.04
a heart that devises wicked p., Pro 6.18
Without counsel p. go wrong, 15.22
The p. of the mind belong to man, 16.01
and your p. will be established. 16.03
A man's mind p. his way, but the LORD 16.09
winks his eyes p. perverse things, 16.03
Many are the p. in the mind of a 19.21
P. are established by counsel; 21.05
The p. of the diligent lead surely 21.05
He who p. to do evil will be called 24.08
out, and I will confound their p.; Is 19.03
p. formed of old, faithful and sure. 25.01
in his heart he p. an ambush for Jer 9.08
We will follow our own p., and 18.12
make void the p. of Judah and 19.07
For I know the p. I have for you, 29.11
p. for welfare and not for evil, to 29.11
He shall devise p. against strongholds, Dan 11.24
Do I make my p. like a worldly man, 2Co 1.17

PLANT
given you every p. yielding seed Gen 1.29
have given every green p. for food. 1.30
when no p. of the field was yet in 2.05
beast and every p. of the field, Ex 9.22
struck down every p. of the field, 9.25
and eat every p. in the land, all 10.12
neither tree nor p. of the field, 10.15
and p. them on thy own mountain, the 15.17
the land and p. all kinds of trees Lev 19.23
olive trees, which you did not p., Deu 6.11
"You shall not p. any tree as an 16.21
you shall p. a vineyard, and you 28.30
You shall p. vineyards and dress 28.39
oliveyards which you did not p. Jos 24.13
and will p. them, that they may 2Sa 7.10
and p. vineyards, and eat their 2Ki 19.29
and will p. them, that they may 1Ch 17.09
they wither before any other p. Job 8.12
put forth branches like a young p. 14.09
nations, but them thou didst p.; Ps 44.02
drive out the nations and p. it. 80.08
and p. vineyards, and get a fruitful 107.37
a time to p., and a time to pluck Ecc 3.02
though you p. pleasant plants and Is 17.10
grow on the day that you p. them, 17.11
and p. vineyards, and eat their 37.30
grew up before him like a young p., 53.02
they shall p. vineyards and eat 65.21
they shall not p. and another eat; 65.22
to overthrow, to build and to p. Jer 1.10
that I will build and p. it, 18.09
I will p. them, and not uproot them. 24.06
p. gardens and eat their produce. 29.05
and p. gardens and eat their 29.28
Again you shall p. vineyards upon 31.05
the planters shall p., and shall 31.05
to build and to p., says the LORD. 31.28
and I will p. them in this land in 32.41
you shall not p. or have a vineyard; 35.07
I will p. you, and not pluck you up; 42.10
and p. battering rams against it Eze 4.02
and grow up like a p. of the field. 16.07
I myself will p. it upon a high 17.22
height of Israel will I p. it, 17.23
build houses and p. vineyards. 28.26
Though he may flourish as the reed p., Hos 13.15
they shall p. vineyards and drink Amo 9.14
I will p. them upon their land, and 9.15
And the LORD God appointed a p., Jon 4.06
exceedingly glad because of the p. 4.06
a worm which attacked the p., 4.07
you do well to be angry for the p.?" 4.09
"You pity the p., for which you did 4.10
though they p. vineyards, they shall Zep 1.13
"Every p. which my heavenly Father Mt 15.13

PLANTATIONS
them prosperous p. so that they shall Eze 34.29

PLANTED
And the LORD God p. a garden in Gen 2.08
tiller of the soil. He p. a vineyard; 9.20
Abraham p. a tamarisk tree in 21.33
like aloes that the LORD has p., Num 24.06
there that has p. a vineyard and Deu 20.06
He is like a tree p. by streams of Ps 1.03
the stock which thy right hand p. 80.15
They are p. in the house of the 92.13
He who p. the ear, does he not hear 94.09
the cedars of Lebanon which he p. 104.16
houses and p. vineyards for myself; Ecc 2.04
and p. in them all kinds of fruit 2.05
and a time to pluck up what is p.; 3.02
of stones, and p. it with choice vines; Is 5.02
Scarcely are they p., scarcely sown, 40.24
Yet I p. you a choice vine, wholly Jer 2.21
who p. you, has pronounced evil 11.17
He is like a tree p. by water, 17.08
and what I have p. I am plucking 45.04
of the land p. it in fertile Eze 17.05
From the bed where it was p. 17.07
you have p. pleasant vineyards, but Amo 5.11
Father has not p. will be rooted Mt 15.13
a householder who p. a vineyard, 21.33
"A man p. a vineyard, and set a Mk 12.01
had a fig tree p. in his vineyard; Lk 13.06
and be p. in the sea,' and it would 17.06
they sold, they p., they built, 17.28
"A man p. a vineyard, and let it out 20.09
I p., Apollos watered, but God gave 1Co 3.06

PLANTERS
the p. shall plant, and shall enjoy Jer 31.05

PLANTEST
Thou p. them, and they take root; Jer 12.02

PLANTING
men of Judah are his pleasant p.; Is 5.07
land for ever, the shoot of my p., 60.21
the p. of the LORD, that he may be 61.03
flow round the place of its p., Eze 31.04
country, a place for p. vineyards; Mic 1.06

PLANTS
p. yielding seed, and fruit trees Gen 1.11
p. yielding seed according to their 1.12
you shall eat the p. of the field. 3.18
and as I gave you the green p., 9.03
ate all the p. in the land and all Ex 10.15
have become like p. of the field, 2Ki 19.26
or the p. of the earth, and they Job 12.08
Under the lotus p. he lies, 40.21
and p. for man to cultivate, that he Ps 104.14
their youth be like p. full grown, 144.12
of her hands she p. vineyard. Pro 31.16
plant pleasant p. and set out Is 17.10
become like p. of the field and 37.27
he p. a cedar and the rain nourishes 44.14
So when the p. came up and bore Mt 13.26
So neither he who p. nor he who 1Co 3.07
He who p. and he who waters are 3.08
Who p. a vineyard without eating 9.07

PLASTER
and the p. that they scrap off Lev 14.41
take other p. and p. the house. 14.42
timber and all the p. of the house; 14.45
large stones, and p. them with p.; Deu 27.02
Ebal, and you shall p. them with p. 27.04
wrote on the p. of the wall of the Dan 5.05

PLASTERED
and scraped the house and p. it, Lev 14.43
the house after the house was p., 14.48

PLATE
"And you shall make a p. of pure gold, Ex 28.36
And they made the p. of the holy 39.30
in front, he set the golden p., Lev 8.09
was one silver p. whose weight was Num 7.13
for his offering one silver p., 7.19
his offering was one silver p., 7.25
was one silver p. whose weight was 7.31
his offering was one silver p., 7.37
his offering was one silver p., 7.43
his offering was one silver p., 7.49
his offering was one silver p., 7.55
his offering was one silver p., 7.61
his offering was one silver p., 7.67
his offering was one silver p., 7.73
his offering was one silver p., 7.79
each silver p. weighing a hundred 7.85
And take an iron p., and place Eze 4.03

PLATE (cont.)
outside of the cup and of the p., Mt 23.25
inside of the cup and of the p., 23.26

PLATES
shall make its p. and dishes for Ex 25.29
its p. and dishes for incense, and 37.16
of blue, and put upon it the p., Num 4.07
twelve silver p., twelve silver 7.84
into hammered p. as a covering for 16.38

PLATFORM
made a bronze p. five cubits long, 2Ch 6.13
temple had a raised p. round about; Eze 41.08
the part of the p. which was left 41.09
Between the p. of the temple and 41.09
the part of the p. that was left 41.11

PLATTER
of John the Baptist here on a p." Mt 14.08
brought on a p. and given to the 14.11
head of John the Baptist on a p." Mk 6.25
and brought his head on a p., 6.28

PLAUSIBLE
were not in p. words of wisdom, but 1Co 2.04

PLAY
all those who p. the lyre and pipe. Gen 4.21
sojourn, and he would p. the judge! 19.09
eat and drink, and rose up to p. Ex 32.06
and when they p. the harlot after 34.15
their daughters p. the harlot 34.16
make your sons p. the harlot after 34.16
after whom they p. the harlot. Lev 17.07
people began to p. the harlot with Num 25.01
will rise and p. the harlot after Deu 31.16
he will p. it, and you will be well." 1Sa 16.16
for me a man who can p. well, 16.17
this fellow to p. the madman in my 21.15
young men arise and p. before us." 2Sa 2.14
and let us p. the man for our 10.12
who should p. loudly on musical 1Ch 15.16
Benaiah were to p. harps according 15.20
who were to p. harps and lyres; 16.05
and let us p. the man for our 19.13
him where all the wild beasts p. Job 40.20
Will you p. with him as with a bird, 41.05
p. skilfully on the strings, with Ps 33.03
stringed harp I will p. to thee, 144.09
child shall p. over the hole of Is 11.08
and will p. the harlot with all the 23.17
solicited you to p. the harlot; Eze 16.34
you shall not p. the harlot, or Hos 3.03
they shall p. the harlot, but not 4.10
left their God to p. the harlot. 4.12
your daughters p. the harlot, 4.13
daughters when they p. the harlot, 4.14
Though you p. the harlot, O Israel, 4.15

PLAYED
daughter-in-law has p. the harlot; Gen 38.24
for they p. the harlot after other Ju 2.17
and all Israel p. the harlot after 8.27
again and p. the harlot after the 8.33
the lyre and p. it with his hand; 1Sa 16.23
I have p. the fool, and have erred 26.21
And when the minstrel p., 2Ki 3.15
and p. the harlot after the gods of 1Ch 5.25
and p. the harlot in their doings. Ps 106.39
You have p. the harlot with many Jer 3.01
tree, and there p. the harlot? 3.06
but she too went and p. the harlot. 3.08
and p. the harlot because of your Eze 16.15
shrines, and on them p. the harlot; 16.16
men, and with them p. the harlot; 16.17
You also p. the harlot with the 16.26
You p. the harlot also with the 16.28
yea, you p. the harlot with them, and 16.28
they p. the harlot in Egypt; 23.03
they p. the harlot in their youth; 23.03
"Oholah p. the harlot while she was 23.05
when she p. the harlot in the land 23.19
because you p. the harlot with the 23.30
For their mother has p. the harlot; Hos 2.05
you have p. the harlot, Israel is 5.03
for you have p. the harlot, forsaking 9.01
how will any one know what is p.? 1Co 14.07
glorified herself and p. the wanton, Rev 18.07

PLAYERS
ruler's house, and saw the flute p., Mt 9.23
of flute p. and trumpeters, shall be Rev 18.22

PLAYING
Abraham, p. with her son Isaac. Gen 21.09
follow him in p. the harlot after Lev 20.05
p. the harlot after them, I will set 20.06
profanes herself by p. the harlot, 21.09
in Israel by p. the harlot in her Deu 22.21
man who is skilful in p. they lyre; 1Sa 16.16
Bethlehemite, who is skilful in p., 16.18
house, while David was p. the lyre, 18.10
and David was p. the lyre. 19.09
p. on pipes, and rejoicing with 1Ki 1.40
between them maidens p. timbrels: Ps 68.25
I will make you stop p. the harlot, Eze 16.41
boys and girls p. in its streets. Zec 8.05
sound of harpers p. on their harps, Rev 14.02

PLAYMATES
market places and calling to their p., Mt 11.16

PLAYS
than one who p. the great man but Pro 12.09
voice and p. well on an instrument, Eze 33.32

PLEA
with an empty p. turn aside him Is 29.21
even when the p. of the needy is 32.07
me, O LORD, and hearken to my p. Jer 18.19
let my humble p. come before you, 37.20
'I made a humble p. to the king 38.26
thou didst hear my p., "Do not close Lam 3.56

PLEAD
that I may p. with you before the 1Sa 12.07
and p. my cause, and deliver me from 24.15
will you p. the case for God? Job 13.08
Arise, O God, p. thy cause; Ps 74.22
P. my cause and redeem me; 119.154
for the LORD will p. their cause Pro 22.23
he will p. their cause against you. 23.11
the fatherless, p. for the widow. Is 1.17
yet I would p. my case before thee. Jer 12.01
He will surely p. their cause, 50.34
I will p. your cause and take 51.36
"P. with your mother, p.—for she is Hos 2.02
p. your case before the mountains, Mic 6.01

PLEADED
if I have not p. with thee on behalf Jer 15.11

PLEADING
the weeping and p. of Israel's sons, Jer 3.21
arguing and p. about the kingdom of Ac 19.08

PLEADINGS
and listen to the p. of my lips. Job 13.06

PLEADS
your God who p. the cause of his Is 51.22
until he p. my cause and executes Mic 7.09
how he p. with God against Israel? Rom 11.02

PLEAS
they rely on empty p., they speak Is 59.04

PLEASANT

tree that is p. to the sight and Gen 2.09
was good, and that the land was p.; 49.15
very p. have you been to me; 2Sa 1.26
discern what is p. and what is not? 19.35
the situation of this city is p., 2Ki 2.19
have fallen for me in p. places; Ps 16.06
Then they despised the p. land, 106.24
how good and p. it is when brothers 133.01
knowledge will be p. to your soul; Pro 2.10
and bread eaten in secret is p. 9.17
and p. speech increases persuasiveness. 16.21
P. words are like a honeycomb, 16.24
for it will be p. if you keep them 22.18
eaten, and waste your p. words. 23.08
with all precious and p. riches. 24.04
How fair and p. you are, O loved one, Sol 7.06
and it is p. for the eyes to behold Ecc 11.07
men of Judah are his p. planting; Is 5.07
and jackals in the p. palaces; 13.22
you plant p. plants and set out 17.10
"A p. vineyard, sing of it! 27.02
your breasts for the p. fields, 32.12
and all our p. places have become 64.11
my sons, and give you a p. land, Jer 3.19
have made my p. portion a desolate 12.10
looked, and my sleep was p. to me. 31.26
walls and destroy your p. houses; Eze 26.12
you have planted p. vineyards, Amo 5.11
you drive out from their p. houses; Mic 2.09
and the p. land was made desolate. Zec 7.14
seems painful rather than p.; Heb 12.11

PLEASANTNESS

prosperity and their years in p. Job 36.11
Her ways are ways of p., and all her Pro 3.17

PLEASE

your power; do to her as you p." Gen 16.06
to you, and do to them as you p.; 19.08
women did not p. Isaac his father, 28.08
may it p. my lord, we will be slaves 47.25
If she does not p. her master, Ex 21.08
perhaps it will p. God that you may Num 23.27
"P. tell me wherein your great Ju 16.06
p. tell me how you might be bound." 16.10
But should it p. my father to do 1Sa 20.13
therefore may it p. thee to bless 2Sa 7.29
had given him, they did not p. him. 1Ki 9.12
if it p. you, I will give you 21.06
therefore may it p. thee to bless 1Ch 17.27
be kind to this people and p. them, 2Ch 10.07
If it p. the king, let a royal order Est 1.19
If it p. the king, let it be decreed 3.09
"If it p. the king, let the king and 5.04
and if it p. the king to grant my 5.08
and if it p. the king, let my life 7.03
"If it p. the king, and if I have 8.05
write as you p. with regard to the 8.08
"If it p. the king, let the Jews who 9.13
that it would p. God to crush me, Job 6.09
This will p. the LORD more than an Ps 69.31
When a man's ways p. the LORD, Pro 16.07
not up nor awaken love until it p. Sol 2.07
not up nor awaken love until it p. 3.05
not up nor awaken love until it p. 8.04
the things that p. me and hold Is 56.04
they shall not p. him with their Hos 9.04
"P. come to us without delay." Ac 9.38
who are in the flesh cannot p. God. Rom 8.08
the weak, and not to p. ourselves; 15.01
let each of us p. his neighbor for 15.02
For Christ did not p. himself; 15.03
of the Lord, how to p. the Lord; 1Co 7.32
affairs, how to p. his wife, 7.33
affairs, how to p. her husband. 7.34
just as I try to p. all men in 10.33
away, we make it our aim to p. him. 2Co 5.09
Or am I trying to p. men? If I were Gal 1.10
not to p. men, but to p. God who tests 1Th 2.04
you ought to live and to p. God, 4.01
faith it is impossible to p. him. Heb 11.06
"Have a seat here, p.," while you say Jas 2.03

PLEASED

Their words p. Hamor and Hamor's son Gen 34.18
it p. Pharaoh and his servants 45.16
"Be p. to command me when I am to Ex 8.09
saw that it p. the LORD to bless Num 24.01
Manassites spoke, it p. them well. Jos 22.30
And the report p. the people of 22.33
the woman; and she p. Samson well. Ju 14.07
"Be p. to spend the night, and let 19.06
because it has p. the LORD to make 1Sa 12.22
told Saul, and the thing p. him. 18.20
it p. David well to be the king's 18.26
took notice of it, and it p. them; 2Sa 3.36
the king did p. all the people. 3.36
And the advice p. Absalom and all 17.04
dead today, then you would be p. 19.06
It p. the Lord that Solomon had 1Ki 3.10
"Be p. to accept two talents." 2Ki 5.23
"Be p. to go with your servants." 6.03
So it p. the king to send me; Neh 2.06
This advice p. the king and the Est 1.21
This p. the king, and he did so. 2.04
And the maiden p. him and won his 2.09
This counsel p. Haman, and he had 5.14
and did as they p. to those who 9.05
"But now, be p. to look at me; Job 6.28
Be p., O LORD, to deliver me! Ps 40.13
I know that thou art p. with me, 41.11
those who are p. with their 49.13
offering, thou wouldst not be p. 51.16
Be p., O God, to deliver me! 70.01
The LORD was p., for his righteousness' Is 42.21
It p. Darius to set over the Dan 6.01
he did as he p. and magnified 8.04
O LORD, hast done as it p. thee." Jon 1.14
Will the LORD be p. with thousands Mic 6.07
will he be p. with you or show you Mal 1.08
Son, with whom I am well p." Mt 3.17
with whom my soul is well p. 12.18
before the company, and p. Herod, 14.06
Son, with whom I am well p.; 17.05
but did to him whatever they p. 17.12
Son; with thee I am well p." Mk 1.11
she p. Herod and his guests; 6.22
they did to him whatever they p., 9.13
peace among men with whom he is p.!" Lk 2.14
Son; with thee I am well p." 3.22
And what they said p. the whole Ac 6.05
and when he saw that it p. the Jews, 12.03
have been p. to make some contribution Rom 15.26
they were p. to do it, and indeed 15.27
it p. God through the folly of what 1Co 1.21
with most of them God was not p.; 10.05
was p. to reveal his Son to me, in Gal 1.16
fulness of God was p. to dwell, Col 1.19
he was attested as having p. God. Heb 11.05
Son, with whom I am well p.," 2Pe 1.17

PLEASES

you; dwell where it p. you." Gen 20.15
your towns, where it p. him best; Deu 23.16
"Get her for me; for she p. me well." Ju 14.03
and lay hands on whatever p. them, 1Ki 20.06
"If it p. the king, and if your Neh 2.05
"If it p. the king, let letters be 2.07
the maiden who p. the king be Est 2.04
the heavens; he does whatever he p. Ps 115.03
Whatever the LORD p. he does, 135.06
For to the man who p. him God gives Ecc 2.26
only to give to one who p. God. 2.26

PLEASES (cont.)
he who p. God escapes her, but the Ecc 7.26
unpleasant, for he does whatever he p. 8.03
everything, for this p. the Lord. Col 3.20
commandments and do what p. him. 1Jn 3.22

PLEASING
And when the LORD smelled the p. odor, Gen 8.21
it is a p. odor, an offering by fire Ex 29.18
as a p. odor before the LORD; 29.25
for a p. odor, an offering by fire 29.41
offering by fire, a p. odor to the LORD. Lev 1.09
offering by fire, a p. odor to the LORD. 1.13
offering by fire, a p. odor to the LORD. 1.17
offering by fire, a p. odor to the LORD. 2.02
offering by fire, a p. odor to the LORD. 2.09
offered on the altar for a p. odor. 2.12
offering by fire, a p. odor to the LORD. 3.05
food offered by fire for a p. odor. 3.16
the altar for a p. odor to the 4.31
portion on the altar, a p. odor to the LORD. 6.15
offer it for a p. odor to the LORD. 6.21
a p. odor, an offering by fire to 8.21
a p. odor, an offering by fire to 8.28
the fat for a p. odor to the LORD. 17.06
by fire to the LORD, a p. odor; 23.13
offering by fire, a p. odor to the LORD. 23.18
and I will not smell your p. odors. 26.31
to make a p. odor to the LORD, Num 15.03
a hin of wine, a p. odor to the LORD. 15.07
offering by fire, a p. odor to the LORD. 15.10
offering by fire, a p. odor to the LORD. 15.13
a p. odor to the LORD, he shall do 15.14
a p. odor to the LORD, with its 15.24
offering by fire, a p. odor to the LORD; 18.17
my p. odor, you shall take heed to 28.02
at Mount Sinai for a p. odor, 28.06
offering by fire, a p. odor to the LORD. 28.08
for a burnt offering of p. odor, 28.13
offering by fire, a p. odor to the LORD; 28.24
a p. odor to the LORD: two young 28.27
a p. odor to the LORD: one young 29.02
a p. odor, an offering by fire to 29.06
a p. odor: one young bull, one ram, 29.08
a p. odor to the LORD, thirteen 29.13
a p. odor to the LORD: one bull, one 29.36
is found something p. to the LORD, 1Ki 14.13
that they may offer p. sacrifices Ez 6.10
and I be p. in his eyes, let an Est 8.05
May my meditation be p. to him, Ps 104.34
words of the pure are p. to him. Pro 15.26
The Preacher sought to find p. words, Ecc 12.10
nor your sacrifices p. to me. Jer 6.20
they offered p. odor to all their Eze 6.13
you set before them for a p. odor, 16.19
As a p. odor I will accept you, when 20.41
Jerusalem will be p. to the LORD as Mal 3.04
for I always do what is p. to him." Jn 8.29
If I were still p. men, Gal 1.10
to learn what is p. to the Lord. Eph 5.10
sacrifice acceptable and p. to God. Php 4.18
fully p. to him, bearing fruit in Col 1.10
for such sacrifices are p. to God. Heb 13.16
you that which is p. in his sight, 13.21

PLEASURE
my husband is old, shall I have p.?" Gen 18.12
'I have no p. in you,' behold, here 2Sa 15.26
king's household, and to do his p. 19.18
sons he took p. in me to make me 1Ch 28.04
heart, and hast p. in uprightness; 29.17
king send us his p. in this matter. Ez 5.17
and over our cattle at their p., Neh 9.37
Is it any p. of the Almighty if you Job 22.03
Do good to Zion in thy good p.; Ps 51.18
They take p. in falsehood. 62.04
to instruct his princes at his p., 105.22
studied by all who have p. in them. 111.02
nor his p. in the legs of a man; 147.10
but the LORD takes p. in those who 147.11
For the LORD takes p. in his people; 149.04
wise conduct is p. to a man of Pro 10.23
A fool takes no p. in understanding, 18.02
He who loves p. will be a poor man; 21.17
"Come now, I will make a test of p.; Ecc 2.01
and of p., "What use is it?" 2.02
I kept my heart from no p., 2.10
my heart found p., in all my toil, 2.10
drink and take p. in all his toil. 3.31
toiling and depriving myself of p.?" 4.08
for he has no p. in fools. 5.04
will say, "I have no p. in them"; 12.01
of your fast you seek your own p., Is 58.03
from doing your p. on my holy day, 58.13
own ways, or seeking your own p., 58.13
of scorn, they take no p. in it. Jer 6.10
your lovers, with whom you took p., Eze 16.37
Have I any p. in the death of the 18.23
For I have no p. in the death of 18.32
I have no p. in the death of the 33.11
that I may take p. in it and that Hag 1.08
I have no p. in you, says the LORD Mal 1.10
Father's good p. to give you the Lk 12.32
so that you might have a double p.; 2Co 1.15
will and to work for his good p. Php 2.13
truth but had p. in unrighteousness. 2Th 2.12
lovers of p. rather than lovers of 2Ti 3.04
offerings thou hast taken no p. Heb 10.06
nor taken p. in sacrifices and 10.08
back, my soul has no p. in him." 10.38
us for a short time at their p., 12.10
on the earth in luxury and in p.; Jas 5.05
They count it p. to revel in the 2Pe 2.13

PLEASURES
thy right hand are p. for evermore. Ps 16.11
you lover of p., who sit securely, Is 47.08
cares and riches and p. of life, Lk 8.14
slaves to various passions and p., Tit 3.03
to enjoy fleeting p. of sin. Heb 11.25

PLEDGE
she said, "Will you give me a p., Gen 38.17
He said, "What p. shall I give you?" 38.18
to receive the p. from the woman's 38.20
take your neighbor's garment in p., Ex 22.26
an oath to bind himself by a p., Num 30.02
LORD, and binds herself by a p., 30.03
vow and of her p. by which she has 30.04
and every p. by which she has bound 30.04
no p. by which she has bound 30.05
herself by a p. with an oath, 30.10
and every p. by which she bound 30.11
or concerning her p. of herself, 30.12
a mill or an upper millstone in p.; Deu 24.06
he would be taking a life in p. 24.06
go into his house to fetch his p. 24.10
loan shall bring the p. out to you. 24.11
man, you shall not sleep in his p.; 24.12
to him the p. that he may sleep in 24.13
or take a widow's garment in p.; 24.17
"Lay down a p. for me with thyself; Job 17.03
they take the widow's ox for a p. 24.03
and take in p. the infant of the 24.09
have given your p. for a stranger; Pro 6.01
A man without sense gives a p., 17.18
and hold him in p. when he gives 20.16
and hold him in p. when he gives 27.13
but restores to the debtor his p., Eze 18.07
robbery, does not restore the p., 18.12
exacts no p., commits no robbery, 18.16
if the wicked restores the p., 33.15
altar upon garments taken in p.; Amo 2.08
for having violated their first p. 1Ti 5.12

PLEDGED
p. their allegiance to King Solomon. 1Ch 29.24
They p. themselves to put away Ez 10.19

PLEDGES
and her p. by which she has bound Num 30.07
or all her p., that are upon her; 30.14
have exacted p. of your brothers Job 22.06
Be not one of those who give p., Pro 22.26
how long?—and loads himself with p.! Hab 2.06

PLEIADES
the P. and the chambers of the Job 9.09
"Can you bind the chains of the P., 38.31
He who made the P. and Orion, Amo 5.08

PLENTEOUS
of Egypt during the seven p. years. Gen 41.34
During the seven p. years the earth 41.47
and with him is p. redemption. Ps 130.07
ground, which will be rich and p. Is 30.23

PLENTIFUL
made cedar as p. as the sycamore 1Ki 10.27
made cedar as p. as the sycamore 2Ch 1.15
and cedar as p. as the sycamore of 9.27
you into a p. land to enjoy its Jer 2.07
his disciples, "The harvest is p., Mt 9.37
he said to them, "The harvest is p., Lk 10.02

PLENTIFULLY
and p. declared sound knowledge! Job 26.03
of a rich man brought forth p.; Lk 12.16

PLENTY
the earth, and p. of grain and wine. Gen 27.28
years of great p. throughout all 41.29
and all the p. will be forgotten in 41.30
and the p. will be unknown in the 41.31
when there was p. in the land of 41.48
The seven years of p. that prevailed 41.53
and had enough and have p. left; 2Ch 31.10
will be contempt and wrath in p. Est1.18
then your barns will be filled with p., Pro 3.10
his land will have p. of bread, 12.11
and you will have p. of bread. 20.13
his land will have p. of bread, 28.19
pursuits will have p. of poverty. 28.19
for then we had p. of food, Jer 44.17
"You shall eat in p. and be satisfied, Joe 2.26
the secret of facing p. and hunger, Php 4.12

PLIGHT
saw that they were in evil p., when Ex 5.19
courage melted away in their evil p.; Ps 107.26

PLIGHTED
I p. my troth to you and entered Eze 16.08

PLOT
there was a p. of ground full of 2Sa 23.11
his stand in the midst of the p., 23.12
cast him on the p. of ground 2Ki 9.25
requite you on this p. of ground.' 9.26
and cast him on the p. of ground, 9.26
There was a p. of ground full of 1Ch 11.13
his stand in the midst of the p., 11.14
Agagite and the p. which he had Est 8.03
that his wicked p. which he had 9.25
conspire, and the peoples p. in vain? Ps 2.01
as they p. to take my life. 31.13
of those who treacherously p. evil. 59.05
out a cunningly conceived p. 64.06
do not further his evil p.! 140.08
Of this a square p. of five hundred Eze 45.02
What do you p. against the LORD? Nah 1.09
but their p. became known to Saul. Ac 9.24
and when a p. was made against him 20.03
the Jews made a p. and bound 23.12
would be a p. against the man, I 23.30

PLOTS
hidest them from the p. of men; Ps 31.20
He p. mischief while on his bed; 36.04
The wicked p. against the righteous, 37.12
from the secret p. of the wicked, 64.02
A worthless man p. evil, and his Pro 16.27
and his mind p. iniquity: to practice Is 32.06
let us make p. against Jeremiah, for Jer 18.18
for p. shall be devised against him. Dan 11.25
me through the p. of the Jews; Ac 20.19

PLOTTED
and they all p. together to come Neh 4.08
had p. against the Jews to destroy Est 9.24
who p. evil against the LORD, and Nah 1.11
passed, the Jews p. to kill him, Ac 9.23

PLOTTING
that Saul was p. evil against him; 1Sa 23.09
All the day you are p. destruction. Ps 52.01
Even though princes sit p. against me, 119.23
knowest all their p. to slay me. Jer 18.23

PLOW
You shall not p. with an ox and an Deu 22.10
and some of p. his ground and to 1Sa 8.12
those who p. iniquity and sow Job 4.08
sluggard does not p. in the autumn; Pro 20.04
plows for sowing p. continually? Is 28.24
Judah must p., Jacob must harrow Hos 10.11
Does one p. the sea with oxen? Amo 6.12
his hand to the p. and looks back Lk 9.62
plowman should p. in hope and the 1Co 9.10

PLOWED
which is neither p. nor sown, Deu 21.04
"If you had not p. with my heifer, Ju 14.18
The plowers p. upon my back; they Ps 129.03
hosts, Zion shall be p. as a field; Jer 26.18
You have p. iniquity, you have Hos 10.13
of you Zion shall be p. as a field; Mic 3.12

PLOWERS
The p. plowed upon my back; they made Ps 129.03

PLOWING
will be neither p. nor harvest. Gen 45.06
in p. time and in harvest you shall Ex 34.21
who was p., with twelve yoke of 1Ki 19.19
"The oxen were p. and the asses Job 1.14
has a servant p. or keeping sheep, Lk 17.07

PLOWMAN
"when the p. shall overtake the Amo 9.13
because the p. should plow in hope 1Co 9.10

PLOWMEN
the land to be vinedressers and p. 2Ki 25.12
shall be your p. and vinedressers; Is 61.05
the land to be vinedressers and p. Jer 52.16

PLOWS
Does he who p. for sowing plow Is 28.24

PLOWSHARE
The Philistines to sharpen his p., 1Sa 13.20

PLOWSHARES
a pim for the p. and for the 1Sa 13.21
shall beat their swords into p., Is 2.04
Beat your p. into swords, and your Joe 3.10
shall beat their swords into p., Mic 4.03

PLUCK
you may p. the ears with your hand, Deu 23.25
then I will p. you up from the land 2Ch 7.20

PLUCK (cont.)
for he will p. my feet out of the Ps 25.15
pass along the way p. its fruit? 80.12
and a time to p. up what is planted, Ecc 3.02
to p. up and to break down, to Jer 1.10
I will p. them up from their land, 12.14
and I will p. up the house of Judah 12.14
I will utterly p. it up and 12.17
that I will p. up and break down 18.07
over them to p. up and break down, 31.28
will plant you, and not p. you up; 42.10
and p. out your hair, and tear your Eze 23.34
p. it out and throw it away; Mt 5.29
they began to p. ears of grain and 12.01
p. it out and throw it from you; 18.09
disciples began to p. ears of grain. Mk 2.23
eye causes you to sin, p. it out; 9.47

PLUCKED
her mouth a freshly p. olive leaf; Gen 8.11
you shall be p. off the land which Deu 28.63
tent-cord is p. up within them, Job 4.21
whose stakes will never be p. up, Is 33.20
My dwelling is p. up and removed 38.12
And after I have p. them up, Jer 12.15
But the vine was p. up in fury, Eze 19.12
as I looked its wings were p. off, Dan 7.04
horns were p. up by the roots; 7.08
shall be p. up and go to others 11.04
were as a brand p. out of the Amo 4.11
never again be p. up out of the 9.15
not this a brand p. from the fire?" Zec 3.02
his disciples p. and ate some ears Lk 6.01
you would have p. out your eyes Gal 4.15

PLUCKING
what I have planted I am p. up— Jer 45.04

PLUMAGE
they the pinions and p. of love? Job 39.13
rich in p. of many colors, came to Eze 17.03
eagle with great wings and much p.; 17.07

PLUMB
beside a wall built with a p. line, Amo 7.07
with a p. line in his hand. 7.07
And I said, "A p. line." 7.08
I am setting a p. line in the 7.08

PLUMMET
and the p. of the house of Ahab; 2Ki 21.13
the line, and righteousness the p.; Is 28.17
and the p. of chaos over its nobles. 34.11
shall see the p. in the hand of Zec 4.10

PLUMP
p. and good, were growing on one Gen 41.05
up the seven p. and full ears. 41.07

PLUNDER
for there was much p. in them. 2Ch 14.14
of Adar, and to p. their goods. Est 3.13
and women, and to p. their goods, 8.11
but they laid no hand on the p. 9.10
but they laid no hands on the p. 9.15
but they laid no hands on the p. 9.16
may strangers p. the fruits of his Ps 109.11
him, to take spoil and seize p., Is 10.06
they shall p. the people of the 11.14
us, and the lot of those who p. us. 17.14
who shall p. them, and seize them, Jer 20.05
all who p. her shall be sated, says 50.10
wealth and despoil it and p. it; Eze 29.19
they might possess it and p. it. 36.05
to seize spoil and carry off p.; 38.12
assembled your hosts to carry off p., 38.13
and p. those who plundered them, 39.10
done, scattering among them p., Dan 11.24
by captivity and p., for some days. 11.33
P. the silver, p. the gold! Nah 2.09
lies and booty—no end to the p.! 3.01
of the peoples shall p. you, Hab 2.08
remnant of my people shall p. them, Zep 2.09
shall become p. for those who Zec 2.09
man's house and p. his goods, Mt 12.29
Then indeed he may p. his house. 12.29
man's house and p. his goods, Mk 3.27
then indeed he may p. his house. 3.27

PLUNDERED
and p. the city, because their Gen 34.27
over to plunderers, who p. them; Ju 2.14
of the power of those who p. them. 2.16
of the hands of those who p. them. 1Sa 14.48
Philistines, and they p. their camp. 17.53
and p. the camp of the Syrians. 2Ki 7.16
They p. all the cities, for there 2Ch 14.14
them up to be p. in a land where Neh 4.04
with evil or p. my enemy without Ps 7.04
and have p. their treasures; Is 10.13
houses will be p. and their wives 13.16
But this is a people robbed and p., 42.22
Chaldea shall be p.; all who Jer 50.10
her treasures, that they may be p.! 50.37
and plunder those who p. them, Eze 39.10
and your strongholds shall be p. Amo 3.11
Because you have p. many nations, Hab 2.08
Their goods shall be p., and their houses Zep 1.13
sent me to the nations who p. you, Zec 2.08
and the houses p. and the women 14.02

PLUNDERER
the p. plunders, and the destroyer Is 21.02

PLUNDERERS
and he gave them over to p., Ju 2.14
O p. of my heritage, though you are Jer 50.11
if p. by night—how you have been Ob 1.05
for p. have stripped them and Nah 2.02

PLUNDERING
to p., and to utter shame, as at Ez 9.07
accepted the p. of your property, Heb 10.34

PLUNDERS
the plunderer p., and the destroyer Is 21.02

PLUNGE
yet thou wilt p. me into a pit, and Job 9.31
desires that p. men into ruin and 1Ti 6.09

PLUNGES
A bad messenger p. men into trouble, Pro 13.17

PLUNGING
like a horse p. headlong into Jer 8.06

PLY
and priest p. their trade through Jer 14.18

POCHERETHHAZZEBAIM
the sons of P., and the sons of Ami Ez 2.57
the sons of P., the sons of Amon. Neh 7.59

PODS
have fed on the p. that the swine Lk 15.16

POETS
even some of your p. have said, Ac 17.28

POINT
of our kinsmen p. out what I have Gen 31.32
sick and was at the p. of death. 2Ki 20.01
it came to the p. in Jerusalem and 24.20
sick and was at the p. of death, 2Ch 32.24
repaired to a p. opposite the Neh 3.16
repaired to a p. opposite the 3.26

POINT (cont.)
the glittering p. comes out of his Job 20.25
I was at the p. of utter ruin in Pro 5.14
sick and was at the p. of death. Is 38.01
with a p. of diamond it is engraved Jer 17.01
boundary to a p. opposite the Eze 47.20
disciples came to p. out to him the Mt 24.01
daughter is at the p. of death. Mk 5.23
was sick and at the p. of death. Lk 7.02
son, for he was at the p. of death. Jn 4.47
no one from a human p. of view, 2Co 5.16
Christ from a human p. of view, 5.16
At every p. you have proved yourselves 7.11
The p. is this: he who sows sparingly 9.06
already on the p. of being sacrificed; 2Ti 4.06
Now the p. in what we are saying is Heb 8.01
resisted to the p. of shedding 12.04
fails in one p. has become guilty Jas 2.10
remains and is on the p. of death, Rev 3.02

POINTED
prophetic utterances which p. to you, 1Ti 1.18

POINTING
the p. of the finger, and speaking Is 58.09
p. to judgment, but the sins of 1Ti 5.24

POINTS
with his feet, p. with his finger, Pro 6.13
had certain p. of dispute with him Ac 25.19
But on some p. I have written to Rom 15.15

POISON
their grapes are grapes of p., Deu 32.32
their wine is the p. of serpents, 32.33
my spirit drinks their p.; the terrors Job 6.04
He will such the p. of asps; the tongue 20.16
They gave me p. for food, and for my Ps 69.21
their lips is the p. of vipers. 140.03
justice into p. and the fruit of Amo 6.12
a restless evil, full of deadly p. Jas 3.08

POISONED
and has given us p. water to drink, Jer 8.14
and give them p. water to drink; 23.15
Gentiles and p. their minds Ac 14.02

POISONOUS
a root bearing p. and bitter fruit, Deu 29.18
burning heat and p. pestilence; 32.24
and give them p. water to drink. Jer 9.15
springs up like p. weeds in the Hos 10.04

POLE
carried it on a p. between two of Num 13.23
fiery serpent, and set it on a p.; 21.08
bronze serpent, and set it on a p.; 21.09

POLES
You shall make p. of acacia wood, Ex 25.13
shall put the p. into the rings on 25.14
The p. shall remain in the rings of 25.15
holders for the p. to carry the 25.27
You shall make the p. of acacia wood, 25.28
And you shall make p. for the altar, 27.06
p. of acacia wood, and overlay them 27.06
and the p. shall be put through the 27.07
so that the p. shall be upon the 27.07
be holders for p. with which to 30.04
You shall make the p. of acacia wood, 30.05
the ark with its p., the mercy seat 35.12
the table with its p. and all its 35.13
with its p., and the anointing oil 35.15
its p., and all its utensils, the 35.16
And he made p. of acacia wood, and 37.04
and put the p. into the rings on 37.05
holders for the p. to carry the 37.14
He made the p. of acacia wood to 37.15
holders for the p. with which to 37.27
And he made the p. of acacia wood, 37.28
grating as holders for the p.; 38.05
he made the p. of acacia wood, and 38.06
And he put the p. through the rings 38.07
with its p. and the mercy seat; 39.35
its p., and all its utensils; 39.39
up its frames, and put in its p., 40.18
and put the p. on the ark, and set 40.20
of blue, and shall put in its p. Num 4.06
goatskin, and shall put in its p. 4.08
goatskin, and shall put in its p.; 4.11
goatskin, and shall put in its p. 4.14
covering above the ark and its p. 1Ki 8.07
And the p. were so long that the 8.08
the ends of the p. were seen from 8.08
upon their shoulders with the p., 1Ch 15.15
covering above the ark and its p. 2Ch 5.08
And the p. were so long that the 5.09
the ends of the p. were seen from 5.09

POLICE
day, the magistrates sent the p., Ac 16.35
The p. reported these words to the 16.38

POLISH
p. your spears, put on your coats of Jer 46.04

POLISHED
he made me a p. arrow, in his quiver Is 49.02
a sword is sharpened and also p., Eze 21.09
p. to flash like lightning! 21.10
So the sword is given to be p., 21.11
sharpened and p. to be given into 21.11
lightning, it is p. for slaughter. 21.15
it is p. to glitter and to flash 21.28

POLLUTE
You shall not thus p. the land in Num 35.33

POLLUTED
but because he p. his father's couch, 1Ch 5.01
and they p. the house of the LORD 2Ch 36.14
and the land was p. with blood. Ps 106.38
spring or a p. fountain is a Pro 25.26
The earth lies p. under its inhabitants Is 24.05
deeds are like a p. garment. 64.06
would not that land be greatly p.? Jer 3.01
You have p. the land with your vile 3.02
she p. the land, committing adultery 3.09
they have p. my land with the 16.18
with which you have p. yourselves; Eze 20.43
and after she was p. by them, 23.17
and p. yourself with their idols. 23.30
By offering p. food upon my altar. Mal 1.07
And you say, 'How have we p. it?' 1.07
say that the LORD's table is p., 1.12
the p., as for murderers, fornicators, Rev 21.08

POLLUTES
for blood p. the land, and no Num 35.33

POLLUTIONS
from the p. of the peoples of the Ez 6.21
with the p. of the peoples of the 9.11
from the p. of idols and from Ac 15.20

POMEGRANATE
and a p., a golden bell and a p., Ex 28.34
a bell and a p., a bell and a p. round 39.26
under the p. tree which is at 1Sa 14.02
halves of a p. behind your veil. Sol 4.03
halves of a p. behind your veil. 6.07
P., palm, and apple, all the trees of Joe 1.12
the p., and the olive tree still Hag 2.19

POMEGRANATES
you shall make p. of blue and Ex 28.33
robe they made p. of blue and 39.24
between the p. upon the skirts of 39.25
robe round about, between the p.; 39.25
they brought also some p. and figs. Num 13.23
grain, or figs, or vines, or p.; 20.05
of vines and fig trees and p., Deu 8.08
Likewise he made p.; in two rows 1Ki 7.18
there were two hundred p., 7.20
four hundred p. for the two 7.42
two rows of p. for each network, to 7.42
a network and p., all of bronze, 2Ki 25.17
and he made a hundred p., 2Ch 3.16
four hundred p. for the two 4.13
two rows of p. for each network, to 4.13
an orchard of p. with all choicest Sol 4.13
whether the p. were in bloom. 6.11
opened and the p. are in bloom. 7.12
wine to drink, the juice of my p. 8.02
a network and p., all of bronze, Jer 52.22
pillar had the like, with p. 52.22
There were ninety-six p. on the sides: 52.23
all the p. were a hundred upon the 52.23

POMMEL
but I p. my body and subdue it, lest 1Co 9.27

POMP
splendor and p. of his majesty for Est 1.04
Man cannot abide in his p., Ps 49.12
Man cannot abide in his p., 49.20
Your p. is brought down to Sheol, Is 14.11
and Bernice came with great p., Ac 25.23

PONDER
has wrought, and p. what he has done. Ps 64.09
and p. over you: 'Is this the man Is 14.16

PONDERING
these things, p. them in her heart. Lk 2.19
And while Peter was p. the vision, Ac 10.19

PONDERS
of the righteous p. how to answer, Pro 15.28

PONDS
and their p., and all their pools Ex 7.19

PONTIUS
P. Pilate being governor of Judea, Lk 3.01
anoint, both Herod and P. Pilate, Ac 4.27
testimony before P. Pilate made the 1Ti 6.13

PONTUS
Judea and Cappadocia, P. and Asia, Ac 2.09
a native of P., lately come from 18.02
the exiles of the dispersion in P., 1Pe 1.01

POOL
and met them at the p. of Gibeon; 2Sa 2.13
the one on the one side of the p., 2.13
other on the other side of the p. 2.13
them beside the p. at Hebron. 4.12
the chariot by the p. of Samaria, 1Ki 22.38
by the conduit of the upper p., 2Ki 18.17
how he made the p. and the conduit 20.20
Fountain Gate and to the King's P.; Neh 2.14
the wall of the P. of Shelah of 3.15
of David, to the artificial p., 3.16
who turns the rock into a p. of water, Ps 114.08
of the upper p. on the highway to Is 7.03
the waters of the lower p., 22.09
walls for the water of the old p. 22.11
the burning sand shall become a p., 35.07
of the upper p. on the highway to 36.02
make the wilderness a p. of water, 41.18
at the great p. which is in Gibeon. Jer 41.12
Nineveh is like a p. whose waters Nah 2.08
Jerusalem by the sheep gate a p., Jn 5.02
at certain seasons into the p., * 5.04
put me into the p. when the water 5.07
wash in the p. of Siloam" (which 9.07

POOLS
and all their p. of water, that they Ex 7.19
and over the p., and cause frogs to 8.05
this dry stream-bed full of p. 2Ki 3.16
early rain also covers it with p. Ps 84.06
He turns a desert into p. of water, 107.35
I made myself p. from which to Ecc 2.06
Your eyes are p. in Heshbon, by the Sol 7.04
and p. of water, and I will sweep it Is 14.23
into islands, and dry up the p. 42.15

POOR
p. and very gaunt and thin, such as Gen 41.19
of my people with you who is p., Ex 22.25
be partial to a p. man in his suit. 23.03
justice due to your p. in his suit. 23.06
that the p. of your people may eat; 23.11
and the p. shall not give less, than 30.15
"But if he is p. and cannot afford Lev 14.21
them for the p. and for the 19.10
partial to the p. or defer to the 19.15
them for the p. and for the 23.22
"If your brother becomes p., 25.25
"And if your brother becomes p., 25.35
your brother becomes p. beside you, 25.39
him becomes p. and sells himself 25.47
And if a man is too p. to pay your 27.08
and whether the land is rich or p., Num 13.20
will be no p. among you (for the Deu 15.04
"If there is among you a p. man, 15.07
your hand against your p. brother, 15.07
eye be hostile to your p. brother, 15.09
For the p. will never cease out of 15.11
needy and to the p., in the land. 15.11
And if he is a p. man, you shall not 24.12
hired servant who is p. and needy, 24.14
the sun goes down (for he is p., 24.15
young men, whether p. or rich. Ru 3.10
The Lord makes p. and makes rich; 1Sa 2.07
He raises up the p. from the dust; 2.08
that I am a p. man and of no 18.23
the one rich and the other p. 2Sa 12.01
but the p. man had nothing but one 12.03
him, but he took the p. man's lamb, 12.04
to one another and gifts to the p. Est 9.22
So the p. have hope, and injustice Job 5.16
will seek the favor of the p., 20.10
has crushed and abandoned the p., 20.19
They thrust the p. off the road; 24.04
the p. of the earth all hide 24.04
in pledge the infant of the p. 24.09
that he may kill the p. and needy; 24.14
because I delivered the p. who cried, 29.12
I was a father to the p., 29.16
Was not my soul grieved for the p.? 30.25
anything that the p. desired, 31.16
or a p. man without covering; 31.19
regards the rich more than the p., 34.19
the cry of the p. to come to him, 34.28
the hope of the p. shall not Ps 9.18
the wicked hotly pursue the p.; 10.02
he lurks that he may seize the p., 10.09
he seizes the p. when he draws him 10.09
"Because the p. are despoiled, 12.05
would confound the plans of the p., 14.06
This p. man cried, and the Lord 34.06
to bring down the p. and needy, 37.14
As for me, I am p. and needy; 40.17
Blessed is he who considers the p.! 41.01
low and high, rich and p. together! 49.02
But I am p. and needy; 70.05
righteousness, and thy p. with justice! 72.02

POOR (cont.)
the cause of the p. of the people, Ps 72.04
the p. and him who has no helper. 72.12
forget the life of thy p. for ever. 74.19
let the p. and needy praise thy 74.21
answer me, for I am p. and needy. 86.01
but pursued the p. and needy and 109.16
For I am p. and needy, and my heart 109.22
freely, he has given to the p.; 112.09
He raises the p. from the dust, and 113.07
I will satisfy her p. with bread. 132.15
poverty of the p. is their ruin. Pro 10.15
another pretends to be p., 13.07
but a p. man has no means of 13.08
ground of the p. yields much food, 13.23
The p. is disliked even by his 14.20
happy is he who is kind to the p. 14.21
He who oppresses a p. man insults 14.31
spirit with the p. than to divide 16.19
He who mocks the p. insults his 17.05
The p. use entreaties, but the rich 18.23
Better is a p. man who walks in his 19.01
but a p. man is deserted by his 19.04
All a p. man's brothers hate him; 19.07
is kind to the p. lends to the 19.17
and a p. man is better than a liar. 19.22
the cry of the p. will himself cry 21.13
loves pleasure will be a p. man; 21.17
The rich and the p. meet together; 22.02
The rich rules over the p., 22.07
he shares his bread with the p. 22.09
oppresses the p. to increase his 22.16
Do not rob the p., because he is p., 22.22
A p. man who oppresses the p. is 28.03
Better is a p. man who walks in his 28.06
it for him who is kind to the p. 28.08
but a p. man who has understanding 28.11
is a wicked ruler over a p. people. 28.15
He who gives to the p. will not want, 28.27
man knows the rights of the p.; 29.07
The p. man and the oppressor meet 29.13
king judges the p. with equity his 29.14
or lest I be p., and steal, and 30.09
to devour the p. from off the earth, 30.14
the rights of the p. and needy. 31.09
She opens her hand to the p., 31.20
Better is a p. and wise youth than Ecc 4.13
his own kingdom had been born p. 4.14
a province the p. oppressed and 5.08
what does the p. man have who 6.08
was found in it a p. wise man, 9.15
yet no one remembered that p. man. 9.15
though the p. man's wisdom is 9.16
spoil of the p. is in your houses. Is 3.14
by grinding the face of the p.?" 3.15
and to rob the p. of my people of 10.02
righteousness he shall judge the p., 11.04
the first-born of the p. will feed, 14.30
hast been a stronghold to the p., 25.04
tramples it, the feet of the p., 26.06
and the p. among men shall exult in 29.19
to ruin the p. with lying words, 32.07
When the p. and needy seek water, 41.17
the homeless p. into your house; 58.07
the lifeblood of guiltless p.; Jer 2.34
Then I said, "These are only the p., 5.04
the cause of the p. and needy; 22.16
some of the p. people who owned 39.10
but did not aid the p. and needy. Eze 16.49
oppresses the p. and needy, commits 18.12
have oppressed the p. and needy, 22.29
the head of the p. into the dust Amo 2.07
of Samaria, who oppress the p., 4.01
upon the p., and take from him 5.11
and bring the p. of the land to an 8.04
that we may buy the p., for silver 8.06
as if to devour the p. in secret. Hab 3.14
fatherless, the sojourner, or the p.; Zec 7.10
"Blessed are the p. in spirit, Mt 5.03
and the p. have good news preached 11.05
you possess and give to the p., 19.21
a large sum, and given to the p." 26.09
For you always have the p. with you, 26.11
what you have, and give to the p., Mk 10.21
And a p. widow came, and put in two 12.42
this p. widow has put in more than 12.43
denarii, and given to the p." 14.05
For you always have the p. with you, 14.07
me to preach good news to the p. Lk 4.18
and said: "Blessed are you p., 6.20
the p., have good news preached to 7.22
invite the p., the maimed, the lame, 14.13
bring in the p., and maimed and 14.21
his gate lay a p. man named Lazarus, 16.20
The p. man died and was carried by 16.22
you have and distribute to the p., 18.22
half of my goods I give to the p.; 19.08
and he saw a p. widow put in two 21.02
this p. widow has put in more than 21.03
drunk freely, then the p. wine; Jn 2.10
denarii and given to the p.?" 12.05
cared for the p. but because he 12.06
The p. you always have with you, but 12.08
he should give something to the p. 13.29
contribution for the p. among the Rom 15.26
as p., yet making many rich; 2Co 6.10
yet for your sake he became p., 8.09
scatters abroad, he gives to the p.; 9.09
they would have us remember the p., Gal 2.10
and a p. man in shabby clothing Jas 2.02
while you say to the p. man, 2.03
those who are p. in the world to 2.05
But you have dishonored the p. man. 2.06
wretched, pitiable, p., blind, and naked. Rev 3.17
both rich and p., both free and 13.16

POORER
you were in p. condition than the Dan 1.10

POOREST
except the p. people of the land. 2Ki 24.14
some of the p. of the land to be 25.12
those of the p. of the land who had Jer 40.07
some of the p. of the people and 52.15
some of the p. of the land to be 52.16

POPLAR
fresh rods of p. and almond and Gen 30.37
p., and terebinth, because their Hos 4.13
he shall strike root as the p.; Hos 14.05

POPULAR
the Jews and p. with the multitude Est 10.03

POPULATION
the whole p. was involved in the Num 15.26

POPULOUS
a nation, great, mighty, and p. Deu 26.05
be forsaken, the p. city deserted; Is 32.14

PORATHA
and P. and Adalia and Aridatha Est 9.08

PORCH
there was a p. in front with 1Ki 7.06
between the p. and the altar, were Eze 8.16
And when he went out to the p., Mt 26.71

PORCIUS
Felix was succeeded by P. Festus; Ac 24.27

PORCUPINE
hawk and the p. shall possess it, Is 34.11

PORPHYRY
silver on a mosaic pavement of p., Est 1.06

PORTALS
entrance of the p. she cries aloud: Pro 8.03

PORTENT
I have been as a p. to many; Ps 71.07
as a sign and a p. against Egypt Is 20.03
And a great p. appeared in heaven, a Rev 12.01
And another p. appeared in heaven; 12.03
Then I saw another p. in heaven, 15.01

PORTENTS
are signs and p. in Israel from Is 8.18
"And I will give p. in the heavens Joe 2.30

PORTICO
the temple, in the p. of Solomon. Jn 10.23
to them in the p. called Solomon's, Ac 3.11
were all together in Solomon's P. 5.12

PORTICOES
Bethzatha, which was five p. Jn 5.02

PORTION
"Is there any p. or inheritance Gen 31.14
but Benjamin's p. was five times 43.34
and gather a day's p. every day, Ex 16.04
the LORD; and it shall be your p. 29.26
and the thigh of the priests' p., 29.27
is the priests' p. to be offered 29.28
as its memorial p. upon the altar, Lev 2.02
its memorial p. and burn this on 2.09
as its memorial p. part of the 2.16
as its memorial p. and burn this 5.12
as its memorial p. on the altar, 6.15
it as their p. of my offerings by 6.17
have the right thigh for a p. 7.33
This is the p. of Aaron and of his 7.35
it was Moses' p. of the ram of 8.29
as a memorial p. to be offered by 24.07
him a most holy p. out of the 24.09
offering, as its memorial p., Num 5.26
they are a holy p. for the priest, 6.20
I have given them to you as a p., 18.08
shall you have any p. among them; 18.20
I am your p. and your inheritance 18.20
the p. of those who had gone out to 31.36
Therefore Levi has no p. or inheritance Deu 10.09
since he has no p. or inheritance 12.12
for he has no p. or inheritance 14.27
he has no p. or inheritance with 14.29
shall have no p. or inheritance 18.01
him a double p. of all that he has, 21.17
the sacred p. out of my house, and 26.13
For the LORD's p. is his people, 32.09
a commander's p. was reserved; 33.21
and no p. was given to the Levites Jos 14.04
of Jephunneh a p. among the people 15.13
one lot and one p. as an inheritance, 17.14
The Levites have no p. among you, 18.07
people of Israel, to each his p. 18.10
because the p. of the tribe of 19.09
you have no p. in the LORD. 22.25
come, "You have no p. in the LORD."' 22.27
in the p. of ground which Jacob 24.32
he would give Hannah only one p., 1Sa 1.05
"Bring the p. I gave you, of which I 9.23
and the upper p. and set them 9.24
a p. of meat, and a cake of raisins. 2Sa 6.19
"We have no p. in David, and we have 20.01
"What p. have we in David? We have 1Ki 12.16
every day a p., as long as he lived. 2Ki 25.30
a p. of meat, and a cake of raisins. 1Ch 16.03
as your p. for an inheritance. 16.18
"What p. have we in David? We have 2Ch 10.16
to give the p. due to the priests 31.04
but you have no p. or right or Neh 2.20
her ointments and her p. of food, Est 2.09
This is the wicked man's p. from God, Job 20.29
their p. is cursed in the land; 24.18
"This is the p. of a wicked man 27.13
What would be my p. from God above, 31.02
wind shall be the p. of their cup. Ps 11.06
The LORD is my chosen p. and my cup; 16.05
from men whose p. in life is of 17.14
who are pleased with their p. 49.13
up Shechem and p. out the Vale of 60.06
may have their p. from the foe. 68.23
of my heart and my p. for ever. 73.26
Canaan as your p. for an inheritance." 105.11
and p. out the Vale of Succoth. 108.07
The LORD is my p.; I promise 119.57
my p. in the land of the living. 142.05
that is your p. in the life and in Ecc 9.09
Give a p. to seven, or even to eight, 11.02
This is the p. of those who despoil Is 17.14
divide him a p. with the great, 53.12
stones of the valley is your p.; 57.06
shame you shall have a double p., 61.07
land you shall possess a double p.; 61.07
these is he who is the p. of Jacob, Jer 10.16
they have trampled down my p., 12.10
my pleasant p. a desolate wilderness. 12.10
the p. I have measured out to you, 13.25
to receive his p. there among the 37.12
these is he who is the p. of Jacob, 51.19
"The LORD is my p.," says my soul, Lam 3.24
and diminished your allotted p., Eze 16.27
for the LORD a p. of the land as a 45.01
It shall be the holy p. of the land; 45.04
"Alongsde the p. set apart as the 45.06
and as the fixed p. of oil, 45.14
east side to the west, Dan, one p. 48.01
side to the west, Asher, one p. 48.02
side the west, Naphtali, one p. 48.03
side to the west, Manasseh, one p. 48.04
side to the west, Ephraim, one p. 48.05
side to the west, Reuben, one p. 48.06
side to the west, Judah, one p. 48.07
shall be the p. which you shall set 48.08
The p. which you shall set apart 48.09
be the allotments of the holy p.: 48.10
as a special p. from the holy 48.12
from the holy p. of the land, 48.12
alienate this choice p. of the land, 48.14
the holy p. shall be ten thousand 48.18
it shall be alongside the holy p. 48.18
The whole p. which you shall set 48.20
the holy p. together with the 48.20
of the holy p. and of the property 48.21
of the holy p. to the east border, 48.21
The holy p. with the sanctuary of 48.21
The p. of the prince shall lie 48.22
side to the west, Benjamin, one p. 48.23
side to the west, Simeon, one p. 48.24
side to the west, Issachar, one p. 48.25
side to the west, Zebulun, one p. 48.26
east side to the west, Gad, one p. 48.27
them a daily p. of the rich food Dan 1.05
he changes the p. of my people; Mic 2.04
Judah as his p. in the holy land, Zec 2.12
Mary has chosen the good p., Lk 10.42
give them their p. of food at the 12.42

PORTIONED
his hand was p. it out to them with Is 34.17

PORTIONS
of his flock and of their fat p. Gen 4.04
P. were taken to them from Joseph's 43.34
They shall have equal p. to eat, Deu 18.08
Thus there fell to Manasseh ten p., Jos 17.05
They shall divide it into seven p., 18.05
he would give p. to Peninnah his 1Sa 1.04

PORTIONS (cont.)
distribute the p. to their brethren, 2Ch 31.15
to distribute p. to every male 31.19
wine and send p. to him for whom Neh 8.10
and to send p. and to make great 8.12
into them the p. required by the 12.44
gave the daily p. for the singers 12.47
out that the p. of the Levites had 13.10
they send choice p. to one another. Est 9.19
sending choice p. to one another 9.22
in length to one of the tribal p., Eze 45.07
tribes of Israel. Joseph shall have two p. 47.13
equal to one of the tribal p., 48.08
border, parallel to the tribal p., 48.21
and these are their several p., 48.29

PORTRAY
and p. upon it a city, even Jerusalem; Eze 4.01
p. the temple, its arrangement, its 43.11

PORTRAYED
and there, p. upon the wall round Eze 8.10
she saw men p. upon the wall, the 23.14
of the Chaldeans p. in vermilion, 23.14
was publicly p. as crucified? Gal 3.01

PORTS
to sail to the p. along the coast Ac 27.02

POSITION
each in p., standard by standard. Num 2.17
take your p., stand still, and see 2Ch 20.17
give her royal p. to another who Est 1.19
you do not regard the p. of men. Mt 22.16
you do not regard the p. of men, Mk 12.14
any one in the p. of an outsider 1Co 14.16
on a man's p. and not on his heart. 2Co 5.12
keep their own p. but left their Jud 1.06

POSITIONS
he said to his men, "Take your p." 1Ki 20.12
they took their p. against the 20.12
for kings and all who are in high p., 1Ti 2.02

POSSESS
to give you this land to p." Gen 15.07
am I to know that I shall p. it?" 15.08
descendants shall p. the gate of 22.17
descendants p. the gate of those 24.60
and herds and all that they p., 47.01
the Hittite to p. as a burying 49.30
the Hittite, to p. as a burying place. 50.13
you are increased and p. the land. Ex 23.30
and I will give it to you to p., Lev 20.24
And in all the country you p., 25.24
and his descendants shall p. it. Num 14.24
of his family, and he shall p. it. 27.11
given the land to you to p. it. 33.53
of Israel may p. the inheritance 36.08
will give it, and they shall p. it. Deu 1.39
God has given you this land to p.; 3.18
which you are going over to p. 4.14
are going over the Jordan to p.; 4.26
the land which I give them to p.' 5.31
in the land which you shall p. 5.33
which you are going over, to p. it; 6.01
and go in and p. the land which the 8.01
has brought me in to p. this land'; 9.04
are you going in to p. their land; 9.05
good land to p. because of your 9.06
they may go in and p. the land, 10.11
which you are going over to p., 11.08
going over to p. is a land of 11.11
and when you p. it and live in it, 11.31
your fathers, has given you to p., 12.01
you for an inheritance to p.), 15.04
and you p. it and dwell in it, and 17.14
the LORD your God gives you to p. 19.02
the LORD your God gives you to p., 19.14
the LORD your God gives you to p., 21.01
gives you an inheritance to p., 25.19
of your ground the locust shall p. 28.42
possessed, that you may p. it; 30.05
over the Jordan to enter and p. 30.18
are going over the Jordan to p." 31.13
are going over the Jordan to p." 32.47
p. the lake and the south." 33.23
the LORD your God gives you to p.' " Jos 1.11
and shall p. it, the land which 1.15
clear it and p. it to its farthest 17.18
and you shall p. their land, as the 23.05
the hill country of Seir to p., 24.04
Will you not p. what Chemosh your Ju 11.24
Chemosh your god gives you to p.? 11.24
dispossessed before us, we will p. 11.24
go, and enter in and p. the land. 18.09
that you may p. this good land, 1Ch 28.08
to go in to p. the land which thou Neh 9.15
told their fathers to enter and p. 9.23
and his children shall p. the land. Ps 25.13
for the LORD shall p. the land. 37.09
But the meek shall p. the land, 37.11
by the LORD shall p. the land, 37.22
The righteous shall p. the land, 37.29
he will exalt you to p. the land; 37.34
shall dwell there and p. it; 69.35
of Israel will p. them in the Is 14.02
lest they rise and p. the earth, 14.21
hawk and the porcupine shall p. it, 34.11
they shall p. it for ever, from 34.17
descendants will p. the nations and 54.03
refuge in me shall p. the land, 57.13
they shall p. the land for ever, the 60.21
land you shall p. a double portion; 61.07
the land is surely given us to p.' Eze 33.24
shed blood; shall you then p. the land? 33.25
wife; shall you then p. the land? 33.26
that they might p. it and plunder 36.05
and they shall p. you, and you shall 36.12
and p. the kingdom for ever, for Dan 7.18
Nettles shall p. their precious Hos 9.06
to p. the land of the Amorite. Amo 2.10
that they may p. the remnant of 9.12
of Jacob shall p. their own Ob 1.17
Those of the Negeb shall p. Mount Esau, 1.19
they shall p. the land of Ephraim 1.19
of Samaria and Benjamin shall p. Gilead. 1.19
of Israel shall p. Phoenicia as 1.20
Sepharad shall p. the cities of the 1.20
survivors of my nation shall p. them." Zep 2.09
this people to p. all these things. Zec 8.12
sell what you p. and give to the Mt 19.21
truths to those who p. the Spirit. 1Co 2.13
know that "all of us p. knowledge." 8.01
However, not all p. this knowledge. 8.07
Do all p. gifts of healing? Do all 12.30

POSSESSED
left to him; and they p. his land. Num 21.35
the land which your fathers p., Deu 30.05
yet very much land to be p. Jos 13.01
which they had p. themselves by 22.09
descendants went in and p. the land, Neh 9.24
The man with power p. the land, Job 22.08
Thy holy people p. thy sanctuary a Is 63.18
a land p. by nettles and salt pits, Zep 2.09
him many who were p. with demons; Mt 8.16
daughter is severely p. by a demon." 15.22
who were sick or p. with demons. Mk 1.32
"He is p. by Beelzebul, and by the 3.22
who had been p. with demons begged 5.18
daughter was p. by an unclean 7.25
he who had been p. with demons was Lk 8.36
the things which he p. was his own, Ac 4.32
came out of many who were p., 8.07

POSSESSES

daughter who p. an inheritance in Num 36.08

POSSESSING

and p. wealth, and how they were far Ju 18.07
nothing, and yet p. everything. 2Co 6.10

POSSESSION

of Canaan, for an everlasting p.; Gen 17.08
presence as a p. for a burying 23.09
to Abraham as a p. in the presence 23.18
to Abraham as a p. for a burying 23.20
that you take p. of the land of 28.04
cattle in his p. which he had 31.18
places in the land of their p. 36.43
and gave them a p. in the land of 47.11
after you for an everlasting p.' 48.04
I will give it to you for a p. Ex 6.08
shall be my own p. among all 19.05
sells him or is found in p. of him, 21.16
beast is found alive in his p., 22.04
Canaan, which I give you for a p., Lev 14.34
in a house in the land of your p., 14.34
houses in the cities of their p., 25.32
a city of their p. shall be 25.33
are there p. among the people of 25.33
for that is their perpetual p. 25.34
return to the p. of his fathers. 25.41
you, to inherit as a p. for ever; 25.46
the priest shall be in p. of it. 27.21
a part of his p. by inheritance, 27.22
belongs as a p. by inheritance. 27.24
and took p. of his land from the Num 21.24
Give to us a p. among our father's 27.04
shall give them p. of an inheritance 27.07
be given to your servants for a p.; 32.05
shall be your p. before the LORD. 32.22
them the land of Gilead for a p.; 32.29
and the p. of our inheritance shall 32.32
and you shall take p. of the land 33.53
from the inheritance of their p., 35.02
give from the p. of the people of 35.08
may return to the land of his p. 35.28
go in and take p. of the land which Deu 1.08
go up, take p., as the LORD, the God 1.21
given Mount Seir to Esau as a p. 2.05
you any of their land for a p., 2.09
Ar to the sons of Lot for a p.' 2.09
Israel did to the land of their p., 2.12
land of the sons of Ammon as a p., 2.19
it to the sons of Lot for a p.' 2.19
begin to take p., and contend with 2.24
begin to take p., that you may 2.31
"When we took p. of this land at 3.12
man to his p. which I have given 3.20
put them in p. of the land which 3.28
go in and take p. of the land 4.01
you are entering to take p. of it. 4.05
to be a people of his own p., 4.20
over and take p. of that good land. 4.22
And they took p. of his land and 4.47
go in and take p. of the good land 6.18
you are entering to take p. of it, 7.01
you to be a people for his own p., 7.06
'Go up and take p. of the land 9.23
go in and take p. of the land 11.08
entering to take p. of it is not 11.10
you are entering to take p. of it, 11.29
go in and take p. of the land which 11.31
you to be a people for his own p., 14.02
LORD your God gives you as a p., 19.03
you are entering to take p. of it. 23.20
inheritance, and have taken p. of it, 26.01
you are a people for his own p., 26.18
you are entering to take p. of it. 28.21
you are entering to take p. of it. 28.63
you are entering to take p. of it. 30.16
and you shall put them in p. of it. 31.07
to the people of Israel for a p.; 32.49
as a p. for the assembly of Jacob. 33.04
go in to take p. of the land which Jos 1.11
they also take p. of the land 1.15
return to the land of your p., 1.15
and took p. of their land beyond 12.01
land for a p. to the Reubenites 12.06
of Israel as a p. according to 12.07
could not take p. of those cities; 17.12
to go in and take p. of the land, 18.03
sword they took p. of it and 19.47
the son of Jephunneh as his p. 21.12
midst of the p. of the people of 21.41
and having taken p. of it, 21.43
in the land where your p. lies, 22.04
Moses had given a p. in Bashan; 22.07
had given a p. beside their 22.07
take for yourselves a p. among us; 22.19
and you took p. of their land, and I 24.08
and he took p. of the hill country, Ju 1.19
inheritance to take p. of the land. 2.06
and they took p. of the city of 3.13
of the LORD took p. of Gideon; 6.34
so Israel took p. of all the land 11.21
And they took p. of all the territory 11.22
and are you to take p. of them? 11.23
take p. of the vineyard of Naboth 1Ki 21.15
the Jezreelite, to take p. of it. 21.16
where he has gone to take p. 21.18
"Have you killed, and also taken p.?"' 21.19
and they took p. of Samaria, and 2Ki 17.24
coming to drive us out of thy p., 2Ch 20.11
of God took p. of Zechariah the 24.20
their cities, every man to his p. 31.01
then have no p. in the province Ez 4.16
to take p. of it, is a land unclean 9.11
so they took p. of the land of Neh 9.22
and took p. of houses full of all 9.25
and the ends of the earth your p. Ps 2.08
them for a p. and settled the 78.55
"Let us take p. for ourselves of 83.12
and they took p. of the fruit of 105.44
for himself, Israel as his own p. 135.04
will make it a p. of the hedgehog, Is 14.23
and they shall take p. of it." Jer 30.03
the right of p. and redemption is 32.08
and they entered and took p. of it. 32.23
nations to take p. of their houses; Eze 7.24
to us this land is given for a p.' 11.15
to the people of the East for a p., 25.04
to the people of the East as a p., 25.10
one man, yet he got p. of the land; 33.24
mine, and we will take p. of them, 35.10
heights have become our p.,' 36.02
you became the p. of the rest of 36.03
themselves as a p. with wholehearted 36.05
no p. in Israel; I am their p. 44.28
"When you allot the land as a p., 45.01
as their p. for cities to live in. 45.05
assign for the p. of the city an 45.06
child, and he who got p. of her. Dan 11.06
become the p. of the remnant of Zep 2.07
land has been my p. since my youth.' Zec 13.05
my special p. on the day when I act, Mal 3.17
it to him in p. and to his posterity Ac 7.05
inheritance until we acquire p. of it, Eph 1.14
had a better p. and an abiding one Heb 10.34

POSSESSIONS

and all their p. which they had Gen 12.05
for their p. were so great that 13.06
they shall come out with great p. 15.14
He had p. of flocks and herds, and a 26.14
For their p. were too great for 36.07
and they gained p. in it, and were 47.27
they shall have p. among you in Num 32.30

POSSESSIONS (cont.)

he assigns his p. as an inheritance Deu 21.16
Their p. and settlements were 1Ch 7.28
again in their p. in their cities 9.02
heart, and you have not asked p., 2Ch 1.11
p., and honor, and such as none of the 1.12
and valuable p., together with 21.03
your wives, and all your p., 21.14
away all the p. they found that 21.17
from his own p. was for the burnt 31.03
God had given him very great p. 32.29
these were from the king's p. 35.07
and his p. have increased in the Job 1.10
The p. of his house will be carried 20.28
house, and ruler of all his p., Ps 105.21
had also great p. of herds and Ecc 2.07
wealth and p. and power to enjoy 5.19
p., and honor, so that he lacks 6.02
Jacob shall possess their own p. Ob 1.17
her of her p. and hurl her wealth Zec 9.04
sorrowful; for he had great p. Mt 19.22
he will set him over all his p. 24.47
sorrowful; for he had great p. Mk 10.22
consist in the abundance of his p." Lk 12.15
Sell your p., and give alms; 12.33
he will set him over all his p. 12.44
and they sold their p. and goods Ac 2.45

POSSESSORS

it takes away the life of its p. Pro 1.19
as many as were p. of lands or Ac 4.34

POSSIBLE

but with God all things are p." Mt 19.26
lead astray, if p., even the elect. 24.24
if it be p., let this cup pass from 26.39
All things are p. to him who Mk 9.23
for all things are p. with God." 10.27
to lead astray, if p., the elect. 13.22
if it were p., the hour might pass 14.35
Father, all things are p. to thee; 14.36
impossible with men is p. with God." Lk 18.27
it was not p. for him to be held Ac 2.24
if p., the intent of your heart may 8.22
him as soon as p., they departed. 17.15
if p., on the day of Pentecost. 20.16
they planned if p. to bring the 27.39
If p., so far as it depends upon Rom 12.18
if p., you would have plucked out Gal 4.15
that if p. I may attain the resurrection Php 3.11

POST

each from his p., and put commanders 1Ki 20.24
and at my p. I am stationed whole Is 21.08
his stand by the p. of the gate. Eze 46.02

POSTED

And the priest p. watchmen over the 2Ki 11.18
And Jehoiada p. watchmen for the 2Ch 23.18

POSTERITY

or with my offspring or with my p., Gen 21.23
So their p. perished from Heshbon, Num 21.30
P. shall serve him; men shall tell Ps 22.30
for there is p. for the man of 37.37
the p. of the wicked shall be cut 37.38
their p. shall be established 102.28
May his p. be cut off; may his name 109.13
offspring and p., says the LORD. Is 14.22
winds of heaven, but not to his p., Dan 11.04
to Abraham and to his p., for ever." Lk 1.55
'And in his p. shall all the Ac 3.25
possession and to his p. after him, 7.05
that his p. would be aliens in a 7.06
Of this man's p. God has brought to 13.23

POSTS

gate of the city and the two p., Ju 16.03
The priests stood at their p.; 2Ch 7.06
accustomed p. according to the law 30.16
He made its p. of silver, its back Sol 3.10
and the p. of the gate of the inner Eze 45.19

POT

a smoking fire p. and a flaming Gen 15.17
and the broth he put in a p., Ju 6.19
pan, or kettle, or cauldron, or p.; 1Sa 2.14
his servant, "Set on the great p., 2Ki 4.38
cut them up into the p. of pottage, 4.39
of God, there is death in the p.!" 4.40
And he threw it into the p., 4.41
And there was no harm in the p. 4.41
from a boiling p. and burning Job 41.20
He makes the deep boil like a p.; 41.31
the sea like a p. of ointment. 41.31
the crackling of thorns under a p., Ecc 7.06
And I said, "I see a boiling p., Jer 1.13
broken p., a vessel no one cares 22.28
Set on the p., set it on, pour in Eze 24.03
to the p. whose rust is in it, and 24.06
like a blazing p. in the midst of Zec 12.06
and every p. in Jerusalem and Judah 14.21

POTIPHAR

had sold him in Egypt to P., Gen 37.36
and P., an officer of Pharaoh, the 39.01

POTIPHERA

the daughter of P. priest of On. Gen 41.45
the daughter of P. priest of On, 41.50
the daughter of P. the priest of 46.20

POTS

You shall make p. for it to receive Ex 27.03
the p., the shovels, the basins, the 38.03
it in mortars, and boiled it in p., Num 11.08
Hiram also made the p., the shovels, 1Ki 7.40
Now the p., the shovels, and the 7.45
And they took away the p., and the 2Ki 25.14
Huram also made the p., the shovels, 2Ch 4.11
The p., the shovels, the forks, and 4.16
boiled the holy offerings in p., 35.13
Sooner than your p. can feel the Ps 58.09
And they took away the p., and the Jer 52.18
and the p., and the lampstands, and 52.19
they are reckoned as earthen p., Lam 4.02
"And the p. in the house of the Zec 14.20
of cups and p. and vessels of Mk 7.04
as when earthen p. are broken in Rev 2.27

POTSHERD

And he took a p. with which to Job 2.08
my strength is dried up like a p., Ps 22.15
at the entry of the P. Gate, Jer 19.02

POTSHERDS

His underparts are like sharp p.; Job 41.30

POTTAGE

Once when Jacob was boiling p., Gen 25.29
"Let me eat some of that red p., 25.30
gave Esau bread and p. of lentils, 25.34
and boil p. for the sons of the 2Ki 4.38
and cut them up into the pot of p., 4.39
while they were eating of the p., 4.40
or p., or wine, or oil, or any kind Hag 2.12

POTTER

Shall the p. be regarded as the Is 29.16
on mortar, as the p. treads clay. 41.25
an earthen vessel with the p.! 45.09
are the clay, and thou art our p.; 64.08
as it seemed good to the p. to do. Jer 18.04
do with you as this p. has done? 18.06
Has the p. no right over the clay, Rom 9.21

POTTER'S

them in pieces like a p. vessel. Ps 2.09
like that of a p. vessel which is Is 30.14
"Arise, and go down to the p. house, Jer 18.02
So I went down to the p. house, 18.03
of clay was spoiled in the p. hand, 18.04
like the clay in the p. hand, 18.06
buy a p. earthen flask, and take 19.01
city, as one breaks a p. vessel, 19.11
pots, the work of a p. hands! Lam 4.02
toes partly of p. clay and partly Dan 2.41
and bought with them the p. field, Mt 27.07
and they gave them for the p. field, 27.10

POTTERS

These were the p. and inhabitants 1Ch 4.23

POUND

your p. has made ten pounds more.' Lk 19.16
'Lord, your p. has made five pounds.' 19.18
here is your p., which I kept laid 19.20
'Take the p. from him, and give it 19.24
Mary took a p. of costly ointment Jn 12.03

POUNDS

his servants, he gave them ten p., Lk 19.13
your pound has made ten p. more.' 19.16
'Lord, your pound has made five p.' 19.18
give it to him who has the ten p.' 19.24
said to him, 'Lord, he has ten p.!' 19.25

POUNDS'

aloes, about a hundred p. weight. Jn 19.39

POUR

the Nile and p. it upon the dry Ex 4.09
bowls with which to p. libations; 25.29
and p. it on his head and anoint 29.07
blood you shall p. out at the base 29.12
and you shall p. no libation thereon 30.09
flagons with which to p. libations. 37.16
he shall p. oil upon it, and put Lev 2.01
it in pieces, and p. oil on it; 2.06
bull he shall p. out at the base 4.07
blood he shall p. out at the base 4.18
and p. out the rest of its blood at 4.25
and p. out the rest of its blood at 4.30
and p. out the rest of its blood at 4.34
and p. it into the palm of his own 14.15
priest shall p. some of the oil 14.26
off they shall p. into an unclean 14.41
be eaten shall p. out its blood 17.13
he shall p. no oil upon it and put Num 5.15
place you shall p. out a drink 28.07
you shall p. it out upon the earth Deu 12.16
you shall p. it out upon the earth 12.24
you shall p. it out on the ground 15.23
and p. the broth over them." And he did Ju 6.20
and p. it on the burnt offering, and 1Ki 18.33
and p. into all these vessels; 2Ki 4.04
"P. out for the men, that they may 4.41
and p. it on his head, and say, 'Thus 9.03
Didst thou not p. me out like milk Job 10.10
which the skies p. down, and drop 36.28
P. forth the overflowings of your 40.11
I will not p. out or take their Ps 16.04
as I p. out my soul: how I went with 42.04
p. out your heart before him; 62.08
P. out thy indignation upon them, 69.24
and he will p. a draught from it, 75.08
P. out thy anger on the nations 79.06
They p. out their arrogant words, 94.04
My lips will p. forth praise that 119.171
I p. out my complaint before him, I 142.02
They shall p. forth the fame of thy 145.07
I will p. out my thoughts to you; Pro 1.23
the mouths of fools p. out folly. 15.02
For I will p. water on the thirsty Is 44.03
I will p. my Spirit upon your 44.03
if you p. yourself out for the 58.10
"P. it out upon the children in the Jer 6.11
and they p. out drink offerings to 7.18
P. out thy wrath upon the nations 10.25
For I will p. out their wickedness 14.16
of heaven and p. out libations to 44.17
heaven and to p. out libations to 44.25
P. out your heart like water before Lam 2.19
Now I will soon p. out my wrath Eze 7.08
and p. out my wrath upon it with 14.19
thought I would p. out my wrath 20.08
thought I would p. out my wrath 20.13
thought I would p. out my wrath 20.21
And I will p. out my indignation 21.31
pot, set it on, p. in water also; 24.03
she did not p. it upon the ground 24.07
And I will p. my wrath upon Pelusium, 30.15
when I p. out my Spirit upon the 39.29
them I will p. out my wrath like Hos 5.10
They shall not p. libations of wine 9.04
that I will p. out my spirit on all Joe 2.28
days, I will p. out my spirit. 2.29
and I will p. down her stones into Mic 1.06
to p. out upon them my indignation, Zep 3.08
"And I will p. out on the house of Zec 12.10
for you and p. down for you an Mal 3.10
that I will p. out my Spirit upon Ac 2.17
those days I will p. out my Spirit; 2.18
Does a spring p. forth from the Jas 3.11
"Go and p. out on the earth the Rev 16.01

POURED

a pillar and p. oil on the top of Gen 28.18
and he p. out a drink offering on 35.14
offering on it, and p. oil on it. 35.14
rain no longer p. upon the earth. Ex 9.33
It shall not be p. upon the bodies 30.32
place, where the ashes are p. out, Lev 4.12
the ashes are p. out it shall be 4.12
And he p. some of the anointing oil 8.12
and p. out the blood at the base of 8.15
and p. out the blood at the base of 9.09
whose head the anointing oil is p., 21.10
shall be p. out on the altar of Deu 12.17
drew water and p. it out before 1Sa 7.06
vial of oil and p. it on his head, 10.01
of it; he p. it out to the LORD, 2Sa 23.16
that are upon it shall be p. out. 1Ki 13.03
and the ashes p. out from the altar, 13.05
who p. water on the hands of Elijah." 2Ki 3.11
and as she p. they brought the 4.05
And they p. out for the men to eat. 4.40
the young man p. the oil on his 9.06
the p. his drink offering, and threw 16.13
of it; he p. it out to the LORD, 1Ch 11.18
shall not be p. out upon Jerusalem 2Ch 12.07
of the LORD that is p. out on us, 34.21
wrath will be p. out upon this 34.25
my groanings are p. out like water. Job 3.24
and the rock p. out for me streams 29.06
"And now my soul is p. out within me; 30.16
I am p. out like water, and all my Ps 22.14
grace is p. upon your lips; 45.02
the heavens p. down rain, at the 68.08
The clouds p. out water; the skies 77.17
They have p. out their blood like 79.03
thou hast p. over me fresh oil. 92.10
they p. out innocent blood, the 106.38
fragrant, your name is oil p. out; Sol 1.03
they p. out a prayer when thy Is 26.16
For the LORD has p. out upon you a 29.10
until the Spirit is p. upon us from 32.15
So he p. upon him the heat of his 42.25
because he p. out his soul to death, 53.12
them you have p. out a drink 57.06
and I p. out their lifeblood on the 63.06

POURED (cont.)
wrath will be p. out on this place, Jer 7.20
have been p. out to other gods— 19.13
have been p. out to other gods, to 32.29
my wrath were p. out on the 42.18
wrath will be p. out on you when 42.18
my anger were p. forth and kindled 44.06
of heaven and p. out libations to 44.19
her image and p. out libations to 44.19
he has p. out his fury like fire. Lam 2.04
my heart is p. out in grief because 2.11
their life is p. out on their 2.12
he p. out his hot anger; and he 4.11
and there they p. out their drink Eze 20.28
outstretched arm, and with wrath p. out, 20.33
outstretched arm, and with wrath p. out; 20.34
I the LORD have p. out my wrath 22.22
Therefore I have p. out my indignation 22.31
bosom and p. out their lust upon 23.08
So I p. out my wrath upon them for 36.18
of God have been p. out upon us, Dan 9.11
decreed end is p. out on the 9.27
he has p. down for you abundant Joe 2.23
like waters p. down a steep place. Mic 1.04
His wrath is p. out like fire, and Nah 1.06
blood shall be p. out like dust, Zep 1.17
pipes from which the oil is p. out?" Zec 4.12
and she p. it on his head, as he sat Mt 26.07
which is p. out for many for the 26.28
the jar and p. it over his head. Mk 14.03
covenant, which is p. out for many. 14.24
cup which is p. out for you is the *Lk 22.20
and he p. out the coins of the Jn 2.15
Then he p. water into a basin, and 13.05
he has p. out this which you see Ac 2.33
Spirit had been p. out even on the 10.45
love has been p. into our hearts Rom 5.05
Even if I am to be p. as a libation Php 2.17
which he p. out upon us richly Tit 3.06
The serpent p. water like a river Rev 12.15
the dragon had p. from his mouth. 12.16
p. unmixed into the cup of his 14.10
angel went and p. his bowl on the 16.02
The second angel p. his bowl into 16.03
The third angel p. his bowl into 16.04
The fourth angel p. his bowl on the 16.08
The fifth angel p. his bowl on the 16.10
The sixth angel p. his bowl on the 16.12
The seventh angel p. his bowl into 16.17

POURING
but I have been p. out my soul 1Sa 1.15
of heaven and p. out libations to Jer 44.18
In p. this ointment on my body she Mt 26.12
p. on oil and wine; then he set him Lk 10.34

POURS
He p. contempt on princes, and Job 12.21
he p. out my gall on the ground. 16.13
scorn me; my eye p. out tears to God, 16.20
Day to day p. forth speech, and Ps 19.02
he p. contempt upon princes and 107.40
of the wicked p. out evil things. Pro 15.28
and p. them out upon the surface of Amo 5.08
and p. them out upon the surface of 9.06
fire p. from their mouth and Rev 11.05

POVERTY
and all that you have, come to p.' Gen 45.11
and p. will come upon you like a Pro 6.11
A slack hand causes p., but the hand 10.04
the p. of the poor is their ruin. 10.15
P. and disgrace come to him who 13.18
Love not sleep, lest you come to p.; 20.13
and the glutton will come to p., 23.21
and p. will come upon you like a 24.34
pursuits will have plenty of p. 28.19

give me neither p. nor riches; 30.08
let them drink and forget their p., 31.07
she out of her p. has put in Mk 12.44
she out of her p. put in all the Lk 21.04
their extreme p. have overflowed 2Co 8.02
so that by his p. you might become 8.09
and your p. (but you are rich) and Rev 2.09

POWDER
it with fire, and ground it to p., Ex 32.20
the rain of your land p. and dust; Deu 28.24
the Asherim and the images into p., 2Ch 34.07

POWDERS
the fragrant p. of the merchant? Sol 3.06

POWER
"Behold, your maid is in your p.; Gen 16.06
It is in my p. to do you harm; 31.29
in pride and pre-eminent in p. 49.03
which I have put in your p.; Ex 4.21
I let you live, to show you my p., 9.16
glorious in p., thy right hand, O 15.06
with great p. and with a mighty 32.11
and I will break the pride of your p., Lev 26.19
shall have no p. to stand before 26.37
let the p. of the LORD be great as Num 14.17
Have I now any p. at all to speak 22.38
his own presence, by his great p., Deu 4.37
'My p. and the might of my hand 8.17
he who gives you p. to get wealth; 8.18
by thy great p. and by thy outstretched 9.29
not be in the p. of your hand to 28.32
when he sees that their p. is gone, 32.36
all the mighty p. and all the 34.12
and they had no p. to flee this way Jos 8.20
numerous people, and have great p.; 17.17
them into the p. of their enemies Ju 2.14
them out of the p. of those who 2.16
give them into the p. of Joshua. 2.23
and exalt the p. of his anointed." 1Sa 2.10
save us from the p. of our enemies." 4.03
us from the p. of these mighty 4.08
to restore his p. at the river 2Sa 8.03
him from the p. of his enemies." 18.19
day from the p. of all who rose up 18.31
the p. of the LORD came upon him. 2Ki 3.15
as the royal p. was firmly in his 14.05
confirm his hold of the royal p. 15.19
with great p. and with an outstretched 17.36
and the p., and the glory, and the 1Ch 29.11
In thy hand are p. and might; 29.12
not recover his p. in the days of 2Ch 13.20
In thy hand are p. and might, 20.06
as the royal p. was firmly in his 25.03
for God has p. to help or to cast 25.08
who could make war with mighty p., 26.13
by force and p. made them cease. Ez 4.23
and the p. of his wrath is against 8.22
by thy great p. and by thy strong Neh 1.10
but it is not in our p. to help it, 5.05
they have p. also over our bodies 9.37
And all the acts of his p. and might, Est 10.02
all that he has is in your p.; Job 1.12
to Satan, "Behold, he is in your p.; 2.06
in war from the p. of the sword. 5.20
them into the p. of their transgression. 8.04
old age, and grow mighty in p.? 21.07
The man with p. possessed the land, 22.08
with me in the greatness of his p.? 23.06
the life of the mighty by his p.; 24.22
"How you have helped him who has no p.! 26.02
By his p. he stilled the sea; 26.12
thunder of his p. who can understand?" 26.14
flees from its p. in headlong 27.22
Behold, God is exalted in his p.; 36.22
he is great in p. and justice, 37.23
and his p. in the muscles of his 40.16

POWER (cont.)
We will sing and praise thy p. Ps 21.13
my life from the p. of the dog! 22.20
will not abandon him to his p., 37.33
my soul from the p. of Sheol, 49.15
make them totter by thy p., and bring 59.11
heard this: that p. belongs to God; 62.11
sanctuary, beholding thy p. and glory. 63.02
given over to the p. of the sword, 63.10
So great is thy p. that thy enemies 66.03
thy saving p. among all nations. 67.02
Ascribe p. to God, whose majesty is 68.34
and his p. is in the skies. 68.34
he gives p. and strength to his 68.35
Thy p. and thy righteousness, O God, 71.19
and did not trust his saving p. 78.22
and by his p. he led out the south 78.26
They did not keep in mind his p., 78.42
and delivered his p. to captivity, 78.61
to thy great p. preserve those 79.11
his soul from the p. of Sheol? 89.48
Who considers the p. of thy anger, 90.11
thy glorious p. to their children. 90.16
he might make known his mighty p. 106.08
them from the p. of the enemy. 106.10
into subjection under their p. 106.42
his people the p. of his works, 111.06
thy kingdom, and tell of thy p., 145.11
Great is our LORD, and abundant in p.; 147.05
when it is in your p. to do it. Pro 3.27
have come into your neighbor's p.: 6.03
life are in the p. of the tongue, 18.21
of their oppressors there was p., Ecc 4.01
possessions and p. to enjoy them, 5.19
does not give him p. to enjoy them, 6.02
No man has p. to retain the spirit, 8.08
lop the boughs with terrifying p.; Is 10.33
words are strategy and p. for war? 36.05
he is strong in p. not one is 40.26
He gives p. in the faint, and to him 40.29
and the great p. of your enchantments. 47.09
themselves from the p. of the flame. 47.14
Or have I no p. to deliver? Behold, 50.02
is he who made the earth by his p., Jer 10.12
make them know my p. and my might, 16.21
them over to the p. of the sword, 18.21
who by my great p. and my outstretched 27.05
by thy great p. and by thy outstretched 32.17
is he who made the earth by his p., 51.15
you, every one according to his p., Eze 22.06
my sanctuary, the pride of your p., 24.21
Israel to the p. of the sword at 35.05
the p., and the might, and the glory, Dan 2.37
had not had any p. over the bodies 3.27
by his mighty p. as a royal residence 4.30
Daniel from the p. of the lions." 6.27
one who could rescue from his p.; 8.04
the ram had no p. to stand before 8.07
could rescue the ram from his p. 8.07
his nation, but not with his p. 8.22
His p. shall be great, and he shall 8.24
and all of it shall be in his p. 11.16
stir up his p. and his courage 11.25
shattering of the p. of the holy 12.07
I ransom them from the p. of Sheol? Hos 13.14
it is in the p. of their hand. Mic 2.01
But as for me, I am filled with p., 3.08
from his hand; and there he veiled his p. Hab 3.04
nor by p., but by my Spirit, says Zec 4.06
kingdom and the p. and the glory, *Mt 6.13
the scriptures nor the p. of God. 22.29
of heaven with p. and great glory; 24.30
man seated at the right hand of P., 26.64
in himself that p. had gone forth Mk 5.30
the kingdom of God come with p." 9.01
the scriptures nor the p. of God? 12.24
in clouds with great p. and glory. 13.26
sitting at the right hand of P., 14.62
him in the spirit and p. of Elijah, Lk 1.17
and the p. of the Most High will 1.35
returned in the p. of the Spirit 4.14
authority and p. he commands the 4.36
and the p. of the Lord was with him 5.17
for p. came forth from him and 6.19
I perceive that p. has gone forth 8.46
and gave them p. and authority 9.01
and over all the p. of the enemy; 10.19
has p. to cast into hell; yes, I tell you, 12.05
receive kingly p. and then return. 19.12
having received the kingly p., 19.15
in a cloud with p. and great glory 21.27
your hour, and the p. of darkness." 22.53
at the right hand of the p. of God." 22.69
me when you come in your kingly p." 23.42
are clothed with p. from on high." 24.49
he gave p. to become children of Jn 1.12
I have p. to lay it down, and I have 10.18
and I have p. to take it again; 10.18
is coming. He has no p. over me; 14.30
hast given him p. over all flesh, 17.02
that I have p. to release you, and p. 19.10
would have no p. over me unless it 19.11
shall receive p. when the Holy Ac 1.08
by our own p. or piety we had made 3.12
"By what p. or by what name did you 4.07
And with great p. the apostles gave 4.33
And Stephen, full of grace and p., 6.08
man is that p. of God which is 8.10
saying 'Give me also this p., 8.19
with the Holy Spirit and with p.; 10.38
and from the p. of Satan to God, 26.18
Son of God in p. according to the Rom 1.04
it is the p. of God for salvation 1.16
his eternal p. and deity, has been 1.20
Greeks, are under the p. of sin, 3.09
purpose of showing my p. in you, 9.17
his wrath and to make known his p., 9.22
for God has the p. to graft them 11.23
so that by the p. of the Holy 15.13
p. of signs and wonders, by the p. 15.19
of Christ be emptied of its p. 1Co 1.17
being saved it is the p. of God. 1.18
Christ the p. of God and the wisdom 1.24
demonstration of the Spirit and p., 2.04
wisdom of men but in the p. of God. 2.05
these arrogant people but their p. 4.19
does not consist in talk but in p. 4.20
is present, with the p. of our Lord Jesus, 5.04
will also raise us up by his p. 6.14
pray for the p. to interpret. 14.13
rule and every authority and p. 15.24
in weakness, it is raised in p. 15.43
and the p. of sin is the law. 15.56
transcendent p. belongs to God and 2Co 4.07
truthful speech, and the p. of God; 6.07
but have divine p. to destroy 10.04
for my p. is made perfect in 12.09
that the p. of Christ may rest upon 12.09
weakness but lives by the p. of God. 13.04
live with him by the p. of God. 13.04
greatness of his p. in us who Eph 1.19
and authority and p. and dominion, 1.21
the prince of the p. of the air, 2.02
given me by the working of his p. 3.07
may have p. to comprehend with all 3.18
him who by the p. at work within 3.20
him and the p. of his resurrection, Php 3.10
by the p. which enables him even to 3.21
May you be strengthened with all p., Col 1.11
but also in p. and in the Holy 1Th 1.05
and work of faith by his p., 2Th 1.11
be with all p. and with pretended 2.09
but a spirit of p. and love and 2Ti 1.07
for the gospel in the p. of God, 1.08

POWER (cont.)

religion but denying the p. of it. 2Ti 3.05
the universe by his word of p. Heb 1.03
him who has the p. of death, 2.14
but by the p. of an indestructible 7.16
herself received p. to conceive, 11.11
man has great p. in its effects. Jas 5.16
who by God's p. are guarded through 1Pe 1.05
His divine p. has granted to us all 2Pe 1.03
to you the p. and coming of our 1.16
though greater in might and p., 2.11
world is in the p. of the evil one. 1Jn 5.19
I will give him p. over the nations. Rev 2.26
have received p. from my Father; 2.27
I know that you have but little p., 3.08
to receive glory and honor and p., 4.11
to receive p. and wealth and wisdom 5.12
they were given p. over a fourth 6.08
had been given p. to harm earth 7.02
and honor and p. and might be to 7.12
given p. like the p. of scorpions 9.03
and their p. of hurting men for 9.10
For the p. of the horses is in 9.19
two witnesses p. to prophesy for 11.03
They have p. to shut the sky, that 11.06
and they have p. over the waters to 11.06
taken thy great p. and begun to 11.17
salvation and the p. and the 12.10
dragon gave his p. and his throne 13.02
the angel who has p. over fire, 14.18
the glory of God and from his p., 15.08
of God who had p. over these 16.09
who have not yet received royal p., 17.12
give over their p. and authority 17.13
over their royal p. to the beast, 17.17
and glory and p. belong to our God, 19.01
such the second death has no p., 20.06

POWERFUL

man Mordecai grew more and more p. Est 9.04
The voice of the LORD is p., the voice Ps 29.04
and decides between p. contenders. Pro 18.18
no great and p. king has asked Dan 2.10
p. and without number; its teeth Joe 1.06
mountains a great and p. people; 2.02
like a p. army drawn up for battle. 2.05
he that executes his word is p. 2.11
not many were p., not many were of 1Co 1.26
dealing with you, but is p. in you. 2Co 13.03

POWERFULLY

for he p. confuted the Jews in Ac 18.28

POWERLESS

For we are p. against this great 2Ch 20.12

POWERS

is why these p. are at work in him." Mt 14.02
and the p. of death shall not 16.18
and the p. of the heavens will be 24.29
is why these p. are at work in him." Mk 6.14
and the p. in the heavens will be 13.25
for the p. of the heavens will be Lk 21.26
present, nor things to come, nor p., Rom 8.38
And if I have prophetic p., and understand 1Co 13.02
principalities and p. in the Eph 3.10
against the p., against the world 6.12
principalities and p. and made a Col 2.15
of God and the p. of the age to Heb 6.05
authorities, and p. subject to him. 1Pe 3.22

PRACTICE

charge never to p. any of these Lev 18.30
You shall not p. augury or witchcraft. 19.26
the peoples who p. these abominations? Ez 9.14
understanding have all those who p. it. Ps 111.10
to p. ungodliness, to utter error Is 32.06
that I am the LORD who p. kindness, Jer 9.24
delusive visions nor p. divination; Eze 13.23
when they p. harlotry with her? 23.43
so p. and observe whatever they Mt 23.03
for they preach, but do not p. 23.03
for us Romans to accept or p." Ac 16.21
them but approve those who p. them. Rom 1.32
of the saints, p. hospitality. 12.13
Consider the p. of Israel; 1Co 10.18
contentious, we recognize no other p., 11.16
we refuse to p. cunning or to tamper 2Co 4.02
greedy to p. every kind of uncleanness. Eph 4.19
P. these duties, devote yourself to 1Ti 4.15
trained by p. to distinguish good Heb 5.14
will be disorder and every vile p. Jas 3.16
P. hospitality ungrudgingly to one 1Pe 4.09
sacrificed to idols and p. immorality. Rev 2.14
my servants to p. immorality and 2.20

PRACTICED

customs which were p. before you, Lev 18.30
and p. soothsaying and augury, and 2Ki 21.06
and p. soothsaying and augury and 2Ch 33.06
oppressions that are p. under the sun. Ecc 4.01
because he p. extortion, robbed his Eze 18.18
the land have p. extortion and 22.29
which she had p. since her days in 23.08
treachery they have p. against me, 39.26
had previously p. magic in the Ac 8.09
of those who p. magic arts brought 19.19
licentiousness which they have p. 2Co 12.21

PRACTICES

the abominable p. of those nations Deu 18.09
any one who p. divination, a soothsayer, 18.10
abominable p. the LORD your God is 18.12
abominable p. which they have done 20.18
with abominable p. they provoked 32.16
any of their p. or their stubborn Ju 2.19
the abominable p. of the nations 2Ki 16.03
the abominable p. of the nations 21.02
people still followed corrupt p. 2Ch 27.02
the abominable p. of the nations 28.03
the abominable p. of the nations 33.02
Esther fixed these p. of Purim, Est 9.32
No man who p. deceit shall dwell in Ps 101.07
confessing and divulging their p. Ac 19.18
the man who p. the righteousness Rom 10.05
put off the old nature with its p. Col 3.09
nor any one who p. abomination or Rev 21.27
one who loves and p. falsehood. 22.15

PRACTICING

and for p. oppression and violence. Jer 22.17
off your sins by p. righteousness, Dan 4.27
"Beware of p. your piety before men Mt 6.01

PRAETORIAN

the whole p. guard and to all the Php 1.13

PRAETORIUM

governor took Jesus into the p., Mt 27.27
inside the palace (that is, the p.); Mk 15.16
the house of Caiaphas to the p. Jn 18.28
themselves did not enter the p., 18.28
Pilate entered the p. again and 18.33
he entered the p. again and said to 19.09
him to be guarded in Herod's p. Ac 23.35

PRAISE

"This time I will p. the LORD"; Gen 29.35
Judah, your brothers shall p. you; 49.08
and I will p. him, my father's God, Ex 15.02
an offering of p. to the LORD. Lev 19.24
He is your p.; he is your God; Deu 10.21
in p. and in fame and in honor, and 26.19
"P. his people, O you nations; 32.43
of Israel, and render p. to him; Jos 7.19
and to p. the LORD, the God of 1Ch 16.04

PRAISE (cont.)

thy holy name, and glory in thy p. 1Ch 16.35
instruments which have made for p." 23.05
in thanksgiving and p. to the LORD. 25.03
our God, and p. thy glorious name. 29.13
in unison in p. and thanksgiving 2Ch 5.13
in p. to the LORD, "For he is good, 5.13
offices of p. and ministry before 8.14
stood up to p. the LORD, the God of 20.19
to the LORD and p. him in holy 20.21
And when they began to sing and p., 20.22
the LORD and to give thanks and p. 31.02
to p. the LORD, according to the Ez 3.10
exalted above all blessing and p." Neh 9.05
to p. and to give thanks, according 12.24
were songs of p. and thanksgiving 12.46
in Sheol who can give thee p.? Ps 6.05
and I will sing p. to the name of 7.17
I will sing p. to thy name, O Most 9.02
We will sing and p. thy power. 21.13
the congregation I will p. thee: 22.22
You who fear the LORD, p. him! 22.23
From thee comes my p. in the great 22.25
who seek him shall p. the LORD! 22.26
Will the dust p. thee? Will it tell 30.09
that my soul may p. thee and not be 30.12
righteous! P. befits the upright. 33.01
P. the LORD with the lyre, make 33.02
his p. shall continually be in my 34.01
the mighty throng I will p. thee. 35.18
and of thy p. all the day long. 35.28
my mouth, a song of p. to our God. 40.03
for I shall again p. him, my help 42.05
for I shall again p. him, my help 42.11
and I will p. thee with the lyre, O 43.04
for I shall again p. him, my help 43.05
peoples will p. you for ever and 45.17
so thy p. reaches to the ends of 48.10
a man gets p. when he does well 49.18
my mouth shall show forth thy p. 51.15
whose word I p., in God I trust 56.04
I p., in the LORD, whose word I p., 56.10
than life, my lips will p. thee. 63.03
P. is due to thee, O God, in Zion; 65.01
his name; give to him glorious p.! 66.02
let the sound of his p. be heard, 66.08
Let the peoples p. thee, O God; 67.03
let all the peoples p. thee! 67.03
Let the peoples p. thee, O God; 67.05
let all the peoples p. thee! 67.05
I will p. the name of God with a 69.30
Let heaven and earth p. him, 69.34
My p. is continually of thee. 71.06
My mouth is filled with thy p., 71.08
and will p. thee yet more and more. 71.14
I will p. thy righteousness, thine 71.16
I will also p. thee with the harp 71.22
Therefore the people turn and p. them; 73.10
let the poor and needy p. thy name. 74.21
Surely the wrath of men shall p. thee; 76.10
generation we will recount thy p. 79.13
in thy house, ever singing thy p.! 84.04
Do the shades rise up to p. thee? 88.10
Let the heavens p. thy wonders, 89.05
and Hermon joyously p. thy name. 89.12
noise to him with songs of p.! 95.02
Let them p. thy great and terrible 99.03
thanksgiving, and his courts with p.! 100.04
people yet unborn may p. the LORD: 102.18
the LORD, and in Jerusalem his p., 102.21
I will sing p. to my God while I 104.33
O my soul! P. the LORD! 104.35
observe his laws. P. the LORD! 105.45
P. the LORD! O give thanks 106.01
the LORD, or show forth all his p.? 106.02
his words; they sang his p. 106.12
thy holy name and glory in thy p. 106.47
people say, "Amen!" P. the LORD! 106.48
and p. him in the assembly of the 107.32
Be not silent, O God of my p.! 109.01
I will p. him in the midst of the 109.30
P. the LORD. I will give thanks 111.01
practice it. His p. endures for ever! 111.10
P. the LORD. Blessed is the man 112.01
P. the LORD! P., O servants of the LORD, 113.01
p. the name of the LORD! 113.01
mother of children. P. the LORD! 113.09
The dead do not p. the LORD, 115.17
and for evermore. P. the LORD! 115.18
O Jerusalem. P. the LORD! 116.19
P. the LORD, all nations! 117.01
endures for ever. P. the LORD! 117.02
I will p. thee with an upright 119.07
At midnight I rise to p. thee, 119.62
Accept my offerings of p., 119.108
Seven times a day I p. thee for thy 119.164
will pour forth p. that thou dost 119.171
that I may p. thee, and let thy 119.175
P. the LORD. P. the name of the LORD, 135.01
give p., O servants of the LORD, 135.01
P. the LORD, for the LORD is good; 135.03
in Jerusalem! P. the LORD! 135.21
before the gods I sing thy p.; 138.01
kings of the earth shall p. thee, 138.04
I p. thee, for thou art fearful and 139.14
and p. thy name for ever and ever. 145.02
will speak the p. of the LORD, 145.21
P. the LORD! P. the LORD, O my soul! 146.01
I will p. the LORD as long as I 146.02
all generations. P. the LORD! 146.10
P. the LORD! For it is good 147.01
gracious, and a song of p. is seemly. 147.01
P. the LORD, O Jerusalem! 147.12
P. your God, O Zion! 147.12
his ordinances. P. the LORD! 147.20
P. the LORD! P. the LORD from the 148.01
heavens, p. him in the heights! 148.01
P. him, all his angels, p. him, all his 148.02
P, him, sun and moon, p. him all you 148.03
P. him, you highest heavens, and you 148.04
Let them p. the name of the LORD! 148.05
P the LORD from the earth, you sea 148.07
Let them p. the name of the LORD, 148.13
p. for all his saints, for the 148.14
who are near to him. P. the LORD! 148.14
P. the LORD! Sing to the LORD 149.01
his p. in the assembly of the 149.01
Let them p. his name with dancing, 149.03
his faithful ones, P. the LORD! 149.09
P. the LORD! P. God in his 150.01
p. him in his mighty firmament! 150.01
P. him for his mighty deeds; 150.02
p. him according to his exceeding 150.02
P. him with trumpet sound; 150.03
p. him with lute and harp! 150.03
P. him with timbrel and dance; 150.04
p. him with strings and pipe! 150.04
P. him with sounding cymbals; 150.05
p. him with loud clashing cymbals! 150.05
breathes p. the LORD! P. the LORD! 150.06
Let another p. you, and not your own Pro 27.02
and a man is judged by his p. 27.21
Those who forsake the law p. the wicked, 28.04
let her works p. her in the gates. 31.31
of the earth we hear songs of p., Is 24.16
exalt thee, I will p. thy name; 25.01
thank thee, death cannot p. thee; 38.18
nor my p. to graven images. 42.08
his p. from the end of the earth! 42.10
and declare his p. in the coastlands. 42.12
that they might declare my p. 43.21
the sake of my p. I restrain it 48.09
shall proclaim the p. of the LORD. 60.06
walls Salvation, and your gates P. 60.18

PRAISE (cont.)
the mantle of p. instead of a faint Is 61.03
righteousness and p. to spring 61.11
and makes it a p. in the earth. 62.07
it shall eat it and p. the LORD, 62.09
a p., and a glory, but they would Jer 13.11
shall be saved; for thou art my p. 17.14
p. the LORD! For he has delivered 20.13
give p., and say, 'The LORD has 31.07
a p. and a glory before all the 33.09
the p. of the whole earth seized! 51.41
my fathers, I give thanks and p., Dan 2.23
p. and extol and honor the King of 4.37
and p. the name of the LORD your Joe 2.26
and the earth was full of his p. Hab 3.03
shame into p. and renown in all Zep 3.19
thou hast brought perfect p.'?" Mt 21.16
return and give p. to God except Lk 17.18
when they saw it, gave p. to God. 18.43
to rejoice and p. God with a loud 19.37
and said to him, "Give God the p.; Jn 9.24
for they loved the p. of men more 12.43
of men more than the p. of God. 12.43
His p. is not from men but from God. Rom 2.29
every tongue shall give p. to God." 14.11
"Therefore I will p. thee among the 15.09
and again, "P. the Lord all Gentiles, 15.11
and let all the peoples p. him"; 15.11
to the p. of his glorious grace Eph 1.06
to live for the p. of his glory. 1.12
of it, to the p. of his glory. 1.14
Christ, to the glory and p. of God. Php 1.11
if there is anything worthy of p., 4.08
of the congregation I will p. thee." Heb 2.12
offer up a sacrifice of p. to God, 13.15
Is any cheerful? Let him sing p. Jas 5.13
may redound to p. and glory and 1Pe 1.07
do wrong and to p. those who do 2.14
"P. our God, all you his servants, Rev 19.05

PRAISED
saw her, they p. her to Pharaoh. Gen 12.15
people saw him, they p. their God; Jn 16.24
so much to be p. for his beauty as 2Sa 14.25
the LORD, who is worthy to be p., 22.04
is the LORD, and greatly to be p., 1Ch 16.25
said "Amen!" and p. the LORD. 16.36
and the priests p. the LORD day by 2Ch 30.21
when they p. the LORD, because the Ez 3.11
assembly said "Amen" and p. the LORD. Neh 5.13
the LORD, who is worthy to be p., Ps 18.03
greatly to be p. in the city of 48.01
is the LORD, and greatly to be p.; 96.04
the name of the LORD is to be p.! 113.03
Great is the LORD, and greatly to be p., 145.03
who fears the LORD, is to be p. Pro 31.30
and were p. in the city where they Ecc 8.10
concubines also, and they p. her. Sol 6.09
house, where our fathers p. thee, Is 64.11
and p. and honored him who lives Dan 4.34
and p. the gods of gold and silver, 5.04
and you have p. the gods of silver 5.23
renowned and p. among all the Zep 3.20
streets, that they may be p. by men. Mt 6.02
was made straight, and she p. God. Lk 13.13
he p. God, and said, "Certainly this 23.47
for all men p. God for what had Ac 4.21

PRAISES
nations, and sing p. to thy name. 2Sa 22.50
sing p. to him, tell of all his 1Ch 16.09
shall offer p. to the LORD with 23.05
David offered p. by their ministry 2Ch 7.06
Levites to sing p. to the LORD 29.30
And they sang p. with gladness, and 29.30
Sing p. to the LORD, who dwells in Ps 9.11
that I may recount all thy p., 9.14
nations, and sing p. to thy name. 18.49
enthroned on the p. of Israel. 22.03
Sing p. to the LORD, O you his 30.04
Sing p. to God, sing p.! 47.06
Sing p. to our King, sing p.! 47.06
all the earth; sing p. with a psalm! 47.07
I will sing p. to thee among the 57.09
Strength, I will sing p. to thee; 59.09
I will sing p. to thee, for thou, O 59.17
So will I ever sing p. to thy name, 61.08
and my mouth p. thee with joyful 63.05
sing p. to thee, sing p. to thy name." 66.04
Sing to God, sing p. to his name; 68.04
sing p. to the Lord, 68.32
I will sing p. to thee with the 71.22
for joy, when I sing p. to thee; 71.23
I will sing p. to the God of Jacob. 75.09
to sing p. to thy name, O Most High; 92.01
forth into joyous song and sing p.! 98.04
Sing p. to the LORD with the lyre, 98.05
sing p. to him, tell of all his 105.02
I will sing, I will sing p.! 108.01
I will sing p. to thee among the 108.03
I will sing p. to my God while I 146.02
it is good to sing p. to our God; 147.01
Let the high p. of God be in their 149.06
her husband also, and he p. her: Pro 31.28
"Sing p. to the LORD, for he has Is 12.05
the p. of the LORD, according to all 63.07

PRAISING
thanking and p. the LORD, and 1Ch 23.30
the people running and p. the king, 2Ch 23.12
p. and giving thanks to the LORD, Ez 3.11
heavenly host p. God and saying, 2.13
glorifying and p. God for all they 2.20
turned back, p. God with a loud voice; 17.15
p. God and having favor with all Ac 2.47
walking and leaping and p. God. 3.08
people saw him walking and p. God, 3.09

PRANCE
mustered in array; the chargers p. Nah 2.03

PRATING
but a p. fool will come to ruin. Pro 10.08
p. against me with evil words. 3Jn 1.10

PRAY
I p. you, to your servant's house and Gen 19.02
and he will p. for you, and you 20.07
I p. thee, and show steadfast love 24.12
'P. let down your jar that I may 24.14
"P. give me a little water to drink 24.17
"P. give me a little water from 24.43
I said to her, 'P. let me drink.' 24.45
I p., some of your son's mandrakes." 30.14
Deliver me, I p. thee, from the hand 32.11
him, "Tell me, I p., your name." 32.29
I p. you, if I have found favor in 33.10
Accept, I p. you, my gift that is 33.11
I p. you, give her to him in marriage. 34.08
I p. you, where they are pasturing 37.16
I p. you, whose these are, the signet 38.25
Tell them to me, I p. you." 40.08
I p. you, to make mention of me to 40.14
I p. you, speak a word in my lord's 44.18
I p. you, remain instead of the lad 44.33
brothers, "Come near to me, I p. you." 45.04
and now, we p. you, let your servants 47.04
I p. you, that I may bless them." 48.09
I p. you, in the ears of Pharaoh, 50.04
I p. you, and bury my father; 50.05
I p. you, the transgression of your 50.17
And now, we p. you, forgive the 50.17
and now, we p. you, let us go a three Ex 3.18
I p., some other person." 4.13
I p., to my kinsmen in Egypt and 4.18
let us go, we p., a three days' 5.03

PRAY (cont.)

you and I will p. to the LORD that Ex 8.29
I p. you, only this once, and entreat 10.17
I p. thee, out of thy book which 32.32
I p. thee, if I have found favor in 33.13
Moses said, "I p. thee, show me thy 33.18
I p. thee, go in the midst of us, 34.09
I p. you, for you know how we are to Num 10.31
And now, I p. thee, let the power of 14.17
I p. thee, according to the greatness 14.19
I p. you, from the tents of these 16.26
p. to the LORD, that he take away 21.07
P., now, tarry here this night also, 22.19
I p. and see the good land beyond Deu 3.25
"P. show us the way into the city, Ju 1.24
"P., give me a little water to 4.19
"P., sir, if the LORD is with us, why 6.13
"P., Lord, how can I deliver Israel? 6.15
I p. thee, until I come to thee, and 6.18
p., let me make trial only this 6.39
p., let it be dry only on the 6.39
"P., give loaves of bread to the 8.05
deliver us, we p. thee, this day." 10.15
we p., through your land'; but the 11.17
we p., through your land to our 11.19
I p. thee, let the man of God whom 13.08
"P., let us detain you, and prepare 13.15
fairer than she? P. take her instead." 15.02
I p. thee, and strengthen me, I p. 16.28
we p. thee, that we may know whether 18.05
p. tarry all night. Behold, the day 19.09
She said, 'P., let me glean and Ru 2.07
I p. you, in one of the priest's 1Sa 2.36
and I will p. to the LORD for you." 7.05
"P., tell me what Samuel said to 10.15
"P. for your servants to the LORD 12.19
the LORD by ceasing to p. for you; 12.23
I p., pardon my sin, and return with 15.25
"P. let my father and my mother 22.03
P., give whatever you have at hand 25.08
p. let your handmaid speak in your 25.24
P. forgive the trespass of your 25.28
courage to p. this prayer to thee. 2Sa 7.27
"P. let my sister Tamar come and 13.06
I p. you, speak to the king; 13.13
p. let the king and his servants go 13.24
p. let my brother Amnon go with us." 13.26
"P. let the king invoke the LORD 14.11
"P. let your handmaid speak a word 14.12
"P. let me go and pay my vow, which 15.07
I p. thee, turn the counsel of 15.31
P. let your servant return, that I 19.37
I p. thee, take away the iniquity of 24.10
I p. thee, be against me and against 24.17
And he said, "P. ask King Solomon— 1Ki 2.17
when they p. toward this place; 8.30
and p. and make supplication to 8.33
if they p. toward this place, and 8.35
and they p. to the LORD toward the 8.44
and p. to thee toward their land, 8.48
and p. for me, that my hand may be 13.06
Benhadad says, 'P., let me live.'" 20.32
of the LORD, "Strike me I p." 20.35
man, and said, "Strike me, I p." 20.37
I p. you, let my life, and the life 2Ki 1.13
to Elisha, "Tarry here, I p. you; 2.02
him, "Elisha, tarry here, I p. you; 2.04
said to him, "Tarry here, I p. you; 2.06
"I p. you, let me inherit a double 2.09
p., let them go, and seek your 2.16
I p. you, let there be given to your 5.17
p., give them a talent of silver 5.22
I p. thee, open his eyes that he may 6.17
I p. thee, with blindness." 6.18
"P., speak to your servants in the 18.26
found courage to p. before thee. 1Ch 17.25
But now, I p. thee take away the 21.08
I p. thee, O LORD my God, be against 21.17
when they p. toward this place; 2Ch 6.21
and p. and make supplication to 6.24
if they p. toward this place, and 6.26
and they p. to thee toward this 6.34
and p. toward their land, which thou 6.38
and p. and seek my face, and turn 7.14
and p. for the life of the king and Ez 6.10
which I now p. before thee day and Neh 1.06
Turn, I p., let no wrong be done. Job 6.29
I p. you, of bygone ages, and consider 8.08
profit do we get if we p. to him?' 21.15
my servant Job shall p. for you, 42.08
and my God, for to thee do I p. Ps 5.02
For I p., "Only let them not 38.16
P. for the peace of Jerusalem! 122.06
I p. you, between me and my vineyard. Is 5.03
he comes to his sanctuary to p., 16.12
"P., speak to your servants in 36.11
do not p. for this people, or lift Jer 7.16
"Therefore do not p. for this 11.14
"Do not p. for the welfare of this 14.11
and p. to the LORD on its behalf, 29.07
call upon me and come and p. to me, 29.12
"P. for us to the LORD our God." 37.03
Now hear, I p. you, O my lord the 37.20
and p. to the LORD your God for us, 42.02
I will p. to the LORD your God 42.04
'P. for us to the LORD our God, and 42.20
"I p. thee, LORD, is not this what I Jon 4.02
P. now, consider what will come to Hag 2.15
enemies and p. for those who Mt 5.44
"And when you p., you must not be 6.05
to stand and p. in the synagogues 6.05
But when you p. go into your room 6.06
the door and p. of your Father who 6.06
P. then like this: Our Father who 6.09
p. therefore the Lord of the 9.38
up into the hills by himself to p. 14.23
might lay his hands on them and p. 19.13
P. that your flight may not be in 24.20
"Sit here, while I go yonder and p." 26.36
Watch and p. that you may not enter 26.41
them, he went into the hills to p. Mk 6.46
P. that it may not happen in winter. 13.18
disciples, "Sit here, while I p." 14.32
Watch and p. that you may not enter 14.38
he went out into the hills to p.; Lk 6.12
p. for those who abuse you. 6.28
and went up on the mountain to p. 9.28
p. therefore the Lord of the 10.02
teach us to p., as John taught his 11.01
"When you p., say: "Father, hallowed 11.02
and see it; I p. you, have me excused.' 14.18
examine them; I p. you, have me excused.' 14.19
ought always to p. and not lose 18.01
"Two men went up into the temple to p., 18.10
"P. that you may not enter into 22.40
Rise and p. that you may not enter 22.46
And I will p. the Father, and he Jn 14.16
that I shall p. the Father for you; 16.26
I do not p. that thou shouldst take 17.15
"I do not p. for these only, but 17.20
and p. to the Lord that, if possible, Ac 8.22
"P. for me to the Lord, that nothing 8.24
p., does the prophet say this, about 8.34
went up on the housetop to p., 10.09
do not know how to p. as we ought, Rom 8.26
for a woman to p. to God with her 1Co 11.13
a tongue should p. for the power 14.13
For if I p. in a tongue, my spirit 14.14
I will p. with the spirit and I 14.15
and I will p. with the mind also; 14.15
while they long for you and p. for you, 2Co 9.14
But we p. God that you may not do 13.07
What we p. for is your improvement. 13.09
P. at all times in the Spirit, with Eph 6.18

PRAY (cont.)

Jesus Christ, when we p. for you,	Col 1.03
we have not ceased to p. for you,	1.09
and p. for us also, that God may	4.03
p. constantly,	1Th 5.17
Brethren, p. for us.	5.25
To this end we always p. for you,	2Th 1.11
p. for us, that the word of the Lord	3.01
in every place the men should p.,	1Ti 2.08
and I p. that the sharing of your	Phm 1.06
P. for us, for we are sure that we	Heb 13.18
Let him p. Is any cheerful?	Jas 5.13
and let them p. over him, anointing	5.14
and p. for one another, that you may	5.16
not say that one is to p. for that.	1Jn 5.16
Beloved, I p. that all may go well	3Jn 1.02
most holy faith; p. in the Holy Spirit;	Jud 1.20

PRAYED

Then Abraham p. to God; and God healed	Gen 20.17
And Isaac p. to the LORD for his	25.21
from Pharaoh and p. to the LORD.	Ex 8.30
and Moses p. to the LORD, and the	Num 11.02
So Moses p. for the people.	21.07
and I p. for Aaron also at the same	Deu 9.20
And I p. to the LORD, 'O LORD GOD,	9.26
distressed and p. to the LORD,	1Sa 1.10
For this child I p.; and the LORD	1.27
Hannah also p. and said, "My heart	2.01
And Samuel p. to the LORD.	8.06
two of them, and p. to the LORD.	2Ki 4.33
Then Elisha p., and said, "O LORD, I	6.17
Elisha p. to the LORD, and said,	6.18
And Hezekiah p. before the LORD, and	19.15
and p. to the LORD, saying,	20.02
For Hezekiah had p. for them,	2Ch 30.18
p. because of this and cried to	32.20
of death, and he p. to the LORD;	32.24
He p. to him, and God received his	33.13
While Ezra p. and made confession,	Ez 10.01
So I p. to the God of heaven.	Neh 2.04
And we p. to our God, and set a	4.09
when he had p. for his friends;	Job 42.10
I p. with head bowed on my bosom,	Ps 35.13
And Hezekiah p. to the LORD:	Is 37.15
you have p. to me concerning	37.21
to the wall, and p. to the LORD,	38.02
I p. to the LORD, saying:	Jer 32.16
times a day and p. and gave thanks	Dan 6.10
I p. to the LORD my God and made	9.04
Then Jonah p. to the LORD his God	Jon 2.01
And he p. to the LORD and said, "I	4.02
farther he fell on his face and p.,	Mt 26.39
second time, he went away and p.,	26.42
went away and p. for the third	26.44
to a lonely place, and there he p.	Mk 1.35
he fell on the ground and p. that,	14.35
And again he went away and p.,	14.39
withdrew to the wilderness and p.	Lk 5.16
stood and p. thus with himself,	18.11
but I have p. for you that your	22.32
throw, and knelt down and p.,	22.41
in an agony he p. more earnestly;	22.44
And they p. and said, "Lord, who	Ac 1.24
And when they had p., the place	4.31
and they p. and laid their hands	6.06
he p., "Lord Jesus, receive my	7.59
who came down and p. for them that	8.15
all outside and knelt down and p.;	9.40
to the people, and p. constantly to God.	10.02
he knelt down and p. with them all.	20.36
on the beach we p. and bade one	21.05
from the stern, and p. for day to come.	27.29
and Paul visited him and p.,	28.08
ourselves and he p. fervently that	Jas 5.17
Then he p. again and the heaven	5.18

PRAYER

and the LORD granted his p.,	Gen 25.21
courage to pray this p. to thee.	2Sa 7.27
regard to the p. of thy servant	1Ki 8.28
cry and to the p. which thy	8.28
hearken to the p. which thy	8.29
whatever p., whatever supplication	8.38
in heaven their p. and their	8.45
place their p. and their supplication,	8.49
all this p. and supplication to	8.54
have heard your p. and your	9.03
accordance with the p. of Elisha.	2Ki 6.18
lift up your p. for the remnant	19.04
Your p. to me about Sennacherib	19.20
your father: I have head your p.,	20.05
regard to the p. of thy servant	2Ch 6.19
cry and to the p. which thy	6.19
hearken to the p. which thy	6.20
whatever p., whatever supplication	6.29
heaven their p. and their supplication,	6.35
place their p. and their supplications,	6.39
attentive to a p. of this place.	6.40
When Solomon had ended his p.,	7.01
said to him: "I have heard your p.,	7.12
attentive to the p. that is made in	7.15
and their p. came to his holy	30.27
and his p. to his God, and the words	33.18
And his p., and how God received	33.19
to hear the p. of thy servant which	Neh 1.06
attentive to the p. of thy servant,	1.11
and to the p. of thy servants who	1.11
to begin the thanksgiving in p.,	11.17
in my hands, and my p. is pure.	Job 16.17
You will make your p. to him,	22.27
God pays no attention to their p.	24.12
will accept his p. not to deal	42.08
and the LORD accepted Job's p.	42.09
be gracious to me, and hear my p.	Ps 4.01
the LORD accepts my p.	6.09
Give ear to my p. from lips free of	17.01
one who is godly offer p. to thee;	32.06
"Hear my p., O LORD, and give ear to	39.12
a p. to the God of my life.	42.08
Hear my p., O God; give ear to the	54.02
Give ear to my p., O God;	55.01
Hear my cry, O God, listen to my p.;	61.01
O thou who hearest p.! To thee shall	65.02
given heed to the voice of my p.	66.19
not rejected my p. or removed his	66.20
my p. is to thee, O LORD. At an acceptable	69.13
May p. be made for him continually,	72.15
O LORD God of hosts, hear my p.;	84.08
Give ear, O LORD, to my p.;	86.06
Let my p. come before thee, incline	88.02
the morning my p. comes before	88.13
Hear my p., O LORD; let my cry	102.01
he will regard the p. of the	102.17
me, even as I make p. for them.	109.04
let his p. be counted as sin!	109.07
Let my p. be counted as incense	141.02
for my p. is continually against	141.05
Hear my p., O LORD; give ear to	143.01
but the p. of the upright is his	Pro 15.08
he hears the p. of the righteous.	15.29
even his p. is an abomination.	28.09
poured out a p. when thy chastening	Is 26.16
lift up your p. for the remnant	37.04
your father: I have heard your p.,	38.05
make them joyful in my house of p.;	56.07
a house of p. for all peoples.	56.07
or lift up cry or p. for them,	Jer 7.16
up a cry or p. on their behalf, for	11.14
cry for help, he shuts out my p.;	Lam 3.08
so that no p. can pass through	3.44
seeking him by p. and supplications	Dan 9.03
hearken to the p. of thy servant	9.17
while I was speaking in p.,	9.21

PRAYER (cont.)
and my p. came to thee, into thy Jon 2.07
A p. of Habakkuk the prophet, Hab 3.01
comes out except by p. and fasting *Mt 17.21
shall be called a house of p.'; 21.13
And whatever you ask in p., 21.22
be driven out by anything but p." Mk 9.29
a house of p. for all the nations'? 11.17
I tell you, whatever you ask in p., 11.24
for your p. is heard, and your wife Lk 1.13
with fasting and p. night and day. 2.37
night he continued in p. to God. 6.12
'My house shall be a house of p.'; 19.46
And when he rose from p., he came to 22.45
accord devoted themselves to p., Ac 1.14
up to the temple at the hour of p., 3.01
ourselves to p. and to the ministry 6.04
the ninth hour of p. in my house; 10.30
your p. has been heard and your 10.31
but earnest p. for him was made to 12.05
with p. and fasting, they committed 14.23
supposed there was a place of p.; 16.13
As we were going to the place of p., 16.16
desire and p. to God for them is Rom 10.01
in tribulation, be constant in p. 12.12
you may devote yourselves to p.; 1Co 7.05
You also must help us by p., 2Co 1.11
with all p. and supplication. Eph 6.18
always in every p. of mine for you Php 1.04
for you all making my p. with joy, 1.04
And it is my p. that your love may 1.09
everything by p. and supplication 4.06
Continue steadfastly in p., Col 4.02
consecrated by the word of God and p. 1Ti 4.05
and the p. of faith will save the Jas 5.15
The p. of a righteous man has great 5.16
and his ears are open to their p. 1Pe 3.12

PRAYERS
The p. of David, the son of Jesse, Ps 72.20
thou be angry with thy people's p.? 80.04
even though you make many p., I will not Is 1.15
for a pretense you make long p.; *Mt 23.14
and for a pretense make long p. Mk 12.40
of John fast often and offer p., Lk 5.33
and for a pretense make long p. 20.47
the breaking of bread and the p. Ac 2.42
"Your p. and your alms have ascended 10.04
I mention you always in my p., Rom 1.09
with me in your p. to God on my 15.30
granted us in answer to many p. 2Co 1.11
for you, remembering you in my p., Eph 1.16
through your p. and the help of Php 1.19
remembering you earnestly in his p., Col 4.12
constantly mentioning you in our p., 1Th 1.02
p., intercessions, and thanksgivings 1Ti 2.01
supplications and p. night and day; 5.05
I remember you constantly in my p., 2Ti 1.03
when I remember you in my p., Phm 1.04
through your p. to be granted to 1.22
offered up p. and supplications, Heb 5.07
order that your p. may not be 1Pe 3.07
keep sane and sober for your p. 4.07
which are the p. of the saints; Rev 5.08
mingle with the p. of all the 8.03
rose with the p. of the saints 8.04

PRAYING
As she continued p. before the LORD, 1Sa 1.12
in your presence, p. to the LORD. 1.26
fasting and p. before the God of Neh 1.04
and keep on p. to a god that cannot Is 45.20
While I was speaking and p., Dan 9.20
"And in p. do not heap up empty Mt 6.07
And whenever you stand p., Mk 11.25
the people were p. outside at the Lk 1.10
also had been baptized and was p., 3.21
that as he was p. alone the 9.18
And as he was p., the appearance of 9.29
He was p. in a certain place, and 11.01
p. that you may have strength to 21.36
I am p. for them; Jn 17.09
I am not p. for the world but for 17.09
for behold, he is p., Ac 9.11
"I was in the city of Joppa p.; 11.05
were gathered together and were p. 12.12
fasting and p. they laid their 13.03
and Silas were p. and singing 16.25
Jerusalem and was p. in the temple, 22.17
p. earnestly night and day that we 1Th 3.10

PRAYS
thy servant p. before thee this 1Ki 8.28
he comes and p. toward this house, 8.42
which thy servant p. before thee; 2Ch 6.19
he comes and p. toward this house, 6.32
Then man p. to God, and he accepts Job 33.26
he p. to it and says, "Deliver me, Is 44.17
Any man who p. or prophesies with 1Co 11.04
but any woman who p. or prophesies 11.05
my spirit p. but my mind is unfruitful. 14.14

PREACH
p. against the south, and prophesy Eze 20.46
Jerusalem and p. against the 21.02
and do not p. against the house of Amo 7.16
"Do not p."—thus they p.— Mic 2.06
"one should not p. of such things; 2.06
"I will p. to you of wine and 2.11
From that time Jesus began to p., Mt 4.17
And p. as you go, saying, 'The 10.07
to teach and p. in their cities. 11.01
for they p., but do not practice. 23.03
towns, that I may p. there also; Mk 1.38
him, and to be sent out to p. 3.14
p. the gospel to the whole creation. * 16.15
anointed me to p. good news to the Lk 4.18
"I must p. the good news of the 4.43
them out to p. the kingdom of God 9.02
commanded us to p. to the people, Ac 10.42
had in every city those who p. him, 15.21
called us to p. the gospel to them. 16.10
so I am eager to p. the gospel to Rom 1.15
While you p. against stealing, do 2.21
is, the word of faith which we p.); 10.08
And how can men p. unless they are 10.15
the feet of those who p. good news!" 10.15
it my ambition to p. the gospel, 15.20
me to baptize but to p. the gospel, 1Co 1.17
of what we p. to save those who 1.21
but we p. Christ crucified, a 1.23
For if I p. the gospel, that gives 9.16
to me if I do not p. the gospel! 9.16
so we p. and so you believed. 15.11
to Troas to p. the gospel of 2Co 2.12
For what we p. is not ourselves, but 4.05
so that we may p. the gospel in 10.16
should p. to you a gospel contrary Gal 1.08
that I might p. him among the 1.16
gospel which I p. among the 2.02
still p. circumcision, why am I 5.11
to p. to the Gentiles the unsearchable Eph 3.08
Some indeed p. Christ from envy and Php 1.15
p. the word, be urgent in season and 2Ti 4.02

PREACHED
the poor have good news p. to them. Mt 11.05
kingdom will be p. throughout the 24.14
this gospel is p. in the whole 26.13
And he p., saying, "After he comes Mk 1.07
went out and p. that men should 6.12
must first be p. to all nations. 13.10
the gospel is p. in the whole 14.09
they went forth and p. everywhere, * 16.19
he p. good news to the people. Lk 3.18

PREACHED (cont.)
the poor have good news p. to them. Lk 7.22
news of the kingdom of God is p., 16.16
sins should be p. in his name to 24.47
Philip as he p. good news about Ac 8.12
passing on he p. the gospel to all 8.40
Damascus he had p. boldly in the 9.27
after the baptism which John p.: 10.37
coming John had p. a baptism of 13.24
and there they p. the gospel. 14.07
When they had p. the gospel to that 14.21
because he p. Jesus and the resurrection. 17.18
I have fully p. the gospel of Rom 15.19
in what terms I p. to you the 1Co 15.01
Now if Christ is p. as raised from 15.12
whom we p. among you, Silvanus and 2Co 1.19
another Jesus than the one we p., 11.04
because I p. God's gospel without 11.07
contrary to that which we p. to you, Gal 1.08
which was p. by me is not man's 1.11
p. the gospel beforehand to Abraham, 3.08
ailment that I p. the gospel to 4.13
And he came and p. peace to you who Eph 2.17
which has been p. to every creature Col 1.23
while we p. to you the gospel of 1Th 2.09
p. amount the nations, believed on in 1Ti 3.16
from David, as p. in my gospel, 2Ti 2.08
by those who p. the good news to 1Pe 1.12
the good news which was p. to you. 1.25
he went and p. to the spirits in 3.19
the gospel was p. even to the dead, 4.06

PREACHER
The words of the P., the son of Ecc 1.01
says the P., vanity of vanities! 1.02
I the P. have been king over Israel 1.12
says the P., adding one thing to 7.27
Vanity of vanities, says the P.; 12.08
the P. also taught the people 12.09
The P. sought to find pleasing 12.10
he would be the p. for this people! Mic 2.11
seems to be a p. of foreign Ac 17.18
how are they to hear without a p.? Rom 10.14
was appointed a p. and apostle (I 1Ti 2.07
was appointed a p. and apostle and 2Ti 1.11

PREACHES
you by the Jesus whom Paul p. Ac 19.13
one comes and p. another Jesus 2Co 11.04

PREACHING
p. in the wilderness of Judea, Mt 3.01
synagogues and p. the gospel of 4.23
synagogues and p. the gospel of 9.35
they repented at the p. of Jonah, 12.41
p. a baptism of repentance for the Mk 1.04
came into Galilee p. the gospel of God, 1.14
p. in their synagogues and casting 1.39
and he was p. the word to them. 2.02
p. a baptism of repentance for the Lk 3.03
And he was p. in the synagogues of 4.44
p. and bringing the good news of 8.01
p. the gospel and healing everywhere. 9.06
they repented at the p. of Jonah, 11.32
in the temple and p. the gospel, 20.01
teaching and p. Jesus as the Ac 5.42
should give up p. the word of God 6.02
scattered went about p. the word. 8.04
p. the gospel to many villages of 8.25
p. boldly in the name of the Lord. 9.29
p. good news of peace by Jesus 10.36
the Greeks also, p. the Lord Jesus. 11.20
teaching and p. the word of the 15.35
Macedonia, Paul was occupied with p., 18.05
have gone about p. the kingdom 20.25
p. the kingdom of God and teaching 28.31
is heard comes by the p. of Christ. Rom 10.17
gospel and the p. of Jesus Christ, 16.25
that in my p. I may make the gospel 1Co 9.18
lest after p. to others I myself 9.27
then our p. is in vain and your 15.14
churches for his p. of the gospel; 2Co 8.18
If any one is p. to you a gospel Gal 1.09
us is now p. the faith he once 1.23
of scripture, to p., to teaching. 1Ti 4.13
those who labor in p. and teaching; 5.17
through the p. with which I have Tit 1.03

PRECEDE
shall not p. those who have fallen 1Th 4.15

PRECEDED
The prophets who p. you and me from Jer 28.08

PRECEPT
For it is p. upon p., p. upon p., Is 28.10
will be to them p. upon p., p. upon p., 28.13
"Not all men can receive this p., Mt 19.11

PRECEPTS
the p. of the LORD are right, Ps 19.08
all his p. are trustworthy, 111.07
commanded thy p. to be kept 119.04
I will meditate on thy p., 119.15
Make me understand the way of thy p., 119.27
Behold, I long for thy p.; 119.40
liberty, for I have sought thy p. 119.45
to me, that I have kept thy p. 119.56
thee, of those who keep thy p. 119.63
with my whole heart I keep thy p.; 119.69
for me, I will meditate on thy p. 119.78
but I have not forsaken thy p. 119.87
I will never forget thy p. 119.93
for I have sought thy p. 119.94
than the aged, for I keep thy p. 119.100
Through thy p. I get understanding; 119.104
me, but I do not stray from thy p. 119.110
Therefore I direct my steps by all thy p.; 119.128
oppression, that I may keep thy p. 119.134
despised, yet I do not forget thy p. 119.141
Consider how I love thy p.! 119.159
I keep thy p. and testimonies, for 119.168
help me, for I have chosen thy p. 119.173
for I give you good p.: Pro 4.02
your father, and kept all his p., Jer 35.18
teaching as doctrines the p. of men.'" Mt 15.09
teaching as doctrines the p. of men.' Mk 7.07
uncircumcised keeps the p. of the law, Rom 2.26
according to human p. and doctrines? Col 2.22

PRECINCTS
chamberlain, which was in the p.; 2Ki 23.11

PRECIOUS
my life was p. in your eyes this 1Sa 26.21
your life was p. this day in my 26.24
may my life be p. in the sight of 26.24
of gold, and in it was a p. stone; 2Sa 12.30
and very much gold, and p. stones; 1Ki 10.02
quantity of spices, and p. stones; 10.10
amount of almug wood and p. stones. 10.11
of yours, be p. in your sight. 2Ki 1.13
let my life be p. in your sight." 1.14
the p. oil, his armory, all that was 20.13
of gold, and in it was a p. stone; 1Ch 20.02
all sorts of p. stones, and marble. 29.02
And whoever had p. stones gave them 29.08
house with settings of p. stones. 2Ch 3.06
and very much gold and p. stones. 9.01
and p. stones: there were no spices 9.09
brought algum wood and p. stones. 9.10
and p. things, which they took for 20.25
Jerusalem and p. things to Hezekiah 32.23
for p. stones, for spices, for 32.27
with the p. vessels of the house of 36.10
and destroyed all its p. vessels. 36.19

PRECIOUS (cont.)
fine bright bronze as p. as gold. Ez 8.27
mother-of-pearl and p. stones. Est 1.06
is your gold, and your p. silver; Job 22.25
and his eye sees every p. thing. 28.10
in p. onyx or sapphire. 28.16
How p. is thy steadfast love, O God! Ps 36.07
and p. is their blood in his sight. 72.14
P. in the sight of the LORD is the 116.15
It is like the p. oil upon the head, 133.02
How p. to me are thy thoughts, O God! 139.17
we shall find all p. goods, Pro 1.13
She is more p. than jewels, and 3.15
diligent man will get p. wealth. 12.27
lips of knowledge are a p. jewel. 20.15
P. treasure remains in a wise man's 21.20
filled with all p. and pleasant 24.04
She is far more p. than jewels. 31.10
name is better than p. ointment; Ecc 7.01
a p. cornerstone of a sure foundation: Is 28.16
the p. oil, his whole armory, all 39.02
Because you are p. in my eyes, 43.04
and all your wall of p. stones. 54.12
If you utter what is p., and not what Jer 15.19
bitterness all the p. things that Lam 1.07
his hands over all her p. things. 1.10
The p. sons of Zion, worth their 4.02
that they may profane my p. place; Eze 7.22
have taken treasure and p. things; 22.25
and all p. stones, and gold. 27.22
every p. stone was your covering, 28.13
and with their p. vessels of Dan 11.08
with p. stones and costly gifts. 11.38
and all the p. things of Egypt; 11.43
possess their p. things of silver; Hos 9.06
his treasury of every p. thing. 13.15
or wealth of every p. thing. Nah 2.09
of any value nor as p. to myself, Ac 20.24
p. stones, wood, hay, stubble— 1Co 3.12
waits for the p. fruit of the Jas 5.07
more p. than gold which though 1Pe 1.07
but with the p. blood of Christ, 1.19
but in God's sight chosen and p.; 2.04
stone, a cornerstone chosen and p., 2.06
he is p., but for those who do not 2.07
which in God's sight is very p. 3.04
to us his p. and very great 2Pe 1.04

PREDESTINED
and thy plan had p. to take place. Ac 4.28
foreknew he also p. to be conformed Rom 8.29
And those whom he p. he also called; 8.30

PREDICT
the new moons p. what shall befall Is 47.13

PREDICTED
proclaimed, who had p. these things. 2Ki 23.16
from Judah and p. these things 23.17
And as Isaiah p., "If the Lord of Rom 9.29

PREDICTING
them when p. the sufferings of 1Pe 1.11

PREDICTIONS
remember the p. of the holy 2Pe 3.02
the p. of the apostles of our Lord Jud 1.17

PRE-EMINENCE
shall not have p. because you went Gen 49.04
shall there be p. among them. Eze 7.11

PRE-EMINENT
p. in pride and p. in power. Gen 49.03
that in everything he might be p. Col 1.18

PREFECT
and chief p. over all the wise men Dan 2.48

PREFECTS
the p., and the governors, the Dan 3.02
the p., and the governors, the 3.03
the p., the governors, and the king's 3.27
the p. and the satraps, the counselors 6.07

PREFER
love's sake I p. to appeal to you— Phm 1.09

PREFERENCE
first-born in p. to the son of the Deu 21.16

PREFERRED
Death shall be p. to life by all Jer 8.03
but I p. to do nothing without your Phm 1.14

PREGNANCY
no birth, no p., no conception! Hos 9.11

PREGNANT
and is p. with mischief and brings Ps 7.14
and their p. women ripped open. Hos 13.16

PREPARATION
brethren had made p. for them. 1Ch 12.39
I will therefore make p. for it." 22.05
Next day, that is, after the day of P., Mt 27.62
come, since it was the day of P., Mk 15.42
It was the day of P., and the sabbath Lk 23.54
was the day of P. for the Passover; Jn 19.14
Since it was the day of P., 19.31
So because of the Jewish day of P., 19.42

PREPARATIONS
for I made p. for building. 1Ch 28.02
These p. having thus been made, the Heb 9.06

PREPARE
the servant, who hastened to p. it. Gen 18.07
and p. for me savory food, such as I 27.04
and p. for me savory food, that I 27.07
that I may p. from them savory food 27.09
when they p. what they bring in, it Ex 16.05
you shall p. with the burnt offering, Num 15.05
you shall p. for a cereal offering 15.06
And when you p. a bull for a burnt 15.08
According to the number that you p., 15.12
You shall p. the roads, and divide Deu 19.03
'P. your provisions; for within Jos 1.11
detain you, and p. a kid for you." Ju 13.15
take and p. a new cart and two 1Sa 6.07
or herd to p. for the wayfarer who 2Sa 12.04
and p. the food in my sight, that I 13.05
Amnon's house, and p. food for him." 13.07
I may go in and p. it for myself 1Ki 17.12
and I will p. the other bull and 18.23
yourselves one bull and p. it first, 18.25
'P. your chariot and go down, lest 18.44
the showbread, to p. it every Sabbath. 1Ch 9.32
stonecutters to p. dressed stones 22.02
to p. timber for me in abundance, 2Ch 2.09
commanded them to p. chambers in 31.11
P. yourselves according to your 35.04
and p. for your brethren, to do 35.06
dinner which I will p. for them, Est 5.08
the morning I p. a sacrifice for Ps 5.03
P. your work outside, get everything Pro 24.27
P. slaughter for his sons because Is 14.21
They p. the table, they spread the 21.05
the wilderness p. the way of the 40.03
p. the way, remove every obstruction 57.14
p. the way for the people; build up, 62.10
"P. war against her; up and let us Jer 6.04
I will p. destroyers against you, 22.07
"P. buckler and shield, and advance 46.03
P. yourselves baggage for exile, O 46.19
p. the ambushes; for the LORD has 51.12
p. the nations for war against her, 51.27

PREPARE (cont.)
P. the nations for war against her, Jer 51.28
inflamed I will p. them a feast 51.39
on which you may p. your bread." Eze 4.15
p. for yourself an exile's baggage, 12.03
I will p. you for blood, and blood 35.06
P. war, stir up the mighty men. Joe 3.09
p. to meet your God, O Israel!" Amo 4.12
my messenger to p. the way before Mal 3.01
P. the way of the Lord, make his Mt 3.03
who shall p. thy way before thee.' 11.10
has done it to p. me for burial. 26.12
you have us p. for you to eat the 26.17
thy face, who shall p. thy way; Mk 1.02
P. the way of the Lord, make his 1.03
have us go and p. for you to eat 14.12
furnished and ready; there p. for us." 14.15
go before the Lord to p. his ways, Lk 1.76
P. the way of the Lord, make his 3.04
who shall p. thy way before thee.' 7.27
'P. supper for me, and gird yourself 17.08
"Go and p. the passover for us, that 22.08
him, "Where will you have us p. it?" 22.09
that I go to p. a place for you? Jn 14.02
And when I go and p. a place for 14.03
p. a guest room for me, for I am Phm 1.22
to p. the way for the kings from Rev 16.12

PREPARED
milk, and the calf which he had p., Gen 18.08
For I have p. the house and a place 24.31
and his mother p. savory food, 27.14
which she had p., into the hand of 27.17
He also p. savory food, and brought 27.31
eat, that only may be p. by you. Ex 12.16
had they p. for themselves any 12.39
you to the place which I have p. 23.20
The onyx stones were p., enclosed 39.06
and all that is p. on a pan or a Lev 7.09
"I have p. the seven altars, and I Num 23.04
went into his house and p. a kid, Ju 6.19
in the morning, and he p. to go; 19.05
and p. it for the man who had come 2Sa 12.04
and he p. for himself chariots and 1Ki 1.05
the hewing and p. the timber and 5.18
it was with stone p. at the quarry; 6.07
sanctuary he p. in the innermost 6.19
and they p. it, and called on the 18.26
So he p. for them a great feast; 2Ki 6.23
the Syrians have p. against us. 7.12
p. the mixing of the spices, 1Ch 9.30
and he p. a place for the ark of 15.01
its place, which he had p. for it. 15.03
to the place that I have p. for it. 15.12
the place that David had p. for it, 2Ch 1.04
kinds of spices p. by the perfumer's 16.14
And Uzziah p. for all the army 26.14
house of the LORD; and they p. them. 31.11
When the service had been p. for, 35.10
And afterward they p. for themselves 35.14
so the Levites p. for themselves 35.14
brethren the Levites p. for them. 35.15
of the LORD was p. that day, 35.16
when Josiah had p. the temple, 35.20
Now that which was p. for one day Neh 5.18
fowls likewise were p. for me, 5.18
to him for whom nothing is p.; 8.10
p. for Tobiah a large chamber where 13.05
dinner that I have p. for the king." Est 5.04
to the dinner that Esther had p. 5.05
to the banquet she p. but myself. 5.12
the gallows that he had p. for him. 6.04
to the banquet that Esther had p. 6.14
which Haman has p. for Mordecai, 7.09
which he had p. for Mordecai. 7.10
Behold, I have p. my case; I know Job 13.18
him, like a king p. for battle. 15.24
when I p. my seat in the square, 29.07
he has p. his deadly weapons, making Ps 7.13
grain, for so thou hast p. it. 65.09
I have p. a lamp for my anointed. 132.17
For a burning place has long been p.; Is 30.33
Say, 'Stand ready and be p., Jer 46.14
that you were created they were p. Eze 28.13
the LORD has p. a sacrifice and Zep 1.07
and when this is p., they will set Zec 5.11
whom it has been p. by my Father." Mt 20.23
the kingdom p. for you from the 25.34
eternal fire p. for the devil and 25.41
them, and they p. the passover. 26.19
for those for whom it has been p." Mk 10.40
had told them; and they p. the passover. 14.16
ready for the Lord a people p." Lk 1.17
which thou hast p. in the presence 2.31
and the things you have p., 12.20
and they p. the passover. 22.13
and p. spices and ointments. 23.56
the spices which they had p. 24.01
which he has p. beforehand for glory, Rom 9.23
what God has p. for those who love 1Co 2.09
He who has p. us for this very 2Co 5.05
which God p. beforehand, that we Eph 2.10
For a tent was p., the outer one, in Heb 9.02
but a body hast thou p. for me; 10.05
for he has p. for them a city. 11.16
Always be p. to make a defense to 1Pe 3.15
where she has a place p. by God, Rev 12.06
p. as a bride adorned for her 21.02

PREPARES
evil and their heart p. deceit." Job 15.35
he p. rain for the earth, he makes Ps 147.08
she p. her food in summer, and Pro 6.08

PREPAREST
Thou p. a table before me in the Ps 23.05

PREPARING
p. for him a chamber in the courts Neh 13.07
feast which I am p. for you, Eze 39.17
feast which I am p. for you. 39.19
but while they were p. it, Ac 10.10
affliction is p. for us an eternal 2Co 4.17

PRESCRIBED
made ten golden lampstands as p., 2Ch 4.07
before the inner sanctuary, as p.; 4.20
not kept it in great numbers as p. 30.05
the passover otherwise than as p. 30.18
Who has p. for him his way, or who Job 36.23
and p. bounds for it, and set bars 38.10

PRESCRIBING
oil, and salt without p. how much. Ez 7.22

PRESENCE
from the p. of the LORD God among Gen 3.08
went away from the p. of the LORD, 4.16
to me in your p. as a possession 23.09
in the p. of the sons of my people 23.11
possession in the p. of the Hittites, 23.18
out from the p. of Isaac his 27.30
In the p. of our kinsmen point out 31.32
went out from the p. of Pharaoh, 41.46
for they were dismayed at his p. 45.03
went out from the p. of Pharaoh. 47.10
were driven out from Pharaoh's p. Ex 10.11
bread of the P. on the table 25.30
"My p. will go with you, and I will 33.14
"If thy p. will not go with me, do 33.15
utensils, and the bread of the P.; 35.13
departed from the p. of Moses. 35.20
utensils, and the bread of the P.; 39.36
forth from the p. of the LORD and Lev 10.02
cut off from my p.: I am the LORD. 22.03

PRESENCE (cont.)

bread of the P. they shall spread Num 4.07
went from the p. of the assembly 20.06
you out of Egypt with his own p., Deu 4.37
beaten in his p. with a number of 25.02
up to him in the p. of the elders, 25.09
in the p. of the people of Israel, Jos 8.32
the LORD in his p. with our burnt 22.27
attendants went out from his p. Ju 3.19
Buy it in the p. of those sitting Ru 4.04
and in the p. of the elders of my 4.04
may appear in the p. of the LORD, 1Sa 1.22
who was standing here in your p., 1.26
in the p. of Eli the priest. 2.11
Samuel grew in the p. of the LORD. 2.21
in speech, and a man of good p.; 16.18
So Saul removed him from his p., 18.13
and he was in his p. as before. 19.07
there but the bread of the P., 21.06
fellow to play the madman in my p.? 21.15
earth away from the p. of the LORD; 26.20
When Joab came out from David's p., 2Sa 3.26
and he ate in his p. and drank, 11.13
said, "Put this woman out of my p., 13.17
he is not to come into my p." 14.24
did not come into the king's p. 14.24
without coming into the king's p. 14.28
let me go into the p. of the king; 14.32
out from the p. of the king to 24.04
So she came into the king's p., 1Ki 1.28
table for the bread of the P., 7.48
the LORD in the p. of all the 8.22
sought the p. of Solomon to hear 10.24
in the p. of the people, saying, 21.13
So he went out from his p. a leper, 2Ki 5.27
had dispatched a man from his p.; 6.32
he cast them from his p. until now. 13.23
that he cast them out from his p. 24.20
strength, seek his p. continually! 1Ch 16.11
recorded them in the p. of the king, 24.06
in the p. of King David, Zadok, 24.31
the LORD in the p. of all the 29.10
tables for the bread of the P., 2Ch 4.19
the LORD in the p. of all the 6.12
knees in the p. of all the assembly 6.13
sought the p. of Solomon to hear 9.23
in the p. of the priests in the 26.19
has chosen you to stand in his p., 29.11
the altars of the Baals in his p.; 34.04
Now I had not been sad in his p. Neh 2.01
And he said in the p. of his 4.02
spoke of his good deeds in my p., 6.19
in the p. of the men and the women 8.03
Then Memucan said in p. of the king Est 1.16
Chronicles in the p. of the king. 2.23
he even assault the queen in my p., 7.08
out from the p. of the king in 8.15
went forth from the p. of the LORD. Job 1.12
went forth from the p. of the LORD, 2.07
are established in their p., 21.08
Therefore I am terrified at his p.; 23.15
have cast off restraint in my p. 30.11
him, he comes into his p. with joy. 33.26
in thy p. there is fullness of joy, Ps 16.11
him glad with the joy of thy p. 21.06
before me in the p. of my enemies; 23.05
covert of thy p. thou hidest them 31.20
so long as the wicked are in my p." 39.01
and set me in thy p. for ever. 41.12
Cast me not away from thy p., 51.11
it is good, in the p. of the godly. 52.09
poured down rain, at the p. of God; 68.08
on Sinai quaked at the p. of God, 68.08
come into his p. with thanksgiving; 95.02
Come into his p. with singing! 100.02
lies shall continue in my p. 101.07
strength, seek his p. continually! 105.04
at the p. of the LORD, at the 114.07
at the p. of the God of Jacob, 114.07
the LORD in the p. of all his 116.14
the LORD in the p. of all his 116.18
whither shall I flee from thy p.? 139.07
he upright shall dwell in thy p. 140.13
Leave the p. of a fool, for there Pro 14.07
surety in the p. of his neighbor. 17.18
the wicked from the p. of the king, 25.05
in the king's p. or stand in the 25.06
put lower in the p. of the prince. 25.07
go from his p., do not delay when Ecc 8.03
in your very p. aliens devour your Is 1.07
the LORD, defying his glorious p. 3.08
of Egypt will tremble at his p., 19.01
and the angel of his p. saved them; 63.09
mountains might quake at thy p.— 64.01
nations might tremble at thy p.! 64.02
the mountains quaked at thy p. 64.03
to the p. of the LORD in Jerusalem, Jer 3.17
your abominations from my p., 4.01
up and cast you away from my p., 23.39
in the p. of the priests and all 28.01
prophet in the p. of the priests 28.05
spoke in the p. of all the people, 28.11
in the p. of Hanamel my cousin, in 32.12
in the p. of the witnesses who 32.12
and in the p. of all the Jews who 32.12
Baruch in their p., saying, 32.13
a man in my p. to offer burnt 33.18
that he cast them out from his p. 52.03
water before the p. of the Lord! Lam 2.19
of a man in the p. of the Most 3.35
in the p. of those who slay you, Eze 28.09
of the earth, shall quake at my p., 38.20
"Then from his p. the hand was sent, Dan 5.24
Tarshish from the p. of the LORD. Jon 1.03
away from the p. of the LORD. 1.03
fleeing from the p. of the LORD, 1.10
I said, 'I am cast out from thy p.; 2.04
and I will put you out of my p. Mal 2.03
of God and ate the bread of the P., Mt 12.04
and ate the bread of the P., Mk 2.26
Gabriel, who stand in the p. of God; Lk 1.19
prepared in the p. of all peoples, 2.31
took and ate the bread of the P., 6.04
declared in the p. of all the 8.47
say, 'We ate and drank in your p., 13.26
honored in the p. of all who sit 14.10
not able in the p. of the people 20.26
me in thy own p. with the glory Jn 17.05
signs in the p. of the disciples, 20.30
me full of gladness with thy p. Ac 2.28
up and denied in the p. of Pilate, 3.13
health in the p. of you all. 3.16
may come from the p. of the Lord, 3.19
Then they left the p. of the council, 5.41
to God in the p. of all he broke 27.35
in the p. of the God in whom he Rom 4.17
being might boast in the p. of God. 1Co 1.29
for your sake in the p. of Christ, 2Co 2.10
and bring us with you into his p. 4.14
strong, but his bodily p. is weak, 10.10
only as in my p. but much more in Php 2.12
from the p. of the Lord and from 2Th 1.09
sin, rebuke them in the p. of all, 1Ti 5.20
In the p. of God and of Christ 5.21
confession in the p. of many 6.12
In the p. of God who gives life to 6.13
you in the p. of God and of Christ 2Ti 4.01
the table and the bread of the P.; Heb 9.02
appear in the p. of God on our 9.24
before the p. of his glory with Jud 1.24
will shelter them with his p. Rev 7.15
of the first beast in its p., 13.12
to work in the p. of the beast, 13.14
brimstone in the p. of the holy 14.10

PRESENCE (cont.)
angels and in the p. of the Lamb. Rev 14.10
who in its p. had worked the signs 19.20
from his p. earth and sky fled away, 20.11

PRESENT
had with him a p. for his brother Gen 32.13
they are a p. sent to my lord Esau; 32.18
him with the p. that goes before 32.20
So the p. passed on before him; 32.21
then accept my p. from my hand; 33.10
so much as marriage p. and gift, 34.12
and carry down to the man a p., 43.11
So the men took the p., and they took 43.15
they made ready the p. for Joseph's 43.25
to him the p. which they had with 43.26
shall give the marriage p. for her, Ex 22.16
to the marriage p. for virgins. 22.17
and p. yourself there to me on the 34.02
the priests shall p. the blood, Lev 1.05
And Aaron shall p. the goat on 16.09
"Aaron shall p. the bull as a sin 16.11
altar, he shall p. the live goat; 16.20
short you may p. for a freewill 22.23
But you shall p. an offering by 23.08
then you shall p. a cereal offering 23.16
And you shall p. with the bread 23.18
and you shall p. an offering by 23.25
yourselves and p. an offering by 23.27
Seven days you shall p. offerings 23.36
convocation and p. an offering by 23.36
priest shall p. them before the Num 6.16
And you shall p. the Levites before 8.09
When you p. the Levites before the 8.10
you shall p. an offering to the 15.19
meal you shall p. a cake as an 15.20
threshing floor, so shall you p. it. 15.20
"Be p., you and all your company, 16.16
of Israel p. to the Lord I give to 18.19
which they p. as an offering to the 18.24
then you shall p. an offering from 18.26
So shall you also p. an offering to 18.28
you shall p. every offering due to 18.29
and the offering that you p., Deu 12.06
and the offering that you p., 12.11
or the offering that you p.; 12.17
and p. yourselves in the tent of 31.14
She said to him, "Give me a p.; Jos 15.19
She said to him, "Give me a p.; Ju 1.15
come to thee, and bring out my p., 6.18
and there is no p. to bring to the 1Sa 9.07
Now therefore p. yourselves before 10.19
despised him, and brought him no p. 10.27
the people who were p. with him, 13.15
the people who were p. with them, 13.16
no marriage p. except a hundred 18.25
And now let this p. which your 25.27
"Here is a p. for you from the 30.26
followed him a p. from the king. 2Sa 11.08
Every one of them brought his p., 1Ki 10.25
to you a p. of silver and gold; 15.19
so accept now a p. from your 2Ki 5.15
"Take a p. with you and go to meet 8.08
and took a p. with him, all kinds of 8.09
and sent a p. to the king of 16.08
with letters and a p. to Hezekiah; 20.12
who are p. here, offering freely and 1Ch 29.17
who were p. had sanctified themselves, 2Ch 5.11
Every one of them brought his p., 9.24
addition to our p. sins and guilt. 28.13
all who were p. with him bowed 29.29
that were p. at Jerusalem kept the 30.21
Israel who were p. went out to the 31.01
all who were p. in Jerusalem and 34.32
offerings for all that were p., 35.07
Israel who were p. kept the 35.17
all Judah and Israel who were p., 35.18
all Israel there p. had offered; Ez 8.25
all the people p. in Susa the Est 1.05
of God came to p. themselves Job 1.06
of God came to p. themselves 2.01
among them to p. himself before 2.01
a very p. help in trouble. Ps 46.01
with letters and a p. to Hezekiah, Is 39.01
Declare and p. your case; 45.21
him an allowance of food and a p., Jer 40.05
and incense to p. at the temple of 41.05
you sent me to p. your supplication 42.09
You shall p. them before the Lord, Eze 43.24
for we do not p. our supplications Dan 9.18
now he does not p. himself at the Hos 13.13
do not go up and p. themselves, Zec 14.18
P. that to your governor; Mal 1.08
till they p. right offerings to the 3.03
to Jerusalem to p. him to the Lord Lk 2.22
know how to interpret the p. time? 12.56
There were some p. at that very 13.01
So in the p. case I tell you, keep Ac 5.38
we are all here p. in the sight of 10.33
this new teaching is which you p.? 17.19
and all the elders were p. 21.18
and said, "Go away for the p.; 24.25
Agrippa and all who are p. with us, 25.24
to prove at the p. time that he Rom 3.26
sufferings of this p. time are not 8.18
nor things p., nor things to come, 8.38
So too at the p. time there is a 11.05
to p. your bodies as a living 12.01
At p., however, I am going to 15.25
or death or the p. or the future, 1Co 3.22
To the p. hour we hunger and thirst, 4.11
absent in body I am p. in spirit, 5.03
and as if p., I have already 5.03
are assembled, and my spirit is p., 5.04
abundance at the p. time should 2Co 8.14
that when I am p. I may not have 10.02
letter when absent, we do when p. 10.11
to Christ to p. you as a pure 11.02
as I did when p. on my second visit, 13.02
to deliver us from the p. evil age, Gal 1.04
and not only when I am p. with you. 4.18
wish to be p. with you now and to 4.20
corresponds to the p. Jerusalem, 4.25
world rulers of this p. darkness, Eph 6.12
in order to p. you holy and blameless Col 1.22
that we may p. every man mature in 1.28
promise for the p. life and also 1Ti 4.08
Do your best to p. yourself to God 2Ti 2.15
For Demas, in love with this p. world, 4.10
(which is symbolic for the p. age). Heb 9.09
falling and to p. you without Jud 1.24

PRESENTABLE
which our more p. parts do not 1Co 12.24

PRESENTED
and he p. himself to him, and fell Gen 46.29
five men and p. them to Pharaoh. 47.02
and when it is p. to the priest, Lev 2.08
day they were p. to serve as 7.35
Then he p. the ram of the burnt 8.18
Then he p. the other ram, the ram of 8.22
sons of Aaron p. the blood to him, 9.09
Then he p. the people's offering, and 9.15
And he p. the burnt offering, and 9.16
And he p. the cereal offering, and 9.17
Azazel shall be p. alive before 16.10
Joshua went and p. themselves in Deu 31.14
and they p. themselves before God. Jos 24.01
And he p. the tribute to Eglon king Ju 3.17
to him under the oak and p. them. 6.19
p. themselves in the assembly of 20.02
to the Lord and p. burnt offerings 1Ch 21.26
sacrifices and p. the provocation Eze 20.28
of Days and was p. before him. Dan 7.13

PRESENTED (cont.)
To them he p. himself alive after Ac 1.03
saints and widows he p. her alive. 9.41
the offering p. for every one of 21.26
they p. Paul also before him. 23.33
They p. many gifts to us; 28.10
church might be p. before him in Eph 5.27

PRESENTING
for p. to the LORD offerings by Lev 23.37
Ehud had finished p. the tribute, Ju 3.18
and p. my supplication before the Dan 9.20
after p. themselves before the LORD Zec 6.05

PRESENTS
sojourners in Israel p. his offering, Lev 22.18
Philistines brought Jehoshaphat p., 2Ch 17.11
And when Moab p. himself, when he Is 16.12
he who p. a cereal offering, like 66.03
and make merry and exchange p., Rev 11.10

PRESERVE
that we may p. offspring through Gen 19.32
that we may p. offspring through 19.34
God sent me before you to p. life. 45.05
before you to p. for you a remnant 45.07
that he might p. us alive, as at Deu 6.24
P. me, O God, for in thee I take Ps 16.01
May integrity and uprightness p. me, 25.21
and thy faithfulness ever p. me! 40.11
p. my life from dread of the enemy, 64.01
thy great power p. those doomed to 79.11
P. my life, for I am godly; 86.02
O LORD, in thy justice p. my life. 119.149
P. my life according to thy steadfast 119.159
of trouble, thou dost p. my life; 138.07
from evil men; p. me from violent men, 140.01
p. me from violent men, who have 140.04
name's sake, O LORD, p. my life! 143.11
to p. you from the evil woman, from Pro 6.24
to p. you from the loose woman, from 7.05
the lips of the wise will p. them. 14.03
Loyalty and faithfulness p. the king, 20.28
whoever loses his life will p. it. Lk 17.33

PRESERVED
to face, and yet my life is p." Gen 32.30
and p. us in all the way that we Jos 24.17
he has p. us and given into our 1Sa 30.23
and thy care has p. my spirit. Job 10.12
The righteous shall be p. for ever, Ps 37.28
and to restore the p. of Israel; Is 49.06
is left and is p. shall die of Eze 6.12
Egypt, and by a prophet he was p. Hos 12.13
wineskins, and so both are p." Mt 9.17
of the gospel might be p. for you. Gal 2.05
but p. Noah, a herald of righteousness, 2Pe 2.05

PRESERVES
The LORD p. the faithful, but Ps 31.23
he p. the lives of his saints; 97.10
The LORD p. the simple; 116.06
The LORD p. all who love him; 145.20
He who guards his mouth p. his life; Pro 13.03
He who guards his way p. his life. 16.17
is that wisdom p. the life of him Ecc 7.12

PRESERVEST
in them; and thou p. all of them; Neh 9.06
thou p. me from trouble; thou dost Ps 32.07

PRESERVING
of justice and p. the way of his Pro 2.08

PRESIDENTS
and over them three p., Dan 6.02
above all the other p. and satraps, 6.03
Then the p. and the satraps sought 6.04
Then these p. and satraps came by 6.06
All the p. of the kingdom, the 6.07

PRESS
and as the fulness of the wine p. Num 18.27
and as produce of the wine p.; 18.30
floor, and out of your wine p.; Deu 15.14
threshing floor and your wine p.; 16.13
beating out wheat in the wine p., Ju 6.11
they killed at the wine p. of Zeeb, 7.25
threshing floor, or from the wine p.?" 2Ki 6.27
or p. down his tongue with a cord? Job 41.01
bow, and from the p. of battle. Is 21.15
his that treads in the wine p.? 63.02
"I have trodden the wine p. alone, 63.03
as in a wine p. the virgin daughter Lam 1.15
and p. the siege against it. Eze 4.03
let us p. on to know the LORD; Hos 6.03
in, tread, for the wine p. is full. Joe 3.13
I will p. you down in your place, as Amo 2.13
their horsemen p. proudly on. Hab 1.08
around it, and dug a wine p. in it, Mt 21.33
it, and dug a pit for the wine p., Mk 12.01
surround you and p. upon you!" Lk 8.45
the Pharisees began to p. him hard, 11.53
but I p. on to make it my own, Php 3.12
I p. on toward the goal for the 3.14
the great wine p. of the wrath of Rev 14.19
and the wine p. was trodden outside 14.20
and blood flowed from the wine p., 14.20
tread the wine p. of the fury of 19.15

PRESSED
Then they p. hard against the man Gen 19.09
the grapes and p. them into 40.11
and p. Balaam's foot against the Num 22.25
The Amorites p. the Danites back Ju 1.34
told her, because she p. him hard. 14.17
And when she p. him hard with her 16.16
(for the people were hard p.), 1Sa 13.06
The battle p. hard upon Saul, and 31.03
He p. him, but he would not go but 2Sa 13.25
But Absalom p. him until he let 13.27
The battle p. hard upon Saul, and 1Ch 10.03
they are not p. out, or bound up, or Is 1.06
I have not p. thee to send evil, nor Jer17.16
breasts were p. and their virgin Eze 23.03
your bosom and p. your young breasts." 23.21
had diseases p. upon him to touch Mk 3.10
While the people p. upon him to Lk 5.01
good measure, p. down, shaken together, 6.38
he went, the people p. round him. 8.42
I am hard p. between the two. Php 1.23

PRESSES
and from the outflow of your p. Ex 22.29
treading wine p. on the sabbath, Neh 13.15
they tread the wine p., but suffer Job 24.11
treader treads out wine in the p.; Is 16.10
the wine cease from the wine p.; Jer 48.33
as a cart full of sheaves p. down. Amo 2.13
of Hananel to the king's wine p. Zec 14.10

PRESSING
For p. milk produces curds, Pro 30.33
p. the nose produces blood, and 30.33
and p. anger produces stife. 30.33
"You see the crowd p. around you, Mk 5.31

PRESSURE
my p. will not be heavy upon you. Job 33.07
is the daily p. upon me of my 2Co 11.28

PRESUME
is he that would p. to do this?" Est 7.05
and do not p. to say to yourselves, Mt 3.09
therefore I did not p. to come to you. Lk 7.07

PRESUME (cont.)
Or do you p. upon the riches of his — Rom 2.04
he did not p. to pronounce a reviling — Jud 1.09

PRESUMED
But they p. to go up to the heights — Num 14.44

PRESUMES
But the prophet who p. to speak a — Deu 18.20

PRESUMPTION
I know your p., and the evil of your — 1Sa 17.28

PRESUMPTUOUS
and were p. and went up into the — Deu 1.43
back thy servant also from p. sins; — Ps 19.13

PRESUMPTUOUSLY
The man who acts p., by not obeying — Deu 17.12
and fear, and not act p. again. — 17.13
the prophet has spoken it p., — 18.22
fathers acted p. and stiffened — Neh 9.16
Yet they acted p. and did not obey — 9.29

PRETEND
down on your bed, and p. to be ill; — 2Sa 13.05
"P. to be a mourner, and put on — 14.02
why do you p. to be another? For — 1Ki 14.06
There are friends who p. to be friends, — Pro 18.24

PRETENDED
So Amnon lay down, and p. to be ill; — 2Sa 13.06
she came, she p. to be another woman. — 1Ki 14.05
who p. to be sincere, that they — Lk 20.20
power and with p. signs and wonders, — 2Th 2.09

PRETENDS
One man p. to be rich, yet has nothing; — Pro 13.07
another p. to be poor, yet has great — 13.07

PRETENSE
Israel made a p. of being beaten — Jos 8.15
heart, but in p., says the LORD." — Jer 3.10
and for a p. you make long prayers; — *Mt 23.14
and for a p. make long prayers. — Mk 12.40
and for a p. make long prayers. — Lk 20.47
under p. of laying out anchors from — Ac 27.30
whether in p. or in truth, Christ is — Php 1.18

PRETENSIONS
through the p. of liars whose consciences — 1Ti 4.02

PRETEXT
using your freedom as a p. for evil; — 1Pe 2.16

PRETEXTS
who is estranged seeks p. to break out — Pro 18.01

PREVAIL
that he did not p. against Jacob, — Gen 32.25
shall not p. against a man for any — Deu 19.15
for not by might shall a man p. — 1Sa 2.09
but if I p. against him and kill — 17.09
let not man p. against thee." — 2Ch 14.11
you will not p. against him but — Est 6.13
they p. against him, like a king — Job 15.24
Let not man p.; let the nations be — Ps 9.19
say, "With our tongue we will p., — 12.04
When our transgressions p. over us, — 65.03
a man might p. against one who is — Ecc 4.12
sanctuary to pray, he will not p. — Is 16.12
but they shall not p. against you, — Jer 1.19
they cannot p., though they roar, — 5.22
but they shall not p. over you, — 15.20
shall deal with them and shall p. — Dan 11.07
of thousands, but he shall not p. — 11.12
of death shall not p. against it. — Mt 16.18
words, and p. when thou art judged." — Rom 3.04

PREVAILED
The waters p. and increased greatly — Gen 7.18
And the waters p. so mightily upon — 7.19
the waters p. above the mountains, — 7.20
And the waters p. upon the earth a — 7.24
with my sister, and have p."; — 30.08
with God and with men, and have p." — 32.28
of plenty that p. in the land of — 41.53
Moses held up his hand, Israel p.; — Ex 17.11
he lowered his hand, Amalek p. — 17.11
and his hand p. over Cushanrishathaim. — Ju 3.10
And the hand of Midian p. over Israel; — 6.02
So David p. over the Philistine with — 1Sa 17.50
But the king's word p. against Joab — 2Sa 24.04
But the king's word p. against Joab. — 1Ch 21.04
that time, and the men of Judah p., — 2Ch 13.18
the Ammonites and p. against them. — 27.05
lest my enemy say, "I have p. over him"; — Ps 13.04
yet they have not p. against me. — 129.02
stronger than I, and thou hast p. — Jer 20.07
deceived you and p. against you; — 38.22
are desolate, for the enemy has p. — Lam 1.16
with the saints, and p. over them, — Dan 7.21
He strove with the angel and p., — Hos 12.04
confederates have p. against you; — Ob 1.07
be crucified. And their voices p. — Lk 23.23
house and stay." And she p. upon us. — Ac 16.15
of the Lord grew and p. mightily. — 19.20

PREVAILEST
Thou p. for ever against him, and he — Job 14.20

PREVENT
in the power of your hand to p. it. — Deu 28.32
of our God to p. the taunts of the — Neh 5.09
in order to p. the bodies from — Jn 19.31
What is to p. my being baptized?" — Ac 8.36
to p. you from doing what you would. — Gal 5.17

PREVENTED
the LORD has p. me from bearing — Gen 16.02
John would have p. him, saying, — Mt 3.14
should be p. from attending to his — Ac 24.23
to you (but thus far have been p.), — Rom 1.13
they were p. by death from continuing — Heb 7.23

PREVIOUSLY
where they had p. put the cereal — Neh 13.05
before his God, as he had done p. — Dan 6.10
Simon who had p. practiced magic — Ac 8.09
For they had p. seen Trophimus the — 21.29
a covenant p. ratified by God, so — Gal 3.17

PREY
And when birds of p. came down upon — Gen 15.11
they captured and made their p. — 34.29
from the p., my son, you have gone — 49.09
in the morning devouring the p., — 49.27
our little ones will become a p.; — Num 14.03
who you said would become a p., — 14.31
lie down till it devours the p., — 23.24
who you said would become a p., — Deu 1.39
shall become a p. and a spoil to — 2Ki 21.14
lion perishes for lack of p., — Job 4.11
like an eagle swooping on the p. — 9.26
seeking p. in the wilderness as — 24.05
"That path no bird of p. knows, — 28.07
him drop his p. from his teeth. — 29.17
"Can you hunt the p. for the lion, — 38.39
Who provides for the raven its p., — 38.41
Thence he spies out the p.; — 39.29
they shall be p. for jackals. — Ps 63.10
The young lions roar for their p., — 104.21
not given us as p. to their teeth! — 124.06
slothful man will not catch his p., — Pro 12.27
they growl and seize their p., — Is 5.29
may make the fatherless their p.! — 10.02
to the birds of p. of the mountains — 18.06

PREY (cont.)
the birds of p. will summer upon Is 18.06
or a young lion growls over his p., 31.04
Then p. and spoil in abundance will 33.23
even the lame will take the p. 33.23
have become a p. with none to 42.22
calling a bird of p. from the east, 46.11
Can the p. be taken from the mighty, 49.24
and the p. of the tyrant be rescued, 49.25
from evil makes himself a p. 59.15
Why then has he become a p.? Jer 2.14
to me like a speckled bird of p.? 12.09
the birds of p. against her round 12.09
and all who p. on you I will make a p. 30.16
the hands of foreigners for a p., Eze 7.21
be no more in your hand as p.; 13.21
lion, and he learned to catch p.; 19.03
lion, and he learned to catch p.; 19.06
like a roaring lion tearing the p.; 22.25
her are like wolves tearing the p., 22.27
riches and a p. of your merchandise; 26.12
because my sheep have become a p., 34.08
they shall no longer be a p.; 34.22
no more be a p. to the nations, 34.28
have become a p. and derision to 36.04
you to birds of p. of every sort 39.04
I have seen, are destined for a p.; Hos 9.13
in the forest, when he has no p.? Amo 3.04
where the lion brought his p., Nah 2.11
and strangled p. for his lionesses; 2.12
his caves with p. and his dens 2.12
cut off your p. from the earth, 2.13
and breasts of p. and reptiles and Ac 11.06
no one makes a p. of you by Col 2.08

PREYS
or p. upon you, or takes advantage 2Co 11.20

PRICE
For the full p. let him give it to Gen 23.09
I will give the p. of the field; 23.13
live ox and divide the p. of it; Ex 21.35
by you at the p. for a guilt Lev 5.18
by you at the p. for a guilt 6.06
are many you shall increase the p., 25.16
are few you shall diminish the p., 25.16
and the p. of his release shall be 25.50
out of the p. paid for him the 25.51
for him the p. for his redemption. 25.51
redemption p. (at a month old you Num 18.16
betrothed at the p. of a hundred 2Sa 3.14
but I will buy it of you for a p.; 24.24
received them from Kue at a p. 1Ki 10.28
LORD—give it to me at its full p.— 1Ch 21.22
but I will buy it for the full p.; 21.24
received them from Kue for a p. 2Ch 1.16
silver cannot be weighed as its p. Job 28.15
the p. of wisdom is above pearls. 28.18
demanding no high p. for them. Ps 44.12
or give to God the p. of his life, 49.07
a fool have a p. in his hand to Pro 17.16
and the goats the p. of a field; 27.26
not for p. or reward," says the LORD Is 45.13
milk without money and without p. 55.01
without p., for all your sins, Jer 15.13
spoil as the p. of your sin 17.03
and shall divide the land for a p. Dan 11.39
the lordly p. at which I was paid Zec 11.13
p. of him on whom a p. had been set Mt 27.09
you were bought with a p. So glorify 1Co 6.20
You were bought with a p.; do not 7.23
water without p. from the fountain Rev 21.06
take the water of life without p. 22.17

PRICK
more a brier to p. or a thorn to Eze 28.24

PRICKED
embittered, when I was p. in heart, Ps 73.21

PRICKS
shall be as p. in your eyes and Num 33.55

PRIDE
pre-eminent in p. and pre-eminent Gen 49.03
and I will break the p. of your power, Lev 26.19
himself for the p. of his heart, 2Ch 32.26
his deed, and cut off p. from man; Job 33.17
because of the p. of evil men. 35.12
he is king over all the sons of p." 41.34
In the p. of his countenance the Ps 10.04
the righteous in p. and contempt. 31.18
the p. of Jacob whom he loves. 47.04
let them be trapped in their p. 59.12
Therefore p. is their necklace; 73.06
P. and arrogance and the way of Pro 8.13
When p. comes, then comes disgrace; 11.02
P. goes before destruction, and a 16.18
man who acts with arrogant p. 21.24
A man's p. will bring him low, but he 29.23
and the p. of men shall be humbled; Is 2.11
and the p. of men shall be brought 2.17
shall be the p. and glory of the 4.02
who say in p. and in arrogance of heart: 9.09
king of Assyria and his haughty p. 10.12
an end to the p. of the arrogant, 13.11
splendor and p. of the Chaldeans, 13.19
We have heard of the p. of Moab, 16.06
his p., and his insolence—his 16.06
to defile the p. of all glory, to 23.09
lay low his p. together with the 25.11
I spoil the p. of Judah and the Jer 13.09
and the great p. of Jerusalem. 13.09
will weep in secret for your p.; 13.17
We have heard of the p. of Moab— 48.29
his p., and his arrogance, and the 48.29
and the p. of your heart, you who 49.16
slain all the p. of our eyes in Lam 2.04
has blossomed, p. has budded. Eze 7.10
she and her daughters had p., 16.49
your mouth in the day of your p., 16.56
the p. of your power, the delight of 24.21
bring to nought the p. of Egypt, 32.12
who walk in p. he is able to abase. Dan 4.37
The p. of Israel testifies to his Hos 5.05
The p. of Israel witnesses against 7.10
"I abhor the p. of Jacob, and hate Amo 6.08
The LORD has sworn by the p. of Jacob: 8.07
The p. of your heart has deceived Ob 1.03
their lot in return for their p., Zep 2.10
make an end of the p. of Philistia. Zec 9.06
The p. of Assyria shall be laid low, 10.11
envy, slander, p., foolishness. Mk 7.22
woman has long hair, it is her p.? 1Co 11.15
by my p. in you which I have in 15.31
those who p. themselves on a man's 2Co 5.12
I have great p. in you; I am filled 7.04
expressed to him some p. in you, 7.14
our confidence and p. in our hope. Heb 3.06
of the eyes and the p. of life, 1Jn 2.16

PRIEST
he was p. of God Most High. Gen 14.18
the daughter of Potiphera p. of On. 41.45
the daughter of Potiphera p. of On, 41.50
daughter of Potiphera the p. of On, 46.20
Now the p. of Midian had seven Ex 2.16
father-in-law, Jethro, the p. of Midian; 3.01
Jethro, the p. of Midian, Moses' 18.01
The son who is p. in his place 29.30
for Aaron the p. and the garments 31.10
the holy garments for Aaron the p., 35.19
of Ithamar the son of Aaron the p. 38.21
the holy garments for Aaron the p., 39.41
him, that he may serve me as p. 40.13

PRIEST (cont.)
of Aaron the p. shall put fire on Lev 1.07
And the p. shall burn the whole on 1.09
and the p. shall lay them in order 1.12
And the p. shall offer the whole, 1.13
And the p. shall bring it to the 1.15
And the p. shall burn it on the 1.17
and the p. shall burn this as its 2.02
and when it is presented to the p., 2.08
And the p. shall take from the 2.09
And the p. shall burn as its 2.16
And the p. shall burn it on the 3.11
And the p. shall burn them on the 3.16
if it is the anointed p. who sins, 4.03
And the anointed p. shall take some 4.05
and the p. shall dip his finger in 4.06
And the p. shall put some of the 4.07
and the p. shall burn them upon the 4.10
Then the anointed p. shall bring 4.16
and the p. shall dip his finger in 4.17
and the p. shall make atonement for 4.20
Then the p. shall take some of the 4.25
so the p. shall make atonement for 4.26
And the p. shall take some of its 4.30
and the p. shall burn it upon the 4.31
and the p. shall make atonement for 4.31
Then the p. shall take some of the 4.34
and the p. shall burn it on the 4.35
and the p. shall make atonement for 4.35
and the p. shall make atonement for 5.06
He shall bring them to the p., 5.08
and the p. shall make atonement for 5.10
And he shall bring it to the p., 5.12
and the p. shall take a handful of 5.12
Thus the p. shall make atonement 5.13
the remainder shall be for the p., 5.13
fifth to it and give it to the p.; 5.16
and the p. shall make atonement for 5.16
bring to the p. a ram without 5.18
and the p. shall make atonement for 5.18
bring to the p. his guilt offering 6.06
and the p. shall make atonement for 6.07
And the p. shall put on his linen 6.10
the p. shall burn wood on it every 6.12
The p. from among Aaron's sons, who 6.22
offering of a p. shall be wholly 6.23
The p. who offers it for sin shall 6.26
the p. shall burn them on the altar 7.05
the p. who makes atonement with it 7.07
And the p. who offers any man's 7.08
belong to the p. who offers it. 7.09
belong to the p. who throws the 7.14
The p. shall burn the fat on the 7.31
give to the p. as an offering from 7.32
to Aaron the p. and to his sons, as 7.34
bring to the p. at the door of the 12.06
and the p. shall make atonement for 12.08
to Aaron the p. or to one of his 13.02
and the p. shall examine the 13.03
when the p. has examined him he 13.03
the p. shall shut up the diseased 13.04
and the p. shall examine him on the 13.05
then p. shall shut him up seven 13.05
and the p. shall examine him again 13.06
then the p. shall pronounce him 13.06
himself to the p. for his cleansing, 13.07
shall appear again before the p.; 13.07
and the p. shall make an examination, 13.08
then the p. shall pronounce him 13.06
he shall be brought to the p.; 13.09
and the p. shall make an examination, 13.10
and the p. shall pronounce him 13.11
to foot, so far as the p. can see, 13.12
then the p. shall make an examination, 13.13
And the p. shall examine the raw 13.15
then he shall come to the p., 13.16
and the p. shall examine him, and if 13.17
then the p. shall pronounce the 13.17
then it shall be shown to the p.; 13.19
and the p. shall make an examination, 13.20
then the p. shall pronounce him 13.20
But if the p. examines it, and the 13.21
then the p. shall shut him up seven 13.21
then the p. shall pronounce him 13.22
and the p. shall pronounce him 13.23
the p. shall examine it, and if the 13.25
and the p. shall pronounce him 13.25
But if the p. examines it, and the 13.26
the p. shall shut up seven days, 13.26
and the p. shall examine him the 13.27
then the p. shall pronounce him 13.27
and the p. shall pronounce him 13.28
the p. shall examine the disease; 13.30
then the p. shall pronounce him 13.30
And if the p. examines the itching 13.31
then the p. shall shut up the 13.31
seventh day the p. shall examine 13.32
and the p. shall shut up the person 13.33
seventh day the p. shall examine 13.34
then the p. shall pronounce him 13.34
then the p. shall examine him, and 13.36
the p. need not seek for the yellow 13.36
and the p. shall pronounce him 13.37
the p. shall make an examination, 13.39
Then the p. shall examine him, and 13.43
the p. must pronounce him unclean; 13.44
and shall be shown to the p. 13.49
And the p. shall examine the 13.50
"And if the p. examines, and the 13.53
then the p. shall command that they 13.54
and the p. shall examine the 13.55
"But if the p. examines, and the 13.56
He shall be brought to the p.; 14.02
and the p. shall go out of the camp, 14.03
and the p. shall make an examination. 14.03
the p. shall command them to take 14.04
and the p. shall command them to 14.05
And the p. who cleanses him shall 14.11
And the p. shall take one of the 14.12
sin offering, belongs to the p.; 14.13
The p. shall take some of the blood 14.14
and the p. shall put it on the tip 14.14
Then the p. shall take some of the 14.15
in his hand the p. shall put on 14.17
Then the p. shall make atonement 14.18
The p. shall offer the sin offering, 14.19
and the p. shall offer the burnt 14.20
Thus the p. shall make atonement 14.20
them for his cleansing to the p., 14.23
and the p. shall take the lamb of 14.24
and the p. shall wave them for a 14.24
and the p. shall take some of the 14.25
And the p. shall pour some of the 14.26
and the p. shall put some of the 14.28
and the p. shall make atonement 14.31
house shall come and tell the p., 14.35
Then the p. shall command that they 14.36
before the p. goes to examine the 14.36
afterward the p. shall go in to 14.36
then the p. shall go out of the 14.38
And the p. shall come again on the 14.39
then the p. shall command that they 14.40
then the p. shall go and look; 14.44
"But if the p. comes and makes an 14.48
then the p. shall pronounce the 14.48
meeting, and give them to the p.; 15.14
and the p. shall offer them, one for 15.15
and the p. shall make atonement for 15.15
pigeons, and bring them to the p., 15.29
And the p. shall offer one for a 15.30
and the p. shall make atonement for 15.30
And the p. who is anointed and 16.32
consecrated as p. in his father's 16.32
to the p. at the door of the tent 17.05
and the p. shall sprinkle the blood 17.06
And the p. shall make atonement for 19.22

PRIEST (cont.)

for the p. is holy to his God. Lev 21.07
And the daughter of any p., 21.09
"The p. who is chief among his 21.10
of Aaron the p. who has a blemish 21.21
sojourner of the p. or a hired 22.10
but if a p. buys a slave as his 22.11
and give the holy thing to the p. 22.14
fruits of your harvest to the p.; 23.10
the sabbath the p. shall wave it. 23.11
And the p. shall wave them with the 23.20
be holy to the LORD for the p. 23.20
bring the person before the p., 27.08
and the p. shall value him; 27.08
who vowed the p. shall value him. 27.08
bring the animal before the p., 27.11
and the p. shall value it as either 27.12
as you, the p., value it, so it shall 27.12
the p. shall value it as either 27.14
as the p. values it, so it shall 27.14
then the p. shall compute the 27.18
the p. shall be in possession of it. 27.21
then the p. shall compute the 27.23
and set them before Aaron the p., Num 3.06
of Aaron the p. was to be chief 3.32
of Aaron the p. shall have charge 4.16
of Ithamar the son of Aaron the p. 4.28
of Ithamar the son of Aaron the p. 4.33
shall go to the LORD for the p., 5.08
they bring to the p., shall be his; 5.09
man gives to the p. shall be his. 5.10
man shall bring his wife to the p., 5.15
"And the p. shall bring her near, 5.16
and the p. shall take holy water in 5.17
And the p. shall set the woman 5.18
in his hand the p. shall have the 5.18
Then the p. shall make her take an 5.19
then' (let the p. make the woman 5.21
"Then the p. shall write these 5.23
And the p. shall take the cereal 5.25
and the p. shall take a handful of 5.26
and the p. shall execute upon her 5.30
pigeons to the p. to the door of 6.10
and the p. shall offer one for a 6.11
And the p. shall present them 6.16
the p. shall offer also its cereal 6.17
And the p. shall take the shoulder 6.19
and the p. shall wave them for a 6.20
they are a holy portion for the p., 6.20
of Ithamar the son of Aaron the p. 7.08
And the p. shall make atonement for 15.25
And the p. shall make atonement 15.28
of Aaron the p. to take up the 16.37
So Eleazar the p. took the bronze 16.39
so that no one who is not a p., 16.40
LORD's offering to Aaron the p. 18.28
shall give her to Eleazar the p., 19.03
and Eleazar the p. shall take some 19.04
and the p. shall take cedarwood 19.06
Then the p. shall wash his clothes 19.07
and the p. shall be unclean until 19.07
of Eleazar, son of Aaron the p., 25.07
of Eleazar, son of Aaron the p., 25.11
Eleazar the son of Aaron, the p., 26.01
and Eleazar the p. spoke with them 26.03
by Moses and Eleazar the p., 26.63
numbered by Moses and Aaron the p., 26.64
Moses, and before Eleazar the p., 27.02
Eleazar the p. and all the congregation, 27.19
shall stand before Eleazar the p., 27.21
Eleazar the p. and the whole 27.22
Phinehas the son of Eleazar the p., 31.06
to Moses, and to Eleazar the p., 31.12
Moses, and Eleazar the p., 31.13
And Eleazar the p. said to the men 31.21
and Eleazar the p. and the heads 31.26
to Eleazar the p. as an offering 31.29
and Eleazar the p. did as the LORD 31.31
for the LORD, to Eleazar the p., 31.41
and Eleazar the p. received from 31.51
and Eleazar the p. received the 31.54
to Eleazar the p. and to the 32.02
concerning them to Eleazar the p., 32.28
And Aaron the p. went up Mount Hor 33.38
Eleazar the p. and Joshua the son 34.17
of the high p. who was anointed 32.25
until the death of the high p.; 35.28
of the high p. the manslayer may 35.28
before the death of the high p. 35.32
ministered as p. in his stead. Deu 10.06
not obeying the p. who stands to 17.12
give to the p. the shoulder and 18.03
the p. shall come forward and speak 20.02
shall go to the p. who is in 26.03
Then the p. shall take the basket 26.04
of Canaan, which Eleazar the p., Jos 14.01
Eleazar the p. and Joshua the son 17.04
Eleazar the p. and Joshua the son 19.51
of him who is high p. at the time: 20.06
to Eleazar the p. and to Joshua 21.01
of Aaron the p. received by lot 21.04
of Aaron the p. they gave Hebron, 21.13
Phinehas the son of Eleazar the p., 22.13
When Phinehas the p. and the chiefs 22.30
of Eleazar the p. said to the 22.31
Phinehas the son of Eleazar the p., 22.32
one of his sons, who became his p. Ju 17.05
me, and be to me a father and a p., 17.10
and the young man became his p., 17.12
me, because I have a Levite as p." 17.13
hired me, and I have become his p." 18.04
succeed." And the p. said to them, 18.05
while the p. stood by the entrance 18.17
the p. said to them, "What are you 18.18
us, and be to us a father and a p. 18.19
for you to be p. to the house of 18.19
or to be p. to a tribe and family 18.19
and the p., and go away, and what 18.24
and the p. who belonged to him, the 18.27
Now Eli the p. was sitting on the 1Sa 1.09
in the presence of Eli the p. 2.11
brought up the p. would take for 2.14
"Give meat for the p. to roast; 2.15
the tribes of Israel to be my p., 2.28
raise up for myself a faithful p., 2.35
the p. of the LORD in Shiloh, 14.03
And while Saul was talking to the p., 14.19
and Saul said to the p., "Withdraw 14.19
But the p. said, "Let us draw near 14.36
David to Nob to Ahimelech the p.; 21.01
And David said to Ahimelech the p., 21.02
And the p. answered David, "I have 21.04
And David answered the p., "Of a 21.05
So the p. gave him the holy bread; 21.06
And the p. said, "The sword of 21.09
sent to summon Ahimelech the p., 22.11
and he said to Abiathar the p., 23.09
And David said to Abiathar the p., 30.07
The king also said to Zadok the p., 2Sa 15.27
the Jairite was also David's p. 20.26
Zeruiah and with Abiathar the p.; 1Ki 1.07
But Zadok the p., and Benaiah the 1.08
Abiathar the p., and Joab the 1.19
of the army, and Abiathar the p.; 1.25
and Zadok the p., and Benaiah the 1.26
said, "Call to me Zadok the p., 1.32
and let Zadok the p., and Nathan the 1.34
So Zadok the p., Nathan the prophet, 1.38
There Zadok the p. took the horn of 1.39
the son of Abiathar the p. came; 1.42
has sent with him Zadok the p., 1.44
and Zadok the p. and Nathan the 1.45
Abiathar the p. and Joab the son 2.22
And to Abiathar the p. the king said, 2.26
Abiathar from being p. to the LORD, 2.27
put Zadok the p. in the place of 2.35

PRIEST (cont.)
the son of Zadok was the p.; 1Ki 4.02
of Nathan was p. and king's friend; 4.05
all that Jehoiada the p. commanded, 2Ki 11.09
and came to Jehoiada the p. 11.09
And the p. delivered to the captains 11.10
Then Jehoiada the p. commanded the 11.15
For the p. said, "Let her not be 11.15
slew Mattan the p. of Baal before 11.18
And the p. posted watchmen over the 11.18
Jehoiada the p. instructed him. 12.02
Jehoiada the p. and the other 12.07
Then Jehoiada the p. took a chest 12.09
and the high p. came up and they 12.10
to Urijah the p. a model of the 16.10
And Urijah the p. built the altar; 16.11
so Urijah the p. made it, before 16.11
And King Ahaz commanded Urijah the p., 16.15
Urijah the p. did all this, as King 16.16
"Go up to Hilkiah the high p., 22.04
the high p. said to Shaphan the 22.08
"Hilkiah the p. has given me a book 22.10
And the king commanded Hilkiah the p., 22.12
So Hilkiah the p., and Ahikam, and 22.14
the high p., and the priests of the 23.04
Hilkiah the p. found in the house 23.24
guard took Seraiah the chief p., 25.18
and Zephaniah the second p., and the 25.18
who served as p. in the house that 1Ch 6.10
left Zadok the p. and his brethren 16.39
and Zadok the p., and Ahimelech the 24.06
son of Jehoiada the p., as chief; 27.05
for the LORD, and Zadok as p. 29.22
rams becomes a p. of what are no 2Ch 13.09
God, and without a teaching p., 15.03
the chief p. is over you in all 19.11
and wife of Jehoiada the p., 22.11
all that Jehoiada the p. commanded. 23.08
Jehoiada the p. did not dismiss 23.08
And Jehoiada the p. delivered to 23.09
Then Jehoiada the p. brought out 23.14
For the p. said, "Do not slay her 23.14
slew Mattan the p. of Baal before 23.17
all the days of Jehoiada the p. 24.02
of the chief p. would come and 24.11
Zechariah the son of Jehoiada the p.; 24.20
of the son of Jehoiada the p., 24.25
But Azariah the p. went in after 26.17
And Azariah the chief p., and all 26.20
Azariah the chief p., who was of 31.10
the high p. and delivered the 34.09
Hilkiah the p. found the book of 34.14
"Hilkiah the p. has given me a book 34.18
should be a p. to consult Urim and Eze 2.63
Eleazar, son of Aaron the chief p.— 7.05
Artaxerxes gave to Ezra the p., 7.11
to Ezra the p., the scribe of the 7.12
the River: Whatever Ezra the p., 7.21
into the hands of Meremoth the p., 8.33
And Ezra the p. stood up and said 10.10
Ezra the p. selected men, heads of 10.16
the high p. rose up with his Neh 3.01
the house of Eliashib the high p. 3.20
until a p. with Urim and Thummim 7.65
And Ezra the p. brought the law 8.02
and Ezra the p. and scribe, and the 8.09
And the p., the son of Aaron, shall 10.38
and of Ezra the p. the scribe. 12.26
Eliashib the p., who was appointed 13.04
the storehouses Shelemiah the p., 13.13
the son of Eliashib the high p., 13.28
"You are a p. ever after the Ps 110.04
Uriah the p. and Zechariah the son Is 8.02
as with the people, so with the p.; 24.02
the p. and the prophet reel with 28.07
and from prophet to p., every one Jer 6.13
from prophet to p. every one deals 8.10
prophet and p. ply their trade 14.18
law shall not perish from the p., 18.18
Now Pashhur the p., the son of 21.01
of Malchiah and Zephaniah the p., 21.01
"Both prophet and p. are ungodly; 23.11
or a p. asks you, 'What is the 23.33
prophet, p., or one of the people 23.34
Zephaniah the son of Maaseiah the p., 29.25
made you p. instead of Jehoiada the p., 29.26
Zephaniah the p. read this letter 29.29
of Shelemiah, and Zephaniah the p., 37.03
guard took Seraiah the chief p., 52.24
and Zephaniah the second p., 52.24
indignation has spurned king and p. Lam 2.06
Or should p. and prophet be slain 2.20
of the LORD came to Ezekiel the p., Eze 1.03
but the law perishes from the p., 7.26
come near to me, to serve me as p., 44.13
No p. shall drink wine, when he 44.21
a widow who is the widow of a p. 44.22
The p. shall take some of the blood 45.19
with you is my contention, O p. Hos 4.04
I reject you from being a p. to me. 4.06
And it shall be like people, like p.; 4.09
Then Amaziah the p. of Bethel sent Amo 7.10
the son of Jehozadak, the high p., Hag 1.01
the high p., with all the remnant 1.12
the high p., and the spirit of all 1.14
the high p., and to all the remnant 2.02
son of Jehozadak, the high p.; 2.04
Joshua the high p. standing before Zec 3.01
Hear now, O Joshua the high p., 3.08
the son of Jehozadak, the high p.; 6.11
there shall be a p. by his throne, 6.13
For the lips of a p. should guard Mal 2.07
but go, show yourself to the p., Mt 8.04
in the palace of the high p., 26.03
struck the slave of the high p., 26.51
led him to Caiaphas the high p., 26.57
as the courtyard of the high p., 26.58
And the high p. stood up and said. 26.62
And the high p. said to him, "I adjure 26.63
Then the high p. tore his robes, and 26.65
but go, show yourself to the p., Mk 1.44
of God, when Abiathar was high p., 2.26
of the high p. and cut off his ear. 14.47
And they led Jesus to the high p.; 14.53
into the courtyard of the high p.; 14.54
And the high p. stood up in the 14.60
Again the high p. asked him, 14.61
And the high p. tore his mantle, and 14.63
of the maids of the high p. came; 14.66
there was a p. named Zechariah, of Lk 1.05
was serving as p. before God when 1.08
but "go and show yourself to the p., 5.14
Now by chance a p. was going down 10.31
of the high p. and cut off his 22.50
who was high p. that year, said to Jn 11.49
but being high p. that year he 11.51
Caiaphas, who was high p. that year. 18.13
disciple was known to the high p., 18.15
of the high p. along with Jesus, 18.15
who was known to the high p., 18.16
The high p. then questioned Jesus 18.19
"Is that how you answer the high p.?" 18.22
him bound to Caiaphas the high p. 18.24
One of the servants of the high p., 18.26
with Annas the high p. and Caiaphas Ac 4.06
But the high p. rose up and all who 5.17
Now the high p. came and those who 5.21
And the high p. questioned them, 5.27
And the high p. said, "Is this so?" 7.01
the Lord, went to the high p. 9.01
And the p. of Zeus, whose temple was 14.13
a Jewish high p. named Sceva were 19.14
as the high p. and the whole 22.05
And the high p. Ananias commanded 23.02
"Would you revile God's high p.?" 23.04
brethren, that he was the high p.; 23.05

PRIEST (cont.)

days the high p. Ananias came down Ac 24.01
faithful high p. in the service of Heb 2.17
and high p. of our confession. 3.01
a great high p. who has passed 4.14
have not a high p. who is unable 4.15
For every high p. chosen from among 5.01
exalt himself to be made a high p., 5.05
"Thou art a p. for ever, after the 5.06
by God a high p. after the order 5.10
become a high p. for ever after 6.20
p. of the most high God, met Abraham 7.01
of God he continues a p. for ever. 7.03
for another p. to arise after the 7.11
when another p. arises in the 7.15
who has become a p., not according 7.16
"Thou art a p. for ever, after the 7.17
his mind, 'Thou art a p. for ever.'" 7.21
that we should have such a high p., 7.26
is this: we have such a high p., 8.01
For every high p. is appointed to 8.03
for this p. also to have something 8.03
earth, he would not be a p. at all, 8.04
the second only the high p. goes, 9.07
as a high p. of the good things 9.11
as the high p. enters the Holy 9.25
And every p. stands daily at his 10.11
we have a great p. over the house 10.21
by the high p. as a sacrifice for 13.11

PRIESTHOOD

to consecrate him for my p. Ex 28.03
and the p. shall be theirs by a 29.09
to a perpetual p. throughout their 40.15
and they shall attend to their p.; Num 3.10
And would you seek the p. also? 16.10
iniquity in connection with your p. 18.01
attend to your p. for all that 18.07
I give your p. as a gift, and any 18.07
the covenant of a perpetual p., 25.13
for the p. of the LORD is their Jos 18.07
excluded from the p. as unclean; Ez 2.62
excluded from the p. as unclean; Neh 7.64
defiled the p. and the covenant of 13.29
covenant of the p. and the Levites 13.29
according to the custom of the p., Lk 1.09
the Levitical p. (for under it the Heb 7.11
For when there is a change in the p., 7.12
but he holds his p. permanently, 7.24
to be a holy p., to offer spiritual 1Pe 2.05
a royal p., a holy nation, God's own 2.09

PRIESTLY

Gentiles in the p. service of the Rom 15.16
who receive the p. office have a Heb 7.05

PRIEST'S

that is in the p. hand he shall Lev 14.18
that is in the p. hand he shall 14.29
If a p. daughter is married to an 22.12
But if a p. daughter is a widow or 22.13
to minister in the p. office. Num 3.03
And the p. heart was glad; Ju 18.20
the p. servant would come, while the 1Sa 2.13
the p. servant would come and say 2.15
in one of the p. places, that I may 2.36
bringing him into the high p. house. Lk 22.54
struck the high p. slave and cut Jn 18.10

PRIESTS

Only the land of the p. he did not buy; Gen 47.22
for the p. had a fixed allowance 47.22
the land of the p. alone did not 47.26
me a kingdom of p. and a holy Ex 19.06
And also let the p. who come near 19.22
do not let the p. and the people 19.24
people of Israel, to serve me as p.— 28.01
and his sons to serve me as p. 28.04
them, that they may serve me as p. 28.41
them, that they may serve me as p. 29.01
will consecrate, to serve me as p. 29.44
them that they may serve me as p. 30.30
his sons, for their service as p., 31.10
his sons, for their service as p. 35.19
garments of his sons to serve as p. 39.41
that they may serve me as p.: 40.15
sons the p. shall present the Lev 1.05
sons the p. shall lay the pieces, 1.08
sons the p. shall throw it blood 1.11
and bring it to Aaron's sons the p. 2.02
sons the p. shall throw the blood 3.02
every male among the p. may eat of it; 6.29
Every male among the p. may eat of it; 7.06
presented to serve as p. of the LORD; 7.35
or to one of his sons the p., 13.02
atonement for the p. and for all 16.33
"Speak to the p., the sons of Aaron, 21.01
The p. shall not profane the holy 22.15
the anointed p., whom he ordained Num 3.03
served as p. in the lifetime of 3.04
sanctuary with which the p. minister, 3.31
the p., shall blow the trumpets. 10.08
and coming to the Levitical p., Deu 17.09
is in charge of the Levitical p.; 17.18
"The Levitical p., that is, all the 18.01
before the p. and the judges who 19.17
And the p. the sons of Levi shall 21.05
the Levitical p. shall direct you; 24.08
the Levitical p. said to all 27.09
gave it to the p. the sons of Levi, 31.09
being carried by the Levitical p., Jos 3.03
And Joshua said to the p., 3.06
command the p. who bear the ark of 3.08
the feet of the p. who bear the 3.13
Jordan with the p. bearing the ark 3.14
the feet of the p. bearing the ark 3.15
the p. who bore the ark of the 3.17
the feet of the p. bearing the ark 4.09
For the p. who bore the ark stood 4.10
LORD and the p. passed over before 4.11
"Command the p. who bear the ark of 4.16
Joshua therefore commanded the p., 4.17
And when the p. bearing the ark of 4.18
And seven p. shall bear seven 6.04
the p. blowing the trumpets. 6.04
Nun called the p. and said to them, 6.06
and let seven p. bear seven trumpets 6.06
the seven p. bearing the seven 6.08
went before the p. who blew the 6.09
and the p. took up the ark of the 6.12
And the seven p. bearing the seven 6.13
when the p. had blown the trumpets, 6.16
the Levitical p. who carried the 8.33
the p., were in all thirteen cities 21.19
his sons were p. to the tribe of Ju 18.30
and Phinehas, were p. of the LORD. 1Sa 1.03
The custom of the p. with the 2.13
This is why the p. of Dagon and all 5.05
called for the p. and the diviners 6.02
house, the p. who were at Nob; 22.11
"Turn and kill the p. of the LORD; 22.17
to fall upon the p. of the LORD. 22.17
"You turn and fall upon the p." 22.18
turned and fell upon the p., 22.18
And Nob, the city of the p., 22.19
Saul had killed the p. of the LORD. 22.21
the son of Abiathar were p.; 2Sa 8.17
Pelethites; and David's sons were p. 8.18
and Abiathar the p. with you there? 15.35
it to Zadok and Abiathar the p. 15.35
said to Zadok and Abiathar the p., 17.15
to Zadok and Abiathar the p., 19.11
and Zadok and Abiathar were p.; 20.25
Zadok and Abiathar were p.; 1Ki 4.04
and the p. took up the ark. 8.03
the p. and the Levites brought them 8.04

PRIESTS (cont.)

Then the p. brought the ark of the 1Ki 8.06
And when the p. came out of the 8.10
so that the p. could not stand to 8.11
and appointed p. from among all the 12.31
in Bethel the p. of the high 12.32
upon you the p. of the high places 13.02
but made p. for the high places 13.33
consecrated to be p. of the high 13.33
and his p., until he left him none 2Ki 10.11
all his worshipers and all his p.; 10.19
Jehoash said to the p., "All the 12.04
let the p. take, each from his 12.05
Jehoash the p. had made no repairs 12.06
and the other p. and said to them, 12.07
So the p. agreed that they should 12.08
and the p. who guarded the threshold 12.09
of the LORD; it belonged to the p. 12.16
one of the p. whom you carried 17.27
So one of the p. whom they had 17.28
of people as p. of the high places, 17.32
the secretary, and the senior p., 19.02
and the p. and the prophets, all the 23.02
and the p. of the second order, and 23.04
the idolatrous p. whom the kinds 23.05
brought all the p. out of the 23.08
where the p. had burned incense, 23.08
However, the p. of the high places 23.09
And he slew all the p. of the high 23.20
the p., the Levites, and the temple 1Ch 9.02
Of the p.: Jedaiah, Jehoiarib, Jachin, 9.10
Others, of the sons of the p., 9.30
them to the p. and Levites in the 13.02
summoned the p. Zadok and Abiathar, 15.11
So the p. and the Levites sanctified 15.14
the p., should blow the trumpets 15.24
Jahaziel the p. were to blow 16.06
brethren the p. before the tabernacle 16.39
the son of Abiathar were p.; 18.16
Israel and the p. and the Levites. 23.02
However, the p. of the high places 23.09
Eleazar and Ithamar became the p. 24.02
houses of the p. and of the 24.06
houses of the p. and of the 24.31
divisions of the p. and of the 28.13
divisions of the p. and the Levites 28.21
the sea was for the p. to wash in. 2Ch 4.06
He made the court of the p., 4.09
the p. and the Levites brought 5.05
So the p. brought the ark of the 5.07
Now when the p. came out of the 5.11
(for all the p. who were present 5.11
and twenty p. who were trumpeters; 5.12
so that the p. could not stand to 5.14
Let thy p., O LORD God, be clothed 6.41
And the p. could not enter the 7.02
The p. stood at their posts; 7.06
them the p. sounded trumpets; 7.06
divisions of the p. for their 8.14
before the p. as the duty of each 8.14
commanded the p. and Levites 8.15
And the p. and the Levites that 11.13
from serving as p. of the LORD, 11.14
appointed his own p. for the high 11.15
not driven out the p. of the LORD, 13.09
and made p. for yourselvs like the 13.09
We have p. ministering to the LORD 13.10
and his p. with their battle 13.12
and the p. blew the trumpets. 13.14
the p. Elishama and Jerhoram 17.08
Levites and p. and heads of families 19.08
of you p. and Levites who come off 23.04
LORD except the p. and ministering 23.06
the Levitical p. and the Levites 23.18
And he gathered the p. and the 24.05
with eighty p. of the LORD who were 26.17
but for the p. the sons of Aaron, 26.18
angry with the p. leprosy broke 26.19
presence of the p. in the house of 26.19
and all the p., looked at him, and 26.20
He brought in the p. and the 29.04
The p. went into the inner part of 29.16
commanded the p. the sons of Aaron 29.21
and the p. received the blood and 29.22
and the p. killed them and made a 29.24
and the p. with the trumpets. 29.26
But the p. were too few and could 29.34
so until other p. had sanctified 29.34
heart than the p. in sanctifying 29.34
because the p. had not sanctified 30.03
And the p. and the Levites were put 30.15
the p. threw the blood which they 30.16
Levites and the p. praised the 30.21
And the p. sanctified themselves in 30.24
and the p. and the Levites, and the 30.25
Then the p. and the Levites arose 30.27
divisions of the p. and of the 31.02
the p. and the Levites, for burnt 31.02
due to the p. and the Levites, that 31.04
questioned the p. and the Levites 31.09
him in the cities of the p., 31.15
enrollment of the p. was according 31.17
The p. were enrolled with all their 31.18
the p., who were in the fields of 31.19
male among the p. and to every one 31.19
bones of the p. on their altars, 34.05
Jerusalem and the p. and the 34.30
He appointed the p. to their 35.02
to the p., and to the Levites. 35.08
gave to the p. for the passover 35.08
the p. stood in their place, and the 35.10
and the p. sprinkled the blood 35.11
for themselves and for the p., 35.14
because the p. the sons of Aaron 35.14
and for the p. the sons of Aaron. 35.14
and the p. and the Levites, and all 34.18
All the leading p. and the people 36.14
and the p. and the Levites, every Ez 1.05
The p.: the sons of Jedaiah, of the 2.36
Also, of the sons of the p.: 2.61
The p., the Levites, and some of the 2.70
son of Jozadak, with his fellow p., 3.02
the p. and the Levites and all who 3.08
the p. in their vestments came 3.10
But many of the p. and Levites and 3.12
as the p. at Jerusalem require—let 6.09
the p. and the Levites, and the rest 6.16
And they set the p. in their 6.18
For the p. and the Levites had 6.20
exiles, for their fellow p., 6.20
and some of the p. and Levites, 7.07
Israel or their p. or Levites in 7.13
offerings of the people and the p., 7.16
or toll upon any one of the p., 7.24
I reviewed the people and the p., 8.15
set apart twelve of the leading p.: 8.24
the chief p. and the Levites and 8.29
So the p. and the Levites took over 8.30
Israel and the p. and the Levites, 9.01
and our p. have been given into the 9.07
the leading p. and Levites and all 10.05
Of the sons of the p. who had 10.18
the p., the nobles, the officials, Neh 2.16
brethren the p. and they built the 3.01
After him the p., the men of the 3.22
Above the Horse Gate and p. repaired, 3.28
And I called the p., and took an 5.12
The p.: the sons of Jedaiah, namely 7.39
Also, of the p.: the sons of Hobaiah, 7.63
So the p., the Levites, the gatekeepers, 7.73
with the p. and the Levites, came 8.13
our p., our prophets, our fathers, 9.32
our p., and our fathers have not 9.34
and our p. set their seal to it. 9.38
Bilgai, Shemaiah; these are the p. 10.08
the p., the Levites, the gatekeepers, 10.28

PRIESTS (cont.)
the p., the Levites, and the people, Neh 10.34
to the p. who minister in the house 10.36
to the p., to the chambers of the 10.37
and the p. that minister, and the 10.39
the p., the Levites, the temple 11.03
Of the p.: Jedaiah the son of 11.10
and of the p. and the Levites, were 11.20
These are the p. and the Levites 12.01
chiefs of the p. and of their 12.07
And in the days of Joiakim were p., 12.12
also the p. until the reign of 12.22
And the p. and the Levites purified 12.30
and the p. Eliakim, Maaseiah, Miniamin, 12.41
the law for the p. and for the 12.44
over the p. and the Levites who 12.44
and the contributions for the p. 13.05
the duties of the p. and Levites, 13.30
He leads p. away stripped, and Job 12.19
Their p. fell by the sword, and Ps 78.64
Moses and Aaron were among his p., 99.06
Let thy p. be clothed with righteousness, 132.09
Her p. I will clothe with salvation, 132.16
the secretary, and the senior p., Is 37.02
shall be called the p. of the LORD, 61.06
I will take for p. and for Levites, 66.21
of the p. who were in Anathoth in Jer 1.01
its p., and the people of the land. 1.18
The p. did not say, 'Where is the 2.08
their p., and their prophets, 2.26
the p. shall be appalled and the 4.09
and the p. rule at their direction; 5.31
its princes, the bones of the p., 8.01
the p., the prophets, and all the 13.13
people and some of the senior p., 19.01
The p. and the prophets and all the 26.07
then the p. and the prophets and 26.08
Then the p. and the prophets said 26.11
said to the p. and the prophets, 26.16
Then I spoke to the p. and to all 27.16
presence of the p. and all the 28.01
presence of the p. and all the 28.05
and to the p., the prophets, and all 29.01
priest, and to all the p., saying, 29.25
the soul of the p. with abundance, 31.14
their p. and their prophets, the men 32.32
and the Levitical p. shall never 33.18
with the Levitical p. my ministers. 33.21
the Levitical p. who minister to 33.22
the p., and all the people of the 34.19
with his p. and his princes. 48.07
with his p. and his princes. 49.03
gates are desolate, her p. groan; Lam 1.04
my p. and elders perished in the 1.19
and the iniquities of her p., 4.13
no honor was shown to the p., 4.16
Her p. have done violence to my law Eze 22.26
is for the p. who have charge of 40.45
is for the p. who have charge of 40.46
where the p. who approach the LORD 42.13
When the p. enter the holy place, 42.14
the Levitical p. of the family of 43.19
and the p. shall sprinkle salt upon 43.24
day onward the p. shall offer upon 43.27
"But the Levitical p., the sons of 44.15
offerings, shall belong to the p.; 44.30
give to the p. the first of your 44.30
The p. shall not eat of anything, 44.31
it shall be for the p., who minister 45.04
The p. shall offer his burnt offering 46.02
of the holy chambers for the p., 46.19
place where the p. shall boil the 46.20
the p. shall have an allotment 48.10
This shall be for the consecrated p., 48.11
And alongside the territory of the p., 48.13
Hear this, O p.! Give heed, O Hos 5.01
so the p. are banded together; 6.09
its idolatrous p. shall wail over 10.05
The p. mourn, the ministers of the Joe 1.09
O p., wail, O ministers of the altar. 1.13
vestibule and the altar let the p., 2.17
its p. teach for hire, its prophets Mic 3.11
and the name of the idolatrous p.; Zep 1.04
her p. profane what is sacred, they 3.04
hosts; Ask the p. to decide this Hag 2.11
holy?' " The p. answered, "No." 2.12
The p. answered, "It does become 2.13
and to ask the p. of the house of Zec 7.03
the people of the land and the p., 7.05
O p., who despise my name. You Mal 1.06
"And now, O p., this command is for 2.01
all the chief p. and scribes of Mt 2.04
were with him, but only for the p.? 12.04
the sabbath the p. in the temple 12.05
elders and chief p. and scribes, 16.21
to the chief p. and scribes, 20.18
But when the chief p. and the 21.15
the chief p. and the elders of the 21.23
When the chief p. and the Pharisees 21.45
Then the chief p. and the elders of 26.03
Iscariot, went to the chief p. 26.14
from the chief p. and the elders 26.47
Now the chief p. and the whole 26.59
all the chief p. and the elders of 27.01
to the chief p. and the elders, 27.03
But the chief p., taking the pieces 27.06
accused by the chief p. and elders, 27.12
Now the chief p. and the elders 27.20
So also the chief p., with the 27.41
the chief p. and the Pharisees 27.62
told the chief p. all that had 28.11
lawful for any but the p. to eat, Mk 2.26
and the chief p. and the scribes, 8.31
to the chief p. and the scribes, 10.33
And the chief p. and the scribes 11.18
the chief p. and the scribes and 11.27
And the chief p. and the scribes 14.01
to the chief p. in order to betray 14.10
from the chief p. and the scribes 14.43
all the chief p. and the elders 14.53
Now the chief p. and the whole 14.55
as it was morning the chief p., 15.01
And the chief p. accused him of 15.03
that the chief p. had delivered 15.10
But the chief p. stirred up the 15.11
So also the chief p. mocked him to 15.31
lawful for any but the p. to eat, Lk 6.04
elders and chief p. and scribes, 9.22
"Go and show yourselves to the p." 17.14
The chief p. and the scribes and 19.47
the chief p. and the scribes with 20.01
and the chief p. tried to lay 20.19
And the chief p. and the scribes 22.02
with the chief p. and captains how 22.04
to the chief p. and captains of 22.52
together, both chief p. and scribes; 22.66
to the chief p. and the multitudes, 23.04
The chief p. and the scribes stood 23.10
the chief p. and the rulers and 23.13
and how our chief p. and rulers 24.20
the Jews sent p. and Levites from Jn 1.19
and the chief p. and Pharisees sent 7.32
back to the chief p. and Pharisees, 7.45
So the chief p. and the Pharisees 11.47
Now the chief p. and the Pharisees 11.57
So the chief p. planned to put 12.10
from the chief p. and the Pharisees, 18.03
and the chief p. have handed you 18.35
When the chief p. and the officers 19.06
The chief p. answered, "We have no 19.15
The chief p. of the Jews then said 19.21
the p. and the captain of the Ac 4.01
what the chief p. and the elders 4.23
and the chief p. heard these words, 5.24
many of the p. were obedient to 6.07
from the chief p. to bind all who 9.14

PRIESTS (cont.)

them bound before the chief p. Ac 9.21
the chief p. and all the council 22.30
went to the chief p. and elders, 23.14
And the chief p. and the principal 25.02
the chief p. and the elders of the 25.15
by authority from the chief p., 26.10
and commission of the chief p. 26.12
tribe Moses said nothing about p. Heb 7.14
formerly became p. took their 7.21
The former p. were many in number, 7.23
He has no need, like those high p., 7.27
men in their weakness as high p., 7.28
since there are p. who offer gifts 8.04
the p. go continually into the 9.06
p. to his God and Father, to him be Rev 1.06
them a kingdom and p. to our God. 5.10
they shall be p. of God and of 20.06

PRIESTS'

and the thigh of the p. portion, Ex 29.27
for it is the p. portion to be 29.28
shall be the p. due from the Deu 18.03
very place where the p. feet stood, Jos 4.03
soles of the p. feet were lifted 4.18
silver, and one hundred p. garments. Ez 2.69
five hundred and thirty p. garments. Neh 7.70
of silver, and sixty-seven p. garments. 7.72
and certain of the p. sons with 12.35

PRIMEVAL

among p. ruins. with those who go Eze 26.20

PRINCE

you are a mighty p. among us. Gen 23.06
the p. of the land, saw her, he 34.02
"Who made you a p. and a judge over Ex 2.14
also make yourself a p. over us? Num 16.13
the daughter of the p. of Midian, 25.18
of him that is p. among his Deu 33.16
him to be p. over my people Israel. 1Sa 9.16
you to be p. over his people 10.01
you to be p. over his heritage. 10.01
him to be p. over his people, 13.14
has appointed you p. over Israel, 25.30
not know that a p. and a great man 2Sa 3.38
and you shall be p. over Israel.'" 5.02
to appoint me as p. over Israel, 6.21
you should be p. over my people 7.08
to Hezekiah the p. of my people, 2Ki 20.05
Nahshon, p. of the sons of Judah. 1Ch 2.10
his brothers and a p. was from him, 5.02
you shall be p. over my people 11.02
The p. Jehoiada, of the house of 12.27
you should be p. over my people 17.07
anointed him as p. for the LORD, 29.22
chose no man as p. over my people 2Ch 6.05
Maacah as chief p. among his 11.22
out to Sheshbazzar the p. of Judah. Ez 1.08
say, 'Where is the house of the p.? Job 21.28
like a p. I would approach him. 31.37
die like men, and fall like any p." Ps 82.07
but without people a p. is ruined. Pro 14.28
still less is false speech to a p. 17.07
lower in the presence of the p. 25.07
set me in a chariot beide my p. Sol 6.12
Everlasting Father, P. of Peace." Is 9.06
Their p. shall be one of themselves, Jer 30.21
the p. is wrapped in despair, and Eze 7.27
concerns the p. in Jerusalem and 12.10
And the p. who is among them shall 12.12
p. of Israel, whose day has come, the 21.25
say to the p. of Tyre, Thus says the 28.02
no longer be a p. in the land of 30.13
David shall be p. among them; 34.24
servant shall be their p. for ever. 37.25
the chief p. of Meshech and Tubal; 38.02
chief p. of Meshech and Tubal; 38.03
chief p. of Meshech and Tubal; 39.01
Only the p. may sit in it to eat 44.03
"And to the p. shall belong the 45.07
this offering to the p. in Israel. 45.16
On that day the p. shall provide 45.22
The p. shall enter by the vestibule 46.02
that the p. offers to the LORD on 46.04
When the p. enters, he shall go in 46.08
the p. shall go in with them; 46.10
When the p. provides a freewill 46.12
If the p. makes a gift to any of 46.16
then it shall revert to the p.; 46.17
The p. shall not take any of the 46.18
of the city shall belong to the p. 48.21
portions, it shall belong to the p. 48.21
of that which belongs to the p. 48.22
portion of the p. shall lie 48.22
even up to the P. of the host; Dan 8.11
rise up against the P. of princes; 8.25
a p., there shall be seven weeks. 9.25
people of the p. who is to come 9.26
The p. of the kingdom of Persia 10.13
there with the p. of the kingdom 10.13
to fight against the p. of Persia; 10.20
the p. of Greece will come. 10.20
these except Michael, your p. 10.21
and the p. of the covenant also. 11.22
the great p. who has charge of your 12.01
dwell many days without king or p., Hos 3.04
the p. and the judge ask for a Mic 7.03
out demons by the p. of demons." Mt 9.34
the p. of demons, that this man 12.24
and by the p. of demons he casts Mk 3.22
by Beelzebul, the p. of demons"; Lk 11.15
following the p. of the power of Eph 2.02

PRINCE'S

It shall be the p. duty to furnish Eze 45.17

PRINCES

And when the p. of Pharaoh saw her, Gen 12.15
shall be the father of twelve p., 17.20
twelve p. according to their tribes. 25.16
the well which the p. dug, Num 21.18
so the p. of Moab stayed with 22.08
and said to the p. of Balak, 22.13
So the p. of Moab rose and went to 22.14
Once again Balak sent p., 22.15
ass, and went with the p. of Moab. 22.21
went on with the p. of Balak. 22.35
and to the p. who were with him. 22.40
he and all the p. of Moab were 23.06
and the p. of Moab with him. 23.17
the p. of Sihon, who dwelt in the Jos 13.21
give ear, O p.; to the LORD I will Ju 5.03
the p. of Issachar came with 5.15
And they took the two p. of Midian, 7.25
into your hands the p. of Midian, 8.03
them sit with p. and inherit a 1Sa 2.08
Then the p. of the Philistines came 18.30
But the p. of the Ammonites said to 2Sa 10.03
visit the royal p. and the sons of 2Ki 10.13
and his p., and his palace officials. 24.12
and all the p., and all the mighty 24.14
by name were p. in their families, 1Ch 4.38
mighty warriors, chief of the p. 7.40
But the p. of the Ammonites said to 19.03
and the p., and Zadok the priest, 24.06
to Rehoboam and to the p. of Judah, 2Ch 12.05
Then the p. of Israel and the king 12.06
year of his reign he sent his p., 17.07
and also some of the p. of Judah. 21.04
he met the p. of Judah and the sons 22.08
And all the p. and all the people 24.10
of Jehoiada the p. of Judah came 24.17
destroyed all the p. of the people 24.23
before the p. and all the assembly. 28.14
house of the king and of the p., 28.21

PRINCES (cont.)
king and the p. commanded the 2Ch 29.30
king and his p. and all the 30.02
letters from the king and his p., 30.06
king and the p. commanded by the 30.12
and the p. gave the assembly a 30.24
Hezekiah and the p. came and saw 31.08
of the envoys of the p. of Babylon, 32.31
And his p. contributed willingly to 35.08
treasures of the king and of his p., 36.18
our p., our priests, our prophets, Neh 9.32
our kings, our p., our priests, and 9.34
and our p., our Levites, and our 9.38
brought up the p. of Judah upon 12.31
and half of the p. of Judah, 12.32
for all his p. and servants. Est 1.03
the peoples and the p. her beauty; 1.11
the seven p. of Persia and Media, 1.14
in presence of the king and the p., 1.16
also to all the p. and all the 1.16
be telling it to all the king's p., 1.18
advice pleased the king and the p., 1.21
banquet to all his p. and servants; 2.18
above all the p. who were with him. 3.01
and to the p. of all the peoples, 3.12
him above the p. and the servants 5.11
to one of the king's most noble p.; 6.09
governors and the p. of the provinces 8.09
All the p. of the provinces and the 9.03
or with p. who had gold, who filled Job 3.15
He pours contempt on p., 12.21
the p. refrained from talking, and 29.09
who shows no partiality to p., 34.19
will make them p. in all the earth. Ps 45.16
The p. of the peoples gather as the 47.09
the p. of Judah in their throng, the 68.27
the p. of Zebulun, the p. of Naphtali. 68.27
who cuts off the spirit of p., 76.12
all their p. like Zebah and Zalmunna, 83.11
to instruct his p. at his pleasure, 105.22
contempt upon p. and makes them 107.40
sit with p., with the p. of his people. 113.08
LORD than to put confidence in p. 118.09
Even though p. sit plotting against 119.23
P. persecute me without cause, but 119.161
Put not your trust in p., 146.03
p. and all rulers of the earth! 148.11
by me p. rule, and nobles govern the Pro 8.16
less for a slave to rule over p. 19.10
and p. walking on foot like slaves. Ecc 10.07
and your p. feast in the morning! 10.16
and your p. feast at the proper 10.17
Your p. are rebels and companions Is 1.23
And I will make boys their p., 3.04
the elders and p. of his people: 3.14
The p. of Zoan are utterly foolish; 19.11
The p. of Zoan have become fools, 19.13
and the p. of Memphis are deluded; 19.13
Arise, O p., oil the shield! 21.05
of crowns, whose merchants were p., 23.08
and p. will rule in justice. 32.01
and all its p. shall be nothing. 34.12
who brings p. to nought, and makes 40.23
Therefore I profaned the p. of the 43.28
p., and they shall prostrate 49.07
its p., its priests, and the people Jer 1.18
their p., their priests, and their 2.26
shall fail both king and p.; 4.09
of Judah, the bones of its p., 8.01
and on horses, they and their p., 17.25
together with the p. of Judah, 24.01
his p., the remnant of Jerusalem 24.08
its kings and p., to make them a 25.18
his servants, his p., all his people, 25.19
When the p. of Judah heard these 26.10
said to the p. and to all the 26.11
to all the p. and all the people, 26.12
Then the p. and all the people said 26.16
all his warriors and all the p., 26.21
the p. of Judah and Jerusalem, the 29.02
to anger—their kings and their p., 32.32
all the p. and all the people who 34.10
the p. of Judah, the p. of Jerusalem, 34.19
and his p. I will give into the 34.21
was near the chamber of the p., 35.04
and all the p. were sitting there: 36.12
son of Hananiah, and all the p. 36.12
Then all the p. sent Jehudi the son 36.14
Then the p. said to Baruch, "Go and 36.19
and all the p. who stood beside 36.21
Jeremiah and brought him to the p. 37.14
And the p. were enraged at Jeremiah, 37.15
Then the p. said to the king, "Let 38.04
surrender to the p. of the king of 38.17
surrender to the p. of the king of 38.18
led out to the p. of the king of 38.22
If the p. hear that I have spoken 38.25
Then all the p. came to Jeremiah 38.27
all the p. of the king of Babylon 39.03
our fathers, our kings and our p., 44.17
fathers, your kings and your p., 44.21
exile, with his priests and his p. 48.07
exile, with his priests and his p. 49.03
their king and p., says the LORD. 49.38
and upon her p. and her wise men! 50.35
make drunk her p. and her wise men, 51.57
slew all the p. of Judah at Riblah. 52.10
Her p. have become like harts that Lam 1.06
her king and p. are among the 2.09
Her p. were purer than snow, whiter 4.07
P. are hung up by their hands; 5.12
son of Benaiah, p. of the people. Eze 11.01
king and her p. and brought them 17.12
lamentation for the p. of Israel, 19.01
it is against all the p. of Israel; 21.12
"Behold, the p. of Israel in you, 22.06
Her p. in the midst of her are like 22.25
Her p. in the midst of her are like 22.27
Then all the p. of the sea will 26.16
Arabia and all the p. of Kedar were 27.21
is there, her kings and all her p., 32.29
"The p. of the north are there, all 32.30
the blood of the p. of the earth— 39.18
And my p. shall no more oppress my 45.08
Lord GOD: Enough, O p. of Israel! 45.09
rise up against the prince of p.; Dan 8.25
our p., and our fathers, and to all 9.06
to our p., and to our fathers, 9.08
but Michael, one of the chief p., 10.13
but one of his p. shall be stronger 11.05
The p. of Judah have become like Hos 5.10
and the p. by their treachery. 7.03
of our king the p. became sick 7.05
their p. shall fall by the sword 7.16
They set up p., but without my 8.04
while from anointing king and p. 8.10
them no more; all their p. are rebels. 9.15
where are all your p., to defend 13.10
you said, "Give me a king and p."? 13.10
he and his p. together," says the Amo 1.15
and will slay all its p. with him, 2.03
shepherds and eight p. of men; Mic 5.05
Your p. are like grasshoppers, your Nah 3.17

PRINCESS
The p. is decked in her chamber Ps 45.13
She that was a p. among the cities Lam 1.01

PRINCESSES
p., and three hundred concubines; 1Ki 11.03
children, the p., and every person whom Jer 43.06

PRINCIPAL
scribes and the p. men of the people Lk 19.47
priests and the p. men of the Jews Ac 25.02

PRINCIPALITIES
nor p., nor things present, nor Rom 8.38
known to the p. and powers in the Eph 3.10
and blood, but against the p., 6.12
or dominions or p. or authorities— Col 1.16
He disarmed the p. and powers and 2.15

PRINCIPLE
On what p.? On the p. of works? Rom 3.27
No, but on the p. of faith. 3.27

PRINCIPLES
again the first p. of God's word. Heb 5.12

PRINT
in his hands the p. of the nails, Jn 20.25

PRISCA
Greet P. and Aquila, my fellow Rom 16.03
Aquila and P., together with the 1Co 16.19
Greet P. and Aquila, and the household 2Ti 4.19

PRISCILLA
come from Italy with his wife P., Ac 18.02
Syria, and with him P. and Aquila. 18.18
but when P. and Aquila heard him, 18.26

PRISON
took him and put him into the p., Gen 39.20
confined, and he was there in p. 39.20
the sight of the keeper of the p. 39.21
keeper of the p. committed to 39.22
the prisoners who were in the p.; 39.22
the keeper of the p. paid no heed 39.23
in the p. where Joseph was confined. 40.03
Egypt, who were confined in the p.— 40.05
brother, while you remain in p., 42.16
all together in p. for three days. 42.17
brothers remain confined in your p., 42.19
he ground at the mill in the p. Ju 16.21
they called Samson out of the p., 16.25
the king, "Put this fellow in p., 1Ki 22.27
shut him up, and bound him in p. 2Ki 17.04
Jehoiachin king of Judah from p.; 25.27
Jehoiachin put off his p. garments. 25.29
in p., for he was in a rage with 2Ch 16.10
the king, Put this fellow in p., 18.26
Bring me out of p., that I may Ps 142.07
had gone from p. to the throne or Ecc 4.14
they will be shut up in a p., Is 24.22
from the p. those who sit in 42.07
opening of the p. to those who are 61.01
for he had not yet been put in p. Jer 37.04
secretary, for it had been made a p. 37.15
people, that you have put me in p.? 37.18
and put him in p. till the day of 52.11
of Judah and brought him out of p.; 52.31
Jehoiachin put off his p. garments. 52.33
to the guard, and you be put in p.; Mt 5.25
John heard in p. about the deeds 11.02
and bound him and put him in p., 14.03
and had John beheaded in the p., 14.10
and put him in p. till he should 18.30
I was in p. and you came to me.' 25.36
thee sick or in p. and visit thee?' 25.39
sick and in p. and you did not 25.43
stranger or naked or sick or in p., 25.44
bound him in p. for the sake of Mk 6.17
went and beheaded him in the p., 6.27
And among the rebels in p., 15.07
all, that he shut up John in p. Lk 3.20
and the officer put you in p. 12.58
to go with you to p. and to death." 22.33
thrown into p. for an insurrection 23.19
thrown into p. for insurrection 23.25
For John had not yet been put in p. Jn 3.24
and put them in the common p. Ac 5.18
Lord opened the p. doors and 5.19
and sent to the p. to have them 5.21
they did not find them in the p., 5.22
"We found the p. securely locked 5.23
whom you put in p. are standing in 5.25
and women and committed them to p. 8.03
he put him in p., and delivered him 12.04
So Peter was kept in p.; but earnest 12.05
the door were guarding the p.; 12.06
Lord had brought him out of the p. 12.17
upon them, they threw them into p., 16.23
into the inner p. and fastened 16.24
foundations of the p. were shaken; 16.26
saw that the p. doors were open, he 16.27
citizens, and have thrown us into p.; 16.37
So they went out of the p., and 16.40
delivering to p. both men and 22.04
a favor, Felix left Paul in p. 24.27
shut up many of the saints in p., 26.10
on account of which I am in p., Col 4.03
Remember those who are in p., Heb 13.03
prison, as though in p. with them; 13.03
and preached to the spirits in p., 1Pe 3.19
about to throw some of you into p., Rev 2.10
Satan will be loosed from his p. 20.07

PRISONER
took him p. in the eighth year of 2Ki 24.12
crowd any one p. whom they wanted. Mt 27.15
And they had then a notorious p, 27.16
them any one p. whom they asked. Mk 15.06
"Paul the p. called me and asked me Ac 23.18
"There is a man left p by Felix; 25.14
in sending a p., not to indicate 25.27
I was delivered p. from Jerusalem 28.17
a p. for Christ Jesus on behalf of Eph 3.01
I therefore. a p. for the Lord, beg 4.01
Aristarchus my fellow p. greets you, Col 4.10
nor of me his p., but take your 2Ti 1.08
Paul, a p. for Christ Jesus, and Phm 1.01
and now a p. also for Christ Jesus— 1.09
my fellow p. in Christ Jesus, sends 1.23

PRISONERS
where the king's p. were confined, Gen 39.20
care all the p. who were in the 39.22
There the p. are at ease together; Job 3.18
he leads out the p. to prosperity; Ps 68.06
groans of the p. come before thee; 79.11
to hear the groans of the p., 102.20
p. in affliction and in irons, 107.10
The LORD sets the p. free; 146.07
among the p. or fall among the Is 10.04
who did not let his p. go home?' 14.17
gathered together as p. in a pit; 24.22
bring out the p. from the dungeon, 42.07
saying to the p., 'Come forth,' to 49.09
foot all the p. of the earth, Lam 3.34
Return to your stronghold, O p. of hope; Zec 9.12
and the p. were listening to them, Ac 16.25
supposing that the p. had escaped. 16.27
and some other p. to a centurion 27.01
The soldier's plan was to kill the p, 27.42
my kinsmen and my fellow p.; Rom 16.07
For you had compassion on the p., Heb 10.34

PRISONS
trapped in holes and hidden in p.; Is 42.22
you up to the synagogues and p., Lk 21.12

PRIVATE
and seizes him by the p. parts, Deu 25.11
"Speak to David in p. and say, 1Sa 18.22
whispered in p. rooms shall be Lk 12.03
went up, not publicly but in p. Jn 7.10

PRIVATELY
of the gate to speak with him p.. 2Sa 3.27
disciples came to Jesus p. and said, Mt 17.19
the disciples came to him p., 24.03

PRIVATELY (cont.)
but p. to his own disciples he Mk 4.34
him aside from the multitude p., 7.33
house, his disciples asked him p., 9.28
and John and Andrew aked him p., 13.03
to the disciples he said p., Lk 10.23
hand, and going aside asked him p., Ac 23.19
before them (but p. before those Gal 2.02

PRIZE
P. her highly, and she will exalt Pro 4.08
shall have his life as a p. of war. Jer 21.09
shall have his life as a p. of war, 38.02
have your life as a p. of war, 39.18
your life as a p. of war in all 45.05
but only one receives the p.? 1Co 9.24
goal for the p. of the upward call Php 3.14

PRIZED
all its p. belongings, and all the Jer 20.05

PROBLEMS
and solve p. were found in this Dan 5.12
give interpretations and solve p. 5.16

PROCEDURE
according to the p. established for 1Ch 24.19
was the king's p. toward all who Est 1.13

PROCEED
Let Pharaoh p. to appoint overseers Gen 41.34
twice, but I will p. no further." Job 40.05
for they p. from evil to evil, and Jer 9.03
and dignity p. from themselves. Hab 1.07
does not p. from faith is sin. Rom 14.23

PROCEEDED
words which p. out of his mouth; Lk 4.22
he p. to tell a parable, because he 19.11
for I p. and came forth from God; Jn 8.42
he p. to arrest Peter also. Ac 12.03

PROCEEDING
it were an error p. from the ruler: Ecc 10.05

PROCEEDS
to all that p. out of his mouth. Num 30.02
then whatever p. out of her lips 30.12
everything that p. out of the Deu 8.03
for from me p. the spirit, and I Is 57.16
every word that p. from the mouth Mt 4.04
out of the mouth p. from the heart, 15.18
who p. from the Father, he will bear Jn 15.26
and brought the p. of what was Ac 4.34
he kept back some of the p., 5.02
back part of the p. of the land? 5.03

PROCESSION
which gave thanks and went in p. Neh 12.31
and led them in p. to the house of Ps 42.04
Bind the festal p. with branches, 118.27
nations, with their kings led in p. Is 60.11

PROCESSIONS
Thy solemn p. are seen, O God, the Ps 68.24
the p. of my God, my King, into the 68.24

PROCHORUS
and P, and Nicanor, and Timon, and Ac 6.05

PROCLAIM
and will p. before you my name 'The Ex 33.19
which you shall p. as holy convocations, Lev 23.02
which you shall p. at the time 23.04
which you shall p. as times of 23.37
and p. liberty throughout the land 25.10
For I will p. the name of the LORD. Deu 32.03
Now therefore p. in the ears of the Ju 7.03
"P. a fast, and set Naboth on high 1Ki 21.09
up prophets to p. concerning you Neh 6.07
publish and p. in all their towns 8.15
and p. his deliverance to a people Ps 22.31
Were I to p. and tell of them, they 40.05
I will p. thy name, for it is good, 52.09
and I still p. thy wondrous deeds. 71.17
till I p. thy might to all the 71.18
my mouth I will p. thy faithfulness 89.01
The heavens p. his righteousness; 97.06
Men shall p. the might of thy 145.06
knowledge, but fools p. their folly. Pro 12.23
they p. their sin like Sodom, they Is 3.09
p. that his name is exalted. 12.04
Let him p. it, let him declare and 44.07
p. it, send it forth to the end of 48.20
and shall p. the praise of the LORD. 60.06
to p. liberty to the captives, and 61.01
to p. the year of the LORD's favor, 61.02
"Go and p. in the hearing of Jer 2.02
Go, and p. these words toward the 3.12
and p. in Jerusalem, and say, "Blow 4.05
house of Jacob, p. it in Judah: 5.20
and p. there this word, and say, Hear 7.02
"P. all these words in the cities 11.06
and p. there the words that I tell 19.02
p., give praise, and say, 'The LORD 31.07
behold, I p. to you liberty to the 34.17
"Declare in Egypt, and p. in Migdol; 46.14
p. in Memphis and Tahpanhes; 46.14
and p., set up a banner and p., 50.02
P. this among the nations: Prepare Joe 3.09
P. to the strongholds in Assyria, Amo 3.09
and p. freewill offerings, publish 4.05
and p. to it the message that I Jon 3.02
whispered, p. upon the housetops. Mt 10.27
and he shall p. justice to the 12.18
and began to p. in the Decapolis Mk 5.20
has sent me to p. release to the Lk 4.18
to p. the acceptable year of the 4.19
go and p. the kingdom of God." 9.60
who p. to you the way of salvation." Ac 16.17
whom I p. to you, is the Christ." 17.03
as unknown, this I p. to you. 17.23
he would p. light both to the 26.23
that those who p. the gospel 1Co 9.14
you p. the Lord's death until he 11.26
mouth boldly to p. the mystery of Eph 6.19
the former p. Christ out of partisanship, Php 1.17
Him we p., warning every man and Col 1.28
me strength to p. the word fully, 2Ti 4.17
"I will p. thy name to my brethren, Heb 2.12
and p. to you the eternal life 1Jn 1.02
seen and heard we p. also to you, 1.03
have heard from him and p. to you, 1.05
gospel to p. to those who dwell on Rev 14.06

PROCLAIMED
there, and p. the name of the LORD. Ex 34.05
and p., "The LORD, the LORD, a God 34.06
and word was p. throughout the camp, 36.06
a memorial p. with blast of trumpets, Lev 23.24
the LORD's release has been p. Deu 15.02
of Rimmon, and p. peace to them. Ju 21.13
they p. a fast, and set Naboth on 1Ki 21.12
the trumpet, and p., "Jehu is king." 2Ki 9.13
assembly for Baal." So they p. it. 10.20
and they p. him king, and anointed 11.12
the LORD which the man of God p., 23.16
and p. a fast throughout all Judah. 2Ch 20.03
and they p. him king, and Jehoiada 23.11
Then I p. a fast there, at the river Ez 8.21
by the king is p. throughout all Est 1.20
king's order and his edict were p., 2.08
none who p., none who heard your Is 41.26
I declared and saved and p., 43.12
the LORD has p. to the end of the 62.11
they would have p. my words to my Jer 23.22
to Jerusalem p. a fast before the 36.09

PROCLAIMED (cont.)
And the herald p. aloud, "You are Dan 3.04
they p. a fast, and put on sackcloth, Jon 3.05
which the LORD p. by the former Zec 7.07
the more zealously they p. it. Mk 7.36
rooms shall be p. upon the housetops. Lk 12.03
So Jesus p., as he taught in the Jn 7.28
great day, Jesus stood up and p., 7.37
afterwards, also p. these days. Ac 3.24
Samaria, and p. to them the Christ. 8.05
synagogues immediately he p. Jesus, 9.20
the word which was p. throughout 10.37
they p. the word of God in the 13.05
forgiveness of sins is p. to you, 13.38
city where we p. the word of the 15.36
word of God was p. by Paul at 17.13
your faith is p. in all the world. Rom 1.08
my name may be p. in all the earth." 9.17
pretense or in truth, Christ is p.; Php 1.18

PROCLAIMING
p. before him: 'Thus shall it be Est 6.09
p., "Thus shall it be done to the 6.11
was right in my eyes by p. liberty, Jer 34.15
have not obeyed me by p. liberty, 34.17
p. throughout the whole city how Lk 8.39
the people and p. in Jesus the Ac 4.02
I did not come p. to you the 1Co 2.01
temple of God, p. himself to be God. 2Th 2.04
a strong angel p. with a loud Rev 5.02

PROCLAIMS
and the firmament p. his handiwork. Ps 19.01
Many a man p. his own loyalty, but a Pro 20.06
from Dan and p. evil from Mount Jer 4.15
brings good tidings, who p. peace! Nah 1.15

PROCLAMATION
before it; and Aaron made p. and said, Ex 32.05
And you shall make p. on the same Lev 23.21
Then King Asa made a p. to all Judah, 1Ki 15.22
And p. was made throughout Judah 2Ch 24.09
to make a p. throughout all Israel, 30.05
that he made a p. throughout all 36.22
that he made a p. throughout all Ez 1.01
And a p. was made throughout Judah 10.07
province by p. to all the peoples Est 3.14
and by p. to all peoples, and the 8.13
to make a p. of liberty to them, Jer 34.08
and p. was made concerning him, that Dan 5.29
And he made p. and published through Jon 3.07
sacred and imperishable p. of eternal *Mk 16.08

PROCONSUL
He was with the p., Sergius Paulus, Ac 13.07
to turn away the p. from the faith. 13.08
Then the p. believed, when he saw 13.12
But when Gallio was p. of Achaia, 18.12

PROCONSULS
courts are open, and there are p.; Ac 19.38

PROCURED
provisions, and p. wives for them. 2Ch 11.23

PROCURING
So Judas, p. a band of soldiers and Jn 18.03

PRODUCE
part of the p. of the land of Gen 41.34
gathered in the p. of the land, Lev 23.39
year, you will be eating old p.; 25.22
when its p. comes in, you shall eat 25.22
the Levites as p. of the threshing Num 18.30
and as p. of the wine press; 18.30
tithe of your p. in the same year. Deu 14.28
you in all your p. and in all the 16.15
tithe of your p. in the third year, 26.12
and he ate the p. of the field; 32.13
with the finest p. of the ancient 33.15
they ate of the p. of the land, Jos 5.11
they ate of the p. of the land; 5.12
and destroy the p. of the land, Ju 6.04
for him, and shall bring in the p., 2Sa 9.10
with all the p. of the fields from 2Ki 8.06
and over the p. of the vineyards 1Ch 27.27
and of all the p. of the field; 2Ch 31.05
the first fruits of all your p.; Pro 3.09
the p. of the ground, which will be Is 30.23
plant gardens and eat their p. Jer 29.05
and plant gardens and eat their p. 29.28
Its p. shall be food for the Eze 48.18
the p. of the olive fail and the Hab 3.17
and the earth has withheld its p. Hag 1.10
through us will p. thanksgiving to 2Co 9.11
which p. envy, dissension, slander, 1Ti 6.04

PRODUCED
nothing that is p. by the grapevine, Num 6.04
and p. blossoms, and it bore ripe 17.08
this godly grief has p. in you, 2Co 7.11

PRODUCES
For pressing milk p. curds, Pro 30.33
curds, pressing the nose p. blood, 30.33
and pressing anger p. strife. 30.33
and p. a weapon for its purpose. Is 54.16
The earth p. of itself, first the Mk 4.28
good treasure of his heart p. good, Lk 6.45
out of his evil treasure p. evil; 6.45
that suffering p. endurance, Rom 5.03
and endurance p. character, and 5.04
character, and character p. hope, 5.04
For godly grief p. a repentance 2Co 7.10
regret, but worldly grief p. death. 7.10
of your faith p. steadfastness. Jas 1.03

PRODUCING
to a nation p. the fruits of it. Mt 21.43

PRODUCTS
you and all the p. of your toil Hag 2.17

PROFANE
wield your tool upon it you p. it. Ex 20.25
and so p. the name of your God: I am Lev 18.21
and so p the name of your God: I am 19.12
"Do not p. your daughter by making 19.29
among his people and so p. himself. 21.04
and not p. the name of their God; 21.06
nor p. the sanctuary of his God; 21.12
that he may not p. his children 21.15
that he may not p. my sanctuaries; 21.23
that they may not p. my holy name; 22.02
it and die thereby when they p. it: 22.09
shall not p. the holy things of 22.15
And you shall not p. my holy name, 22.32
you shall not p. the holy things Num 18.32
steal, and p. the name of my God. Pro 30.09
and does not p. it, and holds fast Is 56.06
for a spoil; and they shall p. it. Eze 7.21
that they may p. my precious place; 7.22
robbers shall enter and p. it, 7.22
shall no more p. with your gifts 20.39
came into my sanctuary to p. it. 23.39
I will p. my sanctuary, the pride of 24.21
I cast you as a p. thing from the 28.16
appear and p. the temple and Dan 11.31
her priests p. what is sacred, they Zep 3.04
But you p. it when you say that the Mal 1.12
in the temple p. the sabbath, Mt 12.05
He even tried to p. the temple, Ac 24.06
and sinners, for the unholy and p., 1Ti 1.09

PROFANED
because he has p. a holy thing of Lev 19.08
Therefore I p. the princes of the Is 43.28
with my people. I p. my heritage; 47.06

PROFANED (cont.)

it, for how should my name be p.? Is 48.11
and have p. this place by burning Jer 19.04
around and p. my name when each of 34.16
and their holy places shall be p. Eze 7.24
You have p. me among my people for 13.19
should not be p. in the sight of 20.09
and my sabbaths they greatly p. 20.13
should not be p. in the sight of 20.14
in my statutes, and p. my sabbaths; 20.16
man shall live; they p. my sabbaths. 20.21
should not be p. in the sight of 20.22
my statutes and p. my sabbaths, 20.24
my holy things, and p. my sabbaths. 22.08
And I shall be p. through you in 22.16
my law and have p. my holy things; 22.26
sabbaths, so that I am p. among them. 22.26
on the same day and p. my sabbaths. 23.38
over my sanctuary when it was p., 25.03
your trade you p. your sanctuaries; 28.18
they p. my holy name, in that men 36.20
caused to be p. among the nations 36.21
which you have p. among the 36.22
which has been p. among the 36.23
and which you have p. among them; 36.23
let my holy name be p. any more; 39.07
maiden, so that my holy name is p.; Amo 2.07
"Let her be p., and let our eyes Mic 4.11
for Judah has p. the sanctuary of Mal 2.11
and p. the blood of the covenant by Heb 10.29

PROFANES

every one who p. it shall be put to Ex 31.14
of any priest, if she p. herself by Lev 21.09
playing the harlot, p. her father; 21.09

PROFANING

my sanctuary and p. my holy name. Lev 20.03
you are doing, p. the sabbath day?" Neh 13.17
upon Israel by p. the sabbath." 13.18
not p. it, and keeps his hand from Is 56.02
p. it, when you offer to me my food, Eze 44.07
p. the covenant of our fathers? Mal 2.10
be guilty of p. the body and blood 1Co 11.27

PROFESS

as befits women who p. religion. 1Ti 2.10
They p. to know God, but they deny Tit 1.16

PROFESSING

for by p. it some have missed the 1Ti 6.21

PROFIT

"What p. is it if we slay our Gen 37.26
nor give him your food for p. Lev 25.37
things which cannot p. or save, 1Sa 12.21
for the king's p. to tolerate them. Est 3.08
from the p. of his trading he will Job 20.18
And what p. do we get if we pray to 21.15
"What p. is there in my death, if I Ps 30.09
silver and its p. better than gold. Pro 3.14
Treasures gained by wickedness do not p., 10.02
Riches do not p. in the day of wrath, 11.04
In all toil there is p., but mere talk 14.23
a people that cannot p. them, Is 30.05
that brings neither help nor p., 30.05
to a people that cannot p. them. 30.06
things they delight in do not p.; 44.09
your God, who teaches you to p., 48.17
went after things that do not p. Jer 2.08
glory for that which does not p. 2.11
themselves out but p. nothing. 12.13
things in which there is no p. 16.19
so they do not p. this people at 23.32
keep other souls alive for your p.? Eze 13.18
What p. is an idol when its maker Hab 2.18
For what will it p. a man, if he Mt 16.26
For what does it p. a man, to gain Mk 8.36
For what does it p. a man if he Lk 9.25
What does it p.. my brethren, if a Jas 2.14
for the body, what does it p.? 2.16

PROFITABLE

"Can a man be p. to God? Surely he Job 22.02
he who is wise is p. to himself. 22.02
perceives that her merchandise is p. Pro 31.18
an image, that is p. for nothing? Is 44.10
to you anything that was p.. Ac 20.20
inspired by God and p. for teaching, 2Ti 3.16
these are excellent and p. to men. Tit 3.08

PROFITS

'It p. a man nothing that he should Job 34.09

PROFLIGACY

now join them in the same wild p., 1Pe 4.04

PROFLIGATE

charge of being p. or insubordinate. 1Tit 1.06

PROFLIGATES

slanderers, p., fierce, haters of good, 2Ti 3.03

PROFUSE

friend; p. are the kisses of an enemy. Pro 27.06

PROGRESS

for your p. and joy in the faith, Php 1.25
them, so that all may see your p. 1Ti 4.15

PROJECTED

a crown which p. upward one cubit; 1Ki 7.31

PROJECTING

and the tower p. from the upper Neh 3.25
Gate on the east and the p. tower. 3.26
the great p. tower as far as the 3.27
from the altar hearth p. upward, Eze 43.15

PROJECTION

the rounded p. which was beside 1Ki 7.20

PROLONG

that you may p. your days in the Deu 4.40
P. the life of the king; may his Ps 61.06
Wilt thou p. thy anger to all 85.05
hates unjust gain will p. his days. Pro 28.16
neither will he p. his days like a Ecc 8.13
offspring, he shall p. his days; Is 53.10

PROLONGED

that your days may be p., and that Deu 5.16
life; and that your days may be p. 6.02
days may be p. in the land which 25.15
hand and its days will not be p. Is 13.22
lives were p. for a season and a Dan 7.12
and he p. his speech until midnight Ac 20.07

PROLONGS

Yet God p. the life of the mighty Job 24.22
The fear of the LORD p. life, Pro 10.27
wicked man who p. his life in his Ecc 7.15
a hundred times and p. his life, 8.12

PROMINENT

tribunes and the p. men of the city. Ac 25.23

PROMISE

and p. to deal loyally and truly Gen 47.29
and I p. that I will bring you up Ex 3.17
Because of thy p., and according to 2Sa 7.21
the p. of the LORD proves true; 22.31
has fulfilled his p. which he made; 1Ki 8.20
word has failed of all his good p., 8.56
(This was the p. of the LORD which 2Ki 15.12
Abraham, his sworn p. to Isaac, 1Ch 16.16
according to the p. of God to exalt 25.05
let thy p. to David my father be 2Ch 1.09

PROMISE (cont.)

has fulfilled his p. which he made; 2Ch 6.10
labor who does not perform this p. Neh 5.13
and thou hast fulfilled thy p., 9.08
the p. of the LORD proves true; Ps 18.30
Abraham, his sworn p. to Isaac, 105.09
For he remembered his holy p., 105.42
land, having no faith in his p. 106.24
Confirm to thy servant thy p., 119.38
thy salvation according to thy p.; 119.41
affliction that thy p. gives me life. 119.50
my portion; I p. to keep thy words. 119.57
gracious to me according to thy p. 119.58
according to thy p. to thy servant. 119.76
eyes fail with watching for thy p.; 119.82
Uphold me according to thy p., 119.116
the fulfilment of thy righteous p. 119.123
my steps according to thy p., 119.133
Thy p. is well tried, and thy 119.140
that I may meditate upon thy p. 119.148
give me life according to thy p.! 119.154
to you my p. and bring you back to Jer 29.10
them all the good that I p. them. 32.42
will fulfil the p. I made to the 33.14
according to the p. that I made you Hag 2.05
I send the p. of my Father upon you Lk 24.49
to wait for the p. of the Father, Ac 1.04
the Father the p. of the Holy 2.33
For the p. is to you and to your 2.39
"But as the time of the p. drew near, 7.17
ready, waiting for the p. from you." 23.21
for hope in the p. made by God to 26.06
The p. to Abraham and his descendants, Rom 4.13
faith is null and the p. is void. 4.14
order that the p. may rest on 4.16
him waver concerning the p. of God, 4.20
children of the p. are reckoned as 9.08
For this is what the p. said, 9.09
receive the p. of the Spirit Gal 3.14
by God, so as to make the p. void. 3.17
by the law, it is no longer by p.; 3.18
but God gave it to Abraham by a p. 3.18
come to whom the p. had been made; 3.19
offspring, heirs according to p. 3.29
son of the free woman through p. 4.23
like Isaac, are children of p. 4.28
strangers to the covenants of p., Eph 2.12
partakers of the p. in Christ Jesus 3.06
the first commandment with a p.), 6.02
as it holds p. for the present life 1Ti 4.08
according to the p. of the life 2Ti 1.01
while the p. of entering his rest Heb 4.01
For when God made a p. to Abraham, 6.13
patiently endured, obtained the p. 6.15
heirs of the p. the unchangeable 6.17
he sojourned in the land of p., 11.09
heirs with him of the same p. 11.09
They p. them freedom, but they 2Pe 2.19
"Where is the p. of his coming? For 3.04
not slow about his p. as some count 3.09
according to his p. we wait for new 3.13

PROMISED

to Abraham what he has p. him." Gen 18.19
the LORD did to Sarah as he had p. 21.01
as he has p., you shall keep this Ex 12.25
that I have p. I will give to your 32.13
for the LORD has p. good to Israel." Num 10.29
be great as thou hast p., saying, 14.17
to the place which the LORD has p.; 14.40
your sheep; and do what you have p." 32.24
and bless you, as he has p. you! Deu 1.11
has p. you, in a land flowing with 6.03
before you, as the LORD has p. 6.19
quickly, as the LORD has p. you. 9.03
into the land which he p. them, 9.28
that you shall tread, as he p. you. 11.25
as he has p. you, and you say, 'I 12.20
as he p. you, and you shall lend to 15.06
their inheritance, as he p. them. 18.02
land which he p. to give to your 19.08
what you have p. with your mouth. 23.23
as he has p. you, and that you are 26.18
God of your fathers, has p. you. 27.03
journey which I p. that you should 28.68
as he p. you, and as he swore to 29.13
given to you, as I p. to Moses. Jos 1.03
to your brethren, as he p. them; 22.04
land, as the LORD your God p. you. 23.05
who fights for you, as he p. you. 23.10
LORD your God p. concerning you; 23.14
LORD your God p. concerning you 23.15
'I p. that your house and the house 1Sa 2.30
for the LORD has p. David, 2Sa 3.18
and thou hast p. this good thing to 7.28
as he p., Adonijah shall be put to 1Ki 2.24
gave Solomon wisdom, as he p. him; 5.12
fulfilled what he p. with his mouth 8.15
as the LORD p., and I have built 8.20
my father what thou hast p. him, 8.25
according to all that he p.; 8.56
as I p. David your father, saying, 9.05
since he p. to give a lamp to him 2Ki 8.19
will do the thing that he has p.: 20.09
and thou hast p. this good thing to 1Ch 17.26
the LORD had p. to make Israel a 27.23
fulfilled what he p. with his mouth 2Ch 6.04
as the LORD p., and I have built 6.10
my father what thou hast p. him, 6.16
where thou hast p. to set thy name, 6.20
since he had p. to give a lamp to 21.07
oath of them to do as they had p. Neh 5.12
and the people did as they had p. 5.13
that Haman had p. to pay into the Est 4.07
and my mouth p. when I was in Ps 66.14
God has p. in his sanctuary: "With 108.07
will do this thing that he has p.: Is 38.07
so that he p. with an oath to give Mt 14.07
and p. to give him money. And he Mk 14.11
perform the mercy p. to our fathers, Lk 1.72
but p. to give it to him in possession Ac 7.05
Israel a Savior, Jesus, as he p. 13.23
that what God p. to the fathers, 13.32
which he p. beforehand through his Rom 1.02
God was able to do what he had p. 4.21
commandment which p. life proved to 7.10
advance for this gift you have p., 2Co 9.05
that what was p. to faith in Jesus Gal 3.22
sealed with the p. Holy Spirit, Eph 1.13
God, who never lies, p. ages ago Tit 1.02
may receive the p. eternal inheritance, Heb 9.15
wavering, for he who p. is faithful; 10.23
will of God and receive what is p. 10.36
considered him faithful who had p. 11.11
not having received what was p., 11.13
did not receive what was p., 11.39
but now he has p., "Yet once more 12.26
which God has p. to those who love Jas 1.12
which he has p. to those who love 2.05
And this is what he has p. us, 1Jn 2.25

PROMISES

of all the good p. which the LORD Jos 21.45
p. of the LORD are p. that are pure, Ps 12.06
Are his p. at an end for all time? 77.80
the law, the worship, and the p.; Rom 9.04
to confirm the p. given to the 15.08
For all the p. of God find their 2Co 1.20
Since we have these p., beloved, 7.01
Now the p. were made to Abraham and Gal 3.16
the law then against the p. of God? 3.21
faith and patience inherit the p. Heb 6.12
and blessed him who had the p. 7.06
since it is enacted on better p. 8.06
received the p. was ready to offer 11.17

PROMISES (cont.)
received p., stopped the mouths of Heb 11.33
us his precious and very great p., 2Pe 1.04

PROMISING
deceive you by p. that Jerusalem 2Ki 19.10
deceive you by p. that Jerusalem Is 37.10

PROMOTE
us my path, that they p. my calamity; Job 30.13
but to p. good order and to secure 1Co 7.35
genealogies which p. speculations 1Ti 1.04
your faith may p. the knowledge of Phm 1.06

PROMOTED
King Ahasuerus p. Haman the son of Est 3.01
Then the king p. Shadrach, Meshach, Dan 3.30

PROMOTING
of wisdom in p. rigor of devotion Col 2.23

PROMOTIONS
all the p. with which the king had Est 5.11

PROMPTED
P. by her mother, she said, "Give me Mh 14.08
Some of the crowd p. Alexander, Ac 19.33

PROMPTS
a man's heart p. him to bring into 2Ki 12.04

PRONOUNCE
"By you Israel will p. blessing, Gen 48.20
him he shall p. him unclean. Lev 13.03
then the priest shall p. him clean; 13.06
the priest shall p. him unclean; 13.08
the priest shall p. him unclean; 13.11
he shall p. him clean of the 13.13
the raw flesh, and p. him unclean; 13.15
priest shall p. the diseased person clean; 13.17
the priest shall p. him unclean; 13.20
the priest shall p. him unclean; 13.22
and the priest shall p. him clean. 13.23
the priest shall p. him unclean; 13.25
the priest shall p. him unclean; 13.27
and the priest shall p. him clean; 13.28
the priest shall p. him unclean; 13.30
then the priest shall p. him clean; 13.34
and the priest shall p. him clean. 13.37
the priest must p. him unclean; 13.44
then he shall p. him clean, and 14.07
priest shall p. the house clean, 14.48
the decision which they p. to you, Deu 17.11
for he could not p. it right; Ju 12.06
Throne where he was to p. judgment, 1Ki 7.07
to him and p. blessings in his 1Ch 23.13
judgment you p. you will be judged, Mt 7.02
undertook to p. the name of the Ac 19.13
Therefore do not p. judgment before 1Co 4.05
do not p. a reviling judgment upon 2Pe 2.11
not presume to p. a reviling Jud 1.09

PRONOUNCED
but he had p. the prophecy against Neh 6.12
has p. evil against you, because of Jer 11.17
has the LORD p. all this great 16.10
the evil that I have p. against it, 19.15
evil which he has p. against you. 26.13
evil which he had p. against them? 26.19
evil that I have p. against them; 35.17
the LORD has p. against this 36.07
evil that I have p. against them, 36.31
LORD your God p. this evil against 40.02
Is this blessing p. only upon the Rom 4.09
present, I have already p. judgment 1Co 5.03

PRONOUNCES
So also David p. a blessing upon Rom 4.06

PROOF
why do you put the LORD to the p.?" Ex 17.02
put the LORD to the p. by saying, 17.07
put me to the p. these ten times Num 14.22
tested me, and put me to the p., Ps 95.09
commanded, for a p. of the people." Mt 8.04
commanded, for a p. of the people." Mk 1.44
commanded, for a p. to the people." Lk 5.14
So give p., before the churches, of 2Co 8.24
since you desire p. that Christ is 13.03

PROOFS
bring your p., says the King of Is 41.21
alive after his passion by many p., Ac 1.03

PROPER
offerings, each on its p. day; Lev 23.37
of God to its p. condition and 2Ch 24.13
your princes feast at the p. time, Ecc 10.17
in rows and barley in its p. place, Is 28.25
them their food at the p. time? Mt 24.45
portion of food at the p. time? Lk 12.42
is it p. for a woman to pray to God 1Co 11.13
to which was borne at the p. time. 1Ti 2.06
manifest at the p. time by the 6.15
and at the p. time manifested in Tit 1.03
but left their p. dwelling have Jud 1.06

PROPERLY
that he is not behaving p. toward his 1Co 7.36
when each part is working p., makes Eph 4.16

PROPERTY
give me p. among you for a burying Gen 23.04
All the p. which God has taken away 31.16
and trade in it, and get p. in it." 34.10
their p. and all their beasts be 34.23
and all his p. which he had acquired 36.06
put his hand to his neighbor's p.; Ex 22.11
buys a slave as his p. for money, Lev 22.11
return to his p. and each of you 25.10
each of you shall return to his p. 25.13
poor, and sells part of his p., 25.25
and he shall return to his p. 25.27
and he shall return to his p. 25.28
your land; and they may be your p. 25.45
met him at the p. of Naboth the 2Ki 9.21
were stewards of King David's p. 1Ch 27.31
of all the p. and cattle of the 28.01
elders all his p. should be forfeited, Ez 10.08
one lived on his p. in their towns: Neh 11.03
friends to get a share of their p., Job 17.05
district and the p. of the city, Eze 45.07
district and the p. of the city, 45.07
It is to be his p. in Israel. And 45.08
sons, it is their p. by inheritance. 46.16
thrusting them out of their p.; 46.18
inheritance out of his own p., 46.18
shall be dispossessed of his p. 46.18
together with the p. of the city. 48.20
and of the p. of the city shall 48.21
and the p. of the city, shall be in 48.22
and entrusted to them his p.; Mt 25.14
me the share of p. that falls to Lk 15.12
squandered his p. in loose living. 15.13
wife Sapphira sold a piece of p., Ac 5.01
accepted the plundering of your p., Heb 10.34

PROPHECY
and in the p. of Ahijah the Shilonite, 2Ch 9.29
the p. of Azariah the son of Oded, 15.08
he had pronounced the p. against me Neh 6.12
Where there is no p. the people 29.18
fulfilled the p. of Isaiah which Mt 13.14
if p., in proportion to our faith; Rom 12.06
to another p., to another the 1Co 12.10
as for p., it will pass away; 13.08
imperfect and our p. is imperfect; 13.09

PROPHECY (cont.)

or knowledge or p. or teaching? 1Co 14.06
while p. is not for unbelievers but 14.22
that no p. of scripture is a matter 2Pe 1.20
because no p. ever came by the 1.21
reads aloud the words of the p., Rev 1.03
of Jesus is the spirit of p. 19.10
the words of the p. of this book. 22.07
the words of the p. of this book, 22.10
the words of the p. of this book: 22.18
the words of the book of this p., 22.19

PROPHESIED

spirit rested upon them, they p. Num 11.25
tent, and so they p. in the camp. 11.26
upon him, and he p. among them. 1Sa 10.10
saw how he p. with the prophets, 10.11
messengers of Saul, and they also p. 19.20
other messengers, and they also p. 19.21
the third time, and they also p. 19.21
him also, and as he went he p., 19.23
and he too p. before Samuel, and lay 19.24
And all the prophets p. so, 1Ki 22.12
who p. under the direction of the 1Ch 25.02
who p. with the lyre in thanksgiving 25.03
And all the prophets p. so, 2Ch 18.11
of Mareshah p. against Jehoshaphat, 20.37
p. to the Jews who were in Judah Ez 5.01
the prophets p. by Baal, and went Jer 2.08
to whom you have p. falsely." 20.06
they p. by Baal and led my people 23.13
did not speak to them, yet they p. 23.21
which Jeremiah p. against all the 25.13
Why have you p. in the name of the 26.09
because he has p. against this 26.11
"Micah of Moresheth p. in the days 26.18
another man who p. in the name of 26.20
He p. against this city and against 26.20
words which you have p. come true, 28.06
and me from ancient times p. war, 28.08
Shemaiah has p. to you when I did 29.31
Where are your prophets who p. to you, 37.19
of Israel who p. concerning Jerusalem Eze 13.16
So I p. as I was commanded; 37.07
and as I p., there was a noise, and 37.07
So I p. as he commanded me, and the 37.10
in those days p. for years that I 38.17
prophets and the law p. until John; Mt 11.13
the Holy Spirit, and p., saying, Lk 1.67
that year he p. that Jesus should Jn 11.51
and they spoke with tongues and p. Ac 19.06
four unmarried daughters, who p. 21.09
The prophets who p. of the grace 1Pe 1.10
seventh generation from Adam p., Jud 1.14

PROPHESIES

for he never p. good concerning me, 1Ki 22.08
for he never p. good concerning me, 2Ch 18.07
As for the prophet who p. peace, Jer 28.09
the LORD over every madman who p., 29.26
hence, and he p. of times far off.' Eze 12.27
pierce him through when he p. Zec 13.03
ashamed of hs vision when he p.; 13.04
who prays or p. with his head 1Co 11.04
who prays or p. with her head 11.05
he who p. speaks to men for their 14.03
but he who p. edifies the church. 14.04
He who p. is greater than he who 14.05

PROPHESY

and you shall p. with them and be 1Sa 10.06
he would not p. good concerning me, 1Ki 22.18
who should p. with lyres, with harps, 1Ch 25.01
he would not p. good concerning me, 2Ch 18.17
"P. not to us what is right; Is 30.10
to us smooth things, p. illusions, 30.10
the prophets p. falsely, and the Jer 5.31
"Do not p. in the name of the LORD, 11.21
prophets who p. in my name although 14.15
to whom they p. shall be cast out 14.16
where the LORD had sent him to p., 19.14
of the prophets who p. to you, 23.16
have said who p. lies in my name, 23.25
heart of the prophets who p. lies, 23.26
and who p. the deceit of their own 23.26
against those who p. lying dreams, 23.32
shall p. against them all these 25.30
LORD sent me to p. against this 26.12
"Why do you p. and say, 'Thus says 32.03
and you shall p. against the city. Eze 4.07
of Israel, and p. against them, 6.02
p. against them, p., O son of man." 11.04
"Son of man, p. against the prophets 13.02
p. and say to those who prophesy 13.02
to those who p. out of their own 13.02
who p. out of their own minds; 13.17
own minds; p. against them 13.17
and p. against the forest land in 20.46
p. against the land of Israel 21.02
"Son of man, p. and say, Thus says 21.09
"P. therefore, son of man; clap your 21.14
p., and say, Thus says the Lord GOD 21.28
the Ammonites, and p. against them. 25.02
toward Sidon, and p. against her 28.21
and p. against him and against all 29.02
"Son of man, p., and say, Thus says 30.02
"Son of man, p. against the shepherds 34.02
p., and say to them, even to the 34.02
Mount Seir, and p. against it, 35.02
p. to the mountains of Israel, and 36.01
therefore p., and say, Thus says the 36.03
Therefore p. concerning the land of 36.06
"P. to these bones, and say to them, 37.04
"P. to the breath, p., son of man, and say 37.09
Therefore p., and say to them, Thus 37.12
and Tubal, and p. against him 38.02
p., and say to Gog, Thus says the 38.14
p. against Gog, and say, Thus says 39.01
sons and your daughters shall p., Joe 2.28
prophets, saying, 'You shall not p.' Amo 2.12
GOD has spoken; who can but p.?" 3.08
and eat bread there, and p. there; 7.12
but never again p. at Bethel, 7.13
me, 'Go, p. to my people Israel.' 7.15
'Do not p. against Israel, and do 7.16
did we not p. in your name, and cast Mt 7.22
Well did Isaiah p. of you, when 15.07
saying, "P. to us, you Christ! Who 26.68
"Well did Isaiah p. of you hypocrites, Mk 7.06
to strike him, saying to him, "P.!" 14.65
blindfolded him and asked him, "P.! Lk 22.64
sons and your daughters shall p., Ac 2.17
pour out my Spirit; and they shall p. 2.18
gifts, especially that you may p. 1Co 14.01
in tongues, but even more to p. 14.05
But if all p., and an unbeliever or 14.24
For you can all p. one by one, 14.31
brethren, earnestly desire to p., 14.39
"You must again p. about many Rev 10.11
power to p. for one thousand two 11.03

PROPHESYING

"Eldad and Medad are p. in the camp." Num 11.27
flute, and lyre before them, p. 1Sa 10.05
When he had finished p., he came 10.13
saw the company of the prophets p., 19.20
the prophets were p. before them. 1Ki 22.10
the prophets were p. before them. 2Ch 18.09
through the p. of Haggai the Ez 6.14
prophets are p. lies in my name; Jer 14.14
They are p. to you a lying vision, 14.14
heard Jeremiah p. these things. 20.01
is a lie which they are p. to you, 27.10
is a lie which they are p. to you. 27.14
but they are p. falsely in my name. 27.15
and the prophets who are p. to you. 27.15

PROPHESYING (cont.)
of your prophets who are p. to you, Jer 27.16
is a lie which they are p. to you. 27.16
which they are p. to you in my 29.09
who are p. a lie to you in my name: 29.21
of Anathoth who is p. to you? 29.27
while I was p., that Pelatiah the Eze 11.13
do not despise p., 1Th 5.20
fall during the days of their p., Rev 11.06

PROPHET
for he is a p., and he will pray Gen 20.07
your brother shall be your p. Ex 7.01
If there is a p. among you, I the Num 12.06
"If a p. arises among you, or a Deu 13.01
words of that p. or to that 13.03
But that p. or that dreamer of 13.05
up for you a p. like me from among 18.15
up for them a p. like you from 18.18
But the p. who presumes to speak a 18.20
other gods, that same p. shall die.' 18.20
when a p. speaks in the name of the 18.22
the p. has spoken it presumptuously, 18.22
not arisen a p. since in Israel 34.10
the LORD sent a p. to the people of Ju 6.08
established as a p. of the LORD. 1Sa 3.20
is now called a p. was formerly 9.09
Then the p. Gad said to David, "Do 22.05
the king said to Nathan the p., 2Sa 7.02
and sent a message by Nathan the p.; 12.25
of the LORD came to the p. Gad, 24.11
son of Jehoiada, and Nathan the p., 1Ki 1.08
Nathan the p. or Benaiah or the 1.10
the king, Nathan the p. came in. 1.22
the king, "Here is Nathan the p." 1.23
Nathan the p., and Benaiah the son 1.32
and Nathan the p. there anoint him 1.34
Nathan the p., and Benaiah the son 1.38
Nathan the p., and Benaiah the son 1.44
and Nathan the p. have anointed 1.45
the p. Ahijah the Shilonite found 11.29
Now there dwelt an old p. in Bethel. 13.11
"I also am a p. as you are, and an 13.18
came to the p. who had brought him 13.20
the ass for the p. whom he had 13.23
in the city where the old p. dwelt. 13.25
And when the p. who had brought him 13.26
And the p. took up the body of the 13.29
Ahijah the p. is there, who said of 14.02
spoke by his servant Ahijah the p. 14.18
came by the p. Jehu the son of 16.07
against Baasha by Jehu the p., 16.12
I only, am left a p. of the LORD; 18.22
Elijah the p. came near and said, "O 18.36
anoint to be p. in your place. 19.16
And behold, a p. came near to Ahab 20.13
Then the p. came near to the king 20.22
So the p. departed, and waited for 20.38
here another p. of the LORD of 22.07
"Is there no p. of the LORD here, 2Ki 3.11
were with the p. who is in Samaria! 5.03
know that there is a p. in Israel." 5.08
if the p. had commanded you to do 5.13
the p. who is in Israel, tells the 6.12
Then Elisha the p. called one of 9.01
the p., went to Ramothgilead. 9.04
the p., who was from Gathhepher. 14.25
Judah by every p. and every seer, 17.13
to the p. Isaiah the son of Amoz. 19.02
And Isaiah the p. the son of Amoz 20.01
And Isaiah the p. cried to the LORD; 20.11
Then Isaiah the p. came to King 20.14
bones of the p. who came out of 23.18
house, David said to Nathan the p., 1Ch 17.01
in the Chronicles of Nathan the p., 29.29
in the history of Nathan the p., 2Ch 9.29
Then Shemaiah the p. came to 12.05
of Shemaiah the p. and of Iddo the 12.15
in the story of the p. Iddo. 13.22
here another p. of the LORD of 18.06
came to him from Elijah the p., 21.12
with Amaziah and sent to him a p., 25.15
So the p. stopped, but said, "I 25.16
Isaiah the p. the son of Amoz wrote 26.22
But a p. of the LORD was there, 28.09
king's seer and of Nathan the p.; 29.25
Hezekiah the king and Isaiah the p., 32.20
of Isaiah the p. the son of Amoz, 32.32
since the days of Samuel the p.; 35.18
himself before Jeremiah the p., 36.12
of Haggai the p. and Zechariah the Ez 6.14
there is no longer any p., and there Ps 74.09
the soldier, the judge and the p., Is 3.02
and the p. who teaches lies is the 9.15
priest and the p. reel with strong 28.07
to the p. Isaiah the son of Amoz. 37.02
And Isaiah the p. the son of Amoz 38.01
Then Isaiah the p. came to King 39.03
appointed you a p. to the nations." Jer 1.05
and from p. to priest, every one 6.13
from p. to priest, every one deals 8.10
For both p. and priest ply their 14.18
the wise, nor the word from the p. 18.18
Then Pashhur beat Jeremiah the p., 20.02
"Both p. and priest are ungodly; 23.11
Let the p. who has a dream tell the 23.28
or a p., or a priest asks you, "What 23.33
And as for the p., priest, or one of 23.34
Thus you shall say to the p., 23.37
which Jeremiah the p. spoke to all 25.02
the p. from Gibeon, spoke to me in 28.01
Then the p. Jeremiah spoke to 28.05
to Hananiah the p. in the presence 28.05
and the p. Jeremiah said, "Amen! 28.06
As for the p. who prophesies peace, 28.09
the word of that p. comes to pass, 28.09
the LORD has truly sent the p." 28.09
Then the p. Hananiah took the yoke-bars 28.10
from the neck of Jeremiah the p., and 28.10
but Jeremiah the p. went his way. 28.11
Sometime after the p. Hananiah had 28.12
off the neck of Jeremiah the p., 28.12
Jeremiah the p. said to the p. Hananiah, 28.15
month, the p. Hananiah died. 28.17
Jeremiah the p. sent from Jerusalem 29.01
in the hearing of Jeremiah the p. 29.29
Jeremiah the p. was shut up in the 32.02
Then Jeremiah the p. spoke all 34.06
Jeremiah the p. ordered him about 36.08
the secretary and Jeremiah the p., 36.26
he spoke through Jeremiah the p. 37.02
Maaseiah, to Jeremiah the p. saying, 37.03
the LORD came to Jeremiah the p.: 37.06
Hananiah, seized Jeremiah the p., 37.13
to Jeremiah the p. by casting him 38.09
Jeremiah the p. out of the cistern 38.10
Jeremiah the p. and received him 38.14
and said to Jeremiah the p., 42.02
Jeremiah the p. said to them, "I 42.04
Jeremiah the p. and Baruch the son 43.06
Jeremiah the p. spoke to Baruch 45.01
to Jeremiah the p. concerning the 46.01
to Jeremiah the p. about the 46.13
to Jeremiah the p. concerning the 47.01
to Jeremiah the p. concerning Elam, 49.34
the Chaldeans, by Jeremiah the p.: 50.01
Jeremiah the p. commanded Seraiah 51.59
priest and p. be slain in the Lam 2.20
there has been a p. among them. Eze 2.05
they seek a vision from the p., 7.26
his face, and yet comes to the p., 14.04
yet comes to a p. to inquire for 14.07
And if the p. be deceived and speak 14.09
I, the LORD, have deceived that p., 14.09
punishment of the p. and the 14.10
know that a p. has been among them." 33.33

PROPHET (cont.)
of the LORD of Jeremiah the p., Dan 9.02
righteousness, to seal both vision and p., 9.24
the p. also shall stumble with you Hos 4.05
The p. is a fool, the man of the 9.07
The p. is the watchman of Ephraim, 9.08
By a p. the LORD brought Israel up 12.13
and by a p. he was preserved. 12.13
"I am no p., nor a prophet's son; Amo 7.14
of God which Habakkuk the p. saw. Hab 1.01
A prayer of Habakkuk the p., 3.01
by Haggai the p. to Zerubbabel the Hag 1.01
of the LORD came by Haggai the p., 1.03
and the words of Haggai the p., 1.12
of the LORD came by Haggai the p., 2.01
of the LORD came by Haggai the p., 2.10
son of Iddo, the p., saying, Zec 1.01
of Berechiah, son of Iddo, the p.; 1.07
And if any one again appears as a p., 13.03
On that day every p. will be 13.04
'I am no p., I am a tiller of the 13.05
you Elijah the p. before the great Mal 4.05
the Lord had spoken by the p.: Mt 1.22
for so it is written by the p.: 2.05
what the Lord had spoken by the p., 2.15
was spoken by the p. Jeremiah: 2.17
of by the p. Isaiah when he said, 3.03
spoken by the p. Isaiah might be 4.14
what was spoken by the p. Isaiah, 8.17
He who receives a p. because he is a p. 10.41
then did you go out? To see a p.? 11.09
I tell you, and more than a p. 11.09
what was spoken by the p. Isaiah: 12.17
it except the sign of the p. Jonah. 12.39
fulfil what was spoken by the p.: 13.35
"A p. is not without honor except 13.57
because they held him to be a p. 14.05
what was spoken by the p., saying, 21.04
"This is the p. Jesus from Nazareth 21.11
for all hold that John was a p." 21.26
because they held him to be a p. 21.46
sacrilege spoken of by the p. Daniel, 24.15
had been spoken by the p. Jeremiah, 27.09
As it is written in Isaiah the p., Mk 1.02
"A p. is not without honor, except 6.04
"It is a p., like one of the 6.15
all held that John was a real p. 11.32
be called the p. of the Most High; Lk 1.76
book of the words of Isaiah the p., 3.04
to him the book of the p. Isaiah. 4.17
no p. is acceptable in his own 4.24
in the time of the p. Elisha; 4.27
"A great p. has arisen among us!" and 7.16
What then did you go out to see? A p.? 7.26
Yes, I tell you, and more than a p. 7.26
to himself, "If this man were a p., 7.39
be that a p. should perish away 13.33
and convinced that John was a p. 20.06
who was a p. mighty in deed and 24.19
"Are you the p.?" And he answered, Jn 1.21
the Lord,' as the p. Isaiah said." 1.23
the Christ, nor Elijah, nor the p.?" 1.25
"Sir, I perceive that you are a p. 4.19
testified that a p. has no honor in 4.44
is indeed the p. who is to come 6.14
people said, "This is really the p." 7.40
see that no p. is to rise from 7.52
opened your eyes?" He said, "He is a p." 9.17
spoken by the p. Isaiah might be 12.38
is what was spoken by the p. Joel: Ac 2.16
Being therefore a p., and knowing 2.30
up for you a p. from your brethren 3.22
listen to that p. shall be destroyed 3.23
up for you a p. from your brethren 7.37
houses made with hands; as the p. says, 7.48
he was reading the p. Isaiah. 8.28
heard him reading Isaiah the p., 8.30
does the p. say this, about himself 8.34
magician, a Jewish false p., named 13.06
them judges until Samuel the p. 13.20
a p. named Agabus came down from 21.10
fathers through Isaiah the p.: 28.25
If any one thinks that he is a p., 1Co 14.37
a p. of their own, said, Cretans are Tit 1.12
and from the mouth of the false p., Rev 16.13
it the false p. who in its presence 19.20
the beast and the false p. were, 20.10

PROPHETESS
the p., the sister of Aaron, took a Ex 15.20
Now Deborah, a p., the wife of Ju 4.04
and Asaiah went to Huldah the p., 2Ki 22.14
had sent went to Huldah the p.. 2Ch 34.22
and also the p. Noadiah and the Neh 6.14
And I went to the p., and she Is 8.03
And there was a p., Anna, the Lk 2.36
calls herself a p. and is teaching Rev 2.20

PROPHETIC
and through the p. writings is made Rom 16.26
And if I have p. powers, and understand 1Co 13.02
with the p. utterances which 1Ti 1.18
given you by p. utterance when the 4.14
And we have the p. word made more 2Pe 1.19

PROPHET'S
"I am no prophet, nor a p. son; Amo 7.14
prophet shall receive a p. reward, Mt 10.41
and restrained the p. madness. 2Pe 2.16

PROPHETS
that all the LORD's people were p., Num 11.29
meet a band of p. coming down from 1Sa 10.05
behold, a band of p. met him; 10.10
saw how he prophesied with the p., 10.11
of Kish? Is Saul also among the p.?" 10.11
proverb, "Is Saul also among the p.?" 10.12
the company of the p. prophesying, 19.20
is said, "Is Saul also among the p.?" 19.24
by dreams, or by Urim, or by p. 28.06
no more, either by p. or by dreams; 28.15
Jezebel cut off the p. of the LORD, 1Ki 18.04
took a hundred p. and hid them by 18.04
Jezebel killed the p. of the LORD, 18.13
of the LORD's p. by fifties in a 18.13
and fifty p. of Baal and the four 18.19
and the four hundred p. of Asherah, 18.19
gathered the p. together at Mount 18.20
but Baal's p. are four hundred and 18.22
Then Elijah said to the p. of Baal. 18.25
said to them, "Seize the p. of Baal; 18.40
slain all the p. with the sword. 19.01
and slain thy p. with the sword; 19.10
and slain thy p. with the sword; 19.14
the sons of the p. said to his 20.35
recognized him as one of the p. 20.41
of Israel gathered the p. together, 22.06
and all the p. were prophesying 22.10
And all the p. prophesied so, and 22.12
words of the p. with one accord 22.13
spirit in the mouth of all his p.' 22.22
in the mouth of all these your p.; 22.23
And the sons of the p. who were in 2Ki 2.03
The sons of the p. who were at 2.05
of the sons of the p. also went, 2.07
the sons of the p. who were at 2.15
Go to the p. of your father and the 3.13
the p. of your mother." But the king 3.13
the sons of the p. cried to Elisha, 4.01
the sons of the p. were sitting 4.38
pottage for the sons of the p." 4.38
young men of the sons of the p.; 5.22
Now the sons of the p. said to Elisha, 6.01
the sons of the p. and said to him, 9.01
the blood of my servants the p., 9.07
call to me all the p. of Baal, 10.19

PROPHETS (cont.)

sent to you by my servants the p." 2Ki 17.13
spoken by all his servants the p. 17.23
LORD said by his servants the p., 21.10
Jerusalem, and the priests and the p., 23.02
he spoke by his servants the p. 24.02
my anointed ones, do my p. no harm!" 1Ch 16.22
of Israel gathered the p. together, 2Ch 18.05
and all the p. were prophesying 18.09
And all the p. prophesied so, and 18.11
words of the p. with one accord 18.12
spirit in the mouth of all his p.' 18.21
in the mouth of these your p.; 18.22
believe his p., and you will 20.20
Yet he sent p. among them to bring 24.19
was from the LORD through his p. 29.25
his words, and scoffing at his p., 36.16
Now the p., Haggai and Zechariah Ez 5.01
and with them were the p. of God, 5.02
command by thy servants the p., 9.11
also set up p. to proclaim concerning Neh 6.07
the rest of the p. who wanted to 6.14
their back and killed thy p., 9.26
them by thy Spirit through thy p.; 9.30
our p., our fathers, and all thy 9.32
my anointed ones, do my p. no harm!" Ps 105.15
the p., and covered your heads, the Is 29.10
and to the p., "Prophesy not to us 30.10
the p. prophesied by Baal, and went Jer 2.08
their priests, and their p., 2.26
devoured your p. like a ravening 2.30
be appalled and the p. astounded." 4.09
The p. will become wind; the word 5.13
the p. prophesy falsely, and the 5.31
all my servants the p. to them, 7.25
the priests, the bones of the p., 8.01
the p., and all the inhabitants of 13.13
the p. say to them, 'You shall not 14.13
"The p. are prophesying lies in my 14.14
concerning the p. who prophesy in 14.15
famine those p. shall be consumed. 14.15
Concerning the p.: My heart is 23.09
In the p. of Samaria I saw an 23.13
But in the p. of Jerusalem I have 23.14
LORD of hosts concerning the p.: 23.15
for from the p. of Jerusalem 23.15
words of the p. who prophesy to 23.16
"I did not send the p., yet they ran; 23.21
heard what the p. have said who 23.25
heart of the p. who prophesy lies, 23.26
Therefore, behold, I am against the p., 23.30
Behold, I am against the p., 23.31
to you all his servants the p., 25.04
my servants the p. whom I send to 26.05
The priests and the p. and all the 26.07
priests and the p. and all the 26.08
priests and the p. said to the 26.11
said to the priests and the p., 26.16
So do not listen to your p., 27.09
words of the p. who are saying to 27.14
you and the p. who are prophesying 27.15
words of your p. who are prophesying 27.16
If they are p., and if the word of 27.18
The p. who preceded you and me from 28.08
the p., and all the people, whom 29.01
Do not let your p. and your 29.08
has raised up p. for us in Babylon, 29.15
sent to you by my servants the p., 29.19
princes, their priests and their p., 32.32
sent to you all my servants the p., 35.15
Where are your p. who prophesied to 37.19
sent to you all my servants the p., 44.04
and her p. obtain no vision from Lam. 2.09
Your p. have seen for you false and 2.14
the sins of her p. and the iniquities 4.13
prophesy against the p. of Israel, Eze 13.02
to the foolish p. who follow their 13.03
Your p. have been like foxes among 13.04
be against the p. who see delusive 13.09
these p. daub it with whitewash; 13.10
the p. of Israel who prophesied 13.16
And her p. have daubed for them 22.28
by my servants the p. of Israel, 38.17
listened to thy servants the p., Dan 9.06
before us by his servants the p. 9.10
Therefore I have hewn them by the p., Hos 6.05
I spoke to the p.; it was I who 12.10
and through the p. gave parables. 12.10
raised up some of your sons for p., Amo 2.11
drink wine, and commanded the p., 2.12
his secret to his servants the p. 3.07
concerning the p. who lead my Mic 3.05
the sun shall go down upon the p., 3.06
for hire, its p. divine for money; 3.11
Her p. are wanton, faithless men; Zep 3.04
to whom the former p. cried out, Zec 1.04
And the p., do they live for ever? 1.05
I commanded my servants the p., 1.06
of the LORD of hosts and the p., 7.03
LORD proclaimed by the former p.?" 7.07
his Spirit through the former p. 7.12
words from the mouth of the p., 8.09
the land the p. and the unclean 13.02
spoken by the p. might be fulfilled, Mt 2.23
persecuted the p. who were before 5.12
come to abolish the law and the p.; 5.17
for this is the law and the p. 7.12
"Beware of false p., who come to 7.15
For all the p. and the law prophesied 11.13
many p. and righteous men longed to 13.17
others Jeremiah or one of the p." 16.14
depend all the law and the p." 22.40
tombs of the p. and adorn the 23.29
in shedding the blood of the p.' 23.30
sons of those who murdered the p. 23.31
Therefore I send you p. and wise 23.34
killing the p. and stoning those 23.37
And many false p. will arise and 24.11
and false p. will arise and show 24.24
scriptures of the p. might be 26.56
prophet, like one of the p. of old." Mk 6.15
and others one of the p." 8.28
and false p. will arise and show 13.22
mouth of his holy p. from of old, Lk 1.70
for so their fathers did to the p. 6.23
their fathers did to the false p. 6.26
that one of the old p. had risen. 9.08
that one of the old p. has risen." 9.19
you that many p. and kings desired 10.24
tombs of the p. whom your fathers 11.47
'I will send them p. and apostles, 11.49
that the blood of all the p., 11.50
and all the p. of the kingdom of 13.28
killing the p. and stoning those 13.34
"The law and the p. were until John; 16.16
said, 'They have Moses and the p.; 16.29
they do not hear Moses and the p., 16.31
of man by the p. will be accomplished. 18.31
all that the p. have spoken! 24.25
beginning with Moses and all the p., 24.27
Moses and the p. and the psalms 24.44
in the law and also the p. wrote, Jn 1.45
It is written in the p., 'And they 6.45
Abraham died, as did the p.; and I 8.52
And the p. died! Who do you claim 8.53
foretold by the mouth of all the p., Ac 3.18
mouth of his holy p. from of old. 3.21
And all the p. who have spoken, from 3.24
the sons of the p. and of the 3.25
is written in the book of the p.: 7.42
Which of the p. did not your 7.52
To him all the p. bear witness that 10.43
Now in these days p. came down from 11.27
Antioch there were p. and teachers, 13.01
After the reading of the law and the p., 13.15
utterances of the p. which are read 13.27

PROPHETS (cont.)
upon you what is said in the p.: Ac 13.40
this the words of the p. agree, 15.15
and Silas, who were themselves p., 15.32
by the law or written in the p., 24.14
but what the p. and Moses said 26.22
King Agrippa, do you believe the p.? 26.27
the law of Moses and from the p. 28.23
through his p. in the holy scriptures, Rom 1.02
the law and the p. bear witness to 3.21
"Lord, they have killed thy p., 11.03
second p., third teachers, then 1Co 12.28
Are all p.? Are all teachers? Do 12.29
Let two or three p. speak, and let 14.29
and the spirits of p. are subject to p. 14.32
foundation of the apostles and p., Eph 2.20
holy apostles and p. by the Spirit; 3.05
some p., some evangelists, some 4.11
both the Lord Jesus and the p., 1Th 2.15
of old to our fathers by the p.; Heb 1.01
of David and Samuel and the p.— 11.32
take the p. who spoke in the name Jas 5.10
The p. who prophesied of the grace 1Pe 1.10
But false p. also arose among the 2Pe 2.01
of the holy p. and the commandment 3.02
for many false p. have gone out 1Jn 4.01
announced to his servants the p., Rev 10.07
these two p. had been a torment to 11.10
the p. and saints, and those who 11.18
shed the blood of saints and p., 16.06
O saints and apostles and p., 18.20
the blood of p. and of saints, 18.24
the God of the spirits of the p., 22.06
with you and your brethren the p., 22.09

PROPORTION
each, the p. to the inheritance which Num 35.08
of stripes in p. of his offence. Deu 25.02
if prophecy, in p. to our faith; Rom 12.06

PROPOSAL
This p. seemed good to Pharaoh and Gen 41.37

PROPOSE
that they p. to do will now be Gen 11.06
for you p. to bring upon us guilt 2Ch 28.13

PROPOSED
and the king did as Memucan p.; Est 1.21

PROPOUND
"Son of man, p. a riddle, and speak Eze 17.02

PROPPED
the king was p. up in his chariot 1Ki 22.35
king of Israel p. himself up in 2Ch 18.34

PROSELYTE
single p., and when he became a p., Mt 23.15
and Nicolaus, a p. of Antioch. Ac 6.05

PROSELYTES
visitors from Rome, both Jews and p., Ac 2.10

PROSPECT
but a fearful p. of judgment, and a Heb 10.27

PROSPER
his angel with you and p. your way; Gen 24.40
now thou wilt p. the way which I 24.42
all that he did to p. in his hands. 39.03
he did, the LORD made it p. 39.23
and you shall not p. in your ways; Deu 28.29
that you may p. in all that you do. 29.09
I know that the LORD will p. me, Ju 17.13
May you p. in Ephrathah and be Ru 4.11
he not cause to p. all my help and 2Sa 23.05
that you may p. in all that you do 1Ki 2.03
Then you will p. if you are careful 1Ch 22.13
of the LORD, so that you cannot p.? 2Ch 24.20
sought the LORD, God made him p. 26.05
"The God of heaven will make us p., Neh 2.20
His ways p. at all times; thy Ps 10.05
"May they p. who love you! 122.06
who gives heed to the word will p., Pro 16.20
A man of crooked mind does not p., 17.20
he who keeps understanding will p. 19.08
his transgressions will not p., 28.13
or you do not know which will p., Ecc 11.06
him, and he will p. in his way. Is 48.15
Behold, my servant shall p., 52.13
of the LORD shall p. in his hand; 53.10
is fashioned against you shall p., 54.17
and p. in the thing for which I 55.11
trust, and you will not p. by them. Jer 2.37
to make it p., and they do not 5.28
why does the way of the wicked p.? 12.01
her enemies p., because the LORD Lam 1.05
make deceit p. under his hand, Dan 8.25
He shall p. till the indignation is 11.36
not only p. but when they put God Mal 3.15
as he may p., so that contributions 1Co 16.02

PROSPERED
the LORD had p. his journey or not. Gen 24.21
me, since the LORD has p. my way; 24.56
people fared, and how the war p. 2Sa 11.07
wherever he went forth, he p. 2Ki 18.07
and he p., and all Israel obeyed 1Ch 29.23
every side." So they built and p. 2Ch 14.07
he did with all his heart, and p. 31.21
And Hezekiah p. in all his works. 32.30
elders of the Jews built and p., Ez 6.14
therefore they have not p., Jer 10.21
of food, and p., and saw no evil. 44.17
So this Daniel p. during the reign Dan 6.28
ground, and the horn acted and p. 8.12
I have p., and I need nothing; Rev 3.17

PROSPERING
will again take delight in p. you, Deu 30.09
in my house and p. in my palace. Dan 4.04

PROSPERITY
peace or their p. all your days Deu 23.06
LORD will make you abound in p., 28.11
eye on all the p. which shall be 1Sa 2.32
your wisdom and p. surpass the 1Ki 10.07
and never seek their peace or p., Ez 9.12
in p. the destroyer will come upon Job 15.21
therefore his p. will not endure. 20.21
They spend their days in p., 21.13
Behold, is not their p. in their hand? 21.16
One dies in full p., being wholly 21.23
and my p. has passed away like a 30.15
they complete their days in p., 36.11
He himself shall abide in p., Ps 25.13
I said in my p., "I shall never be 30.06
delight themselves in abundant p. 37.11
he leads out the prisoners to p.; 68.06
mountains bear p. for the people, 72.03
when I saw the p. of the wicked. 73.03
that I may see the p. of thy chosen 106.05
May you see the p. of Jerusalem all 128.05
with me, enduring wealth and p. Pro 8.18
but p. rewards the righteous. 13.21
In the day of p. be joyful, and in Ecc 7.14
great shall be the p. of your sons. Is 54.13
I will extend p. to her like a 66.12
I spoke to you in your p., but you Jer 22.21
them abundance of p. and security. 33.06
and all the p. I provide for it. 33.09
and in this place I will give p., Hag 2.09
shall again overflow with p., Zec 1.17
When Jerusalem was inhabited and in p., 7.07
shall be a sowing of peace and p.; 8.12

PROSPEROUS
himself becomes p. and finds Lev 25.26
make you more p. and numerous than Deu 30.05
you abundantly p. in all the work 30.09
then you shall make your way p., Jos 1.08
and p. ease, but did not aid the Eze 16.49
for them p. plantations so that 34.29

PROSPERS
diligently and p. in their hands. Ez 5.08
wither. In all that he does, he p. Ps 1.03
yourself over him who p. in his way, 37.07
gives it; wherever he turns he p. Pro 17.08

PROSTITUTE
be no cult p. of the daughters of Deu 23.17
there a cult p. of the sons of 23.17
and make them members of a p.? 1Co 6.15
himself to a p. becomes one body 6.16

PROSTITUTED
lofty place and p. your beauty, Eze 16.25

PROSTITUTES
were also male cult p. in the land. 1Ki 14.24
the male cult p. out of the land, 15.12
the male cult p. who remained in 22.46
of the cult p. which were in the 2Ki 23.07
harlots, and sacrifice with cult p., Hos 4.14

PROSTRATE
Then I lay p. before the LORD as Deu 9.18
"So I lay p. before the LORD for 9.25
There the evildoers lie p., they Ps 36.12
I am utterly bowed down and p.; 38.06
princes, and they shall p. themselves; Is 49.07

PROTECT
'For my sake p. the young man 2Sa 18.12
and horsemen to p. us against the Ez 8.22
p. us, guard us ever from this Ps 12.07
name of the God of Jacob p. you! 20.01
p. me from those who rise up 59.01
I will p. him, because he knows my 91.14
LORD of hosts will p. Jerusalem; Is 31.05
he will p. and deliver it, he will 31.05
The LORD of hosts will p. them, Zec 9.15

PROTECTED
you will be p. and take your rest Job 11.18
together against thy p. ones. Ps 83.03

PROTECTING
city, and like a high wall p. him. Pro 18.11

PROTECTION
their p. is removed from them, and Num 14.09
and help you, let them be your p.! Deu 32.38
and to give us p. in Judea and Ez 9.09
a guard as a p. against them day Neh 4.09
For the p. of wisdom is like the Ecc 7.12
of wisdom is like the p. of money; 7.12
Or let them lay hold of my p., Is 27.05
take refuge in the p. of Pharaoh, 30.02
Therefore shall the p. of Pharaoh 30.03

PROTECTOR
fatherless and p. of widows is God Ps 68.05

PROTECTS
the LORD p. him and keeps him alive; Ps 41.02
on the earth: a woman p. a man." Jer 31.22

PROTEST
I p., brethren, by my pride in you 1Co 15.31

PROUD
But when he was strong he grew p.. 2Ch 26.16
done to him, for his heart was p. 32.25
For God abases the p., but he saves Job 22.29
The p. beasts have not trodden it; 28.08
here shall your p. waves be stayed'? 38.11
one that is p., and abase him. 40.11
Look on every one that is p., 40.12
shall all the p. of the earth bow Ps 22.29
trust, who does not turn to the p., 40.04
render to the p. their deserts! 94.02
at ease, the contempt of the p. 123.04
tears down the house of the p., Pro 15.25
to divide the spoil with the p. 16.19
Haughty eyes and a p. heart, 21.04
"Scoffer" is the name of the p., 21.24
is better than the p. in spirit. Ecc 7.08
against all that is p. and lofty, Is 2.12
the pride of Moab, how p. he was; 16.06
Woe to the p. crown of the drunkards 28.01
The p. crown of the drunkards of 28.03
be not p., for the LORD has spoken. Jer 13.15
he is very p.—of his loftiness, his 48.29
O p. one, says the Lord GOD of hosts; 50.31
The p. one shall stumble and fall, 50.32
will put an end to their p. might, Eze 7.24
Lord God: "Because your heart is p., 28.02
has become p. in your wealth— 28.05
Your heart was p. because of your 28.17
and her p. might shall come down; 30.06
and her p. might shall come to an 30.18
its heart was p. of its height, 31.10
and her p. might shall come to an 33.28
them like his p. steed in battle. Zec 10.03
scattered the p. in the imagination Lk 1.51
So do not become p., but stand in Rom 11.20
reason to be p. of my work for God. 15.17
that you can be p. of us as we can 2Co 1.14
giving you cause to be p. of us, 5.12
and every p. obstacle to the 10.05
Christ I may be p. that I did not Php 2.16
p., arrogant, abusive, disobedient to 2Ti 3.02
it says, "God opposes the p., Jas 4.06
another, for "God opposes the p., 1Pe 5.05

PROUDLY
Talk no more so very p., 1Sa 2.03
"The wings of the ostrich wave p.; Job 39.13
long, for many fight against me p. Ps 56.02
my anger, my p. exulting ones. Is 13.03
for she has p. defiled the LORD, the Jer 50.29
was hardened so that he dealt p., Dan 5.20
their horsemen press p. on. Hab 1.08
your midst your p. exultant ones, Zep 3.11

PROVE
'P. yourselves by working a miracle, Ex 7.09
that I may p. them, whether they 16.04
for God has come to p. you, 20.20
"If he p. to be a worthy man, not 1Ki 1.52
they could not p. their fathers' Ez 2.59
they could not p. their fathers' Neh 7.61
blameless, he would p. me perverse. Job 9.20
who will p. me a liar, and show that 24.25
P. me, O LORD, and try me; Ps 26.02
and so p. to be my disciples. Jn 15.08
Neither can they p. to you what Ac 24.13
charges which they could not p. 25.07
it was to p. at the present time Rom 3.26
that you may p. what is the will of 12.02
but to p. by the earnestness of 2Co 8.08
you may not p. vain in this case, 9.03
then I p. myself a transgressor. Gal 2.18
then if they p. themselves blameless 1Ti 3.10
impossible that God should p. false, Heb 6.18
which comes upon you to p. you, 1Pe 4.12

PROVED
an ordinance and there he p. them, Ex 15.25
case, that you may be p. right. Is 43.26
p. neighbor to the man who fell Lk 10.36

PROVED (cont.)
promised life p. to be death to me. Rom 7.10
point you have p. yourselves guiltless 2Co 7.11
boasting before Titus has p. true. 7.14
kind of men we p. to be among you 1Th 1.05

PROVENDER
"We have both straw and p. enough, Gen 24.25
him straw and p. for the camels, 24.32
to give his ass p. at the lodging 42.47
when he had given their asses p., 43.24
We have straw and p. for our asses, Ju 19.19
his house, and gave the asses p.; 19.21
till the ground will eat salted p., Is 30.24

PROVERB
a p., and a byword, among all the Deu 28.37
Therefore it became a p., 1Sa 10.12
As the p. of the ancients says, 'Out 24.13
will become a p. and a byword 1Ki 9.07
will make it a p. and a byword 2Ch 7.20
I will incline my ear to a p.; Ps 49.04
to understand a p. and a figure, Pro 1.06
is a p. in the mouth of fools. 26.07
a drunkard is a p. in the mouth of 26.09
what is this p. that you have about Eze 12.22
GOD: I will put an end to this p., 12.23
no more use it as a p. in Israel.' 12.23
proverbs will use this p. about you, 16.44
repeating this p. concerning the 18.02
this p. shall no more be used by 18.03
you will quote to me this p., Lk 4.23
to them according to the true p., 2Pe 2.22

PROVERBS
He also uttered three thousand p.; 1Ki 4.32
Your maxims are p. of ashes, Job 13.12
The p. of Solomon, son of David, king Pro 1.01
These also are p. of Solomon which 25.01
and arranging p. with great care. Ecc 12.09
one who uses p. will use this Eze 16.44

PROVES
the promise of the LORD p. true; 2Sa 22.31
the promise of the LORD p. true; Ps 18.30
Every word of God p. true; he is a Pro 30.05
the word, and it p. unfruitful. Mt 13.22
the word, and it p. unfruitful. Mk 4.19

PROVIDE
"God will p. himself the lamb for a Gen 22.08
of that place The LORD will p.; 22.14
when shall I p. for my own household 30.30
and there I will p. for you, 45.11
I will p. for you and your little 50.21
of the land shall p. food for you, Lev 25.06
and p. for me here seven bulls and Num 23.01
and p. for me here seven bulls and 23.29
P. three men from each tribe, and I Jos 18.04
"P. for me a man who can play well, 1Sa 16.17
and I will p. for you with me in 2Sa 19.33
God, which you have occasion to p., Ez 7.20
you may p. it out of the king's 7.20
O God, thou didst p. for the needy. Ps 68.10
bread, or p. meat for his people?" 78.20
the lambs will p. your clothing, and Pro 27.26
yet they p. their food in the 30.25
and all the prosperity I p. for it. Jer 33.09
And I will p. for them prosperous Eze 34.29
days you shall p. daily a goat for 43.25
he shall p. the sin offerings, 45.17
prince shall p. for himself and 45.22
he shall p. as a burnt offering to 45.23
And he shall p. as a cereal offering 45.24
he shall p. an ephah with the bull 46.07
"He shall p. a lamb a year old 46.13
morning by morning he shall p. it. 46.13
And he shall p. a cereal offering 46.14
eating and drinking what they p., Lk 10.07
p. yourselves with purses that do 12.33
Also p. mounts for Paul to ride, and Ac 23.24
will also p. the way of escape, 1Co 10.13
And God is able to p. you with 2Co 9.08
everything and may p. in abundance 9.08
one does not p. for his relatives, 1Ti 5.08

PROVIDED
mount of the LORD it shall be p." Gen 22.14
And Joseph p. his father, his 47.12
So there were p., out of the Num 31.05
p. you are careful to keep all this Deu 19.09
for I have p. for myself a king 1Sa 16.01
and he had p. the king with food 2Sa 19.32
and p. for them, but did not go in 20.03
who p. food for the king and his 1Ki 4.07
And there I have p. a place for the 8.21
David also p. great stores of iron 1Ch 22.03
So David p. materials in great 22.05
pains I have p. for the house of 22.14
timber and stone too I have p. 22.14
So I have p. for the house of my 29.02
all that I have p. for the holy 29.03
that we have p. for building thee 29.16
Jerusalem, whom David my father p. 2Ch 2.07
p. them with food and drink, and 28.15
He likewise p. cities for himself, 32.29
and I p. for the wood offering, at Neh 13.31
and he quickly p. her with her Est 2.09
without blemish, shall be p. Eze 43.25
offering and the oil shall be p., 46.15
who p. for them out of their means. Lk 8.03
p. we suffer with him in order that Rom 8.17
p. you continue in his kindness; 11.22
p. that you continue in the faith, Col 1.23
will be richly p. for you an 2P 1.11

PROVIDES
Who p. for the raven its prey, when Job 38.41
He p. food for those who fear him; Ps 111.05
yet night and p. food for her household Pro 31.15
When the prince p. a freewill offering, Eze 46.12

PROVIDEST
thou p. their grain, for so thou Ps 65.09

PROVIDING
your God is p. you a place of rest, Jos 1.13
my wishes by p. food for my household." 1Ki 5.09
p. all manner of store; may our Ps 144.13

PROVINCE
people of the p. who came up out Ez 2.01
the rest of the p. Beyond the 4.10
the men of the p. Beyond the River, 4.11
possession of the p. Beyond the 4.16
the rest of the p. Beyond the 4.17
over the whole p. Beyond the River, 4.20
governor of the p. Beyond the 5.03
governor of the p. Beyond the 5.06
who were in the p. Beyond the 5.06
that we went to the p. of Judah, 5.08
which is in the p. of Media, 6.02
governor of the p. Beyond the 6.06
who are in the p. Beyond the River, 6.06
tribute of the p. from Beyond the 6.08
governor of the p. Beyond the 6.13
find in the whole p. of Babylonia, 7.16
treasurers in the p. Beyond the 7.21
people of the p. Beyond the River, 7.25
governors of the p. Beyond the 8.36
there in the p. who escaped exile Neh 1.03
governors of the p. Beyond the 2.07
governors of the p. Beyond the 2.09
governor of the p. Beyond the 3.07
people of the p. who came up out 7.06
chiefs of the p. who lived in 11.03

PROVINCE (cont.)
to every p. in its own script and Est 1.22
to every p. in its own script and 3.12
decree in every p. by proclamation 3.14
And in every p., wherever the king's 4.03
to every p. in its own script and 8.09
any people or p. that might attack 8.11
be issued as a decree in every p., 8.13
And in every p. and in every city, 8.17
p., and city, and that these days of 9.28
If you see in a p. the poor oppressed Ecc 5.08
ruler over the whole p. of Babylon, Dan 2.48
the affairs of the p. of Babylon; 2.49
of Dura, in the p. of Babylon. 3.01
the affairs of the p. of Babylon: 3.12
and Abednego in the p. of Babylon. 3.30
capital, which is in the p. of Elam; 8.02
into the richest parts of the p.; 11.24
he asked to what p. he belonged. Ac 23.34
Now when Festus had come into his p., 25.01

PROVINCES
city, hurtful of kings and p., Ez 4.15
one hundred and twenty-seven p., Est 1.01
governors of the p. being before 1.03
are in all the p. of King Ahasuerus. 1.16
he sent letters to all the royal p., 1.22
in all the p. of his kingdom to 2.03
a remission of taxes to the p., 2.18
in all the p. of your kingdom; 3.08
over all the p. and to the princes 3.12
by couriers to all the king's p., 3.13
of the king's p. know that *if* any 4.11
who are in all the p. of the king. 8.05
princes of the p. from India to 8.09
a hundred and twenty-seven p., 8.09
throughout all the p. of King 8.12
throughout all the p. of King 9.02
princes of the p. and the satraps 9.03
fame spread throughout all the p.; 9.04
done in the rest of the king's p.! 9.12
in the king's p. also gathered to 9.16
were in all the p. of King Ahasuerus, 9.20
twenty-seven p. of the kingdom of 9.30
and the treasure of kings and p.; Ecc 2.08
officials of the p. to come to the Dan 3.02
and all the officials of the p., 3.03

PROVING
in Damascus by p. that Jesus was Ac 9.22
explaining and p. that it was 17.03

PROVISION
and p. for his father on the Gen 45.23
"This is the p. for the manslayer, Deu 19.04
man had to make p. for one month 1Ki 4.07
Solomon's p. for one day was thirty 4.22
palace for which I have made p." 1Ch 29.19
and a settled p. for the singers, as Neh 11.23
make the same p. for sin offerings, Eze 45.25
much peace, and since by your p., Ac 24.02
and make no p. for the flesh, to Rom 13.14
writing this to secure any such p. 1Co 9.15

PROVISIONED
and were p., and went against them; 1Ki 20.27

PROVISIONS
and all their p., and went their Gen 14.11
to give them p. for the journey. 42.25
and gave them p. for the journey. 45.21
prepared for themselves any p. Ex 12.39
the people. 'Prepare your p.; Jos 1.11
cunning, and went and made ready p., 9.04
and all their p. were dry and moldy. 9.05
'Take p. in your hand for the 9.11
So the men partook of their p., 9.14
to bring p. for the people, that Ju 20.10
and took the p., and went, as Jesse 1Sa 17.20
and gave him p., and gave him the 22.10
supplied p. for King Solomon, and 1Ki 4.27
abundant p. of meal, cakes of figs, 1Ch 12.40
and he gave them abundant p., 2Ch 11.23
I will abundantly bless her p.; Ps 132.15
round about, to lodge and get p.; Lk 9.12

PROVOCATION
because of the p. of his sons and Deu 32.19
had I not feared p. by the enemy, 32.27
me, and my eye dwells on their p. Job 17.02
but a fool's p. is heavier than both. Pro 27.03
presented the p. of their offering; Eze 20.28
Ephraim has given bitter p.; Hos 12.14

PROVOCATIONS
of all the p. with which Manasseh 2Ki 23.26

PROVOKE
God, so as to p. him to anger, Deu 4.25
of the LORD, to p. him to anger. 9.18
I will p. them with a foolish 32.21
And her rival used to p. her sorely, 1Sa 1.06
of the LORD, she used to p. her. 1.07
Ahab did more to p. the LORD, 1Ki 16.33
why should you p. trouble so that 2Ki 14.10
that they might p. me to anger 22.17
why should you p. trouble so that 2Ch 25.19
that they might p. me to anger 34.25
and those who p. God are secure, who Job 12.06
a people who p. me to my face Is 65.03
to other gods, to p. me to anger. Jer 7.18
Is it I whom they p.? says the LORD. 7.19
or p. me to anger with the work of 25.06
that you might p. me to anger with 25.07
to other gods, to p. me to anger. 32.29
nothing but p. me to anger by the 32.30
which they did to p. me to anger— 32.32
Why do you p. me to anger with the 44.08
with violence, and p. me further to anger? Eze 8.17
your harlotry, to p. me to anger. 16.26
and to p. him to speak of many Lk 11.53
Shall we p. the Lord to jealousy? 1Co 10.22
do not p. you rchildren to anger, Eph 6.04
do not p. your children, lest they Col 3.21

PROVOKED
forget how you p. the LORD your Deu 9.07
Even at Horeb you p. the LORD to 9.08
you p. the LORD to wrath. 9.22
practices they p. him to anger. 32.16
they have p. me with their idols. 32.21
and they p. the LORD to anger. Ju 2.12
and they p. him to jealousy with 1Ki 14.22
the anger to which he p. the LORD, 15.30
the anger to which you have p. me, 21.22
and p. the LORD, the God of Israel, 22.53
my sight and have p. me to anger, 2Ki 21.15
with which Manasseh had p. him. 23.26
for they have p. thee to anger Neh 4.05
and p. the Holy One of Israel. Ps 78.41
For they p. him to anger with their 78.58
they p. the LORD to anger with 106.29
"Why have they p. me to anger Jer 8.19
when your fathers p. me to wrath, Zec 8.14
his spirit was p. within him as he Ac 17.16
Therefore I was p. with that Heb 3.10
And with whom was he p. forty years? 3.17

PROVOKES
Or what p. you that you answer? Job 16.03
he who p. him to anger forfeits his Pro 20.02
of jealousy, which p. to jealousy. Eze 8.03

PROVOKING
p. him to anger through the work of Deu 31.29
p. me to anger, and have cast me 1Ki 14.09

PROVOKING (cont.)
their Asherim, p. the LORD to anger. 1Ki 14.15
p. me to anger with their sins, 16.02
p. him to anger with the work of 16.07
p. the LORD God of Israel to anger 16.13
p. the LORD, the God of Israel, to 16.26
wicked things, p. the LORD to anger, 2Ki 17.11
sight of the LORD, p. him to anger. 17.17
sight of the LORD, p. him to anger. 21.06
p. the LORD to anger, Joshiah removed 23.19
p. to anger the LORD, the God of his 2Ch 28.25
sight of the LORD, p. him to anger. 33.06
p. me to anger by burning incense Jer 11.17
p. me to anger, in that they went to 44.03
no p. of one another, no envy of one Gal 5.26

PROWL
On every side the wicked p., Ps 12.08
lies desolate, jackals p. over it. Lam 5.18

PROWLED
He p. among the lions; he became a Eze 19.06

PROWLING
like dogs and p. about the city. Ps 59.06
like dogs and p. about the city. 59.14

PROWLS
the devil p. around like a roaring 1Pe 5.08

PRUDENCE
that p. may be given to the simple, Pro 1.04
O simple ones, learn p.; O foolish men, 8.05
dwell in p., and I find knowledge 8.12
and the simple will learn p.; 19.25
replied with p. and discretion to Dan 2.14
the dishonest steward for his p.; Lk 16.08

PRUDENT
p. in speech, and a man of good 1Sa 16.18
A son who gathers in summer is p., Pro 10.05
he who restrains his lips is p. 10.19
but the p. man ignores an insult. 12.16
A p. man conceals his knowledge, but 12.23
In everything a p. man acts with 13.16
The wisdom of a p. man is to 14.08
but the p. looks where he is going. 14.15
but the p. are crowned with knowledge. 14.18
but he who heeds admonition is p. 15.05
but a p. wife is from the LORD. 19.14
A p. man sees danger and hides 22.03
A p. man sees danger and hides 27.12
Has counsel perished from the p.? Jer 49.07
Therefore he who is p. will keep Amo 5.13

PRUNE
years you shall p. your vineyard, Lev 25.03
sow your field or p. your vineyard. 25.04

PRUNED
it shall not be p. or hoed, and briers and Is 5.06

PRUNES
branch that does bear fruit he p.. Jn 15.02

PRUNING
and their spears into p. hooks; Is 2.04
cut off the shoots with p. hooks, 18.05
and your p. hooks into spears; Joe 3.10
and their spears into p. hooks; Mic 4.03

PSALM
the earth; sing praises with a p.! Ps 47.07
it is written in the second p., Ac 13.33
Therefore he says also in another p., 13.35

PSALMIST
of Jacob, the sweet p. of Israel: 2Sa 23.01

PSALMS
himself says in the Book of P., Lk 20.42
prophets and the p. must be fulfilled 24.44
For it is written in the Book of P., Ac 1.20
addressing one another in p. and Eph 5.19
and as you sing p. and hymns and Col 3.16

PTOLEMAIS
voyage from Tyre, we arrived at P.; Ac 21.07

PUAH
named Shiphrah and the other P., Ex 1.15
deliver Israel Tola the son of P., Ju 10.01
P., Jashub, and Shimron, four. 1Ch 7.01

PUBLIC
that he hears a p. adjuration to Lev 5.01
them from the p. square of Bethshan, 2Sa 21.12
truth has fallen in the p. squares, Is 59.14
powerfully confuted the Jews in p.. Ac 18.28
teaching you in p. and from house 20.20
and made a p. example of them, Col 2.15
attend to the p. reading of scripture, 1Ti 4.13

PUBLICLY
went up, not p. but in private. Jn 7.10
to them, "They have beaten us p., Ac 16.37
Christ was p. portrayed as crucified? Gal 3.01
sometimes being p. exposed to abuse Heb 10.33

PUBLISH
p. it not in the streets of Ashkelon; 2Sa 1.20
they should p. and proclaim in all Neh 8.15
freewill offerings, p. them; Amo 4.05

PUBLISHED
proclamation and p. through Nineveh, Jon 3.07

PUBLISHES
who p. peace, who brings good Is 52.07
who p. salvation, who says to Zion, 52.07

PUBLIUS
named P., who received us and Ac 28.07
the father of P. lay sick with 28.08

PUDENS
as do P. and Linus and Claudia and 2Ti 4.21

PUFFED
of you may be p. up in favor of 1Co 4.06
p. up without reason by his sensuous Col 2.18
or he may be p. up with conceit and 1Ti 3.06
he is p. up with conceit, he knows 6.04

PUFFS
as for all his foes, he p. at them. Ps 10.05
"Knowledge" p. up, but love builds 1Co 8.01

PUL
P. the king of Assyria came against 2Ki 15.19
Menahem gave P. a thousand talents 15.19
the spirit of P. king of Assyria, 1Ch 5.26

PULL
and p. his sandal off his foot, and Deu 25.09
and p. down the altar of Baal which Ju 6.25
And also p. out some from the Ru 2.16
P. them out like sheep for the Jer 12.03
build you up and not p. you down; 42.10
Will he not p. up its roots and cut Eze 17.09
many people to p. it from its 17.09
I will p. down my barns, and build Lk 12.18
not immediately p. him out on a 14.05

PULLED
and which has not p. in the yoke. Deu 21.03
of him that had his sandal p. off. 25.10
for he has p. down the altar of Ju 6.30

PULLED (cont.)

because his altar has been p. down." Ju 6.31
him," because he p. down his altar. 6.32
and p. them up, bar and all, and put 16.03
and p. away the pin, the loom, and 16.14
he p. down and broke in pieces, and 2Ki 23.12
high place he p. down and he broke 23.15
a beam shall be p. out of his Ez 6.11
and p. hair from my head and beard, 9.03
some of them and p. out their hair; Neh 13.25
my hope has he p. up like a tree. Job 19.10
to those who p. out the beard; Is 50.06

PULPIT

on a wooden p. which they had made Neh 8.04

PUNISH

do not p. us because we have done Num 12.11
I am about to p. his house for 1Sa 3.13
'I will p. what Amalek did to 15.02
now, because his anger does not p., Job 35.15
Awake to p. all the nations; Ps 59.05
then I will p. their transgression 89.32
Jerusalem he will p. the arrogant Is 10.12
I will p. the world for its evil, 13.11
the LORD will p. the host of 24.21
of his place to p. the inhabitants 26.21
sword will p. Leviathan the 27.01
Shall I not p. them for these Jer 5.09
Shall I not p. them for these 5.29
at the time that I p. them, 6.15
when I p. them, they shall be 8.12
Shall I not p. them for these 9.09
when I will p. all those who are 9.25
of hosts: "Behold. I will p. them; 11.22
their iniquity and p. their sins." 14.10
I will p. you according to the 21.14
I will p. that man and his 23.34
I will p. the king of Babylon and 25.12
I will p. that nation with the 27.08
I will p. Shemaiah of Nehelam and 29.32
and I will p. all who oppress them. 30.20
And I will p. him and his offspring 36.31
I will p. those who dwell in the 44.13
that I will p. you in this place, in 44.29
upon him, the time when I p. him. 49.08
come, the time when I will p. you. 50.31
And I will p. Bel in Babylon, and 51.44
when I will p. the images of 51.47
he will p., he will uncover your Lam 4.22
and I will p. you for all your Eze 7.03
but I will p. you for your ways, 7.04
and I will p. you for all your 7.08
I will p. you according to your 7.09
and I will p. the house of Jehu for Hos 1.04
And I will p. her for the feast 2.13
I will p. them for their ways, and 4.09
I will not p. your daughters when 4.14
their iniquity, and p. their sins; 8.13
iniquity, he will p. their sins. 9.09
and will p. Jacob according to his 12.02
therefore I will p. you for all Amo 3.02
"that on the day I p. Israel for 3.14
I will p. the altars of Bethel, and 3.14
"I will p. the officials and the Zep 1.08
On that day I will p. every one who 1.09
and I will p. the men who are 1.12
shepherds, and I will p. the leaders; Zec 10.03
and will p. him, and put him with Mt 24.51
and will p. him, and put him with Lk 12.46
them go, finding no way to p. them, Ac 4.21
being ready to p. every disobedience, 2Co 10.06
sent by him to p. those who do 1Pe 2.14

PUNISHABLE

committed a crime p. by death and Deu 21.22
there is no offence p. by death, 22.26

PUNISHED

under his hand, he shall be p. Ex 21.20
a day or two, he is not to be p.; 21.21
so that I p. its iniquity, and the Lev 18.25
hast p. us less than our iniquities Ez 9.13
an iniquity to be p. by the judges; Job 31.11
an iniquity to be p. by the judges, 31.28
When a scoffer is p., the simple becomes Pro 21.11
after many days they will be p. Is 24.22
this is the city which must be p.; Jer 6.06
as I have p. Jerusalem, with the 44.13
as I p. the king of Assyria. 50.18
in bonds of Jerusalem to be p. Ac 22.05
And I p. them often in all the 26.11
as p., and yet not killed; 2Co 6.09
courage when you are p. by him. Heb 22.05

PUNISHMENT

"My p. is greater than I can bear. Gen 4.13
be consumed in the p. of the city." 19.15
no p. shall come upon you for this 1Sa 28.10
p. will overtake us; now therefore come, 2Ki 7.09
wrath brings the p. of the sword, Job 19.29
Add to them p. upon p.; Ps 69.27
What will you do on the day of p., Is 10.03
of the staff of p. which the LORD 30.32
time of their p. they shall perish. Jer 10.15
of Anathoth, the year of their p." 11.23
year of their p., says the LORD. 23.12
the p. of a merciless foe, because 30.14
upon them, the time of their p. 46.21
I am bringing p. upon Amon of 46.25
year of their p., says the LORD. 48.44
I am bringing p. on the king of 50.18
day has come, the time of their p. 50.27
Be not cut off in her p., 51.06
time of their p. they shall perish. 51.18
a man, about the p. of his sins? Lam 3.39
been greater than the p. of Sodom, 4.06
The p. of your iniquity, O daughter 4.22
I will lay the p. of the house of Eze 4.04
upon it, you shall bear their p. 4.04
number of the years of their p.; 4.05
you bear the p. of the house of 4.05
and bear the p. of the house of 4.06
and waste away under their p. 4.17
And they shall bear their p.— 14.10
the p. of the prophet and the 14.10
prophet and the p. of the inquirer 14.10
come, the time of your final p., 21.25
come, the time of their final p. 21.29
at the time of their final p.; 35.05
went astray, shall bear their p. 44.10
GOD, that they shall bear their p. 44.12
a desolation in the day of p.; Hos 5.09
The days of p. have come, the days 9.07
for four, I will not revoke the p.; Amo 1.03
for four, I will not revoke the p.; 1.06
for four, I will not revoke the p.; 1.09
for four, I will not revoke the p.; 1.11
for four, I will not revoke the p.; 1.13
for four, I will not revoke the p.; 2.01
for four, I will not revoke the p.; 2.04
for four, I will not revoke the p.; 2.06
watchmen, of their p., has come; Mic 7.04
shall be the p. to Egypt and the p. to all Zec 14.19
And they will go away into eternal p., Mt 25.46
For such a one this p. by the 2Co 2.06
what longing, what zeal, what p.! 7.11
suffer the p. of eternal destruction 2Th 1.09
How much worse p. do you think will Heb 10.29
unrighteous under p. until the day 2Pe 2.09
For fear has to do with p., 1Jn 4.18
by undergoing a p. of eternal fire. Jud 1.07

PUNITES

of Puvah, the family of the P.; Num 26.23

PUNON
from Zalmonah, and encamped at P. Num 33.42
And they set out from P., 33.43

PUPIL
and great, teacher and p. alike. 1Ch 25.08

PUR
they cast P., that is the lot, Est 3.07
and had cast P., that is the lot, to 9.24
days Purim, after the term P. 9.26

PURAH
to the camp with P. your servant; Ju 7.10
went down with P. his servant to 7.11

PURCHASE
You shall p. food from them for Deu 2.06
right of redemption by p. is yours.' Jer 32.07
Then I took the sealed deed of p., 32.11
the deed of p. to Baruch the son 32.12
witnesses who signed the deed of p., 32.12
sealed deed of p. and this open 32.14
the deed of p. to Baruch the son 32.16

PURCHASED
which Abraham p. from the Hittites. Gen 25.10
is in it were p. from the Hittites." 49.32
people pass by whom thou hast p. Ex 15.16

PURE
And you shall overlay it with p. gold, Ex 25.11
shall make a mercy seat of p. gold; 25.17
You shall overlay it with p. gold, 25.24
of p. gold you shall make them. 25.29
shall make a lampstand of p. gold. 25.31
piece of hammered work of p. gold. 25.36
their trays shall be of p. gold. 25.38
Of a talent of p. gold shall it be 25.39
bring to you p. beaten olive oil 27.20
and two chains of p. gold, twisted 28.14
chains like cords, of p. gold; 28.22
"And you shall make a plate of p. gold, 28.36
And you shall overlay it with p. gold, 30.03
spices with p. frankincense (of 30.34
seasoned with salt, p. and holy; 30.35
and the p. lampstand with all its 31.08
overlaid it with p. gold within and 37.02
And he made a mercy seat of p. gold; 37.06
and he overlaid it with p. gold, 37.11
the vessels of p. gold which were 37.16
also made the lampstand of p. gold. 37.17
piece of hammered work of p. gold. 37.22
snuffers and its trays of p. gold. 37.23
utensils of a talent of p. gold. 37.24
He overlaid it with p. gold, 37.26
and the p. fragrant incense, blended 37.29
chains like cords, of p. gold; 39.15
They also made bells of p. gold, 39.25
plate of the holy crown of p. gold, 39.30
the lampstand of p. gold and its 39.37
to bring you p. oil from beaten Lev 24.02
lampstand of p. gold before the 24.04
a row, upon the table of p. gold. 24.06
And you shall put p. frankincense 24.07
with the p. thou dost show thyself p., 2Sa 22.27
and he overlaid it with p. gold. 1Ki 6.20
inside of the house with p. gold, 6.21
the lampstands of p. gold, 7.49
incense, and firepans, of p. gold; 7.50
Forest of Lebanon were of p. gold; 10.21
and p. gold for the forks, the 1Ch 28.17
it on the inside with p. gold. 2Ch 3.04
their lamps of p. gold to burn 4.20
incense, and firepans, of p. gold; 4.22
and overlaid it with p. gold. 9.17
Forest of Lebanon were of p. gold; 9.20
showbread on the table of p. gold, 13.11
Can a man be p. before his Maker? Job 4.17
if you are p. and upright, surely 8.06
For you say, 'My doctrine is p., 11.04
in my hands, and my prayer is p. 16.17
nor can it be valued in p. gold. 28.19
I am p., and there is no iniquity 33.09
the LORD are promises that are p., Pro 12.06
with the p. thou dost show thyself 18.26
the pure thou dost show thyself p.; 18.26
the commandment of the LORD is p., 19.08
who has clean hands and a p. heart, 24.04
to those who are p. in heart. 73.01
How can a young man keep his way p.? 119.09
words of the p. are pleasing to Pro 15.26
of a man are p. in his own eyes, 16.02
heart clean; I am p. from my sin"? 20.09
what he does is p. and right. 20.11
but the conduct of the p. is right. 21.08
those who are p. in their own eyes 30.12
a choice vine, wholly of p. seed. Jer 2.21
how the p. gold is changed! Lam 4.01
the hair of his head like p. wool; Dan 7.09
long will it be till they are p. Hos 8.05
of the peoples to a p. speech, Zep 3.09
to my name. and a p. offering; Mal 1.11
"Blessed are the p. in heart, Mt 5.08
alabaster jar of ointment of p. nard, Mk 14.03
ointment of p. nard and anointed Jn 12.03
you as a p. bride to her one 2Co 11.02
a sincere and p. devotion to 11.03
and may be p. and blameless for the Php 1.10
whatever is p., whatever is lovely, 4.08
issues from a p. heart and a good 1Ti 1.05
another man's sins; keep yourself p. 5.22
call upon the LORD from a p. heart. 2Ti 2.22
To the p. all things are p., but to the Tit 1.15
and unbelieving nothing is p.; 1.15
our bodies washed with p. water. Heb 10.22
Religion that is p. and undefiled Jas 1.27
But the wisdom from above is first p., 3.17
long for the p. spiritual milk, that 1Pe 2.02
him purifies himself as he is p. 1Jn 3.03
robed in p. bright linen, and their Rev 15.06
bright and p."—for the fine linen 19.08
white and p., followed him on white 19.14
jasper, while the city was p. gold, 21.18
the street of the city was p. gold. 21.21

PURER
Her princes were p. than snow, Lam 4.07
thou who art of p. eyes than to Hab 1.13

PUREST
lamps, and the tongs, of p. gold; 2Ch 4.21

PURGE
So you shall p. the evil from the Deu 13.05
So you shall p. the evil from the 17.07
so you shall p. the evil from 17.12
but you shall p. the guilt of 19.13
so you shall p. the evil from the 19.19
So you shall p. the guilt of 21.09
so you shall p. the evil from your 21.21
so you shall p. the evil from the 22.21
so you shall p. the evil from 22.22
so you shall p. the evil from the 22.24
so you shall p. the evil from the 24.07
he began to p. Judah and Jerusalem 2Ch 34.03
P. me with hyssop, and I shall be Ps 51.07
I will p. out the rebels from among Eze 20.38

PURGED
and p. Judah and Jerusalem. 2Ch 34.05
when he had p. the land and the 34.08

PURIFICATION
of their God and the service of p., Neh 12.45
came for their p. according to the Lk 2.22
there, for the Jewish rites of p., Jn 2.06

PURIFICATION (cont.)
the days of p. would be fulfilled Ac 21.26
When he had made p. for sins, Heb 1.03
sanctifies for the p. of the flesh, 9.13

PURIFIED
and p. the altar, and poured out the Lev 8.15
And the Levites p. themselves from Num 8.21
shall also be p. with the water of 31.23
the Levites had p. themselves Ez 6.20
and the Levites p. themselves; Neh 12.30
and they p. the people and the 12.30
on the ground, p. seven times. Ps 12.06
the next day he p. himself with Ac 21.26
they found me p. in the temple, 24.18
almost everything is p. with blood. Heb 9.22
things to be p. with these rites, 9.23
Having p. your souls by your 1Pe 1.22

PURIFIER
sit as a refiner and p. of silver, Mal 3.03

PURIFIES
If any one p. himself from what is 2Ti 2.21
hopes in him p. himself as he is 1Jn 3.03

PURIFY
and p. yourselves, and change your Gen 35.02
p. yourselves and your captives on Num 31.19
You shall p. every garment, every 31.20
they should p. themselves and come Neh 13.22
p. yourselves, you who bear the Is 52.11
sanctify and p. themselves to go 66.17
atonement for the altar and p. it, Eze 43.26
Many shall p. themselves, and make Dan 12.10
and he will p. the sons of Levi and Mal 3.03
not eat unless they p. themselves; Mk 7.04
the Passover, to p. themselves. Jn 11.55
take these men and p. yourself Ac 21.24
iniquity and to p. for himself a Tit 2.14
p. your conscience from dead works Heb 9.14
and p. your hearts, you men of Jas 4.08

PURIFYING
days in the blood of her p.; Lev 12.04
the days of her p. are completed. 12.04
blood of her p. for sixty-six days. 12.05
the days of her p. are completed, 12.06
(now she was p. herself from her 2Sa 11.04
John's disciples and a Jew over p. Jn 3.25

PURIM
Therefore they called these days P., Est 9.26
these days of P. should never fall 9.28
confirming this second letter about P. 9.29
that these days of P. should be 9.31
Esther fixed these practices of P., 9.32

PURITY
He who loves p. of heart, and whose Pro 22.11
by p., knowledge, forebearance, 2Co 6.06
conduct, in love, in faith, in p. 1Ti 4.12
women like sisters, in all p. 5.02

PURPLE
blue and p. and scarlet stuff and Ex 25.04
and blue and p. and scarlet stuff; 26.01
of blue and p. and scarlet stuff 26.31
of blue and p. and scarlet stuff 26.36
of blue and p. and scarlet stuff 27.16
blue and p. and scarlet stuff, and 28.05
of blue and p. and scarlet stuff, 28.06
blue and p. and scarlet stuff, and 28.08
blue and p. and scarlet stuff, and 28.15
of blue and p. and scarlet stuff, 28.33
blue and p. and scarlet stuff and 35.06
found blue or p. or scarlet stuff 35.23
in blue and p. and scarlet stuff 35.25
in blue and p. and scarlet stuff 35.35
and blue and p. and scarlet stuff, 36.08
of blue and p. and scarlet stuff 36.35
of blue and p. and scarlet stuff 36.37
in blue and p. and scarlet stuff 38.18
in blue and p. and scarlet stuff 38.23
And of the blue and p. and scarlet 39.01
blue and p. and scarlet stuff, and 39.02
the blue and p. and the scarlet 39.03
blue and p. and scarlet stuff, and 39.05
blue and p. and scarlet stuff, and 39.08
of blue and p. and scarlet stuff 39.24
and of blue and p. and scarlet 39.29
and spread a p. cloth over it. Num 4.13
pendants and the p. garments worn Ju 8.26
and in p., crimson, and blue fabrics, 2Ch 2.07
and in p., blue, and crimson fabrics 2.14
of blue and p. and crimson fabrics 3.14
fine linen and p. to silver rings Est 1.06
and a mantle of fine linen and p., 8.15
her clothing is fine linen and p. Pro 31.22
its back of gold, its seat of p.; Sol 3.10
and your flowing locks are like p.; 7.05
their clothing is violet and p.; Jer 10.09
brought up in p. lie on ash heaps. Lam 4.05
warriors clothed in p., governors and Eze 23.06
blue and p. from the coasts of 27.07
p., embroidered work, fine linen, 27.16
interpretation, shall be clothed with p., Dan 5.07
you shall be clothed with p., 5.16
and Daniel was clothed with p., 5.29
And they clothed him in a p. cloak, Mk 15.17
they stripped him of the p. cloak, 15.20
was clothed in p. and fine linen Lk 16.19
head, and arrayed him in a p. robe; Jn 19.02
crown of thorns and the p. robe. 19.05
a seller of p. goods, who was a Ac 16.14
was arrayed in p. and scarlet, Rev 17.04
p., silk and scarlet, all kinds of 18.12
in p. and scarlet, bedecked with 18.16

PURPORTING
or by letter p. to be from us, to 2Th 2.02

PURPOSE
but for this p. have I let you live, Ex 9.16
you have some evil p. in mind. 10.10
any vessel that is used for any p.; Lev 11.32
And so I p. to build a house for 1Ki 5.05
help David with singleness of p. 1Ch 12.33
against them to frustrate their p., Ez 4.05
For this p. he was hired, that I Neh 6.13
which they had made for the p.; 8.04
I know that this was thy p. Job 10.13
and that no p. of thine can be 42.02
to God who fulfils his p. for me. Ps 57.02
They hold fast to their evil p.; 64.05
near who persecute me with evil p.; 119.150
The LORD will fulfil his p. for me; 138.08
has made everything for its p., Pro 16.04
but it is the p. of the LORD that will 19.21
The p. in a man's mind is like deep 20.05
let the p. of the Holy One of Is 5.19
This is the p. that is purposed 14.26
because of the p. which the LORD 19.17
and he shall fulfil all my p.'; 44.28
and I will accomplish all my p.,' 46.10
he shall perform his p. on Babylon, 48.14
and produces a weapon for its p. 54.16
shall accomplish that which I p., 55.11
To what p. does frankincense come Jer 6.20
you, and formed a p. against you. 49.30
because his p. concerning Babylon 51.11
other cities also; for I was sent for this p." Lk 4.43
rejected the p. of God for themselves, 7.30
not consented to their p. and deed, 23.51
No, for this p. I have come to this Jn 12.27
And he has come here for this p., Ac 9.21
to the Lord with steadfast p.; 11.23

PURPOSE (cont.)

I have appeared to you for this p., Ac 26.16
that they had obtained their p., 27.13
them from carrying out their p. 27.43
The p. was to make him the father Rom 4.11
who are called according to his p. 8.28
that God's p. of election might 9.11
up for the very p. of showing my 9.17
the law, then Christ died to no p. Gal 2.21
much of you, but for no good p.; 4.17
For a good p. it is always good to 4.18
according to the p. of his will, Eph 1.05
according to his p. which he set 1.09
according to the p. of him who 1.11
to the eternal p. which he has 3.11
sent him to you for this very p., 6.22
sent him to you for this very p., Col 4.08
of his own p. and the grace which 2Ti 1.09
unchangeable character of his p., Heb 6.17
you have seen the p. of the Lord, Jas 5.11
carry out his p. by being of one Rev 17.17

PURPOSED

Now Solomon p. to build a temple 2Ch 2.01
and as I have p., so shall it stand, Is 14.24
purpose that is p. concerning the 14.26
For the LORD of hosts has p., 14.27
LORD of hosts has p. against Egypt. 19.12
LORD of hosts has p. against them. 19.17
Who has p this against Tyre, the 23.08
The LORD of hosts has p. it, 23.09
I have p., and I will do it. 46.11
for I have spoken, I have p.; Jer 4.28
The LORD has done what he p., Lam 2.17
LORD of hosts p. to deal with us Zec 1.06
"As I p. to do evil to you, when 8.14
so again have I p. in these days to 8.15

PURPOSES

for I know the p. which they are Deu 31.21
for ever such p. and thoughts in 1Ch 29.18
they were rebellious in their p.. Ps 106.43
Edom and the p. which he has Jer 49.20
and the p. which he has formed 50.45
for the LORD's p. against Babylon 51.29
will disclose the p. of the heart. 1Co 4.05

PURSE

us, we will all have one p."— Pro 1.14
Those who lavish gold from the p., Is 46.06
Carry no p., no bag, no sandals; Lk 10.04
you out with no p. or bag or 22.35
now, let him who has a p. take it, 22.36

PURSES

yourselves with p. that do not Lk 12.33

PURSLANE

any taste in the slime of the p.? Job 6.06

PURSUE

they did not p. the sons of Jacob. Gen 35.05
and he will p. them and I will get Ex 14.04
'I will p., I will overtake, I will 15.09
in hot anger p. the manslayer and Deu 19.06
they shall p. you until you perish. 28.22
upon you and p. you and overtake 28.45
p. them quickly, for you will Jos 2.05
were called together to p. them, 8.16
p. your enemies, fall upon their 10.19
After whom do you p.? After a dead dog! 1Sa 24.14
If men rise up to p. you and to 25.29
does my lord p. after his servant? 26.18
"Shall I p. after this band? Shall I overtake 30.08
He answered him, "P.; for you shall 30.08
will set out and p. David tonight. 2Sa 17.01
your lord's servants and p. him, 20.06
Jerusalem to p. Sheba the son of 20.07
after Joab to p. Sheba the son of 20.13
before your foes while they p. you? 24.13
a driven leaf and p. dry chaff? Job 13.25
Why do you, like God, p. me? 19.22
If you say, 'How we will p. him!' 19.28
let the enemy p. me and overtake me, Ps 7.05
the wicked hotly p. the poor; 10.02
and do good; seek peace, and p. it. 34.14
p. and seize him, for there is none 71.11
so do thou p. them with thy tempest 83.15
you who p. deliverance, you who seek Is 51.01
I will p. them with sword, famine, Jer 29.18
to silence; the sword shall p. you. 48.02
Thou wilt p. them in anger and Lam 3.66
for blood, and blood shall p. you; Eze 35.06
therefore blood shall p. you. 35.06
She shall p. her lovers, but not Hos 2.07
the good; the enemy shall p. him. 8.03
and will p. his enemies into Nah 1.08
who did not p. righteousness have Rom 9.30
they did not p. it through faith, 9.32
Let us then p. what makes for peace 14.19
let him seek peace and p. it. 1Pe 3.11

PURSUED

routed them and p. them to Hobath, Gen 14.15
with him and p. him for seven days 31.23
my sin, that you have hotly p. me? 31.36
of Egypt and he p. the people of Ex 14.08
The Egyptians p. them, all Pharaoh's 14.09
The Egyptians p., and went in after 14.23
and defeated them and p. them, Num 14.45
overflow them as they p. after you, Deu 11.04
So the men p. after them on the way Jos 2.07
and as they p. Joshua they were 8.16
left the city open, and p. Israel. 8.17
where they p. them and all of them 8.24
the Egyptians p. your fathers with 24.06
but they p. him, and caught him, and Ju 1.06
And Barak p. the chariots and the 4.16
as Barak p. Sisera, Jael went out to 4.22
Manasseh, and they p. after Midian. 7.23
press of Zeeb, as they p. Midian; 7.25
and he p. them and took the two 8.12
they p. them and trod them down 20.43
and they were p. hard to Gidom, and 20.45
of Mizpah and p. the Philistines, 1Sa 7.11
a shout and p. the Philistines as 17.52
he p. after David in the wilderness 23.25
and Asahel p. Abner, and as he went 2Sa 2.19
But Joab and Abishai p. Abner; 2.24
and p. Israel no more, nor did they 2.28
his brother p. Sheba the son of 20.10
I p. my enemies and destroyed them, 22.38
Syrians fled and Israel p. them. 1Ki 20.20
And Jehu p. him, and said, "Shoot him 2Ki 9.27
army of the Chaldeans p. the king, 25.05
And Abijah p. Jeroboam, and took 2Ch 13.19
were with him p. them as far as 14.13
my honor is p. as by the wind, and Job 30.15
I p. my enemies and overtook them; Ps 18.37
but p. the poor and needy and the 109.16
For the enemy has p. me; he has crushed 143.03
But the army of the Chaldeans p. them, Jer 39.05
army of the Chaldeans p. the king, 52.08
thyself with anger and p. us, Lam 3.43
because he p. his brother with the Amo 1.11
but that Israel who p. the righteousness Rom 9.31
he p. the woman who had borne the Rev 12.13

PURSUER

without strength before the p. Lam 1.06

PURSUERS

and as soon as the p. had gone out, Jos 2.07
the hills, lest the p. meet you; 2.16
days, until the p. have returned; 2.16
three days, until the p. returned; 2.22

PURSUERS (cont.)
for the p. had made search all Jos 2.22
wilderness turned back upon the p. 8.20
cast their p. into the depths, as a Neh 9.11
save me from all my p., and deliver me, Ps 7.01
spear and javelin against my p.! 35.03
therefore your p. shall be swift. Is 30.16
her p. have all overtaken her in Lam 1.03
Our p. were swifter than the 4.19

PURSUES
you shall flee when none p. you. Lev 26.17
and they shall fall when none p. 26.36
to escape a sword, though none p.; 26.37
And if the avenger of blood p. him, Jos 20.05
live, but he who p. evil will die. Pro 11.19
Misfortune p. sinners, but prosperity 13.21
he loves him who p. righteousness. 15.09
He p. them with words, but does not 19.07
He who p. righteousness and kindness 21.21
The wicked flee when no one p., 28.01
He p. them and passes on safely, by Is 41.03
and p. the east wind all day long; Hos 12.01

PURSUING
who were with him, faint yet p. Ju 8.04
and I am p. after Zebah and Zalmunna, 8.05
went up from p. the Philistines; 1Sa 14.46
So Saul returned from p. after David, 23.28
troops came back from p. Israel; 2Sa 18.16
they turned back from p. him. 1Ki 22.33
they turned back from p. him. 2Ch 18.32
with the angel of the LORD p. them! Ps 35.06

PURSUIT
them, and went in p. as far as Dan. Gen 14.14
But David went on with the p., 1Sa 30.10
turn from the p. of their brethren?" 2Sa 2.26
given up the p. of their brethren 2.27
Joab returned from the p. of Abner; 2.30

PURSUITS
follows worthless p. has no sense. Pro 12.11
worthless p. will have plenty of 28.19
gets entangled in civilian p., 2Ti 2.04
fade away in the midst of his p. Jas 1.11

PUSH
with them he shall p. the peoples, Deu 33.17
your God will p. them back before Jos 23.05
these you shall p. the Syrians 1Ki 22.11
these you shall p. the Syrians 2Ch 18.10
Through thee we p. down our foes; Ps 44.05
Because you p. with side and Eze 34.21

PUSHED
she p. against the wall, and pressed Num 22.25
I was p. hard, so that I was falling, Ps 118.13

PUT
"Let the earth p. forth vegetation, Gen 1.11
and there he p. the man whom he had 2.08
the man and p. him in the garden 2.15
I will p. enmity between you and 3.15
lest he p. forth his hand and take 3.22
And the LORD p. a mark on Cain, lest 4.15
So he p. forth his hand and took 8.09
Ham: Cush, Egypt, P., and Canaan. 10.06
But the men p. forth their hands 19.10
Then Abraham p. forth his hand, and 22.10
"P. your hand under my thigh, 24.02
So the servant p. his hand under 24.09
So I p. the ring on her nose, and 24.47
or his wife shall be p. to death." 26.11
and p. them on Jacob her younger 27.15
of the kids she p. upon his hands 27.16
he p. it under his head and lay 28.11
which he had p. under his head and 28.18
and p. the stone back in its place 29.03
and p. them in charge of his sons; 30.35
and he p. his own droves apart, and 30.40
and did not p. them with Laban's 30.40
gods and p. them n the camel's 31.34
and p. a space between drove and 32.16
thigh was p. out of joint as he 32.25
And he p. the maids with their 33.02
"P. away the foreign gods that are 35.02
and p. sackcloth upon his loins, and 37.34
she p. off her widow's garments, and 38.14
and p. on a veil, wrapping herself 38.14
her veil she p. on the garments of 38.19
was in labor, one p. out a hand; 38.28
his house and p. him in charge of 39.04
and he has p. everything that he 39.08
took him and p. him into the 39.20
and he p. them in custody in the 40.03
they should p. me into the dungeon." 40.15
and p. me and the chief baker in 41.10
his hand and p. it on Joseph's hand, 41.42
and p. a gold chain about his neck; 41.42
And he p. them all together in 42.17
brothers, "My money has been p. back; 42.28
p. him in my hands, and I will bring 42.37
do not know who p. our money in 43.22
must have p. treasure in your 43.23
and p. each man's money in the mouth 44.01
and p. my cup, the silver cup, in the 44.02
p. them in charge of my cattle." 47.06
p. your hand under my thigh, and 47.29
p. your right hand upon his head." 48.18
and thus he p. Ephraim before 48.20
and he was p. in a coffin in Egypt. 50.26
and she p. the child in it and Ex 2.03
p. off your shoes from your feet, 3.05
and you shall p. them on your sons 3.22
"P. out your hand, and take it by 4.04
so he p. out his hand and caught it, 4.04
"P. your hand into your bosom. 4.06
And he p. his hand into his bosom; 4.06
"P. your hand back into your bosom. 4.07
So he p. his hand back into his 4.07
to him and p. the words in his 4.15
which I have p. in your power; 4.21
and have p. a sword in their hand 5.21
Thus I will p. a division between 8.23
I could have p. forth my hand and 9.15
and p. it on the two doorposts and 12.07
day you shall p. away leaven out 12.15
I will p. none of the diseases upon 15.26
you which I p. upon the Egyptians; 15.26
and p. an omer of manna in it, and 16.33
Why do you p. the LORD to the proof? 17.02
because they p. the LORD to the 17.07
took a stone and p. it under him, 17.12
the mountain shall be p. to death; 19.12
that he dies shall be p. to death. 21.12
or his mother shall be p. to death. 21.15
of him, shall be p. to death. 21.16
or his mother shall be p. to death. 21.17
owner also shall be p. to death. 21.29
or not he has p. his hand to his 22.08
he has not p. his hand to his 22.11
with a beast shall be p. to death. 22.19
of the blood and p. it in basins, 24.06
gold for it and p. them on its 25.12
And you shall p. the poles into the 25.14
And you shall p. into the ark the 25.16
And you shall p. the mercy seat on 25.21
ark you shall p. the testimony 25.21
and p. the clasps into the loops, 26.11
And you shall p. the mercy seat upon 26.34
and you shall p. the table on the 26.35
poles shall be p. through the 27.07
and p. the two rings on the two 28.23
And you shall p. the two cords of 28.24
and p. them at the two ends of the 28.26

PUT (cont.)

you shall p. the Urim and the Ex 28.30
And you shall p. them upon Aaron 28.41
And you shall p. them in one basket 29.03
and p. on Aaron the coat and the 29.05
and p. the holy crown upon the 29.06
his sons, and p. coats on them, 29.08
of the bull and p. it upon the 29.12
and p. them with its pieces and its 29.17
its blood and p. it upon the tip 29.20
and you shall p. all these in the 29.24
And you shall p. it before the veil 30.06
And you shall p. it between the 30.18
and you shall p. water in it, 30.18
and p. part of it before the 30.36
profanes it shall be p. to death; 31.14
sabbath day shall be p. to death. 31.15
'P. every man his sword on his side, 32.27
and no man p. on his ornaments. 33.04
So now p. off your ornaments from 33.05
by I will p. you in a cleft of the 33.22
he p. a veil on his face; 34.33
and Moses would p. the veil upon 34.35
work on it shall be p. to death; 35.02
the LORD has p. ability and 36.01
whose mind the LORD had p. ability, 36.02
and p. the poles into the rings on 37.05
And he p. the poles through the 38.07
and p. the two rings on the two 39.16
and they p. the two cords of gold 39.17
and p. them at the two ends of the 39.19
and p. the bells between the 39.25
And you shall p. in it the ark of 40.03
And you shall p. the golden altar 40.05
and the altar, and p. water in it. 40.07
and p. upon Aaron the holy garments, 40.13
sons also and p. coats on them, 40.14
and p. in its poles, and raised up 40.18
and p. the covering of the tent 40.19
testimony and p. it into the ark, 40.20
and p. the poles on the ark, and set 40.20
And he p. the table in the tent of 40.22
And he p. the lampstand in the tent 40.24
And he p. the golden altar in the 40.26
And he p. in place the screen for 40.28
and p. water in it for washing, 40.30
priest shall p. fire on the altar, Lev 1.07
and p. frankincense on it, 2.01
And you shall p. oil upon it, and 2.15
priest shall p. some of the blood 4.07
And he shall p. some of the blood 4.18
his finger and p. it on the horns 4.25
his finger and p. it on the horns 4.30
his finger and p. it on the horns 4.34
he shall p. no oil upon it, and 5.11
and shall p. no frankincense on it, 5.11
priest shall p. on his linen 6.10
and p. his linen breeches upon his 6.10
and p. them beside the altar. 6.10
Then he shall p. off his garments, 6.11
and p. on other garments, and carry 6.11
may be p. to any other use, but on 7.24
he p. on him the coat, and p. the ephod 8.07
breastpiece he p. the Urim and the 8.08
with his finger p. it on the horns 8.15
its blood and p. it on the tip of 8.23
and Moses p. some of the blood on 8.24
and he p. all these in the hands of 8.27
the blood and p. it on the horns 9.09
and they p. the fat upon the 9.20
and p. fire in it, and laid incense 10.01
it must be p. into water, and it 11.32
but if water is p. on the seed and 11.38
priest shall p. it on the tip of 14.14
priest shall p. on the tip of the 14.17
hand he shall p. on the head of 14.18
and p. it on the tip of the right 14.25
priest shall p. some of the oil 14.28
blood of the guilt offering was p.; 14.28
hand he shall p. on the head of 14.29
and I p. a leprous disease in a 14.34
stones and p. them in the place of 14.42
He shall p. on the holy linen coat, 16.04
body in water, and then p. them on. 16.04
and p. the incense on the fire 16.13
and p. it on the horns of the altar 16.18
and he shall p. them upon the head 16.21
and shall p. off the linen garments 16.23
which he p. on when he went into 16.23
and p. on his garments, and come 16.24
the deaf or p. a stumbling block 19.14
They shall not be p. to death, 19.20
to Molech shall be p. to death; 20.02
and do not p. him to death, 20.04
or his mother shall be p. to death; 20.09
adulteress shall be p. to death. 20.10
both of them shall be p. to death, 20.11
both of them shall be p. to death; 20.12
they shall be p. to death, their 20.13
a beast, he shall be p. to death; 20.15
they shall be p. to death, their 20.16
or a wizard shall be p. to death; 20.27
And you shall p. pure frankincense 24.07
And they p. him in custody, till the 24.12
of the LORD shall be p. to death; 24.16
the Name, shall be p. to death. 24.16
kills a man shall be p. to death. 24.17
kills a man shall be p. to death. 24.21
leaf shall p. them to flight, 26.36
he shall be p. to death. 27.29
hear, he shall be p. to death. Num 1.51
near, he shall be p. to death. 3.10
came near was to be p. to death. 3.38
then they shall p. on it a covering 4.06
of blue, and shall p. in its poles. 4.06
and p. upon it the plates, the 4.07
goatskin, and shall p. in its poles. 4.08
and they shall p. it with all its 4.10
of goatskin and p. it upon the 4.10
goatskin, and shall p. in its poles; 4.11
and p. them in a cloth of glue, and 4.12
and p. them on the carrying frame. 4.12
and they shall p. on it all the 4.14
goatskin, and shall p. in its poles. 4.14
that they p. out of the camp every 5.02
you shall p. out both male and 5.03
oil upon it and p. no frankincense 5.15
tabernacle and p. it into the 5.17
head and p. it on the fire which 6.18
and shall p. them upon the hands of 6.19
"So shall they p. my name upon the 6.27
is upon you and p. it upon them; 11.17
upon him and p. it upon the 11.25
the LORD would p. his spirit upon 11.29
and yet have p. me to the proof 14.22
They p. him in custody, because it 15.34
"the man shall be p. to death; 15.35
and to p. upon the tassel of each 15.38
p. fire in them and put incense 16.07
in them and p. incense upon them 16.07
Will you p. out the eyes of these 16.14
and p. incense upon it, and every 16.17
and they p. fire in them and laid 16.18
and p. fire therein from off the 16.46
and he p. on the incense, and made 16.47
had sprouted and p. forth buds, 17.08
"P. back the rod of Aaron before 17.10
comes near shall be p. to death." 18.07
and p. them upon Eleazar his son; 20.26
and p. them upon Eleazar his son; 20.28
And the LORD p. a word in Balaam's 23.05
and p. a word in his mouth, and said, 23.16
the murderer shall be p. to death. 35.16
the murderer shall be p. to death. 35.17
the murderer shall be p. to death. 35.18
shall himself p. the murderer to 35.19

PUT (cont.)
him, he shall p. him to death. Num 35.19
the blow shall be p. to death; 35.21
of blood shall p. the murderer to 35.21
shall be p. to death on the 35.30
person shall be p. to death on the 35.30
but he shall be p. to death. 35.31
I will begin to p. the dread and Deu 2.25
and he shall p. them in possession 3.28
"You shall not p. the LORD your God 6.16
and you shall p. them in the ark.' 10.02
and p. the tables in the ark which 10.05
your tribes to p. his name and 12.05
will choose to p. his name there 12.21
of dreams shall be p. to death, 13.05
against him to p. him to death, 13.09
you shall surely p. the inhabitants 13.15
time you first p. the sickle to 16.09
is to die shall be p. to death; 17.06
shall not be p. to death on the 17.06
against him to p. him to death, 17.07
you may not be a foreigner over you, 17.15
and I will p. my words in my mouth, 18.18
hand you shall p. all its males to 20.13
And she shall p. off her captive's 21.13
by death and he is p. to death, 21.22
nor shall a man p. on a woman's 22.05
he may not p. her away all his days. 22.19
he may not p. her away all his days. 22.29
you shall not p. any in your 23.24
you shall not p. a sickle to your 23.25
shall not be p. to death for the 24.16
the children be p. to death for 24.16
man shall be p. to death for his 24.16
and you shall p. it in a basket, and 26.02
and he will p. a yoke of iron upon 28.48
your God will p. all these curses 30.07
and you shall p. them in possession 31.07
p. it in their mouths, that this 31.19
and p. it by the side of the ark of 31.26
and two p. ten thousand to flight, 32.30
they shall p. incense before thee, 33.10
command him, shall be p. to death. Jos 1.18
"P. off your shoes from your feet; 5.15
they p. into the treasury of the 6.24
and they p. dust upon their heads. 7.06
and p. them among their own stuff. 7.11
p. your feet upon the necks of 10.24
and p. their feet on their necks. 10.24
smote them and p. them to death, 10.26
And they p. to the sword all who 11.11
smote them, and p. them to death. 11.17
they p. the Canaanites to forced 17.13
he p. darkness between you and the 24.07
p. away the gods which your fathers 24.14
He said, "Then p. away the foreign 24.23
they p. the Canaanites to forced Ju 1.28
She p. her hand to the tent peg and 5.26
the Israelites p. in seed the 6.03
the meat he p. in a basket, and the 6.19
and the broth he p. in a pot, 6.19
and p. them on this rock, and pour 6.20
him shall be p. to death by 6.31
and p. trumpets into the hands of 7.16
ephod of it and p. it in his city, 8.27
men of Shechem p. men in ambush 9.25
men of Shechem p. confidence in 9.26
Abimelech p. it against the 9.49
So they p. away the foreign gods 10.16
"Let me now p. a riddle to you; 14.12
"P. your riddle, that we may hear it." 14.13
you have p. a riddle to my countrymen, 14.16
and p. a torch between each pair of 15.04
and p. out his hand and seized it, 15.15
and p. them on his shoulders and 16.03
p. your hand upon your mouth, and 18.19
and p. her out to them; 19.25
Then he p. her upon the ass; 19.28
that we may p. them to death, and 20.13
and p. away evil from Israel." 20.13
saying, "He shall be p. to death." 21.05
and p. on your best clothes and go Ru 3.03
P. away your wine from you." 1Sa 1.14
"P. me, I pray you, in one of the 2.36
has the LORD p. us to rout today 4.03
took Dagon and p. him back in his 5.03
and p. in a box at its side the 6.08
And they p. the ark of the LORD on 6.11
then p. away the foreign gods and 7.03
So Israel p. away the Baals and the 7.04
and your asses, and p. them to his work. 8.16
which I said to you, 'P. it aside.'" 9.23
and thus p. disgrace upon all 11.02
the morrow Saul p. the people in 11.11
men, that they may p. them to death." 11.12
a man shall be p. to death this 11.13
but no man p. his hand to his mouth; 14.26
so he p. forth the tip of the staff 14.27
and p. his hand to his mouth; 14.27
he turned he p. them to the worse. 14.47
he p. a helmet of bronze on his 17.38
used to them." And David p. them off. 17.39
and p. them in his shepherd's bag, in 17.40
And David p. his hand in his bag 17.49
but he p. his armor in his tent. 17.54
lives, he shall not be p. to death." 19.06
on the bed and p. a pillow of 19.13
"Why should he be p. to death? 20.32
determined to p. David to death. 20.33
king would not p. forth their hand 22.17
of the priests, he p. to the sword; 22.19
and sheep, he p. to the sword. 22.19
to p. forth my hand against him, 24.06
'I will not p. forth my hand 24.10
when the LORD p. me into your 24.18
for who can p. forth his hand 26.09
that I should p. forth my hand 26.11
and I would not p. forth my hand 26.23
And Saul had p. the mediums and the 28.03
himself and p. on other garments, 28.08
and she p. it before Saul and his 28.25
They p. his armor in the temple of 31.10
not afraid to p. forth your hand 2Sa 1.14
who p. ornaments of gold upon your 1.24
Uzzah p. out his hand to the ark of 6.06
because he p. forth his hand to 6.07
whom I p. away from before you, 7.15
he measured to be p. to death, 8.02
Then David p. garrisons in Aram of 8.06
And he p. garrisons in Edom; 8.14
throughout all Edom he p. garrisons, 8.14
of his men he p. in the charge of 10.10
"The LORD also has p. away your sin; 12.13
"P. this woman out of my presence, 13.17
So his servant p. her out, and bolted the 13.18
And Tamar p. ashes on her head, and 13.19
and p. on mourning garments; 14.02
So Joab p. the words in her mouth. 14.03
it was he who p. all these words in 14.19
he would p. out his hand, and take 15.05
I would not p. forth my hand 18.12
not Shimei be p. to death for this, 19.21
any one be p. to death in Israel 19.22
and p. them in a house under guard, 20.03
because he p. the Gibeonites to 21.01
is it for us to p. any man to 21.04
They were p. to death in the first 21.09
'I will not p. you to death with 1Ki 2.08
shall be p. to death this day." 2.24
not at this time p. you to death, 2.26
The king p. Benaiah the son of 2.35
and the king p. Zadok the priest in 2.35
until the LORD p. them under the 5.03
He p. the cherubim in the innermost 6.27
which Moses p. there at Horeb, 8.09
and p. my name there for ever; 9.03

PUT (cont.)

and the king p. them in the House	1Ki 10.17
which God had p. into his mind.	10.24
where I have chosen to p. my name.	11.36
yoke that your father p. upon us'?"	12.09
Bethel, and the other he p. in Dan.	12.29
of Israel, to p. his name there.	14.21
He p. away the male cult prostitutes	15.12
on the wood, but p. no fire to it;	18.23
on the wood, and put no fire to it.	18.23
of your god, but p. no fire to it."	18.25
And he p. the wood in order, and cut	18.33
and p. his face between his knees.	18.42
and p. commanders in their places;	20.24
let us p. sackcloth on our loins	20.31
and p. ropes on their heads, and	20.32
and p. sackcloth upon his flesh, and	21.27
the LORD has p. a lying spirit in	22.23
"P. this fellow in prison, and feed	22.27
me a new bowl, and p. salt in it."	2Ki 2.20
for he p. away the pillar of Baal	3.02
all who were able to p. on armor,	3.21
and p. there for him a bed, a table,	4.10
and p. them in the house; and he sent	5.24
and p. it under him on the bare	9.13
and p. their heads in baskets, and	10.07
So when they p. them to the sword,	10.25
and she p. him and his nurse in a	11.02
with them and p. them under oath	11.04
and p. the crown upon him, and gave	11.12
the threshold p. in it all the	12.09
But he did not p. to death the	14.06
shall not be p. to death for the	14.06
the children be p. to death for	14.06
and p. it on the north side of his	16.14
and p. it upon a pediment of stone.	16.17
and p. them in the shrines of the	17.29
and p. them in Halah, and on the	18.11
Behold, I will p. a spirit in him, so	19.07
I will p. my hook in your nose and	19.28
"In Jerusalem will I p. my name."	21.04
of Israel, I will p. my name for ever;	21.07
Moreover Josiah p. away the mediums	23.24
And Pharaoh Neco p. him in bonds at	23.33
and p. out the eyes of Zedekiah, and	25.07
and put them to death at Riblah in	25.21
So Jehoiachin p. off his prison	25.29
Ham: Cush, Egypt, P., and Canaan.	1Ch 1.08
men whom David p. in charge of the	6.31
who p. to flight the inhabitants of	8.13
And they p. his armor in the temple	10.10
and p. to flight all those in the	12.15
Uzzah p. out his hand to hold the	13.09
him because he p. forth his hand	13.10
Then David p. garrisons in Syria of	18.06
And he p. garrisons in Edom;	18.13
of his men he p. in the charge of	19.11
and he p. his sword back into its	21.27
a necklace and p. them on the tops	2Ch 3.16
and p. them on the chains.	3.16
which Moses p. there at Horeb,	5.10
and the king p. them in the House	9.16
which God had p. into his mind.	9.23
yoke that your father p. upon us'?"	10.09
and p. commanders in them, and	11.11
And he p. shields and spears in all	11.12
of Israel to p. his name there.	12.13
and p. away the abominable idols	15.08
should be p. to death, whether young	15.13
and p. him in the stocks, in prison,	16.10
the LORD has p. a lying spirit in	18.22
P. this fellow in prison, and feed	18.26
brought to Jehu and p. to death.	22.09
and she p. him and his nurse in a	22.11
and p. the crown upon him, and gave	23.11
But he did not p. their children to	25.04
shall not be p. to death for the	25.04
the children be p. to death for	25.04
Why should you be p. to death?"	25.16
the vestibule and p. out the lamps,	29.07
and the Levites were p. to shame,	30.15
of Israel, I will p. my name for ever;	33.07
he also p. commanders of the army	33.14
"P. the holy ark in the house which	35.03
to Babylon and p. them in his	36.07
kingdom and also p. it in writing:	36.22
kingdom and also p. it in writing:	Ez 1.01
go and p. them in the temple which	5.15
you shall p. them in the house of	6.05
that shall p. forth a hand to	6.12
who p. such a thing as this into	7.27
with our God to p. away all these	10.03
themselves to p. away their wives,	10.19
and they p. them away with their	10.44
what my God had p. into my heart	Neh 2.12
nobles did not p. their necks to	3.05
Then God p. it into my mind to	7.05
had previously p. the cereal	13.05
palace and p. in custody of Hegai,	Est 2.08
that they may p. it into the king's	3.09
his clothes and p. on sackcloth	4.01
all alike are to be p. to death,	4.11
day Esther p. on her royal robes	5.01
Hast thou not p. a hedge about him	Job 1.10
But p. forth thy hand now, and touch	1.11
himself do not p. forth your hand."	1.12
But p. forth thy hand now, and touch	2.05
I will p. off my sad countenance,	9.27
p. it far away, and let not wickedness	11.14
in my teeth, and p. my life in my hand.	13.14
it will bud and p. forth branches	14.09
"Yea, the light of the wicked is p. out,	18.05
and his lamp above him is p. out.	18.06
that God has p. me in the wrong,	19.06
"He has p. my brethren far from me,	19.13
the lamp of the wicked is p. out?	21.17
die I will not p. away my integrity	27.05
Men p. an end to darkness, and	28.03
I p. on righteousness, and it	29.14
my Maker soon p. an end to me.	32.22
to make the ground p. forth grass?	38.27
Who has p. wisdom in the clouds, or	38.36
Will you even p. me in the wrong?	40.08
Can you p. a rope in his nose, or	41.02
or will you p. him on leash for	41.05
and p. your trust in the LORD.	Ps 4.05
Thou hast p. more joy in my heart	4.07
and be p. to shame in a moment.	6.10
thou hast p. all things under his	8.06
know thy name p. their trust in	9.10
P. them in fear, O LORD! Let the nations	9.20
who does not p. out his money at	15.05
statutes I did not p. away from me.	18.22
For you will p. them to flight;	21.12
I trust, let me not be p. to shame;	25.02
that wait for thee be p. to shame;	25.03
let me not be p. to shame, for I	25.20
let me never be p. to shame; in thy	31.01
Let me not be p. to shame, O LORD,	31.17
let the wicked be p. to shame,	31.17
he p. the deeps in storehouses.	33.07
Let them be p. to shame and dishonor	35.04
Let them be p. to shame and confusion	35.26
they are not p. to shame in evil	37.19
He p. a new song in my mouth, a song	40.03
and p. their trust in the LORD.	40.03
Let them be p. to shame and confusion	40.14
and hast p. to confusion those who	44.07
and p. a new and right spirit	51.10
they will be p. to shame, for God	53.05
thy faithfulness p. an end to them.	54.05
am afraid, I p. my trust in thee.	56.03
p. thou my tears in thy bottle!	56.08
he will p. to shame those who	57.03
P. no confidence in extortion, set	62.10
hope in thee be p. to shame	69.06

PUT (cont.)
Let them be p. to shame and confusion Ps 70.02
let me never be p. to shame! 71.01
May my accusers be p. to shame and 71.13
they have been p. to shame and 71.24
thou dost p. an end to those who 73.27
not the downtrodden be p. to shame; 74.21
And he p. his adversaries to rout; 78.66
he p. them to everlasting shame. 78.66
Let them be p. to shame and dismayed 83.17
and p. away thy indignation toward 85.04
may see and be p. to shame because 86.17
Thou hast p. me in the depths of 88.06
and p. me to the proof, though they 95.09
worshipers of images are p. to shame, 97.07
his neck was p. in a collar of iron; 105.18
and p. God to the test in the 106.14
Let my assailants be p. to shame; 109.28
p. your trust in the LORD! He is their 115.10
LORD than to p. confidence in man. 118.08
LORD than to p. confidence in 118.09
Then I shall not be p. to shame, 119.06
P. false ways far from me; and 119.29
O LORD let me not be p. to shame! 119.31
and shall not be p. to shame; 119.46
Let the godless be p. to shame. 119.78
that I may not be p. to shame! 119.80
let me not be p. to shame in my 119.116
the righteous p. forth their hands 125.03
He shall not be p. to shame when he 127.05
hate Zion be p. to shame and 129.05
love, for in thee I p. my trust. 143.08
P. not your trust in princes, in a 146.03
P. away from you crooked speech, and Pro 4.24
and p. devious talk far from you. 4.24
slothful will be p. to forced labor. 12.24
lamp of the wicked will be p. out. 13.09
lamp will be p. out in utter 20.20
and p. a knife to your throat if 23.02
lamp of the wicked will be p. out. 24.20
Do not p. yourself forward in the 25.06
than to be p. lower in the 25.07
p. your hand on your mouth. 30.32
also he has p. eternity into man's Ecc 3.11
he must p. forth more strength; 10.10
and p. away pain from your body; 11.10
I had p. off my garment, how could I Sol 5.03
my garment, how could I p. it on? 5.03
My beloved p. his hand to the latch, 5.04
who p. darkness for light and light Is 5.20
who p. bitter for sweet and sweet 5.20
and I will not p. the LORD to the 7.12
but we will p. cedars in their place." 9.10
child shall p. his hand on the 11.08
They shall p. forth their hand 11.14
I will p. an end to the pride of 13.11
shall blossom and p. forth shoots, 27.06
and p. in wheat in rows and barley 28.25
men shall be p. to forced labor. 31.08
Behold, I will p. a spirit in him, so 37.07
I will p. my hook in your nose and 37.29
you shall be p. to shame and 41.11
I will p. in the wilderness the 41.19
I have p. my spirit upon him, he 42.01
back and utterly p. to shame, 42.17
P. me in remembrance, let us argue 43.26
know, that they may be p. to shame. 44.09
his fellows shall be p. to shame, 44.11
they shall be p. to shame together. 44.11
All of them are p. to shame and 45.16
shall not be p. to shame or 45.17
I will p. salvation in Zion, for 46.13
p. off your veil, strip off your 47.02
you shall p. them all on as an 49.18
exiled and p. away, but who has 49.21
for me shall not be p. to shame. 49.23
divorce, with which I p. her away? 50.01
transgressions your mother was p. away. 50.01
that I shall not be p. to shame; 50.07
Awake, awake, p. on strength, O arm of 51.09
And I have p. my words in your 51.16
and I will p. it into the hand of 51.23
Awake, awake, p. on your strength, O 52.01
p. on your beautiful garments, O 52.01
he has p. him to grief; when he makes 53.10
for you will not be p. to shame; 54.04
mouth wide and p. out your tongue? 57.04
He p. on righteousness as a breastplate, 59.17
he p. on garments of vengeance for 59.17
which I have p. in your mouth, 59.21
You who p. the LORD in remembrance, 62.06
Where is he who p. in the midst of 63.11
but you shall be p. to shame; 65.13
is they who shall be p. to shame. 66.05
P., and Lud, who draw the bow, to 66.19
Then the LORD p. forth his hand and Jer 1.09
I have p. my words in your mouth. 1.09
You shall be p. to shame by Egypt 2.36
as you were p. to shame by Assyria 2.36
The wise men shall be p. to shame, 8.09
and p. no trust in any brother; 9.04
goldsmith is p. to shame by his 10.14
and p. it on your loins, and do not 13.01
of the LORD, and p. it on my loins. 13.02
forsake thee shall be p. to shame; 17.13
Let those be p. to shame who 17.18
me, but let me not be p. to shame; 17.18
and p. him in the stocks that were 20.02
the wicked he will p. to the sword, 25.31
certain that if you p. me to death, 26.15
and all Judah p. him to death? 26.19
the king sought to p. him to death; 26.21
to the people to be p. to death. 26.24
yoke-bars, and p. them on your neck. 27.02
and p. its neck under the yoke of 27.08
I have p. upon the neck of all 28.14
to p. him in the stocks and collar. 29.26
I will p. my law within them, and I 31.33
and p. them in an earthenware 32.14
and I will p. the fear of me in 32.40
having p. the scroll in the chamber 36.20
he had not yet been p. in prison. 37.04
that you have p. me in prison? 37.18
king, "Let this man be p. to death, 38.04
that they had p. Jeremiah into 38.07
"P. the rags and clothes between 38.12
you not be sure to p. me to death? 38.15
I will not p. you to death or 38.16
and we will not p. you to death,' 38.25
He p. out the eyes of Zedekiah, and 39.07
you have p. your trust in me, says 39.18
p. on your coats of mail! 46.04
of Ethiopia and P. who handle the 46.09
of Egypt shall be p. to shame, 46.24
P. yourself into your scabbard, rest 47.06
Kiriathaim is p. to shame, it is 48.01
the fortress is p. to shame and 48.01
Moab is p. to shame, for it is 48.20
Bel is p. to shame, Merodach is 50.02
Her images are p. to shame, 50.02
goldsmith is p. to shame by his 51.17
whole land shall be p. to shame, 51.47
'We are p. to shame, for we have 51.51
He p. out the eyes of Zedekiah, and 52.11
and p. him in prison till the day 52.11
and p. them to death at Riblah in 52.27
So Jehoiachin p. off his prison 52.33
on their heads and p. on sackcloth; Lam 2.10
he has p. heavy chains on me; 3.07
let him p. his mouth in the dust— 3.29
and p. siegeworks against it, and Eze 4.02
I will p. cords upon you, so that 4.08
and p. them into a single vessel, 4.09
I will p. an end to their proud 7.24
He p. forth the form of a hand, and 8.03

PUT (cont.)

Lo, they p. the branch to their nose Eze 8.17
and p. a mark upon the foreheads of 9.04
and p. it into the hands of the man 10.07
and p. a new spirit within them; 11.19
I will p. an end to this proverb, 12.23
and p. bracelets on your arms, and a 16.11
And I p. a ring on your nose, and 16.12
branches and p. forth foliage. 17.06
With hooks they p. him in a cage, 19.09
and I will p. you in and melt you. 22.20
Thus I will p. an end to your 23.27
and they p. bracelets upon the 23.42
Thus will I p. an end to lewdness 23.48
p. in it the pieces of flesh, all 24.04
she p. it on the bare rock, she did 24.07
and p. your shoes on you feet; 24.17
"Persia and Lud and P. were in your 27.10
I will p. hooks in your jaws, and 29.04
Ethiopia, and P., and Lud, and all 30.05
I will p. an end to the wealth of 30.10
and p. an end to the images, in 30.13
so I will p. fear in the land of 30.13
and p. my sword in his hand: but I 30.24
When I p. my sword into the hand of 30.25
and p. darkness upon your land, says 32.08
and p. a stop to their feeding the 34.10
a new spirit I will p. within you; 36.26
And I will p. my spirit within you, 36.27
and p. breath in you, and you shall 37.06
And I will p. my Spirit within you, 37.14
and p. hooks into your jaws, and I 38.04
and P. are with them, all of them 38.05
they shall p. the most holy 42.13
they shall p. on other garments 42.14
Now let them p. away their idolatry 43.09
and p. it on the four horns of the 43.20
they shall p. off the garments in 44.19
and they shall p. on other garments, 44.19
P. away violence and oppression, and 45.09
offering and p. it on the doorposts 45.19
up, and whom he would me p. down. Dan 5.19
of gold was p. about his neck, 5.29
and shall p. down three kings. 7.24
to p. an end to sin, and atone 9.24
commander shall p. an end to his 11.18
and I will p. an end to the kingdom Hos 1.04
that she p. away her harlotry from 2.02
And I will p. an end to all her 2.11
Ephraim shall be p. to shame, 10.06
but I will p. Ephraim to the yoke, 10.11
shall never again be p. to shame. Joe 2.26
shall never again be p. to shame. 2.27
P. in the sickle, for the harvest is 3.13
O you who p. far away the evil day, Amo 6.03
and p. on sackcloth, from the Jon 3.05
and the diviners p. to shame; Mic 3.07
you shall p. away, but not save, and 6.14
P. no trust in a neighbor, have no 7.05
P. and the Libyans were her helpers. Nah 3.09
and p. the arrows to the string. Hab 3.09
shall not be p. to shame because Zep 3.11
earns wages to p. them into a bag Hag 1.06
"Let them p. a clean turban on his Zec 3.05
So they p. a clean turban on his 3.05
the LORD will p. a shield about 12.08
he will not p. on a hairy mantle in 13.04
And I will p. this third into the 13.09
and I will p. you out of my presence. Mal 2.03
and thereby p. me to the test, says 3.10
but when they p. God to the test 3.15
and unwilling to p. her to shame, Mt 1.19
a lamp and p. it under a bushel, 5.15
the guard, and you be p. in prison; 5.25
your body, what you shall p. on. 6.25
Neither is new wine p. into old 9.17
but new wine is p. into fresh 9.17
when the crowd had been p. outside, 9.25
parents and have them p. to death; 10.21
I will p. my Spirit upon him, and he 12.18
it empty, swept, and p. in order. 12.44
Another parable he p. before them, 13.24
Another parable he p. before them, 13.31
and bound him and p. him in prison, 14.03
he wanted to p. him to death, 14.05
and they p. them at his feet, and he 15.30
he p. him in the midst of them, 18.02
and went and p. him in prison till 18.30
together, let no man p. asunder." 19.06
of divorce, and to p. her away?" 19.07
and p. their garments on them, and 21.07
"He will p. those wretches to a 21.41
"Why p. me to the test, you hypocrites?" 22.18
till I p. thy enemies under thy 22.44
tribulation, and p. you to death; 24.09
and p. him with the hypocrites; 24.51
"P. your sword back into its place; 26.52
that they might p. him to death, 26.59
against Jesus to p. him to death; 27.01
not lawful to p. them into the 27.06
stripped him and p. a scarlet robe 27.28
of thorns they p. it on his head, 27.29
and p. a reed in his right hand. 27.29
and p. his own clothes on him, and 27.31
over his head they p. the charge 27.37
and p. it on a reed, and gave it to 27.48
brought in to be p. under a bushel, Mk 4.21
But he p. them all outside, and took 5.40
sandals and not p. on two tunics. 6.09
he p. his fingers into his ears, and 7.33
and p. him in the midst of them; 9.36
of divorce, and to p. her away." 10.04
together, let not man p. asunder." 10.09
to them, "Why p. me to the test? 12.15
till I p. thy enemies under thy 12.36
Many rich people p. in large sums. 12.41
and p. in two copper coins, which 12.42
poor widow has p. in more than all 12.43
her poverty has p. in everything 12.44
parents and have them p. to death; 13.12
against Jesus to p. him to death; 14.55
crown of thorns they p. it on him. 15.17
and p. his own clothes on him. 15.20
p. it on a reed and gave it to him 15.36
he has p. down the mighty from Lk 1.52
rose up and p. him out of the city, 4.29
he asked him to p. out a little 5.03
"P. out into the deep and let down 5.04
wine must be p. into fresh wineskins. 5.38
over, will be p. into your lap. 6.38
a child and p. him by his side, 9.47
stood up to p. him to the test, 10.25
he finds it swept that p. in order. 11.25
your body, what you shall p. on. 12.22
and p. him with the unfaithful. 12.46
and the officer p. you in prison. 12.58
I dig about it and p. on manure. 13.08
his adversaries were p. to shame; 13.17
the best robe, and p. it on him; 15.22
and p. a ring on his hand, and shoes 15.22
when I am p. out of the stewardship.' 16.04
did you not p. my money into the 19.23
a poor widow p. in two copper 21.02
poor widow has p. in more than all 21.03
of her poverty p. in all the 21.04
some of you they will p. to death; 21.16
seeking how to p. him to death; 22.02
led away to be p. to death with 23.32
John had not yet been p. in prison. Jn 3.24
have no man to p. me into the pool 5.07
"He p. clay on my eyes, and I washed, 9.15
he was to be p. out of the synagogue. 9.22
counsel how to p. him to death. 11.53
used to take what was p. into it. 12.06
planned to p. Lazarus also to 12.10

PUT (cont.)

they should be p. out of the Jn 12.42
had already p. it into the heart 13.02
They will p. you out of the synagogues; 16.02
"P. your sword into its sheath; 18.11
for us to p. any man to death." 18.31
and p. it on his head, and arrayed 19.02
a title and p. it on the cross; 19.19
so they p. a sponge full of the 19.29
"P. your finger here, and see my 20.27
and p. out your hand, and place it 20.27
he p. on his clothes, for he was 21.07
And they p. forward two, Joseph Ac 1.23
them and p. them in custody until 4.03
apostles and p. them in the common 5.18
men whom you p. in prison are 5.25
the men to be p. outside for a 5.34
But Peter p. them all outside and 9.40
They p. him to death by hanging him 10.39
he p. him in prison, and delivered 12.04
yourself and p. on your sandals." 12.08
that they should be p. to death. 12.19
day Herod p. on his royal robes, 12.21
he p. them into the inner prison 16.24
whom the Jews had p. forward. 19.33
p. them off, saying, "When Lysias the 24.22
when they were p. to death I cast 26.10
we p. to sea, accompanied by Aristarchus, 27.02
The next day we p. in at Sidon; 27.03
for Italy, and p. us on board. 27.06
advised to p. to sea from there, on 27.12
of sticks and p. them on the fire, 28.03
they p. on board whatever we needed 28.10
whom God p. forward as an expiation Rom 3.25
who was p. to death for our trespasses 4.25
the Spirit you p. to death the 8.13
in him will not be p. to shame. 9.33
believes in him will be p. to shame. 10.11
of darkness and p. on the armor of 13.12
But p. on the Lord Jesus Christ, and 13.14
decide never to p. a stumbling 14.13
rather than p. an obstacle in the 1Co 9.12
We must not p. the Lord to the test, 10.09
until he has p. all his enemies 15.25
"For God has p. all things in 15.27
"All things are p. in subjection 15.27
is excepted who p. all things 15.27
to him who p. all things under him, 15.28
nature must p. on the imperishable, 15.53
nature must p. on immortality. 15.53
of you is to p. something aside 16.02
see that you p. him at ease among 16.10
he has p. his seal upon us and 2Co 1.22
not to p. it too severely—to you 2.05
who p. a veil over his face so that 3.13
and long to p. on our heavenly 5.02
We p. no obstacle in any one's way, 6.03
in you, I was not p. to shame; 7.14
you, I shall not be p. to shame. 10.08
into Christ have p. on Christ. Gal 3.27
and he has p. all things under his Eph 1.22
P. off your old nature which 4.22
and p. on the new nature, created 4.24
and slander be p. away from you, 4.31
P. on the whole armor of God, that 6.11
and having p. on the breastplate of 6.14
that I am p. here for the defense Php 1.16
and p. no confidence in the flesh. 3.03
P. to death therefore what is Col 3.05
But now p. them all away: anger, 3.08
that you have p. off the old 3.09
and have p. on the new nature, which 3.10
P. on then, as God's chosen ones, holy 3.12
And above all these p. on love, 3.14
and p. on the breastplate of faith 1Th 5.08
If you p. these instructions before 1Ti 4.06
an opponent may be p. to shame, Tit 2.08
"I will p. my trust in him." And again Heb 2.13
where your fathers p. me to the 3.09
I will p. my laws into their minds, 8.10
of the age to p. away sin by the 9.26
I will p. my laws on their hearts, 10.16
in war, p. foreign armies to flight. 11.34
lame may not be p. out of joint 12.13
Therefore p. away all filthiness Jas 1.21
If we p. bits into the mouths of 3.03
So p. away all malice and all guile 1Pe 2.01
in him will not be p. to shame. 2.06
you should p. to silence the 2.15
in Christ may be p. to shame. 3.16
being p. to death in the flesh but 3.18
who likes to p. himself first, does 3Jn 1.09
taught Balak to p. a stumbling Rev 2.14
"P. in your sickle, and reap, for the 14.15
"P. in your sickle, and gather the 14.18
for God has p. it into their hearts 17.17

PUTEOLI

on the second day we came to P. Ac 28.13

PUTHITES

the P., the Shumathites, and the 1Ch 2.53

PUTIEL

to wife one of the daughters of P.; Ex 6.25

PUTS

it or whoever p. any of it on an Ex 30.33
The word that God p. in my mouth, Num 22.38
speak what the LORD p. in my mouth?" 23.12
of divorce and p. it in her hand Deu 24.01
of divorce and p. it in her hand 24.03
and p. out her hand and seizes him 25.11
One man of you p. to flight a Jos 23.10
boast himself as he that p. it off. 1Ki 20.11
Even in his servants he p. no trust, Job 4.18
Behold, God p. no trust in his holy 15.15
"Man p. his hand to the flinty rock, 28.09
he p. my feet in the stocks, and 33.11
The lot p. an end to disputes and Pro 18.18
A wicked man p. on a bold face, but 21.29
when your neighbor p. you to shame? 25.08
She p. her hands to the distaff, and 31.19
The fig tree p. forth its figs, and Sol 2.13
against him who p. nothing into Mic 3.05
And no one p. a piece of unshrunk Mt 9.16
tender and p. forth its leaves, you 24.32
And no one p. new wine into old Mk 2.22
at once he p. in the sickle, because 4.29
and p. forth large branches, so that 4.32
tender and p. forth its leaves, you 13.28
leaves home and p. his servants in 13.34
new garment and p. it upon an old Lk 5.36
And no one p. new wine into old 5.37
or p. it under a bed, but puts it on 8.16
but p. it on a stand, that those who 8.16
"No one who p. his hand to the plow 9.62
lighting a lamp p. it in a cellar 11.33
When the perishable p. on the 1Co 15.54
and the mortal p. on immortality, 15.54
be to God who p. the same earnest 2Co 8.16
or p. on airs, or strikes you in the 11.20
them and p. them out of the church. 3Jn 1.10

PUTTEST

Thou p. my feet in the stocks, and Job 13.27

PUTTING

p. it on her shoulder, along with Gen 21.14
p. them outside the camp, that they Num 5.03
capturing it and p. it to the sword Jos 19.47
p. their hands to their mouths, was Ju 7.06
p. the little ones and the cattle 18.21
and p. innocent blood upon the 1Ki 2.05
p. his mouth and upon his mouth, his 2Ki 4.34
p. down one and lifting up another. Ps 75.07

PUTTING (cont.)
p. to death persons who should not Eze 13.19
his heart and p. the stumbling 14.07
with him, p. him under oath. (The chief 17.13
the multitude p. money into the Mk 12.41
saw the rich p. their gifts into Lk 21.01
trial of God by p. a yoke upon the Ac 15.10
And p. to sea from there we sailed 27.04
and p. his hands on him healed him. 28.08
P. in at Syracuse, we stayed there 28.12
so that by p. it on we may not be 2Co 5.03
Therefore, p. away falsehood, let Eph 4.25
by p. off the body of flesh in the Col 2.11
p. everything in subjection under Heb 2.08
"Now in p. everything in subjection 2.08
since I know that the p. off of my 2Pe 1.14

PUVAH
Lola, P., Iob, and Shimron. Gen 46.13
of P., the family of the Punites; Num 26.23

PYRE
its p. made deep and wide, with fire Is 30.33

PYRRHUS
the son of P., accompanied him; Ac 20.04

Q

QUAILS
In the evening q. came up and Ex 16.13
and it brought q. from the sea, Num 11.31
the next day, and gathered the q.; 11.32
They asked, and he brought q., Ps 105.40

QUAKE
Thou hast made the land to q., Ps 60.02
the cherubim; let the earth q.! 99.01
mountains might q. at thy presence— Is 64.01
the nations q. at the sound of its Eze 31.16
shall q. at my presence, and the 38.20
The mountains q. before him, the Nah 1.05

QUAKED
and the whole mountain q. greatly. Ex 19.18
The mountains q. before the LORD, Ju 5.05
the earth q.; and it became 1Sa 14.15
of the heavens trembled and q., 2Sa 22.08
of the mountains trembled and q., Ps 18.07
the earth q., the heavens poured 68.08
yon Sinai q. at the presence of God, 68.08
smote them, and the mountains q.; Is 5.25
the mountains q. at thy presence. 64.03

QUAKES
their stallions the whole land q. Jer 8.16
At his wrath the earth q., and the nations 10.10
The earth q. before them, the Joe 2.10

QUAKING
they were q., and all the hills Jer 4.24
"Son of man, eat your bread with q., Eze 12.18

QUALIFIED
able men q. for the service; 1Ch 26.08
who has q. us to be ministers of a 2Co 3.06
who has q. us to share in the Col 1.12

QUANTITIES
as bronze in q. beyond weighing, 1Ch 22.03
brought great q. of cedar to David. 22.04
besides great q. of onyx and stones 29.02
Solomon made all these things in great q., 2Ch 4.18

QUANTITY
measures of length or weight or q. Lev 19.35
and a very great q. of spices, 1Ki 10.10
in great q. before his death. 1Ch 22.05
and all measures of q. or size. 23.29
and a very great q. of spices, 2Ch 9.09
to haul it in, for the q. of fish. Jn 21.06

QUARREL
and over that they did not q.; Gen 26.22
said to them, "Do not q. on the way." 45.24
"When men q. and one strikes the Ex 21.18
see how he is seeking a q. with me." 2Ki 5.07
so quit before the q. breaks out. Pro 17.14
meddles in a q. not his own is 26.17
fast only to q. and to fight and Is 58.04

QUARRELED
of Gerar q. with Isaac's herdsmen, Gen 26.20
well, and they q. over that also; 26.21
a man of Israel q. in the camp, Lev 24.10
and they q. with one another in the 2Sa 14.06

QUARRELING
but q. is like the bars of a castle. Pro 18.19
and a wife's q. is a continual 19.13
from strife; but every fool will be q. 20.03
and q. and abuse will cease. 22.10
there is no whisperer, q. ceases. 26.20
as they were q. and would have Ac 7.26
licentiousness, not in q. and jealousy. Rom 13.13
people that there is q. among you, 1Co 1.11
that perhaps there may be q., 2Co 12.20
holy hands without anger or q.; 1Ti 2.08
to avoid q., to be gentle, and to Tit 3.02

QUARRELS
you know that they breed q. 2Ti 2.23
and q. over the law, for they are Tit 3.09

QUARRELSOME
so is a q. man for kindling strife. Pro 26.21
not q., and no lover of money. 1Ti 3.03
must not be q. but kindly to every 2Ti 2.24

QUARRIED
they q. out great, costly stones in 1Ki 5.17
buy timber and q. stone for making 2Ki 12.12
timber and q. stone to repair the 22.06
and the builders to buy q. stone, 2Ch 34.11

QUARRIES
He who q. stones is hurt by them; Ecc 10.09

QUARRY
was with stone prepared at the q.; 1Ki 6.07
thousand to q. in the hill country, 2Ch 2.02
thousand to q. in the hill country, 2.18
and to the q. from which you were Is 51.01

QUART
"A q. of wheat for a denarius, and Rev 6.06

QUARTER
in Jerusalem in the Second Q.); 2Ki 22.14
in the Second Q.) and spoke to her 2Ch 34.22
rise for the Jews from another q., Est 4.14
Come against her from every q.; Jer 50.26
Gate, a wail from the Second Q., Zep 1.10
people came to him from every q. Mk 1.45

QUARTERMASTER
of his reign. Seraiah was the q. Jer 51.59

QUARTERS
winds from the four q. of heaven; Jer 49.36

QUARTS
and three q. of barley for a denarius; Rev 6.06

QUARTUS
and our brother Q., greet you. Rom 16.23

QUEEN
Now when the q. of Sheba heard of 1Ki 10.01
And when the q. of Sheba had seen 10.04
these which the q. of Sheba gave 10.10
gave to the q. of Sheba all that 10.13
the sister of Tahpenes the q. 11.19
from being q. mother because she 15.13
and the sons of the q. mother. 2Ki 10.13
Now when the q. of Sheba heard of 2Ch 9.01
And when the q. of Sheba had seen 9.03
those which the q. of Sheba gave 9.09
gave to the q. of Sheba all that 9.12
from being q. mother because she 15.16
said to me (the q. sitting beside Neh 2.06
Q. Vashti also gave a banquet for Est 1.09
to bring Q. Vashti before the king 1.11
But Q. Vashti refused to come at 1.12
what is to be done to Q. Vashti, 1.15
to the king has Q. Vashti done 1.16
deed of the q. will be made known 1.17
commanded Q. Vashti to be brought 1.17
pleases the king be q. instead of Vashti." 2.04
and made her q. instead of Vashti. 2.17
and he told it to Q. Esther, 2.22
the q. was deeply distressed; 4.04
the king saw Q. Esther standing in 5.02
said to her, "What is it, Q. Esther? 5.03
"Even Q. Esther let no one come 5.12
went in to feast with Q. Esther. 7.01
"What is your petition, Q. Esther? 7.02
Then Q. Esther answered, "If I have 7.03
Then King Ahasuerus said to Q. Esther, 7.05
terror before the king and the q. 7.06
to beg his life from Q. Esther, 7.07
even assault the q. in my presence, 7.08
Ahasuerus gave to Q. Esther the 8.01
Ahasuerus said to Q. Esther and to 8.07
And the king said to Q. Esther, 9.12
Then Q. Esther, the daughter of 9.29
the Jew and Q. Esther enjoined 9.31
The command of Q. Esther fixed 9.32
hand stands the q. in gold of Ps 45.09
to make cakes for the q. of heaven; Jer 7.18
Say to the king and the q. mother: 13.18
and the q. mother, the eunuchs, the 29.02
incense to the q. of heaven and 44.17
incense to the q. of heaven and 44.18
incense to the q. of heaven and 44.19
incense to the q. of heaven and to 44.25
The q., because of the words of the Dan 5.10
and the q. said, "O king, live for 5.10
The q. of the South will arise at Mt 12.42
The q. of the South will arise at Lk 11.31
of Candace the q. of the Ethiopians, Ac 8.27
'A q. I sit, I am no widow, mourning Rev 18.07

QUEENLY
your feet in sandals, O q. maiden! Sol 7.01

QUEEN'S
heard of the q. behavior will be Est 1.18

QUEENS
There are sixty q. and eighty Sol 6.08
the q. and concubines also, and they 6.09
and their q. your nursing mothers. Is 49.23

QUENCH
Thus they would q. my coal which is 2Sa 14.07
lest you q. the lamp of Israel." 21.17
the wild asses q. their thirst. Ps 104.11
Many waters cannot q. love, neither can Sol 8.07
together, with none to q. them. Is 1.31
dimly burning wick he will not q.; 42.03
fire, and burn with none to q. it, Jer 4.04
fire, and burn with none to q. it, 21.12
with none to q. it for Bethel, Amo 5.06
bruised reed or q. a smoldering Mt 12.20
which you can q. all the flaming Eph 6.16
Do not q. the Spirit, 1Th 5.19

QUENCHED
this place, and it will not be q. 2Ki 22.17
upon this place and will not be q. 2Ch 34.25
faint, with his thirst not q., Is 29.08
Night and day it shall not be q.; 34.10
are extinguished, q. like a wick: 43.17
die, their fire shall not be q., 66.24
ground; it will burn and not be q." Jer 7.20
of Jerusalem and shall not be q.' " 17.27
the blazing flame shall not be q., Eze 20.47
kindled it; it shall not be q." 20.48
not die, and the fire is not q. *Mk 9.44
not die, and the fire is not q. * 9.46
not die, and the fire is not q. 9.48
q. raging fire, escaped the edge of Heb 11.34

QUESTION
I will q. you, and you shall declare Job 38.03
I will q. you, and you declare to me. 40.07
I will q. you, and you declare to me.' 42.04
"Will you q. me about my children, Is 45.11
to Jeremiah, "I will ask you a q.; Jer 38.14
Ask the priests to decide this q., Hag 2.11
them, "I also will ask you a q.; Mt 21.24
and they asked him a q., 22.23
asked him a q., to test him. 22.35
together, Jesus asked them a q., 22.41
"Why do you q. thus in your hearts? Mk 2.08
Jesus said to them, "I will ask you a q.; 11.29
and they asked him a q., saying, 12.18
no one dared to ask him any q. 12.34
and the Pharisees began to q., Lk 5.21
them, "Why do you q. in your hearts? 5.22
them, "I also will ask you a q.; 20.03
and they asked him a q., saying, 20.28
no longer dared to ask him any q. 20.40
And they began to q. one another, 22.23
things, and need none to q. you; Jn 16.30
apostles and the elders about this q. Ac 15.02
raising any q. on the ground of 1Co 10.25
raising any q. on the ground of 10.27

QUESTIONED
"The man q. us carefully about Gen 43.07
a young man of Succoth, and q. him; Ju 8.14
And Hezekiah q. the priests and the 2Ch 31.09
The king q. him secretly in his Jer 37.17
so that they q. among themselves, Mk 1.27
that they thus q. within themselves, 2.08
and all men q. in their hearts Lk 3.15
So he q. him at some length; 23.09
priest then q. Jesus about his Jn 18.19
And the high priest q. them, Ac 5.27

QUESTIONING
sitting there, q. in their hearts, Mk 2.06
q. what the rising from the dead 9.10
things without grumbling or q., Php 2.14

QUESTIONINGS
When Jesus perceived their q., Lk 5.22
and why do q. rise in your hearts? 24.38

QUESTIONS

told him was in answer to these q.; Gen 43.07
she came to test him with hard q. 1Ki 10.01
And Solomon answered all her q.; 10.03
Jerusalem to test him with hard q., 2Ch 9.01
And Solomon answered all her q.; 9.02
one dare to ask him any more q. Mt 22.46
listening to them and asking them q.; Lk 2.46
In that day you will ask me no q. Jn 16.23
is a matter of q. about words and Ac 18.15
was accused about q. of their law, 23.29
a loss how to investigate these q., 25.20
on you in q. of food and drink or Col 2.16

QUICK

and there is q. raw flesh in the Lev 13.10
the wily are brought to a q. end. Job 5.13
A man of q. temper acts foolishly, Pro 14.17
Be not q. to anger, for anger lodges Ecc 7.09
Let every man be q. to hear, Jas 1.19

QUICKLY

"Make ready q. three measures of Gen 18.06
and she q. let down her jar upon 24.18
So she q. emptied her jar into the 24.20
She q. let down her jar from her 24.46
you have found it so q., my son?" 27.20
Then every man q. lowered his sack 44.11
turned aside q. out of the way Ex 32.08
and carry it q. to the congregation, Num 16.46
you, and he would destroy you q. Deu 7.04
them out, and make them perish q., 9.03
me, 'Arise, go down q. from here; 9.12
turned aside q. out of the way 9.12
turned aside q. from the way which 9.16
and you perish q. off the good 11.17
you are destroyed and perish q., 28.20
pursue them q., for you will Jos 2.05
And the ambush rose q. out of their 8.19
come up to us q., and save us, and 10.06
shall perish q. from off the good 23.16
and carry them q. to the camp to 1Sa 17.17
David ran q. toward the battle line 17.48
and she q. killed it, and she took 28.24
in haste, lest he overtake us q., 2Sa 15.14
Now therefore send q. and tell David, 17.16
so both of them went away q., 17.18
"Arise, and go q. over the water; 17.21
and they q. took it up from him and 1Ki 20.33
"Bring q. Micaiah the son of Imlah." 22.09
is the king's order, 'Come down q.!'" 2Ki 1.11
that I may q. go to the man of God, 4.22
"Bring q. Micaiah the son of Imlah." 2Ch 18.08
And they thrust him out q., and he himself 26.20
carried them q. to all the lay 35.13
and he q. provided her with her Est 2.09
"Bring Haman q., that we may do as 5.05
for his wrath is q. kindled. Ps 2.12
a threefold cord is not q. broken. Ecc 4.12
Make friends q. with your accuser, Mt 5.25
Then go q. and tell his disciples 28.07
So they departed q. from the tomb 28.08
'Go out q. to the streets and lanes Lk 14.21
'Bring q. the best robe, and put it 15.22
and sit down q. and write fifty.' 16.06
she rose q. and went to him. Jn 11.29
saw Mary rise q. and go out, they 11.31
"What you are going to do, do q." 13.27
and woke him, saying, "Get up q." Ac 12.07
haste and get q. out of Jerusalem, 22.18
that you are so q. deserting him Gal 1.06
not to be q. shaken in mind or 2Th 2.02

QUICK-TEMPERED

be arrogant or q. or a drunkard or Tit 1.07

QUIET

field, while Jacob was a q. man, Gen 25.27
They kept q. all night, saying, "Let Ju 16.02
q. and unsuspecting, lacking nothing 18.07
"Keep q., put your hand upon your 18.19
to a people q. and unsuspecting, and 18.27
and we keep q. and do not take it 1Ki 22.03
the city was q. after Athaliah had 2Ki 11.20
was very broad, q., and peaceful; 1Ch 4.40
give peace and q. to Israel in his 22.09
So the realm of Jehoshaphat was q., 2Ch 20.30
and the city was q., after Athaliah 23.21
"Be q., for this day is holy; Neh 8.11
should have lain down and been q.; Job 3.13
I am not at ease, nor am I q.; 3.26
When he is q., who can condemn? 34.29
those who are q. in the land they Ps 35.20
they were glad because they had q., 107.30
dry morsel with q. than a house Pro 17.01
and laughs, and there is no q. 29.09
wise heard in q. are better than Ecc 9.17
be q., do not fear, and do not let Is 7.04
The whole earth is at rest and q.; 14.07
dwellings, and in q. resting places. 32.18
a q. habitation, an immovable tent, 33.20
shall return and have q. and ease, Jer 30.10
shall return and have q. and ease, 46.27
How long till you are q.? 47.06
How can it be q., when the LORD has 47.07
like the sea which cannot be q. 49.23
fall upon the q. people who dwell Eze 38.11
that the sea may q. down for us?" Jon 1.11
then the sea will q. down for you; 1.12
you ought to be q. and do nothing Ac 19.36
language, they were the more q. 22.02
we may lead a q. and peaceable 1Ti 2.02
jewel of a gentle and q. spirit, 1Pe 3.04

QUIETED

But Caleb q. the people before Num 13.30
But I have calmed and q. my soul, Ps 131.02
like a child q. at its mother's 131.02
like a child that is q. is my soul. 131.02
the town clerk had q. the crowd, Ac 19.35

QUIETLY

but a wise man q. holds it back. Pro 29.11
"I will q. look from my dwelling Is 18.04
one should wait q. for the salvation Lam 3.26
I will q. wait for the day of trouble Hab 3.16
shame, resolved to divorce her q. Mt 1.19
saying q., "The Teacher is here and Jn 11.28
to aspire to live q., to mind 1Th 4.11

QUIETNESS

Better is a handful of q. than two Ecc 4.06
in q. and in trust shall be your Is 30.15
righteousness, q. and trust for ever. 32.17
their work in q. and to earn their 2Th 3.12

QUIETS

who is slow to anger q. contention. Pro 15.18

QUIRINIUS

when Q. was governor of Syria. Lk 2.02

QUIT

upon you, and after that I will q." Ju 15.07
so q. before the quarrel breaks out. Pro 17.14
The old men have q. the city gate, Lam 5.14

QUITE

of the living; you are q. wrong." Mk 12.27
Jesus Christ q. openly and unhindered Ac 18.31

QUIVER
your q. and your bow, and go out to Gen 27.03
Upon him rattle the q., the flashing Job 39.23
man who has his q. full of them! Ps 127.05
And Elam bore the q. with chariots Is 22.06
arrow, in his q. he hid me away. 49.02
Their q. is like an open tomb, they Jer 5.16
into my heart the arrows of his q.; Lam 3.13
trembles, my lips q. at the sound; Hab 3.16

QUOTE
you will q. to me this proverb, Lk 4.23

QUOTED
afterward, in the words already q., Heb 4.07

R

RAAMA
Havilah, Sabta, R., and Sabteca. 1Ch 1.09

RAAMAH
Havilah, Sabtah, R., and Sabteca. Gen 10.07
The sons of R.: Sheba and Dedan. 10.07
The sons of R.: Sheba and Dedan. 1Ch 1.09
of Sheba and R. traded with you; Eze 27.22

RAAMIAH
R., Nahamani, Mordecai, Bilshan, Neh 7.07

RAAMSES
store cities, Pithom and R. Ex 1.11

RABBAH
is it not in R. of the Ammonites? Deu 3.11
to Aroer, which is east of R., Jos 13.25
and R.: two cities with their 15.60
the Ammonites, and besieged R. 2Sa 11.01
fought against R. of the Ammonites, 12.26
and said, "I have fought against R.; 12.27
the people together and went to R., 12.29
of Nahash from R. of the Ammonites, 17.27
Ammonites, and came and besieged R. 1Ch 20.01
And Joab smote R., and overthrew it. 20.01
heard against R. of the Ammonites; Jer 49.02
Cry, O daughters of R.! Gird yourselves 49.03
to come to R. of the Ammonites and Eze 21.20
I will make R. a pasture for camels 25.05
kindle a fire in the wall of R., Amo 1.14

RABBI
places, and being called r. by men. Mt 23.07
But you are not to be called r., 23.08
"R. (which means Teacher), where are Jn 1.38
"R., you are the Son of God! You are 1.49
"R., we know that you are a teacher 3.02
"R., he who was with you beyond the 3.26
besought him, saying, "R., eat." 4.31
said to him, "R., when did you come here?" 6.25
"R., who sinned, this man or his 9.02
"R., the Jews were but now seeking 11.08

RABBITH
R., Kishion, Ebez, Jos 19.20

RABBLE
Now the r. that was among them had Num 11.04
On my right hand the r. rise, Job 30.12
some wicked fellows of the r., Ac 17.05

RABBONI
and said to him in Hebrew, "R.!" Jn 20.16

RABMAG
Rabsaris, Nergalsharezer the R., Jer 39.03
Rabsaris, Nergalsharezer the R., 39.13

RABSARIS
the R., and the Rabshakeh with a 2Ki 18.17
Sarsechim the R., Nergalsharezer Jer 39.03
of the guard, Nebushazban the R., 39.13

RABSHAKEH
and the R. with a great army from 2Ki 18.17
And the R. said to them, "Say to 18.19
said to the R., "Pray, speak to your 18.26
But the R. said to them, "Has my 18.27
Then the R. stood and called out in 18.28
and told him the words of the R. 18.37
God heard all the words of the R., 19.04
The R. returned, and found the king 19.08
sent the R. from Lachish to King Is 36.02
And the R. said to them, "Say to 36.04
Shebna, and Joah said to the R., 36.11
But the R. said, "Has my master sent 36.12
Then the R. stood and called out in 36.13
and told him the words of the R. 36.22
your God heard the words of the R., 37.04
The R. returned, and found the king 37.08

RACAL
in R., in the cities of the Jerahmeelites, 1Sa 30.29

RACE
that the holy r. has mixed itself Ez 9.02
the sun the r. is not to the swift, Ecc 9.11
with our r. and forced our fathers Ac 7.19
of my brethren, my kinsmen by r. Rom 9.03
and of their r., according to the 9.05
know that in a r. all the runners 1Co 9.24
good fight, I have finished the r., 2Ti 4.07
perseverance the r. that is set Heb 12.01
But you are a chosen r., a royal 1Pe 2.09

RACED
"If you have r. with men on foot, Jer 12.05

RACHEL
and see, R. his daughter is coming Gen 29.06
R. came with her father's sheep; 29.09
Now when Jacob saw R. the daughter 29.10
Then Jacob kissed R., and wept 29.11
And Jacob told R. that he was her 29.12
and the name of the younger was R. 29.16
but R. was beautiful and lovely. 29.17
Jacob loved R.; and he said, 29.18
years for your younger daughter R." 29.18
So Jacob served seven years for R., 29.20
Did I not serve with you for R.? 29.25
gave him his daughter R. to wife. 29.28
to his daughter R. to be her maid. 29.29
So Jacob went in to R. also, 29.30
and he loved R. more than Leah, and 29.30
opened her womb; but R. was barren. 29.31
When R. saw that she bore Jacob no 30.01
Jacob's anger was kindled against R., 30.02
Then R. said, "God has judged me, and 30.06
Then R. said, "With mighty wrestlings 30.08
Then R. said to Leah, "Give me, I 30.14
R. said, "Then he may lie with you 30.15
Then God remembered R., and God 30.22
When R. had borne Joseph, Jacob said 30.25
sent and called R. and Leah into 31.04
Then R. and Leah answered him, "Is 31.14
and R. stole her father's household 31.19
not know that R. had stolen them. 31.32
Now R. had taken the household gods 31.34
among Leah and R. and the two 33.01
and R. and Joseph last of all. 33.02
and last Joseph and R. drew near, 33.07
R. travailed, and she had hard labor 35.16

RACHEL (cont.)
So R. died, and she was buried on Gen 35.19
The sons of R.: Joseph and Benjamin. 35.24
The sons of R., Jacob's wife: Joseph 46.19
(these are the sons of R., who were 46.22
whom Laban gave to R. his daughter, 46.25
R. to my sorrow died in the land of 48.07
like R. and Leah, who together built Ru 4.11
R. is weeping for her children; Jer 31.15
R. weeping for her children; she refused Mt 2.18

RACHEL'S
R. maid Bilhah conceived again and Gen 30.07
out of Leah's tent, and entered R. 31.33
it is the pillar of R. tomb, 35.20
of Bilhah, R. maid: Dan and Naphtali. 35.25
meet two men by R. tomb in the 1Sa 10.02

RACKS
The night r. my bones, and the pain Job 30.17

RADDAI
Nethanel the fourth, R. the fifth, 1Ch 2.14

RADIANCE
its r. like a most rare jewel, like Rev 21.11

RADIANT
Look to him, and be r.; so your faces Ps 34.05
My beloved is all r. and ruddy, Sol 5.10
Then you shall see and be r., Is 60.05
they shall be r. over the goodness Jer 31.12
my r. appearance was fearfully Dan 10.08

RAFTERS
the house to the r. of the ceiling, 1Ki 6.15
of cedar from the floor to the r., 6.16
with cedar from floor to r. 7.07
house are cedar, our r. are pine. Sol 1.17

RAFTS
make it into r. to go by sea to 1Ki 5.09
it to you in r. by sea to Joppa, so 2Ch 2.16

RAGE
So he turned and went away in a r. 2Ki 5.12
for he was in a r. with him 2Ch 16.10
slain them in a r. which has 28.09
With fierceness and r. he swallows Job 39.24
The nations r., the kingdoms totter; Ps 46.06
Advance, O horses, and r., O chariots! Jer 46.09
in furious r. commanded that Dan 3.13
The sword shall r. against their Hos 11.06
The chariots r. in the streets, they Nah 2.04
the wise men, was in a furious r., Mt 2.16
Spirit, 'Why did the Gentiles r., Ac 4.25

RAGED
Because you have r. against me and 2Ki 19.28
Because you have r. against me and Is 37.29
The nations r., but thy wrath came, Rev 11.18

RAGES
his heart r. against the LORD. Pro 19.03
the fool only r. and laughs, and 29.09

RAGING
coming in, and your r. against me. 2Ki 19.27
from the r. wind and tempest. Ps 55.08
Thou dost rule the r. of the sea; 89.09
us would have gone the r. waters. 124.05
coming in, and your r. against me. Is 37.28
and the sea ceased from its r. Jon 1.15
the r. waters swept on; the deep gave Hab 3.10
rebuked the wind and the r. waves; Lk 8.24
and in r. fury against them, I Ac 26.11
quenched r. fire, escaped the edge Heb 11.34

RAGS
drowsiness will clothe a man with r. Pro 23.21
from there old r. and worn-out Jer 38.11
"Put the r. and clothes between 38.12

RAHAB
of a harlot whose name was R., Jos 2.01
Then the king of Jericho sent to R., 2.03
only R. the harlot and all who are 6.17
spies went in, and brought out R., 6.23
But R. the harlot, and her father's 6.25
him bowed the helpers of R. Job 9.13
by his understanding he smote R. 26.12
know me I mention R. and Babylon; Ps 87.04
Thou didst crush R. like a carcass, 89.10
have called her "R. who sits still." Is 30.07
thou that didst cut R. in pieces, 51.09
and Salmon the father of Boaz by R., Mt 1.05
By faith R. the harlot did not Heb 11.31
was not also R. the harlot justified Jas 2.25

RAHAM
Shema was the father of R., the father 1Ch 2.44

RAID
Raiders shall r. Gad, but he shall r. Gen 49.19
in Judah, and made a r. on Lehi. Ju 15.09
have made a r. upon the land. 1Sa 23.27
whom have you made a r. today? 27.10
had made a r. upon the Negeb and 30.01
We had made a r. upon the Negeb of 30.14
David arrived with Joab from a r., 2Sa 3.22
they came down to r. their cattle. 1Ch 7.21
come and made a r. in the valley 14.09
yet again made a r. in the valley. 14.13
and made a r. upon the camels and Job 1.17
in, and the bandits r. without. Hos 7.01

RAIDERS
R. shall raid Gad, but he shall raid Gen 49.19
And r. came out of the camp of the 1Sa 13.17
garrison and even the r. trembled; 14.15
David against the band of r.; 1Ch 12.21

RAIDING
Jephthah, and went r. with him. Ju 11.03
men who were captains of r. bands; 2Sa 4.02

RAIDS
and made r. upon the Geshurites, the 1Sa 27.08
on one of their r. had carried off 2Ki 5.02
came no more on r. into the land 6.23
had made r. on the cities in the 2Ch 28.18

RAIL
All your enemies r. against you; Lam 2.16
"All our enemies r. against us; 3.46

RAILED
our master; and he r. at them. 1Sa 25.14
criminals who were hanged r. at him, Lk 23.39

RAIMENT
and r., and gave them to Rebekah; Gen 24.53
them, and for my r. they cast lots. Ps 22.18
Thou changest them like r., and they 102.26
and I have stained all my r. Is 63.03
and your r. was of fine linen, and Eze 16.13
his r. was white as snow, and the Dan 7.09
To see a man clothed in soft r.? Mt 11.08
who wear soft r. are in kings' 11.08
lightning, and his r. white as snow. 28.03
A man clothed in soft r.? Behold, Lk 7.25
and his r. became dazzling white. 9.29

RAIN
not caused it to r. upon the earth, Gen 2.05
I will send r. upon the earth 7.04
And r. fell upon the earth forty 7.12

RAIN (cont.)
the r. from the heavens was restrained, Gen 8.02
and the r. no longer poured upon Ex 9.33
saw that the r. and the hail and 9.34
I will r. bread from heaven for you 16.04
water by the r. from heaven, Deu 11.11
he will give the r. for your land 11.14
the early r. and the latter r., 11.14
heavens, so that there be no r., 11.17
to give the r. of your land in its 28.12
will make the r. of your land 28.24
May my teaching drop as the r., 32.02
as the gentle r. upon the tender 32.02
that he may send thunder and r.; 1Sa 12.17
LORD sent thunder and r. that day; 12.18
let there be no dew or r. upon you, 2Sa 1.21
harvest until r. fell upon them 21.10
like r. that makes grass to sprout 23.04
and there is no r. because they 1Ki 8.35
and grant r. upon thy land, which 8.36
be neither dew nor r. these years, 17.01
there was no r. in the land. 17.07
the LORD sends r. upon the earth. 17.14
and I will send r. upon the earth. 18.01
is a sound of the rushing of r. 18.41
and go down, lest the r. stop you. 18.44
and wind, and there was a great r. 18.45
'You shall not see wind or r., 2Ki 3.17
and there is no r. because they 2Ch 6.26
and grant r. upon thy land, which 6.27
the heavens so that there is no r., 7.13
matter and because of the heavy r. Ez 10.09
many, and it is a time of heavy r.; 10.13
he gives r. upon the earth and Job 5.10
and r. it upon him as his food. 20.23
wet with the r. of the mountains, 24.08
when he made a decree for the r., 28.26
They waited for me as for the r.; 29.23
their mouths as for the spring r. 29.23
water, he distils his mist in r. 36.27
the shower and the r., 'Be strong.' 37.06
a channel for the torrents of r., 38.25
to bring r. on a land where no man 38.26
"Has the r. a father, or who has 38.28
wicked he will r. coals of fire Ps 11.06
quaked, the heavens poured down r., 68.08
R. in abundance, O God, thou didst 68.09
May he be like r. that falls on the 72.06
the early r. also covers it with 84.06
He gave them hail for r., and lightning 105.32
lightnings for the r. and brings 135.07
he prepares r. for the earth, he 147.08
clouds that bring the spring r. Pro 16.15
is a continual dripping of r. 19.13
clouds and wind without r. is a man who 25.14
The north wind brings forth r.; 25.23
Like snow in summer or r. in harvest, 26.01
is a beating r. that leaves no 28.03
If the clouds are full of r., they empty Ecc 11.03
and the clouds return after the r.; 12.02
is past, the r. is over and gone. Sol 2.11
a shelter from the storm and r. Is 4.06
that they r. no r. upon it. 5.06
And he will give r. for the seed 30.23
a cedar and the r. nourishes it. 44.14
let the skies r. down righteousness 45.08
"For as the r. and the snow come 55.10
and the spring r. has not come; Jer 3.03
who gives the r. in its season, the 5.24
the autumn r. and the spring r., 5.24
He makes lightnings for the r., 10.13
since there is no r. on the land, 14.04
of the nations that can bring r.? 14.22
He makes lightnings for the r., 51.16
is in the cloud on the day of r., Eze 1.28
There will be a deluge of r., 13.11
be a deluge of r. in my anger, 13.13
and I will r. upon him and his 38.22
he may come and r. salvation upon Hos 10.12
for he has given the early r. for your Joe 2.23
poured down for you abundant r., 2.23
early and the latter r., as before. 2.23
withheld the r. from you when Amo 4.07
I would send r. upon one city, and 4.07
and send no r. upon another city; 4.07
on which it did not r. withered; 4.07
Ask r. from the LORD in the season Zec 10.01
in the season of the spring r., 10.01
who gives men showers of r., to every 10.01
there will be no r. upon them. 14.17
and sends r. on the just and on the Mt 5.45
and the r. fell, and the floods came, 7.25
and the r. fell, and the floods came, 7.27
it had begun to r. and was cold. Ac 28.02
has drunk the r. that often falls Heb 6.07
receives the early and the late r. Jas 5.07
fervently that it might not r., 5.17
months it did not r. on the earth. 5.17
again and the heaven gave r., 5.18
that no r. may fall during the days Rev 11.06

RAINBOW
throne was a r. that looked like Rev 4.03
with a r. over his head, and his 10.01

RAINED
Then the LORD r. on Sodom and Gen 19.24
And the LORD r. hail upon the land Ex 9.23
and he r. down upon them manna to Ps 78.24
he r. flesh upon them like dust, 78.27
or r. upon in the day of indignation Eze 22.24
one field would be r. upon, and the Amo 4.07
and brimstone r. from heaven and Lk 17.29

RAINS
give you your r. in their season, Lev 26.04
torrential r. and hailstones, fire Eze 38.22
as the spring r. that water the Hos 6.03
you from heaven r. and fruitful Ac 14.17

RAINY
dripping on a r. day and a contentious Pro 27.15

RAISE
and r. up offspring for your Gen 38.08
your God will r. up for you a Deu 18.15
I will r. up for them a prophet 18.18
And I will r. up for myself a 1Sa 2.35
I will r. up your son after you, who 2Sa 7.12
I will r. up evil against you out 12.11
to r. him from the ground; but he would 12.17
Moreover the LORD will r. up for 1Ki 14.14
and cymbals, to r. sounds of joy. 1Ch 15.16
I will r. up your offspring after 17.11
and r. me up, that I may requite Ps 41.10
R. a song, sound the timbrel, the 81.02
for insight and r. your voice for Pro 2.03
not understanding r. her voice? 8.01
He will r. a signal for a nation Is 5.26
He will r. an ensign for the 11.12
On a bare hill r. a signal, cry 13.02
Horonaim they r. a cry of destruction 15.05
and I will r. siegeworks against 29.03
and I will r. up their ruins'; 44.26
my servant to r. up the tribes of 49.06
and r. my signal to the peoples; 49.22
you shall r. up the foundations of 58.12
they shall r. up the former devastations 61.04
R. a standard toward Zion, flee for Jer 4.06
and r. a signal on Bethhaccherem; 6.01
r. a lamentation on the bare 7.29
make haste and r. a wailing over 9.18
when I will r. up for David a 23.05
king, whom I will r. up for them. 30.09
and r. shouts for the chief of the 31.07

RAISE (cont.)

R. a shout against her round about, Jer 50.15
with none to r. him up, and I will 50.32
and they shall r. the shout of 51.14
and r. a roof of shields against Eze 26.08
And they will r. a lamentation over 26.17
r. a lamentation over Tyre, 27.02
wailing they r. a lamentation for 27.32
"Son of man, r. a lamentation over 28.12
"Son of man, r. a lamentation over 32.02
and r. you from your graves, O my 37.12
and r. you from your graves, O my 37.13
and he shall r. a great multitude, Dan 11.11
north shall again r. a multitude, 11.13
on the third day he will r. us up, Hos 6.02
her land, with none to r. her up. Amo 5.02
I will r. up against you a nation, O 6.14
"In that day I will r. up the booth 9.11
and r. up its ruins, and rebuild it 9.11
that we will r. against him seven Mic 5.05
these stones to r. up children to Mt 3.09
Heal the sick, r. the dead, cleanse 10.08
and r. up children for his brother. 22.24
and r. up children for his brother. Mk 12.19
these stones to r. up children to Lk 3.08
the wife and r. up children for 20.28
look up and r. your heads, because 21.28
and in three days I will r. it up. Jn 2.19
and will you r. it up in three days?" 2.20
but r. it up at the last day. 6.39
and I will r. him up at the last 6.40
and I will r. him up at the last 6.44
and I will r. him up at the last 6.54
Lord God will r. up for you a Ac 3.22
'God will r. up for you a prophet 7.37
and will also r. us up by his 1Co 6.14
whom he did not r. if it is true 15.15
Lord Jesus will r. us also with 2Co 4.14
God was able to r. men even from Heb 11.19
man, and the Lord will r. him up; Jas 5.15

RAISED

And when Esau r. his eyes and saw Gen 33.05
its poles, and r. up its pillars; Ex 40.18
all the congregation r. a loud cry; Num 14.01
whom he r. up in their stead, that Jos 5.07
the people r. a great shout, and the 6.20
And they r. over him a great heap 7.26
and r. over it a great heap of 8.29
Then the LORD r. up judges, who Ju 2.16
Whenever the LORD r. up judges for 2.18
the LORD r. up a deliverer for the 3.09
the LORD r. up for them a deliverer, 3.15
were with him r. their voices and 1Sa 30.04
and r. over him a very great heap 2Sa 18.17
up the men who r. their hand 18.28
of the man who was r. on high, 23.01
King Solomon r. a levy of forced 1Ki 5.13
And the LORD r. up an adversary 11.14
God also r. up as an adversary to 11.23
whom have you r. your voice and 2Ki 19.22
LORD), and when the song was r., 2Ch 5.13
men of Judah r. the battle shout. 13.15
and r. towers upon it, and outside 32.05
and r. it to a very great height; 33.14
and they r. their voices and wept; Job 2.12
if I have r. my hand against the 31.21
who hate thee have r. their heads. Ps 83.02
Therefore he r. his hand and swore 106.26
and r. the stormy wind, which lifted 107.25
up, my eyes are not r. too high; 131.01
He has r. up a horn for his people, 148.14
and shall be r. above the hills; Is 2.02
songs are sung, no shouts are r.; 16.10
a signal is r. on the mountains, 18.03
whom have you r. your voice and 37.23
and my highways shall be r. up. 49.11

'The LORD has r. up prophets for us Jer 29.15
the noise of their voice is r.; 51.55
a clamor was r. in the house of the Lam 2.07
temple had a r. platform round Eze 41.08
whom he would he r. up, and whom Dan 5.19
It was r. up on one side; it had 7.05
I r. my eyes and saw, and behold, a 8.03
r. his right hand and his left hand 12.07
And I r. up some of your sons for Amo 2.11
and shall be r. up above the hills; Mic 4.01
Judah, so that no man r. his head; Zec 1.21
the one will be r. against the 14.13
deaf hear, and the dead are r. up, Mt 11.05
he has been r. from the dead; 14.02
killed, and on the third day be r. 16.21
the Son of man is r. from the dead." 17.09
and he will be r. on the third day." 17.23
and he will be r. on the third day." 20.19
But after I am r. up, I will go 26.32
who had fallen asleep were r., 27.52
baptizer has been r. from the dead; Mk 6.14
"John, whom I beheaded, has been r." 6.16
And as for the dead being r., 12.26
But after I am r. up, I will go 14.28
and has r. up a horn of salvation Lk 1.69
the dead are r. up, the poor have 7.22
John had been r. from the dead, 9.07
killed, and on the third day be r." 9.22
in the crowd r. her voice and said 11.27
But that the dead are r., even Moses 20.37
When therefore he was r. from the dead, Jn 2.22
whom Jesus had r. from the dead. 12.01
whom he had r. from the dead. 12.09
of the tomb and r. him from the 12.17
after he was r. from the dead. 21.14
But God r. him up, having loosed the Ac 2.24
This Jesus God r. up, and of that we 2.32
by the right hand and r. him up; 3.07
of life, whom God r. from the dead. 3.15
from your brethren as he r. me up. 3.22
God, having r. up his servant, sent 3.26
whom God r. from the dead, by him 4.10
of our fathers r. Jesus whom you 5.30
from your brethren as he r. me up.' 7.37
but God r. him on the third day and 10.40
he r. up David to be their king; 13.22
But God r. him from the dead; 13.30
fact that he r. him from the dead, 13.34
but he whom God r. up saw no 13.37
in him that r. from the dead Jesus Rom 4.24
trespasses and r. for our justification. 4.25
as Christ was r. from the dead by 6.04
Christ being r. from the dead will 6.09
who has been r. from the dead in 7.04
of him who r. Jesus from the dead 8.11
he who r. Christ Jesus from the 8.11
who was r. from the dead, who is at 8.34
"I have r. you up for the very 9.17
heart that God r. him from the 10.09
delivered to them what has been r., 15.28
And God r. the Lord and will also 1Co 6.14
that he was r. on the third day in 15.04
is preached as r. from the dead, 15.12
dead, then Christ has not been r.; 15.13
if Christ has not been r., then our 15.14
testified of God that he r. Christ, 15.15
is true that the dead are not r. 15.15
For if the dead are not r., 15.16
then Christ has not been r. 15.16
If Christ has not been r., 15.17
Christ has been r. from the dead, 15.20
If the dead are not r. at all, 15.29
If the dead are not r., "Let us eat 15.32
one will ask, "How are the dead r.? 15.35
perishable, what is r. is imperishable. 15.42
in dishonor, it is r. in glory. 15.43
in weakness, it is r. in power. 15.43

RAISED (cont.)
it is r. a spiritual body. If there is 1Co 15.44
the dead will be r. imperishable, 15.52
knowing that he who r. the Lord 2Co 4.14
who for their sake died and was r. 5.15
Father, who r. him from the dead— Gal 1.01
Christ when he r. him from the Eph 1.20
and r. us up with him, and made us 2.06
you were also r. with him through Col 2.12
of God, who r. him from the dead. 2.12
If then you have been r. with Christ, 3.01
whom he r. from the dead, Jesus who 1Th 1.10
who r. him from the dead and gave 1Pe 1.21

RAISES
he brings down to Sheol and r. up. 1Sa 2.06
He r. up the poor from the dust; 2.08
When he r. himself up the mighty Job 41.25
but he r. up the needy out of Ps 107.41
He r. the poor from the dust, and 113.07
and r. up all who are bowed down. 145.14
in the markets she r. her voice; Pro 1.20
So the LORD r. adversaries against Is 9.11
it r. from their thrones all who 14.09
For as the Father r. the dead and Jn 5.21
by any of you that God r. the dead? Ac 26.08
ourselves but on God who r. the dead; 2Co 1.09

RAISIN-CAKES
stricken, for the r. of Kirhareseth. Is 16.07

RAISING
For lo, I am r. up in the land a Zec 11.16
to us their children by r. Jesus; Ac 13.33
to all men by r. him from the dead." 17.31
market without r. any question on 1Co 10.25
you without r. any question on the 10.27

RAISINS
and a hundred clusters of r., 1Sa 25.18
of figs and two clusters of r. 30.12
portion of meat, and a cake of r. 2Sa 6.19
of bread, a hundred bunches of r., 16.01
clusters of r., and wine and oil, 1Ch 12.40
portion of meat, and a cake of r. 16.03
Sustain me with r., refresh me Sol 2.05
to other gods and love cakes of r. Hos 3.01

RAKEM
and his sons were Ulam and R. 1Ch 7.16

RAKKATH
Zer, Hammath, R., Chinnereth, Jos 19.35

RAKKON
and Mejarkon and R. with the Jos 19.46

RALLIED
were with him r. and went into the 1Sa 14.20

RALLY
of the trumpet, r. to us there. Neh 4.20
fear thee, to r. to it from the bow. Ps 60.04

RAM
a r. three years old, a turtledove, Gen 15.09
and behold, behind him was a r., 22.13
and Abraham went and took the r., 22.13
hands upon the head of the r., Ex 29.15
and you shall slaughter the r., 29.16
Then you shall cut the r. into pieces, 29.17
and burn the whole r. upon the altar; 29.18
"You shall take the other r.; 29.19
hands upon the head of the r., 29.19
and you shall kill the r., 29.20
"You shall also take the fat of the r., 29.22
(for it is a r. of ordination), 29.22
breast of the r. of Aaron's ordination 29.26
offered from the r. of ordination, 29.27
"You shall take the r. of ordination, 29.31
flesh of the r. and the bread that 29.32
a r. without blemish out of the Lev 5.15
him with the r. of the guilt 5.16
to the priest a r. without blemish 5.18
a r. without blemish out of the 6.06
presented the r. of the burnt 8.18
their hands on the head of the r. 8.18
And when the r. was cut into pieces, 8.20
burned the whole r. on the altar, 8.21
the other r., the r. of ordination; 8.22
their hands on the head of the r. 8.22
portion of the r. of ordination, 8.29
and a r. for a burnt offering, both 9.02
and an ox and a r. for peace 9.04
He killed the ox also and the r., 9.18
and the fat of the ox and of the r., 9.19
offering and a r. for a burnt 16.03
and one r. for a burnt offering. 16.05
of meeting, a r. for a guilt offering. 19.21
him with the r. of the guilt 19.22
addition to the r. of atonement Num 5.08
and one r. without blemish as a 6.14
shall offer the r. as a sacrifice 6.17
shall take the shoulder of the r., 6.19
one r., one male lamb a year old, 7.15
one r., one male lamb a year old, 7.21
one r., one male lamb a year old, 7.27
one r., one male lamb a year old, 7.33
one r., one male lamb a year old, 7.39
one r., one male lamb a year old, 7.45
one r., one male lamb a year old, 7.51
one r., one male lamb a year old, 7.57
one r., one male lamb a year old, 7.63
one r., one male lamb a year old, 7.69
one r., one male lamb a year old, 7.75
one r., one male lamb a year old, 7.81
Or for a r., you shall prepare for 15.06
shall be done for each bull or r., 15.11
on each altar a bull and a r. 23.02
upon each altar a bull and a r. 23.04
a bull and a r. on each altar. 23.14
a bull and a r. on each altar. 23.30
one r., seven male lambs a year old 28.11
mixed with oil, for the one r.; 28.12
a bull, a third of a hin for a r., 28.14
one r., and seven male lambs a year 28.19
a bull, and two tenths for a r.; 28.20
one r., seven male lambs a year old; 28.27
each bull, two tenths for one r., 28.28
one r., seven male lambs a year old 29.02
the bull, two tenths for the r., 29.03
one r., seven male lambs a year old; 29.08
bull, two tenths for the one r., 29.09
one r., seven male lambs a year old 29.36
for the r., and for the lambs by 29.37
Hezron of R., R. of Amminadab, Ru 4.19
him: Jerahmeel, R., and Chelubai. 1Ch 2.09
R. was the father of Amminadab, and 2.10
R., his first-born, Bunah, Oren, Ozem, 2.25
The sons of R., the first-born of 2.27
offering was a r. of the flock for Ez 10.19
of the family of R., became angry. Job 32.02
blemish and a r. from the flock Eze 43.23
a bull and a r. from the flock, 43.25
each bull, an ephah for each r., 45.24
blemish and a r. without blemish; 46.04
with the r. shall be an ephah, and 46.05
blemish, and six lambs and a r., 46.06
the bull and an ephah with the r., 46.07
and with a r. an ephah, and with the 46.11
a r. standing on the bank of the Dan 8.03
I saw the r. charging westward and 8.04
He came to the r. with the two 8.06
I saw him come close to the r., 8.07
and struck the r. and broke his 8.07

RAM (cont.)

and the r. had no power to stand Dan 8.07
could rescue the r. from his power. 8.07
As for the r. which you saw with 8.20
and Hezron the father of R., Mt 1.03
and R. the father of Amminadab, and 1.04

RAMAH

Gibeon, R., Beeroth, Jos 18.25
as Baalathbeer, R. of the Negeb. 19.08
then the boundary turns to R., 19.29
Adamah, R., Hazor, 19.36
Deborah between R. and Bethel in Ju 4.05
spend the night at Gibeah or at R. 19.13
went back to their house at R. 1Sa 1.19
Then Elkanah went home to R. 2.11
Then he would come back to R., 7.17
together and came to Samuel at R., 8.04
Then Samuel went to R.; and Saul 15.34
And Samuel rose up, and went to R. 16.13
and he came to Samuel at R., and told 19.18
"Behold, David is at Naioth in R." 19.19
Then he himself went to R., 19.22
"Behold, they are at Naioth in R." 19.22
he went from there to Naioth in R.; 19.23
until he came to Naioth in R. 19.23
Then David fled from Naioth in R., 20.01
they buried him in his house at R. 25.01
and buried him in R., his own city. 28.03
and built R., that he mght permit 1Ki 15.17
of it, he stopped building R., 15.21
the stones of R. and its timber, 15.22
the Syrians had given him at R., 2Ki 8.29
and built R., that he might permit 2Ch 16.01
of it, he stopped building R., 16.05
the stones of R. and its timber, 16.06
wounds which he had received at R., 22.06
The sons of R. and Geba, six hundred Ez 2.26
The men of R. and Geba, six hundred Neh 7.30
Hazor, R., Gittaim, 11.33
R. trembles, Gibeah of Saul has fled Is 10.29
the LORD: "A voice is heard in R., Jer 31.15
the guard had let him go from R., 40.01
horn in Gibeah, the trumpet in R. Hos 5.08
"A voice was heard in R., wailing Mt 2.18

RAMATHAIMZOPHIM

certain man of R. of the hill 1Sa 1.01

RAMATHITE

the vineyards was Shimei the R.; 1Ch 27.27

RAMATHLEHI

hand; and that place was called R. Ju 15.17

RAMATHMIZPEH

and from Heshbon to R. and Betonim, Jos 13.26

RAMESES

of the land, in the land of R., Gen 47.11
journeyed from R. to Succoth, Ex 12.37
They set out from R. in the first Num 33.03
people of Israel set out from R., 33.05

RAMIAH

R., Izziah, Malchijah, Mijamin, Ez 10.25

RAMOTH

and R. in Gilead for the Gadites, Deu 4.43
and R. in Gilead, from the tribe of Jos 20.08
R. in Gilead with its pasture lands, 21.38
in R. of the Negeb, in Jattir, 1Sa 30.27
R. with its pasture lands, and Anem 1Ch 6.73
R. in Gilead with its pasture lands, 6.80

RAMOTHGILEAD

Bengeber, in R. (he had the villages 1Ki 4.13
"Do you know that R. belongs to us, 22.03
you go with me to battle at R.?" 22.04
"Shall I go to battle against R., 22.06
and said, "Go up to R. and triumph; 22.12
shall we go to R. to battle, or shall we 22.15
that he may go up and fall at R.?' 22.20
the king of Judah went up to R. 22.29
against Hazael king of Syria at R., 2Ki 8.28
of oil in your hand, and go to R. 9.01
young man, the prophet, went to R. 9.04
on guard at R. against Hazael king 9.14
induced him to go up against R. 2Ch 18.02
Judah, "Will you go with me to R.?" 18.03
"Shall we go to battle against R., 18.05
and said, "Go up to R. and triumph; 18.11
shall we go to R. to battle, 18.14
that he may go up and fall at R.?' 18.19
the king of Judah went up to R. 18.28
against Hazael king of Syria at R. 22.05

RAMPART

city, and it stood against the r.; 2Sa 20.15
the caused r. and wall to lament, Lam 2.08
her r. a sea, and water her wall? Nah 3.08
Tyre has built herself a r., and heaped Zec 9.03

RAMPARTS

consider well her r., go through Ps 48.13
Man the r.; watch the road; gird your Nah 2.01

RAM'S

make a long blast with the r. horn, Jos 6.05

RAMS

not eaten the r. of your flocks. Gen 31.38
two hundred ewes and twenty r., 32.14
bull and two r. without blemish, Ex 29.01
and bring the bull and the two r. 29.03
"Then you shall take one of the r., 29.15
and the two r., and the basket of Lev 8.02
and one young bull, and two r.; 23.18
five r., five male goats, and five Num 7.17
five r., five male goats, and five 7.23
five r., five male goats, and five 7.29
five r., five male goats, and five 7.35
five r., five male goats, and five 7.41
five r., five male goats, and five 7.47
five r., five male goats, and five 7.53
five r., five male goats, and five 7.59
five r., five male goats, and five 7.65
five r., five male goats, and five 7.71
five r., five male goats, and five 7.77
five r., five male goats, and five 7.83
twelve r., twelve male lambs a year 7.87
the r. sixty, the male goats sixty, 7.88
me here seven bulls and seven r. 23.01
me here seven bulls and seven r. 23.29
two r., fourteen male lambs a year 29.13
two tenths for each of the two r., 29.14
two r., fourteen male lambs a year 29.17
for the r., and for the lambs by 29.18
two r., fourteen male lambs a year 29.20
for the r., and for the lambs by 29.21
two r., fourteen male lambs a year 29.23
for the r., and for the lambs by 29.24
two r., fourteen male lambs a year 29.26
for the r., and for the lambs by 29.27
two r., fourteen male lambs a year 29.29
for the r., and for the lambs by 29.30
two r., fourteen male lambs a year 29.32
for the r., and for the lambs by 29.33
flock, with fat of lambs and r., Deu 32.14
and to hearken than the fat of r. 1Sa 15.22
the wool of a hundred thousand r. 2Ki 3.04
sacrificed seven bulls and seven r. 1Ch 15.26
a thousand r., and a thousand lambs, 29.21
bull or seven r. becomes a priest 2Ch 13.09
seven hundred r. and seven thousand 17.11
seven r., seven lambs, and seven he-goats 29.21

RAMS (cont.)
they killed the r. and their blood 2Ch 29.22
a hundred r., and two hundred lambs 29.32
r., or sheep for burnt offerings to Ez 6.09
two hundred r., four hundred lambs, 6.17
r., and lambs, with their cereal 7.17
ninety-six r., seventy-seven lambs, 8.35
take seven bulls and seven r., Job 42.08
the smoke of the sacrifice of r.; Ps 66.15
The mountains skipped like r.; 114.04
O mountains, that you skip like r.? 114.06
offerings of r. and the fat of fed Is 1.11
with the fat of the kidneys of r. 34.06
the r. of Nebaioth shall minister 60.07
and you shall fall like choice r. Jer 25.34
slaughter, like r. and he-goats. 51.40
plant battering r. against it Eze 4.02
set battering r. against the gates, 21.22
his battering r. against your 26.09
dealers in lambs, r., and goats; 27.21
sheep and sheep, r. and he-goats. 34.17
of r., of lambs, and of goats, of 39.18
bulls and seven r. without blemish, 45.23
be pleased with thousands of r., Mic 6.07

RAMS'
tanned r. skins, goatskins, acacia Ex 25.05
of tanned r. skins and goatskins. 26.14
tanned r. skins, and goatskins; 35.07
hair or tanned r. skins or goatskins, 35.23
of tanned r. skins and goatskins. 36.19
of tanned r. skins and goatskins, 39.34
trumpets of r. horns before the Jos 6.04
trumpets of r. horns before the 6.06
trumpets of r. horns before the 6.08
trumpets of r. horns before the 6.13

RAN
he r. from the tent door to meet Gen 18.02
And Abraham r. to the herd, and took 18.07
Then the servant r. to meet her, 24.17
the trough and r. again to the 24.20
Then the maiden r. and told her 24.28
and Laban r. out to the man, to the 24.29
and she r. and told her father. 29.12
he r. to meet him, and embraced him 29.13
But Esau r. to meet him, and embraced 33.04
and fire r. down to the earth. Ex 9.23
And a young man r. and told Moses, Num 11.27
and r. into the midst of the 16.47
messengers, and they r. to the tent; Jos 7.22
they r. and entered the city and 8.19
south boundary r. from the end of 15.02
And its boundary r. from Heleph, 19.33
of the Amorites r. from the ascent Ju 1.36
the camp, and all the army r.; 7.21
And Jotham r. away and fled, and 9.21
And the woman r. in haste and told 13.10
and r. to Eli, and said, "Here I am, 1Sa 3.05
A man of Benjamin r. from the 4.12
Then they r. and fetched him from 10.23
and r. to the ranks, and went and 17.22
David r. quickly toward the battle 17.48
Then David r. and stood over the 17.51
As the lad r., he shot an arrow 20.36
Cushite bowed before Joab, and r. 2Sa 18.21
Then Ahimaaz r. by the way of the 18.23
Shimei's slaves r. away to Achish, 1Ki 2.39
And the water r. round about the 18.35
his loins and r. before Ahab to 18.46
and r. after Elijah, and said, "let 19.20
not send the prophets, yet they r.; Jer 23.21
And the pavement r. along the side Eze 40.18
and he r. at him in his mighty Dan 8.06
of them at once r. and took a Mt 27.48
and r. to tell his disciples. 28.08
from afar, he r. and worshiped him; Mk 5.06
and they r. there on foot from all 6.33
and r. about the whole neighborhood 6.55
and r. up to him and greeted him. 9.15
a man r. up and knelt before him, 10.17
the linen cloth and r. away naked. 14.52
And one r. and, filling a sponge 15.36
and r. and embraced him and kissed Lk 15.20
So he r. on ahead and climbed up 19.04
But Peter rose and r. to the tomb; * 24.12
So she r., and went to Simon Peter Jn 20.02
They both r., but the other disciple 20.04
all the people r. together to them Ac 3.11
So Philip r. to him, and heard him 8.30
the gate but r. in and told that 12.14
aroused, and the people r. together; 21.30
centurions, and r. down to them; 21.32
a shoal they r. the vessel aground 27.41

RANGE
feet of the ox and the ass r. free. Is 32.20
which r. through the whole earth. Zec 4.10

RANGES
He r. the mountains as his pasture, Job 39.08

RANK
Jew was next in r. to King Ahasuerus, Est 10.03
king, yet all of them march in r.; Pro 30.27
captain of fifty and the man of r., Is 3.03
filthiness and r. growth of Jas 1.21

RANKS
and shouted to the r. of Israel, 1Sa 17.08
"I defy the r. of Israel this day; 17.10
of the baggage, and ran to the r., 17.22
up out of the r. of the Philistines, 17.23
approaches the r. is to be slain. 2Ki 11.08
army, "Bring her out between the r.; 11.15
them, "Bring her out between the r.; 2Ch 23.14
there is no straggler in his r. Is 14.31
He who comes after me r. before me, Jn 1.15
me comes a man who r. before me, 1.30

RANSOM
If a r. is laid on him, then he Ex 21.30
shall give a r. for himself to the 30.12
shall accept no r. for the life of Num 35.31
shall accept no r. for him who has 35.32
Or, 'R. me from the hand of oppressors'? Job 6.23
into the Pit, I have found a r.; 33.24
greatness of the r. turn you aside. 36.18
Truly no man can r. himself, or give to Ps 49.07
for the r. of his life is costly, 49.08
But God will r. my soul from the 49.15
The r. of a man's life is his wealth, Pro 13.08
The wicked is a r. for the righteous, 21.18
I give Egypt as your r., Ethiopia Is 43.03
Shall I r. them from the power of Hos 13.14
to give his life as a r. for many. Mt 20.28
to give his life as a r. for many. Mk 10.45
who gave himself as a r. for all, 1Ti 2.06
thy blood didst r. men for God Rev 5.09

RANSOMED
man and not yet r. or given her Lev 19.20
from among men, shall be r.; 27.29
So the people r. Jonathan, that he did 1Sa 14.45
And the r. of the LORD shall return, Is 35.10
And the r. of the LORD shall return, 51.11
For the LORD has r. Jacob, Jer 31.11
that you were r. from the futile 1Pe 1.18

RAPACITY
they are full of extortion and r. Mt 23.25

RAPHA
Nohah the fourth, and R. the fifth. 1Ch 8.02

RAPHAH
R. was his son, Eleasah his son, 1Ch 8.37

RAPHU
of Benjamin, Palti the son of R.; Num 13.09

RARE
of the LORD was r. in those days; 1Sa 3.01
make men more r. than fine gold, Is 13.12
its radiance like a most r. jewel, Rev 21.11

RASE
how they said, "R. it, r. it! Ps 137.07

RASH
with his lips a r. oath to do evil Lev 5.04
any sort of r. oath that men swear, 5.04
therefore my words have been r. Job 6.03
and he spoke words that were r. Ps 106.33
There is one whose r. words are Pro 12.18
Be not r. with your mouth, nor let Ecc 5.02
The mind of the r. will have good Is 32.04
to be quiet and do nothing r. Ac 19.36

RASHLY
It is a snare for a man to say r., Pro 20.25

RATED
owner shall be r. as the time of a Lev 25.50

RATHER
given to you r. than to your Gen 48.22
but r. the anger of the LORD and Deu 29.20
How much r., then, when he says to 2Ki 5.13
r. let the shadow go back ten 20.10
strangling and death r. than my bones. Job 7.15
he justified himself r. than God; 32.02
you have chosen r. than affliction 36.21
I would r. be a doorkeeper in the Ps 84.10
and knowledge r. than choice gold; Pro 8.10
is to be chosen r. than silver. 16.16
her cubs, r. than a fool in his folly. 17.12
is to be chosen r. than great 22.01
yet it finds rest r. than he. Ecc 6.05
and not r. that he should turn from Eze 18.23
up their bodies r. than serve and Dan 3.28
of God, r. than burnt offerings. Hos 6.06
but go r. to the lost sheep of the Mt 10.06
r. fear him who can destroy both 10.28
go r. to the dealers and buy for 25.09
but r. that a riot was beginning, he 27.24
was no better but r. grew worse. Mk 5.26
"Blessed r. are those who hear the Lk 11.28
No, I tell you, but r. division; 12.51
Will he not r. say to him, 'Prepare 17.08
house justified r. than the other; 18.14
r. let the greatest among you 22.26
men loved darkness r. than light, Jn 3.19
to listen to you r. than to God, Ac 4.19
"We must obey God r. than men. 5.29
having a r. accurate knowledge of 24.22
the creature r. than the Creator, Rom 1.25
but r. decide never to put a 14.13
Ought you not r. to mourn? Let him 1Co 5.02
But r. I wrote to you not to 5.11
r. suffer wrong? Why not r. be defrauded? 6.07
endure anything r. than put an 9.12
For I would r. die than have any 9.15
church I would r. speak five words 14.19
so you should r. turn to forgive 2Co 2.07
and we would r. be away from the 5.08
or r. to be known by God, how can Gal 4.09
R., speaking the truth in love, we Eph 4.15
but r. let him labor, doing honest 4.28
speculations r. than the divine 1Ti 1.04
r. they must serve all the better 6.02
of pleasure r. than lovers of God, 2Ti 3.04
r. than one named after the order Heb 7.11
choosing r. to share ill-treatment 11.25
seems painful r. than pleasant; 12.11
put out of joint but r. be healed. 12.13
I would r. not use paper and ink, 2Jn 1.12
but I would r. not write with pen 3Jn 1.13

RATIFIED
or adds to it, once it has been r. Gal 3.15
a covenant previously r. by God, 3.17
covenant was not r. without blood. Heb 9.18

RATTLE
Upon him r. the quiver, the flashing Job 39.23
he laughs at the r. of javelins. 41.29

RATTLING
was a noise, and behold, a r.; Eze 37.07

RAVAGE
of your mice that r. the land, 1Sa 6.05
and they r. it, and it be made Eze 14.15

RAVAGED
and they r. the Ammonites, and 2Sa 11.01
and r. the country of the Ammonites, 1Ch 20.01
r., she shall sit upon the ground. Is 3.26
And he r. their strongholds, and Eze 19.07

RAVAGER
the r. of our country, who has slain Ju 16.24
also created the r. to destroy; Is 54.16

RAVAGES
Rescue me from their r., my life Ps 35.17
The boar from the forest r. it, 80.13

RAVED
and he r. within his house, while 1Sa 18.10
they r. on until the time of the 1Ki 18.29

RAVEN
and sent forth a r.; and it went Gen 8.07
every r. according to its kind, Lev 11.15
every r. after its kind; Deu 14.14
Who provides for the r. its prey, Job 38.41
his locks are wavy, black as a r. Sol 5.11
the owl and the r. shall dwell in Is 34.11
the r. croak on the threshold; Zep 2.14

RAVENING
like a r. and roaring lion. Ps 22.13
your prophets like a r. lion. Jer 2.30

RAVENOUS
Benjamin is a r. wolf, in the Gen 49.27
nor shall any r. beast come up on Is 35.09
clothing but inwardly are r. wolves. Mt 7.15

RAVENS
commanded the r. to feed you there 1Ki 17.04
And the r. brought him bread and 17.06
and to the young r. which cry. Ps 147.09
out by the r. of the valley and Pro 30.17
Consider the r.: they neither sow Lk 12.24

RAVINE
with a r. between them and Ai. Jos 8.11

RAVINES
come and settle in the steep r., Is 7.19
to the r. and the valleys: Behold, I, Eze 6.03
and in all your r. those slain 35.08
the r. and the valleys, the desolate 36.04
to the r. and valleys, Thus says the 36.06

RAVISH
R. them and do with them what seems Ju 19.24

RAVISHED
and they r. my concubine, and she is Ju 20.05
You have r. my heart, my sister, my Sol 4.09
you have r. my heart with a glance 4.09
be plundered and their wives r. Is 13.16
Women are r. in Zion, virgins in the Lam 5.11
houses plundered and the women r.; Zec 14.02

RAW
eat any of it r. or boiled with Ex 12.09
there is quick r. flesh in the Lev 13.10
But when r. flesh appears on him, he 13.14
priest shall examine the r. flesh, 13.15
r. flesh is unclean, for it is 13.15
But if the r. flesh turns again and 13.16
skin and the r. flesh of the burn 13.24
boiled meat from you, but r. 1Sa 2.15

RAYS
r. flashed from his hand; Hab 3.04
a lamp with its r. gives you light Lk 11.36

RAZED
and he r. the city and sowed it Ju 9.45
they r. her palaces, they made her a Is 23.13

RAZOR
separation no r. shall come upon Num 6.05
them go with a r. over all their 8.07
No r. shall come upon his head, for Ju 13.05
"A r. has never come upon my head; 16.17
and no r. shall touch his head." 1Sa 1.11
Your tongue is like a sharp r., Ps 52.02
shave with a r. which is hired Is 7.20
as a barber's r. and pass it over Eze 5.01

REACH
loins to the thighs they shall r.; Ex 28.42
and r. to the shoulder of the sea Num 34.11
shall r. from the wall of the city 35.04
a report should r. Darius and then Ez 5.05
and his head r. to the clouds, Job 20.06
r. old age, and grow mighty in power? 21.07
waters, they shall not r. him. Ps 32.06
O God, r. the high heavens. 71.19
at Zoan and his envoys r. Hanes, Is 30.04
salvation may r. to the end of the 49.06
drink water may r. up to them in Eze 31.14
to be safe from the r. of harm! Hab 2.09
they could not r. him for the Lk 8.19
that somehow they could r. Phoenix, Ac 27.12
apportioned us, to r. even to you. 2Co 10.13
as though we did not r. you; 10.14
be judged to have failed to r. it. Heb 4.01
but that all should r. repentance. 2Pe 3.09

REACHED
and the top of it r. to heaven; Gen 28.12
set out and r. their cities on the Jos 9.17
their families r. southward to the 15.01
of Manasseh r. from Asher to 17.07
on the north Asher is r., and on the 17.10
its inheritance r. as far as Sarid; 19.10
And Ehud r. with his left hand, took Ju 3.21
of the Lord r. out the tip of the 6.21
"He r. from on high, he took me, he 2Sa 22.17
So he r. out his hand and took it. 2Ki 6.07
saying, "The messenger r. them, 9.18
"He r. them, but he is not coming 9.20
a rage which has r. up to heaven. 2Ch 28.09
and my cry to him r. his ears. Ps 18.06
He r. from on high, he took me, he 18.16
till they r. a city to dwell in. 107.07
As my hand has r. to the kingdoms Is 10.10
which r. to Jazer and strayed to 16.08
all joy has r. its eventide; 24.11
the sword has r. their very life. Jer 4.10
is bitter; it has r. your very heart." 4.18
r. as far as Jazer; upon your summer 48.32
judgment has r. up to heaven and 51.09
and its top r. to heaven, and it was Dan 4.11
so that its top r. to heaven, 4.20
and before they r. the bottom of 6.24
transgressors have r. their full 8.23
Then tidings r. the king of Nineveh, Jon 3.06
it has r. to the gate of my people, Mic 1.09
Jesus immediately r. out his hand Mt 14.31
When the disciples r. the other side, 16.05
outran Peter and r. the tomb first; Jn 20.04
who r. the tomb first, also went in, 20.08
which had been r. by the apostles Ac 16.04
or are you the only ones it has r.? 1Co 14.36
harvesters have r. the ears of the Jas 5.04

REACHES
read, "When this letter r. you, 2Ki 5.06
Though the sword r. him, it does not Job 41.26
so thy praise r. to the ends of the Ps 48.10
thy faithfulness r. to the clouds. 108.04
and r. out her hands to the needy. Pro 31.20
r. to Eglaim, the wailing r. to Beerelim. Is 15.08
stream that r. up to the neck; 30.28
greatness has grown and r. to heaven, Dan 4.22

REACHING
r. to the fortified city of Tyre; Jos 19.29
r. even to the neck; and its outspread Is 8.08

READ
and r. it in the hearing of the Ex 24.07
and he shall r. in it all the days Deu 17.19
you shall r. this law before all 31.11
And afterward he r. all the words Jos 8.34
Joshua did not r. before all the 8.35
which r., "When this letter reaches 2Ki 5.06
the king of Israel r. the letter, 5.07
hand of the messengers, and r. it; 19.14
the book to Shaphan, and he r. it. 22.08
And Shaphan r. it before the king. 22.10
which the king of Judah has r. 22.16
and he r. in their hearing all 23.02
And Shaphan r. it before the king. 2Ch 34.18
book which was r. before the king 34.24
and he r. in their hearing all 34.30
us has been plainly r. before me. Ez 4.18
letter was r. before Rehum and 4.23
And he r. from it facing the square Neh 8.03
And they r. from the book, from the 8.08
he r. from the book of the law of 8.18
their place and r. from the book 9.03
On that day they r. from the book 13.01
and they were r. before the king. Est 6.01
one who can r., saying, "R. this," Is 29.11
give the book to one who cannot r., 29.12
"R. this," he says, "I cannot r." 29.12
Seek and r. from the book of the 34.16
hand of the messengers, and r. it; 37.14
Zephaniah the priest r. this letter Jer 29.29
house you shall r. the words of 36.06
You shall r. them also in the 36.06
Baruch r. the words of Jeremiah 36.10
when Baruch r. the scroll in the 36.13
scroll that you r. in the hearing 36.14
and r. it." So Baruch r. it to them. 36.15
and Jehudi r. it to the king and 36.21
As Jehudi r. three or four columns, 36.23
see that you r. all these words, 51.61
they could not r. the writing or Dan 5.08
in before me to r. this writing 5.15
Now if you can r. the writing and 5.16
nevertheless I will r. the writing 5.17
"Have you not r. what David did, Mt 12.03
Or have you not r. in the law how 12.05
"Have you not r. that he who made 19.04
have you never r., 'Out of the 21.16

READ (cont.)
"Have you never r. in the scriptures: Mt 21.42
have you not r. what was said to 22.31
which r., "This is Jesus the King 27.37
"Have you never r. what David did, Mk 2.25
Have you not r. this scripture: 'The 12.10
have you not r. in the book of 12.26
of the charge against him r., 15.26
sabbath day. And he stood up to r.; Lk 4.16
"Have you not r. what David did 6.03
in the law? How do you r.?" 10.26
it r., "Jesus of Nazareth, the King Jn 19.19
Many of the Jews r. this title, 19.20
prophets which are r. every sabbath, Ac 13.27
for he is r. every sabbath in the 15.21
And when they r. it, they rejoiced 15.31
but what you can r. and understand; 2Co 1.13
to be known and r. by all men; 3.02
when they r. the old covenant, that 3.14
Moses is r. a veil lies over their 3.15
When you r. this you can perceive Eph 3.04
this letter has been r. among you, Col 4.16
have it r. also in the church of 4.16
see that you r. also the letter 4.16
this letter be r. to all the 1Th 5.27

READER
holy place (let the r. understand), Mt 24.15
not to be (let the r. understand), Mk 13.14

READILY
stammerers will speak r. and distinctly. Is 32.04
accepted, you submit to it r. enough. 2Co 11.04

READINESS
by the hand of a man who is in r. Lev 16.21
but hold yourselves all in r.; Jos 8.04
so that your r. in desiring it may 2Co 8.11
For if the r. is there, it is 8.12
for I know your r., of which I 9.02

READING
that the people understood the r. Neh 8.08
him about r. from the scroll the Jer 36.08
When you finish r. this book, 51.63
he was r. the prophet Isaiah. Ac 8.28
and heard him r. Isaiah the prophet, 8.30
"Do you understand what you are r.?" 8.30
scripture which he was r. was this: 8.32
After the r. of the law and the 13.15
On r. the letter, he asked to what 23.34
to the public r. of scripture, 1Ti 4.13

READS
"Whoever r. this writing, and shows Dan 5.07
tablets, so he may run who r. it. Hab 2.02
Blessed is he who r. aloud the Rev 1.03

READY
"Make r. quickly three measures of Gen 18.06
slaughter an animal and make r., 43.16
they made r. the present for 43.25
Then Joseph made r. his chariot and 46.29
So he made r. his chariot and took Ex 14.06
They are almost r. to stone me. 17.04
and be r. by the third day; 19.11
"Be r. by the third day; do not go 19.15
Be r. in the morning, and come up in 34.02
r. to go before the people of Num 32.17
you that he was r. to destroy you. Deu 9.08
so that he was r. to destroy you. 9.19
that he was r. to destroy him; 9.20
about forty thousand r. armed for Jos 4.13
and went and made r. provisions, 9.04
but if you make r. a burnt offering, Ju 13.16
of wine, and five sheep r. dressed, 1Sa 25.18
servants are r. to do whatever my 2Sa 15.15
I am r. to do all you desire in the 1Ki 5.08
"Make r." And they made r. his chariot. 2Ki 9.21
side, and if you are r. to obey me, 10.06
hundred and sixty, r. for service. 1Ch 5.18
two hundred, r. for service in war. 7.11
seasoned troops r. for battle. 12.36
we have made r. and sanctified; 2Ch 29.19
But thou art a God r. to forgive, Neh 9.17
the peoples to be r. for that day. Est 3.14
Jews were to be r. on that day to 8.13
it is r. for those whose feet slip. Job 12.05
day of darkness is r. at his hand; 15.23
extinct, the grave is r. for me. 17.01
and calamity is r. for his stumbling 18.12
new wineskins, it is r. to burst. 32.19
For I am r. to fall, and my pain is Ps 38.17
is like the pen of a r. scribe. 45.01
of mine, they run and make r. 59.04
My heart is r., O God, my heart is r.! 108.01
steadfast love be r. to comfort me 119.76
Let thy hand be r. to help me, 119.173
Condemnation is r. for scoffers, Pro 19.29
The horse is made r. for the day of 21.31
if all of them are r. on your lips. 22.18
get everything r. for you in the 24.27
yea, for the king it is made r., Is 30.33
I was r. to be sought by those who 65.01
I was r. to be found by those who 65.01
Say, 'Stand r. and be prepared, for Jer 46.14
blown the trumpet and made all r.; Eze 7.14
"Be r. and keep r., you and all 38.07
Now if you are r. when you hear the Dan 3.15
LORD has kept r. the calamity and 9.14
I have made r. my dinner, my oxen Mt 22.04
are killed, and everything is r.; 22.04
his servants, 'The wedding is r., 22.08
Therefore you also must be r.; 24.44
those who were r. went in with him 25.10
to have a boat r. for him because Mk 3.09
large upper room furnished and r.; 14.15
to make r. for the Lord a people Lk 1.17
the Samaritans, to make r. for him; 9.52
You also must be r.; for the Son 12.40
did not make r. or act according 12.47
'Come; for all is now r.' 14.17
furnished; there make r." 22.12
I am r. to go with you to prison 22.33
For I am r. not only to be imprisoned Ac 21.13
days we made r. and went up to 21.15
And we are r. to kill him before he 23.15
and now they are r., waiting for 23.21
the night get r. two hundred 23.23
for you were not r. for it; 1Co 3.02
and even yet you are not r., 3.02
sound, who will get r. for battle? 14.08
r. to day Yes and No at once? 2Co 1.17
Achaia has been r. since last year 9.02
this case, so that you may be r., 9.03
me and find that you are not r., 9.04
that it may be r. not as an 9.05
being r. to punish every disobedience, 10.06
third time I am r. to come to you. 12.14
we were r. to share with you not 1Th 2.08
of the house, r. for any good work. 2Ti 2.21
to be r. for any honest work, Tit 3.01
growing old is r. to vanish away. Heb 8.13
promises was r. to offer up his 11.17
for a salvation r. to be revealed 1Pe 1.05
to him who is r. to judge the 4.05
trumpets made r. to blow them. Rev 8.06
who had been held r. for the hour, 9.15
and his Bride has made herself r.; 19.07

REAFFIRM
So I beg you to r. your love for 2Co 2.08

REAIAH
R. the son of Shobal was the father 1Ch 4.02
Micah his son, R. his son, Baal his 5.05

REAIAH (cont.)
the sons of Gahar, the sons of R., Ez 2.47
the sons of R., the sons of Rezin, Neh 7.50

REAL
held that John was a r. prophet. Mk 11.32
what was done by the angel was r., Ac 12.09
to know the r. reason why the Jews 22.30
For he is not a r. Jew who is one Rom 2.28
and r. circumcision is a matter of 2.29
that "an idol has no r. existence," 1Co 8.04
Honor widows who are r. widows. 1Ti 5.03
She who is a r. widow, and is left 5.05
may assist those who are r. widows. 5.16

REALITIES
of the true form of these r., Heb 10.01

REALIZE
Do you not r. that Jesus Christ is 2Co 13.05

REALIZED
When he r. this, he went to the Ac 12.12
for he r. that Paul was a Roman 22.29
which he has r. in Christ Jesus Eph 3.11

REALIZING
"R. that for many years you have Ac 24.10
earnestness in r. the full assurance Heb 6.11

REALLY
"Have I r. seen God and remained Gen 16.13
whether you are r. my son Esau or 27.21
He said, "Are you r. my son Esau?" 27.24
"I r. thought that you utterly Ju 15.02
the authorities r. know that this Jn 7.26
said, "This is r. the prophet." 7.40
the Spirit of God r. dwells in you. Rom 8.09
dough, as you r. are unleavened. 1Co 5.07
eat food as r. offered to an idol; 8.07
declare that God is r. among you. 14.25
in vain?—if it r. is in vain. Gal 3.04
to me has r. served to advance the Php 1.12
word of men but as what it r. is, 1Th 2.13
If you r. fulfil the royal law, Jas 2.08

REALM
or in all his r. that Hezekiah did 2Ki 20.13
So the r. of Jehoshaphat was quiet, 2Ch 20.30
be against the r. of the king and Ez 7.23
or in all his r. that Hezekiah did Is 39.02
king over the r. of the Chaldeans— Dan 9.01
come into the r. of the king of 11.09

REAP
"When you r. the harvest of your Lev 19.09
you shall not r. your field to its 19.09
I give you and r. its harvest, 23.10
"And when you r. the harvest of 23.22
you shall not r. your field to its 23.22
in your harvest you shall not r., 25.05
nor r. what grows of itself, nor 25.11
"When you r. your harvest in your Deu 24.19
his ground and to r. his harvest, 1Sa 8.12
and r., and plant vineyards, and eat 2Ki 19.29
iniquity and sow trouble r. the same. Job 4.08
sow in tears r. with shouts of joy Ps 126.05
sows injustice will r. calamity, Pro 22.08
who regards the clouds will not r. Ecc 11.04
then in the third year sow and r., Is 37.30
and they shall r. the whirlwind. Hos 8.07
r. the fruit of steadfast love; 10.12
You shall sow, but not r.; you shall Mic 6.15
neither sow nor r. nor gather into Mt 6.26
You knew that I r. where I have not 25.26
ravens: they neither sow nor r., Lk 12.24
and r. what you did not sow. 19.21
I sent you to r. that for which you Jn 4.38
that I may r. some harvest among Rom 1.13
too much if we r. your material 1Co 9.11
sparingly will also r. sparingly, 2Co 9.06
bountifully will also r. bountifully. 9.06
a man sows, that he will also r. Gal 6.07
will from the flesh r. corruption; 6.08
from the Spirit r. eternal life. 6.08
for in due season we shall r., 6.09
and r., for the hour to r. has come, Rev 14.15

REAPED
and r. in the same year a hundredfold Gen 26.12
have sown wheat and have r. thorns, Jer 12.13
you have r. injustice, you have Hos 10.13
on the earth, and the earth was r. Rev 14.16

REAPER
with which the r. does not fill his Ps 129.07
be as when the r. gathers standing Is 17.05
field, like sheaves after the r., Jer 9.22
overtake the r. and the treader of Amo 9.13
that sower and r. may rejoice together. Jn 4.36

REAPERS
gleaned in the field after the r.; Ru 2.03
and he said to the r., "The LORD 2.04
who was in charge of the r., 2.05
was in charge of the r. answered, 2.06
among the sheaves after the r. 2.07
So she sat beside the r., and he 2.14
one day to his father among the r. 2Ki 4.18
at harvest time I will tell the r., Mt 13.30
of the age, and the r. are angels. 13.39

REAPING
upon the field which they are r., Ru 2.09
Bethshemesh were r. their wheat 1Sa 6.13
r. where you did not sow, and Mt 25.24
lay down and r. what I did not sow? Lk 19.22

REAPS
He who r. receives wages, and Jn 4.36
true, 'One sows and another r.' 4.37

REAR
and for the r. of the tabernacle Ex 26.22
of the tabernacle in the r.; 26.23
the tabernacle at the r. westward. 26.27
And for the r. of the tabernacle 36.27
of the tabernacle in the r. 36.28
the tabernacle at the r. westward. 36.32
acting as the r. guard of all the Num 10.25
cut off at your r. all who lagged Deu 25.18
and the r. guard came after the ark, Jos 6.09
and the r. guard came after the ark 6.13
city and its r. guard west of the 8.13
your enemies, fall upon their r., 10.19
passing on in the r. with Achish, 1Sa 29.02
go around to their r., and come 2Sa 5.23
him both in front and in the r., 10.09
r. an altar to the LORD on the 24.18
cubits of the r. of the house with 1Ki 6.16
him both in front and in the r., 1Ch 19.10
go up and r. an altar to the LORD 21.18
of Israel will be your r. guard. Is 52.12
of the LORD shall be your r. guard. 58.08
and his r. into the western sea; Joe 2.20

REARED
his youth I r. him as a father, and Job 31.18
"Sons have I r. and brought up, but Is 1.02
I have neither r. young men nor 23.04
I dandled and r. my enemy destroyed Lam 2.22

REARING
of young lions, r. her whelps. Eze 19.02

REASON

in the land by r. of that famine Gen 41.31
languished by r. of the famine. 47.13
land was ruined by r. of the flies. Ex 8.24
makes atonement, by r. of the life. Lev 17.11
but you shall r. with your neighbor, 19.17
he sinned by r. of the dead body. Num 6.11
And you shall bear no sin by r. of it, 18.32
is not clean by r. of what chances Deu 23.10
by r. of the abundance of all 28.47
And this is the r. why Joshua Jos 5.04
For this r. he has not come to the 1Sa 20.29
And this was the r. why he lifted 1Ki 11.27
There an upright man could r. with him, Job 23.07
or even by r. of strength fourscore Ps 90.10
Do not contend with a man for no r., Pro 3.30
let us r. together, says the LORD: Is 1.18
of branches by r. of abundant water. Eze 19.10
and my r. returned to me, and I Dan 4.34
the same time my r. returned to me; 4.36
by r. of the vision pains have come 10.16
'For this r. a man shall leave his Mt 19.05
'For this r. a man shall leave his Mk 10.07
the r. why you do not hear them is Jn 8.47
For this r. the Father loves me, 10.17
The r. why the crowd went to meet 12.18
what is the r. for your coming?" Ac 10.21
I should have r. to bear with you, O 18.14
know the real r. why the Jews 22.30
For this r. the Jews seized me in 26.21
there was no r. for the death 28.18
For this r. therefore I have asked 28.20
For this r. God gave them up to Rom 1.26
For the same r. you also pay taxes, 13.06
he who has no r. to judge himself 14.22
I have r. to be proud of my work 15.17
This is the r. why I have so often 15.22
and then his r. to boast will be in Gal 6.04
For this r., because I have heard Eph 1.15
For this r. I, Paul, a prisoner for 3.01
For this r. I bow my knees before 3.14
"For this r. a man shall leave his 5.31
Though I myself have r. for confidence Php 3.04
thinks he has r. for confidence in 3.04
up without r. by his sensuous mind, Col 2.18
For this r., when I could bear it 1Th 3.05
for this r., brethren, in all our 3.07
but I received mercy for this r., 1Ti 1.16
open to r., full of mercy and good Jas 3.17
For this very r. make every effort 2Pe 1.05
The r. why the world does not know 1Jn 3.01
The r. the Son of God appeared was 3.08

REASONED

like a child, I r. like a child; 1Co 13.11

REASONING

Hear now my r., and listen to the Job 13.06

REASSURE

and r. our hearts before him 1Jn 3.19

REASSURED

Thus he r. them and comforted them. Gen 50.21

REBA

and R., the five kings of Midian; Num 31.08
and Rekem and Zur and Hur and R., Jos 13.21

REBECCA

but also when R. had conceived children Rom 9.10

REBEKAH

Bethuel became the father of R. Gen 22.23
R., who was born to Bethuel the son 24.15
R. had a brother whose name was 24.29
heard the words of R. his sister, 24.30
R. came out with her water jar on 24.45
Behold, R. is before you, take her 24.51
and raiment, and gave them to R.; 24.53
And they called R., and said to 24.58
So they sent away R. their sister 24.59
And they blessed R., and said to 24.60
Then R. and her maids arose, and 24.61
thus the servant took R., and went 24.61
And R. lifted up her eyes, and when 24.64
and took R., and she became his 24.67
years old when he took to wife R., 25.20
and R. his wife conceived. 25.21
his game; but R. loved Jacob. 25.28
should kill me for the sake of R."; 26.07
and saw Isaac fondling R. his wife. 26.08
made life bitter for Isaac and R. 26.35
Now R. was listening when Isaac 27.05
R. said to her son Jacob, "I heard 27.06
But Jacob said to R. his mother, 27.11
Then R. took the best garments of 27.15
Esau her older son were told to R.; 27.42
Then R. said to Isaac, "I am weary 27.46
the Aramean, the brother of R., 28.05
they buried Isaac and R. his wife; 49.31

REBEKAH'S

kinsman, and that he was R. son; Gen 29.12
And Deborah, R. nurse, died, and she 35.08

REBEL

do not r. against him, for he will Ex 23.21
Only, do not r. against the LORD; Num 14.09
And if you r. against the LORD Jos 22.18
only do not r. against the LORD, or 22.19
that we should r. against the LORD, 22.29
voice and not r. against the 1Sa 12.14
but r. against the commandment of 12.15
that you and the Jews intend to r.; Neh 6.06
"There are those who r. against the Job 24.13
smitten, that you continue to r.? Is 1.05
But if you refuse and r., 1.20
from birth you were called a r. 48.08
themselves, they r. against me. Hos 7.14

REBELLED

but in the thirteenth year they r. Gen 14.04
because you r. against my command Num 20.24
you r. against my word in the 27.14
but r. against the command of the Deu 1.26
but you r. against the command of 1.43
then you r. against the commandment 9.23
of Ahab, Moab r. against Israel. 2Ki 1.01
king of Moab r. against the king 3.05
"The king of Moab has r. against me; 3.07
He r. against the king of Assyria, 18.07
rely, that you have r. against me? 18.20
then he turned and r. against him. 24.01
And Zedekiah r. against the king of 24.20
rose up and r. against his lord; 2Ch 13.06
He also r. against King Nebuchadnezzar, 36.13
disobedient and r. against thee Neh 9.26
out, for they have r. against thee. Ps 5.10
How often they r. against him in 78.40
Yet they tested and r. against the 78.56
they r. against his words. 105.28
but r. against the Most High at the 106.07
for they had r. against the words 107.11
up, but they have r. against me. Is 1.02
rely, that you have r. against me? 36.05
But they r. and grieved his holy 63.10
of the men that have r. against me; 66.24
You have all r. against me, says the Jer 2.29
that you r. against the LORD your 3.13
because she has r. against me, 4.17
And Zedekiah r. against the king of 52.03
for I have r. against his word; Lam 1.18
"We have transgressed and r., 3.42
of rebels, who have r. against me; Eze 2.03
has wickedly r. against my ordinances 5.06

REBELLED (cont.)

But he r. against him by sending Eze 17.15
But they r. against me and would 20.08
house of Israel r. against me in 20.13
But the children r. against me; 20.21
wrong and acted wickedly and r., Dan 9.05
because we have r. against him, 9.09
them, for they have r. against me! Hos 7.13
because she has r. against her God 13.16
by which you have r. against me; Zep 3.11

REBELLING

Are you r. against the king?" Neh 2.19
r. against the Most High in the Ps 78.17

REBELLION

he has taught r. against the LORD Deu 13.05
this day in r. against the LORD? Jos 22.16
If it was in r. or in breach of 22.22
For r. is as the sin of divination, 1Sa 15.23
has been in r. against the house 1Ki 12.19
has been in r. against the house 2Ch 10.19
and that r. and sedition have been Ez 4.19
For he adds r. to his sin; Job 34.37
An evil man seeks only r., Pro 17.11
have uttered r. against the LORD. Jer 28.16
he has talked r. against the LORD. 29.32
of their sin and r. against me. 33.08
unless the r. comes first, and the 2Th 2.03
harden your hearts as in the r., Heb 3.08
harden your hearts as in the r. 3.15
error, and perish in Korah's r. Jud 1.11

REBELLIOUS

you have been r. against the LORD. Deu 9.07
You have been r. against the LORD 9.24
"If a man has a stubborn and r. son, 21.18
'This our son is stubborn and r., 21.20
For I know how r. and stubborn you 31.27
you have been r. against the LORD; 31.27
r. woman, do I not know that you 1Sa 20.30
rebuilding that r. and wicked city Ez 4.12
learn that this city is a r. city, 4.15
let not the r. exalt themselves. Ps 66.07
but the r. dwell in a parched land. 68.06
gifts among men, even among the r., 68.18
a stubborn and r. generation, 78.08
but they were r. in their purposes, 106.43
"Woe to the r. children," says the Is 30.01
For they are a r. people, lying sons, 30.09
and I was not r., I turned not 50.05
hands all the day to a r. people, 65.02
people has a stubborn and r. heart; Jer 5.23
They are all stubbornly r., going about 6.28
me, because I have been very r. Lam 1.20
(for they are a r. house) they will Eze 2.05
looks, for they are a r. house. 2.06
to hear; for they are a r. house. 2.07
be not r. like that r. house; open your 2.08
looks, for they are a r. house." 3.09
reprove them; for they are a r. house. 3.26
him refuse; for they are a r. house. 3.27
dwell in the midst of a r. house, 12.02
for they are a r. house. Therefore, 12.03
understand, though they are a r. house. 12.03
the r. house, said to you, 'What are 12.09
O r. house, I will speak the word 12.25
"Say now to the r. house, Do you not 17.12
allegory to the r. house and say 24.03
And say to the r. house, to the 44.06
Woe to her that is r. and defiled, Zep 3.01
they that heard and yet were r.? Heb 3.16

REBELS

to be kept as a sign for the r., Num 17.10
he said to them, "Hear now, you r.; 20.10
Whoever r. against your commandment Jos 1.18
or make us as r. by building yourselves 22.19
Your princes are r. and companions Is 1.23
But r. and sinners shall be destroyed 1.28
of Israel, to a nation of r., Eze 2.03
purge out the r. from among you, 20.38
love them no more; all their princes are r. Hos 9.15
And among the r. in prison, who had Mk 15.07

REBUILD

and r. the house of the LORD, the Ez 1.03
to go up to r. the house of the 1.05
and began to r. the house of God 5.02
of the Jews r. this house of God 6.07
sepulchres, that I may r. it. Neh 2.05
If he tears down, none can r.; Job 12.14
r. the walls of Jerusalem, Ps 51.18
save Zion and r. the cities of 69.35
and r. them as they were at first. Jer 33.07
and r. it as in the days of old; Amo 9.11
and they shall r. the ruined 9.14
not yet come to r. the house of Hag 1.02
shattered but we will r. the ruins, Mal 1.04
and I will r. the dwelling of David, Ac 15.16
I will r. its ruins, and I will set 15.16

REBUILDING

and of the r. of the house of God 2Ch 24.27
They are r. that rebellious and Ez 4.12
and we are r. the house that was 5.11
king for the r. of this house of 5.17
Jews for the r. of this house of 6.08

REBUILDS

man that rises up and r. this city, Jos 6.26

REBUILT

and he r. the city, and settled in Jos 19.50
And they r. the city, and dwelt in Ju 18.28
and r. the towns, and dwelt in them. 21.23
so Solomon r. Gezer) and Bethhoron 1Ki 9.17
For he r. the high places which 2Ki 21.03
Solomon r. the cities which Huram 2Ch 8.02
For he r. the high places which his 33.03
if this city is r. and the walls Ez 4.13
if this city is r. and its walls 4.16
and that this city be not r., 4.21
this house of God should be r. 5.13
the house of God be r. on its site. 5.15
at Jerusalem, let the house be r., 6.03
they r. it and set its doors, its Neh 3.13
he r. it and set its doors, its 3.14
he r. it and covered it and set its 3.15
the earth who r. ruins for themselves, Job 3.14
city no more, it will never be r. Is 25.02
And your ancient ruins shall be r.; 58.12
city shall be r. upon its mound, Jer 30.18
city shall be r. for the LORD from 31.38
you shall never be r.; for I the LORD Eze 26.14
inhabited and the waste places r.; 36.10
and the waste places shall be r. 36.33
have r. the ruined places, and 36.36

REBUKE

her to glean, and do not r. her. Ru 2.16
at the r. of the LORD, at the blast 2Sa 22.16
day of distress, of r., and of disgrace; 2Ki 19.03
and will r. the words which the 19.04
God of our fathers see and r. you. 1Ch 12.17
He will surely r. you if in secret Job 13.10
tremble, and are astounded at his r. 26.11
O LORD, r. me not in thy anger, nor Ps 6.01
at thy r., O LORD, at the blast of 18.15
O LORD, r. me not in thy anger, nor 38.01
But now I r. you, and lay the charge 50.21
R. the beasts that dwell among the 68.30
At thy r., O God of Jacob, both 76.06
perish at the r. of thy countenance 80.16
At thy r. they fled; at the sound 104.07
Thou dost r. the insolent, accursed 119.21

REBUKE (cont.)
man strike or r. me in kindness, Ps 141.05
a scoffer does not listen to r. Pro 13.01
A r. goes deeper into a man of 17.10
but those who r. the wicked will 24.25
Better is open r. than hidden love. 27.05
lest he r. you, and you be found a 30.06
man to hear the r. of the wise Ecc 7.05
but he will r. them, and they will Is 17.13
day of distress, of r., and of disgrace; 37.03
and will r. the words which the 37.04
Behold, by my r. I dry up the sea, I 50.02
of the LORD, the r. of your God. 51.20
angry with you and will not r. you. 54.09
and his r. with flames of fire. 66.15
to Satan, "The LORD r. you, O Satan! Zec 3.02
who has chosen Jerusalem r. you! 3.02
Behold, I will r. your offspring, and Mal 2.03
I will r. the devourer for you, so 3.11
Peter took him and began to r. him, Mt 16.22
took him, and began to r. him. Mk 8.32
r. him, and if he repents, forgive Lk 17.03
to him, "Teacher, r. your disciples. 19.39
Do not r. an older man but exhort 1Ti 5.01
r. them in the presence of all, so 5.20
r., and exhort, be unfailing in 2Ti 4.02
Therefore r. them sharply, that they Tit 1.13
him, but said, "The Lord r. you." Jud 1.09

REBUKED
of my hands, and r. you last night. Gen 31.42
his father r. him, and said to him, 37.10
he r. kings on their account, 1Ch 16.21
Thou hast r. the nations, thou hast Ps 9.05
he r. kings on their account, 105.14
He r. the Red Sea, and it became dry 106.09
have you not r. Jeremiah of Jer 29.27
he rose and r. the winds and the Mt 8.26
And Jesus r. him, and the demon came 17.18
The disciples r. the people; 19.13
The crowd r. them, telling them to 20.31
But Jesus r. him, saying, "Be silent, Mk 1.25
And he awoke and r. the wind, 4.39
he r. Peter, and said, "Get behind me, 8.33
he r. the unclean spirit, saying to 9.25
and the disciples r. them. 10.13
And many r. him, telling him to be 10.48
But Jesus r. him, saying, "Be silent, Lk 4.35
he stood over her and r. the fever, 4.39
"But he r. them, and would not 4.41
he awoke and r. the wind and the 8.24
But Jesus r. the unclean spirit, and 9.42
But he turned and r. them. 9.55
the disciples saw it, they r. them. 18.15
And those who were in front r. him, 18.39
But the other r. him, saying, "Do you 23.40
but was r. for his own transgression 2Pe 2.16

REBUKES
hear, and in whose mouth are no r. Ps 38.14
dost chasten man with r. for sin, 39.11
He who r. a man will afterward find Pro 28.23
He r. the sea and makes it dry, he Nah 1.04

RECAH
of Irnahash. These are the men of R. 1Ch 4.12

RECALL
r. it to mind, you transgressors, Is 46.08
But r. the former days when, after Heb 10.32
at any time to r. these things. 2Pe 1.15

RECALLING
r. their iniquity, when they turn to Eze 29.16

RECEDED
and the waters r. from the earth Gen 8.03

RECEIVE
its mouth to r. your brother's Gen 4.11
to r. the pledge from the woman's 38.20
you shall r. the offering for me. Ex 25.02
which you shall r. from them: 25.03
make pots for it to r. its ashes, 27.03
"They shall r. gold, blue and purple 28.05
which you r. from the people of Num 18.28
the mountain to r. the tables of Deu 9.09
and should r. no mercy but be Jos 11.20
up there, and you shall r. it; 1Ki 5.09
too small to r. the burnt offering 8.64
whom I serve, I will r. none. 2Ki 5.16
when the Levites r. the tithes; Neh 10.38
Shall we r. good at the hand of God, Job 2.10
of God, and shall we not r. evil? 2.10
Why did the knees r. me? Or why the 3.12
R. instruction from his mouth, and 22.22
oppressors r. from the Almighty: 27.13
or what does he r. from your hand? 35.07
He will r. blessing from the LORD, Ps 24.05
power of Sheol, for he will r. me. 49.15
afterward thou wilt r. me to glory. 73.24
r. instruction in wise dealing, Pro 1.03
My son, if you r. my words and 2.01
let your ear r. the word of his Jer 9.20
might not hear and r. instruction. 17.23
not listened to r. instruction. 32.33
Will you not r. instruction and 35.13
of Benjamin to r. his portion 37.12
speak to you r. in your heart, Eze 3.10
you shall r. from me gifts and Dan 2.06
the Most High shall r. the kingdom, 7.18
fall, they shall r. a little help. 11.34
one will not r. you or listen to Mt 10.14
a prophet shall r. a prophet's 10.41
man shall r. a righteous man's 10.41
the blind r. their sight and the 11.05
"Not all men can r. this precept, 19.11
who is able to r. this, let him r. it." 19.12
will r. a hundredfold, and inherit 19.29
they thought they would r. more; 20.10
you will r., if you have faith. 21.22
you will r. greater condemnation. * 23.14
word, immediately r. it with joy; Mk 4.16
place will not r. you and they 6.11
does not r. the kingdom of God 10.15
who will not r. a hundredfold now 10.30
to him, "Master, let me r. my sight." 10.51
in prayer, believe that you r. it, 11.24
They will r. the greater condemnation 12.40
to those from whom you hope to r., Lk 6.34
to sinners, to r. as much again. 6.34
the blind r. their sight, the lame 7.22
they hear the word, r. it with joy; 8.13
And wherever they do not r. you, 9.05
but the people would not r. him, 9.53
Whenever you enter a town and they r. you, 10.08
a town and they do not r. you, 10.10
his will, shall r. a severe beating. 12.47
a beating, shall r. a light beating. 12.48
that people may r. me into their 16.04
fails they may r. you into the 16.09
does not r. the kingdom of God 18.17
who will not r. manifold more in 18.30
He said, "Lord, let me r. my sight. 18.41
And Jesus said to him, "R. your sight; 18.42
far country to r. kingly power and 19.12
They will r. the greater condemnation 20.47
but you do not r. our testimony. Jn 3.11
"No one can r. anything except what 3.27
testimony which I r. is from man; 5.34
I do not r. glory from men. 5.41
Father's name, and you do not r. me; 5.43
in his own name, him you will r. 5.43
who r. glory from one another and 5.44
who believed in him were to r.; 7.39

RECEIVE (cont.)

me and does not r. my sayings has Jn 12.48
of truth, whom the world cannot r., 14.17
and you will r., that your joy may 16.24
said to them, "R. the Holy Spirit. 20.22
But you shall r. power when the Ac 1.08
and you shall r. the gift of the 2.38
expecting to r. something from them 3.05
whom heaven must r. until the time 3.21
prayed, "Lord Jesus, r. my spirit. 7.59
that they might r. the Holy Spirit 8.15
my hands may r. the Holy Spirit. 8.19
wrote to the disciples to r. him. 18.27
"Did you r. the Holy Spirit when 19.02
is more blessed to give than to r. 20.35
me, 'Brother Saul, r. your sight.' 22.13
that they may r. forgiveness of 26.18
will those who r. the abundance of Rom 5.17
For you did not r. the spirit of 8.15
to you they also may r. mercy. 11.31
and you will r. his approval, 13.03
that you may r. her in the Lord as 16.02
man does not r. the gifts of the 1Co 2.14
and each shall r. his wages 3.08
survives, he will r. a reward. 3.14
every man will r. his commendation 4.05
what have you that you did not r.? 4.07
They do it to r. a perishable 9.25
that each one may r. good or evil, 2Co 5.10
or if you r. a different spirit 11.04
For I did not r. it from man, nor Gal 1.12
Did you r. the Spirit by words of 3.02
that we might r. the promise of the 3.14
that we might r. adoption as sons. 4.05
to you that if you r. circumcision, 5.02
For even those who r. circumcision 6.13
he will r. the same again from the Eph 6.08
So r. him in the Lord with all joy; Php 2.29
Lord you will r. the inheritance Col 3.24
if he comes to you, r. him), 4.10
r. him as you would r. me. Phm 1.17
that we may r. mercy and find grace Heb 4.16
of Levi who r. the priestly office 7.05
are called may r. the promised 9.15
will of God and r. what is promised 10.36
which he was to r. as an inheritance 11.08
speaking, he did r. him back. 11.19
did not r. what was promised, 11.39
will r. anything from the Lord. Jas 1.07
test he will r. the crown of life 1.12
wickedness and r. with meekness 1.21
You ask and do not r., because you 4.03
and we r. from him whatever we ask, 1Jn 3.22
If we r. the testimony of men, the 5.09
do not r. him into the house or 2Jn 1.10
to r. glory and honor and power, for Rev 4.11
to r. power and wealth and wisdom 5.12
but they are to r. authority as 17.12

RECEIVED

with such favor have you r. me. Gen 33.10
your sacks for you; I r. your money." 43.23
And he r. the gold at their hand, Ex 32.04
and they r. from Moses all the 36.03
Behold, I r. a command to bless: he Num 23.20
the priest r. from them the gold, 31.51
the priest r. the gold from the 31.54
houses have r. their inheritance, 34.14
half-tribe have r. their inheritance 34.15
and the Gadites r. their inheritance, Jos 13.08
of Israel r. in the land of Canaan, 14.01
and Ephraim, r. their inheritance. 16.04
of Manasseh r. an inheritance 17.06
Manasseh have r. their inheritance 18.07
the priest r. by lot from the 21.04
the Kohathites r. by lot from the 21.05
The Gershonites r. by lot from the 21.06
their families r. from the tribe 21.07
Then David r. from her hand what 1Sa 25.35
the insult I r. at the hand of 25.39
king's traders r. them from Kue at 1Ki 10.28
Hezekiah r. the letter from the 2Ki 19.14
and when they r. help against them, 1Ch 5.20
Then David r. them, and made them 12.18
king's traders r. them from Kue 2Ch 1.16
wounds which he had r. at Ramah, 22.06
and the priests r. the blood and 29.22
which they r. from the hand of the 30.16
and God r. his entreaty and heard 33.13
and how God r. his entreaty, and all 33.19
which they r. from them while the 35.11
my ear r. the whisper of it. Job 4.12
I looked and r. instruction. Pro 24.32
Hezekiah r. the letter from the Is 37.14
that she has r. from the LORD's hand 40.02
King Zedekiah sent for him, and r. him. Jer 37.17
the prophet and r. him at the 38.14
And Darius the Mede r. the kingdom, Dan 5.31
when the saints r. the kingdom. 7.22
'The wounds I r. in the house of my Zec 13.06
You r. without pay, give without pay Mt 10.08
came, each of them r. a denarius. 20.09
each of them also r. a denarius. 20.10
immediately they r. their sight and 20.34
He who had r. the five talents went 25.16
But he who had r. the one talent, 25.18
And he who had r. the five talents 25.20
He also who had r. the one talent 25.24
I should have r. what was my own 25.27
immediately he r. his sight and Mk 10.52
and the guards r. him with blows. 14.65
for you have r. your consolation. Lk 6.24
days drew near for him to be r. up, 9.51
named Martha r. him into her house 10.38
because he has r. him safe and 15.27
your lifetime r. your good things, 16.25
And immediately he r. his sight and 18.43
and came down, and r. him joyfully. 19.06
having r. the kingly power, he 19.15
and his own people r. him not. Jn 1.11
But to all who r. him, who believed 1.12
And from his fulness have we all r., 1.16
I went and washed and r. my sight. 9.11
asked him how he had r. his sight. 9.15
been blind and had r. his sight, 9.18
of the man who had r. his sight, 9.18
charge I have r. from my Father. 10.18
and they have r. them and know in 17.08
When Jesus had r. the vinegar, he 19.30
and having r. from the Father the Ac 2.33
So those who r. his word were 2.41
and he r. living oracles to give to 7.38
you who r. the law as delivered by 7.53
Samaria had r. the word of God, 8.14
them and they r. the Holy Spirit. 8.17
people who have r. the Holy Spirit 10.47
also had r. the word of God. 11.01
Having r. this charge, he put them 16.24
and Jason has r. them; 17.07
for they r. the word with all 17.11
ministry which I r. from the Lord 20.24
Jerusalem, the brethren r. us gladly. 21.17
From them I r. letters to the 22.05
very hour I r. my sight and saw 22.13
who r. us and entertained us 28.07
"We have r. no letters from Judea 28.21
through whom we have r. grace and Rom 1.05
by his blood, to be r. by faith. 3.25
He r. circumcision as a sign or 4.11
we have now r. our reconciliation. 5.11
but you have r. the spirit of 8.15
but now have r. mercy because of 11.30
Now we have r. not the spirit of 1Co 2.12
If then you r. it, why do you boast 4.07

RECEIVED (cont.)
For I r. from the Lord what I also 1Co 11.23
which you r., in which you stand, 15.01
of first importance what I also r., 15.03
that we had r. the sentence of 2Co 1.09
trembling with which you r. him. 7.15
different spirit from the one you r., 11.04
Five times I have r. at the hands 11.24
contrary to that which you r., Gal 1.09
but r. me as an angel of God, as 4.14
learned and r. and heard and seen Php 4.09
I have r. full payment, and more; 4.18
having r. from Epaphroditus the 4.18
As therefore you r. Christ Jesus Col 2.06
whom you have r. instructions— 4.10
which you have r. in the Lord. 4.17
for you r. the word in much affliction, 1Th 1.06
that when you r. the word of God 2.13
the tradition that you r. from us. 2Th 3.06
but I r. mercy because I had acted 1Ti 1.13
but I r. mercy for this reason, that 1.16
created to be r. with thanksgiving 4.03
if it is r. with thanksgiving; 4.04
or disobedience r. a just retribution, Heb 2.02
who formerly r. the good news 4.06
their genealogy r. tithes from 7.06
Here tithes are r. by mortal men; 7.08
under it the people r. the law), 7.11
the men of old r. divine approval. 11.02
which he r. approval as righteous, 11.04
Sarah herself r. power to conceive, 11.11
not having r. what was promised, but 11.13
and he who had r. the promises was 11.17
r. promises, stopped the mouths of 11.33
Women r. their dead by resurrection 11.35
works when she r. the messengers Jas 2.25
had not r. mercy but now you r. mercy. 1Pe 2.10
As each has r. a gift, employ it for 4.10
For when he r. honor and glory from 2Pe 1.17
which you r. from him abides in 1Jn 2.27
I myself have r. power from my Rev 2.27
Remember then what you r. and heard; 3.03
who have not yet r. royal power, 17.12
those who had r. the mark of the 19.20
and had not r. its mark on their 20.04

RECEIVES
besides what he r. from the sale Deu 18.08
who r. strangers instead of her Eze 16.32
For every one who asks r., and he who Mt 7.08
"He who r. you r. me, and he 10.40
and he who r. me r. him who 10.40
He who r. a prophet because he is a 10.41
and he who r. a righteous man 10.41
and immediately r. it with joy; 13.20
"Whoever r. one such child in my 18.05
one such child in my name r. me; 18.05
r. one such child in my name r. me; Mk 9.37
r. me, r. not me but him who sent me." 9.37
"Whoever r. this child in my name r. me, Lk 9.48
whoever r. me r. him who sent me; 9.48
For every one who asks r., 11.10
"This man r. sinners and eats with 15.02
heard, yet no one r. his testimony; Jn 3.32
he who r. his testimony sets his 3.33
He who reaps r. wages, and gathers 4.36
the sabbath a man r. circumcision, 7.23
he who r. any one whom I send r. me; 13.20
and he who r. me r. him who sent me." 13.20
believes in him r. forgiveness of Ac 10.43
compete, but only one r. the prize? 1Co 9.24
every man who r. circumcision that Gal 5.03
cultivated, r. a blessing from God. Heb 6.07
who r. tithes, paid tithes through 7.09
and chastises every son whom he r. 12.06
it until it r. the early and the Jas 5.07
no one knows except him who r. it. Rev 2.17

and r. a mark on his forehead or on 14.09
and whoever r. the mark of its name 14.11

RECEIVING
in thy steps, r. direction from thee, Deu 33.03
and r. gifts among men, even among Ps 68.18
And on r. it they grumbled at the Mt 20.11
for we are r. the due reward of our Lk 23.41
So, after r. the morsel, he immediately Jn 13.30
and r. a command for Silas and Ac 17.15
with men and r. in their own Rom 1.27
in giving and r. except you only; Php 4.15
deliberately after r. the knowledge Heb 10.26
be grateful for r. a kingdom that 12.28

RECENT
He must not be a r. convert, 1Ti 3.06

RECENTLY
You r. repented and did what was Jer 34.15
who r. stirred up a revolt and led Ac 21.38

RECESSED
the house windows with r. frames. 1Ki 6.04
three had windows with r. frames. Eze 41.16
And there were r. windows and palm 41.26

RECESSES
mountains, to the far r. of Lebanon; 2Ki 19.23
or walked in the r. of the deep? Job 38.16
mountains, to the far r. of Lebanon; Is 37.24

RECHAB
and the name of the other R., 2Sa 4.02
R. and Baanah, set out, and about the 4.05
so R. and Baanah his brother 4.06
But David answered R. and Baanah 4.09
the son of R. coming to meet him; 2Ki 10.15
Baal with Jehonadab the son of R.; 10.23
the father of the house of R. 1Ch 2.55
Malchijah the son of R., Neh 3.14
no wine, for Jonadab the son of R., Jer 35.06
the voice of Jonadab the son of R., 35.08
the son of R. gave to his sons, to 35.14
the son of R. have kept the 35.16
the son of R. shall never lack a 35.19

RECHABITES
"Go to the house of the R., Jer 35.02
and the whole house of the R. 35.03
set before the R. pitchers full of 35.05
the house of the R. Jeremiah said, 35.18

RECITE
in a book and r. it in the ears of Ex 17.14
right have you to r. my statutes, Ps 50.16

RECITED
Moses came and r. all the words of Deu 32.44

RECKLESS
hired worthless and r. fellows, Ju 9.04
treacherous, r., swollen with 2Ti 3.04

RECKLESSNESS
astray by their lies and their r., Jer 23.32

RECKON
let him r. the years since he sold Lev 25.27
He shall r. with him who bought him 25.50
that he may r. the amount of the 2Ki 22.04
whom the Lord will not r. his sin. Rom 4.08
understanding r. the number of the Rev 13.18

RECKONED
and he r. it to him as righteousness. Gen 15.06
them shall be r. with the fields Lev 25.31
r. by the shekel of the sanctuary; Num 3.50
shall be r. to you as though it 18.27

RECKONED (cont.)
rest shall be r. to the Levites as Num 18.30
of Ekron, it is r. as Canaanite; Jos 13.03
(for Beeroth also is r. to Benjamin; 2Sa 4.02
of their generations was r.: 1Ch 5.07
I am r. among those who go down to Ps 88.04
And that has been r. to him as 106.31
how they are r. as earthen pots, the Lam 4.02
"He was r. with the transgressors" *Mk 15.28
'And he was r. with transgressors'; Lk 22.37
and it was r. to him as righteousness." Rom 4.03
wages are not r. as a gift but as 4.04
his faith is r. as righteousness. 4.05
that faith was r. to Abraham as 4.09
How then was it r. to him? 4.10
have righteousness r. to them, 4.11
his faith was "r. to him as 4.22
"it was r. to him," were written not 4.23
It will be r. to us who believe in 4.24
the promise are r. as descendants. 9.08
and it was r. to him as righteousness." Gal 3.06
and it was r. to him as righteousness"; Jas 2.23

RECKONING
lifeblood I will surely require a r.; Gen 9.05
now there comes a r. for his blood." 42.22
he shall make a r. with him; Lev 25.52
r. by the shekel of the sanctuary, Num 3.47
and not r. itself among the nations! 23.09
became a father's house in one r. 1Ch 23.11
for he is like one who is inwardly r. Pro 23.07
When he began the r., one was Mt 18.24

RECKONS
man to whom God r. righteousness Rom 4.06

RECOGNITION
well as yours. Give r. to such men. 1Co 16.18

RECOGNIZE
And he did not r. him, because his Gen 27.23
arose before one could r. another; Ru 3.14
him from afar, they did not r. him; Job 2.12
they did not r. him nor understand Ac 13.27
they did not r. the land, but they 27.39
we r. no other practice, nor do the 1Co 11.16
If any one does not r. this, he is 14.38

RECOGNIZED
And he r. it, and said, "It is my Gen 37.33
they r. the voice of the young Ju 18.03
Saul r. David's voice, and said, "Is 1Sa 26.17
and Obadiah r. him, and fell on his 1Ki 18.07
king of Israel r. him as one of 20.41
they are not r. in the streets; Lam 4.08
And when the men of that place r. him, Mt 14.35
immediately the people r. him, Mk 6.54
eyes were opened and they r. him; Lk 24.31
and r. him as the one who sat for Ac 3.10
and they r. that they had been with 4.13
But when they r. that he was a Jew, 19.34
are genuine among you may be r. 1Co 11.19
not recognize this, he is not r. 14.38

RECOGNIZING
But their eyes were kept from r. him. Lk 24.16
R. Peter's voice, in her joy she did Ac 12.14

RECOILS
My heart r. within me, my compassion Hos 11.08

RECOMMENDATION
letters of r. to you, or from you? 2Co 3.01
You yourselves are our letter of r., 3.02

RECOMPENSE
and r., for the time when their Deu 32.35
The LORD r. you for what you have Ru 2.12
should the king r. me with such a 2Sa 19.36
for emptiness will be his r. Job 15.31
Let him r. it to themselves, that 21.19
so r. them for their crime; Ps 56.07
eyes and see the r. of the wicked. 91.08
a year of r. for the cause of Zion. Is 34.08
with vengeance, with the r. of God. 35.04
is with him, and his r. before him. 40.10
the LORD, and my r. with my God." 49.04
will faithfully give them their r., 61.08
is with him, and his r. before him." 62.11
LORD, rendering r. to his enemies! 66.06
And I will doubly r. their iniquity Jer 16.18
Is evil a r. for good? Yet they have 18.20
and I will r. them according to 25.14
for the LORD is a God of r., 51.56
of Egypt as his r. for which he Eze 29.20
come, the days of r. have come; Hos 9.07
bringing my r., to repay every one Rev 22.12

RECOMPENSED
the cleanness of my hands he r. me. 2Sa 22.21
Therefore the LORD has r. me 22.25
the cleanness of my hands he r. me. Ps 18.20
Therefore the LORD has r. me 18.24

RECONCILE
this fellow r. himself to his lord? 1Sa 29.04
and might r. us both to God in one Eph 2.16
and through him to r. to himself Col 1.20

RECONCILED
first be r. to your brother, and Mt 5.24
quarreling and would have r. them, Ac 7.26
enemies we were r. to God by the Rom 5.10
Son, much more, now that we are r., 5.10
or else be r. to her husband)—and 1Co 7.11
through Christ r. us to himself 2Co 5.18
on behalf of Christ, be r. to God. 5.20
he has now r. in his body of flesh Col 1.22

RECONCILIATION
whom we have now received our r. Rom 5.11
rejection means the r. of the world, 11.15
and gave us the ministry of r.; 2Co 5.18
entrusting to us the message of r. 5.19

RECONCILING
was in Christ r. the world to 2Co 5.19

RECORD
and they kept a genealogical r. 1Ch 4.33
on which this was written: "A r. Ez 6.02

RECORDED
which is not r. in the book of Deu 28.61
r. them in the presence of the king, 1Ch 24.06
which are r. in the Book of the 2Ch 20.34
the weight of everything was r. Ez 8.34
there were r. the heads of fathers' Neh 12.22
And it was r. in the Book of the Est 2.23
And Mordecai r. these things, and 9.20
of Purim, and it was r. in writing. 9.32
Let this be r. for a generation to Ps 102.18
who has been r. for life in Is 4.03

RECORDER
Jehoshaphat the son of Ahilud was r.; 2Sa 8.16
the son of Ahilud was the r.; 20.24
Jehoshaphat the son of Ahilud was r.; 1Ki 4.03
and Joah the son of Asaph, the r. 2Ki 18.18
the r., came to Hezekiah with their 18.37
Jehoshaphat the son of Ahilud was r.; 1Ch 18.15
the r., to repair the house of the 2Ch 34.08
and Joah the son of Asaph, the r. Is 36.03
the r., came to Hezekiah with their 36.22

RECORDS
to Lehem (now the r. are ancient). 1Ch 4.22
the book of the r. of your fathers. Ez 4.15
the book of the r. and learn that 4.15
The LORD r. as he registers the Ps 87.06

RECOUNT
that I may r. all thy praises, that Ps 9.14
on thy name and r. thy wondrous 75.01
generation we will r. thy praise. 79.13
and r. the deeds of the LORD. 118.17
I will r. the steadfast love of the Is 63.07

RECOUNTED
deeds which our fathers r. to us, Ju 6.13
And Haman r. to them the splendor Est 5.11

RECOUNTS
with joy. He r. to men his salvation, Job 33.26

RECOVER
why did you not r. them within Ju 11.26
whether I shall r. from this 2Ki 1.02
'Shall I r. from this sickness?' 8.08
'Shall I r. from this sickness?' 8.09
to him, 'You shall certainly r.'; 8.10
me that you would certainly r." 8.14
you shall die, you shall not r.' " 20.01
lay it on the boil, that he may r." 20.07
Jeroboam did not r. his power in 2Ch 13.20
second time to r. the remnant Is 11.11
you shall die, you shall not r." 38.01
it to the boil, that he may r." 38.21
hands on the sick; and they will r." *Mk 16.18
he has fallen asleep, he will r." Jn 11.12

RECOVERED
another, until David r. himself. 1Sa 20.41
David r. all that the Amalekites 30.18
any of the spoil which we have r., 30.22
defeated him and r. the cities of 2Ki 13.25
and how he r. for Israel Damascus 14.28
the king of Edom r. Elath for Edom, 16.06
sick and had r. from his sickness: Is 38.09
that he had been sick and had r. 39.01

RECOVERING
captives and r. of sight to the Lk 4.18

RED
The first came forth r., all his body Gen 25.25
"Let me eat some of that r. pottage, 25.30
his eyes shall be r. with wine, 49.12
and drove them into the R. Sea; Ex 10.19
the wilderness toward the R. Sea. 13.18
officers are sunk in the R. Sea. 15.04
led Israel onward from the R. Sea, 15.22
bounds from the R. Sea to the sea 23.31
wilderness by the way to the R. Sea. Num 14.25
to bring you a r. heifer without 19.02
set out by the way to the R. Sea, 21.04
Elim, and encamped by the R. Sea. 33.10
And they set out from the R. Sea, 33.11
in the direction of the R. Sea. Deu 1.40
in the direction of the R. Sea, 2.01
water of the R. Sea overflow them 11.04
water of the R. Sea before you Jos 2.10
LORD your God did to the R. Sea, 4.23
chariots and horsemen to the R. Sea. 24.06
wilderness to the R. Sea and came Ju 11.16
Eloth on the shore of the R. Sea, 1Ki 9.26
water opposite them as r. as blood. 2Ki 3.22
and hear their cry at the R. Sea, Neh 9.09
My face is r. with weeping, and on Job 16.16
the Most High at the R. Sea. Ps 106.07
He rebuked the R. Sea, and it became 106.09
and terrible things by the R. Sea. 106.22
who divided the R. Sea in sunder, 136.13
Pharaoh and his host in the R. Sea, 136.15
Do not look at wine when it is r., Pro 23.31
though they are r. like crimson, Is 1.18
Why is thy apparel r., and thy garments 63.02
cry shall be heard at the R. Sea. Jer 49.21
The shield of his mighty men is r., Nah 2.03
a man riding upon a r. horse! Zec 1.08
and behind him were r., sorrel, and 1.08
The first chariot had r. horses, 6.02
fair weather; for the sky is r.' Mt 16.02
for the sky is r. and threatening.' 16.03
signs in Egypt and at the R. Sea, Ac 7.36
crossed the R. Sea as if on dry Heb 11.29
And out came another horse, bright r.; Rev 6.04
behold a great r. dragon, with seven 12.03

REDDISH
greenish or r. in the garment, Lev 13.49
house with greenish or r. spots, 14.37

REDDISH-WHITE
a white swelling or a r. spot, Lev 13.19
burn becomes a spot, r. or white, 13.24
bald forehead a r. diseased spot, 13.42
swelling is r. on his bald head or 13.43

REDEEM
and I will r. you with an outstretched Ex 6.06
of an ass you shall r. with a lamb, 13.13
if you will not r. it you shall 13.13
man among your sons you shall r. 13.13
all the first-born of my sons I r. 13.15
of an ass you shall r. with a lamb, 34.20
if you will not r. it you shall 34.20
first-born of your sons you shall r. 34.20
shall come and r. what his brother Lev 25.25
If a man has no one to r. it, 25.26
finds sufficient means to r. it, 25.26
he may r. it within a whole year 25.29
the Levites may r. at any time. 25.32
one of his brothers may r. him, 25.48
uncle, or his cousin may r. him, 25.49
belonging to his family may r. him; 25.49
if he grows rich he may r. himself. 25.49
But if he wishes to r. it, 27.13
dedicates it wishes to r. his house, 27.15
dedicates the field wishes to r. it, 27.19
he does not wish to r. the field, 27.20
If a man wishes to r. any of his 27.31
the first-born of man you shall r., Num 18.15
of unclean beasts you shall r. 18.15
old you shall r. them) you shall 18.16
of a goat, you shall not r.; 18.17
If you will r. it, r. it; Ru 4.04
is no one besides you to r. it, 4.04
And he said, "I will r. it." 4.04
"I cannot r. it for myself, lest I 4.06
yourself, for I cannot r. it. 4.06
God went to r. to be his people, 2Sa 7.23
God went to r. to be his people, 1Ch 17.21
whom thou didst r. from Egypt? 17.21
In famine he will r. you from death, Job 5.20
R. Israel, O God, out of all his Ps 25.22
r. me, and be gracious to me. 26.11
r. me, set me free because of my 69.18
Thou didst with thy arm r. thy people, 77.15
R. me from man's oppression, that I 119.134
Plead my cause and r. me; 119.154
And he will r. Israel from all his 130.08
hand shortened, that it cannot r.? Is 50.02
and r. you from the grasp of the Jer 15.21
I would r. them, but they speak lies Hos 7.13
Shall I r. them from Death? 13.14
the LORD will r. you from the hand Mic 4.10
that he was the one to r. Israel. Lk 24.21
to r. those who were under the law, Gal 4.05
for us to r. us from all iniquity Tit 2.14

REDEEMED

the angel who has r. me from all Gen 48.16
love the people whom thou hast r., Ex 15.13
then he shall let her be r.; 21.08
If it is not r. within a full year, Lev 25.30
they may be r., and they shall be 25.31
then after he is sold he may be r.; 25.48
And if he is not r. by these means, 25.54
man, it shall not be r. any more; 27.20
if it is not r., it shall be sold 27.27
inherited field, shall be sold or r.; 27.28
be holy: it shall not be r." 27.33
of them is r. to Aaron and his Num 3.48
and above those r. by the Levites; 3.49
and r. you from the house of Deu 7.08
whom thou hast r. through thy 9.26
of Egypt and r. you out of the 13.05
and the LORD your God r. you; 15.15
people Israel, whom thou hast r., 21.08
LORD your God r. you from there; 24.18
who has r. my life out of every 2Sa 4.09
who has r. my soul out of every 1Ki 1.29
whom thou hast r. by thy great Neh 1.10
He has r. my soul from going down Job 33.28
thou hast r. me, O LORD, faithful God Ps 31.05
which thou hast r. to be the tribe 74.02
the day when he r. them from the 78.42
Let the r. of the LORD say so, whom 107.02
so, whom he has r. from trouble 107.02
Zion shall be r. by justice, and Is 1.27
who r. Abraham, concerning the house 29.22
but the r. shall walk there. 35.09
"Fear not, for I have r. you; 43.01
return to me, for I have r. you. 44.22
For the LORD has r. Jacob, 44.23
"The LORD has r. his servant Jacob!" 48.20
sea a way for the r. to pass over? 51.10
and you shall be r. without money. 52.03
his people, he has r. Jerusalem. 52.09
holy people, The r. of the LORD; 62.12
love and in his pity he r. them; 63.09
and has r. him from hands too Jer 31.11
O Lord, thou hast r. my life. Lam 3.58
and r. you from the house of Mic 6.04
for I have r. them, and they shall Zec 10.08
he has visited and r. his people, Lk 1.68
Christ r. us from the curse of the Gal 3.13
who had been r. from the earth. Rev 14.03
these have been r. from mankind as 14.04

REDEEMER

For I know that my R. lives, Job 19.25
sight, O LORD, my rock and my r. Ps 19.14
rock, the Most High God their r. 78.35
for their R. is strong; he will plead Pro 23.11
your R. is the Holy One of Israel. Is 41.14
your R., the Holy One of Israel: 43.14
the King of Israel and his R., 44.06
your R., who formed you from the 44.24
Our R.—the LORD of hosts is his 47.04
your R., the Holy One of Israel: "I 48.17
the R. of Israel and his Holy One, 49.07
and your R., the Mighty One of 49.26
the Holy One of Israel is your R., 54.05
on you, says the LORD, your R. 54.08
"And he will come to Zion as R., 59.20
LORD, am your Savior and your R., 60.16
our R. from of old is thy name. 63.16
Their R. is strong; the LORD of hosts Jer 50.34

REDEEMING

concerning r. and exchanging: Ru 4.07

REDEEMS

The LORD r. the life of his servants Ps 34.22
and violence he r. their life; 72.14
who r. your life from the Pit, who 103.04
occurred which r. them from the Heb 9.15

REDEMPTION

give for the r. of his life Ex 21.30
you shall grant a r. of the land. Lev 25.24
year he shall have the right of r. 25.29
does not exercise his right of r., 25.33
paid for him the price for his r. 25.51
shall refund the money for his r. 25.52
And for the r. of the two hundred Num 3.46
So Moses took the r. money from 3.49
and Moses gave the r. money to 3.51
And their r. price (at a month old 18.16
Take my right of r. yourself, Ru 4.06
He sent r. to his people; Ps 111.09
love, and with him is plenteous r. 130.07
but a poor man has no means of r. Pro 13.08
heart, and my year of r. has come. Is 63.04
the right of r. by purchase is Jer 32.07
of possession and r. is yours; 32.08
looking for the r. of Jerusalem. Lk 2.38
because your r. is drawing near. 21.28
through the r. which is in Christ Rom 3.24
as sons, the r. of our bodies. 8.23
righteousness and sanctification and r.; 1Co 1.30
In him we have r. through his blood, Eph 1.07
you were sealed for the day of r. 4.30
in whom we have r., the forgiveness Col 1.14
blood, thus securing an eternal r. Heb 9.12

REDNESS

without cause? Who has r. of eyes? Pro 23.29

REDOUND

and it will r. to their honor on Eze 39.13
may r. to praise and glory and 1Pe 1.07

REDRESS

from the sojourner without r. Eze 22.29

REED

fat, and they fed in the r. grass. Gen 41.02
the Nile and fed in the r. grass; 41.18
as a r. is shaken in the water, and 1Ki 14.15
that broken r. of a staff, which 2Ki 18.21
They go by like skiffs of r., Job 9.26
palm branch and r. in one day— Is 9.14
or tail, palm branch or r., may do. 19.15
that broken r. of a staff, which 36.06
a bruised r. he will not break, and 42.03
been a staff of r. to the house of Eze 29.06
and a measuring r. in his hand; 40.03
the measuring r. in the man's hand 40.05
the thickness of the wall, one r.; 40.05
and the height, one r. 40.05
threshold of the gate, one r. deep; 40.06
rooms, one r. long, and one r. broad; 40.07
the gate at the inner end, one r. 40.07
measured a full r. of six long 41.08
east side with the measuring r., 42.16
hundred cubits by the measuring r. 42.16
hundred cubits by the measuring r. 42.17
hundred cubits by the measuring r. 42.18
hundred cubits by the measuring r. 42.19
Though he may flourish as the r. plant, Hos 13.15
A r. shaken by the wind? Mt 11.07
break a bruised r. or quench a 12.20
and put a r. in his right hand. 27.29
and took the r. and struck him on 27.30
with vinegar, and put it on a r., 27.48
And they struck his head with a r., Mk 15.19
put it on a r. and gave it to him 15.36
to behold? A r. shaken by the wind? Lk 7.24

REEDS

it among the r. at the river's Ex 2.03
among the r. and sent her maid to 2.05

REEDS (cont.)

Can r. flourish where there is no Job 8.11
covert of the r. and in the marsh. 40.21
the beasts that dwell among the r., Ps 68.30
r. and rushes will rot away. Is 19.06
grass shall become r. and rushes. 37.05

REEL

us wine to drink that made us r. Ps 60.03
These also r. with wine and stagger Is 28.07
and the prophet r. with strong 28.07

REELAIAH

R., Mordecai, Bilshan, Mispar, Bigvai, Ez 2.02

REELED

"Then the earth r. and rocked; 2Sa 22.08
Then the earth r. and rocked; Ps 18.07
they r. and staggered like drunken 107.27

REELING

a cup of r. to all the peoples Zec 12.02

REELS

My mind r., horror has appalled me; Is 21.04

REFERRING

offsprings," r. to many; but, r. to one, Gal 3.16
(r. to things which all perish as Col 2.22

REFINE

and a place for gold which they r. Job 28.01
I will r. them and test them, for Jer 9.07
to r. and to cleanse them and to Dan 11.35
and r. them as one refines silver, Zec 13.09
of Levi and r. them like gold and Mal 3.03

REFINED

altar of incense made of r. gold, 1Ch 28.18
thousand talents of r. silver, 29.04
silver r. in a furnace on the Ps 12.06
of wine on the lees well r. Is 25.06
Behold, I have r. you, but not like 48.10
make themselves white, and be r.; Dan 12.10
r. as in a furnace, and his voice Rev 1.15
you to buy from me gold r. by fire, 3.18

REFINER

he will sit as a r. and purifier of Mal 3.03

REFINER'S

he is like a r. fire and like fullers' Mal 3.02

REFINES

and refine them as one r. silver, Zec 13.09

REFINING

in vain the r. goes on, for the Jer 6.29

REFLECT

and to r. only after making his Pro 20.25

REFLECTS

so the mind of man r. the man. Pro 27.19
He r. the glory of God and bears Heb 1.03

REFORMATION

body imposed until the time of r. Heb 9.10

REFORMS

r. are introduced on behalf of this Ac 24.02

REFRACTORY

every respect; they are not to be r., Tit 2.09

REFRAIN

you shall r from leaving him with Ex 23.05
But if you r. from vowing, it shall Deu 23.22
you therefore r. from marrying? Ru 1.13
R. from anger, and forsake wrath! Ps 37.08
and a time to r. from embracing; Ecc 3.05
years he shall r. from attacking Dan 11.08
no right to r. from working for a 1Co 9.06
and will r. from burdening you in 2Co 11.09
But I r. from it, so that no one may 12.06

REFRAINED

the princes r. from talking, and Job 29.09
So he r. and did not kill them Jer 41.08
you that I r. from coming to 2Co 1.23
So I r. and will refrain from 11.09

REFRAINS

yet r. from keeping the passover, Num 9.13
and he who r. from marriage will do 1Co 7.38

REFRESH

that you may r. yourselves, and Gen 18.05
and r. yourself, and I will give you 1Ki 13.07
me with raisins, r. me with apples; Sol 2.05
in the Lord. R. my heart in Christ. Phm 1.20

REFRESHED

bondmaid, and the alien, may be r. Ex 23.12
seventh day he rested, and was r. 31.17
so Saul was r., and was well, and 1Sa 16.23
the Jordan; and there he r. himself. 2Sa 16.14
with joy and be r. in your company Rom 15.32
for they r. my spirit as well as 1Co 16.18
of Onesiphorus, for he often r. me; 2Ti 1.16
saints have been r. through you. Phm 1.07

REFRESHES

heart, and good news r. the bones. Pro 15.30
he r. the spirit of his masters. 25.13

REFRESHING

that times of r. may come from the Ac 3.19

REFRESHMENT

to your flesh and r. to your bones. Pro 3.08

REFUGE

shall be the six cities of r., Num 35.06
cities to be cities of r. for you, 35.11
be for you a r. from the avenger, 35.12
shall be your six cities of r. 35.13
land of Canaan, to be cities of r. 35.14
shall be for r. for the people of 35.15
restore him to his city of r., 35.25
of his city of r. to which he fled, 35.26
the bounds of his city of r., 35.27
in his city of r. until the death 35.28
him who has fled to his city of r., 35.32
the rock in which they took r. Deu 32.37
Israel, 'Appoint the cities of r., Jos 20.02
be for you a r. from the avenger 20.03
the city of r. for the slayer, with 21.13
the city of r. for the slayer, with 21.21
the city of r. for the slayer, and 21.27
the city of r. for the slayer, 21.32
the city of r. for the slayer, 21.38
then come and take r. in my shade; Ju 9.15
wings you have come to take r.! Ru 2.12
my God, my rock, in whom I take r., 2Sa 22.03
my stronghold and my r., my savior; 22.03
for all those who take r. in him. 22.31
This God is my strong r., and has 22.33
Aaron they gave the cities of r.: 1Ch 6.57
They were given the cities of r.: 6.67
Blessed are all who take r. in him. Ps 2.12
all who take r. in thee rejoice, 5.11
O LORD my God, in thee do I take r.; 7.01
In the LORD I take r.; how can you 11.01
the poor, but the LORD is his r. 14.06
Preserve me, O God, for in thee I take r. 16.01
those who seek r. from their 17.07

REFUGE (cont.)
my God, my rock, in whom I take r., Ps 18.02
for all those who take r. in him. 18.30
to shame, for I take r. in thee. 25.20
is the saving r. of his anointed. 28.08
In thee, O LORD, do I seek r.; 31.01
Be thou a rock of r. for me, 31.02
hidden for me, for thou art my r. 31.04
for those who take r. in thee, 31.19
is the man who takes r. in him! 34.08
those who take r. in him will be 34.22
of men take r. in the shadow of 36.07
he is their r. in the time of 37.39
them, because they take r. in him. 37.40
thou art the God in whom I take r.; 43.02
God is our r. and strength, a very 46.01
the God of Jacob is our r. 46.07
the God of Jacob is our r. 46.11
man who would not make God his r., 52.07
and sought r. in his wealth!" 52.07
me, for in thee my soul takes r.; 57.01
shadow of thy wings I will take r., 57.01
fortress and a r. in the day of my 59.16
for thou art my r., a strong tower 61.03
my mighty rock, my r. is God. 62.07
before him; God is a r. for us. 62.08
in the LORD, and take r. in him! 64.10
In thee, O LORD, do I take r.; 71.01
Be thou to me a rock of r., 71.03
but thou art my strong r. 71.07
I have made the Lord GOD my r., 73.28
"My r. and my fortress; 91.02
under his wings you will find r.; 91.04
Because you have made the LORD your r., 91.09
and my God the rock of my r. 94.22
the rocks are a r. for the badgers. 104.18
better to take r. in the LORD than 118.08
better to take r. in the LORD than 118.09
in thee I seek r.; leave me not 141.08
no r. remains to me, no man cares 142.04
Thou art my r., my portion in the 142.05
I have fled to thee for r.! 143.09
my shield and he in whom I take r., 144.02
and his children will have a r. Pro 14.26
righteous finds r. through his 14.32
shield to those who take r. in him. 30.05
and for a r. and a shelter from the Is 4.06
afflicted of his people find r. 14.32
be a r. to them from the destroyer. 16.04
not remembered the Rock of your r.; 17.10
for we have made lies our r., 28.15
will sweep away the r. of lies, 28.17
to take r. in the protection of 30.02
he who takes r. in me shall 57.13
my r. in the day of trouble, to thee Jer 16.19
thou art my r. in the day of evil. 17.17
No r. will remain for the shepherds, 25.35
But the LORD is a r. to his people, Joe 3.16
he knows those who take r. in him. Nah 1.07
you will seek a r. from the enemy. 3.11
They shall seek r. in the name of Zep 3.12
have fled for r. might have strong Heb 6.18

REFUND
them he shall r. out of the price Lev 25.51
him he shall r. the money for his 25.52

REFUSE
if you r. to let him go, behold, I Ex 4.23
But if you r. to let them go, behold, 8.02
For if you r. to let them go and 9.02
long will you r. to humble yourself 10.03
For if you r. to let my people go, 10.04
"How long do you r. to keep my 16.28
to make of you; do not r. me." 1Ki 2.16
he will not r. you—to give me 2.17
make of you; do not r. me." 2.20
my mother; for I will not r. you." 2.20
and my gold, and I did not r. him." 20.07
because they r. to do what is just. Pro 21.07
him for his hands r. to labor. 21.25
But if you r. and rebel, you shall Is 1.20
corpses were as r. in the midst of 5.25
he knows how to r. the evil and 7.15
knows how to r. the evil and 7.16
harlot's brow, you r. to be ashamed. Jer 3.03
R. silver they are called, for the 6.30
fast to deceit, they r. to return. 8.05
they r. to know me, says the LORD. 9.06
who r. to hear my words, who stubbornly 13.10
"And if they r. to accept the cup 25.28
But if you r. to surrender, this is 38.21
them fast, they r. to let them go. 50.33
offscouring and r. among the Lam 3.45
they hear or r. to hear (for they Eze 2.05
whether they hear or r. to hear; 2.07
whether they hear or r. to hear. 3.11
and he that will r. to hear, let him r.; 3.27
and sell the r. of the wheat?" Amo 8.06
and do not r. him who would borrow Mt 5.42
you and they r. to hear you, Mk 6.11
yet you r. to come to me that you Jn 5.40
I r. to be a judge of these things." Ac 18.15
as the r. of the world, the offscouring 1Co 4.13
Do not r. one another except 7.05
we r. to practice cunning or to 2Co 4.02
all things, and count them as r., Php 3.08
But r. to enrol younger widows; 1Ti 5.11
See that you do not r. him who is Heb 12.25
dead bodies and r. to let them be Rev 11.09

REFUSED
but he r. to be comforted, and said, Gen 37.35
But he r. and said to his master's 39.08
But his father r., and said, "I know, 48.19
Pharaoh stubbornly r. to let us go, Ex 13.15
Thus Edom r. to give Israel passage Num 20.21
the LORD has r. to let me go with 22.13
But the people r. to listen to the 1Sa 8.19
He r., and said, "I will not eat." 28.23
But he r. to turn aside; therefore Abner 2Sa 2.23
out before him, but he r. to eat. 13.09
But the man r. to strike him. 1Ki 20.35
which he r. to give you for money; 21.15
he urged him to take it, but he r. 2Ki 5.16
they r. to obey, and were not Neh 9.17
But Queen Vashti r. to come at the Est 1.12
but r. to walk according to his law Ps 78.10
I have called and you r. to listen, Pro 1.24
people have r. the waters of Is 8.06
but they r. to take correction. Jer 5.03
than rock; they have r. to repent. 5.03
who r. to hear my words; they have gone 11.10
they have r. to return to me. Hos 11.05
But they r. to hearken, and turned a Zec 7.11
she r. to be consoled, because they Mt 2.18
He r. and went and put him in 18.30
But he r., and said to him, "Go home Mk 5.19
But he was angry and r. to go in. Lk 15.28
For a while he r.; but afterward 18.04
"This Moses whom they r., saying, Ac 7.35
Our fathers r. to obey him, but 7.39
because they r. to love the truth 2Th 2.10
r. to be called the son of Pharaoh's Heb 11.24
when they r. him who warned them 12.25

REFUSES
he r. to let the people go. Ex 7.14
father utterly r. to give her to 22.17
"Balaam r. to come with us." Num 22.14
husband's brother r. to perpetuate Deu 25.07
My appetite r. to touch them; Job 6.07
my soul r. to be comforted. Ps 77.02
she r. to be comforted for her Jer 31.15

REFUSES (cont.)
If he r. to listen to them, tell it Mt 18.17
and if he r. to listen even to the 18.17
If any one r. to obey what we say 2Th 3.14
he r. himself to welcome the 3Jn 1.10
but she r. to repent of her immorality Rev 2.21

REFUSING
wound incurable, r. to be healed? Jer 15.18
stubborn evil will, r. to listen to me; 16.12
their neck r. to hear my words." 19.15
turned aside, r. to obey thy voice. Dan 9.11
r. to accept release, that they Heb 11.35

REGAIN
nor do they r. the paths of life. Pro 2.19
him so that he might r. his sight. Ac 9.12
me that you may r. your sight and 9.17

REGAINED
from his eyes and he r. his sight. Ac 9.18

REGAL
beautiful, and came to r. estate. Eze 16.13

REGARD
the LORD had r. for Abel and his Gen 4.04
Cain and his offering he had no r. 4.05
Laban did not r. him with favor as 31.02
father does not r. me with favor 31.05
at it and pay no r. to lying words. Ex 5.09
but he who did not r. the word of 9.21
And I will have r. for you and make Lev 26.09
needs to be done with r. to them. Num 4.26
do not r. the stubbornness of this Deu 9.27
who shall not r. the person of the 28.50
father and mother, 'I r. them not'; 33.09
broke faith in r. to the devoted Jos 7.01
be blameless in r. to the Philistines, Ju 15.03
Do not r. your maidservant as a 1Sa 1.16
they had no r. for the LORD. 2.12
Let not my lord r. this ill-natured 25.25
Yet have r. to the prayer of thy 1Ki 8.28
not that I have r. for Jehoshaphat 2Ki 3.14
without r. to their divisions; 2Ch 5.11
Yet have r. to the prayer of thy 6.19
as you please with r. to the Jews, Est 8.08
with r. to their fasts and their 9.31
I r. not myself; I loathe my life. Job 9.21
and had no r. for any of his ways, 34.27
cry, nor does the Almighty r. it. 35.13
he does not r. any who are wise in 37.24
With r. to the works of men, by the Ps 17.04
and r. with favor your burnt 20.03
Because they do not r. the works of 28.05
those who pay r. to vain idols; 31.06
Have r. for thy covenant; for the dark 74.20
heaven, and see; have r. for this vine, 80.14
heart, and they do not r. my ways. 95.10
he will r. the prayer of the 102.17
safe and have r. for thy statutes 119.117
what is man that thou dost r. him, 144.03
righteous man has r. for the life Pro 12.10
my heart with r. to the sons of Ecc 3.18
but they do not r. the deeds of the Is 5.12
of hosts, him you shall r. as holy; 8.13
who have no r. for silver and do 13.17
In that day men will r. their Maker, 17.07
they will not have r. for the altars, 17.08
or have r. for him who planned it 22.11
despised, there is no r. for man. 33.08
so I will r. as good the exiles Jer 24.05
them, he will r. them no more; Lam 4.16
Daniel with r. to the kingdom; Dan 6.04
Those who pay r. to vain idols Jon 2.08
for you do not r. the position of Mt 22.16
for you do not r. the position of Mk 12.14
I neither fear God nor r. man, Lk 18.04
for with r. to this sect we know Ac 28.22
were free in r. to righteousness. Rom 6.20
This is how one should r. us, 1Co 4.01
we r. no one from a human point of 2Co 5.16
we r. him thus no longer. 5.16
drink or with r. to a festival or Col 2.16
yoke of slavery r. their masters 1Ti 6.01
do not r. lightly the discipline of Heb 12.05
a faithful brother as I r. him, 1Pe 5.12

REGARDED
Are we not r. by him as foreigners Gen 31.15
Nevertheless he r. their distress, Ps 106.44
Shall the potter be r. as the clay; Is 29.16
field shall be r. as a forest? 29.17
they would be r. as a strange thing Hos 8.12
for he has r. the low estate of his Lk 1.48
who neither feared God nor r. man; 18.02
them was to be r. as the greatest. 22.24
uncircumcision be r. as circumcision? Rom 2.26
we are r. as sheep to be slaughtered 8.36
though we once r. Christ from a 2Co 5.16

REGARDING
R. the words which you have heard, 2Ki 22.18
R. the words which you have heard, 2Ch 34.26
Moreover I make a decree r. what Ez 6.08
perish for ever without any r. it. Job 4.20
Jerusalem and be tried there r. them. Ac 25.20

REGARDS
only as r. the throne will I be Gen 41.40
nor r. the rich more than the poor, Job 34.19
the LORD is high, he r. the lowly; Ps 138.06
and he who r. the clouds will not Ecc 11.04
he no longer r. the offering or Mal 2.13
As r. the gospel they are enemies Rom 11.28
but as r. election they are beloved 11.28
missed the mark as r. the faith. 1Ti 6.21

REGEM
R., Jotham, Geshan, Pelet, Ephah, and 1Ch 2.47

REGEMMELECH
sent Sharezer and R. and their men, Zec 7.02

REGENERATION
the washing of r. and renewal in Tit 3.05

REGION
lying in the r. of Moab by the top Num 21.20
the whole r. of Argob, the kingdom Deu 3.04
all the r. of Argob, I gave to the 3.13
Manassite took all the r. of Argob, 3.14
and the r. of the Geshurites and Jos 13.11
Their r. extended from Mahanaim, 13.30
came to the r. about the Jordan, 22.10
in the r. about the Jordan, on the 22.11
served in the r. beyond the River, 24.15
didst march from the r. of Edom, Ju 5.04
Gilead, and he had the r. of Argob, 1Ki 4.13
over all the r. west of the 4.24
throughout all the r. east of Gilead. 1Ch 5.10
and from the r. of Geba and Neh 12.29
the eastern r. and goes down into Eze 47.08
and in all that r. who were two Mt 2.16
and all the r. about the Jordan, 3.05
who sat in the r. and shadow of 4.16
to all that r. and brought to him 14.35
woman from that r. came out and 15.22
boat and went to the r. of Magadan. 15.39
and entered the r. of Judea beyond 19.01
all the surrounding r. of Galilee. Mk 1.28
away to the r. of Tyre and Sidon. 7.24
Then he returned from the r. of Tyre, 7.31
through the r. of the Decapolis. 7.31
and went to the r. of Judea and 10.01
And in that r. there were shepherds Lk 2.08

REGION (cont.)
tetrarch of the r. of Ituraea and Lk 3.01
into all the r. about the Jordan, 3.03
every place in the surrounding r. 4.37
throughout the r. of Judea and Ac 8.01
Lord spread throughout all the r. 13.49
through the r. of Phrygia and 16.06
through the r. of Galatia and 18.23

REGIONS
all the r. of the Philistines, and Jos 13.02
the Pit, in the r. dark and deep. Ps 88.06
Sidon, and all the r. of Philistia? Joe 3.04
have any room for work in these r., Rom 15.23
be silenced in the r. of Achaia. 2Co 11.10
Then I went into the r. of Syria Gal 1.21

REGISTER
enrolled in the r. of the house of Eze 13.09

REGISTERED
who r. themselves by families, by Num 1.18
upon them; they were among those r., 11.26
These, r. by name, came in the days 1Ch 4.41
as they were r. according to the 23.24
with whom were r. one hundred and Ez 8.03

REGISTERS
The LORD records as he r. the peoples, Ps 87.06

REGISTRATION
These sought their r. among those Ez 2.62
These sought their r. among those Neh 7.64

REGRET
and he departed with no one's r. 2Ch 21.20
I do not r. it (though I did r. it), 2Co 7.08
to salvation and brings no r., 7.10

REGULAR
fine flour as a r. cereal offering, Lev 6.20
which is her r. discharge from her 15.19
a r. allowance was given him by the 2Ki 25.30
this was the r. period of their Est 2.12
a r. allowance was given him by the Jer 52.34
be settled in the r. assembly. Ac 19.39

REGULARLY
life he dined r. at the king's 2Ki 25.29
life he dined r. at the king's Jer 52.33

REGULATIONS
months under the r. for the women, Est 2.12
Why do you submit to r., Col 2.20
covenant had r. for worship and an Heb 9.01
r. for the body imposed until the 9.10

REHABIAH
The sons of Eliezer: R. the chief; 1Ch 23.17
but the sons of R. were very many. 23.17
Of R.: of the sons of R., Isshiah the 24.21
from Eliezer were his son R., 26.25

REHOB
from the wilderness of Zin to R., Num 13.21
Ebron, R., Hammon, Kanah, as far as Jos 19.28
Aphek and R.—twenty-two cities 19.30
and R. with its pasture lands—four 21.31
of Helbah, or of Aphik, or of R.; Ju 1.31
defeated Hadadezer the son of R., 2Sa 8.03
the son of R., king of Zobah. 8.12
and the Syrians of Zobah and of R., 10.08
and R. with its pasture lands; 1Ch 6.75
Mica, R., Hashabiah, Neh 10.11

REHOBOAM
and R. his son reigned in his stead. 1Ki 11.43
R. went to Shechem, for all Israel 12.01
of Israel came and said to R., 12.03
Then King R. took counsel with the 12.06
people came to R. the third day, 12.12
But R. reigned over the people of 12.17
Then King R. sent Adoram, who was 12.18
And King R. made haste to mount his 12.18
When R. came to Jerusalem, he 12.21
the kingdom to R. the son of 12.21
"Say to R. the son of Solomon, king 12.23
to R. king of Judah, and they will 12.27
me and return to R. king of Judah." 12.27
Now R. the son of Solomon reigned 14.21
R. was forty-one years old when he 14.21
In the fifth year of King R., 14.25
and King R. made in their stead 14.27
Now the rest of the acts of R., 14.29
was war between R. and Jeroboam 14.30
And R. slept with his fathers and 14.31
was war between R. and Jeroboam 15.06
R., Abijah his son, Asa his son, 1Ch 3.10
and R. his son reigned in his 2Ch 9.31
R. went to Shechem, for all Israel 10.01
all Israel came and said to R., 10.03
Then King R. took counsel with the 10.06
people came to R. the third day, 10.12
King R. spoke to them according to 10.14
But R. reigned over the people of 10.17
Then King R. sent Hadoram, who was 10.18
And King R. made haste to mount his 10.18
When R. came to Jerusalem, he 11.01
to restore the kingdom to R. 11.01
"Say to R. the son of Solomon king 11.03
R. dwelt in Jerusalem, and he built 11.05
years they made R. the son of 11.17
R. took as wife Mahalath the 11.18
R. loved Maacah the daughter of 11.21
and R. appointed Abijah the son of 11.22
When the rule of R. was established 12.01
In the fifth year of King R., 12.02
prophet came to R. and to the 12.05
and King R. made in their stead 12.10
So King R. established himself in 12.13
R. was forty-one years old when he 12.13
Now the acts of R., from first to last, 12.15
wars between R. and Jeroboam. 12.15
And R. slept with his fathers, and 12.16
him and defied R. the son of 13.07
when R. was young and irresolute 13.07
and Solomon the father of R., and R. Mt 1.07

REHOBOTH
so he called its name R., Gen 26.22
and Shaul of R. on the Euphrates 36.37
Shaul of R. on the Euphrates 1Ch 1.48

REHOBOTH-IR
and built Nineveh, R., Calah, and Gen 10.11

REHUM
Mispar, Bigvai, R., and Baanah. Ez 2.02
R. the commander and Shimshai the 4.08
then wrote R. the commander, Shimshai 4.09
"To R. the commander and Shimshai 4.17
was read before R. and Shimshai 4.23
R. the son of Bani; next to him Neh 3.17
R., Hashabnah, Maaseiah, 10.25
Shecaniah, R., Meremoth, 12.03

REI
and R., and David's mighty men were 1Ki 1.08

REIGN
him, "Are you indeed to r. over us? Gen 37.08
The LORD will r. for ever and ever. Ex 15.18
to the olive tree, 'R. over us.' Ju 9.08
tree, 'Come you, and r. over us.' 9.10
vine, 'Come you, and r. over us.' 9.12
bramble, 'Come you, and r. over us.' 9.14

REIGN (cont.)

of the king who shall r. over them. 1Sa 8.09
of the king who will r. over you: 8.11
And you shall r. over the people of 10.01
that said, 'Shall Saul r. over us?' 11.12
'No, but a king shall r. over us,' 12.12
years old when he began to r.; 13.01
when he began to r. over Israel, 2Sa 2.10
that you may r. over all that your 3.21
years old when he began to r., 5.04
"Solomon your son shall r. after me, 1Ki 1.13
Solomon your son shall r. after me, 1.17
said, 'Adonijah shall r. after me, 1.24
Solomon your son shall r. after me, 1.30
all Israel fully expected me to r.; 2.15
year of Solomon's r. over Israel, 6.01
and you shall r. over all that your 11.37
years old when he began to r., 14.21
Abijam began to r. over Judah. 15.01
Israel Asa began to r. over Judah, 15.09
began to r. over Israel in the 15.25
Ahijah began to r. over all Israel 15.33
Baasha began to r. over Israel in 16.08
When he began to r., as soon as he 16.11
Omri began to r. over Israel, and 16.23
of Omri began to r. over Israel, 16.29
as Asa began to r. over Judah in 22.41
years old when he began to r., 22.42
Ahab began to r. over Israel in 22.51
son who was to r. in his stead, 2Ki 3.27
Jehoshaphat, king of Judah, began to r. 8.16
Jehoram, king of Judah, began to r. 8.25
years old when he began to r., 8.26
Ahaziah began to r. over Judah. 9.29
years old when he began to r. 11.21
year of Jehu Jehoash began to r., 12.01
Jehu began to r. over Israel in 13.01
began to r. over Israel in Samaria, 13.10
Joash, king of Judah, began to r. 14.01
years old when he began to r., 14.02
began to r. in Samaria, and he 14.23
Amaziah, king of Judah, began to r. 15.01
years old when he began to r., 15.02
Jabesh began to r. in the thirty-ninth 15.13
of Gadi began to r. over Israel, 15.17
began to r. over Israel in Samaria, 15.23
began to r. over Israel in Samaria, 15.27
Uzziah, king of Judah, began to r. 15.32
years old when he began to r., 15.33
Jotham, king of Judah, began to r. 16.01
years old when he began to r., 16.02
Elah began to r. in Samaria over 17.01
Ahaz, king of Judah, began to r. 18.01
years old when he began to r., 18.02
years old when he began to r., 21.01
years old when he began to r., 21.19
years old when he began to r., 22.01
years old when he began to r., 23.31
that he might not r. in Jerusalem, 23.33
years old when he began to r., 23.36
in the eighth year of his r., 24.12
And in the ninth year of his r., 25.01
in the year that he began to r., 25.27
year of David's r. search was made 1Ch 26.31
month of the fourth year of his r. 2Ch 3.02
years old when he began to r., 12.13
Abijah began to r. over Judah. 13.01
fifteenth year of the r. of Asa. 15.10
thirty-fifth year of the r. of Asa. 15.19
thirty-sixth year of the r. of Asa, 16.01
year of his r. Asa was diseased in 16.12
in the forty-first year of his r. 16.13
year of his r. he sent his princes, 17.07
years old when he began to r., 20.31
years old when he began to r., 21.20
years old when he began to r., 22.02
Let him r., as the LORD spoke 23.03
years old when he began to r., 24.01
years old when he began to r., 25.01
years old when he began to r., 26.03
years old when he began to r., 27.01
years old when he began to r., 27.08
years old when he began to r., 28.01
Hezekiah began to r. when he was 29.01
In the first year of his r., 29.03
discarded in his r. when he was 29.19
years old when he began to r., 33.01
years old when he began to r., 33.21
years old when he began to r., 34.01
For in the eighth year of his r., 34.03
Now in the eighteenth year of his r., 34.08
year of the r. of Josiah this 35.19
years old when he began to r.; 36.02
years old when he began to r., 36.05
years old when he began to r., 36.09
years old when he began to r., 36.11
even until the r. of Darius king Ez 4.05
r. of Ahasuerus, in the beginning of his r., 4.06
year of the r. of Darius king of 4.24
year of the r. of Darius the king. 6.15
in the r. of Artaxerxes king of 7.01
in the r. of Artaxerxes the king: 8.01
until the r. of Darius the Persian Neh 12.22
year of his r. he gave a banquet Est 1.03
in the seventh year of his r., 2.16
that a godless man should not r., Job 34.30
The LORD will r. for ever, thy God, O Ps 146.10
By me kings r., and rulers decree Pro 8.15
of hosts will r. on Mount Zion and Is 24.23
a king will r. in righteousness, and 32.01
in the thirteenth year of his r. Jer 1.02
and he shall r. as king and deal 23.05
beginning of the r. of Jehoiakim 26.01
beginning of the r. of Zedekiah the 27.01
beginnng of the r. of Zedekiah 28.01
not have a son to r. on his throne, 33.21
beginning of the r. of Zedekiah 49.34
in the fourth year of his r. 51.59
And in the ninth year of his r., 52.04
But thou, O LORD, dost r. for ever; Lam 5.19
year of the r. of Jehoiakim king Dan 1.01
year of the r. of Nebuchadnezzar, 2.01
during the r. of Darius and the 6.28
Darius and the r. of Cyrus the 6.28
year of the r. of King Belshazzar 8.01
in the first year of his r., 9.02
the LORD will r. over them in Mic 4.07
and he will r. over the house of Lk 1.33
year of the r. of Tiberius Caesar, 3.01
do not want this man to r. over us. 19.14
did not want me to r. over them, 19.27
righteousness r. in life through Rom 5.17
also might r. through righteousness 5.21
sin therefore r. in your mortal 6.12
And would that you did r., 1Co 4.08
For he must r. until he has put all 15.25
endure, we shall also r. with him; 2Ti 2.12
God, and they shall r. on earth. Rev 5.10
and he shall r. for ever and ever. 11.15
thy great power and begun to r. 11.17
and they shall r. with him a 20.06
and they shall r. for ever and 22.05

REIGNED

the kings who r. in the land of Gen 36.31
before any king r. over the 36.31
Bela the son of Beor r. in Edom, 36.32
of Zerah of Bozrah r. in his stead. 36.33
of the Temanites r. in his stead. 36.34
r. in his stead, the name of his 36.35
Samlah of Masrekah r. in his stead. 36.36
on the Euphrates r. in his stead. 36.37
the son of Achbor r. in his stead. 36.38
and Hadar r. in his stead, the name 36.39

REIGNED (cont.)

who r. in Heshbon, as far as the	Jos 13.10
who r. in Ashtaroth and in Edrei	13.12
who r. in Heshbon, whom Moses	13.21
king of Canaan, who r. in Hazor;	Ju 4.02
and he r. . . . and two years over Israel.	1Sa 13.01
over Israel, and he r. two years.	2Sa 2.10
to reign, and he r. forty years.	5.04
At Hebron he r. over Judah seven	5.05
at Jerusalem he r. over all Israel	5.05
So David r. over all Israel;	8.15
and Hanun his son r. in his stead.	10.01
Saul, in whose place you have r.;	16.08
time that David r. over Israel was	1Ki 2.11
he r. seven years in Hebron, and	2.11
abhorred Israel, and r. over Syria.	11.25
that Solomon r. in Jerusalem over	11.42
Rehoboam his son r. in his stead.	11.43
But Rehoboam r. over the people of	12.17
how he warred and how he r.,	14.19
that Jeroboam r. was twenty-two	14.20
and Nadab his son r. in his stead.	14.20
the son of Solomon r. in Judah.	14.21
and he r. seventeen years in	14.21
And Abijam his son r. in his stead.	14.31
He r. for three years in Jerusalem.	15.02
And Asa his son r. in his stead.	15.08
and he r. forty-one years in	15.10
Jehoshaphat his son r. in his stead.	15.24
and he r. over Israel two years.	15.25
king of Judah, and r. in his stead.	15.28
and r. twenty-four years.	15.33
and Elah his son r. in his stead.	16.06
Israel in Tirzah, and r. two years.	16.08
king of Judah, and r. in his stead.	16.10
of Judah Zimri r. seven days in	16.15
and r. for twelve years; six years he r.	16.23
and Ahab his son r. in his stead.	16.28
the son of Omri r. over Israel in	16.29
Ahaziah his son r. in his stead.	22.40
and he r. twenty-five years in	22.42
Jehoram his son r. in his stead.	22.50
and he r. two years over Israel.	22.51
in Samaria, and he r. twelve years.	2Ki 3.01
and he r. eight years in Jerusalem.	8.17
Ahaziah his son r. in his stead.	8.24
and he r. one year in Jerusalem.	8.26
Jehoahaz his son r. in his stead.	10.35
The time that Jehu r. over Israel	10.36
while Athaliah r. over the land.	11.03
and he r. forty years in Jerusalem.	12.01
Amaziah his son r. in his stead.	12.21
and he r. seventeen years.	13.01
and Joash his son r. in his stead.	13.09
Samaria, and he r. sixteen years.	13.10
and he r. twenty-nine years in	14.02
Jeroboam his son r. in his stead.	14.16
and he r. forty-one years.	14.23
Zechariah his son r. in his stead.	14.29
and he r. fifty-two years in	15.02
and Jotham his son r. in his stead.	15.07
son of Jeroboam r. over Israel in	15.08
killed him, and r. in his stead.	15.10
and he r. one month in Samaria.	15.13
and slew him, and r. in his stead.	15.14
and he r. ten years in Samaria.	15.17
Pekahiah his son r. in his stead.	15.22
in Samaria, and he r. two years.	15.23
he slew him, and r. in his stead.	15.25
in Samaria, and r. twenty years.	15.27
and r. in his stead, in the twentieth	15.30
and he r. sixteen years in Jerusalem	15.33
and Ahaz his son r. in his stead.	15.38
and he r. sixteen years in Jerusalem	16.02
Hezekiah his son r. in his stead.	16.20
over Israel, and he r. nine years.	17.01
and he r. twenty-nine years in	18.02
Esarhaddon his son r. in his stead.	19.37
Manasseh his son r. in his stead.	20.21
and he r. fifty-five years in	21.01
and Amon his son r. in his stead.	21.18
and he r. two years in Jerusalem.	21.19
and Josiah his son r. in his stead.	21.26
and he r. thirty-one years in	22.01
and he r. three months in Jerusalem	23.31
and he r. eleven years in Jerusalem	23.36
Jehoiachin his son r. in his stead.	24.06
and he r. three months in Jerusalem	24.08
and he r. eleven years in Jerusalem	24.18
the kings who r. in the land of	1Ch 1.43
before any king r. over the	1.43
of Zerah of Bozrah r. in his stead.	1.44
of the Temanites r. in his stead.	1.45
country of Moab, r. in his stead;	1.46
Samlah of Masrekah r. in his stead.	1.47
on the Euphrates r. in his stead.	1.48
the son of Achbor, r. in his stead.	1.49
died, Hadad r. in his stead;	1.50
where he r. for seven years and six	3.04
And he r. thirty-three years in	3.04
were their cities until David r.	4.31
So David r. over all Israel;	18.14
died, and his son r. in his stead.	19.01
son of Jesse r. over all Israel.	29.26
The time that he r. over Israel was	29.27
he r. seven years in Hebron, and	29.27
Solomon his son r. in his stead.	29.28
And he r. over Israel.	2Ch 1.13
Solomon r. in Jerusalem over all	9.30
Rehoboam his son r. in his stead.	9.31
But Rehoboam r. over the people of	10.17
himself in Jerusalem and r.	12.13
and he r. seventeen years in	12.13
and Abijah his son r. in his stead.	12.16
He r. for three years in Jerusalem.	13.02
and Asa his son r. in his stead.	14.01
Jehoshaphat his son r. in his stead,	17.01
Thus Jehoshaphat r. over Judah.	20.31
and he r. twenty-five years in	20.31
Jehoram his son r. in his stead.	21.01
and he r. eight years in Jerusalem.	21.05
and he r. eight years in Jerusalem;	21.20
son of Jehoram king of Judah r.	22.01
and he r. one year in Jerusalem.	22.02
while Athaliah r. over the land.	22.12
and he r. forty years in Jerusalem;	24.01
Amaziah his son r. in his stead.	24.27
and he r. twenty-nine years in	25.01
and he r. fifty-two years in	26.03
And Jotham his son r. in his stead.	26.23
and he r. sixteen years in Jerusalem	27.01
and he r. sixteen years in Jerusalem	27.08
and Ahaz his son r. in his stead.	27.09
and he r. sixteen years in Jerusalem	28.01
Hezekiah his son r. in his stead.	28.27
and he r. twenty-nine years in	29.01
Manasseh his son r. in his stead.	32.33
and he r. fifty-five years in	33.01
and Amon his son r. in his stead.	33.20
and he r. two years in Jerusalem.	33.21
and he r. thirty-one years in	34.01
and he r. three months in Jerusalem	36.02
and he r. eleven years in Jerusalem	36.05
Jehoiachin his son r. in his stead.	36.08
and he r. three months and ten days	36.09
and he r. eleven years in Jerusalem	36.11
Ahasuerus who r. from India to	Est 1.01
Esarhaddon his son r. in his stead.	Is 37.38
who r. instead of Josiah his father,	Jer 22.11
r. instead of Coniah the son of	37.01
and he r. eleven years in Jerusalem	52.01
that Archelaus r. over Judea in	Mt 2.22
Yet death r. from Adam to Moses,	Rom 5.14
death r. through that one man, much	5.17

REIGNED (cont.)
as sin r. in death, grace also might Rom 5.21
and r. with Christ a thousand years Rev 20.04

REIGNS
the king who r. over you will 1Sa 12.14
say among the nations, "The LORD r.!" 1Ch 16.31
God r. over the nations; God sits Ps 47.08
The LORD r.; he is robed in majesty; 93.01
Say among the nations, "The LORD r.! 96.10
The LORD r.; let the earth rejoice; 97.01
The LORD r.; let the peoples tremble! 99.01
who says to Zion, "Your God r." Is 52.07
the Lord our God the Almighty r. Rev 19.06

REIN
"You give your mouth free r. for evil, Ps 50.19

REINED
Then Joram r. about and fled, saying 2Ki 9.23

REJECT
God will not r. a blameless man, nor Job 8.20
to suit you, because you r. it? 34.33
and r. not your mother's teaching; Pro 1.08
then I will r. the descendants of Jer 33.26
I r. you from being a priest to me. Hos 4.06
commands of men who r. the truth. Tit 1.14
we escape if we r. him who warns Heb 12.25
r. authority, and revile the glorious Jud 1.08

REJECTED
you have r. the LORD who is among Num 11.20
have not r. you, but they have r. me 1Sa 8.07
But you have this day r. your God, 10.19
you have r. the word of the LORD, 15.23
he has also r. you from being king. 15.23
for you have r. the word of the 15.26
the LORD has r. you from being 15.26
seeing I have r. him from being 16.01
his stature, because I have r. him; 16.07
And the LORD r. all the descendants 2Ki 17.20
"If I have r. the cause of my Job 31.13
put to shame, for God has r. them. Ps 53.05
thou hast r. us, broken our defenses 60.01
Hast thou not r. us, O God? 60.10
he has not r. my prayer or removed 66.20
of wrath, and he utterly r. Israel. 78.59
He r. the tent of Joseph, he did not 78.67
But now thou hast cast off and r., 89.38
Hast thou not r. us, O God? 108.11
the builders r. has become the 118.22
For thou hast r. thy people, the Is 2.06
for they have r. the law of the 5.24
He was despised and r. by men; 53.03
the LORD has r. those in whom you Jer 2.37
and as for my law, they have r. it. 6.19
called, for the LORD has r. them. 6.30
the LORD has r. and forsaken the 7.29
lo, they have r. the word of the 8.09
Hast thou utterly r. Judah? 14.19
You have r. me, says the LORD, you 15.06
'The LORD has r. the two families 33.24
Or hast thou utterly r. us? Lam 5.22
my statutes but r. my ordinances, Eze 20.13
because they r. my ordinances and 20.16
but had r. my statutes and profaned 20.24
because you have r. knowledge, Hos 4.06
they have r. the law of the LORD, Amo 2.04
be as though I had not r. them; Zec 10.06
the builders r. has become the Mt 21.42
and be r. by the elders and the Mk 8.31
the builders r. has become the 12.10
and the lawyers r. the purpose of Lk 7.30
and be r. by the elders and chief 9.22
things and be r. by this generation 17.25
the builders r. has become the 20.17
stone which was r. by you builders, Ac 4.11
I ask, then, has God r. his people? Rom 11.01
God has not r. his people whom he 11.02
is to be r. if it is received with 1Ti 4.04
he was r., for he found no chance Heb 12.17
r. by men but in God's sight chosen 1Pe 2.04
the builders r. has become the 2.07

REJECTING
by r. my ordinances and not walking Eze 5.06
a fine way of r. the commandment Mk 7.09
By r. conscience, certain persons 1Ti 1.19

REJECTION
For if their r. means the reconciliation Rom 11.15

REJECTS
but he who r. reproof goes astray. Pro 10.17
you hears me, and he who r. you r. me, Lk 10.16
he who r. me r. him who sent me." 10.16
He who r. me and does not receive Jn 12.48

REJOICE
and you shall r. before the LORD Lev 23.40
and you shall r., you and your Deu 12.07
And you shall r. before the LORD 12.12
and you shall r. before the LORD 12.18
before the LORD your God and r., 14.26
and you shall r. before the LORD 16.11
you shall r. in your feast, you and 16.14
and you shall r. in all the good 26.11
and you shall r. before the LORD 27.07
"R., Zebulun, in your going out; 33.18
r. in Abimelech, and let him also r. Ju 9.19
to Dagon their god, and to r.; 16.23
because I r. in thy salvation. 1Sa 2.01
daughters of the Philistines r., 2Sa 1.20
of those who seek the LORD r.! 1Ch 16.10
be glad, and let the earth r., 16.31
let thy saints r. in thy goodness. 2Ch 6.41
had made them r. over their 20.27
had made them r. with great joy; Neh 12.43
let it not r. among the days of the Job 3.06
who r. exceedingly, and are glad, 3.22
and r. to the sound of the pipe. 21.12
let all who take refuge in thee r., Ps 5.11
of Zion I may r. in thy deliverance 9.14
lest my foes r. because I am shaken 13.04
my heart shall r. in thy salvation. 13.05
Jacob shall r., Israel shall be 14.07
hast not let my foes r. over me. 30.01
I will r. and be glad for thy 31.07
and r., O righteous, and shout for 32.11
R. in the LORD, O you righteous! 33.01
Then my soul shall r. in the LORD, 35.09
Let not those r. over me who are 35.19
and let them not r. over me! 35.24
altogether who r. at my calamity! 35.26
pray, "Only let them not r. over me, 38.16
who seek thee r. and be glad in 40.16
of Judah r. because of thy judgments 48.11
bones which thou hast broken r. 51.08
Jacob will r. and Israel be glad. 53.06
The righteous will r. when he sees 58.10
But the king shall r. in God; 63.11
Let the righteous r. in the LORD, 64.10
river on foot. There did we r. in him, 66.06
who seek thee r. and be glad in 70.04
But I will r. for ever, I will sing 75.09
that thy people may r. in thee? 85.06
thou hast made all his enemies r. 89.42
that we may r. and be glad all our 90.14
be glad, and let the earth r.; 96.11
let the earth r.; let the many coastlands 97.01
and the daughters of Judah r., 97.08
R. in the LORD, O you righteous, and 97.12
may the LORD r. in his works, 104.31
to him, for I r. in the LORD. 104.34
of those who seek the LORD r.! 105.03

REJOICE (cont.)

that I may r. in the gladness of Ps 106.05
let us r. and be glad in it. 118.24
Those who fear thee shall see me and r., 119.74
I r. at thy word like one who finds 119.162
the sons of Zion r. in their King! 149.02
who r. in doing evil and delight in Pro 2.14
and r. in the wife of your youth, 5.18
My soul will r. when your lips 23.16
of the righteous will greatly r.; 23.24
be glad, let her who bore you r. 23.25
Do not r. when your enemy falls, and 24.17
are in authority, the people r.: 29.02
who come later will not r. in him. Ecc 4.16
many years, let him r. in them all; 11.08
R., O young man, in your youth, and 11.09
We will exult and r. in you; Sol 1.04
they r. before thee as with joy at Is 9.03
as men r. when they divide the 9.03
Lord does not r. over their young 9.17
The cypresses r. at you, the cedars 14.08
"R. not, O Philistia, all of you, that 14.29
us be glad and r. in his salvation 25.09
the desert shall r. and blossom; 35.01
and r. with joy and singing. 35.02
And you shall r. in the LORD; 41.16
your heart shall thrill and r.; 60.05
dishonor you shall r. in your lot; 61.07
I will greatly r. in the LORD, my 61.10
so shall your God r. over you. 62.05
behold, my servants shall r., 65.13
But be glad and r. for ever in that 65.18
I will r. in Jerusalem, and be glad 65.19
"R. with Jerusalem, and be glad for 66.10
r. with her in joy, all you who 66.10
shall see, and your heart shall r.; 66.14
of merrymakers, nor did I r.; Jer 15.17
Then shall the maidens r. in the dance, 31.13
I will r. in doing them good, and I 32.41
"Though you r., though you exult, O 50.11
he has made the enemy r. over you, Lam 2.17
R. and be glad, O daughter of Edom, 4.21
Let not the buyer r., nor the seller mourn, Eze 7.12
R. not, O Israel! Exult not like Hos 9.01
be glad and r., for the LORD has Joe 2.21
and r. in the LORD, your God; 2.23
you who r. in Lodebar, who say, "Have Amo 6.13
R. not over me, O my enemy; Mic 7.08
yet I will r. in the LORD, I will Hab 3.18
R. and exult with all your heart, O Zep 3.14
he will r. over you with gladness, 3.17
Sing and r., O daughter of Zion; Zec 2.10
the day of small things shall r., 4.10
R. greatly, O daughter of Zion! 9.09
Their children shall see it and r., 10.07
R. and be glad, for your reward is Mt 5.12
and many will r. at his birth; Lk 1.14
R. in that day, and leap for joy, for 6.23
Nevertheless do not r. in this, 10.20
but r. that your names are written 10.20
'R. with me, for I have found my 15.06
'R. with me, for I have found the 15.09
began to r. and praise God with a 19.37
sower and reaper may r. together. Jn 4.36
were willing to r. for a while in 5.35
and lament, but the world will r.; 16.20
you again and your hearts will r., 16.22
and we r. in our hope of sharing Rom 5.02
we r. in our sufferings, knowing 5.03
but we also r. in God through our 5.11
R. in your hope, be patient in 12.12
R. with those who r., weep with those 12.15
"R., O Gentiles, with his people"; 15.10
so that I r. over you, I would have 16.19
and those who r. as though they 1Co 7.30
member is honored, all r. together. 12.26
it does not r. at wrong, but rejoices 13.06
I r. at the coming of Stephanas and 16.17
those who should have made me r., 2Co 2.03
As it is, I r., not because you were 7.09
I r., because I have perfect 7.16
"R., O barren one that dost not Gal 4.27
is proclaimed; and in that I r. Php 1.18
Yes, and I shall r. For I know 1.19
I am glad and r. with you all. 2.17
also should be glad and r. with me. 2.18
that you may r. at seeing him again, 2.28
Finally, my brethren, r. in the Lord. 3.01
R. in the Lord always; again I will say, R. 4.04
I r. in the Lord greatly that now 4.10
Now I r. in my sufferings for your Col 1.24
R. always, 1Th 5.16
In this you r., though now for a 1Pe 1.06
in him and r. with unutterable and 1.08
But r. in so far as you share 4.13
you may also r. and be glad when 4.13
the earth will r. over them and Rev 11.10
R. then, O heaven and you that dwell 12.12
R. over her, O heaven, O saints and 18.20
Let us r. and exult and give him 19.07

REJOICED

And Jethro r. for all the good Ex 18.09
and saw the ark, they r. to see it. 1Sa 6.13
all the men of Israel r. greatly. 11.15
You saw it, and r.; why then will you 19.05
he r. greatly, and said, "Blessed be 1Ki 5.07
So all the people of the land r.; 2Ki 11.20
Then the people r. because these 1Ch 29.09
David the king also r. greatly. 29.09
And all Judah r. over the oath; 2Ch 15.15
So all the people of the land r.; 23.21
all the people r. and brought 24.10
all the people r. because of what 29.36
sojourners who dwelt in Judah, r. 30.25
great sacrifices that day and r., Neh 12.43
the women and children also r. 12.43
for Judah r. over the priests and 12.44
the city of Susa shouted and r. Est 8.15
if I have r. because my wealth was Job 31.25
"If I have r. at the ruin of him 31.29
of the forces with him, they r. Jer 41.13
your feet and r. with all the Eze 25.06
As you r. over the inheritance of 35.15
should not have r. over the people Ob 1.12
they r. exceedingly with great joy; Mt 2.10
mercy to her, and they r. with her. Lk 1.58
same hour he r. in the Holy Spirit 10.21
all the people r. at all the 13.17
Your father Abraham r. that he was Jn 8.56
If you loved me, you would have r., 14.28
heart was glad, and my tongue r.; Ac 2.26
to the idol and r. in the works of 7.41
they read it, they r. at the exhortation. 15.31
and he r. with all his household 16.34
for me, so that I r. still more. 2Co 7.07
own comfort we r. still more at 7.13
I r. greatly to find some of your 2Jn 1.04
For I greatly r. when some of the 3Jn 1.03

REJOICES

Therefore my heart is glad, and my soul r.; Ps 16.09
In thy strength the king r., O LORD; 21.01
with the righteous, the city r.; Pro 11.10
The light of the righteous r., 13.09
The light of the eyes r. the heart, 15.30
but a righteous man sings and r. 29.06
the bridegroom r. over the bride, Is 62.05
in his seine; so he r. and exults. Hab 1.15
he r. over it more than over the Mt 18.13
and my spirit r. in God my Savior, Lk 1.47
r. greatly at the bridegroom's voice Jn 3.29
at wrong, but r. in the right. 1Co 13.06

REJOICING
to the city of David with r.; 2Sa 6.12
and r. with great joy, so that the 1Ki 1.40
they have gone up from there r., 1.45
of the land r. and blowing trumpets 2Ki 11.14
from the house of Obededom with r. 1Ch 15.25
of the land r. and blowing trumpets, 2Ch 23.13
with r. and with singing, according 23.18
send portions and to make great r., Neh 8.12
And there was very great r. 8.17
the LORD are right, r. the heart; Ps 19.08
r. before him always, Pro 8.30
r. in his inhabited world and 8.31
behold, I create Jerusalem a r., Is 65.18
For the r. of the whole earth I Eze 35.14
r. as if to devour the poor in Hab 3.14
he lays it on his shoulders, r. Lk 15.05
r. that they were counted worthy to Ac 5.41
no more, and went on his way r. 8.39
rejoice as though they were not r., 1Co 7.30
as sorrowful, yet always r.; 2Co 6.10
r. to see your good order and the Col 2.05
the presence of his glory with r., Jud 1.24

REKEM
R., Zur, Hur, and Reba, the five kings Num 31.08
Evi and R. and Zur and Hur and Reba, Jos 13.21
R., Irpeel, Taralah, 18.27
Korah, Tappuah, R., and Shema. 1Ch 2.43
and R. was the father of Shammai. 2.44

REKINDLE
Hence I remind you to r. the gift 2Ti 1.06

RELATED
and having r. everything to them, he Ac 10.08
Paul as they r. what signs and 15.12
Symeon has r. how God first visited 15.14
he r. one by one the things that 21.19

RELATION
law and boast of your r. to God Rom 2.17
act on behalf of men in r. to God, Heb 5.01

RELATIONS
exchanged natural r. for unnatural, Rom 1.26
gave up natural r. with women and 1.27

RELATIVE
"The man is a r. of ours, one of our Ru 2.20

RELATIVES
one does not provide for his r., 1Ti 5.08
woman has r. who are widows, 5.16

RELAX
"Do not r. your hand from your Jos 10.06

RELAXES
Whoever then r. one of the least of Mt 5.19

RELAYS
Lebanon, ten thousand a month in r.; 1Ki 5.14

RELEASE
price of his r. shall be according Lev 25.50
seven years you shall grant a r. Deu 15.01
of the r.: every creditor shall r. 15.02
the LORD's r. has been proclaimed. 15.02
your brother your hand shall r. 15.03
the year of r. is near,' and your 15.09
at the set time of the year of r., 31.10
would wait, till my r. should come. Job 14.14
Now, behold, I r. you today from the Jer 40.04
accustomed to r. for the crowd any Mt 27.15
"Whom do you want me to r. for you, 27.17
two do you want me to r. for you? 27.21
he used to r. for them any one Mk 15.06
you want me to r. for you the King 15.09
to have him r. for them Barabbas 15.11
me to proclaim r. to the captives Lk 4.18
therefore chastise him and r. him. 23.16
Now he was obliged to r. one man to * 23.17
with this man, and r. to us Barabbas"— 23.18
once more, desiring to r. Jesus; 23.20
therefore chastise him and r. him. 23.22
that I should r. one man for you Jn 18.39
you have me r. for you the King of 18.39
know that I have power to r. you, 19.10
Upon this Pilate sought to r. him, 19.12
"If you r. this man, you are not 19.12
when he had decided to r. him. Ac 3.13
tortured, refusing to accept r., Heb 11.35
"R. the four angels who are bound Rev 9.14

RELEASED
in the jubilee it shall be r., Lev 25.28
it shall not be r. in the jubilee. 25.30
they shall be r. in the jubilee. 25.31
possession shall be r. in the jubilee; 25.33
he shall be r. in the year of 25.54
when it is r. in the jubilee, shall 27.21
The king sent and r. him, the ruler of the Ps 105.20
is bowed down shall speedily be r.; Is 51.14
when Pashhur r. Jeremiah from the Jer 20.03
of that servant r. him and forgave Mt 18.27
Then he r. for them Barabbas, and 27.26
were opened, his tongue was r., Mk 7.35
r. for them Barabbas; and having scourged 15.15
He r. the man who had been thrown Lk 23.25
When they were r. they went to Ac 4.23
our brother Timothy has been r., Heb 13.23
So the four angels were r., Rev 9.15

RELENT
and I did not r., says the LORD of Zec 8.14

RELENTED
and r. according to the abundance Ps 106.45
I have not r. nor will I turn back. Jer 4.28

RELENTING
and destroyed you;—I am weary of r. Jer 15.06

RELIABLE
And I got r. witnesses, Uriah the Is 8.02

RELIANCE
again be the r. of the house of Eze 29.16

RELIED
because they r. upon the LORD, the 2Ch 13.18
"Because you r. on the king of 16.07
Yet because you r. on the LORD, 16.08

RELIEF
shall bring us r. from our work Gen 5.29
r. and deliverance will rise for Est 4.14
and got r. from their enemies, and 9.16
the Jews got r. from their enemies, 9.22
I must speak, that I may find r.; Job 32.20
to send r. to the brethren who Ac 11.29
part in the r. of the saints— 2Co 8.04

RELIES
of the LORD and r. upon his God? Is 50.10

RELIEVE
and Saul went in to r. himself. 1Sa 24.03
R. the troubles of my heart, and Ps 25.17

RELIEVED
"I r. your shoulder of the burden; Ps 81.06
r. the afflicted, and devoted 1Ti 5.10

RELIEVING
"He is only r. himself in the closet Ju 3.24

RELIGION
party of our r. I have lived as a Ac 26.05
as befits women who profess r. 1Ti 2.10
confess, is the mystery of our r.: 3.16
holding the form of r. but denying 2Ti 3.05
his heart, this man's r. is vain. Jas 1.26
R. that is pure and undefiled 1.27

RELIGIOUS
that in every way you are very r. Ac 17.22
learn their r. duty to their own 1Ti 5.04
If any one thinks he is r., Jas 1.26

RELUCTANTLY
not r. or under compulsion, for God 2Co 9.07

RELY
On whom do you now r., that you have 2Ki 18.20
king of Egypt to all who r. on him. 18.21
"We r. on the LORD our God," is it 18.22
when you r. on Egypt for chariots 18.24
make you to r. on the LORD by 18.30
God on whom you r. deceive you by 19.10
for we r. on thee, and in thy name 2Ch 14.11
and did not r. on the LORD your God, 16.07
and do not r. on your own insight. Pro 3.05
and perverseness, and r. on them; Is 30.12
to Egypt for help and r. on horses, 31.01
On whom do you now r., that you have 36.05
king of Egypt to all who r. on him. 36.06
"We r. on the LORD our God," is it 36.07
when you r. on Egypt for chariots 36.09
make you r. on the LORD by saying, 36.15
God on whom you r. deceive you by 37.10
they r. on empty pleas, they speak 59.04
a Jew and r. upon the law and Rom 2.17
was to make us r. not on ourselves 2Co 1.09
For all who r. on works of the law Gal 3.10

RELYING
you are r. now on Egypt, that broken 2Ki 18.21
of Assyria, 'On what are you r., 2Ch 32.10
you are r. on Egypt, that broken Is 36.06

REMAIN
"Let the maiden r. with us a while, Gen 24.55
"R. a widow in your father's house, 38.11
while you r. in prison, that your 42.16
your brothers r. confined in your 42.19
r. instead of the lad as a slave to 44.33
flocks and your herds r. behind. Ex 10.24
let none of it r. until the 12.10
r. every man of you in his place, 16.29
fat of my feast r. until the 23.18
The poles shall r. in the rings of 25.15
r. until the morning, then you shall 29.34
you shall r. day and night for Lev 8.35
They shall r. an abomination to you 11.11
He shall r. unclean as long as he 13.46
shall not r. with you all night 19.13
it shall r. seven days with its 22.27
he sold shall r. in the hand of 25.28
If there r. but a few years until 25.52
the years that r. until the year 27.18
money to it, and it shall r. his. 27.19
shall r. there in the cities of Num 32.26
inheritance shall r. with us beyond 32.32
whom you let r. shall be as pricks 33.55
For the man must r. in his city of 35.28
cattle) shall r. in the cities Deu 3.19
the first day r. all night until 16.04
and shall r. in your house and 21.13
his body shall not r. all night 21.23
last of the children who r. to him; 28.54
cattle shall r. in the land which Jos 1.14
which r. to this very day. 10.27
Gath, and in Ashdod, did some r. 11.22
a place, and he shall r. with them. 20.04
And he shall r. in that city until 20.06
your tribes those nations that r., 23.04
R. this night, and in the morning, if Ru 3.13
God of Israel must not r. with us; 1Sa 5.07
"Let David r. in my service, for he 16.22
and r. beside yonder stone heap. 20.19
"Do not r. in the stronghold; 22.05
"R. at Jericho until your beards 2Sa 10.05
"R. here today also, and tomorrow I 11.12
I will be, and with him I will r. 16.18
brethren who r. in all the land of 1Ch 13.02
"R. at Jericho until your beards 19.05
their lairs, and r. in their dens. Job 37.08
and men of integrity will r. in it; Pro 2.21
And though a tenth r. in it, Is 6.13
or incense altars will r. standing. 27.09
I will make shall r. before me, 66.22
your descendants and your name r. 66.22
comes, for its leaves r. green, Jer 17.08
of Jerusalem who r. in this land, 24.08
No refuge will r. for the shepherds, 25.35
to Babylon and r. there until the 27.22
there he shall r. until I visit 32.05
If you r., then return to Gedaliah 40.05
If you will r. in this land, then I 42.10
you and let you r. in your own 42.12
'We will not r. in this land,' 42.13
to r. in the land of Judah. 43.04
they r. in their strongholds; 51.30
none of them shall r., nor their abundance, Eze 7.11
things shall not r. as they are; 21.26
to me, "This gate shall r. shut; 44.02
therefore it shall r. shut. 44.02
They shall not r. in the land of Hos 9.03
And if ten men r. in one house, they Amo 6.09
Jerusalem shall r. aloft upon its Zec 14.10
and r. there till I tell you; Mt 2.13
r. here, and watch with me. 26.38
even to death; r. here, and watch." Mk 14.34
And r. in the same house, eating and Lk 10.07
you see the Spirit descend and r., Jn 1.33
in me may not r. in darkness. 12.46
is my will that he r. until I come, 21.22
is my will that he r. until I come, 21.23
unsold, did it not r. your own? Ac 5.04
they asked him to r. for some days. 10.48
them all to r. faithful to the 11.23
well for them to r. single as I do. 1Co 7.08
let her r. single or else be 7.11
Every one should r. in the state in 7.20
called, there let him r. with God. 7.24
well for a person to r. as he is. 7.26
But to r. in the flesh is more Php 1.24
that I shall r. and continue with 1.25
r. at Ephesus that you may charge 1Ti 1.03
are not, they cannot r. hidden. 5.25
that what cannot be shaken may r. Heb 12.27
comes he must r. only a little Rev 17.10

REMAINDER
you shall burn the r. with fire; Ex 29.34
And the r. shall be for the priest, Lev 5.13
the r. of the families of the Jos 21.40
and the r. of the archers of the Is 21.17
"The r., five thousand cubits in Eze 48.15
The r. of the length alongside the 48.18

REMAINED
seen God and r. alive after seeing Gen 16.13
yet his bow r. unmoved, his arms 49.24
so Pharaoh's heart r. hardened, Ex 7.22
from his people; not one r. 8.31
not a green thing r., neither tree nor 10.15
not so much as one of them r. 14.28
the tabernacle, they r. in camp. Num 9.18
of the LORD they r. in camp; 9.20
the cloud r. from evening until 9.21

REMAINED (cont.)

of Israel r. in camp and did not Num 9.22
Now two men r. in the camp, one 11.26
to Hazeroth; and they r. at Hazeroth. 11.35
the son of Jephunneh r. alive, 14.38
inheritance r. in the tribe of the 36.12
So you r. at Kadesh many days, the Deu 1.46
days, the days that you r. there. 1.46
So we r. in the valley opposite 3.29
I r. on the mountain forty days and 9.09
and r. there three days, until the Jos 2.22
they r. in their places in the camp 5.08
remnant which r. of them had 10.20
There r. among the people of Israel 18.02
returned, and ten thousand r. Ju 7.03
not consent. So Israel r. at Kadesh. 11.17
and he r. with him three days; 19.04
the country of Moab and r. there. Ru 1.02
So the woman r. and nursed her son, 1Sa 1.23
And David r. in the strongholds in 23.14
David r. at Horesh, and Jonathan 23.18
two hundred r. with the baggage. 25.13
But David r. in the wilderness; 26.03
David r. two days in Ziklag; 2Sa 1.01
ark of the LORD r. in the house of 6.11
But David r. at Jerusalem. 11.01
So Uriah r. in Jerusalem that day, 11.12
back to Jerusalem; and they r. there. 15.29
and all Israel r. there six months, 1Ki 11.16
prostitutes who r. in the days of 22.46
slew all that r. of the house of 2Ki 10.11
slew all that r. to Ahab in 10.17
and he r. with her six years, hid in 11.03
and the Asherah also r. in Samaria. 13.06
none r., except the poorest people 24.14
the people who r. in the land of 25.22
And the ark of God r. with the 1Ch 13.14
But David r. at Jerusalem. And Joab smote 20.01
Ethiopians fell until none r. alive; 2Ch 14.13
and he r. with them six years, hid 22.12
Jerusalem, and there we r. three days. Ez 8.32
the people r. in their places. Neh 8.07
nine tenths r. in the other towns. 11.01
in Jerusalem; also my wisdom r. with me. Ecc 2.09
fortified cities of Judah that r. Jer 34.07
and there r. of them only wounded 37.10
the dungeon cells, and r. there many days, 37.16
So Jeremiah r. in the court of the 37.21
And Jeremiah r. in the court of the 38.13
And Jeremiah r. in the court of the 38.28
to him, and the people who r. 39.09
and its roots r. where it stood. Eze 17.06
but Daniel r. at the king's court. Dan 2.49
and r. there until the death of Mt 2.15
it would have r. until this day. 11.23
he made signs to them and r. dumb. Lk 1.22
And Mary r. with her about three 1.56
dove from heaven, and it r. on him. Jn 1.32
there he r. with them and baptized. 3.22
the people who r. on the other 6.22
So saying, he r. in Galilee. 7.09
at first baptized, and there he r. 10.40
While it r. unsold, did it not Ac 5.04
Judea to Caesarea, and r. there. 12.19
So they r. for a long time, speaking 14.03
And they r. no little time with the 14.28
But Paul and Barnabas r. in Antioch, 15.35
We r. in this city some days; 16.12
but Silas and Timothy r. there. 17.14
the bow stuck and r. immovable, 27.41
and r. with him fifteen days. Gal 1.18
Erastus r. at Corinth; Trophimus I 2Ti 4.20

REMAINEST

they will perish, but thou r.; Heb 1.11

REMAINING

names of the r. six on the other Ex 28.10
Now the booty r. of the spoil that Num 31.32
women, and children; we left none r.; Deu 2.34
and there is none r., bond or free. 32.36
person in it, he left none r.; Jos 10.28
he left none r. in it; and he did 10.30
his people, until he left none r. 10.33
he left none r., as he had done to 10.37
he left none r.; as he had done 10.39
he left none r., but utterly 10.40
them, until they left none r. 11.08
men take five of the r. horses, 2Ki 7.13
priests, until he left him none r. 10.11
and bury those r. upon the face of Eze 39.14
none of them r. among the nations 39.28
the bodies from r. on the cross on Jn 19.31

REMAINS

While the earth r., seedtime and Gen 8.22
anything that r. until the morning Ex 12.10
And the part that r. of the curtains 26.12
the tent, the half curtain that r., 26.12
of what r. in the length of the 26.13
the morrow what r. of it shall be Lev 7.16
but what r. of the flesh of the 7.17
and what r. of the flesh and the 8.32
offering that r. of the offerings 10.12
But if the spot r. in one place and 13.23
But if the spot r. in one place and 13.28
of the oil that r. in his hand the 14.17
heap of stones that r. to this day; Jos 7.26
and there r. yet very much land to 13.01
This is the land that yet r.: 13.02
"There r. yet the youngest, but 1Sa 16.11
king, "Behold, he r. in Jerusalem; 2Sa 16.03
son of Shaphat r. on his shoulders 2Ki 6.31
erred, my error r. with myself. Job 19.04
no refuge r. to me, no man cares for Ps 142.04
a man of understanding r. silent. Pro 11.12
Precious treasure r. in a wise man's 21.20
comes, but the earth r. for ever. Ecc 1.04
in Zion and r. in Jerusalem will Is 4.03
whose stump r. standing when it is 6.13
Nothing r. but to crouch among the 10.04
remnant that r. of this evil Jer 8.03
and Sidon every helper that r. 47.04
so his taste r. in him, and his 48.11
all that r. of Israel in the Eze 9.08
so that there r. in it no strong 19.14
"What r. on both sides of the holy 48.21
For now no strength r. in me, Dan 10.17
behold, all the earth r. at rest. Zec 1.11
you say, 'We see,' your guilt r. Jn 9.41
the earth and dies, it r. alone; 12.24
law that the Christ r. for ever. 12.34
she is happier if she r. as she is. 1Co 7.40
covenant, that same veil r. unlifted, 2Co 3.14
he r. faithful—for he cannot deny 2Ti 2.13
promise of entering his rest r., Heb 4.01
Since therefore it r. for some to 4.06
So then, there r. a sabbath rest for 4.09
there no longer r. a sacrifice for 10.26
He who does not love r. in death. 1Jn 3.14
strengthen what r. and is on the Rev 3.02

REMALIAH

And Pekah the son of R., his captain, 2Ki 15.25
the son of R. began to reign over 15.27
against Pekah the son of R., 15.30
second year of Pekah the son of R., 15.32
Pekah the son of R. against Judah. 15.37
year of Pekah the son of R., 16.01
of Syria and Pekah the son of R., 16.05
the son of R. slew a hundred and 2Ch 28.06
the son of R. the king of Israel Is 7.01
Rezin and Syria and the son of R. 7.04
with Ephraim and the son of R., 7.05

REMALIAH (cont.)
head of Samaria is the son of R. Is 7.09
before Rezin and the son of R.; 8.06

REMEDY
his people, till there was no r. 2Ch 36.16

REMEMBER
I will r. my covenant which is Gen 9.15
upon it and r. the everlasting 9.16
r., God is witness between you and 31.50
But r. me, when it is well with you, 40.14
the chief butler did not r. Joseph, 40.23
to Pharaoh, "I r. my faults today. 41.09
"R. this day, in which you came out Ex 13.03
"R. the sabbath day, to keep it holy 20.08
R. Abraham, Isaac, and Israel, thy 32.13
I will r. my covenant with Jacob, Lev 26.42
I will r. my covenant with Isaac 26.42
Abraham, and I will r. the land. 26.42
for their sake r. the covenant 26.45
We r. the fish we ate in Egypt for Num 11.05
look upon and r. all the commandments 15.39
So you shall r. and do all my 15.40
You shall r. that you were a Deu 5.15
but you shall r. what the LORD your 7.18
And you shall r. all the way which 8.02
You shall r. the LORD your God, for 8.18
R. and do not forget how you 9.07
R. thy servants, Abraham, Isaac, and 9.27
You shall r. that you were a slave 15.15
life you may r. the day when you 16.03
You shall r. that you were a slave 16.12
R. what the LORD your God did to 24.09
but you shall r. that you were a 24.18
You shall r. that you were a slave 24.22
"R. what Amalek did to you on the 25.17
R. the days of old, consider the 32.07
"R. the word which Moses the Jos 1.13
Israel did not r. the LORD their Ju 8.34
R. also that I am your bone and 9.02
r. me, I pray thee, and strengthen me, 16.28
and r. me, and not forget thy 1Sa 1.11
my lord, then r. your handmaid." 25.31
me guilty or r. how your servant 2Sa 19.19
for r., when you and I rode side by 2Ki 9.25
"R. now, O LORD, I beseech thee, how I 20.03
R. the wonderful works that he has 1Ch 16.12
R. thy steadfast love for David thy 2Ch 6.42
king did not r. the kindness which 24.22
R. the word which thou didst Neh 1.08
R. the Lord, who is great and 4.14
R. for my good, O my God, all that I 5.19
R. Tobiah and Sanballat, O my God, 6.14
R. me, O my God, concerning this, and 13.14
R. this also in my favor, O my God, 13.22
R. them, O my God, because they have 13.29
fruits. R. me, O my God, for good. 13.31
"R. that my life is a breath; Job 7.07
R. that thou hast made me of clay; 10.09
you will r. it as waters that have 11.16
appoint me a set time, and r. me! 14.13
"R. to extol his work, of which men 36.24
May he r. all your offerings, and Ps 20.03
the earth shall r. and turn to the 22.27
R. not the sins of my youth, or my 25.07
to thy steadfast love r. me, 25.07
These things I r., as I pour out my 42.04
therefore I r. thee from the land 42.06
R. thy congregation, which thou hast 74.02
R. Mount Zion, where thou hast dwelt 74.02
R. this, O LORD, how the enemy scoffs, 74.18
r. how the impious scoff at thee 74.22
days of old, I r. the years long ago. 77.05
yea, I will r. thy wonders of old. 77.11
Do not r. against us the iniquities 79.08
those whom thou dost r. no more, 88.05
R., O Lord, what the measure of life 89.47
R., O Lord, how thy servant is 89.50
covenant and r. to do his commandments 103.18
R. the wonderful works that he has 105.05
R. me, O LORD, when thou showest 106.04
they did not r. the abundance of 106.07
For he did not r. to show kindness, 109.16
R. thy word to thy servant, in which 119.49
I r. thy name in the night, O LORD, 119.55
R., O LORD, in David's favor, all the 132.01
if I do not r. you, if I do not set 137.06
R., O LORD, against the Edomites the 137.07
I r. the days of old, I meditate on 143.05
and r. their misery no more. Pro 31.07
will not much r. the days of his Ecc 5.20
but let him r. that the days of 11.08
R. also your Creator in the days of 12.01
and said, "R. now, O LORD, I beseech Is 38.03
"R. not the former things, nor 43.18
sake, and I will not r. your sins. 43.25
R. these things, O Jacob, and Israel, 44.21
"R. this and consider, recall it to 46.08
r. the former things of old; 46.09
things to heart or r. their end. 47.07
your widowhood you will r. no more. 54.04
and did not r. me, did not give me a 57.11
those that r. thee in thy ways. 64.05
and r. not iniquity for ever. 64.09
I r. the devotion of your youth, Jer 2.02
now he will r. their iniquity and 14.10
r. and do not break thy covenant 14.21
r. me and visit me, and take vengeance 15.15
while their children r. their 17.02
R. how I stood before thee to speak 18.20
against him, I do r. him still. 31.20
and I will r. their sin no more. 31.34
the land, did not the LORD r. it? 44.21
R. the LORD from afar, and let 51.50
R. my affliction and my bitterness, Lam 3.19
R., O LORD, what has befallen us; 5.01
who escape will r. me among the Eze 6.09
you did not r. the days of your 16.22
yet I will r. my covenant with you 16.60
Then you will r. your ways, and be 16.61
that you may r. and be confounded, 16.63
And there you shall r. your ways 20.43
the Egyptians or r. them any more. 23.27
Then you will r. your evil ways, and 36.31
consider that I r. all their evil Hos 7.02
Now he will r. their iniquity, and 8.13
he will r. their iniquity, he will 9.09
and did not r. the covenant of Amo 1.09
O my poeple, r. what Balak king of Mic 6.05
make it known; in wrath r. mercy. Hab 3.02
in far countries they shall r. me, Zec 10.09
"R. the law of my servant Moses, the Mal 4.04
and there r. that your brother has Mt 5.23
Do you not r. the five loaves of 16.09
we r. how that impostor said, while 27.63
do you not hear? And do you not r.? Mk 8.18
fathers, and to r. his holy covenant, Lk 1.72
'Son, r. that you in your lifetime 16.25
R. Lot's wife. 17.32
r. me when you come in your kingly 23.42
R. how he told you, while he was 24.06
R. the word that I said to you, 'A Jn 15.20
comes you may r. that I told you 16.04
r. it is not you that support the Rom 11.18
you because you r. me in everything 1Co 11.02
only they would have us r. the poor, Gal 2.10
Therefore r. that at one time you Eph 2.11
r. that you were at that time 2.12
R. my fetters. Grace be with you. Col 4.18
For you r. our labor and toil, 1Th 2.09
that you always r. us kindly and 3.06
Do you not r. that when I was still 2Th 2.05
when I r. you constantly in my 2Ti 1.03

REMEMBER (cont.)
As I r. your tears, I long night and 2Ti 1.04
R. Jesus Christ, risen from the dead, 2.08
always when I r. you in my prayers, Phm 1.04
and I will r. their sins no more." Heb 8.12
"I will r. their sins and their 10.17
R. those who are in prison, as 13.03
R. your leaders, those who spoke to 13.07
that you should r. the predictions 2Pe 3.02
But you must r., beloved, the Jud 1.17
R. then from what you have fallen, Rev 2.05
R. then what you received and heard 3.03

REMEMBERED
But God r. Noah and all the beasts Gen 8.01
God r. Abraham, and sent Lot out of 19.29
Then God r. Rachel, and God hearkened 30.22
And Joseph r. the dreams which he 42.09
and God r. his covenant with Ex 2.24
thus I am to be r. throughout all 3.15
bondage and I have r. my covenant. 6.05
my name to be r. I will come to 20.24
that you may be r. before the LORD Num 10.09
his wife, and the LORD r. her; 1Sa 1.19
he r. Vashti and what she had done Est 2.01
days should be r. and kept throughout 9.28
their name is no longer r.; Job 24.20
They r. that God was their rock, the Ps 78.35
He r. that they were but flesh, a 78.39
the name of Israel be r. no more! 83.04
He has r. his steadfast love and 98.03
For he r. his holy promise, and 105.42
He r. for their sake his covenant, 106.45
his fathers be r. before the LORD, 109.14
his wonderful works to be r.; 111.04
be moved; he will be r. for ever. 112.06
It is he who r. us in our low 136.23
sat down and wept, when we r. Zion. 137.01
Yet no one r. that poor man. Ecc 9.15
and have not r. the Rock of your Is 17.10
many songs, that you may be r. 23.16
Then he r. the days of old, of Moses 63.11
shall not be r. or come into mind. 65.17
come to mind, or be r., or missed; Jer 3.16
that his name be r. no more. 11.19
he has not r. his footstool in the Lam 2.01
which he has done shall not be r.; Eze 3.20
Because you have not r. the days of 16.43
committed shall be r. against him; 18.22
which he has done shall be r.; 18.24
you have made your guilt to be r., 21.24
you shall be no more r.; 21.32
that it may be r. no more among 25.10
of his righteous deeds shall be r.; 33.13
committed shall be r. against him; 33.16
fainted within me, I r. the LORD; Jon 2.07
so that they shall be r. no more; Zec 13.02
And Peter r. the saying of Jesus, Mt 26.75
And Peter r. and said to him, Mk 11.21
And Peter r. how Jesus had said to 14.72
And Peter r. the word of the Lord, Lk 22.61
And they r. his words, 24.08
His disciples r. that it was Jn 2.17
his disciples r. that he had said 2.22
then they r. that this had been 12.16
your alms have been r. before God. Ac 10.31
And I r. the word of the Lord, how 11.16
and God r. great Babylon, to make Rev 16.19
and God has r. her iniquities. 18.05

REMEMBERING
r. the days of her youth, when she Eze 23.19
r. that for three years I did not Ac 20.31
r. the words of the Lord Jesus, how 20.35
for you, r. you in my prayers, Eph 1.16
always r. you earnestly in his Col 4.12
r. before our God and Father your 1Th 1.03

REMEMBERS
our frame; he r. that we are dust. Ps 103.14
Jerusalem r. in the days of her Lam 1.07
she no longer r. the anguish, for Jn 16.21
as he r. the obedience of you all, 2Co 7.15

REMEMBRANCE
blot out the r. of Amalek from Ex 17.14
as stones of r. for the sons of 28.12
LORD upon his two shoulders for r. 28.12
to continual r. before the LORD. 28.29
of Israel to r. before the LORD, so 30.16
to be stones of r. for the sons of 39.07
offering of r., bringing iniquity to r. Num 5.15
hands the cereal offering of r., 5.18
serve you for r. before your God: I 10.10
blot out the r. of Amalek from Deu 25.19
I will make the r. of them cease 32.26
have no son to keep my name in r."; 2Sa 18.18
come to me to bring my sin to r., 1Ki 17.18
For in death there is no r. of thee; Ps 6.05
to cut off the r. of them from the 34.16
There is no r. of former things, nor Ecc 1.11
there be any r. of later things 1.11
the fool there is no enduring r., 2.16
and wiped out all r. of them. Is 26.14
Put me in r., let us argue together 43.26
put the LORD in r., take no rest, 62.06
but he brings their guilt to r., Eze 21.23
appear—because you have come to r., 21.24
and a book of r. was written before Mal 3.16
Israel, in r. of his mercy, Lk 1.54
given for you. Do this in r. of me. * 22.19
bring to your r. all that I have Jn 14.26
is for you. Do this in r. of me." 1Co 11.24
often as you drink it, in r. of me." 11.25
I thank my God in all my r. of you, Php 1.03

REMETH
R., Engannim, Enhaddah, Bethpazzez; Jos 19.21

REMIND
to r. you of my ways in Christ, as I 1Co 4.17
Now I would r. you, brethren, in what 15.01
let him r. himself that as he is 2Co 10.07
Hence I r. you to rekindle the gift 2Ti 1.06
R. them of this, and charge them 2.14
R. them to be submissive to rulers Tit 3.01
always to r. you of these things, 2Pe 1.12
Now I desire to r. you, though you Jud 1.05

REMINDED
I am r. of your sincere faith, a 2Ti 1.05

REMINDER
to be a r. to the people of Israel, Num 16.40
of the LORD as a r. to Heldai, Zec 6.14
to you very boldly by way of r., Rom 15.15
there is a r. of sin year after Heb 10.03
body, to arouse you by way of r., 2Pe 1.13
your sincere mind by way of r.; 3.01

REMISSION
also granted a r. of taxes to the Est 2.18

REMNANT
to preserve for you a r. on earth, Gen 45.07
was left of the r. of the Rephaim; Deu 3.11
and when the r. which remained of Jos 10.20
one of the r. of the Rephaim, who 12.04
was left of the r. of the Rephaim); 13.12
and join the r. of these nations 23.12
Then down marched the r. of the noble; Ju 5.13
name nor r. upon the face of the 2Sa 14.07
but of the r. of the Amorites; 21.02
And the r. of the male cult prostitutes 1Ki 22.46
prayer for the r. that is left. 2Ki 19.04
And the surviving r. of the house 19.30

REMNANT (cont.)
of Jerusalem shall go forth a r., 2Ki 19.31
cast off the r. of my heritage, 21.14
destroyed the r. of the Amalekites 1Ch 4.43
again to the r. of you who have 2Ch 30.06
from all the r. of Israel and from 34.09
to leave us a r., and to give us a Ez 9.08
hast given us such a r. as this, 9.13
us, so that there should be no r., 9.14
we are left a r. that has escaped, 9.15
The r. of the trees of his forest Is 10.19
In that day the r. of Israel and 10.20
A r. will return, the r. of Jacob, 10.21
only a r. of them will return. 10.22
to recover the r. which is left of 11.11
Assyria for the r. which is left 11.16
cut off from Babylon name and r., 14.22
with famine, and your r. I will slay. 14.30
who escape, for the r. of the land. 15.09
and the r. of Syria will be like 17.03
of beauty, to the r. of his people; 28.05
prayer for the r. that is left. 37.04
And the surviving r. of the house 37.31
of Jerusalem shall go forth a r., 37.32
all the r. of the house of Israel, 46.03
thoroughly as a vine the r. of Israel; Jer 6.09
life by all the r. that remains of 8.03
will gather the r. of my flock out 23.03
the r. of Jerusalem who remain in 24.08
Gaza, Ekron, and the r. of Ashdod); 25.20
saved his people, the r. of Israel. 31.07
had left a r. in Judah and had 40.11
and the r. of Judah would perish?" 40.15
for all this r. (for we are left 42.02
word of the LORD, O r. of Judah, 42.15
shall have no r. or survivor from 42.17
O r. of Judah, 'Do not go to Egypt.' 42.19
took all the r. of Judah who had 43.05
midst of Judah, leaving you no r.? 44.07
I will take the r. of Judah who 44.12
none of the r. of Judah who have 44.14
and all the r. of Judah, who came to 44.28
the r. of the coastland of Caphtor. 47.04
O r. of the Anakim, how long will 47.05
pardon those whom I leave as a r. 50.20
a full end of the r. of Israel? Eze 11.13
and the r. of the Philistines shall Amo 1.08
be gracious to the r. of Joseph. 5.15
may possess the r. of Edom and all 9.12
I will gather the r. of Israel; Mic 2.12
and the lame I will make the r.; 4.07
Then the r. of Jacob shall be in 5.07
And the r. of Jacob shall be among 5.08
transgression for the r. of his 7.18
all the r. of the peoples shall Hab 2.08
this place the r. of Baal and the Zep 1.04
possession of the r. of the house 2.07
The r. of my people shall plunder 2.09
with all the r. of the people, Hag 1.12
spirit of all the r. of the people; 1.14
and to all the r. of the people, 2.02
sight of the r. of this people in Zec 8.06
deal with the r. of this people as 8.11
will cause the r. of this people 8.12
it too shall be a r. for our God; 9.07
only a r. of them will be saved; Rom 9.27
at the present time there is a r., 11.05

REMONSTRATED
So I r. with the officials and said, Neh 13.11
Then I r. with the nobles of Judah 13.17

REMOTE
sojourning in the r. parts of the Ju 19.01
in Judah to the r. parts of the 19.18

REMOTEST
I came to its r. height, its densest Is 37.24

REMOVAL
for impurity, for the r. of sin. Num 19.09
full fruit of the r. of his sin: Is 27.09
indicates the r. of what is shaken, Heb 12.27
not as a r. of dirt from the body 1Pe 3.21

REMOVE
to r. it from Ephraim's head to Gen 48.17
God only to r. this death from me. Ex 10.17
And all its fat he shall r., Lev 4.31
fat he shall r. as the fat of the 4.35
and I will r. evil beasts from the 26.06
you shall not r. your neighbor's Deu 19.14
then I would r. Abimelech. Ju 9.29
And do this: r. the kings, each from 1Ki 20.24
"I will r. Judah also out of my 2Ki 23.27
to r. them out of his sight, for the 24.03
and I will no more r. the foot of 2Ch 33.08
if you r. unrighteousness far from Job 22.23
Men r. landmarks; they seize flocks 24.02
R. thy stroke from me; I am spent Ps 39.10
but I will not r. from him my 89.33
so far does he r. our transgressions 103.12
R. not the ancient landmark which Pro 22.28
Do not r. an ancient landmark or 23.10
R. far from me falsehood and lying; 30.08
R. vexation from your mind, and put Ecc 11.10
r. the evil of your doings from Is 1.16
as with lye and r. all your alloy. 1.25
I will r. its hedge, and it shall be 5.05
r. every obstruction from my 57.14
If you r. your abominations from my Jer 4.01
r. the foreskin of your hearts, O 4.04
I will r. you from the face of the 28.16
so that I will r. it from my sight 32.31
they will r. from it all its Eze 11.18
R. the turban, and take off the 21.26
and r. their robes, and strip off 26.16
For I will r. the names of the Hos 2.17
like those who r. the landmark; 5.10
to the yoke, and none shall r. it. 11.07
"I will r. the northerner far from Joe 2.20
which you cannot r. your necks; Mic 2.03
for then I will r. from your midst Zep 3.11
"I will r. disaster from you, so 3.18
"R. the filthy garments from him." Zec 3.04
and I will r. the guilt of this 3.09
and also I will r. from the land 13.02
r. this cup from me; yet not what Mk 14.36
r. this cup from me; nevertheless Lk 22.42
and I will r. you beyond Babylon. Ac 7.43
him not seek to r. the marks of 1Co 7.18
so as to r. mountains, but have not 13.02
come to you and r. your lampstand Rev 2.05

REMOVED
and Noah r. the covering of the ark, Gen 8.13
Thence he r. to the mountain on the 12.08
But that day Laban r. the he-goats 30.35
Then Joseph r. them from his knees, 48.12
and r. the swarms of flies from Ex 8.31
as the fat is r. from the peace Lev 4.31
of the lamb is r. from the sacrifice 4.35
and when the cloud r. from over the Num 12.10
their protection is r. from them, 14.09
'I have r. the sacred portion out Deu 26.13
or r. any of it while I was unclean, 26.14
So Saul r. him from his presence, 1Sa 18.13
which is r. from before the LORD, to 21.06
and r. all the idols that his 1Ki 15.12
He also r. Maacah his mother from 15.13
But the high places were not r.; 2Ki 14.04
Nevertheless the high places were not r.; 15.35
the LORD he r. from the front of 16.14
and r. the laver from them, and he 16.17
for the king he r. from the house 16.18
and r. them out of his sight; 17.18

REMOVED (cont.)
until the LORD r. Israel out of his 2Ki 17.23
He r. the high places, and broke the 18.04
places and altars Hezekiah has r., 18.22
And he r. the horses that the kings 23.11
the LORD to anger, Josiah r.; 23.19
as I have r. Israel, and I will cast 23.27
King Asa r. from being queen mother 2Ch 15.16
They set to work and r. the altars 30.14
and the rock is r. from its place; Job 14.18
or the rock be r. out of its place? 18.04
my prayer or r. his steadfast love Ps 66.20
Thou hast r. the scepter from his 89.44
The righteous will never be r., Pro 10.30
I have r. the boundaries of peoples, Is 10.13
he r. them with his fierce blast in 27.08
places and altars Hezekiah has r., 36.07
plucked up and r. from me like a 38.12
may depart and the hills be r., 54.10
covenant of peace shall not be r., 54.10
goes on, for the wicked are not r. Jer 6.29
you will be r. far from your land, 27.10
Though I r. them far off among the Eze 11.16
therefore I r. them, when I saw it. 16.50
r. his robe, and covered himself Jon 3.06
they r. the roof above him; Mk 2.04
God r. him from there into this Ac 7.04
And when he had r. him, he raised 13.22
has done this be r. from among you. 1Co 5.02
turns to the Lord the veil is r. 2Co 3.16
block of the cross has been r. Gal 5.11
and island was r. from its place. Rev 6.14

REMOVES
be he who r. his neighbor's landmark.' Deu 27.17
he who r. mountains, and they know Job 9.05
and the LORD r. men far away, and Is 6.12
he r. kings and sets up kings; Dan 2.21
my people; how he r. it from me! Mic 2.04

REMOVING
r. from it every speckled and Gen 30.32
r. them far from their own border. Joe 3.06

REND
and do not r. your clothes, lest you Lev 10.06
hang loose, nor r. his clothes; 21.10
"R. your clothes, and gird on 2Sa 3.31
lest like a lion they r. me, Ps 7.02
lest I r., and there be none to 50.22
a time to r., and a time to sew; Ecc 3.07
thou wouldst r. the heavens and Is 64.01
nor did they r. their garments. Jer 36.24
will r. and go away, I will carry Hos 5.14
as a wild beast would r. them. 13.08
and r. your hearts and not your Joe 2.13

RENDER
which they r. to me, shall be most Num 18.09
of Israel, and r. praise to him; Jos 7.19
of God was in him, to r. justice. 1Ki 3.28
and r. to each whose heart thou 8.39
and r. to each whose heart thou 2Ch 6.30
r. them their due reward. Ps 28.04
Those who r. me evil for good are 38.20
I will r. thank offerings to thee. 56.12
and of the isles r. him tribute, 72.10
r. to the proud their deserts! 94.02
What shall I r. to the LORD for all 116.12
the coastlands he will r. requital. Is 59.18
to r. his anger in fury, and his 66.15
and we will r. the fruit of our Hos 14.02
R. true judgments, show kindness and Zec 7.09
r. in your gates judgments that are 8.16
men will r. account for every Mt 12.36
"R. therefore to Caesar the things 22.21
"R. to Caesar the things that are Mk 12.17
"Then r. to Caesar the things that Lk 20.25
For he will r. to every man according Rom 2.06
thanksgiving can we r. to God for you, 1Th 3.09
you do when you r. any service to 3Jn 1.05
R. to her as she herself has Rev 18.06

RENDERED
the judgment which the king had r.; 1Ki 3.28
all the service he r. at Ephesus. 2Ti 1.18
Render to her as she herself has r., Rev 18.06

RENDERING
r. recompense to his enemies! Is 66.06
vengeance, the requital he is r. her. Jer 51.06
for the r. of this service not only 2Co 9.12
r. service with a good will as to Eph 6.07

RENDERS
oracles of God; whoever r. service, 1Pe 4.11
as one who r. it by the strength which 4.11

RENEW
to Gilgal and there r. the kingdom. 1Sa 11.14
thou dost r. thy witnesses against Job 10.17
the LORD shall r. their strength, Is 40.31
let the peoples r. their strength; 41.01
be restored! R. our days as of old! Lam 5.21
In the midst of the years r. it; Hab 3.02
gladness, he will r. you in his love; Zep 3.17

RENEWAL
transformed by the r. of your mind, Rom 12.02
regeneration and r. in the Holy Tit 3.05

RENEWED
grass which is r. in the morning: Ps 90.05
morning it flourishes and is r.; 90.06
your youth is r. like the eagle's. 103.05
inner nature is being r. every day. 2Co 4.16
and be r. in the spirit of your Eph 4.23
which is being r. in knowledge Col 3.10

RENEWEST
and thou r. the face of the ground. Ps 104.30

RENOUNCE
Why does the wicked r. God, and say Ps 10.13
of you does not r. all that he has Lk 14.33
training us to r. irreligion and Tit 2.12

RENOUNCED
Thou hast r. the covenant with thy Ps 89.39
We have r. disgraceful, underhanded 2Co 4.02

RENOUNCES
greedy for gain curses and r. the LORD. Ps 10.03

RENOWN
that were of old, the men of r. Gen 6.04
thy r., O LORD, throughout all ages. Ps 135.13
the r. of Moab is no more. In Jer 48.02
And your r. went forth among the Eze 16.14
the harlot because of your r., 16.15
into praise and r. in all the Zep 3.19

RENOWNED
Ephrathah and be r. in Bethlehem; Ru 4.11
and may his name be r. in Israel! 4.14
He was the most r. of the thirty, 2Sa 23.19
He was r. among the thirty, but he 23.23
He was the most r. of the thirty, 1Ch 11.21
He was r. among the thirty, but he 11.25
O city r., that was mighty on the Eze 26.17
I will make you r. and praised Zep 3.20

RENT
not in the pit, he r. his clothes Gen 37.29
Then Jacob r. his garments, and put 37.34
Then they r. their clothes, and 44.13
out the land, r. their clothes, Num 14.06

RENT (cont.)
Then Joshua r. his clothes, and fell Jos 7.06
he r. his clothes, and said, "Alas, my Ju 11.35
his clothes r. and with earth upon 1Sa 4.12
his clothes r. and earth upon his 2Sa 1.02
hold of his clothes, and r. them; 1.11
and r. the long-sleeved robe which 13.19
and r. his garments, and lay on the 13.31
were standing by r. their garments. 13.31
with his coat r. and earth upon 15.32
and strong wind r. the mountains, 1Ki 19.11
he r. his clothes, and put sackcloth 21.27
own clothes and r. them in two 2Ki 2.12
he r. his clothes and said, "Am I 5.07
king of Israel had r. his clothes, 5.08
"Why have you r. your clothes? Let 5.08
of the woman he r. his clothes— 6.30
And Athaliah r. her clothes, and 11.14
to Hezekiah with their clothes r., 18.37
he r. his clothes, and covered 19.01
book of the law, he r. his clothes. 22.11
and you have r. your clothes and 22.19
And Athaliah r. her clothes, and 2Ch 23.13
words of the law he r. his clothes. 34.19
and have r. your clothes and wept 34.27
I r. my garments and my mantle, and Ez 9.03
with my garments and my mantle r., 9.05
Mordecai r. his clothes and put on Est 4.01
and r. his robe, and shaved his head, Job 1.20
and they r. their robes and sprinkled 2.12
and the cloud is not r. under them. 26.08
to quake, thou hast r. it open; Ps 60.02
the earth is r. asunder, the earth Is 24.19
to Hezekiah with their clothes r., 36.22
he r. his clothes, and covered 37.01

REPAID
r. me good, whereas I have r. you evil. 1Sa 24.17
invite you in return, and you be r. Lk 14.12
You will be r. at the resurrection 14.14
a gift to him that he might be r.?" Rom 11.35

REPAIR
and let them r. the house wherever 2Ki 12.05
it over for the r. of the house." 12.07
that they should not r. the house. 12.08
and quarried stone to r. the house. 22.06
Israel money to r. the house of 2Ch 24.05
and bronze to r. the house of the 24.12
to r. the house of the LORD his God 34.08
to r. its ruins, and to give us Ez 9.09
r. its breaches, for it totters. Ps 60.02
they shall r. the ruined cities, the Is 61.04
that is fallen and r. its breaches, Amo 9.11

REPAIRED
And he r. the altar of the LORD 1Ki 18.30
and Joab r. the rest of the city. 1Ch 11.08
and he r. the altar of the LORD 2Ch 15.08
the house of the LORD, and r. them. 29.03
the son of Uriah, son of Hakkoz r. Neh 3.04
of Berechiah, son of Meshezabel r. 3.04
to them Zadok the son of Baana r. 3.04
And next to them the Tekoites r.; 3.05
son of Besodeiah r. the Old Gate; 3.06
And next to them r. Melatiah the 3.07
son of Harhaiah, goldsmiths, r. 3.08
Hananiah, one of the perfumers, r.; 3.08
half the district of Jerusalem, r. 3.09
son of Harumaph r. opposite his 3.10
Hattush the son of Hashabneiah r. 3.10
of Pahathmoab r. another section 3.11
Jerusalem, r., he and his daughters. 3.12
of Zanoah r. the Valley Gate; they 3.13
and r. a thousand cubits of the 3.13
of Bethhaccherem, r. the Dung Gate; 3.14
r. the Fountain Gate; he rebuilt 3.15
r. to a point opposite the sepulchres 3.16
After him the Levites r.: Rehum the 3.17
of Keilah, r. for his district. 3.17
After him their brethren r.: Bavvai 3.18
r. another section opposite the 3.19
son of Zabbai r. another section 3.20
son of Hakkoz r. another section 3.21
priests, the men of the Plain, r. 3.22
and Hasshub r. opposite their 3.23
son of Ananiah r. beside his own 3.23
son of Henadad r. another section, 3.24
the son of Uzai r. opposite the 3.25
living on Ophel r. to a point 3.26
the Tekoites r. another section 3.27
Above the Horse Gate the priests r., 3.28
son of Immer r. opposite his own 3.29
the keeper of the East Gate, r. 3.29
son of Zalaph r. another section. 3.30
of Berechiah r. opposite his 3.30
r. as far as the house of the 3.31
goldsmiths and the merchants r. 3.32

REPAIRER
be called the r. of the breach, the Is 58.12

REPAIRING
them, "Why are you not r. the house? 2Ki 12.07
who were r. the house of the LORD 12.14
house of the LORD, r. the house, 22.05
and the r. went forward in their 2Ch 24.13
gave it for r. and restoring the 34.10
the walls and r. the foundations. Ez 4.12
heard that the r. of the walls of Neh 4.07

REPAIRS
wherever any need of r. is discovered." 2Ki 12.05
priests had made no r. on the house. 12.06
for making r. on the house of the 12.12
outlay upon the r. of the house. 12.12

REPAY
the LORD will r. me with good for 2Sa 16.12
given to me, that I should r. him? Job 41.11
and he will r. him for his deed. Pro 19.17
Do not say, "I will r. evil"; 20.22
so will he r., wrath to his adversaries, Is 59.18
I will r., yea, I will r. into their 65.06
then he will r. every man for what Mt 16.27
I will r. you when I come back.' Lk 10.35
blessed, because they cannot r. you. 14.14
R. no one evil for evil, but take Rom 12.17
is mine, I will r., says the Lord. 12.19
it just to r. with affliction 2Th 1.06
I will r. it—to say nothing of Phm 1.19
said, "Vengeance is mine, I will r." Heb 10.30
and r. her double for her deeds; Rev 18.06
to r. every one for what he has 22.12

REPAYS
See that none of you r. evil for evil, 1Th 5.15

REPEAT
there they r. the triumphs of the Ju 5.11
I r., let no one think me foolish; 2Co 11.16

REPEATED
he r. them in the ears of the LORD. 1Sa 8.21
they r. them before Saul; and he 17.31
So he r., "Give them to the men, 2Ki 4.43

REPEATEDLY
which my mind has sought r., but I Ecc 7.28
Nor was it to offer himself r., Heb 9.25
had to suffer r. since the foundation 9.26
offering r. the same sacrifices, 10.11

REPEATING
"What do you mean by r. this proverb Eze 18.02

REPEATS
but he who r. a matter alienates a Pro 17.09
vomit is a fool that r. his folly. 26.11

REPENT
"Lest the people r. when they see Ex 13.17
and r. of this evil against thy 32.12
or a son of man, that he should r. Num 23.19
"I r. that I have made Saul king; 1Sa 15.11
Glory of Israel will not lie or r.; 15.29
he is not a man, that he should r." 15.29
and r., and make supplication to 1Ki 8.47
if they r. with all their mind and 8.48
and r., and make supplication to 2Ch 6.37
if they r. with all their mind and 6.38
myself, and r. in dust and ashes. Job 42.06
If a man does not r., he has bent Ps 7.12
justice, and those in her who r., Is 1.27
than rock; they have refused to r. Jer 5.03
iniquity and are too weary to r. 9.05
I will r. of the evil that I 18.08
then I will r. of the good which I 18.10
that I may r. of the evil which I 26.03
the LORD will r. of the evil which 26.13
not the LORD r. of the evil which 26.19
for I r. of the evil which I did to 42.10
R. and turn away from your idols; Eze 14.06
R. and turn from all your transgressions, 18.30
I will not spare, I will not r.; 24.14
whether he will not turn and r., Joe 2.14
God may yet r. and turn from his Jon 3.09
"R., for the kingdom of heaven is Mt 3.02
"R., for the kingdom of heaven is 4.17
been done, because they did not r. 11.20
not afterward r. and believe him. 21.32
r., and believe in the gospel." Mk 1.15
and preached that men should r. 6.12
but unless you r. you will all Lk 13.03
but unless you r. you will all 13.05
them from the dead, they will r. 16.30
'I r.,' you must forgive him." 17.04
"R., and be baptized every one of Ac 2.38
R. therefore, and turn again, that 3.19
R. therefore of this wickedness of 8.22
commands all men everywhere to r., 17.30
they should r. and turn to God and 26.20
that they will r. and come to know 2Ti 2.25
for he found no chance to r., Heb 12.17
r. and do the works you did at Rev 2.05
from its place, unless you r. 2.05
R. then. If not, I will come 2.16
time to r., but she refuses to r. of 2.21
unless they r. of her doings; 2.22
keep that, and r. If you will 3.03
and chasten; so be zealous and r. 3.19
did not r. of the works of their 9.20
nor did they r. of their murders or 9.21
they did not r. and give him glory 16.09
and did not r. of their deeds. 16.11

REPENTANCE
Bear fruit that befits r., Mt 3.08
"I baptize you with water for r., 3.11
a baptism of r. for the forgiveness Mk 1.04
a baptism of r. for the forgiveness Lk 3.03
Bear fruits that befit r., and do 3.08
the righteous, but sinners to r. 5.32
righteous persons who need no r. 15.07
and that r. and forgiveness of sins 24.47
to give r. to Israel and forgiveness Ac 5.31
also God has granted r. unto life. 11.18
a baptism of r. to all the people 13.24
baptized with the baptism of r., 19.04
to Greeks of r. to God and of 20.21
perform deeds worthy of their r. 26.20
kindness is meant to lead you to r.? Rom 2.04
produces a r. that leads to 2Co 7.10
a foundation of r. from dead works Heb 6.01
again to r. those who have once 6.04
but that all should reach r. 2Pe 3.09

REPENTED
And the LORD r. of the evil which Ex 32.14
And the LORD r. that he had made 1Sa 15.35
the LORD r. of the evil, and said to 2Sa 24.16
LORD saw, and he r. of the evil; 1Ch 21.15
they r. and sought God earnestly. Ps 78.34
For after I had turned away I r.; Jer 31.19
You recently r. and did what was 34.15
The LORD r. concerning this; Amo 7.03
The LORD r. concerning this; 7.06
God r. of the evil which he had Jon 3.10
So they r. and said, As the LORD of Zec 1.06
they would have r. long ago in Mt 11.21
for they r. at the preaching of 12.41
but afterward he r. and went. 21.29
he r. and brought back the thirty 27.03
Sidon, they would have r. long ago, Lk 10.13
for they r. at the preaching of 11.32
and have not r. of the impurity, 2Co 12.21

REPENTEST
in steadfast love, and r. of evil. Jon 4.02

REPENTING
because you were grieved into r.; 2Co 7.09

REPENTS
no man r. of his wickedness, saying, Jer 8.06
in steadfast love, and r. of evil. Joe 2.13
one sinner who r. than over Lk 15.07
of God over one sinner who r. 15.10
him, and if he r., forgive him; 17.03

REPHAEL
R., Obed, and Elzabad, whose brethren 1Ch 26.07

REPHAH
R. was his son, Resheph his son, Telah 1Ch 7.25

REPHAIAH
his son R., his son Arnan, his son 1Ch 3.21
R., and Uzziel, the sons of Ishi; 4.42
R., Jeriel, Jahmai, Ibsam, and Shemuel, 7.02
and R. was his son, Eleasah his 9.43
Next to them R. the son of Hur, Neh 3.09

REPHAIM
and subdued the R. in Ashterothkarnaim, Gen 14.05
the Hittites, the Perizzites, the R., 15.20
Anakim they are also known as R., Deu 2.11
(That also is known as a land of R.; 2.20
R. formerly lived there, but the 2.20
was left of the remnant of the R.; 3.11
Bashan is called the land of R. 3.13
one of the remnant of the R., Jos 12.04
was left of the remnant of the R.); 13.12
northern end of the valley of R.; 15.08
land of the Perizzites and the R., 17.15
the north end of the valley of R.; 18.16
and spread out in the valley of R. 2Sa 5.18
and spread out in the valley of R. 5.22
was encamped in the valley of R. 23.13
was encamped in the valley of R. 1Ch 11.15
made a raid in the valley of R. 14.09
ears of grain in the Valley of R. Is 17.05

REPHAN
Moloch, and the star of the god R., Ac 7.43

REPHIDIM
of the LORD, and camped at R.; Ex 17.01
and fought with Israel at R. 17.08
set out from R. and came into the 19.02
out from Alush, and encamped at R., Num 33.14
And they set out from R., and 33.15

REPLACE
and to r. every man's money in his Gen 42.25

REPLACED
which was r. in our sacks the first Gen 43.18
to be r. by hot bread on the day it 1Sa 21.06

REPLANTED
places, and r. that which was desolate; Eze 36.36

REPLENISH
soul, every languishing soul I will r. Jer 31.25

REPLENISHED
I shall be r., now that she is laid Eze 26.02

REPLIED
She r., "Your signet and your cord, Gen 38.18
And Judah r., "Let her keep the 38.23
They r., "The man questioned us 43.07
He r., "Rest assured, do not be 43.23
And she r., "All that you say I Ru 3.05
She r., "Wait, my daughter, until you 3.18
But David r., "Your father knows 1Sa 20.03
The king r. to him, "Do as he has 1Ki 2.31
Then I r. to them, "The God of Neh 2.20
Then Daniel r. with prudence and Dan 2.14
But he r. to the man who told him, Mt 12.48
Simon Peter r., "You are the Christ, 16.16
He r., "Elijah does come, and he is 17.11
But he r. to one of them, 'Friend, I 20.13
But the wise r., 'Perhaps there 25.09
But he r., 'Truly, I say to you, I do 25.12
And he r., "Who are my mother and Mk 3.33
He r., "My name is Legion; for we 5.09
Jesus r., "A man was going down Lk 10.30
They r., "Are you from Galilee too? Jn 7.52
And he r., "I believe that Jesus *Ac 8.37
James r., "Brethren, listen to me. 15.13
Paul r., "I am a Jew, from Tarsus in 21.39
Paul r.: "Realizing that for many 24.10
Festus r. that Paul was being kept 25.04

REPLY
if any one salutes you, do not r.; 2Ki 4.29
And this was their r. to us: 'We are Ez 5.11
Esther told them to r. to Mordecai, Est 4.15
let me speak, and do thou r. to me. Job 13.22
Then Peter said in r., "Lo, we have Mt 19.27
And they could not r. to this. Lk 14.06
But what is God's r. to him? "I have Rom 11.04

REPORT
brought an ill r. of them to their Gen 37.02
When the r. was heard in Pharaoh's 45.16
"You shall not utter a false r. Ex 23.01
Israel an evil r. of the land Num 13.32
up an evil r. against the land, 14.36
brought up an evil r. of the land, 14.37
shall hear the r. of you and shall Deu 2.25
for we have heard a r. of him, Jos 9.09
And the r. pleased the people of 22.33
said to them, "What do you r.?" Ju 18.08
it is no good r. that I hear the 1Sa 2.24
"The r. was true which I heard in 1Ki 10.06
surpass the r. which I heard. 10.07
Beersheba to Dan, and bring me a r., 1Ch 21.02
"The r. was true which I heard in 2Ch 9.05
you surpass the r. which I heard. 9.06
them till a r. should reach Darius Ez 5.05
they sent him a r., in which was 5.07
their king, according to this r. Neh 6.06
When the r. comes to Egypt, they Is 23.05
in anguish over the r. about Tyre. 23.05
We have heard the r. of it, Jer 6.24
"We must r. all these words to the 36.16
of Babylon heard the r. of them, 50.43
fearful at the r. heard in the 51.46
when a r. comes in one year and 51.46
and afterward a r. in another year, 51.46
come to you to r. to you the news. Eze 24.26
O LORD, I have heard the r. of thee, Hab 3.02
And the r. of this went through all Mt 9.26
and a r. concerning him went out Lk 4.14
the more the r. went abroad 5.15
And this r. concerning him spread 7.17
"Lord, who has believed our r., Jn 12.38
For they themselves r. concerning 1Th 1.09

REPORTED
And Moses r. the words of the Ex 19.08
they r. the matter in the ears of 1Sa 11.04
and they r. to him, "Men are coming 1Ki 20.17
And the watchman r., saying, "The 2Ki 9.18
Again the watchman r., "He reached 9.20
and r. to the king, "Your servants 22.09
and further r. to the king, "All 2Ch 34.16
Now when it was r. to Sanballat and Neh 6.01
"It is r. among the nations, and 6.06
now it will be r. to the king 6.07
presence, and r. my words to him. 6.19
the capital was r. to the king. Est 9.11
and they r. all the words to the Jer 36.20
they went and r. to their lord all Mt 18.31
it was r. that he was at home. Mk 2.01
they r. briefly to Peter and those with * 16.08
came and r. this to his master. Lk 14.21
friends and r. what the chief Ac 4.23
prison, and they returned and r., 5.22
And the jailer r. the words to Paul, 16.36
The police r. these words to the 16.38
coming here has r. or spoken any 28.21
For it has been r. to me by Chloe's 1Co 1.11
It is actually r. that there is 5.01
and love and r. that you always 1Th 3.06

REPORTING
r. the conversion of the Gentiles, Ac 15.03

REPORTS
not believe the r. until I came 1Ki 10.07
not believe the r. until I came 2Ch 9.06
She had heard the r. about Jesus, Mk 5.27
And r. of him went out into every Lk 4.37

REPOSE
rest to the weary; and this is r."; Is 28.12

REPRESENT
You shall r. the people before God, Ex 18.19

REPRESENTATION
a r. by the art and imagination of Ac 17.29

REPRESENTING
twelve men, each r. his fathers' house. Num 1.44

REPROACH
said, "God has taken away my r."; Gen 30.23
rolled away the r. of Egypt from Jos 5.09
the sheaves, and do not r. her. Ru 2.15
and takes away the r. from Israel? 1Sa 17.26
ten times you have cast r. upon me; Job 19.03
heart does not r. me for any of my 27.06
nor takes up a r. against his Ps 15.03
for thy sake that I have borne r., 69.07
soul with fasting, it became my r. 69.10
Thou knowest my r., and my shame 69.19
Turn away the r. which I dread; 119.39
but sin is a r. to any people. Pro 14.34
son who causes shame and brings r. 19.26
by your name; take away our r." Is 4.01
and the r. of his people he will 25.08
fear not the r. of men, and be not 51.07
and the r. of your widowhood you 54.04
know that for thy sake I bear r. Jer 15.15

REPROACH (cont.)
become for me a r. and derision Jer 20.08
you everlasting r. and perpetual 23.40
to be a r., a byword, a taunt, and a 24.09
a hissing, and an everlasting r. 25.09
and a r. among all the nations 29.18
put to shame, for we have heard r.; 51.51
an object of r. among the nations Eze 5.14
You shall be a r. and a taunt, a 5.15
an object of r. for the daughters 16.57
Ammonites, and concerning their r.; 21.28
have made you a r. to the nations, 22.04
suffer the r. of the nations. 34.29
suffered the r. of the nations; 36.06
you shall themselves suffer r. 36.07
any more the r. of the nations, 36.15
and make not thy heritage a r., Joe 2.17
more make you a r. among the 2.19
that you will not bear r. for it. Zep 3.18
me, to take away my r. among men. Lk 1.25
in saying this you r. us also. 11.45
Now a bishop must be above r., 1Ti 3.02
may fall into r. and the snare of 3.07
so that they may be without r. 5.07
and free from r. until the appearing 6.14

REPROACHED
to the poor." And they r. her. Mk 14.05
of those who r. thee fell on me. Rom 15.03
If you are r. for the name of 1Pe 4.14

REPROACHES
that I may answer him who r. me. Pro 27.11
and will turn back upon him his r. Hos 12.14
"The r. of those who reproached Rom 15.03

REPROACHING
all men generously and without r., Jas 1.05

REPROBATE
in whose eyes a r. is despised, but Ps 15.04

REPROOF
But what does r. from you reprove? Job 6.25
Give heed to my r.; behold, I Pro 1.23
and would have none of my r., 1.25
counsel, and despised all my r., 1.30
discipline or be weary of his r., 3.11
discipline, and my heart despised r.! 5.12
but he who rejects r. goes astray. 10.17
but he who hates r. is stupid. 12.01
but he who heeds r. is honored. 13.18
the way; he who hates r. will die. 15.10
The rod and r. give wisdom, but a 29.15
for r., for correction, and for 2Ti 3.16

REPROOFS
and the r. of discipline are the way Pro 6.23

REPROVE
but what does reproof from you r.? Job 6.25
Do you think that you can r. words, 6.26
I do not r. you for your sacrifices Ps 50.08
Do not r. a scoffer, or he will hate Pro 9.08
r. a wise man, and he will love you. 9.08
r. a man of understanding, and he 19.25
you, and your apostasy will r. you. Jer 2.19
be dumb and unable to r. them; Eze 3.26
exhort and r. with all authority. Tit 2.15
Those whom I love, I r. and chasten; Rev 3.19

REPROVED
A scoffer does not like to be r.; Pro 15.12
He who is often r., yet stiffens 29.01
who had been r. by him for Herodias, Lk 3.19

REPROVER
of gold is a wise r. to a listening Pro 25.12

REPROVES
"Behold, happy is the man whom God r.; Job 5.17
your fear of him that he r. you, 22.04
for the LORD r. him whom he loves, Pro 3.12
and he who r. a wicked man incurs 9.07
but he who boldly r. makes peace. 10.10
a snare for him who r. in the gate, Is 29.21
They hate him who r. in the gate, Amo 5.10

REPTILE
of r. and sea creature, can be tamed Jas 3.07

REPTILES
of birds, and of r., and of fish. 1Ki 4.33
of animals and r. and birds of the Ac 10.12
of prey and r. and birds of the 11.06
man or birds or animals or r. Rom 1.23

REPULSE
How then can you r. a single captain 2Ki 18.24
How then can you r. a single captain Is 36.09

REPULSIVE
I am r. to my wife, loathsome to the Job 19.17

REPUTE
that I am a poor man and of no r.?" 1Sa 18.23
Solomon great r. in the sight of 1Ch 29.25
favor and good r. in the sight of Pro 3.04
you, and your ill r. have no end. 25.10
among you seven men of good r., Ac 6.03
and dishonor, in ill r. and good r. 2Co 6.08
who were of r.) the gospel which I Gal 2.02
who were of r. added nothing to me; 2.06

REPUTED
those who were r. to be something Gal 2.06
who were r. to be pillars, gave to 2.09

REQUEST
to them, "Let me make a r. of you; Ju 8.24
will perform the r. of his servant. 2Sa 14.15
has granted the r. of his servant. 14.22
And now I have one r. to make of you; 1Ki 2.16
"I have one small r. to make of you; 2.20
to her, "Make your r., my mother; 2.20
to me, "For what do you make r.?" Neh 2.04
What is your r.? It shall be given Est 5.03
And what is your r.? Even to the 5.06
said, "My petition and my r. is: 5.07
grant my petition and fulfil my r., 5.08
And what is your r.? Even to the 7.02
petition, and my people at my r. 7.03
And what further is your r.? It 9.12
"O that I might have my r., Job 6.08
not withheld the r. of his lips. Ps 21.02
LORD your God according to your r., Jer 42.04
Daniel made r. of the king, and he Dan 2.49

REQUESTED
earrings that he r. was one thousand Ju 8.26

REQUESTS
let your r. be made known to God. Php 4.06
have obtained the r. made of him. 1Jn 5.15

REQUIRE
I will surely r. a reckoning; Gen 9.05
beast I will r. it and of man; 9.05
brother I will r. the life of man. 9.05
of my hand you shall r. him. 43.09
does the LORD your God r. of you, Deu 10.12
name, I myself will r. it of him. 18.19
your God will surely r. it of you, 23.21
but one thing I r. of you; 2Sa 3.13
shall I not now r. his blood at 4.11
Why then should my lord r. this? 1Ch 21.03
as the priests at Jerusalem r.— Ez 6.09

REQUIRE (cont.)
these and r. nothing from them. Neh 5.12
his blood I will r. at your hand. Eze 3.18
his blood I will r. at your hand. 3.20
there I will r. your contributions 20.40
blood I will r. at the watchman's 33.06
his blood I will r. at your hand. 33.08
and I will r. my sheep at their 34.10
does the LORD r. of you but to do Mic 6.08
in whatever she may r. from you, Rom 16.02
more presentable parts do not r. 1Co 12.24

REQUIRED
of my hand you r. it, whether Gen 31.39
forty days were r. for it, for 50.03
for so many are r. for embalming. 50.03
objects which they are r. to carry. Num 4.32
and bring the offering r. of her, 5.15
the king's business r. haste. 1Sa 21.08
to the place where it was r., 1Ki 4.28
king of Assyria r. of Hezekiah 2Ki 18.14
for they were r. to count them when 1Ch 9.28
before the ark as each day r., 16.37
according to the number r. of them, 23.31
as the duty of each day r., 2Ch 8.13
priests as the duty of each day r., 8.14
have you not r. the Levites to 24.06
LORD as the duty of each day r., 31.16
to the ordinance, as each day r., Ez 3.04
whatever else is r. for the house 7.20
for the singers, as every day r. Neh 11.23
the portions r. by the law for the 12.44
and sin offering thou hast not r. Ps 40.06
For there our captors r. of us songs, 137.03
may be r. of this generation, Lk 11.50
it shall be r. of this generation. 11.51
this night your soul is r. of you; 12.20
is given, of him will much be r.; 12.48
Moreover it is r. of stewards that 1Co 4.02
to command you to do what is r., Phm 1.08
of suffering is r. of your brotherhood 1Pe 5.09

REQUIREMENT
that the just r. of the law might Rom 8.04
to a legal r. concerning bodily Heb 7.16

REQUIRES
his people Israel, as each day r.; 1Ki 8.59
r. of you, be it done with all Ez 7.21
who r. of you this trampling of my Is 1.12
law do by nature what the law r., Rom 2.14
what the law r. is written on 2.15

REQUIRING
"If any case arises r. decision Deu 17.08

REQUITAL
Will he then make r. to suit you, Job 34.33
his adversaries, r. to his enemies; Is 59.18
the coastlands he will render r. 59.18
the r. he is rendering her. Jer 51.06

REQUITE
him, he will r. him to his face. Deu 7.10
Do you thus r. the LORD, you foolish 32.06
and will r. those who hate me. 32.41
come they may r. Gibeah of Benjamin, Ju 20.10
The LORD r. the evildoer according 2Sa 3.39
I will r. you on this plot of 2Ki 9.26
the work of a man he will r. him, Job 34.11
R. them according to their work, and Ps 28.04
r. them according to the work of 28.04
They r. me evil for good; my soul 35.12
raise me up, that I may r. them! 41.10
He will r. my enemies with evil; 54.05
For thou dost r. a man according to 62.12
nor r. us according to our iniquities 103.10
and will he not r. man according Pro 24.12
lead him and r. him with comfort, Is 57.18
but dost r. the guilt of fathers to Jer 32.18
R. her according to her deeds, do to 50.29
"I will r. Babylon and all the 51.24
of recompense, he will surely r. 51.56
"Thou wilt r. them, O LORD, according Lam 3.64
but I will r. their deeds upon Eze 9.10
I will r. their deeds upon their 11.21
I will r. your deeds upon your head, 16.43
he broke, I will r. upon his head. 17.19
and r. them for their deeds. Hos 4.09
and r. him according to his deeds. 12.02
I will r. your deed upon your own Joe 3.04
and I will r. your deed upon your 3.07
the Lord will r. him for his deeds. 2Ti 4.14

REQUITED
as I have done, so God has r. me. Ju 1.07
Thus God r. the crime of Abimelech, 9.56
was right, and it was not r. to me. Job 33.27
if I have r. my friend with evil or Ps 7.04
If the righteous is r. on earth, Pro 11.31
way have I r. upon their heads, Eze 22.31
your lewdness shall be r. upon you, 23.49

REQUITES
and r. to their face those who hate Deu 7.10
and who r. him for what he has done? Job 21.31
but abundantly r. him who acts Ps 31.23
shall he be who r. you with what 137.08

REQUITING
r. the guilty by bringing his conduct 2Ch 6.23

RESCUE
that he might r. him out of their Gen 37.22
congregation shall r. the manslayer Num 35.25
help there was no one to r. her. Deu 22.27
draws near to r. her husband from 25.11
overtake and shall surely r. 1Sa 30.08
Come up, and r. me from the hand of 2Ki 16.07
dragging me away, with none to r. Ps 7.02
let him r. him, for he delights in 22.08
Incline thy ear to me, r. me speedily! 31.02
R. me from their ravages, my life 35.17
faithful help r. me from sinking 69.14
righteousness deliver me and r. me; 71.02
R. me, O my God, from the hand of the 71.04
R. the weak and the needy; 82.04
I will r. him and honor him. 91.15
r. me and deliver me from the many 144.07
R. me from the cruel sword, and 144.11
R. those who are being taken away Pro 24.11
they carry it off, and none can r. Is 5.29
it, he will spare and r. it. 31.05
have become a prey with none to r., 42.22
I will r. my sheep from their Eze 34.10
and I will r. them from all places 34.12
till the sun went down to r. him. Dan 6.14
no one who could r. from his power; 8.04
one who could r. the ram from his 8.07
no one shall r. her out of my hand Hos 2.10
will carry off, and none shall r. 5.14
The Lord will r. me from every evil 2Ti 4.18
knows how to r. the godly from 2Pe 2.09

RESCUED
who had r. them from the hand of Ju 8.34
and r. you from the hand of Midian; 9.17
and Israel r. their territory from 1Sa 7.14
taken; and David r. his two wives. 30.18
that he is r. in the day of wrath? Job 21.30
my soul also, which thou hast r. Ps 71.23
and r. us from our foes, for his 136.24
or the captives of a tyrant be r.? Is 49.24
and the prey of the tyrant be r., 49.25
Israel who dwell in Samaria be r., Amo 3.12
There you shall be r., there the Mic 4.10

RESCUED (cont.)
and r. him out of all his afflictions, Ac 7.10
his angel and r. me from the hand 12.11
them with the soldiers and r. him, 23.27
yet from them all the Lord r. me. 2Ti 3.11
So I was r. from the lion's mouth. 4.17
and if he r. righteous Lot, greatly 2Pe 2.07

RESCUES
He delivers and r., he works Dan 6.27
"As the shepherd r. from the mouth Amo 3.12

RESCUEST
to kings, who r. David thy servant. Ps 144.10

RESEMBLED
of them; they r. the sons of a king." Ju 8.18

RESEMBLING
a sapphire, in form r. a throne. Eze 10.01
of the holy place was something r. 41.21
God for images r. mortal man or Rom 1.23
but r. the Son of God he continues Heb 7.03

RESEN
R. between Nineveh and Calah; that is Gen 10.12

RESENTFUL
went to his house r. and sullen, 1Ki 20.43
own way; it is not irritable or r.; 1Co 13.05

RESENTMENT
in much vexation and sickness and r.? Ecc 5.17

RESERVE
That food shall be a r. for the land Gen 41.36

RESERVED
"Have you not r. a blessing for me Gen 27.36
most holy things, r. from the fire; Num 18.09
there a commander's portion was r.; Deu 33.21
contribution r. for the LORD and 2Ch 31.14
which I have r. for the time of Job 38.23
gloom of darkness has been r. 2Pe 2.17
of darkness has been r. for ever. Jud 1.13

RESERVOIR
You made a r. between the two walls Is 22.11

RESHEPH
R. his son, Telah his son, Tahan his 1Ch 7.25

RESIDE
for the aliens who r. among you and Eze 47.22

RESIDENCE
as a royal r. and for the glory of Dan 4.30

RESIDENTS
and Elamites and r. of Mesopotamia, Ac 2.09
And all the r. of Lydda and Sharon 9.35
so that all the r. of Asia heard 19.10
became known to all r. of Ephesus, 19.17

RESIDES
In whatever tribe the alien r., there Eze 47.23

RESIDUE
the r. of wrath thou wilt gird upon Ps 76.10
I make the r. of it an abomination? Is 44.19
and stamped the r. with its feet. Dan 7.07
and stamped the r. with its feet; 7.19

RESIST
Do not r. one who is evil. But if Mt 5.39
you always r. the Holy Spirit. Ac 7.51
fault? For who can r. his will?" Rom 9.19
and those who r. will incur judgment 13.02
R. the devil and he will flee from Jas 4.07
righteous man; he does not r. you. 5.06
R. him, firm in your faith, knowing 1Pe 5.09

RESISTED
you have not yet r. to the point of Heb 12.04

RESISTS
he who r. the authorities r. what God Rom 13.02

RESOLUTE
if he continues r. in keeping my 1Ch 28.07

RESOLUTELY
He set to work r. and built up all 2Ch 32.05

RESOLVE
every good r. and work of faith by 2Th 1.11

RESOLVED
But Daniel r. that he would not Dan 1.08
shame, r. to divorce her quietly. Mt 1.19
events Paul r. in the Spirit to Ac 19.21

RESORT
You r. to the sword, you commit Eze 33.26

RESORTED
in all Israel r. to him from all 2Ch 11.13
"Why have you r. to the gods of a 25.15

RESOUND
The clamor will r. to the ends of Jer 25.31

RESOUNDED
mighty shout, so that the earth r. 1Sa 4.05

RESOURCE
in me, and any r. is driven from me. Job 6.13

RESOURCES
multiply your r. and increase the 2Co 9.10

RESPECT
the LORD, "Do not r. their offering. Num 16.15
guiltless with r. to this oath of Jos 2.17
guiltless with r. to your oath 2.20
no r. is shown to the elders. Lam 5.12
them, saying, 'They will r. my son.' Mt 21.37
them, saying, 'They will r. my son.' Mk 12.06
it may be they will r. him. Lk 20.13
with r. to the hope and the resurrection Ac 23.06
'With r. to the resurrection of the 24.21
r. to whom r. is due, honor to whom Rom 13.07
may command the r. of outsiders, 1Th 4.12
to r. those who labor among you and 5.12
to give satisfaction in every r.; Tit 2.09
made like his brethren in every r., Heb 2.17
who in every r. has been tempted 4.15
to your masters with all r., 1Pe 2.18

RESPECTED
a r. member of the council, who was Mk 15.43
to discipline us and we r. them. Heb 12.09

RESPECTFUL
life, godly and r. in every way. 1Ti 2.02
submissive and r. in every way; 3.04

RESPECTS
but he who r. the commandment will Pro 13.13
wife see that she r. her husband. Eph 5.33
Show yourself in all r. a model of Tit 2.07

RESPITE
Pharaoh saw that there was a r., Ex 8.15
us seven days r. that we may send 1Sa 11.03
to give him r. from days of trouble, Ps 94.13
yourself no rest, your eyes no r.! Lam 2.18
flow without ceasing, without r., 3.49

RESPOND
and the beam from the woodwork r. Hab 2.11

RESPONSE
"And you shall make r. before the Deu 26.05

RESPONSIVELY
and they sang r., praising and giving Ez 3.11

REST
the ark came to r. upon the mountains Gen 8.04
and the r. fled to the mountain. 14.10
and r. yourselves under the tree, 18.04
Jacob fed the r. of Laban's flock. 30.36
and let the r. go and carry grain 42.19
He replied, "R. assured, do not be 42.23
and the r. of you shall be blameless." 44.10
restored like the r. of his flesh. Ex 4.07
you make them r. from their 5.05
'Tomorrow is a day of solemn r., 16.23
you shall let it r. and lie fallow, 23.11
on the seventh day you shall r.; 23.12
your ox and your ass may have r., 23.12
and the r. of the blood you shall 29.12
and throw the r. of the blood 29.20
day is a sabbath of solemn r., 31.15
with you, and I will give you r." 33.14
on the seventh day you shall r.; 34.21
time and in harvest you shall r. 34.21
sabbath of solemn r. to the LORD; 35.02
and the r. of the blood of the bull Lev 4.07
and the r. of the blood he shall 4.18
pour out the r. of its blood at 4.25
pour out the r. of its blood at 4.30
pour out the r. of its blood at 4.34
while the r. of the blood shall be 5.09
And the r. of it Aaron and his sons 6.16
and the r. of the oil that is in 14.18
and the r. of the oil that is in 14.29
It is a sabbath of solemn r. to you, 16.31
day is a sabbath of solemn r., 23.03
shall observe a day of solemn r., 23.24
be to you a sabbath of solemn r., 23.32
the first day shall be a solemn r., 23.39
eighth day shall be a solemn r. 23.39
sabbath of solemn r. for the land, 25.04
a year of solemn r. for the land. 25.05
then the land shall r., 26.34
it lies desolate it shall have r., 26.35
the r. which it had not in your 26.35
then the r. shall be reckoned to Num 18.30
Midian with the r. of their slain, 31.08
the r. of Gilead, and all Bashan, the Deu 3.13
until the LORD gives r. to your 3.20
maidservant may r. as well as you. 5.14
yet come to the r. and to the 12.09
he gives you r. from all your 12.10
And the r. shall hear, and fear, and 19.20
has given you r. from all your 25.19
shall be no r. for the sole of 28.65
God is providing you a place of r., Jos 1.13
until the LORD gives r. to your 1.15
shall r. in the waters of the 3.13
And the land had r. from war. 11.23
sword among the r. of their slain. 13.22
the r. of the kingdom of Sihon king 13.27
And the land had r. from war. 14.15
made to the r. of the tribe of 17.02
allotted to the r. of the Manassites 17.06
And the r. of the Kohathites 21.05
As to the r. of the Kohathites 21.20
families of the r. of the Kohathites 21.26
And to the r. of the Levites, the 21.34
LORD gave them r. on every side 21.44
God has given r. to your brethren, 22.04
LORD had given r. to Israel from 23.01
So the land had r. forty years. Ju 3.11
the land had r. for eighty years. 3.30
the land had r. for forty years. 5.31
but all the r. of the people knelt 7.06
he sent all the r. of Israel every 7.08
the land had r. forty years in the 8.28
turns out, for the man will not r., Ru 3.18
the r. of the people he sent home, 1Sa 13.02
and the r. we have utterly destroyed 15.15
as he was taking his noonday r. 2Sa 4.05
had given him r. from all his 7.01
I will give you r. from all your 7.11
the r. of his men he put in the 10.10
gather the r. of the people together, 12.28
lord the king will set me at r.'; 14.17
God has given me r. on every side; 1Ki 5.04
who has given r. to his people 8.56
Now the r. of the acts of Solomon, 11.41
and to the r. of the people, 12.23
Now the r. of the acts of Jeroboam, 14.19
Now the r. of the acts of Rehoboam, 14.29
The r. of the acts of Abijam, and 15.07
Now the r. of all the acts of Asa, 15.23
Now the r. of the acts of Nadab, and 15.31
Now the r. of the acts of Baasha, 16.05
Now the r. of the acts of Elah, and 16.14
Now the r. of the acts of Zimri, and 16.20
Now the r. of the acts of Omri 16.27
And the r. fled into the city of 20.30
Now the r. of the acts of Ahab, and 22.39
Now the r. of the acts of Jehoshaphat, 22.45
Now the r. of the acts of Ahaziah 2Ki 1.18
and your sons can live on the r." 4.07
Now the r. of the acts of Joram, and 8.23
Now the r. of the acts of Jehu, and 10.34
Now the r. of the acts of Joash, and 12.19
Now the r. of the acts of Jehoahaz 13.08
Now the r. of the acts of Joash, and 13.12
Now the r. of the acts of Jehoash 14.15
Now the r. of the deeds of Amaziah, 14.18
Now the r. of the acts of Jeroboam, 14.28
Now the r. of the acts of Azariah, 15.06
Now the r. of the deeds of Zechariah, 15.11
Now the r. of the deeds of Shallum, 15.15
Now the r. of the deeds of Menahem, 15.21
Now the r. of the deeds of Pekahiah, 15.26
Now the r. of the acts of Pekah, and 15.31
Now the r. of the acts of Jotham, 15.36
Now the r. of the acts of Ahaz 16.19
On what do you r. this confidence 18.19
The r. of the deeds of Hezekiah, and 20.20
Now the r. of the acts of Manasseh, 21.17
Now the r. of the acts of Amon 21.25
Now the r. of the acts of Josiah, 23.28
Now the r. of the deeds of Jehoiakim, 24.05
And the r. of the people who were 25.11
with the r. of the multitude, 25.11
To the r. of the Kohathites were 1Ch 6.61
for the r. of the families of the 6.70
To the r. of the Merarites were 6.77
Joab repaired the r. of the city. 11.08
likewise all the r. of Israel were 12.38
and the r. of those chosen and 16.41
the r. of his men he put in the 19.11
And of the r. of the sons of Levi: 24.20
a house of r. for the ark of the 28.02
Now the r. of the acts of Solomon, 2Ch 9.29
The r. of the acts of Abijah, his 13.22
days the land had r. for ten years. 14.01
And the kingdom had r. under him. 14.05
in Judah, for the land had r. 14.06
the LORD gave them r. round about. 15.15
his God gave him r. round about. 20.30
Now the r. of the acts of Jehoshaphat, 20.34
brought the r. of the money before 24.14
Now the r. of the deeds of Amaziah, 25.26
Now the r. of the acts of Uzziah, 26.22
Now the r. of the acts of Jotham, 27.07

REST (cont.)
Now the r. of his acts and all his 2Ch 28.26
and he gave them r. on every side. 32.22
Now the r. of the acts of Hezekiah, 32.32
Now the r. of the acts of Manasseh, 33.18
Now the r. of the acts of Josiah, 35.26
Now the r. of the acts of Jehoiakim, 36.08
with the r. of their brethren, the Ez 3.08
and the r. of the heads of fathers' 4.03
Tabeel and the r. of their associates 4.07
and the r. of their associates, the 4.09
and the r. of the nations whom the 4.10
and in the r. of the province 4.10
scribe and the r. of their associates 4.17
and in the r. of the province 4.17
and the r. of the returned exiles, 6.16
to do with the r. of the silver 7.18
and the r. that were to do the work Neh 2.16
and to the r. of the people, 4.14
and to the r. of the people, 4.19
Arab and to the r. of our enemies 6.01
Noadiah and the r. of the prophets 6.14
And what the r. of the people gave 7.72
But after they had r. they did evil 9.28
The r. of the people, the priests, 10.28
and the r. of the people cast lots 11.01
And the r. of Israel, and of the 11.20
done in the r. of the king's Est 9.12
then I should have been at r., Job 3.13
and there the weary are at r. 3.17
I have no r.; but trouble comes." 3.26
protected and take your r. in safety. 11.18
"Because his greed knew no r., 20.20
the pain that gnaws me takes no r. 30.17
and by night, but find no r. Ps 22.02
I would fly away and be at r.; 55.06
that they should not enter my r. 95.11
Return, O my soul, to your r.; 116.07
shall not r. upon the land allotted 125.03
to go late to r., eating the bread 127.02
little folding of the hands to r., Pro 6.10
understanding will r. in the 21.16
folding of the hands to r.," 24.33
Discipline your son, and he will give you r.; 29.17
in the night his mind does not r. Ecc 2.23
yet it finds r. rather than he. 6.05
of the LORD shall r. upon him, Is 11.02
has given you r. from your pain 14.03
The whole earth is at r. and quiet; 14.07
even there you will have no r. 23.12
the LORD will r. on this mountain, 25.10
"This is r.; give r. to the weary; 28.12
returning and r. you shall be 30.15
On what do you r. this confidence 36.04
of Sheol for the r. of my years. 38.10
And the r. of it he makes into a 44.17
they r. in their beds who walk in 57.02
for it cannot r., and its waters 57.20
for Jerusalem's sake I will not r., 62.01
LORD in remembrance, take no r., 62.06
and give him no r. until he establishes 62.07
Spirit of the LORD gave them r. 63.14
me, and what is the place of my r.? 66.01
in it, and find r. for your souls. Jer 6.16
And the r. of them I will give to 15.09
and the r. of the vessels which are 27.19
when Israel sought for r., 31.02
with all the r. of the officers of 39.03
to Babylon the r. of the people 39.09
captive all the r. of the people 41.10
took all the r. of the people whom 41.16
with my groaning, and I find no r. 45.03
your scabbard, r. and be still! 47.06
that he may give r. to the earth, 50.34
people and the r. of the people 52.15
with the r. of the artisans. 52.15
Give yourself no r., your eyes no Lam 2.18
we are weary, we are given no r. 5.05
and destroy the r. of the seacoast Eze 25.16
your feet the r. of your pasture; 34.18
must foul the r. with your feet? 34.18
possession of the r. of the nations, 36.03
derision to the r. of the nations 36.04
against the r. of the nations, 36.05
a blessing may r. on your house. 44.30
"As for the r. of the tribes: from 48.23
perish with the r. of the wise men Dan 2.18
As for the r. of the beasts, their 7.12
was different from all the r., 7.19
and you shall r., and shall stand 12.13
and go, for this is no place to r.; Mic 2.10
then the r. of his brethren shall 5.03
all the earth remains at r. Zec 1.11
my Spirit at r. in the north 6.08
Hadrach and will r. upon Damascus. 9.01
but the r. of the people shall not 14.02
till it came to r. over the place Mt 2.09
heavy-laden, and I will give you r. 11.28
you will find r. for your souls. 11.29
waterless places seeking r., 12.43
while the r. seized his servants, 22.06
still sleeping and taking your r.? 26.45
to a lonely place, and r. a while. Mk 6.31
still sleeping and taking your r.? 14.41
they went back and told the r., but they * 16.13
your peace shall r. upon him; Lk 10.06
waterless places seeking r.; 11.24
why are you anxious about the r.? 12.26
to the eleven and to all the r. 24.09
that he meant taking r. in sleep. Jn 11.13
Peter and the r. of the apostles, Ac 2.37
None of the r. dared join them, but 5.13
or what is the place of my r.? 7.49
that the r. of men may seek the 15.17
security from Jason and the r., 17.09
and the r. on planks or on pieces 27.44
the r. of the people on the island 28.09
as among the r. of the Gentiles. Rom 1.13
the promise may r. on grace and be 4.16
it, but the r. were hardened, 11.07
faith might not r. in the wisdom 1Co 2.05
To the r. I say, not the Lord, that 7.12
mind could not r. because I did 2Co 2.13
bodies had no r. but we were 7.05
mind has been set at r. by you all. 7.13
the power of Christ may r. upon me. 12.09
than the r. of the churches, except 12.13
And with him the r. of the Jews Gal 2.13
but the law does not r. on faith, 3.12
of wrath, like the r. of mankind. Eph 2.03
and to all the r. that my imprisonment Php 1.13
Clement and the r. of my fellow 4.03
and to grant r. with us to you who 2Th 1.07
so that the r. may stand in fear. 1Ti 5.20
'They shall never enter my r.'" Heb 3.11
they should never enter his r., 3.18
promise of entering his r. remains, 4.01
we who have believed enter that r., 4.03
'They shall never enter my r.,'" 4.03
said, "They shall never enter my r." 4.05
For if Joshua had given them r., 4.08
a sabbath r. for the people of God 4.09
enters God's r. also ceases from 4.10
therefore strive to enter that r., 4.11
to live for the r. of the time in 1Pe 4.02
But to the r. of you in Thyatira, Rev 2.24
and told to r. a little longer, 6.11
The r. of mankind, who were not 9.20
and the r. were terrified and gave 11.13
make war on the r. of her offspring, 12.17
and they have no r., day or night, 14.11
"that they may r. from their labors, 14.13
And the r. were slain by the sword 19.21
The r. of the dead did not come to 20.05

RESTED

and he r. on the seventh day from Gen 2.02
on it God r. from all his work 2.03
So the people r. on the seventh day Ex 16.30
is in them, and r. the seventh day; 20.11
and on the seventh day he r., 31.17
as the cloud r. over the tabernacle, Num 9.18
And when it r., he said, "Return, O 10.36
and when the spirit r. upon them, 11.25
Medad, and the spirit r. upon them; 11.26
house of Joseph r. heavily upon Ju 1.35
pillars upon which the house r., 16.29
and r. there. And he said to 2Ki 4.12
the LORD, after the ark r. there. 1Ch 6.31
day they r. and made that a day of Est 9.17
and r. on the fifteenth day, making 9.18
on which it r. to the threshold of Eze 9.03
sabbath they r. according to the Lk 23.56
"And God r. on the seventh day from Heb 4.04

RESTING

he saw that a r. place was good, and Gen 49.15
to seek out a r. place for them. Num 10.33
without r. even for a moment. Ru 2.07
and go to thy r. place, thou and the 2Ch 6.41
and let my cry find no r. place. Job 16.18
and go to thy r. place, thou and the Ps 132.08
"This is my r. place for ever; here 132.14
dwellings, and in quiet r. places. Is 32.18
and find for herself a r. place. 34.14
of shepherds r. their flocks. Jer 33.12
the nations, but finds no r. place; Lam 1.03
distributed and r. on each one of Ac 2.03

RESTITUTION

He shall make r.; if he has nothing Ex 22.01
he shall make r. from the best in 22.05
kindled the fire shall make full r. 22.06
the oath, and he shall not make r. 22.11
him, he shall make r. to its owner. 22.12
shall not make r. for what has 22.13
with it, he shall make full r. 22.14
was with it, he shall not make r.; 22.15
He shall also make r. for what he Lev 5.16
shall make full r. for his wrong, Num 5.07
kinsman to whom r. may be made for 5.08
the r. for wrong shall go to the 5.08

RESTIVE

a r. young camel interlacing her Jer 2.23

RESTLESS

a r. evil, full of deadly poison. Jas 3.08

RESTORE

Now then r. the man's wife; for he is Gen 20.07
But if you do not r. her, know that 20.07
their hand, to r. him to his father. 37.22
your head and r. you to your 40.13
you shall r. it to him before the Ex 22.26
he shall r. what he took by robbery, Lev 6.04
he shall r. it in full, and shall 6.05
congregation shall r. him to his Num 35.25
then you shall r. it to him. Deu 22.02
you shall r. to him the pledge that 24.13
your God will r. your fortunes, 30.03
now therefore r. it peaceably. Ju 11.13
now therefore I will r. it to you. 17.03
in order to r. the name of the dead Ru 4.05
against me and I will r. it to you. 1Sa 12.03
as he went to r. his power at the 2Sa 8.03
and I will r. to you all the land 9.07
and he shall r. the lamb fourfold, 12.06
to r. the kingdom to Rehoboam the 1Ki 12.21
took from your father I will r.; 20.34
"R. all that was hers, together with 2Ki 8.06
to r. the kingdom to Rehoboam. 2Ch 11.01
decided to r. the house of the 24.04
carpenters to r. the house of the 24.12
Will they r. things? Will they Neh 4.02
"We will r. these and require 5.12
R. to me the joy of thy salvation, Ps 51.12
thou hast been angry; oh, r. us. 60.01
thou didst r. thy heritage as it 68.09
What I did not steal must I now r.? 69.04
R. us, O God; let thy face shine, 80.03
R. us, O God of hosts; let thy 80.07
R. us, O LORD God of hosts! 80.19
thou didst r. the fortunes of Jacob 85.01
R. us again, O God of our salvation, 85.04
R. our fortunes, O LORD, like the 126.04
And I will r. your judges as at the Is 1.26
Oh, r. me to health and make me live 38.16
a spoil with none to say, "R.!" 42.22
of Jacob and to r. the preserved 49.06
I will r. you, and you shall stand Jer 15.19
them back and r. them to this 27.22
and I will r. your fortunes and 29.14
when I will r. the fortunes of my 30.03
For I will r. health to you, and 30.17
I will r. the fortunes of the tents 30.18
when I r. their fortunes: 'The LORD 31.23
for I will r. their fortunes, says 32.44
I will r. the fortunes of Judah and 33.07
For I will r. the fortunes of the 33.11
For I will r. their fortunes, and 33.26
Yet I will r. the fortunes of Moab 48.47
afterward I will r. the fortunes of 49.06
days I will r. the fortunes of 49.39
I will r. Israel to his pasture, and 50.19
sea is your ruin; who can r. you? Lam 2.13
your iniquity to r. your fortunes, 2.14
R. us to thyself, O LORD, that we may 5.21
"I will r. their fortunes, both the Eze 16.53
and I will r. your own fortunes in 16.53
does not r. the pledge, lifts up his 18.12
and I will r. the fortunes of Egypt, 29.14
Now I will r. the fortunes of Jacob, 39.25
of the word to r. and build Dan 9.25
When I would r. the fortunes of my Hos 6.11
I will r. to you the years which Joe 2..25
when I r. the fortunes of Judah and 3.01
I will r. the fortunes of my people Amo 9.14
of them and r. their fortunes. Zep 2.07
when I r. your fortunes before your 3.20
that I will r. to you double. Zec 9.12
come, and he is to r. all things; Mt 17.11
does come first to r. all things; Mk 9.12
one of anything, I r. it fourfold. Lk 19.08
at this time r. the kingdom to Ac 1.06
spiritual should r. him in a spirit Gal 6.01
impossible to r. again to repentance Heb 6.04
will himself r., establish, and 1Pe 5.10

RESTORED

and r. Sarah his wife to him. Gen 20.14
He r. the chief butler to his 40.21
I was r. to my office, and the baker 41.13
it was r. like the rest of his Ex 4.07
face, and shall not be r. to you; Deu 28.31
And he r. the eleven hundred pieces Ju 17.03
So when he r. the money to his 17.04
from Israel were r. to Israel, 1Sa 7.14
me, that my hand may be r. to me. 1Ki 13.06
and the king's hand was r. to him, 13.06
times, and your flesh shall be r., 2Ki 5.10
his flesh was r. like the flesh of 5.14
woman whose son he had r. to life, 8.01
how Elisha had r. the dead to life, 8.05
son he had r. to life appealed to 8.05
is her son whom Elisha r. to life. 8.05
He built Elath and r. it to Judah, 14.22
He r. the border of Israel from the 14.25
and they r. the house of God to its 2Ch 24.13

RESTORED (cont.)
He built Eloth and r. it to Judah, 2Ch 26.02
of the house of the LORD was r. 29.35
He also r. the altar of the LORD 33.16
be r. and brought back to the Ez 6.05
and they r. Jerusalem as far as the Neh 3.08
And the LORD r. the fortunes of Job, Job 42.10
r. me to life from among those gone Ps 30.03
When the LORD r. the fortunes of 126.01
daughter of my people not been r.? Jer 8.22
bring me back that I may be r., 31.18
thyself, O LORD, that we may be r.! Lam 5.21
the land that is r. from war, Eze 38.08
shall be r. to its rightful state. Dan 8.14
how shall its saltness be r.? Mt 5.13
and it was r., whole like the other 12.13
it out, and his hand was r. Mk 3.05
and he looked intently and was r., 8.25
And he did so, and his hand was r. Lk 6.10
how shall its saltness be r.? 14.34
that I may be r. to you the sooner Heb 13.19

RESTORER
He shall be to you a r. of life and Ru 4.15
breach, the r. of streets to dwell in. Is 58.12

RESTORES
When the LORD r. the fortunes of Ps 14.07
he r. my soul. He leads me in 23.03
When God r. the fortunes of his 53.06
but r. to the debtor his pledge, Eze 18.07
if the wicked r. the pledge, gives 33.15

RESTORING
it for repairing and r. the house. 2Ch 34.10
(For the LORD is r. the majesty of Nah 2.02

RESTRAIN
God, and he did not r. them. 1Sa 3.13
"Therefore I will not r. my mouth; Job 7.11
and he does not r. the lightnings 37.04
to r. her is to restrain the wind Pro 27.16
her is to r. the wind or to grasp 27.16
sake of my praise I r. it for you, Is 48.09
Wilt thou r. thyself at these 64.12
Who can r. her lust? None who Jer 2.24
and r. its rivers, and many waters Eze 31.15

RESTRAINED
the rain from the heavens was r., Gen 8.02
the people were r. from bringing; Ex 36.06
the LORD has r. you from bloodguilt, 1Sa 25.26
who has r. me from hurting you, 25.34
pursuing Israel; for Joab r. them. 2Sa 18.16
Nevertheless Haman r. himself, Est 5.10
I have not r. my lips, as thou Ps 40.09
he r. his anger often, and did not 78.38
I have kept still and r. myself; Is 42.14
thus, they have not r. their feet; Jer 14.10
he r. not his hand from destroying; Lam 2.08
they scarcely r. the people from Ac 14.18
human voice and r. the prophet's 2Pe 2.16

RESTRAINING
know what is r. him now so that he 2Th 2.06

RESTRAINS
promote my calamity; no one r. them. Job 30.13
but he who r. his lips is prudent. Pro 10.19
He who r. his words has knowledge, 17.27
only he who now r. it will do so 2Th 2.07

RESTRAINT
have cast off r. in my presence. Job 30.11
fool throws off r. and is careless Pro 14.16
no prophecy the people cast off r., 29.18
there is no r. any more. Is 23.10
benefit, not to lay any r. upon you, 1Co 7.35
kept under r. until faith should be Gal 3.23

RESTRICTED
You are not r. by us, but you are 2Co 6.12
but you are r. in your own affections 6.12

RESTS
the pillars on which the house r., Ju 16.26
seat were arm r. and two lions 1Ki 10.19
lions standing beside the arm r., 10.19
"The spirit of Elijah r. on Elisha." 2Ki 2.15
seat were arm r. and two lions 2Ch 9.18
lions standing beside the arm r., 9.18
On God r. my deliverance and my Ps 62.07
and he who has it r. satisfied; Pro 19.23
but the wrath of God r. upon him. Jn 3.36
of glory and of God r. upon you. 1Pe 4.14

RESULT
and the r. of righteousness, quietness Is 32.17
with the r. that you will be Jer 27.10
with the r. that I will drive you 27.15

RESUMED
and r. his place, he said to them, Jn 13.12

RESURRECTION
him, who say that there is no r.; Mt 22.23
In the r., therefore, to which of 22.28
For in the r. they neither marry 22.30
And as for the r. of the dead, have 22.31
tombs after his r. they went into 27.53
him, who say that there is no r.; Mk 12.18
In the r. whose wife will she be? 12.23
be repaid at the r. of the just. Lk 14.14
those who say that there is no r., 20.27
In the r., therefore, whose wife 20.33
age and to the r. from the dead 20.35
sons of God, being sons of the r. 20.36
to the r. of life, and those who Ju 5.29
done evil, to the r. of judgment. 5.29
again in the r. at the last day. 11.24
to her, "I am the r. and the life; 11.25
become with us a witness to his r. Ac 1.22
and spoke of the r. of the Christ, 2.31
in Jesus the r. from the dead. 4.02
testimony to the r. of the Lord 4.33
he preached Jesus and the r. 17.18
they heard of the r. of the dead, 17.32
hope and the r. of the dead I am 23.06
Sadducees say that there is no r., 23.08
there will be a r. of both the 24.15
respect to the r. of the dead I am 24.21
holiness by his r. from the dead, Rom 1.04
united with him in a r. like his. 6.05
that there is no r. of the dead? 1Co 15.12
But if there is no r. of the dead, 15.13
has come also the r. of the dead. 15.21
So is it with the r. of the dead. 15.42
know him and the power of his r., Php 3.10
I may attain the r. from the dead. 3.11
that the r. is past already. 2Ti 2.18
the r. of the dead, and eternal Heb 6.02
Women received their dead by r. 11.35
through the r. of Jesus Christ 1Pe 1.03
through the r. of Jesus Christ, 3.21
were ended. This is the first r. Rev 20.05
is he who shares in the first r.! 20.06

RETAIN
No man has power to r. the spirit, Ecc 8.08
come upon me, and I r. no strength. Dan 10.16
she shall not r. the strength of 11.06
strong shall not r. his strength, Amo 2.14
He does not r. his anger for ever Mic 7.18
if you r. the sins of any, they are Jn 20.23

RETAINED
tent, but r. the three hundred men; Ju 7.08
changed, and I r. no strength. Dan 10.08
retain the sins of any, they are r." Ju 20.23

RETINUE
to Jerusalem with a very great r., 1Ki 10.02
a very great r. and camels bearing 2Ch 9.01

RETORT
At this r. Moses fled, and became an Ac 7.29

RETREAT
I entered its farthest r., its densest 2Ki 19.23

RETRIBUTION
trap, a pitfall and a r. for them; Rom 11.09
disobedience received a just r., Heb 2.02

RETURN
bread till you r. to the ground, Gen 3.19
are dust, and to dust you shall r. 3.19
and she did not r. to him any more. 8.12
After his r. from the defeat of 14.17
"R. to your mistress, and submit to 16.09
"I will surely r. to you in the 18.10
appointed time I will r. to you, 18.14
other also in r. for serving me 29.27
"R. to the land of your fathers and 31.03
and r. to the land of your birth.'" 31.13
'R. to your country and to your 32.09
bury my father; then I will r." 50.05
when they see war, and r. to Egypt. Ex 13.17
of you shall r. to his property Lev 25.10
each of you shall r. to his family. 25.10
of you shall r. to his property. 25.13
and he shall r. to his property. 25.27
and he shall r. to his property. 25.28
and r. to the possession of his 25.41
the field shall r. to him from 27.24
"R., O Lord, to the ten thousand Num 10.36
in r. for their service which they 18.21
your reward in r. for your service 18.31
"R. to Balak, and thus you shall 23.05
"R. to Balak, and thus shall you 23.16
We will not r. to our homes until 32.18
that you shall r. and be free of 32.22
manslayer may r. to the land of 35.28
that he may r. to dwell in the land 35.32
then you shall r. every man to his Deu 3.20
you will r. to the Lord your God 4.30
Go and say to them, "R. to your tents." 5.30
the people to r. to Egypt in order 17.16
'You shall never r. that way again.' 17.16
and r. to the Lord your God, you and 30.02
then you shall r. to the land of Jos 1.15
he said, "I will stay till you r." Ju 6.18
and trembling, let him r. home. 7.03
Gideon) in r. for all the good that 8.35
when I r. victorious from the 11.31
none of us will r. to his house. 20.08
daughters-in-law to r. from the Ru 1.06
on the way to r. to the land of 1.07
r. each of you to her mother's house 1.08
we will r. with you to your people. 1.10
gods; r. after your sister-in-law." 1.15
leave you or to r. from following 1.16
then they would r. to their home. 1Sa 2.20
and let it r. to its own place, that 5.11
by all means r. him a guilt 6.03
offering that we shall r. to him?" 6.04
and r. with me, that I may worship 15.25
to Saul, "I will not r. with you; 15.26
and r. with me, that I may worship 15.30
not let him r. to his father's 18.02
r., my son David, for I will no more 26.21
that he may r. to the place to 29.04
to r. to the land of the Philistines 29.11
Then Abner said to him, "Go, r."; 2Sa 3.16
beards have grown, and then r." 10.05
to him, but he will not r. to me." 12.23
But if you r. to the city, and say 15.34
"R., both you and all your servants 19.14
Pray let your servant r., that I 19.37
answer I shall r. to him who sent 24.13
R. every man to his home, for this 1Ki 12.24
kill me and r. to Rehoboam king of 12.27
nor r. by the way that you came. 13.09
and did not r. by the way that he 13.10
"I may not r. with you, or go in 13.16
nor r. by the way that you came.'" 13.17
r. on your way to the wilderness of 19.15
let each r. to his home in peace.'" 22.17
"If you r. in peace, the Lord has 22.28
a rumor and r. to his own land; 2Ki 19.07
he came, by the same he shall r., 19.33
beards have grown, and then r." 1Ch 19.05
answer I shall r. to him who sent 21.12
R. every man to his home, for this 2Ch 11.04
let each r. to his home in peace.'" 18.16
and water, until I r. in peace.'" 18.26
"If you r. in peace, the Lord has 18.27
and take it and r. it to its place 24.11
r. to the Lord, the God of Abraham, 30.06
For if you r. to the Lord, your 30.09
their captors, and r. to this land. 30.09
face from you, if you r. to him." 30.09
did not make r. according to the 32.25
but if you r. to me and keep my Neh 1.09
you be gone, and when will you r.?" 2.06
R. to them this very day their 5.11
a leader to r. to their bondage in 9.17
told them to r. answer to Esther, Est 4.13
mother's womb, and naked shall I r.; Job 1.21
before I go whence I shall not r., 10.21
that he will r. out of darkness, 15.22
go the way whence I shall not r. 16.22
If you r. to the Almighty and 22.23
let him r. to the days of his 33.25
together, and man would r. to dust. 34.15
commands that they r. from iniquity. 36.10
go forth, and do not r. to them. 39.04
have faith in him that he will r., 39.12
ways, and sinners will r. to thee. Ps 51.13
R. sevenfold into the bosom of our 79.12
R., O Lord! How long? Have 90.13
for justice will r. to the righteous, 94.15
they die and r. to their dust. 104.29
In r. for my love they accuse me, 109.04
R., O my soul, to your rest; 116.07
and the clouds r. after the rain; Ecc 12.02
R., r., O Shulammite, r., r., that we Sol 6.13
A remnant will r., the remnant of Is 10.21
only a remnant of them will r. 10.22
and they will r. to the Lord, and he 19.22
and she will r. to her hire, and 23.17
And the ransomed of the Lord shall r., 35.10
and r. to his own land; 37.07
he came, by the same he shall r., 37.34
I give men in r. for you, peoples in 43.04
r. to me, for I have redeemed you. 44.22
righteousness a word that shall not r.: 45.23
And the ransomed of the Lord shall r., 51.11
they see the r. of the Lord to 52.08
let him r. to the Lord, that he may 55.07
and r. not thither but water the 55.10
it shall not r. to me empty, but it 55.11
R. for the sake of thy servants, the 63.17
man's wife, will he r. to her? Jer 3.01
and would you r. to me? says the 3.01
done all this she will r. to me'; 3.07
but she did not r., and her false 3.07
Judah did not r. to me with her 3.10
'R., faithless Israel, says the Lord. 3.12
R., O faithless children, says the 3.14

RETURN (cont.)

"R., O faithless sons, I will heal Jer 3.22
"If you r., O Israel, says the LORD, 4.01
says the LORD, to me you should r. 4.01
if one turns away, does he not r.? 8.04
fast to deceit, they refuse to r. 8.05
they r. with their vessels empty; 14.03
"If you r., I will restore you, and 15.19
R., every one from his evil way, and 18.11
for he shall r. no more to see his 22.10
place: "He shall r. here no more, 22.11
land to which they will long to r., 22.27
to return, there they shall not r. 22.27
for they shall r. to me with their 24.07
Jacob shall r. and have quiet and 30.10
great company, they shall r. here. 31.08
R., O virgin Israel, r. to these your 31.21
help you is about to r. to Egypt, 37.07
then r. to Gedaliah the son of 40.05
or survive or r. to the land of 44.14
they desire to r. to dwell there; 44.14
for they shall not r., except some 44.14
the sword shall r. from the land 44.28
Jacob shall r. and have quiet and 46.27
who does not r. empty-handed. 50.09
our ways, and r. to the LORD! Lam 3.40
shall not r. to what he has sold, Eze 7.13
Sodom and her daughters shall r. to 16.55
Samaria and her daughters shall r. 16.55
your daughters shall r. to your former 16.55
R. it to its sheath. In the place 21.30
no one shall r. by way of the gate 46.09
But now I will r. to fight against Dan 10.20
south but shall r. into his own 11.09
And he shall r. to his land with 11.28
his will, and r. to his own land. 11.28
he shall r. and come into the 11.29
'I will go and r. to my first Hos 2.07
of Israel shall r. and seek the 3.05
not permit them to r. to their God. 5.04
I will r. again to my place, until 5.15
"Come, let us r. to the LORD; 6.01
yet they do not r. to the LORD 7.10
their sins; they shall r. to Egypt. 8.13
but Ephraim shall r. to Egypt, 9.03
They shall r. to the land of Egypt, 11.05
they have refused to r. to me. 11.05
and I will r. them to their homes, 11.11
r., hold fast to love and justice, 12.06
R., O Israel, to the LORD your God, 14.01
Take with you words and r. to the LORD; 14.02
They shall r. and dwell beneath my 14.07
"r. to me with all your heart, with Joe 2.12
R. to the LORD, your God, for he is 2.13
places, yet you did not r. to me, Amo 4.06
yet you did not r. to me," says the 4.08
yet you did not r. to me," says the 4.09
yet you did not r. to me," says the 4.10
yet you did not r. to me," says the 4.11
deeds shall r. on your own head. Ob 1.15
the hire of a harlot they shall r. Mic 1.07
brethren shall r. to the people of 5.03
be their lot in r. for their pride, Zep 2.10
yet you did not r. to me, says the Hag 2.17
R. to me, says the LORD of hosts, and Zec 1.03
and I will r. to you, says the LORD 1.03
R. from your evil ways and from 1.04
I will r. to Zion, and will dwell in 8.03
R. to your stronghold, O prisoners 9.12
children they shall live and r. 10.09
R. to me, and I will return to you, Mal 3.07
and I will r. to you, says the LORD 3.07
But you say, 'How shall we r.?' 3.07
in a dream not to r. to Herod, Mt 2.12
worthy, let your peace r. to you. 10.13
'I will r. to my house from which I 12.44
a man give in r. for his life? 16.26
can a man give in r. for his life? Mk 8.37
and lend, expecting nothing in r.; Lk 6.35
"R. to your home, and declare how 8.39
On their r. the apostles told him 9.10
but if not, it shall r. to you. 10.06
'I will r. to my house from which I 11.24
lest they also invite you in r., 14.12
Was no one found to r. and give 17.18
receive kingly power and then r. 19.12
no more to r. to corruption, he Ac 13.34
'After this I will r., and I will 15.16
let us r. and visit the brethren in 15.36
"I will r. to you if God wills," and 18.21
determined to r. through Macedonia 20.03
But then what r. did you get from Rom 6.21
the r. you get is sanctification 6.22
time I will r. and Sarah shall 9.09
way in peace, that he may r. to me; 1Co 16.11
In r.—I speak as to children— 2Co 6.13
and make some r. to their parents; 1Ti 5.04
would have had opportunity to r. Heb 11.15
reviled, he did not revile in r.; 1Pe 2.23
Do not r. evil for evil or reviling 3.09

RETURNED

and she r. to him to the ark, for Gen 8.09
and Abraham r. to his place. 18.33
rose up and r. to the land of the 21.32
So Abraham r. to his young men, and 22.19
then he departed and r. home. 31.55
And the messengers r. to Jacob, 32.06
So Esau r. that day on his way to 33.16
When Reuben r. to the pit and saw 37.29
and r. to his brothers, and said, 37.30
So he r. to Judah, and said, "I have 38.22
and he r. to them and spoke to them 42.24
delayed, we would now have r. twice." 43.10
money that was r. in the mouth of 43.12
'Why have you r. evil for good? Why 44.04
his ass, and they r. to the city. 44.13
Joseph r. to Egypt with his brothers 50.14
and the sea r. to its wonted flow Ex 14.27
The waters r. and covered the 14.28
So Moses r. to the LORD and said, 32.31
of the congregation r. to him, 34.31
elders of Israel r. to the camp. Num 11.30
forty days they r. from spying out 13.25
and who r. and made all the congregation 14.36
And Aaron r. to Moses at the 16.50
And he r. to him, and lo, he and all 23.06
And you r. and wept before the LORD Deu 1.45
days, until the pursuers have r.; Jos 2.16
three days, until the pursuers r.; 2.22
of the Jordan r. to their place 4.18
city once, and r. into the camp. 6.14
And they r. to Joshua, and said to 7.03
all Israel r. to Ai, and smote it 8.24
Then Joshua r., and all Israel with 10.15
all the people r. safe to Joshua in 10.21
Then Joshua r., and all Israel with 10.43
the half-tribe of Manasseh r. home, 22.09
r. from the Reubenites and the 22.32
twenty-two thousand r., and ten Ju 7.03
and he r. to the camp of Israel, and 7.15
son of Joash r. from the battle by 8.13
she r. to her father, who did with 11.39
And after a while he r. to take her; 14.08
his spirit r., and he revived. 15.19
And Benjamin r. at that time; 21.14
they went and r. to their inheritance, 21.23
So Naomi r., and Ruth the Moabitess Ru 1.22
who r. from the country of Moab. 1.22
they r. that day to Ekron. 1Sa 6.16
the Philistines r. as a guilt 6.17
Philistines have r. the ark of the 6.21
And as David r. from the slaughter 17.57
when David r. from slaying the 18.06

RETURNED (cont.)

So Saul r. from pursuing after 1Sa 23.28
When Saul r. from following the 24.01
and he has r. me evil for good. 25.21
the LORD has r. the evil-doing of 25.39
his way, and Saul r. to his place. 26.25
when David had r. from the slaughter 2Sa 1.01
and the sword of Saul r. not empty. 1.22
Joab r. from the pursuit of Abner; 2.30
to him, "Go, return"; and he r. 3.16
And when Abner r. to Hebron, Joab 3.27
And David r. to bless his household 6.20
When he r., he slew eighteen 8.13
Then Joab r. from fighting against 10.14
Then she r. to her house. 11.04
and all the people r. to Jerusalem. 12.31
find them, they r. to Jerusalem. 17.20
him, and he r. to his own home. 19.39
And Joab r. to Jerusalem to the 20.22
and the men r. after him only to 23.10
from Jerusalem to Gath and r., 1Ki 2.41
then Jeroboam r. from Egypt. 12.02
Israel heard that Jeroboam had r., 12.20
And he r. from following him, and 19.21
The messengers r. to the king, and 2Ki 1.05
he said to them, "Why have you r.?" 1.05
and thence he r. to Samaria. 2.25
from him and r. to their own land. 3.27
Therefore he r. to meet him, and 4.31
Then he r. to the man of God, he and 5.15
And the messengers r., and told the 7.15
when the woman r. from the land of 8.03
And King Joram r. to be healed in 8.29
but King Joram had r. to be healed 9.15
hostages, and he r. to Samaria. 14.14
The Rabshakeh r., and found the 19.08
them. Then he r. to Jerusalem. 23.20
in Moab and r. to Lehem (now the 1Ch 4.22
and all the people r. to Jerusalem. 20.03
then Jeroboam r. from Egypt. 2Ch 10.02
and r. and did not go against 11.04
camels. Then they r. to Jerusalem. 14.15
king of Judah r. in safety to his 19.01
Then they r., every man of Judah 20.27
and he r. to be healed in Jezreel 22.06
and r. home in fierce anger. 25.10
and hostages, and he r. to Samaria. 25.24
trees. Then they r. to Samaria. 28.15
of Israel r. to their cities, every 31.01
So he r. with shame of face to his 32.21
Israel. Then he r. to Jerusalem. 34.07
they r. to Jerusalem and Judah, Ez 2.01
heard that the r. exiles were 4.01
then answer be r. by letter 5.05
and the rest of the r. exiles, 6.16
first month the r. exiles kept the 6.19
passover lamb for all the r. exiles, 6.20
of Israel who had r. from exile, 6.21
the r. exiles, offered burnt offerings 8.35
the faithlessness of the r. exiles, 9.04
to all the r. exiles that they 10.07
Then the r. exiles did so. 10.16
by the Valley Gate, and so r. Neh 2.15
we all r. to the wall, each to his 4.15
they r. to Jerusalem and Judah, each 7.06
those who had r. from the captivity 8.17
Then Mordecai r. to the king's gate. Est 6.12
And the king r. from the palace 7.08
The Rabshakeh r., and found the Is 37.08
then all the Jews r. from all the Jer 40.12
Judah who had r. to live in the 43.05
and my reason r. to me, and I Dan 4.34
At the same time my reason r. to me; 4.36
my majesty and splendor r. to me. 4.36
I have r. to Jerusalem with Zec 1.16
And when he r. to Capernaum after Mk 2.01
The apostles r. to Jesus, and told 6.30
Then he r. from the region of Tyre, 7.31
three months, and r. to her home. Lk 1.56
And the shepherds r., glorifying 2.20
they r. into Galilee, to their own 2.39
they r. to Jerusalem, seeking him. 2.45
r. from the Jordan, and was led by 4.01
And Jesus r. in the power of the 4.14
who had been sent r. to the house, 7.10
so he got into the boat and r. 8.37
Now when Jesus r., the crowd 8.40
And her spirit r., and she got up 8.55
The seventy r. with joy, saying, 10.17
When he r., having received the 19.15
r. home beating their breasts. 23.48
then they r., and prepared spices 23.56
that same hour and r. to Jerusalem; 24.33
And they r. to Jerusalem with great 24.52
Then they r. to Jerusalem from the Ac 1.12
prison, and they r. and reported, 5.22
they r. to Jerusalem, preaching the 8.25
and Saul r. from Jerusalem when 12.25
John left them and r. to Jerusalem; 13.13
they r. to Lystra and to Iconium 14.21
board the ship, and they r. home. 21.06
"When I had r. to Jerusalem and was 22.17
the morrow they r. to the barracks, 23.32
and again I r. to Damascus. Gal 1.17
but have now r. to the Shepherd and 1Pe 2.25

RETURNING

which you are r. to him as a guilt 1Sa 6.08
"If you are r. to the LORD with all 7.03
r. to Jerusalem with joy, for the 2Ch 20.27
"In r. and rest you shall be saved; Is 30.15
as he was r. to the city, he was Mt 21.18
as they were r., the boy Jesus Lk 2.43
and r. from the tomb they told all 24.09
and was r.; seated in his chariot, Ac 8.28
met Abraham r. from the slaughter Heb 7.01

RETURNS

and r. to her father's house, as in Lev 22.13
he r. no more to his house, nor does Job 7.10
His mischief r. upon his own head, Ps 7.16
breath departs he r. to his earth; 146.04
If a man r. evil for good, evil will Pro 17.13
Like a dog that r. to his vomit is 26.11
and on its circuits the wind r. Ecc 1.06
and the dust r. to the earth as it 12.07
and the spirit r. to God who gave 12.07

REU

years, he became the father of R.; Gen 11.18
the birth of R. two hundred and 11.19
When R. had lived thirty-two years, 11.20
and R. lived after the birth of 11.21
Eber, Peleg, R.; 1Ch 1.25
the son of R., the son of Peleg, the Lk 3.35

REUBEN

a son, and she called his name R.; Gen 29.32
wheat harvest R. went and found 30.14
in that land R. went and lay with 35.22
R. (Jacob's first-born), Simeon, Levi, 35.23
But when R. heard it, he delivered 37.21
And R. said to them, "Shed no blood; 37.22
When R. returned to the pit and saw 37.29
And R. answered them, "Did I not 42.22
Then R. said to his father, "Slay my 42.37
and his sons. R., Jacob's first-born, 46.08
and the sons of R.: Hanoch, Pallu, 46.09
shall be mine, as R. and Simeon are. 48.05
R., you are my first-born, my might, 49.03
R., Simeon, Levi, and Judah, Ex 1.02
the sons of R., the first-born of 6.14
these are the families of R. 6.14
From R., Elizur the son of Shedeur; Num 1.05
The people of R., Israel's first-born, 1.20

REUBEN (cont.)

of the tribe of R. was forty-six	Num 1.21
of the camp of R. by their companies,	2.10
the people of R. being Elizur the	2.10
The whole number of the camp of R.,	2.16
the leader of the men of R.:	7.30
of the camp of R. set out by their	10.18
their names: From the tribe of R.,	13.04
On the son of Peleth, sons of R.,	16.01
R., the first-born of Israel;	26.05
the sons of R.: of Hanoch, the family	26.05
Now the sons of R. and the sons of	32.01
and the sons of R. came and said	32.02
sons of Gad and to the sons of R.,	32.06
and the sons of R. said to Moses,	32.25
the sons of Gad and the sons of R.,	32.29
of Gad and the sons of R. answered,	32.31
and to the sons of R. and to the	32.33
And the sons of R. built Heshbon,	32.37
of the sons of R. by fathers'	34.14
the sons of Eliab, son of R.;	Deu 11.06
R., Gad, Asher, Zebulun, Dan, and	27.13
"Let R. live, and not die,	33.06
The sons of R. and the sons of Gad	Jos 4.12
the people of R. was the Jordan as	13.23
the stone of Bohan the son of R.;	15.06
and Gad and R. and half the tribe	18.07
the Stone of Bohan the son of R.;	18.17
tableland, from the tribe of R.,	20.08
received from the tribe of R.,	21.07
and out of the tribe of R.,	21.36
the clans of R. there were great	Ju 5.15
the clans of R. there were great	5.16
R., Simeon, Levi, Judah, Issachar,	1Ch 2.01
The sons of R. the first-born of	5.01
the sons of R., the first-born of	5.03
cities out of the tribes of R.,	6.63
the Jordan, out of the tribe of R.:	6.78
side to the west, R., one portion.	Eze 48.06
Adjoining the territory of R.,	48.07
the gate of R., the gate of Judah,	48.31
twelve thousand of the tribe of R.,	Rev 7.05

REUBENITE

Adina the son of Shiza the R.,	1Ch 11.42

REUBENITES

These are the families of the R.;	Num 26.07
I gave to the R. and the Gadites	Deu 3.12
and to the R. and the Gadites I	3.16
wilderness on the tableland for the R.,	4.43
it for an inheritance to the R.,	29.08
And to the R., the Gadites, and the	Jos 1.12
land for a possession to the R. and	12.06
of Manasseh the R. and the Gadites	13.08
tribe of the R. according to their	13.15
This was the inheritance of the R.,	13.23
Then Joshua summoned the R., and the	22.01
So the R. and the Gadites and the	22.09
the R. and the Gadites and the half	22.10
the R. and the Gadites and the half	22.11
sent to the R. and the Gadites and	22.13
And they came to the R., the Gadites,	22.15
Then the R., the Gadites, and the	22.21
us and you, you R. and Gadites;	22.25
words that the R. and the Gadites	22.30
said to the R. and the Gadites and	22.31
from the R. and the Gadites in the	22.32
land where the R. and the Gadites	22.33
The R. and the Gadites called the	22.34
and the R., and the Manassites, from	2Ki 10.33
exile; he was a chieftain of the R.	1Ch 5.06
R., the Gadites, and the half-tribe	5.18
R., the Gadites, and the half-tribe	5.26
the Reubenite, a leader of the R.,	11.42
the R. and Gadites and the half-tribe	12.37
to have the oversight of the R.,	26.32
for the R. Eliezer the son of	27.16

REUEL

Esau, Eliphaz; Basemath bore R.;	Gen 36.04
R. the son of Basemath the wife of	36.10
These are the sons of R.: Nahath,	36.13
These are the sons of R., Esau's son:	36.17
the chiefs of R. in the land of Edom;	36.17
When they came to their father R.,	Ex 2.18
Gad being Eliasaph the son of R.,	Num 2.14
Hobab the son of R. the Midianite,	10.29
Eliphaz, R., Jeush, Jalam, and Korah.	1Ch 1.35
The sons of R.: Nahath, Zerah, Shammah,	1.37
Shephatiah, son of R., son of Ibnijah;	9.08

REUMAH

his concubine, whose name was R.,	Gen 22.24

REVEAL

The heavens will r. his iniquity,	Job 20.27
heal them and r. to them abundance	Jer 33.06
have been able to r. this mystery.	Dan 2.47
to whom the Son chooses to r. him.	Mt 11.27
to whom the Son chooses to r. him.	Lk 10.22
was pleased to r. his Son to me, in	Gal 1.16
God will r. that also to you.	Php 3.15

REVEALED

there God had r. himself to him	Gen 35.07
God has r. to Pharaoh what he is	41.25
things that are r. belong to us	Deu 29.29
'I r. myself to the house of your	1Sa 2.27
LORD had not yet been r. to him.	3.07
for the LORD r. himself to Samuel	3.21
came, the LORD had r. to Samuel:	9.15
hast r. to thy servant that thou	1Ch 17.25
Have the gates of death been r. to you,	Job 38.17
he has r. his vindication in the	Ps 98.02
of hosts has r. himself in my ears:	Is 22.14
land of Cyprus it is r. to them.	23.01
And the glory of the LORD shall be r.,	40.05
has the arm of the LORD been r.?	53.01
come, and my deliverance be r.	56.01
Then the mystery was r. to Daniel	Dan 2.19
has this mystery been r. to me,	2.30
of Persia a word was r. to Daniel,	10.01
the corruption of Ephraim is r.,	Hos 7.01
is covered that will not be r.,	Mt 10.26
understanding and r. them to babes;	11.25
and blood has not r. this to you,	16.17
And it had been r. to him by the	Lk 2.26
out of many hearts may be r.	2.35
understanding and r. them to babes;	10.21
Nothing is covered up that will not be r.,	12.02
the day when the Son of man is r.	17.30
that he might be r. to Israel.	Jn 1.31
has the arm of the Lord been r.?"	12.38
After this Jesus r. himself again	21.01
and he r. himself in this way.	21.01
that Jesus was r. to the disciples	21.14
of God is r. through faith for	Rom 1.17
wrath of God is r. from heaven	1.18
righteous judgment will be r.	2.05
the glory that is to be r. to us.	8.18
God has r. to us through the Spirit	1Co 2.10
because it will be r. with fire,	3.13
for us might be r. to you in the	2Co 7.12
restraint until faith should be r.	Gal 3.23
it has now been r. to his holy	Eph 3.05
Lord Jesus is r. from heaven with	2Th 1.07
and the man of lawlessness is r.,	2.03
so that he may be r. in his time.	2.06
And then the lawless one will be r.,	2.08
ready to be r. in the last time.	1Pe 1.05
It was r. to them that they were	1.12
and be glad when his glory is r.	4.13
in the glory that is to be r.	5.01
for thy judgments have been r.	Rev 15.04

REVEALER

and a r. of mysteries, for you have	Dan 2.47

REVEALING
without r. his secret to his Amo 3.07
longing for the r. of the sons of Rom 8.19
wait for the r. of our Lord Jesus 1Co 1.07

REVEALS
about as a talebearer r. secrets, Pro 11.13
goes about gossiping r. secrets; 20.19
he r. deep and mysterious things; Dan 2.22
a God in heaven who r. mysteries, 2.28
and he who r. mysteries made known 2.29

REVEL
it pleasure to r. in the daytime. 2Pe 2.13

REVELATION
hast made this r. to thy servant, 2Sa 7.27
Can this give r.? Behold, it is Hab 2.19
a light for r. to the Gentiles, and Lk 2.32
according to the r. of the mystery Rom 16.25
bring you some r. or knowledge or 1Co 14.06
a r., a tongue, or an interpretation 14.26
If a r. is made to another sitting 14.30
came through a r. of Jesus Christ. Gal 1.12
I went up by r.; and I laid before 2.02
wisdom and of r. in the knowledge Eph 1.17
mystery was made known to me by r., 3.03
honor at the r. of Jesus Christ. 1Pe 1.07
to you at the r. of Jesus Christ. 1.13
The r. of Jesus Christ, which God Rev 1.01

REVELATIONS
on to visions and r. of the Lord. 2Co 12.01
too elated by the abundance of r., 12.07

REVELING
not in r. and drunkenness, not in Rom 13.13
r. in their dissipation, carousing 2Pe 2.13

REVELRY
and the r. of those who stretch themselves Amo 6.07

REVELS
r., carousing, and lawless idolatry. 1Pe 4.03

REVENGE
he will not spare when he takes r. Pro 6.34
him, and take our r. on him. Jer 20.10

REVENGEFULLY
Edom acted r. against the house of Eze 25.12
the Philistines acted r. and took 25.15

REVENUE
and the royal r. will be impaired. Ez 4.13
without delay from the royal r., 6.08
your r. was the grain of Shihor, the Is 23.03
r. to whom r. is due, respect to whom Rom 13.07

REVENUES
than great r. with injustice. Pro 16.08

REVERE
of you shall r. his mother and his Lev 19.03
you did not r. me as holy in the Deu 32.51
I r. thy commandments, which I love, Ps 119.48

REVERED
(Now Obadiah r. the Lord greatly; 1Ki 18.03
your servant have r. the Lord from my 18.12

REVERENCE
my sabbaths and r. my sanctuary: Lev 19.30
my sabbaths and r. my sanctuary: 26.02
shall not pay r. to the gods of Ju 6.10
one another out of r. for Christ. Eph 5.21
acceptable worship, with r. and awe; Heb 12.28
but in your hearts r. Christ as Lord. 1Pe 3.15
yet do it with gentleness and r.; 3.15

REVERENT
likewise to be r. in behavior, Tit 2.03
when they see your r. and chaste 1Pe 3.02

REVERT
then it shall r. to the prince; only Eze 46.17

REVIEWED
As I r. the people and the priests, Ez 8.15

REVILE
"You shall not r. God, nor curse a Ex 22.28
Is the enemy to r. thy name for Ps 74.10
you when men r. you and persecute Mt 5.11
when they exclude you and r. you, Lk 6.22
"Would you r. God's high priest?" Ac 23.04
the enemy no occasion to r. us. 1Ti 5.14
reviled, he did not r. in return; 1Pe 2.23
those who r. your good behavior in 3.16
not afraid to r. the glorious ones, 2Pe 2.10
authority, and r. the glorious ones. Jud 1.08
But these men r. whatever they do 1.10

REVILED
and ate and drank and r. Abimelech. Ju 9.27
of the king of Assyria have r. me. 2Ki 19.06
"Whom have you mocked and r.? 19.22
of the king of Assyria have r. me. Is 37.06
'Whom have you mocked and r.? 37.23
mountains and r. me upon the hills, 65.07
with him also r. him in the same Mt 27.44
crucified with him also r. him. Mk 15.32
And they r. him, saying, "You are his Jn 9.28
was spoken by Paul, and r. him. Ac 13.45
And when they opposed and r. him, 18.06
When r., we bless; when persecuted, 1Co 4.12
When he was r., he did not revile 1Pe 2.23
them the way of truth will be r. 2Pe 2.02

REVILER
r., drunkard, or robber—not even to 1Co 5.11

REVILERS
at the words of the taunters and r., Ps 44.16
nor r., nor robbers will inherit 1Co 6.10

REVILES
r. the Lord, and that person shall Num 15.30
and an impious people r. thy name. Ps 74.18

REVILING
utter destruction and Israel to r. Is 43.28
other words against him, r. him. Lk 22.65
return evil for evil or r. for r.; 1Pe 3.09
not pronounce a r. judgment upon 2Pe 2.11
r. in matters of which they are 2.12
to pronounce a r. judgment upon Jud 1.09

REVILINGS
men, and be not dismayed at their r. Is 51.07
heard all the r. which you uttered Eze 35.12
of Moab and the r. of the Ammonites, Zep 2.08

REVIVE
Will they r. the stones out of the Neh 4.02
who seek God, let your hearts r. Ps 69.32
sore troubles wilt r. me again; 71.20
Wilt thou not r. us again, that thy 85.06
dust; r. me according to thy word! 119.25
to r. the spirit of the humble, and Is 57.15
and to r. the heart of the contrite 57.15
for food to r. their strength. Lam 1.11
far from me, one to r. my courage; 1.16
sought food to r. their strength. 1.19
After two days he will r. us; Hos 6.02

REVIVED
spirit of their father Jacob r.; Gen 45.27
his spirit returned, and he r. Ju 15.19

REVIVED (cont.)
when he had eaten, his spirit r.; 1Sa 30.12
came into him again, and he r. 1Ki 17.22
he r., and stood on his feet. 2Ki 13.21
commandment came, sin r. and I died; Rom 7.09
length you have r. your concern Php 4.10

REVIVING
us a little r. in our bondage. Ez 9.08
grant us some r. to set up the 9.09
the LORD is perfect, r. the soul; Ps 19.07

REVOKE
he has blessed, and I cannot r. it. Num 23.20
be written to r. the letters devised Est 8.05
four, I will not r. the punishment; Amo 1.03
four, I will not r. the punishment; 1.06
four, I will not r. the punishment; 1.09
four, I will not r. the punishment; 1.11
four, I will not r. the punishment; 1.13
four, I will not r. the punishment; 2.01
four, I will not r. the punishment; 2.04
four, I will not r. the punishment; 2.06

REVOKED
with the king's ring cannot be r. Est 8.08
the Persians, which cannot be r. Dan 6.08
and Persians, which cannot be r. 6.12

REVOLT
God, speaking oppression and r., Is 59.13
"There is r. among the men of Judah Jer 11.09
stirred up a r. and led the four Ac 21.38

REVOLTED
In his days Edom r. from the rule 2Ki 8.20
So Edom r. from the rule of Judah 8.22
Then Libnah r. at the same time. 8.22
In his days Edom r. from the rule 2Ch 21.08
So Edom r. from the rule of Judah 21.10
time Libnah also r. from his rule, 21.10
him from whom you have deeply r., Is 31.06

REWARD
your r. shall be very great. Gen 15.01
for it is your r. in return for Num 18.31
and a full r. be given you by the Ru 2.12
So may the LORD r. you with good 1Sa 24.19
which was the r. I gave him for his 2Sa 4.10
will have no r. for the tidings 18.22
king recompense me with such a r.? 19.36
yourself, and I will give you a r." 1Ki 13.07
behold, they r. us by coming to 2Ch 20.11
for you and r. you with a rightful Job 8.06
in keeping them there is great r. Ps 19.11
hands; render them their due r. 28.04
there is a r. for the righteous; 58.11
So they r. me evil for good, and 109.05
May this be the r. of my accusers 109.20
LORD, the fruit of the womb a r. 127.03
sows righteousness gets a sure r. Pro 11.18
The r. for humility and fear of the 22.04
his head, and the LORD will r. you. 25.22
and this was my r. for all my toil Ecc 2.10
they have a good r. for their toil. 4.09
nothing, and they have no more r.; 9.05
behold, his r. is with him, and his Is 40.10
exiles free, not for price or r., 45.13
behold, his r. is with him, and his 62.11
for your r. is great in heaven, for Mt 5.12
who love you, what r. have you? 5.46
will have no r. from your Father 6.01
I say to you, they have their r. 6.02
who sees in secret will r. you. 6.04
I say to you, they have their r. 6.05
who sees in secret will r. you. 6.06
I say to you, they have their r. 6.16
who sees in secret will r. you. 6.18
shall receive a prophet's r., 10.41
shall receive a righteous man's r. 10.41
to you, he shall not lose his r." 10.42
will by no means lose his r. Mk 9.41
your r. is great in heaven; Lk 6.23
and your r. will be great, and you 6.35
receiving the due r. of our deeds; 23.41
field with the r. of his wickedness Ac 1.18
survives, he will receive a r. 1Co 3.14
this of my own will, I have a r.; 9.17
What then is my r.? Just this: 9.18
receive the inheritance as your r.; Col 3.24
confidence, which has a great r. Heb 10.35
of Egypt, for he looked to the r. 11.26
worked for, but may win a full r. 2Jn 1.08

REWARDED
"The LORD r. me according to my 2Sa 22.21
be weak, for your work shall be r. 2Ch 15.07
The LORD r. me according to my Ps 18.20
respects the commandment will be r. Pro 13.13
for your work shall be r., says the Jer 31.16

REWARDING
righteous by r. him according to 1Ki 8.32
righteous by r. him according to 2Ch 6.23
r. every man according to his ways Jer 32.19
for r. thy servants, the prophets Rev 11.18

REWARDS
The LORD r. every man for his 1Sa 26.23
but prosperity r. the righteous. Pro 13.21
me gifts and r. and great honor. Dan 2.06
yourself, and give your r. to another; 5.17
and that he r. those who seek him. Heb 11.06

REWORKED
and he r. it into another vessel, as Jer 18.04

REZEPH
R., and the people of Eden who were 2Ki 19.12
R., and the people of Eden who were Is 37.12

REZIN
began to send R. the king of Syria 2Ki 15.37
Then R. king of Syria and Pekah the 16.05
captive to Kir, and he killed R. 16.09
the sons of R., the sons of Nekoda, Ez 2.48
the sons of R., the sons of Nekoda, Neh 7.50
R. the king of Syria and Pekah the Is 7.01
fierce anger of R. and Syria and 7.04
and the head of Damascus is R. 7.08
in fear before R. and the son of 8.06

REZON
R. the son of Eliada, who had fled 1Ki 11.23

RHEGIUM
we made a circuit and arrived at R.; Ac 28.13

RHESA
the son of R., the son of Zerubbabel, Lk 3.27

RHODA
gateway, a maid named R. came to answer. Ac 12.13

RHODES
The men of R. traded with you; many Eze 27.15
to Cos, and the next day to R., and Ac 21.01

RIB
and the r. which the LORD God had Gen 2.22

RIBAI
the son of R. of Gibeah of the 2Sa 23.29
Ithai the son of R. of Gibeah of 1Ch 11.31

RIBLAH

from Shepham to R. on the east Num 34.11
him in bonds at R. in the land of 2Ki 23.33
up to the king of Babylon at R., 25.06
them to the king of Babylon at R. 25.20
to death at R. in the land of 25.21
at R., in the land of Hamath; Jer 39.05
of Zedekiah at R. before his eyes; 39.06
of Babylon at R. in the land of 52.09
all the princes of Judah at R. 52.10
them to the king of Babylon at R. 52.26
to death at R. in the land of 52.27
habitations, from the wilderness to R. Eze 6.14

RIBS

took one of his r. and closed up Gen 2.21
it had three r. in its mouth between Dan 7.05

RICH

Now Abram was very r. in cattle, Gen 13.02
should say, 'I have made Abram r.' 14.23
and the man became r., and gained 26.13
Thus the man grew exceedingly r., 30.43
Asher's food shall be r., and he 49.20
The r. shall not give more, and the Ex 30.15
or sojourner with you becomes r., Lev 25.47
or if he grows r. he may redeem 25.49
and whether the land is r. or poor, Num 13.20
and the r. yield of the months, Deu 33.14
you who sit on r. carpets and you Ju 5.10
young men, whether poor or r. Ru 3.10
The LORD makes poor and makes r.; 1Sa 2.07
The man was very r.; he had 25.02
the one r. and the other poor. 2Sa 12.01
The r. man had very many flocks and 12.02
came a traveler to the r. man, 12.04
where they found r., good pasture, 1Ch 4.40
fortified cities and a r. land, Neh 9.25
the large and r. land which thou 9.35
And its r. yield goes to the kings 9.37
he will not be r., and his wealth Job 15.29
He goes to bed r., but will do so 27.19
nor regards the r. more than the 34.19
low and high, r. and poor together! Ps 49.02
Be not afraid when one becomes r., 49.16
the hand of the diligent makes r. Pro 10.04
A r. man's wealth is his strong city 10.15
The blessing of the LORD makes r., 10.22
One man pretends to be r., 13.07
but the r. has many friends. 14.20
A r. man's wealth is his strong city, 18.11
entreaties, but the r. answer roughly. 18.23
loves wine and oil will not be r. 21.17
The r. and the poor meet together; 22.02
The r. rules over the poor, and the 22.07
his own wealth, or gives to the r., 22.16
integrity than a r. man who is 28.06
A r. man is wise in his own eyes, 28.11
hastens to be r. will not go 28.20
surfeit of the r. will not let him Ecc 5.12
and the r. sit in a low place. 10.06
in your bedchamber curse the r.; 10.20
and instead of a r. robe, Is 3.24
the head of the r. valley of those 28.01
is on the head of the r. valley, 28.04
which will be r. and plenteous. 30.23
and their soil made r. with fat. 34.07
and with a r. man in his death, 53.09
they have become great and r., Jer 5.27
let not the r. man glory in his 9.23
r. in treasures, your end has come, 51.13
r. in plumage of many colors, came Eze 17.03
portion of the r. food which the Dan 1.05
himself with the king's r. food, 1.08
eat the king's r. food be observed 1.13
youths who ate the king's r. food. 1.15
took away their r. food and the 1.16
who eat his r. food shall be his 11.26
but I am r., I have gained wealth Hos 12.08
have carried my r. treasures into Joe 3.05
Your r. men are full of violence; Mic 6.12
in luxury, and his food is r. Hab 1.16
I will clothe you with r. apparel. Zec 3.04
be the LORD, I have become r.'; 11.05
be hard for a r. man to enter the Mt 19.23
than for a r. man to enter the 19.24
there came a r. man from Arimathea, 27.57
than for a r. man to enter the Mk 10.25
Many r. people put in large sums. 12.41
and the r. he has sent empty away. Lk 1.53
"But woe to you that are r., 6.24
"The land of a r. man brought forth 12.16
himself, and is not r. toward God." 12.21
or your kinsmen or r. neighbors, 14.12
"There was a r. man who had a 16.01
"There was a r. man, who was clothed 16.19
what fell from the r. man's table; 16.21
The r. man also died and was buried 16.22
he became sad, for he was very r. 18.23
than for a r. man to enter the 18.25
was a chief tax collector, and r. 19.02
up and saw the r. putting their 21.01
Already you have become r.! Without 1Co 4.08
as poor, yet making many r.; as 2Co 6.10
Christ, that though he was r., yet 8.09
by his poverty you might become r. 8.09
who is r. in mercy, out of the great Eph 2.04
desire to be r. fall into temptation, 1Ti 6.09
As for the r. in this world, charge 6.17
to be r. in good deeds, liberal and 6.18
and the r. in his humiliation, Jas 1.10
So will the r. man fade away in the 1.11
the world to be r. in faith and 2.05
Is it not the r. who oppress you, is 2.06
Come now, you r., weep and howl for 5.01
(but you are r.) and the slander of Rev 2.09
I am r., I have prospered, and I 3.17
refined by fire, that you may be r., 3.18
generals and the r. and the strong, 6.15
both r. and poor, both free and 13.16
have grown r. with the wealth of 18.03
ships at sea grew r. by her wealth! 18.19

RICHER

gives freely, yet grows all the r.; Pro 11.24
shall be far r. than all of them; Dan 11.02

RICHES

the king will enrich with great r., 1Sa 17.25
long life or r. or the life of your 1Ki 3.11
both r. and honor, so that no other 3.13
of the earth in r. and in wisdom. 10.23
Both r. and honor come from thee, 1Ch 29.12
age, full of days, r., and honor; 29.28
I will also give you r., possessions, 2Ch 1.12
of the earth in r. and in wisdom. 9.22
and he had great r. and honor. 17.05
Jehoshaphat had great r. and honor; 18.01
had very great r. and honor; 32.27
while he showed the r. of his royal Est 1.04
to them the splendor of his r., 5.11
He swallows down r. and vomits them Job 20.15
boast of the abundance of their r.? Ps 49.06
trusted in the abundance of his r., 52.07
if r. increase, set not your heart 62.10
at ease, they increase in r. 73.12
Wealth and r. are in his house; 112.03
I delight as much as in all r. 119.14
in her left hand are r. and honor. Pro 3.16
R. and honor are with me, enduring 8.18
R. do not profit in the day of 11.04
gets honor, and violent men get r. 11.16
He who trusts in his r. will wither, 11.28
to be chosen rather than great r., 22.01

RICHES (cont.)
of the LORD is r. and honor and Pro 22.04
with all precious and pleasant r. 24.04
for r. do not last for ever; 27.24
give me neither poverty nor r.; 30.08
eyes are never satisfied with r., Ecc 4.08
r. were kept by their owner to his 5.13
and those r. were lost in a bad 5.14
nor r. to the intelligent, nor favor 9.11
carry their r. on the backs of Is 30.06
and in their r. you shall glory. 61.06
not the rich man glory in his r.; Jer 9.23
is he who gets r. but not by right 17.11
therefore the r. they gained have 48.36
a spoil of your r. and a prey of Eze 26.12
Your r., your wares, your merchandise, 27.27
has become strong through his r., Dan 11.02
but all his r. can never offset the Hos 12.08
the delight in r. choke the word, Mt 13.22
the world, and the delight in r., Mk 4.19
those who have r. to enter the 10.23
the cares and r. and pleasures of Lk 8.14
will entrust to you the true r.? 16.11
those who have r. to enter the 18.24
upon the r. of his kindness and Rom 2.04
make known the r. of his glory for 9.23
and bestows his r. upon all who 10.12
trespass means r. for the world, 11.12
failure means r. for the Gentiles, 11.12
depth of the r. and wisdom and 11.33
according to the r. of his grace Eph 1.07
what are the r. of his glorious 1.18
immeasurable r. of his grace in 2.07
the unsearchable r. of Christ, 3.08
according to the r. of his glory he 3.16
according to his r. in glory in Php 4.19
Gentiles are the r. of the glory of Col 1.27
to have all the r. of assured 2.02
on uncertain r. but on God who 1Ti 6.17
Your r. have rotted and your Jas 5.02

RICHEST
with gifts, the r. of the people Ps 45.12
come into the r. parts of the Dan 11.24

RICHLY
they may yield more r. for you: Lev 19.25
of the diligent is r. supplied. Pro 13.04
the word of Christ dwell in you r., Col 3.16
but on God who r. furnishes us 1Ti 6.17
out upon us r. through Jesus Tit 3.06
so there will be r. provided for 2Pe 1.11

RICHNESS
to share the r. of the olive tree, Rom 11.17

RIDDEN
which you have r. all your life long Num 22.30
and the horse which the king has r., Est 6.08

RIDDLE
them, "Let me now put a r. to you; Ju 14.12
"Put your r., that we may hear it." 14.13
in three days tell what the r. was. 14.14
husband to tell us what the r. is, 14.15
you have put a r. to my countrymen, 14.16
she told the r. to her countrymen. 14.17
you would not have found out my r." 14.18
to those who had told the r. 14.19
I will solve my r. to the music of Ps 49.04
propound a r., and speak an allegory Eze 17.02

RIDDLES
the words of the wise and their r. Pro 1.06
explain r., and solve problems were Dan 5.12
who understands r., shall arise. 8.23

RIDE
and he made him to r. in his second Gen 41.43
He made him r. on the high places Deu 32.13
you who r. on tawny asses, you who Ju 5.10
for the king's household to r. on, 2Sa 16.02
that I may r. upon it and go with 19.26
my son to r. on my own mule, 1Ki 1.33
Solomon to r. on King David's mule, 1.38
caused him to r. on the king's mule 1.44
Turn round and r. behind me." And 2Ki 9.18
peace? Turn round and r. behind me." 9.19
So he had him r. in his chariot. 10.16
and made him r. through the open Est 6.11
the wind, thou makest me r. on it, Job 30.22
In your majesty r. forth victoriously Ps 45.04
thou didst let men r. over our heads; 66.12
and, "We will r. upon swift steeds," Is 30.16
I will make you r. upon the heights 58.14
they r. upon horses, set in array as Jer 6.23
they r. upon horses, arrayed as a 50.42
us, we will not r. upon horses; Hos 14.03
when thou didst r. upon thy horses, Hab 3.08

RIDE
Also provide mounts for Paul to r., Ac 23.24

RIDER
heels so that his r. falls backward. Gen 49.17
horse and his r. he has thrown into Ex 15.01
horse and his r. he has thrown into 15.21
she laughs at the horse and his r. Job 39.18
both r. and horse lay stunned. Ps 76.06
in pieces the horse and his r.; Jer 51.21
panic, and its r. with madness. Zec 12.04
white horse, and its r. had a bow; Rev 6.02
its r. was permitted to take peace 6.04
and its r. had a balance in his 6.05

RIDER'S
and its r. name was Death, and Hades Rev 6.08

RIDERS
on your part to set r. upon them. 2Ki 18.23
When he sees r., horsemen in pairs, Is 21.07
r. on asses, r. on camels, let him listen 21.07
here come r., horsemen in pairs! 21.09
on your part to set r. upon them. 36.08
at my table with horses and r., Eze 39.20
overthrow the chariots and their r.; Hag 2.22
horses and their r. shall go down, 2.22
shall confound the r. on horses. Zec 10.05
the r. wore breastplates the color Rev 9.17
the flesh of horses and their r., 19.18

RIDES
the discharge r. shall be unclean. Lev 15.09
who r. through the heavens to your Deu 33.26
song to him who r. upon the clouds Ps 68.04
to him who r. in the heavens, the 68.33
shall he who r. the horse save his Amo 2.15

RIDEST
who r. on the wings of the wind, Ps 104.03

RIDGES
settling its r., softening it with Ps 65.10

RIDICULED
greatly enraged, and he r. the Jews. Neh 4.01

RIDING
Now he was r. on the ass, and his Num 22.22
Absalom was r. upon his mule, and 2Sa 18.09
couriers r. on swift horses that Est 8.10
the LORD is r. on a swift cloud and Is 19.01
r. in chariots and on horses, they Jer 17.25
r. in chariots and on horses, they, 22.04
young men, horsemen r. on horses. Eze 23.06

RIDING (cont.)
horsemen r. on horses, all of them Eze 23.12
warriors, all of them r. on horses. 23.23
with you in saddlecloths for r. 27.20
all of them r. on horses, a great 38.15
behold, a man r. upon a red horse! Zec 1.08
humble and r. on an ass, on a colt 9.09

RIGHT
hand, then I will go to the r.; Gen 13.09
or if you take the r. hand, 13.09
the Judge of all the earth do r.? 18.25
led me by the r. way to take the 24.48
may turn to the r. hand or to the 24.49
Ephraim in his r. hand toward 48.13
left hand toward Israel's r. hand, 48.13
stretched out his r. hand and laid 48.14
father laid his r. hand upon the 48.17
put your r. hand upon his head. 48.18
said, "It would not be r. to do so; Ex 8.26
the LORD is in the r., and I and 9.27
them on their r. hand and on their 14.22
them on their r. hand and on their 14.29
Thy r. hand, O LORD, glorious in 15.06
thy r. hand, O LORD, shatters the 15.06
Thou didst stretch out thy r. hand, 15.12
do that which is r. in his eyes, 15.26
shall have no r. to sell her to a 21.08
cause of those who are in the r. 23.08
the tip of the r. ear of Aaron and 29.20
the tips of the r. ears of his 29.20
upon the thumbs of their r. hands, 29.20
the great toes of their r. feet, 29.20
and the r. thigh (for it is a ram 29.22
And the r. thigh you shall give to Lev 7.32
shall have the r. thigh for a 7.33
tip of Aaron's r. ear and on the 8.23
thumb of his r. hand and on the 8.23
on the great toe of his r. foot. 8.23
tips of their r. ears and on the 8.24
thumbs of their r. hands and on 8.24
on the great toes of their r. feet; 8.24
with their fat, and the r. thigh; 8.25
on the fat and on the r. thigh; 8.26
breasts and the r. thigh Aaron 9.21
the tip of the r. ear of him who 14.14
and on the thumb of his r. hand, 14.14
on the great toe of his r. foot. 14.14
and dip his r. finger in the oil 14.16
the tip of the r. ear of him who 14.17
and on the thumb of his r. hand, 14.17
on the great toe of his r. foot, 14.17
the tip of the r. ear of him who 14.25
and on the thumb of his r. hand, 14.25
on the great toe of his r. foot. 14.25
with his r. finger some of the oil 14.27
that is in his r. hand on the tip 14.28
the tip of the r. ear of him who 14.28
and on the thumb of his r. hand, 14.28
and the great toe of his r. foot, 14.28
he shall have the r. of redemption. 25.29
not exercise his r. of redemption, 25.33
and as the r. thigh are yours. Num 18.18
aside to the r. hand or to the 20.17
either to the r. or to the left. 22.26
"The daughters of Zelophehad are r.; 27.07
tribe of the sons of Joseph is r. 36.05
neither to the r. nor to the left. Deu 2.27
aside to the r. hand or to the 5.32
do what is r. and good in the 6.18
whatever is r. in his own eyes; 12.08
you do what is r. in the sight of 12.25
is good and r. in the sight of the 12.28
doing what is r. in the sight of 13.18
one kind of legal r. and another, 17.08
either to the r. hand or to the 17.11
either to the r. hand or to the 17.20
you do what is r. in the sight of 21.09
the r. of the first-born is his. 21.17
to the r. hand or to the left, to go 28.14
iniquity, just and r. is he. 32.04
with flaming fire at his r. hand. 33.02
there they offer r. sacrifices; 33.19
from it to the r. hand or to the Jos 1.07
seems good and r. in your sight to 9.25
neither to the r. hand nor to the 23.06
it on his r. thigh under his Ju 3.16
took the sword from his r. thigh, 3.21
peg and her r. hand to the workmen's 5.26
and in their r. hands the trumpets 7.20
for he could not pronounce it r.; 12.06
his r. hand on the one and his left 16.29
did what was r. in his own eyes. 17.06
did what was r. in his own eyes. 21.25
Take my r. of redemption yourself, Ru 4.06
neither to the r. nor to the left, 1Sa 6.12
that I gouge out all your r. eyes, 11.02
you in the good and the r. way. 12.23
to me it seems r. that you should 29.06
neither to the r. hand nor to the 2Sa 2.19
aside to your r. hand or to your 2.21
turn to the r. hand or to the left 14.19
"See, your claims are good and r.; 15.03
men were on his r. hand and on his 16.06
What further r. have I, then, to cry 19.28
beard with his r. hand to kiss him 20.09
mother; and she sat on his r. 1Ki 2.19
understanding to discern what is r., 3.11
doing what is r. in my sight and 11.33
and do what is r. in my eyes by 11.38
only that which was r. in my eyes, 14.08
did what was r. in the eyes of the 15.05
did what was r. in the eyes of the 15.11
him on his r. hand and on his left 22.19
doing what was r. in the sight of 22.43
one another, "We are not doing r. 2Ki 7.09
carrying out what is r. in my eyes, 10.30
did what was r. in the eyes of the 12.02
altar on the r. side as one entered 12.09
And he did what was r. in the eyes 14.03
And he did what was r. in the eyes 15.03
And he did what was r. in the eyes 15.34
not do what was r. in the eyes of 16.02
their God things that were not r. 17.09
And he did what was r. in the eyes 18.03
And he did what was r. in the eyes 22.02
aside to the r. hand or to the 22.02
Asaph, who stood on his r. hand, 1Ch 6.39
with either the r. or the left 12.02
the thing was r. in the eyes of 13.04
was good and r. in the eyes of the 2Ch 14.02
standing on his r. hand and on his 18.18
he did what was r. in the sight of 20.32
did what was r. in the eyes of the 24.02
And he did what was r. in the eyes 25.02
And he did what was r. in the eyes 26.04
And he did what was r. in the eyes 27.02
not do what was r. in the eyes of 28.01
And he did what was r. in the eyes 29.02
and the plan seemed r. to the king 30.04
was good and r. and faithful 31.20
He did what was r. in the eyes of 34.02
aside to the r. or to the left. 34.02
no portion or r. or memorial in Neh 2.20
and Maaseiah on his r. hand; 8.04
and give them r. ordinances and 9.13
One went to the r. upon the wall to 12.31
the thing seem r. before the king, Est 8.05
does the Almighty pervert the r.? Job 8.03
maintain the r. of a man with God, 16.21
I turn to the r. hand, but I cannot 23.09
lives, who has taken away my r., 27.02
it from me to say that you are r.; 27.05
On my r. hand the rabble rise, they 30.12

RIGHT (cont.)
aged that understand what is r. Job 32.09
"Behold, in this you are not r. 33.12
declare to man what is r. for him; 33.23
sinned, and perverted what was r., 33.27
Let us choose what is r.; let us 34.04
and God has taken away my r.; 34.05
in spite of my r. I am counted a 34.06
you say, 'It is my r. before God,' 35.02
but gives the afflicted their r. 36.06
that your own r. hand can give you 40.14
have not spoken of me what is r., 42.07
have not spoken of me what is r., 42.08
Answer me when I call, O God of my r.! Ps 4.01
Offer r. sacrifices, and put your 4.05
blamelessly, and does what is r., 15.02
because he is at my r. hand, 16.08
in thy r. hand are pleasures for 16.11
come! Let thy eyes see the r.! 17.02
their adversaries at thy r. hand. 17.07
and thy r. hand supported me, and 18.35
the precepts of the LORD are r., 19.08
mighty victories by his r. hand. 20.06
your r. hand will find out those 21.08
He leads the humble in what is r., 25.09
and whose r. hands are full of 26.10
Bestir thyself, and awake for my r., 35.23
light, and your r. as the noonday. 37.06
but thy r. hand, and thy arm, and the 44.03
of truth and to defend the r.; 45.04
let your r. hand teach you dread 45.04
at your r. hand stands the queen in 45.09
God will help her r. early. 46.05
Thy r. hand is filled with victory; 48.10
"What r. have you to recite my 50.16
put a new and r. spirit within me. 51.10
wilt thou delight in r. sacrifices, 51.19
indeed decree what is r., you gods? 58.01
victory by thy r. hand and answer 60.05
to thee; thy r. hand upholds me. 63.08
thee; thou dost hold my r. hand. 73.23
thou keep thy r. hand in thy bosom? 74.11
grief that the r. hand of the Most 77.10
mountain which his r. hand had won. 78.54
the stock which thy r. hand planted. 80.15
be upon the man of thy r. hand, 80.17
maintain the r. of the afflicted 82.03
is thy hand, high thy r. hand. 89.13
the sea and his r. hand on the 89.25
exalted the r. hand of his foes; 89.42
side, ten thousand at your r. hand; 91.07
His r. hand and his holy arm have 98.01
delivered, give help by thy r. hand, 108.06
stands at the r. hand of the needy, 109.31
"Sit at my r. hand, till I make your 110.01
The Lord is at your r. hand; 110.05
"The r. hand of the LORD does 118.15
the r. hand of the LORD is exalted, 118.16
the r. hand of the LORD does 118.16
O LORD, that thy judgments are r., 119.75
I have done what is just and r.; 119.121
O LORD, and r. are thy judgments. 119.137
for all thy commandments are r. 119.172
LORD is your shade on your r. hand. 121.05
O Jerusalem, let my r. hand wither! 137.05
enemies, and thy r. hand delivers me. 138.07
and thy r. hand shall hold me. 139.10
thy works! Thou knowest me r. well; 139.14
I look to the r. and watch, but 142.04
whose r. hand is a r. hand of falsehood 144.08
whose r. hand is a r. hand of falsehood 144.11
Long life is in her r. hand; Pro 3.16
swerve to the r. or to the left; 4.27
from my lips will come what is r.; 8.06
understands and r. to those who 8.09
of a fool is r. in his own eyes, 12.15
There is a way which seems r. to a man, 14.12
he loves him who speaks what is r. 16.13
there is a way which seems r. to a man, 16.25
who states his case first seems r., 18.17
his acts, what he does is pure and r. 20.11
Every way of a man is r. in his own 21.02
but the conduct of the pure is r. 21.08
to show you what is r. and true, 22.21
when your lips speak what is r. 23.16
He who gives a r. answer kisses the 24.26
or to grasp oil in his r. hand. 27.16
and justice and r. violently taken Ecc 5.08
heart inclines him toward the r., 10.02
and that his r. hand embraced me! Sol 2.06
and that his r. hand embraced me! 8.03
and deprive the innocent of his r.! Is 5.23
They snatch on the r., but are still 9.20
the poor of my people of their r., 10.02
turn aside him who is in the r. 29.21
"Prophesy not to us what is r.; 30.10
you turn to the r. or when you 30.21
when the plea of the needy is r. 32.07
and my r. is disregarded by my God"? 40.27
you with my victorious r. hand. 41.10
LORD your God, hold your r. hand; 41.13
that we might say, "He is r."? 41.26
case, that you may be proved r. 43.26
"Is there not a lie in my r. hand?" 44.20
whose r. hand I have grasped, to 45.01
the truth, I declare what is r. 45.19
of Israel, but not in truth or r. 48.01
and my r. hand spread out the 48.13
yet surely my r. is with the LORD, 49.04
abroad to the r. and to the left, 54.03
sworn by his r. hand and by his 62.08
arm to go at the r. hand of Moses, 63.12
What r. has my beloved in my house, Jer 11.15
he who gets riches but not by r.; 17.11
were the signet ring on my r. hand, 22.24
is evil, and their might is not r. 23.10
me as seems good and r. to you. 26.14
it to whomever it seems r. to me. 27.05
for the r. of redemption by purchase 32.07
for the r. of possession and 32.08
did what was r. in my eyes by 34.15
you think it good and r. to go. 40.04
go wherever you think it r. to go. 40.05
"The LORD is in the r., for I have Lam 1.18
from them his r. hand in the face 2.03
with his r. hand set like a foe; 2.04
to turn aside the r. of a man in 3.35
the face of a lion on the r. side, Eze 1.10
but on your r. side, and bear the 4.06
they are more in the r. than you. 16.52
and does what is lawful and r.— 18.05
son has done what is lawful and r., 18.19
and does what is lawful and r., 18.21
and does what is lawful and r., 18.27
Cut sharply to r. and left where 21.16
Into his r. hand comes the lot for 21.22
it until he comes whose r. it is; 21.27
and does what is lawful and r., 33.14
he has done what is lawful and r., 33.16
and does what is lawful and r., 33.19
arrows drop out of your r. hand. 39.03
his works are r. and his ways are Dan 4.37
raised his r. hand and his left 12.07
for the ways of the LORD are r., Hos 14.09
"They do not know how to do r.," Amo 3.10
not know their r. hand from their Jon 4.11
in the LORD's r. hand will come Hab 2.16
standing at his r. hand to accuse Zec 3.01
give you the r. of access among 3.07
one on the r. of the bowl and the 4.03
trees on the r. and the left of 4.11
"If it seems r. to you, give me my 11.12
sword smite his arm and his r. eye! 11.17
his r. eye utterly blinded!" 11.17

RIGHT (cont.)
devour to the r. and to the left Zec 12.06
they present r. offerings to the Mal 3.03
If your r. eye causes you to sin, Mt 5.29
And if your r. hand causes you to 5.30
one strikes you on the r. cheek, 5.39
know what your r. hand is doing, 6.03
and whatever is r. I will give you 20.04
one at your r. hand and one at your 20.21
to sit at my r. hand and at my 20.23
Sit at my r. hand, till I put thy 22.44
place the sheep at his r. hand, 25.33
will say to those at his r. hand, 25.34
man seated at the r. hand of Power, 26.64
and put a reed in his r. hand. 27.29
one on the r. and one on the left. 27.38
there, clothed and in his r. mind, Mk 5.15
for it is not r. to take the 7.27
one at your r. hand and one at your 10.37
but to sit at my r. hand or at my 10.40
said to him, "You are r., Teacher; 12.32
Sit at my r. hand, till I put thy 12.36
r. into the courtyard of the high 14.54
sitting at the r. hand of Power, 14.62
one on his r. and one on his left. 15.27
a young man sitting on the r. side, 16.05
standing on the r. side of the Lk 1.11
was there whose r. hand was 6.06
clothed and in his r. mind; and 8.35
said to him, "You have answered r.; 10.28
judge for yourselves what is r.? 12.57
to my Lord, Sit at my r. hand, 20.42
high priest and cut off his r. ear. 22.50
seated at the r. hand of the power 22.69
one on the r. and one on the left. 23.33
"You are r. in saying, 'I have no Jn 4.17
appearances, but judge with r. judgment." 7.24
"Are we not r. in saying that you 8.48
and you are r., for so I am. 13.13
slave and cut off his r. ear. 18.10
the net on the r. side of the boat, 21.06
for he is at my r. hand that I may Ac 2.25
exalted at the r. hand of God, 2.33
to my Lord, Sit at my r. hand, 2.34
took him by the r. hand and raised 3.07
"Whether it is r. in the sight of 4.19
him at his r. hand as Leader and 5.31
"It is not r. that we should give 6.02
standing at the r. hand of God; 7.55
man standing at the r. hand of God." 7.56
your heart is not r. before God. 8.21
does what is r. is acceptable to 10.35
Holy Spirit was r. in saying to 28.25
at the r. time Christ died for the Rom 5.06
I can will what is r., but I cannot 7.18
be a law that when I want to do r., 7.21
who is at the r. hand of God, who 8.34
Has the potter no r. over the clay, 9.21
it is r. not to eat meat or drink 14.21
Do we not have the r. to our food 1Co 9.04
Do we not have the r. to be accompanied 9.05
I who have no r. to refrain from 9.06
we have not made use of this r., 9.12
full use of my r. in the gospel. 9.18
at wrong, but rejoices in the r. 13.06
Come to your r. mind, and sin no 15.34
if we are in our r. mind, it is 2Co 5.13
righteousness for the r. hand and 6.07
but that you may do what is r., 13.07
Barnabas the r. hand of fellowship, Gal 2.09
him sit at his r. hand in the Eph 1.20
all that is good and r. and true), 5.09
in the Lord, for this is r. 6.01
It is r. for me to feel thus about Php 1.07
is, seated at the r. hand of God. Col 3.01
not because we have not that r., 2Th 3.09
gain what they have no r. to teach. Tit 1.11
sat down at the r. hand of the Heb 1.03
"Sit at my r. hand, till I make thy 1.13
seated at the r. hand of the 8.01
he sat down at the r. hand of God, 10.12
seated at the r. hand of the 12.02
serve the tent have no r. to eat. 13.10
Whoever knows what is r. to do and Jas 4.17
and to praise those who do r. 1Pe 2.14
that by doing r. you should put to 2.15
if when you do r. and suffer for 2.20
if you do r. and let nothing 3.06
let him turn away from evil and do r.; 3.11
if you are zealous for what is r.? 3.13
is better to suffer for doing r., 3.17
and is at the r. hand of God, 3.22
God's will do r. and entrust their 4.19
I think it r., as long as I am in 2Pe 1.13
Forsaking the r. way they have gone 2.15
one who does r. is born of him. 1Jn 2.29
He who does r. is righteous, as he 3.07
does not do r. is not of God, 3.10
in his r. hand he held seven stars, Rev 1.16
But he laid his r. hand upon me, 1.17
stars which you saw in my r. hand, 1.20
the seven stars in his r. hand, 2.01
And I saw in the r. hand of him who 5.01
scroll from the r. hand of him who 5.07
And he set his r. foot on the sea, 10.02
lifted up his r. hand to heaven 10.05
marked on the r. hand or the 13.16
and the righteous still do r., 22.11
may have the r. to the tree of 22.14

RIGHTED
you; and before every one you are r." Gen 20.16

RIGHTEOUS
Noah was a r. man, blameless in his Gen 6.09
that you are r. before me in this 7.01
destroy the r. with the wicked 18.23
Suppose there are fifty r. within 18.24
it for the fifty r. who are in it? 18.24
to slay the r. with the wicked, so 18.25
so that the r. fare as the wicked! 18.25
find at Sodom fifty r. in the city, 18.26
Suppose five of the fifty r. are lacking? 18.28
"She is more r. than I, inasmuch as 38.26
do not slay the innocent and r., Ex 23.07
Let me die the death of the r., Num 23.10
ordinances so r. as all this law Deu 4.08
judge the people with r. judgment. 16.18
and subverts the cause of the r. 16.19
to David, "You are more r. than I; 1Sa 24.17
have slain a r. man in his own 2Sa 4.11
two men more r. and better than 1Ki 2.32
vindicating the r. by rewarding 8.32
vindicating the r. by rewarding 2Ch 6.23
themselves and said, "The LORD is r." 12.06
thy promise, for thou art r. Neh 9.08
'Can mortal man be r. before God? Job 4.17
If I am r., I cannot lift up my 10.15
born of a woman, that he can be r.? 15.14
Yet the r. holds to his way, and he 17.09
to the Almighty if you are r., 22.03
The r. see it and are glad; 22.19
How then can man be r. before God? 25.04
because he was r. in his own eyes. 32.01
condemn him who is r. and mighty, 34.17
If you are r., what do you give to 35.07
not withdraw his eyes from the r., 36.07
in the congregation of the r.; Ps 1.05
for the LORD knows the way of the r., 1.06
For thou dost bless the r., O LORD; 5.12
an end, but establish thou the r., 7.09
the minds and hearts, thou r. God. 7.09
God is a r. judge, and a God who has 7.11
on the throne giving r. judgment. 9.04
are destroyed, what can the r. do"? 11.03

RIGHTEOUS (cont.)
The LORD tests the r. and the wicked, Ps 11.05
For the LORD is r., he loves r. deeds; 11.07
is with the generation of the r. 14.05
LORD are true, and r. altogether. 19.09
against the r. in pride and 31.18
O r., and shout for joy, all you 32.11
Rejoice in the LORD, O you r.! 33.01
eyes of the LORD are toward the r., 34.15
When the r. cry for help, the LORD 34.17
Many are the afflictions of the r.; 34.19
who hate the r. will be condemned. 34.21
The wicked plots against the r., 37.12
little that the r. has than the 37.16
but the LORD upholds the r. 37.17
but the r. is generous and gives; 37.21
not seen the r. forsaken or his 37.25
The r. shall be preserved for ever, 37.28
The r. shall possess the land, and 37.29
The mouth of the r. utters wisdom, 37.30
The wicked watches the r., and 37.32
salvation of the r. is from the 37.39
The r. shall see, and fear, and shall 52.06
never permit the r. to be moved. 55.22
The r. will rejoice when he sees 58.10
there is a reward for the r.; 58.11
Let the r. rejoice in the LORD, and 64.10
But let the r. be joyful; let them 68.03
them not be enrolled among the r. 69.28
My mouth will tell of thy r. acts, 71.15
talk of thy r. help all the day 71.24
horns of the r. shall be exalted. 75.10
The r. flourish like the palm tree, 92.12
for justice will return to the r., 94.15
together against the life of the r., 94.21
Light dawns for the r., and joy 97.11
O you r., and give thanks to his 97.12
LORD is gracious, merciful, and r. 112.04
For the r. will never be moved; 112.06
Gracious is the LORD, and r.; 116.05
of victory in the tents of the r.: 118.15
the r. shall enter through it. 118.20
when I learn thy r. ordinances. 119.07
thee, because of thy r. ordinances. 119.62
it, to observe thy r. ordinances. 119.106
the fulfilment of thy r. promise. 119.123
R. art thou, O LORD, and right are 119.137
Thy righteousness is r. for ever, 119.142
Thy testimonies are r. for ever; 119.144
one of thy r. ordinances endures 119.160
praise thee for thy r. ordinances. 119.164
upon the land allotted to the r. 125.03
lest the r. put forth thier hands 125.03
The LORD is r.; he has cut the 129.04
Surely the r. shall give thanks to 140.13
The r. will surround me; for thou 142.07
no man living is r. before thee. 143.02
bowed down; the LORD loves the r. 146.08
and keep to the paths of the r. Pro 2.20
but he blesses the abode of the r. 3.33
But the path of the r. is like the 4.18
All the words of my mouth are r.; 8.08
teach a r. man and he will increase 9.09
LORD does not let the r. go hungry, 10.03
Blessings are on the head of the r., 10.06
The memory of the r. is a blessing, 10.07
The mouth of the r. is a fountain 10.11
The wage of the r. leads to life, 10.16
The tongue of the r. is choice 10.20
The lips of the r. feed many, 10.21
desire of the r. will be granted. 10.24
but the r. is established for ever. 10.25
The hope of the r. ends in gladness, 10.28
The r. will never be removed, but 10.30
The mouth of the r. brings forth 10.31
The lips of the r. know what is 10.32
The r. is delivered from trouble, 11.08
by knowledge the r. are delivered. 11.09
When it goes well with the r., 11.10
those who are r. will be delivered 11.21
The desire of the r. ends only in 11.23
but the r. will flourish like a 11.28
The fruit of the r. is a tree of 11.30
If the r. is requited on earth, how 11.31
the root of the r. will never be 12.03
The thoughts of the r. are just; 12.05
but the house of the r. will stand. 12.07
A r. man has regard for the life of 12.10
but the root of the r. stands firm. 12.12
but the r. escapes from trouble. 12.13
No ill befalls the r., but the wicked 12.21
A r. man turns away from evil, but 12.26
A r. man hates falsehood, but a 13.05
The light of the r. rejoices, 13.09
but prosperity rewards the r. 13.21
wealth is laid up for the r. 13.22
The r. has enough to satisfy his 13.25
the wicked at the gates of the r. 14.19
but the r. finds refuge through his 14.32
house of the r. there is much 15.06
The mind of the r. ponders how to 15.28
but he hears the prayer of the r. 15.29
R. lips are the delight of a king, 16.13
it is gained in a r. life. 16.31
condemns the r. are both alike an 17.15
a fine on a r. man is not good; 17.26
or to deprive a r. man of justice. 18.05
the r. man runs into it and is safe 18.10
A r. man who walks in his integrity 20.07
The r. observes the house of the 21.12
is done, it is a joy to the r., 21.15
The wicked is a ransom for the r., 21.18
but the r. gives and does not hold 21.26
The father of the r. will greatly 23.24
man against the dwelling of the r.; 24.15
for a r. man falls seven times, and 24.16
fountain is a r. man who gives way 25.26
but the r. are bold as a lion. 28.01
When the r. triumph, there is great 28.12
when they perish, the r. increase. 28.28
When the r. are in authority, the 29.02
but a r. man sings and rejoices. 29.06
A r. man knows the rights of the 29.07
but the r. will look upon their 29.16
man is an abomination to the r., 29.27
will judge the r. and the wicked, Ecc 3.17
there is a r. man who perishes in 7.15
Be not r. overmuch, and do not make 7.16
Surely there is not a r. man on 7.20
that there are r. men to whom it 8.14
according to the deeds of the r. 8.14
how the r. and the wise and their 9.01
to the r. and the wicked, to the 9.02
Tell the r. that it shall be well Is 3.10
of praise, of glory to the R. One. 24.16
that the r. nation which keeps 26.02
The way of the r. is level; 26.07
make smooth the path of the r. 26.07
a r. God and a Savior; there is 45.21
by his knowledge shall the r. one, 53.11
make many to be accounted r.; 53.11
The r. man perishes, and no one lays 57.01
For the r. man is taken away from 57.01
they ask of me r. judgments, 58.02
Your people shall all be r.; 60.21
and all our r. deeds are like a 64.06
R. art thou, O LORD, when I complain Jer 12.01
O LORD of hosts, who triest the r., 20.12
raise up for David a r. Branch, 23.05
I will cause a r. Branch to spring 33.15
midst of her the blood of the r. Lam 4.13
Again, if a r. man turns from his Eze 3.20
and his r. deeds which he has done 3.20
Nevertheless if you warn the r. man not to sin, 3.21
have disheartened the r. falsely, 13.22

RIGHTEOUS (cont.)

sisters appear r. by all the Eze 16.51
have made your sisters appear r. 16.52
"If a man is r. and does what is 18.05
he is r., he shall surely live, says 18.09
righteousness of the r. shall be 18.20
But when a r. man turns away from 18.24
None of the r. deeds which he has 18.24
When a r. man turns away from his 18.26
off from you both r. and wicked. 21.03
off from you both r. and wicked, 21.04
But r. men shall pass judgment on 23.45
righteousness of the r. shall not 33.12
and the r. shall not be able to 33.12
Though I say to the r. that he 33.13
none of his r. deeds shall be 33.13
When the r. turns from his righteousness, 33.18
LORD our God is r. in all the Dan 9.14
Lord, according to all thy r. acts, 9.16
they sell the r. for silver, Amo 2.06
your sins—you who afflict the r., 5.12
For the wicked surround the r., Hab 1.04
swallows up the man more r. than he? 1.13
but the r. shall live by his faith. 2.04
The LORD within her is r., Zep 3.05
between the r. and the wicked, Mal 3.18
not to call the r., but sinners. Mt 9.13
who receives a r. man because he 10.41
because he is a r. man shall 10.41
shall receive a r. man's reward. 10.41
prophets and r. men longed to see 13.17
Then the r. will shine like the sun 13.43
and separate the evil from the r., 13.49
also outwardly appear r. to men, 23.28
and adorn the monuments of the r., 23.29
come all the r. blood shed on 23.35
Then the r. will answer him, 'Lord, 25.37
but the r. into eternal life. 25.46
nothing to do with that r. man, 27.19
not to call the r., but sinners. Mk 2.17
that he was a r. and holy man, 6.20
And they were both r. before God, Lk 1.06
and this man was r. and devout, 2.25
I have not come to call the r., 5.32
ninety-nine r. persons who need no 15.07
that they were r. and despised 18.09
of the council, a good and r. man, 23.50
O r. Father, the world has not known Jn 17.25
But you denied the Holy and R. One, Ac 3.14
beforehand the coming of the R. One, 7.52
who through faith is r. shall live. Rom 1.17
when God's r. judgment will be 2.05
of the law who are r. before God, 2.13
written: "None is r., no, not one; 3.10
he himself is r. and that he 3.26
Why, one will hardly die for a r. man— 5.07
obedience many will be made r. 5.19
through faith is r. shall live"; Gal 3.11
how holy and r. and blameless was 1Th 2.10
evidence of the r. judgment of God, 2Th 1.05
the r. judge, will award to me on 2Ti 4.08
the r. scepter is the scepter of Heb 1.08
but my r. one shall live by faith, 10.38
which he received approval as r., 11.04
condemned, you have killed the r. man; Jas 5.06
The prayer of a r. man has great 5.16
eyes of the Lord are upon the r., 1Pe 3.12
the r. for the unrighteous, that he 3.18
And "If the r. man is scarcely 4.18
and if he rescued r. Lot, 2Pe 2.07
(for by what that r. man saw and 2.08
vexed in his r. soul day after day 2.08
the Father, Jesus Christ the r.; 1Jn 2.01
If you know that he is r., 2.29
He who does right is r., as he is r. 3.07
were evil and his brother's r. 3.12
linen is the r. deeds of the Rev 19.08
and the r. still do right, and the 22.11

RIGHTEOUSLY

and judge r. between a man and his Deu 1.16
judge r., maintain the rights of Pro 31.09
He who walks r. and speaks uprightly Is 33.15
who judgest r., who triest the Jer 11.20

RIGHTEOUSNESS

and he reckoned it to him as r. Gen 15.06
the LORD by doing r. and justice; 18.19
but in r. shall you judge your Lev 19.15
And it will be r. for us, if we are Deu 6.25
because of my r. that the LORD has 9.04
Not because of your r. or the 9.05
land to possess because of your r.; 9.06
and it shall be r. to you before 24.13
man for his r. and his faithfulness 1Sa 26.23
rewarded me according to my r.; 2Sa 22.21
recompensed me according to my r., 22.25
in r., and in uprightness of heart 1Ki 3.06
rewarding him according to his r. 8.32
you may execute justice and r. 10.09
rewarding him according to his r. 2Ch 6.23
you may execute justice and r. 9.08
I hold fast my r., and will not let Job 27.06
I put on r., and it clothed me; 29.14
yourself, and your r. a son of man. 35.08
afar, and ascribe r. to my Maker. 36.03
and abundant r. he will not violate 37.23
in thy r. because of my enemies; Ps 5.08
according to my r. and according 7.08
the LORD the thanks due to his r., 7.17
and he judges the world with r., 9.08
me, I shall behold thy face in r.; 17.15
rewarded me according to my r.; 18.20
recompensed me according to my r., 18.24
me in paths of r. for his name's 23.03
to shame; in thy r. deliver me! 31.01
He loves r. and justice; the earth 33.05
LORD, my God, according to thy r.; 35.24
tell of thy r. and of thy praise 35.28
Thy r. is like the mountains of God, 36.06
you love r. and hate wickedness. 45.07
The heavens declare his r., 50.06
In thy r. deliver me and rescue me; 71.02
I will praise thy r., thine alone. 71.16
Thy power and thy r., O God, reach 71.19
and thy r. to the royal son! 72.01
May he judge thy people with r., 72.02
the people, and the hills, in r.! 72.03
In his days may r. flourish, 72.07
r. and peace will kiss each other. 85.10
and r. will look down from the sky. 85.11
R. will go before him, and make his 85.13
R. and justice are the foundation 89.14
name all the day, and extol thy r. 89.16
He will judge the world with r., 96.13
r. and justice are the foundation 97.02
The heavens proclaim his r.; 97.06
He will judge the world with r., 98.09
executed justice and r. in Jacob. 99.04
and his r. to children's children, 103.17
justice, who do r. at all times! 106.03
to him as r. from generation to 106.31
his work, and his r. endures for ever. 111.03
his house; and his r. endures for ever. 112.03
to the poor; his r. endures for ever; 112.09
Open to me the gates of r., that I 118.19
thy precepts; in thy r. give me life! 119.40
thy testimonies in r. and in all 119.138
Thy r. is righteous for ever, and 119.142
Let thy priests be clothed with r., 132.09
faithfulness answer me, in thy r.! 143.01
In thy r. bring me out of trouble! 143.11
and shall sing aloud of thy r. 145.07
dealing, r., justice, and equity; Pro 1.03
will understand r. and justice and 2.09
I walk in the way of r., in the 8.20
profit, but r. delivers from death. 10.02

RIGHTEOUSNESS (cont.)

wrath, but r. delivers from death.	Pro 11.04
The r. of the blameless keeps his	11.05
The r. of the upright delivers them,	11.06
one who sows r. gets a sure reward	11.18
He who is steadfast in r. will live,	11.19
In the path of r. is life, but the	12.28
R. guards him whose way is upright,	13.06
R. exalts a nation, but sin is a	14.34
but he loves him who pursues r.	15.09
a little with r. than great	16.08
the throne is established by r.	16.12
and his throne is upheld by r.	20.28
To do r. and justice is more	21.03
He who pursues r. and kindness will	21.21
throne will be established in r.	25.05
wickedness, and in the place of r.,	Ecc 3.16
righteous man who perishes in his r.,	7.15
R. lodged in her, but now murderers.	Is 1.21
you shall be called the city of r.,	1.26
and those in her who repent, by r.	1.27
for r., but behold, a cry!	5.07
Holy God shows himself holy in r.	5.16
and with r. from this time forth	9.07
is decreed, overflowing with r.	10.22
but with r. he shall judge the poor,	11.04
R. shall be the girdle of his waist,	11.05
justice and is swift to do r.	16.05
inhabitants of the world learn r.	26.09
the wicked, he does not learn r.;	26.10
the line, and r. the plummet;	28.17
Behold, a king will reign in r.,	32.01
and r. abide in the fruitful field.	32.16
And the effect of r. will be peace,	32.17
be peace, and the result of r.,	32.17
will fill Zion with justice and r.;	33.05
the LORD, I have called you in r.,	42.06
and let the skies rain down r.;	45.08
let it cause r. to spring up also;	45.08
I have aroused him in r.,	45.13
gone forth in r. a word that shall	45.23
be said of me, are r. and strength;	45.24
and your r. like the waves of the	48.18
you who know r., the people in	51.07
In r. you shall be established;	54.14
and do r., for soon my salvation	56.01
tell of your r. and your doings,	57.12
nation that did r. and did not	58.02
your r. shall go before you, the	58.08
and r. does not overtake us;	59.09
turned back, and r. stands afar off;	59.14
him victory, and his r. upheld him.	59.16
He put on r. as a breastplate, and a	59.17
peace and your taskmasters r.	60.17
that they may be called oaks of r.,	61.03
has covered me with the robe of r.,	61.10
GOD will cause r. and praise to	61.11
meetest him that joyfully works r.,	64.05
justice, and r. in the earth;	Jer 9.24
Thus says the LORD: Do justice and r.,	22.03
and drink and do justice and r.?	22.15
execute justice and r. in the land.	23.05
be called: 'The LORD is our r.'	23.06
O habitation of r., O holy hill!	31.23
execute justice and r. in the land.	33.15
be called: 'The LORD is our r.'	33.16
turns from his r. and commits	Eze 3.20
but their own lives by their r.,	14.14
but their own lives by their r.	14.20
the r. of the righteous shall be	18.20
for the r. which he has done he	18.22
away from his r. and commits	18.24
away from his r. and commits	18.26
The r. of the righteous shall not	33.12
to live by his r. when he sins.	33.12
trusts in his r. and commits	33.13
When the righteous turns from his r.,	33.18
oppression, and execute justice and r.;	45.09
off your sins by practicing r.,	Dan 4.27
belongs r., but to us confusion of	9.07
thee on the ground of our r.,	9.18
iniquity, to bring in everlasting r.,	9.24
and those who turn many to r.,	12.03
you to me in r. and in justice,	Hos 2.19
Sow for yourselves r., reap the fruit	10.12
and cast down r. to the earth!	Amo 5.07
and r. like an everflowing stream.	5.24
and the fruit of r. into wormwood—	6.12
seek r., seek humility; perhaps	Zep 2.03
God, in faithfulness and in r.	Zec 8.08
my name the sun of r. shall rise,	Mal 4.02
is fitting for us to fulfil all r.	Mt 3.15
those who hunger and thirst for r.,	5.06
unless your r. exceeds that of the	5.20
But seek first his kingdom and his r.,	6.33
For John came to you in the way of r.,	21.32
in holiness and r. before him all	Lk 1.75
of sin and of r. and of judgment:	Jn 16.08
of r., because I go to the Father,	16.10
of the devil, you enemy of all r.,	Ac 13.10
the world in r. by a man whom he	17.31
For in it the r. of God is revealed	Rom 1.17
But now the r. of God has been	3.21
the r. of God through faith in	3.22
This was to show God's r., because	3.25
and it was reckoned to him as r.	4.03
his faith is reckoned as r.	4.05
God reckons r. apart from works:	4.06
was reckoned to Abraham as r.	4.09
or seal of the r. which he had by	4.11
who thus have r. reckoned to them,	4.11
law but through the r. of faith.	4.13
faith was "reckoned to him as r."	4.22
free gift of r. reign in life	5.17
man's act of r. leads to acquittal	5.18
reign through r. to eternal life	5.21
to God as instruments of r.	6.13
or of obedience, which leads to r.?	6.16
from sin, have become slaves of r.	6.18
your members to r. for sanctification	6.19
sin, you were free in regard to r.	6.20
spirits are alive because of r.	8.10
did not pursue r. have attained it,	9.30
it, that is, r. through faith;	9.30
who pursued the r. which is based	9.31
ignorant of the r. that comes from	10.03
they did not submit to God's r.	10.03
practices the r. which is based on	10.05
But the r. based on faith says, Do	10.06
and drink but r. and peace and joy	14.17
our r. and sanctification and	1Co 1.30
dispensation of r. must far exceed	2Co 3.09
him we might become the r. of God.	5.21
the weapons of r. for the right	6.07
partnership have r. and iniquity?	6.14
the poor; his r. endures for ever."	9.09
increase the harvest of your r.	9.10
disguise themselves as servants of r.	11.15
and it was reckoned to him as r."	Gal 3.06
then r. would indeed be by the law.	3.21
faith, we wait for the hope of r.	5.05
of God in true r. and holiness.	Eph 4.24
put on the breastplate of r.,	6.14
the fruits of r. which come	Php 1.11
as to r. under the law blameless.	3.06
not having a r. of my own, based on	3.09
the r. from God that depends on	3.09
aim at r., godliness, faith, love,	1Ti 6.11
youthful passions and aim at r.,	2Ti 2.22
correction, and for training in r.,	3.16
is laid up for me the crown of r.,	4.08
because of deeds done by us in r.,	Tit 3.05
Thou hast loved r. and hated	Heb 1.09
is unskilled in the word of r.,	5.13
king of r., and then he is also	7.02

RIGHTEOUSNESS (cont.)

an heir of the r. which comes by Heb 11.07
fruit of r. to those who have been 12.11
of man does not work the r. of God. Jas 1.20
and it was reckoned to him as r."; 2.23
And the harvest of r. is sown in 3.18
we might die to sin and live to r. 1Pe 2.24
ours in the r. of our God and 2Pe 1.01
a herald of r., with seven other 2.05
the way of r. than after knowing 2.21
and a new earth in which r. dwells. 3.13
and in r. he judges and makes war. Rev 19.11

RIGHTEOUSNESS'

for his r. sake, to magnify his law Is 42.21
who are persecuted for r. sake, Mt 5.10
But even if you do suffer for r. sake, 1Pe 3.14

RIGHTFUL

fire to the LORD, and his r. dues. Deu 18.01
reward you with a r. habitation. Job 8.06
shall be restored to its r. state. Dan 8.14
share this r. claim upon you, 1Co 9.12

RIGHTLY

Esau said, "Is he not r. named Jacob? Gen 27.36
they have r. said all that they Deu 5.28
'They have r. said all that they 18.17
than wine; r. do they love you. Sol 1.04
he said to him, "You have judged r." Lk 7.43
know that you speak and teach r., 20.21
but if I have spoken r., why do Jn 18.23
judgment of God r. falls upon Rom 2.02
r. handling the word of truth. 2Ti 2.15

RIGHTS

her clothing, or her marital r. Ex 21.10
the people the r. and duties of 1Sa 10.25
man knows the r. of the poor; Pro 29.07
and pervert the r. of all the 31.05
for the r. of all who are left 31.08
maintain the r. of the poor and 31.09
do not defend the r. of the needy. Jer 5.28
give to his wife her conjugal r., 1Co 7.03
made no use of any of these r., 9.15

RIGID

grinds his teeth and becomes r.; Mk 9.18

RIGOR

people of Israel serve with r., Ex 1.13
work they made them serve with r. 1.14
in promoting r. of devotion and Col 2.23

RIM

with a r. of one span around its Eze 43.13
with a r. around it half a cubit 43.17
ledge, and upon the r. round about; 43.20

RIMMON

and R.: in all, twenty-nine cities, Jos 15.32
and going on to R. it bends toward 19.13
the wilderness to the rock of R.; Ju 20.45
the wilderness to the rock of R., 20.47
at the rock of R. four months. 20.47
Benjaminites who were at the rock of R., 21.13
sons of R. a man of Benjamin from 2Sa 4.02
Now the sons of R. the Beerothite, 4.05
the sons of R. the Beerothite, "As 4.09
the house of R. to worship there, 2Ki 5.18
and I bow myself in the house of R., 5.18
when I bow myself in the house of R., 5.18
R., Tochen, and Ashan, five cities, 1Ch 4.32
He has gone up from R., Is 10.27
from Geba to R. south of Jerusalem Zec 14.10

RIMMONO

R. with its pasture lands, Tabor 1Ch 6.77

RIMMONPEREZ

from Rithmah, and encamped at R. Num 33.19
And they set out from R., and 33.20

RIMS

their r., their spokes, and their 1Ki 7.33
The four wheels had r. and they had Eze 1.18
and their r. were full of eyes 1.18
And their r., and their spokes, and 10.12

RING

man took a gold r. weighing a half Gen 24.22
When he saw the r., and the bracelets 24.30
So I put the r. on her nose, and the 24.47
took his signet r. from his hand 41.42
joined at the top, at the first r.; Ex 26.24
joined at the top, at the first r.; 36.29
took his signet r. from his hand Est 3.10
and sealed with the king's r. 3.12
and the king took off his signet r., 8.02
and seal it with the king's r.; 8.08
with the king's r. cannot be 8.08
and sealed with the king's r., 8.10
a piece of money and a r. of gold. Job 42.11
Like a gold r. in a swine's snout is Pro 11.22
Like a gold r. or an ornament of 25.12
were the signet r. on my right Jer 22.24
And I put a r. on your nose, and Eze 16.12
herself with her r. and jewelry, Hos 2.13
and make you like a signet r.; Hag 2.23
and put a r. on his hand, and shoes Lk 15.22

RINGLEADER

and a r. of the sect of the Nazarenes Ac 24.05

RINGS

and the r. that were in their ears; Gen 35.04
shall cast four r. of gold for it Ex 25.12
two r. on the one side of it, and 25.12
and two r. on the other side of it. 25.12
poles into the r. on the sides of 25.14
shall remain in the r. of the ark; 25.15
shall make for it four r. of gold, 25.26
and fasten the r. to the four 25.26
Close to the frame the r. shall lie, 25.27
make their r. of gold for holders 26.29
four bronze r. at its four corners 27.04
poles shall be put through the r., 27.07
for the breastpiece two r. of gold, 28.23
and put the two r. on the two 28.23
gold in the two r. at the edges of 28.24
And you shall make two r. of gold, 28.26
And you shall make two r. of gold, 28.27
of the breastpiece by its r. to the 28.28
to the r. of the ephod with a lace 28.28
And two golden r. shall you make 30.04
"Take off the r. of gold which are 32.02
took off the r. of gold which were 32.03
earrings and signet r. and armlets, 35.22
and made their r. of gold for 36.34
for it four r. of gold for its 37.03
two r. on its one side and two r. on 37.03
poles into the r. on the sides of 37.05
He cast for it four r. of gold, 37.13
fastened the r. to the four 37.13
Close to the frame were the r., 37.14
and made two r. of gold on it under 37.27
He cast four r. on the four corners 38.05
through the r. on the sides of the 38.07
of gold filigree and two gold r., 39.16
and put the two r. on the two 39.16
gold in the two r. at the edges of 39.17
Then they made two r. of gold, 39.19
And they made two r. of gold, 39.20
breastpiece by its r. to the rings 39.21
rings to the r. of the ephod with 39.21
signet r., earrings, and beads, to Num 31.50
to silver r. and marble pillars, Est 1.06

RINGS (cont.)
the signet r. and nose r.; Is 3.21
a man with gold r. and in fine Jas 2.02

RINNAH
Shimon: Amnon, R., Benhanan, and Tilon. 1Ch 4.20

RINSE
they were to r. off what was used 2Ch 4.06

RINSED
shall be scoured, and r. in water. Lev 6.28
without having r. his hands in 15.11
of wood shall be r. in water. 15.12
my delicacies, he has r. me out. Jer 51.34

RIOT
but rather that a r. was beginning, Mt 27.24

RIOTING
danger of being charged with r. today, Ac 19.40

RIP
ones, and r. up their women with child." 2Ki 8.12

RIPE
the season of the first r. grapes. Num 13.20
blossoms, and it bore r. almonds. 17.08
The first r. fruits of all that is 18.13
come to your grave in r. old age, Job 5.26
the sickle, for the harvest is r. Joe 3.13
But when the grain is r., at once Mk 4.29
harvest of the earth is fully r. Rev 14.15
the earth, for its grapes are r. 14.18

RIPENED
forth, and the clusters r. into grapes. Gen 40.10

RIPENING
and the flower becomes a r. grape, Is 18.05

RIPHATH
Gomer: Ashkenaz, R., and Togarmah. Gen 10.03

RIPPED
and he r. up all the women in it 2Ki 15.16
and their pregnant women r. open. Hos 13.16
they have r. up women with child Amo 1.13

RISE
then you may r. up early and go on Gen 19.02
angry that I cannot r. before you, 31.35
"R. up early in the morning and Ex 8.20
"R. up early in the morning and 9.13
nor did any r. from his place for 10.23
"R. up, go forth from among my 12.31
the people would r. up and worship, 33.10
"You shall r. up before the hoary Lev 19.32
come to call you, r., go with them; Num 22.20
"R., Balak, and hear; hearken to 23.18
a scepter shall r. out of Israel; 24.17
'Now r. up, and go over the brook Deu 2.13
'R. up, take your journey, and go 2.24
when you lie down, and when you r. 6.07
when you lie down, and when you r. 11.19
enemies who r. against you to be 28.07
your children who r. up after you, 29.22
people will r. and play the harlot 31.16
Let them r. up and help you, let 32.38
hate him, that they r. not again. 33.11
then you shall r. up from the Jos 8.07
his first-born, "R., and slay them." Ju 8.20
"R. yourself, and fall upon us; 8.21
r. early and rush upon the city; 9.33
cloud of smoke r. up out of the 20.38
signal began to r. out of the city 20.40
If men r. up to pursue you and to 1Sa 25.29
Now then r. early in the morning 29.10
And Absalom used to r. early and 2Sa 15.02
and all who r. up against you for 18.32
through, so that they did not r.; 22.39
in and bid him r. from among his 2Ki 9.02
they said, "Let us r. up and build." Neh 2.18
deliverance will r. for the Jews Est 4.14
and he would r. early in the Job 1.05
the sun, and it does not r.; 9.07
when I r. they talk against me. 19.18
the earth will r. up against him. 20.27
they r. up when they despair of 24.22
On my right hand the rabble r., 30.12
so that they were not able to r.; Ps 18.38
but we shall r. and stand upright. 20.08
and buckler, and r. for my help! 35.02
Malicious witnesses r. up; 35.11
they are thrust down, unable to r. 36.12
he will not r. again from where he 41.08
R. up, come to our help! Deliver 44.26
from those who r. up against me, 59.01
Do the shades r. up to praise thee? 88.10
when its waves r., thou stillest 89.09
R. up, O judge of the earth; 94.02
At midnight I r. to praise thee, 119.62
I r. before dawn and cry for help; 119.147
It is in vain that you r. up early, 127.02
the clouds r. at the end of the 135.07
when I sit down and when I r. up; 139.02
them that r. up against thee? 139.21
be cast into pits, no more to r.! 140.10
disaster from them will r. suddenly, Pro 24.22
but when the wicked r., men 28.12
When the wicked r., men hide 28.28
Her children r. up and call her 31.28
"I will r. now and go about the Sol 3.02
Woe to those who r. early in the Is 5.11
and it will r. over all its channels 8.07
lest they r. and possess the earth, 14.21
"I will r. up against them," says 14.22
it falls, and will not r. again. 24.20
shall live, their bodies shall r. 26.19
For the LORD will r. up as on Mount 28.21
R. up, you women who are at ease, 32.09
stench of their corpses shall r.; 34.03
they cannot r., they are extinguished, 43.17
your light r. in the darkness and 58.10
men fall, do they not r. again? Jer 8.04
makes the mist r. from the ends of 10.13
fall and r. no more, because of the 25.27
they would r. up and burn this city 37.10
I will r., I will cover the earth, I 46.08
against her, and r. up for battle! 49.14
"R. up, advance against Kedar! 49.28
"R. up, advance against a nation at 49.31
makes the mist r. from the ends of 51.16
to r. no more, because of the evil 51.64
he shall even r. up against the Dan 8.25
many shall r. against the king of 11.14
and foul smell of him will r., Joe 2.20
no more to r., is the virgin Israel Amo 5.02
and I will r. against the house of 7.09
and all of it r. like the Nile, and 8.08
shall fall, and never r. again. 8.14
"R. up! let us r. against her for battle!" Ob 1.01
But you r. against my people as an Mic 2.08
when I fall, I shall r.; 7.08
the sun of righteousness shall r., Mal 4.02
"R., take the child and his mother, Mt 2.13
"R., take the child and his mother, 2.20
makes his sun r. on the evil and 5.45
forgiven,' or to say, 'R. and walk'? 9.05
"R., take up your bed and go home." 9.06
children will r. against parents 10.21
them, saying, "R., and have no fear." 17.07
For nation will r. against nation, 24.07
R., let us be going; see, my 26.46
'After three days I will r. again.' 27.63
'R., take up your pallet and walk'? Mk 2.09
"I say to you, r., take up your 2.11

RISE (cont.)
and should sleep and r. night and day, Mk 4.27
and after three days r. again. 8.31
after three days he will r." 9.31
and after three days he will r." 10.34
heart; r., he is calling you." 10.49
For when they r. from the dead, they 12.25
For nation will r. against nation, 13.08
children will r. against parents 13.12
R., let us be going; see, my 14.42
you,' or to say, 'R. and walk'? Lk 5.23
r., take up your bed and go home." 5.24
importunity he will r. and give him 11.08
some one should r. from the dead." 16.31
"R. and go your way; your faith 17.19
and on the third day he will r." 18.33
"Nation will r. against nation, and 21.10
R. and pray that you may not enter 22.46
crucified, and on the third day r." 24.07
do questionings r. in your hearts? 24.38
on the third day r. from the dead, 24.46
"R., take up your pallet, and walk." Jn 5.08
no prophet is to r. from Galilee." 7.52
to her, "Your brother will r. again." 11.23
"I know that he will r. again in the 11.24
saw Mary r. quickly and go out, they 11.31
love the Father. R., let us go hence. 14.31
that he must r. from the dead. 20.09
"R. and go toward the south to the Ac 8.26
but r. and enter the city, and you 9.06
"R. and go to the street called 9.11
r. and make your bed." And 9.34
to the body he said, "Tabitha, r." 9.40
came a voice to him, "R., Peter; 10.13
R. and go down, and accompany them 10.20
a voice saying to me, 'R., Peter; 11.07
to suffer and to r. from the dead, 17.03
'R., and go into Damascus, and there 22.10
R. and be baptized, and wash away 22.16
But r. and stand upon your feet; 26.16
the first to r. from the dead, 26.23
the dead in Christ will r. first; 1Th 4.16
that they might r. again to a Heb 11.35
"R. and measure the temple of God Rev 11.01

RISEN
The sun had r. on the earth when Gen 19.23
but if the sun has r. upon him, Ex 22.03
you have r. in your fathers' stead, Num 32.14
and you have r. up against my Ju 9.18
him, so that he has r. against me, 1Sa 22.13
family has r. against your handmaid, 2Sa 14.07
for I have r. in the place of David 1Ki 8.20
for I have r. in the place of 2Ch 6.10
from of old has r. against kings, Ez 4.19
iniquities have r. higher than our 9.06
my leanness has r. up against me, Job 16.08
false witnesses have r. against me, Ps 27.12
For insolent men have r. against me, 54.03
insolent men have r. up against me; 86.14
glory of the LORD has r. upon you. Is 60.01
pass through, for the water had r.; Eze 47.05
women there has r. no one greater Mt 11.11
'He has r. from the dead,' and the 27.64
not here; for he has r., as he said. 28.06
that he has r. from the dead, and 28.07
And if Satan has r. up against Mk 3.26
man should have r. from the dead. 9.09
to the tomb when the sun had r. 16.02
He has r., he is not here; see the 16.06
those who saw him after he had r. *16.14
one of the old prophets had r. Lk 9.08
one of the old prophets has r. 9.19
householder has r. up and shut the 13.25
"The Lord has r. indeed, and has 24.34
r. from the dead, descended from 2Ti 2.08

RISES
then if the man r. again and walks Ex 21.19
As a lioness it r. up and as a lion Num 23.24
malicious witness r. against any Deu 19.16
be the man that r. up and rebuilds Jos 6.26
that r. toward Seir, as far as 11.17
that r. toward Seir (and Joshua 12.07
like the sun as he r. in his might. Ju 5.31
then, if the king's anger r., 2Sa 11.20
So man lies down and r. not again; Job 14.12
The murderer r. in the dark, that he 24.14
let him that r. up against me be 27.07
what then shall I do when God r. up? 31.14
Who r. up for me against the wicked? Ps 94.16
When the sun r., they get them away 104.22
Light r. in the darkness for the 112.04
falls seven times, and r. again; Pro 24.16
She r. while it is yet night and 31.15
The sun r. and the sun goes down, Ecc 1.05
hastens to the place where it r. 1.05
anger of the ruler r. against you, 10.04
and one r. up at the voice of a 12.04
when he r. to terrify the earth. Is 2.19
when he r. to terrify the earth. 2.21
tongue that r. against you in 54.17
Egypt r. like the Nile, like rivers Jer 46.08
and all of it r. like the Nile, and Amo 9.05
the daughter r. up against her Mic 7.06
—when the sun r., they fly away; Nah 3.17
he who r. to rule the Gentiles; Rom 15.12
For the sun r. with its scorching Jas 1.11
the morning star r. in your hearts. 2Pe 1.19

RISING
a man's hand is r. out of the sea. 1Ki 18.44
are my foes! Many are r. against me; Ps 3.01
Its r. is from the end of the 19.06
earth from the r. of the sun to 50.01
From the r. of the sun to its 113.03
r. early in the morning, will be Pro 27.14
be dark at its r. and the moon Is 13.10
his anger, and in thick r. smoke; 30.27
from the r. of the sun, and he shall 41.25
from the r. of the sun and from the 45.06
his glory from the r. of the sun; 59.19
kings to the brightness of your r. 60.03
"Who is this, r. like the Nile, like Jer 46.07
waters are r. out of the north, and 47.02
Behold their sitting and their r.; Lam 3.63
shall come, r. from the wilderness; Hos 13.15
For from the r. of the sun to its Mal 1.11
what the r. from the dead meant. Mk 9.10
the fall and r. of many in Israel, Lk 2.34
you see a cloud r. in the west, 12.54
ascend from the r. of the sun, Rev 7.02
And I saw a beast r. out of the sea, 13.01

RISK
who went at the r. of their lives? 2Sa 23.17
For at the r. of their lives they 1Ch 11.19

RISKED
and r. his life, and rescued you Ju 9.17
men who have r. their lives for the Ac 15.26
who r. their necks for my life, to Rom 16.04

RISKING
r. his life to complete your service Php 2.30

RISSAH
from Libnah, and encamped at R. Num 33.21
And they set out from R., and 33.22

RITE
observe this r. as an ordinance for Ex 12.24

RITES
having charge of the r. within the Num 3.38

RITES (cont.)

for the Jewish r. of purification, Jn 2.06
things to be purified with these r., Heb 9.23

RITHMAH

from Hazeroth, and encamped at R. Num 33.18
And they set out from R., and 33.19

RITUAL

tent, performing their r. duties; Heb 9.06

RIVAL

a woman as a r. wife to her sister, Lev 18.18
And her r. used to provoke her 1Sa 1.06
the garden of God could not r. it, Eze 31.08

RIVALRY

indeed preach Christ from envy and r., Php 1.15

RIVER

A r. flowed out of Eden to water Gen 2.10
The name of the second r. is Gihon; 2.13
name of the third r. is Hiddekel, 2.14
And the fourth r. is the Euphrates. 2.14
give this land, from the r. of Egypt 15.18
to the great r., the r. Euphrates, 15.18
came down to bathe at the r., Ex 2.05
her maidens walked beside the r.; 2.05
at Pethor, which is near the R., Num 22.05
afar, like gardens beside a r., 24.06
far as the great r., the r. Euphrates. Deu 1.07
banks of the r. Jabbok and the 2.37
as far over as the r. Jabbok, 3.16
and from the R., the r. Euphrates, to the 11.24
far as the great r., the r. Euphrates, Jos 1.04
the valley as far as the r. Jabbok, 12.02
from beyond the R. and led him 24.03
your fathers served beyond the R., 24.14
served in the region beyond the R., 24.15
meet you by the r. Kishon with his Ju 4.07
Haroshethhagoiim to the r. Kishon. 4.13
his power at the r. Euphrates. 2Sa 8.03
the r. of Gozan, and in the cities 2Ki 17.06
the r. of Gozan, and in the cities 18.11
of Assyria to the r. Euphrates. 23.29
Brook of Egypt to the r. Euphrates. 24.07
and the r. Gozan, to this day. 1Ch 5.26
his monument at the r. Euphrates. 18.03
of the province Beyond the R., Ez 4.10
Beyond the R., send greeting. 4.11
in the province Beyond the R. 4.16
province Beyond the R., greeting. 4.17
the whole province Beyond the R. 4.20
Beyond the R. and Shetharbozenai 5.03
Beyond the R. and Shetharbozenai 5.06
Beyond the R. sent to Darius the 5.06
of the province Beyond the R. 6.06
province Beyond the R., keep away; 6.06
of the province from Beyond the R. 6.08
of the province Beyond the R., 6.13
in the province Beyond the R.: 7.21
in the province Beyond the R., 7.25
them to the r. that runs to Ahava, 8.15
at the r. Ahava, that we might 8.21
from the r. Ahava on the twelfth 8.31
of the province Beyond the R.; 8.36
of the province Beyond the R., Neh 2.07
of the province Beyond the R., 2.09
of the province Beyond the R. 3.07
and a r. wastes away and dries up, Job 14.11
Behold, if the r. is turbulent he is 40.23
drink from the r. of thy delights. Ps 36.08
There is a r. whose streams make 46.04
the r. of God is full of water; 65.09
men passed through the r. on foot. 66.06
and from the R. to the ends of the 72.08
the sea, and its shoots to the R. 80.11
Sisera and Jabin at the r. Kishon, 83.09
through the desert like a r. 105.41
which is hired beyond the R.— Is 7.20
against them the waters of the R., 8.07
hand over the R. with his scorching 11.15
and the r. will be parched and dry; 19.05
day from the r. Euphrates to the 27.12
peace would have been like a r., 48.18
extend prosperity to her like a r., 66.12
was by the r. Euphrates at Carchemish Jer 46.02
north by the r. Euphrates they 46.06
north country by the r. Euphrates. 46.10
among the exiles by the r. Chebar, Eze 1.01
of the Chaldeans by the r. Chebar; 1.03
Telabib, who dwelt by the r. Chebar. 3.15
which I had seen by the r. Chebar; 3.23
that I saw by the r. Chebar. 10.15
the God of Israel by the r. Chebar; 10.20
I had seen by the r. Chebar. 10.22
which I had seen by the r. Chebar; 43.03
and it was a r. that I could not 47.05
a r. that could not be passed 47.05
me back along the bank of the r. 47.06
the bank of the r. very many trees 47.07
And wherever the r. goes every 47.09
will live where the r. goes. 47.09
the banks, on both sides of the r., 47.12
vision, and I was at the r. Ulai. Dan 8.02
ram standing on the bank of the r. 8.03
standing on the bank of the r., 8.06
on the bank of the great r., 10.04
to Egypt, and from Egypt to the R., Mic 7.12
The r. gates are opened, the palace Nah 2.06
and from the R. to the ends of the Zec 9.10
baptized by him in the r. Jordan, Mt 3.06
baptized by him in the r. Jordan, Mk 1.05
bound at the great r. Euphrates. Rev 9.14
water like a r. out of his mouth 12.15
swallowed the r. which the dragon 12.16
his bowl on the great r. Euphrates, 16.12
showed me the r. of the water of 22.01
also, on either side of the r., 22.02

RIVER'S

it among the reeds at the r. brink. Ex 2.03
wait for him by the r. brink, 7.15

RIVERS

there it divided and became four r. Gen 2.10
over their r., their canals, and Ex 7.19
hand with your rod over the r., 8.05
the seas or in the r., you may eat. Lev 11.09
the seas or the r. that has not 11.10
the r. of Damascus, better than all 2Ki 5.12
He will not look upon the r., Job 20.17
and established it upon the r. Ps 24.02
caused waters to flow down like r. 78.16
He turned their r. to blood, 78.44
sea and his right hand on the r. 89.25
He turns r. into a desert, springs 107.33
which is beyond the r. of Ethiopia; Is 18.01
conquering, whose land the r. divide. 18.02
conquering, whose land the r. divide, 18.07
us a place of broad r. and streams, 33.21
I will open r. on the bare heights, 41.18
I will turn the r. into islands, 42.15
and through the r., they shall not 43.02
wilderness and r. in the desert. 43.19
r. in the desert, to give drink to 43.20
'Be dry, I will dry up your r.'; 44.27
your legs, pass through the r. 47.02
up the sea, I make the r. a desert; 50.02
like r. whose waters surge? Jer 46.07
like r. whose waters surge. 46.08
my eyes flow with r. of tears Lam 3.48
making its r. flow round the place Eze 31.04
mourn for it, and restrain its r., 31.15
you burst forth in your r., 32.02
with your feet, and foul their r. 32.02

RIVERS (cont.)
and cause their r. to run like oil, Eze 32.14
with ten thousands of r. of oil? Mic 6.07
it dry, he dries up all the r.; Nah 1.04
Was thy wrath against the r., O LORD? Hab 3.08
Was thy anger against the r., 3.08
didst cleave the earth with r. 3.09
From beyond the r. of Ethiopia my Zep 3.10
shall flow r. of living water. Jn 7.38
journeys, in danger from r., 2Co 11.26
a third of the r. and on the Rev 8.10
bowl into the r. and the fountains 16.04

RIVERSIDE
we went outside the gate to the r., Ac 16.13

RIZIA
The sons of Ulla: Arah, Hanniel, and R. 1Ch 7.39

RIZPAH
had a concubine, whose name was R., 2Sa 3.07
the two sons of R. the daughter of 21.08
Then R. the daughter of Aiah took 21.10
was told what R. the daughter of 21.11

ROAD
which is on the r. to Timnah; Gen 38.14
He went over to her at the r. side, 38.16
of the LORD standing in the r., Num 22.23
the ass turned aside out of the r., 22.23
the ass, to turn her into the r. 22.23
didst stand in the r. against me. 22.34
from the Arabah r. from Elath and Deu 2.08
I will go only by the r., 2.27
west of the r., toward the going 11.30
who misleads a blind man on the r. 27.18
the r. on which you are going will Ju 4.09
upon his seat by the r. watching, 1Sa 4.13
is beside the r. on the east of 26.03
the Horonaim r. by the side of the 2Sa 13.34
So David and his men went on the r., 16.13
the Shilonite found him on the r. 1Ki 11.29
met him on the r. and killed him. 13.24
and his body was thrown in the r., 13.24
and saw the body thrown in the r., 13.25
found his body thrown in the r., 13.28
Shallecheth on the r. that goes up. 1Ch 26.16
four at the r. and two at the 26.18
They thrust the poor off the r.; Job 24.04
corner, taking the r. to her house Pro 7.08
says, "There is a lion in the r.! 26.13
Even when the fool walks on the r., Ecc 10.03
on the r. to Horonaim they raise a Is 15.05
into the field, nor walk on the r.; Jer 6.25
highway, the r. by which you went. 31.21
Man the ramparts; watch the r.; Nah 2.01
spread their garments on the r., Mt 21.08
trees and spread them on the r. 21.08
And they were on the r., Mk 10.32
spread their garments on the r., 11.08
As they were going along the r., Lk 9.57
and salute no one on the r. 10.04
a priest was going down that r.; 10.31
spread their garments on the r. 19.36
us while he talked to us on the r., 24.32
told what had happened on the r., 24.35
south to the r. that goes down Ac 8.26
to Gaza." This is a desert r. 8.26
went along the r. they came to 8.36
to you on the r. by which you came, 9.17
them how on the r. he had seen the 9.27

ROADS
You shall prepare the r., and Deu 19.03
not asked those who travel the r., Job 21.29
they have made their r. crooked, Is 59.08
"Stand by the r., and look, and ask Jer 6.16
in their ways, in the ancient r., 18.15
The r. to Zion mourn, for none come Lam 1.04

ROADSIDE
two blind men sitting by the r., Mt 20.30
of Timaeus, was sitting by the r. Mk 10.46
man was sitting by the r. begging; Lk 18.35

ROAM
They r. about for food, and growl if Ps 59.15

ROAMED
places where David and his men had r. 1Sa 30.31

ROAR
Let the sea r., and all that fills 1Ch 16.32
The r. of the lion, the voice of the Job 4.10
me about in the r. of the storm. 30.22
though its waters r. and foam, Ps 46.03
let the sea r., and all that fills 96.11
Let the sea r., and all that fills 98.07
The young lions r. for their prey, 104.21
a lion, like young lions they r.; Is 5.29
Ah, the r. of nations, they r. like the 17.12
The nations r. like the roaring of 17.13
Let the sea r. and all that fills 42.10
up the sea so that its waves r.— 51.15
though they r., they cannot pass Jer 5.22
but with the r. of a great tempest 11.16
'The LORD will r. from on high, 25.30
he will r. mightily against his 25.30
up the sea so that its waves r.— 31.35
"They shall r. together like lions; 51.38
Their waves r. like many waters, the 51.55
the LORD, he will r. like a lion; Hos 11.10
yea, he will r., and his sons shall 11.10
Does a lion r. in the forest, when Amo 3.04
Hark, the r. of the lions, for the Zec 11.03

ROARED
behold, a young lion r. against him; Ju 41.05
Thy foes have r. in the midst of Ps 74.04
The lions have r. against him, they Jer 2.15
against him, they have r. loudly. 2.15
The lion has r.; who will not fear? Amo 3.08

ROARING
at me, like a ravening and r. lion. Ps 22.13
who dost still the r. of the seas, 65.07
the r. of their waves, the tumult of 65.07
voice, the floods lift up their r. 93.03
Like a r. lion or a charging bear Pro 28.15
Their r. is like a lion, like young Is 5.29
that day, like the r. of the sea. 5.30
roar like the r. of mighty waters! 17.12
roar like the r. of many waters, 17.13
sound of them is like the r. sea; Jer 6.23
of them is like the r. of the sea; 50.42
were in it at the sound of his r. Eze 19.07
her are like a r. lion tearing the 22.25
Her officials within her are r. lions; Zep 3.03
perplexity at the r. of the sea and Lk 21.25
devil prowls around like a r. lion, 1Pe 5.08
with a loud voice, like a lion r.; Rev 10.03

ROARS
After it his voice r.; he thunders Job 37.04
And the LORD r. from Zion, and Joe 3.16
"The LORD r. from Zion, and utters Amo 1.02

ROAST
"Give meat for the priest to r.; for 1Sa 2.15

ROASTED
shall eat the flesh that night, r.; Ex 12.08
but r., its head with its legs and 12.09
And they r. the passover lamb with 2Ch 35.13
I r. flesh and have eaten; and shall Is 44.19
king of Babylon r. in the fire," Jer 29.22

ROASTS

eats flesh, he r. meat and is satisfied; Is 44.16

ROB

oppress your neighbor or r. him. Lev 19.13
which shall r. you of your children, 26.22
Do not r. the poor, because he is Pro 22.22
justice and to r. the poor of my Is 10.02
and they will r. you of your Eze 5.17
Will man r. God? Yet you are Mal 3.08
"R. no one by violence or by false Lk 3.14
who abhor idols, do you r. temples? Rom 2.22

ROBBED

only oppressed and r. continually, Deu 28.29
and they r. all who passed by them Ju 9.25
like a bear r. of her cubs in the 2Sa 17.08
they are r. of sleep unless they Pro 4.16
man meet a she-bear r. of her cubs, 17.12
But this is a people r. and plundered, Is 42.22
the oppressor him who has been r., Jer 21.12
the oppressor him who has been r. 22.03
r. his brother, and did what is not Eze 18.18
them like a bear r. of her cubs, Hos 13.08
I r. other churches by accepting 2Co 11.08

ROBBER

in wait like a r. and increases Pro 23.28
will come upon you like a r., 24.34
"If he begets a son who is a r., Eze 18.10
"Have you come out as against a r., Mt 26.55
"Have you come out as against a r., Mk 14.48
"Have you come out as against a r., Lk 22.52
way, that man is a thief and a r.; Jn 10.01
but Barabbas!" Now Barabbas was a r. 18.40
or r.—not even to eat with such a 1Co 5.11

ROBBERS

The tents of r. are at peace, and Job 12.06
the spoiler, and Israel to the r.? Is 42.24
become a den of r. in your eyes? Jer 7.11
r. shall enter and profane it, Eze 7.22
As r. lie in wait for a man, so the Hos 6.09
but you make it a den of r." Mt 21.13
Then two r. were crucified with him, 27.38
And the r. who were crucified with 27.44
But you have made it a den of r." Mk 11.17
And with him they crucified two r., 15.27
to Jericho, and he fell among r., Lk 10.30
to the man who fell among the r.?" 10.36
but you have made it a den of r." 19.46
came before me are thieves and r.; Jn 10.08
this world, or the greedy and r., 1Co 5.10
nor r. will inherit the kingdom of 6.10
danger from r., danger from my own 2Co 11.26

ROBBERY

or through r., or if he has oppressed Lev 6.02
shall restore what he took by r., 6.04
extortion, set no vain hopes on r.; Ps 62.10
love justice, I hate r. and wrong; Is 61.08
commits no r., gives his bread to Eze 18.07
commits r., does not restore the 18.12
commits no r., but gives his bread 18.16
practiced extortion and committed r.; 22.29
gives back what he had taken by r., 33.15
up violence and r. in their Amo 3.10

ROBBING

and are r. the threshing floors. 1Sa 23.01
man rob God? Yet you are r. me. Mal 3.08
But you say, 'How are we r. thee?' 3.08
with a curse, for you are r. me; 3.09

ROBE

he made him a long r. with sleeves. Gen 37.03
they stripped him of his r., the 37.23
the long r. with sleeves that he 37.23
Then they took Joseph's r., and 37.31
and dipped the r. in the blood; 37.31
sent the long r. with sleeves and 37.32
whether it is your son's r. or not." 37.32
it, and said, "It is my son's r.; 37.33
a r., a coat of checker work, a Ex 28.04
shall make the r. of the ephod all 28.31
about on the skirts of the r. 28.34
the coat and the r. of the ephod, 29.05
He also made the r. of the ephod 39.22
opening of the r. in it was like 39.23
skirts of the r. they made pomegranates 39.24
the skirts of the r. round about, 39.25
skirts of the r. for ministering; 39.26
and clothed him with the r., Lev 8.07
him a little r. and take it to him 1Sa 2.19
the skirt of his r., and it tore. 15.27
himself of the r. that was upon 18.04
cut off the skirt of Saul's r. 24.04
the skirt of your r. in my hand; 24.11
I cut off the skirt of your r., 24.11
and he is wrapped in a r. 28.14
was wearing a long r. with sleeves; 2Sa 13.18
the long-sleeved r. which she wore; 13.19
clothed with a r. of fine linen, 1Ch 15.27
and rent his r., and shaved his Job 1.20
justice was like a r. and a turban. 29.14
and instead of a rich r., Is 3.24
and I will clothe him with your r., 22.21
off your veil, strip off your r., 47.02
me with the r. of righteousness, as 61.10
bind them in the skirts of your r. Eze 5.03
removed his r., and covered himself Jon 3.06
you strip the r. from the peaceful, Mic 2.08
shall take hold of the r. of a Jew, Zec 8.23
him and put a scarlet r. upon him, Mt 27.28
him, they stripped him of the r., 27.31
right side, dressed in a white r.; Mk 16.05
servants, 'Bring quickly the best r., Lk 15.22
and arrayed him in a purple r.; Jn 19.02
crown of thorns and the purple r. 19.05
with a long r. and with a golden Rev 1.13
given a white r. and told to rest 6.11
He is clad in a r. dipped in blood, 19.13
On his r. and on his thigh he has a 19.16

ROBED

The LORD reigns; he is r. in majesty; Ps 93.01
the LORD is r., he is girded with 93.01
r. in pure bright linen, and their Rev 15.06

ROBES

their thrones, arrayed in their r., 1Ki 22.10
into battle, but you wear your r. 22.30
their thrones, arrayed in their r.; 2Ch 18.09
into battle, but you wear your r. 18.29
on her royal r. and stood in the Est 5.01
let royal r. be brought, which the 6.08
and let the r. and the horse be 6.09
take the r. and the horse, as you 6.10
So Haman took the r. and the horse, 6.11
king in royal r. of blue and white, 8.15
they rent their r. and sprinkled Job 2.12
your r. are all fragrant with myrrh Ps 45.08
in her chamber with gold-woven r.; 45.13
in many-colored r. she is led to 45.14
down on the collar of his r.! 133.02
the festal r., the mantles, the Is 3.22
their thrones, and remove their r., Eze 26.16
Then the high priest tore his r., Mt 26.65
who like to go about in long r., Mk 12.38
who like to go about in long r., Lk 20.46
two men stood by them in white r., Ac 1.10
day Herod put on his royal r., 12.21
of gold, and wearing of r., 1Pe 3.03
the Lamb, clothed in white r., Rev 7.09
"Who are these, clothed in white r., 7.13

ROBES (cont.)
washed their r. and made them Rev 7.14
Blessed are those who wash their r., 22.14

ROBS
He who r. his father or his mother Pro 28.24

ROCK
the Shepherd, the R. of Israel), Gen 49.24
you there on the r. at Horeb; Ex 17.06
and you shall strike the r., 17.06
where you shall stand upon the r.; 33.21
will put you in a cleft of the r., 33.22
And the r. badger, because it chews Lev 11.05
and tell the r. before their eyes Num 20.08
bring water out of the r. for them; 20.08
assembly together before the r., 20.10
forth water for you out of this r.? 20.10
and struck the r. with his rod 20.11
and your nest is set in the r.; 24.21
you water out of the flinty r., Deu 8.15
and the r. badger, because they chew 14.07
"The R., his work is perfect; 32.04
made him suck honey out of the r., 32.13
and oil out of the flinty r. 32.13
scoffed at the R. of his salvation 32.15
unmindful of the R. that begot you, 32.18
unless their R. had sold them, and 32.30
For their r. is not as our R., even 32.31
the r. in which they took refuge. 32.37
cakes, and put them on this r., Ju 6.20
fire from the r. and consumed the 6.21
they killed Oreb at the r. of Oreb, 7.25
offered it upon the r. to the LORD, 13.19
in the cleft of the r. of Etam. 15.08
to the cleft of the r. of Etam, 15.11
and brought him up from the r. 15.13
the wilderness to the r. of Rimmon; 20.45
the wilderness to the r. of Rimmon, 20.47
abode at the r. of Rimmon four 20.47
who were at the r. of Rimmon, 21.13
there is no r. like our God. 1Sa 2.02
down to the r. which is in the 23.25
place was called the R. of Escape. 23.38
spread it for herself on the r., 2Sa 21.10
He said, "The LORD is my r., 22.02
my God, my r., in whom I take refuge, 22.03
And who is a r., except our God 22.32
"The LORD lives; and blessed be my r., 22.47
be my God, the r. of my salvation, 22.47
the R. of Israel has said to me: 23.03
down to the r. to David at the 1Ch 11.15
to the top of a r. and threw them 2Ch 25.12
them down from the top of the r.; 25.12
them from the r. for their thirst, Neh 9.15
and the r. is removed from its Job 14.18
or the r. be removed out of its 18.04
were graven in the r. for ever! 19.24
cling to the r. for want of 24.08
"Man puts his hand to the flinty r., 28.09
and the r. poured out for me 29.06
On the r. he dwells and makes his 39.28
The LORD is my r., and my fortress, Ps 18.02
my r., in whom I take refuge, my 18.02
And who is a r., except our God?— 18.31
The LORD lives; and blessed be my r., 18.46
O LORD, my r. and my redeemer. 19.14
he will set me high upon a r. 27.05
my r., be not deaf to me, lest, if 28.01
Be thou a r. of refuge for me, a 31.02
thou art my r. and my fortress; 31.03
bog, and set my feet upon a r., 40.02
I say to God, my r.; "Why hast 42.09
thou me to the r. that is higher 61.02
He only is my r. and my salvation, 62.02
He only is my r. and my salvation, 62.06
my mighty r., my refuge is God. 62.07
Be thou to me a r. of refuge, 71.03
for thou art my r. and my fortress 71.03
He made streams come out of the r., 78.16
He smote the r. so that water 78.20
They remembered that God was their r., 78.35
honey from the r. I would satisfy 81.16
and the R. of my salvation. 89.26
he is my r., and there is no 92.15
and my God the r. of my refuge. 94.22
noise to the r. of our salvation! 95.01
He opened the r., and water gushed 105.41
who turns the r. into a pool of 114.08
As a r. which one cleaves and 141.07
my r., who trains my hands for war, 144.01
my r. and my fortress, my stronghold 144.02
sky, the way of a serpent on a r., Pro 30.19
O my dove, in the clefts of the r., Sol 2.14
Enter into the r., and hide in the Is 2.10
and a r. of stumbling to both 8.14
he smote Midian at the r. of Oreb; 10.26
remembered the R. of your refuge; 17.10
habitation for yourself in the r.? 22.16
the LORD GOD is an everlasting r. 26.04
of the LORD, to the R. of Israel. 30.29
His r. shall pass away in terror, 31.09
of a great r. in a weary land. 32.02
There is no R.; I know not any." 44.08
water flow for them from the r.; 48.21
he cleft the r. and the water 48.21
look to the r. from which you were 51.01
made their faces harder than r.; Jer 5.03
hide it there in a cleft of the r. 13.04
O r. of the plain, says the LORD; 21.13
which breaks the r. in pieces? 23.29
"Leave the cities, and dwell in the r., 48.28
who live in the clefts of the r., 49.16
she put it on the bare r., she did Eze 24.07
set on the bare r. the blood she 24.08
from her, and make her a bare r. 26.04
I will make you a bare r.; you 26.14
who live in the clefts of the r., Ob 1.03
and thou, O R., hast established Hab 1.12
who built his house upon the r.; Mt 7.24
it had been founded on the r. 7.25
and on this r. I will build my 16.18
tomb, which he had hewn in the r.; 27.60
which had been hewn out of the r.; Mk 15.46
and laid the foundation upon r.; Lk 6.48
And some fell on the r.; and as 8.06
And the ones on the r. are those who, 8.13
a r. that will make them fall; Rom 9.33
supernatural R. which followed 1Co 10.04
them, and the R. was Christ. 10.04
a r. that will make them fall"; for 1Pe 2.08

ROCKED
"Then the earth reeled and r.; the 2Sa 22.08
Then the earth reeled and r.; the Ps 18.07

ROCK-HEWN
shroud, and laid him in a r. tomb, Lk 23.53

ROCKS
in holes and in r. and in tombs 1Sa 13.06
men in front of the Wildgoats' R. 24.02
in pieces the r. before the LORD, 1Ki 19.11
stoneheap; he lives among the r. Job 8.17
He cuts out channels in the r., 28.10
holes of the earth and of the r. 30.06
He cleft r. in the wilderness, and Ps 78.15
the r. are a refuge for the badgers 104.18
and dashes them against the r.! 137.09
they make their homes in the r.; Pro 30.26
caves of the r. and the holes of Is 2.19
caverns of the r. and the clefts 2.21
and in the clefts of the r., 7.19
will be the fortresses of r.; 33.16
valleys, under the clefts of the r.? 57.05
they enter thickets; they climb among r.; Jer 4.29

ROCKS (cont.)
and out of the clefts of the r. Jer 16.16
Do horses run upon r.? Does one Amo 6.12
and the r. are broken asunder by Nah 1.06
earth shook, and the r. were split; Mt 27.51
that we might run on the r., Ac 27.29
and among the r. of the mountains, Rev 6.15
calling to the mountains and r., 6.16

ROCKY
there was a r. crag on the one side 1Sa 14.04
one side and a r. crag on the 14.04
in the fastness of the r. crag. Job 39.28
Other seeds fell on r. ground, Mt 13.05
As for what was sown on r. ground, 13.20
Other seed fell on r. ground, Mk 4.05
are the ones sown upon r. ground, 4.16

ROD
that in your hand?" He said, "A r." Ex 4.02
and it became a r. in his hand— 4.04
shall take in your hand this r., 4.17
his hand Moses took the r. of God. 4.20
'Take your r. and cast it down 7.09
cast down his r. before Pharaoh 7.10
For every man cast down his r., 7.12
But Aaron's r. swallowed up their 7.12
your hand the r. which was turned 7.15
Nile with the r. that is in my 7.17
'Take your r. and stretch out your 7.19
lifted up the r. and struck the 7.20
hand with your r. over the rivers, 8.05
out your r. and strike the dust of 8.16
stretched out his hand with his r., 8.17
stretched forth his r. toward heaven; 9.23
forth his r. over the land of 10.13
Lift up your r., and stretch out 14.16
your hand the r. with which you 17.05
hill with the r. of God in my hand 17.09
with a r. and the slave dies under 21.20
Write each man's name upon his r., Num 17.02
Aaron's name upon the r. of Levi. 17.03
shall be one r. for the head of 17.03
And the r. of the man whom I choose 17.05
and the r. of Aaron was among their 17.06
the r. of Aaron for the house of 17.08
looked, and each man took his r. 17.09
"Put back the r. of Aaron before 17.10
"Take the r., and assemble the 20.08
And Moses took the r. from before 20.09
struck the rock with his r. twice; 20.11
chasten him with the r. of men, 2Sa 7.14
Let him take his r. away from me, Job 9.34
and no r. of God is upon them. 21.09
shall break them with a r. of iron, Ps 2.09
thy r. and thy staff, they comfort 23.04
with the r. and their iniquity 89.32
but a r. is for the back of him who Pro 10.13
He who spares the r. hates his son, 13.24
of a fool is a r. for his back, 14.03
and the r. of his fury will fail. 22.08
but the r. of discipline drives it 22.15
if you beat him with a r., he will 23.13
him with the r. you will save his 23.14
and a r. for the back of fools. 26.03
The r. and reproof give wisdom, but 29.15
the r. of his oppressor, thou hast Is 9.04
the r. of my anger, the staff of my 10.05
As if a r. should wield him who 10.15
smite with the r. and lift up 10.24
and his r. will be over the sea, and 10.26
the earth with the r. of his mouth, 11.04
that the r. which smote you is 14.29
with a stick, and cummin with a r. 28.27
LORD, when he smites with his r. 30.31
and I said, "I see a r. of almond." Jer 1.11
affliction under the r. of his wrath; Lam 3.01
grown up into a r. of wickedness; Eze 7.11
I will make you pass under the r., 20.37
You have despised the r., my son, 21.10
could it do if you despise the r.? 21.13
with a r. they strike upon the Mic 5.01
Shall I come to you with a r., 1Co 4.21
and Aaron's r. that budded, and the Heb 9.04
shall rule them with a r. of iron, Rev 2.27
given a measuring r. like a staff, 11.01
all the nations with a r. of iron, 12.05
will rule them with a r. of iron; 19.15
had a measuring r. of gold to 21.15
he measured the city with his r., 21.16

RODANIM
Elishah, Tarshish, Kittim, and R. 1Ch 1.07

RODE
and r. upon the camels and followed Gen 24.61
thirty sons who r. on thirty asses Ju 10.04
grandsons, who r. on seventy asses; 12.14
And as she r. on the ass, and came 1Sa 25.20
He r. on a cherub, and flew; 2Sa 22.11
And Ahab r. and went to Jezreel. 1Ki 18.45
when you and I r. side by side 2Ki 9.25
me but the beast on which I r. Neh 2.12
r. out in haste, urged by the king's Est 8.14
He r. on a cherub, and flew; Ps 18.10
And as he r. along, they spread Lk 19.36

RODS
took fresh r. of poplar and almond Gen 30.37
them, exposing the white of the r. 30.37
He set the r. which he had peeled 30.38
in front of the r. and so the 30.39
Jacob laid the r. in the runnels 30.41
they might breed among the r., 30.41
Aaron's rod swallowed up their r. Ex 7.12
of Israel, and get from them r., Num 17.02
their fathers' houses, twelve r. 17.02
and all their leaders gave him r., 17.06
their fathers' houses, twelve r.; 17.06
rod of Aaron was among their r. 17.06
deposited the r. before the LORD 17.07
out all the r. from before the 17.09
gave orders to beat them with r. Ac 16.22
Three times I have been beaten with r.; 2Co 11.25

ROEBUCK
the r., the wild goat, the ibex, the Deu 14.05

ROEBUCKS
harts, gazelles, r., and fatted fowl. 1Ki 4.23

ROGELIM
Barzillai the Gileadite from R., 2Sa 17.27
Gileadite had come down from R.; 19.31

ROHGAH
Shemer his brother: R., Jehubbah, and Aram. 1Ch 7.34

ROLL
shepherds would r. the stone from Gen 29.03
"R. great stones against the mouth Jos 10.18
r. a great stone to me here." 1Sa 14.33
they come; amid the crash they r. on. Job 30.14
in the r. of the book it is written Ps 40.07
and they r. upward in a column of Is 9.18
and the skies r. up like a scroll. 34.04
gird on sackcloth, and r. in ashes; Jer 6.26
and r. in ashes, you lords of the 25.34
and r. you down from the crags, and 51.25
But let justice r. down like waters, Amo 5.24
in Bethleaphrah r. yourselves in Mic 1.10
"Who will r. away the stone for us Mk 16.03
like a mantle thou wilt r. them up, Heb 1.12
written of me in the r. of the book." 10.07

ROLLED
the stone is r. from the mouth of Gen 29.08
went up and r. the stone from the 29.10
"This day I have r. away the Jos 5.09
and r. it up, and struck the water, 2Ki 2.08
every garment r. in blood will be Is 9.05
nor is a cart wheel r. over cummin; 28.27
like a weaver I have r. up my life; 38.12
and he r. a great stone to the door Mt 27.60
and came and r. back the stone, 28.02
he fell on the ground and r. about, Mk 9.20
and he r. a stone against the door 15.46
saw that the stone was r. back; 16.04
found the stone r. away from the Lk 24.02
cloths but r. up in a place by Jn 20.07
like a scroll that is r. up, Rev 6.14

ROLLING
will come back upon him who starts it r. Pro 26.27

ROMAMTIEZER
and R., Joshbekashah, Mallothi, Hothir, 1Ch 25.04
to R., his sons and his brethren, twelve. 25.31

ROMAN
district of Macedonia, and a R. colony. Ac 16.12
men who are R. citizens, and have 16.37
heard that they were R. citizens; 16.38
scourge a man who is a R. citizen, 22.25
For this man is a R. citizen." 22.26
him, "Tell me, are you a R. citizen?" 22.27
that Paul was a R. citizen and 22.29
learned that he was a R. citizen. 23.27

ROMANS
and the R. will come and destroy both Jn 11.48
not lawful for us R. to accept or Ac 16.21
custom of the R. to give up any 25.16
Jerusalem into the hands of the R. 28.17

ROME
to Cyrene, and visitors from R., Ac 2.10
commanded all the Jews to leave R. 18.02
been there, I must also see R. 19.21
you must bear witness also at R. 23.11
seven days. And so we came to R. 28.14
And when we came into R., Paul was 28.16
To all God's beloved in R., who are Rom 1.07
gospel to you also who are in R. 1.15
he arrived in R. he searched for 2Ti 1.17

ROOF
Make a r. for the ark, and finish it Gen 6.16
come under the shelter of my r. 19.08
shall make a parapet for your r., Deu 22.08
But she had brought them up to the r., Jos 2.06
she had laid in order on the r. 2.06
she came up to them on the r., 2.08
alone in his cool r. chamber. Ju 3.20
doors of the r. chamber upon him, 3.23
doors of the r. chamber were 3.24
open the doors of the r. chamber, 3.25
they went to the r. of the tower. 9.51
and on the r. there were about 16.27
was spread for Saul upon the r., 1Sa 9.25
Samuel called to Saul upon the r., 9.26
upon the r. of the king's house, 2Sa 11.02
he saw from the r. a woman bathing 11.02
a tent for Absalom upon the r.; 16.22
went up to the r. of the gate by 18.24
Let us make a small r. chamber with 2Ki 4.10
altars on the r. of the upper 23.12
each on his r., and in their courts Neh 8.16
cleaved to the r. of their mouth. Job 29.10
cleave to the r. of my mouth, Ps 137.06
Through sloth the r. sinks in, Ecc 10.18
cleaves to the r. of its mouth for Lam 4.04
cleave to the r. of your mouth, Eze 3.26
and raise a r. of shields against 26.08
walking on the r. of the royal Dan 4.29
to have you come under my r.; Mt 8.08
they removed the r. above him; Mk 2.04
went up on the r. and let him down Lk 5.19
to have you come under my r.; 7.06

ROOFS
upon whose r. incense has been Jer 19.13
houses on whose r. incense has 32.29
bow down on the r. to the host of Zep 1.05

ROOM
Is there r. in your father's house Gen 24.23
provender enough, and r. to lodge in." 24.25
now the LORD has made r. for us, 26.22
man of Israel into the inner r., Num 25.08
into the inner r. of the house of 2Ki 10.25
and of the r. for the mercy seat; 1Ch 28.11
hast given me r. when I was in Ps 4.01
gift makes r. for him and brings Pro 18.16
field, until there is no more r., Is 5.08
make r. for me to dwell in. 49.20
because there is no r. elsewhere. Jer 7.32
every man in his r. of pictures? Eze 8.12
of the one side r. to the back of 40.13
into the inner r. and measured the 41.03
And he measured the length of the r., 41.04
and the inner r. and the outer 41.15
the door, even to the inner r., 41.17
in the inner r. and the nave were 41.17
Let the bridegroom leave his r., Joe 2.16
till there is no r. for them. Zec 10.10
go into your r. and shut the door Mt 6.06
there was no longer r. for them, Mk 2.02
Teacher says, Where is my guest r., 14.14
a large upper r. furnished and 14.15
been done, and still there is r.' Lk 14.22
says to you, Where is the guest r., 22.11
you a large upper r. furnished; 22.12
they went up to the upper r., Ac 1.13
her, they laid her in an upper r. 9.37
they took him to the upper r. 9.39
longer have any r. for work in Rom 15.23
time, prepare a guest r. for me, Phm 1.22

ROOMS
make r. in the ark, and cover it Gen 6.14
flowers, in the inner and outer r. 1Ki 6.29
gold in the inner and outer r. 6.30
its upper r., and its inner chambers, 1Ch 28.11
by knowledge the r. are filled with Pro 24.04
and his upper r. by injustice; Jer 22.13
great house with spacious upper r., 22.14
and the side r., one reed long, and Eze 40.07
between the side r., five cubits; 40.07
were three side r. on either side 40.10
There was a barrier before the side r., 40.12
and the side r. were six cubits on 40.12
into their jambs in the side r., 40.16
Its side r., three on either side, 40.21
Its side r., its jambs, and its 40.29
Its side r., its jambs, and its 40.33
Its side r., its jambs, and its 40.36
say, 'Lo, he is in the inner r., Mt 24.26
in private r. shall be proclaimed Lk 12.03
In my Father's house are many r.; Jn 14.02

ROOT
be among you a r. bearing poisonous Deu 29.18
and r. up Israel out of this good 1Ki 14.15
Judah shall again take r. downward, 2Ki 19.30
I have seen the fool taking r., Job 5.03
Though its r. grow old in the earth, 14.08
nor will he strike r. in the earth; 15.29
and, 'The r. of the matter is 19.28
burn to the r. all my increase. 31.12
it took deep r. and filled the land Ps 80.09

ROOT (cont.)

but the r. of the righteous will Pro 12.03
but the r. of the righteous stands 12.12
so their r. will be as rottenness, Is 5.24
In that day the r. of Jesse shall 11.10
the serpent's r. will come forth 14.29
I will kill your r. with famine, 14.30
In days to come Jacob shall take r., 27.06
Judah shall again take r. downward, 37.31
their stem taken r. in the earth, 40.24
and like a r. out of dry ground; 53.02
Thou plantest them, and they take r.; Jer 12.02
their r. is dried up, they shall Hos 9.16
he shall strike r. as the poplar; 14.05
and I will r. out your Asherim from Mic 5.14
leave them neither r. nor branch. Mal 4.01
axe is laid to the r. of the trees; Mt 3.10
they had no r. they withered away. 13.06
yet he has no r. in himself, but 13.21
the weeds you r. up the wheat 13.29
since it had no r. it withered Mk 4.06
and they have no r. in themselves, 4.17
axe is laid to the r. of the trees; Lk 3.09
but these have no r., they believe 8.13
and if the r. is holy, so are the Rom 11.16
it is not you that support the r., 11.18
but the r. that supports you. 11.18
"The r. of Jesse shall come, he who 15.12
of money is the r. of all evils; 1Ti 6.10
that no "r. of bitterness" spring up Heb 12.15
the R. of David, has conquered, so Rev 5.05
I am the r. and the offspring of 22.16

ROOTED

let what grows for me be r. out. Job 31.08
their cities thou hast r. out; Ps 9.06
treacherous will be r. out of it. Pro 2.22
has not planted will be r. up. Mt 15.13
'Be r. up, and be planted in the sea, Lk 17.06
being r. and grounded in love, Eph 3.17
r. and built up in him and established Col 2.07

ROOTS

His r. twine about the stone-heap; Job 8.17
His r. dry up beneath, and his 18.16
and overturns mountains by the r. 28.09
my r. spread out to the waters, with 29.19
themselves the r. of the broom. 30.04
him, and covers the r. of the sea. 36.30
a branch shall grow out of his r. Is 11.01
sends out its r. by the stream, Jer 17.08
and its r. remained where it stood. Eze 17.06
this vine bent its r. toward him, 17.07
not pull up its r. and cut off its 17.09
many people to pull it from its r. 17.09
for its r. went down to abundant 31.07
the stump of its r. in the earth, Dan 4.15
the stump of its r. in the earth, 4.23
the stump of the r. of the tree, 4.26
horns were plucked up by the r.; 7.08
branch from her r. shall arise in 11.07
fruit above, and his r. beneath. Amo 2.09
at the r. of the mountains. Jon 2.06
fig tree withered away to its r. Mk 11.20

ROPE

them down by a r. through the Jos 2.15
A r. is hid for him in the ground, a Job 18.10
Can you put a r. in his nose, or 41.02
and instead of a girdle, a r.; Is 3.24

ROPES

So they bound him with two new r., Ju 15.13
and the r. which were on his arms 15.14
me with new r. that have not been 16.11
took new r. and bound him with 16.12
he snapped the r. off his arms 16.12
Israel will bring r. to that city, 2Sa 17.13
on our loins and r. upon our heads, 1Ki 20.31
and put r. on their heads, and went 20.32
you bind him in the furrow with r., Job 39.10
who draw sin as with cart r., Is 5.18
guard, letting Jeremiah down by r. Jer 38.06
to Jeremiah in the cistern by r. 38.11
between your armpits and the r. 38.12
Jeremiah up with r. and lifted him 38.13
cut away the r. of the boat, Ac 27.32
loosening the r. that tied the 27.40

ROSE

Cain r. up against his brother Abel, Gen 4.08
and it r. high above the earth. 7.17
he r. to meet them, and bowed 19.01
So Abimelech r. early in the 20.08
So Abraham r. early in the morning, 21.14
of his army r. up and returned to 21.32
So Abraham r. early in the morning, 22.03
And Abraham r. up from before his 23.03
Abraham r. and bowed to the Hittites, 23.07
and drank, and r. and went his way. 25.34
morning they r. early and took 26.31
So Jacob r. early in the morning, 28.18
The sun r. upon him as he passed 32.31
his daughters r. up to comfort him 37.35
And Pharaoh r. up in the night, he, Ex 12.30
And he r. early in the morning, and 24.04
So Moses r. with his servant Joshua, 24.13
And they r. up early on the morrow, 32.06
eat and drink, and r. up to play. 32.06
to the tent, all the people r. up, 33.08
and he r. early in the morning and 34.04
And the people r. all that day, and Num 11.32
And they r. early in the morning, 14.40
and they r. up before Moses, with a 16.02
Then Moses r. and went to Dathan 16.25
So Balaam r. in the morning, and 22.13
princes of Moab r. and went to 22.14
So Balaam r. in the morning, and 22.21
Then Balaam r., and went back to 24.25
he r. and left the congregation, and 25.07
morning Joshua r. and set out from Jos 3.01
above stood and r. up in a heap 3.16
Then Joshua r. early in the morning, 6.12
day they r. early at the dawn of 6.15
So Joshua r. early in the morning, 7.16
And the ambush r. quickly out of 8.19
men of the town r. early in the Ju 6.28
When he r. early next morning and 6.38
were with him r. early and encamped 7.01
that were with him r. up by night, 9.34
were with him r. from the ambush. 9.35
and he r. against them and slew 9.43
And when the man r. up to go, 19.07
and his servant r. up to depart, 19.09
he r. up and departed, and arrived 19.10
And her master r. up in the morning, 19.27
and the man r. up and went away to 19.28
And the men of Gibeah r. against me, 20.05
people of Israel r. in the morning, 20.19
men of Israel r. up out of their 20.33
And on the morrow the people r. early, 21.04
When she r. to glean, Boaz instructed Ru 2.15
and drunk in Shiloh, Hannah r. 1Sa 1.09
They r. early in the morning and 1.19
of Ashdod r. early the next day, 5.03
But when they r. early on the next 5.04
The one crag r. on the north in 14.05
And Samuel r. early to meet Saul in 15.12
And Samuel r. up, and went to Ramah. 16.13
And David r. early in the morning, 17.20
and Judah r. with a shout and 17.52
And Jonathan r. from the table in 20.34
David r. from beside the stone heap 20.41
And he r. and departed; 20.42
And David r. and fled that day from 21.10
r., and went to David at Horesh, and 23.

ROSE (cont.)

And Saul r. up and left the cave, 1Sa 24.07
Then David r. and went down to the 25.01
And she r. and bowed with her face 25.41
made haste and r. and mounted on 25.42
Then David r. and came to the place 26.05
Then they r. and went away that 28.25
power of all who r. up against you." 2Sa 18.31
He r. and struck down the Philistines 23.10
and r., and each went his own way. 1Ki 1.49
And the king r. to meet her, and 2.19
When I r. in the morning to nurse 3.21
And when they r. early in the 2Ki 3.22
the Israelites r. and attacked the 3.24
the man of God r. early in the 6.15
And the king r. in the night, and 7.12
and r. by night, and he and his 8.21
Then King David r. to his feet and 1Ch 28.02
r. up and rebelled against his lord 2Ch 13.06
And they r. early in the morning 20.20
Ammon and Moab r. against the 20.23
and he r. by night and smote the 21.09
mentioned by name r. and took the 28.15
the king r. early and gathered the 29.20
of the LORD r. against his people, 36.16
Then r. up the heads of the fathers' Ez 1.05
sacrifice I r. from my fasting, 9.05
the high priest r. up with his Neh 3.01
that he neither r. nor trembled Est 5.09
And the king r. from the feast in 7.07
and Esther r. and stood before the 8.05
withdrew, and the aged r. and stood; Job 29.08
the anger of God r. against them Ps 78.31
The mountains r., the valleys sank 104.08
side, when men r. up against us, 124.02
I am a r. of Sharon, a lily of the Sol 2.01
men with him r. up and struck down Jer 41.02
living creatures r. from the earth, Eze 1.19
rose from the earth, the wheels r. 1.19
and the wheels r. along with them; 1.20
and when those r. from the earth, 1.21
the wheels r. along with them; 1.21
broader as they r. from story to 41.07
was astonished and r. up in haste. Dan 3.24
then I r. and went about the king's 8.27
But Jonah r. to flee to Tarshish Jon 1.03
When the sun r., God appointed a 4.08
And he r. and took the child and Mt 2.14
And he r. and took the child and 2.21
her, and she r. and served him. 8.15
Then he r. and rebuked the winds 8.26
And he r. and went home. 9.07
And he r. and followed him. 9.09
And Jesus r. and followed him, with 9.19
but when the sun r. they were 13.06
those maidens r. and trimmed their 25.07
he r. and went out to a lonely Mk 1.35
And he r., and immediately took up 2.12
And he r. and followed him. 2.14
and when the sun r. it was scorched, 4.06
when he r. early on the first day of the * 16.09
And they r. up and put him out of Lk 4.29
immediately she r. and served them 4.39
And immediately he r. before them, 5.25
and r. and followed him. 5.28
And he r. and stood there. 6.08
And when he r. from prayer, he came 22.45
But Peter r. and ran to the tomb; * 24.12
And they r. that same hour and 24.33
The sea r. because a strong wind Jn 6.18
she r. quickly and went to him. 11.29
r. from supper, laid aside his 13.04
The young men r. and wrapped him up Ac 5.06
But the high priest r. up and all 5.17
And he r. and went. And behold, 8.27
Then he r. and was baptized, 9.18
make your bed." And immediately he r. 9.34
So Peter r. and went with them. 9.39
The next day he r. and went off 10.23
with him after he r. from the dead. 10.41
he r. up and entered the city; 14.20
the party of the Pharisees r. up, 15.05
Peter r. and said to them, "Brethren, 15.07
Then the king r., and the governor 26.30
eat and drink and r. up to dance. 1Co 10.07
that Jesus died and r. again, 1Th 4.14
of the incense r. with the prayers Rev 8.04
from the shaft r. smoke like the 9.02
beast which r. out of the earth; 13.11

ROSH

Ehi, R., Muppim, Huppim, and Ard Gen 46.21

ROT

but the name of the wicked will r. Pro 10.07
but passion makes the bones r. 14.30
up, reeds and rushes will r. away. Is 19.06
All the host of heaven shall r. away, 34.04
an offering wood that will not r.; 40.20
and like dry r. to the house of Hos 5.12
flesh shall r. while they are Zec 14.12
eyes shall r. in their sockets, and 14.12
tongues shall r. in their mouths. 14.12

ROTE

a commandment of men learned by r.; Is 29.13

ROTTED

Your riches have r. and your garments Jas 5.02

ROTTEN

Man wastes away like a r. thing, like Job 13.28
iron as straw, and bronze as r. wood. 41.27

ROTTENNESS

shame is like r. in his bones. Pro 12.04
Instead of perfume there will be r.; Is 3.24
flame, so their root will be as r., 5.24
r. enters into my bones, my steps Hab 3.16

ROUGH

level, and the r. places a plain. Is 40.04
the r. places into level ground. 42.16
and the r. ways shall be made smooth; Lk 3.05

ROUGHLY

like strangers and spoke r. to them. Gen 42.07
spoke r. to us, and took us to be 42.30
me if your father answers you r.? 1Sa 20.10
entreaties, but the rich answer r. Pro 18.23

ROUND

the cities that were r. about them, Gen 35.05
your sheaves gathered r. it, 37.07
Egyptians dug r. about the Nile Ex 7.24
led the people r. by the way of 13.18
morning dew lay r. about the camp. 16.13
set bounds for the people r. about, 19.12
upon it a molding of gold r. about. 25.11
r. about on the skirts of the robe. 28.34
it against the altar r. about. 29.16
blood against the altar r. about. 29.20
and its sides r. about and its 30.03
for it a molding of gold r. about. 30.03
and its sides r. about, and its 37.26
a molding of gold r. about it, 37.26
All the hangings r. about the court 38.16
for the court r. about were of 38.20
the bases r. about the court, and 38.31
and all the pegs r. about the court. 38.31
the skirts of the robe r. about, 39.25
a pomegranate r. about upon the 39.26
shall set up the court r. about, 40.08
the court r. the tabernacle and 40.33
throw the blood r. about against Lev 1.05
blood against the altar r. about. 1.11
blood against the altar r. about. 3.02

ROUND (cont.)

blood against the altar r. about. Lev 3.08
blood against the altar r. about. 3.13
be thrown on the altar r. about. 7.02
on the horns of the altar r. about, 8.15
the blood upon the altar r. about. 8.19
the blood upon the altar r. about. 8.24
he threw it on the altar r. about. 9.12
he threw upon the altar r. about, 9.18
the house to be scraped r. about, 14.41
on the horns of the altar r. about. 16.18
You shall not r. off the hair on 19.27
the nations that are r. about you. 25.44
Also the pillars of the court r. about, Num 3.37
of the court r. about with their 4.32
and placed them r. about the tent. 11.24
r. about the camp, and about two 11.31
that were r. about them fled at 16.34
lick up all that is r. about us, 22.04
land with its boundaries all r. 34.12
pasture lands r. about the cities. 35.02
outward a thousand cubits all r. 35.04
the peoples who are r. about you; Deu 6.14
from all your enemies r. about, 12.10
the peoples that are r. about you, 13.07
the nations that are r. about me'; 17.14
from all your enemies r. about, 25.19
boundary bends r. to Baalah (that Jos 15.09
the boundary bends r. to Shikkeron, 15.11
is the boundary r. about the people 15.12
boundary turns r. toward Taanathshiloh, 16.06
boundary by boundary r. about. 18.20
the villages r. about these cities 19.08
with the pasture lands r. about it. 21.11
each its pasture lands r. about it; 21.42
from all their enemies r. about, 23.01
the peoples who were r. about them, Ju 2.12
power of their enemies r. about, 2.14
man in his place r. about the camp, 7.21
fellows collected r. Jephthah, 11.03
who turned r. and said to Micah, 18.23
fellows, beset the house r. about, 19.22
beset the house r. about me by 20.05
set men in ambush r. about Gibeah. 20.29
the hand of their enemies r. about. 1Sa 10.01
built the city r. about from the 2Sa 5.09
from all his enemies r. about, 7.01
peace on all sides r. about him. 1Ki 4.24
was in all the nations r. about. 4.31
running r. the walls of the house, 6.05
of the house r. about with carved 6.29
courses of hewn stone r. about, 7.12
in two rows r. about upon the one 7.18
pomegranates, in two rows r. about; 7.20
it was r., ten cubits from brim to 7.23
compassing the sea r. about; 7.24
its opening was r., as a pedestal 7.31
and its panels were square, not r. 7.31
there was a r. band half a cubit 7.35
of each, with wreaths r. about. 7.36
And the water ran r. about the 18.35
season, when the time comes r., 2Ki 4.16
and chariots was r. about the city. 6.15
chariots of fire r. about Elisha. 6.17
Turn r. and ride behind me." And 9.18
peace? Turn r. and ride behind me." 9.19
nations that were r. about them, 17.15
of Judah and r. about Jerusalem; 23.05
siegeworks against it r. about. 25.01
were upon the capital r. about. 25.17
which were r. about these cities 1Ch 4.33
And they lodged r. about the house 9.27
built the city r. about from the 11.08
from all his enemies r. about; 22.09
it was r., ten cubits from brim 2Ch 4.02
compassing the sea r. about; 4.03
all the cities r. about Gerar, 14.14
the Lord gave them rest r. about. 15.15
the lands that were r. about Judah, 17.10
for his God gave him rest r. about. 20.30
Fish Gate, and carried it r. Ophel, 33.14
Naphtali, in their ruins r. about, 34.06
gathered r. me while I sat appalled Ez 9.04
all the nations r. about us were Neh 6.16
the circuit r. Jerusalem and from 12.28
me, and encamp r. about my tent. Job 19.12
Therefore snares are r. about you, 22.10
They turn r. and r. by his guidance, 37.12
R. about his teeth is terror. 41.14
set themselves against me r. about. Ps 3.06
Yea, dogs are r. about me; 22.16
up above my enemies r. about me; 27.06
go r. about her, number her towers, 48.12
r. about him a mighty tempest. 50.03
like water r. about Jerusalem, and 79.03
and derided by those r. about us. 79.04
above all that are r. about him? 89.07
thy faithfulness r. about thee? 89.08
thick darkness are r. about him; 97.02
burns up his adversaries r. about. 97.03
a garment which he wraps r. him, 109.19
mountains are r. about Jerusalem, 125.02
so the Lord is r. about his people, 125.02
south, and goes r. to the north; Ecc 1.06
r. and r. goes the wind, and on its 1.06
For a cry has gone r. the land of Is 15.08
and whirl you r. and r., and throw 22.18
let the feasts run their r. 29.01
I will encamp against you r. about, 29.03
it set him on fire r. about, 42.25
Lift up your eyes r. about and see; 49.18
Lift up your eyes r. about, and see; 60.04
against all its walls r. about, Jer 1.15
are they against her r. about, 4.17
birds of prey against her r. about? 12.09
and the places r. about Jerusalem, 17.26
devour all that is r. about her. 21.14
against all these nations r. about; 25.09
sword shall devour r. about you. 46.14
Bemoan him, all you who are r. about him, 48.17
to all that are r. about him. 48.39
from all who are r. about you, 49.05
in array against Babylon r. about, 50.14
Raise a shout against her r. about, 50.15
Encamp r. about her; let no one 50.29
devour all that is r. about him. 50.32
siegeworks against it r. about. 52.04
Chaldeans were r. about the city. 52.07
all the walls r. about Jerusalem. 52.14
were upon the capital r. about. 52.22
hundred upon the network r. about. 52.23
cloud, with brightness r. about it, Eze 1.04
rims were full of eyes r. about. 1.18
appearance of fire enclosed r. about; 1.27
there was brightness r. about him. 1.27
appearance of the brightness r. about. 1.28
battering rams against it r. about. 4.02
with the sword r. about the city; 5.02
with countries r. about her. 5.05
than the countries r. about her, 5.06
the nations that are r. about you, 5.07
the nations that are r. about you; 5.07
fall by the sword r. about you; 5.12
the nations r. about you and in 5.14
to the nations r. about you, 5.15
your bones r. about your altars. 6.05
their idols r. about their altars, 6.13
portrayed upon the wall r. about, 8.10
wheels were full of eyes r. about— 10.12
the nations that are r. about you. 11.12
wind all who are r. about him, 12.14
those r. about who despise you. 16.57
were upon your walls r. about, 27.11
shields upon your walls r. about; 27.11
its rivers flow r. the place of 31.04
their graves r. about her, all of 32.22

ROUND (cont.)
her company is r. about her grave; Eze 32.23
their graves r. about her, all of 32.25
their graves r. about them, all of 32.26
and the places r. about my hill a 34.26
the rest of the nations r. about; 36.04
that are r. about you shall 36.07
that are left r. about you shall 36.36
And he led me r. among them; 37.02
and r. about the vestibule of the 40.14
And the gateway had windows r. about, 40.16
had windows r. about inside, 40.16
a pavement, r. about the court; 40.17
were windows r. about in it and in 40.25
were windows r. about in it and in 40.29
And there were vestibules r. about, 40.30
were windows r. about in it and in 40.33
and it had windows r. about; 40.36
were fastened r. about within. 40.43
four cubits, r. about the temple. 41.05
story to story r. about the temple 41.07
had a raised platform r. about; 41.08
twenty cubits r. about the temple 41.10
left free was five cubits r. about. 41.11
was five cubits thick r. about, 41.12
were paneled and r. about all three 41.16
was paneled with wood r. about, 41.16
all the walls r. about in the 41.17
on the whole temple r. about; 41.19
measured the temple area r. about. 42.15
whole territory r. about upon the 43.12
and its base one cubit r. about. 43.17
ledge, and upon the rim r. about; 43.20
at the bottom of the rows r. about. 46.23
and led me r. on the outside to the 47.02
among all who are r. about us. Dan 9.16
and come, all you nations r. about, Joe 3.11
to judge all the nations r. about. 3.12
all the nations r. about shall Ob 1.16
and the flood was r. about me; Jon 2.03
over me, the deep was r. about me; 2.05
be to her a wall of fire r. about, Zec 2.05
with her cities r. about her, 7.07
to all the peoples r. about; 12.02
the left all the peoples r. about, 12.06
all the nations r. about shall be 14.14
they sent r. to all that region and Mt 14.35
fastened r. his neck and to be 18.06
and villages r. about and buy Mk 6.36
were hung r. his neck and he were 9.42
he had looked r. at everything, 11.11
he went, the people pressed r. him. Lk 8.42
the villages and country r. about, 9.12
were hung r. his neck and he were 17.02
Jews gathered r. him and said to Jn 10.24
she turned r. and saw Jesus standing, 20.14
shining r. me and those who journeyed Ac 26.13
and as far r. as Illyricum I have Rom 15.19
with a golden girdle r. his breast; Rev 1.13
and r. the throne was a rainbow 4.03
R. the throne were twenty-four 4.04
And r. the throne, on each side of 4.06
are full of eyes all r. and within, 4.08
angels stood r. the throne and 7.11
the throne and r. the elders and 7.11

ROUNDED
also above the r. projection which 1Ki 7.20
His arms are r. gold, set with Sol 5.14
Your r. thighs are like jewels, the 7.01
Your navel is a r. bowl that never 7.02

ROUSE
and as a lioness; who dares r. him up? Gen 49.09
and like a lioness; who will r. him up Num 24.09
who are skilled to r. up Leviathan. Job 3.08
then he will r. himself for you 8.06
R. thyself! Why sleepest thou, O Ps 44.23
R. thyself, come to my help, and see! 59.04
R. yourself, r. yourself, stand up, O Is 51.17
I will r. against you your lovers Eze 23.22
To r. my wrath, to take vengeance, I 24.08

ROUSED
awake, or be r. out of his sleep. Job 14.12
thee when once thy anger is r.? Ps 76.07
the Lord God, my wrath will be r. Eze 38.18
for he has r. himself from his holy Zec 2.13

ROUSES
When she r. herself to flee, she Job 39.18
it r. the shades to greet you, all Is 14.09

ROUSING
For lo, I am r. the Chaldeans, that Hab 1.06

ROUT
Lord put us to r. today before the 1Sa 4.03
And he put his adversaries to r.; Ps 78.66
send out thy arrows and r. them! 144.06

ROUTE
by the caravan r. east of Nobah and Ju 8.11

ROUTED
and r. them and pursued them to Gen 14.15
and the Lord r. the Egyptians in Ex 14.27
And the Lord r. Sisera and all his Ju 4.15
"They are r. before us, as at the 20.32
and they were r. before Israel. 1Sa 7.10
scattered them; lightning, and r. them. 2Sa 22.15
Judah, so that they were r. 2Ch 20.22
flashed forth lightnings, and r. them. Ps 18.14

ROW
A r. of sardius, topaz, and carbuncle Ex 28.17
carbuncle shall be the first r.; 28.17
and the second r. an emerald, a 28.18
and the third r. a jacinth, an agate, 28.19
and the fourth r. a beryl, an onyx, 28.20
A r. of sardius, topaz, and carbuncle 39.10
and carbuncle was the first r.; 39.10
and the second r., an emerald, a 39.11
and the third r., a jacinth, an 39.12
and the fourth r., a beryl, an onyx, 39.13
six in a r., upon the table of pure Lev 24.06
put pure frankincense with each r., 24.07
pillars, fifteen in each r. 1Ki 7.03
to the north r. of the holy chambers Eze 46.19
four courts was a r. of masonry, 46.23

ROWED
Nevertheless the men r. hard to bring Jon 1.13
When they had r. about three or four Jn 6.19

ROWERS
of Sidon and Arvad were your r.; skilled Eze 27.08
Your r. have brought you out into the 27.26

ROWING
that they were distressed in r., for Mk 6.48

ROWS
shall set in it four r. of stones. Ex 28.17
And they set in it four r. of stones. 39.10
And you shall set them in two r., Lev 24.06
upon three r. of cedar pillars, 1Ki 7.02
There were window frames in three r., 7.04
in two r. round about upon the one 7.18
pomegranates, in two r. round about; 7.20
the gourds were in two r., cast with 7.24
two r. of pomegranates for each 7.42
the gourds were in two r., cast with 2Ch 4.03
two r. of pomegranates for each 4.13
among the olive r. of the wicked Job 24.11
His back is made of r. of shields, 41.15
put in wheat in r. and barley in Is 28.25
the bottom of the r. round about. Eze 46.23

ROYAL
and he shall yield r. dainties. Gen 49.20
city, like one of the r. cities, Jos 10.02
dwell in the r. city with you? 1Sa 27.05
Ammonites, and took the r. city. 2Sa 12.26
and all the r. officials of Judah, 1Ki 1.09
Solomon sits upon the r. throne. 1.46
establish your r. throne over 9.05
he was of the r. house in Edom. 11.14
to visit the r. princes and the 2Ki 10.13
and destroyed all the r. family. 11.01
And as soon as the r. power was 14.05
confirm his hold of the r. power. 15.19
of the r. family, came with ten men, 25.25
establish his r. throne in Israel 1Ch 22.10
upon him such r. majesty as had 29.25
and a r. palace for himself. 2Ch 2.01
and a r. palace for himself. 2.12
then I will establish your r. throne, 7.18
destroyed all the r. family of the 22.10
set the king upon the r. throne. 23.20
And as soon as the r. power was 25.03
"Have we made you a r. counselor? 25.16
and the r. revenue will be impaired Ez 4.13
be made in the r. archives there 5.17
cost be paid from the r. treasury. 6.04
without delay from the r. revenue, 6.08
sat on his r. throne in Susa the Est 1.02
riches of his r. glory and the 1.04
and the r. wine was lavished 1.07
before the king with her r. crown, 1.11
let a r. order go forth from him, 1.19
king give her r. position to 1.19
letters to all the r. provinces, 1.22
into his r. palace in the tenth 2.16
that he set the r. crown on her 2.17
and gave gifts with r. liberality. 2.18
put on her r. robes and stood in 5.01
sitting on his r. throne inside 5.01
let r. robes be brought, which the 6.08
on whose head a r. crown is set; 6.08
service, bred from the r. stud. 8.10
of the king in r. robes of blue 8.15
governors and the r. officials also 9.03
Your r. scepter is a scepter of Ps 45.06
thy righteousness to the r. son! 72.01
and a r. diadem in the hand of your Is 62.03
of the r. family, one of the chief Jer 41.01
will spread his r. canopy over 43.10
one of the seed r. and made a Eze 17.13
both of the r. family and of the Dan 1.03
the roof of the r. palace of 4.29
power as a r. residence and for 4.30
that in all my r. dominion men 6.26
person to whom r. majesty has not 11.21
the LORD, and shall bear r. honor, Zec 6.13
day Herod put on his r. robes, Ac 12.21
If you really fulfil the r. law, Jas 2.08
a r. priesthood, a holy nation, God's 1Pe 2.09
who have not yet received r. power, Rev 17.12
over their r. power to the beast, 17.17

RUBBED
nor r. with salt, nor swathed with Eze 16.04
and every shoulder was r. bare; 29.18

RUBBING
ears of grain, r. them in their hands. Lk 6.01

RUBBISH
the stones out of the heaps of r., Neh 4.02
is failing, and there is much r.; 4.10

RUDDER
guided by a very small r. wherever the Jas 3.04

RUDDERS
loosening the ropes that tied the r.; Ac 27.40

RUDDY
Now he was r., and had beautiful 1Sa 16.12
youth, r. and comely in appearance. 17.42
My beloved is all radiant and r., Sol 5.10
bodies were more r. than coral, Lam 4.07

RUDE
it is not arrogant or r. Love does 1Co 13.05

RUE
tithe mint and r. and every herb, Lk 11.42

RUFUS
the father of Alexander and R., Mk 15.21
Greet R., eminent in the Lord, also Rom 16.13

RUG
the tent, and she covered him with a r. Ju 4.18

RUGGED
or a young stag upon r. mountains. Sol 2.17

RUGS
prepare the table, they spread the r., Is 21.05

RUIN
delight in bringing r. upon you and Deu 28.63
See, your r. is on you; for you 2Sa 16.08
and r. every good piece of land 2Ki 3.19
But they were the r. of him, and 2Ch 28.23
kings of Judah had let go to r. 34.11
rejoiced at the r. of him that Job 31.29
Let r. come upon them unawares! Ps 35.08
let them fall therein to r.! 35.08
those who seek my hurt speak of r., 38.12
r. is in its midst; oppression 55.11
tongue he will bring them to r.; 64.08
thou dost make them fall to r. 73.18
way of the wicked he brings to r. 146.09
or of the r. of the wicked, when it Pro 3.25
point of utter r. in the assembled 5.14
but a prating fool will come to r. 10.08
babbling of a fool brings r. near. 10.14
poverty of the poor is their r. 10.15
tower of the wicked comes to r., 12.12
opens wide his lips comes to r. 13.03
way of the faithless is their r. 13.15
A fool's mouth is his r., and his 18.07
a man's folly brings his way to r., 19.03
A foolish son is r. to his father, 19.13
the wicked are cast down to r. 21.12
who knows the r. that will come 24.22
and a flattering mouth works r. 26.28
her palaces, they made her a r. Is 23.13
a heap, the fortified city a r.; 25.02
devices to r. the poor with lying 32.07
and r. shall come on you suddenly, 47.11
land shall become a r. and a waste, Jer 25.11
a r., without inhabitant. 46.19
For vast as the sea is your r.; Lam 2.13
transgressions, lest iniquity be your r. Eze 18.30
A r., r., r. I will make it; there 21.27
of the seas on the day of your r. 27.27
Upon its r. will dwell all the 31.13
understanding shall come to r. Hos 4.14
not grieved over the r. of Joseph! Amo 6.06
of Judah in the day of their r.; Ob 1.12
Desolation and r.! Hearts faint Nah 2.10
a day of r. and devastation, a day Zep 1.15
and the r. of that house was great. Lk 6.49
in their paths are r. and misery, Rom 3.16
eat cause the r. of one for whom 14.15
plunge men into r. and destruction 1Ti 6.09

RUINED
the land was r. by reason of the Ex 8.24
(The flax and the barley were r., 9.31
wheat and the spelt were not r., 9.32
yet understand that Egypt is r.? 10.07

RUINED (cont.)
but without people a prince is r. Pro 14.28
they shall repair the r. cities, Is 61.04
eagles—woe to us, for we are r.! Jer 4.13
Why is the land r. and laid waste 9.12
is heard from Zion: 'How we are r.! 9.19
he has r. and broken her bars; Lam 2.09
be waste and your high places r., Eze 6.06
your altars will be waste and r., 6.06
desolate and r. cities are now 36.35
LORD, have rebuilt the r. places, 36.36
granaries are r. because the grain Joe 1.17
rebuild the r. cities and inhabit Amo 9.14
lamentation, and say, "We are utterly r.; Mic 2.04
stripped them and r. their branches. Nah 2.02
for the glorious trees are r.! Zec 11.02

RUINS
and made it for ever a heap of r., Jos 8.28
house will become a heap of r.; 1Ki 9.08
fortified cities into heaps of r., 2Ki 19.25
Naphtali, in their r. round about, 2Ch 34.06
to repair its r., and to give us Ez 9.09
Jerusalem lies in r. with its gates Neh 2.17
who rebuilt r. for themselves, Job 3.14
destined to become heaps of r.; 15.28
in a heap of r. stretch out his 30.24
have vanished in everlasting r.; Ps 9.06
Direct thy steps to the perpetual r.; 74.03
they have laid Jerusalem in r. 79.01
hast laid his strongholds in r. 89.40
driven out of the r. they inhabit! 109.10
but one who exacts gifts r. it. Pro 29.04
this heap of r. shall be under Is 3.06
and kids shall feed among the r. 5.17
city, and will become a heap of r. 17.01
the gates are battered into r. 24.12
cities crash into heaps of r., 37.26
built, and I will raise up their r.'; 44.26
And your ancient r. shall be 58.12
They shall build up the ancient r., 61.04
our pleasant places have become r. 64.11
cities are in r., without inhabitant. Jer 2.15
cities will be r. without inhabitant 4.07
were laid in r. before the LORD, 4.26
I will make Jerusalem a heap of r., 9.11
Jerusalem shall become a heap of r., 26.18
and Babylon shall become a heap of r., 51.37
laid in r. its strongholds; Lam 2.05
laid in r. the place of his appointed 2.06
to lay in r. the wall of the 2.08
been like foxes among r., O Israel. Eze 13.04
nether world, among primeval r., 26.20
your houses shall be laid in r. Dan 2.05
limb, and their houses laid in r.; 3.29
its breaches, and raise up its r., Amo 9.11
Jerusalem shall become a heap of r., Mic 3.12
their battlements are in r.; Zep 3.06
while this house lies in r.? Hag 1.04
of my house that lies in r., 1.09
shattered but we will rebuild the r., Mal 1.04
I will rebuild its r., Ac 15.16
deceived: "Bad company r. good morals." 1Co 15.33
no good, but only r. the hearers. 2Ti 2.14

RULE
the greater light to r. the day, Gen 1.16
the lesser light to r. the night; 1.16
to r. over the day and over the 1.18
husband, and he shall r. over you. 3.16
with according to this same r. Ex 21.31
You shall not r. over him with Lev 25.43
people of Israel you shall not r., 25.46
he shall not r. with harshness over 25.53
who hate you shall r. over you, 26.17
and you shall r. over many nations, Deu 15.06
but they shall not r. over you. 15.06
"R. over us, you and your son and Ju 8.22
"I will not r. over you, and my son 8.23
and my son will not r. over you; 8.23
the LORD will r. over you. 8.23
the sons of Jerubbaal r. over you, 9.02
over you, or that one r. over you?' 9.02
it is who shall r. over my people. 1Sa 9.17
Edom revolted from the r. of Judah, 2Ki 8.20
from the r. of Judah to this day. 8.22
of all his r. and his might and of 1Ch 29.30
for who can r. this thy people, that 2Ch 1.10
that you may r. my people over 1.11
not fail you a man to r. Israel. 7.18
When the r. of Rehoboam was established 12.01
Dost thou not r. over all the 20.06
Edom revolted from the r. of Judah, 21.08
from the r. of Judah to this day. 21.10
Libnah also revolted from his r., 21.10
had no one able to r. the kingdom. 22.09
establish their r. on the earth? Job 38.33
Thou dost r. the raging of the sea; Ps 89.09
LORD, for he comes to r. the earth. 98.09
R. in the midst of your foes! 110.02
the sun to r. over the day, for his 136.08
and stars to r. over the night, 136.09
by me princes r., and nobles govern Pro 8.16
The hand of the diligent will r., 12.24
wisely will r. over a son who acts 17.02
for a slave to r. over princes. 19.10
but when the wicked r., the people 29.02
and babes shall r. over them. Is 3.04
of ruins shall be under your r."; 3.06
oppressors, and women r. over them. 3.12
and r. over those who oppressed 14.02
a fierce king will r. over them, 19.04
who r. this people in Jerusalem! 28.14
and princes will r. in justice. 32.01
and my arms will r. the peoples; 51.05
and the priests r. at their Jer 5.31
descendants to r. over the seed of 33.26
Slaves r. over us; there is none Lam 5.08
never again r. over the nations. Eze 29.15
making you r. over them all—you Dan 2.38
which shall r. over all the earth. 2.39
And at the latter end of their r., 8.23
who shall r. with great dominion 11.03
up to Mount Zion to r. Mount Esau; Ob 1.21
they shall r. the land of Assyria Mic 5.06
then you shall r. my house and Zec 3.07
shall sit and r. upon his throne. 6.13
are supposed to r. over the Mk 10.42
he who rises to r. the Gentiles; Rom 15.12
we might share the r. with you! 1Co 4.08
wife does not r. over her own body, 7.04
does not r. over his own body, but 7.04
This is my r. in all the churches. 7.17
destroying every r. and every 15.24
be upon all who walk by this r., Gal 6.16
far above all r. and authority and Eph 1.21
the head of all r. and authority. Col 2.10
peace of Christ r. in your hearts, 3.15
r. their households, and give the 1Ti 5.14
Let the elders who r. well be 5.17
and he shall r. them with a rod of Rev 2.27
one who is to r. all the nations 12.05
and he will r. them with a rod of 19.15

RULED
and r. from Aroer, which is on the Jos 12.02
and r. over Mount Hermon and 12.05
Abimelech r. over Israel three Ju 9.22
when the judges r. there was a Ru 1.01
Solomon r. over all the kingdoms 1Ki 4.21
who r. in Moab and returned to 1Ch 4.22
And he r. over all the kings from 2Ch 9.26
who r. over the whole province Ez 4.20
those who hated them r. over them. Ps 106.41
that r. the nations in anger with Is 14.06
lords besides thee have r. over us, 26.13

RULED (cont.)
those over whom thou hast never r., Is 63.19
and harshness you have r. them. Eze 34.04
and against our rulers who r. us, Dan 9.12
to the dominion with which he r.; 11.04

RULER
his house and r. over all the land Gen 45.08
and he is r. over all the land of 45.26
God, nor curse a r. of your people. Ex 22.28
"When a r. sins, doing unwittingly Lev 4.22
When Zebul the r. of the city heard Ju 9.30
him to be r. over Israel and over 1Ki 1.35
I will make him r. all the days of 11.34
Eleazar was the r. over them in 1Ch 9.20
r. of half the district of Jerusalem, Neh 3.09
r. of half the district of Jerusalem, 3.12
r. of the district of Bethhaccherem, 3.14
r. of the district of Mizpah, 3.15
r. of half the district of Bethzur, 3.16
r. of half the district of Keilah, 3.17
r. of half the district of Keilah; 3.18
r. of Mizpah, repaired another 3.19
son of Ahitub, r. of the house of God, 11.11
the r. of the peoples set him free; Ps 105.20
and r. of all his possessions, 105.21
Without having any chief, officer or r., Pro 6.07
When you sit down to eat with a r., 23.01
With patience a r. may be persuaded, 25.15
is a wicked r. over a poor people. 28.15
A r. who lacks understanding is a 28.16
If a r. listens to falsehood, all 29.12
Many seek the favor of a r., 29.26
the shouting of a r. among fools. Ecc 9.17
anger of the r. rises against you, 10.04
an error proceeding from the r.: 10.05
sent lambs to the r. of the land, Is 16.01
is our judge, the LORD is our r., 33.22
their r. shall come forth from Jer 30.21
is in the land, and r. is against r. 51.46
strong stem, no scepter for a r. Eze 19.14
and made him r. over the whole Dan 2.48
be the third r. in the kingdom. 5.07
be the third r. in the kingdom. 5.16
be the third r. in the kingdom. 5.29
He shall become r. of the treasures 11.43
will cut off the r. from its midst, Amo 2.03
upon the cheek the r. of Israel. Mic 5.01
me one who is to be r. in Israel, 5.02
crawling things that have no r. Hab 1.14
battle bow, out of them every r. Zec 10.04
shall come a r. who will govern my Mt 2.06
a r. came in and knelt before him, 9.18
said to the r. of the synagogue, Mk 5.36
house of the r. of the synagogue, 5.38
who was a r. of the synagogue; Lk 8.41
But the r. of the synagogue, indignant 13.14
the house of a r. who belonged to 14.01
And a r. asked him, "Good Teacher, 18.18
named Nicodemus, a r. of the Jews. Jn 3.01
now shall the r. of this world be 12.31
for the r. of this world is coming. 14.30
because the r. of this world is 16.11
'Who made you a r. and a judge Ac 7.27
'Who made you a r. and a judge?' 7.35
sent as both r. and deliverer by 7.35
Crispus, the r. of the synagogue, 18.08
the r. of the synagogue, and beat 18.17
speak evil of a r. of your people. 23.05
dead, and the r. of kings on earth. Rev 1.05

RULER'S
nor the r. staff from between his Gen 49.10
strongest stem became a r. scepter; Eze 19.11
And when Jesus came to the r. house, Mt 9.23
came from the r. house some who Mk 5.35
a man from the r. house came and Lk 8.49

RULERS
over the people as r. of thousands, Ex 18.21
r. of thousands, of hundreds, of 18.25
there are five r. of the Philistines, Jos 13.03
the Philistines are r. over us? What Ju 15.11
to the r. of the city, to the elders, 2Ki 10.01
for the r. of the Philistines took 1Ch 12.19
who were r. in their fathers' houses, 26.06
and the r. take counsel together, Ps 2.02
wise; be warned, O r. of the earth. 2.10
Can wicked r. be allied with thee, 94.20
princes and all r. of the earth! 148.11
reign, and r. decree what is just; Pro 8.15
a land transgresses it has many r.; 28.02
or for r. to desire strong drink; 31.04
more than ten r. that are in a Ecc 7.19
word of the LORD, you r. of Sodom! Is 1.10
of the wicked, the scepter of r., 14.05
All your r. have fled together, 22.03
and makes the r. of the earth as 40.23
shall trample on r. as on mortar, 41.25
by the nations, the servant of r.: 49.07
Their r. wail, says the LORD, and 52.05
the r. transgressed against me; Jer 2.08
in dishonor the kingdom and its r. Lam 2.02
us and against our r. who ruled us, Dan 9.12
shall make them r. over many and 11.39
an oven, and they devour their r. Hos 7.07
of Jacob and r. of the house of Mic 3.01
of Jacob and r. of the house of 3.09
and of r. they make sport. Hab 1.10
means least among the r. of Judah; Mt 2.06
know that the r. of the Gentiles 20.25
Then came one of the r. of the Mk 5.22
synagogues and the r. and the Lk 12.11
priests and the r. and the people, 23.13
but the r. scoffed at him, saying, 23.35
priests and r. delivered him up to 24.20
in ignorance, as did also your r. Ac 3.17
morrow their r. and elders and 4.05
"R. of the people and elders, 4.08
and the r. were gathered together, 4.26
the r. of the synagogue sent to 13.15
who live in Jerusalem and their r., 13.27
with their r., to molest them and 14.05
the market place before the r.; 16.19
For r. are not a terror to good Rom 13.03
this age or of the r. of this age, 1Co 2.06
None of the r. of this age understood 2.08
the world r. of this present Eph 6.12
submissive to r. and authorities, Tit 3.01

RULES
When one r. justly over men ruling 2Sa 23.03
to the sanctuary's r. of cleanness. 2Ch 30.19
and he r. over the nations. Ps 22.28
know that God r. over Jacob to the 59.13
who r. by his might for ever, whose 66.07
and his kingdom r. over all. 103.19
and he who r. his spirit than he Pro 16.32
The rich r. over the poor, and the 22.07
with might, and his arm r. for him; Is 40.10
the Most High r. the kingdom of Dan 4.17
the Most High r. the kingdom of 4.25
time that you know that Heaven r. 4.26
the Most High r. the kingdom of 4.32
Most High God r. the kingdom of 5.21
you to keep these r. without favor, 1Ti 5.21
he competes according to the r. 2Ti 2.05

RULEST
come from thee, and thou r. over all. 1Ch 29.12

RULING
justly over men r. in the fear of 2Sa 23.03
of David, and r. again in Judah. Jer 22.30

RUMAH
Zebidah the daugher of Pedaiah of R. 2Ki 23.36

RUMBLE
and r. of wheel, galloping horse and Nah 3.02

RUMBLING
voice and the r. that comes from Job 37.02
at the r. of their wheels, the Jer 47.03
As with the r. of chariots, they Joe 2.05

RUMOR
he shall hear a r. and return to 2Ki 19.07
'We have heard a r. of it with our Job 28.22
in him, so that he shall hear a r., Is 37.07
Hark, a r.! Behold, it comes!— Jer 10.22
comes upon disaster, r. follows r.; Eze 7.26

RUMORS
will hear of wars and r. of wars; Mt 24.06
you hear of wars and r. of wars, Mk 13.07

RUN
his branches r. over the wall. Gen 49.22
and to r. before his chariots; 1Sa 8.11
leave of me to r. to Bethlehem his 20.06
"R. and find the arrows which I 20.36
let his spittle r. down his beard. 21.13
and fifty men to r. before him. 2Sa 15.01
"Let me r., and carry tidings to 18.19
let me also r. after the Cushite. 18.22
"Why will you r., my son, seeing 18.22
"Come what may," he said, "I will r." 18.23
So he said to him, "R." Then 18.23
and fifty men to r. before him. 1Ki 1.05
r. at once to meet her, and say to 2Ki 4.26
I will r. after him, and get something 5.20
of the LORD r. to and fro throughout 2Ch 16.09
of the feast had r. their course, Job 1.05
of mine, they r. and make ready. Ps 59.04
I will r. in the way of thy commandments 119.32
for their feet r. to evil, and they Pro 1.16
and if you r., you will not stumble 4.12
that make haste to r. to evil, 6.18
All streams r. to the sea, but the Ecc 1.07
that they may r. after strong drink, Is 5.11
let the feasts r. their round. 29.01
they shall r. and not be weary, they 40.31
that knew you not shall r. to you, 55.05
Their feet r. to evil, and they make 59.07
R. to and fro through the streets Jer 5.01
our eyes may r. down with tears, 9.18
bitterly and r. down with tears, 13.17
'Let my eyes r. down with tears 14.17
Do the mountain waters r. dry, 18.14
and r. to and fro among the hedges! 49.03
suddenly make them r. away from her; 49.19
suddenly make them r. away from her; 50.44
weep nor shall your tears r. down. Eze 24.16
cause their rivers to r. like oil, 32.14
boundary shall r. from the sea to 47.17
boundary shall r. from Hazarenon 47.18
it shall r. from Tamar as far as 47.19
boundary shall r. from Tamar to 48.28
Many shall r. to and fro, and Dan 12.04
horses, and like war horses they r. Joe 2.04
the city, they r. upon the walls; 2.09
Do horses r. upon rocks? Does one Amo 6.12
they shall r. to and fro, to seek 8.12
like a pool whose waters r. away. Nah 2.08
tablets, so he may r. who reads it. Hab 2.02
"R., say to that young man, 'Jerusalem Zec 2.04
that they should r. on the Syrtis, Ac 27.17
we shall have to r. on some island. 27.26
that we might r. on the rocks, 27.29
prize? So r. that you may obtain it. 1Co 9.24
Well, I do not r. aimlessly, I do not 9.26
should be running or had r. in vain. Gal 2.02
that I did not r. in vain or labor Php 2.16
and let us r. with perseverance the Heb 12.01

RUNNELS
in front of the flocks in the r., Gen 30.38
the rods in the r. before the eyes 30.41

RUNNER
"My days are swifter than a r.; Job 9.25
One r. runs to meet another, and one Jer 51.31

RUNNERS
that in a race all the r. compete, 1Co 9.24

RUNNING
in an earthen vessel over r. water. Lev 14.05
that was killed over the r. water; 14.06
an earthen vessel over r. water, 14.50
was killed and in the r. water, 14.51
and with the r. water, and with the 14.52
shall bathe his body in r. water, 15.13
and r. water shall be added in a Num 19.17
down to a valley with r. water, Deu 21.04
and looked, he saw a man r. alone. 2Sa 18.24
And the watchman saw another man r.; 18.26
said, "See, another man r. alone!" 18.26
"I think the r. of the foremost is 18.27
is like the r. of Ahimaaz the son 18.27
r. round the walls of the house, 1Ki 6.05
Naaman saw some one r. after him, 2Ki 5.21
of the people r. and praising the 2Ch 23.12
r. stubbornly against him with a Job 15.26
r. down upon the beard, upon the Ps 133.02
r. down on the collar of his robes! 133.02
there will be brooks r. with water, Is 30.25
saw that a crowd came r. together, Mk 9.25
r. over, will be put into your lap. Lk 6.38
And r. under the lee of a small Ac 27.16
I should be r. or had run in vain. Gal 2.02
You were r. well; who hindered 5.07

RUNS
his body r. with his discharge, or Lev 15.03
the north side r. from the bay of Jos 15.05
them to the river that r. to Ahava, Ez 8.15
he r. upon me like a warrior. Job 16.14
when the dust r. into a mass and 38.38
a strong man r. its course with joy. Ps 19.05
them vanish like water that r. away; 58.07
to the earth; his word r. swiftly. 147.15
righteous man r. into it and is Pro 18.10
loves a bribe and r. after gifts. Is 1.23
One runner r. to meet another, and Jer 51.31

RURAL
collect the tithes in all our r. towns. Neh 10.37

RUSH
rise early and r. upon the city; Ju 9.33
in the r. of great waters, they Ps 32.06
it to bow down his head like a r., Is 58.05
the north shall r. upon him like a Dan 11.40
they r. to and fro through the squares; Nah 2.04
heaven like the r. of a mighty wind, Ac 1.02

RUSHED
the valley they r. forth at his Ju 5.15
was with him r. forward and stood 9.44
two companies r. upon all who were 9.44
were in ambush r. out of their 20.33
made haste and r. upon Gibeah; 20.37
evil spirit from God r. upon Saul, 1Sa 18.10
r. down to the Jordan before the 2Sa 19.17
the whole herd r. down the steep Mt 8.32
r. down the steep bank into the sea, Mk 5.13
and the herd r. down the steep bank Lk 8.33
their ears and r. together upon Ac 7.57
garments and r. out among the 14.14

RUSHED (cont.)
And he called for lights and r. in, Ac 16.29
and they r. together into the 19.29

RUSHES
though Jordan r. against his mouth Job 40.23
from a boiling pot and burning r. 41.20
as a bird r. into a snare; he does Pro 7.23
dry up, reeds and r. will rot away. Is 19.06
grass shall become reeds and r. 35.07

RUSHING
there is a sound of the r. of rain. 1Ki 18.41
or he will come like a r. stream, Is 59.19
at the r. of his chariots, at the Jer 47.03
chariots with horses r. into battle; Rev 9.09

RUST
city, to the pot whose r. is in it, Eze 24.06
and whose r. has not gone out of it 24.06
be melted in it, its r. consumed. 24.11
its thick r. does not go out of it 24.12
Its r. is your filthy lewdness. 24.13
earth, where moth and r. consume and Mt 6.19
heaven, where neither moth nor r. consumes 6.20
and their r. will be evidence against Jas 5.03

RUSTED
Your gold and silver have r., and Jas 5.03

RUTH
Orpah and the name of the other R. Ru 1.04
mother-in-law, but R. clung to her. 1.14
But R. said, "Entreat me not to 1.16
and R. the Moabitess her daughter-in-law 1.22
And R. the Moabitess said to Naomi, 2.02
Then Boaz said to R., "Now, listen, 2.08
And R. the Moabitess said, "Besides, 2.21
And Naomi said to R., her daughter-in-law, 2.22
"I am R., your maidservant; spread 3.09
are also buying R. the Moabitess, 4.05
Also R. the Moabitess, the widow of 4.10
So Boaz took R. and she became his 4.13
and Boaz the father of Obed by R., Mt 1.05

RUTHLESS
years that are laid up for the r. Job 15.20
r. men seek my life; they do not Ps 54.03
a band of r. men seek my life, and 86.14
lay low the haughtiness of the r. Is 13.11
cities of r. nations will fear thee 25.03
blast of the r. is like a storm 25.04
so the song of the r. is stilled. 25.05
multitude of the r. like passing 29.05
For the r. shall come to nought and 29.20
you from the grasp of the r. Jer 15.21
foolish, faithless, heartless, r. Rom 1.31

RUTHLESSLY
smashed so r. that among its fragments Is 30.14

S

SABACHTHANI
a loud voice, "Eli, Eli, lama s.?" Mt 27.46
a loud voice, "Eloi, Eloi, lama s.?" Mk 15.34

SABBATH
solemn rest, a holy s. to the LORD; Ex 16.23
for today is a s. to the LORD; 16.25
which is a s., there will be none." 16.26
The LORD has given you the s., 16.29
"Remember the s. day, to keep it 20.08
day is a s. to the LORD your God; 20.10
blessed the s. day and hallowed it 20.11
You shall keep the s., because it is 31.14
seventh day is a s. of solemn rest, 31.15
any work on the s. day shall be 31.15
people of Israel shall keep the s., 31.16
observing the s. throughout their 31.16
have a holy s. of solemn rest to 35.02
all your habitations on the s. day." 35.03
It is a s. of solemn rest to you, Lev 16.31
seventh day is a s. of solemn rest, 23.03
it is a s. to the LORD in all your 23.03
after the s. the priest shall wave 23.11
count from the morrow after the s., 23.15
to the morrow after the seventh s.; 23.16
be to you a s. of solemn rest, 23.32
to evening shall you keep your s." 23.32
Every s. day Aaron shall set it in 24.08
land shall keep a s. to the LORD. 25.02
shall be a s. of solemn rest for 25.04
for the land, a s. to the LORD; 25.04
The s. of the land shall provide 25.06
man gathering sticks on the s. day. Num 15.32
"On the s. day two male lambs a 28.09
this is the burnt offering of every s., 28.10
" 'Observe the s. day, to keep it Deu 5.12
day is a s. to the LORD your God; 5.14
commanded you to keep the s. day. 5.15
today? It is neither new moon nor s." 2Ki 4.23
off duty on the s. and guard the 11.05
in force on the s. and guard the 11.07
who were to go off duty on the s., 11.09
who were to come on duty on the s., 11.09
way for the s. which had been 16.18
showbread, to prepare it every s. 1Ch 9.32
who come off duty on the s., 2Ch 23.04
who were to go off duty on the s., 23.08
who were to come on duty on the s.; 23.08
that it lay desolate it kept s., 36.21
them thy holy s. and command them Neh 9.14
or any grain on the s. day to sell, 10.31
them on the s. or on a holy day; 10.31
treading wine presses on the s., 13.15
into Jerusalem on the s. day; 13.15
them on the s. to the people of 13.16
are doing, profaning the s. day? 13.17
upon Israel by profaning the s." 13.18
gates of Jerusalem before the s., 13.19
not be opened until after the s. 13.19
might be brought in on the s. day. 13.19
on they did not come on the s. 13.21
the gates, to keep the s. day holy. 13.22
New moon and s. and the calling of Is 1.13
who keeps the s., not profaning it, 56.02
servants, every one who keeps the s., 56.06
turn back your foot from the s., 58.13
and call the s. a delight and the 58.13
moon to new moon, and from s. to s., 66.23
a burden on the s. day or bring it Jer 17.21
houses on the s. or do any work, 17.22
but keep the s. day holy, as I 17.22
gates of this city on the s. day, 17.24
but keep the s. day holy and do no 17.24
to keep the s. day holy, and not to 17.27
gates of Jerusalem on the s. day, 17.27
end in Zion appointed feast and s., Lam 2.06
but on the s. day it shall be Eze 46.01
the LORD on the s. day shall be 46.04
offerings as he does on the s. day. 46.12
And the s., that we may offer wheat Amo 8.05
through the grainfields on the s.; Mt 12.01
what is not lawful to do on the s." 12.02
law how on the s. the priests in 12.05
in the temple profane the s., 12.05
For the Son of man is lord of the s." 12.08
"Is it lawful to heal on the s.?" 12.10

SABBATH (cont.)

and it falls into a pit on the s., Mt 12.11
it is lawful to do good on the s." 12.12
may not be in winter or on a s. 24.20
Now after the s., toward the dawn 28.01
immediately on the s. he entered Mk 1.21
One s. he was going through the 2.23
doing what is not lawful on the s.?" 2.24
"The s. was made for man, not man 2.27
made for man, not man for the s.; 2.27
Son of man is lord even of the s." 2.28
he would heal him on the s., 3.02
lawful on the s. to do good or to 3.04
And on the s. he began to teach in 6.02
that is, the day before the s., 15.42
And when the s. was past, Mary 16.01
as his custom was, on the s. day. Lk 4.16
And he was teaching them on the s.; 4.31
On a s., while he was going through 6.01
what is not lawful to do on the s.?" 6.02
"The Son of man is lord of the s." 6.05
On another s., when he entered the 6.06
whether he would heal on the s., 6.07
lawful on the s. to do good or to 6.09
in one of the synagogues on the s. 13.10
because Jesus had healed on the s., 13.14
be healed, and not on the s. day." 13.14
of you on the s. untie his ox or 13.15
from this bond on the s. day?" 13.16
One s. when he went to dine at the 14.01
lawful to heal on the s., or not?" 14.03
immediately pull him out on a s. day?" 14.05
Preparation, and the s. was beginning. 23.54
On the s. they rested according to 23.56
Now that day was the s. Jn 5.09
"It is the s., it is not lawful for 5.10
because he did this on the s. 5.16
only broke the s. but also called 5.18
you circumcise a man upon the s. 7.22
If on the s. a man receives circumcision, 7.23
because on the s. I made a man's 7.23
Now it was a s. day when Jesus made 9.14
God, for he does not keep the s." 9.16
cross on the s. (for that s. was a 19.31
near Jerusalem, a s. day's journey away Ac 1.12
And on the s. day they went into 13.14
prophets which are read every s., 13.27
might be told them the next s. 13.42
The next s. almost the whole city 13.44
is read every s. in the synagogues." 15.21
and on the s. day we went outside 16.13
argued in the synagogue every s., 18.04
a festival or a new moon or a s. Col 2.16
there remains a s. rest for the Heb 4.09

SABBATHS

of Israel, 'You shall keep my s., Ex 31.13
father, and you shall keep my s.: Lev 19.03
You shall keep my s. and reverence 19.30
besides the s. of the LORD, and 23.38
You shall keep my s. and reverence 26.02
shall enjoy its s. as long as it 26.34
land shall rest, and enjoy its s. 26.34
had not in your s. when you dwelt 26.35
and enjoy its s. while it lies 26.43
are offered to the LORD on s., 1Ch 23.31
on the s. and the new moons and the 2Ch 2.04
commandment of Moses for the s., 8.13
and the burnt offerings for the s., 31.03
until the land had enjoyed its s. 36.21
the s., the new moons, the appointed Neh 10.33
"To the eunuchs who keep my s., Is 56.04
Moreover I gave them my s., Eze 20.12
and my s. they greatly profaned. 20.13
in my statutes, and profaned my s.; 20.16
and hallow my s. that they may be a 20.20
man shall live; they profaned my s. 20.21
my statutes and profaned my s., 20.24
my holy things, and profaned my s. 22.08
and they have disregarded my s., 22.26
on the same day and profaned my s. 23.38
and they shall keep my s. holy. 44.24
and the s., all the appointed 45.17
the LORD on the s. and on the new 46.03
her s., and all her appointed Hos 2.11

SABEANS

and the S. fell upon them and took Job 1.15
and the S., men of stature, shall Is 45.14
and they will sell them to the S., Joe 3.08

SABTA

S., Raama, and Sabteca. The sons of 1Ch 1.09

SABTAH

S., Raamah, and Sabteca. The sons of Gen 10.07

SABTECA

Sabtah, Raamah, and S. The sons of Gen 10.07
Sabta, Raama, and S. The sons of 1Ch 1.09

SACHAR

Ahiam the son of S. the Hararite, 1Ch 11.35
S. the fourth, Nethanel the fifth, 26.04

SACHIA

Jeuz, S., and Mirmah. These were his 1Ch 8.10

SACK

every man's money in his s., Gen 42.25
them opened his s. to give his ass 42.27
his money in the mouth of his s.; 42.27
here it is in the mouth of my s.!" 42.28
bundle of money was in his s.; 42.35
man's money in the mouth of his s., 43.21
money in the mouth of his s., 44.01
mouth of the s. of the youngest, 44.02
lowered his s. to the ground, 44.11
and every man opened his s. 44.11
the cup was found in Benjamin's s. 44.12
or a garment or a skin or a s., Lev 11.32
and fresh ears of grain in his s. 2Ki 4.42

SACKCLOTH

and put s. upon his loins, and Gen 37.34
and gird on s., and mourn before 2Sa 3.31
the daughter of Aiah took s., 21.10
let us put s. on our loins and 1Ki 20.31
So they girded s. on their loins, 20.32
and put s. upon his flesh, and 21.27
flesh, and fasted and lay in s., 21.27
he had s. beneath upon his body— 2Ki 6.30
and covered himself with s., 19.01
covered with s., to the prophet 19.02
clothed in s., fell upon their 1Ch 21.16
assembled with fasting and in s., Neh 9.01
clothes and put on s. and ashes, Est 4.01
the king's gate clothed with s. 4.02
most of them lay in s. and ashes. 4.03
so that he might take off his s., 4.04
I have sewed s. upon my skin, and Job 16.15
hast loosed my s. and girded me Ps 30.11
I wore s., I afflicted myself with 35.13
When I made s. my clothing, I became 69.11
of a rich robe, a girding of s.; Is 3.24
in the streets they gird on s.; 15.03
and loose the s. from your loins 20.02
to baldness and girding with s.; 22.12
and gird s. upon your loins. 32.11
and covered himself with s., 37.01
clothed with s., to the prophet 37.02
blackness, and make s. their covering." 50.03
and to spread s. and ashes under 58.05
For this gird you with s., Jer 4.08
gird on s., and roll in ashes; 6.26
are gashes, and on the loins is s. 48.37

SACKCLOTH (cont.)
Gird yourselves with s., lament, and run Jer 49.03
dust on their heads and put on s.; Lam 2.10
They gird themselves with s., Eze 7.18
you, and gird themselves with s., 27.31
with fasting and s. and ashes. Dan 9.03
girded with s. for the bridegroom Joe 1.08
Gird on s. and lament, O priests, 1.13
Go in, pass the night in s., 1.13
I will bring s. upon all loins, and Amo 8.10
and put on s., from the greatest of Jon 3.05
robe, and covered himself with s., 3.06
man and beast be covered with s., 3.08
repented long ago in s. and ashes. Mt 11.21
long ago, sitting in s. and ashes. Lk 10.13
and the sun become black as s., Rev 6.12
and sixty days, clothed in s. 11.03

SACKED
time Menahem s. Tappuah and all 2Ki 15.16
therefore he s. it, and he ripped up 15.16

SACKS
As they emptied their s., behold, every Gen 42.35
returned in the mouth of your s.; 43.12
replaced in our s. the first time, 43.18
the lodging place we opened our s., 43.21
know who put our money in our s." 43.22
put treasure in your s. for you; 43.23
house, "Fill the men's s. with food, 44.01
we found in the mouth of our s., 44.08
took worn-out s. upon their asses, Jos 9.04
For the bread in our s. is gone, 1Sa 9.07

SACRED
make of these a s. anointing oil Ex 30.25
removed the s. portion out of my Deu 26.13
and iron, are s. to the LORD; they shall go Jos 6.19
servant into a s. covenant with 1Sa 20.08
music and instruments for s. song. 1Ch 16.42
because of your s. oath be not Ecc 8.02
the east, shall be s. to the LORD. Jer 31.40
gifts, with all your s. offerings. Eze 20.40
to the temple, outside the s. area. 43.21
near any of my s. things and the 44.13
and the things that are most s.; 44.13
her priests profane what is s., Zep 3.04
Judah shall be s. to the LORD of Zec 14.21
temple that has made the gold s.? Mt 23.17
the altar that makes the gift s.? 23.19
the s. and imperishable proclamation * Mk 16.08
and of the s. stone that fell from Ac 19.35
with the s. writings which are 2Ti 3.15

SACRIFICE
and Jacob offered a s. on the Gen 31.54
that we may s. to the LORD our God.' Ex 3.18
and s. to the LORD our God, lest he 5.03
'Let us go and offer s. to our God.' 5.08
say, 'Let us go and s. to the LORD.' 5.17
the people go to s. to the LORD." 8.08
s. to your God within the land." 8.25
for we shall s. to the LORD our God 8.26
If we s. offerings abominable to 8.26
wilderness and s. to the LORD our 8.27
to s. to the LORD your God in the 8.28
the people go to s. to the LORD." 8.29
that we may s. to the LORD our God. 10.25
'It is the s. of the LORD's passover, 12.27
Therefore I s. to the LORD all the 13.15
make for me and s. on it your burnt 20.24
the blood of my s. with leavened 23.18
their gods and s. to their gods 34.15
invites you, you eat of his s., 34.15
the blood of my s. with leaven; 34.25
shall the s. of the feast of the 34.25
offering is a s. of peace offering, Lev 3.01
And from the s. of the peace offering, 3.03
offering for a s. of peace offering 3.06
Then from the s. of the peace offering 3.09
the ox of the s. of the peace offerings), 4.10
the fat of the s. of peace offerings; 4.26
from the s. of peace offerings, and 4.35
the law of the s. of peace offerings 7.11
With the s. of his peace offerings 7.13
flesh of the s. of his peace offerings 7.15
But if the s. of his offering is a 7.16
on the day that he offers his s., 7.16
flesh of the s. on the third day 7.17
flesh of the s. of his peace offering 7.18
flesh of the s. of the LORD's peace 7.20
flesh of the s. of the LORD's peace 7.21
that offers the s. of his peace offerings 7.29
from the s. of his peace offerings 7.29
from the s. of your peace offerings; 7.32
to s. before the LORD, and a cereal 9.04
the s. of peace offerings for the 9.18
who offers a burnt offering or s., 17.08
of meeting, to s. it to the LORD; 17.09
"When you offer a s. of peace offerings 19.05
one offers a s. of peace offerings 22.21
to the LORD or s. within your land; 22.24
you s. a s. of thanksgiving 22.29
you shall s. it so that you may be 22.29
a year old as a s. of peace offerings, 23.19
the ram as a s. of peace offering Num 6.17
is under the s. of the peace 6.18
and for the s. of peace offerings, 7.17
and for the s. of peace offerings, 7.23
and for the s. of peace offerings, 7.29
and for the s. of peace offerings, 7.35
and for the s. of peace offerings, 7.41
and for the s. of peace offerings, 7.47
and for the s. of peace offerings, 7.53
and for the s. of peace offerings, 7.59
and for the s. of peace offerings, 7.65
and for the s. of peace offerings, 7.71
and for the s. of peace offerings, 7.77
and for the s. of peace offerings, 7.83
cattle for the s. of peace offerings 7.88
fire or a burnt offering or a s., 15.03
offering, or for the s., for each lamb. 15.05
or for a s., to fulfil a vow, or for 15.08
you shall not s. it to the LORD Deu 15.21
the passover s. to the LORD your 16.02
flesh which you s. on the evening 16.04
the passover s. within any of your 16.05
you shall offer the passover s., 16.06
"You shall not s. to the LORD your 17.01
people, from those offering a s., 18.03
and you shall s. peace offerings, 27.07
for burnt offering, nor for s., Jos 22.26
nor for s., but to be a witness 22.28
or s., other than the altar of the 22.29
offer a great s. to Dagon their Ju 16.23
worship and to s. to the LORD of 1Sa 1.03
to offer to the LORD the yearly s., 1.21
was that when any man offered s., 2.13
her husband to offer the yearly s. 2.19
be expiated by s. or offering for 3.14
people have a s. today on the high 9.12
comes, since he must bless the s.; 9.13
offerings and to s. peace offerings. 10.08
to s. to the LORD your God; and the 15.15
to s. to the LORD your God in Gilgal." 15.21
behold, to obey is better than s., 15.22
'I have come to s. to the LORD.' 16.02
And invite Jesse to the s., and I will also 16.03
I have come to s. to the LORD; consecrate 16.05
yourselves, and come with me to the s." 16.05
sons, and invited them to the s. 16.05
is a yearly s. there for all the 20.06
our family holds a s. in the city, 20.29
king went to Gibeon to s. there, 1Ki 3.04
with him, offered s. before the LORD. 8.62
and he shall s. upon you the priest 13.02
about the time of offering the s., 2Ki 3.20

SACRIFICE (cont.)

offering or s. to any god but the	2Ki 5.17
I have a great s. to offer to Baal;	10.19
continued to s. and burn incense	12.03
and all the blood of the s.; but the	16.15
them or serve them or s. to them;	17.35
to him, and to him you shall s.	17.36
people offered s. before the LORD.	2Ch 7.04
offered as a s. twenty-two thousand	7.05
place for myself as a house of s.	7.12
to Jerusalem to s. to the LORD,	11.16
I will s. to them that they may	28.23
sat appalled until the evening s.	Ez 9.04
And at the evening s. I rose from	9.05
Will they s.? Will they finish	Neh 4.02
morning I prepare a s. for thee,	Ps 5.03
S. and offering thou dost not	40.06
who made a covenant with me by s.!"	50.05
Offer to God a s. of thanksgiving,	50.14
thanksgiving as his s. honors me;	50.23
For thou hast no delight in s.;	51.16
The s. acceptable to God is a	51.17
freewill offering I will s. to thee;	54.06
with the smoke of the s. of rams;	66.15
to thee the s. of thanksgiving and	116.17
up of my hands as an evening s.!	141.02
The s. of the wicked is an abomination	Pro 15.08
acceptable to the LORD than s.	21.03
The s. of the wicked is an abomination	21.27
than to offer the s. of fools;	Ecc 5.01
sacrifices and him who does not s.	9.02
worship with s. and burnt offering,	Is 19.21
For the LORD has a s. in Bozrah,	34.06
thither you went up to offer s.	57.07
hosts holds a s. in the north	Jer 46.10
him who offers s. in the high	48.35
your gifts and s. your sons by	Eze 20.31
children in s. to their idols,	23.39
offering and the s. for the people,	44.11
at the time of the evening s.	Dan 9.21
he shall cause s. and offering to	9.27
without s. or pillar, without ephod	Hos 3.04
They s. on the tops of the mountains,	4.13
and s. with cult prostitutes, and a	4.14
I desire steadfast love and not s.,	6.06
They love s.; they s. flesh and eat it;	8.13
if in Gilgal they s. bulls, their altars	12.11
S. to these, they say. Men kiss	13.02
offer a s. of thanksgiving of that	Amo 4.05
they offered a s. to the LORD and	Jon 1.16
of thanksgiving will s. to thee;	2.09
has prepared a s. and consecrated	Zep 1.07
And on the day of the LORD's s.—	1.08
so that all who s. may come and	Zec 14.21
boil the flesh of the s. in them.	14.21
When you offer blind animals in s.,	Mal 1.08
means, 'I desire mercy, and not s.'	Mt 9.13
and not s.,' you would not have	12.07
and to offer a s. according to what	Lk 2.24
and offered a s. to the idol and	Ac 7.41
wanted to offer s. with the people	14.13
people from offering s. to them.	14.18
present your bodies as a living s.,	Rom 12.01
what pagans s. they offer to	1Co 10.20
you, "This has been offered in s.,	10.28
a fragrant offering and s. to God.	Eph 5.02
a s. acceptable and pleasing to God.	Php 4.18
bound to offer s. for his own sins	Heb 5.03
put away sin by the s. of himself.	9.26
for all time a single s. for sins,	10.12
no longer remains a s. for sins,	10.26
God a more acceptable s. than Cain,	11.04
priest as a s. for sin are burned	13.11
offer up a s. of praise to God,	13.15

SACRIFICED

offerings and s. peace offerings	Ex 24.05
and have worshiped it and s. to it,	32.08
And Balak s. oxen and sheep, and	Num 22.40
They s. to demons which were no	Deu 32.17
to the LORD, and s. peace offerings.	Jos 8.31
and they s. there to the LORD.	Ju 2.05
On the day when Elkanah s.,	1Sa 1.04
offerings and s. sacrifices on	6.15
There they s. peace offerings	11.15
six paces, he s. an ox and a fatling.	2Sa 6.13
Adonijah s. sheep, oxen, and fatlings	1Ki 1.09
He has s. oxen, fatlings, and sheep	1.19
and has s. oxen, fatlings, and sheep	1.25
only, he s. and burnt incense at the	3.03
incense and s. to their gods.	11.08
people still s. and burned incense	22.43
people still s. and burned incense	2Ki 14.04
people still s. and burned incense	15.04
people still s. and burned incense	15.35
And he s. and burned incense on the	16.04
who s. for them in the shrines of	17.32
they s. seven bulls and seven rams.	1Ch 15.26
They s. to the LORD on that day,	2Ch 15.11
And he s. and burned incense on the	28.04
For he s. to the gods of Damascus	28.23
people still s. at the high places,	33.17
Amon s. to all the images that	33.22
graves of those who had s. to them.	34.04
They s. their sons and their	Ps 106.37
whom they s. to the idols of Canaan;	106.38
and these you s. to them to be	Eze 16.20
when they s. the passover lamb, his	Mk 14.12
the passover lamb had to be s.	Lk 22.07
what has been s. to idols and from	Ac 15.29
what has been s. to idols and from	21.25
our paschal lamb, has been s.	1Co 5.07
already on the point of being s.;	2Ti 4.06
might eat food s. to idols and	Rev 2.14
and to eat food s. to idols.	2.20

SACRIFICES

and offered s. to the God of his	Gen 46.01
let us have s. and burnt offerings,	Ex 10.25
a burnt offering and s. to God;	18.12
"Whoever s. to any god, save to the	22.20
out of the s. of their peace	Lev 7.34
from the s. of the peace offerings	10.14
may bring their s. which they slay	17.05
slay them as s. of peace offerings	17.05
no more slay their s. for satyrs,	17.07
s. and drink offerings, each on its	23.37
and over the s. of your peace	Num 10.10
the people to the s. of their gods,	25.02
your burnt offerings and your s.,	Deu 12.06
your burnt offerings and your s.,	12.11
blood of your s. shall be poured	12.27
who ate the fat of their s.,	32.38
there they offer right s.;	33.19
offerings and s. and peace offerings;	Jos 22.27
eye at my s. and my offerings	1Sa 2.29
and sacrificed s. on that day to	6.15
delight in burnt offerings and s.,	15.22
And while Absalom was offering the s.,	2Sa 15.12
go up to offer s. in the house of	1Ki 12.27
and he offered s. upon the altar;	12.32
in to offer s. and burnt offerings	2Ki 10.24
the Jebusite, he made his s. there.	1Ch 21.28
And they performed s. to the LORD,	29.21
and s. in abundance for all Israel;	29.21
the burnt offering and the s.,	2Ch 7.01
bring s. and thank offerings to the	29.31
assembly brought s. and thank	29.31
upon it you shall burn your s."?	32.12
offered upon it s. of peace	33.16
the place where s. are offered and	Ez 6.03
offer pleasing s. to the God of	6.10
offered great s. that day and	Neh 12.43
Offer right s., and put your trust	Ps 4.05
regard with favor your burnt s.!	20.03
in his tent s. with shouts of joy;	27.06

SACRIFICES (cont.)
I do not reprove you for your s.; Ps 50.08
then wilt thou delight in right s., 51.19
and ate s. offered to the dead; 106.28
And let them offer s. of thanksgiving, 107.22
"I had to offer s., and today I Pro 7.14
to him who s. and him who does not Ecc 9.02
"What to me is the multitude of your s.? Is 1.11
offerings, or honored me with your s. 43.23
satisfied me with the fat of your s. 43.24
and their s. will be accepted on 56.07
he who s. a lamb, like him who 66.03
acceptable, nor your s. pleasing to me. Jer 6.20
your burnt offerings to your s., 7.21
concerning burnt offerings and s. 7.22
bringing burnt offerings and s., 17.26
offerings, and to make s. for ever." 33.18
offered their s. and presented the Eze 20.28
Like the flock for s., like the flock 36.38
on which the s. were to be slaughtered. 40.41
offerings and the s. were slaughtered. 40.42
shall boil the s. of the people." 46.24
shall not please him with their s. Hos 9.04
bring your s. every morning, your Amo 4.04
"Did you bring to me s. and offerings 5.25
Therefore he s. to his net and Hab 1.16
and yet s. to the Lord what is Mal 1.14
all whole burnt offerings and s." Mk 12.33
Pilate had mingled with their s. Lk 13.01
offer to me slain beasts and s., Ac 7.52
who eat the s. partners in the 1Co 10.18
to offer gifts and s. for sins. Heb 5.01
to offer s. daily, first for his own 7.27
is appointed to offer gifts and s.; 8.03
gifts and s. are offered which 9.09
themselves with better s. than these. 9.23
by the same s. which are continually 10.01
But in these s. there is a reminder 10.03
"S. and offerings thou hast not 10.05
pleasure in s. and offerings and 10.08
offering repeatedly the same s., 10.11
for such s. are pleasing to God. 13.16
offer spiritual s. acceptable to 1Pe 2.05

SACRIFICIAL
let their s. feasts be a trap. Ps 69.22
Can vows and s. flesh avert your Jer 11.15
sides to the s. feast which I am Eze 39.17
a great s. feast upon the mountains 39.17
at the s. feast which I am preparing 39.19
altar share in the s. offerings? 1Co 9.13
upon the s. offering of your faith, Php 2.17

SACRIFICING
come and say to the man who was s., 1Sa 2.15
The people were s. at the high 1Ki 3.02
s. so many sheep and oxen that they 8.05
s. to the calves that he had made. 12.32
s. so many sheep and oxen that they 2Ch 5.06
s. peace offerings and giving 30.22
we have been s. to him ever since Ez 4.02
s. in gardens and burning incense Is 65.03
they kept s. to the Baals, and Hos 11.02

SACRILEGE
the desolating s. spoken of by the Mt 24.15
the desolating s. set up where it Mk 13.14

SACRILEGIOUS
who are neither s. nor blasphemers Ac 19.37

SAD
And why is your heart s.? Am I not 1Sa 1.08
her countenance was no longer s. 1.18
I had not been s. in his presence. Neh 2.01
said to me, "Why is your face s., 2.02
Why should not my face be s., 2.03
I will put off my s. countenance, Job 9.27
Even in laughter the heart is s., Pro 14.13
But when he heard this he became s., Lk 18.23
and they stood still, looking s. 24.17

SADDLE
and put them in the camel's s., Gen 31.34
And any s. on which he who has the Lev 15.09
'S. an ass for me, that I may ride 2Sa 19.26
to his sons, "S. the ass for me." 1Ki 13.13
to his sons, "S. the ass for me." 13.27

SADDLECLOTHS
Dedan traded with you in s. for riding. Eze 27.20

SADDLED
s. his ass, and took two of his Gen 22.03
and s. his ass, and went with the Num 22.21
had with him a couple of s. asses, Ju 19.10
met him, with a couple of asses s., 2Sa 16.01
he s. his ass, and went off home to 17.23
Shimei arose and s. an ass, 1Ki 2.40
So they s. the ass for him and he 13.13
he s. the ass for the prophet whom 13.23
ass for me." And they s. it. 13.27
Then she s. the ass, and she said to 2Ki 4.24

SADDUCEES
Pharisees and S. coming for Mt 3.07
And the Pharisees and S. came, 16.01
the leaven of the Pharisees and S. 16.06
the leaven of the Pharisees and S. 16.11
teaching of the Pharisees and S. 16.12
The same day S. came to him, who say 22.23
heard that he had silenced the S., 22.34
And S. came to him, who say that Mk 12.18
There came to him some S., Lk 20.27
temple and the S. came upon them, Ac 4.01
him, that is, the party of the S., 5.17
one part were S. and the other 23.06
between the Pharisees and the S.; 23.07
For the S. say that there is no 23.08

SADLY
and not s., for that would be of no Heb 13.17

SADNESS
nothing else but s. of the heart. Neh 2.02
for by s. of countenance the heart Ecc 7.03

SAFE
have in the field into s. shelter; Ex 9.19
'I shall be s., though I walk in Deu 29.19
people returned s. to Joshua in Jos 10.21
it is s. for you and there is no 1Sa 20.21
enemy, will he let him go away s.? 24.19
refuge, and has made my way s. 2Sa 22.33
You shall know that your tent is s., Job 5.24
Their houses are s. from fear, 21.09
with strength, and made my way s. Ps 18.32
didst keep me s. upon my mother's 22.09
holdest them s. under thy shelter 31.20
Oh to be s. under the shelter of 61.04
that I may be s. and have regard 119.117
righteous man runs into it and is s. Pro 18.10
he who trusts in the LORD is s. 29.25
And if in a s. land you fall down, Jer 12.05
to be s. from the reach of harm! Hab 2.09
and holy man, and kept him s. Mk 6.20
he has received him s. and sound.' Lk 15.27
irksome to me, and is s. for you. Php 3.01

SAFEKEEPING
your life; with me you shall be in s." 1Sa 22.23

SAFELY
And Jacob came s. to the city of Gen 33.18
my lord the king has come s. home." 2Sa 19.30
He pursues them and passes on s., Is 41.03
seize him and lead him away s." Mk 14.44

SAFELY (cont.)
charging the jailer to keep them s. Ac 16.23
and bring him s. to Felix the 23.24

SAFETY
about, so that you live in s., Deu 12.10
the LORD, he dwells in s. by him; 33.12
So Israel dwelt in s., the fountain of 33.28
on every side; and you dwelt in s. 1Sa 12.11
you away, that you may go in s. 20.13
until the day he came back in s. 2Sa 19.24
And Judah and Israel dwelt in s., 1Ki 4.25
returned in s. to his house in 2Ch 19.01
His sons are far from s., they are crushed Job 5.04
those who mourn are lifted to s. 5.11
protected and take your rest in s. 11.18
O LORD, makest me dwell in s. Ps 4.08
him in the s. for which he longs. 12.05
my soul in s. from the battle that 55.18
He led them in s., so that they 78.53
abundance of counselors there is s. Pro 11.14
inhabitants of Gebim flee for s. Is 10.31
feed, and the needy lie down in s.; 14.30
flee for s., stay not, for I bring Jer 4.06
Flee for s., O people of Benjamin, 6.01
and I will make them dwell in s. 32.37
and I will make you lie down in s. Hos 2.18
was there any s. from the foe for Zec 8.10

SAFFRON
nard and s., calamus and cinnamon, Sol 4.14

SAIL
place, or keep the s. spread out. Is 33.23
linen from Egypt was your s., Eze 27.07
and his company set s. from Paphos, Ac 13.13
Setting s. therefore from Troas, we 16.11
wills," and he set s. from Ephesus. 18.21
he was about to set s. for Syria, 20.03
we set s. for Assos, intending to 20.13
had decided to s. past Ephesus, 20.16
we had parted from them and set s., 21.01
Phoenicia, we went aboard, and set s. 21.02
that we should s. for Italy, they delivered 27.01
was about to s. to the ports along 27.02
not have set s. from Crete and 27.21
you all those who s. with you.' 27.24
months we set s. in a ship which 28.11

SAILED
and as they s. he fell asleep. Lk 8.23
and from there they s. to Cyprus. Ac 13.04
and from there they s. to Antioch, 14.26
with him and s. away to Cyprus, 15.39
of the brethren and s. for Syria, 18.18
but we s. away from Philippi after 20.06
it on the left we s. to Syria, 21.03
from there we s. under the lee of 27.04
And when we had s. across the sea 27.05
We s. slowly for a number of days, 27.07
we s. under the lee of Crete off 27.07
weighed anchor and s. along Crete, 27.13
and when we s., they put on board 28.10

SAILING
And s. from there we came the Ac 20.15
a ship of Alexandria s. for Italy, 27.06

SAILORS
midnight the s. suspected that Ac 27.27
And as the s. were seeking to 27.30
s. and all whose trade is on the Rev 18.17

SAINT
Greet every s. in Christ Jesus. Php 4.21

SAINTS
and let thy s. rejoice in thy 2Ch 6.41
As for the s. in the land, they are Ps 16.03
O you his s., and give thanks to 30.04
Love the LORD, all you his s.! 31.23
you his s., for those who fear him 34.09
he will not forsake his s. The righteous 37.28
flesh of thy s. to the beasts of 79.02
to his s., to those who turn to him 85.08
he preserves the lives of his s.; 97.10
of the LORD is the death of his s. 116.15
and let thy s. shout for joy. 132.09
and her s. will shout for joy. 132.16
and all thy s. shall bless thee! 145.10
his people, praise for all his s., 148.14
and preserving the way of his s. Pro 2.08
But the s. of the Most High shall Dan 7.18
this horn made war with the s., 7.21
given for the s. of the Most High, 7.22
came when the s. received the 7.22
wear out the s. of the Most High, 7.25
people of the s. of the Most High; 7.27
mighty men and the people of the s. 8.24
bodies of the s. who had fallen Mt 27.52
he has done to thy s. at Jerusalem; Ac 9.13
also to the s. that lived at Lydda. 9.32
calling the s. and widows he 9.41
shut up many of the s. in prison, 26.10
in Rome, who are called to be s.: Rom 1.07
intercedes for the s. according to 8.27
Contribute to the needs of the s., 12.13
to Jerusalem with aid for the s. 15.25
the poor among the s. at Jerusalem; 15.26
Jerusalem may be acceptable to the s., 15.31
her in the Lord as befits the s., 16.02
and all the s. who are with them. 16.15
called to be s. together with all 1Co 1.02
the unrighteous instead of the s.? 6.01
know that the s. will judge the 6.02
as in all the churches of the s., 14.33
the contribution for the s.: 16.01
themselves to the service of the s.; 16.15
with all the s. who are in the 2Co 1.01
part in the relief of the s.— 8.04
you about the offering for the s., 9.01
wants of the s. but also overflows 9.12
All the s. greet you. 13.13
To the s. who are also faithful in Eph 1.01
and your love toward all the s., 1.15
glorious inheritance in the s., 1.18
with the s. and members of the 2.19
I am the very least of all the s., 3.08
with all the s. what is the 3.18
for the equipment of the s., 4.12
among you, as is fitting among s. 5.03
supplication for all the s., 6.18
To all the s. in Christ Jesus who Php 1.01
All the s. greet you, especially 4.22
To the s. and faithful brethren in Col 1.02
which you have for all the s., 1.04
the inheritance of the s. in light. 1.12
but now made manifest to his s. 1.26
of our Lord Jesus with all his s. 1Th 3.13
that day to be glorified in his s., 2Th 1.10
hospitality, washed the feet of the s., 1Ti 5.10
the Lord Jesus and all the s., Phm 1.05
hearts of the s. have been refreshed 1.07
for his sake in serving the s., Heb 6.10
Greet all your leaders and all the s. 13.24
once for all delivered to the s. Jud 1.03
which are the prayers of the s.; Rev 5.08
of all the s. upon the golden 8.03
prayers of the s. from the hand of 8.04
thy servants, the prophets and s., 11.18
make war on the s. and to conquer 13.07
the endurance and faith of the s. 13.10
a call for the endurance of the s., 14.12
shed the blood of s. and prophets, 16.06
blood of the s. and the blood of 17.06
O s. and apostles and prophets, for 18.20
the blood of prophets and of s., 18.24

SAINTS (cont.)

is the righteous deeds of the s. Rev 19.08
the camp of the s. and the beloved 20.09
the Lord Jesus be with all the s. 22.21

SAKE

And for her s. he dealt well with Gen 12.16
spare the whole place for their s. 18.26
"For the s. of forty I will not do 18.29
"For the s. of twenty I will not 18.31
"For the s. of ten I will not 18.32
kill me for the s. of Rebekah"; 26.07
descendants for my servant Abraham's s." 26.24
Egyptian's house for Joseph's s.; 39.05
to the Egyptians for Israel's s., Ex 18.08
the slave go free for the eye's s. 21.26
slave go free for the tooth's s. 21.27
will for their s. remember the Lev 26.45
to him, "Are you jealous for my s.? Num 11.29
to all these nations for your s., Jos 23.03
to me for your s. that the hand of Ru 1.13
people, for his great name's s., 1Sa 12.22
kingdom for the s. of his people 2Sa 5.12
him kindness for Jonathan's s.?" 9.01
kindness for the s. of your father 9.07
gently for my s. with the young 18.05
'For my s. protect the young man 18.12
a far country for thy name's s. 1Ki 8.41
Yet for the s. of David your father 11.12
for the s. of David my servant and 11.13
and for the s. of Jerusalem which 11.13
for the s. of my servant David and 11.32
David and for the s. of Jerusalem, 11.32
for the s. of David my servant whom 11.34
Nevertheless for David's s. the LORD 15.04
for the s. of David his servant, 2Ki 8.19
for my own s. and for the sake of 19.34
and for the s. of my servant David." 19.34
own s. and for my servant David's s." 20.06
exalted for the s. of his people 1Ch 14.02
For thy servant's s., O LORD, and 17.19
country for the s. of thy great 2Ch 6.32
me for the s. of thy steadfast Ps 6.04
of righteousness for his name's s. 23.03
me, for thy goodness' s., O LORD! 25.07
For thy name's s., O LORD, pardon my 25.11
for thy name's s. lead me and guide 31.03
Nay, for thy s. we are slain all the 44.22
us for the s. of thy steadfast 44.26
For it is for thy s. that I have 69.07
our sins, for thy name's s.! 79.09
Yet he saved them for his name's s., 106.08
remembered for their s. his covenant, 106.45
on my behalf for thy name's s.; 109.21
for the s. of thy steadfast love 115.01
and companions' s. I will say, 122.08
For the s. of the house of the LORD 122.09
servant David's s. do not turn 132.10
For thy name's s., O LORD, preserve 143.11
this city to save it, for my own s. Is 37.35
and for the s. of my servant David." 37.35
pleased, for his righteousness' s., 42.21
"For your s. I will send to Babylon 43.14
your transgressions for my own s., 43.25
For the s. of my servant Jacob, and 45.04
"For my name's s. I defer my anger, 48.09
for the s. of my praise I restrain 48.09
For my own s., for my own s., I do 48.11
For Zion's s. I will not keep silent, 62.01
for Jerusalem's s. I will not rest, 62.01
Return for the s. of thy servants, 63.17
so I will do for my servants' s., 65.08
you out for my name's s. have said, 66.05
us, act, O LORD, for thy name's s.; Jer 14.07
Do not spurn us, for thy name's s.; 14.21
that for thy s. I bear reproach. 15.15
Take heed for the s. of your lives, 17.21

But I acted for the s. of my name, Eze 20.09
But I acted for the s. of my name, 20.14
and acted for the s. of my name, 20.22
I deal with you for my name's s., 20.44
wisdom for the s. of your splendor. 28.17
Lord GOD: It is not for your s., 36.22
but for the s. of my holy name, 36.22
It is not for your s. that I will 36.32
supplications, and for thy own s., Dan 9.17
for thy own s., O my God, because 9.19
persecuted for righteousness' s., Mt 5.10
governors and kings for my s., 10.18
be hated by all for my name's s. 10.22
his life for my s. will find it. 10.39
for the s. of Herodias, his brother 14.03
of God for the s. of your tradition? 15.03
So, for the s. of your tradition, you 15.06
his life for my s. will find it. 16.25
eunuchs for the s. of the kingdom 19.12
for my name's s., will receive a 19.29
by all nations for my name's s. 24.09
but for the s. of the elect those 24.22
in prison for the s. of Herodias, Mk 6.17
his life for my s. and the gospel's 8.35
or lands, for my s. and for the gospel, 10.29
governors and kings for my s., to bear 13.09
be hated by all for my name's s. 13.13
but for the s. of the elect, whom he 13.20
whoever loses his life for my s., Lk 9.24
for the s. of the kingdom of God, 18.29
and governors for my name's s. 21.12
be hated by all for my name's s. 21.17
and for your s. I am glad that I Jn 11.15
has come for you s., not for mine. 12.30
me for the s. of the works themselves. 14.11
And for their s. I consecrate myself, 17.19
must suffer for the s. of my name." Ac 9.16
lives for the s. of our Lord Jesus 15.26
faith for the s. of his name among Rom 1.05
were written not for his s. alone, 4.23
"For thy s. we are being killed all 8.36
Christ for the s. of my brethren, 9.03
are enemies of God, for your s.; 11.28
beloved for the s. of their forefathers. 11.28
but also for the s. of conscience. 13.05
for the s. of food, destroy the work 14.20
We are fools for Christ's s., but you are 1Co 4.10
Does he not speak entirely for our s.? 9.10
It was written for our s., because the 9.10
do it all for the s. of the gospel, 9.23
informed you, and for conscience' s.— 10.28
been for your s. in the presence 2Co 2.10
as your servants for Jesus' s. 4.05
given up to death for Jesus' s., 4.11
For it is all for your s., so that as 4.15
who for their s. died and was 5.15
For our s. he made him to be sin 5.21
yet for your s. he became poor, so 8.09
For the s. of Christ, then, I am 12.10
that for the s. of Christ you Php 1.29
in him but also suffer for his s., 1.29
as loss for the s. of Christ. 3.07
For his s. I have suffered the loss 3.08
in my sufferings for your s., Col 1.24
afflictions for the s. of his body, 1.24
proved to be among you for your s. 1Th 1.05
we feel for your s. before our God, 3.09
wine for the s. of your stomach 1Ti 5.23
everything for the s. of the elect, 2Ti 2.10
yet for love's s. I prefer to appeal Phm 1.09
for the s. of those who are to Heb 1.14
those for whose s. it is cultivated, 6.07
showed for his s. in serving the 6.10
the end of the times for your s. 1Pe 1.20
for the Lord's s. to every human 2.13
do suffer for righteousness' s., 3.14
your sins are forgiven for his s. 1Jn 2.12
set out for his s. and have 3Jn 1.07

SAKE (cont.)
themselves for the s. of gain to Jud 1.11
and bearing up for my name's s., Rev 2.03

SAKKUTH
You shall take up S. your king, Amo 5.26

SALA
the son of S., the son of Nahshon, Lk 3.32

SALAMIS
When they arrived at S., they proclaimed Ac 13.05

SALE
within a whole year after its s.; Lev 25.29
from the s. of his patrimony. Deu 18.08
yourselves for s. to your enemies 28.68
that we may offer wheat for s., Amo 8.05

SALECAH
as far as S. and Edrei, cities of Deu 3.10
Hermon and S. and all Bashan to Jos 12.05
Mount Hermon, and all Bashan to S.; 13.11
the land of Bashan as far as S.: 1Ch 5.11

SALEM
Melchizedek king of S. brought out Gen 14.18
His abode has been established in S., Ps 76.02
king of S., priest of the most high Heb 7.01
and then he is also king of S., 7.02

SALIM
was baptizing at Aenon near S., because Jn 3.23

SALLAI
S., nine hundred and twenty-eight. Neh 11.08
of S., Kallai; of Amok, Eber; 12.20

SALLU
S. the son of Meshullam, son of 1Ch 9.07
S. the son of Meshullam, son of Joed, Neh 11.07
S., Amok, Hilkiah, Jedaiah. 12.07

SALMA
Nahshon was the father of S., 1Ch 2.11
the father of Salma, S. of Boaz, 2.11
S., the father of Bethlehem, and 2.51
The sons of S.: Bethlehem, the 2.54

SALMON
Amminadab of Nahshon, Nahshon of S., Ru 4.20
S. of Boaz, Boaz of Obed, 4.21
and Nahshon the father of S., Mt 1.04
and S. the father of Boaz by Rahab, 1.05

SALMONE
under the lee of Crete off S. Ac 27.07

SALOME
the younger and of Joses, and S., Mk 15.40
and S., bought spices, so that they 16.01

SALT
of Siddim (that is, the S. Sea). Gen 14.03
and she became a pillar of s. 19.26
seasoned with s., pure and holy; Ex 30.35
all your cereal offerings with s.; Lev 2.13
not let the s. of the covenant 2.13
your offerings you shall offer s. 2.13
a covenant of s. for ever before Num 18.19
the end of the S. Sea on the east; 34.03
and its end shall be at the S. Sea. 34.12
the S. Sea, under the slopes of Deu 3.17
the whole land brimstone and s., 29.23
the S. Sea, were wholly cut off; Jos 3.16
the S. Sea, southward to the foot of 12.03
ran from the end of the S. Sea, 15.02
And the east boundary is the S. Sea, 15.05
the City of S., and Engedi: six 15.62
at the northern bay of the S. Sea, 18.19
the city and sowed it with s. Ju 9.45
Edomites in the Valley of S. 2Sa 8.13
me a new bowl, and put s. in it." 2Ki 2.20
spring of water and threw s. in it, 2.21
the Valley of S. and took Sela by 14.07
Edomites in the Valley of S. 1Ch 18.12
and his sons by a covenant of s.? 2Ch 13.05
the Valley of S. and smote ten 25.11
we eat the s. of the palace and it Ez 4.14
s., wine, or oil, as the priests at 6.09
and s. without prescribing how much 7.22
is tasteless be eaten without s., Job 6.06
and the s. land for his dwelling 39.06
wilderness, in an uninhabited s. land. Jer 17.06
to cleanse you, nor rubbed with s., Eze 16.04
shall sprinkle s. upon them and 43.24
become fresh; they are to be left for s. 47.11
possessed by nettles and s. pits, Zep 2.09
"You are the s. of the earth; Mt 5.13
but if s. has lost its taste, how 5.13
"S. is good; but if the s. has lost Mk 9.50
Have s. in yourselves, and be at 9.50
"S. is good; but if s. has lost Lk 14.34
seasoned with s., so that you may Col 4.06
No more can s. water yield fresh. Jas 3.12

SALTED
the ground will eat s. provender, Is 30.24
For every one will be s. with fire. Mk 9.49

SALTNESS
how shall its s. be restored? Mt 5.13
but if the salt has lost its s., Mk 9.50
how shall its s. be restored? Lk 14.34

SALTY
a fruitful land into a s. waste, Ps 107.34

SALU
woman, was Zimri the son of S., Num 25.14

SALUTATIONS
and s. in the market places, and Mt 23.07
and to have s. in the market places Mk 12.38
synagogues and s. in the market Lk 11.43
and love s. in the market places 20.46

SALUTE
went out to meet him and s. him. 1Sa 13.10
And thus you shall s. him: 25.06
of the wilderness to s. our master; 25.14
If you meet any one, do not s. him; 2Ki 4.29
And if you s. only your brethren, Mt 5.47
As you enter the house, s. it. 10.12
And they began to s. him, "Hail, King Mk 15.18
no sandals, and s. no one on the road. Lk 10.04

SALUTED
drew near to the people he s. them. 1Sa 30.21

SALUTES
and if any one s. you, do not reply; 2Ki 4.29

SALVATION
I wait for thy s., O LORD. Gen 49.18
and see the s. of the LORD, which he Ex 14.13
my song, and he has become my s.; 15.02
and scoffed at the Rock of his s. Deu 32.15
because I rejoice in thy s. 1Sa 2.01
my shield and the horn of my s., 2Sa 22.03
hast given me the shield of thy s., 22.36
be my God, the rock of my s., 22.47
Tell of his s. from day to day. 1Ch 16.23
O God of our s., and gather and 16.35
O LORD God, be clothed with s., 2Ch 6.41
This will be my s., that a godless Job 13.16
with joy. He recounts to men his s., 33.26
my heart shall rejoice in thy s. Ps 13.05

SALVATION (cont.)
the horn of my s., my stronghold. Ps 18.02
hast given me the shield of thy s., 18.35
and exalted be the God of my s., 18.46
vindication from the God of his s. 24.05
me, for thou art the God of my s.; 25.05
The LORD is my light and my s.; 27.01
forsake me not, O God of my s.! 27.09
and thy s. to the upright of heart! 36.10
The s. of the righteous is from the 37.39
Make haste to help me, O Lord, my s.! 38.22
of thy faithfulness and thy s.; 40.10
who love thy s. say continually, 40.16
aright I will show the s. of God! 50.23
Restore to me the joy of thy s., 51.12
bloodguiltiness, O God, thou God of my s., 51.14
in silence; from him comes my s. 62.01
is my rock and my s., my fortress; 62.02
is my rock and my s., my fortress; 62.06
O God of our s., who art the hope 65.05
daily bears us up; God is our s. 68.19
Our God is a God of s.; and to God 68.20
let thy s., O God, set me on high! 69.29
those who love thy s. say evermore, 70.04
of thy deeds of s. all the day, 71.15
working s. in the midst of the 74.12
O God of our s., for the glory of 79.09
O God of our s., and put away thy 85.04
love, O LORD, and grant us thy s. 85.07
Surely his s. is at hand for those 85.09
my God, and the Rock of my s. 89.26
satisfy him, and show him my s. 91.16
joyful noise to the rock of our s.! 95.01
tell of his s. from day to day. 96.02
up the cup of s. and call on the 116.13
and my song; he has become my s. 118.14
answered me and hast become my s. 118.21
thy s. according to thy promise; 119.41
My soul languishes for thy s.; 119.81
eyes fail with watching for thy s., 119.123
S. is far from the wicked, for they 119.155
I hope for thy s., O LORD, and I do 119.166
I long for thy s., O LORD, and thy 119.174
Her priests I will clothe with s., 132.16
"Behold, God is my s.; I will trust, Is 12.02
my song, and he has become my s. 12.02
draw water from the wells of s. 12.03
have forgotten the God of your s., 17.10
us be glad and rejoice in his s." 25.09
he sets up s. as walls and bulwarks 26.01
our s. in the time of trouble. 33.02
abundance of s., wisdom, and knowledge; 33.06
that s. may sprout forth, and let it 45.08
by the LORD with everlasting s.; 45.17
far off, and my s. will not tarry; 46.13
I will put s. in Zion, for Israel my 46.13
that my s. may reach to the end of 49.06
in a day of s. I have helped you; 49.08
my s. has gone forth, and my arms 51.05
but my s. will be for ever, and my 51.06
and my s. to all generations." 51.08
who publishes s., who says to Zion, 52.07
earth shall see the s. of our God. 52.10
for soon my s. will come, and my 56.01
for s., but it is far from us. 59.11
and a helmet of s. upon his head; 59.17
you shall call your walls S., 60.18
clothed me with the garments of s., 61.10
and her s. as a burning torch. 62.01
of Zion, "Behold, your s. comes; 62.11
LORD our God is the s. of Israel. Jer 3.23
quietly for the s. of the LORD. Lam 3.26
he may come and rain s. upon you. Hos 10.12
I will wait for the God of my s.; Mic 7.07
forth for the s. of thy people, Hab 3.13
for the s. of thy anointed. 3.13
I will joy in the God of my s. 3.18
imperishable proclamation of eternal s. * Mk 16.08
up a horn of s. for us in the Lk 1.69
knowledge of s. to his people in 1.77
for mine eyes have seen thy s. 2.30
and all flesh shall see the s. of God." 3.06
"Today s. has come to this house, 19.09
what we know, for s. is from the Jews. Jn 4.22
And there is s. in no one else, for Ac 4.12
been sent the message of this s. 13.26
you may bring s. to the uttermost 13.47
who proclaim to you the way of s." 16.17
then that this s. of God has been 28.28
of God for s. to every one who has Rom 1.16
their trespass s. has come to the 11.11
For s. is nearer to us now than 13.11
it is for your comfort and s.; 2Co 1.06
and helped you on the day of s." 6.02
behold, now is the day of s. 6.02
that leads to s. and brings no 7.10
of truth, the gospel of your s., Eph 1.13
And take the helmet of s., 6.17
but of your s., and that from God. Php 1.28
out your own s. with fear and 2.12
and for a helmet the hope of s. 1Th 5.08
but to obtain s. through our Lord 5.09
may obtain the s. which in Christ 2Ti 2.10
instruct your for s. through faith 3.15
appeared for the s. of all men, Tit 2.11
sake of those who are to obtain s.? Heb 1.14
if we neglect such a great s.? 2.03
of their s. perfect through suffering. 2.10
of eternal s. to all who obey him, 5.09
of better things that belong to s. 6.09
faith for a s. ready to be revealed 1Pe 1.05
you obtain the s. of your souls. 1.09
searched and inquired about this s.; 1.10
that by it you may grow up to s.; 2.02
the forbearance of our Lord as s. 2Pe 3.15
to write to you of our common s., Jud 1.03
"S. belongs to our God who sits Rev 7.10
"Now the s. and the power and the 12.10
S. and glory and power belong to 19.01

SALVE
and s. to anoint your eyes, that you Rev 3.18

SAMARIA
which are in the cities of S., 1Ki 13.32
the hill of S. from Shemer for two 16.24
S., after the name of Shemer, the 16.24
his fathers, and was buried in S.; 16.28
over Israel in S. twenty-two years 16.29
house of Baal, which he built in S. 16.32
to Ahab. Now the famine was severe in S. 18.02
and he went up and besieged S., and fought 20.01
if the dust of S. shall suffice 20.10
to him, "Men are coming out from S." 20.17
Damascus, as my father did in S." 20.34
resentful and sullen, and came to S. 20.43
beside the palace of Ahab king of S. 21.01
Ahab king of Israel, who is in S.; 21.18
at the entrance of the gate of S.; 22.10
king died, and was brought to S.; 22.37
and they buried the king in S. 22.37
the chariot by the pool of S., 22.38
over Israel in S. in the seventeenth 22.51
upper chamber in S., and lay sick; 2Ki 1.02
the messengers of the king of S., 1.03
Mount Carmel, and thence he returned to S. 2.25
Ahab became king over Israel in S., 3.01
marched out of S. at that time and 3.06
were with the prophet who is in S.! 5.03
you seek." And he led them to S. 6.19
As soon as they entered S., Elisha said, 6.20
lo, they were in the midst of S. 6.20
army, and went up, and besieged S. 6.24
And there was a great famine in S., 6.25
for a shekel, at the gate of S." 7.01
time tomorrow in the gate of S.," 7.18

SAMARIA (cont.)

Now Ahab had seventy sons in S. 2Ki 10.01
wrote letters, and sent them to S., 10.01
Then he set out and went to S. 10.12
And when he came to S., he slew all 10.17
all that remained to Ahab in S., 10.17
fathers, and they buried him in S. 10.35
over Israel in S. was twenty-eight 10.36
began to reign over Israel in S., 13.01
the Asherah also remained in S. 13.06
fathers, and they buried him in S.; 13.09
began to reign over Israel in S., 13.10
was buried in S. with the kings of 13.13
hostages, and he returned to S. 14.14
was buried in S. with the kings of 14.16
of Israel, began to reign in S., 14.23
over Israel in S. six months. 15.08
and he reigned one month in S. 15.13
came up from Tirzah and came to S., 15.14
son of Jabesh in S. and slew him, 15.14
and he reigned ten years in S. 15.17
began to reign over Israel in S., 15.23
the Gileadites, and slew him in S., 15.25
began to reign over Israel in S., 15.27
began to reign in S. over Israel, 17.01
all the land and came to S., and for three 17.05
the king of Assyria captured S., and he 17.06
the cities of S. instead of the 17.24
and they took possession of S., 17.24
the cities of S. do not know the 17.26
away from S. came and dwelt in 17.28
came up against S. and besieged it 18.09
of Hoshea king of Israel, S. was taken. 18.10
they delivered S. out of my hand? 18.34
Jerusalem the measuring line of S., 21.13
of the prophet who came out of S. 23.18
that were in the cities of S., 23.19
years he went down to Ahab in S. 2Ch 18.02
at the entrance of the gate of S.; 18.09
he was captured while hiding in S., 22.09
from S. to Bethhoron, and killed 25.13
hostages, and he returned to S. 25.24
them and brought the spoil to S. 28.08
to meet the army that came to S., 28.09
of palm trees. Then they returned to S. 28.15
the cities of S. and in the rest Ez 4.10
who live in S. and in the rest of 4.17
his brethren and of the army of S., Neh 4.02
And the head of Ephraim is S., Is 7.09
and the head of S. is the son of 7.09
the spoil of S. will be carried 8.04
Ephraim and the inhabitants of S., 9.09
like Arpad? Is not S. like Damascus? 10.09
than those of Jerusalem and S., 10.10
I have done to S. and her images?" 10.11
they delivered S. out of my hand? 36.19
In the prophets of S. I saw an Jer 23.13
vineyards upon the mountains of S.; 31.05
from Shechem and Shiloh and S., 41.05
And your elder sister is S., Eze 16.46
S. has not committed half your sins; 16.51
the fortunes of S. and her daughters, 16.53
and S. and her daughters shall 16.55
Oholah is S., and Oholibah is 23.04
is the cup of your sister S.; 23.33
revealed, and the wicked deeds of S.; Hos 7.01
I have spurned your calf, O S. 8.05
The calf of S. shall be broken to 8.06
The inhabitants of S. tremble for 10.05
S. shall bear her guilt, because she 13.16
yourselves upon the mountains of S., Amo 3.09
Israel who dwell in S. be rescued, 3.12
who are in the mountain of S., 4.01
feel secure on the mountain of S., 6.01
Those who swear by Ashimah of S., 8.14
and the land of S. and Benjamin Ob 1.19
he saw concerning S. and Jerusalem. Mic 1.01
Is it not S.? And what is 1.05
Therefore I will make S. a heap in 1.06
along between S. and Galilee. Lk 17.11
He had to pass through S. Jn 4.04
So he came to a city of S., called Sychar, 4.05
There came a woman of S. to draw water. 4.07
ask a drink of me, a woman of S.?" 4.09
all Judea and S. and to the end of Ac 1.08
throughout the region of Judea and S., 8.01
Philip went down to a city of S., 8.05
city and amazed the nation of S., 8.09
heard that S. had received the 8.14
and Galilee and S. had peace and 9.31
through both Phoenicia and S., 15.03

SAMARIA'S

S. king shall perish, like a chip on Hos 10.07

SAMARITAN

But a S., as he journeyed, came to Lk 10.33
him thanks. Now he was a S. 17.16
The S. woman said to him, "How is it Jn 4.09
that you are a S. and have a demon?" 8.48

SAMARITANS

high places which the S. had made, 2Ki 17.29
and enter no town of the S., Mt 10.05
and entered a village of the S., Lk 9.52
For Jews have no dealings with S. Jn 4.09
Many S. from that city believed in 4.39
So when the S. came to him, they 4.40
gospel to many villages of the S. Ac 8.25

SAME

On the very s. day Noah and his Gen 7.13
reaped in the s. year a hundredfold 26.12
to him the s. night and said, 26.24
That s. day Isaac's servants came 26.32
shall say the s. thing to Esau 32.19
The s. night he arose and took his 32.22
and she told him the s. story, 39.17
we dreamed on the s. night, 41.11
The s. day Pharaoh commanded the Ex 5.06
deliver the s. number of bricks. 5.18
did the s. by their secret arts. 7.11
Egypt did the s. by their secret 7.22
magicians did the s. by their secret arts, 8.07
so this s. night is a night of 12.42
with according to this s. rule. 21.31
curtains shall have the s. measure. 26.08
shall be of the s. workmanship and 28.08
the curtains had the s. measure. 36.09
eleven curtains had the s. measure. 36.15
was of the s. materials and workmanship, 39.05
be eaten the s. day you offer it, Lev 19.06
It shall be eaten on the s. day, 22.30
day of the s. month is the feast 23.06
parched or fresh until this s. day, 23.14
make proclamation on the s. day; 23.21
shall do no work on this s. day; 23.28
afflicted on this s. day shall be 23.29
does any work on this s. day, 23.30
and cover the s. with a covering of Num 4.08
consecrate his head that s. day, 6.11
do to us, the s. will we do to you." 10.32
In the s. way you shall offer daily, 28.24
for Aaron also at the s. time. Deu 9.20
of your produce in the s. year, 14.28
other gods, that s. prophet shall die.' 18.20
but you shall bury him the s. day, 21.23
the people the s. day, saying, 27.11
So Moses wrote this song the s. day, 31.22
the city in the s. manner seven Jos 6.15
shoulder of Luz (the s. is Bethel), 18.13
That s. night the Lord said to him, Ju 7.09
and spoke to them in the s. way; 8.08
line in the s. place where they 20.22
of them shall die on the s. day. 1Sa 2.34

SAME (cont.)

and came to Shiloh the s. day, 1Sa 4.12
for the s. plague was upon all of 6.04
and spoke the s. words as before. 17.23
people answered him in the s. way, 17.27
another, and spoke in the s. way; 17.30
his men, on the s. day together. 31.06
But that s. night the word of the 2Sa 7.04
woman and I dwell in the s. house; 1Ki 3.17
had the s. measure and the s. form. 6.25
the second pillar was the s. 7.15
and he did the s. with the other 7.18
of the s. measure and the s. form. 7.37
The s. day the king consecrated the 8.64
And he gave a sign the s. day, 13.03
Libnah revolted at the s. time. 2Ki 8.22
second year what springs of the s.; 19.29
by the s. he shall return, and he 19.33
But that s. night the word of the 1Ch 17.03
some of the people at the s. time. 2Ch 16.10
paid him the s. amount in the 27.05
to the LORD—this s. King Ahaz. 28.22
Has not this s. Hezekiah taken away 32.12
This s. Hezekiah closed the upper 32.30
At the s. time Tattenai the governor Ez 5.03
I answered them in the s. manner. Neh 6.04
In the s. way Sanballat for the 6.05
on the thirteenth day of the s., Est 9.01
day of the s., year by year, 9.21
and sow trouble reap the s. Job 4.08
but thou art the s., and thy years Ps 102.27
and the fate of beasts is the s.; Ecc 3.19
They all have the s. breath, 3.19
second year what springs of the s.; Is 37.30
by the s. he shall return, and he 37.34
In that s. year, at the beginning of Jer 28.01
In that s. year, in the seventh 28.17
vineyards and fields at the s. time. 39.10
and the four had the s. likeness, Eze 1.16
the four had the s. likeness, 10.10
and does the s. abominable things 18.24
shall come forth from the s. land. 21.19
defiled; they both took the s. way. 23.13
sanctuary on the s. day and profaned 23.38
on the s. day they came into my 23.39
the three were of the s. size; 40.10
on either side were of the s. size. 40.10
were of the s. size as those of 40.21
were of the s. size as those of 40.22
they had the s. size as the others. 40.24
it was of the s. size as the others. 40.28
were of the s. size as the others; 40.29
it was of the s. size as the others. 40.32
were of the s. size as the others; 40.33
it had the s. size as the others. 40.35
were of the s. size as the others; 40.36
of the s. length and breadth, with 42.11
with the s. exits and arrangements 42.11
and shall go out by the s. way." 44.03
bath shall be of the s. measure, 45.11
You shall do the s. on the seventh 45.20
shall make the s. provision for 45.25
and he shall go out by the s. way. 46.08
the four were of the s. size. 46.22
At the s. time my reason returned Dan 4.36
shall speak lies at the s. table, 11.27
his father go in to the s. maiden, Amo 2.07
and go the s. day to the house of Zec 6.10
even the tax collectors do the s.? Mt 5.46
Do not even the Gentiles do the s.? 5.47
That s. day Jesus went out of the 13.01
But that s. servant, as he went out, 18.28
and the ninth hour, he did the s. 20.05
went to the second and said the s.; 21.30
and they did the s. to them. 21.36
The s. day Sadducees came to him, 22.23
third time, saying the s. words. 26.44
him also reviled him in the s. way. 27.44
bread in the s. dish with me. Mk 14.20
not deny you." And they all said the s. 14.31
and prayed, saying the s. words. 14.39
that to you? For even sinners do the s. Lk 6.33
And remain in the s. house, eating and 10.07
In that s. hour he rejoiced in the 10.21
are under the s. sentence of 23.40
And they rose that s. hour and 24.33
come in the s. way as you saw him Ac 1.11
God gave the s. gift to them as he 11.17
tell you the s. things by word of 15.27
took them the s. hour of the night, 16.33
he was of the s. trade he stayed 18.03
At the s. time he hoped that money 24.26
at the s. time loosening the ropes 27.40
are doing the very s. things. Rom 2.01
make out of the s. lump one vessel 9.21
the s. Lord is Lord of all and 10.12
do not have the s. function, 12.04
For the s. reason you also pay 13.06
in the s. mind and the s. judgment. 1Co 1.10
Does not the law say the s.? 9.08
In the s. way, the Lord commanded 9.14
and all ate the s. supernatural 10.03
and all drank the s. supernatural 10.04
for we all partake of the s. loaf. 10.17
it is the s. as if her head were 11.05
In the s. way also the cup, after 11.25
varieties of gifts, but the s. Spirit; 12.04
varieties of service, but the s. Lord; 12.05
but it is the s. God who inspires 12.06
knowledge according to the s. Spirit, 12.08
to another faith by the s. Spirit, 12.09
inspired by one and the s. Spirit, 12.11
may have the s. care for one 12.25
endure the s. sufferings that we 2Co 1.06
that s. veil remains unlifted, 3.14
Since we have the s. spirit of 4.13
who puts the s. earnest care for 8.16
they work on the s. terms as we do. 11.12
Did we not act in the s. spirit? 12.18
Did we not take the s. steps? 12.18
heirs, members of the s. body, Eph 3.06
receive the s. again from the Lord, 6.08
do the s. to them, and forbear 6.09
engaged in the s. conflict which Php 1.30
being of the s. mind, having the s. love, 2.02
To write the s. things to you is 3.01
suffered the s. things from your 1Th 2.14
At the s. time, prepare a guest room Phm 1.22
But thou art the s., and thy years Heb 1.12
likewise partook of the s. nature, 2.14
one fall by the s. sort of disobedience 4.11
you to show the s. earnestness in 6.11
And in the s. way he sprinkled with 9.21
by the s. sacrifices which are 10.01
repeatedly the s. sacrifices, 10.11
heirs with him of the s. promise. 11.09
attempted to do the s., were drowned. 11.29
Jesus Christ is the s. yesterday 13.08
And in the s. way was not also Jas 2.25
From the s. mouth come blessing and 3.10
forth from the s. opening fresh 3.11
arm yourselves with the s. thought, 1Pe 4.01
them in the s. wild profligacy, and 4.04
that the s. experience of suffering 5.09
destroyed in the s. destruction 2Pe 2.12
But by the s. word the heavens and 3.07
to walk in the s. way in which he 1Jn 2.06
its length the s. as its breadth; Rev 21.16

SAMGARNEBO

S., Sarsechim the Rabsaris, Nergalsharezer Jer 39.03

SAMLAH

and S. of Masrekah reigned in his Gen 36.36
S. died, and Shaul of Rehoboth on 36.37

SAMLAH (cont.)
S. of Masrekah reigned in his stead 1Ch 1.47
When S. died, Shaul of Rehoboth on 1.48

SAMOS
the next day we touched at S.; Ac 20.15

SAMOTHRACE
we made a direct voyage to S., Ac 16.11

SAMSON
bore a son, and called his name S.; Ju 13.24
S. went down to Timnah, and at 14.01
But S. said to his father, "Get her 14.03
Then S. went down with his father 14.05
the woman; and she pleased S. well. 14.07
and S. made a feast there; for so the 14.10
And S. said to them, "Let me now put 14.12
S. went to visit his wife with a 15.01
And S. said to them, "This time I 15.03
So S. went and caught three hundred 15.04
"S., the son-in-law of the Timnite, 15.06
And S. said to them, "If this is 15.07
said, "We have come up to bind S., 15.10
and said to S., "Do you not know 15.11
And S. said to them, "Swear to me 15.12
And S. said, "With the jawbone of an 15.16
S. went to Gaza, and there he saw a 16.01
"S. has come here," and they surrounded 16.02
But S. lay till midnight, and at 16.03
And Delilah said to S., "Please tell 16.06
And S. said to her, "If they bind me 16.07
"The Philistines are upon you, S.!" 16.09
And Delilah said to S., "Behold, 16.10
"The Philistines are upon you, S.!" 16.12
And Delilah said to S., "Until now 16.13
"The Philistines are upon you, S.!" 16.14
"The Philistines are upon you, S.!" 16.20
god has given S. our enemy into 16.23
"Call S., that he may make sport 16.25
So they called S. out of the prison, 16.25
and S. said to the lad who held him 16.26
who looked on while S. made sport. 16.27
Then S. called to the LORD and said, 16.28
And S. grasped the two middle 16.29
And S. said, "Let me die with the 16.30
S., Jephthah, of David and Samuel Heb 11.32

SAMSON'S
fourth day they said to S. wife, Ju 14.15
And S. wife wept before him, and 14.16
And S. wife was given to his 14.20

SAMUEL
a son, and she called his name S., 1Sa 1.20
S. was ministering before the LORD, 2.18
And the boy S. grew in the presence 2.21
Now the boy S. continued to grow 2.26
Now the boy S. was ministering to 3.01
and S. was lying down within the 3.03
Then the LORD called, "S.! S.!" 3.04
And the LORD called again, "S.! 3.06
And S. arose and went to Eli, and 3.06
Now S. did not yet know the LORD, 3.07
And the LORD called S. again the 3.08
Therefore Eli said to S., "Go, lie down; 3.09
So S. went and lay down in his 3.09
calling as at other times, "S.! S.!" 3.10
And S. said, "Speak, for thy servant 3.10
Then the LORD said to S., "Behold, 3.11
S. lay until morning; then he opened 3.15
And S. was afraid to tell the 3.15
But Eli called S. and said, "S., my son." 3.16
So S. told him everything and hid 3.18
And S. grew, and the LORD was with 3.19
knew that S. was established as a 3.20
himself to S. at Shiloh by the 3.21
And the word of S. came to all 4.01
Then S. said to all the house of 7.03
Then S. said, "Gather all Israel at 7.05
And S. judged the people of Israel 7.06
And the people of Israel said to S., 7.08
So S. took a sucking lamb and 7.09
and S. cried to the LORD for Israel, 7.09
As S. was offering up the burnt 7.10
Then S. took a stone and set it up 7.12
the Philistines all the days of S. 7.13
S. judged Israel all the days of 7.15
When S. became old, he made his sons 8.01
together and came to S. at Ramah, 8.04
thing displeased S. when they said, 8.06
And S. prayed to the LORD. 8.06
And the LORD said to S., "Hearken to 8.07
So S. told all the words of the LORD 8.10
to listen to the voice of S.; and they said, 8.19
And when S. had heard all the words 8.21
And the LORD said to S., "Hearken to 8.22
S. then said to the men of Israel, 8.22
they saw S. coming out toward them 9.14
came, the LORD had revealed to S.: 9.15
When S. saw Saul, the LORD told him, 9.17
Then Saul approached S. in the gate, 9.18
S. answered Saul, "I am the seer; 9.19
Then S. took Saul and his servant 9.22
And S. said to the cook, "Bring the 9.23
and S. said, "See, what was kept is 9.24
So Saul ate with S. that day. 9.24
break of dawn S. called to Saul 9.26
and both he and S. went out into 9.26
S. said to Saul, "Tell the servant 9.27
Then S. took a vial of oil and 10.01
When he turned his back to leave S., 10.09
not to be found, we went to S." 10.14
"Pray, tell me what S. said to you." 10.15
of which S. had spoken, he did not 10.16
Now S. called the people together 10.17
Then S. brought all the tribes of 10.20
And S. said to all the people, "Do 10.24
Then S. told the people the rights 10.25
Then S. sent all the people away, 10.25
not come out after Saul and S., 11.07
Then the people said to S., 11.12
Then S. said to the people, "Come, 11.14
And S. said to all Israel, "Behold, I 12.01
And S. said to the people, "The LORD 12.06
and S., and delivered you out of 12.11
So S. called upon the LORD, and the 12.18
greatly feared the LORD and S. 12.18
And all the people said to S., 12.19
And S. said to the people, "Fear not 12.20
days, the time appointed by S.; 13.08
but S. did not come to Gilgal, and 13.08
burnt offering, behold, S. came; 13.10
S. said, "What have you done?" 13.11
And S. said to Saul, "You have done 13.13
And S. arose, and went up from 13.15
And S. said to Saul, "The LORD sent 15.01
The word of the LORD came to S.: 15.10
And S. was angry; and he cried 15.11
And S. rose early to meet Saul in 15.12
and it was told S., "Saul came to 15.12
And S. came to Saul, and Saul said 15.13
And S. said, "What then is this 15.14
Then S. said to Saul, "Stop! I will tell 15.16
And S. said, "Though you are little 15.17
And Saul said to S., "I have obeyed 15.20
And S. said, "Has the LORD as great 15.22
And Saul said to S., "I have sinned; 15.24
And S. said to Saul, "I will not 15.26
As S. turned to go away, Saul laid 15.27
And S. said to him, "The LORD has 15.28
So S. turned back after Saul; 15.31
Then S. said, "Bring here to me Agag 15.32
And S. said, "As your sword has made 15.33
And S. hewed Agag in pieces before 15.33
Then S. went to Ramah; and Saul went 15.34

SAMUEL (cont.)

And S. did not see Saul again until	1Sa 15.35
but S. grieved over Saul.	15.35
The LORD said to S., "How long will	16.01
And S. said, "How can I go? If Saul	16.02
S. did what the LORD commanded, and	16.04
But the LORD said to S., "Do not look	16.07
and made him pass before S. And he said,	16.08
seven of his sons pass before S.	16.10
And S. said to Jesse, "The LORD has	16.10
And S. said to Jesse, "Are all your	16.11
And S. said to Jesse, "Send and	16.11
Then S. took the horn of oil, and	16.13
And S. rose up, and went to Ramah.	16.13
escaped, and he came to S. at Ramah,	19.18
And he and S. went and dwelt at	19.18
and S. standing as head over them,	19.20
he asked, "Where are S. and David?"	19.22
and he too prophesied before S.,	19.24
Now S. died; and all Israel	25.01
Now S. had died, and all Israel had	28.03
He said, "Bring up S. for me."	28.11
When the woman saw S., she cried out	28.12
And Saul knew that it was S.,	28.14
Then S. said to Saul, "Why have you	28.15
And S. said, "Why then do you ask me,	28.16
fear because of the words of S.;	28.20
The sons of S.: Joel his first-born,	1Ch 6.28
singer the son of Joel, son of S.,	6.33
David and S. the seer established	9.22
to the word of the LORD by S.	11.03
Also all that S. the seer, and Saul	26.28
in the Chronicles of S. the seer,	29.29
since the days of S. the prophet;	2Ch 35.18
S. also was among those who called	Ps 99.06
Moses and S. stood before me, yet	Jer 15.01
from S. and those who came afterwards,	Ac 3.24
them judges until S. the prophet.	13.20
of David and S. and the prophets—	Heb 11.32

SANBALLAT

But when S. the Horonite and Tobiah	Neh 2.10
But when S. the Horonite and Tobiah	2.19
Now when S. heard that we were	4.01
But when S. and Tobiah and the	4.07
was reported to S. and Tobiah and	6.01
S. and Geshem sent to me, saying,	6.02
In the same way S. for the fifth	6.05
Tobiah and S. had hired him.	6.12
Remember Tobiah and S., O my God,	6.14
the son-in-law of S. the Horonite;	13.28

SANCTIFICATION

members to righteousness for s.	Rom 6.19
return you get is s. and its end,	6.22
righteousness and s. and redemption;	1Co 1.30
your s.: that you abstain from	1Th 4.03
through s. by the Spirit and belief	2Th 2.13

SANCTIFIED

and it shall be s. by my glory;	Ex 29.43
and the Levites s. themselves to	1Ch 15.14
who were present had s. themselves,	2Ch 5.11
and s. themselves, and went in as	29.15
eight days they s. the house of	29.17
faithless, we have made ready and s.;	29.19
priests had s. themselves their	29.34
priests had not s. themselves in	30.03
which he has s. for ever, and serve	30.08
so that they s. themselves, and	30.15
assembly who had not s. themselves;	30.17
And the priests s. themselves in	30.24
inheritance among all those who are s	Ac 20.32
those who are s. by faith in me.'	26.18
acceptable, s. by the Holy Spirit.	Rom 15.16
to those s. in Christ Jesus, called	1Co 1.02
you were s., you were justified in	6.11
those who are s. have all one	Heb 2.11
we have been s. through the offering	10.10
for all time those who are s.	10.14
of the covenant by which he was s.,	10.29
the Father and s. by the Spirit	1Pe 1.02

SANCTIFIES

For he who s. and those who are	Heb 2.11
of a heifer s. for the purification	9.13

SANCTIFY

may know that I, the LORD, s. you.	Ex 31.13
do them; I am the LORD who s. you.	Lev 20.08
I the LORD, who s. you, am holy.	21.08
for I am the LORD who s. him."	21.15
for I am the LORD who s. them."	21.23
it: I am the LORD who s. them.	22.09
for I am the LORD who s. them."	22.16
of Israel; I am the Lord who s. you,	22.32
to s. me in the eyes of the people	Num 20.12
to s. me at the waters before their	27.14
said to the people, "S. yourselves;	Jos 3.05
s. the people, and say, 'S. yourselves	7.13
"S. a solemn assembly for Baal."	2Ki 10.20
s. yourselves, you and your brethren,	1Ch 15.12
Now s. yourselves, and s. the house	2Ch 29.05
They began to s. on the first day	29.17
and s. yourselves, and prepare for	35.06
course, Job would send and s. them,	Job 1.05
in his midst, they will s. my name;	Is 29.23
they will s. the Holy One of Jacob,	29.23
"Those who s. and purify themselves	66.17
might know that I the LORD s. them.	Eze 20.12
know that I the LORD s. Israel,	37.28
S. a fast, call a solemn assembly.	Joe 1.14
s. a fast; call a solemn assembly;	2.15
S. the congregation; assemble the elders;	2.16
S. them in the truth; thy word is	Jn 17.17
that he might s. her, having cleansed	Eph 5.26
God of peace himself s. you wholly;	1Th 5.23
in order to s. the people through	Heb 13.12

SANCTIFYING

than the priests in s. themselves.	2Ch 29.34

SANCTUARIES

that he may not profane my s.;	Lev 21.23
and will make your s. desolate,	26.31
Jerusalem and preach against the s.;	Eze 21.02
of your trade you profaned your s.;	28.18
and the s. of Israel shall be laid	Amo 7.09

SANCTUARY

the s., O LORD, which thy hands have	Ex 15.17
And let them make me a s.,	25.08
shekel of the s. (the shekel is	30.13
according to the shekel of the s.,	30.24
construction of the s. shall work	36.01
for doing the work on the s.	36.03
every sort of task on the s. came,	36.04
more for the offering for the s."	36.06
in all the construction of the s.,	38.24
shekels, by the shekel of the s.	38.24
shekels, by the shekel of the s.:	38.25
a shekel, by the shekel of the s.),	38.26
for casting the bases of the s.,	38.27
in front of the veil of the s.	Lev 4.06
according to the shekel of the s.;	5.15
from before the s. out of the camp	10.04
offering in the place of the s.,	10.17
into the inner part of the s.,	10.18
ought to have eaten it in the s.,	10.18
thing, nor come into the s.,	12.04
he shall make atonement for the s.,	16.33
and reverence my s.: I am the LORD.	19.30
defiling my s. and profaning my	20.03
neither shall he go out of the s.,	21.12
nor profane the s. of his God;	21.12
and reverence my s.: I am the LORD.	26.02

SANCTUARY (cont.)

according to the shekel of the s. Lev 27.03
according to the shekel of the s.: 27.25
attending to the duties of the s. Num 3.28
vessels of the s. with which the 3.31
of those who had charge of the s. 3.32
charge of the rites within the s., 3.38
reckoning by the shekel of the s., 3.47
reckoned by the shekel of the s.; 3.50
service which are used in the s., 4.12
covering the s. and all the 4.15
and all the furnishings of the s., 4.15
in it, of the s. and its vessels." 4.16
according to the shekel of the s., 7.13
according to the shekel of the s., 7.19
according to the shekel of the s., 7.25
according to the shekel of the s., 7.31
according to the shekel of the s., 7.37
according to the shekel of the s., 7.43
according to the shekel of the s., 7.49
according to the shekel of the s., 7.55
according to the shekel of the s., 7.61
according to the shekel of the s., 7.67
according to the shekel of the s., 7.73
according to the shekel of the s., 7.79
according to the shekel of the s., 7.85
according to the shekel of the s., 7.86
of Israel should come near the s. 8.19
iniquity in connection with the s.; 18.01
vessels of the s. or to the altar, 18.03
duties of the s. and the duties of 18.05
according to the shekel of the s., 18.16
he has defiled the s. of the LORD; 19.20
vessels of the s. and the trumpets 31.06
whole yield be forfeited to the s., Deu 22.09
the oak in the s. of the LORD. Jos 24.26
both the nave and the inner s.; 1Ki 6.05
built this within as an inner s., 6.16
the nave in front of the inner s., 6.17
The inner s. he prepared in the 6.19
The inner s. was twenty cubits long, 6.20
across, in front of the inner s., 6.21
to the inner s. he overlaid with 6.22
In the inner s. he made two cherubim 6.23
to the inner s. he made doors of 6.31
on the north, before the inner s.; 7.49
in the inner s. of the house, in the 8.06
the holy place before the inner s.; 8.08
and build the s. of the LORD God, 1Ch 22.19
of the tent of meeting and the s., 23.32
officers of the s. and officers of 24.05
you to build a house for the s.; 28.10
before the inner s., as prescribed; 2Ch 4.20
in the inner s. of the house, in the 5.07
the holy place before the inner s.; 5.09
built thee in it a s. for thy name, 20.08
Go out of the s.; for you have 26.18
and for the s. and for Judah. 29.21
to the LORD, and come to his s., 30.08
the sword in the house of their s., 36.17
where are the vessels of the s., Neh 10.39
May he send you help from the s., Ps 20.02
my hands toward thy most holy s. 28.02
God has spoken in his s.: "With exultation 60.06
So I have looked upon thee in the s., 63.02
of my God, my King, into the s.— 68.24
Terrible is God in his s., the God of 68.35
until I went into the s. of God; 73.17
has destroyed everything in the s.! 74.03
They set thy s. on fire; to the ground 74.07
He built his s. like the high heavens 78.69
strength and beauty are in his s. 96.06
God has promised in his s.: 108.07
Judah became his s., Israel his 114.02
Praise God in his s.; praise him in 150.01
And he will become a s., and a stone Is 8.14
when he comes to his s. to pray, 16.12
Therefore I profaned the princes of the s., 43.28
to beautify the place of my s.; 60.13
drink it in the courts of my s. 62.09
possessed thy s. a little while; 63.18
beginning is the place of our s. Jer 17.12
has seen the nations invade her s., Lam 1.10
scorned his altar, disowned his s.; 2.07
be slain in the s. of the Lord? 2.20
have defiled my s. with all your Eze 5.11
here, to drive me far from my s.? 8.06
And begin at my s." So they began 9.06
I have been a s. to them for a 11.16
have defiled my s. on the same day 23.38
they came into my s. to profane it. 23.39
GOD: Behold, I will profane my s., 24.21
over my s. when it was profaned, 25.03
and will set my s. in the midst of 37.26
when my s. is in the midst of them 37.28
back to the outer gate of the s., 44.01
who are to be excluded from the s. 44.05
to be in my s., profaning it, when 44.07
foreigners to keep my charge in my s. 44.08
of Israel, shall enter my s. 44.09
They shall be ministers in my s., 44.11
charge of my s. when the people of 44.15
they shall enter my s., and they shall 44.16
hundred cubits shall be for the s., 45.02
broad, in which shall be the s., 45.03
minister in the s. and approach 45.04
houses and a holy place for the s. 45.04
blemish, and cleanse the s. 45.18
water for them flows from the s. 47.12
with the s. in the midst of it. 48.08
with the s. of the LORD in the 48.10
with the s. of the temple in its 48.21
the place of his s. was overthrown. Dan 8.11
over of the s. and host to be 8.13
then the s. shall be restored to 8.14
thy face to shine upon thy s., 9.17
shall destroy the city and the s. 9.26
at Bethel, for it is the king's s., Amo 7.13
has profaned the s. of the LORD, Mal 2.11
between the s. and the altar. Mt 23.35
between the altar and the s. Lk 11.51
a minister in the s. and the true Heb 8.02
copy and shadow of the heavenly s.; 8.05
for worship and an earthly s. 9.01
way into the s. is not yet opened 9.08
not into a s. made with hands, a 9.24
to enter the s. by the blood of 10.19
into the s. by the high priest as 13.11

SANCTUARY'S

according to the s. rules of 2Ch 30.19

SAND

and as the s. which is on the Gen 22.17
descendants as the s. of the sea, 32.12
like the s. of the sea, until he 41.49
the Egyptian and hid him in the s. Ex 2.12
the s. lizard, and the chameleon. Lev 11.30
and the hidden treasures of the s." Deu 33.19
number like the s. that is upon Jos 11.04
as the s. which is upon the seashore Ju 7.12
troops like the s. on the seashore 1Sa 13.05
as the s. by the sea for multitude, 2Sa 17.11
were as many as the s. by the sea; 1Ki 4.20
mind like the s. on the seashore, 4.29
be heavier than the s. of the sea; Job 6.03
shall multiply my days as the s., 29.18
birds like the s. of the seas; Ps 78.27
them, they are more than the s. 139.18
and s. is weighty, but a fool's Pro 27.03
Israel be as the s. of the sea, Is 10.22
the burning s. shall become a pool, 35.07
would have been like the s., 48.19
I placed the s. as the bound for Jer 5.22
in number than the s. of the seas; 15.08
shall be like the s. of the sea, Hos 1.10

SAND (cont.)
They gather captives like s. Hab 1.09
who built his house upon the s.; Mt 7.26
of Israel be as the s. of the sea, Rom 9.27
grains of s. by the seashore. Heb 11.12
and he stood on the s. of the sea. Rev 12.17
number is like the s. of the sea. 20.08

SANDAL
and pull his s. off his foot, and Deu 25.09
of him that had his s. pulled off. 25.10
drew off his s. and gave it to the Ru 4.07
for yourself," he drew off his s. 4.08
thong of whose s. I am not worthy Jn 1.27

SANDALS
your s. on your feet, and your staff Ex 12.11
and your s. have not worn off your Deu 29.05
patched s. on their feet, and Jos 9.05
loins, and upon the s. on my feet. 1Ki 2.05
gave them s., provided them with 2Ch 28.15
How graceful are your feet in s., Sol 7.01
and the needy for a pair of s., Amo 8.06
whose s. I am not worthy to carry; Mt 3.11
two tunics, nor s., nor a staff; 10.10
thong of whose s. I am not worthy Mk 1.07
but to wear s. and not put on two 6.09
thong of whose s. I am not worthy Lk 3.16
Carry no purse, no bag, no s.; 10.04
you out with no purse or bag or s., 22.35
"Dress yourself and put on your s." Ac 12.08
the s. of whose feet I am not 13.25

SANDAL-THONG
a thread or a s. or anything that Gen 14.23
waistcloth is loose, not a s. broken; Is 5.27

SANDS
numbered and the s. of the sea Jer 33.22

SANE
therefore keep s. and sober for 1Pe 4.07

SANG
of Israel s. this song to the LORD, Ex 15.01
And Miriam s. to them: "Sing to the 15.21
Then Israel s. this song: "Spring up, Num 21.17
Then s. Deborah and Barak the son Ju 5.01
And the women s. to one another as 1Sa 18.07
worshiped, and the singers s., 2Ch 29.28
And they s. praises with gladness, 29.30
and they s. responsively, praising Ez 3.11
And the singers s. with Jezrahiah Neh 12.42
when the morning stars s. together, Job 38.07
his words; they s. his praise. Ps 106.12
and they s. a new song, saying, Rev 5.09

SANK
they s. as lead in the mighty Ex 15.10
He s., he fell, he lay still at her Ju 5.27
he s., he fell; where he s., there 5.27
the stone s. into his forehead, and 1Sa 17.49
heart, and he s. in his chariot. 2Ki 9.24
they s. into sleep; all the men of war Ps 76.05
the valleys s. down to the place 104.08
mire, and Jeremiah s. in the mire. Jer 38.06
the everlasting hills s. low. Hab 3.06
He s. into a deep sleep as Paul Ac 20.09

SANSANNAH
Ziklag, Madmannah, S., Jos 15.31

SAP
in old age, are ever full of s. and green, Ps 92.14

SAPH
Sibbecai the Hushathite slew S., 2Sa 21.18

SAPPHIRA
with his wife S. sold a piece of Ac 5.01

SAPPHIRE
as it were a pavement of s. stone, Ex 24.10
an emerald, a s., and a diamond; 28.18
an emerald, a s., and a diamond; 39.11
of Ophir, in precious onyx or s. Job 28.16
beauty of their form was like s. Lam 4.07
of a throne, in appearance like s.; Eze 1.26
above them something like a s., 10.01
s., carbuncle, and emerald; 28.13
of fire and of s. and of sulphur, Rev 9.17
the second s., the third agate, the 21.19

SAPPHIRES
Its stones are the place of s., Job 28.06
is ivory work, encrusted with s. Sol 5.14
and lay your foundations with s. Is 54.11

SARAH
her name, Sarai, but S. shall be her Gen 17.15
Shall S., who is ninety years old, 17.17
but S. your wife shall bear you a 17.19
whom S. shall bear to you at this 17.21
hastened into the tent to S., 18.06
said to him, "Where is S. your wife?" 18.09
and S. your wife shall have a son." 18.10
And S. was listening at the tent 18.10
Now Abraham and S. were old, 18.11
to be with S. after the manner of 18.11
So S. laughed to herself, saying, 18.12
"Why did S. laugh, and say, 'Shall I 18.13
and S. shall have a son." 18.14
But S. denied, saying, "I did not 18.15
And Abraham said of S. his wife, 20.02
king of Gerar sent and took S. 20.02
and restored S. his wife to him. 20.14
To S. he said, "Behold, I have given 20.16
house of Abimelech because of S., 20.18
The LORD visited S. as he had said, 21.01
the LORD did to S. as he had 21.01
And S. conceived, and bore Abraham a 21.02
whom S. bore him, Isaac. 21.03
And S. said, "God has made laughter 21.06
to Abraham that S. would suckle 21.07
But S. saw the son of Hagar the 21.09
whatever S. says to you, do as she 21.12
S. lived a hundred and twenty-seven 23.01
were the years of the life of S. 23.01
And S. died at Kiriatharba (that is, 23.02
in to mourn for S. and to weep for 23.02
Abraham buried S. his wife in the 23.19
And S. my master's wife bore a son 24.36
was buried, with S. his wife. 25.10
buried Abraham and S. his wife; 49.31
your father and to S. who bore you; Is 51.02
will return and S. shall have a Rom 9.09
By faith S. herself received power Heb 11.11
as S. obeyed Abraham, calling him 1Pe 3.06

SARAH'S
the Egyptian S. maid, bore to Abraham. Gen 25.12
considered the barrenness of S. womb. Rom 4.19

SARAI
the name of Abram's wife was S., Gen 11.29
Now S. was barren; she had no child. 11.30
and S. his daughter-in-law, his son 11.31
And Abram took S. his wife, and Lot 12.05
he said to S. his wife, "I know that 12.11
because of S., Abram's wife. 12.17
Now S., Abram's wife, bore him no 16.01
and S. said to Abram, "Behold now, 16.02
Abram hearkened to the voice of S. 16.02
S., Abram's wife, took Hagar the 16.03
And S. said to Abram, "May the wrong 16.05
But Abram said to S., "Behold your 16.06

SARAI (cont.)
Then S. dealt harshly with her, and Gen 16.06
maid of S., where have you come 16.08
"I am fleeing from my mistress S." 16.08
"As for S. your wife, you shall not 17.15
you shall not call her name S., 17.15

SARAPH
and S., who ruled in Moab and 1Ch 4.22

SARDIS
Thyatira and to S. and to Philadelphia Rev 1.11
angel of the church in S. write: 3.01
Yet you have still a few names in S., 3.04

SARDIUS
A row of s., topaz, and carbuncle Ex 28.17
A row of s., topaz, and carbuncle 39.10

SARGON
who was sent by S. the king of Is 20.01

SARID
inheritance reached as far as S.; Jos 19.10
from S. it goes in the other 19.12

SARSECHIM
S. the Rabsaris, Nergalsharezer the Jer 39.03

SASHES
the s., the perfume boxes, and the Is 3.20

SAT
as he s. at the door of his tent in Gen 18.01
and s. down over against him a good 21.16
And as she s. over against him, the 21.16
camel's saddle, and s. upon them. 31.34
Then thy s. down to eat; and looking 37.25
and s. at the entrance to Enaim, 38.14
And they s. before him, the first-born 43.33
his strength, and s. up in bed. 48.02
of Midian; and he s. down by a well. Ex 2.15
of Pharaoh who s. on his throne to 12.29
when we s. by the fleshpots and ate 16.03
and he s. upon it, and Aaron and Hur 17.12
morrow Moses s. to judge the people, and 18.13
and the people s. down to eat and 32.06
discharge has s. shall wash his Lev 15.06
Asher s. still at the coast of the Ju 5.17
LORD came and s. under the oak at 6.11
the woman as she s. in the field; 13.09
So the two men s. and ate and drank 19.06
he went in and s. down in the open 19.15
they s. there before the LORD, and 20.26
and s. there till evening before 21.02
So she s. beside the reapers, and he Ru 2.14
up to the gate and s. down there; 4.01
and he turned aside and s. down. 4.01
"Sit down here"; so they s. down. 4.02
as he s. in his house with his 1Sa 19.09
the king s. down to eat food. 20.24
The king s. upon the seat, as at 20.25
Jonathan s. opposite, and Abner 20.25
and Abner s. by Saul's side, but 20.25
the earth, and s. upon the bed. 28.23
and they s. down, the one on the one 2Sa 2.13
went in and s. before the LORD, and 7.18
So Solomon s. upon the throne of 1Ki 2.12
then he s. on his throne, and had a 2.19
king's mother, and she s. on his right. 2.19
And as they s. at the table, the 13.20
and came and s. down under a broom 19.04
came in and s. opposite him; and the base 21.13
the child s. on her lap till noon, 2Ki 4.20
and Jeroboam s. upon his throne; 13.13
went in and s. before the LORD, and 1Ch 17.16
Then Solomon s. on the throne of 29.23
my head and beard, and s. appalled. Ez 9.03
me while I s. appalled until the 9.04
all the people s. in the open 10.09
month they s. down to examine the 10.16
these words I s. down and wept, Neh 1.04
King Ahasuerus s. on his royal Est 1.02
king's face, and s. first in the kingdom—: 1.14
king and Haman s. down to drink; 3.15
scrape himself, and s. among the ashes. Job 2.08
And they s. with him on the ground 2.13
and s. as chief, and I dwelt like a 29.25
thou hast s. on the throne giving Ps 9.04
Some s. in darkness and in gloom, 107.10
there we s. down and wept, when we 137.01
great delight I s. in his shadow, Sol 2.03
down those who s. on thrones. Is 10.13
you have s. awaiting lovers like Jer 3.02
I s. alone, because thy hand was 15.17
came and s. in the middle gate: 39.03
And I s. there overwhelmed among Eze 3.15
as I s. in my house, with the elders 8.01
there s. women weeping for Tammuz. 8.14
of Israel to me, and s. before me. 14.01
of the LORD, and s. before me. 20.01
you s. upon a stately couch, with a 23.41
the court s. in judgment, and the Dan 7.10
with sackcloth, and s. in ashes. Jon 3.06
of the city and s. to the east of 4.05
He s. under it in the shade, till he 4.05
than Thebes that s. by the Nile, Nah 3.08
the people who s. in darkness have Mt 4.16
for those who s. in the region and 4.16
and when he s. down his disciples 5.01
And as he s. at table in the house, 9.10
came and s. down with Jesus and 9.10
of the house and s. beside the sea. 13.01
he got into a boat and s. there; 13.02
it ashore and s. down and sorted 13.48
into the hills, and s. down there. 15.29
garments on them, and he s. thereon. 21.07
As he s. on the Mount of Olives, the 24.03
it on his head, as he s. at table. 26.07
he s. at table with the twelve 26.20
Day after day I s. in the temple 26.55
going inside he s. with the guards 26.58
then they s. down and kept watch 27.36
back the stone, and s. upon it. 28.02
And as he s. at table in his house, Mk 2.15
around on those who s. about him, 3.34
into a boat and s. in it on the 4.01
So they s. down in groups, by 6.40
And he s. down and called the 9.35
tied, on which no one has ever s.; 11.02
garments on it; and he s. upon it. 11.07
And he s. down opposite the treasury, 12.41
And as he s. on the Mount of Olives 13.03
as he s. at table, a woman came with 14.03
eleven themselves as they s. at table; * 16.14
and s. down at the right hand of God. * 16.19
back to the attendant, and s. down; Lk 4.20
And he s. down and taught the 5.03
And the dead man s. up, and began to 7.15
Pharisee's house, and s. at table. 7.36
who s. at the Lord's feet and 10.39
so he went in and s. at table. 11.37
of those who s. at table with him 14.15
on which no one has ever yet s.; 19.30
he s. at table, and the apostles 22.14
the courtyard and s. down together, 22.55
down together, Peter s. among them. 22.55
him as he s. in the light and 22.56
s. down beside the well. Jn 4.06
and there s. down with his disciples 6.03
so the men s. down, in number about 6.10
and he s. down and taught them. * 8.02
him, while Mary s. in the house. 11.20
found a young ass and s. upon it; 12.14
Jesus out and s. down on the 19.13
as the one who s. for alms at the Ac 3.10

SAT (cont.)
all who s. in the council saw that Ac 6.15
and when she saw Peter she s. up. 9.40
into the synagogue and s. down. 13.14
and we s. down and spoke to the 16.13
"The people s. down to eat and 1Co 10.07
he s. down at the right hand of the Heb 1.03
he s. down at the right hand of God, 10.12
conquered and s. down with my Rev 3.21
And he who s. there appeared like 4.03
voice to him who s. upon the cloud, 14.15
So he who s. upon the cloud swung 14.16
He who s. upon it is called Faithful 19.11
throne and him who s. upon it; 20.11
And he who s. upon the throne said, 21.05

SATAN
S. stood up against Israel, and 1Ch 21.01
and S. also came among them. Job 1.06
The LORD said to S., "Whence have you 1.07
S. answered the LORD, "From going 1.07
And the LORD said to S., "Have you 1.08
Then S. answered the LORD, "Does Job 1.09
And the LORD said to S., "Behold, 1.12
So S. went forth from the presence 1.12
and S. also came among them to 2.01
And the LORD said to S., "Whence have 2.02
S. answered the LORD, "From going 2.02
And the LORD said to S., "Have you 2.03
Then S. answered the LORD, "Skin for 2.04
And the LORD said to S., "Behold, he 2.06
So S. went forth from the presence 2.07
and S. standing at his right hand Zec 3.01
And the LORD said to S., "The LORD 3.02
"The LORD rebuke you, O S.! 3.02
Then Jesus said to him, "Begone, S.! Mt 4.10
and if S. casts out S., he is 12.26
said to Peter, "Get behind me, S.! 16.23
wilderness forty days, tempted by S.; Mk 1.13
parables, "How can S. cast out S.? 3.23
And if S. has risen up against 3.26
S. immediately comes and takes away 4.15
Peter, and said, "Get behind me, S.! 8.33
"I saw S. fall like lightning from Lk 10.18
And if S. also is divided against 11.18
of Abraham whom S. bound for 13.16
Then S. entered into Judas called 22.03
S. demanded to have you, that he 22.31
S. entered into him. Jesus said to him, Jn 13.27
why has S. filled your heart to lie Ac 5.03
and from the power of S. to God, 26.18
will soon crush S. under your feet Rom 16.20
this man to S. for the destruction 1Co 5.05
lest S. tempt you through lack of 7.05
to keep S. from gaining the advantage 2Co 2.11
for even S. disguises himself as an 11.14
me in the flesh, a messenger of S., 12.07
again and again—but S. hindered us. 1Th 2.18
the activity of S. will be with 2Th 2.09
delivered to S. that they may 1Ti 1.20
some have already strayed after S. 5.15
are not, but are a synagogue of S. Rev 2.09
killed among you, where S. dwells. 2.13
some call the deep things of S., 2.24
synagogue of S. who say that they 3.09
who is called the Devil and S., 12.09
serpent, who is the Devil and S., 20.02
S. will be loosed from his prison 20.07

SATAN'S
you dwell, where S. throne is; Rev 2.13

SATED
But before they had s. their craving, Ps 78.30
soul has been s. with the scorn of 123.04
way and be s. with their own devices. Pro 1.31
lest you be s. with it and vomit it 25.16
He who is s. loathes honey, but to 27.07

it is s. with blood, it is gorged Is 34.06
The sword shall devour and be s., Jer 46.10
her shall be s., says the LORD. 50.10
bitterness, he has s. me with wormwood. Lam 3.15
You will be s. with contempt instead of Hab 2.16

SATISFACTION
What has become of the s. you felt? Gal 4.15
and to give s. in every respect; Tit 2.09

SATISFIED
and you shall eat, and not be s. Lev 26.26
s. with favor, and full of the Deu 33.23
and she ate until she was s., Ru 2.14
she had left over after being s. 2.18
Why are you not s. with my flesh? Job 19.22
I shall be s. with beholding thy Ps 17.15
The afflicted shall eat and be s.; 22.26
We shall be s. with the goodness of 65.04
the earth is s. with the fruit of 104.13
of his words a man is s. with good, Pro 12.14
the fruit of his mouth a man is s.; 18.20
he is s. by the yield of his lips. 18.20
and he who has it rests s.; 19.23
Sheol and Abaddon are never s., 27.20
and never s. are the eyes of man. 27.20
Three things are never s.; 30.15
the eye is not s. with seeing, Ecc 1.08
his eyes are never s. with riches, 4.08
money will not be s. with money; 5.10
mouth, yet his appetite is not s. 6.07
devour on the left, but are not s.; Is 9.20
and awakes with his hunger not s., 29.08
or s. me with the fat of your 43.24
flesh, he roasts meat and is s.; 44.16
the travail of his soul and be s.; 53.11
may suck and be s. with her 66.11
people shall be s. with my goodness, Jer 31.14
desire shall be s. on the hills of 50.19
them, and still you were not s. Eze 16.28
and even with this you were not s. 16.29
till I have s. my fury upon you. 24.13
from the seas, you s. many peoples; 27.33
They shall eat, but not be s.; Hos 4.10
wine, and oil, and you will be s.; Joe 2.19
"You shall eat in plenty and be s., 2.26
to drink water, and were not s.; Amo 4.08
but not be s., and there shall be Mic 6.14
righteousness, for they shall be s. Mt 5.06
And they all ate and were s. And they took up 14.20
And they all ate and were s.; and they took 15.37
And they all ate and were s. Mk 6.42
And they ate, and were s.; and they took 8.08
hunger now, for you shall be s. Lk 6.21
And all ate and were s. And they took 9.17
us the Father, and we shall be s." Jn 14.08
I myself am s. about you, my brethren, Rom 15.14

SATISFIES
who s. you with good as long as you Ps 103.05
For he s. him who is thirsty, and 107.09

SATISFIEST
thou s. the desire of every living Ps 145.16

SATISFY
to s. the waste and desolate land, Job 38.27
or s. the appetite of the young 38.39
honey from the rock I would s. you." Ps 81.16
S. us in the morning with thy 90.14
With long life I will s. him, 91.16
I will s. her poor with bread. 132.15
if he steals to s. his appetite Pro 6.30
has enough to s. his appetite, 13.25
labor for that which does not s.? Is 55.02
the hungry and s. the desire of 58.10
and s. your desire with good things, 58.11
For I will s. the weary soul, and Jer 31.25

SATISFY (cont.)
my fury upon them and s. myself; Eze 5.13
they cannot s. their hunger or fill 7.19
So will I s. my fury on you, and my 16.42
my hands, and I will s. my fury; 21.17
we will s. him and keep you out of Mt 28.14
wishing to s. the crowd, released Mk 15.15
his aim is to s. the one who 2Ti 2.04

SATISFYING
s. your hearts with food and Ac 14.17

SATRAPS
to the king's s. and to the Ez 8.36
to the king's s. and to the Est 3.12
the Jews to the s. and the governors 8.09
provinces and the s. and the 9.03
Nebuchadnezzar sent to assemble the s., Dan 3.02
Then the s., the prefects, and the 3.03
And the s., the prefects, the 3.27
kingdom a hundred and twenty s., 6.01
to whom these s. should give 6.02
all the other presidents and s., 6.03
presidents and the s. sought to 6.04
presidents and s. came by agreement 6.06
kingdom, the prefects and the s., 6.07

SATYR
the s. shall cry to his fellow; Is 34.14

SATYRS
more slay their sacrifices for s., Lev 17.07
and for the s., and for the calves 2Ch 11.15
dwell, and there s. will dance. Is 13.21

SAUL
and he had a son whose name was S., 1Sa 9.02
So Kish said to S. his son, 9.03
S. said to his servant who was with 9.05
Then S. said to his servant, "But if 9.07
The servant answered S. again, 9.08
And S. said to his servant, "Well 9.10
Now the day before S. came, 9.15
When Samuel say S., the LORD told 9.17
Then S. approached Samuel in the 9.18
Samuel answered S., "I am the seer; 9.19
S. answered, "Am I not a Benjaminite, 9.21
Then Samuel took S. and his servant 9.22
portion and set them before S.; 9.24
So S. ate with Samuel that day. 9.24
was spread for S. upon the roof, 9.25
Samuel called to S. upon the roof, 9.26
So S. arose, and both he and Samuel 9.26
of the city, Samuel said to S., 9.27
Is S. also among the prophets?" 10.11
"Is S. also among the prophets?" 10.12
And S. said to his uncle, "He told 10.16
and S. the son of Kish was taken by 10.21
S. also went to his home at Gibeah, 10.26
messengers came to Gibeah of S., 11.04
Now S. was coming from the field 11.05
and S. said, "What ails the people, 11.05
mightily upon S. when he heard 11.06
not come out after S. and Samuel, 11.07
And on the morrow S. put the people 11.11
that said, 'Shall S. reign over us? 11.12
But S. said, "Not a man shall be put 11.13
there they made S. king before the 11.15
and there S. and all the men of 11.15
S. was . . . years old when he began 13.01
S. chose three thousand men of 13.02
were with S. in Michmash and the 13.02
And S. blew the trumpet throughout 13.03
it said that S. had defeated the 13.04
called out to join S. at Gilgal. 13.04
S. was still at Gilgal, and all the 13.07
So S. said, "Bring the burnt offering 13.09
and S. went out to meet him and 13.10
And S. said, "When I saw that the 13.11
And Samuel said to S., "You have done 13.13
And S. numbered the people who were 13.15
And S., and Jonathan his son, and 13.16
of the people with S. and Jonathan; 13.22
but S. and Jonathan his son had 13.22
the son of S. said to the young 14.01
S. was staying in the outskirts of 14.02
And the watchmen of S. in Gibeah of 14.16
Then S. said to the people who were 14.17
And S. said to Ahijah, "Bring hither 14.18
And while S. was talking to the 14.19
and S. said to the priest, "Withdraw 14.19
Then S. and all the people who were 14.20
who were with S. and Jonathan. 14.21
for S. laid an oath on the people, 14.24
Then they told S., "Behold, the 14.33
And S. said, "Disperse yourselves 14.34
And S. built an altar to the LORD; 14.35
Then S. said, "Let us go down after 14.36
And S. inquired of God, "Shall I go 14.37
And S. said, "Come hither, all you 14.38
And the people said to S., "Do what 14.40
Therefore S. said, "O LORD God of 14.41
And Jonathan and S. were taken, 14.41
Then S. said, "Cast the lot between 14.42
Then S. said to Jonathan, "Tell me 14.43
And S. said, "God do so to me and 14.44
Then the people said to S., 14.45
Then S. went up from pursuing the 14.46
When S. had taken the kingship over 14.47
Now the sons of S. were Jonathan, 14.49
Kish was the father of S., and Ner the 14.51
The Philistines all the days of S.; 14.52
and when S. saw any strong man, or 14.52
And Samuel said to S., "The LORD sent 15.01
So S. summoned the people, and 15.04
And S. came to the city of Amalek, 15.05
And S. said to the Kenites, "Go, 15.06
And S. defeated the Amalekites, from 15.07
But S. and the people spared Agag, 15.09
"I repent that I have made S. king; 15.11
early to meet S. in the morning; 15.12
"S. came to Carmel, and behold, he 15.12
And Samuel came to S., 15.13
and S. said to him, "Blessed be you 15.13
S. said, "They have brought them 15.15
Then Samuel said to S., "Stop! 15.16
And S. said to Samuel, "I have 15.20
And S. said to Samuel, "I have 15.24
And Samuel said to S., "I will not 15.26
S. laid hold upon the skirt of his 15.27
So Samuel turned back after S.; 15.31
and S. worshiped the LORD. 15.31
and S. went up to his house in 15.34
up to his house in Gibeah of S. 15.34
did not see S. again until the day 15.35
death, but Samuel grieved over S. 15.35
he had made S. king over Israel. 15.35
"How long will you grieve over S., 16.01
If S. hears it, he will kill me. 16.02
of the LORD departed from S., and an 16.14
So S. said to his servants, "Provide 16.17
Therefore S. sent messengers to 16.19
sent them by David his son to S. 16.20
And David came to S., and entered 16.21
And S. loved him greatly, and he 16.21
And S. sent to Jesse, saying, "Let 16.22
evil spirit from God was upon S., 16.23
so S. was refreshed, and was well, 16.23
And S. and the men of Israel were 17.02
and are you not servants of S.? 17.08
When S. and all Israel heard these 17.11
In the days of S. the man was 17.12
had followed S. to the battle; 17.13
the three eldest followed S., 17.14
and forth from S. to feed his 17.15

SAUL (cont.)
Now S., and they, and all the men of 1Sa 17.19
they repeated them before S.; 17.31
And David said to S., "Let no man's 17.32
And S. said to David, "You are not 17.33
But David said to S., "Your servant 17.34
And S. said to David, "Go, and the 17.37
Then S. clothed David with his 17.38
Then David said to S., "I cannot go 17.39
When S. saw David go forth against 17.55
him before S with the head of the 17.57
And S. said to him, "Whose son are 17.58
When he had finished speaking to S., 18.01
And S. took him that day, and would 18.02
successful wherever S. sent him; 18.05
so that S. set him over the men of 18.05
to meet King S., with timbrels, with 18.06
"S. has slain his thousands, And 18.07
And S. was very angry, and this 18.08
And S. eyed David from that day on. 18.09
spirit from God rushed upon S., 18.10
S. had his spear in his hand; 18.10
and S. cast the spear, for he 18.11
S. was afraid of David, because the 18.12
with him but had departed from S. 18.12
So S. removed him from his presence, 18.13
And when S. saw that he had great 18.15
Then S. said to David, "Here is my 18.17
For S. thought, "Let not my hand be 18.17
And David said to S., "Who am I, 18.18
and they told S., and the thing 18.20
Therefore S. said to David a second 18.21
And S. commanded his servants, 18.22
And the servants of S. told him, 18.24
Then S. said, "Thus shall you say to 18.25
Now S. thought to make David fall 18.25
And S. gave him his daughter Michal 18.27
But when S. saw and knew that the 18.28
S. was still more afraid of David. 18.29
So S. was David's enemy continually. 18.29
than all the servants of S.; 18.30
And S. spoke to Jonathan his son 19.01
"S. my father seeks to kill you; 19.02
well of David to S. his father, 19.04
And S. hearkened to the voice of 19.06
S. swore, "As the LORD lives, he 19.06
And Jonathan brought David to S., 19.07
spirit from the LORD came upon S., 19.09
And S. sought to pin David to the 19.10
but he eluded S., so that he struck 19.10
That night S. sent messengers to 19.11
And when S. sent messengers to take 19.14
Then S. sent the messengers to see 19.15
S. said to Michal, "Why have you 19.17
And Michal answered S., "He said to me, 19.17
him all that S. had done to him. 19.18
And it was told S., "Behold, David is at 19.19
Then S. sent messengers to take 19.20
God came upon the messengers of S, 19.20
When it was told S., he sent other 19.21
And S. sent messengers again the 19.21
"Is S. also among the prophets?" 19.24
Yet S. did not say anything that 20.26
And S. said to Jonathan his son, 20.27
Jonathan answered S., "David earnestly 20.28
Then Jonathan answered S. his father, 20.32
But S. cast his spear at him to 20.33
the servants of S. was there that 21.07
rose and fled that day from S., 21.10
'S. has slain his thousands, And 21.11
Now S. heard that David was discovered, 22.06
S. was sitting at Gibeah, under the 22.06
And S. said to his servants who 22.07
who stood by the servants of S., 22.09
And S. said, "Hear now, son of Ahitub." 22.12
And S. said to him, "They have you 22.13
told David that S. had killed the 22.21
that he would surely tell S. 22.22
Now it was told S. that David had 23.07
And S. said, "God has given him into 23.07
And S. summoned all the people to 23.08
David knew that S. was plotting 23.09
heard that S. seeks to come to 23.10
Will S. come down, as thy servant 23.11
me and my men into the hand of S.?" 23.12
When S. was told that David had 23.13
And S. tought him every day, but God 23.14
afraid because S. had come out to 23.15
for the hand of S. my father shall 23.17
S. my father also knows this." 23.17
Ziphites went up to S. at Gibeah, 23.19
And S. said, "May you be blessed by 23.21
and went to Ziph ahead of S. 23.24
And when S. heard that, he pursued 23.25
S. went on one side of the mountain, 23.26
making haste to get away from S., 23.26
as S. and his men were closing in 23.26
when a messenger came to S., 23.27
So S. returned from pursuing after 23.28
When S. returned from following the 24.01
Then S. took three thousand chosen 24.02
and S. went in to relieve himself. 24.03
did not permit them to attack S. 24.07
And S. rose up and left the cave, 24.07
of the cave, and called after S., 24.08
And when S. looked behind him, David 24.08
And David said to S., "Why do you 24.09
finished speaking these words to S., 24.16
S. said, "Is this your voice, my son 24.16
And S. lifted up his voice and wept 24.16
And David swore this to S. 24.22
Then S. went home; but David and 24.22
S. had given Michal his daughter, 25.44
Then the Ziphites came to S. at Gibeah, 26.01
So S. arose and went down to the 26.02
And S. encamped on the hill of 26.03
he saw that S. came after him into 26.03
of a certainty that S. had come. 26.04
to the place where S. had encamped; 26.05
David saw the place where S. lay, 26.05
S. was lying within the encampment, 26.05
down with me into the camp to S.?" 26.06
and there lay S. sleeping within 26.07
S. recognized David's voice, and said, 26.17
Then S. said, "I have done wrong; 26.21
Then S. said to David, "Blessed be 26.25
and S. returned to his place. 26.25
perish one day by the hand of S.; 27.01
then S. will despair of seeking me 27.01
it was told S. that David had fled 27.04
And S. had put the mediums and the 28.03
and S. gathered all Israel, and they 28.04
When S. saw the army of the Philistines, 28.05
And when S. inquired of the LORD, 28.06
Then S. said to his servants, "Seek 28.07
So S. disguised himself and put on 28.08
"Surely you know what S. has done, 28.09
But S. wore to her by the LORD, "As 28.10
and the woman said to S., "Why have you 28.12
deceived me? You are S." 28.12
And the woman said to S., "I see a god 28.13
And S. knew that it was Samuel, and 28.14
Then Samuel said to S., "Why have you 28.15
S. answered, "I am in great distress 28.15
Then S. fell at once full length 28.20
And the woman came to S., and when she 28.21
put it before S. and his servants; 28.25
not this David, the servant of S., 29.03
'S. has slain his thousands, And 29.05
Philistines overtook S. and his sons; 31.02
and Malchishua, the sons of S. 31.02
The battle pressed hard upon S., 31.03
Then S. said to his armor-bearer, 31.04
Therefore S. took his own sword, and 31.04
armor-bearer saw that S. was dead, 31.05
Thus S. died, and his three sons, and 31.06

SAUL (cont.)
fled and that S. and his sons were 1Sa 31.07
they found S. and his three sons 31.08
the Philistines had done to S., 31.11
the body of S. and the bodies of 31.12
After the death of S., when David had 2Sa 1.01
and S. and his son Jonathan are 1.04
you know that S. and his son 1.05
and there was S. leaning upon his 1.06
evening for S. and for Jonathan 1.12
lamentation over S. and Jonathan 1.17
the shield of S., not anointed with 1.21
the sword of S. returned not empty 1.22
"S. and Jonathan, beloved and lovely 1.23
weep over S., who clothed you 1.24
of Jabeshgilead who buried S.," 2.04
this loyalty to S. your lord, 2.05
for S. your lord is dead, and the 2.07
had taken Ishbosheth the son of S., 2.08
of Ishbosheth the son of S., 2.12
and Ishbosheth the son of S., 2.15
the house of S. and the house of 3.01
the house of S. became weaker and 3.01
the house of S. and the house of 3.06
himself strong in the house of S. 3.06
Now S. had a concubine, whose name 3.07
to the house of S. your father, 3.08
the kingdom from the house of S., 3.10
the son of S., had a son who was 4.04
the news about S. and Jonathan 4.04
the son of S., your enemy, who 4.08
this day on S. and on his offspring 4.08
S. is dead,' and thought he was 4.10
when S. was king over us, it was you 5.02
the daughter of S. looked out of 6.16
the daughter of S. came out to 6.20
the daughter of S. had no child to 6.23
from him, as I took it from S., 7.15
any one left of the house of S., 9.01
of the house of S. whose name was 9.02
still some one of the house of S., 9.03
son of S., came to David, and fell 9.06
you all the land of S. your father; 9.07
belonged to S. and to all his 9.09
delivered you out of the hand of S.; 12.07
of the family of the house of S., 16.05
all the blood of the house of S., 16.08
the servant of the house of S., 19.17
the son of S. came down to meet 19.24
blood guilt on S. and on his house, 21.01
S. had sought to slay them in his 21.02
between us and S. or his house; 21.04
David and Jonathan the son of S. 21.07
of Aiah, whom she bore to S., 21.08
Sons of Merob the daughter of S., 21.08
the concubine of S., had done, 21.11
the bones of S. and the bones of 21.12
Philistines killed S. on Gilboa; 21.12
the bones of S. and the bones of 21.13
the bones of S. and his son 21.14
enemies, and from the hand of S. 22.01
And in the days of S. they made war 1Ch 5.10
Kish of S., S. of Jonathan, Malchishua, 8.33
Kish of S., S. of Jonathan, Malchishua, 9.39
Philistines overtook S. and his sons; 10.02
and Malchishua, the sons of S. 10.02
The battle pressed hard upon S., 10.03
Then S. said to his armor-bearer, 10.04
Therefore S. took his own sword, and 10.04
armor-bearer saw that S. was dead, 10.05
Thus S. died; he and his three sons 10.06
fled and that S. and his sons were 10.07
they found S. and his sons fallen 10.08
the Philistines had done to S., 10.11
the body of S. and the bodies of 10.12
So S. died for his unfaithfulness; 10.13
even when S. was king, it was you 11.02
because of S. the son of Kish; 12.01
Philistines for the battle against S. 12.19
he will desert to his master S. 12.19
turn the kingdom of S. over to him, 12.23
Benjaminites, the kinsmen of S., 12.29
allegiance to the house of S. 12.29
we neglected it in the days of S. 13.03
the daughter of S. looked out of 15.29
and S. the son of Kish, and Abner 26.28
trembles, Gibeah of S. has fled. Is 10.29
the feet of a young man named S. Ac 7.58
And S. was consenting to his death. 8.01
But S. laid waste the chuch, and 8.03
But S., still breathing threats and 9.01
"S., S., why do you persecute me?" 9.04
S. arose from the ground; and when his eyes 9.08
Judas for a man of Tarsus named S.; 9.11
"Brother S., the Lord Jesus who 9.17
But S. increased all the more in 9.22
but their plot became known to S. 9.24
went to Tarsus to look for S.; 11.25
by the hand of Barnabas and S. 11.30
And Barnabas and S. returned from 12.25
of Herod the tetrarch, and S. 13.01
me Barnabas and S. for the work to 13.02
Barnabas and S. and sought to hear 13.07
But S., who is also called Paul, 13.09
God gave them S. the son of Kish, a 13.21
'S., S., why do you persecute me?' 22.07
'Brother S., receive your sight. 22.13
'S., S., why do you persecute me? 26.14

SAUL'S
S. father, were lost. So Kish said 1Sa 9.03
S. uncle said to him and to his 10.14
And S. uncle said, "Pray, tell me 10.15
and the name of S. wife was Ahinoam 14.50
was Abner the son of Ner, S. uncle; 14.50
And S. servants said to him, "Behold 16.15
also in the sight of S. servants. 18.05
S. daughter, should have been given 18.19
Now S. daughter Michal loved David; 18.20
And S. servants spoke those words 18.23
But Jonathan, S. son, delighted much 19.01
opposite, and Abner sat by S. side, 20.25
Then S. anger was kindled against 20.30
Edomite, the chief of S. herdsmen. 21.07
And Jonathan, S. son, rose, and went 23.16
cut off the skirt of S. robe. 24.04
because he had cut off S. skirt. 24.05
and the jar of water from S. head; 26.12
behold, a man came from S. camp, 2Sa 1.02
commander of S. army, had taken 2.08
Ishbosheth, S. son, was forty years 2.10
S. daughter, when you come to see my 3.13
messengers to Ishbosheth S. son, 3.14
S. son, heard that Abner had died at 4.01
Now S. son had two men who were 4.02
S. servant, and said to him, "All 9.09
the son of S. son Jonathan, because 21.07
they were Benjaminites, S. kinsmen. 1Ch 12.02

SAVE
s. to the LORD only, shall be Ex 22.20
these cities he might s. his life: Deu 4.42
by fleeing there may s. his life. 19.04
of these cities and s. his life; 19.05
you shall s. alive nothing that 20.16
to s. you and to give up your 23.14
and s. alive my father and mother, Jos 2.13
and s. us, and help us; for all the 10.06
among us and s. us from the power 1Sa 4.03
that he may s. us from the hand of 7.08
He shall s. my people from the hand 9.16
and you will s. them from the hand 10.01
said, "How can this man s. us?" 10.27
then, if there is no one to s. us, 11.03
things which cannot profit or s., 12.21

SAVE (cont.)

"If you do not s. your life tonight, 1Sa 19.11
the Philistines and s. Keilah. 23.02
David I will s. my people Israel 2Sa 3.18
They looked, but there was none to s.; 22.42
that you may s. your own life and 1Ki 1.12
find grass and s. the horses and 18.05
s. us, I beseech thee, from his hand, 2Ki 19.19
For I will defend this city to s. it, 19.34
and gather and s. us from among 1Ch 16.35
affliction, and thou wilt hear and s. 2Ch 20.09
he will not s. anything in which he Job 20.20
Turn, O LORD, s. my life; deliver me Ps 6.04
s. me from all my pursuers, and 7.01
for help, but there was none to s., 18.41
S. me from the mouth of the lion, my 22.21
O s. thy people, and bless thy 28.09
for me, a strong fortress to s. me! 31.02
s. me in thy steadfast love! 31.16
by its great might it cannot s. 33.17
do I trust, nor can my sword s. me. 44.06
S. me, O God, by thy name, and vindicate 54.01
I call upon God; and the LORD will s. me. 55.16
He will send from heaven and s. me, 57.03
and s. me from bloodthirsty men. 59.02
S. me, O God! For the waters have 69.01
For God will s. Zion and rebuild 69.35
incline thy ear to me, and s. me! 71.02
to s. me, for thou art my rock and 71.03
judgment to s. all the oppressed 76.09
up thy might, and come to s. us! 80.02
s. thy servant who trusts in thee. 86.02
and s. the son of thy handmaid. 86.16
S. us, O LORD our God, and gather us 106.47
S. me according to thy steadfast 109.26
to s. him from those who condemn 109.31
LORD, I beseech thee, s. my life! 116.04
S. us, we beseech thee, O LORD! 118.25
I am thine, s. me; for I have sought 119.94
s. me, that I may observe thy 119.146
and s. yourself, for you have come Pro 6.03
s. yourself like a gazelle from the 6.05
rod you will s. his life from 23.14
for him, that he might s. us. Is 25.09
is our king; he will s. us. 33.22
of God. He will come and s. you." 35.04
s. us from his hand, that all the 37.20
For I will defend this city to s. it, 37.35
The LORD will s. me, and we will 38.20
on praying to a god that cannot s. 45.20
they cannot s. the burden, but 46.02
I will bear; I will carry and will s. 46.04
not answer or s. him from his 46.07
let them stand forth and s. you, 47.13
there is no one to s. you. 47.15
you, and I will s. your children. 49.25
not shortened, that it cannot s., 59.01
announcing vindication, mighty to s." 63.01
trouble they say, 'Arise and s. us!' Jer 2.27
if they can s. you, in your time of 2.28
but they cannot s. them in the 11.12
like a mighty man who cannot s.? 14.09
am with you to s. you and deliver 15.20
s. me, and I shall be saved; 17.14
I will s. you from afar, and your 30.10
For I am with you to s. you, 30.11
For I will surely s. you, 39.18
to s. you and to deliver you from 42.11
I will s. you from afar, and your 46.27
S. yourselves! Be like a wild 48.06
Babylon, let every man s. his life! 51.06
Let every man s. his life from the 51.45
for a nation which could not s. Lam 4.17
in order to s. his life, that wicked Eze 3.18
from his wicked way to s. his life; 13.22
and right, he shall s. his life. 18.27
I will s. my flock, they shall no 34.22
but I will s. them from all the 37.23
Where now is your king, to s. you; Hos 13.10
Assyria shall not s. us, we will not 14.03
nor shall the mighty s. his life; Amo 2.14
swift of foot shall not s. himself, 2.15
he who rides the horse s. his life; 2.15
to s. him from his discomfort. Jon 4.06
but not s., and what you s. I will give Mic 6.14
"Violence!" and thou wilt not s.? Hab 1.02
And I will s. the lame and gather Zep 3.19
I will s. my people from the east Zec 8.07
so will I s. you and you shall be a 8.13
their God will s. them for they 9.16
and I will s. the house of Joseph. 10.06
for he will s. his people from Mt 1.21
and woke him, saying, "S., Lord; 8.25
to sink he cried out, "Lord, s. me." 14.30
For whoever would s. his life will 16.25
Son of man came to s. the lost. * 18.11
it in three days, s. yourself! 27.40
he cannot s. himself. He is the King 27.42
whether Elijah will come to s. him. 27.49
to s. life or to kill?" But they were Mk 3.04
For whoever would s. his life will 8.35
sake and the gospel's will s. it. 8.35
s. yourself, and come down from the 15.30
"He saved others; he cannot s. himself. 15.31
to s. life or to destroy it?" Lk 6.09
For whoever would s. his life will 9.24
life for my sake, he will s. it. 9.24
not to destroy men's lives but to s. * 9.55
came to seek and to s. the lost." 19.10
let him s. himself, if he is the 23.35
the King of the Jews, s. yourself!" 23.37
the Christ? S. yourself and us!" 23.39
s. me from this hour'? No, for this Jn 12.27
the world but to s. the world. 12.47
"S. yourselves from this crooked Ac 2.40
wishing to s. Paul, kept them from 27.43
jealous, and thus s. some of them. Rom 11.14
we preach to s. those who believe. 1Co 1.21
whether you will s. your husband? 7.16
know whether you will s. your wife? 7.16
that I might by all means s. some. 9.22
came into the world to s. sinners. 1Ti 1.15
doing you will s. both yourself 4.16
every evil and s. me for his 2Ti 4.18
who was able to s. him from death, Heb 5.07
for all time to s. those who draw 7.25
with sin but to s. those who are 9.28
which is able to s. your souls. Jas 1.21
but has not work? Can his faith s. him? 2.14
who is able to s. and to destroy. 4.12
of faith will s. the sick man, 5.15
of his way will s. his soul from 5.20
s. some, by snatching them out of Jud 1.23

SAVED

little one?—and my life will be s.!" Gen 19.20
And they said, "You have s. our lives; 47.25
Thus the LORD s. Israel that day Ex 14.30
you shall be s. from your enemies. Num 10.09
a people s. by the LORD, the shield Deu 33.29
belonged to her, Joshua s. alive; Jos 6.25
now you have s. the people of 22.31
who s. them out of the power of Ju 2.16
and he s. them from the hand of 2.18
if you had s. them alive, I would 8.19
whom they had s. alive of the 21.14
And David s. neither man nor woman 1Sa 27.11
who have this day s. your life, 2Sa 19.05
and s. us from the hand of the 19.09
and I am s. from my enemies. 22.04
so that he s. himself there more 2Ki 6.10
so he s. them by the hand of 14.27
and the LORD s. them by a great 1Ch 11.14
So the LORD s. Hezekiah and the 2Ch 32.22
saviors who s. them from the hand Neh 9.27

SAVED (cont.)

whose word s. the king, is standing Est 7.09
How you have s. the arm that has no Job 26.02
and I am s. from my enemies. Ps 18.03
To thee they cried, and were s.; 22.05
A king is not s. by his great army; 33.16
and s. him out of all his troubles. 34.06
But thou hast s. us from our foes, 44.07
thy face shine, that we may be s.! 80.03
thy face shine, that we may be s.! 80.07
thy face shine, that we may be s.! 80.19
Yet he s. them for his name's sake, 106.08
So he s. them from the hand of the 106.10
when I was brought low, he s. me. 116.06
You will be s. from the loose woman, Pro 2.16
returning and rest you shall be s.; Is 30.15
I declared and s. and proclaimed, 43.12
But Israel is s. by the LORD with 45.17
"Turn to me and be s., all the ends 45.22
the angel of his presence s. them; 63.09
a long time, and shall we be s.? 64.05
wickedness, that you may be s. Jer 4.14
summer is ended, and we are not s." 8.20
save me, and I shall be s.; 17.14
In his days Judah will be s., 23.06
yet he shall be s. out of it. 30.07
'The LORD has s. his people, the 31.07
Judah will be s. and Jerusalem 33.16
but you will have s. your life. Eze 3.19
and you will have s. your life." 3.21
warning, he would have s. his life. 33.05
but you will have s. your life. 33.09
he who has s. Daniel from the power Dan 6.27
who endures to the end will be s. Mt 10.22
astonished, saying, "Who then can be s.?" 19.25
who endures to the end will be s. 24.13
shortened, no human being would be s.; 24.22
"He s. others; he cannot sense 27.42
said to him, "Then who can be s.?" Mk 10.26
who endures to the end will be s. 13.13
days, no human being would be s. 13.20
the scribes, saying, "He s. others; 15.31
believes and is baptized will be s.; * 16.16
that we should be s. from our Lk 1.71
the woman, "Your faith has s. you; 7.50
they may not believe and be s. 8.12
"Lord, will those who are s. be few?" 13.23
heard it said, "Then who can be s.?" 18.26
at him, saying, "He s. others; 23.35
the world might be s. through him. Jn 3.17
but I say this that you may be s. 5.34
he will be s., and will go in and 10.09
the name of the Lord shall be s.' Ac 2.21
day by day those who were being s. 2.47
among men by which we must be s." 4.12
a message by which you will be s., 11.14
custom of Moses, you cannot be s." 15.01
we shall be s. through the grace 15.11
said, "Men, what must I do to be s.?" 16.30
the Lord Jesus, and you will be s., 16.31
of our being s. was at last 27.20
stay in the ship, you cannot be s." 27.31
shall we be s. by him from the Rom 5.09
reconciled, shall we be s. by his life. 5.10
For in this hope we were s. 8.24
only a remnant of them will be s.; 9.27
for them is that they may be s. 10.01
him from the dead, you will be s. 10.09
confesses with his lips and so is s. 10.10
the name of the Lord will be s." 10.13
and so all Israel will be s.; 11.26
who are being s. it is the power 1Co 1.18
loss, though he himself will be s., 3.15
spirit may be s. in the day of the 5.05
that of many, that they may be s. 10.33
by which you are s., if you hold 15.02
who are being s. and among those 2Co 2.15
Christ (by grace you have been s.), Eph 2.05
you have been s. through faith; 2.08
the Gentiles that they may be s.— 1Th 2.16
to love the truth and so be s. 2Th 2.10
you from the beginning to be s., 2.13
all men to be s. and to come to 1Ti 2.04
Yet woman will be s. through 2.15
who s. us and called us with a holy 2Ti 1.09
he s. us, not because of deeds done Tit 3.05
persons, were s. through water. 1Pe 3.20
the righteous man is scarcely s., 4.18
that he who s. a people out of the Jud 1.05

SAVES

who s. you from all your calamities 1Sa 10.19
For as the LORD lives who s. Israel, 14.39
that the LORD s. not with sword 17.47
But he s. the fatherless from their Job 5.15
the proud, but he s. the lowly. 22.29
who s. the upright in heart. Ps 7.10
and s. the crushed in spirit. 34.18
and s. them, because they take 37.40
and s. the lives of the needy. 72.13
also hears their cry, and s. them. 145.19
A truthful witness s. lives, Pro 14.25
now s. you, not as a removal of dirt 1Pe 3.21

SAVEST

thou s. me from violence. 2Sa 22.03
man and beast thou s., O LORD. Ps 36.06

SAVING

me great kindness in s. my life; Gen 19.19
concerning all the s. deeds of the 1Sa 12.07
the LORD from s. by many or by few 14.06
he is the s. refuge of his anointed Ps 28.08
not hid thy s. help within my 40.10
thy s. power among all nations. 67.02
and did not trust his s. power. 78.22
or thy s. help in the land of 88.12
may know the s. acts of the LORD." Mic 6.05
an ark for the s. of his household; Heb 11.07

SAVIOR

my stronghold and my refuge, my s.; 2Sa 22.03
(Therefore the LORD gave Israel a s., 2Ki 13.05
O s. of those who seek refuge from Ps 17.07
their S., who had done great things 106.21
oppressors he will send them a s., Is 19.20
the Holy One of Israel, your S. 43.03
and besides me there is no s. 43.11
thyself, O God of Israel, the S. 45.15
me, a righteous God and a S.; 45.21
know that I am the LORD your S., 49.26
am your S. and your Redeemer, the 60.16
not deal falsely: and he became their S. 63.08
its s. in time of trouble, why Jer 14.08
me, and besides me there is no s. Hos 13.04
and my spirit rejoices in God my S., Lk 1.47
this day in the city of David a S., 2.11
this is indeed the S. of the world." Jn 4.42
at his right hand as Leader and S., Ac 5.31
God has brought to Israel a S., 13.23
his body, and is himself its S. Eph 5.23
heaven, and from it we await a S., Php 3.20
of God our S. and of Christ Jesus 1Ti 1.01
in the sight of God our S., 2.03
who is the S. of all men, especially 4.10
appearing of our S. Christ Jesus, 2Ti 1.10
entrusted by command of God our S.; Tit 1.03
the Father and Christ Jesus our S. 1.04
adorn the doctrine of God our S. 2.10
our great God and S. Jesus Christ, 2.13
kindness of God our S. appeared, 3.04
through Jesus Christ our S., 3.06
of our God and S. Jesus Christ: 2Pe 1.01
of our Lord and S. Jesus Christ. 1.11
of our Lord and S. Jesus Christ, 2.20
of the Lord and S. through your 3.02

SAVIOR (cont.)
of our Lord and S. Jesus Christ. 2Pe 3.18
his Son as the S. of the world. 1Jn 4.14
our S. through Jesus Christ our Jud 1.25

SAVIORS
didst give them s. who saved them Neh 9.27
S. shall go up to Mount Zion to Ob 1.21

SAVORY
and prepare for me s. food, Gen 27.04
came, and prepare for me s. food, 27.07
from them s. food for your father, 27.09
and his mother prepared s. food, 27.14
and she gave the s. food and the 27.17
He also prepared s. food, and brought it 27.31

SAWED
s. with saws, back and front, even 1Ki 7.09

SAWN
they were s. in two, they were Heb 11.37

SAWS
to labor with s. and iron picks 2Sa 12.31
sawed with s., back and front, even 1Ki 7.09
to labor with s. and iron picks 1Ch 20.03

SAYINGS
of Abijah, his ways and his s., 2Ch 13.22
words, I listened for your wise s., Job 32.11
I will utter dark s. from of old, Ps 78.02
to my words: incline your ear to my s. Pro 4.20
for you thirty s. of admonition 22.20
These also are s. of the wise. 24.23
The s. of the wise are like goads, Ecc 12.11
the collected s. which are given 12.11
And when Jesus finished these s., Mt 7.28
Now when Jesus had finished these s., 19.01
When Jesus had finished all these s., 26.01
ended all his s. in the hearing of Lk 7.01
after these s. he took with him 9.28
are not the s. of one who has a Jn 10.21
one hears my s. and does not keep 12.47
does not receive my s. has a judge; 12.48

SCAB
smite with a s. the heads of the Is 3.17

SCABBARD
Put yourself into your s., rest and be Jer 47.06

SCABS
disease or s. or crushed testicles Lev 21.20
a discharge or an itch or s., 22.22

SCALE
between the s. armor and the 1Ki 22.34
between the s. armor and the 2Ch 18.33
like soldiers they s. the wall. Joe 2.07

SCALES
in the waters that has fins and s., Lev 11.09
rivers that has not fins and s., 11.10
not fins and s. is an abomination 11.12
whatever has fins and s. you may eat. Deu 14.09
have fins and s. you shall not eat 14.10
just balance and s. are the LORD's; Pro 16.11
LORD, and false s. are not good. 20.23
A wise man s. the city of the 21.22
mountains in s. and the hills in a Is 40.12
accounted as the dust on the s.; 40.15
and weigh out silver in the s., 46.06
and weighed the money on s. Jer 32.10
of your streams stick to your s.; Eze 29.04
streams which stick to your s. 29.04

man with wicked s. and with a bag Mic 6.11
something like s. fell from his Ac 9.18
they had s. like iron breastplates, Rev 9.09

SCANT
feed him with s. fare of bread and 1Ki 22.27
feed him with s. fare of bread and 2Ch 18.26
and the s. measure that is accursed? Mic 6.10

SCAR
spread, it is the s. of the boil; Lev 13.23
for it is the s. of the burn. 13.28

SCARCELY
when Jacob had s. gone out from Gen 27.30
S. had I passed them, when I found Sol 3.04
S. are they planted, s. sown, s. has Is 40.24
words they s. restrained the Ac 14.18
And "If the righteous man is s. saved, 1Pe 4.18

SCARCITY
you will eat bread without s., Deu 8.09

SCARE
then thou dost s. me with dreams Job 7.14

SCARECROWS
Their idols are like s. in a Jer 10.05

SCARFS
pendants, the bracelets, and the s.; Is 3.19

SCARLET
and bound on his hand a s. thread, Gen 38.28
out with the s. thread upon his 38.30
blue and purple and s. stuff and Ex 25.04
and blue and purple and s. stuff; 26.01
and purple and s. stuff and fine 26.31
and purple and s. stuff and fine 26.36
and purple and s. stuff and fine 27.16
gold, blue and purple and s. stuff, 28.05
of blue and purple and s. stuff, 28.06
gold, blue and purple and s. stuff, 28.08
gold, blue and purple and s. stuff, 28.15
of blue and purple and s. stuff, 28.33
blue and purple and s. stuff and 35.06
or purple or s. stuff or fine 35.23
and purple and s. stuff and fine 35.25
and purple and s. stuff and fine 35.35
and blue and purple and s. stuff, 36.08
and purple and s. stuff and fine 36.35
and purple and s. stuff and fine 36.37
and purple and s. stuff and fine 38.18
and purple and s. stuff and fine 38.23
and purple and s. stuff they made 39.01
gold, blue and purple and s. stuff, 39.02
blue and purple and the s. stuff, 39.03
gold, blue and purple and s. stuff, 39.05
gold, blue and purple and s. stuff, 39.08
and purple and s. stuff and fine 39.24
of blue and purple and s. stuff, 39.29
cedarwood and s. stuff and hyssop; Lev 14.04
cedarwood and the s. stuff and the 14.06
cedarwood and s. stuff and hyssop, 14.49
and the hyssop and the s. stuff, 14.51
cedarwood and hyssop and s. stuff; 14.52
spread over them a cloth of s., Num 4.08
cedarwood and hyssop and s. stuff, 19.06
shall bind this s. cord in the Jos 2.18
she bound the s. cord in the 2.21
who clothed you daintily in s., 2Sa 1.24
her household are clothed in s. Pro 31.21
Your lips are like a s. thread, Sol 4.03
LORD: though your sins are like s., Is 1.18
do you mean that you dress in s., Jer 4.30
his soldiers are clothed in s. Nah 2.03
him and put a s. robe upon him, Mt 27.28
with water and s. wool and hyssop, Heb 9.19

SCARLET (cont.)
sitting on a s. beast which was Rev 17.03
woman was arrayed in purple and s., 17.04
silk and s., all kinds of scented 18.12
in purple and s., bedecked with 18.16

SCATTER
in Jacob and s. them in Israel. Gen 49.07
And I will s. you among the nations, Lev 26.33
then s. the fire far and wide. Num 16.37
And the LORD will s. you among the Deu 4.27
And the LORD will s. you among all 28.64
"I will s. them afar, I will make 32.26
and s. them beyond the Euphrates, 1Ki 14.15
I will s. you among the peoples; Neh 1.08
the clouds s. his lightning. Job 37.11
For God will s. the bones of the Ps 53.05
s. the peoples who delight in war. 68.30
thou didst s. thy enemies with thy 89.10
Flash forth the lightning and s. them, 144.06
its surface and s. its inhabitants Is 24.01
does he not s. dill, sow cummin, and 28.25
You will s. them as unclean things; 30.22
and the tempest shall s. them. 41.16
I will s. them among the nations Jer 9.16
I will s. you like chaff driven by 13.24
wind I will s. them before the 18.17
who destroy and s. the sheep of my 23.01
I will s. to every wind those who 49.32
and I will s. them to all those 49.36
part you shall s. to the wind, Eze 5.02
survive I will s. to all the winds 5.10
part I will s. to all the winds 5.12
and I will s. your bones round 6.05
the cherubim, and s. them over the city. 10.02
And I will s. toward every wind all 12.14
the nations and s. them through 12.15
that I would s. them among the 20.23
I will s. you among the nations and 22.15
I will s. the Egyptians among the 29.12
I will s. the Egyptians among the 30.23
and I will s. the Egyptians among 30.26
off its leaves and s. its fruit; Dan 4.14
who came like a whirlwind to s. me, Hab 3.14
against the land of Judah to s. it. Zec 1.21
if a man should s. seed upon the Mk 4.26

SCATTERED
lest we be s. abroad upon the face Gen 11.04
So the LORD s. them abroad from 11.08
there the LORD s. them abroad over 11.09
So the people were s. abroad Ex 5.12
and s. it upon the water, and made 32.20
O LORD, and let thy enemies be s.; Num 10.35
where the LORD your God has s. you. Deu 30.03
and those who survived were s., 1Sa 11.11
well's mouth, and s. grain upon it; 2Sa 17.19
And he sent out arrows, and s. them; 22.15
saw all Israel s. upon the mountains, 1Ki 22.17
and all his army was s. from him. 2Ki 25.05
saw all Israel s. upon the mountains, 2Ch 18.16
certain people s. abroad and Est 3.08
the whelps of the lioness are s. Job 4.11
brimstone is s. upon his habitation 18.15
the east wind is s. upon the earth? 38.24
sent out his arrows, and s. them; Ps 18.14
and hast s. us among the nations. 44.11
Let God arise, let his enemies be s.; 68.01
When the Almighty s. kings there, 68.14
shall perish; all evildoers shall be s. 92.09
Should your springs be s. abroad, Pro 5.16
like s. nestlings, so are the Is 16.02
up of thyself nations are s.; 33.03
your God and s. your favors among Jer 3.13
prospered, and all their flock is s. 10.21
"You have s. my flock, and have 23.02
the nations among whom I s. you, 30.11
say, 'He who s. Israel will gather 31.10
are gathered about you would be s., 40.15
and all his army was s. from him. 52.08
holy stones lie s. at the head of Lam 4.01
The LORD himself has s. them, 4.16
when you are s. through the Eze 6.08
and though I s. them among the 11.16
countries where you have been s., 11.17
survivors shall be s. to every wind; 17.21
of the countries where you are s., 20.34
countries where you have been s.; 20.41
the peoples among whom they are s., 28.25
peoples among whom they were s.; 29.13
So they were s., because there was 34.05
My sheep were s., they wandered 34.06
my sheep were s. over all the face 34.06
of his sheep have been s. abroad, 34.12
they have been s. on a day of 34.12
till you have s. them abroad, 34.21
I s. them among the nations, and 36.19
they have s. them among the nations, Joe 3.02
Your people are s. on the mountains Nah 3.18
then the eternal mountains were s., Hab 3.06
are the horns which have s. Judah, Zec 1.19
"These are the horns which s. Judah, 1.21
"and I s. them with a whirlwind 7.14
Though I s. them among the nations, 10.09
shepherd, that the sheep may be s.; 13.07
the sheep of the flock will be s.' Mt 26.31
shepherd, and the sheep will be s.' Mk 14.27
he has s. the proud in the imagination Lk 1.51
children of God who are s. abroad. Jn 11.52
it has come, when you will be s., 16.32
and all who followed him were s. Ac 5.37
they were all s. throughout the 8.01
Now those who were s. went about 8.04
Now those who were s. because of 11.19

SCATTERING
and the people were s. from him. 1Sa 13.08
that the people were s. from me, 13.11
whirlwind, and cold from the s. winds. Job 37.09
the nations, s. them over the lands. Ps 106.27
s. among them plunder, spoil, and Dan 11.24

SCATTERS
Behold, he s. his lightning about Job 36.30
wool; he s. hoarfrost like ashes. Ps 147.16
he who does not gather with me s. Mt 12.30
he who does not gather with me s. Lk 11.23
the wolf snatches them and s. them. Jn 10.12
"He s. abroad, he gives to the poor; 2Co 9.09

SCENT
yet at the s. of water it will bud Job 14.09
the s. of your garments is like the Sol 4.11
garments is like the s. of Lebanon. 4.11
and the s. of your breath like 7.08
in him, and his s. is not changed. Jer 48.11

SCENTED
all kinds of s. wood, all articles of Rev 18.12

SCEPTER
The s. shall not depart from Judah, Gen 49.10
with the s. and with their staves. Num 21.18
and a s. shall rise out of Israel; 24.17
out the golden s. that he may live Est 4.11
the golden s. that was in his hand 5.02
and touched the top of the s. 5.02
held out the golden s. to Esther, 8.04
Your royal s. is a s. of equity; Ps 45.06
Ephraim is my helmet; Judah is my s. 60.07
Thou hast removed the s. from his hand, 89.44
Ephraim is my helmet; Judah my s. 108.08
forth from Zion your mighty s. 110.02
For the s. of wickedness shall not 125.03
of the wicked, the s. of rulers, Is 14.05
say, 'How the mighty s. is broken, Jer 48.17

SCEPTER (cont.)
strongest stem became a ruler's s.; Eze 19.11
no strong stem, no s. for a ruler. 19.14
that holds the s. from Betheden; Amo 1.05
that holds the s. from Ashkelon; 1.08
and the s. of Egypt shall depart. Zec 10.11
righteous s. is the s. of thy kingdom. Heb 1.08

SCEVA
high priest named S. were doing this. Ac 19.14

SCHEME
as they s. together against me, as Ps 31.13
mind, and you will devise an evil s. Eze 38.10

SCHEMES
and the s. of the wily are brought Job 5.13
and his own s. throw him down. 18.07
thoughts, and your s. to wrong me. 21.27
caught in the s. which they have Ps 10.02
it was against me they devised s., Jer 11.19

SCHEMING
the wicked, from the s. of evildoers, Ps 64.02

SCOFF
They s. and speak with malice; Ps 73.08
How long, O God, is the foe to s.? 74.10
how the impious s. at thee all the 74.22
if you s., you alone will bear it. Pro 9.12
Now therefore do not s., lest your Is 28.22
At kings they s., and of rulers Hab 1.10

SCOFFED
and s. at the Rock of his salvation. Deu 32.15
because they s. and boasted against Zep 2.10
heard all this, and they s. at him. Lk 16.14
but the rulers s. at him, saying, 23.35

SCOFFER
He who corrects a s. gets himself Pro 9.07
Do not reprove a s., or he will 9.08
but a s. does not listen to rebuke. 13.01
A s. seeks wisdom in vain, but 14.06
A s. does not like to be reproved; 15.12
Strike a s., and the simple will 19.25
When a s. is punished, the simple 21.11
"S." is the name of the proud, 21.24
Drive out a s., and strife will go 22.10
and the s. is an abomination to men 24.09
come to nought and the s. cease, Is 29.20

SCOFFERS
sinners, nor sits in the seat of s.; Ps 1.01
How long will s. delight in their Pro 1.22
Condemnation is ready for s., 19.29
S. set a city aflame, but wise men 29.08
you s., who rule this people in Is 28.14
'Behold, you s., and wonder, and Ac 13.41
that s. will come in the last days 2Pe 3.03
"In the last time there will be s., Jud 1.18

SCOFFING
and s. at his prophets, till the 2Ch 36.16
Job, who drinks up s. like water, Job 34.07
Beware lest wrath entice you into s.; 36.18
in their s. and fools hate knowledge? Pro 1.22
in s. derision of him, and say, "Woe Hab 2.06
will come in the last days with s., 2Pe 3.03

SCOFFS
how the enemy s., and an impious people Ps 74.18

SCORCH
it was allowed to s. men with fire; Rev 16.08

SCORCHED
hot coals and his feet not be s.? Pro 6.28
swarthy, because the sun has s. me. Sol 1.06
inhabitants of the earth are s., Is 24.06
south to north shall be s. by it. Eze 20.47
but when the sun rose they were s.; Mt 13.06
and when the sun rose it was s., Mk 4.06
men were s. by the fierce heat, and Rev 16.09

SCORCHING
a s. wind shall be the portion of Ps 11.06
and his speech is like a s. fire. Pro 16.27
over the River with his s. wind, Is 11.15
neither s. wind nor sun shall smite 49.10
burden of the day and the s. heat. Mt 20.12
you say, 'There will be s. heat'; Lk 12.55
rises with its s. heat and withers Jas 1.11
not strike them, nor any s. heat. Rev 7.16

SCORN
but they laughed them to s., and 2Ch 30.10
My friends s. me; my eye pours Job 16.20
the innocent laugh them to s., 22.19
I am the s. of all my adversaries, a Ps 31.11
Make me not the s. of the fool! 39.08
derision and s. of those about us. 44.13
with s. and disgrace may they be 71.13
make us the s. of our neighbors; 80.06
has become the s. of his neighbors. 89.41
I am an object of s. to my accusers; 109.25
away from me their s. and contempt, 119.22
sated with the s. of those who are 123.04
LORD is to them an object of s., Jer 6.10
shall bear the s. of the peoples. Mic 6.16
you did not s. or despise me, but Gal 4.14

SCORNED
deed you have utterly s. the LORD, 2Sa 12.14
s. by men, and despised by the Ps 22.06
Remember, O Lord, how thy servant is s.; 89.50
his house, it would be utterly s. Sol 8.07
The Lord has s. his altar, disowned Lam 2.07
like a harlot, because you s. hire. Eze 16.31

SCORNERS
Toward the s. he is scornful, but to Pro 3.34

SCORNFUL
Toward the scorners he is s., but to Pro 3.34

SCORNS
she s. you—the virgin daughter of 2Ki 19.21
He s. the tumult of the city; Job 39.07
God s. the wicked, but the upright Pro 14.09
a father and s. to obey a mother 30.17
she s. you—the virgin daughter of Is 37.22

SCORPION
asks for an egg, will give him a s.? Lk 11.12
was like the torture of a s., when Rev 9.05

SCORPIONS
serpents and s. and thirsty ground Deu 8.15
but I will chastise you with s.'" 1Ki 12.11
but I will chastise you with s." 12.14
but I will chastise you with s.'" 2Ch 10.11
but I will chastise you with s." 10.14
are with you and you sit upon s.; Eze 2.06
to tread upon serpents and s., Lk 10.19
like the power of s. of the earth; Rev 9.03
they have tails like s., and stings, 9.10

SCOUNDRELS
worthless s. gathered about him and 2Ch 13.07

SCOURED
that shall be s., and rinsed in water. Lev 6.28

SCOURGE
a s. on your sides, and thorns in Jos 23.13
be hid from the s. of the tongue, Job 5.21
you, no s. come near your tent. Ps 91.10

SCOURGE (cont.)

hosts will wield against them a s., Is 10.26
overwhelming s. passes through it 28.15
overwhelming s. passes through you 28.18
some you will s. in your synagogues Mt 23.34
upon him, and s. him, and kill him; Mk 10.34
they will s. him and kill him, and Lk 18.33
for you to s. a man who is a Roman Ac 22.25

SCOURGED

to be mocked and s. and crucified, Mt 20.19
and having s. Jesus, delivered him 27.26
and having s. Jesus, he delivered Mk 15.15
Then Pilate took Jesus and s. him. Jn 19.01

SCOURGES

the rod and their iniquity with s.; Ps 89.32

SCOURGING

ordered him to be examined by s., Ac 22.24
Others suffered mocking and s., and Heb 11.36

SCOUTS

And Benhadad sent out s., and they 1Ki 20.17

SCRAPE

that they s. off they shall pour Lev 14.41
potsherd with which to s. himself, Job 2.08
and I will s. her soil from her, and Eze 26.04

SCRAPED

of the house to be s. round about, Lev 14.41
the stones and s. the house and 14.43
He s. it out into his hands, and Ju 14.09

SCRAPES

s. with his feet, points with his Pro 6.13

SCRAPS

used to pick up s. under my table; Ju 1.07

SCREEN

shall make a s. for the door of Ex 26.36
make for the s. five pillars of 26.37
shall be a s. twenty cubits long, 27.16
mercy seat, and the veil of the s.; 35.12
and the s. for the door, at the door 35.15
and the s. for the gate of the 35.17
He also made a s. for the door of 36.37
And the s. for the gate of the 38.18
goatskins, and the veil of the s.; 39.34
and the s. for the door of the tent 39.38
and the s. for the gate of the 39.40
and you shall s. the ark with the 40.03
and set up the s. for the door of 40.05
and hang up the s. for the gate of 40.08
and set up the veil of the s., 40.21
in place the s. for the door of 40.28
and set up the s. of the gate of 40.33
the s. for the door of the tent of Num 3.25
the s. for the door of the court 3.26
the priests minister, and the s.; 3.31
and take down the veil of the s., 4.05
and the s. for the door of the tent 4.25
and the s. for the entrance of the 4.26

SCREENED

and s. the ark of the testimony; as the Ex 40.21

SCRIBE

And the s. Shemaiah the son of 1Ch 24.06
a man of understanding and a s.; 27.32
Shimshai the s. wrote a letter Ez 4.08
Shimshai the s., and the rest of 4.09
Shimshai the s. and the rest of 4.17
Shimshai the s. and their associates, 4.23
He was a s. skilled in the law of 7.06
the s., learned in matters of the 7.11
the s. of the law of the God of 7.12
the s. of the law of the God of 7.21
told Ezra the s. to bring the book Neh 8.01
And Ezra the s. stood on a wooden 8.04
governor, and Ezra the priest and s., 8.09
to Ezra the s. in order to study 8.13
and of Ezra the priest the s. 12.26
and Ezra the s. went before them. 12.36
Zadok the s., and Pedaiah of the 13.13
is like the pen of a ready s. Ps 45.01
and gave it to Baruch the s., Jer 36.32
And a s. came up and said to him, Mt 8.19
"Therefore every s. who has been 13.52
And the s. said to him, "You are Mk 12.32
Is the wise man? Where is the s.? 1Co 1.20

SCRIBES

also of the s. that dwelt at Jabez: 1Ch 2.55
and some of the Levites were s., 2Ch 34.13
pen of the s. has made it into a Jer 8.08
your s. like clouds of locusts Nah 3.17
chief priests and s. of the people, Mt 2.04
that of the s. and Pharisees, 5.20
had authority, and not as their s. 7.29
some of the s. said to themselves, 9.03
Then some of the s. and Pharisees 12.38
Then Pharisees and s. came to Jesus 15.01
elders and chief priests and s., 16.21
"Then why do the s. say that first 17.10
to the chief priests and s., 20.18
priests and the s. saw the wonderful 21.15
"The s. and the Pharisees sit on 23.02
to you, s. and Pharisees, hypocrites! 23.13
you, s. and Pharisees, hypocrites! * 23.14
Woe to you, s. and Pharisees, hypocrites! 23.15
"Woe to you, s. and Pharisees, hypocrites! 23.23
"Woe to you, s. and Pharisees, hypocrites! 23.25
"Woe to you, s. and Pharisees, hypocrites! 23.27
"Woe to you, s. and Pharisees, hypocrites! 23.29
you prophets and wise men and s., 23.34
where the s. and the elders had 26.57
with the s. and elders, mocked him, 27.41
had authority, and not as the s. Mk 1.22
Now some of the s. were sitting 2.06
And the s. of the Pharisees, when 2.16
And the s. who came down from Jerusalem 3.22
to him, with some of the s., who 7.01
the Pharisees and the s. asked him, 7.05
and the chief priests and the s., 8.31
"Why do the s. say that first Elijah 9.11
about them, and s. arguing with them. 9.14
to the chief priests and the s., 10.33
priests and the s. heard it and 11.18
priests and the s. and the elders 11.27
And one of the s. came up and heard 12.28
"How can the s. say that the Christ 12.35
teaching he said, "Beware of the s., 12.38
priests and the s. were seeking 14.01
priests and the s. and the elders. 14.43
elders and the s. were assembled. 14.53
priests, with the elders and s., 15.01
him to one another with the s., 15.31
And the s. and the Pharisees began Lk 5.21
and their s. murmured against his 5.30
And the s. and the Pharisees watched 6.07
elders and chief priests and s., 9.22
the s. and the Pharisees began to 11.53
And the Pharisees and the s. murmured, 15.02
priests and the s. and the principal 19.47
priests and the s. with the elders 20.01
The s. and the chief priests tried 20.19
And some of the s. answered, 20.39
"Beware of the s., who like to go 20.46
priests and the s. were seeking 22.02
together, both chief priests and s.; 22.66
The chief priests and the s. stood by, 23.10
The s. and the Pharisees brought *Jn 8.03
and elders and s. were gathered Ac 4.05

SCRIBES (cont.)
people and the elders and the s. Ac 6.12
and some of the s. of the Pharisees' 23.09

SCRIPT
in its own s. and to every people Est 1.22
in its own s. and every people in 3.12
in its own s. and to every people 8.09
Jews in their s. and their language 8.09

SCRIPTURE
Have you not read this s.: Mk 12.10
And the s. was fulfilled which says * 15.28
"Today this s. has been fulfilled Lk 4.21
you that this s. must be fulfilled 22.37
believed the s. and the word which Jn 2.22
as the s. has said, 'Out of his 7.38
Has not the s. said that the Christ 7.42
of God came (and s. cannot be 10.35
it is that the s. may be fulfilled, 13.18
that the s. might be fulfilled. 17.12
This was to fulfil the s. "They 19.24
said (to fulfil the s.), "I thirst." 19.28
place that the s. might be fulfilled, 19.36
And again another s. says, "They 19.37
for as yet they did not know the s., 20.09
"Brethren, the s. had to be fulfilled, Ac 1.16
passage of the s. which he was 8.32
with this s. he told him the good 8.35
For what does the s. say? "Abraham Rom 4.03
For the s. says to Pharaoh, "I have 9.17
The s. says, "No one who believes in 10.11
know what the s. says of Elijah, 11.02
by us to live according to s., 1Co 4.06
And the s., foreseeing that God Gal 3.08
But the s. consigned all things to 3.22
But what does the s. say? "Cast 4.30
attend to the public reading of s., 1Ti 4.13
for the s. says, "You shall not 5.18
All s. is inspired by God and 2Ti 3.16
the royal law, according to the s., Jas 2.08
and the s. was fulfilled which says, 2.23
it is in vain that the s. says, 4.05
For it stands in s.: "Behold, I am 1Pe 2.06
no prophecy of s. is a matter of 2Pe 1.20

SCRIPTURES
"Have you never read in the s.: Mt 21.42
neither the s. nor the power of 22.29
then should the s. be fulfilled, 26.54
that the s. of the prophets might 26.56
neither the s. nor the power of Mk 12.24
But let the s. be fulfilled." 14.49
them in all the s. the things Lk 24.27
road, while he opened to us the s.?" 24.32
their minds to understand the s., 24.45
You search the s., because you Jn 5.39
he argued with them from the s., Ac 17.02
examining the s. daily to see if 17.11
eloquent man, well versed in the s. 18.24
showing by the s. that the Christ 18.28
his prophets in the holy s., Rom 1.02
encouragement of the s. we might 15.04
sins in accordance with the s., 1Co 15.03
day in accordance with the s., 15.04
destruction, as they do the other s. 2Pe 3.16

SCROLL
a s. was found on which this was Ez 6.02
and the skies roll up like a s. Is 34.04
"Take a s. and write on it all the Jer 36.02
wrote upon a s. at the dictation 36.04
LORD from the s. which you have 36.06
from the s. words of the LORD 36.08
the words of Jeremiah from the s., 36.10
the words of the LORD from the s., 36.11
Baruch read the s. in the hearing 36.13
your hand the s. that you read in 36.14
Neriah took the s. in his hand and 36.14
I wrote them with ink on the s. 36.18
having put the s. in the chamber 36.20
the king sent Jehudi to get the s., 36.21
the entire s. was consumed in the 36.23
urged the king not to burn the s., 36.25
had burned the s. with the words 36.27
"Take another s. and write on it 36.28
words that were in the first s., 36.28
the LORD, You have burned this s., 36.29
took another s. and gave it to 36.32
words of the s. which Jehoiakim 36.32
and, lo, a written s. was in it; Eze 2.09
eat this s., and go, speak to the 3.01
and he gave me the s. to eat. 3.02
eat this s. that I give you and 3.03
and saw, and behold, a flying s.! Zec 5.01
I answered, "I see a flying s.; 5.02
on the throne a s. written within Rev 5.01
to open the s. and break its seals?" 5.02
to open the s. or to look into it, 5.03
to open the s. or to look into it. 5.04
he can open the s. and its seven 5.05
and took the s. from the right 5.07
And when he had taken the s., 5.08
to take the s. and to open its 5.09
vanished like a s. that is rolled 6.14
He had a little s. open in his hand. 10.02
take the s. which is open in the 10.08
told him to give me the little s.; 10.09
took the little s. from the hand 10.10

SCRUPLES
be determined by another man's s.? 1Co 10.29

SCULPTURED
back at the s. stones near Gilgal, Ju 3.19
and passed beyond the s. stones, 3.26

SCURVY
the ulcers and the s. and the itch, Deu 28.27

SCYTHIAN
S., slave, free man, but Christ is Col 3.11

SEA
dominion over the fish of the s., Gen 1.26
the fish of the s. and over the 1.28
ground and all the fish of the s.; 9.02
of Siddim (that is, the Salt S.). 14.03
descendants as the sand of the s., 32.12
abundance, like the sand of the s., 41.49
shall dwell at the shore of the s.; 49.13
and drove them into the Red S.; Ex 10.19
the wilderness toward the Red S. 13.18
Pihahiroth, between Migdol and the s., 14.02
encamp over against it, by the s. 14.02
overtook them encamped at the s., 14.09
hand over the s. and divide it, 14.16
go on dry ground through the s. 14.16
stretched out his hand over the s.; 14.21
LORD drove the s. back by a strong 14.21
and made the s. dry land, and the 14.21
the midst of the s. on dry ground, 14.22
them into the midst of the s., 14.23
"Stretch out your hand over the s., 14.26
stretched forth his hand over the s., 14.27
and the s. returned to its wonted 14.27
Egyptians in the midst of the s. 14.27
that had followed them into the s.; 14.28
on dry ground through the s., 14.29
rider he has thrown into the s. 15.01
and his host he cast into the s.; 15.04
officers are sunk in the Red S. 15.04
congealed in the heart of the s. 15.08
with thy wind, the s. covered them; 15.10
and his horsemen went into the s., 15.19
the waters of the s. upon them; 15.19

SEA (cont.)

ry ground in the midst of the s. Ex 15.19
rider he has thrown into the s. 15.21
led Israel onward from the Red S., 15.22
the s., and all that is in them, and 20.11
the Red S. to the s. of the Philistines, 23.31
the s. gull, the hawk according to Lev 11.16
the fish of the s. be gathered Num 11.22
and it brought quails from the s., 11.31
and the Canaanites dwell by the s., 13.29
wilderness by the way to the Red S. 14.25
set out by the way to the Red S., 21.04
midst of the s. into the wilderness, 33.08
Elim, and encamped by the Red S. 33.10
And they set out from the Red S., 33.11
the end of the Salt S. on the east; 34.03
its termination shall be at the S. 34.05
have the Great S. and its coast; 34.06
from the Great S. you shall mark 34.07
shoulder of the s. of Chinnereth 34.11
its end shall be at the Salt S. 34.12
in the direction of the Red S. Deu 1.40
in the direction of the Red S., 2.01
as far as the s. of the Arabah, 3.17
the Salt S., under the slopes of 3.17
as far as the S. of the Arabah, 4.49
of the Red S. overflow them as 11.04
river Euphrates, to the western s. 11.24
the s. gull, the hawk, after their 14.15
Neither is it beyond the s., 30.13
'Who will go over the s. for us, 30.13
of Judah as far as the Western S., 34.02
to the Great S. toward the going Jos 1.04
of the Red S. before you when you 2.10
down toward the s. of the Arabah, 3.16
the Salt S., were wholly cut off; 3.16
LORD your God did to the Red S., 4.23
the Canaanites that were by the s., 5.01
of the Great S. toward Lebanon, 9.01
Arabah to the S. of Chinneroth 12.03
to the s. of the Arabah, the Salt S., 12.03
lower end of the S. of Chinnereth, 13.27
ran from the end of the Salt S., 15.02
and comes to its end at the s. 15.04
And the east boundary is the Salt S., 15.05
the bay of the s. at the mouth of 15.05
boundary comes to an end at the s. 15.11
was the Great S. with its coast-line 15.12
from Ekron to the s., all that were 15.46
and the great s. with its coast-line 15.47
to Gezer, and it ends at the s. 16.03
the boundary goes thence to the s.; 16.06
brook Kanah, and ends at the s. 16.08
of the brook and ends at the s.; 17.09
with the s. forming its boundary; 17.10
at the northern bay of the Salt S., 18.19
to Hosah, and it ends at the s.; 19.29
Jordan to the Great S. in the west. 23.04
of Egypt, and you came to the s.; 24.06
chariots and horsemen to the Red S. 24.06
and made the s. come upon them and 24.07
sat still at the coast of the s., Ju 5.17
to the Red S. and came to Kadesh. 11.16
the sand by the s. for multitude, 2Sa 17.11
Then the channels of the s. were seen, 22.16
were as many as the sand by the s.; 1Ki 4.20
it down to the s. from Lebanon; 5.09
rafts to go by s. to the place you 5.09
Then he made the molten s.; 7.23
compassing the s. round about; 7.24
the s. was set upon them, and all 7.25
and he set the s. on the southeast 7.39
and the one s., and the twelve oxen 7.44
the twelve oxen underneath the s. 7.44
Eloth on the shore of the Red S., 9.26
who were familiar with the s., 9.27
of Tarshish at s. with the fleet 10.22

"Go up now, look toward the s." 18.43
man's hand is rising out of the s." 18.44
as far as the S. of the Arabah, 2Ki 14.25
took down the s. from off the 16.17
and the bronze s. that were in the 25.13
the one s., and the stands, which 25.16
Let the s. roar, and all that fills 1Ch 16.32
made the bronze s. and the pillars 18.08
it to you in rafts by s. to Joppa, 2Ch 2.16
Then he made the molten s.; 4.02
compassing the s. round about; 4.03
the s. was set upon them, and all 4.04
and the s. was for the priests to 4.06
and he set the s. at the southeast 4.10
and the one s., and the twelve oxen 4.15
and Eloth on the shore of the s., 8.17
and servants familiar with the s., 8.18
you from Edom, from beyond the s.; 20.02
cedar trees from Lebanon to the s., Ez 3.07
and hear their cry at the Red S., Neh 9.09
didst divide the s. before them, 9.11
the midst of the s. on dry land; 9.11
and on the coastlands of the s. Est 10.01
be heavier than the sand of the s.; Job 6.03
Am I the s., or a s. monster, that thou 7.12
and trampled the waves of the s.; 9.08
the earth, and broader than the s. 11.09
the fish of the s. will declare to 12.08
By his power he stilled the s.; 26.12
and the s. says, 'It is not with 28.14
and covers the roots of the s. 36.30
"Or who shut in the s. with doors, 38.08
entered into the springs of the s., 38.16
he makes the s. like a pot of 41.31
of the air, and the fish of the s., Ps 8.08
passes along the paths of the s. 8.08
Then the channels of the s. were seen, 18.15
waters of the s. as in a bottle; 33.07
shake in the heart of the s.; 46.02
He turned the s. into dry land; 66.06
back from the depths of the s., 68.22
May he have dominion from s. to s., 72.08
Thou didst divide the s. by thy might; 74.13
Thy way was through the s., 77.19
He divided the s. and let them pass 78.13
but the s. overwhelmed their 78.53
it sent out its branches to the s., 80.11
Thou dost rule the raging of the s.; 89.09
his hand on the s. and his right 89.25
mightier than the waves of the s., 93.04
The s. is his, for he made it; 95.05
let the s. roar, and all that fills 96.11
Let the s. roar, and all that fills 98.07
Yonder is the s., great and wide, 104.25
the Most High at the Red S. 106.07
He rebuked the Red S., and it 106.09
and terrible things by the Red S. 106.22
Some went down to the s. in ships, 107.23
lifted up the waves of the s. 107.25
the waves of the s. were hushed. 107.29
The s. looked and fled, Jordan 114.03
What ails you, O S., that you flee? 114.05
who divided the Red S. in sunder, 136.13
Pharaoh and his host in the Red S., 136.15
in the uttermost parts of the s., 139.09
the s., and all that is in them; 146.06
you s. monsters and all deeps, 148.07
when he assigned to the s. its limit, Pro 8.29
lies down in the midst of the s., 23.34
streams run to the s., but the s. is not full; Ecc 1.07
day, like the roaring of the s. Is 5.30
make glorious the way of the s., 9.01
Israel be as the sand of the s., 10.22
and his rod will be over the s., 10.26
LORD as the waters cover the s. 11.09
and from the coastlands of the s. 11.11
the tongue of the s. of Egypt; 11.15
abroad and passed over the s. 16.08

SEA (cont.)
like the thundering of the s.! Is 17.12
concerning the wilderness of the s. 21.01
passed over the s. and were on 23.02
s. has spoken, the stronghold of the s., 23.04
stretched out his hand over the s., 23.11
in the coastlands of the s., 24.15
slay the dragon that is in the s. 27.01
Let the s. roar and all that fills 42.10
LORD, who makes a way in the s., 43.16
righteousness like the waves of the s.; 48.18
by my rebuke I dry up the s., 50.02
not thou that didst dry up the s., 51.10
depths of the s. a way for the 51.10
stirs up the s. so that its waves 51.15
the wicked are like the tossing s.; 57.20
abundance of the s. shall be turned 60.05
up out of the s. the shepherds of 63.11
the sand as the bound for the s., Jer 5.22
of them is like the roaring s.; 6.23
of the coastland across the s.; 25.22
the s., the stands, and the rest of 27.19
stirs up the s. so that its waves 31.35
sands of the s. cannot be measured, 33.22
mountains, and like Carmel by the s., 46.18
Your branches passed over the s., 48.32
cry shall be heard at the Red S. 49.21
like the s. which cannot be quiet. 49.23
them is like the roaring of the s.; 50.42
will dry up her s. and make her 51.36
The s. has come up on Babylon; 51.42
and the bronze s. that were in the 52.17
the one s., the twelve bronze bulls 52.20
bulls which were under the s., 52.20
For vast as the s. is your ruin; Lam 2.13
as the s. brings up its waves. Eze 26.03
midst of the s. a place for the 26.05
princes of the s. will step down 26.16
renowned, that was mighty on the s., 26.17
that are in the s. are dismayed at 26.18
dwells at the entrance to the s., 27.03
ships of the s. with their mariners 27.09
pilots of the s. stand on the 27.29
like Tyre in the midst of the s.? 27.32
the fish of the s., and the birds 38.20
of the Travelers east of the s.; 39.11
the stagnant waters of the s., 47.08
waters of the s. may become fresh; 47.09
Fishermen will stand beside the s.; 47.10
like the fish of the Great S. 47.10
from the Great S. by way of 47.15
shall run from the s. to Hazarenon, 47.17
to the eastern s. and as far as 47.18
the Brook of Egypt to the Great S. 47.19
the Great S. shall be the boundary 47.20
from the s. by way of Hethlon to 48.01
the Brook of Egypt to the Great S. 48.28
were stirring up the great s. Dan 7.02
great beasts came up out of the s., 7.03
between the s. and the glorious 11.45
shall be like the sand of the s., Hos 1.10
the fish of the s. are taken away. 4.03
his front into the eastern s., Joe 2.20
and his rear into the western s.; 2.20
who calls for the waters of the s., Amo 5.08
Does one plow the s. with oxen? 6.12
They shall wander from s. to s., and 8.12
my sight at the bottom of the s., 9.03
who calls for the waters of the s., 9.06
hurled a great wind upon the s., Jon 1.04
was a mighty tempest on the s., 1.04
that were in the ship into the s., 1.05
who made the s. and the dry land. 1.09
that the s. may quiet down for us?" 1.11
For the s. grew more and more 1.11
me up and throw me into the s.; 1.12
then the s. will quiet down for you 1.12
for the s. grew more and more 1.13
up Jonah and threw him into the s.; 1.15
and the s. ceased from its raging. 1.15
from s. to s. and from mountain to Mic 7.12
our sins into the depths of the s. 7.19
He rebukes the s. and makes it dry, Nah 1.04
her rampart a s., and water her 3.08
makest men like the fish of the s., Hab 1.14
LORD, as the waters cover the s. 2.14
or thy indignation against the s., 3.08
trample the s. with thy horses, the 3.15
of the air and the fish of the s. Zep 1.03
earth and the s. and the dry land; Hag 2.06
and hurl her wealth into the s., Zec 9.04
dominion shall be from s. to s., 9.10
shall pass through the s. of Egypt, 10.11
waves of the s. shall be smitten, 10.11
to the eastern s. and half of them 14.08
and half of them to the western s.; 14.08
and dwelt in Capernaum by the s., Mt 4.13
toward the s., across the Jordan. 4.15
As he walked by the S. of Galilee, 4.18
brother, casting a net into the s.; 4.18
arose a great storm on the s., 8.24
and rebuked the winds and the s.; 8.26
that even winds and s. obey him?" 8.27
down the steep bank into the s., 8.32
of the house and sat beside the s. 13.01
thrown into the s. and gathered 13.47
he came to them, walking on the s. 14.25
disciples saw him walking on the s., 14.26
and passed along the S. of Galilee. 15.29
go to the s. and cast a hook, and 17.27
be drowned in the depth of the s. 18.06
'Be taken up and cast into the s.,' 21.21
you traverse s. and land to make a 23.15
passing along by the S. of Galilee, Mk 1.16
of Simmon casting a net in the s.; 1.16
He went out again beside the s.; 2.13
with his disciples to the s., 3.07
Again he began to teach beside the s. 4.01
a boat and sat in it on the s.; 4.01
was beside the s. on the land. 4.01
wind, and said to the s., "Peace! 4.39
that even wind and s. obey him?" 4.41
They came to the other side of the s., 5.01
into the s., and were drowned in the s. 5.13
about him; and he was beside the s. 5.21
came, the boat was out on the s., 6.47
he came to them, walking on the s. 6.48
walking on the s. they thought it 6.49
through Sidon to the S. of Galilee, 7.31
and he were thrown into the s. 9.42
'Be taken up and cast into the s.,' 11.23
neck and he were cast into the s., Lk 17.02
up, and be planted in the s.,' 17.06
roaring of the s. and the waves, 21.25
other side of the S. of Galilee, Jn 6.01
which is the S. of Tiberias. 6.01
his disciples went down to the s., 6.16
started across the s. to Capernaum. 6.17
The s. rose because a strong wind 6.18
walking on the s. and drawing near 6.19
side of the s. saw that there had 6.22
him on the other side of the s., 6.25
disciples by the S. of Tiberias; 21.01
for work, and sprang into the s. 21.07
earth and the s. and everything in Ac 4.24
signs in Egypt and at the Red S., 7.36
earth and the s. and all that is 14.15
sent Paul off on his way to the s., 17.14
we put to s., accompanied by 27.02
And putting to s. from there we 27.04
across the s. which is off Cilicia 27.05
advised to put to s. from there, 27.12
drifting across the s. of Adria, 27.27
had lowered the boat into the s., 27.30
throwing out the wheat into the s. 27.38
anchors and left them in the s., 27.40

SEA (cont.)

though he has escaped from the s., Ac 28.04
of Israel be as the sand of the s., Rom 9.27
and all passed through the s., 1Co 10.01
Moses in the cloud and in the s., 10.02
and a day I have been adrift at s.; 2Co 11.25
danger at s., danger from false 11.26
crossed the Red S. as if on dry Heb 11.29
a wave of the s. that is driven Jas 1.06
bird, of reptile and s. creature, 3.07
wild waves of the s., casting up Jud 1.13
there is as it were a s. of glass, Rev 4.06
and under the earth and in the s., 5.13
on earth or s. or against any tree 7.01
given power to harm earth and s., 7.02
the earth or the s. or the trees, 7.03
with fire, was thrown into the s.; 8.08
and a third of the s. became blood, 8.09
living creatures in the s. died, 8.09
he set his right foot on the s., 10.02
saw standing on s. and land lifted 10.05
and the s. and what is in it, that 10.06
standing on the s. and on the land 10.08
O earth and s., for the devil has 12.12
And he stood on the sand of the s. 12.17
I saw a beast rising out of the s., 13.01
the s. and the fountains of water. 14.07
appeared to be a s. of glass 15.02
beside the s. of glass with harps 15.02
angel poured his bowl into the s., 16.03
thing died that was in the s. 16.03
trade is on the s., stood far off 18.17
had ships at s. grew rich by her 18.19
millstone and threw it into the s., 18.21
number is like the sand of the s. 20.08
And the s. gave up the dead in it, 20.13
passed away, and the s. was no more. 21.01

SEACOAST

the s., the land of the Canaanites, Deu 1.07
and destroy the rest of the s. Eze 25.16
Woe to you inhabitants of the s., Zep 2.05
And you, O s., shall be pastures, 2.06
The s. shall become the possession 2.07
Jerusalem and the s. of Tyre and Lk 6.17

SEAFARING

And all shipmasters and s. men, sailors Rev 18.17

SEAL

name and sealed them with his s., 1Ki 21.08
and our priests set their s. to it. Neh 9.38
Those who set their s. are Nehemiah 10.01
and s. it with the king's ring; Est 8.08
It is changed like clay under the s., Job 38.14
shut up closely as with a s. 41.15
Set me as a s. upon your heart, as a Sol 8.06
your heart, as a s. upon your arm; 8.06
s. the teaching among my disciples. Is 8.16
but s. up the vision, for it pertains Dan 8.26
to s. both vision and prophet, and 9.24
and s. the book, until the time of 12.04
his testimony set his s. to this, Jn 3.33
him has God the Father set his s." 6.27
as a sign or s. of the righteousness Rom 4.11
for you are the s. of my apostleship 1Co 9.02
he has put his s. upon us and given 2Co 1.22
bearing this s.: "The Lord knows 2Ti 2.19
When he opened the second s., Rev 6.03
When he opened the third s., 6.05
When he opened the fourth s., 6.07
When he opened the fifth s., 6.09
When he opened the sixth s., 6.12
with the s. of the living God, and 7.02
When the Lamb opened the seventh s., 8.01
have not the s. of God upon their 9.04
"S. up what the seven thunders have 10.04
"Do not s. up the words of the 22.10

SEALED

with me, s. up in my treasuries Deu 32.34
Ahab's name and s. them with his 1Ki 21.08
Ahasuerus and s. with the king's Est 3.12
of the king and s. with the king's 8.08
Ahasuerus and s. with the king's 8.10
transgression would be s. up in a bag, Job 14.17
a garden locked, a fountain s. Sol 4.12
the words of a book that is s. Is 29.11
he says, "I cannot, for it is s." 29.11
s. it, got witnesses, and weighed the Jer 32.10
Then I took the s. deed of purchase, 32.11
both this s. deed of purchase and 32.14
be signed and s. and witnessed, 32.44
and the king s. it with his own Dan 6.17
are shut up and s. until the time 12.09
were s. with the promised Holy Eph 1.13
whom you were s. for the day of 4.30
on the back, s. with seven seals; Rev 5.01
till we have s. the servants of our 7.03
And I heard the number of the s., 7.04
hundred and forty-four thousand s., 7.04
twelve thousand s. out of the tribe 7.05
twelve thousand s. out of the tribe 7.08
the pit, and shut it and s. it over him, 20.03

SEALING

secure by s. the stone and setting Mt 27.66

SEALS

does not rise; who s. up the stars; Job 9.07
He s. up the hand of every man, that 37.07
on the back, sealed with seven s.; Rev 5.01
open the scroll and break its s.?" 5.02
open the scroll and break its s." 5.05
take the scroll and to open its s., 5.09
Lamb opened one of the seven s., 6.01

SEAM

But his tunic was without s., woven Jn 19.23

SEAMEN

s. who were familiar with the sea, 1Ki 9.27

SEAMS

men were in you, caulking your s.; Eze 27.09

SEARCH

if you s. after him with all your Deu 4.29
and make s. and ask diligently; 13.14
here tonight to s. out the land." Jos 2.02
have come to s. out all the land." 2.03
had made s. all along the way and 2.22
they had made s. and inquired, Ju 6.29
I will s. him out among all the 1Sa 23.23
Philistines went up in s. of David; 2Sa 5.17
his servants to you to s. the city, 10.03
and they shall s. your house and 1Ki 20.06
"S., and see that there is no 2Ki 10.23
Philistines went up in s. of David; 1Ch 14.08
come to you to s. and to overthrow 19.03
David's reign s. was made and men 26.31
in order that s. may be made in the Ez 4.15
and s. has been made, and it has 4.19
let s. be made in the royal archives 5.17
and s. was made in Babylonia, in the 6.01
out my iniquity and s. for my sin, Job 10.06
and s. out to the farthest bound 28.03
Who can s. out our crimes? We have Ps 64.06
night; I meditate and s. my spirit: 77.06
S. me, O God, and know my heart! 139.23
like silver and s. for it as for Pro 2.04
glory of kings is to s. things out. 25.02
to seek and to s. out by wisdom Ecc 1.13
to know and to s. out and to seek 7.25
S. her squares to see if you can Jer 5.01
"I the LORD s. the mind and try the 17.10
people groan as they s. for bread; Lam 1.11

SEARCH (cont.)
with none to s. or seek for them. Eze 34.06
I myself will s. for my sheep, and 34.11
months they will make their s. 39.14
there I will s. out and take them; Amo 9.03
time I will s. Jerusalem with Zep 1.12
"Go and s. diligently for the child, Mt 2.08
Herod is about to s. for the child, 2.13
a merchant in s. of fine pearls, 13.45
hills and go in s. of the one that 18.12
You s. the scriptures, because you Jn 5.39
S. and you will see that no prophet 7.52

SEARCHED
So he s., but did not find the Gen 31.35
And he s.. beginning with the 44.12
He s. for Ahaziah, and he was 2Ch 22.09
Lo, this we have s. out; it is true. Job 5.27
he established it, and s. it out. 28.27
and I s. out the cause of him whom 29.16
while you s. out what to say. 32.11
thou hast s. me and known me! Ps 139.01
I s. with my mind how to cheer my Ec 2.03
a land that I had s. out for them, Eze 20.06
shepherds have not s. for my sheep, 34.08
in Rome he s. for me eagerly and 2Ti 1.17
was to be yours s. and inquired 1Pe 1.10

SEARCHES
for the LORD s. all hearts, and 1Ch 28.09
well with you when he s. you out? Job 13.09
and he s. after every green thing. 39.08
evil comes to him who s. for it. Pro 11.27
And he who s. the hearts of men Rom 8.27
For the Spirit s. everything, 1Co 2.10
that I am he who s. mind and heart, Rev 2.23

SEARCHEST
Thou s. out my path and my lying Ps 139.03

SEARCHING
the LORD, s. all his innermost parts. Pro 20.27
to him, "Every one is s. for you." Mk 1.37

SEARCHINGS
Reuben there were great s. of heart. Ju 5.15
Reuben there were great s. of heart. 5.16

SEARED
of liars whose consciences are s., 1Ti 4.02

SEAS
were gathered together he called S. Gen 1.10
and fill the waters in the s., 1.22
whether in the s. or in the rivers, Lev 11.09
But anything in the s. or the 11.10
affluence of the s. and the hidden Deu 33.19
the s. and all that is in them; Neh 9.06
for he has founded it upon the s., Ps 24.02
the earth, and of the farthest s.; 65.05
who dost still the roaring of the s., 65.07
the s. and everything that moves 69.34
birds like the sand of the s.; 78.27
on earth, in the s. and all deeps. 135.06
the way of a ship on the high s., Pro 30.19
in number than the sand of the s.; Jer 15.08
'How you have vanished from the s., Eze 26.17
borders are in the heart of the s.; 27.04
laden in the heart of the s. 27.25
brought you out into the high s. 27.26
wrecked you in the heart of the s. 27.26
heart of the s. on the day of your 27.27
When your wares came from the s., 27.33
Now you are wrecked by the s., 27.34
the gods, in the heart of the s., 28.02
the slain in the heart of the s. 28.08
you are like a dragon in the s.; 32.02
the deep, into the heart of the s., Jon 2.03

SEASHORE
and as the sand which is on the s. Gen 22.17
saw the Egyptians dead upon the s. Ex 14.30
like the sand that is upon the s., Jos 11.04
which is upon the s. for multitude. Ju 7.12
the sand on the s. in multitude; 1Sa 13.05
of mind like the sand on the s., 1Ki 4.29
and against the s. he has appointed Jer 47.07
innumerable grains of sand by the s. Heb 11.12

SEASIDE
a tanner, whose house is by the s." Ac 10.06
house of Simon, a tanner, by the s.' 10.32

SEASON
bear to you at this s. next year." Gen 17.21
In the mating s. of the flock 31.10
You shall s. all your cereal Lev 2.13
give you your rains in their s., 26.04
time was the s. of the first-ripe Num 13.20
heed to offer to me in its due s.' 28.02
the rain for your land in its s., Deu 11.14
land in its s. and to bless all 28.12
"At this s., when the time comes 2Ki 4.16
to the threshing floor in its s. Job 5.26
forth the Mazzaroth in their s., 38.32
that yields its fruit in its s., Ps 1.03
to give them their food in due s. 104.27
givest them their food in due s. 145.15
and a word in s., how good it is! Pro 15.23
For everything there is a s., Ecc 3.01
God, who gives the rain in its s., Jer 5.24
send down the showers in their s.; Eze 34.26
were prolonged for a s. and a time. Dan 7.12
in its time, and my wine in its s.; Hos 2.09
in its first s., I saw your fathers 9.10
the LORD in the s. of the spring Zec 10.01
When the s. of fruit drew near, he Mt 21.34
its saltness, how will you s. it? Mk 9.50
for it was not the s. for figs. 11.13
perhaps by agreement for a s., 1Co 7.05
for in due s. we shall reap, if we Gal 6.09
be urgent in s. and out of s., 2Ti 4.02

SEASONED
s. with salt, pure and holy; Ex 30.35
Of Zebulun fifty thousand s. troops, 1Ch 12.33
forty thousand s. troops ready for 12.36
men, and all the s. warriors. 28.01
s. with salt, so that you may know Col 4.06

SEASONS
signs and for s. and for days and Gen 1.14
be observed at their appointed s., Est 9.31
Thou hast made the moon to mark the s.; Ps 104.19
the appointed s. the cereal offering Eze 46.11
He changes times and s.; he removes Dan 2.21
house of Judah s. of joy and Zec 8.19
give him the fruits in their s." Mt 21.41
down at certain s. into the pool, *Jn 5.04
know times or s. which the Father Ac 1.07
from heaven rains and fruitful s., 14.17
and months, and s., and years! Gal 4.10
But as to the times and the s., 1Th 5.01

SEAT
shall make a mercy s. of pure gold; Ex 25.17
on the two ends of the mercy s. 25.18
with the mercy s. shall you make 25.19
the mercy s. with their wings, 25.20
the mercy s. shall the faces of 25.20
put the mercy s. on the top of the 25.21
you, and from above the mercy s., 25.22
put the mercy s. upon the ark of 26.34
the mercy s. that is over the 30.06
and the mercy s. that is thereon, 31.07
the mercy s., and the veil of the 35.12
And he made a mercy s. of pure gold; 37.06

SEAT (cont.)
ends of the mercy s. he made them. Ex 37.07
with the mercy s. he made the 37.08
the mercy s. with their wings, with 37.09
the mercy s. were the faces of the 37.09
with its poles and the mercy s.; 39.35
set the mercy s. above on the ark; 40.20
the mercy s. which is upon the ark, Lev 16.02
in the cloud upon the mercy s. 16.02
cover the mercy s. which is upon 16.13
on the front of the mercy s., 16.14
the mercy s. he shall sprinkle the 16.14
upon the mercy s. and before the mercy s.; 16.15
above the mercy s. that was upon Num 7.89
that extends to the s. of Ar, 21.15
for you." And he arose from his s. Ju 3.20
sitting on the s. beside the 1Sa 1.09
princes and inherit a s. of honor. 2.08
upon his s. by the road watching, 4.13
from his s. by the side of the 4.18
because your s. will be empty. 20.18
The king sat upon the s., as at 20.25
times, upon the s. by the wall; 20.25
arose, and took his s. in the gate. 2Sa 19.08
and had a s. brought for the king's 1Ki 2.19
side of the s. were arm rests and 10.19
And he took his s. on the throne of 2Ki 11.19
and gave him a s. above the seats 25.28
and of the room for the mercy s.; 1Ch 28.11
side of the s. were arm rests and 2Ch 9.18
They had their s. at Jerusalem. 19.08
him and set his s. above all the Est 3.01
that I might come even to his s.! Job 23.03
I prepared my s. in the square, 29.07
nor sits in the s. of scoffers; Ps 1.01
and over it take thy s. on high. 7.07
she takes a s. on the high places Pro 9.14
its back of gold, its s. of purple; Sol 3.10
"Take a lowly s., for your beautiful Jer 13.18
and took their s. in the entry of 26.10
and gave him a s. above the seats 52.32
where was the s. of the image of Eze 8.03
I sit in the s. of the gods, in the 28.02
was ancient of days took his s.; Dan 7.09
and bring near the s. of violence? Amo 6.03
and the Pharisees sit on Moses' s.; Mt 23.02
he was sitting on the judgment s., 27.19
love the best s. in the synagogues Lk 11.43
on the judgment s. at a place Jn 19.13
took his s. upon the throne, and Ac 12.21
day he took his s. on the tribunal 25.06
day took my s. on the tribunal and 25.17
before the judgment s. of God; Rom 14.10
before the judgment s. of Christ, 2Co 5.10
he takes his s. in the temple of 2Th 2.04
glory overshadowing the mercy s. Heb 9.05
"Have a s. here, please," while you Jas 2.03

SEATED
soon as he had s. himself on his 1Ki 16.11
LORD our God, who is s. on high, Ps 113.05
and s. above the likeness of a Eze 1.26
the Son of man s. at the right Mt 26.64
of man shall be s. at the right Lk 22.69
distributed them to those who were s.; Jn 6.11
s. in his chariot, he was reading Ac 8.28
s. at the right hand of God. Col 3.01
one who is s. at the right hand of Heb 8.01
and is s. at the right hand of the 12.02
heaven, with one s. on the throne! Rev 4.02
and s. on the thrones were twenty-four 4.04
to him who is s. on the throne, 4.09
him who is s. on the throne and 4.10
of him who was s. on the throne a 5.01
of him who was s. on the throne. 5.07
of him who is s. on the throne, 6.16
and s. on the cloud one like a son 14.14
harlot who is s. upon many waters. 17.01
hills on which the woman is s.; 17.09
you saw, where the harlot is s., 17.15
God who is s. on the throne, 19.04
and s. on them were those to whom 20.04

SEATING
the s. of his officials, and the 1Ki 10.05
the s. of his officials, and the 2Ch 9.04

SEATS
seat above the s. of the kings who 2Ki 25.28
seat above the s. of the kings who Jer 52.32
money-changers and the s. of those Mt 21.12
and the best s. in the synagogues, 23.06
money-changers and the s. of those Mk 11.15
and the best s. in the synagogues 12.39
and the best s. in the synagogues Lk 20.46

SEBA
S., Havilah, Sabtah, Raamah, and Gen 10.07
S., Havilah, Sabta, Raama, and Sabteca 1Ch 1.09
kings of Sheba and S. bring gifts! Ps 72.10
Ethiopia and S. in exchange for you Is 43.03

SEBAM
Elealeh, S., Nebo, and Beon, Num 32.03

SECACAH
wilderness, Betharabah, Middin, S., Jos 15.61

SECOND
and there was morning, a s. day. Gen 1.08
The name of the s. river is Gihon; 2.13
it with lower, s., and third decks. 6.16
in the s. month, on the seventeenth 7.11
In the s. month, on the twenty-seventh 8.14
to Abraham a s. time from heaven, 22.15
again and bore Jacob a s. son. 30.07
Leah's maid Zilpah bore Jacob a s. son 30.12
instructed the s. and the third 32.19
fell asleep and dreamed a s. time; 41.05
made him to ride in his s. chariot; 41.43
The name of the s. he called 41.52
day of the s. month after they had Ex 16.01
the outmost curtain in the s. set. 26.04
the curtain that is in the s. set; 26.05
which is outmost in the s. set. 26.10
and for the s. side of the tabernacle, 26.20
and the s. row an emerald, a sapphire, 28.18
the outmost curtain of the s. set; 36.11
the curtain that was in the s. set; 36.12
And for the s. side of the tabernacle, 36.25
and the s. row, an emerald, a sapphire, 39.11
And in the first month in the s. year, 40.17
shall offer the s. for a burnt Lev 5.10
it, shall then be washed a s. time, 13.58
on the first day of the s. month, Num 1.01
in the s. year after they had come 1.01
and on the first day of the s. month, 1.18
and fifty. They shall set out s. 2.16
On the s. day Nethanel the son of 7.18
month of the s. year after they 9.01
In the s. month on the fourteenth 9.11
when you blow an alarm the s. time, 10.06
In the s. year, in the s. month, on 10.11
"On the s. day twelve young bulls, 29.17
people of Israel again the s. time." Jos 5.02
And the s. day they marched around 6.14
and he took it on the s. day, 10.32
The s. lot came out for Simeon, for 19.01
the s. bull seven years old, and Ju 6.25
then take the s. bull, and offer it 6.26
and the s. bull was offered upon 6.28
the Benjaminites the s. day. 20.24
them out of Gibeah the s. day, 20.25
and the name of his s., Abijah; 1Sa 8.02
Saul said to David a s. time, 18.21
But on the s. day, the morrow after 20.27

SECOND (cont.)

ate no food the s. day of the 1Sa 20.34
and his s., Chileab, of Abigail the 2Sa 3.03
And he sent a s. time, but Joab 14.29
ground, without striking a s. blow; 20.10
which is the s. month, he began to 1Ki 6.01
the s. pillar was the same. 7.15
LORD appeared to Solomon a s. time, 9.02
Israel in the s. year of Asa king 15.25
And he said, "Do it a s. time"; 18.34
and they did it a s. time. 18.34
of the LORD came again a s. time, 19.07
stead in the s. year of Jehoram 2Ki 1.17
Then he sent out a s. horseman, 9.19
Then he wrote to them a s. letter, 10.06
In the s. year of Joash the son of 14.01
In the s. year of Pekah the son of 15.32
and in the s. year what springs of 19.29
in Jerusalem in the S. Quarter); 22.14
and the priests of the s. order, 23.04
And the s. pillar had the like, with 25.17
and Zephaniah the s. priest, 25.18
Abinadab the s., Shemea the third, 1Ch 2.13
the s. Daniel, by Abigail the 3.01
the s. Jehoiakim, the third Zedekiah, 3.15
Shapham the s., Janai, and Shaphat 5.12
Joel his first-born, the s. Abijah. 6.28
the name of the s. was Zelophehad; 7.15
Ashbel the s., Aharah the third, 8.01
Jeush the s., and Eliphelet the 8.39
chief, Obadiah s., Eliab third, 12.09
their brethren of the s. order, 15.18
and s. to him were Zechariah, Jeiel, 16.05
Jahath was the chief, and Zizah the s.; 23.11
Amariah the s., Jahaziel the third, 23.19
Micah the chief and Isshiah the s. 23.20
to Jehoiarib, the s. to Jedaiah, 24.07
Amariah the s., Jahaziel the third, 24.23
the s. to Gedaliah, to him and his 25.09
Jediael the s., Zebadiah the third, 26.02
Jehozabad the s., Joah the third, 26.04
Hilkiah the s., Tebaliah the third, 26.11
of the division of the s. month; 27.04
the son of David king the s. time, 29.22
to build in the s. month of the 2Ch 3.02
amount in the s. and the third 27.05
the passover in the s. month— 30.02
unleavened bread in the s. month, 30.13
the fourteenth day of the s. month. 30.15
with Shimei his brother as s.; 31.12
Jerusalem in the S. Quarter) and 34.22
him in his s. chariot and brought 35.24
Now in the s. year of their coming Ez 3.08
in the s. month, Zerubbabel the son 3.08
until the s. year of the reign of 4.24
On the s. day the heads of fathers' Neh 8.13
of Hassenuah was s. over the city. 11.09
the s. among his brethren; 11.17
back to the s. harem in custody of Est 2.14
were gathered together the s. time, 2.19
And on the s. day, as they were 7.02
confirming this s. letter about 9.29
and the name of the s. Keziah; Job 42.14
blotted out in the s. generation! Ps 109.13
his hand yet a s. time to recover Is 11.11
and in the s. year what springs of 37.30
of the LORD came to me a s. time, Jer 1.13
of the LORD came to me a s. time, 13.03
LORD came to Jeremiah a s. time, 33.01
And the s. pillar had the like, with 52.22
and Zephaniah the s. priest, 52.24
you shall lie down a s. time, Eze 4.06
and the s. face was the face of a 10.14
And on the s. day you shall offer a 43.22
In the s. year of the reign of Dan 2.01
They answered a s. time, "Let the 2.07
another beast, a s. one, like a bear. 7.05
came to Jonah the s. time, saying, Jon 3.01
Gate, a wail from the S. Quarter, Zep 1.10
In the s. year of Darius the king, Hag 1.01
In the s. year of Darius the king, 2.01
in the s. year of Darius, the word 2.10
the LORD came a s. time to Haggai 2.20
in the s. year of Darius, the word Zec 1.01
in the s. year of Darius, the word 1.07
And a s. time I said to him, "What 4.12
red horses, the s. black horses, 6.02
Then I broke my s. staff Union, 11.14
And he went to the s. and said the Mt 21.30
So too the s. and third, down to the 22.26
And a s. is like it, You shall love 22.39
Again, for the s. time, he went away 26.42
and the s. took her, and died, Mk 12.21
The s. is this, 'You shall love your 12.31
immediately the cock crowed a s. time. 14.72
If he comes in the s. watch, or in Lk 12.38
And the s. came, saying, 'Lord, your 19.18
and the s. 20.30
Can he enter a s. time into his Jn 3.04
This was now the s. sign that Jesus 4.54
So for the s. time they called the 9.24
A s. time he said to him, "Simon, son 21.16
And at the s. visit Joseph made Ac 7.13
voice came to him again a s. time, 10.15
answered a s. time from heaven, 11.09
passed the first and the s. guard, 12.10
also it is written in the s. psalm, 13.33
and on the s. day we came to 28.13
s. prophets, third teachers, then 1Co 12.28
the s. man is from heaven. 15.47
I did when present on my s. visit, 2Co 13.02
have been no occasion for a s. Heb 8.07
Behind the s. curtain stood a tent 9.03
but into the s. only the high 9.07
will appear a s. time, not to deal 9.28
first in order to establish the s. 10.09
This is now the s. letter that I 2Pe 3.01
shall not be hurt by the s. death. Rev 2.11
the s. living creature like an ox, 4.07
When he opened the s. seal, 6.03
I heard the s. living creature say, 6.03
The s. angel blew his trumpet, and 8.08
The s. woe has passed; 11.14
a s., followed, saying, "Fallen, 14.08
The s. angel poured his bowl into 16.03
Over such the s. death has no power, 20.06
This is the s. death, the lake of 20.14
brimstone, which is the s. death. 21.08
the s. sapphire, the third agate, the 21.19

SECRET

of Egypt did the same by their s. arts. Ex 7.11
of Egypt did the same by their s. arts; 7.22
magicians did the same by their s. arts, 8.07
magicians tried by their s. arts to bring 8.18
a craftsman, and sets it up in s.' Deu 27.15
be he who slays his neighbor in s.' 27.24
"The s. things belong to the LORD 29.29
"I have a s. message for you, O king." Ju 3.19
So the s. of his strength was not 16.09
stay in a s. place and hide yourself; 1Sa 19.02
But Absalom sent s. messengers 2Sa 15.10
you if in s. you show partiality. Job 13.10
he lurks in s. like a lion in his Ps 10.09
teach me wisdom in my s. heart. 51.06
hide me from the s. plots of the 64.02
you in the s. place of thunder; 81.07
our s. sins in the light of thy 90.08
thee, when I was being made in s., 139.15
and bread eaten in s. is pleasant." Pro 9.17
A gift in s. averts anger; and a 21.14
and do not disclose another's s.; 25.09
with every s. thing, whether good or Ecc 12.14
LORD will lay bare their s. parts. Is 3.17
darkness and the hoards in s. places, 45.03
I did not speak in s., in a land of 45.19

SECRET (cont.)

beginning I have not spoken in s., Is 48.16
and spend the night in s. places; 65.04
will weep in s. for your pride; Jer 13.17
hide himself in s. places so that 23.24
Daniel; no s. is hidden from you; Eze 28.03
revealing his s. to his servants Amo 3.07
as if to devour the poor in s. Hab 3.14
so that your alms may be in s.; Mt 6.04
who sees in s. will reward you. 6.04
pray to your Father who is in s.; 6.06
who sees in s. will reward you. 6.06
but by your Father who is in s.; 6.18
who sees in s. will reward you. 6.18
been given the s. of the kingdom Mk 4.11
nor is anything s., except to come 4.22
nor anything s. that shall not be Lk 8.17
For no man works in s. if he seeks Jn 7.04
which was kept s. for long ages Rom 16.25
But we impart a s. and hidden 1Co 2.07
of the things that they do in s.; Eph 5.12
learned the s. of facing plenty Php 4.12

SECRETARIES

Ahijah the sons of Shisha were s.; 1Ki 4.03
Then the king's s. were summoned on Est 3.12
The king's s. were summoned at that 8.09

SECRETARY

Abiathar were priests; and Seraiah was s.; 2Sa 8.17
and Sheva was s.; and Zadok and 20.25
the king's s. and the high priest 2Ki 12.10
the household, and Shebnah the s., 18.18
the household, and Shebna the s., 18.37
the household, and Shebna the s., 19.02
the s., to the house of the LORD, 22.03
high priest said to Shaphan the s., 22.08
And Shaphan the s. came to the king, 22.09
Then Shaphan the s. told the king, 22.10
son of Micaiah, and Shaphan the s., 22.12
and the s. of the commander of 25.19
Abiathar were priests; and Shavsha was s.; 1Ch 18.16
the king's s. and the officer of the 2Ch 24.11
by Jeiel the s. and Maaseiah the 26.11
Then Hilkiah said to Shaphan the s., 34.15
Then Shaphan the s. told the king, 34.18
Shaphan the s., and Asaiah the 34.20
the household, and Shebna the s., Is 36.03
the household, and Shebna the s., 36.22
the household, and Shebna the s., 37.02
Gemariah the son of Shaphan the s., Jer 36.10
Elishama the s., Delaiah the son of 36.12
in the chamber of Elishama the s.; 36.20
the chamber of Elishama the s.; 36.21
Baruch the s. and Jeremiah the 36.26
in the house of Jonathan the s., 37.15
to the house of Jonathan the s., 37.20
and the s. of the commander of the 52.25

SECRETARY'S

king's house, into the s. chamber; Jer 36.12

SECRETLY

Why did you flee s., and cheat me, Gen 31.27
entices you s., saying, 'Let us go Deu 13.06
because she will eat them s., 28.57
sent two men s. from Shittim as Jos 2.01
For you did it s.; but I will 2Sa 12.12
of Israel did s. against the LORD 2Ki 17.09
and my heart has been s. enticed, Job 31.27
they talk of laying snares s., Ps 64.05
his neighbor s. I will destroy. 101.05
questioned him s. in his house, Jer 37.17
King Zedekiah swore s. to Jeremiah, 38.16
of Kareah spoke s. to Gedaliah at 40.15
the wise men s. and ascertained Mt 2.07
together; I have said nothing s. Jn 18.20
but s., for fear of the Jews, asked 19.38
Then they s. instigated men, who Ac 6.11
and do they now cast us out s.? 16.37
of false brethren s. brought in, Gal 2.04
who will s. bring in destructive 2Pe 2.01
has been s. gained by some who Jud 1.04

SECRETS

he would tell you the s. of wisdom! Job 11.06
For he knows the s. of the heart. Ps 44.21
about as a talebearer reveals s., Pro 11.13
goes about gossiping reveals s.; 20.19
to know the s. of the kingdom of Mt 13.11
to know the s. of the kingdom of Lk 8.10
God judges the s. of men by Christ Rom 2.16
the s. of his heart are disclosed; 1Co 14.25

SECT

ringleader of the s. of the Nazarenes. Ac 24.05
to the Way, which they call a s., 24.14
regard to this s. we know that 28.22

SECTION

repaired another s. and the Tower Neh 3.11
repaired another s. opposite the 3.19
repaired another s. from the Angle 3.20
repaired another s. from the door 3.21
son of Henadad repaired another s., 3.24
repaired another s. opposite the 3.27
son of Zalaph repaired another s. 3.30
measure off a s. twenty-five Eze 45.03
Another s., twenty-five thousand 45.05

SECU

came to the great well that is in S.; 1Sa 19.22

SECUNDUS

of the Thessalonians, Aristarchus and S.; Ac 20.04

SECURE

feet, and set me s. on the heights. 2Sa 22.34
ordered in all things and s. 23.05
Rehoboam the son of Solomon s., 2Ch 11.17
to give us a s. hold within his Ez 9.08
you will be s., and will not fear. Job 11.15
and those who provoke God are s., 12.06
being wholly at ease and s., 21.23
rejoices; my body also dwells s. Ps 16.09
feet, and set me s. on the heights. 18.33
upon a rock, making my steps s. 40.02
of thy servants shall dwell s.; 102.28
me will dwell s. and will be at Pro 1.33
but he who hates suretyship is s. 11.15
in s. dwellings, and in quiet Is 32.18
You felt s. in your wickedness, you 47.10
bound with cords and made s.; Eze 27.24
and they shall be s. in their land; 34.27
those who feel s. on the mountain Amo 6.01
And they shall dwell s., for now Mic 5.04
is the exultant city that dwelt s., Zep 2.15
to be made s. until the third day, Mt 27.64
go, make it as s. as you can." 27.65
the sepulchre s. by sealing the 27.66
with difficulty to s. the boat; Ac 27.16
order and to s. your undivided 1Co 7.35
writing this to s. any such provision. 9.15

SECURELY

so you will dwell in the land s. Lev 25.18
eat your fill, and dwell in it s. 25.19
full, and dwell in your land s. 26.05
on your way s. and your foot will Pro 3.23
He who walks in integrity walks s., 10.09
who sit s., who say in your heart, Is 47.08
be saved, and Israel will dwell s. Jer 23.06
saved and Jerusalem will dwell s. 33.16
that dwells s., says the LORD, that 49.31
And they shall dwell s. in it, and Eze 28.26
They shall dwell s., when I execute 28.26
they may dwell s. in the wilderness 34.25

SECURELY (cont.)
they shall dwell s., and none Eze 34.28
and now dwell s., all of them. 38.08
upon the quiet people who dwell s., 38.11
my people Israel are dwelling s., 38.14
those who dwell s. in the coastlands 39.06
when they dwell s. in their land 39.26
the prison s. locked and the Ac 5.23

SECURING
blood, thus s. an eternal redemption. Heb 9.12

SECURITY
neighbor in a matter of deposit or s., Lev 6.02
were there, how they dwelt in s., Ju 18.07
will be peace and s. in my days?" 2Ki 20.19
He gives them s., and they are Job 24.23
dwell in the land, and enjoy s. Ps 37.03
and s. within your towers! 122.07
I am oppressed; be thou my s.! Is 38.14
will be peace and s. in my days." 39.08
abundance of prosperity and s. Jer 33.06
Jerusalem shall dwell in s. Zec 14.11
they had taken s. from Jason and Ac 17.09
When people say, "There is peace and s.," 1Th 5.03

SEDITION
and that s. was stirred up in it Ez 4.15
rebellion and s. have been made in 4.19

SEDUCE
He shall s. with flattery those who Dan 11.32

SEDUCED
and Manasseh s. them to do more 2Ki 21.09
Manasseh s. Judah and the inhabitants 2Ch 33.09

SEDUCES
"If a man s. a virgin who is not Ex 22.16

SEDUCTIVE
With much s. speech she persuades Pro 7.21

SEED
vegetation, plants yielding s., and Gen 1.11
bearing fruit in which is their s., 1.11
plants yielding s. according to 1.12
bearing fruit in which is their s., 1.12
plant yielding s. which is upon 1.29
every tree with s. in its fruit; 1.29
woman, and between your s. and her s.; 3.15
and give us s., that we may live, 47.19
Now here is s. for you, and you 47.23
as s. for the field and as food for 47.24
it was like coriander s., white, Ex 16.31
falls upon any s. for sowing that Lev 11.37
is put on the s. and any part of 11.38
your field with two kinds of s.; 19.19
and you shall sow your s. in vain, 26.16
be according to the s. for it; 27.16
whether of the s. of the land or 27.30
Now the manna was like coriander s., Num 11.07
and his s. shall be in many waters, 24.07
you sowed your s. and watered it Deu 11.10
tithe all the yield of your s., 14.22
your vineyard with two kinds of s., 22.09
shall carry much s. into the field, 28.38
Israelites put in s. the Midianites Ju 6.03
would contain two measures of s. 1Ki 18.32
bearing the s. for sowing, shall Ps 126.06
In the morning sow your s., and at Ecc 11.06
and a homer of s. shall yield but Is 5.10
is felled." The holy s. is its stump. 6.13
rain for the s. with which you sow 30.23
giving s. to the sower and bread to 55.10
a choice vine, wholly of pure s. Jer 2.21
the s. of man and the s. of beast. 31.27
to rule over the s. of Abraham, 33.26
you shall not sow s.; you shall 35.07
We have no vineyard or field or s.; 35.09
Then he took of the s. of the land Eze 17.05
took one of the s. royal and made 17.13
I swore to the s. of the house of 20.05
The s. shrivels under the clods, the Joe 1.17
of grapes him who sows the s.; Amo 9.13
Is the s. yet in the barn? Do the Hag 2.19
man who sowed good s. in his field; Mt 13.24
you not sow good s. in your field? 13.27
of mustard s. which a man took and 13.31
sows the good s. is the Son of man; 13.37
and the good s. means the sons of 13.38
faith as a grain of mustard s., 17.20
some s. fell along the path, and the Mk 4.04
Other s. fell on rocky ground, where 4.05
Other s. fell among thorns and the 4.07
should scatter s. upon the ground, 4.26
and the s. should sprout and grow, 4.27
It is like a grain of mustard s., 4.31
"A sower went out to sow his s.; Lk 8.05
is this: The s. is the word of God. 8.11
of mustard s. which a man took and 13.19
had faith as a grain of mustard s., 17.06
to each kind of s. its own body. 1Co 15.38
He who supplies s. to the sower and 2Co 9.10
of perishable s. but of imperishable, 1Pe 1.23

SEEDS
not even the s. or the skins. Num 6.04
some s. fell along the path, and the Mt 13.04
Other s. fell on rocky ground, where 13.05
Other s. fell upon thorns, and the 13.07
Other s. fell on good soil and brought 13.08
it is the smallest of all s., but 13.32
And other s. fell into good soil Mk 4.08
smallest of all the s. on earth; 4.31

SEEDTIME
s. and harvest, cold and heat, summer Gen 8.22

SEEK
so that he may s. occassion against 43.18
priest need not s. for the yellow Lev 13.36
do not s. them out, to be defiled by 19.31
to s. out a resting place for them. Num 10.33
And would you s. the priesthood 16.10
his enemy, and did not s. his harm; 35.23
in the way to s. you out a place Deu 1.33
there you will s. the LORD your 4.29
But you shall s. the place which 12.05
You shall not s. their peace or 23.06
should I not s. a home for you, that Ru 3.01
which you went to s. are found, 1Sa 10.02
And he said, "To s. the asses; 10.14
to s. out a man who skilful in 16.16
Saul had come out to s. his life. 23.15
And Saul and his men went to s. him. 23.25
and went to s. David and his men in 24.02
and those who s. to do evil to my 25.26
to pursue you and to s. your life, 25.29
to s. David in the wilderness of 26.02
Israel has come out to s. my life, 26.20
"S. out for me a woman who is a 28.07
You s. the life of only one man, and 2Sa 17.03
you s. to destroy a city which is a 20.19
Gath to Achish, to s. his slaves; 1Ki 2.40
my lord has not sent to s. you; 18.10
and they s. my life, to take it away." 19.10
and they s. my life, to take it away." 19.14
let them go, and s. your master; 2Ki 2.16
bring you to the man whom you s." 6.19
to s. pasture for their flocks, 1Ch 4.39
and did not s. guidance from the 10.14
of those who s. the LORD rejoice! 16.10
S. the LORD and his strength, 16.11
s. his presence continually! 16.11
and heart to s. the LORD your God. 22.19
observe and s. out all the commandments 28.08

SEEK (cont.)

If you s. him, he will be found by	1Ch 28.09
and pray and s. my face, and turn	2Ch 7.14
their hearts to s. the LORD God of	11.16
not set his heart to s. the LORD.	12.14
and commanded Judah to s. the LORD,	14.04
If you s. him, he will be found by	15.02
into a covenant to s. the LORD,	15.12
that whoever would not s. the LORD,	15.13
his disease he did not s. the LORD,	16.12
his father; he did not s. the Baals,	17.03
and have set your heart to s. God."	19.03
and set himself to s. the LORD,	20.03
assembled to s. help from the LORD;	20.04
of Judah they came to s. the LORD.	20.04
He set himself to s. God in the	26.05
who sets his heart to s. God,	30.19
he began to s. the God of David his	34.03
to s. from him a straight way for	Ez 8.21
is for good upon all that s. him,	8.22
and never s. their peace or prosperity,	9.12
one had come to s. the welfare of	Neh 2.10
May God above not s. it, nor light	Job 3.04
I would s. God, and to God would I	5.08
thou wilt s. me, but I shall not be."	7.21
If you will s. God and make supplication	8.05
that thou dost s. out my iniquity	10.06
His children will s. the favor of	20.10
on the left hand I s. him, but I cannot	23.09
love vain words and s. after lies?	Ps 4.02
not forsaken those who s. thee.	9.10
countenance the wicked does not s. him;	10.04
s. out his wickedness till thou	10.15
that act wisely, that s. after God.	14.02
of those who s. refuge from their	17.07
those who s. him shall praise the	22.26
the generation of those who s. him,	24.06
who s. the face of the God of Jacob	24.06
of the LORD, that will I s. after;	27.04
Thou hast said, "S. ye my face."	27.08
to thee, "Thy face, LORD, do I s."	27.08
In thee, O LORD, do I s. refuge;	31.01
but those who s. the LORD lack no	34.10
do good; s. peace, and pursue it.	34.14
and dishonor who s. after my life!	35.04
Those who s. my life lay their	38.12
those who s. my hurt speak of ruin,	38.12
altogether who s. to snatch away	40.14
But may all who s. thee rejoice and	40.16
that are wise, that s. after God.	53.02
against me, ruthless men s. my life;	54.03
All day long they s. to injure my	56.05
I s. thee, my soul thirsts for thee;	63.01
But those who s. to destroy my life	63.09
not those who s. thee be brought	69.06
you who s. God, let your hearts	69.32
shame and confusion who s. my life!	70.02
May all who s. thee rejoice and be	70.04
may they be covered who s. my hurt.	71.13
day of my trouble I s. the Lord;	77.02
that they may s. thy name, O LORD.	83.16
band of ruthless men s. my life,	86.14
of those who s. the LORD rejoice!	105.03
S. the LORD and his strength,	105.04
s. his presence continually!	105.04
who s. him with their whole heart,	119.02
With my whole heart I s. thee;	119.10
for they do not s. thy statutes.	119.155
s. thy servant, for I do not forget	119.176
LORD our God, I will s. your good.	122.09
in thee I s. refuge; leave me not	141.08
they will s. me diligently but will	Pro 1.28
if you s. it like silver and search	2.04
to s. you eagerly, and I have found	7.15
and those who s. me diligently find	8.17
Many s. the favor of a generous man,	19.06
he will s. at harvest and have nothing.	20.04
I awake? I will s. another drink."	23.35
but those who s. the LORD understand	28.05
blameless, and the wicked s. his life.	29.10
Many s. the favor of a ruler, but	29.26
my mind to s. and to search out by	Ecc 1.13
a time to s., and a time to lose;	3.06
out and to s. wisdom and the sum	7.25
"I will s. him whom my soul loves."	Sol 3.02
that we may s. him with you?	6.01
s. justice, correct oppression;	Is 1.17
smote them, nor s. the LORD of hosts.	9.13
him shall the nations s., and his	11.10
and to s. shelter in the shadow of	30.02
S. and read from the book of the	34.16
You shall s. those who contend with	41.12
When the poor and needy s. water,	41.17
offspring of Jacob, 'S. me in chaos.'	45.19
deliverance, you who s. the LORD;	51.01
"S. the LORD while he may be found,	55.06
Yet they s. me daily, and delight to	58.02
your fast you s. your own pleasure,	58.03
found by those who did not s. me.	65.01
None who s. her need weary themselves	Jer 2.24
direct your course to s. lovers!	2.33
lovers despise you; they s. your life.	4.30
who s. your life, and say, "Do not	11.21
hand of those who s. their life.	19.07
and those who s. their life afflict	19.09
hand of those who s. their lives.	21.07
the hand of those who s. your life,	22.25
But s. the welfare of the city	29.07
You will s. me and find me;	29.13
when you s. me with all your heart,	29.13
hand of those who s. their lives.	34.20
hand of those who s. their lives,	34.21
hand of these men who s. your life.	38.16
the hand of those who s. his life,	44.30
And do you s. great things for	45.05
S. them not; for, behold, I am	45.05
hand of those who s. their life,	46.26
and before those who s. their life;	49.37
and they shall s. the LORD their	50.04
they will s. peace, but there shall	Eze 7.25
they s. a vision from the prophet,	7.26
with none to search or s. for them.	34.06
for my sheep, and will s. them out.	34.11
abroad, so will I s. out my sheep;	34.12
I will s. the lost, and I will bring	34.16
and told them to s. mercy of the	Dan 2.18
and she shall s. them, but shall not	Hos 2.07
return and s. the LORD their God,	3.05
herds they shall go to s. the LORD,	5.06
acknowledge their guilt and s. my face,	5.15
their distress they s. me, saying,	5.15
their God, nor s. him, for all this.	7.10
for it is the time to s. the LORD,	10.12
house of Israel: "S. me and live;	Amo 5.04
but do not s. Bethel, and do not	5.05
S. the LORD and live, lest he break	5.06
S. good, and not evil, that you may	5.14
to s. the word of the LORD, but they	8.12
whence shall I s. comforters for	Nah 3.07
you will s. a refuge from the enemy	3.11
who do not s. the LORD or inquire	Zep 1.06
S. the LORD, all you humble of the	2.03
s. righteousness, s. humility; perhaps	2.03
They shall s. refuge in the name of	3.12
and to s. the LORD of hosts;	Zec 8.21
shall come to s. the LORD of hosts	8.22
or s. the wandering, or heal the	11.16
that day I will s. to destroy all	12.09
and men should s. instruction from	Mal 2.07
Lord whom you s. will suddenly	3.01
For the Gentiles s. all these	Mt 6.32
But s. first his kingdom and his	6.33
s., and you will find; knock, and	7.07
I know that you s. Jesus who was	28.05
"Why does this generation s. a sign?	Mk 8.12
you s. Jesus of Nazareth, who was	16.06

SEEK (cont.)

s., and you will find; knock, and Lk 11.09
And do not s. what you are to eat 12.29
of the world s. these things; 12.30
Instead, s. his kingdom, and these 12.31
will s. to enter and will not be 13.24
the house and s. diligently until 15.08
of man came to s. and to save the 19.10
"Why do you s. the living among the 24.05
and said to them, "What do you s.?" Jn 1.38
because I s. not my own will but 5.30
and do not s. the glory that comes 5.44
you s. me, not because you saw signs, 6.26
the law. Why do you s. to kill me?" 7.19
this the man whom they s. to kill?" 7.25
you will s. me and you will not 7.34
'You will s. me and you will not 7.36
and you will s. me and die in your 8.21
yet you s. to kill me, because my 8.37
but now you s. to kill me, a man who 8.40
Yet I do not s. my own glory; there is 8.50
You will s. me; and as I said to 13.33
and said to them, "Whom do you s.?" 18.04
Again he asked them, "Whom do you s.?" 18.07
so, if you s. me, let these men go." 18.08
are you weeping? Whom do you s.?" 20.15
that the rest of men may s. the Lord, Ac 15.17
that they should s. God, in the hope 17.27
But if you s. anything further, it 19.39
I do not s. to escape death; but if 25.11
in well-doing s. for glory and honor Rom 2.07
found by those who did not s. me; 10.20
alone am left, and they s. my life." 11.03
demand signs and Greeks s. wisdom, 1Co 1.22
Let him not s. to remove the marks 7.18
Let him not s. circumcision. 7.18
bound to a wife? Do not s. to be free. 7.27
free from a wife? Do not s. marriage. 7.27
Let no one s. his own good, but the 10.24
for I s. now what is yours but you; 2Co 12.14
that I s. the gift; but I s. the fruit Php 4.17
s. the things that are above, where Col 3.01
nor did we s. glory from men, 1Th 2.06
but always s. to do good to one 5.15
that he rewards those who s. him. Heb 11.06
but we s. the city which is to come 13.14
let him s. peace and pursue it. 1Pe 3.11
days men will s. death and will Rev 9.06

SEEKING

the man asked him, "What are you s.?" Gen 37.15
"I am s. my brothers," he said, 37.16
men who were s. your life are dead Ex 4.19
show you the man whom you are s." Ju 4.22
for he was s. an occasion against 14.04
the Danites was s. for itself an 18.01
will despair of s. me any longer 1Sa 27.01
you have been s. David as king 2Sa 3.17
you are now s. to go to your own 1Ki 11.22
and see how this man is s. trouble; 20.07
see how he is s. a quarrel with me 2Ki 5.07
consulted a medium, s. guidance, 1Ch 10.13
s. his God, he did with all his 2Ch 31.21
s. prey in the wilderness as food Job 24.05
their prey, s. their food from God. Ps 104.21
However much man may toil in s., Ecc 8.17
or s. your own pleasure, or talking Is 58.13
this man is not s. the welfare of Jer 38.04
s. him by prayer and supplications Dan 9.03
through waterless places s. rest, Mt 12.43
s. from him a sign from heaven, to Mk 8.11
scribes were s. how to arrest him 14.01
they returned to Jerusalem, s. him. Lk 2.45
through waterless places s. rest; 11.24
and he came s. fruit on it and 13.06
I have come s. fruit on this fig 13.07
scribes were s. how to put him to 22.02
and went to Capernaum, s. Jesus. Jn 6.24
a demon! Who is s. to kill you?" 7.20
Jews were but now s. to stone you, 11.08
but they were s. to kill him. Ac 9.29
s. to turn away the proconsul from 13.08
he went about s. people to lead 13.11
s. to bring them out to the people. 17.05
sailors were s. to escape from the 27.30
and s. to establish their own, they Rom 10.03
not s. my own advantage, but that of 1Co 10.33
Am I now s. the favor of men, or of Gal 1.10
clear that they are s. a homeland. Heb 11.14
roaring lion, s. some one to devour. 1Pe 5.08

SEEKS

with you until your brother s. it; Deu 22.02
"Saul my father s. to kill you; 1Sa 19.02
your father, that he s. my life?" 20.01
for he that s. my life s. your life; 22.23
heard that Saul s. to come to 23.10
say, 'Behold, David s. your hurt'? 24.09
"Behold, my own son s. my life; 2Sa 16.11
the righteous, and s. to slay him. Ps 37.32
He who diligently s. good s. favor, Pro 11.27
A scoffer s. wisdom in vain, but 14.06
who has understanding s. knowledge, 15.14
He who forgives an offense s. love, 17.09
An evil man s. only rebellion, and a 17.11
makes his door high s. destruction. 17.19
is estranged s. pretexts to break 18.01
the ear of the wise s. knowledge. 18.15
She s. wool and flax, and works with 31.13
and God s. what has been driven Ecc 3.15
who judges and s. justice and is Is 16.05
spirit within me earnestly s. thee. 26.09
he s. out a skilful craftsman to 40.20
one who does justice and s. truth; Jer 5.01
for him, to the soul that s. him. Lam 3.25
As a shepherd s. out his flock when Eze 34.12
and he who s. finds, and to him who Mt 7.08
adulterous generation s. for a sign; 12.39
adulterous generation s. for a sign, 16.04
and he who s. finds, and to him who Lk 11.10
it s. a sign, but no sign shall be 11.29
Whoever s. to gain his life will 17.33
such the Father s. to worship him. Jn 4.23
in secret if he s. to be known 7.04
his own authority s. his own glory; 7.18
but he who s. the glory of him who 7.18
is One who s. it and he will be 8.50
one understands, no one s. for God. Rom 3.11

SEEM

and I shall s. to be mocking him, Gen 27.12
It shall not s. hard to you, when Deu 15.18
"Does it s. to you a little thing 1Sa 18.23
to him as it shall s. good to you.'" 24.04
if it s. good to the king, let Ez 5.17
the hardship s. little to thee Neh 9.32
if the thing s. right before the Est 8.05
Does it s. good to thee to oppress, Job 10.03
their horses' hoofs s. like flint, Is 5.28
But to them it will s. like a false Eze 21.23
If it s. slow, wait for it; Hab 2.03
the body which s. to be weaker are 1Co 12.22
I would not s. to be frightening 2Co 10.09
though we may s. to have failed. 13.07

SEEMED

But he s. to his sons-in-law to be Gen 19.14
and they s. to him but a few days 29.20
This proposal s. good to Pharaoh 41.37
and we s. to ourselves like grasshoppers, Num 13.33
grasshoppers, and so we s. to them." 13.33
The thing s. good to me, and I took Deu 1.23
and it s. impossible to Amnon to do 2Sa 13.02
and the plan s. right to the king 2Ch 30.04
it s. to me a wearisome task, Ps 73.16
the sun, and it s. great to me. Ecc 9.13

SEEMED (cont.)
as it s. good to the potter to do. Jer 18.04
It has s. good to me to show the Dan 4.02
and which s. greater than its 7.20
it s. good to me also, having Lk 1.03
but these words s. to them an idle 24.11
Then it s. good to the apostles and Ac 15.22
it has s. good to us in assembly to 15.25
For it has s. good to the Holy 15.28
and I heard what s. to be a voice Rev 6.06
One of its heads s. to have a 13.03
I heard what s. to be the mighty 19.01
Then I heard what s. to be the 19.06

SEEMLY
gracious, and a song of praise is s. Ps 147.01
modestly and sensibly in s. apparel, 1Ti 2.09

SEEMS
'There s. to me to be some sort of Lev 14.35
do as it s. good and right in your Jos 9.25
Do to us whatever s. good to thee; Ju 10.15
do with them what s. good to you; 19.24
"Do what s. best to you, wait until 1Sa 1.23
let him do what s. good to him." 3.18
do to us whatever s. good to you." 11.10
said, "Do whatever s. good to you." 14.36
to Saul, "Do what s. good to you." 14.40
and to me it s. right that you 29.06
the LORD do what s. good to him." 2Sa 10.12
him do to me what s. good to him." 15.26
"Whatever s. best to you I will do." 18.04
do therefore what s. good to you. 19.27
do for him whatever s. good to you." 19.37
do for him whatever s. good to you; 19.38
and offer up what s. good to him; 24.22
or, if it s. good to you, I will give 1Ki 21.02
"If it s. good to you, and if it is 1Ch 13.02
the LORD do what s. good to him." 19.13
the king do what s. good to him; 21.23
Whatever s. good to you and your Ez 7.18
do with them as it s. good to you." Est 3.11
There is a way which s. right to a man, Pro 14.12
there is a way which s. right to a man, 16.25
who states his case first s. right, 18.17
Do with me as s. good and right to Jer 26.14
it to whomever it s. right to me. 27.05
If it s. good to you to come with 40.04
but if it s. wrong to you to come 40.04
"If it s. right to you, give me my Zec 11.12
"He s. to be a preacher of foreign Ac 17.18
For it s. to me unreasonable, in 25.27
If it s. advisable that I should go 1Co 16.04
all discipline s. painful rather Heb 12.11

SEER
said, "Come, let us go to the s."; 1Sa 9.09
a prophet was formerly called a s. 9.09
and said to them, "Is the s. here?" 9.11
me where is the house of the s.?" 9.18
Samuel answered Saul, "I am the s.; 9.19
prophet Gad, David's s., saying, 2Sa 24.11
by every prophet and every s., 2Ki 17.13
and Samuel the s. established them 1Ch 9.22
spoke to Gad, David's s., saying, 21.09
the sons of Heman the king's s., 25.05
also all that Samuel the s., 26.28
in the Chronicles of Samuel the s., 29.29
in the Chronicles of Gad the s., 29.29
of Iddo the s. concerning Jeroboam 2Ch 9.29
the prophet and of Iddo the s.? 12.15
time Hanani the s. came to Asa 16.07
Then Asa was angry with the s., 16.10
of Hanani the s. went out to meet 19.02
Gad the king's s. and of Nathan 29.25
words of David and of Asaph the s. 29.30
Heman, and Jeduthun the king's s.; 35.15
"O s., go, flee away to the land of Amo 7.12

SEERS
words of the s. who spoke to him 2Ch 33.18
written in the Chronicles of the S. 33.19
and covered your heads, the s. Is 29.10
who say to the s., "See not"; and to 30.10
the s. shall be disgraced, and the Mic 3.07

SEES
when he s. that the lad is not with Gen 44.31
and when he s. you he will be glad Ex 4.14
and when he s. the blood on the 12.23
s. her nakedness, and she s. his nakedness, Lev 20.17
bitten, when he s. it, shall live. Num 21.08
who s. the vision of the Almighty, 24.04
who s. the vision of the Almighty, 24.16
when he s. that their power is gone, Deu 32.36
for the LORD s. not as man s.; man 1Sa 16.07
city is pleasant,as my lord s.; 2Ki 2.19
The eye of him who s. me will Job 7.08
of flesh? Dost thou see as man s.? 10.04
when he s. iniquity, will he not 11.11
and his eye s. every precious thing 28.10
and s. everything under the heavens 28.24
of a man, and he s. all his steps. 34.21
of the ear, but now my eye s. thee; 42.05
he s. all the sons of men; Ps 33.13
for he s. that his day is coming. 37.13
birth that never s. the sun. 58.08
rejoice when he s. the vengeance; 58.10
the earth s. and trembles. 97.04
until he s. his desire on his 112.08
The wicked man s. it and is angry; 112.10
A prudent man s. danger and hides Pro 22.03
A prudent man s. danger and hides 27.12
let him announce what he s. Is 21.06
When he s. riders, horsemen in pairs, 21.07
when a man s. it, he eats it up as 28.04
the dark, and who say, "Who s. us? 29.15
For when he s. his children, the 29.23
He s. many things, but does not 42.20
wickedness, you said, "No one s. me"; 47.10
LORD from heaven looks down and s.; Lam 3.50
vision that he s. is for many days Eze 12.27
a son who s. all the sins which 18.14
"When Pharaoh s. them, he will 32.31
and if he s. the sword coming upon 33.03
But if the watchman s. the sword 33.06
land and any one s. a man's bone, 39.15
your Father who s. in secret will Mt 6.04
your Father who s. in secret will 6.06
your Father who s. in secret will 6.18
only what he s. the Father doing; Jn 5.19
every one who s. the Son and 6.40
but how he now s. we do not know, 9.21
s. the wolf coming and leaves the 10.12
because he s. the light of this 11.09
And he who s. me s. him who sent me. 12.45
it neither s. him nor knows him; 14.17
For who hopes for what he s.? Rom 8.24
For who s. anything different in 1Co 4.07
For if any one s. you, a man of 8.10
of me than he s. in me or hears 2Co 12.06
goods and s. his brother in need, 1Jn 3.17
If any one s. his brother committing 5.16

SEETHE
its pieces, s. also its bones in it. Eze 24.05

SEGUB
at the cost of his youngest son S., 1Ki 16.34
sixty years old; and she bore him S.; 1Ch 2.21
and S. was the father of Jair, who 2.22

SEIGE
neighbor in the s. and in the distress, Jer 19.09

SEINE
his net, he gathers them in his s.; Hab 1.15
net and burns incense to his s.; 1.16

SEIR

Horites in their Mount S. as far as Gen 14.06
Esau his brother in the land of S., 32.03
until I come to my lord in S." 33.14
returned that day on his way to S. 33.16
dwelt in the hill country of S.; 36.08
Edomites in the hill country of S. 36.09
These are the sons of S. the Horite, 36.20
the sons of S. in the land of Edom. 36.21
to their clans in the land of S. 36.30
S. also, his enemies, shall be Num 24.18
way of Mount S. to Kadeshbarnea. Deu 1.02
you down in S. as far as Hormah. 1.44
many days we went about Mount S. 2.01
the sons of Esau, who live in S.; 2.04
given Mount S. to Esau as a 2.05
the sons of Esau who live in S., 2.08
The Horites also lived in S. formerly, 2.12
who live in S., when he destroyed 2.22
who live in S. and the Moabites 2.29
Sinai, and dawned from S. upon us; 33.02
from Mount Halak, that rises toward S., Jos 11.17
rises toward S. (and Joshua gave 12.07
circles west of Baalah to Mount S., 15.10
the hill country of S. to possess, 24.04
"LORD, when thou didst go forth from S., Ju 5.04
The sons of S.: Lotan, Shobal, Zibeon, 1Ch 1.38
went to Mount S., having as their 4.42
men of Ammon and Moab and Mount S., 2Ch 20.10
and Mount S., who had come against 20.22
the inhabitants of Mount S., 20.23
an end of the inhabitants of S., 20.23
and smote ten thousand men of S. 25.11
brought the gods of the men of S., 25.14
One is calling to me from S., Is 21.11
set your face against Mount S., Eze 35.02
Mount S., and I will stretch out my 35.03
I will make Mount S. a waste and a 35.07
Mount S., and all Edom, all of it. 35.15

SEIRAH

sculptured stones, and escaped to S. Ju 3.26

SEIZE

make slaves of us and s. our asses." Gen 43.18
from the ambush, and s. the city; Jos 8.07
Midianites and s. the waters Ju 7.24
vineyards and s. each man his wife 21.21
and s. one of the young men, and 2Sa 2.21
"S. the prophets of Baal; let not 1Ki 18.40
"S. Micaiah, and take him back to 22.26
he is, that I may send and s. him." 2Ki 6.13
"S. Micaiah, and take him back to 2Ch 18.25
That night—let thick darkness s. it! Job 3.06
they s. flocks and pasture them. 24.02
wicked; judgment and justice s. you. 36.17
he lurks that he may s. the poor, Ps 10.09
pursue and s. him, for there is none 71.11
days be few; may another s. his goods! 109.08
May the creditor s. all that he has 109.11
they growl and s. their prey, Is 5.29
him, to take spoil and s. plunder, 10.06
Pangs and agony will s. them; 13.08
He will s. firm hold on you, 22.17
and s. them, and carry them to Jer 20.05
of Abdeel to s. Baruch the secretary 36.26
They shall s. your sons and your Eze 23.25
to s. spoil and carry off plunder; 38.12
to you, 'Have you come to s. spoil? 38.13
cattle and goods, to s. great spoil?' 38.13
They covet fields, and s. them; Mic 2.02
to s. habitations not their own. Hab 1.06
I shall kiss is the man; s. him." Mt 26.48
teaching, and you did not s. me. 26.55
heard it, they went out to s. him, Mk 3.21
s. him and lead him away safely. 14.44
teaching, and you did not s. me. 14.49
of Damascus in order to s. me, 2Co 11.32
encouragement to s. the hope set Heb 6.18
so that no one may s. your crown. Rev 3.11

SEIZED

so the men s. him and his wife and Gen 19.16
which Abimelech's servants had s., 21.25
he s. her and lay with her and 34.02
pangs have s. on the inhabitants of Ex 15.14
and s. the fords of the Jordan Ju 3.28
and they s. the waters as far as 7.24
then they s. him and slew him at 12.06
and put out his hand and s. it, 15.15
And the Philistines s. him and 16.21
So the man s. his concubine, and put 19.25
for the anguish has s. me, and yet my 2Sa 1.09
I s. him and slew him at Ziklag, 4.10
And they s. them; and Elijah brought 1Ki 18.40
And he s. all the gold and silver, 2Ki 14.14
And he s. all the gold and silver, 2Ch 25.24
he s. also the treasuries of the 25.24
he s. me by the neck and dashed me Job 16.12
he has s. a house which he did not 20.19
pangs have s. me, like the pangs of Is 21.03
trembling his s. the godless: "Who 33.14
s. Jeremiah the prophet, saying, "You Jer 37.13
and s. Jeremiah and brought him to 37.14
but shall be s. by the king of 38.23
be taken and the strongholds s. 48.41
turned to flee, and panic s. her; 49.24
anguish s. him, pain as of a woman 50.43
the fords have been s., the bulwarks 51.32
the praise of the whole earth s.! 51.41
they s. her sons and her daughters; Eze 23.10
that pangs have s. you like a Mic 4.09
For Herod had s. John and bound him Mt 14.03
while the rest s. his servants, 22.06
and laid hands on Jesus and s. him. 26.50
Then those who had s. Jesus led him 26.57
For Herod had sent and s. John, Mk 6.17
And they laid hands on him and s. him. 14.46
cloth about his body; and they s. him, 14.51
And amazement s. them all, and they Lk 5.26
Fear s. them all; and they glorified 7.16
(For many a time it had s. him; 8.29
for they were s. with great fear; 8.37
Then they s. him and led him away, 22.54
they s. one Simon of Cyrene, who was 23.26
of the Jews s. Jesus and bound him Jn 18.12
upon him and s. him and brought Ac 6.12
And when he had s. him, he put him 12.04
they s. Paul and Silas and dragged 16.19
And they all s. Sosthenes, the ruler 18.17
they s. Paul and dragged him out of 21.30
This man was s. by the Jews, and was 23.27
profane the temple, but we s. him. 24.06
reason the Jews s. me in the 26.21
And he s. the dragon, that ancient Rev 20.02

SEIZES

leaders of Moab, trembling s. them; Ex 15.15
and the man s. her and lies with Deu 22.25
and s. her and lies with her, and 22.28
her hand and s. him by the private 25.11
A trap s. him by the heel, a snare Job 18.09
and horror s. them of the east. 18.20
dismayed, and shuddering s. my flesh. 21.06
With violence it s. my garment; 30.18
he s. the poor when he draws him Ps 10.09
Hot indignation s. me because of 119.53
She s. him and kisses him, and with Pro 7.13
and wherever it s. him, it dashes Mk 9.18
a spirit s. him, and he suddenly Lk 9.39

SEIZING

and s. him by the throat he said, Mt 18.28

SELA

of Akrabbim, from S. and upward. Ju 1.36
of Salt and took S. by storm, 2Ki 14.07

SELA (cont.)
from S., by way of the desert, to Is 16.01
the inhabitants of S. sing for joy, 42.11

SELDOM
Let your foot be s. in your neighbor's Pro 25.17

SELECT
let Pharaoh s. a man discreet and Gen 41.33
"S. lambs for yourselves according Ex 12.21
then you shall s. cities to be Num 35.11
s. the best and fittest of your 2Ki 10.03

SELECTED
Ezra the priest s. men, heads of Ez 10.16

SELED
The sons of Nadab: S. and Appaim; 1Ch 2.30
Appaim; and S. died childless. 2.30

SELEUCIA
Holy Spirit, they went down to S.; Ac 13.04

SELF
thou didst swear by thine own s., Ex 32.13
that our old s. was crucified with Rom 6.06
the law of God, in my inmost s., 7.22
For men will be lovers of s., 2Ti 3.02
of your owing me even your own s. Phm 1.19

SELF-ABASEMENT
insisting on s. and worship of angels, Col 2.18
of devotion and s. and severity to 2.23

SELF-CONCEIT
Let us have no s., no provoking of Gal 5.26

SELF-CONDEMNED
person is perverted and sinful; he is s. Tit 3.11

SELF-CONTROL
A man without s. is like a city Pro 25.28
justice and s. and future judgment, Ac 24.25
Satan tempt you through lack of s. 1Co 7.05
But if they cannot exercise s., 7.09
athlete exercises s. in all things. 9.25
gentleness, s.; against such Gal 5.23
a spirit of power and love and s. 2Ti 1.07
and knowledge with s., 2Pe 1.06
and s. with steadfastness, and 1.06

SELF-CONTROLLED
master of himself, upright, holy, and s.; Tit 1.08

SELF-INDULGENT
whereas she who is s. is dead even while 1Ti 5.06

SELFISH
kind to the ungrateful and the s. Lk 6.35
jealousy and s. ambition in your Jas 3.14
where jealousy and s. ambition exist, 3.16

SELFISHNESS
s., slander, gossip, conceit, and 2Co 12.20
anger, s., dissension, party spirit, Gal 5.20
Do nothing from s. or conceit, but in Php 2.03

SELL
said, "First s. me your birthright." Gen 25.31
Come, let us s. him to the Ishmaelites, 37.27
therefore they did not s. their land. 47.22
no right to s. her to a foreign Ex 21.08
then they shall s. the live ox and 21.35
And if you s. to your neighbor or Lev 25.14
years for crops he shall s. to you. 25.15
You shall s. me food for money, that Deu 2.28
or you may s. it to a foreigner; 14.21
but you shall not s. her for money, 21.14
the LORD will s. Sisera into the Ju 4.09
s. the oil and pay your debts, and 2Ki 4.07
but you even s. your brethren that Neh 5.08
any grain on the sabbath day to s., 10.31
Buy truth, and do not s. it; Pro 23.23
and will s. the land into the hand Eze 30.12
They shall not s. or exchange any 48.14
I will s. your sons and your Joe 3.08
and they will s. them to the 3.08
because they s. the righteous for Amo 2.06
moon be over, that we may s. grain? 8.05
and s. the refuse of the wheat?" 8.06
and those who s. them say, 'Blessed Zec 11.05
s. what you possess and give to the Mt 19.21
go. s. what you have, and give to the Mk 10.21
S. your possessions, and give alms; Lk 12.33
S. all that you have and distribute 18.22
has no sword s. his mantle and buy 22.36
one can buy or s. unless he has Rev 13.17

SELLER
as with the buyer, so with the s.; Is 24.02
nor the s. mourn, for wrath is upon Eze 7.12
For the s. shall not return to what 7.13
a s. of purple goods, who was a Ac 16.14

SELLERS
merchants and s. of all kinds of wares Neh 13.20

SELLING
of the crops that he is s. to you. Lev 25.16
is s. the parcel of land which Ru 4.03
those who were s. oxen and ship Jn 2.14

SELLS
"When a man s. his daughter as a Ex 21.07
whether he s. him or is found in 21.16
or a sheep, and kills it or s. it, 22.01
and s. part of his property, then Lev 25.25
"If a man s. a dwelling house in a 25.29
and s. himself to you, you shall not 25.39
poor and s. himself to the stranger 25.47
he treats him as a slave or s. him, Deu 24.07
is on the head of him who s. it. Pro 11.26
She makes linen garments and s. them; 31.24
joy he goes and s. all that he has Mt 13.44

SELVES
among your own s. will arise men Ac 20.30
gospel of God but also our own s., 1Th 2.08

SEMACHIAH
brethren were able men, Elihu and S. 1Ch 26.07

SEMBLANCE
beyond human s., and his form beyond Is 52.14
their wings the s. of human hands. Eze 10.21

SEMEIN
the son of S., the son of Josech, Lk 3.26

SEMEN
he spilled the s. on the ground, lest Gen 38.09
"And if a man has an emission of s., Lev 15.16
on which the s. comes shall be washed 15.17
a woman and has an emission of s., 15.18
for him who has an emission of s., 15.32
man who has had an emission of s., 22.04

SENAAH
The sons of S., three thousand six Ez 2.35
The sons of S., three thousand nine Neh 7.38

SENATE
the council and all the s. of Israel, Ac 5.21

SEND
days I will s. rain upon the earth Gen 7.04
he will s. his angel before you, 24.07
will s. his angel with you and 24.40

SEND (cont.)
he said, "S. me back to my master." Gen 24.54
then I will s., and fetch you from 27.45
"S. me away, that I may go to my own 30.25
Come, I will s. you to them." And 37.13
"I will s. you a kid from the flock." 38.17
give me a pledge, till you s. it?" 38.17
But Jacob did not s. Benjamin, 42.04
S. one of you, and let him bring 42.16
If you will s. our brother with us, 43.04
but if you will not s. him, 43.05
"S. the lad with me, and we will 43.08
that he may s. back your other 43.14
Come, I will s. you to Pharaoh that Ex 3.10
s., I pray, some other person." 4.13
people? Why didst thou ever s. me? 5.22
a strong hand he will s. them out, 6.01
I will s. swarms of flies on you 8.21
time I will s. all my plagues upon 9.14
Now therefore s., get your cattle 9.19
to s. them out of the land in haste 12.33
"Behold, I s. an angel before you, to 23.20
I will s. my terror before you, and 23.27
And I will s. hornets before you, 23.28
And I will s. an angel before you, 33.02
me know whom thou wilt s. with me. 33.12
and s. him away into the wilderness Lev 16.21
Then you shall s. abroad the loud 25.09
you shall s. abroad the trumpet 25.09
cities I will s. pestilence among 26.25
I will s. faintness into their 26.36
"S. men to spy out the land of Num 13.02
their fathers shall you s. a man, 13.02
"Did I not s. to you to call you 22.37
You shall s. a thousand from each 31.04
'Let us s. men before us, that they Deu 1.22
your God will s. hornets among 7.20
his city shall s. and fetch him 19.12
"The LORD will s. upon you curses, 28.20
whom the LORD will s. against you, 28.48
and I will s. the teeth of beasts 32.24
and wherever you s. us we will go. Jos 1.16
and I will s. them out that they 18.04
hand of Midian; do not I s. you?" Ju 6.14
whom thou didst s. come again to 13.08
"S. away the ark of the God of 1Sa 5.11
what we shall s. it to its place." 6.02
"If you s. away the ark of the God 6.03
do not s. it empty, but by all means 6.03
Then s. it off, and let it go its 6.08
time I will s. to you a man from 9.16
that I may s. you on your way." 9.26
that we may s. messengers through 11.03
that he may s. thunder and rain; 12.17
I will s. you to Jesse the Bethlehemite, 16.01
said to Jesse, "S. and fetch him; 16.11
"S. me David your son, who is with 16.19
I not then s. and disclose it to 20.12
and s. you away, that you may go in 20.13
I will s. the lad, saying, 'Go, find 20.21
Therefore s. and fetch him to me, 20.31
of the matter about which I s. you, 21.02
"S. the man back, that he may return 29.04
"S. me Uriah the Hittite." And Joab 2Sa 11.06
"S. out every one from me." So 13.09
sent for Joab, to s. him to the king; 14.29
that I may s. you to the king, to 14.32
them you shall s. to me everything 15.36
Now therefore s. quickly and tell 17.16
better that you s. us help from 18.03
by whatever way thou shalt s. them, 1Ki 8.44
and I will s. rain upon the earth." 18.01
Now therefore s. and gather all 18.19
nevertheless I will s. my servants 20.06
And he said, "You shall not s." 2Ki 2.16
till he was ashamed, he said, "S." 2.17
"S. me one of the servants and one 4.22
and I will s. a letter to the king 5.05
he is, that I may s. and seize him." 6.13
already perished; let us s. and see." 7.13
and s. to meet them, and let him say, 9.17
LORD began to s. Rezin the king of 15.37
"S. there one of the priests whom 17.27
let us s. abroad to our brethren 1Ch 13.02
So now s. me a man skilled to work 2Ch 2.07
S. me also cedar, cypress, and algum 2.08
let him s. to his servants; 2.15
by whatever way thou shalt s. them, 6.34
or s. pestilence among my people, 7.13
and s. back the captives from your 28.11
Beyond the River, s. greeting. Ez 4.11
therefore we s. and inform the king, 4.14
let the king s. us his pleasure in 5.17
to s. us ministers for the house of 8.17
that you s. me to Judah, to the city Neh 2.05
So it pleased the king to s. me; 2.06
sweet wine and s. portions to him 8.10
drink and to s. portions and to 8.12
on which they s. choice portions Est 9.19
and they would s. and invite their Job 1.04
Job would s. and sanctify them, and 1.05
full God will s. his fierce anger 20.23
They s. forth their little ones 21.11
Can you s. forth lightnings, that 38.35
May he s. you help from the sanctuary, Ps 20.02
Oh s. out thy light and thy truth; 43.03
He will s. from heaven and save me, 57.03
God will s. forth his steadfast 57.03
s. out thy arrows and rout them! 144.06
the sluggard to those who s. him. Pro 10.26
messenger to those who s. him, 25.13
"Whom shall I s., and who will go Is 6.08
I said, "Here I am! S. me." 6.08
Against a godless nation I s. him, 10.06
will s. wasting sickness among his 10.16
oppressors he will s. them a savior, 19.20
or deaf as my messenger whom I s.? 42.19
sake I will s. to Babylon and 43.14
s. it forth to the end of the earth; 48.20
them I will s. survivors to the 66.19
all to whom I s. you you shall go, Jer 1.07
or s. to Kedar and examine with 2.10
and I will s. the sword after them, 9.16
s. for the skilful women to come; 9.17
Her nobles s. their servants for 14.03
I did not s. them, nor did I command 14.14
my name although I did not s. them, 14.15
S. them out of my sight, and let 15.01
afterwards I will s. for many 16.16
I have not pressed thee to s. evil, 17.16
"I did not s. the prophets, yet they 23.21
when I did not s. them or charge 23.32
And I will s. sword, famine, and 24.10
behold, I will s. for all the tribes 25.09
nations to whom I s. you drink it. 25.15
prophets whom I s. to you urgently, 26.05
S. word to the king of Edom, the 27.03
I did not s. them, says the LORD. 29.09
"S. to all the exiles, saying, 'Thus 29.31
to you when I did not s. him, 29.31
and do not s. me back to the house 37.20
he would not s. me back to the 38.26
LORD our God did not s. you to say, 43.02
I will s. and take Nebuchadrezzar 43.10
when I shall s. to him tilters who 48.12
I will s. the sword after them, 49.37
and I will s. to Babylon winnowers, 51.02
I s. you to the people of Israel, to Eze 2.03
and stubborn: I s. you to them; 2.04
I will s. famine and wild beasts 5.17
of bread and s. famine upon it, 14.13
Or if I s. a pestilence into that 14.19
more when I s. upon Jerusalem my 14.21
for I will s. pestilence into her, 28.23
and s. them down, her and the 32.18

SEND (cont.)
and I will s. down the showers in Eze 34.26
I will s. fire on Magog and on 39.06
one who shall s. an exactor of Dan 11.20
but I will s. a fire upon his Hos 8.14
So I will s. a fire upon the house Amo 1.04
So I will s. a fire upon the wall 1.07
So I will s. a fire upon the wall 1.10
So I will s. a fire upon Teman, and 1.12
So I will s. a fire upon Moab, and 2.02
So I will s. a fire upon Judah, and 2.05
I would s. rain upon one city, and 4.07
and s. no rain upon another city; 4.07
"when I will s. a famine on the 8.11
I will s. it forth, says the LORD of Zec 5.04
then I will s. the curse upon you Mal 2.02
"Behold, I s. my messenger to 3.01
I will s. you Elijah the prophet 4.05
s. us away into the herd of swine." Mt 8.31
the harvest to s. out laborers 9.38
"Behold, I s. you out as sheep in 10.16
I s. my messenger before thy face, 11.10
The Son of man will s. his angels, 13.41
s. the crowds away to go into the 14.15
"S. her away, for she is crying 15.23
am unwilling to s. them away 15.32
and he will s. them immediately." 21.03
Therefore I s. you prophets and 23.34
and he will s. out his angels with 24.31
he will at once s. me more than 26.53
I s. my messenger before thy face, Mk 1.02
eagerly not to s. them out of the 5.10
"S. us to the swine, let us enter 5.12
and began to s. them out two by two, 6.07
s. them away, to go into the country 6.36
and if I s. them away hungry to 8.03
of it and will s. it back here • 11.03
And then he will s. out the angels, 13.27
I s. my messenger before thy face, Lk 7.27
"S. the crowd away, to go into the 9.12
the harvest to s. out laborers 10.02
behold, I s. you out as lambs in the 10.03
'I will s. them prophets and 11.49
and s. Lazarus to dip the end of 16.24
to s. him to my father's house, 16.27
I will s. my beloved son; 20.13
And behold, I s. the promise of my 24.49
may believe that thou didst s. me." Jn 11.42
any one whom I s. receives me; 13.20
whom the Father will s. in my name, 14.26
whom I shall s. to you from the 15.26
but if I go, I will s. him to you. 16.07
believed that thou didst s. me. 17.08
As thou didst s. me into the world, 17.18
has sent me, even so I s. you." 20.21
and that he may s. the Christ Ac 3.20
now come, I will s. you to Egypt." 7.34
And now s. men to Joppa, and bring 10.05
a holy angel to s. for you to come 10.22
S. therefore to Joppa and ask for 10.32
'S. to Joppa and bring Simon called 11.13
to s. relief to the brethren who 11.29
among them and s. them to Antioch 15.22
choose men and s. them to you with 15.25
for I will s. you far away to the 22.21
until I could s. him to Ceasar." 25.21
the emperor, I decided to s. him. 25.25
from the Gentiles—to whom I s. you 26.17
For Christ did not s. me to baptize 1Co 1.17
I will s. those whom you accredit 16.03
The churches of Asia s. greetings. 16.19
s. you hearty greetings in the Lord 16.19
All the brethren s. greetings. 16.20
and have you s. me on my way to 2Co 1.16
Lord Jesus to s. Timothy to you Php 2.19
therefore to s. him just as soon 2.23
it necessary to s. to you Epaphroditus 2.25
I am the more eager to s. him, 2.28
When I s. Artemas or Tychicus to Tit 3.12
All who are with me s. greetings to 3.15
come from Italy s. you greetings. Heb 13.24
will do well to s. them on their 3Jn 1.06
in a book and s. it to the seven Rev 1.11

SENDEST
thou s. forth thy fury, it consumes Ex 15.07
his countenance, and s. him away. Job 14.20
When thou s. forth thy Spirit, they Ps 104.30

SENDING
this wrong in s. me away is greater 2Sa 13.16
I am s. to you a present of silver 1Ki 15.19
that you are s. to inquire of 2Ki 1.06
behold, I am s. to you silver and 2Ch 16.03
days for s. choice portions to one Est 9.22
I am a. among you serpents, adders Jer 8.17
"Behold, I am s. for many fishers, 16.16
the sword which I am s. among them." 25.16
the sword which I am s. among you.' 25.27
I am s. on them sword, famine, and 29.17
s. them persistently, saying, 'Turn 35.15
LORD our God to whom we are s. you, 42.06
against him by s. ambassadors to Eze 17.15
s. forth its streams to all the 31.04
I am s. to you grain, wine, and oil, Joe 2.19
And s. away the crowds, he got into Mt 15.39
s. it to the elders by the hand of Ac 11.30
in s. a prisoner, not to indicate 25.27
s. his own Son in the likeness of Rom 8.03
With him we are s. the brother who 2Co 8.18
them we are s. our brother whom we 8.22
But I am s. the brethren so that 9.03
I am s. him back to you, sending my Phm 1.12
him back to you, s. my very heart. 1.12
it known by s. his angel to his Rev 1.01

SENDS
in her hand and s. her out of his Deu 24.01
in her hand and s. her out of his 24.03
that the LORD s. rain upon the 1Ki 17.14
that this man s. word to me to cure 2Ki 5.07
the earth and s. waters upon the Job 5.10
if he s. them out, they overwhelm 12.15
lo, he s. forth his voice, his mighty Ps 68.33
The LORD s. forth from Zion your 110.02
He s. forth his command to the 147.15
He s. forth his word, and melts them 147.18
He who s. a message by the hand of Pro 26.06
which s. ambassadors by the Nile, in Is 18.02
that s. out its roots by the stream, Jer 17.08
the LORD your God s. you to us. 42.05
and s. rain on the just and on the Mt 5.45
he s. an embassy and asks terms of Lk 14.32
Therefore God s. upon them a strong 2Th 2.11
Eubulus s. greetings to you, as do 2Ti 4.21
in Christ Jesus, s. greetings to you, Phm 1.23
likewise chosen, s. you greetings; 1Pe 5.13

SENEH
was Bozez, and the name of the other S. 1Sa 14.04

SENIOR
and the s. priests, covered with 2Ki 19.02
and the s. priests, clothed with Is 37.02
people and some of the s. priests, Jer 19.01

SENIR
Sirion, while the Amorites call it S.), Deu 3.09
Baalhermon, S., and Mount Hermon. 1Ch 5.23
from the peak of S. and Hermon, Sol 4.08
your planks of fir trees from S.; Eze 27.05

SENNACHERIB
King Hezekiah S. king of Assyria 2Ki 18.13
and hear the words of S., which he 19.16

SENNACHERIB (cont.)
to me about S. king of Assyria I have 2Ki 19.20
Then S. king of Assyria departed, 19.36
of faithfulness S. king of Assyria 2Ch 32.01
saw that S. had come and intended 32.02
After this S. king of Assyria, who 32.09
"Thus says S. king of Assyria, 'On 32.10
the hand of S. king of Assyria and 32.22
S. king of Assyria came up against Is 36.01
and hear all the words of S., 37.17
me concerning S. king of Assyria, 37.21
Then S. king of Assyria departed, 37.37

SENSE
and they gave the s., so that the Neh 8.08
He who commits adultery has no s.; Pro 6.32
youths, a young man without s., 7.07
To him who is without s. she says, 9.04
to him who is without s. she says, 9.16
for the back of him who lacks s. 10.13
many, but fools die for lack of s. 10.21
belittles his neighbor lacks s., 11.12
commended according to his good s., 12.08
worthless pursuits has no s. 12.11
Good s. wins favor, but the way of 13.15
Folly is a joy to him who has no s., 15.21
A man without s. gives a pledge, and 17.18
Good s. makes a man slow to anger, 19.11
the vineyard of a man without s.; 24.30
he lacks s., and he says to every Ecc 10.03
are only the poor, they have no s.; Jer 5.04
like a dove, silly and without s., Hos 7.11
where would be the s. of smell? 1Co 12.17

SENSELESS
LORD, you foolish and s. people Deu 32.06
A s., a disreputable brood, they Job 30.08
O foolish and s. people, who have Jer 5.21
and their s. minds were darkened. Rom 1.21
into many s. and hurtful desires 1Ti 6.09
do with stupid, s. controversies; 2Ti 2.23

SENSIBLE
I speak as to s. men; judge for 1Co 10.15
s., dignified, hospitable, an apt teacher, 1Ti 3.02
s., sound in faith, in love, and in Tit 2.02
to be s., chaste, domestc, kind, and 2.05

SENSIBLY
modestly and s. in seemly apparel, not 1Ti 2.09

SENSUOUS
puffed up without reason by his s. mind, Col 2.18

SENT
therefore the LORD God s. him forth Gen 3.23
and s. forth a raven; and it went 8.07
Then he s. forth a dove from him, to 8.08
and again he s. forth the dove out 8.10
seven days, and s. forth the dove; 8.12
the LORD has s. us to destroy it." 19.13
and s. Lot out of the midst of the 19.29
king of Gerar s. and took Sarah. 20.02
with the child, and s. her away. 21.14
So they s. away Rebekah their 24.59
still living he s. them away from 25.06
me and have s. me away from you 26.27
good and have s. you away in peace 26.29
so she s. and called Jacob her 27.42
Thus Isaac s. Jacob away; and he 28.05
Jacob and s. him away to Paddan-aram 28.06
So Jacob s. and called Rachel and 31.04
I might have s. you away with 31.27
you would have s. me away empty-handed 31.42
And Jacob s. messengers before him 32.03
and I have s. to tell my lord, in 32.05
are a present s. to my lord Esau; 32.18
He took them and s. them across the 32.23
So he s. him from the valley of 37.14
and they s. the long robe with 37.32
When Judah s. the kid by his friend 38.20
you see, I s. this kid, and you could 38.23
she s. word to her father-in-law, 38.25
and he s. and called for all the 41.08
Then Pharaoh s. and called Joseph, 41.14
the men were s. away with their 44.03
for God s. me before you to preserve 45.05
And God s. me before you to preserve 45.07
So it was not you who s. me here, 45.08
To his father he s. as follows: 45.23
Then he s. his brothers away, and as 45.24
which Joseph had s. to carry him, 45.27
which Pharaoh had s. to carry him. 46.05
He s. Judah before him to Joseph, to 46.28
So they s. a message to Joseph, 50.16
the reeds and s. her maid to fetch Ex 2.05
that I have s. you: when you have 3.12
of your fathers has s. me to you,' 3.13
of Israel, 'I am has s. me to you.'" 3.14
the God of Jacob, has s. me to you': 3.15
the LORD with which he had s. him, 4.28
s. me to you, saying, "Let my people 7.16
And Pharaoh s., and behold, not one 9.07
and the LORD s. thunder and hail, 9.23
Then Pharaoh s., and called Moses 9.27
wife, after he had s. her away, 18.02
And he s. young men of the people 24.05
And the LORD s. a plague upon the 32.35
that it may be s. away into the Lev 16.10
So Moses s. them from the wilderness Num 13.03
men whom Moses s. to spy out the 13.16
Moses s. them to spy out the land 13.17
to the land to which you s. us; 13.27
men whom Moses s. to spy out the 14.36
And Moses s. to call Dathan and 16.12
the LORD has s. me to do all these 16.28
men, then the LORD has not s. me. 16.29
Moses s. messengers from Kadesh to 20.14
and s. an angel and brought us 20.16
Then the LORD s. fiery serpents 21.06
Then Israel s. messengers to Sihon 21.21
And Moses s. to spy out Jazer; 21.32
s. messengers to Balaam the son of 22.05
of Moab, has s. to me, saying, 22.10
Once again Balak s. princes, 22.15
and s. to Balaam and to the princes 22.40
your messengers whom you s. to me, 24.12
And Moses s. them to the war, a 31.06
when I s. them from Kadeshbarnea to 32.08
"So I s. messengers from the Deu 2.26
And when the LORD s. you from 9.23
who s. her away, may not take her 24.04
which the LORD s. him to do in the 34.11
the son of Nun s. two men secretly Jos 2.01
Then the king of Jericho s. to Rahab, 2.03
Then she s. them away, and they 2.21
she hid the messengers that we s. 6.17
whom Joshua s. to spy out Jericho. 6.25
Joshua s. men from Jericho to Ai, 7.02
So Joshua s. messengers, and they 7.22
valor, and s. them forth by night. 8.03
So Joshua s. them forth; and they 8.09
of Jerusalem s. to Hoham king of 10.03
men of Gibeon s. to Joshua at the 10.06
he s. to Jobab king of Madon, and to 11.01
of the LORD s. me from Kadeshbarnea 14.07
I was in the day that Moses s. me; 14.11
blessed them, and s. them away; 22.06
And when Joshua s. them away to 22.07
of Israel s. to the Reubenites and 22.13
And I s. Moses and Aaron, and I 24.05
and he s. and invited Balaam the 24.09
And I s. the hornet before you, 24.12
So Joshua s. the people away, every 24.28
house of Joseph s. to spy out Ju 1.23

SENT (cont.)

of Israel s. tribute by him to Ju 3.15
he s. away the people that carried 3.18
She s. and summoned Barak the son 4.06
the LORD s. a prophet to the people 6.08
And he s. messengers throughout all 6.35
And he s. messengers to Asher, 6.35
and he s. all the rest of Israel 7.08
And Gideon s. messengers throughout 7.24
And God s. an evil spirit between 9.23
And he s. messengers to Abimelech 9.31
Then Jephthah s. messengers to the 11.12
And Jephthah s. messengers again to 11.14
Israel then s. messengers to the 11.17
And they s. also to the king of 11.17
Israel then s. messengers to Sihon 11.19
of Jephthah which he s. to him. 11.28
And he s. her away for two months; 11.38
she s. and called the lords of the 16.18
So the Danites s. five able men 18.02
and s. her throughout all the 19.29
and s. her throughout all the 20.06
of Israel s. men through all the 20.12
congregation s. thither twelve 21.10
congregation s. word to the 21.13
So the people s. to Shiloh, and 1Sa 4.04
So they s. and gathered together 5.08
So they s. the ark of God to Ekron. 5.10
They s. therefore and gathered 5.11
So they s. messengers to the 6.21
Then Samuel s. all the people away, 10.25
in pieces and s. them throughout 11.07
and the LORD s. Moses and Aaron, 12.08
And the LORD s. Jerubbaal and Barak, 12.11
and the LORD s. thunder and rain 12.18
the rest of the people he s. home, 13.02
"The LORD s. me to anoint you king 15.01
And the LORD s. you on a mission, 15.18
mission on which the LORD s. me, 15.20
And he s., and brought him in. Now 16.12
Therefore Saul s. messengers to 16.19
and s. them by David his son to 16.20
And Saul s. to Jesse, saying, "Let 16.22
them before Saul; and he s. for him. 17.31
successful wherever Saul s. him; 18.05
That night Saul s. messengers to 19.11
And when Saul s. messengers to take 19.14
Then Saul s. the messengers to see 19.15
Then Saul s. messengers to take 19.20
he s. other messengers, and they 19.21
And Saul s. messengers again the 19.21
for the LORD has s. you away. 20.22
Then the king s. to summon Ahimelech 22.11
So David s. ten young men; 25.05
David s. messengers out of the 25.14
young men of my lord, whom you s. 25.25
who s. you this day to meet me! 25.32
Then David s. and wooed Abigail, to 25.39
"David has s. us to you to take you 25.40
David s. out spies, and learned of a 26.04
he s. part of the spoil to his 30.26
and s. messengers throughout the 31.09
David s. messengers to the men of 2Sa 2.05
And Abner s. messengers to David at 3.12
Then David s. messengers to Ishbosheth 3.14
And Ishbosheth s., and took her 3.15
So David s. Abner away; and he went 3.21
for he had s. him away, and he had 3.22
is it that you have s. him away, 3.24
he s. messengers after Abner, and 3.26
king of Tyre s. messengers to 5.11
Tou s. his son Joram to King David, 8.10
Then King David s. and brought him 9.05
So David s. by his servants to 10.02
David has s. comforters to you, 10.03
Has not David s. his servants to 10.03
at their hips, and s. them away. 10.04
he s. to meet them, for the men were 10.05
the Ammonites s. and hired the 10.06
he s. Joab and all the host of the 10.07
And Hadadezer s., and brought out 10.16
David s. Joab, and his servants with 11.01
And David s. and inquired about the 11.03
So David s. messengers, and took her 11.04
and she s. and told David, "I am 11.05
So David s. word to Joab, "Send me 11.06
And Joab s. Uriah to David. 11.06
and s. it by the hand of Uriah. 11.14
Then Joab s. and told David all the 11.18
all that Joab had s. him to tell. 11.22
David s. and brought her to his 11.27
And the LORD s. Nathan to David. 12.01
and s. a message by Nathan the 12.25
And Joab s. messengers to David, and 12.27
Then David s. home to Tamar, saying, 13.07
And Joab s. to Tekoa, and fetched 14.02
Then Absalom s. for Joab, to send 14.29
And he s. a second time, but Joab 14.29
I s. word to you, 'Come here, that I 14.32
But Absalom s. secret messengers 15.10
he s. for Ahithophel the Gilonite, 15.12
And David s. forth the army, one 18.02
"When Joab s. your servant, I saw a 18.29
And King David s. this message to 19.11
so that they s. word to the king, 19.14
And he s. out arrows, and scattered 22.15
I shall return to him who s. me." 24.13
So the LORD s. a pestilence upon 24.15
and the king has s. with him Zadok 1Ki 1.44
So King Solomon s., and they brought 1.53
So King Solomon s. Benaiah the son 2.25
Solomon s. Benaiah the son of 2.29
Then the king s. and summoned 2.36
the king s. and summoned Shimei, and 2.42
king of Tyre s. his servants to 5.01
And Solomon s. word to Hiram, 5.02
And Hiram s. to Solomon, saying, "I 5.08
message which you have s. to me; 5.08
And he s. them to Lebanon, ten 5.14
And King Solomon s. and brought 7.13
eighth day he s. the people away; 8.66
Hiram had s. to the king one 9.14
And Hiram s. with the fleet his 9.27
And they s. and called him; 12.03
Then King Rehoboam s. Adoram, 12.18
they s. and called him to the 12.20
and King Asa s. them to Benhadad 15.18
and s. the commanders of his armies 15.20
my lord has not s. to seek you; 18.10
So Ahab s. to all the people of 18.20
Then Jezebel s. a messenger to 19.02
And he s. messengers into the city 20.02
'I s. to you, saying, "Deliver to me 20.05
for he s. to me for my wives and my 20.07
Benhadad s. to him and said, "The 20.10
And Benhadad s. out scouts, and they 20.17
and she s. the letters to the 21.08
did as Jezebel had s. word to them. 21.11
letters which she had s. to them, 21.11
Then they s. to Jezebel, saying, 21.14
so he s. messengers, telling them 2Ki 1.02
'Go back to the king who s. you, 1.06
Then the king s. to him a captain 1.09
Again the king s. to him another 1.11
Again the king s. the captain of a 1.13
you have s. messengers to inquire 1.16
the LORD has s. me as far as 2.02
for the LORD has s. me to Jericho." 2.04
the LORD has s. me to the Jordan." 2.06
They s. therefore fifty men; and for 2.17
And he went and s. word to Jehoshaphat 3.07
That I have s. to you Naaman my 5.06
he s. to the king, saying, "Why have 5.08
And Elisha s. a messenger to him, 5.10

SENT (cont.)

My master has s. me to say, 'There 2Ki 5.22
and he s. the men away, and they 5.24
But the man of God s. word to the 6.09
king of Israel s. to the place of 6.10
So he s. there horses and chariots 6.14
he s. them away, and they went to 6.23
murderer has s. to take off my 6.32
and the king s. them after the army 7.14
king of Syria has s. me to you, 8.09
Then he s. out a second horseman, 9.19
and s. them to Samaria, to the 10.01
s. to Jehu, saying, "We are your 10.05
and s. them to him at Jezreel. 10.07
And Jehu s. throughout all Israel; 10.21
year Jehoiada s. and brought the 11.04
and s. these to Hazael king of 12.18
Then Amaziah s. messengers to 14.08
king of Israel s. word to Amaziah 14.09
on Lebanon s. to a cedar on 14.09
But they s. after him to Lachish, 14.19
So Ahaz s. messengers to Tiglathpileser 16.07
and s. a present to the king of 16.08
And King Ahaz s. to Urijah the 16.10
King Ahaz had s. from Damascus, 16.11
for he had s. messengers to So, 17.04
and which I s. to you by my servants 17.13
the LORD s. lions among them, which 17.25
therefore he has s. lions among 17.26
king of Judah s. to the king of 18.14
And the king of Assyria s. the Tartan, 18.17
"Has my master s. me to speak these 18.27
And he s. Eliakim, who was over the 19.02
of Assyria has s. to mock the 19.04
he s. messengers again to Hezekiah, 19.09
which he has s. to mock the living 19.16
the son of Amoz s. to Hezekiah, 19.20
s. envoys with letters and a 20.12
the king s. Shaphan the son of 22.03
'Tell the man who s. you to me, 22.15
who s. you to inquire of the LORD, 22.18
Then the king s., and all the 23.01
and he s. and took the bones out 23.16
And the LORD s. against him bands 24.02
and s. them against Judah to 24.02
when the LORD s. Judah and Jerusalem 1Ch 6.15
after he had s. away Hushim and 8.08
and s. messengers throughout the 10.09
took counsel and s. him away, 12.19
king of Tyre s. messengers to 14.01
he s. his son Hadoram to King David, 18.10
And he s. all sorts of articles of 18.10
So David s. messengers to console 19.02
David has s. comforters to you, 19.03
at their hips, and s. them away; 19.04
he s. to meet them, for the men were 19.05
the Ammonites s. a thousand 19.06
he s. Joab and all the army of the 19.08
they s. messengers and brought out 19.16
I shall return to him who s. me." 21.12
So the LORD s. a pestilence upon 21.14
And God s. the angel to Jerusalem 21.15
And Solomon s. word to Huram the 2Ch 2.03
my father and s. him cedar to 2.03
in a letter which he s. to Solomon, 2.11
"Now I have s. a skilled man, endued 2.13
month he s. the people away to 7.10
And Huram s. him by his servants 8.18
And they s. and called him; 10.03
Then King Rehoboam s. Hadoram, 10.18
Jeroboam had s. an ambush around to 13.13
and s. them to Benhadad king of 16.02
and s. the commanders of his armies 16.04
of his reign he s. his princes, 17.07
Yet he s. prophets among them to 24.19
and s. all their spoil to the king 24.23
of the army whom Amaziah s. back, 25.13
Amaziah and s. to him a prophet, 25.15
counsel and s. to Joash the son of 25.17
king of Israel s. word to Amaziah 25.18
on Lebanon s. to a cedar on 25.18
But they s. after him to Lachish, 25.27
time King Ahaz s. to the king of 28.16
Hezekiah s. to all Israel and Judah, 30.01
s. her servants to Jerusalem to 32.09
And the LORD s. an angel, who cut 32.21
who had been s. to him to inquire 32.31
he s. Shaphan the son of Azaliah, 34.08
the king had s. went to Huldah the 34.22
'Tell the man who s. you to me, 34.23
who s. you to inquire of the LORD, 34.26
Then the king s. and gathered 34.29
But he s. envoys to him, saying, 35.21
Nebuchadnezzar s. and brought him 36.10
s. persistently to them by his 36.15
a copy of the letter that they s.— Ez 4.11
The king s. an answer: "To Rehum the 4.17
which you s. to us has been 4.18
the River s. to Darius the king; 5.06
they s. him a report, in which was 5.07
to the word s. by Darius the king, 6.13
For you are s. by the king and his 7.14
Then I s. for Eliezer, Ariel, Shemaiah, 8.16
and s. them to Iddo, the leading man 8.17
the king had s. with me officers Neh 2.09
Sanballat and Geshem s. to me, 6.02
And I s. messengers to them, saying, 6.03
And they s. to me four times in 6.04
the fifth time s. his servant to 6.05
Then I s. to him, saying, "No such 6.08
and saw that God had not s. him, 6.12
nobles of Judah s. many letters to 6.17
And Tobiah s. letters to make me 6.19
he s. letters to all the royal Est 1.22
Letters were s. by couriers to all 3.13
she s. garments to clothe Mordecai, 4.04
and he s. and fetched his friends 5.10
letters were s. by mounted couriers 8.10
and s. letters to all Jews who 9.20
Letters were s. to all the Jews, to 9.30
You have s. widows away empty, and Job 22.09
And he s. out his arrows, and Ps 18.14
he s. them food in abundance. 78.25
He s. among them swarms of flies, 78.45
it s. out its branches to the sea, 80.11
he had s. a man ahead of them, 105.17
The king s. and released him, the 105.20
He s. Moses his servant, and Aaron 105.26
He s. darkness, and made the land 105.28
but s. a wasting disease among them 106.15
he s. forth his word, and healed 107.20
He s. redemption to his people; 111.09
s. signs and wonders against 135.09
She has s. out her maids to call Pro 9.03
messenger will be s. against him. 17.11
a true answer to those who s. you? 22.21
The Lord has s. a word against Is 9.08
They have s. lambs to the ruler of 16.01
who was s. by Sargon the king of 20.01
king of Assyria s. the Rabshakeh 36.02
"Has my master s. me to speak these 36.12
And he s. Eliakim, who was over the 37.02
of Assyria has s. to mock the 37.04
he s. messengers to Hezekiah, saying, 37.09
which he has s. to mock the living 37.17
the son of Amoz s. to Hezekiah, 37.21
s. envoys with letters and a 39.01
Lord GOD has s. me and his Spirit. 48.16
in the thing for which I s. it. 55.11
you s. your envoys far off, and s. down 57.09
he has s. me to bind up the brokenhearted, 61.01
I had s. her away with a decree of Jer 3.08
persistently s. all my servants 7.25
the LORD had s. him to prophesy, 19.14

SENT (cont.)
King Zedekiah s. to him Pashhur Jer 21.01
when I s. to you, saying, "You shall 23.38
whom I have s. away from this place 24.05
persistently s. to you all his 25.04
to whom the Lord s. me drink it: 25.17
"The LORD s. me to prophesy against 26.12
truth the LORD s. me to you to 26.15
Then King Jehoiakim s. to Egypt 26.22
I have not s. them, says the LORD, 27.15
the LORD has truly s. the prophet." 28.09
Hananiah, the LORD has not s. you, 28.15
the prophet s. from Jerusalem to 29.01
The letter was s. by the hand of 29.03
king of Judah s. to Babylon to 29.03
whom I have s. into exile from 29.04
where I have s. you into exile, 29.07
from which I s. you into exile. 29.14
I persistently s. to you by my 29.19
exiles whom I s. away from Jerusalem 29.20
You have s. letters in your name to 29.25
For he has s. to us in Babylon, 29.28
I have s. to you all my servants 35.15
Then all the princes s. Jehudi the 36.14
Then the king s. Jehudi to get the 36.21
King Zedekiah s. Jehucal the son of 37.03
of Judah who s. you to me to 37.07
King Zedekiah s. for him, and 37.17
King Zedekiah s. for Jeremiah the 38.14
s. and took Jeremiah from the court 39.14
Ammonites has s. Ishmael the son 40.14
to whom you s. me to present your 42.09
For you s. me to the LORD your God, 42.20
anything that he s. me to tell you. 42.21
LORD their God had s. him to them, 43.01
Yet I persistently s. to you all my 44.04
has been s. among the nations: 49.14
"From on high he s. fire; Lam 1.13
For you are not s. to a people of Eze 3.05
Surely, if I s. you to such, they 3.06
when the LORD has not s. them, 13.06
there they s. up their soothing 20.28
and s. messengers to them in 23.16
They even s. for men to come from 23.40
far, to whom a messenger was s., 23.40
God because I s. them into exile 39.28
Nebuchadnezzar s. to assemble the Dan 3.02
who has s. his angel and delivered 3.28
"Then from his presence the hand was s., 5.24
My God s. his angel and shut the 6.22
for now I have been s. to you." 10.11
to Assyria, and s. to the great king. Hos 5.13
great army, which I s. among you. Joe 2.25
"I s. among you a pestilence after Amo 4.10
of Bethel s. to Jeroboam king of 7.10
has been s. among the nations: Ob 1.01
and I s. before you Moses, Aaron, and Mic 6.04
as the LORD their God had s. him; Hag 1.12
the LORD has s. to patrol the Zec 1.10
after his glory s. me to the 2.08
that the LORD of hosts has s. me. 2.09
the LORD of hosts has s. me to you. 2.12
the LORD of hosts has s. me to you. 4.09
the LORD of hosts has s. me to you. 6.15
of Bethel had s. Sharezer and 7.02
of hosts had s. by his Spirit 7.12
that I have s. this command to you, Mal 2.04
and he s. them to Bethlehem, saying, Mt 2.08
and he s. and killed all the male 2.16
These twelve Jesus s. out, 10.05
receives me receives him who s. me. 10.40
he s. word by his disciples 11.02
he s. and had John beheaded in the 14.10
they s. round to all that region 14.35
"I was s. only to the lost sheep of 15.24
he s. them into his vineyard. 20.02
then Jesus s. two disciples, 21.01
he s. his servants to the tenants, 21.34
Again he s. other servants, more 21.36
Afterward he s. his son to them, 21.37
and s. his servants to call those 22.03
Again he s. other servants, saying, 22.04
and he s. his troops and destroyed 22.07
And they s. their disciples to him, 22.16
stoning those who are s. to you! 23.37
his wife s. word to him, "Have 27.19
him, and s. him away at once, Mk 1.43
him, and to be s. out to preach 3.14
outside they s. to him and called 3.31
For Herod had s. and seized John, 6.17
the king s. a soldier of the guard 6.27
And he s. them away; and immediately 8.10
And he s. him away to his home, 8.26
receives not me but him who s. me." 9.37
he s. two of his disciples, 11.01
he s. a servant to the tenants, to 12.02
and s. him away empty-handed. 12.03
Again he s. to them another servant, 12.04
And he s. another, and him they 12.05
finally he s. him to them, saying, 12.06
And they s. to him some of the 12.13
And he s. two of his disciples, and 14.13
Jesus himself s. out by means of them, * 16.08
and I was s. to speak to you, and to Lk 1.19
Gabriel was s. from God to a city 1.26
and the rich he was s. empty away, 1.53
He has s. me to proclaim release to 4.18
and Elijah was s. to none of them 4.26
for I was s. for this purpose." 4.43
he s. to him elders of the Jews, 7.03
the centurion s. friends to him, 7.06
who had been s. returned to the 7.10
s. them to the Lord, saying, "Are you 7.19
"John the Baptist has s. us to you, 7.20
but he s. him away, saying, 8.38
and he s. them out to preach the 9.02
receives me receives him who s. me; 9.48
And he s. messengers ahead of him, 9.51
and s. them on ahead of him, two by 10.01
rejects me rejects him who s. me." 10.16
stoning those who are s. to you! 13.34
the banquet he s. his servant to 14.17
who s. him into his fields to feed 15.15
hated him and s. an embassy after 19.14
he s. two of the disciples, 19.29
So those who were s. went away and 19.32
he s. a servant to the tenants, that 20.10
and s. him away empty-handed. 20.10
And he s. another servant; him also 20.11
and s. him away empty-handed. 20.11
And he s. yet a third; this one 20.12
and s. spies, who pretended to be 20.20
So Jesus s. Peter and John, saying, 22.08
"When I s. you out with no purse or 22.35
he s. him over to Herod, who was 23.07
apparel, he s. him back to Pilate. 23.11
Herod, for he s. him back to us. 23.15
There was a man s. from God, Jn 1.06
when the Jews s. priests and 1.19
have an answer for those who s. us. 1.22
Now they had been s. from the 1.24
but he who s. me to baptize with 1.33
For God s. the Son into the world, 3.17
but I have been s. before him. 3.28
For he whom God has s. utters the 3.34
is to do the will of him who s. me, 4.34
I s. you to reap that for which you 4.38
not honor the Father who s. him. 5.23
my word and believes him who s. me, 5.24
will but the will of him who s. me. 5.30
You s. to John, and he has borne 5.33
witness that the Father has s. me. 5.36
And the Father who s. me has 5.37
do not believe him whom he has s. 5.38

SENT (cont.)
you believe in him whom he has s." Jn 6.29
but the will of him who s. me; 6.38
and this is the will of him who s. me, 6.39
the Father who s. me draws him; 6.44
As the living Father s. me, 6.57
is not mine, but his who s. me; 7.16
glory of him who s. him is true, 7.18
he who s. me is true, and him you do 7.28
for I come from him, and he s. me. 7.29
and Pharisees s. officers to 7.32
and then I go to him who s. me; 7.33
that judge, but I and he who s. me. 8.16
the Father who s. me bears witness 8.18
but he who s. me is true, and I 8.26
And he who s. me is with me; 8.29
not of my own accord, but he s. me. 8.42
work the works of him who s. me, 9.04
pool of Siloam" (which means S.). 9.07
consecrated and s. into the world, 10.36
So the sisters s. to him, saying, 11.03
not in me but in him who s. me. 12.44
And he who sees me sees him who s. me. 12.45
the Father who s. me has himself 12.49
who is s. greater than he who s. him. 13.16
receives me receives him who s. me." 13.20
mine but the Father's who s. me. 14.24
they do not know him who s. me. 15.21
But now I am going to him who s. me; 16.05
and Jesus Christ whom thou hast s. 17.03
so I have s. them into the world. 17.18
may believe that thou hast s. me. 17.21
that thou hast s. me and hast 17.23
these know that thou hast s. me. 17.25
Annas then s. him bound to Caiaphas 18.24
As the Father has s. me, even so I 20.21
s. him to you first, to bless you in Ac 3.26
and s. to the prison to have them 5.21
he s. forth our fathers the first 7.12
And Joseph s. and called to him 7.14
God s. as both ruler and deliverer 7.35
they s. to them Peter and John, 8.14
has s. me that you may regain your 9.17
Caesarea, and s. him off to Tarsus. 9.30
s. two men to him entreating him, 9.38
to them, he s. them to Joppa. 10.08
the men that were s. by Cornelius, 10.17
hesitation; for I have s. them." 10.20
So when I was s. for, I came without 10.29
I ask then why you s. for me." 10.29
So I s. to you at once, and you have 10.33
the word which he s. to Israel, 10.36
which we were, s. to me from Caesarea. 11.11
and they s. Barnabas to Antioch. 11.22
the Lord has s. his angel and 12.11
hands on them and s. them off. 13.03
So, being s. out by the Holy Spirit, 13.04
rulers of the synagogue s. to them, 13.15
to us has been s. the message of 13.26
So, being s. on their way by the 15.03
They s. Judas called Barsabbas, and 15.22
We have therefore s. Judas and 15.27
So when they were s. off, 15.30
they were s. off in peace by the 15.33
brethren to those who had s. them. 15.33
day, the magistrates s. the police, 16.35
magistrates have s. to let you go; 16.36
immediately s. Paul and Silas away 17.10
immediately s. Paul off on his way 17.14
And having s. into Macedonia two of 19.22
s. to him and begged him not to 19.31
Paul s. for the disciples and 20.01
And from Miletus he s. to Ephesus 20.17
we have s. a letter with our 21.25
I s. him to you at once, ordering 23.30
and he s. for Paul and heard him 24.24
So he s. for him often and conversed 24.26
to have the man s. to Jerusalem, 25.03
of God has been s. to the Gentiles 28.28
can men preach unless they are s.? Rom 10.15
Therefore I s. to you Timothy, my 1Co 4.17
any of those whom I s. to you? 2Co 12.17
and s. the brother with him. 12.18
God s. forth his Son, born of woman, Gal 4.04
God has s. the Spirit of his Son 4.06
I have s. him to you for this very Eph 6.22
Thessalonica you s. me help once Php 4.16
from Epaphroditus the gifts you s., 4.18
I have s. him to you for this very Col 4.08
and we s. Timothy, our brother and 1Th 3.02
I s. that I might know your faith, 3.05
Tychicus I have s. to Ephesus. 2Ti 4.12
ministering spirits s. forth to serve, Heb 1.14
messengers and s. them out another Jas 2.25
the Holy Spirit s. from heaven, 1Pe 1.12
or to governors as s. by him to 2.14
that God s. his only Son into the 1Jn 4.09
he loved us and s. his Son to be 4.10
the Father has s. his Son as the 4.14
spirits of God s. out into all the Rev 5.06
has s. his angel to show his 22.06
"I Jesus have s. my angel to you 22.16

SENTENCE
and give s. between me and you, and 1Sa 24.15
at Riblah, who passed s. upon him. 2Ki 25.06
justified in thy s. and blameless Ps 51.04
Because s. against an evil deed is Ecc 8.11
"This man deserves the s. of death, Jer 26.11
does not deserve the s. of death, 26.16
of Hamath; and he passed s. upon him. 39.05
Hamath, and he passed s. upon him. 52.09
s. of adulteresses, and with the s. of women Eze 23.45
to me, there is but one s. for you. Dan 2.09
The s. is by the decree of the 4.17
So Pilate gave s. that their demand Lk 23.24
under the same s. of condemnation? 23.40
him, asking for s. against him. Ac 25.15
execute his s. upon the earth with Rom 9.28
commandment, are summed up in this s., 13.09
we had received the s. of death; 2Co 1.09

SENTENCED
are you to escape being s. to hell? Mt 23.33
last of all, like men s. to death; 1Co 4.09

SENTRIES
locked and the s. standing at the Ac 5.23
and s. before the door were guarding 12.06
he examined the s. and ordered 12.19

SENTRY
a s. there named Irijah the son of Jer 37.13

SEORIM
the third to Harim, the fourth to S., 1Ch 24.08

SEPARATE
and let it s. the waters from the Gen 1.06
the heavens to s. the day from the 1.14
and to s. the light from the 1.18
S. yourself from me. If you take the 13.09
of him who was s. from his brothers 49.26
they shall be s. beneath, but joined Ex 26.24
the veil shall s. for you the holy 26.33
And they were s. beneath, but joined 36.29
of Israel s. from their uncleanness, Lev 15.31
of a Nazirite, to s. himself to the LORD, Num 6.02
he shall s. himself from wine and 6.03
and s. himself to the LORD for the 6.12
"Thus you shall s. the Levites from 8.14
"S. yourselves from among this 16.21
For thou didst s. them from among 1Ki 8.53
death, and he dwelt in a s. house. 2Ki 15.05
being a leper dwelt in a s. house, 2Ch 26.21

SEPARATE (cont.)
s. yourselves from the peoples of Ez 10.11
will surely s. me from his people"; Is 56.03
come out and s. the evil from the Mt 13.49
and he will s. them one from 25.32
Who shall s. us from the love of Rom 8.35
will be able to s. us from the 8.39
wife should not s. from her 1Co 7.10
desires to s., let it be so; 7.15
and be s. from them, says the Lord, 2Co 6.17

SEPARATED
and God s. the light from the Gen 1.04
firmament and s. the waters which 1.07
thus they s. from each other. 13.11
after Lot had s. from him, "Lift up 13.14
And Jacob s. the lambs, and set the 30.40
who have s. you from the peoples. Lev 20.24
and have s. you from the peoples, 20.26
of Israel has s. you from the Num 16.09
which Moses s. from that of the men 31.42
when he s. the sons of men, he fixed Deu 32.08
the Kenite had s. from the Kenites, Ju 4.11
horses of fire s. the two of them. 2Ki 2.11
joined them and s. himself from Ez 6.21
have not s. themselves from the 9.01
and we are s. on the wall, far from Neh 4.19
And the Israelites s. themselves 9.02
all who have s. themselves from 10.28
they s. from Israel all those of 13.03
clasp each other and cannot be s. Job 41.17
so that they s. from each other; Ac 15.39
came he drew back and s. himself, Gal 2.12
were at that time s. from Christ, Eph 2.12
s. from sinners, exalted above the Heb 7.26

SEPARATES
for which he s. himself to the Num 6.05
days that he s. himself to the 6.06
and a whsiperer s. close friends. Pro 16.28
who s. himself from me, taking his Eze 14.07
as a shepherd s. the sheep from Mt 25.32

SEPARATION
All the days of his s. he shall eat Num 6.04
of his vow of s. no razor shall 6.05
because his s. to God is upon his 6.07
All the days of his s. he is holy 6.08
to the LORD for the days of his s., 6.12
void, because his s. was defiled. 6.12
the time of his s. has been 6.13
the law for his s. as a Nazirite. 6.21
have made a s. between you and Is 59.02
to make a s. between the holy and Eze 42.20

SEPHAR
direction of S. to the hill Gen 10.30

SEPHARAD
who are in S. shall possess the Ob 1.20

SEPHARVAIM
and S., and placed them in the 2Ki 17.24
and Anammelech, the gods of S. 17.31
Where are the gods of S., Hena, and 18.34
Arpad, the king of the city of S., 19.13
Where are the gods of S.? Have they Is 36.19
Arpad, the king of the city of S., 37.13

SEPHARVITES
and the S. burned their children 2Ki 17.31

SEPULCHRE
us will withhold from you his s., Gen 23.06
destruction, their throat is an open s., Ps 5.09
are cast out, away from your s., Is 14.19
there, sitting opposite the s. Mt 27.61
Therefore order the s. to be made 27.64
and made the s. secure by sealing 27.66
the other Mary went to see the s. 28.01

SEPULCHRES
dead in the choicest of our s.; Gen 23.06
city, the place of my fathers' s., Neh 2.03
to the city of my fathers' s., 2.05
a point opposite the s. of David, 3.16

SERAH
Beriah, with S. their sister. Gen 46.17
of the daughter of Asher was S. Num 26.46
Ishvi, Beriah, and their sister S. 1Ch 7.30

SERAIAH
were priests; and S. was secretary; 2Sa 8.17
the guard took S. the chief priest, 2Ki 25.18
and S. the son of Tanhumeth the 25.23
The sons of Kenaz: Othniel and S.; 1Ch 4.13
and S. was the father of Joab the 4.14
Joshibiah, son of S., son of Asiel, 4.35
Azariah of S., S. of Jehozadak 6.14
S., Reelaiah, Mordecai, Bilshan, Ez 2.02
king of Persia, Ezra the son of S., 7.01
S., Azariah, Jeremiah, Neh 10.02
S. the son of Hilkiah, son of 11.11
and Joshua: S., Jeremiah, Ezra, 12.01
of fathers' houses: of S., Meraiah; 12.12
king's son and S. the son of Jer 36.26
S. the son of Tanhumeth, the sons of 40.08
commanded S. the son of Neriah, son 51.59
S. was the quartermaster. 51.59
And Jeremiah said to S.: 51.61
the guard took S. the chief priest, 52.24

SERAPHIM
Above him stood the s.; each had Is 6.02
Then flew one of the s. to me, 6.06

SERED
of Zebulun: S., Elon, and Jahleel Gen 46.14
of S., the family of the Seredites; Num 26.26

SEREDITES
of Sered, the family of the S.; Num 26.26

SERGIUS
S. Paulus, a man of intelligence, who Ac 13.07

SERIOUS
or has any s. blemish whatever, you Deu 15.21
him many s. charges which they Ac 25.07
Deacons likewise must be s., 1Ti 3.08
The women likewise must be s., 3.11
s., sensible, sound in faith, in love, Tit 2.02

SERPENT
Now the s. was more subtle than any Gen 3.01
And the woman sad to the s., 3.02
But the s. said to the woman, "You 3.04
"The s. beguiled me, and I ate." 3.13
The LORD God said to the s., Because you have 3.14
Dan shall be a s. in the way, a 49.17
on the ground, and it became a s.; Ex 4.03
Pharaoh, that it may become a s.' " 7.09
his servants, and it became a s. 7.10
the rod which was turned into a s. 7.15
"Make a fiery s., and set it on a Num 21.08
So Moses made a bronze s., and set it on 21.09
and if a s. bit any man, he would 21.09
look at the bronze s. and live. 21.09
the bronze s. that Moses had made, 2Ki 18.04
his hand pierced the fleeing s. Job 26.13
They have venom like the venom of a s., Ps 58.04
lion and the s. you will trample 91.13
At the last it bites like a s., Pro 23.32
the way of a s. on a rock, the way 30.19
and a s. will bite him who breaks Ecc 10.08

SERPENT (cont.)

If the s. bites before it is Ecc 10.11
and its fruit will be a flying s. Is 14.29
punish Leviathan the fleeing s., 27.01
Leviathan the twisting s., and he 27.01
lion, the viper and the flying s., 30.06
a sound like a s. gliding away; Jer 46.22
against the wall, and a s. bit him. Amo 5.19
sea, there I will command the s., 9.03
they shall lick the dust like a s., Mic 7.17
for a fish, will give him a s.? Mt 7.10
instead of a fish give him a s.; Lk 11.11
lifted up the s. in the wilderness, Jn 3.14
that as the s. deceived Eve by his 2Co 11.03
that ancient s., who is called the Rev 12.09
fly from the s. into the wilderness, 12.14
The s. poured water like a river 12.15
that ancient s., who is the Devil 20.02

SERPENT'S

oxen, and fatlings by the S. Stone, 1Ki 1.09
They make their tongue sharp as a s. Ps 140.03
for from the s. root will come Is 14.29
and dust shall be the s. food. 65.25

SERPENTS

down his rod, and they became s. Ex 7.12
LORD sent fiery s. among the Num 21.06
that he take away the s. from us." 21.07
with its fiery s. and scorpions Deu 8.15
their wine is the poison of s., 32.33
For behold, I am sending among you s., Jer 8.17
so be wise as s. and innocent as Mt 10.16
You s., you brood of vipers, how are 23.33
they will pick up s., and if *Mk 16.18
to tread upon s. and scorpions, Lk 10.19
them did and were destroyed by s.; 1Co 10.09
their tails are like s., with heads, and Rev 9.19

SERUG

years, he became the father of S.; Gen 11.20
the birth of S. two hundred and 11.21
When S. had lived thirty years, he 11.22
and S. lived after the birth of 11.23
S., Nahor, Terah; 1Ch 1.26
the son of S., the son of Reu, the Lk 3.35

SERVANT

your sight, do not pass by your s. Gen 18.03
on—since you have come to your s." 18.05
and good, and gave it to the s., 18.07
behold, your s. has found favor in 19.19
And Abraham said to his s., 24.02
The s. said to him, "Perhaps the 24.05
So the s. put his hand under the 24.09
Then the s. took ten of his master's 24.10
hast appointed for thy s. Isaac. 24.14
Then the s. ran to meet her, and 24.17
So he said, "I am Abraham's s. 24.34
When Abraham's s. heard their words, 24.52
And the s. brought forth jewelry of 24.53
and Abraham's s. and his men. 24.59
thus the s. took Rebekah, and went 24.61
and said to the s., "Who is the 24.65
The s. said, "It is my master." 24.65
And the s. told Isaac all the 24.66
descendants for my s. Abraham's sake." 26.24
lord Esau: Thus says your s. Jacob, 32.04
which thou hast shown to thy s., 32.10
say, 'They belong to your s. Jacob; 32.18
'Moreover your s. Jacob is behind 32.20
God has graciously given your s." 33.05
Let my lord pass on before his s., 33.14
"The Hebrew s., whom you have 39.17
"This is the way your s. treated me," 39.19
a s. of the captain of the guard; 41.12
"Your s. our father is well, he is 43.28
let your s., I pray you, speak a 44.18
your anger burn against your s.; 44.18
back to your s. my father we told 44.24
Then your s. my father said to us, 44.27
when I come to your s. my father, 44.30
hairs of your s. our father with 44.31
For your s. became surety for the 44.32
let your s., I pray you, remain 44.33
since thou hast spoken to thy s.; Ex 4.10
sojourner or hired s. may eat of it. 12.45
in the LORD and in his s. Moses. 14.31
So Moses rose with his s. Joshua, 24.13
his s. Joshua the son of Nun, a 33.11
of a hired s. shall not remain Lev 19.13
or a hired s. shall not eat of a 22.10
for your hired s. and the sojourner 25.06
you as a hired s. and as a sojourner. 25.40
be rated as the time of a hired s. 25.50
As a s. hired year by year shall he 25.53
hast thou dealt ill with thy s.? Num 11.11
Not so with my s. Moses; he is entrusted 12.07
to speak against my s. Moses?" 12.08
But my s. Caleb, because he has a 14.24
to show thy s. thy greatness and Deu 3.24
that you were a s. in the land of 5.15
cost of a hired s. he has served 15.18
oppress a hired s. who is poor and 24.14
So Moses the s. of the LORD died 34.05
death of Moses the s. of the LORD, Jos 1.01
"Moses my s. is dead; now therefore, 1.02
which Moses my s. commanded you; 1.07
which Moses the s. of the LORD 1.13
which Moses the s. of the LORD 1.15
him, "What does my lord bid his s.?" 5.14
as Moses the s. of the LORD had 8.31
as Moses the s. of the LORD had 8.33
commanded his s. Moses to give you 9.24
as Moses the s. of the LORD had 11.12
LORD had commanded Moses his s., 11.15
Moses, the s. of the LORD, and the 12.06
and Moses the s. of the LORD gave 12.06
as Moses the s. of the LORD gave 13.08
when Moses the s. of the LORD sent 14.07
which Moses the s. of the LORD 18.07
that Moses the s. of the LORD 22.02
which Moses the s. of the LORD 22.04
which Moses the s. of the LORD 22.05
the s. of the LORD, died, being a 24.29
the s. of the LORD, died at the age Ju 2.08
to the camp with Purah your s.; 7.10
with Purah his s. to the outposts 7.11
deliverance by the hand of thy s.; 15.18
with him his s. and a couple of 19.03
concubine and his s. rose up to 19.09
and the s. said to his master, "Come 19.11
And he said to his s., "Come and let us 19.13
said to his s. who was in charge Ru 2.05
And the s. who was in charge of the 2.06
the priest's s. would come, while the 1Sa 2.13
the priest's s. would come and say 2.15
'Speak, LORD, for thy s. hears.' " 3.09
said, "Speak, for thy s. hears." 3.10
said to his s. who was with him, 9.05
Then Saul said to his s., "But if we go 9.07
The s. answered Saul again, "Here, I 9.08
And Saul said to his s., "Well said; 9.10
Saul and his s. and brought them 9.22
"Tell the s. to pass on before us, 9.27
Saul's uncle said to him and to his s., 10.14
thou not answered thy s. this day 14.41
your s. will go and fight with this 17.32
"Your s. used to keep sheep for his 17.34
Your s. has killed both lions and 17.36
the son of your s. Jesse the 17.58
the king sin against his s. David; 19.04
it will be well with your s.; 20.07
Therefore deal kindly with your s., 20.08
brought your s. into a sacred 20.08

SERVANT (cont.)
has stirred up my s. against me, 1Sa 22.08
anything to his s. or to all the 22.15
for your s. has known nothing of 22.15
thy s. has surely heard that Saul 23.10
come down, as thy s. has heard? 23.11
I beseech thee, tell thy s." 23.11
which your s. has brought to my 25.27
and has kept back his s. from evil; 25.39
handmaid is a s. to wash the feet 25.41
does my lord pursue after his s.? 26.18
the king hear the words of his s. 26.19
why should your s. dwell in the 27.05
therefore he shall be my s. always." 27.12
you shall know what your s. can do." 28.02
the s. of Saul, king of Israel, who 29.03
found in your s. from the day I 29.08
s. to an Amalekite; and my master 30.13
the hand of my s. David I will 2Sa 3.18
"Go and tell my s. David, 7.05
thus you shall say to my s. David, 7.08
thou knowest thy s., O Lord GOD! 7.20
greatness, to make thy s. know it. 7.21
concerning thy s. and concerning 7.25
house of thy s. David will be 7.26
made this revelation to thy s., 7.27
therefore thy s. has found courage 7.27
promised this good thing to thy s.; 7.28
thee to bless the house of thy s., 7.29
house of thy s. be blessed for 7.29
Now there was a s. of the house of 9.02
And he said, "Your s. is he." 9.02
and he answered, "Behold, your s." 9.06
"What is your s., that you should 9.08
Saul's s., and said to him, "All that 9.09
my lord the king commands his s., 9.11
his servant, so will your s. do." 9.11
'Your s. Uriah the Hittite is dead 11.21
and your s. Uriah the Hittite is 11.24
So his s. put her out, and bolted 13.18
your s. has sheepshearers; pray let the 13.24
and his servants go with your s. 13.24
as your s. said, so it has come 13.35
will perform the request of his s. 14.15
and deliver his s. from the hand 14.16
It was your s. Joab who bade me; 14.19
of affairs your s. Joab did this. 14.20
"Today your s. knows that I have 14.22
has granted the request of his s." 14.22
"Your s. is of such and such a 15.02
For your s. vowed a vow while I 15.08
life, there also will your s. be." 15.21
Absalom, 'I will be your s., O king; 15.34
been your father's s. in time past, 15.34
past, so now I will be your s.,' 15.34
Ziba the s. of Mephibosheth met him, 16.01
answered, "When Joab sent your s., 18.29
And Ziba the s. of the house of 19.17
how your s. did wrong on the day 19.19
For your s. knows that I have 19.20
"My lord, O king, my s. deceived me; 19.26
for your s. said to him, 'Saddle an 19.26
with the king.' For your s. is lame. 19.26
slandered your s. to my lord the 19.27
you set your s. among those who 19.28
Can your s. taste what he eats or 19.35
should your s. be an added burden 19.35
Your s. will go a little way over 19.36
Pray let your s. return, that I may 19.37
But here is your s. Chimham; 19.37
take away the iniquity of thy s.; 24.10
my lord the king come to his s.?" 24.21
Solomon your s. he has not invited. 1Ki 1.19
But me, your s., and Zadok the 1.26
and your s. Solomon, he has not 1.26
not slay his s. with the sword.'" 1.51
king has said, so will your s. do." 2.38
love to thy s. David my father, 3.06
hast made thy s. king in place of 3.07
And thy s. is in the midst of thy 3.08
Give thy s. therefore an understanding 3.09
kept with thy s. David my father 8.24
keep with thy s. David my father 8.25
spoken to thy s. David my father. 8.26
prayer of thy s. and to his 8.28
which thy s. prays before thee 8.28
which thy s. offers toward this 8.29
supplication of thy s. and of thy 8.30
open to the supplication of thy s., 8.52
thy s., when thou didst bring our 8.53
which he uttered by Moses his s. 8.56
he maintain the cause of his s., 8.59
to David his s. and to Israel his 8.66
you and will give it to your s. 11.11
of David my s. and for the sake of 11.13
a s. of Solomon, whose mother's name 11.26
the sake of my s. David and for 11.32
sake of David my s. whom I chose, 11.34
that David my s. may always have a 11.36
as David my s. did, I will be with 11.38
you will be a s. to this people 12.07
you have not been like my s. David, 14.08
he spoke by his s. Ahijah the 14.18
he spoke by his s. Ahijah the 15.29
But his s. Zimri, commander of half 16.09
would give your s. into the hand 18.09
although I your s. have revered 18.12
in Israel, and that I am thy s., 18.36
And he said to his s., "Go up now, 18.43
to Judah, and left his s. there. 19.03
demanded of your s. I will do; 20.09
"Your s. Benhadad says, 'Pray, let me 20.32
"Your s. went out into the midst of 20.39
And as your s. was busy here and 20.40
"Your s. my husband is dead; 2Ki 4.01
know that your s. feared the LORD, 4.01
and he said to Gehazi his s., 4.12
The father said to his s., 4.19
the ass, and she said to her s., 4.24
coming, he said to Gehazi his s., 4.25
before him, he said to his s., 4.38
But his s. said, "How am I to set 4.43
I have sent to you Naaman my s., 5.06
accept now a present from your s." 5.15
given to your s. two mules' burden 5.17
henceforth your s. will not offer 5.17
matter may the LORD pardon your s.: 5.18
LORD pardon your s. in this matter." 5.18
Gehazi, the s. of Elisha the man of 5.20
And he said, "Your s. went nowhere." 5.25
When the s. of the man of God rose 6.15
And the s. said, "Alas, my master! 6.15
with Gehazi the s. of the man of 8.04
"What is your s., who is but a dog, 8.13
for the sake of David his s., 8.19
he spoke by his s. Elijah the 9.36
done what he said by his s. Elijah." 10.10
there is no s. of the LORD here 10.23
he spoke by his s. Jonah the son 14.25
saying, "I am your s. and your son. 16.07
that Moses the s. of the LORD 18.12
and for the sake of my s. David." 19.34
sake and for my s. David's sake." 20.06
the law that my s. Moses commanded 21.08
and Asaiah the king's s., saying, 22.12
Jehoiakim became his s. three years; 24.01
a s. of the king of Babylon, came to 25.08
that Moses the s. of God had 1Ch 6.49
O offspring of Abraham his s., 16.13
"Go and tell my s. David, 17.04
thus shall you say to my s. David, 17.07
say to thee for honoring thy s.? 17.18
For thou knowest thy s. 17.18
concerning thy s. and concerning 17.23

SERVANT (cont.)
house of thy s. David will be 1Ch 17.24
revealed to thy s. that thou wilt 17.25
therefore thy s. has found 17.25
promised this good thing to thy s.; 17.26
thee to bless the house of thy s., 17.27
take away the iniquity of thy s.; 21.08
which Moses the s. of the LORD had 2Ch 1.03
kept with thy s. David my father 6.15
keep with thy s. David my father 6.16
thou hast spoken to thy s. David. 6.17
prayer of thy s. and to his 6.19
which thy s. prays before thee; 6.19
which thy s. offers toward this 6.20
supplications of thy s. and of thy 6.21
steadfast love for David thy s." 6.42
a s. of Solomon the son of David, 13.06
the s. of the LORD, on the congregation 24.06
that Moses the s. of God laid upon 24.09
GOD and against his s. Hezekiah. 32.16
and Asaiah the king's s., saying, 34.20
prayer of thy s. which I now pray Neh 1.06
thou didst command thy s. Moses. 1.07
thou didst command thy s. Moses, 1.08
attentive to the prayer of thy s., 1.11
and give success to thy s. today, 1.11
and if your s. has found favor in 2.05
the Horonite and Tobiah the s., 2.10
the Horonite and Tobiah the s., 2.19
man and his s. pass the night 4.22
time sent his s. to me with an 6.05
statutes and a law by Moses thy s. 9.14
was given by Moses the s. of God, 10.29
"Have you considered my s. Job, Job 1.08
"Have you considered my s. Job, 2.03
I call to my s., but he gives me no 19.16
to take him for your s. for ever? 41.04
me what is right, as my s. Job has. 42.07
and go to my s. Job, and offer up 42.08
and my s. Job shall pray for you, 42.08
me what is right, as my s. Job has. 42.08
Moreover by them is thy s. warned; Ps 19.11
Keep back thy s. also from presumptuous 19.13
Turn not thy s. away in anger, thou 27.09
Let thy face shine on thy s.; 31.16
delights in the welfare of his s.! 35.27
Hide not thy face from thy s.; 69.17
He chose David his s., and took him 78.70
save thy s. who trusts in thee. 86.02
Gladden the soul of thy s., 86.04
give thy strength to thy s., 86.16
one, I have sworn to David my s.: 89.03
I have found David, my s.; 89.20
renounced the covenant with thy s.; 89.39
Remember, O Lord, how thy s. is scorned; 89.50
O offspring of Abraham his s., 105.06
He sent Moses his s., and Aaron whom 105.26
holy promise, and Abraham his s. 105.42
put to shame; may thy s. be glad! 109.28
O LORD, I am thy s.; I am thy s., 116.16
Deal bountifully with thy s., 119.17
thy s. will meditate on thy statutes 119.23
Confirm to thy s. thy promise, which 119.38
Remember thy word to thy s., 119.49
Thou hast dealt well with thy s., 119.65
according to thy promise to thy s. 119.76
How long must thy s. endure? 119.84
Be surety for thy s. for good; 119.122
Deal with thy s. according to thy 119.124
I am thy s.; give me understanding, 119.125
Make thy face shine upon thy s., 119.135
is well tried, and thy s. loves it. 119.140
seek thy s., for I do not forget 119.176
For thy s. David's sake do not turn 132.10
a heritage to Israel his s., 136.22
Enter not into judgment with thy s.; 143.02
my adversaries, for I am thy s. 143.12
kings, who rescuest David thy s. 144.10
the fool will be s. to the wise. Pro 11.29
A s. who deals wisely has the king's 14.35
By mere words a s. is not disciplined, 29.19
He who pampers his s. from childhood, 29.21
Do not slander a s. to his master, 30.10
lest you hear your s. cursing you; Ecc 7.21
"As my s. Isaiah has walked naked Is 20.03
I will call my s. Eliakim the son 22.20
and for the sake of my s. David." 37.35
my s., Jacob, whom I have chosen, the 41.08
"You are my s., I have chosen you 41.09
Behold my s., whom I uphold, my 42.01
Who is blind but my s., or deaf as my 42.19
or blind as the s. of the LORD? 42.19
"and my s. whom I have chosen, that 43.10
O Jacob my s., Israel whom I have 44.01
O Jacob my s., Jeshurun whom I have 44.02
and Israel, for you are my s.; 44.21
I formed you, you are my s.; 44.21
who confirms the word of his s., 44.26
For the sake of my s. Jacob, 45.04
"The LORD has redeemed his s. Jacob!" 48.20
"You are my s., Israel, in whom I 49.03
me from the womb to be his s., 49.05
should be my s. to raise up the 49.06
the s. of rulers: "Kings shall see 49.07
LORD and obeys the voice of his s., 50.10
Behold, my s. shall prosper, he shall 52.13
my s., make many to be accounted 53.11
the days of old, of Moses his s. 63.11
Is he a homeborn s.? Why then Jer 2.14
my s., and I will bring them 25.09
my s., and I have given him also 27.06
O Jacob my s., says the LORD, nor be 30.10
with David my s. may be broken, 33.21
the descendants of David my s., 33.22
and David my s. and will not 33.26
my s., and he will set his throne 43.10
O Jacob my s., nor be dismayed, O 46.27
O Jacob my s., says the LORD, for I 46.28
land which I gave to my s. Jacob. Eze 28.25
my s. David, and he shall feed them: 34.23
and my s. David shall be prince 34.24
"My s. David shall be king over 37.24
dwelt that I gave to my s. Jacob; 37.25
and David my s. shall be their 37.25
s. of the living God, has your God, Dan 6.20
of Moses the s. of God have been 9.11
prayer of thy s. and to his 9.17
How can my lord's s. talk with my 10.17
will take you, O Zerubbabel my s., Hag 2.23
I will bring my s. the Branch. Zec 3.08
his father, and a s. his master. Mal 1.06
"Remember the law of my s. Moses, 4.04
my s. is lying paralyzed at home, in Mt 8.06
the word, and my s. will be healed. 8.08
And the s. was healed at that 8.13
his teacher, nor a s. above his master; 10.24
and the s. like his master. If they have 10.25
"Behold, my s. whom I have chosen, my 12.18
So the s. fell on his knees, imploring 18.26
lord of that s. released him and 18.27
But that same s., as he went out, 18.28
So his fellow s. fell down and 18.29
and said to him, 'You wicked s.! 18.32
have had mercy on your fellow s., 18.33
great among you must be your s., 20.26
greatest among you shall be your s.; 23.11
"Who then is the faithful and wise s., 24.45
Blessed is that s. whom his master 24.46
But if that wicked s. says to 24.48
the master of that s. will come on 24.50
'Well done, good and faithful s.; 25.21
'Well done, good and faithful s.; 25.23
him, 'You wicked and slothful s.! 25.26
the worthless s. into the outer 25.30

SERVANT (cont.)

must be last of all and s. of all." Mk 9.35
great among you must be your s., 10.43
he sent a s. to the tenants, to get 12.02
Again he sent to them another s., 12.04
He has helped his s. Israel, Lk 1.54
us in the house of his s. David, 1.69
thou thy s. depart in peace, 2.29
the word, and let my s. be healed. 7.07
Blessed is that s. whom his master 12.43
But if that s. says to himself, 'My 12.45
the master of that s. will come on 12.46
And that s. who knew his master's 12.47
he sent his s. to say to those who 14.17
So the s. came and reported this to 14.21
householder in anger said to his s., 14.21
And the s. said, 'Sir, what you 14.22
And the master said to the s., 14.23
No s. can serve two masters; 16.13
who has a s. plowing or keeping 17.07
Does he thank the s. because he did 17.09
said to him, 'Well done, good s.! 19.17
of your own mouth, you wicked s.! 19.22
he sent a s. to the tenants, that 20.10
And he sent another s.; him also they 20.11
I am, there shall my s. be also; Jn 12.26
a s. is not greater than his master 13.16
for the s. does not know what his 15.15
'A s. is not greater than his 15.20
glorified his s. Jesus, whom you Ac 3.13
God, having raised up his s., 3.26
thy s., didst say by the Holy 4.25
together against thy holy s. Jesus, 4.27
the name of thy holy s. Jesus." 4.30
Paul, a s. of Jesus Christ, called to Rom 1.01
for he is God's s. for your good. 13.04
he is the s. of God to execute his 13.04
pass judgment on the s. of another? 14.04
Christ became a s. to the circumcised 15.08
I should not be a s. of Christ. Gal 1.10
himself, taking the form of a s., Php 2.07
Epaphras our beloved fellow s. Col 1.07
minister and fellow s. in the Lord. 4.07
a s. of Christ Jesus, greets you, 4.12
and God's s. in the gospel of 1Th 3.02
And the Lord's s. must not be 2Ti 2.24
Paul, a s. of God and an apostle of Tit 1.01
faithful in all God's house as a s., Heb 3.05
James, a s. of God and of the Lord Jas 1.01
Simon Peter, a s. and apostle of 2Pe 1.01
Jude, a s. of Jesus Christ and Jud 1.01
sending his angel to his s. John, Rev 1.01
the s. of God, and the song of the 15.03
I am a fellow s. with you and your 19.10
I am a fellow s. with you and your 22.09

SERVANT'S

to your s. house and spend the Gen 19.02
also of thy s. house for a great 2Sa 7.19
spoken of thy s. house for a great 1Ch 17.17
For thy s. sake, O LORD, and according 17.19

SERVANTS

he and his s., and routed them and Gen 14.15
the morning, and called all his s., 20.08
which Abimelech's s. had seized, 21.25
his father's s. had dug in the 26.15
But when Isaac's s. dug in the 26.19
And there Isaac's s. dug a well. 26.25
day Isaac's s. came and told him 26.32
brothers I have given to him for s., 27.37
delivered into the hand of his s., 32.16
by itself, and said to his s., 32.16
he made a feast for all his s., 40.20
of the chief baker among his s. 40.20
When Pharaoh was angry with his s., 41.10
good to Pharaoh and to all his s. 41.37
And Pharaoh said to his s., 41.38
but to buy food have your s. come. 42.10
honest men, your s. are not spies." 42.11
your s., are twelve brothers, the 42.13
be it from your s. that they 44.07
With whomever of your s. it be found, 44.09
has found out the guilt of your s.; 44.16
My lord asked his s., saying, 'Have you 44.19
Then you said to your s., 'Bring him 44.21
Then you said to your s., "Unless your 44.23
and your s. will bring down the 44.31
it pleased Pharaoh and his s. well. 45.16
'Your s. have been keepers of cattle 46.34
"Your s. are shepherds, as our 47.03
let your s. dwell in the land of 47.04
commanded his s. the physicians to 50.02
him went up all the s. of Pharaoh, 50.07
transgression of the s. of the God 50.17
and said, "Behold, we are your s." 50.18
"Why do you deal thus with your s.? Ex 5.15
No straw is given to your s., 5.16
And behold, your s. are beaten; 5.16
in the sight of Pharaoh and his s., 5.21
his rod before Pharaoh and his s., 7.10
Pharaoh and in the sight of his s., 7.20
houses of your s. and of your 8.03
on your people and on all your s."'" 8.04
and for your s. and for your 8.09
houses and your s. and your people; 8.11
on you and your s. and your people, 8.21
from his s., and from his people, 8.29
from his s., and from his people; 8.31
and upon your s. and your people, 9.14
LORD among the s. of Pharaoh made 9.20
But as for you and your s., 9.30
hardened his heart, he and his s. 9.34
his heart and the heart of his s., 10.01
of all your s. and of all the 10.06
And Pharaoh's s. said to him, "How 10.07
of Pharaoh's s. and in the sight 11.03
And all these your s. shall come 11.08
and all his s., and all the Egyptians; 12.30
Pharaoh and his s. was changed 14.05
thy s., to whom thou didst swear by 32.13
For they are my s., whom I brought Lev 25.42
For to me the people of Israel are s., 25.55
they are my s. whom I brought forth 25.55
and said to the s. of Balak, Num 22.18
ass, and his two s. were with him. 22.22
"Your s. have counted the men of 31.49
land for cattle; and your s. have cattle." 32.04
given to your s. for a possession; 32.05
"Your s. will do as my lord commands. 32.25
but your s. will pass over, every 32.27
has said to your s., so we will do. 32.31
Remember thy s., Abraham, Isaac, and Deu 9.27
and to all his s. and to all his 29.02
and have compassion on his s., 32.36
for he avenges the blood of his s., 32.43
and to all his s. and to all his 34.11
They said to Joshua, "We are your s." Jos 9.08
very far country your s. have come, 9.09
and say to them, "We are your s.; 9.11
told to your s. for a certainty 9.24
not relax your hand from your s.; 10.06
When he had gone, the s. came; Ju 3.24
So Gideon took ten men of his s., 6.27
and the young man with your s.; 19.19
me, 'You shall keep close by my s., Ru 2.21
orchards and give them to his s. 1Sa 8.14
it to his officers and to his s. 8.15
son, "Take one of the s. with you, 9.03
"Pray for your s. to the LORD your 12.19
And Saul's s. said to him, "Behold 16.15
Let our lord now command your s., 16.16
So Saul said to his s., "Provide for me 16.17
Philistine, and are you not s. of Saul? 17.08

SERVANTS (cont.)

kill me, then we will be your s.; 1Sa 17.09
you shall be our s. and serve us." 17.09
and also in the sight of Saul's s. 18.05
And Saul commanded his s., 18.22
in you, and all his s. love you; 18.22
And Saul's s. spoke those words in 18.23
And the s. of Saul told him, "Thus 18.24
And when his s. told David these 18.26
success than all the s. of Saul; 18.30
Jonathan his son and to all his s., 19.01
man of the s. of Saul was there 21.07
And the s. of Achish said to him, 21.11
Then said Achish to his s., 21.14
and all his s. were standing about 22.06
said to his s. who stood about him, 22.07
who stood by the s. of Saul, 22.09
among all your s. is so faithful 22.14
But the s. of the king would not 22.17
at hand to your s. and to your son 25.08
answered David's s., "Who is David? 25.10
There are many s. nowadays who are 25.10
And when the s. of David came to 25.40
wash the feet of the s. of my lord." 25.41
Then Saul said to his s., 28.07
And his s. said to him, "Behold, 28.07
But his s., together with the woman, 28.23
and she put it before Saul and his s.; 28.25
with the s. of your lord who came 29.10
and the s. of Ishbosheth the son of 2Sa 2.12
and the s. of David, went out and 2.13
and twelve of the s. of David. 2.15
were beaten before the s. of David. 2.17
of David's s. nineteen men besides 2.30
But the s. of David had slain of 2.31
Just then the s. of David arrived 3.22
And the king said to his s., 3.38
Moabites became s. to David and 8.02
Syrians became s. to David and 8.06
carried by the s. of Hadadezer, 8.07
all the Edomites became David's s. 8.14
sons and your s. shall till the 9.10
had fifteen sons and twenty s. 9.10
house became Mephibosheth's s. 9.12
sent by his s. to console him 10.02
And David's s. came into the land of 10.02
David sent his s. to you to search 10.03
So Hanun took David's s., and shaved off 10.04
kings who were s. of Hadadezer saw 10.19
and his s. with him, and all Israel; 11.01
house with all the s. of his lord, 11.09
Joab and the s. of my lord are 11.11
his couch with the s. of his lord, 11.13
and some of the s. of David among 11.17
shot at your s. from the wall; 11.24
some of the king's s. are dead; 11.24
And the s. of David feared to tell 12.18
saw that his s. were whispering 12.19
and David said to his s., "Is the child 12.19
Then his s. said to him, "What is 12.21
king and hs s. go with your 13.24
Then Absalom commanded his s., 13.28
So the s. of Absalom did to Amnon 13.29
and all his s. who were standing by 13.31
and all his s. wept very bitterly. 13.36
Then he said to his s., "See, Joab's field 14.30
So Absalom's s. set the field on 14.30
"Why have your s. set my field on 14.31
said to all his s. who were with 15.14
And the king's s. said to the king, 15.15
your s. are ready to do whatever my 15.15
And all his s. passed by him; 15.18
and at all the s. of King David; 16.06
said to Abishai and to all his s., 16.11
When Absalom's s. came to the woman 17.20
defeated there by the s. of David, 18.07
chanced to meet the s. of David. 18.09

shame the faces of all your s., 19.05
commanders and s. are nothing to 19.06
go out and speak kindly to your s.; 19.07
"Return, both you and all your s." 19.14
his fifteen sons and his twenty s., 19.17
take your lord's s. and pursue him, 20.06
went down together with his s., 21.15
of David and by the hand of his s. 21.22
king and his s. coming on toward 24.20
Therefore his s. said to him, "Let a 1Ki 1.02
not told your s. who should sit on 1.27
"Take with you the s. of your lord, 1.33
Moreover the king's s. came to 1.47
and made a feast for all his s. 3.15
of Tyre sent his s. to Solomon, 5.01
and my s. will join your s., 5.06
you for your s. such wages as you 5.06
My s. shall bring it down to the 5.09
love to thy s. who walk before 8.23
and judge thy s., condemning the 8.32
and forgive the sin of thy s., 8.36
And Hiram sent with the fleet his s., 9.27
together with the s. of Solomon; 9.27
and the attendance of his s., 10.05
Happy are these your s., 10.08
back to her own land, with her s. 10.13
Edomites of his father's s., 11.17
then they will be your s. for ever." 12.07
gave them into the hands of his s.; 15.18
nevertheless I will send my s. to 20.06
house and the houses of your s., 20.06
By the s. of the governors of the 20.14
Then he mustered the s. of the 20.15
The s. of the governors of the 20.17
the s. of the governors of the 20.19
And the s. of the king of Syria 20.23
And his s. said to him, "Behold now, 20.31
And the king of Israel said to his s., 22.03
"Let my s. go with your s. in 22.49
life of these fifty s. of yours, 2Ki 1.13
are with your s. fifty strong men; 2.16
the king of Israel's s. answered, 3.11
me one of the s. and one of the 4.22
But his s. came near and said to 5.13
and laid them upon two of his s.; 5.23
"Be pleased to go with your s." 6.03
he took counsel with his s., 6.08
he called his s. and said to them, 6.11
And one of his s. said, "None, my 6.12
in the night, and said to his s., 7.12
And one of his s. said, "Let some 7.13
the blood of my s. the prophets, 9.07
blood of all the s. of the LORD. 9.07
came out to the s. of his master, 9.11
His s. carried him in a chariot to 9.28
"We are your s., and we will do all 10.05
His s. arose and made a conspiracy, 12.20
his s., who struck him down, so that 12.21
he killed his s. who had slain the 14.05
sent to you by my s. the prophets." 17.13
spoken by all his s. the prophets. 17.23
among the least of my master's s., 18.24
speak to your s. in the Aramaic 18.26
When the s. of King Hezekiah came 19.05
with which the s. of the king of 19.06
LORD said by his s. the prophets, 21.10
And the s. of Amon conspired 21.23
"Your s. have emptied out the money 22.09
And his s. carried him dead in a 23.30
he spoke by his s. the prophets. 24.02
At that time the s. of Nebuchadnezzar 24.10
while his s. were besieging it; 24.11
and his s., and his princes, and his 24.12
the Levites, and the temple s. 1Ch 9.02
Moabites became s. to David and 18.02
and the Syrians became s. to David, 18.06
carried by the s. of Hadadezer, 18.07

SERVANTS (cont.)
all the Edomites became David's s. 1Ch 18.13
And David's s. came to Hanun in the 19.02
Have not his s. come to you to 19.03
So Hanun took David's s., 19.04
And when the s. of Hadadezer saw 19.19
of David and by the hand of his s. 20.08
the king, all of them my lord's s.? 21.03
know that your s. know how to cut 2Ch 2.08
And my s. will be with your s., 2.08
I will give you for your s., the hewers 2.10
has spoken, let him send to his s.; 2.15
love to thy s. who walk before 6.14
and judge thy s., requiting the 6.23
and forgive the sin of thy s., 6.27
sent him by his s. ships and s. familiar 8.18
together with the s. of Solomon, 8.18
and the attendance of his s., 9.04
Happy are these your s., who continually 9.07
Moreover the s. of Huram and the s. of 9.10
back to her own land, with her s. 9.12
to Tarshish with the s. of Huram; 9.21
then they will be your s. for ever." 10.07
Nevertheless they shall be s. to him, 12.08
his s. conspired against him because of 24.25
he killed his s. who had slain the 25.03
sent his s. to Jerusalem to Hezekiah 32.09
And his s. said still more against 32.16
And his s. conspired against him 33.24
committed to your s. they are doing. 34.16
and the king said to his s., 35.23
So his s. took him out of the 35.24
and they became s. to him and to 36.20
The temple s.: the sons of Ziha, the Ez 2.43
the sons of Solomon's s.: the sons of 2.55
All the temple s. and the sons of 2.58
of Solomon's s. were three hundred 2.58
and the temple s. lived in their 2.70
Your s., the men of the province 4.11
'We are the s. of the God of heaven 5.11
and gatekeepers, and the temple s. 7.07
the temple s., or other s. of this 7.24
the temple s. at the place Casiphia, 8.17
and twenty of the temple s., 8.20
command by thy s. the prophets, 9.11
for the people of Israel thy s., Neh 1.06
They are thy s. and thy people, whom 1.10
prayer of thy s. who delight to 1.11
and we his s. will arise and build; 2.20
and the temple s. living on Ophel 3.26
of the temple s. and of the 3.31
half of my s. worked on construction, 4.16
brethren nor my s. nor the men of 4.23
brethren and my s. are lending 5.10
Even their s. lorded it over the 5.15
and all my s. were gathered there 5.16
The temple s.: the sons of Ziha, the 7.46
The sons of Solomon's s.: the sons of 7.57
temple s. and the sons of Solomon's s. 7.60
the temple s., and all Israel, lived 7.73
and all his s. and all the people 9.10
the temple s., and all who have 10.28
the temple s., and the descendants 11.03
the descendants of Solomon's s. 11.03
But the temple s. lived on Ophel; 11.21
and Gishpa were over the temple s. 11.21
I set some of my s. over the gates, 13.19
banquet for all his princes and s., Est 1.03
Then the king's s. who attended him 2.02
banquet to all his princes and s.; 2.18
And all the king's s. who were at 3.02
Then the king's s. who were at the 3.03
"All the king's s. and the people of 4.11
the princes and the s. of the king. 5.11
The king's s. who attended him 6.03
So the king's s. told him, "Haman is 6.05
she-asses, and very many s.; Job 1.03
and slew the s. with the edge of 1.15
and burned up the sheep and the s., 1.16
and slew the s. with the edge of 1.17
Even in his s. he puts no trust, and 4.18
The LORD redeems the life of his s.; Ps 34.22
and his s. shall dwell there and 69.35
the children of his s. shall 69.36
bodies of thy s. to the birds of 79.02
blood of thy s. be known among the 79.10
How long? Have pity on thy s.! 90.13
Let thy work be manifest to thy s., 90.16
For thy s. hold her stones dear, and 102.14
The children of thy s. shall dwell 102.28
to deal craftily with his s. 105.25
Praise, O s. of the LORD, praise the 113.01
stand this day; for all things are thy s. 119.91
Behold, as the eyes of s. look to 123.02
all you s. of the LORD, who stand by 134.01
give praise, O s. of the LORD, 135.01
against Pharaoh and all his s.; 135.09
and have compassion on his s. 135.14
among the least of my master's s., Is 36.09
speak to your s. in Aramaic, for we 36.11
When the s. of King Hezekiah came 37.05
with which the s. of the king of 37.06
By your s. you have mocked the Lord, 37.24
heritage of the s. of the LORD and 54.17
and to be his s., every one who 56.06
Return for the sake of thy s., 63.17
and my s. shall dwell there. 65.09
my s. shall eat, but you shall be 65.13
behold, my s. shall drink, but you 65.13
behold, my s. shall rejoice, but you 65.13
behold, my s. shall sing for gladness 65.14
but his s. he will call by a 65.15
hand of the LORD is with his s., 66.14
sent all my s. the prophets to Jer 7.25
Her nobles send their s. for water; 14.03
and his s., and the people in this 21.07
and your s., and your people who 22.02
and their s., and their people. 22.04
to you all his s. the prophets, 25.04
his s., his princes, all his people, 25.19
the words of my s. the prophets 26.05
sent to you by my s. the prophets, 29.19
shall no more make s. of them. 30.08
sent to you all my s. the prophets, 35.15
nor any of his s. who heard all 36.24
offspring and his s. for their 36.31
he nor his s. nor the people of 37.02
to you or your s. or this people, 37.18
sent to you all my s. the prophets, 44.04
days by my s. the prophets of Eze 38.17
his inheritance to one of his s., 46.17
"Test your s. for ten days; Dan 1.12
to what you see deal with your s." 1.13
Tell your s. the dream, and we will 2.04
"Let the king tell his s. the dream, 2.07
s. of the Most High God, come forth, 3.26
his angel and delivered his s., 3.28
listened to thy s. the prophets, 9.06
before us by his s. the prophets. 9.10
his secret to his s. the prophets. Amo 3.07
I commanded my s. the prophets, Zec 1.06
And the s. of the householder came Mt 13.27
The s. said to him, 'Then do you 13.28
and he said to his s., "This is 14.02
to settle accounts with his s. 18.23
of his fellow s. who owed him a 18.28
When his fellow s. saw what had 18.31
he sent his s. to the tenants, to 21.34
tenants took his s. and beat one, 21.35
Again he sent other s., more than 21.36
and sent his s. to call those who 22.03
Again he sent other s., saying, 22.04
while the rest seized his s., 22.06
Then he said to his s., "The wedding 22.08

SERVANTS (cont.)

And those s. went out into the Mt 22.10
and begins to beat his fellow s., 24 49
called his s. and entrusted to 25.14
master of those s. came and settled 25.19
in the boat with the hired s., Mk 1.20
home and puts his s. in charge, 13.34
Blessed are those s. whom the Lk 12.37
them so, blessed are those s.! 12.38
father's hired s. have bread 15.17
treat me as one of your hired s." 15.19
But the father said to his s., 15.22
one of the s. and asked what this 15.26
you, say, 'We are unworthy s.; 17.10
Calling ten of his s., he gave them 19.13
power, he commanded these s., 19.15
His mother said to the s., Jn 2.05
from (though the s. who had drawn 2.09
his s. met him and told him that 4.51
No longer do I call you s., 15.15
Now the s. and officers had made a 18.18
One of the s. of the high priest, a 18.26
my s. would fight, that I might not 18.36
grant to thy s. to speak thy word Ac 4.29
two of his s. and a devout soldier 10.07
"These men are s. of the Most High 16.17
S. through whom you believed, as the 1Co 3.05
as s. of Christ and stewards of the 4.01
ourselves as your s. for Jesus' 2Co 4.05
but as s. of God we commend ourselves 6.04
strange if his s. also disguise 11.15
themselves as s. of righteousness. 11.15
Are they s. of Christ? I am a 11.23
through love be s. of one another. Gal 5.13
but as s. of Christ, doing the will Eph 6.06
s. of Christ Jesus, To all the Php 1.01
winds, and his s. flames of fire." Heb 1.07
for evil; but live as s. of God. 1Pe 2.16
S., be submissive to your masters 2.18
to show to his s. what must soon Rev 1.01
beguiling my s. to practice 2.20
of their fellow s. and their 6.11
have sealed the s. of our God upon 7.03
announced to his s. the prophets, 10.07
to be judged, for rewarding thy s., 11.18
avenged on her the blood of his s. 19.02
all you his s., you who fear him, 19.05
and his s. shall worship him; 22.03
to show his s. what must soon take 22.06

SERVANTS'

is no pasture for your s. flocks, Gen 47.04
of Pharaoh and into his s. houses, Ex 8.24
before the eyes of his s. maids, 2Sa 6.20
it,' so I will do for my s. sake, Is 65.08

SERVE

and it shall s. as food for you and Gen 6.21
on the nation which they s., and afterward 15.14
the elder shall s. the younger. 25.23
Let peoples s. you, and nations bow 27.29
and you shall s. your brother; 27.40
you therefore s. me for nothing? 29.15
"I will s. you seven years for your 29.18
Did I not s. with you for Rachel 29.25
people of Israel s. with rigor, Ex 1.13
work they made them s. with rigor. 1.14
"When you s. as midwife to the 1.16
you shall s. God upon this mountain 3.12
"Let my son go that he may s. me"; 4.23
that they may s. me in the wilderness 7.16
my people go, that they may s. me. 8.01
my people go, that they may s. me. 8.20
my people go, that they may s. me. 9.01
my people go, that they may s. me. 9.13
my people go, that they may s. me. 10.03
that they may s. the LORD their God 10 07
s. the LORD your God; 10.08
and s. the LORD, for that is what 10.11
Moses, and said, "Go, s. the LORD; 10.24
take of them to s. the LORD our 10 26
what we must s. the LORD until we 10.26
and go, s. the LORD, as you have said 12.31
alone and let us s. the Egyptians'? 14.12
for us to s. the Egyptians than to 14.12
not bow down to them or s. them; 20 05
he shall s. six years, and in the 21.02
and he shall s. him for life. 21.06
nor s. them, nor do according to 23.24
You shall s. the LORD your God, and 23.25
for if you s. their gods, it will 23.33
to s. me as priests—Aaron and 28.01
and his sons to s. me as priests. 28.04
that they may s. me as priests. 28.41
that they may s. me as priests. 29.01
consecrate, to s. me as priests. 29.44
that they may s. me as priests. 30.30
of his sons to s. as priests. 39.41
him, that he may s. me as priest. 40.13
that they may s. me as priests: and 40.15
presented to s. as priests of the Lev 7.35
shall not make him s. as a slave: 25.39
He shall s. with you until the year 25.40
of the service and s. no more, Num 8.25
they shall s. you for remembrance 10.10
and you will s. as eyes for us. 10.31
and you shall s. I give your 18.07
for their service which they s., 18.21
away and worship them and s. them, Deu 4.19
And there you will s. gods of wood 4.28
not bow down to them or s. them; 5.09
you shall s. him, and swear by his 6.13
following me, to s. other gods; 7.04
neither shall you s. their gods, 7.16
other gods and s. them and worship 8.19
to s. the LORD your God with all 10.12
you shall s. him and cleave to him, 10.20
and to s. him with all your heart 11.13
turn aside and s. other gods and 11.16
did these nations s. their gods? 12.30
not known, 'and let us s. them,' 13.02
and you shall s. him and cleave to 13.04
'Let us go and s. other gods,' which 13.06
'Let us go and s. other gods,' which 13.13
he shall s. you six years, and in 15.12
labor for you and shall s. you. 20.11
to go after other gods to s. them. 28.14
and there you shall s. other gods, 28.36
"Because you did not s. the LORD 28.47
therefore you shall s. your enemies 28.48
and there you shall s. other gods, 28.64
God to go and s. the gods of those 29.18
to worship other gods and s. them, 30.17
turn to other gods and s. them, 31.20
and to s. him with all your heart Jos 22.05
or s. them, or bow down yourselves 23.07
and go and s. other gods and bow 23.16
and s. him in sincerity and in 24.14
and in Egypt, and s. the LORD. 24.14
if you be unwilling to s. the LORD, 24.15
choose this day whom you will s., 24.15
and my house, we will s. the LORD. 24.15
forsake the LORD, to s. other gods; 24.16
therefore we also will s. the LORD, 24.18
the people, "You cannot s. the LORD, 24.18
the people, "You cannot s. the LORD; 24.19
the LORD and s. foreign gods, 24.20
"Nay, but we will s. the LORD." 24.21
have chosen the LORD, to s. him." 24.22
"The LORD our God we will s., 24.24
of Shechem, that we should s. him? Ju 9.28
his officer s. the men of Hamor 9.28
Why then should we s. him? 9.28

SERVE (cont.)

Abimelech, that we should s. him?' Ju 9.38
the LORD, and did not s. him. 10.06
and s. him only, and he will deliver 1Sa 7.03
treaty with us, and we will s. you. 11.01
our enemies, and we will s. thee. 12.10
the LORD and s. him and hearken to 12.14
but s. the LORD with all your heart 12.20
and s. him faithfully with all your 12.24
shall be our servants and s. us. 17.09
LORD saying, 'Go, s. other gods.' 26.19
And again, whom should I s.? 2Sa 16.19
your father, so I will s. you." 16.19
but go and s. other gods and 1Ki 9.06
yoke upon us, and we will s. you." 12.04
to this people today and s. them, 12.07
whom I s., were it not that I have 2Ki 3.14
whom I s., I will receive none." 5.16
but Jehu will s. him much. 10.18
to them or s. them or sacrifice to 17.35
of Assyria, and would not s. him. 18.07
and s. the king of Babylon, and it 25.24
and s. him with a whole heart and 1Ch 28.09
and go and s. other gods and 2Ch 7.19
yoke upon us, and we will s. you. 10.04
Levites will s. you as officers. 19.11
and s. the LORD your God, that his 30.08
Judah to s. the LORD the God of 33.16
were in Israel s. the LORD their 34.33
Now s. the LORD your God and his 35.03
They did not s. thee in their Neh 9.35
Almighty, that we should s. him? Job 21.15
If they hearken and s. him, 36.11
"Is the wild ox willing to s. you? 39.09
S. the LORD with fear, with trembling Ps 2.11
Posterity shall s. him; men shall 22.30
before him, all nations s. him! 72.11
S. the LORD with gladness! 100.02
with which you were made to s., Is 14.03
Their webs will not s. as clothing; 59.06
that will not s. you shall perish; 60.12
and you said, 'I will not s.' Yea, upon Jer 2.20
so you shall s. strangers in a land 5.19
gone after other gods to s. them; 11.10
other gods to s. them and worship 13.10
I will make you s. your enemies in 15.14
there you shall s. other gods day 16.13
I will make you s. your enemies in 17.04
his neighbor s. him for nothing, 22.13
other gods to s. and worship them, 25.06
nations shall s. the king of 25.11
the beasts of the field to s. him. 27.06
nations shall s. him and his son 27.07
will not s. this Nebuchadnezzar 27.08
'You shall not s. the king of 27.09
of the king of Babylon and s. him, 27.11
and s. him and his people, and live. 27.12
which will not s. the king of 27.13
'You shall not s. the king of 27.14
s. the king of Babylon and live. 27.17
of Babylon, and they shall s. him, 28.14
But they shall s. the LORD their 30.09
not go after other gods to s. them, 35.15
not be afraid to s. the Chaldeans. 40.09
and s. the king of Babylon, and it 40.09
incense and s. other gods that 44.03
Go s. every one of you his idols, Eze 20.39
of them, shall s. me in the land; 20.40
the temple to s. as supports for 41.06
attend on the people, to s. them. 44.11
to s. me as priest, nor come near 44.13
competent to s. in the king's Dan 1.04
they do not s. your gods or worship 3.12
that you do not s. my gods or 3.14
our God whom we s. is able to 3.17
we will not s. your gods or 3.18
rather than s. and worship any god 3.28
whom you s. continually, deliver you 6.16
whom you s. continually, been able 6.20
and languages should s. him; 7.14
dominions shall s. and obey them.' 7.27
of the LORD and s. him with one Zep 3.09
You have said, 'It is vain to s. God. Mal 3.14
God and one who does not s. him. 3.18
your God and him only shall you s.'" Mt 4.10
"No one can s. two masters; 6.24
You cannot s. God and mammon. 6.24
came not to be served but to s., 20.28
came not to be served but to s., Mk 10.45
might s. him without fear, Lk 1.74
God, and him only shall you s. 4.08
my sister has left me to s. alone? 10.40
and he will come and s. them. 12.37
No servant can s. two masters; 16.13
You cannot s. God and mammon." 16.13
me, and gird yourself and s. me, 17.08
the word of God to s. tables. Ac 6.02
judge the nation which they s., 7.07
appoint you to s. and bear witness 26.16
whom I s. with my spirit in the Rom 1.09
so that we s. not under the old 7.06
I of myself s. the law of God with 7.25
with my flesh I s. the law of sin. 7.25
"The elder will s. the younger." 9.12
aglow with the Spirit, s. the Lord. 12.11
persons do not s. our Lord Christ, 16.18
and those who s. at the altar share 1Co 9.13
from them in order to s. you. 2Co 11.08
to s. a living and true God, 1Th 1.09
blameless let them s. as deacons. 1Ti 3.10
for those who s. well as deacons 3.13
they must s. all the better since 6.02
God whom I s. with a clear conscience, 2Ti 1.03
that he might s. me on your behalf Phm 1.13
ministering spirits sent forth to s., Heb 1.14
They s. a copy and shadow of the 8.05
dead works to s. the living God. 9.14
which those who s. the tent have 13.10
s. as an example by undergoing a Jud 1.07
and s. him day and night within his Rev 7.15

SERVED

Twelve years they had s. Chedorlaomer, Gen 14.04
So Jacob s. seven years for Rachel, 29.20
and s. Laban for another seven 29.30
my children for whom I have s. you, 30.26
yourself know how I have s. you, 30.29
that I have s. your father with 31.06
I s. you fourteen years for your 31.41
himself he said, "Let food be s." 43.31
They s. him by himself, and them by 43.32
and Ithamar s. as priests in the Num 3.04
all who s. in the tent of meeting, 4.37
all who s. in the tent of meeting, 4.41
you shall dispossess s. their gods, Deu 12.02
servant he has s. you six years. 15.18
and has gone and s. other gods and 17.03
and went and s. other gods and 29.26
and of Nahor; and they s. other gods. Jos 24.02
your fathers s. beyond the River, 24.14
your fathers s. in the region 24.15
And Israel s. the LORD all the days 24.31
And the people s. the LORD all the Ju 2.07
sight of the LORD and s. the Baals; 2.11
and s. the Baals and the Ashtaroth. 2.13
their sons; and they s. their gods. 3.06
of Israel s. Cushanrishathaim 3.08
of Israel s. Eglon the king of 3.14
and s. the Baals and the Ashtaroth, 10.06
our God and have s. the Baals. 10.10
have forsaken me and s. other gods; 10.13
from among them and s. the LORD; 10.16
the women who s. at the entrance 1Sa 2.22
Ashtaroth, and they s. the LORD only. 7.04

SERVED (cont.)

and have s. the Baals and the 1Sa 12.10
the young man who s. him and said, 2Sa 13.17
As I have s. your father, so I will 16.19
people whom I had not known s. me. 22.44
tribute and s. Solomon all the 1Ki 4.21
and worshiped them and s. them; 9.09
and went and s. Baal, and worshiped 16.31
He s. Baal and worshiped him, and 22.53
to them, "Ahab s. Baal a little; 2Ki 10.18
and they s. idols, of which the LORD 17.12
the host of heaven, and s. Baal. 17.16
LORD but also s. their own gods, 17.33
and also s. their graven images; 17.41
the host of heaven, and s. them. 21.03
and s. the idols that his father 21.21
the idols that his father s., 21.21
(it was he who s. as priest in the 1Ch 6.10
These are the men who s. and their sons. 6.33
officers who s. the king in all 27.01
of the divisions that s. the king, 28.01
and worshiped them and s. them; 2Ch 7.22
and s. the Asherim and the idols. 24.18
the host of heaven, and s. them. 33.03
his father had made, and s. them. 33.22
Drinks were s. in golden goblets, Est 1.07
eunuchs who s. King Ahasuerus as 1.10
people whom I had not known s. me. Ps 18.43
They s. their idols, which became a 106.36
forsaken me and s. foreign gods in Jer 5.19
which they have loved and s., 8.02
gods and have s. and worshiped 16.11
worshiped other gods and s. them. 22.09
to you and has s. you six years; 34.14
bodyguard who s. the king of 52.12
a thousand thousands s. him, Dan 7.10
plunder for those who s. them. Zec 2.09
left her, and she rose and s. him. Mt 8.15
man came not to be s. but to serve, 20.28
fever left her; and she s. them. Mk 1.31
came not to be s. but to serve, 10.45
immediately she rose and s. them. Lk 4.39
Lo, these many years I have s. you, 15.29
Martha s., but Lazarus was one of Jn 12.02
after he had s. the counsel of God Ac 13.36
nor is he s. by human hands, as 17.25
worshiped and s. the creature Rom 1.25
me has really s. to advance the Php 1.12
a father he has s. with me in the 2.22
no one has ever s. at the altar. Heb 7.13

SERVES

as a man spares his son who s. him. Mal 3.17
between one who s. God and one who 3.18
and the leader as one who s. Lk 22.26
who sits at table, or one who s.? 22.27
But I am among you as one who s. 22.27
"Every man s. the good wine first, Jn 2.10
If any one s. me, he must follow me; 12.26
If any one s. me, the Father will 12.26
our wickedness s. to show the Rom 3.05
he who thus s. Christ is acceptable 14.18
Who s. as a soldier at his own 1Co 9.07

SERVICE

you know the s. which I have given Gen 30.26
he entered the s. of Pharaoh king 41.46
their lives bitter with hard s., Ex 1.14
promised, you shall keep this s. 12.25
you, 'What do you mean by this s.?' 12.26
shall keep this s. in this month. 13.05
it for the s. of the tent of 30.16
his sons, for their s. as priests, 31.10
yourselves for the s. of the LORD, 32.29
his sons, for their s. as priests." 35.19
of meeting, and for all its s., 35.21
utensils for the s. of the tabernacle, 39.40
to the years of s. due from him he Lev 25.52
all the s. pertaining to these. Num 3.26
all the s. pertaining to these. 3.31
all the s. pertaining to these. 3.36
old, all who can enter the s., 4.03
This is the s. of the sons of 4.04
vessels of the s. which are used 4.12
which are used for the s. there, 4.14
them, all who can enter for s., 4.23
This is the s. of the families of 4.24
and all the equipment for their s.; 4.26
All the s. of the sons of the 4.27
This is the s. of the families of 4.28
every one that can enter the s., 4.30
whole of their s. in the tent of 4.31
This is the s. of the families of 4.33
whole of their s. in the tent of 4.33
every one that could enter the s., 4.35
could enter the s. for work in the 4.39
every one that could enter the s., 4.43
do the work of s. and the work of 4.47
in doing the s. of the tent of 7.05
to each man according to his s." 7.05
of Gershon, according to their s.; 7.07
of Merari, according to their s., 7.08
be theirs to do the s. of the LORD. 8.11
go in to do s. at the tent of 8.15
to do the s. for the people of 8.19
in to do their s. in the tent of 8.22
the work in the s. of the tent of 8.24
the work of the s. and serve no 8.25
charge, and they shall do no s. 8.26
to do s. in the tabernacle of the 16.09
meeting, for all the s. of the tent; 18.04
to do the s. of the tent of meeting 18.06
for their s. which they serve, 18.21
their s. in the tent of meeting. 18.21
shall do the s. of the tent of 18.23
return for your s. in the tent of 18.31
who had come from s. in the war. 31.14
have done in the s. of their gods, Deu 20.18
do perform the s. of the LORD in Jos 22.27
came to Saul, and entered his s. 1Sa 16.21
saying, "Let David remain in my s., 16.22
deeds have been of good s. to you; 19.04
day I entered your s. until now, 29.08
the hard s. of your father and his 1Ki 12.04
of bronze used in the temple s., 2Ki 25.14
hundred and sixty, ready for s. 1Ch 5.18
charge of the s. of song in the 6.31
performed their s. in due order. 6.32
for all the s. of the tabernacle 6.48
two hundred, ready for s. in war. 7.11
for s. in war, was twenty-six 7.40
the work of the s. of the house of 9.13
in charge of the work of the s., 9.19
had charge of the utensils of s., 9.28
of the temple free from other s., 9.33
officials in the s. of the king. 18.17
work for the s. of the house of 23.24
or any of the things for its s."— 23.26
Aaron for the s. of the house of 23.28
work for the s. of the house of 23.28
for the s. of the house of the LORD 23.32
the appointed duties in their s. 24.03
duty in their s. to come into the 24.19
chiefs of the s. also set apart 25.01
apart for the s. certain of the 25.01
lyres for the s. of the house of 25.06
able men qualified for the s.; 26.08
LORD and for the s. of the king. 26.30
the work of the s. in the house of 28.13
vessels for the s. in the house of 28.13
for all golden vessels for each s., 28.14
of silver vessels for each s., 28.14
use of each lampstand in the s., 28.15
work for the s. of the house of 28.20

SERVICE (cont.)
for all the s. of the house of God 1Ch 28.21
who has skill for any kind of s.; 28.21
They gave for the s. of the house 29.07
of the priests for their s., 2Ch 8.14
the hard s. of your father and his 10.04
may know my s. and the service of 12.08
service and the s. of kingdoms 12.08
of Aaron, and Levites for their s. 13.10
a volunteer for the s. of the LORD, 17.16
These were in the s. of the king, 17.19
both for the s. and for the burnt 24.14
Thus the s. of the house of the 29.35
good skill in the s. of the LORD. 30.22
division, each according to his s., 31.02
for their s. according to their 31.16
undertook in the s. of the house of 31.21
who did work in every kind of s.; 34.13
them in the s. of the house of the 35.02
When the s. had been prepared for, 35.10
not need to depart from their s., 35.15
So all the s. of the LORD was 35.16
for the s. of God at Jerusalem, as Ez 6.18
you for the s. of the house of 7.19
shekel for the s. of the house of Neh 10.32
stood opposite them in the s. 12.09
performed the s. of their God and 12.45
God and the s. of purification, as 12.45
the house of my God and for his s. 13.14
that were used in the king's s., Est 8.10
that were used in the king's s., 8.14
"Has not man a hard s. upon earth, Job 7.01
All the days of my s. I would wait, 14.14
and the hard s. with which you Is 14.03
you must set him free from your s. Jer 34.14
of bronze used in the temple s.; 52.18
to do all its s. and all that is to Eze 44.14
there Israel did s. for a wife, Hos 12.12
And when his time of s. was ended, Lk 1.23
think he is offering s. to God. Jn 16.02
if s., in our serving; he who teaches, Rom 12.07
in the priestly s. of the gospel 15.16
also to be of s. to them in 15.27
and that my s. for Jerusalem may be 15.31
in the temple s. get their food 1Co 9.13
and there are varieties of s., 12.05
themselves to the s. of the saints; 16.15
and fellow worker in your s.; 2Co 8.23
rendering of this s. not only 9.12
Under the test of this s., 9.13
rendering s. with a good will as to Eph 6.07
his life to complete your s. to me. Php 2.30
by appointing me to his s., 1Ti 1.12
by their s. are believers and 6.02
know all the s. he rendered at 2Ti 1.18
No soldier on s. gets entangled in 2.04
high priest in the s. of God, Heb 2.17
priest stands daily at his s., 10.11
whoever renders s., as one who 1Pe 4.11
you render any s. to the brethren, 3Jn 1.05
their journey as befits God's s. 1.06
and faith and s. patient Rev 2.19

SERVING
in return for s. me another seven Gen 29.27
we have let Israel go from s. us?" Ex 14.05
Gershonites, in s. and bearing burdens: Num 4.24
each to his task of s. or carrying; 4.49
s. them and bowing down to them; Ju 2.19
and s. the Baals and the Asheroth. 3.07
forsaking me and s. other gods, 1Sa 8.08
them out from s. as priests of the 2Ch 11.14
was your sail, s. as your ensign; Eze 27.07
the temple, and s. in the temple; 44.11
Now while he was s. as priest Lk 1.08
Martha was distracted with much s.; 10.40
s. the Lord with all humility and Ac 20.19
if service, in our s.; he who teaches, Rom 12.07
as s. the Lord and not men, Col 3.23
you are s. the Lord Christ. 3.24
for he is very useful in s. me. 2Ti 4.11
for his sake is s. the saints, Heb 6.10
that they were s. not themselves 1Pe 1.12

SERVITUDE
because the s. was heavy upon this Neh 5.18
an iron yoke of s. to Nebuchadnezzar Jer 28.14
because of affliction and hard s.; Lam 1.03

SET
And God s. them in the firmament of Gen 1.17
and s. the door of the ark in its 6.16
dove found no place to s. her foot, 8.09
I s. my bow in the cloud, and it 9.13
and they s. forth to go to the land 12.05
and they s. him on the way, with his 12.20
prepared, and s. it before them; 18.08
Then the men s. out from there, and 18.16
with them to s. them on their way. 18.16
him forth and s. him outside the 19.16
Abraham s. seven ewe lambs of the 21.28
ewe lambs which you have s. apart? 21.29
Then food was s. before him to eat; 24.33
and Isaac s. them on their way, and 26.31
that night, because the sun had s. 28.11
was a ladder s. up on the earth, 28.12
his head and s. it up for a pillar 28.18
which I have s. up for a pillar, 28.22
and he s. a distance of three days' 30.36
He s. the rods which he had peeled 30.38
and s. the faces of the flocks 30.40
and s. his sons and his wives on 31.17
and s. his face toward the hill 31.21
S. it here before my kinsmen and 31.37
and s. it up as a pillar. 31.45
which I have s. between you and me. 31.51
And Jacob s. up a pillar in the 35.14
and Jacob s. up a pillar upon her 35.20
and s. him over the land of Egypt. 41.33
I have s. you over all the land of 41.41
Thus he s. him over all the land of 41.43
back to you and s. him before you, 43.09
that I may s. my eyes upon him.' 44.21
Then Jacob s. out from Beersheba; 46.05
and s. him before Pharaoh, and Jacob 47.07
Therefore they s. taskmasters over Ex 1.11
and his sons and s. them on an ass, 4.20
taskmasters had s. over them, 5.14
that day I will s. apart the land 8.22
And the LORD s. a time, saying, 9.05
you shall s. apart to the LORD all 13.12
They s. out from Elim, and all the 16.01
And when they s. out from Rephidim 19.02
and s. before them all these words 19.07
And you shall s. bounds for the 19.12
'S. bounds about the mountain, and 19.23
which you shall s. before them. 21.01
And I will s. your bounds from the 23.31
And you shall s. the bread of the 25.30
lamps shall be s. up so as to give 25.37
outmost curtain in the first s.; 26.04
outmost curtain in the second s. 26.04
curtain that is in the second s.; 26.05
curtain that is outmost in one s., 26.10
which is outmost in the second s. 26.10
And you shall s. the table outside 26.35
And you shall s. it under the ledge 27.05
a lamp may be s. up to burn 27.20
And you shall s. the two stones 28.12
And you shall s. in it four rows of 28.17
they shall be s. in gold filigree. 28.20
and you shall s. the turban on his 29.06
people, that they are s. on evil. 32.22
onyx stones and stones to be s., 35.27

SET (cont.)
outmost curtain of the first s.; Ex 36.11
outmost curtain of the second s.; 36.11
curtain that was in the second s.; 36.12
the outsmost curtain of the one s., 36.17
And he s. them on the shoulder-pieces 39.07
And the s. in it four rows of 39.10
with the lamps s. and all its 39.37
and s. its arrangements in order; 40.04
the lampstand, and s. up its lamps. 40.04
and s. up the screen for the door 40.05
You shall s. the altar of burnt 40.06
And you shall s. up the court round 40.08
and s. up its frames, and put in its 40.18
and s. the mercy seat above on the 40.20
and s. up the veil of the screen, 40.21
and s. the bread in order on it 40.23
and s. up the lamps before the LORD 40.25
And he s. the altar of burnt 40.29
And he s. the laver between the 40.30
and s. up the screen of the gate of 40.33
And he s. the turban upon his head, Lev 8.09
he s. the golden plate, the holy 8.09
him shall s. the man who is to be 14.11
and s. them before the LORD at the 16.07
I will s. my face against that 17.10
I myself will s. my face against 20.03
then I will s. my face against that 20.05
I will s. my face against that 20.06
which I have s. apart for you to 20.25
And you shall s. them in two rows, 24.06
day Aaron shall s. it in order 24.08
you shall not s. up a figured 26.01
I will s. my face against you, and 26.17
When the tabernacle is to s. out, Num 1.51
pitched, the Levites shall s. it up. 1.51
they shall s. out first on the 2.09
They shall s. out second. 2.16
"Then the tent of meeting shall s. out, 2.17
so shall they s. out, each in 2.17
They shall s. out third on the 2.24
They shall s. out last, standard by 2.31
and so they s. out, every one in his 2.34
and s. them before Aaron the priest, 3.06
When the camp is s. out, 4.05
and s. her before the LORD; 5.16
priest shall s. the woman before 5.18
then he shall s. the woman before 5.30
When you s. up the lamps, the seven 8.02
he s. up its lamps to give light in 8.03
day that the tabernacle was s. up, 9.15
that the people of Israel s. out; 9.17
LORD the people of Israel s. out, 9.18
of the LORD, and did not s. out. 9.19
command of the LORD they s. out. 9.20
they s. out, or if it continued for 9.21
the cloud was taken up they s. out. 9.21
remained in camp and did not s. out; 9.22
when it was taken up they s. out. 9.22
command of the LORD they s. out; 9.23
are on the east side shall s. out. 10.05
are on the south side shall s. out. 10.06
blown whenever they are to s. out. 10.06
of Israel s. out by stages from 10.12
They s. out for the first time at 10.13
men of Judah s. out first by their 10.14
who carried the tabernacle, s. out. 10.17
camp of Reuben s. out by their 10.18
Then the Kohathites s. out, 10.21
tabernacle was s. up before their 10.21
men of Ephraim s. out by their 10.22
s. out by their companies; 10.25
to their hosts, when they s. out. 10.28
So they s. out from the mount of 10.33
whenever they s. out from the camp. 10.34
And whenever the ark s. out, 10.35
people did not s. out on the march 12.15
After that the people s. out from 12.16
tomorrow and s. out for the 14.25
From Mount Hor they s. out by the 21.04
fiery serpent, and s. it on a pole; 21.08
serpent, and s. it on a pole; 21.09
And the people of Israel s. out, 21.10
And they s. out from Oboth, and 21.11
From there they s. out, and encamped 21.12
From there they s. out, and encamped 21.13
Then the people of Israel s. out, 22.01
but s. his face toward the wilderness 24.01
and your nest is s. in the rock; 24.21
They s. out from Rameses in the 33.03
of Israel s. out from Rameses, and 33.05
And they s. out from Succoth, and 33.06
And they s. out from Etham, and 33.07
And they s. out from before Hahiroth, 33.08
And they s. out from Marah, and came 33.09
And they s. out from Elim, and 33.10
And they s. out from the Red Sea, 33.11
And they s. out from the wilderness 33.12
And they s. out from Dophkah, and 33.13
And they s. out from Alush, and 33.14
And they s. out from Rephidim, and 33.15
And they s. out from the wilderness 33.16
And they s. out from Kibrothhattaavah, 33.17
And they s. out from Hazeroth, and 33.18
And they s. out from Rithmah, and 33.19
And they s. out from Rimmonperez, 33.20
And they s. out from Libnah, and 33.21
And they s. out from Rissah, and 33.22
And they s. out from Kehelathah, and 33.23
And they s. out from Mount Shepher, 33.24
And they s. out from Haradah, and 33.25
And they s. out from Makheloth, and 33.26
And they s. out from Tahath, and 33.27
And they s. out from Terah, and 33.28
And they s. out from Mithkah, and 33.29
And they s. out from Hashmonah, and 33.30
And they s. out from Moseroth, and 33.31
And they s. out from Benejaakan, and 33.32
And they s. out from Horhaggidgad, 33.33
And they s. out from Jotbathah, and 33.34
And they s. out from Abronah, and 33.35
And they s. out from Eziongeber, and 33.36
And they s. out from Kadesh, and 33.37
And they s. out from Mount Hor, and 33.41
And they s. out from Zalmonah, and 33.42
And they s. out from Punon, and 33.43
And they s. out from Oboth, and 33.44
And they s. out from Ilyim, and 33.45
And they s. out from Dibongad, and 33.46
And they s. out from Almondiblathaim, 33.47
And they s. out from the mountains 33.48
Behold, I have s. the land before Deu 1.08
and s. them as heads over you, 1.15
"And we s. out from Horeb, and went 1.19
your God has s. the land before 1.21
law which I s. before you this day? 4.08
Then Moses s. apart three cities in 4.41
law which Moses s. before the 4.44
that the LORD s. his love upon you 7.07
time the LORD s. apart the tribe 10.08
yet the LORD s. his heart in love 10.15
"Behold, I s. before you this day a 11.26
you shall s. the blessing on Mount 11.29
ordinances which I s. before you 11.32
God chooses, to s. his name there, 14.24
And you shall not s. up a pillar, 16.22
'I will s. a king over me, like all, 17.14
you may indeed s. as king over you 17.15
you shall s. as king over you; 17.15
you shall s. apart three cities for 19.02
You shall s. apart three cities. 19.07
which the men of old have s. 19.14
and s. not the guilt of innocent 21.08
and s. it down before the altar of 26.04

SET (cont.)

'And you shall s. it down before Deu 26.10
that he will s. you high above all 26.19
you shall s. up large stones, and 27.02
you shall s. up these stones, 27.04
your God will s. you high above 28.01
and your king whom you s. over you, 28.36
not venture to s. the sole of her 28.56
which I have s. before you, and you 30.01
"See, I have s. before you this day 30.15
that I have s. before you life and 30.19
at the s. time of the year of 31.10
Joshua rose and s. out from Jos 3.01
then you shall s. out from your 3.03
So, when the people s. out from 3.14
And Joshua s. up twelve stones in 4.09
the Jordan, Joshua s. up in Gilgal. 4.20
and s. them outside the camp of 6.23
son shall he s. up its gates. 6.26
you shall s. the city on fire, doing 8.08
and s. them in ambush between 8.12
made haste to s. the city on fire. 8.19
on the day we s. forth to come to 9.12
of Israel s. out and reached their 9.17
and s. men by it to guard them; 10.18
and they s. great stones against 10.27
since you have s. me in the land of 15.19
which were s. apart for the 16.09
and s. up the tent of the meeting there 18.01
that they may s. out and go up and 18.04
in the land and s. down in a book 18.09
So they s. apart Kedesh in Galilee 20.07
and s. it up there under the oak in 24.26
the sword, and s. the city on fire. Ju 1.08
since you have s. me in the land of 1.15
From Ephraim they s. out thither 5.14
my present, and s. it before thee. 6.18
dog laps, you shall s. by himself; 7.05
when they had just s. the watch; 7.19
the LORD s. every man's sword 7.22
and they s. the stronghold on fire 9.49
And when he had s. fire to the 15.05
s. forth from Zorah and Eshtaol, 18.11
And the Danites s. up the graven 18.30
So they s. up Micah's graven image 18.31
So Israel s. men in ambush round 20.29
and s. themselves in array against 20.30
their place and s. themselves in array at 20.33
whom they had s. against Gibeah. 20.36
which they found they s. on fire. 20.48
So she s. out from the place where Ru 1.07
So she s. forth and went and 2.03
and on them he has s. the world. 1Sa 2.08
years old and his eyes were s., 4.15
of Dagon and s. it up beside Dagon 5.02
and s. them upon the great stone; 6.15
which they s. down the ark of the 6.18
a stone and s. it up between 7.12
journey on which we have s. out." 9.06
do not s. your mind on them, for 9.20
portion and s. them before Saul; 9.24
what was kept is s. before you. 9.24
but s. a king over us.' now therefore 10.19
the LORD has s. a king over you. 12.13
he s. up a monument for himself and 15.12
so that Saul s. him over the men of 18.05
let me s. a morsel of bread before 28.22
So David s. out with his men early 29.11
So David s. out, and the six hundred 30.09
and s. up the throne of David over 2Sa 3.10
s. out, and about the heat of the 4.05
and s. it in its place, inside the 6.17
the battle was s. against him both 10.09
"S. Uriah in the forefront of the 11.15
they s. food before him, and he ate. 12.20
and s. them to labor with saws and 12.31
lord the king will s. me at rest'; 14.17
go and s. it on fire." So Akalom's 14.30
servants s. the field on fire. 14.30
your servants s. my field on fire?" 14.31
and they s. down the ark of God, 15.24
and I will s. out and pursue David 17.01
And he s. his house in order, and 17.23
Now Absalom had s. Amasa over the 17.25
and s. over them commanders of 18.01
had taken and s. up for himself 18.18
but you s. your servant among those 19.28
beyond the s. time which had been 20.05
and s. me secure on the heights. 22.34
And David s. him over his bodyguard 23.23
whom I will s. upon your throne in 1Ki 5.05
your servants such wages as you s.; 5.06
to s. there the ark of the covenant 6.19
to s. upon the tops of the pillars; 7.16
He s. up the pillars at the vestibule 7.21
he s. up the pillar on the south 7.21
and he s. up the pillar on the 7.21
the sea was s. upon them, and all 7.25
the panels were s. in the frames 7.28
that were s. in the frames were 7.29
And he s. the stands, gve on the 7.39
and he s. the sea on the southeast 7.39
"The LORD has s. the sun in the 8.12
statutes which I have s. before you, 9.06
in you and s. you on the throne of 10.09
They s. out from Midian and came to 11.18
And he s. one in Bethel, and the 12.29
and s. up its gates at the cost of 16.34
and s. Naboth on high among the 21.09
and s. two base fellows opposite 21.10
and s. Naboth on high among the 21.12
and when one is full, s. it aside." 2Ki 4.04
So she s. out, and came to the man 4.25
"S. on the great pot, and boil 4.38
"How am I to s. this before a 4.43
So he s. it before them. And they ate, 4.44
S. bread and water before them, that 6.22
you will s. on fire their fortresses, 8.12
and s. up a king of their own. 8.20
and Ahaziah king of Judah s. out, 9.21
sons and s. him on his father's 10.03
Then he s. out and went to Samaria. 10.12
captains who were s. over the army, 11.15
and s. it beside the altar on the 12.09
But when Hazael s. his face to go 12.17
they s. up for themselves pillars 17.10
on your part to s. riders upon 18.23
he has s. out to fight against you," 19.09
'S. your house in order; for you shall die, 20.01
he had made he s. in the house of 21.07
And David s. him over his bodyguard 1Ch 11.25
and s. it inside the tent which 16.01
as he went to s. up his monument at 18.03
the battle was s. against him both 19.10
And when David s. the battle in 19.17
and s. them to labor with saws and 20.03
and he s. stonecutters to prepare 22.02
Now s. your mind and heart to seek 22.19
Aaron was s. apart to consecrate 23.13
service also s. apart for the 25.01
He s. up the pillars in front of 2Ch 3.17
the sea was s. upon them, and all 4.04
and s. five on the south side, and 4.06
and s. them in the temple, five on 4.07
and he s. the sea at the southeast 4.10
And there I have s. the ark, 6.11
and had s. it in the court; 6.13
thou hast promised to s. thy name, 6.20
commandments which I have s. before you, 7.19
in you and s. you on his throne as 9.08
And those who had s. their hearts 11.16
for he did not s. his heart to 12.14
s. out the showbread on the table 13.11
and s. garrisons in the land of 17.02

SET (cont.)

and have s. your heart to seek God." 2Ch 19.03
and s. himself to seek the LORD, and 20.03
the LORD s. an ambush against the 20.22
had not yet s. their hearts upon 20.33
and s. up a king of their own. 21.08
and he s. all the people as a guard 23.10
captains who were s. over the army, 23.14
And they s. the king upon the royal 23.20
and s. it outside the gate of the 24.08
and s. them by fathers' houses 25.05
and s. them up as his gods, and 25.14
He s. himself to seek God in the 26.05
They s. to work and removed the 30.14
He s. to work resolutely and built 32.05
And he s. combat commanders over 32.06
he had made he s. in the house of 33.07
high places and s. up the Asherim 33.19
Over them were s. Jahath and 34.12
And they s. aside the burnt offerings 35.12
They s. the altar in its place, for Ez 3.03
And they s. the priests in their 6.18
For Ezra had s. his heart to study 7.10
officials had s. apart to attend 8.20
Then I s. apart twelve of the 8.24
reviving to s. up the house of our 9.09
to send me; and I s. him a time. Neh 2.06
consecrated it and s. its doors; 3.01
laid its beams and s. its doors, 3.03
laid its beams and s. its doors, 3.06
they rebuilt it and s. it doors, 3.13
he rebuilt it and s. its doors, 3.14
it and covered it and s. its doors, 3.15
and s. a guard as a protection 4.09
time I had not s. up the doors in 6.01
And you have also s. up prophets to 6.07
built and I had s. up the doors, 7.01
which thou didst s. before them; 9.35
whom thou hast s. over us because 9.37
and our priests s. their seal to 9.38
Those who s. their seal are Nehemiah 10.01
and they s. apart that which was 12.47
and the Levites s. apart that which 12.47
together and s. them in their 13.11
And I s. some of my servants over 13.19
so that he s. the royal crown on Est 2.17
advanced him and s. his seat above 3.01
on whose head a royal crown is s.; 6.08
And Esther s. Mordecai over the 8.02
that thou dost s. thy mind upon Job 7.17
"If you s. your heart aright, you 11.13
thou wouldest appoint me a s. time, 14.13
he s. me up as his target, 16.12
and he has s. darkness upon my 19.08
disdained to s. with the dogs of 30.01
s. your words in order before me; 33.05
and what was s. on your table was 36.16
bounds for it, and s. bars and doors, 38.10
The kings of the earth s. themselves, Ps 2.02
"I have s. my king on Zion, my holy 2.06
people who have s. themselves 3.06
the LORD has s. apart the godly 4.03
they s. their eyes to cast me to 17.11
and s. me secure on the heights. 18.33
In them he has s. a tent for the 19.04
name of our God s. up our banners! 20.05
thou dost s. a crown of fine gold 21.03
he will s. me high upon a rock. 27.05
thou hast s. my feet in a broad 31.08
and s. my feet upon a rock, making 40.02
and s. me in thy presence for ever. 41.12
but them thou didst s. free; 44.02
they do not s. God before them. 54.03
They s. a net for my steps; 57.06
Thou hast s. up a banner for those 60.04
How long will you s. upon a man to 62.03
s. no vain hopes on robbery; 62.10
increase, s. not your heart on them. 62.10
s. me free because of my enemies! 69.18
salvation, O God, s. me on high! 69.29
They s. their mouths against the 73.09
Truly though dost s. them in slippery 73.18
they s. up their own signs for 74.04
They s. thy sanctuary on fire; 74.07
At the s. time which I appoint I 75.02
they should s. their hope in God, 78.07
and they do not s. thee before 86.14
"I have s. the crown upon one who 89.19
I will s. his hand on the sea and 89.25
Thou hast s. our iniquities before 90.08
I will not s. before my eyes 101.03
to s. free those who were doomed to 102.20
Thou didst s. the earth on its 104.05
Thou didst s. a bound which they 104.09
ruler of the peoples s. him free; 105.20
LORD answered me and s. me free. 118.05
I s. thy ordinances before me. 119.30
There thrones for judgment were s., 122.05
your body I will s. on your throne. 132.11
if I do not s. Jerusalem above my 137.06
wayside they have s. snares for me. 140.05
S. a guard over my mouth, O LORD, 141.03
they s. an ambush for their own Pro 1.18
Ages ago I was s. up, at the first, 8.23
she has s. up her seven pillars. 9.01
wine, she has also s. her table. 9.02
do not s. your heart on his destruction 19.18
landmark which your fathers have s. 22.28
Scoffers s. a city aflame, but wise 29.08
sons of men is fully s. to do evil. Ecc 8.11
folly is s. in many high places, and 10.06
of water, bathed in milk, fitly s. Sol 5.12
are rounded gold, s. with jewels. 5.14
s. upon bases of gold. His appearance 5.15
my fancy s. me in a chariot beside 6.12
S. me as a seal upon your heart, as 8.06
and s. up the son of Tabeel as king Is 7.06
and will s. them in their own land, 14.01
of God I will s. my throne on high 14.13
plants and s. out slips of an 17.10
s. a watchman, let him announce what 21.06
I would s. out against them, I would 27.04
who s. out to go down to Egypt, 30.02
on your part to s. riders upon 36.08
"He has s. out to fight against you." 37.09
S. your house in order; for you shall die, 38.01
craftsman to s. up an image that 40.20
I will s. in the desert the cypress, 41.19
S. forth your case, says the LORD; 41.21
it s. him on fire round about, but 42.25
s. forth your case, that you may be 43.26
him declare and s. it forth before 44.07
my city and s. my exiles free, 45.13
they s. it in its place, and it 46.07
therefore I have s. my face like a 50.07
a fire, who s. brands alight! 50.11
I will s. your stones in antimony, 54.11
mountain you have s. your bed, 57.07
doorpost you have s. up your symbol; 57.08
O Jerusalem, I have s. watchmen; 62.06
me, for I am s. apart from you." 65.05
who s. a table for Fortune and fill 65.11
and I will s. a sign among them. 66.19
See, I have s. you this day over Jer 1.10
every one shall s. his throne at 1.15
how I would s. you among my sons, 3.19
a destroyer of nations has s. out; 4.07
They s. a trap; they catch men. 5.26
I s. watchmen over you, saying, 'Give 6.17
s. in array as a man for battle, 6.23
they have s. their abominations in 7.30
my law which I s. before them, 9.13
again, and to s. up my curtains. 10.20

SET (cont.)

the altars you have s. up to shame, Jer 11.13
tempest he will s. fire to it, 11.16
and s. them apart for the day of 12.03
saw when they s. as head over you 13.21
We s. our hope on thee, for thou 14.22
A glorious throne s. on high from 17.12
I s. before you the way of life and 21.08
For I have s. my face against this 21.10
I will s. shepherds over them who 23.04
I will s. my eyes upon them for 24.06
my law which I have s. before you, 26.04
"S. up waymarks for yourself, make 31.21
children's teeth are s. on edge.' 31.29
his teeth shall be s. on edge. 31.30
shall come and s. this city on 32.29
They s. up their abominations in 32.34
one should s. free his Hebrew 34.09
every one would s. free his slave, 34.10
they obeyed and s. them free. 34.10
and female slaves they had s. free, 34.11
of you must s. free the fellow 34.14
you must s. him free from your 34.14
whom you had s. free according to 34.16
Then I s. before the Rechabites 35.05
Jeremiah s. out from Jerusalem to 37.12
captive and s. out to cross over 41.10
If you s. your faces to enter Egypt 42.15
All the men who s. their faces to 42.17
of Neriah has s. you against us, 43.03
and he will s. his throne above 43.10
statutes which I s. before you and 44.10
I will s. my face against you for 44.11
Judah who have s. their faces to 44.12
and I will s. my throne in Elam, and 49.38
s. up a banner and proclaim, conceal 50.02
S. yourselves in array against 50.14
I s. a snare for you and you were 50.24
S. up a standard against the walls 51.12
s. up watchmen; prepare the 51.12
"S. up a standard on the earth, blow 51.27
they were s. upon my neck; Lam 1.14
his anger has s. the daughter of 2.01
with his right hand s. like a foe; 2.04
his bow and s. me as a mark for 3.12
into me and s. me upon my feet; Eze 2.02
and s. me upon my feet; 3.24
s. camps also against it, and plant 4.02
and s. your face toward it, and let 4.03
And you shall s. your face toward 4.07
I have s. her in the center of the 5.05
"Son of man, s. your face toward the 6.02
s. your face against the daughters 13.17
and s. the stumbling block of their 14.03
and I will s. my face against that 14.08
And I will s. my face against them; 15.07
when I s. my face against them. 15.07
and s. my oil and my incense before 16.18
you s. before them for a pleasing 16.19
and s. it in a city of merchants. 17.04
He s. it like a willow twig, 17.05
of the cedar, and will s. it out; 17.22
children's teeth are s. on edge'? 18.02
Then the nations s. against him 19.08
their eyes were s. on their 20.24
"Son of man, s. your face toward the 20.46
"Son of man, s. your face toward 21.02
to s. battering rams against the 21.22
they shall s. themselves against 23.24
S. on the pot, set it on, pour in 24.03
s. it on, pour in water also; 24.03
I have s. on the bare rock the 24.08
Then s. it empty upon the coals, 24.11
"Son of man, s. your face toward the 25.02
and they shall s. their encampments 25.04
he will s. up a siege wall against 26.08
"Son of man, s. your face toward 28.21
"Son of man, s. your face against 29.02
when I have s. fire to Egypt, and 30.08
and will s. fire to Zoan, and will 30.14
And I will s. fire to Egypt; 30.16
high and s. its top among the 31.10
lofty height or s. their tops 31.14
whose graves are s. in the uttermost 32.23
their heart is s. on their gain. 33.31
And I will s. up over them one 34.23
"Son of man, s. your face against 35.02
and s. me down in the midst of the 37.01
and will s. my sanctuary in the 37.26
"Son of man, s. your face toward Gog, 38.02
They will s. apart men to pass 39.14
then he shall s. up a sign by it, 39.15
"And I will s. my glory among the 39.21
and s. me down upon a very high 40.02
and s. your mind upon all that I 40.04
chambers were s. back from the 42.06
but you have s. foreigners to keep 44.08
you shall s. apart for the LORD a 45.01
"Alongside the portion s. apart as 45.06
portion which you shall s. apart, 48.08
which you shall s. apart for the 48.09
which you shall s. apart shall be 48.20
of heaven will s. up a kingdom Dan 2.44
He s. it up on the plain of Dura, in 3.01
King Nebuchadnezzar had s. up. 3.02
the King Nebuchadnezzar had s. up; 3.03
that Nebuchadnezzar had s. up. 3.03
that King Nebuchadnezzar has s. up; 3.05
King Nebuchadnezzar had s. up. 3.07
golden image which you have s. up." 3.12
golden image which I have s. up? 3.14
golden image which you have s. up." 3.18
and s. at nought the king's command, 3.28
Darius to s. over the kingdom a 6.01
king planned to s. him over the 6.03
and s. his mind to deliver Daniel; 6.14
he touched me and s. me on my feet. 8.18
which he s. before us by his 9.10
touched me and s. me trembling on 10.10
day that you s. your mind to 10.12
He shall s. his face to come with 11.17
heart shall be s. against the holy 11.28
And they shall s. up the abomination 11.31
that makes desolate is s. up, 12.11
and s. her like a parched land, and Hos 2.03
S. the trumpet to your lips, for a 8.01
They s. up princes, but without my 8.04
and I will s. my eyes upon them for Amo 9.04
your nest is s. among the stars, Ob 1.04
friends have s. a trap under you— 1.07
I will s. them together like sheep Mic 2.12
to the wall, the mantelet is s. up. Nah 2.05
to s. his nest on high, to be safe Hab 2.09
which I have s. before Joshua, Zec 3.09
they will s. the ephah down there 5.11
country have s. my Spirit at rest 6.08
and s. it upon the head of Joshua, 6.11
for I s. every man against his 8.10
I will s. your captives free from 9.11
and s. him on the pinnacle of the Mt 4.05
A city s. on a hill cannot be hid. 5.14
For I have come to s. a man against 10.35
and s. a hedge around it, and dug a 21.33
his master has s. over his household, 24.45
he will s. him over all his possessions. 24.47
a little, I will s. you over much; 25.21
a little, I will s. you over much; 25.23
price had been s. by some of the 27.09
disciples to s. before the people; Mk 6.41
disciples to s. before the people; 8.06
and they s. them before the crowd. 8.06
also should be s. before them. 8.07
and s. a hedge around it, and dug a 12.01
sacrilege s. up where it ought not 13.14

SET (cont.)
And the disciples s. out and went Mk 14.16
this child is s. for the fall and Lk 2.34
and s. him on the pinacle of the 4.09
to s. at liberty those who are oppressed, 4.18
For I am a man s. under authority, 7.08
side of the lake." So they s. out, 8.22
disciples to s. before the crowd. 9.16
he s. his face to go to Jerusalem. 9.51
his face was s. toward Jerusalem. 9.53
you, eat what is s. before you; 10.08
then he s. him on his own beast and 10.34
I have nothing to s. before him'; 11.06
his master will s. over his 12.42
he will s. him over all his possessions 12.44
on the colt they s. Jesus upon it. 19.35
you, on whom you s. your hope. Jn 5.45
him has God the Father s. his seal." 6.27
that he would s. one of his Ac 2.30
And when they had s. them in the 4.07
of the earth s. themselves in 4.26
they s. them before the council. 5.27
These they s. before the apostles, 6.06
and s. up false witnesses who said, 6.13
"S. apart for me Barnabas and Saul 13.02
and his company s. sail from 13.13
'I have s. you to be a light for 13.47
its ruins, and I will s. it up, 15.16
and s. food before them; and he rejoiced 16.34
s. the city in an uproar, and 17.05
and he s. sail from Ephesus. 18.21
he was about to s. sail for Syria, 20.03
we s. sail for Assos, intending to 20.13
first day that I s. foot in Asia, 20.18
had parted from them and s. sail, 21.01
we went aboard, and s. sail. 21.02
Paul down and s. him before them. 22.30
could have been s. free if he had 26.32
should not have s. sail from Crete 27.21
After three months we s. sail in a 28.11
they wished to s. me at liberty, 28.18
s. apart for the gospel of God Rom 1.01
having been s. free from sin, have 6.18
you have been s. free from sin and 6.22
Jesus has s. me free from the law 8.02
to the flesh s. their minds on the 8.05
to the Spirit s. their minds on 8.05
To s. the mind on the flesh is 8.06
but to s. the mind on the Spirit is 8.06
mind that is s. on the flesh is 8.07
itself will be s. free from its 8.21
eat whatever is s. before you 1Co 10.27
on him we have s. our hope that he 2Co 1.10
mind has been s. at rest by you 7.13
But when he who had s. me apart Gal 1.15
until the date s. by the father. 4.02
For freedom Christ has s. us free; 5.01
which he s. forth in Christ Eph 1.09
with minds s. on earthly things. Php 3.19
this he s. aside, nailing it to the Col 2.14
S. your minds on things that are 3.02
have our hope s. on the living God, 1Ti 4.10
but s. the believers an example in 4.12
has s. her hope on God and continues 5.05
nor to s. their hopes on uncertain 6.17
to seize the hope s. before us. Heb 6.18
commandment is s. aside because of 7.18
tent which is s. up not by man but 8.02
the race that is s. before us, 12.01
joy that was s. before him endured 12.02
a forest is s. ablaze by a small Jas 3.05
and s. on fire by hell. 3.06
s. your hope fully upon the grace 1Pe 1.13
For they have s. out for his sake 3Jn 1.07
It is these who s. up divisions, Jud 1.19
I have s. before you an open door, Rev 3.08
And he s. his right foot on the sea, 10.02

SETH
bore a son and called his name S., Gen 4.25
To S. also a son was born, and he 4.26
after his image, and named him S. 5.03
the father of S. were eight 5.04
When S. had lived a hundred and 5.06
S. lived after the birth of Enosh 5.07
Thus all the days of S. were nine 5.08
Adam, S., Enosh; 1Ch 1.01
the son of S., the son of Adam, the Lk 3.38

SETHUR
tribe of Asher. S. the son of Michael; Num 13.13

SETS
and when Aaron s. up the lamps in Ex 30.08
as the camp s. out, after that the Num 4.15
and s. his heart upon it); lest he Deu 24.15
and s. it up in secret.' And all the 27.15
and s. on fire the foundations of 32.22
who s. his heart to seek God, the 2Ch 30.19
he s. on high those who are lowly, Job 5.11
and s. others in their place. 34.24
the throne he s. them for ever, 36.07
he s. himself in a way that is not Ps 36.04
as the flame s. the mountains 83.14
The LORD s. the prisoners free; 146.07
understanding s. his face toward Pro 17.24
he s. up salvation as walls and Is 26.01
as when one s. out to the sound of 30.29
when he s. himself to destroy? 51.13
his heart and s. the stumbling Eze 14.04
he removes kings and s. up kings; Dan 2.21
and s. over it the lowliest of men.' 4.17
and s. over it whom he will. 5.21
his testimony s. his seal to this, Jn 3.33
himself a king s. himself against 19.12
again he s. a certain day, "Today," Heb 4.07

SETTEST
that thou s. a guard over me? Job 7.12
thou s. a bound to the soles of my 13.27

SETTING
onyx stones, and stones for s., Ex 25.07
in cutting stones for s., 31.05
and onyx stones and stones for s., 35.09
in cutting stones for s., 35.33
had finished s. up the tabernacle, Num 7.01
"We are s. out for the place of 10.29
on which we are s. out will Ju 18.05
the axes and for s. the goads. 1Sa 13.21
s. up his son after him, and establishing 1Ki 15.04
quantities of onyx and stones for s., 1Ch 29.02
the rising of the sun to its s. Ps 50.01
the sun knows its time for s. 104.19
the sun to its s. the name of the 113.03
apples of gold in a s. of silver. Pro 25.11
by s. their threshold by my threshold Eze 43.08
I am s. a plumb line in the midst Amo 7.08
the sun to its s. my name is great Mal 1.11
sealing the stone and s. a guard. Mt 27.66
And as he was s. out on his journey, Mk 10.17
Now when the sun was s., all those Lk 4.40
S. sail therefore from Troas, we Ac 16.11
s. on fire the cycle of nature, and Jas 3.06

SETTINGS
enclose them in s. of gold filigree Ex 28.11
And you shall make s. of gold 28.13
attach the corded chains to the s. 28.14
attach to the two s. of filigree, 28.25
enclosed in s. of gold filigree and 39.06
enclosed in s. of gold filigree. 39.13
and they made two s. of gold 39.16
attached to the two s. of filigree; 39.18
the house with s. of precious 2Ch 3.06
gold were your s. and your engravings Eze 28.13

SETTLE

s. your father and your brothers in Gen 47.06
enemies who s. in it shall be Lev 26.32
possession of the land and s. in it, Num 33.53
in this book would s. upon him, Deu 29.20
but will s. the matter today." Ru 3.18
all come and s. in the steep Is 7.19
whose feet carried her to s. afar? 23.07
the birds of the air to s. on you, Eze 32.04
who wished to s. accounts with his Mt 18.23
an effort to s. with him on the Lk 12.58
S. it therefore in your minds, not 21.14

SETTLED

in the land of Shinar and s. there. Gen 11.02
they came to Haran, they s. there. 11.31
he s. over against all his people. 25.18
Then Joseph s. his father and his 47.11
and s. on the whole country of Ex 10.14
of the LORD s. on Mount Sinai, 24.16
the place where the cloud s. down, Num 9.17
and the cloud s. down in the 10.12
and Israel s. in all the cities of 21.25
son of Manasseh, and he s. in it. 32.40
before them, and s. in their stead; Deu 2.12
them, and s. in their stead; 2.21
and s. in their stead even to this 2.22
destroyed them and s. in their stead. 2.23
and every assault shall be s. 21.05
took possession of it and s. in it, Jos 19.47
he rebuilt the city, and s. in it. 19.50
possession of it, they s. there. 21.43
Reubenites and the Gadites were s. 22.33
they went and s. with the people. Ju 1.16
and so they s. a matter. 2Sa 20.18
and s. in their place, because there 1Ch 4.41
and s. the people of Israel in them 2Ch 8.02
with its villages; and they s. there. 28.18
deported and s. in the cities of Ez 4.10
and a s. provision for the singers, Neh 11.23
possession and s. the tribes of Ps 78.55
his youth and has s. on his lees; Jer 48.11
and his people s. in its cities? 49.01
came and s. accounts with them. Mt 25.19
it shall be s. in the regular Ac 19.39

SETTLEMENTS

These were their s., and they kept 1Ch 4.33
to their s. within their borders: 6.54
Their possessions and s. were 7.28

SETTLING

s. down by his landings. Ju 5.17
s. its ridges, softening it with Ps 65.10
of locusts s. on the fences in a Nah 3.17

SEVEN

Enosh eight hundred and s. years, Gen 5.07
birth of Lamech s. hundred and eighty-two 5.26
of Lamech were s. hundred and seventy-seven 5.31
Take with you s. pairs of all clean 7.02
and s. pairs of the birds of the 7.03
For in s. days I will send rain 7.04
And after s. days the waters of the 7.10
He waited another s. days, and again 8.10
Then he waited another s. days, 8.12
of Serug two hundred and s. years, 11.21
Abraham set s. ewe lambs of the 21.28
of these s. ewe lambs which you 21.29
"These s. ewe lambs you will take 21.30
will serve you s. years for your 29.18
So Jacob served s. years for Rachel, 29.20
for serving me another s. years." 29.27
served Laban for another s. years. 29.30
pursued him for s. days and 31.23
himself to the ground s. times, 33.03
out of the Nile s. cows sleek and 41.02
And behold, s. other cows, gaunt and 41.03
cows ate up the s. sleek and fat 41.04
and behold, s. ears of grain, plump 41.05
after them sprouted s. ears, 41.06
swallowed up the s. plump and full 41.07
and s. cows, fat and sleek, came up 41.18
and s. other cows came up after 41.19
cows ate up the first s. fat cows, 41.20
saw in my dream s. ears growing on 41.22
and s. ears, withered, thin, and 41.23
ears swallowed up the s. good ears. 41.24
The s. good cows are seven years, 41.26
The seven good cows are s. years, 41.26
and the s. good ears are seven 41.26
the seven good ears are s. years; 41.26
The s. lean and gaunt cows that 41.27
came up after them are s. years, 41.27
and the s. empty ears blighted by 41.27
wind are also s. years of famine. 41.27
There will come s. years of great 41.29
will arise s. years of famine, and 41.30
during the s. plenteous years. 41.34
against the s. years of famine 41.36
During the s. plenteous years the 41.47
the food of the s. years when 41.48
The s. years of plenty that prevailed 41.53
and the s. years of famine began to 41.54
bone to Jacob—s. persons in all). 46.25
a mourning for his father s. days. 50.10
priest of Midian had s. daughters; Ex 2.16
S. days passed after the LORD had 7.25
S. days you shall eat unleavened 12.15
For s. days no leaven shall be 12.19
S. days you shall eat unleavened 13.06
Unleavened bread shall be eaten for s. days; 13.07
s. days it shall be with its dam; 22.30
bread for s. days at the appointed 23.15
you shall make the s. lamps for it; 25.37
his place shall wear them s. days, 29.30
through s. days shall you ordain 29.35
S. days you shall make atonement 29.37
S. days you shall eat unleavened 34.18
And he made its s. lamps and its 37.23
talents and s. hundred and thirty 38.24
and a thousand s. hundred and 38.25
And of the thousand s. hundred and 38.28
of the blood s. times before the Lev 4.06
and sprinkle it s. times before 4.17
some of it on the altar s. times, 8.11
of the tent of meeting for s. days, 8.33
it will take s. days to ordain you 8.33
remain day and night for s. days, 8.35
then she shall be unclean s. days; 12.02
up the diseased person for s. days; 13.04
shall shut him up s. days more; 13.05
priest shall shut him up s. days; 13.21
priest shall shut him up s. days, 13.26
the itching disease for s. days, 13.31
itching disease for s. days more; 13.33
which has the disease for s. days; 13.50
he shall shut it up s. days more; 13.54
sprinkle it s. times upon him who 14.07
dwell outside his tent s. days. 14.08
with his finger s. times before 14.16
his left hand s. times before the 14.27
and shut up the house s. days 14.38
and sprinkle the house s. times. 14.51
for himself s. days for his 15.13
be in her impurity for s. days, 15.19
him, he shall be unclean s. days; 15.24
shall count for herself s. days, 15.28
the blood with his finger s. times. 16.14
upon it with his finger s. times, 16.19
it shall remain s. days with its 22.27
s. days you shall eat unleavened 23.06
by fire to the LORD s. days; 23.08
s. full weeks shall you be, 23.15

SEVEN (cont.)
with the bread s. lambs a year old Lev 23.18
month and for s. days is the feast 23.34
S. days you shall present offerings. 23.36
keep the feast of the LORD s. days; 23.39
before the LORD your God s. days. 23.40
to the LORD s. days in the year; 23.41
You shall dwell in booths for s. days; 23.42
"And you shall count s. weeks of years, 25.08
s. times s. years, so that the time of 25.08
the time of the s. weeks of years 25.08
was sixty-two thousand s. hundred. Num 1.39
sixty-two thousand s. hundred. 2.26
and upward was s. thousand five 3.22
two thousand s. hundred and fifty. 4.36
the s. lamps shall give light in 8.02
should she not be shamed s. days? 12.14
shut up outside the camp s. days, 12.14
shut up outside the camp s. days; 12.15
was built s. years before Zoan in 13.22
were fourteen thousand s. hundred, 16.49
of the tent of meeting s. times. 19.04
person shall be unclean s. days; 19.11
the tent, shall be unclean s. days. 19.14
a grave, shall be unclean s. days. 19.16
Balak, "Build for me here s. altars, 23.01
for me here s. bulls and s. rams." 23.01
him, "I have prepared the s. altars, 23.04
and built s. altars, and offered a 23.14
Balak, "Build for me here s. altars, 23.29
for me here s. bulls and s. rams." 23.29
thousand s. hundred and thirty. 26.07
was fifty-two thousand s. hundred. 26.34
one thousand s. hundred and thirty 26.51
s. male lambs a year old without 28.11
s. days shall unleavened bread be 28.17
and s. male lambs a year old; 28.19
you offer for each of the s. lambs; 28.21
for s. days, the food of an offering 28.24
s. male lambs a year old; 28.27
a tenth for each of the s. lambs; 28.29
s. male lambs a year old without 29.02
one tenth for each of the s. lambs; 29.04
s. male lambs a year old; 29.08
a tenth for each of the s. lambs: 29.10
keep a feast to the LORD s. days; 29.12
"On the seventh day s. bulls, 29.32
s. male lambs a year old without 29.36
Encamp outside the camp s. days; 31.19
thousand s. hundred and fifty 31.52
s. nations greater and mightier Deu 7.01
end of every s. years you shall 15.01
s. days you shall eat it with 16.03
in all your territory for s. days; 16.04
"You shall count s. weeks; 16.09
to count the s. weeks from the 16.09
keep the feast of booths s. days, 16.13
For s. days you shall keep the 16.15
way, and flee before you s. ways. 28.07
and flee s. ways before them; 28.25
them, "At the end of every s. years, 31.10
And s. priests shall bear s. trumpets Jos 6.04
march around the city s. times, 6.04
and let s. priests bear s. trumpets 6.06
the s. priests bearing the s. trumpets 6.08
the s. priests bearing the s. trumpets 6.13
city in the same manner s. times: 6.15
marched around the city s. times. 6.15
of Israel s. tribes whose inheritance 18.02
They shall divide it into s. portions, 18.05
the land in s. divisions and bring 18.06
of it by towns in s. divisions; 18.09
into the hand of Midian s. years. Ju 6.01
bull, the second bull s. years old, 6.25
one thousand s. hundred shekels of 8.26
And he judged Israel s. years. 12.09
within the s. days of the feast, and 14.12
before him the s. days that their 14.17
bind me with s. fresh bowstrings 16.07
brought her s. fresh bowstrings 16.08
you weave the s. locks of my head 16.13
took the s. locks of his head and 16.14
shave off the s. locks of his head. 16.19
who mustered s. hundred picked men. 20.15
Among all these were s. hundred 20.16
who is more to you than s. sons, Ru 4.15
The barren has borne s., 1Sa 2.05
of the Philistines s. months. 6.01
S. days you shall wait, until I come 10.08
"Give us s. days respite that we 11.03
He waited s. days, the time appointed 13.08
And Jesse made s. of his sons pass 16.10
tree in Jabesh, and fasted s. days. 31.13
of Judah was s. years and six 2Sa 2.11
over Judah s. years and six months 5.05
a thousand and s. hundred horsemen, 8.04
the men of s. hundred chariots, and 10.18
let s. of his sons be given to us, 21.06
and the s. of them perished together 21.09
he reigned s. years in Hebron, and 1Ki 2.11
and the third was s. cubits broad; 6.06
He was s. years in building it. 6.38
before the LORD our God, s. days. 8.65
He had s. hundred wives, princesses, 11.03
Zimri reigned s. days in Tirzah. 16.15
And he said, "Go again s. times." 18.43
Yet I will leave s. thousand in 19.18
the people of Israel, s. thousand. 20.15
opposite one another s. days. 20.29
made a circuitous march of s. days, 2Ki 3.09
took with him s. hundred swordsmen 3.26
the child sneezed s. times, 4.35
"Go and wash in the Jordan s. times, 5.10
dipped himself s. times in the 5.14
come upon the land for s. years." 8.01
land of the Philistines s. years. 8.02
And at the end of the s. years, 8.03
Jehoash was s. years old when he 11.21
s. thousand, and the craftsmen and 24.16
he reigned for s. years and six 1Ch 3.04
Johanan, Delaiah, and Anani, s. 3.24
Jorai, Jacan, Zia, and Eber, s. 5.13
thousand s. hundred and sixty, 5.18
one thousand s. hundred and sixty, 9.13
obliged to come in every s. days, 9.25
oak in Jabesh, and fasted s. days. 10.12
valor for war, s. thousand one hundred. 12.25
with him three thousand s. hundred. 12.27
they sacrificed s. bulls and s. rams. 15.26
s. thousand horsemen, and twenty 18.04
the men of s. thousand chariots, 19.18
one thousand s. hundred men of 26.30
two thousand s. hundred men of 26.32
and s. thousand talents of refined 29.04
he reigned s. years in Hebron, and 29.27
Solomon held the feast for s. days, 2Ch 7.08
altar s. days and the feast s. days. 7.09
a young bull or s. rams becomes a 13.09
s. hundred oxen and s. thousand sheep. 15.11
brought him s. thousand s. hundred rams 17.11
and s. thousand s. hundred he-goats. 17.11
Joash was s. years old when he 24.01
hundred and s. thousand five 26.13
they brought s. bulls, s. rams, 29.21
s. lambs, and s. he-goats for a sin 29.21
unleavened bread s. days with great 30.21
food of the festival for s. days, 30.22
keep the feast for another s. days; 30.23
it for another s. days with 30.23
bulls and s. thousand sheep for 30.24
feast of unleavened bread s. days. 35.17
of Arab, s. hundred and seventy-five. Ez 2.05
of Zaccai, s. hundred and sixty. 2.09

SEVEN (cont.)
and Beeroth, s. hundred and forty-three. Ez 2.25
and Ono, s. hundred and twenty-five. 2.33
whom there were s. thousand three 2.65
Their horses were s. hundred and 2.66
six thousand s. hundred and twenty 2.67
unleavened bread s. days with joy; 6.22
king and his s. counselors to make 7.14
of Zaacai, s. hundred and sixty. Neh 7.14
and Beeroth, s. hundred and forty-three. 7.29
and Ono, s. hundred and twenty-one. 7.37
whom there were s. thousand three 7.67
Their horses were s. hundred and 7.68
six thousand s. hundred and twenty 7.69
They kept the feast s. days; 8.18
a banquet lasting for s. days, Est 1.05
the s. eunuchs who served King 1.10
the s. princes of Persia and Media, 1.14
and with s. chosen maids from the 2.09
born to him s. sons and three Job 1.02
He had s. thousand sheep, three 1.03
the ground s. days and s. nights, 2.13
in s. there shall no evil touch you 5.19
therefore take s. bulls and s. rams, 42.08
He had also s. sons and three 42.13
on the ground, purified s. times. Ps 12.06
S. times a day I praise thee for 119.164
s. which are an abomination to him: Pro 6.16
she has set up her s. pillars. 9.01
for a righteous man falls s. times, 24.16
own eyes than s. men who can 26.16
for there are s. abominations in 26.25
Give a portion to s., or even to Ecc 11.02
And s. women shall take hold of one Is 4.01
smite it into s. channels that men 11.15
sevenfold, as the light of s. days, 30.26
She who bore s. has languished; Jer 15.09
and s. men of the king's council, who 52.25
of the Jews s. hundred and forty-five 52.30
overwhelmed among them s. days. Eze 3.15
And at the end of s. days, 3.16
make fires of them for s. years; 39.09
For s. months the house of Israel 39.12
at the end of s. months they will 39.14
and s. steps led up to it; 40.22
And there were s. steps leading up 40.26
sidewalls of the entrance, s. cubits. 41.03
For s. days you shall provide daily 43.25
S. days shall they make atonement 43.26
he shall count for himself s. days, 44.26
and for s. days unleavened bread 45.21
And on the s. days of the festival 45.23
LORD s. young bulls and s. rams 45.23
blemish, on each of the s. days; 45.23
and for the s. days of the feast, 45.25
furnace heated s. times more than Dan 3.19
and let s. times pass over him. 4.16
till s. times pass over him; 4.23
and s. times shall pass over you, 4.25
and s. times shall pass over you, 4.32
a prince, there shall be s. weeks. 9.25
against him s. shepherds and eight Mic 5.05
upon a single stone with s. facets, Zec 3.09
and s. lamps on it, with s. lips 4.02
"These s. are the eyes of the LORD, 4.10
brings with him s. other spirits Mt 12.45
They said, "S., and a few small 15.34
he took the s. loaves and the fish, 15.36
they took up s. baskets full of 15.37
Or the s. loaves of the four thousand, 16.10
I forgive him, As many as s. times?" 18.21
"I do not say to you s. times, but seventy times. 18.22
Now there were s. brothers among us 22.25
to which of the s. will she be 22.28
loaves have you?" They said, "S. Mk 8.05
and he took the s. loaves, and having 8.06
pieces left over, s. baskets full. 8.08
"And the s. for the four thousand, 8.20
And they said to him, "S." 8.20
There were s. brothers; the first took 12.20
and the s. left no children. 12.22
For the s. had her as wife. 12.23
from whom he had cast out s. demons. * 16.09
her husband s. years from her Lk 2.36
from whom s. demons had gone out, 8.02
goes and brings s. other spirits 11.26
against you s. times in the day, 17.04
the day, and turns to you s. times, 17.04
Now there were s. brothers; 20.29
likewise all s. left no children 20.31
For the s. had her as wife. 20.33
about s. miles from Jerusalem, 24.13
from among you s. men of good Ac 6.03
had destroyed s. nations in the 13.19
S. sons of a Jewish high priest 19.14
Troas, where we stayed for s. days. 20.06
we stayed there for s. days. 21.04
evangelist, who was one of the s., 21.08
When the s. days were almost 21.27
to stay with them for s. days. 28.14
kept for myself s. thousand men Rom 11.04
had been encircled for s. days. Heb 11.30
with s. other persons, when he 2Pe 2.05
John to the s. churches that are in Rev 1.04
and from the s. spirits who are 1.04
and send it to the s. churches, 1.11
turning I saw s. golden lampstands, 1.12
in his right hand he held s. stars, 1.16
mystery of the s. stars which you 1.20
and the s. golden lampstands, the 1.20
the s. stars are the angels of the 1.20
angels of the s. churches and the 1.20
s. lampstands are the s. churches. 1.20
who holds the s. stars in his right hand, 2.01
among the s. golden lampstands. 2.01
s. spirits of God and the s. stars. 3.01
the throne burn s. torches of fire, 4.05
which are the s. spirits of God; 4.05
on the back, sealed with s. seals; 5.01
open the scroll and its s. seals." 5.05
with s. horns and with s. eyes, 5.06
which are the s. spirits of God 5.06
Lamb opened one of the s. seals, 6.01
Then I saw the s. angels who stand 8.02
and s. trumpets were given to them. 8.02
s. angels who had the s. trumpets 8.06
called out, the s. thunders sounded. 10.03
And when the s. thunders had sounded 10.04
up what the s. thunders have said, 10.04
s. thousand people were killed in 11.13
with s. heads and ten horns, and 12.03
and s. diadems upon his heads. 12.03
sea, with ten horns and s. heads, 13.01
s. angels with s. plagues, which 15.01
came the s. angels with the s. plagues, 15.06
gave the s. angels s. golden bowls full 15.07
until the s. plagues of the s. angels 15.08
the temple telling the s. angels, 16.01
the earth the s. bowls of the 16.01
the s. angels who had the s. bowls 17.01
and it had s. heads and ten horns. 17.03
the beast with s. heads and ten 17.07
the s. heads are s. hills on 17.09
they are also s. kings, five of whom 17.10
an eighth but it belongs to the s., 17.11
the s. angels who had the s. bowls 21.09
s. bowls full of the s. last plagues, 21.09

SEVENFOLD
vengeance shall be taken on him s. Gen 4.15
If Cain is avenged s., truly Lamech 4.24
you again s. for your sins, Lev 26.18
s. as many as your sins. 26.21
will smite you s. for your sins. 26.24
you myself s. for your sins. 26.28

SEVENFOLD (cont.)
Return s. into the bosom of our Ps 79.12
And if he is caught, he will pay s.; Pro 6.31
the light of the sun will be s., Is 30.26

SEVENTEEN
Joseph, being s. years old, was Gen 37.02
in the land of Egypt s. years; 47.28
and he reigned s. years in Jerusalem, 1Ki 14.21
Samaria, and he reigned s. years. 2Ki 13.01
s. thousand and two hundred, ready 1Ch 7.11
and he reigned s. years in Jerusalem, 2Ch 12.13
sons of Harim, one thousand and s. Ez 2.39
The sons of Harim, a thousand and s. Neh 7.42
money to him, s. shekels of silver. Jer 32.09

SEVENTEENTH
on the s. day of the month, on that Gen 7.11
on the s. day of the month, the ark 8.04
Samaria in the s. year of Jehoshaphat 1Ki 22.51
In the s. year of Pekah the son of 2Ki 16.01
the s. to Hezir, the eighteenth to 1Ch 24.15
to the s., to Joshbekashah, his sons 25.24

SEVENTH
And on the s. day God finished his Gen 2.02
rested on the s. day from all his 2.02
So God blessed the s. day and 2.03
in the s. month, on the seventeenth 8.04
the first day until the s. day, Ex 12.15
and on the s. day a holy assembly; 12.16
and on the s. day there shall be a 13.06
but on the s. day, which is a 16.26
On the s. day some of the people 16.27
go out of his place on the s. day." 16.29
So the people rested on the s. day. 16.30
but the s. day is a sabbath to the 20.10
is in them, and rested the s. day; 20.11
and in the s. he shall go out free, 21.02
but the s. year you shall let it 23.11
but on the s. day you shall rest; 23.12
and on the s. day he called to 24.16
but the s. day is a sabbath of 31.15
and on the s. day he rested, and was 31.17
but on the s. day you shall rest; 34.21
but on the s. day you shall have a 35.02
shall examine him on the s. day, Lev 13.05
examine him again on the s. day, 13.06
shall examine him the s. day; 13.27
and on the s. day the priest shall 13.32
and on the s. day the priest shall 13.34
examine the disease on the s. day. 13.51
And on the s. day he shall shave 14.09
come again on the s. day, and look; 14.39
you for ever that in the s. month, 16.29
but on the s. day is a sabbath of 23.03
on the s. day is a holy convocation 23.08
to the morrow after the s. sabbath; 23.16
In the s. month, on the first day of 23.24
day of this s. month is the day of 23.27
day of this s. month and for seven 23.34
"On the fifteenth day of the s. month, 23.39
you shall keep it in the s. month. 23.41
but in the s. year there shall be a 25.04
on the tenth day of the s. month; 25.09
'What shall we eat in the s. year, 25.20
on the s. day he shall shave it. Num 6.09
On the s. day Elishama the son of 7.48
on the third day and on the s. day, 19.12
on the third day and on the s. day; 19.19
thus on the s. day he shall cleanse 19.19
And on the s. day you shall have a 28.25
day of the s. month you shall have 29.01
day of this s. month you shall 29.07
day of the s. month you shall have 29.12
"On the s. day seven bulls, two rams, 29.32
on the third day and on the s. day. 31.19
wash your clothes on the s. day, 31.24
but the s. day is a sabbath to the Deu 5.14
'The s. year, the year of release is 15.09
and in the s. year you shall let 15.12
and on the s. day there shall be a 16.08
and on the s. day you shall march Jos 6.04
On the s. day they rose early at 6.15
And at the s. time, when the priests 6.16
The s. lot came out for the tribe 19.40
and on the s. day he told her, Ju 14.17
to him on the s. day before the 14.18
On the s. day the child died. 2Sa 12.18
Ethanim, which is the s. month. 1Ki 8.02
And at the s. time he said, "Behold, 18.44
Then on the s. day the battle was 20.29
But in the s. year Jehoiada sent 2Ki 11.04
In the s. year of Jehu Jehoash 12.01
which was the s. year of Hoshea son 18.09
on the s. day of the month—which 25.08
But in the s. month, Ishmael the son 25.25
Ozem the sixth, David the s.; 1Ch 2.15
Attai sixth, Eliel s., 12.11
the s. to Hakkoz, the eighth to 24.10
the s. to Jesharelah, his sons and 25.14
the sixth, Eliehoenai the s. 26.03
Issachar the s., Peullethai the 26.05
S., for the s. month, was Helez 27.10
the feast which is in the s. month. 2Ch 5.03
day of the s. month he sent the 7.10
But in the s. year Jehoiada took 23.01
and finished them in the s. month. 31.07
When the s. month came, and the sons Ez 3.01
day of the s. month they began to 3.06
in the s. year of Artaxerxes the 7.07
was in the s. year of the king; 7.08
And when the s. month had come, the Neh 7.73
on the first day of the s. month. 8.02
during the feast of the s. month, 8.14
crops of the s. year and the 10.31
On the s. day, when the heart of the Est 1.10
in the s. year of his reign, 2.16
in the s. month, the prophet Hananiah Jer 28.17
In the s. month, Ishmael the son of 41.01
in the s. year, three thousand and 52.28
In the s. year, in the fifth month, Eze 20.01
on the s. day of the month, the word 30.20
the same on the s. day of the 45.20
In the s. month, on the fifteenth 45.25
in the s. month, on the twenty-first Hag 2.01
in the fifth month and in the s., Zec 7.05
the fifth, and the fast of the s., 8.19
second and third, down to the s. Mt 22.26
"Yesterday at the s. hour the fever Jn 4.52
spoken of the s. day in this way, Heb 4.04
rested on the s. day from all his 4.04
Enoch in the s. generation from Jud 1.14
When the Lamb opened the s. seal, Rev 8.01
call to be sounded by the s. angel, 10.07
Then the s. angel blew his trumpet, 11.15
The s. angel poured his bowl into 16.17
the s. chrysolite, the eighth beryl, 21.20

SEVENTY
When Kenan had lived s. years, Gen 5.12
When Terah had lived s. years, 11.26
that came into Egypt, were s. 46.27
the Egyptians wept for him s. days. 50.03
offspring of Jacob were s. persons; Ex 1.05
springs of water and s. palm trees; 15.27
and s. of the elders of Israel, and 24.01
and s. of the elders of Israel went 24.09
was contributed was s. talents, 38.29
one silver basin of s. shekels, Num 7.13
one silver basin of s. shekels, 7.19
one silver basin of s. shekels, 7.25
one silver basin of s. shekels, 7.31
one silver basin of s. shekels, 7.37
one silver basin of s. shekels, 7.43
one silver basin of s. shekels, 7.49

SEVENTY (cont.)
one silver basin of s. shekels, Num 7.55
one silver basin of s. shekels, 7.61
one silver basin of s. shekels, 7.67
one silver basin of s. shekels, 7.73
one silver basin of s. shekels, 7.79
thirty shekels and each basin s., 7.85
"Gather for me s. men of the elders 11.16
and he gathered s. men of the 11.24
him and put it upon the s. elders; 11.25
springs of water and s. palm trees, 33.09
went down to Egypt s. persons; Deu 10.22
"S. kings with their thumbs and Ju 1.07
Now Gideon had s. sons, his own 8.30
that all s. of the sons of Jerubbaal 9.02
And they gave him s. pieces of 9.04
s. men, upon one stone; but Jotham 9.05
s. men on one stone, and have made 9.18
done to the s. sons of Jerubbaal 9.24
father in killing his s. brothers; 9.56
grandsons, who rode on s. asses; 12.14
he slew s. men of them, and the 1Sa 6.19
Dan to Beersheba s. thousand men. 2Sa 24.15
Solomon also had s. thousand burden 1Ki 5.15
Nod Ahab had s. sons in Samaria. 2Ki 10.01
s. persons, were with the great men 10.06
s. persons, and put their heads in 10.07
hundred and s. thousand who drew 1Ch 21.05
and there fell s. thousand men of 21.14
assigned s. thousand men to bear 2Ch 2.02
S. thousand of them he assigned to 2.18
the assembly brought was s. bulls, 29.32
kept sabbath, to fulfill s. years. 36.21
of Athaliah, and with him s. men. Ez 8.07
and Zakkur, and with them s. men. 8.14
will be forgotten for s. years, Is 23.15
At the end of s. years, it will 23.15
At the end of s. years, the LORD 23.17
serve the king of Babylon s. years. Jer 25.11
Then after s. years are completed, I 25.12
When s. years are completed for 29.10
them stood s. men of the elders of Eze 8.11
the west side was s. cubits broad; 41.12
of Jerusalem, namely, s. years. Dan 9.02
"S. weeks of years are decreed 9.24
had indignation these s. years?' Zec 1.12
for these s. years, was it for me 7.05
seven times, but s. times seven. Mt.18.22
After this the Lord appointed s. others, Lk 10.01
The s. returned with joy, saying, 10.17
soldiers with s. horsemen and two Ac 23.23

SEVENTY-FIVE
Abram was s. years old when he Gen 12.04
life, a hundred and s. years. 25.07
seven hundred and s. shekels, Ex 38.25
hundred and s. shekels he made 38.28
six hundred and s. thousand sheep, Num 31.32
of sheep was six hundred and s. 31.37
sons of Arah, seven hundred and s. Ez 2.05
and slew s. thousand of those who Est 9.16
and all his kindred, s. souls; Ac 7.14

SEVENTY-FOUR
of Judah was s. thousand six Num 1.27
numbered being s. thousand six 2.04
of the sons of Hodoviah, s. Ez 2.40
Kadmiel of the sons of Hodevah, s. Neh 7.43

SEVENTY-SEVEN
were seven hundred and s. years; Gen 5.31
and elders of Succoth, s. men. Ju 8.14
s. lambs, and as a sin offering Ez 8.35

SEVENTY-SEVENFOLD
avenged sevenfold, truly Lamech s." Gen 4.24

SEVENTY-SIX
s. thousand five hundred. Num 26.22
two hundred and s. persons in the Ac 27.37

SEVENTY-THREE
thousand two hundred and s. Num 3.43
two hundred and s. of the first-born 3.46
of Jeshua, nine hundred and s. Ez 2.36
of Jeshua, nine hundred and s. Neh 7.39

SEVENTY-TWO
s. thousand cattle, Num 31.33
of which the LORD's tribute was s. 31.38
two thousand one hundred and s. Ez 2.03
Shephatiah, three hundred and s. 2.04
two thousand a hundred and s. Neh 7.08
Shephatiah, three hundred and s. 7.09
the gates, were a hundred and s. 11.19

SEVER
its neck, but shall not s. it, Lev 5.08

SEVERAL
distributing the s. territories of Jos 19.49
The cities of the s. families of 21.33
cities of the s. Merarite families, 21.40
their divisions for the s. gates; 2Ch 8.14
were men in the s. cities who were 31.19
and these are their s. portions, Eze 48.29
For s. days he was with the disciples Ac 9.19

SEVERE
for the famine was s. in the land. Gen 12.10
the famine was s. in the land of 41.56
the famine was s. over all the 41.57
Now the famine was s. in the land. 43.01
the famine is s. in the land of 47.04
for the famine was very s., 47.13
the famine was s. upon them. 47.20
with a very s. plague upon your Ex 9.03
afflictions s. and lasting, and Deu 28.59
illness was so s. that there was 1Ki 17.17
Now the famine was s. in Samaria. 18.02
famine was so s. in the city that 2Ki 25.03
feet, and his disease became s.; 2Ch 16.12
will have a s. sickness with a 21.15
There is s. discipline for him who Pro 15.10
the famine was so s. in the city, Jer 52.06
is the decree of the king so s.?" Dan 2.15
will, shall receive a s. beating. Lk 12.47
of you, because you are a s. man; 19.21
You knew that I was a s. man, 19.22
for in a s. test of affliction, 2Co 8.02
not have to be s. in my use of the 13.10

SEVERED
You are s. from Christ, you who Gal 5.04

SEVERELY
leaving him s. wounded, his servants 2Ch 24.25
my daughter is s. possessed by a Mt 15.22
not to put it too s.—to you all. 2Co 2.05

SEVERITY
the kindness and the s. of God: Rom 11.22
s. toward those who have fallen, but 11.22
self-abasement and s. to the body, Col 2.23

SEW
a time to rend, and a time to s.; Ecc 3.07
the women who s. magic bands upon Eze 13.18

SEWED
and they s. fig leaves together and Gen 3.07
I have s. sackcloth upon my skin, Job 16.15

SEWS
No one s. a piece of unshrunk cloth Mk 2.21

SEX
on the woman as the weaker s., 1Pe 3.07

SHAALABBIN
S., Aijalon, Ithlah, Jos 19.42

SHAALBIN
and in S., but the hand of the Ju 1.35
S., Bethshemesh, and Elonbethhanan; 1Ki 4.09

SHAALBON
Eliahba of S., the sons of Jashen, 2sa 23.32
Azmaveth of Baharum, Eliahba of S., 1Ch 11.33

SHAALIM
they passed through the land of S., 1Sa 9.04

SHAAPH
Geshan, Pelet, Ephah, and S. 1Ch 2.47
She also bore S. the father of 2.49

SHAARAIM
S., Adithaim, Gederah, Gederothaim: Jos 15.36
on the way from S. as far as Gath 1Sa 17.52
Hazarsusim, Bethbiri, and S. 1Ch 4.31

SHAASHGAZ
in custody of S. the king's eunuch Est 2.14

SHABBETHAI
Meshullam and S. the Levite Ez 10.15
S., Hodiah, Maaseiah, Kelita, Azariah, Neh 8.07
and S. and Jozabad, of the chiefs of 11.16

SHABBY
a poor man in s. clothing also Jas 2.02

SHADE
then come and take refuge in my s.; Ju 9.15
For his s. the lotus trees cover Job 40.22
mountains were covered with its s., Ps 80.10
LORD is your s. on your right hand 121.05
It will be for a s. by day from the Is 4.06
make your s. like night at the 16.03
the storm and a s. from the heat; 25.04
as heat by the s. of a cloud, 25.05
like the s. of a great rock in a 32.02
in the s. of its branches birds of Eze 17.23
with fair branches and forest s., 31.03
of the field found s. under it, Dan 4.12
which beasts of the field found s., 4.21
terebinth, because their s. is good. Hos 4.13
He sat under it in the s., Jon 4.05
it might be a s. over his head, 4.06
the air can make nests in its s." Mk 4.32

SHADES
The s. below tremble, the waters and Job 26.05
Do the s. rise up to praise thee? Ps 88.10
to death, and her paths to the s.; Pro 2.18
it rouses the s. to greet you, all Is 14.09
they are s., they will not arise; 26.14
the land of the s. thou wilt let 26.19

SHADOW
"You see the s. of the mountains as Ju 9.36
shall the s. go forward ten steps, 2Ki 20.09
thing for the s. to lengthen ten 20.10
rather let the s. go back ten steps." 20.10
he brought the s. back ten steps, 20.11
days on the earth are like a s., 1Ch 29.15
Like a slave who longs for the s., Job 7.02
for our days on earth are a s. 8.09
he flees like a s., and continues not. 14.02
and all my members are like a s. 17.07
hide me in the s. of thy wings, Ps 17.08
the valley of the s. of death, 23.04
take refuge in the s. of thy wings. 36.07
Surely man goes about as a s.! 39.06
in the s. of thy wings I will take 57.01
and in the s. of thy wings I sing 63.07
abides in the s. of the Almighty, 91.01
My days are like an evening s.; 102.11
I am gone, like a s. at evening; 109.23
his days are like a passing s. 144.04
life, which he passes like a s.? Ecc 6.12
will he prolong his days like a s., 8.13
With great delight I sat in his s., Sol 2.03
to seek shelter in the s. of Egypt! Is 30.02
shelter in the s. of Egypt to your 30.03
and gather her young in her s.; 34.15
Behold, I will make the s. cast by 38.08
in the s. of his hand he hid me; 49.02
and hid you in the s. of my hand, 51.16
"In the s. of Heshbon fugitives Jer 48.45
"Under his s. we shall live among Lam 4.20
and under its s. dwelt all great Eze 31.06
will go from its s. and leave it. 31.12
dwelt under its s. among the 31.17
return and dwell beneath my s., Hos 14.07
the region and s. of death light Mt 4.16
in darkness and in the s. of death, Lk 1.79
by at least his s. might fall on Ac 5.15
These are only a s. of what is to Col 2.17
a copy and s. of the heavenly Heb 8.05
law has but a s. of the good 10.01
no variation or s. due to change. Jas 1.17

SHADOWS
Until the day breathes and the s. flee, Sol 2.17
Until the day breathes and the s. flee, 4.06
for the s. of evening lengthen!" Jer. 6.04

SHADRACH
Belteshazzar, Hananiah he called S., Dan 1.07
of the king, and he appointed S., 2.49
of Babylon: S., Meshach, and Abednego. 3.12
in furious rage commanded that S., 3.13
O S., Meshach, and Abednego, that you 3.14
S., Meshach, and Abednego answered 3.16
of his face was changed against S., 3.19
mighty men of his army to bind S., 3.20
fire slew those men who took up S., 3.22
S., Meshach, and Abednego, fell bound 3.23
"S., Meshach, and Abednego, servants 3.26
Then S., Meshach, and Abednego came 3.26
said, "Blessed be the God of S., 3.28
anything against the God of S., 3.29
Then the king promoted S., Meshach, 3.30

SHAFT
base and the s. of the lampstand Ex 25.31
base and the s. of the lampstand 37.17
And the s. of his spear was like a 1Sa 17.07
up the water s. to attack the lame 2Sa 5.08
the s. of whose spear was like a 21.19
with iron and the s. of a spear, 23.07
the s. of whose spear was like a 1Ch 20.05
the key of the s. of the bottomless Rev 9.01
he opened the s. of the bottomless 9.02
and from the s. rose smoke like the 9.02
darkened with the smoke from the s. 9.02

SHAFTS
They open s. in a valley away from Job 28.04
weapons, making his arrows fiery s. Ps 7.13
pierce with thy s. the head of his Hab 3.14

SHAGEE
Jonathan the son of S. the Hararite, 1Ch 11.34

SHAHARAIM
And S. had sons in the country of 1Ch 8.08

SHAHAZUMAH
S., and Bethshemesh, and its boundary Jos 19.22

SHAKE

at other times, and s. myself free." Ju 16.20
"So may God s. out every man from Neh 5.13
trembling, which made all my bones s. Job 4.14
He will s. off his unripe grape, 15.33
against you, and s. my head at you. 16.04
the mountains s. in the heart of Ps 46.02
of the forest s. before the wind. Is 7.02
he will s. his fist at the mount of 10.32
and Carmel s. off their leaves. 33.09
S. yourself from the dust, arise; 52.02
broken within me, all my bones s.; Jer 23.09
your walls will s. at the noise of Eze 26.10
the coastlands s. at the sound of 26.15
and made all their loins to s.; 29.07
and the heavens and the earth s. Joe 3.16
capitals until the thresholds s., Amo 9.01
and s. the house of Israel among 9.09
I will s. the heavens and the earth Hag 2.06
and I will s. all nations, so that 2.07
I am about to s. the heavens and 2.21
I will s. my hand over them, and Zec 2.09
s. off the dust from your feet as Mt 10.14
s. off the dust that is on your Mk 6.11
and could not s. it, because it had Lk 6.48
leave that town s. off the dust 9.05
more I will s. not only the earth Heb 12.26

SHAKEN

as a reed is s. in the water, and 1Ki 14.15
So may he be s. out and emptied." Neh 5.13
the people are s. and pass away, Job 34.20
and the wicked be s. out of it? 38.13
my foes rejoice because I am s. Ps 13.04
my fortress; I shall not be s. 62.06
foundations of the earth are s. 82.05
so that it should never be s. 104.05
I am s. off like a locust. 109.23
earth will be s. out of its place, Is 13.13
the sea, he has s. the kingdoms; 23.11
asunder, the earth is violently s. 24.19
if s. they fall into the mouth of Nah 3.12
to behold? A reed s. by the wind? Mt 11.07
powers of the heavens will be s.; 24.29
powers in the heavens will be s. Mk 13.25
s. together, running over, will be Lk 6.38
to behold? A reed s. by the wind? 7.24
powers of the heavens will be s. 21.26
my right hand that I may not be s.; Ac 2.25
they were gathered together was s.; 4.31
foundations of the prison were s.; 16.26
not to be quickly s. in mind or 2Th 2.02
indicates the removal of what is s., Heb 12.27
that what cannot be s. may remain. 12.27
a kingdom that cannot be s., 12.28
its winter fruit when s. by a gale; Rev 6.13

SHAKES

who s. the earth out of its place, Job 9.06
of the LORD s. the wilderness, Ps 29.08
the LORD s. the wilderness of 29.08
the LORD of hosts s. over them. Is 19.16
who s. his hands, lest they hold a 33.15
by it is horrified and s. his head. Jer 18.16
he s. the arrows, he consults the Eze 21.21
of your pilots the countryside s., 27.28
the nations as one s. with a sieve, Amo 9.09
by her hisses and s. his fist. Zep 2.15

SHAKING

be a great s. in the land of Israel; Eze 38.19

SHALISHA

and passed through the land of S., 1Sa 9.04

SHALLECHETH

at the gate of S. on the road that 1Ch 26.16

SHALLUM

S. the son of Jabesh conspired 2Ki 15.10
S. the son of Jabesh began to reign 15.13
he struck down S. the son of 15.14
Now the rest of the deeds of S., 15.15
the wife of S. the son of Tikvah, 22.14
father of Sismai, and Sismai of S. 1Ch 2.40
S. was the father of Jekamiah, and 2.41
the third Zedekiah, the fourth S. 3.15
S. was his son, Mibsam his son, 4.25
Ahitub of Zadok, Zadok of S., 6.12
S. of Hilkiah, Hilkiah of Azariah, 6.13
and S., the offspring of Bilhah. 7.13
S., Akkub, Talmon, Ahiman, and their 9.17
their kinsmen (S. being the chief), 9.17
S. the son of Kore, son of Ebiasaph, 9.19
the first-born of S. the Korahite, 9.31
Meshillemoth, Jehizkiah the son of S., 2Ch 28.12
the wife of S. the son of Tokhath, 34.22
the sons of S., the sons of Ater, Ez 2.42
son of S., son of Zadok, son of 7.02
the gatekeepers: S., Telem, and Uri. 10.24
S., Amariah, and Joseph. 10.42
Next to him S. the son of Hallohesh, Neh 3.12
And S. the son of Colhozeh, ruler of 3.15
the sons of S., the sons of Ater, 7.45
LORD concerning S. the son of Jer 22.11
the son of S. your uncle will come 32.07
chamber of Maaseiah the son of S., 35.04

SHALMAI

the sons of Hagaba, the sons of S., Neh 7.48

SHALMAN

as S. destroyed Betharbel on the day Hos 10.14

SHALMANESER

Against him came up S. king of 2Ki 17.03
S. king of Assyria came up against 18.09

SHAMA

S. and Jeiel the sons of Hotham the 1Ch 11.44

SHAME

to their s. among their enemies), Ex 32.25
the son of Jesse to your own s., 1Sa 20.30
and to the s. of your mother's 20.30
As for me, where could I carry my s.? 2Sa 13.13
covered with s. th faces of all 19.05
and the Levites were put to s., 2Ch 30.15
returned with s. of face to his 32.21
and to utter s., as at this day. Ez 9.07
exile are is great trouble and s.; Neh 1.03
hate you will be clothed with s., Job 8.22
when you mock, shall no one s. you? 11.03
youth, and their life ends in s. 36.14
how long shall my honor suffer s.? Ps 4.02
back, and be put to s. in a moment. 6.10
I trust, let me not be put to s.; 25.02
that wait for thee be put to s.; 25.03
let me not be put to s., 25.20
let me never be put to s.; 31.01
Let me not be put to s., 31.17
let the wicked be put to s., 31.17
Let them be put to s. and dishonor 35.04
Let them be put to s. and confusion 35.26
be clothed with s. and dishonor 35.26
they are not put to s. in evil times, 37.19
Let them be put to s. and confusion 40.14
because of their s. who say to me, 40.15
before me., and s. has covered my face, 44.15
they will be put to s., for God has 53.05
he will put to s. those who trample 57.03
in thee be put to s. through me, 69.06
reproach, that s. has covered my face. 69.07
and my s. and my dishonor; my foes 69.19
Let them be put to s. and confusion 70.02
appalled because of their s. who say, 70.03

SHAME (cont.)
refuge; let me never be put to s.! Ps 71.01
accusers be put to s. and consumed; 71.13
been put to s. and disgraced who 71.24
Let not the downtrodden be put to s.; 74.21
he put them to everlasting s. 78.66
Fill their faces with s., that they 83.16
Let them be put to s. and dismayed 83.17
see and be put to s. because thou, 86.17
thou hast covered him with s. 89.45
worshipers of images are put to s., 97.07
Let my assailants be put to s.; 109.28
in their own s. as in a mantle! 109.29
Then I shall not be put to s., 119.06
O LORD; let me not be put to s.! 119.31
kings, and shall not be put to s.; 119.46
Let the godless be put to s., 119.78
that I may not be put to s.! 119.80
let me not be put to s. in my hope! 119.116
not be put to s. when he speaks 127.05
Zion be put to s. and turned 129.05
His enemies I will clothe with s., 132.18
she is wanton and knows no s. Pro 9.13
who sleeps in harvest brings s. 10.05
she who brings s. is like rottenness 12.04
he hears, it is his folly and s. 18.13
son who causes s. and brings 19.26
when your neighbor puts you to s.? 25.08
he who hears you bring s. upon you, 25.10
to himself brings s. to his mother. 29.15
of sackcloth; instead of beauty, s. Is 3.24
uncovered, to the s. of Egypt. 20.04
you s. of your master's house. 22.18
protection of Pharaoh turn to your s., 30.03
every one comes to s. through a 30.05
nor profit, but s. and disgrace." 30.05
shall be put to s. and confounded; 41.11
turned back and utterly put to s., 42.17
nor know, that they may be put to s. 44.09
all his fellows shall be put to s., 44.11
they shall be put to s. together. 44.11
them are put to s. and confounded, 45.16
not be put to s. or counfounded to 45.17
uncovered, and your s. shall be seen. 47.03
wait for me shall not be put to s." 49.23
not my face from s. and spitting. 50.06
know that I shall not be put to s.; 50.07
for you will not be put to s.; 54.04
will forget the s. of your youth, 54.04
Instead of your s. you shall have a 61.07
rejoice, but you shall be put to s.; 65.13
it is they who shall be put to s. 66.05
shall be put to s. by Egypt as you Jer 2.36
as you were put to s. by Assyria. 2.36
Let us lie down in our s., and let 3.25
The wise men shall be put to s., 8.09
goldsmith is put to s. by his idols; 10.14
the altars you have set up to s., 11.13
face, and your s. will be seen. 13.26
forsake thee shall be put to s.; 17.13
Let those be put to s. who persecute 17.18
me, but let me not be put to s.; 17.18
sorrow, and spend my days in s.? 20.18
everlasting reproach and perpetual s., 23.40
The nations have heard of your s., 46.12
of Egypt shall be put to s., 46.24
Kiriathaim is put to s., it is taken; 48.01
is put to s. and broken down; 48.01
Moab is put to s., for it is broken 48.20
How Moab has turned his back in s.! 48.39
Bel is put to s., Merodach is 50.02
Her images are put to s., her idols 50.02
goldsmith is put to s. by his idols; 51.17
her whole land shall be put to s., 51.47
'We are put to s., for we have 51.51
s. is upon all faces, and baldness Eze 7.18
Because your s. was laid bare and 16.36
mouth again because of your s., 16.63
they bear their s. with those who 32.24
they bear their s. with those who 32.25
gone down in s. with the slain, 32.30
and bear their s. with those who 32.30
They shall forget their s., 39.26
but they shall bear their s., 44.13
and some to s. and everlasting Dan 12.02
I will change their glory into s. Hos 4.07
they love s. more than their glory. 4.18
Ephraim shall be put to s., 10.06
shall never again be put to s. Joe 2.26
shall never again be put to s. 2.27
s. shall cover you, and you shall be Ob 1.10
of Shaphir, in nakedness and s.; Mic 1.11
disgraced, and the diviners put to s.; 3.07
and s. will cover her who said to 7.10
nakedness and kingdoms on your s. Nah 3.05
You have devised s. to your house Hab 2.10
them drunk, to gaze on their s.! 2.15
and s. will come upon your glory! 2.16
but the unjust knows no s. Zep 3.05
not be put to s. because of the 3.11
change their s. into praise and 3.19
man and unwilling to put her to s., Mt 1.19
all his adversaries were put to s.; Lk 13.17
will begin with s. to take the 14.09
in him will not be put to s." Rom 9.33
believes in him will be put to s." 10.11
in the world to s. the wise, 1Co 1.27
in the world to s. the strong, 1.27
I say this to your s. Can it be 6.05
of God. I say this to your s. 15.34
pride in you, I was not put to s.; 2Co 7.14
you, I shall not be put to s. 10.08
To my s., I must say, we were too 11.21
For it is a s. even to speak of the Eph 5.12
belly, and they glory in their s., Php 3.19
that an opponent may be put to s., Tit 2.08
despising the s., and is seated at Heb 12.02
in him will not be put to s." 1Pe 2.06
behavior in Christ may be put to s. 3.16
from him in s. at his coming. 1Jn 2.28
up the foam of their own s.; Jud 1.13
and to keep the s. of your nakedness Rev 3.18

SHAMED
should she not be s. seven days? Num 12.14
"As a thief is s. when caught, so Jer 2.26
so the house of Israel shall be s.: 2.26
We are utterly s., because we 9.19
she has been s. and disgraced. 15.09
They will be greatly s., for they 20.11
your mother shall be utterly s., 50.12

SHAMEFUL
it is a s. thing, and they shall be Lev 20.17
and charges her with s. conduct, Deu 22.14
he has made s. charges against her, 22.17
he has done a s. thing in Israel.'" Jos 7.15
our youth the s. thing has devoured Jer 3.24
For it is s. for a woman to speak 1Co 14.35
not for s. gain but eagerly, 1Pe 5.02

SHAMEFULLY
wicked man acts s. and disgracefully. Pro 13.05
his wrath falls on one who acts s. 14.35
will rule over a son who acts s., 17.02
that conceived them has acted s. Hos 2.05
treated them s., and killed them. Mt 22.06
in the head, and treated him s. Mk 12.04
be mocked and s. treated and spit Lk 18.32
him also they beat and treated s., 20.11
and been s. treated at Philippi, as 1Th 2.02

SHAMELESS
together and hold assembly, O s. nation, Zep 2.01
men committing s. acts with men and Rom 1.27

SHAMELESSLY
the vulgar fellows s. uncovers himself!" 2Sa 6.20

SHAMES
companion of gluttons s. his father. Pro 28.07

SHAMGAR
After him was S. the son of Anath, Ju 3.31
"In the days of S., son of Anath, 5.06

SHAMHUTH
fifth month, was S., the Izrahite; 1Ch 27.08

SHAMIR
in the hill country, S., Jattir, Soco, Jos 15.48
and he lived at S. in the hill country Ju 10.01
Then he died, and was buried at S. 10.02
Uzziel, Micah; of the sons of Micah, S. 1Ch 24.24

SHAMLAI
the sons of S., the sons of Hanan, Ez 2.46

SHAMMA
Bezer, Hod, S., Shilshah, Ithran, and 1Ch 7.37

SHAMMAH
of Reuel: Nahath, Zerah, S., and Mizzah. Gen 36.13
the chiefs Nahath, Zerah, S., and Mizzah; 36.17
Then Jesse made S. pass by. And he 1Sa 16.09
to him Abinadab, and the third S. 17.13
And next to him was S., the son of 2Sa 23.11
S. of Harod, Elika of Harod, 23.25
S. the Hararite, ahiam the son of 23.33
of Reuel: Nahath, Zerah S., and Mizzah. 1Ch 1.37

SHAMMAI
The sons of Onam: S. and Jada. The 1Ch 2.28
The sons of S.: Nadab and Abishur. 2.28
and Rekem was the father of S. 2.44
The son of S.: Maon; and Maon was 2.45
Miriam, S., and Ishbah, the father of 4.17

SHAMMAI'S
the sons of Jada, S. brother: Jether and 1Ch 2.32

SHAMMOTH
S. of Harod, Helez the Pelonite, 1Ch 11.27

SHAMMUA
tribe of Reuben, S. the son of Zaccur; Num 13.04
Jerusalem: S., Shobab, Nathan, Solomon, 2Sa 5.14
Jerusalem: S., Shobab, Nathan, Solomon, 1Ch 14.04
and Abda the son of S., son of Galal, Neh 11.17
of Bilgah, S.; of Shamaiah, Jehonathan; 12.18

SHAMSHERAI
S., Shehariah, Athaliah, 1Ch 8.26

SHAPED
Before the mountains had been s., Pro 8.25
an idol when its maker has s. it, Hab 2.18

SHAPES
he s. it with hammers, and forges it Is 44.12
he s. it into the figure of a man, 44.13

SHAPHAM
S. the second, Janai, and Shaphat in 1Ch 5.12

SHAPHAN
the king sent S. the son of Azaliah, 2Ki 22.03
priest said to S. the secretary, 22.08
And Hilkiah gave the book to S., 22.08
And S. the secretary came to the 22.09
Then S. the secretary told the king, 22.10
And S. read it before the king. 22.10
priest, and Ahikam the son of S., 22.12
and S. the secretary, and Asaiah the 22.12
and S., and Asaiah went to Huldah 22.14
son of Ahikam, son of S., governor. 25.22
he sent S. the son of Azaliah, and 2Ch 34.08
Then Hilkiah said to S. the secretary, 34.15
and Hilkiah gave the book to S. 34.15
S. brought the book to the king, and 34.16
Then S. the secretary told the king, 34.18
And S. read it before the king. 34.18
Hilkiah, Ahikam the son of S., 34.20
S. the secretary, and Asaiah the 34.20
the son of S. was with Jeremiah so Jer 26.24
the son of S. and Gemariah the son 29.03
the son of S. the secretary, 36.10
son of S., heard all the words of 36.11
of Achbor, Gemariah the son of S., 36.12
son of S., that he should take him 39.14
son of S., whom the king of Babylon 40.05
son of S., swore to them and their 40.09
son of S., as governor over them, 40.11
son of S., with the sword, and 41.02
the son of Ahikam, son of S.; 43.06
the son of S. standing among them. Eze 8.11

SHAPHAT
tribe of Simeon, S. the son of Hori; Num 13.05
the son of S. of Abelmeholah you 1Ki 19.16
and found Elisha the son of S., 19.19
"Elisha the son of S. is here, 2Ki 3.11
the son of S. remains on his 6.31
Igal, Bariah Neariah, and S., six. 1Ch 3.22
second, Janai, and S. in Bashan. 5.12
the valleys was S. the son of Adlai. 27.29

SHAPHIR
Pass on your way, inhabitants of S., Mic 1.11

SHAPING
I am s. evil against you and devising Jer 18.11

SHARAI
Machnadebai, Shashai, S., Ez 10.40

SHARAR
Ahiam the son of S. the Hararite, 2Sa 23.33

SHARE
and the s. of the men who went with Gen 14.24
Eshcol, and Mamre take their s." 14.24
should have no s. in the heritage 1Sa 26.19
For as his s. is who goes down into 30.24
battle, so shall his s. be who stays 30.24
by the baggage; they shall s. alike." 30.24
inherit a double s. of your spirit." 2Ki 2.09
to get a s. of their property, the Job 17.05
given her no s. in understanding. 39.17
and will s. the inheritance as one Pro 17.02
for ever any s. in all that is Ecc 9.06
Is it not to s. your bread with the Is 58.07
let him s. with him who has none; Lk 3.11
give me the s. of property that 15.12
allotted his s. in this ministry. Ac 1.17
to those who s. the faith of Rom 4.16
their place to s. the richness of 11.17
have come to s. in their spiritual 15.27
that we might s. the rule with you! 1Co 4.08
thresh in hope of a s. in the crop. 9.10
If others s. this rightful claim 9.12
at the altar s. in the sacrificial 9.13
that I may s. in its blessings. 9.23
For as we s. abundantly in Christ's 2Co 1.05
Christ we s. abundantly in comfort 1.05
that as you s. in our sufferings, 1.07
you will also s. in our comfort. 1.07
taught the word s. all good things Gal 6.06
and may s. his sufferings, becoming Php 3.10
was kind of you to s. my trouble. 4.14
qualified us to s. in the inheritance Col 1.12
were ready to s. with you not only 1Th 2.08
but take your s. of suffering for 2Ti 1.08

SHARE (cont.)
Take your s. of suffering as a good 2Ti 2.03
to have the first s. of the crops. 2.06
the children s. in flesh and blood, Heb 2.14
who s. in a heavenly call, consider 3.01
For we s. in Christ, if only we hold 3.14
choosing rather to s. ill-treatment 11.25
good, that we may s. his holiness. 12.10
to do good and to s. what you have, 13.16
so far as you s. Christ's sufferings, 1Pe 4.13
who s. with you in Jesus the Rev 1.09
sins, lest you s. in her plagues; 18.04
take away his s. in the tree of 22.19

SHARED
and because you s. in all the 1Ki 2.26
than in a house s. with a contentious Pro 21.09
than in a house s. with a contentious 25.24

SHARES
"We have ten s. in the king, and in 2Sa 19.43
bitterness, and no stranger s. its joy. Pro 14.10
for he s. his bread with the poor. 22.09
who greets him s. his wicked work. 2Jn 1.11
holy is he who s. in the first Rev 20.06

SHAREZER
Adrammelech and S., his sons, slew him 2Ki 19.37
his god, Adrammelech and S., his sons, Is 37.38
Bethel had sent S. and Regemmelech Zec 7.02

SHARING
in our hope of s. the glory of God. Rom 5.02
and I pray that the s. of your Phm 1.06

SHARON
pasture lands of S. to their limits. 1Ch 5.16
that pastured in S. was Shitrai the 27.29
I am a rose of S., a lily of the Sol 2.01
S. is like a desert; and Bashan Is 33.09
to it, the majesty of Carmel and S. 35.02
S. shall become a pasture for flocks, 65.10
residents of Lydda and S. saw him, Ac 9.35

SHARONITE
pastured in Sharon was Shitrai the S.; 1Ch 27.29

SHARP
His underparts are like s. potsherds; Job 41.30
Your arrows are s. in the heart of Ps 45.05
Your tongue is like a s. razor, 52.02
arrows, their tongues s. swords. 57.04
A warrior's s. arrows, with glowing 120.04
their tongue s. as a serpent's 140.03
wormwood, s. as a two-edged sword. Pro 5.04
club, or a sword, or a s. arrow. 25.18
their arrows are s., all their bows Is 5.28
sledge, new, s., and having teeth; 41.15
He made my mouth like a s. sword, 49.02
you, O son of man, take a s. sword; Eze 5.01
And there arose a s. contention, Ac 15.39
mouth issued a s. two-edged sword, Rev 1.16
him who has the s. two-edged sword. 2.12
his head, and a s. sickle in his hand. 14.14
heaven, and he too had a s. sickle. 14.17
voice to him who had the s. sickle, 14.18
mouth issues a s. sword with which 19.15

SHARPEN
Philistines to s. his plowshare, his 1Sa 13.20
"S. the arrows! Take up the shields! Jer 51.11

SHARPENED
a sword is s. and also polished, Eze 21.09
s. for slaughter, polished to flash 21.10
it is s. and polished to be given 21.11

SHARPENING
third of a shekel for s. the axes and 1Sa 13.21

SHARPENS
my adversary s. his eyes against me Job 16.09
Iron s. iron, and one man s. another. Pro 27.17

SHARPER
s. than any two-edged sword, piercing Heb 4.12

SHARPLY
Cut s. to right and left where your Eze 21.16
Therefore rebuke them s., that they Tit 1.13

SHARUHEN
and S.—thirteen cities with their Jos 19.06

SHASHAI
Machnadebai, S., Sharai, Ez 10.40

SHASHAK
and Ahio, S., and Jeremoth. 1Ch 8.14
Iphdeiah, and Penuel were the sons of S. 8.25

SHATTER
wind thou didst s. the ship of Ps 48.07
will you set upon a man to s. him, 62.03
But God will s. the heads of his 68.21
he will s. kings on the day of his 110.05
he will s. chiefs over the wide 110.06
and s. them on the heads of all the Amo 9.01

SHATTERED
and s. every tree of the field. Ex 9.25
she s. and pierced his temple. Ju 5.26
and s. the trees of their country. Ps 105.33
her gods he has s. to the ground." Is 21.09
"We are s. but we will rebuild the Mal 1.04

SHATTERER
The s. has come up against you. Man Nah 2.01

SHATTERING
that when the s. of the power of the Dan 12.07

SHATTERS
right hand, O LORD, s. the enemy. Ex 15.06
He s. the mighty without investigation, Job 34.24
and s. the spear, he burns the Ps 46.09
For he s. the doors of bronze, and 107.16
one cleaves and s. on the land, 141.07
breaks to pieces and s. all things; Dan 2.40
and s. him, and will hardly leave Lk 9.39

SHAUL
and S. of Rehoboth on the Euphrates Gen 36.37
S. died, and Baalhanan the son of 36.38
and S., the son of Canaanitish 46.10
and S., the son of Canaanite Ex 6.15
of S., the family of the Shaulites. Num 26.13
S. of Rehoboth on the Euphrates 1Ch 1.48
When S. died, Baalhanan, the son of 1.49
Nemuel, Jamin, Jarib, Zerah, S.; 4.24
Uzziah his son, and S. his son. 6.24

SHAULITES
Zerahites; of Shaul, the family of the S. Num 26.13

SHAVE
then he shall s. himself, but the Lev 13.33
but the itch he shall not s.; 13.33
and s. off all his hair, and bathe 14.08
day he shall s. all his hair off 14.09
he shall s. off his beard and his 14.09
nor s. off the edges of their 21.05
then he shall s. his head on the Num 6.09
on the seventh day he shall s. it. 6.09
Nazirite shall s. his consecrated 6.18
and she shall s. her head and pare Deu 21.12
and had him s. off the seven locks Ju 16.19
the Lord will s. with a razor Is 7.20

SHAVE (cont.)
They shall not s. their heads or Eze 44.20
so that they may s. their heads. Ac 21.24

SHAVED
and when he had s. himself and Gen 41.14
If I be s., then my strength will Ju 16.17
to grow again after it had been s. 16.22
and s. off half the beard of each, 2Sa 10.04
and s. them, and cut off their 1Ch 19.04
and s. his head, and fell upon the Job 1.20
their beards s. and their clothes Jer 41.05
"For every head is s. and every 48.37

SHAVEH
him at the Valley of S. (that is, the Gen 14.17

SHAVEHKIRIATHAIM
the Zuzim in Ham, the Emim in S., Gen 14.05

SHAVEN
after he has s. the hair of his Num 6.19
is the same as if her head were s. 1Co 11.05
for a woman to be shorn or s., 11.06

SHAVSHA
Abiathar were priests; and S. was 1Ch 18.16

SHEAF
and lo, my s. arose and stood upright; Gen 37.07
round it, and bowed down to my s." 37.07
shall bring the s. of the first Lev 23.10
shall wave the s. before the LORD, 23.11
And on the day when you wave the s., 23.12
you brought the s. of the wave 23.15
have forgotten a s. in the field, Deu 24.19

SHEAL
Adaiah, Jashub, S., and Jeremoth. Ez 10.29

SHEALTIEL
Jeconiah, the captive: S. his son, 1Ch 3.17
the son of S. with his kinsmen, and Ez 3.02
the son of S. and Jeshua the son 3.08
the son of S. and Jeshua the son 5.02
up with Zerubbabel the son of S., Neh 12.01
to Zerubbabel the son of S., Hag 1.01
Then Zerubbabel the son of S., 1.12
spirit of Zerubbabel the son of S., 1.14
"Speak now of Zerubbabel the son of S., 2.02
the son of S., says the LORD, and 2.23
Jechoniah was the father of S., Mt 1.12
and S. the father of Zerubbabel, 1.12
the son of S., the son of Neri, Lk 3.27

SHEAR
Laban had gone to s. his sheep, and Gen 31.19
going up to Timnah to s. his sheep," 38.13
nor s. the firstlings of your flock. Deu 15.19

SHEARER
or a lamb before its s. is dumb, so he Ac 8.32

SHEARERS
I hear that you have s.; now your 1Sa 25.07
meat that I have killed for my s., 25.11
a sheep that before its s. is dumb, Is 53.07

SHEARIAH
Bocheru, Ishmael, S., Obadiah, and Hanan. 1Ch 8.38
Bocheru, Ishmael, S., Obadiah, and Hanan; 9.44

SHEARING
goats. He was s. his sheep in Carmel. 1Sa 25.02
wilderness that Nabal was s. his sheep. 25.04

SHEARJASHUB
you and S. your son, at the end of Is 7.03

SHE-ASSES
maidservants, s., and camels. Gen 12.16
ten bulls, twenty s. and ten he-asses. 32.15
and ten s. loaded with grain, bread, 45.23
and over the s. was Jehdeiah the 1Ch 27.30
yoke of oxen, and five hundred s., Job 1.03
yoke of oxen, and a thousand s. 42.12

SHEATH
his sword and drew it out of its s., 1Sa 17.51
with a sword in its s. fastened upon 2Sa 20.08
he put his sword back into its s. 1Ch 21.27
draw forth my sword out of its s., Eze 21.03
go out of its s. against all flesh 21.04
have drawn my sword out of its s.; 21.05
Return it to its s. In the place 21.30
Thou didst strip the s. from thy bow, Hab 3.09
Peter, "Put your sword into its s.; Jn 18.11

SHEATHED
its sheath; it shall not be s. again. Eze 21.05

SHEAVES
behold, we were binding s. in the field, Gen 37.07
your s. gathered round it, and bowed 37.07
among the s. after the reapers.' Ru 2.07
"Let her glean even among the s., 2.15
clothing; hungry, they carry the s.; Job 24.10
of joy, bringing his s. with him. Ps 126.06
or the binder of s. his bosom, 129.07
like s. after the reaper, and none Jer 9.22
as a cart full of s. presses down. Amo 2.13
gathered them as s. to the threshing Mic 4.12
like a flaming torch among s.; Zec 12.06

SHEBA
The sons of Raamah: S. and Dedan. Gen 10.07
Obal, Abimael, S., 10.28
Jokshan was the father of S. and Dedan. 25.03
inheritance Beersheba, S., Moladah, Jos 19.02
worthless fellow, whose name was S., 2Sa 20.01
and followed S. the son of Bichri; 20.02
"Now S. the son of Bichri will do 20.06
to pursue S. the son of Bichri. 20.07
brother pursued S. the son of 20.10
Joab to pursue S. the son of 20.13
And S. passed through all the 20.14
called as. the son of Bichri, has 20.21
off the head of S. the son of 20.22
the queen of S. heard of the fame 1Ki 10.01
the queen of S. had seen all the 10.04
the queen of S. gave to King 10.10
to the queen of S. all that she 10.13
The sons of Raamah: S. and Dedan. 1Ch 1.09
Ebal, Abimael, S., 1.22
the sons of Jokshan: S. and Dedan. 1.32
S., Jorai, Jacan, Zia, and Eber, seven. 5.13
the queen of S. heard of the fame 2Ch 9.01
the queen of S. had seen the 9.03
the queen of S. gave to King 9.09
to the queen of S. all that she 9.12
look, the travelers of S. hope. Job 6.19
the kings of S. and Seba bring Ps 72.10
may gold of S. be given to him! 72.15
all those from S. shall come. Is 60.06
frankincense come to me from S., Jer 6.20
The traders of S. and Raamah traded Eze 27.22
S. and Dedan and the merchants of 38.13

SHEBANIAH
S., Joshaphat, Nethanel, Amasai, 1Ch 15.24
S., Bunni, Sherebiah, Bani, and Neh 9.04
S., and Pethahiah, said, "Stand up 9.05
Hattush, S., Malluch, 10.04

SHEBANIAH (cont.)
S., Hodiah, Kelita, Pelaiah, Hanan, Neh 10.10
Zaccur, Sherebiah, S., 10.12
of Malluchi, Jonathan, of S., Joseph; 12.14

SHEBARIM
them before the gate as far as S., Jos 7.05

SHEBAT
eleventh month which is the month of S., Zec 1.07

SHE-BEAR
Let a man meet a s. robbed of her cubs, Pro 17.12

SHE-BEARS
And two s. came out of the woods and 2Ki 2.24

SHEBER
Caleb's concubine, bore S. and Tirhanah. 1Ch 2.48

SHEBNA
and S. the secretary, and Joah the 2Ki 18.37
and S. the secretary, and the senior 19.02
to S., who is over the household, Is 22.15
and S. the secretary, and Joah the 36.03
Then Eliakim, S., and Joah said to 36.11
and S. the secretary, and Joah the 36.22
and S. the secretary, and the senior 37.02

SHEBNAH
and S. the secretary, and Joah the 2Ki 18.18
Hilkiah, and S., and Joah, said to the 18.26

SHEBUEL
The sons of Gershom: S. the chief. 1Ch 23.16
S., and Jerimoth, Hananiah, Hanani, 25.04
and S. the son of Gershom, son of 26.24

SHECANIAH
Arnan, his son Obadiah, his son S. 1Ch 3.21
The sons of S.: Shemaiah. And the 3.22
the ninth to Jeshua, the tenth to S., 24.11
and S. were faithfully assisting 2Ch 31.15
of the sons of S. Of the sons of Ez 8.03
S. the son of Jahaziel, and with him 8.05
And S. the son of Jehiel, of the 10.02
After him Shemaiah the son of S., Neh 3.29
son-in-law of S. the son of Arah: 6.18
S., Rehum, Meremoth, 12.03

SHECHEM
the land to the place at S., Gen 12.06
came safely to the city of S., 33.18
and when S. the son of Hamor the 34.02
So S. spoke to his fathe Hamor, 34.04
the father of S. went out to Jacob 34.06
soul of my son S. longs for your 34.08
S. also said to her father and to 34.11
Jacob answered S. and his father 34.13
pleased Hamor and Hamor's son S. 34.18
and his son S. came to the gate of 34.20
hearkened to Hamor and his son S.; 34.24
and his son S. with the sword, 34.26
under the oak which was near S. 35.04
their father's flock near S. 37.12
brothers pasturing the flock at S.? 37.13
of Hebron, and he came to S. 37.14
and of S., the family of the Num 26.31
Helek, Asriel, S., Hepher, and Shemida; Jos 17.02
Michmethath, which is east of S.; 17.07
and S. in the hill country of 20.07
To them were given S., the city of 21.21
all the tribes of Israel to S., 24.01
and ordinances for them at S. 24.25
up from Egypt were buried at S., 24.32
the father of S. for a hundred 24.32
who was in S. also bore him a son, Ju 8.31
Jerubbaal went to S. to his mother's 9.01
the ears of all the citizens of S., 9.02
in the ears of all the men of S.; 9.03
the citizens of S. came together, 9.06
by the oak of the pillar at S. 9.06
you men of S., that God may listen 9.07
king over the citizens of S., 9.18
the citizens of S., and Bethmillo; 9.20
come out from the citizens of S., 9.20
Abimelech and the men of S.; 9.23
and the men of S. dealt treacherously 9.23
slew them, and upon the men of S., 9.24
And the men of S. put men in ambush 9.25
Ebed moved into S. with his 9.26
and the men of S. put confidence in 9.26
is Abimelech, and who are we of S., 9.28
the men of Hamor the father of S.? 9.28
and his kinsmen have come to S., 9.31
wait against S. in four companies. 9.34
out at the head of the men of S., 9.39
that they could not live on at S. 9.41
of the Tower of S. heard of it, 9.46
of the Tower of S. were gathered 9.47
of the Tower of S. also died, 9.49
of the men of S. fall back upon 9.57
that goes up from Bethel to S., 21.19
Rehoboam went to S., for all Israel 1Ki 12.01
had come to S. to make him king. 12.01
Then Jeroboam built S. in the hill 12.25
S. with its pasture lands in the 1Ch 6.67
were Ahian, S., Likhi, and Aniam. 7.19
S. and its towns, and Ayyah and its 7.28
Rehoboam went to S., for all Israel 2Ch 10.01
had come to S. to make him king. 10.01
will divide up S. and portion out Ps 60.06
exultation I will divide up S., 108.07
arrived from S. and Shiloh and Jer 41.05
they murder on the way to S., Hos 6.09
carried back to S. and laid in the Ac 7.16
from the sons of Hamor in S. 7.16

SHECHEM'S
S. father, he bought for a hundred Gen 33.19
and took Dinah out to S. house, 34.26

SHECHEMITES
of Shechem, the family of the S.; Num 26.31

SHED
man, by man shall his blood be s.; Gen 9.06
And Reuben said to them, "S. no blood; 37.22
he has s. blood; and that man Lev 17.04
for the blood that is s. in it, Num 35.33
by the blood of him who s. it. 35.33
blood be s. in your land which the Deu 19.10
'Our hands did not s. this blood, 21.07
neither did our eyes see it s. 21.07
for having s. blood without cause 1Sa 25.31
and s. his bowels to the ground, 2Sa 20.10
blood which had been s. in war, 1Ki 2.05
blood which Joab s. without cause. 2.31
Moreover Manasseh s. very much 2Ki 21.16
the innocent blood that he had s.; 24.04
'You have s. much blood and have 1Ch 22.08
you have s. so much blood before 22.08
are a warrior and have s. blood.' 28.03
O God, thou didst s. abroad; Ps 68.09
My eyes s. streams of tears, because 119.136
his crown will s. its luster. 132.18
and they make haste to s. blood. Pro 1.16
and hands that s. innocent blood, 6.17
and the moon will not s. its light. Is 13.10
disclose the blood s. upon her, 26.21
make haste to s. innocent blood; 59.07
or s. innocent blood in this place, Jer 7.06
nor s. innocent blood in this place 22.03
who s. in the midst of her the Lam 4.13
wedlock and s. blood are judged, Eze 16.38

SHED (cont.)
by the blood which you have s., Eze 22.04
men in you who slander to s. blood, 22.09
In you men take bribes to s. blood; 22.12
sentence of women that s. blood; 23.45
blood she has s. is still in the 24.07
the bare rock the blood she has s., 24.08
eyes to your idols, and s. blood; 33.25
which they had s. in the land, 36.18
they have s. innocent blood in Joe 3.19
the righteous blood s. on earth, Mt 23.35
s. from the foundation of the world, Lk 11.50
of Stephen thy witness was s., Ac 22.20
"Their feet are swift to s. blood, Rom 3.15
For men have s. the blood of saints Rev 16.06

SHEDDER
a s. of blood, who does none of Eze 18.10

SHEDDING
for s. innocent blood, and for Jer 22.17
power, have been bent on s. blood. Eze 22.06
s. blood, destroying lives to get 22.27
with them in s. the blood of the Mt 23.30
and without the s. of blood there Heb 9.22
to the point of s. your blood. 12.04

SHEDEUR
from Reuben, Elizur the son of D.; Num 1.05
Reuben being Elizur the son of S., 2.10
fourth day Elizur the son of S., 7.30
offering of Elizur the son of S. 7.35
host was Elizur the son of S. 10.18

SHEDS
Whoever s. the blood of man, by man Gen 9.06
A city that s. blood in the midst Eze 22.03
as the fig tree s. its winter fruit Rev 6.13

SHEEP
Now Abel was a keeper of s., and Gen 4.02
and he had s., oxen, he-asses, 12.16
Then Abimelech took s. and oxen, 20.14
So Abraham took s. and oxen and 21.27
three flocks of s. lying beside it 29.02
and water the s., and put the stone 29.03
his daughter is coming with the s.!" 29.06
water the s., and go, pasture them." 29.07
of the well; then we water the s." 29.08
Rachel came with her father's s.; 29.09
and the s. of Laban his mother's 29.10
and spotted s. and every black 30.32
Laban had gone to shear his s., 31.19
up to Timnah to shear his s.," 38.13
it from the s. or from the goats; Ex 12.05
offerings, your s. and your oxen; 20.24
"If a man steals an ox or a s., 22.01
five oxen for an ox, and four s. for a s. 22.01
it is an ox or an ass or a s., 22.04
for s., for clothing, or for any 22.09
or an ox or a s. or any beast to 22.10
with your oxen and with your s.: 22.30
the firstlings of cow and s. 34.19
from the s. or goats, he shall offer Lev 1.10
eat no fat, of ox, or s., or goat. 7.23
the bulls or the s. or the goats. 22.19
"When a bull or s. or goat is born, 22.27
whether ox or s., it is the LORD's 27.26
of a cow, or the firstling of a s., Num 18.17
And Balak sacrificed oxen and s., 22.40
may not be as s. which have no 27.17
and seventy-five thousand s., 31.32
thirty-seven thousand five hundred s., 31.36
tribute of s. was six hundred and 31.37
thirty-seven thousand five hundred s., 31.43
little ones, and folds for your s.; 32.24
fortified cities, and folds for s. 32.36
may eat: the ox, the s., the goat, Deu 14.04
or s., or wine or strong drink, 14.26
God an ox or a s. in which is a 17.01
sacrifice, whether it be ox or s.: 18.03
the first of the fleece of your s., 18.04
brother's ox or his s. go astray, 22.01
your s. shall be given to your 28.31
s., and asses, with the edge of the Jos 6.21
and his oxen and asses and s., 7.24
in Israel, and no s. or ox or ass. Ju 6.04
and took s. and oxen and calves, and 1Sa 14.32
every man bring his ox or his s., 14.34
suckling, ox and s., camel and ass.'" 15.03
the best of the s. and of the oxen 15.09
this bleating of the s. in my ears, 15.14
the best of the s. and of the oxen, 15.15
s. and oxen, the best of the things 15.21
but behold, he is keeping the s." 16.11
David your son, who is with the s." 16.19
feed his father's s. at Bethlehem. 17.15
and left the s. with a keeper, and 17.20
left those few s. in the wilderness? 17.28
used to keep s. for his father; 17.34
asses and s., he put to the sword. 22.19
three thousand s. and a thousand 25.02
He was shearing his s. in Carmel. 25.02
that Nabal was shearing his s. 25.04
we were with them keeping the s. 25.16
and five s. ready dressed, and five 25.18
woman alive, but took away the s., 27.09
the pasture, from following the s., 2Sa 7.08
honey and curds and s. and cheese 17.29
but these s., what have they done 24.17
Adonijah sacrificed s., oxen, and 1Ki 1.09
and s. in abundance, and has invited 1.19
and s. in abundance, and has invited 1.25
a hundred s., besides harts, gazelles, 4.23
sacrificing so many s. and oxen 8.05
a hundred and twenty thousand s. 8.63
as s. that have no shepherd; 22.17
king of Moab was a s. breeder; 2Ki 3.04
s. and oxen, menservants and maidservants? 5.26
two hundred and fifty thousand s., 1Ch 5.21
oxen and s., for there was joy in 12.40
the pasture, from following the s., 17.07
But these s., what have they done? 21.17
sacrificing so many s. and oxen 2Ch 5.06
a hundred and twenty thousand s. 7.05
carried away s. in abundance and 14.15
hundred oxen and seven thousand s. 15.11
an abundance of s. and oxen for 18.02
as s. that have no shepherd; 18.16
bulls and three thousand s. 29.33
seven thousand s. for offerings, 30.24
thousand bulls and ten thousand s. 30.24
in the tithe of cattle and s., 31.06
or s. for burnt offerings to the Ez 6.09
priests and they built the S. Gate. Neh 3.01
corner and the S. Gate the goldsmiths 3.32
day was one ox and six choice s.; 5.18
of the Hundred, to the S. Gate; 12.39
He had seven thousand s., three Job 1.03
burned up the s. and the servants, 1.16
warmed with the fleece of my s.; 31.20
and he had fourteen thousand s., 42.12
all s. and oxen, and also the beasts Ps 8.07
hast made us like s. for slaughter, 44.11
accounted as s. for the slaughter. 44.22
Like s. they are appointed for 49.14
against the s. of thy pasture? 74.01
Then he led forth his people like s., 78.52
pasture, and the s. of his hand. 95.07
people, and the s. of his pasture. 100.03
I have gone astray like a lost s.; 119.176
may our s. bring forth thousands 144.13
keep alive a young cow and two s.; Is 7.21
are let loose and where s. tread. 7.25
or like s. with none to gather them, 13.14

SHEEP (cont.)
slaying oxen and killing s., Is 22.13
brought me your s. for burnt 43.23
All we like s. have gone astray; 53.06
and like a s. that before its 53.07
them out like s. for the slaughter, Jer 12.03
and scatter the s. of my pasture!" 23.01
"My people have been lost s.; 50.06
"Israel is a hunted s. driven away 50.17
Should not shepherds feed the s.? Eze 34.02
but you do not feed the s. 34.03
My s. were scattered, they wandered 34.06
my s. were scattered over all the 34.06
because my s. have become a prey, 34.08
and my s. have become food for all 34.08
have not searched for my s., 34.08
themselves, and have not fed my s.; 34.08
I will require my s. at their hand, 34.10
put a stop to their feeding the s.; 34.10
will rescue my s. from their 34.10
I, I myself will search for my s., 34.11
some of his s. have been scattered 34.12
abroad, so will I seek out my s.; 34.12
will be the shepherd of my s., 34.15
I judge between s. and s., rams 34.17
And must my s. eat what you have 34.19
between the fat s. and the lean s. 34.20
and I will judge between s. and s. 34.22
And you are my s., the s. of my pasture, 34.31
and one s. from every flock of two 45.15
wife, and for a wife he herded s.) Hos 12.12
even the flocks of s. are dismayed. Joe 1.18
them together like s. in a fold, Mic 2.12
young lion among the flocks of s., 5.08
Therefore the people wander like s.; Zec 10.02
for those who trafficked in the s. 11.07
named Union. And I tended the s. 11.07
day, and the traffickers in the s., 11.11
that the s. may be scattered; 13.07
like s. without a shepherd. Mt 9.36
to the lost s. of the house of 10.06
send you out as s. in the midst of 10.16
if he has one s. and it falls into 12.11
much more value is a man than a s.! 12.12
to the lost s. of the house of 15.24
If a man has a hundred s., and one 18.12
separates the s. from the goats, 25.32
will place the s. at his right 25.33
and the s. of the flock will be 26.31
they were like s. without a shepherd; Mk 6.34
and the s. will be scattered.' 14.27
"What man of you, having a hundred s., Lk 15.04
I have found my s. which was lost.' 15.06
a servant plowing or keeping s., 17.07
selling oxen and s. and pigeons, Jn 2.14
with the s. and oxen, out of the 2.15
in Jerusalem by the s. gate a pool, 5.02
the door is the shepherd of the s. 10.02
the s. hear his voice, and he calls 10.03
calls his own s. by name and leads 10.03
and the s. follow him, for they know 10.04
to you, I am the door of the s. 10.07
but the s. did not heed them. 10.08
lays down his life for the s. 10.11
whose own the s. are not, sees the 10.12
coming and leaves the s. and flees; 10.12
and cares nothing for the s. 10.13
and I lay down my life for the s. 10.15
And I have other s., that are not 10.16
because you do not belong to my s. 10.26
My s. hear my voice, and I know them, 10.27
He said to him, "Tend my s." 21.16
Jesus said to him, "Feed my s." 21.17
"As a s. led to the slaughter or a Ac 8.32
are regarded as s. to be slaughtered Rom 8.36
about in skins of s. and goats, Heb 11.37
the great shepherd of the s., 13.20
For you were straying like s., 1Pe 2.25
cattle and s., horses and chariots, Rev 18.13

SHEEPFOLD
of the Jordan against a strong s., Jer 49.19
of the Jordan against a strong s., 50.44
not enter the s. by the door but Jn 10.01

SHEEPFOLDS
ass, crouching between the s.; Gen 49.14
"We will build s. here for our Num 32.16
Why did you tarry among the s., Ju 5.16
And he came to the s. by the way, 1Sa 24.03
for all kinds of cattle, and s. 2Ch 32.28
though they stay among the s.— Ps 68.13
servant, and took him from the s.; 78.70

SHEEP'S
who come to you in s. clothing but Mt 7.15

SHEEPSHEARERS
he went up to Timnah to his s., Gen 38.12
years Abslon had s. at Baalhazor, 2Sa 13.23
said, "Behold, your servant has s.; 13.24

SHEEPSKIN
the covering of s. that is on top of it, Num 4.25

SHEER
and it will be s. terror to understand Is 28.19

SHEERAH
His daughter was S., who built both 1Ch 7.24

SHEET
like a great s., let down by four Ac 10.11
like a great s., let down from heaven 11.05

SHE-GOAT
a s. three years old, a ram three years Gen 15.09

SHE-GOATS
and all the s. that were speckled Gen 30.35
ewes and your s. have not miscarried, 31.38
two hundred s. and twenty he-goats, 32.14

SHEHARIAH
Shamsherai, S., Athaliah, 1Ch 8.26

SHEKEL
a gold ring weighing a half s., Gen 24.22
half a s. according to the s. of the Ex 30.13
(the s. is twenty gerahs), half a s. as 30.13
than the half s., when you give the 30.15
according to the s. of the sanctuary, 30.24
shekels, by the s. of the sanctuary. 38.24
shekels, by the s. of the sanctuary: 38.25
half the s., by the s. of the sanctuary), 38.26
according to the s. of the sanctuary; Lev 5.15
according to the s. of the sanctuary. 27.03
according to the s. of the sanctuary: 27.25
twenty gerahs shall make a s. 27.25
reckoning by the s. of the sanctuary, Num 3.47
the s. of twenty gerahs, you shall 3.47
reckoned by the s. of the sanctuary; 3.50
according to the s. of the sanctuary, 7.13
according to the s. of the sanctuary, 7.19
according to the s. of the sanctuary, 7.25
according to the s. of the sanctuary, 7.31
according to the s. of the sanctuary, 7.37
according to the s. of the sanctuary, 7.43
according to the s. of the sanctuary, 7.49
according to the s. of the sanctuary, 7.55
according to the s. of the sanctuary, 7.61
according to the s. of the sanctuary, 7.67
according to the s. of the sanctuary, 7.73
according to the s. of the sanctuary, 7.79
according to the s. of the sanctuary, 7.85
according to the s. of the sanctuary, 7.86
according to the s. of the sanctuary, 18.16

SHEKEL (cont.)

the fourth part of a s. of silver, 1Sa 9.08
a third of a s. for sharpening the 13.21
fine meal shall be sold for a s., 2Ki 7.01
two measures of barledy for a s., 7.01
of fine meal was sold for a s., 7.16
two measures of barley for a s., 7.16
of barley shall be sold for a s., 7.18
a measure of fine meal for a s., 7.18
nails was one s. to fifty shekels 2Ch 3.09
third part of a s. for the service Neh 10.32
The s. shall be twenty gerahs; Eze 45.12
the ephah small and the s. great, Amo 8.05
open its mouth you will find a s.; Mt 17.27

SHEKELS

worth four hundred s. of silver, Gen 23.15
four hundred s. of silver, according 23.16
for her arms weighing ten gold s., 24.22
Ishmaelites for twenty s. of silver; 37.28
three hundred s. of silver and 45.22
their master thirty s. of silver, Ex 21.32
of liquid myrrh five hundred s., 30.23
and seven hundred and thirty s., 38.24
seven hundred and seventy-five s., 38.25
seventy-five s. he made hooks for 38.28
two thousand and four hundred s.; 38.29
valued by you in s. of silver, Lev 5.15
old shall be fifty s. of silver, 27.03
your valuation shall be thirty s. 27.04
shall be for a male twenty s., 27.05
and for a female ten s. 27.05
be for a male five s. of silver, 27.06
shall be three s. of silver. 27.06
for a male shall be fifteen s., 27.07
and for a female ten s. 27.07
be valued at fifty s. of silver. 27.16
you shall take five s. apiece; Num 3.47
three hundred and sixty-five s., 3.50
weight was a hundred and thirty s., 7.13
one silver basin of seventy s., 7.13
one golden dish of ten s., full of 7.14
weight was a hundred and thirty s., 7.19
one silver basin of seventy s., 7.19
one golden dish of ten s., full of 7.20
weight was a hundred and thirty s., 7.25
one silver basin of seventy s., 7.25
one golden dish of ten s., full of 7.26
weight was a hundred and thirty s., 7.31
one silver basin of seventy s., 7.31
one golden dish of ten s., full of 7.32
weight was a hundred and thirty s., 7.37
one silver basin of seventy s., 7.37
one golden dish of ten s., full of 7.38
weight was a hundred and thirty s., 7.43
one silver basin of seventy s., 7.43
one golden dish of ten s., full of 7.44
weight was a hundred and thirty s., 7.49
one silver basin of seventy s., 7.49
one golden dish of ten s., full of 7.50
weight was a hundred and thirty s., 7.55
one silver basin of seventy s., 7.55
one golden dish of ten s., full of 7.56
weight was a hundred and thirty s., 7.61
one silver basin of seventy s., 7.61
one golden dish of ten s., full of 7.62
weight was a hundred and thirty s., 7.67
one silver basin of seventy s., 7.67
one golden dish of ten s., full of 7.68
weight was a hundred and thirty s., 7.73
one silver basin of seventy s., 7.73
one golden dish of ten s., full of 7.74
weight was a hundred and thirty s., 7.79
one silver basin of seventy s., 7.79
one golden dish of ten s., full of 7.80
and thirty s. and each basin 7.85
four hundred s. according to the 7.85
weighing ten s. apiece according to 7.86
being a hundred and twenty s.; 7.86
you shall fix at five s. in silver, 18.16
thousand seven hundred and fifty s. 31.52
fine him a hundred s. of silver, Deu 22.19
the young woman fifty s. of silver, 22.29
and two hundred s. of silver, Jos 7.21
a bar of gold weighing fifty s., 7.21
thousand seven hundred s. of gold; Ju 8.26
was five thousand s. of bronze. 1Sa 17.05
weighed six hundred s. of iron; 17.07
two hundred s. by the king's weight. 2Sa 14.26
weighed three hundred s. of bronze, 21.16
the oxen for fifty s. of silver. 24.24
six hundred s. of gold went into 1Ki 10.16
Egypt for six hundred s. of silver, 10.29
six thousand s. of gold, and ten 2Ki 5.05
was sold for eighty s. of silver, 6.25
dove's dung for five s. of silver. 6.25
fifty s. of silver from every man, 15.20
six hundred s. of gold by weight 1Ch 21.25
Egypt for six hundred s. of silver, 2Ch 1.17
was one shekel to fifty s. of gold. 3.09
six hundred s. of beaten gold 9.15
three hundred s. of gold went 9.16
wine, besides forty s. of silver. Neh 5.15
worth a thousand s. of silver, Is 7.23
to him, seventeen s. of silver. Jer 32.09
be by weight, twenty s. a day; Eze 4.10
five s. shall be five s., and 45.12
and ten s. shall be ten s., and 45.12
and your mina shall be fifty s. 45.12
her for fifteen s. of silver and a Hos 3.02
as my wages thirty s. of silver. Zec 11.12
took the thirty s. of silver and 11.13

SHELAH

Arpachshad became the father of S.; Gen 10.24
and S. became the father of Eber. 10.24
years he became the father of S.; 11.12
the birth of S. four hundred and 11.13
When S. had lived thirty years, he 11.14
and S. lived after the birth of 11.15
a son, and she called his name S. 38.05
till S. my son grows up"—for he 38.11
for she saw that S. was grown up, 38.14
as I did not give her to my son S." 38.26
S., Perez, and Zerah (but Er and 46.12
of S., the family of the Shelanites; Num 26.20
Arpachshad was the father of S.; 1Ch 1.18
and S. was the father of Eber. 1.18
Shem, Arpachshad, S.; 1.24
The sons of Judah: Er, Onan, and S.; 2.03
The sons of S. the son of Judah: Er 4.21
of the Pool of S. of the king's Neh 3.15
the son of Eber, the son of S., Lk 3.35

SHELANITES

of Shelah, the family of the S.; Num 26.20

SHELEMIAH

The lot for the east fell to S. 1Ch 26.14
S., Nathan, Adaiah, Ez 10.39
Azarel, S., Shemariah, 10.41
the son of S. and Hanun the sixth Neh 3.30
over the storehouses S. the priest, 13.13
son of S., son of Cushi, to say to Jer 36.14
of Azriel and S. the son of Abdeel 36.26
Zedekiah sent Jehucal the son of S., 37.03
there named Irijah the son of S., 37.13
of Pashhur, Jucal the son of S., 38.01

SHELEPH

father of Almodad, S., Hazarmaveth, Jerah Gen 10.26
father of Almodad, S., Hazarmaveth, Jerah, 1Ch 1.20

SHELESH

brother: Zophah, Imna, S., and Amal. 1Ch 7.35

SHELOMI
of Asher a leader, Ahihud the son of S. Num 34.27

SHELOMITH
His mother's name was S., the daughter Lev 24.11
Hananiah, and S. was their sister; 1Ch 3.19
The sons of Izhar: S. the chief. 23.18
him Abijah, Attai, Ziza, and S. 2Ch 11.20
S. the son of Josiphiah, and with Ez 8.10

SHELOMOTH
of Shimei: S., Haziel, and Haran, three. 1Ch 23.09
Izharites, S.; of the sons of S., Jahath. 24.22
and his son Zichri, and his son S. 26.25
This S. and his brethren were in 26.26
in the care of S. and his brethren 26.28

SHELTER
have come under the s. of my roof." Gen 19.08
you have in the field into safe s.; Ex 9.19
cling to the rock for want of s. Job 24.08
hide me in his s. in the day of Ps 27.05
safe under thy s. from the strife 31.20
to find me a s. from the raging 55.08
be safe under the s. of thy wings! 61.04
dwells in the s. of the Most High, 91.01
a refuge and a s. from the storm Is 4.06
a s. from the storm and a shade 25.04
and in falsehood we have taken s."; 28.15
and waters will overwhelm the s." 28.17
and to seek s. in the shadow of 30.02
and the s. in the shadow of Egypt 30.03
the throne will s. them with his Rev 7.15

SHELUMIEL
from Simeon, S. the son of Zurishaddai; Num 1.06
tribe of Simeon being S. the son of 2.12
On the fifth day S. the son of 7.36
this was the offering of S. the son of 7.41
the men of Simeon was S. the son of 10.19

SHEM
old, Noah became the father of S., Gen 5.32
three sons, S., Ham, and Japheth. 6.10
S. and Ham and Japheth, and Noah's 7.13
went forth from the ark were S., 9.18
Then S. and Japheth took a garment, 9.23
"Blessed by the LORD my God be S.; 9.26
let him dwell in the tents of S.; 9.27
sons of Noah, S., Ham, and Japheth; 10.01
To S. also, the father of all the 10.21
The sons of S.: Elam, Asshur, Arpachshad, 10.22
These are the sons of S., by their 10.31
These are the descendants of S. 11.10
When S. was a hundred years old, he 11.10
and S. lived after the birth of 11.11
Noah, S., Ham, and Japheth. 1Ch 1.04
The sons of S.: Elam, Asshur, Arpachshad, 1.17
S., Arpachshad, Shelah; 1.24
the son of S., the son of Noah, the Lk 3.36

SHEMA
Amam, S., Moladah, Jos 15.26
of Hebron: Korah, Tappuah, Rekem, and S. 1Ch 2.43
S. was the father of Raham, the 2.44
son of S., son of Joel, who dwelt in 5.08
and Beriah and S. (they were heads 8.13
S., Anaiah, Uriah, Hilkiah, and Neh 8.04

SHEMAAH
Joash, both sons of S. of Gibeah; 1Ch 12.03

SHEMAIAH
of God came to S. the man of God: 1Ki 12.22
The sons of Shecaniah: And the 1Ch 3.22
And the sons of S.: Hattush, Igal, 3.22
Jedaiah, son of Shimri, son of S.— 4.37
S. his son, Gog his son, Shimei his 5.04
S. the son of Hasshub, son of 9.14
and Obadiah the son of S., 9.16
S. the chief, with two hundred of 15.08
S., Eliel, and Amminadab, 15.11
And the scribe S. the son of 24.06
S. the first-born, Jehozabad the 26.04
Also to his son S. were sons born, 26.06
The sons of S.: Othni, Rephael, Obed, 26.07
the LORD came to S. the man of God: 2Ch 11.02
Then S. the prophet came to Rehoboam 12.05
the word of the LORD came to S.: 12.07
chronicles of S. the prophet and 12.15
S., Nethaniah, Zebadiah, Asahel, 17.08
sons of Jeduthun, S. and Uzziel. 29.14
S., Amariah, and Shecaniah were 31.15
and S. and Nethanel his brothers, 35.09
and S., and with them sixty men. Ez 8.13
S., Elnathan, Jarib, Elnathan, Nathan, 8.16
S., Jehiel, and Uzziah. 10.21
Isshijah, Malchijah, S., Shimeon, 10.31
After him S. the son of Shecaniah, Neh 3.29
the house of S. the son of Delaiah, 6.10
Maaziah, Bilgai, S.; 10.08
S. the son of Hasshub, son of 11.15
S., Joiarib, Jedaiah, 12.06
of Bilgah, Shammua; of S., Jehonathan; 12.18
Judah, Benjamin, S., and Jeremiah, 12.34
son of S., son of Mattaniah, son of 12.35
S., Azarel, Milalai, Gilalai, Maai, 12.36
and Maaseiah, S., Eleazar, Uzzi, 12.42
the son of S. from Kiriathjearim. Jer 26.20
To S. of Nehelam you shall say: 29.24
the LORD concerning S. of Nehelam: 29.31
Because S. has prophesied to you 29.31
I will punish S. of Nehelam and his 29.32
secretary, Delaiah the son of S., 36.12

SHEMARIAH
Bealiah, S., Shephatiah the Haruphite; 1Ch 12.05
bore him sons, Jeush, S., and Zaham. 2Ch 11.19
Benjamin, Malluch, and S. Ez 10.32
Azarel, Shelemiah, S., 10.41

SHEMEBER
S. king of Zeboiim, and the king of Gen 14.02

SHEMED
and S., who built Ono and Lod with 1Ch 8.12

SHEMER
of Samaria from S. for two talents 1Ki 16.24
Samaria, after the name of S., 16.24
son of Amzi, son of Bani, son of S., 1Ch 6.46
The sons of S. his brother: Rohgah, 7.34

SHEMIDA
and of S., the family of the Num 26.32
Asriel, Shechem, Hepher, and S.; Jos 17.02
The sons of S. were Ahian, Shechem, 1Ch 7.19

SHEMIDAITES
and of Shemida, the family of the S.; Num 26.32

SHEMINITH
to lead with lyres according to the S. 1Ch 15.21

SHEMIRAMOTH
S., Jehiel, Unni, Eliab, Benaiah, 1Ch 15.18
S., Jehiel, Unni, Eliab, Maaseiah, and 15.20
S., Jehiel, Mattithiah, Eliab, Benaiah, 16.05
S., Jehonathan, Adonijah, Tobijah, and 2Ch 17.08

SHEMUEL
of Simeon, S. the son of Ammihud. Num 34.20
and S., heads of their fathers' houses, 1Ch 7.02

SHENAZZAR
S., Jekamiah, Hoshama, and Nedabiah; 1Ch 3.18

SHEOL

I shall go down to S. to my son, Gen 37.35
my gray hairs with sorrow to S." 42.38
down my gray hairs in sorrow to S.' 44.29
our father with sorrow to S. 44.31
and they go down alive into S., Num 16.30
to them went down alive into S.; 16.33
and it burns to the depths of S., Deu 32.22
he brings down to S. and raises up. 1Sa 2.06
the cords of S. entangled me, the 2Sa 22.06
his head go down to S. in peace. 1Ki 2.06
goes down to S. does not come up; Job 7.09
Deeper than S.—what can you know? 11.08
Oh that thou wouldest hide me in S., 14.13
If I look for S. as my house, if I 17.13
Will it go down to the bars of S.? 17.16
and in peace they go down to S. 21.13
so does S. those who have sinned. 24.19
S. is naked before God, and Abaddon 26.06
in S. who can give thee praise? Ps 6.05
The wicked shall depart to S., 9.17
For thou dost not give me up to S., 16.10
the cords of S. entangled me, the 18.05
hast brought up my soul from S., 30.03
let them go dumbfounded to S. 31.17
Like sheep they are appointed for S.; 49.14
waste away; S. shall be their home. 49.14
my soul from the power of S., 49.15
let them go down to S. alive; 55.15
my soul from the depths of S. 86.13
and my life draws near to S. 88.03
his soul from the power of S.? 89.48
the pangs of S. laid hold on me; 116.03
If I make my bed in S., thou art 139.08
bones be strewn at the mouth of S. 141.07
like S. let us swallow them alive Pro 1.12
her steps follow the path to S.; 5.05
Her house is the way to S., 7.27
her guests are in the depths of S. 9.18
S. and Abaddon lie open before the 15.11
life, that he may avoid S. beneath. 15.24
rod you will save his life from S. 23.14
S. and Abaddon are never satisfied, 27.20
S., the barren womb, the earth ever 30.16
or knowledge or wisdom in S., Ecc 9.10
Therefore S. has enlarged its Is 5.14
it be deep as S. or high as heaven." 7.11
S. beneath is stirred up to meet 14.09
Your pomp is brought down to S., 14.11
But you are brought down to S., 14.15
and with S. we have an agreement; 28.15
agreement with S. will not stand; 28.18
to the gates of S. for the rest of 38.10
For S. cannot thank thee, death 38.18
far off, and sent down even to S. 57.09
it goes down to S. I will make the Eze 31.15
cast it down to S. with those who 31.16
They also shall go down to S. with it, 31.17
helpers, out of the midst of S.: 32.21
went down to S. with their weapons 32.27
I ransom them from the power of S.? Hos 13.14
O S., where is your destruction? Compassion 13.14
"Thou they dig into S., from there Amo 9.02
out of the belly of S. I cried, Jon 2.02
His greed is as wide as S.; like Hab 2.05

SHEPHAM

eastern boundary from Hazarenan to S.; Num 34.10
go down from S. to Riblah on the east 34.11

SEPHATIAH

and the fifth, S. the son of Abital; 2Sa 3.04
the fifth S., by Abital; the sixth 1Ch 3.03
and Meshullam the son of S., son 9.08
Bealiah, Shemariah, S. the Haruphite; 12.05
Simeonites, S. the son of Maacah; 27.16
Zechariah, Azariah, Michael, and S.; 2Ch 21.02
The sons of S., three hundred and Ez 2.04
the sons of S., the sons of Hattil, 2.57
Of the sons of S., Zebadiah the son 8.08
The sons of S., three hundred and Neh 7.09
the sons of S., the sons of Hattil, 7.59
son of S., son of Mahalalel, of the 11.04
Now S. the son of Mattan, Gedaliah Jer 38.01

SHEPHELAH

plentiful as the sycamore of the S. 1Ki 10.27
trees in the S. was Baalhanan the 1Ch 27.28
plentiful as the sycamore of the S. 2Ch 1.15
plentiful as the sycamore of the S. 9.27
both in the S. and in the plain, and 26.10
cities in the S. and the Negeb of 28.18
from the S., from the hill country, Jer 17.26
country, in the cities of the S., 32.44
country, in the cities of the S., 33.13
those of the S. the land of the Ob 1.19

SHEPHER

Kehelathah, and encamped at Mount S. Num 33.23
And they set out from Mount S., 33.24

SHEPHERD

for every s. is an abomination to Gen 46.34
One of Jacob (by the name of the S., 49.24
not be as sheep which have no s." Num 27.17
'You shall be s. of my people 2Sa 5.02
I commanded to s. my people Israel, 7.07
mountains, as sheep that have no s.; 1Ki 22.17
'You shall be s. of my people 1Ch 11.02
whom I commanded to s. my people, 17.06
mountains, as sheep that have no s.; 2Ch 18.16
The LORD is my s., I shall not want Ps 23.01
be thou their s., and carry them 28.09
Death shall be their s.; straight 49.14
him to be the s. of Jacob his 78.71
Give ear, O S. of Israel, thou who 80.01
sayings which are given by one S. Ecc 12.11
He will feed his flock like a s., Is 40.11
'He is my s., and he shall fulfil 44.28
The wind shall s. all your shepherds, Jer 22.22
keep him as a s. keeps his flock.' 31.10
as a s. cleans his cloak of vermin; 43.12
What s. can stand before me? 49.20
What s. can stand before me? 50.44
in pieces the s. and his flock; 51.23
scattered, because there was no s.; Eze 34.05
wild beasts, since there was no s.; 34.08
As a s. seeks out his flock when 34.12
I myself will be the s. of my sheep, 34.15
And I will set up over them one s., 34.23
he shall feed them and be their s. 34.23
and they shall all have one s. 37.24
"As the s. rescues from the mouth Amo 3.12
S. thy people with thy staff, the Mic 7.14
are afflicted for want of a s. Zec 10.02
"Become s. of the flock doomed to 11.04
fall each into the hand of his s., 11.06
So I became the s. of the flock 11.07
So I said, "I will not be your s. 11.09
the implements of a worthless s. 11.15
in the land a s. who does not care 11.16
Woe to my worthless s., who deserts 11.17
against my s., against the man who 13.07
"Strike the s., that the sheep may 13.07
helpless, like sheep without a s. Mt 9.36
another as a s. separates the 25.32
is written, 'I will strike the s., 26.31
they were like sheep without a s.; Mk 6.34
is written, 'I will strike the s., 14.27
by the door is the s. of the sheep. Jn 10.02
I am the good s. The good s. lays down 10.11
He who is a hireling and not a s., 10.12
I am the good s.; I know my own 10.14
there shall be one flock, one s. 10.16
the great s. of the sheep, by the Heb 13.20

SHEPHERD (cont.)

returned to the S. and Guardian of 1Pe 2.25
And when the chief S. is manifested 5.04
of the throne will be their s., Rev 7.17

SHEPHERDING

was s. the flock with his brothers; Gen 37.02

SHEPHERD'S

brook, and put them in his s. bag, 1Sa 17.40
and removed from me like a s. tent; Is 38.12

SHEPHERDS

the s. would roll the stone from the Gen 29.03
and the men are s., for they have 46.32
to Pharaoh, "Your servants are s., 47.03
The s. came and drove them away; Ex 2.17
us out of the hand of the s., 2.19
shall be s. in the wilderness Num 14.33
now your s. have been with us, and 1Sa 25.07
when he was at Betheked of the S., 2Ki 10.12
no s. will make their flocks lie Is 13.20
when a band of s. is called forth 31.04
The s. also have no understanding; 56.11
out of the sea the s. of his flock? 63.11
I will give you s. after my own Jer 3.15
S. with their flocks shall come 6.03
For the s. are stupid, and do not 10.21
Many s. have destroyed my vineyard, 12.10
The wind shall shepherd all your s., 22.22
"Woe to the s. who destroy and 23.01
concerning the s. who care for my 23.02
I will set s. over them who will 23.04
"Wail, you s., and cry, and roll in 25.34
No refuge will remain for the s., 25.35
Hark, the cry of the s., and the 25.36
habitations of s. resting their 33.12
their s. have led them astray, 50.06
prophesy against the s. of Israel, Eze 34.02
even to the s., Thus says the Lord 34.02
s. of Israel who have been feeding 34.02
Should not s. feed the sheep? 34.02
you s., hear the word of the LORD: 34.07
and because my s. have not searched 34.08
but the s. have fed themselves, and 34.08
therefore, you s., hear the word of 34.09
GOD, Behold, I am against the s.; 34.10
shall the s. feed themselves. 34.10
who was among the s. of Tekoa, Amo 1.01
the pastures of the s. mourn, 1.02
him seven s. and eight princes of Mic 5.05
Your s. are asleep, O king of Nah 3.18
meadows for s. and folds for flocks. Zep 2.06
"My anger is hot against the s., Zec 10.03
Hark, the wail of the s., for their 11.03
and their own s. have no pity on 11.05
one month I destroyed the three s. 11.08
there were s. out in the field, Lk 2.08
the s. said to one another, "Let us 2.15
wondered at what the s. told them. 2.18
And the s. returned, glorifying and 2.20

SHEPHERDS'

pasture your kids beside the s. tents. Sol 1.08

SHEPHI

Shobal: Alian, Manahath, Ebal, S., and Onam. 1Ch 1.40

SHEPHO

Shobal: Alvan, Manahath, Ebal, S., and Onam. Gen 36.23

SHEPHUPHAM

of S., the family of the Shuphamites; Num 26.39

SHEPHUPHAN

Gera, S., and Huram. 1Ch 8.05

SHERD

its fragments not a s. is found with Is 30.14

SHEREBIAH

namely S. with his sons and kinsmen, Ez 8.18
S., Hashabiah, and ten of their 8.24
S., Jamin, Akkub, Shabbethai, Hodiah, Neh 8.07
Shebaniah, S., Bani, and Chenani; 9.04
S., Hodiah, Shebaniah, and Pethahiah, 9.05
Zaccur, S., Shebaniah, 10.12
S., Judah, and Mattaniah, who with 12.08
S., and Jeshua the son of Kadmiel, 12.24

SHERESH

and the name of his brother was S.; 1Ch 7.16

SHESHAI

and Ahiman, S., and Talmai, the Num 13.22
S. and Ahiman and Talmai, the Jos15.14
they defeated S. and Ahiman and Ju 1.10

SHESHAN

sons of Ishi: S. The sons of S.: Ahlai. 1Ch 2.31
Now S. had no sons, only daughters; 2.34
but S. had an Egyptian slave, 2.34
So S. gave his daughter in marriage 2.35

SHESHBAZZAR

them out to S. the prince of Judah. Ez 1.08
All these did S. bring up, when the 1.11
delivered to one whose name was S., 5.14
Then this S. came and laid the 5.16

SHETH

Moab, and break down all the sons of S. Num 24.17

SHETHAR

S., Admatha, Tarshish, Meres, Marsena, Est 1.14

SHETHARBOZENAI

the River and S. and their associates Ez 5.03
the River and S. and his associates 5.06
S., and your associates the governors 6.06
S., and their associatees did with 6.13

SHEVA

and S. was secretary; and Zadok and 2Sa 20.25
S. the father of Machbenah and the 1Ch 2.49

SHIBAH

He called it S.; therefore the name Gen 26.33

SHIBBOLETH

"Then say, S.," and he said "Sibboleth," Ju 12.06

SHIELD

"Fear not, Abram, I am your s.; Gen 15.01
the s. of your help, and the sword Deu 33.29
Was s. or spear to be seen among Ju 5.08
For there the s. of the mighty was 2Sa 1.21
the s. of Saul, was anointed with 1.21
my s. and the horn of my salvation, 22.03
he is a s. for all those who take 22.31
given me the s. of thy salvation, 22.36
shekels of gold went into each s. 1Ki 10.16
minas of gold went into each s.; 10.17
it with a s. or cast up a mound 2Ki 19.32
who carried s. and sword, and drew 1Ch 5.18
expert with s. and spear, whose 12.08
Judah bearing s. and spear were 12.24
men armed with s. and spear. 12.34
of beaten gold went into each s. 2Ch 9.15
shekels of gold went into each s.; 9.16
thousand men armed with bow and s., 17.17
war, able to handle spear and s. 25.05
against him with a thick-bossed s.; Job 15.26
art a s. about me, my glory, and the Ps 3.03
cover him with favor as with a s. 5.12
My s. is with God, who saves the 7.10
my s., and the horn of my salvation, 18.02
he is a s. for all those who take 18.30

SHIELD (cont.)
given me the s. of thy salvation, Ps 18.35
The LORD is my strength and my s.; 28.07
for the LORD; he is our help and s. 33.20
Take hold of s. and buckler, and 35.02
bring them down, O Lord, our s.! 59.11
the s., the sword, and the weapons 76.03
Behold our s., O God; look upon 84.09
For the LORD God is a sun and s.; 84.11
For our s. belongs to the LORD, our 89.18
faithfulness is a s. and buckler. 91.04
He is their help and their s. 115.09
He is their help and their s. 115.10
He is their help and their s. 115.11
Thou art my hiding-place and my s.; 119.114
my s. and he in whom I take refuge, 144.02
he is a s. to those who walk in Pro 2.07
he is a s. to those who take refuge 30.05
Arise, O princes, oil the s.! Is 21.05
horsemen, and Kir uncovered the s. 22.06
there, or come before it with a s., 37.33
"Prepare buckler and s., and advance Jer 46.03
Ethiopia and Put who handle the s., 46.09
s., and helmet, and I will commit Eze 23.24
they hung the s. and helmet in you; 27.10
all of them with buckler and s., 38.04
all of them with s. and helmet; 38.05
The s. of his mighty men is red, his Nah 2.03
LORD will put a s. about the Zec 12.08
above all taking the s. of faith, Eph 6.16

SHIELD-BEARER
shekels of iron; and his s. went before him. 1Sa 17.07
near to David, with his s. in front of him. 17.41

SHIELDS
And David took the s. of gold which 2Sa 8.07
hundred large s. of beaten gold; 1Ki 10.16
three hundred s. of beaten gold; 10.17
away all the s. of gold which 14.26
made in their stead s. of bronze, 14.27
the spears and s. that had been 2Ki 11.10
And David took the s. of gold which 1Ch 18.07
hundred large s. of beaten gold; 2Ch 9.15
three hundred s. of beaten gold; 9.16
And he put s. and spears in all the 11.12
took away the s. of gold which 12.09
made in their stead s. of bronze, 12.10
that carried s. and drew bows; 14.08
large and small s. that had been 23.09
prepared for all the army s., 26.14
made weapons and s. in abundance. 32.05
for s., and for all kinds of costly 32.27
s., bows, and coats of mail; Neh 4.16
His back is made of rows of s., Job 41.15
For the s. of the earth belong to Ps 47.09
bucklers, all of them s. of warriors. Sol 4.04
"Sharpen the arrows! Take up the s.! Jer 51.11
and raise a roof of s. against you. Eze 26.08
they hung their s. upon your walls 27.11
and whose s. are upon their bones; 32.27
s. and bucklers, bows and arrows, 39.09

SHIFTING
not s. from the hope of the gospel Col 1.23

SHIGIONOTH
Habakkuk the prophet, according to S. Hab 3.01

SHIHOR
(from the S., which is east of Egypt, Jos 13.03
Israel from the S. of Egypt to the 1Ch 13.05
your revenue was the grain of S., Is 23.03

SHIHORLIBNATH
on the west it touches Carmel and S., Jos 19.26

SHIKKERON
then the boundary bends round to S., Jos 15.11

SHILHI
name was Azubah the daughter of S. 1Ki 22.42
name was Azubah the daughter of S. 2Ch 20.31

SHILHIM
Lebaoth, S., Ain, and Rimmon: in all, Jos 15.32

SHILLEM
Jahzeel, Guni, Jezer, and S. Gen 46.24
of S., the family of the Shillemites. Num 26.49

SHILLEMITES
of Shillem, the family of the S. Num 26.49

SHILOAH
the waters of S. that flow gently, Is 8.06

SHILOH
people of Irael assembled at S., Jos 18.01
for you here before the LORD in S." 18.08
came to Joshua in the camp at S., 18.09
for them in S. before the LORD: 18.10
by lot at S. before the LORD, at 19.51
said to them at S. in the land of 21.02
from the people of Israel at S., 22.09
people of Israel gathered at S., 22.12
long as the house of God was at S. Ju 18.31
brought them to the camp at S., 21.12
the yearly feast of the LORD at S., 21.19
daughters of S. come out to dance 21.21
his wife from the daughters of S., 21.21
sacrifice to the LORD of hosts at S., 1Sa 1.03
eaten and drunk in S., Hannah rose. 1.09
him to the house of the LORD at S.; 1.24
So they did at S. to all the 2.14
And the LORD appeared again at S., 3.21
to Samuel at S. by the word of the 3.21
covenant of the LORD here from S., 4.03
So the people sent to S., 4.04
and came to S. the same day, with 4.12
Eli, the priest of the LORD in S., 14.03
concerning the house of Eli in S. 1Ki 2.27
the wife of Jeroboam, and go to S.; 14.02
and went to S., and came to the 14.04
He forsook his dwelling at S., Ps 78.60
Go now to my place that was in S., Jer 7.12
to your fathers, as I did to S. 7.14
then I will make this house like S., 26.06
'This house shall be like S., and 26.09
from Shechem and S. and Samaria, 41.05

SHILONITE
Ahijah the S. found him on the road. 1Ki 11.29
by Ahijah the S. to Jeroboam the 12.15
spoke by his servant Ahijah the S.; 15.29
in the prophecy of Ahijah the S., 2Ch 9.29
by Ahijah the S. to Jeroboam the 10.15
son of Zechariah, son of the S. Neh 11.05

SHILONITES
And of the S.: Asaiah the first-born, 1Ch 9.05

SHILSHAH
Hod, Shamma, S., Ithran, and Beera. 1Ch 7.37

SHIMEA
Abinadab the second, S. the third, 1Ch 2.13
S., Shobab, Nathan, and Solomon, four 3.05
S. his son, Haggiah his son, and 6.30
the son of Berechiah, son of S., 6.39
Israel, Jonathan the son of S., 20.07

SHIMEAH
the son of S., David's brother; 2Sa 13.03
But Jonadab the son of S., David's 13.32
and Mikloth (he was the father of S.). 1Ch 8.32

SHIMEAM
and Mikloth was the father of S.; and 1Ch 9.38

SHIMEATH
the son of S. and Jehozabad the 2Ki 12.21
Zabad the son of S. the Ammonitess, 2Ch 24.26

SHIMEATHITES
Tirathites, and S., and the Sucathites. 1Ch 2.55

SHIMEI
Libni and S., by their families. Ex 6.17
by their families: Libni and S. Num 3.18
house of Saul, whose name was S., 2Sa 16.05
And S. said as he cursed, "Begone, 16.07
while S. went along on the hillside 16.13
And S. the son of Gera, the Benjaminite, 19.16
And S. the son of Gera fell down 19.18
"Shall not S. be put to death for 19.21
And the king said to S., "You shall 19.23
Israel, Jonathan the son of S., 21.21
and S., and Rei, and David's mighty 1Ki 1.08
also with you S. the son of Gera, 2.08
Then the king sent and summoned S., 2.36
And S. said to the king, "What you 2.38
So S. dwelt in Jerusalem many days. 2.38
And when it was told S., "Behold, 2.39
S. arose and saddled an ass, and 2.40
S. went and brought his slaves from 2.40
was told that S. had gone from 2.41
the king sent and summoned S., 2.42
The king also said to S., "You know 2.44
S. the son of Ela, in Benjamin; 4.18
sons of Pedaiah: Zerubbabel and S.; 1Ch 3.19
son, Zaccur his son, S. his son. 4.26
S. had sixteen sons and six daughters; 4.27
his son, Gog his son, S. his son, 5.04
the sons of Gershom: Libni and S. 6.17
S. his son, Uzzah his son, 6.29
Ethan, son of Zimmah, son of S., 6.42
and Shimrath were the sons of S. 8.21
The sons of Gershom were Ladan and S. 23.07
The sons of S.: Shelomoth, Haziel, and 23.09
And the sons of S.: Jahath, Zina, and 23.10
These four were the sons of S. 23.10
S., Hashabiah, and Mattithiah, six, 25.03
the tenth to S., his sons and his 25.17
the vineyards was S. the Ramathite; 27.27
the sons of Heman, Jehuel and S.; 2Ch 29.14
with S. his brother as second; 31.12
Conaniah and S. his brother, 31.13
S., Kelaiah (that is, Kelita), Ez 10.23
Eliphelet, Jeremai, Manasseh, and S. 10.33
Of the sons of Binnui: S., 10.38
son of S., son of Kish, a Benjaminite, Est 2.05

SHIMEI'S
two of S. slaves ran away to Achish, 1Ki 2.39

SHIMEITES
Libnites and the family of the S.; Num 3.21
the family of the S. by itself, and Zec 12.13

SHIMEON
Isshijah, Malchijah, Shemaiah, S., Ez 10.31

SHIMON
The sons of S.: Amnon, Rinnah, Benhanan, 1Ch 4.20

SHIMRATH
Beraiah, and S. were sons of Shimei. 1Ch 8.21

SHIMRI
Jedaiah, son of S., son of Shemaiah— 1Ch 4.37
Jediael the son of S., and Joha 11.45
S. the chief (for though he was not 26.10
sons of Elizaphan, S. and Jeuel; 2Ch 29.13

SHIMRITH
Jehozabad the son of S. the Moabitess. 2Ch 24.26

SHIMRON
Issachar: Tola, Puvah, Iob, and S. Gen 46.13
of S., the family of the Shimronites. Num 26.24
of Madon, and to the king of S., Jos 11.01
S., Idalah, and Bethlehem—twelve 19.15
Tola, Puah, Jashub, and S., four. 1Ch 7.01

SHIMRONITES
of Shimron, the family of the S. Num 26.24

SHIMRONMERON
the king of S., one; the king of Jos 12.20

SHIMSHAI
commander and S. the scribe wrote Ez 4.08
S. the scribe, and the rest of their 4.09
commander and S. the scribe and 4.17
Rehum and S. the scribe and their 4.23

SHINAB
S. king of Admah, Shemeber king of Gen 14.02

SHINAR
Accad, all of them in the land of S. Gen 10.10
in the land of S. and settled there. 11.02
In the days of Amraphel king of S., 14.01
king of Goiim, Amraphel king of S., 14.09
spoil a beautiful mantle from S., Jos 7.21
from S., from Hamath, and from the Is 11.11
he brought them to the land of S., Dan 1.02
He said to me, "To the land of S., Zec 5.11

SHINE
The LORD make his face to s. upon you, Num 6.25
not seek it, nor light s. upon it. Job 3.04
the flame of his fire does not s. 18.05
and light will s. on your ways. 22.28
the lightning of his cloud to s.? 37.15
Let thy face s. on thy servant; Ps 31.16
and make his face to s. upon us, 67.01
upon the cherubim, s. forth 80.01
let thy face s., that we may be 80.03
let thy face s., that we may be 80.07
let thy face s., that we may be 80.19
thou God of vengeance, s. forth! 94.01
of man, oil to make his face s., 104.15
Make thy face s. upon thy servant, 119.135
A man's wisdom makes his face s., Ecc 8.01
Arise, s.; for your light has Is 60.01
thy face to s. upon thy sanctuary, Dan 9.17
are wise shall s. like the brightness 12.03
a crown they shall s. on his land. Zec 9.16
Let your light so s. before men, Mt 5.16
righteous will s. like the sun in 13.43
"Let light s. out of darkness," who 2Co 4.06
among whom you s. as lights in the Php 2.15
of a lamp shall s. in thee no more Rev 18.23
need of sun or moon to s. upon it, 21.23

SHINED
of deep darkness, on them has light s. Is 9.02

SHINES
perfection of beauty, God s. forth. Ps 50.02
which s. brighter and brighter Pro 4.18
the east and s. as far as the west, Mt 24.27
The light s. in the darkness, and Jn 1.05

SHINING
like the sun s. forth upon a 2Sa 23.04
Behind him he leaves a s. wake; Job 41.32
moon, praise him, all you s. stars! Ps 148.03
smoke and the s. of a flaming fire Is 4.05
s. like crystal, spread out above Eze 1.22
and the stars withdraw their s. Joe 2.10

SHINING (cont.)
and the stars withdraw their s. Joe 3.15
He was a burning and s. lamp, Jn 5.35
s. round me and those who journeyed Ac 26.13
as to a lamp s. in a dark place, 2Pe 1.19
and the true light is already s. 1Jn 2.08
like the sun s. in full strength. Rev 1.16
third of the day was kept from s., 8.12

SHION
Hapharaim, S., Anaharath, Jos 19.19

SHIP
the way of a s. on the high seas, Pro 30.19
can go, nor stately s. can pass. Is 33.21
and found a s. going to Tarshish; Jon 1.03
so that the s. threatened to break 1.04
that were in the s. into the sea, 1.05
part of the s. and had lain down, 1.05
hard to bring the s. back to land, 1.13
But going ahead to the s., Ac 20.13
And they brought him to the s. 20.38
And having found a s. crossing to 21.02
for there the s. was to unload its 21.03
Then we went on board the s., 21.06
And embarking in a s. of Adramyttium, 27.02
centurion found a s. of Alexandria 27.06
not only of the cargo and the s., 27.10
owner of the s. than to what Paul 27.11
and when the s. was caught and 27.15
took measures to undergird the s.; 27.17
own hands the tackle of the s. 27.19
life among you, but only of the s. 27.22
were seeking to escape from the s., 27.30
"Unless these men stay in the s., 27.31
and seventy-six persons in the s.) 27.37
enough, they lightened the s., 27.38
if possible to bring the s. ashore. 27.39
on planks or on pieces of the s. 27.44
set sail in a s. which had wintered 28.11
a s. of Alexandria, with the Twin 28.11

SHIPHI
Ziza the son of S., son of Allon, 1Ch 4.37

SHIPHMITE
for the wine cellars was Zabdi the S. 1Ch 27.27

SHIPHRAH
whom was named S. and the other Puah, Ex 1.15

SHIPHTAN
Ephraim a leader, Kemuel the son of S. Num 34.24

SHIPMASTERS
And all s. and seafaring men, sailors Rev 18.17

SHIPS
he shall become a haven for s., Gen 49.13
But s. shall come from Kittim and Num 24.24
will bring you back in s. to Egypt, Deu 28.68
Dan, why did he abide with the s.? Ju 5.17
built a fleet of s. at Eziongeber, 1Ki 9.26
had a fleet of s. of Tarshish at 10.22
the fleet of s. of Tarshish used 10.22
Jehoshaphat made s. of Tarshish to 22.48
for the s. were wrecked at Eziongeber. 22.48
go with your servants in the s., 22.49
by his servants s. and servants 2Ch 8.18
For the king's s. went Tarshish 9.21
three years the s. of Tarshish 9.21
him in building s. to go to 20.36
they built the s. in Eziongeber. 20.36
And the s. were wrecked and were 20.37
didst shatter the s. of Tarshish. Ps 48.07
There go the s., and Leviathan 104.26
Some went down to the sea in s., 107.23
She is like the s. of the merchant, Pro 31.14
against all the s. of Tarshish, Is 2.16
Wail, O s. of Tarshish, for Tyre is 23.01
Wail, O s. of Tarshish, for your 23.14
the s. of Tarshish first, to bring 60.09
all the s. of the sea with their Eze 27.09
The s. of Tarshish traveled for you 27.25
and down from their s. come all 27.29
For s. of Kittim shall come against Dan 11.30
and horsemen, and with many s.; 11.40
Look at the s. also; though they Jas 3.04
a third of the s. were destroyed. Rev 8.09
all who had s. at sea grew rich by 18.19

SHIPWRECK
persons have made s. of their faith, 1Ti 1.19

SHIPWRECKED
Three times I have been s.; a night 2Co 11.25

SHISHA
Ahijah the sons of S. were secretaries; 1Ki 4.03

SHISHAK
to S. king of Egypt, and was in 1Ki 11.40
S. king of Egypt came up against 14.25
S. king of Egypt came up against 2Ch 12.02
gathered at Jerusalem because of S., 12.05
abandoned you to the hand of S. 12.05
upon Jerusalem by the hand of S. 12.07
So S. king of Egypt came up against 12.09

SHITRAI
pastured in Sharon was S. the Sharonite; 1Ch 27.29

SHITTIM
While Israel dwelt in S. the people Num 25.01
two men secretly from S. as spies, Jos 2.01
Joshua rose and set out from S. 3.01
And they have made deep the pit of S.; Hos 5.02
LORD and water the valley of S. Joe 3.18
what happened from S. to Gilgal, Mic 6.05

SHIZA
Adina the son of S. the Reubenite, 1Ch 11.42

SHOA
Pekod and S. and Koa, and all the Eze 23.23

SHOAL
they enclosed a great s. of fish; Lk 5.06
But striking a s. they ran the vessel Ac 27.41

SHOBAB
Shammua, S., Nathan, Solomon, 2Sa 5.14
her sons: Jesher, S., and Ardon. 1Ch 2.18
S., Nathan, and Solomon, four by 3.05
Shammua, S., Nathan, Solomon, 14.04

SHOBACH
Helam, with S. the commander of the army 2Sa 10.16
and wounded S. the commander of their 10.18

SHOBAI
sons of Hatita, and the sons of S., Ez 2.42
Akkub, the sons of Hatita, the sons of S., Neh 7.45

SHOBAL
the land: Lotan, S., Zibeon, Anah, Gen 36.20
These are the sons of S.: Alvan, 36.23
chiefs Lotan, S., Zibeon, Anah, 36.29
S., Zibeon, Anah, Dishon, Ezer, and 1Ch 1.38
The sons of S.: Alian, Manahath, Ebal, 1.40
S. the father of Kiriathjearim, 2.50
S. the father of Kiriathjearim had 2.52
Perez, Hezron, Carmi, Hur, and S. 4.01
Reaiah the son of S. was the father 4.02

SHOBEK
Hallohesh, Pilha, S., Neh 10.24

SHOBI
S. the son of Nahash from Rabbah of 2Sa 17.27

SHOCK
as a s. of grain comes up to the Job 5.26
will direct the s. of his battering Eze 26.09

SHOCKED
be s., be utterly desolate, says the Jer 2.12

SHOCKS
and burned up the s. and the standing Ju 15.05

SHOD
cloth and s. you with leather, I Eze 16.10
and having s. your feet with the Eph 6.15

SHOE
my washbasin; upon Edom I cast my s.; Ps 60.08
my washbasin; upon Edom I cast my s.; 108.09

SHOES
put off your s. from your feet, for Ex 3.05
"Put off your s. from your feet; Jos 5.15
garments and s. of ours are worn 9.13
take off your s. from your feet, Is 20.02
and put your s. on your feet; Eze 24.17
heads and your s. on your feet; 24.23
and the needy for a pair of s.— Amo 2.06
on his hand, and s. on his feet; Lk 15.22
'Take off the s. from your feet, for Ac 7.33

SHOHAM
Jaaziah, Beno, S., Zaccur, and Ibri. 1Ch 24.27

SHOMER
and Jehozabad the son of S., 2Ki 12.21
S., Hotham, and their sister Shua. 1Ch 7.32

SHONE
of his face s. because he had been Ex 34.29
behold, the skin of his face s., 34.30
that the skin of Moses' face s.; 34.35
he s. forth from Mount Paran, he Deu 33.02
and the sun s. upon the water, the 2Ki 3.22
when his lamp s. upon my head, and Job 29.03
have looked at the sun when it s., 31.26
and the earth s. with his glory. Eze 43.02
and his face s. like the sun, and Mt 17.02
glory of the Lord s. around them, Lk 2.09
appeared, and a light s. in the cell; Ac 12.07
from heaven suddenly s. about me. 22.06
who has s. in our hearts to give 2Co 4.06

SHOOK
I also s. out my lap and said, "So Neh 5.13
the world; the earth trembled and s. Ps 77.18
the thresholds s. at the voice of Is 6.04
of his people s. as the trees of 7.02
earth tremble, who s. kingdoms, 14.16
he looked and s. the nations; Hab 3.06
and the earth s., and the rocks Mt 27.51
But they s. off the dust from their Ac 13.51
he s. out his garments and said to 18.06
He, however, s. off the creature into 28.05
His voice then s. the earth; but now Heb 12.26

SHOOT
And I will s. three arrows to the side 1Sa 20.20
"Run and find the arrows which I s." 20.36
that they would s. from the wall? 2Sa 11.20
him, and said, "S. him also"; and 2Ki 9.27
Then Elisha said, "S."; and he shot. 13.17
to this city or s. an arrow there, 19.32
and could s. arrows and sling 1Ch 12.02
to s. arrows and great stones. 2Ch 26.15
to s. in the dark at the upright in Ps 11.02
But God will s. his arrow at them; 64.07
come forth a s. from the stump of Is 11.01
or s. an arrow there, or come before 37.33
the s. of my planting, the work of 60.21
s. at her, spare no arrows, for she Jer 50.14
shall s. forth your branches, and Eze 36.08
a wild olive s., were grafted in Rom 11.17

SHOOTING
s. from ambush at the blameless, Ps 64.04
s. at him suddenly and without fear 64.04
beginning of the s. up of the Amo 7.01

SHOOTS
and his s. spread over his garden. Job 8.16
and that its s. will not cease. 14.07
the flame will dry up his s., 15.30
the sea, and its s. to the River. Ps 80.11
be like olive s. around your table 128.03
Your s. are an orchard of pomegranates Sol 4.13
its s. spread abroad and passed Is 16.08
cut off the s. with pruning hooks, 18.05
shall blossom and put forth s., 27.06
For as the earth brings forth its s., 61.11
from abundant water in its s. Eze 31.05
his s. shall spread out; his beauty Hos 14.06

SHOPHACH
with S. the commander of the army 1Ch 19.16
and killed also S. the commander 19.18

SHORE
Zebulun shall dwell at the s. of the sea; Gen 49.13
Eloth on the s. of the Red Sea, 1Ki 9.26
and Eloth on the s. of the sea, 2Ch 8.17
pilots of the sea stand on the s. Eze 27.29
Gennesaret, and moored to the s. Mk 6.53

SHORN
s. of strength, are dismayed and 2Ki 19.26
like a flock of s. ewes that have Sol 4.02
in baldness, every beard is s.; Is 15.02
s. of strength, are dismayed and 37.27
for a woman to be s. or shaven, 1Co 11.06

SHORT
had gone but a s. distance from Gen 44.04
too long or too s. you may present Lev 22.23
had gone from him a s. distance, 2Ki 5.19
that the exulting of the wicked is s., Job 20.05
Thou hast cut s. the days of his Ps 89.45
the years of the wicked will be s. Pro 10.27
For the bed is too s. to stretch Is 28.20
"In a s. time you think to make me Ac 26.28
"Whether s. or long, I would to God 26.29
sinned and fall s. of the glory of Rom 3.23
appointed time has grown very s.; 1Co 7.29
for a s. time, in person not in 1Th 2.17
us for a s. time at their pleasure, Heb 12.10
he knows that his time is s.! Rev 12.12

SHORTENED
to Moses, "Is the LORD's hand s.? Num 11.23
steps are s. and his own schemes Job 18.07
in midcourse; he has s. my days. Ps 102.23
Is my hand s., that it cannot Is 50.02
Behold, the LORD's hand is not s., 59.01
And if those days had not been s., Mt 24.22
of the elect those days will be s. 24.22
And if the Lord had not s. the days, Mk 13.20
whom he chose, he s. the days. 13.20

SHORTLY
and God will s. bring it to pass. Gen 41.32
house will now s. be brought back Jer 27.16
he himself intended to go there s. Ac 25.04
the Lord that s. I myself shall Php 2.24

SHORTSIGHTED
is blind and s. and has forgotten 2Pe 1.09

SHOT

its blossoms s. forth, and the Gen 40.10
s. at him, and harassed him sorely; 49.23
him, but he shall be stoned or s.; Ex 19.13
of it, as though I s. at a mark. 1Sa 20.20
he s. an arrow beyond him. 20.36
of the arrow which Jonathan had s., 20.37
Then the archers s. at your servants 2Sa 11.24
and s. Joram between the shoulders, 2Ki 9.24
and they s. him in the chariot at 9.27
Elisha said, "Shoot"; and he s. 13.17
And the archers s. King Josiah; 2Ch 35.23
and s. forth its branches toward Eze 17.07

SHOULDER

it to Hagar, putting it on her s., Gen 21.14
out with her water jar upon her s. 24.15
out with her water jar on her s.; 24.45
let down her jar from her s., 24.46
so he bowed his s. to bear, 49.15
shall take the s. of the ram, Num 6.19
which had to be carried on the s. 7.09
reach to the s. of the sea of 34.11
the priest the s. and the two Deu 18.03
up each of you a stone upon his s., Jos 4.05
at the southern s. of the Jebusite 15.08
to the northern s. of Mount Jearim 15.10
goes out to the s. of the hill 15.11
goes up to the s. north of Jericho, 18.12
to the s. of Luz (the same is 18.13
south of the s. of the Jebusites, 18.16
north of the s. of Betharabah it 18.18
the north of the s. of Bethhoglah; 18.19
took it up and laid it on his s. Ju 9.48
a stubborn s. and stiffened their Neh 9.29
my s. blade fall from my s., Job 31.22
Surely I would carry it on my s.; 31.36
"I relieved your s. of the burden; Ps 81.06
burden, and the staff for his s., Is 9.04
the government will be upon his s., 9.06
burden will depart from your s., 10.27
down upon the s. of the Philistines 11.14
them, and his burden from their s. 14.25
place on his s. the key of the 22.22
lift the baggage upon your s., Eze 12.06
outfit upon my s. in their sight. 12.07
baggage upon his s. in the dark, 12.12
good pieces, the thigh and the s.; 24.04
bald and every s. was rubbed bare; 29.18
Because you push with side and s., 34.21
hearken, and turned a stubborn s., Zec 7.11

SHOULDER-PIECE

It shall have two s. attached to Ex 29.07
stones upon the s. of the ephod, 28.12
it in front of the s. of the ephod. 28.25
part of the two s. of the ephod, 28.27
They made for the ephod s., 39.04
he set them on the s. of the ephod, 39.07
it in front of the s. of the ephod. 39.18
part of the two s. of the ephod, 39.20

SHOULDERS

garment, laid it upon both their s., Gen 9.23
up in their mantles on their s. Ex 12.34
upon his two s. for remembrance. 28.12
makes his dwelling between his s. Deu 33.12
put them on his s. and carried Ju 16.03
from his s. upward he was taller 1Sa 9.02
of the people from his s. upward. 10.23
of bronze slung between his s. 17.06
of Shaphat remains on his s. today. 2Ki 6.31
and shot Joram between the s., 9.24
God upon their s. with the poles, 1Ch 15.15
no longer carry it upon your s. 2Ch 35.03
They lift it upon their s., Is 46.07
shall be carried on their s. 49.22
you broke, and tore all their s.; Eze 29.07
to bear, and lay them on men's s.; Mt 23.04
he lays it on his s., rejoicing. Lk 15.05

SHOUT

and the s. of a king is among them. Num 23.21
the people shall s. with a great s.; Jos 6.05
"You shall not s. or let your voice 6.10
day I bid you s.; then you shall s." 6.10
Joshua said to the people, "S.; for 6.16
the people raised a great s., and 6.20
and s., 'For the LORD and for Ju 7.18
camp, all Israel gave a mighty s., 1Sa 4.05
rose with a s. and pursued the 17.52
men of Judah raised the battle s. 2Ch 13.15
the people shouted with a great s., Ez 3.11
of the joyful s. from the sound of 3.13
the people shouted with a great s. 3.13
they s. after them as after a thief Job 30.05
May we s. for joy over your victory, Ps 20.05
and s. for joy, all you upright in 32.11
my vindication s. for joy and be 35.27
S. to God with loud songs of joy! 47.01
God has gone up with a s., the LORD 47.05
over Philistia I s. in triumph. 60.08
and the evening to s. for joy. 65.08
they s. and sing together for joy. 65.13
My lips will s. for joy, when I sing 71.23
s. for joy to the God of Jacob! 81.01
the people who know the festal s., 89.15
over Philistia I s. in triumph. 108.09
and let thy saints s. for joy. 132.09
and her saints will s. for joy. 132.16
S., and sing for joy, O inhabitant Is 12.06
harvest the battle s. has fallen. 16.09
the vintage s. is hushed. 16.10
of the LORD they s. from the west. 24.14
let them s. from the top of the 42.11
done it; s., O depths of the earth; 44.23
declare this with a s. of joy, 48.20
they s. against the cities of Judah. Jer 4.16
I s., "Violence and destruction!" 20.08
and s., like those who tread grapes, 25.30
the shouting is not the s. of joy. 48.33
Raise a s. against her round about, 50.15
shall raise the s. of victory over 51.14
O daughter of Zion; s., O Israel! Zep 3.14
S. aloud, O daughter of Jerusalem! Zec 9.09
break forth and s., thou who Gal 4.27

SHOUTED

the noise of the people as they s., Ex 32.17
they s., and fell on their faces. Lev 9.24
So the people s., and the trumpets Jos 6.20
And they s. to the Danites, who Ju 18.23
And all the people s., "Long live 1Sa 10.24
He stood and s. to the ranks of 17.08
And when the men of Judah s., 2Ch 13.15
And they s. it with a loud voice in 32.18
all the people s. with a great Ez 3.11
laid, though many s. aloud for joy; 3.12
for the people s. with a great 3.13
the city of Susa s. and rejoiced. Est 8.15
and all the sons of God s. for joy? Job 38.07
him and that followed him s., Mt 21.09
But they s. all the more, "Let him 27.23
But they s. all the more, "Crucify Mk 15.14
they s. out, "Crucify, crucify him!" Lk 23.21
And the people s., "The voice of a Ac 12.22
Some in the crowd s. one thing, 21.34
out why they s. thus against him. 22.24

SHOUTING

is not the sound of s. for victory, Ex 32.18
Philistines came s. to meet him; Ju 15.14
Philistines heard the noise of the s., 1Sa 4.06
does this great s. in the camp of 4.06

SHOUTING (cont.)

to the battle line, s. the war cry. 1Sa 17.20
up the ark of the LORD with s., 2Sa 6.15
the covenant of the LORD with s., 1Ch 15.28
and with s., and with trumpets, and 2Ch 15.14
laughter, and your lips with s. Job 8.21
of the captains, and the s. 39.25
a strong man s. because of wine. Ps 78.65
better than the s. of a ruler Ecc 9.17
of walls and a s. to the mountains. Is 22.05
by their s. or daunted at their 31.04
and the s. of the Chaldeans will be 43.14
the s. is not the shout of joy. Jer 48.33
not of joyful s. upon the mountains. Eze 7.07
cry, to lift up the voice with s., 21.22
with s. in the day of battle, with a Amo 1.14
amid s. and the sound of the 2.02
s. that he ought not to live any Ac 52.54

SHOUTINGS

you who are full of s., tumultuous Is 22.02

SHOUTS

he hears not the s. of the driver. Job 39.07
his tent sacrifices with s. of joy; Ps 27.06
on the strings, with loud s. 33.03
with glad s. and songs of thanksgiving, 42.04
and our tongue with s. of joy; 126.02
sow in tears reap with s. of joy! 126.05
shall come home with s. of joy, 126.06
perish there are s. of gladness. Pro 11.10
songs are sung, no s. are raised; Is 16.10
he s. aloud, he shows himself mighty 42.13
and raise s. for the chief of the Jer 31.07
no one treads them with s. of joy; 48.33
the top stone amid s. of 'Grace, Zec 4.07

SHOVEL

has been winnowed with s. and fork. Is 30.34

SHOVELS

and s. and basins and forks and Ex 27.03
the s., the basins, the forks, and 38.03
the s., and the basins, all the Num 4.14
made the pots, the s., and the basins. 1Ki 7.40
the s., and the basins, all these 7.45
and the s., and the snuffers, and 2Ki 25.14
made the pots, the s., and the basins. 2Ch 4.11
The pots, the s., the forks, and all 4.16
and the s., and the snuffers, and Jer 52.18

SHOW

to the land that I will s. you. Gen 12.01
and s. steadfast love to my master 24.12
to s. you my power, so that my name Ex 9.16
that I may s. these signs of mine 10.01
to s. whether or not he has put his 22.08
According to all that I s. you 25.09
s. me now thy ways, that I may know 33.13
said, "I pray thee, s. me thy glory." 33.18
will s. mercy on whom I will s. mercy. 33.19
'I will s. myself holy among those Lev 10.03
to s. when it is unclean and when 14.57
the LORD will s. who is his, Num 16.05
to s. you by what way you should go, Deu 1.33
only begun to s. thy servant thy 3.24
with them, and s. no mercy to them. 7.02
and s. you mercy, and have compassion 13.17
you shall not s. partiality; 16.19
of the old or s. favor to the 28.50
your father, and he will s. you; 32.07
s. us the way into the city, and we Ju 1.24
and I will s. you the man whom you 4.22
then s. me a sign that it is thou 6.17
and they did not s. kindness to the 8.35
and s. them the ways of the king 1Sa 8.09
come to you and s. you what you 10.08
and we will s. ourselves to them. 14.08
to us, and we will s. you a thing." 14.12
and I will s. you what you shall do; 16.03
s. me the loyal love of the LORD, 20.14
Now may the LORD s. steadfast love 2Sa 2.06
that I may s. him kindness for 9.01
that I may s. the kindness of God 9.03
for I will s. you kindness for the 9.07
may the LORD s. steadfast love and 15.20
loyal thou dost s. thyself loyal; 22.26
man thou dost s. thyself blameless; 22.26
the pure thou dost s. thyself pure, 22.27
thou dost s. thyself perverse. 22.27
Be strong, and s. yourself a man, 1Ki 2.02
s. yourself to Ahab; and I will 18.01
So Elijah went to s. himself to 18.02
I will surely s. myself to him 18.15
"Will you not s. me who of us is 2Ki 6.11
that Hezekiah did not s. them. 20.13
storehouses that I did not s. them." 20.15
to s. his might in behalf of those 2Ch 16.09
in order to s. the peoples and the Est 1.11
that he might s. it to Esther and 4.08
Will you s. partiality toward him, Job 13.08
you if in secret you s. partiality. 13.10
"I will s. you, hear me; and what 15.17
and s. that there is nothing in 24.25
I will not s. partiality to any 32.21
and I will s. you, for I have yet 36.02
Thou dost s. me the path of life; Ps 16.11
Wondrously s. thy steadfast love, O 17.07
loyal thou dost s. thyself loyal; 18.25
man thou dost s. thyself blameless; 18.25
the pure thou dost s. thyself pure; 18.26
thou dost s. thyself perverse. 18.26
aright I will s. the salvation of 50.23
my mouth shall s. forth thy praise. 51.15
s. thy strength, O God, thou who hast 68.28
unjustly and s. partiality to the 82.02
S. us thy steadfast love, O LORD, and 85.07
S. me a sign of thy favor, that 86.17
satisfy him, and s. him my salvation. 91.16
to s. that the LORD is upright; 92.15
or s. forth all his praise? 106.02
he did not remember to s. kindness, 109.16
to s. you what is right and true, Pro 22.21
To s. partiality is not good; 28.21
testing them to s. them that they Ecc 3.18
formed them will s. them no favor. Is 27.11
exalts himself to s. mercy to you. 30.18
that Hezekiah did not s. them. 39.02
storehouses that I did not s. them." 39.04
and s. us the former things? 43.09
then thou didst s. me their evil Jer 11.18
night, for I will s. you no favor.' 16.13
I will s. them my back, not my face, 18.17
your God may s. us the way we 42.03
spare, and you shall s. no pity; Eze 9.05
with their lips they s. much love, 33.31
'Will you not s. us what you mean 37.18
So I will s. my greatness and my 38.23
on the day that I s. my glory, 39.13
mind upon all that I shall s. you, 40.04
in order that I might s. it to you; 40.04
and s. them how to distinguish 44.23
and we will s. the interpretation." Dan 2.04
But if you s. the dream and its 2.06
Therefore s. me the dream and its 2.06
and we will s. its interpretation." 2.07
that you can s. me its interpretation." 2.09
and none can s. it to the king 2.11
that he might s. to the king the 2.16
and I will s. the king the interpretation." 2.24
astrologers can s. to the king the 2.27
good to me to s. the signs and 4.02
and he will s. the interpretation." 5.12
they could not s. the interpretation 5.15
"And now I will s. you the truth. 11.02

SHOW (cont.)

of Egypt I will s. them marvelous Mic 7.15
Thou wilt s. faithfulness to Jacob 7.20
'I will s. you what they are.' Zec 1.09
s. kindness and mercy each to his 7.09
pleased with you or s. you favor? Mal 1.08
will he s. favor to any of you? 1.09
but go, s. yourself to the priest, Mt 8.04
asked him to s. them a sign from 16.01
Jesus began to s. his disciples 16.21
S. me the money for the tax." 22.19
will arise and s. great signs and 24.24
but go, s. yourself to the priest, Mk 1.44
will arise and s. signs and 13.22
And he will s. you a large upper 14.15
but "go and s. yourself to the Lk 5.14
I will s. you what he is like: 6.47
"Go and s. yourselves to the 17.14
and s. no partiality, but truly 20.21
"S. me a coin. Whose likeness 20.24
And he will s. you a large upper 22.12
have you to s. us for doing this?" Jn 2.18
he comes, he will s. us all things." 4.25
works than these will he s. him, 5.20
things, s. yourself to the world." 7.04
He said this to s. by what death he 12.33
s. us the Father, and we shall be 14.08
can you say, 'S. us the Father'? 14.09
had spoken to s. by what death he 18.32
(This he said to s. by what death 21.19
s. which one of these two thou hast Ac 1.24
And I will s. wonders in the heaven 2.19
into the land which I will s. you.' 7.03
for I will s. him how much he must 9.16
They s. that what the law requires Rom 2.15
serves to s. the justice of God, 3.05
This was to s. God's righteousness, 3.25
desiring to s. his wrath and to 9.22
circumcised to s. God's truthfulness, 15.08
And I will s. you a still more 1Co 12.31
and you s. that you are a letter 2Co 3.03
to s. that the transcendent power 4.07
the Lord and to s. our good will. 8.19
may not have to s. boldness with 10.02
of the things that s. my weakness. 11.30
ages he might s. the immeasurable Eph 2.07
S. yourself in all respects a model Tit 2.07
and in your teaching s. integrity, 2.07
but to s. entire and true fidelity, 2.10
and to s. perfect courtesy toward 3.02
one of you to s. the same earnestness Heb 6.11
God desired to s. more convincingly 6.17
Do not neglect to s. hospitality to 13.02
My brethren, s. no partiality as you Jas 2.01
But if you s. partiality, you commit 2.09
S. me your faith apart from your 2.18
I by my works will s. you my faith. 2.18
life let him s. his works in the 3.13
God gave him to s. to his servants Rev 1.01
and I will s. you what must take 4.01
I will s. you the judgment of the 17.01
I will s. you the Bride, the wife of 21.09
his angel to s. his servants what 22.06

SHOWBREAD

Kohathites had charge of the s., 1Ch 9.32
to assist also with the s., the flour 23.29
of gold for each table for the s., 28.16
the continual offering of the s., 2Ch 2.04
set out the s. on the table of pure 13.11
table for the s. and all its 29.18
for the s., the continual cereal Neh 10.33

SHOWED

with Joseph and s. him steadfast Gen 39.21
and the LORD s. him a tree, and he Ex 15.25
and s. them the fruit of the land. Num 13.26
and he s. himself holy among them. 20.13
and the LORD s. signs and wonders, Deu 6.22
And the LORD s. him all the land, 34.01
And he s. them the way into the Ju 1.25
she s. her mother-in-law what she Ru 2.18
So both of them s. themselves to 1Sa 14.11
for you s. kindness to all the 15.06
and Jonathan s. him all these things. 19.07
because you s. this loyalty to Saul 2Sa 2.05
And his sons s. him the way which 1Ki 13.12
he did, and the might that he s., 16.27
Jehoshaphat, and his might that he s., 22.45
When he s. him the place, he cut 2Ki 6.06
and he s. them the king's son. 11.04
and he s. them all his treasure 20.13
the Levites who s. good skill in 2Ch 30.22
while he s. the riches of his royal Est 1.04
and they s. him sympathy and Job 42.11
and he s. them his treasure house, Is 39.02
and s. him the way of understanding? 40.14
your hand, you s. them no mercy; 47.06
the LORD s. this vision: Behold, Jer 24.01
the things that the LORD had s. me. Eze 11.25
my statutes and s. them my ordinances, 20.11
envy which you s. because of your 35.11
Thus the Lord GOD s. me: behold, he Amo 7.01
Thus the Lord GOD s. me: behold, the 7.04
He s. me: behold, the Lord was 7.07
Thus the Lord GOD s. me: behold, a 8.01
He has s. you, O man, what is good; Mic 6.08
Then the LORD s. me four smiths. Zec 1.20
Then he s. me Joshua the high 3.01
and s. him all the kingdoms of the Mt 4.08
and s. him all the kingdoms of the Lk 4.05
He said, "The one who s. mercy on him." 10.37
even Moses s., in the passage about 20.37
he s. them his hands and his feet. * 24.40
he s. them his hands and his side. Jn 20.20
And the natives s. us unusual Ac 28.02
love which you s. for his sake in Heb 6.10
as our LORD Jesus Christ s. me. 2Ps 1.14
and s. me the holy city Jerusalem Rev 21.10
Then he s. me the river of the 22.01
of the angel who s. them to me; 22.08

SHOWER

and to the s. and the rain, 'Be Job 37.06
"S., O heavens, from above, and let Is 45.08
you say at once, 'A s. is coming'; Lk 12.54

SHOWERS

grass, and as the s. upon the herb. Deu 32.02
its ridges, softening it with s., Ps 65.10
like s. that water the earth! 72.06
Therefore the s. have been withheld, Jer 3.03
Or can the heavens give s.? 14.22
send down the s. in their season; Eze 34.26
they shall be s. of blessing. 34.26
he will come to us as the s., Hos 6.03
like s. upon the grass, which tarry Mic 5.07
who gives men s. of rain, to every Zec 10.01

SHOWEST

when thou s. favor to thy people; Ps 106.04
who s. steadfast love to thousands, Jer 32.18

SHOWING

but s. steadfast love to thousands Ex 20.06
but s. steadfast love to thousands Deu 5.10
This day I keep s. loyalty to the 2Sa 3.08
covenant and s. steadfast love to 1Ki 8.23
covenant and s. steadfast love to 2Ch 6.14
iniquities by s. mercy to the Dan 4.27
and s. coats and garments which Ac 9.39
s. by the scriptures that the 18.28
very purpose of s. my power in you, Rom 9.17
outdo one another in s. honor. 12.10

SHOWING (cont.)
as I count on s. against some who 2Co 10.02
to make a good s. in the flesh Gal 6.12

SHOWN
and you have s. me great kindness Gen 19.19
that thou hast s. steadfast love 24.14
which thou hast s. to thy servant, 32.10
God has s. to Pharaoh what he is 41.28
"Since God has s. you all this, 41.39
which is being s. you on the Ex 25.40
which has been s. you on the 26.30
as it has been s. you on the 27.08
after he has s. himself to the Lev 13.07
then it shall be s. to the priest; 13.19
and shall be s. to the priest. 13.49
which the LORD had s. Moses, Num 8.04
To you it was s., that you might Deu 4.35
our God has s. us his glory and 5.24
or s. us all these things, or now Ju 13.23
and hast s. me future generations, O 2Sa 7.19
"Thou hast s. great and steadfast 1Ki 3.06
the LORD had s. to David his 8.66
the LORD has s. me that he shall 2Ki 8.10
"The LORD has s. me that you are to 8.13
and hast s. me future generations, O 1Ch 17.17
"Thou hast s. great and steadfast 2Ch 1.08
the LORD had s. to David and to 7.10
had s. him, but killed his son. 24.22
favor has been s. by the LORD our Ez 9.08
has wondrously s. his steadfast Ps 31.21
citadels God has s. himself a sure 48.03
the miracles that he had s. them. 78.11
He has s. his people the power of 111.06
If favor is s. to the wicked, he Is 26.10
Israel has s. herself less guilty Jer 3.11
who hast s. signs and wonders in 32.20
which the LORD has s. to me: 38.21
no honor was s. to the priests, no Lam 4.16
no respect is s. to the elders. 5.12
ways but have s. partiality in Mal 2.09
He has s. strength with his arm, he Lk 1.51
the LORD had s. great mercy to her, 1.58
"I have s. you many good works from Jn 10.32
but God has s. me that I should not Ac 10.28
things I have s. you that by so 20.35
because God has s. it to them. Rom 1.19
that sin might be s. to be sin, 7.13
I have s. myself to those who did 10.20
by the mercy s. to you they also 11.31
which has been s. in the churches 2Co 8.01
s. hospitality, washed the feet of 1Ti 5.10
which was s. you on the mountain." Heb 8.05
mercy to one who has s. no mercy; Jas 2.13
Do you want to be s., you foolish 2.20

SHOWS
if the disease s. greenish or Lev 13.49
and whatever he s. me I will tell Num 23.03
and s. steadfast love to his 2Sa 22.51
who s. no partiality to princes, nor Job 34.19
and s. steadfast love to his Ps 18.50
the God who s. me steadfast love. 59.17
but to the humble he s. favor. Pro 3.34
the Holy God s. himself holy in Is 5.16
he s. himself mighty against his 42.13
and s. me its interpretation, shall Dan 5.07
morning he s. forth his justice, Zep 3.05
and s. him all that he himself is Jn 5.20
perceive that God s. no partiality, Ac 10.34
For God s. no partiality. Rom 2.11
But God s. his love for us in that 5.08
God s. no partiality)—those, I say, Gal 2.06

SHREWD
a s. counselor, and his lot came out 1Ch 26.14
own eyes, and s. in their own sight! Is 5.21

SHREWDLY
let us deal s. with them, lest they Ex 1.10

SHRINE
And the man Micah had a s., and he Ju 17.05
into the inner s. behind the curtain, Heb 6.19

SHRINES
put them in the s. of the high places 2Ki 17.29
for them in the s. of the high places. 17.32
And all the s. also of the high places 23.19
made for yourself daily decked s., Eze 16.16
does not live in s. made by man, Ac 17.24
who made silver s. of Artemis, 19.24

SHRINK
on you will s. from you and say, Nah 3.07
how I did not s. from declaring to Ac 20.20
for I did not s. from declaring to 20.27
of those who s. back and are destroyed, Heb 10.39
confidence and not s. from him in 1Jn 2.28

SHRINKS
and if he s. back, my soul has no Heb 10.38

SHRIVELED
And he has s. me up, which is a Job 16.08
their skin has s. upon their bones, Lam 4.08

SHRIVELS
The seed s. under the clods, the Joe 1.17

SHROUD
wrapped it in a clean linen s., Mt 27.59
And he bought a linen s., and taking Mk 15.46
down, wrapped him in the linen s., 15.46
down and wrapped it in a linen s., Lk 23.53

SHRUB
He is like a s. in the desert, and Jer 17.06

SHRUBS
the greatest of s. and becomes a Mt 13.32
and becomes the greatest of all s., Mk 4.32

SHUA
certain Canaanite whose name was S.; Gen 38.02
Shomer, Hotham, and their sister S. 1Ch 7.32

SHUAH
Jokshan, Medan, Midian, Ishbak, and S. Gen 25.02
Jokshan, Medan, Midian, Ishbak, and S. 1Ch 1.32

SHUAL
toward Ophrah, to the land of S., 1Sa 13.17
Suah, Harnepher, S., Beri, Imrah, 1Ch 7.36

SHUA'S
the wife of Judah, S. daughter, died; Gen 38.12

SHUBAEL
Amram, S.; of the sons of S., Jehdeiah. 1Ch 24.20
S., his sons and his brethren, 25.20

SHUDDER
little more than a year you will s., Is 32.10
are at ease, s., you complacent ones; 32.11
their kings shall s. because of you, Eze 32.10
do well. Even the demons believe—and s. Jas 2.19

SHUDDERING
am dismayed, and s. seizes my flesh. Job 21.06

SHUHAH
Chelub, the brother of S., was the 1Ch 4.11

SHUHAM
of S., the family of the Shuhamites. Num 26.42

SHUHAMITES
families: of Shuham, the family of the S. Num 26.42
All the families of the S., according 26.43

SHUHITE
Temanite, Bildad the S., and Zophar the Job 2.11
Then Bildad the S. answered: 8.01
Then Bildad the S. answered: 18.01
Then Bildad the S. answered: 25.01
Temanite, and Bildad the S. and Zophar the 42.09

SHULAMMITE
O S., return, return, that we may Sol 6.13
Why should you look upon the s., 6.13

SHUMATHITES
Puthites, the S., and the Mishraites; 1Ch 2.53

SHUN
hast caused my companions to s. me; Ps 88.08
caused lover and friend to s. me; 88.18
S. immorality. Every other sin 1Co 6.18
beloved, s. the worship of idols. 10.14
for you, man of God, s. all this; 1Ti 6.11
So s. youthful passions and aim at 2Ti 2.22

SHUNAMMITE
Israel, and found Abishag the S., 1Ki 1.03
and Abishag the S. was ministering 1.15
give me Abishag the S. as my wife. 2.17
"Let Abishag the S. be given to 2.21
ask Abishag the S. for Adonijah? 2.22
Gehazi his servant, "Call this S." 2Ki 4.12
servant, "Look, yonder is the S.; 4.25
Gehazi and said, "Call this S." 4.36

SHUNEM
included Jezreel, Chesulloth, S., Jos 19.18
and came and encamped at S.; and 1Sa 28.04
One day Elisha went on to S., where 2Ki 4.08

SHUNI
S., Ezbon, Eri, Arodi, and Areli. Gen 46.16
of S., the family of the Shunites; Num 26.15

SHUNITES
of Shuni, the family of the S.; Num 26.15

SHUNS
who swears is as he who s. an oath. Ecc 9.02

SHUPHAMITES
of Shephupham, the family of the S.; Num 26.39

SHUPPIM
And S. and Huppim were the sons of 1Ch 7.12
took a wife for Huppim and for S. 7.15
For S. and Hosah it came out for 26.16

SHUR
wilderness, the spring on the way to S. Gen 16.07
and dwelt between Kadesh and S.; and 20.01
They dwelt from Havilah to S., which 25.18
went into the wilderness of S.; Ex 15.22
Amalekites, from Havilah as far as S., 1Sa 15.07
as far as S., to the land of Egypt. 27.08

SHUT
commanded him; and the LORD s. him in. Gen 7.16
door to the men, s. the door after him, 19.06
the house to them, and s. the door. 19.10
land; the wilderness has s. them in.' Ex 14.03
priest shall s. up the diseased Lev 13.04
priest shall s. him up seven days 13.05
he shall not s. him up, for he is 13.11
priest shall s. him up seven days; 13.21
priest shall s. him up seven days, 13.26
priest shall s. up the person with 13.31
priest shall s. up the person with 13.33
and s. up that which has the disease 13.50
and he shall s. it up seven days 13.54
and s. up the house seven days. 14.38
while it is s. up shall be unclean 14.46
Let her be s. up outside the camp Num 12.14
So Miriam was s. up outside the 12.15
and he s. up the heavens, so that Deu 11.17
your heart or s. your hand against 15.07
had gone out, the gate was s. Jos 2.07
Now Jericho was s. up from within 6.01
and women, and s. themselves in; Ju 9.51
and s. up their calves at home. 1Sa 6.10
for he has s. himself in by entering 23.07
So they were s. up until the day of 2Sa 20.03
"When heaven is s. up and there is 1Ki 8.35
and s. the door upon yourself and 2Ki 4.04
from him and s. the door upon 4.05
and s. the door upon him, and went 4.21
So he went in and s. the door upon 4.33
s. the door, and hold the door fast 6.32
the king of Assyria s. him up, 17.04
"When heaven is s. up and there is 2Ch 6.26
When I s. up the heavens so that 7.13
and he s. up the doors of the house 28.24
They also s. the doors of the 29.07
who was s. up, he said, "Let us meet Neh 6.10
guard let them s. and bar the doors. 7.03
doors should be s. and gave orders 13.19
because it did not s. the doors of Job 3.10
by day they s. themselves up; 24.16
"Or who s. in the sea with doors, 38.08
s. up closely as with a seal. 41.15
Has he in anger s. up his compassion?" Ps 77.09
I am s. in so that I cannot escape; 88.08
and the doors on the street are s.; Ecc 12.04
ears heavy, and s. their eyes; Is 6.10
and none shall s.; and he shall s., 22.22
every house is s. up so that none 24.10
they will be s. up in a prison, and 24.22
and s. your doors behind you; 26.20
for he has s. their eyes, so that 44.18
kings shall s. their mouths because 52.15
day and night they shall not be s.; 60.11
cause to bring forth, s. the womb? 66.09
The cities of the Negeb are s. up, Jer 13.19
a burning fire s. up in my bones, 20.09
the prophet was s. up in the court 32.02
he was still s. up in the court of 33.01
while he was s. up in the court of 39.15
s. yourself within your house. Eze 3.24
which faces east; and it was s. 44.01
to me, "This gate shall remain s.; 44.02
therefore it shall remain s. 44.02
east shall be s. on the six 46.01
gate shall not be s. until evening. 46.02
has gone out the gate shall be s. 46.12
his angel and s. the lions' mouths, Dan 6.22
s. up the words, and seal the book, 12.04
the words are s. up and sealed 12.09
among you who would s. the doors, Mal 1.10
your room and s. the door and pray Mt 6.06
because you s. the kingdom of 23.13
marriage feast; and the door was s. 25.10
that he s. up John in prison. Lk 3.20
the heaven was s. up three years 4.25
the door is now s., and my 11.07
has risen up and s. the door, 13.25
the doors being s. where the Jn 20.19
The doors were s., but Jesus came 20.26
and at once the gates were s. Ac 21.30
I not only s. up many of the saints 26.10
they want to s. you out, that you Gal 4.17
who opens and no one shall s., Rev 3.07
door, which no one is able to s.; 3.08
They have power to s. the sky, 11.06
and s. it and sealed it over him, 20.03
gates shall never be s. by day— 21.25

SHUTHELAH
of S., the family of the Shuthelahites; Num 26.35
And these are the sons of S.: 26.36
S., and Bered his son, Tahath his 1Ch 7.20
Zabad his son, S. his son, and Ezer 7.21

SHUTHELAHITES
of Shuthelah, the family of the S.; Num 26.35

SHUTS
hope, and injustice s. her mouth. Job 5.16
if he s. a man in, none can open. 12.14
and s. his eyes from looking upon Is 33.15
cry for help, he s. out my prayer; Lam 3.08
shall shut, who s. and no one opens. Rev 3.07

SHUTTLE
days are swifter than a weaver's s., Job 7.06

SIA
the sons of S., the sons of Padon, Neh 7.47

SIAHA
the sons of S., the sons of Padon, Ez 2.44

SIBBECAI
then S. the Hushathite slew Saph, 2Sa 21.18
S. the Hushathite, Ilai the Ahohite, 1Ch 11.29
then S. the Hushathite slew Sippai, 20.04
was S. the Hushathite, of the Zerahites; 27.11

SIBBOLETH
and he said "S.," for he could not Ju 12.06

SIBMAH
(their names to be changed), and S.; Num 32.38
and S., and Zerethshahar on the Jos 13.19
Heshbon languish, and the vine of S.; Is 16.08
weeping of Jazer for the vine of S.; 16.09
Jazer I weep for you, O vine of S.! Jer 48.32

SIBRAIM
Berothah, S. (which lies on the border Eze 47.16

SICK
also for her who is s. with her Lev 15.33
which the LORD has made it s.— Deu 29.22
to take David, she said, "He is s." 1Sa 19.14
because I fell s. three days ago. 30.13
bore to David, and it became s. 2Sa 12.15
Abijah the son of Jeroboam fell s. 1Ki 14.01
concerning her son; for he is s. 14.05
chamber in Samaria, and lay s.; 2Ki 1.02
Benhadad the king of Syria was s.; 8.07
Ahab in Jezreel, because he was s. 8.29
had fallen s. with the illness of 13.14
Hezekiah became s. and was at the 20.01
he heard that Hezekiah had been s. 20.12
Ahab in Jezreel, because he was s. 2Ch 22.06
Hezekiah became s. and was at the 32.24
face sad, seeing you are not s.? Neh 2.02
But I, when they were s.—I wore Ps 35.13
Some were s. through their sinful 107.17
Hope deferred makes the heart s., Pro 13.12
with apples; for I am s. with love. Sol 2.05
that you tell him I am s. with love. 5.08
The whole head is s., and the Is 1.05
be as when a s. man wastes away. 10.18
And no inhabitant will say, "I am s."; 33.24
Hezekiah became s. and was at the 38.01
he had been s. and had recovered 38.09
he had been s. and had recovered. 39.01
healing, my heart is s. within me. Jer 8.18
For this our heart has become s., Lam 5.17
the s. you have not healed, the Eze 34.04
overcome and lay s. for some days; Dan 8.27
princes became s. with the heat of Hos 7.05
offer those that are lame or s., Mal 1.08
taken by violence or is lame or s., 1.13
and they brought him all the s., Mt 4.24
mother-in-law lying s. with a fever; 8.14
a word, and healed all who were s. 8.16
a physician, but those who are s. 9.12
Heal the s., raise the dead, cleanse 10.08
on them, and healed their s. 14.14
brought to him all that were s., 14.35
I was s. and you visited me, I was 25.36
did we see thee s. or in prison 25.39
s. and in prison and you did not 25.43
or naked or s. or in prison, 25.44
mother-in-law lay s. with a fever, Mk 1.30
all who were s. or possessed with 1.32
many who were s. with various 1.34
a physician, but those who are s.; 2.17
upon a few s. people and healed 6.05
many that were s. and healed them. 6.13
began to bring s. people on their 6.55
they laid the s. in the market 6.56
lay their hands on the s.; and they will * 16.18
any that were s. with various Lk 4.40
a physician, but those who are s.; 5.31
who was s. and at the point of 7.02
heal the s. in it and say to them, 10.09
The s. man answered him, "Sir, I have Jn 5.07
carried out the s. into the Ac 5.15
bringing the s. and those afflicted 5.16
In those days she fell s. and died; 9.37
away from his body to the s., 19.12
of Publius lay s. with fever and 28.08
Is any among you s.? Let him call Jas 5.14
of faith will save the s. man, 5.15

SICKBED
The LORD sustains him on his s.; Ps 41.03
Behold, I will throw her on a s., Rev 2.22

SICKLE
first put the s. to the standing Deu 16.09
shall not put a s. to your neighbor's 23.25
his mattock, his axe, or his s.; 1Sa 13.20
who handles the s. in time of Jer 50.16
Put in the s., for the harvest is Joe 3.13
is ripe, at once he puts in the s., Mk 4.29
head, and a sharp s. in his hand. Rev 14.14
"Put in your s., and reap, for the 14.15
cloud swung his s. on the earth, 14.16
heaven, and he too had a sharp s. 14.17
voice to him who had the sharp s., 14.18
"Put in your s., and gather the 14.18
angel swung his s. on the earth 14.19

SICKNESS
and I will take s. away from the Ex 23.25
lies with a woman having her s., Lev 20.18
will take away from you all s.; Deu 7.15
Every s. also, and every affliction 28.61
plague, whatever s. there is; 1Ki 8.37
whether I shall recover from this s." 2Ki 1.02
'Shall I recover from this s.?' " 8.08
"Shall I recover from this s.?' " 8.09
plague, whatever s. there is; 2Ch 6.28
have a severe s. with a disease of 21.15
A man's spirit will endure s.; Pro 18.14
vexation and s. and resentment? Ecc 5.17
send wasting s. among his stout Is 10.16
and had recovered from his s.: 38.09
s. and wounds are ever before me. Jer 6.07
When Ephraim saw his s., and Hos 5.13

SICKNESSES
lasting, and s. grievous and lasting. Deu 28.59
land and the s. with which the LORD 29.22

SIDDIM
forces in the Valley of S. (that is, Gen 14.03

SIDDIM (cont.)

joined battle in the Valley of S. Gen 14.08
Now the Valley of S. was full of 14.10

SIDE

set the door of the ark in its s.; Gen 6.16
of Isaac, had not been on my s., 31.42
He went over to her at the road s., 38.16
to the west s. of the wilderness, Ex 3.01
one s., and the other on the other s.; 17.12
two rings on the one s. of it, 25.12
two rings on the other s. of it. 25.12
out of one s. of it and three 25.32
lampstand out of the other s. of it; 25.32
And the cubit on the one s., 26.13
and the cubit on the other s., 26.13
on this s. and that s., to cover it. 26.13
twenty frames for the south s.; 26.18
and for the second s. of the 26.20
on the north s. twenty frames, 26.20
of the one s. of the tabernacle, 26.27
of the other s. of the tabernacle, 26.27
frames of the s. of the tabernacle 26.27
on the south s. of the tabernacle 26.35
put the table on the north s. 26.35
On the south s. the court shall 27.09
a hundred cubits long for one s.; 27.09
on the north s. there shall be 27.11
on the west s. there shall be 27.12
for the one s. of the gate shall 27.14
On the other s. the hangings shall 27.15
on the one s. and on the other were 32.15
and said, "Who is on the LORD's s.? 32.26
'Put every man his sword on his s., 32.27
twenty frames for the south s.; 36.23
And for the second s. of the 36.25
on the north s., he made twenty 36.25
of the one s. of the tabernacle, 36.31
of the other s. of the tabernacle, 36.32
one s. and two rings on its other s. 37.03
out of one s. of it and three 37.18
lampstand out of the other s. of it; 37.18
for the south s. the hangings of 38.09
And for the north s. a hundred 38.11
And for the west s. were hangings 38.12
hangings for one s. of the gate 38.14
And so for the other s.; on this 38.15
on the north s. of the tabernacle, 40.22
on the south s. of the tabernacle, 40.24
it on the north s. of the altar Lev 1.11
drained out on the s. of the altar; 1.15
it beside the altar on the east s., 1.16
offering on the s. of the altar, 5.09
the tent of meeting on every s. Num 2.02
on the east s. toward the sunrise 2.03
"On the south s. shall be the 2.10
"On the west s. shall be the 2.18
"On the north s. shall be the 2.25
on the south s. of the tabernacle, 3.29
on the north s. of the tabernacle. 3.35
are on the east s. shall set out. 10.05
are on the south s. shall set out. 10.06
about a day's journey on this s. and 11.31
a day's journey on the other s., 11.31
on the other s. of the Arnon, 21.13
vineyards, with a wall on either s. 22.24
on the other s. of the Jordan and 32.19
to us on this s. of the Jordan to 32.19
your south s. shall be from the 34.03
of Zin along the s. of Edom, 34.03
to Riblah on the east s. of Ain; 34.11
for the east s. two thousand cubits, 35.05
for the south s. two thousand cubits, 35.05
for the west s. two thousand cubits, 35.05
for the north s. two thousand cubits, 35.05
on the east s. of the Jordan as Deu 4.49
put it by the s. of the ark of the 31.26
and encamped on the north s. of Ai, Jos 8.11
some on this s., and some on that s.; 8.22
on the west s. of the Jordan, 12.07
on the north s. runs from the bay 15.05
is on the south s. of the valley; 15.07
all that were by the s. of Ashdod, 15.46
is on the other s. of the Jordan; 17.05
on the north s. of the brook and 17.09
On the north s. their boundary 18.12
on the western s. southward from 18.14
of Judah. This forms the western s. 18.14
And the southern s. begins at the 18.15
its boundary on the eastern s. 18.20
rest on every s. just as he had 21.44
you on the other s. of the Jordan. 22.04
on the s. that belongs to the 22.11
on the other s. of the Jordan; 24.08
also on every s. of all the camp, Ju 7.18
of all their enemies on every s.; 8.34
on the east s. of the land of Moab, 11.18
on the other s. of the Arnon; 11.18
his seat by the s. of the gate; 1Sa 4.18
in a box at its s. the figures of 6.08
hand of your enemies on every s.; 12.11
Philistine garrison on yonder s. 14.01
one s. and a rocky crag on the other s.; 14.04
all Israel, "You shall be on one s., 14.40
my son will be on the other s." 14.40
all his enemies on every s., 14.47
on the mountain on the one s., 17.03
on the mountain on the other s., 17.03
shoot three arrows to the s. of it, 20.20
the arrows are on this s. of you, 20.21
opposite, and Abner sat by Saul's s., 20.25
Saul went on one s. of the mountain, 23.26
on the other s. of the mountain; 23.26
Then David went over to the other s., 26.13
on the other s. of the valley and 31.07
the one on the one s. of the pool, 2Sa 2.13
other on the other s. of the pool. 2.13
his sword in his opponent's s.; 2.16
road by the s. of the mountain. 13.34
kind stood at the s. of the gate, 18.04
and on his s. are Abiathar the 1Ki 2.22
as far as the other s. of Jokmeam; 4.12
God has given me rest on every s.; 5.04
and he made s. chambers all around. 6.05
was on the south s. of the house; 6.08
with wreaths at the s. of each. 7.30
five on the south s. of the house, 7.39
five on the north s. of the house; 7.39
on the south s. and five on the 7.49
and on each s. of the seat were arm 10.19
to the one s. and to the other, 2Ki 2.08
to the one s. and to the other; 2.14
you and I rode s. by s. behind Ahab 9.25
window, and said, "Who is on my s.? 9.32
saying, "If you are on my s., 10.06
from the south s. of the house to 11.11
house to the north s. of the house, 11.11
on the right s. as one entered the 12.09
it on the north s. of his altar. 16.14
to the east s. of the valley, 1Ch 4.39
the desert this s. of the Euphrates, 5.09
on the east s. of the Jordan, out of 6.78
in the king's gate on the east s. 9.18
he not given you peace on every s.? 22.18
wash, and set five on the south s., 2Ch 4.06
side, and five on the north s. 4.06
on the south s. and five on the north. 4.07
on the south s. and five on the north. 4.08
and on each s. of the seat were arm 9.18
he has given us peace on every s. 14.07
from the south s. of the house to 23.10
house to the north s. of the house, 23.10
and he gave them rest on every s. 32.22
to the west s. of the city of 32.30

SIDE (cont.)
girded at his s. while he built. Neh 4.18
and all that he has, on every s.? Job 1.10
Terrors frighten him on every s., 18.11
He breaks me down on every s., 19.10
whom I shall see on my s., 19.27
On every s. the wicked prowl, as Ps 12.08
of many—terror on every s.! 31.13
thy arrows flashed on every s. 77.17
A thousand may fall at your s., 91.07
With the LORD on my s. I do not fear. 118.06
The LORD is on my s. to help me; 118.07
me, surrounded me on every s.; 118.11
been the LORD who was on our s., 124.01
been the LORD who was on our s., 124.02
On the s. of their oppressors there Ecc 4.01
has a sword, terror is on every s. Jer 6.25
Pashhur, but Terror on every s. 20.03
whispering. Terror is on every s.! 20.10
look not back—terror on every s.! 46.05
cry to them: 'Terror on every s.!' 49.29
calamity from every s. of them, 49.32
her from every s. on the day of 51.02
that his city is taken on every s.; 51.31
feast my terrors on every s.; Lam 2.22
the face of a lion on the right s., Eze 1.10
the face of an ox on the left s., 1.10
"Then lie upon your left s., 4.04
second time, but on your right s., 4.06
turn from one s. to the other, 4.08
of days that you lie upon your s., 4.09
with a writing case at his s. 9.02
who had the writing case at his s. 9.03
with the writing case at his s., 9.11
on the south s. of the house, 10.03
is on the east s. of the city. 11.23
you from every s. for your harlotries 16.33
them against you from every s., 16.37
set against him snares on every s.; 19.08
them against you from every s.: 23.22
you on every s. with buckler, 23.24
that is against her on every s. 28.23
Because you push with s. and shoulder, 34.21
and the s. rooms, one reed long, and 40.07
and the space between the s. rooms, 40.07
were three s. rooms on either s. of 40.10
jambs on either s. were of the 40.10
There was a barrier before the s. rooms, 40.12
rooms, one cubit on either s.: and the 40.12
rooms were six cubits on either s. 40.12
back of the one s. room to the 40.13
into their jambs in the s. rooms, 40.16
ran along the s. of the gates, 40.18
Its s. rooms, three on either s., 40.21
on its jambs, one on either s. 40.26
Its s. rooms, its jambs, and its 40.29
to the inner court on the east s., 40.32
Its s. rooms, its jambs, and its 40.33
on its jambs, one on either s.; 40.34
Its s. rooms, its jambs, and its 40.36
on its jambs, one on either s.; 40.37
gate were two tables on either s., 40.39
on the other s. of the vestibule 40.40
the outside of the s. of the gate, 40.41
one at the s. of the north gate 40.44
other at the s. of the south gate 40.44
vestibule, five cubits on either s.; 40.48
were three cubits on either s. 40.48
beside the jambs on either s. 40.49
on each s. six cubits was the 41.01
were five cubits on either s.; 41.02
and the breadth of the s. chambers, 41.05
And the s. chambers were in three 41.06
as supports for the s. chambers, 41.06
And the s. chambers became broader 41.07
on the s. of the temple a stairway 41.07
foundations of the s. chambers 41.08
wall of the s. chambers was five 41.09
round about the temple on every s. 41.10
doors of the s. chambers opened on 41.11
on the west s. was seventy cubits 41.12
west and its walls on either s., 41.15
toward the palm tree on the one s., 41.19
the palm tree on the other s. 41.19
and palm trees on either s., 41.26
on the north s. was a hundred 42.02
was an entrance on the east s., 42.09
was an entrance on the east s., 42.12
the east s. with the measuring 42.16
turned and measured the north s., 42.17
turned and measured the south s., 42.18
turned to the west s. and measured, 42.19
which was at the s. of the gate, 46.19
was coming out on the south s. 47.02
on the one s. and on the other. 47.07
On the north s., from the Great Sea 47.15
This shall be the north s. 47.17
"On the east s., the boundary shall 47.18
This shall be the east s. 47.18
"On the south s., it shall run from 47.19
This shall be the south s. 47.19
"On the west s., the Great Sea 47.20
of Hamath. This shall be the west s. 47.20
from the east s. to the west, 48.01
from the east s. to the west, Asher, 48.02
from the east s. to the west, 48.03
from the east s. to the west, 48.04
from the east s. to the west, 48.05
from the east s. to the west, Reuben, 48.06
from the east s. to the west, Judah, 48.07
from the east s. to the west, shall 48.08
from the east s. to the west, with 48.08
thousand cubits on the northern s., 48.10
in breadth on the western s., 48.10
in breadth on the eastern s., 48.10
in length on the southern s., 48.10
the north s. four thousand five 48.16
the south s. four thousand five 48.16
the east s. four thousand five 48.16
and the west s. four thousand five 48.16
from the east s. to the west, 48.23
from the east s. to the west, Simeon, 48.24
from the east s. to the west, 48.25
from the east s. to the west, 48.26
from the east s. to the west, Gad, 48.27
On the north s., which is to be 48.30
On the east s., which is to be four 48.32
On the south s., which is to be 48.33
On the west s., which is to be four 48.34
It was raised up on one s.; Dan 7.05
contends by my s. against these 10.21
mountains shall touch the s. of it; Zec 14.05
orders to go over to the other s. Mt 8.18
And when he came to the other s., 8.28
and go before him to the other s., 14.22
the disciples reached the other s., 16.05
for your are not on the s. of God, 16.23
took a spear and pierced his s., * 27.49
"Let us go across to the other s." Mk 4.35
They came to the other s. of the sea, 5.01
again in the boat to the other s., 5.21
and go before him to the other s., 6.45
again he departed to the other s. 8.13
For you are not on the s. of God, 8.33
young man sitting on the right s., 16.05
on the right s. of the altar of Lk 1.11
across to the other s. of the lake." 8.22
a child and put him by his s., 9.47
him he passed by on the other s. 10.31
saw him, passed by on the other s. 10.32
the sky from one s. to the other, 17.24
you, and hem you in on every s., 19.43
to the other s. of the Sea of Jn 6.01
on the other s. of the sea saw 6.22

SIDE (cont.)
him on the other s. of the sea, Jn 6.25
one on either s., and Jesus between 19.18
pierced his s. with a spear, 19.34
showed them his hands and his s. 20.20
nails, and place my hand in his s., 20.25
your hand, and place it in my s.; 20.27
net on the right s. of the boat, 21.06
Peter on the s. and woke him, Ac 12.07
mind striving s. by s. for the Php 1.27
have labored s. by s. with me in 4.03
on each s. of the throne, are four Rev 4.06
on either s. of the river, the tree 22.02

SIDED
some s. with the Jews, and some with Ac 14.04

SIDES
the rings on the s. of the ark, Ex 25.14
six branches going out of its s., 25.32
hang over the s. of the tabernacle, 26.13
be upon the two s. of the altar, 27.07
its top and its s. round about and 30.03
on two opposite s. of it shall you 30.04
that were written on both s.; 32.15
the rings on the s. of the ark, 37.05
six branches going out of its s., 37.18
and its s. round about, and its 37.26
molding, on two opposite s. of it, 37.27
the rings on the s. of the altar, 38.07
in your eyes and thorns in your s., Num 33.55
on opposite s. of the ark before Jos 8.33
trap for you, a scourge on your s., 23.13
peace on all s. round about him. 1Ki 4.24
The gatekeepers were on the four s., 1Ch 9.24
nests in the s. of the mouth of a Jer 48.28
ninety-six pomegranates on the s.: 52.23
on their four s. they had human Eze 1.08
and crushed you from all s., 36.03
and will gather them from all s., 37.21
gather from all s. to the sacrificial 39.17
He measured it on the four s. 42.20
land on both s. of the holy 45.07
on both s. of the river, there will 47.12
"What remains on both s. of the 48.21
covered on all s. with gold, Heb 9.04

SIDEWALLS
and the s. of the gate were three Eze 40.48
and the s. of the entrance were 41.02
and the s. of the entrance, seven 41.03
on the s. of the vestibule. 41.26

SIDON
the father of S. his first-born, Gen 10.15
on the Canaanites extended from S., 10.19
and his border shall be at S. 49.13
as far as Great S. and Misrephothmaim, Jos 11.08
Kanah, as far as S. the Great; 19.28
of Acco, or the inhabitants of S., Ju 1.31
the gods of S., the gods of Moab, 10.06
deliverer because it was far from S., 18.28
from Dan they went around to S., 2Sa 24.06
to Zarephath, which belongs to S., 1Ki 17.09
the father of S. his first-born, 1Ch 1.13
of the coast, O merchants of S., Is 23.02
Be ashamed, O S., for the sea has 23.04
O oppressed virgin daughter of S.; 23.12
kings of Tyre, all the kings of S., Jer 25.22
and the king of S. by the hand of 27.03
from Tyre and S. every helper that 47.04
The inhabitants of S. and Arvad Eze 27.08
"Son of man, set your face toward S., 28.21
O S., and I will manifest my glory 28.22
O Tyre and S., and all the regions Joe 3.04
Tyre and S., though they are very Zec 9.02
you had been done in Tyre and S., Mt 11.21
for Tyre and S. than for you. 11.22
to the district of Tyre and S. 15.21
about Tyre and S. a great multitude, Mk 3.08
away to the region of Tyre and S. 7.24
went through S. to the Sea of 7.31
to Zarephath, in the land of S., Lk 4.26
and the seacoast of Tyre and S., 6.17
you had been done in Tyre and S., 10.13
for Tyre and S. than for you. 10.14
with the people of Tyre and S.; Ac 12.20
The next day we put in at S.; 27.03

SIDONIAN
Edomite, S., and Hittite women, 1Ki 11.01

SIDONIANS
(the S. call Hermon Sirion, while Deu 3.09
and Mearah which belongs to the S., Jos 13.04
to Misrephothmaim, even all the S. 13.06
and the S., and the Hivites who Ju 3.03
The S. also, and the Amalekites, and 10.12
security, after the manner of the S., 18.07
far from the S. and had no dealings 18.07
how to cut timber like the S." 1Ki 5.06
Ashtoreth the goddess of the S., 11.05
Ashtoreth the goddess of the S., 11.33
daughter of Ethbaal king of the S., 16.31
Ashtoreth the abomination of the S., 2Ki 23.13
for the S. and Tyrians brought 1Ch 22.04
and oil to the S. and the Tyrians Ez 3.07
and all the S., who have gone down Eze 32.30

SIEGE
in the s. and in the distress with Deu 28.53
in the s. and in the distress with 28.55
in the s. and in the distress with 28.57
and laid s. to it, and assaulted it: Jos 10.31
and they laid s. to it, and assaulted 10.34
Israel were laying s. to Gibbethon. 1Ki 15.27
Jerusalem, and laid s. to it; 2Ki 25.01
that you stand s. in Jerusalem? 2Ch 32.10
Go up, O Elam, lay s., O Media; Is 21.02
They erected their s. towers, they razed 23.13
shield, or cast up a s. mound against it. 37.33
cast up a s. mound against Jerusalem Jer 6.06
ground, O you who dwell under s.! 10.17
Behold, the s. mounds have come up 32.24
against the s. mounds and before 33.04
and they laid s. to it and built 52.04
and build a s. wall against it, and Eze 4.02
of s., and press the s. against it. 4.03
face toward the s. of Jerusalem, 4.07
have completed the days of your s. 4.08
the days of the s. are completed; 5.02
are cast up and s. walls built to 17.17
cast up mounds, to build s. towers. 21.22
has laid s. to Jerusalem this very 24.02
will set up a s. wall against you, 26.08
s. is laid against us; with a rod Mic 5.01
Draw water for the s., strengthen Nah 3.14
also in the s. against Jerusalem. Zec 12.02

SIEGEWORKS
you may build s. against the city Deu 20.20
and they built s. against it round 2Ki 25.01
they have cast up s. against me, Job 19.12
it, building great s. against it. Ecc 9.14
and I will raise s. against you. Is 29.03
to it and built s. against it Jer 52.04
and put s. against it, and build a Eze 4.02
north shall come and throw up s., Dan 11.15

SIEVE
nations with the s. of destruction, Is 30.28
nations as one shakes with a s., Amo 9.09

SIFT
to s. the nations with the sieve of Is 30.28
that he might s. you like wheat, Lk 22.31

SIGH
our years come to an end like a s. Ps 90.09
languishes, all the merry-hearted s. Is 24.07
of the men who s. and groan over Eze 9.04
S. therefore, son of man; s. with 21.06
they say to you, 'Why do you s.?' 21.07
S., but not aloud; make no mourning 24.17
in this tent, we s. with anxiety; 2Co 5.04

SIGHED
he s., and said to him, "Ephphatha," Mk 7.34
And he s. deeply in his spirit, and 8.12

SIGHING
For my s. comes as my bread, and my Job 3.24
with sorrow, and my years with s.; Ps 31.10
my s. is not hidden from thee. 38.09
all the s. she has caused I bring Is 21.02
and sorrow and s. shall flee away. 35.10
and sorrow and s. shall flee away. 51.11

SIGHS
for us with s. too deep for words. Rom 8.26

SIGHT
pleasant to the s. and good for Gen 2.09
Now the earth was corrupt in God's s., 6.11
that Ishmael might live in thy s.!" 17.18
if I have found favor in your s., 18.03
servant has found favor in your s., 19.19
I may bury my dead out of my s." 23.04
I should bury my d. out of my s., 23.08
that I may find favor in your s." 32.05
"To find favor in the s. of my lord." 33.08
if I have found favor in your s., 33.10
me find favor in the s. of my lord." 33.15
was wicked in the s. of the LORD; 38.07
displeasing in the s. of the LORD, 38.10
favor in his s. and attended him, 39.04
favor in the s. of the keeper of 39.21
blame in the s. of my father all 44.32
left in the s. of my lord but our 47.18
now I have found favor in your s., 47.29
turn aside and see this great s., Ex 3.03
favor in the s. of the Egyptians; 3.21
the signs in the s. of the people. 4.30
offensive in the s. of Pharaoh and 5.21
in the s. of Pharaoh and in the s. of 7.20
toward heaven in the s. of Pharaoh. 9.08
favor in the s. of the Egyptians. 11.03
in the s. of Pharaoh's servants and 11.03
and in the s. of the people. 11.03
favor in the s. of the Egyptians, 12.36
in the s. of the elders of Israel. 17.06
Sinai in the s. of all the people. 19.11
mountain in the s. of the people 24.17
you have also found favor in my s.' 33.12
if I have found favor in thy s., 33.13
know thee and find favor in thy s. 33.13
that I have found favor in thy s., 33.16
or you have found favor in my s., 33.17
now I have found favor in thy s.," 34.09
in the s. of all the house of 40.38
acceptable in the s. of the LORD?" Lev 10.19
cut off in the s. of the children 20.17
a defect in his s. or an itching 21.20
with harshness over him in your s. 25.53
of Egypt in the s. of the nations, 26.45
have I not found favor in thy s., Num 11.11
at once, if I find favor in thy s., 11.15
heifer shall be burned in his s.; 19.05
Hor in the s. of all the congregation 20.27
therefore, if it is evil in thy s., 22.34
woman to his family, in the s. of Moses 25.06
and in the s. of the whole congregation 25.06
shall commission him in their s. 27.19
"If we have found favor in your s., 32.05
evil in the s. of the LORD was 32.13
triumphantly in the s. of all the 33.03
understanding in the s. of the peoples, Deu 4.06
is evil in the s. of the LORD, your 4.25
and good in the s. of the LORD, 6.18
was evil in the s. of the LORD, 9.18
is right in the s. of the LORD. 12.25
right in the s. of the LORD your 12.28
is right in the s. of the LORD 13.18
is evil in the s. of the LORD your 17.02
is right in the s. of the LORD. 21.09
brother be degraded in your s. 25.03
mad by the s. which your eyes 28.34
to him in the s. of all Israel, 31.07
what is evil in the s. of the LORD, 31.29
wrought in the s. of all Israel. 34.12
exalt you in the s. of all Israel, Jos 3.07
Joshua in the s. of all Israel; 4.14
and right in your s. to do to us." 9.25
and he said in the s. of Israel, 10.12
you, and drive them out of your s.; 23.05
did those great signs in our s., 24.17
was evil in the s. of the LORD and Ju 2.11
was evil in the s. of the LORD, 3.07
was evil in the s. of the LORD; 3.12
was evil in the s. of the LORD. 3.12
was evil in the s. of the LORD, 4.01
was evil in the s. of the LORD; 6.01
of the LORD vanished from his s. 6.21
was evil in the s. of the LORD, 10.06
was evil in the s. of the LORD; 13.01
him in whose s. I shall find favor." Ru 2.02
very great in the s. of the LORD; 1Sa 2.17
have done in the s. of the LORD, 12.17
was evil in the s. of the LORD?" 15.19
for he has found favor in my s." 16.22
was good in the s. of all the 18.05
and also in the s. of Saul's 18.05
was precious this day in my s., 26.24
be precious in the s. of the LORD, 26.24
blameless in my s. as an angel of 29.09
LORD, to do what is evil in his s.? 2Sa 12.09
your wives in the s. of this sun. 12.11
eat, and prepare the food in my s., 13.05
make a couple of cakes in my s., 13.06
it, and made cakes in his s. 13.08
that I have found favor in your s., 14.22
let me ever find favor in your s., 16.04
concubines in the s. of all Israel. 16.22
according to my cleanness in his s. 22.25
compassion in the s. of those who 1Ki 8.50
my name I will cast out of my s.; 9.07
was evil in the s. of the LORD, 11.06
great favor in the s. of Pharaoh, 11.19
is right in my s. and keeping my 11.33
was evil in the s. of the LORD, 14.22
was evil in the s. of the LORD, 15.26
was evil in the s. of the LORD, 15.34
that he did in the s. of the LORD, 16.07
doing evil in the s. of the LORD, 16.19
was evil in the s. of the LORD, 16.25
did evil in the s. of the LORD 16.30
what is evil in the s. of the LORD. 21.20
was evil in the s. of the LORD 21.25
was right in the s. of the LORD; 22.43
was evil in the s. of the LORD, 22.52
of yours, be precious in your s. 2Ki 1.13
let my life be precious in your s." 1.14
was evil in the s. of the LORD, 3.02
light thing in the s. of the LORD; 3.18
was evil in the s. of the LORD. 8.18
was evil in the s. of the LORD, 8.27
was evil in the s. of the LORD, 13.02
was evil in the s. of the LORD; 13.11
was evil in the s. of the LORD; 14.24
was evil in the s. of the LORD, 15.09
was evil in the s. of the LORD; 15.18

SIGHT (cont.)
was evil in the s. of the LORD; 2Ki 15.24
was evil in the s. of the LORD; 15.28
was evil in the s. of the LORD, 17.02
to do evil in the s. of the LORD, 17.17
and removed them out of his s.; 17.18
he had cast them out of his s. 17.20
LORD removed Israel out of his s., 17.23
have done what is good in thy s." 20.03
was evil in the s. of the LORD, 21.02
much evil in the s. of the LORD, 21.06
is evil in my s. and have provoked 21.15
was evil in the s. of the LORD. 21.16
was evil in the s. of the LORD, 21.20
remove Judah also out of my s., 23.27
was evil in the s. of the LORD, 23.32
was evil in the s. of the LORD, 23.37
LORD, to remove them out of his s., 24.03
was evil in the s. of the LORD, 24.09
was evil in the s. of the LORD, 24.19
was wicked in the s. of the LORD, 1Ch 2.03
Now therefore in the s. of all Israel, 28.08
repute in the s. of all Israel, 29.25
my name, I will cast out of my s., 2Ch 7.20
was right in the s. of the LORD. 20.32
was evil in the s. of the LORD. 21.06
was evil in the s. of the LORD, 22.04
was evil in the s. of the LORD our 29.06
exalted in the s. of all nations 32.23
was evil in the s. of the LORD, 33.02
much evil in the s. of the LORD, 33.06
was evil in the s. of the LORD, 33.22
was evil in the s. of the LORD his 36.05
was evil in the s. of the LORD. 36.09
was evil in the s. of the LORD his 36.12
him mercy in the s. of this man." Neh 1.11
servant has found favor in your s., 2.05
sin be blotted out from thy s.; 4.05
the book in the s. of all the 8.05
favor in his s. more than all the Est 2.17
favor in his s. and he held out to 5.02
found favor in the s. of the king, 5.08
"If I have found favor in your s., 7.03
if I have found favor in his s., 8.05
heavens are not clean in his s.; Job 15.15
Why are we stupid in your s.? 18.03
the stars are not clean in his s.; 25.05
hesitate to spit at the s. of me. 30.10
their wickedness in the s. of men, 34.26
is laid low even at the s. of him. 41.09
judgments are on high, out of his s.; Ps 10.05
cleanness of my hands in his s. 18.24
my heart be acceptable in thy s., 19.14
in the s. of the sons of men! 31.19
alarm, "I am driven far from thy s." 31.22
lifetime is as nothing in thy s. 39.05
at the s. of the enemy and the 44.16
done that which is evil in thy s., 51.04
precious is their blood in his s. 72.14
In the s. of their fathers he 78.12
years in thy s. are but as yesterday 90.04
vindication in the s. of the nations. 98.02
Precious in the s. of the LORD is 116.15
a net spread in the s. of any bird; Pro 1.17
repute in the s. of God and man. 3.04
let them not escape from your s., 3.21
only one in the s. of my mother, 4.03
Let them not escape from your s.; 4.21
Better is the s. of the eyes than Ecc 6.09
your heart and the s. of your eyes. 11.09
eyes, and shrewd in their own s.! Is 5.21
have done what is good in thy s." 38.03
And I will cast you out of my s., Jer 7.15
done evil in my s., says the LORD; 7.30
Send them out of my s., and let them go! 15.01
and if it does evil in my s., 18.10
nor blot out their sin from thy s. 18.23
flask in the s. of the men who go 19.10
but evil in my s. from their youth; 32.30
I will remove it from my s. 32.31
are no longer a nation in their s. 33.24
in the s. of the men of Judah, 43.09
was evil in the s. of the LORD, 52.02
it in their s. on human dung." Eze 4.12
of you in the s. of the nations. 5.08
you and in the s. of all that pass 5.14
in their own s. for the evils 6.09
the earth in my s. as they went 10.19
go into exile by day in their s.; 12.03
place to another place in their s. 12.03
your baggage by day in their s., 12.04
yourself at evening in their s., 12.04
Dig through the wall in their s., 12.05
In their s. you shall lift the 12.06
upon my shoulder in their s. 12.07
upon you in the s. of many women; 16.41
profaned in the s. of the nations 20.09
in whose s. I made myself known to 20.09
profaned in the s. of the nations, 20.14
in whose s. I had brought them out. 20.14
profaned in the s. of the nations, 20.22
in whose s. I had brought them out. 20.22
among you in the s. of the nations. 20.41
you in the s. of the nations; 22.16
earth in the s. of all who saw you 28.18
in them in the s. of the nations, 28.25
it was in the s. of all who passed 36.34
holiness in the s. of many nations. 39.27
and write it down in their s., 43.11
compassion in the s. of the chief Dan 1.09
lewdness in the s. of her lovers, Hos 2.10
hide from my s. at the bottom of Amo 9.03
will not lose s. of all that I Zep 3.07
Is it not in your s. as nothing? Hag 2.03
marvelous in the s. of the remnant Zec 8.06
it also be marvelous in my s., 8.06
evil is good in the s. of the LORD, Mal 2.17
receive their s. and the lame walk, Mt 11.05
received their s. and folowed him. 20.34
him, "Master, let me receive my s." Mk 10.51
he received his s. and followed 10.52
and recovering of s. to the blind, Lk 4.18
that were blind he bestowed s. 7.21
heard: the blind receive their s., 7.22
is an abomination in the s. of God. 16.15
said, "Lord, let me receive my s." 18.41
Jesus said to him, "Receive your s.; 18.42
he received his s. and followed 18.43
who assembled to see the s., 23.48
and he vanished out of their s. 24.31
went and washed and received my s." Jn 9.11
him how he had received his s. 9.15
been blind and had received his s., 9.18
the man who had received his s., 9.18
a cloud took him out of their s. Ac 1.09
is right in the s. of God to 4.19
Moses saw it he wondered at the s.; 7.31
favor in the s. of God and asked 7.46
And for three days he was without s., 9.09
him so that he might regain his s." 9.12
may regain your s. and be filled 9.17
his eyes and he regained his s. 9.18
all here present in the s. of God, 10.33
and burned them in the s. of all; 19.19
When we had come in s. of Cyprus, 21.03
me, 'Brother Saul, receive your s.' 22.13
hour I received my s. and saw him. 22.13
justified in his s. by works of the Rom 3.20
for what is noble in the s. of all. 12.17
in the s. of God we speak in Christ. 2Co 2.17
man's conscience in the s. of God. 4.02
walk by faith, not by s. 5.07
revealed to you in the s. of God. 7.12
Lord's s. but also in the s. of men. 8.21

SIGHT (cont.)
It is in the s. of God that we have 2Co 12.19
not known by s. to the churches of Gal 1.22
acceptable in the s. of God our 1Ti 2.03
is acceptable in the s. of God. 5.04
terrifying was the s. that Moses Heb 12.21
that which is pleasing in his s., 13.21
but in God's s. chosen and precious 1Pe 2.04
which in God's s. is very precious. 3.04
works perfect in the s. of my God. Rev 3.02
And in the s. of their foes they 11.12
heaven to earth in the s. of men; 13.13

SIGHTS
and the s. which your eyes shall Deu 28.67

SIGN
"This is the s. of the covenant Gen 9.12
it shall be a s. of the covenant 9.13
"This is the s. of the covenant 9.17
it shall be a s. of the covenant 17.11
and this shall be the s. for you, Ex 3.12
God said, "or heed the first s., 4.08
they may believe the latter s. 4.08
By tomorrow shall this s. be."'" 8.23
The blood shall be a s. for you, 12.13
be to you as a s. on your hand and 13.09
for this is a s. between me and you 31.13
It is a s. for ever between me and 31.17
they shall be a s. to the people Num 16.38
to be kept as a s. for the rebels, 17.10
bind them as a s. upon your hand, Deu 6.08
bind them as a s. upon your hand, 11.18
and gives you a s. or a wonder, 13.01
and the s. or wonder which he tells 13.02
be upon you as a s. and a wonder, 28.46
house, and give me a sure s., Jos 2.12
that this may be a s. among you, 4.06
then show me a s. that it is thou Ju 6.17
shall be the s. to you: both of them 1Sa 2.34
shall be the s. to you that the 10.01
And this shall be the s. to us." 14.10
And he gave a s. the same day, 1Ki 13.03
"This is the s. that the LORD has 13.03
according to the s. which the man 13.05
there was no sound or s. of life. 2Ki 4.31
"And this shall be the s. for you: 19.29
shall be the s. that the LORD will 20.08
"This is the s. to you from the 20.09
he answered him and gave him a s. 2Ch 32.24
about the s. that had been done in 32.31
Show me a s. of thy favor, that Ps 86.17
"Ask a s. of the LORD your God; Is 7.11
Lord himself will give you a s. 7.14
It will be a s. and a witness to 19.20
years as a s. and a portent 20.03
"And this shall be the s. for you: 37.30
"This is the s. to you from the 38.07
"What is the s. that I shall go up 38.22
an everlasting s. which shall not 55.13
and I will set a s. among them. 66.19
This shall be the s. to you, Jer 44.29
This is a s. for the house of Eze 4.03
have made you a s. for the house 12.06
Say, 'I am a s. for you: as I have 12.11
will make him a s. and a byword 14.08
as a s. between me and them, that 20.12
they may be a s. between me and 20.20
Thus shall Ezekiel be to you a s.; 24.24
So you will be a s. to them; 24.27
then he shall set up a s. by it, 39.15
the interdict and s. the document, Dan 6.08
Did you not s. an interdict, that 6.12
we wish to see a s. from you." Mt 12.38
seeks for a s.; but no s. shall be given 12.39
it except the s. of the prophet 12.39
him to show them a s. from heaven. 16.01
seeks for a s., but no s. shall be given 16.04
given to it except the s. of Jonah." 16.04
will be the s. of your coming and 24.03
then will appear the s. of the Son 24.30
Now the betrayer had given them a s., 26.48
seeking from him a s. from heaven, Mk 8.11
"Why does this generation seek a s.? Truly 8.12
no s. shall be given to this generation." 8.12
will be the s. when these things 13.04
Now the betrayer had given them a s., 14.44
And this will be a s. for you: Lk 2.12
and for a s. that is spoken against 2.34
sought from him a s. from heaven. 11.16
it seek a s. but no s. shall be 11.29
given to it except the s. of Jonah. 11.29
Jonah became a s. to the men of 11.30
will be the s. when this is about 21.07
hoping to see some s. done by him. 23.08
"What s. have you to show us for Jn 2.18
now the second s. that Jesus did 4.54
people saw the s. which he had 6.14
"Then what s. do you do, that we may 6.30
"John did no s., but everything 10.41
they heard he had done this s. 12.18
that a notable s. has been performed Ac 4.16
on whom this s. of healing was 4.22
circumcision as a s. or seal of the Rom 4.11
tongues are a s. not for believers 1Co 14.22

SIGNAL
Now the appointed s. between the Ju 20.38
But when the s. began to rise out 20.40
He will raise a s. for a nation Is 5.26
On a bare hill raise a s., 13.02
when a s. is raised on the mountains, 18.03
of a mountain, like a s. on a hill. 30.17
and raise my s. to the peoples; 49.22
and raise a s. on Bethhaccherem; Jer 6.01
"I will s. for them and gather them Zec 10.08

SIGNATURE
(Here is my s.! let the Almighty Job 31.35

SIGNED
I s. the deed, sealed it, got witnesses, Jer 32.10
witnesses who s. the deed of 32.12
deeds shall be s. and sealed and 32.44
Therefore King Darius s. the Dan 6.09
knew that the document had been s., 6.10
king, or the interdict you have s., 6.13

SIGNET
"Your s. and your cord, and your Gen 38.18
the s. and the cord and the staff." 38.25
took his s. ring from his hand and 41.42
on it, like the engraving of a s., Ex 28.36
earrings and s. rings and armlets, 35.22
like the engravings of a s., 39.06
inscription, like the engraving of a s., 39.30
s. rings, earrings, and beads, to make Num 31.50
king took his s. ring from his Est 3.10
and the king took off his s. ring, 8.02
the s. rings and nose rings; Is 3.21
were the s. ring on my right hand, Jer 22.24
"You were the s. of perfection, full Eze 28.12
own s. and with the s. of his lords, Dan 6.17
LORD, and make you like a s. ring; Hag 2.23

SIGNETS
As a jeweler engraves s., so shall you Ex 28.11
they shall be like s., each engraved 28.21
they were like s., each engraved 39.14

SIGNPOST
And make a s., make it at the head Eze 21.19

SIGNS

let them be for s. and for seasons Gen 1.14
even these two s. or heed your Ex 4.09
with which you shall do the s." 4.17
and all the s. which he had charged 4.28
and did the s. in the sight of the 4.30
I multiply my s. and wonders in 7.03
may show these s. of mine among 10.01
and what s. I have done among them; 10.02
of all the s. which I have wrought Num 14.11
my glory and my s. which I wrought 14.22
by s., by wonders, and by war, by a Deu 4.34
and the LORD showed s. and wonders, 6.22
the s., the wonders, the mighty hand, 7.19
his s. and his deeds which he did 11.03
great terror, with s. and wonders; 26.08
the s., and those great wonders; 29.03
him for all the s. and the wonders 34.11
did those great s. in our sight, Jos 24.17
Now when these s. meet you, do 1Sa 10.07
and all these s. came to pass that 10.09
and didst perform s. and wonders Neh 9.10
bounds are afraid at thy s.; Ps 65.08
they set up their own s. for s. 74.04
We do not see our s.; there is no longer 74.09
when he wrought his s. in Egypt, 78.43
They wrought his s. among them, 105.27
sent s. and wonders against Pharaoh 135.09
given me are s. and portents in Is 8.18
dismayed at the s. of the heavens Jer 10.02
who hast shown s. and wonders in 32.20
land of Egypt with s. and wonders, 32.21
me to show the s. and wonders that Dan 4.02
How great are his s., how mighty 4.03
he works s. and wonders in heaven 6.27
interpret the s. of the times. Mt 16.03
and show great s. and wonders, 24.24
will arise and show s. and wonders, Mk 13.22
And these s. will accompany those * 16.17
the message by the s. that attended it. * 16.20
and he made s. to them and remained Lk 1.22
And they made s. to his father, 1.62
not coming with s. to be observed; 17.20
terrors and great s. from heaven. 21.11
"And there will be s. in sun and 21.25
This, the first of his s., Jesus did at Jn 2.11
when they saw his s. which he did; 2.23
no one can do these s. that you do, 3.02
"Unless you see s. and wonders you 4.48
they saw the s. which he did on 6.02
seek me, not because you saw s., 6.26
will he do more s. than this man 7.31
a man who is a sinner do such s.?" 9.16
For this man performs many s. 11.47
he had done so many s. before them, 12.37
did many other s. in the presence 20.30
above and s. on the earth beneath, Ac 2.19
and wonders and s. which God did 2.22
wonders and s. were done through 2.43
and s. and wonders are performed 4.30
Now many s. and wonders were done 5.12
wonders and s. among the people. 6.08
wonders and s. in Egypt and at the 7.36
him and saw the s. which he did. 8.06
And seeing s. and great miracles 8.13
granting s. and wonders to be done 14.03
related what s. and wonders God 15.12
by the power of s. and wonders, Rom 15.19
For Jews demand s. and Greeks seek 1Co 1.22
The s. of a true apostle were 2Co 12.12
with s. and wonders and mighty 12.12
and with pretended s. and wonders, 2Th 2.09
bore witness by s. and wonders and Heb 2.04
It works great s., even making fire Rev 13.13
and by the s. which it is allowed 13.14
performing s., who go abroad to the 16.14
had worked the s. by which he 19.20

SIHON

messengers to S. king of the Num 21.21
But S. would not allow Israel to 21.23
was the city of S. the king of the 21.26
let the city of S. be established. 21.27
Heshbon, flame from the city of S. 21.28
captives, to an Amorite king, S. 21.29
as you did to S. king of the 21.34
the kingdom of S. king of the 32.33
after he had defeated S. the king Deu 1.04
into your hand S. the Amorite, 2.24
of Kedemoth to S. the king of 2.26
But S. the king of Heshbon would 2.30
begun to give S. and his land over 2.31
Then S. came out against us, he and 2.32
as you did to S. the king of the 3.02
as we did to S. the king of Heshbon, 3.06
in the land of S. the king of the 4.46
S. the king of Heshbon and Og the 29.07
do to them as he did to S. and Og, 31.04
to S. and Og, whom you utterly Jos 2.10
S. the king of Heshbon, and Og king 9.10
S. king of the Amorites who dwelt 12.02
the boundary of S. king of Heshbon. 12.05
the cities of S. king of the 13.10
the kingdom of S. king of the 13.21
Hur and Reba, the princes of S., 13.21
the kingdom of S. king of Heshbon, 13.27
messengers to S. king of the Ju 11.19
But S. did not trust Israel to pass 11.20
so S. gathered all his people 11.20
gave S. and all his people into the 11.21
the country of S. king of the 1Ki 4.19
of the land of S. king of Heshbon Neh 9.22
S., king of the Amorites, and Og, Ps 135.11
S., king of the Amorites, for his 136.19
a flame from the house of S.; Jer 48.45

SILAS

and S., leading men among the Ac 15.22
We have therefore sent Judas and S., 15.27
And Judas and S., who were themselves 15.32
but Paul chose S. and departed, 15.40
seized Paul and S. and dragged 16.19
Paul and S. were praying and 16.25
he fell down before Paul and S., 16.29
persuaded, and joined Paul and S.; 17.04
sent Paul and S. away by night to 17.10
but S. and Timothy remained there. 17.14
a command for S. and Timothy to 17.15
When S. and Timothy arrived from 18.05

SILENCE

gazed at her in s. to learn Gen 24.21
"Keep s. and hear, O Israel: this day Deu 27.09
And he commanded, "S." And all his Ju 3.19
For if you keep s. at such a time Est 4.14
there was s., then I heard a voice: Job 4.16
Should your babble s. men, and when 11.03
"Let me have s., and I will speak, 13.13
waited, and kept s. for my counsel. 29.21
terrified me, so that I kept s., 31.34
"I will not keep s. concerning his 41.12
Our God comes, he does not keep s., Ps 50.03
For God alone my soul waits in s.; 62.01
For God alone my soul waits in s., 62.05
O God, do not keep s.; do not hold 83.01
soon have dwelt in the land of s. 94.17
nor do any that go down into s. 115.17
a time to keep s., and a time Ecc 3.07
Listen to me in s., O coastlands; Is 41.01
Sit in s., and go into darkness, O 47.05
O Madmen, shall be brought to s.; Jer 48.02
of Zion sit on the ground in s.; Lam 2.10
sit alone in s. when he has laid 3.28
place they shall be cast out in s." Amo 8.03
all the earth keep s. before him. Hab 2.20

SILENCE (cont.)

And they kept s. and told no one in Lk 9.36
And all the assembly kept s.; Ac 15.12
of them keep s. in church and 1Co 14.28
should keep s. in the churches. 14.34
Let a woman learn in s. with all 1Ti 2.11
should put to s. the ignorance of 1Pe 2.15
there was s. in heaven for about Rev 8.01

SILENCED

heard that he had s. the Sadducees, Mt 22.34
When they heard this they were s. Ac 11.18
shall not be s. in the regions of 2Co 11.10
they must be s., since they are Tit 1.11

SILENT

if we are s. and wait until the 2Ki 7.09
But the people were s. and answered 18.36
They were s., and could not find Neh 5.08
"Teach me, and I will be s.; Job 6.24
Oh that you would keep s., 13.05
For then I would be s. and die. 13.19
be s., and I will speak. 33.31
be s., and I will teach you wisdom." 33.33
own hearts on your beds, and be s. Ps 4.04
if thou be s. to me, I become like 28.01
soul may praise thee and not be s. 30.12
be not s.! O Lord, be not far 35.22
I was dumb and s., I held my peace 39.02
you have done and I have been s.; 50.21
Be not s., O God of my praise! 109.01
a man of understanding remains s. Pro 11.12
fool who keeps s. is considered 17.28
But they were s. and answered him Is 36.21
For Zions sake I will not keep s., 62.01
the night they shall never be s. 62.06
Wilt thou keep s., and afflict us 64.12
before me: "I will not keep s., 65.06
I cannot keep s.; for I hear Jer 4.19
will keep s. in such a time; Amo 5.13
and art s. when the wicked swallows Hab 1.13
Be s. before the Lord GOD! Zep 1.07
Be s., all flesh, before the LORD; Zec 2.13
them, telling them to be s.; Mt 20.31
But Jesus was s. And the high priest 26.63
"Be s., and come out of him!" Mk 1.25
or to kill?" But they were s. 3.04
But they were s.; for on the way 9.34
rebuked him, telling him to be s.; 10.48
But he was s. and made no answer. 14.61
you will be s. and unable to speak Lk 1.20
"Be s., and come out of him!" 4.35
But they were s. Then he took 14.04
rebuked him, telling him to be s.; 18.39
if these were s., the very stones 19.40
marveling at his answer they were s. 20.26
to them with his hand to be s., Ac 12.17
afraid, but speak and do not be s.; 18.09
sitting by, let the first be s. 1Co 14.30
over men; she is to keep s. 1Ti 2.12

SILK

fine linen and covered you with s. Eze 16.10
and s., and embroidered cloth; 16.13
s. and scarlet, all kinds of scented Rev 18.12

SILLA

on the way that goes down to S. 2Ki 12.20

SILLY

s. and without sense, calling to Hos 7.11
nor s. talk, nor levity, which are Eph 5.04
to do with godless and s. myths. 1Ti 4.07

SILOAM

the tower in S. fell and killed Lk 13.04
in the pool of S." (which means Jn 9.07
said to me, 'Go to S. and wash'; 9.11

SILVANUS

S. and Timothy and I, was not Yes 2Co 1.19
Paul, S., and Timothy, To the church 1Th 1.01
Paul, S., and Timothy, To the church 2Th 1.01
By S., a faithful brother as I 1Pe 5.12

SILVER

rich in cattle, in s., and in gold. Gen 13.02
brother a thousand pieces of s.; 20.16
worth four hundred shekels of s.; 23.15
for Ephron the s. which he had 23.16
Hittites, four hundred shekels of s., 23.16
s. and gold, menservants and maidservants, 24.35
forth jewelry of s. and of gold, 24.53
Ishmaelites for twenty shekels of s., 37.28
the s. cup, in the mouth of the sack 44.02
Why have you stolen my s. cup? 44.04
should we steal s. or gold from 44.08
shekels of s. and five festal 45.22
jewelry of s. and of gold, and Ex 3.22
neighbor, jewelry of s. and of gold." 11.02
Egyptians jewelry of s. and of gold, 12.35
not make gods of s. to be with me, 20.23
their master thirty shekels of s., 21.32
from them: gold, s, and bronze, 25.03
and forty bases of s. you shall 26.19
and their forty bases of s., 26.21
their bases of s., sixteen bases; 26.25
of gold, upon four bases of s. 26.32
and their fillets shall be of s. 27.10
and their fillets shall be of s. 27.11
court shall be filleted with s.; 27.17
their hooks shall be of s., 27.17
to work in gold, s., and bronze, 31.04
offering: gold, s., and bronze; 35.05
an offering of s. or bronze 35.24
to work in gold and s. and bronze, 35.32
forty bases of s. under the twenty 36.24
and their forty bases of s., 36.26
frames with their bases of s.: 36.30
he cast for them four bases of s. 36.36
and their fillets were of s. 38.10
pillars and their fillets of s. 38.11
and their fillets were of s. 38.12
and their fillets were of s.; 38.17
of their capitals was also of s., 38.17
of the court were filleted with s. 38.17
were of bronze, their hooks of s., 38.19
capitals and their fillets of s. 38.19
And the s. from those of the 38.25
talents of s. were for casting the 38.27
valued by you in shekels of s., Lev 5.15
old shall be fifty shekels of s., 27.03
be for a male five shekels of s., 27.06
shall be three shekels of s. 27.06
be valued at fifty shekels of s. 27.16
offering was one s. plate whose Num 7.13
one s. basin of seventy shekels, 7.13
for his offerin one s. plate, 7.19
one s. basin of seventy shekels, 7.19
his offering was one s. plate, 7.25
one s. basin of seventy shekels, 7.25
offering was one s. plate whose 7.31
one s. basin of seventy shekels, 7.31
his offering was one s. plate, 7.37
one s. basin of seventy shekels, 7.37
his offering was one s. plate, 7.43
one s. basin of seventy shekels, 7.43
his offering was one s. plate, 7.49
one s. basin of seventy shekels, 7.49
his offering was one s. plate, 7.55
one s. basin of seventy shekels, 7.55
his offering was one s. plate, 7.61
one s. basin of seventy shekels, 7.61
his offering was one s. plate, 7.67
one s. basin of seventy shekels, 7.67
his offering was one s. plate, 7.73

SILVER (cont.)
one s. basin of seventy shekels, Num 7.73
his offering was one s. plate, 7.79
one s. basin of seventy shekels, 7.79
twelve s. plates, twelve s. basins, 7.84
each s. plate weighing a hundred 7.85
all the s. of the vessels two 7.85
"Make two s. trumpets; of hammered work 10.02
shall fix at five shekels in s., 18.16
me his house full of s. and gold, 22.18
me his house full of s. and gold, 24.13
the s., the bronze, the iron, the tin, 31.22
not covet the s. or the gold that Deu 7.25
and your s. and gold is multiplied, 8.13
multiply for himself s. and gold. 17.17
fine him a hundred shekels of s., 22.19
young woman fifty shekels of s., 22.29
of s. and gold, which were among 29.17
But all s. and gold, and vessels of Jos 6.19
only the s. and gold, and the 6.24
and two hunderd shekels of s., 7.21
my tent, with the s. underneath." 7.21
in his tent with the s. underneath. 7.22
and the s. and the mantle and the 7.24
with s., gold, bronze, and iron, and 22.08
of Megiddo; they got no spoils of s. Ju 5.19
pieces of s. out of the house of 9.04
you eleven hundred pieces of s." 16.05
pieces of s. which were taken from 17.02
my ears, behold, the s. is with me; 17.02
hundred pieces of s. to his mother; 17.03
consecrate the s. to the LORD from 17.03
took two hundred pieces of s., 17.04
give you ten pieces of s. a year, 17.10
for a piece of s. or a loaf of 1Sa 2.36
the fourth part of a shekel of s., 9.08
brought with him articles of s., 2Sa 8.10
with the s. and gold which he 8.11
you ten pieces of s. and a girdle." 18.11
weight of a thousand pieces of s., 18.12
not a matter of s. or gold between 21.04
the oxen for fifty shekels of s. 24.24
the s., the gold, and the vessels, 1Ki 7.51
none were of s., it was not considered 10.21
s., ivory, apes, and peacocks. 10.22
articles of s. and gold, garments, 10.25
And the king made s. as common in 10.27
for six hundred shekels of s., 10.29
votive gifts, s., and gold, and vessels. 15.15
took all the s. and the gold that 15.18
to you a present of s. and gold; 15.19
from Shemer for two talents of s.; 16.24
'Your s. and your gold are mine; 20.03
to me your s. and your gold, 20.05
and for my s. and my gold, and I did 20.07
else you shall pay a talent of s.' 20.39
taking with him ten talents of s., 2Ki 5.05
a talent of s. and two festal 5.22
up two talents of s. in two bags, 5.23
was sold for eighty shekels of s., 6.25
dove's dung for five shekels of s. 6.25
carried off s. and gold and clothing, 7.08
the house of the LORD basins of s., 12.13
or of s., from the money that was 12.13
And he seized all the gold and s., 14.14
gave Pul a thousand talents of s., 15.19
fifty shekels of s. from every man, 15.20
Ahaz also took the s. and gold that 16.08
talents of s. and thirty talents 18.14
him all the s. that was found in 18.15
the s., the gold, the spices, the 20.13
talents of s. and a talent of gold 23.33
gave the s. and the gold to Pharaoh, 23.35
he exacted the s. and the gold of 23.35
and what was of s., as s. 25.15
of gold, of s., and of bronze; 1Ch 18.10
with the s. and gold which he had 18.11
talents of s. to hire chariots and 19.06
of gold, a million talents of s., 22.14
gold, s., bronze, and iron. 22.16
the weight of s. vessels for each 28.14
the weight of s. for a lampstand 28.15
the s. for the s. tables, 28.16
for the s. bowls and the weight 28.17
the s. for the things of s., and 29.02
treasure of my own of gold and s., 29.03
thousand talents of refined s., 29.04
of gold and s. for the things of 29.05
and s. for the things of s. 29.05
gold, ten thousand talents of s., 29.07
And the king made s. and gold as 2Ch 1.15
for six hundred shekels of s., 1.17
s., bronze, and iron, and in purple, 2.07
s., bronze, iron, stone, and wood, and 2.14
had dedicated, and stored the s., 5.01
brought gold and s. to Solomon. 9.14
s. was not considered as anything 9.20
s., ivory, apes, and peacocks. 9.21
articles of s. and of gold, garments, 9.24
And the king made s. as common in 9.27
s., and gold, and vessels. 15.18
Then Asa took s. and gold from the 16.02
I am sending to you s. and gold; 16.03
presents, and s. for tribute; 17.11
of s., gold, and valuable possessions, 21.03
incense, and vessels of gold and s. 24.14
Israel for a hundred talents of s. 25.06
And he seized all the gold and s., 25.24
that year a hundred talents of s., 27.05
made for himself treasuries for s., 32.27
talents of s. and a talent of gold 36.03
men of his place with s. and gold, Ez 1.04
them aided them with vessels of s., 1.06
of gold, a thousand basins of s., 1.09
four hundred and ten bowls of s., 1.10
of gold and of s. were five 1.11
of gold, five thousand minas of s., 2.69
And the gold and s. vessels of the 5.14
the gold and s. vessels of the 6.05
to convey the s. and gold which 7.15
with all the s. and gold which you 7.16
with the rest of the s. and gold, 7.18
up to a hundred talents of s., 7.22
out to them the s. and the gold 8.25
hundred and fifty talents of s., 8.26
and s. vessels worth a hundred 8.26
and the s. and the gold are a 8.28
weight of the s. and the gold and 8.30
the s. and the gold and the vessels 8.33
wine, besides forty shekels of s. Neh 5.15
thousand two hundred minas of s. 7.71
of gold, two thousand minas of s., 7.72
and purple to s. rings of marble Est 1.06
of gold and s. on a mosaic pavement 1.06
talents of s. into the hands of 3.09
who filled their houses with s. Job 3.15
is your gold, and your precious s.; 22.25
Though he heap up s. like dust, 27.16
the innocent will divide the s. 27.17
"Surely there is a mine for s., 28.01
and s. cannot be weighed as its 28.15
s. refined in a furnace on the Ps 12.06
thou hast tried us as s. is tried. 66.10
wings of a dove covered with s., 68.13
led forth Israel wit s. and gold, 105.37
Their idols are s. and gold, 115.04
thousands of gold and s. pieces, 119.72
of the nations are s. and gold, 135.15
seek it like s. and search for it Pro 2.04
than gain from s. and its profit 3.14
Take my instruction instead of s., 8.10
gold, and my yield than choice s. 8.19
of the righteous is choice s.; 10.20
is to be chosen rather than s. 16.16

SILVER (cont.)

The crucible is for s., and the furnace Pro 17.03
favor is better than s. or gold. 22.01
Take away the dross from the s., 25.04
apples of gold in a setting of s. 25.11
The crucible is for s., and the furnace 27.21
for myself s. and gold and the Ecc 2.08
before the s. cord is snapped, or 12.06
ornaments of gold, studded with s. Sol 1.11
He made its posts of s., 3.10
build upon her a battlement of s.; 8.09
its fruit a thousand pieces of s. 8.11
Your s. has become dross, your wine Is 1.22
Their land is filled with s. and gold, 2.07
their idols of s. and their idols 2.20
worth a thousand shekels of s., 7.23
no regard for s. and do not 13.17
his idols of s. and his idols of 31.07
the s., the gold, the spices, the 39.02
gold, and casts for it s. chains. 40.19
and weigh out s. in the scales, hire 46.06
have refined you, but not like s.; 48.10
their s. and gold with them, for the 60.09
instead of iron I will bring s.; 60.17
Refuse s. they are called, for the Jer 6.30
Men deck it with s. and gold; 10.04
Beaten s. is brought from Tarshish, 10.09
to him, seventeen shekels of s. 32.09
and what was of s., as s. 52.19
They cast their s. into the streets, Eze 7.19
their s. and gold are not able to 7.19
Thus you were decked with gold and s.; 16.13
jewels of my gold and of my s., 16.17
all of them, s. and bronze and tin 22.18
As men gather s. and bronze and 22.20
As s. is melted in a furnace, so you 22.22
s., iron, tin, and lead they exchanged 27.12
gold and s. into your treasuries; 28.04
to carry away s. and gold, to take 38.13
gold, its breast and arms of s., Dan 2.32
the s., and the gold, all together 2.35
the clay, the s., and the gold. 2.45
of gold and of s. which Nebuchadnezzar 5.02
the golden and s. vessels which 5.03
praised the gods of gold and s., 5.04
praised the gods of s. and gold, 5.23
precious vessels of s. and of gold; 11.08
he shall honor with gold and s., 11.38
of the treasures of gold and of s., 11.43
upon her s. and gold which they Hos 2.08
shekels of s. and a homer and a 3.02
With their s. and gold they made 8.04
their precious things of s.; 9.06
idols skilfully made of their s., 13.02
For you have taken my s. and my gold, Joe 3.05
they sell the righteous for s., Amo 2.06
the poor for s. and the needy for 8.06
Plunder the s., plunder the gold! Nah 2.09
it is overlaid with gold and s., Hab 2.19
all who weigh out s. are cut off. Zep 1.11
Neither their s. nor their gold 1.18
The s. is mine, and the gold is mine, Hag 2.08
Take from them s. and gold, and make Zec 6.11
and heaped up s. like dust, and gold 9.03
as my wages thirty shekels of s. 11.12
shekels of s. and cast them into 11.13
and refine them as one refines s., 13.09
s., and garments in great abundance 14.14
as a refiner and purifier of s., Mal 3.03
and refine them like gold and s., 3.03
nor s., nor copper in your belts, Mt 10.09
they paid him thirty pieces of s. 26.15
pieces of s. to the chief priests 27.03
the pieces of s. in the temple, 27.05
priests, taking the pieces of s., 27.06
they took the thirty pieces of s., 27.09
having ten s. coins, if she loses Lk 15.08
"I have no s. and gold, but I give Ac 3.06
for a sum of s. from the sons of 7.16
"Your s. perish with you, because 8.20
or s., or stone, a representation by 17.29
to fifty thousand pieces of s. 19.19
who made s. shrines of Artemis, 19.24
no one's s. or gold or apparel. 20.33
s., precious stones, wood, hay, 1Co 3.12
of gold and s. but also of wood 2Ti 2.20
Your gold and s. have rusted, and Jas 5.03
perishable things such as s. or gold, 1Pe 1.18
of gold and s. and bronze and Rev 9.20
cargo of gold, s., jewels and pearls, 18.12

SILVER-COVERED

defile your s. graven images and Is 30.22

SILVERSMITH

of silver, and gave it to the s., Ju 17.04
a s., who made silver shrines of Ac 19.24

SIMEON

son also"; and she called his name S. Gen 29.33
S. and Levi, Dinah's brothers, took 34.25
Then Jacob said to S. and Levi, 34.30
S., Levi, Judah, Issachar, and Zebulun. 35.23
And he took S. from them and bound 42.24
and S. is no more, and now you would 42.36
Then he brought S. out to them. 43.23
The sons of S.: Jemuel, Jamin, Ohad, 46.10
be mine, as Reuben and S. are. 48.05
S. and Levi are brothers; weapons of 49.05
Reuben, S., Levi, and Judah, Ex 1.02
The sons of S.: Jemuel, Jamin, Ohad, 6.15
these are the families of S. 6.15
from S., Shelumiel the son of Num 1.06
Of the people of S., their generations, 1.22
of the tribe of S. was fifty-nine 1.23
to him shall be the tribe of S., 2.12
the people of S. being Shelumiel 2.12
the leader of the men of S.: 7.36
of the men of S. was Shelumiel the 10.19
from the tribe of S., Shephat the son 13.05
The sons of S. according to their 26.12
Of the tribe of the sons of S., 34.20
S., Levi, Judah, Issachar, Joseph, and Deu 27.12
The second lot came out for S., Jos 19.01
for the tribe of S., according to 19.01
of the tribe of S. according to 19.08
of the tribe of S. formed part of 19.09
the tribe of S. obtained an inheritance 19.09
S., and Benjamin, thirteen cities. 21.04
the tribe of S. they gave the 21.09
And Judah said to S. his brother, Ju 1.03
allotted to you." So S. went with him. 1.03
And Judah went with S. his brother, 1.17
S., Levi, Judah, Issachar, Zebulun, 1Ch 2.01
The sons of S.: Nemuel, Jamin, Jarib, 4.24
S., and Benjamin these cities which 6.65
and S. who were sojourning with 2Ch 15.09
and S., and as far as Naphtali, in 34.06
side to the west, S., one portion. Eze 48.24
Adjoining the territory of S., 48.25
the gate of S., the gate of Issachar, 48.33
in Jerusalem, whose name was S., Lk 2.25
and S. blessed them and said to 2.34
twelve thousand of the tribe of S., Rev 7.07

SIMEONITES

fathers' house belonging to the S. Num 25.14
These are the families of the S., 26.14
them, five hundred men of the S., 1Ch 4.42
Of the S., mighty men of valor for 12.25
for the S., Shephatiah the son of 27.16

SIMILAR

and many s. words were added to Jer 36.32
they were s. to the chambers on the Eze 42.11

SIMON
S. who is called Peter and Andrew Mt 4.18
S., who is called Peter, and Andrew 10.02
S. the Cananaean, and Judas Iscariot, 10.04
James and Joseph and S. and Judas? 13.55
S. Peter replied, "You are the 16.16
him, "Blessed are you, S. Bar-Jona! 16.17
saying, "What do you think, S.? 17.25
in the house of S. the leper, 26.06
upon a man of Cyrene, S. by name; 27.32
S. and Andrew the brother of S. Mk 1.16
entered the house of S. and Andrew, 1.29
And S. and those who were with him 1.36
S. whom he surnamed Peter; 3.16
Thaddaeus, and S. the Cananaean, 3.18
James and Joses and Judas and S., 6.03
in the house of S. the leper, 14.03
"S., are you asleep? Could you not 14.37
S. of Cyrene, who was coming in from 15.21
he said to S., "Put out into the Lk 5.04
And S. answered, "Master, we toiled 5.05
But when S. Peter saw it, he fell 5.08
Zebedee, who were partners with S. 5.10
And Jesus said to S., "Do not be 5.10
S., whom he named Peter, and Andrew 6.14
and S. who was called the Zealot, 6.15
"S., I have something to say to you 7.40
S. answered, "The one, I suppose, to 7.43
toward the woman he said to S., 7.44
"S., S., behold, Satan demanded to 22.31
away, they seized one S. of Cyrene, 23.26
indeed, and has appeared to S.!" 24.34
was Andrew, S. Peter's brother. Jn 1.40
He first found his brother S., 1.41
"So you are S. the son of John? 1.42
S. Peter's brother, said to him, 6.08
S. Peter answered him, "Lord, to whom 6.68
of Judas the son of S. Iscariot, 6.71
He came to S. Peter; and Peter said 13.06
S. Peter said to him, "Lord, not my 13.09
so S. Peter beckoned to him and 13.24
to Judas, the son of S. Iscariot. 13.26
S. Peter said to him, "LORD, where 13.36
Then S. Peter, having a sword, drew 18.10
S. Peter followed Jesus, and so did 18.15
Now S. Peter was standing and 18.25
and went to S. Peter and the other 20.02
Then S. Peter came, following him, 20.06
S. Peter, Thomas called the Twin, 21.02
S. Peter said to them, "I am going 21.03
When S. Peter heard that it was 21.07
So S. Peter went aboard and hauled 21.11
breakfast, Jesus said to S. Peter, 21.15
"S., son of John, do you love me 21.15
"S., son of John, do you love me?" 21.16
"S., son of John, do you love me?" 21.17
of Alphaeus and S. the Zealot and Ac 1.13
was a man named S. who had previously 8.09
Even S. himself believed, and after 8.13
Now when S. saw that the Spirit was 8.18
And S. answered, "Pray for me to the 8.24
many days with one S., a tanner. 9.43
and bring one S. who is called 10.05
he is lodging with S., a tanner 10.06
to ask whether S. who was called 10.18
and ask for S. who is called Peter 10.32
he is lodging in the house of S., 10.32
to Joppa and bring S. called Peter; 11.13
S. Peter, a servant and apostle of 2Pe 1.01

SIMON'S
Now S. mother-in-law lay sick with Mk 1.30
synagogue, and entered S. house. Lk 4.38
Now S. mother-in-law was ill with a 4.38
which was S., he asked him to put 5.03
Iscariot, S. son, to betray him, Jn 13.02
having made inquiry for S. house, Ac 10.17

SIMPLE
fool, and jealousy slays the s. Job 5.02
LORD is sure, making wise the s.; Ps 19.07
The LORD preserves the s.; 116.06
it imparts understanding to the s. 119.130
that prudence may be given to the s., Pro 1.04
O s. ones, will you love being s.? 1.22
For the s. are killed by their 1.32
and I have seen among the s., 7.07
O s. ones, learn prudence; 8.05
"Whoever is s., let him turn in 9.04
"Whoever is s., let him turn in 9.16
The s. believes everything, but the 14.15
The s. acquire folly, but the 14.18
and the s. will learn prudence; 19.25
is punished, the s. becomes wise; 21.11
but the s. go on, and suffer for it. 22.03
but the s. go on, and suffer for it. 27.12

SIMPLE-MINDED
they deceive the hearts of the s. Rom 16.18

SIMPLENESS
Leave s., and live, and walk in the Pro 9.06

SIMPLICITY
guests, and they went in their s., 2Sa 15.11

SIMPLY
Let what you say be s. 'yes' or 'no'; Mt 5.37

SIN
s. is couching at the door; Gen 4.07
great and their s. is very grave, 18.20
on me and my kingdom a great s.? 20.09
What is my s., that you have hotly 31.36
wickedness, and s. against God?" 39.09
tell you not to s. against the lad? 42.22
of your brothers and their s., 50.17
forgive my s., I pray you, only this Ex 10.17
came to the wilderness of S., 16.01
the wilderness of S. by stages, 17.01
your eyes, that you may not s." 20.20
lest they make you s. against me; 23.33
outside the camp; it is a s. offering. 29.14
a bull as a s. offering for 29.36
shall offer a s. offering for the 29.36
blood of the s. offering of 30.10
have brought a great s. upon them?" 32.21
people, "You have sinned a great s. 32.30
I can make atonement for your s." 32.30
this people have sinned a great s.; 32.31
if thou wilt forgive their s.— 32.32
I will visit their s. upon them." 32.34
iniquity and transgression and s., 34.07
and pardon our iniquity and our s., 34.09
offer for the s. which he has Lev 4.03
to the LORD for a s. offering. 4.03
the bull of the s. offering he 4.08
commits a s. unwittingly and the 4.13
when the s. which they have committed 4.14
bull for a s. offering and bring 4.14
with the bull of the s. offering, 4.20
it is the s. offering for the 4.21
if the s. which he has committed is 4.23
the LORD; it is a s. offering. 4.24
blood of the s. offering with his 4.25
make atonement for him for his s., 4.26
when the s. which he has committed 4.28
for his s. which he has committed. 4.28
on the head of the s. offering, 4.29
and kill the s. offering in the 4.29
as his offering for a s. offering, 4.32
upon the head of the s. offering, 4.33
kill it for a s. offering in the 4.33
blood of the s. offering with his 4.34
for him for the s. which he has 4.35
confess the s. he has committed, 5.05

SIN (cont.)

LORD for the s. which he has Lev 5.06
lamb or a goat, for a s. offering; 5.06
make atonement for him for his s. 5.06
LORD for the s. which he has 5.07
one for a s. offering and the other 5.07
first the one for the s. offering; 5.08
blood of the s. offering on the 5.09
the altar; it is a s. offering. 5.09
for him for the s. which he has 5.10
offering for the s. which he has 5.11
of fine flour for a s. offering; 5.11
on it, for it is a s. offering. 5.11
to the LORD; it is a s. offering. 5.12
for him for the s. where he has 5.13
which men do and s. therein, 6.03
like the s. offering and the guilt 6.17
This is the law of the s. offering. 6.25
shall the s. offering be killed 6.25
who offers it for s. shall eat it; 6.26
But no s. offering shall be eaten 6.30
offering is like the s. offering, 7.07
of the s. offering, of the guilt 7.37
and the bull of the s. offering, 8.02
the bull of the s. offering; 8.14
of the bull of the s. offering. 8.14
"Take a bull calf for a s. offering, 9.02
'Take a male goat for a s. offering, 9.03
and offer your s. offering and 9.07
killed the calf of the s. offering, 9.08
liver from the s. offering he 9.10
the goat of the s. offering which 9.15
killed it, and offered it for s., 9.15
like the first s. offering. 9.15
offering the s. offering and the 9.22
about the goat of the s. offering, 10.16
not eaten the s. offering in the 10.17
offered their s. offering and 10.19
I had eaten the s. offering today, 10.19
or a turtledove for a s. offering, 12.06
and the other for a s. offering; 12.08
they kill the s. offering and the 14.13
like the s. offering, belongs to the 14.13
priest shall offer the s. offering, 14.19
one shall be a s. offering and the 14.22
one for a s. offering and the other 14.31
one for a s. offering and the other 15.15
offer one for a s. offering and 15.30
bull for a s. offering and a ram 16.03
two male goats for a s. offering, 16.05
the bull as a s. offering for 16.06
and offer it as a s. offering; 16.09
the bull as a s. offering for 16.06
and offer it as a s. offering; 16.09
the bull as a s. offering for 16.11
the goat as the s. offering which 16.15
And the fat of the s. offering he 16.25
bull for the s. offering and the 16.27
and the goat for the s. offering, 16.27
lest you bear s. because of him. 19.17
LORD for his s. which he has 19.22
and the s. which he has committed 19.22
they shall bear their s., they shall die 20.20
lest they bear s. for it and die 22.09
one male goat for a s. offering, 23.19
curses his God shall bear his s. 24.15
confess his s. which he has Num 5.07
offer one for a s. offering and 6.11
without blemish as a s. offering, 6.14
and offer his s. offering and his 6.16
one male goat for a s. offering; 7.16
one male goat for a s. offering; 7.22
one male goat for a s. offering; 7.28
one male goat for a s. offering; 7.34
one male goat for a s. offering; 7.40
one male goat for a s. offering; 7.46
one male goat for a s. offering; 7.52
one male goat for a s. offering; 7.58
one male goat for a s. offering; 7.64
one male goat for a s. offering; 7.70
one male goat for a s. offering; 7.76
one male goat for a s. offering; 7.82
male goats for a s. offering; 7.87
young bull for a s. offering. 8.08
the one for a s. offering and the 8.12
purified themselves from s., 8.21
that man shall bear his s. 9.13
one male goat for a s. offering. 15.24
and their s. offering before the 15.25
goat a year old for a s. offering. 15.27
shall one man s., and wilt thou be 16.22
and every s. offering of theirs 18.09
meeting, lest they bear s. and die. 18.22
shall bear no s. by reason of it, 18.32
impurity, for the removal of s. 19.09
ashes of the burnt s. offering, 19.17
of Korah, but died for his own s.; 27.03
male goat for a s. offering to the 28.15
also one male goat for a s. offering, 28.22
with one male goat for a s. offering, 29.05
also one male goat for a s. offering, 29.11
besides the s. offering of atonement, 29.11
also one male goat for a s. offering, 29.16
also one male goat for a s. offering, 29.19
also one male goat for a s. offering, 29.22
also one male goat for a s. offering, 29.25
also one male goat for a s. offering; 29.28
also one male goat for a s. offering; 29.31
also one male goat for a s. offering; 29.34
also one male goat for a s. offering; 29.38
be sure your s. will find you out. 32.23
encamped in the wilderness of S. 33.11
set out from the wilderness of S., 33.12
of all the s. which you had in doing Deu 9.18
or their wickedness, or their s., 9.27
against you, and it be s. in you. 15.09
and so to s. against the LORD your 20.18
of you, and it would be s. in you. 23.21
vowing, it shall be no s. in you. 23.22
to the LORD, and it be s. in you. 24.15
be put to death for his own s. 24.16
enough of the s. at Peor from Jos 22.17
Thus the s. of the young men was 1Sa 2.17
that I should s. against the LORD 12.23
and do not s. against the LORD by 14.34
see how this s. has arisen today. 14.38
rebellion is as the s. of divination, 15.23
pardon my s., and return with me, 15.25
not the king s. against his 19.04
then will you s. against innocent 19.05
And what is my s. before your 20.01
"The LORD also has put away your s.; 2Sa 12.13
and forgive the s. of thy people 1Ki 8.34
thy name, and turn from their s., 8.35
and forgive the s. of thy servants, 8.36
"If they s. against thee—for there 8.46
there is no man who does not s.— 8.46
And this thing became a s., 12.30
thing became s. to the house of 13.34
and which he made Israel to s." 14.16
his s. which he made Israel to s. 15.26
and which he made Israel to s. 15.30
his s. which he made Israel to s. 15.34
have made my people Israel to s., 16.02
and which they made Israel to s., 16.13
and for his s. which he committed, 16.19
he committed, making Israel to s. 16.19
sins which he made Israel to s., 16.26
me to bring my s. to remembrance, 17.18
because you have made Israel to s. 21.22
of Nebat, who made Israel to s. 22.52
Nevertheless he clung to the s. of 2Ki 3.03
Nebat, which he made Israel to s.; 3.03
Nebat, which he made Israel to s., 10.29

SIN (cont.)

Jeroboam, which he made Israel to s. 2Ki 10.31
money from the s. offerings was 12.16
Nebat, which he made Israel to s.; 13.02
Jeroboam, which he made Israel to s., 13.06
Nebat, which he made Israel to s., 13.11
every man shall die for his own s." 14.06
Nebat, which he made Israel to s. 14.24
Nebat, which he made Israel to s. 15.09
Nebat, which he made Israel to s. 15.18
Nebat, which he made Israel to s. 15.24
Nebat, which he made Israel to s. 15.28
LORD and made them commit great s. 17.21
Judah also to s. with his idols; 21.11
the s. which he made Judah to s. 21.16
and the s. that he committed, are 21.17
of Nebat, who made Israel to s., 23.15
and forgive the s. of thy people 2Ch 6.25
thy name, and turn from their s., 6.26
and forgive the s. of thy servants, 6.27
"If they s. against thee—for there 6.36
there is no man who does not s.— 6.36
forgive their s. and heal their 7.14
every man shall die for his own s." 25.04
he-goats for a s. offering for the 29.21
he-goats for the s. offering were 29.23
them and made a s. offering with 29.24
offering and the s. offering should 29.24
and all his s. and his faithlessness, 33.19
and as a s. offering for all Israel Ez 6.17
and as a s. offering twelve he-goats; 8.35
let not their s. be blotted out Neh 4.05
afraid and act in this way and s., 6.13
and the s. offerings to make 10.33
king of Israel s. on account of 13.26
foreign women made even him to s. 13.26
Job did not s. or charge God with Job 1.22
this Job did not s. with his lips. 2.10
If I s., what do I do to thee, thou 7.20
my iniquity and search for my s., 10.06
If I s., thou dost mark me, and dost 10.14
me know my transgression and my s. 13.23
wouldest not keep watch over my s.; 14.16
let my mouth s. by asking for his 31.30
For he adds rebellion to his s.; 34.37
Be angry, but s. not; commune Ps 4.04
is forgiven, whose s. is covered. 32.01
When I declared not my s., 32.03
I acknowledged my s. to thee, 32.05
didst forgive the guilt of my s. 32.05
in my bones because of my s. 38.03
my iniquity, I am sorry for my s. 38.18
that I may not s. with my tongue; 39.01
chasten man with rebukes for s., 39.11
offering and s. offering thou hast 40.06
iniquity, and cleanse me from my s.! 51.02
and my s. is ever before me. 51.03
and in s. did my mother conceive me. 51.05
For no transgression or s. of mine, 59.03
For the s. of their mouths, the 59.12
thou didst pardon all their s. 85.02
let his prayer be counted as s.! 109.07
and let not the s. of his mother 109.14
that I might not s. against thee. 119.11
is caught in the toils of his s. Pro 5.22
life, the gain of the wicked to s. 10.16
but s. overthrows the wicked. 13.06
but s. is a reproach to any people. 14.34
is mouth does not s. in judgment. 16.10
I am pure from my s."? 20.09
the lamp of the wicked, are s. 21.04
The devising of folly is s., 24.09
Let not your mouth lead you into s., Ecc 5.06
they proclaim their s. like Sodom, Is 3.09
who draw s. as with cart ropes, 5.18
taken away, and your s. forgiven." 6.07
fruit of the removal of his s.: 27.09
that they may add s. to s.; 30.01

makes himself an offering for s., 53.10
yet he bore the s. of many, 53.12
What is the s. that we have committed Jer 16.10
their iniquity and their s., 16.18
"The s. of Judah is written with a 17.01
price of your s. throughout all 17.03
blot out their s. from thy sight. 18.23
every one shall die for his own s.; 31.30
I will remember their s. no more." 31.34
abomination, to cause Judah to s. 32.35
the guilt of their s. against me, 33.08
guilt of their s. and rebellion 33.08
their iniquity and their s. 36.03
and s. in Judah, and none shall be 50.20
him, he shall die for his s., Eze 3.20
man not to s., and he does not s., 3.21
guilty and the s. he has committed, 18.24
turns from his s. and does what is 33.14
offering and the s. offering and 40.39
the s. offering, and the guilt 42.13
Lord GOD, a bull for a s. offering. 43.19
take the bull of the s. offering, 43.21
without blemish for a s. offering; 43.22
daily a goat for a s. offering; 43.25
he shall offer his s. offering, 44.27
the s. offering, and the guilt 44.29
he shall provide the s. offerings, 45.17
blood of the s. offering and put 45.19
a young bull for a s. offering. 45.22
a he-goat daily for a s. offering. 45.23
same provision for s. offerings, 45.25
guilt offering and the s. offering, 46.20
my s. and the s. of my people Dan 9.20
transgression, to put an end to s., 9.24
They feed on the s. of my people; Hos 4.08
the s. of Israel, shall be destroyed 10.08
And now they s. more and more, and 13.02
bound up his s. is kept in store. 13.12
And what is the s. of the house of Mic 1.05
beginning of s. to the daughter of 1.13
transgression and to Israel his s. 3.08
of my body for the s. of my soul?" 6.07
them from s. and uncleanness. Zec 13.01
If your right eye causes you to s., Mt 5.29
your right hand causes you to s., 5.30
every s. and blasphemy will be 12.31
all causes of s. and all evildoers, 13.41
ones who believe in me to s., 18.06
to the world for temptations to s.! 18.07
hand or your foot causes you to s., 18.08
And if your eye causes you to s., 18.09
shall my brother s. against me, 18.21
but is guilty of an eternal s."— Mk 3.29
ones who believe in me to s., 9.42
hand causes you to s., cut it off; 9.43
foot causes you to s., cut it off; 9.45
eye causes you to s., pluck it out; 9.47
"Temptations to s. are sure to come; Lk 17.01
one of these little ones to s. 17.02
who takes away the s. of the world! Jn 1.29
S. no more, that nothing worse 5.14
"Let him who is without s. among * 8.07
condemn you; go, and do not s. again." *8.11
will seek me and die in your s.; 8.21
who commits s. is a slave to s. 8.34
Which of you convicts me of s.? 8.46
him, "You were born in utter s., 9.34
to them, they would not have s.; 15.22
they have no excuse for their s. 15.22
else did, they would not have s.; 15.24
the world of s. and of righteousness 16.08
of s., because they do not believe 16.09
me to you has the greater s." 19.11
do not hold this s. against them." Ac 7.60
Greeks, are under the power of s., Rom 3.09
the law comes knowledge of s. 3.20
the Lord will not reckon his s." 4.08
Therefore as s. came into the world 5.12

SIN (cont.)
one man and death through s., Rom 5.12
s. indeed was in the world before 5.13
but s. is not counted where there 5.13
the effect of that one man's s. 5.16
but where s. increased, grace 5.20
so that, as s. reigned in death, 5.21
to continue in s. that grace may 6.01
we who died to s. still live in it? 6.02
might no longer be enslaved to s. 6.06
For he who has died is freed from s. 6.07
The death he died he died to s., 6.10
yourselves dead to s. and alive to 6.11
Let not s. therefore reign in your 6.12
your members to s. as instruments 6.13
For s. will have no dominion over 6.14
Are we to s. because we are not 6.15
either of s., which leads to death, 6.16
once slaves of s. have become 6.17
and, having been set free from s., 6.18
When you were slaves of s., 6.20
set free from s. and have become 6.22
For the wages of s. is death, 6.23
That the law is s.? By no means 7.07
law, I should not have known s. 7.07
But s., finding opportunity in the 7.08
Apart from the law s. lies dead. 7.08
came, s. revived and I died; 7.09
For s., finding opportunity in the 7.11
It was s., working death in me 7.13
that s. might be shown to be s., 7.13
but I am carnal, sold under s. 7.14
but s. which dwells within me. 7.17
but s. which dwells within me. 7.20
to the law of s. which dwells in 7.23
my flesh I serve the law of s. 7.25
free from the law of s. and death. 8.02
likeness of sinful flesh and for s., 8.03
he condemned s. in the flesh, 8.03
your bodies are dead because of s., 8.10
does not proceed from faith is s. 14.23
Every other s. which a man commits 1Co 6.18
But if you marry, you do not s., 7.28
But if you marry, you do not s., 7.28
wishes: let them marry—it is no s. 7.36
it is weak, you s. against Christ. 8.12
to your right mind, and s. no more. 15.34
The sting of death is s., 15.56
and the power of s. is the law. 15.56
made him to be s. who knew no s., 2Co 5.21
Did I commit a s. in abasing myself 11.07
is Christ then an agent of s.? Gal 2.17
scripture consigned all things to s., 3.22
Be angry but do not s.; Eph 4.26
As for those who persist in s., 1Ti 5.20
hardened by the deceitfulness of s. Heb 3.13
age to put away s. by the sacrifice 9.26
to deal with s. but to save those 9.28
have any consciousness of s. 10.02
a reminder of s. year after year. 10.03
offerings and s. offerings thou 10.06
offerings and s. offerings" (these 10.08
is no longer any offering for s. 10.18
For if we s. deliberately after 10.26
enjoy the fleeting pleasures of s. 11.25
and s. which clings so closely, and 12.01
struggle against s. you have not 12.04
a sacrifice for s. are burned 13.11
it has conceived gives birth to s.; Jas 1.15
and s. when it is full-grown brings 1.15
you commit s., and are convicted by 2.09
fails to do it, for him it is s. 4.17
He committed no s.; no guile was 1Pe 2.22
we might die to s. and live to 2.24
in the flesh has ceased from s., 4.01
of adultery, insatiable for s. 2Pe 2.14
his Son cleanses us from all s. 1Jn 1.07
If we say we have no s., we deceive 1.08
this to you so that you may not s.; 2.01
but if any one does s., we have an 2.01
Every one who commits s. is guilty 3.04
of lawlessness; s. is lawlessness. 3.04
sins, and in him there is no s. 3.05
He who commits s. is of the devil; 3.08
No one born of God commits s.; 3.09
and he cannot s. because he is born 3.09
committing what is not a mortal s., 5.16
for those whose s. is not mortal. 5.16
There is s. which is mortal; 5.16
All wrongdoing is s., 5.17
but there is s. which is not mortal. 5.17
any one born of God does not s., 5.18

SINAI
Sin, which is between Elim and S., Ex 16.01
came into the wilderness of S. 19.01
and came into the wilderness of S., 19.02
down upon Mount S. in the sight of 19.11
And Mount S. was wrapped in smoke, 19.18
And the LORD came down upon Mount S., 19.20
people cannot come up to Mount S.; 19.23
of the LORD settled on Mount S., 24.16
of speaking with him upon Mount S., 31.18
come up in the morning to Mount S., 34.02
morning and went up on Mount S., 34.04
When Moses came down from Mount S., 34.29
had spoken with him in Mount S. 34.32
LORD commanded Moses on Mount S., Lev 7.38
the LORD, in the wilderness of S. 7.38
The LORD said to Moses on Mount S., 25.01
of Israel on Mount S. by Moses. 26.46
the people of Israel on Mount S. 27.34
to Moses in the wilderness of S., Num 1.01
them in wilderness of S. 1.19
LORD spoke with Moses on Mount S.; 3.01
the LORD in the wilderness of S.; 3.04
to Moses in the wilderness of S., 3.14
to Moses in the wilderness of S., 9.01
evening, in the wilderness of S.; 9.05
stages from the wilderness of S.; 10.12
of Israel in the wilderness of S.; 26.64
at Mount S. for a pleasing odor, an 28.06
encamped in the wilderness of S. 33.15
set out from the wilderness of S. 33.16
He said, "The LORD came from S., Deu 33.02
yon S. before the LORD, the God of Ju 5.05
Thou didst come down upon Mount S., Neh 9.13
yon S. quaked at the presence of Ps 68.08
Lord came from S. into the holy 68.17
him in the wilderness of Mount S., Ac 7.30
angel who spoke to him at Mount S., 7.38
One is from Mount S., bearing children Gal 4.24
Now Hagar is Mount S. in Arabia; 4.25

SINCE
s. you have come to your servant." Gen 18.05
s. the LORD has prospered my way; 24.56
And s. they bred when they came to 30.38
"S. God has shown you all this, 41.39
and I have never seen him s. 44.28
s. I have seen your face and know 46.30
heretofore or s. thou hast spoken Ex 4.10
For s. I came to Pharaoh to speak 5.23
land of Egypt s. it became a 9.24
s. he dealt faithlessly with 21.08
s. it is for Aaron and for his sons 29.27
s. it is a thing most holy and has Lev 10.17
your father, s. she is your sister. 18.11
s. he has a blemish, he shall not 21.21
S. there is a blemish in them, 22.25
s. it is for him a most holy 24.09
the years s. he sold it and pay 25.27
s. she was not taken in the act; Num 5.13
Now, s. the Amalekites and the 14.15
s. he has defiled the sanctuary of 19.20

SINCE (cont.)
s. they are too mighty for me; Num 22.06
S. you saw no form on the day that Deu 4.15
s. the day that God created man 4.32
this day (s. I am not speaking to 11.02
s. he has no portion or inheritance 12.12
s. he fares well with you, 15.16
s. the LORD has said to you, 'You 17.16
s. he was not at enmity with his 19.06
s. you have humiliated her. 21.14
a prophet s. in Israel like Moses, 34.10
been no day like it before or s., Jos 10.14
forty-five years s. the time that 14.10
s. you have set me in the land of 15.19
s. hitherto the LORD has blessed me?" 17.14
s. the hill country of Ephraim is 17.15
s. the lot fell to them first. 21.10
s. it is the LORD your God who 23.10
s. you have set me in the land of Ju 1.15
s. we have sworn by the LORD that 21.07
s. the women are destroyed out of 21.16
mother-in-law s. the death of your Ru 2.11
s. he must bless the sacrifice; 1Sa 9.13
s. the LORD has turned from you and 28.16
and s. he deserted me I have 29.03
in a house s. the day I brought up 2Sa 7.06
s. my lord the king has come safely 19.30
'S. the day that I brought my 1Ki 8.16
"S. this has been your mind and you 11.11
"S. I exalted you out of the dust 16.02
s. he promised to give a lamp to 2Ki 8.19
s. the day their fathers came out 21.15
had been kept s. the days of the 23.22
in a house s. the day I led up 1Ch 17.05
S. more chief men were found among 24.04
s. heaven, even highest heaven, 2Ch 2.06
'S. the day that I brought my 6.05
and s. he had promised to give a 21.07
for s. the time of Solomon the son 30.26
"S. they began to bring the contributions 31.10
kept in Israel s. the days of 35.18
to him ever s. the days of Esarhaddon Ez 4.02
s. we had told the king, "The hand 8.22
s. the time of the kings of Assyria Neh 9.32
s. they will say, 'King Ahasuerus Est 1.17
s. this was the regular period of 2.12
S. his days are determined, and the Job 14.05
S. thou hast closed their minds to 17.04
s. man was placed upon earth, 20.04
the morning s. your days began, and 38.12
and s. my mother bore me thou hast Ps 22.10
S. he is your lord, bow to him; 45.11
s. one fate comes to all, to the Ecc 9.02
have not come s. the day the Is 7.17
'S. you were laid low, no hewer 14.08
s. there is no rain on the land, the Jer 14.04
But s. we left off burning incense 44.18
had practiced s. her days in Egypt; Eze 23.08
s. there was no shepherd; 34.08
never has been s. there was a Dan 12.01
And s. you have forgotten the law Hos 4.06
S. the day that the foundation of Hag 2.18
s. the day that the foundation of Zec 8.09
has been my possession s. my youth.' 13.05
s. they had no depth of soil, Mt 13.05
and s. they had no root they 13.06
has been hidden s. the foundation 13.35
treasury, s. they are blood money." 27.06
s. it had no depth of soil; Mk 4.05
and s. it had no root it withered 4.06
s. it enters, not his heart but his 7.19
s. it was the day of Preparation, 15.42
this be, s. I have no husband?" Lk 1.34
s. my master is taking the stewardship 16.03
s. then the good news of the 16.16
s. he also is a son of Abraham. 19.09
s. you are under the same sentence 23.40
now the third day s. this happened. 24.21
s. he says, 'Where I am going, you Jn 8.22
s. he has opened your eyes?" 9.17
Never s. the world began has it 9.32
s. thou hast given him power over 17.02
S. it was the day of Preparation, in 19.31
s. it is only the third hour of the Ac 2.15
S. Lydda was near Joppa, the disciples, 9.38
S. you thrust it from you, and judge 13.46
S. we have heard that some persons 15.24
s. he himself gives to all men life 17.25
but s. it is a matter of questions 18.15
"S. through you we enjoy much peace, 24.02
and s. by your provision, most 24.02
twelve days s. I went up to 24.11
s. not a hair is to perish from the 27.34
s. it is because of the hope of 28.20
Ever s. the creation of the world Rom 1.20
And s. they did not see fit to 1.28
of the law s. through the law 3.20
s. all have sinned and fall short 3.23
s. God is one; and he will 3.30
Therefore, s. we are justified by 5.01
S., therefore, we are now justified 5.09
s. you are not under law but under 6.14
s. he gives thanks to God; 14.06
But now, s. I no longer have any 15.23
and s. I have longed for many years 15.23
For s., in wisdom of God, the 1Co 1.21
s. then you would need to go out of 5.10
s. he is the image and glory of God 11.07
s. you are eager for manifestations 14.12
S. we have such a hope, we are very 2Co 3.12
S. we have the same spirit of faith 4.13
S. we have these promises, beloved, 7.01
Achaia has been ready s. last year; 9.02
s. many boast of worldly things, I 11.18
s. you desire proof that Christ is 13.03
But s. we are bereft of you, 1Th 2.17
For s. we belive that Jesus died 4.14
But, s. we belong to the day, let us 5.08
s. indeed God deems it just to 2Th 1.06
all the better s. those who 1Ti 6.02
s. his aim is to satisfy the one 2Ti 2.04
s. they are upsetting whole families Tit 1.11
S. therefore the children share in Heb 2.14
S. therefore it remains for some to 4.06
S. then we have a great high priest 4.14
s. he himself is beset with weakness 5.02
s. you have become dull of hearing. 5.11
s. they crucify the Son of God on 6.06
s. he had no one greater by whom to 6.13
s. he always lives to make interecession 7.25
s. there are priests who offer 8.04
s. it is enacted on better promises 8.06
s. a death has occurred which 9.15
s. it is not in force as long as 9.17
repeatedly s. the foundation of 9.26
For s. the law but a shadow of 10.01
s. we have confidence to enter the 10.19
and s. we have a great priest over 10.21
s. you knew that you yourselves had 10.34
s. she considered him faithful who 11.11
s. God had foreseen something 11.40
Therefore, s. we are surrounded by 12.01
s. you also are in the body. 13.03
s. it is written, "You shall be holy, 1Pe 1.16
s. you are joint heirs of the grace 3.07
S. therefore Christ suffered in the 4.01
s. love covers a multitude of sins. 4.08
s. I know that the putting off of 2Pe 1.14
For ever s. the fathers fell asleep, 3.04
S. all these things are thus to be 3.11
s. you wait for these, be zealous to 3.14
had never been s. men were on the Rev 16.18
S. in her heart she says, 'A queen I 18.07
s. no one buys their cargo any more, 18.11

SINCERE
sent spies, who pretended to be s., Lk 20.20
astray from a s. and pure devotion 2Co 11.03
and a good conscience and s. faith. 1Ti 1.05
I am reminded of your s. faith, 2Ti 1.05
the truth for a s. love of the 1Pe 1.22
aroused your s. mind by way of 2Pe 3.01

SINCERELY
what my lips know they speak s. Job 33.03
not s. but thinking to afflict me Php 1.17

SINCERITY
serve him in s. and in faithfulness; Jos 24.14
unleavened bread of s. and truth. 1Co 5.08
you, with holiness and godly s., 2Co 1.12
but as men of s., as commissioned 2.17

SINEW
do not eat the s. of the hip which Gen 32.32
Jacob's thigh on the s. of the hip. 32.32
neck is an iron s. and your Is 48.04

SINEWS
knit me together with bones and s. Job 10.11
the s. of his thighs are knit 40.17
And I will lay s. upon you, and will Eze 37.06
there were s. on them, and flesh had 37.08

SINFUL
a brood of s. men, to increase still Num 32.14
Then I took the s. thing, Deu 9.21
Some were sick through their s. ways, Ps 107.17
Ah, s. nation, a people laden with Is 1.04
the penalty for your s. idolatry; Eze 23.49
Lord God are upon the s. kingdom, Amo 9.08
this adulterous and s. generation, Mk 8.38
from me, for I am a s. man, O Lord." Lk 5.08
delivered into the hands of s. men, 24.07
him so that the s. body might be Rom 6.06
our s. passions, aroused by the law, 7.05
might become s. beyond measure. 7.13
the likeness of s. flesh and for 8.03
such a person is perverted and s.; Tit 3.11

SINFULLY
your hands have s. made for you. Is 31.07

SING
"I will s. to the Lord, for he has Ex 15.01
"S. to the Lord, for he has triumphed 15.21
"Spring up, O well!—s. to it!— Num 21.17
to the Lord I will s., Ju 5.03
Did they not s. to one another of 1Sa 21.11
of whom they s. to one another in 29.05
and s. praises to thy name. 2Sa 22.50
S. to him, s. praises to him, tell 1Ch 16.09
S. to the Lord, all the earth! 16.23
of the wood s. for joy before the 16.33
who were to s. to the Lord and 2Ch 20.21
And when they began to s. and praise, 20.22
the Levites to s. praises to the 29.30
They s. to the tambourine and the Job 21.12
the widow's heart to s. for joy. 29.13
rejoice, let them ever s. for joy; Ps 5.11
and I will s. praise to the name of 7.17
I will s. praise to thy name, O Most 9.02
S. praises, to the Lord, who dwells 9.11
I will s. to the Lord, because he 13.06
and s. praises to thy name. 18.49
We will s. and praise thy power. 21.13
I will s. and make melody to the 27.06
S. praises to the Lord, O you his 30.04
S. to him a new song, play skilfully 33.03
S. praises to God, s. praises! 47.06
S. praises to our King, s. praises! 47.06
the earth; s. praises with a psalm! 47.07
my tongue will s. aloud of thy 51.14
I will s. and make melody! 57.07
I will s. praises to thee among the 57.09
I will s. praises to thee; 59.09
But I will s. of thy might; 59.16
I will s. aloud of thy steadfast 59.16
I will s. praises to thee, for thou, 59.17
So will I ever s. praises to thy 61.08
shadow of thy wings I s. for joy. 63.07
they shout and s. together for joy 65.13
s. the glory of his name; 66.02
they s. praises to thee, s. praises 66.04
the nations be glad and s. for joy, 67.04
S. to God, s. praises to his name; 68.04
S. to God, O kingdoms of the earth; 68.32
s. praises to the Lord, 68.32
I will s. praises to thee with the 71.22
when I s. praises to thee; 71.23
I will s. praises to the God of 75.09
S. aloud to God our strength; 81.01
heart and flesh s. for joy to the 84.02
I will s. of thy steadfast love, O 89.01
to s. praises to thy name, O Most 92.01
works of thy hands I s. for joy. 92.04
O come, let us s. to the Lord; 95.01
O s. to the Lord a new song; 96.01
s. to the Lord, all the earth! 96.01
S. to the Lord, bless his name; 96.02
the trees of the wood s. for joy 96.12
O s. to the Lord a new song, for he 98.01
into joyous song and s. praises! 98.04
S. praises to the Lord with the 98.05
let the hills s. for joy together 98.08
I will s. of loyalty and of justice 101.01
to thee, O Lord, I will s. 101.01
habitation; they s. among the branches. 104.12
I will s. to the Lord as long as I 104.33
I will s. praise to my God while I 104.33
S. to him, s. praises to him, tell 105.02
I will s., I will s. praises! 108.01
I will s. praises to thee among the 108.03
My tongue will s. of thy word, for 119.172
s. to his name, for he is gracious! 135.03
"S. us one of the songs of Zion! 137.03
How shall we s. the Lord's song in a 137.04
before the gods I s. thy praise; 138.01
And they shall s. of the ways of 138.05
I will s. a new song to thee, O God; 144.09
and shall s. aloud of thy righteousness. 145.07
I will s. praises to my God while I 146.02
it is good to s. praises to our 147.01
S. to the Lord with thanksgiving; 147.07
S. to the Lord a new song, his 149.01
let them s. for joy on their 149.05
Let me s. for my beloved a love Is 5.01
"S. praises to the Lord, for he has 12.05
Shout, and s. for joy, O inhabitant 12.06
s. many songs, that you may be 23.16
up their voices, they s. for joy; 24.14
in the dust, awake and s. for joy; 24.14
in the dust, awake and s. for joy! 26.19
day: "A pleasant vineyard, s. of it! 27.02
the tongue of the dumb s. for joy. 35.06
and we will s. to stringed instruments 38.20
S. to the Lord a new song, his 42.10
the inhabitants of Sela s. for joy, 42.11
S., O heavens, for the Lord has done 44.23
S. for joy, O heavens, and exult, O 49.13
voice, together they s. for joy; 52.08
"S., O barren one, who did not bear; 54.01
servants shall s. for gladness of 65.14
S. to the Lord; praise the Lord! Jer 20.13
"S. aloud with gladness for Jacob, 31.07
They shall come and s. aloud on the 31.12
bride, the voices of those who s., 33.11
shall s. for joy over Babylon; 51.48
who s. idle songs to the sound of Amo 6.05
S. aloud, O daughter of Zion; Zep 3.14
S. and rejoice, O daughter of Zion; Zec 2.10

SING (cont.)
the Gentiles, and s. to thy name"; Rom 15.09
I will s. with the spirit and I 1Co 14.15
and I will s. with the mind also. 14.15
and as you s. psalms and hymns and Col 3.16
Is any cheerful? Let him s. praise. Jas 5.13
and night they never cease to s., Rev 4.08
and they s. a new song before the 14.03
And they s. the song of Moses, the 15.03

SINGED
the hair of their heads was not s., Dan 3.27

SINGER
Heman the s. the son of Joel, son of 1Ch 6.33

SINGERS
Therefore the ballad s. say, Num 21.17
lyres also the harps for the s.; 1Ki 10.12
Now these are the s., the heads of 1Ch 9.33
brethren as the s. who should play 15.16
The s., Heman, Asaph, and Ethan, were 15.19
and the s., and Chenaniah the 15.27
the leader of the music of the s.; 15.27
and all the Levitical s., 2Ch 5.12
trumpeters and s. to make themselves 5.13
lyres also and harps for the s.; 9.11
and the s. with their musical 23.13
and the s. sang, and the trumpeters 29.28
The s., the sons of Asaph, were in 35.15
The s.: the sons of Asaph, one Ez 2.41
had two hundred male and female s. 2.65
and the s., the gatekeepers, and 2.70
the s. and gatekeepers, and the 7.07
the s., the doorkeepers, the temple 7.24
Of the s.: Eliashib. Of the gatekeepers 10.24
the s., and the Levites had been Neh 7.01
The s.: the sons of Asaph, a hundred 7.44
had two hundred and forty-five s., 7.67
the s., some of the people, the 7.73
the s., the temple servants, and all 10.28
and the gatekeepers and the s. 10.39
the s., over the work of the house 11.22
and a settled provision for the s., 11.23
And the sons of the s. gathered 12.28
for the s. had built for themselves 12.29
And the s. sang with Jezrahiah as 12.42
as did the s. and the gatekeepers, 12.45
of old there was a chief of the s., 12.46
portions for the s. and the gatekeepers; 12.47
s., and gatekeepers, and the contributions 13.05
so that the Levites and the s., 13.10
the s. in front, the minstrels last, Ps 68.25
S. and dancers alike say, "All my 87.07
I got s., both men and women, and Ecc 2.08

SINGING
but the sound of s. that I hear." Ex 32.18
s. and dancing, to meet the King Saul, 1Sa 18.06
voice of s. men and s. women? 2Sa 19.35
who were trained in s. to the LORD, 1Ch 25.07
Moses, with rejoicing and with s., 2Ch 23.18
s. with all their might to the LORD. 30.21
s. men and s. women have 35.25
with thanksgiving and with s., Neh 12.27
s. aloud a song of thanksgiving, and Ps 26.07
in thy house, ever s. thy praise! 84.04
Come into his presence with s.! 100.02
with joy, his chosen ones with s. 105.43
the time of s. has come, and the Sol 2.12
they break forth into s. Is 14.07
No more do they drink wine with s.; 24.09
and rejoice with joy and s. 35.02
return, and come to Zion with s., 35.10
break forth into s., 44.23
break forth, O mountains, into s.! 49.13
return, and come with s. to Zion; 51.11
Break forth together into s., 52.09
break forth into s. and cry aloud, 54.01
you shall break forth into s., 55.12
will exult over you with loud s. Zep 3.17
were praying and s. hymns to God, Ac 16.25
s. and making melody to the Lord Eph 5.19
crowns before the throne, s., Rev 4.10

SINGLE
not a s. locust was left in all the Ex 11.90
If he comes in s., he shall go out s.; 21.03
if for a s. moment I should go up 33.05
a branch with a s. cluster of Num 13.23
"A s. witness shall not prevail Deu 19.15
And the LORD would s. him out from 29.21
not leave him a s. male of his 1Ki 16.11
you repulse a s. captain among the 2Ki 18.24
were of a s. mind to make David 1Ch 12.38
you repulse a s. captain among the Is 36.09
and put them into a s. vessel, Eze 4.09
upon a s. stone with seven facets, I Zec 3.09
the guilt of this land in a s. day. 3.09
and land to make a s. proselyte Mt 23.15
no answer, not even to a s. charge; 27.14
well for them to remain s. as I do. 1Co 7.08
let her remain s. or else be 7.11
twenty-three thousand fell in a s. day. 10.08
If all were a s. organ, where would 12.19
for all time a s. sacrifice for Heb 10.12
For by a s. offering he has perfected 10.14
sold his birthright for a s. meal. 12.16
shall her plagues come in a s. day, Rev 18.08
of the gates made of a s. pearl, 21.21

SINGLENESS
to help David with s. of purpose. 1Ch 12.33
in s. of heart, as to Christ; Eph 6.05
but in s. of heart, fearing the Lord Col 3.22

SINGS
and he s. before men, and says: 'I Job 33.27
He who s. songs to a heavy heart is Pro 25.20
a righteous man s. and rejoices. 29.06
like one who s. love songs with a Eze 33.32

SINITES
the Hivites, the Arkites, the S., Gen 10.17
the Hivites, the Arkites, the S., 1Ch 1.15

SINK
make my assailants s. under me. 2Sa 22.40
make my assailants s. under me. Ps 18.39
I s. in deep mire, where there is no 69.02
and say, 'Thus shall Babylon s., Jer 51.64
s. into the heart of the seas on Eze 27.27
and be tossed about and s. again, Amo 8.08
and beginning to s. he cried out, Mt 14.30
boats, so that they began to s. Lk 5.07
"Let these words s. into your ears; 9.44

SINKING
help rescue me from s. in the mire; Ps 69.14

SINKS
s. down, and falls by his might. Ps 10.10
for her house s. down to death, and Pro 2.18
Through sloth the roof s. in, Ecc 10.18
as dry grass s. down in the flame, Is 5.24
and s. again, like the Nile of Egypt; Amo 9.05

SINNED
And how have I s. against you, Gen 20.09
said to them, "I have s. this time; Ex 9.27
he s. yet again, and hardened his 9.34
"I have s. against the LORD your 10.16
people, "You have s. a great sin. 32.30
this people have s. a great sin; 32.31
"Whoever has s. against me, him will 32.33
when one has s. and become guilty, Lev 6.04
because he s. by reason of the dead Num 6.11

SINNED (cont.)
we have done foolishly and have s. Num 12.11
LORD has promised; for we have s." 14.40
men who have s. at the cost of 16.38
"We have s., for we have spoken 21.07
"I have s., for I did not know that 22.34
you have s. against the LORD; 32.23
'We have s. against the LORD; Deu 1.41
you had s. against the LORD your 9.16
Israel has s.; they have transgressed Jos 7.11
a truth I have s. against the LORD 7.20
"We have s. against thee, because we Ju 10.10
said to the LORD, "We have s.; 10.15
I therefore have not s. against you, 11.27
"We have s. against the LORD." 1Sa 7.06
'We have s., because we have 12.10
And Saul said to Samuel, "I have s.; 15.24
Then he said, "I have s.; 15.30
because he has not s. against you, 19.04
I have not s. against you, though 24.11
"I have s. against the LORD." 2Sa 12.13
For your servant knows that I have s.; 19.20
"I have s. greatly in what I have 24.10
I have s., and I have done wickedly; 24.17
because they have s. against thee, 1Ki 8.33
because they have s. against thee, 8.35
'We have s., and have acted perversely 8.47
people who have s. against thee, 8.50
which he s. and which he made 14.16
which he s. and which he made 15.30
sins of Elah his son which they s., 16.13
And he said, "Wherein have I s., 18.09
of Israel had s. against the LORD 2Ki 17.07
"I have s. greatly in that I have 1Ch 21.08
is I who have s. and done very 21.17
because they have s. against thee, 2Ch 6.24
because they have s. against thee, 6.26
'We have s., and have acted perversely 6.37
people who have s. against thee. 6.39
which we have s. against thee. Neh 1.06
I and my father's house have s. 1.06
but s. against thy ordinances, by 9.29
"It may be that my sons have s., Job 1.05
If your children have s. against him, 8.04
so does Sheol those who have s. 24.19
'I s., and perverted what was right, 33.27
am I better off than if I had s.?' 35.03
If you have s., what do you accomplish 35.06
me, for I have s. against thee!" Ps 41.04
have I s., and done that which is 51.04
Yet they s. still more against him, 78.17
In spite of all this they still s.; 78.32
Both we and our fathers have s.; 106.06
the LORD, against whom we have s., Is 42.24
Your first father s., and your 43.27
Behold, thou wast angry, and we s.; 64.05
judgment for saying, 'I have not s.' Jer 2.35
for we have s. against the LORD our 3.25
because we have s. against the 8.14
are many, we have s. against thee. 14.07
for we have s. against thee. 14.20
Because you s. against the LORD, and 40.03
and because you s. against the 44.23
for they have s. against the LORD, 50.07
for she has s. against the LORD. 50.14
Jerusalem s. grievously, therefore Lam 1.08
Our fathers s., and are no more; 5.07
woe to us, for we have s.! 5.16
filled with violence, and you s.; Ez 28.16
backslidings in which they have s., 37.23
any one who has s. through error 45.20
we have s. and done wrong and acted Dan 9.05
because we have s. against thee. 9.08
us, because we have s. against him. 9.11
we have s., we have done wickedly. 9.15
the more they s. against me; Hos 4.07
of Gibeah, you have s., O Israel; 10.09
LORD because I have s. against him, Mic 7.09
they have s. against the LORD; Zep 1.17
"I have s. in betraying innocent Mt 27.04
I have s. against heaven and before Lk 15.18
I have s. against heaven and before 15.21
who s., this man or his parents, Jn 9.02
"It was not that this man s., 9.03
All who have s. without the law Rom 2.12
all who have s. under the law will 2.12
since all have s. and fall short of 3.23
to all men because all men s.— 5.12
of those who s. before and have 2Co 12.21
those who s. before and all the 13.02
Was it not with those who s., Heb 3.17
not spare the angels when they s., 2Pe 2.04
If we say we have not s., 1Jn 1.10
the devil has s. from the beginning. 3.08

SINNER
much more the wicked and the s.! Pro 11.31
He who despises his neighbor is a s., 14.21
but to the s. he gives the work of Ecc 2.26
but the s. is taken by her. 7.26
though a s. does evil a hundred 8.12
As is the good man, so is the s.; 9.02
but one s. destroys much good. 9.18
and the s. a hundred years old Is 65.20
who was a s., when she learned that Lk 7.37
is touching him, for she is a s." 7.39
heaven over one s. who repents 15.07
of God over one s. who repents." 15.10
'God, be merciful to me a s.!' 18.13
be the guest of a man who is a s." 19.07
a man who is a s. do such signs?" Jn 9.16
we know that this man is a s." 9.24
"Whether he is a s., I do not know; 9.25
am I still being condemned as a s.? Rom 3.07
brings back a s. from the error of Jas 5.20
will the impious and s. appear?" 1Pe 4.18

SINNER'S
but the s. wealth is laid up for Pro 13.22

SINNERS
great s. against the LORD. Gen 13.13
said, 'Go, utterly destroy the s., 1Sa 15.18
nor stands in the way of s., Ps 1.01
nor s. in the congregation of the 1.05
therefore he instructs s. in the way. 25.08
Sweep me not away with s., 26.09
and s. will return to thee. 51.13
Let s. be consumed from the earth, 104.35
My son, if s. entice you, do not Pro 1.10
Misfortune pursues s., but prosperity 13.21
Let not your heart envy s., but continue 23.17
But rebels and s. shall be destroyed Is 1.28
and to destroy its s. from it. 13.09
The s. in Zion are afraid; 33.14
All the s. of my people shall die Amo 9.10
collectors and s. came and sat Mt 9.10
eat with tax collectors and s.?" 9.11
not to call the righteous, but s." 9.13
a friend of tax collectors and s.!' 11.19
is betrayed into the hands of s. 26.45
collectors and s. were sitting Mk 2.15
was eating with s. and tax collectors, 2.16
he eat with tax collectors and s.?" 2.16
not to call the righteous, but s." 2.17
is betrayed into the hands of s. 14.41
drink with tax collectors and s.?" Lk 5.30
righteous, but s. to repentance." 5.32
For even s. love those who love 6.32
that to you? For even s. do the same. 6.33
Even s. lend to s., to receive 6.34
a friend of tax collectors and s.!" 7.34
were worse s. than all the other 13.02
collectors and s. were all drawing 15.01
man receives s. and eats with them." 15.02
that God does not listen to s., Jn 9.31

SINNERS (cont.)

we were yet s. Christ died for us. Rom 5.08
disobedience many were made s., 5.19
Jews by birth and not Gentile s., Gal 2.15
we ourselves were found to be s., 2.17
disobedient, for the ungodly and s., 1Ti 1.09
came into the world to save s. 1.15
And I am the foremost of s.; 1.15
unstained, separated from s., Heb 7.26
endured from s. such hostility 12.03
you s., and purify your hearts, you Jas 4.08
which ungodly s. have spoken Jud 1.15

SINNING

I who kept you from s. against me; Gen 20.06
the people are s. against the LORD, 1Sa 14.33
has multiplied altars for s., Hos 8.11
have become to him altars for s. 8.11
Thus, s. against your brethren and 1Co 8.12
tempted as we are, yet without s. Heb 4.15

SINS

If any one s. unwittingly in any of Lev 4.02
if it is the anointed priest who s., 4.03
"When a ruler s., doing unwittingly 4.22
common people s. unwittingly in 4.27
"If any one s. in that he hears a 5.01
of faith and s. unwittingly in any 5.15
"If any one s., doing any of the 5.17
"If any one s. and commits a breach 6.02
their transgressions, all their s.; 16.16
their transgressions, all their s.; 16.21
from all your s. you shall be clean 16.30
the year because of all their s." 16.34
you again sevenfold for your s., 26.18
you, sevenfold as many as your s. 26.21
smite you sevenfold for your s. 26.24
you myself sevenfold for your s. 26.28
any of the s. that men commit by Num 5.06
"If one person s. unwittingly, he 15.27
when he s. unwittingly, to make 15.28
be swept away with all their s." 16.26
your trangressions or your s. Jos 24.19
If a man s. against a man, God will 1Sa 2.25
but if a man s. against the LORD, 2.25
have added to all our s. this evil, 12.19
"If a man s. against his neighbor 1Ki 8.31
up because of the s. of Jeroboam, 14.16
with their s. which they committed, 14.22
in all the s. which his father did 15.03
it was for the s. of Jeroboam which 15.30
provoking me to anger with their s., 16.02
for all the s. of Baasha and the 16.13
Baasha and the s. of Elah his son 16.13
because of his s. which he committed, 16.19
and in the s. which he made Israel 16.26
to walk in the s. of Jeroboam the 16.31
aside from the s. of Jeroboam the 2Ki 10.29
not turn from the s. of Jeroboam, 10.31
followed the s. of Jeroboam the 13.02
depart from the s. of the house of 13.06
from all the s. of Jeroboam the 13.11
from all the s. of Jeroboam the 14.24
depart from the s. of Jeroboam the 15.09
from all the s. of Jeroboam the 15.18
away from the s. of Jeroboam the 15.24
depart from the s. of Jeroboam the 15.28
in all the s. which Jeroboam did; 17.22
for the s. of Manasseh, according to 24.03
"If a man s. against his neighbor 2Ch 6.22
Have you not s. of your own against 28.10
to our present s. and guilt. 28.13
confessing the s. of the people of Neh 1.06
confessed their s. and the iniquities 9.02
hast set over us because of our s.; 9.37
many are my iniquities and my s.? Job 13.23
servant also from presumptuous s.; Ps 19.13
Remember not the s. of my youth, 25.07
my trouble, and forgive all my s. 25.18
Hide thy face from my s., and blot out 51.09
on account of s. When our transgressions 65.03
deliver us, and forgive our s., 79.09
our secret s. in the light of thy 90.08
deal with us according to our s., 103.10
earth who does good and never s. Ecc 7.20
though your s. are like scarlet, Is 1.18
cast all my s. behind thy back. 38.17
LORD's hand double for all her s. 40.02
you have burdened me with your s., 43.24
and I will not remember your s. 43.25
a cloud, and your s. like mist; 44.22
to the house of Jacob their s. 58.01
and your s. have hid his face from 59.02
and our s. testify against us; 59.12
in our s. we have been a long time, Is 64.05
and your s. have kept good from you. Jer 5.25
their iniquity and punish their s." 14.10
for all your s., throughout all 15.13
because your s. are flagrant. 30.14
because your s. are flagrant, I have 30.15
about the punishment of his s.? Lam 3.39
This was for the s. of her prophets 4.13
punish, he will uncover your s. 4.22
when a land s. against me by acting Eze 14.13
Samaria has not committed half your s.; 16.51
because of your s. in which you 16.52
mine: the soul that s. shall die. 18.04
sees all the s. which his father 18.14
The soul that s. shall die. 18.20
from all his s. which he has 18.21
in all your doings your s. appear— 21.24
transgressions and our s. are upon us, 33.10
by his righteousness when he s. 33.12
None of the s. that he has committed 33.16
break off your s. by practicing Dan 4.27
because for our s., and for the 9.16
iniquity, and punish their s.; Hos 8.13
iniquity, he will punish their s. 9.09
transgressions, and how great are your s.— Amo 5.12
and for the s. of the house of Mic 1.05
you desolate because of your s. 6.13
cast all our s. into the depths of 7.19
will save his people from their s." Mt 1.21
river Jordan, confessing their s. 3.06
heart, my son; your s. are forgiven." 9.02
'Your s. are forgiven,' or to say, 9.05
authority on earth to forgive s." 9.06
"If your brother s. against you, 18.15
for many for the forgiveness of s. 26.28
repentance for the forgiveness of s. Mk 1.04
river Jordan, confessing their s. 1.05
"My son, your s. are forgiven." 2.05
Who can forgive s. but God alone?" 2.07
'Your s. are forgiven,' or to say, 2.09
authority on earth to forgive s."— 2.10
all s. will be forgiven the sons of 3.28
in the forgiveness of their s., Lk 1.77
repentance for the forgiveness of s. 3.03
your s. are forgiven you." 5.20
Who can forgive s. but God only?" 5.21
'Your s. are forgiven you,' or to 5.23
authority on earth to forgive s."— 5.24
her s., which are many, are forgiven, 7.47
said to her, "Your s. are forgiven." 7.48
"Who is this, who even forgives s.?" 7.49
and forgive us our s., for we ourselves 11.04
if your brother s., rebuke him, 17.03
and if he s. against you seven 17.04
forgiveness of s. should be 24.47
you that you would die in your s., Jn 8.24
die in your s. unless you believe 8.24
If you forgive the s. of any, 20.23
if you retain the s. of any, 20.23
for the forgiveness of your s.; Ac 2.38

SINS (cont.)
that your s. may be blotted out, Ac 3.19
to Israel and forgiveness of s. 5.31
forgiveness of s. through his name." 10.43
forgiveness of s. is proclaimed to 13.38
be baptized, and wash away your s., 22.16
forgiveness of s. and a place 26.18
he had passed over former s.; Rom 3.25
forgiven, and whose s. are covered; 4.07
those whose s. were not like the 5.14
them when I take away their s." 11.27
the immoral man s. against his own 1Co 6.18
died for our s. in accordance with 15.03
and you are still in your s. 15.17
himself for our s. to deliver us Gal 1.04
through the trespasses and s. Eph 2.01
redemption, the forgiveness of s. Col 1.14
to fill up the measure of their s. 1Th 2.16
participate in another man's s.; 1Ti 5.22
The s. of some men are conspicuous, 5.24
but the s. of others appear later. 5.24
burdened with s. and swayed by 2Ti 3.06
he had made purification for s., Heb 1.03
expiation for the s. of the people. 2.17
offer gifts and sacrifices for s. 5.01
for his own s. as well as for 5.03
for his own s. and then for those 7.27
I will remember their s. no more." 8.12
there is no forgiveness of s. 9.22
once to bear the s. of many, 9.28
and goats should take away s. 10.04
which can never take away s. 10.11
all time a single sacrifice for s., 10.12
remember their s. and their 10.17
longer remains a sacrifice for s., 10.26
and if he has committed s., Jas 5.15
Therefore confess your s. to one another, 5.16
and will cover a multitude of s. 5.20
bore our s. in his body on the 1Pe 2.24
also died for s. once for all, 3.18
love covers a multitude of s. 4.08
he was cleansed from his old s. 2Pe 1.09
If we confess our s., he is faithful 1Jn 1.09
forgive our s. and cleanse us from 1.09
and he is the expiation for our s., 2.02
also for the s. of the whole world 2.02
because your s. are forgiven for 2.12
that he appeared to take away s., 3.05
No one who abides in him s.; 3.06
no one who s. has either seen him 3.06
Son to be the expiation for our s. 4.10
freed us from our s. by his blood Rev 1.05
lest you take part in her s., 18.04
for her s. are heaped high as 18.05

SIPHMOTH
in Aroer, in S., in Eshtemoa, 1Sa 30.28

SIPPAI
Sibbecai the Hushathite slew S., 1Ch 20.24

SIR
s., if the LORD is with us, why then Ju 6.13
'S., did you not sow good seed in Mt 13.27
'I go, s.,' but did not go. 21.30
and said, "S., we remember how that 27.63
s., this year also, till I dig about Lk 13.08
'S., what you commanded has been 14.22
"S., you have nothing to draw with, Jn 4.11
"S., give me this water, that I may 4.15
"S., I perceive that you are a 4.19
"S., come down before my child dies." 4.49
"S., I have no man to put me into 5.07
s., that I may believe in him?" 9.36
to him, "S., we wish to see Jesus." 12.21
"S., if you have carried him away, 20.15
I said to him, "S., you know." Rev 7.14

SIRAH
him back from the cistern of S.; 2Sa 3.26

SIRION
(the Sidonians call Hermon S., Deu 3.09
Arnon, as far as Mount S. (that is, 4.48
and S. like a young wild ox. Ps 29.06
of Lebanon leave the crags of S.? Jer 18.14

SIRS
saying, "S., I perceive that the Ac 27.10

SISERA
the commander of his army was S., Ju 4.02
And I will draw out S., the general 4.07
LORD will sell S. into the hand of 4.09
When S. was told that Barak the son 4.12
S. called out all his chariots, nine 4.13
LORD has given S. into your hand. 4.14
And the LORD routed S. and all his 4.15
and S. alighted from his chariot 4.15
all the army of S. fell by the 4.16
But S. fled away on foot to the 4.17
And Jael came out to meet S., 4.18
And behold, as Barak pursued S., 4.22
and there lay S. dead, with the tent 4.22
courses they fought against S. 5.20
she struck S. a blow, she crushed 5.26
the mother of S. gazed through the 5.28
spoil of dyed stuffs for S., 5.30
he sold them into the hand of S., 1Sa 12.09
the sons of S., the sons of Temah, Ez 2.53
the sons of S., the sons of Temah, Neh 7.55
as to S. and Jabin at the river Ps 83.09

SISMAI
Eleasah was the father of S., and S. of 1Ch 2.40

SISTER
The s. of Tubalcain was Naamah. Gen 4.22
Say you are my s., that it may go 12.13
'She is my s.,' so that I took her 12.19
of Sarah his wife, "She is my s." 20.02
himself say to me, 'She is my s.'? 20.05
Besides she is indeed my s., the daughter 20.12
heard the words of Rebekah his s., 24.30
Rebekah their s. and her nurse, 24.59
"Our s., be the mother of thousands 24.60
the s. of Laban the Aramean. 25.20
his wife, he said, "She is my s."; 26.07
then could you say, 'She is my s.'? 26.09
Abraham's son, the s. of Nebaioth. 28.09
no children, she envied her s.; 30.01
wrestlings I have wrestled with my s., 30.08
he had defiled their s. Dinah. 34.13
to give our s. to one who is 34.14
because their s. had been defiled; 34.27
"Should he treat our s. as a harlot?" 34.31
daughter, the s. of Nebaioth. 36.03
Heman; and Lotan's s. was Timna. 36.22
Ishvi, Beriah, with Serah their s. 46.17
And his s. stood at a distance, to Ex 2.04
Then his s. said to Pharaoh's 2.07
his father's s. and she bore him 6.20
of Amminadab and the s. of Nahshon; 6.23
the s. of Aaron, took a timbrel in 15.20
uncover the nakedness of your s., Lev 18.09
your father, since she is your s. 18.11
the nakedness of your father's s.; 18.12
the nakedness of your mother's s., 18.13
a woman as a rival wife to her s., 18.18
nakedness while her s. is yet alive. 18.18
"If a man takes his s., a daughter 20.17
your mother's s. or of your 20.19
sister or of your father's s., 20.19
or his virgin s. (who is near to 21.03
his mother, nor for brother or s., Num 6.07
their s., who was slain on the day 25.18

SISTER (cont.)

and Moses and Miriam their s. Num 26.59
" 'Cursed be he who lies with his s., Deu 27.22
not her younger s. fairer than she? Ju 15.02
David's son, had a beautiful s., 2Sa 13.01
ill because of his s. Tamar; 13.02
Tamar, my brother Absalom's s." 13.04
'Let my s. Tamar come and give me 13.05
"Pray let my s. Tamar come and make 13.06
to her, "Come, lie with me, my s." 13.11
Now hold your peace, my s.; 13.20
because he had forced his s. Tamar. 13.22
the day he forced his s. Tamar. 13.32
s. of Zeruiah, Joab's mother. 17.25
in marriage the s. of his own wife, 1Ki 11.19
the s. of Tahpenes the queen. 11.19
And the s. of Tahpenes bore him 11.20
s. Ahaziah, took Joash the son of 2Ki 11.02
Homam; and Lotan's s. was Timna. 1Ch 1.39
concubines; and Tamar was their s. 3.09
Hananiah, and Shelomith was their s.; 3.19
name of their s. was Hazzelelponi, 4.03
the s. of Naham, were the fathers of 4.19
The name of his s. was Maacah. 7.15
And his s. Hammolecheth bore Ishhod, 7.18
Ishvi, Beriah, and their s. Serah. 7.30
Shomer, Hotham, and their s. Shua. 7.32
because she was a s. of Ahaziah, 2Ch 22.11
the worm, 'My mother,' or 'My s.,' Job 17.14
"You are my s.," and call insight Pro 7.04
my s., my bride, you have ravished Sol 4.09
is your love, my s., my bride! 4.10
A garden locked is my s., my bride, 4.12
my s., my bride, I gather my myrrh 5.01
my s., my love, my dove, my perfect 5.02
We have a little s., and she has 8.08
What shall we do for our s., 8.08
and her false s. Judah saw it. Jer 3.07
yet her false s. Judah did not fear, 3.08
this her false s. Judah did not 3.10
'Ah my brother!' or 'Ah s.!' 22.18
and you are the s. of your sisters, Eze 16.45
And your elder s. is Samaria, who 16.46
and your younger s., who lived 16.46
your s. Sodom and her daughters 16.48
was the guilt of your s. Sodom: 16.49
Was not your s. Sodom a byword in 16.56
another in you defiles his s., 22.11
and Oholibah the name of her s. 23.04
"Her s. Oholibah saw this, yet she 23.11
was worse than that of her s. 23.11
her, as I had turned from her s. 23.18
You have gone the way of your s.; 23.31
is the cup of your s. Samaria; 23.33
or unmarried s. they may defile 44.25
and to your s., "She has obtained Hos 2.01
is my brother, and s., and mother." Mt 12.50
is my brother, and s., and mother." Mk 3.35
And she had a s. called Mary, who Lk 10.39
care that my s. has left me to 10.40
village of Mary and her s. Martha. Jn 11.01
Martha and her s. and Lazarus. 11.05
she went and called her s. Mary, 11.28
"Martha, the s. of the dead man, 11.39
his mother, and his mother's s., 19.25
son of Paul's s. heard of their Ac 23.16
I commend to you our s. Phoebe, Rom 16.01
Philologus, Julia, Nereus and his s., 16.15
the brother or s. is not bound. 1Co 7.15
and Apphia our s. and Archippus our Phm 1.02
If a brother or s. is ill-clad and Jas 2.15
children of your elect s. greet you. 2Jn 1.13

SISTER-IN-LAW

your s. has gone back to her people Ru 1.15
her gods; return after your s." 1.15

SISTER'S

and the bracelets on his s. arms, Gen 24.30
the tidings of Jacob his s. son, Gen 29.13
he has uncovered his s. nakedness, Lev 20.17
drink your s. cup which is deep Eze 23.32

SISTERS

and mother, my brothers and s., Jos 2.13
and their s. were Zeruiah and 1Ch 2.16
their three s. to eat and drink Job 1.04
brothers and s. and all who had 42.11
and you are the sister of your s., Eze 16.45
have made your s. appear righteous 16.51
made judgment favorable to your s.; 16.52
have made your s. appear righteous 16.52
As for your s., Sodom and her 16.55
and be ashamed when I take your s., 16.61
And are not all his s. with us? Mt 13.56
or brothers or s. or father or 19.29
and are not his s. here with us?" Mk 6.03
or brothers or s. or mother or 10.29
brothers and s. and mothers and 10.30
and children and brothers and s., Lk 14.26
So the s. sent to him, saying, "Lord, Jn 11.03
women like s., in all purity. 1Ti 5.02

SIT

now s. up and eat of my game, that Gen 27.19
Why do you s. alone, and all the Ex 18.14
go to the war while you s. here? Num 32.06
of them when you s. in your house, Deu 6.07
and when you s. down outside, you 23.13
She used to s. under the palm of Ju 4.05
you who s. on rich carpets and you 5.10
s. down here"; and he turned aside Ru 4.01
the city, and said, "S. down here"; 4.02
to make them s. with princes and 1Sa 2.08
for we will not s. down till he 16.11
not fail to s. at table with the 20.05
and he shall s. upon my throne"? 1Ki 1.13
me, and he shall s. upon my throne.' 1.17
them who shall s. on the throne of 1.20
and he shall s. upon my throne'? 1.24
who should s. on the throne of my 1.27
and he shall s. upon my throne in 1.30
shall come and s. upon my throne; 1.35
my offspring to s. on my throne 1.48
him a son to s. on his throne this 3.06
and s. on the throne of Israel, as 8.20
before me to s. upon the throne of 8.25
"Why do we s. here till we die? 2Ki 7.03
and if we s. here, we die also. 7.04
generation shall s. on the throne 10.30
"Your sons shall s. upon the throne 15.12
my son to s. upon the throne of 1Ch 28.05
and s. on the throne of Israel, as 2Ch 6.10
before me to s. upon the throne of 6.16
I do not s. with false men, nor do I Ps 26.04
and I will not s. with the wicked. 26.05
You s. and speak against your 50.20
talk of those who s. in the gate, 69.12
"S. at my right hand, till I make 110.01
to make them s. with princes, with 113.08
Even though princes s. plotting 119.23
for ever shall s. upon your throne." 132.12
Thou knowest when I s. down and 139.02
he has made me s. in darkness like 143.03
If you s. down, you will not be Pro 3.24
When you s. down to eat with a 23.01
and the rich s. in a low place. Ecc 10.06
she shall s. upon the ground. Is 3.26
I will s. on the mount of assembly 14.13
and on it will s. in faithfulness 16.05
prison those who s. in darkness. 42.07
Come down and s. in the dust, O 47.01
s. on the ground without a throne, O 47.01
S. in silence, and go into darkness, 47.05

SIT (cont.)

who s. securely, who say in your Is 47.08
I shall not s. as a widow or know 47.08
is this, no fire to s. before! 47.14
who s. in tombs, and spend the night 65.04
Why do we s. still? Gather together, Jer 8.14
the kings who s. on David's throne, 13.13
I did not s. in the company of 15.17
house of feasting to s. with them, 16.08
city kings who s. on the throne of 17.25
who s. on the throne of David, you, 22.02
house kings who s. on the throne 22.04
lack a man to s. on the throne of 33.17
"S. down and read it." So Baruch 36.15
have none to s. upon the throne of 36.30
and s. on the parched ground, O 48.18
daughter of Zion s. on the ground Lam 2.10
Let him s. alone in silence when he 3.28
with you and you s. upon scorpions; Eze 2.06
they will s. upon the ground and 26.16
I s. in the seat of the gods, in the 28.02
and they s. before you as my people, 31.31
Only the prince may s. in it to eat 44.03
But the court shall s. in judgment, Dan 7.26
there I will s. to judge all the Joe 3.12
but they shall s. every man under Mic 4.04
when I s. in darkness, the LORD will 7.08
and your friends who s. before you, Zec 3.08
and shall s. and rule upon his 6.13
shall again s. in the streets of 8.04
he will s. as a refiner and purifier Mal 3.03
and west and s. at table with Mt 8.11
the crowds to s. down on the grass; 14.19
the crowd to s. down on the ground, 15.35
of man shall s. on his glorious 19.28
me will also s. on twelve thrones, 19.28
that these two sons of mine may s., 20.21
but to s. at my right hand and at 20.23
S. at my right hand, till I put thy 22.44
the Pharisees s. on Moses' seat; 23.02
then he will s. on his glorious 25.31
"S. here, while I go yonder and pray." 26.36
them all to s. down by companies Mk 6.39
the crowd to s. down on the ground; 8.06
"Grant us to s., one at your right 10.37
but to s. at my right hand or at my 10.40
S. at my right hand, till I put thy 12.36
his disciples, "S. here, while I pray." 14.32
to those who s. in darkness and in Lk 1.79
"Make them s. down in companies, 9.14
did so, and made them all s. down. 9.15
himself and have them s. at table, 12.37
and s. at table in the kingdom of 13.29
do not s. down in a place of honor, 14.08
go and s. in the lowest place, so 14.10
of all who s. at table with you. 14.10
does not first s. down and count 14.28
will not s. down first and take 14.31
and s. down quickly and write fifty.' 16.06
'Come at once and s. down at table'? 17.07
to my Lord, S. at my right hand, 20.42
and s. on thrones judging the 22.30
Jesus said, "Make the people s. down." Jn 6.10
the man who used to s. and beg?" 9.08
to my Lord, S. at my right hand, Ac 2.34
Philip to come up and s. with him. 8.31
and made him s. at his right hand Eph 1.20
and made us s. with him in the 2.06
"S. at my right hand, till I make Heb 1.13
"Stand there," or, "S. at my feet," Jas 2.03
grant him to s. with me on my Rev 3.21
elders who s. on their thrones 11.16
'A queen I s., I am no widow, 18.07

SITE

"Give me the s. of the threshing 1Ch 21.22
of gold by weight for the s. 21.25
of God, to erect it on its s.; Ez 2.68
house of God be rebuilt on its s." 5.15
rebuild this house of God on its s. 6.07
over the whole s. of Mount Zion Is 4.05
aloft upon its s. from the Gate of Zec 14.10

SITES

and the s. on which he built high 2Ch 33.19

SITHRI

Uzziel: Mishael, Elzaphan, and S. Ex 6.22

SITNAH

that also; so he called its name S. Gen 26.21

SITS

of Pharaoh who s. upon his throne, Ex 11.05
on which he s. shall be unclean. Lev 15.04
And whoever s. on anything on which 15.06
upon which she s. shall be unclean. 15.20
upon which she s. shall wash his 15.22
bed or anything upon which she s., 15.23
on which she s. shall be unclean, 15.26
"And when he s. on the throne of Deu 17.18
of hosts who s. enthroned on the 2Sa 6.02
Solomon s. upon the royal throne. 1Ki 1.46
of the LORD who s. enthroned above 1Ch 13.06
the Jew who s. at the king's gate. Est 6.10
nor s. in the seat of scoffers; Ps 1.01
He who s. in the heavens laughs; 2.04
But the LORD s. enthroned for ever, 9.07
He s. in ambush in the villages; 10.08
The LORD s. enthroned over the 29.10
The LORD s. enthroned as king for 29.10
from where he s. enthroned he looks 33.14
the nations; God s. on his holy throne. 47.08
He s. enthroned upon the cherubim; 99.01
She s. at the door of her house, she Pro 9.14
A king who s. on the throne of 20.08
when he s. among the elders of the 31.23
justice to him who s. in judgment, Is 28.06
have called her "Rahab who s. still." 30.07
It is he who s. above the circle of 40.22
the king who s. on the throne of Jer 29.16
How lonely s. the city that was Lam 1.01
of God and by him who s. upon it. Mt 23.22
one who s. at table, or one who Lk 22.27
is it not the one who s. at table? 22.27
"To him who s. upon the throne and Rev 5.13
to our God who s. upon the throne, 7.10
and he who s. upon the throne will 7.15
against him who s. upon the horse 19.19
sword of him who s. upon the horse, 19.21

SITTING

and Lot was s. in the gate of Sodom. Gen 19.01
Now Ephron was s. among the Hittites; 23.10
them when you are s. in your house, Deu 11.19
and the mother s. upon the young 22.06
as he was s. alone in his cool roof Ju 3.20
in the presence of those s. here, Ru 4.04
the priest was s. on the seat 1Sa 1.09
Eli was s. upon his seat by the 4.13
Saul was s. at Gibeah, under the 22.06
his men were s. in the innermost 24.03
Now David was s. between the two 2Sa 18.24
the king is s. in the gate"; 19.08
God, and found him s. under an oak; 1Ki 13.14
of Judah were s. on their thrones, 22.10
I saw the LORD s. on his throne, 22.19
who was s. on the top of a hill, and 2Ki 1.09
of the prophets were s. before him, 4.38
Elisha was s. in his house, and the 6.32
and the elders were s. with him. 6.32
and not to the men s. on the wall, 18.27
"But I know you s. down and your 19.27
of Judah were s. on their thrones, 2Ch 18.09
and they were s. at the threshing 18.09

SITTING (cont.)

I saw the LORD s. on his throne, 2Ch 18.18
to me (the queen s. beside him), Neh 2.06
Mordecai was s. at the king's gate. Est 2.19
as Mordecai was s. at the king's 2.21
The king was s. on his royal throne 5.01
Mordecai the Jew s. at the king's 5.13
I saw the Lord s. upon a throne, Is 6.01
and not to the men s. on the wall, 36.12
'I know your s. down and your going 37.28
succeed in s. on the throne of Jer 22.30
Jews who were s. in the court of 32.12
and all the princes were s. there: 36.12
the king was s. in the winter 36.22
the king was s. in the Benjamin 38.07
Behold their s. and their rising; Lam 3.63
the elders of Judah s. before me, Eze 8.01
there was a woman s. in the ephah! Zec 5.07
called Matthew s. at the tax Mt 9.09
like children s. in the market 11.16
two blind men s. by the roadside, 20.30
Now Peter was s. outside in the 26.69
while he was s. on the judgment 27.19
s. opposite the sepulchre. 27.61
Now some of the scribes were s. there, Mk 2.06
son of Alphaeus s. at the tax 2.14
sinners were s. with Jesus and his 2.15
And a crowd was s. about him; 3.32
and saw the demoniac s. there, 5.15
of Timaeus, was s. by the roadside. 10.46
and he was s. with the guards, and 14.54
the Son of man s. at the right 14.62
saw a young man s. on the right 16.05
s. among the teachers, listening to Lk 2.46
and teachers of the law s. by, 5.17
s. at the tax office; and he said 5.27
and others s. at table with them. 5.29
like children s. in the market 7.32
that he was s. at table in the 7.37
s. at the feet of Jesus, clothed and 8.35
long ago, s. in sackcloth and ashes. 10.13
a blind man was s. by the roadside 18.35
is coming, s. on an ass's colt!" Jn 12.15
s. where the body of Jesus had lain, 20.12
all the house where they were s. Ac 2.02
Now at Lystra there was a man s., 14.08
Eutychus was s. in the window. 20.09
Are you s. to judge me according to 23.03
and those who were s. with them; 26.30
revelation is made to another s. by, 1Co 14.30
I saw a woman s. on a scarlet Rev 17.03

SITUATION

the s. of this city is pleasant, as 2Ki 2.19

SIVAN

month, which is the month of S., Est 8.09

SIX

Noah was s. hundred years old when Gen 7.06
In the s. hundredth year of Noah's 7.11
In the s. hundred and first year, in 8.13
because I have borne him s. sons"; 30.20
and s. years for your flock, and you 31.41
about s. hundred thousand men on Ex 12.37
and took s. hundred picked chariots 14.07
S. days you shall gather it; 16.26
S. days you shall labor, and do all 20.09
for in s. days the LORD made heaven 20.11
slave, he shall serve s. years, 21.02
"For s. years you shall sow your 23.10
"S. days you shall do your work, but 23.12
and the cloud covered it s. days; 24.16
and there shall be s. branches 25.32
so for the s. branches going out of 25.33
pair of the s. branches going out 25.35
and s. curtains by themselves, and 26.09
westward you shall make s. frames. 26.22
s. of their names on the one stone, 28.10
the remaining s. on the other 28.10
S. days shall work be done, but the 31.15
Israel that in s. days the LORD 31.17
"S. days you shall work, but on the 34.21
S. days shall work be done, but on 35.02
and s. curtains by themselves. 36.16
tabernacle westward he made s. frames. 36.27
And there were s. branches going 37.18
so for the s. branches going out of 37.19
pair of the s. branches going out 37.21
for s. hundred and three thousand, 38.26
S. days shall work be done; Lev 23.03
s. in a row, upon the table of pure 24.06
S. years you shall sow your field, 25.03
and s. years you shall prune your 25.03
thousand s. hundred and fifty. Num 1.25
seventy-four thousand s. hundred. 1.27
number was s. hundred and three 1.46
seventy-four thousand s. hundred. 2.04
thousand s. hundred and fifty. 2.15
fifty-seven thousand s. hundred. 2.31
companies were s. hundred and 2.32
were eight thousand s. hundred, 3.28
and upward was s. thousand two 3.34
two thousand s. hundred and thirty 4.40
s. covered wagons and twelve oxen, a 7.03
I am number s. hundred thousand on 11.21
was forty-five thousand s. hundred. 26.41
s. hundred and one thousand seven 26.51
s. hundred and seventy-five thousand 31.32
of sheep was s. hundred and 31.37
shall be the s. cities of refuge, 35.06
shall be your s. cities of refuge. 35.13
These s. cities shall be for refuge 35.15
S. days you shall labor, and do all Deu 5.13
you, he shall serve you s. years, 15.12
servant he has served you s. years. 15.18
For s. days you shall eat unleavened 16.08
Thus shall you do for s. days. Jos 6.03
into the camp. So they did for s. days. 6.14
s. cities with their villages. 15.59
s. cities with their villages. 15.62
who killed s. hundred of the Ju 3.31
Jephthah judged Israel s. years. 12.07
And s. hundred men of the tribe of 18.11
Now the s. hundred men of the 18.16
gate with the s. hundred men armed 18.17
But s. hundred men turned and fled 20.47
he measured out s. measures of Ru 3.15
saying, "These s. measures of barley 3.17
and s. thousand horsemen, and troops 1Sa 13.05
with him, about s. hundred men. 13.15
him were about s. hundred men, 14.02
height was s. cubits and a span. 17.04
head weighed s. hundred shekels of 17.07
his men, who were about s. hundred, 23.13
he and the s. hundred men who were 27.02
and the s. hundred men who were 30.09
was seven years and s. months. 2Sa 2.11
Judah seven years and s. months; 5.05
ark of the LORD had gone s. paces, 6.13
and all the s. hundred Gittites who 15.18
who had s. fingers on each hand, and 21.20
and s. toes on each foot, twenty-four 21.20
the middle one was s. cubits broad, 1Ki 6.06
in one year was s. hundred and 10.14
s. hundred shekels of gold went 10.16
The throne had s. steps, and at the 10.19
each end of a step on the s. steps. 10.20
from Egypt for s. hundred shekels 10.29
Israel remained there s. months, 11.16
s. years he reigned in Tirzah. 16.23
s. thousand shekels of gold, and ten 2Ki 5.05
and he remained with her s. years, 11.03
have struck five or s. times; 13.19
over Israel in Samaria s. months. 15.08

SIX (cont.)
s. were born to him in Hebron, where 1Ch 3.04
for seven years and s. months. 3.04
Bariah, Neariah, and Shaphat, s. 3.22
Shimei had sixteen sons and s. daughters; 4.27
twenty-two thousand s. hundred. 7.02
Azel had s. sons, and these are 8.38
their kinsmen, s. hundred and ninety. 9.06
Azel had s. sons and these are 9.44
and spear were s. thousand eight 12.24
Levites four thousand s. hundred. 12.26
thousand s. hundred men equipped 12.35
who had s. fingers on each hand, and 20.06
and s. toes on each foot, twenty-four 20.06
paid Ornan s. hundred shekels of 21.25
s. thousand shall be officers and 23.04
s., under the direction of their 25.03
On the east there were s. each day, 26.17
form Egypt for s. hundred shekels 2Ch 1.17
three thousand s. hundred to 2.02
fifty-three thousand s. hundred. 2.17
three thousand s. hundred as 2.18
overlaid it with s. hundred talents 3.08
in one year was s. hundred and 9.13
s. hundred shekels of beaten gold 9.15
The throne had s. steps and a 9.18
each end of a step on the s. steps. 9.19
and he remained with them s. years, 22.12
valor was two thousand s. hundred. 26.12
offerings were s. hundred bulls 29.33
two thousand s. hundred lambs and 35.08
of Bani, s. hundred and forty-two. Ex 2.10
s. hundred and twenty-three. 2.11
Adonikam, s. hundred and sixty-six. 2.13
and Geba, s. hundred and twenty-one 2.26
three thousand s. hundred and 2.35
of Nekoda, s. hundred and fifty-two. 2.60
asses were s. thousand seven hundred 2.67
into their hand s. hundred and 8.26
day was one ox and s. choice sheep; Neh 5.18
of Arah, s. hundred and fifty-two. 7.10
of Binnui, s. hundred and forty-eight. 7.15
of Bebai, s. hundred and twenty-eight. 7.16
Adonikam, s. hundred and sixty-seven. 7.18
of Adin, s. hundred and fifty-five. 7.20
and Geba, s. hundred and twenty-one. 7.30
Nekoda, s. hundred and forty-two. 7.62
and their asses s. thousand seven 7.69
s. months with oil of myrrh and Est 2.12
s. months with spices and ointments 2.12
He will deliver you from s. troubles; Job 5.19
s. thousand camels, a thousand yoke 42.12
There are s. things which the LORD Pro 6.16
each had s. wings: with two he Is 6.02
'At the end of s. years each of you Jer 34.14
to you and has served you s. years; 34.14
were four thousand and s. hundred. 52.30
And lo, s. men came from the direction Eze 9.02
the man's hand was s. long cubits, 40.05
side rooms were s. cubits on 40.12
on each side s. cubits was the 41.01
breadth of the entrance, s. cubits; 41.03
of the temple, s. cubits thick; 41.05
a full reed of s. long cubits. 41.08
be shut on the s. working days; 46.01
day shall be s. lambs without 46.04
and s. lambs and a ram, which shall 46.06
cubits and its breadth s. cubits. Dan 3.01
And after s. days Jesus took with Mt 17.01
And after s. days Jesus took with Mk 9.02
shut up three years and s. months, Lk 4.25
"There are s. days on which work 13.14
Now s. stone jars were standing Jn 2.06
S. days before the Passover, Jesus 12.01
These s. brethren also accompanied Ac 11.12
And he stayed a year and s. months, 18.11
three years and s. months it did Jas 5.17
creatures, each of them with s. wings, Rev 4.08
its number is s. hundred and sixty-six. 13.18
for one thousand s. hundred stadia. 14.20

SIXTEEN
these she bore to Jacob—s. persons). Gen 46.18
their bases of silver, s. bases; Ex 26.25
s. bases, under every frame two 36.30
The persons were s. thousand, Num 31.40
and s. thousand persons— 31.46
was s. thousand seven hundred and 31.52
s. cities with their villages. Jos 15.41
s. cities with their vllages. 19.22
Samaria, and he reigned s. years. 2Ki 13.10
who was s. years old, and made him 14.21
He was s. years old when he began 15.02
and he reigned s. years in Jerusalem 15.33
and he reigned s. years in Jerusalem 16.02
Shimei had s. sons and six daughters; 1Ch 4.27
them under s. heads of fathers' 24.04
twenty-two sons and s. daughters. 2Ch 13.21
who was s. years old, and made him 26.01
Uzziah was s. years old, and made him 26.01
Uzziah was s. years old when he 26.03
and he reigned s. years in Jerusalem. 27.01
and he reigned s. years in Jerusalem. 27.08
and he reigned s. years in Jerusalem. 28.01

SIXTEENTH
to Bilgah, the s. to Immer, 1Ch 24.14
to the s., to Hananiah, his sons and 25.23
and on the s. day of the first 2Ch 29.17

SIXTH
and there was morning, a s. day. Gen 1.31
again, and she bore Jacob a s. son." 30.19
On the s. day, when they prepare Ex 16.05
On the s. day they gathered twice 16.22
therefore on the s. day he gives 16.29
and the s. curtain you shall double 26.09
blessing upon you in the s. year, Lev 25.21
On the s. day Eliasaph the son of Num 7.42
"On the s. day eight bulls, two rams, 29.29
The s. lot came out for the tribe Jos 19.32
and the s., Ithream of Eglah, David's 2Sa 3.05
In the s. year of Hezekiah, which 2Ki 18.10
Ozem the s., David the seventh; 1Ch 2.15
the s. Ithream, by his wife Eglah; 3.03
Attai s., Eliel seventh, 12.11
to Malchijah, the s. of Mijamin, 24.09
the s. of Bukkiah, his sons and his 25.13
Jehohanan the s., Eliehoenai the 26.03
Ammiel the s., Issachar the seventh, 26.05
S., for the s. month, was Ira, the son 27.09
in the s. year of the reign of Ez 6.15
and Hanun the s. son of Zalaph Neh 3.30
by measure, the s. part of a hin; Eze 4.11
In the s. year, in the s. month, on the 8.01
one s. of an ephah from each homer 45.13
and one s. of an ephah from each 45.13
one s. of an ephah, and one third of 46.14
in the s. month, on the first day of Hag 1.01
day of the month, in the s. month. 1.15
again about the s. hour and the Mt 20.05
Now from the s. hour there was 27.45
And when the s. hour had come, there Mk 15.33
In the s. month the angel Gabriel Lk 1.26
and this is the s. month with her 1.36
It was now about the s. hour, and 23.44
the well. It was about the s. hour. Jn 4.06
Passover; it was about the s. hour. 19.14
housetop to pray, about the s. hour. Ac 10.09
When he opened the s. seal, I looked, Rev 6.12
Then the s. angel blew his trumpet, 9.13
saying to the s. angel who had the 9.14
The s. angel poured his bowl on the 16.12
the s. carnelian, the seventh 21.20

SIXTY
Isaac was s. years old when she Gen 25.26
years old up to s. years old shall Lev 27.03
the person is s. years old and 27.07
bulls, the rams s., the male goats s., Num 7.88
the male lambs a year old s. This 7.88
number, s. thousand five hundred. 26.27
s. cities, the whole region of Argob, Deu 3.04
which are in Bashan, s. cities, Jos 13.30
three hundred and s. of Abner's men. 2Sa 2.31
s. great cities with walls and 1Ki 4.13
flour and s. measures of meal, 4.22
built for the LORD was s. cubits long, 6.02
and s. men of the people of the 2Ki 25.19
married when he was s. years old; 1Ch 2.21
Kenath and its villages, s. towns. 2.23
thousand seven hundred and s., 5.18
one thousand seven hundred and s., 9.13
was s. cubits, and the breadth 2Ch 3.03
eighteen wives and s. concubines, 11.21
twenty-eight sons and s. daughters); 11.21
chariots and s. thousand horsemen. 12.03
of Zaccai, seven hundred and s. Ez 2.09
forty-two thousand three hundred and s., 2.64
height shall be s. cubits and its 6.03
cubits and its breadth s. cubits, 6.03
and with him a hundred and s. men. 8.10
and Shemaiah, and with them s. men. 8.13
of Zaccai, seven hundred and s. Neh 7.14
forty-two thousand three hundred and s., 7.66
About it are s. mighty men of the Sol 3.07
are s. queens and eighty concubines, 6.08
and s. men of the people of the Jer 52.25
height was s. cubits and its breadth Dan 3.01
hundredfold, some s., some thirty. Mt 13.08
in another s., and in another thirty." 13.23
widow who is under s. years of age, 1Ti 5.09
thousand two hundred and s. days, Rev 11.03
thousand two hundred and s. days. 12.06

SIXTY-EIGHT
and also Obededom and his s. brethren; 1Ch 16.38
four hundred and s. valiant men. Neh 11.06

SIXTY-FIVE
When Mahalalel had lived s. years, Gen 5.15
When Enoch had lives s. years, he 5.21
were three hundred and s. years. 5.23
thousand, three hundred and s. shekels, Num 3.50
(within s. years Ephraim will be Is 7.08

SIXTYFOLD
thirtyfold and s. and a hundredfold." Mk 4.08
thirtyfold and s. and a hundredfold." 4.20

SIXTY-FOUR
number, s. thousand three hundred. Num 26.25
number, were s. thousand four hundred. 26.43

SIXTY-NINE
were nine hundred and s. years; Gen 5.27
five thousand four hundred and s. Ez 1.11

SIXTY-ONE
s. thousand asses, Num 31.34
of which the LORD's tribute was s. 31.39
of the work s. thousand darics of Ez 2.69

SIXTY-SEVEN
sons of Adonikam, six hundred and s. Neh 7.18
sons of Bigvai, two thousand and s. 7.19
of silver, and s. priests' garments. 7.72

SIXTY-SIX
sons' wives, were s. persons in all; Gen 46.26
blood of her purifying for s. days. Lev 12.05
six hundred and s. talents of gold, 1Ki 10.14
six hundred and s. talents of gold, 2Ch 9.13
of Adonikam, six hundred and s. Ez 2.13
its number is six hundred and s. Rev 13.18

SIXTY-TWO
hold a hundred and s. years he became Gen 5.18
Jared were nine hundred and s. years; 5.20
of Dan was s. thousand seven hundred. Num 1.39
numbered being s. thousand seven 2.26
for the service; s. of Obededom. 1Ch 2608
kingdom, being about s. years old. Dan 5.31
Then for s. weeks it shall be built 9.25
And after the s. weeks, an anointed 9.26

SIZE
the Jordan, an altar of great s. Jos 22.10
and all measures of quantity or s. 1Ch 23.29
and three were of the same s.; Eze 40.10
on either side were the same s. 40.10
of the same s. as those of the 40.21
of the same s. as those of the 40.22
they had the same s. as the others. 40.24
was of the same s. as the others. 40.28
were of the same s. as the others; 40.29
was of the same s. as the others. 40.32
were of the same s. as the others; 40.33
it had the same s. as the others. 40.35
were of the same s. as the others; 40.36
broad; the four were of the same s. 46.22

SKIES
and in his majesty through the s. Deu 33.26
dispersed be under the farthest s., Neh 1.09
which the s. pour down, and drop Job 36.28
Can you, like him, spread out the s., 37.18
light when it is bright in the s., 37.21
Israel, and his power is in the s. Ps 68.34
water; the s. gave forth thunder; 77.17
Yet he commanded the s. above, 78.23
For who in the s. can be compared 89.06
stand firm while the s. endure. 89.37
when he made firm the s. above, Pro 8.28
and the s. roll up like a scroll. Is 34.04
and let the s. rain down righteousness; 45.08
has been lifted up even to the s. Jer 51.09

SKIFFS
They go by like s. of reed, like an Job 9.26

SKILFUL
Esau was a s. hunter, a man of the Gen 25.27
a man who is s. in playing the 1Sa 16.16
who is s. in playing, a man of valor, 16.18
all who were s., was two hundred 1Ch 25.07
invented by s. men, to be on the 2Ch 26.15
all who were s. with instruments of 34.12
them, and guided them with s. hand. Ps 78.72
Do you see a man s. in his work? Pro 22.29
counselor and the s. magician and Is 3.03
he seeks out a s. craftsman to set 40.20
send for the s. women to come; Jer 9.17
hands of brutal men, s. to destroy. Eze 21.31
handsome and s. in all wisdom, Dan 1.04

SKILFULLY
with cherubim s. worked shall you Ex 26.01
of fine twined linen, s. worked. 28.06
And the s. woven band upon it, to 28.08
above the s. woven band of the 28.27
lie upon the s. woven band of the 28.28
him with the s. woven band of the 29.05
stuff, with cherubim s. worked. 36.08
with cherubim s. worked he made it. 36.35
And the s. woven band upon it, to 39.05
above the s. woven band of the 39.20
lie upon the s. woven band of the 39.21
him with the s. woven band of the Lev 8.07

SKILFULLY (cont.)
play s. on the strings, with loud Ps 33.03
idols s. made of their silver, all Hos 13.02

SKILL
and s., for making any work in 1Ki 7.14
man who has s. for any kind of 1Ch 28.21
who showed good s. in the service 2Ch 30.22
man of understanding acquire s., Pro 1.05
knowledge and s. must leave all to Ecc 1.21
toil and all s. in work come from 4.04
intelligent, no favor to the men of s.; 9.11
together with the s. of his hands. Is 25.11
learning and s. in all letters and Dan 1.17

SKILLED
in s. work shall it be made, with Ex 26.31
breastpiece of judgment, in s. work; 28.15
wood, for work in every s. craft. 35.33
any sort of workman or s. designer. 35.35
fine twined linen, in s. design. 39.03
in s. work, like the work of the 39.08
without number, s. in working 1Ch 22.15
send me a man s. to work in gold, 2Ch 2.07
to be with the s. workers who are 2.07
"Now I have sent a s. man, endued 2.13
He was a scribe s. in the law of Ez 7.06
who are s. to rouse up Leviathan. Job 3.08
They are s. in doing evil, but how Jer 4.22
they are all the work of s. men. 10.09
men of Lud, s. in handling the bow. 46.09
are like a s. warrior who does not 50.09
s. men of Zemer were in you, they Eze 27.08
Gebal and her s. men were in you, 27.09
those who are s. in lamentation, Amo 5.16
like a s. master builder I laid a 1Co 3.10

SKIN
and took bread and a s. of water, Gen 21.14
When the water in the s. was gone, 21.15
went, and filled the s. with water, 21.19
and its s., and its dung, you shall Ex 29.14
know that the s. of his face shone 34.29
the s. of his face shone, and they 34.30
that the s. of Moses' face shone; 34.35
But the s. of the bull and all its Lev 4.11
for himself the s. of the burnt 7.08
and its s., and its flesh, and its 8.17
The flesh and the s. he burned with 9.11
or a garment or a s. or a sack, 11.32
man has on the s. of his body a 13.02
disease on the s. of his body, 13.02
diseased spot on the s. of his body; 13.03
be deeper than the s. of his body, 13.03
is white in the s. of his body, 13.04
and appears no deeper than the s., 13.04
disease has not spread in the s., 13.05
disease has not spread in the s., 13.06
But if the eruption spreads in the s., 13.07
the eruption has spread in the s., 13.08
is a white swelling in the s., 13.10
leprosy in the s. of his body, 13.11
the leprosy breaks out in the s., 13.12
covers all the s. of the diseased 13.12
there is in the s. of one's body a 13.18
deeper than the s. and its hair 13.20
and it is not deeper than the s., 13.21
and if it spreads in the s., 13.22
a burn on its s. and the raw flesh 13.24
and it appears deeper than the s., 13.25
and it is no deeper than the s., 13.26
if it is spreading in the s., 13.27
and does not spread in the s., 13.28
if it appears deeper than the s., 13.30
deeper than the s. and there is no 13.31
to be no deeper than the s., 13.32
spread in the s. and it appears to 13.34
to be no deeper than the s., 13.34
spreads in the s. after his 13.35
if the itch has spread in the s., 13.36
has spots on the s. of the body, 13.38
spots on the s. of the body are of 13.39
that has broken out in the s.; 13.39
of leprosy in the s. of the body, 13.43
or in a s. or in anything made of s., 13.48
or in s. or in anything made of s., 13.49
or in the s., whatever be the use 13.51
whatever be the use of the s., 13.51
woolen or linen, or anything of s., 13.52
warp or woof or in anything of s., 13.53
garment or the s. or the warp or 13.56
warp or woof, or in anything of s., 13.57
or anything of s. from which the 13.58
warp or woof, or in anything of s., 13.59
and every s. on which the semen 15.17
their s. and their flesh and their 16.27
her s., her flesh, and her blood, Num 19.05
every garment, every article of s., 31.20
So she opened a s. of milk and gave Ju 4.19
ephah of flour, and a s. of wine; 1Sa 1.24
and another carrying a s. of wine. 10.03
and a s. of wine and a kid, and sent 16.20
of summer fruits, and a s. of wine. 2Sa 16.01
answered the LORD, "S. for s.! All that Job 2.04
my s. hardens, then breaks out 7.05
Thou didst clothe me with s. and flesh, 10.11
I have sewed sackcloth upon my s., 16.15
By disease his s. is consumed, the 18.13
cleave to my s. and to my flesh, 19.20
have escaped by the s. of my teeth. 19.20
and after my s. has been thus 19.26
My s. turns black and falls from me, 30.30
Can you fill his s. with harpoons, 41.07
change his s. or the leopard his Jer 13.23
made my flesh and my s. waste away, Lam 3.04
their s. has shriveled upon their 4.08
Our s. is hot as an oven with the 5.10
upon you, and cover you with s., Eze 37.06
upon them, and s. had covered them; 37.08
who tear the s. from off my people, Mic 3.02
and flay their s. from off them, 3.03

SKINS
and for his wife garments of s., Gen 3.21
and the s. of the kids she put upon 27.16
tanned rams' s., goatskins, acacia Ex 25.05
of tanned rams' s. and goatskins. 26.14
tanned rams' s., and goatskins; 35.07
or tanned rams' s. or goatskins, 35.23
of tanned rams' s. and goatskins. 36.19
of tanned rams' s. and goatskins, 39.34
not even the seeds or the s. Num 6.04
and two s. of wine, and five sheep 1Sa 25.18
every ten days s. of wine in Neh 5.18
if it is, the s. burst, and the wine Mt 9.17
spilled, and the s. are destroyed; 9.17
does, the wine will burst the s., Mk 2.22
wine is lost, and so are the s.; 2.22
but new wine is for fresh s." 2.22
will burst the s. and it will be Lk 5.37
and the s. will be destroyed. 5.37
went about in s. of sheep and Heb 11.37

SKIP
He makes Lebanon to s. like a calf, Ps 29.06
O mountains, that you s. like rams? 114.06

SKIPPED
The mountains s. like rams, the hills Ps 114.04

SKIRT
spread your s. over your maidservant, Ru 3.09
laid hold upon the s. of his robe, 1Sa 15.27
cut off the s. of Saul's robe. 24.04
because he had cut off Saul's s. 24.05
see the s. of your robe in my hand; 24.11

SKIRT (cont.)
that I cut off the s. of your robe, 1Sa 24.11
and I spread my s. over you, and Eze 16.08
flesh in the s. of his garment, Hag 2.12
garment, and touches with his s. 2.12

SKIRTS
On its s. you shall make pomegranates Ex 28.33
around its s., with bells of gold 28.33
round about on the s. of the robe. 28.34
On the s. of the robe they made 39.24
upon the s. of the robe round 39.25
about upon the s. of the robe for 39.26
take hold of the s. of the earth, Job 38.13
Also on your s. is found the Jer 2.34
iniquity that you s. are lifted up, 13.22
lift up your s. over your face, 13.26
Her uncleanness was in her s.; Lam 1.09
bind them in the s. of your robe. Eze 5.03
lift up your s. over your face; Nah 3.05

SKULL
Abimelech's head, and crushed his s. Ju 9.53
of her than the s. and the feet 2Ki 9.35
(which means the place of a s.), Mt 27.33
(which means the place of a s.). Mk 15.22
the place which is called The S., Lk 23.33
the place called the place of a s., Jn 19.17

SKY
righteousness will look down from the s. Ps 85.11
the way of an eagle is the s., the way Pro 30.19
be fair weather; for the s. is red.' Mt 16.02
for the s. is red and threatening.' 16.03
interpret the appearance of the s., 16.03
the appearance of earth and s.; Lk 12.56
lights up the s. from one side to 17.24
sacred stone that fell from the s.? Ac 19.35
stars of the s. fell to the earth Rev 6.13
the s. vanished like a scroll that 6.14
They have power to shut the s., 11.06
presence earth and s. fled away, 20.11

SLACK
he will not be s. with him who Deu 7.10
God, you shall not be s. to pay it; 23.21
will you be s. to go in and take Jos 18.03
care not to be s. in this matter; Ez 4.22
A s. hand causes poverty, but the Pro 10.04
He who is s. in his work is a brother 18.09

SLACKED
So the law is s. and justice never Hab 1.04

SLACKEN
do not s. the pace for me unless I 2Ki 4.24

SLACKNESS
does the work of the LORD with s.; Jer 48.10

SLAIN
I have s. a man for wounding me, a Gen 4.23
the sons of Jacob came upon the s., 34.27
therefore he has s. them in the Num 14.16
touches one who is s. with a sword, 19.16
or the s., or the dead, or the grave 19.18
I would have s. you and let her 22.33
and drinks the blood of the s." 23.24
The name of the s. man of Israel, 25.14
who was s. with the Midianite women, 25.14
woman who was s. was Cozbi the 25.15
who was s. on the day of the plague 25.18
Midian with the rest of their s., 31.08
and whoever has touched any s., 31.19
to possess, any one is found s., Deu 21.01
which are around him that is s.; 21.02
nearest to the s. man shall take a 21.03
nearest to the s. man shall wash 21.06
Your ox shall be s. before your Deu 28.31
blood of the s. and the captives, 32.42
over all of them, s., to Israel; Jos 11.06
sword among the rest of their s. 13.22
and have s. his sons, seventy men on Ju 9.18
of an ass have I s. a thousand men." 15.16
our country, who has s. many of us." 16.24
whom he had s. during his life. 16.30
two thousand men of them were s. 20.45
Eli, Hophni and Phinehas, were s. 1Sa 4.11
"Saul has s. his thousands, And 18.07
'Saul has s. his thousands, And 21.11
'Saul has s. his thousands, And 29.05
Philistines, and fell s. on Mount Gilboa. 31.01
Philistines came to strip the s., 31.08
'I have s. the LORD's anointed.'" 2Sa 1.16
Israel, is s. upon thy high places! 1.19
"From the blood of the s., from the 1.22
"Jonathan lies s. upon thy high 1.25
of David had s. of Benjamin three 2.31
or who is s. by the sword, or who 3.29
wicked men have s. a righteous man 4.11
Uriah the Hittite was s. also. 11.17
and have s. him with the sword of 12.09
"Absalom has s. all the king's sons, 13.30
after him only to strip the s. 23.10
and had s. the Canaanites who dwelt 1Ki 9.16
of the army went up to bury the s., 11.15
which has torn him and s. him, 13.26
and how he had s. all the prophets 19.01
and s. thy prophets with the sword; 19.10
and s. thy prophets with the sword; 19.14
together, and s. one another. 2Ki 3.23
sons who were about to be s., 11.02
Athaliah, so that he was not s.; 11.02
approaches the ranks is to be s. 11.08
"Let her not be s. in the house of 11.15
king's house, and there she was s. 11.16
had been s. with the sword at the 11.20
servants who had s. the king his 14.05
For many fell s., because the war 1Ch 5.22
and fell s. on Mount Gilboa. 10.01
Philistines came to strip the s., 10.08
so there fell s. of Israel five 2Ch 13.17
to the camp had s. all the older 22.01
sons who were about to be s., 22.11
enters the house shall be s. 23.07
her is to be s. with the sword." 23.14
Athaliah had been s. with the sword. 23.21
servants who had s. the king his 25.03
but you have s. them in a rage 28.09
to be s., and to be annihilated. Est 7.04
number of those s. in Susa the 9.11
the Jews have s. five hundred men 9.12
and where the s. are, there is he." Job 39.30
thy sake we are s. all the day Ps 44.22
like the s. that lie in the grave, 88.05
yea, all her s. are a mighty host. Pro 7.26
I shall be s. in the streets! 22.13
the prisoners or fall among the s. Is 10.04
untimely birth, clothed with the s., 14.19
your land, you have s. your people. 14.20
Your s. are not s. with the sword 22.02
her, and will no more cover her s. 26.21
they been s. as their slayers were s.? 27.07
Their s. shall be cast out, and the 34.03
and those s. by the LORD shall be 66.16
night for the s. of the daughter Jer 9.01
behold, those s. by the sword! 14.18
their youths be s. by the sword in 18.21
"And those s. by the LORD on that 25.33
men whom he had s. was the large 41.09
of Nethaniah filled it with the s. 41.09
after he had s. Gedaliah the son 41.16
Nethaniah had s. Gedaliah the son 41.18
They shall fall down s. in the land 51.04
and all her s. shall fall in the 51.47

SLAIN (cont.)
Babylon must fall for the s. of Israel, Jer 51.49
have fallen the s. of all the 51.49
and he has s. all the pride of our Lam 2.04
and prophet be s. in the sanctuary 2.20
day of thy anger thou hast s. them, 2.21
cast down your s. before your Eze 6.04
And the s. shall fall in the midst 6.07
when their s. lie among their idols 6.13
and fill the courts with the s. 9.07
multiplied your s. in this city, 11.06
filled its streets with the s. 11.06
Your s. whom you have laid in the 11.07
the sword for those to be s.; 21.14
mainland shall be s. by the sword. 26.06
death of the s. in the heart of 28.08
and the s. shall fall in the midst 28.23
when the s. fall in Egypt, and her 30.04
and fill the land with the s. 30.11
to those who are s. by the sword; 31.17
with those who are s. by the sword. 31.18
amid those who are s. by the sword, 32.20
the uncircumcised, s. by the sword.' 32.21
all of them s., fallen by the sword; 32.22
all of them s., fallen by the sword, 32.23
all of them s., fallen by the sword, 32.24
a bed among the s. with all her 32.25
uncircumcised, s. by the sword; 32.25
they are placed among the s. 32.25
uncircumcised, s. by the sword; 32.26
with those who are s. by the sword. 32.28
with those who are s. by the sword; 32.29
gone down in shame with the s., 32.30
with those who are s. by the sword, 32.30
s. by the sword, says the LORD GOD. 32.31
with those who are s. by the sword, 32.32
fill your mountains with the s.; 35.08
ravines those s. with the sword 35.08
breath, and breathe upon these s., 37.09
that the wise men were to be s., Dan 2.13
Belshazzar the Chaldean king was s. 5.30
the beast was s., and its body 7.11
away, and many shall fall down s. 11.26
I have s. them by the words of my Hos 6.05
hosts of s., heaps of corpses, dead Nah 3.03
Ethiopians, shall be s. by my sword. Zep 2.12
doomed to be s. for those who Zec 11.07
but he was s. and all who followed Ac 5.36
you offer to me s. beasts and 7.42
standing, as though it had been s., Rev 5.06
for thou wast s. and by thy blood 5.09
"Worthy is the Lamb who was s., 5.12
who had been s. for the word of 6.09
of life of the Lamb that was s. 13.08
with the sword must he be s. 13.10
the image of the beast to be s. 13.15
of all who have been s. on earth." 18.24
And the rest were s. by the sword 19.21

SLANDER
who does not s. with his tongue, and Ps 15.03
brother; you s. your own mother's son. 50.20
and he who utters s. is a fool. Pro 10.18
Do not s. a servant to his master, 30.10
men in you who s. to shed blood, Eze 22.09
fornication, theft, false witness, s. Mt 15.19
envy, s., pride, foolishness. Mk 7.22
s., gossip, conceit, and disorder. 2Co 12.20
and clamor and s. be put away from Eph 4.31
s., and foul talk from your mouth. Col 3.08
dissension, s., base suspicions, 1Ti 6.04
insincerity and envy and all s. 1Pe 2.01
rich) and the s. of those who say Rev 2.09

SLANDERED
He has s. your servant to my lord 2Sa 19.27
whom I knew not s. me without Ps 35.15
when s., we try to conciliate; we 1Co 4.13

SLANDERER
and down as a s. among your people, Lev 19.16
Let not the s. be established in Ps 140.11
every neighbor goes about as a s. Jer 9.04

SLANDERERS
s., haters of God, insolent, haughty, Rom 1.30
no s., but temperate, faithful in 1Ti 3.11
s., profligates, fierce, haters of 2Ti 3.03
not to be s. or slaves to drink; Tit 2.03

SLANDEROUSLY
as some people s. charge us with Rom 3.08

SLANDERS
uttering s. against me, my adversaries Ps 27.02
Him who s. his neighbor secretly I 101.05
rebellious, going about with s.; Jer 6.28

SLAPPED
face, and struck him; and some s. him, Mt 26.67

SLASHES
He s. open my kidneys, and does not Job 16.13

SLAUGHTER
and s. an animal and make ready, for Gen 43.16
and you shall s. the ram, and shall Ex 29.16
you may s. and eat flesh within any Deu 12.15
them with a great s. at Gibeon, Jos 10.10
slaying them with a very great s., 10.20
Abelkeramim, with a very great s. Ju 11.33
them hip and thigh with great s.; 15.08
and there was a very great s., 1Sa 4.10
been a great s. among the people; 4.17
made a great s. among the people. 6.19
and that first s., which Jonathan 14.14
for now the s. among the Philistines 14.30
from the s. of the Philistine, 17.57
and made a great s. among them, 19.08
and made a great s. among them. 23.05
from the s. of the Amalekites, 2Sa 1.01
has been a s. among the people who 17.09
and the s. there was great on that 18.07
band, after the s. by David; 1Ki 11.24
killed the Syrians with a great s. 20.21
people slew them with a great s.; 2Ch 13.17
came from the s. of the Edomites, 25.14
who defeated him with great s. 28.05
Thou hast made us like sheep for s., Ps 44.11
and accounted as sheep for the s. 44.22
her, as an ox goes to the s., Pro 7.22
those who are stumbling to the s. 24.11
Their bows will s. the young men; Is 13.18
Prepare s. for his sons because of 14.21
water, in the day of the great s., 30.25
them, has given them over for s. 34.02
a great s. in the land of Edom. 34.06
like a lamb that is led to the s., 53.07
of you shall bow down to the s.; 65.12
of Hinnom, but the valley of S.: Jer 7.32
like a gentle lamb led to the s. 11.19
them out like sheep for the s., 12.03
set them apart for the day of s. 12.03
of Benhinnom but the Valley of S. 19.06
days of your s. and dispersion 25.34
his young men have gone to s., 48.15
bulls, let them go down to the s. 50.27
them down like lambs to the s., 51.40
with his weapon for s. in his hand, Eze 9.02
sharpened for s., polished to flash 21.10
it is the sword for the great s., 21.14
lightning, it is polished for s. 21.15
sword, a sword is drawn for the s., 21.28
when s. is made in the midst of you? 26.15
with the wool, you s. the fatlings; 34.03
must lead forth his sons to s. Hos 9.13
Mount Esau will be cut off by s. Ob 1.09

SLAUGHTER (cont.)
shepherd of the flock doomed to s. Zec 11.04
led to the s. or a lamb before its Ac 8.32
from the s. of the kings and Heb 7.01
fattened your hearts in a day of s. Jas 5.05

SLAUGHTERED
Shall flocks and herds be s. for them, Num 11.22
outside the camp and s. before him; 19.03
She has s. her beasts, she has mixed Pro 9.02
that you s. my children and delivered Eze 16.21
For when they had s. their children 23.39
the guilt offering were to be s. 40.39
which the sacrifices were to be s. 40.41
offerings and the sacrifices were s. 40.42
we are regarded as sheep to be s. Rom 8.36

SLAUGHTERING
had finished s. all the inhabitants Jos 8.24
s. the Moabites as they went. 2Ki 3.24
s., and destroying them, and did as Est 9.05
hast slain them, s. without mercy. Lam 2.21

SLAUGHTERS
"He who s. an ox is like him who Is 66.03

SLAVE
a s. of slaves shall he be to his Gen 9.25
be Shem; and let Canaan be his s. 9.26
of Shem; and let Canaan be his s." 9.27
and a s. born in his house will be 15.03
"Cast out this s. woman with her 21.10
the son of this s. woman shall not 21.10
lad and because of your s. woman; 21.12
of the son of the s. woman also, 21.13
whom it is found shall be my s., 44.10
the cup was found shall be my s.; 44.17
of the lad as a s. to my lord; 44.33
and became a s. at forced labor. 49.15
but every s. that is bought for Ex 12.44
When you buy a Hebrew s., he shall 21.02
But if the s. plainly says, 'I love 21.05
"When a man sells his daughter as a s., 21.07
"When a man strikes his s., male or 21.20
a rod and the s. dies under his 21.20
But if the s. survives a day or two, 21.21
punished; for the s. is his money. 21.21
"When a man strikes the eye of his s., 21.26
shall let the s. go free for the 21.26
If he knocks out the tooth of his s., 21.27
shall let the s. go free for the 21.27
If the ox gores a s., male or 21.32
carnally with a woman who is a s., Lev 19.20
a priest buys a s. as his property 22.11
for money, the s. may eat of it; 22.11
shall not make him serve as a s.: 25.39
that you were a s. in the land of Deu 15.15
remember that you were a s. in Egypt; 16.12
you shall not treat her as a s., 21.14
to his master a s. who has escaped 23.15
he treats him as a s. or sells him, 24.07
that you were a s. in Egypt and 24.18
that you were a s. in the land of 24.22
but Sheshan had an Egyptian s., 1Ch 2.34
in marriage to Jarha his s.; 2.35
and the s. is free from his master. Job 3.19
Like a s. who longs for the shadow, 7.02
them, Joseph, who was sold as a s. Ps 105.17
A s. who deals wisely will rule Pro 17.02
much less for a s. to rule over 19.10
borrower is the s. of the lender. 22.07
a s. when he becomes king, and a 30.22
as with the s., so with his master; Is 24.02
"Is Israel a s.? Is he a homeborn Jer 2.14
kings shall make him their s. 27.07
every one would set free his s., 34.10
and to my s., 'Do this,' and he does Mt 8.09
be first among you must be your s.; 20.27
and struck the s. of the high 26.51
first among you must be s. of all. Mk 10.44
and struck the s. of the high 14.47
centurion had a s. who was dear to Lk 7.02
asking him to come and heal his s. 7.03
and to my s., 'Do this,' and he does 7.08
the house, they found the s. well. 7.10
them struck the s. of the high 22.50
one who commits sin is a s. to sin. Jn 8.34
The s. does not continue in the 8.35
high priest's s. and cut off his 18.10
were met by a s. girl who had a Ac 16.16
Were you a s. when called? Never 1Co 7.21
the Lord as a s. is a freedman of 7.22
free when called is a s. of Christ. 7.22
I have made myself a s. to all, 9.19
there is neither s. nor free, Gal 3.28
is a child, is no better than a s., 4.01
you are no longer a s. but a son, 4.07
one by a s. and one by a free woman. 4.22
But the son of the s. was born 4.23
"Cast out the s. and her son; 4.30
the son of the s. shall not 4.30
children of the s. but of the free 4.31
Lord, whether he is a s. or free. Eph 6.08
s., free man, but Christ is all, and Col 3.11
no longer as a s. but more than a s., Phm 1.16
s. and free, hid in the caves and Rev 6.15
both free and s., to be marked on 13.16
both free and s., both small and 19.18

SLAVERY
the spirit of s. to fall back into Rom 8.15
Sinai, bearing children for s.; Gal 4.24
for she is in s. with her children. 4.25
not submit again to a yoke of s. 5.01
the yoke of s. regard their masters 1Ti 6.01

SLAVE'S
his right ear. The s. name was Malchus. Jn 18.10

SLAVES
a slave of s. shall he be to his Gen 9.25
and will be s. there, and they will 15.13
son and all the s. born in his 17.23
and oxen, and male and female s., 20.14
wife and female s. so that they 20.17
to make s. of us and seize our 43.18
and we also will be my lord's s." 44.09
behold, we are my lord's s., 44.16
our land will be s. to Pharaoh; 47.19
he made s. of them from one end of 47.21
my lord, we will be s. to Pharaoh." 47.25
made his s. and his cattle flee Ex 9.20
LORD left his s. and his cattle in 9.21
shall not go out as the male s. do. 21.07
male and female s. and for your Lev 25.06
they shall not be sold as s. 25.42
male and female s. whom you may 25.44
male and female s. from among the 25.44
you may make s. of them, but over 25.46
that you should not be their s.; 26.13
"We were Pharaoh's s. in Egypt; Deu 6.21
your enemies as male and female s., 28.68
and some of you shall always be s., Jos 9.23
but have become s. to do forced 16.10
lest you become s. to the Hebrews 1Sa 4.09
flocks, and you shall be his s. 8.17
two of Shimei's s. ran away to 1Ki 2.39
"Behold, your s. are in Gath," 2.39
to Gath to Achish, to seek his s.; 2.40
went and brought his s. from Gath. 2.40
Solomon made a forced levy of s., 9.21
of Israel Solomon made no s.; 9.22
take my two children to be his s." 2Ki 4.01
Solomon made no s. for his work; 2Ch 8.09
male and female, as your s. 28.10
sons and our daughters to be s., Neh 5.05

SLAVES (cont.)

Behold, we are s. this day; Neh 9.36
its good gifts, behold, we are s. 9.36
If we had been sold merely as s., Est 7.04
I bought male and female s., Ecc 2.07
and had s. who were born in my 2.07
I have seen s. on horses, and 10.07
princes walking on foot like s. 10.07
LORD's land as male and female s.; Is 14.02
kings shall make s. even of them; Jer 25.14
one should set free his Hebrew s., 34.09
male and female s. they had set 34.11
brought them into subjection as s. 34.11
took back his male and female s., 34.16
them into subjection to be your s. 34.16
S. rule over us; there is none to Lam 5.08
yourselves to any one as obedient s., Rom 6.16
you are s. of the one whom you obey, 6.16
who were once s. of sin have 6.17
have become s. of righteousness. 6.18
When you were s. of sin, you were 6.20
from sin and have become s. of God, 6.22
a price; do not become s. of men. 1Co 7.23
s. or free—and all were made to 12.13
bear it if a man makes s. of you, 2Co 11.20
we were s. to the elemental spirits Gal 4.03
whose s. you want to be once more? 4.09
S., be obedient to those who are Eph 6.05
S., obey in everything those who Col 3.22
treat your s. justly and fairly, 4.01
to be slanderers or s. to drink; Tit 2.03
Bid s. to be submissive to their 2.09
s. to various passions and pleasures, 3.03
themselves are s. of corruption; 2Pe 2.19
chariots, and s., that is, human souls. Rev 18.13

SLAY

and whoever finds me will s. me." Gen 4.14
to s. the righteous with the wicked, 18.25
wilt thou s. an innocent people 20.04
and took the knife to s. his son. 22.10
him, lest he come and s. us all, 32.11
is it if we s. our brother and 37.26
"S. my two sons if I do not bring 42.37
for in their anger they s. men, 49.06
I will s. your first-born son.'" Ex 4.23
pass through to s. the Egyptians; 12.23
to enter your houses to s. you. 12.23
and do not s. the innocent and 23.07
to s. them in the mountains, and to 32.12
and s. every man his brother, and 32.27
which they s. in the open field, Lev 17.05
and s. them as sacrificed of peace 17.05
shall no more s. their sacrifices 17.07
one of you s. his men who have Num 25.05
them out to s. them in the wilderness." Deu 9.28
a bribe to s. an innocent person.' 27.25
them alive, I would not s. you." Ju 8.19
his first-born, "Rise, and s. them." 8.20
his hands to s. his brothers. 9.24
the will of the LORD to s. them. 1Sa 2.25
of Israel to s. us and our people." 5.10
that it may not s. us and our 5.11
sheep, and s. them here, and eat; 14.34
is guilt in me, s. me yourself; 20.08
to me, 'Stand beside me and s. me; 2Sa 1.09
king's will to s. Abner the son of 3.37
the avenger of blood s. no more, 14.11
had sought to s. them in his zeal 21.02
he will not s. his servant with 1Ki 1.51
child, and by no means s. it." 3.26
first woman, and by no means s. it; 3.27
the sword of Hazael shall Jehu s.; 19.17
the sword of Jehu shall Elisha s. 19.17
father, shall I s. them? Shall I s. them?" 2Ki 6.21
He answered, "You shall not s. them. 6.22
Would you s. those whom you have 6.22
and you will s. their young men 8.12
to the officers, "Go in and s. them; 10.25
and s. with the sword any one who 11.15
Athaliah, so that she did not s. him; 2Ch 22.11
"Do not s. her in the house of the 23.14
to s., and to annihilate all Jews, Est 3.13
to s., and to annihilate any armed 8.11
Behold, he will s. me; I have no Job 13.15
Evil shall s. the wicked; and those Ps 34.21
to s. those who walk uprightly; 37.14
the righteous, and seeks to s. him. 37.32
S. them not, lest my people forget; 59.11
They s. the widow and the sojourner, 94.06
O that thou wouldst s. the wicked, 139.19
of his lips he shall s. the wicked. Is 11.04
famine, and your remnant I will s. 14.30
and he will s. the dragon that is 27.01
who s. your children in the valleys, 57.05
and the Lord GOD will s. you; 65.15
lion from the forest shall s. them, Jer 5.06
the sword to s., the dogs to tear, 15.03
all their plotting to s. me. 18.23
and shall s. them with the sword. 20.04
and he shall s. them before your 29.21
"Let me go and s. Ishmael the son 40.15
S., and utterly destroy after them, 50.21
S. all her bulls, let them go down 50.27
s. old men outright, young men and Eze 9.06
they shall s. their sons and their 23.47
He will s. with the sword your 26.08
he will s. your people with the 26.11
the presence of those who s. you, 28.09
they shall s. the burnt offering 44.11
and his companions, to s. them. Dan 2.13
had gone out to s. the wise men of 2.14
land, and s. her with thirst. Hos 2.03
I will s. their beloved children. 9.16
and will s. all its princes with Amo 2.03
of them I will s. with the sword; 9.01
the sword, and it shall s. them; 9.04
Those who buy them s. them and go Zec 11.05
them here and s. them before me." Lk 19.27
Lord Jesus will s. him with the 2Th 2.08
so that men should s. one another; Rev 6.04

SLAYER

not give up the s. into his hand; Jos 20.05
then the s. may go again to his own 20.06
the city of refuge for the s., 21.13
the city of refuge for the s., 21.21
the city of refuge for the s., 21.27
the city of refuge for the s., 21.32
the city of refuge for the s., 21.38
be given into the hand of the s. Eze 21.11

SLAYERS

been slain as their s. were slain? Is 27.07

SLAYING

had finished s. them with a very Jos 10.20
returned from s. the Philistine, 1Sa 18.06
with whom I sojourn, by s. her son?" 1Ki 17.20
s. oxen and killing sheep, eating Is 22.13
and pursued us, s. without pity; Lam 3.43
and mercilessly s. nations for Hab 1.17

SLAYS

If any one s. Cain, vengeance shall Gen 4.15
avenger of blood s. the manslayer, Num 35.27
be he who s. his neighbor in Deu 27.24
fool, and jealously s. the simple. Job 5.02
if any one s. with the sword, with Rev 13.10

SLEDGE

like a threshing s. on the mire. Job 41.30
not threshed with a threshing s., Is 28.27
Behold, I will make of you a threshing s., 41.15

SLEDGES

the threshing s. and the yokes of	2Sa 24.22
and the threshing s. for the wood,	1Ch 21.23
Gilead with threshing s. of iron.	Amo 1.03

SLEEK

of the Nile seven cows s. and fat,	Gen 41.02
ate up the seven s. and fat cows.	41.04
fat and s., came up out of the Nile	41.18
fat, you grew thick, you became s.;	Deu 32.15
pangs; their bodies are sound and s.	Ps 73.04
they have grown fat and s. They know	Jer 5.28

SLEEP

caused a deep s. to fall upon the	Gen 2.21
down, a deep s. fell on Abram;	15.12
and lay down in that place to s.	28.11
Then Jacob awoke from his s. and said,	28.16
night, and my s. fled from my eyes.	31.40
his body; in what else shall he s.?	Ex 22.27
you shall not s. in his pledge;	Deu 24.12
that he may s. in his cloak and	24.13
are about to s. with your fathers;	31.16
But he awoke from his s., and	Ju 16.14
She made him s. upon her knees;	16.19
And he awoke from his s., and	16.20
the roof, and he lay down to s.	1Sa 9.25
because a deep s. from the LORD	26.12
On that night the king could not s.;	Est 6.01
night, when deep s. falls on men,	Job 4.13
awake, or be roused out of his s.	14.12
when deep s. falls upon men, while	33.15
I lie down and s.; I wake again,	Ps 3.05
In peace I will both lie down and s.;	4.08
my eyes, lest I s. the s. of death;	13.03
of their spoil; they sank into s.;	76.05
Then the Lord awoke as from s.,	78.65
Israel will neither slumber nor s.	121.04
or he gives to his beloved in s.	127.02
I will not give s. to my eyes or	132.04
lie down, your s. will be sweet.	Pro 3.24
For they cannot s. unless they have	4.16
are robbed of s. unless they have	4.16
Give your eyes no s. and your	6.04
When will you arise from your s.?	6.09
A little s., a little slumber, a	6.10
Slothfulness casts into a deep s.,	19.15
Love not s., lest you come to	20.13
"A little s., a little slumber, a	24.33
Sweet is the s. of a laborer,	Ecc 5.12
of the rich will not let him s.	5.12
day nor night one's eyes see s.;	8.16
out upon you a spirit of deep s.,	Is 29.10
All my s. has fled because of the	38.15
and my s. was pleasant to me.	Jer 31.26
swoon away and s. a perpetual s. and	51.39
they shall s. a perpetual s. and not	51.57
the wilderness and s. in the woods.	Eze 34.25
was troubled, and his s. left him.	Dan 2.01
to him, and s. fled from him.	6.18
into a deep s. with my face to the	8.18
face in a deep s. with my face to	10.09
of those who s. in the dust of the	12.02
man that is wakened out of his s.	Zec 4.01
When Joseph woke from s., he did	Mt 1.24
and should s. and rise night and	Mk 4.27
were heavy with s. but kept awake,	Lk 9.32
and he said to them, "Why do you s.?	22.46
but I go to awake him out of s."	Jn 11.11
that he meant taking rest in s.	11.13
sank into a deep s. as Paul talked	Ac 20.09
longer; and being overcome by s.,	20.09
time now for you to wake from s.	Rom 13.11
We shall not all s., but we shall	1Co 15.51
So then let us not s., as others do,	1Th 5.06
For those who s. s. at night, and those	5.07
we wake or s. we might live with	5.10

SLEEPER

to him, "What do you mean, you s.?	Jon 1.06
O s., and arise from the dead, and	Eph 5.14

SLEEPEST

Rouse thyself! Why s. thou, O Lord?	Ps 44.23

SLEEPING

and there lay Saul s. within the	1Sa 26.07
for the girl is not dead but s."	Mt 9.24
but while men were s., his enemy	13.25
to the disciples and found them s.;	26.40
And again he came and found them s.,	26.43
"Are you still s. and taking your	26.45
weep? The child is not dead but s."	Mk 5.39
And he came and found them s.,	14.37
And again he came and found them s.,	14.40
"Are you still s. and taking your	14.41
weep; for she is not dead but s."	Lk 8.52
and found them s. for sorrow,	22.45
Peter was s. between two soldiers,	Ac 12.06

SLEEPLESS

hardship, through many a s. night,	2Co 11.27

SLEEPS

lord the king s. with his fathers,	1Ki 1.21
but a son who s. in harvest brings	Pro 10.05
none stumbles, none slumbers or s.,	Is 5.27

SLEEVES

he made him a long robe with s.	Gen 37.03
the long robe with s. that he wore;	37.23
long robe with s. and brought it	37.32
was wearing a long robe with s.;	2Sa 13.18

SLEPT

and while he s. took one of his	Gen 2.21
So while he s., Delilah took the	Ju 16.14
wheat, but she grew drowsy and s.;	2Sa 4.06
But Uriah s. at the door of the	11.09
Then David s. with his fathers, and	1Ki 2.10
me, while your maidservant s.,	3.20
that David s. with his fathers and	11.21
And Solomon s. with his fathers, and	11.43
and he s. with his fathers, and	14.20
And Rehoboam s. with his fathers	14.31
And Abijam s. with his fathers;	15.08
And Asa s. with his fathers, and was	15.24
And Baasha s. with his fathers, and	16.06
And Omri s. with his fathers, and	16.28
And he lay down and s. under a	19.05
So Ahab s. with his fathers;	22.40
And Jehoshaphat s. with his fathers,	22.50
So Joram s. with his fathers, and	2Ki 8.24
So Jehu s. with his fathers, and	10.35
So Jehoahaz s. with his fathers, and	13.09
So Joash s. with his fathers, and	13.13
And Jehoash s. with his fathers, and	14.16
after the king s. with his fathers	14.22
And Jeroboam s. with his fathers,	14.29
And Azariah s. with his fathers, and	15.07
And Menahem s. with his fathers, and	15.22
Jotham s. with his fathers, and was	15.38
And Ahaz s. with his fathers, and	16.20
And Hezekiah s. with his fathers;	20.21
And Manasseh s. with his fathers,	21.18
So Jehoiakim s. with his fathers,	24.06
And Solomon s. with his fathers, and	2Ch 9.31
And Rehoboam s. with his fathers,	12.16
So Abijah s. with his fathers, and	14.01
And Asa s. with his fathers, dying	16.13
Jehoshaphat s. with his fathers, and	21.01
after the king s. with his fathers	26.02
And Uzziah s. with his fathers, and	26.23
And Jotham s. with his fathers, and	27.09
And Ahaz s. with his fathers, and	28.27
And Hezekiah s. with his fathers,	32.33

SLEPT (cont.)

So Manasseh s. with his fathers, and 2Ch 33.20
I should have s.; then I should Job 3.13
I s., but my heart was awake. Sol 5.02
delayed, they all slumbered and s. Mt 25.05

SLEW

instead of Abel, for Cain s. him." Gen 4.25
They s. Hamor and his son Shechem 34.26
of the LORD; and the LORD s. him. 38.07
of the LORD, and he s. him also. 38.10
when he s. the Egyptians but spared Ex 12.27
the LORD s. all the first-born in 13.15
the day that I s. all the first-born Num 3.13
the day that I s. all the first-born 8.17
And Israel s. him with the edge of 21.24
So they s. him, and his sons, and all 21.35
commanded Moses, and s. every male. 31.07
They s. the kings of Midian with 31.08
and they also s. Balaam the son of 31.08
Shebarim, and s. them at the descent. Jos 7.05
who s. them with a great slaughter 10.10
Penuel and s. the men of the city. Ju 8.17
are the men whom you s. at Tabor?" 8.18
arose and s. Zebah and Zalmunna; 8.21
and s. his brothers the sons of 9.05
who s. them, and upon the men of 9.24
he rose against them and s. them. 9.43
who were in the fields and s. them. 9.44
seized him and s. him at the fords 12.06
and with it he s. a thousand men. 15.15
dead whom he s. at his death were 16.30
Then they s. the bull, and they 1Sa 1.25
who s. about four thousand men on 4.02
And he s. some of the men of 6.19
he s. seventy men of them, and the 6.19
and s. them on the ground; 14.32
him that night, and s. them there. 14.34
his hand and he s. the Philistine, 19.05
the Philistines s. Jonathan and 31.02
and s. him, because I was sure that 2Sa 1.10
and Abishai his brother s. Abner, 3.30
and s. him, and beheaded him. 4.07
I seized him and s. him at Ziklag, 4.10
David s. twenty-two thousand men of 8.05
he s. eighteen thousand Edomites in 8.13
and David s. of the Syrians the men 10.18
life of his brother whom he s.'; 14.07
Sibbecai the Hushathite s. Saph, 21.18
s. Goliath the Gittite, the shaft of 21.19
of Shimei, David's brother, s. him. 21.21
hundred whom he s. at one time. 23.08
defended it, and s. the Philistines; 23.12
three hundred men and s. them, 23.18
went down and s. a lion in a pit 23.20
And he s. an Egyptian, a handsome 23.21
and s. with his own spear. 23.21
he attacked and s. with the sword 1Ki 2.32
the slain, he s. every male in Edom 11.15
and s. them, and boiled their flesh 19.21
and s. them, seventy persons, and put 2Ki 10.07
against my master, and s. him; 10.09
So Jehu s. all that remained of the 10.11
and s. them at the pit of Betheked, 10.14
he s. all that remained to Ahab in 10.17
and they s. Mattan the priest of 11.18
and s. Joash in the house of Millo, 12.20
him to Lachish, and s. him there. 14.19
of Jabesh in Samaria and s. him, 15.14
and s. him in Samaria, in the 15.25
he s. him, and reigned in his 15.25
and s. him, and reigned in his stead, 15.30
and s. a hundred and eighty-five 19.35
s. him with the sword, and escaped 19.37
of the land s. all those who had 21.24
And he s. all the priests of the 23.20
and Pharaoh Neco s. him at Megiddo, 23.29
They s. the sons of Zedekiah before 25.07
sight of the LORD, and he s. him. 1Ch 2.03
Gath who were born in the land s., 7.21
and the Philistines s. Jonathan and 10.02
Therefore the LORD s. him, and 10.14
three hundred whom he s. at one time. 11.11
defended it, and s. the Philistines; 11.14
three hundred men and s. them, 11.20
went down and s. a lion in a pit 11.22
And he s. an Egyptian, a man of 11.23
and s. him with his own spear. 11.23
David s. twenty-two thousand men of 18.05
s. eighteen thousand Edomites in 18.12
and David s. of the Syrians the 19.18
Sibbecai the Hushathite s. Sippai, 20.04
the son of Jair s. Lahmi the 20.05
of Shimea, David's brother, s. him. 20.07
Abijah and his people s. them with 2Ch 13.17
he s. all his brothers with the 21.04
house, and they s. her there. 23.15
and they s. Mattan the priest of 23.17
the priest, and s. him on his bed. 24.25
him to Lachish, and s. him there. 25.27
son of Remaliah s. a hundred and 28.06
s. Maaseiah the king's son and 28.07
of the land s. all those who had 33.25
who s. their young men with the 36.17
itself the Jews s. and destroyed Est 9.06
and also s. Parshandatha and 9.07
Adar and they s. three hundred men 9.15
and s. seventy-five thousand of 9.16
and s. the servants with the edge Job 1.15
and s. the servants with the edge 1.17
them and he s. the strongest of Ps 78.31
When he s. them, they sought for him; 78.34
many nations and s. mighty kings, 135.10
and s. famous kings, for his steadfast 136.18
and s. a hundred and eighty-five Is 37.36
s. him with the sword, and escaped 37.38
who s. him with the sword and cast Jer 26.23
The king of Babylon s. the sons of 39.06
king of Babylon s. all the nobles 39.06
Ishmael also s. all the Jews who 41.03
and the men with him s. them, 41.07
The king of Babylon s. the sons of 52.10
and also s. all the princes of 52.10
and her they s. with the sword; Eze 23.10
of the fire s. those men who took Dan 3.22
whom he would he s., and whom 5.19
I s. your young men with the sword; Amo 4.10

SLIGHT

Is it too s. a thing for the house Eze 8.17
For this s. momentary affliction is 2Co 4.17

SLIME

taste in the s. of the purslane? Job 6.06
the snail which dissolves into s., Ps 58.08

SLING

every one could s. a stone at a hair, Ju 20.16
his s. was in his hand, and he drew 1Sa 17.40
Philistine with a s. and with a 17.50
s. out as from the hollow of a s. 25.29
arrows and s. stones with either 1Ch 12.02
the stone in the s. is he who gives Pro 26.08

SLINGERS

and the s. surrounded and conquered 2Ki 3.25
shall devour and tread down the s.; Zec 9.15

SLINGING

of mail, bows, and stones for s. 2Ch 26.14
I am s. out the inhabitants of the Jer 10.18

SLINGSTONES

flee; for him s. are turned to stubble. Job 41.28

SLIP
the time when their foot shall s.; Deu 32.35
under me, and my feet did not s.; 2Sa 22.37
then let no one s. out of the city 2Ki 9.15
is ready for those whose feet s. Job 12.05
under me, and my feet did not s. Ps 18.36
in his heart; his steps do not s. 37.31
and has not let our feet s. 66.09

SLIPPED
and Baanah his brother s. in. 2Sa 4.06
to thy paths, my feet have not s. Ps 17.05
stumbled, my steps had well nigh s. 73.02
who s. in to spy out our freedom Gal 2.04

SLIPPERY
Let their way be dark and s., with Ps 35.06
Truly thou dost set them in s. places; 73.18
be to them like s. paths in the Jer 23.12

SLIPS
and the head s. from the handle and Deu 19.05
boast against me when my foot s.! Ps 38.16
"My foot s.," thy steadfast love, O 94.18
like a bad tooth or a foot that s. Pro 25.19
and set out s. of an alien god, Is 17.10

SLOPE
one mountain s. which I took from Gen 48.22
and the s. of the valleys that Num 21.15

SLOPES
under the s. of Pisgah on the east. Deu 3.17
the Arabah, under the s. of Pisgah. 4.49
Negeb and the lowland and the s., Jos 10.40
to the foot of the s. of Pisgah; 12.03
in the s., in the wilderness, and in 12.08
and the s. of Pisgah, and Bethjeshimoth, 13.20
moving down the s. of Gilead. Sol 4.01
moving down the s. of Gilead. 6.05

SLOTH
Through s. the roof sinks in, and Ecc 10.18

SLOTHFUL
while the s. will be put to forced Pro 12.24
A s. man will not catch his prey, 12.27
him, 'You wicked and s. servant! You Mt 25.26

SLOTHFULNESS
S. casts into a deep sleep, and an Pro 19.15

SLOW
but I am s. of speech and of tongue Ex 4.10
s. to anger, and abounding in 34.06
'The LORD is s. to anger, and Num 14.18
Do not be s. to go, and enter in and Ju 18.09
s. to anger and abounding in Neh 9.17
s. to anger and abounding in Ps 86.15
s. to anger and abounding in 103.08
s. to anger and abounding in 145.08
He who is s. to anger has great Pro 14.29
but he who is s. to anger quiets 15.18
He who is s. to anger is better 16.32
Good sense makes a man s. to anger, 19.11
s. to anger, and abounding in Joe 2.13
s. to anger, and abounding in Jon 4.02
The LORD is s. to anger and of Nah 1.03
If it seem s., wait for it; Hab 2.03
and s. of heart to believe all that LK 24.25
quick to hear, s. to speak, s. to anger, Jas 1.19
The LORD is not s. about his promise 2Pe 3.09

SLOWLY
his servant, and I will lead on s., Gen 33.14
We sailed s. for a number of days, Ac 27.07

SLOWNESS
about his promise as some count s., 2Pe 3.09

SLUGGARD
Go to the ant, O s.; consider her Pro 6.06
How long will you lie there, O s.? 6.09
so is the s. to those who send him. 10.26
The soul of the s. craves, and gets 13.04
The way of a s. is overgrown with 15.19
The s. buries his hand in the dish, 19.24
The s. does not plow in the autumn; 20.04
The desire of the s. kills him for 21.25
The s. says, "There is a lion 22.13
the field of a s. by the vineyard 24.30
The s. says, "There is a lion in the 26.13
hinges, so does a s. on his bed. 26.14
The s. buries his hand in the dish; 26.15
The s. is wiser in his own eyes than 26.16

SLUGGISH
that you may not be s., but imitators Heb 6.12

SLUMBER
men, while they s. on their beds, Job 33.15
moved, he who keeps you will not s. Ps 121.03
Israel will neither s. nor sleep. 121.04
to my eyes or s. to my eyelids, 132.04
no sleep and your eyelids no s.; Pro 6.04
a little s., a little folding of 6.10
a little s., a little folding of 24.33
dreaming, lying down, loving to s. Is 56.10
O king of Assyria; your nobles s. Nah 3.18

SLUMBERED
was delayed, they all s. and slept. Mt 25.05

SLUMBERS
none s. or sleeps, not a waistcloth Is 5.27

SLUNG
of bronze s. between his shoulders. 1Sa 17.06
and s. it, and struck the Philistine 17.49

SMALL
both s. and great, so that they Gen 19.11
"Is it a s. matter that you have 30.15
the household is too s. for a lamb, Ex 12.04
but any s. matter they shall decide 18.22
but any s. matter they decided 18.26
and you shall beat some of it very s., 30.36
house he shall take two s. birds, Lev 14.49
handfuls of sweet incense beaten s.; 16.12
is it too s. a thing for you that Num 16.09
Is it a s. thing that you have 16.13
and to a s. tribe you shall give a 26.54
you shall give a s. inheritance; 26.54
and to a s. tribe you shall give a 33.54
you shall give a s. inheritance; 33.54
shall hear the s. and the great Deu 1.17
crushed it, grinding it very s., 9.21
kinds of weights, a large and a s. 25.13
of measures, a large and a s. 25.14
either great or s. without disclosing 1Sa 20.02
who were in it, both s. and great; 30.02
whether s. or great, sons or daughters, 30.19
And yet this was a s. thing in thy 2Sa 7.19
"I have one s. request to make of 1Ki 2.20
LORD was too s. to receive the 8.64
after the fire a still s. voice. 19.12
"Fight with neither s. nor great, 22.31
some s. boys came out of the city 2Ki 2.23
Let us make a s. roof chamber with 4.10
under your charge is too s. for us. 6.01
all the people, both s. and great; 23.02
both s. and great, and the captains 25.26
And this was a s. thing in thy eyes, 1Ch 17.17
s. and great, teacher and pupil 25.08
s. and great alike, for their gates. 26.13
"Fight with neither s. nor great, 2Ch 18.30
the large and s. shields that had 23.09
all the people both great and s.; 34.30

SMALL (cont.)
great and s., and the treasures of 2Ch 36.18
the capital, both great and s., Est 1.05
The s. and the great are there, and Job 3.19
And though your beginning was s., 8.07
consolations of God too s. for you, 15.11
and how s. a whisper do we hear of 26.14
"Behold, I am of s. account; what 40.04
living things both s. and great. Ps 104.25
fear the LORD, both s. and great. 115.13
I am s. and despised, yet I do not 119.141
of adversity, your strength is s. Pro 24.10
Four things on earth are s., 30.24
every s. vessel, from the cups to Is 22.24
of your foes shall be like s. dust, 29.05
Both great and s. shall die in this Jer 16.06
honored, and they shall not be s. 30.19
I will make you s. among the 49.15
also the s. bowls, and the firepans, 52.19
shall take from these a s. number, Eze 5.03
your harlotries so s. a matter 16.20
make them so s. that they will 29.15
of the court were s. courts, 46.22
become strong with a s. people. Dan 11.23
How can Jacob stand? He is so s.! Amo 7.02
How can Jacob stand? He is so s.! 7.05
make the ephah s. and the shekel 8.05
Behold, I will make you s. among the Ob 1.02
the day of s. things shall rejoice, Zec 4.10
said, "Seven, and a few s. fish." Mt 15.34
And they had a few s. fish; Mk 8.07
able to do as s. a thing as that, Lk 12.26
crowd, because he was s. of stature. 19.03
there was no s. stir among the Ac 12.18
Barnabas had no s. dissension and 15.02
testifying both to s. and great, 26.22
the lee of a s. island called 27.16
and no s. tempest lay on us, all 27.20
me it is a very s. thing that I 1Co 4.03
by a very s. rudder wherever the Jas 3.04
forest is set ablaze by a s. fire! 3.05
both s. and great, and for destroying Rev 11.18
both s. and great, both rich and 13.16
you who fear him, s. and great. 19.05
free and slave, both s. and great. 19.18
great and s., standing before the 20.12

SMALLER
lot between the larger and the s. Num 26.56
and from the s. tribes you shall 35.08
and from the s. ledge to the larger Eze 43.14

SMALLEST
and the s. one a mighty nation; Is 60.22
it is the s. of all seeds, but when Mt 13.32
is the s. of all the seeds on earth; Mk 4.31

SMART
surety for a stranger will s. for it, Pro 11.15

SMASHED
trumpets and s. the jars that were Ju 7.19
vessel which is s. so ruthlessly Is 30.14

SMELL
he smelled the s. of his garments, Gen 27.27
s. of my son is as the s. of a field 27.27
and I will not s. your pleasing Lev 26.31
see, nor hear, nor eat, nor s. Deu 4.28
not hear; noses, but do not s. Ps 115.06
and no s. of fire had come upon Dan 3.27
stench and foul s. of him will Joe 2.20
where would be the sense of s.? 1Co 12.17

SMELLED
And when the LORD s. the pleasing Gen 8.21
and he s. the smell of his garments, 27.27

SMELLS
He s. the battle from afar, the thunder Job 39.25

SMELT
you and will s. away your dross as Is 1.25

SMELTED
earth, and copper is s. from the ore. Job 28.02

SMILED
I s. on them when they had no confidence; Job 29.24

SMITE
out my hand and s. Egypt with all Ex 3.20
and I will s. all the first-born in 12.12
you, when I s. the land of Egypt. 12.13
I myself will s. you sevenfold for Lev 26.24
"Harass the Midianites, and s. them; Num 25.17
The LORD will s. you with consumption, Deu 28.22
The LORD will s. you with the boils 28.27
The LORD will s. you with madness 28.28
The LORD will s. you on the knees 28.35
and help me, and let us s. Gibeon; Jos 10.04
and you shall s. the Midianites as Ju 6.16
they began to s. and kill some of 20.31
had begun to s. and kill about 20.39
"Go and s. the inhabitants of 21.10
Now go and s. Amalek, and utterly 1Sa 15.03
cast his spear at him to s. him; 20.33
LORD lives, the LORD will s. him; 26.10
why would I s. you to the ground? 2Sa 2.22
"Whoever would s. the Jebusites, 5.08
before you to s. the army of the 5.24
and s. the city with the edge of 15.14
the LORD will s. Israel, as a reed 1Ki 14.15
"Whoever shall s. the Jebusites 1Ch 11.06
before you to s. the army of the 14.15
For thou dost s. all my enemies on Ps 3.07
The sun shall not s. you by day, 121.06
the LORD will s. with a scab the Is 3.17
when they s. with the rod and lift 10.24
and he shall s. the earth with the 11.04
and s. it into seven channels that 11.15
And the LORD will s. Egypt, smiting 19.22
scorching wind nor sun shall s. them, 49.10
Come, let us s. him with the tongue, Jer 18.18
And I will s. the inhabitants of 21.06
He shall s. them with the edge of 21.07
whom I shall s. in my anger and my 33.05
He shall come and s. the land of 43.11
of Babylon to s. the land of Egypt: 46.13
know that I am the LORD, who s. Eze 7.09
through the city after him, and s.; 9.05
S. therefore upon your thigh. 21.12
when I s. all who dwell in it, then 32.15
I will s. the winter house with the Amo 3.15
"S. the capitals until the thresholds 9.01
Therefore I have begun to s. you, Mic 6.13
May the sword s. his arm and his Zec 11.17
the LORD will s. all the peoples 14.12
lest I come and s. the land with a Mal 4.06
and to s. the earth with every Rev 11.06
sword with which to s. the nations, 19.15

SMITER
let him give his cheek to the s., and Lam 3.30

SMITERS
I gave my back to the s., and my Is 50.06

SMITES
"Whoever s. Kiriathsepher, and takes Jos 15.16
binds up; he s., but his hands heal. Job 5.18
the LORD, when he s. with his rod. Is 30.31

SMITH
Now there was no s. to be found 1Sa 13.19
and the s. has material for a Pro 25.04
created the s. who blows the fire Is 54.16

SMITHS

and all the craftsmen and the s.; 2Ki 24.14
and the craftsmen and the s., 24.16
and the s., and had brought them to Jer 24.01
and the s. had departed from 29.02
Then the LORD showed me four s. Zec 1.20

SMITING

the angel who was s. the people, 2Sa 24.17
struck him, s. and wounding him. 1Ki 20.37
s. and healing, and they will return Is 19.22
And while they were s., and I was Eze 9.08

SMITTEN

you shall be s. before your enemies; Lev 26.17
"Surely they are s. down before us, Ju 20.39
You have s. Uriah the Hittite with 2Sa 12.09
You have indeed s. Edom, and your 2Ki 14.10
I have s. Edom,' and your heart has 2Ch 25.19
out, because the LORD has s. him. 26.20
persecute him whom thou hast s., Ps 69.26
My heart is s. like grass, and 102.04
Why will you still be s., that you Is 1.05
Has he s. them as he smote those 27.07
stricken, s. by God, and afflicted. 53.04
In vain have I s. your children, Jer 2.30
Thou hast s. them, but they felt no 5.03
of my people is s. with a great 14.17
Why hast thou s. us so that there 14.19
house shall be s. into fragments, Amo 6.11
the waves of the sea shall be s., Zec 10.11

SMOKE

the s. of the land went up like the Gen 19.28
went up like the s. of a furnace. 19.28
And Mount Sinai was wrapped in s., Ex 19.18
and the s. of it went up like the s. 19.18
jealousy would s. against that man, Deu 29.20
the s. of the city went up to Jos 8.20
and that the s. of the city went up, 8.21
great cloud of s. rise up out of Ju 20.38
out of the city in a column of s., 20.40
the city went up in s. to heaven. 20.40
S. went up from his nostrils, and 2Sa 22.09
Out of his nostrils comes forth s., Job 41.20
S. went up from his nostrils, and Ps 18.08
vanish—like s. they vanish away. 37.20
with the s. of the sacrifice of 66.15
As s. is driven away, so drive them 68.02
does thy anger s. against the 74.01
For my days pass away like s., 102.03
touches the mountains and they s.! 104.32
become like a wineskin in the s., 119.83
Touch the mountains that they s.! 144.05
and s. to the eyes, so is the Pro 10.26
wilderness, like a column of s., Sol 3.06
and s. and the shining of a flaming Is 4.05
and the house was filled with s. 6.04
they roll upward in a column of s. 9.18
For s. comes out of the north, and 14.31
his anger, and in thick rising s.; 30.27
its s. shall go up for ever. 34.10
the heavens will vanish like s., 51.06
These are a s. in my nostrils, a 65.05
and the s. of the cloud of incense Eze 8.11
floor or like s. from a window. Hos 13.03
blood and fire and columns of s. Joe 2.30
I will burn your chariots in s., Nah 2.13
blood, and fire, and vapor of s.; Ac 2.19
and the s. of the incense rose with Rev 8.04
rose s. like the s. of a great furnace, 9.02
darkened with the s. from the shaft. 9.02
Then from the s. came locusts on 9.03
and fire and s. and sulphur issued 9.17
by the fire and s. and sulphur 9.18
And the s. of their torment goes up 14.11
was filled with s. from the glory 15.08
they see the s. of her burning; 18.09
as they saw the s. of her burning, 18.18
The s. from her goes up for ever 19.03

SMOKING

a s. fire pot and a flaming torch Gen 15.17
of the trumpet and the mountain s., Ex 20.18

SMOLDERING

of these two s. stumps of firebrands, Is 7.04
a bruised reed or quench a s. wick, Mt 12.20

SMOLDERS

all night their anger s.; in the Hos 7.06

SMOOTH

is a hairy man, and I am a s. man. Gen 27.11
and upon the s. part of his neck; 27.16
and chose five s. stones from the 1Sa 17.40
the adventuress with her s. words, Pro 2.16
from the s. tongue of the adventuress 6.24
the adventuress with her s. words. 7.05
with her s. talk she compels him. 7.21
vessel are s. lips with an evil 26.23
tall and s., to a people feared Is 18.02
of hosts from a people tall and s., 18.07
thou dost make s. the path of the 26.07
speak to us s. things, prophesy 30.10
Among the s. stones of the valley 57.06
the rough ways shall be made s.; Lk 3.05

SMOOTHER

His speech was s. than butter, yet Ps 55.21
honey, and her speech is s. than oil; Pro 5.03

SMOOTHLY

sparkles in the cup and goes down s. Pro 23.31
like the best wine that goes down s., Sol 7.09

SMOOTHS

and he who s. with the hammer him who Is 41.07

SMOTE

the LORD s. all the first-born in Ex 12.29
and the LORD s. the people with a Num 11.33
land which the LORD s. before the 32.04
and we s. him until no survivor was Deu 3.03
turned back and s. the men of Ai. Jos 8.21
and Israel s. them, until there was 8.22
and s. it with the edge of the 8.24
and s. them as far as Azekah and 10.10
afterward Joshua s. them and put 10.26
and s. it and its king with the 10.28
and he s. it with the edge of the 10.30
and s. it with the edge of the 10.32
and Joshua s. him and his people, 10.33
and s. it with the edge of the 10.35
and s. it with the edge of the 10.37
and they s. them with the edge of 10.39
who s. them and chased them as far 11.08
and they s. them, until they left 11.08
and s. its king with the sword; 11.10
and s. them with the edge of the 11.12
every man they s. with the edge of 11.14
and s. them, and put them to death. 11.17
and s. it with the edge of the Ju 1.08
and they s. the city with the edge 1.25
And he s. them from Aroer to the 11.33
and the men of Gilead s. Ephraim, 12.04
And he s. them hip and thigh with 15.08
and s. them with the edge of the 18.27
moved out and s. all the city with 20.37
and s. them with the edge of the 20.48
the gods who s. the Egyptians with 1Sa 4.08
and s. them, as far as below Bethcar 7.11
and s. the Amalekites, and delivered 14.48
after him and s. him and delivered 17.35
beard, and s. him and killed him. 17.35
And afterward David's heart s. him, 24.05
ten days later the LORD s. Nabal; 25.38

SMOTE (cont.)
And David s. the land, and left 1Sa 27.09
And David s. them from twilight 30.17
And he s. him so that he died. 2Sa 1.15
therefore Abner s. him in the belly 2.23
and there he s. him in the belly, so 3.27
they s. him, and slew him, and 4.07
and s. the Philistines from Geba to 5.25
and God s. him there because he put 6.07
deeds; he s. two ariels of Moab. 23.20
But David's heart s. him after he 24.10
of Israel s. of the Syrians a 1Ki 20.29
commanders s. the Edomites who had 2Ki 8.21
And the LORD s. the king, so that he 15.05
He s. the Philistines as far as 18.08
And the king of Babylon s. them, 25.21
deeds; he s. two ariels of Moab. 1Ch 11.22
and he s. him because he put forth 13.10
and they s. the Philistine army 14.16
And Joab s. Rabbah, and overthrew it 20.01
with this thing, and he s. Israel. 21.07
and the LORD s. him, and he died. 2Ch 13.20
And they s. all the cities round 14.14
And they s. the tents of those who 14.15
by night and s. the Edomites who 21.09
this the LORD s. him in his bowels 21.18
of Salt and s. ten thousand men of 25.11
So the Jews s. all their enemies Est 9.05
by his understanding he s. Rahab. Job 26.12
He s. the rock so that water gushed Ps 78.20
He s. all the first-born in Egypt, 78.51
He s. their vines and fig trees, and 105.33
He s. all the first-born in their 105.36
He it was who s. the first-born of 135.08
who s. many nations and slew mighty 135.10
to him who s. the first-born of 136.10
to him who s. great kings, for his 136.17
his hand against them and s. them, Is 5.25
did not turn to him who s. them, 9.13
no more lean upon him that s. them, 10.20
as when he s. Midian at the rock of 10.26
that s. the peoples in wrath with 14.06
the rod which s. you is broken, 14.29
smitten them as he s. those who s. them? 27.07
I s. him, I hid my face and was 57.17
for in my wrath I s. you, but in 60.10
was instructed, I s. upon my thigh; Jer 31.19
Philistines, before Pharaoh s. Gaza. 47.01
Nebuchadrezzar king of Babylon s. 49.28
And the king of Babylon s. them, 52.27
went forth, and s. in the city. Eze 9.07
and it s. the image on its feet of Dan 2.34
"I s. you with blight and mildew; Amo 4.07
I s. you and all the products of Hag 2.17
Immediately an angel of the Lord s. him, Ac 12.23

SMYRNA
Ephesus and to S. and to Pergamum Rev 1.11
angel of the church in S. write: 2.08

SNAIL
be like the s. which dissolves into Ps 58.08

SNAPPED
But he s. the bowstrings, as a string Ju 16.09
But he s. the ropes off his arms 16.12
before the silver cord is s., or the Ecc 12.06

SNAPS
a string of tow s. when it touches the Ju 16.09

SNARE
long shall this man be a s. to us? Ex 10.07
gods, it will surely be a s. to you." 23.33
it become a s. in the midst of you. 34.12
gods, for that would be a s. to you. Deu 7.16
they shall be a s. and a trap for Jos 23.13
their gods shall be a s. to you." Ju 2.03
and it became a s. to Gideon and 8.27
him, that she may be a s. for him, 1Sa 18.21
you laying a s. for my life to 28.09
by the heel, a s. lays hold of him. Job 18.09
hooks, or pierce his nose with a s.? 40.24
own table before them become a s.; Ps 69.22
you from the s. of the fowler and 91.03
idols, which became a s. to them. 106.36
The wicked have laid a s. for me, 119.110
s. of the fowlers; the s. is broken, 124.07
as a bird rushes into a s.; he does Pro 7.23
and his lips are a s. to himself. 18.07
It is a s. for a man to say rashly, 20.25
a fleeting vapor and a s. of death. 21.06
ways and entangle yourself in a s. 22.25
The fear of man lays a s.; but he 29.25
birds which are caught in a s., Ecc 9.12
a trap and a s. to the inhabitants Is 8.14
and the s. are upon you, O inhabitant 24.17
the pit shall be caught in the s. 24.18
and lay a s. for him who reproves 29.21
and s. are before you, O inhabitant Jer 48.43
the pit shall be caught in the s. 48.44
I set a s. for you and you were 50.24
and he shall be taken in my s.; Eze 12.13
and he shall be taken in my s., 17.20
for you have been a s. at Mizpah, Hos 5.01
yet a fowler's s. is on all his 9.08
Does a bird fall in a s. on the earth, Amo 3.05
Does a s. spring up from the ground, 3.05
come upon you suddenly like a s.; Lk 21.34
their feast become a s. and a trap, Rom 11.09
reproach and the s. of the devil. 1Ti 3.07
into a s., into many senseless and 6.09
escape from the s. of the devil, 2Ti 2.26

SNARED
the wicked are s. in the work of Ps 9.16
if you are s. in the utterance of Pro 6.02
sons of men are s. at an evil time, Ecc 9.12
broken, they shall be s. and taken." Is 8.15
and be broken, and s., and taken. 28.13

SNARES
the s. of death confronted me. 2Sa 22.06
Therefore s. are round about you, Job 22.10
the s. of death confronted me. Ps 18.05
Those who seek my life lay their s., 38.12
they talk of laying s. secretly, 64.05
The s. of death encompassed me; 116.03
wayside they have set s. for me. 140.05
me, and from the s. of evildoers! 141.09
that one may avoid the s. of death. Pro 13.14
that one may avoid the s. of death. 14.27
Thorns and s. are in the way of the 22.05
woman whose heart is s. and nets, Ecc 7.26
take me, and laid s. for my feet. Jer 18.22
set against him s. on every side; Eze 19.08

SNARLING
and s. with their lips—for "Who," Ps 59.07

SNATCH
(There are those who s. the fatherless Job 24.09
Drought and heat s. away the snow 24.19
who seek to s. away my life; let Ps 40.14
he will s. and tear you from your 52.05
They s. on the right, but are still Is 9.20
no one shall s. them out of my Jn 10.28
one is able to s. them out of the 10.29

SNATCHED
and s. the spear out of the Egyptian's 2Sa 23.21
and s. the spear out of the Egyptian's 1Ch 11.23
They were s. away before their time Job 22.16

SNATCHES
Behold, he s. away; who can hinder Job 9.12
one comes and s. away what is sown Mt 13.19
and the wolf s. them and scatters Jn 10.12

SNATCHING
save some, by s. them out of the fire; Jud 1.23

SNEEZED
the child s. seven times, and the child 2Ki 4.35

SNEEZINGS
His s. flash forth light, and his eyes Job 41.18

SNIFF
and you s. at me, says the LORD of Mal 1.13

SNIFFING
wilderness, in her heat s. the wind! Jer 2.24

SNORTING
locust? His majestic s. is terrible. Job 39.20
"The s. of their horses is heard from Jer 8.16

SNOUT
ring in a swine's s. is a beautiful Pro 11.22

SNOW
hand was leprous, as white as s. Ex 4.06
Miriam was leprous, as white as s. Num 12.10
a pit on a day when s. had fallen. 2Sa 23.20
presence a leper, as white as s. 2Ki 5.27
a pit on a day when s. had fallen. 1Ch 11.22
ice, and where the s. hides itself. Job 6.16
If I wash myself with s., and 9.30
and heat snatch away the s. waters; 24.19
For to the s. he says, 'Fall on the 37.06
entered the storehouses of the s., 38.22
me, and I shall be whiter than s. Ps 51.07
kings there, s. fell on Zalmon. 68.14
He gives s. like wool; he scatters 147.16
fire and hail, s. and frost, stormy 148.08
Like the cold of s. in the time of Pro 25.13
Like s. in summer or rain in 26.01
not afraid of s. for her household, 31.21
they shall be as white as s.; Is 1.18
rain and the s. come down from 55.10
Does the s. of Lebanon leave the Jer 18.14
Her princes were purer than s., Lam 4.07
his raiment was white as s., and the Dan 7.09
lightning, and his raiment white as s. Mt 28.03
white as white wool, white as s.; Rev 1.14

SNUFFERS
Its s. and their trays shall be of Ex 25.38
lamps and its s. and its trays of 37.23
its s., its trays, and all the Num 4.09
the cups, s., basins, dishes for 1Ki 7.50
s., bowls, trumpets, or any vessels 2Ki 12.13
and the s., and the dishes for 25.14
the s., basins, dishes for incense, 2Ch 4.22
and the s., and the basins, and the Jer 52.18

SOAK
may it s. into his body like water, Ps 109.18

SOAKED
their land shall be s. with blood, Is 34.07

SOAP
yourself with lye and use much s., Jer 2.22
refiner's fire and like fullers' s.; Mal 3.02

SOAR
Though you s. aloft like the eagle, Ob 1.04

SOARS
it by your wisdom that the hawk s., Job 39.26

SOBER
Festus, but I am speaking the s. truth. Ac 26.25
but to think with s. judgment, each Rom 12.03
but let us keep awake and be s. 1Th 5.06
let us be s., and put on the breastplate 5.08
and to live s., upright, and godly Tit 2.12
be s., set your hope fully upon the 1Pe 1.13
keep sane and s. for your prayers. 4.07
Be s., be watchful. Your adversary 5.08

SO-CALLED
s. because they were craftsmen. 1Ch 4.14
there may be s. gods in heaven or 1Co 8.05
against every s. god or object of 2Th 2.04

SOCKET
let my arm be broken from its s. Job 31.22

SOCKETS
their pillars ten, and their s. ten; Ex 38.12
and the s. of gold, for the doors of 1Ki 7.50
and the s. of the temple, for the 2Ch 4.22
their eyes shall rot in their s., Zec 14.12

SOCO
Jarmuth, Adullam, S., Azekah, Jos 15.35
hill country, Shamir, Jattir, S., 15.48
and they were gathered at S., 1Sa 17.01
and encamped between S. and Azekah, 17.01
(to him belonged S. and all the 1Ki 4.10
of Gedor, Heber the father of S., 1Ch 4.18
Bethzur, S., Adullam, 2Ch 11.07
S. with its villages, Timnah with 28.18

SODI
of Zebulun, Gaddiel the son of S.; Num 13.10

SODOM
Gaza, and in the direction of S., Gen 10.19
the LORD destroyed S. and Gomorrah. 13.10
and moved his tent as far as S. 13.12
Now the men of S. were wicked, great 13.13
made war with Bera king of S., 14.02
Then the king of S., the king of 14.08
as the kings of S. and Gomorrah 14.10
all the goods of S. and Gomorrah, 14.11
who dwelt in S., and his goods, and 14.12
the king of S. went out to meet him 14.17
And the king of S. said to Abram, 14.21
But Abram said to the king of S., 14.22
there, and they looked toward S.; 18.16
outcry against S. and Gomorrah is 18.20
from there, and went toward S.; 18.22
"If I find at S. fifty righteous in 18.26
angels came to S. in the evening; 19.01
Lot was sitting in the gate of S. 19.01
the men of S., both young and old, 19.04
LORD rained on S. and Gomorrah 19.24
down toward S. and Gomorrah and 19.28
like that of S. and Gomorrah, Deu 29.23
vine comes from the vine of S., 32.32
we should have been like S., Is 1.09
word of the LORD, you rulers of S.! 1.10
they proclaim their sin like S., 3.09
will be like S. and Gomorrah when 13.19
of them have become like S. to me, Jer 23.14
As when S. and Gomorrah and their 49.18
God overthrew S. and Gomorrah and 50.40
greater than the punishment of S., Lam 4.06
of you, is S. with her daughters. Eze 16.46
your sister S. and her daughters 16.48
was the guilt of your sister S.: 16.49
the fortunes of S. and her daughters, 16.53
S. and her daughters shall return 16.55
Was not your sister S. a byword in 16.56
when God overthrew S. and Gomorrah, Amo 4.11
Israel, "Moab shall become like S., Zep 2.09
for the land of S. and Gomorrah Mt 10.15
done in you had been done in S., 11.23
for the land of S. than for you." 11.24
on that day for S. than for that Lk 10.12
went out from S. fire and brimstone 17.29
have fared like S. and been made Rom 9.29

SODOM (cont.)
the cities of S. and Gomorrah to 2Pe 2.06
just as S. and Gomorrah and the Jud 1.07
allegorically called S. and Egypt, Rev 11.08

SODOMITES
s., kidnapers, liars, perjurers, and 1Ti 1.10

SOFT
Will he speak to you s. words? Job 41.03
A s. answer turns away wrath, but a Pro 15.01
and a s. tongue will break a bone. 25.15
To see a man clothed in s. raiment? Mt 11.08
those who wear s. raiment are in 11.08
A man clothed in s. raiment? Lk 7.25

SOFTENED
out, or bound up, or s. with oil. Is 1.06

SOFTENING
s. it with showers, and blessing its Ps 65.10

SOFTER
his words were s. than oil, yet they Ps 55.21

SOFTLY
and went s. to him and drove the Ju 4.21
Then she came s., and uncovered his Ru 3.07

SOIL
Noah was the first tiller of the s. Gen 9.20
for tilling the s. was Ezri the 1Ch 27.26
fertile lands, for he loved the s. 2Ch 26.10
wash away the s. of the earth; Job 14.19
my feet, how could I s. them? Sol 5.03
for the s. of my people growing up Is 32.13
and their s. made rich with fat. 34.07
pitch, and her s. into brimstone; 34.09
land and planted it in fertile s.; Eze 17.05
it to good s. by abundant waters, 17.08
and I will scrape her s. from her, 26.04
and timber and s. they will cast 26.12
Be confounded, O tillers of the s., Joe 1.11
our land and treads upon our s., Mic 5.05
prophet, I am a tiller of the s.; Zec 13.05
not destroy the fruits of your s.; Mal 3.11
ground, where they had not much s., Mt 13.05
up, since they had no depth of s., 13.05
fell on good s. and brought forth 13.08
As for what was sown on good s., 13.23
ground, where it had not much s., Mk 4.05
up, since it had no depth of s.; 4.05
fell into good s. and brought 4.08
upon the good s. are the ones who 4.20
And some fell into good s. and grew, Lk 8.08
And as for that in the good s., 8.15

SOILED
people who have not s. their garments; Rev 3.04

SOJOURN
Abram went down to Egypt to s. there, Gen 12.10
they said, "This fellow came to s., 19.09
S. in this land, and I will be with 26.03
"We have come to s. in the land; 47.04
stranger shall s. with you and Ex 12.48
the strangers that s. among them, Lev 17.08
strangers that s. among them eats 17.10
the strangers that s. among them, 17.13
of the strangers that s. in Israel, 20.02
strangers who s. with you and 25.45
I am going to s. where I may find Ju 17.09
Judah went to s. in the country of Ru 1.01
even upon the widow with whom I s., 1Ki 17.20
and s. wherever you can; for the 2Ki 8.01
wickedness; evil may not s. with thee. Ps 5.04
O LORD, who shall s. in thy tent? 15.01
that I s. in Meshech, that I dwell 120.05
let the outcasts of Moab s. among you; Is 16.04
the first into Egypt to s. there, 52.04
many days in the land where you s. Jer 35.07
there, no man shall s. in her. 49.18
there, no man shall s. in her." 49.33
and no son of man shall s. in her. 50.40
of the strangers that s. in Israel, Eze 14.07
them out of the land where they s., 20.38

SOJOURNED
Kadesh and Shur; and he s. in Gerar. Gen 20.01
with the land where you have s." 21.23
And Abraham s. many days in the 21.34
'I have s. with Laban, and stayed 32.04
where Abraham and Isaac had s. 35.27
went down into Egypt and s. there, Deu 26.05
who was a Levite; and he s. there. Ju 17.07
household and s. in the land of 2Ki 8.02
Jacob s. in the land of Ham. Ps 105.23
By faith he s. in the land of Heb 11.09

SOJOURNER
"I am a stranger and a s. among you; Gen 23.04
"I have been a s. in a foreign land." Ex 2.22
whether he is a s. or a native of 12.19
No s. or hired servant may eat of 12.45
"I have been a s. in a foreign land"), 18.03
or the s. who is within your gates; 20.10
whether he is a native or a s., Lev 17.15
them for the poor and for the s.: 19.10
A s. of the priest or a hired 22.10
the s. as well as the native, when 24.16
one law for the s. and for the 24.22
servant and the s. who lives with 25.06
stranger and a s. he shall live 25.35
you as a hired servant and as a s. 25.40
"If a stranger or s. with you 25.47
to the stranger or s. with you, 25.47
both for the s. and for the native." Num 9.14
so shall the s. be before the LORD. 15.15
hand, whether he is native or a s., 15.30
stranger and for the s. among them, 35.15
or the s. who is within your gates, Deu 5.14
and loves the s., giving him food 10.18
Love the s. therefore; for you were 10.19
and the s., the fatherless, and the 14.29
the s., the fatherless, and the 16.11
the s., the fatherless, and the 16.14
because you were a s. in his land. 23.07
due to the s. or to the fatherless, 24.17
it shall be for the s., the fatherless, 24.19
it shall be for the s., the fatherless, 24.20
it shall be for the s., the fatherless, 24.21
and the s. who is among you. 26.11
the s., the fatherless, and the 26.12
the s., the fatherless, and the 26.13
perverts the justice due to the s., 27.19
The s. who is among you shall mount 28.43
and the s. who is in your camp, both 29.11
and the s. within your towns, that 31.12
s. as well as homeborn, with their Jos 8.33
"I am the son of a s., an Amalekite." 2Sa 1.13
(the s. has not lodged in the Job 31.32
guest, a s., like all my fathers. Ps 39.12
They slay the widow and the s., 94.06
I am a s. on earth; hide not thy 119.19
the s. suffers extortion in your Eze 22.07
extorted from the s. without redress. 22.29
fatherless, the s., or the poor; Zec 7.10
those who thrust aside the s., Mal 3.05

SOJOURNERS
descendants will be s. in a land Gen 15.13
the land in which they dwelt as s. Ex 6.04
or of the s. in Israel presents Lev 22.18
you are strangers and s. with me. 25.23
for you were s. in the land of Deu 10.19
or one of the s. who are in your 24.14

SOJOURNERS (cont.)

and the s. who lived among them. Jos 8.35
and have been s. there to this day). 2Sa 4.03
of little account, and s. in it, 1Ch 16.19
and s., as all our fathers were; 29.15
and the s. who came out of the land 2Ch 30.25
and the s. who dwelt in Judah, 30.25
of little account, and s. in it, Ps 105.12
The LORD watches over the s., 146.09
you are no longer strangers and s., Eph 2.19

SOJOURNING

the years of my s. are a hundred Gen 47.09
my fathers in the days of their s. 47.09
And if a stranger is s. with you, Num 15.14
and for the stranger s. among them, Jos 20.09
Levite was s. in the remote parts Ju 19.01
Ephraim, and he was s. in Gibeah; 19.16
and Simeon who were s. with them, 2Ch 15.09

SOJOURNINGS

after you, the land of your s., Gen 17.08
land of your s. which God gave to 28.04
land of their s. could not support 36.07
in the land of his father's s., 37.01

SOJOURNS

and of her who s. in her house, Ex 3.22
for the stranger who s. among you." 12.49
or the stranger who s. among you; Lev 16.29
stranger who s. among you eat 17.12
or the stranger who s. among you 18.26
"When a stranger s. with you in 19.33
The stranger who s. with you shall 19.34
And if a stranger s. among you, Num 9.14
for the stranger who s. with you, 15.15
for the stranger who s. with you." 15.16
and the stranger who s. among them, 15.26
for the stranger who s. among them. 15.29
to the stranger who s. among them, 19.10
survivor, in whatever place he s., Ez 1.04

SOLACE

and the s. of my lips would assuage Job 16.05

SOLD

and s. his birthright to Jacob. Gen 25.33
For he has s. us, and he has been 31.15
and s. him to the Ishmaelites for 37.28
Midianites had s. him in Egypt to 37.36
and s. to the Egyptians, for the 41.56
he it was who s. to all the people 42.06
Joseph, whom you s. into Egypt. 45.04
yourselves, because you s. me here; 45.05
all the Egyptians s. their fields, 47.20
then he shall be s. for his theft. Ex 22.01
land shall not be s. in perpetuity, Lev 25.23
and redeem what his brother has s. 25.25
years since he s. it and pay back 25.27
to the man to whom he s. it; 25.27
then what he s. shall remain in the 25.28
house that was s. in a city of 25.33
to their cities may not be s.; 25.34
they shall not be s. as slaves. 25.42
then after he is s. he may be 25.48
year when he s. himself to him 25.50
or if he has s. the field to 27.20
it shall be s. at its valuation. 27.27
field, shall be s. or redeemed; 27.28
is s. to you, he shall serve you six Deu 15.12
unless their Rock had s. them, 32.30
and he s. them into the power of Ju 2.14
and he s. them into the hand of 3.08
And the LORD s. them into the hand 4.02
and he s. them into the hand of the 10.07
and he s. them into the hand of 1Sa 12.09
you have s. yourself to do what is 1Ki 21.20
There was none who s. himself to do 21.25
ass's head was s. for eighty 2Ki 6.25
fine meal shall be s. for a shekel, 7.01
of fine meal was s. for a shekel, 7.16
of barley shall be s. for a shekel, 7.18
and s. themselves to do evil in the 17.17
who have been s. to the nations; Neh 5.08
brethren that they may be s. to us!" 5.08
them on the day when they s. food. 13.15
of wares and s. them on the 13.16
For we are s., I and my people, to Est 7.04
If we had been s. merely as slaves, 7.04
Thou hast s. thy people for a Ps 44.12
Joseph, who was s. as a slave. 105.17
is it to whom I have s. you? Is 50.01
for your iniquities you were s., 50.01
"You were s. for nothing, and you 52.03
who has been s. to you and has Jer 34.14
shall not return to what he has s., Eze 7.13
and have s. a girl for wine, and Joe 3.03
You have s. the people of Judah and 3.06
place to which you have s. them, 3.07
Are not two sparrows s. for a penny? Mt 10.29
went and s. all that he had and 13.46
pay, his lord ordered him to be s., 18.25
out all who s. and bought in the 21.12
the seats of those who s. pigeons. 21.12
might have been s. for a large sum, 26.09
out those who s. and those who Mk 11.15
the seats of those who s. pigeons; 11.15
might have been s. for more than 14.05
five sparrows s. for two pennies? Lk 12.06
they s., they planted, they built, 17.28
began to drive out those who s., 19.45
And he told those who s. the pigeons, Jn 2.16
ointment not s. for three hundred 12.05
and they s. their possessions and Ac 2.45
possessors of lands or houses s. them, 4.34
the proceeds of what was s. 4.34
s. a field which belonged to him, 4.37
wife Sapphira s. a piece of property, 5.01
And after it was s., was it not at 5.04
me whether you s. the land for so 5.08
of Joseph, s. him into Egypt; 7.09
but I am carnal, s. under sin. Rom 7.14
Eat whatever is s. in the meat 1Co 10.25
who s. his birthright for a single Heb 12.16

SOLDERING

anvil, saying of the s., "It is good"; Is 41.07

SOLDIER

and behold, a s. turned and brought 1Ki 20.39
the mighty man and the s., the Is 3.02
the king sent a s. of the guard Mk 6.27
made four parts, one for each s. Jn 19.23
and a devout s. from among those Ac 10.07
with the s. that guarded him. 28.16
Who serves as a s. at his own 1Co 9.07
and fellow worker and fellow s., Php 2.25
as a good s. of Christ Jesus. 2Ti 2.03
No s. on service gets entangled in 2.04
sister and Archippus our fellow s., Phm 1.02

SOLDIER'S

now Joab was wearing a s. garment, 2Sa 20.08

SOLDIERS

of Israel thirty thousand foot s. 1Sa 4.10
and twenty thousand foot s.; 2Sa 8.04
of Zobah, twenty thousand foot s., 10.06
they were the s., they were his 1Ki 9.22
thousand foot s. in one day. 20.29
and twenty thousand foot s.; 1Ch 18.04
chariots, and forty thousand foot s., 19.18
they were s., and his officers, 2Ch 8.09
He had s., mighty men of valor, in 17.13
Moreover Uzziah had an army of s., 26.11
for a band of s. and horsemen to Ez 8.22

SOLDIERS (cont.)

hands of the s. who are left in — Jer 38.04
of Judah and all the s. saw them, — 39.04
the Chaldean s. who happened to be — 41.03
s., women, children, and eunuchs, whom — 41.16
Even her hired s. in her midst are — 46.21
and all her s. shall be destroyed — 49.26
and all her s. shall be destroyed — 50.30
with fire, and the s. are in panic. — 51.32
horsemen and a host of many s. — Eze 26.07
like s. they scale the wall. — Joe 2.07
his s. are clothed in scarlet. — Nah 2.03
under authority, with s. under me; — Mt 8.09
Then the s. of the governor took — 27.27
to them, "You have a guard of s.; — 27.65
they gave a sum of money to the s. — 28.12
And the s. led him away inside the — Mk 15.16
S. also asked him, "And we, what — Lk 3.14
with s. under me: and I say to one, — 7.08
And Herod with his s. treated him — 23.11
The s. also mocked him, coming up — 23.36
a band of s. and some officers — Jn 18.03
So the band of s. and their captain — 18.12
And the s. plaited a crown of — 19.02
When the s. had crucified Jesus — 19.23
So the s. did this; but standing — 19.25
So the s. came and broke the legs — 19.32
But one of the s. pierced his side — 19.34
to four squads of s. to guard him, — Ac 12.04
Peter was sleeping between two s., — 12.06
stir among the s. over what had — 12.18
He at once took s. and centurions, — 21.32
they saw the tribune and the s., — 21.32
carried by the s. because of the — 21.35
commanded the s. to go down and — 23.10
two hundred s. with seventy — 23.23
them with the s. and rescued him, — 23.27
So the s., according to their — 23.31
Paul said to the centurion and the s., — 27.31
Then the s. cut away the ropes of — 27.32

SOLDIERS'

The s. plan was to kill the prisoners, — Ac 27.42

SOLE

much as for the s. of the foot to — Deu 2.05
on which the s. of your foot treads — 11.24
from the s. of your foot to the — 28.35
to set the s. of her foot upon the — 28.56
be no rest for the s. of your foot; — 28.65
Every place that the s. of your — Jos 1.03
from the s. of his foot to the — 2Sa 14.25
up with the s. of my foot all the — 2Ki 19.24
sores from the s. of his foot to — Job 2.07
From the s. of the foot even to the — Is 1.06
up with the s. of my foot all the — 37.25
were like the s. of a calf's foot; — Eze 1.07

SOLEMN

'Tomorrow is a day of s. rest, — Ex 16.23
seventh day is a sabbath of s. rest, — 31.15
holy sabbath of s. rest to the — 35.02
It is a sabbath of s. rest to you, — Lev 16.31
seventh day is a sabbath of s. rest, — 23.03
you shall observe a day of s. rest, — 23.24
be to you a sabbath of s. rest, — 23.32
it is a s. assembly; you shall do — 23.36
the first day shall be a s. rest, — 23.39
the eighth day shall be a s. rest. — 23.39
be a sabbath of s. rest for the — 25.04
be a year of s. rest for the land. — 25.05
day you shall have a s. assembly: — Num 29.35
shall be a s. assembly to the LORD — Deu 16.08
"Sanctify a s. assembly for Baal." — 2Ki 10.20
eighth day they held a s. assembly; — 2Ch 7.09
eighth day there was a s. assembly, — Neh 8.18
Thy s. processions are seen, O God, — Ps 68.24
endure iniquity and s. assembly. — Is 1.13
they have sworn s. oaths; but he — Eze 21.23
Sanctify a fast, call a s. assembly. — Joe 1.14
sanctify a fast; call a s. assembly; — 2.15
no delight in your s. assemblies. — Amo 5.21

SOLEMNLY

"The man s. warned us, saying, 'You — Gen 43.03
for Joseph had s. sworn the people — Ex 13.19
I s. warn you this day that you — Deu 8.19
you shall s. warn them, and show — 1Sa 8.09
and s. admonish you, saying, 'Know for — 1Ki 2.42
For I s. warned your fathers when I — Jer 11.07
things, as we s. forewarned you. — 1Th 4.06

SOLES

And when the s. of the feet of the — Jos 3.13
and the s. of the priests' feet — 4.18
put them under the s. of his feet. — 1Ki 5.03
settest a bound to the s. of my feet. — Job 13.27
and the s. of their feet were like — Eze 1.07
and the place of the s. of my feet, — 43.07
be ashes under the s. of your feet, — Mal 4.03

SOLICITED

none s. you to play the harlot; and — Eze 16.34

SOLID

I fed you with milk, not s. food; — 1Co 3.02
word. You need milk, not s. food; — Heb 5.12
But s. food is for the mature, for — 5.14

SOLITARY

iniquities upon him to a s. land; — Lev 16.22
For the fortified city is s., a — Is 27.10

SOLOMON

Shammua, Shobab, Nathan, S., — 2Sa 5.14
a son, and he called his name S. — 12.24
the mighty men or S. his brother. — 1Ki 1.10
said to Bathsheba the mother of S., — 1.11
life and the life of your son S. — 1.12
"S. your son shall reign after me, — 1.13
'S. your son shall reign after me, — 1.17
but S. your servant he has not — 1.19
I and my son S. will be counted — 1.21
of Jehoiada, and your servant S., — 1.26
'S. your son shall reign after me, — 1.30
and cause S. my son to ride on my — 1.33
and say, 'Long live King S.!' — 1.34
king, even so may he be with S., — 1.37
down and caused S. to ride on King — 1.38
oil from the tent, and anointed S. — 1.39
the people said, "Long live King S.!" — 1.39
lord King David has made S. king; — 1.43
S. sits upon the royal throne. — 1.46
the name of S. more famous than — 1.47
And Adonijah feared S.; and he — 1.50
And it was told S., "Behold, — 1.51
"Behold, Adonijah fears King S.; — 1.51
'Let King S. swear to me first that — 1.51
And S. said, "If he prove to be a — 1.52
So King S. sent, and they brought — 1.53
came and did obeisance to King S.; — 1.53
and S. said to him, "Go to your — 1.53
he charged S. his son, saying, — 2.01
So S. sat upon the throne of David — 2.12
came to Bathsheba the mother of S. — 2.13
And he said, "Pray ask King S.— — 2.17
So Bathsheba went to King S., to — 2.19
King S. answered his mother, "And — 2.22
Then King S. swore by the LORD, — 2.23
So King S. sent Benaiah the son of — 2.25
So S. expelled Abiathar from being — 2.27
And when it was told King S., "Joab — 2.29
S. sent Benaiah the son of Jehoiada, — 2.29
And when S. was told that Shimei — 2.41
But King S. shall be blessed, and — 2.45
was established in the hand of S. — 2.46

SOLOMON (cont.)
S. made a marriage alliance with 1Ki 3.01
S. loved the LORD, walking in the 3.03
S. used to offer a thousand burnt 3.04
appeared to S. in a dream by night 3.05
And S. said, "Thou hast shown great 3.06
the Lord that S. had asked this. 3.10
And S. awoke, and behold, it was a 3.15
King S. was king over all Israel, 4.01
S. had twelve officers over all 4.07
the daughter of S. as his wife); 4.11
the daughter of S. as his wife); 4.15
S. ruled over all the kingdoms from 4.21
and served S. all the days of his 4.21
his fig tree, all the days of S. 4.25
S. also had forty thousand stalls 4.26
supplied provisions for King S., 4.27
And God gave S. wisdom and understanding 4.29
peoples to hear the wisdom of S., 4.34
of Tyre sent his servants to S., 5.01
And S. sent word to Hiram, 5.02
When Hiram heard the words of S., 5.07
And Hiram sent to S., saying, 5.08
So Hiram supplied S. with all the 5.10
while S. gave Hiram twenty thousand 5.11
S. gave this to Hiram year by year. 5.11
And the LORD gave S. wisdom, 5.12
was peace between Hiram and S.; 5.12
King S. raised a levy of forced 5.13
S. also had seventy thousand burden 5.15
which King S. built for the LORD 6.02
Now the word of the LORD came to S., 6.11
So S. built the house, and finished 6.14
And S. overlaid the inside of the 6.21
S. was building his own house 7.01
S. also made a house like this hall 7.08
And King S. sent and brought Hiram 7.13
He came to King S., and did all 7.14
he did for King S. on the house of 7.40
LORD, which Hiram made for King S., 7.45
And S. left all the vessels unweighed, 7.47
So S. made all the vessels that 7.48
work that King S. did on the house 7.51
And S. brought in the things which 7.51
Then S. assembled the elders of 8.01
before King S. in Jerusalem, to 8.01
assembled to King S. at the feast 8.02
And King S. and all the congregation 8.05
Then S. said, "The LORD has set the 8.12
Then S. stood before the altar of 8.22
Now as S. finished offering all 8.54
S. offered as peace offerings to 8.63
So S. held the feast at that time, 8.65
When S. had finished building the 9.01
and all that S. desired to build, 9.01
the LORD appeared to S. a second time, 9.02
in which S. had built the two 9.10
had supplied S. with cedar and 9.11
King S. gave to Hiram twenty cities 9.11
the cities which S. had given him, 9.12
which King S. levied to build the 9.15
so S. rebuilt Gezer) and Bethhoron 9.17
and all the store-cities that S. had, 9.19
and whatever S. desired to build in 9.19
these S. made a forced levy of 9.21
people of Israel S. made no slaves; 9.22
own house which S. had built for 9.24
Three times a year S. used to offer 9.25
King S. built a fleet of ships at 9.26
together with the servants of S.; 9.27
and they brought it to King S. 9.28
of the fame of S. concerning the 10.01
and when she came to S., she told 10.02
And S. answered all her questions; 10.03
had seen all the wisdom of S., 10.04
the queen of Sheba gave to King S. 10.10
And King S. gave to the queen of 10.13
given her by the bounty of King S. 10.13
that came to S. in one year was 10.14
King S. made two hundred large 10.16
as anything in the days of S. 10.21
Thus King S. excelled all the kings 10.23
the presence of S. to hear his 10.24
And S. gathered together chariots 10.26
Now King S. loved many foreign 11.01
S. clung to these in love. 11.02
For when S. was old his wives 11.04
For S. went after Ashtoreth the 11.05
So S. did what was evil in the 11.06
Then S. built a high place for 11.07
And the LORD was angry with S., 11.09
Therefore the LORD said to S., 11.11
raised up an adversary against S., 11.14
of Israel all the days of S., 11.25
a servant of S., whose mother's name 11.26
S. built the Millo, and closed up 11.27
and when S. saw that the young man 11.28
the kingdom from the hand of S., 11.31
S. sought therefore to kill Jeroboam 11.40
was in Egypt until the death of S. 11.40
Now the rest of the acts of S., 11.41
in the book of the acts of S.? 11.41
And the time that S. reigned in 11.42
And S. slept with his fathers, and 11.43
wither he had fled from King S.), 12.02
stood before S. his father while 12.06
kingdom to Rehoboam the son of S. 12.21
"Say to Rehoboam the son of S., 12.23
the son of S. reigned in Judah. 14.21
shields of gold which S. had made; 14.26
said to David and to S. his son, 2Ki 21.07
which S. the king of Israel had 23.13
which S. king of Israel had made, as 24.13
which S. had made for the house of 25.16
and S., four by Bathshua, the 1Ch 3.05
The descendants of S.: Rehoboam, 3.10
the house that S. built in Jerusalem) 6.10
until S. had built the house of the 6.32
Shammua, Shobab, Nathan, S., 14.04
with it S. made the bronze sea 18.08
"S. my son is young and inexperienced, 22.05
Then he called for S. his son, 22.06
David said to S., "My son, I had it 22.07
for his name shall be S., and I will 22.09
of Israel to help S. his son, 22.17
he made S. his son king over Israel 23.01
he has chosen S. my son to sit 28.05
'It is S. your son who shall build 28.06
"And you, S. my son, know the God of 28.09
Then David gave S. his son the plan 28.11
Then David said to S. his son, 28.20
"S. my son, whom alone God has 29.01
Grant to S. my son that with a 29.19
And they made S. the son of David 29.22
Then S. sat on the throne of the 29.23
their allegiance to King S. 29.24
And the LORD gave S. great repute 29.25
and S. his son reigned in his 29.28
S. the son of David established 2Ch 1.01
S. spoke to all Israel, to the 1.02
And S., and all the assembly with 1.03
And S. and the assembly sought the 1.05
And S. went up there to the bronze 1.06
In that night God appeared to S., 1.07
And S. said to God, "Thou hast shown 1.08
God answered S., "Because this was 1.11
So S. came from the high place at 1.13
S. gathered together chariots and 1.14
Now S. purposed to build a temple 2.01
And S. assigned seventy thousand 2.02
And S. sent word to Huram the king 2.03
in a letter which he sent to S., 2.11
Then S. took a census of all the 2.17
Then S. began to build the house of 3.01

SOLOMON (cont.)
he did for King S. on the house of 2Ch 4.11
bronze for King S. for the house 4.16
S. made all these things in great 4.18
So S. made all the things that were 4.19
the work that S. did for the house 5.01
And S. brought in the things which 5.01
Then S. assembled the elders of 5.02
And King S. and all the congregation 5.06
Then S. said, "The LORD has said 6.01
Then S. stood before the altar of 6.12
S. had made a bronze platform five 6.13
When S. had ended his prayer, fire 7.01
King S. offered as a sacrifice 7.05
And S. consecrated the middle of 7.07
bronze altar S. had made could not 7.07
At that time S. held the feast for 7.08
to David and to S. and to Israel 7.10
Thus S. finished the house of the 7.11
all that S. had planned to do in 7.11
appeared to S. in the night and 7.12
in which S. had built the house of 8.01
S. rebuilt the cities which Huram 8.02
And S. went to Hamathzobah, and took 8.03
all the store-cities that S. had, 8.06
and whatever S. desired to build in 8.06
these S. made a forced levy and so 8.08
of Israel S. made no slaves for 8.09
were the chief officers of King S., 8.10
S. brought Pharaoh's daughter up 8.11
Then S. offered up burnt offerings 8.12
all the work of S. from the day 8.16
Then S. went to Eziongeber and 8.17
together with the servants of S., 8.18
of gold and brought it to King S. 8.18
of the fame of S. she came to 9.01
When she came to S., she told him 9.01
And S. answered all her questions; 9.02
hidden from S. which he could not 9.02
of Sheba had seen the wisdom of S., 9.03
the queen of Sheba gave to King S. 9.09
of Huram and the servants of S., 9.10
And King S. gave to the queen of 9.12
that came to S. in one year was 9.13
land brought gold and silver to S. 9.14
King S. made two hundred large 9.15
as anything in the days of S. 9.20
Thus King S. excelled all the kings 9.22
the presence of S. to hear his 9.23
and S. had four thousand stalls for 9.25
imported for S. from Egypt and 9.28
Now the rest of the acts of S., 9.29
S. reigned in Jerusalem over all 9.30
And S. slept with his fathers, and 9.31
whither he had fled from King S.), 10.02
stood before S. his father while 10.06
the son of S. king of Judah, 11.03
made Rehoboam the son of S. secure, 11.17
years in the way of David and S. 11.17
shields of gold which S. had made; 12.09
a servant of S. the son of David, 13.06
and defied Rehoboam the son of S., 13.07
the time of S. the son of David 30.26
said to David and to S. his son, 33.07
the house which S. the son of 35.03
and the directions of S. his son. 35.04
command of David and his son S. Neh 12.45
Did not S. king of Israel sin on 13.26
The proverbs of S., son of David, Pro 1.01
are proverbs of S. which the men 25.01
of Kedar, like the curtains of S. Sol 1.05
Behold, it is the litter of S.! 3.07
King S. made himself a palanquin 3.09
of Zion, and behold King S., 3.11
S. had a vineyard at Baalhamon; 8.11
you, O S., may have the thousand, and 8.12
which S. the king had made for the Jer 52.20
the father of S. by the wife of Mt 1.06
and S. the father of Rehoboam, and 1.07
even S. in all his glory was not 6.29
the earth to hear the wisdom of S., 12.42
something greater than S. is here. 12.42
the earth to hear the wisdom of S., Lk 11.31
something greater than S. is here. 11.31
even S. in all his glory was not 12.27
the temple, in the portico of S. Jn 10.23
But it was S. who built a house for Ac 7.47

SOLOMON'S
S. provision for one day was thirty 1Ki 4.22
for all who came to King S. table, 4.27
so that S. wisdom surpassed the 4.30
besides S. three thousand three 5.16
So S. builders and Hiram's builders 5.18
fourth year of S. reign over 6.01
as dowry to his daughter, S. wife; 9.16
officers who were over S. work: 9.23
All King S. drinking vessels were 10.21
And S. import of horses was from 10.28
And S. import of horses was from 2Ch 1.16
These are S. measurements for 3.03
All King S. drinking vessels were 9.20
The sons of S. servants: the sons of Ez 2.55
and the sons of S. servants were 2.58
The sons of S. servants: the sons of Neh 7.57
and the sons of S. servants were 7.60
and the descendants of S. servants. 11.03
The Song of Songs, which is S. Sol 1.01
the portico called S., astounded. Ac 3.11
were all together in S. Portico. 5.12

SOLVE
I will s. my riddle to the music of Ps 49.04
and s. problems were found in this Dan 5.12
interpretations and s. problems. 5.16

SOME
she also gave s. to her husband, Gen 3.06
s. fell into them, and the rest fled 14.10
"Let me eat s. of that red pottage, 25.30
pray, s. of your son's mandrakes." 30.14
leave with you s. of the men who 33.15
they were still s. distance from 35.16
S. time after this, the butler of 40.01
continued for s. time in custody. 40.04
take s. of the choice fruits of the 43.11
there was still s. distance to go 48.07
you shall take s. water from the Ex 4.09
send, I pray, s. other person." 4.13
you have s. evil purpose in mind. 10.10
Then they shall take s. of the blood, 12.07
they gathered, s. more, s. less. 16.17
s. left part of it till the morning, 16.20
On the seventh day s. of the people 16.27
taking with you s. of the elders 17.05
and you shall beat s. of it very 30.36
shall take s. of the blood of the Lev 4.05
shall put s. of the blood on the 4.07
shall bring s. of the blood of the 4.16
And he shall put s. of the blood on 4.18
shall take s. of the blood of the 4.25
shall take s. of its blood with 4.30
shall take s. of the blood of the 4.34
shall sprinkle s. of the blood of 5.09
And he sprinkled s. of it on the 8.11
And he poured s. of the anointing 8.12
and took s. of its blood and put it 8.23
and Moses put s. of the blood on 8.24
Then Moses took s. of the anointing 8.30
shall take s. of the blood of the 14.14
shall take s. of the log of oil, 14.15
and sprinkle s. oil with his finger 14.16
And s. of the oil that remains in 14.17
shall take s. of the blood of the 14.25
shall pour s. of the oil into the 14.26

SOME (cont.)

right finer s. of the oil that is Lev 14.27
shall put s. of the oil that is in 14.28
to me to be s. sort of disease in 14.35
and he shall take s. of the blood 16.14
and shall take s. of the blood of 16.18
shall sprinkle s. of the blood 16.19
and take s. of the dust that is on Num 5.17
and s. man other than your husband 5.20
and consumed s. outlying parts of 11.01
and I will take s. of the spirit 11.17
and took s. of the spirit that was 11.25
and bring s. of the fruit of the 13.20
brought also s. pomegranates and 13.23
shall take s. of her blood with 19.04
and sprinkle s. of her blood toward 19.04
they shall take s. ashes of the 19.17
and took s. of them captive. 21.01
invest him with s. of your authority, 27.20
in their hands s. of the fruit of Deu 1.25
s. of the gods of the peoples that 13.07
he has found s. indecency in her, 24.01
you shall take s. of the first of 26.02
took s. of the devoted things; Jos 7.01
they have taken s. of the devoted 7.11
s. on this side, and s. on that side; 8.22
and s. of you shall always be 9.23
Gath, and in Ashdod, did s. remain. 11.22
and gave s. to them, and they ate. Ju 14.09
and was there s. four months. 19.02
to smite and kill s. of the people, 20.31
and eat s. bread, and dip your Ru 2.14
satisfied, and she had s. left over. 2.14
And also pull out s. from the 2.16
And he slew s. of the men of 1Sa 6.19
s. twenty years, and all the house 7.02
and s. to plow his ground and to 8.12
But s. worthless fellows said, "How 10.27
and bring s. token from them." 17.18
and s. bade me kill you, but I 24.10
"For s. time past you have been 2Sa 3.17
there not still s. one of the 9.03
he chose s. of the picked men of 10.09
and s. of the servants of David 11.17
s. of the king's servants are dead; 11.24
dead? He may do himself s. harm." 12.18
of the pits, or in s. other place. 17.09
And when s. of the people fall at 17.09
upon him in s. place where he is 17.12
"O that s. one would give me water 23.15
s. cakes, and a jar of honey, and go 1Ki 14.03
and not lose s. of the animals." 18.05
and stood at s. distance from them, 2Ki 2.07
upon s. mountain or into s. valley." 2.16
s. small boys came out of the city 2.23
who urged him to eat s. food. 4.08
'They shall eat and have s. left.'" 4.43
and had s. left, according to the 4.44
commanded you to do s. great thing, 5.13
when Naaman saw s. one running 5.21
"Let s. men take five of the 7.13
and s. of her blood spattered on 9.33
them, which killed s. of them. 17.25
And s. of your own sons, who are 20.18
the guard left s. of the poorest 25.12
And s. of them, five hundred men of 1Ch 4.42
And s. of the families of the sons 6.66
And s. of the people of Judah, 9.03
S. of them had charge of the 9.28
Also s. of their kinsmen of the 9.32
"O that s. one would give me water 11.17
And s. of the men of Benjamin and 12.16
S. of the men of Manasseh deserted 12.19
he chose s. of the picked men of 19.10
and distributed s. of his sons 2Ch 11.23
I will grant them s. deliverance, 12.07
cruelties upon s. of the people at 16.10
S. of the Philistines brought 17.11
After s. years he went down to Ahab 18.02
Nevertheless s. good is found in 19.03
and with them s. of the Meunites, 20.01
S. men came and told Jehoshaphat, "A 20.02
and also s. of the princes of Judah 21.04
s. of his own sons struck him down 32.21
and s. of the Levites were scribes, 34.13
S. of the heads of families, when Ez 2.68
and s. of the people lived in 2.70
s. of the people of Israel, and 7.07
and s. of the priests and Levites, 7.07
For they have taken s. of their 9.02
to grant us s. reviving to set up 9.09
greatly that s. one had come to Neh 2.10
and s. of our daughters have 5.05
Now s. of the heads of fathers' 7.70
And s. of the heads of fathers' 7.71
s. of the people, the temple servants, 7.73
s. of the people of Judah lived in 11.25
And after s. time I asked leave of 13.06
And I set s. of my servants over 13.19
them and beat s. of them and 13.25
say, "O that we might see s. good! Ps 4.06
S. boast of chariots, and s. of horses; 20.07
S. wandered in desert wastes, 107.04
S. sat in darkness and in gloom, 107.10
S. were sick through their sinful 107.17
S. went down to the sea in ships, 107.23
they have made s. one stumble. Pro 4.16
or s. winged creature tell the Ecc 10.20
And s. of your own sons, who are Is 39.07
And s. of them also I will take for 66.21
and take s. of the elders of the Jer 19.01
the people and s. of the senior 19.01
land of Judah s. of the poor 39.10
not return, except s. fugitives. 44.14
away captive s. of the poorest of 52.15
the guard left s. of the poorest 52.16
And of these again you shall take s., Eze 5.04
"Yet I will leave s. of you alive. 6.08
the nations s. who escape the 6.08
and took s. of it, and put it into 10.07
You took s. of your garments, and 16.16
his flock when s. of his sheep 34.12
And you shall take s. of its blood, 43.20
shall take s. of the blood of the 45.19
with s. of the vessels of the house Dan 1.02
to bring s. of the people of Israel, 1.03
but s. of the firmness of iron 2.41
and s. of the host of the stars it 8.10
overcome and lay sick for s. days; 8.27
After s. years they shall make an 11.06
and for s. years he shall refrain 11.08
and after s. years he shall come on 11.13
captivity and plunder, for s. days. 11.33
and s. of those who are wise shall 11.35
shall awake, s. to everlasting life, 12.02
and s. to shame and everlasting 12.02
And I raised up s. of your sons for Amo 2.11
and s. of your men for 2.11
"I overthrew s. of you, as when God 4.11
was feeding at s. distance from Mt 8.30
And behold, s. of the scribes said 9.03
Then s. of the scribes and Pharisees 12.38
S. one told him, "Your mother and * 12.47
s. seeds fell along the path, and 13.04
s. a hundredfold, s. sixty, s. thirty. 13.08
"S. say John the Baptist, others say 16.14
there are s. standing here who will 16.28
s. of whom you will kill and 23.34
and s. you will scourge in your 23.34
'Give us s. of your oil, for our 25.08
and struck him; and s. slapped him, 26.67
had been set by s. of the sons of 27.09
And s. of the bystanders hearing it 27.47
s. of the guard went into the city 28.11

SOME (cont.)

they worshipped him; but s. doubted. Mt 28.17
returned to Capernaum after s. days, Mk 2.01
Now s. of the scribes were sitting 2.06
s. seed fell along the path, and the 4.04
from the ruler's house s. who said, 5.35
S. said, "John the baptizer has been 6.14
with s. of the scribes, who had come 7.01
they saw that s. of his disciples 7.02
and s. of them have come a long way 8.03
And s. people brought to him a 8.22
there are s. standing here who will 9.01
get from them s. of the fruit of 12.02
others, s. they beat and s. they killed. 12.05
sent to him s. of the Pharisees 12.13
Pharisees and s. of the Herodians, 12.13
But there were s. who said to 14.04
And s. stood up and bore false 14.57
And s. began to spit on him, and to 14.65
And s. of the bystanders hearing it 15.35
things closely for s. time past, Lk 1.03
plucked and ate s. ears of grain, 6.01
But s. of the Pharisees said, "Why 6.02
and also s. women who had been 8.02
s. fell along the path, and was 8.05
And s. fell on the rock; and as it 8.06
And s. fell among thorns; and the 8.07
And s. fell into good soil and grew, 8.08
But Jesus said, "S. one touched me; 8.46
it was said by s. that John had 9.07
by s. that Elijah had appeared, and 9.08
there are s. standing here who will 9.27
But s. of them said, "He casts out 11.15
s. of whom they will kill and 11.49
There were s. present at that very 13.01
And s. one said to him, "Lord, will 13.23
And behold, s. are last who will be 13.30
and s. are first who will be last." 13.30
At that very hour s. Pharisees came, 13.31
but if s. one goes to them from the 16.30
be convinced if s. one should rise 16.31
this parable to s. who trusted in 18.09
And s. of the Pharisees in the 19.39
should give him s. of the fruit of 20.10
There came to him s. Sadducees, 20.27
And s. of the scribes answered, 20.39
And as s. spoke of the temple, how 21.05
and s. of you they will put to 21.16
And a little later s. one else saw 22.58
hoping to see s. sign done by him. 23.08
So he questioned him at s. length; 23.09
Moreover, s. women of our company 24.22
S. of those who were with us went 24.24
"Now draw s. out, and take it to the Jn 2.08
But there are s. of you that do not 6.64
While s. said, "He is a good man," 7.12
S. of the people of Jerusalem 7.25
s. of the people said, "This is 7.40
But s. said, "Is the Christ to come 7.41
S. of them wanted to arrest him, but 7.44
S. said, "It is he"; others said, "No, 9.09
S. of the Pharisees said, "This man 9.16
S. of the Pharisees near him heard 9.40
But s. of them said, "Could not he 11.37
but s. of them went to the Pharisees 11.46
at the feast were s. Greeks. 12.20
S. thought that, because Judas had 13.29
S. of his disciples said to one 16.17
of soldiers and s. officers from 18.03
of the boat, and you will find s." 21.06
"Bring s. of the fish that you have 21.10
he kept back s. of the proceeds, Ac 5.02
shadow might fall on s. of them. 5.15
And s. one came and told them, "The 5.25
and drew away s. of the people 5.37
Then s. of those who belonged to 6.09
"How can I, unless s. one guides me?" 8.31
about himself or about s. one else?" 8.34
the road they came to s. water, 8.36
and s. of the brethren from Joppa 10.23
asked him to remain for s. days. 10.48
But there were s. of them, men of 11.20
hands upon s. who belonged to the 12.01
divided; s. sided with the Jews, 14.04
and s. with the apostles. 14.04
But s. men came down from Judea and 15.01
Barnabas and s. of the others were 15.02
But s. believers who belonged to 15.05
have heard that s. persons from us 15.24
And after they had spent s. time, 15.33
And after s. days Paul said to 15.36
We remained in this city s. days; 16.12
And s. of them were persuaded, and 17.04
and taking s. wicked fellows of the 17.05
Jason and s. of the brethren 17.06
S. also of the Epicurean and Stoic 17.18
And s. said, "What would this 17.18
For you bring s. strange things to 17.20
as even s. of your poets have said, 17.28
resurrection of the dead, s. mocked; 17.32
But s. men joined him and believed, 17.34
After spending s. time there he 18.23
There he found s. disciples. 19.01
but when s. were stubborn and 19.09
Then s. of the itinerant Jewish 19.13
s. of the Asiarchs also, who were 19.31
Now s. cried one thing, s. another; for 19.32
S. of the crowd prompted Alexander, 19.33
While we were staying for s. days, 21.10
And s. of the disciples from 21.16
S. in the crowd shouted one thing, 21.34
s. another; and as he could not 21.34
and s. of the scribes of the 23.09
came down with s. elders and a 24.01
Now after s. years I came to bring 24.17
or tumult. But s. Jews from Asia— 24.18
custody but should have s. liberty, 24.23
After s. days Felix came with his 24.24
Now when s. days had passed, Agrippa 25.13
Paul and s. other prisoners to a 27.01
But we shall have to run on s. island." 27.26
urged them all to take s. food, 27.33
Therefore I urge you to take s. food; 27.34
encouraged and ate s. food themselves 27.36
And s. were convinced by what he 28.24
impart to you s. spiritual gift to Rom 1.11
that I may reap s. harvest among 1.13
What if s. were unfaithful? Does 3.03
—as s. people slanderously charge 3.08
jealous, and thus save s. of them. 11.14
But if s. of the branches were 11.17
But on s. points I have written to 15.15
pleased to make s. contribution 15.26
S. are arrogant, as though I were 1Co 4.18
And such were s. of you. But you 6.11
But s., through being hitherto 8.07
without getting s. of the milk? 9.07
that I might by all means save s. 9.22
be idolaters as s. of them were; 10.07
in immorality as s. of them did, 10.08
as s. of them did and were destroyed 10.09
as s. of them did and were destroyed 10.10
(But if s. one says to you, "This 10.28
are weak and ill, and s. have died. 11.30
unless s. one interprets, so that 14.05
I bring you s. revelation or 14.06
though s. have fallen asleep. 15.06
how can s. of you say that there is 15.12
For s. have no knowledge of God. 15.34
But s. one will ask, "How are the 15.35
of wheat or of s. other grain. 15.37
I hope to spend s. time with you, 16.07
but in s. measure—not to put it 2Co 2.05
as s. do, letters of recommendation 3.01

SOME (cont.)
expressed to him s. pride in you, 2Co 7.14
lest if s. Macedonians come with me 9.04
showing against s. who suspect us 10.02
ourselves with s. of those who 10.12
For if s. one comes and preaches 11.04
but there are s. who trouble you Gal 1.07
that s. should be apostles, s. prophets, Eph 4.11
s. evangelists, s. pastors and teachers, 4.11
S. indeed preach Christ from envy Php 1.15
For we hear that s. of you are 2Th 3.11
in later times s. will depart from 1Ti 4.01
bodily training is of s. value, 4.08
family and make s. return to their 5.04
For s. have already strayed after 5.15
The sins of s. men are conspicuous, 5.24
craving that s. have wandered away 6.10
professing it s. have missed the 6.21
They are upsetting the faith of s. 2Ti 2.18
and s. for noble use, s. for ignoble. 2.20
I want s. benefit from you in the Phm 1.20
(For every house is built by s. one, Heb 3.04
it remains for s. to enter it, 4.06
you need s. one to teach you again 5.12
together, as is the habit of s., 10.25
S. were tortured, refusing to accept 11.35
for thereby s. have entertained 13.02
But s. one will say, "You have faith Jas 2.18
the truth and s. one brings him 5.19
so that s., though they do not obey 1Pe 3.01
lion, seeking s. one to devour. 5.08
his promise as s. count slowness, 2Pe 3.09
There are s. things in them hard to 3.16
greatly to find s. of your children 2Jn 1.04
rejoiced when s. of the brethren 3Jn 1.03
gained by s. who long ago were Jud 1.04
And convince s., who doubt; 1.22
save s., by snatching them out of 1.23
on s. have mercy with fear, hating 1.23
about to throw s. of you into Rev 2.10
you have s. there who hold the 2.14
So you also have s. who hold the 2.15
I will give s. of the hidden manna, 2.17
learned what s. call the deep 2.24

SOMEBODY
arose, giving himself out to be s., Ac 5.36
saying that he himself was s. great. 8.09

SOMEHOW
the chance that s. they could Ac 27.12
asking that s. by God's will I may Rom 1.10
of yours s. become a stumbling 1Co 8.09
lest s. I should be running or had Gal 2.02
for fear that s. the tempter had 1Th 3.05

SOMETHING
But if the LORD creates s. new, Num 16.30
"Out of the eater came s. to eat. Ju 14.14
Out of the strong came s. sweet." 14.14
"S. has befallen him; he is not 1Sa 20.26
Then he said, "I have s. to say to you." 1Ki 2.14
there is found s. pleasing to the 14.13
run after him, and get s. from him." 2Ki 5.20
for I have yet s. to say on God's Job 36.02
may they leave s. over to their Ps 17.14
there was s. that looked like Eze 1.13
above them s. like a sapphire, in 10.01
the holy place was s. resembling 41.21
Are you paying me back for s.? If Joe 3.04
"Peace" when they have s. to eat, Mic 3.05
your brother has s. against you, Mt 5.23
I tell you, s. greater than the 12.06
s. greater than Jonah is here. 12.41
s. greater than Solomon is here. 12.42
go away; you give them s. to eat." 14.16
before him she asked him for s. 20.20
told them to give her s. to eat. Mk 5.43
about and buy themselves s. to eat." 6.36
them, "You give them s. to eat." 6.37
"Simon, I have s. to say to you." Lk 7.40
directed that s. should be given 8.55
to them, "You give them s. to eat." 9.13
s. greater than Solomon is here. 11.31
s. greater than Jonah is here. 11.32
him, to catch at s. he might say. 11.54
that he should give s. to the poor. Jn 13.29
expecting to receive s. from them. Ac 3.05
And immediately s. like scales fell 9.18
hungry and desired s. to eat; 10.10
and s. descending, like a great 10.11
s. descending, like a great sheet, 11.05
except telling or hearing s. new. 17.21
the tribune, "May I say s. to you?" 21.37
for he has s. to tell him." 23.17
to you, as he has s. to say to you." 23.18
him, I may have s. to write. 25.26
circumcision s. external and Rom 2.28
he has s. to boast about, but not 4.02
If any one imagines that he knows s., 1Co 8.02
you is to put s. aside and store 16.02
reputed to be s. (what they were Gal 2.06
For if any one thinks he is s., 6.03
priest also to have s. to offer. Heb 8.03
since God had foreseen s. better for us, 11.40
as though s. strange were happening 1Pe 4.12
I have written s. to the church; 3Jn 1.09
and s. like a great mountain, Rev 8.08

SOMETIME
S. after the prophet Hananiah had Jer 28.12

SOMETIMES
S. the cloud was a few days over Num 9.20
And s. the cloud remained from 9.21
because s. a man who has toiled Ecc 2.21
s. being publicly exposed to abuse Heb 10.33
and s. being partners with those so 10.33

SOMEWHAT
to inquire s. more closely about him. Ac 23.20

SOMEWHERE
It has been testified s., "What is Heb 2.06
For he has s. spoken of the seventh 4.04

SON
city after the name of his s., Enoch. Gen 4.17
bore a s. and called his name Seth, 4.25
To Seth also a s. was born, and he 4.26
the father of a s. in his own likeness, 5.03
he became the father of a s., 5.28
his youngest s. had done to him, 9.24
Abram his s. and Lot the s. of Haran, 11.31
his s. Abram's wife, and they went 11.31
his wife, and Lot his brother's s., 12.05
the s. of Abram's brother, who dwelt 14.12
your own s. shall be your heir." 15.04
with child, and shall bear a s.; 16.11
And Hagar bore Abram a s.; 16.15
Abram called the name of his s., 16.15
I will give you a s. by her; 17.16
your wife shall bear you a s., 17.19
Ishmael his s. and all the slaves 17.23
And Ismel his s. was thirteen 17.25
Abraham and his s. Ishmael were 17.26
Sarah your wife shall have a s." 18.10
spring, and Sarah shall have a s." 18.14
The first-born bore a s., and 19.37
The younger also bore a s., 19.38
bore Abraham a s. in his old age 21.02
the name of his s. who was born to 21.03
circumcised his s. Isaac when he 21.04
old when his s. Isaac was born to 21.05
have borne him a s. in his old age." 21.07
But Sarah saw the s. of Hagar the 21.09

SON (cont.)

Abraham, playing with her s. Isaac. Gen 21.09
out this slave woman with her s.; 21.10
for the s. of this slave woman 21.10
shall not be heir with my s. Isaac." 21.10
to Abraham on account of his s. 21.11
a nation of the s. of the slave 21.13
"Take your s., your only s. Isaac, whom 22.02
men with him, and his s. Isaac; 22.03
and laid it on Isaac his s.; 22.06
And he said, "Here am I, my s." 22.07
lamb for a burnt offering, my s." 22.08
in order, and bound Isaac his s., 22.09
and took the knife to slay his s. 22.10
have not withheld your s., your only s., 22.12
a burnt offering instead of his s. 22.13
have not withheld your s., your only s., 22.16
for me Ephron the s. of Zohar, 23.08
a wife for my s. from the daughters 24.03
and take a wife for my s. Isaac." 24.04
then take your s. back to the land 24.05
you do not take my s. back there. 24.06
take a wife for my s. from there. 24.07
you must not take my s. back there." 24.08
born to Bethuel the s. of Milcah, 24.15
of Bethuel the s. of Milcah, 24.24
wife bore a s. to my master when 24.36
a wife for my s. from the daughters 24.37
kindred, and take a wife for my s.' 24.38
a wife for my s. from my kindred 24.40
has appointed for my master's s.' 24.44
Nahor's s., whom Milcah bore to him.' 24.47
of my master's kinsman for his s. 24.48
be the wife of your master's s., 24.51
sent them away from his s. Isaac, 25.06
of Ephron the s. of Zohar the 25.09
Abraham God blessed Isaac his s. 25.11
Abraham's s., whom Hagar the Egyptian, 25.12
Abraham's s.: Abraham was the father 25.19
his older s., and said to him, "My s."; 27.01
when Isaac spoke to his s. Esau. 27.05
Rebekah said to her s. Jacob, 27.06
my s., obey my word as I command 27.08
him, "Upon me be your curse, my s.; 27.13
best garments of Esau her older s., 27.15
put them on Jacob her younger s.; 27.15
into the hand of her s. Jacob. 27.17
"Here I am; who are you, my s.?" 27.18
But Isaac said to his s., "How is 27.20
have found it so quickly, my s.?" 27.20
my s., to know whether you are 27.21
you are really my s. Esau or not." 27.21
He said, "Are you really my s. Esau?" 27.24
him, "Come near and kiss me, my s." 27.26
the smell of my s. is as the smell 27.27
"I am your s., your first-born, Esau." 27.32
what then can I do for you, my s.?" 27.37
Esau her older s. were told to 27.42
and called Jacob her younger s., 27.42
Now therefore, my s., obey my voice; 27.43
the s. of Bethuel the Aramean, the 28.05
daughter of Ishmael Abraham's s., 28.09
"Do you know Laban the s. of Nahor?" 29.05
and that he was Rebekah's s.; 29.12
tidings of Jacob his sister's s., 29.13
And Leah conceived and bore a s., 29.32
She conceived again and bore a s., 29.33
he has given me this s. also"; 29.33
Again she conceived and bore a s., 29.34
And she conceived again and bore a s., 29.35
conceived and bore Jacob a s. 30.05
heard my voice and given me a s."; 30.06
again and bore Jacob a second s. 30.07
Leah's maid Zilpah bore Jacob a s. 30.10
maid Zilpah bore Jacob a second s. 30.12
conceived and bore Jacob a fifth s. 30.17
and she bore Jacob a sixth s. 30.19
She conceived and bore a s., 30.23
"May the LORD add to me another s.!" 30.24
Shechem the s. of Hamor the Hivite, 34.02
"The soul of my s. Shechem longs 34.08
pleased Hamor and Hamor's s. Shechem. 34.18
So Hamor and his s. Shechem came to 34.20
hearkened to Hamor and his s. Shechem; 34.24
Hamor and his s. Shechem with the 34.26
for now you will have another s." 35.17
of Anah the s. of Zibeon the 36.02
Eliphaz the s. of Adah the wife of 36.10
Reuel the s. of Basemath the wife 36.10
a concubine of Eliphaz, Esau's s.; 36.12
daughter of Anah the s. of Zibeon, 36.14
Esau's s.: the chiefs Nahath, Zerah, 36.17
Bela the s. of Beor reigned in Edom, 36.32
and Jobab the s. of Zerah of Bozrah 36.33
and Hadad the s. of Bedad, who 36.35
Baalhanan the s. of Achbor reigned 36.38
Baalhanan the s. of Achbor died, and 36.39
he was the s. of his old age; 37.03
and mourned for his s. many days. 37.34
down to Sheol to my s., mourning." 37.35
and she conceived and bore a s., 38.03
Again she conceived and bore a s., 38.04
Yet again she bore a s., and she 38.05
till Shelah my s. grows up"—for he 38.11
I did not give her to my s. Shelah." 38.26
"My s. shall not go down with you, 42.38
his mother's s., and said, "Is this 43.29
God be gracious to you, my s.!" 43.29
to him, 'Thus says your s. Joseph, 45.09
Joseph my s. is still alive; 45.28
the s. of a Canaanitish woman. 46.10
he called his s. Joseph and said to 47.29
"Your s. Joseph has come to you"; 48.02
and said, "I know, my s., I know; 48.19
the prey, my s., you have gone up. 49.09
of Machir the s. of Manasseh were 50.23
if it is a s., you shall kill him; Ex 1.16
"Every s. that is born to the 1.22
The woman conceived and bore a s.; 2.02
daughter, and he became her s.; 2.10
She bore a s., and he called his 2.22
LORD, Israel is my first-born s., 4.22
"Let my s. go that he may serve me"; 4.23
I will slay your first-born s.'" 4.23
the s. of a Canaanite woman; 6.15
Aaron's s., took to wife one of the 6.25
hearing of your s. and of your son's s. 10.02
you shall tell your s. on that day, 13.08
in time to come your s. asks you, 13.14
or your s., or your daughter, your 20.10
If he designates her for his s., 21.09
If it gores a man's s. or daughter, 21.31
and the s. of your bondmaid, and the 23.12
The s. who is priest in his place 29.30
name Bezalel the s. of Uri, s. of Hur, 31.02
the s. of Ahisamach, of the tribe of 31.06
the cost of his s. and of his 32.29
his servant Joshua the s. of Nun, 33.11
by name Bezalel the s. of Uri, s. of Hur, 35.30
and Oholiab the s. of Ahisamach of 35.34
of Ithamar the s. of Aaron the 38.21
Bezalel the s. of Uri, s. of Hur, of 38.22
was Oholiab the s. of Ahisamach, 38.23
whether for a s. or for a daughter, Lev 12.06
his s., his daughter, his brother, 21.02
Now an Israelite woman's s., 24.10
Israelite woman's s. and a man of 24.10
Israelite woman's s. blasphemed the 24.11
Reuben, Elizur the s. of Shedeur; Num 1.05
Shelumiel the s. of Zurishaddai; 1.06
Judah, Nahshon the s. of Amminadab; 1.07
from Issachar, Nethanel the s. of Zuar; 1.08
from Zebulun, Eliab the s. of Helon; 1.09
Elishama the s. of Ammihud, and from 1.10

SON (cont.)
Manasseh, Gamaliel the s. of Pedahzur; Num 1.10
Benjamin, Abidan the s. of Gideoni; 1.11
Dan, Ahiezer the s. of Ammishaddai; 1.12
from Asher, Pagiel the s. of Ochran; 1.13
from Gad, Eliasaph the s. of Deuel; 1.14
from Naphtali, Ahira the s. of Enan. 1.15
being Nahshon the s. of Amminadab, 2.03
being Nethanel the s. of Zuar, 2.05
being Eliab the s. of Helon, 2.07
being Elizur the s. of Shedeur, 2.10
Shelumiel the s. of Zurishaddai, 2.12
being Eliasaph the s. of Reuel, 2.14
being Elishama the s. of Ammihud, 2.18
being Gamaliel the s. of Pedahzur, 2.20
being Abidan the s. of Gideoni, 2.22
Ahiezer the s. of Ammishaddai, 2.25
being Pagiel the s. of Ochran, 2.27
being Ahira the s. of Enan, 2.29
the s. of Lael as head of the 3.24
with Elizaphan the s. of Uzziel as 3.30
And Eleazar the s. of Aaron the 3.32
was Zuriel the s. of Abihail; 3.35
"And Eleazar the s. of Aaron the 4.16
of Ithamar the s. of Aaron the 4.28
of Ithamar the s. of Aaron the 4.33
of Ithamar the s. of Aaron the 7.08
was Nahshon the s. of Amminadab, 7.12
of Nahshon the s. of Amminadab. 7.17
second day Nethanel the s. of Zuar, 7.18
offering of Nethanel the s. of Zuar. 7.23
third day Eliab the s. of Helon, 7.24
offering of Eliab the s. of Helon. 7.29
day Elizur the s. of Shedeur, 7.30
of Elizur the s. of Shedeur. 7.35
Shelumiel the s. of Zurishaddai, 7.36
of Shelumiel the s. of Zurishaddai. 7.41
sixth day Eliasaph the s. of Deuel, 7.42
of Eliasaph the s. of Deuel. 7.47
day Elishama the s. of Ammihud, 7.48
of Elishama the s. of Ammihud. 7.53
day Gamaliel the s. of Pedahzur, 7.54
of Gamaliel the s. of Pedahzur. 7.59
ninth day Abidan the s. of Gideoni, 7.60
of Abidan the s. of Gideoni. 7.65
day Ahiezer the s. of Ammishaddai, 7.66
of Ahiezer the s. of Ammishaddai. 7.71
day Pagiel the s. of Ochran, 7.72
offering of Pagiel the s. of Ochran. 7.77
twelfth day Ahira the s. of Enan, 7.78
offering of Ahira the s. of Enan. 7.83
was Nahshon the s. of Amminadab. 10.14
was Nethanel the s. of Zuar. 10.15
Zebulun was Eliab the s. of Helon. 10.16
host was Elizur the s. of Shedeur. 10.18
Shelumiel the s. of Zurishaddai. 10.19
Gad was Eliasaph the s. of Deuel. 10.20
was Elishama the s. of Ammihud. 10.22
was Gamaliel the s. of Pedahzur. 10.23
was Abidan the s. of Gideoni. 10.24
was Ahiezer the s. of Ammishaddai. 10.25
Asher was Pagiel the s. of Ochran. 10.26
Naphtali was Ahira the s. of Enan. 10.27
to Hobab the s. of Reuel the 10.29
And Joshua the s. of Nun, the 11.28
Reuben, Shammua the s. of Zaccur; 13.04
of Simeon, Shaphat the s. of Hori; 13.05
Judah, Caleb the s. of Jephunneh; 13.06
of Issachar, Igal the s. of Joseph; 13.07
of Ephraim, Hoshea the s. of Nun; 13.08
of Benjamin, Palti the s. of Raphu; 13.09
of Zebulun, Gaddiel the s. of Sodi; 13.10
of Manasseh, Gaddi the s. of Susi; 13.11
of Dan, Ammiel the s. of Gemalli; 13.12
of Asher, Sethur the s. of Michael; 13.13
Naphtali, Nahbi the s. of Vophsi; 13.14
of Gad, Geuel the s. of Machi. 13.15
called Hoshea the s. of Nun Joshua. 13.16
And Joshua the s. of Nun and 14.06
Caleb the s. of Jephunneh, who were 14.06
Caleb the s. of Jephunneh and 14.30
Jephunneh and Joshua the s. of Nun. 14.30
But Joshua the s. of Nun and 14.38
and Caleb the s. of Jephunneh 14.38
Now Korah the s. of Izhar, s. of Kohath, 16.01
s. of Levi, and Dathan and Abiram 16.01
and On the s. of Peleth, sons of 16.01
"Tell Eleazar the s. of Aaron the 16.37
Take Aaron and Eleazar his s., 20.25
and put them upon Eleazar his s.; 20.26
and put them upon Eleazar his s.; 20.28
And Balak the s. of Zippor saw all 22.02
So Balak the s. of Zippor, who was 22.04
to Balaam the s. of Beor at Pethor, 22.05
"Balak the s. of Zippor, king of 22.10
"Thus says Balak the s. of Zippor: 22.16
hearken to me, O s. of Zippor: 23.18
or a s. of man, that he should 23.19
oracle of Balaam the s. of Beor, 24.03
oracle of Balaam the s. of Beor, 24.15
When Phinehas the s. of Eleazar, 25.07
s. of Aaron the priest, saw it, he 25.07
"Phinehas the s. of Eleazar, s. of Aaron 25.11
was Zimri the s. of Salu, head of a 25.14
and to Eleazar the s. of Aaron, 26.01
Now Zelophehad the s. of Hepher had 26.33
Caleb the s. of Jephunneh and 26.65
Jephunneh and Joshua the s. of Nun. 26.65
of Zelophehad the s. of Hepher, 27.01
s. of Gilead, s. of Machir, s. of Manasseh, 27.01
families of Manasseh the s. of Joseph. 27.01
his family, because he had no s.? 27.04
and has no s., then you shall cause 27.08
Moses, "Take Joshua the s. of Nun, 27.18
Phinehas the s. of Eleazar the 31.06
slew Balaam the s. of Beor with 31.08
Caleb the s. of Jephunneh the 32.12
Kenizzite and Joshua the s. of Nun, 32.12
and to Joshua the s. of Nun, 32.28
of Manasseh the s. of Joseph, 32.33
of Machir the s. of Manasseh went 32.39
to Machir the s. of Manasseh, 32.40
And Jair the s. of Manasseh went 32.41
priest and Joshua the s. of Nun. 34.17
Judah, Caleb the s. of Jephunneh. 34.19
Simeon, Shemuel the s. of Ammihud. 34.20
Benjamin, Elidad the s. of Chislon. 34.21
a leader, Bukki the s. of Jogli. 34.22
a leader, Hanniel the s. of Ephod. 34.23
leader, Kemuel the s. of Shiphtan. 34.24
Elizaphan the s. of Parnach. 34.25
a leader, Paltiel the s. of Azzan. 34.26
a leader, Ahihud the s. of Shelomi. 34.27
leader, Pedahel the s. of Ammihud. 34.28
sons of Gilead the s. of Machir, 36.01
s. of Manasseh, of the fathers' 36.01
sons of Manasseh the s. of Joseph, 36.12
bore you, as a man bears his s., Deu 1.31
except Caleb the s. of Jephunneh; 1.36
Joshua the s. of Nun, who stands 1.38
or your s., or your daughter, or 5.14
you and your s. and your son's s., 6.02
"When your s. asks you in time to 6.20
then you shall say to your s., 6.21
that, as a man disciplines his s., 8.05
and his s. Eleazar ministered as 10.06
the sons of Eliab, s. of Reuben; 11.06
you and your s. and your daughter, 12.18
the s. of your mother, or your s., or 13.06
you and your s. and your daughter, 16.11
you and your s. and your daughter, 16.14
who burns his s. or his daughter 18.10
the first-born s. is hers that is 21.15
not treat the s. of the loved as 21.16

SON (cont.)

preference to the s. of the disliked,	Deu 21.16
the s. of the disliked, by giving	21.17
has a stubborn and rebellious s.,	21.18
'This our s. is stubborn and	21.20
you Balaam the s. of Beor from	23.04
and one of them dies and has no s.,	25.05
And the first s. whom she bears	25.06
to her s. and to her daughter,	28.56
Joshua the s. of Nun and said, "Be	31.23
he and Joshua the s. of Nun.	32.44
And Joshua the s. of Nun was full	34.09
LORD said to Joshua the s. of Nun,	Jos 1.01
And Joshua the s. of Nun sent two	2.01
and came to Joshua the s. of Nun;	2.23
So Joshua the s. of Nun called the	6.06
of his youngest s. shall he set up	6.26
for Achan the s. of Carmi, s. of Zabdi,	7.01
s. of Zerah, of the tribe of Judah,	7.01
and Achan the s. of Carmi, s. of Zabdi,	7.18
s. of Zerah, of the tribe of Judah,	7.18
"My s., give glory to the LORD God	7.19
him took Achan the s. of Zerah,	7.24
the s. of Beor, the soothsayer, the	13.22
of Machir the s. of Manasseh for	13.31
priest, and Joshua the s. of Nun,	14.01
and Caleb the s. of Jephunneh the	14.06
to Caleb the s. of Jephunneh for	14.13
of Caleb the s. of Jephunneh the	14.14
stone of Bohan the s. of Reuben;	15.06
valley of the s. of Hinnom at the	15.08
to Caleb the s. of Jephunneh a	15.13
And Othniel the s. of Kenaz,	15.17
of Manasseh the s. of Joseph,	17.02
Now Zelophehad the s. of Hepher,	17.03
s. of Gilead, s. of Machir, s. of Manasseh,	17.03
and Joshua the s. of Nun and the	17.04
the valley of the s. of Hinnom,	18.16
Stone of Bohan the s. of Reuben;	18.17
among them to Joshua the s. of Nun.	19.49
asd Joshua the s. of Nun and the	19.51
to Joshua the s. of Nun and to the	21.01
to Caleb the s. of Jephunneh as	21.12
Phinehas the s. of Eleazar the	22.13
Did not Achan the s. of Zerah break	22.20
And Phinehas the s. of Eleazar the	22.31
Then Phinehas the s. of Eleazar the	22.32
Then Balak the s. of Zippor, king of	24.09
Balaam the s. of Beor to curse you,	24.09
After these things Joshua the s. of Nun,	24.29
And Eleazar the s. of Aaron died;	24.33
the town of Phinehas his s.,	24.33
And Othniel the s. of Kenaz,	Ju 1.13
And Joshua the s. of Nun, the	2.08
Othniel the s. of Kenaz, Caleb's	3.09
then Othniel the s. of Kenaz died.	3.11
the s. of Gera, the Benjaminite, a	3.15
After him was Shamgar the s. of Anath,	3.31
Barak the s. of Abinoam from	4.06
that Barak the s. of Abinoam had	4.12
and Barak the s. of Abinoam on	5.01
s. of Anath, in the days of Jael,	5.06
your captives, O s. of Abinoam.	5.12
as his s. Gideon was beating out	6.11
"Gideon the s. of Joash has done	6.29
said to Joas, "Bring out your s.,	6.30
sword of Gideon the s. of Joash,	7.14
Then Gideon the s. of Joash returned	8.13
you and your s. and your grandson	8.22
and my s. will not rule over you;	8.23
Jerubbaal the s. of Joash went and	8.29
was in Shechem also bore him a s.,	8.31
And Gideon the s. of Joash died in	8.32
Now Abimelech the s. of Jerubbaal	9.01
the youngest s. of Jerubbaal was	9.05
the s. of his maidservant, king over	9.18
And Gaal the s. of Ebed moved into	9.26

And Gaal the s. of Ebed said, "Who	9.28
Did not the s. of Jerubbaal and	9.28
the words of Gaal the s. of Ebed,	9.30
Gaal the s. of Ebed and his kinsmen	9.31
And Gaal the s. of Ebed went out	9.35
of Jotham the s. of Jerubbaal.	9.57
deliver Israel Tola the s. of Puah,	10.01
s. of Dodo, a man of Issachar;	10.01
but he was the s. of a harlot.	11.01
for you are the s. of another woman	11.02
better than Balak the s. of Zippor,	11.25
her he had neither s. nor daughter.	11.34
After him Abdon the s. of Hillel	12.13
Then Abdon the s. of Hillel the	12.15
you shall conceive and bear a s.	13.03
you shall conceive and bear a s.	13.05
you shall conceive and bear a s.;	13.07
And the woman bore a s., and called	13.24
said, "Blessed be my s. by the LORD."	17.02
to the LORD from my hand for my s.,	17.03
and Jonathan the s. of Gershom,	18.30
s. of Moses, and his sons were	18.30
and Phinehas the s. of Eleazar,	20.28
s. of Aaron, ministered before it in	20.28
her conception, and she bore a s.	Ru 4.13
"A s. has been born to Naomi."	4.17
name was Elkanah the s. of Jeroham,	1Sa 1.01
s. of Elihu, s. of Tohu, s. of Zuph,	1.01
wilt give to thy maidservant a s.,	1.11
Hannah conceived and bore a s.,	1.20
woman remained and nursed her s.,	1.23
But he said, "I did not call, my s.;	3.06
Samuel and said, "Samuel, my s."	3.16
And he said, "How did it go, my s.?"	4.16
"Fear not, for you have borne a s."	4.20
and they consecrated his s., Eleazar,	7.01
name of his first-born s. was Joel,	8.02
the s. of Abiel, s. of Zeror, s. of Becorath,	9.01
s. of Aphiah, a Benjaminite, a man of	9.01
and he had a s. whose name was Saul,	9.02
So Kish said to Saul his s., "Take me	9.03
"What shall I do about my s.?"	10.02
"What has come over the s. of Kish?	10.11
and Saul the s. of Kish was taken	10.21
And Saul, and Jonathan his s.,	13.16
Saul and Jonathan his s. had them.	13.22
Jonathan the s. of Saul said to	14.01
and Ahijah the s. of Ahitub, Ichabod's	14.03
s. of Phinehas, s. of Eli, the priest of	14.03
though it be in Jonathan my s.,	14.39
and Jonathan my s. will be on the	14.40
is in me or in Jonathan my s.,	14.41
lot between me and my s. Jonathan."	14.42
his army was Abner the s. of Ner,	14.50
of Abner was the s. of Abiel.	14.51
I have seen a s. of Jesse the	16.18
and said, "Send me David your s.,	16.19
sent them by David his s. to Saul.	16.20
Now David was the s. of an Ephrathite	17.12
And Jesse said to David his s.,	17.17
"Abner, whose s. is this youth?"	17.55
"Inquire whose s. the stripling is."	17.56
"Whose s. are you, young man?"	17.58
"I am the s. of your servant Jesse	17.58
to Jonathan his s. and to all his	19.01
Saul's s., delighted much in David.	19.01
And Saul said to Jonathan his s.,	20.27
"Why has not the s. of Jesse come	20.27
"You s. of a perverse, rebellious	20.30
have chosen the s. of Jesse to	20.30
For as long as the s. of Jesse	20.31
will the s. of Jesse give every one	22.07
to me when my s. makes a league	22.08
a league with the s. of Jesse,	22.08
to me that my s. has stirred up my	22.08
"I saw the s. of Jesse coming to	22.09
to Ahimelech the s. of Ahitub,	22.09

SON (cont.)
the s. of Ahitub, and all his 1Sa 22.11
And Saul said, "Hear now, s. of Ahitub." 22.12
you and the s. of Jesse, in that you 22.13
sons of Ahimelech the s. of Ahitub, 22.20
When Abiathar the s. of Ahimelech 23.06
Saul's s., rose, and went to David at 23.16
"Is this your voice, my s. David?" 24.16
your servants and to your s. David.'" 25.08
Who is the s. of Jesse? There are 25.10
to Palti the s. of Laish, who was of 25.44
Saul lay, with Abner the s. of Ner, 26.05
brother Abishai the s. of Zeruiah, 26.06
army, and to Abner the s. of Ner, 26.14
"Is this your voice, my s. David? 26.17
return, my s. David, for I will no 26.21
David, "Blessed be you, my s. David! 26.25
to Achish the s. of Maoch, king of 27.02
the s. of Ahimelech, "Bring me the 30.07
Saul and his s. Jonathan are also 2Sa 1.04
Saul and his s. Jonathan are dead 1.05
Jonathan his s. and for the people 1.12
"I am the s. of a sojourner, an 1.13
over Saul and Jonathan his s., 1.17
Now Abner the s. of Ner, commander 2.08
taken Ishbosheth the s. of Saul, 2.08
Saul's s., was forty years old when 2.10
Abner the s. of Ner, and the servants 2.12
of Ishbosheth the s. of Saul, 2.12
And Joab the s. of Zeruiah, and the 2.13
and Ishbosheth the s. of Saul, 2.15
Absalom the s. of Maacah the 3.03
fourth, Adonijah the s. of Haggith; 3.04
fifth, Shephatiah the s. of Abital; 3.04
messengers to Ishbosheth Saul's s., 3.14
husband Paltiel the s. of Laish. 3.15
"Abner the s. of Ner came to the 3.23
that Abner the s. of Ner came to 3.25
the blood of Abner the s. of Ner. 3.28
will to slay Abner the s. of Ner. 3.37
Saul's s., heard that Abner had died 4.01
Now Saul's s. had two men who were 4.02
Jonathan, the s. of Saul, had a s. 4.04
the s. of Saul, your enemy, who 4.08
I will raise up your s. after you, 7.12
his father, and he shall be my s. 7.14
defeated Hadadezer the s. of Rehob, 8.03
Tou sent his s. Joram to King David, 8.10
spoil of Hadadezer the s. of Rehob, 8.12
And Joab the s. of Zeruiah was over 8.16
Jehoshaphat the s. of Ahilud was 8.16
and Zadok the s. of Ahitub and 8.17
Ahimelech the s. of Abiathar were 8.17
and Benaiah the s. of Jehoiada was 8.18
"There is still a s. of Jonathan; 9.03
house of Machir the s. of Ammiel, 9.04
house of Machir the s. of Ammiel, 9.05
And Mephibosheth the s. of Jonathan, 9.06
s. of Saul, came to David, and fell 9.06
I have given to your master's s. 9.09
your master's s. may have bread to 9.10
your master's s. shall always eat 9.10
And Mephibosheth had a young s., 9.12
and Hanum his s. reigned in his 10.01
with Hanum the s. of Nahash, 10.02
Abimelech the s. of Jerubbesheth 11.21
became his wife, and bore him a s. 11.27
and she bore a s., and he called 12.24
David's s., had a beautiful sister, 13.01
time Amnon, David's s., loved her. 13.01
the s. of Shimeah, David's brother; 13.03
"O s. of the king, why are you so 13.04
my s., let us not all go, lest we be 13.25
But Jonadab the s. of Shimeah, 13.32
went to Talmai the s. of Ammihud, 13.37
mourned for his s. day after day. 13.37
Now Joab the s. of Zeruiah perceived 14.01
and my s. be not destroyed." He said, 14.11
hair of your s. shall fall to the 14.11
me and my s. together from the 14.16
Ahimaaz your s., and Jonathan the 15.27
and Jonathan the s. of Abiathar. 15.27
Zadok's s., and Jonathan Abiathar's s.; 15.36
"And where is your master's s.? 16.03
name was Shimei, the s. of Gera; 16.05
into the hand of your s. Absalom. 16.08
Then Abishai the s. of Zeruiah said 16.09
"Behold, my own s. seeks my life; 16.11
Should it not be his s.? As I have 16.19
Amasa was the s. of a man named 17.25
Shobi the s. of Nahash from Rabbah 17.27
and Machir the s. of Ammiel from 17.27
of Abishai the s. of Zeruiah, 18.02
my hand against the king's s.; 18.12
"I have no s. to keep my name in 18.18
Then said Ahimaaz the s. of Zadok, 18.19
because the king's s. is dead." 18.20
Then Ahimaaz the s. of Zadok said 18.22
my s., seeing that you will have no 18.22
running of Ahimaaz the s. of Zadok. 18.27
"O my s. Absalom, my s., my s. Absalom! 18.33
of you, O Absalom, my s., my s.!" 18.33
"The king is grieving for his s. 19.02
"O my s. Absalom, O Absalom, my s., my s.!" 19.04
And Shimei the s. of Gera, the 19.16
And Shimei the s. of Gera fell down 19.18
Abishai the s. of Zeruiah answered, 19.21
Mephiosheth the s. of Saul came 19.24
the s. of Bichri, a Benjaminite; 20.01
no inheritance in the s. of Jesse; 20.01
followed Sheba the s. of Bichri; 20.02
"Now Sheba the s. of Bichri will do 20.06
to pursue Sheba the s. of Bichri. 20.07
pursued Sheba the s. of Bichri. 20.10
to pursue Sheba the s. of Bichri. 20.13
called Sheba the s. of Bichri, 20.21
the head of Sheba the s. of Bichri, 20.22
and Benaiah the s. of Jehoiada was 20.23
Jehoshaphat the s. of Ahilud was 20.24
the s. of Saul's s. Jonathan, 21.07
David and Jonathan the s. of Saul. 21.07
to Adriel the s. of Barzillai the 21.08
bones of his s. Jonathan from the 21.12
and the bones of his s. Jonathan; 21.13
of Saul and his s. Jonathan in the 21.14
But Abishai the s. of Zeruiah came 21.17
and Elhanan the s. of Jaareoregim, 21.19
Jonathan the s. of Shimei, David's 21.21
the s. of Jesse, the oracle of the 23.01
Eleazar the s. of Dodo, s. of Ahohi. 23.09
the s. of Agee the Hararite. 23.11
the s. of Zeruiah, was chief of the 23.18
And Benaiah the s. of Jehoiada was 23.20
did Benaiah the s. of Jehoiada, 23.22
Elhahan the s. of Dodo of Bethlehem, 23.24
Ira the s. of Ikkesh of Tekoa, 23.26
Heleb the s. of Baanah of Netophah, 23.29
Ittai the s. of Ribai of Gibeah of 23.29
Ahiam the s. of Sharar the Hararite, 23.33
Eliphelet the s. of Ahasbai of 23.34
Eliam the s. of Ahithophel of Gilo, 23.34
Igal the s. of Nathan of Zobah, Bani 23.36
armor-bearer of Joab the s. of Zeruiah, 23.37
Now Adonijah the s. of Haggith 1Ki 1.05
with Joab the s. of Zeruiah and 1.07
and Benaiah the s. of Jehoiada, 1.08
Adonijah the s. of Haggith has 1.11
and the life of your s. Solomon. 1.12
"Solomon your s. shall reign after 1.13
'Solomon your s. shall reign after 1.17
that I and my s. Solomon will be 1.21
and Benaiah the s. of Jehoiada, 1.26
'Solomon your s. shall reign after 1.30
and Benaiah the s. of Jehoiada." 1.32

SON (cont.)

Solomon my s. to ride on my own	1Ki 1.33
And Benaiah the s. of Jehoiada	1.36
and Benaiah the s. of Jehoiada,	1.38
Jonathan the s. of Abiathar the	1.42
and Benaiah the s. of Jehoiada,	1.44
he charged Solomon his s., saying,	2.01
what Joab the s. of Zeruiah did to	2.05
Abner and the s. of Ner, and Amasa the	2.05
and Amasa the s. of Jether, whom he	2.05
with you Shimei the s. of Gera,	2.08
Then Adonijah the s. of Haggith	2.13
priest and Joab the s. of Zeruiah."	2.22
sent Benaiah the s. of Jehoiada;	2.25
sent Benaiah the s. of Jehoiada,	2.29
Abner the s. of Ner, commander of	2.32
and Amasa the s. of Jether, commander	2.32
Then Benaiah the s. of Jehoiada	2.34
put Benaiah the s. of Jehoiada	2.35
s. of Maacah, king of Gath.	2.39
commanded Benaiah the s. of Jehoiada;	2.46
given him a s. to sit on his	3.06
And this woman's s. died in the	3.19
and took my s. from beside me, while	3.20
and laid her dead s. in my bosom.	3.20
'This is my s. that is alive, and	3.23
is alive, and your s. is dead';	3.23
but your s. is dead, and my s. is	3.23
Then the woman whose s. was alive	3.26
her heart yearned for her s.,	3.26
Azariah the s. of Zadok was the	4.02
Jehoshaphat the s. of Ahilud was	4.03
Benaiah the s. of Jehoiada was in	4.04
Azariah the s. of Nathan was over	4.05
Zabud the s. of Nathan was priest	4.05
Adoniram the s. of Abda was in	4.06
Baana the s. of Ahilud, in Taanach,	4.12
villages of Jair the s. of Manasseh,	4.13
Ahinadab the s. of Iddo, in Mahanaim	4.14
Baana the s. of Hushai, in Asher and	4.16
Jehoshaphat the s. of Paruah,	4.17
Shimei the s. of Ela, in Benjamin;	4.18
Geber the s. of Uri, in the land of	4.19
your s., whom I will set upon your	5.05
to David a wise s. to be over this	5.07
He was the s. of a widow of the	7.14
but your s. who shall be born to	8.19
tear it out of the hand of your s.	11.12
I will give one tribe to your s.,	11.13
Tahpenes bore him Genubath his s.,	11.20
Rezon the s. of Eliada, who had fled	11.23
Jeroboam the s. of Nebat, an Ephraimite	11.26
Yet to his s. I will give one tribe,	11.36
Rehoboam his s. reigned in his	11.43
Jeroboam the s. of Nebat heard of	12.02
to Jeroboam the s. of Nebat.	12.15
no inheritance in the s. of Jesse.	12.16
to Rehoboam the s. of Solomon.	12.21
"Say to Rehoboam the s. of Solomon,	12.23
a s. shall be born to the house of	13.02
time Abijah the s. of Jeroboam	14.01
inquire of you concerning her s.;	14.05
and Nadab his s. reigned in his	14.20
Now Rehoboam the s. of Solomon	14.21
And Abijam his s. reigned in his	14.31
of King Jeroboam the s. of Nebat,	15.01
setting up his s. after him,	15.04
And Asa his s. reigned in his stead	15.08
to Benhadad the s. of Tabrimmon,	15.18
the s. of Hezion, king of Syria, who	15.18
Jehoshaphat his s. reigned in his	15.24
Nadab the s. of Jeroboam began to	15.25
Baasha the s. of Ahijah, of the	15.27
Baasha the s. of Ahijah began to	15.33
to Jehu the s. of Hanania against	16.01
house of Jeroboam the s. of Nebat.	16.03
and Elah his s. reigned in his	16.06

Jehu the s. of Hanani against	16.07
Elah the s. of Baasha began to	16.08
of Elah his s. which they sinned,	16.13
followed Tibni the s. of Ginath,	16.21
followed Tibni the s. of Ginath;	16.22
way of Jeroboam the s. of Nebat,	16.26
and Ahab his s. reigned in his	16.28
Ahab the s. of Omri began to reign	16.29
and Ahab the s. of Omri reigned	16.29
And Ahab the s. of Omri did evil in	16.30
sins of Jeroboam the s. of Nebat,	16.31
the cost of his youngest s. Segub,	16.34
he spoke by Joshua the s. of Nun.	16.34
prepare it for myself and my s.,	17.12
make for yourself and your s.	17.13
After this the s. of the woman, the	17.17
and to cause the death of my s.!	17.18
And he said to her, "Give me your s."	17.19
whom I sojourn, by slaying her s.?"	17.20
Elijah said, "See, your s. lives."	17.23
and Jehu the s. of Nimshi you shall	19.16
and Elisha the s. of Shaphat of	19.16
and found Elisha the s. of Shaphat,	19.19
house of Jeroboam the s. of Nebat,	21.22
house of Baasha the s. of Ahijah,	21.22
the LORD, Micaiah the s. of Imlah;	22.08
quickly Micaiah the s. of Imlah.	22.09
And Zedekiah the s. of Chenaanah	22.11
Then Zedekiah the s. of Chenaanah	22.24
city and to Joash the king's s.;	22.26
and Ahaziah his s. reigned in his	22.40
Jehoshaphat the s. of Asa began to	22.41
Then Ahaziah the s. of Ahab said to	22.49
and Jehoram his s. reigned in his	22.50
Ahaziah the s. of Ahab began to	22.51
way of Jeroboam the s. of Nebat,	22.52
of Jehoram the s. of Jehoshaphat,	2Ki 1.17
Judah, because Ahaziah had no s.	1.17
Jehoram the s. of Ahab became king	3.01
sin of Jeroboam the s. of Nebat,	3.03
"Elisha the s. of Shaphat is here,	3.11
took his eldest s. who was to	3.27
were full, she said to her s.,	4.06
she has no s., and her husband is	4.14
round. you shall embrace a s."	4.16
and she bore a s. about that time	4.17
said, "Did I ask my lord for a s.?	4.28
to him, he said, "Take up your s."	4.36
she took up her s. and went out.	4.37
'Give your s., that we may eat him	6.28
and we will eat my s. tomorrow.'	6.28
So we boiled my s., and ate him.	6.29
'Give your s., that we may eat him';	6.29
but she has hidden her s."	6.29
of Elisha the s. of Shaphat	6.31
the woman whose s. he had restored	8.01
the woman whose s. he had restored	8.05
and here is her s. whom Elisha	8.05
"Your s. Benhadad king of Syria has	8.09
fifth year of Joram the s. of Ahab,	8.16
Jehoram the s. of Jehoshaphat, king	8.16
and Ahaziah his s. reigned in his	8.24
year of Joram the s. of Ahab,	8.25
Ahaziah the s. of Jehoram, king of	8.25
with Joram the s. of Ahab to make	8.28
And Ahaziah the s. of Jehoram king	8.29
see Joram the s. of Ahab in	8.29
the s. of Jehoshaphat, s. of Nimshi;	9.02
house of Jeroboam the s. of Nebat,	9.09
house of Baasha the s. of Ahijah.	9.09
the s. of Jehoshaphat the s. of Nimsi	9.14
driving of Jehu the s. of Nimshi;	9.20
year of Joram the s. of Ahab,	9.29
Jehonadab the s. of Rechab coming	10.15
with Jehonadab the s. of Rechab;	10.23
sins of Jeroboam the s. of Nebat,	10.29
Jehoahaz his s. reigned in his	10.35

SON (cont.)

Ahaziah saw that her s. was dead,	2Ki 11.01
took Joash the s. of Ahaziah,	11.02
and he showed them the king's s.	11.04
Then he brought out the king's s.,	11.12
It was Jozacar the s. of Shimeath	12.21
and Jehozabad the s. of Shomer,	12.21
and Amaziah his s. reigned in his	12.21
year of Joash the s. of Ahaziah,	13.01
Jehoahaz the s. of Jehu began to	13.01
sins of Jeroboam the s. of Nebat,	13.02
hand of Benhadad the s. of Hazael.	13.03
and Joash his s. reigned in his	13.09
Jehoash the s. of Jehoahaz began	13.10
sins of Jeroboam the s. of Nebat,	13.11
Benhadad his s. became king in his	13.24
Then Jehoash the s. of Jehoahaz	13.25
Benhadad the s. of Hazael the	13.25
year of Joash the s. of Joahaz,	14.01
Amaziah the s. of Joash, king of	14.01
Jehoash the s. of Jehoahaz, s. of Jehu,	14.08
your daughter to my s. for a wife';	14.09
the s. of Jehoash, s. of Ahaziah, at	14.13
Jeroboam his s. reigned in his	14.16
Amaziah the s. of Joash, king of	14.17
death of Jehoash s. of Jehoahaz,	14.17
year of Amaziah the s. of Joash,	14.23
Jeroboam the s. of Joash, king of	14.23
sins of Jeroboam the s. of Nebat,	14.24
servant Jonah the s. of Amittai,	14.25
hand of Jeroboam the s. of Joash.	14.27
Zechariah his s. reigned in his	14.29
Azariah the s. of Amaziah, king of	15.01
the king's s. was over the household,	15.05
and Jotham his s. reigned in his	15.07
Zechariah the s. of Jeroboam	15.08
sins of Jeroboam the s. of Nebat,	15.09
Shallum the s. of Jabesh conspired	15.10
Shallum the s. of Jabesh began to	15.13
Then Menahem the s. of Gadi came up	15.14
Shallum the s. of Jabesh in	15.14
Menahem the s. of Gadi began to	15.17
sins of Jeroboam the s. of Nebat,	15.18
Pekahiah his s. reigned in his	15.22
Pekahiah the s. of Menahem began	15.23
sins of Jeroboam the s. of Nebat,	15.24
And Pekah the s. of Remaliah, his	15.25
Pekah the s. of Remaliah began to	15.27
sins of Jeroboam the s. of Nebat,	15.28
Then Hoshea the s. of Elah made a	15.30
against Pekah the s. of Remaliah,	15.30
year of Jotham the s. of Uzziah.	15.30
year of Pekah the s. of Remaliah,	15.32
Jotham the s. of Uzziah, king of	15.32
and Pekah the s. of Remaliah	15.37
and Ahaz his s. reigned in his	15.38
year of Pekah the s. of Remaliah,	16.01
Ahaz the s. of Jotham, king of Judah,	16.01
even burned his s. as an offering,	16.03
Syria and Pekah the s. of Remaliah,	16.05
"I am your servant and your s.	16.07
Hezekiah his s. reigned in his	16.20
Hoshea the s. of Elah began to	17.01
made Jeroboam the s. of Nebat king.	17.21
third year of Hoshea s. of Elah,	18.01
Hezekiah the s. of Ahaz, king of	18.01
seventh year of Hoshea s. of Elah,	18.09
to them Eliakim the s. of Hilkiah,	18.18
and Joah the s. of Asaph, the	18.18
Then Eliakim the s. of Hilkiah,	18.26
Then Eliakim the s. of Hilkiah,	18.37
and Joah the s. of Asaph, the	18.37
the prophet Isaiah the s. of Amoz.	19.02
Then Isaiah the s. of Amoz sent to	19.20
Esarhaddon his s. reigned in his	19.37
the prophet the s. of Amoz came to	20.01
Merodachbaladan the s. of Baladan,	20.12
Manasseh his s. reigned in his	20.21
And he burned his s. as an offering,	21.06
to David and to Solomon his s.,	21.07
and Amon his s. reigned in his	21.18
made Josiah his s. king in his	21.24
and Josiah his s. reigned in his	21.26
Shaphan the s. of Azaliah, s. of Meshullam,	22.03
and Ahikam the s. of Shaphan,	22.12
and Achbor the s. of Micaiah,	22.12
Shallum the s. of Tikvah, s. of Harhas,	22.14
might burn his s. or his daughter	23.10
by Jeroboam the s. of Nebat,	23.15
took Jehoahaz the s. of Josiah,	23.30
Eliakim the s. of Josiah king in	23.34
Jehoiachin his s. reigned in his	24.06
Gedalah the s. of Ahikam, s. of Shaphan,	25.22
Ishmael the s. of Nethaniah, and	25.23
and Johanan the s. of Kareah,	25.23
and Seraiah the s. of Tanhumeth	25.23
Jaazaniah the s. of the Maacathite.	25.23
Ishmael the s. of Nethaniah, s. of Elishama,	25.25
Bela the s. of Beor, the name of	1Ch 1.43
Jobab the s. of Zerah of Bozrah	1.44
Hadad the s. of Bedad, who defeated	1.46
the s. of Achbor, reigned in his	1.49
and Ethan's s. was Azariah.	2.08
Caleb the s. of Hezron had children	2.18
The s. of Shammai: Maon;	2.45
Abijah his s., Asa his s., Jehoshaphat his s.,	3.10
Joram his s., Ahaziah his s., Joash his s.,	3.11
Amaziah his s., Azariah his s., Jotham his s.,	3.12
Ahaz his s., Hezekiah his s., Manasseh his s.,	3.13
Amon his s., Josiah his s.	3.14
Jeconiah his s., Zedekiah his s.;	3.16
the captive: Shealtiel his s.,	3.17
his s. Rephaiah, his s. Arnan, his	3.21
his s. Obadiah, his s. Shecaniah.	3.21
Reaiah the s. of Shobal was the	4.02
families of Aharhel the s. of Harum.	4.08
The sons of Caleb the s. of Jephunneh:	4.15
The sons of Shelah the s. of Judah:	4.21
Shallum was his s.,	4.25
Mibsam his s., Mishma his s.	4.25
Hammuel his s., Zaccur his s., Shimei his s.	4.26
Jamlech, Joshah the s. of Amaziah,	4.34
s. of Joshibiah, s. of Seraiah, s. of Asiel,	4.35
Ziza the s. of Shiphi, s. of Allon,	4.37
s. of Jedaiah, s. of Shimri, s. of Shemaiah—	4.37
sons of Joseph the s. of Israel,	5.01
Shemaiah his s., Gog his s., Shimei his s.,	5.04
Micah his s., Reaiah his s., Baal his s.,	5.05
Beerha his s., whom Tilgathpilneser	5.06
s. of Azaz, s. of Shema, s. of Joel,	5.08
the sons of Abihail the s. of Huri,	5.14
s. of Jaroah, s. of Gilead, s. of Michael,	5.14
s. of Jeshishai, s. of Jahdo, s. of Buz;	5.14
Ahi the s. of Abdiel, s. of Guni,	5.15
Libni his s., Jahath his s., Zimmah his s.,	6.20
Joah his s., Iddo his s.,	6.21
Zerah his s., Jeatherai his s.	6.21
Amminadab his s., Korah his s., Assir his s.,	6.22
Elkanah his s., Ebiasaph his s., Assir his s.,	6.23
Tahath his s., Uriel his s., Uzziah	6.24
Uzziah his s., and Shaul his s.	6.24
Elkanah his s., Zophai his s., Nahath his s.,	6.26
Eliab his s., Jeroham his s., Elkana his s.	6.27
Libni his s., Shimei his s., Uzziah his s.,	6.29
Shimea his s., Haggiah his s., and Asaiah his s.	6.30
the singer the s. of Joel, s. of Samuel,	6.33
s. of Elkanah, s. of Jeroham, s. of	6.34
s. of Eliel, s. of Toah,	6.34
s. of Zuph, s. of Elkanah, s. of	6.35
s. of Mahath, s. of Amasai,	6.35
s. of Elkanah, s. of Joel, s. of	6.36
s. of Azariah, s. of Zephaniah,	6.36
s. of Tahath, s. of Assir, s. of	6.37
s. of Ebiasaph, s. of Korah,	6.37

SON (cont.)

s. of Izhar, s. of Kohath, s. of Levi, s. of Israel; 1Ch 6.38
Asaph the s. of Berechiah, s. of Shimea, 6.39
s. of Michael, s. of Baaseiah, s. of Malchijah, 6.40
s. of Ethni, s. of Zerah, s. of Adaiah, 6.41
s. of Ethan, s. of Zimmah, s. of Shimei, 6.42
s. of Jahath, s. of Gershom, s. of Levi. 6.43
the s. of Kishi, s. of Abdi, s. of Malluch, 6.44
s. of Hashabiah, s. of Amaziah, s. of Hilkiah, 6.45
s. of Amzi, s. of Bani, s. of Shemer, 6.46
s. of Mahli, s. of Mushi, s. of 6.47
s. of Merari, s. of Levi; 6.47
the sons of Aaron: Eleazar his s., 6.50
Phinehas his s., Abishua his s., 6.50
Bukki his s., Uzzi his s., Zerahiah his s., 6.51
Meraioth his s., Amariah his s., Ahitub his s., 6.52
Zadok his s., Ahimaaz his s. 6.53
gave to Caleb the s. of Jephunneh. 6.56
the wife of Machir bore a s., 7.16
the s. of Machir, s. of Manasseh. 7.17
and Bered his s., Tahath his s., 7.20
Eleadah his s., Tahath his s., 7.20
Zabad his s., Shuthelah his s., and 7.21
and she conceived and bore a s.; 7.23
Rephah was his s., Resheph his s., 7.25
Telah his s., Tahan his s., 7.25
Ladan his s., Ammihud his s., Elishama his s., 7.26
Nun his s., Joshua his s. 7.27
sons of Joseph the s. of Israel. 7.29
His first-born s.: Abdon, then Zur, 8.30
and the s. of Jonathan was Meribbaal; 8.34
his s., Eleasah his s., Azel his s. 8.37
Uthai the s. of Ammihud, s. of Omri, 9.04
s. of Imri, s. of Bani, from the 9.04
the sons of Perez the s. of Judah. 9.04
Sallu the s. of Meshullam, s. of 9.07
s. of Hodaviah, s. of Hassenuah, 9.07
Ibneiah the s. of Jeroham, Elah the 9.08
Elah the s. of Uzzi, s. of Michri, 9.08
and Meshullam the s. of Shephatiah, 9.08
s. of Reuel, s. of Ibnijah; 9.08
and Azariah the s. of Hilkiah, 9.11
s. of Meshullam, s. of Zadok, s. of 9.11
s. of Meraioth, s. of Ahitub, the 9.11
s. of Jeroham, s. of Pashhur, s. of Malchijah, 9.12
s. of Adiel, s. of Jahzerah, s. of Meshullam, 9.12
s. of Meshillemith, s. of Immer; 9.12
s. of Hasshub, s. of Azrikam, s. of Hashabiah, 9.14
s. of Mica, s. of Zichri, s. of Asaph; 9.15
s. of Shemaiah, s. of Galal, s. of Jeduthun, 9.16
Berechiah the s. of Asa, s. of Elkanah, 9.16
s. of Kore, s. of Ebiasaph, s. of Korah, 9.19
And Phinehas the s. of Eleazar was 9.20
Zechariah the s. of Meshelemiah was 9.21
and his first-born s. Abdon, 9.36
and the s. of Jonathan was Meribbaal; 9.40
Rephaiah was his s., Eleasah his s., Azel his s. 9.43
over to David the s. of Jesse. 10.14
And Joab the s. of Zeruiah went 11.06
men was Eleazar the s. of Dodo, 11.12
And Benaiah the s. of Jehoiada was 11.22
did Benaiah the s. of Jehoiada, 11.24
Elhanan the s. of Dodo of Bethlehem, 11.26
Ira the s. of Ikkesh of Tekoa, 11.28
Heled the s. of Baanah of Netophah, 11.30
Ithai the s. of Ribai of Gibeah of 11.31
Jonathan the s. of Shagee the 11.34
Ahiam the s. of Sachar the Hararite, 11.35
Hararite, Eliphal the s. of Ur, 11.35
of Carmel, Naarai the s. of Ezbai, 11.37
of Nathan, Mibhar the s. of Habri, 11.38
armor-bearer of Joab the s. of Zeruiah, 11.39
Hittite, Zabad the s. of Ahlai, 11.41
Adina the s. of Shiza the Reubenite, 11.42
Hanan the s. of Maacah, and Joshaphat 11.43
Jediael the s. of Shimri, and Joha 11.45
because of Saul the s. of Kish; 12.01
and with you, O s. of Jesse! 12.18
appointed Heman of s. of Joel; 15.17
brethren Asaph the s. of Berechiah; 15.17
brethren, Ethan the s. of Kushaiah; 15.17
the s. of Jeduthun, and Hosah were 16.38
his father, and he shall be my s.; 17.13
he set his s. Hadoram to King 18.10
the s. of Zeruiah, slew eighteen 18.12
And Joab the s. of Zeruiah was over 18.15
Jehoshaphat the s. of Ahilud was 18.15
and Zadok the s. of Ahitub and 18.16
Ahimelech the s. of Abiathar were 18.16
and Benaiah the s. of Jehoiada was 18.17
and his s. reigned in his stead. 19.01
with Hanun the s. of Nahash, 19.02
and Elhanan the s. of Jair slew 20.05
Jonathan the s. of Shimea, David's 20.07
"Solomon my s. is young and inexperienced, 22.05
Then he called for Solomon his s., 22.06
"My s., I had it in my heart to 22.07
Behold, a s. shall be born to you; 22.09
He shall be my s., and I will be 22.10
Now, my s., the LORD be with you, so 22.11
to help Solomon his s., saying, 22.17
Solomon his s. king over Israel. 23.01
scribe Shemaiah the s. of Nethanel, 24.06
and Ahimelech the s. of Abiathar, 24.06
Korahites, Meshelemiah the s. of Kore, 26.01
Also to his s. Shemaiah were sons 26.06
lots also for his s. Zechariah, 26.14
and Shebuel the s. of Gershom, 26.24
s. of Moses, was chief officer in 26.24
from Eliezer were his s. Rehabiah, 26.25
and his s. Jeshaiah, and his s. Joram, 26.25
his s. Zichri, and his s. Shelomoth. 26.25
and Saul the s. of Kish, and Abner 26.28
and Abner the s. of Ner, and Joab 26.28
and Joab the s. of Zeruiah had 26.28
Jashobeam the s. of Zabdiel was in 27.02
the s. of Jehoiada the priest, as 27.05
Ammizabad his s. was in charge of 27.06
and his s. Zebadiah after him; 27.07
the s. of Ikkesh the Tekoite; 27.09
Eliezer the s. of Zichri was chief 27.16
Shephatiah the s. of Maacah; 27.16
for Levi, Hashabiah the s. of Kemuel; 27.17
Issachar, Omri the s. of Michael; 27.18
Zebulun, Ishmaiah the s. of Obadiah; 27.19
Naphtali, Jeremoth the s. of Azriel; 27.19
Ephraimites, Hoshea the s. of Azaziah; 27.20
Manasseh, Joel the s. of Pedaiah; 27.20
Gilead, Iddo the s. of Zechariah; 27.21
Benjamin, Jaasiel the s. of Abner; 27.21
for Dan, Azarel the s. of Jeroham. 27.22
Joab the s. of Zeruiah began to 27.24
was Azmaveth the s. of Adiel; 27.25
was Jonathan the s. of Uzziah; 27.25
the soil was Ezri the s. of Chelub; 27.26
was Shaphat the s. of Adlai. 27.29
and Jehiel the s. of Hachmoni 27.32
by Jehoiada the s. of Benaiah, 27.34
Solomon my s. to sit upon the 28.05
is Solomon your s. who shall build 28.06
for I have chosen him to be my s., 28.06
Solomon my s., know the God of your 28.09
Solomon his s. the plan of the 28.11
Then David said to Solomon his s., 28.20
"Solomon my s., whom alone God has 29.01
Grant to Solomon my s. that with a 29.19
Solomon the s. of David king the 29.22
Thus David the s. of Jesse reigned 29.26
and Solomon his s. reigned in his 29.28
Solomon the s. of David established 2Ch 1.01
that Bezalel the s. of Uri, s. of Hur, 1.05
who has given King David a wise s., 2.12
the s. of a woman of the daughters 2.14
but your s. who shall be born to 6.09

SON (cont.)

concerning Jeroboam the s. of Nebat? 2Ch 9.29
Rehoboam his s. reigned in his 9.31
Jeroboam the s. of Nebat heard of 10.02
to Jeroboam the s. of Nebat. 10.15
no inheritance in the s. of Jesse. 10.16
"Say to Rehoboam the s. of Solomon 11.03
Rehoboam the s. of Solomon secure, 11.17
of Jerimoth the s. of David, 11.18
daughter of Eliab the s. of Jesse; 11.18
Abijah the s. of Maacah as chief 11.22
and Abijah his s. reigned in his 12.16
Yet Jeroboam the s. of Nebat 13.06
servant of Solomon the s. of David, 13.06
defied Rehoboam the s. of Solomon, 13.07
and Asa his s. reigned in his 14.01
came upon Azariah the s. of Oded, 15.01
prophecy of Azariah the s. of Oded, 15.08
Jehoshaphat his s. reigned in his 17.01
to him Amasiah the s. of Zichri, 17.16
the LORD, Micaiah the s. of Imlah; 18.07
quickly Micaiah the s. of Imlah." 18.08
And Zedekiah the s. of Chenaanah 18.10
Then Zedekiah the s. of Chenaanah 18.23
city and to Joash the king's s.; 18.25
But Jehu the s. of Hanani the seer 19.02
and Zebadiah the s. of Ishmael, 19.11
Jahaziel the s. of Zechariah, s. of Benaiah, 20.14
s. of Jeiel, s. of Mattaniah, a Levite 20.14
chronicles of Jehu the s. of Hanani, 20.34
Then Eliezer the s. of Dodavahu of 20.37
and Jehoram his s. reigned in his 21.01
so that no s. was left to him 21.17
except Jehoahaz, his youngest s. 21.17
his youngest s. king in his stead; 22.01
So Ahiziah the s. of Jehoram king 22.01
Jehoram the s. of Ahab king of 22.05
And Ahiziah the s. of Jehoram king 22.06
see Joram the s. of Ahab in 22.06
to meet Jehu the s. of Nimshi, 22.07
Ahaziah saw that her s. was dead, 22.10
king, took Joash the s. of Ahaziah, 22.11
Azariah the s. of Jeroham, Ishmael 23.01
Ishmael the s. of Jehohanan, Azariah 23.01
Azariah the s. of Obed, Maaseiah the 23.01
Maaseiah the s. of Adaiah, and 23.01
and Elishaphat the s. of Zichri. 23.01
to them, "Behold, the king's s.! 23.03
Then he brought out the king's s., 23.11
Zechariah the s. of Jehoiada the 24.20
had shown him, but killed his s. 24.22
blood of the s. of Jehoiada the 24.25
were Zabad the s. of Shimeath the 24.26
Jehozabad the s. of Shimrith the 24.26
And Amaziah his s. reigned in his 24.27
Joash the s. of Jehoahaz, s of Jehu, king 25.17
your daughter to my s. for a wife'; 25.18
the s. of Joash, s. of Ahaziah, at 25.23
Amaziah the s. of Joash king of 25.25
death of Joash the s. of Jehoahaz, 25.25
And Jotham his s. was over the 26.21
the prophet the s. of Amoz wrote. 26.22
And Jotham his s. reigned in his 26.23
and Ahaz his s. reigned in his 27.09
in the valley of the s. of Hinnom, 28.03
For Pekah the s. of Remaliah slew a 28.06
the king's s. and Azrikam the 28.07
Azariah the s. of Johanan, Berechiah 28.12
Berechiah the s. of Meshillemoth, 28.12
Jehizkiah the s. of Shallum, and 28.12
and Amasa the s. of Hadlai, stood up 28.12
Hezekiah his s. reigned in his 28.27
s. of Amasai, and Joel the s. of Azariah, 29.12
s. of Abdi, and Azariah the s. of Jehallelel; 29.12
s. of Zimmah, and Eden the s. of Joah; 29.12
of Solomon the s. of David king of 30.26
And Kore the s. of Imnah the Levite, 31.14
the s. of Amoz, prayed because of 32.20
Isaiah the prophet the s. of Amoz, 32.32
Manasseh his s. reigned in his 32.33
in the valley of the s. of Hinnom, 33.06
to David and to Solomon his s., 33.07
and Amon his s. reigned in his 33.20
made Josiah his s. king in his 33.25
he sent Shaphan the s. of Azaliah, 34.08
and Joah the s. of Joahaz, the 34.08
Ahikam the s. of Shaphan, Abdon the s. 34.20
Shallum the s. of Tokhath, s. of Basra, 34.22
which Solomon the s. of David, 35.03
the directions of Solomon his s. 35.04
Jehoahaz the s. of Josiah and made 36.01
Jehoiachin his s. reigned in his 36.08
Then arose Jeshua the s. of Jozadak, Ez 3.04
Zerubbabel the s. of Shealtiel 3.02
Zerubbabel the s. of Shealtiel and 3.08
and Jeshua the s. of Jozadak made 3.08
and Zechariah the s. of Iddo, 5.01
Then Zerubbabel the s. of Shealtiel 5.02
and Jeshua the s. of Jozadak arose 5.02
and Zechariah the s. of Iddo. 6.14
the s. of Seraiah, s. of Azariah, s. of Hilkiah, 7.01
s. of Shallum, s. of Zadok, s. of Ahitub, 7.02
s. of Amariah, s. of Azariah, s. of Meraioth, 7.03
s. of Zerahiah, s. of Uzzi, s. of Bukki, 7.04
s. of Abishua, s. of Phinehas, s. 7.05
s. of Eleazar, s. of Aaron the 7.05
Eliehoenai the s. of Zerahiah, 8.04
Shecaniah the s. of Jahaziel, and 8.05
Ebed the s. of Jonathan, and with 8.06
Jeshaiah the s. of Athaliah, and 8.07
Zebadiah the s. of Michael, and with 8.08
Obadiah the s. of Jehiel, and with 8.09
Shelomith the s. of Josiphiah, and 8.10
Zechariah the s. of Bebai, and with him 8.11
Johanan the s. of Hakkatan, and with 8.12
of Mahli the s. of Levi, s. of Israel, 8.18
Meremoth the priest, s. of Uriah, and 8.33
him was Eleazar the s. of Phinehas, 8.33
s. of Jeshua and Noadiah the s. of Binnui. 8.33
And Shecaniah the s. of Jehiel, 10.02
of Jehohanan the s. of Eliashib, 10.06
Only Jonathan the s. of Asahel and 10.15
Jahzeiah the s. of Tikvah opposed 10.15
of Jeshua the s. of Jozadak and 10.18
of Nehemiah the s. of Hacaliah. Neh 1.01
them Zaccur the s. of Imri built. 3.02
Meremoth the s. of Uriah, s. of Hakkoz 3.04
s. of Berechiah, s. of Meshezabel repaired. 3.04
them Zadok the s. of Baana repaired. 3.04
And Joiada the s. of Paseah and 3.06
Meshullam the s. of Besodeiah 3.06
Next to them Uzziel the s. of Harhaiah, 3.08
Next to them Rephaiah the s. of Hur, 3.09
Jedaiah the s. of Harumaph repaired 3.10
him Hattush the s. of Hashabneiah 3.10
Malchijah the s. of Harim and 3.11
and Hasshub the s. of Pahathmoab 3.11
to him Shallum the s. of Hallohesh, 3.12
Malchijah the s. of Rechab, ruler of 3.14
And Shallum the s. of Colhozeh, 3.15
After him Nehemiah the s. of Azbuk, 3.16
repaired: Rehum the s. of Bani; 3.17
Bavvai the s. of Henadad, ruler of 3.18
next to him Ezer the s. of Joshua, 3.19
After him Baruch the s. of Zabbai 3.20
Meremoth the s. of Uriah, s. of Hakkoz 3.21
Azariah the s. of Maaseiah, s. of Ananiah 3.23
After him Binnui the s. of Henadad 3.24
Palal the s. of Uzai repaired 3.25
After him Pedaiah the s. of Parosh 3.25
After them Zadok the s. of Immer 3.29
him Shemaiah the s. of Shecaniah, 3.29
Hananiah the s. of Shelemiah and 3.30
Hanun the sixth s. of Zalaph 3.30

SON (cont.)

Meshullam the s. of Berechiah Neh 3.30
Shemaiah the s. of Delaiah, s. of Mehetabel, 6.10
of Shecaniah the s. of Arah: 6.18
and his s. Jehohanan had taken the 6.18
Meshullam the s. of Berechiah as 6.18
of Jeshua the s. of Nun to that 8.17
the s. of Hacaliah, Zedekiah, 10.01
Jeshua the s. of Azaniah, Binnui of 10.09
the s. of Aaron, shall be with the 10.38
s. of Uzziah, s. of Zechariah, s. of Amariah, 11.04
s. of Shephatiah, s. of Mahalalel, 11.04
s. of Baruch, s. of Colhozeh, s. of Hazaiah, 11.05
s. of Adaiah, s. of Joiarib, s. of 11.05
s. of Zechariah, s. of the Shilonite. 11.05
Sallu the s. of Meshullam, s. of 11.07
s. of Joed, s. of Pedaiah, s. of Kolaiah, 11.07
s. of Maaseiah, s. of Ithiel, s. of Jeshaiah. 11.07
Joel the s. of Zichri was their 11.09
and Judah the s. of Hassenuah was 11.09
Jedaiah the s. of Joiarib, Jachin, 11.10
Seraiah the s. of Hilkiah, s. of Meshullam, 11.11
s. of Zadok, s. of Meraioth, s. of Ahitub, 11.11
and Adaiah the s. of Jeroham, 11.12
s. of Pelaliah, s. of Amzi, s. of Zechariah, 11.12
s. of Pashhur, s. of Malchijah, 11.12
the s. of Azarel, s. of Ahzai, s. 11.13
s. of Meshillemoth, s. of Immer, 11.13
was Zabdiel the s. of Haggedolim. 11.14
Shemaiah the s. of Hasshub, s. of 11.15
s. of Azrikam, s. of Hashabiah, s. of Bunni; 11.15
and Mattaniah the s. of Mica, 11.17
s. of Zabdi, s. of Asaph, who was 11.17
s. of Shammua, s. of Galal, s. of Jeduthun. 11.17
Uzzi the s. of Bani, s. of Hashabiah, 11.22
s. of Mattaniah, s. of Mica, of the 11.22
And Pethahiah the s. of Meshezabel, 11.24
the sons of Zerah the s. of Judah, 11.24
Zerubbabel the s. of Shealtiel, 12.01
days of Johanan the s. of Eliashib. 12.23
and Jeshua the s. of Kadmiel, 12.24
Joiakim the s. of Jeshua s. of Jozadak, 12.26
Zechariah the s. of Jonathan, s. of 12.35
s. of Shemaiah, s. of Mattaniah, s. 12.35
s. of Micaiah, s. of Zaccur, s. of Asaph; 12.35
of David and his s. Solomon. 12.45
Hanan the s. of Zaccur, s. of Mattaniah, 13.13
the s. of Eliashib the high priest, 13.28
the s. of Jair, s. of Shimei, s. of Kish, Est 2.05
Haman the s. of Hammedatha the 3.01
the s. of Hammedatha, the enemy of 3.10
he s. of Hammedatha, which he wrote 8.05
sons of Haman the s. of Hammedatha, 9.10
the s. of Hammedatha, the enemy of 8.24
and the s. of man, who is a worm! Job 25.06
Then Elihu the s. of Barachel the 32.02
And Elihu the s. of Barachel the 32.06
and your righteousness a s. of man. 35.08
"You are my s., today I have Ps 2.07
and the s. of man that thou dost 8.04
you slander your own mother's s. 50.20
thy rightousness to the royal s.! 72.01
the s. of Jesse, are ended. 72.20
the s. of man whom thou hast made 80.17
and save the s. of thy handmaid. 86.16
servant, the s. of thy handmaid. 116.16
or the s. of man that thou dost 144.03
in a s. of man, in whom there is no 146.03
s. of David, king of Israel: Pro 1.01
Hear, my s., your father's instruction, 1.08
My s., if sinners entice you, do not 1.10
my s., do not walk in the way with 1.15
My s., if you receive my words and 2.01
My s., do not forget my teaching, 3.01
My s., do not despise the LORD's 3.11
as a father the s. in whom he 3.12
My s., keep sound wisdom and 3.21
When I was a s. with my father, 4.03
Hear, my s., and accept my words, 4.10
My s., be attentive to my words; 4.20
My s., be attentive to my wisdom, 5.01
my s., with a loose woman and 5.20
My s., if you have become surety 6.01
my s., and save yourself, for you 6.03
My s., keep your father's commandment, 6.20
My s., keep my words and treasure 7.01
A wise s. makes a glad father, but a 10.01
but a foolish s. is a sorrow to his 10.01
A s. who gathers in summer is 10.05
but a s. who sleeps in harvest 10.05
A wise s. hears his father's instruction, 13.01
He who spares the rod hates his s., 13.24
A wise s. makes a glad father, but a 15.20
rule over a s. who acts shamefully, 17.02
A stupid s. is grief to a father; 17.21
A foolish s. is a grief to his 17.25
A foolish s. is ruin to his father, 19.13
Discipline your s. while there is 19.18
his mother is a s. who causes 19.26
Cease, my s., to hear instruction 19.27
My s., if your heart is wise, my 23.15
Hear, my s., and be, and direct 23.19
begets a wise s. will be glad in 23.24
My s., give me your heart, and let 23.26
My s., eat honey, for it is good, 24.13
My s., fear the LORD and the king, 24.21
Be wise, my s., and make my heart 27.11
He who keeps the law is a wise s., 28.07
Discipline your s., and he will give 29.17
The words of Agur s. of Jakeh of 30.01
What, my s.? What, s. of my womb? 31.02
What, s. of my vows? 31.02
the s. of David, king in Jerusalem. Ecc 1.01
either s. or brother, yet there is 4.08
and he is father of a s., 5.14
your king is the s. of free men, 10.17
My s., beware of anything beyond 12.12
The vision of Isaiah the s. of Amoz, Is 1.01
Isaiah the s. of Amoz saw concerning 2.01
In the days of Ahaz the s. of Jotham, 7.01
s. of Uzziah, king of Judah, Rezin 7.01
and Pekah the s. of Remaliah the 7.01
Ahaz, you and Shearjashub your s., 7.03
and Syria and the s. of Remaliah. 7.04
Ephraim and the s. of Remaliah, 7.05
and set up the s. of Tabeel as 7.06
of Samaria is the s. of Remaliah. 7.09
woman shall conceive and bear a s., 7.14
Zechariah the s. of Jeberechiah, 8.02
and she conceived and bore a s. 8.03
Rezin and the s. of Remaliah; 8.06
child is born, to us a s. is given; 9.06
which Isaiah the s. of Amoz saw. 13.01
heaven, O Day Star, s. of Dawn! 14.12
I am a s. of the wise, a s. of ancient kings"? 19.11
spoken by Isaiah the s. of Amoz, 20.02
servant Eliakim the s. of Hilkiah, 22.20
to him Eliakim the s. of Hilkiah, 36.03
and Joah the s. of Asaph, the 36.03
Then Eliakim the s. of Hilkiah, 36.22
and Joah the s. of Asaph, the 36.22
the prophet Isaiah the s. of Amoz. 37.02
Then Isaiah the s. of Amoz sent to 37.21
Esarhaddon his s. reigned in his 37.38
the prophet the s. of Amoz came to 38.01
Merodachbaladan the s. of Baladan, 39.01
compassion on the s. of her womb?" 49.15
of the s. of man who is made like 51.12
and the s. of man who holds it fast, 56.02
upon her she was delivered of a s. 66.07
the s. of Hilkiah, of the priests Jer 1.01
the days of Josiah the s. of Amon, 1.02
days of Jehoiakim the s. of Josiah, 1.03

SON (cont.)

Zedekiah, the s. of Josiah, king of Judah, Jer 1.03
make mourning as for an only s., 6.26
in the valley of the s. of Hinnom, 7.31
or the valley of the s. of Hinnom, 7.32
what Manasseh the s. of Hezekiah, 15.04
the s. of Immer, who was chief 20.01
"A s. is born to you," making him 20.15
him Pashhur the s. of Malchiah and 21.01
the priest, the s. of Maaseiah, saying, 21.01
concerning Shallum the s. of Josiah, 22.11
concerning Jehoiakim the s. of Josiah, 22.18
though Coniah the s. of Jehoiakim, 22.24
Jeconiah the s. of Jehoiakim, 24.01
year of Jehoiakim the s. of Josiah, 25.01
year of Josiah the s. of Amon, 25.03
of Jehoiakim the s. of Josiah, 26.01
Uriah the s. of Shemaiah from 26.20
Elnathan the s. of Achbor and 26.22
of Ahikam the s. of Shaphan was 26.24
reign of Zedekiah the s. of Josiah, 27.01
him and his s. and his grandson, 27.07
Jeconiah the s. of Jehoiakim, 27.20
Hananiah the s. of Azzur, the 28.01
place Jeconiah the s. of Jehoiakim, 28.04
of Elasah the s. of Shaphan and 29.03
and Gemariah the s. of Hilkiah, 29.03
concerning Ahab the s. of Kolaiah and 29.21
and Zedekiah the s. of Maaseiah, 29.21
Zephaniah the s. of Maaseiah the 29.25
Is Ephraim my dear s. 31.20
Hanamel the s. of Shallum your 32.07
to Baruch the s. of Neriah s. of Mahseiah, 32.12
purchase to Baruch the s. of Neriah, 32.16
in the valley of the s. of Hinnom, 32.35
not have a s. to reign on his 33.21
days of Jehoiakim the s. of Josiah, 35.01
Jaazaniah the s. of Jeremiah, s. of Habazziniah, 35.03
sons of Hanan the s. of Igdaliah, 35.04
of Maaseiah the s. of Shallum, 35.04
wine, for Jonadab the s. of Rechab, 35.06
voice of Jonadab the s. of Rechab, 35.08
Jonadab the s. of Rechab gave to 35.14
of Jonadab the s. of Rechab have 35.16
Jonadab the s. of Rechab shall 35.19
year of Jehoiakim the s. of Josiah, 36.01
called Baruch the s. of Neriah, 36.04
And Baruch the s. of Neriah did all 36.08
year of Jehoiakim the s. of Josiah 36.09
of Gemariah the s. of Shaphan the 36.10
Micaiah the s. of Gemariah, s. of Shaphan, 36.11
Delaiah the s. of Shemaiah, Elnathan 36.12
Elnathan the s. of Achbor, Gemariah 36.12
Gemariah the s. of Shaphan, Zedekiah 36.12
Zedekiah the s. of Hahaniah, and all 36.12
sent Jehudi the s. of Nethaniah, 36.14
s. of Shelemiah, s. of Cushi, to say 36.14
So Baruch the s. of Neriah took 36.14
the king's s. and Seraiah the s. of Azriel 36.26
Shelemiah the s. of Abdeel to 36.26
the s. of Neriah, who wrote on it at 36.32
Zedekiah the s. of Josiah, whom 37.01
of Coniah the s. of Jehoiakim. 37.01
sent Jehucal the s. of Shelemiah, 37.03
priest, the s. of Maaseiah, to Jeremiah 37.03
Irijah the s. of Shelemiah, s. of Hananiah, 37.13
Now Shephatiah the s. of Mattan, 38.01
Gedaliah the s. of Pashhur, Jucal 38.01
Jucal the s. of Shelemiah, and 38.01
and Pashhur the s. of Malchiah 38.01
the king's s., which was in the 38.06
Gedaliah the s. of Ahikam, s. of Shaphan, 39.14
to Gedaliah the s. of Ahikam, s. of Shaphan, 40.05
went to Gedaliah the s. of Ahikam, 40.06
Gedaliah the s. of Ahikam governor 40.07
Ishmael the s. of Nethaniah, Johanan 40.08
Jonanan the s. of Kareah, Seraiah 40.08
Seraiah the s. of Tanhumeth, the 40.08
Jezaniah the s. of the Maacathite, 40.08
Gedaliah the s. of Ahikam, s. of Shaphan, 40.09
Gedaliah the s. of Ahikam, s. of Shaphan, 40.11
Now Johanan the s. of Kareah and 40.13
Ishmael the s. of Nethaniah to 40.14
Gedaliah the s. of Ahikam would 40.14
Then Johanan the s. of Kareah spoke 40.15
slay Ishmael the s. of Nethaniah, 40.15
But Gedaliah the s. of Ahikam said 40.16
said to Johanan the s. of Kareah, 40.16
Ishmael the s. of Nethaniah, s. of Elishama, 41.01
men to Gedaliah the s. of Ahikam, 41.01
Ishmael the s. of Nethaniah and the 41.02
Gedaliah the s. of Ahikam, s. of Shaphan, 41.02
And Ishmael the s. of Nethaniah 41.06
"Come in to Gedaliah the s. of Ahikam." 41.06
Ishmael the s. of Nethaniah and the 41.07
Ishmael the s. of Nethaniah filled 41.09
to Gedaliah the s. of Ahikam. 41.10
Ishmael the s. of Nethaniah took 41.10
Johahan the s. of Kareah and all 41.11
Ishmael the s. of Nethaniah had 41.11
Ishmael the s. of Nethaniah. 41.12
saw Johanan the s. of Kareah and 41.13
went to Johanan the s. of Kareah. 41.14
But Ishmael the s. of Nethaniah 41.15
Then Johanan the s. of Kareah and 41.16
Ishmael the s. of Nethaniah had 41.16
slain Gedaliah the s. of Ahikam— 41.16
Ishmael the s. of Nethaniah had 41.18
slain Gedaliah the s. of Ahikam, 41.18
and Johanan the s. of Kareah and 42.01
and Azariah the s. of Hoshaiah, 42.01
Johanan the s. of Kareah and all 42.08
Azariah the s. of Hoshaiah and 43.02
and Johanan the s. of Kareah and 43.02
but Baruch the s. of Neriah has set 43.03
So Johanan the s. of Kareah and all 43.04
But Johanan the s. of Kareah and 43.05
Gedaliah the s. of Ahikam, s. of Shaphan; 43.06
and Baruch the s. of Neriah. 43.06
spoke to Baruch the s. of Neriah, 45.01
year of Jehoiakim the s. of Josiah, 45.01
year of Jehoiakim the s. of Josiah, 46.02
and no s. of man shall sojourn in 50.40
through which no s. of man passes. 51.43
Seraiah the s. of Neriah, s. of Mahseiah, 51.59
the s. of Buzi, in the land of the Eze 1.03
"S. of man, stand upon your feet, and 2.01
"S. of man, I sent you to the people 2.03
And you, s. of man, be not afraid of 2.06
"But you, s. of man, hear what I say 2.08
"S. of man, eat what is offered to 3.01
"S. of man, eat this scroll that I 3.03
"S. of man, go, get you to the house 3.04
"S. of man, all my words that I 3.10
"S. of man, I have made you a 3.17
And you, O s. of man, behold, cords 3.25
"And you, O s. of man, take a brick 4.01
"S. of man, behold, I will break the 4.16
"And you, O s. of man, take a sharp 5.01
"S. of man, set your face toward the 6.02
"And you, O s. of man, thus says the 7.02
"S. of man, lift up your eyes now in 8.05
"S. of man, do you see what they are 8.06
"S. of man, dig in the wall"; and 8.08
Jaazaniah the s. of Shaphan 8.11
"S. of man, have you seen what the 8.12
"Have you seen this, O s. of man? 8.15
"Have you see this, O s. of man? 8.17
them Jaazaniah the s. of Azzur, 11.01
and Pelatiah the s. of Benaiah, 11.01
"S. of man, these are the men who 11.02
them, prophesy, O s. of man." 11.04
Pelatiah the s. of Benaiah died. 11.13
"S. of man, your brethren, even your 11.15

SON (cont.)

"S. of man, you dwell in the midst Eze 12.02
Therefore, s. of man, prepare for 12.03
"S. of man, has not the house of 12.09
"S. of man, eat your bread with 12.18
"S. of man, what is this proverb 12.22
"S. of man, behold, they of the house 12.27
"S. of man, prophesy against the 13.02
"And you, s. of man, set your face 13.17
"S. of man, these men have taken 14.03
"S. of man, when a land sins against 14.13
deliver neither s. nor daughter; 14.20
"S. of man, how does the wood of the 15.02
"S. of man, make known to Jerusalem 16.02
"S. of man, propound a riddle, and 17.02
well as the soul of the s. is mine: 18.04
"If he begets a s. who is a robber, 18.10
man begets a s. who sees all the 18.14
should not the s. suffer for the 18.19
'When the s. has done what is 18.19
The s. shall not suffer for the 18.20
suffer for the iniquity of the s.; 18.20
"S. of man, speak to the elders of 20.03
s. of man, will you judge them? 20.04
"Therefore. s. of man, speak to the 20.27
"S. of man, set your face toward the 20.46
"S. of man, set your face toward 21.02
Sigh therefore, s. of man; 21.06
"S. of man, prophesy and say, Thus 21.09
my s., with everything of wood. 21.10
Cry and wail, s. of man, for it is 21.12
"Prophesy therefore, s. of man; 21.14
"S. of man, mark two ways for the 21.19
"And you, s. of man, prophesy, and say, 21.28
"And you, s. of man, will you judge, 22.02
"S. of man, the house of Israel has 22.18
"S. of man, say to her, You are a 22.24
"S. of man, there were two women, the 23.02
"S. of man, will you judge Oholah 23.36
"S. of man, write down the name of 24.02
"S. of man, behold, I am about to 24.16
"And you, s. of man, on the day when 24.25
"S. of man, set your face toward the 25.02
"S. of man, because Tyre said 26.02
"Now you, s. of man, raise a lamentation 27.02
"S. of man, say to the prince of 28.02
"S. of man, raise a lamentation over 28.12
"S. of man, set your face toward 28.21
"S. of man, set your face against 29.02
"S. of man, Nebuchadrezzar king of 29.18
"S. of man, prophesy, and say, Thus 30.02
"S. of man, I have broken the arm of 30.21
"S. of man, say to Pharaoh king of 31.02
"S. of man, raise a lamentation over 32.02
"S. of man, wail over the multitude 32.18
"S. of man, speak to your people and 33.02
"So you, s. of man, I have made a 33.07
"And you, s. of man, say to the house 33.10
And you, s. of man, say to your 33.12
"S. of man, the inhabitants of these 33.24
"As for you, s. of man, your people 33.30
"S. of man, prophesy against the 34.02
"S. of man, set your face against 35.02
"And you, s. of man, prophesy to the 36.01
"S. of man, when the house of Israel 36.17
"S. of man, can these bones live?" 37.03
s. of man, and say to the breath, 37.09
"S. of man, these bones are the 37.11
"S. of man, take a stick and write 37.16
"S. of man, set your face toward Gog, 38.02
"Therefore, s. of man, prophesy, and 38.14
"And you, s. of man, prophesy against 39.01
"As for you, s. of man, thus says the 39.17
"S. of man, look with your eyes, and 40.04
"S. of man, this is the place of my 43.07
"And you, s. of man, describe to the 43.10
"S. of man, thus says the Lord GOD: 43.18
"S. of man, mark well, see with your 44.05
for s. or daughter, for brother or 44.25
"S. of man, have you seen this?" 47.06
fourth is like a s. of the gods." Dan 3.25
And you his s., Belshazzar, have not 5.22
there came one like a s. of man, 7.13
O s. of man, that the vision is for 8.17
year of Darius the s. of Ahasuerus, 9.01
that came to Hosea the s. of Beeri, Hos 1.01
days of Jeroboam the s. of Joash, 1.01
she conceived and bore him a s. 1.03
she conceived and bore a s. 1.08
and out of Egypt I called my s. 11.01
for him, but he is an unwise s.; 3.13
came to Joel, the s. of Pethuel: Joe 1.01
days of Jeroboam the s. of Joash, Amo 1.01
am no prophet, nor a prophet's s.; 7.14
like the mourning for an only s., 8.10
came to Jonah the s. of Amittai, Jon 1.01
what Balaam the s. of Beor answered Mic 6.05
for the s. treats the father with 7.06
Zephaniah the s. of Cushi, s. of Gedaliah, Zep 1.01
s. of Amariah, s. of Hezekiah, in 1.01
the days of Josiah the s. of Amon, 1.01
to Zerubbabel the s. of Shealtiel, Hag 1.01
and to Joshua the s. of Jehozadak, 1.01
Then Zerubbabel the s. of Shealtiel, 1.12
and Joshua the s. of Jehozadak, 1.12
of Zerubbabel the s. of Shealtiel, 1.14
of Joshua the s. of Jehozadak, 1.14
to Zerubbabel the s. of Shealtiel, 2.02
and to Joshua the s. of Jehozadak, 2.02
s. of Jehozadak, the high priest; 2.04
the s. of Shealtiel, says the LORD, 2.23
Zechariah the s. of Berechiah, s. of Iddo, Zec 1.01
to Zechariah the s. of Berechiah, s. of Iddo, 1.07
of Josiah, the s. of Zephaniah. 6.10
the s. of Jehozadak, the high priest; 6.11
and Josiah the s. of Zephaniah. 6.14
a s. honors his father, and a Mal 1.06
a man spares his s. who serves him. 3.17
the s. of David, the s. of Abraham. Mt 1.01
s. of David, do not fear to take 1.20
she will bear a s., and you shall 1.21
shall conceive and bear a s., 1.23
her not until she had bore a s.; 1.25
"Out of Egypt have I called my s." 2.15
saying, "This is my beloved S., 3.17
to him, "If you are the S. of God, 4.03
to him, "If you are the S. of God, 4.06
James the s. of Zebedee and John 4.21
if his s. asks him for a loaf, will 7.09
but the S. of man has nowhere to 8.20
you to do with us, O S. of God? 8.29
the paralytic, take heart, my s.; 9.02
know that the S. of man has 9.06
"Have mercy on us, S. of David." 9.27
James the s. of Zebedee, and John 10.02
James the s. of Alphaeus, and 10.03
Israel, before the S. of man comes. 10.23
he who loves s. or daughter more 10.37
the S. of man came eating and 11.19
one knows the S. except the Father, 11.27
except the S. and any one to whom 11.27
one to whom the S. chooses to 11.27
For the S. of man is lord of the 12.08
said, "Can this be the S. of David?" 12.23
against the S. of man will be 12.32
so will the S. of man be three days 12.40
the good seed is the S. of man; 13.37
The S. of man will send his angels, 13.41
Is not this the carpenter's s.? 13.55
truly you are the S. of God." 14.33
mercy on me, O Lord, S. of David; 15.22
do men say that the S. of man is?" 16.13
the S. of the living God." 16.16

SON (cont.)

For the S. of man is to come with Mt 16.27
they see the S. of man coming in 16.28
cloud said, this is my beloved S., 17.05
until the S. of man is raised from 17.09
So also the S. of man will suffer 17.12
"Lord, have mercy on my s., 17.15
"The S. of man is to be delivered 17.22
For the S. of man came to save the * 18.11
when the S. of man shall sit on his 19.28
and the S. of man will be delivered 20.18
even as he S. of man came not to 20.28
out, "Have mercy on us, S. of David!" 20.30
have mercy on us, S. of David!" 20.31
shouted "Hosanna to the S. of David! 21.09
temple, "Hosanna to the S. of David!" 21.15
'S., go and work in the vineyard 21.28
Afterward he sent his s. to them, 21.37
saying, 'They will respect my s.' 21.37
But when the tenants saw the s., 21.38
gave a marriage feast for his s., 22.02
of the Christ? "Whose s. is he?" 22.42
They said to him, "The s. of David." 22.42
calls him Lord, how is he his s.?" 22.45
of Zechariah the s. of Barachiah, 23.35
be the coming of the S. of man. 24.27
the sign of the S. of man in 24.30
will see the S. of man coming on 24.30
nor the S., but the Father only. 24.36
be the coming of the S. of man. 24.37
be the coming of the S. of man. 24.39
for the S. of man is coming at an 24.44
"When the S. of man comes in his 25.31
and the S. of man will be delivered 26.02
The S. of man goes as it is written 26.24
man by whom the S. of man is 26.24
and the S. of man is betrayed into 26.45
you are the Christ, the S. of God." 26.63
will see the S. of man seated at 26.64
If you are the S. of God, 27.40
for he said, 'I am the S. of God.'" 27.43
said, "Truly this was a S. of God!" 27.54
and of the S. and of the Holy 28.19
of Jesus Christ, the S. of God. Mk 1.01
heaven, thou art my beloved S.; 1.11
saw James the s. of Zebedee and 1.19
"My s., your sins are forgiven." 2.05
know that the S. of man has 2.10
he saw Levi the s. of Alphaeus 2.14
so the S. of man is lord even of 2.28
cried out, "You are the S. of God." 3.11
James the s. of Zebedee and John 3.17
and James the s. of Alphaeus, and 3.18
S. of the Most High God? 5.07
the s. of Mary and brother of James 6.03
them that the S. of man must 8.31
of him will the S. of man also be 8.38
the cloud, "This is my beloved S.; 9.07
until the S. of man should have 9.09
how is it written of the S. of man, 9.12
I brought my s. to you, for he has a 9.17
"The S. of man will be delivered 9.31
and the S. of man will be delivered 10.33
For the S. of man also came not to 10.45
the s. of Timaeus, was sitting by 10.46
S. of David, have mercy on me!" 10.47
"S. of David, have mercy on me!" 10.48
He had still one other, a beloved s.; 12.06
saying, 'They will respect my s.' 12.06
that the Christ is he s. of David? 12.35
so how is he his s.?" 12.37
will see the S. of man coming in 13.26
nor the S., but only the Father. 13.32
For the S. of man goes as it is 14.21
man by whom the S. of man is 14.21
the S. of man is betrayed into the 14.41
the Christ, the S. of the Blessed?" 14.61
will see the S. of man sitting at 14.62
"Truly this man was a s. of God!" 15.39
wife Elizabeth will bear you a s., Lk 1.13
conceive in your womb and bear a s., 1.31
be called the S. of the Most High; 1.32
will be called holy, the S. of God. 1.35
old age has also conceived a s.; 1.36
delivered, and she gave birth to a s. 1.57
her first-born s. and wrapped him 2.07
"S., why have you treated us so? 2.48
to John the s. of Zechariah in the 3.02
heaven, "Thou art my beloved S.; 3.22
s. (as was supposed) of Joseph, the s. of Heli, 3.23
s. of Matthat, the s. of Levi, the s. of Melchi, 3.24
s. of Jannai, the s. of Joseph, 3.24
the s. of Mattathias, the s. of Amos, 3.25
s. of Nahum, the s. of Esli, the s. of Naggai, 3.25
the s. of Maath, the s. of Mattathias, 3.26
s. of Semein, the s. of Josech, the s. of Joda, 3.26
the s. of Jonan, the s. of Rhesa, 3.27
s. of Zerubbabel, the s. of Shealtiel, the s. 3.27
the s. of Melchi, the s. of Addi, the s. of Cosam, 3.28
the s. of Elmadam, the s. of Er, 3.28
s. of Jesus, the s. of Eliezer, the s. of Jorim, 3.29
the s. of Matthat, the s. of Levi, 3.29
s. of Symeon, the s. of Judas, the s. of Joseph, 3.30
the s. of Jonam, the s. of Eliakim, 3.30
s. of Melea, the s. of Menna, the s. of Mattatha, 3.31
the s. of Nathan, the s. of David, 3.31
s. of Jesse, the s. of Obed, the s. of Boaz, 3.32
the s. of Sala, the s. of Nahshon, 3.32
the s. of Amminadab, the s. of Admin, 3.33
the s. of Arni, the s. of Hezron, 3.33
the s. of Perez, the s. of Judah, 3.33
s. of Jacob, the s. of Isaac, the s. of Abraham, 3.34
the s. of Terah, the s. of Nahor, 3.34
s. of Serug, the s. of Reu, the s. of Peleg, 3.35
the s. of Eber, the s. of Shelah, 3.35
the s. of Cainan, the s. of Arphaxad, 3.36
s. of Shem, the s. of Noah, the s. of Lamech, 3.36
the s. of Methuselah, the s. of Enoch, 3.37
the s. of Jared, the s. of Mahaleleel, 3.37
of Mahalaleel, the s. of Cainan, 3.37
the s. of Enos, the s. of Seth, the 3.38
the s. of Adam, the s. of God. 3.38
to him, "If you are the S. of God, 4.03
to him, "If you are the S. of God, 4.09
they said, "Is not this Joseph's s.?" 4.22
crying, "You are the S. of God!" 4.41
know that the S. of man has 5.24
"The S. of man is lord of the 6.05
and James the s. of Alphaeus, and 6.15
and Judas the s. of James, and Judas 6.16
evil, on account of the S. of man! 6.22
the only s. of his mother and she 7.12
The S. of man has come eating and 7.34
S. of the Most High God? 8.28
saying, the S. of man must suffer 9.22
of him will the S. of man be 9.26
saying, "This is my S., my Chosen; 9.35
I beg you to look upon my s., 9.38
bear with you? Bring your s. here." 9.41
for the S. of man is to be delivered 9.44
the S. of man came not to destroy * 9.55
but the S. of man has nowhere to 9.58
And if a s. of peace is there, your 10.06
knows who the S. is except the 10.22
is except the S. and any one to 10.22
one to whom the S. chooses to 10.22
if his s. asks for a fish, will 11.11
so will the S. of man be to this 11.30
the S. of man also will acknowledge 12.08
against the S. of man will be 12.10
for the S. of man is coming at an 12.40
father against s. and s. against father, 12.53
the younger s. gathered all he had 15.13
longer worthy to be called your s.; 15.19

SON (cont.)

And the s. said to him, 'Father, I Lk 15.21
longer worthy to be called your s.' 15.21
for this my s. was dead, and is 15.24
"Now his elder s. was in the field; 15.25
But when this s. of yours came, who 15.30
'S., you are always with me, and all 15.31
'S., remember that you in your 16.25
one of the days of the S. of man, 17.22
so will the S. of man be in his day. 17.24
it be in the days of the S. of man. 17.26
day when the S. of man is revealed. 17.30
when the S. of man comes, will he 18.08
written of the S. of man by the 18.31
S. of David, have mercy on me!" 18.38
"S. of David, have mercy on me!" 18.39
since he also is a s. of Abraham. 19.09
For the S. of man came to seek and 19.10
I will send my beloved s.; 20.13
say that the Christ is David's s.? 20.41
him Lord; so how is he his s.?" 20.44
will see the S. of man coming in a 21.27
and to stand before the S. of man." 21.36
For the S. of man goes as it has 22.22
you betray the S. of man with a 22.48
But from now on the S. of man shall 22.69
said, "Are you the S. of God, then?" 22.70
that the S. of man must be delivered 24.07
as of the only S. from the Father. Jn 1.14
the only S., who is in the bosom of 1.18
witness that this is the S. of God." 1.34
"So you are Simon of the s. of John? 1.42
of Nazareth, the s. of Joseph." 1.45
him, "Rabbi, you are the S. of God! 1.49
and descending upon the S. of man." 1.51
descended from heaven, the S. of man. 3.13
so must the S. of man be lifted up, 3.14
the world that he gave his only S., 3.16
For God sent the S. into the world, 3.17
in the name of the only S. of God. 3.18
the Father loves the S., 3.35
believes in the S. has eternal 3.36
not obey the S. shall not see life, 3.36
that Jacob gave to his s. Joseph. 4.05
was an official whose s. was ill. 4.46
him to come down and heal his s., 4.47
"Go; your s. will live." The man 4.50
told him that his s. was living. 4.51
said to him, "Your s. will live"; 4.53
the S. can do nothing of his own 5.19
he does, that the S. does likewise. 5.19
For the Father loves the S., 5.20
so also the S. gives life to whom 5.21
has given all judgment to the S., 5.22
that all may honor the S., 5.23
not honor the S. does not honor 5.23
hear the voice of the S. of God, 5.25
has granted the S. also to have 5.26
because he is the S. of man. 5.27
which the S. of man will give to 6.27
who sees the S. and believes in 6.40
the s. of Joseph, whose father and 6.42
flesh of the S. of man and drink 6.53
were to see the S. of man ascending 6.62
of Judas the s. of Simon Iscariot, 6.71
you have lifted up the S. of man, 8.28
the s. continues for ever. 8.35
So if the S. makes you free, you 8.36
"Is this your s., who you say was 9.19
"We know that this is our s., 9.20
"Do you believe in the S. of man?" 9.35
I said, 'I am the S. of God'? 10.36
so that the S. of God may be 11.04
the S. of God, he who is coming into 11.27
come for the S. of man to be 12.23
say that the S. of man must be 12.34
Who is this S. of man?" 12.34
Simon's s., to betray him, 13.02
the s. of Simon Iscariot. 13.26
"Now is the S. of man glorified, and 13.31
Father may be glorified in the S.; 14.13
glorify thy S. that the S. may 17.01
is lost but the s. of perdition, 17.12
he has made himself the S. of God." 19.07
his mother, "Woman, behold your s.!" 19.26
the S. of God, and that believing 20.31
s. of John, do you love me more than 21.15
s. of John, do you love me?" 21.16
s. of John, do you love me?" 21.17
James the s. of Alphaeus and Simon Ac 1.13
Zealot and Judas the s. of James. 1.13
S. of encouragement), a Levite, a 4.36
and brought him up as her own s. 7.21
and the S. of man standing at the 7.56
that Jesus Christ is the S. of God." * 8.37
Jesus, saying, "He is the S. of God." 9.20
and said, "You s. of the devil, you 13.10
God gave them Saul the s. of Kish, 13.21
in David the s. of Jesse a man 13.22
'Thou art my S., today I have 13.33
the s. of a Jewish woman who was a 16.01
the s. of Pyrrhus, accompanied him; 20.04
I am a Pharisee, a s. of Pharisees; 23.06
Now the s. of Paul's sister heard of 23.16
the gospel concerning his S., Rom 1.03
and designated S. of God in power 1.04
my spirit in the gospel of his S., 1.09
to God by the death of his S., 5.10
sending his own S. in the likeness 8.03
conformed to the image of his S., 8.29
spare his own S. but gave him up 8.32
return and Sarah shall have a s." 9.09
into the fellowship of his S., 1Co 1.09
then the S. himself will also be 15.28
For the S. of God, Jesus Christ, whom 2Co 1.19
was pleased to reveal his S. to me, Gal 1.16
I live by faith in the S. of God, 2.20
fully come, God sent forth his S., 4.04
Spirit of his S. into our hearts, 4.06
but a s., and if a s. then an heir. 4.07
But the s. of the slave was born 4.23
the s. of the free woman through 4.23
"Cast out the slave and her s.; for the s. 4.30
with the s. of the free woman." 4.30
of the knowledge of the S. of God, Eph 4.13
how as a s. with a father he has Php 2.22
to the kingdom of his beloved S., Col 1.13
and to wait for his S. from heaven, 1Th 1.10
is revealed, the s. of perdition, 2Th 2.03
my s., in accordance with the 1Ti 1.18
You then, my s., be strong in the 2Ti 2.01
days he has spoken to us by a S., Heb 1.02
"Thou art my S., today I have 1.05
and he shall be to me a s.?" 1.05
But of the S. he says, "Thy throne, O 1.08
or the s. of man, that thou carest 2.06
faithful over God's house as a s. 3.06
the S. of God, let us hold fast our 4.14
"Thou art my S., today I have 5.05
Although he was a S., 5.08
crucify the S. of God on their own 6.06
resembling the S. of God he 7.03
appoints a S. who has been made 7.28
man who has spurned the S. of God, 10.29
was ready to offer up his only s., 11.17
be called the s. of Pharaoh's 11.24
"My s., do not regard lightly the 12.05
chastises every s. whom he receives." 12.06
for what s. is there whom his 12.07
he offered his s. Isaac upon the Jas 2.21
and so does my s. Mark. 1Pe 5.13
Glory, "This is my beloved S., 2Pe 1.17
the s. of Beor, who loved gain from 2.15
and with his S. Jesus Christ. 1Jn 1.03

SON (cont.)
of Jesus his S. cleanses us from 1Jn 1.07
who denies the Father and the S. 2.22
who denies the S. has the Father. 2.23
confesses the S. has the Father 2.23
abide in the S. and in the Father. 2.24
The reason the S. of God appeared 3.08
the name of his S. Jesus Christ 3.23
sent his only S. into the world, 4.09
us and sent his S. to be the 4.10
has sent his S. as the Savior of 4.14
that Jesus is the S. of God, 4.15
that Jesus is the S. of God? 5.05
he has borne witness to his S. 5.09
believes in the S. of God has the 5.10
that God has borne to his S. 5.10
life, and this life is in his S. 5.11
He who has the S. has life; 5.12
he who has not the S. has not life. 5.12
in the name of the S. of God, 5.13
know that the S. of God has come 5.20
is true, in his S. Jesus Christ. 5.20
from Jesus Christ the Father's S. 2Jn 1.03
has both the Father and the S. 1.09
lampstands one like a s. of man, Rev 1.13
write: 'The words of the S. of God, 2.18
on the cloud one like a s. of man, 14.14
be his God and he shall be my s. 21.07

SONG
of Israel sang this s. to the LORD, Ex 15.01
The LORD is my strength and my s., 15.02
Then Israel sang this s.: Num 21.17
Now therefore write this s., Deu 31.19
that this s. may be a witness for 31.19
this s. shall confront them as a 31.21
So Moses wrote this s. the same day, 31.22
words of this s. until they were 31.30
words of this s. in the hearing of 32.44
Awake, awake, utter a s.! Jc 5.12
words of this s. on the day when 2Sa 22.01
the service of s. in the house of 1Ch 6.31
They ministered with s. before the 6.32
with s. and lyres and harps and 13.08
and instruments for sacred s. 16.42
and when the s. was raised, with 2Ch 5.13
the s. to the LORD began also, and 29.27
"And now I have become their s., Job 30.09
singing aloud a s. of thanksgiving, Ps 26.07
and with my s. I give thanks to him. 28.07
Sing to him a new s., 33.03
new s. in my mouth, a s. of praise 40.03
and at night his s. is with me, 42.08
lift up a s. to him who rides upon 68.04
praise the name of God with a s.; 69.30
their maidens had no marriage s. 78.63
Raise a s., sound the timbrel, the 81.02
O sing to the LORD a new s.; 96.01
O sing to the LORD a new s., 98.01
into joyous s. and sing praises! 98.04
The LORD is my strength and my s.; 118.14
sing the LORD's s. in a foreign 137.04
I will sing a new s. to thee, O God; 144.09
and a s. of praise is seemly. 147.01
Sing to the LORD a new s., 149.01
wise than to hear the s. of fools. Ecc 7.05
daughters of s. are brought low; 12.04
The S. of Songs, which is Solomon's. Sol 1.01
beloved a love s. concerning his Is 5.01
LORD GOD is my strength and my s., 12.02
Tyre as in the s. of the harlot: 23.15
so the s. of the ruthless is 25.05
In that day this s. will be sung in 26.01
You shall have a s. as in the night 30.29
Sing to the LORD a new s., 42.10
thanksgiving and the voice of s. 51.03
take up a taunt s. against you, Mic 2.04
and they sang a new s., Rev 5.09
and they sing a new s. before the 14.03
learn that s. except the hundred 14.03
And they sing the s. of Moses, 15.03
and the s. of the Lamb, saying, 15.03

SONGS
sent you away with mirth and s., Gen 31.27
with s. of joy, and with instruments 1Sa 18.06
with s. and lyres and harps and 2Sa 6.05
and his s. were a thousand and five 1Ki 4.32
charge of the s. of thanksgiving. Neh 12.08
and there were s. of praise and 12.46
Maker, who gives s. in the night, Job 35.10
glad shouts and s. of thanksgiving, Ps 42.04
Shout to God with loud s. of joy! 47.01
and the drunkards make s. about me. 69.12
noise to him with s. of praise! 95.02
and tell of his deeds in s. of joy! 107.22
Hark, glad s. of victory in the 118.15
have been my s. in the house of my 119.54
our captors required of us s., 137.02
"Sing us one of the s. of Zion!" 137.03
He who sings s. to a heavy heart is Pro 25.20
The Song of S., which is Solomon's. Sol 1.01
in the vineyards no s. are sung, Is 16.10
sing many s., that you may be 23.16
of the earth we hear s. of praise, 24.16
them shall come s. of thanksgiving, Jer 30.19
burden of their s. all day long. Lam 3.14
I am the burden of their s. 3.63
And I will stop the music of your s., Eze 26.13
who sings love s. with a beautiful 33.32
Take away from me the noise of your s.; Amo 5.23
who sing idle s. to the sound of 6.05
The s. of the temple shall become 8.03
and all your s. into lamentation; 8.10
psalms and hymns and spiritual s., Eph 5.19
and spiritual s. with thankfulness Col 3.16

SON-IN-LAW
the s. of the Timnite, because he Ju 15.06
the girl's father said to his s., 19.05
that I should be s. to the king?" 1Sa 18.18
time, "You shall now be my s." 18.21
now then become the king's s.'" 18.22
thing to become the king's s., 18.23
David well to be the king's s. 18.26
that he might become the king's s. 18.27
as David, who is the king's s., 22.14
for he was s. to the house of Ahab. 2Ki 8.27
he was the s. of Shecaniah the son Neh 6.18
was the s. of Sanballat the Horonite; 13.28

SON'S
I may eat of my s. game and bless Gen 27.25
arise, and eat of his s. game, 27.31
I pray, some of your s. mandrakes." 30.14
you take away my s. mandrakes also?" 30.15
you tonight for your s. mandrakes." 30.15
hired you with my s. mandrakes." 30.16
whether it is your s. robe or not." 37.32
it, and said, "It is my s. robe; 37.33
flint and cut off her s. foreskin, Ex 4.25
son and of your s. son how I have 10.02
nakedness of your s. daughter or of Lev 18.10
she is your s. wife, you shall not 18.15
not take her s. daughter or her 18.17
you and your son and your s. son, Deu 6.02
the kingdom out of his s. hand, 1Ki 11.35
but in his s. days I will bring the 21.29
his name, and what is his s. name? Pro 30.04

SONS
and he had other s. and daughters. Gen 5.04
and had other s. and daughters. 5.07
and had other s. and daughters. 5.10

SONS (cont.)

and had other s. and daughters.	Gen 5.13
and had other s. and daughters.	5.16
and had other s. and daughters.	5.19
and had other s. and daughters.	5.22
and had other s. and daughters.	5.26
and had other s. and daughters.	5.30
the s. of God saw that the daughters	6.02
when the s. of God came in to the	6.04
And Noah had three s.,	6.10
your s., your wife, and your sons'	6.18
And Noah and his s. and his wife	7.07
On the very same day Noah and his s.,	7.13
wives of his s. with them entered	7.13
and your s. and your sons' wives	8.16
and his s. and his wife and his	8.18
And God blessed Noah and his s.,	9.01
to Noah and to his s. with him,	9.08
The s. of Noah who went forth from	9.18
These three were the s. of Noah;	9.19
the generations of the s. of Noah,	10.01
s. were born to them after the	10.01
The s. of Japheth: Gomer, Magog, Madai,	10.02
The s. of Gomer: Ashkenaz, Riphath,	10.03
The s. of Javan: Elishah, Tarshish,	10.04
These are the s. of Japheth in	10.05
The s. of Ham: Cush, Egypt, Put, and	10.06
The s. of Cush: Seba, Havilah, Sabtah,	10.07
The s. of Raamah: Sheba and Dedan.	10.07
These are the s. of Ham, by their	10.20
The s. of Shem: Elam, Asshur, Arpachshad,	10.22
The s. of Aram: Uz, Hul, Gether, and	10.23
To Eber were born two s.:	10.25
all these were the s. of Joktan.	10.29
These are the s. of Shem, by their	10.31
are the families of the s. of Noah,	10.32
which the s. of men had built.	11.05
and had other s. and daughters.	11.11
and had other s. and daughters.	11.13
and had other s. and daughters.	11.15
and had other s. and daughters.	11.17
and had other s. and daughters.	11.19
and had other s. and daughters.	11.21
and had other s. and daughters.	11.23
and had other s. and daughters.	11.25
Sons-in-law, s., daughters, or any	19.12
presence of the s. of my people I	23.11
The s. of Dedan were Asshurim,	25.03
The s. of Midian were Ephah, Epher,	25.04
But to the s. of his concubines	25.06
Isaac and Ismael his s. buried him	25.09
are the names of the s. of Ishmael,	25.13
These are the s. of Ismael and	25.16
your mother's s. bow down to you.	27.29
because I have borne him three s.";	29.34
because I have borne him six s.";	30.20
and put them in charge of his s.;	30.35
heard that the s. of Laban were	31.01
and set his s. and his wives on	31.17
me to kiss my s. and my daughters	31.28
And from the s. of Hamor, Shechem's	33.19
but his s. were with his cattle in	34.05
The s. of Jacob came in from the	34.07
The s. of Jacob answered Shechem	34.13
two of the s. of Jacob, Simeon and	34.25
And the s. of Jacob came upon the	34.27
did not pursue the s. of Jacob.	35.05
Now the s. of Jacob were twelve.	35.22
The s. of Leah: Reuben (Jacob's	35.23
The s. of Rachel: Joseph and Benjamin	35.24
The s. of Bilhah, Rachel's maid: Dan	35.25
The s. of Zilpah, Leah's maid: Gad and	35.26
These were the s. of Jacob who were	35.26
and his s. Esau and Jacob buried	35.29
These are the s. of Esau who were	36.05
his s., his daughters, and all the	36.06
These are the names of Esau's s.:	36.10
The s. of Eliphaz were Teman, Omar,	36.11
These are the s. of Adah,	36.12
These are the s. of Reuel: Nahath,	36.13
These are the s. of Basemath, Esau's	36.13
These are the s. of Oholibamah the	36.14
These are the chiefs of the s. of Esau.	36.15
The s. of Eliphaz the first-born of	36.15
they are the s. of Adah.	36.16
These are the s. of Reuel, Esau's son:	36.17
they are the s. of Basemath, Esau's	36.17
These are the s. of Oholibamah,	36.18
These are the s. of Esau (that is,	36.19
These are the s. of Seir the Horite,	36.20
the s. of Seir in the land of Edom.	36.21
the s. of Lotan were Hori and Heman;	36.22
These are the s. of Shobal: Alvan,	36.23
These are the s. of Zibeon: Aiah and	36.24
These are the s. of Dishon: Hemdan,	36.26
These are the s. of Ezer: Bilhan,	36.27
These are the s. of Dishan: Uz and	36.28
a lad with the s. of Bilhah and	37.02
All his s. and all his daughters	37.35
of famine came, Joseph had two s.,	41.50
grain in Egypt, he said to his s.,	42.01
Thus the s. of Israel came to buy	42.05
We are all s. of one man, we are	42.11
the s. of one man in the land of	42.13
twelve brothers, s. of our father;	42.32
"Slay my two s. if I do not bring	42.37
know that my wife bore me two s.;	44.27
The s. of Israel did so;	45.21
and the s. of Israel carried Jacob	46.05
his s., and his sons' s. with him,	46.07
came into Egypt, Jacob and his s.	46.08
and the s. of Reuben: Hanoch, Pallu,	46.09
The s. of Simeon: Jemuel, Jamin, Ohad,	46.10
The s. of Levi: Gershon, Kohath, and	46.11
The s. of Judah: Er, Onan, Shelah,	46.12
and the s. of Perez were Hezron and	46.12
The s. of Issachar: Tola, Puvah, Iob,	46.13
The s. of Zebulun: Sered, Elon, and	46.14
(these are the s. of Leah, whom she	46.15
altogether his s. and his daughters	46.15
The s. of Gad: Ziphion, Haggi, Shuni,	46.16
The s. of Asher: Imnah, Ishvah, Ishvi,	46.17
And the s. of Beriah: Heber and	46.17
(these are the s. of Zilpah, whom	46.18
The s. of Rachel, Jacob's wife: Joseph	46.19
And the s. of Benjamin: Bela, Becher,	46.21
(these are the s. of Rachel, who	46.22
The s. of Dan: Hushim.	46.23
The s. of Naphtali: Jahzeel, Guni,	46.24
(these are the s. of Bilhah, whom	46.25
and the s. of Joseph, who were born	46.27
so he took with him his two s.,	48.01
And now your two s.,	48.05
When Israel saw Joseph's s.,	48.08
"They are my s., whom God has given	48.09
Then Jacob called his s.,	49.01
O s. of Jacob, and hearken to Israel	49.02
your father's s. shall bow down	49.08
When Jacob finished charging his s.,	49.33
Thus his s. did for him as he had	50.12
for his s. carried him to the land	50.13
took an oath of the s. of Israel,	50.25
names of the s. of Israel who came	Ex 1.01
the s. of Israel, out of Egypt."	3.10
and bring the s. of Israel out of	3.11
them on your s. and on your	3.22
wife and his s. and set them on an	4.20
the s. of Reuben, the first-born of	6.14
The s. of Simeon: Jemuel, Jamin, Ohad,	6.15
names of the s. of Levi according	6.16
The s. of Gershon: Libni and Shimei,	6.17
The s. of Kohath: Amram, Izhar, Hebron	6.18
The s. of Merari: Mahli and Mushi.	6.19

SONS (cont.)
The s. of Izhar: Korah, Nepheg, and Ex 6.21
And the s. of Uzziel: Mishael, 6.22
The s. of Korah: Assir, Elkanah, and 6.24
my people the s. of Israel, out of 7.04
go with our s. and daughters and 10.09
for you and for your s. for ever. 12.24
man among your s. you shall redeem 13.13
the first-born of my s. I redeem.' 13.15
and her two s., of whom the name of 18.03
came with his s. and his wife to 18.05
wife and her two s. with her," 18.06
and she bears him s. or daughters, 21.04
first-born of your s. you shall 22.29
Aaron and his s. shall tend it from 27.21
and his s. with him, from among the 28.01
me as priests—Aaron and Aaron's s., 28.01
brother and his s. to serve me as 28.04
the names of the s. of Israel, 28.09
with the names of the s. of Israel; 28.11
remembrance for the s. of Israel; 28.12
to the names of the s. of Israel; 28.21
names of the s. of Israel in the 28.29
"And for Aaron's s. you shall make 28.40
and upon his s. with him, and shall 28.41
and upon his s., when they go into 28.43
Aaron and his s. to the door of 29.04
Then you shall bring his s., 29.08
you shall ordain Aaron and his s. 29.09
Aaron and his s. shall lay their 29.10
Aaron and his s. shall lay their 29.15
Aaron and his s. shall lay their 29.19
tips of the right ears of his s., 29.20
and upon his s. and his sons' 29.21
and his s. and his sons' garments 29.21
Aaron and in the hands of his s., 29.24
it is for Aaron and for his s. 29.27
Aaron and his s. as a perpetual 29.28
shall be for his s. after him, 29.29
and Aaron and his s. shall eat the 29.32
shall do to Aaron and to his s., 29.35
also and his s. I will consecrate, 29.44
Aaron and his s. shall wash their 30.19
And you shall anoint Aaron and his s., 30.30
priest and the garments of his s., 31.10
your s., and your daughters, and 32.02
And all the s. of Levi gathered 32.26
And the s. of Levi did according to 32.28
of their daughters for your s., 34.16
and make your s. play the harlot 34.16
first-born of your s. you shall 34.20
priest, and the garments of his s., 35.19
to the names of the s. of Israel. 39.06
remembrance for the s. of Israel; 39.07
to the names of the s. of Israel; 39.14
fine linen, for Aaron and his s., 39.27
garments of his s. to serve as 39.41
Aaron and his s. to the door of 40.12
You shall bring his s. also and put 40.14
Aaron and his s. washed their 40.31
and Aaron's s. the priests shall Lev 1.05
and the s. of Aaron the priest 1.07
and Aaron's s. the priests shall lay 1.08
and Aaron's s. the priests shall 1.11
bring it to Aaron's s. the priests. 2.02
shall be for Aaron and his s.; 2.03
shall be for Aaron and his s.; 2.10
and Aaron's s. the priests shall 3.02
Then Aaron's s. shall burn it on the 3.05
and Aaron's s. shall throw its blood 3.08
and the s. of Aaron shall throw its 3.13
"Command Aaron and his s., 6.09
The s. of Aaron shall offer it 6.14
of it Aaron and his s. shall eat; 6.16
Aaron and his s. shall offer to 6.20
The priest from among Aaron's s., 6.22
"Say to Aaron and his s., 6.25
shall be for all the s. of Aaron, 7.10
shall be for Aaron and his s. 7.31
he among the s. of Aaron who offers 7.33
to Aaron the priest and to his s., 7.34
and of his s. from the offerings 7.35
"Take Aaron and his s. with him 8.02
And Moses brought Aaron and his s., 8.06
And Moses brought Aaron's s., 8.13
Aaron and his s. laid their hands 8.14
Aaron and his s. laid their hands 8.18
Aaron and his s. laid their hands 8.22
And Aaron's s. were brought, and 8.24
Aaron and in the hands of his s., 8.27
also upon his s. and his sons' 8.30
and his s. and his sons' garments 8.30
And Moses said to Aaron and his s., 8.31
'Aaron and his s. shall eat it'; 8.31
And Aaron and his s. did all the 8.36
Aaron and his s. and the elders of 9.01
And the s. of Aaron presented the 9.09
and Aaron's s. delivered to him the 9.12
and Aaron's s. delivered to him the 9.18
the s. of Aaron, each took his 10.01
the s. of Uzziel the uncle of Aaron, 10.04
his s., "Do not let the hair of 10.06
you nor your s. with you, when you 10.09
his s. who were left, "Take the 10.12
you and your s. and your daughters 10.14
the s. of Aaron who were left, 10.16
or to one of his s. the priests, 13.02
the death of the two s. of Aaron, 16.01
"Say to Aaron and his s., 17.02
against the s. of your own people, 19.18
the s. of Aaron, and say to them 21.01
and to his s. and to all the 21.24
"Tell Aaron and his s. to keep away 22.02
Aaron and his s. and all the 22.18
And it shall be for Aaron and his s., 24.09
bequeath them to your s. after you, 25.46
You shall eat the flesh of your s., 26.29
from the s. of Joseph, from Ephraim, Num 1.10
These are the names of the s. of Aaron: 3.02
these are the names of the s. of Aaron, 3.03
the Levites to Aaron and his s.; 3.09
you shall appoint Aaron and his s., 3.10
'Number the s. of Levi, by fathers' 3.15
And these were the s. of Levi by 3.17
names of the s. of Gershon by 3.18
And the s. of Kohath by their 3.19
And the s. of Merari by their 3.20
charge of the s. of Gershon in the 3.25
The families of the s. of Kohath 3.29
charge of the s. of Merari was to 3.36
were Moses and Aaron and his s., 3.38
is redeemed to Aaron and his s. 3.48
redemption money to Aaron and his s., 3.51
"Take a census of the s. of Kohath 4.02
Kohath from among the s. of Levi, 4.02
service of the s. of Kohath in the 4.04
Aaron and his s. shall go in and 4.05
Aaron and his s. have finished 4.15
after that the s. of Kohath shall 4.15
which the s. of Kohath are to 4.15
Aaron and his s. shall go in and 4.19
"Take a census of the s. of Gershon 4.22
service of the s. of the Gershonites 4.27
at the command of Aaron and his s., 4.27
families of the s. of the Gershonites 4.28
"As for the s. of Merari, you shall 4.29
the families of the s. of Merari, 4.33
numbered the s. of Kohathites, 4.34
The number of the s. of Gershon, 4.38
the families of the s. of Gershon, 4.41
the families of the s. of Merari, 4.42
the families of the s. of Merari, 4.45
"Say to Aaron and his s., 6.23
oxen he gave to the s. of Gershon, 7.07

SONS (cont.)

oxen he gave to the s. of Merari, Num 7.08
But to the s. of Kohath he gave 7.09
Levites to attend Aaron and his s., 8.13
Aaron and his s. from among the 8.19
attendance upon Aaron and his s.; 8.22
And the s. of Aaron, the priests, 10.08
the s. of Gershon and the s. of Merari, 10.17
we saw the Nephilim (the s. of Anak, 13.33
Dathan and Abiram the s. of Eliab, 16.01
the son of Peleth, s. of Reuben, 16.01
You have gone too far, s. of Levi!" 16.07
Korah, "Hear now, you s. of Levi: 16.08
brethren the s. of Levi with you? 16.10
Dathan and Abiram the s. of Eliab; 16.12
their s., and their little ones. 16.27
"You and your s. and your fathers' 18.01
you and your s. with you shall 18.01
you and your s. with you are 18.02
And you and your s. with you shall 18.07
and to your s. as a perpetual due. 18.08
be most holy to you and to your s. 18.09
and to your s. and daughters with 18.11
and to your s. and daughters with 18.19
He has made his s. fugitives, 21.29
and his s., and all his people, 21.35
and break down all the s. of Sheth. 24.17
the s. of Reuben: of Hanoch, the 26.05
And the s. of Pallu: Eliab. 26.08
The s. of Eliab: Nemuel, Dathan, and 26.09
the s. of Korah did not die. 26.11
The s. of Simeon according to their 26.12
The s. of Gad according to their 26.15
families of the s. of Gad according 26.18
The s. of Judah were Er and Onan; 26.19
And the s. of Judah according to 26.20
And the s. of Perez were: of Hezron, 26.21
The s. of Issachar according to 26.23
The s. of Zebulun, according to 26.26
The s. of Joseph according to their 26.28
The s. of Manasseh: of Machir, the 26.29
These are the s. of Gilead: of Iezer, 26.30
the son of Hepher had no s., 26.33
These are the s. of Ephraim according 26.35
And these are the s. of Shuthelah: 26.36
families of the s. of Ephraim 26.37
These are the s. of Joseph according 26.37
The s. of Benjamin according to 26.38
And the s. of Bela were Ard and 26.40
These are the s. of Benjamin 26.41
These are the s. of Dan according 26.42
The s. of Asher according to their 26.44
Of the s. of Beriah: of Heber, the 26.45
families of the s. of Asher 26.47
The s. of Naphtali according to 26.48
for his own sin; and he had no s. 27.03
Now the s. of Reuben and the s. of Gad 32.01
the s. of Gad and the s. of Reuben came 32.02
said to the s. of Gad and to the s. of Reuben, 32.06
the s. of Gad and the s. of Reuben said 32.25
"If the s. of Gad and the s. of Reuben, 32.29
And the s. of Gad and the s. of Reuben 32.31
to the s. of Gad and to the s. of Reuben 32.33
And the s. of Gad built Dibon, 32.34
And the s. of Reuben built Heshbon, 32.37
And the s. of Machir the son of 32.39
tribe of the s. of Reuben by 34.14
tribe of the s. of Gad by their 34.14
Of the tribe of the s. of Simeon, 34.20
tribe of the s. of Dan a leader, 34.22
Of the s. of Joseph: of the tribe of 34.23
tribe of the s. of Manasseh a 34.23
tribe of the s. of Ephraim a 34.24
tribe of the s. of Zebulun a 34.25
tribe of the s. of Issachar a 34.26
tribe of the s. of Asher a leader, 34.27
tribe of the s. of Naphtali a 34.28
families of the s. of Gilead the 36.01
fathers' houses of the s. of Joseph, 36.01
to any of the s. of the other 36.03
tribe of the s. of Joseph is right. 36.05
were married to s. of their 36.11
families of the s. of Manasseh the 36.12
have seen the s. of the Anakim Deu 1.28
of your brethren the s. of Esau, 2.04
brethren the s. of Esau who live 2.08
given Ar to the s. of Lot for a 2.09
but the s. of Esau dispossessed 2.12
the frontier of the s. of Ammon, 2.19
the land of the s. of Ammon as a 2.19
given it to the s. of Lot for a 2.19
as he did for the s. of Esau, 2.22
as the s. of Esau who live in Seir 2.29
him and his s. and all his people. 2.33
the land of the s. of Ammon you 2.37
to their s. or taking their 7.03
taking their daughters for your s. 7.03
turn away your s. from following 7.04
the s. of the Anakim, whom you know, 9.02
can stand before the s. of Anak?' 9.02
Dathan and Abiram the s. of Eliab, 11.06
you and your s. and your daughters, 12.12
even burn their s. and their 12.31
"You are the s. of the LORD your 14.01
the LORD, him and his s. for ever. 18.05
And the priests the s. of Levi 21.05
as an inheritance to his s., 21.16
prostitute of the s. of Israel. 23.17
Your s. and your daughters shall be 28.32
You shall beget s. and daughters, 28.41
the flesh of your s. and daughters, 28.53
it to the priests the s. of Levi, 31.09
when he separated the s. of men, 32.08
to the number of the s. of God. 32.08
provocation of his s. and his 32.19
he said, "Blessed above s. be Asher; 33.24
The s. of Reuben and the s. of Gad Jos 4.12
and his s. and daughters, and his 7.24
from there the three s. of Anak, 15.14
and no s., but only daughters; 17.03
an inheritance along with his s. 17.06
belonged to the s. of Ephraim. 17.08
Yet the s. of Manasseh could not 17.12
bought from the s. of Hamor the 24.32
out from it the three s. of Anak. Ju 1.20
daughters they gave to their s.; 3.06
they resembled the s. of a king." 8.18
my brothers, the s. of my mother; 8.19
Now Gideon had seventy s., 8.30
seventy of the s. of Jerubbaal, 9.05
his brothers the s. of Jerubbaal, 9.05
this day, and have slain his s., 9.18
to the seventy s. of Jerubbaal 9.24
And he had thirty s. who rode on 10.04
And Gilead's wife also bore him s.; 11.02
and when his wife's s. grew up, 11.02
He had thirty s.; and thirty 12.09
brought in from outside for his s. 12.09
He had forty s. and thirty grandsons, 12.14
and installed one of his s., 17.05
became to him like one of his s. 17.11
and his s. were priests to the 18.30
he and his wife and his two s. Ru 1.01
of his two s. were Mahlon and 1.02
and she was left with her two s. 1.03
of her two s. and her husband. 1.05
Have I yet s. in my womb that they 1.11
this night and should bear s., 1.12
you than seven s., has borne him." 4.15
where the two s. of Eli, Hophni and 1Sa 1.03
and to all her s. and daughters; 1.04
Am I not more to you than ten s.?" 1.08
Now the s. of Eli were worthless 2.12
and bore three s. and two daughters. 2.21

SONS (cont.)

all that his s. were doing to all 1Sa 2.22
No, my s.; it is no good report 2.24
and honor your s. above me by 2.29
which shall befall your two s., 2.34
because his s. were blaspheming God, 3.13
and the two s. of Eli, Hophni and 4.04
and the two s. of Eli, Hophni and 4.11
two s. also, Hophni and Phinehas, 4.17
he made his s. judges over Israel. 8.01
Yet his s. did not walk in his ways, 8.03
old and your s. do not walk in 8.05
will take your s. and appoint them 8.11
and behold, my s. are with you; 12.02
Now the s. of Saul were Jonathan, 14.49
for myself a king among his s." 16.01
he consecrated Jesse and his s., 16.05
seven of his s. pass before Samuel. 16.10
to Jesse, "Are all your s. here?" 16.11
named Jesse, who had eight s. 17.12
The three eldest s. of Jesse had 17.13
of his three s. who went to the 17.13
But one of the s. of Ahimelech the 22.20
you and your s. shall be with me; 28.19
their wives and s. and daughters 30.03
each for his s. and daughters. 30.06
s. or daughters, spoil or anything 30.19
Philistines overtook Saul and his s.; 31.02
and Malchishua, the s. of Saul. 31.02
and his three s., and his armor-bearer, 31.06
and that Saul and his s. were dead, 31.07
and his three s. fallen on Mount 31.08
bodies of his s. from the wall of 31.12
And the three s. of Zeruiah were 2Sa 2.18
And s. were born to David at Hebron: 3.02
these men the s. of Zeruiah are too 3.39
s. of Rimmon a man of Benjamin from 4.02
Now the s. of Rimmon the Beerothite, 4.05
the s. of Rimmon the Beerothite, "As 4.09
and more s. and daughters were born 5.13
the s. of Abinadab, were driving the 6.03
with the stripes of the s. of men; 7.14
and David's s. were priests. 8.18
And you and your s. and your 9.10
had fifteen s. and twenty servants 9.10
table, like one of the king's s. 9.11
Absalom invited all the king's s. 13.23
and all the king's s. go with him. 13.27
Then all the king's s. arose, 13.29
has slain all the king's s., 13.30
all the young men the king's s., 13.32
that all the king's s. are dead; 13.33
"Behold, the king's s. have come; 13.35
the king's s. came, and lifted up 13.36
And your handmaid had two s., 14.06
There were born to Absalom three s., 14.27
with your two s., Ahimaaz your son, 15.27
their two s. are with them there, 15.36
to do with you, you s. of Zeruiah? 16.10
lives of your s. and your daughters, 19.05
his fifteen s. and his twenty 19.17
you s. Zeruiah, that you should 19.22
let seven of his s. be given to us, 21.06
took the two s. of Rizpah the 21.08
and the five s. of Merob the 21.08
the s. of Jashen, Jonathan 23.32
the king's s., and all the royal 1Ki 1.09
has invited all the s. of the king, 1.19
and has invited all the king's s., 1.25
"If your s. take heed to their way, 2.04
with the s. of Barzillai the 2.07
Elihoreph and Ahijah the s. of 4.03
Calcol, and Darda, the s. of Mahol; 4.31
if only your s. take heed to their 8.25
house among the s. of Pharaoh. 11.20
And his s. came and told him all 13.11
And his s. showed him the way which 13.12
And he said to his s., "Saddle the 13.13
And he said to his s., "Saddle the 13.27
had buried him, he said to his s., 13.31
of the tribes of the s. of Jacob, 18.31
man of the s. of the prophets said 20.35
And the s. of the prophets who were 2Ki 2.03
The s. of the prophets who were at 2.05
Fifty men of the s. of the prophets 2.07
Now when the s. of the prophets who 2.15
of one of the s. of the prophets 4.01
the door upon yourself and your s., 4.04
the door upon herself and her s.; 4.05
you and your s. can live on the 4.07
And as the s. of the prophets were 4.38
pottage for the s. of the prophets 4.38
men of the s. of the prophets; 5.22
Now the s. of the prophets said to 6.01
lamp to him and to his s. for ever. 8.19
one of the s. of the prophets and 9.01
of Naboth and the blood of his s.— 9.26
Now Ahab had seventy s. in Samaria. 10.01
to the guardians of the s. of Ahab, 10.01
your master's s. are with you, 10.02
your master's s. and set him on 10.03
take the heads of your master's s., 10.06
Now the king's s., seventy persons, 10.06
to them, they took the king's s., 10.07
brought the heads of the king's s., 10.08
princes and the s. of the queen 10.13
your s. of the fourth generation 10.30
the king's s. who were about to be 11.02
"Your s. shall sit upon the throne 15.12
burned their s. and their daughters 17.17
his s., slew him with the sword, and 19.37
And some of your own s., who are born 20.18
in the valley of the s. of Hinnom, 23.10
They slew the s. of Zedekiah before 25.07
The s. of Japheth: Gomer, Magog, Madai, 1Ch 1.05
The s. of Gomer: Ashkenaz, Diphath, 1.06
The s. of Javan: Elishah, Tarshish, 1.07
The s. of Ham: Cush, Egypt, Put, and 1.08
The s. of Cush: Seba, Havilah, Sabta, 1.09
The s. of Raamah: Sheba and Dedan. 1.09
The s. of Shem: Elam, Asshur, Arpachshad, 1.17
To Eber were born two s.: the name of 1.19
all these were the s. of Joktan. 1.23
The s. of Abraham: Isaac and Ishmael. 1.28
These are the s. of Ishmael. 1.31
The s. of Keturah, Abraham's concubine: 1.32
The s. of Jokshan: Sheba and Dedan. 1.32
The s. of Midian: Ephah, Epher, Hanoch, 1.33
The s. of Isaac: Esau and Israel. 1.34
The s. of Esau: Eliphaz, Reuel, Jeush, 1.35
The s. of Eliphaz: Teman, Omar, Zephi, 1.36
The s. of Reuel: Nahath, Zerah, 1.37
The s. of Seir: Lotan, Shobal, Zibeon, 1.38
The s. of Lotan: Hori and Homam; 1.39
The s. of Shobal: Alian, Manahath, 1.40
The s. of Zibeon: Aiah and Anah. 1.40
The s. of Anah: Dishon. 1.41
The s. of Dishon: Hamran, Eshban, 1.41
The s. of Ezer: Bilhan, Zaavan, and 1.42
The s. of Dishan: Uz and Aran. 1.42
These are the s. of Israel: Reuben, 2.01
The s. of Judah: Er, Onan, and Shelah; 2.03
Judah had five s. in all. 2.04
The s. of Perez: Hezron and Hamul. 2.05
The s. of Zerah: Zimri, Ethan, Heman, 2.06
The s. of Carmi: Achar, the troubler 2.07
The s. of Hezron, that were born to 2.09
Nahshon, prince of the s. of Judah. 2.10
The s. of Zeruiah: Abishai, Joab, and 2.16
and these were her s.: 2.18
The s. of Jerahmeel, the first-born 2.25
The s. of Ram, the first-born of 2.27
The s. of Onam: Shammai and Jada. 2.28
The s. of Shammai: Nadab and Abishur. 2.28

SONS (cont.)

The s. of Nadab: Seled and Appaim; 1Ch 2.30
The s. of Appaim: Ishi. 2.31
The s. of Ishi: Sheshan. 2.31
The s. of Sheshan: Ahlai. 2.31
The s. of Jada, Shammai's brother: 2.32
The s. of Jonathan: Peleth and Zaza. 2.33
Now Sheshan had no s., 2.34
The s. of Caleb the brother of 2.42
The s. of Mareshah: Hebron. 2.42
The s. of Hebron: Korah, Tappuah, 2.43
The s. of Jahdai: Regem, Jotham, 2.47
The s. of Hur the first-born of 2.50
of Kiriathjearim had other s.: 2.52
The s. of Salma: Bethlehem, the 2.54
These are the s. of David that were 3.01
All these were David's s., 3.09
besides the s. of the concubines; 3.09
The s. of Josiah: Johanan the first-born, 3.15
and the s. of Jeconiah, the captive: 3.17
and the s. of Pedaiah: Zerubbabel 3.19
and the s. of Zerubbabel: Meshullam 3.19
The s. of Hananiah: Pelatiah and 3.21
The s. of Shecaniah: Shemaiah. 3.22
And the s. of Shemaiah: Hattush, Igal, 3.22
The s. of Neariah: Elioenai, Hizkiah, 3.23
The s. of Elioenai: Hodaviah, Eliashib, 3.24
The s. of Judah: Perez, Hezron, Carmi, 4.01
These were the s. of Etam: Jezreel, 4.03
These were the s. of Hur, 4.04
These were the s. of Naarah. 4.06
The s. of Helah: Zereth, Izhar, and 4.07
The s. of Kenaz: Othniel and Seraiah; 4.13
and the s. of Othniel: Hathath and 4.13
The s. of Caleb the son of Jephunneh: 4.15
and the s. of Elah: Kenaz. 4.15
The s. of Jehallelel: Ziph, Ziphah, 4.16
The s. of Ezrah: Jether, Mered, Epher, 4.17
These are the s. of Bithiah, the 4.17
The s. of the wife of Hodiah, the 4.19
The s. of Shimon: Amnon, Rinnah, 4.20
The s. of Ishi: Zoheth and Benzoheth. 4.20
The s. of Shelah the son of Judah: 4.21
The s. of Simeon: Nemuel, Jamin, Jarib, 4.24
The s. of Mishma: Hammuel his son, 4.26
Shimei had sixteen s. and six 4.27
Rephaiah, and Uzziel, the s. of Ishi; 4.42
The s. of Reuben the first-born of 5.01
given to the s. of Joseph the son 5.01
the s. of Reuben, the first-born of 5.03
The s. of Joel: Shemaiah his son, Gog 5.04
The s. of Gad dwelt over against 5.11
These were the s. of Abihail the 5.14
The s. of Levi: Gershom, Kohath, and 6.01
The s. of Kohath: Amram, Izhar, Hebron, 6.02
The s. of Aaron: Nadab, Abihu, Eleazar, 6.03
The s. of Levi: Gershom, Kohath, and 6.16
are the names of the s. of Gershom: 6.17
The s. of Kohath: Amram, Izhar, Hebron, 6.18
The s. of Merari: Mahli and Mushi. 6.19
The s. of Kohath: Amminadab his son, 6.22
The s. of Elkanah: Amasai and 6.25
The s. of Samuel: Joel his first-born, 6.28
The s. of Merari: Mahli, Libni his 6.29
the men who served and their s. 6.33
Of the s. of the Kohathites: Heman 6.33
their brethren the s. of Merari: 6.44
But Aaron and his s. made offerings 6.49
These are the s. of Aaron: Eleazar 6.50
to the s. of Aaron of the families 6.54
To the s. of Aaron they gave the 6.57
families of the s. of Kohath had 6.66
The s. of Issachar: Tola, Puah, Jashub, 7.01
The s. of Tola: Uzzi, Rephaiah, Jeriel, 7.02
The s. of Uzzi: Izrahiah. 7.03
And the s. of Izrahiah: Michael, 7.03
for they had many wives and s. 7.04
The s. of Benjamin: Lecher, and 7.06
The s. of Bela: Ezbon, Uzzi, Uzziel, 7.07
The s. of Becher: Zemirah, Joash, 7.08
All these were the s. of Becher; 7.09
The s. of Jediael: Bilhan. 7.10
And the s. of Bilhan: Jeush, Benjamin, 7.10
All these were the s. of Jediael 7.11
and Huppim were the s. of Ir, 7.12
s. of Ir, Hushim the s. of Aher. 7.12
The s. of Naphtali: Jahziel, Guni, 7.13
The s. of Manasseh: Asriel, whom his 7.14
and his s. were Ulam and Rakem. 7.16
The s. of Ulam: Bedan. 7.17
These were the s. of Gilead the son 7.17
The s. of Shemida were Ahian, 7.19
The s. of Ephraim: Shuthelah, and 7.20
these dwelt the s. of Joseph the 7.29
The s. of Asher: Imnah, Ishvah, Ishvi, 7.30
The s. of Beriah: Heber and Malchiel, 7.31
The s. of Japhlet: Pasach, Bimhal, and 7.33
These are the s. of Japhlet. 7.33
The s. of Shemer his brother: Rohgah, 7.34
The s. of Heler his brother: Zophah, 7.35
The s. of Zophah: Suah, Harnepher, 7.36
The s. of Jether: Jephunneh, Pispa, 7.38
The s. of Ulla: Arah, Hanniel, and 7.39
And Bela had s.: Addar, Gera, Abihud, 8.03
These are the the s. of Ehud (they were 8.06
And Shaharaim had s. in the country 8.08
He had s. by Hodesh his wife: Jobab, 8.09
These were his s., heads of fathers' 8.10
He also had s. by Hushim: Abitub and 8.11
The s. of Elpaal: Eber, Misham, and 8.12
Ishpah, and Joha were s. of Beriah. 8.16
and Jobab were the s. of Elpaal. 8.18
and Shimrath were the s. of Shimei. 8.21
Iphdeiah, and Penuel were the s. of Shashak. 8.25
and Zichri were the s. of Jeroham. 8.27
The s. of Micah: Pithon, Melech, Tarea, 8.35
Azel had six s., and these are 8.38
All these were the s. of Azel. 8.38
The s. of Eshek his brother: Ulam 8.39
The s. of Ulam were men who were 8.40
having many s. and grandsons, one 8.40
from the s. of Perez the son of 9.04
Asaiah the first-born, and his s. 9.05
Of the s. of Zerah: Jeuel and their 9.06
of Hashabiah, of the s. of Merari; 9.14
So they and their s. were in charge 9.23
Others, of the s. of the priests, 9.30
The s. of Micah: Pithon, Melech, 9.41
Azel had six s. and these are their 9.44
these were the s. of Azel. 9.44
Philistines overtook Saul and his s.; 10.02
and Malchishua, the s. of Saul. 10.02
and his three s. and all his house 10.06
and that Saul and his s. were dead, 10.07
Saul and his s. fallen on Mount 10.08
of Saul and the bodies of his s., 10.12
and Jeiel the s. of Hotham the 11.44
the s. of Elnaam, and Ithmah the 11.46
both s. of Shemaah of Gibeah; 12.03
and Pelet the s. of Azmaveth; 12.03
the s. of Jeroham of Gedor. 12.07
David begot more s. and daughters. 14.03
together the s. of Aaron and the 15.04
of the s. of Kohath, Uriel the chief, 15.05
of the s. of Merari, Asaiah the 15.06
of the s. of Gershom, Joel the chief, 15.07
of the s. of Elizaphan, Shemaiah the 15.08
of the s. of Hebron, Eliel the chief, 15.09
of the s. of Uzziel, Amminadab the 15.10
and of the s. of Merari, their 15.17
s. of Jacob, his chosen ones! 16.13
The s. of Jeduthun were appointed 16.42
after you, one of your own s., 17.11
and David's s. were the chief 18.17

SONS (cont.)
and his four s. who were with him 1Ch 21.20
corresponding to the s. of Levi: 23.06
The s. of Gershom were Ladan and 23.07
The s. of Ladan: Jehiel the chief, 23.08
The s. of Shimei: Shelomoth, Haziel, 23.09
And the s. of Shimei: Jahath, Zina, 23.10
These four were the s. of Shimei. 23.10
Jeush and Beriah had not many s., 23.11
The s. of Kohath: Amram, Izhar, Hebron, 23.12
The s. of Amram: Aaron and Moses. 23.13
that he and his s. for ever should 23.13
But the s. of Moses the man of God 23.14
The s. of Moses: Gershom and Eliezer. 23.15
The s. of Gershom: Shebuel the chief 23.16
The s. of Eliezer: Rehabiah the 23.17
Eliezer had no other s., 23.17
but the s. of Rehabiah were very 23.17
The s. of Izhar: Shelomith the chief. 23.18
The s. of Hebron: Jeriah the chief, 23.19
The s. of Uzziel: Micah the chief 23.20
The s. of Merari: Mahli and Mushi. 23.21
The s. of Mahli: Eleazar and Kish. 23.21
Eleazar died having no s., but only 23.22
the s. of Kish, married them. 23.22
The s. of Mushi: Mahli, Eder, and 23.23
These were the s. of Levi by their 23.24
to assist the s. of Aaron for the 23.28
and shall attend the s. of Aaron, 23.32
divisions of the s. of Aaron were 24.01
The s. of Aaron: Nadab, Abihu, Eleazar, 24.01
help of Zadok of the s. of Eleazar, 24.03
and Ahimelech of the s. of Ithamar, 24.03
found among the s. of Eleazar than 24.04
than among the s. of Ithamar, 24.04
houses of the s. of Eleazar, 24.04
and eight of the s. of Ithamar. 24.04
among both the s. of Eleazar and 24.05
of Eleazar and the s. of Ithamar. 24.05
And of the rest of the s. of Levi: 24.20
of the s. of Amam, Shubael; 24.20
of the s. of Shubael, Jehdeiah. 24.20
of the s. of Rehabiah, Isshiah the 24.21
of the s. of Shelomoth, Jahath. 24.22
The s. of Hebron: Jeriah the chief, 24.23
The s. of Uzziel, Micah; 24.24
of the s. of Micah, Shamir. 24.24
of the s. of Isshiah, Zechariah. 24.25
The s. of Merari: Mahli and Mushi. 24.26
The s. of Jaaziah: Beno. 24.26
The s. of Merari: of Jaaziah, Beno, 24.27
Of Mahli: Eleazar, who had no s. 24.28
Of Kish, the s. of Kish: Jerahmeel. 24.29
The s. of Mushi: Mahli, Eder, and 24.30
These were the s. of the Levites 24.30
as their brethren the s. of Aaron, 24.31
service certain of the s. of Asaph, 25.01
Of the s. of Asaph: Zaccur, Joseph, 25.02
s. of Asaph, under the direction of 25.02
the s. of Jeduthun: Gedaliah, Zeri, 25.03
Of Heman, the s. of Heman: Bukkiah, 25.04
All these were the s. of Heman the 25.05
Heman fourteen s. and three 25.05
his brethren and his s., twelve; 25.09
his s. and his brethren, twelve; 25.10
his s. and his brethren, twelve; 25.11
his s. and his brethren, twelve; 25.12
his s. and his brethren, twelve; 25.13
his s. and his brethren, twelve; 25.14
his s. and his brethren, twelve; 25.15
his s. and his brethren, twelve; 25.16
his s. and his brethren, twelve; 25.17
his s. and his brethren, twelve; 25.18
his s. and his brethren, twelve; 25.19
his s. and his brethren, twelve; 25.20
his s. and his brethren, twelve; 25.21
his s. and his brethren, twelve; 25.22
his s. and his brethren, twelve; 25.23
his s. and his brethren, twelve; 25.24
his s. and his brethren, twelve; 25.25
his s. and his brethren, twelve; 25.26
his s. and his brethren, twelve; 25.27
his s. and his brethren, twelve; 25.28
his s. and his brethren, twelve; 25.29
his s. and his brethren, twelve; 25.30
his s. and his brethren, twelve. 25.31
son of Kore, of the s. of Asaph. 26.01
And Meshelemiah had s.: Zechariah 26.02
And Obededom had s.: Shemaiah 26.04
Also to his son Shemaiah were s. born, 26.06
The s. of Shemaiah: Othni, Rephael, 26.07
were of the s. of Obededom with their s. 26.08
And Meshelemiah had s. and brethren, 26.09
Hosah, of the s. of Merari, had s.: 26.10
all the s. and brethren of Hosah 26.11
and to his s. was allotted the 26.15
the Korahites and the s. of Merari. 26.19
The s. of Ladan, the s. of the Gershonites 26.21
The s. of Jehieli, Zetham and Joel 26.22
Chenaniah and his s. were appointed 26.29
the Pelonite, of the s. of Ephraim; 27.10
of Pirathon, of the s. of Ephraim; 27.14
of Hachmoni attended the king's s. 27.32
and cattle of the king and his s., 28.01
my father's s. he took pleasure in 28.04
And of all my s. (for the LORD has 28.05
given me many s.) he has chosen 28.05
and also all the s. of King David, 29.24
their s. and kinsmen, arrayed in 2Ch 5.12
if only your s. take heed to their 6.16
Jeroboam and his s. cast them out 11.14
and she bore him s., Jeush, 11.19
twenty-eight s. and sixty daughters); 11.21
some of his s. through all the 11.23
David and his s. by a covenant of 13.05
in the hand of the s. of David, 13.08
the s. of Aaron, and the Levites, and 13.09
to the LORD who are s. of Aaron, 13.10
O s. of Israel, do not fight against 13.12
had twenty-two s. and sixteen 13.21
a Levite of the s. of Asaph, 20.14
he s. of Jehoshaphat: Azariah, 21.02
these were the s. of Jehoshaphat 21.02
lamp to him and to his s. for ever. 21.07
and also his s. and his wives, so 21.17
camp had slain all the older s. 22.01
Judah and the s. of Ahaziah's 22.08
the king's s. who were about to be 22.11
spoke concerning the s. of David. 23.03
Jehoiada and his s. anointed him, 23.11
wives, and he had s. and daughters. 24.03
For the s. of Athaliah, that wicked 24.07
Accounts of his s., and of the many 24.27
for the priests the s. of Aaron, 26.18
and burned his s. as an offering, 28.03
kinsfolk, women, s., and daughters; 28.08
sword and our s. and our daughters 29.09
My s., do not now be negligent, for 29.11
of the s. of the Kohathites; 29.12
and of the s. of Merari, Kish the 29.12
and of the s. of Elizaphan, Shimri 29.13
and of the s. of Asaph, Zechariah 29.13
and of the s. of Heman, Jehuel and 29.14
and of the s. of Jeduthun, Shemaiah 29.14
the priests the s. of Aaron to 29.21
their s., and their daughters, the 31.18
And for the s. of Aaron, the priests, 31.19
some of his own s. struck him down 32.21
of the tombs of the s. of David; 32.33
And he burned his s. as an offering 33.06
of the s. of Merari, and Zechariah 34.12
of the s. of the Kohathites, to have 34.12
the priests the s. of Aaron were 35.14

SONS (cont.)
for the priests the s. of Aaron. 2Ch 35.14
the s. of Asaph, were in their place 35.15
him and to his s. until the 36.20
the s. of Parosh, two thousand one Ez 2.03
The s. of Shephatiah, three hundred 2.04
The s. of Arah, seven hundred and 2.05
The s. of Pahathmoab, namely the 2.06
namely the s. of Jeshua and Joab, 2.06
The s. of Elam, one thousand two 2.07
The s. of Zattu, nine hundred and 2.08
The s. of Zaccai, seven hundred and 2.09
The s. of Bani, six hundred and 2.10
The s. of Bebai, six hundred and 2.11
The s. of Azgad, one thousand two 2.12
The s. of Adonikam, six hundred and 2.13
The s. of Bigvai, two thousand and 2.14
The s. of Adin, four hundred and 2.15
The s. of Ater, namely of Hezekiah, 2.16
The s. of Bezai, three hundred and 2.17
The s. of Jorah, one hundred and 2.18
The s. of Hashum, two hundred and 2.19
The s. of Gibbar, ninety-five. 2.20
The s. of Bethlehem, one hundred and 2.21
The s. of Azmaveth, forty-two 2.24
The s. of Kiriatharim, Chephirah, and 2.25
The s. of Ramah and Geba, six 2.26
The s. of Nebo, fifty-two. 2.29
The s. of Magbish, one hundred and 2.30
The s. of the other Elam, one 2.31
The s. of Harim, three hundred and 2.32
The s. of Lod, Hadid and Ono, seven 2.33
The s. of Jericho, three hundred and 2.34
The s. of Senaah, three thousand six 2.35
The s. of Jedaiah, of the house of 2.36
The s. of Immer, one thousand and 2.37
The s. of Pashhur, one thousand two 2.38
The s. of Harim, one thousand and 2.39
the s. of Jeshua and Kadmiel, of the 2.40
of the s. of Hodaviah, seventy-four. 2.40
the s. of Asaph, one hundred and 2.41
The s. of the gatekeepers: the s. 2.42
the s. of Shallum, the s. of Ater, 2.42
the s. of Talmon, the s. of 2.42
the s. of Akkub, the s. of Hatita, 2.42
and the s. of Shobai, in all one 2.42
the s. of Ziha, the s. of Hasupha, 2.43
of Hasupha, the s. of Tabbaoth, 2.43
the s. of Keros, the s. of 2.44
the s. of Siaha, the s. of Padon, 2.44
the s. of Lebanah, the s. of 2.45
the s. of Hagabah, the s. of Akkub, 2.45
the s. of Hagab, the s. of 2.46
the s. of Shamlai, the s. of Hanan, 2.46
the s. of Giddel, the s. of 2.47
the s. of Gahar, the s. of Reaiah, 2.47
the s. of Rezin, the s. of 2.48
the s. of Nekoda, the s. of Gazzam, 2.48
the s. of Uzza, the s. of 2.49
the s. of Paseah, the s. of Besai, 2.49
the s. of Asnah, the s. of 2.50
s. of Meunim, the s. of Nephisim, 2.50
the s. of Bakbuk, the s. of 2.51
the s. of Hapupha, the s. of Harhur, 2.51
the s. of Bazluth, the s. of 2.52
the s. of Mehida, the s. of Harsha, 2.52
the s. of Barkos, the s. of 2.53
the s. of Sisera, the s. of Temah, 2.53
the s. of Neziah, and the s. of Hatipha. 2.54
The s. of Solomon's servants: the 2.55
the s. of Sotai, the s. of Hassophereth, 2.55
the s. of Hassophereth, the s. of Peruda, 2.55
the s. of Jaalah, the s. of 2.56
the s. of Darkon, the s. of Giddel, 2.56
the s. of Shephatiah, the s. of Hattil, 2.57
s. of Pocherethhazzebaim, and the s. of Ami. 2.57
servants and the s. of Solomon's 2.58
the s. of Delaiah, the s. of Tobiah, 2.60
and the s. of Nekoda, six hundred 2.60
Also, of the s. of the priests: the 2.61
the s. of Habaiah, the s. of Hakkoz, 2.61
and the s. of Barzillai (who had 2.61
and the s. of Israel were in the 3.01
And Jeshua with his s. and his 3.09
kinsmen and Kadmiel and his s., 3.09
the s. of Judah, together took the 3.09
along with the s. of Henadad and 3.09
the Levites, their s. and kinsmen. 3.09
the s. of Asaph, with cymbals, to 3.10
the life of the king and his s. 6.10
the realm of the king and his s. 7.23
Of the s. of Phinehas, Gershom. 8.02
Of the s. of Ithamar, Daniel. 8.02
Of the s. of David, Hattush, 8.02
of the s. of Shecaniah. 8.03
Of the s. of Parosh, Zechariah, with 8.03
Of the s. of Pahathmoab, Eliehoenai 8.04
Of the s. of Zattu, Shecaniah the 8.05
Of the s. of Adin, Ebed the son of 8.06
Of the s. of Elam, Jeshaiah the son 8.07
Of the s. of Shephatiah, Zebadiah 8.08
Of the s. of Joab, Obadiah the son 8.09
Of the s. of Bani, Shelomith the son 8.10
Of the s. of Bebai, Zechariah the 8.11
Of the s. of Azgad, Johanan the son 8.12
Of the s. of Adonikam, those who 8.13
Of the s. of Bigvai, Uthai and 8.14
found there none of the s. of Levi. 8.15
of the s. of Mahli the son of Levi, 8.18
Serebiah with his s. and kinsmen, 8.18
him Jeshaiah of the s. of Merari, 8.19
his kinsmen and their s., twenty; 8.19
for themselves and for their s.; 9.02
not your daughters to their s., 9.12
take their daughters for your s., 9.12
of the s. of Elam, addressed Ezra: 10.02
Of the s. of the priests who had 10.18
of the s. of Jeshua the son of 10.18
Of the s. of Immer: Hanani and 10.20
Of the s. of Harim: Maaseiah, Elijah, 10.21
Of the s. of Pashhur: Elioenai, 10.22
of the s. of Parosh: Ramiah, Izziah, 10.25
Of the s. of Elam: Mattaniah, Zechariah, 10.26
Of the s. of Zattu: Elioenai, Eliashib, 10.27
Of the s. of Bebai were Jehohanan, 10.28
Of the s. of Bani were Meshullam, 10.29
Of the s. of Pahathmoab: Adna, Chelal, 10.30
Of the s. of Harim: Eliezer, Isshijah, 10.31
Of the s. of Hashum: Mattenai, 10.33
Of the s. of Bani: Maadai, Amram, Uel, 10.34
Of the s. of Binnui: Shimei, 10.38
Of the s. of Nebo: Jeiel, Mattithiah, 10.43
And the s. of Hassenaah built the Neh 3.03
your s., your daughters, your wives, 4.14
"With our s. and our daughters, we 5.02
are forcing our s. and our daughters 5.05
the s. of Parosh, two thousand a 7.08
The s. of Shephatiah, three hundred 7.09
The s. of Arah, six hundred and 7.10
The s. of Pahathmoab, namely the 7.11
namely the s. of Jeshua and Joab, 7.11
The s. of Elam, a thousand two 7.12
The s. of Zattu, eight hundred and 7.13
The s. of Zaccai, seven hundred and 7.14
The s. of Binnui, six hundred and 7.15
The s. of Bebai, six hundred and 7.16
The s. of Azgad, two thousand three 7.17
The s. of Adonikam, six hundred and 7.18
The s. of Bigvai, two thousand and 7.19
The s. of Adin, six hundred and 7.20
The s. of Ater, namely of Hezekiah, 7.21
The s. of Hashum, three hundred and 7.22
The s. of Bezai, three hundred and 7.23

SONS (cont.)
The s. of Hariph, a hundred and Neh 7.24
The s. of Gibeon, ninety-five. 7.25
The s. of the other Elam, a thousand 7.34
The s. of Harim, three hundred and 7.35
The s. of Jericho, three hundred and 7.36
The s. of Lod, Hadid, and Ono, seven 7.37
The s. of Senaah, three thousand 7.38
the s. of Jedaiah, namely the house 7.39
The s. of Immer, a thousand and 7.40
The s. of Pashhur, a thousand two 7.41
The s. of Harim, a thousand and 7.42
The Levites: the s. of Jeshua, namely 7.43
of Kadmiel of the s. of Hodevah, 7.43
the s. of Asaph, a hundred and forty 7.44
the s. of Shallum, the s. of 7.45
the s. of Ater, the s. of Talmon, 7.45
the s. of Akkub, the s. of Hatita, 7.45
the s. of Shobai, a hundred and 7.45
the s. of Ziha, the s. of 7.46
the s. of Hasupha, the s. of Tabbaoth 7.46
the s. of Keros, the s. of 7.47
the s. of Sia, the s. of Padon, 7.47
the s. of Lebana, the s. of 7.48
s. of Hagaba, the s. of Shalmai, 7.48
the s. of Hanan, the s. of 7.49
the s. of Giddel, the s. of Gahar, 7.49
the s. of Reaiah, the s. of 7.50
the s. of Rezin, the s. of Nekoda, 7.50
the s. of Gazzam, the s. of 7.51
the s. of Uzza, the s. of Paseah, 7.51
the s. of Besai, the s. of Meunim, 7.52
the s. of Nephushesim, 7.52
the s. of Bakbuk, the s. of 7.53
the s. of Hakupha, the s. of Harhur, 7.53
the s. of Bazlith, the s. of 7.54
s. of Mehida, the s. of Harsha, 7.54
the s. of Barkos, the s. of 7.55
the s. of Sisera, the s. of Temah, 7.55
the s. of Neziah, the s. of Hatipha. 7.56
The s. of Solomon's servants: the 7.57
the s. of Sotai, the s. of 7.57
the s. of Sophereth, the s. of Perida, 7.57
the s. of Jaala, the s. of 7.58
the s. of Darkon, the s. of Giddel, 7.58
the s. of Shephatiah, the s. of 7.59
the s. of Hattil, the s. of Pocherethhazzebaim, 7.59
Pocherethhazzebaim, the s. of Amon. 7.59
servants and the s. of Solomon's 7.60
the s. of Delaiah, the s. of 7.62
the s. of Tobiah, the s. of Nekoda, 7.62
the s. of Hobaiah, the s. of Hakkoz, 7.63
the s. of Barzillai (who had taken 7.63
Binnui of the s. of Henadad, Kadmiel 10.09
their s., their daughters, all who 10.28
or take their daughters for our s.; 10.30
first-born of our s. and our 10.36
Israel and the s. of Levi shall 10.39
certain of the s. of Judah and of 11.04
of Judah and of the s. of Benjamin. 11.04
Of the s. of Judah: Athaiah the son 11.04
of Mahalalel of the s. of Perez; 11.04
All the s. of Perez who lived in 11.06
And these are the s. of Benjamin: 11.07
of the s. of Asaph, the singers, over 11.22
of the s. of Zerah the son of Judah, 11.24
The s. of Levi, heads of fathers' 12.23
And the s. of the singers gathered 12.28
of the priests' s. with trumpets: 12.35
that which was for the s. of Aaron. 12.47
give your daughters to their s., 13.25
for your s. or for yourselves. 13.25
And one of the s. of Jehoiada, the 13.28
his riches, the number of his s., Est 5.11
the ten s. of Haman the son of 9.10
men and also the ten s. of Haman. 9.12
And let the ten s. of Haman be 9.13
and the ten s. of Haman were hanged 9.14
that he and his s. should be 9.25
to him seven s. and three daughters. Job 1.02
His s. used to go and hold a feast 1.04
"It may be that my s. have sinned, 1.05
a day when the s. of God came to 1.06
a day when his s. and daughters 1.13
"Your s. and daughters were eating 1.18
a day when the s. of God came to 2.01
His s. are far from safety, they are 5.04
His s. come to honor, and he does 14.21
loathsome to the s. of my own 19.17
up their iniquity for their s. 21.19
and all the s. of God shouted for 38.07
is king over all the s. of pride. 41.34
He had also seven s. and three 42.13
and saw his s., and his sons' s., 42.16
vanished from among the s. of men. Ps 12.01
is exalted among the s. of men. 12.08
children from among the s. of men. 21.10
all you s. of Jacob, glorify him, and 22.23
awe of him all you s. of Israel! 22.23
in the sight of the s. of men! 31.19
heaven he sees all the s. of men; 33.13
Come O s., listen to me, I will 34.11
You are the fairest of the s. of men; 45.02
Instead of your fathers shall be your s.; 45.16
heaven upon the s. of men to see 53.02
that greedily devour the s. of men; 57.04
you judge the s. of men uprightly? 58.01
brethren, an alien to my mother's s. 69.08
the s. of Jacob and Joseph. 77.15
s. of the Most High, all of you; 82.06
hast created all the s. of men! 89.47
s. of Jacob, his chosen ones! 105.06
sacrificed their s. and their 106.37
blood of their s. and daughters, 106.38
wonderful works to the s. of men! 107.08
wonderful works to the s. of men! 107.15
wonderful works to the s. of men! 107.21
wonderful works to the s. of men! 107.31
he has given to the s. of men. 115.16
Lo, s. are a heritage from the LORD, 127.03
warrior are the s. of one's youth. 127.04
"One of the s. of your body I will 132.11
If your s. keep my covenant and my 132.12
their s. also for ever shall sit 132.12
May our s. in their youth be like 144.12
known to the s. of men thy mighty 145.12
he blesses your s. within you. 147.13
let the s. of Zion rejoice in their 149.02
Hear, O s. a father's instruction, Pro 4.01
And now, O s., listen to me, and do 5.07
And now, O s., listen to me, and be 7.24
and my cry is to the s. of men. 8.04
and delighting in the s. of men. 8.31
And now my s., listen to me: happy 8.32
the glory of the s. is their fathers. 17.06
blessed are his s. after him! 20.07
given to the s. of men to be busy Ecc 1.13
good for the s. of men to do under 2.03
given to the s. of men to be busy 3.10
regard to the s. of men that God 3.18
For the fate of the s. of men and 3.19
heart of the s. of men is fully 8.11
so the s. of men are snared at an 9.12
My mother's s. were angry with me, Sol 1.06
"S. have I reared and brought up, Is 1.02
s. who deal corruptly! They have 1.04
slaughter for his s. because of the 14.21
men of the s. of Kedar will be few 21.17
they are a rebellious people, lying s., 30.09
s. who will not hear the instruction 30.09
his s., slew him with the sword, and 37.38
And some of your own s., 39.07
bring my s. from afar and my 43.06
shall bring your s. in their bosom, 49.22

SONS (cont.)

her among all the s. she has borne; Is 51.18
among all the s. she has brought 51.18
Your s. have fainted, they lie at 51.20
beyond that of the s. of men— 52.14
all your s. shall be taught by the 54.13
shall be the prosperity of your s. 54.13
name better than s. and daughters; 56.05
s. of the sorceress, offspring of 57.03
your s. shall come from far, and 60.04
to bring your s. from far, their 60.09
The s. of those who oppressed you 60.14
so shall your s. marry you, and as 62.05
s. who will not deal falsely; 63.08
in labor she brought forth her s. 66.08
how I would set you among my s., Jer 3.19
and pleading of Israel's s., 3.21
O faithless s., I will heal your 3.22
their s. and their daughters. 3.24
eat up your s. and your daughters; 5.17
fathers and s. together, neighbor 6.21
"For the s. of Judah have done evil 7.30
to burn their s. and their daughters 7.31
to s. of Ammon, Moab, and all who 9.26
their s. and their daughters shall 11.22
fathers and s. together, says the 13.14
their s., and their daughters. 14.16
shall you have s. or daughters in 16.02
concerning the s. and daughters 16.03
to burn their s. in the fire as 19.05
flesh of their s. and their 19.09
Edom, Moab, and the s. of Ammon; 25.21
Moab, the king of the s. of Ammon, 27.03
Take wives and have s. and daughters; 29.06
take wives for your s., and give 29.06
they may bear s. and daughters; 29.06
s. of Israel and the s. of Judah 32.30
the s. of Israel have done nothing 32.30
the evil of the s. of Israel and 32.32
Israel and the s. of Judah which 32.32
offer up their s. and daughters to 32.35
and all his s., and the whole house 35.03
chamber of the s. of Hanan the 35.04
neither you nor your s. for ever; 35.06
wives, our s., or our daughters, 35.08
the son of Rechab gave to his s., 35.14
The s. of Jonadab the son of 35.16
wives and your s. shall be led out 38.23
slew the s. of Zedekiah at Riblah 39.06
the s. of Ephai the Netophathite, 40.08
the crown of the s. of tumult. 48.45
for your s. have been taken 48.46
says the LORD: "Has Israel no s? 49.01
slew the s. of Zedekiah before his 52.10
afflict or grieve the s. of men. Lam 3.33
The precious s. of Zion, worth their 4.02
shall eat their s. in the midst of Eze 5.10
and s. shall eat their fathers; 5.10
deliver neither s. nor daughters; 14.16
deliver neither s. nor daughters, 14.18
to lead out s. and daughters, 14.22
And you took your s. and your 16.20
and sacrifice your s. by fire, 20.31
and they bore s. and daughters. 23.04
they seized her s. and her daughters; 23.10
seize your s. and your daughters, 23.25
for food the s. whom they had 23.37
slay their s. and their daughters, 23.47
and your s. and your daughters whom 24.21
and also their s. and daughters, 24.25
these are the s. of Zadok, who alone 40.46
alone among the s. of Levi may 40.46
the s. of Zadok, who kept the charge 44.15
to any of his s. out of his 46.16
inheritance, it shall belong to his s., 46.16
only his s. may keep a gift from 46.17
shall give his s. their inheritance 46.18

to you as a native-born s. of Israel; 47.22
the s. of Zadok, who kept my charge, 48.11
the s. of men, the beasts of the Dan 2.38
likeness of the s. of men touched 10.16
"His s. shall wage war and assemble 11.10
to them, "S. of the living God." Hos 1.10
Ephraim's s., as I have seen, are 9.13
lead forth his s. to slaughter. 9.13
and his s. shall come trembling 11.10
gladness fails from the s. of men. Joe 1.12
"Be glad, O s. of Zion, and rejoice 2.23
your s. and your daughters shall 2.28
I will sell your s. and your 3.08
into the hand of the s. of Judah, 3.08
up some of your s. for prophets, Amo 2.11
and your s. and your daughters 7.17
for men nor wait for the s. of men. Mic 5.07
and the king's s. and all who Zep 1.08
I will brandish your s., O Zion, Zec 9.13
over your s., O Greece, and wield 9.13
will purify the s. of Levi and Mal 3.03
O s. of Jacob, are not consumed. 3.06
for they shall be called s. of God. Mt 5.09
so that you may be s. of your 5.45
while the s. of the kingdom will be 8.12
by whom do your s. cast them out? 12.27
seed means the s. of the kingdom; 13.38
weeds are the s. of the evil one, 13.38
From their s. or from others?" 17.25
said to him, "Then the s. are free. 17.26
mother of the s. of Zebedee came 20.20
with her s., and kneeling before 20.20
that these two s. of mine may sit, 20.21
A man had two s.; and he went 21.28
that you are s. of those who 23.31
Peter and the two s. of Zebedee, 26.37
set by some of the s. of Israel, 27.09
the mother of the s. of Zebedee. 27.56
Boanerges, that is, s. of thunder; Mk 3.17
will be forgiven the s. of men, 3.28
the s. of Zebedee, came forward to 10.35
many of the s. of Israel to the Lk 1.16
s. of Zebedee, who were partners 5.10
and you will be s. of the Most 6.35
by whom do your s. cast them out? 11.19
"There was a man who had two s.; 15.11
for the s. of this world are wiser 16.08
generation than the s. of light. 16.08
"The s. of this age marry and are 20.34
equal to angels and are s. of God, 20.36
being s. of the resurrection. 20.36
and his s., and his cattle?" Jn 4.12
that you may become s. of light." 12.36
the s. of Zebedee, and two others of 21.02
and your s. and your daughters Ac 2.17
You are the s. of the prophets and 3.25
silver from the s. of Hamor in 7.16
his brethren, the s. of Israel. 7.23
he became the father of two s. 7.29
and kings and the s. of Israel; 9.15
"Brethren, s. of the family of 13.26
Seven s. of a Jewish high priest 19.14
by the Spirit of God are s. of God. Rom 8.14
for the revealing of the s. of God; 8.19
as we wait for adoption as s., 8.23
will be called 's. of the living 9.26
number of the s. of Israel be as 9.27
you shall be my s. and daughters, 2Co 6.18
of faith who are the s. of Abraham. Gal 3.07
Christ Jesus you are all s. of God, 3.26
we might receive adoption as s. 4.05
And because you are s., God has 4.06
is written that Abraham had two s., 4.22
love to be his s. through Jesus Eph 1.05
at work in the s. of disobedience. 2.02
known to the s. of men in other 3.05
comes upon the s. of disobedience. 5.06

SONS (cont.)
For you are all s. of light and 1Th 5.05
and s. of the day; we are not of 5.05
in bringing many s. to glory, Heb 2.10
blessed each of the s. of Joseph, 11.21
exhortation which addresses you as s.?— 12.05
God is treating you as s.; for what 12.07
illegitimate children and not s. 12.08
block before the s. of Israel, Rev 2.14
every tribe of the s. of Israel, 7.04
tribes of the s. of Israel were 21.12

SONS'
wife, and your s. wives with you. Gen 6.18
wife and his s. wives with him 7.07
sons and your s. wives with you. 8.16
his wife and his s. wives with him. 8.18
and his s. sons with him, his 46.07
daughters, and his s. daughters; 46.07
not including Jacob's s. wives, 46.26
sons and his s. garments with him; Ex 29.21
sons and his s. garments with him. 29.21
upon his sons and his s. garments; Lev 8.30
sons and his s. garments with him. 8.30
it is your due and your s. due, 10.13
given as your due and your s. due, 10.14
and your s. with you, as a due for 10.15
and his s. sons, four generations. Job 42.16

SONSHIP
you have received the spirit of s. Rom 8.15
Israelites, and to them belong the s., 9.04

SONS-IN-LAW
S., sons, daughters, or any one you Gen 19.12
So Lot went out and said to his s., 19.14
he seemed to his s. to be jesting. 19.14

SOON
As s. as Isaac had finished blessing Gen 27.30
but as s. as I lifted up my voice 39.18
as s. as it budded, its blossoms 40.10
As s. as the morning was light, the 44.03
it that you have come so s. today?" Ex 2.18
"As s. as I have gone out of the 9.29
And as s. as he came near the camp 32.19
that you will s. utterly perish Deu 4.26
and as s. as the pursuers had gone Jos 2.07
And as s. as we heard it, our hearts 2.11
as s. as you hear the sound of the 6.05
As s. as the people heard the sound 6.20
and as s. as he had stretched out 8.19
they s. turned aside from the way Ju 2.17
As s. as Gideon died, the people of 8.33
as s. as the sun is up, rise early 9.33
"As s. as the child is weaned, I 1Sa 1.22
As s. as you enter the city, you 9.13
As s. as he had finished offering 13.10
And as s. as the lad had gone, David 20.41
and depart as s. as you have light." 29.10
And as s. as he had finished 2Sa 13.36
"As s. as you hear the sound of the 15.10
as s. as they heard of me, they 22.45
And as s. as he was king, he killed 1Ki 15.29
as s. as he had seated himself on 16.11
And as s. as I have gone from you, 18.12
as s. as you have gone from me, a 20.36
And as s. as he had departed from 20.36
As s. as Jezebel heard that Naboth 21.15
And as s. as Ahab heard that Naboth 21.16
As s. as they entered Samaria, 2Ki 6.20
"Now then, as s. as this letter 10.02
So as s. as he had made an end of 10.25
and as s. as the man touched the 13.21
And as s. as the royal power was 14.05
And as s. as the royal power was 2Ch 25.03
As s. as the command was spread 31.05
would my Maker s. put an end to me. Job 32.22
As s. as they heard of me they Ps 18.44
For they will s. fade like the 37.02
As s. as they saw it, they were 48.05
I would s. subdue their enemies, and 81.14
they are s. gone, and we fly away. 90.10
my soul would s. have dwelt in the 94.17
But they s. forgot his works; 106.13
eats it up as s. as it is in his Is 28.04
for s. my salvation will come, and 56.01
For as s. as Zion was in labor she 66.08
Now I will s. pour out my wrath Eze 7.08
for they will s. come home. 36.08
Therefore, as s. as all the peoples Dan 3.07
nations, I will s. gather them up. Hos 8.10
as s. as its branch becomes tender Mt 24.32
will be able s. after to speak Mk 9.39
as s. as its branch becomes tender 13.28
And as s. as it was morning the 15.01
S. afterward he went to a city Lk 7.11
S. afterward he went on through 8.01
as s. as they come out in leaf, you 21.30
to come to him as s. as possible, Ac 17.15
But s. a tempestuous wind, called 27.14
of peace will s. crush Satan under Rom 16.20
But I will come to you s., 1Co 4.19
Jesus to send Timothy to you s., Php 2.19
him just as s. as I see how it 2.23
I hope to come to you s., but I am 1Ti 3.14
Do your best to come to me s. 2Ti 4.09
I shall see you if he comes s. Heb 13.23
putting off of my body will be s., 2Pe 1.14
I hope to see you s., and we will 3Jn 1.14
servants what must s. take place; Rev 1.01
come to you s. and war against 2.16
I am coming s.; hold fast to what 3.11
behold, the third woe is s. to come. 11.14
servants what must s. take place. 22.06
And behold, I am coming s." 22.07
I am coming s., bringing my recompense, 22.12
things says, "Surely I am coming s." 22.20

SOONER
S. than your pots can feel the heat Ps 58.09
I may be restored to you the s. Heb 13.19

SOOT
Now their visage is blacker than s., Lam 4.08

SOOTHING
here they sent up their s. odors, Eze 20.28

SOOTHSAYER
a s. or an augur, or a sorcerer, Deu 18.10
the s., the people of Israel killed Jos 13.22

SOOTHSAYERS
give heed to s. and to diviners; Deu 18.14
east and of s. like the Philistines, Is 2.06
your s., or your sorcerers, who are Jer 27.09
and you shall have no more s.; Mic 5.12

SOOTHSAYING
and practiced s. and augury, and 2Ki 21.06
and practiced s. and augury and 2Ch 33.06
brought her owners much gain by s. Ac 16.16

SOPATER
S. of Beroea, the son of Pyrrhus, Ac 20.04

SOPHERETH
the sons of S., the sons of Perida, Neh 7.57

SORCERER
soothsayer, or an augur, or a s., Deu 18.10

SORCERERS
summoned the wise men and the s.; Ex 7.11
will consult the idols and the s., Is 19.03
or your s., who are saying to you, Jer 27.09

SORCERERS (cont.)
enchanters, the s., and the Chaldeans Dan 2.02
be a swift witness against the s., Mal 3.05
s., idolaters, and all liars, their Rev 21.08
the dogs and s. and fornicators 22.15

SORCERESS
"You shall not permit a s. to live. Ex 22.18
sons of the s., offspring of the Is 57.03

SORCERIES
harlotries and the s. of your mother 2Ki 9.22
of your many s. and the great power Is 47.09
your enchantments and your many s., 47.12
and I will cut off s. from your hand, Mic 5.12
or their s. or their immorality or Rev 9.21

SORCERY
offerings, and used divination and s., 2Ki 17.17
soothsaying and augury and s., 2Ch 33.06
idolatry, s., enmity, strife, jealousy, Gal 5.20
nations were deceived by thy s. Rev 18.23

SORE
On the third day, when they were s., Gen 34.25
them; and they were in s. straits. Ju 2.15
hast made me see many s. troubles wilt Ps 71.20
this is vanity; it is a s. affliction. Ecc 6.02
upon Jerusalem my four s. acts of Eze 14.21

SOREK
loved a woman in the valley of S., Ju 16.04

SORELY
shot at him, and harassed him s.; Gen 49.23
so that Israel was s. distressed. Ju 10.09
And her rival used to provoke her s., 1Sa 1.06
my lord I am a woman s. troubled; 1.15
My soul also is s. troubled. But Ps 6.03
shall be ashamed and s. troubled; 6.10
The LORD has chastened me s., 118.18
I am s. afflicted; give me life, O 119.107
"S. have they afflicted me from my 129.01
"S. have they afflicted me from my 129.02
keep silent, and afflict us s.? Is 64.12

SORES
breaking out in s. on man and Ex 9.09
breaking out in s. on man and 9.10
with loathsome s. from the sole of Job 2.07
but bruises and s. and bleeding Is 1.06
man named Lazarus, full of s., Lk 16.20
the dogs came and licked his s. 16.21
foul and evil s. came upon the men Rev 16.02
of heaven for their pain and s., 16.11

SORREL
him were red, s., and white horses. Zec 1.08

SORROW
my gray hairs with s. to Sheol." Gen 42.38
down my gray hairs in s. to Sheol." 44.29
our father with s. to Sheol. 44.31
Rachel to my s. died in the land of 48.07
and his own s. and stretching out 2Ch 6.29
for them from s. into gladness and Est 9.22
and have s. in my heart all the day? Ps 13.02
For my life is spent with s., and 31.10
my eye grows dim through s. Every 88.09
through oppression, trouble, and s., 107.39
My soul melts away for s.; strengthen 119.28
foolish son is a s. to his mother. Pro 10.01
rich, and he adds no s. with it. 10.22
but by s. of heart the spirit is 15.13
Who has s.? Who has strife? 23.29
increases knowledge increases s. Ecc 1.18
S. is better than laughter, for by 7.03
and s. and sighing shall flee away. Is 35.10
and s. and sighing shall flee away. 51.11
from the womb to see toil and s., Jer 20.18
and give them gladness for s. 31.13
the LORD has added s. to my pain; 45.03
see if there is any s. like my s. Lam 1.12
be filled with drunkenness and s. Eze 23.33
and found them sleeping for s., Lk 22.45
to you, s. has filled your hearts. Jn 16.06
but your s. will turn into joy. 16.20
When a woman is in travail she has s., 16.21
So you have s. now but I will see 16.22
that I have great s. and unceasing Rom 9.02
may be overwhelmed by excessive s. 2Co 2.07
me also, lest I should have s. upon s. Php 2.27

SORROWFUL
a very great and s. lamentation; Gen 50.10
man heard this he went away s.; Mt 19.22
And they were very s., and began 26.22
he began to be s. and troubled. 26.37
"My soul is very s., even to death; 26.38
countenance fell, and he went away s.; Mk 10.22
They began to be s., and to say to 14.19
"My soul is very s., even to death; 14.34
you will be s., but your sorrow Jn 16.20
as s., yet always rejoicing; 2Co 6.10

SORROWING
s. most of all because of the word Ac 20.38

SORROWS
another god multiply their s.; Ps 16.04
a man of s., and acquainted with Is 53.03
our griefs and carried our s.; 53.04
anguish and s. have taken hold of Jer 49.24

SORRY
And the LORD was s. that he had Gen 6.06
for I am s. that I have made them." 6.07
none of you is s. for me or 1Sa 22.08
my iniquity, I am s. for my sin. Ps 38.18
And the king was s.; but because Mt 14.09
And the king was exceedingly s.; Mk 6.26
if I made you s. with my letter, 2Co 7.08

SORT
bring two of every s. into the ark, Gen 6.19
two of every s. shall come in to 6.20
with you every s. of food that is 6.21
its kind, every bird of every s. 7.14
to do every s. of work done by a Ex 35.35
by any s. of workman or skilled 35.35
doing every s. of task on the 36.04
of whatever s. the uncleanness may Lev 5.03
any s. of rash oath that men swear, 5.04
me to be some s. of disease in my 14.35
your neighbor a loan of any s., Deu 24.10
with every s. of plague in the 1Sa 4.08
them with every s. of distress. 2Ch 15.06
birds of every s. will nest. Eze 17.23
of the common s. drunkards were 23.42
prey of every s. and to the wild 39.04
birds of every s. and to all 39.17
"What s. of man is this, that even Mt 8.27
her mind what s. of greeting this Lk 1.29
who and what s. of woman this is 7.39
will test what s. of work each one 1Co 3.13
by the same s. of disobedience. Heb 4.11
what s. of persons ought you to be 2Pe 3.11

SORTED
sat down and s. the good into vessels Mt 13.48

SORTS
taking all s. of choice gifts from Gen 24.10
there were all s. of baked food 40.17
all s. of gold objects, every man Ex 35.22
themselves all s. of people as 2Ki 17.32

SORTS (cont.)
And he sent all s. of articles of 1Ch 18.10
all s. of precious stones, and 29.02
and to do all s. of engraving and 2Ch 2.14

SOSIPATER
Lucius and Jason and S., my kinsmen. Rom 16.21

SOSTHENES
And they all seized S., the ruler Ac 18.17
Christ Jesus, and our brother S., 1Co 1.01

SOTAI
the sons of S., the sons of Hassophereth, Ez 2.55
the sons of S., the sons of Sophereth, Neh 7.57

SOUGHT
brother, and he s. a place to weep. Gen 43.30
heard of it, he s. to kill Moses. Ex 2.15
LORD met him and s. to kill him. 4.24
every one who s. the LORD would go 33.07
because he s. to draw you away from Deu 13.10
But when they s. him, he could not 1Sa 10.21
the LORD has s. out a man after his 13.14
which Jonathan s. to go over to 14.04
And Saul s. to pin David to the 19.10
And Saul s. him every day, but God 23.14
fled to Gath, he s. for him no more. 27.04
Saul, your enemy, who s. your life; 2Sa 4.08
when they had s. and could not 17.20
and David s. the face of the LORD. 21.01
Saul had s. to slay them in his 21.02
young maiden be s. for my lord the 1Ki 1.02
So they s. for a beautiful maiden 1.03
And the whole earth s. the presence 10.24
Solomon s. therefore to kill 11.40
three days they s. him but did not 2Ki 2.17
and the assembly s. the LORD. 2Ch 1.05
of the earth s. the presence of 9.23
because he have s. the LORD our 14.07
we have s. him, and he has given 14.07
and s. him, he was found by them. 15.04
and had s. him with their whole 15.15
but s. help from physicians. 16.12
but s. the God of his father and 17.04
who s. the LORD with all his heart." 22.09
they had s. the gods of Edom. 25.20
and as long as he s. the LORD, 26.05
These s. their registration among Ez 2.62
These s. their registration among Neh 7.64
Jerusalem they s. the Levites in 12.27
virgins be s. out for the king. Est 2.02
angry and s. to lay hands on King 2.21
Haman s. to destroy all the Jews, 3.06
and who had s. to lay hands upon 6.02
lay hands on such as s. their hurt. 9.02
for he s. the welfare of his people 10.03
I s. the LORD, and he answered me, Ps 34.04
though I s. him, he could not be 37.36
and s. refuge in his wealth!" 52.07
and disgraced who s. to do me hurt. 71.24
When he slew them, they s. for him; 78.34
they repented and s. God earnestly. 78.34
liberty, for I have s. thy precepts. 119.45
for I have s. thy precepts. 119.94
which my mind has s. repeatedly, Ecc 7.28
but they have s. out many devices. 7.29
The Preacher s. to find pleasing 12.10
bed by night I s. him whom my soul Sol 3.01
I s. him, but found him not; 3.01
I s. him, but found him not. 3.02
I s. him, but found him not; 5.06
O LORD, in distress they s. thee, Is 26.16
and you shall be called S. out, 62.12
I was ready to be s. by those who 65.01
down, for my people who have s. me. 65.10
which they have s. and worshiped; Jer 8.02
the king s. to put him to death; 26.21
wilderness; when Israel s. for rest, 31.02
who was his enemy and s. his life." 44.30
iniquity shall be s. in Israel, 50.20
while they s. food to revive their Lam 1.19
And I s. for a man among them who Eze 22.30
though you be s. for, you will never 26.21
back, the lost you have not s., 34.04
and they s. Daniel and his companions, Dan 2.13
counselors and my lords s. me, 4.36
and the satraps s. to find a 6.04
the vision, I s. to understand it; 8.15
prevailed he wept and s. his favor. Hos 12.04
pillaged, his treasures s. out! Ob 1.06
for those who s. the child's life Mt 2.20
that moment he s. an opportunity 26.16
whole council s. false testimony 26.59
heard it and s. a way to destroy Mk 11.18
And he s. an opportunity to betray 14.11
whole council s. testimony against 14.55
and they s. him among their kinsfolk Lk 2.44
to them, "How is it that you s. me? 2.49
And the people s. him and came to 4.42
and they s. to bring him in and lay 5.18
And all the crowd s. to touch him, 6.19
things?" And he s. to see him. 9.09
s. from him a sign from heaven. 11.16
And he s. to see who Jesus was, but 19.03
of the people s. to destroy him; 19.47
and s. an opportunity to betray him 22.06
why the Jews s. all the more to Jn 5.18
because the Jews s. to kill him. 7.01
So they s. to arrest him; but no one 7.30
Upon this Pilate s. to release him, 19.12
And when Herod had s. for him and Ac 12.19
and Saul and s. to hear the word 13.07
immediately we s. to go on into 16.10
And having s. out the disciples, we 21.04
Israel failed to obtain what it s. Rom 11.07
repent, though he s. it with tears. Heb 12.17

SOUL
And his s. was drawn to Dinah the Gen 34.03
"The s. of my son Shechem longs for 34.08
And as her s. was departing (for 35.18
that we saw the distress of his s., 42.21
O my s., come not into their 49.06
that s. shall be cut off from among Ex 31.14
and my s. shall not abhor you. Lev 26.11
and if your s. abhors my ordinances, 26.15
idols; and my s. will abhor you. 26.30
and their s. abhorred my statutes. 26.43
and keep your s. diligently, lest Deu 4.09
your heart and with all your s. 4.29
your heart, and with all your s., 6.05
your heart and with all your s., 10.12
your heart and with all your s., 11.13
mine in your heart and in your s.; 11.18
your heart and with all your s. 13.03
your friend who is as your own s., 13.06
your heart and with all your s. 26.16
failing eyes, and a languishing s.; 28.65
your heart and with all your s.; 30.02
your heart and with all your s., 30.06
your heart and with all your s. 30.10
your heart and with all your s." Jos 22.05
March on, my s., with might! Ju 5.21
urged him, his s. was vexed to death. 16.16
pouring out my s. before the LORD. 1Sa 1.15
"As your s. lives, O king, I cannot 17.55
the s. of Jonathan was knit to the 18.01
was knit to the s. of David, 18.01
Jonathan loved him as his own s. 18.01
because he loved him as his own s. 18.03
LORD lives and as your s. lives, 20.03
loved him as he loved his own s. 20.17
and as your s. lives, seeing the 25.26
all the people were bitter in s., 30.06

SOUL (cont.)

blind, who are hated by David's s." 2Sa 5.08
and as your s. lives, I will not do 11.11
has redeemed my s. out of every 1Ki 1.29
their heart and with all their s., 2.04
over all that your s. desires, 11.37
this child's s. come into him 17.21
and the s. of the child came into 17.22
with all his heart and all his s., 2Ki 23.03
with all his s. and with all his 23.25
their heart and with all their s.; 2Ch 15.12
with all his heart and all his s., 34.31
and life to the bitter in s., Job 3.20
complain in the bitterness of my s. 7.11
speak in the bitterness of my s. 10.01
Another dies in bitterness of s., 21.25
and the s. of the wounded cries for 24.12
Almighty, who has made my s. bitter; 27.02
"And now my s. is poured out within 30.16
Was not my s. grieved for the poor? 30.25
he keeps back his s. from the Pit, 33.18
His s. draws near the Pit, and his 33.22
He has redeemed my s. from going 33.28
to bring back his s. from the Pit, 33.30
My s. also is sorely troubled. Ps 6.03
ground and lay my s. in the dust. 7.05
and his s. hates him that loves 11.05
How long must I bear pain in my s., 13.02
heart is glad, and my s. rejoices; 16.09
LORD is perfect, reviving the s.; 19.07
Deliver my s. from the sword, my 22.20
my afflicted s. from the horns of 22.21
he restores my s. He leads me 23.03
not lift up his s. to what is 24.04
To thee, O LORD, I lift up my s. 25.01
hast brought up my s. from Sheol, 30.03
that my s. may praise thee and not 30.12
from grief, my s. and my body also. 31.09
he may deliver their s. from death, 33.19
Our s. waits for the LORD; 33.20
My s. makes its boast in the LORD; 34.02
Say to my s. "I am your deliverance 35.03
Then my s. shall rejoice in the 35.09
evil for good; my s. is forlorn. 35.12
so longs my s. for thee, O God. 42.01
My s. thirsts for God, for the 42.02
I remember, as I pour out my s.: 42.04
O my s., and why are you disquieted 42.05
My s. is cast down within me, 42.06
O my s., and why are you disquieted 42.11
O my s., and why are you disquieted 43.05
For our s. is bowed down to the 44.25
will ransom my s. from the power 49.15
He will deliver my s. in safety 55.18
hast delivered my s. from death, 56.13
me for in thee my s. takes refuge; 57.01
for my steps; my s. was bowed down. 57.06
Awake, my s.! Awake, O harp and 57.08
For God alone my s. waits in silence; 62.01
For God alone my s. waits in silence, 62.05
my s. thirsts for thee; my flesh 63.01
My s. is feasted as with marrow and 63.05
My s. clings to thee; thy right 63.08
When I rumbled my s. with fasting, 69.10
my s. also, which thou hast rescued. 71.23
When my s. was embittered, when I 73.21
Do not deliver the s. of thy dove 74.19
my s. refuses to be comforted. 77.02
My s. longs, yea, faints for the 84.02
Gladden the s. of thy servant for 86.04
thee, O Lord, do I lift up my s. 86.04
delivered my s. from the depths of 86.13
For my s. is full of troubles, and 88.03
can deliver his s. from the power 89.48
my s. would soon have dwelt in the 94.17
many, thy consolations cheer my s. 94.19
Bless the LORD, O my s.; and all 103.01
O my s., and forget not all his 103.02
dominion. Bless the LORD, O my s.! 103.22
Bless the LORD, O my s.! O LORD my 104.01
Bless the LORD, O my s.! Praise the 104.35
their s. fainted within them. 107.05
I will sing praises! Awake, my s.! 108.01
Return, O my s., to your rest; 116.07
hast delivered my s. from death, 116.08
My s. is consumed with longing for 119.20
My s. cleaves to the dust; 119.25
My s. melts away for sorrow; 119.28
My s. languishes for thy salvation; 119.81
therefore my s. keeps them. 119.129
My s. keeps thy testimonies; 119.167
Too long our s. has been sated with 123.04
my s. waits, and in his word I hope; 130.05
my s. waits for the LORD more than 130.06
But I have calmed and quieted my s., 131.02
a child that is quieted is my s. 131.02
my strength of s. thou didst 138.03
my s. thirsts for thee like a 143.06
go, for to thee I lift up my s. 143.08
Praise the LORD, O my s.! 146.01
will be pleasant to your s.; Pro 2.10
life for your s. and adornment for 3.22
The s. of the sluggard craves, and 13.04
while the s. of the diligent is 13.04
fulfilled is sweet to the s.; 13.19
sweetness to the s. and health to 16.24
The s. of the wicked desires evil; 21.10
My s. will rejoice when your lips 23.16
keeps watch over your s. know it, 24.12
Know that wisdom is such to your s.; 24.14
Like cold water to a thirsty s., 25.25
but the s. is torn by trouble. 27.09
you whom my s. loves, where you Sol 1.07
I sought him whom my s. loves; 3.01
I will seek him whom my s. loves." 3.02
"Have you seen him whom my s. loves?" 3.03
when I found him whom my s. loves. 3.04
My s. failed me when he spoke. 5.06
your appointed feasts my s. hates; Is 1.14
both s. and body, and it will be as 10.18
of Moab cry aloud; his s. trembles. 15.04
Therefore my s. moans like a lyre 16.11
name is the desire of our s. 26.08
My s. yearns for thee in the night, 26.09
because of the bitterness of my s. 38.15
my chosen, in whom my s. delights; 42.01
travail of his s. and be satisfied 53.11
he poured out his s. to death, 53.12
hear, that your s. may live; 55.03
my s. shall exult in my God; 61.10
and their s. delights in their 66.03
beloved of my s. into the hands of Jer 12.07
my s. will weep in secret for your 13.17
Does thy s. loathe Zion? Why hast 14.19
I will feast the s. of the priests 31.14
For I will satisfy the weary s., 31.25
languishing s. I will replenish." 31.25
with all my heart and all my s. 32.41
my s. is in tumult, my heart is Lam 1.20
my s. is in tumult; my heart is 2.11
me s. is bereft of peace, I have 3.17
My s. continually thinks of it and 3.20
says my s., "therefore I will hope 3.24
for him, to the s. that seeks him. 3.25
the s. of the father as well as the Eze 18.04
as well as the s. of the son is 18.04
the s. that sins shall die. 18.04
The s. that sins shall die. 18.20
eyes, and the desire of your s.; 24.21
weep over you in bitterness of s., 27.31
When my s. fainted within me, I Jon 2.07
of my body for the sin of my s.?" Mic 6.07
first-ripe fig which my s. desires. 7.01
utters the evil desire of his s.; 7.03

SOUL (cont.)

he whose s. is not upright in him Hab 2.04
the body but cannot kill the s.; Mt 10.28
destroy both s. and body in hell. 10.28
with whom my s. is well pleased. 12.18
your heart, and with all your s., 22.37
"My s. is very sorrowful, even to 26.38
your heart, and with all your s., Mk 12.30
"My s. is very sorrowful, even to 14.34
said, "My s. magnifies the Lord, Lk 1.46
pierce through your own s. also), 2.35
your heart, and with all your s., 10.27
And I will say to my s., S., you have 12.19
This night your s. is required of 12.20
"Now is my s. troubled. And what Jn 12.27
wilt not abandon my s. to Hades, Ac 2.27
And fear came upon every s.; 2.43
be that every s. that does not 3.23
believed were of one heart and s., 4.32
your spirit and s. and body be 1Th 5.23
to the division of s. and spirit, Heb 4.12
and steadfast anchor of the s., 6.19
my s. has no pleasure in him. 10.38
will save his s. from death and Jas 5.20
that wage war against your s. 1Pe 2.11
his righteous s. day after day 2Pe 2.08
know that it is well with your s. 3Jn 1.02
for which thy s. longed has gone Rev 18.14

SOULS

to make atonement for your s.; Lev 17.11
and you know in your hearts and s., Jos 23.14
in it, and find rest for your s. Jer 6.16
who made our s., I will not put you 38.16
every stature, in the hunt for s.! Eze 13.18
you hunt down s. belonging to my 13.18
and keep other s. alive for your 13.18
bands with which you hunt the s., 13.20
I will let the s. that you hunt go 13.20
Behold, all s. are mine; the soul 18.04
and you will find rest for your s. Mt 11.29
that day about three thousand s. Ac 2.41
all his kindred, seventy-five s.; 7.14
strengthening the s. of the disciples, 14.22
spend and be spent for your s. 2Co 12.15
who have faith and keep their s. Heb 10.39
are keeping watch over your s., 13.17
which is able to save your s. Jas 1.21
obtain the salvation of your s. 1Pe 1.09
Having purified your s. by your 1.22
Shepherd and Guardian of your s. 2.25
entrust their s. to a fatihful 4.19
They entice unsteady s. They have 2Pe 2.14
the altar the s. of those who had Rev 6.09
and slaves, that is, human s. 18.13
Also I saw the s. of those who had 20.04

SOUND

And they heard the s. of the LORD Gen 3.08
"I heard the s. of thee in the 3.10
And as the s. of the trumpet grew Ex 19.19
lightnings and the s. of the 20.18
and its s. shall be heard when he 28.35
"It is not the s. of shouting for 32.18
or the s. of the cry of defeat, but 32.18
but the s. of singing that I hear." 32.18
the s. of a driven leaf shall put Lev 26.36
but you shall not s. an alarm. Num 10.07
then you shall s. an alarm with 10.09
you heard the s. of words, but saw Deu 4.12
as you hear the s. of the trumpet, Jos 6.05
people heard the s. of the trumpet, 6.20
To the s. of musicians at the Ju 5.11
When Eli heard the s. of the outcry, 1Sa 4.14
you hear the s. of marching in the 2Sa 5.24
and with the s. of the horn. 6.15
as you hear the s. of the trumpet, 15.10
Joab heard the s. of the trumpet, 1Ki 1.41
Ahijah heard the s. of her feet, 14.06
for there is a s. of the rushing of 18.41
there was no s. or sign of life. 2Ki 4.31
Is not the s. of his master's feet 6.32
Syrians hear the s. of chariots, 7.06
the s. of a great army, so that they 7.06
you hear the s. of marching in the 1Ch 14.15
Ethan, were to s. bronze cymbals; 15.19
to the s. of the horn, trumpets, and 15.28
Asaph was to s. the cymbals, 16.05
trumpets to s. the call to battle 2Ch 13.12
distinguish the s. of the joyful Ez 3.13
shout from the s. of the people's 3.13
shout, and the s. was heard afar. 3.13
you hear the s. of the trumpet, Neh 4.20
and rejoice to the s. of the pipe. Job 21.12
plentifully declared s. knowledge! 26.03
I have heard the s. of your words. 33.08
still at the s. of the trumpet. 39.24
Hearken to the s. of my cry, my King Ps 5.02
has heard the s. of my weeping. 6.08
the LORD with the s. of a trumpet. 47.05
let the s. of his praise be heard, 66.08
their bodies are s. and sleek. 73.04
Raise a song, s. the timbrel, the 81.02
with the lyre and the s. of melody! 98.05
trumpets and the s. of the horn 98.06
at the s. of thy thunder they took 104.07
do not make a s. in their throat. 115.07
Praise him with trumpet s.; 150.03
he stores up s. wisdom for the Pro 2.07
My son, keep s. wisdom and discretion 3.21
I have counsel and s. wisdom, 8.14
break out against all s. judgment. 18.01
when the s. of the grinding is low, Ecc 12.04
to Sheol, the s. of your harps; Is 14.11
flees at the s. of the terror 24.18
to you at the s. of your cry; 30.19
sets out to the s. of the flute to 30.29
will be to the s. of timbrels and 30.32
heard in it the s. of weeping and 65.19
for I hear the s. of the trumpet, Jer 4.19
and hear the s. of the trumpet? 4.21
'Give heed to the s. of the trumpet!' 6.17
the s. of them is like the roaring 6.23
at the s. of the neighing of their 8.16
For a s. of wailing is heard from 9.19
or hear the s. of the trumpet, or be 42.14
"She makes a s. like a serpent 46.22
At the s. of their fall the earth 49.21
the s. of their cry shall be heard 49.21
The s. of them is like the roaring 50.42
At the s. of the capture of Babylon 50.46
I heard the s. of their wings like the s. Eze 1.24
a s. of tumult like the s. of a host; 1.24
behind me the s. of a great 3.12
it was the s. of the wings of the 3.13
and the s. of the wheels beside 3.13
And the s. of the wings of the 10.05
in it at the s. of his roaring. 19.07
The s. of a carefree multitude was 23.42
and the s. of your lyres shall be 26.13
shake at the s. of your fall, 26.15
At the s. of the cry of your pilots 27.28
quake at the s. of its fall, 31.16
who hears the s. of the trumpet 33.04
He heard the s. of the trumpet, and 33.05
and the s. of his coming was like the s. 43.02
that when you hear the s. of the horn, Dan 3.05
peoples heard the s. of the horn, 3.07
man who hears the s. of the horn, 3.10
when you hear the s. of the horn, 3.15
because of the s. of the great 7.11
and the s. of his words like the 10.06
Then I heard the s. of his words; 10.09
when I heard the s. of his words, 10.09
S. the alarm at Bethaven; Hos 5.08
s. the alarm on my holy mountain! Joe 2.01

SOUND (cont.)

shouting and the s. of the trumpet; Amo 2.02
idle songs to the s. of the harp, 6.05
and it is s. wisdom to fear thy Mic 6.09
trembles, my lips quiver at the s.; Hab 3.16
the s. of the day of the LORD is Zep 1.14
the Lord GOD will s. the trumpet, Zec 9.14
heal the maimed, or nourish the s., 11.16
s. no trumpet before you, as the Mt 6.02
So, if your eye is s., your whole 6.22
but if your eye is not s., your 6.23
So, every s. tree bears good fruit, 7.17
A s. tree cannot bear evil fruit, 7.18
when your eye is s., your whole body Lk 11.34
but when it is not s., your body 11.34
he has received him safe and s.' 15.27
wills, and you hear the s. of it, Jn 3.08
And suddenly a s. came from heaven Ac 2.02
And at this s. the multitude came 2.06
the bugle gives an indistinct s., 1Co 14.08
For the trumpet will s., 15.52
and with the s. of the trumpet of 1Th 4.16
body be kept s. and blameless at 5.23
else is contrary to s. doctrine, 1Ti 1.10
agree with the s. words of our 6.03
pattern of the s. words which you 2Ti 1.13
people will not endure s. teaching, 4.03
instruction in s. doctrine and Tit 1.09
that they may be s. in the faith, 1.13
you, teach what befits s. doctrine. 2.01
s. in faith, in love, and in steadfastness 2.02
and s. speech that cannot be 2.08
and the s. of a trumpet, and a voice Heb 12.19
was like the s. of many waters; Rev 1.15
heaven like the s. of many waters 14.02
and like the s. of loud thunder; 14.02
was like the s. of harpers playing 14.02
and the s. of harpers and minstrels, 18.22
and the s. of the millstone shall 18.22
like the s. of many waters and like 19.06
and like the s. of mighty thunderpeals, 19.06

SOUNDED

he s. the trumpet in the hill country Ju 3.27
and he s. the trumpet, and the 6.34
When I have s. my father, about this 1Sa 20.12
them the priests s. trumpets; 2Ch 7.06
singers sang, and the trumpeters s.; 29.28
The man who s. the trumpet was Neh 4.18
that s. like a great earthquake. Eze 3.13
The nations s. an alarm against him 19.04
So they s. and found twenty fathoms Ac 27.28
farther on they s. again and found 27.28
of the Lord s. forth from you in 1Th 1.08
called out, the seven thunders s. Rev 10.03
And when the seven thunders had s., 10.04
call to be s. by the seventh angel, 10.07

SOUNDING

Praise him with s. cymbals; praise Ps 150.05

SOUNDNESS

There is no s. in my flesh because Ps 38.03
and there is no s. in my flesh. 38.07
there is no s. in it, but bruises Is 1.06

SOUNDS

when the trumpet s. a long blast, Ex 19.13
and cymbals, to raise s. of joy. 1Ch 15.16
Terrifying s. are in his ears; Job 15.21
When the trumpet s., he says 'Aha!' 39.25

SOUR

'The fathers have eaten s. grapes, and Jer 31.29
each man who eats s. grapes, his teeth 31.30
'The fathers have eaten s. grapes, Eze 18.02

SOURCE

He is the s. of your life in Christ 1Co 1.30
he became the s. of eternal salvation Heb 5.09

SOURCES

which is at the s. of the streams of Is 7.18

SOUTH

and to the north and to the s.; Gen 28.14
twenty frames for the s. side; Ex 26.18
lampstand on the s. side of the 26.35
On the s. side the court shall have 27.09
twenty frames for the s. side; 36.23
for the s. side the hangings of the 38.09
table on the s. side of the 40.24
"On the s. side shall be the Num 2.10
encamp on the s. side of the 3.29
that are on the s. side shall set 10.06
your s. side shall be from the 34.03
shall turn s. of the ascent of 34.04
end shall be s. of Kadeshbarnea; 34.04
and for the s. side two thousand 35.05
LORD, possess the lake and the s." Deu 33.23
and in the Arabah s. of Chinneroth, Jos 11.02
in the s., all the land of the 13.04
wilderness of Zin at the fatherest s. 15.01
And their s. boundary ran from the 15.02
and goes up s. of Kadeshbarnea, 15.03
This shall be your s. boundary. 15.04
which is on the s. side of the 15.07
people of Judah in the extreme S., 15.21
to the s. of the brook, among the 17.09
the land to the s. being Ephraim's 17.10
continuing in his territory on the s., 18.05
that lies s. of Lower Bethhoron. 18.13
the mountain that lies to the s., 18.14
s. of the shoulder of the Jebusites, 18.16
at the s. of the Jordan: this is 18.19
Hukok, touching Zebulun at the s., 19.34
to Shechem, and s. of Lebonah." Ju 21.29
other on the s. in front of Geba. 1Sa 14.05
Hachilah, which is s. of Jeshimon? 23.19
the Arabah to the s. of Jeshimon. 23.24
was on the s. side of the house; 1Ki 6.08
pillar on the s. and called its 7.21
three facing s., and three facing 7.25
five on the s. side of the house, 7.39
five on the s. side and five on the 7.49
from the s. side of the house to 2Ki 11.11
to the s. of the mount of corruption, 23.13
sides, east, west, north, and s.; 1Ch 9.24
Obededom's came out for the s., 26.15
on the s. four each day, as well as 26.17
one on the s., the other on the 2Ch 3.17
that on the s. he called Jachin, 3.17
three facing s., and three facing 4.04
wash, and set five on the s. side, 4.06
five on the s. side and five on the 4.07
five on the s. side and five on the 4.08
from the s. side of the house to 23.10
Pleiades and the chambers of the s.; Job 9.09
is still because of the s. wind? 37.17
spreads his wings toward the s.? 39.26
his power he led out the s. wind; Ps 78.26
The north and the s., thou hast 89.12
from the north and from the s. 107.03
The wind blows to the s., and goes Ecc 1.06
falls to the s. or to the north, in 11.03
Awake, O north wind, and come, O s. wind! Sol 4.16
and to the s., Do not withhold; Is 43.06
standing on the s. side of the Eze 10.03
sister, who lived to the s. of you, 16.46
man, set your face toward the s., 20.46
the south, preach against the s., 20.46
all faces from s. to north shall 20.47
against all flesh from s. to north; 21.04
And he led me toward the s., 40.24
behold, there was a gate on the s.; 40.24

SOUTH (cont.)

a gate on the s. of the inner	Eze 40.27
from gate to gate toward the s.,	40.27
to the inner court by the s. gate,	40.28
gate, and he measured the s. gate;	40.28
side of the north gate facing s.,	40.44
the side of the s. gate facing	40.44
which faces s. is for the priests	40.45
and another door toward the s.;	41.11
On the s. also, opposite the yard	42.10
And below the s. chambers was an	42.12
chambers and the s. chambers	42.13
he turned and measured the s. side,	42.18
shall go out by the s. gate;	46.09
enters by the s. gate shall go out	46.09
from below the s. end of the	47.01
of the temple, s. of the altar.	47.01
was coming out on the s. side.	47.02
"On the s. side, it shall run from	47.19
Great Sea. This shall be the s. side.	47.19
the s. side four thousand five	48.16
on the s. two hundred and fifty, on	48.17
the territory of Gad to the s.,	48.28
On the s. side, which is to be four	48.33
exceedingly great toward the s.,	Dan 8.09
"Then the king of the s. shall be	11.05
the king of the s. shall come to	11.06
the king of the s. but shall	11.09
Then the king of the s., moved	11.11
rise against the king of the s.;	11.14
forces of the s. shall not stand,	11.15
the king of the s. with a great	11.25
the king of the s. shall wage war	11.25
shall return and come into the s.;	11.29
the king of the s. shall attack	11.40
ones go toward the s. country."	Zec 6.06
and the S. and the lowland were	7.07
forth in the whirlinds of the s.	9.14
Geba to Rimmon s. of Jerusalem.	14.10
The queen of the S. will arise at	Mt 12.42
The queen of the S. will arise at	Lk 11.31
And when you see the s. wind blowing,	12.55
and west, and from north and s.,	13.29
go toward the s. to the road that	Ac 8.26
And when the s. wind blew gently,	27.13
after one day a s. wind sprang up,	28.13
on the s. three gates, and on the	Rev 21.13

SOUTHEAST

the sea on the s. corner of the	1Ki 7.39
the sea at the s. corner of the	2Ch 4.10
of Crete, looking northeast and s.,	Ac 27.12

SOUTHERN

and your s. boundary shall be from	Num 34.03
Hinnom at the s. shoulder of the	Jos 15.08
And the s. side begins at the	18.15
the Jordan: this is the s. border.	18.19
thousand in length on the s. side,	Eze 48.10

SOUTHWARD

northward and s. and eastward and	Gen 13.14
and northward and s. and eastward,	Deu 3.27
s. to the foot of the slopes of	Jos 12.03
families reached s. to the boundary	15.01
Sea, from the bay that faces s.;	15.02
it goes out s. of the ascent of	15.03
goes along s. to the inhabitants	17.07
passes along s. in the direction	18.13
western side s. from the mountain	18.14
westward and northward and s.;	Dan 8.04
northward, and the other half s.	Zec 14.04

SOVEREIGN

"S. Lord, who didst make the heaven	Ac 4.24
time by the blessed and only S.,	1Ti 6.15
"O S. Lord, holy and true, how long	Rev 6.10

SOVEREIGNTY

nor shall its s. be left to another	Dan 2.44

SOW

for you, and you shall s. the land.	Gen 47.23
years you shall s. your land and	Ex 23.10
labor, of what you s. in the field.	23.16
you shall not s. your field with	Lev 19.19
Six years you shall s. your field,	25.03
you shall not s. your field or	25.04
in it you shall neither s., nor reap	25.11
if we may not s. or gather in our	25.20
When you s. in the eighth year, you	25.22
And you shall s. your seed in vain,	26.16
"You shall not s. your vineyard	Deu 22.09
then in the third year s.,	2Ki 19.29
iniquity and s. trouble reap the	Job 4.08
then let me s., and another eat;	31.08
they s. fields, and plant vineyards,	Ps 107.37
May those who s. in tears reap with	126.05
He who observes the wind will not s.;	Ecc 11.04
In the morning s. your seed, and at	11.06
blossom in the morning that you s.;	Is 17.11
s. cummin, and put in wheat in rows	28.25
seed with which you s. the ground,	30.23
Happy are you who s. beside all	32.20
then in the third year s. and reap,	37.30
fallow ground, and s. not among thorns.	Jer 4.03
when I will s. the house of Israel	31.27
you shall not s. seed; you shall not	35.07
and I will s. him for myself in the	Hos 2.23
For they s. the wind, and they shall	8.07
S. for yourselves righteousness,	10.12
You shall s., but not reap; you shall	Mic 6.15
they neither s. nor reap nor gather	Mt 6.26
saying: "A sower went out to s.	13.03
did you not s. good seed in your	13.27
man, reaping where you did not s.,	25.24
"Listen! A sower went out to s.	Mk 4.03
"A sower went out to s. his seed;	Lk 8.05
they neither s. nor reap, they have	12.24
down, and reap what you did not s.'	19.21
down and reaping what I did not s.?	19.22
What you s. does not come to life	1Co 15.36
And what you s. is not the body	15.37
and the s. is washed only to wallow	2Pe 2.22

SOWED

And Isaac s. in that land, and	Gen 26.12
where you s. your seed and watered	Deu 11.10
razed the city and s. it with salt.	Ju 9.45
And as he s., some seeds fell along	Mt 13.04
to a man who s. good seed in his	13.24
enemy came and s. weeds among the	13.25
a man took and s. in his field;	13.31
and the enemy who s. them is the	13.39
that I reap where I have not s.,	25.26
And as he s., some seed fell along	Mk 4.04
and as he s., some fell along the	Lk 8.05
a man took and s. in his garden;	13.19

SOWER

seed to the s. and bread to the eater,	Is 55.10
Cut off from Babylon the s., and	Jer 50.16
saying, "A s. went out to sow.	Mt 13.03
"Hear then the parable of the s.	13.18
"Listen! A s. went out to sow.	Mk 4.03
The s. sows the word.	4.14
"A s. went out to sow his seed;	Lk 8.05
so that s. and reaper may rejoice	Jn 4.36
seed to the s. and bread for food	2Co 9.10

SOWING

any seed for s. that is to be sown,	Lev 11.37
shall last to the time for s.;	26.05
a s. of a homer of barley shall be	27.16
weeping, bearing the seed for s.,	Ps 126.06
evil, continually s. discord;	Pro 6.14

SOWING (cont.)

who plows for s. plow continually? Is 28.24
shall be a s. of peace and prosperity Zec 8.12

SOWN

that is to be s., it is clean; Lev 11.37
which is neither plowed nor s., Deu 21.04
which you have s. and the yield of 22.09
and all that is s. by the Nile Is 19.07
scarcely s., scarcely has their 40.24
causes what is s. in it to spring 61.11
the wilderness, in a land not s. Jer 2.02
They have s. wheat and have reaped 12.13
and you shall be tilled and s.; Eze 36.09
You have s. much, and harvested Hag 1.06
away what is s. in his heart; Mt 13.19
this is what was s. along the path. 13.19
As for what was s. on rocky ground, 13.20
As for what was s. among thorns, 13.22
As for what was s. on good soil, 13.23
the path, where the word is s.; Mk 4.15
away the word which is s. in them. 4.15
are the ones s. upon rocky ground, 4.16
are the ones s. among thorns; 4.18
But those that were s. upon the 4.20
when s. upon the ground, is the 4.31
yet when it is s. it grows up and 4.32
If we have s. spiritual good among 1Co 9.11
What is s. is perishable, what is 15.42
It is s. in dishonor, it is raised 15.43
It is s. in weakness, it is raised 15.43
It is s. a physical body, it is 15.44
righteousness is s. in peace by Jas 3.18

SOWS

and a man who s. discord among Pro 6.19
but one who s. righteousness gets a 11.18
He who s. injustice will reap 22.08
of grapes him who s. the seed; Amo 9.13
"He who s. the good seed is the Son Mt 13.37
The sower s. the word. Mk 4.14
true, 'One s. and another reaps.' Jn 4.37
he who s. sparingly will also reap 2Co 9.06
and he who s. bountifully will also 9.06
not mocked, for whatever a man s., Gal 6.07
For he who s. to his own flesh will 6.08
but he who s. to the Spirit will 6.08

SPACE

and put a s. between drove and Gen 32.16
light upon the s. in front of it. Ex 25.37
shall be a s. between you and it, a Jos 3.04
with a great s. between them; 1Sa 26.13
trees, according to the s. of each, 1Ki 7.36
parts of the s. behind the wall, in Neh 4.13
and the s. between the side rooms, Eze 40.07
to the s. above the door, even to 41.17
cubits for an open s. around it. 45.02

SPACIOUS

hast brought us forth to a s. place. Ps 66.12
a great house with s. upper rooms, Jer 22.14

SPAIN

see you in passing as I go to S., Rom 15.24
I shall go on by way of you to S.; 15.28

SPAN

a s. its length and a s. its breadth. Ex 28.16
a s. its length and a s. its breadth 39.09
height was six cubits and a s. 1Sa 17.04
yet their s. is but toil and Ps 90.10
marked off the heavens with a s., Is 40.12
a rim of one s. around its edge. Eze 43.13
add one cubit to his s. of life? Mt 6.27
can add a cubit to his s. of life? Lk 12.25

SPARE

place and not s. it for the fifty Gen 18.24
I will s. the whole place for their 18.26
nor shall you s. him, nor shall you Deu 13.08
toward the LORD, s. us not today Jos 22.22
do not s. them, but kill both man 1Sa 15.03
of Israel had sworn to s. them, 2Sa 21.02
perhaps he will s. your life." 1Ki 20.31
if they s. our lives we shall live, 2Ki 7.04
and s. me according to the greatness Neh 13.22
he is in your power; only s. his life." Job 2.06
open my kidneys, and does not s.; 16.13
s. none of those who treacherously Ps 59.05
he did not s. them from death, but 78.50
In thy steadfast love s. my life, 119.88
and he will not s. when he takes Pro 6.34
it, he will s. and rescue it. Is 31.05
vengeance, and I will s. no man. 47.03
"Cry aloud, s. not, lift up your 58.01
not pity or s. or have compassion, Jer 13.14
or s. them, or have compassion.' 21.07
shoot at her, s. no arrows, for she 50.14
S. not her young men; utterly destroy 51.03
my eye will not s., and I will Eze 5.11
And my eye will not s. you, nor 7.04
And my eye will not s., nor will 7.09
my eye will not s., nor will I have 8.18
your eye shall not s., and you 9.05
As for me, my eye will not s., 9.10
I will not s., I will not repent; 24.14
"S. thy people, O LORD, and make not Joe 2.17
and I will s. them as a man spares Mal 3.17
have bread enough and to s., Lk 15.17
He who did not s. his own Son but Rom 8.32
For if God did not s. the natural 11.21
branches, neither will he s. you. 11.21
troubles, and I would s. you that. 1Co 7.28
it was to s. you that I refrained 2Co 1.23
I come again I will not s. them— 13.02
For if God did not s. the angels 2Pe 2.04
if he did not s. the ancient world, 2.05

SPARED

my life may be s. on your account." Gen 12.13
the Egyptians but s. our houses.'" Ex 12.27
altar shall be s. to weep out his 1Sa 2.33
But Saul and the people s. Agag, 15.09
for the people s. the best of the 15.15
bade me kill you, but I s. you. 24.10
death, and one full line to be s. 2Sa 8.02
But the king s. Mephibosheth, the 21.07
my master has s. this Naaman the 2Ki 5.20
persons, and he s. none of them. 10.14
wicked man is s. in the day of Job 21.30
Babylon, then your life shall be s., Jer 38.17
you, and your life shall be s. 38.20
Nevertheless my eye s. them, Eze 20.17
to thresh, and I s. her fair neck; Hos 10.11

SPARES

He who s. the rod hates his son, but Pro 13.24
for the fire; no man s. his brother. Is 9.19
them as a man s. his son who serves Mal 3.17

SPARING

so be s. of complimentary words. Pro 25.27
in among you, not s. the flock; Ac 20.29

SPARINGLY

he who sows s. will also reap s., and 2Co 9.06

SPARK

shall become tow, and his work a s., Is1.31

SPARKLED

and they s. like burnished bronze. Eze 1.07

SPARKLES

when it s. in the cup and goes down Pro 23.31

SPARKLING
the wheels was like s. chrysolite. Eze 10.09

SPARKS
born to trouble as the s. fly upward. Job 5.07
flaming torches; s. of fire leap forth. 41.19

SPARROW
Even the s. finds a home, and the Ps 84.03
Like a s. in its flitting, like a Pro 26.02

SPARROWS
Are not two s. sold for a penny? Mt 10.29
you are of more value than many s. 10.31
Are not five s. sold for two pennies? Lk 12.06
you are of more value than many s. 12.07

SPAT
Then they s. in his face, and struck Mt 26.67
And they s. upon him, and took the 27.30
and he s. and touched his tongue; Mk 7.33
and s. upon him, and they knelt down 15.19
he s. on the ground and made clay Jn 9.06

SPATTERED
of her blood s. on the wall and on 2Ki 9.33

SPEAK
upon myself to s. to the LORD, Gen 18.27
the LORD be angry, and I will s. 18.30
upon myself to s. to the LORD. 18.31
and I will s. again but this once. 18.32
told my errand." He said, "S. on." 24.33
we cannot s. to you bad or good. 24.50
your father s. to your brother 27.06
heed that you s. to Jacob neither 31.29
went out to Jacob to s. with him. 34.06
and could not s. peaceably to him. 37.04
does my lord s. such words as 44.07
What shall we s.? Or how can we 44.16
s. a word in my lord's ears, and let 44.18
s., I pray you, in the ears of 50.04
and teach you what you shall s." Ex 4.12
I know that he can s. well; 4.14
And you shall s. to him and put the 4.15
He shall s. for you to the people; 4.16
came to Pharaoh to s. in thy name, 5.23
You shall s. all that I command you; 7.02
S. now in the hearing of the people, 11.02
which you shall s. to the children 19.06
people may hear when I s. with you, 19.09
"You s. to us, and we will hear; 20.19
but let not God s. to us, lest we 20.19
"S. to the people of Israel, that 25.02
I will s. with you of all that I 25.22
And you shall s. to all who have 28.03
meet with you, to s. there to you. 29.42
and the LORD would s. with Moses. 33.09
LORD used to s. to Moses face to 33.11
in before the LORD to s. with him, 34.34
until he went in to s. with him. 34.35
"S. to the people of Israel, and say Lev 1.02
yet does not s., he shall bear his 5.01
"S. to the priests, the sons of 21.01
of meeting to s. with the LORD, Num 7.89
vision, I s. with him in a dream. 12.06
With him I s. mouth to mouth, clearly, 12.08
not afraid to s. against my servant 12.08
"S. to the people of Israel, and bid 15.38
"S. to the people of Israel, and get 17.02
which I bid you, that shall you s." 22.35
any power at all to s. anything? 22.38
puts in my mouth, that must I s." 22.38
to Balak, and thus you shall s." 23.05
take heed to s. what the LORD puts 23.12
to Balak, and thus shall you s." 23.16
the LORD speaks, that will I s.?' 24.13
s. no more to me of this matter. Deu 3.26
ordinances which I s. in your 5.01
day seen God s. with man and man 5.24
and s. to us all that the LORD our 5.27
the LORD our God will s. to you; 5.27
and he shall s. to them all that I 18.18
words which he shall s. in my name, 18.19
who presumes to s. a word in my 18.20
I have not commanded him to s., 18.20
come forward and s. to the people, 20.02
officers shall s. to the people, 20.05
officers shall s. further to the 20.08
and s. to him: and if he persists, 25.08
continued to s. these words to all 31.01
that I may s. these words in their 31.28
"Give ear, O heavens, and I will s.; 32.01
me, let me s. but this once; Ju 6.39
to s. kindly to her and bring her 19.03
consider it, take counsel, and s." 19.30
'S., LORD, for thy servant hears.'" 1Sa 3.09
"S., for thy servant hears." 3.10
"S. to David in private and say, 18.22
told him, "Thus and so did David s." 18.24
and I will s. to my father about 19.03
ill-natured that one cannot s. to him." 25.17
let your handmaid s. in your ears, 25.24
of the gate to s. with him privately, 2Sa 3.27
did I s. a word with any of the 7.07
therefore, I pray you, s. to the king; 13.13
go to the king, and s. thus to him." 14.03
"Pray let your handmaid s. a word to 14.12
my lord the king." He said, "S." 14.12
thought, 'I will s. to the king; 14.15
said, "Let my lord the king s." 14.18
do as he advises? If not, you s." 17.06
go out and s. kindly to your servants; 19.07
"Why s. any more of your affairs 19.29
the first to s. of bringing back 19.43
'Come here, that I may s. to you.'" 20.16
I will s. for you to the king." 1Ki 2.18
to s. to him on behalf of Adonijah. 2.19
thou didst s. with thy mouth, and 8.24
and s. good words to them when you 12.07
"Thus shall you s. to this people 12.10
of one of them, and s. favorably." 22.13
LORD says to me, that I will s." 22.14
you that you s. to me nothing but 22.16
the LORD go from me to s. to you?" 22.24
words that you s. in your bedchamber 2Ki 6.12
s. to your servants in the Aramaic 18.26
do not s. to us in the language 18.26
sent me to s. these words to your 18.27
"Thus shall you s. to Hezekiah king 19.10
did I s. a word with any of the 1Ch 17.06
thou didst s. with thy mouth, and 2Ch 6.15
and s. good words to them, then they 10.07
"Thus shall you s. to the people 10.10
of one of them, and s. favorably." 18.12
what my God says, that I will s." 18.13
you that you s. to me nothing but 18.15
the LORD go from me to s. to you?" 18.23
of Israel and to s. against him, 32.17
and s. with them from heaven and Neh 9.13
they could not s. the language of 13.24
own house and s. according to the Est 1.22
palace to s. to the king about 6.04
"You s. as one of the foolish women Job 2.10
one of the foolish women would s. 2.10
I will s. in the anguish of my 7.11
Then I would s. without fear of him, 9.35
I will s. in the bitterness of my 10.01
But oh, that God would s., 11.05
But I would s. to the Almighty, and 13.03
Will you s. falsely for God, and 13.07
and s. deceitfully for him? 13.07
and I will s., and let come on me 13.13
or let me s., and do thou reply to 13.22
I also could s. as you do, if you 16.04
"If I s., my pain is not assuaged, 16.06

SPEAK (cont.)
Consider, and then we will s. Job 18.02
and I will s., and after I have 21.03
my lips will not s. falsehood, 27.04
After I spoke they did not s. again, 29.22
had waited to s. to Job because 32.04
'Let days s., and many years teach 32.07
I wait, because they do not s., 32.16
I must s., that I may find relief; 32.20
my lips know they s. sincerely. 33.03
to me; be silent, and I will s. 33.31
s., for I desire to justify you. 33.32
Shall it be told him that I would s.? 37.20
Will he s. to you soft words? 41.03
'Hear, and I will s.; I will question 42.04
Then he will s. to them in his Ps 2.05
Thou destroyest those who s. lies; 5.06
lips and a double heart they s. 12.02
their mouths they s. arrogantly. 17.10
who s. peace with their neighbors, 28.03
which s. insolently against the 31.18
For they do not s. peace, but 35.20
those who seek my hurt s. of ruin, 38.12
My mouth shall s. wisdom; the 49.03
and I will s., O Israel, I will 50.07
You sit and s. against your brother 50.20
For my enemies s. concerning me, 71.10
They scoff and s. with malice; 73.08
"I will s. thus," I would have been 73.15
on high, or s. with insolent neck." 75.05
I am so troubled that I cannot s. 77.04
God the LORD will s., for he will s. peace 85.08
Of old thou didst s. in a vision to 89.19
of those who s. evil against my 109.20
They have mouths, but do not s.; 115.05
I will also s. of thy testimonies 119.46
but when I s., they are for war! 120.07
but they s. not, they have eyes, but 135.16
whose mouths s. lies, and whose 144.08
whose mouths s. lies, and whose 144.11
They shall s. of the glory of thy 145.11
My mouth will s. the praise of the 145.21
for I will s. noble things, and from Pro 8.06
Do not s. in the hearing of a fool, 23.09
when your lips s. what is right. 23.16
to keep silence, and a time to s.; Ecc 3.07
in that day he will s. out, Is 3.07
s. a word, but it will not stand, for 8.10
word which they s. there is no 8.20
All of them will s. and say to you: 14.10
of Egypt which s. the language of 19.18
the LORD will s. to this people, 28.11
Then deep from the earth you shall s., 29.04
s. to us smooth things, prophesy 30.10
stammerers will s. readily and 32.04
s. to your servants in Aramaic, for 36.11
do not s. to us in the language of 36.11
sent me to s. these words to your 36.12
"Thus shall you s. to Hezekiah king 37.10
S. tenderly to Jerusalem, and cry to 40.02
and s., O Israel, "My way is hid 40.27
them approach, then let them s.; 41.01
I did not s. in secret, in a land of 45.19
I the LORD s. the truth, I declare 45.19
shall know that it is I who s.; 52.06
they s. lies, they conceive mischief 59.04
men shall s. of you as the ministers 61.06
Behold, I do not know how to s., Jer 1.06
whatever I command you you shall s. 1.07
Now it is I who s. in judgment upon 4.12
to the great, and will s. to them; 5.05
To whom shall I s. and give warning, Jer 6.10
I did not s. to your fathers or 7.22
"So you shall s. all these words to 7.27
taught their tongue to s. lies; 9.05
S., "Thus says the LORD: 'The dead 9.22
cucumber field, and they cannot s.; 10.05
and s. to the men of Judah and the 11.02
though they s. fair words to you." 12.06
"You shall s. to them this word: 13.12
did I command them or s. to them. 14.14
before thee to s. good for them, 18.20
For whenever I s., I cry out, I 20.08
him, or s. any more in his name," 20.09
king of Judah, and s. there this word, 22.01
they s. visions of their own minds, 23.16
I did not s. to them, yet they 23.21
who has my word s. my word faithfully 23.28
and s. to all the cities of Judah 26.02
that I command you to s. to them; 26.02
commanded him to s. to all the 26.08
me to you to s. all these words in 26.15
word which I s. in your hearing 28.07
For as often as I s. against him, 31.20
and shall s. with him face to face 32.04
What thou didst s. has come to pass, 32.24
Go and s. to Zedekiah king of Judah 34.02
eye to eye and s. with him face to 34.03
and s. with them, and bring them to 35.02
your feet, and I will s. with you." Eze 2.01
And you shall s. my words to them, 2.07
and go, s. to the house of Israel." 3.01
and s. with my words to them. 3.04
that I shall s. to you receive in 3.10
nor s. to warn the wicked from his 3.18
and there I will s. with you." 3.22
But when I s. with you, I will open 3.27
I the LORD will s. the word which I will s., 12.25
I will s. the word and perform it, 12.25
word which I s. will be performed, 12.28
Therefore s. to them, and say to 14.04
prophet be deceived and s. a word, 14.09
and s. an allegory to the house of 17.02
"Son of man, s. to the elders of 20.03
s. to the house of Israel and say 20.27
and you shall s. and be no longer 24.27
s., and say, Thus says the Lord GOD: 29.03
The mighty chief shall s. of them, 32.21
"Son of man, s. to your people and 33.02
and you do not s. to warn the 33.08
I s. in my hot jealousy against the 36.05
I s. in my jealous wrath, because 36.06
S. to the birds of every sort and 39.17
have agreed to s. lying and Dan 2.09
He shall s. words against the Most 7.25
heed to the words that I s. to you, 10.11
"Let my lord s., for you have 10.19
they shall s. lies at the same 11.27
and shall s. astonishing things 11.36
wilderness, and s. tenderly to her. Hos 2.14
them, but they s. lies against me. 7.13
your inhabitants s. lies, and Mic 6.12
"S. now to Zerubbabel the son of Hag 2.02
"S. to Zerubbabel, governor of Judah, 2.21
S. the truth to one another, render Zec 8.16
for you s. lies in the name of the 13.03
how you are to s. or what you are Mt 10.19
for it is not you who s., but the 10.20
Jesus began to s. to the crowds 11.07
how can you s. good, when you are 12.34
stood outside, asking to s. to him. 12.46
outside, asking to s. to you." * 12.47
"Why do you s. to them in parables?" 13.10
This is why I s. to them in parables, 13.13
that I did not s. about bread? 16.11
would not permit the demons to s., Mk 1.34
"Why does this man s. thus? It is 2.07
he did not s. to them without a 4.34
the deaf hear and the dumb s." 7.37
able soon after to s. evil of me. 9.39
And he began to s. to them in 12.01
hour, for it is not you who s., 13.11
not know this man of whom you s." 14.71
demons; they will s. in new tongues; * 16.17
and I was sent to s. to you, Lk 1.19

SPEAK (cont.)

and unable to s. until the day Lk 1.20
he could not s. to them, and they 1.22
and would not allow them to s., 4.41
when all men s. well of you, for so 6.26
dead man sat up, and began to s. 7.15
he began to s. to the crowds 7.24
provoke him to s. of many things, 11.53
know that you s. and teach rightly, 20.21
One of the two who heard John s., Jn 1.40
we s. of what we know, and bear 3.11
said to her, "I who s. to you am he." 4.26
authority but s. thus as the 8.28
I s. of what I have seen with my 8.38
is of age, he will s. for himself." 9.21
commandment what to say and what to s. 12.49
to you I do not s. on my own 14.10
for he will not s. on his own 16.13
but whatever he hears he will s., 16.13
shall no longer s. to you in 16.25
and these things I s. in the world, 17.13
said to him, "You will not s. to me? 19.10
and began to s. in other tongues, Ac 2.04
us warn them to s. no more to any 4.17
them not to s. or teach at all in 4.18
for we cannot but s. of what we 4.20
thy servants to s. thy word with 4.29
the temple and s. to the people 5.20
them not to s. in the name of 5.40
have heard him s. blasphemous 6.11
never ceases to s. words against 6.13
As I began to s., the Holy Spirit 11.15
Holy Spirit to s. the word in Asia 16.06
but s. and do not be silent; 18.09
He began to s. boldly in the 18.26
I beg you, let me s. to the people." 21.39
'You shall not s. evil of a ruler 23.05
governor had motioned to him to s., 24.10
and heard him s. upon faith in 24.24
have permission to s. for yourself." 26.01
things, and to him I s. freely; 26.26
asked to see you and s. with you, 28.20
on us? (I s. in a human way.) Rom 3.05
not venture to s. of anything 15.18
Does he not s. entirely for our 1Co 9.10
I s. as to sensible men; judge for 10.15
Do all s. with tongues? Do all 12.30
If I s. in the tongues of men and 13.01
Now I want you all to s. in tongues, 14.05
God that I s. in tongues more than 14.18
I would rather s. five words with 14.19
foreigners will I s. to this people, 14.21
assembles and all s. in tongues, 14.23
If any s. in a tongue, let there be 14.27
in church and s. to himself and to 14.28
Let two or three prophets s., 14.29
For they are not permitted to s., 14.34
for a woman to s. in church. 14.35
the sight of God we s. in Christ. 2Co 2.17
we too believe, and so we s., 4.13
In return—I s. as to children— 6.13
let every one s. the truth with his Eph 4.25
a shame even to s. of the things 5.12
declare it boldly, as I ought to s. 6.20
more bold to s. the word of God Php 1.14
make it clear, as I ought to s. Col 4.04
so we s., not to please men, but to 1Th 2.04
to s. evil of no one, to avoid Tit 3.02
God would not s. later of another Heb 4.08
Though we s. thus, yet in your case, 6.09
things we cannot now s. in detail. 9.05
For people who s. thus make it 11.14
slow to s., slow to anger, Jas 1.19
So s. and so act as those who are 2.12
Do not s. evil against one another, 4.11
in case they s. against you as 1Pe 2.12
image of the beast should even s., Rev 13.15

SPEAKER

Paul because he was the chief s., Ac 14.12
I shall be a foreigner to the s. 1Co 14.11
and the s. a foreigner to me. 14.11

SPEAKERS

s. in various kinds of tongues. 1Co 12.28

SPEAKEST

a sign that it is thou who s. with me. Ju 6.17

SPEAKING

when he had finished s. to Abraham; Gen 18.33
Before he had done s., behold, 24.15
"Before I had done s. in my heart, 24.45
While he was still s. with them, 29.09
made an end of s. with him upon Ex 31.18
Moses had finished s. with them, 34.33
heard the voice s. to him from Num 7.89
And as he finished s. all these 16.31
voice of a god s. out of the midst Deu 4.33
the living God s. out of the midst 5.26
(since I am not s. to your children 11.02
made an end of s. to the people, 20.09
had finished s. all these words to 32.45
When he had finished s., he threw Ju 15.17
Hannah was s. in her heart; only 1Sa 1.13
I have been s. out of my great 1.16
When he had finished s. to Saul, 18.01
had finished s. these words to 24.16
And as soon as he had finished s., 2Sa 13.36
you are still s. with the king, 1Ki 1.14
While she was still s. with the king, 1.22
While he was still s., behold, 1.42
And while he was still s. with them, 2Ki 6.33
But as he was s. the king said to 2Ch 25.16
While he was yet s., there came Job 1.16
While he was yet s., there came 1.17
While he was yet s., there came 1.18
Yet who can keep from s.? 4.02
evil, and your lips from s. deceit. Ps 34.13
and lying more than s. the truth. 52.03
they err from their birth, s. of lies. 58.03
s. against me with lying tongues. 109.02
of the finger, and s. wickedness, Is 58.09
s. oppression and revolt, conceiving 59.13
while they are yet s. I will hear. 65.24
heard Jeremiah s. these words in Jer 26.07
had finished s. all that the LORD 26.08
by s. such words to them. 38.04
So they left off s. with him, 38.27
for you are s. falsely of Ishmael." 40.16
finished s. to all the people all 43.01
and I heard the voice of one s. Eze 1.28
and I heard him s. to me. 2.02
I heard one s. to me out of the 43.06
a man, and a mouth s. great things. Dan 7.08
great words which the horn was s. 7.11
Then I heard a holy one s.; 8.13
As he was s. to me, I fell into a 8.18
While I was s. and praying, confessing 9.20
while I was s. in prayer, the man 9.21
While he was s. this word to me, I 10.11
While he was thus s. to them, Mt 9.18
of your Father s. through you. 10.20
While he was still s. to the people, 12.46
wondered, when they saw the dumb s., 15.31
He was still s., when lo, a bright 17.05
that he was s. to them of John the 17.13
perceived that he was s. about them. 21.45
While he was still s., Judas came, 26.47
While he was still s., there came Mk 5.35
immediately, while he was still s., 14.43
And when he had ceased s., he said Lk 5.04
While he was still s., a man from 8.49
While he was s., a Pharisee asked 11.37
While he was still s., there came 22.47
immediately, while he was still s., 22.60

SPEAKING (cont.)

or whether I am s. on my own Jn 7.17
s. openly, and they say nothing to 7.26
I am not s. of you all; I know 13.18
now you are s. plainly, not in any 16.29
and s. of the kingdom of God. Ac 1.03
one heard them s. in his own 2.06
not all these who are s. Galileans? 2.07
And as they were s. to the people, 4.01
For they heard them s. in tongues 10.46
s. the word to none except Jews. 11.19
s. boldly for the Lord, who bore 14.03
He listened to Paul s.; and Paul, 14.09
After they finished s., James 15.13
s. evil of the Way before the 19.09
will arise men s. perverse things, 20.30
voice of the one who was s. to me. 22.09
but I am s. the sober truth. 26.25
I am s. in human terms, because of Rom 6.19
for I am s. to those who know the 7.01
I am s. the truth in Christ, I am 9.01
Now I am s. to you Gentiles. 11.13
that no one s. by the Spirit of 1Co 12.03
if I come to you s. in tongues, 14.06
For you will be s. into the air. 14.09
and do not forbid s. in tongues; 14.39
humanly s., I fought with beasts at 15.32
Even if I am unskilled in s., 2Co 11.06
I am s. as a fool—I also dare to 11.21
fool, for I shall be s. the truth. 12.06
God that we have been s. in Christ, 12.19
proof that Christ is s. in me. 13.03
Rather, s. the truth in love, we are Eph 4.15
hindering us from s. to the Gentiles 1Th 2.16
world to come, of which we are s. Heb 2.05
In s. of a new covenant he treats 8.13
through his faith he is still s. 11.04
figuratively s., he did receive him 11.19
you do not refuse him who is s. 12.25
evil and his lips from s. guile; 1Pe 3.10
s. of this as he does in all his 2Pe 3.16
to see the voice that was s. to me, Rev 1.12
I had heard s. to me like a trumpet, 4.01

SPEAKS

that it is my mouth that s. to you. Gen 45.12
to face, as a man s. to his friend. Ex 33.11
word to you, as the LORD s. to me"; Num 22.08
what the LORD s., that will I speak' 24.13
or who s. in the name of other gods, Deu 18.20
when a prophet s. in the name of 18.22
"The Spirit of the LORD s. by me, 2Sa 23.02
the tongue in my mouth s. Job 33.02
For God s. in one way, and in two, 33.14
'Job s. without knowledge, his words 34.35
and s. truth from his heart; Ps 15.02
Transgression s. to the wicked deep 36.01
wisdom, and his tongue s. justice. 37.30
s. and summons the earth from the 50.01
shame when he s. with his enemies 127.05
entrance of the city gates she s.: Pro 1.21
He who s. the truth gives honest 12.17
he loves him who s. what is right. 16.13
associate with one who s. foolishly. 20.19
when he s. graciously, believe him 26.25
My beloved s. and says to me: "Arise, Sol 2.10
evildoer, and every mouth s. folly. Is 9.17
For the fool s. folly, and his mind 32.06
walks righteously and s. uprightly; 33.15
neighbor, and no one s. the truth; Jer 9.05
a deadly arrow; it s. deceitfully; 9.08
his mouth each s. peaceably to his 9.08
Hear the word which the LORD s. to you, 10.01
voice of God Almighty when he s. Eze 10.05
language that s. anything against Dan 3.29
they abhor him who s. the truth. Amo 5.10
but whoever s. against the Holy Mt 12.32
abundance of the heart the mouth s. 12.34
'He who s. evil of father or mother, 15.04
and, 'He who s. evil of father or Mk 7.10
"Who is this that s. blasphemies? Lk 5.21
abundance of the heart his mouth s. 6.45
And every one who s. a word against 12.10
the earth, and of the earth he s.; Jn 3.31
He who s. on his own authority 7.18
he s. according to his own nature 8.44
him, and it is he who s. to you." 9.37
"Tell us who it is of whom he s." 13.24
the law says it s. to those who Rom 3.19
For one who s. in a tongue speaks 1Co 14.02
in a tongue s. not to men but to 14.02
who prophesies s. to men for their 14.03
He who s. in a tongue edifies 14.04
greater than he who s. in tongues, 14.05
he who s. in a tongue should pray 14.13
blood that s. more graciously than Heb 12.24
He that s. evil against a brother Jas 4.11
s. evil against the law and judges 4.11
whoever s., as one who utters 1Pe 4.11

SPEAR

congregation, and took a s. in his hand Num 25.07
Was shield or s. to be seen among Ju 5.08
sword nor s. found in the hand of 1Sa 13.22
shaft of his s. was like a weaver's 17.07
and with a s. and with a javelin; 17.45
LORD saves not with sword and s.; 17.47
Saul had his s. in his hand; 18.10
and Saul cast the s., for he thought, 18.11
his house with his s. in his hand; 19.09
pin David to the wall with the s.; 19.10
he struck the s. into the wall. 19.10
But Saul cast his s. at him to 20.33
you not here a s. or a sword at 21.08
with his s. in his hand, and all his 22.06
with his s. stuck in the ground at 26.07
earth with one stroke of the s., 26.08
take now the s. that is at his 26.11
So David took the s. and the jar of 26.12
And now see where the king's s. is, 26.16
answer, "Here is the s., O king! 26.22
there was Saul leaning upon his s.; 2Sa 1.06
the belly with the butt of his s., 2.23
so that the s. came out at his back 2.23
whose s. weighed three hundred 21.16
shaft of whose s. was like a 21.19
with iron and the shaft of a s., 23.07
he wielded his s. against eight 23.08
he wielded his s. against three 23.18
the Egyptian had a s. in his hand; 23.21
snatched the s. out of the Egyptian's 23.21
hand, and slew him with his own s. 23.21
he wielded his s. against three 1Ch 11.11
he wielded his s. against three 11.20
in his hand a s. like a weaver's 11.23
snatched the s. out of the Egyptian's 11.23
hand, and slew him with his own s. 11.23
warriors, expert with shield and s., 12.08
shield and s. were six thousand 12.24
men armed with shield and s. 12.34
shaft of whose s. was like a 20.05
war, able to handle s. and shield. 2Ch 25.05
the flashing s. and the javelin. Job 39.23
nor the s., the dart, or the javelin 41.26
Draw the s. and javelin against my Ps 35.03
the bow, and shatters the s., 46.09
They lay hold on bow and s., Jer 6.23
They lay hold of bow and s.; 50.42
flashing sword and glittering s., Nah 3.03
at the flash of thy glittering s. Hab 3.11
another took a s. and pierced his *Mt 27.49
soldiers pierced his side with a s., Jn 19.34

SPEAR'S

and his s. head weighed six hundred 1Sa 17.07

SPEARMEN
and two hundred s. to go as far as Ac 23.23

SPEARS
Hebrews make themselves swords or s."; 1Sa 13.19
captains the s. and shields that 2Ki 11.10
put shields and s. in all the cities, 2Ch 11.12
Judah, armed with bucklers and s., 14.08
captains the s. and the large and 23.09
s., helmets, coats of mail, bows, and 26.14
swords, their s., and their bows. Neh 4.13
construction, and half held the s., 4.16
them held the s. from the break of 4.21
or his head with fishing s.? Job 41.07
their teeth are s. and arrows, Ps 57.04
and their s. into pruning hooks; Is 2.04
polish your s., put on your coats Jer 46.04
handpikes and s., and they will Eze 39.09
and your pruning hooks into s.; Joe 3.10
and their s. into pruning hooks; Mic 4.03

SPECIAL
a man makes a s. vow of persons to Lev 27.02
a man or a woman makes a s. vow, Num 6.02
coastlands were your own s. markets, Eze 27.15
to them as a s. portion from the 48.12
my s. possession on the day when I Mal 3.17
each has his own s. gift from God, 1Co 7.07

SPECIFICATIONS
all its parts, and according to all its s. 1Ki 6.38

SPECK
Why do you see the s. that is in Mt 7.03
Let me take the s. out of your eye, 7.04
to take the s. out of your brother's 7.05
Why do you see the s. that is in Lk 6.41
me take out the s. that is in your 6.42
to take out the s. that is in your 6.42

SPECKLED
from it every s. and spotted sheep and Gen 30.32
and the spotted and s. among the goats; 30.32
Every one that is not s. and spotted 30.33
all she-goats that were s. and spotted, 30.35
brought forth striped, s., and spotted. 30.39
heritage to me like a s. bird of prey? Jer 12.09

SPECTACLE
because we have become a s. to the world, 1Co 4.09

SPECULATIONS
which promote s. rather than the divine 1Ti 1.04

SPED
at the light of thine arrows as they s., Hab 3.11
and to be s. on my journey there by you, Rom 15.24

SPEECH
may not understand one another's s." Gen 11.07
but I am slow of s. and of tongue." Ex 4.10
mouth, clearly, and not in dark s.; Num 12.08
my s. distil as the dew, as the Deu 32.02
prudent in s., and a man of good 1Sa 16.18
when the s. of a despairing man is Job 6.26
He deprives of s. those who are 12.20
hear my s., O Job, and listen to all 33.01
Day to day pours forth s., and Ps 19.02
There is no s., nor are there words 19.03
His s. was smoother than butter, yet 55.21
of evil, from men of perverted s., Pro 2.12
Put away from you crooked s., 4.24
and her s. is smoother than oil; 5.03
man, goes about with crooked s., 6.12
With much seductive s. she persuades 7.21
of evil and perverted s. I hate. 8.13
and pleasant s. increases persuasiveness 16.21
of the wise makes his s. judicious, 16.23
and his s. is like a scorching fire 16.27
Fine s. is not becoming to a fool; 17.07
still less is false s. to a prince. 17.07
is perverse in s., and is a fool. 19.01
and whose s. is gracious, will have 22.11
His s. is most sweet, and he is Sol 5.16
because their s. and their deeds Is 3.08
my voice; hearken, and hear my s. 28.23
and your s. shall whisper out of 29.04
daughters, give ear to my s. 32.09
of an obscure s. which you cannot 33.19
of foreign s. and a hard language, Eze 3.05
of foreign s. and a hard language, 3.06
will change the s. of the peoples Zep 3.09
to a pure s., that all of them may 3..09
and had an impediment in his s.; Mk 7.32
he prolonged his s. until midnight. Ac 20.07
in him with all s. and all knowledge 1Co 1.05
and my s. and my message were not 2.04
a tongue utter s. that is not 14.09
truthful s., and the power of God; 2Co 6.07
is weak, and his s. of no account. 10.10
may delude you with beguiling s. Col 2.04
Let your s. always be gracious, 4.06
an example in s. and conduct, 1Ti 4.12
and sound s. that cannot be censured, Tit 2.08
love in word or s. but in deed and 1Jn 3.18

SPEECHES
I will not answer him with your s. Job 32.14

SPEECHLESS
a wedding garment?' And he was s. Mt 22.12
who were traveling with him stood s., Ac 9.07

SPEED
let him s. his work that we may see Is 5.19
"No! We will s. upon horses," therefore 30.16
therefore you shall s. away; and, 30.16
so that you may s. me on my journey, 1Co 16.06
S. him on his way in peace, that he 16.11
of the Lord may s. on and triumph, 2Th 3.01
Do your best to s. Zenas the lawyer Tit 3.13

SPEEDILY
Incline thy ear to me, rescue me s.! Ps 31.02
thy compassion come s. to meet us, 79.08
answer me s. in the day when I call 102.02
evil hunt down the violent man s.! 140.11
an evil deed is not executed s., Ecc 8.11
and lo, swiftly, s. it comes! Is 5.26
My deliverance draws near s., 51.05
is bowed down shall s. be released; 51.14
your healing shall spring up s.; 58.08
upon your own head swiftly and s. Joe 3.04
tell you, he will vindicate them s. Lk 18.08

SPELT
wheat and the s. were not ruined, Ex 9.32
proper place, and s. as the border? Is 28.25
millet and s., and put them into a Eze 4.09

SPEND
servant's house and s. the night, Gen 19.02
we will s. the night in the street." 19.02
and s. the money for whatever you Deu 14.26
I will s. my arrows upon them; 32.23
man, "Be pleased to s. the night, Ju 19.06
But the man would not s. the night; 19.10
Jebusites, and s. the night in it." 19.11
and s. the night at Gibeah or at 19.13
to go in and s. the night at Gibeah. 19.15
into his house to s. the night. 19.15
only, do not s. the night in the 19.20
and my concubine, to s. the night. 20.04
he will not s. the night with the 2Sa 17.08
They s. their days in prosperity, Job 21.13
Will he s. the night at your crib? 39.09

SPEND (cont.)
Why do you s. your money for that Is 55.02
and s. the night in secret places; 65.04
sorrow, and s. my days in shame? Jer 20.18
"Thus shall my anger s. itself, Eze 5.13
when I s. my fury upon them. 5.13
Thus I will s. my fury upon them. 6.12
and s. my anger against you, and 7.08
Thus will I s. my wrath upon the 13.15
upon them and s. my anger against 20.08
upon them and s. my anger against 20.21
and whatever more you s., Lk 10.35
might not have to s. time in Asia; Ac 20.16
with you or even s. the winter, 1Co 16.06
I hope to s. some time with you, if 16.07
most gladly s. and be spent for 2Co 12.15
have decided to s. the winter Tit 3.12
to s. it on your passions. Jas 4.03
such a town and s. a year there 4.13

SPENDING
After s. some time there he departed Ac 18.23

SPENT
drank, and they s. the night there. Gen 24.54
money was all s. in the land of 47.15
my lord that our money is all s.; 47.18
and your strength shall be s. in vain, Lev 26.20
and s. the night in the camp. Jos 6.11
but Joshua s. that night among the 8.09
But Joshua s. that night in the 8.13
near Jebus, the day was far s., Ju 19.11
'The jar of meal shall not be s., 1Ki 17.14
The jar of meal was not s., 17.16
where he s. the night, neither Ez 10.06
For my life is s. with sorrow, and Ps 31.10
I am utterly s. and crushed; 38.08
I am s. by the blows of thy hand. 39.10
me not when my strength is s. 71.09
and the toil I had s. in doing it, Ecc 2.11
and s. all his days in darkness and 5.17
I have s. strength for nothing Is 49.04
My eyes are s. with weeping; Lam 2.11
palace, and s. the night fasting; Dan 6.18
and had s. all that she had, and was Mk 5.26
And when he had s. everything, Lk 15.14
evening and the day is now far s." 24.29
And after they had s. some time, Ac 15.33
who lived there s. their time in 17.21
There he s. three months, and when a 20.03
s. from the beginning among my own 26.04
spend and be s. for your souls. 2Co 12.15

SPEW
nor hot, I will s. you out of my mouth. Rev 3.16

SPICE
fragrance of your oils than any s.! Sol 4.10
I gather my myrrh with my s., I eat 5.01
cinnamon, s., incense, myrrh, frankincense, Rev 18.13

SPICED
I would give you s. wine to drink, the Sol 8.02

SPICES
s. for the anointing oil and for Ex 25.06
"Take the finest s.: of liquid 30.23
"Take sweet s., stacte, and onycha, 30.34
sweet s. with pure frankincense (of 30.34
s. for the anointing oil and for 35.08
and s. and oil for the light, and 35.28
retinue, with camels bearing s., 1Ki 10.02
and a very great quantitty of s., 10.10
an abundance of s. as these which 10.10
s., horses, and mules, so much year 10.25
the s., the precious oil, his armory, 2Ki 20.13
the oil, the incense, and the s. 1Ch 9.29
prepared the mixing of the s., 9.30
of incense of sweet s. before him, 2Ch 2.04
camels bearing s. and very much 9.01
and a very great quantity of s., 9.09
there were no s. such as those 9.09
s., horses, and mules, so much year 9.24
offerings and incense of sweet s., 13.11
kinds of s. prepared by the 16.14
for s., for shields, and for all 32.27
six months with s. and ointments Est 2.12
and aloes, with all chief s.— Sol 4.14
His cheeks are like beds of s., 5.13
to his garden, to the beds of s., 6.02
stag upon the mountains of s. 8.14
the s., the precious oil, his whole Is 39.02
And as s. were burned for your Jer 34.05
men shall burn s. for you and 34.05
wares the best of all kinds of s., Eze 27.22
bought s., so that they might go Mk 16.01
and prepared s. and ointments. Lk 23.56
taking the s. which they had 24.01
it in linen cloths with the s., Jn 19.40

SPIDER'S
sunder, and his trust is a s. web, Job 8.14
which he builds is like a s. web, 27.18
eggs, they weave the s. web; Is 59.05

SPIED
went up and s. out the land from Num 13.21
of the land which they had s. out, 13.32
those who had s. out the land, 14.06
days in which you s. out the land, 14.34
the Valley of Eshcol and s. it out. Deu 1.24
two men who had s. out the land, Jos 6.22
And the men went up and s. out Ai. 7.02
and he s. the company of Jehu as he 2Ki 9.17

SPIES
"You are s., you have come to see Gen 42.09
men, your servants are not s." 42.11
"It is as I said to you, you are s. 42.14
life of Pharaoh, surely you are s." 42.16
and took us to be s. of the land. 42.30
'We are honest men, we are not s.; 42.31
that you are not s. but honest men, 42.34
men secretly from Shittim as s., Jos 2.01
young men who had been s. went in, 6.23
And the s. saw a man coming out of Ju 1.24
David sent out s., and learned of a 1Sa 26.04
Thence he s. out the prey; Job 39.29
and sent s., who pretended to be Lk 20.20
given friendly welcome to the s. Heb 11.31

SPILLED
brother's wife he s. the semen on Gen 38.09
skins burst, and the wine is s., Mt 9.17
burst the skins and it will be s., Lk 5.37

SPILT
we are like water s. on the ground, 2Sa 14.14

SPIN
they grow; they neither toil nor s.; Mt 6.28
they grow; they neither toil nor s.; Lk 12.27

SPINDLE
who is leprous, or who holds a s., 2Sa 3.29
distaff, and her hands hold the s. Pro 31.19

SPIRIT
and the S. of God was moving over Gen 1.02
"My s. shall not abive in man for 6.03
in the morning his s. was troubled; 41.08
as this, in whom is the S. of God?" 41.38
the s. of their father Jacob 45.27
O my s., be not joined to their 49.06
of their broken s. and their cruel Ex 6.09
have filled him with the S. of God, 31.03
and every one whose s. moved him, 35.21

SPIRIT (cont.)

has filled him with the S. of God,	Ex 35.31
and if the s. of jealousy comes	Num 5.14
or if the s. of jealousy comes upon	5.14
or when the s. of jealousy comes	5.30
some of the s. which is upon you	11.17
some of the s. that was upon him	11.25
and when the s. rested upon them,	11.25
and the s. rested upon them;	11.26
LORD would put his s. upon them!"	11.29
has a different s. and has followed	14.24
And the S. of God came upon him,	24.02
of Nun, a man in whom is the s.,	27.18
hardened his s. and made his heart	Deu 2.30
Nun was full of the s. of wisdom,	34.09
there was no longer any s. in them,	Jos 5.01
The S. of the LORD came upon him,	Ju 3.10
But the S. of the LORD took possession	6.34
sent an evil s. between Abimelech	9.23
Then the S. of the LORD came upon	11.29
And the S. of the LORD began to	13.25
and the S. of the LORD came mightily	14.06
And the S. of the LORD came mightily	14.19
and the S. of the LORD came mightily	15.14
his s. returned, and he revived.	15.19
Then the s. of the LORD will come	1Sa 10.06
and the s. of God came mightily	10.10
And the s. of God came mightily	11.06
and the S. of the LORD came mightily	16.13
Now the S. of the LORD departed	16.14
and an evil s. from the LORD	16.14
an evil s. from God is tormenting	16.15
when the evil s. from God is upon	16.16
the evil s. from God was upon Saul,	16.23
and the evil s. departed from him.	16.23
morrow an evil s. from God rushed	18.10
Then an evil s. from the LORD came	19.09
the S. of God came upon the messengers	1Sa 19.20
and the S. of God came upon him	19.23
And he said, "Divine for me by a s.,	28.08
when he had eaten, his s. revived;	30.12
And the s. of the king longed to go	2Sa 13.39
"The S. of the LORD speaks by me,	23.02
LORD, there was no more s. in her.	1Ki 10.05
the S. of the LORD will carry you	18.12
"Why is your s. so vexed that you	21.05
Then a s. came forward and stood	22.21
will be a lying s. in the mouth of	22.22
has put a lying s. in the mouth of	22.23
"How did the S. of the LORD go from	22.24
inherit a double share of your s."	2Ki 2.09
"The s. of Elijah rests on Elisha."	2.15
may be that the S. of the LORD has	2.16
go with you in s. when the man	5.26
I will put a s. in him, so that he	19.07
stirred up the s. of Pul king of	1Ch 5.26
the s. of Tilgathpilneser king of	5.26
Then the S. came upon Amasai, chief	12.18
LORD, there was no more s. in her.	2Ch 9.04
The s. of God came upon Azariah the	15.01
Then a s. came forward and stood	18.20
will be a lying s. in the mouth of	18.21
has put a lying s. in the mouth of	18.22
way did the S. of the LORD go from	18.23
And the S. of the LORD came upon	20.14
Then the S. of God took possession	24.20
stirred up the s. of Cyrus king of	36.22
stirred up the s. of Cyrus king of	Ez 1.01
every one whose s. God had stirred	1.05
Thou gavest thy good S. to instruct	Neh 9.20
them by thy S. through thy prophets	9.30
A s. glided past my face; the hair	Job 4.15
my s. drinks their poison; the	6.04
will speak in the anguish of my s.;	7.11
and thy care has preserved my s.	10.12
that you turn your s. against God,	15.13
My s. is broken, my days are extinct,	17.01

my understanding a s. answers me.	20.03
and whose s. has come forth from	26.04
and the s. of God is in my nostrils	27.03
But it is the s. in a man, the	32.08
the s. within me constrains me.	32.18
The s. of God has made me, and the	33.04
should take back his s. to himself,	34.14
Into thy hand I commit my s.;	Ps 31.05
and in whose s. there is no deceit.	32.02
and saves the crushed in s.	34.18
put a new and right s. within me.	51.10
and take not thy holy S. from me.	51.11
and uphold me with a willing s.	51.12
acceptable to God is a broken s.;	51.17
who cuts off the s. of princes,	76.12
moan; I meditate, and my s. faints.	77.03
night; I meditate and search my s.:	77.06
whose s. was not faithful to God.	78.08
When thou sendest forth thy S.,	104.30
for they made his s. bitter, and	106.33
Whither shall I go from thy S.?	139.07
When my s. is faint, thou knowest my	142.03
Therefore my s. faints within me;	143.04
My s. fails! Hide not thy face	143.07
Let thy good s. lead me on a level	143.10
trustworthy in s. keeps a thing	Pro 11.13
perverseness in it breaks the s.	15.04
sorrow of heart the s. is broken.	15.13
eyes, but the LORD weighs the s.	16.02
and a haughty s. before a fall.	16.18
be of a lowly s. with the poor	16.19
who rules his s. than he who takes	16.32
but a downcast s. dries up the	17.22
who has a cool s. is a man of	17.27
A man's s. will endure sickness;	18.14
but a broken s. who can bear?	18.14
The s. of man is the lamp of the	20.27
he refreshes the s. of his masters.	25.13
who is lowly in s. will obtain	29.23
whether the s. of man goes upward	Ecc 3.21
upward and the s. of the beast	3.21
the patient in s. is better than	7.08
is better than the proud in s.	7.08
No man has power to retain the s.,	8.08
know how the s. comes to the bones	11.05
and the s. returns to God who gave	12.07
s. of judgment and by a s. of burning.	Is 4.04
And the S. of the LORD shall rest	11.02
the s. of wisdom and understanding,	11.02
the s. of counsel and might, the	11.02
the s. of knowledge and the fear of	11.02
and the s. of the Egyptians within	19.03
within her a s. of confusion;	19.14
my s. within me earnestly seeks	26.09
and a s. of justice to him who sits	28.06
out upon you a s. of deep sleep,	29.10
who err in s. will come to understanding,	29.24
but not of my s., that they may add	30.01
their horses are flesh, and not s.	31.03
until the S. is poured upon us from	32.15
and his S. has gathered them.	34.16
I will put a s. in him, so that he	37.07
in all these is the life of my s.	38.16
Who has directed he S. of the LORD,	40.13
I have put my s. upon him, he will	42.01
upon it and s. to those who walk	42.05
I will pour my S. upon your descendants,	44.03
Lord GOD has sent me and his S.	48.16
a wife forsaken and grieved in s.,	54.06
who is of a contrite and humble s.,	57.15
to revive the s. of the humble, and	57.15
for from me proceeds the s.,	57.16
my s. which is upon you, and my	59.21
The S. of the Lord GOD is upon me,	61.01
of praise instead of a faint s.;	61.03
rebelled and grieved his holy S.;	63.10
in the midst of them his holy S.,	63.11
the S. of the LORD gave them rest.	63.14

SPIRIT (cont.)
and shall wail for anguish of s. Is 65.14
that is humble and contrite in s., 66.02
stir up the s. of a destroyer Jer 51.01
stirred up the s. of the kings of 51.11
wherever the s. would go, they went, Eze 1.12
Wherever the s. would go, they went, 1.20
for the s. of the living creatures 1.20
for the s. of the living creatures 1.21
the S. entered into me and set me 2.02
Then the S. lifted me up, and as the 3.12
The S. lifted me up and took me 3.14
in bitterness in the heat of my s., 3.14
But the S. entered into me, and set 3.24
and the S. lifted me up between 8.03
for the s. of the living creatures 10.17
The S. lifted me up, and brought me 11.01
And the S. of the LORD fell upon me, 11.05
and put a new s. within them; 11.19
And the S. lifted me up and brought 11.24
vision by the S. of God into 11.24
prophets who follow their own s., 13.03
yourselves a new heart and a new s.! 18.31
every s. will faint and all knees 21.07
and a new s. I will put within you; 36.26
And I will put my s. within you, 36.27
me out by the S. of the LORD, 37.01
And I will put my S. within you, 37.14
I pour out my S. upon the house of 39.29
the S. lifted me up, and brought me 43.05
and his s. was troubled, and his Dan 2.01
and my s. is troubled to know the 2.03
in whom is the s. of the holy gods 4.08
I know that the s. of the holy 4.09
for the s. of the holy gods is in 4.18
in whom is the s. of the holy gods 5.11
because an excellent s., 5.12
of you that the s. of the holy 5.14
up and his s. was hardened so that 5.20
because an excellent s. was in him; 6.03
my s. within me was anxious and the 7.15
For a s. of harlotry has led them Hos 4.12
For the s. of harlotry is within 5.04
a fool, the man of the s. is mad, 9.07
I will pour out my s. on all flesh; Joe 2.28
those days, I will pour out my s. 2.29
Is the S. of the LORD impatient? Mic 2.07
with the S. of the LORD, and with 3.08
stirred up the s. of Zerubbabel Hag 1.14
and the s. of Joshua the son of 1.14
and the s. of all the remnant of 1.14
My S. abides among you; fear not. 2.05
but my by S., says the LORD of Zec 4.06
have set my S. at rest in the 6.08
had sent by his S. through the 7.12
and formed the s. of man within 12.01
of Jerusalem a s. of compassion 12.10
the prophets and the unclean s. 13.02
sustained for us the s. of life? Mal 2.15
to be with child of the Holy S.; Mt 1.18
conceived in her is of the Holy S.; 1.20
you with the Holy S. and with fire. 3.11
and he saw the S. of God descending 3.16
led up by the S. into the wilderness 4.01
"Blessed are the poor in s., 5.03
but the S. of your Father speaking 10.20
I will put my S. upon him, and he 12.18
But if it is by the S. of God that 12.28
against the S. will not be forgiven 12.31
the Holy S. will not be forgiven, 12.32
"When the unclean s. has gone out 12.43
that David, inspired by the S., 22.43
the s. indeed is willing, but the 26.41
a loud voice and yielded up his s. 27.50
and of the Son and of the Holy S., 28.19
will baptize you with the Holy S." Mk 1.08
opened and the S. descending upon 1.10
The S. immediately drove him out 1.12
synagogue a man with an unclean s.; 1.23
And the unclean s., convulsing him 1.26
perceiving in his s. that they thus 2.08
the Holy S. never has forgiveness, 3.29
had said, "He has an unclean s." 3.30
tombs a man with an unclean s., 5.02
out of the man, you unclean s.!" 5.08
was possessed by an unclean s., 7.25
And he sighed deeply in his s., 8.12
son to you, for he has a dumb s.; 9.17
and when the s. saw him, immediately 9.20
together, he rebuked the unclean s., 9.25
saying to it, "You dumb and deaf s., 9.25
David himself, inspired by the Holy S., 12.36
not you who speak, but the Holy S. 13.11
the s. indeed is willing, but the 14.38
he will be filled with the Holy S., Lk 1.15
him in the s. and power of Elijah, 1.17
"The Holy S. will come upon you, and 1.35
was filled with the Holy S. 1.41
and my s. rejoices in God my Savior, 1.47
was filled with the Holy S., 1.67
child grew and became strong in s., 1.80
and the Holy S. was upon him. 2.25
him by the Holy S. that he should 2.26
And inspired by the S. he came into 2.27
you with the Holy S. and with fire. 3.16
and the Holy S. descended upon him 3.22
And Jesus, full of the Holy S., 4.01
Jordan, and was led by the S. 4.01
the power of the S. into Galilee, 4.14
"The S. of the Lord is upon me, 4.18
man who had the s. of an unclean 4.33
the unclean s. to come out of the 8.29
And her s. returned, and she got up 8.55
and behold, a s. seizes him, and he 9.39
But Jesus rebuked the unclean s., 9.42
not know what manner of s. you are * 9.55
rejoiced in the Holy S. and said, 10.21
give the Holy S. to those who ask 11.13
"When the unclean s. has gone out 11.24
the Holy S. will not be forgiven. 12.10
for the Holy S. will teach you in 12.12
who had had a s. of infirmity for 13.11
into thy hands I commit my s.!" 23.46
and supposed that they saw a s. 24.37
for a s. has not flesh and bones as 24.39
"I saw the S. descend as a dove Jn 1.32
you see the S. descend and remain, 1.33
he who baptizes with the Holy S.' 1.33
one is born of water and the S., 3.05
that which is born of the S. is s. 3.06
every one who is born of the S." 3.08
by measure that he gives the S.; 3.34
worship the Father in s. and truth, 4.23
God is s., and those who worship 4.24
him must worship in s. and truth." 4.24
It is the s. that gives life, the 6.63
have spoken to you are s. and life. 6.63
Now this he said about the S., 7.39
for as yet the S. had not been 7.39
deeply moved in s. and troubled; 11.33
thus spoken, he was troubled in s., 13.21
even the s. of truth, whom the world 14.17
the Holy S., whom the Father will 14.26
even the S. of truth, who proceeds 15.26
When the S. of truth comes, he will 16.13
bowed his head and gave up his s. 19.30
said to them, "Receive the Holy S. 20.22
the Holy S. to the apostles whom Ac 1.02
shall be baptized with the Holy S." 1.05
when the Holy S. has come upon you 1.08
which the Holy S. spoke beforehand 1.16
with the Holy S. and began to 2.04
as the S. gave them utterance. 2.04
will pour out my S. upon all flesh, 2.17
those days I will pour out my S.; 2.18

SPIRIT (cont.)

Father the promise of the Holy S., Ac 2.33
receive the gift of the Holy S. 2.38
Then Peter, filled with the Holy S., 4.08
servant, didst say by the Holy S., 4.25
with the Holy S. and spoke the 4.31
lie to the Holy S. and to keep 5.03
to tempt the S. of the Lord? 5.09
so is the Holy S. whom God has 5.32
full of the S. and of wisdom, whom 6.03
full of faith and of the Holy S., 6.05
wisdom and the S. with which he 6.10
you always resist the Holy S. 7.51
But he, full of the Holy S., 7.55
prayed, "Lord Jesus, receive my s." 7.59
they might receive the Holy S.; 8.15
them and they received the Holy S. 8.17
saw that the S. was given through 8.18
my hands may receive the Holy S." 8.19
And the S. said to Philip, "Go up 8.29
the S. of the Lord caught up Philip 8.39
and be filled with the Holy S." 9.17
of the Holy S. it was multiplied. 9.31
the S. said to him, "Behold, three 10.19
with the Holy S. and with power; 10.38
the Holy S. fell on all who heard 10.44
of the Holy S. had been poured out 10.45
the Holy S. just as we have?" 10.47
And the S. told me to go with them 11.12
the Holy S. fell on them just as on 11.15
shall be baptized with the Holy S.' 11.16
full of the Holy S. and of faith. 11.24
foretold by the S. that there 11.28
the Holy S. said, "Set apart for me 13.02
So, being sent out by the Holy S., 13.04
Paul, filled with the Holy S., 13.09
with joy and with the Holy S. 13.52
them the Holy S. just as he did to 15.08
to the Holy S. and to us to lay 15.28
by the Holy S. to speak the word 16.06
but the S. of Jesus did not allow 16.07
girl who had a s. of divination 16.16
and turned and said to the s., 16.18
his s. was provoked within him as 17.16
and being fervent in s., he spoke 18.25
the Holy S. when you believed?" 19.02
even heard that there is a Holy S." 19.02
them, the Holy S. came on them; 19.06
But the evil s. answered them, 19.15
whom the evil s. was leaped on 19.16
resolved in the S. to pass through 19.21
bound in the S., not knowing what 20.22
except that the Holy S. testifies 20.23
which the Holy S. has made you 20.28
Through the S. they told Paul not 21.04
and said, "Thus says the Holy S., 21.11
no resurrection, nor angel, nor s.; 23.08
What if a s. or an angel spoke to 23.09
"The Holy S. was right in saying to 28.25
according to the S. of holiness by Rom 1.04
I serve with my s. in the gospel 1.09
the Holy S. which has been given 5.05
code but in the new life of the S. 7.06
For the law of the S. of life in 8.02
the flesh but according to the S. 8.04
according to the S. set their minds 8.05
minds on the things of the S. 8.05
the mind on the S. is life and 8.06
in the flesh, you are in the S., 8.09
if the S. of God really dwells in 8.09
not have the S. of Christ does not 8.09
If the S. of him who raised Jesus 8.11
through his S. which dwells in you 8.11
but if by the S. you put to death 8.13
are led by the S. of God are sons 8.14
not receive the s. of slavery to 8.15
have received the s. of sonship. 8.15
it is the S. himself bearing 8.16
with our s. that we are children 8.16
have the first fruits of the S., 8.23
Likewise the S. helps us in our 8.26
but the S. himself intercedes for 8.26
knows what is the mind of the S., 8.27
because the S. intercedes for the 8.27
bears me witness in the Holy S., 9.01
"God gave them a s. of stupor, 11.08
flag in zeal, be aglow with the S., 12.11
and peace and joy in the Holy S.; 14.17
of the Holy S. you may abound in 15.13
acceptable, sanctified by the Holy S. 15.16
by the power of the Holy S., 15.19
Christ and by the love of the S., 15.30
demonstration of the S. and power, 1Co 2.04
God has revealed to us through the S. 2.10
For the S. searches everything, even 2.10
except the s. of the man which is 2.11
of God except the S. of God. 2.11
received not the s. of the world, 2.12
but the S. which is from God, that 2.12
human wisdom but taught by the S., 2.13
truths to those who possess the S. 2.13
receive the gifts of the S. of God, 2.14
and that God's S. dwells in you? 3.16
or with love in a s. of gentleness? 4.21
absent in body I am present in s., 5.03
and my s. is present, with the power 5.04
that his s. may be saved in the day 5.05
Christ and in the S. of our God. 6.11
the Lord becomes one s. with him. 6.17
a temple of the Holy S. within you, 6.19
how to be holy in body and s.; 7.34
I think that I have the S. of God. 7.40
speaking by the S. of God ever 12.03
is Lord" except by the Holy S. 12.03
varieties of gifts, but the same S.; 12.04
manifestation of the S. for the 12.07
through the S. the utterance of 12.08
knowledge according to the same S., 12.08
to another faith by the same S., 12.09
gifts of healing by the one S., 12.09
inspired by one and the same S., 12.11
For by one S. we were all baptized 12.13
all were made to drink of one S. 12.13
but he utters mysteries in the S. 14.02
eager for manifestations of the S., 14.12
my s. prays but my mind is unfruitful. 14.14
pray with the s. and I will pray 14.15
sing with the s. and I will sing 14.15
Otherwise, if you bless with the s., 14.16
last Adam became a life-giving s. 15.45
refreshed my s. as well as yours. 16.18
given us his S. in our hearts as a 2Co 1.22
but with the S. of the living God, 3.03
in a written code but in the S.; 3.06
code kills, but the S. gives life. 3.06
dispensation of the S. be attended 3.08
Now the Lord is the S., and 3.17
and where the S. of the Lord is, 3.17
comes from the Lord who is the S. 3.18
have the same s. of faith as he 4.13
has given us the S. as a guarantee. 5.05
kindness, the Holy S., genuine love, 6.06
every defilement of body and s., 7.01
a different s. from the one you 11.04
Did we not act in the same s.? 12.18
of the Holy S. be with you all. 13.14
you receive the S. by works of the Gal 3.02
Having begun with the S., are you 3.03
supplies the S. to you and works 3.05
promise of the S. through faith. 3.14
has sent the S. of his Son into 4.06
according to the S., so it is now. 4.29
For through the S., by faith, 5.05
walk by the S., and do not gratify 5.16
of the flesh are against the S., 5.17

SPIRIT (cont.)
desires of the S. are against the Gal 5.17
are led by the S. you are not 5.18
selfishness, dissension, party s., 5.20
But the fruit of the S. is love, 5.22
If we live by the S., let us 5.25
let us also walk by the S. 5.25
restore him in a s. of gentleness. 6.01
who sows to the S. will from the 6.08
will from the S. reap eternal life 6.08
Christ be with your s., brethren. 6.18
sealed with the promised Holy S., Eph 1.13
may give you a s. of wisdom and of 1.17
the s. that is now at work in the 2.02
access in one S. to the Father. 2.18
a dwelling place of God in the S. 2.22
apostles and prophets by the S; 3.05
through his S. in the inner man, 3.16
unity of the S. in the bond of 4.03
There is one body and one S., 4.04
renewed in the s. of your minds, 4.23
And do not grieve the Holy S. of God, 4.30
but be filled with the S., 5.18
salvation, and the sword of the S., 6.17
Pray at all times in the S., 6.18
the help of the S. of Jesus Christ Php 1.19
you that you stand firm in one s., 1.27
love, any participation in the S., 2.01
circumcision, who worship God in s., 3.03
Lord Jesus Christ be with your s. 4.23
known to us your love in the S. Col 1.08
in body, yet I am with you in s., 2.05
and in the Holy S. and with full 1Th 1.05
with joy inspired by the Holy S.; 1.06
God, who gives his Holy S. to you. 4.08
Do not quench the S., 5.19
and may your s. and soul and body 5.23
either by s. or by word, or by 2Th 2.02
sanctification by the S. and belief 2.13
in the flesh, vindicated in the S., 1Ti 3.16
Now the S. expressly says that in 4.01
not give us a s. of timidity but a 2Ti 1.07
timidity but a s. of power and 1.07
you by the Holy S. who dwells 1.14
The Lord be with your s. Grace 4.22
and renewal in the Holy S., Tit 3.05
Lord Jesus Christ be with your s. Phm 1.25
of the Holy S. distributed according Heb 2.04
as the Holy S. says, "Today, when you 3.07
to the division of soul and s., 4.12
become partakers of the Holy S., 6.04
By this the Holy S. indicates that 9.08
the eternal S. offered himself 9.14
And the Holy S. also bears witness 10.15
and outraged the S. of grace? 10.29
the body apart from the s. is dead, Jas 2.26
over the s. which he has made to 4.05
sanctified by the S. for obedience 1Pe 1.02
indicated by the S. of Christ 1.11
the Holy S. sent from heaven, 1.12
jewel of a gentle and quiet s., 3.04
have unity of s., sympathy, love of 3.08
the flesh but made alive in the s.; 3.18
they might live in the s. like God. 4.06
because the S. of glory and of God 4.14
by the Holy S. spoke from God. 2Pe 1.21
by the S. which he has given us. 1Jn 3.24
Beloved, do not believe every s., 4.01
By this you know the S. of God: 4.02
every s. which confesses that Jesus 4.02
and every s. which does not confess 4.03
This is the s. of antichrist, of 4.03
we know the s. of truth and the 4.06
of truth and the s. of error. 4.06
he has given us of his own S. 4.13
And the S. is the witness, because 5.07
because the S. is the truth. 5.07
the S., the water, and the blood; 5.08
worldly people, devoid of the S. Ju 1.19
holy faith; pray in the Holy S.; 1.20
I was in the S. on the Lord's day, Rev 1.10
hear what the S. says to the 2.07
hear what the S. says to the 2.11
hear what the S. says to the 2.17
hear what the S. says to the 2.29
hear what the S. says to the 3.06
hear what the S. says to the 3.13
hear what the S. says to the 3.22
At once I was in the S., and lo, 4.02
says the S., "that they may rest 14.13
me away in the S. into a wilderness, 17.03
demons, a haunt of every foul s., 18.02
of Jesus is the s. of prophecy. 19.10
And in the S. he carried me away to 21.10
The S. and the Bride say, "Come." 22.17

SPIRITS
the God of the s. of all flesh, Num 16.22
the God of the s. of all flesh, 27.16
and he cast out the s. with a word, Mt 8.16
them authority over unclean s., 10.01
him seven other s. more evil than 12.45
he commands even the unclean s., Mk 1.27
whenever the unclean s. beheld him, 3.11
And the unclean s. came out, 5.13
them authority over the unclean s. 6.07
power he commands the unclean s., Lk 4.36
troubled with unclean s. were cured. 6.18
diseases and plagues and evil s., 7.21
healed of evil s. and infirmities: 8.02
that the s. are subject to you; 10.20
seven other s. more evil than 11.26
those afflicted with unclean s., Ac 5.16
For unclean s. came out of many who 8.07
and the evil s. came out of them. 19.12
Jesus over those who had evil s., 19.13
your s. are alive because of Rom 8.10
ability to distinguish between s., 1Co 12.10
and the s. of prophets are subject 14.32
the elemental s. of the universe. Gal 4.03
the weak and beggarly elemental s., 4.09
the elemental s. of the universe, Col 2.08
the elemental s. of the universe, 2.20
to deceitful s. and doctrines of 1Ti 4.01
all ministering s. sent forth to Heb 1.14
to the Father of s. and live? 12.09
and to the s. of just men made 12.23
and preached to the s. in prison, 1Pe 3.19
but test the s. to see whether they 1Jn 4.01
from the seven s. who are before Rev 1.04
has the seven s. of God and the 3.01
which are the seven s. of God; 4.05
are the seven s. of God sent out 5.06
prophet, three foul s. like frogs; 16.13
for they are demonic s., performing 16.14
the God of the s. of the prophets, 22.06

SPIRITUAL
to you some s. gift to strengthen Rom 1.11
of the heart, s. and not literal. 2.29
We know that the law is s.; 7.14
to God, which is your s. worship. 12.01
to share in their s. blessings, 15.27
you are not lacking in any s. gift, 1Co 1.07
interpreting s. truths to those who 2.13
The s. man judges all things, but is 2.15
could not address you as s. men, 3.01
If we have sown s. good among you, 9.11
Now concerning s. gifts, brethren, I 12.01
and earnestly desire the s. gifts, 14.01
or s., he should acknowledge that 14.37
body, it is raised a s. body. 15.44
body, there is also a s. body. 15.44
But it is not the s. which is first 15.46
but the physical, and then the s. 15.46

SPIRITUAL (cont.)
you who are s. should restore him Gal 6.01
with every s. blessing in the Eph 1.03
in psalms and hymns and s. songs, 5.19
against the s. hosts of wickedness 6.12
his will in all s. wisdom and Col 1.09
and hymns and s. songs with 3.16
babes, long for the pure s. milk, 1Pe 2.02
yourselves built into a s. house, 2.05
to offer s. sacrifices acceptable 2.05

SPIRITUALLY
them because they are s. discerned. 1Co 2.14

SPIT
her father had but s. in her face, Num 12.14
off his foot, and s. in his face; Deu 25.09
and I am one before whom men s. Job 17.06
not hesitate to s. at the sight of 30.10
and when he had s. on his eyes and Mk 8.23
and s. upon him, and scourge him, and 10.34
And some began to s. on him, 14.65
and shamefully treated and s. upon; Lk 18.32

SPITE
And if in s. of this you will not Lev 26.18
"And if in s. of this you will not 26.27
in s. of all the signs which I have Num 14.11
Yet in s. of this word you did not Deu 1.32
is hope for Israel in s. of this. Ez 10.02
hand is heavy in s. of my groaning. Job 23.02
in s. of my right I am counted a 34.06
In s. of all this they still sinned Ps 78.32
in s. of all his great multitide, Is 16.14
in s. of your many sorceries and 47.09
Yet in s. of all these things Jer 2.34

SPITS
he who has the discharge s. on one who Lev 15.08

SPITTING
I hid not my face from shame and s. Is 50.06

SPITTLE
and let his s. run down his beard. 1Sa 21.13
let me alone till I swallow my s.? Job 7.19
clay of the s. and anointed the Jn 9.06

SPLENDID
and there shall be your s. chariots, Is 22.18

SPLENDOR
tell my father of all my s. in Egypt, Gen 45.13
royal glory and the s. and pomp of his Est 1.04
recounted to them the s. of his riches, 5.11
shone, on the moon moving in s., Job 31.26
Out of the north comes golden s.; 37.22
clothe yourself with glory and s. 40.10
s. and majesty thou dost bestow Ps 21.05
Of the glorious s. of thy majesty, 145.05
and the glorious s. of thy kingdom. 145.12
the s. and pride of the Chaldeans, Is 13.19
heaven to earth the s. of Israel; Lam 2.01
through the s. which I had bestowed Eze 16.14
helmet in you; they gave you s. 27.10
of your wisdom and defile your s. 28.07
wisdom for the sake of your s. 28.17
my majesty and s. returned to me. Dan 4.36
and I will fill this house with s., Hag 2.07
The latter s. of this house shall 2.09
came with such s. that the Israelites 1Co 3.07
Spirit be attended with greater s.? 3.08
For if there was s. in the dispensation 3.09
righteousness must far exceed it in s. 3.09
what once had s. has come to have 3.10
has come to have no s. at all, 3.10
because of the s. that surpasses 3.10
For if what faded away came with s., 3.11
permanent must have much more s. 3.11
not see the end of the fading s. 3.13
be presented before him in s., Eph 5.27
dainties and thy s. are lost to 18.14
earth was made bright with his s. Rev 18.01

SPLINTERED
waste my vines, and s. my fig trees; Joe 1.07

SPLIT
the ground under them s. asunder; Num 16.31
And God s. open the hollow place Ju 15.19
and they s. up the wood of the cart 1Sa 6.14
the earth was s. by their noise. 1Ki 1.40
Olives shall be s. in two from Zec 14.04
earth shook, and the rocks were s.; Mt 27.51
The great city was s. into three Rev 16.19

SPLITS
and he who s. logs is endangered by Ecc 10.09

SPOIL
prey, and at even dividing the s." Gen 49.27
overtake, I will divide the s., Ex 15.09
and took all the s. and all the Num 31.11
and the booty and the s. to Moses, 31.12
remaining of the s. that the men of 31.32
cattle we took as s. for ourselves, Deu 2.35
cattle and the s. of the cities we 3.07
gather all its s. into the midst 13.16
the city and all its s. with fire, 13.16
all its s., you shall take as booty 20.14
shall enjoy the s. of your enemies, 20.14
when I say among the s. a beautiful Jos 7.21
only its s. and its cattle you 8.02
cattle and the s. of that city 8.27
And all the s. of these cities and 11.14
divide the s. of your enemies with 22.08
not finding and dividing the s.?— Ju 5.30
s. of dyed stuffs for Sisera, s. of 5.30
work embroidered for my neck as s.?' 5.30
man of you the earrings of his s." 8.24
cast in it the earrings of his s. 8.25
and took their s. and gave the 14.19
today of the s. of their enemies 1Sa 14.30
the people flew upon the s., 14.32
Why did you swoop on the s., 15.19
But the people took of the s., 15.21
all the great s. they had taken 30.16
s. or anything that had been taken; 30.19
him, and said, "This is David's s." 30.20
them any of the s. which we have 30.22
sent part of the s. to his freinds, 30.26
you from the s. of the enemies of 30.26
of the young men, and take his s." 2Sa 2.21
a raid, bringing much s. with them. 3.22
and from the s. of Hadadezer the 8.12
brought forth the s. of the city, 12.30
another. Now then, Moab, to the s.!" 2Ki 3.23
a prey and a s. to all their enemies, 21.14
brought forth the s. of the city, 1Ch 20.02
From s. won in battles they dedicated 26.27
from the s. which they had brought, 2Ch 15.11
came to take the s. from them, 20.25
were three days in taking the s., 20.25
sent all their s. to the king of 24.23
people in them, and took much s. 25.13
also took much s. from them and 28.08
them and brought the s. to Samaria. 28.08
captives and the s. before the 28.14
and with the s. they clothed all 28.15
and our enemies have gotten s. Ps 44.10
The women at home divide the s., 68.12
stouthearted were stripped of their s.; 76.05
word like one who finds great s. 119.162
we shall fill our houses with s.; Pro 1.13
to divide the s. with the proud. 16.19
that s. the vineyards, for our Sol 2.15

SPOIL (cont.)
the s. of the poor is in your Is 3.14
Damascus and the s. of Samaria will 8.04
rejoice when they divide the s. 9.03
right, that widows may be their s., 10.02
to take s. and seize plunder, and to 10.06
and s. is gathered as the caterpillar 33.04
Then prey and s. in abundance will 33.23
a s. with none to say, "Restore!" 42.22
divide the s. with the strong; 53.12
Even so will I s. the pride of Jer 13.09
your treasures I will give as s., 15.13
I will give for s. as the price of 17.03
who despoil you shall become a s., 30.16
booty, their herds of cattle a s. 49.32
the wicked of the earth for a s.; Eze 7.21
them an object of terror and a s. 23.46
hand you over as s. to the nations; 25.07
shall become a s. to the nations; 26.05
They will make a s. of your riches 26.12
to seize s. and carry off plunder; 38.12
to you, 'Have you come to seize s.? 38.13
and goods, to seize great s.?' 38.13
among them plunder, s., and goods. Dan 11.24
when the s. taken from you will be Zec 14.01
he trusted, and divides his s. Lk 11.22

SPOILED
and behold, the waistcloth was s.; Jer 13.07
of clay was s. in the potter's hand, 18.04

SPOILER
Who gave up Jacob to the s., and Is 42.24

SPOILERS
and gave them into the hand of s., 2Ki 17.20

SPOILS
of Megiddo; they got no s. of silver. Ju 5.19
patriarch gave him a tithe of the s. Heb 7.04

SPOKE
the name of the LORD who s. to her, Gen 16.13
Again he s. to him, and said, "Suppose 18.29
and who s. to me and swore to me, 24.07
"Thus the man s. to me," he went to 24.30
when Isaac s. to his son Esau. 27.05
of your father s. to me last night, 31.29
the maiden and s. tenderly to her. 34.03
So Shechem s. to his father Hamor, 34.04
But Hamor s. with them, saying, "The 34.08
their city and s. to the men of 34.20
And although she s. to Joseph day 39.10
the words which his wife s. to him, 39.19
strangers and s. roughly to them. 42.07
he returned to them and s. to them. 42.24
s. roughly to us, and took us to be 42.30
and s. with him at the door of the 43.19
well, the old man of whom you s.? 43.27
brother, of whom you s. to me? 43.29
them, he s. to them these words. 44.06
And God s. to Israel in visions of 46.02
Joseph s. to the household of 50.04
Joseph wept when they s. to him. 50.17
And Aaron s. all the words which Ex 4.30
Moses s. thus to the people of 6.09
But the LORD s. to Moses and Aaron, 6.13
It was they who s. to Pharaoh king 6.27
when the LORD s. to Moses in the 6.28
years old, when they s. to Pharaoh. 7.07
And as Aaron s. to the whole 16.10
Moses s., and God answered him in 19.19
And God s. all these words, saying, 20.01
and s. to him from the tent of Lev 1.01
And the LORD s. to Aaron, saying, 10.08
The LORD s. to Moses, after the 16.01
So Moses s. to Aaron and to his 21.24
So Moses s. to the people of Israel 24.23
The LORD s. to Moses in the wilderness Num 1.01
when the LORD s. with Moses on 3.01
two cherubim; and it s. to him. 7.89
And the LORD s. to Moses in the 9.01
down in the cloud and s. to him, 11.25
Miriam and Aaron s. against Moses 12.01
Moses s. to the people of Israel; 17.06
And the people s. against God and 21.05
the priest s. with them in the 26.03
came near and s. before Moses and 36.01
that Moses s. to all Israel beyond Deu 1.01
Moses s. to the people of Israel 1.03
So I s. to you, and you would not 1.43
Then the LORD s. to you out of the 4.12
that the LORD s. to you at Horeb 4.15
which Moses s. to the children of 4.45
The LORD s. with you face to face 5.04
"These words the LORD s. to all 5.22
your words, when you s. to me; 5.28
Then Moses s. the words of this 31.30
Then s. Joshua to the LORD in the Jos 10.12
that the LORD s. this word to 14.10
of which the LORD s. on that day; 14.12
And the tribe of Joseph s. to Joshua, 17.14
of which I s. to you through Moses, 20.02
the Gadites and the Manassites s., 22.30
blessed God and s. no more of 22.33
of the LORD which he s. to us; 24.27
of the LORD s. these words to all Ju 2.04
and s. to them in the same way; 8.08
mother's kinsmen s. all these words 9.03
Gaal s. again and said, "Look, men 9.37
and Jephthah s. all his words 11.11
you the man who s. to this womans?" 13.11
and also s. it in my ears, behold, 17.02
is the man of whom I s. to you! 1Sa 9.17
and s. the same words as before. 17.23
heard when he s. to the men; 17.28
another, and s. in the same way; 17.30
words which David s. were heard, 17.31
And Saul's servants s. those words 18.23
And Saul s. to Jonathan his son and 19.01
And Jonathan s. well of David to 19.04
has done to you as he s. by me; 28.17
for the people s. of stoning him, 30.06
Abner also s. to Benjamin; 2Sa 3.19
this vision, Nathan s. to David. 7.17
we s. to him, and he did not listen 12.18
But Absalom s. to Amnon neither 13.22
And David s. to the LORD the words 22.01
Then David s. to the LORD when he 24.17
his word which he s. concerning me, 1Ki 2.04
Thus they s. before the king. 3.22
He s. of trees, from the cedar that 4.33
he s. also of beasts, and of birds, 4.33
which I s. to David your father. 6.12
he s. to them according to the 12.14
which the LORD s. by Ahijah the 12.15
and an angel s. to me by the word 13.18
the word which the LORD s. to him." 13.26
which he s. by his servant Ahijah 14.18
LORD which he s. by his servant 15.29
which he s. against Baasha by Jehu 16.12
which he s. by Joshua the son of 16.34
of the LORD which he s. by Elijah. 17.16
"Because I s. to Naboth the Jezreelite, 21.06
to the word which Elisha s. 2Ki 2.22
"Thus and so s. the maiden from the 5.04
he said, "Thus and so he s. to me, 9.12
which he s. by his servant Elijah 9.36
which the LORD s. concerning the 10.10
of the LORD which he s. to Elijah. 10.17
which he s. by his servant Jonah 14.25
you heard how I s. against this 22.19
LORD which he s. by his servants 24.02
and he s. kindly to him, and gave 25.28
this vision, Nathan s. to David. 1Ch 17.15
And the LORD s. to Gad, David's seer, 21.09

SPOKE (cont.)

Solomon s. to all Israel, to the 2Ch 1.02
King Rehoboam s. to them according 10.14
which he s. by Ahijah the Shilonite 10.15
as the LORD s. concerning the sons 23.03
And Hezekiah s. encouragingly to 30.22
of the city and s. encouragingly 32.06
And they s. of the God of Jerusalem 32.19
Jerusalem as they s. of the gods of 32.19
The LORD s. to Manasseh and to his 33.10
the seers who s. to him in the 33.18
Quarter) and s. to her to that 34.22
who s. from the mouth of the LORD. 36.12
came to them and s. to them thus, Ez 5.03
those elders and s. to them thus, 5.09
Also they s. of his good deeds in Neh 6.19
their children s. the language of 13.24
And when they s. to him day after Est 3.04
Then Esther s. to Hathach and gave 4.10
Then Esther s. again to the king; 8.03
his people and s. peace to all his 10.03
and no one s. a word to him, for Job 2.13
After I s. they did not speak again, 29.22
For he s., and it came to be; Ps 33.09
then I s. with my tongue: 39.03
They s. against God, saying, "Can God 78.19
He s. to them in the pillar of 99.07
He s., and there came swarms of 105.31
He s., and the locusts came, and 105.34
and he s. words that were rash. 106.33
My soul failed me when he s. Sol 5.06
Again the LORD s. to Ahaz, Is 7.10
The LORD s. to me again: 8.05
For the LORD s. thus to me with his 8.11
which the LORD s. concerning Moab 16.13
when I s., you did not listen, but 65.12
when I s. they did not listen; 66.04
and when I s. to you persistently Jer 7.13
I s. to you in your prosperity, but 22.21
the prophet s. to all the people 25.02
Then Jeremiah s. to all the princes 26.12
land arose and s. to all the 26.17
king of Judah I s. in like manner: 27.12
Then I s. to the priests and to all 27.16
s. to me in the house of the LORD, 28.01
Jeremiah s. to Hananiah the 28.05
And Hananiah s. in the presence of 28.11
which the LORD s. concerning 30.04
the prophet s. all these words to 34.06
nations, from the day I s. to you, 36.02
LORD which he s. through Jeremiah 37.02
son of Kareah s. secretly to 40.15
the prophet s. to Baruch the son 45.01
which the LORD s. to Jeremiah the 46.13
whenever you s. of him you wagged 48.27
which the LORD s. concerning 50.01
done what he s. concerning the 51.12
and he s. kindly to him, and gave 52.32
And when he s. to me, the Spirit Eze 2.02
and he s. with me and said to me, 3.24
So I s. to the people in the 24.18
he of whom I s. in former days by 38.17
And the king s. with them, and among Dan 1.19
and a mouth that s. great things, 7.20
holy one said to the one that s., 8.13
who s. in thy name to our kings, our 9.06
which he s. against us and against 9.12
then I opened my mouth and s. 10.16
And when he s. to me, I was 10.19
When the LORD first s. through Hosea, Hos 1.02
and there God s. with him— 12.04
I s. to the prophets; it was I 12.10
When Ephraim s., men trembled; 13.01
And the LORD s. to the fish, and it Jon 2.10
s. to the people with the LORD's Hag 1.13
feared the LORD s. with one Mal 3.16
had been cast out, the dumb man s.; Mt 9.33
so that the dumb man s. and saw. 12.22
But immediately he s. to them, 14.27
Jesus s. to him first, saying, "What 17.25
And again Jesus s. to them in 22.01
parables he s. the word to them, as Mk 4.33
immediately he s. to them and said, 6.50
was released, and he s. plainly. 7.35
Lord Jesus, after he had s. to them, * 16.19
as he s. to our fathers, to Abraham Lk 1.55
loosed, and he s., blessing God. 1.64
as he s. by the mouth of his holy 1.70
and s. of him to all who were 2.38
the saying which he s. to them. 2.50
And all s. well of him, and wondered 4.22
them and s. to them of the kingdom 9.11
in glory and s. of his departure, 9.31
the dumb man s., and the people 11.14
And Jesus s. to the lawyers and 14.03
And as some s. of the temple, how it 21.05
And they s. many other words 22.65
are my words which I s. to you, 24.44
But he s. of the temple of his body Jn 2.21
word that Jesus s. to him and went 4.50
He s. of Judas the son of Simon 6.71
the Jews no one s. openly of him. 7.13
"No man ever s. like this man!" 7.46
Again Jesus s. to them, saying, "I am 8.12
These words he s. in the treasury, 8.20
understand that he s. to them of 8.27
As he s. thus, many believed in him. 8.30
Thus he s., and then he said to 11.11
he saw his glory and s. of him. 12.41
another, uncertain of whom he s. 13.22
went out and s. to the maid who 18.16
the Holy Spirit s. beforehand by Ac 1.16
he foresaw and s. of the resurrection 2.31
that all that God s. by the mouth of 3.21
Holy Spirit and s. the word of God 4.31
and the Spirit with which he s. 6.10
And God s. to this effect, that his 7.06
the angel who s. to him at Mount 7.38
even as he who s. to Moses directed 7.44
who s. to him, and how at Damascus 9.27
And he s. and disputed against the 9.29
When the angel who s. to him had 10.07
to Antioch s. to the Greeks also, 11.20
he s. in this way, 'I will give you 13.34
who s. to them and urged them to 13.43
And Paul and Barnabas s. out boldly, 13.46
and so s. that a great company 14.01
we sat down and s. to the women 16.13
And they s. the word of the Lord to 16.32
he s. and taught accurately the 18.25
and they s. with tongues and 19.06
and for three months s. boldly, 19.08
he s. to them in the Hebrew language, 21.40
if a spirit or an angel s. to him?" 23.09
I s. like a child, I thought like a 1Co 13.11
and so I s.," we too believe, and so 2Co 4.13
ways God s. of old to our fathers Heb 1.01
those who s. to you the word of God 13.07
prophets who s. in the name of the Jas 5.10
by the Holy Spirit s. from God. 2Pe 1.21
a dumb ass s. with human voice and 2.16
heard from heaven s. to me again, Rev 10.08
a lamb and it s. like a dragon. 13.11
and s. to me, saying, "Come, I will 21.09

SPOKEN

overthrow the city of which you have s. Gen 19.21
the time of which God had s. to him. 21.02
master's son, as the LORD has s." 24.51
that of which I have s. to you." 28.15
the place where he had s. with him. 35.13
the place where he had s. with him, 35.14
place where God had s. with him, 35.15
since thou hast s. to thy servant; Ex 4.10
which the LORD had s. to Moses, 4.30

SPOKEN (cont.)
as the LORD had s. to Moses. Ex 9.12
as the LORD had s. through Moses. 9.35
that the LORD has s. we will do." 19.08
which the LORD has s. we will do." 24.03
that the LORD has s. we will do, 24.07
place of which I have s. to you; 32.34
thing that you have s. I will do; 33.17
the LORD had s. with him in Mount 34.32
the LORD has s. to them by Moses." Lev 10.11
the LORD indeed s. only through Num 12.02
Has he not s. through us also 12.02
I, the LORD, have s.; surely this 14.35
which the LORD has s. to Moses, 15.22
for we have s. against the LORD and 21.07
said to him, "What has the LORD s.?" 23.17
Or has he s., and will he not 23.19
that you have s. is good for us to Deu 1.14
people, which they have s. to you; 5.28
rightly said all that they have s. 5.28
the LORD had s. with you on the 9.10
the LORD had s. to you on the 10.04
rightly said all that they have s. 18.17
the word which the LORD has not s.?' 18.21
a word which the LORD has not s.; 18.22
the prophet has s. it presumptuously, 18.22
to the LORD your God, as he has s." 26.19
at your head, as the LORD has s. 31.03
all that the LORD had s. to Moses; Jos 11.23
comforted me and s. kindly to your Ru 2.13
kin, of whom Boaz had s., came by. 4.01
all that I have s. concerning his 1Sa 3.12
then have you s. to me in this way?" 9.21
kingdom, of which Samuel had s., 10.16
matter of which you and I have s., 20.23
good that he has s. concerning you, 25.30
"As God lives, if you had not s., 2Sa 2.27
by the maids of whom you have s., 6.22
thou hast s. also of thy servant's 7.19
which thou hast s. concerning thy 7.25
his house, and do as thou hast s.; 7.25
hast s., and with thy blessing 7.29
to him, "Thus has Ahithophel s.; 17.06
The God of Israel has s., the Rock 23.03
which he had s. concerning the 1Ki 2.27
which thou hast s. to thy servant 8.26
is the sign that the LORD has s.: 13.03
also which he had s. to the king, 13.11
eat; for the LORD has s. it."' 14.11
the people answered, "It is well s." 18.24
the LORD has s. evil concerning you 22.23
peace, the LORD has not s. by me." 22.28
word of the LORD which he had s. 22.38
of the LORD which Elijah had s. 2Ki 1.17
you have a word s. on your behalf 4.13
as he had s. by all his servants 17.23
the LORD has s. concerning him: 19.21
the LORD which you have s. is good." 20.19
thou hast also s. of thy servant's 1Ch 17.17
which thou hast s. concerning thy 17.23
for ever, and do as thou hast s.; 17.23
which he had s. in the name of the 21.19
God, as he has s. concerning you. 22.11
and wine, of which my lord has s., 2Ch 2.15
which thou hast s. to thy servant 6.17
the LORD has s. evil concerning 18.22
peace, the LORD has not s. by me." 18.27
women have s. of Josiah in their 35.25
words which the king had s. to me. Neh 2.18
and after I have s., mock on. Job 21.03
you have s. in my hearing, and I 33.08
I have s. once, and I will not 40.05
After the LORD had s. these words 42.07
you have not s. of me what is 42.07
you have not s. of me what is 42.08
I have s. of thy faithfulness and Ps 40.10
God has s. in his sanctuary: "With 60.06
Once God has s.; twice have I 62.11
Glorious things are s. of you, 87.03
A word fitly s. is like apples of Pro 25.11
on the day when she is s. for? Sol 8.08
ear, O earth; for the LORD has s.: Is 1.02
for the mouth of the LORD has s." 1.20
the LORD had s. by Isaiah the son 20.02
LORD, the God of Israel, has s." 21.17
be cut off, for the LORD has s." 22.25
O Sidon, for the sea has s., 23.04
for the LORD has s. this word. 24.03
all the earth; for the LORD has s. 25.08
the LORD has s. concerning him: 37.22
For he has s. to me, and he himself 38.15
the LORD which you have s. is good." 39.08
for the mouth of the LORD has s." 40.05
I have s., and I will bring it to 46.11
have s. and called him, I have 48.15
beginning I have not s. in secret, 48.16
for the mouth of the LORD has s." 58.14
your lips have s. lies, your tongue 59.03
you have s., but you have done all Jer 3.05
for I have s., I have purposed; 4.28
They have s. falsely of the LORD, 5.12
"Because they have s. this word, 5.14
but they have not s. aright; 8.06
whom has the mouth of the LORD s., 9.12
be not proud, for the LORD has s. 13.15
nation, concerning which I have s., 18.08
answered?' or 'What has the LORD s.?' 23.35
you?' or 'What has the LORD s.?' 23.37
and I have s. persistently to you, 25.03
for he has s. to us in the name of 26.16
as the LORD has s. concerning any 27.13
and they have s. in my name lying 29.23
the words that I have s. to you. 30.02
For I have s. the word, says the 34.05
I have s. to you persistently, but 35.14
because I have s. to them and they 35.17
that I have s. to you against 36.02
of the LORD which he had s. to him. 36.04
that I have s. with you and come 38.25
which you have s. to us in the 44.16
be destroyed, as the LORD has s. 48.08
have s. in my jealousy, when I spend Eze 5.13
chastisements—I, the LORD, have s.— 5.15
upon you. I, the LORD, have s." 5.17
They have s. falsehood and divined 13.06
the LORD,' although I have not s.?" 13.07
know that I, the LORD, have s." 17.21
I the LORD have s., and I will do it." 17.24
satisfy my fury; I the LORD have s." 21.17
remembered; for I the LORD have s." 21.32
I the LORD have s., and I will do it. 22.14
Lord GOD,' when the LORD has not s. 22.28
for I have s., says the Lord GOD. 23.34
I the LORD have s.; it shall come to 24.14
for I have s., says the Lord GOD; 26.05
for I the LORD have s., says the 26.14
for I have s., says the Lord GOD." 28.10
of foreigners; I, the LORD, have s. 30.12
among them; I, the LORD, have s. 34.24
the LORD, have s., and I will do it. 36.36
have s., and I have done it, says 37.14
for I have s., says the Lord GOD. 39.05
That is the day of which I have s. 39.08
to you it is s.: The kingdom has Dan 4.31
When he had s. to me according to 10.15
nation far off; for the LORD has s." Joe 3.08
that the LORD has s. against you, Amo 3.01
The Lord GOD has s.; who can but 3.08
house of Esau; for the LORD has s. Ob 1.18
mouth of the LORD of hosts has s. Mic 4.04
say, 'How have we s. against thee?' Mal 3.13
the Lord had s. by the prophet: Mt 1.22
the Lord had s. by the prophet, 2.15
what was s. by the prophet Jeremiah: 2.17

SPOKEN (cont.)

that what was s. by the prophets Mt 2.23
is he who was s. of by the prophet 3.03
that what was s. by the prophet 4.14
fulfil what was s. by the prophet 8.17
fulfil what was s. by the prophet 12.17
fulfil what was s. by the prophet: 13.35
fulfil what was s. by the prophet, 21.04
sacrilege s. of by the prophet 24.15
what had been s. by the prophet 27.09
after he had s. to them, was taken *Mk 16.19
of what was s. to her from the Lk 1.45
and for a sign that is s. against 2.34
And when the voice had s., Jesus 9.36
answered, "Teacher, you have s. well." 20.39
all that the prophets have s.! 24.25
and the word which Jesus had s. Jn 2.22
that I have s. to you are spirit 6.63
We know that God has s. to Moses, 9.29
Now Jesus had s. of his death, but 11.13
said, "An angel has s. to him." 12.29
that the word s. by the prophet 12.38
that I have s. will be his judge 12.48
For I have not s. on my own authority 12.49
When Jesus had thus s., he was troubled 13.21
"These things I have s. to you, 14.25
by the word which I have s. to you. 15.03
These things I have s. to you, 15.11
If I had not come and s. to them, 15.22
When Jesus had s. these words, he 17.01
When Jesus had s. these words, he 18.01
to fulfil the word which he had s., 18.09
"I have s. openly to the world; 18.20
"If I have s. wrongly, bear witness 18.23
but if I have s. rightly, why do you 18.23
which Jesus had s. to show by what 18.32
is what was s. by the prophet Joel: Ac 2.16
And all the prophets who have s., 3.24
testified and s. the word of the 8.25
who is well s. of by the whole 10.22
contradicted what was s. by Paul, 13.45
of God should be s. first to you. 13.46
And when they had s. the word in 14.25
He was well s. of by the brethren 16.02
And when he had s. thus, he knelt down 20.36
all because of the word he had s., 20.38
well s. of by all the Jews who 22.12
has reported or s. any evil about 28.21
that everywhere it is s. against." 28.22
is good to you be s. of as evil. Rom 14.16
last days he has s. to us by a Son, Heb 1.02
things that were to be s. later, 3.05
has somewhere s. of the seventh 4.04
things are s. belonged to another 7.13
no further messages be s. to them. 12.19
which ungodly sinners have s. against him. Jud 1.15

SPOKES

their s., and their hubs, were all 1Ki 7.33
wheels had rims and they had s.; Eze 1.18
and their s., and the wheels were 10.12

SPOKESMAN

elders and a s., one Tertullus. Ac 24.01

SPONGE

of them at once ran and took a s., Mt 27.48
filling a s. full of vinegar, put it Mk 15.36
so they put a s. full of the Jn 19.29

SPORT

how I have made s. of the Egyptians Ex 10.02
"Because you have made s. of me. Num 22.29
Samson, that he may make s. for us." Ju 16.25
prison, and he made s. before them. 16.25
who looked on while Samson made s. 16.27
After he had made s. of them, 1Sa 6.06
me through, and make s. of me." 31.04
uncircumcised come and make s. of me. 1Ch 10.04
"But now they make s. of me, Job 30.01
which thou didst form to s. in it. Ps 104.26
It is like s. to a fool to do wrong, Pro 10.23
Of whom are you making s.? Against whom Is 57.04
scoff, and of rulers they make s. Hab 1.10

SPOT

a swelling or an eruption or a s., Lev 13.02
the diseased s. on the skin of his 13.03
in the diseased s. has turned 13.03
But if the s. is white in the skin 13.04
if the diseased s. is dim and the 13.06
swellng or a reddish-white s., 13.19
But if the s. remains in one place 13.23
raw flesh of the burn becomes a s., 13.24
the hair in the s. has turned 13.25
the hair in the s. is not white 13.26
But if the s. remains in one place 13.28
a reddsh-white diseased s., 13.42
if the diseased s. has not changed 13.55
the leprous s. is on the back or 13.55
shall tear the s. out of the 13.56
a swelling or an eruption or a s., 14.56
and if any s. has cleaved to my Job 31.07
without s. or wrinkle or any such Eph 5.27
of a lamb without blemish or s. 1Pe 1.19
found by him without s. or blemish, 2Pe 3.14

SPOTLESS

no lie was found, for they are s. Rev 14.05

SPOTS

or a woman has s. on the skin of Lev 13.38
on the skin of the body, white s., 13.38
and if the s. on the skin of the 13.39
house with greenish or reddish s., 14.37
his skin or the leopard his s.? Jer 13.23

SPOTTED

speckled and s. sheep and every Gen 30.32
and the s. and speckled among the 30.32
speckled and s. among the goats 30.33
he-goats that were striped and s., 30.35
she-goats that were speckled and s., 30.35
forth striped, speckled, and s. 30.39
'The s. shall be your wages,' then 31.08
wages,' then all the flock bore s.; 31.08
were striped, s., and mottled. 31.10
upon the flock are striped, s., and mottled; 31.12
even the garment s. by the flesh. Jud 1.23

SPRANG

and there s. up fire from the rock Ju 6.21
soil, and immediately they s. up, Mt 13.05
soil, and immediately it s. up, Mk 4.05
his mantle he s. up and came to 10.50
for work, and s. into the sea. Jn 21.07
your feet." And he s. up and walked. Ac 14.10
after one day a south wind s. up, 28.13

SPREAD

From these the coastland peoples s. Gen 10.05
of the Canaanites s. abroad. 10.18
the nations s. abroad on the earth 10.32
and you shall s. abroad to the west 28.14
the famine had s. over all the 41.56
and the more they s. abroad. Ex 1.12
The cherubim shall s. out their 25.20
and unleavened wafers s. with oil. 29.02
The cherubim s. out their wings 37.09
and he s. the tent over the tabernacle, 40.19
or unleavened wafers s. with oil. Lev 2.04
oil, unleavened wafers s. with oil, 7.12
the disease has not s. in the skin, 13.05
the disease has not s. in the skin, 13.06
if the eruption has s. in the skin, 13.08

SPREAD (cont.)

in one place and does not s., Lev 13.23
place and does not s. in the skin, 13.28
and if the itch has not s., 13.32
itch has not s. in the skin and it 13.34
and if the itch has s. in the skin, 13.36
the disease has s. in the garment, 13.51
disease has not s. in the garment 13.53
disease has not s., it is unclean; 13.55
the disease has s. in the walls of 14.39
if the disease has s. in the house, 14.44
disease has not s. in the house 14.48
and s. over that a cloth all of Num 4.06
they shall s. a cloth of blue, and 4.07
then they shall s. over them a 4.08
they shall s. a cloth of blue, and 4.11
and s. a purple cloth over it; 4.13
and they shall s. upon it a covering 4.14
and unleavened wafers s. with oil, 6.15
and they s. them out for themselves 11.32
laid waste until fire s. to Medeba." 21.30
'And they shall s. the garment Deu 22.17
And they s. a garment, and every man Ju 8.25
s. your skirt over your maidservant, Ru 3.09
Israel, and when the battle s., 1Sa 4.02
a bed was s. for Saul upon the roof, 9.25
they were s. abroad over all the 30.16
had come and s. out in the valley 2Sa 5.18
and s. out in the valley of Rephaim 5.22
woman took and s. a covering over 17.19
The battle s. over the face of all 18.08
and s. it for herself on the rock, 21.10
cherubim were s. out so that a 1Ki 6.27
and s. gold upon the cherubim and 6.32
For the cherubim s. out their wings 8.07
and s. forth his hands toward 8.22
it in water and s. it over his 2Ki 8.15
and s. it before the LORD. 19.14
cherubim that s. their wings and 1Ch 28.18
For the cherubim s. out their wings 2Ch 5.08
of Israel, and s. forth his hands. 6.12
and s. forth his hands toward heaven; 6.13
and his fame s. even to the border 26.08
And his fame s. far, for he was 26.15
As soon as the command was s. abroad, 31.05
my knees and s. out my hands to Ez 9.05
"The work is great and widely s., Neh 4.19
and his fame s. throughout all the Est 9.04
and his shoots s. over his garden. Job 8.16
if I s. my couch in darkness, 17.13
my roots s. out to the waters, with 29.19
s. out the skies, hard as a molten 37.18
or s. forth our hands to a strange Ps 44.20
"Can God s. a table in the wilderness? 78.19
O LORD; I s. out my hands to thee. 88.09
He s. a cloud for a covering, and 105.39
to him who s. out the earth upon 136.06
and with cords they have s. a net, 140.05
vain is a net s. in the sight of Pro 1.17
The lips of the wise s. knowledge; 15.07
When you s. forth your hands, I will Is 1.15
its shoots s. abroad and passed 16.08
languish who s. nets upon the 19.08
they s. the rugs, they eat, they 21.05
veil that is s. over all nations. 25.07
And he will s. out his hands in the 25.11
its place, or keep the sail s. out. 33.23
the LORD, and s. it before the LORD. 37.14
who s. forth the earth and what 42.05
who s. out the earth—Who was with 44.24
my right hand s. out the heavens; 48.13
For you will s. abroad to the right 54.03
and to s. sackcloth and ashes under 58.05
I s. out my hands all the day to a 65.02
and they shall be s. before the sun Jer 8.02
is no one to s. my tent again, and to set up 10.20
and he will s. his royal canopy over them 43.10
an eagle, and s. his wings against Moab; 48.40
and s. his wings against Bozrah, and 49.22
he s. a net for my feet; he turned me Lam 1.13
and their wings were s. out above; Eze 1.11
like crystal, s. out above their heads. 1.22
and he s. it before me; and it had 2.10
And I will s. my net over him, and 12.13
and I s. my skirt over you, and 16.08
I will s. my net over him, and he 17.20
they s. their net over him; 19.08
with a table s. before it on which 23.41
who s. terror in the land of the 32.23
who s. terror in the land of the 32.24
of them was s. in the land of the 32.25
for they s. terror in the land of 32.26
For he s. terror in the land of the 32.32
at Mizpah, and a net s. upon Tabor. Hos 5.01
I will s. over them my net; I will bring 7.12
his shoots shall s. out; his beauty 14.06
there is s. upon the mountains a Joe 2.02
for I have s. you abroad as the Zec 2.06
and s. dung upon your faces, the Mal 2.03
So his fame s. throughout all Syria, Mt 4.24
went away and s. his fame through 9.31
Most of the crowd s. their garments 21.08
the trees and s. them on the road. 21.08
story has been s. among the Jews 28.15
once his fame s. everywhere throughout Mk 1.28
and to s. the news, so that Jesus 1.45
And many s. their garments on the 11.08
and others s. leafy branches which 11.08
concerning him s. through the Lk 7.17
they s. their garments on the road. 19.36
The saying s. abroad among the Jn 21.23
that it may s. no further among Ac 4.17
of the Lord s. throughout all the 13.49
and so death s. to all men because Rom 5.12

SPREADING

if it is s. in the skin, then the Lev 13.27
or in anything of skin, it is s.; 13.57
s. out its wings, catching them, Deu 32.11
the people of the LORD s. abroad. 1Sa 2.24
understand the s. of the clouds, Job 36.29
and the s. branches he will hew Is 18.05
sprouted and became a low s. vine, Eze 17.06
the sea a place for the s. of nets; 26.05
be a place for the s. of nets; 26.14
will be a place for the s. of nets; 47.10

SPREADS

But if the eruption s. in the skin, Lev 13.07
and if it s. in the skin, then the 13.22
But if the itch s. in the skin 13.35
of the moon, and s. over it his cloud. Job 26.09
and s. his wings toward the south? 39.26
he s. himself like a threshing 41.30
colored s. of Egyptian linen; Pro 7.16
A perverse man s. strife, and a 16.28
his neighbor s. a net for his feet 29.05
it as a swimmer s. his hands out Is 25.11
and s. them like a tent to dwell in 40.22
The locust s. its wings and flies Nah 3.16
and through us s. the fragrance of 2Co 2.14

SPRIG

will take a s. from the lofty top Eze 17.22

SPRING

found her by a s. of water in the Gen 16.07
the s. on the way to Shur. 16.07
surely return to you in the s., 18.10
in the s., and Sarah shall have a 18.14
Behold, I am standing by the s. of water, 24.13
She went down to the s., and filled 24.16
ran out to the man, to the s. 24.29
standing by the camels at the s. 24.30
"I came today to the s., and said, 24.42

SPRING (cont.)
behold, I am standing by the s. of water; Gen 24.43
she went down to the s., and drew. 24.45
you, and kings shall s. from you. 35.11
bough, a fruitful bough by a s.; 49.22
Nevertheless a s. or a cistern Lev 11.36
sang this song: "S. up, O well! Num 21.17
mountain to the s. of the Waters Jos 15.09
to the s. of the Waters of Nephtoah 18.15
encamped beside the s. of Harod; Ju 7.01
In the s. of the year, the time when 2Sa 11.01
for in the s. the king of Syria 1Ki 20.22
In the s. Benhadad mustered the 20.26
Then he went to the s. of water and 2Ki 2.21
they stopped every s. of water, 3.25
about that time the following s., 4.17
the land in the s. of the year. 13.20
In the s. of the year, the time when 1Ch 20.01
In the s. of the year King Nebuchadnezzar 2Ch 36.10
out of the earth others will s. Job 8.19
their mouths as for the s. rain. 29.23
Faithfulness will s. up from the Ps 85.11
the flint into a s. of water. 114.08
the clouds that bring the s. rain. Pro 16.15
Like a muddied s. or a polluted 25.26
before they s. forth I tell you of Is 42.09
They shall s. up like grass amid 44.04
cause righteousness to s. up also; 45.08
your healing shall s. up speedily; 58.08
like a s. of water, whose waters 58.11
causes what is sown in it to s. up, 61.11
and praise to s. forth before all 61.11
and the s. rain has not come; Jer 3.03
the autumn rain and the s. rain, 5.24
Branch to s. forth for David; 33.15
cause a horn to s. forth to the Eze 29.21
as the s. rains that water the Hos 6.03
his s. shall be parched; it shall strip 13.15
Does a snare s. up from the ground, Amo 3.05
LORD in the season of the s. rain, Zec 10.01
become in him a s. of water Jn 4.14
appeal does not s. from error or 1Th 2.03
of bitterness" s. up and cause Heb 12.15
Does a s. pour forth from the same Jas 3.11

SPRINGING
found there a well of s. water, Gen 26.19

SPRINGS
found the hot s. in the wilderness, Gen 36.24
were twelve s. of water and Ex 15.27
were twelve s. of water and Num 33.09
of water, of fountains and s., Deu 8.07
Negeb, give me also s. of water." Jos 15.19
her the upper s. and the lower s." 15.19
Negeb, give me also s. of water. Ju 1.15
her the upper s. and the lower s. 1.15
land to all the s. of water and to 1Ki 18.05
tree, and stop up all s. of water, 2Ki 3.19
second year what s. of the same; 19.29
water of the s. that were outside 2Ch 32.03
stopped all the s. and the brook 32.04
you entered into the s. of the sea, Job 38.16
Thou didst cleave open s. and brooks; Ps 74.15
of Baca they make it a place of s.; 84.06
alike say, "All my s. are in you." 87.07
Thou makest s. gush forth in the 104.10
s. of water into thirsty ground, 107.33
a parched land into s. of water. 107.35
for from it flow the s. of life. Pro 4.23
Should your s. be scattered abroad, 5.16
there were no s. abounding with 8.24
are like doves beside s. of water, Sol 5.12
and the thirsty ground s. of water; Is 35.07
second year what s. of the same; 37.30
and the dry land s. of water. 41.18
now it s. forth, do you not perceive 43.19
and by s. of water will guide them. 49.10
so judgment s. up like poisonous Hos 10.04
These are waterless s. and mists 2Pe 2.17
guide them to s. of living water; Rev 7.17

SPRINKLE
and s. it upon Aaron and his Ex 29.21
the blood and s. part of the blood Lev 4.06
the blood and s. it seven times 4.17
and he shall s. some of the blood 5.09
and he shall s. it seven times upon 14.07
and s. some oil with his finger 14.16
and shall s. with his right finger 14.27
and s. the house seven times. 14.51
and s. it with his finger on the 16.14
seat he shall s. the blood with 16.14
And he shall s. some of the blood 16.19
priest shall s. the blood on the 17.06
s. the water of expiation upon them, Num 8.07
You shall s. their blood upon the 18.17
and s. some of her blood toward the 19.04
and s. it upon the tent, and upon 19.18
person shall s. upon the unclean 19.19
I will s. clean water upon you, and Eze 36.25
priests shall s. salt upon them 43.24

SPRINKLED
of its blood is s. on a garment, Lev 6.27
on which it was s. in a holy place 6.27
And he s. some of it on the altar 8.11
and s. it upon Aaron and his 8.30
and the priests s. the blood which 2Ch 35.11
their robes and s. dust upon their Job 2.12
lifeblood is s. upon my garments, Is 63.03
gray hairs are s. upon him, Hos 7.09
and s. both the book itself and all Heb 9.19
the same way he s. with the blood 9.21
with our hearts s. clean from an 10.22
kept the Passover and s. the blood, 11.28
and to the s. blood that speaks 12.24

SPRINKLES
He who s. the water for impurity Num 19.21

SPRINKLING
s. it upon the mercy seat and Lev 16.15
For if the s. of defiled persons Heb 9.13
Christ and for s. with his blood: 1Pe 1.02

SPROUT
of the man whom I choose shall s.; Num 17.05
nothing, where no grass can s., Deu 29.23
makes grass to s. from the earth. 2Sa 23.04
does trouble s. from the ground; Job 5.06
that it will s. again, and that its 14.07
the wicked s. like grass and all Ps 92.07
I will make a horn to s. for David; 132.17
open, that salvation may s. forth, Is 45.08
making it bring forth and s., 55.10
and the seed should s. and grow, Mk 4.27

SPROUTED
after them s. seven ears, thin and Gen 41.06
by the east wind, s. after them, 41.23
of Levi had s. and put forth buds, Num 17.08
and it s. and became a low spreading Eze 17.06

SPROUTING
all its fresh s. leaves wither? Eze 17.09

SPRUNG
herb of the field had yet s. up— Gen 2.05

SPUN
who had ability s. with their Ex 35.25
what they had s. in blue and 35.25
with ability s. the goats' hair. 35.26

SPURN
if you s. my statutes, and if your Lev 26.15
I will not s. them, neither will I 26.44
"Will the Lord s. for ever, and Ps 77.07
Thou dost s. all who go astray from 119.118
Do not s. us, for thy name's sake; Jer 14.21

SPURNED
because they s. my ordinances, and Lev 26.43
and s. them, because of the provocation Deu 32.19
and s. the counsel of the Most High Ps 107.11
indignation has s. king and priest Lam 2.06
Israel has s. the good; the enemy Hos 8.03
I have s. your calf, O Samaria. 8.05
the man who has s. the Son of God, Heb 10.29

SPURNS
goes in to her, and then s. her, Deu 22.13
to this man to wife, and he s. her; 22.16
that is not good; he s. not evil. Ps 36.04

SPY
"Send men to s. out the land of Num 13.02
whom Moses sent to s. out the land. 13.16
Moses sent them to s. out the land 13.17
to s. it out, is a land that devours 13.32
we passed through to s. it out, 14.07
whom Moses sent to s. out the land, 14.36
men who went to s. out the land. 14.38
And Moses sent to s. out Jazer; 21.32
whom Joshua sent to s. out Jericho. Jos 6.25
to them, "Go up and s. out the land." 7.02
Kadeshbarnea to s. out the land; 14.07
of Joseph sent to s. out Bethel. Ju 1.23
to s. out the land and to explore 18.02
who had gone to s. out the country 18.14
who had gone to s. out the land 18.17
and to s. it out, and to overthrow 2Sa 10.03
overthrow and to s. out the land?" 1Ch 19.03
slipped in to s. out our freedom Gal 2.04

SPYING
they returned from s. out the land. Num 13.25

SQUADS
him to four s. of soldiers to Ac 12.04

SQUANDERED
and there he s. his property in Lk 15.13

SQUANDERS
with harlots s. his substance. Pro 29.03

SQUARE
the altar shall be s., and its height Ex 27.01
It shall be s. and double, a span 28.16
it shall be s., and two cubits 30.02
it was s., and two cubits was its 37.25
it was s., and three cubits was its 38.01
It was s.; the breastpiece 39.09
into the midst of its open s., Deu 13.16
down in the open s. of the city; Ju 19.15
wayfarer in the open s. of the city; 19.17
do not spend the night in the s." 19.20
from the public s. of Bethshan, 2Sa 21.12
of olivewood, in the form of a s., 1Ki 6.33
doorways and windows had s. frames, 7.05
and its panels were s., not round. 7.31
them in the s. on the east, 2Ch 29.04
to him in the s. at the gate of 32.06
sat in the open s. before the Ez 10.09
man into the s. before the Water Neh 8.01
it facing the s. before the Water 8.03
and in the s. at the Water Gate and 8.16
Gate and in the s. at the Gate of 8.16
in the open s. of the city in Est 4.06
through the open s. of the city, 6.09
through the open s. of the city, 6.11
when I prepared my seat in the s., Job 29.07
yourself a lofty place in every s.; Eze 16.24
your lofty place in every s.; Eze 16.24
your lofty place in every s., 16.31
The altar hearth shall be s., 43.16
The ledge also shall be s., 43.17
Of this a s. plot of five hundred 45.02
be twenty-five thousand cubits s., 48.20

SQUARED
The doorposts of the nave were s.; Eze 41.21

SQUARES
The s. of the town forget them; Job 24.20
city, in the streets and in the s.; Sol 3.02
and in the s. every one wails and Is 15.03
truth has fallen in the public s., 59.14
Search her s. to see if you can Jer 5.01
and the young men from the s. 9.21
Moab and in the s. there is nothing 48.38
her young men shall fall in her s., 49.26
her young men shall fall in her s., 50.30
be built again with s. and moat, Dan 9.25
"In all the s. there shall be Amo 5.16
rush to and fro through the s.; Nah 2.04

SQUEEZED
next morning and s. the fleece, Ju 6.38

STABBED
And if he s. him from hatred, or Num 35.20
"But if he s. him suddenly without 35.22

STABILITY
knowledge its s. will long continue. Pro 28.02
By justice a king gives s. to the land, 29.04
and he will be the s. of your times, Is 33.06
lawless men and lose your own s. 2Pe 3.17

STABLE
s. and steadfast, not shifting from Col 1.23

STACHYS
fellow worker in Christ, and my beloved S. Rom 16.09

STACKED
so that the s. grain or the standing Ex 22.06

STACTE
s., and onycha, and galbanum, sweet Ex 30.34

STADIA
for one thousand six hundred s. Rev 14.20
with his rod, twelve thousand s.; 21.16

STAFF
with only my s. I crossed this Gen 32.10
and your s. that is in your hand." 38.18
the signet and the cord and the s." 38.25
nor the ruler's from between 49.10
feet, and your s. in your hand; Ex 12.11
again and walks abroad with his s., 21.19
When I break your s. of bread, Lev 26.26
that pass under the herdsman's s., 27.32
and he struck the ass with his s. Num 22.27
those who bear the marshal's s.; Ju 5.14
the tip of the s. that was in his 6.21
the tip of the s. that was in his 1Sa 14.27
the tip of the s. that was in my 14.43
Then he took his s. in his hand, 17.40
Benaiah went down to him with a s., 2Sa 23.21
and take my s. in your hand, and go. 2Ki 4.29
and lay my s. upon the face of the 4.29
and laid the s. upon the face of 4.31
on Egypt, that broken reed of a s., 18.21
Benaiah went down to him with a s., 1Ch 11.23
thy rod and thy s., they comfort me. Ps 23.04
land, and broke every s. of bread, 105.16

STAFF (cont.)
Jerusalem and from Judah stay and s., Is 3.01
and the s. for his shoulder, the rod 9.04
rod of my anger, the s. of my fury! 10.05
or as if a s. should lift him who 10.15
lift up their s. against you as 10.24
has broken the s. of the wicked, 14.05
stroke of the s. of punishment 30.32
on Egypt, that broken reed of a s., 36.06
scepter is broken, the glorious s.' Jer 48.17
will break the s. of bread in Eze 4.16
you, and break your s. of bread. 5.16
and break its s. of bread and send 14.13
you have been a s. of reed to the 29.06
and their s. gives them oracles. Hos 4.12
Shepherd thy people with thy s., Mic 7.14
each with s. in hand for very age. Zec 8.04
And I took my s. Grace, and I broke 11.10
Then I broke my second s. Union, 11.14
two tunics, nor sandals, nor a s.; Mt 10.10
for their journey except a s.; Mk 6.08
no s., nor bag, nor bread, nor money; Lk 9.03
in worship over the head of his s. Heb 11.21
given a measuring rod like a s., Rev 11.01

STAFFS
And I took two s.; one I named Zec 11.07

STAG
slaughter, or as a s. is caught fast Pro 7.22
is like a gazelle, or a young s. Sol 2.09
or a young s. upon rugged mountains. 2.17
or a young s. upon the mountains 8.14

STAGE
s. by s., by command of the LORD; Num 33.02

STAGES
from the wilderness of Sin by s., Ex 17.01
set out by s. from the wilderness Num 10.12
These are the s. of the people of 33.01
these are their s. according to 33.02

STAGGER
he makes them s. like a drunken Job 12.25
have made Egypt s. in all her Is 19.14
with wine and s. with strong drink; 28.07
they are confused with wine, they s. 28.07
s., but not with strong drink! 29.09
They shall drink and s. and be Jer 25.16
and boys s. under loads of wood. Lam 5.13
and s., and shall be as though they Ob 1.16
Drink, yourself, and s.! The cup in the Hab 2.16

STAGGERED
they reeled and s. like drunken men, Ps 107.27

STAGGERING
drunk to the dregs the bowl of s. Is 51.17
taken from your hand the cup of s.; 51.22

STAGGERS
as a drunken man s. in his vomit. Is 19.14
The earth s. like a drunken man, it 24.20

STAGNANT
it enters the s. waters of the sea, Eze 47.08

STAIN
the s. of your guilt is still Jer 2.22

STAINED
and I have s. all my raiment. Is 63.03

STAINING
s. the whole body, setting on fire Jas 3.06

STAIRS
one went up by s. to the middle 1Ki 6.08
as far as the s. that go down from Neh 3.15
Upon the s. of the Levites stood 9.04
them by the s. of the city of 12.37

STAIRWAY
and its s. had eight steps. Eze 40.31
and its s. had eight steps. 40.34
and its s. had eight steps. 40.37
side of the temple a s. led upward, 41.07

STAKE
turn now, my vindication is at s. Job 6.29

STAKES
whose s. will never be plucked up, Is 33.20
your cords and strengthen your s. 54.02

STALK
and good, were growing on one s. Gen 41.05
growing on one s., full and good; 41.22

STALKS
them with the s. of flax which she Jos 2.06
the pestilence that s. in darkness, Ps 91.06
an adulteress s. a man's very life. Pro 6.26

STALL
calves from the midst of the s.; Amo 6.04
leaping like calves from the s. Mal 4.02

STALLIONS
They were well-fed lusty s., Jer 5.08
of their s. the whole land quakes. 8.16
stamping of the hoofs of his s., 47.03
at grass, and neigh like s., 50.11

STALLS
forty thousand s. of horses for 1Ki 4.26
four thousand s. for horses and 2Ch 9.25
and s. for all kinds of cattle, 32.28
and there be no herd in the s., Hab 3.17

STAMMERERS
tongue of the s. will speak readily Is 32.04

STAMMERING
s. in a tongue which you cannot understand. Is 33.19

STAMP
and s. your foot, and say, Alas! Eze 6.11
bears the very s. of his nature, Heb 1.03

STAMPED
them and s. them down like the 2Sa 22.43
your hands and s. your feet and Eze 25.06
and s. the residue with its feet. Dan 7.07
and s. the residue with its feet; 7.19

STAMPING
noise of the s. of the hoofs of Jer 47.03

STAND
But they said, "S. back!" Gen 19.09
why do you s. outside? For I have 24.31
also the ground on which they s. Ex 8.21
could not s. before Moses because 9.11
the morning and s. before Pharaoh, 9.13
s. firm, and see the salvation of 14.13
Behold, I will s. before you there 17.06
tomorrow I will s. on the top of 17.09
all the people s. about you from 18.14
they took their s. at the foot of 19.17
descend and s. at the door of the 33.09
where you shall s. upon the rock; 33.21
you shall not s. forth against the Lev 19.16
no power to s. before your enemies. 26.37
priest values it, so it shall s. 27.14
it shall s. at your full valuation; 27.17
them take their s. there with you. Num 11.16
and to s. before the congregation 16.09

STAND (cont.)

LORD took his s. in the way as his Num 22.22
that thou didst s. in the road 22.34
"S. beside your burnt offering, and 23.03
"S. here beside your burnt offering, 23.15
cause him to s. before Eleazar the 27.19
And he shall s. before Eleazar the 27.21
caused him to s. before Eleazar 27.22
then all her vows shall s., 30.04
she has bound herself shall s. 30.04
she has bound herself, shall s.; 30.05
then her vows shall s., and her pledges 30.07
she has bound herself shall s. 30.07
herself, shall s. against her. 30.09
oppose her; then all her vows shall s., 30.11
which she bound herself shall s. 30.11
shall not s.: her husband has made 30.12
everything that can s. the fire, 31.23
and whatever cannot s. the fire, 31.23
But you, s. here by me, and I will Deu 5.31
shall be able to s. against you, 7.24
'Who can s. before the sons of Anak?' 9.02
to s. before the LORD to minister 10.08
shall be able to s. against you; 11.25
to s. and minister in the name of 18.05
Levites who s. to minister there 18.07
You shall s. outside, and the man to 24.11
these shall s. upon Mount Gerizim 27.12
And these shall s. upon Mount Ebal 27.13
"You s. this day all of you before 29.10
be able to s. before you all the Jos 1.05
you shall s. still in the Jordan.'" 3.08
from above shall s. in one heap." 3.13
for the place where you s. is holy." 5.15
Israel cannot s. before their 7.12
you cannot s. before your enemies, 7.13
not a man of them s. before you." 10.08
s. thou still at Gibeon, and thou 10.12
and shall s. at the entrance of 20.04
"S. at the door of the tent, and if Ju 4.20
They made him s. between the 16.25
"Who is able to s. before the LORD, 1Sa 6.20
Now therefore s. still, that I may 12.07
Now therefore s. still and see this 12.16
then we will s. still in our place, 14.09
came forward and took his s., 17.16
will go out and s. beside my father 19.03
'S. beside me and slay me; for anguish 2Sa 1.09
and took their s. on the top of a 2.25
rise early and s. beside the way 15.02
king said, "Turn aside, and s. here." 18.30
of Joab's men took his s. by Amasa, 20.11
Yea, does not my house s. so with God? 23.05
But he took his s. in the midst of 23.12
each s. was four cubits long, four 1Ki 7.27
Moreover each s. had four bronze 7.30
at the four corners of each s.; 7.34
the top of the s. there was a 7.35
the top of the s. its stays and 7.35
could not s. to minister because 8.11
who continually s. before you and 10.08
before whom I s., there shall be 17.01
before whom I s., I will surely 18.15
and s. upon the mount before the 19.11
and s., and call on the name of the 2Ki 5.11
two kings could not s. before him; 10.04
how then can we s.?" 10.04
But he took his s. in the midst of 1Ch 11.14
And they shall s. every morning, 12.30
could not s. to minister because 2Ch 5.14
who continually s. before you and 9.07
we will s. before this house, and 20.09
s. still, and see the victory of the 20.17
chosen you to s. in his presence, 29.11
that you s. siege in Jerusalem? 32.10
Jerusalem and in Benjamin s. to it. 34.32
And s. in the holy place according 35.05
for none can s. before thee because Ez 9.15
we cannot s. in the open. Nor is this 10.13
Let our officials s. for the whole 10.14
"S. up and bless the LORD your God Neh 9.05
one could make a s. against them, Est 9.02
his house, but it does not s.; Job 8.15
at last he will s. upon the earth; 19.25
I s., and thou dost not heed me. 30.20
I s. up in the assembly, and cry for 30.28
because they s. there, and answer no 32.16
before me; take your s. 33.05
he cannot s. still at the sound of 39.24
down the wicked where they s. 40.12
then is he that can s. before me? 41.10
wicked will not s. in the judgment, Ps 1.05
boastful may not s. before thy eyes 5.05
Why dost thou s. afar off, O LORD? 10.01
but we shall rise and s. upright. 20.08
and s. in awe of him, all you sons 22.23
And who shall s. in his holy place? 24.03
of the world s. in awe of him! 33.08
and companions s. aloof from my 38.11
plague, and my kinsmen s. afar off. 38.11
Who can s. before thee when once 76.07
and made the waters s. like a heap. 78.13
my covenant will s. firm for him. 89.28
it shall s. firm while the skies 89.37
hast not made him s. in battle. 89.43
By thy appointment they s. this day; 119.91
iniquities, Lord, who could s.? 130.03
who s. by night in the house of the 134.01
you that s. in the house of the 135.02
who can s. before his cold? 147.17
way, in the paths she takes her s.; Pro 8.02
the house of the righteous will s. 12.07
his work? he will s. before kings; 22.29
he will not s. before obscure men. 22.29
presence or s. in the place of the 25.06
but who can s. before jealousy? 27.04
youth, who was to s. in his place; Ecc 4.15
It shall not s., and it shall not Is 7.07
speak a word, but it will not s., 8.10
of Jesse shall s. as an ensign to 11.10
I have purposed, so shall it s., 14.24
saw cried: "Upon a watchtower I s., 21.08
horsemen took their s. at the gates. 22.07
agreement with Sheol will not s.; 28.18
and will s. in awe of the God of 29.23
word of our God will s. for ever. 40.08
let them s. forth, they shall be 44.11
done, saying, 'My counsel shall s., 46.10
S. fast in your enchantments and 47.12
let them s. forth and save you, 47.13
to them, they s. forth together. 48.13
Let us s. up together. Who is my 50.08
s. up, O Jerusalem, you who have 51.17
Aliens shall s. and feed your 61.05
"S. by the roads, and look, and ask Jer 6.16
"S. in the gate of the LORD's house, 7.02
and then come and s. before me in 7.10
The wild asses s. on the bare 14.06
you, and you shall s. before me. 15.19
"Go and s. in the Benjamin Gate, by 17.19
S. in the court of the LORD's house, 26.02
palace shall s. where it used to 30.18
never lack a man to s. before me." 35.19
to s. for you before the Chaldeans 40.10
shall know whose word will s., 44.28
will surely s. against you for 44.29
Say, 'S. ready and be prepared, for 46.14
Why did not your bull s.? Jer 46.15
and fled together, they did not s.; 46.21
S. by the way and watch, O inhabitant 48.19
What shepherd can s. before me? 49.20
What shepherd can s. before me? 50.44
and let him not s. up in his coat 51.03
LORD's purposes against Babylon s., 51.29

STAND (cont.)
from the sword, go, s. not still! Jer 51.50
s. upon your feet, and I will speak Eze 2.01
that it might s. in battle in the 13.05
keeping his covenant it might s.) 17.14
up the wall and s. in the breach 22.30
pilots of the sea s. on the shore 27.29
shall take his s. by the post of 46.02
Fishermen will s. beside the sea; 47.10
they were to s. before the king. Dan 1.05
an end, and it shall s. for ever; 2.44
and made to s. upon two feet like 7.04
no beast could s. before him, 8.04
ram had no power to s. before him, 8.07
and s. upright, for now I have been 10.11
forces of the south shall not s., 11.15
there shall be no strength to s. 11.15
will, and none shall s. before him; 11.16
and he shall s. in the glorious 11.16
it shall not s. or be to his 11.17
but he shall not s., for plots shall 11.25
their God shall s. firm and take 11.32
and shall s. in your allotted place 12.13
he who handles the bow shall not s., Amo 2.15
How can Jacob s.? He is so small!" 7.02
How can Jacob s.? He is so small!" 7.05
And he shall s. and feed his flock Mic 5.04
Who can s. before his indignation? Nah 1.06
I will take my s. to watch, and Hab 2.01
anointed who s. by the LORD of the Zec 4.14
his feet shall s. on the Mount of 14.04
and who can s. when he appears? Mal 3.02
but on a s., and it gives light to Mt 5.15
they love to s. and pray in the 6.05
divided against itself will s.; 12.25
how then will his kingdom s.? 12.26
'Why do you s. here idle all day?' 20.06
itself, that kingdom cannot s. Mk 3.24
that house will not be able to s. 3.25
he cannot s., but is coming to an 3.26
or under a bed, and not on a s.? 4.21
And whenever you s. praying, 11.25
and you will s. before governors 13.09
who s. in the presence of God; Lk 1.19
withered hand, "Come and s. here." 6.08
under a bed, but puts it on a s., 8.16
himself, how will his kingdom s.? 11.18
but on a s., that those who enter 11.33
will begin to s. outside and to 13.25
and to s. before the Son of man." 21.36
why do you s. looking into heaven?" Ac 1.11
"Go and s. in the temple and speak 5.20
Peter lifted him up, saying, "S. up; 10.26
"S. upright on your feet." 14.10
And now I s. here on trial for hope 26.06
But rise and s. upon your feet; 26.16
and so I s. here testifying both to 26.22
you must s. before Caesar; and lo, God 27.24
to this grace in which we s., Rom 5.02
but you s. fast only through faith. 11.20
do not become proud, but s. in awe. 11.20
the Master is able to make him s. 14.04
we shall all s. before the judgment 14.10
you received, in which you s., 1Co 15.01
Be watchful, s. firm in your faith, 16.13
for you s. firm in your faith. 2Co 1.24
s. fast therefore, and do not submit Gal 5.01
may be able to s. against the Eph 6.11
day, and having done all, to s. 6.13
S. therefore, having girded your 6.14
of you that you s. firm in one Php 1.27
s. firm thus in the Lord, my beloved 4.01
taking his s. on visions, puffed up Col 2.18
that you may s. mature and fully 4.12
if you s. fast in the Lord. 1Th 3.08
s. firm and hold to the traditions 2Th 2.15
so that the rest may s. in fear. 1Ti 5.20
"S. there," or, "Sit at my feet," Jas 2.03
grace of God; s. fast in it. 1Pe 5.12
Behold, I s. at the door and knock; Rev 3.20
has come, and who can s. before it?" 6.17
the seven angels who s. before God, 8.02
lampstands which s. before the Lord 11.04
they will s. far off, in fear of her 18.10
will s. far off, in fear of her 18.15

STANDARD
camp and every man by his own s.; Num 1.52
shall encamp each by his own s., 2.02
shall be of the s. of the camp of 2.03
shall be the s. of the camp of 2.10
each in position, s. by s. 2.17
shall be the s. of the camp of 2.18
shall be the s. of the camp of Dan 2.25
shall set out last, s. by s. 2.31
The s. of the camp of the men of 10.14
And the s. of the camp of Reuben 10.18
And the s. of the camp of the men 10.22
Then the s. of the camp of the men 10.25
length, in cubits of the old s., 2Ch 3.03
officers desert the s. in panic, Is 31.09
Raise a s. toward Zion, flee for Jer 4.06
How long must I see the s., 4.21
Set up a s. against the walls of 51.12
"Set up a s. on the earth, blow the 51.27
the homer shall be the s. measure. Eze 45.11
heart to the s. of teaching to Rom 6.17

STANDARDS
so they encamped by their s., Num 2.34
were wise according to worldly s., 1Co 1.26

STANDING
Behold, I am s. by the spring of Gen 24.13
he was s. by the camels at the 24.30
behold, I am s. by the spring of 24.43
that he was s. by the Nile, 41.01
my dream I was s. on the banks of 41.17
on which you are s. is holy ground." Ex 3.05
grain or the s. grain or the field 22.06
pillar of cloud s. at the door of 33.10
angel of the LORD s. in the road, Num 22.23
angel of the LORD s. in the way, 22.31
of Moab were s. beside his burnt 23.06
he was s. beside his burnt offering, 23.17
put the sickle to the s. grain. Deu 16.09
go into your nieghbor's s. grain, 23.25
sickle to your neighbor's s. grain. 23.25
go into the s. grain of the Ju 15.05
up the shocks and the s. grain, 15.05
woman who was s. here in your 1Sa 1.26
and Samuel s. as head over them, the 19.20
all his servants were s. about him. 22.06
who were s. by rent their garments 2Sa 13.31
and two lions s. beside the arm 1Ki 10.19
Jeroboam was s. by the altar to 13.01
road, and the lion s. by the body. 13.25
and the lion s. beside the body. 13.28
host of heaven s. beside him on 22.19
as they both were s. by the Jordan. 2Ki 2.07
watchman was s. on the tower in 9.17
was the king s. by the pillar, 11.14
of the LORD was s. by the threshing 1Ch 21.15
of the LORD s. between earth and 21.16
and two lions s. beside the arm 2Ch 9.18
host of heaven s. on his right 18.18
was the king s. by his pillar at 23.13
they are still s. guard let them Neh 7.03
gatekeepers s. guard at the 12.25
saw Queen Esther s. in the court, Est 5.02
"Haman is there, s. in the court." 6.05
is s. in Haman's house, fifty cubits 7.09
Our feet have been s. within your Ps 122.02
a man of humble s. who works for Pro 12.09
stump remains s. when it is felled Is 6.13

STANDING (cont.)

reaper gathers s. grain and his Is 17.05
or incense altars will remain s. 27.09
people who were s. in the house of Jer 28.05
the son of Shaphan s. among them. Eze 8.11
cherubim were s. on the south side 10.03
and he was s. in the gateway. 40.03
While the man was s. beside me, 43.06
a ram s. on the bank of the river. Dan 8.03
I had seen s. on the bank of the 8.06
as I was s. on the bank of the 10.04
The s. grain has no heads, it shall Hos 8.07
the Lord was s. beside a wall built Amo 7.07
I saw the LORD s. beside the altar, 9.01
take away from you its s. place. Mic 1.11
He was s. among the myrtle trees in Zec 1.08
So the man who was s. among the 1.10
LORD who was s. among the myrtle 1.11
the high priest s. before the 3.01
and Satan s. at his right hand to 3.01
Now Joshua was s. before the angel, 3.03
to those who were s. before him, 3.04
the angel of the LORD was s. by. 3.05
access among those who are s. here. 3.07
and your brothers are s. outside, *Mt 12.47
there are some s. here who will 16.28
he saw others s. idle in the 20.03
he went out and found others s.; 20.06
s. in the holy place (let the 24.15
and s. outside they sent to him and Mk 3.31
there are some s. here who will 9.01
of the Lord s. on the right side Lk 1.11
he was s. by the lake of Gennesaret. 5.01
and s. behind him at his feet, 7.38
and your brothers are s. outside, 8.20
there are some s. here who will 9.27
s. far off, would not even lift up 18.13
again John was s. with two of his Jn 1.35
Now six stone jars were s. there, 2.06
alone with the woman s. before him. * 8.09
on account of the people s. by, 11.42
The crowd s. by heard it and said 12.29
who betrayed him, was s. with them. 18.05
and they were s. and warming 18.18
was with them, s. and warming himself. 18.18
of the officers s. by struck Jesus 18.22
Now Simon Peter was s. and warming 18.25
but s. by the cross of Jesus were 19.25
the disciple whom he loved s. near, 19.26
she turned round and saw Jesus s., 20.14
But Peter, s. with the eleven, lifted Ac 21.4
him this man is s. before you well. 4.10
had been healed s. beside them, 4.14
and the sentries s. at the doors, 5.23
in prison are s. in the temple and 5.25
where you are s. is holy ground. 7.33
and Jesus s. at the right hand of 7.55
the Son of man s. at the right 7.56
seen the angel s. in his house and 11.13
told that Peter was s. at the gate. 12.14
women of high s. and the leading 13.50
Macedonia was s. beseeching him 16.09
women of high s. as well as men. 17.12
So Paul, s. in the middle of the 17.22
s. on the steps, motioned with his 21.40
and s. by me said to me, 'Brother 22.13
I also was s. by and approving, and 22.20
to the centurion who was s. by, 22.25
I cried out while s. among them, 24.21
"I am s. before Caesar's tribunal, 25.10
gain a good s. for themselves and 1Ti 3.13
as long as the outer tent is still s. Heb 9.08
the Judge is s. at the doors. Jas 5.09
faith of equal s. with ours in the 2Pe 1.01
I saw a Lamb s., as though it had Rev 5.06
saw four angels s. at the four 7.01
s. before the throne and before the 7.09
whom I saw s. on sea and land 10.05
angel who is s. on the sea and on 10.08
s. beside the sea of glass with 15.02
Then I saw an angel s. in the sun, 19.17
s. before the throne, and books were 20.12

STANDS

and it s. to this day, that Pharaoh Gen 47.26
and thy cloud s. over them and thou Num 14.14
die until he s. before the congregation 35.12
who s. before you, he shall enter; Deu 1.38
the priest who s. to minister 17.12
as with him who s. here with us 29.15
which s. there to this day. Jos 8.29
where the LORD's tabernacle s., 22.19
our God that s. before his tabernacle!" 22.29
to this day it still s. at Ophrah, Ju 6.24
He also made the ten s. of bronze; 1Ki 7.27
This was the construction of the s.: 7.28
were of one piece with the s.; 7.32
were of one piece with the s. 7.34
After this manner he made the ten s.; 7.37
was a laver for each of the ten s. 7.38
And he set the s., five on the 7.39
the ten s., and the ten lavers upon the s.; 7.43
Ahaz cut off the frames of the s., 2Ki 16.17
and the s. and the bronze sea that 25.13
and the s., which Solomon had made 25.16
the world s. firm, never to be moved 1Ch 16.30
s. also, and the lavers upon the s., 2Ch 4.14
nor s. in the way of sinners, nor Ps 1.01
My foot s. on level ground; in the 26.12
The counsel of the LORD s. for ever, 33.11
every man s. as a mere breath! 39.05
your right hand s. the queen in 45.09
On the holy mount s. the city he 87.01
Who s. up for me against evildoers? 94.16
For he s. at the right hand of the 109.31
established the earth, and it s. fast. 119.90
but my heart s. in awe of thy words 119.161
the root of the righteous s. firm. Pro 12.12
there he s. behind our wall, gazing Sol 2.09
contend, he s. to judge his people. Is 3.13
things, and by noble things he s. 32.08
it in its place, and it s. there; 46.07
and righteousness s. afar off; 59.14
the s., and the rest of the vessels Jer 27.19
and the s. and the bronze sea that 52.17
and the s., which Solomon the king 52.20
king of Babylon s. at the parting Eze 21.21
"The thing s. fast, according to the Dan 6.12
against the man who s. next to me, Zec 13.07
but among you s. one whom you do Jn 1.26
who s. and hears him, rejoices 3.29
his own master that he s. or falls. Rom 14.04
thinks that he s. take heed lest 1Co 10.12
But God's firm foundation s., 2Ti 2.19
And every priest s. daily at his Heb 10.11
For it s. in scripture: "Behold, I am 1Pe 2.06

STANK

together in heaps, and the land s. Ex 8.14

STAR

a s. shall come forth out of Jacob, Num 24.17
from heaven, O Day S., son of Dawn! Is 14.12
we have seen his s. in the East, Mt 2.02
them what time the s. appeared; 2.07
and lo, the s. which they had seen 2.09
When they saw the s., they rejoiced 2.10
and the s. of the god Rephan, the Ac 7.43
for s. differs from s. in glory. 1Co 15.41
and the morning s. rises in your 2Pe 1.19
and I will give him the morning s. Rev 2.28
and a great s. fell from heaven, 8.10
The name of the s. is Wormwood. 8.11
and I saw a s. fallen from heaven 9.01
of David, the bright morning s." 22.16

STARE
they s. and gloat over me; Ps 22.17
Those who see you will s. at you, Is 14.16
or why do you s. at us, as though by Ac 3.12

STARED
And he fixed his gaze and s. at him, 2Ki 8.11
And he s. at him in terror, and said, Ac 10.04

STAR-GOD
your king, and Kaiwan your s., Amo 5.26

STARS
rule the night; he made the s. also. Gen 1.16
toward heaven, and number the s., 15.05
descendants as the s. of heaven and 22.17
descendants as the s. of heaven, 26.04
and eleven s. were bowing down to 37.09
descendants as the s. of heaven, Ex 32.13
this day as the s. of heaven for Deu 1.10
the sun and the moon and the s., 4.19
made you as the s. of heaven for 10.22
Whereas you were as the s. of 28.62
From heaven fought the s., Ju 5.20
Israel as many as the s. of heaven. 1Ch 27.23
break of dawn till the s. came out. Neh 4.21
descendants as the s. of heaven, 9.23
Let the s. of its dawn be dark; Job 3.09
does not rise; who seals up the s.; 9.07
See the highest s., how lofty 22.12
bright and the s. are not clean in 25.05
when the morning s. sang together, 38.07
moon and the s. which thou hast Ps 8.03
the moon and s. to rule over the 136.09
He determines the number of the s., 147.04
praise him, all you shining s.! 148.03
and the s. are darkened and the Ecc 12.02
For the s. of the heavens and their Is 13.10
above the s. of God I will set my 14.13
the heavens, who gaze at the s., 47.13
moon and the s. for light by night, Jer 31.35
heavens, and make their s. dark; Eze 32.07
the host of the s. it cast down to Dan 8.10
like the s. for ever and ever. 12.03
and the s. withdraw their shining. Joe 2.10
and the s. withdraw their shining. 3.15
your nest is set among the s., Ob 1.04
more than the s. of the heavens. Nah 3.16
and the s. will fall from heaven, Mt 24.29
and the s. will be falling from Mk 13.25
be signs in sun and moon and s., Lk 21.25
neither sun nor s. appeared for Ac 27.20
moon, and another glory of the s.; 1Co 15.41
as many as the s. of heaven and as Heb 11.12
wandering s. for whom the nether Jud 1.13
in his right hand he held seven s., Rev 1.16
of the seven s. which you saw in 1.20
the seven s. are the angels of the 1.20
holds the seven s. in his right 2.01
spirits of God and the seven s. 3.01
and the s. of the sky fell to the 6.13
of the moon, and a third of the s., 8.12
on her head a crown of twelve s.; 12.01
down a third of the s. of heaven, 12.04

START
and s. early in the morning, and 1Sa 29.10

STARTED
So the men s. on their way; and Joshua Jos 18.08
Then she s. with her daughters-in-law Ru 1.06
for an insurrection s. in the city, Lk 23.19
and s. across the sea to Capernaum. Jn 6.17

STARTING
Moses wrote down their s. places, Num 33.02
according to their s. places. 33.02

STARTLE
so shall he s. many nations; kings shall Is 52.15

STARTLED
At midnight the man was s., and turned over, Ru 3.08
But they were s. and frightened, and Lk 24.37

STARTS
back upon him who s. it rolling. Pro 26.27

STATE
it, and let it be in a s. of siege, Eze 4.03
be restored to its rightful s." Dan 8.14
and the last s. of that man becomes Mt 12.45
and the last s. of that man becomes Lk 11.26
accusers also to s. before you what Ac 23.30
remain in the s. in which he was 1Co 7.20
in whatever s. each was called, 7.24
in whatever s. I am, to be content. Php 4.11
the last s. has become worse for 2Pe 2.20

STATELY
Three things are s. in their tread; Pro 30.29
four are s. in their stride: 30.29
You are s. as a palm tree, and your Sol 7.07
oars can go, nor s. ship can pass. Is 33.21
you sat upon a s. couch, with a Eze 23.41

STATEMENT
departed, after Paul had made one s.: Ac 28.25
but by the open s. of the truth we 2Co 4.02

STATES
He who s. his case first seems Pro 18.17

STATION
each to his s. and each opposite Neh 7.03
you will be cast down from your s. Is 22.19
and s. myself on the tower, and look Hab 2.01

STATIONED
So they s. the forces, the main Jos 8.13
whom he s. in the chariot cities 1Ki 10.26
Now Jehu had s. eighty men outside, 2Ki 10.24
s. hitherto in the king's gate on 1Ch 9.18
whom he s. in the chariot cities 2Ch 1.14
whom he s. in the chariot cities 9.25
He s. the gatekeepers at the gates 23.19
And he s. the Levites in the house 29.25
I s. the people according to their Neh 4.13
at my post I am s. whole nights. Is 21.08

STATIONS
together and set them in their s. Neh 13.11
Take your s. with your helmets, Jer 46.04

STATURE
we saw in it are men of great s. Num 13.32
to grow both in s. and in favor 1Sa 2.26
appearance or on the height of his s., 16.07
where there was a man of great s., 2Sa 21.20
an Egyptian, a man of great s., 1Ch 11.23
where there was a man of great s., 20.06
men of s., shall come over to you Is 45.14
the heads of persons of every s., Eze 13.18
increased in wisdom and in s., Lk 2.52
crowd, because he was small of s. 19.03
measure of the s. of the fulness Eph 4.13

STATUTE
made it a s. concerning the land Gen 47.26
made for them a s. and an ordinance Ex 15.25
It shall be a s. for ever to be 27.21
be a perpetual s. for him and for 28.43
shall be theirs by a perpetual s. 29.09
it shall be a s. for ever to them, 30.21
be a perpetual s. throughout your Lev 3.17
it shall be a s. for ever throughout 10.09
"And it shall be a s. to you for 16.29

STATUTE (cont.)

yourselves; it is a s. for ever. Lev 16.31
shall be an everlasting s. for you, 16.34
This shall be a s. for ever to them 17.07
it is a s. for ever throughout your 23.14
it is a s. for ever in all your 23.21
it is a s. for ever throughout your 23.31
it is a s. for ever throughout your 23.41
it shall be a s. for ever throughout 24.03
to all the s. for the passover Num 9.12
according to the s. of the passover 9.14
you shall have one s., both for the 9.14
for a perpetual s. throughout your 10.08
shall be one s. for you and for 15.15
a perpetual s. throughout your 15.15
be a perpetual s. throughout your 18.23
"This is the s. of the law which 19.02
sojourns among them, a perpetual s. 19.10
shall be a perpetual s. for them. 19.21
of Israel a s. and ordinance, 27.11
"This is the s. of the law which 31.21
shall be for a s. and ordinance to 35.29
he made it a s. and an ordinance 1Sa 30.25
which he confirmed as a s. to Jacob, 1Ch 16.17
For it is a s. for Israel, an Ps 81.04
thee, who frame mischief by s.? 94.20
which he confirmed to Jacob as a s., 105.10

STATUTES

commandments, my s., and my laws." Gen 26.05
commandments and keep all his s., Ex 15.26
them know the s. of God and his 18.16
teach them the s. and the decisions, 18.20
Israel all the s. which the LORD Lev 10.11
You shall not walk in their s. 18.03
and keep my s. and walk in them. 18.04
therefore keep my s. and my ordinances, 18.05
shall keep my s. and my ordinances 18.26
"You shall keep my s. You shall not 19.19
observe all my s. and all my 19.37
Keep my s., and do them; 20.08
keep all my s. and all my ordinances, 20.22
"Therefore you shall do my s., 25.18
"If you walk in my s. and observe 26.03
if you spurn my s., and if your 26.15
and their soul abhorred my s. 26.43
These are the s. and ordinances and 26.46
to all its s. and all its ordinances Num 9.03
These are the s. which the LORD 30.16
heed to the s. and the ordinances Deu 4.01
have taught you s. and ordinances, 4.05
who, when they hear all these s., 4.06
there that has s. and ordinances 4.08
to teach you s. and ordinances, 4.14
shall keep his s. and his commandments, 4.40
the s., and the ordinances, which 4.45
the s. and the ordinances which I 5.01
commandment and the s. and the 5.31
the s. and the ordinances which the 6.01
keeping all his s. and his commandments, 6.02
and his s., which he has commanded 6.17
testimonies and the s. and the 6.20
commanded us to do all these s., 6.24
and the s., and the ordinances, 7.11
and his ordinances and his s., 8.11
commandments and s. of the LORD, 10.13
his s., his ordinances, and his 11.01
to do all the s. and the ordinances 11.32
"These are the s. and ordinances 12.01
be careful to observe these s. 16.12
the words of this law and these s., 17.19
you to do these s. and ordinances; 26.16
and keep his s. and his commandments 26.17
his commandments and his s., 27.10
commandments and his s. which I 28.15
commandments and his s. which he 28.45
commandments and his s. which are 30.10
commandments and his s. and his 30.16
and made s. and ordinances for them Jos 24.25
and from his s. I did not turn 2Sa 22.23
in his ways and keeping his s., 1Ki 2.03
walking in the s. of David his 3.03
keeping my s. and my commandments, 3.14
will walk in my s. and obey my 6.12
his s., and his ordinances, which he 8.58
walking in his s. and keeping his 8.61
and keeping my s. and my ordinances, 9.04
commandments and my s. which I have 9.06
covenant and my s. which I have 11.11
and keeping my s. and my ordinances, 11.33
who kept my commandments and my s.; 11.34
by keeping my s. and my commandments, 11.38
and keep my commandments and my s., 2Ki 17.13
They despised his s., and his covenant 17.15
not follow the s. or the ordinances 17.34
And the s. and the ordinances and 17.37
and his testimonies and his s., 23.03
to observe the s. and the ordinances 1Ch 22.13
and thy s., performing all, and that 29.19
and keeping my s. and my ordinances, 2Ch 7.17
and forsake my s. and my commandments 7.19
s. or ordinances, then you shall 19.10
the s., and the ordinances given 33.08
and his testimonies and his s., 34.31
to teach his s. and ordinances in Ez 7.10
of the LORD and his s. for Israel: 7.11
the s., and the ordinances which Neh 1.07
true laws, good s. and commandments, 9.13
commandments and s. and a law by 9.14
Lord and his ordinances and his s. 10.29
and his s. I did not put away from Ps 18.22
right have you to recite my s., 50.16
if they violate my s. and do not 89.31
and the s. that he gave them. 99.07
end that they should keep his s., 105.45
may be steadfast in keeping thy s.! 119.05
I will observe thy s.; O forsake me 119.08
thou, O LORD; teach me thy s.! 119.12
I will delight in thy s.; I will not 119.16
servant will meditate on thy s. 119.23
answer me; teach me thy s.! 119.26
Teach me, O LORD, the way of thy s.; 119.33
and I will meditate on thy s. 119.48
Thy s. have been my songs in the 119.54
steadfast love; teach me thy s.! 119.64
dost good; teach me thy s. 119.68
afflicted, that I might learn thy s. 119.71
May my heart be blameless in thy s., 119.80
yet I have not forgotten thy s. 119.83
heart to perform thy s. for ever, 119.112
have regard for thy s. continually! 119.117
all who go astray from thy s.; 119.118
steadfast love, and teach me thy s. 119.124
thy servant, and teach me thy s. 119.135
me, O LORD! I will keep thy s. 119.145
for they do not seek thy s. 119.155
that thou dost teach me thy s. 119.171
his s. and ordinances to Israel. 147.19
violated the s., broken the everlasting Is 24.05
my law and my s. which I set before you Jer 44.10
law and in his s. and in his testimonies; 44.23
and against my s. more than the Eze 5.06
ordinances and not walking in my s. 5.06
walked in my s. or kept my ordinances, 5.07
for you have not walked in my s., 11.12
may walk in my s. and keep my 11.20
walks in my s., and is careful to 18.09
my ordinances, and walks in my s.; 18.17
been careful to observe all my s., 18.19
keeps all my s. and does what is 18.21
I gave them my s. and showed them 20.11
not walk in my s. but rejected my 20.13
ordinances and did not walk in my s., 20.16
not walk in the s. of your fathers, 20.18
walk in my s., and be careful to 20.19
they did not walk in my s., and were not 20.21

STATUTES (cont.)

had rejected my s. and profaned my Eze 20.24
Moreover I gave them s. that were 20.25
and walks in the s. of life, 33.15
to walk in my s. and be careful to 36.27
and be careful to observe my s. 37.24
my laws and my s. in all my 44.24
the LORD, and have not kept his s., Amo 2.04
For you have kept the s. of Omri, Mic 6.16
But my words and my s., which I Zec 1.06
aside from my s. and have not kept Mal 3.07
the s. and ordinances that I 4.04

STAVES

with the scepter and with their s." Num 21.18

STAY

"S. here with the ass; I and the lad Gen 22.05
and s. with him a while, until your 27.44
any other man; s. with me." 29.19
you go, and you shall s. no longer." Ex 9.28
but do not s. there yourselves, Jos 10.19
"I will s. till you return." Ju 6.18
"S. with me, and be to me a father 17.10
made him s., and he remained with 19.04
s. in a secret place and hide 1Sa 19.02
the lad, "Hurry, make haste, s. not." 20.38
father and my mother s. with you, 22.03
S. with me, fear not; for he that 22.23
Go back, and s. with the king; 2Sa 15.19
not a man will s. with you this 19.07
my calamity; but the LORD was my s. 22.19
now s. your hand." And the angel 24.16
with your glory, and s. at home; 2Ki 14.10
and did not s. there in the land. 15.20
now s. your hand." And the angel 1Ch 21.15
But now s. at home; why should you 2Ch 25.19
ways, and do not s. in its paths. Job 24.13
my calamity; but the LORD was my s. Ps 18.18
for the LORD is the s. of his hand. 37.24
though they s. among the sheepfolds— 68.13
wayward, her feet do not s. at home; Pro 7.11
and from Judah s. and staff, Is 3.01
the whole s. of bread, and the whole s. of 3.01
and s. themselves on the God of 48.02
s. not, for I bring evil from the Jer 4.06
will surely s. away from us," 37.09
for they will not s. away. 37.09
"They shall s. with us no longer." Lam 4.15
and none can s. his hand or say to Dan 4.35
and s. with him until you depart. Mt 10.11
s. there until you leave the place. Mk 6.10
s. there, and from there depart. Lk 9.04
for I must s. at your house today." 19.05
"S. with us, for it is toward 24.29
So he went in to s. with them. 24.29
but s. in the city, until you are 24.49
they asked him to s. with them; Jn 4.40
during their s. in the land of Ac 13.17
the Lord, come to my house and s." 16.15
asked him to s. for a longer 18.20
"Unless these men s. in the ship, 27.31
were invited to s. with them for 28.14
Paul was allowed to s. by himself, 28.16
and perhaps I will s. with you or 1Co 16.06
But I will s. in Ephesus until 16.08

STAYED

and s. there that night, because the Gen 28.11
And he s. with him a month. 29.14
with Laban, and s. until now; 32.04
So no one s. with him when Joseph 45.01
and s. in the land of Midian; Ex 2.15
month, and the people s. in Kadesh; Num 20.01
the princes of Moab s. with Balaam. 22.08
the plague was s. from the people 25.08
'You have s. long enough at this Deu 1.06
"I s. on the mountain, as at the 10.10
and the moon s., until the nation Jos 10.13
The sun s. in the midst of heaven, 10.13
Gilead s. beyond the Jordan; Ju 5.17
went down and s. in the cleft of 15.08
s. in Geba of Benjamin; but the Philistines 1Sa 13.16
and they s. with him all the time 22.04
where those s. who were left behind. 30.09
two hundred s. behind, who were too 30.10
with food while he s. at Mahanaim; 2Sa 19.32
but Haman s. to beg his life from Est 7.07
here shall your proud waves be s.'? Job 38.11
interposed, and the plague was s. Ps 106.30
whose mind is s. on thee, because he Is 26.03
And they went and s. at Geruth Jer 41.17
the boy Jesus s. behind in Jerusalem. Lk 2.43
and they s. with him that day, for Jn 1.39
and there they s. for a few days. 2.12
with them; and he s. there two days. 4.40
he s. two days longer in the place 11.06
and there he s. with the disciples. 11.54
And he s. in Joppa for many days Ac 9.43
of the same trade he s. with them, 18.03
And he s. a year and six months, 18.11
After this Paul s. many days longer, 18.18
he himself s. in Asia for a while. 19.22
Troas, where we s. for seven days. 20.06
we s. there for seven days. 21.04
brethren and s. with them for one 21.07
one of the seven, and s. with him. 21.08
When he had s. among them not more 25.06
And as they s. there many days, 25.14
we s. there for three days. 18.12

STAYING

Saul was s. in the outskirts of 1Sa 14.02
means Teacher), where are you s.?" Jn 1.38
They came and saw where he was s.; 1.39
And while s. with them he charged Ac 1.04
the upper room, where they were s., 1.13
While we were s. for some days, a 21.10

STAYS

his share be who s. by the baggage; 1Sa 30.24
the stand its s. and its panels 1Ki 7.35
surfaces of its s. and on its 7.36
the watchman s. awake in vain. Ps 127.01
He who s. in this city shall die by Jer 21.09
He who s. in this city shall die by 38.02

STEAD

Zerah of Bozrah reigned in his s. Gen 36.33
of the Temanites reigned in his s. 36.34
country of Moab, reigned in his s., 36.35
of Masrekah reigned in his s. 36.36
on the Euphrates reigned in his s. 36.37
son of Achbor reigned in his s. 36.38
died, and Hadar reigned in his s., 36.39
you have risen in your fathers' s., Num 32.14
them, and settled in their s.; Deu 2.12
them, and settled in their s.; 2.21
in their s. even to this day. 2.22
them and settled in their s.) 2.23
ministered as priest in his s. 10.06
whom he raised up in their s., Jos 5.07
Hanun his son reigned in his s. 2Sa 10.01
shall sit upon my throne in my s.'; 1Ki 1.30
for he shall be king in my s.; 1.35
Rehoibiam his son reigned in his s. 11.43
Nadab his son reigned in his s. 14.20
made in their s. shields of bronze, 14.27
Abijam his son reigned in his s. 14.31
and Asa his son reigned in his s. 15.08
Jehoshaphat his son reigned in his s. 15.24
of Judah, and reigned in his s. 15.28
and Elah his son reigned in his s. 16.06
of Judah, and reigned in his s. 16.10
and Ahab his son reigned in his s. 16.28
Ahaziah his son reigned in his s. 22.40

STEAD (cont.)
Jehoram his son reigned in his s. 1Ki 22.50
king in his s. in the second year 2Ki 1.17
son who was to reign in his s., 3.27
And Hazael became king in his s. 8.15
Ahaziah his son reigned in his s. 8.24
Jehoahaz his son reigned in his s. 10.35
Amaziah his son reigned in his s. 12.21
Joash his son reigned in his s. 13.09
his son became king in his s. 13.24
Jeroboam his son reigned in his s. 14.16
Zechariah his son reigned in his s. 14.29
Jotham his son reigned in his s. 15.07
killed him, and reigned in his s. 15.10
slew him, and reigned in his s. 15.14
Pekahiah his son reigned in his s. 15.22
he slew him, and reigned in his s. 15.25
slew him, and reigned in his s., 15.30
and Ahaz his son reigned in his s. 15.38
Hezekiah his son reigned in his s. 16.20
Esarhaddon his son reigned in his s. 19.37
Manasseh his son reigned in his s. 20.21
and Amon his son reigned in his s. 21.18
made Josiah his son king in his s. 21.24
Josiah his son reigned in his s. 21.26
made him king in his father's s. 23.30
Jehoiachin his son reigned in his s. 24.06
king in his s., and changed his 24.17
Zerah of Bozrah reigned in his s. 1Ch 1.44
of the Temanites reigned in his s. 1.45
country of Moab, reigned in his s.; 1.46
of Masrekah reigned in his s. 1.47
on the Euphrates reigned in his s. 1.48
son of Achbor, reigned in his s. 1.49
died, Hadad reigned in his s.; 1.50
and his son reigned in his s. 19.01
Solomon his son reigned in his s. 29.28
and hast made me king in his s. 2Ch 1.08
Rehoboam his son reigned in his s. 9.31
made in their s. shields of bronze, 12.10
Abijah his son reigned in his s. 12.16
and Asa his son reigned in his s. 14.01
Jehoshaphat his son reigned in his s., 17.01
Jehoram his son reigned in his s. 21.01
his youngest son king in his s.; 22.01
Amaziah his son reigned in his s. 24.27
Jotham his son reigned in his s. 26.23
and Ahaz his son reigned in his s. 27.09
Hezekiah his son reigned in his s. 28.27
Manasseh his son reigned in his s. 32.33
and Amon his son reigned in his s. 33.20
made Josiah his son king in his s. 33.25
in his father's s. in Jerusalem. 36.01
Jehoiachin his son reigned in his s. 36.08
Esarhaddon his son reigned in his s. Is 37.38

STEADFAST
and show s. love to my master Gen 24.12
thou hast shown s. love to my 24.14
forsaken his s. love and his 24.27
of all the s. love and all the 32.10
with Joseph and showed him s. love, 39.21
"Thou hast led in thy s. love the Ex 15.13
but showing s. love to thousands of 20.06
abounding in s. love and faithfulness, 34.06
keeping s. love for thousands, 34.07
to anger, and abounding in s. love, Num 14.18
to the greatness of thy s. love, 14.19
but showing s. love to thousands of Deu 5.10
covenant and s. love with those 7.09
covenant and the s. love which he 7.12
Therefore be very s. to keep and do Jos 23.06
the LORD show s. love and faithfulness 2Sa 2.06
will not take my s. love from him, 7.15
the LORD show s. love and faithfulness 15.20
and shows s. love to his anointed, 22.51
shown great and s. love to thy 1Ki 3.06
for him this great and s. love, 3.06
and showing s. love to thy servants 8.23
for his s. love endures for ever! 1Ch 16.34
for his s. love endures for ever. 16.41
will not take my s. love from him, 17.13
shown great and s. love to David 2Ch 1.08
for his s. love endures for ever," 5.13
and showing s. love to thy servants 6.14
Remember thy s. love for David thy 6.42
for his s. love endures for ever." 7.03
for his s. love endures for ever— 7.06
for his s. love endures for ever." 20.21
for his s. love endures for ever Ez 3.11
to me his s. love before the king 7.28
to us his s. love before the kings 9.09
covenant and s. love with those Neh 1.05
to anger and abounding in s. love, 9.17
who keepest covenant and s. love, 9.32
to the greatness of thy s. love. 13.22
Thou hast granted me life and s. love; Job 10.12
abundance of thy s. love will enter Ps 5.07
me for the sake of thy s. love. 6.04
But I have trusted in thy s. love; 13.05
Wondrously show thy s. love, 17.07
and shows s. love to his anointed, 18.50
and through the s. love of the Most 21.07
and of thy s. love, for they have 25.06
according to thy s. love remember 25.07
of the LORD are s. love and 25.10
For thy s. love is before my eyes, 26.03
and be glad for thy s. love, 31.07
save me in thy s. love! 31.16
shown his s. love to me when I was 31.21
but s. love surrounds him who 32.10
is full of the s. love of the LORD 33.05
on those who hope in his s. love, 33.18
Let thy s. love, O LORD, be upon us, 33.22
Thy s. love, O LORD, extends to the 36.05
How precious is thy s. love, O God! 36.07
O continue thy s. love to those who 36.10
concealed thy s. love and thy 40.10
let thy s. love and thy faithfulness 40.11
By day the LORD commands his s. love; 42.08
us for the sake of thy s. love! 44.26
We have thought on thy s. love, 48.09
O God, according to thy s. love; 51.01
I trust in the s. love of God for 52.08
send forth his s. love and his 57.03
My heart is s., O God, my heart is s.! 57.07
For thy s. love is great to the 57.10
My God in his s. love will meet me; 59.10
aloud of thy s. love in the 59.16
the God who shows me s. love. 59.17
bid s. love and faithfulness watch 61.07
to thee, O Lord, belongs s. love. 62.12
Because thy s. love is better than 63.03
or removed his s. love from me! 66.20
abundance of thy s. love answer me. 69.13
O LORD, for thy s. love is good; 69.16
Has his s. love for ever ceased? 77.08
generation whose heart was not s., 78.08
Their heart was not s. toward him; 78.37
Show us thy s. love, O LORD, and 85.07
S. love and faithfulness will meet; 85.10
abounding in s. love to all who 86.05
For great is thy s. love toward me; 86.13
abounding in s. love and faithfulness 86.15
Is thy s. love declared in the 88.11
I will sing of thy s. love, 89.01
For thy s. love was established for 89.02
s. love and faithfulness go before 89.14
faithfulness and my s. love shall 89.24
My s. love I will keep for him for 89.28
not remove from him my s. love, 89.33
where is thy s. love of old, which 89.49
us in the morning with thy s. love, 90.14
to declare thy s. love in the 92.02
thy s. love, O LORD, held me up. 94.18
remembered his s. love and faithfulness 98.03

STEADFAST (cont.)

his s. love endures for ever, and Ps 100.05
crowns you with s. love and mercy, 103.04
to anger and abounding in s. love. 103.08
so great in his s. love toward 103.11
But the s. love of the LORD is from 103.17
for his s. love endures for ever! 106.01
the abundance of thy s. love, 106.07
to the abundance of his s. love. 106.45
for his s. love endures for ever! 107.01
thank the LORD for his s. love, 107.08
thank the LORD for his s. love, 107.15
thank the LORD for his s. love, 107.21
thank the LORD for his s. love, 107.31
consider the s. love of the LORD. 107.43
For thy s. love is great above the 108.04
because thy s. love is good, deliver 109.21
Save me according to thy s. love! 109.26
the sake of thy s. love and thy 115.01
For great is his s. love toward us; 117.02
his s. love endures for ever! 118.01
"His s. love endures for ever." 118.02
"His s. love endures for ever." 118.03
"His s. love endures for ever." 118.04
for his s. love endures for ever! 118.29
my ways may be s. in keeping thy 119.05
Let thy s. love come to me, O LORD, 119.41
O LORD, is full of thy s. love; 119.64
Let thy s. love be ready to comfort 119.76
In thy s. love spare my life, that I 119.88
servant according to thy s. love, 119.124
Hear my voice in thy s. love; 119.149
my life according to thy s. love. 119.159
For with the LORD there is s. love, 130.07
for his s. love endures for ever. 136.01
for his s. love endures for ever. 136.02
for his s. love endures for ever; 136.03
for his s. love endures for ever; 136.04
for his s. love endures for ever; 136.05
for his s. love endures for ever; 136.06
for his s. love endures for ever; 136.07
for his s. love endures for ever; 136.08
for his s. love endures for ever; 136.09
for his s. love endures for ever; 136.10
for his s. love endures for ever; 136.11
for his s. love endures for ever; 136.12
for his s. love endures for ever; 136.13
for his s. love endures for ever; 136.14
for his s. love endures for ever; 136.15
for his s. love endures for ever; 136.16
for his s. love endures for ever; 136.17
for his s. love endures for ever; 136.18
for his s. love endures for ever; 136.19
for his s. love endures for ever; 136.20
for his s. love endures for ever; 136.21
for his s. love endures for ever. 136.22
for his s. love endures for ever; 136.23
for his s. love endures for ever; 136.24
for his s. love endures for ever. 136.25
for his s. love endures for ever. 136.26
name for thy s. love and thy 138.02
thy s. love, O LORD, endures for ever 138.08
hear in the morning of thy s. love, 143.08
And in thy s. love cut off my 143.12
to anger and abounding in s. love. 145.08
in those who hope in his s. love. 147.11
He who is s. in righteousness will Pro 11.19
established in s. love and on it Is 16.05
but my s. love shall not depart 54.10
my s., sure love for David. 55.03
recount the s. love of the LORD, 63.07
to the abundance of his s. love. 63.07
the LORD, my s. love and mercy. Jer 16.05
who showest s. love to thousands, 32.18
for his s. love endures for ever!' 33.11
The s. love of the LORD never Lam 3.22
to the abundance of his s. love; 3.32
covenant and s. love with those Dan 9.04
in s. love, and in mercy. Hos 2.19
For I desire s. love and not 6.06
righteousness, reap the fruit of s. love; 10.12
to anger, and abounding in s. love, Joe 2.13
to anger, and abounding in s. love, Jon 4.02
because he delights in s. love. Mic 7.18
to Jacob and s. love to Abraham, as 7.20
to the Lord with s. purpose; Ac 11.23
be s., immovable, always abounding 1Co 15.58
stable and s., not shifting from Col 1.23
as a sure and s. anchor of the Heb 6.19
Behold, we call those happy who were s. Jas 5.11

STEADFASTLY

their king s. from the Jordan to 2Sa 20.02
Continue s. in prayer, being watchful Col 4.02

STEADFASTNESS

that by s. and by the encouragement Rom 15.04
May the God of s. and encouragement 15.05
of love and s. of hope in our Lord 1Th 1.03
of God for your s. and faith in 2Th 1.04
of God and to the s. of Christ. 3.05
faith, love, s., gentleness. 1Ti 6.11
my patience, my love, my s., 2Ti 3.10
sound in faith, in love, and in s. Tit 2.02
testing of your faith produces s. Jas 1.03
And let s. have its full effect, 1.04
You have heard of the s. of Job, 5.11
self-control, and self-control with s., 2Pe 1.06
and s. with godliness, 1.06

STEADILY

And Jehoshaphat grew s. greater. 2Ch 17.12

STEADY

his hands were s. until the going Ex 17.12
it is I who keep s. its pillars. Ps 75.03
His heart is s., he will not be 112.08
Keep s. my steps according to thy 119.133
always be s., endure suffering, do 2Ti 4.05

STEAL

house, but why did you s. my gods?" Gen 31.30
then should we s. silver or gold 44.08
"You shall not s. Ex 20.15
"You shall not s., nor deal falsely, Lev 19.11
"'Neither shall you s. Deu 5.19
day as people s. in who are ashamed 2Sa 19.03
What I did not s. must I now Ps 69.04
and s., and profane the name of my Pro 30.09
Will you s., murder, commit adultery, Jer 7.09
who s. my words from one another. 23.30
would they not s. only enough for Ob 1.05
and where thieves break in and s., Mt 6.19
thieves do not break in and s. 6.20
You shall not s., You shall not 19.18
his disciples go and s. him away, 27.64
Do not s., Do not bear false Mk 10.19
Do not s., Do not bear false Lk 18.20
comes only to s. and kill and Jn 10.10
preach against stealing, do you s.? Rom 2.21
You shall not s., You shall not 13.09
Let the thief no longer s., Eph 4.28

STEALING

"If a man is found s. one of his Deu 24.07
s., and committing adultery; Hos 4.02
preach against s., do you steal? Rom 2.21

STEALS

"Whoever s. a man, whether he sells Ex 21.16
"If a man s. an ox or a sheep, and 22.01
a thief if he s. to satisfy his Pro 6.30
every one who s. shall be cut off Zec 5.03

STEALTH

to arrest Jesus by s. and kill him. Mt 26.04
to arrest him by s., and kill him; Mk 14.01

STEALTHILY
David arose and s. cut off the 1Sa 24.04
"Now a word was brought to me s., Job 4.12
His eyes s. watch for the hapless, Ps 10.08

STEED
them like his proud s. in battle. Zec 10.03

STEEDS
the galloping, galloping of his s. Ju 5.22
and swift s. they brought to the 1Ki 4.28
and, "We will ride upon swift s., Is 30.16
Harness the s. to the chariots, Mic 1.13
When the s. came out, they were Zec 6.07

STEEP
come and settle in the s. ravines, Is 7.19
like waters poured down a s. place. Mic 1.04
rushed down the s. bank into the Mt 8.32
rushed down the s. bank into the Mk 5.13
rushed down the s. bank into the Lk 8.33

STEERS
and young s. with the mighty bulls. Is 34.07

STEM
has their s. taken root in the Is 40.24
Its strongest s. became a ruler's Eze 19.11
off, its strong s. was withered; 19.12
And fire has gone out from its s., 19.14
there remains in it no strong s., 19.14

STENCH
and the s. of their corpses shall Is 34.03
the s. and foul smell of him will Joe 2.20
and I made the s. of your camp go Amo 4.10

STEP
there is but a s. between me and 1Sa 20.03
each end of a s. on the six steps. 1Ki 10.20
each end of a s. on the six steps. 2Ch 9.19
if my s. has turned aside from the Job 31.07
your s. will not be hampered; Pro 4.12
whom victory meets at every s.? Is 41.02
of the sea will s. down from their Eze 26.16

STEPHANAS
baptize also the household of S. 1Co 1.16
household of S. were the first 16.15
the coming of S. and Fortunatus 16.17

STEPHEN
whole multitude, and they chose S., Ac 6.05
And S., full of grace and power, did 6.08
Asia, arose and disputed with S. 6.09
And S. said: "Brethren and fathers, 7.02
And as they were stoning S., he prayed, 7.59
Devout men buried S., and made great 8.02
that arose over S. traveled as far 11.19
the blood of S. thy witness was 22.20

STEPPE
Bezer in the s. with its pasture 1Ch 6.78
I have given the s. for his home, Job 39.06

STEPPED
And as he s. out on land, there met Lk 8.27
whoever s. in first after the *Jn 5.04

STEPS
shall not go up by s. to my altar, Ex 20.26
so they followed in thy s., Deu 33.03
a wide place for my s. under me, 2Sa 22.37
The throne had six s., and at the 1Ki 10.19
each end of a step on the six s. 10.20
put it under him on the bare s., 2Ki 9.13
forward ten s., or go back ten s.?" 20.09
for the shadow to lengthen ten s.; 20.10
let the shadow go back ten s." 20.10
he brought the shadow back ten s., 20.11
the algum wood s. for the house of 2Ch 9.11
The throne had six s. and a footstool 9.18
each end of a step on the six s. 9.19
For then thou wouldest number my s., Job 14.16
His strong s. are shortened and his 18.07
My foot has held fast to his s.; 23.11
when my s. were washed with milk, 29.06
see my ways, and number all my s.? 31.04
give him an account of all my s.; 31.37
of a man, and he sees all his s. 34.21
My s. have held fast to thy paths, Ps 17.05
a wide place for my s. under me, 18.36
The s. of a man are from the LORD, 37.23
in his heart; his s. do not slip. 37.31
upon a rock, making my s. secure. 40.02
nor have our s. departed from thy 44.18
they lurk, they watch my s. 56.06
They set a net for my s.; 57.06
my s. had well nigh slipped. 73.02
Direct thy s. to the perpetual 74.03
Therefore I direct my s. by all thy 119.128
Keep steady my s. according to thy 119.133
her s. follow the path to Sheol; Pro 5.05
way, but the LORD directs his s. 16.09
A man's s. are ordered by the LORD; 20.24
Guard your s. when you go to the Ecc 5.01
of the poor, the s. of the needy." Is 26.06
the dial of Ahaz turn back ten s." 38.08
dial the ten s. by which it had 38.08
in man who walks to direct his s. Jer 10.23
Men dogged our s. so that we could Lam 4.18
going up its s., and measured the Eze 40.06
and seven s. led up to it; 40.22
were seven s. leading up to it, and 40.26
and its stairway had eight s. 40.31
and its stairway had eight s. 40.34
and its stairway had eight s. 40.37
and ten s. led up to it; and there were 40.49
The s. of the altar shall face east." 43.17
my s. totter beneath me. I will quietly Hab 3.16
am going another s. down before me." Jn 5.07
And when he came to the s., he was Ac 21.35
leave, Paul, standing on the s., 21.40
Did we not take the same s.? 2Co 12.18
that you should follow in his s. 1Pe 2.21

STERN
a nation of s. countenance, who Deu 28.50
A s. vision is told to me; the plunderer Is 21.02
But he was in the s., asleep on the Mk 4.38
let out four anchors from the s., Ac 27.29
and the s. was broken up by the 27.41

STERNLY
And Jesus s. charged them, "See that Mt 9.30
And he s. charged him, and sent him Mk 1.43

STEWARD
he said to the s. of his house, Gen 43.16
went up to the s. of Joseph's house, 43.19
Then he commanded the s. of his house, 44.01
the city, Joseph said to his s., 44.04
go to this s., to Shebna, who is Is 22.15
said to the s. whom the chief of Dan 1.11
So the s. took away their rich food 1.16
of the vineyard said to his s., Mt 20.08
Herod's s., and Susanna, and many Lk 8.03
then is the faithful and wise s., 12.42
"There was a rich man who had a s., 16.01
stewardship, for you can no longer be s.' 16.02
And the s. said to himself, 'What 16.03
the dishonest s. for his prudence; 16.08
and take it to the s. of the feast." Jn 2.08
When the s. of the feast tasted the 2.09
the s. of the feast called the 2.09
as God's s., must be blameless; Tit 1.07

STEWARDS
All these were s. of King David's 1Ch 27.31
the s. of all the property and 28.01
of Christ and s. of the mysteries 1Co 4.01
is required of s. that they be 4.02
as good s. of God's varied grace: 1Pe 4.10

STEWARDSHIP
Turn in the account of your s., Lk 16.02
is taking the s. away from me? 16.03
houses when I am put out of the s.' 16.04
heard of the s. of God's grace that Eph 3.02

STICK
shall have a s. with your weapons; Deu 23.13
he cut off a s., and threw it in 2Ki 6.06
bones which were not seen s. out. Job 33.21
but dill is beaten out with a s., Is 28.27
of your streams s. to your scales; Eze 29.04
streams which s. to your scales. 29.04
take a s. and write on it, 'For 37.16
take another s. and write upon it, 37.16
'For Joseph (the s. of Ephraim) and 37.16
and join them together into one s., 37.17
to take the s. of Joseph (which is 37.19
will join with it the s. of Judah, 37.19
of Judah, and make them one s., 37.19

STICKS
a man gathering s. on the sabbath Num 15.32
him gathering s. brought him to 15.33
a dog, that you come to me with s.?" 1Sa 17.43
a widow was there gathering s.; 1Ki 17.10
now, I am gathering a couple of s., 17.12
is a friend who s. closer than a Pro 18.24
When the s. on which you write are Eze 37.20
a bundle of s. and put them on the Ac 28.03

STIFF
He makes his tail s. like a cedar; Job 40.17

STIFFENED
he s. his neck and hardened his 2Ch 36.13
presumptuously and s. their neck Neh 9.16
but they s. their neck and appointed 9.17
shoulder and s. their neck and 9.29
their ear, but s. their neck. Jer 7.26
but s. their neck, that they might 17.23
because they have s. their neck, 19.15

STIFFENS
yet s. his neck will suddenly be Pro 29.01

STIFF-NECKED
and behold, it is a s. people; Ex 32.09
the way, for you are a s. people." 33.03
of Israel, 'You are a s. people; 33.05
of us, although it is a s. people; 34.09
Do not now be s. as your fathers 2Ch 30.08
"You s. people, uncircumcised in Ac 7.51

STILL
the waters were s. on the face of Gen 8.09
s. going toward the Negeb. 12.09
but Abraham s. stood before the 18.22
while he was s. living he sent 25.06
it is s. high day, it is not time 29.07
While he was s. speaking with them, 29.09
when they were s. some distance 35.16
for they were s. as gaunt as at the 41.21
saying, 'Is your father s. alive? 43.07
whom you spoke? Is he s. alive?" 43.27
our father is well, he is s. alive." 43.28
to Joseph's house, he was s. there; 44.14
is my father s. alive?" But his brothers 45.03
"Joseph is s. alive, and he is ruler 45.26
Joseph my son is s. alive; I will go 45.28
and know that you are s. alive." 46.30
when there was s. some distance to 48.07
and see whether they are s. alive." Ex 4.18
S. Pharaoh's heart was hardened, and 7.13
to let them go and s. hold them, 9.02
You are s. exalting yourself 9.17
you, and you have only to be s." 14.14
they are as s. as a stone, till thy 15.16
They s. kept bringing him freewill 36.03
If there are s. many years, according Lev 25.51
he shall s. keep the passover to Num 9.10
his uncleanness is s. on him. 19.13
to increase s. more the fierce 32.14
as you have heard, and s. live? Deu 4.33
God speak with man and man s. live. 5.24
fire, as we have, and has s. lived? 5.26
you shall stand s. in the Jordan.'" Jos 3.08
it was s. warm when we took it from 9.12
stand thou s. at Gibeon, and thou 10.12
And the sun stood s., and the moon 10.13
I am s. as strong to this day as I 14.11
but when he s. did not open the Ju 3.25
Asher sat s. at the coast of the 5.17
he fell, he lay s. at her feet; 5.27
To this day it s. stands at Ophrah, 6.24
Gideon, "The people are s. too many; 7.04
afraid, because he was s. a youth. 8.20
Now therefore stand s., that I may 1Sa 12.07
Now therefore stand s. and see this 12.16
But if you s. do wickedly, you shall 12.25
Saul was s. at Gilgal, and all the 13.07
then we will stand s. in our place, 14.09
Saul was s. more afraid of David. 18.29
If I am s. alive, show me the loyal 20.14
me, and yet my life s. lingers." 2Sa 1.09
had fallen and died, stood s. 2.23
"Is there s. any one left of the 9.01
"Is there not s. some one of the 9.03
"There is s. a son of Jonathan; 9.03
said, "While the child was s. alive, 12.22
be better for me to be there s." 14.32
while he was s. alive in the oak. 18.14
so he turned aside, and stood s. 18.30
"How many years have I s. to live, 19.34
Can I s. listen to the voice of 19.35
eyes of my lord the king s. see it; 24.03
Then while you are s. speaking with 1Ki 1.14
While she was s. speaking with the 1.22
While he was s. speaking, behold, 1.42
heard of it (for he was s. in Egypt, 12.02
after the fire a s. small voice. 19.12
And he said, "Does he s. live? 20.32
and the people s. sacrificed and 22.43
And as they s. went on and talked, 2Ki 2.11
And while he was s. speaking with 6.33
the people s. sacrificed and 14.04
the people s. sacrificed and 15.04
the people s. sacrificed and 15.35
But every nation s. made gods of 17.29
S. the LORD did not turn from the 23.26
the land is s. ours, because we 2Ch 14.07
stand s., and see the victory of 20.17
But the people s. followed corrupt 27.02
servants said s. more against the 32.16
Nevertheless the people s. sacrificed 33.17
while they are s. standing guard Neh 7.03
He s. holds fast his integrity, Job 2.03
"Do you s. hold fast your integrity? 2.09
It stood s., but I could not 4.16
is in turmoil, and is never s.; 30.27
the earth is s. because of the 37.17
he cannot stand s. at the sound of 39.24
to s. the enemy and the avenger. Ps 8.02
He leads me beside s. waters; 23.02
Be s. before the LORD, and wait 37.07
"Be s., and know that I am God. 46.10
who dost s. the roaring of the seas, 65.07
hast wounded, they afflict s. more. 69.26
and I s. proclaim thy wondrous 71.17

STILL (cont.)
the earth feared and was s., Ps 76.08
Yet they sinned s. more against him, 78.17
the food was s. in their mouths, 78.30
In spite of all this they s. sinned; 78.32
not hold thy peace or be s., O God! 83.01
They s. bring forth fruit in old 92.14
he made the storm be s., and the waves 107.29
When I awake, I am s. with thee. 139.18
wise man, and he will be s. wiser; Pro 9.09
s. less is false speech to a prince 17.07
my mind s. guiding me with wisdom— Ecc 2.03
than the living who are s. alive; 4.02
Why will you s. be smitten, that you Is 1.05
and his hand is stretched out s. 5.25
and his hand is stretched out s. 9.12
and his hand is stretched out s. 9.17
but are s. hungry, and they devour 9.20
and his hand is stretched out s. 9.21
and his hand is stretched out s. 10.04
Be s., O inhabitants of the coast, O 23.02
have called her "Rahab who sits s." 30.07
I have kept s. and restrained 42.14
"Therefore I s. contend with you, Jer 2.09
of your guilt is s. before me, 2.22
Why do we sit s.? Gather together 8.14
against him, I do remember him s. 31.20
while he was s. shut up in the 33.01
Now Jeremiah was s. going in and 37.04
into your scabbard, rest and be s.! 47.06
from the sword, go, stand not s.! 51.50
when they stood s., they let down Eze 1.24
when they stood s., they let down 1.25
you will see s. greater abominations 8.06
"You will see s. greater abominations 8.13
You will see s. greater abominations 8.15
When they stood s., these stood s., 10.17
and s. you were not satisfied. 16.28
she has shed is s. in the midst of 24.07
Will you s. say, 'I am a god,' in the 28.09
they lie s., the uncircumcised, 32.21
While the words were s. in the Dan 4.31
and s. more greatness was added to 4.36
but Judah is s. known by God, and is Hos 11.12
"Is there s. any one with you?" Amo 6.10
For s. the vision awaits its time; Hab 2.03
and moon stood s. in their habitation 3.11
the olive tree s. yield nothing? Hag 2.19
Jerusalem shall s. be inhabited in Zec 12.06
while they are s. on their feet, 14.12
While he was s. speaking to the Mt 12.46
"Are you also s. without understanding? 15.16
He was s. speaking, when lo, a bright 17.05
have observed; what do I s. lack?" 19.20
"Are you s. sleeping and taking 26.45
While he was s. speaking, Judas came, 26.47
Why do we s. need witnesses? 26.65
while he was s. alive, 'After three 27.63
and s. more will be given you. Mk 4.24
"Peace! Be s.!" And the wind 4.39
While he was s. speaking, there came 5.35
He had s. one other, a beloved son; 12.06
"Are you s. sleeping and taking 14.41
while he was s. speaking, Judas came, 14.43
said, "Why do we s. need witnesses? 14.63
the bier, and the bearers stood s. Lk 7.14
While he was s. speaking, a man from 8.49
been done, and s. there is room.' 14.22
said to him, "One thing you s. lack. 18.22
While he was s. speaking, there came 22.47
about an hour s. another insisted, 22.59
while he was s. speaking, the cock 22.60
you, while he was s. in Galilee, 24.06
And they stood s., looking sad. 24.17
And while they s. disbelieved for 24.41
while I was s. with you, that 24.44
them, "My Father is working s., Jn 5.17
but was s. in the place where 11.30
to you, while I am s. with you. 14.25
while it was s. dark, and saw that 20.01
But Saul, s. breathing threats and Ac 9.01
While Peter was s. saying this, 10.44
sleep as Paul talked s. longer; 20.09
why am I s. being condemned as a Rom 3.07
while he was s. uncircumcised. 4.11
we who died to sin s. live in it? 6.02
me then, "Why does he s. find fault? 9.19
for you are s. of the flesh. 1Co 3.03
claim upon you, do not we s. more? 9.12
will show you a s. more excellent 12.31
time, most of whom are s. alive, 15.06
futile and you are s. in your sins. 15.17
and s. more toward you, with holiness 2Co 1.12
For while we are s. in this tent, 5.04
for me, so that I rejoiced s. more. 7.07
we rejoiced s. more at the joy of 7.13
If I were s. pleasing men, I should Gal 1.10
And I was s. not known by sight to 1.22
s. preach circumcision, why am I s. 5.11
live as if you s. belonged to the Col 2.20
that when I was s. with you I told 2Th 2.05
serving the saints, as you s. do. Heb 6.10
for he was s. in the loins of his 7.10
as the outer tent is s. standing 9.08
his faith he is s. speaking. 11.04
his brother is in the darkness s. 1Jn 2.09
Yet you have s. a few names in Rev 3.04
behold, two woes are s. to come. 9.12
Let the evildoer s. do evil, 22.11
evil, and the filthy s. be filthy, 22.11
and the righteous s. do right, 22.11
do right, and the holy s. be holy." 22.11

STILLED
So the Levites s. all the people, Neh 8.11
By his power he s. the sea; Job 26.12
The mirth of the timbrels is s., Is 24.08
the mirth of the lyre is s. 24.08
so the song of the ruthless is s. 25.05

STILLEST
when its waves rise, thou s. them. Ps 89.09

STILLING
and s. her mighty voice. Their waves roar Jer 51.55

STING
"O death, where is thy s.? O death, where 1Co 15.55
The s. of death is sin, and the 15.56

STINGS
a serpent, and s. like an adder. Pro 23.32
of a scorpion, when it s. a man. Rev 9.05
and s., and their power of hurting 9.10

STINGY
eat the bread of a man who is s.; Pro 23.06

STINK
their fish s. for lack of water, and Is 50.02

STIR
So I will s. them to jealousy with Deu 32.21
LORD began to s. him in Mahanehdan, Ju 13.25
fierce that he dares to s. him up. Job 41.10
and did not s. up all his wrath. Ps 78.38
S. up thy might, and come to save us! 80.02
their heart, and s. up wars continually. 140.02
that you s. not up nor awaken love Sol 2.07
that you s. not up nor awaken love 3.05
that you s. not up nor awaken love 8.04
And I will s. up Egyptians against Is 19.02
I will s. up the spirit of a Jer 51.01
he shall s. up all against the Dan 11.02
And he shall s. up his power and 11.25
whose baker ceases to s. the fire, Hos 7.04
But now I will s. them up from the Joe 3.07

STIR (cont.)
s. up the mighty men. Let all the Joe 3.09
was no small s. among the soldiers Ac 12.18
arose no little s. concerning the 19.23
consider how to s. up one another Heb 10.24

STIRRED
came, every one whose heart s. him, Ex 35.21
one whose heart s. him up to come 36.02
They s. him to jealousy with Deu 32.16
They have s. me to jealousy with 32.21
whole town was s. because of them; Ru 1.19
that my son has s. up my servant 1Sa 22.08
LORD who has s. you up against me, 26.19
God of Israel s. up the spirit of 1Ch 5.26
And the LORD s. up against Jehoram 2Ch 21.16
the LORD s. up the spirit of Cyrus 36.22
the LORD s. up the spirit of Cyrus Ez 1.01
spirit God had s. to go up to 1.05
sedition was s. up in it from of 4.15
Sheol beneath is s. up to meet you Is 14.09
Who s. up one from the east whom Is 41.02
I s. up one from the north, and he 41.25
The LORD has s. up the spirit of Jer 51.11
And the LORD s. up the spirit of Hag 1.14
Jerusalem, all the city was s., Mt 21.10
chief priests s. up the crowd to Mk 15.11
And they s. up the people and the Ac 6.12
and s. up persecution against Paul 13.50
unbelieving Jews s. up the Gentiles 14.02
s. up all the crowd, and laid hands 21.27
who recently s. up a revolt and led 21.38
your zeal has s. up most of them. 2Co 9.02

STIRRING
and they are s. up the city against Ju 9.31
Behold, I am s. up the Medes against Is 13.17
great nation is s. from the farthest Jer 6.22
tempest is s. from the farthest 25.32
I am s. up and bringing against 50.09
many kings are s. from the farthest 50.41
of heaven were s. up the great sea Dan 7.02
s. up and inciting the crowds. Ac 17.13
with any one or s. up a crowd, 24.12

STIRS
Like an eagle that s. up its nest, Deu 32.11
the innocent s. himself up against Job 17.08
Hatred s. up strife, but love covers Pro 10.12
but a harsh word s. up anger. 15.01
A hot-tempered man s. up strife, 15.18
A greedy man s. up strife, but he 28.25
A man of wrath s. up strife, and a 29.22
against them, and s. up their enemies. Is 9.11
a man of war he s. up his fury; 42.13
who s. up the sea so that its waves 51.15
If any one s. up strife, it is not 54.15
whoever s. up strife with you shall 54.15
who s. up the sea so that its waves Jer 31.35
"He s. up the people, teaching Lk 23.05

STOCK
the s. which thy right hand planted Ps 80.15
a virgin of the s. of the house of Eze 44.22

STOCKS
the seer, and put him in the s., 2Ch 16.10
Thou puttest my feet in the s., Job 13.27
he puts my feet in the s., 33.11
put him in the s. that were in the Jer 20.02
released Jeremiah from the s., 20.03
to put him in the s. and collar. 29.26
and fastened their feet in the s. Ac 16.24

STOIC
Epicurean and S. philosophers met Ac 17.18

STOLE
and Rachel s. her father's household Gen 31.19
so Absalom s. the hearts of the men 2Sa 15.06
And the people s. into the city 19.03
and s. him away from among the 2Ki 11.02
and s. him away from among the 2Ch 22.11
by night and s. him away while we Mt 28.13

STOLEN
found with me, shall be counted s." Gen 30.33
not know that Rachel had s. them. 31.32
whether s. by day or s. by night. 31.39
For I was indeed s. out of the land 40.15
Why have you s. my silver cup? 44.04
If the s. beast is found alive in Ex 22.04
and it is s. out of the man's house, 22.07
But if it is s. from him, he shall 22.12
they have s., and lied, and put them Jos 7.11
the men of Judah s. you away, 2Sa 19.41
who had s. them from the public 21.12
"S. water is sweet, and bread eaten Pro 9.17

STOMACH
and the two cheeks and the s. Deu 18.03
yet his food is turned in his s.; Job 20.14
give you and fill your s. with it." Eze 3.03
into the mouth passes into the s., Mt 15.17
enters, not his heart but his s., Mk 7.19
meant for the s. and the s. for food"— 1Co 6.13
sake of your s. and your frequent 1Ti 5.23
it will be bitter to your s., Rev 10.09
had eaten it my s. was made bitter 10.10

STOMACHS
hunger or fill their s. with it. Eze 7.19

STONE
bdellium and onyx s. are there. Gen 2.12
And they had brick for s., 11.03
and he took the s. which he had 28.18
and this s., which I have set up 28.22
The s. on the well's mouth was large, 29.02
would roll the s. from the mouth 29.03
and put the s. back in its place 29.03
and the s. is rolled from the mouth 29.08
and rolled the s. from the well's 29.10
So Jacob took a s., and set it up 31.45
spoken with him, a pillar of s.; 35.14
of wood and in vessels of s.'" Ex 7.19
their eyes, will they not s. us? 8.26
down into the depths like a s. 15.05
thy arm, they are as still as a s., 15.16
They are almost ready to s. me." 17.04
so they took a s. and put it under 17.12
And if you make me an altar of s., 20.25
other with a s. or with his fist 21.18
it were a pavement of sapphire s., 24.10
I will give you the tables of s., 24.12
six of their names on the one s., 28.10
the remaining six on the other s., 28.10
tables of s., written with the 31.18
two tables of s. like the first; 34.01
two tables of s. like the first; 34.04
took in his hand two tables of s. 34.04
the land shall s. him with stones. Lev 20.02
let all the congregation s. him. 24.14
all the congregation shall s. him; 24.16
set up a figured s. in your land, 26.01
congregation said to s. them with Num 14.10
congregation shall s. him with 15.35
him down with a s. in the hand, 35.17
or used a s., by which a man may 35.23
wrote them upon two tables of s. Deu 4.13
you will serve gods of wood and s., 4.28
wrote them upon two tables of s., 5.22
to receive the tables of s., 9.09
two tables of s. written with the 9.10
LORD gave me the two tables of s., 9.11

STONE (cont.)
two tables of s. like the first, Deu 10.01
two tables of s. like the first, 10.03
You shall s. him to death with 13.10
and you shall s. that man or woman 17.05
the city shall s. him to death 21.21
her city shall s. her to death 22.21
and you shall s. them to death with 22.24
serve other gods, of wood and s. 28.36
of wood and s., which neither you 28.64
things, their idols of wood and s., 29.17
each of you a s. upon his shoulder, Jos 4.05
goes up to the s. of Bohan the son 15.06
down to the S. of Bohan the son of 18.17
and he took a great s., 24.26
this s. shall be a witness against 24.27
Jerubbaal, seventy men, upon one s.; Ju 9.05
his sons, seventy men on one s., 9.18
one could sling a s. at a hair, 20.16
A great s. was there; and they split 1Sa 6.14
and set them upon the great s.; 6.15
The great s., beside which they set 6.18
Then Samuel took a s. and set it up 7.12
roll a great s. to me here." 14.33
hand in his bag and took out a s., 17.49
the s. sank into his forehead, and 17.49
Philistine with a sling and with a s., 17.50
and remain beside yonder s. heap. 20.19
from beside the s. heap and fell 20.41
within him, and he became as a s. 25.37
gold, and in it was a precious s.; 2Sa 12.30
at the great s. which is in Gibeon, 20.08
and fatlings by the Serpent's S., 1Ki 1.09
hewers of s. in the hill country, 5.15
timber and the s. to build the 5.18
it was with s. prepared at the 6.07
all was cedar, no s. was seen. 6.18
courses of hewn s. and one course 6.36
courses of hewn s. round about, 7.12
two tables of s. which Moses put 8.09
as common in Jerusalem as s., 10.27
take him out, and s. him to death." 21.10
piece of land every man threw a s., 2Ki 3.25
and quarried s. for making repairs 12.12
and put it upon a pediment of s. 16.17
work of men's hands, wood and s.; 19.18
and quarried s. to repair the 22.06
gold, and in it was a precious s.; 1Ch 20.02
timber and s. too I have provided 22.14
gold as common in Jerusalem as s., 2Ch 1.15
s., and wood, and in purple, blue, and 2.14
as common in Jerusalem as s., 9.27
the builders to buy quarried s., 34.11
he will break down their s. wall!" Neh 4.03
into the depths, as a s. into mighty waters. 9.11
The waters become hard like s., Job 38.30
His heart is hard as a s., 41.24
you dash your foot against a s. Ps 91.12
The s. which the builders rejected 118.22
is like a magic s. in the eyes of Pro 17.08
and its s. wall was broken down. 24.31
who binds the s. in the sling is 26.08
and a s. will come back upon him 26.27
A s. is heavy, and sand is weighty, 27.03
and a s. of offense, and a rock of Is 8.14
in Zion for a foundation a s., 28.16
a tested s., a precious cornerstone, 28.16
work of men's hands, wood and s.; 37.19
and to a s., 'You gave me birth.' Jer 2.27
committing adultery with s. and tree. 3.09
No s. shall be taken from you for a 51.26
a corner and no s. for a foundation, 51.26
bind a s. to it, and cast it into 51.63
and they shall s. you and cut you Eze 16.40
countries, and worship wood and s.' 20.32
And the host shall s. them and 23.47
every precious s. was your covering, 28.13
the heart of s. and give you a 36.26
tables of hewn s. for the burnt 40.42
a s. was cut out by no human hand, Dan 2.34
But the s. that struck the image 2.35
you saw that a s. was cut from a 2.45
silver, bronze, iron, wood, and s. 5.04
and s., which do not see or hear or 5.23
And a s. was brought and laid upon 6.17
shall be like s. heaps on the Hos 12.11
you have built houses of hewn s., Amo 5.11
For the s. will cry out from the Hab 2.11
to a dumb s., Arise! Can this give 2.19
Before a s. was placed upon a s. Hag 2.15
upon the s. which I have set before Zec 3.09
upon a single s. with seven facets, 3.09
forward the top s. amid shouts of 4.07
Jerusalem a heavy s. for all the 12.03
you strike your foot against a s.'" Mt 4.06
him for a loaf, will give him a s.? 7.09
'The very s. which the builders 21.42
who falls on this s. will be broken * 21.44
be left here one s. upon another, 24.02
rolled a great s. to the door of 27.60
by sealing the s. and setting a 27.66
and came and rolled back the s., 28.02
'The very s. which the builders Mk 12.10
be left here one s. upon another, 13.02
and he rolled a s. against the door 15.46
roll away the s. for us from the 16.03
saw that the s. was rolled back; 16.04
command this s. to become bread." Lk 4.03
you strike your foot against a s.'" 4.11
not leave one s. upon another in 19.44
men,' all the people will s. us; 20.06
'The very s. which the builders 20.17
falls on that s. will be broken to 20.18
left here one s. upon another that 21.06
And they found the s. rolled away 24.02
Now six s. jars were standing there, Jn 2.06
law Moses commanded us to s. such. * 8.05
be the first to throw a s. at her." * 8.07
took up stones again to s. him. 10.31
for which of these do you s. me?" 10.32
"We s. you for no good work but for 10.33
were but now seeking to s. you, 11.08
was a cave, and a s. lay upon it. 11.38
Jesus said, "Take away the s." Martha the sister 11.39
So they took away the s. And Jesus lifted 11.41
saw that the s. had been taken 20.01
This is the s. which was rejected Ac 4.11
to molest them and to s. them, 14.05
or s., a representation by the art 17.29
of the sacred s. that fell from 19.35
stumbled over the stumbling s., Rom 9.32
in Zion a s. that will make men 9.33
on tablets of s. but on tablets of 2Co 3.03
of death, carved in letters on s., 3.07
Come to him, to that living s., 1Pe 2.04
"Behold, I am laying in Zion a s., 2.06
"The very s. which the builders 2.07
and "A s. that will make men 2.08
and I will give him a white s., Rev 2.17
written on the s. which no one 2.17
silver and bronze and s. and wood, 9.20
angel took up a s. like a great 18.21

STONECUTTERS
and to the masons and the s., 2Ki 12.12
and he set s. to prepare dressed 1Ch 22.02
s., masons, carpenters, and all kinds 22.15

STONED
him, but he shall be s. or shot; Ex 19.13
woman to death, the ox shall be s., 21.28
man or a woman, the ox shall be s., 21.29
of silver, and the ox shall be s. 21.32
they shall be s. with stones, their Lev 20.27
and s. him with stones. Thus the people 24.23
and s. him to death with stones, as Num 15.36

STONED (cont.)

And all Israel s. him with stones; Jos 7.25
with fire, and s. them with stones. 7.25
and all Israel s. him to death 1Ki 12.18
and s. him to death with stones. 21.13
Jezebel, saying, "Naboth has been s.; 21.14
Naboth had been s. and was dead, 21.15
of Israel s. him to death with 2Ch 10.18
the king they s. him with stones 24.21
killed another, and s. another. Mt 21.35
afraid of being s. by the people. Ac 5.26
him out of the city and s. him; 7.58
they s. Paul and dragged him out of 14.19
once I was s. Three times I have been 2Co 11.25
They were s., they were sawn in two, Heb 11.37
the mountain, it shall be s." 12.20

STONE-HEAP

His roots twine about the s.; Job 8.17

STONE'S

withdrew from them about a s. throw, Lk 22.41

STONES

taking one of the s. of the place, Gen 28.11
"Gather s.," and they took s., 31.46
you shall not build it of hewn s.; Ex 20.25
onyx s., and s. for setting, for the 25.07
And you shall take two onyx s., 28.09
engrave the two s.; two s. with the names 28.11
set the two s. upon the shoulder-pieces 28.12
as s. of remembrance for the sons 28.12
shall set in it four rows of s. 28.17
There shall be twelve s. with their 28.21
in cutting s. for setting, and in 31.05
and onyx s. and s. for setting, 35.09
brought onyx s. and s. to be 35.27
in cutting s. for setting, and in 35.33
The onyx s. were prepared, enclosed 39.06
to be s. of remembrance for the 39.07
And they set in it four rows of s. 39.10
There were twelve s. with their 39.14
take out the s. in which is the Lev 14.40
take other s. and put them in the 14.42
put them in the place of those s., 14.42
taken out the s. and scraped the 14.43
its s. and timber and all the 14.45
the land shall stone him with s. 20.02
they shall be stoned with s., 20.27
the camp, and stoned him with s. 24.23
congregation said to stone them with s. Num 14.10
stone him with s. outside the camp 15.35
and stoned him to death with s., 15.36
and destroy all their figured s., 33.52
a land whose s. are iron, and out of Deu 8.09
You shall stone him to death with s., 13.10
that man or woman to death with s. 17.05
shall stone him to death with s.; 21.21
shall stone her to death with s., 22.21
shall stone them to death with s., 22.24
you, you shall set up large s., 27.02
Jordan, you shall set up these s., 27.04
the LORD your God, an altar of s.; 27.05
to the LORD your God of unhewn s.; 27.06
write upon the s. all the words of 27.08
'Take twelve s. from here out of Jos 4.03
'What do those s. mean to you?' 4.06
So these s. shall be to the people 4.07
took up twelve s. out of the midst 4.08
set up twelve s. in the midst of 4.09
And those twelve s., which they 4.20
to come, 'What do these s. mean?' took 4.21
And all Israel stoned him with s.; 7.25
with fire, and stoned them with s. 7.25
a great heap of s. that remains to 7.26
raised over it a great heap of s., 8.29
of Moses, "an altar of unhewn s., 8.31
wrote upon the s. a copy of the 8.32
down great s. from heaven upon 10.11
"Roll great s. against the mouth of 10.18
they set great s. against the 10.27
at the sculptured s. near Gilgal, Ju 3.19
passed beyond the sculptured s., 3.26
with s. laid in due order; 6.26
five smooth s. from the brook, 1Sa 17.40
And he threw s. at David, and at all 2Sa 16.06
and threw s. at him and flung dust. 16.13
over him a very great heap of s.; 18.17
costly s. in order to lay the 1Ki 5.17
of the house with dressed s. 5.17
All these were made of costly s., 7.09
The foundation was of costly s., 7.10
huge s., s. of eight and ten 7.10
And above were costly s., 7.11
very much gold, and precious s.; 10.02
quantity of spices, and precious s.; 10.10
of almug wood and precious s. 10.11
Israel stoned him to death with s. 12.18
away the s. of Ramah and its 15.22
Elijah took twelve s., according to 18.31
and with the s. he built an altar 18.32
and the s., and the dust, and licked 18.38
baked on hot s. and a jar of water 19.06
and stoned him to death with s. 21.13
every good piece of land with s." 2Ki 3.19
till only its s. were left in 3.25
down and he broke in pieces its s., 23.15
and sling s. with either the right 1Ch 12.02
prepare dressed s. for building 22.02
quantities of onyx and s. for setting, 29.02
colored s., all sorts of precious s., 29.02
had precious s. gave them to the 29.08
house with settings of precious s. 2Ch 3.06
and very much gold and precious s. 9.01
and precious s.: there were no 9.09
brought algum wood and precious s. 9.10
Israel stoned him to death with s. 10.18
away the s. of Ramah and its 16.06
stoned him with s. in the court of 24.21
of mail, bows, and s. for slinging. 26.14
to shoot arrows and great s. 26.15
for precious s., for spices, for 32.27
It is being built with huge s., Ez 5.08
of great s. and one course of 6.04
they revive the s. out of the Neh 4.02
mother-of-pearl and precious s. Est 1.06
in league with the s. of the field, Job 5.23
Is my strength the strength of s., 6.12
the waters wear away the s.; 14.19
Ophir among the s. of the torrent 22.24
Its s. are the place of sapphires, 28.06
For thy servants hold her s. dear, Ps 102.14
gold, and abundance of costly s.; Pro 20.15
a time to cast away s., and a time Ecc 3.05
and a time to gather s. together; 3.05
He who quarries s. is hurt by them; 10.09
He digged it and cleared it of s., Is 5.02
but we will build with dressed s.; 9.10
who go down to the s. of the Pit, 14.19
makes all the s. of the altars 27.09
I will set your s. in antimony, 54.11
and all your wall of precious s. 54.12
Among the smooth s. of the valley 57.06
wood, bronze, instead of s., iron. 60.17
clear it of s., lift up an ensign 62.10
"Take in your hands large s., Jer 43.09
above these s. which I have hid, 43.10
he has blocked my ways with hewn s., Lam 3.09
into the pit and cast s. on me; 3.53
The holy s. lie scattered at the 4.01
your s. and timber and soil they Eze 26.12
and all precious s., and gold. 27.22
midst of the s. of fire you walked 28.14
from the midst of the s. of fire. 28.16
with precious s. and costly gifts. Dan 11.38

STONES (cont.)

pour down her s. into the valley, Mic 1.06
and consume it, both timber and s." Zec 5.04
able from these s. to raise up Mt 3.09
command these s. to become loaves 4.03
out, and bruising himself with s. Mk 5.05
what wonderful s. and what wonderful 13.01
able from these s. to raise up Lk 3.08
silent, the very s. would cry out." 19.40
with noble s. and offerings, 21.05
So they took up s. to throw at him; Jn 8.59
The Jews took up s. again to stone 10.31
precious s., wood, hay, stubble— 1Co 3.12
and like living s. be yourselves 1Pe 2.05

STONING

for the people spoke of s. him, 1Sa 30.06
prophets and s. those who are sent Mt 23.37
prophets and s. those who are sent Lk 13.34
And as they were s. Stephen, Ac 7.59

STONY

I will take the s. heart out of Eze 11.19

STOOD

three men s. in front of him. Gen 18.02
and he s. by them under the tree 18.08
Abraham still s. before the LORD. 18.22
where he had s. before the LORD; 19.27
the LORD s. above it and said, "I am 28.13
lo, my sheaf arose and s. upright; 37.07
and s. by the other cows on the 41.03
to Egypt, and s. before Joseph. 43.15
before all those who s. by him; 45.01
And his sister s. at a distance, to Ex 2.04
but Moses s. up and helped them, and 2.17
and s. before Pharaoh, and Moses 9.10
before them and s. behind them, 14.19
up, the floods s. up in a heap; 15.08
and the people s. about Moses from 18.13
and trembled; and they s. afar off, 20.18
And the people s. afar off, while 20.21
then Moses s. in the gate of the 32.26
and every man s. at his tent door, 33.08
in the cloud and s. with him there, 34.05
drew near and s. before the LORD. Lev 9.05
and s. at the door of the tent, and Num 12.05
and they s. at the entrance of the 16.18
came out and s. at the door of 16.27
And he s. beween the dead and the 16.48
of the LORD s. in a narrow path 22.24
and s. in a narrow place, where 22.26
And they s. before Moses, and before 27.02
day that you s. before the LORD Deu 4.10
came near and s. at the foot of 4.11
while I s. between the LORD and you 5.05
pillar of cloud s. by the door of 31.15
down from above s. and rose up in Jos 3.16
of the LORD s. on dry ground in 3.17
place where the priests' feet s., 4.03
the ark of the covenant had s.; 4.09
bore the ark s. in the midst of 4.10
and they s. in awe of him, as they 4.14
as they had s. in awe of Moses, all 4.14
a man s. before him with his drawn 5.13
s. on opposite sides of the ark 8.33
And the sun s. still, and the moon 10.13
the cities that s. on mounds did 11.13
until he has s. before the congregation 20.06
till he s. before the congregation. 20.09
They s. every man in his place Ju 7.21
he went and s. on the top of Mount 9.07
went out and s. in the entrance of 9.35
forward and s. at the entrance of 9.44
s. by the entrance of the gate; 18.16
the priest s. by the enrance of 18.17
And the LORD came and s. forth, 1Sa 3.10
and when he s. among the people, he 10.23
And the Philistines s. on the 17.03
and Israel s. on the mountain on 17.03
He s. and shouted to the ranks of 17.08
said to the men who s. by him, 17.26
Then David ran and s. over the 17.51
great success, he s. in awe of him. 18.15
to his servants who s. about him, 22.07
who s. by the servants of Saul, "I 22.09
said to the guard who s. about him, 22.17
and s. afar off on the top of the 26.13
So I s. beside him, and slew him, 2Sa 1.10
had fallen and died, s. still. 2.23
elders of his house s. beside him, 12.17
So the king s. at the side of the 18.04
you yourself would have s. aloof." 18.13
so he turned aside, and s. still. 18.30
and it s. against the rampart; 20.15
king's presence, and s. before the king. 1Ki 1.28
and s. before the ark of the 3.15
to the king, and s. before him. 3.16
and they s. in awe of the king, 3.28
It s. upon twelve oxen, three facing 7.25
all the assembly of Israel s. 8.14
Then Solomon s. before the altar of 8.22
and he s., and blessed all the 8.55
while twelve lions s. there, 10.20
who had s. before Solomon his 12.06
up with him and s. before him. 12.08
the road, and the ass s. beside it; 13.24
the lion also s. beside the body. 13.24
went out and s. at the entrance of 19.13
forward and s. before the LORD, 22.21
and s. at some distance from them, 2Ki 2.07
went back and s. on the bank of 2.13
had called her, she s. before him. 4.12
called her, she s. in the doorway. 4.15
and he came and s. before him; 5.15
and s. before his master, and Elisha 5.25
When he came and s. before him, 8.09
he s., and said to all the people, 10.09
and the guards s., every man with 11.11
he revived, and s. on his feet. 13.21
they came and s. by the conduit of 18.17
Then the Rabshakeh s. and called 18.28
And the king s. by the pillar and 23.03
who s. on his right hand, namely, 1Ch 6.39
Satan s. up against Israel, and 21.01
the cherubim s. on their feet, 2Ch 3.13
It s. upon twelve oxen, three facing 4.04
s. east of the altar with a hundred 5.12
all the assembly of Israel s. 6.03
Then Solomon s. before the altar of 6.12
and he s. upon it. Then he knelt 6.13
The priests s. at their posts; 7.06
sounded trumpets, and all Israel s. 7.06
while twelve lions s. there, 9.19
who had s. before Solomon his 10.06
up with him and s. before him. 10.08
Then Abijah s. up on Mount Zemaraim 13.04
forward and s. before the LORD, 18.20
And Jehoshaphat s. in the assembly 20.05
men of Judah s. before the LORD, 20.13
s. up to praise the LORD, the God of 20.19
Jehoshaphat s. and said, "Hear me, 20.20
and he s. above the people, and 24.20
s. up against those who were coming 28.12
The Levites s. with the instruments 29.26
incense altars which s. above them; 34.04
And the king s. in his place and 34.31
the priests s. in their place, and 35.10
And Ezra the priest s. up and said Ez 10.10
and the leaders s. behind all the Neh 4.16
And Ezra the scribe s. on a wooden 8.04
and beside him s. Mattithiah, 8.04
he opened it all the people s. 8.05
and s. and confessed their sins and 9.02

STOOD (cont.)
And they s. up in their place and Neh 9.03
stairs of the Levites s. Jeshua, 9.04
their brethren s. opposite them in 12.09
who gave thanks s. in the house of 12.40
royal robes and s. in the inner Est 5.01
and Esther rose and s. before the 8.05
the hair of my flesh s. up. Job 4.15
It s. still, but I could not discern 4.16
withdrew, and the aged rose and s.; 29.08
because I s. in great fear of the 31.34
he commanded, and it s. forth. Ps 33.09
the waters s. above the mountains. 104.06
s. in the breach before him, to turn 106.23
Then Phinehas s. up and interposed, 106.30
Above him s. the seraphim; each had six Is 6.02
And he s. by the conduit of the 36.02
Then the Rabshakeh s. and called 36.13
Moses and Samuel s. before me, Jer 15.01
Remember how I s. before thee to 18.20
and he s. in the court of the LORD's 19.14
among them has s. in the council 23.18
But if they had s. in my council, 23.22
the princes who s. beside the king 36.21
gods, and all the women who s. by, 44.15
and when those s., these s.; Eze 1.21
when they s. still, they let down 1.24
when they s. still, they let down 1.25
lo, the glory of the LORD s. there, 3.23
And before them s. seventy men of 8.11
went in and s. beside the bronze 9.02
he went in and s. beside a wheel. 10.06
When they s. still, these s. 10.17
of the house and s. over the cherubim. 10.18
and they s. at the door of the east 10.19
and s. upon the mountain which is 11.23
and its roots remained where it s. 17.06
and s. upon their feet, an exceedingly 37.10
therefore they s. before the king. Dan 1.19
came in and s. before the king. 2.02
s. before you, and its appearance 2.31
and they s. before the image that 3.03
times ten thousand s. before him; 7.10
of those who s. there and asked 7.16
there s. before me one having the 8.15
So he came near where I s.; 8.17
this word to me, I s. up trembling. 10.11
I said to him who s. before me, 10.16
I s. up to confirm and strengthen 11.01
two others s., one on this bank of 12.05
On the day that you s. aloof, Ob 1.11
You should not have s. at the 1.14
He s. and measured the earth; Hab 3.06
The sun and moon s. still in their 3.11
feared me, he s. in awe of my name. Mal 2.05
mother and his brothers s. outside, Mt 12.46
the whole crowd s. on the beach. 13.02
And the high priest s. up and said, 26.62
Now Jesus s. before the governor; 27.11
And those who s. there said to them, Mk 11.05
of those who s. by drew his sword, 14.47
And some s. up and bore false 14.57
And the high priest s. up in the 14.60
who s. facing him, saw that he thus 15.39
the sabbath day. And he s. up to read; Lk 4.16
And he s. over her and rebuked the 4.39
stand here." And he rose and s. there. 6.08
with them and s. on a level place, 6.17
the bier, and the bearers s. still. 7.14
and the two men who s. with him. 9.32
a lawyer s. up to put him to the 10.25
ten lepers, who s. at a distance 17.12
The Pharisee s. and prayed thus 18.11
And Zacchaeus s. and said to the 19.08
And he said to those who s. by, 19.24
priests and the scribes s. by, 23.10
And the people s. by, watching; 23.35
from Galilee s. at a distance and 23.49
two men s. by them in dazzling 24.04
And they s. still, looking sad. 24.17
this, Jesus himself s. among them. 24.36
Jesus s. up and proclaimed, "If any Jn 7.37
he s. up and said to them, "Let him * 8.07
another as they s. in the temple, 11.56
while Peter s. outside at the door. 18.16
A bowl full of vinegar s. there; 19.29
But Mary s. weeping outside the 20.11
Jesus came and s. among them and 20.19
but Jesus came and s. among them, 20.26
breaking, Jesus s. on the beach; 21.04
two men s. by them in white robes, Ac 1.10
days Peter s. up among the brethren 1.15
And leaping up he s. and walked and 3.08
s. up and ordered the men to be put 5.34
traveling with him s. speechless, 9.07
All the widows s. beside him 9.39
for Simon's house, s. before the gate 10.17
a man s. before me in bright 10.30
named Agabus s. up and foretold by 11.28
So Paul s. up, and motioning with 13.16
those who s. by him to strike him 23.02
Those who s. by said, "Would you 23.04
Pharisees' party s. up and contended, 23.09
night the Lord s. by him and said, 23.11
found when I s. before the council, 24.20
down from Jerusalem s. about him, 25.07
When the accusers s. up, they brought no 25.18
night there s. by me an angel of 27.23
his face, because he s. condemned. Gal 2.11
the bond which s. against us with Col 2.14
But the Lord s. by me and gave me 2Ti 4.17
second curtain s. a tent called Heb 9.03
for when he has s. the test he Jas 1.12
a throne s. in heaven, with one Rev 4.02
And all the angels s. round the 7.11
angel came and s. at the altar 8.03
and they s. up on their feet, and 11.11
And the dragon s. before the woman 12.04
And he s. on the sand of the sea. 12.17
on Mount Zion s. the Lamb, and with 14.01
trade is on the sea, s. far off 18.17

STOOL
make thy enemies a s. for thy feet.' Lk 20.43
make thy enemies a s. for thy feet.' Ac 2.35
thy enemies a s. for thy feet"? Heb 1.13
should be made a s. for his feet. 10.13

STOOP
They s., they bow down together, Is 46.02
am not worthy to s. down and untie. Mk 1.07

STOOPED
He s. down, he couched as a lion, and Gen 49.09
as she wept she s. to look into Jn 20.11

STOOPING
s. and looking in, he saw the linen *Lk 24.12
and s. to look in, he saw the linen Jn 20.05

STOOPS
Nebo s., their idols are on beasts Is 46.01

STOP
look back or s. anywhere in the Gen 19.17
has passed on s. here yourself for 1Sa 9.27
Then Samuel said to Saul, "S.! I will tell 15.16
and go down, lest the rain s. you.'" 1Ki 18.44
and s. up all springs of water, and 2Ki 3.19
S.! Why should you be put 2Ch 25.16
mighty men to s. the water of the 32.03
they did not s. them till a report Ez 5.05
them and kill them and s. the work." Neh 4.11
should the work s. while I leave 6.03
s. and consider the wondrous works Job 37.14
fugitives s. without strength; Jer 48.45

STOP (cont.)

I will make you s. playing the Eze 16.41
And I will s. the music of your 26.13
and put a s. to their feeding the 34.10
And he commanded the chariot to s., Ac 8.38
will you not s. making crooked the 13.10

STOPPED

Philistines had s. and filled with Gen 26.15
Philistines had s. them after the 26.18
or his body is s. from discharge, Lev 15.03
and the living and the plague was s. Num 16.48
of meeting, when the plague was s. 16.50
Jordan shall be s. from flowing, Jos 3.13
of Bethshemesh, and s. there. 1Sa 6.14
and all the men s., and pursued 2Sa 2.28
one who came by, seeing him, s.; 20.12
the man saw that all the people s., 20.12
he s. building Ramah, and he dwelt 1Ki 15.21
they s. every spring of water, and 2Ki 3.25
not another." Then the oil s. flowing. 4.06
and he struck three times, and s. 13.18
he s. building Ramah, and let his 2Ch 16.05
So the prophet s., but said, "I know 25.16
and they s. all the springs and the 32.04
of God which is in Jerusalem s.; Ez 4.24
for the mouths of liars will be s. Ps 63.11
and many waters shall be s.; Eze 31.15
and s. their ears that they might Zec 7.11
of my mountains shall be s. up, 14.05
And Jesus s. and called them, saying, Mt 20.32
And Jesus s. and said, "Call him." Mk 10.49
And Jesus s., and commanded him to Lk 18.40
loud voice and s. their ears and Ac 7.57
the soldiers, they s. beating Paul. 21.32
law, so that every mouth may be s., Rom 3.19
promises, s. the mouths of lions, Heb 11.33

STOPS

the deaf adder that s. its ear, Ps 58.04
and all wickedness s. its mouth. 107.42
who s. his ears from hearing of Is 33.15
and also s. those who want to 3Jn 1.10

STORE

food that is eaten, and s. it up; Gen 6.21
And you shall eat old s. long kept, Lev 26.10
"Is not this laid up in s. with me, Deu 32.34
so that we have this great s. left." 2Ch 31.10
full, providing all manner of s.; Ps 144.13
and s. them in your vessels, and Jer 40.10
is bound up, his sin is kept in s. Hos 13.12
"those who s. up violence and Amo 3.10
for I have nowhere to s. my crops?' Lk 12.17
there I will s. all my grain and 12.18
put something aside and s. it up, 1Co 16.02

STORE-CITIES

they built for Pharaoh s., Pithom and Ex 1.11
and all the s. that Solomon had, and 1Ki 9.19
and all the s. which he built in 2Ch 8.04
and all the s. that Solomon had, and 8.06
Abelmaim, and all the s. of Naphtali. 16.04
built in Judah fortresses and s., 17.12

STORED

and s. up food in the cities; Gen 41.48
he s. up in every city the food 41.48
And Joseph s. up grain in great 41.49
and s. them in the treasuries of 1Ki 7.51
fathers have s. up till this day, 2Ki 20.17
and s. the silver, the gold, and all 2Ch 5.01
where the documents were s. Ez 6.01
with what thou hast s. up for them; Ps 17.14
it will not be s. or hoarded, Is 23.18
fathers have s. up till this day, 39.06
now exist have been s. up for fire, 2Pe 3.07

STOREHOUSE

to his sons was allotted the s. 1Ch 26.15
as well as two and two at the s.; 26.17
God, to the chambers, to the s. Neh 10.38
the king, to a wardrobe of the s., Jer 38.11
Bring the full tithes into the s., Mal 3.10
they have neither s. nor barn, Lk 12.24

STOREHOUSES

the land, Joseph opened all the s., Gen 41.56
all that was found in his s.; 2Ki 20.13
nothing in my s. that I did not 20.15
s. also for the yield of grain, wine, 2Ch 32.28
guard at the s. of the gates. Neh 12.25
grain, wine, and oil into the s. 13.12
over the s. Shelemiah the priest, 13.13
"Have you entered the s. of the snow, Job 38.22
have you seen the s. of the hail, 38.22
in a bottle; he put the deeps in s. Ps 33.07
brings forth the wind from his s. 135.07
all that was found in his s. Is 39.02
nothing in my s. that I did not 39.04
brings forth the wind from his s. Jer 10.13
brings forth the wind from his s. 51.16
the clods, the s. are desolate; Joe 1.17

STORES

provided great s. of iron for 1Ch 22.03
and over the s. of oil was Joash. 27.28
and s. of food, oil, and wine. 2Ch 11.11
and he had great s. in the cities 17.13
over the chambers for the s., Neh 12.44
You say, 'God s. up their iniquity Job 21.19
he s. up sound wisdom for the Pro 2.07
at Michmash he s. his baggage; Is 10.28
for we have s. of wheat, barley, oil, Jer 41.08

STORIES

the side chambers were in three s., Eze 41.06
against gallery in three s. 42.03
For they were in three s., 42.06

STORING

heart you are s. up wrath for Rom 2.05

STORK

the s., the heron according to its Lev 11.19
the s., the heron, after their kinds; Deu 14.18
the s. has her home in the fir trees. Ps 104.17
Even the s. in the heavens knows Jer 8.07
had wings like the wings of a s., Zec 5.09

STORM

Valley of Salt and took Sela by s., 2Ki 14.07
chaff that the s. carries away? Job 21.18
me about in the roar of the s. 30.22
he made the s. be still, and the Ps 107.29
when panic strikes you like a s., Pro 1.27
and a shelter from the s. and rain. Is 4.06
in the s. which will come from afar? 10.03
and whirling dust before the s. 17.13
from the s. and a shade from the 25.04
is like a s. against a wall, 25.04
like a s. of hail, a destroying 28.02
like a s. of mighty, overflowing 28.02
Behold, the s. of the LORD! Wrath Jer 23.19
Behold the s. of the LORD! Wrath 30.23
You will advance, coming on like a s., Eze 38.09
In the s. the king of Israel shall Hos 10.15
His way is in whirlwind and s., Nah 1.03
the LORD who makes the s. clouds, Zec 10.01
there arose a great s. on the sea, Mt 8.24
And a great s. of wind arose, and Mk 4.37
And a s. of wind came down on the Lk 8.23
springs and mists driven by a s.; 2Pe 2.17

STORMS

till the s. of destruction pass by. Ps 57.01

STORM-TOSSED
s., and not comforted, behold, I will Is 54.11
As we were violently s., they began next Ac 27.18

STORMWIND
fire, and his chariots like the s., Is 66.15

STORMY
commanded, and raised the s. wind, Ps 107.25
s. wind fulfilling his command! 148.08
a s. wind came out of the north, and Eze 1.04
will fall, and a s. wind break out; 13.11
I will make a s. wind break out in 13.13
'It will be s. today, for the sky is Mt 16.03

STORY
and she told him the same s., Gen 39.17
The lowest s. was five cubits broad, 1Ki 6.06
for the lowest s. was on the south 6.08
went up by stairs to the middle s., 6.08
from the middle s. to the third. 6.08
each s. five cubits high, and it was 6.10
written in the s. of the prophet 2Ch 13.22
over another, thirty in each s. Eze 41.06
as they rose from s. to s., 41.07
from s. to s. round about the 41.07
from the lowest s. to the top 41.07
to the top s. through the middle s. 41.07
and this s. has been spread among Mt 28.15
from the third s. and was taken up Ac 20.09

STOUT
sickness among his s. warriors, Is 10.16
and he who is s. of heart among the Amo 2.16
"Your words have been s. against me, Mal 3.13

STOUTHEARTED
The s. were stripped of their spoil; Ps 76.05

STOVE
whether oven or s., it shall be Lev 11.35

STRAGGLER
and there is no s. in his ranks." Is 14.31

STRAIGHT
go up every man s. before him." Jos 6.05
every man s. before him, and they 6.20
And the cows went s. in the direction 1Sa 6.12
seek from him a s. way for ourselves, Ez 8.21
they went up s. before them by the Neh 12.37
make thy way s. before me. Ps 5.08
s. to the grave they descend, and 49.14
he led them by a s. way, till they 107.07
and he will make s. your paths. Pro 3.06
and your gaze be s. before you. 4.25
They are all s. to him who understands 8.09
by, who are going s. on their way, 9.15
of the blameless keeps his way s., 11.05
he whose way is s. is an abomination 29.27
What is crooked cannot be made s., Ecc 1.15
who can make s. what he has made 7.13
make s. in the desert a highway for Is 40.03
and I will make s. all his ways; 45.13
in a s. path in which they shall Jer 31.09
s. to the hill Gareb, and shall then 31.39
every man s. before him, with none 49.05
Their legs were s., and the soles of Eze 1.07
they went every one s. forward, 1.09
And each went s. forward; 1.12
their wings were stretched out s., 1.23
They went every one s. forward. 10.22
but each shall go out s. ahead. 46.09
breaches, every one s. before her; Amo 4.03
way of the Lord, make his paths s." Mt 3.03
of the Lord, make his paths s.—" Mk 1.03
way of the Lord, make his paths s. Lk 3.04
and the crooked shall be made s., 3.05
and immediately she was made s., 13.13
'Make s. the way of the Lord,' as Jn 1.23
and go to the street called S., Ac 9.11
crooked the s. paths of the Lord? 13.10
we came by a s. course to Cos, and 21.01
and make s. paths for your feet, so Heb 12.13

STRAIGHTEN
and could not fully s. herself. Lk 13.11

STRAIGHTFORWARD
they were not s. about the truth Gal 2.14

STRAIN
the toil and s. with which he Ecc 2.22

STRAINING
s. out a gnat and swallowing a Mt 23.24
lies behind and s. forward to what Php 3.13

STRAITS
to them; and they were in sore s. Ju 2.15
they were in s. (for the people 1Sa 13.06
his sufficiency he will be in s.; Job 20.22

STRANGE
after the s. gods of the land, Deu 31.16
him to jealousy with s. gods; 32.16
forth our hands to a s. god, Ps 44.20
There shall be no s. god among you; 81.09
from a people of s. language, 114.01
Your eyes will see s. things, Pro 23.33
but by men of s. lips and with an Is 28.11
to do his deed—s. is his deed! 28.21
when there was no s. god among you; 43.12
would be regarded as a s. thing. Hos 8.12
"We have seen s. things today." Lk 5.26
For you bring some s. things to our Ac 17.20
"By men of s. tongues and by the 1Co 14.21
So it is not s. if his servants 2Co 11.15
away by diverse and s. teachings; Heb 13.09
something s. were happening to you. 1Pe 4.12

STRANGER
"I am a s. and a sojourner among Gen 23.04
And when a s. shall sojourn with Ex 12.48
and for the s. who sojourns among 12.49
not wrong a s. or oppress him, 22.21
"You shall not oppress a s.; 23.09
you know the heart of a s., 23.09
native or the s. who sojourns Lev 16.29
shall any s. who sojourns among 17.12
native or the s. who sojourns 18.26
"When a s. sojourns with you in 19.33
The s. who sojourns with you shall 19.34
them for the poor and for the s.: 23.22
as a s. and a sojourner he shall 25.35
"If a s. or sojourner with you 25.47
himself to the s. or sojourner 25.47
And if a s. sojourns among you, and Num 9.14
And if a s. is sojourning with you, 15.14
you and for the s. who sojourns 15.15
you and for the s. who sojourns 15.16
and the s. who sojourns among them, 15.26
and for the s. who sojourns among 15.29
and to the s. who sojourns among 19.10
and for the s. and for the sojourner 35.15
married outside the family to a s.; Deu 25.05
and for the s. sojourning among Jos 20.09
and no s. passed among them). Job 15.19
my maidservants count me as a s.; 19.15
I have become a s. to my brethren, Ps 69.08
have given your pledge for a s.; Pro 6.01
surety for a s. will smart for it, 11.15
bitterness, and no s. shares its joy. 14.10
when he has given surety for a s., 20.16
a s., and not your own lips. 27.02
when he has given surety for a s., 27.13
enjoy them, but a s. enjoys them; Ecc 6.02
thou be like a s. in the land, Jer 14.08

STRANGER (cont.)
I was a s. and you welcomed me, Mt 25.35
we see thee a s. and welcome thee, 25.38
I was a s. and you did not welcome 25.43
or thirsty or a s. or naked or 25.44
A s. they will not follow, but they Jn 10.05

STRANGER'S
or to a member of the s. family, Lev 25.47

STRANGERS
them like s. and spoke roughly to Gen 42.07
for you were s. in the land of Ex 22.21
for you were s. in the land of 23.09
or of the s. that sojourn among Lev 17.08
or of the s. that sojourn among 17.10
or of the s. that sojourn among 17.13
for you were s. in the land of 19.34
or of the s. that sojourn in Israel, 20.02
for you are s. and sojourners with 25.23
from among the s. who sojourn with 25.45
For we are s. before thee, and 1Ch 29.15
may s. plunder the fruits of his Ps 109.11
lest s. take their fill of your Pro 5.10
alone, and not for s. with you. 5.17
is hopeless, for I have loved s., Jer 2.25
favors among s. under every green 3.13
you shall serve s. in a land that 5.19
and s. shall no more make servants 30.08
inheritance has been turned over to s., Lam 5.02
or of the s. that sojourn in Israel, Eze 14.07
who receives s. instead of her 16.32
I will bring s. upon you, the most 28.07
be holy and s. shall never again Joe 3.17
on the day that s. carried off his Ob 1.11
the potter's field, to bury s. in. Mt 27.07
they do not know the voice of s." Jn 10.05
and s. to the covenants of promise, Eph 2.12
are no longer s. and sojourners, 2.19
that they were s. and exiles on Heb 11.13
neglect to show hospitality to s., 13.02
to the brethren, especially to s., 3Jn 1.05

STRANGLED
his whelps and s. prey for his Nah 2.12
and from what is s. and from blood. Ac 15.20
from what is s. and from unchastity. 15.29
from what is s. and from unchastity." 21.25

STRANGLING
I would choose s. and death rather Job 7.15

STRATEGY
mere words are s. and power for war? Is 36.05

STRAW
"We have both s. and provender enough, Gen 24.25
and gave him s. and provender for 24.32
give the people s. to make bricks, Ex 5.07
go and gather s. for themselves. 5.07
Pharaoh, 'I will not give you s. 5.10
get your s. wherever you can find 5.11
of Egypt, to gather stubble for s. 5.12
daily task, as when there was s." 5.13
No s. is given to your servants, yet 5.16
for no s. shall be given you, yet 5.18
We have s. and provender for our Ju 19.19
Barley also and s. for the horses 1Ki 4.28
That they are like s. before the Job 21.18
He counts iron as s., and bronze 41.27
the lion shall eat s. like the ox. Is 11.07
as s. is trodden down in a dung-pit. 25.10
the lion shall eat s. like the ox; 65.25
What has s. in common with wheat? Jer 23.28

STRAY
but I do not s. from thy precepts. Ps 119.110
her ways, do not s. into her paths; Pro 7.25
instruction only to s. from the 19.27

STRAYED
reached to Jazer and s. to the desert; Is 16.08
the s. you have not brought back, Eze 34.04
lost, and I will bring back the s., 34.16
Woe to them, for they have s. from me! Hos 7.13
For some have already s. after Satan. 1Ti 5.15

STRAYING
For you were s. like sheep, but have 1Pe 2.25

STRAYS
Like a bird that s. from its nest, Pro 27.08
nest, is a man who s. from his home. 27.08

STREAKS
and plane, and peeled white s. in them, Gen 30.37

STREAM
them and sent them across the s., Gen 32.23
fountain of wisdom is a gushing s. Pro 18.04
heart is a s. of water in the hand 21.01
an overflowing s. that reaches up Is 30.28
like a s. of brimstone, kindles it. 30.33
for he will come like a rushing s., 59.19
the nations like an overflowing s.; 66.12
that sends out its roots by the s., Jer 17.08
Let ears s. down like a torrent Lam 2.18
A s. of fire issued and came forth Dan 7.10
stood, one on this bank of the s. 12.05
and one on that bank of the s. 12.05
who was above the waters of the s., 12.06
who was above the waters of the s., 12.07
and all the s. beds of Judah shall Joe 3.18
righteousness like an everflowing s. Amo 5.24
the s. broke against that house, and Lk 6.48
against which the s. broke, 6.49

STREAM-BED
'I will make this dry s. full of pools.' 2Ki 3.16
but that s. shall be filled with water, 3.17

STREAMS
sole of my foot all the s. of Egypt.' 2Ki 19.24
the s. flowing with honey and curds. Job 20.17
He binds up the s. so that they do 28.11
rock poured out for me s. of oil! 29.06
like a tree planted by s. of water, Ps 1.03
As a hart longs for flowing s., 42.01
a river whose s. make glad the 46.04
thou didst dry up ever-flowing s. 74.15
He made s. come out of the rock, and 78.16
water gushed out and s. overflowed. 78.20
they could not drink of their s. 78.44
My eyes shed s. of tears, because 119.136
s. of water in the streets? Pro 5.16
All s. run to the sea, but the sea Ecc 1.07
to the place where the s. flow, 1.07
water, and flowing s. from Lebanon. Sol 4.15
at the sources of the s. of Egypt, Is 7.18
like s. of water in a dry place, 32.02
us a place of broad rivers and s., 33.21
And the s. of Edom shall be turned 34.09
wilderness, and s. in the desert; 35.06
of my foot all the s. of Egypt. 37.25
land, and s. on the dry ground; 44.03
waters, like willows by flowing s. 44.04
run dry, the cold flowing s.? Jer 18.14
that lies in the midst of his s., Eze 29.03
fish of your s. stick to your 29.04
you up out of the midst of your s., 29.04
fish of your s. which stick to 29.04
you and all the fish of your s.; 29.05
against you, and against your s., 29.10
forth its s. to all the trees of 31.04

STREET
we will spend the night in the s." Gen 19.02
doors of your house into the s., Jos 2.19
he and Samuel went out into the s. 1Sa 9.26

STREET (cont.)
and he has no name in the s. Job 18.17
sojourner has not lodged in the s.; 31.32
who see me in the s. flee from me. Ps 31.11
Wisdom cried aloud in the s.; in the Pro 1.20
passing along the s. near her corner, 7.08
now in the s., now in the market, 7.12
and the doors on the s. are shut; Ecc 12.04
voice, or make it heard in the s.; Is 42.02
head of every s. like an antelope 51.20
and like the s. for them to pass 51.23
it out upon the children in the s., Jer 6.11
him daily from the bakers' s., 37.21
In the s. the sword bereaves; in the Lam 1.20
for hunger at the head of every s. 2.19
scattered at the head of every s. 4.01
head of every s. you built your Eze 16.25
chamber at the head of every s., 16.31
in pieces at the head of every s.; Nah 3.10
synagogues and at the s. corners, Mt 6.05
at the door out in the open s.; Mk 11.04
and go to the s. called Straight, Ac 9.11
out and passed on through one s.; 12.10
will lie in the s. of the great Rev 11.08
and the s. of the city was pure 21.21
through the middle of the s. of the city; 22.02

STREETS
publish it not in the s. of Ashkelon; 2Sa 1.20
them down like the mire of the s. 22.43
them out like the mire of the s. Ps 18.42
be no cry of distress in our s.! 144.14
abroad, streams of water in the s.? Pro 5.16
outside! I shall be slain in the s.!" 22.13
the road! There is a lion in the s.!" 26.13
and the mourners go about the s.; Ecc 12.05
in the s. and in the squares; Sol 3.02
as refuse in the midst of the s. Is 5.25
them down like the mire of the s. 10.06
in the s. they gird on sackcloth; 15.03
outcry in the s. for lack of wine; 24.11
the restorer of s. to dwell in. 58.12
fro through the s. of Jerusalem, Jer 5.01
Judah and in the s. of Jerusalem? 7.17
and from the s. of Jerusalem the 7.34
from the s. and the young men from 9.21
and in the s. of Jerusalem: Hear the 11.06
as many as the s. of Jerusalem are 11.13
be cast out in the s. of Jerusalem, 14.16
Judah and the s. of Jerusalem that 33.10
Judah and in the s. of Jerusalem; 44.06
Judah and in the s. of Jerusalem? 44.09
Judah and in the s. of Jerusalem; 44.17
Judah and in the s. of Jerusalem, 44.21
Chaldeans, and wounded in her s. 51.04
babes faint in the s. of the city. Lam 2.11
wounded men in the s. of the city, 2.12
In the dust of the s. lie the young 2.21
on dainties perish in the s.; 4.05
they are not recognized in the s.; 4.08
through the s., so defiled with 4.14
that we could not walk in our s.; 4.18
They cast their silver into the s., Eze 7.19
have filled its s. with the slain. 11.06
horses he will trample all your s.; 26.11
into her, and blood into her s.; 28.23
and in all the s. they shall say, Amo 5.16
down like the mire of the s. Mic 7.10
The chariots rage in the s., Nah 2.04
waste their s. so that none walks Zep 3.06
again sit in the s. of Jerusalem, Zec 8.04
And the s. of the city shall be 8.05
boys and girls playing in its s. 8.05
and gold like the dirt of the s. 9.03
the foe in the mud of the s.; 10.05
do in the synagogues and in the s., Mt 6.02
any one hear his voice in the s.; 12.19
out into the s. and gathered all 22.10
you, go into its s. and say, Lk 10.10
presence, and you taught in our s.' 13.26
quickly to the s. and lanes of the 14.21
carried out the sick into the s., Ac 5.15

STRENGTH
shall no longer yield to you its s.; Gen 4.12
served your father with all my s.; 31.06
then Israel summoned his s., and sat 48.02
might, and the first fruits of my s., 49.03
for by s. of hand the LORD brought Ex 13.03
'By s. of hand the LORD brought us 13.14
The LORD is my s. and my song, and 15.02
them by thy s. to thy holy abode. 15.13
and your s. shall be spent in vain, Lev 26.20
but now our s. is dried up, and Num 11.06
he is the first issue of his s.; Deu 21.17
as your days, so shall your s. be. 33.25
my s. now is as my s. was then, Jos 14.11
for as the man is, so is his s." Ju 8.21
and see wherein his great s. lies, 16.05
tell me wherein your great s. lies, 16.06
the secret of his s. was not known. 16.09
told me wherein your great s. lies." 16.15
then my s. will leave me, and I 16.17
torment him, and his s. left him. 16.19
my s. is exalted in the LORD. 1Sa 2.01
broken, but the feeble gird on s. 2.04
he will give s. to his king, and 2.10
when I will cut off your s. and the s. 2.31
and there was no s. in him, 28.20
you may have s. when you go on 28.22
until they had no more s. to weep. 30.04
gird me with s. for the battle; 2Sa 22.40
and went in the s. of that food 1Ki 19.08
Jehu drew his bow with his full s., 2Ki 9.24
words are counsel and s. for war! 18.20
and there is no s. to bring them 19.03
shorn of s., are dismayed and 19.26
Seek the LORD and his s., seek his 1Ch 16.11
him; s. and joy are in his place. 16.27
ascribe to the LORD glory and s.! 16.28
make great and to give s. to all. 29.12
"The s. of the burden-bearers is Neh 4.10
for the joy if the LORD is your s." 8.10
What is my s., that I should wait? Job 6.11
Is my s. the s. of stones, or is my 6.12
and mighty in s.—who has hardened 9.04
If it is a contest of s., behold him! 9.19
With him are s. and wisdom; the 12.16
and have laid my s. in the dust. 16.15
His s. is hunger-bitten, and calamity 18.12
have saved the arm that has no s.! 26.02
I gain from the s. of their hands, 30.02
he is mighty in s. of understanding 36.05
or all the force of your s.? 36.19
on him because his s. is great, 39.11
Do you clothe his neck with s.? 39.19
the valley, and exults in his s.; 39.21
Behold, his s. in his loins, and his 40.16
or his mighty s., or his goodly 41.12
In his neck abides s., and terror 41.22
I love thee, O LORD, my s. Ps 18.01
the God who girded me with s., 18.32
gird me with s. for the battle; 18.39
In thy s. the king rejoices, O LORD; 21.01
Be exalted, O LORD, in thy s.! 21.13
my s. is dried up like a potsherd, 22.15
The LORD is my s. and my shield; 28.07
The LORD is the s. of his people, 28.08
ascribe to the LORD glory and s. 29.01
May the LORD give s. to his people! 29.11
my s. fails because of my misery, 31.10
my s. was dried up as by the heat 32.04
is not delivered by his great s. 33.16
My heart throbs, my s. fails me; 38.10
God is our refuge and s., 46.01
O my S., I will sing praises to 59.09

STRENGTH (cont.)
O my S., I will sing praises to Ps 59.17
who by thy s. hast established the 65.06
show thy s., O God, thou who hast 68.28
gives power and s. to his people. 68.35
forsake me not when my s. is spent. 71.09
but God is the s. of my heart and 73.26
issue of their s. in the tents of 78.51
Sing aloud to God our s.; shout for 81.01
Blessed are the men whose s. is in thee, 84.05
They go from s. to s.; the God of gods 84.07
give thy s. to thy servant, and save 86.16
to the Pit; I am a man who has no s., 88.04
For thou art the glory of their s.; 89.17
or even by reason of s. fourscore; 90.10
is robed, he is girded with s. 93.01
s. and beauty are in his sanctuary. 96.06
ascribe to the LORD glory and s.! 96.07
He has broken my s. in mid-course; 102.23
Seek the LORD and his s., seek his 105.04
the first issue of all their s. 105.36
The LORD is my s. and my song; 118.14
my s. of soul thou didst increase. 138.03
is not in the s. of the horse, 147.10
strangers take their fill of your s., Pro 5.10
wisdom, I have insight, I have s. 8.14
crops come by the s. of the ox. 14.04
The glory of young men is their s., 20.29
of knowledge than he who has s.; 24.05
day of adversity, your s. is small. 24.10
Give not your s. to women, your ways 31.03
her loins with s. and makes her 31.17
S. and dignity are her clothing, and 31.25
Wisdom gives s. to the wise man Ecc 7.19
edge, he must put forth more s.; 10.10
for s., and not for drunkenness! 10.17
"By the s. of my hand I have done Is 10.13
the LORD GOD is my s. and my song, 12.02
and s. to those who turn back the 28.06
and in trust shall be your s." 30.15
and there is no s. to bring them 37.03
shorn of s., are dismayed and 37.27
lift up your voice with s., 40.09
who has no might he increases s. 40.29
for the LORD shall renew their s., 40.31
let the peoples renew their s.; 41.01
he becomes hungry and his s. fails, 44.12
of me, are righteousness and s.; 45.24
I have spent my s. for nothing and 49.04
and my God has become my s.— 49.05
put on s., O arm of the LORD; 51.09
Awake, awake, put on your s., O Zion; 52.01
you found new life for your s., 57.10
marching in the greatness of his s.? 63.01
O LORD, my s. and my stronghold, my Jer 16.19
Heshbon fugitives stop without s.; 48.45
their s. has failed, they have 51.30
fled without s. before the pursuer Lam 1.06
treasures for food to revive their s. 1.11
he caused my s. to fail; the Lord 1.14
sought food to revive their s. 1.19
thou hast given me wisdom and s., Dan 2.23
vision, and no s. was left in me; 10.08
changed, and I retained no s. 10.08
come upon me, and I retain no s. 10.16
For now no s. remains in me, and no 10.17
shall not retain the s. of her arm, 11.06
for there shall be no s. to stand. 11.15
come with the s. of his whole 11.17
Aliens devour his s., and he knows Hos 7.09
the strong shall not retain his s., Amo 2.14
not by our own s. taken Karnaim 6.13
his flock in the s. of the LORD, Mic 5.04
gird your loins; collect all your s. Nah 2.01
Ethiopia was her s., Egypt too, 3.09
GOD, the Lord, is my s.; he makes Hab 3.19
to destroy the s. of the kingdoms Hag 2.22
Jerusalem have s. through the LORD Zec 12.05
no one had the s. to subdue him. Mk 5.04
your mind, and with all your s.' 12.30
understanding, and with all the s., 12.33
He has shown s. with his arm, he has Lk 1.51
your soul, and with all your s., 10.27
you may have s. to escape all 21.36
But Saul increased all the more in s., Ac 9.22
it will give you s., since not a 27.34
let you be tempted beyond your s., 1Co 10.13
Lord and in the s. of his might. Eph 6.10
him who has given me s. for this, 1Ti 1.12
me and gave me s. to proclaim the 2Ti 4.17
won s. out of weakness, became Heb 11.34
it by the s. which God supplies; 1Pe 4.11
face was like the sun shining in full s. Rev 1.16

STRENGTHEN
Joshua, and encourage and s. him; Deu 3.28
and s. me, I pray thee, only this Ju 16.28
"S. your heart with a morsel of 19.05
"S. your heart, and tarry until the 19.08
s. your attack upon he city, and 2Sa 11.25
s. yourself, and consider well what 1Ki 20.22
but now, O God, s. thou my hands. Neh 6.09
I could s. you with my mouth, and Job 16.05
thou wilt s. their heart, thou wilt Ps 10.17
with him, my arm also shall s. him. 89.21
shine, and bread to s. man's heart. 104.15
s. me according to thy word! 119.28
S. the weak hands, and make firm the Is 35.03
I will s. you, I will help you, I 41.10
your cords and s. your stakes. 54.02
they s. the hands of evildoers, so Jer 23.14
And I will s. the arms of the king Eze 30.24
I will s. the arms of the king of 30.25
and I will s. the weak, and the fat 34.16
I stood up to confirm and s. him. Dan 11.01
water for the siege, s. your forts; Nah 3.14
"I will s. the house of Judah, and I Zec 10.06
turned again, s. your brethren." Lk 22.32
you some spiritual gift to s. you, Rom 1.11
who is able to s. you according to 16.25
he will s. you and guard you from 2Th 3.03
hands and s. your weak knees, Heb 12.12
restore, establish, and s. you. 1Pe 5.10
Awake, and s. what remains and is on Rev 3.02

STRENGTHENED
and the LORD s. Eglon the king of Ju 3.12
hands shall be s. to go down against 7.11
who s. his hands to slay his brothers. 9.24
at Horesh, and s. his hand in God. 1Sa 23.16
But David s. himself in the LORD 30.06
of all who are with you will be s. 2Sa 16.21
They s. the kingdom of Judah, and 2Ch 11.17
stead, and s. himself against Israel. 17.01
to its proper condition and s. it. 24.13
and he s. the Millo in the city 32.05
So they s. their hands for the Neh 2.18
and you have s. the weak hands. Job 4.03
The weak you have not s., the sick Eze 34.04
of a man touched me and s. me. Dan 10.18
I was s. and said, "Let my lord 10.19
my lord speak, for you have s. me." 10.19
Although I trained and s. their arms, Hos 7.15
and took food and was s. for several Ac 9.19
brethren with many words and s. them. 15.32
So the churches were s. in the faith, 16.05
grant you to be s. with might Eph 3.16
May you be s. with all power, Col 1.11
well that the heart be s. by grace, Heb 13.09

STRENGTHENING
afflicted him instead of s. him. 2Ch 28.20
him an angel from heaven, s. him. Lk 22.43
s. the souls of the disciples, Ac 14.22
Syria and Cilicia, s. the churches. 15.41
and Phrygia, s. all the disciples. 18.23

STRENGTHENS
For he s. the bars of your gates; Ps 147.13
can do all things in him who s. me. Php 4.13

STRESS
last days there will come times of s. 2Ti 3.01

STRETCH
So I will s. out my hand and smite Ex 3.20
when I s. forth my hand upon Egypt 7.05
your rod and s. out your hand over 7.19
'S. out your hand with your rod 8.05
'S. out your rod and strike the 8.16
"S. forth your hand toward heaven, 9.22
I will s. out my hands to the LORD; 9.29
"S. out your hand over the land of 10.12
"S. out your hand toward heaven 10.21
and s. out your hand over the sea 14.16
"S. out your hand over the sea, that 14.26
Thou didst s. out thy right hand, 15.12
Like valleys that s. afar, like Num 24.06
"S. out the javelin that is in your Jos 8.18
And I will s. over Jerusalem the 2Ki 21.13
you will s. out your hands toward Job 11.13
in a heap of ruins s. out his hand, 30.24
hasten to s. out her hands to God. Ps 68.31
thou dost s. out thy hand against 138.07
I s. out my hands to thee; 143.06
S. forth thy hand from on high, 144.07
is too short to s. oneself on it, Is 28.20
He shall s. the line of confusion 34.11
for I will s. out my hand against Jer 6.12
I will s. out my hand against you, 51.25
And I will s. out my hand against Eze 6.14
and I will s. out my hand against 14.09
and I s. out my hand against it, and 14.13
I will s. out my hand against Edom, 25.13
I will s. out my hand against the 25.16
he shall s. it out against the land 30.25
and I will s. out my hand against 35.03
He shall s. out his hand against Dan 11.42
and s. themselves upon their Amo 6.04
of those who s. themselves shall 6.07
"I will s. out my hand against Zep 1.04
And he will s. out his hand against 2.13
said to the man, "S. out your hand." Mt 12.13
said to the man, "S. out your hand." Mk 3.05
and said to him, "S. out your hand." Lk 6.10
you will s. out your hands, and Jn 21.18

STRETCHED
And Israel s. out his right hand Gen 48.14
So Aaron s. out his hand over the Ex 8.06
Aaron s. out his hand with his rod, 8.17
Then Moses s. forth his rod toward 9.23
and s. out his hands to the LORD; 9.33
So Moses s. forth his rod over the 10.13
So Moses s. out his hand toward 10.22
Then Moses s. out his hand over the 14.21
So Moses s. forth his hand over the 14.27
And Joshua s. out the javelin that Jos 8.18
as soon as he had s. out his hand, 8.19
with which he s. out the javelin, 8.26
And when the angel s. forth his 2Sa 24.16
Jeroboam s. out his hand from the 1Ki 13.04
which he s. out against him, dried 13.04
Then he s. himself upon the child 17.21
and as he s. himself upon him, the 2Ki 4.34
and s. himself upon him; 4.35
a drawn sword s. out over Jerusalem 1Ch 21.16
who alone s. out the heavens, and Job 9.08
Because he has s. forth his hand 15.25
Or who s. the line upon it? 38.05
My companion s. out his hand Ps 55.20
my hand is s. out without wearying 77.02
who hast s. out the heavens like a 104.02
have s. out my hand and no one has Pro 1.24
and he s. out his hand against them Is 5.25
away and his hand is s. out still. 5.25
away and his hand is s. out still. 9.12
away and his hand is s. out still. 9.17
away and his hand is s. out still. 9.21
away and his hand is s. out still. 10.04
hand that is s. out over all the 14.26
His hand is s. out, and who will 14.27
He has s. out his hand over the sea, 23.11
the heavens and s. them out, 42.05
who s. out the heavens alone, who 44.24
my hands that s. out the heavens, 45.12
who s. out the heavens and laid the 51.13
of your habitations be s. out; 54.02
understanding s. out the heavens. Jer 10.12
so I have s. out my hand against 15.06
understanding s. out the heavens. 51.15
The enemy has s. out his hands over Lam 1.10
their wings were s. out straight, Eze 1.23
a hand was s. out to me, and, lo, a 2.09
And a cherub s. forth his hand from 10.07
I s. out my hand against you, and 16.27
I have s. out my hand against you, 25.07
he s. out his hand with mockers. Hos 7.05
line shall be s. out over Jerusalem Zec 1.16
who s. out the heavens and founded 12.01
And he s. out his hand and touched Mt 8.03
And the man s. it out, and it was 12.13
were with Jesus s. out his hand 26.51
he s. out his hand and touched him, Mk 1.41
He s. it out, and his hand was 3.05
And he s. out his hand, and touched Lk 5.13
Then Paul s. out his hand and Ac 26.01

STRETCHES
He s. out the north over the void, Job 26.07
When the LORD s. out his hand, the Is 31.03
will behold a land that s. afar. 33.17
who s. out the heavens like a 40.22
The carpenter s. a line, he marks it 44.13
Zion s. out her hands, but there is Lam 1.17

STRETCHEST
while thou s. out thy hand to heal, Ac 4.30

STRETCHING
own heart and s. out his hands toward 1Ki 8.38
own sorrow and s. out his hands 2Ch 6.29
s. out the heavens and laying the Is 51.16
s. out her hands, "Woe is me! I am Jer 4.31
And s. out his hand toward his Mt 12.49

STREW
I will s. your flesh upon the mountains, Eze 32.05

STREWED
dust of them and s. it over the graves 2Ch 34.04

STREWN
their bones be s. at the mouth of Sheol. Ps 141.07

STRICKEN
did not die were s. with tumors, 1Sa 5.12
they are not s. like other men. Ps 73.05
For all the day long I have been s., 73.14
and my heart is s. within me. 109.22
utterly s., for the raisin-cakes of Is 16.07
yet we esteemed him s., smitten by 53.04
s. for the transgression of my 53.08
s. by want of the fruits of the Lam 4.09
he has s., and he will bind us up. Hos 6.01
Ephraim is s., their root is dried 9.16

STRICT
order was s. and the furnace very Dan 3.22
according to the s. manner of the law Ac 22.03

STRICTEST
according to the s. party of our religion Ac 26.05

STRICTLY
"Your father s. charged the people 1Sa 14.28
let judgment be s. executed upon Ez 7.26
Then he s. charged the disciples to Mt 16.20
And he s. ordered them not to make Mk 3.12
And he s. charged them that no one 5.43
saying, "We s. charged you not to Ac 5.28
"We have s. bound ourselves by an 23.14

STRICTNESS
teach shall be judged with greater s. Jas 3.01

STRIDE
their tread; four are stately in their s.: Pro 30.29

STRIDING
he-goat, and a king s. before his people. Pro 30.31

STRIFE
and there was s. between the herdsmen Gen 13.07
"Let there be no s. between you and 13.08
Zin during the s. of the congregation, Num 27.14
and burden of you and your s.? Deu 1.12
people were at s. throughout all 2Sa 19.09
deliver me from s. with the peoples; 22.44
and with continual s. in his bones; Job 33.19
deliver me from s. with the Ps 18.43
thy shelter from the s. of tongues. 31.20
I see violence and s. in the city. 55.09
Hatred stirs up s., but love Pro 10.12
By insolence the heedless make s., 13.10
A hot-tempered man stirs up s., 15.18
A perverse man spreads s., and a 16.28
a house full of feasting with s. 17.01
The beginning of s. is like letting 17.14
He who loves transgression loves s.; 17.19
A fool's lips bring s., and his 18.06
for a man to keep aloof from s.; 20.03
and s. will go out, and quarreling 22.10
Who has s.? Who has complaining? 23.29
a quarrelsome man for kindling s. 26.21
A greedy man stirs up s., 28.25
A man of wrath stirs up s., 29.22
and pressing anger produces s. 30.33
If any one stirs up s., it is not Is 54.15
stirs up s. with you shall fall 54.15
a man of s. and contention to the Jer 15.10
before me; s. and contention arise. Hab 1.03
s., deceit, malignity, they are Rom 1.29
there is jealousy and s. among you, 1Co 3.03
s., jealousy, anger, selfishness, Gal 5.20

STRIKE
wrong, "Why do you s. your fellow?" Ex 2.13
I will s. the water that is in the 7.17
your rod and s. the dust of the 8.16
and you shall s. the rock, and water 17.06
I will s. them with the pestilence Num 14.12
and I will s. you down, and cut off 1Sa 17.46
spear, and I will not s. him twice." 26.08
you, 'S. Amnon,' then kill him. 2Sa 13.28
I will s. down the king only, 17.02
did you not s. him there to the 18.11
Jehoiada, saying, "Go, s. him down." 1Ki 2.29
s. him down and bury him; and thus 2.31
command of the LORD, "S. me, I pray." 20.35
But the man refused to s. him. 20.35
man, and said, "S. me, I pray." 20.37
"S. this people, I pray thee, with 2Ki 6.18
And you shall s. down the house of 9.07
"S. the ground with them"; and he 13.18
now you will s. down Syria only 13.19
nor will he s. root in the earth; Job 15.29
a bronze arrow will s. him through. 20.24
and commands it to s. the mark. 36.32
of the earth may s. terror no more. Ps 10.18
before him and s. down those who 89.23
Let a good man s. or rebuke me in 141.05
S. a scoffer, and the simple will Pro 19.25
and they s. hands with foreigners. Is 2.06
shall take and s. with the sword Eze 5.02
I s. my hands together at the 22.13
then I will s. your bow from your 39.03
he shall s. root as the poplar; Hos 14.05
with a rod they s. upon the cheek Mic 5.01
I will s. every horse with panic, Zec 12.04
when I s. every horse of the 12.04
"S. the shepherd, that the sheep may 13.07
lest you s. your foot against a Mt 4.06
'I will s. the shepherd and the 26.31
'I will s. the shepherd, and the Mk 14.27
and to s. him, saying to him, "Prophesy 14.65
lest you s. your foot against a Lk 4.11
"Lord, shall we s. with the sword?" 22.49
spoken rightly, why do you s. me?" Jn 18.23
stood by him to s. him on the Ac 23.02
"God shall s. you, you whitewashed 23.03
and I will s. her children dead. Rev 2.23
the sun shall not s. them, nor any 7.16

STRIKES
"Whoever s. a man so that he dies Ex 21.12
"Whoever s. his father or his 21.15
quarrel and one s. the other with 21.18
"When a man s. his slave, male or 21.20
"When a man s. the eye of his slave, 21.26
the handle and s. his neighbor so Deu 19.05
He s. them for their wickedness in Job 34.26
I will mock when panic s. you, Pro 1.26
when panic s. you like a storm, and 1.27
the hammer him who s. the anvil, Is 41.07
wither when the east wind s. it— Eze 17.10
But if any one s. you on the right Mt 5.39
To him who s. you on the cheek, Lk 6.29
puts on airs, or s. you in the face. 2Co 11.20

STRIKING
wounding me, a young man for s. me. Gen 4.23
ground, without s. a second blow; 2Sa 20.10
and avenged him by s. the Egyptian. Ac 7.24
But s. a shoal they ran the vessel 27.41

STRING
as a s. of tow snaps when it Ju 16.09
have fitted their arrow to the s., Ps 11.02
born your navel s. was not cut, Eze 16.04
bow, and put the arrows to the s. Hab 3.09

STRINGED
ivory palaces s. instruments make Ps 45.08
upon a ten s. harp I will play to 144.09
we will sing to s. instruments all Is 38.02

STRINGS
to him with the harp of ten s.! Ps 33.02
new song, play skilfully on the s., 33.03
dance; praise him with s. and pipe! 150.04
ornaments, your neck with s. of jewels. Sol 1.10

STRIP
And you shall not s. your vineyard Lev 19.10
and s. Aaron of his garments, and Num 20.26
Philistines came to s. the slain, 1Sa 31.08
after him only to s. the slain. 2Sa 23.10
Philistines came to s. the slain, 1Ch 10.08
Who can s. off his outer garment? Job 41.13
s., and make yourselves bare, and Is 32.11
s. off your robe, uncover your legs, 47.02
s. away her branches, for they are Jer 5.10
become drunk and s. yourself bare. Lam 4.21
they shall s. you of your clothes Eze 16.39
They shall also s. you of your 23.26
and s. off their embroidered 26.16
s. off its leaves and scatter its Dan 4.14
lest I s. her naked and make her as Hos 2.03
it shall s. his treasury of every 13.15
you s. the robe from the peaceful, Mic 2.08

STRIP (cont.)
Thou didst s. the sheath from thy Hab 3.09
the Lord will s. her of her possessions Zec 9.04

STRIPE
burn for burn, wound for wound, s. for s. Ex 21.25

STRIPED
he-goats that were s. and spotted, Gen 30.35
and so the flocks brought forth s., 30.39
toward the s. and all the black in 30.40
'The s. shall be your wages,' then 31.08
wages,' then all the flock bore s. 31.08
leaped upon the flock were s., 31.10
that leap upon the flock are s., 31.12

STRIPES
a number of s. in proportion to Deu 25.02
Forty s. may be given him, but not 25.03
beat him with more s. than these, 25.03
with the s. of the sons of men; 2Sa 7.14
and with his s. we are healed. Is 53.05

STRIPLING
said, "Inquire whose son the s. is." 1Sa 17.56

STRIPPED
they s. him of his robe, the long Gen 37.23
of Israel s. themselves of their Ex 33.06
And Moses s. Aaron of his garments, Num 20.28
And Jonathan s. himself of the robe 1Sa 18.04
And he too s. offhis clothes, and 19.24
and s. off his armor, and sent 31.09
time Hezekiah s. the gold from the 2Ki 18.16
And they s. him and took his head 1Ch 10.09
He leads counselors away s. Job 12.17
He leads priests away s., and overthrows 12.19
He has s. from me my glory, and 19.09
and s. the naked of their clothing. 22.06
stouthearted were s. of their spoil; Ps 76.05
But I have s. Esau bare, I have Jer 49.10
land will be s. of all it contains, Eze 12.19
its fruit was s. off, its strong 19.12
the land is s. of all that fills 32.15
it has s. off their bark and thrown Joe 1.07
I will go s. and naked; I will make Mic 1.08
plunderers have s. them and ruined Nah 2.02
its mistress is s., she is carried off, 2.07
And they s. him and put a scarlet Mt 27.28
they s. him of the robe, and put his 27.31
they s. him of the purple cloak, and Mk 15.20
who s. him and beat him, and departed, Lk 10.30
for he was s. for work, and sprang Jn 21.07

STRIPS
and s. the forests bare; and in his Ps 29.09
he lies down, and s. its branches. Is 27.10

STRIVE
"When men s. together, and hurt a Ex 21.22
whom thou didst s. at the waters Deu 33.08
Did he ever s. against Israel, or Ju 11.25
who keep the law s. against them. Pro 28.04
those who s. against you shall be Is 41.11
"S. to enter by the narrow door; Lk 13.24
to s. together with me in your Rom 15.30
s. to excel in building up the 1Co 14.12
to know now greatly I s. for you, Col 2.01
For to this end we toil and s., 1Ti 4.10
Let us therefore s. to enter that Heb 4.11
S. for peace with all men, and for 12.14

STRIVEN
for you have s. with God and with Gen 32.28

STRIVES
"Woe to him who s. with his Maker, Is 45.09

STRIVING
all is vanity and a s. after wind. Ecc 1.14
this also is but a s. after wind. 1.17
all was vanity and a s. after wind, 2.11
all is vanity and a s. after wind. 2.17
also is vanity and s. after wind. 2.26
also is vanity and a s. after wind. 4.04
full of toil and a s. after wind. 4.06
also is vanity and a s. after wind. 4.16
also is vanity and a s. after wind. 6.09
with one mind s. side by side for Php 1.27
s. with all the energy which he Col 1.29

STROKE
the earth with one s. of the spear, 1Sa 26.08
Remove thy s. from me; I am spent Ps 39.10
And every s. of the staff of Is 30.23
of your eyes away from you at a s.; Eze 24.16

STROKES
evil; s. make clean the innermost parts. Pro 20.30

STRONG
Issachar is a s. ass, crouching Gen 49.14
multiplied and grew exceedingly s.; Ex 1.07
people multiplied and grew very s. 1.20
for with a s. hand he will send 6.01
with a s. hand he will drive them 6.01
LORD turned a very s. west wind, 10.19
for with a s. hand the LORD has 13.09
for by a s. hand the LORD brought 13.16
sea back by a s. east wind all 14.21
"Drink no wine nor s. drink, Lev 10.09
himself from wine and s. drink; Num 6.03
vinegar made from wine or s. drink, 6.03
was among them had a s. craving; 11.04
who dwell in it are s. or weak, 13.18
who dwell in the land are s., 13.28
with many men, and with a s. force. 20.20
offering of s. drink to the LORD. 28.07
you this day, that you may be s., Deu 11.08
or wine or s. drink, whatever your 14.26
have not drunk wine or s. drink; 29.06
Be s. and of good courage, do not 31.06
"Be s. and of good courage; for you 31.07
"Be s. and of good courage; for you 31.23
Be s. and of good courage; for you Jos 1.06
Only be s. and very courageous, 1.07
Be s. and of good courage; be not 1.09
Only be s. and of good courage." 1.18
be s. and of good courage; for thus 10.25
I am still as s. to this day as I 14.11
But when the people of Israel grew s., 17.13
of iron, and though they are s." 17.18
before you great and s. nations; 23.09
When Israel grew s., they put the Ju 1.28
all s., able-bodied men; not a man 3.29
But there was a s. tower within the 9.51
and drink no wine or s. drink, 13.04
so then drink no wine or s. drink, 13.07
let her drink wine or s. drink, 13.14
Out of the s. came something sweet." 14.14
saw that they were too s. for him, 18.26
drunk neither wine nor s. drink, 1Sa 1.15
and when Saul saw any s. man, 14.52
Now therefore let your hands be s., 2Sa 2.07
making himself s. in the house of 3.06
"If the Syrians are too s. for me, 10.11
the Ammonites are too s. for you, 10.11
And the conspiracy grew s., 15.12
He delivered me from my s. enemy, 22.18
This God is my s. refuge, and has 22.33
Be s., and show yourself a man, 1Ki 2.02
and a great and s. wind rent the 19.11
with your servants fifty s. men; 2Ki 2.16
all of them s. and fit for war. 24.16
though Judah became s. among his 1Ch 5.02
who gave him s. support in his 11.10

STRONG (cont.)

"If the Syrians are too s. for me, 1Ch 19.12
the Ammonites are too s. for you, 19.12
Be s., and of good courage. Fear 22.13
the sanctuary; be s., and do it." 28.10
"Be s. and of good courage, and do 28.20
He made the fortresses s., and put 2Ch 11.11
the cities, and made them very s. 11.12
Rehoboam was established and was s., 12.01
in this way you will be s. for war, 25.08
of Egypt, for he became very s. 26.08
marvelously helped, till he was s. 26.15
But when he was s. he grew proud, 26.16
"Be s. and of good courage. Do 32.07
or prosperity, that you may be s., Ez 9.12
we are with you; be s. and do it." 10.04
thy great power and by thy s. hand. Neh 1.10
The s. lion perishes for lack of Job 4.11
and looses the belt of the s. 12.21
His s. steps are shortened and his 18.07
to the shower and the rain, 'Be s.' 37.06
Their young ones become s., they 39.04
He delivered me from my s. enemy, Ps 18.17
and like a s. man runs its course 19.05
s. bulls of Bashan surround me; 22.12
The LORD, s. and mighty, the LORD, Ps 24.08
be s., and let your heart take 27.14
established me as a s. mountain; 30.07
a s. fortress to save me! 31.02
Be s., and let your heart take 31.24
from him who is too s. for him, 35.10
a s. tower against the enemy. 61.03
a s. fortress, to save me, for thou 71.03
but thou art my s. refuge. 71.07
like a s. man shouting because of 78.65
whom thou hast made s. for thyself! 80.17
they are the s. arm of the children 83.08
s. is thy hand, high thy right hand. 89.13
with a s. hand and an outstretched 136.12
my s. deliverer, thou hast covered 140.07
for they are too s. for me! 142.06
A rich man's wealth is his s. city; Pro 10.15
The s. tower of the wicked comes to 12.12
of the LORD one has s. confidence, 14.26
The name of the LORD is a s. tower; 18.10
A rich man's wealth is his s. city, 18.11
A brother helped is like a s. city, 18.19
Wine is a mocker; s. drink a brawler; 20.01
and a bribe in the bosom, s. wrath. 21.14
for their Redeemer is s.; he will 23.11
wise man is mightier than a s. man, 24.05
the ants are a people not s., 30.25
or for rulers to desire s. drink; 31.04
Give s. drink to him who is perishing, 31.06
strength and makes her arms s. 31.17
swift, nor the battle to the s., Ecc 9.11
and the s. men are bent, and the 12.03
for love is s. as death, jealousy is Sol 8.06
And the s. shall become tow, and his Is 1.31
that they may run after s. drink, 5.11
valiant men in mixing s. drink, 5.22
to me with his s. hand upon me, 8.11
In that day their s. cities will be 17.09
you away violently, O you s. man. 22.17
s. drink is bitter to those who 24.09
Therefore s. peoples will glorify 25.03
land of Judah: "We have a s. city; 26.01
and great and s. sword will punish 27.01
Lord has one who is mighty and s.; 28.02
wine and stagger with s. drink; 28.07
and the prophet reel with s. drink, 28.07
wine, they stagger with s. drink; 28.07
scoff, lest your bonds be made s.; 28.22
stagger, but not with s. drink! 29.09
horsemen because they are very s., 31.01
a fearful heart, "Be s., fear not! 35.04
because he is s. in power not one 40.26
and forges it with his s. arm; 44.12
lets it grow s. among the trees of 44.14
shall divide the spoil with the s.; 53.12
us fill ourselves with s. drink; 56.12
things, and make your bones s.; 58.11
not truth has grown s. in the land; Jer 9.03
with outstretched hand and s. arm, 21.05
him from hands to s. for him. 31.11
with a s. hand and outstretched arm, 32.21
the Jordan against a s. sheepfold, 49.19
Their Redeemer is s.; the LORD of 50.34
the Jordan against a s. sheepfold, 50.44
make the watch s.; set up watchmen; 51.12
she should fortify her s. height, 51.53
hand of the LORD being s. upon me; Eze 3.14
will not take a s. arm or many 17.09
its s. stem was withered; the 19.12
there remains in it no s. stem, 19.14
endure, or can your hands be s., 22.14
it may become s. to wield the 30.21
both the s. arm and the one that 30.22
the fat and he s. I will watch 34.16
s. as iron, because iron breaks to Dan 2.40
shall be partly s. and partly 2.42
The tree grew and became s., and 4.11
you saw, which grew and became s., 4.20
king, who have grown and become s. 4.22
and dreadful and exceedingly s.; 7.07
but when he was s., the great horn 8.08
And he shall make a s. covenant 9.27
you; be s. and of good courage." 10.19
when he has become s. through his 11.02
"Then the king of the south shall be s., 11.05
he shall become s. with a small 11.23
and who was as s. as the oaks; Amo 2.09
and the s. shall not retain his 2.14
destruction flash forth against the s., 5.09
preach to you of wine and s. drink, Mic 2.11
decide for s. nations afar off; 4.03
who were cast off, a s. nation; 4.07
LORD, "Though they be s. and many, Nah 1.12
of hosts: "Let your hands be s., Zec 8.09
Fear not, but let your hands be s." 8.13
Many peoples and s. nations shall 8.22
I will make them s. in the LORD and 10.12
can one enter a s. man's house and Mt 12.29
unless he first binds the s. man? 12.29
one can enter a s. mans' house and Mk 3.27
unless he first binds the s. man; 3.27
shall drink no wine nor s. drink, Lk 1.15
child grew and became s. in spirit, 1.80
And the child grew and became s., 2.40
When a s. man, fully armed, guards 11.21
I am not s. enough to dig, and I am 16.03
rose because a s. wind was blowing Jn 6.18
his feet and ankles were made s. Ac 3.07
made this man s. whom you see and 3.16
but he grew s. in his faith as he Rom 4.20
We who are s. ought to bear with 15.01
weak in the world to shame the s., 1Co 1.27
We are weak, but you are s. 4.10
betrothed, if his passions are s., 7.36
your faith, be courageous, be s. 16.13
"His letters are weighty and s., 2Co 10.10
for when I am weak, then I am s. 12.10
when we are weak and you are s. 13.09
Finally, be s. in the Lord and in Eph 6.10
Therefore God sends upon them a s. delusion, 2Th 2.11
be s. in the grace that is in 2Ti 2.01
might have s. encouragement to Heb 6.18
great and are driven by s. winds, Jas 3.04
you, young men, because you are s., 1Jn 2.14
and I saw a s. angel proclaiming Rev 5.02
generals and the rich and the s., 6.15

STRONGER

the one shall be s. than the other, Gen 25.23
Whenever the s. of the flock were 30.41
were Laban's, and the s. Jacob's. 30.42

STRONGER (cont.)
people; for they are s. than we." Num 13.31
than honey? What is s. than a lion?" Ju 14.18
eagles, they were s. than lions. 2Sa 1.23
and David grew s. and s., while the 3.01
and being s. than she, he forced her, 13.14
hills, and so they were s. than we; 1Ki 20.23
surely we shall be s. than they. 20.23
surely we shall be s. than they." 20.25
he that has clean hands grows s. and s. Job 17.09
and made them s. than their foes. Ps 105.24
to dispute with one s. than he. Ecc 6.10
thou art s. than I, and thou hast Jer 20.07
shall be s. than he and his Dan 11.05
but when one s. than he assails him Lk 11.22
the weakness of God is s. than men. 1Co 1.25
to jealousy? Are we s. than he? 10.22

STRONGEST
them and he slew the s. of them, Ps 78.31
Its s. stem became a ruler's scepter Eze 19.11
deal with the s. fortresses by the Dan 11.39

STRONGHOLD
your God on the top of the s. here, Ju 6.26
entered the s. of the house of 9.46
Abimelech put it against the s., 9.49
they set the s. on fire over them, 9.49
the time that David was in the s. 1Sa 22.04
to David, "Do not remain in the s.; 22.05
and his men went up to the s. 24.22
Nevertheless David took the s. of Zion, 2Sa 5.07
And David dwelt in the s., and called 5.09
heard of it and went down to the s. 5.17
my s. and my refuge, my savior; 22.03
David was then in the s.; and the 23.14
Nevertheless David took the s. of Zion, 1Ch 11.05
And David dwelt in the s.; therefore 11.07
David was then in the s.; and the 11.16
to David at the s. in the wilderness 12.08
and Judah came to the s. to David. 12.16
The LORD is a s. for the oppressed, Ps 9.09
oppressed, a s. in times of trouble. 9.09
the horn of my salvation, my s. 18.02
The LORD is the s. of my life; 27.01
But the LORD has become my s., 94.22
my s. and my deliverer, my shield 144.02
The LORD is a s. to him whose way Pro 10.29
brings down the s. in which they 21.22
the s. of the sea, saying: "I have Is 23.04
Tarshish, for your s. is laid waste. 23.14
For thou hast been a s. to the poor, 25.04
a s. to the needy in his distress, a 25.04
her and her s. and distress her, 29.07
O LORD, my strength and my s., my Jer 16.19
day when I take from them their s., Eze 24.25
the s. of Egypt, and cut off the 30.15
people, a s. to the people of Israel. Joe 3.16
a s. in the day of trouble; he knows Nah 1.07
Return to your s., O prisoners of Zec 9.12

STRONGHOLDS
they dwell in are camps or s., Num 13.19
mountains, and the caves and the s. Ju 6.02
remained in the s. in the wilderness, 1Sa 23.14
hide among us in the s. at Horesh, 23.19
and dwelt in the s. of Engedi. 23.29
thou hast laid his s. in ruins. Ps 89.40
concerning Canaan to destroy its s. Is 23.11
Thorns shall grow over its s., 34.13
trusted in your s. and your Jer 48.07
against you; he has destroyed your s. 48.18
shall be taken and the s. seized. 48.41
fighting, they remain in their s.; 51.30
broken down the s. of the daughter Lam 2.02
its palaces, laid in ruins its s.; 2.05
And he ravaged their s., and laid Eze 19.07
who are in s. and in caves shall 33.27
He shall devise plans against s., Dan 11.24
cities, and it shall devour his s. Hos 8.14
it shall devour the s. of Benhadad. Amo 1.04
Gaza, and it shall devour her s. 1.07
Tyre, and it shall devour her s." 1.10
it shall devour the s. of Bozrah." 1.12
Rabbah, and it shall devour her s., 1.14
it shall devour the s. of Kerioth, 2.02
shall devour the s. of Jerusalem." 2.05
Proclaim to the s. in Assyria, 3.09
and to the s. in the land of Egypt, 3.09
violence and robbery in their s." 3.10
and your s. shall be plundered. 3.11
pride of Jacob, and hate his s.; 6.08
land and throw down all your s.; Mic 5.11
come trembling out of their s., 7.17
have divine power to destroy s. 2Co 10.04

STRONGLY
But he urged them s.; so turned Gen 19.03
I s. urged him to visit you with 1Co 16.12
for he s. opposed our message. 2Ti 4.15

STROVE
because you s. against the LORD. Jer 50.24
and in his manhood he s. with God. Hos 12.03
He s. with the angel and prevailed, 12.04

STRUCK
And they s. with blindness the men Gen 19.11
up the rod and s. the water that Ex 7.20
after the LORD had s. the Nile. 7.25
and s. the dust of the earth, and 8.17
my hand and s. you and your people 9.15
The hail s. down everything that 9.25
and the hail s. down every plant of 9.25
the rod with which you s. the Nile, 17.05
he that s. him shall be clear; 21.19
and is s. so that he dies, there 22.02
up lest you be s. down before your Num 14.42
up his hand and s. the rock with 20.11
and Balaam s. the ass, to turn her 22.23
against the wall; so he s. her again. 22.25
and he s. the ass with his staff. 22.27
that you have s. me these three 22.28
"Why have you s. your ass these 22.32
and he s. his hands together; 24.10
the LORD had s. down among them; 33.04
"But if he s. him down with an 35.16
And if he s. him down with a stone 35.17
Or if he s. him down with a weapon 35.18
or in enmity s. him down with his 35.21
then he who s. the blow shall be 35.21
she s. Sisera a blow, she crushed Ju 5.26
and s. it so that it fell, and 7.13
that it is not his hand that s. us, 1Sa 6.09
They s. down the Philistines that 14.31
and s. the Philistine on his 17.49
and s. the Philistine, and killed 17.50
so that he s. the spear into the 19.10
that he may be s. down, and die." 2Sa 11.15
And the LORD s. the child that 12.15
and one s. the other and killed him 14.06
Give up the man who s. his brother, 14.07
surrounded Absalom and s. him, 18.15
so Joab s. him with it in the body, 20.10
He rose and s. down the Philistines 23.10
and he s. him down, and he died. 1Ki 2.25
and s. him down and killed him; 2.34
and he went out and s. him down, 2.46
and Baasha s. him down at Gibbethon, 15.27
Zimri came in and s. him down and 16.10
And the man s. him, smiting and 20.37
came near and s. Micaiah on the 22.24
and s. the king of Israel between 22.34
and s. the water, and the water was 2Ki 2.08
and s. the water, saying, "Where is 2.14
And when he had s. the water, 2.14

STRUCK (cont.)
So he s. them with blindness in 2Ki 6.18
him; but who s. down all these? 10.09
who s. him down, so that he died. 12.21
and he s. three times, and stopped 13.18
"You should have s. five or six 13.19
you would have s. down Syria until 13.19
and s. him down at Ibleam, and 15.10
and he s. down Shallum the son of 15.14
and s. him down, and slew him, and 15.30
came near and s. Micaiah on the 2Ch 18.23
and s. the king of Israel between 18.33
of his own sons s. him down there 32.21
and s. the four corners of the Job 1.19
they have s. me insolently upon the 16.10
"They s. me," you will say, "but I Pro 23.35
nations have s. down its branches, Is 16.08
him rose up and s. down Gedaliah Jer 41.02
the stone that s. the image became Dan 2.35
against him and s. the ram and 8.07
and s. the slave of the high priest, Mt 26.51
Then they spat in his face, and s. him; 26.67
you Christ! Who is it that s. you?" 26.68
the reed and s. him on the head. 27.30
and s. the slave of the high priest Mk 14.47
And they s. his head with a reed, 15.19
And one of them s. the slave of the Lk 22.50
"Prophesy! Who is it that s. you?" 22.64
drew it and s. the high priest's Jn 18.10
standing by s. Jesus with his hand, 18.22
and s. him with ther hands. 19.03
and he s. Peter on the side and Ac 12.07
to the law you order me to be s.?" 23.03
northeaster, s. down from the land; 27.14
s. down, but not destroyed; 2Co 4.09
and a third of the sun was s., Rev 8.12

STRUCTURE
He also built a s. against the wall 1Ki 6.05
he built the s. against the whole 6.10
this house and to finish this s.?" Ez 5.03
this house and to finish this s.?' 5.09
cut for the s. of a palace; Ps 144.12
on which was a s. like a city Eze 40.02
in whom the whole s. is joined Eph 2.21

STRUGGLE
endured a hard s. with sufferings, Heb 10.32
In your s. against sin you have not 12.04

STRUGGLED
The children s. together within her Gen 25.22

STRUGGLING
behold, two Hebrews were s. together; Ex 2.13

STRUNG
his sword; he has bent and s. his bow; Ps 7.12

STRUTS
their tongue s. through the earth. Ps 73.09

STRUTTING
the s. cock, the he-goat, and a king Pro 30.31

STUBBLE
of Egypt, to gather s. for straw. Ex 5.12
thy fury, it consumes them like s. 15.07
him slingstones are turned to s. Job 41.28
Clubs are counted as s.; he laughs 41.29
the tongue of fire devours the s., Is 5.24
conceive chaff, you bring forth s.; 33.11
tempest carries them off like s. 40.24
sword, like driven s. with his bow. 41.02
they are like s., the fire consumes 47.14
a flame of fire devouring the s., Joe 2.05
a flame, and the house of Esau s.; Ob 1.18
they are consumed, like dry s. Nah 1.10
and all evildoers will be s.; Mal 4.01
precious stones, wood, hay, s.— 1Co 3.12

STUBBORN
righteousness; for you are a s. people. Deu 9.06
and behold, it is a s. people; 9.13
of your heart, and be no longer s. 10.16
"If a man has a s. and rebellious 21.18
'This our son is s. and rebellious, 21.20
know how rebellious and s. you are; 31.27
their practices or their s. ways. Ju 2.19
but were s., as their fathers had 2Ki 17.14
and turned a s. shoulder and Neh 9.29
a s. and rebellious generation, a Ps 78.08
gave them over to their s. hearts, 81.12
you s. of heart, you who are far Is 46.12
people has a s. and rebellious Jer 5.23
of you follows his s. evil will, 16.12
The people also are impudent and s.: Eze 2.04
a hard forehead and of a s. heart. 3.07
Like a s. heifer, Israel is s.; Hos 4.16
and turned a s. shoulder, and Zec 7.11
but when some were s. and disbelieved, Ac 19.09

STUBBORNLY
For when Pharaoh s. refused to let Ex 13.15
running s. against him with a thick Job 15.26
shall no more s. follow their own Jer 3.17
They are all s. rebellious, going 6.28
but have s. followed their own 9.14
who s. follow their own heart and 13.10
every one who s. follows his own 23.17

STUBBORNNESS
do not regard the s. of this people, Deu 9.27
though I walk in the s. of my heart.' 29.19
and s. is as iniquity and idolatry. 1Sa 15.23
counsels and the s. of their evil Jer 7.24
walked in the s. of his evil heart 11.08
according to the s. of his evil 18.12

STUCK
with his spear s. in the ground at 1Sa 26.07
the bow s. and remained immovable, Ac 27.41

STUD
king's service, bred from the royal s. Est 8.10

STUDDED
you ornaments of gold, s. with silver. Sol 1.11

STUDIED
s. by all who have pleasure in them. Ps 111.02
has learning, when he has never s.?" Jn 7.15

STUDY
his heart to s. the law of the LORD, Ez 7.10
in order to s. the words of the Neh 8.13
much s. is a weariness of the flesh. Ecc 12.12

STUDYING
weighing and s. and arranging proverbs Ecc 12.09

STUFF
and scarlet s. and fine twined Ex 25.04
and blue and purple and scarlet s.; 26.01
and scarlet s. and fine twined 26.31
and scarlet s. and fine twined 26.36
and scarlet s. and fine twined 27.16
blue and purple and scarlet s., 28.05
of blue and purple and scarlet s., 28.06
blue and purple and scarlet s., 28.08
blue and purple and scarlet s., 28.15
of blue and purple and scarlet s., 28.33
and scarlet s. and fine twined 35.06
or scarlet s. or fine linen or 35.23
and scarlet s. and fine twined 35.25
and scarlet s. and fine twined 35.35
for the s. they had was sufficient 36.07

STUFF (cont.)
and blue and purple and scarlet s., Ex 36.08
and scarlet s. and fine twined 36.35
and scarlet s. and fine twined 36.37
and scarlet s. and fine twined 38.18
and scarlet s. and fine twined 38.23
and scarlet s. they made finely 39.01
blue and purple and scarlet s., 39.02
blue and purple and the scarlet s., 39.03
blue and purple and scarlet s., 39.05
blue and purple and scarlet s., 39.08
and scarlet s. and fine twined 39.24
of blue and purple and scarlet s., 39.29
cedarwood and scarlet s. and hyssop; Lev 14.04
and the scarlet s. and the hyssop, 14.06
cedarwood and scarlet s. and hyssop, 14.49
and the hyssop and the scarlet s., 14.51
cedarwood and hyssop and scarlet s. 14.52
of cloth made of two kinds of s. 19.19
cedarwood and hyssop and scarlet s., Num 19.06
You shall not wear a mingled s., Deu 22.11
and put them among their own s. Jos 7.11
work, and in carpets of colored s., Eze 27.24

STUFFS
spoil of dyed s. for Sisera, spoil Ju 5.30
of dyed s. embroidered, two pieces of 5.30

STUMBLE
They shall s. over one another, as Lev 26.37
and foes, they shall s. and fall. Ps 27.02
thy law; nothing can make them s. 119.165
securely and your foot will not s. Pro 3.23
and if you run, you will not s. 4.12
unless they have made some one s. 4.16
they do not know over what they s. 4.19
And many shall s. thereon; they shall Is 8.15
in vision, they s. in giving judgment. 28.07
out his hand, the helper will s., 31.03
we s. at noon as in the twilight, 59.10
in the desert, they did not s. 63.13
blocks against which they shall s.; Jer 6.21
your feet s. on the twilight 13.16
therefore my persecutors will s., 20.11
path in which they shall not s.; 31.09
The proud one shall s. and fall, 50.32
no longer cause your nation to s., Eze 36.15
but he shall s. and fall, and shall Dan 11.19
You shall s. by day, the prophet Hos 4.05
also shall s. with you by night; 4.05
Ephraim shall s. in his guilt; 5.05
Judah also shall s. with them. 5.05
them, but transgressors s. in them. 14.09
they s. as they go, they hasten to Nah 2.05
end—they s. over the bodies! 3.03
caused many to s. by your instruction; Mal 2.08
he does not s., because he sees the Jn 11.09
Zion a stone that will make men s., Rom 9.33
anything that makes your brother s. 14.21
and "A stone that will make men s., 1Pe 2.08
for they s. because they disobey 2.08

STUMBLED
took hold of it, for the oxen s. 2Sa 6.06
to hold the ark, for the oxen s. 1Ch 13.09
they s. and perished before thee. Ps 9.03
But as for me, my feet had almost s., 73.02
was none among his tribes who s. 105.37
For Jerusalem has s., and Judah Is 3.08
they have s. in their ways, in the Jer 18.15
Euphrates they have s. and fallen. 46.06
for warrior has s. against warrior; 46.12
Your multitude s. and fell, and they 46.16
for you have s. because of your Hos 14.01
They have s. over the stumbling Rom 9.32
So I ask, have they s. so as to fall? 11.11

STUMBLES
not your heart be glad when he s.; Pro 24.17
none s., none slumbers or sleeps, Is 5.27
he s., because the light is not in Jn 11.10

STUMBLING
deaf or put a s. block before the Lev 19.14
Your words have upheld him who was s., Job 4.04
and calamity is ready for his s. 18.12
But at my s. they gathered in glee, Ps 35.15
eyes from tears, my feet from s.; 116.08
those who are s. to the slaughter. Pro 24.11
and a rock of s. to both houses of Is 8.14
this people s. blocks against Jer 6.21
and I lay a s. block before him, he Eze 3.20
For it was the s. block of their 7.19
and set the s. block of their 14.03
and sets the s. block of his 14.04
and putting the s. block of his 14.07
and became a s. block of iniquity 44.12
have stumbled over the s. stone, Rom 9.32
never to put a s. block or hindrance 14.13
a s. block to Jews and folly to 1Co 1.23
become a s. block to the weak. 8.09
that case the s. block of the Gal 5.11
and in it there is no cause for s. 1Jn 2.10
Balak to put a s. block before the Rev 2.14

STUMP
and its s. die in the ground, Job 14.08
whose s. remains standing when it Is 6.13
is felled." The holy seed is its s. 6.13
forth a shoot from the s. of Jesse, 11.01
But leave the s. of its roots in Dan 4.15
but leave the s. of its roots in 4.23
leave the s. of the roots of the tree, 4.26

STUMPS
of these two smoldering s. of firebrands, Is 7.04

STUNNED
Jacob, both rider and horse lay s. Ps 76.06
he has left me s., faint all the day Lam 1.13

STUPEFY
S. yourselves and be in a stupor, blind Is 29.09

STUPID
But a s. man will get understanding, Job 11.12
cattle? Why are we s. in your sight? 18.03
fool and the s. alike must perish Ps 49.10
I was s. and ignorant, I was like a 73.22
the s. cannot understand this: 92.06
but he who hates reproof is s. Pro 12.01
A s. son is a grief to a father; 17.21
Surely I am too s. to be a man. 30.02
counselors of Pharaoh give s. counsel. Is 19.11
they are s. children, they have no Jer 4.22
They are both s. and foolish; 10.08
Every man is s. and without knowledge; 10.14
For the shepherds are s., and do 10.21
Every man is s. and without knowledge; 51.17
Have nothing to do with s., senseless, 2Ti 2.23
But avoid s. controversies, genealogies, Tit 3.09

STUPOR
Stupefy yourselves and be in a s., blind Is 29.09
"God gave them a spirit of s., eyes Rom 11.08

SUAH
S., Harnepher, Shual, Beri, Imrah, 1Ch 7.36

SUBDUE
multiply, and fill the earth and s. it; Gen 1.28
them and s. them before you; Deu 9.03
that we may bind him to s. him; Ju 16.05
be bound, that one could s. you." 16.06
and I will s. all your enemies. 1Ch 17.10
and thou didst s. before them the Neh 9.24

SUBDUE (cont.)
themselves, "We will utterly s. them"; Ps 74.08
I would soon s. their enemies, and 81.14
Thou dost s. the noise of the Is 25.05
to s. nations before him and ungird 45.01
no one had the strength to s. him. Mk 5.04
but I pommel my body and s. it, 1Co 9.27

SUBDUED
were with him came and s. the Rephaim Gen 14.05
and s. all the country of the 14.07
and the land is s. before the LORD; Num 32.22
the land shall be s. before you, 32.29
there; the land lay s. before them. Jos 18.01
So Moab was s. that day under the Ju 3.30
So on that day God s. Jabin the 4.23
So Midian was s. before the people 8.28
Ammonites were s. before the 11.33
Philistines were s. and did not 1Sa 7.13
the Philistines and s. them, 2Sa 8.01
from all the nations he s., 8.11
the Philistines and s. them, 1Ch 18.01
and the Philistines were s. 20.04
and the land is s. before the LORD 22.18
men of Israel were s. at that time, 2Ch 13.18
vengeance and s. peoples under me; Ps 18.47
He s. peoples under us, and nations 47.03

SUBDUES
refuge, who s. the peoples under him. Ps 144.02

SUBJECT
and became s. to forced labor. Ju 1.30
Bethanath became s. to forced labor 1.33
and they became s. to forced labor. 1.35
were in Egypt s. to the house of Isa 2.27
with Israel, and became s. to them. 2Sa 10.19
with David, and became s. to him. 1Ch 19.19
the demons are s. to us in your Lk 10.17
that the spirits are s. to you; 10.20
Let every person be s. to the Rom 13.01
Therefore one must be s., 13.05
of prophets are s. to prophets. 1Co 14.32
I urge you to be s. to such men and 16.16
Be s. to one another out of reverence Eph 5.21
Wives, be s. to your husbands, as to 5.22
As the church is s. to Christ, 5.24
wives also be s. in everything to 5.24
him even to s. all things to Php 3.21
Wives, be s. to your husbands, as is Col 3.18
of death were s. to lifelong Heb 2.15
much more be s. to the Father of 12.09
Be s. for the Lord's sake to every 1Pe 2.13
authorities, and powers s. to him. 3.22
are younger be s. to the elders. 5.05

SUBJECTED
for the creation was s. to futility, Rom 8.20
the will of him who s. it in hope; 8.20
When all things are s. to him, 1Co 15.28
will also be s. to him who put all 15.28
angels that God s. the world to Heb 2.05

SUBJECTION
brought into s. under their power. Ps 106.42
and brought them into s. as slaves. Jer 34.11
them into s. to be your slaves. 34.16
all things in s. under his feet. 1Co 15.27
"All things are put in s. under him, 15.27
putting everything in s. under his feet." Heb 2.08
in putting everything in s. to man, 2.08
yet see everything in s. to him. 2.08

SUBJUGATE
now you intend to s. the people of 2Ch 28.10

SUBMISSION
did not yield s. even for a moment, Gal 2.05

SUBMISSIVE
his children s. and respectful in 1Ti 3.04
and s. to their husbands, that the Tit 2.05
Bid slaves to be s. to their masters 2.09
Remind them to be s. to rulers and 3.01
Servants, be s. to your masters with 1Pe 2.18
be s. to your husbands, so that some, 3.01
and were s. to their husbands, 3.05

SUBMISSIVENESS
woman learn in silence with all s. 1Ti 2.11

SUBMIT
to your mistress, and s. to her." Gen 16.09
it does not s. to God's law, indeed Rom 8.07
they did not s. to God's righteousness. 10.03
accepted, you s. to it readily enough. 2Co 11.04
and do not s. again to a yoke of Gal 5.01
Why do you s. to regulations, Col 2.20
Obey your leaders and s. to them; Heb 13.17
S. yourselves therefore to God. Jas 4.07

SUBORDINATE
but should be s., as even the law 1Co 14.34

SUBSEQUENT
sufferings of Christ and the s. glory. 1Pe 1.11

SUBSIDED
over the earth, and the waters s.; Gen 8.01
the waters had s. from the face of 8.08
the waters had s. from the earth. 8.11

SUBSTANCE
his s., and accept the work of his Deu 33.11
lands for their cattle and their s. Jos 14.04
Thy eyes beheld my unformed s.; Ps 139.16
LORD with your s. and with the Pro 3.09
company with harlots squanders his s. 29.03
return to his land with great s., Dan 11.28
to come; but the s. belongs to Christ. Col 2.17

SUBSTITUTE
He shall not s. anything for it or Lev 27.10

SUBTLE
was more s. than any other wild Gen 3.01

SUBVERT
to s. a man in his cause, the Lord Lam 3.36

SUBVERTED
because they have s. me with guile; Ps 119.78

SUBVERTS
and s. the cause of those who are Ex 23.08
of the wise and s. the cause of Deu 16.19

SUCATHITES
and Shimeathites, and the S. These 1Ch 2.55

SUCCEED
sons, who is anointed to s. him, Lev 6.22
of the LORD, for that will not s.? Num 14.41
she bears shall s. to the name of Deu 25.06
which we are setting out will s." Ju 18.05
do many things and will s. in them." 1Sa 26.25
to entice him, and you shall s.; 1Ki 22.22
so that you may s. in building the 1Ch 22.11
of your fathers; for you cannot s." 2Ch 13.12
to entice him, and you shall s.; 18.21
his prophets, and you will s." 20.20
devise mischief, they will not s. Ps 21.11
but with many advisers they s. Pro 15.22
strength; but wisdom helps one to s. Ecc 10.10
perhaps you may be able to s., Is 47.12
shamed, for they will not s. Jer 20.11
a man who shall not s. in his days; 22.30
offspring shall s. in sitting on 22.30

SUCCEED (cont.)
the Chaldeans, you shall not s.'?" Jer 32.05
Will he s.? Can a man escape Eze 17.15
and shall s. in what he does, and Dan 8.24
may now at last s. in coming to Rom 1.10
on law did not s. in fulfilling 9.31

SUCCEEDED
Ahithophel was s. by Jehoiada the 1Ch 27.34
hardened himself against him, and s.?— Job 9.04
Felix was s. by Porcius Festus; and Ac 24.27

SUCCEEDS
and a maid when she s. her mistress. Pro 30.23

SUCCESS
grant me s. today, I pray thee, and Gen 24.12
the LORD your God granted me s.' 27.20
may have good s. wherever you go. Jos 1.07
and then you shall have good s. 1.08
And David had s. in all his undertakings 1Sa 18.14
when Saul saw that he had great s., 18.15
David had more s. than all the 18.30
and give s. to thy servant today, Neh 1.11
so that their hands achieve no s. Job 5.12
LORD, we beseech thee, give us s.! Ps 118.25

SUCCESSFUL
with Joseph, and he became a s. man; Gen 39.02
out and was s. wherever Saul sent 1Sa 18.05

SUCCESSFULLY
his own house he s. accomplished. 2Ch 7.11

SUCCOTH
But Jacob journeyed to S., and built Gen 33.17
the name of the place is called S. 33.17
Israel journeyed from Rameses to S., Ex 12.37
And they moved on from S., and 13.20
from Rameses, and encamped at S. Num 33.05
And they set out from S., and 33.06
S., and Zaphon, the rest of the Jos 13.27
So he said to the men of S., Ju 8.05
And the officials of S. said, 8.06
him as the men of S. had answered. 8.08
And he caught a young man of S., 8.14
him the officials and elders of S., 8.14
And he came to the men of S., 8.15
and with them taught the men of S. 8.16
ground between S. and Zarethan. 1Ki 7.46
clay ground between S. and Zeredah. 2Ch 4.17
and portion out the Vale of S. Ps 60.06
and portion out the Vale of S. 108.07

SUCCOTHBENOTH
the men of Babylon made S., the men 2Ki 17.30

SUCH
took to wife s. of them as they chose. Gen 6.02
Far be it from thee to do s. a thing, 18.25
s. as I love, and bring it to me 27.04
for your father, s. as he loves; 27.09
savory food, s. as his father loved. 27.14
of the Hittite women s. as these, 27.46
goats, and s. shall be my wages. 30.32
with s. favor have you received me. 33.10
your servants s. wages as you set; 1Ki 5.06
again came s. an abundance of 10.10
no s. almug wood has come or been 10.12
"At s. and s. a place shall be my 2Ki 6.08
in heaven, could s. a thing be?" 7.19
S. is Pharaoh king of Egypt to all 18.21
and Judah s. evil that the ears of 21.12
For no s. passover had been kept 23.22
keep for ever s. purposes and 1Ch 29.18
upon him s. royal majesty as had 29.25
s. as none of the kings had who 2Ch 1.12
were no spices s. as those which 9.09
Israel had kept s. a passover as 35.18
all s. as know the laws of your God; Ez 7.25
who put s. a thing as this into the 7.27
hast given us s. a remnant as this, 9.13
were laden in s. a way that each Neh 4.17
"No s. things as you say have been 6.08
"Should s. a man as I flee? And 6.11
And what man s. as I could go into 6.11
Israel sin on account of s. women? 13.26
keep silence at s. a time as this, Est 4.14
the kingdom for s. a time as this?" 4.14
to lay hands on s. as sought their 9.02
S. you have now become to me; Job 6.21
S. are the paths of all who forget 8.13
does not know s. things as these? 12.03
thy eyes upon s. a one and bring 14.03
and let s. words go out of your 15.13
"I have heard many s. things; 16.02
Surely s. are the dwellings of the 18.21
s. is the place of him who knows 18.21
and many s. things are in his mind. 23.14
S. is the generation of those who Ps 24.06
in terror s. as has not been! 53.05
S. knowledge is too wonderful for 139.06
people to whom s. blessings fall! 144.15
S. are the ways of all who get gain Pro 1.19
Know that wisdom is s. to your soul; 24.14
does not understand s. knowledge. 29.07
city where they had done s. things. Ecc 8.10
father's house s. days as have not Is 7.17
S. is Pharaoh king of Egypt to all 36.06
S. to you are those with whom you 47.15
Is s. the fast that I choose, a day 58.05
Who has heard s. a thing? Who 66.08
Who has seen s. things? Shall 66.08
see if there has been s. a thing. Jer 2.10
myself on a nation s. as this? 5.09
myself on a nation s. as this?" 5.29
myself on a nation s. as this? 9.09
for himself gods? S. are no gods!" 16.20
I am bringing s. evil upon this 19.03
by speaking s. words to them. 38.04
things came to s. a pass in 52.03
S. were their faces. And their Eze 1.11
S. was the appearance of the 1.28
Surely, if I sent you to s., 3.06
a man escape who does s. things? 17.15
s. as were carved on the walls; 41.25
king has asked s. a thing of any Dan 2.10
s. as never has been since there 12.01
Has s. a thing happened in your Joe 1.02
will keep silent in s. a time; Amo 5.13
"one should not preach of s. things; Mic 2.06
With s. a gift from your hand, will Mal 1.09
in Israel have I found s. faith. Mt 8.10
who had given s. authority to men. 9.08
for s. was thy gracious will. 11.26
"Whoever receives one s. child in 18.05
"If s. is the case of a man with 19.10
for to s. belongs the kingdom of 19.14
s. as has not been from the beginning 24.21
said, "Go into the city to s. a one, 26.18
With many s. parables he spoke the Mk 4.33
And many s. things you do." 7.13
"Whoever receives one s. child in 9.37
for to s. belongs the kingdom of 10.14
there will be s. tribulation as 13.19
in Israel have I found s. faith." Lk 7.09
this about whom I hear s. things?" 9.09
for s. was thy gracious will. 10.21
for to s. belongs the kingdom of 18.16
for s. the Father seeks to worship Jn 4.23
not s. as the fathers ate and died; 6.58
law Moses commanded us to stone s. * 8.05
a man who is a sinner do s. signs?" 9.16
"Away with s. a fellow from the Ac 22.22
in his case of s. evils as I 25.18
this day might become s. as I am— 26.29
those who do s. things deserve to Rom 1.32

SUCH (cont.)
falls upon those who do s. things. Rom 2.02
those who do s. things and yet do 2.03
you to live in s. harmony with one 15.05
For s. persons do not serve our 16.18
on the man who has done s. a thing. 1Co 5.04
not even to eat with s. a one. 5.11
If then you have s. cases, 6.04
And s. were some of you. But you 6.11
in s. a cast the brother or sister 7.15
this to secure any s. provision. 9.15
s. as the flute or the harp, do not 14.07
be subject to s. men and to every 16.16
Give recognition to s. men. 16.18
For s. a one this punishment by the 2Co 2.06
S. is the confidence that we have 3.04
came with s. splendor that the 3.07
Since we have s. a hope, we are very 3.12
boldness with s. confidence as I 10.02
Let s. people understand that what 10.11
For s. men are false apostles, 11.13
those who do s. things shall not Gal 5.21
against s. there is no law. 5.23
but only s. as is good for edifying, Eph 4.29
spot or wrinkle or any s. thing, 5.27
with all joy; and honor s. men, Php 2.29
Now s. persons we command and 2Th 3.12
Avoid s. godless chatter, for it 2Ti 2.16
the power of it. Avoid s. people. 3.05
knowing that s. a person is perverted Tit 3.11
if we neglect s. a great salvation? Heb 2.03
we should have s. a high priest, 7.26
we have s. a high priest, one who is 8.01
from sinners s. hostility against 12.03
for s. sacrifices are pleasing to 13.16
This wisdom is not s. as comes down Jas 3.15
we will go into s. and such a town 4.13
into such and s. a town and spend 4.13
arrogance. All s. boasting is evil. 4.16
perishable things s. as silver or 1Pe 1.18
s. a one is the deceiver and the 2Jn 1.07
So we ought to support s. men, 3Jn 1.08
committed in s. an ungodly way, Jud 1.15
earthquake s. as had never been Rev 16.18
Over s. the second death has no 20.06

SUCK
herds giving s. are a care to me; Gen 33.13
and he made him s. honey out of the Deu 32.13
for they s. the affluence of the 33.19
why the breasts, that I should s.? Job 3.12
He will s. the poison of asps; 20.16
His young ones s. up blood; 39.30
You shall s. the milk of nations, Is 60.16
you shall s. the breast of kings; 60.16
that you may s. and be satisfied 66.11
and you shall s., you shall be 66.12
those who give s. in those days! Mt 24.19
those who give s. in those days! Mk 13.17
those who give s. in those days! Lk 21.23
and the breasts that never gave s.!' 23.29

SUCKED
bore you, and the breasts that you s.!" Lk 11.27

SUCKING
bosom, as a nurse carries the s. child, Num 11.12
the s. child with the man of gray hairs. Deu 32.25
So Samuel took a s. lamb and offered 1Sa 7.09
The s. child shall play over the Is 11.08
"Can a woman forget her s. child, 49.15

SUCKLE
that Sarah would s. children? Gen 21.07
give the breast and s. their young, Lam 4.03

SUCKLING
infant and s., ox and sheep, camel 1Sa 15.03

SUCKLINGS
children and s., oxen, asses and 1Sa 22.19
of babes and s. thou hast brought Mt 21.16

SUDDEN
I will appoint over you s. terror, Lev 26.16
When disaster brings s. death, Job 9.23
and s. terror overwhelms you; 22.10
Do not be afraid of s. panic, Pro 3.25
s. end he will make of all the Zep 1.18
then s. destruction will come upon 1Th 5.03

SUDDENLY
if any man dies very s. beside him, Num 6.09
And s. the LORD said to Moses and 12.04
he stabbed him s. without enmity, 35.22
So Joshua came upon them s., Jos 10.09
So Joshua came s. upon them with 11.07
for the thing came about s. 2Ch 29.36
but s. I cursed his dwelling. Job 5.03
shooting at him s. and without Ps 64.04
at them; they will be wounded s. 64.07
therefore calamity will come upon him s.; Pro 6.15
for s. it takes to itself wings, 23.05
for disaster from them will rise s., 24.22
his neck will s. be broken beyond 29.01
time, when it s. falls upon them. Ecc 9.12
passing chaff. And in an instant, s., Is 29.05
crash comes s., in an instant; 30.13
and ruin shall come on you s., 47.11
then s. I did them and they came to 48.03
S. my tents are destroyed, my Jer 4.20
for s. the destroyer will come upon 6.26
and terror fall upon them s. 15.08
bringest the marauder s. upon them! 18.22
I will s. make them run away from 49.19
I will s. make them run away from 50.44
S. Babylon has fallen and been 51.08
Will not your debtors s. arise, Hab 2.07
you seek will s. come to his Mal 3.01
And s. looking around they no Mk 9.08
lest he come s. and find you asleep. 13.36
And s. there was with the angel a Lk 2.13
seizes him, and he s. cries out; 9.39
day come upon you s. like a snare; 21.34
And s. a sound came from heaven Ac 2.02
and s. a light from heaven flashed 9.03
and s. there was a great earthquake, 16.26
from heaven s. shone about me. 22.06
to swell up or s. fall down dead; 28.06

SUE
of Tyre will s. your favor with gifts, Ps 45.12
any one would s. you and take your Mt 5.40

SUFFER
and shall s. for your faithlessness, Num 14.33
that we may no longer s. disgrace." Neh 2.17
of their enemies, who made them s.; 9.27
the wine presses, but s. thirst. Job 24.11
how long shall my honor s. shame? Ps 4.02
Behold what I s. from those who 9.13
The young lions s. want and hunger; 34.10
made thy people s. hard things; 60.03
from my youth up, I s. thy terrors; 88.15
companion of fools will s. harm. Pro 13.20
and an idle person will s. hunger. 19.15
the simple go on, and s. for it. 22.03
the simple go on, and s. for it. 27.12
it inhabitants s. for their guilt; Is 24.06
are lifted up, and you s. violence. Jer 13.22
has made her s. for the multitude Lam 1.05
not the son s. for the iniquity of Eze 18.19
son shall not s. for the iniquity 18.20
nor the father s. for the iniquity 18.20
and no longer s. the reproach of 34.29
about you shall themselves s. reproach. 36.07
may never again s. the disgrace of 36.30

SUFFER (cont.)
so that the king might s. no loss. Dan 6.02
Jerusalem and s. many things from Mt 16.21
Son of man will s. at their hands." 17.12
the Son of man must s. many things, Mk 8.31
that he should s. many things and 9.12
"The Son of man must s. many things, Lk 9.22
But first he must s. many things 17.25
this passover with you before I s.; 22.15
Christ should s. these things and 24.26
Christ should s. and on the third 24.46
prophets, that his Christ should s., Ac 3.18
worthy to s. dishonor for the name 5.41
much he must s. for the sake of my 9.16
the Christ to s. and to rise from 17.03
that the Christ must s., and that, 26.23
provided we s. with him in order Rom 8.17
he will s. loss, though he himself 1Co 3.15
Why not rather s. wrong? Why not 6.07
member suffers, all s. together; 12.26
the same sufferings that we s. 2Co 1.06
in him but also s. for his sake, Php 1.29
that we were to s. affliction; 1Th 3.04
They shall s. the punishment of 2Th 1.09
and therefore I s. as I do. But I 2Ti 1.12
have had to s. repeatedly since Heb 9.26
you may have to s. various trials, 1Pe 1.06
do right and s. for it you take it 2.20
But even if you do s. for righteousness 3.14
For it is better to s. for doing 3.17
But let none of you s. as a murderer, 4.15
Therefore let those who s. according 4.19
Do not fear what you are about to s. Rev 2.10

SUFFERED
and we s. no harm, and we did not 1Sa 25.15
of their iniquities s. affliction; Ps 107.17
on me; I s. distress and anguish. 116.03
you have s. the reproach of the Eze 36.06
a woman who had s. from a hemorrhage Mt 9.20
kingdom of heaven has s. violence, 11.12
for I have s. much over him today 27.19
and who had s. much under many Mk 5.26
Galileans, because they s. thus? Lk 13.02
into the fire and s. no harm. Ac 28.05
so that you s. no loss through us. 2Co 7.09
of the one who s. the wrong, 7.12
his sake I have s. the loss of all Php 3.08
we had already s. and been shamefully 1Th 2.02
for you s. the same things from 2.14
he himself has s. and been tempted, Heb 2.18
obedience through what he s.; 5.08
considered abuse s. for the Christ 11.26
Others s. mocking and scourging, and 11.36
So Jesus also s. outside the gate 13.12
because Christ also s. for you, 1Pe 2.21
when he s., he did not threaten; 2.23
Since therefore Christ s. in the flesh, 4.01
for whoever has s. in the flesh 4.01
And after you have s. a little while, 5.10

SUFFERING
time of their s. they cried to Neh 9.27
saw that his s. was very great. Job 2.13
I become afraid if all my s., 9.28
s. no mischance or failure in Ps 144.14
all you peoples, and behold my s.; Lam 1.18
knowing that s. produces endurance, Rom 5.03
heart over what I am s. for you, Eph 3.13
of God, for which you are s.— 2Th 1.05
your share of s. for the gospel in 2Ti 1.08
Take your share of s. as a good 2.03
for which I am s. and wearing 2.09
endure s., do the work of an 4.05
honor because of the s. of death, Heb 2.09
their salvation perfect through s. 2.10
As an example of s. and patience, Jas 5.10
Is any one among you s.? Let him 5.13
he endures pain while s. unjustly. 1Pe 2.19
experience of s. is required of 5.09
s. wrong for their wrongdoing. 2Pe 2.13

SUFFERINGS
their taskmasters; I know their s., Ex 3.07
is but the beginning of the s. Mt 24.08
is but the beginning of the s. Mk 13.08
More than that, we rejoice in our s., Rom 5.03
that the s. of this present time 8.18
we share abundantly in Christ's s. 2Co 1.05
endure the same s. that we suffer. 1.06
know that as you share in our s., 1.07
resurrection, and may share his s., Php 3.10
Now I rejoice in my s. for your sake, Col 1.24
my s., what befell me at Antioch, at 2Ti 3.11
endured a hard struggle with s., Heb 10.32
predicting the s. of Christ and 1Pe 1.11
in so far as you share Christ's s., 4.13
witness of the s. of Christ as 5.01

SUFFERS
is a leper or s. a discharge may Lev 22.04
he should give, and only s. want. Pro 11.24
the belly of the wicked s. want. 13.25
away, and she herself s. bitterly. Lam 1.04
the sojourner s. extortion in your Eze 22.07
is an epileptic and he s. terribly; Mt 17.15
If one member s., all suffer 1Co12.26
yet if one s. as a Christian, let 1Pe 4.16

SUFFICE
slaughtered for them, to s. them? Num 11.22
together for them, to s. them?" 11.22
LORD said to me, 'Let it s. you; Deu 3.26
but they did not s. for them. Ju 21.14
Samaria shall s. for handfuls for 1Ki 20.10
life is costly, and can never s., Ps 49.08
Lebanon would not s. for fuel, Is 40.16
that is past s. for doing what the 1Pe 4.03

SUFFICIENCY
fulness of his s. he will be in Job 20.22
coming from us; our s. is from God, 2Co 3.05

SUFFICIENT
they had was s. to do all the work, Ex 36.07
and finds s. means to redeem it, Lev 25.26
But if he has not s. means to get 25.28
and lend him s. for his need, Deu 15.08
sanctified themselves in s. number, 2Ch 30.03
own trouble be s. for the day. Mt 6.34
to life. Who is s. for these things? 2Co 2.16
Not that we are s. of ourselves to 3.05
"My grace is s. for you, for my 12.09

SUIT
nor shall you bear witness in a s., Ex 23.02
be partial to a poor man in his s. 23.03
justice due to your poor in his s. 23.06
and a s. of apparel, and your living Ju 17.10
any man had a s. to come before 2Sa 15.02
man with a s. or cause might come 15.04
Will he then make requital to s. you, Job 34.33
No one enters s. justly, no one goes Is 59.04
teachers to s. their own likings, 2Ti 4.03

SUITABLE
each with the blessing s. to him. Gen 49.28
the harbor was not s. to winter in, Ac 27.12

SUKKIIM
Egypt—Libyans, S., and Ethiopians. 2Ch 12.03

SULLEN
went to his house resentful and s., 1Ki 20.43
house vexed and s. because of what 21.04

SULPHUR
of fire and of sapphire and of s., Rev 9.17
and smoke and s. issued from their 9.17
fire and smoke and s. issuing from 9.18

SULTRY
rose, God appointed a s. east wind, Jon 4.08

SUM
This is the s. of the things for Ex 38.21
And Joab gave the s. of the numbering 2Sa 24.09
And Joab gave the s. of the numbering 1Ch 21.05
and the exact s. of money that Est 4.07
The s. of thy word is truth; and Ps 119.160
O God, How vast is the s. of them! 139.17
seek wisdom and the s. of things, Ecc 7.25
thing to another to find the s., 7.27
and told the s. of the matter. Dan 7.01
have been sold for a large s. Mt 26.09
they gave a s. of money to the 28.12
bought for a s. of silver from the Ac 7.16
bought this citizenship for a large s." 22.28

SUMMED
are s. up in this sentence, "You shall Rom 13.09

SUMMER
s. and winter, day and night, shall Gen 8.22
a hundred of s. fruits, and a skin 2Sa 16.01
the bread and s. fruit for the 16.02
was dried up as by the heat of s. Ps 32.04
thou hast made s. and winter. 74.17
she prepares her food in s., Pro 6.08
A son who gathers in s. is prudent, 10.05
Like snow in s. or rain in harvest, 26.01
they provide their food in the s.; 30.25
birds of prey will s. upon them, Is 18.06
a first-ripe fig before the s.: 28.04
the s. is ended, and we are not Jer 8.20
gather wine and s. fruits and oil, 40.10
wine and s. fruits in great 40.12
upon your s. fruits and your 48.32
chaff of the s. threshing floors; Dan 2.35
the winter house with the s. house; Amo 3.15
me: behold, a basket of s. fruit. 8.01
and I said, "A basket of s. fruit." 8.02
as when the s. fruit has been Mic 7.01
shall continue in s. as in winter. Zec 14.08
leaves, you know that s. is near. Mt 24.32
leaves, you know that s. is near. Mk 13.28
know that the s. is already near. Lk 21.30

SUMMIT
When David came to the s., where 2Sa 15.32
had passed a little beyond the s., 16.01
as the s. of Lebanon, yet surely I Jer 22.06

SUMMON
king sent to s. Ahimelech the 1Sa 22.11
So Amasa went to s. Judah; but he 2Sa 20.05
who went to s. Micaiah said to him, 1Ki 22.13
who went to s. Micaiah said to him, 2Ch 18.12
matter of justice, who can s. him? Job 9.19
S. thy might, O God; show thy Ps 68.28
who is like me? Who will s. me? Jer 49.19
"S. archers against Babylon, all 50.29
Who will s. me? What shepherd can 50.44
s. against her the kingdoms, Ararat, 51.27
and I will s. the grain and make it Eze 36.29
I will s. every king of terror 38.21
have an opportunity I will s. you." Ac 24.25

SUMMONED
then Israel s. his strength, and sat Gen 48.02
Then Pharaoh s. the wise men and Ex 7.11
And he s. Moses and Aaron by night, 12.31
And Moses s. all Israel, and said to Deu 5.01
And Moses s. all Israel and said to 29.02
Then Moses s. Joshua, and said to 31.07
Joshua s. them, and he said to them, Jos 9.22
Joshua s. all the men of Israel, and 10.24
Then Joshua s. the Reubenites, and 22.01
Joshua s. all Israel their elders 23.02
and s. the elders, the heads, the 24.01
She sent and s. Barak the son of Ju 4.06
And Barak s. Zebulun and Naphtali 4.10
So Saul s. the people, and numbered 1Sa 15.04
And Saul s. all the people to war, 23.08
therefore I have s. you to tell me 28.15
and told him; and he s. Absalom. 2Sa 14.33
Then the king sent and s. Shimei, 1Ki 2.36
the king sent and s. Shimei, 2.42
king of Israel s. an officer and 22.09
Then he s. Gehazi and said, "Call 2Ki 4.36
Therefore King Jehoash s. Jehoiada 12.07
Then David s. the priests Zadok and 1Ch 15.11
king of Israel s. an officer and 2Ch 18.08
So the king s. Jehoiada the chief, 24.06
in her and she was s. by name. Est 2.14
secretaries were s. on the thirteenth 3.12
secretaries were s. at that time, 8.09
If I s. him and he answered me, I Job 9.16
When he s. a famine in the land, and Ps 105.16
have s. my mighty men to execute my Is 13.03
Then he s. Johanan the son of Jer 42.08
he s. an assembly against me to Lam 1.15
sorcerers, and the Chaldeans be s., Dan 2.02
The officers are s., they stumble Nah 2.05
Then Herod s. the wise men secretly Mt 2.07
Then his lord s. him and said to 18.32
And the twelve s. the body of the Ac 6.02
who s. Barnabas and Saul and sought 13.07

SUMMONING
use them for s. the congregation, Num 10.02
for I am s. a sword against all the Jer 25.29
and s. the centurion, he asked him Mk 15.44
So, s. his master's debtors one by Lk 16.05

SUMMONS
speaks and s. the earth from the Ps 50.01

SUMPTUOUSLY
linen and who feasted s. every day. Lk 16.19

SUMS
Many rich people put in large s. Mk 12.41

SUN
As the s. was going down, a deep Gen 15.12
When the s. had gone down and it 15.17
The s. had risen on the earth when 19.23
that night, because the s. had set. 28.11
The s. rose upon him as he passed 32.31
the s., the moon, and eleven stars 37.09
but when the s. grew hot, it melted. Ex 16.21
until the going down of the s. 17.12
but if the s. has risen upon him, 22.03
it to him before the s. goes down; 22.26
When the s. is down he shall be Lev 22.07
them in the s. before the LORD, Num 25.04
you see the s. and the moon and Deu 4.19
toward the going down of the s., 11.30
at the going down of the s., 16.06
or the s. or the moon or any of the 17.03
and when the s. is down, he may come 23.11
when the s. goes down, you shall 24.13
before the s. goes down (for he is 24.15
with the choicest fruits of the s., 33.14
going down of the s. shall be your Jos 1.04
down of the s. Joshua commanded, 8.29
"S., stand thou still at Gibeon, and 10.12
And the s. stood still, and the moon 10.13
The s. stayed in the midst of 10.13
time of the going down of the s., 10.27
be like the s. as he rises in his Ju 5.31

SUN (cont.)

morning, as soon as the s. is up, Ju 9.33
day before the s. went down, 14.18
and the s. went down on them near 19.14
Tomorrow, by the time the s. is hot, 1Sa 11.09
and as the s. was going down they 2Sa 2.24
anything else till the s. goes down!" 3.35
your wives in the sight of this s. 12.11
before all Israel, and before the s.' " 12.12
like the s. shining forth upon a 23.04
LORD has set the s. in the heavens, 1Ki 8.12
and the s. shone upon the water, the 2Ki 3.22
by which the s. had declined on the 20.11
to the s., and the moon, and the 23.05
of Judah had dedicated to the s., 23.11
the chariots of the s. with fire. 23.11
be opened until the s. is hot; Neh 7.03
He thrives before the s., and his Job 8.16
who commands the s., and it does 9.07
about blackened, but not by the s.; 30.28
looked at the s. when it shone, 31.26
them he has set a tent for the s., Ps 19.04
rising of the s. to its setting. 50.01
birth that never sees the s. 58.08
May he live while the s. endures, 72.05
fame continue as long as the s.! 72.17
established the luminaries and the s. 74.16
For the LORD God is a s. and shield; 84.11
throne as long as the s. before me. 89.36
the s. knows its time for setting. 104.19
When the s. rises, they get them 104.22
rising of the s. to its setting 113.03
The s. shall not smite you by day, 121.06
the s. to rule over the day, for his 136.08
Praise him, s. and moon, praise him, 148.03
at which he toils under the s.? Ecc 1.03
The s. rises and the s. goes down, 1.05
there is nothing new under the s. 1.09
everything that is done under the s.; 1.14
nothing to be gained under the s. 2.11
done under the s. was grievous to 2.17
in which I had toiled under the s., 2.18
and used my wisdom under the s. 2.19
toil of my labors under the s., 2.20
with which he toils beneath the s.? 2.22
Moreover I saw under the s. that in 3.16
that are practiced under the s. 4.01
deeds that are done under the s. 4.03
Again, I saw vanity under the s.: 4.07
living who move about under the s., 4.15
which I have seen under the s.: 5.13
toils under the s. the few days of 5.18
which I have seen under the s., 6.01
not seen the s. or known anything; 6.05
will be after him under the s.? 6.12
advantage to those who see the s. 7.11
to all that is done under the s., 8.09
good thing under the s. but to eat, 8.15
which God gives him under the s. 8.15
the work that is done under the s. 8.17
in all that is done under the s., 9.03
in all that is done under the s. 9.06
he has given you under the s., 9.09
at which you toil under the s. 9.09
that under the s. the race is not 9.11
example of wisdom under the s., 9.13
which I have seen under the s., 10.05
for the eyes to behold the s. 11.07
before the s. and the light, and the 12.02
because the s. has scorched me. Sol 1.06
bright as the s., terrible as an 6.10
the s. will be dark at its rising Is 13.10
will be called the City of the S. 19.18
be confounded, and the s. ashamed; 24.23
will be as the light of the s., 30.26
light of the s. will be sevenfold, 30.26
the declining s. on the dial of 38.08
So the s. turned back on the dial 38.08
come, from the rising of the s., 41.25
rising of the s. and from the west, 45.06
wind nor s. shall smite them, for 49.10
glory from the rising of the s.; 59.19
The s. shall be no more your light 60.19
Your s. shall no more go down, nor 60.20
before the s. and the moon and all Jer 8.02
her s. went down while it was yet 15.09
who gives the s. for light by day 31.35
worshiping the s. toward the east. Eze 8.16
I will cover the s. with a cloud, 32.07
till the s. went down to rescue Dan 6.14
The s. and the moon are darkened, Joe 2.10
The s. shall be turned to darkness, 2.31
The s. and the moon are darkened, 3.15
"I will make the s. go down at noon, Amo 8.09
When the s. rose, God appointed a Jon 4.08
and the s. beat upon the head of 4.08
The s. shall go down upon the Mic 3.06
when the s. rises, they fly away; Nah 3.17
The s. and moon stood still in Hab 3.11
rising of the s. to its setting my Mal 1.11
my name the s. of righteousness 4.02
he makes his s. rise on the evil Mt 5.45
but when the s. rose they were 13.06
shine like the s. in the kingdom 13.43
and his face shone like the s., 17.02
those days the s. will be darkened, 24.29
and when the s. rose it was scorched, Mk 4.06
the s. will be darkened, and the 13.24
to the tomb when the s. had risen. 16.02
Now when the s. was setting, all Lk 4.40
be signs in s. and moon and stars, 21.25
the s. shall be turned into darkness Ac 2.20
unable to see the s. for a time." 13.11
from heaven, brighter than the s., 26.13
And when neither s. nor stars 27.20
There is one glory of the s., 1Co 15.41
do not let the s. go down on your Eph 4.26
For the s. rises with its scorching Jas 1.11
was like the s. shining in full Rev 1.16
and the s. became black as sackcloth, 6.12
ascend from the rising of the s., 7.02
the s. shall not strike them, nor 7.16
and a third of the s. was struck, 8.12
and the s. and the air were darkened 9.02
head, and his face was like the s., 10.01
a woman clothed with the s., 12.01
angel poured his bowl on the s., 16.08
Then I saw an angel standing in the s., 19.17
has no need of s. or moon to shine 21.23
they need no light of lamp or s., 22.05

SUNDER

His confidence breaks in s., and Job 8.14
to him who divided the Red Sea in s., Ps 136.13

SUNDOWN

at s., they brought to him all who Mk 1.32

SUNG

thanksgiving be s. to the LORD by 1Ch 16.07
his work, of which men have s. Job 36.24
in the vineyards no songs are s., Is 16.10
song will be s. in the land of 26.01
And when they had s. a hymn, Mt 26.30
And when they had s. a hymn, Mk 14.26

SUNK

picked officers are s. in the Red Sea. Ex 15.04
On what were its bases s., or who Job 38.06
The nations have s. in the pit Ps 9.15
For thy arrows have s. into me, 38.02
that your feet are s. in the mire, Jer 38.22
Her gates have s. into the ground; Lam 2.09
and all your crew have s. with you. Eze 27.34

SUNRISE

side toward the s. shall be of the Num 2.03

SUNRISE (cont.)
the tent of meeting toward the s., Num 3.38
is opposite Moab, toward the s. 21.11
at Jericho eastward, toward the s." 34.15
beyond the Jordan toward the s." Jos 1.15
toward the s. to the boundary of 19.12
east toward the s. to Gathhepher, 19.13

SUNRISING
land beyond the Jordan toward the s., Jos 12.01
toward the s., from Baalgad below 13.05

SUN'S
while the s. light failed; and the Lk 23.45

SUNSET
And about s. a cry went through the 1Ki 22.36
Syrians until evening; then at s. he died. 2Ch 18.34

SUNSHINE
from my dwelling like clear heat in s., Is 18.04

SUPERFLUOUS
Now it is s. for me to write to you 2Co 9.01

SUPERIOR
having become as much s. to angels as Heb 1.04
that the inferior is blessed by the s. 7.07

SUPERLATIVE
least inferior to these s. apostles. 2Co 11.05
all inferior to these s. apostles, 12.11

SUPERNATURAL
and all ate the same s. food and 1Co 10.03
and all drank the same s. drink. 10.04
they drank from the s. rock which 10.04

SUPERSTITION
about their own s. and about one Jesus, Ac 25.19

SUPH
in the Arabah over against S., between Deu 1.01

SUPHAH
"Waheb in S., and the valleys of the Num 21.14

SUPPER
'Prepare s. for me, and gird yourself Lk 17.08
likewise the cup after s., saying, * 22.20
There they made him a s.; Martha Jn 12.02
And during s., when the devil had 13.02
rose from s., laid aside his garments, 13.04
his breast at the s. and had said, 21.20
is not the Lord's s. that you eat. 1Co 11.20
after s., saying, "This cup is the 11.25
to the marriage s. of the Lamb.' Rev 19.09
gather for the great s. of God, 19.17

SUPPLANTED
For he has s. me these two times. He Gen 27.36

SUPPLANTER
for every brother is a s., and every Jer 9.04

SUPPLEMENT
every effort to s. your faith with 2Pe 1.05

SUPPLIANTS
beyond the rivers of Ethiopia my s., Zep 3.10

SUPPLICATION
prayer of thy servant and to his s., 1Ki 8.28
thou to the s. of thy servant and 8.30
pray and make s. to thee in this 8.33
whatever s. is made by any man or 8.38
heaven their prayer and their s., 8.45
and make s. to thee in the land of 8.47
place their prayer and their s., 8.49
be open to the s. of thy servant, 8.52
and to the s. of thy people Israel, 8.52
all this prayer and s. to the LORD, 8.54
I have made s. before the LORD, be 8.59
have heard your prayer and your s., 9.03
of thy servant and to his s., 2Ch 6.19
pray and make s. to thee in this 6.24
whatever s. is made by any man or 6.29
heaven their prayer and their s., 6.35
and make s. to thee in the land of 6.37
and heard his s. and brought him 33.13
king to make s. to him and entreat Est 4.08
God and make s. to the Almighty, Job 8.05
The LORD has heard my s.; the LORD Ps 6.09
Hear the voice of my s., as I cry 28.02
I cried; and to the LORD I made s.: 30.08
and hide not thyself from my s.! 55.01
my prayer; hearken to my cry of s. 86.06
and will not despise their s. 102.17
Let my s. come before thee; deliver 119.170
my voice I make s. to the LORD, 142.01
They will make s. to you, saying: Is 45.14
be that their s. will come before Jer 36.07
"Let our s. come before you, and 42.02
me to present your s. before him: 42.09
petition and s. before his God. Dan 6.11
presenting my s. before the LORD 9.20
a spirit of compassion and s., Zec 12.10
the Spirit, with all prayer and s. Eph 6.18
making s. for all the saints, 6.18
by prayer and s. with thanksgiving Php 4.06

SUPPLICATIONS
that God heeded s. for the land. 2Sa 21.14
So the LORD heeded s. for the land, 24.25
thou to the s. of thy servant and 2Ch 6.21
place their prayer and their s., 6.39
Will he make many s. to you? Job 41.03
he has heard the voice of my s. Ps 28.06
But thou didst hear my s., when 31.22
he has heard my voice and my s. 116.01
be attentive to the voice of my s.! 130.02
ear to the voice of my s., O LORD! 140.06
prayer, O LORD; give ear to my s.! 143.01
will heed their s. and heal them. Is 19.22
by prayer and s. with fasting and Dan 9.03
of thy servant and to his s., 9.17
not present our s. before thee on 9.18
beginning of your s. a word went 9.23
I urge that s., prayers, intercessions, 1Ti 2.01
continues in s. and prayers night 5.05
Jesus offered up prayers and s., Heb 5.07

SUPPLIED
and he s. them with food in exchange Gen 47.17
vessels for oil with which it is s.: Num 4.09
And those officers s. provisions 1Ki 4.27
So Hiram s. Solomon with all the 5.10
of Tyre had s. Solomon with cedar 9.11
soul of the diligent is richly s. Pro 13.04
my needs were s. by the brethren 2Co 11.09
by every joint with which it is s., Eph 4.16

SUPPLIES
with a great army and abundant s. Dan 11.13
He who s. seed to the sower and 2Co 9.10
not only s. the wants of the saints 9.12
Does he who s. the Spirit to you Gal 3.05
it by the strength which God s.; 1Pe 4.11

SUPPLY
her merchandise will s. abundant food Is 23.18
at the present time should s. their want, 2Co 8.14
that their abundance may s. your want, 8.14
for food will s. and multiply your 9.10
And my God will s. every need of yours Php 4.19
to face and s. what is lacking in your 1Th 3.10

SUPPORT
the land could not s. both of them Gen 13.06
could not s. them because of their 36.07

SUPPORT (cont.)
gave him strong s. in his kingdom, 1Ch 11.10
sanctuary, and give you s. from Zion! Ps 20.02
Those who s. Egypt shall fall, and Eze 30.06
remember it is not you that s. the root, Rom 11.18
by accepting s. from them in order 2Co 11.08
So we ought to s. such men, that we 3Jn 1.08

SUPPORTED
for Joab had s. Adonijah although 1Ki 2.28
although he had not s. Absalom— 2.28
and Shabbethai the Levite s. them. Ez 10.15
them security, and they are s.; Job 24.23
salvation, and thy right hand s. me, Ps 18.35
should not be s. by the wall of Eze 41.06

SUPPORTING
order that the s. beams should not 1Ki 6.06

SUPPORTS
four corners were s. for a laver. 1Ki 7.30
The s. were cast, with wreaths at 7.30
There were four s. at the four 7.34
the s. were of one piece with the 7.34
the almug wood s. for the house of 10.12
to serve as s. for the side Eze 41.06
the root, but the root that s. you. Rom 11.18

SUPPOSE
S. here are fifty righteous within Gen 18.24
S. five of the fifty righteous are 18.28
"S. forty are found there." He 18.29
S. thirty are found there." He 18.30
Lord. S. twenty are found there." 18.31
once. S. ten are found there." 18.32
"Let not my lord s. that they have 2Sa 13.32
to heart as to s. that all the 13.33
But if you s. that in this way you 2Ch 25.08
I s., to whom he forgave more." Lk 7.43
I s. that the world itself could Jn 21.25
as you s., since it is only the Ac 2.15
he said, 'What do you s. that I am? 13.25
Do you s., O man, that when you Rom 2.03
person must not s. that a double Jas 1.07
Or do you s. it is in vain that the 4.05

SUPPOSED
those who are s. to rule over the Mk 10.42
being the son (as was s.) of Joseph, Lk 3.23
because they s. that the kingdom 19.11
and s. that they saw a spirit. 24.37
He s. that his brethren understood Ac 7.25
where we s. there was a place of 16.13
and they s. that Paul had brought 21.29
in his case of such evils as I s.; 25.18

SUPPOSING
but s. him to be in the company Lk 2.44
s. that she was going to the tomb Jn 11.31
S. him to be the gardener, she 20.15
of the city, s. that he was dead. Ac 14.19
s. that the prisoners had escaped. 16.27
s. that they had obtained their 27.13

SUPPRESS
men who by their wickedness s. the truth. Rom 1.18

SUPREME
For the word of the king is s., and Ecc 8.04
whether it be to the emperor as s., 1Pe 2.13

SUR
at the gate S. and a third at the 2Ki 11.06

SURE
shall be made s. in perpetuity to Lev 25.30
and be s. your sin will find you Num 32.23
Only be s. that you do not eat the Deu 12.23
house, and give me a s. sign, Jos 2.12
and I will build him a s. house, 1Sa 2.35
Go, make yet more s.; know and 23.22
back to me with s. information. 23.23
certainly make my lord a s. house, 25.28
because I was s. that he could not 2Sa 1.10
shall be made s. for ever before 7.16
you, and will build you a s. house, 1Ki 11.38
the testimony of the LORD is s., Ps 19.07
God has shown himself a s. defense. 48.03
Thy decrees are very s.; 93.05
All thy commandments are s.; 119.86
to David a s. oath from which he 132.11
then all your ways will be s. Pro 4.26
righteousness gets a s. reward. 11.18
him like a peg in a s. place, Is 22.23
fastened in a s. place will give 22.25
plans formed of old, faithful and s. 25.01
of a s. foundation: 'He who believes 28.16
be given him, his water will be s. 33.16
my steadfast, s. love for David. 55.03
will you not be s. to put me to Jer 38.15
Chaldeans, "The word from me is s.: Dan 2.05
see that the word from me is s. 2.08
certain, and its interpretation s." 2.45
shall be s. for you from the time 4.26
of Israel I declare what is s. Hos 5.09
is going forth is s. as the dawn; 6.03
"Temptations to sin are s. to come; Lk 17.01
"Now I am s. that the Lord has sent Ac 12.11
the holy and s. blessings of David.' 13.34
and if you are s. that you are a Rom 2.19
For I am s. that neither death, nor 8.38
Because I was s. of this, I wanted 2Co 1.15
for I felt s. of all of you, that my 2.03
Be s. of this, that no immoral or Eph 5.05
And I am s. that he who began a Php 1.06
The saying is s. and worthy of full 1Ti 1.15
The saying is s.: If any one aspires 3.01
The saying is s. and worthy of full 4.09
and now, I am s., dwells in you. 2Ti 1.05
and I am s. that he is able to 1.12
The saying is s.: If we have died 2.11
hold firm to the s. word as taught, Tit 1.09
The saying is s. I desire you to 3.08
we feel s. of better things that Heb 6.09
We have this as a s. and steadfast 6.19
for we are s. that we have a clear 13.18
the prophetic word made more s. 2Pe 1.19
this we may be s. that we know him, 1Jn 2.03
this we may be s. that we are in 2.05
you may be s. that every one who 2.29

SURELY
lifeblood I will s. require a Gen 9.05
"I will s. return to you in the 18.10
her, know that you shall s. die, 20.07
"S. the LORD is in this place; 28.16
"S. you are my bone and my flesh!" 29.14
s. now my husband will love me." 29.32
s. now you would have sent me away 31.42
life of Pharaoh, s. you are spies." 42.16
S. he has been torn to pieces; 44.28
and thought, "S. the thing is known." Ex 2.14
"S. you are a bridegroom of blood 4.25
to me, I will s. hear their cry; 22.23
it will s. be a snare to you." 23.33
s. this will I do to all this Num 14.35
for I will s. do you great honor, 22.17
s. just now I would have slain you 22.33
'S. none of the men who came up out 32.11
'S. this great nation is a wise and Deu 4.06
this day that you shall s. perish. 8.19
You shall s. destroy all the places 12.02
you shall s. put the inhabitants of 13.15
your God will s. require it of you, 23.21
And I will s. hide my face in that 31.18
my death you will s. act corruptly, 31.29
'S. the land on which your foot has Jos 14.09

SURELY (cont.)

And she said, "I will s. go with you; Ju 4.09
us; we will s. do as you say." 11.10
"We shall s. die, for we have seen 13.22
they said, "S. they are smitten down 20.39
Jonathan my son, he shall s. die." 1Sa 14.39
also; you shall s. die, Jonathan." 14.44
Agag said, "S. the bitterness of 15.32
"S. the LORD's anointed is before 16.06
S. he has come up to defy Israel; 17.25
not clean, s. he is not clean." 20.26
him to me, for he shall s. die." 20.31
"You shall s. die, Ahimelech, you and 22.16
there, that he would s. tell Saul. 22.22
thy servant has s. heard that Saul 23.10
I know that you shall s. be king, 24.20
"S. in vain have I guarded all that 25.21
For as s. as the LORD the God of 25.34
"S. you know what Saul has done, how 28.09
shall s. overtake and shall s. rescue." 30.08
s. the men would have given up the 2Sa 2.27
"As s. as you live, my lord the king, 14.19
for s. they will turn away your 1Ki 11.02
I will s. tear the kingdom from you 11.11
of Samaria, shall s. come to pass." 13.32
I will s. show myself to him today." 18.15
and s. we shall be stronger than 20.23
and s. we shall be stronger than 20.25
"It is s. the king of Israel." 22.32
have gone, but you shall s. die." 2Ki 1.04
you have gone, but shall s. die.'" 1.06
have gone, but you shall s. die.'" 1.16
the kings have s. fought together, 3.23
that he would s. come out to me, 5.11
'As s. as I saw yesterday the blood 9.26
The LORD will s. deliver us, and 18.30
S. this came upon Judah at the 24.03
him but will s. fall before him." Est 6.13
S. vexation kills the fool, and Job 5.02
s. then he will rouse himself for 8.06
S. then you will lift up your face 11.15
He will s. rebuke you if in secret 13.10
S. now God has worn me out; 16.07
S. there are mockers about me, and 17.02
S. such are the dwellings of the 18.21
S. he who is wise is profitable to 22.02
saying, 'S. our adversaries are cut 22.20
"S. there is a mine for silver, and 28.01
S. I would carry it on my shoulder; 31.36
"S., you have spoken in my hearing, 33.08
S. God does not hear an empty cry, 35.13
its measurements—s. you know! 38.05
S. goodness and mercy shall follow Ps 23.06
S. every man stands as a mere 39.05
S. man goes about as a shadow! 39.06
S. for nought are they in turmoil; 39.06
s. every man is a mere breath! 39.11
Men will say, "S. there is a reward 58.11
s. there is a God who judges on 58.11
S. the wrath of men shall praise 76.10
S. his salvation is at hand for 85.09
S. the righteous shall give thanks 140.13
the diligent lead s. to abundance, Pro 21.05
S. there is a future, and your hope 23.18
S. I am too stupid to be a man. 30.02
what is his son's name? S. you know! 30.04
S. this also is vanity and a Ecc 4.16
S. oppression makes the wise man 7.07
S. there is not a righteous man on 7.20
"S. many houses shall be desolate, Is 5.09
s. you shall not be established.'" 7.09
S. for this word which they speak 8.20
"S. this iniquity will not be 22.14
He will s. be gracious to you at 30.19
"The LORD will s. deliver us; 36.15
upon it; s. the people is grass. 40.07
yet s. my right is with the LORD, 49.04
"S. your waste and your desolate 49.19
s. now you will be too narrow for 49.19
S., thus says the LORD: "Even the 49.25
S. he has borne our griefs and 53.04
"The LORD will s. separate me from 56.03
For he said, S. they are my people, 63.08
s. his anger has turned from me.' Jer 2.35
S., as a faithless wife leaves her 3.20
s. thou hast utterly deceived this 4.10
yet s. I will make you a desert, an 22.06
I will s. lift you up and cast you 23.39
I will s. have mercy on him, says 31.20
but shall s. be given into the hand 32.04
but shall s. be captured and 34.03
Chaldeans will s. stay away from 37.09
This city shall s. be given into 38.03
For I will s. save you, and you 39.18
'We will s. perform our vows that 44.25
my words will s. stand against you 44.29
s. their fold shall be appalled at 49.20
He will s. plead their cause, that 50.34
S. the little ones of their flock 50.45
s. their fold shall be appalled at 50.45
S. I will fill you with men, as many 51.14
of recompense, he will s. requite. 51.56
S. because of the anger of the LORD 52.03
s. against me he turns his hand Lam 3.03
S., if I sent you to such, they Eze 3.06
'You shall s. die,' and you give him 3.18
he shall s. live, because he took 3.21
s., because you have defiled my 5.11
s. in the place where the king 17.16
s. my oath which he despised, and my 17.19
he shall s. live, says the Lord GOD. 18.09
he shall s. die; his blood shall be 18.13
his father's iniquity; he shall s. live. 18.17
all my statutes, he shall s. live. 18.19
lawful and right, he shall s. live; 18.21
he shall s. live, he shall not die. 18.28
s. with a mighty hand and an 20.33
he shall s. deal with it as its 31.11
you shall s. die, and you do not 33.08
righteous that he shall s. live, 33.13
'You shall s. die,' yet if he turns 33.14
he shall s. live, he shall not die. 33.15
lawful and right, he shall s. live. 33.16
the land is s. given us to possess.' 33.24
s. those who are in the waste 33.27
they shall s. come to nought; Hos 12.11
S. the Lord GOD does nothing, Amo 3.07
or Gilgal shall s. go into exile, 5.05
Israel shall s. go into exile away 7.17
"S. I will never forget any of 8.07
I will s. gather all of you, O Jacob, Mic 2.12
it will s. come, it will not delay. Hab 2.03
I said, 'S. she will fear me, she Zep 3.07
father or mother, let him s. die.' Mt 15.04
father or mother, let him s. die'; Mk 7.10
I have s. seen the ill-treatment of Ac 7.34
As s. as God is faithful, our word 2Co 1.18
For s. it is not with angels that Heb 2.16
saying, "S. I will bless you and 6.14
"S. I am coming soon." Amen. Come, Rev 22.20

SURETY

"Know of a s. that your descendants Gen 15.13
I will be s. for him; of my hand 43.09
servant became s. for the lad to 44.32
is there that will give s. for me? Job 17.03
Be s. for thy servant for good; Ps 119.122
you have become s. for your Pro 6.01
He who gives s. for a stranger will 11.15
and becomes s. in the presence of 17.18
he has given s. for a stranger, 20.16
when he gives s. for foreigners. 20.16
pledges, who become s. for debts. 22.26
he has given s. for a stranger, 27.13
when he gives s. for foreigners. 27.13
This makes Jesus the s. of a better Heb 7.22

SURETYSHIP
it, but he who hates s. is secure. Pro 11.15

SURF
and the stern was broken up by the s. Ac 27.41

SURFACE
appears to be deeper than the s., Lev 14.37
will twist its s. and scatter its Is 24.01
When he has leveled its s., does 28.25
be as dung on the s. of the ground. Jer 8.02
be as dung on the s. of the ground. 16.04
be dung on the s. of the ground. 25.33
them out upon the s. of the earth, Amo 5.08
them out upon the s. of the earth— 9.06
it from the s. of the ground; 9.08

SURFACES
And on the s. of its stays and on 1Ki 7.36

SURFEIT
but the s. of the rich will not let Ecc 5.12
s. of food, and prosperous ease, but Eze 16.49

SURGE
Nile, like rivers whose waters s.? Jer 46.07
Nile, like rivers whose waters s. 46.08

SURGING
multitude was s. hither and thither. 1Sa 14.16
thy horses, the s. of mighty waters. Hab 3.15

SURNAME
and s. himself by the name of Israel." Is 44.05
I s. you, though you do not know me. 45.04

SURNAMED
Simon whom he s. Peter; Mk 3.16
whom he s. Boanerges, that is, sons 3.17
who was s. Justus, and Matthias. Ac 1.23
Thus Joseph who was s. by the 4.36

SURPASS
and prosperity s. the report which 1Ki 10.07
you s. the report which I heard. 2Ch 9.06
excellently, but you s. them all." Pro 31.29
the wood of the vine s. any wood, Eze 15.02
'Whom do you s. in beauty? Go down, 32.19

SURPASSED
Solomon's wisdom s. the wisdom of 1Ki 4.30
great and s. all who were before Ecc 2.09

SURPASSES
because of the splendor that s. it. 2Co 3.10
love of Christ which s. knowledge, Eph 3.19

SURPASSING
s. all who were over Jerusalem Ecc 1.16
because of the s. grace of God in 2Co 9.14
because of the s. worth of knowing Php 3.08

SURPRISE
for that day to s. you like a thief. 1Th 5.04

SURPRISED
They are s. that you do not now 1Pe 4.04
do not be s. at the fiery ordeal 4.12

SURRENDER
men of Keilah s. me into his hand? 1Sa 23.11
men of Keilah s. me and my men 23.12
the Lord said, "They will s. you." 23.12
shall be to s. him into the king's 23.20
If you will s. to the princes of Jer 38.17
But if you do not s. to the princes 38.18
But if you refuse to s., this is 38.21

SURRENDERED
against her round about, she has s.; Jer 50.15

SURRENDERS
goes out and s. to the Chaldeans Jer 21.09

SURROUND
and will s. us, and cut off our name Jos 7.09
shall s. the king, each with his 2Ki 11.08
and s. them with walls and towers, 2Ch 14.07
The Levites shall s. the king, 23.07
his archers s. me. He slashes open Job 16.13
the willows of the brook s. him. 40.22
me, my deadly enemies who s. me. Ps 17.09
track me down; now they s. me; 17.11
me, strong bulls of Bashan s. me; 22.12
They s. me like a flood all day 88.17
Those who s. me lift up their head, 140.09
The righteous will s. me; 142.07
"An adversary shall s. the land, Amo 3.11
For the wicked s. the righteous, Hab 1.04
the multitudes s. you and press Lk 8.45
up a bank about you and s. you, 19.43

SURROUNDED
to the last man, s. the house; Gen 19.04
and they s. the place and lay in Ju 16.02
s. Absalom and struck him, and 2Sa 18.15
with which his enemies s. him, 1Ki 5.03
the slingers s. and conquered it. 2Ki 3.25
came by night, and s. the city. 6.14
smote the Edomites who had s. him; 8.21
Edomites who had s. him and his 2Ch 21.09
All nations s. me; in the name of Ps 118.10
They s. me, s. me on every side; in the 118.11
They s. me like bees, they blazed 118.12
you see Jerusalem s. by armies, Lk 21.20
since we are s. by so great a cloud Heb 12.01
broad earth and s. the camp of the Rev 20.09

SURROUNDING
of Judah and its s. pasture lands, 1Ch 6.55
all the s. chambers, the treasuries 28.12
throughout all the s. region of Mk 1.28
out through all the s. country. Lk 4.14
into every place in the s. region. 4.37
of Judea and all the s. country. 7.17
people of the s. country of the 8.37
of Lycaonia, and to the s. country; Ac 14.06
and Gomorrah and the s. cities, Jud 1.07

SURROUNDS
steadfast love s. him who trusts Ps 32.10
iniquity of my persecutors s. me, 49.05

SURVIVE
Those who s. him the pestilence Job 27.15
and those who s. will be very few Is 16.14
in this city who s. the pestilence, Jer 21.07
shall escape or s. or return to 44.14
any of you who s. I will scatter Eze 5.10

SURVIVED
was left none that s. or escaped. Jos 8.22
and those who s. were scattered, so 1Sa 11.11
them concerning the Jews that s., Neh 1.02
"The people who s. the sword found Jer 31.02
of the Lord none escaped or s.; Lam 2.22

SURVIVES
But if the slave s. a day or two, Ex 21.21
Then every one that s. of all the Zec 14.16
man has built on the foundation s., 1Co 3.14

SURVIVING
And the s. remnant of the house of 2Ki 19.30
And the s. remnant of the house of Is 37.31

SURVIVOR
there was not one s. left to him; Num 21.35
him until no s. was left to him. Deu 3.03
and let each s., in whatever place Ez 1.04

SURVIVOR (cont.)

and no s. where he used to live. Job 18.19
no remnant or s. from the evil Jer 42.17
shall be no s. to the house of Ob 1.18

SURVIVORS

and to keep alive for you many s. Gen 45.07
and the s. of cities be destroyed!' Num 24.19
inheritance for the s. of Benjamin, Ju 21.17
and out of Mount Zion a band of s. 2Ki 19.31
"The s. there in the province who Neh 1.03
of hosts had not left us a few s., Is 1.09
and glory of the s. of Israel. 4.02
Israel and the s. of the house of 10.20
and out of Mount Zion a band of s. 37.32
together, you s. of the nations! 45.20
them I will send s. to the nations, 66.19
And if any s. escape, they will be Eze 7.16
left in it any s. to lead out sons 14.22
and the s. shall be scattered to 17.21
and your s. shall fall by the sword 23.25
and your s. shall be devoured by 23.25
and among the s. shall be those Joe 2.32
delivered up his s. in the day of Ob 1.14
and the s. of my nation shall Zep 2.09

SUSA

the men of S., that is, the Elamites, Ez 4.09
year, as I was in S. the capital, Neh 1.01
royal throne in S. the capital, Est 1.02
people present in S. the capital, 1.05
to the harem in S. the capital, 2.03
was a Jew in S. the capital whose 2.05
gathered in S. the capital in 2.08
was issued in S. the captal. 3.15
but the city of S. was perplexed. 3.15
issued in S. for their destruction, 4.08
all the Jews to be found in S., 4.16
was issued in S. the capital. 8.14
the city of S. shouted and rejoiced 8.15
In S. the capital itself the Jews 9.06
those slain in S. the capital was 9.11
"In S. the capital the Jews have 9.12
Jews who are in S. be allowed 9.13
a decree was issued in S., 9.14
who were in S. gathered also on 9.15
they slew three hundred men in S.; 9.15
who were in S. gathered on the 9.18
I was in S. the capital, which is in Dan 8.02

SUSANNA

and S., and many others, who provided Lk 8.03

SUSI

of Manasseh), Gaddi the son of S.; Num 13.11

SUSPECT

some who s. us of acting in worldly 2Co 10.02

SUSPECTED

the sailors s. that they were nearing Ac 27.27

SUSPENSE

"How long will you keep us in s. If Ju 10.24
continued in s. and without food, Ac 27.33

SUSPICIONS

envy, dissension, slander, base s., 1Ti 6.04

SUSTAIN

didst thou s. them in the wilderness, Neh 9.21
on the LORD, and he will s. you; Ps 55.22
S. me with raisins, refresh me with Sol 2.05
may know how to s. with a word him Is 50.04
who will s. you to the end, guiltless 1Co 1.08

SUSTAINED

with grain and wine I have s. him. Gen 27.37
witnesses, shall a charge be s. Deu 19.15
God made and s. for us the spirit Mal 2.15
charge must be s. by the evidence 2Co 13.01

SUSTAINS

I wake again, for the LORD s. me. Ps 3.05
The LORD s. him on his sickbed; 41.03

SUSTENANCE

and leave no s. in Israel, and no Ju 6.04
summer, and gathers her s. in harvest. Pro 6.08

SWADDLING

garment, and thick darkness its s. band, Job 38.09
son and wrapped him in s. cloths, and Lk 2.07
babe wrapped in s. cloths and lying 2.12

SWALLOW

they said, "Lest the earth s. us up!" Num 16.34
why will you s. up the heritage of 2Sa 20.19
it, that I should s. up or destroy! 20.20
let me alone till I s. my spittle? Job 7.19
his toil, and will not s. it down; 20.18
The LORD will s. them up in his Ps 21.09
or the deep s. me up, or the pit 69.15
and the s. a nest for herself, where 84.03
like Sheol let us s. them alive and Pro 1.12
like a s. in its flying, a curse 26.02
He will s. up death for ever, and Is 25.08
Like a s. or a crane I clamor, I 38.14
s., and crane keep the time of Jer 8.07
a great fish to s. up Jonah; Jon 1.17

SWALLOWED

And the thin ears s. up the seven Gen 41.07
and the thin ears s. up the seven 41.24
But Aaron's rod s. up their rods. Ex 7.12
thy right hand, the earth s. them. 15.12
opened its mouth and s. them up, Num 16.32
its mouth and s. them up together 26.10
opened its mouth and s. them up, Deu 11.06
people who are with him be s. up.'" 2Sa 17.16
ever wish that he would be s. up? Job 37.20
them not say, "We have s. him up." Ps 35.25
the earth opened and s. up Dathan, 106.17
then they would have s. us up alive, 124.03
who are led by them are s. up. Is 9.16
and those who s. you up will be far 49.19
he has s. me like a monster; Jer 51.34
out of his mouth what he has s. 51.44
Israel is s. up; already they are Hos 8.08
written: "Death is s. up in victory." 1Co 15.54
is mortal may be s. up by life. 2Co 5.04
its mouth and s. the river which Rev 12.16

SWALLOWING

straining out a gnat and s. a camel! Mt 23.24

SWALLOWS

and s. them up, with all that Num 16.30
He s. down riches and vomits them Job 20.15
fierceness and rage he s. the ground; 39.24
when the wicked s. up the man more Hab 1.13

SWAMP

haunt of jackals shall become a s., Is 35.07

SWAMPED

the boat was being s. by the waves; Mt 8.24

SWAMPS

But its s. and marshes will not become Eze 47.11

SWARM

moves, with which the waters s., Gen 1.21
creatures that s. upon the earth, 7.21
the Nile shall s. with frogs which Ex 8.03
such a dense s. of locusts as had 10.14
things that s. upon the earth: Lev 11.29
unclean to you among all that s.; 11.31

SWARM (cont.)
things that s. upon the earth, Lev 11.42
there was a s. of bees in the body Ju 14.08

SWARMED
Their land s. with frogs, even in the Ps 105.30

SWARMING
all s. creatures that swarm upon Gen 7.21
or a carcass of unclean s. things, Lev 5.02
of the s. creatures in the waters 11.10
you among the s. things that swarm 11.29
"Every s. thing that swarms upon 11.41
all the s. things that swarm upon 11.42
with any s. thing that swarms; 11.43
with any s. thing that crawls upon 11.44
the s. locust has eaten. Joe 1.04
What the s. locust left, the hopping 1.04
years which the s. locust has 2.25

SWARMS
bring forth s. of living creatures, Gen 1.20
I will send s. of flies on you and Ex 8.21
shall be filled with s. of flies, 8.21
so that no s. of flies shall be 8.22
came great s. of flies into the 8.24
LORD that the s. of flies may 8.29
and removed the s. of flies from 8.31
thing that s. upon the earth is an Lev 11.41
with any swarming thing that s.; 11.43
creature that s. upon the earth, 11.46
He sent among them s. of flies, Ps 78.45
He spoke, and there came s. of flies, 105.31
living creature which s. will live, Eze 47.09

SWARTHY
Do not gaze at me because I am s., Sol 1.06

SWATHED
rubbed with salt, nor s. with bands. Eze 16.04
I s. you in fine linen and covered 16.10

SWAY
honored, and go to s. over the trees?' Ju 9.09
fruit, and go to s. over the trees?' 9.11
men, and go to s. over the trees?' 9.13

SWAYED
And he s. the heart of all the men 2Sa 19.14
with sins and s. by various impulses, 2Ti 3.06

SWAYS
a drunken man, it s. like a hut; Is 24.20

SWEAR
now therefore s. to me here by God Gen 21.23
And Abraham said, "I will s." 21.24
and I will make you s. by the LORD, 24.03
My master made me s., saying, 'You 24.37
Jacob said, "S. to me first." 25.33
And he said, "S. to me"; and he swore 47.31
My father made me s., saying, 'I am 50.05
your father, as he made you s." 50.06
whom thou didst s. by thine own Ex 32.13
any sort of rash oath that men s., Lev 5.04
And you shall not s. by my name 19.12
thou didst s. to give their Num 11.12
serve him, and s. by his name. Deu 6.13
him, and by his name you shall s. 10.20
as thou didst s. to our fathers, a 26.15
and s., As I live for ever, 32.40
Now then, s. to me by the LORD that Jos 2.12
of yours which you have made us s. 2.17
oath which you have made us s." 2.20
or s. by them, or serve them, or bow 23.07
I s. I will be avenged upon you, and Ju 15.07
"S. to me that you will not fall 15.12
Therefore I s. to the house of Eli 1Sa 3.14
made David s. again by his love 20.17
S. to me therefore by the LORD that 24.21
"S. to me by God, that you will not 30.15
for I s. by the LORD, if you do not 2Sa 19.07
s. to your maidservant, saying, 1Ki 1.13
King Solomon s. to me first that 1.51
"Did I not make you s. by the LORD, 2.42
who had made him s. by God; 2Ch 36.13
false, and does not s. deceitfully. Ps 24.04
all who s. by him shall glory; 63.11
faithfulness thou didst s. to David? 89.49
of Canaan and s. allegiance to the Is 19.18
shall bow, every tongue shall s." 45.23
who s. by the name of the LORD, and 48.01
the land shall s. by the God of 65.16
and if you s., 'As the LORD lives,' Jer 4.02
LORD lives," yet they s. falsely. 5.02
s. falsely, burn incense to Baal, and 7.09
to s. by my name, 'As the LORD lives, 12.16
taught my people to s. by Baal, 12.16
I s. by myself, says the LORD, that 22.05
thou didst s. to their fathers to 32.22
I s. that the nations that are Eze 36.07
and I heard him s. by him who lives Dan 12.07
and s. not, "As the LORD lives." Hos 4.15
Those who s. by Ashimah of Samaria, Amo 8.14
bow down and s. to the LORD and Zep 1.05
to the LORD and yet s. by Milcom; 1.05
against those who s. falsely, Mal 3.05
of old, 'You shall not s. falsely, Mt 5.33
Do not s. at all, either by heaven, 5.34
And do not s. by your head, for you 5.36
a curse on himself and to s., 26.74
a curse on himself and to s., Mk 14.71
And to whom did he s. that they Heb 3.18
had no one greater by whom to s., 6.13
Men indeed s. by a greater than 6.16
do not s., either by heaven or by Jas 5.12

SWEARING
lied about it, s. falsely—in any of all Lev 6.03
there is s., lying, killing, stealing, Hos 4.02

SWEARS
or s. an oath to bind himself by a Num 30.02
and comes and s. his oath before 1Ki 8.31
and comes and s. his oath before 2Ch 6.22
who s. to his own hurt and does not Ps 15.04
and he who s. is as he who shuns an Ecc 9.02
every one who s. falsely shall be Zec 5.03
of him who s. falsely by my name; 5.04
'If any one s. by the temple, it is Mt 23.16
but if any one s. by the gold of 23.16
'If any one s. by the altar, it is 23.18
but if any one s. by the gift that 23.18
he who s. by the altar, s. by it 23.20
he who s. by the temple, s. by it 23.21
he who s. by heaven, s. by the 23.22

SWEAT
In the s. of your face you shall Gen 3.19
with anything that causes s. Eze 44.18
and his s. became like great drops Lk 22.44

SWEEP
behold, I will utterly s. away 1Ki 16.03
I will utterly s. you away, 21.21
S. me not away with sinners, nor my Ps 26.09
or ablaze, may he s. them away! 58.09
Let not the flood s. over me, 69.15
Thou dost s. men away; 90.05
of the wicked will s. them away, Pro 21.07
and it will s. away the beard also. Is 7.20
and it will s. on into Judah, it 8.08
and I will s. it wth the broom of 14.23
As whirlwinds in Negeb s. on, 21.01
and hail will s. away the refuge of 28.17
Then they s. by like the wind and Hab 1.11

SWEEP (cont.)
"I will utterly s. away everything Zep 1.02
"I will s. away man and beast; 1.03
I will s. away the birds of the air 1.03
a lamp and s. the house and seek Lk 15.08
to s. her away with the flood. Rev 12.15

SWEEPING
lead to the s. away of moist and Deu 29.19

SWEEPS
is gone it s. him out of his place. Job 27.21
waters, and the flood s. over me. Ps 69.02

SWEET
the water, and the water became s. Ex 15.25
"Take s. spices, stacte, and onycha, 30.34
s. spices with pure frankincense 30.34
two handfuls of s. incense beaten Lev 16.12
of the strong came something s." Ju 14.14
the s. psalmist of Israel: 2Sa 23.01
of incense of s. spices before him, 2Ch 2.04
offerings and incense of s. spices, 13.11
fat and drink s. wine and send Neh 8.10
"Though wickedness is s. in his mouth, Job 20.12
The clods of the valley are s. to him; 21.33
We used to hold s. converse together Ps 55.14
the s. lyre with the harp. 81.02
How s. are thy words to my taste, 119.103
lie down, your sleep will be s. Pro 3.24
"Stolen water is s., and bread 9.17
desire fulfilled is s. to the soul; 13.19
Bread gained by deceit is s. to a man, 20.17
the honeycomb are s. to your taste. 24.13
is hungry everything bitter is s. 27.07
S. is the sleep of a laborer, Ecc 5.12
Light is s., and it is pleasant for 11.07
and his fruit was s. to my taste. Sol 2.03
your voice, for your voice is s., 2.14
How s. is your love, my sister, my 4.10
His speech is most s., and he is 5.16
bitter for s. and s. for bitter! Is 5.20
Make s. melody, sing many songs, that 23.16
not bought s. cane with money, 43.24
or s. cane from a distant land? Jer 6.20
it was in my mouth as s. as honey. Eze 3.03
of wine, because of the s. wine, Joe 1.05
the mountains shall drip s. wine, 3.18
the mountains shall drip s. wine, Amo 9.13
but s. as honey in your mouth." Rev 10.09
it was s. as honey in my mouth, but 10.10

SWEETER
went down, "What is s. than honey? Ju 14.18
s. also than honey and drippings of Ps 19.10
my taste, s. than honey to my mouth! 119.103

SWEETNESS
I leave my s. and my good fruit, Ju 9.11
s. to the soul and health to the Pro 16.24

SWEET-SMELLING
and of s. cinnamon half as much, that Ex 30.23

SWELL
thigh fall away and your body s.; Num 5.21
make your body s. and your thigh 5.22
bitter pain, and her body shall s., 5.27
upon you, and your foot did not s., Deu 8.04
wear out and their feet did not s. Neh 9.21
Their eyes s. out with fatness Ps 73.07
expecting him to s. up or suddenly Ac 28.06

SWELLING
of his body a s. or an eruption or Lev 13.02
if there is a white s. in the skin, 13.10
there is quick raw flesh in the s., 13.10
comes a white s. or a reddish-white 13.19
it is a s. from the burn, and the 13.28
if the diseased s. is reddish-white 13.43
and for a s. or an eruption or a 14.56

SWEPT
lest you be s. away with all their Num 16.26
The torrent Kishon s. them away, Ju 5.21
you shall be s. away, both you and 1Sa 12.25
blossom will be s. away by the Job 15.30
moment, s. away utterly by terrors! Ps 73.19
Thy wrath has s. over me; thy dread 88.16
then the flood would have s. us away, 124.04
but it is s. away through injustice Pro 13.23
I have s. away your transgressions Is 44.22
beasts and the birds are s. away, Jer 12.04
be utterly s. away before him and Dan 11.22
his army shall be s. away, and many 11.26
the raging waters s. on; the deep Hab 3.10
finds it empty, s., and put in order. Mt 12.44
flood came and s. them all away, 24.39
he finds it s. and put in order. Lk 11.25
His tail s. down a third of the Rev 12.04

SWERVE
but I do not s. from thy testimonies Ps 119.157
Do not s. to the right or to the Pro 4.27
they do not s. from their paths. Joe 2.07

SWERVED
who have s. from the truth by holding 2Ti 2.18

SWERVING
Certain persons by s. from these 1Ti 1.06

SWIFT
as s. as the eagle flies, a nation Deu 28.49
Asahel was as s. of foot as a wild 2Sa 2.18
the horses and s. steeds they 1Ki 4.28
and who were s. as gazelles upon 1Ch 12.08
riding on s. horses that were used Est 8.10
on their s. horses that were used 8.14
loosed the bonds of the s. ass, Job 39.05
the sun the race is not to the s., Ecc 9.11
justice and is s. to do righteousness Is 16.05
Go, you s. messengers, to a nation, 18.02
is riding on a s. cloud and comes 19.01
and, "We will ride upon s. steeds," 30.16
therefore your pursuers shall be s. 30.16
The s. cannot see away, nor the Jer 46.06
"On that day s. messengers shall go Eze 30.09
came to me in s. flight at the time Dan 9.21
Flight shall perish from the s., Amo 2.14
and he who is s. of foot shall not 2.15
fly like an eagle s. to devour. Hab 1.08
I will be a s. witness against the Mal 3.05
"Their feet are s. to shed blood, Rom 3.15
upon themselves s. destruction. 2Pe 2.01

SWIFTER
they were s. than eagles, they were 2Sa 1.23
My days are s. than a weaver's Job 7.06
"My days are s. than a runner; 9.25
his horses are s. than eagles— Jer 4.13
Our pursuers were s. than the Lam 4.19
Their horses are s. than leopards, Hab 1.08

SWIFTLY
at hand, and their doom comes s. Deu 32.35
'They are s. carried away upon the Job 24.18
he came s. upon the wings of the Ps 18.10
to the earth; his word runs s. 147.15
and lo, s., speedily it comes! Is 5.26
one shall fly s. like an eagle, and Jer 48.40
mount up and fly s. like an eagle, 49.22
upon your own head s. and speedily. Joe 3.04

SWIM
spreads his hands out to s.; Is 25.11
it was deep enough to s. in, Eze 47.05

SWIM (cont.)
lest any should s. away and escape Ac 27.42
those who could s. to throw 27.43

SWIMMER
of it as a s. spreads his hands Is 25.11

SWINE
And the s., because it parts the Lev 11.07
And the s., because it parts the Deu 14.08
do not throw your pearls before s., Mt 7.06
Now a herd of many s. was feeding 8.30
send us away into the herd of s." 8.31
they came out and went into the s.; 8.32
Now a great herd of s. was feeding Mk 5.11
they begged him, "Send us to the s., 5.12
came out, and entered the s.; 5.13
to the demoniac and to the s. 5.16
Now a large herd of s. was feeding Lk 8.32
out of the man and entered the s., 8.33
him into his fields to feed s. 15.15
fed on the pods that the s. ate; 15.16

SWINE'S
Like a gold ring in a s. snout is a Pro 11.22
who eat s. flesh, and broth of Is 65.04
like him who offers s. blood; 66.03
eating s. flesh and the abomination 66.17

SWING
afar from men, they s. to and fro. Job 28.04

SWINGING
apiece, two s. leaves for each door. Eze 41.24

SWINGS
and his hand s. the axe to cut down Deu 19.05

SWIRLS
the chaff that s. from the threshing Hos 13.03

SWOLLEN
s. with conceit, lovers of pleasure 2Ti 3.04

SWOON
till they s. away and sleep a Jer 51.39

SWOONED
she has s. away; her sun went Jer 15.09

SWOOP
Why did you s. on the spoil, and do 1Sa 15.19
But they shall s. down upon the Is 11.14

SWOOPING
reed, like an eagle s. on the prey. Job 9.26

SWORD
and a flaming s. which turned every Gen 3.24
By your s. you shall live, and you 27.40
daughters like captives of the s.? 31.26
and his son Shechem with the s., 34.26
Amorites with my s. and with my bow 48.22
us with pestilence or with the s." Ex 5.03
and have put a s. in their hand to 5.21
I will draw my s., 15.09
his people with the edge of the s. 17.13
me from the s. of Pharaoh"). 18.04
and I will kill you with the s., 22.24
'Put every man his s. on his side, 32.27
and the s. shall not go through Lev 26.06
shall fall before you by the s. 26.07
shall fall before you by the s. 26.08
And I will bring a s. upon you, 26.25
I will unsheathe the s. after you; 26.33
flee as one flees from the s., 26.36
one another, as if to escape a s., 26.37
into this land, to fall by the s. Num 14.03
you, and you shall fall by the s.; 14.43
touches one who is slain with a s., 19.16
I come out with the s. against you." 20.18
slew him with the edge of the s., 21.24
road, wth a drawn s. in his hand; 22.23
I wish I had a s. in my hand, 22.29
way, with his drawn s. in his hand; 22.31
Balaam the son of Beor with the s. 31.08
inhabitants of that city to the s., Deu 13.15
cattle, with the edge of the s. 13.15
shall put all its males to the s., 20.13
In the open the s. shall bereave, 32.25
if I whet my glittering s., 32.41
and my s. shall devour flesh—with 32.42
and the s. of your triumph! 33.29
him with his drawn s. in his hand; Jos 5.13
and asses, with the edge of the s. 6.21
had fallen by the edge of the s., 8.24
smote it with the edge of the s. 8.24
men of Israel killed with the s. 10.11
its king with the edge of the s.; 10.28
smote it with the edge of the s., 10.30
smote it with the edge of the s., 10.32
smote it with the edge of the s.; 10.35
smote it with the edge of the s., 10.37
smote them with the edge of the s., 10.39
and smote its king with the s.; 11.10
And they put to the s. all who were 11.11
smote them with the edge of the s., 11.12
they smote with the edge of the s., 11.14
killed with the s. among the rest 13.22
it to the s. they took possession 19.47
was not by your s. or by your bow. 24.12
smote it with the edge of the s., Ju 1.08
the city with the edge of the s., 1.25
for himself a s. with two edges, 3.16
took the s. from his right thigh, 3.21
not draw the s. out of his belly; 3.22
before Barak at the edge of the s.; 4.15
Sisera fell by the edge of the s.; 4.16
other than the s. of Gideon the 7.14
"A. s. for the LORD and for Gideon!" 7.20
set every man's s. against his 7.22
thousand men who drew the s. 8.10
But the youth did not draw his s.; 8.20
"Draw your s. and kill me, lest men 9.54
smote them with the edge of the s., 18.27
men on foot that drew the s. 20.02
thousand men that drew the s., 20.15
hundred thousand men that drew s.; 20.17
all these were men who drew the s. 20.25
all these were men who drew the s. 20.35
the city with the edge of the s. 20.37
thousand men that drew the s., 20.46
smote them with the edge of the s., 20.48
Jabeshgilead with the edge of the s.; 21.10
house shall die by the s. of men. 1Sa 2.33
was neither s. nor spear found in 13.22
every man's s. was against his 14.20
the people with the edge of the s. 15.08
"As your s. has made women childless, 15.33
David girded his s. over his armor, 17.39
to me with a s. and with a spear 17.45
LORD saves not with s. and spear; 17.47
there was no s. in the hand of 17.50
and took his s. and drew it out of 17.51
and even his s. and his bow and his 18.04
not here a spear or a s. at hand? 21.08
neither my s. nor my weapons with 21.08
"The s. of Goliath the Philistine, 21.09
gave him the s. of Goliath the 22.10
you have gven him bread and a s., 22.13
of the priests, he put to the s.; 22.19
asses and sheep, he put to the s. 22.19
his men, "Every man gird on his s.!" 25.13
every man of them girded on his s.; 25.13
David also girded on his s.; 25.13
"Draw your s., and thrust me 31.04

SWORD (cont.)

Therefore Saul took his own s., 1Sa 31.04
was dead, he also fell upon his s., 31.05
because they had fallen by the s. 2Sa 1.12
and the s. of Saul returned not 1.22
and thrust his s. in his opponent's 2.16
"Shall the s. devour for ever 2.26
spindle, or who is slain by the s., 3.29
for the s. devours now one and now 11.25
Uriah the Hittite with the s., 12.09
him with the s. of the Ammonites. 12.09
Now therefore he s. shall never 12.10
the city with the edge of the s." 15.14
more people that day than the s. 18.08
a girdle wih a s. in its sheath 20.08
not observe the s. which was in 20.10
and who was girded with a new s., 21.16
and his hand clove to the s.; 23.10
valiant men who drew the s., 24.09
not slay his servant with the s.'" 1Ki 1.51
not put you to death with the s.' 2.08
slew with the s. two men more 2.32
And the king said, "Bring me a s." 3.24
So a s. was brought before the king 3.24
slain all the prophets with the s. 19.01
and slain thy prophets with the s.; 19.10
and slain thy prophets with the s.; 19.14
from the s. of Hazael shall Jehu 19.17
from the s. of Jehu shall Elisha 19.17
with your s. and with your bow? 2Ki 6.22
slay their young men with the s., 8.12
So when they put them to the s., 10.25
slay with the s. any one who 11.15
slain with the s. at the king's 11.20
to fall by the s. in his own land.'" 19.07
his sons, slew him with the s., 19.37
men, who carried shield and s., 1Ch 5.18
"Draw your s., and thrust me 10.04
Therefore Saul took his own s., 10.04
he also fell upon his s., and died. 10.05
thousand men who drew the s., 21.05
seventy thousand who drew the s. 21.05
while the s. of your enemies 21.12
three days of the s. of the LORD, 21.12
hand a drawn s. stretched out over 21.16
and he put his s. back into its 21.27
afraid of the s. of the angel of 21.30
the s., judgment, or pestilence, or 2Ch 20.09
slew all his brothers with the s., 21.04
her is to be slain with the s." 23.14
Athaliah had been slain with the s. 23.21
fallen by the s. and our sons and 29.09
struck hm down there with the s. 32.21
men with the s. in the house of 36.17
those who had escaped from the s., 36.20
to the s., to captivity, to plundering, Ez 9.07
builders had his s. girded at his Neh 4.18
all their enemies with the s., Est 9.05
servants with the edge of the s.; Job 1.15
servants with the edge of the s.; 1.17
in war from the power of the s. 5.20
and he is destined for the s. 15.22
be afraid of the s., for wrath brings 19.29
brings the punishment of the s., 19.29
are multiplied, it is for the s.; 27.14
his life from perishing by the s. 33.18
not hearken, they perish by the s., 36.12
he does not turn back from the s. 39.22
him who made him bring near his s.! 40.19
Though the s. reaches him, it does 41.26
not repent, God will whet his s.; Ps 7.12
my life from the wicked by thy s., 17.13
Deliver my soul from the s., 22.20
The wicked draw the s. and bend 37.14
their s. shall enter their own 37.15
by their own s. did they win the 44.03
do I trust, nor can my s. save me. 44.06
Gird your s. upon your thigh, O 45.03
given over to the power of the s., 63.10
the s., and the weapons of war. 76.03
He gave his people over to the s., 78.62
Their priests fell by the s., 78.64
turned back the edge of his s., 89.43
Rescue me from the cruel s., 144.11
wormwood, sharp as a two-edged s. Pro 5.04
rash words are like s. thrusts, 12.18
or a s., or a sharp arrow. 25.18
each with his s. at his thigh, Sol 3.08
you shall be devoured by the s.; Is 1.20
not lift up s. against nation, 2.04
fall by the s. and your mighty men 3.25
is caught will fall by the s. 13.15
the slain, those pierced by the s., 14.19
from the swords, from the drawn s., 21.15
slain with the s. or dead in 22.02
and strong s. will punish Leviathan 27.01
shall fall by a s., not of man; 31.08
and a s., not of man, shall devour 31.08
and he shall flee from the s., 31.08
For my s. has drunk its fill in the 34.05
The LORD has a s.; it is sated 34.06
him fall by the s. in his own land.'" 37.07
his sons, slew him with the s., 37.38
makes them like dust with his s., 41.02
He made my mouth like a sharp s., 49.02
and destruction, famine and s.; 51.19
I will destine you to the s., 65.12
and by his s., upon all flesh; 66.16
your own s. devoured your prophets Jer 2.30
whereas the s. has reached their 4.10
us, nor shall we see s. or famine. 5.12
they shall destroy with the s." 5.17
for the enemy has a s., terror is on 6.25
and I will send the s. after them, 9.16
the young men shall die by the s.; 11.22
for the s. of the LORD devours from 12.12
but I will consume them by the s., 14.12
to them, 'You shall not see the s., 14.13
'S. and famine shall not come on 14.15
By s. and famine those prophets 14.15
Jerusalem, victims of famine and s., 14.16
behold, those slain by the s.! 14.18
who are for the s., to the s.; 15.02
the s. to slay, the dogs to tear, and 15.03
give to the s. before their 15.09
perish by the s. and by famine, 16.04
them over to the power of the s., 18.21
be slain by the s. in battle. 18.21
to fall by the s. before their 19.07
fall by the s. of their enemies 20.04
and shall slay them with the s. 20.04
s., and famine, into the hand of 21.07
smite them with the edge of the s.; 21.07
in this city shall die by the s., 21.09
And I will send s., famine, and 24.10
because of the s. which I am 25.16
because of the s. which I am 25.27
am summoning a s. against all the 25.29
will put to the s., says the LORD.' 25.31
because of the s. of the LORD, 25.38
him with the s. and cast his dead 26.23
punish that nation with the s., 27.08
you and your people die by the s., 27.13
'Behold, I am sending on them s., 29.17
I will pursue them with s., 29.18
survived the s. found grace in the 31.02
and because of s. and famine and 32.24
hand of the king of Babylon by s., 32.36
siege mounds and before the s.: 33.04
you: 'You shall not die by the s. 34.04
proclaim to you liberty to the s., 34.17
in this city shall die by the s., 38.02
and you shall not fall by the s.; 39.18
with the s., and killed him, whom 41.02
then the s. which you fear shall 42.16

SWORD (cont.)
to live there shall die by the s., Jer 42.17
that you shall die by the s., 42.22
and to the s. those who are doomed 43.11
those who are doomed to the s. 43.11
by the s. and by famine they shall 44.12
shall die by the s. and by famine; 44.12
with the s., with famine, and with 44.13
consumed by the s. and by famine." 44.18
consumed by the s. and by famine, 44.27
who escape the s. shall return 44.28
The s. shall devour and be sated, 46.10
for the s. shall devour round about 46.14
because of the s. of the oppressor 46.16
Ah, s. of the LORD! How long till 47.06
to silences, the s. shall pursue you. 48.02
keeps back his s. from bloodshed. 48.10
I will send the s. after them, 49.37
because of the s. of the oppressor, 50.16
"A s. upon the Chaldeans, says the 50.35
A s. upon the diviners, that they 50.36
A s. upon her warriors, that they 50.36
A. upon her horses and upon her 50.37
A s. upon all her treasures, that 50.37
"You that have escaped from the s., 51.50
In the street the s. bereaves; Lam 1.20
my young men have fallen by the s.; 2.21
victims of the s. than the victims 4.09
because of the s. in the wilderness 5.09
you, O son of man, take a sharp s.; Eze 5.01
strike with the s. round about the 5.02
I will unsheathe the s. after them. 5.02
fall by the s. round about you; 5.12
will unsheathe the s. after them. 5.12
and I will bring the s. upon you. 5.17
will bring a s. upon you, and I will 6.03
the nations some who escape the s., 6.08
for they shall fall by the s., 6.11
that is near shall fall by the s.; 6.12
The s. is without, pestilence and 7.15
is in the field dies by the s.; 7.15
You have feared the s.; 11.08
and I wll bring the s. upon you, 11.08
You shall fall by the s.; I will judge 11.10
I will unsheathe the s. after them. 12.14
a few of them escape from the s., 12.16
Or if I bring a s. upon that land, 14.17
Let a s. go through the land; 14.17
s., famine, evil beasts, and pestilence, 14.21
of his troops shall fall by the s., 17.21
draw forth my s. out of its sheath, 21.03
therefore my s. shall go out of its 21.04
have drawn my s. out of its sheath; 21.05
A s., a s. is sharpened and also 21.09
So the s. is given to be polished, 21.11
over to the s. with my people. 21.12
and let the s. come down twice, yea 21.14
the s. for those to be slain; 21.14
it is the s. for the great slaughter, 21.14
I have given the glittering s.; 21.15
ways for the s. of the king of 21.19
mark a way for the s. to come to 21.20
say, A s., a s. is drawn for the 21.28
and her they slew with the s.; 23.10
survivors shall fall by the s. 23.25
left behind shall fall by the s. 24.21
to Dedan they shall fall by the s. 25.13
mainland shall be slain by the s. 26.06
slay with the s. your daughters on 26.08
will slay your people with the s.; 26.11
by the s. that is against her on 28.23
Behold, I will bring a s. upon you, 29.08
A s. shall come upon Egypt, and 30.04
shall fall with them by the s. 30.05
shall fall within her by the s., 30.06
of Pibeseth shall fall by the s.; 30.17
may become strong to wield the s. 30.21
I will make the s. fall from his 30.22
and put my s. in his hand: but I 30.24
When I put my s. into the hand of 30.25
to those who are slain by the s.; 31.17
with those who are slain by the s. 31.18
when I brandish my s. before them; 32.10
The s. of the king of Babylon shall 32.11
amid those who are slain by the s., 32.20
the uncircumcised, slain by the s.' 32.21
of them slain, fallen by the s.; 32.22
fallen by the s., who spread terror 32.23
fallen by the s., who went down 32.24
uncircumcised, slain by the s.; 32.25
uncircumcised, slain by the s.; 32.26
with those who are slan by the s. 32.28
with those who are slain by the s.; 32.29
with those who are slain by the s., 32.30
slain by the s., says the Lord GOD. 32.31
with those who are slain by the s., 32.32
If I bring the s. upon a land, 33.02
and if he sees the s. coming upon 33.03
and the s. comes and takes him away, 33.04
sees the s. coming and does not 33.06
and the s. comes, and takes any one 33.06
You resort to the s., you commit 33.26
waste places shall fall by the s.; 33.27
power of the s. at the time of 35.05
those slain with the s. shall fall. 35.08
every man's s. will be against his 38.21
and they all fell by the s. 39.23
they shall fall by s. and flame, Dan 11.33
nor by s., nor by war, nor by horses, Hos 1.07
the s., and war from the land; 2.18
fall by the s. because of the 7.16
The s. shall rage against their 11.06
they shall fall by the s., 13.16
he pursued his brother with the s., Amo 1.11
I slew your young men with the s.; 4.10
the house of Jeroboam with the s." 7.09
'Jeroboam shall die by the s., 7.11
daughters shall fall by the s., 7.17
of them I will slay with the s.; 9.01
there I will command the s., 9.04
of my people shall die by the s., 9.10
not lift up s. against nation; Mic 4.03
the land of Assyria with the s., 5.06
land of Nimrod with the drawn s.; 5.06
you save I will give to the s. 6.14
and the s. shall devour your young Nah 2.13
flashing s. and glittering spear, 3.03
the s. will cut you off. It will devour 3.15
Ethiopians, shall be slain by my s. Zep 2.12
every one by the s. of his fellow. Hag 2.22
and wield you like a warrior's s. Zec 9.13
May the s. smite his arm and his 11.17
"Awake, O s., against my shepherd, 13.07
not come to bring peace, but a s. Mt 10.34
out his hand and drew his s., 26.51
"Put your s. back into its place; 26.52
the s. will perish by the s. 26.52
of those who stood by drew his s., Mk 14.47
(and a s. will pierce through your Lk 2.35
they will fall by the edge of the s., 21.24
him who has no s. sell his mantle 22.36
"Lord, shall we strike with the s.?" 22.49
having a s., drew it and struck the Jn 18.10
"Put your s. into its sheath; 18.11
the brother of John with the s.; Ac 12.02
he drew his s. and was about to 16.27
or nakedness, or peril, or s.? Rom 8.35
he does not bear the s. in vain; 13.04
and the s. of the Spirit, which is Eph 6.17
sharper than any two-edged s., Heb 4.12
fire, escaped the edge of the s., 11.34
two, they were killed with the s.; 11.37
mouth issued a sharp two-edged s., Rev 1.16
him who has the sharp two-edged s. 2.12
them with the s. of my mouth. 2.16

SWORD (cont.)

and he was given a great s. Rev 6.04
to kill with s. and with famine and 6.08
if any one slays with the s., 13.10
with the s. must he be slain. 13.10
wounded by the s. and yet lived; 13.14
issues a sharp s. with which to 19.15
slain by the s. of him who sits 19.21
the s. that issues from hs mouth; 19.21

SWORDS

took their s. and came upon the Gen 34.25
weapons of violence are their s. 49.05
make themselves s. or spears"; 1Sa 13.19
their custom with s. and lances, 1Ki 18.28
with their s., their spears, and Neh 4.13
than oil, yet they were drawn s. Ps 55.21
and arrows, their tongues sharp s. 57.04
who whet their tongues like s., 64.03
and two-edged s. in their hands, 149.06
There are those whose teeth are s. Pro 30.14
all girt with s. and expert in war, Sol 3.08
beat their s. into plowshares, and Is 2.04
For they have fled from the s., 21.15
cut you to pieces with their s. Eze 16.40
and despatch them with their s.; 23.47
draw their s. against the beauty 28.07
shall draw their s. against Egypt, 30.11
to fall by the s. of mighty ones, 32.12
whose s. were laid under their 32.27
buckler and shield, wielding s.; 38.04
Beat your plowshares into s., Joe 3.10
beat their s. into plowshares, and Mic 4.03
a great crowd with s. and clubs, Mt 26.47
with s. and clubs to capture me? 26.55
with him a crowd with s. and clubs, Mk 14.43
with s. and clubs to capture me? 14.48
said, "Look, Lord, here are two s." Lk 22.38
a robber, with s. and clubs? 22.52

SWORDSMEN

seven hundred s. to break through, 1Ki 3.26

SWORE

there both of them s. an oath. Gen 21.31
and who spoke to me and s. to me, 24.07
and s. to him concerning this 24.09
So he s. to him, and sold his 25.33
oath which I s. to Abraham your 26.03
So Jacob s. by the Fear of his 31.53
and he s. to him. Then Israel bowed 47.31
to the land which he s. to Abraham, 50.24
land which I s. to give to Abraham, Ex 6.08
which he s. to your fathers to give 13.05
as he s. to you and your fathers, 13.11
the land of which I s. to Abraham, 33.01
land which he s. to give to them, Num 14.16
land which I s. to give to their 14.23
land where I s. that I would make 14.30
on that day, and he s., saying, 32.10
land which I s. to give to Abraham, 32.11
which the LORD s. to your fathers, Deu 1.08
words, and was angered, and he s., 1.34
land which I s. to give to your 1.35
and he s. that I should not cross 4.21
your fathers which he s. to them. 4.31
land which he s. to your fathers, 6.10
which the LORD s. to give to your 6.18
land which he s. to give to our 6.23
oath which he s. to your fathers, 7.08
love which he s. to your fathers 7.12
land which he s. to your fathers 7.13
which the LORD s. to give to your 8.01
which he s. to your fathers, as at 8.18
which the LORD s. to your fathers, 9.05
which I s. to their fathers to give 10.11
which the LORD s. to your fathers 11.09
which the LORD s. to your fathers 11.21
as he s. to your fathers, 13.17
which the LORD s. to our fathers 26.03
which the LORD s. to your fathers 28.11
and as he s. to your fathers, to 29.13
which the LORD s. to your fathers, 30.20
which I s. to give to their fathers, 31.20
into the land that I s. to give." 31.21
the land which I s. to give them: 31.23
the land of which I s. to Abraham, 34.04
land which I s. to their fathers Jos 1.06
them the LORD s. that he would not 5.06
belong to her, as you s. to her." 6.22
of the congregation s. to them. 9.15
of the oath which we s. to them." 9.20
And Moses s. on that day, saying, 14.09
land which he s. to give to their 21.43
land which I s. to give to your Ju 2.01
Saul s., "As the LORD lives, he 1Sa 19.06
And David s. this to Saul. 24.22
But Saul s. to her by the LORD, "As 28.10
but David s., saying, "God do so to 2Sa 3.35
you s. to your maidservant by the 1Ki 1.17
And the king s., saying, "As the 1.29
as I s. to you by the LORD, the God 1.30
I s. to him by the LORD, saying, 'I 2.08
Then King Solomon s. by the LORD, 2.23
And Gedaliah s. to them and their 2Ki 25.24
Therefore I s. in my anger that Ps 95.11
his hand and s. to them that he 106.26
how he s. to the LORD and vowed to 132.02
The LORD s. to David a sure oath 132.11
as I s. that the waters of Noah Is 54.09
oath which I s. to your fathers to Jer 11.05
Then King Zedekiah s. secretly to 38.16
s. to them and their men, saying, "Do 40.09
I s. to the seed of the house of Eze 20.05
I s. to them, saying, I am the LORD 20.05
On that day I s. to them that I 20.06
Moreover I s. to them in the 20.15
Moreover I s. to them in the 20.23
the land which I s. to give them, 20.28
country which I s. to give to your 20.42
I s. to give it to your fathers, and 47.14
the oath which he s. to our father Lk 1.73
As I s. in my wrath, 'They shall Heb 3.11
"As I s. in my wrath, 'They shall 4.03
whom to swear, he s. by himself, 6.13
and s. by him who lives for ever Rev 10.06

SWORN

"I have s. to the LORD God Most Gen 14.22
and said, "By myself I have s., 22.16
had solemnly s. the people of Ex 13.19
about which he has s. falsely; Lev 6.05
camp, as the LORD had s. to them. Deu 2.14
as he has s. to your fathers, and 19.08
as he has s. to you, if you keep the 28.09
enter into the s. covenant of the 29.12
only that I make his s. covenant, 29.14
the words of his s. covenant, 29.19
the LORD has s. to their fathers 31.07
the LORD had s. to their fathers Jos 5.06
congregation had s. to them by the 9.18
"We have s. to them by the LORD, the 9.19
just as he had s. to their fathers 21.44
and as the LORD had s. to them; Ju 2.15
the men of Israel had s. at Mizpah, 21.01
since we have s. by the LORD that 21.07
For the people of Israel had s., 21.18
as we have s. both of us in the 1Sa 20.42
David what the LORD has s. to him, 2Sa 3.09
of Israel had s. to spare them, 21.02
with Abraham, his s. promise to Isaac, 1Ch 16.16
for they had s. with all their 2Ch 15.15
which thou hadst s. to give them. Neh 9.15
I have s. to David my servant: Ps 89.03
Once for all I have s. by my holiness; 89.35
his s. promise to Isaac, with Abraham, 105.09

SWORN (cont.)
The LORD has s. and will not change Ps 110.04
I have s. an oath and confirmed it, 119.106
LORD of hosts has s. in my hearing: Is 5.09
The LORD of hosts has s.: "As I have 14.24
By myself I have s., from my mouth 45.23
so I have s. that I will not be 54.09
The LORD has s. by his right hand 62.08
and have s. by those who are no Jer 5.07
I have s. by my great name, says the 44.26
For I have s. by myself, says the 49.13
The LORD of hosts has s. by himself: 51.14
they have s. solemn oaths; but he brings Eze 21.23
therefore I have s. concerining them, 44.12
The Lord GOD has s. by his holiness Amo 4.02
The Lord GOD has s. by himself 6.08
The LORD has s. by the pride of 8.07
as thou hast s. to our fathers from Mic 7.20
to the Lord what you have s.' Mt 5.33
that God had s. with an oath to Ac 2.30
"The Lord has s. and will not Heb 7.21

SWUNG
is broken, it has s. open to me; Eze 26.02
upon the cloud s. his sickle on Rev 14.16
So the angel s. his sickle on the 14.19

SYCAMINE
you could say to this s. tree, Lk 17.06

SYCAMORE
plentiful as the s. of the Shephelah. 1Ki 10.27
Over the olive and s. trees in the 1Ch 27.28
plentiful as the s. of the Shephelah. 2Ch 1.15
plentiful as the s. of the Shephelah. 9.27
herdsman, and a dresser of s. trees, Amo 7.14
up into a s. tree to see him, for Lk 19.04

SYCAMORES
with hail, and their s. with frost. Ps 78.47
the s. have been cut down, but we Is 9.10

SYCHAR
called S., near the field that Jn 4.05

SYENE
and these from the land of S." Is 49.12
and desolation, from Migdol to S., Eze 29.10
from Migdol to S. they shall fall 30.06

SYMBOL
doorpost you have set up your s.; Is 57.08

SYMBOLIC
(which is s. for the present age). Heb 9.09

SYMEON
the son of S., the son of Judas, the Lk 3.30
S. who was called Niger, Lucius of Ac 13.01
S. has related how God first 15.14

SYMPATHIZE
is unable to s. with our weaknesses, Heb 4.15

SYMPATHY
they showed him s. and comforted Job 42.11
the Spirit, any affection and s., Php 2.01
s., love of the brethren, a tender 1Pe 3.08

SYNAGOGUE
from there, and entered their s. Mt 12.09
country he taught them in their s., 13.54
he entered the s. and taught. Mk 1.21
was in their s. a man with an 1.23
And immediately he left the s., 1.29
Again he entered the s., 3.01
Then came one of the rulers of the s., 5.22
Jesus said to the ruler of the s., 5.36
the house of the ruler of the s., 5.38
he began to teach in the s.; 6.02
and he went to the s., as his custom Lk 4.16
of all in the s. were fixed on him 4.20
all in the s. were filled with 4.28
And in the s. there was a man who 4.33
And he arose and left the s., 4.38
when he entered the s. and taught, 6.06
our nation, and he built us our s." 7.05
Jairus, who was a ruler of the s.; 8.41
But the ruler of the s., indignant 13.14
This he said in the s., as he taught Jn 6.59
he was to be put out of the s. 9.22
they should be put out of the s.: 12.42
belonged to the s. of the Freedmen Ac 6.09
they went ino the s. and sat down. 13.14
the rulers of the s. sent to them, 13.15
the meeting of the s. broke up, 13.43
together into the Jewish s., 14.01
where there was a s. of the Jews. 17.01
they went into the Jewish s. 17.10
argued in the s. with the Jews and 17.17
And he argued in the s. every sabbath, 18.04
his house was next door to the s. 18.07
Crispus, the ruler of the s., 18.08
Sosthenes, the ruler of the s., 18.17
went into the s. and argued with 18.19
He began to speak boldly in the s.; 18.26
And he entered the s. and for three 19.08
that in every s. I imprisoned and 22.19
and are not, but are a s. of Satan. Rev 2.09
those of the s. of Satan who say 3.09

SYNAGOGUES
in their s. and preaching the Mt 4.23
do in the s. and in the streets, 6.02
and pray in the s. and at the 6.05
in their s. and preaching the 9.35
councils, and flog you in their s., 10.17
and the best seats in the s., 23.06
scourge in your s. and persecute 23.34
in their s. and casting out demons Mk 1.39
seats in the s. and the places of 12.39
and you will be beaten in s.; 13.09
And he taught in their s., being glorified Lk 4.15
was preaching in the s. of Judea. 4.44
seat in the s. and salutations in 11.43
you before the s. and the rulers 12.11
in one of the s. on the sabbath. 13.10
seats in the s. and the places of 20.46
you up to the s. and prisons, 21.12
They will put you out of the s.; Jn 16.02
taught in s. and in the temple, 18.20
for letters to the s. at Damascus, Ac 9.02
And in the s. immediately he 9.20
word of God in the s. of the Jews. 13.05
he is read every sabbath in the s." 15.21
either in the temple or in the s., 24.12
in all the s. and tried to make 26.11

SYNTYCHE
and I entreat S. to agree in the Php 4.02

SYRACUSE
Putting in at S., we stayed there Ac 28.12

SYRIA
the gods of S., the gods of Sidon, Ju 10.06
the Hittites and the kings of S. 1Ki 10.29
Israel, and reigned over S. 11.25
king of S., who dwelt in Damascus, 15.18
anoint Hazael to be king over S.; 19.15
Benhadad the king of S. gathered 20.01
Benhadad king of S. escaped on a 20.20
the king of S. will come up against you." 20.22
of the king of S. said to him, 20.23
For three years S. and Israel 22.01
out of the hand of the king of S.?" 22.03
Now the king of S. had commanded 22.31

SYRIA (cont.)

of the army of the king of S., 2Ki 5.01
the LORD had given victory to S. 5.01
And the king of S. said, "Go now, 5.05
the king of S. was warring against 6.08
of the king of S. was greatly 6.11
Benhadad king of S. mustered his 6.24
Benhadad the king of S. was sick; 8.07
Benhadad king of S. has sent me to 8.09
me that you are to be king over S.' 8.13
Hazael king of S. at Ramothgilead, 8.28
fought against Hazael king of S. 8.29
Ramothgilead against Hazael king of S.; 9.14
he fought with Hazael king of S.) 9.15
Hazael king of S. went up and 12.17
sent these to Hazael king of S. 12.18
Hazael king of S. and into the 13.03
how the king of S. oppressed them. 13.04
for the king of S. had destroyed 13.07
the arrow of victory over S.! 13.17
struck down S. until you had made 13.19
strike down S. only three times." 13.19
Now Hazael king of S. oppressed 13.22
When Hazael king of S. died, 13.24
the king of S. and Pekah the son 15.37
Then Rezin king of S. and Pekah the 16.05
of the king of S. and from the 16.07
put garrisons in S. of Damascus; 1Ch 18.06
the Hittites and the kings of S. 2Ch 1.17
sent them to Benhadad king of S., 16.02
you relied on the king of S., 16.07
of the king of S. has escaped you. 16.07
Now the king of S. had commanded 18.30
Hazael king of S. at Ramothgilead. 22.05
fought against Hazael king of S. 22.06
into the hand of the king of S., 28.05
of the kings of S. helped them, 28.23
the king of S. and Pekah the son Is 7.01
"S. is in league with Ephraim," his 7.02
of Rezin and S. and the son of 7.04
Because S., wth Ephraim and the 7.05
For the head of S. is Damascus, 7.08
the remnant of S. will be like the 17.03
the people of S. shall go into Amo 1.05
So his fame spread through out all S., Mt 4.24
when Quirinius was governor of S. Lk 2.02
in Antioch and S. and Cilicia, Ac 15.23
And he went through S. and Cilicia, 15.41
of the brethren and sailed for S., 18.18
as he was about to set sail for S., 20.03
it on the left we sailed to S., 21.03
into the regions of S. and Cilicia. Gal 1.21

SYRIAN

has spared this Naaman the S., 2Ki 5.20
cleansed, but only Naaman the S." Lk 4.27

SYRIANS

And when the S. of Damascus came to 2Sa 8.05
twenty-two thousand men of the S. 8.05
and the S. became servants to David 8.06
sent and hired the S. of Bethrehob, 10.06
and the S. of Zobah, twenty thousand 10.06
and the S. of Zobah and of Rehob, 10.08
and arrayed them against the S.; 10.09
"If the S. are too strong for me, 10.11
drew near to battle against the S.; 10.13
the Ammonites saw that the S. fled, 10.14
But when the S. saw that they had 10.15
brought out the S. who were beyond 10.16
And the S. arrayed themselves 10.17
And the S. fled before Israel; 10.18
slew of the S. the men of seven 10.18
So the S. feared to help the 10.19
the S. fled and Israel pursued them, 1Ki 20.20
and killed the S. with a great 20.21
spring Benhadad mustered the S., 20.26
but the S. filled the country. 20.27
'Because the S. have said, "The LORD 20.28
smote of the S. a hundred thousand 20.29
shall push the S. until they are 22.11
up in his chariot facing the S., 22.35
Now the S. on one of their raids 2Ki 5.02
for the S. are going down there." 6.09
And when the S. came down against 6.18
And the S. came no more on raids 6.23
us go over to the camp of the S.; 7.04
to go to the camp of the S.; 7.05
to the edge of the camp of the S., 7.05
the army of the S. hear the sound 7.06
"We came to the camp of the S., 7.10
you what the S. have prepared 7.12
sent them after the army of the S., 7.14
which the S. had thrown away in 7.15
and plundered the camp of the S. 7.16
Ramothgilead, where the S. wounded Joram. 8.28
which the S. had given him at 8.29
wounds which the S. had given him, 9.15
escaped from the hand of the S.; 13.05
shall fight the S. in Aphek until 13.17
the Chaldeans, and bands of the S., 24.02
And when the S. of Damascus came to 1Ch 18.05
twenty-two thousand men of the S. 18.05
and the S. became servants to 18.06
and arrayed them against the S.; 19.10
"If the S. are too strong for me, 19.12
drew near before the S. for battle; 19.14
the Ammonites saw that the S. fled, 19.15
But when the S. saw that they had 19.16
brought out the S. who were beyond 19.16
the battle in array against the S., 19.17
And the S. fled before Israel; 19.18
slew of the S. the men of seven 19.18
So the S. were not willing to help 19.19
shall push the S. until they are 2Ch 18.10
facing the S. until evening; 18.34
Ramothgilead. And the S. wounded Joram, 22.05
the army of the S. came up against 24.23
Though the army of the S. had come 24.24
The S. on the east and the Philistines Is 9.12
Chaldeans and the army of the S.' Jer 35.11
from Caphtor and the S. from Kir? Amo 9.07

SYROPHOENICIAN

woman was a Greek, a S. by birth. Mk 7.26

SYRTIS

that they should run on the S., Ac 27.17

T

TAANACH

the king of T., one; the king of Jos 12.21
inhabitants of T. and its villages, 17.11
T. with its pasture lands, and 21.25
or T. and its villages, or the Ju 1.27
at T., by the waters of Megiddo; 5.19
in T., Megiddo, and all Bethshean 1Ki 4.12
T. and its towns, Megiddo and its 1Ch 7.29

TAANATHSHILOH

the boundary turns round toward T., Jos 16.06

TABBAOTH

sons of Hasupha, the sons of T., Ez 2.43
sons of Hasupha, the sons of T., Neh 7.46

TABBATH

the border of Abelmeholah, by T. Ju 7.22

TABEEL
Mithredath and T. and the rest of Ez 4.07
up the son of T. as king in the Is 7.06

TABERAH
name of that place was called T., Num 11.03
"At T. also, and at Massah, and at Deu 9.22

TABERNACLE
concerning the pattern of the t., Ex 25.09
shall make the t. with ten curtains 26.01
the clasps, that the t. may be one whole. 26.06
goats' hair for a tent over the t.; 26.07
shall hang over the back of the t. 26.12
hang over the sides of the t., 26.13
frames for the t. of acacia wood. 26.15
do for all the frames of the t. 26.17
You shall make the frames for the t.: 26.18
and for the second side of the t., 26.20
the rear of the t. westward you 26.22
for corners of the t. in the rear; 26.23
frames of the one side of the t., 26.27
frames of the other side of the t., 26.27
the side of the t. at the rear 26.27
shall erect the t. according to 26.30
side of the t. opposite the table; 26.35
"You shall make the court of the t. 27.09
utensils of the t. for every use, 27.19
the LORD has commanded: the t., 35.10
the door, at the door of the t.; 35.15
the pegs of the t. and the pegs of 35.18
made the t. with ten curtains; 36.08
with clasps; so the t. was one whole. 36.13
goats' hair for a tent over the t.; 36.14
frames for the t. of acacia wood. 36.20
this for all the frames of the t. 36.22
The frames for the t. he made thus: 36.23
And for the second side of the t., 36.25
the rear of the t. westward he 36.27
for corners of the t. in the rear. 36.28
frames of the one side of the t., 36.31
frames of the other side of the t., 36.32
frames of the t. at the rear 36.32
pegs for the t. and for the court 38.20
the sum of the things for the t., 38.21
the t. of the testimony, as they 38.21
the court, all the pegs of the t., 38.31
the work of the t. of the tent of 39.32
And they brought the t. to Moses, 39.33
utensils for the service of the t., 39.40
shall erect the t. of the tent of 40.02
the screen for the door of the t. 40.05
the door of the t. of the tent of 40.06
and anoint the t. and all that is 40.09
of the month, the t. was erected. 40.17
Moses erected the t.; he laid its 40.18
and he spread the tent over the t., 40.19
and he brought the ark into the t., 40.21
on the north side of the t., 40.22
table on the south side of the t., 40.24
the screen for the door of the t. 40.28
the door of the t. of the tent of 40.29
court round the t. and the altar, 40.33
glory of the LORD filled the t. 40.34
glory of the LORD filled the t. 40.35
was taken up from over the t., 40.36
of the LORD was upon the t. by day, 40.38
anointed the t. and all that was Lev 8.10
by defiling my t. that is in their 15.31
the LORD before the t. of the LORD, 17.04
over the t. of the testimony, and Num 1.50
to carry the t. and all its testimony 1.50
it, and shall encamp around the t. 1.50
When the t. is to set out, the 1.51
and when the t. is to be pitched, 1.51
around the t. of the testimony, 1.53
charge of the t. of the testimony. 1.53
meeting, as they minister at the t.; 3.07
Israel as they minister at the t. 3.08
encamp behind the t. on the west, 3.23
tent of meeting was to be the t., 3.25
is around the t. and the altar, 3.26
on the south side of the t., 3.29
encamp on the north side of the t. 3.35
was to be the frames of the t., 3.36
encamp before the t. on the east, 3.38
of all the t. and all that is in 4.16
shall carry the curtains of the t., 4.25
is around the t. and the altar, 4.26
of meeting: the frames of the t., 4.31
floor of the t. and put it into 5.17
had finished setting up the t., 7.01
they offered them before the t. 7.03
On the day that the t. was set up, 9.15
set up, the cloud covered the t., 9.15
it was over the t. like the 9.15
as the cloud rested over the t., 9.18
continued over the t. many days, 9.19
cloud was a few days over the t., 9.20
the cloud continued over the t., 9.22
from over the t. of the testimony, 10.11
And when the t. was taken down, the 10.17
who carried the t., set out. 10.17
and the t. was set up before their 10.21
do service in the t. of the LORD, 16.09
comes near to the t. of the LORD, 17.13
defiles the t. of the LORD, and that 19.13
have charge of the t. of the LORD. 31.30
had charge of the t. of the LORD; 31.47
land where the LORD's t. stands, Jos 22.19
our God that stands before his t.! 22.29
song before the t. of the tent of 1Ch 6.32
service of the t. of the house of 6.48
before the t. of the LORD in the 16.39
For the t. of the LORD, which Moses 21.29
to carry the t. or any of the 23.26
there before the t. of the LORD. 2Ch 1.05

TABERNACLES
of weeks, and the feast of t. 2Ch 8.13
Now the Jews' feast of T. was at hand. Jn 7.02

TABITHA
was at Joppa a disciple named T., Ac 9.36
to the body he said, "T., rise." 9.40

TABLE
taken to them from Joseph's t., Gen 43.34
you shall make a t. of acacia wood; Ex 25.23
for the poles to carry the t. 25.27
and the t. shall be carried with 25.28
Presence on the t. before me 25.30
shall set the t. outside the veil, 26.35
of the tabernacle opposite the t.; 26.35
shall put the t. on the north side 26.35
and the t. and all its utensils, and 30.27
the t. and its utensils, and the 31.08
the t. with its poles and all its 35.13
He also made the t. of acacia wood; 37.10
for the poles to carry the t. 37.14
of acacia wood to carry the t., 37.15
gold which were to be upon the t., 37.16
the t. with all its utensils, and 39.36
And you shall bring in the t., 40.04
And he put the t. in the tent of 40.22
opposite the t. on the south side 40.24
in a row, upon the t. of pure gold. Lev 24.06
the t., the lampstand, the altars, Num 3.31
And over the t. of the bread of the 4.07
used to pick up scraps under my t.; Ju 1.07
fail to sit at t. with the king; 1Sa 20.05
he has not come to the king's t. 20.29
rose from the t. in fierce anger 20.34
and you shall eat at my t. always." 2Sa 9.07

TABLE (cont.)
son shall always eat at my t." 2Sa 9.10
So Mephibosheth ate at David's t., 9.11
for he ate always at the king's t. 9.13
among those who eat at your t. 19.28
be among those who eat at your t.; 1Ki 2.07
all who came to King Solomon's t., 4.27
the golden t. for the bread of the 7.48
the food of his t., the seating of his 10.05
And as they sat at the t., 13.20
Asherah, who eat at Jezebel's t. 18.19
a t., a chair, and a lamp, so that 2Ki 4.10
dined regularly at the king's t.; 25.29
gold for each t. for the showbread, 1Ch 28.16
the food of his t., the seating of his 2Ch 9.04
showbread on the t. of pure gold, 13.11
and the t. for the showbread and 29.18
were at my t. a hundred and fifty Neh 5.17
was set on your t. was full of Job 36.16
Thou preparest a t. before me in Ps 23.05
Let their own t. before them become 69.22
God spread a t. in the wilderness? 78.19
like olive shoots around your t. 128.03
her wine, she has also set her t. Pro 9.02
They prepare the t., they spread the rugs, Is 21.05
who set a t. for Fortune and fill 65.11
dined regularly at the king's t.; Jer 52.33
with a t. spread before it on which Eze 23.41
be filled at my t. with horses and 39.20
"This is the t. which is before the 41.22
and they shall approach my t., 44.16
shall speak lies at the same t., Dan 11.27
that the LORD's t. may be despised Mal 1.07
say that the LORD's t. is polluted, 1.12
west and sit at t. with Abraham, Mt 8.11
And as he sat at t. in the house, 9.10
that fall from their master's t." 15.27
it on his head, as he sat at t. 26.07
he sat at t. with the twelve 26.20
And as he sat at t. in his house, Mk 2.15
dogs under the t. eat the children's 7.28
as he sat at t., a woman came with 14.03
And as they were at t. eating, 14.18
eleven themselves as they sat at t.; * 16.14
and others sitting at t. with them. Lk 5.29
Pharisee's house, and sat at t. 7.36
was sitting at t. in the Pharisee's 7.37
who were at t. with him began to 7.49
so he went in and sat at t. 11.37
himself and have them sit at t., 12.37
and sit at t. in the kingdom of God. 13.29
of all who sit at t. with you. 14.10
who sat at t. with him heard this, 14.15
what fell from the rich man's t.; 16.21
'Come at once and sit down at t.'? 17.07
he sat at t., and the apostles with 22.14
betrays me is with me on the t. 22.21
is the greater, one who sits at t., 22.27
Is it not the one who sits at t.? 22.27
and drink at my t. in my kingdom, 22.30
When he was at t. with them, he took 24.30
was one of those at t. with him. Jn 12.02
Now no one at the t. knew why he 13.28
at t. in an idol's temple, might he 1Co 8.10
partake of the t. of the Lord and 10.21
of the Lord and the t. of demons. 10.21
lampstand and the t. and the bread Heb 9.02

TABLELAND
cities of the t. and all Gilead Deu 3.10
wilderness on the t. for the 4.43
and all the t. of Medeba as far as Jos 13.09
valley, and all the t. by Medeba; 13.16
all its cities that are in the t.; 13.17
that is, all the cities of the t., 13.21
Bezer in the wilderness on the t., 20.08
"Judgment has come upon the t., Jer 48.21

TABLES
I will give you the t. of stone, Ex 24.12
the two t. of the testimony, tables 31.18
t. of stone, written with the finger 31.18
with the two t. of the testimony 32.15
t. that were written on both sides; 32.15
And the t. were the work of God, and 32.16
writing of God, graven upon the t. 32.16
he threw the t. out of his hands 32.19
"Cut two t. of stone like the first 34.01
write upon the t. the words that 34.01
words that were on the first t., 34.01
So Moses cut two t. of stone like 34.04
took in his hand two t. of stone. 34.04
wrote upon the t. the words of the 34.28
with the two t. of the testimony in 34.29
he wrote them upon two t. of stone. Deu 4.13
he wrote them upon two t. of stone, 5.22
mountain to receive the t. of stone, 9.09
the t. of the covenant which the 9.09
gave me the two t. of stone written 9.10
LORD gave me the two t. of stone, 9.11
the t. of the covenant. 9.11
and the two t. of the covenant were 9.15
So I took hold of the two t., 9.17
'Hew two t. of stone like the first, 10.01
write on the t. the words that 10.02
on the first t. which you broke, 10.02
and hewed two t. of stone like the 10.03
mountain with the two t. in my hand. 10.03
And he wrote on the t., as at the 10.04
and put the t. in the ark which I 10.05
except the two t. of stone which 1Ki 8.09
the silver for the silver t., 1Ch 28.16
He also made ten t., and placed 2Ch 4.08
the t. for the bread of the Presence, 4.19
except the two t. which Moses put 5.10
For all t. are full of vomit, no Is 28.08
gate were two t. on either side, Eze 40.39
of the north gate were two t.; 40.40
vestibule of the gate were two t. 40.40
Four t. were on the inside, and four 40.41
and four t. on the outside of the 40.41
eight t., on which the sacrifices 40.41
were also four t. of hewn stone 40.42
And on the t. the flesh of the 40.43
overturned the t. of the money-changers Mt 21.12
overturned the t. of the moneychangers Mk 11.15
money-changers and overturned their t. Jn 2.15
the word of God to serve t. Ac 6.02
and the t. of the covenant; Heb 9.04

TABLET
write them on the t. of your heart. Pro 3.03
write them on the t. of your heart. 7.03
"Take a large t. and write upon it Is 8.01
go, write it before them on a t., 30.08
engraved on the t. of their heart, Jer 17.01
And he asked for a writing t., Lk 1.63

TABLETS
make it plain upon t., so he may run Hab 2.02
not on t. of stone but on t. of human 2Co 3.03

TABOR
the boundary also touches T., Jos 19.22
'Go, gather your men at Mount T., Ju 4.06
Abinoam had gone up to Mount T., 4.12
down from Mount T. with ten 4.14
are the men whom you slew at T.?" 8.18
further and come to the oak of T.; 1Sa 10.03
pasture lands, T. with its pasture lands, 1Ch 6.77
T. and Hermon joyously praise thy Ps 89.12
like T. among the mountains, and Jer 46.18
Mizpah, and a net spread upon T. Hos 5.01

TABRIMMON
them to Benhadad the son of T., 1Ki 15.18

TACKLE
Your t. hangs loose; it cannot hold Is 33.23
their own hands the t. of the ship. Ac 27.19

TADMOR
He built T. in the wilderness and 2Ch 8.04

TAHAN
of T., the family of the Tahanites. Num 26.35
son, Telah his son, T. his son, 1Ch 7.25

TAHANITES
of Tahan, the family of the T. Num 26.35

TAHASH
bore Tebah, Gaham, T., and Maacah. Gen 22.24

TAHATH
from Makheloth, and encamped at T. Num 33.26
And they set out from T., 33.27
T. his son, Uriel his son, Uzziah his 1Ch 6.24
son of T., son of Assir, son of 6.37
T. his son, Eleadah his son, T. his 7.20

TAHCHEMONITE
David had: Joshebbasshebeth a T.; 2Sa 23.08

TAHPANHES
of Memphis and T. have broken the Jer 2.16
And they arrived at T. 43.07
the LORD came to Jeremiah in T.: 43.08
entrance to Pharaoh's palace in T., 43.09
at T., at Memphis, and in the land 44.01
proclaim in Memphis and T.; 46.14

TAHPENES
wife, the sister of T. the queen. 1Ki 11.19
And the sister of T. bore him 11.20
whom T. weaned in Pharaoh's house; 11.20

TAHREA
Pithon, Melech, T., and Ahaz; 1Ch 9.41

TAIL
your hand, and take it by the t."— Ex 4.04
and the fat t., and the fat that 29.22
the fat t. entire, taking it away Lev 3.09
the fat t., the fat that covers the 7.03
and the fat t., and all the fat 8.25
the fat t., and that which covers 9.19
make you the head, and not the t.; Deu 28.13
the head, and you shall be the t. 28.44
and he turned them t. to t., Ju 15.04
He makes his t. stiff like a cedar; Job 40.17
cut off from Israel head and t., Is 9.14
prophet who teaches lies is the t.; 9.15
nothing for Egypt which head or t., 19.15
His t. swept down a third of the Rev 12.04

TAILS
a torch between each pair of t. Ju 15.04
they have t. like scorpions, and Rev 9.10
for five months lies in their t. 9.10
is in their mouths and in their t.; 9.19
their t. are like serpents, with 9.19

TAKE
his hand and t. also of the tree Gen 3.22
Also t. with you every sort of food 6.21
T. with you seven pairs of all 7.02
here is your wife, t. her, and be gone." 12.19
If you t. the left hand, then I will 13.09
or if you t. the right hand, then I 13.09
but t. the goods for yourself." 14.21
that I would not t. a thread or a 14.23
I will t. nothing but what the 14.24
Eshcol, and Mamre t. their share." 14.24
t. your wife and your two daughters 19.15
ewe lambs you will t. from my hand, 21.30
He said, "T. your son, your only son 22.02
you will not t. a wife for my son 24.03
and t. a wife for my son Isaac." 24.04
must I then t. your son back to the 24.05
that you do not t. my son back 24.06
and you shall t. a wife for my son 24.07
you must not t. my son back there." 24.08
'You shall not t. a wife for my 24.37
my kindred, and t. a wife for my son.' 24.38
and you shall t. a wife for my son 24.40
right way to t. the daughter of my 24.48
t. her and go, and let her be the 24.51
Now then, t. your weapons, your 27.03
and t. as wife from there one of 28.02
that you t. possession of the land 28.04
Paddan-aram to t. a wife from there, 28.06
Would you t. away my son's mandrakes 30.15
"T. heed that you say not a word to 31.24
'T. heed that you speak to Jacob 31.29
that you would t. your daughters 31.31
I have that is yours, and t. it." 31.32
or if you t. wives besides my 31.50
and t. our daughters for yourselves. 34.09
and we will t. your daughters to 34.16
then we will t. our daughter, and we 34.17
let us t. their daughters in 34.21
saying, "Let us not t. his life." 37.21
and t. the fifth part of the 41.34
and t. grain for the famine of your 42.33
and now you would t. Benjamin; 42.36
t. some of the choice fruits of the 43.11
T. double the money with you; 43.12
T. also your brother, and arise, go 43.13
If you t. this one also from me, and 44.29
and t. your father and your households, 45.18
t. wagons from the land of Egypt 45.19
"T. this child away, and nurse him Ex 2.09
and t. it by the tail"—so he put 4.04
you shall t. some water from the 4.09
which you shall t. from the Nile 4.09
And you shall t. in your hand this 4.17
why do you t. the people away from 5.04
and I will t. you for my people, and 6.07
'T. your rod and cast it down 7.09
and t. in your hand the rod which 7.15
'T. your rod and stretch out your 7.19
the LORD to t. away the frogs from 8.08
"T. handfuls of ashes from the kiln, 9.08
for we must t. of them to serve the 10.26
t. heed to yourself; never see my 10.28
they shall t. every man a lamb 12.03
his house shall t. according to 12.04
you shall t. it from the sheep or 12.05
Then they shall t. some of the 12.07
T. a bunch of hyssop and dip it in 12.22
T. your flocks and your herds as 12.32
you shall t. an omer apiece, according 16.16
"T. a jar, and put an omer of manna 16.33
and t. in your hand the rod with 17.05
'T. heed that you do not go up into 19.12
"You shall not t. the name of the 20.07
you shall t. him from my altar, that 21.14
If ever you t. your neighbor's 22.26
And you shall t. no bribe, for a 23.08
T. heed to all that I have said to 23.13
and I will t. sickness away from 23.25
that they t. for me an offering; 25.02
And you shall t. two onyx stones, 28.09
and Aaron shall t. upon himself 28.38
T. one young bull and two rams 29.01
And you shall t. the garments, and 29.05
And you shall t. the anointing oil, 29.07
and shall t. part of the blood of 29.12
And you shall t. all the fat that 29.13
"Then you shall t. one of the rams, 29.15
and shall t. its blood and throw it 29.16

TAKE (cont.)
"You shall t. the other ram; Ex 29.19
and t. part of its blood and put it 29.20
Then you shall t. part of the blood 29.21
"You shall also t. the fat of the 29.22
Then you shall t. them from their 29.25
"And you shall t. the breast of the 29.26
"You shall t. the ram of ordination, 29.31
"When you t. the census of the 30.12
And you shall t. the atonement 30.16
"T. the finest spices: of liquid 30.23
"T. sweet spices, stacte, and onycha, 30.34
"T. off the rings of gold which are 32.02
'Let any who have gold t. it off'; 32.24
Now Moses used to t. the tent and 33.07
then I will t. away my hand, and you 33.23
and t. us for thy inheritance." 34.09
T. heed to yourself, lest you make a 34.12
and you t. of their daughters for 34.16
T. from among you an offering to 35.05
Then you shall t. the anointing oil, 40.09
and he shall t. away its crop with Lev 1.16
And he shall t. from it a handful 2.02
priest shall t. from the cereal 2.09
which he shall t. away with the 3.04
which he shall t. away with the 3.10
which he shall t. away with the 3.15
priest shall t. some of the blood 4.05
sin offering he shall t. from it, 4.08
which he shall t. away with the 4.09
fat he shall t. from it and burn 4.19
priest shall t. some of the blood 4.25
priest shall t. some of its blood 4.30
priest shall t. some of the blood 4.34
priest shall t. a handful of it as 5.12
and he shall t. up the ashes to 6.10
And one shall t. from it a handful 6.15
which he shall t. away with the 7.04
"T. Aaron and his sons with him, and 8.02
for it will t. seven days to ordain 8.33
"T. a bull calf for a sin offering, 9.02
'T. a male goat for a sin offering, 9.03
"T. the cereal offering that 10.12
then she shall t. two turtledoves 12.08
command them to t. for him who is 14.04
He shall t. the living bird with 14.06
day he shall t. two male lambs 14.10
priest shall t. one of the male 14.12
The priest shall t. some of the 14.14
priest shall t. some of the log of 14.15
then he shall t. one male lamb for 14.21
priest shall t. the lamb of the 14.24
priest shall t. some of the blood 14.25
that they t. out the stones in 14.40
then they shall t. others stones and 14.42
and he shall t. other plaster and 14.42
house he shall t. two small birds, 14.49
and shall t. the cedarwood and the 14.51
day he shall t. two turtledoves or 15.14
day she shall t. two turtledoves 15.29
And he shall t. from the congregation 16.05
Then he shall t. the two goats, and 16.07
And he shall t. a censer full of 16.12
and he shall t. some of the blood 16.14
and shall t. some of the blood of 16.18
you shall not t. her son's daughter 18.17
And you shall not t. a woman as a 18.18
You shall not t. vengeance or bear 19.18
And he shall t. a wife in her 21.13
but he shall t. to wife a virgin of 21.14
from whom he may t. uncleanness, 22.05
And you shall t. on the first day 23.40
"And you shall t. fine flour, and 24.05
T. no interest from him or increase, 25.36
"T. a census of all the congregation Num 1.02
you shall not t. a census of them 1.49
out, the Levites shall t. it down; 1.51
And you shall t. the Levites for me 3.41
"T. the Levites instead of all the 3.45
you shall t. five shekels apiece; 3.47
twenty gerahs, you shall t. them, 3.47
"T. a census of the sons of Kohath 4.02
shall go in and t. down the veil 4.05
And they shall t. a cloth of blue, 4.09
and they shall t. all the vessels 4.12
And they shall t. away the ashes 4.13
"T. a census of the sons of Gershon 4.22
priest shall t. holy water in an 5.17
and t. some of the dust that is on 5.17
priest shall make her t. an oath, 5.19
make the woman t. the oath of the 5.21
priest shall t. the cereal offering 5.25
priest shall t. a handful of the 5.26
and shall t. the hair from his 6.18
priest shall t. the shoulder of 6.19
"T. the Levites from among the 8.06
Then let them t. a young bull and 8.08
and you shall t. another young bull 8.08
and let them t. their stand there 11.16
and I will t. some of the spirit 11.17
Do this: t. censers, Korah and all 16.06
let every one of you t. his censer, 16.17
the priest to t. up the censers 16.37
"T. your censer, and put fire 16.46
'When you t. from the people of 18.26
priest shall t. some of her blood 19.04
priest shall t. cedarwood and 19.06
they shall t. some ashes of the 19.17
then a clean person shall t. hyssop, 19.18
"T. the rod, and assemble the 20.08
T. Aaron and Eleazar his son, and 20.25
that he t. away the serpents from 21.07
"Must I not t. heed to speak what 23.12
I will t. you to another place; 23.27
shall Asshur t. you away captive 24.22
"T. all the chiefs of the people, 25.04
"T. a census of all the congregation 26.02
"T. a census of the people, from 26.04
"T. Joshua the son of Nun, a man in 27.18
you shall t. heed to offer to me in 28.02
"T. the count of the booty that was 31.26
t. it from their half, and give it 31.29
half you shall t. one drawn out of 31.30
do not t. us across the Jordan." 32.05
but we will t. up arms, ready to go 32.17
if you will t. up arms to go before 32.20
and you shall t. possession of the 33.53
You shall t. one leader of every 34.18
larger tribes you shall t. many, 35.08
smaller tribes you shall t. few; 35.08
turn and t. your journey, and go to Deu 1.07
go in and t. possession of the land 1.08
go up, t. possession, as the LORD, the 1.21
afraid of you. So t. good heed; 2.04
'Rise up, t. your journey, and go 2.24
begin to t. possession, and contend 2.24
begin to t. possession, that you may 2.31
which we did not t. from them— 3.04
and go in and t. possession of the 4.01
I command you, nor t. from it; 4.02
are entering to t. possession of 4.05
"Only t. heed, and keep your soul 4.09
"Therefore t. good heed to yourselves. 4.15
go over and t. possession of that 4.22
T. heed to yourselves, lest you 4.23
to go and t. a nation for himself 4.34
"'You shall not t. the name of the 5.11
then t. heed lest you forget the 6.12
may go in and t. possession of the 6.18
are entering to t. possession of 7.01
And the LORD will t. away from you 7.15
or t. it for yourselves, lest you be 7.25
"T. heed lest you forget the LORD 8.11
'Go up and t. possession of the 9.23

TAKE (cont.)
and go in and t. possession of the Deu 11.08
are entering to t. possession of 11.10
T. heed lest your heart be deceived, 11.16
are entering to t. possession of 11.29
to go in to t. possession of the 11.31
T. heed that you do not offer your 12.13
T. heed that you do not forsake the 12.19
you shall t., and you shall go to 12.36
t. heed that you be not ensnared to 12.30
shall not add to it or t. from it. 12.32
T. heed lest there be a base 15.09
then you shall t. an awl, and thrust 15.17
and you shall not t. a bribe, 16.19
the battle and another man t. her.' 20.07
you shall t. as booty for yourselves; 20.14
war against it in order to t. it, 20.19
slain man shall t. a heifer which 21.03
hands, and you t. them captive, 21.10
her and would t. her for yourself 21.11
mother shall t. hold of him and 21.19
you shall t. them back to your 22.01
you shall not t. the mother with 22.06
the young you may t. to yourself; 22.07
mother shall t. and bring out the 22.15
that city shall t. the man and 22.18
"A man shall not t. his father's 22.30
are entering to t. possession of 23.20
may not t. her again to be his wife, 24.04
"No man shall t. a mill or an upper 24.06
"T. heed, in an attack of leprosy, to 24.08
or t. a widow's garment in pledge; 24.17
and t. her as his wife, and perform 25.05
not wish to t. his brother's wife, 25.07
saying, 'I do not wish to t. her,' 25.08
you shall t. some of the first of 26.02
priest shall t. the basket from 26.04
are entering to t. possession of 28.21
the LORD will t. delight in 28.63
are entering to t. possession of 28.63
LORD will again t. delight in 30.09
are entering to t. possession of 30.16
"T. this book of the law, and put it 31.26
I will t. vengeance on my adversaries, 32.41
to go in to t. possession of the Jos 1.11
and they also t. possession of the 1.15
"T. up the ark of the covenant, and 3.06
Now therefore t. twelve men from 3.12
"T. twelve men from the people, from 4.02
'T. twelve stones from here out of 4.03
and t. up each of you a stone upon 4.05
"T. up the ark of the covenant, and 6.06
them you t. any of the devoted 6.18
until you t. away the devoted 7.13
t. all the fighting men with you, 8.01
you shall t. as booty for yourselves; 8.02
'T. provisions in your hand for the 9.11
could not t. possession of those 17.12
to go in and t. possession of the 18.03
then they shall t. him into the 20.04
T. good care to observe the commandment 22.05
and t. for yourselves a possession 22.19
may the LORD himself t. vengeance. 22.23
T. good heed to yourselves, therefore, 23.11
inheritance to t. possession of Ju 2.06
they will t. care to walk in the 2.22
"T. the meat and the unleavened 6.20
"T. your father's bull, the second 6.25
then t. the second bull, and offer 6.26
t. them down to the water and I 7.04
then come and t. refuge in my shade; 9.15
Israel did not t. away the land of 11.15
and are you to t. possession of 11.23
LORD, and I cannot t. back my vow." 11.35
you must go to t. a wife from the 14.03
a while he returned to t. her; 14.08
fairer than she? Pray t. her instead." 15.02
"You t. my gods which I made, and 18.24
consider it, t. counsel, and speak." 19.30
and we will t. ten men of a hundred 20.10
we did not t. for each man of them 21.22
that you should t. notice of me, Ru 2.10
wings you have come to t. refuge!" 2.12
T. my right of redemption yourself, 4.06
up the priest would t. for himself. 1Sa 2.14
and then t. as much as you wish," 2.16
and if not, I will t. it by force." 2.16
little robe and t. it to him each 2.19
T. courage, and acquit yourselves 4.09
Now then, t. and prepare a new cart 6.07
but t. their calves home, away from 6.07
And t. the ark of the LORD and 6.08
Come down and t. it up to you." 6.21
he will t. your sons and appoint 8.11
He will t. your daughters to be 8.13
He will t. the best of your fields 8.14
He will t. the tenth of your grain 8.15
He will t. your menservants and 8.16
He will t. the tenth of your flocks, 8.17
"T. one of the servants with you, 9.03
"T. a heifer with you, and say, 'I 16.02
"T. for your brothers an ephah of 17.17
also t. these ten cheeses to the 17.18
therefore t. heed to yourself in 19.02
Saul sent messengers to t. David, 19.14
Then Saul sent messengers to t. David; 19.20
may the LORD t. vengeance on 20.16
t. them,' then you are to come, for, 20.21
if you will t. that, t. it, for there 21.09
and t. note of all the lurking 23.23
though you hunt my life to t. it. 24.11
Shall I t. my bread and my water 25.11
us to you to t. you to him as his 25.40
but t. now the spear that is at his 26.11
"Will you t. me down to this band 30.15
and I will t. you down to this band 30.15
of the young men, and t. his spoil." 2Sa 2.21
not willing to t. the ark of the 6.10
but I will not t. my steadfast love 7.15
unwilling to t. one of his own 12.04
and I will t. your wives before 12.11
encamp against the city, and t. it; 12.28
lest I t. the city, and it be called 12.28
your brother; do not t. this to heart." 13.20
the king so t. it to heart as to 13.33
God will not t. away the life of 14.14
and t. hold of him, and kiss him. 15.05
Go back, and t. your brethren with 15.20
Let me go over and t. off his head." 16.09
let him t. it all, since my lord the 19.30
t. your lord's servants and pursue 20.06
in whom I t. refuge, my shield and 22.03
for all those who t. refuge in him. 22.31
t. away the iniquity of thy servant; 24.10
lord the king t. and offer up what 24.22
"T. with you the servants of your 1Ki 1.33
'If your sons t. heed to their way, 2.04
and thus t. away from me and from 2.31
only your sons t. heed to their 8.25
neighbor and is made to t. an oath, 8.31
"T. for yourself ten pieces; 11.31
Nevertheless I will not t. the 11.34
but I will t. the kingdom out of 11.35
And I will t. you, and you shall 11.37
T. with you ten loaves, some cakes, 14.03
he would t. an oath of the 18.10
now, O LORD, t. away my life; 19.04
they seek my life, to t. it away." 19.10
they seek my life, to t. it away." 19.14
pleases them, and t. it away.'" 20.06
said to his men, "T. your positions. 20.12
come out for peace, t. them alive; 20.18
come out for war, t. them alive." 20.18
made haste to t. the bandage away 20.41

TAKE (cont.)
Then t. him out, and stone him to 1Ki 21.10
t. possession of the vineyard of 21.15
Jezrielite, to t. possession of it. 21.16
where he has gone to t. possession. 21.18
and do not t. it out of the hand 22.03
and t. him back to Amon the governor 22.26
was about to t. Elijah up to 2Ki 2.01
the LORD will t. away your master 2.03
the LORD will t. away your master 2.05
has come to t. my two children to 4.01
and t. my staff in your hand, and go 4.29
to him, he said, "T. up your son." 4.36
And he urged him to t. it, 5.16
And he said, "T. it up." 6.07
murderer has sent to t. off my head? 6.32
we shall t. them alive and get into 7.12
"Let some men t. five of the 7.13
"T. a present with you and go to 8.08
and t. this flask of oil in your 9.01
Then t. the flask of oil, and pour 9.03
"T. a horseman, and send to meet 9.17
"T. him up, and cast him on the plot 9.25
Now therefore t. him up and cast 9.26
t. the heads of your master's sons, 10.06
He said, "T. them alive." 10.14
let the priests t., each from his 12.05
Now therefore t. no more money from 12.07
they should t. no more money from 12.08
"T. a bow and arrows"; so he took a 13.15
And he said, "T. the arrows"; and he 13.18
until I come and t. you away to a 18.32
Judah shall again t. root downward, 19.30
And let them t. and lay it on the 20.07
So David did not t. the ark home 1Ch 13.13
I will not t. my steadfast love 17.13
t. away the iniquity of thy servant; 21.08
the LORD, 'T. which you will: 21.11
Then Ornan said to David, "T. it; 21.23
I will not t. for the LORD what 21.24
T. heed now, for the LORD has chosen 28.10
so that you may t. it up to 2Ch 2.16
only your sons t. heed to their 6.16
neighbor and is made to t. an oath, 6.22
But you, t. courage! Do not let your 15.07
and t. him back to Amon the governor 18.25
t. heed what you do, for there is 19.07
t. your position, stand still, and 20.17
people came to t. the spoil from 20.25
the chest and t. it and return it 24.11
order that they might t. the city. 32.18
"T. me away, for I am badly wounded." 35.23
in fetters to t. him to Babylon. 36.06
And t. care not to be slack in this Ez 4.22
"T. these vessels, go and put them 5.15
to t. possession of it, is a land 9.11
neither t. their daughters for your 9.12
and all Israel t. oath that they 10.05
and let us t. counsel together." Neh 6.07
of the land or t. their daughters 10.30
and I made them t. oath in the name 13.25
or t. their daughters for your sons 13.25
she desired to t. with her from Est 2.13
that he might t. off his sackcloth, 4.04
t. the robes and the horse, as you 6.10
transgression and t. away my Job 7.21
nor t. the hand of evildoers. 8.20
Let him t. his rod away from me, and 9.34
protected and t. your rest in 11.18
I will t. my flesh in my teeth, and 13.14
But he knows the way that I t.; 23.10
they t. the widow's ox for a pledge. 24.03
and t. in pledge the infant of the 24.09
Will he t. delight in the Almighty? 27.10
order before me; t. your stand. 33.05
that he should t. delight in God.' 34.09
If he should t. back his spirit to 34.14
T. heed, do not turn to iniquity, for 36.21
that it might t. hold of the skirts 38.13
that you may t. it to its territory 38.20
Can one t. him with hooks, or pierce 40.24
with you to t. him for your servant 41.04
Now therefore t. seven bulls and 42.08
and the rulers t. counsel together, Ps 2.02
are all who t. refuge in him. 2.12
But let all who t. refuge in thee 5.11
my God, in thee do I t. refuge; 7.01
and over it t. thy seat on high. 7.07
thou mayest t. it into thy hands; 10.14
In the LORD I t. refuge; how can 11.01
and does not t. a bribe against the 15.05
me, O God, for in thee I t. refuge. 16.01
not pour out or t. their names 16.04
in whom I t. refuge, my shield, and 18.02
for all those who t. refuge in him. 18.30
to shame, for I t. refuge in thee. 25.20
me, but the LORD will t. me up. 27.10
and let your heart t. courage; 27.14
T. me not off with the wicked, with 28.03
t. me out of the net which is 31.04
me, as they plot to t. my life. 31.13
for those who t. refuge in thee, 31.19
and let your heart t. courage, 31.24
of those who t. refuge in him will 34.22
T. hold of shield and buckler, and 35.02
children of men t. refuge in the 36.07
T. delight in the LORD, and he will 37.04
because they t. refuge in him. 37.40
art the God in whom I t. refuge; 43.02
or t. my covenant on your lips? 50.16
and t. not thy holy Spirit from me. 51.11
of thy wings I will t. refuge, 57.01
They t. pleasure in falsehood. 62.04
in the LORD, and t. refuge in him! 64.10
In thee, O LORD, do I t. refuge; 71.01
"Let us t. possession for ourselves 83.12
Turn to me and t. pity on me; 86.16
"t. me not hence in the midst of my 102.24
It is better to t. refuge in the 118.08
It is better to t. refuge in the 118.09
t. away from me their scorn and 119.22
And t. not the word of truth 119.43
from of old, I t. comfort, O LORD. 119.52
If I t. the wings of the morning 139.09
shield and he in whom I t. refuge, 144.02
T. heed to the path of your feet, Pro 4.26
she does not t. heed to the path of 5.06
lest strangers t. their fill of 5.10
Come, let us t. our fill of love 7.18
T. my instruction instead of silver, 8.10
with those who t. advice is wisdom. 13.10
T. a man's garment when he has given 20.16
T. away the dross from the silver, 25.04
t. away the wicked from the presence 25.05
T. a man's garment when he has given 27.13
to those who t. refuge in him. 30.05
the lizard you can t. in your hands, 30.28
and drink and t. pleasure in all Ecc 3.13
who will no longer t. advice, 4.13
and shall t. nothing for his toil, 5.15
that you should t. hold of this, 7.18
the Lord will t. away the finery Is 3.18
women shall t. hold of one man in 4.01
your name; t. away our reproach." 4.01
'T. heed, be quiet, do not fear, and 7.04
"T. a large tablet and write upon 8.01
T. counsel together, but it will 8.10
to t. spoil and seize plunder, and 10.06
peoples will t. them and bring 14.02
they will t. captive those who were 14.02
you will t. up this taunt against 14.04
your loins and t. off your shoes 20.02
"T. a harp, go about the city, O 23.16
people he will t. away from all 25.08

TAKE (cont.)

In days to come Jacob shall t. root, Is 27.06
it passes through it will t. you; 28.19
to t. refuge in the protection of 30.02
with which to t. fire from the 30.14
even the lame will t. the prey. 33.23
until I come and t. you away to a 36.17
Judah shall again t. root downward, 37.31
"Let them t. a cake of figs, and 38.21
says to his brother, "T. courage!" 41.06
him, but he did not t. it to heart. 42.25
let them t. counsel together! 45.21
T. the millstones and grind meal, 47.02
I will t. vengeance, and I will 47.03
is none to t. her by the hand 51.18
off, a breath will t. them away. 57.13
"If you t. away from the midst of 58.09
then you shall t. delight in the 58.14
LORD in remembrance, t. no rest, 62.06
iniquities, like the wind, t. us away. 64.06
bestirs himself to t. hold of thee; 64.07
also I will t. for priests and for 66.21
I will t. you, one from a city and Jer 3.14
of Jerusalem, look and t. note! 5.01
but they refused to t. correction. 5.03
they t. no pleasure in it. 6.10
"T. up weeping and wailing for the 9.10
Thou plantest them, and they t. root; 12.02
"T. the waistcloth which you have 13.04
and t. from there the waistcloth 13.06
"T. a lowly seat, for your beautiful 13.18
Will not pangs t. hold of you, 13.21
and t. vengeance for me on my 15.15
in thy forbearance t. me not away; 15.15
"You shall not t. a wife, nor shall 16.02
T. heed for the sake of your lives, 17.21
For they have dug a pit to t. me, 18.22
and t. some of the elders of the 19.01
overcome him, and t. our revenge on him." 20.10
"T. from my hand this cup of the 25.15
king of Babylon did not t. away, 27.20
T. wives and have sons and daughters; 29.06
t. wives for your sons, and give 29.06
and they shall t. possession of it 30.03
of Babylon, and he shall t. it; 32.03
and he shall t. Zedekiah to Babylon, 32.05
T. these deeds, both this sealed 32.14
have come up to the city to t. it, 32.24
of Babylon, and he shall t. it. 32.28
and t. it, and burn it with fire. 34.22
"T. a scroll and write on it all 36.02
"T. in your hand the scroll that 36.14
"T. another scroll and write on it 36.28
they shall t. it and burn it with 37.08
"T. three men with you from here, 38.10
in fetters to t. him to Babylon. 39.07
"T. him, look after him well and do 39.12
Shaphan, that he should t. him home. 39.14
son of Nethaniah to t. your life?" 40.14
Why should he t. your life, so that 40.15
may kill us or t. us into exile in 43.03
"T. in your hands large stones, and 43.09
I will send and t. Nebuchadrezzar 43.10
I will t. the remnant of Judah who 44.12
T. your stations with your helmets, 46.04
and t. balm, O virgin daughter of 46.11
t. vengeance on her, do to her as 50.15
T. balm for her pain; perhaps she may 51.08
T. up the shields! The LORD has 51.11
your cause and t. vengeance for 51.36
and t. out of his mouth what he has 51.44
t. a brick and lay it before you, Eze 4.01
And t. an iron plate, and place it 4.03
"And you, t. wheat and barley, beans 4.09
O son of man, t. a sharp sword; 5.01
then t. balances for weighing, and 5.01
part you shall t. and strike with 5.02
And you shall t. from these a small 5.03
And of these again you shall t. some, 5.04
the nations to t. possession of 7.24
"T. fire from between the whirling 10.06
I will t. the stony heart out of 11.19
Do men t. a peg from it to hang any 15.03
clothes and t. your fair jewels, 16.39
be ashamed when I t. your sisters, 16.61
It will not t. a strong arm or many 17.09
"I myself will t. a sprig from the 17.22
an interest or t. any increase, 18.08
And you, t. up a lamentation for the 19.01
the turban, and t. off the crown; 21.26
In you men t. bribes to shed blood; 22.12
you t. interest and increase and 22.12
clothes and t. away your fine 23.26
and t. away all the fruit of your 23.29
all women may t. warning and not 23.48
T. the choicest one of the flock, 24.05
T. out of it piece after piece, 24.06
to t. vengeance, I have set on the 24.08
I am about to t. the delight of 24.16
the day when I t. from them their 24.25
of the land t. a man from among 33.02
of the trumpet does not t. warning, 33.04
trumpet, and did not t. warning; 33.05
and we will t. possession of them,'— 35.10
For I will t. you from the nations, 36.24
and I will t. out of your flesh the 36.26
"Son of man, t. a stick and write on 37.16
then t. another stick and write 37.16
I am about to t. the stick of 37.19
I will t. the people of Israel from 37.21
to t. away cattle and goods, to 38.13
not need to t. wood out of the 39.10
And you shall t. some of its blood, 43.20
You shall also t. the bull of the 43.21
you shall t. a young bull without 45.18
The priest shall t. some of the 45.19
and shall t. his stand by the post 46.02
shall not t. any of the inheritance 46.18
and t. a well-fortified city. Dan 11.15
coastlands, and shall t. many of them; 11.18
be enraged and t. action against 11.30
and shall t. away the continual 11.31
God shall stand firm and t. action. 11.32
t. to yourself a wife of harlotry Hos 1.02
Therefore I will t. back my grain 2.09
and I will t. away my wool and my 2.09
Wine and new wine t. away the 4.11
T. with you words and return to the 14.02
say to him, "T. away all iniquity; 14.02
when they shall t. you away with Amo 4.02
word which I t. up over you in 5.01
the poor and t. from him exactions 5.11
who t. a bribe, and turn aside the 5.12
and I t. no delight in your solemn 5.21
T. away from me the noise of your 5.23
You shall t. up Sakkuth your king, 5.26
therefore I will t. you into exile 5.27
shall t. him up to bring the bones 6.10
from there shall my hand t. them; 9.02
I will search out and t. them; 9.03
"T. me up and throw me into the sea; Jon 1.12
t. my life from me, I beseech thee, 4.03
Bethezel shall t. away from you Mic 1.11
and houses, and t. them away; 2.02
day they shall t. up a taunt song 2.04
children you t. away my glory for 2.09
knows those who t. refuge in him. Nah 1.07
he will not t. vengeance twice on 1.09
t. hold of the brick mold! 3.14
for they heap up earth and t. it. Hab 1.10
I will t. my stand to watch, and 2.01
Shall not all these t. up their 2.06
that I may t. pleasure in it and Hag 1.08
Yet now t. courage, O Zerubbabel, 2.04

TAKE (cont.)

t. courage, O Joshua, son of Jehozadak, Hag 2.04
t. courage, all you people of the 2.04
I will t. you, O Zerubbabel my 2.23
"T. from the exiles Heldai, Tobijah, Zec 6.10
T. from them silver and gold, and 6.11
tongue shall t. hold of the robe 8.23
I will t. away its blood from its 9.07
"T. once more the implements of a 11.15
may come and t. of them and boil 14.21
So t. heed to yourselves, and let Mal 2.15
So t. heed to yourselves and do not 2.16
do not fear to t. Mary your wife, Mt 1.20
t. the child and his mother, and 2.13
"Rise, t. the child and his mother, 2.20
one would sue you and t. your coat, 5.40
'Let me t. the speck out of your 7.04
first t. the log out of your own 7.05
see clearly to t. the speck out of 7.05
to the paralytic, "T. heart, my son; 9.02
t. up your bed and go home." 9.06
"T. heart, daughter; your faith 9.22
T. no gold, nor silver, nor copper in 10.09
and he who does not t. his cross 10.38
and men of violence t. it by force. 11.12
T. my yoke upon you, and learn from 11.29
to them, saying, "T. heart, it is I; 14.27
is not fair to t. the children's 15.26
"T. heed and beware of the leaven 16.06
himself and t. up his cross and 16.24
of the earth t. toll or tribute? 17.25
and t. the first fish that comes up, 17.27
t. that and give it to them for me 17.27
t. one or two others along with you, 18.16
T. what belongs to you, and go; 20.14
"T. heed that no one leads you 24.04
for this must t. place, but the end 24.06
not go down to t. what is in his 24.17
not turn back to t. his mantle. 24.18
till all these things t. place. 24.34
So t. the talent from him, and give 25.28
to the disciples and said, "T., eat; 26.26
for all who t. the sword will 26.52
t. up your pallet and walk'? Mk 2.09
t. up your pallet and go home." 2.11
"T. heed what you hear; the measure 4.24
He charged them to t. nothing for 6.08
them and said, "T. heart, it is I; 6.50
is not right to t. the children's 7.27
"T. heed, beware of the leaven of 8.15
of broken pieces did you t. up?" 8.19
of broken pieces did you t. up?" 8.20
himself and t. up his cross and 8.34
blind man, saying to him, "T. heart; 10.49
the man must t. the wife, and raise 12.19
"T. heed that no one leads you 13.05
this must t. place, but the end is 13.07
"But t. heed to yourselves; 13.09
his house, to t. anything away; 13.15
not turn back to t. his mantle. 13.16
But t. heed; I have told you 13.23
before all these things t. place. 13.30
T. heed, watch; for you do not 13.33
and gave it to them, and said, "T.; 14.22
with myrrh; but he did not t. it. 15.23
to decide what each should t. 15.24
Elijah will come to t. him down." 15.36
to t. away my reproach among men." Lk 1.25
t. up your bed and go home." 5.24
let me t. out the speck that is in 6.42
first t. the log out of your own 6.42
see clearly to t. out the speck 6.42
T. heed then how you hear; 8.18
"T. nothing for your journey, no 9.03
himself and t. up his cross daily 9.23
innkeeper, saying, 'T. care of him; 10.35
"T. heed, and beware of all covetousness; 12.15
t. your ease, eat, drink, be merry.' 12.19
with shame to t. the lowest place. 14.09
down first and t. counsel whether 14.31
'T. your bill, and sit down quickly 16.06
'T. your bill, and write eighty.' 16.07
T. heed to yourselves; if your brother 17.03
not come down to t. them away; 17.31
you t. up what you did not lay down, 19.21
'T. the pound from him, and give it 19.24
that they might t. hold of what he 20.20
the man must t. the wife and raise 20.28
when this is about to t. place?" 21.07
And he said, "T. heed that you are 21.08
for this must first t. place, 21.09
these things begin to t. place, 21.28
"But t. heed to yourselves lest 21.34
these things that will t. place, 21.36
"T. this, and divide it among 22.17
now, let him who has a purse t. it, 22.36
and t. it to the steward of the Jn 2.08
"T. these things away; you shall not 2.16
t. up your pallet, and walk." 5.08
'T. up your pallet, and walk.'" 5.11
'T. up your pallet, and walk'?" 5.12
to come and t. him by force to 6.15
were glad to t. him into the boat, 6.21
"Do you t. offense at this? 6.61
my life, that I may t. it again. 10.17
and I have power to t. it again; 10.18
Jesus said, "T. away the stone." 11.39
box he used to t. what was put 12.06
when it does t. place you may 13.19
again and will t. you to myself, 14.03
so that when it does t. place, 14.29
for he will t. what is mine and 16.14
that he will t. what is mine and 16.15
and no one will t. your joy from 16.22
thou shouldst t. them out of the 17.15
"T. him yourselves and judge him by 18.31
"T. him yourselves and crucify him, 19.06
that he might t. away the body of 19.38
laid him, and I will t. him away." 20.15
and 'His office let another t.' Ac 1.20
to t. the place in this ministry 1.25
plan had predestined to t. place. 4.28
t. care what you do with these men. 5.35
'T. off the shoes from your feet, 7.33
to t. out of them a people for his 15.14
wanted to t. with them John called 15.37
best not to t. with them one who 15.38
them come themselves and t. us out." 16.37
intending to t. Paul aboard there; 20.13
T. heed to yourselves and to all 20.28
t. these men and purify yourself 21.24
to Damascus to t. those also who 22.05
to go down and t. him by force 23.10
"T. courage, for as you have testified 23.11
So I always t. pains to have a 24.16
I now bid you t. heart; for there will 27.22
So t. heart, men, for I have faith in 27.25
urged them all to t. some food, 27.33
Therefore I urge you to t. some food; 27.34
them when I t. away their sins." Rom 11.27
but t. thought for what is noble in 12.17
to t. note of those who create 16.17
Let each man t. care how he builds 1Co 3.10
I therefore t. the members of 6.15
Only t. care lest this liberty of 8.09
that he stands t. heed lest he 10.12
and t. every thought captive to 2Co 10.05
Did I t. advantage of you through 12.17
Did Titus t. advantage of you? 12.18
Did we not t. the same steps? 12.18
that you will t. no other view Gal 5.10
one another t. heed that you are 5.15
T. no part in the unfruitful works Eph 5.11
and I t. it to mean Christ and the 5.32

TAKE (cont.)
Therefore t. the whole armor of God, Eph 6.13
And t. the helmet of salvation, and 6.17
you know how to t. a wife for 1Th 4.04
T. heed to yourself and to your 1Ti 4.16
and we cannot t. anything out of 6.07
t. hold of the eternal life to 6.12
that they may t. hold of the life 6.19
but t. your share of suffering for 2Ti 1.08
T. your share of suffering as a 2.03
T. care, brethren, lest there be in Heb 3.12
And one does not t. the honor upon 5.04
in the law to t. tithes from the 7.05
and goats should t. away sins. 10.04
which can never t. away sins. 10.11
t. the prophets who spoke in the Jas 5.10
beaten for it you t. it patiently? 1Pe 2.20
suffer for it you t. it patiently, 2.20
that he appeared to t. away sins, 1Jn 3.05
servants what must soon t. place; Rev 1.01
and what is to t. place hereafter. 1.19
you what must t. place after this." 4.01
are thou to t. the scroll and to 5.09
permitted to t. peace from the 6.04
t. the scroll which is open in the 10.08
and he said to me, "T. it and eat; 10.09
lest you t. part in her sins, lest 18.04
servants what must soon t. place. 22.06
him who desires t. the water of 22.17
God will t. away his share in the 22.19

TAKEN
Lord God had t. from the man he Gen 2.22
because she was t. out of Man." 2.23
ground, for out of it you were t.; 3.19
the ground from which he was t. 3.23
shall be t. on him sevenfold." 4.15
the woman was t. into Pharaoh's 12.15
his kinsman had been t. captive, 14.14
I have t. upon myself to speak to 18.27
I have t. upon myself to speak to 18.31
of the woman whom you have t.; 20.03
his hand had t. hold of Esau's heel 25.26
and he has t. away your blessing." 27.35
now he has t. away my blessing." 27.36
that you have t. away my husband? 30.15
"God has t. away my reproach": 30.23
"Jacob has t. all that was our 31.01
Thus God has t. away the cattle of 31.09
which God has t. away from our 31.16
Now Rachel had t. the household 31.34
Now Joseph was t. down to Egypt, and 39.01
Portions were t. to them from 43.34
that you have t. us away to die in Ex 14.11
had t. Zipporah, Moses' wife, after 18.02
they shall not be t. from it. 25.15
the cloud was t. up from over the 40.36
but if the cloud was not t. up, 40.37
till the day that it was t. up. 40.37
(just as these are t. from the ox Lev 4.10
offered I have t. from the people 7.34
after he has t. out the stones and 14.43
I have t. the Levites from among Num 3.12
since she was not t. in the act; 5.13
people of Israel, I have t. them for myself. 8.16
and I have t. the Levites instead 8.18
the cloud was t. up from over the 9.17
the cloud was t. up in the morning, 9.21
the cloud was t. up they set out. 9.21
but when it was t. up they set out. 9.22
the cloud was t. up from over the 10.11
And when the tabernacle was t. down, 10.17
I have not t. one ass from them, and 16.15
I have t. your brethren the Levites 18.06
she shall be t. outside the camp 19.03
of Moab and t. all his land out of 21.26
our father be t. away from his 27.04
the count of the booty that was t., 31.26
(The men of war had t. booty, 31.53
inheritance will be t. from the 36.03
so it will be t. away from the lot 36.03
inheritance will be t. from the 36.04
But the Lord has t. you, and brought Deu 4.20
betrothed a wife and has not t. her? 20.07
happy with his wife whom he has t. 24.05
and have t. possession of it, and 26.01
be violently t. away before your 28.31
But the woman had t. the two men Jos 2.04
they have t. some of the devoted 7.11
And he who is t. with the devoted 7.15
and the tribe of Judah was t.; 7.16
the family of the Zerahites was t.; 7.17
man by man, and Zabdi was t.; 7.17
of the tribe of Judah, was t. 7.18
And when you have t. the city, 8.08
that the ambush had t. the city, 8.21
Jerusalem heard how Joshua had t. Ai, 10.01
and having t. possession of it, they 21.43
that he had t. the honey from the Ju 14.09
because he has t. his wife and 15.06
of silver which were t. from you, 17.02
this that has t. place among you? 20.12
For they had t. a great oath 21.05
Philistines had t. from Israel 1Sa 7.14
tribe of Benjamin was t. by lot. 10.20
of the Matrites was t. by lot; 10.21
Saul the son of Kish was t. by lot. 10.21
Whose ox have I t.? Or whose 12.03
Or whose ass have I t.? Or whom 12.03
hand have I t. a bribe to blind my 12.03
oppressed us or t. anything from 12.04
And Jonathan and Saul were t., 14.41
my son Jonathan." And Jonathan was t. 14.42
When Saul had t. the kingship over 14.47
hot bread on the day it is t. away. 21.06
I have t. my life in my hand, and 28.21
and t. captive the women and all 30.02
and sons and daughters t. captive. 30.03
two wives also had been t. captive, 30.05
And when he had t. him down, 30.16
spoil they had t. from the land of 30.16
all that the Amalekites had t.; 30.18
spoil or anything that had been t.; 30.19
had t. Ishbosheth the son of Saul, 2Sa 2.08
and have t. his wife to be your 12.09
and have t. the wife of Uriah the 12.10
I have t. the city of waters. 12.27
lifetime had t. and set up for 18.18
When he was t. out of the highway, 20.13
they cannot be t. with the hand; 23.06
Naphtali (he had t. Basemath the 1Ki 4.15
daughter whom he had t. in marriage. 7.08
But the high places were not t. away. 15.14
Zimri saw that the city was t., 16.18
you killed, and also t. possession?"' 21.19
the high places were not t. away, 22.43
for you, before I am t. from you." 2Ki 2.09
see me as I am being t. from you, 2.10
you have t. all this trouble for us 4.13
whom you have t. captive with your 6.22
Nevertheless the high places were not t. away; 12.03
which he had t. from Jehoahaz his 13.25
Nevertheless the high places were not t. away; 15.04
king of Israel, Samaria was t. 18.10
are born to you, shall be t. away; 20.18
of Babylon had t. all that belonged 24.07
So Judah was t. into exile out of 25.21
And Judah was t. into exile in 1Ch 9.01
they were brought in and t. out. 9.28
them which David his father had t.; 2Ch 2.17
which he had t. in the hill 15.08
places were not t. out of Israel. 15.17
which Asa his father had t. 17.02
And when he had t. counsel with the 20.21

TAKEN (cont.)
places, however, were not t. away; 2Ch 20.33
your kinsfolk whom you have t., 28.11
and had t. Bethshemesh, Aijalon, 28.18
Jerusalem had t. counsel to keep 30.02
same Hezekiah t. away his high 32.12
Barzillai (who had t. a wife from Ez 2.61
Nebuchadnezzar had t. out of the 5.14
For they have t. some of their 9.02
cities who have t. foreign wives 10.14
Jehohanan had t. the daughter of Neh 6.18
Barzillai (who had t. a wife of the 7.63
Esther also was t. into the king's Est 2.08
And when Esther was t. to King 2.16
which he had t. from Haman, and gave 8.02
gave, and the LORD has t. away; Job 1.21
and t. the crown from my head. 19.09
who has t. away my right, and the 27.02
Iron is t. out of the earth, and 28.02
of affliction have t. hold of me. 30.16
and God has t. away my right; 34.05
the mighty are t. away by no human 34.20
thou hast t. heed of my adversities, Ps 31.07
God has t. his place in the divine 82.01
for thou hast t. me up and thrown 102.10
treacherous are t. captive by Pro 11.06
your bed be t. from under you? 22.27
who are being t. away to death; 24.11
to it, nor anything t. from it; Ecc 3.14
and right violently t. away, 5.08
her, but the sinner is t. by her. 7.26
fish which are t. in an evil net, 9.12
The LORD has t. his place to Is 3.13
which he had t. with tongs from 6.06
your guilt is t. away, and your sin 6.07
be broken, they shall be snared and t." 8.15
gladness are t. away from the 16.10
He has t. away the covering of 22.08
the milk, those t. from the breast? 28.09
and be broken, and snared, and t. 28.13
in falsehood we have t. shelter"; 28.15
are born to you, shall be t. away; 39.07
has their stem t. root in the 40.24
I have t. you by the hand and kept 42.06
Can the prey be t. from the mighty, 49.24
captives of the mighty shall be t., 49.25
I have t. from your hand the cup of 51.22
my people are t. away for nothing? 52.05
and judgment he was t. away; 53.08
devout men are t. away, while no one 57.01
righteous man is t. away from 57.01
both husband and wife shall be t., Jer 6.11
anguish has t. hold of us, pain as 6.24
they shall be dismayed and t.; 8.09
and dismay has t. hold on me. 8.21
LORD's flock has been t. captive. 13.17
is t. into exile, wholly t. into exile 13.19
for I have t. away my peace from 16.05
of Babylon had t. into exile from 24.01
Nebuchadnezzar had t. into exile 29.01
of the king of Babylon and be t." 38.03
the day that Jerusalem was t. 38.28
When Jerusalem was t., all the princes 39.03
and when they had t. him, they 39.05
had not been t. into exile to 40.07
in your cities that you have t." 40.10
Kiriathaim is put to shame, it is t.; 48.01
treasures, you also shall be t.; 48.07
joy have been t. away from the 48.33
the cities shall be t. and the 48.41
for your sons have been t. captive, 48.46
and sorrows have t. hold of her, 49.24
tents and their flocks shall be t., 49.29
'Babylon is t., Bel is put to shame, 50.02
from there she shall be t. 50.09
a snare for you and you were t., 50.24
No stone shall be t. from you for a 51.26
that his city is t. on every side; 51.31
"How Babylon is t., the praise 51.41
her warriors are t., their bows 51.56
"Thou hast t. up my cause, O Lord, Lam 3.58
was t. in their pits, he of whom we 4.20
and he shall be t. in my snare; Eze 12.13
these men have t. their idols into 14.03
Is wood t. from it to make anything? 15.03
men of the land he had t. away, 17.13
and he shall be t. in my snare, 17.20
he was t. in their pit; and they 19.04
over him; he was t. in their pit. 19.08
remembrance, you shall be t. in them. 21.24
they have t. treasure and precious 22.25
But if he had t. warning, he would 33.05
that man is t. away in his iniquity, 33.06
back what he had t. by robbery, 33.15
his father had t. out of the Dan 5.02
which had been t. out of the 5.03
and his glory was t. from him; 5.20
that Daniel be t. up out of the 6.23
So Daniel was t. up out of the den, 6.23
beasts, their dominion was t. away, 7.12
and his dominion shall be t. away, 7.26
offering was t. away from him, 8.11
And when the multitude is t., 11.12
continual burnt offering is t. away, 12.11
the fish of the sea are t. away. Hos 4.03
and I have t. them away in my wrath. 13.11
For you have t. my silver and my Joe 3.05
altar upon garments t. in pledge; Amo 2.08
from his den, if he has t. nothing? 3.04
the ground, when it has t. nothing? 3.05
own strength t. Karnaim for 6.13
The LORD has t. away the judgments Zep 3.15
I have t. your iniquity away from Zec 3.04
when the spoil t. from you will be 14.01
city shall be t. and the houses 14.02
what has been t. by violence or is Mal 1.13
bridegroom is t. away from them, Mt 9.15
even what he has will be t. away. 13.12
servants saw what had t. place, 18.31
their lord all that had t. place. 18.31
'Be t. up and cast into the sea,' it 21.21
of God will be t. away from you 21.43
would not have t. part with them 23.30
the field; one is t. and one is left. 24.40
the mill; one is t. and one is left. 24.41
even what he has will be t. away. 25.29
But all this has t. place, 26.56
priests all that had t. place. 28.11
with the elders and t. counsel, 28.12
bridegroom is t. away from them, Mk 2.20
even what he has will be t. away." 4.25
And after he had t. leave of them, 6.46
'Be t. up and cast into the sea,' 11.23
was t. up into heaven, and sat down at * 16.19
catch of fish which they had t.; Lk 5.09
bridegroom is t. away from them, 5.35
thinks that he has will be t. away." 8.18
shall not be t. away from her." 10.42
for you have t. away the key of 11.52
one will be t. and the other left. 17.34
one will be t. and the other left." 17.35
one will be t. and the other left." * 17.36
even what he has will be t. away. 19.26
pass away till all has t. place. 21.32
centurion saw what had t. place, 23.47
when they saw what had t. place, 23.48
"It has t. forty-six years to build Jn 2.20
and t. his garments, and resumed his 13.12
and that they might be t. away. 19.31
stone had been t. away from the 20.01
"They have t. the Lord out of the 20.02
"Because they have t. away my Lord, 20.13
until the day when he was t. up, Ac 1.02
who was t. up from you into heaven, 1.11

TAKEN (cont.)

the day when he was t. up from us— 1.22
For his life is t. up from the Ac 8.33
the thing was t. up at once to 10.16
And when they had t. security from 17.09
the third story and was t. up dead. 20.09
without food, having t. nothing. 27.33
And when this had t. place, 28.09
only through Christ is it t. away. 2Co 3.14
we have t. advantage of no one. 7.02
everything that has t. place here. Col 4.09
on in the world, t. up in glory. 1Ti 3.16
offerings thou hast t. no pleasure. Heb 10.06
desired nor t. pleasure in sacrifices 10.08
By faith Enoch was t. up so that he 11.05
not found, because God had t. him. 11.05
before he was t. he was attested 11.05
And when he had t. the scroll, Rev 5.08
that thou hast t. thy great power 11.17
If any one is to be t. captive, 13.10

TAKES

guiltless who t. his name in vain. Ex 20.07
If he t. another wife to himself, he 21.10
who t. in hunting any beast or bird Lev 17.13
If a man t. a wife and her mother 20.14
"If a man t. his sister, a daughter 20.17
If a man t. his brother's wife, it is 20.21
law for the Nazirite who t. a vow. Num 6.21
accordance with the vow which he t., 6.21
guiltless who t. his name in vain. Deu 5.11
who is not partial and t. no bribe. 10.17
"If any man t. a wife, and goes in 22.13
"When a man t. a wife and marries 24.01
be he who t. a bribe to slay an 27.25
and my hand t. hold on judgment, I 32.41
and t. vengeance on his adversaries, 32.43
tribe which the LORD t. shall come Jos 7.14
family which the LORD t. shall come 7.14
household which the LORD t. shall come 7.14
and t. it, to him will I give Achsah 15.16
attacks Kiriathsepher and t. it, Ju 1.12
and nobody t. me into his house. 19.18
and t. away the reproach from 1Sa 17.26
and he t. it even out of thorns; Job 5.05
He t. the wise in their own craftiness 5.13
and t. away the discernment of the 12.20
He t. away understanding from the 12.24
him off, when God t. away his life? 27.08
the pain that gnaws me t. no rest. 30.17
nor t. up a reproach against his Ps 15.03
is the man who t. refuge in him! 34.08
but the Lord t. thought for me. 40.17
me, for in thee my soul t. refuge; 57.01
Happy shall he be who t. your 137.09
there is none who t. notice of me; 142.04
but the LORD t. pleasure in those 147.11
For the LORD t. pleasure in his 149.04
it t. away the life of its possessors. Pro 1.19
will not spare when he t. revenge. 6.34
way, in the paths she t. her stand; 8.02
she t. a seat on the high places of 9.14
but lawlessness t. away lives. 11.30
his spirit than he who t. a city. 16.32
A fool t. no pleasure in understanding, 18.02
for suddenly it t. to itself wings, 23.05
is like one who t. off a garment 25.20
is like one who t. a passing dog 26.17
a vanity which t. place on earth, Ecc 8.14
When a man t. hold of his brother Is 3.06
behold, he t. up the isles like fine 40.15
he t. a part of it and warms 44.15
But he who t. refuge in me shall 57.13
and he who t. an oath in the land 65.16
and archer every city t. to flight; Jer 4.29
of Israel who t. his idols into Eze 14.04
lends at interest, and t. increase; 18.13
t. no interest or increase, observes 18.17
the sword comes and t. him away, 33.04
and t. any one of them; in his 33.06
the LORD t. vengeance on his Nah 1.02
is he who t. no offense at me." Mt 11.06
comes and t. away the word which Mk 4.15
from him who t. away your cloak do Lk 6.29
and of him who t. away your goods, 6.30
is he who t. no offense at me." 7.23
devil comes and t. away the word 8.12
he t. away his armor in which he 11.22
who t. away the sin of the world! Jn 1.29
No one t. it from me, but I lay it 10.18
before it t. place, that when it 13.19
I have told you before it t. place, 14.29
he t. away, and every branch that 15.02
or t. advantage of you, or puts on 2Co 11.20
so that he t. his seat in the 2Th 2.04
For a will t. effect only at death, Heb 9.17
and if any one t. away from the Rev 22.19

TAKEST

when thou t. away their breath, they Ps 104.29
and thou t. no knowledge of it?' Is 58.03

TAKING

t. all sorts of choice gifts from Gen 24.10
T. one of the stones of the place, 28.11
and t. off her veil she put on the 38.19
t. with you some of the elders of Ex 17.05
t. it away close by the backbone, Lev 3.09
and upward, t. their number by names. Num 3.40
their sons or t. their daughters Deu 7.03
for he would be t. a life in pledge 24.06
t. ten thousand from the tribe of Ju 4.06
And t. what Micah had made, and the 18.27
and from t. vengeance with your own 1Sa 25.26
or for my lord t. vengeance himself 25.31
as he was t. his noonday rest. 2Sa 4.05
"So he went, t. with him ten 2Ki 5.05
God, or partiality, or t. bribes." 2Ch 19.07
were three days in t. the spoil, 20.25
While this was t. place I was not Neh 13.06
I have seen the fool t. root, Job 5.03
her corner t. the road to her house Pro 7.08
is t. away from Jerusalem and from Is 3.01
t. his idols into his heart and Eze 14.07
offended in t. vengeance upon them, 25.12
me, "Where are they t. the ephah?" Zec 5.10
and t. the five loaves and the two Mt 14.19
And t. with him Peter and the two 26.37
still sleeping and t. your rest? 26.45
t. the pieces of silver, sais, "It is 27.06
T. her by the hand he said to her, Mk 5.41
And t. the five loaves and the two 6.41
And t. him aside from the multitude 7.33
and t. him in his arms, he said to 9.36
And t. the twelve again, he began to 10.32
when you see these things t. place, 13.29
still sleeping and t. your rest? 14.41
and t. him down, wrapped him in the 15.46
But t. her by the hand he called, Lk 8.54
And t. the five loaves and the two 9.16
my master is t. the stewardship 16.03
And t. the twelve, he said to them, 18.31
t. up what I did not lay down and 19.22
when you see these things t. place, 21.31
t. the spices which they had 24.01
that he meant t. rest in sleep. Jn 11.13
and t. some wicked fellows of the Ac 17.05
but on t. leave of them he said, "I 18.21
t. the disciples with him, and 19.09
the favor of t. part in the relief 2Co 8.04
Barnabas, t. Titus along with me. Gal 2.01
above all t. the shield of faith, Eph 6.16
t. the form of a servant, being born Php 2.07
t. his stand on visions, puffed up Col 2.18
like a nurse t. care of her children 1Th 2.07

TAKING (cont.)
and not without t. blood which he Heb 9.07
t. not the blood of goats and calves 9.12

TALE
words seemed to them an idle t., Lk 24.11

TALEBEARER
goes about as a t. reveals secrets, Pro 11.13

TALENT
Of a t. of pure gold shall it be Ex 25.39
its utensils of a t. of pure gold. 37.24
hundred talents, a t. for a base. 38.27
the weight of it was a t. of gold, 2Sa 12.30
else you shall pay a t. of silver.' 1Ki 20.39
give them a t. of silver and two 2Ki 5.22
talents of silver and a t. of gold. 23.33
found that it weighed a t. of gold, 1Ch 20.02
talents of silver and a t. of gold. 2Ch 36.03
But he who had received the one t., Mt 25.18
received the one t. came forward, 25.24
went and hid your t. in the ground. 25.25
So take the t. from him, and give it 25.28

TALENTS
was twenty-nine t. and seven Ex 38.24
was a hundred t. and a thousand 38.25
The hundred t. of silver were for 38.27
a hundred bases for the hundred t., 38.27
was contributed was seventy t., 38.29
one hundred and twenty t. of gold. 1Ki 9.14
of four hundred and twenty t.; 9.28
a hundred and twenty t. of gold, 10.10
hundred and sixty-six t. of gold, 10.14
from Shemer for two t. of silver; 16.24
taking with him ten t. of silver, 2Ki 5.05
said, "Be pleased to accept two t." 5.23
and tied up two t. of silver in 5.23
gave Pul a thousand t. of silver, 15.19
three hundred t. of silver and 18.14
of silver and thirty t. of gold. 18.14
of a hundred t. of silver and a 23.33
sent a thousand t. of silver to 1Ch 19.06
LORD a hundred thousand t. of gold, 22.14
a million t. of silver, and bronze 22.14
three thousand t. of gold, of the 29.04
seven thousand t. of refined silver 29.04
five thousand t. and ten thousand 29.07
ten thousand t. of silver, eighteen 29.07
eighteen thousand t. of bronze, 29.07
and a hundred thousand t. of iron. 29.07
with six hundred t. of fine gold. 2Ch 3.08
and fifty t. of gold and brought 8.18
a hundred and twenty t. of gold, 9.09
hundred and sixty-six t. of gold, 9.13
Israel for a hundred t. of silver. 25.06
the hundred t. which I have given 25.09
that year a hundred t. of silver, 27.05
of a hundred t. of silver and a 36.03
up to a hundred t. of silver, Ez 7.22
six hundred and fifty t. of silver, 8.26
silver vessels worth a hundred t., 8.26
talents, and a hundred t. of gold, 8.26
ten thousand t. of silver into the Est 3.09
him who owed him ten thousand t.; Mt 18.24
to one he gave five t., to another 25.15
the five t. went at once and 25.16
with them; and he made five t. more. 25.16
who had the two t. made two t. more. 25.17
received the five t. came forward, 25.20
bringing five t. more, saying, 25.20
you delivered to me five t.; 25.20
here I have made five t. more.' 25.20
who had the two t. came forward, 25.22
'Master, you delivered to me two t.; 25.22
here I have made two t. more.' 25.22
give it to him who has the ten t. 25.28

TALITHA
the hand he said to her, "T. cumi"; Mk 5.41

TALK
come down and t. with you there; Num 11.17
and shall t. of them when you sit Deu 6.07
T. no more so very proudly, let not 1Sa 2.03
"You know the fellow and his t." 2Ki 9.11
and a man full of t. be vindicated? Job 11.02
Should he argue in unprofitable t., 15.03
when I rise they t. against me. 19.18
Job opens his mouth in empty t., 35.16
they t. of laying snares secretly, Ps 64.05
I am the t. of those who sit in the 69.12
And my tongue will t. of thy 71.24
and put devious t. far from you. Pro 4.24
you awake, they will t. with you. 6.22
with her smooth t. she compels him. 7.21
The t. of a fool is a rod for his 14.03
but mere t. tends only to want. 14.23
and their lips t. of mischief. 24.02
the end of his t. is wicked Ecc 10.13
your people who t. together about Eze 33.30
you became the t. and evil gossip 36.03
my lord's servant t. with my lord? Dan 10.17
how to entangle him in his t. Mt 22.15
and began to t. freely about it, Mk 1.45
Herodians, to entrap him in his t. 12.13
I will no longer t. much with you, Jn 14.30
out not the t. of these arrogant 1Co 4.19
not consist in t. but in power. 4.20
Let no evil t. come out of your Eph 4.29
nor silly t., nor levity, which are 5.04
and foul t. from your mouth. Col 3.08
and their t. will eat its way like 2Ti 2.17
to see you and t. with you face to 2Jn 1.12
and we will t. together face to 3Jn 1.14

TALKED
that his brothers t. with him. Gen 45.15
that I have t. with you from Ex 20.22
to him, and Moses t. with them. 34.31
he went down and t. with the woman; Ju 14.07
As he t. with them, behold, the 1Sa 17.23
And as they still went on and t., 2Ki 2.11
Second Quarter); and they t. with her. 22.14
for he has t. rebellion against the Jer 29.32
'The angel who t. with me said to Zec 1.09
words to the angel who t. with me. 1.13
So the angel who t. with me said to 1.14
I said to the angel who t. with me, 1.19
the angel who t. with me came 2.03
And the angel who t. with me came 4.01
I said to the angel who t. with me, 4.04
Then the angel who t. with me 4.05
Then the angel who t. with me came 5.05
I said to the angel who t. with me, 5.10
I said to the angel who t. with me, 6.04
things were t. about through all Lk 1.65
two men t. with him, Moses and 9.30
us while he t. to us on the road, 24.32
And as he t. with him, he went in Ac 10.27
Paul t. with them, intending to 20.07
deep sleep as Paul t. still longer; 20.09
And he who t. to me had a measuring Rev 21.15

TALKERS
empty t. and deceivers, especially Tit 1.10

TALKING
When he had finished t. with him, Gen 17.22
because he had been t. with God. Ex 34.29
t. of them when you are sttting in Deu 11.19
And while Saul was t. to the priest, 1Sa 14.19
Now the king was t. with Gehazi the 2Ki 8.04
While they were yet t. with him, Est 6.14
the princes refrained from t., Job 29.09
your own pleasure, or t. idly; Is 58.13

TALKING (cont.)
them Moses and Elijah, t. with him. Mt 17.03
with Moses; and they were t. to Jesus. Mk 9.04
and t. with each other about all Lk 24.14
While they were t. and discussing 24.15
that he was t. with a woman, Jn 4.27
or, "Why are you t. with her?" 4.27
I am t. like a madman—with far 2Co 11.23

TALL
and many, and t. as the Anakim; Deu 2.10
and many, and t. as the Anakim; 2.21
a people great and t., the sons of the 9.02
of great stature, five cubits t. 1Ch 11.23
t. and smooth, to a people feared Is 18.02
hosts from a people t. and smooth, 18.07
up and became t. and arrived at Eze 16.07
it, the deep made it grow t., 31.04

TALLER
people are greater and t. than we; Deu 1.28
upward he was t. than any of the 1Sa 9.02
he was t. than any of the people 10.23

TALLEST
I felled its t. cedars, its choicest 2Ki 19.23
I felled its t. cedars, its choicest Is 37.24

TALMAI
and T., the descendants of Anak, Num 13.22
of Anak, Sheshai and Ahiman and T., Jos 15.14
defeated Sheshai and Ahiman and T. Ju 1.10
the daughter of T. king of Geshur; 2Sa 3.03
and went to T. the son of Ammihud, 13.37
was Maacah, the daughter of T., 1Ch 3.02

TALMON
T., Ahiman, and their kinsmen 1Ch 9.17
the sons of T., the sons of Akkub, Ez 2.42
the sons of T., the sons of Akkub, Neh 7.45
T. and their brethren, who kept 11.19
T., and Akkub were gatekeepers 12.25

TAMAR
first-born, and her name was T. Gen 38.06
Then Judah said to T. his daughter-in-law, 38.11
So T. went and dwelt in her father's 38.11
And when T. was told, "Your father-in-law 38.13
"T. your daughter-in-law has played 38.24
whom T. bore to Judah, because of Ru 4.12
beautiful sister, whose name was T.; 2Sa 13.01
ill because of his sister T.; 13.02
"I love T., my brother Absalom's 13.04
'Let my sister T. come and give me 13.05
let my sister T. come and make a 13.06
Then David sent home to T., saying, 13.07
So T. went to her brother Amnon's 13.08
Then Amnon said to T., "Bring the food 13.10
And T. took the cakes she had made, 13.10
And T. put ashes on her head, and 13.19
So T. dwelt, a desolate woman, in her 13.20
he had forced his sister T. 13.22
the day he forced his sister T. 13.32
and one daughter whose name was T.; 14.27
And Baalath and T. in the wilderness 1Ki 9.18
His daughter-in-law T. also bore 1Ch 2.04
concubines; and T. was their sister. 3.09
the eastern sea and as far as T. Eze 47.18
shall run from T. as far as the 47.19
shall run from T. to the waters of 48.28
father of Perez and Zerah by T., Mt 1.03

TAMARISK
Abraham planted a t. tree in Gen 21.33
under the t. tree on the height, 1Sa 22.06
them under the t. tree in Jabesh, 31.13

TAMBOURINE
mirth and songs, with t. and lyre? Gen 31.27
t., flute, and lyre before them, 1Sa 10.05
They sing to the t. and the lyre, Job 21.12

TAMBOURINES
and harps and t. and castanets and 2Sa 6.05
and harps and t. and cymbals and 1Ch 13.08

TAME
but no human being can t. the tongue Jas 3.08

TAMED
can be t. and has been t. by humankind Jas 3.07

TAMMUZ
there sat women weeping for T. Eze 8.14

TAMPER
cunning or to t. with God's word, 2Co 4.02

TANHUMETH
the son of T. the Netophathite, and 2Ki 25.23
of Kareah, Seraiah the son of T., Jer 40.08

TANNED
t. rams' skins, goatskins, acacia Ex 25.05
a covering of t. rams' skins and 26.14
t. rams' skins, and goatskins; 35.07
goats' hair or t. rams' skins or 35.23
a covering of t. rams' skins and 36.19
the covering of t. rams' skins and 39.34

TANNER
for many days with one Simon, a t. Ac 9.43
a t., whose house is by the seaside 10.06
of Simon, a t., by the seaside. 10.32

TAPHATH
Naphathdor (he had T. the daughter 1Ki 4.11

TAPPUAH
the king of T., one; the king Jos 12.17
Zanoah, Engannim, T., Enam, 15.34
From T. the boundary goes westward 16.08
The land of T. belonged to Manasseh, 17.08
but the town of T. on the boundary 17.08
Menahem sacked T. and all who were 2Ki 15.16
Korah, T., Rekem, and Shema. 1Ch 2.43

TARALAH
Rekem, Irpeel, T., Jos 18.27

TAREA
Pithon, Melech, T., and Ahaz. 1Ch 8.35

TARGET
he set me up as his t., Job 16.12

TARRIED
ate bread and t. all night on the Gen 31.54
while he t. at Jericho, and he said 2Ki 2.18

TARRY
come down to me, do not t.; Gen 45.09
out of Egypt and could not t., Ex 12.39
"T. here for us, until we come to 24.14
Pray, now, t. here this night also, Num 22.19
Why did you t. among the sheepfolds, Ju 5.16
Why t. the hoofbeats of his chariots?' 5.28
and t. until the day declines." 19.08
pray t. all night. Behold, the 19.09
"T. here, I pray you; for the LORD 2Ki 2.02
t. here, I pray you; for the LORD 2.04
"T. here, I pray you; for the LORD 2.06
and flee; do not t." 9.03
Weeping may t. for the night, but Ps 30.05
my deliverer; do not t., O my God! 40.17
my deliverer; O LORD, do not t.! 70.05

TARRY (cont.)
Those who t. long over wine, those Pro 23.30
who t. late into the evening till Is 5.11
off, and my salvation will not t.; 46.13
who turns aside to t. for a night? Jer 14.08
which t. not for men nor wait for Mic 5.07
one shall come and shall not t.; Heb 10.37

TARSHISH
T., Kittim, and Dodanim. Gen 10.04
of ships of T. at sea with the 1Ki 10.22
of ships of T. used to come 10.22
Jehoshaphat made ships of T. to go 22.48
Elishah, T., Kittim, and Rodanim. 1Ch 1.07
Chenaanah, Zethan, T., and Ahishahar. 7.10
ships went to T. with the servants 2Ch 9.21
the ships of T. used to come 9.21
him in building ships to go to T., 20.36
and were not able to go to T. 20.37
T., Meres, Marsena, and Memucan, the Est 1.14
thou didst shatter the ships of T. Ps 48.07
May the kings of T. and of the 72.10
against all the ships of T., Is 2.16
O ships of T., for Tyre is laid 23.01
Pass over to T., wail, O inhabitants 23.06
like the Nile, O daughter of T.; 23.10
O ships of T., for your stronghold 23.14
the ships of T. first, to bring your 60.09
to T., Put, and Lud, who draw the bow, 66.19
Beaten silver is brought from T., Jer 10.09
"T. trafficked with you because of Eze 27.12
The ships of T. traveled for you 27.25
merchants of T. and all its 38.13
rose to flee to T. from the Jon 1.03
Joppa and found a ship going to T.; 1.03
on board, to go with them to T., 1.03
is why I made hast to flee to T.; 4.02

TARSUS
Judas for a man of T. named Saul; Ac 9.11
Caesarea, and sent him off to T. 9.30
Barnabas went to T. to look for 11.25
from T. in Cilicia, a citizen of no 21.39
born at T. in Cilicia, but brought 22.03

TARTAK
and the Avvites made Nibhaz and T.; 2Ki 17.31

TARTAN
And the king of Assyria sent the T., 2Ki 18.17

TASK
your daily t., as when there was Ex 5.13
done all your t. of making bricks 5.14
every sort of t. on the sanctuary 36.04
each from the t. that he was doing, 36.04
each to his t. and to his burden, Num 4.19
each to his t. of serving or 4.49
Arise, for it is your t., and we are Ez 10.04
it seemed to me a wearisome t., Ps 73.16
Whatever your t., work heartily, as Col 3.23
of bishop, he desires a noble t. 1Ti 3.01

TASKMASTER
who was t. over the forced labor, 1Ki 12.18
who was t. over the forced labor, 2Ch 10.18
they hear not the voice of the t. Job 3.18

TASKMASTERS
Therefore they set t. over them to Ex 1.11
their cry because of their t.; 3.07
commanded the t. of the people and 5.06
So the t. and the foremen of the 5.10
The t. were urgent, saying, "Complete 5.13
whom Pharaoh's t. had set over 5.14
peace and your t. righteousness. Is 60.17

TASKS
household and t. for her maidens. Pro 31.15

TASSEL
to put upon the t. of each corner Num 15.38
be to you a t. to look upon and 15.39

TASSELS
them to make t. on the corners of Num 15.38
make yourself t. on the four Deu 22.12

TASTE
and the t. of it was like wafers Ex 16.31
and the t. of it was like the taste Num 11.08
it was like the t. of cakes baked 11.08
if I t. bread or anything else till 2Sa 3.35
your servant t. what he eats or 19.35
or is there any t. in the slime of Job 6.06
Cannot my t. discern calamity? 6.30
O t. and see that the LORD is good! Ps 34.08
How sweet are thy words to my t., 119.103
the honeycomb are sweet to your t. Pro 24.13
and his fruit was sweet to my t. Sol 2.03
so his t. remains in him, and his Jer 48.11
beast, herd nor flock, t. anything; Jon 3.07
but if salt has lost its t., Mt 5.13
who will not t. death before they 16.28
who will not t. death before they Mk 9.01
who will not t. of death before Lk 9.27
were invited shall t. my banquet.'" 14.24
but if salt has lost its t., 14.34
my word, he will never t. death.' Jn 8.52
by an oath to t. no food till we Ac 23.14
handle, Do not t., Do not touch" Col 2.21
of God he might t. death for every Heb 2.09

TASTED
So none of the people t. food. 1Sa 14.24
because I t. a little of this honey 14.29
"I t. a little honey with the tip 14.43
of soul, never having t. of good. Job 21.25
when he t. the wine, commanded that Dan 5.02
but when he t. it, he would not Mt 27.34
of the feast t. the water now Jn 2.09
who have t. the heavenly gift, and Heb 6.04
and have t. the goodness of the 6.05
for you have t. the kindness of the 1Pe 2.03

TASTELESS
Can that which is t. be eaten Job 6.06

TASTES
try words as the palate t. food? Job 12.11
tests words as the palate t. food. 34.03

TATTENAI
At the same time T. the governor of Ez 5.03
letter which T. the governor of 5.06
T., governor of the province Beyond 6.06
T., the governor of the province 6.13

TATTOO
of the dead or t. any marks upon Lev 19.28

TAUGHT
Behold, I have t. you statutes and Deu 4.05
because he has t. rebellion 13.05
and t. it to the people of Israel. 31.22
and with them t. the men of Ju 8.16
it should be t. to the people of 2Sa 1.18
and t. them how they should fear 2Ki 17.28
And they t. in Judah, having the 2Ch 17.09
of Judah and t. among the people. 17.09
the Levites who t. all Israel and 35.03
the Levites who t. the people said Neh 8.09
God, from my youth thou hast t. me, Ps 71.17
ordinances, for thou hast t. me. 119.102
he t. me, and said to me, "Let your Pro 4.04

TAUGHT (cont.)
I have t. you the way of wisdom; Pro 4.11
of Massa, which his mother t. him: 31.01
Preacher also t. the people Ecc 12.09
and who t. him the path of justice, Is 40.14
and t. him knowledge, and showed him 40.14
me the tongue of those who are t., 50.04
my ear to hear as those who are t. 50.04
All your sons shall be t. by the LORD, 54.13
wicked women you have t. your ways. Jer 2.33
they have t. their tongue to speak 9.05
Baals, as their fathers t. them. 9.14
'even as they t. my people to 12.16
yourself have t. to be friends to 13.21
though I have t. them persistently 32.33
have they t. the difference Eze 22.26
Yet it was I who t. Ephraim to walk, Hos 11.03
his mouth and t. them, saying: Mt 5.02
for he t. them as one who had 7.29
own country he t. them in their 13.54
he entered the synagogue and t. Mk 1.21
for he t. them as one who had 1.22
gathered about him, and he t. them. 2.13
And he t. them many things in 4.02
him all that they had done and t. 6.30
as his custom was, he t. them. 10.01
And he t., and said to them, "Is it 11.17
And as Jesus t. in the temple, he 12.35
And he t. in their synagogues, being Lk 4.15
he sat down and t. the people from 5.03
he entered the synagogue and t., 6.06
he is fully t. will be like his 6.40
to pray, as John t. his disciples." 11.01
presence, and you t. in our streets.' 13.26
'And they shall all be t. by God.' Jn 6.45
synagogue, as he t. at Capernaum. 6.59
went up into the temple and t. 7.14
as he t. in the temple, "You know me, 7.28
and he sat down and t. them. * 8.02
treasury, as he t. in the temple; 8.20
but speak thus as the Father t. me. 8.28
I have always t. in synagogues and 18.20
the temple at daybreak and t. Ac 5.21
and t. a large company of people; 11.26
he spoke and t. accurately the 18.25
doctrine which you have been t.; Rom 16.17
in words not t. by human wisdom 1Co 2.13
human wisdom but t. by the Spirit, 2.13
nor was I t. it, but it came through Gal 1.12
Let him who is t. the word share 6.06
heard about him and were t. in him, Eph 4.21
in the faith, just as you were t., Col 2.07
have been t. by God to love one 1Th 4.09
traditions which you were t. by us, 2Th 2.15
hold firm to the sure word as t., Tit 1.09
is no lie, just as it has t. you, 1Jn 2.27
who t. Balak to put a stumbling Rev 2.14

TAUNT
turn back their t. upon their own Neh 4.04
me an evil name, in order to t. me. 6.13
in my body, my adversaries t. me, Ps 42.10
made us the t. of our neighbors, 44.13
We have become a t. to our neighbors, 79.04
with which thy enemies t., 89.51
All the day my enemies t. me, 102.08
have an answer for those who t. me, 119.42
take up this t. against the king Is 14.04
a t., and a curse in all the places Jer 24.09
a horror, a curse, and a t. 42.18
a curse and a t. among all the 44.08
a horror, a curse, and a t. 44.12
a t., a waste, and a curse; 49.13
You shall be a reproach and a t., Eze 5.15
shall take up a t. song against Mic 2.04
these take up their t. against him, Hab 2.06

TAUNTED
and Zalmunna, about whom you t. me, Ju 8.15
And when he t. Israel, Jonathan the 2Sa 21.21
And when he t. Israel, Jonathan the 1Ch 20.07
which they have t. thee, O Lord! Ps 79.12
how they have t. my people and made Zep 2.08

TAUNTERS
at the words of the t. and revilers, Ps 44.16

TAUNTS
to prevent the t. of the nations Neh 5.09
It is not an enemy who t. me— Ps 55.12
neighbors the t. with which they 79.12
"Thou hast heard their t., Lam 3.61
"I have heard the t. of Moab and Zep 2.08

TAVERNS
of Appius and Three T. to meet us. Ac 28.15

TAWNY
"Tell of it, you who ride on t. asses, Ju 5.10

TAX
Jerusalem the t. levied by Moses, 2Ch 24.06
the LORD the t. that Moses the 24.09
brought their t. and dropped it 24.10
for the king's t. upon our fields Neh 5.04
Do not even the t. collectors do Mt 5.46
Matthew sitting at the t. office; 9.09
many t. collectors and sinners came 9.10
eat with t. collectors and sinners?" 9.11
and Matthew the t. collector; 10.03
a friend of t. collectors and 11.19
the half-shekel t. went up to 17.24
"Does not your teacher pay the t.?" 17.24
as a Gentile and a t. collector. 18.17
the t. collectors and the harlots 21.31
but the t. collectors and the 21.32
Show me the money for the t." 22.19
Alphaeus sitting at the t. office, Mk 2.14
many t. collectors and sinners were 2.15
with sinners and t. collectors, 2.16
he eat with t. collectors and 2.16
T. collectors also came to be Lk 3.12
and saw a t. collector, named Levi, 5.27
Levi, sitting at the t. office; 5.27
company of t. collectors and 5.29
and drink with t. collectors and 5.30
people and the t. collectors 7.29
a friend of t. collectors and 7.34
Now the t. collectors and sinners 15.01
and the other a t. collector. 18.10
or even like this t. collector. 18.11
But the t. collector, standing far 18.13
he was a chief t. collector, 19.02

TAXED
but he t. the land to give the 2Ki 23.35

TAXES
a remission of t. to the provinces, Est 2.18
Is it lawful to pay t. to Caesar, Mt 22.17
Is it lawful to pay t. to Caesar, Mk 12.14
For the same reason you also pay t., Rom 13.06
t. to whom t. are due, revenue to 13.07

TEACH
your mouth and t. you what you Ex 4.12
and will t. you what you shall do. 4.15
and you shall t. them the statutes 18.20
And he has inspired him to t., 35.34
and you are to t. the people of Lev 10.11
and the ordinances which I t. you, Deu 4.01
that they may t. their children so 4.10
at that time to t. you statutes 4.14
ordinances which you shall t. them, 5.31
your God commanded me to t. you, 6.01

TEACH (cont.)

and you shall t. them diligently to Deu 6.07
And you shall t. them to your 11.19
that they may not t. you to do 20.18
and t. it to the people of Israel; 31.19
They shall t. Jacob thy ordinances, 33.10
that he might t. war to such at Ju 3.02
and t. us what we are to do with 13.08
when thou dost t. them the good 1Ki 8.36
and t. them the law of the god of 2Ki 17.27
when thou dost t. them the good 2Ch 6.27
to t. in the cities of Judah; 17.07
and to t. his statutes and ordinances Ez 7.10
who do not know them, you shall t. 7.25
"T. me, and I will be silent; Job 6.24
Will they not t. you, and tell you, 8.10
the beasts, and they will t. you; 12.07
of the earth, and they will t. you; 12.08
Will any t. God knowledge, seeing 21.22
I will t. you concerning the hand 27.11
speak, and many years t. wisdom.' 32.07
silent, and I will t. you wisdom." 33.33
t. me what I do not see; 34.32
T. us what we shall say to him; 37.19
O LORD; t. me thy paths. Ps 25.04
and t. me, for thou art the God of 25.05
T. me thy way, O LORD; and lead me 27.11
instruct you and t. you the way you 32.08
I will t. you the fear of the LORD. 34.11
your right hand t. you dread deeds 45.04
therefore t. me wisdom in my secret 51.06
Then I will t. transgressors thy 51.13
our fathers to t. to their children. 78.05
T. me thy way, O LORD, that I may 86.11
So t. us to number our days that we 90.12
whom thou dost t. out of thy law 94.12
and to t. his elders wisdom. 105.22
O LORD; t. me thy statutes! 119.12
answer me; t. me thy statutes! 119.26
and graciously t. me thy law! 119.29
T. me, O LORD, the way of thy statutes; 119.33
steadfast love; t. me thy statutes! 119.64
T. me good judgment and knowledge, 119.66
doest good; t. me thy statutes. 119.68
and t. me thy ordinances. 119.108
steadfast love, and t. me thy statutes. 119.124
thy servant and t. me thy statutes. 119.135
that thou dost t. me thy statutes. 119.171
testimonies which I shall t. them, 132.12
T. me the way I should go, for to 143.08
T. me to do thy will, for thou art 143.10
t. a righteous man and he will Pro 9.09
that he may t. us his ways and that Is 2.03
"Whom will he t. knowledge, and to 28.09
t. to your daughters a lament, and Jer 9.20
shall each man t. his neighbor and 31.34
They shall t. my people the difference Eze 44.23
and to t. them the letters and Dan 1.04
its priests t. for hire, its prophets Mic 3.11
that he may t. us his ways and we 4.02
from there to t. and preach in Mt 11.01
and t. the way of God truthfully, 22.16
Again he began to t. beside the sea. Mk 4.01
he began to t. in the synagogue; 6.02
and he began to t. them many things. 6.34
And he began to t. them that the 8.31
men, but truly t. the way of God. 12.14
t. us to pray, as John taught his Lk 11.01
Spirit will t. you in that very 12.12
know that you speak and t. rightly, 20.21
but truly t. the way of God. 20.21
among the Greeks and t. the Greeks? Jn 7.35
in utter sin, and would you t. us?" 9.34
he will t. you all things, and bring 14.26
all that Jesus began to do and t., Ac 1.01
not to speak or t. at all in the 4.18
charged you not to t. in this name, 5.28
you that you t. all the Jews who 21.21
you then who t. others, will you not Rom 2.21
others, will you not t. yourself? 2.21
as I t. them everywhere in every 1Co 4.17
nature itself t. you that for a 11.14
as you t. and admonish one another Col 3.16
persons not to t. any different 1Ti 1.03
no woman to t. or to have authority 2.12
Command and t. these things. 4.11
and beloved. T. and urge these duties. 6.02
who will be able to t. others also. 2Ti 2.02
gain what they have no right to t. Tit 1.11
t. what befits sound doctrine. 2.01
they are to t. what is good, 2.03
some one to t. you again the first Heb 5.12
And they shall not t. every one his 8.11
that we who t. shall be judged Jas 3.01
no need that any one should t. you; 1Jn 2.27

TEACHER

and great, t. and pupil alike. 1Ch 25.08
his power; who is a t. like him? Job 36.22
yet your T. will not hide himself Is 30.20
but your eyes shall see your T. 30.20
it, a metal image, a t. of lies? Hab 2.18
"T., I will follow you wherever you Mt 8.19
"Why does your t. eat with tax 9.11
"A disciple is not above his t., 10.24
for the disciple to be like his t., 10.25
"T., we wish to see a sign from you." 12.38
said, "Does not your t. pay the tax?" 17.24
"T., what good deed must I do, to 19.16
"T., we know that you are true, and 22.16
saying, "T., Moses said, 'If a man 22.24
"T., which is the great commandment 22.36
called rabbi, for you have one t., 23.08
'The T. says, My time is at hand; 26.18
"T., do you not care if we perish?" Mk 4.38
Why trouble the T. any further?" 5.35
"T., I brought my son to you, for he 9.17
"T., we saw a man casting out 9.38
"Good T., what must I do to inherit 10.17
"T., all these I have observed from 10.20
"T., we want you to do for us 10.35
"T., we know that you are true, and 12.14
"T., Moses wrote for us that if a 12.19
said to him, "You are right, T.; 12.32
T., what wonderful stones and what 13.01
'The T. says, Where is my guest room, 14.14
"T., what shall we do?" Lk 3.12
A disciple is not above his t., 6.40
fully taught will be like his t. 6.40
And he answered, "What is it, T.?" 7.40
do not trouble the T. any more." 8.49
"T., I beg you to look upon my son, 9.38
"T., what shall I do to inherit 10.25
"T., in saying this you reproach us 11.45
"T., bid my brother divide the 12.13
"Good T., what shall I do to 18.18
"T., rebuke your disciples." 19.39
"T., we know that you speak and 20.21
"T., Moses wrote for us that if a 20.28
"T., you have spoken well." 20.39
"T., when will this be, and what 21.07
'The T. says to you, Where is the 22.11
said to him, "Rabbi (which means T.), Jn 1.38
that you are a t. come from God; 3.02
"Are you a t. of Israel, and yet you 3.10
"T., this woman has been caught in * 8.04
"The T. is here and is calling for 11.28
You call me T. and Lord; and you are 13.13
your Lord and T., have washed your 13.14
"Rabboni!" (which means T.). 20.16
a t. of the law, held in honor by Ac 5.34
a t. of children, having in the law Rom 2.20
a t. of the Gentiles in faith and 1Ti 2.07
dignified, hospitable, an apt t., 3.02

TEACHER (cont.)
a preacher and apostle and t., 2Ti 1.11
every one, an apt t., forbearing, 2.24

TEACHERS
more understanding than all my t., Ps 119.99
the voice of my t. or incline my Pro 5.13
the temple, sitting among the t., Lk 2.46
Pharisees and t. of the law 5.17
Antioch there were prophets and t., Ac 13.01
third t., then workers of miracles, 1Co 12.28
Are all t.? Do all work 12.29
evangelists, some pastors and t., Eph 4.11
desiring to be t. of the law, 1Ti 1.07
for themselves t. to suit their 2Ti 4.03
by this time you ought to be t., Heb 5.12
Let not many of you become t., Jas 3.01
there will be false t. among you, 2Pe 2.01

TEACHES
For your iniquity t. your mouth, Job 15.05
who t. us more than the beasts of 35.11
and t. the humble his way. Ps 25.09
He who t. men knowledge, 94.10
the prophet who t. lies is the Is 9.15
aright; his God t. him. 28.26
who t. you to profit, who leads you 48.17
these commandments and t. men so, Mt 5.19
does them and t. them shall be 5.19
he who t., in his teaching; Rom 12.07
all good things with him who t. Gal 6.06
If any one t. otherwise and does 1Ti 6.03
his anointing t. you about everything, 1Jn 2.27

TEACHING
May my t. drop as the rain, my Deu 32.02
and without a t. priest, and without 2Ch 15.03
Give ear, O my people, to my t.; Ps 78.01
and reject not your mother's t.; Pro 1.08
My son, do not forget my t., 3.01
precepts: do not forsake my t. 4.02
and forsake not your mother's t. 6.20
is a lamp and the t. a light, 6.23
The t. of the wise is a fountain of 13.14
and the t. of kindness is on her 31.26
Give ear to the t. of our God, Is 1.10
seal the t. among my disciples. 8.16
To the t. and to the testimony! 8.20
t. in their synagogues and preaching Mt 4.23
crowds were astonished at his t., 7.28
t. in their synagogues and preaching 9.35
t. as doctrines the precepts of men.'" 15.09
but of the t. of the Pharisees and 16.12
people came up to him as he was t., 21.23
it, they were astonished at his t. 22.33
after day I sat in the temple t., 26.55
t. them to observe all that I have 28.20
And they were astonished at his t., Mk 1.22
A new t.! With authority 1.27
and in his t. he said to them: 4.02
went about among the villages t. 6.06
t. as doctrines the precepts of men.' 7.07
for he was t. his disciples, saying 9.31
multitude was astonished at his t. 11.18
And in his t. he said, "Beware of 12.38
I was with you in the temple t., 14.49
And he was t. them on the sabbath; Lk 4.31
and they were astonished at his t., 4.32
as he was t., there were Pharisees 5.17
Lord's feet and listened to his t. 10.39
Now he was t. in one of the synagogues 13.10
t., and journeying toward Jerusalem 13.22
And he was t. daily in the temple. 19.47
as he was t. the people in the 20.01
And every day he was t. in the temple, 21.37
t. throughout all Judea, from 23.05
"My t. is not mine, but his who sent Jn 7.16
whether the t. is from God or 7.17
about his disciples and his t. 18.19
to the apostles' t. and fellowship, Ac 2.42
they were t. the people and 4.02
in the temple and t. the people. 5.25
with your t. and you intend to 5.28
did not cease t. and preaching 5.42
astonished at the t. of the Lord. 13.12
Judea and were t. the brethren, 15.01
t. and preaching the word of the 15.35
what this new t. is which you 17.19
t. the word of God among them. 18.11
and t. you in public and from house 20.20
the man who is t. men everywhere 21.28
of God and t. about the Lord Jesus 28.31
the standard of t. to which you Rom 6.17
he who teaches, in his t.; 12.07
or knowledge or prophecy or t.? 1Co 14.06
every man and t. every man in all Col 1.28
of scripture, to preaching, to t. 1Ti 4.13
Take heed to yourself and to your t.; 4.16
who labor in preaching and t.; 5.17
of God and the t. may not be 6.01
Christ and the t. which accords 6.03
Now you have observed my t., 2Ti 3.10
by God and profitable for t., 3.16
be unfailing in patience and in t. 4.02
people will not endure sound t., 4.03
families by t. for base gain what Tit 1.11
and in your t. show integrity, 2.07
there who hold the t. of Balaam, Rev 2.14
who hold the t. of the Nicolaitans 2.15
prophetess and is t. and beguiling 2.20
Thyatira, who do not hold this t., 2.24

TEACHINGS
keep my t. as the apple of your eye Pro 7.02
led away by diverse and strange t.; Heb 13.09

TEAM
in pieces the farmer and his t.; Jer 51.23

TEAR
You shall t. down their altars, and Ex 34.13
he shall t. it by its wings, but Lev 1.17
he shall t. the spot out of the 13.56
you shall t. down their altars, and Deu 12.03
I will surely t. the kingdom from 1Ki 11.11
but I will t. it out of the hand of 11.12
However I will not t. away all the 11.13
I am about to t. the kingdom from 11.31
You who t. yourself in your anger, Job 18.04
They are like a lion eager to t., Ps 17.12
will snatch and t. you from your 52.05
t. out the fangs of the young lions, 58.06
the dogs to t., and the birds of Jer 15.03
right hand, yet I would t. you off 22.24
them up, and not t. them down; 24.06
and I will t. them from your arms; Eze 13.20
Your veils also I will t. off, 13.21
out your hair, and t. your breasts; 23.34
I will t. open their breast, and Hos 13.08
who t. the skin from off my people, Mic 3.02
but I will t. down, till they are Mal 1.04
garment, and a worse t. is made. Mt 9.16
the old, and a worse t. is made. Mk 2.21
he will t. the new, and the piece Lk 5.36
"Let us not t. it, but cast lots for Jn 19.24
wipe away every t. from their eyes Rev 7.17
wipe away every t. from their eyes, 21.04

TEARING
like a roaring lion t. the prey; Eze 22.25
of her are like wolves t. the prey, 22.27
fat ones, t. off even their hoofs. Zec 11.16
building up and not for t. down. 2Co 13.10

TEARS
he t. the arm, and the crown of the Deu 33.20
the lion asunder as one t. a kid; Ju 14.06
your prayer, I have seen your t.; 2Ki 20.05
him with t. to avert the evil Est 8.03
If he t. down, none can rebuild; Job 12.14
my eye pours out t. to God, 16.20
every night I flood my bed with t.; Ps 6.06
hold not thy peace at my t.! 39.12
My t. have been my food day and 42.03
put thou my t. in thy bottle! 56.08
hast fed them with the bread of t., 80.05
and given them t. to drink in full 80.05
and mingle t. with my drink, 102.09
my eyes from t., my feet from 116.08
My eyes shed streams of t., 119.136
who sow in t. reap with shouts of 126.05
with her own hands t. it down. Pro 14.01
The LORD t. down the house of the 15.25
the t. of the oppressed, and they Ecc 4.01
every one wails and melts in t. Is 15.03
I drench you with my t., 16.09
from me, let we weep bitter t.; 22.04
will wipe away t. from all faces, 25.08
your prayer, I have seen your t.; 38.05
and my eyes a fountain of t., Jer 9.01
that our eyes may run down with t., 9.18
weep bitterly and run down with t., 13.17
run down with t. night and day, 14.17
weeping, and your eyes from t.; 31.16
in the night, t. on her cheeks; Lam 1.02
my eyes flow with t.; for a 1.16
Let t. stream down like a torrent 2.18
with rivers of t. because of the 3.48
or weep nor shall your t. run down. Eze 24.16
treads down and t. in pieces, Mic 5.08
You cover the LORD's altar with t., Mal 2.13
for the patch t. away from the Mt 9.16
the patch t. away from it, the new Mk 2.21
"No one t. a piece from a new Lk 5.36
began to wet his feet with her t., 7.38
feet with her t. and wiped them 7.44
and with t. and with trials which Ac 20.19
day to admonish every one with t. 20.31
anguish of heart and with many t., 2Co 2.04
you and now tell you even with t., Php 3.18
As I remember your t., I long 2Ti 1.04
supplications, with loud cries and t., Heb 5.07
though he sought it with t. 12.17

TEBAH
bore T., Gaham, Tahash, and Maacah. Gen 22.24

TEBALIAH
T. the third, Zechariah the fourth: 1Ch 26.11

TEBETH
month, which is the month of T., Est 2.16

TEEMS
anything with which the ground t., Lev 20.25
which t. with things innumerable, Ps 104.25

TEETH
with wine, and his t. white with milk. Gen 49.12
While the meat was yet between their t., Num 11.33
I will send the t. of beasts against Deu 32.24
the t. of the young lions, are Job 4.10
I will take my flesh in my t., 13.14
hates me; he has gnashed his t. at me; 16.09
have escaped by the skin of my t. 19.20
made him drop his prey from his t. 29.17
Round about his t. is terror. 41.14
dost break the t. of the wicked. Ps 3.07
more, gnashing at me with their t. 35.16
righteous, and gnashes his t. at him; 37.12
their t. are spears and arrows, 57.04
break the t. in their mouths; 58.06
he gnashes his t. and melts away; 112.10
not given us as prey to their t.! 124.06
Like vinegar to the t., and smoke Pro 10.26
There are those whose t. are swords, 30.14
whose t. are knives, to devour the 30.14
Your t. are like a flock of shorn Sol 4.02
Your t. are like a flock of ewes, 6.06
smoothly, gliding over lips and t. 7.09
sledge, new, sharp, and having t.; Is 41.15
the children's t. are set on edge.' Jer 31.29
his t. shall be set on edge. 31.30
they hiss, they gnash their t., Lam 2.16
He has made my t. grind on gravel, 3.16
the children's t. are set on edge'? Eze 18.02
ribs in its mouth between its t.; Dan 7.05
and it had great iron t.; 7.07
with its t. of iron and claws of 7.19
its t. are lions' t., and it has the Joe 1.06
cleanness of t. in all your cities, Amo 4.06
abominations from between its t.; Zec 9.07
men will weep and gnash their t." Mt 8.12
men will weep and gnash their t. 13.42
men will weep and gnash their t. 13.50
men will weep and gnash their t.' 22.13
men will weep and gnash their t. 24.51
men will weep and gnash their t.' 25.30
and grinds his t. and becomes Mk 9.18
There you will weep and gnash your t., Lk 13.28
they ground their t. against him. Ac 7.54
hair, and their t. like lions' t.; Rev 9.08

TEHAPHNEHES
At T. the day shall be dark, when I Eze 30.18

TEHINNAH
Paseah, and T. the father of Irnahash. 1Ch 4.12

TEKEL
inscribed: MENE, MENE, T., and PARSIN. Dan 5.25
T., you have been weighed in the 5.27

TEKOA
And Joab sent to T., and fetched 2Sa 14.02
When the woman of T. came to the 14.04
And the woman of T. said to the 14.09
Ira the son of Ikkesh of T., 23.26
bore him Ashhur, the father of T. 1Ch 2.24
the father of T., had two wives, 4.05
Ira the son of Ikkesh of T., 11.28
He built Bethlehem, Etam, T., 2Ch 11.06
went out into the wilderness of T.; 20.20
Blow the trumpet in T., and raise Jer 6.01
who was among the shepherds of T., Amo 1.01

TEKOITE
was Ira, the son of Ikkesh the T.; 1Ch 27.09

TEKOITES
And next to them the T. repaired; Neh 3.05
After him the T. repaired another 3.27

TELABIB
and I came to the exiles at T., who Eze 3.15

TELAH
his son, T. his son, Tahan his son, 1Ch 7.25

TELAIM
the people, and numbered them in T., 1Sa 15.04

TELASSAR
the people of Eden who were in T.? 2Ki 19.12
the people of Eden who were in T.? Is 37.12

TELEM
Ziph, T., Bealoth, Jos 15.24
gatekeepers: Shallum, T., and Uri. Ez 10.24

TELHARSHA

T., Cherub, Addan, and Immer, though Ez 2.59
T., Cherub, Addon, and Immer, but they Neh 7.61

TELL

Why did you not t. me that she was Gen 12.18
you did not t. me, and I have not 21.26
mountains of which I shall t. you." 22.02
and said, "T. me whose daughter you 24.23
and truly with my master, t. me; 24.49
and if not, t. me; that I may 24.49
the land of which I shall t. you. 26.02
T. me, what shall your wages be?" 29.15
that he did not t. him that he 31.20
and did not t. me, so that I might 31.27
and I have sent to t. my lord, 32.05
"T. me, I pray, your name." 32.29
"t. me, I pray you, where they are 37.16
T. them to me, I pray you." 40.08
"Did I not t. you not to sin 42.22
me so ill as to t. the man that 43.06
You must t. my father of all my 45.13
"I will go up and t. Pharaoh, 46.31
that I may t. you what shall befall 49.01
"Go in, t. Pharaoh king of Egypt to Ex 6.11
t. Pharaoh king of Egypt all that I 6.29
brother shall t. Pharaoh to let 7.02
and that you may t. in the hearing 10.02
T. all the congregation of Israel 12.03
And you shall t. your son on that 13.08
"T. the people of Israel to turn 14.02
T. the people of Israel to go 14.15
and t. the people of Israel: 19.03
house shall come and t. the priest, Lev 14.35
T. Aaron your brother not to come 16.02
"T. Aaron and his sons to keep away 22.02
and they will t. the inhabitants of Num 14.14
"T. Eleazar the son of Aaron the 16.37
T. the people of Israel to bring 19.02
and t. the rock before their eyes 20.08
whatever he shows me I will t. you." 23.03
"Did I not t. you, 'All that the 23.26
"Did I not t. your messengers whom 24.12
and I will t. you all the commandment Deu 5.31
our elders, and they will t. you. 32.07
If you do not t. this business of Jos 2.14
But if you t. this business of ours, 2.20
Then you shall t. them that the 4.07
commanded Joshua to t. the people, 4.10
and t. me now what you have done; 7.19
"T. of it, you who ride on tawny Ju 5.10
was, and he did not t. me his name; 13.06
But he did not t. his father or his 14.06
But he did not t. them that he had 14.09
if you can t. me what it is, within 14.12
but if you cannot t. me what it is, 14.13
in three days t. what the riddle 14.14
your husband to t. us what the 14.15
nor my mother, and shall I t. you?" 14.16
"Please t. me wherein your great 16.06
please t. me how you might be bound." 16.10
t. me how you might be bound." 16.13
"T. us, how was this wickedness 20.03
and he will t. you what to do." Ru 3.04
So I thought I would t. you of it, 4.04
t. me, that I may know, for there is 4.04
And I t. him that I am about to 1Sa 3.13
was afraid to t. the vision to Eli 3.15
T. us with what we shall send it to 6.02
perhaps he can t. us about the 9.06
the man of God, to t. us our way." 9.08
"T. me where is the house of the 9.18
and will t. you all that is 9.19
"T. the servant to pass on before 9.27
t. me what Samuel said to you." 10.15
spoken, he did not t. him anything. 10.16
But he did not t. his father. 14.01
"T. me what you have done." And 14.43
I will t. you what the LORD said to 15.16
soul lives, O king, I cannot t." 17.55
if I learn anything I will t. you." 19.03
come upon you, would I not t. you?" 20.09
"Who will t. me if your father 20.10
that he would surely t. Saul. 22.22
I beseech thee, t. thy servant." 23.11
young men, and they will t. you. 25.08
But she did not t. her husband 25.19
"Lest they should t. about us, 27.11
summoned you to t. me what I shall 28.15
to him, "How did it go? T. me." 2Sa 1.04
T. it not in Gath, publish it not in 1.20
Abner went to t. David at Hebron 3.19
"Go and t. my servant David, 'Thus 7.05
all that Joab had sent him to t. 11.22
David feared to t. him that the 12.18
after morning? Will you not t. me?" 13.04
t. it to Zadok and Abiathar the 15.35
therefore send quickly and t. David, 17.16
maidservant used to go and t. them, 17.17
they would go and t. King David; 17.17
t. the king what you have seen." 18.21
T. Joab, 'Come here, that I may speak 20.16
to t. them who shall sit on the 1Ki 1.20
he will t. you what shall happen to 14.03
Go, t. Jeroboam, 'Thus says the LORD, 14.07
Go, t. your lord, 'Behold, Elijah is 18.08
t. your lord, "Behold, Elijah is here 18.11
when I come and t. Ahab and he 18.12
t. your lord, "Behold, Elijah is here"'; 18.14
"T. my lord the king, 'All that you 20.09
"T. him, 'Let not him that girds on 20.11
"Did I not t. you that he would not 22.18
T. me; what have you in the 2Ki 4.02
the pace for me unless I t. you." 4.24
let us go and t. the king's household." 7.09
"I will t. you what the Syrians 7.12
"T. me all the great things that Elisha 8.04
said, "That is not true; t. us now." 9.12
city to go and t. the news in 9.15
'T. the man who sent you to me, 22.15
t. of all his wonderful works! 1Ch 16.09
T. of his salvation from day to day. 16.23
"Go and t. my servant David, 'Thus 17.04
"Did I not t. you that he would not 2Ch 18.17
'T. the man who sent you to me, 34.23
and thou didst t. them to go in to Neh 9.15
in the morning t. the king to have Est 5.14
and I alone have escaped to t. you." Job 1.15
and I alone have escaped to t. you." 1.16
and I alone have escaped to t. you." 1.17
and I alone have escaped to t. you." 1.19
and t. you, and utter words out of 8.10
and that he would t. you the 11.06
of the air, and they will t. you; 12.07
T. me, if you have understanding. 38.04
I will t. of the decree of the LORD: Ps 2.07
I will t. of all thy wonderful 9.01
T. among the peoples his deeds! 9.11
I will t. of thy name to my brethren; 22.22
men shall t. of the LORD to the 22.30
Will it t. of thy faithfulness? 30.09
Then my tongue shall t. of thy 35.28
were I to proclaim and t. of them, 40.05
that you may t. the next generation 48.13
"If I were hungry, I would not t. you; 50.12
they will t. what God has wrought, 64.09
and I will t. what he has done for 66.16
My mouth will t. of thy righteous 71.15
that I may t. of all thy works. 73.28
but t. to the coming generation the 78.04
and arise and t. them to their 78.06
t. of his salvation from day to day. 96.02
t. of all his wonderful works! 105.02
and t. of his deeds in songs of joy! 107.22

TELL (cont.)

I t. my trouble before him. Ps 142.02
thy kingdom, and t. of thy power, 145.11
For who can t. man what will be Ecc 6.12
for who can t. him how it will be? 8.07
and who can t. him what will be 10.14
some winged creature t. the matter. 10.20
T. me, you whom my soul loves, where Sol 1.07
that you t. him I am sick with love 5.08
T. the righteous that it shall be Is 3.10
And now I will t. you what I will 5.05
Let them t. you and make known what 19.12
and t. us what is to happen. 41.22
T. us the former things, what they 41.22
T. us what is to come hereafter, 41.23
they spring forth I t. you of them." 42.09
Let them t. us what is yet to be. 44.07
I will t. of your righteousness and 57.12
"And when you t. this people all Jer 16.10
there the words that I t. you. 19.02
dreams which they t. one another, 23.27
who has a dream t. the dream, 23.28
and who t. them and lead my people 23.32
"Go, t. Hananiah, 'Thus says the LORD: 28.13
and will t. you great and hidden 33.03
"T. us, how did you write all these 36.17
"If I t. you, will you not be sure 38.15
'T. us what you said to the king 38.25
the LORD answers you I will t. you; 42.04
anything that he sent me to t. you. 42.21
T. it by the Arnon, that Moab is 48.20
to t. the king of Babylon that his 51.31
T. them therefore, 'Thus says the Eze 12.23
T. them, Behold, the king of Babylon 17.12
"Will you not t. us what these 24.19
that I shall t. you concerning all 44.05
to t. the king his dreams. So they Dan 2.02
T. your servants the dream, and we 2.04
"Let the king t. his servants the 2.07
Therefore t. me the dream, and I 2.09
now we will t. the king its interpretation. 2.36
which I saw; t. me its interpretation. 4.09
and I have come to t. it to you, 9.23
But I will t. you what is inscribed 10.21
T. your children of it, and let your Joe 1.03
your children t. their children, 1.03
"T. us, on whose account this evil Jon 1.08
to it the message that I t. you." 3.02
T. it not in Gath, weep not at all; Mic 1.10
the dreamers t. false dreams, and Zec 10.02
and remain there till I t. you; Mt 2.13
for I t. you, God is able from these 3.09
For I t. you, unless your righteousness 5.20
"Therefore I t. you, do not be 6.25
yet I t. you, even Solomon in all 6.29
I t. you, many will come from east 8.11
What I t. you in the dark, utter in 10.27
"Go and t. John what you hear and 11.04
Yes, I t. you, and more than a 11.09
But I t. you, it shall be more 11.22
But I t. you that it shall be more 11.24
I t. you, something greater than the 12.06
Therefore I t. you, every sin and 12.31
I t. you, on the day of judgment men 12.36
harvest time I will t. the reapers, 13.30
that he did not t. them to beware 16.12
And I t. you, you are Peter, and on 16.18
disciples to t. no one that he was 16.20
"T. no one the vision, until the Son 17.09
but I t. you that Elijah has 17.12
for I t. you that in heaven their 18.10
go and t. him his fault, between you 18.15
listen to them; t. it to the church; 18.17
Again I t. you, it is easier for a 19.24
"T. the daughter of Zion, Behold, 21.05
and if you t. me the answer, then I 21.24
I also will t. you by what authority 21.24
"Neither will I t. you by what 21.27
Therefore I t. you, the kingdom of 21.43
'T. those who are invited, Behold, I 22.04
T. us, then, what you think. Is it 22.17
and observe whatever they t. you, 23.03
For I t. you, you will not see me 23.39
"T. us, when will this be, and what 24.03
I t. you I shall not drink again of 26.29
t. us if you are the Christ, the Son 26.63
But I t. you, hereafter you will see 26.64
and t. the people, 'He has risen 27.64
Then go quickly and t. his disciples 28.07
joy, and ran to t. his disciples. 28.08
go and t. my brethren to go to 28.10
and said, "T. people, 'His disciples 28.13
and t. them how much the Lord has Mk 5.19
And he charged them to t. no one; 7.36
charged them to t. no one about 8.30
charged them to t. no one what 9.09
But I you that Elijah has come, 9.13
he began to t. them what was to 10.32
Therefore I t. you, whatever you ask 11.24
and I will t. you by what authority 11.29
"Neither will I t. you by what 11.33
"T. us, when will this be, and what 13.04
But go, t. his disciples and Peter 16.07
for I t. you, God is able from these Lk 3.08
I t. you, there were many widows in 4.25
And he charged him to t. no one; 5.14
Lord,' and not do what I t. you? 6.46
"I t. you, not even in Israel have I 7.09
"Go and t. John what you have seen 7.22
Yes, I t. you, and more than a 7.26
I t. you, among those born of women 7.28
Therefore I t. you, her sins, which 7.47
charged them to t. no one what had 8.56
commanded them to t. this to no one, 9.21
But I t. you truly, there are some 9.27
I t. you, it shall be more tolerable 10.12
For I t. you that many prophets and 10.24
serve alone? T. her then to help me." 10.40
I t. you, though he will not get up 11.08
And I t. you, Ask, and it will be 11.09
Yes, I t. you, it shall be required 11.51
"I t. you, my friends, do not fear 12.04
into hell; yes, I t. you, fear him! 12.05
"And I t. you, every one who acknowledges 12.08
"Therefore I t. you, do not be anxious 12.22
yet I t. you, even Solomon in all 12.27
Truly I t. you, he will set him over 12.44
No, I t. you, but rather division; 12.51
I t. you, you will never get out 12.59
I t. you, No; but unless you repent 13.03
I t. you, No; but unless you repent 13.05
for many, I t. you, will seek to 13.24
'I t. you, I do not know where you 13.27
"Go and t. that fox, 'Behold, I cast 13.32
And I t. you, you will not see me 13.35
For I t. you, none of those men who 14.24
Even so, I t. you, there will be more 15.07
Even so, I t. you, there is joy 15.10
And I t. you, make friends for 16.09
I t. you, in that night there will 17.34
I t. you, he will vindicate them 18.08
I t. you, this man went down to his 18.14
he proceeded to t. a parable, 19.11
'I t. you, that to every one who has 19.26
"I t. you, if these were silent, the 19.40
"T. us by what authority you do 20.02
will ask you a question; now t. me, 20.03
"Neither will I t. you by what 20.08
And he began to t. the people this 20.09
"Truly I t. you, this poor widow has 21.03
and t. the householder, 'The Teacher 22.11
for I t. you I shall not eat it 22.16
for I t. you that from now on I 22.18
He said, "I t. you, Peter, the cock 22.34

TELL (cont.)
For I t. you that this scripture Lk 22.37
"If you are the Christ, t. us." 22.67
"If I t. you, you will not believe; 22.67
believe if I t. you heavenly Jn 3.12
I t. you, lift up your eyes, and see 4.35
But, because I t. the truth, you do 8.45
If I t. the truth, why do you not 8.46
you are the Christ, t. us plainly." 10.24
"Did I not t. you that if you would 11.40
I t. you this now, before it takes 13.19
"T. us who it is of whom he speaks." 13.24
Nevertheless I t. you the truth: it 16.07
in figures but t. you plainly of 16.25
t. me where you have laid him, and I 20.15
"T. me whether you sold the land Ac 5.08
So in the present case I t. you, 5.38
And he said, "T. this to James and 12.17
themselves will t. you the same 15.27
Do therefore what we t. you. We 21.23
"T. me, are you a Roman citizen?" 22.27
for he has something to t. him." 23.17
"What is it that you have to t. me?" 23.19
"T. no one that you have informed 23.22
For I t. you that Christ became a Rom 15.08
I t. you this, brethren: flesh and 1Co 15.50
I t. you a mystery. We shall not all 15.51
T. me, you who desire to be under Gal 4.21
in the Lord will t. you everything. Eph 6.21
which I shall choose I cannot t. Php 1.22
you and now t. you even with tears, 3.18
Tychicus will t. you all about my Col 4.07
They will t. you of everything that 4.09
time would fail me to t. of Gideon, Heb 11.32
I will t. you the mystery of the Rev 17.07

TELLING
a man was t. a dream to his comrade; Ju 7.13
heard the t. of the dream and its 7.15
have finished t. all the news 2Sa 11.19
t. them, "Go, inquire of Baalzebub, 2Ki 1.02
And while he was t. the king how 8.05
t. them what to say to Iddo and his Ez 8.17
behavior will be t. it to all the Est 1.18
The heavens are t. the glory of God Ps 19.01
and t. all thy wondrous deeds. 26.07
said to Jeremiah, "You are t. a lie. Jer 43.02
t. them to be silent; but they cried Mt 20.31
t. him to be silent; but he cried out Mk 10.48
are you t. this parable for us or Lk 12.41
rebuked him, t. him to be silent; 18.39
Jesus was t. him, "Buy what we need Jn 13.29
we hear them t. in our own tongues Ac 2.11
nothing except t. or hearing 17.21
t. the people to believe in the one 19.04
t. them not to circumcise their 21.21
your enemy by t. you the truth? Gal 4.16
and apostle (I am t. the truth, 1Ti 2.07
from the temple t. the seven Rev 16.01

TELLS
do as she t. you, for through Isaac Gen 21.12
wonder which he t. you comes to Deu 13.02
t. the king of Israel the words 2Ki 6.12
when he t. you, "The LORD our God 2Ch 32.11
when he goes out, he t. it abroad. Ps 41.06
but deal with him as he t. you." Jer 39.12
'If any one t. his father or his Mt 15.05
'If a man t. his father or his Mk 7.11
servants, "Do whatever he t. you." Jn 2.05
and he knows that he t. the truth— 19.35
to him in whatever he t. you. Ac 3.22

TELMELAH
those who came up from T., Telharsha, Ez 2.59
those who came up from T., Telharsha, Neh 7.61

TEMA
Hadad, T., Jetur, Naphish, and Kedemah Gen 25.15
Mishma, Dumah, Massa, Hadad, T., 1Ch 1.30
The caravans of T. look, the travelers Job 6.19
O inhabitants of the land of T. Is 21.14
Dedan, T., Buz, and all who cut the Jer 25.23

TEMAH
the sons of Sisera, the sons of T., Ez 2.53
the sons of Sisera, the sons of T., Neh 7.55

TEMAN
The sons of Eliphaz were T., Omar, Gen 36.11
the chiefs T., Omar, Zepho, Kenaz, 36.15
Kenaz, T., Mibzar, 36.42
T., Omar, Zephi, Gatam, Kenaz, Timna, 1Ch 1.36
Kenaz, T., Mibzar, 1.53
of hosts: "Is wisdom no more in T.? Jer 49.07
against the inhabitants of T.: 49.20
from T. even to Dedan they shall Eze 25.13
So I will send a fire upon T., Amo 1.12
O T., so that every man from Mount Ob 1.09
God came from T., and the Holy One Hab 3.03

TEMANITE
Eliphaz the T., Bildad the Shuhite, Job 2.11
Then Eliphaz the T. answered: 4.01
Then Eliphaz the T. answered: 15.01
Then Eliphaz the T. answered: 22.01
the LORD said to Eliphaz the T.: 42.07
So Eliphaz the T. and Bildad the 42.09

TEMANITES
the land of the T. reigned in his Gen 36.34
the land of the T. reigned in his 1Ch 1.45

TEMENI
Ahuzzam, Hepher, T., and Haahashtari. 1Ch 4.06

TEMPER
A man of quick t. acts foolishly, Pro 14.17
he who has a hasty t. exalts folly. 14.29

TEMPERATE
t., sensible, dignified, hospitable, 1Ti 3.02
but t., faithful in all things. 3.11
Bid the older men be t., serious, Tit 2.02

TEMPEST
For he crushes me with a t., and Job 9.17
fire, round about him a mighty t. Ps 50.03
from the raging wind and t. 55.08
them with thy t. and terrify them 83.15
When the t. passes, the wicked is no Pro 10.25
a destroying t., like a storm of Is 28.02
great noise, with whirlwind and t., 29.06
a cloudburst and t. and hailstones. 30.30
the wind, a covert from the t., 32.02
and the t. carries them off like 40.24
and the t. shall scatter them. 41.16
roar of a great t. he will set Jer 11.16
has gone forth, a whirling t.; 23.19
and a great t. is stirring from the 25.32
has gone forth, a whirling t.; 30.23
with a t. in the day of the whirlwind Amo 1.14
there was a mighty t. on the sea, Jon 1.04
that this great t. has come upon 1.12
and no small t. lay on us, all hope Ac 27.20
and darkness and gloom, and a t., Heb 12.18

TEMPESTUOUS
For the sea grew more and more t. Jon 1.11
grew more and more t. against them. 1.13
But soon a t. wind, called the Ac 27.14

TEMPLE
him and drove the peg into his t., Ju 4.21
dead, with the tent peg in his t. 4.22

TEMPLE (cont.)
she shattered and pierced his t. Ju 5.26
the doorpost of the t. of the LORD. 1Sa 1.09
down within the t. of the LORD, 3.03
his armor in the t. of Ashtaroth; 31.10
From his t. he heard my voice, and 2Sa 22.07
tool of iron was heard in the t., 1Ki 6.07
pillars at the vestibule of the t.; 7.21
the doors of the nave of the t. 7.50
the doors of the t. of the LORD, 2Ki 18.16
out of the t. of the LORD all the 23.04
of gold in the t. of the LORD, 24.13
of bronze used in the t. service, 25.14
the Levites, and the t. servants. 1Ch 9.02
chambers of the t. free from other 9.33
his armor in the t. of their gods, 10.10
his head in the t. of Dagon. 10.10
plan of the vestibule of the t., 28.11
to build a t. for the name of the 2Ch 2.01
who will build a t. for the LORD, 2.12
up the pillars in front of the t., 3.17
prescribed, and set them in the t., 4.07
tables, and placed them in the t., 4.08
and the sockets of the t., 4.22
of the nave of the t. were of gold. 4.22
glory of the LORD filled the t. 7.01
the glory of the LORD upon the t., 7.03
and entered the t. of the LORD to 26.16
did not invade the t. of the LORD. 27.02
found in the t. of the LORD into 29.16
when Josiah had prepared the t., 35.20
The t. servants: the sons of Ziha, Ez 2.43
All the t. servants and the sons of 2.58
and the t. servants lived in their 2.70
foundation of the t. of the LORD 3.06
foundation of the t. of the LORD, 3.10
were building a t. to the LORD, 4.01
out of the t. that was in Jerusalem 5.14
and brought into the t. of Babylon, 5.14
king took out of the t. of Babylon, 5.14
put them in the t. which is in 5.15
took out of the t. that is in 6.05
back to the t. which is in Jerusalem, 6.05
gatekeepers, and the t. servants. 7.07
the t. servants, or other servants 7.24
brethren the t. servants at the 8.17
and twenty of the t. servants, 8.20
gates of the fortress of the t., Neh 2.08
and the t. servants living on Ophel 3.26
house of the t. servants and of 3.31
within the t., and let us close the 6.10
let us close the doors of the t.; 6.10
as I could go into the t. and live? 6.11
The t. servants: the sons of Ziha, 7.46
All the t. servants and the sons of 7.60
the t. servants, and all Israel, 7.73
the t. servants, and all who have 10.28
the t. servants, and the descendants 11.03
But the t. servants lived on Ophel; 11.21
Gishpa were over the t. servants. 11.21
toward thy holy t. in the fear of Ps 5.07
The LORD is in his holy t., the 11.04
From his t. he heard my voice, and 18.06
the LORD, and to inquire in his t. 27.04
and in his t. all cry, "Glory!" 29.09
O God, in the midst of thy t. 48.09
goodness of thy house, thy holy t.! 65.04
Because of thy t. at Jerusalem 68.29
they have defiled thy holy t.; 79.01
toward thy holy t. and give thanks 138.02
and his train filled the t. Is 6.01
and of the t., 'Your foundation shall 44.28
A voice from the t.! The voice of 66.06
'This is the t. of the LORD, the Jer 7.04
the t. of the LORD, the t. of the LORD. 7.04
placed before the t. of the LORD. 24.01
entrance of the t. of the LORD. 38.14
to present at the t. of the LORD. 41.05
LORD our God, vengeance for his t. 50.28
the LORD, the vengeance for his t. 51.11
of bronze used in the t. service; 52.18
at the door of the t. of the LORD, Eze 8.16
their backs to the t. of the LORD, 8.16
around the outside of the t. area, 40.05
priests who have charge of the t., 40.45
the altar was in front of the t. 40.47
vestibule of the t. and measured 40.48
Then he measured the wall of the t., 41.05
four cubits, round about the t. 41.05
the wall of the t. to serve as 41.06
be supported by the wall of the t. 41.06
story to story round about the t.; 41.07
the side of the t. a stairway led 41.07
also that the t. had a raised 41.08
the platform of the t. and the 41.09
round about the t. on every side. 41.10
was facing the t. yard on the west 41.12
Then he measured the t., a hundred 41.13
east front of the t. and the yard, 41.14
The nave of the t. and the inner 41.15
threshold the t. was paneled with 41.16
carved on the whole t. round about; 41.19
opposite the t. yard and opposite 42.01
opposite the t. were a hundred 42.08
the interior of the t. area, 42.15
measured the t. area round about. 42.15
entered the t. by the gate facing 43.04
glory of the LORD filled the t. 43.05
one speaking to me out of the t.; 43.06
of Israel the t. and its appearance 43.10
portray the t., its arrangement, its 43.11
This is the law of the t.: 43.12
behold, this is the law of the t. 43.12
appointed place belonging to the t., 43.21
north gate to the front of the t.; 44.04
the LORD filled the t. of the LORD; 44.04
ordinances of the t. of the LORD 44.05
admitted to the t. and all those 44.05
oversight at the gates of the t., 44.11
the temple, and serving in the t.; 44.11
them to keep charge of the t., 44.14
the Levites who minister at the t., 45.05
put it on the doorposts of the t., 45.19
shall make atonement for the t. 45.20
minister at the t. shall boil the 46.24
me back to the door of the t.; 47.01
threshold of the t. toward the east 47.01
the east (for the t. faced east); 47.01
end of the threshold of the t., 47.01
sanctuary of the t. in its midst, 48.21
out of the t. in Jerusalem be Dan 5.02
which had been taken out of the t., 5.03
and profane the t. and fortress, 11.31
and it is a t. of the kingdom." Amo 7.13
The songs of the t. shall become 8.03
I again look upon thy holy t.?' Jon 2.04
came to thee, into thy holy t. 2.07
you, the Lord from his holy t. Mic 1.02
But the LORD is in his holy t.; Hab 2.20
upon a stone in the t. of the LORD, Hag 2.15
foundation of the LORD's t. was laid, 2.18
he shall build the t. of the LORD. Zec 6.12
who shall build the t. of the LORD, 6.13
shall be in the t. of the LORD as 6.14
help to build the t. of the LORD; 6.15
laid, that the t. might be built. 8.09
seek will suddenly come to his t.; Mal 3.01
set him on the pinnacle of the t., Mt 4.05
priests in the t. profane the 12.05
greater than the t. is here. 12.06
entered the t. of God and drove 21.12
all who sold and bought in the t., 21.12
and the lame came to him in the t., 21.14
the children crying out in the t., 21.15

TEMPLE (cont.)
And when he entered the t., Mt 21.23
swears by the t., it is nothing; 23.16
one swears by the gold of the t., 23.16
the gold or the t. that has made 23.17
and he who swears by the t., 23.21
Jesus left the t. and was going 24.01
out to him the buildings of the t. 24.01
after day I sat in the t. teaching, 26.55
I am able to destroy the t. of God, 26.61
of silver in the t., he departed; 27.05
destroy the t. and build it in 27.40
curtain of the t. was torn in two, 27.51
Jerusalem, and went into the t.; Mk 11.11
he entered the t. and began to 11.15
and those who bought in the t., 11.15
to carry anything through the t. 11.16
And as he was walking in the t., 11.27
And as Jesus taught in the t., 12.35
And as he came out of the t., 13.01
Mount of Olives opposite the t., 13.03
I was with you in the t. teaching, 14.49
destroy this t. that is made with 14.58
destroy the t. and build it in 15.29
curtain of the t. was torn in two, 15.38
to enter the t. of the Lord and Lk 1.09
wondered at his delay in the t. 1.21
he had seen a vision in the t.; 1.22
by the Spirit he came into the t.; 2.27
She did not depart from the t., 2.37
days they found him in the t., 2.46
set him on the pinnacle of the t., 4.09
"Two men went up into the t. to pray, 18.10
And he entered the t. and began to 19.45
And he was teaching daily in the t. 19.47
people in the t. and preaching the 20.01
And as some spoke of the t., 21.05
day he was teaching in the t., 21.37
came to him in the t. to hear him. 21.38
and captains of the t. and elders, 22.52
with you day after day in the t., 22.53
curtain of the t. was torn in two. 23.45
continually in the t. blessing God. 24.53
In the t. he found those who were Jn 2.14
the sheep and oxen, out of the t.; 2.15
"Destroy this t., and in three days 2.19
forty-six years to build this t., 2.20
But he spoke of the t. of his body. 2.21
Afterward, Jesus found him in the t., 5.14
went up into the t. and taught. 7.14
proclaimed, as he taught in the t., 7.28
morning he came again to the t.; *8.02
treasury, as he taught in the t.; 8.20
himself, and went out of the t. 8.59
and Jesus was walking in the t., 10.23
another as they stood in the t., 11.56
taught in synagogues and in the t., 18.20
attending the t. together and Ac 2.46
going up to the t. at the hour of 3.01
gate of the t. which is called 3.02
alms of those who entered the t. 3.02
and John about to go into the t., 3.03
and entered the t. with them, 3.08
at the Beautiful Gate of the t.; 3.10
captain of the t. and the Sadducees 4.01
stand in the t. and speak to the 5.20
entered the t. at daybreak and 5.21
captain of the t. and the chief 5.24
standing in the t. and teaching 5.25
day in the t. and at home they did 5.42
whose t. was in front of the city, 14.13
also that the t. of the great 19.27
Ephesians is t. keeper of the 19.35
with them and went into the t., 21.26
Asia, who had seen him in the t., 21.27
he also brought Greeks into the t., 21.28
Paul had brought him into the t. 21.29
Paul and dragged him out of the t., 21.30
Jerusalem and was praying in the t., 22.17
He even tried to profane the t., 24.06
either in the t. or in the synagogues, 24.12
they found me purified in the t., 24.18
of the Jews, nor against the t., 25.08
me in the t. and tried to kill me. 26.21
you are God's t. and that God's 1Co 3.16
If any one destroys God's t., 3.17
God's t. is holy, and that t. you are. 3.17
your body is a t. of the Holy 6.19
knowledge, at table in an idol's t., 8.10
employed in the t. service get 9.13
service get their food from the t., 9.13
agreement has the t. of God with 2Co 6.16
For we are the t. of the living God; 6.16
grows into a holy t. in the Lord; Eph 2.21
he takes his seat in the t. of God, 2Th 2.04
him a pillar in the t. of my God; Rev 3.12
him day and night within his t.; 7.15
and measure the t. of God and the 11.01
measure the court outside the t.; 11.02
Then God's t. in heaven was opened, 11.19
covenant was seen within his t.; 11.19
And another angel came out of the t., 14.15
angel came out of the t. in heaven, 14.17
and the t. of the tent of witness 15.05
and out of the t. came the seven 15.06
and the t. was filled with smoke 15.08
could enter the t. until the seven 15.08
voice from the t. telling the 16.01
a great voice came out of the t., 16.17
And I saw no t. in the city, for its 21.22
for its t. is the Lord God the 21.22

TEMPLES
fallen from his forehead and t., Lev 13.41
hair on your t. or mar the edges 19.27
a fire in the t. of the gods of Jer 43.12
and the t. of the gods of Egypt he 43.13
my rich treasures into your t. Joe 3.05
You who abhor idols, do you rob t.? Rom 2.22

TEMPT
'You shall not t. the Lord your God.'" Mt 4.07
'You shall not t. the Lord your God.'" Lk 4.12
together to t. the Spirit of the Ac 5.09
lest Satan t. you through lack of 1Co 7.05

TEMPTATION
And lead us not into t., But deliver Mt 6.13
to the man by whom the t. comes! 18.07
that you may not enter into t.; 26.41
that you may not enter into t.; Mk 14.38
And when the devil had ended every t., Lk 4.13
while and in time of t. fall away. 8.13
to us; and lead us not into t." 11.04
that you may not enter into t." 22.40
that you may not enter into t." 22.46
But because of the t. to immorality, 1Co 7.02
No t. has overtaken you that is not 10.13
but with the t. will also provide 10.13
who desire to be rich fall into t., 1Ti 6.09

TEMPTATIONS
"Woe to the world for t. to sin! Mt 18.07
For it is necessary that t. come, 18.07
"T. to sin are sure to come; but woe Lk 17.01

TEMPTED
wilderness to be t. by the devil. Mt 4.01
wilderness forty days, t. by Satan; Mk 1.13
in the wilderness, t. by the devil. Lk 4.02
not let you be t. beyond your 1Co 10.13
to yourself, lest you too be t. Gal 6.01
the tempter had t. you and that 1Th 3.05
himself has suffered and been t., Heb 2.18
is able to help those who are t. 2.18

TEMPTED (cont.)
respect has been t. as we are, Heb 4.15
Let no one say when he is t., Jas 1.13
he is tempted, "I am t. by God"; 1.13
God cannot be t. with evil and he 1.13
but each person is t. when he is 1.14

TEMPTER
And the t. came and said to him, "If Mt 4.03
somehow the t. had tempted you and 1Th 3.05

TEMPTS
with evil and he himself t. no one; Jas 1.13

TEN
Kenan were nine hundred and t. years; Gen 5.14
Abram had dwelt t. years in the land 16.03
this once. Suppose t. are found there." 18.32
"For the sake of t. I will not destroy 18.32
servant took t. of his master's 24.10
her arms weighing t. gold shekels, 24.22
with us a while, at least t. days; 24.55
mother of thousands of t. thousands; 24.60
me and changed my wages t. times, 31.07
you have changed my wages t. times. 31.41
colts, forty cows and t. bulls, 32.15
twenty she-asses and t. he-asses. 32.15
So t. of Joseph's brothers went down 42.03
t. asses loaded with the good 45.23
and t. she-asses loaded with grain, 45.23
lived a hundred and t. years. 50.22
being a hundred and t. years old; 50.26
tabernacle with t. curtains of Ex 26.01
T. cubits shall be the length of a 26.16
fifty cubits, with t. pillars and t. bases. 27.12
the covenant, the t. commandments. 34.28
the tabernacle with t. curtains; 36.08
T. cubits was the length of a frame, 36.21
their pillars t., and their sockets t.; 38.12
of you shall chase t. thousand; Lev 26.08
t. women shall bake your bread in 26.26
and for a female t. shekels. 27.05
and for a female t. shekels. 27.07
one golden dish of t. shekels, Num 7.14
one golden dish of t. shekels, 7.20
one golden dish of t. shekels, 7.26
one golden dish of t. shekels, 7.32
one golden dish of t. shekels, 7.38
one golden dish of t. shekels, 7.44
one golden dish of t. shekels, 7.50
one golden dish of t. shekels, 7.56
one golden dish of t. shekels, 7.62
one golden dish of t. shekels, 7.68
one golden dish of t. shekels, 7.74
one golden dish of t. shekels, 7.80
weighing t. shekels apiece according 7.86
to the t. thousand thousands of 10.36
or t. days, or twenty days, 11.19
gathered least gathered t. homers; 11.32
the proof these t. times and have 14.22
"On the fourth day t. bulls, two 29.23
perform, that is, the t. commandments; Deu 4.13
the t. commandments which the LORD 10.04
and two put t. thousand to flight, 32.30
came from the t. thousands of holy 33.02
such are the t. thousands of Ephraim, 33.17
t. cities with their villages. Jos 15.57
there fell to Manasseh t. portions, 17.05
half-tribe of Manasseh, t. cities. 21.05
Kohathites were t. in all with 21.26
and with him t. chiefs, one from 22.14
being a hundred and t. years old. 24.29
they defeated t. thousand of them Ju 1.04
age of one hundred and t. years. 2.08
that time about t. thousand of the 3.29
taking t. thousand from the tribe 4.06
and t. thousand men went up at his 4.10
Tabor with t. thousand men following 4.14
So Gideon took t. men of his 6.27
returned, and t. thousand remained. 7.03
and he judged Israel t. years. 12.11
I will give you t. pieces of 17.10
and we will take t. men of a 20.10
and a thousand of t. thousand, 20.10
against Gibeah t. thousand picked 20.34
They lived there about t. years; Ru 1.04
And he took t. men of the elders of 4.02
am I not more to you than t. sons?" 1Sa 1.08
and t. thousand men of Judah. 15.04
and these t. loaves, and carry them 17.17
also take these t. cheeses to the 17.18
thousands, And David his t. thousands." 18.07
ascribed to David t. thousands, 18.08
And David his t. thousands'?" 21.11
So David sent t. young men; 25.05
And about t. days later the LORD 25.38
And David his t. thousands'?" 29.05
the king left t. concubines to 2Sa 15.16
you are worth t. thousand of us; 18.03
to give you t. pieces of silver 18.11
And t. young men, Joab's armor-bearers, 18.15
"We have t. shares in the king, and 19.43
king took the t. concubines whom 20.03
t. fat oxen, and twenty pasture-fed 1Ki 4.23
t. thousand a month in relays; 5.14
and t. cubits deep in front of the 6.03
of olivewood, each t. cubits high. 6.23
it was t. cubits from the tip of 6.24
cherub also measured t. cubits; 6.25
height of one cherub was t. cubits, 6.26
stones of eight and t. cubits. 7.10
it was round, t. cubits from brim to 7.23
He also made the t. stands of 7.27
After this manner he made the t. stands; 7.37
And he made t. lavers of bronze; 7.38
a laver for each of the t. stands. 7.38
the t. stands, and the t. lavers upon 7.43
"Take for yourself t. pieces; 11.31
and will give you t. tribes 11.31
and will give it to you, t. tribes. 11.35
Take with you t. loaves, some cakes, 14.03
taking with him t. talents of silver, 2Ki 5.05
of gold, and t. festal garments. 5.05
t. chariots and t. thousand footmen; 13.07
He killed t. thousand Edomites in 14.07
and he reigned t. years in Samaria. 15.17
forward t. steps, or go back t. steps?" 20.09
the shadow to lengthen t. steps; 20.10
let the shadow go back t. steps." 20.10
brought the shadow back t. steps, 20.11
t. thousand captives, and all the 24.14
came with t. men, and attacked and 25.25
the half of Manasseh, t. cities. 1Ch 6.61
talents and t. thousand darics of 29.07
t. thousand talents of silver, 29.07
cubits wide, and t. cubits high. 2Ch 4.01
it was round, t. cubits from brim 4.02
He also made t. lavers in which to 4.06
And he made t. golden lampstands as 4.07
He also made t. tables, and placed 4.08
the land had rest for t. years. 14.01
Salt and smote t. thousand men of 25.11
captured another t. thousand alive, 25.12
and t. thousand cors of wheat and 27.05
of wheat and t. thousand of barley 27.05
bulls and t. thousand sheep. 30.24
months and t. days in Jerusalem. 36.09
hundred and t. bowls of silver, and Ez 1.10
and with him a hundred and t. men. 8.12
and t. of their kinsmen with them. 8.24
them came they said to us t. times, Neh 4.12
and every t. days skins of wine in 5.18
one out of t. to live in Jerusalem 11.01
and I will pay t. thousand talents Est 3.09
the t. sons of Haman the son of 9.10

TEN (cont.)
men and also the t. sons of Haman. Est 9.12
And let the t. sons of Haman be 9.13
and the t. sons of Haman were 9.14
These t. times you have cast Job 19.03
not afraid of t. thousands of Ps 3.06
to him with the harp of t. strings! 33.02
twice t. thousand, thousands upon 68.17
of our life are threescore and t., 90.10
t. thousand at your right hand; 91.07
upon a t. stringed harp I will play 144.09
thousands and t. thousands in our 144.13
man more than t. rulers that are Ecc 7.19
distinguished among t. thousand. Sol 5.10
For t. acres of vineyard shall Is 5.10
dial of Ahaz turn back t. steps." 38.08
on the dial the t. steps by which 38.08
came with t. men to Gedaliah the Jer 41.01
Nethaniah and the t. men with him 41.02
But there were t. men among them 41.08
At the end of t. days the word of 42.07
opening of the gateway, t. cubits; Eze 40.11
and t. steps led up to it; and there 40.49
of the entrance was t. cubits; 41.02
t. cubits wide and a hundred cubits 42.04
cubits long and t. thousand broad, 45.03
cubits long and t. thousand cubits 45.05
and t. shekels shall be t. shekels, 45.12
like the homer, contains t. baths); 45.14
t. thousand cubits in breadth on 48.10
t. thousand in breadth on the 48.10
in length and t. thousand in 48.13
shall be t. thousand cubits to the 48.18
and t. thousand to the west, and it 48.18
"Test your servants for t. days; Dan 1.12
and tested them for t. days. 1.14
At the end of t. days it was seen 1.15
he found them t. times better than 1.20
were before it; and it had t. horns. 7.07
and t. thousand times t. thousand stood 7.10
and concerning the t. horns that 7.20
As for the t. horns, out of this 7.24
of this kingdom t. kings shall 7.24
for him my laws by t. thousands, Hos 8.12
shall have t. left to the house of Amo 5.03
And if t. men remain in one house, 6.09
with t. thousands of rivers of oil? Mic 6.07
twenty measures, there were but t.; Hag 2.16
cubits, and its breadth t. cubits. Zec 5.02
In those days t. men from the 8.23
who owed him t. thousand talents; Mt 18.24
And when the t. heard it, they were 20.24
be compared to t. maidens who took 25.01
it to him who has the t. talents. 25.28
And when the t. heard it, they began Mk 10.41
he is able with t. thousand to Lk 14.31
having t. silver coins, if she loses 15.08
he was met by t. lepers, who stood 17.12
Then said Jesus, "Were not t. cleansed? 17.17
Calling t. of his servants, he gave 19.13
he gave them t. pounds, and said to 19.13
your pound has made t. pounds more.' 19.16
have authority over t. cities.' 19.17
it to him who has the t. pounds.' 19.24
to him, 'Lord, he has t. pounds!') 19.25
not more than eight or t. days, Ac 25.06
than t. thousand words in a tongue. 1Co 14.19
and for t. days you will have Rev 2.10
twice t. thousand times t. thousand; 9.16
with seven heads and t. horns, 12.03
with t. horns and seven heads, with 13.01
with t. diadems upon its horns and 13.01
it had seven heads and t. horns. 17.03
seven heads and t. horns that 17.07
And the t. horns that you saw are 17.12
you saw are t. kings who have not 17.12
And the t. horns that you saw, they 17.16

TENANTS
built a tower, and let it out to t., Mt 21.33
he sent his servants to the t., 21.34
and the t. took his servants and 21.35
But when the t. saw the son, they 21.38
comes, what will he do to those t.?" 21.40
to other t. who will give him the 21.41
a tower, and let it out to t., Mk 12.01
came, he sent a servant to the t., 12.02
But those t. said to one another, 12.07
He will come and destroy the t., 12.09
a vineyard, and let it out to t., Lk 20.09
came, he sent a servant to the t., 20.10
but the t. beat him, and sent him 20.10
But when the t. saw him, they said 20.14
He will come and destroy those t., 20.16

TEND
his sons shall t. it from evening Ex 27.21
furnishings, and they shall t. it, Num 1.50
and you shall t. upward only, and Deu 28.13
He said to him, "T. my sheep." Jn 21.16
T. the flock of God that is your 1Pe 5.02

TENDED
With upright heart he t. them, and Ps 78.72
I named Union. And I t. the sheep. Zec 11.07

TENDER
t. and good, and gave it to the Gen 18.07
who is the most t. and delicately Deu 28.54
The most t. and delicately bred 28.56
because she is so delicate and t., 28.56
the gentle rain upon the t. grass, 32.02
and like t. grass, like grass on the 2Ki 19.26
t., the only one in the sight of my Pro 4.03
of the field and like t. grass, Is 37.27
no more be called t. and delicate. 47.01
the children of their t. care? Lam 2.20
of its young twigs a t. one, Eze 17.22
amid the t. grass of the field. Dan 4.15
in the t. grass of the field; 4.23
my compassion grows warm and t. Hos 11.08
branch becomes t. and puts forth Mt 24.32
branch becomes t. and puts forth Mk 13.28
through the t. mercy of our God, Lk 1.78
a t. heart and a humble mind. 1Pe 3.08

TENDERHEARTED
t., forgiving one another, as God in Eph 4.32

TENDERLY
the maiden and spoke t. to her. Gen 34.03
Speak t. to Jerusalem, and cry to Is 40.02
wilderness, and speak t. to her. Hos 2.14

TENDING
from t. the ewes that had young he Ps 78.71

TENDS
Fret not yourself; it t. only to evil. Ps 37.08
but mere talk t. only to want. Pro 14.23
He who t. a fig tree will eat its 27.18
Who t. a flock without getting some 1Co 9.07

TENONS
There shall be two t. in each frame, Ex 26.17
under one frame for its two t. 26.19
under another frame for its two t.; 26.19
Each frame had two t., for fitting 36.22
under one frame for its two t., 36.24
under another frame for its two t. 36.24

TENS
of hundreds, of fifties, and of t. Ex 18.21
of hundreds, of fifties, and of t. 18.25
commanders of t., and officers, Deu 1.15
he shall cast down t. of thousands, Dan 11.12
And t. of thousands shall fall, but 11.41

TENT

drunk, and lay uncovered in his t. Gen 9.21
east of Bethel, and pitched his t., 12.08
place where his t. had been at the 13.03
and moved his t. as far as Sodom. 13.12
So Abram moved his t., and came 13.18
the door of his t. in the heat of 18.01
he ran from the t. door to meet 18.02
hastened into the t. to Sarah, 18.06
And he said, "She is in the t." 18.09
listening at the t. door behind him. 18.10
Then Isaac brought her into the t., 24.67
the LORD, and pitched his t. there. 26.25
had pitched his t. in the hill 31.25
went into Jacob's t., and into Leah's t., 31.33
and into the t. of the two maidservants, 31.33
And he went out of Leah's t., and 31.33
Laban felt all about the t., but did 31.34
on which he had pitched his t. 33.19
and pitched his t. beyond the 35.21
whom each of you has in his t.'" Ex 16.16
welfare, and went into the t. 18.07
hair for a t. over the tabernacle; 26.07
double over at the front of the t. 26.09
and couple the t. together that it 26.11
remains of the curtains of the t., 26.12
curtains of the t. shall hang over 26.13
make for the t. a covering of 26.14
a screen for the door of the t., 26.36
In the t. of meeting, outside the 27.21
they go into the t. of meeting, 28.43
to the door of the t. of meeting, 29.04
the bull before the t. of meeting. 29.10
at the door of the t. of meeting, 29.11
comes into the t. of meeting to 29.30
at the door of the t. of meeting. 29.32
the door of the t. of meeting 29.42
consecrate the t. of meeting and 29.44
the service of the t. of meeting; 30.16
it between the t. of meeting and 30.18
When they go into the t. of meeting, 30.20
with it the t. of meeting and the 30.26
testimony in the t. of meeting 30.36
the t. of meeting, and the ark of 31.07
and all the furnishings of the t., 31.07
to take the t. and pitch it 33.07
and he called it the t. of meeting. 33.07
would go out to the t. of meeting, 33.07
Whenever Moses went out to the t., 33.08
and every man stood at his t. door, 33.08
until he had gone into the t. 33.08
When Moses entered the t., 33.09
and stand at the door of the t., 33.09
standing at the door of the t., 33.10
worship, every man at his t. door. 33.10
man, did not depart from the t. 33.11
its t. and its covering, its hooks 35.11
to be used for the t. of meeting, 35.21
hair for a t. over the tabernacle; 36.14
to couple the t. together that it 36.18
And he made for the t. a covering 36.19
a screen for the door of the t., 36.37
at the door of the t. of meeting. 38.08
for the door of the t. of meeting, 38.30
tabernacle of the t. of meeting was 39.32
the t. and all its utensils, its 39.33
the screen for the door of the t.; 39.38
tabernacle, for the t. of meeting; 39.40
tabernacle of the t. of meeting. 40.02
tabernacle of the t. of meeting, 40.06
between the t. of meeting and the 40.07
to the door of the t. of meeting, 40.12
and he spread the t. over the 40.19
put the covering of the t. over it, 40.19
put the table in the t. of meeting, 40.22
the lampstand in the t. of meeting, 40.24
altar in the t. of meeting before 40.26
tabernacle of the t. of meeting, 40.29
between the t. of meeting and the 40.30
when they went into the t. of meeting, 40.32
cloud covered the t. of meeting, 40.34
able to enter the t. of meeting, 40.35
to him from the t. of meeting, Lev 1.01
at the door of the t. of meeting, 1.03
at the door of the t. of meeting. 1.05
at the door of the t. of meeting; 3.02
it before the t. of meeting; 3.08
kill it before the t. of meeting; 3.13
the door of the t. of meeting 4.04
and bring it to the t. of meeting; 4.05
LORD which is in the t. of meeting, 4.07
at the door of the t. of meeting. 4.07
bring it before the t. of meeting; 4.14
of the bull to the t. of meeting, 4.16
which is in the t. of meeting 4.18
at the door of the t. of meeting. 4.18
court of the t. of meeting they 6.16
in the court of the t. of meeting. 6.26
into the t. of meeting to make 6.30
at the door of the t. of meeting." 8.03
at the door of the t. of meeting. 8.04
at the door of the t. of meeting, 8.31
the door of the t. of meeting for 8.33
At the door of the t. of meeting 8.35
commanded before the t. of meeting; 9.05
Aaron went into the t. of meeting; 9.23
from the door of the t. of meeting, 10.07
when you go into the t. of meeting, 10.09
the door of the t. of meeting a 12.06
dwell outside his t. seven days. 14.08
at the door of the t. of meeting. 14.11
to the door of the t. of meeting, 14.23
to the door of the t. of meeting, 15.14
to the door of the t. of meeting. 15.29
at the door of the t. of meeting; 16.07
he shall do for the t. of meeting, 16.16
no man in the t. of meeting when 16.17
place and the t. of meeting and 16.20
shall come into the t. of meeting, 16.23
atonement for the t. of meeting and 16.33
to the door of the t. of meeting, 17.04
at the door of the t. of meeting, 17.05
at the door of the t. of meeting, 17.06
to the door of the t. of meeting, 17.09
to the door of the t. of meeting, 19.21
in the t. of meeting, Aaron shall 24.03
in the t. of meeting, on the first Num 1.01
facing the t. of meeting on every 2.02
"Then the t. of meeting shall set 2.17
congregation before the t. of meeting, 3.07
furnishings of the t. of meeting, 3.08
Gershon in the t. of meeting was 3.25
the t. with its covering, the screen 3.25
for the door of the t. of meeting, 3.25
before the t. of meeting toward the 3.38
do the work in the t. of meeting. 4.03
of Kohath in the t. of meeting: 4.04
things of the t. of meeting which 4.15
do the work in the t. of meeting. 4.23
and the t. of meeting with its 4.25
for the door of the t. of meeting, 4.25
Gershonites in the t. of meeting, 4.28
do the work of the t. of meeting. 4.30
their service in the t. of meeting: 4.31
their service in the t. meeting, 4.33
for work in the t. of meeting; 4.35
who served in the t. of meeting, 4.37
for work in the t. of meeting— 4.39
who served in the t. of meeting, 4.41
for work in the t. of meeting— 4.43
burdens in the t. of meeting, 4.47
to the door of the t. of meeting, 6.10
to the door of the t. of meeting, 6.13
at the door of the t. of meeting, 6.18

TENT (cont.)

the service of the t. of meeting, Num 7.05
went into the t. of meeting to 7.89
Levites before the t. of meeting, 8.09
to do service at the t. of meeting, 8.15
of Israel at the t. of meeting, 8.19
service in the t. of meeting in 8.22
the service of the t. of meeting; 8.24
brethren in the t. of meeting, 8.26
tabernacle, the t. of the testimony; 9.15
was taken up from over the t., 9.17
the entrance of the t. of meeting. 10.03
every man at the door of his t.; 11.10
bring them to the t. of meeting, 11.16
and placed them round about the t. 11.24
they had not gone out to the t., 11.26
you three, to the t. of meeting." 12.04
and stood at the door of the t., 12.05
the cloud removed from over the t., 12.10
appeared at the t. of meeting to 14.10
entrance of the t. of meeting with 16.18
the entrance of the t. of meeting. 16.19
turned toward the t. of meeting; 16.42
to the front of the t. of meeting, 16.43
the entrance of the t. of meeting, 16.50
them in the t. of meeting before 17.04
the LORD in the t. of the testimony 17.07
went into the t. of the testimony; 17.08
are before the t. of the testimony 18.02
and attend to all duties of the t.; 18.03
and attend to the t. of meeting, 18.04
for all the service of the t.; 18.04
the service of the t. of meeting. 18.06
their service in the t. of meeting. 18.21
not come near the t. of meeting, 18.22
the service of the t. of meeting, 18.23
your service in the t. of meeting. 18.31
front of the t. of meeting seven 19.04
is the law when a man dies in a t.: 19.14
every one who comes into the t., 19.14
and every one who is in the t., 19.14
water, and sprinkle it upon the t., 19.18
to the door of the t. of meeting, 20.06
at the door of the t. of meeting. 25.06
at the door of the t. of meeting, 27.02
brought it into the t. of meeting, 31.54
yourselves in the t. of meeting, Deu 31.14
themselves in the t. of meeting. 31.14
appeared in the t. in a pillar of 31.15
cloud stood by the door of the t. 31.15
hidden in the earth inside my t., Jos 7.21
messengers, and they ran to the t.; 7.22
hidden in his t. with the silver 7.22
them out of the t. and brought 7.23
and his t., and all that he had; 7.24
and set up the t. of meeting there; 18.01
at the door of the t. of meeting. 19.51
had pitched his t. as far away as Ju 4.11
away on foot to the t. of Jael, 4.17
he turned aside to her into the t., 4.18
her, "Stand at the door of the t., 4.20
the wife of Heber took a t. peg, 4.21
So he went in to her t.; and there 4.22
with the t. peg in his temple. 4.22
her hand to the t. peg and her 5.26
rest of Israel every man to his t., 7.08
camp of Midian, and came to the t., 7.13
down, so that the t. lay flat." 7.13
"We will not any of us go to his t., 20.08
the entrance to the t. of meeting. 1Sa 2.22
he sent home, every man to his t. 13.02
but he put his armor in his t. 17.54
inside the t. which David had 2Sa 6.17
but the ark of God dwells in a t." 7.02
about in a t. for my dwelling. 7.06
So they pitched a t. for Absalom 16.22
took the horn of oil from the t., 1Ki 1.39
fled to the t. of the LORD and 2.28
has fled to the t. of the LORD, 2.29
Benaiah came to the t. of the LORD, 2.30
the t. of meeting, and all the holy 8.04
holy vessels that were in the t.; 8.04
of the damp, they went into a t., 2Ki 7.08
came back, and entered another t., 7.08
tabernacle of the t. of meeting, 1Ch 6.32
of the thresholds of the t., 9.19
the entrance of the t. of meeting. 9.21
is, the house of the t., as guards. 9.23
of God, and pitched a t. for it. 15.01
it inside the t. which David had 16.01
covenant of the LORD is under a t." 17.01
have gone from t. to t. and from 17.05
charge of the t. of meeting and 23.32
for the t. of meeting of God, 2Ch 1.03
had pitched a t. for it in Jerusalem.) 1.04
which was at the t. of meeting, 1.06
from before the t. of meeting, 1.13
the t. of meeting, and all the holy 5.05
holy vessels that were in the t.; 5.05
of Israel for the t. of testimony?" 24.06
You shall know that your t. is safe, Job 5.24
and the t. of the wicked will be no 8.22
The light is dark in his t., 18.06
torn from the t. in which he 18.14
In his t. dwells that which is none 18.15
me, and encamp round about my t. 19.12
is left in his t. will be consumed 20.26
Where is the t. in which the wicked 21.28
friendship of God was upon my t.; 29.04
if the men of my t. have not said, 31.31
O LORD, who shall sojourn in thy t.? Ps 15.01
them he has set a t. for the sun, 19.04
me under the cover of his t., 27.05
offer in his t. sacrifices with 27.06
snatch and tear you from your t.; 52.05
Let me dwell in thy t. for ever! 61.04
the t. where he dwelt among men, 78.60
He rejected the t. of Joseph, 78.67
you, no scourge come near your t. 91.10
stretched out the heavens like a t., 104.02
but the t. of the upright will Pro 14.11
no Arab will pitch his t. there, Is 13.20
faithfulness in the t. of David one 16.05
an immovable t., whose stakes will 33.20
from me like a shepherd's t.; 38.12
spreads them like a t. to dwell in; 40.22
Enlarge the place of your t., 54.02
My t. is destroyed, and all my cords Jer 10.20
is no one to spread my t. again, 10.20
wounded men, every man in his t., 37.10
our eyes in the t. of the daughter Lam 2.04
cornerstone, out of them the t. peg, Zec 10.04
And you took up the t. of Moloch, Ac 7.43
"Our fathers had the t. of witness 7.44
if the earthly t. we live in is 2Co 5.01
For while we are still in this t., 5.04
and the true t. which is set up Heb 8.02
Moses was about to erect the t., 8.05
For a t. was prepared, the outer one, 9.02
curtain stood a t. called the Holy 9.03
go continually into the outer t., 9.06
as the outer t. is still standing 9.08
more perfect t. (not made with 9.11
blood both the t. and all the 9.21
who serve the t. have no right to 13.10
temple of the t. of witness in Rev 15.05

TENT-CORD

If their t. is plucked up within Job 4.21

TENT-DWELLING

the Kenite, of t. women most blessed. Ju 5.24

TENTH
to abate until the t. month; Gen 8.05
in the t. month, on the first day of 8.05
Abram gave him a t. of everything. 14.20
me I will give the t. to thee." 28.22
that on the t. day of this month Ex 12.03
(An omer is the t. part of an ephah.) 16.36
first lamb a t. measure of fine 29.40
a t. of an ephah of fine flour for Lev 5.11
a t. of an ephah of fine flour as a 6.20
and a t. of an ephah of fine flour 14.21
on the t. day of the month, you 16.29
"On the t. day of this seventh 23.27
trumpet on the t. day of the 25.09
every t. animal of all that pass 27.32
a t. of an ephah of barley meal; Num 5.15
On the t. day Ahiezer the son of 7.66
offering of a t. of an ephah of 15.04
also a t. of an ephah of fine flour 28.05
and a t. of fine flour mixed with 28.13
a t. shall you offer for each of 28.21
a t. for each of the seven lambs; 28.29
and one t. for each of the seven 29.04
"On the t. day of this seventh 29.07
a t. for each of the seven lambs: 29.10
and a t. for each of the fourteen 29.15
even to the t. generation none of Deu 23.02
even to the t. generation none 23.03
Jordan on the t. day of the first Jos 4.19
He will take the t. of your grain 1Sa 8.15
He will take the t. of your flocks, 8.17
the t. month, on the t. day of the month, 2Ki 25.01
Jeremiah t., Machbannai eleventh. 1Ch 12.13
to Jeshua, the t. to Shecaniah, 24.11
the t. to Shimei, his sons and his 25.17
T., for the t. month, was Maharai of 27.13
day of the t. month they sat down Ez 10.16
his royal palace in the t. month, Est 2.16
And though a t. remain in it, it Is 6.13
the LORD in the t. year of Zedekiah Jer 32.01
in the t. month, Nebuchadrezzar king 39.01
t. month, on the t. day of the month, 52.04
on the t. day of the month—which 52.12
on the t. day of the month, certain Eze 20.01
the t. month, on the t. day of the month, 24.01
In the t. year, in the t. month, on the 29.01
in the t. month, on the fifth day of 33.21
on the t. day of the month, in the 40.01
bath containing one t. of a homer, 45.11
and the ephah one t. of a homer; 45.11
one t. of a bath from each cor (the 45.14
seventh, and the fast of the t., Zec 8.19
day, for it was about the t. hour. Jn 1.39
apportioned a t. part of everything. Heb 7.02
and a t. of the city fell; Rev 11.13
the t. chrysoprase, the eleventh 21.20

TENTHS
of three t. of an ephah of fine Lev 14.10
it shall be two t. of an ephah of 23.13
waved, made of two t. of an ephah; 23.17
two t. of an ephah shall be in each 24.05
offering two t. of an ephah of Num 15.06
of three t. of an ephah of fine 15.09
and two t. of an ephah of fine 28.09
also three t. of an ephah of fine 28.12
and two t. of fine flour for a 28.12
three t. of an ephah shall you 28.20
for a bull, and two t. for a ram; 28.20
three t. of an ephah for each bull, 28.28
for each bull, two t. for one ram, 28.28
three t. of an ephah for the bull, 29.03
for the bull, two t. for the ram, 29.03
three t. of an ephah for the bull, 29.09
two t. for the one ram, 29.09
three t. of an ephah for each of 29.14
two t. for each of the two rams, 29.14
while nine t. remained in the other Neh 11.01

TENTMAKERS
worked, for by trade they were t. Ac 18.03

TENTS
who dwell in t. and have cattle. Gen 4.20
let him dwell in the t. of Shem; 9.27
also had flocks and herds and t., 13.05
was a quiet man, dwelling in t. 25.27
pitch their t. by their companies, Num 1.52
from the t. of these wicked men, and 16.26
and stood at the door of their t., 16.27
how fair are your t., O Jacob, 24.05
and you murmured in your t., Deu 1.27
you out a place to pitch your t., 1.33
and say to them, "Return to your t." 5.30
their t., and every living thing 11.06
you shall turn and go to your t. 16.07
going out; and Issachar, in your t. 33.18
the people set out from their t., Jos 3.14
up with their cattle and their t., Ju 6.05
every man to his t., O Israel!" 2Sa 20.01
To your t., O Israel! Look now 1Ki 12.16
So Israel departed to their t. 12.16
the twilight and forsook their t., 2Ki 7.07
tied, and the t. as they were." 7.10
destroyed their t. and the Meunim 1Ch 4.41
dwelt in their t. throughout all 5.10
Each of you to your t., O Israel! 2Ch 10.16
So all Israel departed to their t. 10.16
And they smote the t. of those who 14.15
not wickedness dwell in your t. Job 11.14
The t. of robbers are at peace, and 12.06
fire consumes the t. of bribery. 15.34
unrighteousness far from your t., 22.23
let no one dwell in their t. Ps 69.25
of their strength in the t. of Ham. 78.51
the tribes of Israel in their t. 78.55
the t. of Edom and the Ishmaelites, 83.06
than dwell in the t. of wickedness. 84.10
They murmured in their t., 106.25
victory in the t. of the righteous: 118.15
that I dwell among the t. of Kedar! 120.05
like the t. of Kedar, like the Sol 1.05
your kids beside the shepherds' t. 1.08
Suddenly my t. are destroyed, my Jer 4.20
shall pitch their t. around her, 6.03
the fortunes of the t. of Jacob, 30.18
you shall live in t. all your days, 35.07
but we have lived in t., 35.10
Their t. and their flocks shall be 49.29
his palatial t. between the sea Dan 11.45
thorns shall be in their t. Hos 9.06
I will again make you dwell in t., 12.09
I saw the t. of Cushan in affliction; Hab 3.07
victory to the t. of Judah first, Zec 12.07
LORD cut off from the t. of Jacob, Mal 2.12
living in t. with Isaac and Jacob, Heb 11.09

TERAH
years, he became the father of T.; Gen 11.24
the birth of T. a hundred and 11.25
When T. had lived seventy years, he 11.26
Now these are the descendants of T. 11.27
T. was the father of Abram, Nahor, 11.27
his father T. in the land of his 11.28
T. took Abram his son and Lot the 11.31
The days of T. were two hundred and 11.32
five years; and T. died in Haran. 11.32
from Tahath, and encamped at T. Num 33.27
And they set out from T., 33.28
T., the father of Abraham and of Jos 24.02
Serug, Nahor, T.; 1Ch 1.26
the son of T., the son of Nahor, Lk 3.34

TERAPHIM
and he made an ephod and t., and Ju 17.05
t., a graven image, and a molten 18.14
the t., and the molten image, while 18.17
the t., and the molten image, the 18.18
and the t., and the graven image, 18.20
wizards and the t. and the idols 2Ki 23.24
the arrows, he consults the t., Eze 21.21
or pillar, without ephod or t. Hos 3.04
For the t. utter nonsense, and the Zec 10.02

TEREBINTH
like a t. or an oak, whose stump Is 6.13
and t., because their shade is good. Hos 4.13

TERESH
Bigthan and T., two of the king's Est 2.21
had told about Bigthana and T., 6.02

TERM
these days Purim, after the t. Pur. Est 9.26

TERMED
You shall no more be t. Forsaken, Is 62.04
land shall no more be t. Desolate; 62.04

TERMINATION
Egypt, and its t. shall be at the Sea. Num 34.05

TERMS
against it, offer t. of peace to it. Deu 20.10
"I will let you go on these t." 1Ki 20.34
containing the t. and conditions, Jer 32.11
not keep the t. of the covenant 34.18
he shall bring t. of peace and Dan 11.17
an embassy and asks t. of peace. Lk 14.32
I am speaking in human t., Rom 6.19
in what t. I preached to you the 1Co 15.01
they work on the same t. as we do. 2Co 11.12

TERRESTRIAL
celestial bodies and there are t. bodies; 1Co 15.40
one, and the glory of the t. is another. 15.40

TERRIBLE
t. in glorious deeds, doing wonders? Ex 15.11
for it is a t. thing that I will do 34.10
that great and t. wilderness which Deu 1.19
midst of you, a great and t. God. 7.21
the great and t. wilderness, 8.15
and the t. God, who is not partial 10.17
these great and t. things which 10.21
the great and t. deeds which Moses 34.12
of the angel of God, very t.; Ju 13.06
doing for them great and t. things, 2Sa 7.23
a name for great and t. things, 1Ch 17.21
the great and t. God who keeps Neh 1.05
the Lord, who is great and t., 4.14
the great and mighty and t. God, 9.32
God is clothed with t. majesty. Job 37.22
His majestic snorting is t. 39.20
is t., a great king over all the Ps 47.02
Say to God, "How t. are thy deeds! 66.03
he is t. in his deeds among men. 66.05
T. is God in his sanctuary, the God 68.35
But thou, t. art thou! Who can 76.07
who is t. to the kings of the earth. 76.12
great and t. above all that are 89.07
Let them praise thy great and t. name! 99.03
and t. things by the Red Sea. 106.22
for ever. Holy and t. is his name! 111.09
proclaim the might of thy t. acts, 145.06
t. as an army with banners. Sol 6.04
t. as an army with banners?" 6.10
from the desert, from a t. land. Is 21.01
When thou didst t. things which we 64.03
therefore her fall is t., Lam 1.09
you, the most t. of the nations; Eze 28.07
the most t. of the nations, shall be 30.11
the most t. of the nations, will cut 31.12
of them most t. among the nations. 32.12
t. and dreadful and exceedingly Dan 7.07
exceedingly t., with its teeth of 7.19
the great and t. God, who keepest 9.04
of the LORD is great and very t.; Joe 2.11
the great and t. day of the LORD 2.31
Dread and t. are they; Hab 1.07
The LORD will be t. against them; Zep 2.11
the great and t. day of the LORD Mal 4.05
paralyzed at home, in t. distress." Mt 8.06

TERRIBLY
is an epileptic and he suffers t.; Mt 17.15
crying out and convulsing him t., Mk 9.26

TERRIFIED
and he t. and afflicted them with 1Sa 5.06
and when she saw that he was t., 28.21
Therefore I am t. at his presence; Job 23.15
faint; the Almighty has t. me; 23.16
and the contempt of families t. me, 31.34
him is not t. by their shouting or Is 31.04
that we may be dismayed and t. 41.23
they shall be t., they shall be put 44.11
they were t., saying, "It is a ghost!" Mt 14.26
for they all saw him, and were t. Mk 6.50
of wars and tumults, do not be t.; Lk 21.09
the rest were t. and gave glory to Rev 11.13

TERRIFIES
ears of men, and t. them with warnings, Job 33.16

TERRIFY
the wall, to frighten and t. them, 2Ch 32.18
let the blackness of the day t. it. Job 3.05
with dreams and t. me with visions, 7.14
me, and let not dread of him t. me. 9.34
Will not his majesty t. you, 13.11
and let not dread of thee t. me. 13.21
distress and anguish t. him; 15.24
Behold, no fear of me need t. you; 33.07
and t. them in his fury, saying, Ps 2.05
thy tempest and t. them with thy 83.15
when he rises to t. the earth. Is 2.19
when he rises to t. the earth. 2.21
"Let us go up against Judah and t. it, 7.06
I will t. Elam before their enemies, Jer 49.37
from me to t. the unsuspecting Eze 30.09
destruction of the beasts will t. you, Hab 2.17
and these have come to t. them, Zec 1.21
do right and let nothing t. you. 1Pe 3.06

TERRIFYING
T. sounds are in his ears; in prosperity Job 15.21
will lop the boughs with t. power; Is 10.33
Indeed, so t. was the sight that Heb 12.21

TERRITORIES
land and its cities with their t., Num 32.33
distributing the several t. of the land as Jos 19.49

TERRITORY
And the t. of the Canaanites extended Gen 10.19
The t. in which they lived extended 10.30
journeyed toward the t. of the Negeb, 20.01
be seen with you in all your t. Ex 13.07
a city on the edge of your t. Num 20.16
we have passed through your t." 20.17
give Israel passage through his t.; 20.21
we have passed through your t." 21.22
Israel to pass through his t. 21.23
at Iyeabarim, in the t. of Moab. 33.44
through the t. of your brethren Deu 2.04
the Gadites the t. beginning at 3.12
I gave the t. from Gilead as far 3.16
your t. shall be from the wilderness 11.24

TERRITORY (cont.)

the LORD your God enlarges your t., Deu 12.20
you in all your t. for seven days; 16.04
olive trees throughout all your t., 28.40
down of the sun shall be your t. Jos 1.04
So their t. was from Aroer, which is 13.16
Their t. was Jazer, and all the 13.25
from Mahanaim to the t. of Debir, 13.26
to Ataroth, the t. of the Archites; 16.02
westward to the t. of the Japhletites, 16.03
as far as the t. of lower Bethhoron, 16.03
The t. of the Ephraimites by their 16.05
The t. of Manasseh reached from 17.07
continuing in his t. on the south, 18.05
of Joseph in their t. on the north. 18.05
and the t. allotted to it fell 18.11
formed part of the t. of Judah; 19.09
And the t. of its inheritance 19.10
Its t. included Jezreel, Chesulloth, 19.18
Its t. included Helkath, Hali, Beten, 19.25
And the t. of its inheritance 19.41
Rakkon with the t. over against 19.46
When the t. of the Danites was lost 19.47
with me into the t. allotted to me, Ju 1.03
you into the t. allotted to you." 1.03
Judah also took Gaza with its t., 1.18
Ashkelon with its t., and Ekron with its t. 1.18
they did not enter the t. of Moab, 11.18
Israel to pass through his t.; 11.20
of all the t. of the Amorites from 11.22
throughout all the t. of Israel. 19.29
tumors, both Ashdod and its t. 1Sa 5.06
not again enter the t. of Israel. 7.13
rescued their t. from the hand of 7.14
tomb in the t. of Benjamin at 10.02
through all the t. of Israel. 11.03
throughout all the t. of Israel by 11.07
no place in all the t. of Israel, 2Sa 21.05
throughout all the t. of Israel, 1Ki 1.03
eat Jezebel in the t. of Jezreel, 2Ki 9.10
'In the t. of Jezreel the dogs 9.36
of the field in the t. of Jezreel, 9.37
them throughout the t. of Israel: 10.32
in it and its t. from Tirzah on; 15.16
Philistines as far as Gaza and its t., 18.08
cities of their t. out of the 1Ch 6.66
throughout all the t. of Israel.' 21.12
cities in the t. of Ashdod and 2Ch 26.06
from all the t. that belonged to 34.33
take it to its t. and that you may Job 38.20
your sins, throughout all your t. Jer 15.13
of your sin throughout all your t. 17.03
the whole t. round about upon the Eze 43.12
Adjoining the t. of Dan, from the 48.02
Adjoining the t. of Asher, from the 48.03
Adjoining the t. of Naphtali, from 48.04
Adjoining the t. of Manasseh, from 48.05
Adjoining the t. of Ephraim, from 48.06
Adjoining the t. of Reuben, from the 48.07
"Adjoining the t. of Judah, from the 48.08
adjoining the t. of the Levites. 48.12
And alongside the t. of the priests, 48.13
lie between the t. of Judah and 48.22
of Judah and the t. of Benjamin. 48.22
Adjoining the t. of Benjamin, from 48.24
Adjoining the t. of Simeon, from the 48.25
Adjoining the t. of Issachar, from 48.26
Adjoining the t. of Zebulun, from 48.27
And adjoining the t. of Gad to the 48.28
Or is their t. greater than your t., Amo 6.02
and made boasts against their t. Zep 2.08
in the t. of Zebulun and Naphtali, Mt 4.13

TERROR

a t. from God fell upon the cities Gen 35.05
T. and dread fall upon them; Ex 15.16
I will send my t. before you, and 23.27
I will appoint over you sudden t., Lev 26.16
with great t., with signs and Deu 26.08
and in the chambers shall be t., 32.25
Haman was in t. before the king Est 7.06
you, and sudden t. overwhelms you; Job 22.10
For I was in t. of calamity from 31.23
Round about his teeth is t. 41.14
and t. dances before him. 41.22
of the earth may strike t. no more. Ps 10.18
There they shall be in great t., 14.05
whispering of many—t. on every side! 31.13
great t., in t. such as has not been! 53.05
them go away in t. into their 55.15
a breath, and their years in t. 78.33
You will not fear the t. of the night, 91.05
from before the t. of the LORD, Is 2.10
from before the t. of the LORD, 2.19
from before the t. of the LORD, 2.21
At evening time, behold, t.! 17.14
will become a t. to the Egyptians; 19.17
T., and the pit, and the snare are 24.17
sound of the t. shall fall into 24.18
will be sheer t. to understand the 28.19
His rock shall pass away in t., 31.09
Your mind will muse on the t.: 33.18
succeed, perhaps you may inspire t. 47.12
and from t., for it shall not come 54.14
has a sword, t. is on every side. Jer 6.25
a time of healing, but behold, t. 8.15
a time of healing, but behold, t. 14.19
anguish and t. fall upon them 15.08
Be not a t. to me; thou art my 17.17
name Pashhur, but T. on every side. 20.03
will make you a t. to yourself and 20.04
many whispering. T. is on every side! 20.10
a t., a hissing, and a reproach 29.18
cry of panic, of t., and no peace. 30.05
outstretched arm, and with great t.; 32.21
they look not back—t. on every side! 46.05
T., pit, and snare are before you, O 48.43
flees from the t. shall fall into 48.44
I will bring t. upon you, says the 49.05
cry to them: 'T. on every side!' 49.29
of the land are palsied by t. Eze 7.27
them an object of t. and a spoil. 23.46
imposed your t. on all the mainland! 26.17
who spread t. in the land of the 32.23
who spread t. in the land of the 32.24
for t. of them was spread in the 32.25
for they spread t. in the land of 32.26
for the t. of the mighty men was in 32.27
for all the t. which they caused by 32.30
For he spread t. in the land of the 32.32
every kind of t. against Gog, 38.21
t. of them goes before them. Hab 1.09
And he stared at him in t., Ac 10.04
are not a t. to good conduct, but Rom 13.03

TERRORS

and by great t., according to all Deu 4.34
the t. of God are arrayed against Job 6.04
T. frighten him on every side, and 18.11
and is brought to the king of t. 18.14
out of his gall; t. come upon him. 20.25
with the t. of deep darkness. 24.17
T. overtake him like a flood; 27.20
T. are turned upon me; my honor 30.15
the t. of death have fallen upon me Ps 55.04
a moment, swept away utterly by t.! 73.19
from my youth up, I suffer thy t.; 88.15
is high, and t. are in the way; Ecc 12.05
appointed feast my t. on every side; Lam 2.22
there will be t. and great signs Lk 21.11

TERROR-STRICKEN

Assyrians will be t. at the voice of the Is 30.31

TERTIUS
I T., the writer of this letter, greet Rom 16.22

TERTULLUS
some elders and a spokesman, one T. Ac 24.01
T. began to accuse him, saying: "Since 24.02

TEST
put the LORD your God to the t., Deu 6.16
he might humble you and t. you, 8.16
one, whom thou didst t. at Massah, 33.08
that by them I may t. Israel, Ju 2.22
to t. Israel by them, that is, all in 3.01
and I will t. them for you there; 7.04
she came to t. him with hard 1Ki 10.01
to Jerusalem to t. him with hard 2Ch 9.01
and t. him every moment? Job 7.18
his eyelids t., the children of men. Ps 11.04
t. my heart and my mind. 26.02
put God to the t. in the desert; 106.14
now, I will make a t. of pleasure; Ecc 2.01
I will not put the LORD to the t." Is 7.12
I will refine them and t. them, Jer 9.07
Let us t. and examine our ways, and Lam 3.40
"T. your servants for ten days; Dan 1.12
silver, and t. them as gold is tested. Zec 13.09
and thereby put me to the t., Mal 3.10
they put God to the t. they escape." 3.15
and to t. him they asked him to Mt 16.01
malice, said, "Why put me to the t., 22.18
asked him a question, to t. him. 22.35
him a sign from heaven, to t. him. Mk 8.11
up and in order to t. him asked, 10.02
said to them, "Why put me to the t.? 12.15
stood up to put him to the t., Lk 10.25
to t. him, sought from him a sign 11.16
This he said to t. him, for he Jn 6.06
This they said to t. him, that they * 8.06
the fire will t. what sort of work 1Co 3.13
We must not put the Lord to the t., 10.09
that I might t. you and know 2Co 2.09
for in a severe t. of affliction, 8.02
Under the t. of this service, you 9.13
T. yourselves. Do you not realize 13.05
indeed you fail to meet the t.! 13.05
we may appear to have met the t., 13.07
But let each one t. his own work, Gal 6.04
but t. everything; hold fast what 1Th 5.21
put me to the t. and saw my works Heb 3.09
has stood the t. he will receive Jas 1.12
but t. the spirits to whether 1Jn 4.01

TESTED
After these things God t. Abraham, Gen 22.01
By this you shall be t.: 42.15
prison, that your words may be t., 42.16
the test, as you t. him at Massah. Deu 6.16
And Gideon t. them; twenty-two thousand Ju 7.03
For thou, O God, hast t. us; Ps 66.10
They t. God in their heart by 78.18
They t. him again and again, and 78.41
Yet they t. and rebelled against 78.56
I t. you at the waters of Meribah. 81.07
when your fathers t. me, and put me 95.09
pass the word of the LORD t. him. 105.19
All this I have t. by wisdom; Ecc 7.23
a t. stone, a precious cornerstone, Is 28.16
matter, and t. them for ten days. Dan 1.14
silver, and test them as gold is t. Zec 13.09
up to him and t. him by asking, Mt 19.03
we have often t. and found earnest 2Co 8.22
And let them also be t. first; 1Ti 3.10
when he was t., offered up Isaac, Heb 11.17
though perishable is t. by fire, 1Pe 1.07
men but have t. those who call Rev 2.02
into prison, that you may be t., 2.10

TESTER
an assayer and t. among my people, Jer 6.27

TESTEST
if thou t. me, thou wilt find no Ps 17.03

TESTICLES
disease or scabs or crushed t.; Lev 21.20
which has its t. bruised or crushed 22.24
"He whose t. are crushed or whose Deu 23.01

TESTIFIED
your own mouth has t. against you, 2Sa 1.16
these t. against them, but they 2Ch 24.19
For Jesus himself t. that a prophet Jn 4.44
and t., "Truly, truly, I say to you, 13.21
And he t. with many other words and Ac 2.40
Now when they had t. and spoken the 8.25
of whom he t. and said, 'I have 13.22
for as you have t. about me at 23.11
because we t. of God that he raised 1Co 15.15
It has been t. somewhere, "What is Heb 2.06
one of whom it is t. that he lives. 7.08
arrived and t. to the truth of 3Jn 1.03
who have t. to your love before the 1.06

TESTIFIES
up against me, it t. to my face. Job 16.08
The pride of Israel t. to his face; Hos 5.05
the Holy Spirit t. to me in every Ac 20.23
He who t. to these things says, Rev 22.20

TESTIFY
adjuration to t. and though he is Lev 5.01
and they shall t., 'Our hands did Deu 21.07
t. against me before the LORD and 1Sa 12.03
T. against me and I will restore it 12.03
your own lips t. against you. Job 15.06
O Israel, I will t. against you. Ps 50.07
thee, and our sins t. against us; Is 59.12
"Though our iniquities t. against us, Jer 14.07
"Hear, and t. against the house of Amo 3.13
it that these men t. against you?" Mt 26.62
many things they t. against you?" 27.13
it that these men t. against you?" Mk 14.60
me because I t. of it that its Jn 7.07
and to t. that he is the one Ac 10.42
to t. to the gospel of the grace of 20.24
Therefore I t. to you this day that 20.26
time, if they are willing to t., 26.05
as I can t., and beyond their means, 2Co 8.03
I t. again to every man who receives Gal 5.03
Now this I affirm and t. in the Lord, Eph 4.17
to t. the things that were to be Heb 3.05
and t. to it, and proclaim to you 1Jn 1.02
have seen and t. that the Father 4.14
I t. to him too, and you know my 3Jn 1.12

TESTIFYING
t. to the Jews that the Christ was Ac 18.05
t. both to Jews and to Greeks of 20.21
so I stand here t. both to small 26.22
t. to the kingdom of God and trying 28.23
be ashamed then of t. to our Lord, 2Ti 1.08

TESTIMONIES
these are the t., the statutes, and Deu 4.45
and his t., and his statutes, which 6.17
meaning of the t. and the statutes 6.20
and his t., as it is written in the 1Ki 2.03
commandments and his t. and his 2Ki 22.03
thy t., and thy statutes, performing 1Ch 29.19
commandments and his t. and his 2Ch 34.31
who keep his covenant and his t. Ps 25.10
God, and did not observe his t., 78.56
they kept his t., and the statutes 99.07
Blessed are those who keep his t., 119.02
In the way of thy t. I delight as 119.14

TESTIMONIES (cont.)
contempt, for I have kept thy t. Ps 119.22
Thy t. are my delight, they are my 119.24
I cleave to thy t., O LORD; 119.31
Incline my heart to thy t., 119.36
also speak of thy t. before kings, 119.46
thy ways, I turn my feet to thy t.; 119.59
to me, that they may know thy t. 119.79
I may keep the t. of thy mouth. 119.88
to destroy me; but I consider thy t. 119.95
for thy t. are my meditation. 119.99
Thy t. are my heritage for ever; 119.111
as dross; therefore I love thy t. 119.119
understanding, that I may know thy t.! 119.125
Thy t. are wonderful; therefore my 119.129
appointed thy t. in righteousness 119.138
Thy t. are righteous for ever; 119.144
save me, that I may observe thy t. 119.146
known from thy t. that thou hast 119.152
but I do not swerve from thy t. 119.157
My soul keeps thy t.; I love them 119.167
I keep thy precepts and t., for all 119.168
covenant and my t. which I shall 132.12
and in his statutes and in his t., Jer 44.23

TESTIMONY
placed it before the T., to be kept. Ex 16.34
the ark the t. which I shall give 25.16
shall put the t. that I shall give 25.21
that are upon the ark of the t., 25.22
bring the ark of the t. in thither 26.33
the ark of the t. in the most holy 26.34
the veil which is before the t., 27.21
veil that is by the ark of the t., 30.06
the mercy seat that is over the t., 30.06
of meeting and the ark of the t., 30.26
it before the t. in the tent of 30.36
of meeting, and the ark of the t., 31.07
Sinai, the two tables of the t., 31.18
two tables of the t. in his hands, 32.15
tables of the t. in his hand as he 34.29
tabernacle, the tabernacle of the t., 38.21
the ark of the t. with its poles 39.35
shall put in it the ark of the t., 40.03
incense before the ark of the t., 40.05
And he took the t. and put it into 40.20
and screened the ark of the t.; 40.21
which is upon the t., lest he die; Lev 16.13
Outside the veil of the t., 24.03
over the tabernacle of the t., Num 1.50
around the tabernacle of the t., 1.53
charge of the tabernacle of the t. 1.53
cover the ark of the t. with it; 4.05
that was upon the ark of the t., 7.89
the tabernacle, the tent of the t.; 9.15
over the tabernacle of the t., 10.11
the tent of meeting before the t., 17.04
the LORD in the tent of the t. 17.07
Moses went into the tent of the t.; 17.08
the rod of Aaron before the t., 17.10
you are before the tent of the t. 18.02
to death on the t. of one witness. 35.30
the ark of the t. to come up out Jos 4.16
upon him, and gave him the t.; 2Ki 11.12
upon him, and gave him the t.; 2Ch 23.11
of Israel for the tent of t.?" 24.06
do you not accept their t. Job 21.29
the t. of the LORD is sure, making Ps 19.07
He established a t. in Jacob, 78.05
Bind up the t., seal the teaching Is 8.16
To the teaching and to the t.! 8.20
to bear t. before them and the Mt 10.18
world, as a t. to all nations; 24.14
sought false t. against Jesus that 26.59
on your feet for a t. against them." Mk 6.11
my sake, to bear t. before them. 13.09
council sought t. against Jesus to 14.55
Yet not even so did their t. agree. 14.59
your feet as a t. against them." Lk 9.05
This will be a time for you to bear t. 21.13
said, "What further t. do we need? 22.71
He came for t., to bear witness to Jn 1.07
And this is the t. of John, 1.19
but you do not receive our t. 3.11
heard, yet no one receives his t.; 3.32
receives his t. sets his seal to 3.33
in him because of the woman's t., 4.39
to myself, my t. is not true; 5.31
I know that the t. which he bears 5.32
Not that the t. which I receive is 5.34
But the t. which I have is greater 5.36
to yourself; your t. is not true." 8.13
my t. is true, for I know whence I 8.14
that the t. of two men is true; 8.17
his t. is true, and he knows that he 19.35
and we know that his t. is true. 21.24
gave their t. to the resurrection Ac 4.33
will not accept your t. about me.' 22.18
even as the t. to Christ was 1Co 1.06
to you the t. of God in lofty 2.01
the t. of our conscience that we 2Co 1.12
because our t. to you was believed. 2Th 1.10
the t. to which was borne at the 1Ti 2.06
who in his t. before Pontius 6.13
This t. is true. Therefore rebuke Tit 1.13
mercy at the t. of two or three Heb 10.28
If we receive the t. of men, 1Jn 5.09
the t. of God is greater; 5.09
for this is the t. of God that he 5.09
Son of God has the t. in himself. 5.10
believed in the t. that God has 5.10
And this is the t., that God gave 5.11
Demetrius has t. from every one, and 3Jn 1.12
too, and you know my t. is true. 1.12
God and to the t. of Jesus Christ, Rev 1.02
word of God and the t. of Jesus. 1.09
And when they have finished their t., 11.07
Lamb and by the word of their t., 12.11
of God and bear t. to Jesus. 12.17
brethren who hold the t. of Jesus. 19.10
For the t. of Jesus is the spirit 19.10
for their t. to Jesus and for the 20.04
you with this t. for the churches. 22.16

TESTING
t. you to know what was in your Deu 8.02
for the LORD your God is t. you, 13.03
They were for the t. of Israel, Ju 3.04
men that God is t. them to show Ecc 3.18
For it will not be a t.— Eze 21.13
on the day of t. in the wilderness, Heb 3.08
know that the t. of your faith Jas 1.03

TESTS
for the ear t. words as the palate Job 34.03
The LORD t. the righteous and the Ps 11.05
to please God who t. our hearts. 1Th 2.04

TETRARCH
time Herod the t. heard about the Mt 14.01
and Herod being t. of Galilee, Lk 3.01
brother Philip t. of the region of 3.01
and Lysanias t. of Abilene, 3.01
But Herod the t., who had been 3.19
Now Herod the t. heard of all that 9.07
court of Herod the t., and Saul. Ac 13.01

TETTER
it is t. that has broken out in the Lev 13.39

THADDAEUS
James the son of Alphaeus, and T.; Mt 10.03
and T., and Simon the Cananaean, Mk 3.18

THAN

was more subtle t. any other wild Gen 3.01
punishment is greater t. I can bear. 4.13
deal worse with you t. with them." 19.09
one shall be stronger t. the other, 25.23
for you are much mightier t. we." 26.16
is none other t. the house of God, 28.17
give her to you t. that I should 29.19
and he loved Rachel more t. Leah, 29.30
Joseph more t. any other of his 37.03
loved him more t. all his brothers, 37.04
said, "She is more righteous t. I, 38.26
not greater in this house t. I am; 39.09
throne will I be greater t. you." 41.40
brother shall be greater t. he, 48.19
to you rather t. to your brothers 48.22
the Egyptians t. to die in the Ex 14.12
the LORD is greater t. all gods, 18.11
t. the half shekel, when you give 30.15
bring much more t. enough for 36.05
to be deeper t. the skin of his Lev 13.03
and appears no deeper t. the skin, 13.04
appears deeper t. the skin and its 13.20
and it is not deeper t. the skin, 13.21
and it appears deeper t. the skin, 13.25
and it is no deeper t. the skin, 13.26
if it appears deeper t. the skin, 13.30
no deeper t. the skin and there is 13.31
to be no deeper t. the skin, 13.32
to be no deeper t. the skin, 13.34
to be deeper t. the surface, 14.37
some man other t. your husband has Num 5.20
more t. all men that were on the 12.03
for they are stronger t. we." 13.31
greater and mightier t. they." 14.12
number and more honorable t. they. 22.15
his king shall be higher t. Agag, 24.07
are greater and taller t. we; Deu 1.28
greater and mightier t. yourselves, 4.38
and mightier t. yourselves, 7.01
more in number t. any other people 7.07
'These nations are greater t. I; 7.17
greater and mightier t. yourselves, 9.01
mightier and greater t. they.' 9.14
greater and mightier t. yourselves. 11.23
and an army larger t. your own, 20.01
him with more stripes t. these, 25.03
and numerous t. your fathers. 30.05
and because it was greater t. Ai, Jos 10.02
the hailstones t. the men of 10.11
an altar other t. the altar of the 22.19
other t. the altar of the LORD our 22.29
and behaved worse t. their fathers, Ju 2.19
is no other t. the sword of Gideon 7.14
Ephraim better t. the vintage of 8.02
you any better t. Balak the son of 11.25
down, "What is sweeter t. honey? 14.18
What is stronger t. a lion?" 14.18
her younger sister fairer t. she? 15.02
death were more t. those whom he 16.30
last kindness greater t. the first, Ru 3.10
yet there is a kinsman nearer t. I. 3.12
who is more to you t. seven sons, 4.15
Am I not more to you t. ten sons?" 1Sa 1.08
of Israel more handsome t. he; 9.02
he was taller t. any of the people 9.02
he was taller t. any of the people 10.23
to obey is better t. sacrifice, 15.22
and to hearken t. the fat of rams. 15.22
of yours, who is better t. you. 15.28
more success t. all the servants 18.30
David, "You are more righteous t. I; 24.17
better for me t. that I should 27.01
they were swifter t. eagles, 2Sa 1.23
they were stronger t. lions. 1.23
yet more contemptible t. this, 6.22
and being stronger t. she, 13.14
her was greater t. the love with 13.15
away is greater t. the other which 13.16
is better t. the counsel of 17.14
more people that day t. the sword. 18.08
worse for you t. all the evil that 19.07
in David also we have more t. you. 19.43
were fiercer t. the words of the 19.43
will do us more harm t. Absalom; 20.06
throne greater t. the throne of my 1Ki 1.37
of Solomon more famous t. yours, 1.47
his throne greater t. your throne.' 1.47
righteous and better t. himself, 2.32
For he was wiser t. all other men, 4.31
wiser t. Ethan the Ezrahite, and 4.31
is thicker t. my father's loins. 12.10
more t. all that their fathers had 14.22
did more evil t. all who were 16.25
the LORD more t. all that were 16.30
to anger t. all the kings of Israel 16.33
for I am no better t. my fathers." 19.04
and so they were stronger t. we; 20.23
we shall be stronger t. they. 20.23
we shall be stronger t. they." 20.25
better t. all the waters of Israel? 2Ki 5.12
there more t. once or twice. 6.10
us are more t. those who are with 6.16
no more of her t. the skull and 9.35
an army of more t. fifty horsemen 13.07
to do more evil t. the nations had 21.09
more wicked t. all that the 21.11
was more honorable t. his brothers; 1Ch 4.09
sons of Eleazar t. among the sons 24.04
for our God is greater t. all gods. 2Ch 2.05
is thicker t. my father's loins. 10.10
house, who were better t. yourself; 21.13
able to give you much more t. this." 25.09
in heart t. the priests in sanctifying 29.34
passover otherwise t. as prescribed. 30.18
is one greater with us t. with him. 32.07
did more evil t. the nations whom 33.09
have risen higher t. our heads, Ez 9.06
punished us less t. our iniquities 9.13
and God-fearing man t. many. Neh 7.02
to another who is better t. she. Est 1.19
loved Esther more t. all the women, 2.17
his sight more t. all the virgins, 2.17
escape any more t. all the other 4.13
king delight to honor more t. me?" 6.06
dig for it more t. for hid treasures; Job 3.21
be heavier t. the sand of the sea; 6.03
are swifter t. a weaver's shuttle, 7.06
and death rather t. my bones. 7.15
"My days are swifter t. a runner; 9.25
of you less t. your guilt deserves. 11.06
It is higher t. heaven—what can 11.08
Deeper t. Sheol—what can you know? 11.08
Its measure is longer t. the earth, 11.09
the earth, and broader t. the sea. 11.09
will be brighter t. the noonday; 11.17
are among us, older t. your father. 15.10
of me, men who are younger t. I, 30.01
he justified himself rather t. God; 32.02
Job because they were older t. he. 32.04
answer you. God is greater t. man. 33.12
regards the rich more t. the poor, 34.19
am I better off t. if I had sinned?' 35.03
clouds, which are higher t. you. 35.05
who teaches us more t. the beasts 35.11
makes us wiser t. the birds of the 35.11
have chosen rather t. affliction. 36.21
days of Job more t. his beginning; 42.12
joy in my heart t. they have when Ps 4.07
hast made him little less t. God, 8.05
their children have more t. enough; 17.14
More to be desired are they t. gold, 19.10
sweeter also t. honey and drippings 19.10
righteous has t. the abundance of 37.16

THAN (cont.)

would be more t. can be numbered. Ps 40.05
they are more t. the hairs of my 40.12
me, and I shall be whiter t. snow. 51.07
You love evil more t. good, 52.03
and lying more t. speaking the 52.03
His speech was smoother t. butter, 55.21
his words were softer t. oil, 55.21
Sooner t. your pots can feel the 58.09
me to the rock that is higher t. I; 61.02
are together lighter t. a breath. 62.09
steadfast love is better t. life, 63.03
More in number t. the hairs of my 69.04
the LORD more t. an ox or a bull 69.31
more majestic t. the everlasting 76.04
is better t. a thousand elsewhere. 84.10
house of my God t. dwell in the 84.10
of Zion more t. all the dwelling 87.02
Mightier t. the thunders of many 93.04
mightier t. the waves of the sea, 93.04
made them stronger t. their foes. 105.24
in the LORD t. to put confidence 118.08
in the LORD t. to put confidence 118.09
is better to me t. thousands of 119.72
makes me wiser t. my enemies, 119.98
understanding t. all my teachers, 119.99
I understand more t. the aged, 119.100
sweeter t. honey to my mouth! 119.103
have had more t. enough of contempt. 123.03
the LORD more t. watchmen for the 130.06
more t. watchmen for the morning. 130.06
them, they are more t. the sand. 139.18
it is better t. gain from silver Pro 3.14
and its profit better t. gold. 3.14
She is more precious t. jewels, 3.15
and her speech is smoother t. oil; 5.03
knowledge rather t. choice gold; 8.10
for wisdom is better t. jewels, 8.11
My fruit is better t. gold, 8.19
and my yield t. choice silver. 8.19
for himself t. one who plays the 12.09
of the LORD t. great treasure and 15.16
where love is t. a fatted ox and 15.17
righteousness t. great revenues 16.08
To get wisdom is better t. gold; 16.16
is to be chosen rather t. silver. 16.16
with the poor t. to divide the 16.19
to anger is better t. the mighty, 16.32
his spirit t. he who takes a city. 16.32
with quiet t. a house full of 17.01
understanding t. a hundred blows 17.10
rather t. a fool in his folly. 17.12
who sticks closer t. a brother. 18.24
his integrity t. a man who is 19.01
and a poor man is better t. a liar. 19.22
acceptable to the LORD t. sacrifice. 21.03
of the housetop t. in a house 21.09
a desert land t. with a contentious 21.19
be chosen rather t. great riches, 21.20
favor is better t. silver or gold. 22.01
man is mightier t. a strong man, 24.05
of knowledge t. he who has strength; 24.05
t. to be put lower in the presence 25.07
of the housetop t. in a house 25.24
is more hope for a fool t. for him. 26.12
in his own eyes t. seven men who 26.16
provocation is heavier t. both. 27.03
Better is open rebuke t. hidden love. 27.05
who is near t. a brother who is 27.10
his integrity t. a rich man who is 28.06
find more favor t. he who flatters 28.23
is more hope for a fool t. for him. 29.20
She is far more precious t. jewels. 31.10
more t. any who had been before me Ecc 2.07
for a man t. that he should eat 2.24
better for them t. to be happy and 3.12
nothing better t. that a man 3.22
more fortunate t. the living who 4.02
but better t. both is he who has 4.03
of quietness t. two hands full of 4.06
Two are better t. one, because they 4.09
and wise youth t. an old and 4.13
is better t. to offer the sacrifice 5.01
should not vow t. that you should 5.05
untimely birth is better off t. he. 6.03
yet it finds rest rather t. he. 6.05
of the eyes t. the wandering of 6.09
to dispute with one stronger t. he. 6.10
name is better t. precious ointment 7.01
day of death, t. the day of birth. 7.01
of mourning t. to go to the house 7.02
Sorrow is better t. laughter, 7.03
of the wise t. to hear the song of 7.05
end of a thing t. its beginning; 7.08
is better t. the proud in spirit. 7.08
the former days better t. these?" 7.10
wise man more t. ten rulers that 7.19
more bitter t. death the woman 7.26
living dog is better t. a dead lion. 9.04
say that wisdom is better t. might, 9.16
are better t. the shouting of a 9.17
Wisdom is better t. weapons of war, 9.18
For your love is better t. wine, Sol 1.02
will extol your love more t. wine; 1.04
much better is your love t. wine, 4.10
fragrance of your oils t. any spice! 4.10
beloved more t. another beloved, O 5.09
your beloved more t. another beloved, 5.09
were greater t. those of Jerusalem Is 10.10
make men more rare t. fine gold, 13.12
and mankind t. the gold of Ophir. 13.12
In little more t. a year you will 32.10
by him as less t. nothing and 40.17
will be more t. the children of 54.01
heavens are higher t. the earth, 55.09
my ways higher t. your ways and my 55.09
and my thoughts t. your thoughts. 55.09
a name better t. sons and daughters; 56.05
herself less guilty t. false Judah. Jer 3.11
his horses are swifter t. eagles— 4.13
made their faces harder t. rock; 5.03
They did worse t. their fathers. 7.26
more in number t. the sand of the 15.08
have done worse t. your fathers, 16.12
thou art stronger t. I, and thou 20.07
they are more numerous t. locusts; 46.23
More t. for Jazer I weep for you, O 48.32
been greater t. the punishment of Lam 4.06
princes were purer t. snow, whiter t. milk; 4.07
bodies were more ruddy t. coral, the 4.07
Now their visage is blacker t. soot, 4.08
of the sword t. the victims of 4.09
were swifter t. the vultures in 4.19
Like adamant harder t. flint have I Eze 3.09
my ordinances more t. the nations, 5.06
statutes more t. the countries 5.06
more turbulent t. the nations that 5.07
greater abominations t. these." 8.15
more corrupt t. they in all your 16.47
committed more abominations t. they, 16.51
you acted more abominably t. they, 16.52
they are more in the right t. you. 16.52
more corrupt t. she in her doting 23.11
which was worse t. that of her 23.11
you are indeed wiser t. Daniel; 28.03
do more good to you t. ever before. 36.11
away from them t. from the lower 42.05
the ground more t. the lower and 42.06
condition t. the youths who are of Dan 1.10
fatter in flesh t. all the youths 1.15
times better t. all the magicians 1.20
I have more t. all the living has 2.30
times more t. it was wont to be 3.19
bodies rather t. serve and worship 3.28

THAN (cont.)

seemed greater t. its fellows. Dan 7.20
but one was higher t. the other, 8.03
shall be far richer t. all of them; 11.02
be stronger t. he and his dominion 11.05
a multitude, greater t. the former; 11.13
it was better with me then t. now.' Hos 2.07
love shame more t. their glory. 4.18
rather t. burnt offerings. 6.06
Are they better t. these Kingdoms? Amo 6.02
territory greater t. your territory, 6.02
is better for me to die t. to live." Jon 4.03
is better for me to die t. to live." 4.08
there are more t. a hundred and 4.11
Are you better t. Thebes that sat Nah 3.08
merchants more t. the stars of the 3.16
Their horses are swifter t. leopards, Hab 1.08
more fierce t. the evening wolves; 1.08
of purer eyes t. to behold evil 1.13
up the man more righteous t. he? 1.13
shall be greater t. the former, Hag 2.09
coming after me is mightier t. I, Mt 3.11
of your members t. that your whole 5.29
of your members t. that your whole 5.30
anything more t. this comes from 5.37
what more are you doing t. others? 5.47
Is not life more t. food, 6.25
and the body more t. clothing? 6.25
are you not of more value t. they? 6.26
and Gomorrah t. for that town. 10.15
are of more value t. many sparrows. 10.31
or mother more t. me is not worthy 10.37
daughter more t. me is not worthy 10.37
I tell you, and more t. a prophet. 11.09
no one greater t. John the Baptist; 11.11
kingdom of heaven is greater t. he. 11.11
for Tyre and Sidon t. for you. 11.22
for the land of Sodom t. for you." 11.24
something greater t. the temple is 12.06
more value is a man t. a sheep! 12.12
something greater t. Jonah is here. 12.41
something greater t. Solomon is 12.42
other spirits more evil t. himself, 12.45
man becomes worse t. the first. 12.45
maimed or lame t. with two hands 18.08
with one eye t. with two eyes to 18.09
over it more t. over the ninety-nine 18.13
eye of a needle t. for a rich man 19.24
other servants, more t. the first; 21.36
send me more t. twelve legions of 26.53
fraud will be worse t. the first." 27.64
me comes he who is mightier t. I, Mk 1.07
life maimed t. with two hands to 9.43
enter life lame t. with two feet 9.45
with one eye t. with two eyes to 9.47
eye of a needle t. for a rich man 10.25
other commandment greater t. these." 12.31
is much more t. all whole burnt 12.33
has put in more t. all those who 12.43
sold for more t. three hundred 14.05
"Collect no more t. is appointed Lk 3.13
he who is mightier t. I is coming, 3.16
I tell you, and more t. a prophet. 7.26
of women none is greater t. John; 7.28
kingdom of God is greater t. he." 7.28
"We have no more t. five loaves and 9.13
day for Sodom t. for that town. 10.12
for Tyre and Sidon t. for you. 10.14
one stronger t. he assails him and 11.22
other spirits more evil t. himself, 11.26
man becomes worse t. the first." 11.26
something greater t. Solomon is 11.31
something greater t. Jonah is here. 11.32
are of more value t. many sparrows. 12.07
For life is more t. food, 12.23
and the body more t. clothing. 12.23
more value are you t. the birds! 12.24
worse sinners t. all the other 13.02
worse offenders t. all the others 13.04
eminent man t. you be invited by 14.08
who repents t. over ninety-nine 15.07
own generation t. the sons of 16.08
t. for one dot of the law to become 16.17
t. that he should cause one of 17.02
justified rather t. the other; 18.14
eye of a needle t. for a rich man 18.25
has put in more t. all of them; 21.03
shall see greater things t. these." Jn 1.50
men loved darkness rather t. light, 3.19
baptizing more disciples t. John 4.01
Are you greater t. our father Jacob, 4.12
greater works t. these will he 5.20
I have is greater t. that of John; 5.36
do more signs t. this man has done?" 7.31
Are you greater t. our father 8.53
is greater t. all, and no one is 10.29
of men more t. the praise of God. 12.43
is not greater t. his master; 13.16
is sent greater t. he who sent him. 13.16
greater works t. these will he do, 14.12
for the Father is greater t. I. 14.28
Greater love has no man t. this, 15.13
is not greater t. his master.' 15.20
John, do you love me more t. these?" 21.15
to listen to you rather t. to God, Ac 4.19
was more t. forty years old. 4.22
And more t. ever believers were 5.14
"We must obey God rather t. men. 5.29
greater burden t. these necessary 15.28
were more noble t. those in 17.11
more blessed to give t. to receive.'" 20.35
There were more t. forty who made 23.13
for more t. forty of their men lie 23.21
it is not more t. twelve days 24.11
them not more t. eight or ten days, 25.06
brighter t. the sun, shining round 26.13
of the ship t. to what Paul said. 27.11
the creature rather t. the Creator, Rom 1.25
More t. that, we rejoice in our 5.03
we are more t. conquerors through 8.37
more highly t. he ought to think, 12.03
to us now t. when we first believed; 13.11
one day as better t. another, 14.05
foolishness of God is wiser t. men, 1Co 1.25
weakness of God is stronger t. men. 1.25
can any one lay t. that which is 3.11
better to marry t. to be aflame 7.09
anything rather t. put an obstacle 9.12
rather die t. have any one deprive 9.15
to jealousy? Are we stronger t. he? 10.22
is greater t. he who speaks in 14.05
I speak in tongues more t. you all; 14.18
t. ten thousand words in a tongue. 14.19
appeared to more t. five hundred 15.06
I worked harder t. any of them, 15.10
more earnest t. ever because of 2Co 8.22
another Jesus t. the one we 11.04
more of me t. he sees in me or 12.06
less favored t. the rest of the 12.13
intermediary implies more t. one; Gal 3.20
is no better t. a slave, though he 4.01
more children t. she who hath a 4.27
will take no other view t. mine; 5.10
more abundantly t. all that we ask Eph 3.20
count others better t. yourselves. Php 2.03
speculations rather t. the divine 1Ti 1.04
and is worse t. an unbeliever. 5.08
or has been married more t. once; 5.09
pleasure rather t. lovers of God, 2Ti 3.04
as a slave but more t. a slave, Phm 1.16
you will do even more t. I say. 1.21
is more excellent t. theirs. Heb 1.04
a little while lower t. the angels, 2.07
while was made lower t. the angels, 2.09

THAN (cont.)
much more glory t. Moses as the Heb 3.03
house has more honor t. the house. 3.03
sharper t. any two-edged sword, 4.12
swear by a greater t. themselves, 6.16
rather t. one named after the order 7.11
oath, which came later t. the law, 7.28
more excellent t. the old as the 8.06
with better sacrifices t. these. 9.23
more acceptable sacrifice t. Cain, 11.04
people of God t. to enjoy the 11.25
greater wealth t. the treasures of 11.26
seems painful rather t. pleasant; 12.11
more graciously t. the blood of 12.24
more precious t. gold which though 1Pe 1.07
God's will, t. for doing wrong. 3.17
become worse for them t. the first. 2Pe 2.20
righteousness t. after knowing it 2.21
for God is greater t. our hearts, 1Jn 3.20
you is greater t. he who is in the 4.04
No greater joy can I have t. this, 3Jn 1.04

THANK
offer with the t. offering unleavened Lev 7.12
to t., and to praise the LORD, the 1Ch 16.04
And now we t. thee, our God, and 29.13
sacrifices and t. offerings to the 2Ch 29.31
brought sacrifices and t. offerings; 29.31
Then I will t. thee in the great Ps 35.18
I will t. thee for ever, because 52.09
I will render t. offerings to thee. 56.12
Let them t. the LORD for his 107.08
Let them t. the LORD for his 107.15
Let them t. the LORD for his 107.21
Let them t. the LORD for his 107.31
I t. thee that thou hast answered 118.21
For Sheol cannot t. thee, Is 38.18
and bringing t. offerings to the Jer 17.26
as they bring t. offerings to the 33.11
"I t. thee, Father, Lord of heaven Mt 11.25
"I t. thee, Father, Lord of heaven Lk 10.21
Does he t. the servant because he 17.09
I t. thee that I am not like other 18.11
I t. thee that thou hast heard me. Jn 11.41
First, I t. my God through Jesus Rom 1.08
I t. God that I speak in tongues 1Co 14.18
I t. my God in all my remembrance Php 1.03
We always t. God, the Father of our Col 1.03
And we also t. God constantly for 1Th 2.13
I t. him who has given me strength 1Ti 1.12
I t. God whom I serve with a clear 2Ti 1.03
I t. my God always when I remember Phm 1.04

THANKED
them Paul t. God and took courage. Ac 28.15

THANKFUL
I am t. that I baptized none of you 1Co 1.14
t. for your partnership in the gospel Php 1.05
called in the one body. And be t. Col 3.15

THANKFULNESS
If I partake with t., why am I 1Co 10.30
songs with t. in your hearts to God. Col 3.16

THANKING
t. and praising the LORD, and likewise 1Ch 23.30

THANKS
O give t. to the LORD, call on his 1Ch 16.08
O give t. to the LORD, for he is 16.34
we may give t. to thy holy name, 16.35
named to give t. to the LORD, 16.41
worshiped and gave t. to the LORD, 2Ch 7.03
made for giving t. to the LORD— 7.06
"Give t. to the LORD, for his 20.21
and giving t. to the LORD the God 30.22
the LORD and to give t. and praise. 31.02
praising and giving t. to the LORD, Ez 3.11
them, to praise and to give t., Neh 12.24
which gave t. and went in procession 12.31
those who gave t. went to the left, 12.38
those who gave t. stood in the 12.40
to the LORD the t. due to his Ps 7.17
I will give t. to the LORD with my 9.01
and with my song I give t. to him. 28.07
and give t. to his holy name. 30.04
I will give t. to thee for ever. 30.12
we will give t. to thy name for 44.08
I will give t. to thy name, O LORD, 54.06
I will give t. to thee, O Lord, among 57.09
We give t. to thee, O God; we give t.; 75.01
will give t. to thee for ever; 79.13
I give t. to thee, O Lord my God, 86.12
It is good to give t. to the LORD, 92.01
and give t. to his holy name! 97.12
Give t. to him, bless his name! 100.04
O give t. to the LORD, call on his 105.01
O give t. to the LORD, for he is 106.01
we may give t. to thy holy name 106.47
O give t. to the LORD, for he is 107.01
I will give t. to thee, O LORD, among 108.03
I will give great t. to the LORD; 109.30
I will give t. to the LORD with my 111.01
O give t. to the LORD, for he is 118.01
them and give t. to the LORD. 118.19
my God, and I will give t. to thee; 118.28
O give t. to the LORD, for he is 118.29
to give t. to the name of the LORD. 122.04
O give t. to the LORD, for he is 136.01
O give t. to the God of gods, for 136.02
O give t. to the Lord of lords, for 136.03
O give t. to the God of heaven, for 136.26
I give thee t., O LORD, with my 138.01
temple and give t. to thy name for 138.02
righteous shall give t. to thy name; 140.13
that I may give t. to thy name! 142.07
All thy works shall give t. to thee, 145.10
"I will give t. to thee, O LORD, for Is 12.01
"Give t. to the LORD, call upon his 12.04
he t. thee, as I do this day; 38.19
'Give t. to the LORD of hosts, for Jer 33.11
I give t. and praise, for thou hast Dan 2.23
prayed and gave t. before his God, 6.10
having given t. he broke them and Mt 15.36
he had given t. he gave it to them, 26.27
having given t. he broke them and Mk 8.06
he had given t. he gave it to them, 14.23
that very hour she gave t. to God, Lk 2.38
face at Jesus' feet, giving him t. 17.16
and when he had given t. he said, 22.17
he had given t. he broke it and 22.19
loaves, and when he had given t., Jn 6.11
bread after the Lord had given t. 6.23
and giving t. to God in the presence Ac 27.35
honor him as God or give t. to him, Rom 1.21
But t. be to God, that you who were 6.17
T. be to God through Jesus Christ 7.25
the Lord, since he gives t. to God; 14.06
of the Lord and gives t. to God. 14.06
churches of the Gentiles give t.; 16.04
I give t. to God always for you 1Co 1.04
because of that for which I give t.? 10.30
and when he had given t., he broke 11.24
For you may give t. well enough, 14.17
But t. be to God, who gives us the 15.57
many will give t. on our behalf 2Co 1.11
But t. be to God, who in Christ 2.14
But t. be to God who puts the same 8.16
T. be to God for his inexpressible 9.15
I do not cease to give t. for you, Eph 1.16
everything giving t. in the name of 5.20
giving t. to the Father, who has Col 1.12
giving t. to God the Father through 3.17
We give t. to God always for you 1Th 1.02

THANKS (cont.)
give t. in all circumstances; 1Th 5.18
bound to give t. to God always for 2Th 1.03
bound to give t. to God always for 2.13
and honor and t. to him who is Rev 4.09
"We give t. to thee, Lord God 11.17

THANKSGIVING
If he offers it for a t., then he Lev 7.12
offerings for t. he shall bring 7.13
offerings for t. shall be eaten on 7.15
a sacrifice of t. to the LORD, 22.29
appointed that t. be sung to the 1Ch 16.07
the lyre in t. and praise to the 25.03
in praise and t. to the LORD), 2Ch 5.13
of peace offerings and of t.; 33.16
leader to begin the t. in prayer, Neh 11.17
was in charge of the songs of t. 12.08
were songs of praise and t. to God. 12.46
singing aloud a song of t., Ps 26.07
with glad shouts and songs of t., 42.04
Offer to God a sacrifice of t., 50.14
He who brings t. as his sacrifice 50.23
I will magnify him with t. 69.30
Let us come into his presence with t.; 95.02
Enter his gates with t., and his 100.04
And let them offer sacrifices of t., 107.22
sacrifice of t. and call on the 116.17
Sing to the LORD with t.; 147.07
t. and the voice of song. Is 51.03
Out of them shall come songs of t., Jer 30.19
offer a sacrifice of t. of that Amo 4.05
the voice of t. will sacrifice to Jon 2.09
"Amen" to your t. when he does not 1Co 14.16
and more people it may increase t., 2Co 4.15
through us will produce t. to God; 9.11
but instead let there be t. Eph 5.04
supplication with t. let your Php 4.06
you were taught, abounding in t. Col 2.07
being watchful in it with t.; 4.02
For what t. can we render to God 1Th 3.09
received with t. by those who 1Ti 4.03
rejected if it is received with t.; 4.04
and wisdom and t. and honor and Rev 7.12

THANKSGIVINGS
with t. and with singing, with Neh 12.27
also overflows in many t. to God. 2Co 9.12
intercessions, and t. be made for all men, 1Ti 2.01

THEATER
they rushed together into the t., Ac 19.29
him not to venture into the t. 19.31

THEBES
bringing punishment upon Amon of T., Jer 46.25
execute acts of judgment upon T. Eze 30.14
and cut off the multitude of T. 30.15
T. shall be breached, and its walls 30.16
Are you better than T. that sat by Nah 3.08

THEBEZ
Then Abimelech went to T., and Ju 9.50
encamped against T., and took it. 9.50
the wall, so that he died at T.? Why 2Sa 11.21

THEFT
nothing, then he shall be sold for his t. Ex 22.01
fornication, t., false witness, slander. Mt 15.19
fornication, t., murder, adultery, Mk 7.21

THEFTS
or their immorality or their t. Rev 9.21

THEIRS
sojourners in a land that is not t., Gen 15.13
five times as much as any of t. 43.34
shall be t. by a perpetual statute Ex 29.09
that it may be t. to do the Num 8.11
men, and touch nothing of t., 16.26
every offering of t., every cereal 18.09
cereal offering of t. and every sin 18.09
sin offering of t. and every guilt 18.09
and every guilt offering of t., 18.09
The cities shall be t. to dwell in, 35.03
of Kohathites, for t. was the lot, 1Ch 6.54
whose word will stand, mine or t. Jer 44.28
thing in Israel shall be t. Eze 44.29
Every evil of t. is in Gilgal; Hos 9.15
for t. is the kingdom of heaven. Mt 5.03
for t. is the kingdom of heaven. 5.10
obtained is more excellent than t. Heb 1.04

THEME
My heart overflows with a goodly t.; Ps 45.01

THEMSELVES
leaves together and made t. aprons. Gen 3.07
his wife hid t. from the presence 3.08
families of the earth will bless t." 12.03
of the earth shall bless t. by him? 18.18
they wearied t. groping for the 19.11
the nations of the earth bless t., 22.18
of the earth shall bless t.: 26.04
the families of the earth bless t. 28.14
if they gather t. against me and 34.30
shall order t. as you command; 41.40
and bowed t. before him with their 42.06
and them by t., and the Egyptians 43.32
Egyptians who ate with him by t., 43.32
them go and gather straw for t. Ex 5.07
prepared for t. any provisions. 12.39
small matter they shall decide t.; 18.22
any small matter they decided t. 18.26
near to the LORD consecrate t., 19.22
you shall couple five curtains by t., 26.09
and six curtains by t., and the sixth 26.09
they bring guilt upon t. and die. 28.43
people gathered t. together to 32.01
land of Egypt, have corrupted t.; 32.07
have made for t. a molten calf, 32.08
Levi gathered t. together to him. 32.26
they have made for t. gods of gold. 32.31
Israel stripped t. of their ornaments, 33.06
curtains by t., and six curtains by t. 36.16
of them shall bathe t. in water, Lev 15.18
casting out before you defiled t.; 18.24
who registered t. by families, Num 1.18
wash their clothes and cleanse t. 8.07
And the Levites purified t. from sin, 8.21
shall gather t. to you at the 10.03
of Israel, shall gather t. to you. 10.04
them out for t. all around the 11.32
and they assembled t. together 16.03
they assembled t. together against 20.02
who have yoked t. to Baal of Peor. 25.05
who gathered t. together against 27.03
left and hide t. from you are Deu 7.20
they have made t. a molten image. 9.12
and presented t. in the tent of 31.14
even our enemies t. being judges. 32.31
and hid t. in the cave at Makkedah. Jos 10.16
the cave where they had hidden t., 10.27
had possessed t. by command of the 22.09
and they presented t. before God. 24.01
their daughters to t. for wives, Ju 3.06
the people offered t. willingly, 5.02
who offered t. willingly among the 5.09
Israel made for t. the dens which 6.02
lest Israel vaunt t. against me, 7.02
the men and women, and shut t. in; 9.51
set up the graven image for t.; 18.30
presented t. in the assembly of the 20.02
and set t. in array against Gibeah, 20.30
and set t. in array at Baaltamar; 20.33
full have hired t. out for bread, 1Sa 2.05

THEMSELVES (cont.)
the people hid t. in caves and in 1Sa 13.06
Hebrews make t. swords or spears"; 13.19
of them showed t. to the garrison 14.11
the holes where they have hid t." 14.11
who had hid t. in the hill country 14.22
young men have kept t. from women." 21.04
gathered t. together behind Abner, 2Sa 2.25
were by t. in the open country. 10.08
Israel, they gathered t. together. 10.15
Syrians arrayed t. against David, 10.17
they also built for t. high places, 1Ki 14.23
let them choose one bull for t., 18.23
and cut t. after their custom with 18.28
and the harlots washed t. in it, 22.38
camp to hide t. in the open 2Ki 7.12
They built for t. high places at 17.09
they set up for t. pillars and 17.10
and made for t. molten images of 17.16
and sold t. to do evil in the sight 17.17
from among t. all sorts of people 17.32
sanctified t. to bring up the ark 1Ch 15.14
they had made t. odious to David, 19.06
come were by t. in the open 19.09
four sons who were with him hid t. 21.20
who were present had sanctified t., 2Ch 5.11
singers to make t. heard in unison 5.13
are called by my name humble t., 7.14
and the king humbled t. and said, 12.06
When the LORD saw that they humbled t., 12.07
to Shemaiah: "They have humbled t.; 12.07
they took for t. until they could 20.25
their brethren, and sanctified t., 29.15
with him bowed t. and worshiped. 29.29
had sanctified t. their brethren 29.34
then the priests in sanctifying t. 29.34
not sanctified t. in sufficient 30.03
Zebulun humbled t. and came to 30.11
shame, so that they sanctified t., 30.15
assembly who had not sanctified t.; 30.17
and Zebulun, had not cleansed t., 30.18
sanctified t. in great numbers. 30.24
they might give t. to the law of 31.04
were faithful in keeping t. holy. 31.18
prepared for t. and for the priests, 35.14
the Levites prepared for t. 35.14
Levites had purified t. together; Ez 6.20
their fellow priests, and for t.; 6.20
not separated t. from the peoples 9.01
to be wives for t. and for their 9.02
They pledged t. to put away their 10.19
them and made booths for t., Neh 8.16
separated t. from all foreigners, 9.02
had made for t. a molten calf and 9.18
and delighted t. in thy great 9.25
have separated t. from the peoples 10.28
had built for t. villages around 12.29
and the Levites purified t.; 12.30
should purify t. and come and 13.22
day to avenge t. upon their Est 8.13
of the country declared t. Jews, 8.17
took it upon t. and their descendants 9.27
laid down for t. and for their 9.31
came to present t. before the LORD, Job 1.06
came to present t. before the LORD, 2.01
earth who rebuilt ruins for t., 3.14
they mass t. together against me. 16.10
Let him recompense it to t., 21.19
the poor of the earth all hide t. 24.04
by day they shut t. up; 24.16
and to warm t. the roots of the 30.04
where evildoers may hide t. 34.22
at the crashing they are beside t. 41.25
The kings of the earth set t., Ps 2.02
who have set t. against me round 3.06
Let them not say to t., 35.25
dishonor who magnify t. against me! 35.26
and delight t. in abundant prosperity. 37.11
They band t. together, they lurk, 56.06
but they have fallen into it t. 57.06
fierce men band t. against me. 59.03
drip, the hills gird t. with joy, 65.12
the meadows clothe t. with flocks, 65.13
the valleys deck t. with grain, 65.13
let not the rebellious exalt t. 66.07
May men bless t. by him, all nations 72.17
They said to t., "We will utterly 74.08
and our enemies laugh among t. 80.06
Then they attached t. to the Baal 106.28
will offer t. freely on the day 110.03
who lift t. up against thee for 139.20
when the wicked rise, men hide t. Pro 28.12
men hide t., but when they perish, 28.28
happy and enjoy t. as long as they Ecc 3.12
rain, they empty t. on the earth; 11.03
which they made for t. to worship, Is 2.20
For they have brought evil upon t. 3.09
but t. go into captivity. 46.02
cannot deliver t. from the power 47.14
For they call t. after the holy 48.02
and stay t. on the God of Israel; 48.02
and they shall prostrate t.; 49.07
foreigners who join t. to the LORD, 56.06
will not cover t. with what they 59.06
and purify t. to go into the 66.17
and hewed out cisterns for t., Jer 2.13
None who seek her need weary t.; 2.24
then nations shall bless t. in him, 4.02
Is it not t., to their own confusion? 7.19
they have tired t. out but profit 12.13
Their prince shall be one of t., 30.21
not humbled t. even to this day, 44.10
not destroy only enough for t.? 49.09
they shall array t. against her; 50.09
the nations weary t. only for fire. 51.58
They gird t. with sackcloth, and Eze 7.18
nor defile t. any more with all 14.11
they shall set t. against you on [illegible]24
they will clothe t. with trembling[illegible]
they make t. bald for you, and gi[illegible]
and gird t. with sackcloth, and t[illegible]
but the shepherds have fed t., [illegible]
longer shall the shepherds feed t. [illegible]
gave my land to t. as a possessio[illegible]
about you shall t. suffer reproach. [illegible]
not defile t. any more with their [illegible]
shall not gird t. with anything [illegible]
not defile t. by going near to a [illegible]
unmarried sister they may defile t[illegible]
them, and they fled to hide t. Dan 10.0[illegible]
shall lift t. up in order to 11.14
many shall join t. to them with 11.34
Many shall purify t., 12.10
and make t. white, and be refined; 12.10
they shall appoint for t. one head; Hos 1.11
for the men t. go aside with 4.14
drunkards, they give t. to harlotry; 4.18
for grain and wine they gash t., 7.14
corrupted t. as in the days of 9.09
Baalpeor, and consecrated t. to Baal, 9.10
and make for t. molten images, idols 13.02
Let the nations bestir t., Joe 3.12
they lay t. down beside every altar Amo 2.08
and stretch t. upon their couches, 6.04
invent for t. instruments of music; 6.05
and anoint t. with the finest oils, 6.06
who stretch t. shall pass away." 6.07
Though they hide on the top of 9.03
they not steal only enough for t.? Ob 1.05
and dignity proceed from t. Hab 1.07
and nations weary t. for naught? 2.13
all who array t. in foreign attire. Zep 1.08
shall join t. to the LORD in that Zec 2.11
presenting t. before the LORD of 6.05

THEMSELVES (cont.)
lift it shall grievously hurt t. Zec 12.03
the clans of Judah shall say to t., 12.05
David by itself, and their wives by t.; 12.12
Nathan by itself, and their wives by t.; 12.12
Levi by itself, and their wives by t.; 12.13
Simeites by itself, and their wives by t.; 12.13
each by itself, and their wives by t. 12.14
Egypt do not go up and present t., 14.18
some of the scribes said to t., Mt 9.03
the villages and buy food for t." 14.15
And they discussed it among t., 16.07
who have made t. eunuchs for the 19.12
they said to t., 'This is the heir; 21.38
but they t. will not move them with 23.04
so that they questioned among t., Mk 1.27
they thus questioned within t., 2.08
and they have no root in t., 4.17
the boat to a lonely place by t. 6.32
about and buy t. something to eat." 6.36
do not eat unless they purify t.; 7.04
up a high mountain apart by t.; 9.02
So they kept the matter to t., 9.10
some who said to t. indignantly, 14.04
to the eleven t. as they sat at table; * 16.14
rejected the purpose of God for t., Lk 7.30
with him began to say among t., 7.49
who trusted in t. that they were 18.09
they said to t., 'This is the heir; 20.14
he saw the linen cloths by t.; * 24.12
they t. got into the boats and went Jn 6.24
The Jews then disputed among t., 6.52
before the Passover, to purify t. 11.55
me for the sake of the works t. 14.11
may have my joy fulfilled in t. 17.13
they were standing and warming t.; 18.18
They t. did not enter the praetorium, 18.28
one accord devoted t. to prayer, Ac 1.14
And they devoted t. to the apostles' 2.42
kings of the earth set t. in array, 4.26
[illegible] the sa[illegible] 15.27
[illegible] 23.[illegible]
[illegible] 26.16
[illegible]rd 27.31
[illegible]hey 27.31
[illegible] 34.08
[illegible] 34.10
[illegible]h 36.05
[illegible] 36.07
[illegible] 37.23
[illegible] 44.18
[illegible] 44.25
[illegible] 44.25
[illegible] [illegible].07
law requires, they are a law to t., [illegible]
have devoted t. to the service of 1Co [illegible]
those who pride t. on a man's 2Co 5.[illegible]
no longer for t. but for him who 5.15
first they gave t. to the Lord and 8.05
with some of those who commend t. 10.12
they measure t. by one another, 10.12
and compare t. with one another, 10.12
disguising t. as apostles of Christ 11.13
also disguise t. as servants of 11.15
who unsettle you would multilate t.! Gal 5.12
circumcision do not t. keep the law, 6.13
and have given t. up to licentiousness, Eph 4.19
For they t. report concerning us 1Th 1.09
nor to occupy t. with myths and 1Ti 1.04
should adorn t. modestly and 2.09
if they prove t. blameless let 3.10
standing for t. and also great 3.13
thus laying up for t. a good 6.19
accumulate for t. teachers to suit 2Ti 4.03
One of t., a prophet of their own, Tit 1.12
urge the younger men to control t. 2.06
careful to apply t. to good deeds; 3.08
learn to apply t. to good deeds, 3.14
Men indeed swear by a greater than t., Heb 6.16
heavenly things t. with better 9.23
they were serving not t. but you, 1Pe 1.12
used to adorn t. and were submissive 3.05
bringing upon t. swift destruction. 2Pe 2.01
but they t. are slaves of corruption; 2.19
and abandon t. for the sake of gain Jud 1.11
carouse together, looking after t.; 1.12
those who call t. apostles but are Rev 2.02
to be killed as they t. had been. 6.11
who have not defiled t. with women, 14.04

THENCE
T. he removed to the mountain on Gen 12.08
brought you out t. with a mighty Deu 5.15
and the boundary goes t. to the sea; Jos 16.06
and t. goes to Geliloth, which is 18.17
t. it goes to Daberath, then up to 19.13
and t. he returned to Samaria. 2Ki 2.25
priests whom you carried away t.; 17.27
gather them t. and bring them to Neh 1.09
T. he spies out the prey; Job 39.29
go out t., touch no unclean thing; Is 52.11
t. along the Brook of Egypt to the Eze 47.19
t. along the Brook of Egypt to the 48.28
and t. go to Hamath the great; Amo 6.02
t. I will bring you down, says the Ob 1.04

THEOPHILUS
account for you, most excellent T., Lk 1.03
O T., I have dealt with all that Ac 1.01

THEREBY
one may do and t. become guilty. Lev 6.07
of semen, becoming unclean t.; 15.32
for it and die t. when they profane 22.09
and t. you shall live long in the Deu 32.47
peace; t. good will come to you. Job 22.21
and t. put me to the test, says the Mal 3.10
myself, but I am not t. acquitted. 1Co 4.04
t[illegible]g the hostility to an end. Eph 2.16
[illegible]ne have entertained angels Heb 13.02

[illegible]FORE
[illegible]n leaves his father and his Gen 2.24
[illegible]ORD God sent him forth from 3.23
[illegible]said, "Like Nimrod a mighty 10.09
[illegible]name was called Babel, 11.09
[illegible]well was called Beerlahairoi; 16.14
[illegible] name of the city was called 19.22
[illegible]l not let you touch her. 20.06
[illegible] swear to me here by God that 21.23
[illegible]t place was called Beersheba; 21.31
[illegible] name was called Edom.) 25.30
[illegible] name of the city is Beersheba 26.33
[illegible] t., my son, obey my word as I 27.08
[illegible] t., my son, obey my voice; 27.43
sho[illegible]d you t. serve me for nothing? 29.15
t. his name was called Levi. 29.34
t. she called his name Judah; 29.35
t. she called his name Dan. 30.06
me today." T. he named it Galeed, 31.48
T. to this day the Israelites do 32.32
t. the name of the place is called 33.17
T. his name was called Perez. 38.29
Now t. let Pharaoh select a man 41.33
t. is this distress come upon us." 42.21
Now t., when I come to your servant 44.30
Now t., let your servant, I pray you, 44.33
t. they did not sell their land. 47.22
Now t. let me go up, I pray you, and 50.05
T. the place was named Abelmizraim; 50.11
T. they set taskmasters over them Ex 1.11
Now t. go, and I will be with your 4.12
t. they cry, 'Let us go and offer 5.08
t. you say, 'Let us go and sacrifice 5.17
Say t. to the people of Israel, 'I 6.06
Now t. send, get your cattle and all 9.19

THEREFORE (cont.)

Now t., forgive my sin, I pray you, Ex 10.17
t. you shall observe this day, 12.17
You shall t. keep this ordinance at 13.10
T. I sacrifice to the LORD all the 13.15
was bitter; t. it was named Marah. 15.23
t. on the sixth day he gives you 16.29
T. the people found fault with 17.02
Now t., if you will obey my voice 19.05
t. the LORD blessed the sabbath day 20.11
t. you shall not eat any flesh that 22.31
now t. let me alone, that my wrath 32.10
T. the people of Israel stripped 33.06
Now t., I pray thee, if I have found 33.13
consecrate yourselves t., and be Lev 11.44
you shall t. be holy, for I am holy." 11.45
T. I have said to the people of 17.12
t. I have said to the people of 17.14
You shall t. keep my statutes and 18.05
Consecrate yourselves t., and be holy; 20.07
"You shall t. keep all my statutes 20.22
these things, and t. I abhorred them. 20.23
You shall t. make a distinction 20.25
of their God; t. they shall be holy. 21.06
They shall t. keep my charge, lest 22.09
"T. you shall do my statutes, and 25.18
T. the LORD will give you meat, and Num 11.18
T. the name of that place was 11.34
t. he has slain them in the wilderness.' 14.16
T. it is against the LORD that you 16.11
t. they are holy. Thus they shall 16.38
t. I have said of them that they 18.24
T. you shall say to them, 'When you 18.30
t. you shall not bring this assembly 20.12
T. the ballad singers say, "Come to 21.27
Now t., if it is evil in thy sight, 22.34
T. now flee to your place; I said, 24.11
T. say, 'Behold, I give to him my 25.12
Now t., kill every male among the 31.17
"T. take good heed to yourselves. Deu 4.15
know t. this day, and lay it to your 4.39
T. you shall keep his statutes and 4.40
t. the LORD your God commanded you 5.15
Now t. why should we die? For this 5.25
careful to do t. as the LORD your 5.32
Hear t., O Israel, and be careful to 6.03
Know t. that the LORD your God is 7.09
You shall t. be careful to do the 7.11
Know t. this day that he who goes 9.03
"Know t., that the LORD your God is 9.06
T. Levi has no portion or inheritance 10.09
Circumcise t. the foreskin of your 10.16
Love the sojourner t.; for you were 10.19
"You shall t. love the LORD your 11.01
"You shall t. keep all the commandment 11.08
"You shall t. lay up these words of 11.18
t. I command you, You shall open 15.11
t. I command you this today. 15.15
T. I command you, You shall set 19.07
t. your camp must be holy, that he 23.14
t. I command you to do this. 24.18
t. I command you to do this. 24.22
T. when the LORD your God has given 25.19
you shall t. be careful to do them 26.16
You shall t. obey the voice of the 27.10
t. you shall serve your enemies 28.48
T. be careful to do the words of 29.09
t. the anger of the LORD was 29.27
t. choose life, that you and your 30.19
Now t. write this song, and teach it 31.19
now t. arise, go over this Jordan, Jos 1.02
Now t. take twelve men from the 3.12
Joshua t. commanded the priests, 4.17
T. the people of Israel cannot 7.12
In the morning t. you shall be 7.14
T. to this day the name of that 7.26
Now t. you are cursed, and some of 9.23

Now t. divide this land for an 13.07
t. turn and go to your home in the 22.04
T. we said, 'Let us now build an 22.26
T. be very steadfast to keep and do 23.06
t., to love the LORD your God. 23.11
t. he blessed you; so I delivered 24.10
"Now t. fear the LORD, and serve him 24.14
t. we also will serve the LORD, for 24.18
t. it shall be a witness against 24.27
T. the anger of the LORD was Ju 3.08
T. on that day he was called 6.32
Now t. proclaim in the ears of the 7.03
"Now t., if you acted in good faith 9.16
Now t., go by night, you and the men 9.32
t. I will deliver you no more. 10.13
now t. restore it peaceably." 11.13
I t. have not sinned against you, 11.27
T. beware, and drink no wine or 13.04
T. the name of it was called 15.19
now t. I will restore it to you." 17.03
Now t. consider what you will do." 18.14
Now t. give up the men, the base 20.13
T. they turned their backs before 20.42
would you t. wait till they were Ru 1.13
Would you t. refrain from marrying? 1.13
Wash t. and anoint yourself, and put 3.03
T. Hannah wept and would not eat. 1Sa 1.07
t. Eli took her to be a drunken 1.13
T. I have lent him to the LORD; 1.28
T. the LORD the God of Israel 2.30
T. Eli said to Samuel, "Go, lie down; 3.09
T. I swear to the house of Eli that 3.14
They sent t. and gathered together 5.11
T. it became a proverb, 'Is Saul 0.12
Now t. present yourselves before 10.19
T. the men of Jabesh said, "Tomorrow 11.10
Now t. stand still, that I may plead 12.07
Now t. stand still and see this 12.16
T. Saul said, "O LORD God of Israel 14.41
now t. hearken to the words of the 15.01
Now t., I pray, pardon my sin, and 15.25
T. Saul sent messengers to Jesse, 16.19
T. Saul said to David a second time, 18.21
t. take heed to yourself in the 19.02
T. deal kindly with your servant, 20.08
T. send and fetch him to me, for he 20.31
T. David inquired of the LORD, 23.02
See t., and take note of all the 23.23
t. he went down to the rock which 23.25
t. that place was called the Rock 23.28
May the LORD t. be judge, and give 24.15
Swear to me t. by the LORD that you 24.21
T. let my young men find favor in 25.08
Now t. know this and consider what 25.17
now t. let me pin him to the earth 26.08
Now t. let my lord the king hear 26.19
Now t., let not my blood fall to 26.20
t. Ziklag has belonged to the kings 27.06
t. he shall be my servant always." 27.12
t. I have summoned you to tell me 28.15
t. the LORD has done this thing to 28.18
Now t., you also hearken to your 28.22
T. Saul took his own sword, and fell 31.04
Now t. let your hands be strong, and 2Sa 2.07
T. that place was called Helkathhazzurim, 2.16
t. Abner smote him in the belly 2.23
T. it is said, "The blind and the 5.08
T. the name of that place is called 5.20
Now t. thus you shall say to my 7.08
T. thou art great, O LORD God; 7.22
t. thy servant has found courage to 7.27
now t. may it please thee to bless 7.29
Now t. the sword shall never depart 12.10
David t. besought God for the child 12.16
Now t., I pray you, speak to the 13.13
Now t. let not my lord the king so 13.33
Now t. let me go into the presence 14.32

THEREFORE (cont.)
Now t. send quickly and tell David, 2Sa 17.16
t. it is better that you send us 18.03
Now t. arise, go out and speak 19.07
Now t. why do you say nothing about 19.10
t., behold, I have come this day, the 19.20
do t. what seems good to you. 19.27
T. the LORD has recompensed me 22.25
T. he would not drink it. These things 23.17
T. his servants said to him, "Let a 1Ki 1.02
Now t. come, let me give you counsel, 1.12
Act t. according to your wisdom, but 2.06
Now t. hold him not guiltless, for 2.09
Now t. as the LORD lives, who has 2.24
Give thy servant t. an understanding 3.09
Now t. command that cedars of 5.06
Now t., O LORD, God of Israel, keep 8.25
Now t., O God of Israel, let thy 8.26
Let your heart t. be wholly true to 8.61
t. the LORD has brought all this 9.09
T. he said, "What kind of cities are 9.13
T. the LORD said to Solomon, "Since 11.11
Solomon sought t. to kill Jeroboam; 11.40
Now t. lighten the hard service of 12.04
t. the LORD has given him to the 13.26
t. behold, I will bring evil upon 14.10
Arise t., go to your house. When your feet 14.12
t. all Israel made Omri, the commander 16.16
Now t. send and gather all Israel 18.19
t. I will give all this great 20.28
t. your life shall go for his life, 20.42
"T. hear the word of the LORD: I saw 22.19
Now t. behold, the LORD has put a 22.23
t. he said to the driver of his 22.34
Now t. thus says the LORD, 'You 2Ki 1.04
T. you shall not come down from the 1.06
t. you shall not come down from 1.16
They sent t. fifty men; and for three 2.17
T. he returned to meet him, and told 4.31
T. the leprosy of Naaman shall 5.27
now t. come, let us go and tell the 7.09
t. they have gone out of the camp 7.12
Now t. take him up and cast him 9.26
Now t. call to me all the prophets 10.19
T. King Jehoash summoned Jehoiada 12.07
Now t. take no more money from your 12.07
(T. the LORD gave Israel a savior, 13.05
t. he sacked it, and he ripped up 15.16
t. the king of Assyria shut him 17.04
T. the LORD was very angry with 17.18
t. the LORD sent lions among them, 17.25
t. he has sent lions among them, 17.26
t. lift up your prayer for the 19.04
wood and stone, t. they were destroyed. 19.18
"T. thus says the LORD concerning 19.32
t. thus says the LORD, the God of 21.12
t. my wrath will be kindled against 22.17
t., behold, I will gather you to 22.20
T. Saul took his own sword, and fell 1Ch 10.04
T. the LORD slew him, and turned the 10.14
t. it was called the city of 11.07
T. he would not drink it. These things 11.19
T. the name of that place is called 14.11
Now t. thus shall you say to my 17.07
t. thy servant has found courage 17.25
now t. may it please thee to bless 17.27
I will t. make preparation for it 22.05
t. they became a father's house in 23.11
Now t. in the sight of all Israel, 28.08
T. David blessed the LORD in the 29.10
Now t. the wheat and barley, oil and 2Ch 2.15
Now t., O LORD, God of Israel, keep 6.16
Now t., O LORD, God of Israel, let 6.17
t. he has brought all this evil 7.22
Now t. lighten the hard service of 10.04
T. the LORD established the kingdom 17.05
"T. hear the word of the LORD: I saw 18.18
Now t. behold, the LORD has put a 18.22
t. he said to the driver of his 18.33
t. the name of that place has 20.26
T. the LORD was angry with Amaziah 25.15
T. the LORD his God gave him into 28.05
T. the wrath of the LORD came on 29.08
t. the Levites had to kill the 30.17
Now t. do not let Hezekiah deceive 32.15
T. wrath came upon him and Judah 32.25
T. the LORD brought upon them the 33.11
t. my wrath will be poured out upon 34.25
T. he brought up against them the 36.17
t. we send and inform the king, Ez 4.14
T. make a decree that these men be 4.21
T., if it seem good to the king, let 5.17
"Now t., Tattenai, governor of the 6.06
T. give not your daughters to their 9.12
T. let us make a covenant with our 10.03
T. thou didst give them into the Neh 9.27
T. thou didst give them into the 9.30
"Now t., our God, the great and 9.32
the Horonite; t. I chased him from me. 13.28
T. the Jews of the villages, who Est 9.19
T. they called these days Purim, 9.26
And t., because of all that was 9.26
t. despise not the chastening of Job 5.17
t. my words have been rash. 6.03
"T. I will not restrain my mouth; 7.11
t. I say, he destroys both the 9.22
t. thou wilt not let them triumph. 17.04
"T. my thoughts answer me, because 20.02
t. his prosperity will not endure. 20.21
T. snares are round about you, and 22.10
T. you say, 'What does God know? 22.13
T. I am terrified at his presence; 23.15
t. I was timid and afraid to 32.06
T. I say, 'Listen to me; let me also 32.10
"T., hear me, you men of understanding, 34.10
and not I; t. declare what you know. 34.33
T. men fear him; he does not 37.24
T. I have uttered what I did not 42.03
t. I despise myself, and repent in 42.06
Now t. take seven bulls and seven 42.08
T. the wicked will not stand in the Ps 1.05
Now t., O kings, be wise; be warned 2.10
T. my heart is glad, and my soul 16.09
T. the LORD has recompensed me 18.24
t. he instructs sinners in the way. 25.08
T. let every one who is godly offer 32.06
t. I remember thee from the land of 42.06
t. God has blessed you for ever. 45.02
T. God, your God, has anointed you 45.07
t. the peoples will praise you for 45.17
T. we will not fear though the 46.02
t. teach me wisdom in my secret 51.06
T. pride is their necklace; 73.06
T. the people turn and praise them; 73.10
T., when the LORD heard, he was full 78.21
T. I swore in my anger that they 95.11
T. he said he would destroy them— 106.23
T. he raised his hand and swore to 106.26
t. he will lift up his head. 110.07
t. I will call on him as long as I 116.02
understanding; t. I hate every false way. 119.104
as dross; t. I love thy testimonies. 119.119
T. I love thy commandments above 119.127
T. I direct my steps by all thy 119.128
wonderful; t. my soul keeps them. 119.129
T. my spirit faints within me; 143.04
t. they shall eat the fruit of Pro 1.31
t. calamity will come upon him 6.15
t. do not associate with one who 20.19
upon earth; t. let your words be few. Ecc 5.02
poured out; t. the maidens love you. Sol 1.03
T. the Lord says, the LORD of hosts, Is 1.24
T. my people go into exile for want 5.13
T. Sheol has enlarged its appetite 5.14

THEREFORE (cont.)
T., as the tongue of fire devours Is 5.24
T. the anger of the LORD was 5.25
T. the Lord himself will give you a 7.14
t., behold, the Lord is bringing up 8.07
T. the Lord does not rejoice over 9.17
T. the Lord, the LORD of hosts, will 10.16
T. thus says the Lord, the LORD of 10.24
T. all hands will be feeble, and 13.07
T. I will make the heavens tremble, 13.13
t. the armed men of Moab cry aloud; 15.04
T. the abundance they have gained 15.07
T. let Moab wail, let every one wail 16.07
T. I weep with the weeping of Jazer 16.09
T. my soul moans like a lyre for 16.11
t., though you plant pleasant 17.10
T. my loins are filled with anguish; 21.03
T. I said: "Look away from me, let me 22.04
T. a curse devours the earth, and 24.06
t. the inhabitants of the earth are 24.06
T. in the east give glory to the 24.15
T. strong peoples will glorify thee; 25.03
T. by this the guilt of Jacob will 27.09
t. he who made them will not have 27.11
T. the word of the LORD will be to 28.13
T. hear the word of the LORD, you 28.14
t. thus says the Lord GOD, "Behold, I 28.16
Now t. do not scoff, lest your bonds 28.22
t., behold, I will again do marvelous 29.14
T. thus says the LORD, who redeemed 29.22
T. shall the protection of Pharaoh 30.03
t. I have called her "Rahab who 30.07
T. thus says the Holy One of Israel, 30.12
t. this iniquity shall be to you 30.13
t. you shall speed away; 30.16
t. your pursuers shall be swift. 30.16
T. the LORD waits to be gracious to 30.18
t. he exalts himself to show mercy 30.18
t. lift up your prayer for the 37.04
wood and stone; t. they were destroyed. 37.19
"T. thus says the LORD concerning 37.33
T. I profaned the princes of the 43.28
Now t. hear this, you lover of 47.08
t. I have not been confounded; 50.07
t. I have set my face like a flint, 50.07
T. hear this, you who are afflicted, 51.21
Now t. what have I here, says the 52.05
T. my people shall know my name; 52.06
t. in that day they shall know that 52.06
T. I will divide him a portion with 53.12
T. justice is far from us, and 59.09
t. in your land you shall possess a 61.07
t. he turned to be their enemy, and 63.10
T. thus says the Lord GOD: "Behold, 65.13
"T. I still contend with you, says Jer 2.09
T. the showers have been withheld, 3.03
T. a lion from the forest shall 5.06
T. thus says the LORD, the God of 5.14
t. they have become great and rich, 5.27
T. I am full of the wrath of the 6.11
T. they shall fall among those who 6.15
T. hear, O nations, and know, O 6.18
T. thus says the LORD: 'Behold, I 6.21
t. I will do to the house which is 7.14
T. thus says the Lord GOD: Behold, my 7.20
T., behold, the days are coming, says 7.32
T. I will give their wives to 8.10
T. they shall fall among the fallen; 8.12
T. thus says the LORD of hosts: 9.07
T. thus says the LORD of hosts, the 9.15
t. they have not prospered, and all 10.21
T. I brought upon them all the 11.08
T., thus says the LORD, Behold, I am 11.11
"T. do not pray for this people, or 11.14
T. thus says the LORD concerning 11.21
t. thus says the LORD of hosts: 11.22
against me; t. I hate her. 12.08
t. the LORD does not accept them, 14.10
T. thus says the LORD concerning 14.15
T. thus says the LORD: "If you 15.19
t. I will hurl you out of this land 16.13
"T., behold, the days are coming, 16.14
"T., behold, I will make them know, 16.21
Now, t., say to the men of Judah and 18.11
"T. thus says the LORD: Ask among 18.13
T. deliver up their children to 18.21
t., behold, days are coming, says the 19.06
t. my persecutors will stumble, they 20.11
T. thus says the LORD concerning 22.18
T. thus says the LORD, the God of 23.02
"T., behold, the days are coming, 23.07
T. their way shall be to them like 23.12
T. thus says the LORD of hosts 23.15
T., behold, I am against the prophets, 23.30
t., behold, I will surely lift you 23.39
"T. thus says the LORD of hosts: 25.08
"You, t., shall prophesy against 25.30
Now t. amend your ways and your 26.13
T. thus says the LORD: 'Behold, I 28.16
t. thus says the LORD: Behold, I will 29.32
T. all who devour you shall be 30.16
t. I have continued my faithfulness 31.03
T. my heart yearns for him; 31.20
T. thou hast made all this evil 32.23
T., thus says the LORD: Behold, I am 32.28
"Now t. thus says the LORD, the God 32.36
T., thus says the LORD: You have not 34.17
T., thus says the LORD, the God of 35.17
t. thus says the LORD of hosts, the 35.19
T. thus says the LORD concerning 36.30
Now t. know for a certainty that 42.22
T. my wrath and my anger were 44.06
"T. thus says the LORD of hosts, the 44.11
t. your land has become a desolation 44.22
T. hear the word of the LORD, all 44.26
"T., behold, the days are coming, 48.12
T. I wail for Moab; I cry out for 48.31
T. my heart moans for Moab like a 48.36
t. the riches they gained have 48.36
T., behold, the days are coming, says 49.02
T. hear the plan which the LORD has 49.20
T. her young men shall fall in her 49.26
T., thus says the LORD of hosts, the 50.18
T. her young men shall fall in her 50.30
"T. wild beasts and jackals shall 50.39
T. hear the plan which the LORD has 50.45
of her wine, t. the nations went mad. 51.07
T. thus says the LORD: "Behold, I 51.36
"T., behold, the days are coming 51.47
"T., behold, the days are coming, 51.52
t. she became filthy; all who honored Lam 1.08
t. her fall is terrible, she has no 1.09
call to mind, and t. I have hope: 3.21
"t. I will hope in him." 3.24
T. thus says the Lord GOD: Because Eze 5.07
t. thus says the Lord GOD: Behold, I, 5.08
T. fathers shall eat their sons in 5.10
t. I will cut you down; my eye will not 5.11
T. I will make it an unclean thing 7.20
T. I will deal in wrath; my eye will not 8.18
T. prophesy against them, prophesy, O 11.04
T. thus says the Lord GOD: Your 11.07
T. say, 'Thus says the Lord GOD: 11.16
T. say, 'Thus says the Lord: I will 11.17
T., son of man, prepare for yourself 12.03
Tell them t., 'Thus says the Lord 12.23
T. say to them, Thus says the Lord 12.28
T. thus says the Lord GOD: "Because 13.08
t. behold, I am against you, says the 13.08
T. thus says the Lord GOD: I will 13.13
t. you shall no more see delusive 13.23
T. speak to them, and say to them, 14.04
"T. say to the house of Israel, Thus 14.06
T. thus says the Lord GOD: Like the 15.06

THEREFORE (cont.)
Behold, t., I stretched out my hand Eze 16.27
given to you; t. you were different. 16.34
t., behold I will gather all your 16.37
t., behold, I will requite your 16.43
t. I removed them, when I saw it. 16.50
T. thus says the Lord GOD: As I live, 17.19
"T. I will judge you, O house of 18.30
"T., son of man, speak to the house 20.27
t. my sword shall go out of its 21.04
Sigh t., son of man; sigh with 21.06
my people. Smite t. upon your thigh. 21.12
"Prophesy t., son of man; clap your 21.14
"T. thus says the Lord GOD: Because 21.24
T. I have made you a reproach to 22.04
"Behold, t., I strike my hands 22.13
T. thus says the Lord GOD: Because 22.19
t., behold, I will gather you into 22.19
T. I have poured out my indignation 22.31
T. I delivered her into the hands 23.09
T., O Oholibah, thus says the Lord 23.22
t. I will give her cup into your 23.31
T. thus says the Lord GOD: Because 23.35
t. bear the consequences of your 23.35
"T. thus says the Lord GOD: Woe to 24.06
T. thus says the Lord GOD: Woe to 24.09
t. I am handing you over to the 25.04
t., behold, I have stretched out my 25.07
t. I will lay open the flank of 25.09
t. thus says the Lord GOD, I will 25.13
t. thus says the Lord GOD, Behold I 25.16
t. thus says the Lord GOD: Behold, I 26.03
t. thus says the Lord GOD: "Because 28.06
t., behold, I will bring strangers 28.07
t. thus says the Lord GOD: Behold, I 29.08
t., behold, I am against you, and 29.10
T. thus says the Lord GOD: Behold, I 29.19
T. thus says the Lord GOD: Behold, I 30.22
"T. thus says the Lord GOD: Because 31.10
t. he shall be laid among the 32.32
T. say to them, Thus says the Lord 33.25
"T., you shepherds, hear the word of 34.07
t., you shepherds, hear the word of 34.09
"T., thus says the Lord GOD to them: 34.20
t., as I live, says the Lord GOD, I 35.06
of blood, t. blood shall pursue you. 35.06
t., as I live, says the Lord GOD, I 35.11
t. prophesy, and say, Thus says the 36.03
t., O mountains of Israel, hear the 36.04
t. thus says the Lord GOD: I speak 36.05
T. prophesy concerning the land of 36.06
t. thus says the Lord GOD: I swear 36.07
t. you shall no longer devour men 36.14
"T. say to the house of Israel, Thus 36.22
T. prophesy, and say to them, Thus 37.12
"T., son of man, prophesy, and say to 38.14
"T. thus says the Lord GOD: Now I 39.25
entered by it; t. it shall remain shut. 44.02
"T. thus says the Lord GOD: No 44.09
t. I have sworn concerning them, 44.12
t. he asked the chief of the Dan 1.08
t. they stood before the king. 1.19
T. show me the dream and its 2.06
T. tell me the dream, and I shall 2.09
T. Daniel went in to Arioch, whom 2.24
T., as soon as all the peoples 3.07
T. at that time certain Chaldeans 3.08
T. I make a decree: Any people, 3.29
T. I made a decree that all the 4.06
T., O king, let my counsel be 4.27
T. King Darius signed the document 6.09
T. the LORD has kept ready the 9.14
Now t., O our God, hearken to the 9.17
t. consider the word and understand 9.23
Know t. and understand that from 9.25
T. I will hedge up her way with Hos 2.06
T. I will take back my grain in its 2.09
"T., behold, I will allure her, and 2.14
T. the land mourns, and all who 4.03
T. your daughters play the harlot, 4.13
T. I am like a moth to Ephraim, and 5.12
T. I have hewn them by the prophets, 6.05
t. the tumult of war shall arise 10.14
T. they shall be like the morning 13.03
was lifted up; t. they forgot me. 13.06
t. I will punish you for all your Amo 3.02
T. thus says the Lord GOD: "An 3.11
"T. thus I will do to you, O Israel; 4.12
T. because you trample upon the 5.11
T. he who is prudent will keep 5.13
T. thus says the LORD, the God of 5.16
t. I will take you into exile 5.27
T. they shall now be the first of 6.07
"Now t. hear the word of the LORD. 7.16
T. thus says the LORD: 'Your wife 7.17
T. they cried to the LORD, "We Jon 1.14
T. now, O LORD, take my life from me, 4.03
T. I will make Samaria a heap in Mic 1.06
T. you shall give parting gifts to 1.14
T. thus says the LORD: Behold, 2.03
T. you will have none to cast the 2.05
T. it shall be night to you, without 3.06
T. because of you Zion shall be 3.12
T. he shall give them up until the 5.03
T. I have begun to smite you, making 6.13
T. he sacrifices to his net and Hab 1.16
T., as I live," says the LORD of Zep 2.09
"T. wait for me," says the LORD, "for 3.08
Now t. thus says the LORD of hosts: Hag 1.05
T. the heavens above you have 1.10
T. say to them, Thus says the LORD Zec 1.03
T., thus says the LORD, I have 1.16
T. great wrath came from the LORD 7.12
feasts; t. love truth and peace. 8.19
T. the people wander like sheep; 10.02
t. you, O sons of Jacob, are not Mal 3.06
every tree t. that does not bear Mt 3.10
You, t., must be perfect, as your 5.48
"T. I tell you, do not be anxious 6.25
T. do not be anxious, saying, 'What 6.31
"T. do not be anxious about tomorrow, 6.34
pray t. the Lord of the harvest to 9.38
Fear not, t.; you are of more 10.31
T. they shall be your judges. 12.27
T. I tell you, every sin and blasphemy 12.31
"T. every scribe who has been 13.52
"T. the kingdom of heaven may be 18.23
What t. God has joined together, let 19.06
When t. the owner of the vineyard 21.40
T. I tell you, the kingdom of God 21.43
Go t. to the thoroughfares, and 22.09
"Render t. to Caesar the things 22.21
t., to which of the seven will she 22.28
t. you will receive greater condemnation * 23.14
T. I send you prophets and wise men 23.34
Watch t., for you do not know on 24.42
T. you also must be ready; 24.44
Watch t., for you know neither the 25.13
T. that field has been called the 27.08
T. order the sepulchre to be made 27.64
Go t. and make disciples of all 28.19
What t. God has joined together, let Mk 10.09
T. I tell you, whatever you ask in 11.24
Watch t.—for you do not know when 13.35
t. the child to be born will be Lk 1.35
He said t. to the multitudes that 3.07
every tree t. that does not bear 3.09
t. I did not presume to come to you. 7.07
T. I tell you, her sins, which are 7.47
pray t. the Lord of the harvest to 10.02
T. they shall be your judges. 11.19
T. be careful lest the light in you 11.35
T. also the Wisdom of God said, 'I 11.49
"T. I tell you, do not be anxious 12.22

THEREFORE (cont.)
He said t., "What is the kingdom of Lk 13.18
a wife, and t. I cannot come.' 14.20
So t., whoever of you does not 14.33
He said t., "A nobleman went into a 19.12
t., whose wife will the woman be? 20.33
Settle it t. in your minds, not to 21.14
I will t. chastise him and release 23.16
I will t. chastise him and release 23.22
When t. he was raised from the dead, Jn 2.22
t. this joy of mine is now full. 3.29
Jesus t. said to him, "Unless you 4.48
of the people of Jerusalem t. said, 7.25
They said to him t., "Where is your Father?" 8.19
T. his parents said, "He is of age, 9.23
Many of the Jews t., who had come 11.45
Jesus t. no longer went about 11.54
T. they could not believe. 12.39
What I say, t., I say as the Father 12.50
of the world, t. the world hates you. 15.19
t. I said that he will take what is 16.15
Pilate t. said to him, "You will not 19.10
t. he who delivered me to you has 19.11
t. my heart was glad, and my tongue Ac 2.26
Being t. a prophet, and knowing that 2.30
Being t. exalted at the right hand 2.33
house of Israel t. know assuredly 2.36
Repent t., and turn again, that your 3.19
T., brethren, pick out from among 6.03
Repent t. of this wickedness of 8.22
Send t. to Joppa and ask for Simon 10.32
Now t. we are all here present in 10.33
T. he says also in another psalm, 13.35
Let it be known to you t., 13.38
Beware, t., lest there come upon you 13.40
Now t. why do you make trial of God 15.10
T. my judgment is that we should 15.19
We have t. sent Judas and Silas, who 15.27
Setting sail t. from Troas, we made 16.11
now t. come out and go in peace." 16.36
Many of them t. believed, with not a 17.12
we wish to know t. what these 17.20
'What t. you worship as unknown, 17.23
If t. Demetrius and the craftsmen 19.38
T. I testify to you this day that I 20.26
T. be alert, remembering that for 20.31
Do t. what we tell you. We have four 21.23
You t., along with the council, give 23.15
When t. they came together here, I 25.17
T. I have brought him before you, 25.26
t. I beg you to listen to me patiently. 26.03
T. I urge you to take some food; 27.34
For this reason t. I have asked to 28.20
T. God gave them up in the lusts of Rom 1.24
T. you have no excuse, O man, whoever 2.01
T., since we are justified by faith, 5.01
Since, t., we are now justified by 5.09
T. as sin came into the world 5.12
We were buried t. with him by 6.04
Let not sin t. reign in your mortal 6.12
There is t. now no condemnation for 8.01
I appeal to you t., brethren, by 12.01
T. he who resists the authorities 13.02
T. one must be subject, not only to 13.05
t. love is the fulfilling of the 13.10
t., as Christ has welcomed you, for 15.07
"T. I will praise thee among the 15.09
When t. I have completed this, and 15.28
t., as it is written, "Let him who 1Co 1.31
T. do not pronounce judgment before 4.05
T. I sent to you Timothy, my beloved 4.17
Let us, t., celebrate the festival 5.08
Shall I t. take the members of 6.15
T., if food is a cause of my 8.13
T. let any one who thinks that he 10.12
T., my beloved, shun the worship of 10.14
Whoever, t., eats the bread or 11.27
T. I want you to understand that no 12.03
T., he who speaks in a tongue 14.13
If, t., the whole church assembles 14.23
T., my beloved brethren, be steadfast, 15.58
T., having this ministry by the 2Co 4.01
T., knowing the fear of the Lord, we 5.11
I died for all; t. all have died. 5.14
From now on, t., we regard no one 5.16
T., if any one is in Christ, he is a 5.17
T. come out from them, and be 6.17
T. we are comforted. And besides our 7.13
stand fast t., and do not submit Gal 5.01
T. remember that at one time you Eph 2.11
I t., a prisoner for the Lord, beg 4.01
T. it is said, "When he ascended on 4.08
T., putting away falsehood, let 4.25
T. be imitators of God, as beloved 5.01
T. do not associate with them, 5.07
T. it is said, "Awake, O sleeper, and 5.14
T. do not be foolish, but understand 5.17
T. take the whole armor of God, that 6.13
Stand t., having girded your loins 6.14
T. God has highly exalted him and Php 2.09
T., my beloved, as you have always 2.12
I hope t. to send him just as soon 2.23
t., that you may rejoice at seeing 2.28
T., my brethren, whom I love and 4.01
As t. you receive Christ Jesus the Col 2.06
T. let no one pass judgment on you 2.16
Put to death t. what is earthly in 3.05
T. when we could bear it no longer, 1Th 3.01
T. whoever disregards this, disregards 4.08
T. comfort one another with these 4.18
T. encourage one another and build 5.11
T. we ourselves boast of you in the 2Th 1.04
T. God sends upon them a strong 2.11
and t. I suffer as I do. But I am not 2Ti 1.12
T. I endure everything for the sake 2.10
T. rebuke them sharply, that they Tit 1.13
t. God, thy God, has anointed thee Heb 1.09
T. we must pay the closer attention 2.01
Since t. the children share in 2.14
T. he had to be made like his 2.17
T., holy brethren, who share in a 3.01
T., as the Holy Spirit says, "Today, 3.07
T. I was provoked with that generation, 3.10
T., while the promise of entering 4.01
Since t. it remains for some to 4.06
Let us t. strive to enter that rest, 4.11
T. let us leave the elementary 6.01
T. he is the meditator of a new 9.15
T., brethren, since we have confidence 10.19
T. do not throw away your confidence, 10.35
T. from one man, and him as good as 11.12
T. God is not ashamed to be called 11.16
T., since we are surrounded by so 12.01
T. lift your drooping hands and 12.12
T. let us be grateful for receiving 12.28
T. let us go forth to him outside 13.13
T. put away all filthiness and rank Jas 1.21
T. whoever wishes to be a friend of 4.04
t. it says, "God opposes the proud, 4.06
Submit yourselves t. to God. 4.07
Be patient, t., brethren, until the 5.07
T. confess your sins to one another, 5.16
T. gird up your minds, be sober, set 1Pe 1.13
To you t. who believe, he is precious, 2.07
Since t. Christ suffered in the 4.01
t. keep sane and sober for your 4.07
T. let those who suffer according 4.19
Humble yourselves t. under the 5.06
T., brethren, be the more zealous to 2Pe 1.10
T. I intend always to remind you of 1.12
T., beloved, since you wait for 3.14
You t., beloved, knowing this 3.17
t. we know that it is the last hour 1Jn 2.18
t. what they say is of the world, 4.05

THEREFORE (cont.)
T. I counsel you to buy from me Rev 3.18
T. are they before the throne of 7.15

THEREIN
things which men do and sin t., Lev 6.03
and put fire t. from off the altar, Num 16.46
had not built, and you dwell t.; Jos 24.13
the world and those who dwell t.; Ps 24.01
let them fall t. to ruin! 35.08
seas and everything that moves t. 69.34
it, and fools shall not err t. Is 35.08
the world and all that dwell t. Nah 1.05
to cities and all who dwell t. Hab 2.08
to cities and all who dwell t. 2.17
and who keep what is written t.; Rev 1.03
and all t., saying, "To him who sits 5.13
O heaven and you that dwell t.! 12.12

THEREOF
is the LORD's and the fulness t., Ps 24.01

THEREON
You shall offer no unholy incense t., Ex 30.09
and you shall pour no libation t. 30.09
and the mercy seat that is t., 31.07
And many shall stumble t.; Is 8.15
which borders t., Tyre and Sidon, Zec 9.02
garments on them, and he sat t. Mt 21.07

THEREUPON
T. I awoke and looked, and my sleep Jer 31.26

THEREWITH
of the ephod, binding it to him t. Lev 8.07

THESSALONIANS
and of the T., Aristarchus and Ac 20.04
church of the T. in God the Father 1Th 1.01
church of the T. in God our Father 2Th 1.01

THESSALONICA
they came to T., where there was a Ac 17.01
were more noble than those in T. 17.11
the Jews of T. learned that the 17.13
Aristarchus, a Macedonian from T. 27.02
for even in T. you sent me help Php 4.16
has deserted me and gone to T.; 2Ti 4.10

THEUDAS
For before these days T. arose, Ac 5.36

THICK
and there was t. darkness in all Ex 10.22
I am coming to you in a t. cloud, 19.09
and a t. cloud upon the mountain, 19.16
near to the t. cloud where God was 20.21
you grew t., you became sleek; Deu 32.15
went under the t. branches of a 2Sa 18.09
t. darkness was under his feet. 22.10
t. clouds, a gathering of water. 22.12
that he would dwell in t. darkness. 1Ki 8.12
that he would dwell in t. darkness. 2Ch 6.01
let t. darkness seize it! Job 3.06
T. clouds enwrap him, so that he 22.14
and t. darkness covers my face. 23.17
up the waters in his t. clouds, 26.08
He loads the t. cloud with moisture 37.11
and t. darkness its swaddling band, 38.09
t. darkness was under his feet. Ps 18.09
his canopy t. clouds dark with 18.11
Clouds and t. darkness are round 97.02
will be thrust into t. darkness. Is 8.22
his anger, and in t. rising smoke; 30.27
and t. darkness the peoples; 60.02
Israel, or a land of t. darkness? Jer 2.31
towered aloft among the t. boughs; Eze 19.11
its t. rust does not go out of it 24.12
on a day of clouds and t. darkness. 34.12
wall of the temple, six cubits t.; 41.05
was five cubits t. round about, 41.12
a day of clouds and t. darkness! Joe 2.02
a day of clouds and t. darkness, Zep 1.15
for the t. forest has been felled! Zec 11.02

THICK-BOSSED
against him with a t. shield; Job 15.26

THICKENING
the men who are t. upon their lees, Zep 1.12

THICKER
finger is t. than my father's loins. 1Ki 12.10
finger is t. than my father's loins. 2Ch 10.10

THICKET
a ram, caught in a t. by his horns; Gen 22.13
A lion has gone up from his t., Jer 4.07

THICKETS
it kindles the t. of the forest, Is 9.18
cut down the t. of the forest with 10.34
In the t. in Arabia you will lodge, 21.13
they enter t.; They climb upon Jer 4.29

THICKNESS
and its t. was four fingers; 1Ki 7.15
Its t. was a handbreadth; and its brim 7.26
Its t. was a handbreadth; and its brim 2Ch 4.05
and its t. was four fingers, and it Jer 52.21
so he measured the t. of the wall, Eze 40.05
The t. of the outer wall of the 41.09

THIEF
If a t. is found breaking in, and is Ex 22.02
if the t. is found, he shall pay 22.07
If the t. is not found, the owner of 22.08
sells him, then that t. shall die; Deu 24.07
and in the night he is as a t. Job 24.14
shout after them as after a t. 30.05
If you see a t., you are a friend Ps 50.18
men despise a t. if he steals to Pro 6.30
The partner of a t. hates his own 29.24
"As a t. is shamed when caught, so Jer 2.26
the t. breaks in, and the bandits Hos 7.01
through the windows like a t. Joe 2.09
it shall enter the house of the t., Zec 5.04
of the night the t. was coming, Mt 24.43
where no t. approaches and no moth Lk 12.33
at what hour the t. was coming, 12.39
way, that man is a t. and a robber; Jn 10.01
The t. comes only to steal and kill 10.10
the poor but because he was a t., 12.06
Let the t. no longer steal, but Eph 4.28
will come like a t. in the night. 1Th 5.02
that day to surprise you like a t. 5.04
or a t., or a wrongdoer, or a 1Pe 4.15
of the Lord will come like a t., 2Pe 3.10
not awake, I will come like a t., Rev 3.03
("Lo, I am coming like a t.! 16.15

THIEVES
are rebels and companions of t. Is 1.23
Was he found among t., that whenever Jer 48.27
If t. came by night, would they not 49.09
If t. came to you, if plunderers by Ob 1.05
and where t. break in and steal, Mt 6.19
and where t. do not break in and 6.20
came before me are t. and robbers; Jn 10.08
not t., nor the greedy, nor drunkards, 1Co 6.10

THIGH
he had, "Put your hand under my t., Gen 24.02
hand under the t. of Abraham his 24.09
he touched the hollow of his t.; 32.25
and Jacob's t. was put out of joint 32.25
Penuel, limping because of his t. 32.31

THIGH (cont.)
which is upon the hollow of the t., Gen 32.32
of Jacob's t. on the sinew of the 32.32
sight, put your hand under my t., 47.29
and the right t. (for it is a ram Ex 29.22
and the t. of the priests' portion, 29.27
And the right t. you shall give to Lev 7.32
have the right t. for a portion. 7.33
waved and the t. that is offered I 7.34
with their fat, and the right t.; 8.25
on the fat and on the right t.; 8.26
and the right t. Aaron waved for a 9.21
waved and the t. that is offered 10.14
The t. that is offered and the 10.15
LORD makes your t. fall away and Num 5.21
body swell and your t. fall away. 5.22
and her t. shall fall away, and the 5.27
waved and the t. that is offered; 6.20
and as the right t. are yours. 18.18
it on his right t. under his Ju 3.16
took the sword from his right t., 3.21
them hip and t. with great slaughter 15.08
Gird your sword upon your t., Ps 45.03
war, each with his sword at his t., Sol 3.08
was instructed, I smote upon my t.; Jer 31.19
Smite therefore upon your t. Eze 21.12
the t. and the shoulder; fill it with 24.04
laying him bare from t. to neck. Hab 3.13
robe and on his t. he has a name Rev 19.16

THIGHS
loins to the t. they shall reach; Ex 28.42
sinews of his t. are knit together Job 40.17
Your rounded t. are like jewels, the Sol 7.01
of silver, its belly and t. of bronze, Dan 2.32

THIN
gaunt and t., came up out of the Gen 41.03
And the gaunt and t. cows ate up 41.04
t. and blighted by the east wind. 41.06
And the t. ears swallowed up the 41.07
them, poor and very gaunt and t., 41.19
And the t. and gaunt cows ate up 41.20
t., and blighted by the east wind, 41.23
and the t. ears swallowed up the 41.24
the hair in it is yellow and t., Lev 13.30

THINE
thou didst swear by t. own self, Ex 32.13
such works and mighty acts as t.? Deu 3.24
"So perish all t. enemies, O LORD! Ju 5.31
his oath before t. altar in this 1Ki 8.31
T., O LORD, is the greatness, and the 1Ch 29.11
the heavens and in the earth is t.; 29.11
t. is the kingdom, O LORD, and thou 29.11
no purpose of t. can be thwarted. Job 42.02
praise thy righteousness, t. alone. Ps 71.16
T. is the day, t. also the night; 74.16
look upon the face of t. anointed! 84.09
nor are there any works like t. 86.08
The heavens are t., the earth also is t.; 89.11
I am t., save me; for I have 119.94
with them in the time of t. anger. Jer 18.23
'Do not close t. ear to my cry for Lam 3.56
at the light of t. arrows as they Hab 3.11
For t. is the kingdom and the power *Mt 6.13
not my will, but t., be done. Lk 22.42
t. they were, and thou gavest them Jn 17.06
hast given me, for they are t.; 17.09
all mine are t., and t. are mine, 17.10

THING
every creeping t. that creeps upon Gen 1.26
every living t. that moves upon 1.28
And of every living t. of all flesh, 6.19
every creeping t. of the ground 6.20
every living t. that I have made I 7.04
every creeping t. that creeps on 7.14
every living t. that was upon the 7.23
every living t. that is with you 8.17
every creeping t. that creeps on 8.17
And every beast, every creeping t., 8.19
Every moving t. that lives shall be 9.03
Far be it from thee to do such a t., 18.25
thinking of, that you did this t.?" 20.10
And the t. was very displeasing to 21.11
"I do not know who has done this t.; 21.26
"The t. comes from the LORD; 24.50
say the same t. to Esau when you 32.19
for such a t. ought not to be done. 34.07
said to them, "We cannot do this t., 34.14
man did not delay to do the t., 34.19
means that the t. is fixed by God, 41.32
that they should do such a t.! 44.07
thought, "Surely the t. is known." Ex 2.14
LORD will do this t. in the land." 9.05
on the morrow the LORD did this t.; 9.06
not a green t. remained, neither 10.15
flake-like t., fine as hoarfrost on 16.14
for the t. is too heavy for you; 18.18
clothing, or for any kind of lost t., 22.09
"This very t. that you have spoken 33.17
is a terrible t. that I will do 34.10
"This is the t. which the LORD has 35.04
unwittingly and the t. is hidden Lev 4.13
Or if any one touches an unclean t., 5.02
he has done amiss in the holy t., 5.16
or the lost t. which he found, 6.04
it is a t. most holy, like the sin 6.17
any unclean t. shall not be eaten; 7.19
And if any one touches an unclean t., 7.21
"This is the t. which the LORD has 8.05
"This is the t. which the LORD 9.06
since it is a t. most holy and has 10.17
"Every swarming t. that swarms upon 11.41
with any swarming t. that swarms; 11.43
any swarming t. that crawls upon 11.44
shall not touch any hallowed t., 12.04
they wash the t. in which is the 13.54
the diseased t. after it has been 13.55
carries such a t. shall wash his 15.10
This is the t. which the LORD has 17.02
has profaned a holy t. of the LORD; 19.08
his nakedness, it is a shameful t., 20.17
a creeping t. by which he may be 22.05
outsider shall not eat of a holy t. 22.10
servant shall not eat of a holy t.; 22.10
man eats of a holy t. unwittingly, 22.14
and give the holy t. to the priest. 22.14
that day as a holy t. to the LORD. 27.23
"But no devoted t. that a man 27.28
every devoted t. is most holy to 27.28
is it too small a t. for you that Num 16.09
Is it a small t. that you have 16.13
Every devoted t. in Israel shall be 18.14
'The t. that you have spoken is Deu 1.14
The t. seemed good to me, and I took 1.23
such a great t. as this has ever 4.32
an abominable t. into your house, 7.26
abhor it; for it is an accursed t. 7.26
Then I took the sinful t., the calf which 9.21
every living t. that followed them, 11.06
abominable t. which the LORD hates 12.31
an abominable t. has been done 13.14
"You shall not eat any abominable t. 14.03
an abominable t. has been done in 17.04
or woman who has done this evil t., 17.05
with any lost t. of your brother's, 22.03
But if the t. is true, that the 22.20
keep yourself from every evil t. 23.09
a t. made by the hands of a craftsman, 27.15
of Israel a t. for destruction, and Jos 6.18
have become a t. for destruction. 7.12
has done a shameful t. in Israel.'" 7.15
because of you, and did this t. 9.24

THING (cont.)
that not one t. has failed of all Jos 23.14
one another, "Who has done this t.?" Ju 6.29
the son of Joash has done this t." 6.29
father, "Let this t. be done for me; 11.37
drink, or eat any unclean t.; 13.14
my house, do not do this vile t. 19.23
this man do not do so vile a t." 19.24
"Such a t. has never happened or 19.30
I am about to do a t. in Israel, 1Sa 3.11
But the t. displeased Samuel when 8.06
stand still and see this great t., 12.16
to us, and we will show you a t." 14.12
told Saul, and the t. pleased him. 18.20
to you a little t. to become the 18.23
I should do this t. to my lord, 24.06
This t. that you have done is not 26.16
shall come upon you for this t." 28.10
has done this t. to you this day. 28.18
you because you have done this t. 2Sa 2.06
but one t. I require of you; 3.13
this was a small t. in thy eyes, 7.19
this good t. to thy servant; 7.28
soul lives, I will not do this t." 11.11
But the t. that David had done 11.27
fourfold, because he did this t., 12.06
I will do this t. before all 12.12
"What is this t. that you have done? 12.21
for such a t. is not done in Israel; 13.12
planned such a t. against the 14.13
lord the king delight in this t.?" 24.03
Has this t. been brought about by 1Ki 1.27
commanded him concerning this t., 11.10
his home, for this t. is from me.'" 12.24
And this t. became a sin, for the 12.30
After this t. Jeroboam did not turn 13.33
And this t. became sin to the house 13.34
been a light t. for him to walk in 16.31
but this t. I cannot do.'" 20.09
And one said one t., and another 22.20
And he said, "You have asked a hard t.; 2Ki 2.10
This is a light t. in the sight of 3.18
commanded you to do some great t., 5.13
troubled because of this t.; 6.11
in heaven, could this t. be?" 7.02
in heaven, could such a t. be?" 7.19
that he should do this great t.?" 8.13
"This is the t. that you shall do: 11.05
will do the t. that he has promised: 20.09
"It is an easy t. for the shadow to 20.10
in the matter of the devoted t.; 1Ch 2.07
for the t. was right in the eyes of 13.04
And this was a small t. in thy eyes, 17.17
this good t. to thy servant; 17.26
But God was displeased with this t., 21.07
in that I have done this t. 21.08
his home, for this t. is from me.'" 2Ch 11.04
And one said one t., and another 18.19
This is the t. that you shall do: of 23.04
for the t. came about suddenly. 29.36
who put such a t. as this into the Ez 7.27
"What is this t. that you are doing? Neh 2.19
"The t. that you are doing is not 5.09
is this evil t. which you are 13.17
and if the t. seem right before the Est 8.05
For the t. that I fear comes upon Job 3.25
of every living t. and the breath 12.10
Man wastes away like a rotten t., 13.28
bring a clean t. out of an unclean? 14.04
and his eye sees every precious t. 28.10
and the t. that is hid he brings 28.11
he searches after every green t. 39.08
One t. have I asked of the LORD, Ps 27.04
who seek the LORD lack no good t. 34.10
"A deadly t. has fastened upon him; 41.08
No good t. does the LORD withhold 84.11
hast made me a t. of horror to 88.08
the desire of every living t. 145.16
in spirit keeps a t. hidden. Pro 11.13
He who finds a wife finds a good t., 18.22
Is there a t. of which it is said, Ecc 1.10
Better is the end of a t. than its 7.08
adding one t. to another to find 7.27
knows the interpretation of a t.? 8.01
man has no good t. under the sun 8.15
judgment, with every secret t., 12.14
that the t. made should say of its Is 29.16
or the t. formed say of him who 29.16
will do this t. that he has 38.07
Behold, I am doing a new t.; 43.19
is too light a t. that you should 49.06
go out thence, touch no unclean t.; 52.11
prosper in the t. for which I sent 55.11
Who has heard such a t.? 66.08
see if there has been such a t. Jer 2.10
the shameful t. has devoured all 3.24
and horrible t. has happened in 5.30
Israel has done a very horrible t. 18.13
a t. to be hissed at for ever. 18.16
a t. to be hissed at; every one who 19.08
of Samaria I saw an unsavoury t.: 23.13
Jerusalem I have seen a horrible t.: 23.14
has created a new t. on the earth: 31.22
this t. has come upon you. 40.03
Kareah, "You shall not do this t., 40.16
and the t. that we should do." 42.03
do this abominable t. that I hate!' 44.04
has become a filthy t. among them. Lam 1.17
their gold is like an unclean t.; Eze 7.19
will make it an unclean t. to them. 7.20
it too slight a t. for the house 8.17
as a profane t. from the mountain 28.16
every devoted t. in Israel shall 44.29
asked such a t. of any magician or Dan 2.10
The t. that the king asks is 2.11
"The t. stands fast, according to 6.12
My people inquire of a t. of wood, Hos 4.12
Israel I have seen a horrible t.; 6.10
would be regarded as a strange t. 8.12
detestable like the t. they loved. 9.10
Yea, the t. itself shall be carried 10.06
his treasury of every precious t. 13.15
Has such a t. happened in your days, Joe 1.02
be a deceitful t. to the kings of Mic 1.14
or wealth of every precious t. Nah 2.09
him who says to a wooden t., Awake; Hab 2.19
she has done a beautiful t. to me. Mt 26.10
and said to him, "You lack one t.; Mk 10.21
she has done a beautiful t. to me. 14.06
and see this t. that has happened, Lk 2.15
one t. is needful. Mary has chosen 10.42
able to do as small a t. as that, 12.26
said to him, "One t. you still lack. 18.22
one t. I know, that though I was Jn 9.25
and the t. was taken up at once to Ac 10.16
Now some cried one t., some another; 19.32
crowd shouted one t., some another; 21.34
except this one t. which I cried 24.21
want, but I do the very t. I hate. Rom 7.15
of God, attending to this very t. 13.06
is a very small t. that I should 1Co 4.03
on the man who has done such a t. 5.04
prepared us for this very t. is God, 2Co 5.05
which very t. I was eager to do. Gal 2.10
spot or wrinkle or any such t., Eph 5.27
with God a t. to be grasped, Php 2.06
but one t. I do, forgetting what 3.13
It is a fearful t. to fall into the Heb 10.31
it is a loyal t. you do when you 3Jn 1.05
every living t. died that was in Rev 16.03

THINGS
and creeping t. and beasts of the Gen 1.24
and creeping t. and birds of the 6.07
and creeping t. and birds of the 7.23

THINGS (cont.)
After these t. the word of the LORD Gen 15.01
servants, and told them all these t.; 20.08
have done to me t. that ought not 20.09
After these t. God tested Abraham, 22.01
Now after these t. it was told 22.20
LORD had blessed Abraham in all t. 24.01
mother's household about these t. 24.28
Isaac all the t. that he had done. 24.66
Jacob told Laban all these t., 29.13
"Let her keep the t. as her own, 38.23
loaded with the good t. of Egypt, 45.23
does not do these three t. for her, Ex 21.11
They shall eat those t. with which 29.33
"These are the t. which the LORD 35.01
the sum of the t. for the tabernacle, 38.21
is made of these t. to the LORD; Lev 2.08
in any of the t. which the LORD 4.02
any one of the t. which the LORD 4.13
one of all the t. which the LORD 4.22
any one of the t. which the LORD. 4.27
a carcass of unclean swarming t., 5.02
committed in any one of these t., 5.13
in any of the holy t. of the LORD, 5.15
any of the t. which the LORD has 5.17
any of all the t. which men do and 6.03
for any of the t. which one may do 6.07
did all the t. which the LORD 8.36
and yet such t. as these have 10.19
are the living t. which you may 11.02
the swarming t. that swarm upon 11.29
the swarming t. that swarm upon 11.42
and these t. before the LORD, at 14.11
touches these t. shall be unclean, 15.27
yourselves by any of these t., 18.24
for they did all these t., 20.23
the most holy and of the holy t., 21.22
from the holy t. of the people of 22.02
generations approaches the holy t., 22.03
eat of the holy t. until he is 22.04
eat of the holy t. unless he has 22.06
afterward he may eat of the holy t., 22.07
eat of the offering of the holy t. 22.12
the holy t. of the people of Israel, 22.15
and guilt, by eating their holy t.: 22.16
tent of meeting: the most holy t. Num 4.04
touch the holy t., lest they die. 4.15
These are the t. of the tent of 4.15
they come near to the most holy t.: 4.19
upon the holy t. even for a moment, 4.20
all the holy t. of the people of 5.09
and every man's holy t. shall be his; 5.10
of the holy t. which had to be 7.09
set out, carrying the holy t., 10.21
shall do these t. in this way, 15.13
the consecrated t. of the people 18.08
shall be yours of the most holy t., 18.09
the holy t. of the people of 18.32
"And these t. shall be for a statute 35.29
time all the t. that you should do Deu 1.18
you forget the t. which your eyes 4.09
t. which the LORD your God has 4.19
and all these t. come upon you in 4.30
and houses full of all good t., 6.11
and terrible t. which your eyes 10.21
But the holy t. which are due from 12.26
None of the devoted t. shall cleave 13.17
All clean winged t. you may eat. 14.20
does these t. is an abomination to 18.12
does these t. is an abomination to 22.05
For all who do such t., all who act 25.16
reason of the abundance of all t., 28.47
nakedness, and in want of all t.; 28.48
them secretly, for want of all t., 28.57
and you have seen their detestable t., 29.17
"The secret t. belong to the LORD 29.29
but the t. that are revealed belong 29.29
"And when all these t. come upon you, 30.01
venom of crawling t. of the dust. 32.24
Just as we obeyed Moses in all t., Jos 1.17
from the t. devoted to destruction, 6.18
of the devoted t. and make the 6.18
faith in regard to the devoted t.; 7.01
Judah, took some of the devoted t.; 7.01
have taken some of the devoted t.; 7.11
the devoted t. from among you. 7.12
are devoted t. in the midst of you, 7.13
away the devoted t. from among you." 7.13
the devoted t. shall be burned 7.15
in the matter of the devoted t., 22.20
of all the good t. which the LORD 23.14
as all the good t. which the LORD 23.15
bring upon you all the evil t., 23.15
After these t. Joshua the son of 24.29
hands, or shown us all these t., Ju 13.23
announced to us such t. as these." 13.23
to them, "Why do you do such t.? 1Sa 2.23
the men of Ashdod saw how t. were, 5.07
after vain t. which cannot profit 12.21
what great t. he has done for you. 12.24
the best of the t. devoted to 15.21
And David left the t. in charge of 17.22
Jonathan showed him all these t. 19.07
Nabal, his wife told him these t., 25.37
will do many t. and will succeed 26.25
for them great and terrible t., 2Sa 7.23
When King David heard of all these t., 13.21
God to know all t. that are on the 14.20
ordered in all t. and secure. 23.05
These t. did the three mighty men. 23.17
These t. did Benaiah the son of 23.22
the LORD, Three t. I offer you; 24.12
brought in the t. which David his 1Ki 7.51
have done all these t. at thy word. 18.36
to meet you and told you these t.?" 2Ki 1.07
tent, and carried off t. from it, 7.08
all the great t. that Elisha has 8.04
of the holy t. which is brought 12.04
he did in all t. as Joash his 14.03
LORD their God t. that were not 17.09
And they did wicked t., provoking 17.11
and has done t. more wicked than 21.11
proclaimed, who had predicted these t. 23.16
predicted these t. which you have 23.17
These t. did the three mighty men. 1Ch 11.19
These t. did Benaiah the son of 11.24
in making known all these great t. 17.19
a name for great and terrible t., 17.21
the LORD, Three t. I offer you; 21.10
to consecrate the most holy t., 23.13
or any of the t. for its service"— 23.26
able, the gold for the t. of gold, 29.02
the silver for the t. of silver, 29.02
the bronze for the t. of bronze, 29.02
the iron for the t. of iron, 29.02
iron, and wood for the t. of wood, 29.02
gold for the t. of gold and silver 29.05
and silver for the t. of silver. 29.05
For all t. come from thee, and of 29.14
I have freely offered all these t., 29.17
Solomon made all these t. in great 2Ch 4.18
made all the t. that were in the 4.19
brought in the t. which David his 5.01
and precious t., which they took 20.25
the dedicated t. of the house of 24.07
the dedicated t. which had been 31.06
the tithes and the dedicated t. 31.12
After these t. and these acts of 32.01
and precious t. to Hezekiah king 32.23
After these t. had been done, the Ez 9.01
Will they restore t.? Will they sacrifice? Neh 4.02
"No such t. as you say have been 6.08
according to these t. that they did, 6.14
of houses full of all good t., 9.25

THINGS (cont.)
the holy t., and the sin offerings Neh 10.33
After these t., when the anger of Est 2.01
After these t. King Ahasuerus 3.01
And Mordecai recorded these t., 9.20
who does great t. and unsearchable, Job 5.09
marvelous t. without number: 5.09
"How long will you say these t., 8.02
who does great t. beyond understanding, 9.10
and marvelous t. without number. 9.10
Yet these t. thou didst hide in thy 10.13
"Can you find out the deep t. of God? 11.07
Who does not know such t. as these? 12.03
Only grant two t. to me, then I will 13.20
For thou writest bitter t. against me, 13.26
"I have heard many such t.; 16.02
filled their houses with good t.— 22.18
and many such t. are in his mind. 23.14
"Behold, God does all these t., 33.29
he does great t. which we cannot 37.05
"I know that thou canst do all t., 42.02
t. too wonderful for me, which I did 42.03
hast put all t. under his feet, Ps 8.06
who does these t. shall never be 15.05
they ask me of t. that I know not. 35.11
These t. I remember, as I pour out 42.04
These t. you have done and I have 50.21
made thy people suffer hard t.; 60.03
Thou who hast done great t., 71.19
Israel, who alone does wondrous t. 72.18
t. that we have heard and known, 78.03
art great and doest wondrous t., 86.10
Glorious t. are spoken of you, O 87.03
song, for he has done marvelous t.! 98.01
which teems with t. innumerable, 104.25
living t. both small and great. 104.25
hand, they are filled with good t. 104.28
who had done great t. in Egypt, 106.21
and terrible t. by the Red Sea. 106.22
the hungry he fills with good t. 107.09
let him give heed to these t.; 107.43
behold wondrous t. out of thy law. 119.18
for all t. are thy servants. 119.91
LORD has done great t. for them. 126.02
The LORD has done great t. for us; 126.03
myself with t. too great and too 131.01
who plan evil t. in their heart, and 140.02
creeping t. and flying birds! 148.10
There are six t. which the LORD Pro 6.16
Hear, for I will speak noble t., 8.06
of the wicked pours out evil t. 15.28
winks his eyes plans perverse t., 16.30
Your eyes will see strange t., 23.33
and your mind utter perverse t. 23.33
It is the glory of God to conceal t., 25.02
glory of kings is to search t. out. 25.02
Two t. I ask of thee; 30.07
Three t. are never satisfied; 30.15
Three t. are too wonderful for me; 30.18
Under three t. the earth trembles; 30.21
Four t. on earth are small, but they 30.24
Three t. are stately in their tread 30.29
All t. are full of weariness; Ecc 1.08
There is no remembrance of former t., 1.11
of later t. yet to happen among 1.11
he does not enjoy life's good t., 6.03
heed to all the t. that men say, 7.21
to seek wisdom and the sum of t., 7.25
city where they had done such t. 8.10
for all these t. God will bring 11.09
for thou hast done wonderful t., Is 25.01
for all peoples a feast of fat t., 25.06
of fat t. full of marrow, of wine on 25.06
do marvelous t. with this people, 29.14
You turn t. upside down! Shall the potter 29.16
speak to us smooth t., prophesy illusions, 30.10
will scatter them as unclean t.; 30.22

But he who is noble devises noble t., 32.08
things, and by noble t. he stands. 32.08
by these t. men live, and in all 38.16
Tell us the former t., what they are, 41.22
or declare to us the t. to come. 41.22
the former t. have come to pass, and 42.09
to pass, and new t. I now declare; 42.09
These are the t. I will do, and I 42.16
He sees many t., but does not 42.20
this, and show us the former t.? 43.09
"Remember not the former t., 43.18
things, nor consider the t. of old. 43.18
announced from of old the t. to come? 44.07
and the t. they delight in do not 44.09
Remember these t., O Jacob, and 44.21
who made all t., who stretched out 44.24
I am the LORD, who do all these t. 45.07
these t. you carry are loaded as 46.01
remember the former t. of old; 46.09
from ancient times t. not yet done, 46.10
not lay these t. to heart or 47.07
These two t. shall come to you in a 47.09
"The former t. I declared of old, 48.03
time forth I make you hear new t., 48.06
hidden t. which you have not known. 48.06
among them has declared these t.? 48.14
These two t. have befallen you—who 51.19
who choose the t. that please me 56.04
Shall I be appeased for these t.? 57.06
satisfy your desire with good t., 58.11
didst terrible t. which we looked 64.03
thyself at these t., O LORD? Wilt thou 64.12
of abominable t. is in their vessels; 65.04
and the former t. shall not be 65.17
All these t. my hand has made, and 66.02
made, and so all these t. are mine, 66.02
Who has seen such t.? Shall a land 66.08
enjoy its fruits and its good t. Jer 2.07
and went after t. that do not 2.08
Yet in spite of all these t. 2.34
Shall I not punish them for these t.? 5.09
our God done all these t. to us?' 5.19
Shall I not punish them for these t.? 5.29
because you have done all these t., 7.13
Shall I not punish them for these t.? 9.09
for in these t. I delight, says the 9.24
he is the one who formed all t., 10.16
'Why have these t. come upon me?' 13.22
thee, for thou doest all these t. 14.22
worthless t. in which there is no 16.19
The heart is deceitful above all t., 17.09
Jeremiah prophesying these t. 20.01
princes of Judah heard these t., 26.10
I have done these t. to you. 30.15
and hidden t. which you have not 33.03
And do you seek great t. for yourself? 45.05
bring these t. upon Moab in the 48.44
he is the one who formed all t., 51.19
of the LORD t. came to such a pass 52.03
of all these t. was beyond weight. 52.20
the precious t. that were hers Lam 1.07
his hands over all her precious t.; 1.10
"For these t. I weep; my eyes flow 1.16
for these t. our eyes have grown 5.17
your detestable t. and with all Eze 5.11
and their detestable t. of it; 7.20
were all kinds of creeping t., 8.10
for I know the t. that come into 11.05
its detestable t. and all its 11.18
detestable t. and their abominations, 11.21
exiles all the t. that the LORD 11.25
do any of these t. to you out of 16.05
GOD, seeing you did all these t., 16.30
have enraged me with all these t.; 16.43
and did abominable t. before me; 16.50
Do you not know what these t. mean? 17.12
can a man escape who does such t.? 17.15

THINGS (cont.)

his hand and yet did all these t., Eze 17.18
has done all these abominable t.; 18.13
same abominable t. that the wicked 18.24
the detestable t. your eyes feast 20.07
the destestable t. their eyes 20.08
astray after their detestable t.? 20.30
t. shall not remain as they are; 21.26
You have despised my holy t., 22.08
taken treasure and precious t.; 22.25
law and have profaned my holy t.; 22.26
tell us what these t. mean for us, 24.19
idols and their detestable t., 37.23
all creeping t. that creep on the 38.20
have not kept charge of my holy t.; 44.08
nor come near any of my sacred t. 44.13
and the t. that are most sacred; 44.13
he reveals deep and mysterious t.; Dan 2.22
to pieces and shatters all t.; 2.40
man, and a mouth speaking great t. 7.08
to me the interpretation of the t. 7.16
and a mouth that spoke great t., 7.20
astonishing t. against the God of 11.36
and all the precious t. of Egypt; 11.43
end all these t. would be accomplished. 12.07
shall be the issue of these t.?" 12.08
and the creeping t. of the ground; Hos 2.18
their precious t. of silver; 9.06
wise, let him understand these t.; 14.09
rise, for he has done great t. Joe 2.20
for the LORD has done great t.! 2.21
"one should not preach of such t.; Mic 2.06
I will show them marvelous t. 7.15
like the crawling t. of the earth; 7.17
like crawling t. that have no ruler. Hab 1.14
the day of small t. shall rejoice, Zec 4.10
people to possess all these t. 8.12
These are the t. that you shall do: 8.16
for all these t. I hate, says the 8.17
For the Gentiles seek all these t.; Mt 6.32
and all these t. shall be yours as 6.33
give good t. to those who ask him? 7.11
hidden these t. from the wise and 11.25
All t. have been delivered to me by 11.27
And he told them many t. in parables, 13.03
and suffer many t. from the elders 16.21
come, and he is to restore all t.; 17.11
but with God all t. are possible." 19.26
saw the wonderful t. that he did, 21.15
authority are you doing these t., 21.23
by what authority I do these t. 21.24
by what authority I do these t. 21.27
to Caesar the t. that are Caesar's, 22.21
and to God the t. that are God's." 22.21
So also, when you see all these t., 24.33
away till all these t. take place. 24.34
hear how many t. they testify 27.13
he taught them many t. in parables, Mk 4.02
and the desire for other t., 4.19
and he began to teach them many t. 6.34
And many such t. you do." 7.13
but the t. which come out of a man 7.15
All these evil t. come from within, 7.23
saying, "He has done all t. well; 7.37
the Son of man must suffer many t., 8.31
does come first to restore all t.; 9.12
suffer many t. and be treated with 9.12
All t. are possible to him who 9.23
for all t. are possible with God." 10.27
authority are you doing these t., 11.28
by what authority I do these t. 11.29
by what authority I do these t." 11.33
to Caesar the t. that are Caesar's, 12.17
and to God the t. that are God's." 12.17
sign when these t. are all to be 13.04
I have told you all t. beforehand. 13.23
when you see these t. taking place, 13.29
before all these t. take place. 13.30
all t. are possible to thee; 14.36
priests accused him of many t. 15.03
narrative of the t. which have been Lk 1.01
followed all t. closely for some 1.03
concerning the t. of which you 1.04
the day that these t. come to pass, 1.20
is mighty has done great t. for me, 1.49
has filled the hungry with good t., 1.53
And all these t. were talked about 1.65
But Mary kept all these t., 2.19
kept all these t. in her heart. 2.51
all the evil t. that Herod had 3.19
"We have seen strange t. today." 5.26
of John told him of all these t. 7.18
is this about whom I hear such t.?" 9.09
"The Son of man must suffer many t., 9.22
hidden these t. from the wise and 10.21
All t. have been delivered to me by 10.22
anxious and troubled about many t.; 10.41
for alms those t. which are within 11.41
provoke him to speak of many t., 11.53
and the t. you have prepared, whose 12.20
nations of the world seek these t.; 12.30
and these t. shall be yours as well. 12.31
the glorious t. that were done by 13.17
lifetime received your good t., 16.25
and Lazarus in like manner evil t.; 16.25
suffer many t. and be rejected by 17.25
But they understood none of these t.; 18.34
As they heard these t., he proceeded 19.11
you knew the t. that make for 19.42
by what authority you do these t., 20.02
by what authority I do these t." 20.08
to Caesar the t. that are Caesar's, 20.25
and to God the t. that are God's." 20.25
"As for these t. which you see, the 21.06
Now when these t. begin to take 21.28
when you see these t. taking place, 21.31
all these t. that will take place, 21.36
at a distance and saw these t. 23.49
about all these t. that had 24.14
not know the t. that have happened 24.18
And he said to them, "What t.?" 24.19
suffer these t. and enter into his 24.26
scriptures the t. concerning 24.27
You are witnesses of these t. 24.48
all t. were made through him, and Jn 1.03
shall see greater t. than these." 1.50
the pigeons, "Take these t. away; 2.16
you earthly t. and you do not 3.12
believe if I tell you heavenly t.? 3.12
and has given all t. into his hand. 3.35
he comes, he will show us all t." 4.25
If you do these t., show yourself 7.04
had given all t. into his hands, 13.03
If you know these t., blessed are 13.17
"These t. I have spoken to you, 14.25
my name, he will teach you all t., 14.26
These t. I have spoken to you, that 15.11
But I have said these t. to you, 16.04
not say these t. to you from the 16.04
I have said these t. to you, 16.06
"I have yet many t. to say to you, 16.12
to you the t. that are to come. 16.13
Now we know that you know all t., 16.30
and these t. I speak in the world, 17.13
For these t. took place that the 19.36
that he had said these t. to her. 20.18
who is bearing witness to these t., 21.24
and who has written these t.; 21.24
also many other t. which Jesus did 21.25
together and had all t. in common; Ac 2.44
and the peoples imagine vain t.? 4.25
that any of the t. which he 4.32
and upon all who heard of these t. 5.11
And we are witnesses to these t., 5.32

THINGS (cont.)

Did not my hand make all these t.?' Ac 7.50
heard these t. they were enraged, 7.54
that these t. might be told them 13.42
from these vain t. to a living God 14.15
has made these t. known from of 15.18
you the same t. by word of mouth. 15.27
burden than these necessary t.: 15.28
daily to see if these t. were so. 17.11
bring some strange t. to our ears; 17.20
know therefore what these t. mean." 17.20
I refuse to be a judge of these t." 18.15
accurately the t. concerning Jesus, 18.25
Seeing then that these t. cannot be 19.36
arise men speaking perverse t., 20.30
In all t. I have shown you that by 20.35
one by one the t. that God had 21.19
to do many t. in opposing the name 26.09
witness to the t. in which you 26.16
For the king knows about these t., 26.26
none of these t. has escaped his 26.26
perceived in the t. that have been Rom 1.20
who do such t. deserve to die, 1.32
judge, are doing the very same t. 2.01
falls upon those who do such t. 2.02
who do such t. and yet do them 2.03
existence the t. that do not exist 4.17
get from the t. of which you are 6.21
The end of those t. is death. 6.21
their minds on the t. of the flesh, 8.05
minds on the t. of the Spirit. 8.05
not also give us all t. with him? 8.32
in all these t. we are more than 8.37
nor t. present, nor t. to come, nor 8.38
through him and to him are all t. 11.36
even t. that are not, to bring to 1Co 1.28
to bring to nothing t. that are, 1.28
The spiritual man judges all t., 2.15
boast of men. For all t. are yours, 3.21
to light the t. now hidden in 4.05
world, the offscouring of all t. 4.13
"All t. are lawful for me," but not 6.12
me," but not all t. are helpful. 6.12
"All t. are lawful for me," but I 6.12
from whom are all t. and for whom we 8.06
through whom are all t. and through 8.06
I have become all t. to all men, 9.22
exercises self-control in all t. 9.25
Now these t. are warnings for us, 10.06
Now these t. happened to them as a 10.11
"All t. are lawful," but not all 10.23
lawful," but not all t. are helpful. 10.23
"All t. are lawful," but not all t. build up. 10.23
And all t. are from God.) 11.12
About the other t. I will give 11.34
Love bears all t., believes all t., 13.07
hopes all t., endures all t. 13.07
Let all t. be done for edification. 14.26
but all t. should be done decently 14.40
"For God has put all t. in subjection 15.27
"All t. are put in subjection under 15.27
excepted who put all t. under him. 15.27
When all t. are subjected to him, 15.28
to him who put all t. under him, 15.28
Who is sufficient for these t.? 2Co 2.16
look not to the t. that are seen 4.18
seen but to the t. that are unseen; 4.18
for the t. that are seen are 4.18
but the t. that are unseen are 4.18
made this plain to you in all t. 11.06
since many boast of worldly t., 11.18
And, apart from other t., 11.28
boast of the t. that show my 11.30
and he heard t. that cannot be told, 12.04
up again those t. which I tore Gal 2.18
Did you experience so many t. in vain?— 3.04

abide by all t. written in the 3.10
scripture consigned all t. to sin, 3.22
who do such t. shall not inherit 5.21
share all good t. with him who 6.06
all t. in him, t. in heaven and t. on Eph 1.10
accomplishes all t. according to 1.11
and he has put all t. under his 1.22
head over all t. for the church, 1.22
for ages in God who created all t.; 3.09
heavens, that he might fill all t.) 4.10
of these t. that the wrath of God 5.06
to speak of the t. that they do in 5.12
Do all t. without grumbling or Php 2.14
write the same t. to you is not 3.01
I have suffered the loss of all t., 3.08
with minds set on earthly t. 3.19
even to subject all t. to himself. 3.21
of praise, think about these t. 4.08
I can do all t. in him who strengthens 4.13
for in him all t. were created, in Col 1.16
all t. were created through him and 1.16
He is before all t., and in him all t. 1.17
him to reconcile to himself all t., 1.20
(referring to t. which all perish 2.22
seek the t. that are above, where 3.01
Set your minds on t. that are above, 3.02
not on t. that are on earth. 3.02
the same t. from your own countrymen 1Th 2.14
Lord is an avenger in all these t., 4.06
and will do the t. which we 2Th 3.04
saying or the t. about which they 1Ti 1.07
but temperate, faithful in all t. 3.11
Command and teach these t. 4.11
of God who gives life to all t., 6.13
To the pure all t. are pure, Tit 1.15
Declare these t.; exhort and reprove 2.15
I desire you to insist on these t., 3.08
he appointed the heir of all t., Heb 1.02
for whom and by whom all t. exist, 2.10
but the builder of all t. is God.) 3.04
testify to the t. that were to be 3.05
sure of better t. that belong to 6.09
so that through two unchangeable t., 6.18
of whom these t. are spoken 7.13
Of these t. we cannot now speak in 9.05
of the good t. that have come, 9.11
of the heavenly t. to be purified 9.23
the heavenly t. themselves with 9.23
of the good t. to come instead of 10.01
is the assurance of t. hoped for, 11.01
for, the conviction of t. not seen. 11.01
was made out of t. which do not 11.03
desiring to act honorably in all t. 13.18
giving them the t. needed for the Jas 2.16
member and boasts of great t. 3.05
in the t. which have now been 1Pe 1.12
t. into which angels long to look. 1.12
with perishable t. such as silver 1.18
The end of all t. is at hand; 4.07
to us all t. that pertain to life 2Pe 1.03
For if these t. are yours and 1.08
lacks these t. is blind and 1.09
always to remind you of these t., 1.12
at any time to recall these t. 1.15
all t. have continued as they were 3.04
Since all these t. are thus to be 3.11
There are some t. in them hard to 3.16
the world or the t. in the world. 1Jn 2.15
and by those t. that they know by Jud 1.10
all the harsh t. which ungodly 1.15
But I have a few t. against you: Rev 2.14
some call the deep t. of Satan, 2.24
for thou didst create all t., 4.11
for the former t. have passed away." 21.04
said, "Behold, I make all t. new." 21.05
am he who heard and saw these t. 22.08
He who testifies to these t. says, 22.20

THINK
'Let them marry whom they t. best; Num 36.06
"Do you t., because David has sent 2Sa 10.03
"I t. the running of the foremost 18.27
You t. that mere words are counsel 2Ki 18.20
"Do you t., because David has sent 1Ch 19.03
"And now you t. to withstand the 2Ch 13.08
"T. not that in the king's palace Est 4.13
"T. now, who that was innocent ever Job 4.07
Do you t. that you can reprove 6.26
When I t. of it I am dismayed, and 21.06
"Do you t. this to be just? 35.02
t. of the battle; you will not 41.08
one would t. the deep to be hoary. 41.32
for "Who," they t., "will hear us?" Ps 59.07
when I t. of thee upon my bed, and 63.06
I t. of God, and I moan; I meditate 77.03
When I t. of thy ordinances from of 119.52
When I t. of thy ways, I turn my 119.59
of man that thou dost t. of him? 144.03
and his mind does not so t.; Is 10.07
Do you t. that mere words are 36.05
Do you t. you are a king because Jer 22.15
who t. to make my people forget my 23.27
go wherever you t. it good and 40.04
go wherever you t. it right to go." 40.05
So you t., O house of Israel; Eze 11.05
and shall t. to change the times Dan 7.25
"T. not that I have come to abolish Mt 5.17
for they t. that they will be heard 6.07
said "Why do you t. evil in your 9.04
"Do not t. that I have come to 10.34
saying, "What do you t., Simon? 17.25
What do you t.? If a man has 18.12
"What do you t.? A man had 21.28
Tell us, then, what you t. 22.17
saying, "What do you t. of the Christ? 22.42
Do you t. that I cannot appeal to 26.53
do you t., proved neighbor to the Lk 10.36
Do you t. that I have come to give 12.51
"Do you t. that these Galileans 13.02
do you t. that they were worse 13.04
because you t. that in them you Jn 5.39
Do not t. that I shall accuse you 5.45
in the temple, "What do you t.? 11.56
kills you will t. he is offering 16.02
we ought not to t. that the Deity Ac 17.29
"I t. myself fortunate that it is 26.02
short time you t. to make me a 26.28
you not to t. of himself more Rom 12.03
more highly than he ought to t., 12.03
but to t. with sober judgment, each 12.03
For I t. that God has exhibited us 1Co 4.09
I t. that in view of the impending 7.26
And I t. that I have the Spirit of 7.40
body which we t. less honorable we 12.23
I t. that I am not in the least 2Co 11.05
I repeat, let no one t. me foolish; 11.16
that no one may t. more of me than 12.06
abundantly than all that we ask or t., Eph 3.20
of praise, t. about these things. Php 4.08
T. over what I say, for the Lord 2Ti 2.07
punishment do you t. will be Heb 10.29
I t. it right, as long as I am in 2Pe 1.13

THINKING
to Abraham, "What were you t. of, Gen 20.10
t., "Lest the men of the place 26.07
t., "If Esau comes to the one 32.08
t., "Lest they should tell about us, 1Sa 27.11
t., "He has made himself utterly 27.12
t., "David cannot come in here." 2Sa 5.06
t., 'When they come out of the city, 2Ki 7.12
cities, t. to win them for himself. 2Ch 32.01
t., "Their hands will drop from the Neh 6.09
secretly, t., "Who can see us? Ps 64.05
By t. that the LORD's table may be Mal 1.07
futile in their t. and their Rom 1.21
Brethren, do not be children in your t.; 1Co 14.20
babes in evil, but in t. be mature. 14.20
Have you been t. all along that we 2Co 12.19
sincerely but t. to afflict me in Php 1.17
If they had been t. of that land Heb 11.15

THINKS
and he t., 'Let not Jonathan know 1Sa 20.03
He t. in his heart, "I shall not be Ps 10.06
he t. in his heart, "God has forgotten, 10.11
continually t. of it and is bowed Lam 3.20
even what he t. that he has will be Lk 8.18
for any one who t. it unclean. Rom 14.14
one among you t. that he is wise 1Co 3.18
If any one t. that he is not 7.36
Therefore let any one who t. that 10.12
If any one t. that he is a prophet, 14.37
For if any one t. he is something, Gal 6.03
any other man t. he has reason for Php 3.04
If any one t. he is religious, and Jas 1.26

THIRD
and there was morning, a t. day. Gen 1.13
And the name of the t. river is 2.14
with lower, second, and t. decks. 6.16
On the t. day Abraham lifted up his 22.04
Laban on the t. day that Jacob had 31.22
second and the t. and all who 32.19
On the t. day, when they were sore, 34.25
On the t. day, which was Pharaoh's 40.20
On the t. day Joseph said to them, 42.18
children of the t. generation; 50.23
On the t. new moon after the people Ex 19.01
and be ready by the t. day; 19.11
for on the t. day the LORD will 19.11
the people, "Be ready by the t. day; 19.15
morning of the t. day there were 19.16
children to the t. and the fourth 20.05
and the t. row a jacinth, an agate, 28.19
to the t. and the fourth generation." 34.07
and the t. row, a jacinth, an agate, 39.12
sacrifice on the t. day shall be Lev 7.17
offering is eaten on the t. day, 7.18
over until the t. day shall be 19.06
If it is eaten at all on the t. day, 19.07
They shall set out t. on the march. Num 2.24
On the t. day Eliab the son of 7.24
upon the t. and upon the fourth 14.18
mixed with a t. of a hin of oil; 15.06
shall offer a t. of a hin of wine, 15.07
water on the t. day and on the 19.12
himself on the t. day and on the 19.12
unclean on the t. day and on the 19.19
a t. of a hin for a ram, and a 28.14
"On the t. day eleven bulls, two 29.20
captives on the t. day and on the 31.19
children to the t. and fourth Deu 5.09
The children of the t. generation 23.08
of your produce in the t. year, 26.12
reached their cities on the t. day. Jos 9.17
villages; the t. is Naphath. 17.11
The t. lot came up for the tribe of 19.10
the Benjaminites on the t. day, Ju 20.30
called Samuel again the t. time. 1Sa 3.08
and a t. of a shekel for sharpening 13.21
him Abinadab, and the t. Shammah. 17.13
sent messengers again the t. time, 19.21
field till the t. day at evening. 20.05
or the t. day, behold, if he is well 20.12
And on the t. day you will be 20.19
men came to Ziklag on the t. day, 30.01
and on the t. day, behold, a man came 2Sa 1.02
and the t., Absalom the son of 3.03
one t. under the command of Joab, 18.02
one t. under the command of Abishai 18.02
and one t. under the command of 18.02

THIRD (cont.)
Then on the t. day after I was 1Ki 3.18
and the t. was seven cubits broad; 6.06
from the middle story to the t. 6.08
people came to Rehoboam the t. day, 12.12
said, "Come to me again the t. day." 12.12
him in the t. year of Asa king of 15.28
In the t. year of Asa king of Judah, 15.33
in the t. year, saying, "Go, show 18.01
And he said, "Do it a t. time"; 18.34
and they did it a t. time. 18.34
But in the t. year Jehoshaphat the 22.02
captain of a t. fifty with his 2Ki 1.13
And the t. captain of fifty went up, 1.13
one t. of you, those who come off 11.05
(another t. being at the gate Sur 11.06
a t. at the gate behind the guards), 11.06
In the t. year of Hoshea son of 18.01
then in the t. year sow, and reap, 19.29
on the t. day you shall go up to 20.05
house of the LORD on the t. day?" 20.08
Abinadab the second, Shimea the t., 1Ch 2.13
the t. Absalom, whose mother was 3.02
the t. Zedekiah, the fourth Shallum. 3.15
Ashbel the second, Aharah the t., 8.01
the second, and Eliphelet the t. 8.39
chief, Obadiah second, Eliab t., 12.09
Jahaziel the t., and Jekameam the 23.19
the t. to Harim, the fourth to 24.08
Jahaziel the t., Jekameam the 24.23
the t. to Zaccur, his sons and his 25.10
Zebadiah the t., Jathniel the 26.02
Joah the t., Sachar the fourth, 26.04
Tebaliah the t., Zechariah the 26.11
The t. commander, for the t. month, 27.05
people came to Rehoboam the t. day, 2Ch 10.12
said, "Come to me again the t. day." 10.12
Jerusalem in the t. month of the 15.10
In the t. year of his reign he sent 17.07
one t. shall be gatekeepers, 23.04
and one t. shall be at the king's 23.05
house and one t. at the Gate of 23.05
in the second and the t. years. 27.05
In the t. month they began to pile 31.07
finished on the t. day of the Ez 6.15
yearly with the t. part of a Neh 10.32
in the t. year of his reign he gave Est 1.03
On the t. day Esther put on her 5.01
in the t. month, which is the month 8.09
the name of the t. Kerenhappuch. Job 42.14
will be the t. with Egypt and Is 19.24
then in the t. year sow and reap, 37.30
him at the t. entrance of the Jer 38.14
A t. part you shall burn in the Eze 5.02
and a t. part you shall take and 5.02
and a t. part you shall scatter to 5.02
A t. part of you shall die of 5.12
a t. part shall fall by the sword 5.12
and a t. part I will scatter to all 5.12
and the t. the face of a lion, and 10.14
in the t. month, on the first day of 31.01
and one t. of a hin of oil to 46.14
In the t. year of the reign of Dan 1.01
and yet a t. kingdom of bronze, 2.39
shall be the t. ruler in the 5.07
shall be the t. ruler in the 5.16
should be the t. ruler in the 5.29
In the t. year of the reign of King 8.01
In the t. year of Cyrus king of 10.01
on the t. day he will raise us up, Hos 6.02
the t. white horses, and the fourth Zec 6.03
and one t. shall be left alive. 13.08
And I will put this t. into the fire, 13.09
and on the t. day be raised. Mt 16.21
he will be raised on the t. day." 17.23
out about the t. hour he saw 20.03
he will be raised on the t. day." 20.19
So too the second and t., 22.26
away and prayed for the t. time, 26.44
to be made secure until the t. day, 27.64
no children; and the t. likewise; Mk 12.21
And he came the t. time, and said to 14.41
And it was the t. hour, when they 15.25
and on the t. day be raised." Lk 9.22
or in the t., and finds them so, 12.38
and the t. day I finish my course. 13.32
and on the t. day he will rise." 18.33
And he sent yet a t.; this one 20.12
and the t. took her, and likewise 20.31
A t. time he said to them, "Why, what 23.22
crucified, and on the t. day rise." 24.07
it is now the t. day since this 24.21
and on the t. day rise from the 24.46
On the t. day there was a marriage Jn 2.01
This was now the t. time that Jesus 21.14
He said to him the t. time, 21.17
because he said to him the t. time, 21.17
it is only the t. hour of the day; Ac 2.15
him on the t. day and made him 10.40
down from the t. story and was 20.09
"At the t. hour of the night get 23.23
and the t. day they cast out with 27.19
t. teachers, then workers of miracles, 1Co 12.28
raised on the t. day in accordance 15.04
was caught up to the t. heaven— 2Co 12.02
Here for the t. time I am ready to 12.14
This is the t. time I am coming to 13.01
the t. living creature with the Rev 4.07
When he opened the t. seal, 6.05
I heard the t. living creature say, 6.05
and a t. of the earth was burnt up, 8.07
and a t. of the trees were burnt up, 8.07
and a t. of the sea became blood, a 8.09
a t. of the living creatures in the 8.09
and a t. of the ships were destroyed. 8.09
The t. angel blew his trumpet, and a 8.10
it fell on a t. of the rivers and 8.10
A t. of the waters became wormwood, 8.11
and a t. of the sun was struck, and 8.12
and a t. of the moon, and a 8.12
and a t. of the stars, so that a 8.12
so that a t. of their light was 8.12
a t. of the day was kept from 8.12
and likewise a t. of the night. 8.12
the year, to kill a t. of mankind. 9.15
three plagues a t. of mankind was 9.18
behold, the t. woe is soon to come. 11.14
swept down a t. of the stars of 12.04
a t., followed, saying with a loud 14.09
The t. angel poured his bowl into 16.04
the t. agate, the fourth emerald, 21.19

THIRDS
two t. shall be cut off and perish, Zec 13.08

THIRST
children and our cattle with t.?" Ex 17.03
in hunger and t., in nakedness, and Deu 28.48
and shall I now die of t., Ju 15.18
over to die by famine and by t., 2Ch 32.11
them from the rock for their t., Neh 9.15
and gavest them water for their t. 9.20
the wine presses, but suffer t. Job 24.11
and for my t. they gave me vinegar Ps 69.21
the wild asses quench their t. 104.11
their multitude is parched with t. Is 5.13
with his t. not quenched, so shall 29.08
their tongue is parched with t., 41.17
they shall not hunger or t., 49.10
for lack of water, and die of t. 50.02
unshod and your throat from t. Jer 2.25
to the roof of its mouth for t.; Lam 4.04
parched land, and slay her with t. Hos 2.03

THIRST (cont.)
nor a t. for water, but of hearing Amo 8.11
the young men shall faint for t. 8.13
who hunger and t. for righteousness, Mt 5.06
drinks of this water will t. again, Jn 4.13
I shall give him will never t.; 4.14
me this water, that I may not t., 4.15
who believes in me shall never t. 6.35
"If any one t., let him come to me 7.37
(to fulfil the scripture), "I t." 19.28
To the present hour we hunger and t., 1Co 4.11
in hunger and t., often without 2Co 11.27
no more, neither t. any more; Rev 7.16

THIRSTED
But the people t. there for water, Ex 17.03
They t. not when he led them Is 48.21

THIRSTS
My soul t. for God, for the living Ps 42.02
I seek thee, my soul t. for thee; 63.01
my soul t. for thee like a parched 143.06
every one who t., come to the Is 55.01

THIRSTY
scorpions and t. ground where Deu 8.15
little water to drink; for I am t." Ju 4.19
And he was very t., and he called on 15.18
And when you are t., go to the vessels Ru 2.09
and weary and t. in the wilderness." 2Sa 17.29
and the t. pant after his wealth. Job 5.05
hungry and t., their soul fainted Ps 107.05
For he satisfies him who is t., 107.09
springs of water into t. ground, 107.33
and if he is t., give him water to Pro 25.21
Like cold water to a t. soul, 25.25
womb, the earth ever t. for water, 30.16
To the t. bring water, meet the Is 21.14
or as when a t. man dreams he is 29.08
and to deprive the t. of drink. 32.06
and the t. ground springs of water; 35.07
For I will pour water on the t. land, 44.03
shall drink, but you shall be t.; 65.13
wilderness, in a dry and t. land. Eze 19.13
I was t. and you gave me drink, I Mt 25.35
or t. and give thee drink? 25.37
I was t. and you gave me no drink, 25.42
thee hungry or t. or a stranger or 25.44
if he is t., give him drink; Rom 12.20
To the t. I will give water without Rev 21.06
And let him who is t. come, 22.17

THIRTEEN
his son was t. years old when he Gen 17.25
t. young bulls, two rams, fourteen Num 29.13
an ephah for each of the t. bulls, 29.14
t. cities with their villages; Jos 19.06
Simeon, and Benjamin, t. cities. 21.04
of Manasseh in Bashan, t. cities. 21.06
were in all t. cities with their 21.19
were in all t. cities with their 21.33
building his own house t. years, 1Ki 7.01
throughout their families were t. 1Ch 6.60
were allotted t. cities out of the 6.62
sons and brethren of Hosah were t. 26.11
breadth of the gateway, t. cubits. Eze 40.11

THIRTEENTH
but in the t. year they rebelled. Gen 14.04
the t. to Huppah, the fourteenth to 1Ch 24.13
to the t., Shubael, his sons and his 25.20
summoned on the t. day of the Est 3.12
the t. day of the twelfth month, 3.13
on the t. day of the twelfth month, 8.12
on the t. day of the same, when the 9.01
This was on the t. day of the month 9.17
gathered on the t. day and on the 9.18
in the t. year of his reign. Jer 1.02
from the t. year of Josiah the son 25.03

THIRTIETH
In the t. year, in the fourth month, Eze 1.01

THIRTY
had lived a hundred and t. years, Gen 5.03
were nine hundred and t. years; 5.05
Jared eight hundred and t. years, 5.16
cubits, and its height t. cubits. 6.15
When Shelah had lived t. years, 11.14
of Peleg four hundred and t. years, 11.17
When Peleg had lived t. years, 11.18
When Serug had lived t. years, 11.22
Suppose t. are found there." 18.30
will not do it, if I find t. there." 18.30
t. milch camels and their colts, 32.15
Joseph was t. years old when he 41.46
sojourning are a hundred and t. years; 47.09
was four hundred and t. years. Ex 12.40
end of four hundred and t. years, 12.41
to their master t. shekels of 21.32
of each curtain shall be t. cubits, 26.08
of each curtain was t. cubits, 36.15
and seven hundred and t. shekels, 38.24
your valuation shall be t. shekels. Lev 27.04
from t. years old up to fifty years Num 4.03
from t. years old up to fifty years 4.23
from t. years old up to fifty years 4.30
from t. years old up to fifty years 4.35
from t. years old up to fifty years 4.39
two thousand six hundred and t. 4.40
from t. years old up to fifty years 4.43
from t. years old up to fifty years 4.47
was a hundred and t. shekels, 7.13
was a hundred and t. shekels, 7.19
was a hundred and t. shekels, 7.25
was a hundred and t. shekels, 7.31
was a hundred and t. shekels, 7.37
was a hundred and t. shekels, 7.43
was a hundred and t. shekels, 7.49
was a hundred and t. shekels, 7.55
was a hundred and t. shekels, 7.61
was a hundred and t. shekels, 7.67
was a hundred and t. shekels, 7.73
was a hundred and t. shekels, 7.79
a hundred and t. shekels and each 7.85
of Israel wept for Aaron t. days. 20.29
thousand seven hundred and t. 26.07
one thousand seven hundred and t. 26.51
The asses were t. thousand five 31.39
and t. thousand five hundred asses, 31.45
in the plains of Moab t. days; Deu 34.08
Joshua chose t. thousand mighty Jos 8.03
had t. sons who rode on t. asses; Ju 10.04
and they had t. cities, called 10.04
He had t. sons; and t. daughters he gave 12.09
and t. daughters he brought in from 12.09
He had forty sons and t. grandsons, 12.14
they brought t. companions to be 14.11
I will give you t. linen garments 14.12
garments and t. festal garments; 14.12
shall give me t. linen garments 14.13
garments and t. festal garments. 14.13
and killed t. men of the town, and 14.19
country, about t. men of Israel. 20.31
and kill about t. men of Israel; 20.39
fell of Israel t. thousand foot 1Sa 4.10
invited, who were about t. persons. 9.22
and the men of Judah t. thousand. 11.08
t. thousand chariots, and six 13.05
David was t. years old when he 2Sa 5.04
chosen men of Israel, t. thousand. 6.01
And three of the t. chief men went 23.13
of Zeruiah, was chief of the t. 23.18

THIRTY (cont.)
He was the most renowned of the t., 2Sa 23.19
He was renowned among the t., 23.23
brother of Joab was one of the t.; 23.24
for one day was t. measures of 1Ki 4.22
the levy numbered t. thousand men. 5.13
cubits wide, and t. cubits high. 6.02
cubits, and its height t. cubits, 7.02
cubits, and its breadth t. cubits; 7.06
and a line of t. cubits measured 7.23
for t. cubits, compassing the sea 7.24
of silver and t. talents of gold. 2Ki 18.14
Three of the t. chief men went down 1Ch 11.15
of Joab, was chief of the t. 11.20
He was the most renowned of the t., 11.21
He was renowned among the t., 11.25
the Reubenites, and t. with him, 11.42
among the t. and a leader over the t.; 12.04
chief of the t., and he said, "We 12.18
a hundred and t. of his brethren; 15.07
The Levites, t. years old and upward, 23.03
man of the t. and in command of 27.06
thirty and in command of the t.; 27.06
and a line of t. cubits measured 2Ch 4.02
for t. cubits, compassing the sea 4.03
a hundred and t. years old at his 24.15
flock to the number of t. thousand, 35.07
t. bowls of gold, two thousand four Ez 1.10
three thousand six hundred and t. 2.35
three thousand nine hundred and t. Neh 7.38
hundred and t. priests' garments. 7.70
come in to the king these t. days. Est 4.11
written for you t. sayings of Pro 22.20
t. chambers fronted on the pavement. Eze 40.17
one over another, t. in each story. 41.06
forty cubits long and t. broad; 46.22
to any god or man for t. days, Dan 6.07
or man within t. days except to 6.12
out as my wages t. shekels of Zec 11.12
So I took the t. shekels of silver 11.13
a hundredfold, some sixty, some t. Mt 13.08
another sixty, and in another t. 13.23
they paid him t. pieces of silver. 26.15
back the t. pieces of silver to 27.03
they took the t. pieces of silver, 27.09
was about t. years of age, being the Lk 3.23
each holding twenty or t. gallons. Jn 2.06
hundred and t. years afterward, Gal 3.17

THIRTY-EIGHT
the brook Zered was t. years, Deu 2.14
and the total was t. thousand men. 1Ch 23.03
sons of Shobai, a hundred and t. Neh 7.45
who had been ill for t. years. Jn 5.05

THIRTY-EIGHTH
In the t. year of Asa king of Judah, 1Ki 16.29
In the t. year of Azariah king of 2Ki 15.08

THIRTY-FIFTH
war until the t. year of the reign 2Ch 15.19

THIRTY-FIRST
In the t. year of Asa king of Judah, 1Ki 16.23

THIRTY-FIVE
had lived t. years he became the Gen 11.12
of Benjamin was t. thousand four Num 1.37
numbered being t. thousand four 2.23
Jehoshaphat was t. years old when 1Ki 22.42
he made two pillars t. cubits high, 2Ch 3.15
He was t. years old when he began 20.31
their camels were four hundred and t., Ez 2.67
their camels four hundred and t., Neh 7.69
thousand three hundred and t. days. Dan 12.12

THIRTYFOLD
and yielding t. and sixtyfold and Mk 4.08
t. and sixtyfold and a hundredfold. 4.20

THIRTY-FOUR
When Eber had lived t. years, Gen 11.16
was twenty-two thousand and t. 1Ch 7.07

THIRTY-NINE
Shobai, in all one hundred and t. Ez 2.42

THIRTY-NINTH
to reign in the t. year of Uzziah 2Ki 15.13
In the t. year of Azariah king of 15.17
In the t. year of his reign Asa was 2Ch 16.12

THIRTY-ONE
of Tirzah, one: in all, t. kings. Jos 12.24
and he reigned t. years in Jerusalem. 2Ki 22.01
and he reigned t. years in Jerusalem. 2Ch 34.01

THIRTY-SECOND
year to the t. year of Artaxerxes Neh 5.14
for in the t. year of Artaxerxes 13.06

THIRTY-SEVEN
of Ishmael, a hundred and t. years; Gen 25.17
Levi being a hundred and t. years. Ex 6.16
being one hundred and t. years. 6.20
hundred and t. thousand five Num 31.36
hundred and t. thousand five 31.43
Uriah the Hittite: t. in all. 2Sa 23.39
with whom were t. thousand men 1Ch 12.34
thousand three hundred and t.; Ez 2.65
thousand three hundred and t.; Neh 7.67

THIRTY-SEVENTH
In the t. year of Joash king of 2Ki 13.10
And in the t. year of the exile of 25.27
And in the t. year of the captivity Jer 52.31

THIRTY-SIX
The cattle were t. thousand, Num 31.38
t. thousand cattle, 31.44
of Ai killed about t. men of them, Jos 7.05
t. thousand, for they had many wives 1Ch 7.04
Their horses were seven hundred and t., Ez 2.66
Their horses were seven hundred and t., Neh 7.68

THIRTY-SIXTH
In the t. year of the reign of Asa, 2Ch 16.01

THIRTY-THREE
and his daughters numbered t.). Gen 46.15
being a hundred and t. years. Ex 6.18
continue for t. days in the blood Lev 12.04
over all Israel and Judah t. years. 2Sa 5.05
and t. years in Jerusalem. 1Ki 2.11
And he reigned t. years in Jerusalem. 1Ch 3.04
and t. years in Jerusalem. 29.27

THIRTY-TWO
When Reu had lived t. years, Gen 11.20
of Manasseh was t. thousand two Num 1.35
numbered being t. thousand two 2.21
t. thousand five hundred. 26.37
and t. thousand persons in all, 31.35
the LORD's tribute was t. persons. 31.40
t. kings were with him, and horses 1Ki 20.01
and they were two hundred and t.; 20.15
he and the t. kings who helped him. 20.16
commanded the t. captains of his 22.31
He was t. years old when he became 2Ki 8.17
They hired t. thousand chariots and 1Ch 19.07
Jehoram was t. years old when he 2Ch 21.05
He was t. years old when he began 21.20
eight hundred and t. persons; Jer 52.29

THISTLE

"A t. on Lebanon sent to a cedar on 2Ki 14.09
passed by and trampled down the t. 14.09
"A t. on Lebanon sent to a cedar on 2Ch 25.18
passed by and trampled down the t. 25.18
Thorn and t. shall grow up on their Hos 10.08

THISTLES

thorns and t. it shall bring forth Gen 3.18
nettles and t. in its fortresses. Is 34.13
from thorns, or figs from t.? Mt 7.16
But if it bears thorns and t., Heb 6.08

THITHER

testimony in t. within the veil; Ex 26.33
t. you shall go, and t. you shall bring Deu 12.06
t. you shall bring all that I 12.11
they set out t. into the valley, Ju 5.14
And they turned aside t., and came to the 18.15
congregation sent t. twelve thousand 21.10
multitude was surging hither and t. 1Sa 14.16
I brought back t. the vessels of Neh 13.09
they come t. and are confounded. Job 6.20
and return not t. but water the Is 55.10
and t. you went up to offer sacrifice 57.07

THOMAS

T. and Matthew the tax collector; Mt 10.03
and T., and James the son of Mk 3.18
and T., and James the son of Lk 6.15
T., called the Twin, said to his Jn 11.16
T. said to him, "Lord, we do not know 14.05
Now T., one of the twelve, called 20.24
in the house, and T. was with them. 20.26
Then he said to T., "Put your finger 20.27
T. answered him, "My Lord and 20.28
Simon Peter, T. called the Twin, 21.02
Philip and T., Bartholomew and Ac 1.13

THONG

the t. of whose sandals I am not Mk 1.07
the t. of whose sandals I am not Lk 3.16
the t. of whose sandal I am not Jn 1.27

THONGS

to undo the t. of the yoke, to let Is 58.06
me: "Make yourself t. and yoke-bars, Jer 27.02
they had tied him up with the t., Ac 22.25

THORN

Like a t. that goes up into the Pro 26.09
Instead of the t. shall come up the Is 55.13
to prick or a t. to hurt them Eze 28.24
T. and thistle shall grow up on Hos 10.08
most upright of them a t. hedge. Mic 7.04
a t. was given me in the flesh, a 2Co 12.07

THORNBUSHES

of the rocks, and on all the t., Is 7.19

THORNS

t. and thistles it shall bring Gen 3.18
and catches in t. so that the Ex 22.06
in your eyes and t. in your sides, Num 33.55
and t. in your eyes, till you perish Jos 23.13
flesh with the t. of the wilderness Ju 8.07
and he took t. of the wilderness 8.16
are all like t. that are thrown 2Sa 23.06
and he takes it even out of t.; Job 5.05
let t. grow instead of wheat, and 31.40
your pots can feel the heat of t., Ps 58.09
they blazed like a fire of t.; 118.12
of a sluggard is overgrown with t., Pro 15.19
T. and snares are in the way of the 22.05
and lo, it was all overgrown with t.; 24.31
as the crackling of t. under a pot, Ecc 7.06
and briers and t. shall grow up; Is 5.06
silver, will become briers and t. 7.23
all the land will be briers and t.; 7.24
there for fear of briers and t.; 7.25
a fire, it consumes briers and t.; 9.18
and devour his t. and briers in 10.17
that I had t. and briers to battle! 27.04
people growing up in t. and briers; 32.13
like t. cut down, that are burned in 33.12
T. shall grow over its strongholds, 34.13
ground, and sow not among t. Jer 4.03
have sown wheat and have reaped t., 12.13
briers and t. are with you and you Eze 2.06
Therefore I will hedge up her way with t.; Hos 2.06
of silver; t. shall be in their tents. 9.06
Like entangled t. they are consumed, Nah 1.10
Are grapes gathered from t., Mt 7.16
Other seeds fell upon t., 13.07
and the t. grew up and choked them. 13.07
As for what was sown among t., 13.22
a crown of t. they put it on his 27.29
Other seed fell among t. and the Mk 4.07
thorns and the t. grew up and 4.07
And others are the ones sown among t.; 4.18
a crown of t. they put it on him. 15.17
for figs are not gathered from t., Lk 6.44
And some fell among t.; and the t. grew 8.07
And as for what fell among the t., 8.14
the soldiers plaited a crown of t., Jn 19.02
the crown of t. and the purple 19.05
But if it bears t. and thistles, Heb 6.08

THOROUGHFARES

Go therefore to the t., and invite to Mt 22.09

THOROUGHLY

us make bricks, and burn them t." Gen 11.03
time, and shall have him t. healed. Ex 21.19
Wash me t. from my iniquity, and Ps 51.02
"Glean t. as a vine the remnant of Jer 6.09

THOUGH

and t. I multiply my signs and Ex 7.03
to testify and t. he is a witness, Lev 5.01
t. he does not know it, yet he is 5.17
t. the disease has not spread, it is 13.55
to escape a sword, t. none pursues; 26.37
is undetected t. she has defiled Num 5.13
t. she has not defiled herself; 5.14
t. you are under your husband's 5.20
t. under her husband's authority, 5.29
to you as t. it were the grain of 18.27
"T. Balak were to give me his house 22.18
t. he was not his enemy, and did not 35.23
as t. it were a gazelle or a hart. Deu 15.22
t. the man did not deserve to die, 19.06
t. they chastise him, will not give 21.18
cry for help t. she was in the 22.24
and t. the betrothed young woman 22.27
t. I walk in the stubbornness of my 29.19
T. all the people who came out had Jos 5.05
for t. it is a forest, you shall 17.18
t. they have chariots of iron, and 17.18
of iron and t. they are strong." 17.18
t. I am not one of your maidservants." Ru 2.13
t. it be in Jonathan my son, he 1Sa 14.39
"T. you are little in your own eyes, 15.17
side of it, as t. I shot at a mark. 20.20
t. you hunt my life to take it. 24.11
am this day weak, t. anointed king; 2Sa 3.39
t. not like his father and mother, 2Ki 3.02
t. the Chaldeans were around the 25.04
t. Judah became strong among his 1Ch 5.02
the chief (for t. he was not the 26.10
T. the army of the Syrians had come 2Ch 24.24
even t. not according to the 30.19
t. they could not prove their Ez 2.59
t. many shouted aloud for joy; 3.12
t. your dispersed be under the Neh 1.09

THOUGH (cont.)
t. it is against the law; Est 4.16
And t. your beginning was small, Job 8.07
T. I am innocent, I cannot answer 9.15
T. I am innocent, my own mouth would 9.20
t. I am blameless, he would prove me 9.20
and were as t. I had not been, 10.19
T. its root grow old in the earth, 14.08
T. his height mount up to the 20.06
"T. wickedness is sweet in his 20.12
t. he hides it under his tongue, 20.12
t. he is loath to let it go, and 20.13
T. he heap up silver like dust, and 27.16
t. man does not perceive it. 33.14
t. I am without transgression. 34.06
t. her labor be in vain, yet she has 39.16
he is confident t. Jordan rushes 40.23
T. the sword reaches him, it does 41.26
Even t. I walk through the valley Ps 23.04
T. a host encamp against me, my 27.03
t. war arise against me, yet I will 27.03
as t. I grieved for my friend or my 35.14
t. you look well at his place, he 37.10
t. he fall, he shall not be cast 37.24
t. I sought him, he could not be 37.36
t. we have not forgotten thee, or 44.17
will not fear t. the earth should 46.02
t. the mountains shake in the heart 46.02
t. its waters roar and foam, though 46.03
t. the mountains tremble with its 46.03
t. they named lands their own. 49.11
T., while he lives, he counts 49.18
and t. a man gets praise when he 49.18
t. they stay among the sheepfolds— 68.13
that, t. the wicked sprout like 92.07
to the proof, t. they had seen my work. 95.09
Even t. princes sit plotting against me, 119.23
T. the cords of the wicked ensnare 119.61
For t. the LORD is high, he regards 138.06
T. I walk in the midst of trouble, 138.07
nor be appeased t. you multiply Pro 6.35
t. his hatred be covered with guile, 26.26
for t. he understands, he will not 29.19
And t. a man might prevail against Ecc 4.12
even t. he had gone from prison to 4.14
Even t. he should live a thousand 6.06
T. a sinner does evil a hundred 8.12
even t. a wise man claims to know, 8.17
t. the poor man's wisdom is despised, 9.16
t. no man knows what is to be, and 10.14
even t. you make many prayers, I Is 1.15
t. your sins are like scarlet, they 1.18
t. they are red like crimson, they 1.18
And t. a tenth remain in it, it will 6.13
For t. your people Israel be as the 10.22
for t. thou wast angry with me, thy 12.01
therefore, t. you plant pleasant 17.10
t. you make them grow on the day 17.11
captured, t. they had fled far away. 22.03
For t. his officials are at Zoan 30.04
And t. the Lord give you the bread 30.20
surname you, t. you do not know me. 45.04
I gird you, t. you do not know me, 45.05
t. Abraham does not know us and 63.16
even t. they are no gods? But my people Jer 2.11
T. you wash yourself with lye and 2.22
T. they say, "As the LORD lives," yet 5.02
t. the waves toss, they cannot 5.22
t. they roar, they cannot pass over 5.22
t. they cry to me, I will not listen 11.11
t. they speak fair words to you." 12.06
"T. our iniquities testify against 14.07
T. they fast, I will not hear their 14.12
and t. they offer burnt offering 14.12
"T. Moses and Samuel stood before 15.01
t. Coniah the son of Jehoiakim, king 22.24
urgently, t. you have not heeded, 26.05
t. I was their husband, says the 31.32
t. you fight against the Chaldeans, 32.05
t. the city is given into the hands 32.25
and t. I have taught them persistently 32.33
t. I did not command them, nor did 32.35
t. it is impenetrable, because they 46.23
T. you make your nest as high as 49.16
"T. you rejoice, t. you exult, O 50.11
t. you are wanton as a heifer at 50.11
T. Babylon should mount up to 51.53
and t. she should fortify her 51.53
t. I call and cry for help, he shuts Lam 3.08
but, t. he cause grief, he will have 3.32
t. briers and thorns are with you Eze 2.06
and t. they cry in my ears with a 8.18
T. I removed them far off among the 11.16
and t. I scattered them among the 11.16
t. they are a rebellious house. 12.03
t. these three men were in it, as I 14.18
t. they escape from the fire, the 15.07
t. you be sought for, you will never 26.21
t. you consider yourself as wise as 28.02
t. you are but a man, and no god, in 28.09
T. I say to the righteous that he 33.13
Again, t. I say to the wicked, 'You 33.14
your heart, t. you knew all this, Dan 5.22
t. they shall fall by sword and 11.33
t. they turn to other gods and love Hos 3.01
T. you play the harlot, O Israel, let 4.15
T. they hire allies among the 8.10
Even t. they bring forth, I will 9.16
T. he may flourish as the reed 13.15
Even t. you offer me your burnt Amo 5.22
"T. they dig into Sheol, from there 9.02
t. they climb up to heaven, from 9.02
T. they hide themselves on the top 9.03
and t. they hide from my sight at 9.03
And t. they go into captivity 9.04
T. you soar aloft like the eagle, Ob 1.04
t. your nest is set among the stars, 1.04
and shall be as t. they had not 1.16
"T. they be strong and many, they Nah 1.12
T. I have afflicted you, I will 1.12
T. the fig tree do not blossom, nor Hab 3.17
T. they build houses, they shall not Zep 1.13
t. they plant vineyards, they shall 1.13
Tyre and Sidon, t. they are very wise. Zec 9.02
shall be as t. I had not rejected 10.06
T. I scattered them among the 10.09
t. she is your companion and your Mal 2.14
And t. he wanted to put him to Mt 14.05
"T. they all fall away because of 26.33
t. many false witnesses came 26.60
"Even t. they all fall away, I will Mk 14.29
I tell you, t. he will not get up Lk 11.08
'T. I neither fear God nor regard 18.04
it came from (t. the servants who Jn 2.09
that t. I was blind, now I see." 9.25
even t. you do not believe me, 10.38
t. he die, yet shall he live, 11.25
T. he had done so many signs before 12.37
as t. by our own power or piety we Ac 3.12
posterity after him, t. he had no child. 7.05
T. they could charge him with 13.28
as t. he needed anything, since he 17.25
t. he knew only the baptism of John. 18.25
as t. you were going to determine 23.15
as t. they were going to inquire 23.20
T. he has escaped from the sea, 28.04
t. I had done nothing against the 28.17
t. I had no charge to bring against 28.19
T. they know God's decree that those Rom 1.32
even t. they do not have the law. 2.14
Let God be true t. every man be 3.04
t. perhaps for a good man one will 5.07
But it is not as t. the word of God 9.06
t. they were not yet born and had 9.11

THOUGH (cont.)

"T. the number of the sons of Rom 9.27
so we, t. many, are one body in 12.05
t. he himself will be saved, but 1Co 3.15
For t. you have countless guides in 4.15
as t. I were not coming to you. 4.18
For t. absent in body I am present 5.03
wives live as t. they had none, 7.29
who mourn as t. they were not 7.30
who rejoice as t. they were not 7.30
who buy as t. they had no goods, 7.30
the world as t. they had no 7.31
For t. I am free from all men, I 9.19
t. not being myself under the law— 9.20
t. many, are one body, so it is with 12.12
are still alive, t. some have fallen asleep. 15.06
t. it was not I, but the grace of 15.10
T. our outer nature is wasting away, 2Co 4.16
even t. we once regarded Christ 5.16
not regret it (t. I did regret it), 7.08
grieved you, t. only for a while. 7.08
that t. he was rich, yet for your 8.09
For t. we live in the world we are 10.03
as t. we did not reach you; 10.14
T. if I wish to boast, I shall not 12.06
apostles, even t. I am nothing. 12.11
t. we may seem to have failed. 13.07
be circumcised, t. he was a Greek. Gal 2.03
t. a Jew, live like a Gentile and 2.14
t. he is the owner of all the 4.01
and t. my condition was a trial to 4.14
To me, t. I am the very least of all Eph 3.08
who, t. he was in the form of God, Php 2.06
T. I myself have reason for confidence 3.04
For t. I am absent in body, yet I am Col 2.05
but t. we had already suffered and 1Th 2.02
t. we might have made demands as 2.06
t. I formerly blasphemed and 1Ti 1.13
Accordingly, t. I am bold enough in Phm 1.08
For t. by this time you ought to be Heb 5.12
T. we speak thus, yet in your case, 6.09
t. these also are descended from 7.05
And all these, t. well attested by 11.39
to repent, t. he sought it with tears. 12.17
as t. in prison with them; and those who 13.03
t. they are so great and are driven Jas 3.04
t. now for a little while you may 1Pe 1.06
than gold which t. perishable is 1.07
t. you do not now see him you believe 1.08
t. they do not obey the word, may be 3.01
that t. judged in the flesh like 4.06
as t. something strange were 4.12
t. you know them and are established 2Pe 1.12
t. greater in might and power, do 2.11
not as t. I were writing you a new 2Jn 1.05
T. I have much to write to you, I 1.12
t. you were once for all fully Jud 1.05
him, I fell at his feet as t. dead. Rev 1.17
as t. it had been slain, with seven 5.06

THOUGHT

Abraham said, "I did it because I t., Gen 20.11
"Because I t., 'Lest I die because 26.09
for I t. that you would take your 31.31
For he t., "I may appease him with 32.20
he t. her to be a harlot, for she 38.15
Give no t. to your goods, for the 45.20
"I had not t. to see your face; 48.11
and t., "Surely the thing is known." Ex 2.14
evil which he t. to do to his 32.14
do to you as I t. to do to them." Num 33.56
and t. it easy to go up into the Deu 1.41
there be a base t. in your heart, 15.09
And we t., If this should be said Jos 22.28
they t., "He is only relieving Ju 3.24
"I really t. that you utterly hated 15.02
So I t. I would tell you of it, and Ru 4.04
came, he looked on Eliab and t., 1Sa 16.06
for he t., "I will pin David to the 18.11
For Saul t., "Let not my hand be 18.17
Saul t., "Let me give her to him, 18.21
Now Saul t. to make David fall by 18.25
for he t., "Something has befallen 20.26
house of Benjamin t. good to do. 2Sa 3.19
and t. he was bringing good news, 4.10
and your handmaid t., 'I will speak to 14.15
And your handmaid t., 'The word of my 14.17
with a new sword, t. to kill David. 21.16
I t. that he would surely come out 2Ki 5.11
For he t., "Why not, if there will 20.19
and understands every plan and t. 1Ch 28.09
In the t. of one who is at ease Job 12.05
Then I t., 'I shall die in my nest, 29.18
but the Lord takes t. for me. Ps 40.17
We have t. on thy steadfast love, O 48.09
you t. that I was one like yourself. 50.21
We have t. out a cunningly conceived 64.06
But when I t. how to understand 73.16
When I t., "My foot slips," thy 94.18
And I t. the dead who are already Ecc 4.02
is no work or t. or knowledge or 9.10
Even in your t., do not curse the 10.20
For he t., "There will be peace Is 39.08
remember me, did not give me a t.? 57.11
And I t., 'After she has done all Jer 3.07
" 'I t. how I would set you among my 3.19
And I t. you would call me, My 3.19
she took no t. of her doom; Lam 1.09
"Then I t. I would pour out my Eze 20.08
"Then I t. I would pour out my 20.13
"Then I t. I would pour out my 20.21
the t., 'Let us be like the nations, 20.32
and declares to man what is his t.; Amo 4.13
the god will give a t. to us, Jon 1.06
by trustingly with no t. of war. Mic 2.08
feared the LORD and t. on his name. Mal 3.16
they t. they would receive more; Mt 20.10
on the sea they t. it was a ghost, Mk 6.49
perceived the t. of their hearts, Lk 9.47
and he t. to himself, 'What shall I 12.17
but they t. that he meant taking Jn 11.13
Some t. that, because Judas had the 13.29
because you t. you could obtain the Ac 8.20
but t. he was seeing a vision. 12.09
But Paul t. best not to take with 15.38
Why is it t. incredible by any of 26.08
but take t. for what is noble in Rom 12.17
I t. like a child, I reasoned like a 1Co 13.11
So I t. it necessary to urge the 2Co 9.05
and take every t. captive to obey 10.05
I have t. it necessary to send to Php 2.25
moreover he must be well t. of by 1Ti 3.07
arm yourselves with the same t., 1Pe 4.01

THOUGHTLESS

her vows or any t. utterance of Num 30.06
and the t. utterance of her lips, by 30.08

THOUGHTS

imagination of the t. of his heart Gen 6.05
purposes and t. in the hearts of 1Ch 29.18
Amid t. from visions of the night, Job 4.13
"Therefore my t. answer me, because 20.02
I know your t., and your schemes to 21.27
all his t. are, "There is no God." Ps 10.04
the t. of his heart to all generations. 33.11
wondrous deeds and try t. toward us; 40.05
all their t. are against me for 56.05
O LORD, Thy t. are very deep! 92.05
knows the t. of man, that they are 94.11
thou discernest my t. from afar. 139.02
How precious to me are thy t., O God! 139.17
know my heart! Try me and know my t.! 139.23
I will pour out my t. to you; Pro 1.23
The t. of the righteous are just; 12.05

THOUGHTS (cont.)

The t. of the wicked are an abomination Pro 15.26
and the unrighteous man his t.; Is 55.07
For my t. are not your t., neither 55.08
ways and my t. than your t. 55.09
their t. are t. of iniquity, 59.07
"For I know their works and their t., 66.18
shall your evil t. lodge within Jer 4.14
The lips and t. of my assailants Lam 3.62
On that day t. will come into your Eze 38.10
lay in bed came t. of what would Dan 2.29
you may know the t. of your mind. 2.30
long time, and his t. alarmed him. 4.19
changed, and his t. alarmed him; 5.06
Let not your t. alarm you or your 5.10
my t. greatly alarmed me, and my 7.28
do not know the t. of the LORD, Mic 4.12
knowing their t., said "Why do you Mt 9.04
Knowing their t., he said to them, 12.25
For out of the heart come evil t., 15.19
come evil t., fornication, theft, Mk 7.21
that t. out of many hearts may be Lk 2.35
But he knew their t., and he said 6.08
knowing their t., said to them, 11.17
conflicting t. accuse or perhaps Rom 2.15
knows a man's t. except the spirit 1Co 2.11
comprehends the t. of God except 2.11
knows that the t. of the wise are 3.20
your t. will led astray from a 2Co 11.03
discerning the t. and intentions Heb 4.12
and become judges with evil t.? Jas 2.04

THOUSAND

your brother a t. pieces of silver; Gen 20.16
about six hundred t. men on foot, Ex 12.37
people that day about three t. men. 32.28
talents and a t. seven hundred and 38.25
for six hundred and three t., 38.26
And of the t. seven hundred and 38.28
and two t. and four hundred shekels; 38.29
hundred of you shall chase ten t.; Lev 26.08
was forty-six t. five hundred. Num 1.21
was fifty-nine t. three hundred. 1.23
was forty-five t. six hundred and 1.25
was seventy-four t. six hundred. 1.27
was fifty-four t. four hundred. 1.29
was fifty-seven t. four hundred. 1.31
Ephraim was forty t. five hundred. 1.33
was thirty-two t. two hundred. 1.35
was thirty-five t. four hundred. 1.37
Dan was sixty-two t. seven hundred. 1.39
was forty-one t. five hundred. 1.41
was fifty-three t. four hundred. 1.43
and three t. five hundred and 1.46
being seventy-four t. six hundred. 2.04
being fifty-four t. four hundred. 2.06
being fifty-seven t. four hundred. 2.08
and eighty-six t. four hundred. 2.09
being forty-six t. five hundred. 2.11
being fifty-nine t. three hundred. 2.13
forty-five t. six hundred and 2.15
and fifty-one t. four hundred and 2.16
being forty t. five hundred. 2.19
being thirty-two t. two hundred. 2.21
being thirty-five t. four hundred. 2.23
a hundred and eight t. one hundred. 2.24
being sixty-two t. seven hundred. 2.26
being forty-one t. five hundred. 2.28
being fifty-three t. four hundred. 2.30
and fifty-seven t. six hundred. 2.31
and three t. five hundred and 2.32
upward was seven t. five hundred. 3.22
there were eight t. six hundred, 3.28
and upward was six t. two hundred. 3.34
old and upward, were twenty-two t. 3.39
were twenty-two t. two hundred and 3.43

one t. three hundred and sixty-five 3.50
families was two t. seven hundred 4.36
houses was two t. six hundred and 4.40
families was three t. two hundred. 4.44
them were eight t. five hundred 4.48
the vessels two t. four hundred 7.85
to the ten t. thousands of Israel. 10.36
I am number six hundred t. on foot; 11.21
were fourteen t. seven hundred, 16.49
by the plague were twenty-four t. 25.09
was forty-three t. seven hundred 26.07
Simeonites, twenty-two t. two hundred. 26.14
number, forty t. five hundred. 26.18
number, seventy-six t. five hundred. 26.22
number, sixty-four t. three hundred. 26.25
to their number, sixty t. five hundred. 26.27
number was fifty-two t. seven hundred. 26.34
number, thirty-two t. five hundred. 26.37
was forty-five t. six hundred. 26.41
were sixty-four t. four hundred. 26.43
number, fifty-three t. four hundred. 26.47
was forty-five t. four hundred. 26.50
hundred and one t. seven hundred 26.51
of them were twenty-three t., 26.62
You shall send a t. from each of 31.04
a t. from each tribe, twelve thousand 31.05
tribe, twelve t. armed for war. 31.05
a t. from each tribe, together with 31.06
hundred and seventy-five t. sheep, 31.32
seventy-two t. cattle, 31.33
sixty-one t. asses, 31.34
and thirty-two t. persons in all, 31.35
thirty-seven t. five hundred sheep, 31.36
The cattle were thirty-six t., of which 31.38
The asses were thirty t. five hundred, 31.39
The persons were sixteen t., of which 31.40
thirty-seven t. five hundred sheep, 31.43
thirty-six t. cattle, 31.44
and thirty t. five hundred asses, 31.45
and sixteen t. persons— 31.46
was sixteen t. seven hundred and 31.52
city outward a t. cubits all round 35.04
for the east side two t. cubits, 35.05
for the south side two t. cubits, 35.05
for the west side two t. cubits, 35.05
for the north side two t. cubits, 35.05
make you a t. times as many as you Deu 1.11
commandments, to a t. generations, 7.09
How should one chase a t., 32.30
and two put ten t. to flight, 32.30
a distance of about two t. cubits; Jos 3.04
about forty t. ready armed for war 4.13
two or three t. men go up and 7.03
So about three t. went up there 7.04
chose thirty t. mighty men of 8.03
And he took about five t. men, 8.12
were twelve t., all the people of 8.25
One man of you puts to flight a t., 23.10
defeated ten t. of them at Bezek. Ju 1.04
time about ten t. of the Moabites, 3.29
taking ten t. from the tribe of 4.06
and ten t. men went up at his heels; 4.10
Tabor with ten t. men following 4.14
be seen among forty t. in Israel? 5.08
twenty-two t. returned, and ten t. remained. 7.03
about fifteen t. men, all who were 8.10
and twenty t. men who drew the 8.10
requested was one t. seven hundred 8.26
died, about a t. men and women. 9.49
time forty-two t. of the Ephraimites. 12.06
Then three t. men of Judah went 15.11
it, and with it he slew a t. men. 15.15
of an ass have I slain a t. men." 15.16
were about three t. men and women, 16.27
four hundred t. men on foot that 20.02
of Israel, and a hundred of a t., 20.10
and a t. of ten thousand. to bring 20.10

THOUSAND (cont.)
thousand and a thousand of ten t., Ju 20.10
day twenty-six t. men that drew 20.15
four hundred t. men that drew 20.17
day twenty-two t. men of the Israelites. 20.21
ground eighteen t. men of the people 20.25
Gibeah ten t. picked men out of 20.34
twenty-five t. one hundred men of 20.35
Eighteen t. men of Benjamin fell, 20.44
five t. men of them were cut down 20.45
and two t. men of them were slain. 20.45
twenty-five t. men that drew the 20.46
thither twelve t. of their bravest 21.10
slew about four t. men on the 1Sa 4.02
of Israel thirty t. foot soldiers. 4.10
of Israel were three hundred t., 11.08
and the men of Judah thirty t. 11.08
Saul chose three t. men of Israel; 13.02
two t. were with Saul in Michmash 13.02
and a t. were with Jonathan in 13.02
thirty t. chariots, and six t. horsemen, 13.05
two hundred t. men on foot, and ten 15.04
on foot, and ten t. men of Judah. 15.04
coat was five t. shekels of bronze. 17.05
to the commander of their t. See how 17.18
and made him a commander of a t.; 18.13
Then Saul took three t. chosen men 24.02
he had three t. sheep and a t. goats. 25.02
with three t. chosen men of Israel, 26.02
chosen men of Israel, thirty t. 2Sa 6.01
took from him a t. and seven hundred 8.04
and twenty t. foot soldiers; 8.04
slew twenty-two t. men of the Syrians. 8.05
slew eighteen t. Edomites in the 8.13
twenty t. foot soldiers, and the 10.06
the king of Maacah with a t. men, 10.06
and the men of Tob, twelve t. men. 10.06
and forty t. horsemen, and wounded 10.18
"Let me choose twelve t. men, and I will 17.01
But you are worth ten t. of us; 18.03
great on that day, twenty t. men. 18.07
the weight of a t. pieces of silver, 18.12
and with him were a t. men from 19.17
eight hundred t. valiant men who 24.09
men of Judah were five hundred t. 24.09
Dan to Beersheba seventy t. men. 24.15
used to offer a t. burnt offerings 1Ki 3.04
Solomon also had forty t. stalls of 4.26
chariots, and twelve t. horsemen. 4.26
He also uttered three t. proverbs; 4.32
and his songs were a t. and five. 4.32
Hiram twenty t. cors of wheat as 5.11
and twenty t. cors of beaten oil. 5.11
the levy numbered thirty t. men. 5.13
ten t. a month in relays; 5.14
had seventy t. burden-bearers and 5.15
and eighty t. hewers of stone in 5.15
besides Solomon's three t. three 5.16
a lily; it held two t. baths. 7.26
LORD twenty-two t. oxen and a 8.63
and a hundred and twenty t. sheep. 8.63
chariots and twelve t. horsemen, 10.26
and eighty t. chosen warriors, to 12.21
Yet I will leave seven t. in Israel, 19.18
all the people of Israel, seven t. 20.15
a hundred t. foot soldiers in one 20.29
twenty-seven t. men that were left 20.30
king of Israel a hundred t. lambs, 2Ki 3.04
and the wool of a hundred t. rams. 3.04
six t. shekels of gold, and ten 5.05
ten chariots and ten t. footmen; 13.07
He killed ten t. Edomites in the 14.07
gave Pul a t. talents of silver, 15.19
I will give you two t. horses, 18.23
and eighty-five t. in the camp of 19.35
ten t. captives, and all the craftsmen 24.14
seven t., and the craftsmen and the 24.16
one t., all of them strong and fit 24.16
forty-four t. seven hundred and 1Ch 5.18
fifty t. of their camels, two 5.21
two hundred and fifty t. sheep, 5.21
two t. asses, and a hundred 5.21
asses, and a hundred t. men alive. 5.21
being twenty-two t. six hundred. 7.02
thirty-six t., for they had many 7.04
eighty-seven t. mighty warriors, 7.05
was twenty-two t. and thirty-four. 7.07
warriors, was twenty t. two hundred. 7.09
seventeen t. and two hundred, ready 7.11
in war, was twenty-six t. men. 7.40
one t. seven hundred and sixty, very 9.13
hundred and the greater over t. 12.14
spear were six t. eight hundred 12.24
for war, seven t. one hundred. 12.25
Of the Levites four t. six hundred. 12.26
with him three t. seven hundred. 12.27
three t., of whom the majority had 12.29
Ephraimites twenty t. eight hundred, 12.30
half-tribe of Manasseh eighteen t., 12.31
Of Zebulun fifty t. seasoned troops, 12.33
Of Naphtali a t. commanders with 12.34
thirty-seven t. men armed with 12.34
twenty-eight t. six hundred men 12.35
Of Asher forty t. seasoned troops 12.36
and twenty t. men armed with all 12.37
commanded, for a t. generations, 16.15
And David took from him a t. chariots, 18.04
seven t. horsemen, and twenty t. foot soldiers; 18.04
slew twenty-two t. men of the 18.05
slew eighteen t. Edomites in the 18.12
Ammonites sent a t. talents of 19.06
thirty-two t. chariots and the 19.07
the men of seven t. chariots, 19.18
and forty t. foot soldiers, and 19.18
one hundred t. men who drew the 21.05
and seventy t. who drew the sword. 21.05
fell seventy t. men of Israel. 21.14
LORD a hundred t. talents of gold, 22.14
the total was thirty-eight t. men. 23.03
"Twenty-four t. of these," David 23.04
six t. shall be officers and judges, 23.04
four t. gatekeepers, and four 23.05
and four t. shall offer praises to 23.05
one t. seven hundred men of ability, 26.30
two t. seven hundred men of ability, 26.32
division numbering twenty-four t.: 27.01
his division were twenty-four t. 27.02
his division were twenty-four t. 27.04
his division were twenty-four t. 27.05
his division were twenty-four t. 27.07
his division were twenty-four t. 27.08
his division were twenty-four t. 27.09
his division were twenty-four t. 27.10
his division were twenty-four t. 27.11
his division were twenty-four t. 27.12
his division were twenty-four t. 27.13
his division were twenty-four t. 27.14
his division were twenty-four t. 27.15
three t. talents of gold, of the 29.04
and seven t. talents of refined 29.04
of God five t. talents and ten 29.07
talents and ten t. darics of gold, 29.07
ten t. talents of silver, eighteen 29.07
eighteen t. talents of bronze, and a 29.07
and a hundred t. talents of iron. 29.07
a t. bulls, a t. rams, and a t. lambs, 29.21
and offered a t. burnt offerings 2Ch 1.06
chariots and twelve t. horsemen, 1.14
assigned seventy t. men to bear 2.02
and eighty t. to quarry in the 2.02

THOUSAND (cont.)
and three t. six hundred to oversee 2Ch 2.02
twenty t. cors of crushed wheat, 2.10
twenty t. cors of barley, twenty 2.10
twenty t. baths of wine, and twenty 2.10
wine, and twenty t. baths of oil. 2.10
and fifty-three t. six hundred. 2.17
Seventy t. of them he assigned to 2.18
eighty t. to quarry in the hill 2.18
and three t. six hundred as overseers 2.18
it held over three t. baths. 4.05
twenty-two t. oxen and a hundred 7.05
and a hundred and twenty t. sheep. 7.05
had four t. stalls for horses and 9.25
and twelve t. horsemen, whom he 9.25
and eighty t. chosen warriors, to 11.01
chariots and sixty t. horsemen. 12.03
of war, four hundred t. picked men; 13.03
eight hundred t. picked mighty 13.03
Israel five hundred t. picked men. 13.17
of three hundred t. from Judah, 14.08
and eighty t. men from Benjamin, 14.08
hundred oxen and seven t. sheep. 15.11
him seven t. seven hundred rams 17.11
rams and seven t. seven hundred he-goats. 17.11
three hundred t. mighty men of 17.14
with two hundred and eighty t., 17.15
two hundred t. mighty men of valor. 17.16
two hundred t. men armed with bow 17.17
and eighty t. armed for war. 17.18
were three hundred t. picked men, 25.05
also a hundred t. mighty men of 25.06
Salt and smote ten t. men of Seir. 25.11
captured another ten t. alive, 25.12
and killed three t. people in them, 25.13
of valor was two t. six hundred. 26.12
hundred and seven t. five hundred, 26.13
and ten t. cors of wheat and ten 27.05
cors of wheat and ten t. of barley. 27.05
and twenty t. in Judah in one day, 28.06
two hundred t. of their kinsfolk, 28.08
hundred bulls and three t. sheep. 29.33
the assembly a t. bulls and seven t. sheep 30.24
assembly a t. bulls and ten t. sheep. 30.24
flock to the number of thirty t., 35.07
and three t. bulls; these were 35.07
offerings two t. six hundred lambs 35.08
offerings five t. lambs and kids 35.09
a t. basins of gold, a t. basins of silver, Ez 1.09
two t. four hundred and ten bowls 1.10
of silver, and a t. other vessels; 1.10
were five t. four hundred and 1.11
two t. one hundred and seventy-two. 2.03
two t. eight hundred and twelve. 2.06
one t. two hundred and fifty-four. 2.07
one t. two hundred and twenty-two. 2.12
of Bigvai, two t. and fifty-six. 2.14
one t. two hundred and fifty-four. 2.31
three t. six hundred and thirty. 2.35
of Immer, one t. and fifty-two. 2.37
one t. two hundred and forty-seven. 2.38
of Harim, one t. and seventeen. 2.39
was forty-two t. three hundred and 2.64
were seven t. three hundred and 2.65
asses were six t. seven hundred 2.67
work sixty-one t. darics of gold, 2.69
five t. minas of silver, and one 2.69
twenty bowls of gold worth a t. darics, 8.27
and repaired a t. cubits of the Neh 3.13
two t. a hundred and seventy-two. 7.08
two t. eight hundred and eighteen. 7.11
a t. two hundred and fifty-four. 7.12
two t. three hundred and twenty-two 7.17
sons of Bigvai, two t. and sixty-seven. 7.19
a t. two hundred and fifty-four. 7.34
three t. nine hundred and thirty. 7.38
The sons of Immer, a t. and fifty-two. 7.40
a t. two hundred and forty-seven. 7.41
The sons of Harim, a t. and seventeen. 7.42
was forty-two t. three hundred and 7.66
were seven t. three hundred and 7.67
their asses six t. seven hundred 7.69
the treasury a t. darics of gold, 7.70
the work twenty t. darics of gold 7.71
two t. two hundred minas of silver. 7.71
gave was twenty t. darics of gold, 7.72
two t. minas of silver, and sixty-seven 7.72
I will pay ten t. talents of Est 3.09
seventy-five t. of those who hated 9.16
He had seven t. sheep, three Job 1.03
three t. camels, five hundred yoke 1.03
not answer him once in a t. times. 9.03
one of the t., to declare to man 33.23
and he had fourteen t. sheep, 42.12
six t. camels, a t. yoke of oxen, 42.12
yoke of oxen, and a t. she-asses. 42.12
is mine, the cattle on a t. hills. Ps 50.10
twice ten t., thousands upon 68.17
is better than at t. elsewhere. 84.10
For a t. years in thy sight are but 90.04
A t. may fall at your side, ten 91.07
ten t. at your right hand; but it will 91.07
commanded, for a t. generations, 105.08
should live a t. years twice told, Ecc 6.06
One man among a t. I found, 7.28
arsenal, whereon hang a t. bucklers, Sol 4.04
ruddy, distinguished among ten t. 5.10
for its fruit a t. pieces of 8.11
may have the t., and the keepers of 8.12
where there used to be a t. vines, Is 7.23
worth a t. shekels of silver, will 7.23
A t. shall flee at the threat of 30.17
I will give you two t. horses, 36.08
and eighty-five t. in the camp of 37.36
three t. and twenty-three Jews; Jer 52.28
were four t. and six hundred. 52.30
twenty-five t. cubits long and Eze 45.01
long and twenty t. cubits broad; 45.01
twenty-five t. cubits long and ten 45.03
cubits long and ten t. broad, 45.03
twenty-five t. cubits long and ten 45.05
long and ten t. cubits broad, 45.05
city an area five t. cubits broad, 45.06
and twenty-five t. cubits long; 45.06
hand, the man measured a t. cubits, 47.03
Again he measured a t., 47.04
Again he measured a t., and it was 47.05
twenty-five t. cubits in breadth, 48.08
be twenty-five t. cubits in length, 48.09
length, and twenty t. in breadth. 48.09
twenty-five t. cubits on the 48.10
ten t. cubits in breadth on the 48.10
ten t. in breadth on the eastern 48.10
and twenty-five t. in length on 48.10
twenty-five t. cubits in length 48.13
in length and ten t. in breadth. 48.13
be twenty-five t. cubits and the 48.13
cubits and the breadth twenty t. 48.13
five t. cubits in breadth and 48.15
and twenty-five t. in length, 48.15
north side four t. five hundred 48.16
south side four t. five hundred, 48.16
the east side four t. five hundred, 48.16
the west side four t. five hundred. 48.16
shall be ten t. cubits to the east, 48.18
and ten t. to the west, and it shall 48.18
be twenty-five t. cubits square, 48.20
the twenty-five t. cubits of the 48.21
the twenty-five t. cubits to the 48.21
is to be four t. five hundred 48.30
is to be four t. five hundred 48.32
is to be four t. five hundred 48.33
is to be four t. five hundred 48.34

THOUSAND (cont.)
city shall be eighteen t. cubits. Eze 48.35
great feast for a t. of his lords, Dan 5.01
and drank wine in front of the t. 5.01
a t. thousands served him, and ten 7.10
and ten t. times ten t. stood 7.10
"For two t. and three hundred 8.14
shall be a t. two hundred and 12.11
comes to the t. three hundred and 12.12
went forth a t. shall have a Amo 5.03
and twenty t. persons who do not Jon 4.11
who ate were about five t. men, Mt 14.21
Those who ate were four t. men, 15.38
the five loaves of the five t., 16.09
Or the seven loaves of the four t., 16.10
to him who owed him ten t. talents; 18.24
the herd, numbering about two t., Mk 5.13
ate the loaves were five t. men. 6.44
And there were about four t. people. 8.09
the five loaves for the five t., 8.19
"And the seven for the four t., 8.20
For there were about five t. men. Lk 9.14
able with ten t. to meet him who 14.31
comes against him with twenty t.? 14.31
sat down, in number about five t. Jn 6.10
that day about three t. souls. Ac 2.41
of the men came to about five t. 4.04
came to fifty t. pieces of silver. 19.19
led the four t. men of the Assassins 21.38
myself seven t. men who have not Rom 11.04
twenty-three t. fell in a single 1Co 10.08
then ten t. words in a tongue. 14.19
the Lord one day is as a t. years, 2Pe 3.08
and a t. years as one day. 3.08
a hundred and forty-four t. sealed, Rev 7.04
twelve t. sealed out of the tribe 7.05
twelve t. of the tribe of Reuben, 7.05
twelev t. of the tribe of Gad, 7.05
twelve t. of the tribe of Asher, 7.06
twelve t. of the tribe of Naphtali, 7.06
twelve t. of the tribe of Manasseh, 7.06
twelve t. of the tribe of Simeon, 7.07
twelve t. of the tribe of Levi, 7.07
twelve t. of the tribe of Issachar, 7.07
twelve t. of the tribe of Zebulun, 7.08
twelve t. of the tribe of Joseph, 7.08
twelve t. sealed out of the tribe 7.08
was twice ten t. times ten t. 9.16
prophesy for one t. two hundred and 11.03
seven t. people were killed in the 11.13
nourished for one t. two hundred 12.06
and forty-four t. who had his name 14.01
and forty-four t. who had been 14.03
for one t. six hundred stadia. 14.20
and bound him for a t. years, 20.02
till the t. years were ended. 20.03
and reigned with Christ a t. years. 20.04
again until the t. years were 20.05
shall reign with him a t. years. 20.06
And when the t. years are ended, 20.07
with his rod, twelve t. stadia; 21.16

THOUSANDS
the mother of t. of ten t.; Gen 24.60
over the people as rulers of t., Ex 18.21
rulers of t., of hundreds, of 18.25
steadfast love to t. of those who 20.06
keeping steadfast love for t., 34.07
to the ten thousand t. of Israel. Num 10.36
out of the t. of Israel, a thousand 31.05
commanders of t. and the commanders 31.14
who were over the t. of the army, 31.48
the captains of t. and the captains 31.48
commanders of t. and the commanders 31.52
commanders of t. and of hundreds, 31.54
commanders of t., commanders of Deu 1.15
steadfast love to t. of those who 5.10
came from the ten t. of holy ones, 33.02
such are the ten t. of Ephraim, 33.17
and such are the t. of Manasseh. 33.17
commanders of t. and commanders of 1Sa 8.12
LORD by your tribes and by your t. 10.19
"Saul has slain his t., And David his ten t." 18.07
"They have ascribed to David ten t., 18.08
and to me they have ascribed t.; 18.08
'Saul has slain his t., And David his ten t.'?" 21.11
commanders of t. and commanders of 22.07
him out among all the t. of Judah. 23.23
passing on by hundreds and by t. 29.02
'Saul has slain his t., And David his ten t.'?" 29.05
commanders of t. and commanders of 2Sa 18.01
marched out by hundreds and by t. 18.04
Zillethai, chiefs of t. in Manasseh. 1Ch 12.20
commanders of t. and of hundreds, 13.01
Israel, and the commanders of t., 15.25
officers of the t. and the hundreds, 26.26
the commanders of t. and hundreds, 27.01
the king, the commanders of t., 28.01
commanders of t. and of hundreds, 29.06
commanders of t. and of hundreds, 2Ch 1.02
Of Judah, the commanders of t.: 17.14
commanders of t. and of hundreds 25.05
afraid of ten t. of people who Ps 3.06
t. upon t., the Lord came 68.17
to me than t. of gold and silver 119.72
bring forth t. and ten t. in our; 144.13
who showest steadfast love to t., Jer 32.18
a thousand t. served him, and ten Dan 7.10
and he shall cast down tens of t. 11.12
And tens of t. shall fall, but these 11.41
to write for him my laws by ten t., Hos 8.12
LORD be pleased with t. of rams, Mic 6.07
with ten t. of rivers of oil? 6.07
when so many t. of the multitude Lk 12.01
how many t. there are among the Ac 21.20
of myriads and t. of t., Rev 5.11

THREAD
not take a t. or a sandal-thong or Gen 14.23
and bound on his hand a scarlet t., 38.28
with the scarlet t. upon his hand; 38.30
the ropes off his arms like a t. Ju 16.12
Your lips are like a scarlet t., Sol 4.03
the t. of your life is cut. Jer 51.13

THREADS
and cut into t. to work into the Ex 39.03

THREAT
shall flee at the t. of one, Is 30.17
at the t. of five you shall flee, 30.17
purposed, has carried out his t.; Lam 2.17

THREATEN
loftily they t. oppression. Ps 73.08
when he suffered, he did not t.; 1Pe 2.23

THREATENED
so that the ship t. to break up. Jon 1.04
And when they had further t. them, Ac 4.21

THREATENING
today, for the sky is red and t.' Mt 16.03
and forbear t., knowing that he who Eph 6.09

THREATS
And now, Lord, look upon their t., Ac 4.29
still breathing t. and murder against the 9.01

THREE
of Methuselah t. hundred years, Gen 5.22
of Enoch were t. hundred and sixty 5.23
And Noah had t. sons, Shem, Ham, and 6.10
of the ark t. hundred cubits, 6.15
wife and the t. wives of his sons 7.13

THREE (cont.)
These t. were the sons of Noah; Gen 9.19
Noah lived t. hundred and fifty 9.28
Shelah four hundred and t. years, 11.13
of Eber four hundred and t. years, 11.15
t. hundred and eighteen of them, and 14.14
"Bring me a heifer t. years old, 15.09
a she-goat t. years old, a ram t. years 15.09
t. men stood in front of him. 18.02
ready quickly t. measures of fine 18.06
t. flocks of sheep lying beside it; 29.02
because I have borne him t. sons"; 29.34
a distance of t. days' journey 30.36
About t. months later Judah was 38.24
on the vine there were t. branches; 40.10
the t. branches are t. days; 40.12
within t. days Pharaoh will lift up 40.13
there were t. cake baskets on my 40.16
the t. baskets are t. days; 40.18
within t. days Pharaoh will lift up 40.19
all together in prison for t. days. 42.17
Benjamin he gave t. hundred shekels 45.22
child, she hid him t. months. Ex 2.02
let us go a t. days' journey into 3.18
a t. days' journey into the wilderness, 5.03
We must go t. days' journey into 8.27
in all the land of Egypt t. days; 10.22
rise from his place for t. days; 10.23
they went t. days in the wilderness 15.22
not do these t. things for her, 21.11
"T. times in the year you shall 23.14
T. times in the year shall all your 23.17
t. branches of the lampstand out of 25.32
side of it and t. branches of the 25.32
t. cups made like almonds, each with 25.33
and t. cups made like almonds, each 25.33
and its height shall be t. cubits. 27.01
with t. pillars and t. bases. 27.14
with t. pillars and t. bases. 27.15
that day about t. thousand men. 32.28
T. times in the year shall all your 34.23
LORD your God t. times in the year 34.24
t. branches of the lampstand out of 37.18
side of it and t. branches of the 37.18
t. cups made like almonds, each with 37.19
and t. cups made like almonds, each 37.19
and t. cubits was its height. 38.01
with t. pillars and t. bases. 38.14
with t. pillars and t. bases. 38.15
for six hundred and t. thousand, 38.26
offering of t. tenths of an ephah Lev 14.10
t. years it shall be forbidden to 19.23
bring forth fruit for t. years. 25.21
shall be t. shekels of silver. 27.06
was fifty-nine thousand t. hundred. Num 1.23
six hundred and t. thousand five 1.46
fifty-nine thousand t. hundred. 2.13
six hundred and t. thousand five 2.32
one thousand t. hundred and sixty-five 3.50
by families was t. thousand two 4.44
mount of the LORD t. days' journey; 10.33
went before them t. days' journey, 10.33
you t., to the tent of meeting. 12.04
And the t. of them came out. 12.04
offering of t. tenths of an ephah 15.09
you have struck me these t. times?" 22.28
you struck your ass these t. times? 22.32
aside before me these t. times. 22.33
have blessed them these t. times. 24.10
sixty-four thousand t. hundred. 26.25
also t. tenths of an ephah of fine 28.12
t. tenths of an ephah shall you 28.20
t. tenths of an ephah for each bull, 28.28
t. tenths of an ephah for the bull, 29.03
t. tenths of an ephah for the bull, 29.09
t. tenths of an ephah for each of 29.14
was in number t. hundred and 31.36
half was t. hundred and thirty-seven 31.43
and they went a t. days' journey 33.08
You shall give t. cities beyond the 35.14
and t. cities in the land of Canaan, 35.14
Then Moses set apart t. cities in Deu 4.41
end of every t. years you shall 14.28
"T. times a year all your males 16.16
witnesses or of t. witnesses he 17.06
you shall set apart t. cities for 19.02
and divide into t. parts the area 19.03
you, You shall set apart t. cities. 19.07
you shall add t. other cities to 19.09
three other cities to these t., 19.09
or of t. witnesses, shall a charge 19.15
for within t. days you are to pass Jos 1.11
and hide yourselves there t. days, 2.16
hills, and remained there t. days, 2.22
At the end of t. days the officers 3.02
about two or t. thousand men go up 7.03
So about t. thousand went up there 7.04
At the end of t. days after they 9.16
out from there the t. sons of Anak, 15.14
Provide t. men from each tribe, and 18.04
with its pasture lands—t. cities. 21.32
out from it the t. sons of Anak. Ju 1.20
their mouths, was t. hundred men; 7.06
"With the t. hundred men that 7.07
but retained the t. hundred men; 7.08
And he divided the t. hundred men 7.16
hundred men into t. companies, 7.16
And the t. companies blew the 7.20
When they blew the t. hundred 7.22
he and the t. hundred men who were 8.04
Abimelech ruled over Israel t. years. 9.22
and divided them into t. companies, 9.43
t. hundred years, why did you not 11.26
could not in t. days tell what the 14.14
went and caught t. hundred foxes, 15.04
Then t. thousand men of Judah went 15.11
you have mocked me these t. times, 16.15
were about t. thousand men and 16.27
and he remained with him t. days; 19.04
and bore t. sons and two daughters. 1Sa 2.21
asses that were lost t. days ago, 9.20
t. men going up to God at Bethel 10.03
one carrying t. kids, another 10.03
carrying t. loaves of bread, and 10.03
of Israel were t. hundred thousand, 11.08
put the people in t. companies; 11.11
Saul chose t. thousand men of 13.02
of the Philistines in t. companies; 13.17
The t. eldest sons of Jesse had 17.13
names of his t. sons who went to 17.13
the t. eldest followed Saul, 17.14
And I will shoot t. arrows to the 20.20
to the ground, and bowed t. times; 20.41
Then Saul took t. thousand chosen 24.02
he had t. thousand sheep and a 25.02
with t. thousand chosen men of 26.02
drunk water for t. days and t. nights. 30.12
because I fell sick t. days ago. 30.13
and his t. sons, and his armor-bearer, 31.06
Saul and his t. sons fallen on 31.08
And the t. sons of Zeruiah were 2Sa 2.18
of Benjamin t. hundred and sixty 2.31
of Obededom the Gittite t. months; 6.11
to Geshur, and was there t. years. 13.38
There were born to Absalom t. sons, 14.27
And he took t. darts in his hand, 18.14
together to me within t. days, 20.04
in the days of David for t. years, 21.01
spear weighed t. hundred shekels 21.16
he was chief of the t.; 23.08
him among the t. mighty men was 23.09
And t. of the thirty chief men went 23.13
Then the t. mighty men broke 23.16
These things did the t. mighty men. 23.17

THREE (cont.)
spear against t. hundred men and 2Sa 23.18
them, and won a name beside the t. 23.18
but he did not attain to the t. 23.19
a name beside the t. mighty men. 23.22
but he did not attain to the t. 23.23
T. things I offer you; choose one 24.12
"Shall t. years of famine come to 24.13
will you flee t. months before 24.13
shall there be t. days' pestilence 24.13
at the end of t. years that two of 1Ki 2.39
He also uttered t. thousand proverbs; 4.32
besides Solomon's t. thousand t. hundred 5.16
court with t. courses of hewn 6.36
was built upon t. rows of cedar 7.02
There were window frames in t. rows, 7.04
window opposite window in t. tiers. 7.04
was opposite window in t. tiers. 7.05
The great court had t. courses of 7.12
t. facing north, t. facing west, 7.25
t. facing south, and t. facing east; 7.25
cubits wide, and t. cubits high. 7.27
T. times a year Solomon used to 9.25
And he made t. hundred shields of 10.17
t. minas of gold went into each 10.17
Once every t. years the fleet of 10.22
and t. hundred concubines; 11.03
"Depart for t. days, then come again 12.05
He reigned for t. years in Jerusalem. 15.02
himself upon the child t. times, 17.21
For t. years Syria and Israel 22.01
and for t. days they sought him but 2Ki 2.17
called these t. kings to give them 3.10
called these t. kings to give them 3.13
"Two or t. eunuchs looked out at 9.32
and he struck t. times, and 13.18
strike down Syria only t. times. 13.19
T. times Joash defeated him and 13.25
and for t. years he besieged it. 17.05
and at the end of t. years he took 18.10
king of Judah t. hundred talents 18.14
and he reigned t. months in 23.31
became his servant t. years; 24.01
and he reigned t. months in 24.08
of the capital was t. cubits; 25.17
and the t. keepers of the threshold; 25.18
these t. Bathshua the Canaanitess 1Ch 2.03
Abishai, Joab, and Asahel, t. 2.16
Elioenai, Hizkiah, and Azrikam, t. 3.23
Bela, Becher, and Jediael, t. 7.06
he and his t. sons and all his 10.06
a Hachmonite, was chief of the t.; 11.11
spear against t. hundred whom he 11.11
him among the t. mighty men was 11.12
T. of the thirty chief men went 11.15
Then the t. mighty men broke 11.18
These things did the t. mighty men. 11.19
spear against t. hundred men and 11.20
them, and won a name beside the t. 11.20
but he did not attain to the t. 11.21
a name beside the t. mighty men. 11.24
but he did not attain to the t. 11.25
and with him t. thousand seven 12.27
t. thousand, of whom the majority 12.29
were there with David for t. days, 12.39
of Obededom in his house t. months; 13.14
T. things I offer you; choose one 21.10
either t. years of famine; 21.12
or t. months of devastation by 21.12
or else t. days of the sword of 21.12
chief, and Zetham, and Joel, t. 23.08
Shelomoth, Haziel, and Haran, t. 23.09
Mahli, Eder, and Jeremoth, t. 23.23
fourteen sons and t. daughters. 25.05
t. thousand talents of gold, of the 29.04
and t. thousand six hundred to oversee 2Ch 2.02
and t. thousand six hundred as overseers 2.18
t. facing north, three facing west, 4.04
t. facing west, three facing south, 4.04
t. facing south, and three facing 4.04
facing south, and t. facing east; 4.04
it held over t. thousand baths. 4.05
and t. cubits high, and had set it 6.13
and the t. annual feasts—the feast 8.13
And he made t. hundred shields of 9.16
t. hundred shekels of gold went 9.16
once every t. years the ships of 9.21
them, "Come to me again in t. days." 10.05
and for t. years they made Rehoboam 11.17
they walked for t. years in the 11.17
He reigned for t. years in Jerusalem. 13.02
had an army of t. hundred thousand 14.08
million men and t. hundred chariots, 14.09
with t. hundred thousand mighty men 17.14
They were t. days in taking the 20.25
that they were t. hundred thousand 25.05
and killed t. thousand people in 25.13
was an army of t. hundred and 26.13
bulls and t. thousand sheep. 29.33
males from t. years old and upwards, 31.16
thousand, and t. thousand bulls; 35.07
and kids and t. hundred bulls. 35.08
and he reigned t. months in Jerusalem. 36.02
and he reigned t. months and ten 36.09
Shephatiah, t. hundred and seventy-two. Ez 2.04
of Bezai, t. hundred and twenty-three. 2.17
of Harim, t. hundred and twenty. 2.32
Jericho, t. hundred and forty-five. 2.34
t. thousand six hundred and thirty. 2.35
Solomon's servants were t. hundred and 2.58
forty-two thousand t. hundred and sixty, 2.64
seven thousand t. hundred and thirty-seven; 2.65
with t. courses of great stones and 6.04
Jahaziel, and with him t. hundred men. 8.05
and there we encamped t. days. 8.15
and there we remained t. days. 8.32
one did not come within t. days, 10.08
at Jerusalem within the t. days; 10.09
to Jerusalem and was there t. days. Neh 2.11
Shephatiah, t. hundred and seventy-two. 7.09
two thousand t. hundred and twenty-two. 7.17
of Hashum, t. hundred and twenty-eight. 7.22
of Bezai, t. hundred and twenty-four. 7.23
of Harim, t. hundred and twenty. 7.35
Jericho, t. hundred and forty-five. 7.36
t. thousand nine hundred and thirty. 7.38
Solomon's servants were t. hundred and 7.60
forty-two thousand t. hundred and sixty, 7.66
seven thousand t. hundred and thirty-seven; 7.67
neither eat nor drink for t. days, Est 4.16
and they slew t. hundred men in 9.15
to him seven sons and t. daughters. Job 1.02
t. thousand camels, five hundred 1.03
invite their t. sisters to eat and 1.04
"The Chaldeans formed t. companies, 1.17
Now when Job's t. friends heard of 2.11
So these t. men ceased to answer 32.01
also at Job's t. friends because 32.03
in the mouth of these t. men, he became 32.05
twice, t. times, with a man, 33.29
also seven sons and t. daughters. 42.13
T. things are never satisfied; Pro 30.15
T. things are too wonderful for me; 30.18
Under t. things the earth trembles; 30.21
T. things are stately in their 30.29
"In t. years, like the years of a Is 16.14
two or t. berries in the top of the 17.06
barefoot for t. years as a sign 20.03
As Jehudi read t. or four columns, Jer 36.23
"Take t. men with you from here, and 38.10
and the t. keepers of the threshold 52.24
t. thousand and twenty-three Jews; 52.28
t. hundred and ninety days, equal to Eze 4.05
t. hundred and ninety days, you 4.09

THREE (cont.)
even if these t. men, Noah, Daniel, Eze 14.14
even if these t. men were in it, as 14.16
though these t. men were in it, as I 14.18
And there were t. side rooms on 40.10
the t. were of the same size; 40.10
t. on either side, and its jambs and 40.21
the gate were t. cubits on either 40.48
side chambers were in t. stories, 41.06
round about all t. had windows 41.16
t. cubits high, two cubits long, and 41.22
against gallery in t. stories. 42.03
For they were in t. stories, 42.06
t. gates, the gate of Reuben, the 48.31
t. gates, the gate of Joseph, the 48.32
t. gates, the gate of Simeon, the 48.33
t. gates, the gate of Gad, the gate 48.34
were to be educated for t. years, Dan 1.05
And these t. men, Shadrach, Meshach 3.23
and over them t. presidents, of whom 6.02
upon his knees t. times a day and 6.10
makes his petition t. times a day." 6.13
it had t. ribs in its mouth between 7.05
before which t. of the first horns 7.08
and before which t. of them fell, 7.20
ones, and shall put down t. kings. 7.24
thousand and t. hundred evenings 8.14
Daniel, was mourning for t. weeks. 10.02
at all, for the full t. weeks. 10.03
Behold, t. more kings shall arise in 11.02
to the thousand t. hundred and 12.12
"For t. transgressions of Damascus, Amo 1.03
"For t. transgressions of Gaza, and 1.06
"For t. transgressions of Tyre, and 1.09
"For t. transgressions of Edom, and 1.11
"For t. transgressions of the Ammonites, 1.13
"For t. transgressions of Moab, and 2.01
"For t. transgressions of Judah, and 2.04
"For t. transgressions of Israel, 2.06
morning, your tithes every t. days; 4.04
there were yet t. months to the 4.07
so two or t. cities wandered to one 4.08
of the fish t. days and three Jon 1.17
the fish three days and t. nights. 1.17
t. days' journey in breadth. 3.03
month I destroyed the t. shepherds. Zec 11.08
as Jonah was t. days and t. nights Mt 12.40
took and hid in t. measures of 13.33
they have been with me now t. days, 15.32
I will make t. booths here, one for 17.04
evidence of two or t. witnesses. 18.16
For where two or t. are gathered in 18.20
crows, you will deny me t. times." 26.34
of God, and to build it in t. days.'" 26.61
crows, you will deny me t. times." 26.75
the temple and build it in t. days, 27.40
'After t. days I will rise again.' 27.63
they have been with me now t. days, Mk 8.02
and after t. days rise again. 8.31
let us make t. booths, one for you 9.05
after t. days he will rise." 9.31
and after t. days he will rise." 10.34
for more than t. hundred denarii, 14.05
twice, you will deny me t. times." 14.30
and in t. days I will build another, 14.58
twice, you will deny me t. times." 14.72
temple and build it in t. days, 15.29
remained with her about t. months, Lk 1.56
After t. days they found him in the 2.46
was shut up t. years and six 4.25
let us make t. booths, one for you 9.33
Which of these t., do you think, 10.36
to him, 'Friend, lend me t. loaves; 11.05
t. against two and two against t.; 12.52
these t. years I have come seeking 13.07
took and hid in t. measures of 13.21
until you t. times deny that you 22.34
today, you will deny me t. times." 22.61
and in t. days I will raise it up." Jn 2.19
will you raise it up in t. days?" 2.20
had rowed about t. or four miles, 6.19
not sold for t. hundred denarii 12.05
till you have denied me t. times. 13.38
that day about t. thousand souls. Ac 2.41
of about t. hours his wife came in, 5.07
brought up for t. months in his 7.20
And for t. days he was without 9.09
This happened t. times, and the 10.16
"Behold, t. men are looking for you. 10.19
This happened t. times, and all was 11.10
very moment t. men arrived at the 11.11
and for t. weeks he argued with 17.02
synagogue and for t. months spoke 19.08
There he spent t. months, and when a 20.03
that for t. years I did not cease 20.31
after t. days he went up to Jerusalem 25.01
entertained us hospitably for t. days. 28.07
After t. months we set sail in a 28.11
we stayed there for t. days. 28.12
of Appius and T. Taverns to meet 28.15
After t. days he called together 28.17
So faith, hope, love abide, these t.; 1Co 13.13
there be only two or at most t., 14.27
Let two or t. prophets speak, and 14.29
T. times I have been beaten with 2Co 11.25
T. times I have been shipwrecked; 11.25
T. times I besought the Lord about 12.08
evidence of two or t. witnesses. 13.01
Then after t. years I went up to Gal 1.18
evidence of two or t. witnesses. 1Ti 5.19
testimony of two or t. witnesses. Heb 10.28
was hid for t. months by his 11.23
and for t. years and six months it Jas 5.17
There are t. witnesses, the Spirit, 1Jn 5.08
and these t. agree. 5.08
and t. quarts of barley for a Rev 6.06
which the t. angels are about to 8.13
By these t. plagues a third of 9.18
For t. days and a half men from the 11.09
But after the t. and a half days a 11.11
t. foul spirits like frogs; 16.13
great city was split into t. parts, 16.19
on the east t. gates, on the north t. gates, 21.13
on the south t. gates, and on the 21.13
gates, and on the west t. gates. 21.13

THREEFOLD
A t. cord is not quickly broken. Ecc 4.12

THREE-PRONGED
was boiling, with a t. fork in his hand, 1Sa 2.13

THREESCORE
The years of our life are t. and ten, Ps 90.10

THREE-YEAR-OLD
along with a t. bull, an ephah of flour, 1Sa 1.24

THRESH
the LORD will t. out the grain, Is 27.12
No, he does not t. it for ever; 28.28
you shall t. the mountains and 41.15
a trained heifer that loved to t., Hos 10.11
Arise and t., O daughter of Zion, Mic 4.13
the thresher t. in hope of a share 1Co 9.10

THRESHED
O my t. and winnowed one, what I Is 21.10
Dill is not t. with a threshing 28.27
they have t. Gilead with threshing Amo 1.03

THRESHER
in hope and the t. thresh in hope 1Co 9.10

THRESHING

When they came to the t. floor of Atad, Gen 50.10
mourning on the t. floor of Atad, 50.11
And your t. shall last to the time Lev 26.05
as an offering from the t. floor, Num 15.20
it were the grain of the t. floor, 18.27
Levites as produce of the t. floor, 18.30
out of your t. floor, and out of Deu 15.14
from your t. floor and your wine 16.13
a fleece of wool on the t. floor; Ju 6.37
barley tonight at the t. floor. Ru 3.02
and go down to the t. floor; 3.03
down to the t. floor and did just 3.06
the woman came to the t. floor. 3.14
and are robbing the t. floors. 1Sa 23.01
they came to the t. floor of Nacon, 2Sa 6.06
LORD was by the t. floor of Araunah 24.16
the LORD on the t. floor of Araunah 24.18
"To buy the t. floor of you, in 24.21
and the t. sledges and the yokes of 24.22
bought the t. floor and the oxen 24.24
at the t. floor at the entrance of 1Ki 22.10
From the t. floor, or from the wine 2Ki 6.27
and made them like the dust at t. 13.07
came to the t. floor of Chidon, 1Ch 13.09
standing by the t. floor of Ornan 21.15
the LORD on the t. floor of Ornan 21.18
Now Ornan was t. wheat; he turned and saw 21.20
and went forth from the t. floor, 21.21
the site of the t. floor that I 21.22
and the t. sledges for the wood, and 21.23
him at the t. floor of Ornan the 21.28
on the t. floor of Ornan the 2Ch 3.01
sitting at the t. floor at the 18.09
comes up to the t. floor in its Job 5.26
bring your grain to your t. floor? 39.12
himself like a t. sledge on the 41.30
Dill is not threshed with a t. sledge, Is 28.27
Behold, I will make of you a t. sledge, 41.15
is like a t. floor at the time Jer 51.33
the chaff of the summer t. floors; Dan 2.35
a harlot's hire upon all t. floors. Hos 9.01
T. floor and winevat shall not feed 9.02
swirls from the t. floor or like 13.03
"The t. floors shall be full of Joe 2.24
Gilead with t. sledges of iron. Amo 1.03
them as sheaves to the t. floor. Mic 4.12
will clear his t. floor and gather Mt 3.12
to clear his t. floor, and to gather Lk 3.17

THRESHOLD

house, with her hands on the t. Ju 19.27
were lying cut off upon the t.; 1Sa 5.04
tread on the t. of Dagon in Ashdod 5.05
as she came to the t. of the house, 1Ki 14.17
who guarded the t. put in it all 2Ki 12.09
keepers of the t. have collected 22.04
order, and the keepers of the t., 23.04
and the three keepers of the t.; 25.18
the Levites, the keepers of the t., 2Ch 34.09
king's eunuchs, who guarded the t., Est 2.21
king's eunuchs, who guarded the t., 6.02
son of Shallum, keeper of the t. Jer 35.04
and the three keepers of the t.; 52.24
it rested to the t. of the house; Eze 9.03
cherubim to the t. of the house; 10.04
forth from the t. of the house, 10.18
and measured the t. of the gate, 40.06
and the t. of the gate by the 40.07
against the t. the temple was 41.16
by setting their t. by my t. and their 43.08
worship at the t. of the gate. 46.02
from below the t. of the temple 47.01
south end of the t. of the temple, 47.01
every one who leaps over the t., Zep 1.09
window, the raven croak on the t.; 2.14

THRESHOLDS

keepers of the t. of the tent, 1Ch 9.19
chosen as gatekeepers at the t., 9.22
its t., its walls, and its doors; 2Ch 3.07
foundations of the t. shook at the Is 6.04
the capitals until the t. shake, Amo 9.01

THREW

and Moses t. them toward heaven, and Ex 9.10
and he t. it into the water, and the 15.25
of the blood he t. against the 24.06
the blood and t. it upon the people, 24.08
and he t. the tables out of his 32.19
and I t. it into the fire, and there 32.24
and t. the blood upon the altar Lev 8.19
and Moses t. the blood upon the 8.24
and he t. it on the altar round 9.12
which he t. upon the altar round 9.18
and I t. the dust of it into the Deu 9.21
And the LORD t. them into a panic Jos 10.10
the LORD t. down great stones from 10.11
and t. them into the cave where 10.27
and he t. all the army into a panic. Ju 8.12
And a certain woman t. an upper 9.53
he t. away the jawbone out of his 15.17
Philistines and t. them into 1Sa 7.10
And he t. stones at David, and at 2Sa 16.06
and t. stones at him and flung dust. 16.13
and t. him into a great pit in the 18.17
into the field, and t. a garment over him. 20.12
of Bichri, and t. it out to Joab. 20.22
spring of water and t. salt in it, 2Ki 2.21
piece of land every man t. a stone, 3.25
And he t. it into the pot, and 4.41
and t. it in there, and made the 6.06
So they t. her down; and some of her 9.33
and t. the blood of his peace 16.13
of a rock and t. them down from 2Ch 25.12
the blood and t. it against the 29.22
took away and t. into the Kidron 30.14
the priests t. the blood which 30.16
and he t. them outside of the city. 33.15
and I t. all the household furniture Neh 13.08
and they t. the wares that were in Jon 1.05
up Jonah and t. him into the sea; 1.15
into vessels but t. away the bad. Mt 13.48
and t. their garments on it; Mk 11.07
they t. them into prison, charging Ac 16.23
garments and t. dust into the air, 22.23
the altar and t. it on the earth; Rev 8.05
and t. it into the great wine press 14.19
And they t. dust on their heads, as 18.19
millstone and t. it into the sea, 18.21
and t. him into the pit, and shut it 20.03

THRICE

yea t., the sword for those to be Eze 21.14

THRILL

your heart shall t. and rejoice; Is 60.05

THRILLED

and my heart was t. within me. Sol 5.04

THRIVE

why do all who are treacherous t.? Jer 12.01
Thus says the Lord GOD: Will it t.? Eze 17.09
it is transplanted, will it t.? 17.10

THRIVES

He t. before the sun, and his shoots Job 8.16

THROAT

their t. is an open sepulchre, they Ps 5.09
my t. is parched. My eyes grow 69.03
do not make a sound in their t. 115.07
a knife to your t. if you are a Pro 23.02
unshod and your t. from thirst. Jer 2.25

THROAT (cont.)
and seizing him by the t. he said, Mt 18.28
"Their t. is an open grave, they use Rom 3.13

THROATS
God be in their t. and two-edged Ps 149.06

THROBS
My heart t., my strength fails me; Ps 38.10

THRONE
as regards the t. will I be Gen 41.40
of Pharaoh who sits upon his t., Ex 11.05
who sat on his t. to the first-born 12.29
he sits on the t. of his kingdom, Deu 17.18
and set up the t. of David over 2Sa 3.10
establish the t. of his kingdom 7.13
your t. shall be established for 7.16
the king and his t. be guiltless. 14.09
me, and he shall sit upon my t."? 1Ki 1.13
me, and he shall sit upon my t.' 1.17
sit on the t. of my lord the king 1.20
me, and he shall sit upon my t.'? 1.24
sit on the t. of my lord the king 1.27
shall sit upon my t. in my stead'; 1.30
he shall come and sit upon my t.; 1.35
and make his t. greater than the 1.37
than the t. of my lord King David." 1.37
Solomon sits upon the royal t. 1.46
and make his t. greater than your t.' 1.47
offspring to sit on my t. this day, 1.48
fail you a man on the t. of Israel.' 2.04
sat upon the t. of David his father; 2.12
then he sat on his t., and had a 2.19
me on the t. of David my father, 2.24
and to his t., there shall be peace 2.33
and the t. of David shall be 2.45
a son to sit on his t. this day. 3.06
set upon your t. in your place, 5.05
the Hall of the T. where he was to 7.07
and sit on the t. of Israel, 8.20
me to sit upon the t. of Israel, 8.25
your royal t. over Israel for ever, 9.05
you a man upon the t. of Israel.' 9.05
and set you on the t. of Israel! 10.09
The king also made a great ivory t., 10.18
The t. had six steps, and at the 10.19
the back of the t. was a calf's 10.19
as he had seated himself on his t., 16.11
I saw the LORD sitting on his t., 22.19
and set him on his father's t., 2Ki 10.03
shall sit on the t. of Israel." 10.30
his seat on the t. of the kings. 11.19
and Jeroboam sat upon his t.; 13.13
sit upon the t. of Israel to the 15.12
I will establish his t. for ever. 1Ch 17.12
ever and his t. shall be established 17.14
his royal t. in Israel for ever.' 22.10
to sit upon the t. of the kingdom 28.05
sat on the t. of the LORD as king 29.23
and sit on the t. of Israel, 2Ch 6.10
me to sit upon the t. of Israel, 6.16
then I will establish your royal t., 7.18
set you on his t. as king for the 9.08
The king also made a great ivory t., 9.17
The t. had six steps and a footstool 9.18
which were attached to the t., 9.18
I saw the LORD sitting on his t., 18.18
ascended the t. of his father and 21.04
set the king upon the royal t. 23.20
on his royal t. in Susa the capital, Est 1.02
on his royal t. inside the palace 5.01
kings upon the t. he sets them for Job 36.07
hast sat on the t. giving righteous Ps 9.04
established his t. for judgment; 9.07
temple, the LORD's t. is in heaven; 11.04
Your divine t. endures for ever and 45.06
over the nations; God sits on his holy t. 47.08
and build your t. for all generations.'" 89.04
are the foundation of thy t.; 89.14
ever and his t. as the days of the 89.29
his t. as long as the sun before me. 89.36
and cast his t. to the ground. 89.44
thy t. is established from of old; 93.02
are the foundation of his t. 97.02
established his t. in the heavens, 103.19
of your body I will set on your t. 132.11
for ever shall sit upon your t." 132.12
for the t. is established by Pro 16.12
who sits on the t. of judgment 20.08
and his t. is upheld by righteousness. 20.28
and his t. will be established in 25.05
with equity his t. will be established 29.14
prison to the t. or in his own Ecc 4.14
I saw the Lord sitting upon a t., Is 6.01
upon the t. of David, and over his 9.07
of God I will set my t. on high; 14.13
then a t. will be established in 16.05
will become a t. of honor to his 22.23
sit on the ground without a t., 47.01
"Heaven is my t. and the earth is 66.01
shall set his t. at the entrance Jer 1.15
shall be called the t. of the LORD, 3.17
the kings who sit on David's t., 13.13
do not dishonor thy glorious t.; 14.21
A glorious t. set on high from the 17.12
kings who sit on the t. of David, 17.25
Judah, who sit on the t. of David, 22.02
kings who sit on the t. of David, 22.04
in sitting on the t. of David, 22.30
king who sits on the t. of David, 29.16
to sit on the t. of the house of 33.17
not have a son to reign on his t., 33.21
none to sit upon the t. of David, 36.30
he will set his t. above these 43.10
and I will set my t. in Elam, 49.38
thy t. endures to all generations. Lam 5.19
there was the likeness of a t., Eze 1.26
likeness of a t. was a likeness as 1.26
sapphire, in form resembling a t. 10.01
the place of my t. and the place 43.07
he was deposed from his kingly t., Dan 5.20
his t. was fiery flames, its wheels 7.09
Nineveh, and he arose from his t., Jon 3.06
and to overthrow the t. of kingdoms; Hag 2.22
and shall sit and rule upon his t. Zec 6.13
there shall be a priest by his t., 6.13
heaven, for it is the t. of God, Mt 5.34
man shall sit on his glorious t., 19.28
swears by the t. of God and by him 23.22
he will sit on his glorious t. 25.31
give to him the t. of his father Lk 1.32
of his descendants upon his t., Ac 2.30
'Heaven is my t., and earth my 7.49
robes, took his seat upon the t., 12.21
"Thy t., O God, is for ever and ever, Heb 1.08
draw near to the t. of grace, 4.16
hand of the t. of the Majesty in 8.01
at the right hand of the t. of God. 12.02
spirits who are before his t., Rev 1.04
you dwell, where Satan's t. is; 2.13
grant him to sit with me on my t., 3.21
sat down with my Father on his t. 3.21
a t. stood in heaven, with one 4.02
heaven, with one seated on the t.! 4.02
and round the t. was a rainbow that 4.03
Round the t. were twenty-four 4.04
From the t. issue flashes of 4.05
and before the t. burn seven 4.05
and before the t. there is as it 4.06
round the t., on each side of the t., 4.06
to him who is seated on the t., 4.09
seated on the t. and worship him 4.10
crowns before the t., singing, 4.10

THRONE (cont.)

seated on the t. a scroll written	Rev 5.01
And between the t. and the four	5.06
of him who was seated on the t.	5.07
around the t. and the living	5.11
sits upon the t. and to the Lamb	5.13
of him who is seated on the t.,	6.16
before the t. and before the Lamb,	7.09
to our God who sits upon the t.,	7.10
stood round the t. and round the	7.11
before the t. and worshiped God,	7.11
Therefore are they before the t. of God,	7.15
sits upon the t. will shelter them	7.15
midst of the t. will be their	7.17
the golden altar before the t.;	8.03
caught up to God and to his t.,	12.05
power and his t. and great authority.	13.02
song before the t. and before the	14.03
his bowl on the t. of the beast,	16.10
from the t., saying, "It is done!"	16.17
is seated on the t., saying, "Amen.	19.04
And from the t. came a voice crying,	19.05
a great white t. and him who sat	20.11
and small, standing before the t.,	20.12
a great voice from the t. saying,	21.03
And he who sat upon the t. said,	21.05
from the t. of God and of the Lamb	22.01
but the t. of God and of the Lamb	22.03

THRONES

of Judah were sitting on their t.,	1Ki 22.10
of Judah were sitting on their t.,	2Ch 18.09
There t. for judgment were set, the	Ps 122.05
the t. of the house of David.	122.05
brought down those who sat on t.	Is 10.13
from their t. all who were kings	14.09
sea will step down from their t.,	Eze 26.16
As I looked, t. were placed and one	Dan 7.09
me will also sit on twelve t.,	Mt 19.28
put down the mighty from their t.,	Lk 1.52
and sit on t. judging the twelve	22.30
whether t. or dominions or principalities	Col 1.16
Round the throne were twenty-four t.,	Rev 4.04
seated on the t. were twenty-four	4.04
sit on their t. before God fell on	11.16
Then I saw t., and seated on them	20.04

THRONG

in the mighty t. I will praise thee	Ps 35.18
my soul: how I went with the t.,	42.04
the princes of Judah in their t.,	68.27
praise him in the midst of the t.	109.30
her t. and he who exults in her.	Is 5.14
As he went ashore he saw a great t.;	Mt 14.14
so that the t. wondered, when they	15.31
As he landed he saw a great t.,	Mk 6.34
"And the great t. heard him gladly	12.37

THRONGED

great crowd followed him and t. about him.	Mk 5.24

THROUGHOUT

after you t. their generations for	Gen 17.07
after you t. their generations.	17.09
every male t. your generations,	17.12
t. its whole area, was made over	23.17
of great plenty t. all the land of	41.29
be remembered t. all generations.	Ex 3.15
scattered abroad t. all the land of	5.12
shall be blood t. all the land of	7.19
there was blood t. all the land of	7.21
become gnats t. all the land of	8.16
became gnats t. all the land of	8.17
man and beast t. all the land of	9.09
may be declared t. all the earth.	9.16
of the field, t. the land of Egypt."	9.22
in the field t. all the land of	9.25
be a great cry t. all the land of	11.06
t. your generations you shall	12.14
t. your generations, as an ordinance	12.17
of Israel t. their generations.	12.42
of it be kept t. your generations,	16.32
to be kept t. your generations."	16.33
to be observed t. their generations	27.21
burnt offering t. your generations	29.42
before the LORD t. your generations.	30.08
in the year t. your generations;	30.10
his descendants t. their generations."	30.21
anointing oil t. your generations.	30.31
me and you t. your generations,	31.13
the sabbath t. their generations,	31.16
fro from gate to gate t. the camp,	32.27
no man be seen t. all the mountain;	34.03
word was proclaimed t. the camp,	36.06
priesthood t. their generations.	40.15
T. all their journeys, whenever the	40.36
For t. all their journeys the cloud	40.38
perpetual statute t. your generations,	Lev 3.17
for ever t. your generations, from	6.18
a perpetual due t. their generations."	7.36
for ever t. your generations.	10.09
ever to them t. their generations.	17.07
descendants t. their generations	21.17
descendants t. your generations	22.03
for ever t. your generations in	23.14
your dwellings t. your generations.	23.21
for ever t. your generations in	23.31
for ever t. your generations;	23.41
for ever t. your generations.	24.03
the trumpet t. all your land.	25.09
proclaim liberty t. the land to all	25.10
t. his generations; it shall not be	25.30
perpetual statute t. your generations.	Num 10.08
people weeping t. their families,	11.10
is among you t. your generations,	15.14
perpetual statute t. your generations;	15.15
an offering t. your generations.	15.21
and onward t. your generations,	15.23
their garments t. their generations,	15.38
perpetual statute t. your generations;	18.23
of each month t. the months of the	28.14
cities of the land t. the country.	32.33
ordinance to you t. your generations	35.29
tens, and officers, t. your tribes.	Deu 1.15
olive trees t. all your territory,	28.40
trusted, come down t. all your land;	28.52
in all your towns t. all your land,	28.52
all its banks t. the time of	Jos 3.15
he sent messengers t. all Manasseh;	Ju 6.35
sent messengers t. all the hill	7.24
and sent her t. all the territory	19.29
and sent her t. all the country of	20.06
of a hundred t. all the tribes of	20.10
a deathly panic t. the whole city.	1Sa 5.11
and sent them t. all the territory	11.07
blew the trumpet t. all the land,	13.03
to be found t. all the land of	13.19
sent messengers t. the land of the	31.09
t. all Edom he put garrisons, and	2Sa 8.14
messengers t. all the tribes of	15.10
were at strife t. all the tribes	19.09
beautiful maiden t. all the territory	1Ki 1.03
And Jehu sent t. all Israel;	2Ki 10.21
defeated them t. the territory of	10.32
in their tents t. all the region	1Ch 5.10
their cities t. their families	6.60
sent messengers t. the land of the	10.09
departed and went t. all Israel,	21.04
LORD destroying t. all the territory	21.12
of fame and glory t. all lands;	22.05
month after month t. the year,	27.01
run to and fro t. the whole earth,	2Ch 16.09
the fortified cities t. all Judah.	17.19
and proclaimed a fast t. all Judah.	20.03
was made t. Judah and Jerusalem, to	24.09
make a proclamation t. all Israel,	30.05

THROUGHOUT (cont.)
So couriers went t. all Israel and 2Ch 30.06
and the altars t. all Judah and 31.01
Thus Hezekiah did t. all Judah; 31.20
incense altars t. all the land of 34.07
a proclamation t. all his kingdom 36.22
a proclamation t. all his kingdom Ez 1.01
was made t. Judah and Jerusalem to 10.07
is proclaimed t. all his kingdom, Est 1.20
t. the whole kingdom of Ahasuerus. 3.06
upon one day t. all the provinces 8.12
in their cities t. all the provinces 9.02
his fame spread t. all the provinces; 9.04
and kept t. every generation, in 9.28
t. all generations I shall not meet Ps 10.06
as the moon, t. all generations! 72.05
years endure t. all generations!" 102.24
flies, and gnats t. their country. 105.31
thy renown, O LORD, t. all ages. 135.13
dominion endures t. all generations. 145.13
all your sins, t. all your territory. Jer 15.13
of your sin t. all your territory. 17.03
t. all their habitations, from the Eze 6.14
and disperse them t. the lands. 30.23
and disperse them t. the countries. 30.26
shall be holy t. its whole extent. 45.01
to be t. the whole kingdom; Dan 6.01
So his fame spread t. all Syria, Mt 4.24
be preached t. the whole world, as 24.14
everywhere t. all the surrounding Mk 1.28
And he went t. all Galilee, preaching 1.39
proclaiming t. the whole city how Lk 8.39
teaching t. all Judea, from Galilee 23.05
came a famine t. all Egypt and Ac 7.11
all scattered t. the region of 8.01
So the church t. all Judea and 9.31
And it became known t. all Joppa, 9.42
which was proclaimed t. all Judea, 10.37
the Lord spread t. all the region. 13.49
but almost t. all Asia this Paul 19.26
among all the Jews t. the world, 24.05
Jerusalem and t. all the country 26.20
become known t. the whole praetorian Php 1.13
love all the brethren t. Macedonia. 1Th 4.10
with fear t. the time of your 1Pe 1.17
of your brotherhood t. the world. 5.09

THROW
us kill him and t. him into one of Gen 37.20
and let Moses t. them toward heaven Ex 9.08
and will t. into confusion all the 23.27
its blood and t. it against the 29.16
and t. the rest of the blood 29.20
and t. the blood round about Lev 1.05
priests shall t. its blood against 1.11
priests shall t. the blood against 3.02
sons shall t. its blood against 3.08
of Aaron shall t. its blood 3.13
the disease and t. them into an 14.40
and t. them into great confusion, Deu 7.23
and t. him into a panic; and all the 2Sa 17.02
battering the wall, to t. it down. 20.15
He said, "T. her down." So they threw 2Ki 9.33
and t. upon it all the blood of 16.15
and his own schemes t. him down. Job 18.07
t. in your lot among us, we will all Pro 1.14
and t. you like a ball into a wide Is 22.18
a penknife and t. them into the Jer 36.23
and they shall t. down your Eze 16.39
and t. up a mound against you, and 26.08
I will t. my net over you with a 32.03
shall come and t. up siegeworks, Dan 11.15
"Take me up and t. me into the sea; Jon 1.12
your land and t. down all your Mic 5.11
I will t. filth at you and treat Nah 3.06
the Son of God, t. yourself down; Mt 4.06
sin, pluck it out and t. it away; 5.29
to sin, cut it off and t. it away; 5.30
and do not t. your pearls before 7.06
and t. them into the furnace of 13.42
and t. them into the furnace of 13.50
bread and t. it to the dogs. 15.26
sin, cut it off and t. it from you; 18.08
pluck it out and t. it from you; 18.09
bread and t. it to the dogs. Mk 7.27
t. yourself down from here; Lk 4.09
that they might t. him down 4.29
men t. it away. He who has Lk 14.35
from them about a stone's t., 22.41
be the first to t. a stone at her." *Jn 8.07
So they took up stones to t. at him; 8.59
next day to t. the cargo overboard; Ac 27.18
could swim to t. themselves 27.43
Therefore do not t. away your Heb 10.35
is about to t. some of you into Rev 2.10
Behold, I will t. her on a sickbed, 2.22
with her I will t. into great 2.22

THROWING
upon it and for t. blood against Eze 43.18
And t. down the pieces of silver in Mt 27.05
And t. off his mantle he sprang up Mk 10.50
and t. their garments on the colt Lk 19.35
t. out the wheat into the sea. Ac 27.38

THROWN
his rider he has t. into the sea. Ex 15.01
his rider he has t. into the sea." 15.21
blood shall be t. on the altar Lev 7.02
for impurity was not t. upon him, Num 19.13
impurity has not been t. upon him, 19.20
head shall be t. to you over the 2Sa 20.21
all like thorns that are t. away; 23.06
And his body was t. in the road, 1Ki 13.24
and saw the body t. in the road, 13.25
and found his body t. in the road, 13.28
of the LORD that had been t. down; 18.30
t. down thy altars, and slain thy 19.10
t. down thy altars, and slain thy 19.14
the Syrians had t. away in their 2Ki 7.15
their blood was t. against the 2Ch 29.22
their blood was t. against the 29.22
hast taken me up and t. me away. Ps 102.10
have fallen, her walls are t. down. Jer 50.15
and the mountains shall be t. down, Eze 38.20
off their bark and t. it down; Joe 1.07
is cut down and t. into the fire. Mt 3.10
except to be t. out and trodden 5.13
your whole body be t. into hell. 5.29
and tomorrow is t. into the oven, 6.30
is cut down and t. into the fire. 7.19
kingdom will be t. into the outer 8.12
a net which was t. into the sea 13.47
two feet to be t. into the eternal 18.08
two eyes to be t. into the hell of 18.09
another, that will not be t. down." 24.02
neck and he were t. into the sea. Mk 9.42
with two feet to be t. into hell. 9.45
with two eyes to be t. into hell, 9.47
another, that will not be t. down." 13.02
is cut down and t. into the fire." Lk 3.09
the demon had t. him down in the 4.35
and tomorrow is t. into the oven, 12.28
another that will not be t. down." 21.06
who had been t. into prison for an 23.19
who had been t. into prison for 23.25
t. into the fire and burned. Jn 15.06
citizens, and have t. us into prison; Ac 16.37
with fire, was t. into the sea; Rev 8.08
And the great dragon was t. down, 12.09
he was t. down to the earth, and his 12.09
his angels were t. down with him. 12.09
of our brethren has been t. down, 12.10
he had been t. down to the earth, 12.13
great city be t. down with violence, 18.21
These two were t. alive into the 19.20

THROWN (cont.)
them was t. into the lake of fire Rev 20.10
and Hades were t. into the lake of 20.14
he was t. into the lake of fire. 20.15

THROWS
the priest who t. the blood of the Lev 7.14
but a fool t. off restraint and is Pro 14.16
Like a madman who t. firebrands, 26.18

THRUST
they were t. out of Egypt and Ex 12.39
your God has t. them out before Deu 9.04
and t. it through his ear into the 15.17
And he t. out the enemy before you, 33.27
right thigh, and t. it into his belly; Ju 3.21
And his young man t. him through, 9.54
they t. Jephthah out, and said to 11.02
and he would t. it into the pan, or 1Sa 2.14
and t. me through with it, lest 31.04
uncircumcised come and t. me through, 31.04
and t. his sword in his opponent's 2Sa 2.16
and t. them into the heart of 18.14
I t. them through, so that they did 22.39
And Gehazi came to t. her away. 2Ki 4.27
and t. me through with it, lest 1Ch 10.04
And they t. him out quickly, and he 2Ch 26.20
He is t. from light into darkness, Job 18.18
They t. the poor off the road; 24.04
I t. them through, so that they were Ps 18.38
they are t. down, unable to rise. 36.12
They only plan to t. him down from 62.04
they will be t. into thick darkness. Is 8.22
Whoever is found will be t. through, 13.15
I will t. you from your office, and 22.19
Because the Lord t. him down. Jer 46.15
then I will t. you down with those Eze 26.20
They shall t. you down into the Pit, 28.08
and t. at all the weak with your 34.21
And he t. her back into the ephah, Zec 5.08
and t. down the leaden weight upon 5.08
those who t. aside the sojourner, Mal 3.05
of God and you yourselves t. out. Lk 13.28
wronging his neighbor t. him aside, Ac 7.27
but t. him aside, and in their 7.39
which God t. out before our 7.45
Since you t. it from you, and judge 13.46

THRUSTING
by t. out all your enemies from Deu 6.19
t. them out of their property; Eze 46.18

THRUSTS
whose rash words are like sword t., Pro 12.18

THUMB
ear and on the t. of his right Lev 8.23
and on the t. of his right hand, and 14.14
and on the t. of his right hand, and 14.17
and on the t. of his right hand, and 14.25
and on the t. of his right hand, and 14.28

THUMBS
and upon the t. of their right Ex 29.20
ears and on the t. of their right Lev 8.24
and cut off his t. and his great Ju 1.06
with their t. and their great toes 1.07

THUMMIM
you shall put the Urim and the T., Ex 28.30
breastpiece he put the Urim and the T. Lev 8.08
Levi he said, "Give to Levi thy T., Deu 33.08
is in thy people Israel, give T." 1Sa 14.41
be a priest to consult Urim and T. Ez 2.63
with Urim and T. should arise. Neh 7.65

THUNDER
and the Lord sent t. and hail, Ex 9.23
been enough of this t. and hail; 9.28
the t. will cease, and there will be 9.29
and the t. and the hail ceased, and 9.33
and the hail and the t. had ceased, 9.34
spoke, and God answered him in t. 19.19
against them he will t. in heaven. 1Sa 2.10
Lord, that he may send t. and rain; 12.17
the Lord sent t. and rain that day; 12.18
But the t. of his power who can Job 26.14
a way for the lightning of the t.; 28.26
Hearken to the t. of his voice and 37.02
the t. of the captains, and the 39.25
and can you t. with a voice like 40.09
to deep at the t. of thy cataracts; Ps 42.07
the skies gave forth t.; thy arrows 77.17
The crash of thy t. was in the 77.18
you in the secret place of t.; 81.07
sound of thy t. they took to 104.07
Ah, the t. of many peoples, they Is 17.12
they t. like the thundering of the 17.12
of hosts with t. and with earthquake 29.06
like the t. of the Almighty, a sound Eze 1.24
Boanerges, that is, sons of t.; Mk 3.17
lightning, and voices and peals of t., Rev 4.05
say, as with a voice of t., "Come!" 6.01
and there were peals of t., loud noises 8.05
peals of t., an earthquake, and 11.19
and like the sound of loud t.; 14.02
peals of t., and a great earthquake 16.18

THUNDERBOLT
of rain, and a way for the t., Job 38.25

THUNDERBOLTS
the hail, and their flocks to t. Ps 78.48

THUNDERED
but the Lord t. with a mighty voice 1Sa 7.10
The Lord t. from heaven, and the 2Sa 22.14
The Lord also t. in the heavens, and Ps 18.13
heard it and said that it had t. Jn 12.29

THUNDERING
thunder like the t. of the sea! Is 17.12

THUNDERINGS
perceived the t. and the lightnings Ex 20.18
the clouds, the t. of his pavilion? Job 36.29

THUNDEROUS
At the t. noise peoples flee, at the Is 33.03

THUNDERPEALS
and like the sound of mighty t., Rev 19.06

THUNDERS
day there were t. and lightnings, Ex 19.16
he t. with his majestic voice and Job 37.04
God t. wondrously with his voice; 37.05
the God of glory t., the Lord, upon Ps 29.03
Mightier than the t. of many waters, 93.04
called out, the seven t. sounded. Rev 10.03
And when the seven t. had sounded, 10.04
up what the seven t. have said, 10.04

THUS
T. the heavens and the earth were Gen 2.01
T. all the days that Adam lived 5.05
T. all the days of Seth were nine 5.08
T. all the days of Enosh were nine 5.11
T. all the days of Kenan were nine 5.14
T. all the days of Mahalalel were 5.17
T. all the days of Jared were nine 5.20
T. all the days of Enoch were three 5.23
T. all the days of Methuselah were 5.27
T. all the days of Lamech were 5.31
t. they separated from each other. 13.11
T. both the daughters of Lot were 19.36
"T. the man spoke to me," he went 24.30
t. the servant took Rebekah, and 24.61

THUS (cont.)
said, "If it is t., why do I live?" Gen 25.22
T. Esau despised his birthright. 25.34
T. Isaac sent Jacob away; and he went 28.05
T. the man grew exceedingly rich, 30.43
T. God has taken away the cattle of 31.09
T. I was; by day the heat 31.40
"T. you shall say to my lord Esau: 32.04
T. says your servant Jacob, 'I have 32.04
T. he urged him, and he took it. 33.11
T. his father wept for him. 37.35
T. he set him over all the land of 41.43
T. the sons of Israel came to buy 42.05
T. Joseph knew his brothers, but 42.08
'T. says your son Joseph, God has 45.09
T. Israel dwelt in the land of 47.27
and t. he put Ephraim before 48.20
T. his sons did for him as he had 50.12
T. he reassured them and comforted 50.21
and t. I am to be remembered Ex 3.15
t. you shall despoil the Egyptians." 3.22
'T. says the LORD, Israel is my 4.22
"T. says the LORD, the God of Israel, 5.01
"T. says Pharaoh, 'I will not give 5.10
"Why do you deal t. with your 5.15
Moses spoke t. to the people of 6.09
T. says the LORD, "By this you shall 7.17
'T. says the LORD, "Let my people go, 8.01
'T. says the LORD, "Let my people go, 8.20
T. I will put a division between my 8.23
'T. says the LORD, the God of the 9.01
'T. says the LORD, the God of the 9.13
"T. says the LORD, the God of the 10.03
"T. says the LORD: About midnight I 11.04
T. they despoiled the Egyptians. 12.36
T. did all the people of Israel; 12.50
T. the LORD saved Israel that day 14.30
"T. you shall say to the house of 19.03
"T. you shall say to the people of 20.22
t. shall it be with both of them; 26.24
t. Aaron shall bear the judgment of 28.30
T. you shall ordain Aaron and his 29.09
"T. you shall do to Aaron and to 29.35
"T. says the LORD God of Israel, 32.27
T. the LORD used to speak to Moses 33.11
for the tabernacle he made t.: 36.23
he made two of them t., for the two 36.29
t. they attached it in front to the 39.18
T. all the work of the tabernacle 39.32
T. did Moses; according to 40.16
t. bringing guilt on the people, Lev 4.03
T. shall he do with the bull; 4.20
T. the priest shall make atonement 5.13
T. the priest shall make atonement 14.20
T. he shall cleanse the house with 14.52
"T. you shall keep the people of 15.31
But t. shall Aaron come into the 16.03
t. he shall make atonement for the 16.16
T. Moses declared to the people of 23.44
T. the people of Israel did as the 24.23
T. did the people of Israel; Num 1.54
T. did the people of Israel. 2.34
but deal t. with them, that they may 4.19
t. they were numbered by him, as the 4.49
T. you shall bless the people of 6.23
And t. you shall do to them, to 8.07
"T. you shall separate the Levites 8.14
T. did Moses and Aaron and all the 8.20
T. shall you do to the Levites in 8.26
If thou wilt deal t. with me, 11.15
"T. it shall be done for each bull 15.11
T. they shall be a sign to the 16.38
t. I will make to cease from me the 17.05
T. did Moses; as the LORD 17.11
t. on the seventh day he shall 19.19
"T. says your brother Israel: You 20.14
T. Edom refused to give Israel 20.21
T. Israel dwelt in the land of the 21.31
"T. says Balak the son of Zippor 22.16
"Return to Balak, and t. you shall speak." 23.05
"Return to Balak, and t. shall you speak." 23.16
T. the plague was stayed from the 25.08
T. did your fathers, when I sent 32.08
You shall not t. pollute the land 35.33
But t. shall you deal with them: you Deu 7.05
T. you shall do to all the cities 20.15
has the LORD done t. to this land? 29.24
Do you t. requite the LORD, you 32.06
T. the LORD became king in Jeshurun, 33.05
T. shall you do for six days. Jos 6.03
why have you t. fallen upon your 7.10
for t. says the LORD, God of Israel, 7.13
for t. the LORD will do to all your 10.25
T. there fell to Manasseh ten 17.05
T. the LORD gave to Israel all the 21.43
"T. says the whole congregation of 22.16
"T. says the LORD, the God of Israel, 24.02
"T. says the LORD, the God of Israel: Ju 6.08
T. God requited the crime of 9.56
"T. says Jephthah: Israel did not 11.15
"T. and t. has Micah dealt with 18.04
T. the sin of the young men was 1Sa 2.17
"T. the LORD has said, 'I revealed 2.27
"T. says the LORD, the God of Israel, 10.18
and t. put disgrace upon all Israel." 11.02
"T. shall you say to the men of 11.09
T. says the LORD of hosts, 'I will 15.02
"T. and so did David speak." 18.24
"T. shall you say to David, 'The 18.25
"Why have you deceived me t., 19.17
And t. you shall salute him: 'Peace 25.06
T. Saul died, and his three sons, and 31.06
'T. says the LORD: Would you build 2Sa 7.05
Now therefore t. you shall say to 7.08
'T. says the LORD of hosts, I took 7.08
that thou hast brought me t. far? 7.18
"T. shall you say to Joab, 'Do not 11.25
T. says the LORD, the God of Israel, 12.07
T. says the LORD, 'Behold, I will 12.11
and t. he did to all the cities of 12.31
for t. were the virgin daughters of 13.18
to the king, and speak t. to him." 14.03
T. they would quench my coal which 14.07
T. Absalom did to all of Israel who 15.06
"T. has Ahithophel spoken; shall we do 17.06
"T. and so did Ahithophel counsel 17.15
and t. and so have I counseled. 17.15
for t. and so has Ahithophel 17.21
'T. says the LORD, Three things I 24.12
"Why have you done t. and so?" 1Ki 1.06
t. fulfilling the word of the LORD 2.27
"T. said Joab, and t. he answered 2.30
and t. take away from me and from 2.31
T. they spoke before the king. 3.22
T. the work of the pillars was 7.22
T. all the work that King Solomon 7.51
the LORD done t. to this land and 9.08
T. King Solomon excelled all the 10.23
for t. says the LORD, the God of 11.31
"T. shall you speak to this people 12.10
t. shall you say to them, 'My little 12.10
'T. says the LORD, You shall not go 12.24
t. says the LORD: 'Behold, a son 13.02
"T. says the LORD, 'Because you have 13.21
T. and t. shall you say to her. 14.05
'T. says the LORD, the God of Israel: 14.07
T. Zimri destroyed all the house of 16.12
For t. says the LORD the God of 17.14
and said to him, "T. says Benhadad: 20.02
"T. says Benhadad: 'I sent to you, 20.05
"T. says the LORD, Have you seen all 20.13
He said, "T. says the LORD, By the 20.14
"T. says the LORD, 'Because the 20.28
"T. says the LORD, 'Because you have 20.42
'T. says the LORD, "Have you killed, 21.19
'T. says the LORD: "In the place 21.19

THUS (cont.)
"T. says the LORD, 'With these you 1Ki 22.11
and say, 'T. says the king, "Put this 22.27
Now therefore t. says the LORD, 'You 2Ki 1.04
T. says the LORD, Is it because 1.06
"T. says the LORD, 'Because you have 1.16
"T. says the LORD, I have made this 2.21
And he said, "T. says the LORD, 'I 3.16
For t. says the LORD, 'You shall not 3.17
for t. says the LORD, 'They shall 4.43
"T. and so spoke the maiden from 5.04
T. he used to warn him, so that he 6.10
t. says the LORD, Tomorrow about 7.01
'T. says the LORD, I anoint you king 9.03
"T. says the LORD the God of Israel, 9.06
"T. and so he spoke to me, saying, 9.12
'T. says the LORD, I anoint you king 9.12
T. Jehu the son of Jehoshaphat the 9.14
"T. says the king, 'Is it peace?' 9.18
"T. the king has said, 'Is it peace?' 9.19
T. Jehu wiped out Baal from Israel. 10.28
T. she hid him from Athaliah, so 11.02
'T. says the great king, the king of 18.19
T. says the king: 'Do not let 18.29
for t. says the king of Assyria: 18.31
"T. says Hezekiah, This day is a day 19.03
'T. says the LORD: Do not be afraid 19.06
"T. shall you speak to Hezekiah 19.10
"T. says the LORD, the God of Israel: 19.20
"Therefore t. says the LORD concerning 19.32
"T. says the LORD, 'Set your house 20.01
T. says the LORD, the God of David 20.05
therefore t. says the LORD, the God 21.12
'T. says the LORD, the God of Israel: 22.15
T. says the LORD, Behold, I will 22.16
t. shall you say to him, Thus says 22.18
T. says the LORD, the God of Israel: 22.18
T. Saul died; he and his three 1Ch 10.06
'T. says the LORD: You shall not 17.04
Now therefore t. shall you say to 17.07
'T. says the LORD of hosts, I took 17.07
that thou hast brought me t. far? 17.16
and t. David did to all the 20.03
'T. says the LORD, Three things I 21.10
"T. says the LORD, 'Take which you 21.11
T. they shall keep charge of the 23.32
should be able t. to offer willingly? 29.14
T. David the son of Jesse reigned 29.26
T. all the work that Solomon did 2Ch 5.01
T. Solomon finished the house of 7.11
the LORD done t. to this land and 7.21
T. was accomplished all the work of 8.16
T. King Solomon excelled all the 9.22
"T. shall you speak to the people 10.10
t. shall you say to them, 'My 10.10
'T. says the LORD, You shall not go 11.04
"T. says the LORD, 'You abandoned me, 12.05
t. his troops were in front of 13.13
T. the men of Israel were subdued 13.18
"T. says the LORD, 'With these you 18.10
and say, 'T. says the king, Put this 18.26
"T. you shall do in the fear of the 19.09
T. you shall do, and you will not 19.10
T. says the LORD to you, 'Fear not, 20.15
T. Jehoshaphat reigned over Judah. 20.31
"T. says the LORD, the God of David 21.12
T. Jehoshabeath, the daughter of 22.11
T. they did day after day, and 24.11
"T. says God, 'Why do you transgress 24.20
T. Joash the king did not remember 24.22
T. they executed judgment on Joash. 24.24
T. the service of the house of the 29.35
T. Hezekiah did throughout all 31.20
"T. says Sennacherib king of 32.10
"T. says the LORD, the God of Israel: 34.23
T. says the LORD, Behold, I will 34.24
t. shall you say to him, T. says 34.26
T. says the LORD, the God of Israel: 34.26
"T. says Cyrus king of Persia, 'The 36.23
"T. says Cyrus king of Persia: The Ez 1.02
came to them and spoke to them t., 5.03
those elders and spoke to them t., 5.09
T. I cleansed them from everything Neh 13.30
'T. shall it be done to the man Est 6.09
"T. shall it be done to the man 6.11
their hearts." T. Job did continually. Job 1.05
my skin has been t. destroyed, 19.26
T., knowing their works, he overturns 34.25
and said, 'T. far shall you come, and 38.11
"I will speak t.," I would have Ps 73.15
T. they became unclean by their 106.39
Lo, t. shall the man be blessed who 128.04
He has not dealt t. with any other 147.20
beloved, that you t. adjure us? Sol 5.09
t. says the Lord GOD: It shall not Is 7.07
For the LORD spoke t. to me with 8.11
Therefore t. says the Lord, the LORD 10.24
For t. the LORD said to me: "I will 18.04
For t. the Lord said to me: "Go, set 21.06
For t. the Lord said to me, "Within 21.16
T. says the Lord GOD of hosts, "Come, 22.15
For t. it shall be in the midst of 24.13
therefore t. says the Lord GOD, 28.16
Therefore t. says the LORD, who 29.22
Therefore t. says the Holy One of 30.12
For t. says the Lord GOD, the Holy 30.15
For t. the LORD said to me, As a 31.04
'T. says the great king, the king of 36.04
T. says the king: 'Do not let 36.14
for t. says the king of Assyria: 36.16
"T. says Hezekiah, 'This day is a 37.03
'T. says the LORD: Do not be afraid 37.06
"T. shall you speak to Hezekiah 37.10
"T. says the LORD, the God of Israel: 37.21
"Therefore t. says the LORD concerning 37.33
"T. says the LORD: Set your house in 38.01
T. says the LORD, the God of David 38.05
T. says God, the LORD, who created 42.05
But now t. says the LORD, he who 43.01
T. says the LORD, your Redeemer, the 43.14
T. says the LORD, who makes a way in 43.16
T. says the LORD who made you, who 44.02
T. says the LORD, the King of Israel 44.06
T. says the LORD, your Redeemer, who 44.24
T. says the LORD to his anointed, to 45.01
T. says the LORD, the Holy One of 45.11
T. says the LORD: "The wealth of 45.14
For t. says the LORD, who created 45.18
T. says the LORD, your Redeemer, the 48.17
T. says the LORD, the Redeemer of 49.07
T. says the LORD; "In a time of 49.08
T. says the Lord GOD: "Behold, I will 49.22
Surely t. says the LORD: "Even the 49.25
T. says the LORD: "Where is your 50.01
T. says your Lord, the LORD, your God 51.22
For t. says the LORD: "You were sold 52.03
For t. says the Lord GOD: My people 52.04
T. says the LORD: "Keep justice, and 56.01
For t. says the LORD: "To the 56.04
T. says the Lord GOD, who gathers 56.08
For t. says the high and lofty One 57.15
T. says the LORD: "As the wine is 65.08
Therefore t. says the Lord GOD: 65.13
T. says the LORD: "Heaven is my 66.01
For t. says the LORD: "Behold, I will 66.12
T. says the LORD, I remember the Jer 2.02
T. says the LORD: "What wrong did 2.05
For t. says the LORD to the men of 4.03
For t. says the LORD, "The whole 4.27
T. shall it be done to them!'" 5.13
Therefore t. says the LORD, the God 5.14
For t. says the LORD of hosts: "Hew 6.06
T. says the LORD of hosts: "Glean 6.09
T. says the LORD: "Stand by the 6.16
Therefore t. says the LORD: 'Behold, 6.21

THUS (cont.)
T. says the LORD: "Behold, a people Jer 6.22
T. says the LORD of hosts, the God 7.03
Therefore t. says the Lord GOD: 7.20
T. says the LORD of hosts, the God 7.21
T. says the LORD: When men fall, do 8.04
Therefore t. says the LORD of hosts: 9.07
Therefore t. says the LORD of hosts, 9.15
T. says the LORD of hosts: "Consider, 9.17
Speak, "T. says the LORD: 'The dead 9.22
T. says the LORD: "Let not the wise 9.23
T. says the LORD: "Learn not the way 10.02
T. shall you say to them: "The gods 10.11
For t. says the LORD: "Behold, I am 10.18
T. says the LORD, the God of Israel: 11.03
Therefore, t. says the LORD, Behold, I 11.11
Therefore t. says the LORD concerning 11.21
therefore t. says the LORD of hosts: 11.22
T. says the LORD concerning all my 12.14
T. said the LORD to me, "Go and buy 13.01
"T. said the LORD: Even so will I 13.09
'T. says the LORD, the God of Israel, 13.12
'T. says the LORD: Behold, I will 13.13
T. says the LORD concerning this 14.10
"They have loved to wander t., 14.10
Therefore t. says the LORD concerning 14.15
'T. says the LORD: "Those who are 15.02
Therefore t. says the LORD: "If you 15.19
For t. says the LORD concerning the 16.03
"For t. says the LORD: Do not enter 16.05
For t. says the LORD of hosts, the 16.09
T. says the LORD: "Cursed is the man 17.05
T. said the LORD to me: "Go and 17.19
T. says the LORD: Take heed for the 17.21
'T. says the LORD, Behold, I am 18.11
"Therefore t. says the LORD: Ask 18.13
'T. said the LORD, "Go, buy a potter's 19.01
T. says the LORD of hosts, the God 19.03
'T. says the LORD of hosts: So will 19.11
T. will I do this place, says the 19.12
"T. says the LORD of hosts, the God 19.15
For t. says the LORD: Behold, I will 20.04
"T. you shall say to Zedekiah, 'T. 21.04
'T. says the LORD, the God of Israel: 21.04
'T. says the LORD: Behold, I set 21.08
T. says the LORD: "'Execute justice 21.12
T. says the LORD: "Go down to the 22.01
T. says the LORD: Do justice and 22.03
For t. says the LORD concerning the 22.06
the LORD dealt t. with this great 22.08
For t. says the LORD concerning 22.11
Therefore t. says the LORD concerning 22.18
T. says the LORD: "Write this man 22.30
Therefore t. says the LORD, the God 23.02
Therefore t. says the LORD of hosts 23.15
T. says the LORD of hosts: "Do not 23.16
T. shall you say, every one to his 23.35
T. you shall say to the prophet, 23.37
t. says the LORD, 'Because you 23.38
"T. says the LORD, the God of Israel: 24.05
"But t. says the LORD: Like the bad 24.08
"Therefore t. says the LORD of 25.08
T. the LORD, the God of Isrrael, said 25.15
'T. says the LORD of hosts, the God 25.27
'T. says the LORD of hosts: You must 25.28
"T. says the LORD of hosts: Behold, 25.32
"T. says the LORD: Stand in the 26.02
'T. says the LORD: If you will not 26.04
'T. says the LORD of hosts, Zion 26.18
T. the LORD said to me: "Make 27.02
'T. says the LORD of hosts, the God 27.04
"T. says the LORD: Do not listen to 27.16
For t. says the LORD of hosts 27.19
t. says the LORD of hosts, the God 27.21
"T. says the LORD of hosts, the God 28.02
"T. says the LORD: Even so will I 28.11
'T. says the LORD: You have broken 28.13
For t. says the LORD of hosts, the 28.14
Therefore t. says the LORD: 'Behold, 28.16
"T. says the LORD of hosts, the God 29.04
For t. says the LORD of hosts, the 29.08
"For t. says the LORD: When seventy 29.10
T. says the LORD concerning the 29.16
'T. says the LORD of hosts, 'Behold, 29.17
'T. says the LORD of hosts, the God 29.21
"T. says the LORD of hosts, the God 29.25
'T. says the LORD concerning 29.31
therefore t. says the LORD: Behold, I 29.32
"T. says the LORD, the God of Israel: 30.02
"T. says the LORD: We have heard a 30.05
"For t. says the LORD: Your hurt is 30.12
"T. says the LORD: Behold, I will 30.18
T. says the LORD: "The people who 31.02
For t. says the LORD: "Sing aloud 31.07
T. says the LORD: "A voice is heard 31.15
T. says the LORD: "Keep your voice 31.16
T. says the LORD of hosts, the God 31.23
T. says the LORD, who gives the sun 31.35
T. says the LORD: "If the heavens 31.37
'T. says the LORD: Behold I am 32.03
'T. says the LORD of hosts, the God 32.14
For t. says the LORD of hosts, the 32.15
Therefore, t. says the LORD: Behold, I 32.28
"Now therefore t. says the LORD, the 32.36
"For t. says the LORD: Just as I 32.42
"T. says the LORD who made the 33.02
For t. says the LORD, the God of 33.04
"T. says the LORD: In this place of 33.10
"T. says the LORD of hosts: In this 33.12
"For t. says the LORD: David shall 33.17
"T. says the LORD: If you can break 33.20
T. they have despised my people so 33.24
T. says the LORD: If I have not 33.25
"T. says the LORD, the God of Israel: 34.02
'T. says the LORD: Behold, I am 34.02
T. says the LORD concerning you: 34.04
"T. says the LORD, the God of Israel: 34.13
Therefore, t. says the LORD: You have 34.17
"T. says the LORD of hosts, the God 35.13
Therefore, t. says the LORD, the God 35.17
"T. says the LORD of hosts, the God 35.18
therefore t. says the LORD of hosts, 35.19
'T. says the LORD, You have burned 36.29
Therefore t. says the LORD concerning 36.30
"T. says the LORD, God of Israel: 37.07
T. shall you say to the king of 37.07
T. says the LORD, Do not deceive 37.09
"T. says the LORD, He who stays in 38.02
T. says the LORD, This city shall 38.03
"T. says the LORD, the God of hosts, 38.17
'T. says the LORD of hosts, the God 39.16
"T. says the LORD, the God of Israel, 42.09
T. says the LORD of hosts, the God 42.15
"For t. says the LORD of hosts, the God 43.10
"T. says the LORD of hosts, the God 44.02
And now t. says the LORD God of 44.07
"Therefore t. says the LORD of 44.11
T. says the LORD of hosts, the God 44.25
T. says the LORD, Behold I will give 44.30
"T. says the LORD, the God of Israel, 45.02
T. shall you say to him, Thus says 45.04
T. says the LORD: Behold, what I have 45.04
"T. says the LORD: behold, waters are 47.02
"T. says the LORD of hosts, the God 48.01
For t. says the LORD: "Behold, one 48.40
T. far is the judgment on Moab. 48.47
T. says the LORD: "Has Israel no 49.01
T. says the LORD of hosts: "Is 49.07
For t. says the LORD: "If those who 49.12
T. says the LORD: "Rise up, advance 49.28
T. says the LORD of hosts: "Behold, I 49.35
Therefore, t. says the LORD of hosts, 50.18
"T. says the LORD of hosts: The 50.33
T. says the LORD: "Behold, I will 51.01
For t. says the LORD of hosts, the 51.33
Therefore t. says the LORD: "Behold, 51.36

THUS (cont.)

"T. says the LORD of hosts: The — Jer 51.58
and say, 'T. shall Babylon sink, to — 51.64
' "T. far are the words of Jeremiah — 51.64
With whom has thou dealt t.? — Lam 2.20
their faces and their wings t.: — Eze 1.08
to them, 'T. says the Lord GOD.' — 2.04
'T. says the Lord GOD'; whether they — 3.11
'T. says the Lord GOD'; he that will — 3.27
"T. shall the people of Israel eat — 4.13
T. says the Lord GOD: This is — 5.05
Therefore t. says the Lord GOD: — 5.07
therefore t. says the Lord GOD: — 5.08
"T. shall my anger spend itself, and — 5.13
T. says the Lord GOD to the mountains — 6.03
T. says the Lord GOD: "Clap your — 6.11
T. I will spend my fury upon them. — 6.12
t. says the Lord GOD to the land of — 7.02
"T. says the Lord GOD: Disaster — 7.05
T. says the Lord GOD: So you think, O — 11.05
Therefore t. says the Lord GOD: Your — 11.07
'T. says the Lord GOD: Though I — 11.16
'T. says the Lord: I will gather you — 11.17
Say to them, 'T. says the Lord GOD: — 12.10
T. says the Lord GOD concerning the — 12.19
'T. says the Lord GOD: I will put an — 12.23
T. says the Lord GOD: None of my — 12.28
T. says the Lord GOD, Woe to the — 13.03
Therefore t. says the Lord GOD: — 13.08
Therefore t. says the Lord GOD: I — 13.13
T. will I spend my wrath upon the — 13.15
and say, T. says the Lord GOD: Woe to — 13.18
"Wherefore t. says the Lord GOD: — 13.20
T. says the Lord GOD: Any man of the — 14.04
T. says the Lord GOD: Repent and — 14.06
"For t. says the Lord GOD: How much — 14.21
Therefore t. says the Lord GOD: Like — 15.06
and say, T. says the Lord GOD to — 16.03
T. you were decked with gold and — 16.13
T. says the Lord GOD, Because your — 16.36
"Yea, t. says the Lord GOD: I will — 16.59
say, T. says the Lord GOD: A great — 17.03
Say, T. says the Lord GOD: Will it — 17.09
Therefore t. says the Lord GOD: As I — 17.19
T. says the Lord GOD: "I myself will — 17.22
T. says the Lord GOD, Is it to — 20.03
T. says the Lord GOD: On the day — 20.05
T. says the Lord GOD: In this again — 20.27
T. says the Lord GOD: Will you — 20.30
t. says the Lord GOD: Go serve every — 20.39
T. says the Lord GOD, Behold, I will — 20.47
T. says the LORD: Behold, I am — 21.03
T. says the Lord, Say: A sword, a — 21.09
"Therefore t. says the Lord GOD: — 21.24
t. says the Lord GOD: Remove the — 21.26
T. says the Lord GOD concerning the — 21.28
You shall say, T. says the Lord GOD: — 22.03
Therefore t. says the Lord GOD: — 22.19
'T. says the Lord GOD,' when the — 22.28
T. you longed for the lewdness of — 23.21
t. says the Lord GOD: "Behold, I will — 23.22
T. I will put an end to your — 23.27
For t. says the Lord GOD: Behold, I — 23.28
T. says the Lord GOD: "You shall — 23.32
Therefore t. says the Lord GOD: — 23.35
T. they went in to Oholah and to — 23.44
T. says the Lord GOD: "Bring up — 23.46
T. will I put an end to lewdness in — 23.48
T. says the Lord GOD: Set on the pot, — 24.03
"Therefore t. says the Lord GOD: Woe — 24.06
Therefore t. says the Lord GOD: Woe — 24.09
for us, that you are acting t.?" — 24.19
T. says the Lord GOD: Behold, I will — 24.21
T. shall Ezekiel be to you a sign; — 24.24
T. says the Lord GOD, Because you — 25.03
For t. says the Lord GOD: Because — 25.06
"T. says the Lord GOD: Because Moab — 25.08
"T. says the LORD GOD: Because Edom — 25.12
therefore t. says the Lord GOD, I — 25.13
"T. says the Lord GOD: Because the — 25.15
therefore t. says the Lord GOD, — 25.16
therefore t. says the Lord GOD: — 26.03
"For t. says the Lord GOD: Behold, I — 26.07
"T. says the Lord GOD to Tyre: Will — 26.15
"For t. says the Lord GOD: When I — 26.19
t. says the Lord GOD: "O Tyre, you — 27.03
T. says the Lord GOD: "Because your — 28.02
therefore t. says the Lord GOD: — 28.06
T. says the Lord GOD: "You were the — 28.12
and say, T. says the Lord GOD: — 28.22
"T. says the Lord GOD: When I gather — 28.25
T. says the Lord GOD: "Behold I am — 29.03
therefore t. says the Lord GOD: — 29.08
"For t. says the Lord GOD: At the — 29.13
Therefore t. says the Lord GOD: — 29.19
T. says the Lord GOD: "Wail, 'Alas — 30.02
"T. says the LORD: Those who support — 30.06
"T. says the Lord GOD: I will put an — 30.10
"T. says the Lord GOD: I will — 30.13
T. I will execute acts of judgment — 30.19
Therefore t. says the Lord GOD: — 30.22
"Therefore t. says the Lord GOD: — 31.10
"T. says the Lord GOD: When it goes — 31.15
Whom are you t. like in glory and — 31.18
T. says the Lord GOD: I will throw — 32.03
For t. says the Lord GOD: The sword — 32.11
T. have you said: 'Our transgressions — 33.10
T. says the Lord GOD: You eat flesh — 33.25
T. says the Lord GOD: As I live, — 33.27
T. says the Lord GOD: Ho, shepherds — 34.02
T. says the Lord GOD, Behold, I am — 34.10
"For t. says the Lord GOD: Behold, I, — 34.11
t. says the Lord GOD: Behold, I judge — 34.17
"Therefore, t. says the Lord GOD to — 34.20
and say to it, T. says the Lord GOD: — 35.03
T. says the Lord GOD: For the — 35.14
T. says the Lord GOD: Because the — 36.02
T. says the Lord GOD: Because, yea, — 36.03
T. says the Lord GOD to the mountains — 36.04
therefore t. says the Lord GOD: I — 36.05
T. says the Lord GOD: Behold, I speak — 36.06
therefore t. says the Lord GOD: I — 36.07
T. says the Lord GOD: Because men — 36.13
T. says the Lord GOD: It is not for — 36.22
"T. says the Lord GOD: On the day — 36.33
"T. says the Lord GOD: This also I — 36.37
T. says the Lord GOD to these bones: — 37.05
T. says the Lord GOD: Come from the — 37.09
T. says the Lord GOD: "Behold, I will — 37.12
say to them, T. says the Lord GOD: — 37.19
T. says the Lord GOD: Behold, I will — 37.21
and say, T. says the Lord GOD: Behold, — 38.03
"T. says the Lord GOD: On that day — 38.10
T. says the Lord GOD: On that day — 38.14
"T. says the Lord GOD: Are you he of — 38.17
"T. says the Lord GOD: Behold, I am — 39.01
t. shall they cleanse the land. — 39.16
t. says the Lord GOD: Speak to the — 39.17
"Therefore t. says the Lord GOD: Now — 39.25
and t. one went up from the lowest — 41.07
t. says the Lord GOD: These are the — 43.18
t. you shall cleanse the altar and — 43.20
T. says the Lord GOD: O house of — 44.06
"Therefore t. says the Lord GOD: No — 44.09
"T. says the Lord GOD: Enough, O — 45.09
"T. says the Lord GOD: In the first — 45.18
"T. says the Lord GOD: The gate of — 46.01
T. the lamb and the meal offering — 46.15
"T. says the Lord GOD: If the prince — 46.16
T. says the Lord GOD: "These are the — 47.13
he went and said t. to him, — Dan 2.24
and said t. to him: "I have found — 2.25
He cried aloud and said t., — 4.14
"T. he said: 'As for the fourth — 7.23
T. it shall be done to you, O house — Hos 10.15

THUS (cont.)
T. says the LORD: "For three transgressions Amo 1.03
T. says the LORD: "For three transgressions 1.06
T. says the LORD: "For three transgressions 1.09
T. says the LORD: "For three transgressions 1.11
T. says the LORD: "For three transgressions 1.13
T. says the LORD: "For three transgressions 2.01
T. says the LORD: "For three transgressions 2.04
T. says the LORD: "For three transgressions 2.06
Therefore t. says the Lord GOD: "An 3.11
T. says the LORD: "As the shepherd 3.12
"Therefore t. I will do to you, O 4.12
For t. says the Lord GOD: "The city 5.03
For t. says the LORD to the house 5.04
Therefore t. says the LORD, the God 5.16
T. the Lord GOD showed me: behold, he 7.01
T. the Lord GOD showed me: behold, 7.04
For t. Amos has said, 'Jeroboam 7.11
Therefore t. says the LORD: 'Your 7.17
T. the Lord GOD showed me: behold, a 8.01
T. says the Lord GOD concerning Ob 1.01
Therefore t. says the LORD: Behold, Mic 2.03
t. they preach—"one should not 2.06
T. says the LORD concerning the 3.05
t. they weave it together. 7.03
T. says the LORD, "Though they be Nah 1.12
"T. says the LORD of hosts: This Hag 1.02
Now therefore t. says the LORD of 1.05
"T. says the LORD of hosts: Consider 1.07
For t. says the LORD of hosts: Once 2.06
"T. says the LORD of hosts; Ask the 2.11
T. says the LORD of hosts: Return to Zec 1.03
'T. says the LORD of hosts, Return 1.04
T. says the LORD of hosts: I am 1.14
Therefore, t. says the LORD, I have 1.16
Cry again, T. says the LORD of hosts: 1.17
For t. said the LORD of hosts, after 2.08
"T. says the LORD of hosts: If you 3.07
'T. says the LORD of hosts, "Behold, 6.12
"T. says the LORD of hosts, Render 7.09
T. the land they left was desolate, 7.14
"T. says the LORD of hosts: I am 8.02
T. says the LORD: I will return 8.03
T. says the LORD of hosts: Old men 8.04
T. says the LORD of hosts: If it is 8.06
T. says the LORD of hosts: Behold, I 8.07
T. says the LORD of hosts: "Let your 8.09
For t. says the LORD of hosts: "As I 8.14
T. says the LORD of hosts: The fast 8.19
"T. says the LORD of hosts: Peoples 8.20
T. says the LORD of hosts: In those 8.23
T. said the LORD my God: "Become 11.04
T. says the LORD, who stretched out 12.01
for t. it is fitting for us to Mt 3.15
"T., when you give alms, sound no 6.02
T. you will know them by their 7.20
While he was t. speaking to them, 9.18
If David t. calls him Lord, how is 22.45
T. you witness against yourselves, 23.31
"Why does this man speak t.? Mk 2.07
that they t. questioned within 2.08
do you question t. in your hearts? 2.08
t. making void the word of God 7.13
(T. he declared all foods clean.) 7.19
"Why was the ointment t. wasted? 14.04
saw that he t. breathed his last, he 15.39
"T. the Lord has done to me in the Lk 1.25
Galileans, because they suffered t.? 13.02
stood and prayed t. with himself, 18.11
David t. calls him Lord; 20.44
"T. it is written, that the Christ 24.46
heard the crowd t. muttering about Jn 7.32
but speak t. as the Father taught 8.28
As he spoke t., many believed in 8.30
T. he spoke, and then he said to 11.11
If we let him go on t., every one 11.48
When Jesus had t. spoken, he was 13.21
So lying t., close to the breast of 13.25
should suffer, he t. fulfilled. Ac 3.18
T. Joseph who was surnamed by the 4.36
And when he had spoken t., 20.36
"T. says the Holy Spirit, 'So shall 21.11
T. all will know that there is 21.24
why they shouted t. against him. 22.24
"T. I journeyed to Damascus with 26.12
And as he t. made his defense, 26.24
come to you (but t. far have been Rom 1.13
circumcised and who t. have righteousness 4.11
T. a married woman is bound by law 7.02
molder, "Why have you made me t.?" 9.20
jealous, and t. save some of them. 11.14
he who t. serves Christ is acceptable 14.18
t. making it my ambition to preach 15.20
T., sinning against your brethren 1Co 8.12
T., tongues are a sign not for 14.22
T. it is written, "The first man 15.45
view, we regard him t. no longer. 2Co 5.16
T. Abraham "believed God, and it was Gal 3.06
for me to feel t. about you all, Php 1.07
of us who are mature be t. minded; 3.15
stand firm t. in the Lord, my 4.01
t. laying up for themselves a good 1Ti 6.19
Though we speak t., yet in your case Heb 6.09
And t. Abraham, having patiently 6.15
These preparations having t. been made, 9.06
t. securing an eternal redemption. 9.12
T. it was necessary for the copies 9.23
who speak t. make it clear that 11.14
and t. let us offer to God acceptable 12.28
things are t. to be dissolved, what 2Pe 3.11
And every one who t. hopes in him 1Jn 3.03
shall be clad t. in white garments, Rev 3.05
t. he is doomed to be killed. 11.05

THWART
cleverness of the clever I will t. 1Co 1.19

THWARTED
that no purpose of thine can be t. Job 42.02

THWARTS
but he t. the craving of the wicked. Pro 10.03

THYATIRA
named Lydia, from the city of T., Ac 16.14
Pergamum and to T. and to Sardis Rev 1.11
angel of the church in T. write: 2.18
But to the rest of you in T., 2.24

THYSELF
for thou t. didst charge us, saying, Ex 19.23
establish for t. thy people Israel 2Sa 7.24
"With the loyal thou dost show t. loyal; 22.26
man thou dost show t. blameless; 22.26
with the pure thou dost show t. pure, 22.27
crooked thou dost show t. perverse. 22.27
making for t. a name for great and 1Ch 17.21
"Lay down a pledge for me with t.; Job 17.03
lift t. up against the fury of my Ps 7.06
dost thou hide t. in times of 10.01
With the loyal thou dost show t. loyal; 18.25
man thou dost show t. blameless; 18.25
with the pure thou dost show t. pure; 18.26
crooked thou dost show t. perverse. 18.26
Bestir t., and awake for my right, 35.23
Rouse t.! Why sleepest thou, 44.23
and hide not t. from my supplication! 55.01
Rouse t., come to my help, and see! 59.04
whom thou hast made strong for t.! 80.17
Wilt thou hide t. for ever? 89.46
who coverest t. with light as with 104.02
Exalt t., O God, above the heavens! 108.05
lifting up of t. nations are Is 33.03
Truly, thou art a God who hidest t., 45.15
to make for t. a glorious name, 63.14
Wilt thou restrain t. at these 64.12

THYSELF (cont.)
"Thou hast wrapped t. with anger Lam 3.43
thou hast wrapped t. with a cloud 3.44
Restore us to t., O LORD, that we 5.21

TIBERIAS
of Galilee, which is the Sea of T. Jn 6.01
boats from T. came near the place 6.23
to the disciples by the Sea of T.; 21.01

TIBERIUS
year of the reign of T. Caesar, Lk 3.01

TIBHATH
And from T. and from Cun, cities of 1Ch 18.08

TIBNI
people followed T. the son of 1Ki 16.21
who followed T. the son of Ginath; 16.22
so T. died, and Omri became king. 16.22

TIDAL
of Elam, T. king of Goiim, Gen 14.01
T. king of Goiim, Amraphel king of 14.09

TIDINGS
When Laban heard the t. of Jacob Gen 29.13
heard these evil t., they mourned; Ex 33.04
He who brought the t. answered and 1Sa 4.17
she heard the t. that the ark of 4.19
told him the t. of the men of 11.05
to bring t. to Gath, thinking, "Lest 27.11
t. came to David, "Absalom has slain 2Sa 13.30
and carry t. to the king that the 18.19
him, "You are not to carry t. today; 18.20
you may carry t. another day, but 18.20
but today you shall carry no t., 18.20
you will have no reward for the t.?" 18.22
alone, there are t. in his mouth." 18.25
the king said, "He also brings t." 18.26
a good man, and comes with good t." 18.27
"Good t. for my lord the king! 18.31
I am charged with heavy t. for you. 1Ki 14.06
the host of those who bore the t.: Ps 68.11
He is not afraid of evil t.; 112.07
mountain, O Zion, herald of good t.; Is 40.09
O Jerusalem, herald of good t., 40.09
to Jerusalem a herald of good t. 41.27
the feet of him who brings good t., 52.07
peace, who brings good t. of good, 52.07
to bring good t. to the afflicted; 61.01
I have heard t. from the LORD, and a Jer 49.14
for they have heard evil t.; 49.23
you shall say, 'Because of the t. Eze 21.07
But t. from the east and the north Dan 11.44
We have heard t. from the LORD, and Ob 1.01
Then t. reached the king of Nineveh, Jon 3.06
the feet of him who brings good t., Nah 1.15

TIE
heart always, t. them about your neck. Pro 6.21

TIED
And they t. to it a lace of blue, to Ex 39.31
and t. up two talents of silver in 2Ki 5.23
the horses t., and the asses t., 7.10
counted and t. up in bags the 12.10
immediately you will find an ass t., Mt 21.02
enter it you will find a colt t., Mk 11.02
found a colt t. at the door out in 11.04
entering you will find a colt t., Lk 19.30
But when they had t. him up with Ac 22.25
the ropes that t. the rudders; 27.40

TIERS
window opposite window in three t. 1Ki 7.04
was opposite window in three t. 7.05

TIGHT
web and make it t. with the pin, Ju 16.13
and she made them t. with the pin, 16.14

TIGLATHPILESER
king of Israel T. king of Assyria 2Ki 15.29
messengers to T. king of Assyria, 16.07
Damascus to meet T. king of Assyria, 16.10

TIGRIS
the great river, that is, the T., Dan 10.04

TIKVAH
the wife of Shallum the son of T., 2Ki 22.14
Jahzeiah the son of T. opposed this, Ez 10.15

TILES
bed through the t. into the midst Lk 5.19

TILGATHPILNESER
whom T. king of Assyria carried 1Ch 5.06
the spirit of T. king of Assyria, 5.26
So T. kng of Assyria came against 2Ch 28.20

TILL
there was no man to t. the ground; Gen 2.05
of Eden to t. it and keep it. 2.15
shall eat bread t. you return to 3.19
to t. the ground from which he was 3.23
When you t. the ground, it shall no 4.12
can do nothing t. you arrive there." 19.22
t. Shelah my son grows up"—for he 38.11
give me a pledge, t. you send it?" 38.17
t. thy people, O LORD, pass by, Ex 15.16
t. the people pass by whom thou 15.16
man leave any of it t. the morning." 16.19
left part of it t. the morning, 16.20
lay by to be kept t. the morning.'" 16.23
So they laid it by t. the morning, 16.24
t. they came to a habitable land; 16.35
t. they came to the border of the 16.35
Moses from morning t. evening. 18.13
about you from morning t. evening?" 18.14
not go onward t. the day that it 40.37
t. the will of the LORD should be Lev 24.12
on the march t. Miriam was brought Num 12.15
not lie down t. it devours the 23.24
t. you are destroyed, because you Deu 28.45
t. all the nation, the men of war Jos 5.06
in the camp t. they were healed. 5.08
t. we have drawn them away from the 8.06
t. he stood before the congregation. 20.09
t. you perish from off this good 23.13
And they waited t. they were Ju 3.25
t. it went down into the ground, as 4.21
he said, "I will stay t. you return." 6.18
"Let us wait t. the light of the 16.02
But Samson lay t. midnight, and at 16.03
t. he lodged there again. 19.07
her master was, t. it was light. 19.26
and sat there t. evening before God, 21.02
therefore wait t. they were grown? Ru 1.13
t. they have finished all my 2.21
people will not eat t. he comes, 1Sa 9.13
will not sit down t. he comes here." 16.11
in the field t. the third day at 20.05
t. I know what God will do for me." 22.03
anything else t. the sun goes down!" 2Sa 3.35
servants shall t. the land for him, 9.10
t. the two of them could go over on 2Ki 2.08
they urged him t. he was ashamed, 2.17
t. the country was filled with 3.20
t. they fled before them; and they went 3.24
t. only its stones were left in 3.25
the child sat on her lap t. noon, 4.20
"Why do we sit here t. we die? 7.03
it over his face, t. he died. 8.15
t. he had wiped them out, according 10.17

TILL (cont.)
fathers have stored up t. this day, 2Ki 20.17
t. he had filled Jerusalem from one 21.16
was besieged t. the eleventh year 25.02
marvelously helped, t. he was strong. 2Ch 26.15
t. the wrath of the LORD rose 36.16
his people, t. there was no remedy. 36.16
not stop them t. a report should Ez 5.05
angry with us t. thou wouldst 9.14
t. the fierce wrath of our God over 10.14
not know or see t. we come into Neh 4.11
break of dawn t. the stars came 4.21
after month t. the twelfth month, Est 3.07
I am full of tossing t. the dawn. Job 7.04
let me alone t. I swallow my 7.19
t. the heavens are no more he will 14.12
t. my release should come. 14.14
t. I die I will not put away my 27.05
his wickedness t. thou find none. Ps 10.15
not turn back t. they were consumed. 18.37
have overtaken me, t. I cannot see; 40.12
t. the storms of destruction pass 57.01
consume them t. they are no more, 59.13
t. I proclaim thy might to all the 71.18
peace abound, t. the moon be no more! 72.07
t. they reached a city to dwell in. 107.07
t. I make your enemies your footstool." 110.01
our God, t. he have mercy upon us. 123.02
take our fill of love t. morning; Pro 7.18
t. an arrow pierces its entrails; 7.23
t. I might see what was good for Ecc 2.03
the evening t. wine inflames them! Is 5.11
not be forgiven you t. you die, 22.14
t. you are left like a flagstaff on 30.17
the asses that t. the ground will 30.24
fathers have stored up t. this day, 39.06
be discouraged t. he has established 42.04
to t. it and dwell there, says the Jer 27.11
How long t. you are quiet? 47.06
t. they swoon away and sleep a 51.39
was besieged t. the eleventh year 52.05
him in prison t. the day of his 52.11
t. you have completed the days of Eze 4.08
my youth up t. now I have never 4.14
any more t. I have satisfied my 24.13
t. iniquity was found in you. 28.15
t. you have scattered them abroad, 34.21
t. the buriers have buried it in 39.15
shall eat fat t. you are filled, 39.19
and drink blood t. you are drunk, 39.19
the tribes of Israel, shall t. it. 48.19
words before me t. the times Dan 2.09
t. seven times, pass over him; 4.23
t. you know that the Most High 4.25
dew of heaven t. his hair grew as 4.33
and he labored t. the sun went down 6.14
shall prosper t. the indignation 11.36
there was a nation t. that time; 12.01
shall it be t. the end of these 12.06
But go your way t. the end; 12.13
long will it be t. they are pure Hos 8.05
will bereave them t. none is left. 9.12
t. he should see what would become Jon 4.05
destroy you t. no inhabitant is Zep 2.05
that leave nothing t. the morning. 3.03
t. there is no room for them. Zec 10.10
t. they are called the wicked Mal 1.04
t. they present right offerings to 3.03
t. it came to rest over the place Mt 2.09
and remain there t. I tell you; 2.13
t. heaven and earth pass away, not 5.18
never get out t. you have paid the 5.26
t. he brings justice to victory; 12.20
of meal, t. it was all leavened." 13.33
him in prison t. he should pay the 18.30
t. he should pay all his debt. 18.34
t. I put thy enemies under thy feet'? 22.44
not pass away t. all these things 24.34
t. I put thy enemies under thy feet.' Mk 12.36
the wilderness t. the day of his Lk 1.80
and as a widow t. she was eighty-four. 2.37
it convulses him t. he foams, 9.39
never get out t. you have paid the 12.59
t. I dig about it and put on manure. 13.08
of meal, t. it was all leavened." 13.21
t. I eat and drink; and afterward 17.08
them, 'Trade with these t. I come.' 19.13
t. I make thy enemies a stool for 20.43
not pass away t. all has taken 21.32
t. you have denied me three times. Jn 13.38
t. I make thy enemies a stool for Ac 2.35
t. there arose over Egypt another 7.18
all the towns t. he came to 8.40
us on our way t. we were outside 21.05
eat nor drink t. they had killed 23.12
taste no food t. we have killed 23.14
eat nor drink t. they have killed 23.21
to them from morning t. evening, 28.23
t. the offspring should come to Gal 3.19
T. I come, attend to the public 1Ti 4.13
t. I make thy enemies a stool for Heb 1.13
t. we have sealed the servants of Rev 7.03
t. men cursed God for the plague of 16.21
t. the thousand years were ended. 20.03

TILLED
you, and you shall be t. and sown; Eze 36.09
land that was desolate shall be t., 36.34

TILLER
sheep, and Cain a t. of the ground. Gen 4.02
Noah was the first t. of the soil. 9.20
no prophet, I am a t. of the soil; Zec 13.05

TILLERS
O t. of the soil, wail, O vinedressers, Joe 1.11

TILLING
the field for t. the soil was Ezri 1Ch 27.26

TILLS
He who t. his land will have plenty Pro 12.11
He who t. his land will have plenty 28.19

TILON
Amnon, Rinnah, Benhanan, and T. 1Ch 4.20

TILT
Or who can t. the waterskins of the Job 38.37
send to him tilters who will t. him, Jer 48.12

TILTERS
send to him tilters who will t. him, Jer 48.12

TIMAEUS
the son of T., was stting by the Mk 10.46

TIMBER
its stones and t. and all the Lev 14.45
how to cut t. like the Sidonians. 1Ki 5.06
the matter of cedar and cypress t. 5.08
with all the t. of cedar and 5.10
prepared the t. and the stone to 5.18
with cedar and cypress t. and gold, 9.11
the stones of Ramah and its t., 15.22
well as to buy t. and quarried 2Ki 12.12
as for buying t. and quarried 22.06
t. and stone too I have provided. 1Ch 22.14
and algum t. from Lebanon, for I 2Ch 2.08
know how to cut t. in Lebanon. 2.08
to prepare t. for me in abundance, 2.09
servants, the hewers who cut t., 2.10
cut whatever t. you need from 2.16
the stones of Ramah and its t., 16.06
and t. for binders and beams for 34.11
and t. is laid in the walls; Ez 5.08

TIMBER (cont.)
great stones and one course of t.; Ez 6.04
he may give me t. to make beams Neh 2.08
your stones and t. and soil they Eze 26.12
and consume it, both t. and stones." Zec 5.04

TIMBERS
to the house with t. of cedar. 1Ki 6.10
and cedar t. without number; 1Ch 22.04

TIMBREL
of Aaron, took a t. in her hand; Ex 15.20
sound the t., the sweet lyre with Ps 81.02
melody to him with t. and lyre! 149.03
Praise him with t. and dance; 150.04
t. and flute and wine at their Is 5.12

TIMBRELS
out after her with t. and dancing. Ex 15.20
meet him with t. and with dances; Ju 11.34
with t., with songs of joy, and with 1Sa 18.06
between them maidens playing t.: Ps 68.25
The mirth of the t. is stilled, Is 24.08
be to the sound of t. and lyres; 30.32
you shall adorn yourself wth t., Jer 31.04

TIME
In the course of t. Cain brought to Gen 4.03
At that t. men began to call upon 4.26
At that t. the Canaanites were in 12.06
At that t. the Canaanites and the 13.07
the appointed t. I will return to 18.14
old age at the t. of which God had 21.02
At that t. Abimelech and Phicol the 21.22
Abraham a second t. from heaven, 22.15
well of water at the t. of evening, 24.11
the t. when women go out to draw 24.11
When he had been there a long t., 26.08
it is not t. for the animals to be 29.07
in to her, for my t. is completed." 29.21
"Now this t. my husband will be 29.34
"This t. I will praise the LORD"; 29.35
happened at that t. that Judah went 38.01
In course of t. the wife of Judah, 38.12
When the t. of her delivery came, 38.27
From the t. that he made him overseer 39.05
And after a t. his master's wife 39.07
Some t. after this, the butler of 40.01
continued for some t. in custody. 40.04
asleep and dreamed a second t.; 41.05
replaced in our sacks the first t., 43.18
came down the first t. to buy food; 43.20
And when the t. drew near that 47.29
hardened his heart this t. also, Ex 8.32
And the LORD set a t., saying, 9.05
For this t. I will send all my 9.14
about this t. I will cause very 9.18
to them, "I have sinned this t.; 9.27
The t. that the people of Israel 12.40
its appointed t. from year to year. 13.10
And when in t. to come your son 13.14
shall pay for the loss of his t., 21.19
the appointed t. in the month of 23.15
at the t. appointed in the month 34.18
in plowing t. and in harvest you 34.21
as at the t. of her menstruation, Lev 12.02
washed a second t., and be clean." 13.58
not at the t. of her impurity, or if 15.25
beyond the t. of her impurity, all 15.25
proclaim at the t. appointed for 23.04
be for you a t. of holy convocation, 23.27
so that the t. of the seven weeks 25.08
the Levites may redeem at any t. 25.32
the t. he was with his owner shall 25.50
be rated as the t. of a hired 25.50
shall last to the t. of vintage, 26.05
shall last to the t. for sowing; 26.05
Moses at the t. when the LORD Num 3.01
until the t. is completed for which 6.05
but the former t. shall be void, 6.12
when the t. of his separation has 6.13
the passover at its appointed t. 9.02
shall keep it at its appointed t.; 9.03
its appointed t. among the people 9.07
offering at its appointed t.; 9.13
or a longer t., that the cloud 9.22
you blow an alarm the second t., 10.06
for the first t. at the command of 10.13
Now the t. was the season of the 13.20
and we dwelt in Egypt a long t.; 20.15
who was king of Moab at that t., 22.04
shall at any t. go beyond the 35.26
"At that t. I said to you, 'I am not Deu 1.09
And I charged your judges at that t., 1.16
you at that t. all the things that 1.18
And the t. from our leaving Kadeshbarnea 2.14
cities at that t. and utterly 2.34
we took all his cities at that t.— 3.04
land at that t. out of the hand of 3.08
possession of this land at that t., 3.12
"And I commanded you at that t., 3.18
And I commanded Joshua at that t., 3.21
the LORD at that t., saying, 3.23
me at that t. to teach you statutes 4.14
at enmity with him in t. past, 4.42
the LORD and you at that t., 5.05
"When your son asks you in t. to come, 6.20
LORD hearkened to me that t. also. 9.19
for Aaron also at the same t. 9.20
"At that t. the LORD said to me, 10.01
At that t. the LORD set apart the 10.08
the mountain, as at the first t., 10.10
LORD hearkened to me that t. also; 10.10
at the t. you came out of Egypt. 16.06
weeks from the t. you first put 16.09
at enmity with him in t. past— 19.04
with his neighbor in t. past. 19.06
"When you besiege a city for a long t., 20.19
priest who is in office at that t., 26.03
at the set t. of the year of 31.10
for the t. when their foot shall 32.35
throughout the t. of harvest), Jos 3.15
your children ask in t. to come, 4.06
ask their fathers in t. to come, 4.21
At that t. the LORD said to Joshua, 5.02
of Israel again the second t." 5.02
And at the seventh t., when the 6.16
Joshua laid an oath upon them at that t., 6.26
but at the t. of the going down of 10.27
kings and their land at one t., 10.42
tomorrow at this t. I will give 11.06
And Joshua turned back at that t., 11.10
Joshua made war a long t. with all 11.18
And Joshua came at that t., 11.21
years since the t. that the LORD 14.10
him who is high priest at the t.: 20.06
fear that in t. to come your 22.24
say to our children in t. to come, 22.27
to our descendants in t. to come, 22.28
A long t. afterward, when the LORD 23.01
lived in the wilderness a long t. 24.07
killed at that t. about ten Ju 3.29
was judging Israel at that t. 4.04
you in the t. of your distress." 10.14
After a t. the Ammonites made war 11.04
not recover them within that t.? 11.26
fell at that t. forty-two thousand 12.06
At that t. the Philistines had 14.04
at the t. of wheat harvest, Samson 15.01
"This t. I shall be blameless in 15.03
And Benjamin returned at that t.; 21.14
departed from there at that t., 21.24
and in due t. Hannah conceived and 1Sa 1.20
At that t. Eli, whose eyesight had 3.02
called Samuel again the third t, 3.08

TIME (cont.)

And about the t. of her death the 1Sa 4.20
a long t. passed, some twenty years, 7.02
"Tomorrow about this t. I will send 9.16
by the t. the sun is hot, you shall 11.09
the t. appointed by Samuel; 13.08
went at that t. with the people of 14.18
before that t. and who had gone up 14.21
But at the t. when Merab, Saul's 18.19
Saul said to David a second t., 18.21
son-in-law. Before the t. had expired, 18.26
sent messengers again the third t., 19.21
about this t. tomorrow, or the third 20.12
him all the t. that David was in 22.04
Is today the first t. that I have 22.15
all the t. they were in Carmel. 25.07
And the t. that David was king in 2Sa 2.11
"For some t. past you have been 3.17
from the t. that I appointed judges 7.11
the t. when kings go forth to 11.01
and after a t. Amnon, David's son, 13.01
And he sent a second t., but Joab would 14.29
your father's servant in t. past, 15.34
"This t. the counsel which Ahithophel 17.07
will not waste t. like this with 18.14
beyond the set t. which had been 20.05
"They were wont to say in old t., 20.18
hundred whom he slew at one t. 23.08
about harvest t. to David at the 23.13
the morning until the appointed t.; 24.15
never at any t. displeased him by 1Ki 1.06
When David's t. to die drew near, he 2.01
avenging in t. of peace blood which 2.05
And the t. that David reigned over 2.11
not at this t. put you to death, 2.26
So Solomon held the feast at that t., 8.65
appeared to Solomon a second t., 9.02
my heart will be there for all t. 9.03
And at that t., when Jeroboam went 11.29
And the t. that Solomon reigned in 11.42
At that t. Abijah the son of 14.01
And the t. that Jeroboam reigned 14.20
on until the t. of the offering of 18.29
And he said, "Do it a second t."; 18.34
And he said, "Do it a third t."; 18.34
and they did it a third t. 18.34
And at the t. of the offering of 18.36
And at the seventh t. he said, 18.44
of one of them by this t. tomorrow." 19.02
of the LORD came again a second t., 19.07
to you tomorrow about this t., 20.06
Samaria at that t. and mustered 2Ki 3.06
about the t. of offering the 3.20
when the t. comes round, you shall 4.16
son about that t. the following 4.17
Was it a t. to accept money and 5.26
about this t. a measure of fine 7.01
about this t. tomorrow in the gate 7.18
Libnah revolted at the same t. 8.22
me at Jezreel tomorrow at this t." 10.06
The t. that Jehu reigned over 10.36
At that t. Hazael king of Syria 12.17
At that t. Menahem sacked Tappuah 15.16
At that t. the king of Edom recovered 16.06
At that t. Hezekiah stripped the 18.16
At that t. Merodachbaladan the son 20.12
At that t. the servants of Nebuchadnezzar 24.10
was the ruler over them in t. past; 1Ch 9.20
from t. to t., to be with these; 9.25
hundred whom he slew at one t. 11.11
Because you did not carry it the first t., 15.13
from the t. that I appointed judges 17.10
the t. when kings go forth to 20.01
At that t., when David saw that the 21.28
were at that t. in the high place 21.29
son of David king the second t., 29.22
The t. that he reigned over Israel 29.27
At that t. Solomon held the feast 2Ch 7.08
my heart will be there for all t. 7.16
of Israel were subdued at that t., 13.18
For a long t. Israel was without 15.03
At that t. Hanani the seer came to 16.07
some of the people at the same t. 16.10
At that t. Libnah also revolted 21.10
In course of t., at the end of two 21.19
From the t. when he turned away 25.27
At that t. King Ahaz sent to the 28.16
In the t. of his distress he became 28.22
keep it in its t. because the 30.03
for since the t. of Solomon the son 30.26
of all nations from that t. onward. 32.23
kept the passover at that t., 35.17
At the same t. Tattenai the governor Ez 5.03
and from that t. until now it has 5.16
At that t. those who had come from 8.35
many, and it is a t. of heavy rain; 10.13
to send me; and I set him a t. Neh 2.06
also said to the people at that t., 4.22
Moreover from the t. that I was 5.14
up to that t. I had not set up the 6.01
for the fifth t. sent his servant 6.05
and in the t. of their suffering 9.27
since the t. of the kings of 9.32
And after some t. I asked leave of 13.06
"From that t. on they did not come 13.21
gathered together the second t., Est 2.19
keep silence at such a t. as this, 4.14
the kingdom for such a t. as this?" 4.14
secretaries were summoned at that t., 8.09
and at the t. appointed every year, 9.27
In t. of heat they disappear; Job 6.17
thou wouldest appoint me a set t., 14.13
will be paid in full before his t., 15.32
were snatched away before their t.; 22.16
not appointed a t. for any man to 34.23
reserved for the t. of trouble, 38.23
do you know the t. when they bring 39.02
at a t. of distress, in the rush of Ps 32.06
their refuge in the t. of trouble. 37.39
At an acceptable t., O God, 69.13
cast me off in the t. of old age; 71.09
At the set t. which I appoint I 75.02
his promises at an end for all t.? 77.08
t. to favor her; the appointed t. has come. 102.13
the sun knows its t. for setting. 104.19
LORD from this t. forth and for 113.02
LORD from this t. forth and for 115.18
It is t. for the LORD to act, for 119.126
in from this t. forth and for 121.08
from this t. forth and for evermore. 125.02
LORD from this t. forth and for 131.03
at the t. of night and darkness. Pro 7.09
of snow in the t. of harvest is a 25.13
faithless man in t. of trouble is 25.19
and she laughs at the t. to come. 31.25
and a t. for every matter under Ecc 3.01
a t. to be born, and a t. to die; 3.02
a t. to plant, and a t. to pluck up 3.02
a t. to kill, and a t. to heal; 3.03
a t. to break down, and a t. to build up; 3.03
a t. to weep, and a t. to laugh; 3.04
a t. to mourn, and a t. to dance; 3.04
a t. to cast away stones, and a t. 3.05
a. t. to embrace, and a t. to refrain 3.05
a t. to seek, and a t. to lose; 3.06
a t. to keep, and a t. to cast away; 3.06
a t. to rend, and a t. to sew; 3.07
a t. to keep silence, and a t. to speak; 3.07
a t. to love, and a t. to hate; 3.08
a t. for war, and a t. for peace. 3.08
everything beautiful in its t.; 3.11
has appointed a t. for every 3.17
why should you die before your t.? 7.17
wise man will know the t. and way. 8.05

TIME (cont.)

For every matter has its t. and way, Ecc 8.06
but t. and chance happen to them 9.11
For man does not know his t. 9.12
of men are snared at an evil t., 9.12
princes feast at the proper t., 10.17
the t. of singing has come, and the Sol 2.12
In the former t. he brought into Is 9.01
in the latter t. he will make 9.01
from this t. forth and for evermore. 9.07
yet a second t. to recover the 11.11
its t. is close at hand and its 13.22
At evening t., behold, terror! 17.14
At that t. gifts will be brought to 18.07
at that t. the LORD had spoken by 20.02
her pangs, when she is near her t., 26.17
may be for the t. to come as a 30.08
our salvation in the t. of trouble. 33.02
At that t. Merodachbaladan the son 39.01
For a long t. I have held my peace, 42.14
and listen for the t. to come? 42.23
From this t. forth I make you hear 48.06
from the t. it came to be I have 48.16
"In a t. of favor I have answered 49.08
born in the t. of your bereavement 49.20
held my peace, even for a long t., 57.11
from this t. forth and for evermore." 59.21
in its t. I will hasten it. 60.22
in our sins we have been a long t., 64.05
of the LORD came to me a second t., Jer 1.13
But in the t. of their trouble they 2.27
save you, in your t. of trouble; 2.28
At that t. Jerusalem shall be 3.17
At that t. it will be said to this 4.11
at the t. that I punish them, they 6.15
"At that t., says the LORD, the 8.01
crane keep the t. of their coming; 8.07
for a t. of healing, but behold, 8.15
at the t. of their punishment they 10.15
inhabitants of the land at this t., 10.18
them in the t. of their trouble. 11.12
to me in the t. of their trouble. 11.14
the LORD came to me a second t., 13.03
its savior in t. of trouble, why 14.08
for a t. of healing, but behold, 14.19
enemy in the t. of trouble and in 15.11
trouble and in the t. of distress! 15.11
If at any t. I declare concerning a 18.07
And if at any t. I declare concerning 18.09
with them in the t. of thine anger. 18.23
until the t. of his own land comes; 27.07
it is a t. of distress for Jacob; 30.07
"At that t., says the LORD, I will 31.01
At that t. the army of the king of 32.02
that they may last for a long t. 32.14
LORD came to Jeremiah a second t., 33.01
and at that t. I will cause a 33.15
not come at their appointed t., 33.20
vineyards and fields at the same t. 39.10
the t. of their punishment. 46.21
the t. when I punish him. 49.08
"In those days and in that t., 50.04
the sickle in t. of harvest; 50.16
In those days and in that t., 50.20
the t. of their punishment. 50.27
the t. when I will punish you. 50.31
for this is the t. of the LORD's 51.06
at the t. of their punishment they 51.18
floor at the t. when it is trodden 51.33
while and the t. of her harvest 51.33
you shall lie down a second t., Eze 4.06
the t. has come, the day is near, a 7.07
The t. has come, the day draws near. 7.12
who say, 'The t. is not near to 11.03
a very little t. you were more 16.47
a woman in her t. of impurity, 18.06
the t. of your final punishment, 21.25
the t. of their final punishment. 21.29
that her t. may come, and that makes 22.03
the appointed t. of your years has 22.04
a t. of doom for the nations. 30.03
my mouth by the t. the man came to 33.22
sword at the t. of their calamity, 35.05
at the t. of their final punishment; 35.05
the end of that t. they were to Dan 1.05
At the end of the t., when the king 1.18
They answered a second t., 2.07
that you are trying to gain t., 2.08
the king to appoint him a t., 2.16
therefore at that t. certain 3.08
Belteshazzar, was dismayed for a long t., 4.19
you from the t. that you know that 4.26
At the same t. my reason returned 4.36
prolonged for a season and a t. 7.12
and the t. came when the saints 7.22
be given into his hand for a t., 7.25
a t., two times, and half a t. 7.25
vision is for the t. of the end." 8.17
to the appointed t. of the end. 8.19
flight at the t. of the evening 9.21
and moat, but in a troubled t. 9.25
And from the t. that an alliance is 11.23
strongholds, but only for a t. 11.24
is yet to be at the t. appointed. 11.27
"At the t. appointed he shall 11.29
not be this t. as it was before. 11.29
until the t. of the end, for it is 11.35
for it is yet for the t. appointed. 11.35
"At the t. of the end the king of 11.40
"At that t. shall arise Michael, the 12.01
And there shall be a t. of trouble, 12.01
there was a nation till that t.; 12.01
but at that t. your people shall be 12.01
the book, until the t. of the end. 12.04
for ever that it would be for a t., 12.07
a t., two times, and half a t.; 12.07
and sealed until the t. of the end. 12.09
And from the t. that the continual 12.11
will take back my grain in its t., Hos 2.09
as at the t. when she came out of 2.15
for it is the t. to seek the LORD, 10.12
in those days and at that t., Joe 3.01
will keep silent in such a t.; Amo 5.13
for it is an evil t. 5.13
to Jonah the second t., saying, Jon 3.01
haughtily, for it will be an evil t. Mic 2.03
hide his face from them at that t., 3.04
Zion from this t. forth and for 4.07
up until the t. when she who is in 5.03
For still the vision awaits its t.; Hab 2.03
At that t. I will search Jerusalem Zep 1.12
Yea, at that t. I will change the 3.09
at that t. I will deal with all 3.19
At that t. I will bring you home, at 3.20
at the t. when I gather you together; 3.20
people say the t. has not yet come Hag 1.02
"Is it a t. for you yourselves to 1.04
came a second t. to Haggai on the 2.20
And a second t. I said to him, "What Zec 4.12
for at evening t. there shall be 14.07
at the t. of the deportation to Mt 1.11
from them what t. the star appeared; 2.07
according to the t. which he had 2.16
From that t. Jesus began to preach, 4.17
here to torment us before the t.?" 8.29
At that t. Jesus declared, "I thank 11.25
At that t. Jesus went through the 12.01
and at harvest t. I will tell the 13.30
At that t. Herod the tetrarch heard 14.01
boat by this t. was many furlongs 14.24
from that t. Jesus began to show 16.21
At that t. the disciples came to 18.01
them their food at the proper t.? 24.45
Now after a long t. the master of 25.19
The Teacher says, My t. is at hand; 26.18
Again, for the second t., he went away 26.42

TIME (cont.)

away and prayed for the third t., Mt 26.44
"The t. is fulfilled, and the kingdom Mk 1.15
a hundredfold now in this t., 10.30
When the t. came, he sent a servant 12.02
do not know when the t. will come. 13.33
And he came the third t., and said to 14.41
the cock crowed a second t. 14.72
things closely for some t. past, Lk 1.03
which will be fulfilled in their t. 1.20
And when his t. of service was ended, 1.23
Now the t. came for Elizabeth to be 1.57
the t. came for her to be delivered. 2.06
And when the t. came for their 2.22
of the world in a moment of t., 4.05
from him until an opportune t. 4.13
Israel in the t. of the prophet 4.27
but from the t. I came in she has 7.45
a while and in t. of temptation 8.13
for a long t. he had worn no 8.27
(For many a t. it had seized him; 8.29
portion of food at the proper t.? 12.42
how to interpret the present t.? 12.56
at that very t. who told him of 13.01
and at the t. for the banquet he 14.17
receive manifold more in this t., 18.30
not know the t. of your visitation." 19.44
When the t. came, he sent a servant 20.10
and, 'The t. is at hand!' Do not go 21.08
This will be a t. for you to bear 21.13
himself in Jerusalem at that t. 23.07
A third t. he said to them, "Why, 23.22
enter a second t. into his mother's Jn 3.04
he had been lying there a long t., 5.06
"My t. has not yet come, but your 7.06
come, but your t. is always here. 7.06
for my t. has not yet fully come." 7.08
So for the second t. they called 9.24
by this t. there will be an odor, 11.39
now the third t. that Jesus was 21.14
A second t. he said to him, "Simon, 21.16
He said to him the third t., 21.17
you at this t. restore the kingdom Ac 1.06
during all the t. that the Lord 1.21
until the t. for establishing all 3.21
forth our fathers the first t. 7.12
"But as the t. of the promise drew 7.17
at this t. Moses was born, and was 7.20
for a long t. he had amazed them 8.11
came to him again a second t., 10.15
answered a second t. from heaven, 11.09
for the first t. called Christians. 11.26
About that t. Herod the king laid 12.01
and unable to see the sun for a t." 13.11
So they remained for a long t., 14.03
no little t. with the disciples. 14.28
And after they had spent some t., 15.33
spent their t. in nothing except 17.21
After spending some t. there he 18.23
About that t. there arose no little 19.23
might not have to spend t. in Asia; 20.16
you all the t. from the first day 20.18
At the same t. he hoped that money 24.26
They have known for a long t., 26.05
"In a short t. you think to make me 26.28
As much t. had been lost, and the 27.09
at the same t. loosening the ropes 27.40
waited a long t. and saw no 28.06
at the present t. that he himself Rom 3.26
at the right t. Christ died for the 5.06
of this present t. are not worth 8.18
"About this t. I will return and 9.09
at the present t. there is a 11.05
how it is full t. now for you to 13.11
pronounce judgment before the t., 1Co 4.05
Was any one at the t. of his call 7.18
any one at the t. of his call 7.18
the appointed t. has grown very 7.29
five hundred brethren at one t., 15.06
I hope to spend some t. with you, 16.07
the acceptable t. I have listened 2Co 6.02
behold, now is the acceptable t.; 6.02
at the present t. should apply 8.14
Here for the third t. I am ready to 12.14
This is the third t. I am coming to 13.01
But when the t. had fully come, God Gal 4.04
But as at that t. he who was born 4.29
as a plan for the fulness of t., Eph 1.10
that at one t. you Gentiles in the 2.11
were at that t. separated from 2.12
making the most of the t., 5.16
outsiders, making the most of the t. Col 4.05
for a short t., in person not in 1Th 2.17
that he may be revealed in his t. 2Th 2.06
which was borne at the proper t. 1Ti 2.06
at the proper t. by the blessed 6.15
For the t. is coming when people 2Ti 4.03
the t. of my departure has come. 4.06
and at the proper t. manifested in Tit 1.03
At the same t., prepare a guest Phm 1.22
find grace to help in t. of need. Heb 4.16
For though by this t. you ought to 5.12
is able for all t. to save those 7.25
imposed until the t. of reformation. 9.10
of many, will appear a second t., 9.28
offered for all t. a single sacrifice 10.12
perfected for all t. those who are 10.14
For t. would fail me to tell of Gideon, 11.32
us for a short t. at their pleasure, 12.10
for a little t. and then vanishes. Jas 4.14
ready to be revealed in the last t. 1Pe 1.05
what person or t. was indicated by 1.11
throughout the t. of your exile. 1.17
the rest of the t. in the flesh no 4.02
Let the t. that is past suffice for 4.03
For the t. has come for judgment to 4.17
that in due t. he may exalt you. 5.06
be able at any t. to recall these 2Pe 1.15
"In the last t. there will be scoffers, Jud 1.18
before all t. and now and for ever. 1.25
written therein; for the t. is near. Rev 1.03
I gave her t. to repent, but she 2.21
and the t. for the dead to be 11.18
he knows that his t. is short!" 12.12
nourished for a t., and times, and half a t. 12.14
of this book, for the t. is near. 22.10

TIMES

he has supplanted me these two t. Gen 27.36
me and changed my wages ten t., 31.07
you have changed my wages ten t. 31.41
himself to the ground seven t., 33.03
was five t. as much as any of 43.34
them judge the people at all t.; Ex 18.22
And they judged the people at all t.; 18.26
"Three t. in the year you shall 23.14
three t. in the year shall all your 23.17
Three t. in the year shall all your 34.23
LORD your God three t. in the year. 34.24
the blood seven t. before the LORD Lev 4.06
it seven t. before the LORD in 4.17
some of it on the altar seven t., 8.11
it seven t. upon him who is to be 14.07
finger seven t. before the LORD. 14.16
left hand seven t. before the LORD; 14.27
and sprinkle the house seven t. 14.51
to come at all t. into the holy 16.02
the blood with his finger seven t. 16.14
upon it with his finger seven t., 16.19
proclaim as t. of holy convocation, 23.37
seven t. seven years, so that the 25.08
proof these ten t. and have not Num 14.22
of the tent of meeting seven t. 19.04
you have struck me these three t.?" 22.28
you struck your ass these three t.? 22.32
aside before me these three t. 22.33

TIMES (cont.)
as at other t., to meet with omens, Num 24.01
have blessed them these three t. 24.10
you a thousand t. as many as you Deu 1.11
"Three t. a year all your males 16.16
march around the city seven t., Jos 6.04
city in the same manner seven t.: 6.15
marched around the city seven t. 6.15
no enmity against him in t. past. 20.05
you have mocked me these three t., Ju 16.15
said, "I will go out as at other t., 16.20
against Gibeah, as at other t. 20.30
and as at other t. they began to 20.31
in former t. in Israel concerning Ru 4.07
calling as at other t., "Samuel! Samuel!" 1Sa 3.10
as at other t., upon the seat by 20.25
to the ground, and bowed three t.; 20.41
In t. past, when Saul was king over 2Sa 5.02
a hundred t. as many as they are, 24.03
Three t. a year Solomon used to 1Ki 9.25
himself upon the child three t., 17.21
And he said, "Go again seven t." 18.43
"How many t. shall I adjure you 22.16
the child sneezed seven t., 2Ki 4.35
"Go and wash in the Jordan seven t., 5.10
himself seven t. in the Jordan, 5.14
he struck three t., and stopped. 13.18
should have struck five or six t.; 13.19
strike down Syria only three t." 13.19
Three t. Joash defeated him and 13.25
In t. past, even when Saul was king, 1Ch 11.02
who had understanding of the t., 12.32
a hundred t. as many as they are! 21.03
In those t. there was no peace to 2Ch 15.05
"How many t. shall I adjure you 18.15
foreign wives come at appointed t., Ez 10.14
them came they said to us ten t., Neh 4.12
sent to me four t. in this way and 6.04
and many t. thou didst deliver them 9.28
at t. appointed, year by year, to 10.34
at appointed t., and for the first 13.31
to the wise men who knew the t.— Est 1.13
answer him once in a thousand t. Job 9.03
These ten t. you have cast reproach 19.03
"Why are not t. of judgment kept by 24.01
Will he call upon God at all t.? 27.10
twice, three t., with a man, 33.29
a stronghold in t. of trouble. Ps 9.09
thou hide thyself in t. of trouble? 10.01
His ways prosper at all t.; 10.05
on the ground, purified seven t. 12.06
My t. are in thy hand; deliver me 31.15
I will bless the LORD at all t.; 34.01
they are not put to shame in evil t., 37.19
Why should I fear in t. of trouble, 49.05
Trust in him at all t., O people; 62.08
who do righteousness at all t.! 106.03
Many t. he delivered them, but they 106.43
for thy ordinances at all t. 119.20
Seven t. a day I praise thee for 119.164
fill you at all t. with delight, Pro 5.19
A friend loves at all t., and a brother 17.17
for a righteous man falls seven t., 24.16
knows that many t. you have yourself Ecc 7.22
evil a hundred t. and prolongs his 8.12
will be the stability of your t., Is 33.06
from ancient t. things not yet 46.10
stork in the heavens knows her t.; Jer 8.07
me from ancient t. prophesied war, 28.08
and he prophesies of t. far off.' Eze 12.27
be inhabited as in your former t., 36.11
found them ten t. better than all Dan 1.20
words before me till the t. change. 2.09
He changes t. and seasons; he removes 2.21
heated seven t. more than it was 3.19
and let seven t. pass over him. 4.16
field, till seven t. pass over him; 4.23
and seven t. shall pass over you, 4.25
and seven t. shall pass over you, 4.32
his knees three t. a day and 6.10
makes his petition three t. a day." 6.13
ten thousand t. ten thousand stood 7.10
think to change the t. and the law; 7.25
two t., and half a time. 7.25
"In those t. a branch from her 11.07
"In those t. many shall rise 11.14
two t., and half a time; 12.07
interpret the signs of the t. Mt 16.03
forgive him? As many as seven t.?" 18.21
him, "I do not say to you seven t., 18.22
seven t., but seventy t. seven. 18.22
crows, you will deny me three t." 26.34
crows, you will deny me three t." 26.75
twice, you will deny me three t." Mk 14.30
twice, you will deny me three t." 14.72
against you seven t. in the day, Lk 17.04
the day, and turns to you seven t., 17.04
until the t. of the Gentiles are 21.24
But watch at all t., praying 21.36
until you three t. deny that you 22.34
today, you will deny me three t." 22.61
till you have denied me three t. Jn 13.38
for you to know t. or seasons Ac 1.07
that t. of refreshing may come from 3.19
This happened three t., and the thing 10.16
This happened three t., and all was 11.10
The t. of ignorance God overlooked, 17.30
Five t. I have received at the 2Co 11.24
Three t. I have been beaten with 11.25
Three t. I have been shipwrecked; 11.25
Three t. I besought the Lord about 12.08
Pray at all t. in the Spirit, with Eph 6.18
But as to the t. and the seasons, 1Th 5.01
you peace at all t. in all ways. 2Th 3.16
that in later t. some will depart 1Ti 4.01
days there will come t. of stress. 2Ti 3.01
at the end of the t. for your sake. 1Pe 1.20
twice ten thousand t. ten thousand; Rev 9.16
and t., and half a time. 12.14

TIMID
therefore I was t. and afraid to Job 32.06

TIMIDITY
us a spirit of t. but a spirit of 2Ti 1.07

TIMNA
(T. was a concubine of Eliphaz, Gen 36.12
and Heman; and Lotan's sister was T. 36.22
the chiefs T., Alvah, Jetheth, 36.40
Gatam, Kenaz, T., and Amalek. 1Ch 1.36
and Hormam; and Lotan's sister was T. 1.39
chiefs T., Aliah, Jetheth, 1.51

TIMNAH
he went up to T. to his sheepshearers, Gen 38.12
is going up to T. to shear his 38.13
Enaim, which is on the road to T.; 38.14
Bethshemesh, and passes along by T.; Jos 15.10
and T.: ten cities with their 15.57
Elon, T., Ekron, 19.43
Samson went down to T., Ju 14.01
and at T. he saw one of the daughters 14.01
daughters of the Philistines at T.; 14.02
with his father and mother to T., 14.05
and he came to the vineyards of T. 14.05
T. with its villages, and Gimzo with 2Ch 28.18

TIMNATHHERES
the bounds of his inheritance in T., Ju 2.09

TIMNATHSERAH
T. in the hill country of Ephraim; Jos 19.50
him in his own inheritance at T., 24.30

TIMNITE
"Samson, the son-in-law of the T., Ju 15.06

TIMON
and T., and Parmenas, and Nicolaus, a Ac 6.05

TIMOTHY
named T., the son of a Jewish woman Ac 16.01
Paul wanted T. to accompany him; 16.03
but Silas and T. remained there. 17.14
for Silas and T. to come to him as 17.15
When Silas and T. arrived from 18.05
T. and Erastus, he himself stayed in 19.22
and Gaius of Derbe, and T.; 20.04
T., my fellow worker, greets you; Rom 16.21
Therefore I sent to you T., 1Co 4.17
When T. comes, see that you put him 16.10
will of God, and T. our brother. 2Co 1.01
Silvanus and T. and I, was not Yes 1.19
Paul and T., servants of Christ Php 1.01
Lord Jesus to send T. to you soon, 2.19
will of God, and T. our brother, Col 1.01
and T., to the church of the 1Th 1.01
and we sent T., our brother and 3.02
But now that T. has come to us from 3.06
and T., To the church of the 2Th 1.01
To T., my true child in the faith: 1Ti 1.02
T., my son, in accordance with the 1.18
O T., guard what has been entrusted 6.20
To T., my beloved child: Grace, mercy, 2Ti 1.02
and T. our brother, To Philemon our Phm 1.01
our brother T. has been released, Heb 13.23

TIMOTHY'S
But T. worth you know, how as a son Php 2.22

TIN
the iron, the t., and the lead, Num 31.22
and bronze and t. and iron and Eze 22.18
and lead and t. into a furnace, 22.20
silver, iron, t., and lead they 27.12

TINGLE
of every one that hears it will t. 1Sa 3.11
every one who hears of it will t. 2Ki 21.12
every one who hears of it will t. Jer 19.03

TINKLING
as they go, t. with their feet; Is 3.16

TIP
put it upon the t. of the right Ex 29.20
put it on the t. of Aaron's right Lev 8.23
put it on the t. of the right ear 14.14
put on the t. of the right ear of 14.17
put it on the t. of the right ear 14.25
hand on the t. of the right ear of 14.28
reached out the t. of the staff Ju 6.21
put forth the t. of the staff that 1Sa 14.27
honey with the t. of the staff 14.43
cubits from the t. of one wing to 1Ki 6.24
of one wing to the t. of the other. 6.24

TIPHSAH
of the Euphrates from T. to Gaza, 1Ki 4.24

TIPS
and upon the t. of the right ears Ex 29.20
blood on the t. of their right Lev 8.24

TIRAS
Javan, Tubal, Meshech, and T. Gen 10.02
Javan, Tubal, Meshech, and T. 1Ch 1.05

TIRATHITES
the T., and Shimeathites, and the 1Ch 2.55

TIRED
they have t. themselves out but Jer 12.13

TIRHAKAH
concerning T. king of Ethiopia, 2Ki 19.09
concerning T. king of Ethiopa, "He Is 37.09

TIRHANAH
concubine, bore Sheber and T. 1Ch 2.48

TIRIA
Ziph, Ziphah, T., and Asarel. 1Ch 4.16

TIRZAH
Noah, Hoglah, Milcah, and T. Num 26.33
Noah, Hoglah, Milcah, and T. 27.01
for Mahlah, T., Hoglah, Milcah, and 36.11
the king of T., one: in all, thirty-one Jos 12.24
Noah, Hoglah, Milcah, and T. 17.03
and departed, and came to t. 1Ki 14.17
building Ramah, and he dwelt in T. 15.21
to reign over all Israel at T., 15.33
his fathers, and was buried at T.; 16.06
began to reign over Israel in T., 16.08
When he was at T., drinking himself 16.09
who was over the household in T., 16.09
Zimri reigned seven days in T. 16.15
with him, and they besieged T. 16.17
six years he reigned in T. 16.23
came up from T. and came to 2Ki 15.14
in it and its territory from T. on; 15.16
You are beautiful as T., Sol 6.04

TISHBE
of T. in Gilead, said to Ahab, "As 1Ki 17.01

TISHBITE
Now Elijah the T., of Tishbe in 1Ki 17.01
came to Elijah the T., saying, 21.17
came to Elijah the T., saying, 21.28
of the LORD said to Elijah the T., 2Ki 1.03
and he said, "It is Elijah the T." 1.08
spoke by his servant Elijah the T., 9.36

TITHE
"All the t. of the land, whether of Lev 27.30
man wishes to redeem any of his t., 27.31
And all the t. of herds and flocks, 27.32
given every t. in Israel for an Num 18.21
For the t. of the people of Israel, 18.24
of Israel the t. which I have 18.26
it to the LORD, a t. of the t. 18.26
your towns the t. of your grain or Deu 12.17
"You shall t. all the yield of your 14.22
you shall eat the t. of your grain, 14.23
you are not able to bring the t., 14.24
forth all the t. of your produce 14.28
paying all the t. of your produce 26.12
eaten of the t. whole I was mourning, 26.14
in abundantly the t. of everything. 2Ch 31.05
brought in the t. of cattle and 31.06
bring up the t. of the tithes to Neh 10.38
Judah brought the t. of the grain, 13.12
for you t. mint and dill and cummin, Mt 23.23
for you t. mint and rue and every Lk 11.42
gave him a t. of the spoils. Heb 7.04

TITHES
to the LORD from all your t., Num 18.28
your t. and the offering that you Deu 12.06
your t. and the offering that you 12.11
the t. and the dedicated things. 2Ch 31.12
the Levites the t. from our ground, Neh 10.37
who collect the t. in all our 10.37
when the Levites receive the t.; 10.38
tithe of the t. to the house of 10.38
and the t., to gather into them the 12.44
and the t. of grain, wine, and oil, 13.05
morning, your t. every three days; Amo 4.04
robbing thee?" In your t. and offerings. Mal 3.08
Bring the full t. into the storehouse, 3.10

TITHES (cont.)
I give t. of all that I get.' Lk 18.12
the law to take t. from the people, Heb 7.05
received t. from Abraham and 7.06
Here t. are received by mortal men; 7.08
who receives t., paid t. through Abraham, 7.09

TITHING
year, which is the year of t., Deu 26.12

TITIUS
the house of a man named T. Justus, Ac 18.07

TITLE
Pilate also wrote a t. and put it Jn 19.19
Many of the Jews read this t., 19.20

TITUS
I did not find my brother T. there. 2Co 2.13
comforted us by the coming of T., 7.06
still more at the joy of T., 7.13
boasting before T. has proved true 7.14
Accordingly we have urged T. that 8.06
care for you into the heart of T. 8.16
As for T., he is my partner and 8.23
I urged T. to go, and sent the 12.18
Did T. take advantage of you? 12.18
Barnabas, taking T. along with me. Gal 2.01
But even T., who was with me, was 2.03
gone to Galatia, T. to Dalmatia. 2Ti 4.10
To T., my true child in a common Tit 1.04

TIZITE
and Joha his brother, the T., 1Ch 11.45

TOAH
Jeroham, son of Eliel, son of T., 1Ch 6.34

TOB
and dwelt in the land of T.; Ju 11.03
bring Jephthah from the land of T.; 11.05
a thousand men, and the men of T., 2Sa 10.06
and the men of T. and Maacah, 10.08

TOBADONIJAH
Jehonathan, Adonijah, Tobijah, and T.; 2Ch 17.08

TOBIAH
the sons of T., and the sons of Ez 2.60
the Horonite and T. the servant, Neh 2.10
the Horonite and T. the servant, 2.19
T. the Ammonite was by him, and he 4.03
Sanballat and T. and the Arabs and 4.07
Sanballat and T. and to Geshem the 6.01
me because T. and Sanballat had 6.12
Remember T. and Sanballat, O my God, 6.14
of Judah sent many letters to T., 6.17
And T. sent letters to make me 6.19
the sons of T., the sons of Nekoda, 7.62
and who was connected with T., 13.04
prepared for T. a large chamber 13.05
evil that Eliashib had done for T., 13.07
furniture of T. out of the chamber 13.08

TOBIAH'S
and T. letters came to them. Neh 6.17

TOBIJAH
T., and Tobadonijah; and with these 2Ch 17.08
T., and Jedaiah, who have arrived Zec 6.10
T., Jedaiah, and Josiah the son of 6.14

TOCHEN
Rimmon, T., and Ashan, five cities, 1Ch 4.32

TODAY
I have not heard of it until t." Gen 21.26
Abraham, grant me success t., 24.12
"I came t. to the spring, and said, 24.42
let me pass through all your flock t., 30.32
is a witness between you and me t." 31.48
"Why are your faces downcast t.?" 40.07
Pharaoh, "I remember my faults t. 41.09
be kept alive, as they are t. 50.20
it that you have come so soon t.?" Ex 2.18
of making bricks t., as hitherto?" 5.14
which he will work for you t.; 14.13
or the Egyptians whom you see t., 14.13
"Eat it t., for t. is a sabbath 16.25
t. you will not find it in the 16.25
consecrate them t. and tomorrow, 19.10
"T. you have ordained yourselves 32.29
As has been done t., the LORD Lev 8.34
for t. the LORD will appear to you.'" 9.04
t. they have offered their sin 10.19
If I had eaten the sin offering t., 10.19
therefore I command you this t. Deu 15.15
t. you have been rebellious against 31.27
the LORD brings trouble on you t." Jos 7.25
the LORD t. he will be angry with 22.18
the LORD, spare us not t. 22.22
"T. we know that the LORD is in the 22.31
there should be t. one tribe Ju 21.03
to her, "Where did you glean t.? Ru 2.19
name with whom I worked t. is Boaz." 2.19
but will settle the matter t." 3.18
put us to rout t. before the 1Sa 4.03
I fled from the battle t." And he 4.16
a sacrifice t. on the high place. 9.12
for t. you shall eat with me, and in 9.19
depart from me t. you will meet 10.02
for t. the LORD has wrought deliverance 11.13
Is it not wheat harvest t.? 12.17
eaten freely t. of the spoil of 14.30
and see how this sin has arisen t. 14.38
the meal, either yesterday or t.?" 20.27
how much more t. will their vessels 21.05
Is t. the first time that I have 22.15
LORD gave you t. into my hand in 24.10
the LORD gave you into my hand t., 26.23
whom have you made a raid t.?" 27.10
you charge me t. with a fault 2Sa 3.08
king of Israel honored himself t., 6.20
uncovering himself t. before the 6.20
"Remain here t. also, and tomorrow I 11.12
"T. your servant knows that I have 14.22
and shall I t. make you wander 15.20
for he said, 'T. the house of Israel 16.03
good for this cursing of me t." 16.12
"You are not to carry tidings t.; 18.20
but t. you shall carry no tidings, 18.20
"You have t. covered with shame the 19.05
made it clear t. that commanders 19.06
for t. I perceive that if Absalom 19.06
alive and all of us were dead t., 19.06
to this people t. and serve them, 1Ki 12.07
cut off the house of Jeroboam t. 14.14
will surely show myself to him t." 18.15
you know that t. the LORD will 2Ki 2.03
you know that t. the LORD will 2.05
he said, "Why will you go to him t.? 4.23
your son, that we may eat him t., 6.28
of Shaphat remains on his shoulders t." 6.31
and my ordinances, as he is t.' 1Ch 28.07
consecrating himself t. to the LORD?" 29.05
and give success to thy servant t., Neh 1.11
"T. also my complaint is bitter, his Job 23.02
"You are my son, t. I have begotten you. Ps 2.07
O that t. you would hearken to his 95.07
and t. I have paid my vows; Pro 7.14
them known to you t., even to you. 22.19
before t. you have never heard of Is 48.07
from the days of Josiah until t. Jer 36.02
I release you t. from the chains on 40.04
t. I declare that I will restore to Zec 9.12
which t. is alive and tomorrow is Mt 6.30

TODAY (cont.)
the morning, 'It will be stormy t., Mt 16.03
go and work in the vineyard t.' 21.28
much over him t. in a dream." 27.19
"T. this scripture has been fulfilled Lk 4.21
"We have seen strange things t." 5.26
in the field t. and tomorrow is 12.28
and perform cures t. and tomorrow, 13.32
go on my way t. and tomorrow and 13.33
for I must stay at your house t." 19.05
"T. salvation has come to this 19.09
saying, "Would that even t. you knew 19.42
to him, "Before the cock crows t., 22.61
t. you will be with me in Paradise." 23.43
being examined t. concerning a Ac 4.09
'Thou art my Son, t. I have begotten thee.' 13.33
of being charged with rioting t., 19.40
make my defense t. against all the 26.02
"T. is the fourteenth day that you 27.33
t. I have begotten thee"? Or again, Heb 1.05
"T., when you hear his voice, 3.07
day, as long as it is called "t.," 3.13
"T., when you hear his voice do not 3.15
"T.," saying through David so long 4.07
"T., when you hear his voice, do not 4.07
"Thou art my Son, t. I have begotten thee"; 5.05
same yesterday and t. and for ever. 13.08
"T. or tomorrow we will go into Jas 4.13

TOE
on the great t. of his right foot. Lev 8.23
on the great t. of his right foot. 14.14
on the great t. of his right foot, 14.17
on the great t. of his right foot. 14.25
and the great t. of his right foot, 14.28

TOES
upon the great t. of their right Ex 29.20
on the great t. of their right Lev 8.24
off his thumbs and his great t. Ju 1.06
and their great t. cut off used to 1.07
and six t. on each foot, twenty-four 2Sa 21.20
and six t. on each foot, twenty-four 1Ch 20.06
the feet and t. partly of potter's Dan 2.41
And as the t. of the feet were 2.42

TOGARMAH
Gomer: Ashkenaz, Riphath, and T. Gen 10.03
Gomer: Ashkenaz, Diphath, and T. 1Ch 1.06

TOGETHER
be gathered t. into one place, Gen 1.09
were gathered t. he called Seas. 1.10
fig leaves t. and made themselves 3.07
they went forth t. from Ur of the 11.31
support both of them dwelling t.; 13.06
that they could not dwell t., 13.06
So they went both of them t. 22.06
So they went both of them t. 22.08
arose and went t. to Beersheba; 22.19
The children struggled t. within her; 25.22
for the animals to be gathered t.; 29.07
all the flocks are gathered t., 29.08
So Laban gathered t. all the men of 29.22
too great for them to dwell t.; 36.07
And he put them all t. in prison 42.17
t. with his daughter Dinah; 46.15
and said, "Gather yourselves t., 49.01
two Hebrews were struggling t.; Ex 2.13
and gather the elders of Israel t., 3.16
and gathered t. all the elders of 4.29
And they gathered them t. in heaps, 8.14
the people answered t. and said, 19.08
"When men strive t., and hurt a 21.22
couple the tent t. that it may be 26.11
in each frame, for fitting t.; 26.17
edges, that it may be joined t. 28.07
gathered themselves t. to Aaron, 32.01
Levi gathered themselves t. to him. 32.26
couple the tent t. that it might 36.18
had two tenons, for fitting t.; 36.22
assembled the whole congregation t., Num 1.18
t. with the breast that is waved 6.20
the assembly is to be gathered t., 10.07
of the sea be gathered t. for them, 11.22
that are gathered t. against me: 14.35
themselves t. against Moses and 16.03
all your company have gathered t.; 16.11
t. with their wives, their sons, and 16.27
themselves t. against Moses and 20.02
the assembly t. before the rock, 20.10
to Moses, "Gather the people t., 21.16
He gathered all his men t., 21.23
Balaam, and he struck his hands t.; 24.10
swallowed them up t. with Korah, 26.10
themselves t. against the LORD in 27.03
t. with Phinehas the son of Eleazar 31.06
t. with all the Arabah on the east Deu 4.49
not plow with an ox and an ass t. 22.10
a mingled stuff, wool and linen t. 22.11
"If brothers dwell t., and one of 25.05
all the tribes of Israel t. 33.05
city were called t. to pursue them, Jos 8.16
they gathered t. with one accord to 9.02
and encamped t. at the waters of 11.05
t. with the towns which were set 16.09
t. with all the villages round 19.08
and the people of the East came t., Ju 6.33
the citizens of Shechem came t., 9.06
Tower of Shechem were gathered t. 9.47
and the people of Israel came t., 10.17
Sihon gathered all his people t., 11.20
two men sat and ate and drank t.; 19.06
Benjaminites came t. out of the 20.14
who t. built up the house of Israel. Ru 4.11
and gathered t. all the lords of 1Sa 5.08
and gathered t. all the lords of 5.11
Israel gathered t. and came to 8.04
the people t. to the LORD at 10.17
that no two of them were left t. 11.11
me a man, that we may fight t." 17.10
t. with the woman, urged him; 28.23
all his men, on the same day t. 31.06
so they fell down t. Therefore that 2Sa 2.16
gathered themselves t. behind Abner, 2.25
he had gathered all the people t., 2.30
t. with the silver and gold which 8.11
they gathered themselves t. 10.15
David, he gathered all Israel t., 10.17
his servants were whispering t., 12.19
gather the rest of the people t., 12.28
all the people t. and went to 12.29
me and my son t. from the heritage 14.16
men of Judah t. to me within three 20.04
and the seven of them perished t. 21.09
David went down t. with his 21.15
Philistines gathered t. at Lehi, 23.11
t. with the servants of Solomon; 1K 9.27
gathered t. chariots and horsemen; 10.26
t. with certain Edomites of his 11.17
the prophets t. at Mount Carmel. 18.20
of Syria gathered all his army t.; 20.01
of Israel gathered the prophets t., 22.06
the kings have surely fought t., 2Ki 3.23
t. with all the produce of the 8.06
t. with the elders and the guardians, 10.05
t. with the rest of the multitude, 25.11
sons and all his house died t. 1Ch 10.06
Israel gathered t. to David at 11.01
t. with all Israel, to make him king, 11.10
lands, that they may come t. to us. 13.02
And David gathered t. the sons of 15.04
t. with the silver and gold which 18.11
David, he gathered all Israel t., 19.17

TOGETHER (cont.)
to gather t. the aliens who were 1Ch 22.02
t. with the palace officials, the 28.01
Solomon gathered t. chariots and 2Ch 1.14
of the cherubim t. extended twenty 3.11
went to Ophir t. with the servants 8.18
of Israel gathered the prophets t., 18.05
t. with fortified cities in Judah; 21.03
And Ahaz gathered t. the vessels of 28.24
people came t. in Jerusalem to 30.13
assembly agreed t. to keep the 30.23
gathered them t. to him in the 32.06
and gathered t. all the elders of 34.29
The whole assembly t. was forty-two Ez 2.64
t. with the rest of their brethren, 3.08
t. took the oversight of the workmen 3.09
Levites had purified themselves t.; 6.20
wall was joined t. to half its Neh 4.06
all plotted t. to come and fight 4.08
and let us meet t. in one of the 6.02
come, and let us take counsel t." 6.07
"Let us meet t. in the house of God, 6.10
The whole assembly t. was forty-two 7.66
came t. to Ezra the scribe in order 8.13
gathered t. from the circuit round 12.28
I gathered them t. and set them in 13.11
were gathered t. the second time, Est 2.19
am invited by her t. with the king. 5.12
an appointment t. to come to Job 2.11
There the prisoners are at east t.; 3.18
that we should come to trial t. 9.32
and knit me t. with bones and 10.11
I could join words t. against you, 16.04
they mass themselves t. against me. 16.10
shall we descend t. into the dust? 17.16
His troops come on t.; they have cast 19.12
under the nettles they huddle t. 30.07
me, and its furrows have wept t.; 31.38
all flesh would perish t., and man would 34.15
when the morning stars sang t., 38.07
mass and the clods cleave fast t.? 38.38
Hide them all in the dust t.; 40.13
sinews of his thighs are knit t. 40.17
The folds of his flesh cleave t., 41.23
and the rulers take counsel t., Ps 2.02
as they scheme t. against me, 31.13
me, and let us exalt his name t.! 34.03
glee, they gathered t. against me; 35.15
All who hate me whisper t. about me; 41.07
kings assembled, they came on t. 48.04
both low and high, rich and poor t.! 49.02
We used to hold sweet converse t.; 55.14
They band themselves t., they link, 56.06
they are t. lighter than a breath. 62.09
they shout and sing t. for joy. 65.13
who watch for my life consult t., 71.10
they consult t. against thy protected 83.03
all day long; they close in upon me t. 88.17
They band t. against the life of 94.21
hands; let the hills sing for joy t. 98.08
when peoples gather t., and kingdoms 102.22
a city which is bound firmly t., 122.03
didst knit me t. in my mother's 139.13
Let the wicked t. fall into their 141.10
Young men and maidens t., old men and 148.12
The rich and the poor meet t.; Pro 22.02
poor man and the oppressor meet t.; 29.13
and a time to gather stones t.; Ec 3.05
Again, if two lie t., they are warm; 4.11
let us reason t., says the LORD: Is 1.18
and sinners shall be destroyed t., 1.28
and both of them shall burn t., 1.31
Take counsel t., but it will come 8.10
and t. they are against Judah. 9.21
and the lion and the fatling t., 11.06
their young shall lie down t.; 11.07
and t. they shall plunder the 11.14
kingdoms, of nations gathering t.! 13.04
All your rulers have fled t., 22.03
heavens languish t. with the earth. 24.04
be gathered t. as prisoners in a 24.22
low his pride t. with the skill of 25.11
them, I would burn them up t. 27.04
fall, and they will all perish t. 31.03
and all flesh shall see it t., 40.05
let us t. draw near for judgment. 41.01
cypress, the plane and the pine t.; 41.19
may consider and understand t., 41.20
Let all the nations gather t., 43.09
me in remembrance, let us argue t.; 43.26
they shall be put to shame t. 44.11
makers of idols go in confusion t. 45.16
draw near t., you survivors of the 45.20
let them take counsel t.! Who told this 45.21
they bow down t., they cannot save 46.02
call to them, they stand forth t. 48.13
Let us stand up t. Who is my 50.08
t. they sing for joy; for eye to eye 52.08
Break forth t. into singing, you 52.09
they all gather t., they come to you, 60.04
iniquities t., says the LORD; 65.07
The wolf and the lamb shall feed t., 65.25
come to an end t., says the LORD. 66.17
and t. they shall come from the Jer 3.18
others, their fields and wives t.; 6.12
fathers and sons t., neighbor and friend 6.21
Gather t., let us go into the 8.14
fathers and sons t., says the LORD. 13.14
will bring them t. into the midst 21.04
t. with the princes of Judah, the 24.01
and her who is in travail, t.; 31.08
its cities shall dwell there t., 31.24
they ate bread t. there at Mizpah, 41.01
against warrior; they have both fallen t." 46.12
yea, they have turned and fled t., 46.21
yourselves t. and come against her, 49.14
the people of Judah shall come t., 50.04
"They shall roar t. like lions; 51.38
t. with the rest of the artisans. 52.15
by his hand they were fastened t.; Lam 1.14
wall to lament, they languish t. 2.08
strike my hands t. at the dishonest Eze 22.13
people who talk t. about you by 33.30
and the bones came t., bone to its bone. 37.07
and join them t. into one stick, 37.17
t. with a hin of oil to each ephah. 46.05
t. with a hin of oil to each ephah. 46.07
t. with a hin of oil to an ephah. 46.11
holy porton t. with the property 48.20
all t. were broken in pieces, and Dan 2.35
marriage, but they will not hold t., 2.43
gathered t. and saw that the fire 3.27
gave way, and his knees knocked t. 5.06
over to it t. with the continual 8.12
of Israel shall be gathered t., Hos 1.11
man, so the priests are banded t.; 6.09
into exile, he and his princes t., Amo 1.15
"Do two walk t., unless they have 3.03
I will set them t. like sheep in a Mic 2.12
of this soul; thus they weave it t. 7.03
Come t. and hold assembly, O shameless Zep 2.01
at the time when I gather you t.; 3.20
T. they shall be like mighty men in Zec 10.05
the earth will come t. against it. 12.03
they came t. she was found to be Mt 1.18
Let both grow t. until the harvest; 13.30
What therefore God has joined t., 19.06
the Sadducees, they came t. 22.34
the Pharisees were gathered t., 22.41
your children t. as a hen gathers 23.37
the eagles will be gathered t. 24.28
and took counsel t. in order to 26.04
was gathered t. about the door. Mk 1.33
And many were gathered t., so that there 2.02
and the crowd came t. again, so that they 3.20

TOGETHER (cont.)
the Pharisees gathered t. to him, Mk 7.01
saw that a crowd came running t., 9.25
What therefore God has joined t., 10.09
and they called t. the whole 15.16
shaken t., running over, will be put Lk 6.38
crowd came t. and people from town 8.04
the twelve t. and gave them power 9.01
had gathered t. that they trod 12.01
your children t. as a hen gathers 13.34
he calls t. his friends and his 15.06
she calls t. her friends and 15.09
There will be two women grinding t.; 17.35
the eagles will be gathered t. 17.37
of the courtyard and sat down t., 22.55
elders of the people gathered t., 22.66
Pilate then called t. the chief 23.13
But they all cried out t., "Away with 23.18
were talking and discussing t., 24.15
eleven gathered t. and those who 24.33
sower and reaper may rejoice t., Jn 4.36
the temple, were all Jews come t.; 18.20
others of his disciples were t. 21.02
So when they had come t., they asked him, Ac 1.06
t. with the women and Mary the 1.14
they were all t. in one place. 2.01
this sound the multitude came t., 2.06
believed were t. and had all 2.44
the temple t. and breaking bread 2.46
the people ran t. to them in the 3.11
were gathered t. in Jerusalem, 4.05
their voices t. to God and said, 4.24
and the rulers were gathered t., 4.26
were gathered t. against thy holy 4.27
they were gathered t. was shaken; 4.31
you have agreed t. to tempt the 5.09
they were all t. in Solomon's 5.12
him and called t. the council and 5.21
their ears and rushed t. upon him. 7.57
and had called t. his kinsmen and 10.24
were gathered t. and were praying. 12.12
city gathered t. to hear the word 13.44
they entered t. into the Jewish 14.01
the church t. and declared all 14.27
were gathered t. to consider this 15.06
gathered the congregation t., 15.30
spoke to the women who had come t. 16.13
t. with all his household; 18.08
their books t. and burned them in 19.19
These he gathered t., with the workmen 19.25
and they rushed t. into the theater, 19.29
did not know why they had come t. 19.32
we were gathered t. to break bread, 20.07
was aroused, and the people ran t.; 21.30
When therefore they came t. here, 25.17
days he called t. the local leaders 28.17
t. they have gone wrong; no one Rom 3.12
groaning in travail t. until now; 8.22
that t. you may with one voice 15.06
to strive t. with me in your 15.30
to be saints t. with all those who 1Co 1.02
but then come t. again, lest Satan 7.05
when you come t. it is not for the 11.17
When you meet t., it is not the 11.20
when you come t. to eat, wait for 11.33
lest you come t. to be condemned. 11.34
If one member suffers, all suffer t.; 12.26
member is honored, all rejoice t. 12.26
When you come t., each one has a 14.26
t. with the church in their house, 16.19
Working t. with him, then, we entreat 2Co 6.01
to die t. and to live t. 7.03
made us alive t. with Christ (by Eph 2.05
is joined t. and grows into a holy 2.21
joined and knit t. by every joint 4.16
in the gospel t. with Clement and Php 4.03
and in him all things hold t. Col 1.17
as they are knit t. in love, 2.02
flesh, God made alive t. with him, 2.13
and knit t. through its joints and 2.19
everything t. in perfect harmony. 3.14
be caught up t. with them in the 1Th 4.17
not neglecting to meet t., Heb 10.25
and we will talk t. face to face. 3Jn 1.14
feasts, as they boldly carouse t., Jud 1.12
for one hour, t. with the beast. Rev 17.12

TOHU
son of T., son of Zuph, an Ephraimite 1Sa 1.01

TOIL
in t. you shall eat of it all the Gen 3.17
work and from the t. of our hands. 5.29
our t., and our oppression; Deu 26.07
make the whole people t. up there, Jos 7.03
and made them t. at the brickkilns; 2Sa 12.31
will give back the fruit of his t., Job 20.18
desert they go forth to their t., 24.05
their span is but t. and trouble; Ps 90.10
of the fruit of the peoples' t., 105.44
plunder the fruits of his t.! 109.11
eating the bread of anxious t.; 127.02
In all t. there is profit, but mere Pro 14.23
Do not t. to acquire wealth; 23.04
gain by all the t. at which he Ecc 1.03
heart found pleasure in all my t., 2.10
this was my reward for all my t. 2.10
done and the t. I had spent in 2.11
I hated all my t. in which I had 2.18
over all the t. of my labors under 2.20
by a man who did not t. for it. 2.21
from all the t. and strain with 2.22
and find enjoyment in his t. 2.24
What gain has the worker from his t.? 3.09
and take pleasure in all his t. 3.13
Then I saw that all t. and all 4.04
hands full of t. and a striving 4.06
yet there is no end to all his t., 4.08
have a good reward for their t. 4.09
and shall take nothing for his t., 5.15
in all the t. with which one toils 5.18
lot and find enjoyment in his t.— 5.19
All the t. of man is for his mouth, 6.07
with him in his t. through the 8.15
However much man may t. in seeking, 8.17
and in your t. at which you t. under the sun. 9.09
The t. of a fool wearies him, so 10.15
from the womb to see t. and sorrow, Jer 20.18
products of your t. with blight and Hag 2.17
they grow; they neither t. nor spin; Mt 6.28
they grow; they neither t. nor spin; Lk 12.27
in t. and hardship, through many a 2Co 11.27
For this I t., striving with all Col 1.29
remember our labor and t., brethren; 1Th 2.09
but with t. and labor we worked 2Th 3.08
For to this end we t. and strive, 1Ti 4.10
your t. and your patient endurance, Rev 2.02

TOILED
in which I had t. under the sun, Ecc 2.18
all for which I t. and used my 2.19
a man who has t. with wisdom and 2.21
has he that he t. for the wind, 5.16
we t. all night and took nothing! Lk 5.05

TOILING
"For whom am I t. and depriving Ecc 4.08
you that by so t. one must help Ac 20.35

TOILS
he is caught in the t. of his sin. Pro 5.22
toil at which he t. under the sun? Ecc 1.03
with which he t. beneath the sun? 2.22
with which one t. under the sun 5.18

TOKEN
fare, and bring some t. from them. 1Sa 17.18

TOKENS
find in her the t. of virginity.' Deu 22.14
bring out the t. of her virginity 22.15
your daughter the t. of virginity." 22.17
these are the t. of my daughter's 22.17
that the t. of virginity were not 22.20

TOKHATH
the wife of Shallum the son of T., 2Ch 34.22

TOLA
T., Puvah, Iob, and Shimron. Gen 46.13
of T., the family of the Tolaites; Num 26.23
deliver Israel T. the son of Puah, Ju 10.01
T., Puah, Jashub, and Shimron, four. 1Ch 7.01
The sons of T.: Uzzi, Rephaiah, Jeriel, 7.02
namely of T., mighty warriors of 7.02

TOLAD
Bilhah, Ezem, T., 1Ch 4.29

TOLAITES
of Tola, the family of the T.; Num 26.23

TOLD
He said, "Who t. you that you were Gen 3.11
and t. his two brothers outside. 9.22
Abram went, as the LORD had t. him; 12.04
and t. Abram the Hebrew, who was 14.13
and t. them all these things; 20.08
the place of which God had t. him. 22.03
the place of which God had t. him, 22.09
these things it was t. Abraham, 22.20
maiden ran and t. her mother's 24.28
not eat until I have t. my errand." 24.33
And the servant t. Isaac all the 24.66
came and t. him about the well 26.32
I have done as you t. me; now sit up 27.19
her older son were t. to Rebekah; 27.42
And Jacob t. Rachel that he was her 29.12
and she ran and t. her father. 29.12
Jacob t. Laban all these things, 29.13
When it was t. Laban on the third 31.22
and when he t. it to his brothers 37.05
and t. it to his brothers, and said, 37.09
But when he t. it to his father and 37.10
And when Tamar was t., "Your father-in-law 38.13
About three months later Judah was t., 38.24
and she t. him the same story, 39.17
chief butler t. his dream to 40.09
and Pharaoh t. them his dream, but 41.08
and when we t. him, he interpreted 41.12
And I t. it to the magicians, but 41.24
It is as I t. Pharaoh, God has shown 41.28
they t. him all that had befallen 42.29
What we t. him was in answer to 43.07
And he did as Joseph t. him. 44.02
my father we t. him the words of 44.24
And they t. him, "Joseph is still 45.26
But when they t. him all the words 45.27
So Joseph went in and t. Pharaoh, 47.01
After this Joseph was t., 48.01
And it was t. to Jacob, "Your son 48.02
And Moses t. Aaron all the words of Ex 4.28
had also done as Moses t. them, 12.35
of Egypt was t. that the people 14.05
congregation came and t. Moses, 16.22
So Joshua did as Moses t. him, 17.10
And when one t. Moses, "Lo, your 18.06
Then Moses t. his father-in-law all 18.08
Then Moses t. the words of the 19.09
down to the people and t. them. 19.25
Moses came and t. the people all 24.03
and t. the people of Israel that he 34.34
So Moses t. the people of Israel Num 9.04
went out and t. the people the 11.24
And a young man ran and t. Moses, 11.27
And they t. him, "We came to the 13.27
And Moses t. these words to all the 14.39
And Moses t. the people of Israel 29.40
God of your fathers, has t. you; Deu 1.21
of the Red Sea, as the LORD t. me; 2.01
and it is t. you and you hear of it; 17.04
And it was t. the king of Jericho, Jos 2.02
and they t. him all that had 2.23
of Israel, as the LORD t. Joshua; 4.08
"Because it was t. to your servants 9.24
And it was t. Joshua, "The five 10.17
When Sisera was t. that Barak the Ju 4.12
and did as the LORD had t. him; 6.27
When it was t. to Jotham, he went 9.07
along that way; and it was t. Abimelech. 9.25
into the fields, and Abimelech was t. 9.42
Abimelech was t. that all the 9.47
Then the woman came and t. her husband, 13.06
ran in haste and t. her husband, 13.10
and t. his father and mother, "I saw 14.02
and you have not t. me what it is." 14.16
I have not t. my father nor my 14.16
and on the seventh day he t. her, Then she t. 14.17
to those who had t. the riddle. 14.19
The Gazites were t., "Samson has come 16.02
you have mocked me, and t. me lies; 16.10
you have mocked me, and t. me lies; 16.13
you have not t. me wherein your 16.15
And he t. her all his mind, and said 16.17
saw that he had t. her all his 16.18
for he has t. me all his mind." 16.18
your husband has been fully t. me, Ru 2.11
So she t. her mother-in-law with 2.19
as her mother-in-law had t. her. 3.06
Then she t. her all that the man 3.16
said, "What was it that he t. you? 1Sa 3.17
from me of all that he t. you." 3.17
So Samuel t. him everything and hid 3.18
came into the city and t. the news, 4.13
man hastened and came and t. Eli. 4.14
So Samuel t. all the words of the 8.10
the LORD t. him, "Here is the man of 9.17
"He t. us plainly that the asses 10.16
Then Samuel t. the people the 10.25
So they t. him the tidings of the 11.05
came and t. the men of Jabesh, they 11.09
Then they t. Saul, "Behold, the 14.33
And Jonathan t. him, "I tasted a 14.43
and it was t. Samuel, "Saul came to 15.12
and they t. Saul, and the thing 18.20
And the servants of Saul t. him, 18.24
his servants t. David these words, 18.26
And Jonathan t. David, "Saul my 19.02
t. him, "If you do not save your 19.11
and t. him all that Saul had done 19.18
And it was t. Saul, "Behold, David is 19.19
When it was t. Saul, he sent other 19.21
And Abithar t. David that Saul had 22.21
Now they t. David, "Behold, the 23.01
Now it was t. Saul that David had 23.07
When Saul was t. that David had 23.13
for it is t. me that he is very 23.22
And David was t.; therefore he went 23.25
he was t., "Behold, David is in the 24.01
and came back and t. him all this. 25.12
But one of the young men t. Abigail, 25.14
so she t. him nothing at all until 25.36
his wife t. him these things, and 25.37
And when it was t. Saul that Davd 27.04
said to the young man who t. him, 2Sa 1.05
And the young man who t. him said, 1.06
said to the young man who t. him, 1.13
When they t. David, "It was the men 2.04
it was t. Joab, "Abner the son of 3.23
when one t. me, 'Behold, Saul is dead, 4.10
And it was t. King David, "The LORD 6.12

TOLD (cont.)

When it was t. David, he sent to 2Sa 10.05
And when it was t. David, 10.17
and she sent and t. David, 11.05
When they t. David, "Uriah did not 11.10
Then Joab sent and t. David all the 11.18
and came and t. David all that Joab 11.22
Then Joab went to the king, and t. him; 14.33
And it was t. David, "Ahithophel is 15.31
But a lad saw them, and t. Absalom; 17.18
well, and went and t. King David. 17.21
and t. Joab, "Behold, I saw Absalom 18.10
Joab said to the man who t. him, 18.11
watchman called out and t. the king. 18.25
It was t. Joab, "Behold, the king is 19.01
And the people were all t., 19.08
When David was t. what Rizpah the 21.11
So Gad came to David and t. him, 24.13
And they t. the king, "Here is 1Ki 1.23
you have not t. your servants who 1.27
And it was t. Solomon, "Behold, 1.51
And when it was t. King Solomon 2.29
And when it was t. Shimei, 2.39
Solomon was t. that Shimei had 2.41
she t. him all that was on her mind. 10.02
behold, the half was not t. me; 10.07
sons came and t. him all that the 13.11
to the king, they t. to their father. 13.11
they came and t. it in the city 13.25
Has it not been t. my lord what I 18.13
went to meet Ahab, and t. him; 18.16
Ahab t. Jezebel all that Elijah had 19.01
to meet you and t. you these 2Ki 1.07
She came and t. the man of God, and 4.07
it from me, and has not t. me. 4.27
and t. him, "The child has not 4.31
So Naaman went in and t. his lord, 5.04
of which the man of God t. him. 6.10
It was t. him, "Behold, he is in 6.13
and t. them, "We came to the camp of 7.10
and it was t. within the king's 7.11
messengers returned, and t. the king. 7.15
king asked the woman, she t. him. 8.06
and when it was t. him, "The man of God 8.07
"He t. me that you would certainly 8.14
When they came back and t. him, 9.36
When the messenger came and t. him, 10.08
So the king of Assyria was t., 17.26
and t. him the words of the Rabshakeh. 18.37
Then Shaphan the secretary t. the king, 22.10
And the men of the city t. him, 23.17
When David was t. concerning the 1Ch 19.05
And when it was t. David, 19.17
she t. him all that was on her mind. 2Ch 9.01
of your wisdom was not t. me; 9.06
Some men came and t. Jehoshaphat, 20.02
Then Shaphan the secretary t. the king, 34.18
the governor t. them that they were Ez 2.63
since we had t. the king, "The 8.22
and I t. no one what my God had put Neh 2.12
and I had not yet t. the Jews, 2.16
And I t. them of the hand of my God 2.18
the governor t. them that they were 7.65
and they t. Ezra the scribe to 8.01
thou hadst t. their fathers to 9.23
he t. it to Queen Esther, and Esther t. Est 2.22
they t. Haman, in order to see 3.04
for he had t. them that he was a 3.04
and her eunuchs came and t. her, 4.04
and Mordecai t. him all that had 4.07
went and t. Esther what Mordecai 4.09
And they t. Mordecai what Esther 4.12
Then Mordecai t. them to return 4.13
Then Esther t. them to reply to 4.15
Mordecai had t. about Bigthana and 6.02
So the king's servants t. him, 6.05
And Haman t. his wife Zeresh and 6.13
for Esther had t. what he was to 8.01
(what wise men have t., and their fathers Job 15.18
Shall it be t. him that I would 37.20
and did what the LORD had t. them; 42.09
I have t. the glad news of deliverance Ps 40.09
O God, our fathers have t. us, 44.01
known, that our fathers have t. us. 78.03
When I t. of my ways, thou didst 119.26
for it is better to be t., "Come up here," Pro 25.07
live a thousand years twice t., Ecc 6.06
When the house of David was t., Is 7.02
A stern vision is t. to me; 21.02
and t. him the words of the Rabshakeh. 36.22
Has it not been t. you from the 40.21
have I not t. you from of old and 44.08
Who t. this long ago? Who declared it 45.21
has not been t. them they shall 52.15
And Micaiah t. them all the words Jer 36.13
And I t. the exiles all the things Eze 11.25
and t. them to seek mercy of the Dan 2.18
and I t. them the dream, but they 4.07
and I t. him the dream, saying, 4.08
and t. the sum of the matter. 7.01
and it was t., 'Arise, devour much 7.05
So he t. me, and made known to me 7.16
mornings which has been t. is true; 8.26
the LORD, because he had t. them. Jon 1.10
that you would not believe if t. Hab 1.05
They t. him, "In Bethlehem of Judea; Mt 2.05
into the city they t. everything, 8.33
Some one t. him, "Your mother and * 12.47
But he replied to the man who t. him, 12.48
And he t. them many things in parables, 13.03
He t. them another parable. "The 13.33
buried it; and they went and t. Jesus. 14.12
Then Jesus t. his disciples, "If any 16.24
Lo, I have t. you beforehand. 24.25
done will be t. in memory of her." 26.13
you will see him. Lo, I will have t. you." 28.07
the city and t. the chief priests 28.11
and immediately they t. him of her. Mk 1.30
And he t. his disciples to have a 3.09
and t. it in the city and in the 5.14
who had seen it t. what had happened 5.16
before him, and t. him the whole truth. 5.33
and t. them to give her something 5.43
and t. him all that they had done 6.30
And they t. him, "John the Baptist; 8.28
And they t. them what Jesus had 11.06
that he had t. the parable against 12.12
I have t. you all things beforehand 13.23
done will be t. in memory of her." 14.09
and found it as he had t. them; 14.16
you will see him, as he t. you." 16.07
those with him all that they had been t. * 16.08
and t. those who had been with him, * 16.10
and t. the rest, but they did not * 16.13
which had been t. them concerning Lk 2.17
at what the shepherds t. them. 2.18
and seen, as it had been t. them. 2.20
He t. them a parable also: "No one 5.36
He also t. them a parable: "Can a 6.39
disciples of John t. him of all 7.18
And he was t., "Your mother and 8.20
and t. it in the city and in the 8.34
who had seen it t. them how he who 8.36
the apostles t. him what they had 9.10
silence and t. no one in those 9.36
And he t. them a parable, saying, 12.16
very time who t. him of the 13.01
And he t. this parable: "A man had a 13.06
Now he t. a parable to those who 14.07
So he t. them this parable: 15.03
And he t. them a parable, to the 18.01
He also t. this parable to some who 18.09
They t. him, "Jesus of Nazareth is 18.37
and found it as he had t. them. 19.32
that he had t. this parable 20.19

TOLD (cont.)
And he t. them a parable: "Look at Lk 21.29
and found it as he had t. them; 22.13
Remember how he t. you, while he was 24.06
the tomb they t. all this to the 24.09
with them who t. this to the 24.10
Then they t. what had happened on 24.35
And he t. those who sold the Jn 2.16
If I have t. you earthly things and 3.12
see a man who t. me all that I ever 4.29
"He t. me all that I ever did." 4.39
met him and t. him that his son 4.51
went away and t. the Jews that it 5.15
he t. his disciples, "Gather up the 6.12
"This is why I t. you that no one 6.65
I t. you that you would die in your 8.24
what I have t. you from the 8.25
a man who has t. you the truth 8.40
"I have t. you already, and you 9.27
"I t. you, and you do not believe. 10.25
Then Jesus t. them plainly, "Lazarus 11.14
Pharisees and t. them what Jesus 11.46
Philip went and t. Andrew; 12.22
went with Philip and they t. Jesus. 12.22
would I have t. you that I go to 14.02
And now I have t. you before it 14.29
may remember that I t. you of them. 16.04
"I t. you that I am he; so if you seek me, 18.08
and t. them, "I find no crime in him 18.38
and she t. them that he had said 20.18
So the other disciples t. him, 20.25
And some one came and t. them, Ac 5.25
scripture he t. him the good news 8.35
and you will be t. what you are to 9.06
And the Spirit t. me to go with 11.12
And he t. us how he had seen the 11.13
but ran in and t. that Peter was 12.14
things might be t. them the next 13.42
the Spirit they t. Paul not to go 21.04
and they have been t. about you 21.21
they have been t. about you but 21.24
you will be t. all that is appointed 22.10
entered the barracks and t. Paul. 23.16
will be exactly as I have been t. 27.25
as he had been t., "So shall your Rom 4.18
she was t., "The elder will serve 9.12
see who have never been t. of him, 15.21
as he t. us of your longing, your 2Co 7.07
and he heard things that cannot be t., 12.04
I have often t. you and now tell Php 3.18
we t. you beforehand that we were 1Th 3.04
I was still with you I t. you this? 2Th 2.05
white robe and t. to rest a little Rev 6.11
they were t. not to harm the grass 9.04
the angel and t. him to give me 10.09
And I was t., "You must again 10.11
and I was t.: "Rise and measure the 11.01

TOLERABLE
shall be more t. on the day of Mt 10.15
shall be more t. on the day of 11.22
shall be more t. on the day of 11.24
shall be more t. on that day for Lk 10.12
shall be more t. in the judgment 10.14

TOLERATE
for the king's profit to t. them. Est 3.08
that you t. the woman Jezebel, who Rev 2.20

TOLL
or t., and the royal revenue will Ez 4.13
tribute, custom, and t. were paid. 4.20
or t. upon any one of the priests, 7.24
of the earth take t. or tribute? Mt 17.25

TOMB
it is the pillar of Rachel's t., Gen 35.20
in my t. which I hewed out for 50.05
buried in the t. of Joash his Ju 8.32
Eshtaol in the t. of Manoah his 16.31
men by Rachel's t. in the territory 1Sa 10.02
buried him in the t. of his father, 2Sa 2.32
it in the t. of Abner at Hebron. 4.12
was buried in the t. of his father. 17.23
in the t. of Kish his father; and they did 21.14
not come to the t. of your fathers.'" 1Ki 13.22
him in his t. with his fathers in 2Ki 9.28
buried in his t. in the garden of 21.26
"It is the t. of the man of God who 23.17
and buried him in his own t. 23.30
him in the t. which he had hewn 2Ch 16.14
grave, watch is kept over his t. Job 21.32
lie in glory, each in his own t.; Is 14.18
have hewn here a t. for yourself, 22.16
you who hew a t. on the height, and 22.16
Their quiver is like an open t., Jer 5.16
and laid it in his own new t., Mt 27.60
the door of the t., and departed. 27.60
from the t. wth fear and great 28.08
took his body, and laid it in a t. Mk 6.29
laid him in a t. which had been 15.46
a stone against the door of the t. 15.46
went to the t. when the sun had 16.02
for us from the door of the t.?" 16.03
And entering the t., they saw a 16.05
they went out and fled from the t.; 16.08
and laid him in a rock-hewn t., Lk 23.53
and saw the t., and how his body 23.55
at early dawn, they went to the t., 24.01
the stone rolled away from the t., 24.02
from the t. they told all this to 24.09
But Peter rose and ran to the t.; * 24.12
were at the t. early in the 24.22
who were with us went to the t., 24.24
already been in the t. four days. Jn 11.17
was going to the t. to weep there. 11.31
deeply moved again, came to the t.; 11.38
out of the t. and raised him from 12.17
garden a new t. where no one had 19.41
as the t. was close at hand, they 19.42
Magdalene came to the t. early, 20.01
had been taken away from the t. 20.01
have taken the Lord out of the t., 20.02
and they went toward the t. 20.03
Peter and reached the t. first; 20.04
him, and he went into the t.; 20.06
disciple, who reached the t. first, 20.08
But Mary stood weeping outside the t., 20.11
she stooped to look into the t.; 20.11
and his t. is with us to this day. Ac 2.29
and laid in the t. that Abraham 7.16
the tree, and laid him in a t. 13.29
to let them be placed in a t., Rev 11.09

TOMBS
in rocks and in t. and in cisterns, 1Sa 13.06
he saw the t. there on the mount; 2Ki 23.16
and took the bones out of the t., 23.16
but not in the t. of the kings. 2Ch 21.20
bury him in the t. of the kings. 24.25
him into the t. of the kings of 28.27
ascent of the t. of the sons of 32.33
buried in the t. of his fathers. 35.24
who sit in t., and spend the night Is 65.04
shall be brought out of their t.; Jer 8.01
met him, coming out of the t., Mt 8.28
for you are like whitewashed t., 23.27
you build the t. of the prophets 23.29
the t. also were opened, and many 27.52
out of the t. after his resurrection 27.53
him out of the t. a man with an Mk 5.02
who lived among the t.; and no one 5.03
day among the t. and on the 5.05
not in a house but among the t. Lk 8.27
you build the t. of the prophets 11.47

TOMBS (cont.)
them, and you build their t. Lk 11.48
who are in the t. will hear his Jn 5.28

TOMORROW
And he said, "T." Moses said, Ex 8.10
By t. shall this sign be. 8.23
servants, and from his people, T.; 8.29
"T. the LORD will do this thing in 9.05
Behold, t. about this time I will 9.18
t. I will bring locusts into your 10.04
'T. is a day of solemn rest, a holy 16.23
t. I will stand on the top of the 17.09
and consecrate them today and t., 19.10
"T. shall be a feast to the LORD. 32.05
'Consecrate yourselves for t., Num 11.18
turn t. and set out for the wilderness 14.25
upon them before the LORD t., 16.07
LORD, you and they, and Aaron, t.; 16.16
for t. the LORD will do wonders Jos 3.05
say, 'Sanctify yourselves for t.; 7.13
for t. at this time I will give 11.06
whole congregation of Israel t. 22.18
and t. you shall arise early in the Ju 19.09
for t. I will give them into your 20.28
"T. about this time I will send to 1Sa 9.16
'T., by the time the sun is hot, you 11.09
"T. we will give ourselves up to 11.10
life tonight, t. you will be killed." 19.11
t. is the new moon, and I should not 20.05
my father, about this time t., 20.12
"T. is the new moon; and you will be 20.18
and t. you and your sons shall be 28.19
and t. I will let you depart." 2Sa 11.12
of one of them by this time t." 1Ki 19.02
servants to you t. about this time, 20.06
today, and we will eat my son t.' 2Ki 6.28
T. about this time a measure of 7.01
about this time t. in the gate of 7.18
to me at Jezreel t. at this time." 10.06
T. go down against them; behold, they will 2Ch 20.16
t. go out against them, and the 20.17
and Haman come t. to the dinner Est 5.08
and t. I will do as the king has 5.08
And t. also I am invited by her 5.12
Susa be allowed t. also to do 9.13
t. I will give it"—when you have it Pro 3.28
Do not boast about t., for you do not 27.01
us eat and drink, for t. we die." Is 22.13
and t. will be like this day, great 56.12
is alive and t. is thrown into the Mt 6.30
"Therefore do not be anxious about t., 6.34
for t. will be anxious for itself. 6.34
field today and t. is thrown into Lk 12.28
and perform cures today and t., 13.32
way today and t. and the day 13.33
bring Paul down to the council t. Ac 23.20
"T.," said he, "you shall hear him 25.22
us eat and drink, for t. we die." 1Co 15.32
"Today or t. we will go into such Jas 4.13
whereas you do not know about t. 4.14

TONE
cried out in a t. of anguish and Dan 6.20
with you now and to change my t., Gal 4.20

TONGS
the lamps, and the t., of gold; 1Ki 7.49
and the t., of purest gold; 2Ch 4.21
had taken with t. from the altar. Is 6.06

TONGUE
But I am slow of speech and of t." Ex 4.10
a man moved his t. against any of Jos 10.21
that laps the water with his t., Ju 7.05
by me, his word is upon my t. 2Sa 23.02
be hid from the scourge of the t., Job 5.21
Is there any wrong on my t.? 6.30
you choose the t. of the crafty. 15.05
though he hides it under his t., 20.12
the t. of a viper will kill him. 20.16
and my t. will not utter deceit. 27.04
and their t. cleaved to the roof of 29.10
the t. in my mouth speaks. 33.02
or press down his t. with a cord? 41.01
sepulchre, they flatter with their t. Ps 5.09
under his t. are mischief and 10.07
the t. that makes great boasts, 12.03
"With our t. we will prevail, our 12.04
who does not slander with his t., 15.03
and my t. cleaves to my jaws; 22.15
Keep your t. from evil, and your 34.13
Then my t. shall tell of thy 35.28
wisdom, and his t. speaks justice. 37.30
that I may not sin with my t.; 39.01
then I spoke with my t.: 39.03
my t. is like the pen of a ready 45.01
evil, and your t. frames deceit. 50.19
and my t. will sing aloud of thy 51.14
Your t. is like a sharp razor, you 52.02
words that devour, O deceitful t. 52.04
Because of their t. he will bring 64.08
and he was extolled with my t. 66.17
And my t. will talk of thy righteous 71.24
and their t. struts through the 73.09
My t. will sing of thy word, for all 119.172
lying lips, from a deceitful t. 120.02
be done to you, you deceitful t.? 120.03
and our t. with shouts of joy; 126.02
Let my t. cleave to the roof of my 137.06
Even before a word is on my t., 139.04
They make their t. sharp as a 140.03
a lying t., and hands that shed Pro 6.17
from the smooth t. of the adventuress. 6.24
The t. of the righteous is choice 10.20
the perverse t. will be cut off. 10.31
but the t. of the wise brings 12.18
but a lying t. is but for a moment. 12.19
The t. of the wise dispenses 15.02
A gentle t. is a tree of life, but 15.04
answer of the t. is from the LORD. 16.01
gives heed to a mischievous t. 17.04
with a perverse t. falls into 17.20
life are in the power of the t., 18.21
by a lying t. is a fleeting vapor 21.06
mouth and his t. keeps himself out 21.23
and a soft t. will break a bone. 25.15
and a backbiting t., angry looks. 25.23
A lying t. hates its victims, and a 26.28
than he who flatters with his t. 28.23
teaching of kindness is on her t. 31.26
honey and milk are under your t.; Sol 4.11
as the t. of fire devours the Is 5.24
destroy the t. of the sea of Egypt; 11.15
with an alien t. the LORD will 28.11
and his t. is like a devouring fire; 30.27
and the t. of the stammerers will 32.04
stammering in a t. which you 33.19
and the t. of the dumb sing for joy. 35.06
and their t. is parched with thirst, 41.17
shall bow, every t. shall swear." 45.23
given me the t. of those who are 50.04
confute every t. that rises 54.17
mouth wide and put out your t.? 57.04
your t. mutters wickedness. 59.03
They bend their t. like a bow; Jer 9.03
have taught their t. to speak lies; 9.05
Their t. is a deadly arrow; 9.08
Come, let us smite him with the t., 18.18
The t. of the nursling cleaves to Lam 4.04
will make your t. cleave to the Eze 3.26
of the insolence of their t. Hos 7.16
and their t. is deceitful in their Mic 6.12
in their mouth a deceitful t. Zep 3.13
of every t. shall take hold of the Zec 8.23
and he spat and touched his t.; Mk 7.33

TONGUE (cont.)

his t. was released, and he spoke Mk 7.35
mouth was opened and his t. loosed, Lk 1.64
his finger in water and cool my t.; 16.24
heart was glad, and my t. rejoiced; Ac 2.26
and every t. shall give praise to Rom 14.11
who speaks in a t. speaks not to 1Co 14.02
He who speaks in a t. edifies 14.04
if you in a t. utter speech that is 14.09
who speaks in a t. should pray for 14.13
For if I pray in a t., my spirit prays 14.14
than ten thousand words in a t. 14.19
a revelation, a t., or an interpretation. 14.26
If any speak in a t., let there be only 14.27
and every t. confess that Jesus Php 2.11
not bridle his t. but deceives his Jas 1.26
So the t. is a little member and 3.05
the t. is a fire. The t. is an unrighteous 3.06
but no human being can tame the t.— 3.08
him keep his t. from evil and his 1Pe 3.10
every tribe and t. and people and Rev 5.09
and people and t. and nation, 13.07
nation and tribe and t. and people; 14.06

TONGUES

thy shelter from the strife of t. Ps 31.20
plans, O Lord, confuse their t.; 55.09
and arrows, their t. sharp swords. 57.04
who whet their t. like swords, who 64.03
that the t. of your dogs may have 68.23
they lied to him with their t. 78.36
speaking against me with lying t. 109.02
to gather all nations and t.; Is 66.18
who use their t. and say, 'Says the Jer 23.31
and their t. shall rot in their Zec 14.12
out demons; they will speak in new t.; * Mk 16.17
appeared to them t. as of fire, Ac 2.03
and began to speak in other t., 2.04
in our own t. the mighty works of 2.11
speaking in t. and extolling God. 10.46
they spoke with t. and prophesied. 19.06
they use their t. to deceive. Rom 3.13
to another various kinds of t., 1Co 12.10
another the interpretation of t. 12.10
speakers in various kinds of t. 12.28
Do all speak with t.? Do all interpret? 12.30
If I speak in the t. of men and of 13.01
as for t., they will cease; 13.08
Now I want you all to speak in t., 14.05
greater than he who speaks in t., 14.05
if I come to you speaking in t., 14.06
that I speak in t. more than you 14.18
men of strange t. and by the lips 14.21
Thus, t. are a sign not for believers 14.22
assembles and all speak in t., 14.23
and do not forbid speaking in t.; 14.39
from all tribes and peoples and t., Rev 7.09
and nations and t. and kings. 10.11
and tribes and t. and nations gaze 11.09
men gnawed their t. in anguish 16.10
and multitudes and nations and t. 17.15

TONIGHT

are the men who came to you t.? Gen 19.05
let us make him drink wine t. also; 19.34
lie with you t. for your son's 30.15
have come here t. to search out Jos 2.02
in the place where you lodge t.'" 4.03
winnowing barley t. at the threshing Ru 3.02
"If you do not save your life t., 1Sa 19.11
I will set out and pursue David t. 2Sa 17.01
'Do not lodge t. at the fords of 17.16

TONSURES

They shall not make t. upon their Lev 21.05

TOO

Is anything t. hard for the LORD? Gen 18.14
possessions were t. great for them 36.07
are t. many and t. mighty for us. Ex 1.09
household is t. small for a lamb, 12.04
for the thing is t. heavy for you; 18.18
Consider t. that this nation is thy 33.13
mutilated face or a limb t. long, Lev 21.18
has a part t. long or t. short you may 22.23
And if a man is t. poor to pay your 27.08
the burden is t. heavy for me. Num 11.14
said to them, "You have gone t. far! 16.03
You have gone t. far, sons of Levi!" 16.07
is it t. small a thing for you that 16.09
since they are t. mighty for me; 22.06
the case that is t. hard for you, Deu 1.17
was not a city t. high for us; 2.36
beasts grow t. numerous for you. 7.22
his name there is t. far from you, 12.21
And if the way is t. long for you, 14.24
the place is t. far from you, 14.24
towns which is t. difficult for 17.08
this day is not t. hard for you, 30.11
of Ephraim is t. narrow for you." Jos 17.15
of Judah was t. large for them, 19.09
and he t. delivered Israel. Ju 3.31
Naphtali t., on the heights of the 5.18
because he was t. afraid of his 6.27
and they t. were called out to 6.35
with you are t. many for me to 7.02
"The people are still t. many; 7.04
that they were t. strong for him, 18.26
for I am t. old to have a husband. Ru 1.12
they t. followed hard after them in 1Sa 14.22
And he t. stripped off his clothes, 19.24
and he t. prophesied before Samuel, 19.24
who were t. exhausted to cross the 30.10
who had been t. exhausted to follow 30.21
sons of Zeruiah are t. hard for me. 2Sa 3.39
the Syrians are t. strong for me, 10.11
Ammonites are t. strong for you, 10.11
and if this were t. little, I would add 12.08
for they were t. mighty for me. 22.18
the LORD was t. small to receive 1Ki 8.64
journey will be t. great for you." 19.07
empty vessels and not t. few. 2Ki 4.03
your charge is t. small for us. 6.01
the Syrians are t. strong for me, 1Ch 19.12
Ammonites are t. strong for you, 19.12
and stone t. I have provided. 22.14
priests were t. few and could not 2Ch 29.34
consolations of God t. small for you, Job 15.11
I t. was formed from a piece of 33.06
things t. wonderful for me, which I 42.03
for they were t. mighty for me. Ps 18.17
from him who is t. strong for him, 35.10
like a burden t. heavy for me. 38.04
T. long have I had my dwelling 120.06
T. long our soul has been sated 123.04
up, my eyes are not raised t. high; 131.01
with things t. great and t. marvelous 131.01
Such knowledge is t. wonderful for 139.06
for they are t. strong for me! 142.06
is wise, my heart t. will be glad. Pro 23.15
Wisdom is t. high for a fool; 24.07
Surely I am t. stupid to be a man. 30.02
Three things are t. wonderful for 30.18
Is it t. little for you to weary Is 7.13
'You t. have become as weak as we! 14.10
For the bed is t. short to stretch 28.20
the covering t. narrow to wrap 28.20
"It is t. light a thing that you 49.06
now you will be t. narrow for your 49.19
'The place is t. narrow for me; 49.20
From it t. you will come away with Jer 2.37
but she t. went and played the 3.08
a wind t. full for this comes for 4.12
iniquity and are t. weary to repent. 9.05
him from hands t. strong for him. 31.11
Nothing is t. hard for thee, 32.17
is anything t. hard for me? 32.27

TOO (cont.)

and he t. shall be held in derision Jer 48.26
Is it t. slight a thing for the Eze 8.17
Egypt t., and that without limit; Nah 3.09
Gaza t., and shall writhe in Zec 9.05
it t. shall be a remnant for our 9.07
that I t. may come and worship him." Mt 2.08
said, 'You go into the vineyard t., 20.04
them, 'You go into the vineyard t. 20.07
So t. the second and third, down to 22.26
So t., he who had the two talents 25.17
for they t. had gone to the feast. Jn 4.45
They replied, "Are you from Galilee t.? 7.52
Do you t. want to become his disciples?" 9.27
Stand up; I t. am a man." Ac 10.26
at Beroea also, they came there t., 17.13
we t. might walk in newness of life. Rom 6.04
us with sighs t. deep for words. 8.26
So t. at the present time there is 11.05
otherwise you t. will be cut off. 11.22
is it t. much if we reap your 1Co 9.11
we share abundantly in comfort t. 2Co 1.05
not to put it t. severely—to you 2.05
we t. believe, and so we speak, 4.13
boast a little t. much of our 10.08
so that I t. may boast a little. 11.16
of wordly things, I t. will boast.) 11.18
must say, we were t. weak for that! 11.21
to keep me from being t. elated by the 12.07
yourself, lest you t. be tempted. Gal 6.01
I testify to him t., and you know 3Jn 1.12
and he t. had a sharp sickle. Rev 14.17

TOOK

The LORD God t. the man and put him Gen 2.15
while he slept t. one of his ribs 2.21
she t. of its fruit and ate; 3.06
And Lamech t. two wives; the name of the 4.19
and he was not, for God t. him. 5.24
and they t. to wife such of them as 6.02
his hand and t. her and brought 8.09
and t. of every clean animal and of 8.20
Then Shem and Japheth t. a garment, 9.23
And Abram and Nahor t. wives; 11.29
Terah t. Abram his son and Lot the 11.31
And Abram t. Sarai his wife, and Lot 12.05
so that I t. her for my wife? 12.19
So the enemy t. all the goods of 14.11
they also t. Lot, the son of Abram's 14.12
t. Hagar the Egyptian her maid, and 16.03
Then Abraham t. Ishmael his son and 17.23
and t. a calf, tender and good, and 18.07
Then he t. curds, and milk, and the 18.08
king of Gerar sent and t. Sarah. 20.02
Then Abimelech t. sheep and oxen, 20.14
and t. bread and a skin of water, 21.14
and his mother t. a wife for him 21.21
So Abraham t. sheep and oxen and 21.27
and t. two of his young men with 22.03
And Abraham t. the wood of the 22.06
and he t. in his hand the fire and 22.06
and t. the knife to slay his son. 22.10
and Abraham went and t. the ram, 22.13
who t. me from my father's house and 24.07
Then the servant t. ten of his 24.10
the man t. a gold ring weighing a 24.22
thus the servant t. Rebekah, 24.61
So she t. her veil and covered 24.65
and t. Rebekah, and she became his 24.67
Abraham t. another wife, whose name 25.01
old when he t. to wife Rebekah, the 25.20
rose early and t. oath with one 26.31
he t. to wife Judith the daughter 26.34
So he went and t. them and brought 27.14
Then Rebekah t. the best garments 27.15
He t. away my birthright; 27.36
Esau went to Ishmael and t. to wife, 28.09
and he t. the stone which he had 28.18
the evening he t. his daughter 29.23
she t. her maid Zilpah and gave her 30.09
Then Jacob t. fresh rods of poplar 30.37
he t. his kinsmen with him and 31.23
So Jacob t. a stone, and set it up 31.45
and they t. stones, and made a 31.46
and t. from what he had with him a 32.13
he arose and t. his two wives, 32.22
He t. them and sent them across the 32.23
Thus he urged him, and he t. it. 33.11
t. their swords and came upon the 34.25
and t. Dinah out of Shechem's house, 34.26
they t. their flocks and their 34.28
Esau t. his wives from the Canaanites: 36.02
Then Esau t. his wives, his sons, his 36.06
and they t. him and cast him into a 37.24
of silver; and they t. Joseph to Egypt. 37.28
Then they t. Joseph's robe, and 37.31
And Judah t. a wife for Er his 38.06
and the midwife t. and bound on his 38.28
And Joseph's master t. him and put 39.20
and I t. the grapes and pressed 40.11
Then Pharaoh t. his signet ring 41.42
And he t. Simeon from them and 42.24
and t. us to be spies of the land. 42.30
So the men t. the present, and they 43.15
and they t. double the money with 43.15
So Israel t. his journey with all 46.01
They also t. their cattle and their 46.06
his brothers he t. five men and 47.02
so he t. with him his two sons, 48.01
And Joseph t. them both, Ephraim in 48.13
and he t. his father's hand, to 48.17
slope which I t. from the hand of 48.22
Then Joseph t. an oath of the sons 50.25
Levi went and t. to wife a daughter Ex 2.01
no longer she t. for him a basket 2.03
She t. pity on him and said, "This 2.06
So the woman t. the child and 2.09
and when he t. it out, behold, his 4.06
and when he t. it out, behold, it was 4.07
So Moses t. his wife and his sons 4.20
his hand Moses t. the rod of God. 4.20
Then Zipporah t. a flint and cut 4.25
Amram t. to wife Jochebed his 6.20
Aaron t. to wife Elisheba, the 6.23
t. to wife one of the daughters of 6.25
So they t. ashes from the kiln, and 9.10
So the people t. their dough before 12.34
And Moses t. the bones of Joseph 13.19
his chariot and t. his army with 14.06
and t. six hundred picked chariots 14.07
t. a timbrel in her hand; and all the 15.20
so they t. a stone and put it under 17.12
and they t. their stand at the foot 19.17
And Moses t. half of the blood and 24.06
Then he t. the book of the covenant, 24.07
And Moses t. the blood and threw it 24.08
So all the people t. off the rings 32.03
And he t. the calf which they had 32.20
and t. in his hand two tables of 34.04
he t. the veil off, until he came 34.34
And he t. the testimony and put it 40.20
restore what he t. by robbery, Lev 6.04
Then Moses t. the anointing oil, and 8.10
and t. the blood, and with his 8.15
And he t. all the fat that was on 8.16
and t. some of its blood and put it 8.23
Then he t. the fat, and the fat tail, 8.25
the LORD he t. one unleavened cake, 8.26
Then Moses t. them from their hands, 8.28
And Moses t. the breast, and waved 8.29
Then Moses t. some of the anointing 8.30
and t. the goat of the sin offering 9.15
each t. his censer, and put fire in 10.01
Moses and Aaron t. these men who Num 1.17
So Moses t. the redemption money 3.49
people of Israel he t. the money, 3.50

TOOK (cont.)

So Moses t. the wagons and the oxen, Num 7.06
and t. some of the spirit that was 11.25
t. men; and they rose up 16.02
So every man t. his censer, and they 16.18
the priest t. the bronze censers, 16.39
So Aaron t. it as Moses said, and 16.47
looked, and each man t. his rod. 17.09
And Moses t. the rod from before 20.09
and t. some of them captive. 21.01
and t. possession of his land from 21.24
And Israel t. all these cities, and 21.25
and they t. its villages, and 21.32
of the LORD t. his stand in the 22.22
morrow Balak t. Balaam and brought 22.41
And Balaam t. up his discourse, and 23.07
I t. you to curse my enemies, and 23.11
And he t. him to the field of Zophim, 23.14
And Balaam t. up his discourse, and 23.18
So Balak t. Balaam to the top of 23.28
and he t. up his discourse, and said, 24.03
And he t. up his discourse, and said, 24.15
and t. up his discourse, and said, 24.20
and t. up his discourse, and said, 24.21
And he t. up his discourse, and said, 24.23
congregation, and t. a spear in his hand 25.07
he t. Joshua and caused him to 27.22
of Israel t. captive the women of 31.09
and they t. as booty all their 31.09
and t. all the spoil and all the 31.11
spoil that the men of war t. was: 31.32
half Moses t. one of every fifty, 31.47
Manasseh went to Gilead and t. it, 32.39
Manasseh went and t. their villages, 32.41
And Nobah went and t. Kenath and 32.42
So I t. the heads of your tribes, Deu 1.15
and I t. twelve men of you, one man 1.23
And they t. in their hands some of 1.25
only the cattle we t. as spoil for 2.35
And we t. all his cities at that 3.04
of the cities we t. as our booty. 3.07
So we t. the land at that time out 3.08
"When we t. possession of this land 3.12
Jair the Manassite t. all the 3.14
And they t. possession of his land 4.47
So I t. hold of the two tables, and 9.17
Then I t. the sinful thing, the calf 9.21
'I t. this woman, and when I came 22.14
who t. her to be his wife, 24.03
And as the LORD t. delight in doing 28.63
we t. their land, and gave it for an 29.08
as he t. delight in your fathers, 30.09
the rock in which they t. refuge, 32.37
And they t. up the ark of the Jos 3.06
and t. up twelve stones out of the 4.08
which they t. out of the Jordan, 4.20
and the priests t. up the ark of 6.12
before him, and they t. the city. 6.20
t. some of the devoted things; 7.01
then I coveted them, and t. them; 7.21
And they t. them out of the tent 7.23
Israel with him t. Achan the son 7.24
And he t. about five thousand men, 8.12
ran and entered the city and t. it; 8.19
But the king of Ai they t. alive, 8.23
that city Israel t. as their booty, 8.27
and they t. his body down from the 8.29
and t. worn-out sacks upon their 9.04
warm when we t. it from our houses 9.12
the nation t. vengeance on their 10.13
and they t. them down from the 10.27
And Joshua t. Makkedah on that day, 10.28
and he t. it on the second day, and 10.32
and they t. it on that day, and 10.35
and t. it, and smote it with the 10.37
and he t. it with its king and all 10.39
And Joshua t. all these kings and 10.42
and t. Hazor, and smote its king 11.10
Joshua t., and smote them with the 11.12
of Israel t. for their booty; 11.14
So Joshua t. all that land, the hill 11.16
And he t. all their kings, and smote 11.17
of Gibeon; they t. all in battle. 11.19
So Joshua t. the whole land, according 11.23
and t. possession of their land 12.01
Kenaz, the brother of Caleb, t. it; 15.17
the sword they t. possession of it 19.47
Then I t. your father Abraham from 24.03
and you t. possession of their land, 24.08
and he t. a great stone, and set it 24.26
and t. it, and smote it with the Ju 1.08
Caleb's younger brother, t. it; 1.13
Judah also t. Gaza with its territory, 1.18
and he t. possession of the hill 1.19
and they t. their daughters to 3.06
and they t. possession of the city 3.13
t. the sword from his right thigh, 3.21
they t. the key and opened them; 3.25
the wife of Heber t. a tent peg, 4.21
and t. a hammer in her hand, and 4.21
"That the leaders t. the lead in 5.02
So Gideon t. ten men of his servants, 6.27
of the LORD t. possession of Gideon; 6.34
So he t. the jars of the people 7.08
And they t. the two princes of 7.25
them and t. the two kings of 8.12
And he t. the elders of the city 8.16
the city and he t. thorns of the 8.16
and he t. the crescents that were 8.21
He t. his men and divided them into 9.43
he t. the city, and killed the 9.45
and Abimelech t. an axe in his hand, 9.48
and t. it up and laid it on his 9.48
encamped against Thebez, and t. it. 9.50
coming from Egypt t. away my land, 11.13
so Israel t. possession of all the 11.21
And they t. possession of all the 11.22
I t. my life in my hand, and crossed 12.03
And the Gileadites t. the fords of 12.05
So Manoah t. the kid with the 13.19
and t. their spoil and gave the 14.19
hundred foxes, and t. torches; 15.04
he arose and t. hold of the doors 16.03
So Delilah t. new ropes and bound 16.12
Delilah t. the seven locks of his 16.14
came down and t. him and brought 16.31
I t. it." And his mother said, 17.02
his mother t. two hundred pieces of 17.04
and entered and t. the graven 18.17
house and t. the graven image, the 18.18
he t. the ephod, and the teraphim, 18.20
who t. to himself a concubine from 19.01
for no man t. them into his house 19.15
he t. a knife, and laying hold of 19.29
And I t. my concubine and cut her 20.06
t. courage, and again formed the 20.22
and t. their wives, according to 21.23
These t. Moabite wives; the name of the Ru 1.04
And she t. it up and went into the 2.18
be the man who t. notice of you." 2.19
And he t. ten men of the elders of 4.02
So Boaz t. Ruth and she became his 4.13
Then Naomi t. the child and laid 4.16
therefore Eli t. her to be a 1Sa 1.13
she t. him up with her, along with a 1.24
then the Philistines t. the ark of 5.02
So they t. Dagon and put him back 5.03
and t. two milch cows and yoked 6.10
And the Levites t. down the ark of 6.15
came and t. up the ark of the LORD, 7.01
So Samuel t. a sucking lamb and 7.09
Then Samuel t. a stone and set it 7.12
they t. bribes and perverted justice, 8.03
Then Samuel t. Saul and his servant 9.22
So the cook t. up the leg and the 9.24
Then Samuel t. a vial of oil and 10.01

TOOK (cont.)

He t. a yoke of oxen, and cut them 1Sa 11.07
and t. sheep and oxen and calves, 14.32
And he t. Agag the king of the 15.08
But the people t. of the spoil, 15.21
Then Samuel t. the horn of oil, and 16.13
And Jesse t. an ass laden with 16.20
David t. the lyre and played it 16.23
came forward and t. his stand, 17.16
and t. the provisions, and went, as 17.20
and t. a lamb from the flock, 17.34
Then he t. his staff in his hand, 17.40
hand in his bag and t. out a stone, 17.49
and t. his sword and drew it out of 17.51
And David t. the head of the 17.54
Abner t. him, and brought him before 17.57
And Saul t. him that day, and would 18.02
for he t. his life in his hand and 19.05
Michal t. an image and laid it on 19.13
And David t. these words to heart, 21.12
Then Saul t. three thousand chosen 24.02
and t. two hundred loaves, and two 25.18
David also t. Ahinoam of Jezreel; 25.43
So David t. the spear and the jar 26.12
but t. away the sheep, the oxen, the 27.09
and she t. flour, and kneaded it and 28.24
Therefore Saul t. his own sword, 31.04
and t. the body of Saul and the 31.12
And they t. their bones and buried 31.13
and I t. the crown which was on his 2Sa 1.10
Then David t. hold of his clothes, 1.11
and t. their stand on the top of a 2.25
And they t. up Asahel, and buried 2.32
and t. her from her husband Paltiel 3.15
Joab t. him aside into the midst of 3.27
And all the people t. notice of it, 3.36
and his nurse t. him up, and fled; 4.04
They t. his head, and went by the 4.07
But they t. the head of Ishbosheth, 4.12
Nevertheless David t. the stronghold 5.07
And David t. more concubines and 5.13
the ark of God and t. hold of it, 6.06
but David t. it aside to the house 6.10
I t. you from the pasture, from 7.08
as I t. it from Saul, whom I put 7.15
and David t. Metheghammah out of 8.01
And David t. from him a thousand 8.04
And David t. the shields of gold 8.07
King David t. very much bronze. 8.08
So Hanun t. David's servants, and 10.04
So David sent messengers, and t. her; 11.04
but he t. the poor man's lamb, and 12.04
Ammonites, and t. the royal city. 12.26
and fought against it and t. it. 12.29
And he t. the crown of their king 12.30
And she t. dough, and kneaded it, and 13.08
And she t. the pan and emptied it 13.09
And Tamar t. the cakes she had made, 13.10
he t. hold of her, and said to her, 13.11
And the woman t. and spread a 17.19
And he t. three darts in his hand, 18.14
And they t. Absalom, and threw him 18.17
and t. his seat in the gate. 19.08
and the king t. the ten concubines 20.03
And Joab t. Amasa by the beard with 20.09
of Joab's men t. his stand by 20.11
The king t. the two sons of Rizpah 21.08
the daughter of Aiah t. sackcloth, 21.10
David went and t. the bones of Saul 21.12
he t. me, he drew me out of many 22.17
But he t. his stand in the midst of 23.12
and t. and brought it to David. 23.16
the priest t. the horn of oil from 1Ki 1.39
he t. Pharaoh's daughter, and brought 3.01
and t. my son from beside me, while 3.20
and the priests t. up the ark. 8.03
and t. men with them from Paran and 11.18
Then King Rehoboam t. counsel with 12.06
and t. counsel with the young men 12.08
So the king t. counsel, and made two 12.28
And the prophet t. up the body of 13.29
he t. away the treasures of the 14.26
king's house; he t. away everything. 14.26
He also t. away all the shields of 14.26
Then Asa t. all the silver and the 15.18
he t. for wife Jezebel the daughter 16.31
And he t. him from her bosom, and 17.19
And Elijah t. the child, and brought 17.23
Obadiah t. a hundred prophets and 18.04
And they t. the bull which was 18.26
Elijah t. twelve stones, according 18.31
and t. the yoke of oxen, and slew 19.21
And they t. their positions against 20.12
they quickly t. it up from him and 20.33
which my father t. from your 20.34
So they t. him outside the city, and 21.13
Then Elijah t. his mantle, and 2Ki 2.08
Then he t. hold of his own clothes 2.12
And he t. up the mantle of Elijah 2.13
Then he t. the mantle of Elijah 2.14
he t. with him seven hundred 3.26
Then he t. his eldest son who was 3.27
then she t. up her son and went out 4.37
he t. them from their hand, and put 5.24
he reached out his hand and t. it. 6.07
he t. counsel with his servants, 6.08
So they t. two mounted men, and the 7.14
and t. a present with him, all kinds 8.09
the morrow he t. the coverlet and 8.15
every man of them t. his garment, 9.13
they t. the king's sons, and slew 10.07
And they t. them alive, and slew 10.14
And Jehu t. him up with him into 10.15
t. Joash the son of Ahaziah, and 11.02
And he t. the captains, the Carites, 11.19
And he t. his seat on the throne of 11.19
Then Jehoiada the priest t. a chest, 12.09
and fought against Gath, and t. it. 12.17
Jehoash king of Judah t. all the 12.18
bow and arrows"; so he t. a bow and arrows. 13.15
and he t. them. And he said 13.18
son of Jehoahaz t. again from 13.25
of Salt and t. Sela by storm, 14.07
all the people of Judah t. Azariah, 14.21
Ahaz also t. the silver and gold 16.08
and t. it, carrying its people 16.09
and he t. down the sea from off the 16.17
and they t. possession of Samaria, 17.24
at the end of three years he t. it. 18.10
cities of Judah and t. them. 18.13
and he sent and t. the bones out of 23.16
of the land t. Jehoahaz the son of 23.30
But he t. Jehoahaz away; and he came to 23.34
king of Babylon t. him prisoner in 24.12
he t. into captivity from Jerusalem 24.15
in fetters, and t. him to Babylon. 25.07
And they t. away the pots, and the 25.14
of the guard t. away as gold, and what was 25.15
of the guard t. Seraiah the chief 25.18
the city he t. an officer who had 25.19
the captain of the guard t. them, 25.20
But Geshur and Aram t. from them 1Ch 2.23
And Machir t. a wife for Huppim and 7.15
Therefore Saul t. his own sword, 10.04
stripped him and t. his head and 10.09
and t. away the body of Saul and 10.12
Nevertheless David t. the stronghold 11.05
But he t. his stand in the midst of 11.14
and t. and brought it to David. 11.18
the Philistines t. counsel and 12.19
but t. it aside to the house of 13.13
And David t. more wives in Jerusalem, 14.03
I t. you from the pasture, from 17.07
as I t. it from him who was before 17.13
and he t. Gath and its villages out 18.01
And David t. from him a thousand 18.04

TOOK (cont.)
And David t. the shields of gold 1Ch 18.07
David t. very much bronze; with it Solomon 18.08
So Hanun t. David's servants, and 19.04
And David t. the crown of their 20.02
father's sons he t. pleasure in me 28.04
Then Solomon t. a census of all the 2Ch 2.17
and the Levites t. up the ark. 5.04
went to Hamathzobah, and t. it. 8.03
Then King Rehoboam t. counsel with 10.06
and t. counsel with the young men 10.08
Rehoboam t. as wife Mahalath the 11.18
After her he t. Maacah the daughter 11.20
concubines (he t. eighteen wives 11.21
And he t. the fortified cities of 12.04
he t. away the treasures of the 12.09
king's house; he t. away everything. 12.09
He also t. away the shields of gold 12.09
and t. cities from him, Bethel with 13.19
And he t. fourteen wives, and had 13.21
He t. away the foreign altars and 14.03
He also t. out of all the cities of 14.05
he t. courage, and put away the 15.08
They t. oath to the LORD with a 15.14
Then Asa t. silver and gold from 16.02
Then King Asa t. all Judah, and they 16.06
furthermore he t. the high places 17.06
which they t. for themselves until 20.25
t. Joash the son of Ahaziah, and 22.11
seventh year Jehoiada t. courage, 23.01
And he t. the captains, the nobles, 23.20
Spirit of God t. possession of 24.20
But Amaziah t. courage, and led out 25.11
and t. them to the top of a rock 25.12
people in them, and t. much spoil. 25.13
king of Judah t. counsel and sent 25.17
And all the people of Judah t. Uzziah, 26.01
defeated him and t. captive a great 28.05
The men of Israel t. captive two 28.08
they also t. much spoil from them 28.08
by name rose and t. the captives, 28.15
For Ahaz t. from the house of the 28.21
and the Levites t. it and carried 29.16
incense they t. away and threw 30.14
They t. their accustomed posts 30.16
And the people t. confidence from 32.08
who t. Manasseh with hooks and bound him 33.11
And he t. away the foreign gods and 33.15
And Josiah t. away all the abominations 34.33
So his servants t. him out of the 35.24
of the land t. Jehoahaz the son of 36.01
but Neco t. Jehoahaz his brother 36.04
He t. into exile in Babylon those 36.20
together t. the oversight of the Ex 3.09
Cyrus the king t. out of the 5.14
Nebuchadnezzar t. out of the 6.05
I t. courage, for the hand of the 7.28
and the Levites t. over the weight 8.30
been said. So they t. the oath. 10.05
I t. up the wine and gave it to the Neh 2.01
none of us t. off our clothes; 4.23
I t. counsel with myself, and I 5.07
and t. an oath of them to do as 5.12
and t. from them food and wine, 5.15
so they t. possession of the land 9.22
and t. possession of houses full of 9.25
So the king t. his signet ring from Est 3.10
So Haman t. the robes and the horse, 6.11
and the king t. off his signet ring, 8.02
ordained and t. it upon themselves 9.27
Sabeans fell upon them and t. them, Job 1.15
a raid upon the camels and t. them, 1.17
And he t. a potsherd with which to 2.08
And Job again t. up his discourse, 27.01
And Job again t. up his discourse, 29.01
he t. me, he drew me out of many Ps 18.16
Yet thou art he who t. me from the 22.09
were in panic, they t. to flight; 48.05
trembling t. hold of them there, 48.06
thou art he who t. me from my 71.06
and t. him from the sheepfolds; 78.70
it t. deep root and filled the land 80.09
of thy thunder they t. to flight. 104.07
and they t. possession of the fruit 105.44
he t. a bag of money with him; Pro 7.20
they t. away my mantle, those Sol 5.07
and fought against it and t. it,— Is 20.01
the horsemen t. their stand at the 22.07
fortified cities of Judah and t. them. 36.01
you whom I t. from the ends of the 41.09
children, they t. no correction; Jer 2.30
and I t. the waistcloth from the 13.07
So I t. the cup from the LORD's and, 25.17
of the LORD and t. their seat in 26.10
when he t. into exile from Jerusalem 27.20
king of Babylon t. away from this 28.03
Hananiah t. the yoke-bars from the 28.10
fathers when I t. them by the hand 31.32
Then I t. the sealed deed of purchase, 32.11
entered and t. possession of it. 32.23
around and t. back the male and 34.11
each of you t. back his male and 34.16
So I t. Jaazaniah the son of 35.03
son of Neriah t. the scroll in his 36.14
and he t. it from the chamber of 36.21
Then Jeremiah t. another scroll and 36.32
So they t. Jeremiah and cast him 38.06
So Ebedmelech t. the men with him 38.11
and t. from there old rags and worn 38.11
sent and t. Jeremiah from the court 39.14
when he t. him bound in chains along 40.01
of the guard t. Jeremiah and said 40.02
Then Ishmael t. captive all the rest 41.10
of Nethaniah t. them captive and set out 41.10
they t. all their men and went to 41.12
forces with him t. all the rest of 41.16
of the forces t. all the remnant 43.05
all who t. them captive have held 50.33
king of Babylon t. him to Babylon, 52.11
And they t. away the pots, and the 52.18
of the guard t. away as gold, 52.19
of the guard t. Seraiah the chief 52.24
the city he t. an officer who had 52.25
the captain of the guard t. them, 52.26
she t. no thought of her doom; Lam 1.09
Spirit lifted me up and t. me away, Eze 3.14
surely live, because he t. warning; 3.21
and t. me by a lock of my head; 8.03
and t. some of it, and put it into 10.07
who t. it and went out. 10.07
You t. some of your garments, and 16.16
You also t. your fair jewels of my 16.17
and you t. your embroidered garments 16.18
And you t. your sons and your 16.20
with whom you t. pleasure, all those 16.37
to Lebanon and t. the top of the 17.03
Then he t. of the seed of the land 17.05
and t. her king and her princes and 17.12
And he t. one of the seed royal and 17.13
she t. another of her whelps and 19.05
defiled; they both t. the same way. 23.13
revengefully and t. vengeance with 25.15
they t. a cedar from Lebanon to 27.05
the galleries t. more away from 42.05
So the steward t. away their rich Dan 1.16
slew those men who t. up Sadrach, 3.22
was ancient of days t. his seat; 7.09
So he went and t. Gomer the daugher Hos 1.03
I t. them up in my arms; but they did 11.03
In the womb he t. his brother by 12.03
and the LORD t. me from following Amo 7.15
So they t. up Jonah and threw him Jon 1.15
And I t. two staffs; one I named Zec 11.07
And I t. my staff Grace, and I broke 11.10
So I t. the thirty shekels of 11.13
of Jesus Christ t. place in this Mt 1.18

TOOK (cont.)
All this t. place to fulfil what Mt 1.22
commanded him; he t. his wife, 1.24
And he rose and t. the child and 2.14
And he rose and t. the child and 2.21
Then the devil t. him to the holy 4.05
the devil t. him to a very high 4.08
"He t. our infirmities and bore our 8.17
he went in and t. her by the hand, 9.25
went out and t. counsel against 12.14
which a man t. and sowed in his 13.31
which a woman t. and hid in three 13.33
And they t. offense at him. 13.57
came and t. the body and buried it; 14.12
And they t. up twelve baskets full 14.20
he t. the seven loaves and the fish, 15.36
and they t. up seven baskets full 15.37
And Peter t. him and began to 16.22
six days Jesus t. with him Peter 17.01
he t. the twelve disciples aside, 20.17
This t. place to fulfil what was 21.04
and the tenants t. his servants and 21.35
And they t. him and cast him out of 21.39
went and t. counsel how to entangle 22.15
ten maidens who t. their lamps and 25.01
For when the foolish t. their lamps, 25.03
they t. no oil with them; 25.03
but the wise t. flasks of oil with 25.04
and t. counsel together in order to 26.04
Jesus t. bread, and blessed, and 26.26
And he t. a cup, and when he had 26.27
of the people t. counsel against 27.01
So they t. counsel, and bought with 27.07
"And they t. the thirty pieces of 27.09
he t. water and washed his hands 27.24
of the governor t. Jesus into the 27.27
and t. the reed and struck him on 27.30
them at once ran and t. a sponge, 27.48
another t. a spear and pierced his * 27.49
the earthquake and what t. place, 27.54
And Joseph t. the body, and wrapped 27.59
came up and t. hold of his feet 28.09
So they t. the money and did as 28.15
And he came and t. her by the hand Mk 1.31
and immediately t. up the pallet 2.12
they t. him with them, just as he 4.36
and t. the child's father and mother 5.40
with us?" And they t. offense at him. 6.03
they came and t. his body, and laid 6.29
And they t. up twelve baskets full 6.43
and he t. the seven loaves, and 8.06
and they t. up the broken pieces 8.08
And he t. the blind man by the hand, 8.23
And Peter t. him, and began to 8.32
six days Jesus t. with him Peter 9.02
But Jesus t. him by the hand and 9.27
And he t. a child, and put him in 9.36
And he t. them in his arms and 10.16
And they t. him and beat him, and 12.03
And they t. him and killed him, and 12.08
the first t. a wife, and when he 12.20
and the second t. her, and died, 12.21
he t. bread, and blessed, and broke 14.22
And he t. a cup, and when he had 14.23
And he t. with him Peter and James 14.33
t. courage and went to Pilate, and 15.43
he t. him up in his arms and Lk 2.28
And the devil t. him up, and showed 4.05
And he t. him to Jerusalem, and set 4.09
we toiled all night and t. nothing! 5.05
and t. up that on which he lay, and 5.25
and t. and ate the bread of the 6.04
And he t. them and withdrew apart 9.10
And they t. up what was left over, 9.17
sayings he t. with him Peter and 9.28
he t. a child and put him by his 9.47
him to an inn, and t. care of him. 10.34
And the next day he t. out two 10.35
which a man t. and sowed in his 13.19
which a woman t. and hid in three 13.21
Then he t. him and healed him, and 14.04
all he had and t. his journey into 15.13
the first t. a wife, and died 20.29
and the third t. her, and likewise 20.31
And he t. a cup, and when he had 22.17
And he t. bread, and when he had 22.19
Then he t. it down and wrapped it 23.53
he t. the bread and blessed, and 24.30
and he t. it and ate before them. 24.43
This t. place in Bethany beyond the Jn 1.28
of the feast." So they t. it. 2.08
and he t. up his pallet and walked. 5.09
Jesus then t. the loaves, and when 6.11
So they t. up stones to throw at 8.59
The Jews t. up stones again to 10,31
So they t. away the stone. 11.41
day on they t. counsel how to put 11.53
Mary took a pound of costly ointment 12.03
So they t. branches of palm trees 12.13
Then Pilate t. Jesus and scourged 19.01
So they t. Jesus, and he went out, 19.17
Jesus they t. his garments and 19.23
the disciple t. her to his own 19.27
For these things t. place that the 19.36
So he came and t. away his body. 19.38
They t. the body of Jesus, and bound 19.40
Jesus came and t. the bread and 21.13
and a cloud t. him out of their Ac 1.09
And he t. him by the right hand and 3.07
So they t. his advice, and when they 5.40
And you t. up the tent of Moloch, 7.43
and t. food and was strengthened. 9.19
but his disciples t. him by night 9.25
But Barnabas t. him, and brought him 9.27
they t. him to the upper room. 9.39
and this t. place in the days of 11.28
t. his seat upon the throne, and 12.21
they t. him down from the tree, and 13.29
Barnabas t. Mark with him and 15.39
and he t. him and circumcised him 16.03
And he t. them the same hour of the 16.33
And they t. them out and asked them 16.39
And they t. hold of him and brought 17.19
and then t. leave of the brethren 18.18
they t. him and expounded to him 18.26
exhorted them t. leave of them and 20.01
And they t. the lad away alive, and 20.12
we t. him on board and came to 20.14
And coming to us he t. Paul's girdle 21.11
Then Paul t. the men, and the next 21.26
He at once t. soldiers and centurions, 21.32
So he t. him and brought him to the 23.18
The tribune t. him by the hand, and 23.19
t. Paul and brought him by night to 23.31
with great violence t. him out of * 24.07
the next day he t. his seat on the 25.06
on the next day t. my seat on the 25.17
they t. measures to undergird the 27.17
he t. bread, and giving thanks to 27.35
Paul thanked God and t. courage. 28.15
when he was betrayed t. bread, 1Co 11.23
So I t. leave of them and went on 2Co 2.13
my first defense no one t. my part; 2Ti 4.16
became priests t. their office Heb 7.21
the day when I t. them by the hand 8.09
he t. the blood of calves and goats, 9.19
t. heed and constructed an ark for 11.07
and he went and t. the scroll from Rev 5.07
Then the angel t. the censer and 8.05
And I t. the little scroll from the 10.10
Then a mighty angel t. up a stone 18.21

TOOL
you wield your t. upon it you Ex 20.25
and fashioned it with a graving t., 32.04
shall lift up no iron t. upon them. Deu 27.05

TOOL (cont.)
no man has lifted an iron t."; Jos 8.31
nor axe nor any t. of iron was 1Ki 6.07

TOOTH
t. for t., hand for hand, foot for foot, Ex 21.24
If he knocks out the t. of his slave, 21.27
fracture, eye for eye, t. for t.; Lev 24.20
t. for t., hand for hand, foot for Deu 19.21
is like a bad t. or a foot that Pro 25.19
for an eye and a t. for a t. Mt 5.38

TOOTH'S
the slave go free for the t. sake. Ex 21.27

TOP
a tower with its t. in the heavens, Gen 11.04
and the t. of it reached to heaven; 28.12
and poured oil on the t. of it. 28.18
stand on the t. of the hill with Ex 17.09
Hur went up to the t. of the hill. 17.10
to the t. of the mountain; 19.20
Moses to the t. of the mountain, 19.20
fire on the t. of the mountain in 24.17
mercy seat on the t. of the ark; 25.21
beneath, but joined at the t., 26.24
its t. and its sides round about 30.03
to me on the t. of the mountain. 34.02
beneath, but joined at the t., 36.29
its t., and its sides round about, 37.26
of sheepskin that is on t. of it, Num 4.25
there on the t. of the mountain. 20.28
of Moab by the t. of Pisgah which 21.20
For from the t. of the mountains I 23.09
to the t. of Pisgah, and built seven 23.14
took Balaam to the t. of Peor, 23.28
Go up to the t. of Pisgah, and lift Deu 3.27
to the t. of Pisgah, which is 34.01
goes up to the t. of the mountain Jos 15.08
from the t. of the mountain to the 15.09
your God on the t. of the stronghold Ju 6.26
stood on the t. of Mount Gerizim, 9.07
them to the t. of the hill that is 16.03
afar off on the t. of the mountain, 1Sa 26.13
their stand on the t. of a hill. 2Sa 2.25
that was upon the t. of the pillar; 1Ki 7.18
And on the t. of the stand there 7.35
and on the t. of the stand its 7.35
Elijah went up to the t. of Carmel; 18.42
was sitting on the t. of a hill, 2Ki 1.09
of five cubits on the t. of each. 2Ch 3.15
capitals on the t. of the pillars; 4.12
that were on the t. of the pillars; 4.12
them to the t. of a rock and threw 25.12
them down from the t. of the rock; 25.12
and touched the t. of the scepter. Est 5.02
on the t. of the walls she cries Pro 1.21
one who lies on the t. of a mast. 23.34
berries in the t. of the highest Is 17.06
flagstaff on the t. of a mountain, 30.17
shout from the t. of the mountains. 42.11
to Lebanon and took the t. of the cedar; Eze 17.03
from the lofty t. of the cedar, and will 17.22
great height, its t. among the clouds. 31.03
and set its t. among the clouds, 31.10
story to the t. story through the 41.07
about upon the t. of the mountain 43.12
and its t. reached to heaven, and it Dan 4.11
so that its t. reached to heaven, 4.20
and the t. of Carmel withers. Amo 1.02
themselves on the t. of Carmel, 9.03
gold, with a bowl on the t. of it, Zec 4.02
lamps which are on the t. of it. 4.02
forward the t. stone amid shouts 4.07
was torn in two, from t. to bottom; Mt 27.51
was torn in two, from t. to bottom. Mk 15.38
seam, woven from t. to bottom; Jn 19.23

TOPAZ
t., and carbuncle shall be the Ex 28.17
t., and carbuncle was the first row 39.10
The t. of Ethiopia cannot compare Job 28.19
t., and jasper, chrysolite, beryl, and Eze 28.13
the ninth t., the tenth chrysoprase, Rev 21.20

TOPHEL
against Suph, between Paran and T., Deu 1.01

TOPHETH
And he defiled T., which is in the 2Ki 23.10
have built the high place of T., Jer 7.31
when it will no more be called T., 7.32
Slaughter: for they will bury in T., 7.32
place shall no more be called T., 19.06
shall bury in T. because there 19.11
inhabitants, making this city like T. 19.12
be defiled like the place of T. 19.13
Then Jeremiah came from T., 19.14

TOPMOST
he broke off the t. of its young Eze 17.04
off from the t. of its young twigs 17.22

TOPS
the t. of the mountains were seen. Gen 8.05
against him on the mountain t., Ju 9.25
coming down from the mountain t.!" 9.36
marching in the t. of the Balsam 2Sa 5.24
to set upon the t. of the pillars; 1Ki 7.16
capitals upon the t. of the pillars; 7.17
were upon the t. of the pillars in 7.19
And upon the t. of the pillars was 7.22
that were on the t. of the pillars, 7.41
marching in the t. of the balsam 1Ch 14.15
put them on the t. of the pillars; 2Ch 3.16
on the t. of the mountains may it Ps 72.16
or set their t. among the clouds, Eze 31.14
sacrifice on the t. of the mountains, Hos 4.13
leap on the t. of the mountains, Joe 2.05

TORCH
and a flaming t. passed between Gen 15.17
and put a t. between each pair of Ju 15.04
and her salvation as a burning t. Is 62.01
like flaming t. among sheaves; Zec 12.06
from heaven, blazing like a t., Rev 8.10

TORCHES
with t. inside the jars. Ju 7.16
holding in their left hands the t., 7.20
three hundred foxes, and took t.; 15.04
And when he had set fire to the t., 15.05
Out of his mouth go flaming t.; Job 41.19
like t. moving to and fro among the Eze 1.13
lightning, his eyes like flaming t., Dan 10.06
they gleam like t., they dart like Nah 2.04
with lanterns and t. and weapons. Jn 18.03
the throne burn seven t. of fire, Rev 4.05

TORE
and he t. the lion asunder as one Ju 14.06
the skirt of his robe, and it t. 1Sa 15.27
and t. it into twelve pieces. 1Ki 11.30
and t. the kingdom away from the 14.08
the woods and t. forty-two of the 2Ki 2.24
the house of Baal, and t. it down; 11.18
the house of Baal, and t. it down; 2Ch 23.17
me off my way and t. me to pieces; Lam 3.11
and t. all their shoulders; and when Eze 29.07
and his anger t. perpetually, and he Amo 1.11
The lion t. enough for his whelps Nah 2.12
Then the high priest t. his robes, Mt 26.65
And the high priest t. his mantle, Mk 14.63
the demon t. him and convulsed him. Lk 9.42
they t. their garments and rushed Ac 14.14
the magistrates t. the garments 16.22
again those things which I t. down, Gal 2.18

TORMENT
Then she began to t. him, and his strength Ju 16.19
"How long will you t. me, and break me Job 19.02
my hand: you shall lie down in t. Is 50.11
come here to t. us before the time?" Mt 8.29
I adjure you by God, do not t. me?" Mk 5.07
I beseech you, do not t. me." Lk 8.28
being in t., he lifted up his eyes, 16.23
also come into this place of t.' 16.28
had been a t. to those who dwell Rev 11.10
smoke of their t. goes up for ever 14.11
a like measure of t. and mourning. 18.07
stand far off, in fear of her t., 18.10
stand far off, in fear of her t., 18.15

TORMENTED
evil spirit from the LORD t. him. 1Sa 16.14
And Amnon was so t. that he made 2Sa 13.02
and he shall be t. with fire and Rev 14.10
they will be t. day and night for 20.10

TORMENTING
an evil spirit from God is t. you. 1Sa 16.15

TORMENTORS
and our t., mirth, saying, "Sing us Ps 137.03
put it into the hand of your t., Is 51.23

TORN
That which was t. by wild beasts I Gen 31.39
is without doubt t. to pieces. 37.33
Surely he has been t. to pieces; 44.28
If it is t. by beasts, let him bring Ex 22.13
restitution for what has been t. 22.13
flesh that is t. by beasts in the 22.31
a garment, that it may not be t. 28.32
opening, that it might not be t. 39.23
fat of one that is t. by beasts, Lev 7.24
shall wear t. clothes and let the 13.45
of itself or what is t. by beasts, 17.15
of itself or is t. by beasts he 22.08
bruised or crushed or t. or cut, 22.24
worn-out and t. and mended, Jos 9.04
"The LORD has t. the kingdom of 1Sa 15.28
the LORD has t. the kingdom out of 28.17
Behold, the altar shall be t. down, 1Ki 13.03
The altar also was t. down, 13.05
which has t. him and slain him, 13.26
not eaten the body or t. the ass. 13.28
When he had t. Israel from the 2Ki 17.21
He has t. me in his wrath, and hated Job 16.09
He is t. from the tent in which he 18.14
but the soul is t. by trouble. Pro 27.09
out of them shall be t. in pieces; Jer 5.06
which were t. down to make a 33.04
beards shaved and their clothes t., 41.05
died of itself or was t. by beasts, Eze 4.14
and her foundations are t. down. 30.04
that has died of itself or is t. 44.31
you shall be t. limb from limb, and Dan 2.05
Abednego shall be t. limb from limb, 3.29
for he has t., that he may heal us; Hos 6.01
prey and his dens with t. flesh. Nah 2.12
of the temple was t. in two, from top to Mt 27.51
of the temple was t. in two, from top to Mk 15.38
the curtain of the temple was t. in two. Lk 23.45
were so many, the net was not t. Jn 21.11
Paul would be t. in pieces by them, Ac 23.10

TORRENT
The t. Kishon swept them away, the Ju 5.21
the onrushing t., the t. Kishon. 5.21
among the stones of the t. bed, Job 22.24
the t. would have gone over us; Ps 124.04
and shall become an overflowing t.; Jer 47.02
down like a t. day and night! Lam 2.18

TORRENT-BED
My brethren are treacherous as a t., Job 6.15

TORRENTIAL
t. rains and hailstones, fire and Eze 38.22

TORRENTS
the t. of perdition assailed me; 2Sa 22.05
the t. wash away the soil of the Job 14.19
gullies of the t. they must dwell, 30.06
cleft a channel for the t. of rain, 38.25
the t. of perdition assailed me; Ps 18.04

TORTURE
they were allowed to t. them for Rev 9.05
and their t. was like the t. of a scorpion, 9.05

TORTURED
Some were t., refusing to accept Heb 11.35

TOSS
and its waters t. up mire and dirt Is 57.20
though the waves t., they cannot Jer 5.22

TOSSED
and be t. about and sink again, like Amo 8.08
t. to and fro and carried about Eph 4.14
that is driven and t. by the wind. Jas 1.06

TOSSEST
and thou t. me about in the roar of Job 30.22

TOSSING
and I am full of t. till the dawn. Job 7.04
But the wicked are like the t. sea; Is 57.20

TOSSINGS
Thou hast kept count of my t.; Ps 56.08

TOTAL
and the t. was thirty-eight thousand 1Ch 23.03

TOTTER
The nations rage, the kingdoms t.; Ps 46.06
make them t. by thy power, and bring 59.11
my bones, my steps t. beneath me. Hab 3.16

TOTTERING
like a leaning wall, a t. fence? Ps 62.03

TOTTERS
repair its breaches, for it t. Ps 60.02
When the earth t., and all its 75.03

TOU
When T. king of Hamath heard that 2Sa 8.09
T. sent his son Joram to King David, 8.10
had often been at war with T. 8.10
When T. king of Hamath heard that 1Ch 18.09
had often been at war with T. 18.10

TOUCH
garden, neither shall you t. it, Gen 3.03
therefore I did not let you t. her. 20.06
and t. the lintel and the two Ex 12.22
the mountain or t. the border of 19.12
no hand shall t. him, but he shall 19.13
their carcasses you shall not t.; Lev 11.08
she shall not t. any hallowed thing, 12.04
they must not t. the holy things, Num 4.15
and t. nothing of theirs, lest you 16.26
their carcasses you shall not t. Deu 14.08
Israel, and now we may not t. them. Jos 9.19
and no razor shall t. his head." 1Sa 1.11
and he shall never t. you again." 2Sa 14.10
saying, "T. not my anointed ones, do 1Ch 16.22
and t. all that he has, and he will Job 1.11
and t. his bone and his flesh, and 2.05
seven there shall no evil t. you. 5.19
My appetite refuses to t. them; 6.07
saying, "T. not my anointed ones, do Ps 105.15
T. the mountains that they smoke! 144.05

TOUCH (cont.)

t. no unclean thing; go out from Is 52.11
neighbors who t. the heritage Jer 12.14
that none could t. their garments. Lam 4.14
T. not!" So they became 4.15
but t. no one upon whom is the mark Eze 9.06
mountains shall t. the side of it; Zec 14.05
"If I only t. his garment, I shall Mt 9.21
they might only t. the fringe of 14.36
diseases pressed upon him to t. him. Mk 3.10
"If I t. even his garments, I shall 5.28
that they might t. even the fringe 6.56
man, and begged him to t. him. 8.22
to him, that he might t. them; 10.13
And all the crowd sought to t. him, Lk 6.19
yourselves do not t. the burdens 11.46
to him that he might t. them; 18.15
well for a man not to t. a woman. 1Co 7.01
and t. nothing unclean; then I will 2Co 6.17
handle, Do not taste, Do not t." Col 2.21
the first-born might not t. them. Heb 11.28
and the evil one does not t. him. 1Jn 5.18

TOUCHED

as we have not t. you and have Gen 26.29
he t. the hollow of his thigh; 32.25
because he t. the hollow of Jacob's 32.32
and t. Moses' feet with it, and said, Ex 4.25
and upon him who t. the bone, Num 19.18
and whoever has t. any slain, 31.19
and t. the meat and the unleavened Ju 6.21
of valor whose hearts God had t. 1Sa 10.26
that a wing of one t. the one wall, 1Ki 6.27
the other cherub t. the other wall; 6.27
other wings t. each other in the 6.27
an angel t. him, and said to him, 19.05
and t. him, and said, "Arise and eat, 19.07
soon as the man t. the bones of 2Ki 13.21
t. the wall of the house, and its 2Ch 3.11
t. the wing of the other cherub; 3.11
t. the wall of the house, and the 3.12
approached and t. the top of the Est 5.02
for the hand of God has t. me! Job 19.21
And he t. my mouth, and said: "Behold, Is 6.07
"Behold, this has t. your lips; 6.07
put forth his hand and t. my mouth; Jer 1.09
their wings t. one another; Eze 1.09
each of which t. the wing of 1.11
creatures as they t. one another, 3.13
but he t. me and set me on my feet. Dan 8.18
a hand t. me and set me trembling 10.10
of the sons of men t. my lips; 10.16
of a man t. me and strengthened me. 10.18
stretched out his hand and t. him, Mt 8.03
he t. her hand, and the fever left 8.15
behind him and t. the fringe of 9.20
Then he t. their eyes, saying, 9.29
and as many as t. it were made well. 14.36
But Jesus came and t. them, 17.07
And Jesus in pity t. their eyes, 20.34
stretched out his hand and t. him, Mk 1.41
in the crowd and t. his garment. 5.27
and said, "Who t. my garments?" 5.30
you, and yet you say, 'Who t. me?'" 5.31
and as many as t. it were made well. 6.56
and he spat and t. his tongue; 7.33
and t. him, saying, "I will; Lk 5.13
And he came and t. the bier, 7.14
and t. the fringe of his garment; 8.44
And Jesus said, "Who was it that t. me?" 8.45
But Jesus said, "Some one t. me; 8.46
all the people why she had t. him, 8.47
And he t. his ear and healed him. 22.51
the next day we t. at Samos; Ac 20.15
have not come to what may be t., Heb 12.18
looked upon and t. with our hands, 1Jn 1.01

TOUCHES

"Whoever t. this man or his wife Gen 26.11
whoever t. the mountain shall be Ex 19.12
whatever t. the altar shall become 29.37
whatever t. them will become holy. 30.29
Or if any one t. an unclean thing, Lev 5.02
Or if he t. human uncleanness, of 5.03
whoever t. them shall become holy." 6.18
Whatever t. its flesh shall be holy 6.27
"Flesh that t. any unclean thing 7.19
And if any one t. an unclean thing, 7.21
whoever t. their carcass shall be 11.24
every one who t. them shall be 11.26
whoever t. their carcass shall be 11.27
whoever t. them when they are dead 11.31
but whatever t. their carcass shall 11.36
he who t. its carcass shall be 11.39
And any one who t. his bed shall 15.05
And whoever t. the body of him who 15.07
And whoever t. anything that was 15.10
the discharge t. without having 15.11
the discharge t. shall be broken; 15.12
and whoever t. her shall be unclean 15.19
And whoever t. her bed shall wash 15.21
And whoever t. anything upon which 15.22
when he t. it he shall be unclean 15.23
And whoever t. these things shall 15.27
Whoever t. anything that is unclean 22.04
and whoever t. a creeping thing by 22.05
the person who t. any such shall be 22.06
"He who t. the dead body of any Num 19.11
Whoever t. a dead person, the body 19.13
the open field t. one who is slain 19.16
and he who t. the water for impurity 19.21
unclean person t. shall be unclean 19.22
and any one who t. it shall be 19.22
and t. Jericho, ending at the Jordan Jos 16.07
and t. Dabbesheth, then the brook 19.11
the boundary also t. Tabor, 19.22
on the west it t. Carmel and 19.26
and t. Zebulun and the valley of 19.27
of tow snaps when it t. the fire. Ju 16.09
but the man who t. them arms 2Sa 23.07
it t. you, and you are dismayed. Job 4.05
who t. the mountains and they smoke Ps 104.32
none who t. her will go unpunished. Pro 6.29
he who t. the earth and it melts, Amo 9.05
and t. with his skirt bread, or Hag 2.12
with a dead body t. any of these, 2.13
for he who t. you touches the apple Zec 2.08
who touches you t. the apple of 2.08
"If even a beast t. the mountain, Heb 12.20

TOUCHING

unclean through t. the dead body Num 9.06
unclean through t. the dead body 9.07
is unclean through t. a dead body, 9.10
t. Zebulun at the south, and Asher Jos 19.34
whole earth, without t. the ground; Dan 8.05
of woman this is who is t. him, Lk 7.39

TOW

as a string of t. snaps when it Ju 16.09
And the strong shall become t., Is 1.31

TOWARD

on, still going t. the Negeb. Gen 12.09
"Look t. heaven, and number the 15.05
there, and they looked t. Sodom; 18.16
from there, and went t. Sodom; 18.22
and he looked down t. Sodom and 19.28
Gomorrah and t. all the land of 19.28
journeyed t. the territory of the 20.01
and his faithfulness t. my master. 24.27
Jacob left Beersheba, and went t. Haran. 28.10
of the flocks t. the striped and 30.40
set his face t. the hill country 31.21
his right hand t. Israel's left 48.13

TOWARD (cont.)

his left hand t. Israel's right	Gen 48.13
throw them t. heaven in the sight	Ex 9.08
and Moses threw them t. heaven,	9.10
"Stretch forth your hand t. heaven,	9.22
stretched forth his rod t. heaven;	9.23
out your hand t. heaven that there	10.21
stretched out his hand t. heaven,	10.22
of the wilderness t. the Red Sea.	13.18
servants was changed t. the people,	14.05
they looked t. the wilderness, and	16.10
t. the mercy seat shall the faces	25.20
haste to bow his head t. the earth,	34.08
t. the mercy seat were the faces of	37.09
up his hands t. the people and	Lev 9.22
the east side t. the sunrise shall	Num 2.03
the tent of meeting t. the sunrise,	3.38
And Aaron turned t. Miriam, and	12.10
they turned t. the tent of meeting;	16.42
of her blood t. the front of the	19.04
is opposite Moab, t. the sunrise.	21.11
but set his face t. the wilderness.	24.01
Jericho eastward t. the sunrise.	34.15
t. the going down of the sun, in the	Deu 11.30
the Great Sea t. the going down of	Jos 1.04
beyond the Jordan t. the sunrise.	1.15
flowing down t. the sea of the	3.16
to the descent t. the Arabah to	8.14
javelin that is in your hand t. Ai;	8.18
that was in his hand t. the city.	8.18
coast of the Great Sea t. Lebanon,	9.01
that rises t. Seir, as far as	11.17
beyond the Jordan t. the sunrising,	12.01
that rises t. Seir (and Joshua gave	12.07
t. the sunrising, from Baalgad below	13.05
turning t. Gilgal, which is opposite	15.07
t. the boundary of Edom, were	15.21
turns round t. Taanathshiloh,	16.06
eastward t. the sunrise to the	19.12
on the east t. the sunrise to	19.13
on to Rimmon it bends t. Neah;	19.13
or in breach of faith t. the LORD,	22.22
as far as Bethshittah t. Zererah,	Ju 7.22
flame went up t. heaven from the	13.20
now the day has waned t. evening;	19.09
turned and fled t. the wilderness	20.45
turned and fled t. the wilderness	20.47
coming out t. them on his way up	1Sa 9.14
one company turned t. Ophrah,	13.17
another company turned t. Bethhoron,	13.18
company turned t. the border that	13.18
valley of Zeboim t. the wilderness.	13.18
he turned away from him t. another,	17.30
ran quickly t. the battle line to	17.48
if he is well disposed t. David,	20.12
David and his men came down t. her;	25.20
people passed on t. the wilderness.	2Sa 15.23
valley, t. Gad and on to Jazer.	24.05
forth his hand t. Jerusalem to	24.16
and his servants coming on t. him;	24.20
in uprightness of heart t. thee;	1Ki 3.06
spread forth his hands t. heaven;	8.22
open night and day t. this house,	8.29
thy servant offers t. this place.	8.29
when they pray t. this place;	8.30
if they pray t. this place, and	8.35
out his hands t. this house;	8.38
he comes and prays t. this house,	8.42
to the LORD t. the city which thou	8.44
and pray to thee t. their land,	8.48
with hands outstretched t. heaven;	8.54
servant, "Go up now, look t. the sea."	18.43
and he turned t. them, because of	2Ki 13.23
t. Hamath, as he went to set up his	1Ch 18.03
and direct their hearts t. thee.	29.18
spread forth his hands t. heaven;	2Ch 6.13
open day and night t. this house,	6.20
thy servant offers t. this place.	6.20
when they pray t. this place;	6.21
if they pray t. this place, and	6.26
out his hands t. this house;	6.29
he comes and prays t. this house,	6.32
pray to thee t. this city which	6.34
and pray t. their land, which thou	6.38
whose heart is blameless t. him.	16.09
they looked t. the multitude;	20.24
and t. God and his house.	24.16
love endures for ever t. Israel.	Ez 3.11
procedure t. all who were versed	Est 1.13
dust upon their heads t. heaven.	Job 2.12
and increase thy vexation t. me;	10.17
will stretch out your hands t. him.	11.13
Will you show partiality t. him,	13.08
treader turns t. their vineyards.	24.18
person or use flattery t. any man.	32.21
Behold, I am t. God as you are;	33.06
and spreads his wings t. the south?	39.26
I will worship t. thy holy temple	Ps 5.07
My eyes are ever t. the LORD,	25.15
up my hands t. thy most holy	28.02
of the LORD are t. the righteous,	34.15
righteous, and his ears t. their cry.	34.15
deeds and thy thoughts t. us;	40.05
ignorant, I was like a beast t. thee.	73.22
Their heart was not steadfast t. him;	78.37
hate the LORD would cringe t. him,	81.15
and put away thy indignation t. us!	85.04
For great is thy steadfast love t. me;	86.13
steadfast love t. those who fear	103.11
For great is his steadfast love t. us;	117.02
as is thy wont t. those who love	119.132
I bow down t. thy holy temple and	138.02
But my eyes are t. thee,	141.08
T. the scorners he is scornful, but	Pro 3.34
understanding sets his face t. wisdom,	17.24
flying like an eagle t. heaven.	23.05
heart inclines him t. the right,	Ec 10.02
but a fool's heart t. the left.	10.02
proclaim these words t. the north,	Jer 3.12
Raise a standard t. Zion,	4.06
in the desert t. the daughter of	4.11
me, and triest my mind t. thee.	12.03
would not turn t. this people.	15.01
of the Horse Gate t. the east,	31.40
and they went t. the Arabah.	39.04
to Zion, with faces turned t. it,	50.05
out straight, one t. another;	Eze 1.23
and set your face t. it, and let it be	4.03
set your face t. the siege of	4.07
set your face t. the mountains of	6.02
I lifted up my eyes t. the north,	8.05
LORD, and their faces t. the east,	8.16
worshiping the sun t. the east.	8.16
And I will scatter t. every wind	12.14
and its branches turned t. him,	17.06
this vine bent its roots t. him,	17.07
its branches t. him that he might	17.07
set your face t. the south, preach	20.46
set your face t. Jerusalem and	21.02
set your face t. the Ammonites, and	25.02
set your face t. Sidon, and prophesy	28.21
set your face t. Gog, of the land of	38.02
a gate which faced t. the north,	40.20
the gate which faced t. the east;	40.22
And he led me t. the south, and	40.24
from gate to gate t. the south,	40.27
one door t. the north, and another	41.11
and another door t. the south;	41.11
the face of a man t. the palm tree	41.19
of a young lion t. the palm tree	41.19
t. the north, and he brought me to	42.01
t. the outer court, opposite the	42.07
of the temple t. the east (for the	47.01
outer gate, that faces t. the east;	47.02
water flows t. the eastern region	47.08
Most High God has wrought t. me.	Dan 4.02

TOWARD (cont.)

upper chamber open t. Jerusalem;	Dan 6.10
conspicuous horns t. the four winds	8.08
exceedingly great t. the south,	8.09
t. the east, and t. the glorious land.	8.09
turned my face t. the ground and	10.15
and divided t. the four winds of	11.04
his face back t. the fortresses of	11.19
hand and his left hand t. heaven;	12.07
horses goes t. the north country,	Zec 6.06
white ones go t. the west country,	6.06
dappled ones go t. the south	6.06
those who go t. the north country	6.08
t. the sea, across the Jordan,	Mt 4.15
out his hand t. his disciples,	12.49
t. the dawn of the first day of the	28.01
Then turning t. the woman he said	Lk 7.44
his face was set t. Jerusalem.	9.53
himself, and is not rich t. God."	12.21
and journeying t. Jerusalem.	13.22
for it is t. evening and the day is	24.29
day he saw Jesus coming t. him,	Jn 1.29
disciple, and they went t. the tomb.	20.03
"Rise and go t. the south to the	Ac 8.26
conscience t. God and t. men.	24.16
severity t. those who have fallen,	Rom 11.22
behaving properly t. his betrothed,	1Co 7.36
without law t. God but under the	9.21
and his grace t. me was not in vain.	15.10
the world, and still more t. you,	2Co 1.12
that we have through Christ t. God.	3.04
and your love t. all the saints,	Eph 1.15
in kindness t. us in Christ Jesus.	2.07
I press on t. the goal for the	Php 3.14
Conduct yourselves wisely t. outsiders,	Col 4.05
show perfect courtesy t. all men.	Tit 3.02
which you have t. the Lord Jesus	Phm 1.05
dead works and of faith t. God,	Heb 6.01
be merciful t. their iniquities,	8.12
with humility t. one another, for	1Pe 5.05
slowness, but is forbearing t. you,	2Pe 3.09

TOWEL

and girded himself with a t.	Jn 13.04
them with the t. with which he was	13.05

TOWER

and a t. with its top in the	Gen 11.04
down to see the city and the t.,	11.05
his tent beyond the t. of Eder.	35.21
peace, I will break down this t."	Ju 8.09
And he broke down the t. of Penuel,	8.17
people of the T. of Shechem heard	9.46
people of the T. of Shechem were	9.47
people of the T. of Shechem also	9.49
was a strong t. within the city,	9.51
they went to the roof of the t.	9.51
And Abimelech came to the t.,	9.52
the door of the t. to burn it with	9.52
was standing on the t. in Jezreel,	2Ki 9.17
from watch t. to fortified city;	17.09
it as far as the T. of the hundred,	Neh 3.01
as far as the T. of Hananel.	3.01
section and the T. of the Ovens.	3.11
Angle and the t. projecting from	3.25
on the east and the projecting t.	3.26
projecting t. as far as the wall	3.27
above the T. of the Furnaces, to the	12.38
Gate and the T. of Hananel and the	12.39
Hananel and the T. of the Hundred,	12.39
a strong t. against the enemy.	Ps 61.03
The strong t. of the wicked comes	Pro 12.12
The name of the LORD is a strong t.;	18.10
Your neck is like the t. of David,	Sol 4.04
Your neck is like an ivory t.	7.04
your nose is like a t. of Lebanon,	7.04
against every high t., and against	Is 2.15
LORD from the t. of Hananel to the	Jer 31.38
And you, O t. of the flock, hill of	Mic 4.08
and station myself on the t.,	Hab 2.01
and from the T. of Hananel to the	Zec 14.10
and built a t., and let it out to	Mt 21.33
and built a t., and let it out to	Mk 12.01
upon whom the t. in Siloam fell	Lk 13.04
of you, desiring to build a t.,	14.28

TOWERED

it t. aloft among the thick boughs;	Eze 19.11
So it t. high above all the trees	31.05
Because it t. high and set its top	31.10

TOWERING

and t. like a cedar of Lebanon.	Ps 37.35

TOWERS

in the villages and in the t.,	1Ch 27.25
surround them with walls and t.,	2Ch14.07
Moreover Uzziah built t. in Jerusalem	26.09
And he built t. in the wilderness,	26.10
to be on the t. and the corners, to	26.15
and forts and t. on the wooded	27.04
and raised t. upon it, and outside	32.05
go round about her, number her t.,	Ps 48.12
walls, and security within your t.!	122.07
wall, and my breasts were like t.;	Sol 8.10
Hyenas will cry in its t.,	Is 13.22
They erected their siege t., they razed	23.13
you with t. and I will raise	29.03
great slaughter, when the t. fall.	30.25
Where is he who counted the t.?"	33.18
cast up mounds, to build siege t.	Eze 21.22
of Tyre, and break down her t.;	26.04
axes he will break down your t.	26.09
and men of Gamad were in your t.;	27.11

TOWN

but the t. of Tappuah on the	Jos 17.08
to his own t. and his own home, to	20.06
to the t. from which he fled.	20.06
the t. of Phinehas his son, which	24.33
the men of the t. to do it by day,	Ju 6.27
When the men of the t. rose early	6.28
Then the men of the t. said to Joash,	6.30
and killed thirty men of the t.,	14.19
from the t. of Bethlehem in Judah,	17.08
the whole t. was stirred because of	Ru 1.19
by entering a t. that has gates	1Sa 23.07
and Judah, each to his own t.	Ez 2.01
Jerusalem and Judah, each to his t.	Neh 7.06
The squares of the t. forget them;	Job 24.20
beside the gates in front of the t.,	Pro 8.03
from the highest places in the t.,	9.03
seat on the high places of the t.,	9.14
tumultuous city, exultant t.?	Is 22.02
Woe to him who builds a t. with blood,	Hab 2.12
and enter no t. of the Samaritans,	Mt 10.05
And whatever t. or village you	10.11
feet as you leave that house or t.	10.14
and Gomorrah than for that t.	10.15
When they persecute you in one t.,	10.23
and persecute from t. to t.,	23.34
could no longer openly enter a t.,	Mk 1.45
and people from t. after t. came to him,	Lk 8.04
you leave that t. shake off the	9.05
into every t. and place where he	10.01
Whenever you enter a t. and they	10.08
you enter a t. and they do not	10.10
dust of your t. that clings to our	10.11
day for Sodom than for that t.	10.12
from the Jewish t. of Arimathea.	23.50
wilderness, to a t. called Ephraim;	Jn 11.54
And when the t. clerk had quieted	Ac 19.35
elders in every t. as I directed	Tit 1.05
such and such a t. and spend a	Jas 4.13

TOWNS
the Levite that is within your t., Deu 12.12
eat flesh within any of your t., 12.15
eat within your t. the tithe of 12.17
the Levite who is within your t.; 12.18
eat wthin your t. as much as you 12.21
to the alien who is within your t., 14.21
the Levite who is within your t., 14.27
year, and lay it up within your t.; 14.28
the widow, who are within your t., 14.29
in any of your t. within your land 15.07
You shall eat it within your t.; 15.22
any of your t. which the LORD your 16.05
the Levite who is within your t., 16.11
the widow who are within your t. 16.14
in all your t. which the LORD your 16.18
any of your t. which the LORD your 17.02
within your t. which is too 17.08
any of your t. out of all Israel, 18.06
shall choose within one of your t., 23.16
are in your land within your t.; 24.14
eat within your t. and be filled, 26.12
They shall besiege you in all your t., 28.52
you in all your t. throughout all 28.52
shall distress you in all your t. 28.55
shall distress you in your t. 28.57
and the sojourner within your t., 31.12
the sword, and its king and its t., Jos 10.37
it with its king and all its t.; 10.39
and all the t. of Jair, which are in 13.30
with its t. and its villages; 15.45
Ashdod, its t. and its villages; 15.47
Gaza, its t. and its villages; 15.47
together with the t. which were set 16.09
all those t. with their villages 16.09
of it by t. in seven divisons; 18.09
And all the t. which they found Ju 20.48
inheritance, and rebuilt the t., 21.23
given me in one of the country t., 1Sa 27.05
and they dwelt in the t. of Hebron. 2Sa 2.03
high places at all their t., 2Ki 17.09
Kenath and its villages, sixty t. 1Ch 2.23
in Gilead, in Bashan and in its t., 5.16
settlements were Bethel and its t., 7.28
and westward Gezer and its t., 7.28
Shechem and its t., and Ayyah and its t.; 7.28
Bethshean and its t., Taanach and its t., 7.29
Megiddo and its t., Dor and its t. 7.29
who built Ono and Lod with its t., 8.12
temple servants lived in their t., Ez 2.70
towns, and all Israel in their t. 2.70
the sons of Israel were in the t., 3.01
and all Israel, lived in their t. Neh 7.73
children of Israel were in their t. 7.73
in all their t. and in Jerusalem, 8.15
the tithes in all our rural t. 10.37
tenths remained in the other t. 11.01
but in the t. of Judah every one 11.03
lived on his property in their t.: 11.03
were in all the t. of Judah, 11.20
according to the fields of the t.; 12.44
villages, who live in the open t., Est 9.19
upon all its t. all the evil that Jer 19.15
Zion, virgins in the t. of Judah. Lam 5.11
gone through all the t. of Israel, Mt 10.23
followed him on foot from the t. 14.13
them, "Let us go on to the next t., Mk 1.38
ran there on foot from all the t., 6.33
on his way through t. and villages, Lk 13.22
from the t. around Jerusalem, Ac 5.16
to all the t. till he came to 8.40

TOWNSMEN
all my fellow t. know that you are Ru 3.11

TRACE
not be even a t. of it until he Eze 21.27
so that not a t. of them could be Dan 2.35

TRACHONITIS
of the region of Ituraea and T., Lk 3.01

TRACK
They t. me down; now they surround Ps 17.11

TRACKED
A city of evildoers, t. with blood. Hos 6.08

TRACKLESS
and makes them wander in t. wastes; Ps 107.40

TRACKS
the t. of thy chariot drip with Ps 65.11
follow in the t. of the flock, and Sol 1.08
young camel interlacing her t., Je 2.23

TRADE
dwell and t. in it, and get property Gen 34.10
dwell in the land and t. in it, 34.21
and you shall t. in the land. 42.34
ply their t. through the land, and Jer 14.18
they t. their treasures for food to Lam 1.11
and carried it to a land of t., Eze 17.04
great wisdom in t. you have 28.05
abundance of your t. you were 28.16
unrighteousness of your t. you 28.18
'T. with these till I come.' Lk 19.13
my Father's house a house of t." Jn 2.16
was of the same t. he stayed with Ac 18.03
for by t. they were tentmakers. 18.03
only that this t. of ours may come 19.27
a year there and t. and get gain"; Jas 4.13
and all whose t. is on the sea, Rev 18.17

TRADED
Javan, Tubal, and Meshech t. with you; Eze 27.13
The men of Rhodes t. with you; 27.15
and the land of Israel t. with you; 27.17
Dedan t. with you in saddlecloths 27.20
of Sheba and Raamah t. with you; 27.22
Asshur, and Chilmad t. with you. 27.23
These t. with you in choice garments, 27.24
in these they t. with you. 27.24
went at once and t. with them; Mt 25.16

TRADER
A t., in whose hands are false Hos 12.07
no longer be a t. in the house of Zec 14.21

TRADERS
Then Midianite t. passed by; and they drew Gen 37.28
came from the t. and from the traffic 1Ki 10.15
and the king's t. received them 10.28
the king's t. they were exported 10.29
and the king's t. received them 2Ch 1.16
besides that which the t. and 9.14
Will t. bargain over him? Will they divide Job 41.06
whose t. were the honored of the Is 23.08
The t. of Sheba and Raamah traded Eze 27.22
For all the t. are no more; all who Zep 1.11

TRADING
profit of his t. he will get no Job 20.18
also with the t. land of Chaldea; Eze 16.29
know what they had gained by t. Lk 19.15

TRADITION
transgress the t. of the elders? Mt 15.02
of God for the sake of your t.? 15.03
So, for the sake of your t., 15.06
observing the t. of the elders; Mk 7.03
according to the t. of the elders, 7.05
God, and hold fast the t. of men." 7.08
of God, in order to keep your t.! 7.09
through your t. which you hand on. 7.13
deceit, according to human t., Col 2.08
accord with t. that you 2Th 3.06

TRADITIONS
are many other t. which they Mk 7.04
maintain the t. even as I have 1Co 11.02
was I for the t. of my fathers. Gal 1.14
and hold to the t. which you were 2Th 2.15

TRAFFIC
and from the t. of the merchants, 1Ki 10.15

TRAFFICKED
who have t. with you from your Is 47.15
"Tarshish t. with you because of Eze 27.12
Edom t. with you because of your 27.16
Damascus t. with you for your 27.18
in these they t. with you. 27.21
for those who t. in the sheep. Zec 11.07

TRAFFICKERS
and the t. in the sheep, who were Zec 11.11

TRAIN
companions, her escort, in her t. Ps 45.14
mount, leading captives in thy t., 68.18
T. up a child in the way he should Pro 22.06
and his t. filled the temple. Is 6.01
Ethiopians shall follow in his t. Dan 11.43
T. yourself in godliness; 1Ti 4.07
and so t. the young women to love Tit 2.04

TRAINED
captive, he led forth his t. men, Gen 14.14
who were t. in singing to the LORD, 1Ch 25.07
t. also in engraving, to be with the 2Ch 2.07
He is t. to work in gold, silver, 2.14
Although I t. and strengthened Hos 7.15
Ephraim was a t. heifer that loved 10.11
who has been t. for the kingdom of Mt 13.52
their faculties t. by practice to Heb 5.14
to those who have been t. by it. 12.11
They have hearts t. in greed. 2Pe 2.14

TRAINING
than the divine t. that is in 1Ti 1.04
for while bodily t. is of some 4.08
and for t. in righteousness, 2Ti 3.16
t. us to renounce irreligion and Tit 2.12

TRAINS
He t. my hands for war, so that my 2Sa 22.35
He t. my hands for war, so that my Ps 18.34
who t. my hands for war, and my 144.01

TRAITOR
Judas Iscariot, who became a t. Lk 6.16

TRAMPING
boot of the t. warrior in battle Is 9.05

TRAMPLE
that the wild beast may t. them. Job 39.15
and let him t. my life to the Ps 7.05
to me, O God, for men t. upon me; 56.01
my enemies t. upon me all day long, 56.02
put to shame those who t. upon me. 57.03
T. under foot those who lust after 68.30
the serpent you will t. under foot. 91.13
my mountains t. him under foot; Is 14.25
he shall t. on rulers as on mortar, 41.25
horses he will t. all your streets; Eze 26.11
and t. it down, and break it to Dan 7.23
they that t. the head of the poor Amo 2.07
Therefore because you t. upon the 5.11
you who t. upon the needy, and bring 8.04
thou didst t. the nations in anger. Hab 3.12
Thou didst t. the sea with thy 3.15
lest they t. them underfoot and Mt 7.06
and they will t. over the holy city Rev 11.02

TRAMPLED
on the horses, and they t. on her. 2Ki 9.33
passed by and t. down the thistle. 14.09
passed by and t. down the thistle. 2Ch 25.18
and t. the waves of the sea; Job 9.08
its wall, and it shall be t. down. Is 5.05
in my anger and t. them in my 63.03
they have t. down my portion, they Jer 12.10
down to the ground and t. upon him; Dan 8.07
to the ground, and t. upon them. 8.10
and host to be t. under foot?" 8.13

TRAMPLES
and he who t. under foot has Is 16.04
The foot t. it, the feet of the poor, 26.06
so that he t. kings under foot; 41.02

TRAMPLING
of you this t. of my courts? Is 1.12
of tumult and t. and confusion in 22.05
t. the foe in the mud of the Zec 10.05

TRANCE
preparing it, he fell into a t. Ac 10.10
and in a t. I saw a vision, something 11.05
in the temple, I fell into a t. 22.17

TRANSGRESSION
He who loves t. loves strife; Pro 17.19

TRANQUIL
A t. mind gives life to the flesh, Pro 14.30

TRANQUILLITY
perhaps be a lengthening of your t." Dan 4.27

TRANSACTION
to confirm a t., the one drew off Ru 4.07

TRANSCENDENT
show that the t. power belongs to 2Co 4.07

TRANSFER
to t. the kingdom from the house of 2Sa 3.10

TRANSFERRED
shall not be t. from one tribe to Num 36.07
shall be t. from one tribe to 36.09
of darkness and t. us to the Col 1.13

TRANSFIGURED
And he was t. before them, and his Mt 17.02
and he was t. before them, Mk 9.02

TRANSFORMED
world but be t. by the renewal of Rom 12.02

TRANSGRESS
if you t. the covenant of the LORD Jos 23.16
'Why do you t. the commandments of 2Ch 24.20
"Why do you t. the king's command?" Est 3.03
in me; my mouth does not t. Ps 17.03
waters might not t. his command, Pro 8.29
you, and those who t. against me; Eze 20.38
"Come to Bethel, and t.; to Gilgal, Amo 4.04
your disciples t. the tradition of Mt 15.02
"And why do you t. the commandment 15.03
that no man t., and wrong his 1Th 4.06

TRANSGRESSED
I have not t. any of thy commandments, Deu 26.13
they have t. my covenant which Jos 7.11
because he has t. the covenant of 7.15
people have t. my covenant which I Ju 2.20
for I have t. the commandment of 1Sa 15.24
LORD their God but t. his covenant, 2Ki 18.12
who t. in the matter of the devoted 1Ch 2.07
But they t. against the God of 5.25
we have greatly t. in this matter. Ez 10.13

TRANSGRESSED (cont.)
for they have t. the laws, violated Is 24.05
and your mediators t. against me. 43.27
the rulers t. against me; the prophets Jer 2.08
And the men who t. my covenant and 34.18
"We have t. and rebelled, and thou Lam 3.42
fathers have t. against me to this Eze 2.03
All Israel has t. thy law and Dan 9.11
But at Adam they t. the covenant; Hos 6.07
broken my covenant, and t. my law. 8.01

TRANSGRESSES
When a land t. it has many rulers; Pro 28.02
shall not deliver him when he t.; Eze 33.12

TRANSGRESSING
"Why now are you t. the command of Num 14.41
LORD your God, in t. his covenant, Deu 17.02
t., and denying the LORD, and Is 59.13

TRANSGRESSION
the t. of your brothers and their Gen 50.17
forgive the t. of the servants of 50.17
for he will not pardon your t.; Ex 23.21
forgiving iniquity and t. and sin, 34.07
love, forgiving iniquity and t., Num 14.18
not pardon my t. and take away my Job 7.21
them into the power of their t. 8.04
Make me know my t. and my sin. 13.23
my t. would be sealed up in a bag, 14.17
You say, 'I am clean, without t.: I am pure, 33.09
incurable, though I am without t. 34.06
punish, and he does not greatly heed t., 35.15
blameless, and innocent of great t. Ps 19.13
Blessed is he whose t. is forgiven, 32.01
T. speaks to the wicked deep in his 36.01
For no t. or sin of mine, O LORD, 59.03
punish their t. with the rod and 89.32
t. is not lacking, but he who Pro 10.19
is ensnared by the t. of his lips, 12.13
"That is no t.," is the companion 28.24
An evil man is ensnared in his t., 29.06
are in authority, t. increases; 29.16
man given to anger causes much t. 29.22
its t. lies heavy upon it, and it Is 24.20
stricken for the t. of my people? 53.08
Are you not children of t., 57.04
declare to my people their t., 58.01
who turn from t., says the LORD. 59.20
continual burnt offering through t.; Dan 8.12
the t. that makes desolate, and the 8.13
to finish the t., to put an end to 9.24
to Gilgal, and multiply t.; Amo 4.04
All this is for the t. of Jacob and Mic 1.05
What is the t. of Jacob? Is it not 1.05
to Jacob his t. and to Israel his 3.08
I give my first-born for my t., 6.07
passing over t. for the remnant of 7.18
there is no law there is no t. Rom 4.15
sins were not like the t. of Adam, 5.14
valid and every t. or disobedience Heb 2.02
but was rebuked for his own t.; 2Pe 2.16

TRANSGRESSIONS
of Israel, and because of their t., Lev 16.16
and all their t., all their sins; 16.21
not forgive your t. or your sins. Jos 24.19
and all their t. which they have 1Ki 8.50
if I have concealed my t. from men, Job 31.33
And if your t. are multiplied, what 35.06
to them their work and their t., 36.09
of their many t. cast them out, Ps 5.10
not the sins of my youth, or my t.; 25.07
"I will confess my t. to the LORD"; 32.05
Deliver me from all my t. 39.08
thy abundant mercy blot out my t. 51.01
For I know my t., and my sin is 51.03
When our t. prevail over us, thou 65.03
far does he remove our t. from us. 103.12
conceals his t. will not prosper, Pro 28.13
blots out your t. for my own sake, Is 43.25
swept away your t. like a cloud, 44.22
and for your t. your mother was put 50.01
But he was wounded for our t., 53.05
For our t. are multiplied before 59.12
for our t. are with us, and we know 59.12
because their t. are many, their Jer 5.06
suffer for the multitude of her t.; Lam 1.05
"My t. were bound into a yoke; 1.14
dealt with me because of all my t.; 1.22
themselves any more with all their t., Eze 14.11
None of the t. which he has committed 18.22
from all the t. which he had 18.28
Repent and turn from all your t., 18.30
you all the t. which you have 18.31
in that your t. are uncovered, so 21.24
'Our t. and our sins are upon us, 33.10
things, or with any of their t.; 37.23
to their uncleanness and their t., 39.24
"For three t. of Damascus, and for Amo 1.03
"For three t. of Gaza, and for four, 1.06
"For three t. of Tyre, and for four, 1.09
"For three t. of Edom, and for four, 1.11
"For three t. of the Ammonites, and 1.13
"For three t. of Moab, and for four, 2.01
"For three t. of Judah, and for four, 2.04
"For three t. of Israel, and for 2.06
the day I punish Israel for his t., 3.14
For I know how many are your t., 5.12
in you were found the t. of Israel. Mic 1.13
It was added because of t., Gal 3.19
them from the t. under the first Heb 9.15

TRANSGRESSOR
down, then I prove myself a t. Gal 2.18
woman was deceived and became a t. 1Ti 2.14
you have become a t. of the law. Jas 2.11

TRANSGRESSORS
But t. shall be altogether destroyed; Ps 37.38
Then I will teach t. thy ways, 51.13
consider, recall it to mind, you t., Is 46.08
and was numbered with the t.; 53.12
and made intercession for the t. 53.12
when the t. have reached their full Dan 8.23
but t. stumble in them. Hos 14.09
"He was reckoned with the t." *Mk 15.28
me, 'And he was reckoned with t.'; Lk 22.37
and are convicted by the law as t. Jas 2.09

TRANSIENT
the things that are seen are t., 2Co 4.18

TRANSLATED
was written in Aramaic and t. Ez 4.07

TRANSLATION
by t. of his name, king of righteousness, Hab 7.02

TRANSPARENT
city was pure gold, t. as glass. Rev 21.21

TRANSPLANTED
he t. it to good soil by abundant Eze 17.08
when it is t., will it thrive? 17.10
vine in a vineyard t. by the water, 19.10
Now it is t. in the wilderness, in a 19.13

TRAP
shall be a snare and a t. for you, Jos 23.13
A t. seizes him by the heel, a snare Job 18.09
ground, a t. for him in the path. 18.10
their sacrificial feasts be a t. Ps 69.22
Arrogant men have hidden a t. for me, 140.05
Keep me from the t. which they have 141.09

TRAP (cont.)

walk they have hidden a t. for me. Ps 142.03
a t. and a snare to the inhabitants Is 8.14
They set a t.; they catch men. Jer 5.26
earth, when there is no t. for it? Amo 3.05
friends have set a t. under you— Ob 1.07
feast become a snare and a t., Rom 11.09

TRAPPED

let them be t. in their pride. Ps 59.12
are all of them t. in holes and Is 42.22

TRAVAIL

there, anguish as of a woman in t. Ps 48.06
your mother was in t. with you, Sol 8.05
there she who bore you was in t. 8.05
be in anguish like a woman in t. Is 13.08
like the pangs of a woman in t.; 21.03
I will cry out like a woman in t., 42.14
a woman, 'With what are you in t.?'" 45.10
fruit of the t. of his soul and be 53.11
aloud, you who have not been in t.! 54.01
For I heard a cry as of a woman in t., Jer 4.31
of us, pain as of a woman in t. 6.24
you, like those of a woman in t.? 13.21
upon you, pain as of a woman in t.!" 22.23
and her who is in t., together; 31.08
hold of her, as of a woman in t. 49.24
him, pain as of a woman in t. 50.43
have seized you like a woman in t.? Mic 4.09
of Zion, like a woman in t.; 4.10
she who is in t. has brought forth 5.03
When a woman is in t. she has sorrow, Jn 16.21
groaning in t. together until now; Rom 8.22
I am again in t. until Christ be Gal 4.19
and shout, thou who art not in t.; 4.27
upon them as t. comes upon a woman 1Th 5.03

TRAVAILED

Rachel t., and she had hard labor. Gen 35.16
"I have neither t. nor given birth, Is 23.04

TRAVEL

that they might t. by day and by Ex 13.21
not asked those who t. the roads Job 21.29
who were Paul's companions in t. Ac 19.29
the churches to t. with us in this 2Co 8.19

TRAVELED

of Tarshish t. for you with your Eze 27.25
over Stephen t. as far as Phoenicia Ac 11.19

TRAVELER

Now there came a t. to the rich man, 2Sa 12.04

TRAVELERS

ceased and t. kept to the byways. Ju 5.06
of Tema look, the t. of Sheba hope. Job 6.19
they are forgotten by t., they hang 28.04
Valley of the T. east of the sea; Eze 39.11
it will block the t., for there Gog 39.11

TRAVELING

The men who were t. with him stood Ac 9.07

TRAVERSE

for you t. sea and land to make a Mt 23.15

TRAYS

and their t. shall be of pure gold Ex 25.38
snuffers and its t. of pure gold. 37.23
its t., and all the vessels for oil Num 4.09

TREACHEROUS

My brethren are t. as a torrent-bed, Job 6.15
be ashamed who are wantonly t. Ps 25.03
and the t. will be rooted out of it. Pro 2.22
crookedness of the t. destroys them. 11.03
but the t. are taken captive by 11.06
the counsels of the wicked are t. 12.05
desire of the t. is for violence. 13.02
For the t. deal treacherously, the Is 24.16
the t. deal very treacherously." 24.16
you t. one, with whom none has dealt 33.01
adulterers, a company of t. men. Jer 9.02
Why do all who are t. thrive? 12.01
they are like a t. bow, their princes Hos 7.16
Moreover, wine is t.; the arrogant Hab 2.05
t., reckless, swollen with conceit, 2Ti 3.04

TREACHEROUSLY

attacks another to kill him t., Ex 21.14
to act t. against the LORD in the Num 31.16
of Shechem dealt t. with Abimelech; Ju 9.23
And he said, "You have dealt t.; 1Sa 14.33
if I had dealt t. against his life 2Sa 18.13
evil and act t. against our God by Neh 13.27
none of those who t. plot evil. Ps 59.05
away and acted t. like their 78.57
For the treacherous deal t., Is 24.16
the treacherous deal very t." 24.16
one, with whom none has dealt t.! 33.01
you have made an end of dealing t., 33.01
t., you will be dealt with t. 33.01
I knew that you would deal very t., 48.08
even they have dealt t. with you; Jer 12.06
her friends have dealt t. with her, Lam 1.02
blasphemed me, by dealing t. with me. Eze 20.27
they dealt so t. with me that I 39.23

TREACHERY

in their t. which they committed Lev 26.40
'What is this t. which you have Jos 22.16
committed this t. against the LORD; 22.31
saying to Ahaziah, "T., O Ahaziah!" 2Ki 9.23
king of Assyria found t. in Hoshea; 17.04
and meditate t. all the day long. Ps 38.12
a sharp razor, you worker of t. 52.02
of blood and t. shall not live out 55.23
birds, their houses are full of t.; Jer 5.27
for the t. of which he is guilty Eze 18.24
and all the t. they have practiced 39.26
because of the t. which they have Dan 9.07
glad, and the princes of their t. Hos 7.03

TREAD

for the sole of the foot to t. on, Deu 2.05
all the land that you shall t., 11.25
and you shall t. upon their high 33.29
your foot will t. upon I have Jos 1.03
of Dagon do not t. on the threshold 1Sa 5.05
they t. the wine presses, but suffer Job 24.11
the t. down the wicked where they 40.12
thy name we t. down our assailants Ps 44.05
it is he who will t. down our foes. 60.12
You will t. on the lion and the 91.13
it is he who will t. down our foes. 108.13
Three things are stately in their t.; Pro 30.29
are let loose and where sheep t. Is 7.25
and to t. them down like the mire 10.06
shout, like those who t. grapes, Jer 25.30
that you must t. down with your Eze 34.18
Go in, t., for the wine press is Joe 3.13
come down and t. upon the high Mic 1.03
you shall t. olives, but not anoint 6.15
you shall t. grapes, but not drink 6.15
he will t. our iniquities under 7.19
t. the mortar, take hold of the Nah 3.14
he makes me t. upon my high places. Hab 3.19
devour and t. down the slingers; Zec 9.15
And you shall t. down the wicked, Mal 4.03
authority to t. upon serpents and Lk 10.19
he will t. the wine press of the Rev 19.15

TREADER

no t. turns toward their vineyards. Job 24.18
no t. treads out wine in the Is 16.10
reaper and the t. of grapes him Amo 9.13

TREADING
in Judah men t. wine presses on Neh 13.15
an ox when it is t. out the grain. 1Co 9.09
an ox when it is t. out the grain, 1Ti 5.18

TREADS
of your foot t. shall be yours; Deu 11.24
an ox when it t. out the grain. 25.04
no treader t. out wine in the Is 16.10
on mortar, as the potter t. clay. 41.25
like his that t. in the wine press? 63.02
no one t. them with shouts of joy; Jer 48.33
and t. on the heights of the earth— Amo 4.13
into our land and t. upon our soil, Mic 5.05
our land and t. within our border. 5.06
t. down and tears in pieces, and 5.08

TREASON
is no wrong or t. in my hands. 1Sa 24.11
rent her clothes, and cried, "T.! t.!" 2Ki 11.14
rent her clothes, and cried, "T.! T.!" 2Ch 23.13
there for the t. he has committed Eze 17.20

TREASURE
must have put t. in your sacks for Gen 43.23
he showed them all his t. house, 2Ki 20.13
I have a t. of my own of gold and 1Ch 29.03
my words and t. up my commandments Pro 2.01
my words and t. up my commandments 7.01
of the righteous there is much t., 15.06
LORD than great t. and trouble 15.16
Precious t. remains in a wise man's 21.20
gold and the t. of kings and Ecc 2.08
the fear of the LORD is his t. Is 33.06
and he showed them his t. house, 39.02
they have t. and precious Eze 22.25
There is no end of t., or wealth Nah 2.09
For where your t. is, there will Mt 6.21
out of his good t. brings forth 12.35
out of his evil t. brings forth 12.35
heaven is like t. hidden in a 13.44
out of his t. what is new and what 13.52
and you will have t. in heaven; 19.21
and you will have t. in heaven; Mk 10.21
out of the good t. of his heart Lk 6.45
out of his evil t. produces evil; 6.45
So is he who lays up t. for himself, 12.21
with a t. in the heavens that does 12.33
For where your t. is, there will 12.34
and you will have t. in heaven; 18.22
Ethiopians, in charge of all her t., Ac 8.27
But we have this t. in earthen 2Co 4.07
have laid up t. for the last days. Jas 5.03

TREASURED
I have t. in my bosom the words of Job 23.12

TREASURER
out in charge of Mithrdath the t., Ez 1.08
the city t., and our brother Rom 16.23

TREASURERS
to all the t. in the province Ez 7.21
And I appointed as t. over the Neh 13.13
the t., the justices, the magistrates, Dan 3.02
the t., the justices, the magistrates, 3.03

TREASURES
seas and the hidden t. of the sand." Deu 33.19
he took away the t. of the house of 1Ki 14.26
LORD and the t. of the king's house; 14.26
left in the t. of the house of the 15.18
LORD and the t. of the king's house, 15.18
LORD and in the t. of the king's 2Ki 16.08
off all the t. of the house of the 24.13
and the t. of the king's house, and 24.13
chambers and the t. of the house of 1Ch 9.26
took away the t. of the house of 2Ch 12.09
LORD and the t. of the king's house; 12.09
gold from the t. of the house of 16.02
and the t. of the house of the LORD, 36.18
and the t. of the king and of his 36.18
dig for it more than for hid t.; Job 3.21
Utter darkness is laid up for his t.; 20.26
and search for it as for hidden t.; Pro 2.04
T. gained by wickedness do not 10.02
The getting of t. by a lying tongue 21.06
and there is no end to their t.; Is 2.07
and have plundered their t.; 10.13
and their t. on the humps of camels, 30.06
give you the t. of darkness and 45.03
"Your wealth and your t. I will Jer 15.13
and all your t. I will give for 17.03
and all the t. of the kings of 20.05
in your strongholds and your t., 48.07
daughter, who trusted in her t., 49.04
A sword upon all her t., that they may be 50.37
rich in t., your end has come, the 51.13
trade their t. for food to revive Lam 1.11
ruler of the t. of gold and of Dan 11.43
carried my rich t. into your Joe 3.05
been pillaged, his t. sought out! Ob 1.06
Can I forget the t. of wickedness Mic 6.10
so that the t. of all nations shall Hag 2.07
opening their t., they offered him Mt 2.11
lay up for yourselves t. on earth, 6.19
lay up for yourselves t. in heaven, 6.20
are hid all the t. of wisdom and Col 2.03
wealth than the t. of Egypt, Heb 11.26

TREASURIES
store with me, sealed up in my t.? Deu 32.34
them in the t. of the house of the 1Ki 7.51
found in the t. of the house of 2Ki 12.18
LORD and in the t. of the king's 14.14
and in the t. of the king's house. 18.15
charge of the t. of the house of 1Ch 26.20
of God and the t. of the dedicated 26.20
charge of the t. of the house of 26.22
chief officer in charge of the t. 26.24
of all the t. of the dedicated 26.26
Over the king's t. was Azmaveth the 27.25
and over the t. in the country, in 27.25
its t., its upper rooms, and its 28.11
the t. of the house of God, and the 28.12
and the t. for dedicated gifts; 28.12
vessels in the t. of the house of 2Ch 5.01
any matter and concerning the t. 8.15
seized also the t. of the king's 25.24
he made for himself t. for silver, 32.27
they may put it into the king's t." Est 3.09
into the king's t. for the destruction 4.07
who love me, and filling their t. Pro 8.21
gold and silver into your t.; Eze 28.04

TREASURY
to you his good t. the heavens, to give the Deu 28.12
shall go into the t. of the LORD." Jos 6.19
put into the t. of the house of 6.24
them to the t. of the house of the 1Ch 29.08
gave to the t. of the work sixty-one Ez 2.69
the cost be paid from the royal t. 6.04
provide it out of the king's t. 7.20
gave to the t. a thousand darics Neh 7.70
gave into the t. of the work 7.71
the vessels in the t. of his god. Dan 1.02
shall strip his t. of every Hos 13.15
said to me, "Cast it into the t."— Zec 11.13
them into the t. in the house of 11.13
not lawful to put them into the t., Mt 27.06
And he sat down opposite the t., Mk 12.41
multitude putting money into the t. 12.41
who are contributing to the t. 12.43
putting their gifts into the t.; Lk 21.01
These words he spoke in the t., Jn 8.20

TREAT
"Should he t. our sister as a Gen 34.31
"Why did you t. me so ill as to 43.06
you shall not t. her as a slave, Deu 21.14
he may not t. the son of the loved 21.16
so will I t. Zedekiah the king of Jer 24.08
How can I t. you like Zeboiim! Hos 11.08
at you and t. you with contempt, Nah 3.06
t. me as one of your hired servants."' Lk 15.19
Masters, t. your slaves justly and Col 4.01
t. younger men like brothers, 1Ti 5.01

TREATED
"This is the way your servant t. me," Gen 39.19
but he t. them like strangers and 42.07
And the Egyptians t. us harshly, Deu 26.06
for the men t. the offering of the 1Sa 2.17
Father and mother are t. with Eze 22.07
who have t. them with contempt. 28.24
who have t. them with contempt. 28.26
t. them shamefully, and killed them. Mt 22.06
things and be t. with contempt? Mk 9.12
in the head, and t. him shamefully. 12.04
to him, "Son, why have you t. us so? Lk 2.48
and shamefully t. and spit upon; 18.32
also they beat and t. shamefully, 20.11
his soldiers t. him with contempt 23.11
and Julius t. Paul kindly, and gave Ac 27.03
parts are t. with greater modesty, 1Co 12.23
We are t. as impostors, and yet are 2Co 6.08
and been shamefully t. at Philippi, 1Th 2.02
being partners with those so t. Heb 10.33

TREATING
God is t. you as sons; for what son is Heb 12.07

TREATS
and if he t. him as a slave or Deu 24.07
for the son t. the father with Mic 7.06
new covenant he t. the first as Heb 8.13

TREATY
"Make a t. with us, and we will 1Sa 11.01
condition I will make a t. with you, 11.02
and the two of them made a t. 1Ki 5.12

TREE
and every t. with seed in its fruit; Gen 1.29
to grow every t. that is pleasant 2.09
the t. of life also in the midst of 2.09
and the t. of the knowledge of good 2.09
eat of every t. of the garden; 2.16
but of the t. of the knowledge of 2.17
not eat of any t. of the garden'?" 3.01
fruit of the t. which is in the 3.03
saw that the t. was good for food, 3.06
and that the t. was to be desired 3.06
eaten of the t. of which I commanded 3.11
gave me fruit of the t., and I ate." 3.12
eaten of the t. of which I commanded 3.17
and take also of the t. of life, 3.22
to guard the way to the t. of life. 3.24
and rest yourselves under the t., 18.04
them under the t. while they ate. 18.08
planted a tamarisk t. in Beersheba, 21.33
head—from you!—and hang you on a t.; 40.19
shattered every t. of the field. Ex 9.25
shall eat every t. of yours which 10.05
neither t. nor plant of the field, 10.15
and the LORD showed him a t., and he threw 15.25
the hills and under every green t.; Deu 12.02
not plant any t. as an Asherah 16.21
swings the axe to cut down a t., 19.05
death, and you hang him on a t., 21.22
not remain all night upon the t., 21.23
in any t. or on the ground, with 22.06
king of Ai on a t. until evening; Jos 8.29
took his body down from the t., 8.29
and they said to the olive t., Ju 9.08
But the olive t. said to them, 9.09
And the trees said to the fig t., 9.10
But the fig t. said to them, 'Shall 9.11
the pomegranate t. which is at 1Sa 14.02
the tamarisk t. on the height, 22.06
under the tarmarisk t. in Jabesh, 31.13
his vine and under his fig t., 1Ki 4.25
high hill and under every green t.; 14.23
came and sat down under a broom t.; 19.04
down and slept under a broom t.; 19.05
city, and shall fell every good t., 2Ki 3.19
hills, and under every green t. 16.04
high hill and under every green t.; 17.10
and every one of his own fig t., 18.31
hills, and under every green t. 2Ch 28.04
fruits of all fruit of every t., Neh 10.35
contributions, the fruit of every t., 10.37
"For there is hope for a t., Job 14.07
off his blossom, like the olive t. 15.33
my hope has he pulled up like a t. 19.10
so wickedness is broken like a t.' 24.20
He is like a t. planted by streams Ps 1.03
a green olive t. in the house of 52.08
righteous flourish like the palm t., 92.12
with glowing coals of the broom t.! 120.04
She is a t. of life to those who Pro 3.18
of the righteous is a t. of life, 11.30
a desire fulfilled is a t. of life. 13.12
A gentle tongue is a t. of life, 15.04
He who tends a fig t. will eat its 27.18
and if a t. falls to the south or Ecc 11.03
in the place where the t. falls, 11.03
the almond t. blossoms, the grasshopper 12.05
As an apple t. among the trees of Sol 2.03
The fig t. puts forth its figs, and 2.13
You are stately as a palm t., 7.07
climb the palm t. and lay hold of 7.08
under the apple t. I awakened you. 8.05
it, as when an olive t. is beaten— Is 17.06
five on the branches of a fruit t., 17.06
as when an olive t. is beaten, 24.13
leaves falling from the fig t. 34.04
and every one of his own fig t., 36.16
chooses a holm t. or an oak and 44.14
O forest, and every t. in it! 44.23
eunuch say, "Behold, I am a dry t." 56.03
the oaks, under every green t.; who 57.05
the days of a t. shall the days of 65.22
every green t. you bowed down as a Jer 2.20
who say to a t., 'You are my father,' 2.27
high hill and under every green t., 3.06
committing adultery with stone and t. 3.09
strangers under every green t., 3.13
the vine, nor figs on the fig t.; 8.13
A t. from the forest is cut down, 10.03
once called you, 'A green olive t., 11.16
us destroy the t. with its fruit, 11.19
Asherim, beside every green t., 17.02
He is like a t. planted by water, 17.08
mountaintops, under every green t., Eze 6.13
bring low the high t., and make high the low t., 17.24
dry up the green t., and make the dry t. flourish. 17.24
saw any high hill or any leafy t., 20.28
every green t. in you and every dry t.; 20.47
no t. in the garden of God was like 31.08
fruit of the t. and the increase 36.30
a palm t. between cherub and cherub. 41.18
toward the palm t. on the one side, 41.19
toward the palm t. on the other 41.19
a t. in the midst of the earth; Dan 4.10
The t. grew and became strong, and 4.11
'Hew down the t. and cut off its 4.14
The t. you saw, which grew and 4.20
'Hew down the t. and destroy it, but 4.23
the stump of the roots of the t., 4.26
Like the first fruit on the fig t., Hos 9.10
withers, the fig t. languishes. Joe 1.12

TREE (cont.)

the t. bears its fruit, the fig t. and vine give Joe 2.22
his vine and under his fig t., Mic 4.04
Though the fig t. do not blossom, Hab 3.17
the fig t., the pomegranate, and the Hag 2.19
and the olive t. still yield 2.19
his vine and under his fig t. Zec 3.10
every t. therefore that does not Mt 3.10
every sound t. bears good fruit, but 7.17
but the bad t. bears evil fruit. 7.17
A sound t. cannot bear evil fruit, 7.18
nor can a bad t. bear good fruit. 7.18
Every t. that does not bear good 7.19
"Either make the t. good, and its fruit 12.33
or make the t. bad, and its fruit 12.33
for the t. is known by its fruit. 12.33
greatest of shrubs and becomes a t., 13.32
And seeing a fig t. by the wayside 21.19
And the fig t. withered at once. 21.19
"How did the fig t. wither at once?" 21.20
what has been done to the fig t., 21.21
"From the fig t. learn its lesson: 24.32
in the distance a fig t. in leaf, Mk 11.13
saw the fig t. withered away to 11.20
The fig t. which you cursed has 11.21
"From the fig t. learn its lesson: 13.28
every t. therefore that does not Lk 3.09
"For no good t. bears bad fruit, nor 6.43
does a bad t. bear good fruit; 6.43
for each t. is known by its own 6.44
"A man had a fig t. planted in his 13.06
come seeking fruit on this fig t., 13.07
and it grew and became a t., 13.19
you could say to this sycamine t., 17.06
up into a sycamore t. to see him, 19.04
them a parable: "Look at the fig t., 21.29
were under the fig t., I saw you." Jn 1.48
to you, I saw you under the fig t., 1.50
you killed by hanging him on a t. Ac 5.30
to death by hanging him on a t.; 10.39
they took him down from the t., 13.29
the richness of the olive t., Rom 11.17
what is by nature a wild olive t., 11.24
nature, into a cultivated olive t., 11.24
back into their own olive t. 11.24
be every one who hangs on a t."— Gal 3.13
Can a fig t., my brethren, yield Jas 3.12
our sins in his body on the t., 1Pe 2.24
grant to eat of the t. of life, Rev 2.07
as the fig t. sheds its winter 6.13
on earth or sea or against any t. 7.01
or any green growth or any t., 9.04
the t. of life with its twelve 22.02
leaves of the t. were for the 22.02
right to the t. of life and that 22.14
share in the t. of life and in the 22.19

TREES

and fruit t. bearing fruit in which Gen 1.11
and t. bearing fruit in which is 1.12
the fruit of the t. of the garden; 3.02
God among the t. of the garden. 3.08
it and all the t. that were in the 23.17
fruit of the t. which the hail had Ex 10.15
of water and seventy palm t.; 15.27
and plant all kinds of t. for food, Lev 19.23
fruit of goodly t., branches of palm t., 23.40
and boughs of leafy t., and willows 23.40
and the t. of the field shall yield 26.04
and the t. of the land shall not 26.20
the fruit of the t., is the LORD's; 27.30
like cedar t. beside the waters. Num 24.06
of water and seventy palm t., 33.09
hew, and vineyards and olive t., Deu 6.11
vines and fig t. and pomegranates, 8.08
a land of olive t. and honey, 8.08
not destroy its t. by wielding an 20.19
Are the t. in the field men that 20.19
t. which you know are not t. for food 20.20
When you beat your olive t., 24.20
have olive t. throughout all your 28.40
All your t. and the fruit of your 28.42
of Jericho the city of palm t., 34.03
death, and he hung them on five t. Jos 10.26
hung upon the t. until evening; 10.26
they took them down from the t., 10.27
The t. once went forth to anoint a Ju 9.08
honored, and go to sway over the t.?' 9.09
And the t. said to the fig tree, 9.10
fruit, and go to sway over the t.?' 9.11
And the t. said to the vine, 'Come 9.12
men, and go to sway over the t.?' 9.13
Then all the t. said to the bramble, 9.14
And the bramble said to the t., 9.15
and cedar t., also carpenters and 2Sa 5.11
upon them opposite the balsam t. 5.23
in the tops of the balsam t., 5.24
He spoke to t., from the cedar that 1Ki 4.33
and palm t. and open flowers, in 6.29
palm t., and open flowers; he overlay 6.32
the cherubim and upon the palm t. 6.32
and palm t. and open flowers; and he 6.35
and palm t., according to the space 7.36
water, and felled all the good t.; 2Ki 3.25
to the Jordan, they cut down t. 6.04
a land of olive t. and honey, 18.32
and cedar t., also masons and 1Ch 14.01
upon them opposite the balsam t. 14.14
in the tops of the balsam t., 14.15
Then shall the t. of the wood sing 16.33
and sycamore t. in the Shephelah 27.28
at Jericho, the city of palm t. 2Ch 28.15
to bring cedar t. from Lebanon to Ez 3.07
and other leafy t. to make booths, Neh 8.15
orchards and fruit t. in abundance; 9.25
For his shade the lotus t. cover him; Job 40.22
shall all the t. of the wood sing Ps 96.12
The t. of the LORD are watered 104.16
stork has her home in the fir t. 104.17
He smote their vines and fig t., 105.33
shattered the t. of their country. 105.33
all hills, fruit t. and all cedars! 148.09
in them all kinds of fruit t. Ec 2.05
to water the forest of growing t. 2.06
tree among the t. of the wood, so is my Sol 2.03
with all t. of frankincense, myrrh 4.14
shook as the t. of the forest Is 7.02
The remnant of the t. of his forest 10.19
with its majestic t. will fall. 10.34
strong among the t. of the forest; 44.14
and all the t. of the field shall 55.12
eat up your vines and your fig t.; Jer 5.17
the LORD of hosts: "Hew down her t.; 6.06
upon the t. of the field and the 7.20
with axes, like those who fell t. 46.22
is among the t. of the forest? Eze 15.02
vine among the t. of the forest, 15.06
And all the t. of the field shall 17.24
your planks of fir t. from Senir; 27.05
streams to all the t. of the forest. 31.04
above all the t. of the forest; 31.05
nor the fir t. equal its boughts; 31.08
the plane t. were as nothing compared 31.08
and all the t. of Eden envied it, 31.09
order that no t. by the waters may 31.14
and that no t. that drink water may 31.14
and all the t. of the field shall 31.15
and all the t. of Eden, the choice 31.16
in greatness among the t. of Eden? 31.18
down with the t. of Eden to the 31.18
And the t. of the field shall yield 34.27
inside, and on the jambs were palm t. 40.16
and its palm t. were of the same 40.22
and it had palm t. on its jambs, 40.26
and palm t. were on its jambs, and 40.31
and it had palm t. on its jambs, 40.34

TREES (cont.)

and it had palm t. on its jambs, Eze 40.37
of cherubim and palm t., a palm tree 41.18
and palm t. were carved on the 41.20
were carved cherubim and palm t., 41.25
windows and palm t. on either side, 41.26
river very many t. on the one side 47.07
will grow all kinds of t. for food. 47.12
lay waste her vines and her fig t., Hos 2.12
my vines, and splintered my fig t.; Joe 1.07
all the t. of the field are withered 1.12
has burned all the t. of the field. 1.19
your fig t. and your olive t. Amo 4.09
and a dresser of sycamore t., 7.14
are like fig t. with first-ripe Nah 3.12
among the myrtle t. in the glen; Zec 1.08
among the myrtle t. answered, 'These are 1.10
was standing among the myrtle t., 1.11
And there are two olive t. by it, 4.03
these two olive t. on the right 4.11
these two branches of the olive t., 4.12
for the glorious t. are ruined! 11.02
axe is laid to the root of the t.; Mt 3.10
from the t. and spread them on the 21.08
but they look like t., walking. Mk 8.24
axe is laid to the root of the t.; Lk 3.09
at the fig tree, and all the t.; 21.29
branches of palm t. and went out to Jn 12.13
fruitless t. in late autumn, twice Jud 1.12
the earth or the sea or the t., Rev 7.03
a third of the t. were burnt up, 8.07
the two olive t. and the two 11.04

TRELLIS

hacked the wooden t. with axes. Ps 74.05

TREMBLE

The peoples have heard, they t.; Ex 15.14
you and shall t. and be in anguish Deu 2.25
or t., or be in dread of them; 20.03
t. before him, all the earth; 1Ch 16.30
of those who t. at the commandment Ez 10.03
of its place, and its pillars t.; Job 9.06
The shades below t., the waters and 26.05
The pillars of heaven t., and are 26.11
the mountains t. with its tumult. Ps 46.03
make their loins t. continually. 69.23
t. before him, all the earth! 96.09
let the peoples t.! He sits enthroned 99.01
T., O earth, at the presence of the 114.07
when the keepers of the house t., Ecc 12.03
Therefore I will make the heavens t., Is 13.13
this the man who made the earth t., 14.16
of Egypt will t. at his presence, 19.01
and t. with fear before the hand 19.16
the foundations of the earth t. 24.18
T., you women who are at ease, 32.11
afraid, the ends of the earth t.; 41.05
nations might t. at thy presence! 64.02
you who t. at his word: "Your 66.05
Do you not t. before me? says the LORD; Jer 5.22
shall fear and t. because of all 33.09
of their fall the earth shall t.; 49.21
of Babylon the earth shall t., 50.46
the ground and t. every moment, Eze 26.16
Now the isles t. on the day of your 26.18
they shall t. every moment, every 32.10
dominion men t. and fear before Dan 6.26
alarm at Bethaven; t., O Benjamin! Hos 5.08
of Samaria t. for the calf at 10.05
all the inhabitants of the land t., Joe 2.01
quakes before them, the heavens t. 2.10
Shall not the land t. on this account, Amo 8.08
Hearts faint and knees t., anguish is Nah 2.10
those awake who will make you t.? Hab 2.07
curtains of the land of Midian did t. 3.07
that Moses said, "I t. with fear." Heb 12.21

TREMBLED

Then Isaac t. violently, and said, Gen 27.33
the people who were in the camp t. Ex 19.16
the people were afraid and t.; 20.18
the earth t., and the heavens Ju 5.04
for his heart t. for the ark of God. 1Sa 4.13
garrison and even the raiders t.; 14.15
afraid, and his heart t. greatly. 28.05
of the heavens t. and quaked, 2Sa 22.08
Then all the guests of Adonijah t., 1Ki 1.49
Then all who t. at the words of the Ez 9.04
he neither rose nor t. before him, Est 5.09
of the mountains t. and quaked, Ps 18.07
they were afraid, yea, the deep t. 77.16
up the world; the earth t. and shook. 77.18
and languages t. and feared before Dan 5.19
When Ephraim spoke, men t.; Hos 13.01
him the guards t. and became like Mt 28.04
And Moses t. and did not dare to Ac 7.32

TREMBLES

"At this also my heart t., and leaps Job 37.01
the world; the earth sees and t. Ps 97.04
who looks on the earth and it t., 104.32
My flesh t. for fear of thee, and I 119.120
Under three things the earth t.; Pro 30.21
Ramah t., Gibeah of Saul has fled. Is 10.29
Moab cry aloud; his soul t. 15.04
in spirit, and t. at my word. 66.02
The land t. and writhes in pain, for Jer 51.29
and my body t., my lips quiver at Hab 3.16

TREMBLING

and they turned t. to one another, Gen 42.28
leaders of Moab, t. seizes them; Ez 15.15
will give you here a t. heart, Deu 28.65
saying, 'Whoever is fearful and t., Ju 7.03
and all the people followed him t. 1Sa 13.07
of the city came to meet him t., 16.04
Ahimelech came to meet David t., 21.01
and came t. out of their fastnesses. 2Sa 22.46
t. because of this matter and Ez 10.09
and t., which made all my bones Job 4.14
Serve the LORD with fear, with t. Ps 2.11
and came t. out of their fastnesses. 18.45
t. took hold of them there, anguish 48.06
Fear and t. come upon me, and horror 55.05
for has been turned for me into t. Is 21.04
t. has seized the godless: "Who 33.14
water with t. and with fearfulness; Eze 12.18
will clothe themselves with t.; 26.16
but a great t. fell upon them, and Dan 10.07
me and set me t. on my hands and 10.10
this word to me, I stood up t. 10.11
sons shall come t. from the west; Hos 11.10
they shall come t. out of their Mic 7.17
in fear and t. and fell down Mk 5.33
for t. and astonishment had come 16.08
she came t., and falling down Lk 8.47
and t. with fear he fell down Ac 16.29
weakness and in much fear and t.; 1Co 2.03
the fear and t. with which you 2Co 7.15
with fear and t., in singleness of Eph 6.05
own salvation with fear and t.; Php 2.12

TRENCH

And he made a t. about the altar, as 1Ki 18.32
and filled the t. also with water. 18.35
up the water that was in the t. 18.38

TRESPASS

Pray forgive the t. of your handmaid; 1Sa 25.28
But the free gift is not like the t. Rom 5.15
if many died through one man's t., 5.15
following one t. brought condemnation, 5.16
If, because of one man's t., much more 5.17
Then as one man's t. led the condemnation 5.18
Law came in, to increase the t.; 5.20

TRESPASS (cont.)
through their t. salvation has Rom 11.11
Now if their t. means riches for 11.12
Brethren, if a man is overtaken in any t., Gal 6.01

TRESPASSED
"You have t. and married foreign Ez 10.10

TRESPASSES
For if you forgive men their t., Mt 6.14
if you do not forgive men their t., 6.15
will your Father forgive your t. 6.15
in heaven may forgive you your t." Mk 11.25
Father who is in heaven forgive you t. * 11.26
death for our t. and raised for Rom 4.25
following many t. brings justification. 5.16
not counting their t. against them, 2Co 5.19
blood, the forgiveness of our t., Eph 1.07
were dead through the t. and sins 2.01
even when we were dead through our t., 2.05
were dead in t. and the uncircumcision Col 2.13
having forgiven us all our t., 2.13

TRESSES
a king is held captive in the t. Sol 7.05

TRIAL
let me make t. only this once with Ju 6.39
that we should come to t. together. Job 9.32
condemned when he is brought to t. Ps 37.33
let an accuser bring him to t. 109.06
bring you to t. and deliver you up, Mk 13.11
why do you make t. of God by Ac 15.10
resurrection of the dead I am on t." 23.06
dead I am on t. before you this 24.21
I stand here on t. for hope in the 26.06
my condition was a t. to you, Gal 4.14
Blessed is the man who endures t., Jas 1.12
how to rescue the godly from t., 2Pe 2.09
the hour of t. which is coming on Rev 3.10

TRIALS
by t., by signs, by wonders, and by Deu 4.34
the great t. which your eyes saw, 7.19
the great t. which your eyes saw, 29.03
have continued with me in my t.; Lk 22.28
tears and with t. which befell me Ac 20.19
brethren, when you meet various t., Jas 1.02
you may have to suffer various t., 1Pe 1.06

TRIBAL
according to their t. allotments. Jos 11.23
each of the t. families of Israel, 22.14
length to one of the t. portions, Eze 45.07
equal to one of the t. portions, 48.08
parallel to the t. portions, it shall 48.21

TRIBE
son of Hur, of the t. of Judah; Ex 31.02
son of Ahisamach, of the t. of Dan; 31.06
son of Hur, of the t. of Judah; 35.30
son of Ahisamach, of the t. of Dan. 35.34
of the t. of Judah, made all that 38.22
of the t. of Dan, a craftsman and 38.23
daughter of Dibri, of the t. of Dan. Lev 24.11
be with you a man from each t., Num 1.04
the number of the t. of Reuben was 1.21
the number of the t. of Simeon was 1.23
the number of the t. of Gad was 1.25
the number of the t. of Judah was 1.27
the number of the t. of Issachar 1.29
the number of the t. of Zebulun was 1.31
the number of the t. of Ephraim was 1.33
the number of the t. of Manasseh 1.35
the number of the t. of Benjamin 1.37
the number of the t. of Dan was 1.39
the number of the t. of Asher was 1.41
the number of the t. of Naphtali 1.43
their ancestral t. along with them. 1.47
"Only the t. of Levi you shall not 1.49
to him shall be the t. of Issachar, 2.05
Then the t. of Zebulun, the leader 2.07
to him shall be the t. of Simeon, 2.12
Then the t. of Gad, the leader of 2.14
to him shall be the t. of Manasseh, 2.20
Then the t. of Benjamin, the leader 2.22
to him shall be the t. of Asher, 2.27
Then the t. of Naphtali, the leader 2.29
"Bring the t. of Levi near, and set 3.06
"Let not the t. of the families of 4.18
of Amminadab, of the t. of Judah; 7.12
the host of the t. of the men of 10.15
the host of the t. of the men of 10.16
the host of the t. of the men of 10.19
the host of the t. of the men of 10.20
the host of the t. of the men of 10.23
the host of the t. of the men of 10.24
the host of the t. of the men of 10.26
the host of the t. of the men of 10.27
from each t. of their fathers shall 13.02
From the t. of Reuben, Shammua the 13.04
from the t. of Simeon, Shaphat the 13.05
from the t. of Judah, Caleb the son 13.06
from the t. of Issacher, Igal the 13.07
from the t. of Ephraim, Hoshea the 13.08
from the t. of Benjamin, Palti the 13.09
from the t. of Zebulun, Gaddiel the 13.10
from the t. of Joseph (that is from the t. 13.11
from the t. of Dan, Ammiel the son 13.12
from the t. of Asher, Sethur the son 13.13
from the t. of Naphtali, Nahbi the 13.14
from the t. of Gad, Geuel the son of 13.15
the t. of Levi, the tribe of your 18.02
the t. of your father, that they may 18.02
saw Israel encamping t. by t. 24.02
To a large t. you shall give a 26.54
and to a small t. you shall give a 26.54
every t. shall be given its inheritance 26.54
of Israel, a thousand from each t., 31.05
to a large t. you shall give a 33.54
and to a small t. you shall give a 33.54
for the t. of the sons of Reuben by 34.14
houses and the t. of the sons of 34.14
You shall take one leader of every t., 34.18
Of the t. of Judah, Caleb the son of 34.19
Of the t. of the sons of Simeon, 34.20
Of the t. of Benjamin, Elidad the 34.21
Of the t. of the sons of Dan a 34.22
of the t. of the sons of Manasseh a 34.23
And of the t. of the sons of Ephraim 34.24
Of the t. of the sons of Zebulun a 34.25
Of the t. of the sons of Issachar a 34.26
And of the t. of the sons of Asher 34.27
Of the t. of the sons of Naphtali a 34.28
inheritance of the t. to which they 36.03
inheritance of the t. to which they 36.04
inheritance of the t. of our father. 36.04
"The t. of the sons of Joseph is 36.05
family of the t. of their father. 36.06
transferred from one t. to another; 36.07
inheritance of the t. of his fathers. 36.07
inheritance in any t. of the people 36.08
the family of the t. of her father, 36.08
transferred from one t. to another; 36.09
remained in the t. of the family 36.12
men of you, one man for each t.; Deu 1.23
set apart the t. of Levi to carry 10.08
all the t. of Levi, shall have no 18.01
you a man or woman or family or t., 29.18
of Israel, from each t. a man. Jos 3.12
the people, from each t. a man, 4.02
had appointed, a man from each t.; 4.04
and the half t. of Manasseh passed 4.12
of the t. of Judah, took some of the 7.01
and the t. which the LORD takes 7.14

TRIBE (cont.)
brought Israel near t. by t., Jos 7.16
and the t. of Judah was taken; 7.16
of the t. of Judah, was taken. 7.18
tribes and half the t. of Manasseh. 13.07
half of the t. of Manasseh the 13.08
To the t. of Levi alone Moses gave 13.14
inheritance to the t. of the 13.15
also to the t. of the Gadites, 13.24
But to the t. of Levi Moses gave no 13.33
The lot for the t. of the people of 15.01
inheritance of the t. of the people 15.20
belonging to the t. of the people 15.21
inheritance of the t. of the 16.08
was made to the t. of Manasseh, 17.01
to the rest of the t. of Manasseh, 17.02
And the t. of Joseph spoke to 17.14
The t. of Joseph said, "The hill 17.16
Provide three men from each t., 18.04
and half the t. of Manasseh have 18.07
The lot of the t. of Benjamin 18.11
between the t. of Judah and the t. of Joseph. 18.11
city belonging to the t. of Judah. 18.14
inheritance of the t. of Benjamin, 18.20
cities of the t. of Benjamin 18.21
inheritance of the t. of Benjamin 18.28
for the t. of Simeon, according to 19.01
the inheritance of the t. of Judah. 19.01
inheritance of the t. of Simeon 19.08
inheritance of the t. of Simeon 19.09
portion of the t. of Judah was too 19.09
the t. of Simeon obtained an 19.09
lot came up for the t. of Zebulun, 19.10
inheritance of the t. of Zebulun, 19.16
for the t. of Issachar, according to 19.17
inheritance of the t. of Issachar, 19.23
out for the t. of Asher, according 19.24
inheritance of the t. of Asher 19.31
came out for the t. of Napthali, 19.32
for the t. of Naphtali, according to 19.32
inheritance of the t. of Naphtali 19.39
lot came out for the t. of Dan, 19.40
the inheritance of the t. of Dan, 19.48
from the t. of Reuben, and Ramoth in 20.08
from the t. of Gad, and Golan in 20.08
in Bashan, from the t. of Manasseh. 20.08
the families of the t. of Ephraim, 21.05
from the t. of Dan and the half-tribe 21.05
the families of the t. of Ephraim, 21.05
from the t. of Dan and the half-tribe 21.05
the families of the t. of Issachar, 21.06
from the t. of Asher, from the 21.06
from the t. of Naphtali, and from 21.06
received from the t. of Reuben, 21.07
the t. of Gad, and the t. of Zebulun, 21.07
Out of the t. of Judah and the 21.09
Judah and the t. of Simeon they 21.09
then out of the t. of Benjamin, 21.17
them were out of the t. of Ephraim. 21.20
and out of the t. of Dan, Elteke 21.23
and out of the t. of Issachar, 21.28
and out of the t. of Asher, Mishal 21.30
and out of the t. of Naphtali, 21.32
given out of the t. of Zebulun, 21.34
and out of the t. of Reuben, Bezer 21.36
and out of the t. of Gad, Ramoth in 21.38
one half of the t. of Manasseh 22.07
from the t. of Naphtali and the Ju 4.06
of Naphtali and the t. of Zebulun? 4.06
of the t. of the Danites, whose name 13.02
those days the t. of the Danites 18.01
from the whole number of their t., 18.02
And six hundred men of the t. of Dan, 18.11
be priest to a t. and family in 18.19
priests to the t. of the Danites 18.30
men through all the t. of Benjamin, 20.12
be today one t. lacking in Israel?" 21.03
"One t. is cut off from Israel this 21.06
that a t. be not blotted out from 21.17
every man to his t. and family, 21.24
the families of the t. of Benjamin? 1Sa 9.21
and the t. of Benjamin was taken by 10.20
He brought the t. of Benjamin near 10.21
of such and such a t. in Israel," 2Sa 15.02
of a widow of the t. of Naphtali, 1Ki 7.14
but I will give one t. to your son, 11.13
(but he shall have one t., for the sake of 11.32
Yet to his son I will give one t., 11.36
of David, but the t. of Judah only. 12.20
and the t. of Benjamin, a hundred 12.21
was left but the t. of Judah only. 2Ki 17.18
and from the t. of Benjamin, Geba 1Ch 6.60
by lot out of the family of the t., 6.61
territory out of the t. of Ephraim. 6.66
and out of the t. of Issachar: 6.72
out of the t. of Asher: Mashel with 6.74
and out of the t. of Naphtali: 6.76
allotted out of the t. of Zebulun: 6.77
out of the t. of Reuben: Bezer in 6.78
and out of the t. of Gad: Ramoth in 6.80
were named among the t. of Levi. 23.14
to be the t. of thy heritage! Ps 74.02
did not choose the t. of Ephraim; 78.67
but he chose the t. of Judah, 78.68
Israel is the t. of his inheritance Jer 10.16
Israel is the t. of his inheritance 51.19
In whatever t. the alien resides, Eze 47.23
and Azariah of the t. of Judah. Dan 1.06
O t. and assembly of the city! Mic 6.09
of Phanuel, of the t. of Asher; Lk 2.36
a man of the t. of Benjamin, for Ac 13.21
a member of the t. of Benjamin. Rom 11.01
of the t. of Benjamin, a Hebrew born Php 3.05
are spoken belonged to another t., Heb 7.13
with that t. Moses said nothing 7.14
lo, the Lion of the t. of Judah, Rev 5.05
God from every t. and tongue and 5.09
out of every t. of the sons of 7.04
sealed out of the t. of Judah, 7.05
thousand of the t. of Reuben, 7.05
twelve thousand of the t. of Gad, 7.05
twelve thousand of the t. of Asher, 7.06
thousand of the t. of Naphtali, 7.06
thousand of the t. of Manasseh, 7.06
twelve thousand of the t. of Simeon, 7.07
twelve thousand of the t. of Levi, 7.07
thousand of the t. of Issacher, 7.07
twelve thousand of the t. of Zebulun, 7.08
twelve thousand of the t. of Joseph, 7.08
sealed out of the t. of Benjamin. 7.08
it over every t. and people and 13.07
nation and t. and tongue and 14.06

TRIBES
princes according to their t. Gen 25.16
people as one of the t. of Israel. 49.16
All these are the twelve t. if Israel; 49.28
according to the twelve t. of Israel. Ex 24.04
with its name, for the twelve t. 28.21
with its name, for the twelve t. 39.14
the leaders of their ancestral t., Num 1.16
houses, the leaders of the t., 7.02
the heads of the t. of Israel, 10.04
names of the t. of their fathers 26.55
heads of the t. of the people of 30.01
each of the t. of Israel to the 31.04
houses of the t. of the people of 32.28
according to the t. of your fathers 33.54
to the nine t. and to the half-tribe 34.13
the two t. and the half-tribe have 34.15
from the larger t. you shall take 35.08
the smaller t. you shall take few; 35.08

TRIBES (cont.)
of the other t. of the people of Num 36.03
for each of the t. of the people of 36.09
experienced men, according to your t., Deu 1.13
So I took the heads of your t., 1.15
and officers, throughout your t. 1.15
to me, all the heads of your t., 5.23
out of all your t. to put his name 12.05
LORD will choose in one of your t., 12.14
gives you, according to your t.; 16.18
has chosen him out of all your t., 18.05
the heads of your t., your elders, 29.10
from all the t. of Israel for 29.21
Assemble to me all the elders of your t., 31.28
all the t. of Israel together. 33.05
twelve men from the t. of Israel, Jos 3.12
number of the t. of the people of 4.05
number of the t. of the people of 4.08
shall be brought near by your t.; 7.14
land to the t. of Israel as a 12.07
to the nine t. and half the tribe 13.07
houses of the t. of the people of 14.01
Moses for the nine and one-half t. 14.02
and one-half t. beyond the Jordan; 14.03
For the people of Joseph were two t., 14.04
of Israel seven t. whose inheritance 18.02
houses of the t. of the people of 19.51
houses of the t. of the people of 21.01
by lot from the t. of Judah, 21.04
nine cities out of these two t.; 21.16
for your t. those nations that 23.04
gathered all the t. of Israel to 24.01
among the t. of Israel had fallen Ju 18.01
of all the t. of Israel, presented 20.02
throughout all the t. of Israel, 20.10
And the t. of Israel sent men 20.12
of all the t. of Israel did not 21.05
is there of the t. of Israel that 21.08
made a breach in the t. of Israel. 21.15
out of all the t. of Israel to be 1Sa 2.28
from the least of the t. of Israel? 9.21
LORD by your t. and by your thousands." 10.19
brought all the t. of Israel near, 10.20
not the head of the t. of Israel? 15.17
Then all the t. of Israel came to 2Sa 5.01
throughout all the t. of Israel, 15.10
throughout all the t. of Israel, 19.09
through all the t. of Israel to 20.14
"Go through all the t. of Israel, 24.02
Israel and all the heads of the t., 1Ki 8.01
city in all the t. of Israel in 8.16
Solomon, and will give you ten t. 11.31
out of all the t. of Israel), 11.32
and will give it to you, ten t. 11.35
chosen out of all the t. of Israel, 14.21
number of the t. of the sons of 18.31
chosen out of all the t. of Israel, 2Ki 21.07
cities out of the t. of Issachar, 1Ch 6.62
cities out of the t. of Reuben, 6.63
them by lot out of the t. of Judah, 6.65
Over the t. of Israel for the 27.16
the leaders of the t. of Israel. 27.22
of Israel, the officials of the t., 28.01
as did also the leaders of the t., 29.06
Israel and all the heads of the t., 2Ch 5.02
city in all the t. of Israel in 6.05
from all the t. of Israel to 11.16
out of all the t. of Israel to put 12.13
chosen out of all the t. of Israel, 33.07
to the number of the t. of Israel. Ez 6.17
and settled the t. of Israel in Ps 78.55
was none among his t. who stumbled. 105.37
to which the t. go up, the tribes of 122.04
the t. of the LORD, as was decreed 122.04
cornerstones of her t. have led Is 19.13
to raise up the t. of Jacob and to 49.06
thy servants, the t. of thy heritage. 63.17
calling all the t. of the kingdoms Jer 1.15
send for all the t. of the north, 25.09
of the mixed t. that dwell in the 25.24
like the t. of the countries, and Eze 20.32
Ephraim) and the t. of Israel 37.19
the land acording to their t. 45.08
among the twelve t. of Israel. 47.13
you according to the t. of Israel. 47.21
inheritance among the t. of Israel. 47.22
"These are the names of the t.: 48.01
from all the t. of Israel, shall 48.19
"As for the rest of the t.: 48.23
inheritance among the t. of Israel, 48.29
being named after the t. of Israel. 48.31
among the t. of Israel I declare Hos 5.09
Aram, even as all the t. of Israel; Zec 9.01
judging the twelve t. of Israel. Mt 19.28
then all the t. of the earth will 24.30
judging the twelve t. of Israel. Lk 22.30
which our twelve t. hope to attain, Ac 26.07
To the twelve t. in the dispersion: Jas 1.01
and all t. of the earth will wail Rev 1.07
from all t. and peoples and tongues, 7.09
the peoples and t. and tongues and 11.09
of the twelve t. of the sons of 21.12

TRIBULATION
When you are in t., and all these Deu 4.30
may he deliver me out of all t. 1Sa 26.24
enveloped me with bitterness and t.; Lam 3.05
and when t. or persecution arises Mt 13.21
"Then they will deliver you up to t., 24.09
For then there will be great t., 24.21
"Immediately after the t. of those 24.29
then, when t. or persecution arises Mk 4.17
will be such t. as has not been 13.19
after that t., the sun will be 13.24
In the world you have t.; but be of good Jn 16.33
There will be t. and distress for Rom 2.09
Shall t., or distress, or persecution, 8.35
be patient in t., be constant in 12.12
in Jesus the t. and the kingdom Rev 1.09
know your t. and your poverty 2.09
and for ten days you will have t. 2.10
her I will throw into great t., 2.22
who have come out of the great t.; 7.14

TRIBULATIONS
through many t. we must enter the Ac 14.22

TRIBUNAL
and brought him before the t., Ac 18.12
And he drove them from the t. 18.16
and beat him in front of the t. 18.17
his seat on the t. and ordered 25.06
"I am standing before Caesar's t., 25.10
my seat on the t. and ordered the 25.17

TRIBUNE
came to the t. of the cohort that Ac 21.31
they saw the t. and the soldiers, 21.32
Then the t. came up and arrested 21.33
the barracks, he said to the t., 21.37
the t. commanded him to be brought 22.24
he went to the t. and said to him, 22.26
So the t. came and said to him, 22.27
The t. answered, "I bought this 22.28
and the t. also was afraid, for he 22.29
the t., afraid that Paul would be 23.10
now to the t. to bring him down to 23.15
"Bring this young man to the t.; 23.17
and brought him to the t. and said, 23.18
The t. took him by the hand, and 23.19
So the t. dismissed the young man, 23.22
"When Lysias the t. comes down, 24.22

TRIBUNES
the military t. and the prominent Ac 25.23

TRIBUTE
for the LORD a t. from the men of Num 31.28
and the LORD's t. of sheep was six 31.37
the LORD's t. was seventy-two. 31.38
which the LORD's t. was sixty-one. 31.39
the LORD's t. was thirty-two 31.40
And Moses gave the t., which was 31.41
God with the t. of a freewill Deu 16.10
of Israel sent t. by him to Eglon Ju 3.15
presented the t. of Eglon king of 3.17
had finished presenting the t., 3.18
the people that carried the t. 3.18
servants to David and brought t. 2Sa 8.02
servants to David and brought t. 8.06
they brought t. and served Solomon 1Ki 4.21
became his vassal, and paid him t. 2Ki 17.03
and offered no t. to the king of 17.04
upon the land a t. of a hundred 23.33
servants to David and brought t. 1Ch 18.02
servants to David, and brought t. 18.06
Judah brought t. to Jehoshaphat; 2Ch 17.05
presents, and silver for t.; 17.11
The Ammonites paid t. to Uzziah, 26.08
and gave t. to the king of Assyria; 28.21
upon the land a t. of a hundred 36.03
finished, they will not pay t., Ez 4.13
to whom t., custom, and toll were 4.20
the t. of the province from Beyond 6.08
shall not be lawful to impose t., 7.24
King Ahasuerus laid t. on the land Est 10.01
under foot those who lust after t.; Ps 68.30
and of the isles render him t., 72.10
where is he who weighed the t.? Is 33.18
an exactor of t. through the glory Dan 11.20
to Assyria, as t. to the great king. Hos 10.06
kings of the earth take toll or t.? Mt 17.25
lawful for us to give t. to Caesar, Lk 20.22
forbidding us to give t. to Caesar, 23.02

TRICKED
he had been t. by the wise men, was Mt 2.16

TRICKLE
the streams so that they do not t., Job 28.11

TRIED
The magicians t. by their secret Ex 8.18
and he t. in vain to go, for he was 1Sa 17.39
when he has t. me, I shall come Job 23.10
Would that Job were t. to the end, 34.36
thou hast t. us as silver is tried. Ps 66.10
thou hast tried us as silver is t. 66.10
When he is t., let him come forth 109.07
Thy promise is well t., 119.140
I have t. you in the furnace of Is 48.10
But when they t. to arrest him, they Mt 21.46
And they t. to arrest him, but Mk 12.12
chief priests t. to lay hands on Lk 20.19
Again they t. to arrest him, but he Jn 10.39
He even t. to profane the temple, Ac 24.06
and there be t. on these charges 25.09
tribunal, where I ought to be t.; 25.10
Jerusalem and be t. there regarding 25.20
synagogues and t. to make them 26.11
me in the temple and t. to kill me. 26.21
God violently and t. to destroy it; Gal 1.13
the faith he once t. to destroy. 1.23

TRIES
for gold, and the LORD t. hearts. Pro 17.03

TRIEST
that thou t. the heart, and hast 1Ch 29.17
thou who t. the minds and hearts, Ps 7.09
If thou t. my heart, if thou visitest 17.03
who t. the heart and the mind, let Jer 11.20
and t. my mind toward thee. Pull them out 12.03
who t. the righteous, who seest the 20.12

TRIFLE
For it is no t. for you, but it is Deu 32.47
Thou hast sold thy people for a t., Ps 44.12

TRIGON
t., harp, bagpipe, and every kind of Dan 3.05
t., harp, bagpipe, and every kind of 3.07
t., harp, bagpipe, and every kind of 3.10
t., harp, bagpipe, and every kind of 3.15

TRIM
they shall only t. the hair of Eze 44.20

TRIMMED
nor t. his beard, nor washed his 2Sa 19.24
maidens rose and t. their lamps. Mt 25.07

TRIP
who have planned to t. up my feet. Ps 140.04

TRIUMPH
help, and the sword of your t.! Deu 33.29
said, "Go up to Ramothgilead and t.; 1Ki 22.12
And he answered him, "Go up and t.; 22.15
said, "Go up to Ramothgilead and t.; 2Ch 18.11
And answered, "Go up and t.; they 18.14
therefore thou wilt not let them t. Job 17.04
eye has looked in t. on my enemies. Ps 54.07
let me look in t. on my enemies. 59.10
over Philistia I shout in t." 60.08
over Philistia I shout in t." 108.09
I shall look in t. on those who 118.07
When the righteous t., there is great Pro 28.12
of Israel shall t. and glory." Is 45.25
in Christ always leads us in t., 2Co 2.14
of the Lord may speed on and t., 2Th 3.01

TRIUMPHANT
"Our hand is t., the LORD has not Deu 32.27
t. and victorious is he, humble and Zec 9.09

TRIUMPHANTLY
Israel went out t. in the sight of Num 33.03

TRIUMPHED
the LORD, for he has t. gloriously; Ex 15.01
the LORD, for he has t. gloriously; 15.21
that my enemy has not t. over me. Ps 41.11
affliction, for the enemy has t.! Lam 1.09

TRIUMPHING
example of them, t. over them in him. Col 2.15

TRIUMPHS
they repeat the t. of the LORD, Ju 5.11
the t. of his peasantry in Israel. 5.11
Great t. he gives to his king, and 2Sa 22.51
Great t. he gives to his king, and Ps 18.50
yet mercy t. over judgment. Jas 2.13

TRIVIAL
are you incompetent to try t. cases? 1Co 6.02

TROAS
by Mysia, they went down to T. Ac 16.08
Setting sail therefore from T., 16.11
on and were waiting for us at T., 20.05
in five days we came to them at T., 20.06
When I came to T. to preach the 2Co 2.12
that I left with Carpus at T., 2Ti 4.13

TROD
from their vineyards and t. them, Ju 9.27
them and t. them down from Nohah 20.43
and the people t. upon him in the 2Ki 7.17
for the people t. upon him in the 7.20
old way which wicked men have t.? Job 22.15
by paths his feet have not t. Is 41.03
I t. them in my anger and trampled 63.03

TROD (cont.)
I t. down the peoples in my anger, I Is 63.06
that they t. upon one another, he Lk 12.01

TRODDEN
give the land upon which he has t., Deu 1.36
your foot has t. shall be an Jos 14.09
The proud beasts have not t. it; Job 28.08
let them be t. down and wither. Ps 58.07
like a dead body t. under foot. Is 14.19
Moab shall be t. down in his place, 25.10
as straw is t. down in a dung-pit. 25.10
of Ephraim will be t. under foot; 28.03
"I have t. the wine press alone, and 63.03
our adversaries have t. it down. 63.18
floor at the time when it is t.; Jer 51.33
the Lord has t. as in a wine press Lam 1.15
what you have t. with your feet, Eze 34.19
now she will be t. down like the Mic 7.10
thrown out and t. under foot by Mt 5.13
and was t. under foot, and the birds Lk 8.05
Jerusalem will be t. down by the 21.24
wine press was t. outside the city, Rev 14.20

TROOP
Yea, by thee I can crush a t., 2Sa 22.30
Yea, by thee I can crush a t.; Ps 18.29

TROOPED
adultery and t. to the houses of Jer 5.07

TROOPS
And they came out, with all their t., Jos 11.04
with his chariots and his t.; Ju 4.07
And when the t. came to the camp, 1Sa 4.03
and t. like the sand on the seashore 13.05
and the t. came back from pursuing 2Sa 18.16
Now the t. were encamped against 1Ki 16.15
and the t. who were encamped heard 16.16
and made them officers of his t. 1Ch 12.18
of the divisions of the armed t., 12.23
thousand eight hundred armed t. 12.24
Zebulun fifty thousand seasoned t., 12.33
seasoned t. ready for battle. 12.36
thus his t. were in front of 2Ch 13.13
His t. come on together; Job 19.12
I dwelt like a king among his t., 29.25
all the foreign t. in her midst, Jer 50.37
him, his helpers and all his t.; Eze 12.14
the pick of his t. shall fall by 17.21
not stand, or even his picked t., Dan 11.15
Behold your t. are women in your Nah 3.13
and he sent his t. and destroyed Mt 22.07
The number of the t. of cavalry was Rev 9.16

TROPHIMUS
and the Asians, Tychicus and T. Ac 20.04
previously seen T. the Ephesian 21.29
at Corinth; T. I left ill at Miletus. 2Ti 4.20

TROTH
I plighted my t. to you and entered Eze 16.08

TROUBLE
have brought t. on me by making me Gen 34.30
nor has he seen t. in Israel. Num 23.21
and they shall t. you in the land 33.55
destruction, and bring t. upon it. Jos 6.18
said, "Why did you bring t. on us? 7.25
The LORD brings t. on you today." 7.25
come to me now when you are in t.?" Ju 11.07
become the cause of great t. to me; 11.35
"Do not let this matter t. you, 2Sa 11.25
king said to her, "What is your t.?" 14.05
fortified cities, and cause us t." 20.06
and see how this man is seeking t.; 1Ki 20.07
you have taken all this t. for us; 2Ki 4.13
king asked her, "What is your t.?" 6.28
"This t. is from the LORD! Why should 6.33
you provoke t. so that you fall, 14.10
you provoke t. so that you fall, 2Ch 25.19
exile are in great t. and shame; Neh 1.03
"You see the t. we are in, how 2.17
womb, nor hide t. from my eyes. Job 3.10
I have no rest; but t. comes." 3.26
iniquity and sow t. reap the same. 4.08
nor does t. sprout from the ground; 5.06
but man is born to t. as the sparks 5.07
is a few days, and full ot t. 14.01
his cry, when t. comes upon him? 27.09
I have reserved for the time of t., 38.23
the oppressed, a stronghold in times of t. Ps 9.09
thou hide thyself in times of t.? 10.01
thou dost note t. and vexation, 10.14
The LORD answer you in the day of t.! 20.01
for t. is near and there is none to 22.11
Consider my affliction and my t., 25.18
me in his shelter in the day of t.; 27.05
for me, thou preservest me from t.; 32.07
is their refuge in the time of t. 37.39
LORD delivers him in the day of t.; 41.01
strength, a very present help in t. 46.01
Why should I fear in times of t., 49.05
and call upon me in the day of t.; 50.15
hast delivered me from every t., 54.07
answer me; I am overcome by my t. 55.02
For they bring t. upon me, 55.03
and mischief and t. are within it, 55.10
my mouth promised when I was in t. 66.14
They are not in t. as other men are 73.05
In the day of my t. I seek the Lord 77.02
In the day of my t. I call on thee, 86.07
yet their span is but toil and t.; 90.10
I will be with him in t., I will rescue 91.15
to give him respite from days of t., 94.13
whom he has redeemed from t. 107.02
they cried to the LORD in their t., 107.06
they cried to the LORD in their t., 107.13
they cried to the LORD in their t., 107.19
they cried to the LORD in their t., 107.28
low through oppression, t., and sorrow, 107.39
T. and anguish have come upon me, 119.143
Though I walk in the midst of t., 138.07
before him, I tell my t. before him. 142.02
righteousness bring me out of t.! 143.11
He who winks the eye causes t., Pro 10.10
The righteous is delivered from t., 11.08
but the righteous escapes from t. 12.13
but the wicked are filled with t. 12.21
A bad messenger plunges men into t. Pro 13.17
but t. befalls the income of the 15.06
than great treasure and t. with it. 15.16
gain makes t. for his household, 15.27
even the wicked for the day of t. 16.04
his tongue keeps himself out of t. 21.23
man in time of t. is like a bad 25.19
glad, but the soul is torn by t. 27.09
although man's t. lies heavy upon Ecc 8.06
Through a land of t. and anguish, Is 30.06
our salvation in the time of t. 33.02
not answer or save him from his t. 46.07
in the time of their t. they say, Jer 2.27
can save you, in your time of t.; 2.28
save them in the time of their t. 11.12
call to me in the time of their t. 11.14
Isarel, its savior in time ot t., 14.08
in the time of t. and in the time 15.11
stronghold, my refuge in the day of t., 16.19
from every side on the day of t. 51.02
All my enemies have heard of my t.; Lam 1.21
t. the waters with your feet, and Eze 32.02
"I will t. the hearts of many peoples, 32.09
foot of man shall t. them any more, 32.13
shall the hoofs of beasts t. them. 32.13
And there shall be a time of t., Dan 12.01

TROUBLE (cont.)
a stronghold in the day of t.; Nah 1.07
me see wrongs and look upon t.? Hab 1.03
for the day of t. to come upon 3.16
the day's own t. be sufficient for Mt 6.34
to them, "Why do you t. the woman? 26.10
satisfy him and keep you out of t." 28.14
Why t. the Teacher any further?" Mk 5.35
why do you t. her? She has done a 14.06
do not t. youself, for I am not Lk 7.06
do not t. the Teacher any more." 8.49
we should not t. those of the Ac 15.19
are some who t. you and want to Gal 1.07
Henceforth let no man t. me; 6.17
Yet it was kind of you to share my t. Php 4.14
bitterness" spring up and cause t., Heb 12.15

TROUBLED
morning and saw them, they were t. Gen 40.06
So in the morning his spirit was t.; 41.08
my lord, I am a woman sorely t.; 1Sa 1.15
said, "My father has t. the land; 14.29
And he answered, "I have not t. Israel; 1Ki 18.18
was greatly t. because of this 2Ki 6.11
for God t. them with every sort of 2Ch 15.06
LORD, heal me, for my bones are t. Ps 6.02
My soul also is sorely t. But thou, O LORD 6.03
shall be ashamed and sorely t.; 6.10
I am so t. that I cannot speak. 77.04
they are t. like the sea which Jer 49.23
and his spirit was t., and his sleep Dan 2.01
my spirit is t. to know the dream." 2.03
squares and moat, but in a t. time. 9.25
he was t., and all Jerusalem with Mt 2.03
he began to be sorrowful and t. 26.37
to be greatly distressed and t. Mk 14.33
And Zechariah was t. when he saw Lk 1.12
But she was greatly t. at the saying, 1.29
and those who were t. with unclean 6.18
are anxious and t. about many 10.41
"Why are you t., and why do questionings 24.38
into the pool, and t. the water *Jn 5.04
into the pool when the water is t., 5.07
was deeply moved in spirit and t.; 11.33
"Now is my soul t. And what shall I 12.27
he was t. in spirit, and testified, 13.21
"Let not your hearts be t.; 14.01
Let not your hearts be t., 14.27
from us have t. you with words, Ac 15.24
Have no fear of them, nor be t., 1Pe 3.14

TROUBLER
him, "Is it you, you t. of Israel?" 1Ki 18.17
the t. of Israel, who transgressed 1Ch 2.07

TROUBLES
said to her, "What t. you, Hagar? Gen 21.17
many evils and t. will come upon Deu 31.17
many evils and t. have come upon 31.21
He will deliver you from six t.; Job 5.19
Relieve the t. of my heart, and Ps 25.17
Redeem Israel, O God, out of all his t. 25.22
and saved him out of all his t. 34.06
delivers them out of all their t. 34.17
see many sore t. wilt revive me 71.20
For my soul is full of t., and my life 88.03
He who t. his household will inherit Pro 11.29
the former t. are forgotten and Is 65.16
who marry will have worldly t., 1Co 7.28

TROUBLING
There the wicked cease from t., Job 3.17
stepped in first after the t. *Jn 5.04
and he who is t. you will bear his Gal 5.10

TROUGH
jar into the t. and ran again to Gen 24.20

TROUGHS
the watering t., where the flocks Gen 30.38
and filled the t. to water their Ex 2.16

TRUE
word will come t. for you or not." Num 11.23
if it be t. and certain that such Deu 13.14
and if it is t. and certain that 17.04
does not come to pass or come t., 18.22
But if the thing is t., that the 22.20
"T., men came to me, but I did not Jos 2.04
said, "Now when your words come t., Ju 13.12
so that, when your words come t., 13.17
And now it is t. that I am a near Ru 3.12
all that he says comes t. 1Sa 9.06
thou art God, and thy words are t., 2Sa 7.28
That is not t. But a man of 20.21
promise of the LORD proves t.; 22.31
be wholly t. to the LORD our God, 1Ki 8.61
"The report was t. which I heard in 10.06
was not wholly t. to the LORD his 11.04
was not wholly t. to the LORD his 15.03
Asa was wholly t. to the LORD all 15.14
And they said, "That is not t.; 2Ki 9.12
"Is your heart t. to my heart as 10.15
"The report was t. which I heard in 2Ch 9.05
time Israel was without the t. God, 15.03
them right ordinances and t. laws, Neh 9.13
have searched out; it is t. Job 5.27
And even if it be t. that I have 19.04
the promise of the LORD proves t.; Ps 18.30
the ordinances of the LORD are t., 19.09
they were not t. to his covenant. 78.37
for ever, and thy law is t. 119.142
and all thy commandments are t. 119.151
that the word of the LORD is t. 141.06
to show you what is right and t., Pro 22.21
you may give a t. answer to those 22.21
Every word of God proves t.; 30.05
let them hear and say, It is t. Is 43.09
But the LORD is the t. God; Jer 10.10
which you have prophesied come t., 28.06
the LORD be a t. and faithful 42.05
their t. habitation, the LORD, the 50.07
executes t. justice between man and Eze 18.08
"Is it t., O Shadrach, Meshach, and Dan 3.14
They answered the king, "T., O king." 3.24
mornings which has been told is t.; 8.26
And the word was t., and it was a 10.01
idols forsake their t. loyalty. Jon 2.08
Render t. judgments, show kindness Zec 7.09
that are t. and make for peace, 8.16
T. instruction was in his mouth, and Mal 2.06
"Teacher, we know that you are t., Mt 22.16
"Teacher, we know that you are t., Mk 12.14
will entrust to you the t. riches? Lk 16.11
The t. light that enlightens every Jn 1.09
does what is t. comes to the light, 3.21
his seal to this, that God is t. 3.33
when the t. worshipers will worship 4.23
For here the saying holds t., 4.37
to myself, my testimony is not t.; 5.31
testimony which he bears to me is t. 5.32
gives you the t. bread from heaven. 6.32
glory of him who sent him is t., 7.18
he who sent me is t., and him 7.28
to yourself; your testimony is not t." 8.13
to myself, my testimony is t., 8.14
if I do judge, my judgment is t., 8.16
the testimony of two men is t.; 8.17
but he who sent me is t., 8.26
John said about this man was t." 10.41
"I am the t. vine, and my Father is 15.01
they know thee the only t. God, 17.03
borne witness—his testimony is t., 19.35
we know that his testimony is t. 21.24
nor is t. circumcision something Rom 2.28
Let God be t. though every man be 3.04

TRUE (cont.)
That is t. they were broken Rom 11.20
raise if it is t. that the dead 1Co 15.15
as impostors, and yet are t.; 2Co 6.08
everything we said to you was t., 7.14
boasting before Titus has proved t. 7.14
The signs of a t. apostle were 12.12
in God in t. righteousness and Eph 4.24
that is good and right and t.), 5.09
For we are the t. circumcision, who Php 3.03
Only let us hold t. to what we have 3.16
t. yokefellow, help these women, for 4.03
whatever is t., whatever is honorable, Php 4.08
to serve a living and t. God, 1Th 1.09
To Timothy, my t. child in the faith: 1Ti 1.02
To Titus, my t. child in a common Tit 1.04
This testimony is t. Therefore rebuke 1.13
but to show entire and t. fidelity, 2.10
sanctuary and the t. tent which is Heb 8.02
a copy of the t. one, but into 9.24
instead of the t. form of these 10.01
near with a t. heart in full 10.22
that this is the t. grace of God; 1Pe 5.12
them according to the t. proverb, 2Pe 2.22
which is t. in him and in you, 1Jn 2.08
away and the t. light is already 2.08
and is t., and is no lie, just as it 2.27
understanding, to know him who is t.; 5.20
and we are in him who is t., 5.20
This is the t. God and eternal life. 5.20
and you know my testimony is t. 3Jn 1.12
the t. one, who has the key of David, Rev 3.07
Amen, the faithful and t. witness, 3.14
holy and t., how long before thou 6.10
Just and t. are thy ways, O King of 15.03
t. and just are thy judgments! 16.07
for his judgments are t. and just; 19.02
to me, "These are t. words of God." 19.09
upon it is called Faithful and T., 19.11
these words are trustworthy and t." 21.05
"These words are trustworthy and t. 22.06

TRULY
sevenfold, t. Lamech seventy-sevenfold. Gen 4.24
deal loyally and t. with my master, 24.49
for t. to see your face is like 33.10
to deal loyally and t. with me. 47.29
but t., as I live, and as all the Num 14.21
"T. the LORD has given all the land Jos 2.24
But t., as the LORD lives and as 1Sa 20.03
t. by morning there had not been 25.34
"T. I know that it is so: But how Job 9.02
For t. my words are not false; 36.04
T. no man can ransom himself, or Ps 49.07
But t. God has listened; he has given 66.19
T. God is good to the upright, to 73.01
T. thou dost set them in slippery 73.18
beautiful, my beloved, t. lovely. Sol 1.16
T., thou art a God who hidest Is 45.15
T. the hills are a delusion, the Jer 3.23
T. in the LORD our God is the 3.23
"For if you t. amend your ways and 7.05
if you t. execute justice one with 7.05
But I said, "T. this is an affliction, 10.19
the LORD has t. sent the prophet." 28.09
"T., your God is God of gods and Dan 2.47
For t., I say to you, till heaven Mt 5.18
t., I say to you, you will never get 5.26
T., I say to you, they have their 6.02
T., I say to you, they have their 6.05
T., I say to you, they have their 6.16
"T., I say to you, not even in 8.10
T., I say to you, it shall be more 10.15
for t., I say to you, you will not 10.23
t., I say to you, he shall not lose 10.42
T., I say to you, among those born 11.11
T., I say to you, many prophets and 13.17
"T. you are the Son of God." 14.33
T., I say to you, there are some 16.28
For t., I say to you, if you have 17.20
and said, "T., I say to you, unless 18.03
t., I say to you, he rejoices over 18.13
T., I say to you, whatever you bind 18.18
"T., I say to you, it will be hard 19.23
"T., I say to you, in the new world, 19.28
"T., I say to you, if you have faith 21.21
"T., I say to you, the tax collectors 21.31
T., I say to you, all this will come 23.36
T., I say to you, there will not be 24.02
T., I say to you, this generation 24.34
T., I say to you, he will set him 24.47
'T., I say to you, I do not know you.' 25.12
'T., I say to you, as you did it to 25.40
'T., I say to you, as you did it not 25.45
T., I say to you, wherever this 26.13
"T., I say to you, one of you will 26.21
"T., I say to you, this very night, 26.34
"T. this was a son of God!" 27.54
"T., I say to you, all sins will be Mk 3.28
T., I say to you, no sign shall be 8.12
"T., I say to you, there are some 9.01
For t., I say to you, whoever gives 9.41
T., I say to you, whoever does not 10.15
Jesus said, "T., I say to you, there 10.29
T., I say to you, whoever says to 11.23
but t. teach the way of God. Is it 12.14
you have t. said that he is one, and 12.32
"T., I say to you, this poor widow 12.43
T., I say to you, this generation 13.30
And t., I say to you, wherever the 14.09
"T., I say to you, one of you will 14.18
T., I say to you, I shall not drink 14.25
"T., I say to you, this very night, 14.30
"T. this man was a son of God!" 15.39
And he said, "T., I say to you, no Lk 4.24
But I tell you t., there are some 9.27
t., I say to you, he will gird 12.37
T. I tell you, he will set him over 12.44
T., I say to you, whoever does not 18.17
"T., I say to you, there is no man 18.29
but t. teach the way of God. 20.21
And he said, "T. I tell you, this 21.03
T., I say to you, this generation 21.32
"T., I say to you, today you will be 23.43
"T., t., I say to you, you will Jn 1.51
"T., t., I say to you, unless one 3.03
"T., t., I say to you, unless one 3.05
T., t., I say to you, we speak of 3.11
not your husband; this you said t." 4.18
"T., t., I say to you, the Son can 5.19
T., t., I say to you, he who hears 5.24
"T., t., I say to you, the hour is 5.25
"T., t., I say to you, you seek me, 6.26
"T., t., I say to you, it was not 6.32
T., t., I say to you, he who 6.47
"T., t., I say to you, unless you 6.53
my word, you are t. my disciples, 8.31
"T., t., I say to you, every one 8.34
T., t., I say to you, if any one 8.51
"T., t., I say to you, before 8.58
"T., t., I say to you, he who does 10.01
"T., t., I say to you, I am the 10.07
T., t., I say to you, unless a 12.24
T., t., I say to you, a servant is 13.16
T., t., I say to you, he who 13.20
"T., t., I say to you, one of you 13.21
T., t., I say to you, the cock 13.38
"T., t., I say to you, he who 14.12
T., t., I say to you, you will 16.20
T., t., I say to you if you ask 16.23
T., t., I say to you, when you 21.18
for t. in this city there were Ac 4.27
"T. I perceive that God shows no 10.34
But if we judged ourselves t., 1Co 11.31
in him t. love for God is perfected. 1Jn 2.05

TRUMPET
When the t. sounds a long blast, Ex 19.13
mountain, and a very loud t. blast, 19.16
sound of the t. grew louder and 19.19
sound of the t. and the mountain 20.18
abroad the loud t. on the tenth Lev 25.09
send abroad the t. throughout all 25.09
as you hear the sound of the t., Jos 6.05
people heard the sound of the t., 6.20
he sounded the t. in the hill Ju 3.27
and he sounded the t., and the Abiezrites 6.34
When I blow the t., I and all who are 7.18
Saul blew the t. throughout all 1Sa 13.03
So Joab blew the t.; and all the 2Sa 2.28
as you hear the sound of the t., 15.10
Then Joab blew the t., and the troops 18.16
and he blew the t., and said, "We 20.01
So he blew the t., and they dispersed 20.22
then blow the t., and say, 'Long 1Ki 1.34
Then they blew the t.; and all the 1.39
Joab heard the sound of the t., 1.41
bare steps, and they blew the t., 2 Ki 9.13
who sounded the t. was beside me. Neh 4.18
where you hear the sound of the t., 4.20
stand still at the sound of the t. Job 39.24
When the t. sounds, he says 'Aha!' 39.25
the LORD with the sound of a t. Ps 47.05
Blow the t. at the new moon, at the 81.03
Praise him with t. sound; praise him 150.03
look! When a t. is blown, hear! Is 18.03
that day a great t. will be blown, 27.13
not, lift up your voice like a t.; 58.01
"Blow the t. through the land; Jer 4.05
for I hear the sound of the t., 4.19
and hear the sound of the t.? 4.21
Blow the t. in Tekoa, and raise a 6.01
'Give heed to the sound of the t.!' 6.17
war, or hear the sound of the t., 42.14
blow the t. among the nations; 51.27
"They have blown the t. and made Eze 7.14
and blows the t. and warns the 33.03
sound of the t. does not take 33.04
He heard the sound of the t., 33.05
coming and does not blow the t., 33.06
horn in Gibeah, the t. in Ramah. Hos 5.08
Set the t. to your lips, for a 8.01
Blow the t. in Zion; sound the alarm Joe 2.01
Blow the t. in Zion; sanctify a fast; 2.15
shouting and the sound of the t.; Amo 2.02
Is a t. blown in a city, and the 3.06
a day of t. blast and battle cry Zep 1.16
the Lord GOD will sound the t., Zec 9.14
sound no t. before you, as the Mt 6.02
out his angels with a loud t. call, 24.31
twinkling of an eye, at the last t. 1Co 15.52
For the t. will sound, and the dead 15.52
with the sound of the t. of God. 1Th 4.16
and the sound of a t., and a voice Heb 12.19
heard behind me a loud voice like a t. Rev 1.10
had heard speaking to me like a t., 4.01
The first angel blew his t., 8.07
The second angel blew his t., 8.08
The third angel blew his t., 8.10
The fourth angel blew his t., 8.12
And the fifth angel blew his t., 9.01
Then the sixth angel blew his t., 9.13
saying to the sixth angel who had the t., 9.14
the days of the t. call to be 10.07
Then the seventh angel blew his t., 11.15

TRUMPETERS
captains and the t. beside the king, 2Ki 11.14
and twenty priests who were t.; 2Ch 5.12
the duty of the t. and singers to 5.13
captains and the t. beside the king, 23.13
singers sang, and the t. sounded; 29.28
minstrels, of flute players and t., Rev 18.22

TRUMPETS
proclaimed with blast of t., Lev 23.24
"Make two silver t.; of hammered Num 10.02
the priests, shall blow the t. 10.08
The t. shall be to you for a perpetual 10.08
shall sound an alarm with the t., 10.09
shall blow the t. over your burnt 10.10
is a day for you to blow the t., 29.01
sanctuary and the t. for the alarm 31.06
bear seven t. of rams' horns before Jos 6.04
times, the priests blowing the t. 6.04
bear seven t. of rams' horns 6.06
the seven t. of rams' horns before 6.08
blowing the t. with the ark of the 6.08
before the priests who blew the t., 6.09
while the t. blew continually. 6.09
the seven t. of rams' horns before 6.13
on, blowing the t. continually; 6.13
while the t. blew continually. 6.13
when the priests had blown the t., 6.16
shouted, and the t. were blown. 6.20
from their hands, and their t.; Ju 7.08
and put t. into the hands of all of 7.16
then blow the t. also on every side 7.18
they blew the t. and smashed the 7.19
blew the t. and broke the jars, 7.20
their right hands the t. to blow; 7.20
When they blew the three hundred t., 7.22
the land rejoicing and blowing t. 2Ki 11.14
t., or any vessels of gold, or of 12.13
and tambourines and cymbals and t. 1Ch 13.08
should blow the t. before the ark 15.24
t., and cymbals, and made loud music 15.28
were to blow t. continually, 16.06
Jeduthun had t. and cymbals for 16.42
with t. and cymbals and other 2Ch 5.13
them the priests sounded t.; 7.06
their battle t. to sound the call 13.12
LORD, and the priests blew the t. 13.14
and with t., and with horns. 15.14
with harps and lyres and t., 20.28
the land rejoicing and blowing t., 23.13
David, and the priests with the t. 29.26
and the t., accompanied by the 29.27
vestments came forward with t., Ez 3.10
of the priests' sons with t.: Neh 12.35
Zechariah, and Hananiah, with t.; 12.41
With t. and the sound of the horn Ps 98.06
and seven t. were given to them. Rev 8.02
had the seven t. made ready to 8.06
of the other t. which the three 8.13

TRUNK
only the t. of Dagon was left to 1Sa 5.04

TRUST
"For every breach of t., Ex 22.09
But Sihon did not t. Israel to pass Ju 11.20
established them in their office of t. 1Ch 9.22
Even in his servants he puts no t., Job 4.18
in sunder, and his t. in a spider's web. 8.14
God puts no t. in his holy ones, and 15.15
Let him not t. in emptiness, deceiving 15.31
"If I have made gold my t., or called 31.24
and put your t. in the LORD. Ps 4.05
know thy name put their t. in thee, 9.10
in thee I t., let me not be put to 25.02
vain idols; but I t. in the LORD. 31.06
But I t. in thee, O LORD, I say, "Thou 31.14
because we t. in his holy name. 33.21
T. in the LORD, and do good; 37.03
t. in him, and he will act. 37.05
fear, and put their t. in the LORD. 40.03
the man who makes the LORD his t., 40.04
For not in my bow do I t., nor can my 44.06
men who t. in their wealth and 49.06
I t. in the steadfast love of God 52.08
their days, But I will t. in thee. 55.23

TRUST (cont.)
When I am afraid, I put my t. in thee. Ps 56.03
praise, in God I t. without a fear. 56.04
in God I t. without a fear. 56.11
T. in him at all times, O people; 62.08
my t., O LORD, from my youth. 71.05
and did not t. his saving power. 78.22
my fortress; my God, in whom I t. 91.02
so are all who t. in them. 115.08
O Israel, t. in the LORD! 115.09
of Aaron, put your t. in the LORD! 115.10
You who fear the LORD, t. in the LORD! 115.11
who taunt me, for I t. in thy word. 119.42
Those who t. in the LORD are like 125.01
love, for in thee I put my t. 143.08
Put not your t. in princes, in a son 146.03
T. in the LORD with all your heart, Pro 3.05
the stronghold in which they t. 21.22
That your t. may be in the LORD, I 22.19
T. in a faithless man in time of 25.19
I will t., and will not be afraid; Is 12.02
T. in the LORD for ever, for the 26.04
and t. in oppression and perverseness, 30.12
quietness and in t. shall be your 30.15
who t. in chariots because they are 31.01
righteousness, quietness and t. for ever. 32.17
who t. in graven images, who say to 42.17
has rejected those in whom you t., Jer 2.37
in which you t. they shall destroy 5.17
Do not t. in these deceptive words: 7.04
"Behold, you t. in deceptive words 7.08
by my name, and in which you t., 7.14
and put no t. in any brother; 9.04
in the LORD, whose t. is the LORD. 17.07
have made this people t. in a lie. 28.15
him, and has made you t. in a lie, 29.31
because you have put your t. in me, 39.18
Pharaoh and those who t. in him. 46.25
and let your widows t. in me." 49.11
Put no t. in a neighbor, have no Mic 7.05
She does not t. in the LORD, she Zep 3.02
but Jesus did not t. himself to Jn 2.24
and I t. in the Lord that shortly I Php 2.24
And again, "I will put my t. in him." Heb 2.13

TRUSTED
in which you t., come down throughout Deu 28.52
because they t. to the men in Ju 20.36
And Achish t. David, thinking, "He 1Sa 27.12
He t. in the LORD the God of Israel; 2Ki 18.05
entreaty because they t. in him. 1Ch 5.20
deprives of speech those who are t., Job 12.20
torn from the tent in which he t., 18.14
But I have t. in thy steadfast love; Ps 13.05
In thee our fathers t.; 22.04
they t., and thou didst deliver 22.04
in thee they t., and were not 22.05
and I have t. in the LORD without 26.01
Even my bosom friend in whom I t., 41.09
but t. in the abundance of his 52.07
have forgotten me and t. in lies. Jer 13.25
'Your t. friends have deceived you 38.22
because you t. in your strongholds 48.07
who t. in her treasures, saying, 'Who 49.04
"But you t. in your beauty, and Eze 16.15
who t. in him, and set at nought the Dan 3.28
him, because he had t. in his God. 6.23
you have t. in your chariots and Hos 10.13
your t. friends have set a trap Ob 1.07
away his armor in which he t., Lk 11.22
to some who t. in themselves that 18.09
but he t. to him who judges justly. 1Pe 2.23

TRUSTEES
guardians and t. until the date set by Gal 4.02

TRUSTING
his heart is firm, t. in the LORD. Ps 112.07

TRUSTINGLY
neighbor who dwells t. beside you. Pro 3.29
who pass by t. with no thought of Mic 2.08

TRUSTS
For the king t. in the LORD; Ps 21.07
and my shield; in him my heart t.; 28.07
surrounds him who t. in the LORD. 32.10
blessed is the man who t. in thee! 84.12
save thy servant who t. in thee. 86.02
them!—yea, every one who t. in them! 135.18
He who t. in his riches will wither, Pro 11.28
and happy is he who t. in the LORD. 16.20
but he who t. in the LORD will be 28.25
He who t. in his own mind is a fool; 28.26
but he who t. in the LORD is safe. 29.25
The heart of her husband t. in her, 31.11
on thee, because he t. in thee. Is 26.03
yet t. in the name of the LORD and 50.10
is the man who t. in man and makes Jer 17.05
"Blessed is the man who t. in the LORD, 17.07
yet if he t. in his righteousness Eze 33.13
For the workman t. in his own Hab 2.18
He t. in God; let God deliver him Mt 27.43
not work but t. him who justifies Rom 4.05

TRUSTWORTHY
men who are t. and who hate a bribe; Ex 18.21
and just; all his precepts are t., Ps 111.07
but he who is t. in spirit keeps a Pro 11.13
of stewards that they be found t. 1Co 4.02
one who by the Lord's mercy is t. 7.25
for these words are t. and true." Rev 21.05
to me, "These words are t. and true. 22.06

TRUTH
tested, whether there is t. in you; Gen 42.16
"In t. we are guilty concerning our 42.21
"Of a t. I have sinned against the Jos 7.20
"Of a t. women have been kept from 1Sa 21.05
of the LORD in your mouth is t." 1Ki 17.24
nothing but the t. in the name of 22.16
Of a t., O LORD, the kings of 2Ki 19.17
nothing but the t. in the name of 2Ch 18.15
Ahasuerus, in words of peace and t., Est 9.30
In t. I have no help in me, and any Job 6.13
Of a t., God will not do wickedly, 34.12
For there is no t. in their mouth; Ps 5.09
and speaks t. from his heart; 15.02
Lead me in thy t., and teach me, for 25.05
Oh send out thy light and thy t.; 43.03
the cause of t. and to defend the 45.04
thou desirest t. in the inward 51.06
lying more than speaking the t. 52.03
O LORD, that I may walk in thy t.; 86.11
righteousness, and the peoples with his t. 96.13
not the word of t. utterly out of 119.43
The sum of thy word in t.; and every one 119.160
to all who call upon him in t. 145.18
for my mouth will utter t.; Pro 8.07
He who speaks the t. gives honest 12.17
Buy t., and do not sell it; 23.23
and uprightly he wrote words of t. Ec 12.10
the Holy One of Israel, in t. Is 10.20
Of a t., O LORD, the kings of 37.18
I the LORD speak the t., I declare 45.19
of Israel, but not in t. or right. 48.01
for t. has fallen in the public 59.14
T. is lacking, and he who departs 59.15
bless himself by the God of t., 65.16
land shall swear by the God of t.; 65.16
in t., in justice, and in uprightness, Jer 4.02
one who does justice and seeks t.; 5.01
O LORD, do not thy eyes look for t.? 5.03
t. has perished; it is cut off 7.28
falsehood and not t. has grown 9.03
neighbor, and no one speaks the t.; 9.05
for in t. the LORD sent me to you 26.15

TRUTH (cont.)
asked him the t. concerning all Dan 7.16
to know the t. concerning the 7.19
and t. was cast down to the ground, 8.12
iniquities and giving heed to thy t. 9.13
is inscribed in the book of t.: 10.21
"And now I will show you the t. 11.02
they abhor him who speaks the t. Amo 5.10
Speak the t. to one another, render Zec 8.16
therefore love t. and peace. 8.19
him, and told him the whole t. Mk 5.33
may know the t. concerning the Lk 1.04
But in t., I tell you, there were 4.25
among us, full of grace and t.; Jn 1.14
grace and t. came through Jesus 1.17
the Father in spirit and t., 4.23
him must worship in spirit and t." 4.24
and he has borne witness to the t. 5.33
and you will know the t., 8.32
and the t. will make you free." 8.32
told you the t. which I heard from 8.40
and has nothing to do with the t., 8.44
because there is no t. in him. 8.44
But, because I tell the t., 8.45
If I tell the t., why do you not 8.46
the way, and the t., and the life; 14.06
even the Spirit of t., whom the world 14.17
the Father, even the Spirit of t., 15.26
Nevertheless I tell you the t.: 16.07
When the Spirit of t. comes, 16.13
he will guide you into all the t.; 16.13
and know in t. that I came from 17.08
Sanctify them in the t.; thy word is t. 17.17
they also may be consecrated in t. 17.19
world, to bear witness to the t. 18.37
who is of the t. hears my voice." 18.37
Pilate said to him, "What is t.?" 18.38
and he knows that he tells the t.— 19.35
but I am speaking the sober t. Ac 26.25
their wickedness suppress the t. Rom 1.18
exchanged the t. about God for a 1.25
factious and do not obey the t., 2.08
embodiment of knowledge and t.— 2.20
I am speaking the t. in Christ, 9.01
unleavened bread of sincerity and t. 1Co 5.08
statement of the t. we would 2Co 4.02
As the t. of Christ is in me, this 11.10
for I shall be speaking the t. 12.06
against the t., but only for the t. 13.08
that the t. of the gospel might be Gal 2.05
straightforward about the t. of the gospel, 2.14
your enemy by telling you the t.? 4.16
hindered you from obeying the t.? 5.07
who have heard the word of t., Eph 1.13
speaking the t. in love, we are to 4.15
in him, as the t. is in Jesus. 4.21
one speak the t. with his neighbor, 4.25
having girded your loins with t., 6.14
way, whether in pretense or in t., Php 1.18
in the word of the t., the gospel Col 1.05
understood the grace of God in t., 1.06
to love the t. and so be saved. 2Th 2.10
not believe the t. but had pleasure 2.12
by the Spirit and belief in the t. 2.13
to come to the knowledge of the t. 1Ti 2.04
and apostle (I am telling the t., 2.07
of the Gentiles in faith and t. 2.07
the pillar and bulwark of the t. 3.15
those who believe and know the t. 4.03
in mind and bereft of the t., 6.05
guard the t. that has been entrusted 2Ti 1.14
rightly handling the word of t. 2.15
from the t. by holding that the 2.18
repent and come to know the t., 2.25
arrive at a knowledge of the t. 3.07
so these men also oppose the t., 3.08
listening to the t. and wander into 4.04
knowledge of the t. which accords Tit 1.01
commands of men who reject the t. 1.14
receiving the knowledge of the t., Heb 10.26
by the word of t. that we should Jas 1.18
not boast and be false to the t. 3.14
from the t. and some one brings 5.19
obedience to the t. for a sincere 1Pe 1.22
established in the t. that you have. 2Pe 1.12
them the way of t. will be reviled 2.02
do not live according to the t.; 1Jn 1.06
ourselves, and the t. is not in us. 1.08
a liar, and the t. is not in him; 2.04
not because you do not know the t., 2.21
and know that no lie is of the t. 2.21
or speech but in deed and in t. 3.18
shall know that we are of the t., 3.19
the spirit of t. and the spirit of 4.06
because the Spirit is the t. 5.07
children, whom I love in the t., 2Jn 1.01
I but also all who know the t., 1.01
because of the t. which abides in 1.02
the Father's Son, in t. and love. 1.03
of your children following the t., 1.04
Gaius, whom I love in the t. 3Jn 1.01
testified to the t. of your life, 1.03
as indeed you do follow the t. 1.03
that my children follow the t. 1.04
we may be fellow workers in the t. 1.08
every one, and from the t. itself; 1.12

TRUTHFUL
T. lips endure for ever, but a lying Pro 12.19
A t. witness saves lives, but one 14.25
t. speech, and the power of God; 2Co 6.07

TRUTHFULLY
true, and teach the way of God t., Mt 22.16

TRUTHFULNESS
falsehood God's t. abounds to his Rom 3.07
the circumcised to show God's t., 15.08

TRUTHS
spiritual t. to those who possess 1Co 2.13

TRY
in order to t. him and to know all 2Ch 32.31
Does not the ear t. words as the Job 12.11
Prove me, O LORD, and t. me; Ps 26.02
my heart! T. me and know my thoughts! 139.23
those who go to t. mixed wine. Pro 23.30
search the mind and t. the heart, Jer 17.10
when slandered, we t. to conciliate; 1Co 4.13
incompetent to t. trivial cases? 6.02
just as I t. to please all men in 10.33
and t. to learn what is pleasing to Eph 5.10
to t. those who dwell upon the Rev 3.10

TRYING
that you are t. to gain time, Dan 2.08
And as they were t. to kill him, Ac 21.31
of God and t. to convince them 28.23
Or am I t. to please men? If I were Gal 1.10

TRYPHAENA
in the Lord, T. and Tryphosa. Greet the Rom 16.12

TRYPHOSA
in the Lord, Tryphaena, and T. Greet the Rom 16.12

TUBAL
Madai, Javan, T., Meshech, and Tiras. Gen 10.02
Madai, Javan, T., Meshech, and Tiras. 1Ch 1.05
to T. and Javan, to the coastlands Is 66.19
Javan, T., and Meshech traded with Eze 27.13
"Meshech and T. are there, and all 32.26
the chief prince of Meshech and T., 38.02
chief prince of Meshech and T.; 38.03
chief prince of Meshech and T.; 39.01

TUBAL-CAIN
Zillah bore T.; he was the Gen 4.22
The sister of T. was Naamah. 4.22

TUBES
His bones are t. of bronze, his Job 40.18

TUMBLE
every wall shall t. to the ground. Eze 38.20

TUMBLED
of barley bread t. into the camp Ju 7.13

TUMORS
terrified and afflicted them with t., 1Sa 5.06
so that t. broke out upon them. 5.09
did not die were stricken with t., 5.12
"Five golden t. and five golden 6.04
images of your t. and images of 6.05
mice and the images of their t. 6.11
These are the golden t., 6.17

TUMULT
the t. in the camp of the Philistines 1Sa 14.19
I saw a great t., but I do not know 2Sa 18.29
He scorns the t. of the city; Job 39.07
because of the t. of my heart. Ps 38.08
the mountains tremble with its t. 46.03
their waves, the t. of the peoples; 65.07
For lo, thy enemies are in t.; 83.02
in battle t. and every garment Is 9.05
Hark, a t. on the mountains as of a 13.04
has a day of t. and trampling and 22.05
there is a t. of waters in the Jer 10.13
Moab, the crown of the sons of t. 48.45
there is a t. of waters in the 51.16
my soul is in t., my heart is wrung Lam 1.20
my soul is in t.; my heart is 2.11
a sound of t. like the sound of a Eze 1.24
a day of t., and not of joyful 7.07
has a day of t. and trampling and 22.05
therefore the t. of war shall arise Hos 10.14
players, and the crowd making a t., Mt 9.23
lest there be a t. among the 26.05
he saw a t., and people weeping and Mk 5.38
"Why do you make a t. and weep? 5.39
lest there be a t. of the people." 14.02
temple, without any crowd or t. Ac 24.18

TUMULTS
and see the great t. within her, Amo 3.09
And when you hear of wars and t., Lk 21.09
t., labors, watching, hunger; 2Co 6.05

TUMULTUOUS
t. city, exultant town? Is 22.02
she is covered with its t. waves. Jer 51.42

TUNIC
me about like the collar of my t. Job 30.18
But his t. was without seam, woven Jn 19.23

TUNICS
their t., their hats, and their Dan 3.21
nor two t., nor sandals, nor a staff; Mt 10.10
wear sandals and not put on two t. Mk 6.09
nor money; and do not have two t. Lk 9.03

TURBAN
checker work, a t., and a girdle; Ex 28.04
it on the t. of a lace of blue; 28.37
it shall be on the front of the t. 28.37
you shall make a t. of fine linen, 28.39
and you shall set the t. on his head, 29.06
and put the holy crown upon the t. 29.06
and the t. of fine linen, and the 39.28
blue, to fasten it on the t. above; 39.31
And he set the t. upon his head, and Lev 8.09
and on the t., in front, he set the 8.09
girdle, and wear the linen t.; 16.04
justice was like a robe and a t. Job 29.14
Remove the t., and take off the Eze 21.26
Bind on your t., and put your shoes 24.17
them put a clean t. on his head." Zec 3.05
put a clean t. on his head and clothed 3.05

TURBANS
garments, the t., and the veils. Is 3.23
with flowing t. on their heads, all Eze 23.15
Your t. shall be on your heads and 24.23
have linen t. upon their heads, and 44.18

TURBULENT
Behold, if the river is t. he is not Job 40.23
you are more t. than the nations Eze 5.07

TURMOIL
My heart is in t., and is never Job 30.27
Surely for nought are they in t.; Is 39.06
your pain and t. and the hard Is 14.03

TURN
t. aside, I pray you, to your servant's Gen 19.02
that I may t. to the right hand or 24.49
"I will t. aside and see this great Ex 3.03
of Israel to t. back and encamp in 14.02
your enemies t. their backs to you. 23.27
T. from thy fierce wrath, and repent 32.12
Do not t. to idols or make for Lev 19.04
"Do not t. to mediums or wizards; 19.31
t. tomorrow and set out for the Num 14.25
we will not t. aside to the right 20.17
we will not t. aside into field or 21.22
struck the ass, to t. her into the road. 22.23
was no way to t. either to the 22.26
of the LORD may t. away from 25.04
For if you t. away from following 32.15
boundary shall t. south of the 34.04
boundary shall t. from Azmon to 34.05
t. and take your journey, and go to Deu 1.07
t., and journey into the wilderness 1.40
country long enough, t. northward. 2.03
I will t. aside neither to the 2.27
you shall not t. aside to the right 5.32
For they would t. away your sons 7.04
and you t. aside and serve other 11.16
but t. aside from the way which I 11.28
the LORD may t. from the fierceness 13.17
then you shall t. it into money, and 14.25
you shall t. and go to your tents. 16.07
you shall not t. aside from the 17.11
himself, lest his heart t. away; 17.17
that he may not t. aside from the 17.20
and t. back and cover up your 23.13
among you, and t. away from you. 23.14
and if you do not t. aside from any 28.14
if you t. to the LORD your God with 30.10
they will t. to other gods and 30.10
and t. aside from the way which I 31.29
t. not from it to the right hand or Jos 1.07
they t. their backs before their 7.12
therefore t. and go to your home in 22.04
that you must t. away this day from 22.18
an altar to t. away from following 22.23
and t. away this day from following 22.29
For if you t. back, and join the 23.12
then he will t. and do you harm, and 24.20
"T. aside, my lord, t. aside to me; Ju 4.18
let us t. aside to this city of the 19.11
"We will not t. aside into the city 19.12
the men of Israel should t. in battle. 20.39
"T. back, my daughters, why will you Ru 1.11
T. back, my daughters, go your way, 1.12
So Boaz said, "T. aside, friend; 4.01
his hand does not t. away from you." 1Sa 6.03
yet do not t. aside from following 12.20

TURN (cont.)
and do not t. aside after vain 1Sa 12.21
"T. and kill the priests of the 22.17
"You t. and fall upon the priests." 22.18
"T. aside to your right hand or to 2Sa 2.21
would not t. aside from following 2.21
"T. aside from following me; 2.22
But he refused to t. aside; therefore 2.23
bid your people t. from the 2.26
one cannot t. to the right hand or 14.19
t. the counsel of Ahithophel into 15.31
"T. aside, and stand here." So he 18.30
his statutes I did not t. aside. 22.23
and did not t. back until they were 22.38
make my enemies t. their backs to 22.41
that you do and wherever you t.; 1Ki 2.03
if they t. again to thee, and 8.33
and t. from their sin, when thou 8.35
But if you t. aside from following 9.06
they will t. away your heart after 11.02
for it was a t. of affairs brought 12.15
kingdom will t. back to the house 12.26
people will t. again to their lord, 12.27
Jeroboam did not t. from his evil 13.33
and did not t. aside from anything 15.05
"Depart from here and t. eastward, 17.03
"T. about, and carry me out of the 22.34
he did not t. aside from it, doing 22.43
he would t. in there to eat food. 2Ki 4.08
T. round and ride behind me." 9.18
T. round and ride behind me." 9.19
But Jehu did not t. aside from the 10.29
he did not t. from the sins of 10.31
he did not t. away from the sins 15.24
"T. from your evil ways and keep my 17.13
that you should t. fortified 19.25
and I will t. you back on the way 19.28
"T. back, and say to Hezekiah the 20.05
and he did not t. aside to the 22.02
LORD did not t. from the fierceness 23.26
to t. the kingdom of Saul over to 1Ch 12.23
when they t. again and acknowledge 2Ch 6.24
and t. from their sin, when thou 6.26
do not t. away the face of thy 6.42
and t. from their wicked ways, then 7.14
"But if you t. aside and forsake my 7.19
And they did not t. aside from what 8.15
for it was a t. of affairs 10.15
"T. about, and carry me out of the 18.33
and did not t. aside from it; 20.32
fierce anger may t. away from us. 29.10
that he may t. again to the remnant 30.06
fierce anger may t. away from you. 30.08
and will not t. away his face from 30.09
and he did not t. aside to the 34.02
they did not t. away from following 34.33
Josiah would not t. away from him, 35.22
t. back their taunt upon their own Neh 4.04
in order to t. them back to thee, 9.26
in order to t. them back to thy 9.29
they did not t. from their wicked 9.35
Now when the t. came for each Est 2.12
When the t. came for Esther the 2.15
which of the holy ones will you t. Job 5.01
The caravans t. aside from their 6.18
T., I pray, let no wrong be done. 6.29
T. now, my vindication is at stake. 6.29
"God will not t. back his anger; 9.13
now thou dost t. about and destroy 10.08
and wilt thou t. me to dust again 10.09
that you t. your spirit against God, 15.13
I t. to the right hand, but I cannot 23.09
is unchangeable and who can t. him? 23.13
that he may t. man aside from his 33.17
greatness of the ransom t. you aside. 36.18
do not t. to iniquity, for this you 36.21
They t. round and round by his 37.12
he does not t. back from the sword. 39.22
T., O LORD, save my life; Ps 6.04
they shall t. back, and be put to 6.10
and did not t. back till they were 18.37
make my enemies t. their backs to 18.40
shall remember and t. to the LORD; 22.27
T. thou to me, and be gracious to me; 25.16
T. not thy servant away in anger, 27.09
who does not t. to the proud, to 40.04
Thou hast made us t. back from the 44.10
to thy abundant mercy, t. to me. 69.16
Therefore the people t. and praise 73.10
T. again, O God of hosts! 80.14
Then we will never t. back from thee; 80.18
and t. my hand against their foes. 81.14
thou didst t. from thy hot anger. 85.03
to those who t. to him in their 85.08
T. to me and take pity on me; 86.16
"T. back, O children of men!" 90.03
to t. away his wrath from destroying 106.23
O Jordan, that you t. back? 114.05
T. my eyes from looking at vanities; 119.37
T. away the reproach which I dread; 119.39
but I do not t. away from thy law. 119.51
I t. my feet to thy testimonies; 119.59
Let those who fear thee t. to me, 119.79
I do not t. aside from thy ordinances, 119.102
T. to me and be gracious to me, as 119.132
But those who t. aside upon their 125.05
sake do not t. away the face of 132.10
from which he will not t. back: 132.11
the LORD, and t. away from evil. Pro 3.07
and do not t. away from the words 4.05
t. away from it and pass on. 4.15
t. your foot away from evil. 4.27
Let not your heart t. aside to her 7.25
"Whoever is simple, let him t. in here!" 9.04
"Whoever is simple, let him t. in here!" 9.16
but to t. away from evil is an 13.19
and t. away his anger from him. 24.18
aflame, but wise men t. away wrath. 29.08
and does not t. back before any; 30.30
the dust, and all t. to dust again. Ecc 3.20
t., my beloved, be like a gazelle, or Sol 2.17
T. away your eyes from me, for they 6.05
I will t. my hand against you and Is 1.25
T. away from man in whose nostrils 2.22
their hearts, and t. and be healed." 6.10
and their God, and t. their faces upward; 8.21
The people did not t. to him who 9.13
to t. aside the needy from justice 10.02
every man will t. to his own people, 13.14
stretched out, and who will t. it back? 14.27
to those who t. back the battle at 28.06
You t. things upside down! Shall the 29.16
an empty plea t. aside him who is 29.21
of Pharaoh t. to your shame, 30.03
leave the way, t. aside from the 30.11
t. to the right or when you t. to the left. 30.21
T. to him from whom you have deeply 31.06
and I will t. you back on the way 37.29
the dial of Ahaz t. back ten steps." 38.08
I will t. the rivers into islands, 42.15
I will t. the darkness before them 42.16
"T. to me and be saved, all the ends 45.22
"If you t. back your foot from the 58.13
in Jacob who t. from transgression, 59.20
and would not t. from following me. Jer 3.19
not relented nor will I t. back." 4.28
heart would not t. toward this 15.01
Who will t. aside to ask about your 15.05
they did not t. from their ways. 15.07
They shall t to you, but you shall 15.19
you, but you shall not t. to them. 15.19
those who t. away from thee shall 17.13
to t. away thy wrath from them. 18.20
I will t. back the weapons of war 21.04
LORD will not t. back until he has 23.20
saying, 'T. now, every one of you, 25.05

TURN (cont.)

and every one t. from his evil way, Jer 26.03
LORD will not t. back until he has 30.24
I will t. their mourning into joy, I 31.13
Gareb, and shall then t. to Goah. 31.39
that I will not t. away from doing 32.40
that they may not t. from me. 32.40
'T. now every one of you from his 35.15
every one may t. from his evil way, 36.03
every one will t. from his evil 36.07
in the mire, they t. away from you.' 38.22
to t. from their wickedness and 44.05
Flee, t. back, dwell in the depths, O 49.08
every one shall t. to his own 50.16
to t. aside the right of a man in Lam 3.35
he does not t. from his wickedness, Eze 3.19
that you cannot t. from one side 4.08
eyes which t. wantonly after their 6.09
it shall not t. back; and because 7.13
I will t. my face from them, that 7.22
wheels did not t. from beside them. 10.16
he should not t. from his wicked 13.22
Repent and t. away from your idols; 14.06
and t. away your faces from all 14.06
that he should t. from his way and 18.23
Repent and t. from all your transgressions, 18.30
says the Lord GOD; so t., and live." 18.32
when they t. to them for aid. 29.16
warn the wicked to t. from his way, 33.08
warn the wicked to t. from his way, 33.09
and he does not t. from his way; 33.09
that the wicked t. from his way 33.11
t. back, t. back from your evil 33.11
and I will t. to you, and you shall 36.09
and I will t. you about, and put 38.04
and I will t. you about and drive 39.02
and thy wrath t. away from thy Dan 9.16
Afterward he shall t. his face to 11.18
indeed he shall t. his insolence 11.18
Then he shall t. his face back 11.19
and shall t. back and be enraged 11.30
He shall t. back and give heed to 11.30
and those who t. many to righteousness, 12.03
though they t. to other gods and Hos 3.01
They t. to Baal; they are like a 7.16
and will t. back upon him his 12.14
whether he will not t. and repent, Joe 2.14
I will t. my hand against Ekron; Amo 1.08
and t. aside the way of the afflicted 2.07
O you who t. justice to wormwood, 5.07
and t. aside the needy in the gate. 5.12
I will t. your feasts into mourning, 8.10
let every one t. from his evil way Jon 3.08
yet repent and t. from his fierce 3.09
they shall t. in dread to the LORD Mic 7.17
I will t. my hand against the Zec 13.07
And he will t. the hearts of Mal 4.06
t. to him the other also; Mt 5.39
underfoot and t. to attack you. 7.06
and t. for me to heal them.' 13.15
unless you t. and become like 18.03
the field not t. back to take his 24.18
lest they should t. again, Mk 4.12
the field not t. back to take his 13.16
And he will t. many of the sons of Lk 1.16
to t. the hearts of the fathers to 1.17
T. in the account of your stewardship, 16.02
who is in the field not t. back. 17.31
and t. for me to heal them. Jn 12.40
but your sorrow will t. into joy. 16.20
and t. again, that your sins may be Ac 3.19
Our fathers in t. brought it in 7.45
seeking to t. away the proconsul 13.08
life, behold, we t. to the Gentiles. 13.46
that you should t. from these vain 14.15
of the Gentiles who t. to God, 15.19
that they may t. from darkness to 26.18
repent and t. to God and perform 26.20
and t. for me to heal them. 28.27
or at most three, and each in t.; 1Co 14.27
should rather t. to forgive and 2Co 2.07
but we were afflicted at every t.— 7.05
how can you t. back again to the Gal 4.09
this will t. out for my deliverance, Php 1.19
and will t. away from listening to 2Ti 4.04
let him t. away from evil and do 1Pe 3.11
knowing it to t. back from the 2Pe 2.21
the waters to t. them into blood, Rev 11.06

TURNED

a flaming sword which t. every way, Gen 3.24
their faces were t. away, 9.23
then they t. back and came to 14.07
So the men t. from there, and went 18.22
so they t. aside to him and entered 19.03
LORD has blessed you wherever I t. 30.30
and t. in to a certain Adullamite, 38.01
Then he t. away from them and wept; 42.24
and they t. trembling to one 42.28
LORD saw that he t. aside to see, Ex 3.04
Then Moses t. again to the LORD and 5.22
rod which was t. into a serpent. 7.15
hand, and it shall be t. to blood, 7.17
that was in the Nile t. to blood. 7.20
Pharaoh t. and went into his house, 7.23
Then he t. and went out from 10.06
And the LORD t. a very strong west 10.19
they have t. aside quickly out of 32.08
And Moses t., and went down from 32.15
When Moses t. again into the camp, 33.11
spot has t. white and the disease Lev 13.03
the hair in it has not t. white, 13.04
which has t. the hair white, and 13.10
it has all t. white, and he is clean 13.13
and if the disease has t. white, 13.17
the skin and its hair has t. white, 13.20
in the spot has t. white and it 13.25
discipline you are not t. to me, 26.23
if you have not t. aside to Num 5.19
And Aaron t. towards Miriam, and 12.10
you have t. back from following 14.43
they t. toward the tent of meeting; 16.42
so Israel t. away from him. 20.21
Then they t. and went up by the way 21.33
and the ass t. aside out of the 22.23
and t. aside before me these three 22.33
If she had not t. aside from me, 22.33
has t. back my wrath from the 25.11
and t. back to Pihahiroth, which is 33.07
and they t. and went up into the Deu 1.24
"Then we t., and journeyed into the 2.01
"And we t. and went in the direction 2.08
"Then we t. and went up the way to 3.01
they have t. aside quickly out of 9.12
So I t. and came down from the 9.15
you had t. aside quickly from the 9.16
Then I t. and came down from the 10.05
LORD your God t. the curse into a 23.05
because they have t. to other gods. 31.18
when Israel has t. their backs Jos 7.08
then the LORD t. from his burning 7.26
the wilderness t. back upon the 8.20
then they t. back and smote the men 8.21
t. back to Debir and assaulted it, 10.38
And Joshua t. back at that time, and 11.10
they soon t. aside from the way in Ju 2.17
they t. back and behaved worse than 2.19
But he himself t. back at the 3.19
So he t. aside to her into the tent, 4.18
And the LORD t. to him and said, "Go 6.14
and t. it upside down, so that the 7.13
of Israel t. again and played the 8.33
"That is why we have t. to you now, 11.08
and he t. aside to see the carcass 14.08
and he t. them tail to tail, and put 15.04

TURNED (cont.)
and they t. aside and said to him, Ju 18.03
And they t. aside thither, and came 18.15
So they t. and departed, putting the 18.21
who t. round and said to Micah, 18.23
he t. and went back to his home. 18.26
and they t. aside there, to go in 19.15
Then the men of Israel t., and the men 20.41
Therefore they t. their backs 20.42
And they t. and fled toward the 20.45
But six hundred men t. and fled 20.47
men of Israel t. back against the 20.48
and t. over, and behold, a woman lay Ru 3.08
and he t. aside and sat down. 4.01
they t. neither to the right nor to 1Sa 6.12
but t. aside after gain; they took 8.03
them and be t. into another man. 10.06
When he t. his back to leave Samuel, 10.09
one company t. toward Ophrah, to the 13.17
another company t. toward Bethhoron, 13.18
another company t. toward the 13.18
even they also t. to be with the 14.21
wherever he t. he put them to the 14.47
for he has t. back from following 15.11
up a monument for himself and t., 15.12
As Samuel t. to go away, Saul laid 15.27
So Samuel t. back after Saul; 15.31
And he t. away from him toward 17.30
the Edomite t. and fell upon the 22.18
So David's young men t. away, 25.12
and God has t. away from me and 28.15
the LORD has t. from you and 28.16
the bow of Jonathan t. not back, 2Sa 1.22
as he went he t. neither to the 2.19
So he t. aside, and stood still. 18.30
that day was t. into mourning for 19.02
the kingdom has t. about and 1Ki 2.15
So she t. and went back to her own 10.13
and his wives t. away his heart. 11.03
old his wives t. away his heart 11.04
his heart had t. away from the 11.09
that thou hast t. their hearts 18.37
a soldier t. and brought a man to 20.39
and t. away his face, and would eat 21.04
So they t. to fight against him; 22.32
they t. back from pursuing him. 22.33
And he t. around, and when he saw 2Ki 2.24
and he t. into the chamber 4.11
So he t. and went away in a rage. 5.12
when the man t. from his chariot 5.26
and he t. toward them, because of 13.23
So the king of Assyria t. back, 15.20
Then Hezekiah t. his face to the 20.02
And as Josiah t., he saw the tombs 23.16
who t. to the LORD with all his 23.25
then he t. and rebelled against 24.01
and t. the kingdom over to David 1Ch 10.14
he t. and saw the angel, and his 21.20
So she t. and went back to her own 2Ch 9.12
the wrath of the LORD t. from him, 12.12
their distress they t. to the LORD, 15.04
So they t. to fight against him; 18.31
they t. back from pursuing him. 18.32
time when he t. away from the LORD 25.27
and have t. away their faces from 29.06
of the LORD, and t. their backs. 29.06
and had t. the heart of the king of Ez 6.22
and I t. back and entered by the Neh 2.15
yet when they t. and cried to thee 9.28
and t. a stubborn shoulder and 9.29
yet our God t. the curse into a 13.02
that had been t. for them from Est 9.22
feared God, and t. away from evil. Job 1.01
whom I loved have t. against me. 19.19
yet his food is t. in his stomach; 20.14
kept his way and have not t. aside. 23.11
underneath it is t. up as by fire. 28.05
Terrors are t. upon me; my honor is 30.15
Thou hast t. cruel to me; with the 30.21
My lyre is t. to mourning, and my 30.31
if my step has t. aside from the 31.07
because they t. aside from following 34.27
him slingstones are t. to stubble. 41.28
When my enemies t. back, they stumbled Ps 9.03
Thou hast t. for me my mourning 30.11
Let them be t. back and confounded 35.04
let them be t. back and brought to 40.14
Our heart has not t. back, nor have our 44.18
enemies will be t. back in the day 56.09
He t. the sea into dry land; men passed 66.06
Let them be t. back and brought to 70.02
t. back on the day of battle. 78.09
He t. their rivers to blood, so that 78.44
but t. away and acted treacherously 78.57
Yea, thou hast t. back the edge of 89.43
He t. their hearts to hate his 105.25
He t. their waters into blood, and 105.29
looked and fled, Jordan t. back. 114.03
be put to shame and t. backward! 129.05
So I t. to consider wisdom and Ec 2.12
So I t. about and gave my heart up 2.20
I t. my mind to know and to search 7.25
but my beloved had t. and gone. Sol 5.06
Whither has your beloved t., 6.01
anger is not t. away and his hand Is 5.25
anger is not t. away and his hand 9.12
anger is not t. away and his hand 9.17
anger is not t. away and his hand 9.21
anger is not t. away and his hand 10.04
thy anger t. away, and thou didst 12.01
has been t. for me into trembling. 21.04
shall be t. into a fruitful field, 29.17
of Edom shall be t. into pitch, 34.09
Then Hezekiah t. his face to the 38.02
"So the sun t. back on the dial 38.08
They shall be t. back and utterly 42.17
Chaldeans will be t. to lamentations. 43.14
not rebellious, I t. not backward. 50.05
we have t. every one to his own way; 53.06
they have all t. to their own way, 56.11
Justice is t. back, and righteousness 59.14
of the sea shall be t. to you, 60.05
therefore he t. to be their enemy, 63.10
then have you t. degenerate and Jer 2.21
For they have t. their back to me, 2.27
surely his anger has t. from me.' 2.35
the LORD has not t. back from us." 4.08
they have t. aside and gone away. 5.23
Your iniquities have t. these away, 5.25
Their houses shall be t. over to others, 6.12
has this people t. away in perpetual 8.05
They have t. back to the iniquities 11.10
they would have t. them from their 23.22
Why has every face t. pale? 30.06
For after I had t. away I repented; 31.19
They have t. to me their back and 32.33
But afterward they t. around and 34.11
but then you t. around and profaned 34.16
they t. one to another in fear; 36.16
from Mizpah t. about and came back, 41.14
are dismayed and have t. backward. 46.05
they have t. and fled together, they 46.21
How Moab has t. his back in shame! 48.39
she t. to flee, and panic seized her; 49.24
with faces t. toward it, saying, 50.05
he t. me back; he has left Lam 1.13
has been t. over to strangers, our 5.02
dancing has been t. to mourning. 5.15
and its branches t. toward him, Eze 17.06
considered and t. away from all 18.28
she t. from them in disgust. 23.17
I t. in disgust from her, as I had 23.18
as I had t. from her sister. 23.18
lovers from whom you t. in disgust, 23.22
those from whom you t. in disgust; 23.28
and I t. you to ashes upon the 28.18

TURNED (cont.)
Then he t. and measured the north Eze 42.17
Then he t. and measured the south 42.18
Then he t. to the west side and 42.19
Then I t. my face to the Lord God, Dan 9.03
transgressed thy law and t. aside, 9.11
I t. my face toward the ground and 10.15
the peoples; Ephraim is a cake not t. Hos 7.08
for my anger has t. from them. 14.04
The sun shall be t. to darkness, Joe 2.31
But you have t. justice into poison Amo 6.12
how they t. from their evil way, God Jon 3.10
those who have t. back from following Zep 1.06
and t. a stubborn shoulder, and Zec 7.11
land shall be t. into a plain from 14.10
and he t. many from iniquity. Mal 2.06
But you have t. aside from the way; 2.08
you have t. aside from my statutes 3.07
Jesus t., and seeing her he said, Mt 9.22
But he t. and said to Peter, "Get 16.23
immediately t. about in the crowd, Mk 5.30
and t. and said to the multitude Lk 7.09
But he t. and rebuked them. 9.55
him; and he t. and said to them, 14.25
t. back, praising God with a loud 17.15
and when you have t. again, 22.32
And the Lord t. and looked at Peter. 22.61
Jesus t., and saw them following, Jn 1.38
she t. round and saw Jesus standing, 20.14
She t. and said to him in Hebrew, 20.16
Peter t. and saw following them the 21.20
apostleship from which Judas t. aside, Ac 1.25
the sun shall be t. into darkness 2.20
in their hearts they t. to Egypt, 7.39
But God t. and gave them over to 7.42
saw him, and they t. to the Lord. 9.35
that believed t. to the Lord. 11.21
and t. and said to the spirit, "I 16.18
men who have t. the world upside 17.06
persuaded and t. away a considerable 19.26
All have t. aside, together they Rom 3.12
and how you t. to God from idols, to 1Th 1.09
who are in Asia t. away from me, 2Ti 1.15
laughter be t. to mourning and Jas 4.09
Then I t. to see the voice that was Rev 1.12

TURNEST
Thou t. man back to the dust, and Ps 90.03

TURNING
t. aside after a multitude, so as to Ex 23.02
t. toward Gilgal, which is opposite Jos 15.07
t. on the western side southward 18.14
of Israel in t. away this day from 22.16
t. aside from it neither to the 23.06
wiping it and t. it upside down. 2Ki 21.13
his heart against t. to the LORD, 2Ch 36.13
simple are killed by their t. away, Pro 1.32
and t. away from following our God, Is 59.13
t. them away on the mountains; Jer 50.06
forward, without t. as they went. Eze 1.09
they went, without t. as they went. 1.12
directions without t. as they went. 1.17
directions without t. as they went, 10.11
followed without t. as they went. Eze 10.11
t. aside from thy commandments and Dan 9.05
t. from our iniquities and giving 9.13
people are bent on t. away from me; Hos 11.07
But t. and seeing his disciples, he Mk 8.33
Then t. toward the woman he said to Lk 7.44
Then t. to the disciples he said 10.23
But Jesus t. to them said, "Daughters 23.28
to bless you in t. every one of Ac 3.26
then t. to the body he said, "Tabitha, 9.40
your great learning is t. you mad." 26.24
of Christ and t. to a different Gal 1.06
if by t. the cities of Sodom and 2Pe 2.06
and on t. I saw seven golden Rev 1.12

TURNS
until your brother's fury t. away; Gen 27.44
until your brother's anger t. away, 27.45
and it t. into a leprous disease on Lev 13.02
the raw flesh t. again and is 13.16
"If a person t. to mediums and 20.06
whose heart t. away this day from Deu 29.18
But if your heart t. away, 30.17
up to Addar, t. about to Karka, Jos 15.03
the boundary t. round toward 16.06
the boundary t. about to Hannathon, 19.14
then it t. eastward, it goes to 19.27
then the boundary t. to Ramah, 19.29
then the boundary t. to Hosah, 19.29
then the boundary t. westward to 19.34
you learn how the matter t. out, Ru 3.18
fears God and t. away from evil?" Job 1.08
fears God and t. away from evil? 2.03
no treader t. toward their vineyards. 24.18
My skin t. black and falls from me, 30.30
He t. rivers into a desert, springs Ps 107.33
He t. a desert into pools of water, 107.35
who t. the rock into a pool of 114.08
A righteous man t. away from evil, Pro 12.26
is cautious and t. away from evil, 14.16
A soft answer t. away wrath, but a 15.01
of the upright t. aside from evil; 16.17
wherever he t. he prospers. 17.08
the LORD; he t. it wherever he will. 21.01
As a door t. on its hinges, so does 26.14
If one t. away his ear from hearing 28.09
who t. wise men back, and makes Is 44.25
If one t. away, does he not return? Jer 8.04
Every one t. to his own course, 8.06
for light he t. it into gloom and 13.16
a wayfarer who t. aside to tarry 14.08
whose heart t. away from the LORD. 17.05
t. from its evil, I will repent of 18.08
so that no one t. from his wickedness; 23.14
groans, and t. her face away. Lam 1.08
surely against me he t. his hand 3.03
a righteous man t. from his Eze 3.20
"But if a wicked man t. away from 18.21
a righteous man t. away from his 18.24
When a righteous man t. away from 18.26
a wicked man t. away from the 18.27
by it when he t. from his wickedness; 33.12
yet if he t. from his sin and 33.14
When the righteous t. from his 33.18
And when the wicked t. from his 33.19
and t. deep darkness into the Amo 5.08
they cry; but none t. back. Nah 2.08
and t. to you seven times, and says, Lk 17.04
but when a man t. to the Lord the 2Co 3.16
The dog t. back to his own vomit, 2Pe 2.22

TURTLEDOVE
a t., and a young pigeon. Gen 15.09
pigeon or a t. for a sin offering, Lev 12.06
voice of the t. is heard in our Sol 2.12
and the t., swallow, and crane keep Jer 8.07

TURTLEDOVES
his offering of t. or of young Lev 1.14
two t. or two young pigeons, one for 5.07
afford two t. or two young pigeons, 5.11
shall take two t. or two young 12.08
also two t. or two young pigeons, 14.22
of the t. or young pigeons such as 14.30
shall take two t. or two young 15.14
shall take two t. or two young 15.29
shall bring two t. or two young Num 6.10
"a pair of t., or two young pigeons." Lk 2.24

TUSKS
you in payment ivory t. and ebony. Eze 27.15

TWELFTH
On the t. day Ahira the son of Enan, Num 7.78
before him, and he was with the t. 1Ki 19.19
In the t. year of Joram the son of 2Ki 8.25
In the t. year of Ahaz king of 17.01
in the t. month, on the twenty-seventh 25.27
to Elashib, and t. to Jakim, 1Ch 24.12
the t. to Hashabiah, his sons and 25.19
T., for the t. month, was Heldai 27.15
and in the t. year he began to 2Ch 34.03
Ahava on the t. day of the first Ez 8.31
in the t. year of King Ahasuerus, Est 3.07
after month till the t. month, 3.07
the thirteenth day of the t. month, 3.13
the thirteenth day of the t. month, 8.12
Now in the t. month, which is the 9.01
in the t. month, on the twenty-fifth Jer 52.31
on the t. day of the month, the word Eze 29.01
In the t. year, in the twelfth month, 32.01
in the t. month, on the first day of 32.01
In the t. year, in the first month, 32.17
In the t. year of our exile, in the 33.21
eleventh jacinth, the t. amethyst. Rev 21.20

TWELVE
were nine hundred and t. years; Gen 5.08
T. years they had served Chedorlaomer, 14.04
shall be the father of t. princes, 17.20
t. princes according to their 25.16
Now the sons of Jacob were t. 35.22
are t. brothers, the sons of one man 42.13
we are t. brothers, sons of our 42.32
All these are the t. tribes of 49.28
there were t. springs of water and Ex 15.27
and t. pillars, according to the 24.04
according to the t. tribes of 24.04
There shall be t. stones with their 28.21
with its name, for the t. tribes. 28.21
There were t. stones with their 39.14
with its name, for the t. tribes. 39.14
flour, and bake t. cakes of it; Lev 24.05
t. men, each representing his Num 1.44
six covered wagons and t. oxen, 7.03
t. silver plates, t. silver basins, t. golden 7.84
the t. golden dishes, full of 7.86
for the burnt offering t. bulls, 7.87
t. rams, twelve male lambs a year 7.87
t. male lambs a year old, with their 7.87
and t. male goats for a sin offering 7.87
to their fathers' houses, t. rods. 17.02
to their fathers' houses, t. rods; 17.06
"On the second day t. young bulls, 29.17
each tribe, t. thousand armed for war. 31.05
Elim there were t. springs of 33.09
and I took t. men of you, one man Deu 1.23
Now therefore take t. men from the Jos 3.12
"Take t. men from the people, from 4.02
'Take t. stones from here out of 4.03
called the t. men from the people 4.04
and took up t. stones out of the 4.08
And Joshua set up t. stones in the 4.09
And those t. stones, which they took 4.20
were t. thousand, all the people of 8.25
t. cities with their villages; 18.24
t. cities with their villages: 19.15
the tribe of Zebulun, t. cities. 21.07
to them were in all t. cities. 21.40
into t. pieces, and sent her throughout Ju 19.29
sent thither t. thousand of their 21.10
t. for Benjamin and Ishbosheth the 2Sa 2.15
and t. of the servants of David. 2.15
the men of Tob, t. thousand men. 10.06
"Let me choose t. thousand men, and I will 17.01
Solomon had t. officers over all 1Ki 4.07
his chariots, and t. thousand horsemen. 4.26
and a line of t. cubits measured 7.15
It stook upon t. oxen, three facing 7.25
and the t. oxen underneath the sea. 7.44
while t. lions stood there, one on 10.20
chariots and t. thousand horsemen, 10.26
on him, and tore it into t. pieces. 11.30
Israel, and reigned for t. years; 16.23
Elijah took t. stones, according to 18.31
with t. yoke of oxen before him, and 19.19
Samaria, and he reigned t. years. 2Ki 3.01
Manasseh was t. years old when he 21.01
were allotted t. cities out of the 1Ch 6.63
thresholds, were two hundred and t. 9.22
a hundred and t. of his brethren. 15.10
and his brethren and his sons, t.; 25.09
his sons and his brethren, t.; 25.10
his sons and his brethren, t.; 25.11
his sons and his brethren, t.; 25.12
his sons and his brethren, t.; 25.13
his sons and his brethren, t.; 25.14
his sons and his brethren, t.; 25.15
his sons and his brethren, t.; 25.16
his sons and his brethren, t.; 25.17
his sons and his brethren, t.; 25.18
his sons and his brethren, t.; 25.19
his sons and his brethren, t.; 25.20
his sons and his brethren, t.; 25.21
his sons and his brethren, t.; 25.22
his sons and his brethren, t.; 25.23
his sons and his brethren, t.; 25.24
his sons and his brethren, t.; 25.25
his sons and his brethren, t.; 25.26
his sons and his brethren, t.; 25.27
his sons and his brethren, t.; 25.28
his sons and his brethren, t.; 25.29
his sons and his brethren, t.; 25.30
his sons and his brethren, t. 25.31
chariots and t. thousand horsemen, 2Ch 1.14
It stood upon t. oxen, three facing 4.04
and the t. oxen underneath it. 4.15
while t. lions stood there, one on 9.19
and t. thousand horsemen, whom he 9.25
with t. hundred chariots and sixty 12.03
Manasseh was t. years old when he 33.01
two thousand eight hundred and t. Ez 2.06
The sons of Jorah, one hundred and t. 2.18
offering for all Israel t. he-goats, 6.17
Then I set apart t. of the leading 8.24
t. bulls for all Israel, ninety-six 8.35
and as a sin offering t. he-goats; 8.35
t. years, neither I nor my brethren Neh 5.14
The sons of Hariph, a hundred and t. 7.24
after being t. months under the Est 2.12
the t. bronze bulls which were Jer 52.20
its circumference was t. cubits, 52.21
cubits, and the breadth t. cubits; Eze 40.49
t. cubits long by t. broad. 43.16
among the t. tribes of Israel. 47.13
At the end of t. months he was Dan 4.29
hemorrhage for t. years came up Mt 9.20
to him his t. disciples and gave 10.01
The names of the t. apostles are Mt 10.02
These t. Jesus sent out, charging 10.05
instructing his t. disciples, 11.01
they took up t. baskets full of 14.20
me will also sit on t. thrones, 19.28
judging the t. tribes of Israel. 19.28
he took the t. disciples aside, and 20.17
Then one of the t., who was called 26.14
sat at table with the t. disciples; 26.20
one of the t., and with him a great 26.47
me more than t. legions of angels? 26.53
And he appointed t., to be with Mk 3.14
him with the t. asked him concerning 4.10
had a flow of blood for t. years, 5.25
for she was t. years old. And immediately 5.42
And he called to him the t., 6.07
And they took up t. baskets full of 6.43
They said to him, "T." 8.19
And he sat down and called the t.; 9.35

TWELVE (cont.)

And taking the t. again, he began Mk 10.32
he went out to Bethany with the t. 11.11
Iscariot, who was one of the t., 14.10
it was evening he came with the t. 14.17
He said to them, "It is one of the t., 14.20
one of the t., and with him a crowd 14.43
And when he was t. years old, Lk 2.42
disciples, and chose from them t., 6.13
of God. And the t. were with him, 8.01
about t. years of age, and she was 8.42
of blood for t. years and could 8.43
And he called the t. together and 9.01
and the t. came and said to him, 9.12
t. baskets of broken pieces. 9.17
And taking the t., he said to them, 18.31
who was of the number of the t.; 22.03
judging the t. tribes of Israel. 22.30
one of the t., was leading them. 22.47
up and filled t. baskets with Jn 6.13
Jesus said to the t., "Will you also 6.67
the t., and one of you is a devil?" 6.70
one of the t., was to betray him. 6.71
"Are there not t. hours in the day? 11.09
one of the t., called the Twin, was 20.24
And the t. summoned the body of the Ac 6.02
and Jacob of the t. patriarchs 7.08
There were about t. of them in all. 19.07
not more than t. days since I went 24.11
to which our t. tribes hope to 26.07
appeared to Cephas, then to the t. 1Co 15.05
To the t. tribes in the dispersion: Jas 1.01
t. thousand sealed out of the tribe Rev 7.05
t. thousand of the tribe of Reuben, 7.05
t. thousand of the tribe of Gad, 7.05
t. thousand of the tribe of Asher, 7.06
t. thousand of the tribe of Naphtali, 7.06
t. thousand of the tribe of Manasseh, 7.06
t. thousand of the tribe of Simeon, 7.07
t. thousand of the tribe of Levi, 7.07
t. thousand of the tribe of Issachar, 7.07
t. thousand of the tribe of Zebulun, 7.08
t. thousand of the tribe of Joseph, 7.08
t. thousand sealed out of the tribe 7.08
on her head a crown of t. stars; 12.01
with t. gates, and at the gates 21.12
gates, and at the gates t. angels, 21.12
names of the t. tribes of the sons 21.12
of the city had t. foundations, 21.14
and on them the t. names of the 21.14
names of the t. apostles of the 21.14
t. thousand stadia; its length and breadth 21.16
And the t. gates were t. pearls, 21.21
of life with its t. kinds of fruit, 22.02

TWENTIETH

on the t. day of the month, the Num 10.11
In the t. year of Jeroboam king of 1Ki 15.09
in the t. year of Jotham the son of 2Ki 15.30
to Pethahiah, the t. to Jehezkel, 1Ch 24.16
to the t., to Eliathah, his sons and 25.27
on the t. day of the month. Ez 10.09
in the t. year, as I was in Susa the Neh 1.01
in the t. year of King Artaxerxes, 2.01
from the t. year to the thirty-second 5.14

TWENTY

shall be a hundred and t. years." Gen 6.03
Suppose t. are found there." 18.31
"For the sake of t. I will not 18.31
These t. years I have been with you; 31.38
These t. years I have been in your 31.41
two hundred she-goats and t. he-goats, 32.14
two hundred ewes and t. rams, 32.14
t. she-asses and ten he-asses. 32.15
Ishmaelites for t. shekels of 37.28
t. frames for the south side; Ex 26.18
you shall make under the t. frames, 26.19
on the north side t. frames, 26.20
shall be t. and their bases t., 27.10
their pillars t. and their bases t., 27.11
shall be a screen t. cubits long, 27.16
sanctuary (the shekel is t. gerahs), 30.13
from t. years old and upward, shall 30.14
t. frames for the south side; 36.23
of silver under the t. frames, 36.24
the north side, he made t. frames 36.25
their pillars were t. and their bases t., 38.10
their pillars t., their bases t., of bronze, 38.11
it was t. cubits long and five 38.18
from t. years old and upward, for 38.26
of a male from t. years old up to Lev 27.03
five years old up to t. years old, 27.05
shall be for a male t. shekels, 27.05
t. gerahs shall make a shekel. 27.25
from t. years old and upward, all in Num 1.03
of names from t. years old and 1.18
every male from t. years old and 1.20
every male from t. years old and 1.22
from t. years old and upward, all 1.24
from t. years old and upward, every 1.26
from t. years old and upward, every 1.28
from t. years old and upward, every 1.30
from t. years old and upward, every 1.32
from t. years old and upward, every 1.34
from t. years old and upward, every 1.36
from t. years old and upward, every 1.38
from t. years old and upward, every 1.40
from t. years old and upward, every 1.42
from t. years old and upward, every 1.45
the shekel of t. gerahs, you shall 3.47
being a hundred and t. shekels; 7.86
days, or ten days, or t. days, 11.19
numbered from t. years old and 14.29
the sanctuary, which is t. gerahs. 18.16
from t. years old and upward, by 26.02
from t. years old and upward," as 26.04
from t. years old and upward, shall 32.11
a hundred and t. years old this Deu 31.02
a hundred and t. years old when he 34.07
of Israel cruelly for t. years. Ju 4.03
a hundred and t. thousand men who 8.10
t. cities, and as far as Abelkeramim, 11.33
days of the Philistines t. years. 15.20
He had judged Israel t. years. 16.31
some t. years, and all the house of 1Sa 7.02
was of about t. men within as it 14.14
When Abner came with t. men to David 2Sa 3.20
and t. thousand foot soldiers; 8.04
had fifteen sons and t. servants. 9.10
t. thousand foot soldiers, and the 10.06
great on that day, t. thousand men. 18.07
fifteen sons and his t. servants 19.17
the end of nine months and t. days. 24.08
and t. pasture-fed cattle, a hundred 1Ki 4.23
gave Hiram t. thousand cors of 5.11
and t. thousand cors of beaten oil. 5.11
t. cubits wide, and thirty cubits 6.02
of the house was t. cubits long, 6.03
He built t. cubits of the rear of 6.16
inner sanctuary was t. cubits long, 6.20
t. cubits wide, and t. cubits high; 6.20
a hundred and t. thousand sheep. 8.63
At the end of t. years, in which 9.10
gave to Hiram t. cities in the 9.11
one hundred and t. talents of gold 9.14
of four hundred and t. talents, 9.28
a hundred and t. talents of gold, 10.10
t. loaves of barley, and fresh ears 2Ki 4.42
in Samaria, and reigned t. years. 15.27
Ahaz was t. years old when he began 16.02
was t. thousand two hundred. 1Ch 7.09
Of the Ephraimites t. thousand 12.30
one hundred and t. thousand men 12.37
a hundred and t. of his brethren; 15.05
two hundred and t. of his brethren 15.06

TWENTY (cont.)

and t. thousand foot soldiers; 1Ch 18.04
individuals from t. years old and 23.24
Levites from t. years old and 23.27
number those below t. years of age, 27.23
t. thousand cors of crushed wheat, 2Ch 2.10
t. thousand cors of barley, t. 2.10
t. thousand baths of wine, and 2.10
and t. thousand baths of oil. 2.10
cubits, and the breadth t. cubits. 3.03
of the house was t. cubits long, 3.04
height was a hundred and t. cubits. 3.04
t. cubits, and its breadth was t. cubits; 3.08
together extended t. cubits 3.11
these cherubim extended t. cubits; 3.13
t. cubits long, and t. cubits wide, 4.01
a hundred and t. priests who were 5.12
a hundred and t. thousand sheep. 7.05
At the end of t. years, in which 8.01
a hundred and t. talents of gold, 9.09
mustered those t. years old and 25.05
Ahaz was t. years old when he began 28.01
a hundred and t. thousand in Judah 28.06
Levites from t. years old and 31.17
of Harim, three hundred and t. Ez 2.32
six thousand seven hundred and t. 2.67
from t. years old and upward, to 3.08
his kinsmen and their sons, t.; 8.19
besides two hundred and t. of the 8.20
t. bowls of gold worth a thousand 8.27
of Harim, three hundred and t. Neh 7.35
six thousand seven hundred and t. 7.69
of the work t. thousand darics of 7.71
people gave was t. thousand darics 7.72
be by weight, t. shekels a day; Eze 4.10
a breadth of five and t. cubits, 40.13
also the vestibule, t. cubits; 40.14
of the vestibule was t. cubits, 40.49
cubits, and its breadth, t. cubits. 41.02
t. cubits, and its breadth, twenty 41.04
t. cubits, beyond the nave. 41.04
a breadth of t. cubits round about 41.10
Adjoining the t. cubits which 42.03
cubits long and t. thousand cubits 45.01
The shekel shall be t. gerahs; 45.12
and t. thousand in breadth. 48.09
cubits and the breadth t. thousand. 48.13
kingdom a hundred and t. satraps, Dan 6.01
a hundred and t. thousand persons Jon 4.11
When one came to a heap of t. measures, Hag 2.16
fifty measures, there were but t. 2.16
its length is t. cubits, and its Zec 5.02
comes against him with t. thousand Lk 14.31
each holding t. or thirty gallons. Jn 2.06
about a hundred and t.), and said, Ac 1.15
So they sounded and found t. fathoms; 27.28

TWENTY-EIGHT

of each curtain shall be t. cubits, Ex 26.02
of each curtain was t. cubits, 36.09
Israel in Samaria was t. years. 2Ki 10.36
Of the Danites t. thousand six 1Ch 12.35
and had t. sons and sixty daughters); 2Ch 11.21
of Anathoth, one hundred and t. Ez 2.23
sons of Asaph, one hundred and t. 2.41
son of Bebai, and with him t. men. 8.11
The sons of Bebai, six hundred and t. Neh 7.16
of Hashum, three hundred and t. 7.22
The men of Anathoth, a hundred and t. 7.27
Sallai, nine hundred and t. 11.08
men of valor, a hundred and t.; 11.14

TWENTY-FIFTH

finished on the t. day of the Neh 6.15
on the t. day of the month, Jer 52.31
In the t. year of our exile, at the Eze 40.01

TWENTY-FIRST

so until the t. day of the month Ex 12.18
the t. to Jachin, the twenty-second 1Ch 24.17
to the t., to Hothir, his sons and 25.28
on the t. day of the month, the word Hag 2.01

TWENTY-FIVE

from t. years old and upward they Num 8.24
destroyed t. thousand one hundred Ju 20.35
Benjamin were t. thousand men that 20.46
and he reigned t. years in Jerusalem. 1Ki 22.42
He was t. years old when he began 1Ki 14.02
He was t. years old when he began 15.33
He was t. years old when he began 18.02
Jehoiakim was t. years old when he 23.36
and he reigned t. years in Jerusalem. 2Ch 20.31
Amaziah was t. years old when he 25.01
Jotham was t. years old when he 27.01
He was t. years old when he began 27.08
to reign when he was t. years old, 29.01
Jehoiakim was t. years old when he 36.05
and Ono, seven hundred and t. Ez 2.33
were about t. men, with their backs Eze 8.16
of the gateway there were t. men; 11.01
cubits, and its breadth t. cubits. 40.21
cubits, and its breadth t. cubits. 40.25
cubits, and its breadth t. cubits. 40.29
t. cubits long and five cubits 40.30
cubits and its breadth t. cubits. 40.33
cubits and its breadth t. cubits. 40.36
t. thousand cubits long and twenty 45.01
off a section t. thousand cubits 45.03
t. thousand cubits long and ten 45.05
and t. thousand cubits long; 45.06
t. thousand cubits in breadth, and 48.08
LORD shall be t. thousand cubits 48.09
measuring t. thousand cubits on 48.10
and t. thousand in length on the 48.10
an allotment t. thousand cubits in 48.13
length shall be t. thousand cubits 48.13
in breadth and t. thousand in 48.15
apart shall be t. thousand cubits 48.20
from the t. thousand cubits of the 48.21
from the t. thousand cubits to the 48.21

TWENTY-FOUR

of peace offerings t. bulls, Num 7.88
by the plague were t. thousand. 25.09
toes on each foot, t. in number; 2Sa 21.20
at Tirzah, and reigned t. years. 1Ki 15.33
toes on each foot, t. in number; 1Ch 20.06
"T. thousand of these," David said, 23.04
division numbering t. thousand: 27.01
in his division were t. thousand. 27.02
in his division were t. thousand. 27.04
in his division were t. thousand. 27.05
in his division were t. thousand 27.07
in his division were t. thousand. 27.08
in his division were t. thousand. 27.09
in his division were t. thousand. 27.10
in his division were t. thousand. 27.11
in his division were t. thousand. 27.12
in his division were t. thousand. 27.13
in his division were t. thousand. 27.14
in his division were t. thousand. 27.15
of Bezai, three hundred and t. Neh 7.23
Round the throne were t. thrones, Rev 4.04
on the thrones were t. elders, 4.04
the t. elders fall down before him 4.10
creatures and the t. elders fell 5.08
And the t. elders who sit on their 11.16
and the t. elders and the four 19.04

TWENTY-FOURTH

to Delaiah, the t. to Maaziah. 1Ch 24.18
to the t. to Romamtiezer, his sons 25.31
Now on the t. day of this month the Neh 9.01
On the t. day of the first month, as Dan 10.04

TWENTY-FOURTH (cont.)
on the t. day of the month, in the Hag 1.15
On the t. day of the ninth month, in 2.10
from the t. day of the ninth month. 2.18
Haggai on the t. day of the month, 2.20
On the t. day of the eleventh month Zec 1.07

TWENTY-NINE
When Nahor had lived t. years, Gen 11.24
was t. talents and seven hundred Ex 38.24
t. cities, with their villages. Jos 15.32
and he reigned t. years in Jerusalem. 2Ki 14.02
and he reigned t. years in Jerusalem. 18.02
and he reigned t. years in Jerusalem. 2Ch 25.01
and he reigned t. years in Jerusalem. 29.01
basins of silver, t. censers, Ez 1.09

TWENTY-ONE
Zedekiah was t. years old when he 2Ki 24.18
Zedekiah was t. years old when he 2Ch 36.11
Ramah and Geba, six hundred and t. Ez 2.26
Ramah and Geba, sx hundred and t. Neh 7.30
and Ono, seven hundred and t. 7.37
Zedekiah was t. years old when he Jer 52.01
of Persia withstood me t. days; Dan 10.13

TWENTY-SECOND
to Jachin, the t. to Gamul, 1Ch 24.17
to the t., to Giddalti, his sons and 25.29

TWENTY-SEVEN
Sarah lived a hundred and t. years; Gen 23.01
wall fell upon t. thousand men 1Ki 20.30
over one hundred and t. provinces, Est 1.01
a hundred and t. provinces, to every 8.09
the hundred and t. provinces of 9.30

TWENTY-SEVENTH
on the t. day of the month, the Gen 8.14
in the t. year of Asa king of Judah, 1Ki 16.10
In the t. year of Asa king of Judah 16.15
In the t. year of Jeroboam king of 2Ki 15.01
t. day of the month, Evilmerodach 25.27
In the t. year, in the first month, Eze 29.17

TWENTY-SIX
on that day t. thousand men that Ju 20.15
in war, was t. thousand men. 1Ch 7.40

TWENTY-SIXTH
In the t. year of Asa king of Judah, 1Ki 16.08

TWENTY-THIRD
But by the t. year of King Jehoash 2Ki 12.06
In the t. year of Joash the son of 13.01
the t. to Delaiah, the twenty-fourth 1Ch 24.18
to the t., to Mahazioth, his sons 25.30
On the t. day of the seventh month 2Ch 7.10
the month of Sivan, on the t. day; Est 8.09
in the t. year of Nebuchadrezzar, Jer 52.30

TWENTY-THREE
numbered of them were t. thousand, Num 26.62
a hundred and t. years old when he 33.39
And he judged Israel t. years. Ju 10.02
Jehoahaz was t. years old when he 2Ki 23.31
who had t. cities in the land of 1Ch 2.22
Jehoahaz was t. years old when he 2Ch 36.02
The sons of Bebai, six hundred and t. Ez 2.11
of Bezai, three hundred and t. 2.17
sons of Hashum, two hundred and t. 2.19
of Bethlehem, one hundred and t. 2.21
Bethel and Ai, two hundred and t. 2.28
of Bethel and Ai, a hundred and t. Neh 7.32
"For t. years, from the thirteenth Jer 25.03
year, three thousand and t. Jews; 52.28
and t. thousand fell in a single 1Co 10.08

TWENTY-TWO
old and upward, were t. thousand. Num 3.39
numbered were t. thousand two 3.43
the Simeonites, t. thousand two hundred. 26.14
t. cities with their villages. Jos 19.30
t. thousand returned, and ten Ju 7.03
Gileadite, who judged Israel t. years. 10.03
on that day t. thousand men of the 20.21
David slew t. thousand men of the 2Sa 8.05
to the LORD t. thousand oxen and a 1Ki 8.63
that Jeroboam reigned was t. years; 14.20
over Israel in Samaria t. years. 16.29
Ahaziah was t. years old when he 2Ki 8.26
Amon was t. years old when he began 21.19
of David being t. thousand six 1Ch 7.02
genealogies was t. thousand and 7.07
and t. commanders from his own 12.28
David slew t. thousand men of the 18.05
as a sacrifice t. thousand oxen 2Ch 7.05
and had t. sons and sixteen daughters. 13.21
Amon was t. years old when he began 33.21
one thousand two hundred and t. Ez 2.12
men of Michmas, one hundred and t. 2.27
two thousand three hundred and t. Neh 7.17
The men of Michmas, a hundred and t. 7.31
of the house, eight hundred and t.; 11.12

TWICE
we would now have returned t." Gen 43.10
it will be t. as much as they Ex 16.05
day they gathered t. as much bread, 16.22
struck the rock with his rod t.; Num 20.11
to the wall." But David evaded him t. 1Sa 18.11
and I will not strike him t." 26.08
who had appeared to him t., 1Ki 11.09
himself there more than once or t. 2Ki 6.10
outside Jerusalem once or t. Neh 13.20
t., three times, with a man, Job 33.29
t., but I will proceed no further. 40.05
LORD gave Job t. as much as he had 42.10
t. have I heard this: that power Ps 62.11
t. ten thousand, thousands upon 68.17
live a thousand years t. told, Ecc 6.06
and let the sword come down t., Eze 21.14
not take vengeance t. on his foes. Nah 1.09
you make him t. as much a child of Mt 23.15
night, before the cock crows t., Mk 14.30
to him, "Before the cock crows t., 14.72
I fast t. a week, I give tithes of Lk 18.12
after admonishing him once or t., Tit 3.10
in late autumn, t. dead, uprooted; Jud 1.12
of cavalry was t. ten thousand Rev 9.16

TWIG
He set it like a willow t., Eze 17.05

TWIGS
of its young t. and carried it to Eze 17.04
of its young t. a tender one, 17.22

TWILIGHT
'At t. you shall eat flesh, and in Ex 16.12
smote them from t. until the 1Sa 30.17
So they arose at t. to go to the 2Ki 7.05
away in the t. and forsook their 7.07
adulterer also waits for the t., Job 24.15
in the t., in the evening, at the Pro 7.09
the t. I longed for has been turned Is 21.04
we stumble at noon as in the t., 59.10
feet stumble on the t. mountains, Jer 13.16

TWIN
called the T., said to his fellow Jn 11.16
called the T., was not with them 20.24
Simon, Peter, Thomas called the T., 21.02
with the T. Brothers as figurehead. Ac 28.11

TWINE
His roots t. about the stone-heap; Job 8.17

TWINED
scarlet stuff and fine t. linen, Ex 25.04
curtains of fine t. linen and blue 26.01
scarlet stuff and fine t. linen; 26.31
scarlet stuff and fine t. linen, 26.36
hangings of fine t. linen a hundred 27.09
scarlet stuff and fine t. linen, 27.16
hangings of fine t. linen and bases 27.18
scarlet stuff, and fine t. linen. 28.05
and of fine t. linen, skilfully 28.06
scarlet stuff and fine t. linen. 28.08
and fine t. linen shall you make it. 28.15
scarlet stuff and fine t. linen; 35.06
scarlet stuff and fine t. linen; 35.25
scarlet stuff and fine t. linen, 35.35
made of fine t. linen and blue and 36.08
scarlet stuff and fine t. linen; 36.35
scarlet stuff and fine t. linen, 36.37
of the court were of fine t. linen, 38.09
the court were of fine t. linen. 38.16
scarlet stuff and fine t. linen; 38.18
scarlet stuff and fine t. linen. 38.23
scarlet stuff, and fine t. linen. 39.02
stuff, and into the fine t. linen, 39.03
scarlet stuff, and fine t. linen; 39.05
scarlet stuff, fine t. linen. 39.08
scarlet stuff and fine t. linen. 39.24
linen breeches of fine t. linen, 39.28
girdle of fine t. linen and of 39.29

TWINKLING
in the t. of an eye, at the last 1Co 15.52

TWINS
behold, there were t. in her womb. Gen 25.24
came, there were t. in her womb. 38.27
the washing, all of which bear t., Sol 4.02
t. of a gazelle, that feed among the 4.05
the washing, all of them bear t., 6.06
like two fawns, t. of a gazelle. 7.03

TWIST
and he will t. its surface and Is 24.01
and unstable t. to their own 2Pe 3.16

TWISTED
chains of pure gold, t. like cords; Ex 28.14
the breastpiece t. chains like 28.22
the breastpiece t. chains like 39.15
they t. like a deceitful bow. Ps 78.57
is nothing t. or crooked in them. Pro 8.08

TWISTING
Leviathan the t. serpent, and he Is 27.01

TWO
And God made the t. great lights, Gen 1.16
And Lamech took t. wives; 4.19
you shall bring t. of every sort 6.19
t. of every sort shall come in to 6.20
t. and t., male and female, went 7.09
t. and t. of all flesh in which 7.15
and told his t. brothers outside. 9.22
to Eber were born t. sons: the 10.25
of Arpachshad t. years after the 11.10
birth of Reu t. hundred and nine 11.19
birth of Serug t. hundred and 11.21
birth of Nahor t. hundred years, 11.23
of Terah were t. hundred and five 11.32
cut them in t., and laid each half 15.10
but he did not cut the birds in t. 15.10
The t. angels came to Sodom in the 19.01
Behold, I have t. daughters who have 19.08
wife and your t. daughters who are 19.15
wife and his t. daughters by the 19.16
in the hills with his t. daughters, 19.30
in a cave with his t. daughters. 19.30
and the t. men made a covenant. 21.27
and took t. of his young men with 22.03
and t. bracelets for her arms 24.22
"T. nations are in your womb, and 25.23
and t. peoples, born of you, shall be 25.23
and fetch me t. good kids, that I 27.09
has supplanted me these t. times. 27.36
Now Laban had t. daughters; the 29.16
the tent of the t. maidservants, 31.33
that they may decide between us t. 31.37
years for your t. daughters, 31.41
and camels, into t. companies, 32.07
and now I have become t. companies. 32.10
t. hundred she-goats and twenty 32.14
t. hundred ewes and twenty rams, 32.14
he arose and took his t. wives, 32.22
his t. maids, and his eleven children, 32.22
Leah and Rachel and the t. maids. 33.01
t. of the sons of Jacob, Simeon and 34.25
was angry with his t. officers, 40.02
After t. whole years, Pharaoh 41.01
Joseph had t. sons, whom Asenath, the 41.50
"Slay my t. sons if I do not bring 42.37
know that my wife bore me t. sons; 44.27
been in the land these t. years; 45.06
were born to him in Egypt, were t.; 46.27
so he took with him his t. sons, 48.01
And now your t. sons, who were born 48.05
t. Hebrews were struggling together; Ex 2.13
even these t. signs or heed your 4.09
put it on the t. doorposts and the 12.07
lintel and the t. doorposts with 12.22
the lintel and on the t. doorpost, 12.23
as much bread, t. omers apiece; 16.22
day he gives you bread for t. days; 16.29
and her t. sons, of whom the name of 18.03
your wife and her t. sons with her, 18.06
But if the slave survives a day or t., 21.21
t. cubits and a half shall be its 25.10
t. rings on the one side of it, and 25.12
and t. rings on the other side of 25.12
t. cubits and a half shall be its 25.17
And you shall make t. cherubim of 25.18
on the t. ends of the mercy seat. 25.18
make the cherubim on its t. ends. 25.19
between the t. cherubim that are 25.22
t. cubits shall be its length, a 25.23
There shall be t. tenons in each 26.17
t. bases under one frame for its 26.19
another frame for its t. tenons; 26.19
and t. bases under another frame 26.19
another frame for its t. tenons; 26.19
t. bases under one frame, and two 26.21
and t. bases under another frame; 26.21
And you shall make t. frames for 26.23
they shall form the t. corners. 26.24
t. bases under one frame, and two 26.25
and t. bases under another frame. 26.25
be upon the t. sides of the altar, 27.07
It shall have t. shoulder-pieces 28.07
attached to its t. edges, that it 28.07
And you shall take t. onyx stones, 28.09
you engrave the t. stones with the 28.11
shall set the t. stones upon the 28.12
LORD upon his t. shoulders for 28.12
and t. chains of pure gold, twisted 28.14
the breastpiece t. rings of gold, 28.23
and put the t. rings on the two 28.23
rings on the t. edges of the 28.23
shall put the t. cords of gold in 28.24
of gold in the t. rings at the 28.24
the t. ends of the t. cords you 28.25
attach to the t. settings of 28.25
And you shall make t. rings of gold, 28.26
put them at the t. ends of the 28.26
And you shall make t. rings of gold, 28.27
part of the t. shoulder-pieces of 28.27
young bull and t. rams without 29.01
and bring the bull and the t. rams. 29.03

TWO (cont.)

and the t. kidneys with the fat Ex 29.13
and the t. kidneys with the fat 29.22
t. lambs a year old day by day 29.38
and t. cubits shall be its height; 30.02
And t. golden rings shall you make 30.04
its molding on t. opposite sides 30.04
as much, that is, t. hundred and fifty, 30.23
aromatic cane t. hundred and fifty, 30.23
the t. tables of the testimony, 31.18
with the t. tables of the testimony 32.15
"Cut t. tables of stone like the 34.01
So Moses cut t. tables of stone 34.04
in his hand t. tables of stone. 34.04
with the t. tables of the testimony 34.29
Each frame had t. tenons, for 36.22
t. bases under one frame for its t. tenons, 36.24
and t. bases under another frame 36.24
another frame for its t. tenons. 36.24
t. bases under one frame and t. bases under 36.26
And he made t. frames for corners 36.28
he made t. of them thus, for the t. corners. 36.29
bases, under every frame t. bases. 36.30
t. cubits and a half was its length, 37.01
t. rings on its one side and t. rings on 37.03
t. cubits and a half was its length, 37.06
And he made t. cherubim of hammered 37.07
on the t. ends of the mercy seat he 37.07
made the cherubim on its t. ends. 37.08
t. cubits was its length, a cubit 37.10
and t. cubits was its height; 37.25
and made t. rings of gold on it 37.27
on t. opposite sides of it, as 37.27
and t. thousand and four hundred 38.29
joined to it at its t. edges. 39.04
and they made t. settings of gold 39.16
of gold filigree and t. gold rings, 39.16
and put the t. rings on the t. edges of the 39.16
and they put the t. cords of gold 39.17
of gold in the t. rings at the 39.17
T. ends of the t. cords they had 39.18
attached to the t. settings of 39.18
Then they made t. rings of gold, and 39.19
put them at the t. ends of the 39.19
And they made t. rings of gold, and 39.20
part of the t. shoulder-pieces of 39.20
and the t. kidneys with the fat Lev 3.04
and the t. kidneys with the fat 3.10
and the t. kidneys with the fat 3.15
and the t. kidneys with the far 4.09
t. turtledoves or t. young pigeons, 5.07
cannot afford t. turtledoves or t. young 5.11
the t. kidneys with the fat that is 7.04
and the t. rams, and the basket of 8.02
and the t. kidneys with their fat, 8.16
and the t. kidneys with their fat, 8.25
then she shall be unclean t. weeks, 12.05
she shall take t. turtledoves or t. young pigeons, 12.08
to be cleansed t. living clean 14.04
he shall take t. male lambs 14.10
also t. turtledoves or t. young 14.22
house he shall take t. small birds, 14.19
he shall take t. turtledoves or t. young 15.14
she shall take t. turtledoves or t. young 15.29
the death of the t. sons of Aaron, 16.01
of Israel t. male goats for a sin 16.05
Then he shall take the t. goats, 16.07
shall cast lots upon the t. goats, 16.08
and t. handfuls of sweet incense 16.12
your field with t. kinds of seed; 19.19
of cloth made of t. kinds of stuff. 19.19
it shall be t. tenths of an ephah 23.13
your dwellings t. loaves of bread 23.17
made of t. tenths of an ephah; 23.17
and one young bull, and t. rams; 23.18
and t. male lambs a year old as a 23.19
before the LORD, with the t. lambs; 23.20
t. tenths of an ephah shall be in 24.05
And you shall set them in t. rows, 24.06
was thirty-two thousand t. hundred. Num 1.35
being thirty-two thousand t. hundred. 2.21
upward was six thousand t. hundred. 3.34
thousand t. hundred and seventy-three 3.43
redemption of the t. hundred and 3.46
by families was t. thousand seven 4.36
houses was t. thousand six hundred 4.40
was three thousand t. hundred. 4.44
he shall bring t. turtledoves or t. young 6.10
wagon for every t. of the leaders, 7.03
T. wagons and four oxen he gave to 7.07
t. oxen, five rams, five male goats, 7.17
t. oxen, five rams, five male goats, 7.23
t. oxen, five rams, five male goats, 7.29
t. oxen, five rams, five male goats, 7.35
t. oxen, five rams, five male goats, 7.41
t. oxen, five rams, five male goats, 7.47
t. oxen, five rams, five male goats, 7.53
t. oxen, five rams, five male goats, 7.59
t. oxen, five rams, five male goats, 7.65
t. oxen, five rams, five male goats, 7.71
t. oxen, five rams, five male goats, 7.77
t. oxen, five rams, five male goats, 7.83
of the vessels t. thousand four 7.85
from between the t. cherubim; 7.89
Whether it was t. days, or a month, 9.22
"Make t. silver trumpets; of hammered 10.02
or t. days, or five days, or ten days, 11.19
Now t. men remained in the camp, one 11.26
and about t. cubits deep on the 11.31
it on a pole between t. of them; 13.23
cereal offering t. tenths of an 15.06
t. hundred and fifty leaders of the 16.02
t. hundred and fifty censers; 16.17
consumed the t. hundred and fifty 16.35
and his t. servants were with him. 22.22
fire devoured t. hundred and fifty 26.10
twenty-two thousand t. hundred. 26.14
t. male lambs a year old without 28.03
"On the sabbath day t. male lambs a 28.09
and t. tenths of an ephah of fine 28.09
t. young bulls, one ram, seven male 28.11
and t. tenths of fine flour for a 28.12
t. young bulls, one ram, and seven 28.19
for a bull, and t. tenths for a ram; 28.20
t. young bulls, one ram, seven male 28.27
for each bull, t. tenths for one ram, 28.28
for the bull, t. tenths for the ram, 29.03
for the bull, t. tenths for the one ram, 29.09
t. rams, fourteen male lambs a year 29.13
t. tenths for each of the two rams, 29.14
tenths for each of the t. rams, 29.14
t. rams, fourteen male lambs a year 29.17
t. rams, fourteen male lambs a year 29.20
t. rams, fourteen male lambs a year 29.23
t. rams, fourteen male lambs a year 29.26
t. rams, fourteen male lambs a year 29.29
t. rams, fourteen male lambs a year 29.32
and divide the booty into t. parts, 31.27
the t. tribes and the half-tribe 34.15
the east side t. thousand cubits, 35.05
the south side t. thousand cubits, 35.05
the west side t. thousand cubits, 35.05
the north side t. thousand cubits, 35.05
the hand of the t. kings of the Deu 3.08
God has done to these t. kings; 3.21
wrote them upon t. tables of stone 4.13
the t. kings of the Amorites, who 4.47
wrote them upon t. tables of stone, 5.22
gave me the t. tables of stone 9.10
gave me the t. tables of stone, the 9.11
and the t. tables of the covenant 9.15
the covenant were in my t. hands. 9.15
So I took hold of the t. tables, 9.17
and cast them out of my t. hands, 9.17
'Hew t. tables of stone like the 10.01

TWO (cont.)

and hewed t. tables of stone like Deu 10.03
with the t. tables in my hand. 10.03
hoof and has the hoof cloven in t., 14.06
On the evidence of t. witnesses or 17.06
shoulder and the t. cheeks and the 18.03
on the evidence of t. witnesses, 19.15
"If a man has t. wives, the one 21.15
vineyard with t. kinds of seed, 22.09
in your bag t. kinds of weights, a 25.13
in your house t. kinds of measures, 25.14
and t. put ten thousand to flight, 32.30
son of Nun sent t. men secretly Jos 2.01
had taken the t. men and hidden 2.04
you did to the t. kings of the 2.10
Then the t. men came down again 2.23
of about t. thousand cubits; 3.04
said to the t. men who had spied 6.22
but let about t. or three thousand 7.03
and t. hundred shekels of silver, 7.21
he did to the t. kings of the 9.10
inheritance to the t. and one-half 14.03
people of Joseph were t. tribes, 14.04
t. cities with their village 15.60
nine cities out of these t. tribes; 21.16
with its pasture lands—t. cities. 21.25
with its pasture lands—t. cities; 21.27
the t. kings of the Amorites; 24.12
for himself a sword with t. edges, Ju 3.16
A maiden or t. for every man; 5.30
t. pieces of dyed work embroidered 5.30
And they took the t. princes of 7.25
and took the t. kings of Midian, 8.12
while the t. companies rushed upon 9.44
let me alone t. months, that I may 11.37
And he sent her away for t. months; 11.38
And at the end of t. months, 11.39
they bound him with t. new ropes, 15.13
gate of the city and the t. posts, 16.03
Philistines for one of my t. eyes. 16.28
grasped the t. middle pillars upon 16.29
his mother took t. hundred pieces 17.04
So the t. men sat and ate and drank 19.06
and t. thousand men of them were 20.45
he and his wife and his t. sons. Ru 1.01
names of his t. sons were Mahlon 1.02
and she was left with her t. sons. 1.03
bereft of her t. sons and her 1.05
with her t. daughters-in-law, and 1.07
said to her t. daughters-in-law, 1.08
So the t. of them went on until 1.19
He had t. wives; the name of the one 1Sa 1.02
where the t. sons of Eli, Hophni and 1.03
bore three sons and t. daughters. 2.21
which shall befall your t. sons, 2.34
at which the t. ears of every one 3.11
and the t. sons of Eli, Hophni and 4.04
and the t. sons of Eli, Hophni and 4.11
your t. sons also, Hophni and 4.17
a new cart and t. milch cows upon 6.07
and took t. milch cows and yoked 6.10
you will meet t. men by Rachel's 10.02
and give you t. loaves of bread, 10.04
so that no t. of them were left 11.11
he reigned . . . and t. years over Israel. 13.01
t. thousand were with Saul in 13.02
names of his t. daughters were 14.49
t. hundred thousand men on foot, and 15.04
and killed t. hundred of the 18.27
And the t. of them made a covenant 23.18
while t. hundred remained with the 25.13
and took t. hundred loaves, and two 25.18
and t. skins of wine, and five sheep 25.18
and t. hundred cakes of figs, and 25.18
and David with his t. wives, 27.03
and went, he and t. men with him; 28.08
David's t. wives also had been taken 30.05
t. hundred stayed behind, who were 30.10
of figs and t. clusters of raisins 30.12
and David rescued his t. wives. 30.18
Then David came to the t. hundred men, 30.21
David remained t. days in Ziklag; 2Sa 1.01
and his t. wives also, Ahinoam of 2.02
Israel, and he reigned t. years. 2.10
Now Saul's son had t. men who were 4.02
t. lines he measured to be put to 8.02
"There were t. men in a certain 12.01
After t. full years Absalom had 13.23
And your handmaid had t. sons, 14.06
t. hundred shekels by the king's 14.26
So Absalom dwelt t. full years in 14.28
With Absalom went t. hundred men 15.11
with your t. sons, Ahimaaz your son, 15.27
Behold, their t. sons are with them 15.36
bearing t. hundred loaves of bread, 16.01
was sitting between the t. gates; 18.24
The king took the t. sons of Rizpah 21.08
great deeds; he smote t. ariels of Moab. 23.20
dealt with the t. commanders of 1Ki 2.05
with the sword t. men more righteous 2.32
years that t. of Shimei's slaves 2.39
Then t. harlots came to the king, 3.16
only we t. were in the house. 3.18
"Divide the living child in t., 3.25
and the t. of them made a treaty. 5.12
in Lebanon and t. months at home; 5.14
sanctuary he made t. cherubim of 6.23
He covered the t. doors of olivewood 6.32
and t. doors of cypress wood; 6.34
the t. leaves of the one door were 6.34
and the t. leave of the other door 6.34
He cast t. pillars of bronze. 7.15
He also made t. capitals of molten 7.16
Then he made t. nets of checker 7.17
in t. rows round about upon the one 7.18
were upon the t. pillars and also 7.20
there were t. hundred pomegranates, 7.20
in t. rows round about; 7.20
the gourds were in t. rows, 7.24
it held t. thousand baths. 7.26
the t. pillars, the t. bowls of the capitals 7.41
and the t. networks to cover the t. bowls 7.41
pomegranates for the t. networks, 7.42
t. rows of pomegranates for each 7.42
to cover the t. bowls of the 7.42
ark except the t. tables of stone 8.09
Solomon had built the t. houses, 9.10
King Solomon had t. hundred large 10.16
arm rests and t. lions standing 10.19
and the t. of them were alone in 11.29
counsel, and made t. calves of gold. 12.28
he reigned over Israel t. years. 15.25
in Tirzah, and reigned t. years. 16.08
Israel were divided into t. parts; 16.21
from Shemer for t. talents of 16.24
go limping with t. different 18.21
Let t. bulls be given to us; 18.23
would contain t. measures of seed. 18.32
and they were t. hundred and 20.15
them like t. little flocks of 20.27
and set t. base fellows opposite 21.10
And the t. base fellows came in and 21.13
and he reigned t. years over 22.51
consumed the t. former captains of 2Ki 1.14
"So the t. of them went on. 2.06
till the t. of them could go over 2.08
of fire separated the t. of them. 2.11
clothes and rent them in t. pieces. 2.12
And t. she-bears came out of the 2.24
come to take my t. children to be 4.01
shut the door upon the t. of them, 4.33
to your servant t. mules' burden 5.17
of Ephraim t. young men of the 5.22
of silver and t. festal garments. 5.22
"Be pleased to accept t. talents." 5.23

TWO (cont.)

and tied up t. talents of silver in t. bags, 2Ki 5.23
with t. festal garments, and laid 5.23
laid them upon t. of his servants; 5.23
and t. measures of barley for a 7.01
So they took t. mounted men, and the 7.14
and t. measures of barley for a 7.16
"T. measures of barley shall be 7.18
"T. or three eunuchs looked out at 9.32
the t. kings could not stand before 10.04
"Lay them in t. heaps at the 10.08
and the t. divisions of you, which 11.07
Samaria, and he reigned t. years. 15.23
themselves molten images of t. calves; 17.16
I will give you t. thousand horses, 18.23
heaven in the t. courts of the 21.05
and he reigned t. years in Jerusalem 21.19
had made in the t. courts of the 23.12
of the gate between the t. walls, 25.04
As for the t. pillars, the one sea, 25.16
To Eber were born t. sons: 1Ch 1.19
had t. wives, Helah and Naarah; 4.05
t. hundred and fifty thousand sheep, 5.21
t. thousand asses, and a hundred 5.21
was twenty thousand t. hundred. 7.09
seventeen thousand and t. hundred, 7.11
were t. hundred and twelve. 9.22
great deeds; he smote t. ariels of Moab. 11.22
t. hundred chiefs, and all their 12.32
with t. hundred and twenty of his 15.06
with t. hundred of his brethren; 15.08
was t. hundred and eighty-eight. 25.07
as well as t. and t. at the 26.17
at the road and t. at the parbar. 26.18
t. thousand seven hundred men of 26.32
place he made t. cherubim of wood 2Ch 3.10
house he made t. pillars thirty-five 3.15
the gourds were in t. rows, cast with it 4.03
the t. pillars, the bowls, and the 4.12
and the t. capitals on the top of 4.12
and the t. networks to cover the t. bowls 4.12
pomegranates for the t. networks, 4.13
t. rows of pomegranates for each 4.13
to cover the t. bowls of the 4.13
ark except the t. tables which 5.10
t. hundred and fifty, who exercised 8.10
King Solomon made t. hundred large 9.15
arm rests and t. lions standing 9.18
and t. hundred and eighty thousand 14.08
with t. hundred and eighty thousand, 17.15
with t. hundred thousand mighty men 17.16
with t. hundred thousand men armed 17.17
at the end of t. years, his bowels 21.19
Jehoiada got for him t. wives, 24.03
of valor was t. thousand six 26.12
took captive t. hundred thousand 28.08
hundred rams, and t. hundred lambs; 29.32
heaven in the t. courts of the 33.05
and he reigned t. years in Jerusalem. 33.21
offering t. thousand six hundred 35.08
t. thousand four hundred and ten Ez 1.10
t. thousand one hundred and seventy-two. 2.03
t. thousand eight hundred and 2.06
one thousand t. hundred and fifty-four. 2.07
one thousand t. hundred and twenty-two. 2.12
of Bigvai, t. thousand and fifty-six. 2.14
of Hashum t. hundred and twenty-three. 2.19
Bethel and Ai, t. hundred and twenty-three 2.28
one thousand t. hundred and fifty-four. 2.31
one thousand t. hundred and forty-seven. 2.38
and they had t. hundred male and 2.65
mules were t. hundred and forty-five, 2.66
t. hundred rams, four hundred lambs, 6.17
and with him t. hundred men. 8.04
and with him t. hundred and eighteen 8.09
besides t. hundred and twenty of 8.20
and t. vessels of fine bright 8.27
this a work for one day or for t.; 10.13
t. thousand a hundred and seventy-two. Neh 7.08
t. thousand eight hundred and eighteen. 7.11
a thousand t. hundred and fifty-four. 7.12
t. thousand three hundred and twenty-two. 7.17
of Bigvai, t. thousand and sixty-seven. 7.19
a thousand t. hundred and fifty-four. 7.34
a thousand t. hundred and forty-seven. 7.41
and they had t. hundred and forty-five 7.67
their mules t. hundred and forty-five, 7.68
of gold and t. thousand t. hundred minas 7.71
t. thousand minas of silver, and 7.72
fathers' houses, t. hundred and forty-two; 11.13
holy city were t. hundred and 11.18
and appointed t. great companies 12.31
t. of the king's eunuchs, who guarded Est 2.21
t. of the king's eunuchs, who guarded 6.02
keep these t. days according to 9.27
Only grant t. things to me, then I Job 13.20
and in t., though man does not 33.14
you and against your t. friends; 42.07
and cuts in t. the bars of iron. Ps 107.16
T. things I ask of thee; deny them Pro 30.07
The leech has t. daughters; "Give, 30.15
quietness than t. hands full of Ecc 4.06
T. are better than one, because they 4.09
Again, if t. lie together, they are 4.11
t. will withstand him. A threefold 4.12
Your t. breasts are like t. fawns, Sol 4.05
as upon a dance before t. armies? 6.13
Your t. breasts are like t. fawns, 7.03
keepers of the fruit t. hundred. 8.12
with t. he covered his face, and Is 6.02
and with t. he covered his feet, and 6.02
his feet, and with t. he flew. 6.02
of these t. smoldering stumps of 7.04
before whose t. kings you are in 7.16
alive a young cow and t. sheep; 7.21
t. or three berries in the top of 17.06
between the t. walls for the water 22.11
I will give you t. thousand horses, 36.08
These t. things shall come to you 47.09
These t. things have befallen you— 51.19
for my people have committed t. evils: Jer 2.13
from a city and t. from family, 3.14
t. baskets of figs placed before 24.01
Within t. years I will bring back 28.03
of all the nations within t. years. 28.11
rejected the t. families which he 33.24
they cut in t. and passed between 34.18
the gate between the t. walls; 39.04
way of a gate between the t. walls, 52.07
As for the t. pillars, the one sea, 52.20
each creature had t. wings, Eze 1.11
while t. covered their bodies. 1.11
creature had t. wings covering its 1.23
mark t. ways for the sword of the 21.19
way, at the head of the t. ways, 21.21
there were t. women, the daughters 23.02
'These t. nations and these t. countries 35.10
they shall be no longer t. nations, 37.22
no longer divided into t. kingdoms. 37.22
and its jambs, t. cubits; and the 40.09
the gate were t. tables on either 40.39
of the north gate were t. tables; 40.40
vestibule of the gate were t. tables. 40.40
there were t. chambers in the inner 40.44
jambs of the entrance, t. cubits; 41.03
cherub and cherub. Every cherub had t. faces: 41.18
t. cubits long, and t. cubits broad; 41.22
The doors had t. leaves apiece, t. swinging 41.24
t. cubits, with a breadth of one 43.14
from every flock of t. hundred, 45.15
Joseph shall have t. portions. 47.13
on the north t. hundred and fifty 48.17
on the south t. hundred and fifty, 48.17
on the east t. hundred and fifty, 48.17
and on the west t. hundred and 48.17

TWO (cont.)
to stand upon t. feet like a man; Dan 7.04
for a time, t. times, and half a time. 7.25
It had t. horns; and both horns 8.03
He came to the ram with the t. horns, 8.06
the ram and broke his t. horns; 8.07
"For t. thousand and three hundred 8.14
which you saw with the t. horns, 8.20
And as for the t. kings, their minds 11.27
t. others stood, one on this bank of 12.05
for a time, t. times, and half a time; 12.07
be a thousand t. hundred and 12.11
After t. days he will revive us; Hos 6.02
t. years before the earthquake. Amo 1.01
"Do t. walk together, unless they 3.03
from the mouth of the lion t. legs, 3.12
so t. or three cities wandered to 4.08
And there are t. olive trees by it, Zec 4.03
"What are these t. olive trees on 4.11
"What are these t. branches of the 4.12
are beside the t. golden pipes 4.12
"These are the t. anointed who 4.14
t. women coming forward! The wind was 5.09
came out from between t. mountains; 6.01
And I took t. staffs; one I named 11.07
t. thirds shall be cut off and 13.08
be split in t. from east to west 14.04
region who were t. years old or Mt 2.16
he saw t. brothers, Simon who is 4.18
there he saw t. other brothers, 4.21
go one mile, go with him t. miles. 5.41
"No one can serve t. masters; 6.24
t. demoniacs met him, coming out of 8.28
t. blind men followed him, crying 9.27
nor t. tunics, nor sandals, nor a 10.10
Are not t. sparrows sold for a 10.29
only five loaves here and t. fish." 14.17
loaves and the t. fish he looked 14.19
lame than with t. hands or t. feet 18.08
eye than with t. eyes to be thrown 18.09
take one or t. others along with 18.16
the evidence of t. or three 18.16
if t. of you agree on earth about 18.19
For where t. or three are gathered 18.20
and the t. shall become one'? 19.05
So they are no longer t. but one. 19.06
that these t. sons of mine may sit, 20.21
were indignant at the t. brothers. 20.24
And behold, t. blind men sitting by 20.30
then Jesus sent t. disciples, 21.01
A man had t. sons; and he went 21.28
Which of the t. did the will of his 21.31
On these t. commandments depend all 22.40
Then t. men will be in the field; 24.40
T. women will be grinding at the 24.41
to another t., to another one, to 25.15
he who had the t. talents made t. talents more. 25.17
who had the t. talents came 25.22
you delivered to me t. talents; 25.22
here I have made t. talents more.' 25.22
"You know that after t. days the 26.02
Peter and the t. sons of Zebedee, 26.37
came forward. At last t. came forward 26.60
"Which of the t. do you want me to 27.21
Then t. robbers were crucified with 27.38
of the temple was torn in t., 27.51
herd, numbering about t. thousand, Mk 5.13
began to send them out t. by t., 6.07
sandals and not put on t. tunics. 6.09
we go and buy t. hundred denarii 6.37
out, they said, "Five, and t. fish." 6.38
loaves and the t. fish he looked 6.41
he divided the t. fish among them 6.41
than with t. hands to go to hell, 9.43
lame than with t. feet to be 9.45
eye than with t. eyes to be thrown 9.47
and the t. shall become one.' 10.08
so they are no longer t. but one. 10.08
he sent t. of his disciples, 11.01
and put in t. copper coins, which 12.42
It was now t. days before the 14.01
And he sent t. of his disciples, and 14.13
with him they crucified t. robbers, 15.27
of the temple was torn in t., 15.38
appeared in another form to t. of them, * 16.12
turtledoves, or t. young pigeons. Lk 2.24
"He who has t. coats, let him share 3.11
And he saw t. boats by the lake; 5.02
calling to him t. of his disciples, 7.19
"A certain creditor had t. debtors; 7.41
nor money: and do not have t. tunics. 9.03
more than five loaves and t. fish— 9.13
loaves and the t. fish he looked 9.16
And behold, t. men talked with him, 9.30
glory and the t. men who stood 9.32
t. by t., into every town and place 10.01
day he took out t. denarii and 10.35
five sparrows sold for t. pennies? 12.06
three against t. and t. against 12.52
"There was a man who had t. sons; 15.11
No servant can serve t. masters; 16.13
there will be t. men in one bed; 17.34
There will be t. women grinding 17.35
"T. men will be in the field; * 17.36
"T. men went up into the temple to 18.10
he sent t. of the disciples, 19.29
poor widow put in t. copper coins. 21.02
"Look, Lord, here are t. swords. 22.38
T. others also, who were criminals, 23.32
of the temple was torn in t. 23.45
t. men stood by them in dazzling 24.04
That very day t. of them were going 24.13
standing with t. of his disciples; Jn 1.35
The t. disciples heard him say this, 1.37
One of the t. who heard John speak, 1.40
and he stayed there t. days. 4.40
After the t. days he departed to 4.43
"T. hundred denarii would not buy 6.07
has five barley loaves and t. fish; 6.09
the testimony of t. men is true; 8.17
he stayed t. days longer in the 11.06
Jerusalem, about t. miles off, 11.18
and with him t. others, one on 19.18
and she saw t. angels in white, 20.12
and t. others of his disciples were 21.02
t. men stood by them in white robes, Ac 1.10
And they put forward t., Joseph called 1.23
one of these t. thou hast chosen 1.24
he became the father of t. sons. 7.29
sent t. men to him entreating him, 9.38
he called t. of his servants and a 10.07
was sleeping between t. soldiers, 12.06
bound with t. chains, and sentries 12.06
This continued for t. years, 19.10
into Macedonia t. of his helpers, 19.22
for about t. hours they all with 19.34
him to be bound with t. chains. 21.33
Then he called t. of the centurions 23.23
night get ready t. hundred soldiers 23.23
horsemen and t. hundred spearmen 23.23
But when t. years had elapsed, Felix 24.27
(We were in all t. hundred and 27.37
And he lived there t. whole years 28.30
"The t. shall become one. 1Co 6.16
there be only t. or at most three, 14.27
Let t. or three prophets speak, and 14.29
the evidence of t. or three 2Co 13.01
written that Abraham had t. sons, Gal 4.22
these women are t. covenants. 4.24
one new man in place of the t., Eph 2.15
and the t. shall become one. 5.31
I am hard pressed between the t. Php 1.23
the evidence of t. or three 1Ti 5.19
all, as was that of those t. men. 2Ti 3.09
so that through t. unchangeable Heb 6.18

TWO (cont.)

testimony of t. or three witnesses Heb 10.28
They were stoned, they were sawn in t., 11.37
behold, t. woes are still to come. Rev 9.12
And I will grant my t. witnesses 11.03
one thousand t. hundred and sixty 11.03
These are the t. olive trees and 11.04
trees and the t. lampstands which 11.04
because these t. prophets had been 11.10
one thousand t. hundred and sixty 12.06
was given the t. wings of the 12.14
it had t. horns like a lamb and it 13.11
These t. were thrown alive into the 19.20

TWO-EDGED

throats and t. swords in their Ps 149.06
as wormwood, sharp as a t. sword. Pro 5.04
active, sharper than any t. sword, Heb 4.12
his mouth issued a sharp t. sword, Rev 1.16
of him who has the sharp t. sword. 2.12

TYCHICUS

and the Asians, T. and Trophimus. Ac 20.04
T. the beloved brother and faithful Eph 6.21
T. will tell you all about my Col 4.07
T. I have sent to Ephesus. 2Ti 4.12
When I send Artemas or T. to you, Tit 3.12

TYPE

who was a t. of the one who was to Rom 5.14

TYRANNUS

and argued daily in the hall of T. Ac 19.09

TYRANT

or the captives of a t. be rescued? Is 49.24
and the prey of the t. be rescued, 49.25

TYRE

to the fortified city of T.; Jos 19.29
And Hiram king of T. sent messengers 2Sa 5.11
the fortress of T. and to all the 24.07
Now Hiram king of T. sent his 1Ki 5.01
sent and brought Hiram from T. 7.13
and his father was a man of T., 7.14
and Hiram king of T. had supplied 9.11
Hiram came from T. to see the 9.12
And Hiram king of T. send messengers 1Ch 14.01
sent word to Huram the king of T.: 2Ch 2.03
the king of T. answered in a 2.11
and his father was a man of T. 2.14
Men of T. also, who lived in the Neh 13.16
the people of T. will sue your Ps 45.12
Philistia with the inhabitants of T.; 83.07
Philistia and T., with Ethiopia— 87.04
The oracle concerning T. Wail, O ships Is 23.01
for T. is laid waste, without house 23.01
anguish over the report about T. 23.05
Who has purposed this against T., 23.08
They destined T. for wild beasts. 23.13
In that day T. will be forgotten 23.15
will happen to T. as in the song 23.15
years, the LORD will visit T., 23.17
all the kings of T., all the kings Jer 25.22
the king of T., and the king of 27.03
to cut off from T. and Sidon every 47.04
because T. said concerning Jerusalem, Eze 26.02
O T., and will bring up many nations 26.03
They shall destroy the walls of T., 26.04
will bring upon T. from the north 26.07
"Thus says the Lord GOD to T.: 26.15
man, raise a lamentation over T., 27.02
and say to T., who dwells at the 27.03
"O T., you have said, 'I am perfect 27.03
destroyed like T. in the midst of 27.32
"Son of man, say to the prince of T., 28.02
a lamentation over the king of T., 28.12
his army labor hard against T.; 29.18
anything from T. to pay for the 29.18
O T. and Sidon, and all the regions Joe 3.04
"For three transgressions of T., Amo 1.09
send a fire upon the wall of T., 1.10
T. and Sidon, though they are very Zec 9.02
T. has built herself a rampart, and 9.03
you had been done in T. and Sidon, Mt 11.21
of judgment for T. and Sidon than 11.22
to the district of T. and Sidon. 15.21
and from about T. and Sidon a Mk 3.08
away to the region of T. and Sidon. 7.24
Then he returned from the region of T., 7.31
and the seacoast of T. and Sidon, Lk 6.17
you had been done in T. and Sidon, 10.13
judgment for T. and Sidon than for 10.14
with the people of T. and Sidon; Ac 12.20
sailed to Syria, and landed at T.; 21.03
we had finished the voyage from T., 21.07

TYRIANS

Sidonians and T. brought great 1Ch 22.04
Sidonians and the T. to bring cedar Ez 3.07

U

UCAL

says to Ithiel, to Ithiel and U.: Pro 30.01

UEL

sons of Bani: Maadai, Amram, U., Ez 10.34

ULAI

vision, and I was at the river U. Dan 8.02
voice between the banks of the U., 8.16

ULAM

and his sons were U. and Rakem. 1Ch 7.16
The sons of U.: Bedan. These were 7.17
U. his first-born Jeush the second, 8.39
The sons of U. were men who were 8.40

ULCERS

and with the u. and the scurvy and Deu 28.27

ULLA

The sons of U.: Arah, Hanniel, and 1Ch 7.39

UMMAH

U., Aphek and Rehob—twenty-two cities Jos 19.30

UMPIRE

There is no u. between us, who might Job 9.33

UNABLE

of Israel were u. to destroy 1Ki 9.21
they are thrust down, u. to rise. Ps 36.12
men of war were u. to use their 76.05
be dumb and u. to reprove them; Eze 3.26
be silent and u. to speak until Lk 1.20
be blind and u. to see the sun for Ac 13.11
that they were u. to enter because Heb 3.19
priest who is u. to sympathize 4.15

UNANSWERED

"Should a multitude of words go u., Job 11.02

UNAPPROACHABLE

immortality and dwells in u. light, 1Ti 6.16

UNAWARES

swords and came upon the city u., Gen 34.25
Let ruin come upon them u.! Ps 35.08
some have entertained angels u. Heb 13.02

UNBEARABLY
u. crushed that we despaired of 2Co 1.08

UNBELIEF
works there, because of their u. Mt 13.58
And he marveled because of their u. Mk 6.06
"I believe; help my u.!" 9.24
he upbraided them for their u. and * 16.14
broken off because of their u., Rom 11.20
if they do not persist in their u., 11.23
I had acted ignorantly in u., 1Ti 1.13
were unable to enter because of u. Heb 3.19

UNBELIEVER
brother has a wife who is an u., 1Co 7.12
woman has a husband who is an u., 7.13
and an u. or outsider enters, he is 14.24
a believer in common with an u.? 2Co 6.15
the faith and is worse than an u. 1Ti 5.08

UNBELIEVERS
be delivered from the u. in Judea, Rom 15.31
brother, and that before u.? 1Co 6.06
If one of the u. invites you to 10.27
sign not for believers but for u., 14.22
is not for u. but for believers. 14.22
tongues, and outsiders or u. enter, 14.23
has blinded the minds of the u., 2Co 4.04
Do not be mismated with u. For what 6.14

UNBELIEVING
But the u. Jews stirred up the Ac 14.02
For the u. husband is consecrated 1Co 7.14
and the u. wife is consecrated 7.14
But if the u. partner desires to 7.15
the corrupt and u. nothing is pure; Tit 1.15
u. heart, leading you to fall away Heb 3.12

UNBIND
and u. the hair of the woman's head, Num 5.18
to them, "U. him, and let him go." Jn 11.44

UNBLAMABLE
your hearts u. in holiness before 1Th 3.13

UNBORN
his deliverance to a people yet u., Ps 22.31
know them, the children yet u., 78.06
a people yet u. may praise the 102.18

UNBOUND
he u. him, and commanded the chief Ac 22.30

UNCEASING
the peoples in wrath with u. blows, Is14.06
Why is my pain u., my wound incurable, Jer 15.18
whom has not come your u. evil? Nah 3.19
sorrow and u. anguish in my heart. Rom 9.02

UNCERTAIN
at one another, u. of whom he spoke. Jn 13.22
their hopes on u. riches but on 1Ti 6.17

UNCERTAINTY
good fruits, without u. or insincerity. Jas 3.17

UNCHANGEABLE
But he is u. and who can turn him? Job 23.13
the promise the u. character of Heb 6.17
so that through two u. things, 6.18

UNCHASTITY
wife, except on the ground of u., Mt 5.32
except for u., and marries another, 19.09
idols and from u. and from what is Ac 15.20
from what is strangled and from u. 15.29
from what is strangled and from u. 21.25

UNCIRCUMCISED
Any u. male who is not circumcised Gen 17.14
give our sister to one who is u., 34.14
to me, who am a man of u. lips?" Ex 6.12
the LORD, "Behold, I am of u. lips; 6.30
But no u. person shall eat of it. 12.48
if then their u. heart is humbled Lev 26.41
for they were u., because they had Jos 5.07
a wife from the u. Philistines?" Ju 14.03
and fall into the hands of the u.?" 15.18
over to the garrison of these u.; 1Sa 14.06
For who is this u. Philistine, 17.26
and this u. Philistine shall be one 17.36
lest these u. come and thrust me 31.04
lest the daughters of the u. exult. 2Sa 1.20
lest these u. come and make sport 1Ch 10.04
into you the u. and the unclean. Is 52.01
who are circumcised but yet u.— Jer 9.25
for all these nations are u., 9.26
the house of Israel is u. in heart." 9.26
death of the u. by the hand of Eze 28.10
you shall lie among the u., 31.18
Go down, and be laid with the u.' 32.19
the u., slain by the sword.' 32.21
who went down u. into the nether 32.24
all of them u., slain by the sword; 32.25
all of them u., slain by the sword; 32.26
be broken and lie among the u., 32.28
they lie with the u., with those 32.29
they lie u. with those who are 32.30
he shall be laid among the u., 32.32
u. in heart and flesh, to be in my 44.07
u. in heart and flesh, of all the 44.09
u. in heart and ears, you always Ac 7.51
did you go to u. men and eat with 11.03
So, if a man who is u. keeps the Rom 2.26
are physically u. but keep the law 2.27
faith and the u. because of their 3.30
circumcised, or also upon the u.? 4.09
had by faith while he was still u. 4.11
any one at the time of his call u.? 1Co 7.18
entrusted with the gospel to the u., Gal 2.07
Greek and Jew, circumcised and u., Col 3.11

UNCIRCUMCISION
law, your circumcision becomes u. Rom 2.25
will not his u. be regarded as 2.26
circumcision counts for anything nor u., 1Co 7.19
circumcision nor u. is of any avail, Gal 5.06
nor u., but a new creation. 6.15
called the u. by what is called the Eph 2.11
trespasses and the u. of your flesh, Col 2.13

UNCLE
the sons of Uzziel the u. of Aaron, Lev 10.04
or his u., or his cousin may redeem 25.49
Saul's u. said to him and to his 1Sa 10.14
And Saul's u. said, "Pray, tell me 10.15
And Saul said to his u., "He told us 10.16
Abner the son of Ner, Saul's u.; 14.50
Jehoiachin's u., king in his stead, 2Ki 24.17
David's u., was a counselor, being a 1Ch 27.32
is Esther, the daughter of his u., Est 2.07
of Abihail the u. of Mordecai, 2.15
of Shallum your u. will come to Jer 32.07

UNCLEAN
Or if any one touches an u. thing, Lev 5.02
carcass of an u. beast or a 5.02
or a carcass of u. cattle or a 5.02
or a carcass of u. swarming things, 5.02
from him, and he has become u., 5.02
may be with which one becomes u., 5.03
touches any u. thing shall not be 7.19
And if any one touches an u. thing, 7.21
of man or an u. beast or any 7.21
beast or any u. abomination, 7.21
and between the u. and the clean; 10.10

UNCLEAN (cont.)
not part the hoof, is u. to you. Lev 11.04
not part the hoof, is u. to you. 11.05
not part the hoof, is u. to you. 11.06
not chew the cud, is u. to you. 11.07
not touch; they are u. to you. 11.08
"And by these you shall become u.; 11.24
shall be u. until the evening, 11.24
clothes and be u. until the 11.25
does not chew the cud is u. to you; 11.26
one who touches them shall be u. 11.26
go on all fours, are u. to you; 11.27
shall be u. until the evening, 11.27
clothes and be u. until the 11.28
evening; they are u. to you. 11.28
"And these are u. to you among the 11.29
These are u. to you among all that 11.31
dead shall be u. until the evening. 11.31
when they are dead shall be u., 11.32
and it shall be u. until the evening; 11.32
all that is in it shall be u., 11.33
which water may come, shall be u.; 11.34
from every such vessel shall be u. 11.34
of their carcass falls shall be u.; 11.35
they are u., and shall be u. to you. 11.35
touches their carcass shall be u. 11.36
falls on it, it is u. to you. 11.38
shall be u. until the evening, 11.39
clothes and be u. until the 11.40
with them, lest you become u. 11.43
between the u. and the clean and 11.47
then she shall be u. seven days; 12.02
her menstruation, she shall be u. 12.02
then she shall be u. two weeks, 12.05
him he shall pronounce him u. 13.03
the priest shall pronounce him u.; 13.08
the priest shall pronounce him u.; 13.11
not shut him up, for he is u. 13.11
appears on him, he shall be u. 13.14
raw flesh, and pronounce him u.; 13.15
raw flesh is u., for it is leprosy. 13.15
the priest shall pronounce him u.; 13.20
the priest shall pronounce him u.; 13.22
the priest shall pronounce him u.; 13.25
the priest shall pronounce him u.; 13.27
the priest shall pronounce him u.; 13.30
seek for the yellow hair; he is u. 13.36
he is a leprous man, he is u.; 13.44
the priest must pronounce him u.; 13.44
upper lip and cry, 'U., u.' 13.45
He shall remain u. as long as he 13.46
he is u.; he shall dwell alone 13.46
is a malignant leprosy; it is u. 13.51
disease has not spread, it is u.; 13.55
decide whether it is clean or u. 13.59
is in the house be declared u.; 14.36
them into an u. place outside the 14.40
pour into an u. place outside the 14.41
leprosy in the house; it is u. 14.44
out of the city to an u. place. 14.45
up shall be u. until the evening; 14.46
to show when it is u. and when it 14.57
from his body, his discharge is u. 15.02
has the discharge lies shall be u.; 15.04
on which he sits shall be u. 15.04
and be u. until the evening. 15.05
and be u. until the evening. 15.06
and be u. until the evening. 15.07
and be u. until the evening. 15.08
the discharge rides shall be u. 15.09
him shall be u. until the evening; 15.10
and be u. until the evening. 15.10
and be u. until the evening. 15.11
and be u. until the evening. 15.16
and be u. until the evening. 15.17
and be u. until the evening. 15.18
her shall be u. until the evening. 15.19
during her impurity shall be u.; 15.20
upon which she sits shall be u. 15.20
and be u. until the evening. 15.21
and be u. until the evening; 15.22
it he shall be u. until the 15.23
on him, he shall be u. seven days; 15.24
bed on which he lies shall be u. 15.24
of her impurity, she shall be u. 15.25
on which she sits shall be u. 15.26
touches these things shall be u., 15.27
and be u. until the evening. 15.27
the LORD for her u. discharge. 15.30
of semen, becoming u. thereby; 15.32
who lies with a woman who is u. 15.33
and be u. until the evening; 17.15
between the clean beast and the u., 20.25
and between the u. bird and the 20.25
have set apart for you to hold u. 20.25
anything that is u. through contact 22.04
he may be made u. or a man from 22.05
such shall be u. until the evening 22.06
And if it is an u. animal such as 27.11
And if it is an u. animal, 27.27
one that is u. through contact Num 5.02
they die, shall he make himself u.; 6.07
men who were u. through touching 9.06
"We are u. through touching the 9.07
descendants is u. through touching 9.10
firstling of u. beasts you shall 18.15
priests shall be u. until evening. 19.07
and shall be u. until evening. 19.10
clothes, and be u. until evening. 19.10
any person shall be u. seven days; 19.11
thrown upon him, he shall be u.; 19.13
the tent, shall be u. seven days. 19.14
no cover fastened upon it, is u. 19.15
or a grave, shall be u. seven days. 19.16
For the u. they shall take some 19.17
upon the u. on the third day and 19.19
"But the man who is u. and does not 19.20
not been thrown upon him, he is u. 19.20
impurity shall be u. until evening. 19.21
And whatever the u. person touches 19.22
unclean person touches shall be u.; 19.22
it shall be u. until evening. 19.22
the u. and the clean may eat of it, Deu 12.15
the u. and the clean alike may eat 12.22
not part the hoof, are u. for you. 14.07
not chew the cud, is u. for you. 14.08
shall not eat; it is u. for you. 14.10
And all winged insects are u. for you; 14.19
the u. and the clean alike may eat 15.22
removed any of it while I was u., 26.14
But now, if your land is u., Jos 22.19
strong drink, and eat nothing u., Ju 13.04
strong drink, and eat nothing u., 13.07
strong drink, or eat any u. thing; 13.14
should enter who was in any way u. 2Ch 23.19
excluded from the priesthood as u.; Ez 2.62
is a land u. with the pollutions of 9.11
excluded from the priesthood as u.; Neh 7.64
bring a clean thing out of an u.? Job 14.04
Thus they became u. by their acts, Ps 106.39
the evil, to the clean and the u., Ecc 9.02
for I am a man of u. lips, and I dwell Is 6.05
the midst of a people of u. lips; 6.05
You will scatter them as u. things; 30.22
the u. shall not pass over it, and 35.08
you the uncircumcised and the u. 52.01
go out thence, touch no u. thing; 52.11
have all become like one who is u., 64.06
"Away! U.!" men cried at them; Lam 4.15
of Israel eat their bread u., Eze 4.13
and their gold is like an u. thing; 7.19
I will make it an u. thing to them. 7.20
women who are u. in their impurity. 22.10
between the u. and the clean, 22.26

UNCLEAN (cont.)
between the u. and the clean. Eze 44.23
they shall eat u. food in Assyria. Hos 9.03
yourself shall die in an u. land, Amo 7.17
"If one who is u. by contact with a Hag 2.13
any of these, does it become u.?" 2.13
answered, "It does become u." 2.13
and what they offer there is u. 2.14
the prophets and the u. spirit. Zec 13.02
them authority over u. spirits, Mt 10.01
"When the u. spirit has gone out of 12.43
synagogue a man with an u. spirit; Mk 1.23
And the u. spirit, convulsing him 1.26
he commands even the u. spirits, 1.27
And whenever the u. spirits beheld 3.11
they had said, "He has an u. spirit." 3.30
the tombs a man with an u. spirit, 5.02
"Come out of the man, you u. spirit!" 5.08
And the u. spirits came out, and 5.13
them authority over the u. spirits. 6.07
was possessed by an u. spirit, 7.25
together, he rebuked the u. spirit, 9.25
who had the spirit of an u. demon; Lk 4.33
power he commands the u. spirits, 4.36
troubled with u. spirits were 6.18
commanded the u. spirit to come 8.29
But Jesus rebuked the u. spirit, 9.42
"When the u. spirit has gone out of 11.24
those afflicted with u. spirits, Ac 5.16
For u. spirits came out of many who 8.07
anything that is common or u." 10.14
not call any man common or u. 10.28
common or u. has ever entered my 11.08
Jesus that nothing is u. in itself; Rom 14.14
but it is u. for any one who thinks it u. 14.14
Otherwise, your children would be u., 1Co 7.14
the Lord, and touch nothing u.; 2Co 6.17
But nothing u. shall enter it, nor Rev 21.27

UNCLEANNESS
Or if he touches human u., Lev 5.03
sort the u. may be with which one 5.03
offerings while an u. is on him, 7.20
whether the u. of man or an unclean 7.21
who is to be cleansed from his u. 14.19
the law of his u. for a discharge: 15.03
from discharge, it is u. in him. 15.03
discharge she shall continue in u.; 15.25
as in the u. of her impurity. 15.26
of Israel separate from their u., 15.31
die in their u. by defiling my 15.31
while she is in her menstrual u. 18.19
to the LORD, while he has an u., 22.03
or a man from whom he may take u., 22.05
whatever his u. may be— 22.05
if you have not turned aside to u., Num 5.19
be unclean; his u. is still on him. 19.13
was purifying herself from her u. 2Sa 11.04
out all the u. that they found in 2Ch 29.16
it from end to end with their u. Ez 9.11
Her u. was in her skirts; she took no Lam 1.09
me was like the u. of a woman in Eze 36.17
to their u. and their transgressions, 39.24
because of u. that destroys with a Mic 2.10
to cleanse them from sin and u. Zec 13.01
of dead men's bones and all u. Mt 23.27
to practice every kind of u. Eph 4.19
does not spring from error or u., 1Th 2.03
For God has not called us for u., 4.07

UNCLEANNESSES
because of the u. of the people of Lev 16.16
with them in the midst of their u. 16.16
it from the u. of the people of 16.19
shall be clean from all your u., Eze 36.25
will deliver you from all your u.; 36.29

UNCLE'S
If a man lies with his u. wife, Lev 20.20
he has uncovered his u. nakedness; 20.20

UNCLOTHED
not that we would be u., but that we 2Co 5.04

UNCONDEMNED
u., men who are Roman citizens, and Ac 16.37
man who is a Roman citizen, and u.?" 22.25

UNCOVER
near of kin to him to u. nakedness. Lev 18.06
You shall not u. the nakedness of 18.07
you shall not u. her nakedness. 18.07
You shall not u. the nakedness of 18.08
You shall not u. the nakedness of 18.09
You shall not u. the nakedness of 18.10
You shall not u. the nakedness of 18.11
You shall not u. the nakedness of 18.12
You shall not u. the nakedness of 18.13
You shall not u. the nakedness of 18.14
You shall not u. the nakedness of 18.15
you shall not u. her nakedness. 18.15
You shall not u. the nakedness of 18.16
You shall not u. the nakedness of a 18.17
daughter to u. her nakedness; 18.17
a woman to u. her nakedness while 18.19
You shall not u. the nakedness of 20.19
nor shall he u. her who is his Deu 22.30
then, go and u. his feet and lie Ru 3.04
u. your legs, pass through the Is 47.02
will punish, he will u. your sins. Lam 4.22
and will u. your nakedness to them, Eze 16.37
In you men u. their fathers' 22.10
Now I will u. her lewdness in the Hos 2.10
into the valley, and u. her foundations. Mic 1.06

UNCOVERED
drunk, and lay u. in his tent. Gen 9.21
wife has u. his father's nakedness; Lev 20.11
he has u. his sister's nakedness, he 20.17
and she has u. the fountain of her 20.18
he has u. his uncle's nakedness; 20.20
he has u. his brother's nakedness, 20.21
down, but having his eyes u.: Num 24.04
down, but having his eyes u.: 24.16
because he has u. her who is his Deu 27.20
and u. his feet, and lay down. Ru 3.07
with buttocks u., to the shame of Is 20.04
horsemen, and Kir u. the shield. 22.06
Your nakedness shall be u., 47.03
you have u. your bed, you have gone 57.08
I have u. his hiding places, and he Jer 49.10
your nakedness u. in your harlotries Eze 16.36
before your wickedness was u.? 16.57
in that your transgressions are u., 21.24
These u. her nakedness; they seized 23.10
of your harlotry shall be u. 23.29
to pray to God with her head u.? 1Co 11.13

UNCOVERING
u. her nakedness while her sister Lev 18.18
u. himself today before the eyes of 2Sa 6.20

UNCOVERS
and u. her nakedness, he has made Lev 20.18
fellows shamelessly u. himself!" 2Sa 6.20
He u. the deeps out of darkness, and Job 12.22

UNDEFILED
and let the marriage bed be u.; Heb 13.04
is pure and u. before God and the Jas 1.27
u., and unfading, kept in heaven for 1Pe 1.04

UNDERFOOT
trample them u. and turn to attack Mt 7.06

UNDERGIRD

they took measures to u. the ship; Ac 27.17

UNDERGOING

an example by u. a punishment of Jud 1.07

UNDERHANDED

renounced disgraceful, u. ways; we refuse 2Co 4.02

UNDERMINE

in order to u. the claim of those who would 2Co 11.12

UNDERNEATH

and u. are the everlasting arms. Deu 33.27
inside my tent, with the silver u. Jos 7.21
in his tent with the silver u. 7.22
the four wheeels were u. the panels; 1Ki 7.32
and the twelve oxen u. the sea. 7.44
u. the wings of the cherubim. 8.06
one sea, and the twelve oxen u. it. 2Ch 4.15
u. the wings of the cherubim. 5.07
but u. it is turned up as by fire. Job 28.05
whirling wheels u. the cherubim; Eze 10.02
that I saw u. the God of Israel by 10.20
and u. their wings the semblance of 10.21

UNDERPARTS

His u. are like sharp potsherds; Job 41.30

UNDERSTAND

they may not u. one another's Gen 11.07
do you not yet u. that Egypt is Ex 10.07
whose language you do not u., Deu 28.49
has not given you a mind to u., 29.04
they would u. this, they would 32.29
"U. that you and your men are to go 1Sa 28.01
the Aramaic language, for we u. it; 2Ki 18.26
the women and those who could u.; Neh 8.03
helped the people to u. the law, 8.07
make me u. how I have erred. Job 6.24
What do you u. that is not clear to 15.09
and u. what he would say to me. 23.05
thunder of his power who can u.?" 26.14
of the Almighty, that makes him u. 32.08
nor the aged that u. what is right. 32.09
Can any one u. the spreading of the 36.29
I have uttered what I did not u., 42.03
But when I thought how to u. this, Ps 73.16
know, the stupid cannot u. this: 92.06
U., O dullest of the people! Fools, when 94.08
Make me u. the way of thy precepts, 119.27
I u. more than the aged, for I keep 119.100
and instruction, u. words of insight, Pro 1.02
to u. a proverb and a figure, the 1.06
then you will u. the fear of the 2.05
Then you will u. righteousness and 2.09
how then can man u. his way? 20.24
Evil men do not u. justice, 28.05
who seek the LORD u. it completely. 28.05
man does not u. such knowledge. 29.07
for me; four I do not u.: 30.18
not know, my people does not u." Is 1.03
'Hear and hear, but do not u.; 6.09
and u. with their hearts, and turn 6.10
be sheer terror to u. the message. 28.19
in a tongue which you cannot u. 33.19
servants in Aramaic, for we u. it; 36.11
know, may consider and u. together, 41.20
round about, but he did not u.; 42.25
and believe me and u. that I am He. 43.10
minds, so that they cannot u. 44.18
they have not heard they shall u. 52.15
know, nor can you u. what they say. Jer 5.15
man so wise that he can u. this? 9.12
corrupt; who can u. it? 17.09
latter days you will u. it clearly. 23.20
the latter days you will u. this. 30.24
language, whose words you cannot u. Eze 3.06
Perhaps they will u., though they are 12.03
seen the vision, I sought to u. it; Dan 8.15
make this man u. the vision." 8.16
"U., O son of man, that the vision 8.17
by the vision and did not u. it. 8.27
consider the word and u. the vision. 9.23
Know therefore and u. that from the 9.25
your mind to u. and humbled 10.12
to make you u. what is to befall 10.14
who are wise shall make many u., 11.33
I heard, but I did not u. 12.08
and none of the wicked shall u.; 12.10
but those who are wise shall u. 12.10
Whoever is wise, let him u. these things; Hos 14.09
they do not u. his plan, that he has Mic 4.12
they do not hear, nor do they u. Mt 13.13
You shall indeed hear but never u., 13.14
and u. with their heart, and turn 13.15
of the kingdom and does not u. it, 13.19
him and said to them, "Hear and u.: 15.10
the holy place (let the reader u.), 24.15
and may indeed hear but not u.; Mk 4.12
them, "Do you not u. this parable? 4.13
then will you u. all the parables? 4.13
for they did not u. about the 6.52
them, "Hear me, all of you, and u.: 7.14
Do you not yet perceive or u.? 8.17
he said to them, "Do you not yet u.?" 8.21
But they did not u. the saying, 9.32
ought not to be (let the reader u.), 13.14
neither know nor u. what you mean." 14.68
And they did not u. the saying Lk 2.50
see, and hearing they may not u. 8.10
But they did not u. this saying, 9.45
their minds to u. the scriptures, 24.45
Israel, and yet you do not u. this? Jn 3.10
They did not u. that he spoke to 8.27
Why do you not u. what I say? 8.43
they did not u. what he was saying 10.06
may know and u. that the Father is 10.38
you do not u. that it is expedient 11.50
disciples did not u. this at first; 12.16
now, but afterward you will u." 13.07
by his hand, but they did not u. Ac 7.25
"Do you u. what you are reading?" 8.30
recognize him nor u. the utterances 13.27
You shall indeed hear but never u., 28.26
and u. with their heart, and turn 28.27
I do not u. my own actions. Rom 7.15
Again I ask, did Israel not u.? 10.19
I want you to u. this mystery, 11.25
and they shall u. who have never 15.21
that we might u. the gifts bestowed 1Co 2.12
is not able to u. them because 2.14
But I want you to u. that the head 11.03
Therefore I want you to u. that no 12.03
and u. all mysteries and all 13.02
then I shall u. fully, even as I 13.12
but what you can read and u.; 2Co 1.13
I hope you will u. fully, 1.13
Let such people u. that what we say 10.11
but u. what the will of the Lord is Eph 5.17
But u. this, that in the last days 2Ti 3.01
By faith we u. that the world was Heb 11.03
You should u. that our brother 13.23
First of all you must u. this, 2Pe 1.20
First of all you must u. this, 3.03
are some things in them hard to u., 3.16
men revile whatever they do not u., Jud 1.10

UNDERSTANDING

Choose wise, u., and experienced men, Deu 1.13
wisdom and your u. in the sight of 4.06
nation is a wise and u. people.' 4.06
counsel, and there is no u. in them. 32.28
woman was of good u. and beautiful, 1Sa 25.03
therefore an u. mind to govern thy 1Ki 3.09

UNDERSTANDING (cont.)

for yourself u. to discern what is 1Ki 3.11
wisdom and u. beyond measure, 4.29
u., and skill, for making any work 7.14
men who had u. of the times, 1Ch 12.32
LORD grant you discretion and u., 22.12
being a man of u. and a scribe; 27.32
son, endued with discretion and u., 2Ch 2.12
man, endued with u., Huramabi, 2.13
and all who could hear with u., Neh 8.02
all who have knowledge and u., 10.28
and utter words out of their u.? Job 8.10
who does great things beyond u., 9.10
For he is manifold in u. Know then 11.06
But a stupid man will get u., 11.12
But I have u. as well as you; 12.03
and u. in length of days. 12.12
and might; he has counsel and u. 12.13
He takes away u. from the chiefs of 12.24
thou hast closed their minds to u., 17.04
and out of my u. a spirit answers 20.03
by his u. he smote Rahab. 26.12
And where is the place of u.? 28.12
And where is the place of u.? 28.20
and to depart from evil is u. 28.28
you men of u., far be it from God 34.10
"If you have u., hear this; 34.16
Men of u. will say to me, and the 34.34
he is mighty in strength of u. 36.05
of the earth? Tell me, if you have u. 38.04
clouds, or given u. to the mists? 38.36
and given her no share in u. 39.17
without u., which must be curbed Ps 32.09
meditation of my heart shall be u. 49.03
Have those who work evil no u., 53.04
They have neither knowledge nor u., 82.05
a good u. have all those who 111.10
commandments when thou enlargest my u.! 119.32
Give me u., that I may keep thy law 119.34
give me u. that I may learn thy 119.73
I have more u. than all my teachers, 119.99
Through thy precepts I get u.; 119.104
give me u., that I may know thy 119.125
gives light; it imparts u. to the simple. 119.130
righteous for ever; give me u. that I may live. 119.144
give me u. according to thy word! 119.169
to him who by u. made the heavens, 136.05
in power; his u. is beyond measure. 147.05
and the man of u. acquire skill. Pro 1.05
and inclining your heart to u.; 2.02
and raise your voice for u., 2.03
his mouth come knowledge and u.; 2.06
watch over you; u. will guard you; 2.11
wisdom, and the man who gets u., 3.13
by u. he established the heavens; 3.19
wisdom, incline your ear to my u.; 5.01
does not u. raise her voice? 8.01
of him who has u. wisdom is found, 10.13
conduct is pleasure to a man of u. 10.23
but a man of u. remains silent. 11.12
knowledge is easy for a man of u. 14.06
He who is slow to anger has great u., 14.29
Wisdom abides in the mind of a man of u., 14.33
of him who has u. seeks knowledge, 15.14
but a man of u. walks aright. 15.21
he who heeds admonition gains u. 15.32
to get u. is to be chosen rather 16.16
into a man of u. than a hundred 17.10
A man of u. sets his face toward 17.24
has a cool spirit is a man of u. 17.27
A fool takes no pleasure in u., 18.02
he who keeps u. will prosper. 19.08
reprove a man of u., and he will gain 19.25
but a man of u. will draw it out. 20.05
from the way of u. will rest in 21.16
No wisdom, no u., no counsel, can 21.30
buy wisdom, instruction, and u. 23.23
and by u. it is established; 24.03
but with men of u. and knowledge 28.02
man who has u. will find him out. 28.11
A ruler who lacks u. is a cruel 28.16
I have not the u. of a man. 30.02
and by my wisdom, for I have u.; Is 10.13
him, the spirit of wisdom and u., 11.02
him who formed it, "He has no u."? 29.16
who err in spirit will come to u., 29.24
and showed him the way of u.? 40.14
grow weary, his u. is unsearchable. 40.28
The shepherds also have no u.; 56.11
feed you with knowledge and u. Jer 3.15
stupid children, they have no u. 4.22
and by his u. stretched out the 10.12
and by his u. stretched out the 51.15
wisdom and your u. you have gotten Eze 28.04
u. learning, and competent to serve Dan 1.04
and Daniel had u. in all visions 1.17
of wisdom and u. concerning which 1.20
and knowledge to those who have u.; 2.21
father light and u. and wisdom, 5.11
and u. to interpret dreams, explain 5.12
that light and u. and excellent 5.14
come out to give you wisdom and u. 9.22
the word and had u. of the vision. 10.01
Wine and new wine take away the u. Hos 4.11
people without u. shall come to 4.14
trap under you—there is no u. of it. Ob 1.07
out of Edom, and u. out of Mount Esau? 1.08
and peaceful u. shall be between Zec 6.13
the wise and u. and revealed them Mt 11.25
"Are you also still without u.? 15.16
them, "Then are you also without u.? Mk 7.18
all the heart, and with all the u., 12.33
amazed at his u. and his answers. Lk 2.47
the wise and u. and revealed them 10.21
one another, they are without u. 2Co 10.12
they are darkened in their u., Eph 4.18
peace of God, which passes all u., Php 4.07
in all spiritual wisdom and u., Col 1.09
of assured u. and the knowledge of 2.02
without u. either what they are 1Ti 1.07
u. this, that the law is not laid 1.09
will grant you u. in everything. 2Ti 2.07
Who is wise and u. among you? Jas 3.13
God has come and has given us u., 1Jn 5.20
let him who has u. reckon the Rev 13.18

UNDERSTANDS

and u. every plan and thought. 1Ch 28.09
"God u. the way to it, and he knows Job 28.23
to him who u. and right to those Pro 8.09
for though he u., he will not give 29.19
are taken away, while no one u. Is 57.01
that he u. and knows me, that I am Jer 9.24
one who u. riddles, shall arise. Dan 8.23
is he who hears the word and u. it; Mt 13.23
no one u., no one seeks for God. Rom 3.11
for no one u. him, but he utters 1Co 14.02

UNDERSTOOD

They did not know that Joseph u. them, Gen 42.23
and all Israel u. that day that it 2Sa 3.37
direct the music, for he u. it. 1Ch 15.22
And I u., and saw that God had not Neh 6.12
so that the people u. the reading. 8.08
they had u. the words that were 8.12
this, my ear has heard and u. it. Job 13.01
Have you not u. from the foundations Is 40.21
And he u. the word and had understanding Dan 10.01
"Have you u. all this?" They said Mt 13.51
Then they u. that he did not tell 16.12
Then the disciples u. that he was 17.13
But they u. none of these things; Lk 18.34
his brethren u. that God was Ac 7.25
None of the rulers of this age u. this; 1Co 2.08
even as I have been fully u. 13.12

UNDERSTOOD (cont.)
as you have u. in part, that you can 2Co 1.14
you heard and u. the grace of God Col 1.06

UNDERTAKE
households, in all that you u., Deu 12.07
LORD your God in all that you u. 12.18
your work and in all that you u. 15.10
in all that you u. in the land 23.20
your barns, and in all that you u.; 28.08
frustration, in all that you u. to do, 28.20

UNDERTAKEN
Inasmuch as many have u. to compile Lk 1.01

UNDERTAKING
if this plan or this u. is of men, Ac 5.38

UNDERTAKINGS
And David had success in all his u.; 1Sa 18.14

UNDERTOOK
Moses u. to explain this law, saying, Deu 1.05
work that he u. in the service of 2Ch 31.21
So the Jews u. to do as they had Est 9.23
exorcists u. to pronounce the name Ac 19.13

UNDETECTED
and she is u. though she has Num 5.13

UNDIVIDED
to secure your u. devotion to the 1Co 7.35

UNDO
to u. the thongs of the yoke, to let Is 58.06

UNDOING
were his counselors, to his u. 2Ch 22.04
eat his rich food shall be his u.; Dan 11.26

UNDONE
perish, we are u., we are all u. Num 17.12
You are u., O people of Chemosh! 21.29
he left nothing u. of all that the Jos 11.15
Ar is laid waste in a night Moab is u.; Is 15.01
Kir is laid waste in a night Moab is u. 15.01
The people of Chemosh is u.; Jer 48.46

UNDRESSED
grapes of your u. vine you shall Lev 25.05
the grapes from the u. vines. 25.11

UNDYING
our Lord Jesus Christ with love u. Eph 6.24

UNEDUCATED
and perceived that they were u., Ac 4.13

UNEVEN
the u. ground shall become level, Is 40.04

UNFADING
and u., kept in heaven for you, 1Pe 1.04
will obtain the u. crown of glory. 5.04

UNFAILING
be u. in patience and in teaching. 2Ti 4.02
Above all hold u. your love for one 1Pe 4.08

UNFAITHFUL
he was u. to the LORD in that he 1Ch 10.13
they had been u. to the LORD, 2Ch 12.02
have been u. and have done what 29.06
likewise were exceedingly u., 36.14
'If you are u., I will scatter you Neh 1.08
him, and put him with the u. Lk 12.46
What if some were u.? Rom 3.03
U. creatures! Do you not know that Jas 4.04

UNFAITHFULLY
astray and acts u. against him, Num 5.12
and has acted u. against her husband, 5.27

UNFAITHFULNESS
in Babylon because of their u. 1Ch 9.01
So Saul died for his u.; he was 10.13
inhabitants of Jerusalem into u., 2Ch 21.11
inhabitants of Jerusalem into u., 21.13
house of Ahab led Israel into u., 21.13

UNFASTENED
were opened and every one's fetters were u. Ac 16.26

UNFIT
u. to be called an apostle, because 1Co 15.09
disobedient, u. for any good deed. Tit 1.16

UNFOLDING
The u. of thy words gives light; it imparts Ps 119.130

UNFORGOTTEN
for it will live u. in the mouths of Deu 31.21

UNFORMED
Thy eyes beheld my u. substance; Ps 139.16

UNFRUITFUL
water is bad, and the land is u. 2Ki 2.19
choke the word, and it proves u. Mt 13.22
choke the word, and it proves u. Mk 4.19
my spirit prays but my mind is u. 1Co 14.14
Take no part in the u. works of Eph 5.11
of urgent need, and not to be u. Tit 3.14
ineffective or u. in the knowledge 2Pe 1.08

UNGIRD
before him and u. the loins of kings, Is 45.01

UNGIRDED
and Laban u. the camels, and gave him straw Gen 24.32

UNGODLINESS
to practice u., to utter error Is 32.06
of Jerusalem u. has gone forth Jer 23.15
against all u. and wickedness of Rom 1.18
he will banish u. from Jacob"; 11.26
lead people into more and more u., 2Ti 2.16
their deeds of u. which they have Jud 1.15

UNGODLY
God gives me up to the u., Job 16.11
Surely such are the dwellings of the u., 18.21
my cause against an u. people; Ps 43.01
will scatter the bones of the u.; 53.05
"Both prophet and priest are u.; Jer 23.11
trusts him who justifies the u., Rom 4.05
right time Christ died for the u. 5.06
for the u. and sinners, for the 1Ti 1.09
a flood upon the world of the u.; 2Pe 2.05
example to those who were to be u.; 2.06
judgment and destruction of u. men. 3.07
u. persons who pervert the grace of Jud 1.04
convict all the u. of all their 1.15
have committed in such an u. way, 1.15
things which u. sinners have 1.15
following their own u. passions. 1.18

UNGRATEFUL
is kind to the u. and the selfish. Lk 6.35
to their parents, u., unholy, 2Ti 3.02

UNGRUDGINGLY
Practice hospitality u. to one another. 1Pe 4.09

UNHALLOWED
And you, O u. wicked one, prince of Eze 21.25
laid on the necks of the u. wicked, 21.29

UNHAPPY
it is an u. business that God has Ecc 1.13
also is vanity and an u. business. 4.08

UNHEWN
to the LORD your God of u. stores; Deu 27.06
"an altar of u. stones, upon which Jos 8.31

UNHINDERED
Jesus Christ quite openly and u. Ac 28.31

UNHOLY
You shall offer no u. incense thereon, Ex 30.09
and offered u. fire before the LORD, Lev 10.01
they offered u. fire before the Num 3.04
they offered u. fire before the 26.61
for the u. and profane, for murderers 1Ti 1.09
to their parents, ungrateful, u., 2Ti 3.02

UNINFORMED
brethren, I do not want you to be u. 1Co 12.01

UNINHABITED
make you a desolation, an u. land." Jer 6.08
the wilderness, in an u. salt land. 17.06
will make you a desert, an u. city. 22.06
through it; it shall be u. forty years. Eze 29.11
from Gaza; Ashkelon shall be u.; Zec 9.05

UNINTENTIONALLY
there, who kills his neighbor u., Deu 4.42
his neighbor u. without having 19.04

UNION
named Grace, the other I named U. Zec 11.07
Then I broke my second staff U., 11.14

UNISON
heard in u. in praise and thanksgiving 2Ch 5.13

UNITE
u. my heart to fear thy name. Ps 86.11
to u. all things in him, things in Eph 1.10

UNITED
against the city, u. as one man. Ju 20.11
the Jews made a u. attack upon Ac 18.12
For if we have been u. with him in Rom 6.05
certainly be u. with him in a 6.05
but that you be u. in the same 1Co 1.10
But he who is u. to the Lord 6.17

UNITS
were u. of the army for war, thirty-six 1Ch 7.04

UNITY
it is when brothers dwell in u.! Ps 133.01
eager to maintain the u. of the Eph 4.03
attain to the u. of the faith and 4.13
have u. of spirit, sympathy, love of 1Pe 3.08

UNIVERSE
to the elemental spirits of the u. Gal 4.03
to the elemental spirits of the u., Col 2.08
to the elemental spirits of the u., 2.20
upholding the u. by his word of Heb 1.03

UNJUST
deceitful and u. men deliver me! Ps 43.01
the grasp of the u. and cruel man. 71.04
is greedy for u. gain makes Pro 15.27
he who hates u. gain will prolong 28.16
An u. man is an abomination to the 29.27
every one is greedy for u. gain; Jer 6.13
every one is greedy for u. gain; 8.10
but the u. knows no shame. Zep 3.05
rain on the just and on the u. Mt 5.45
u., adulterers, or even like this Lk 18.11
of both the just and the u. Ac 24.15
That God is u. to inflict wrath on Rom 3.05
For God is not so u. as to overlook Heb 6.10

UNJUSTLY
will you judge u. and show partiality Ps 82.02
he endures pain while suffering u. 1Pe 2.19

UNKNOWN
plenty will be u. in the land by Gen 41.31
this inscription, 'To an u. god.' Ac 17.23
what therefore you worship as u., 17.23
as u., and yet well known; 2Co 6.09

UNLAWFUL
know how u. it is for a Jew to Ac 10.28

UNLEAVENED
and baked u. bread, and they ate. Gen 19.03
with u. bread and bitter herbs they Ex 12.08
Seven days you shall eat u. bread; 12.15
observe the feast of u. bread, 12.17
you shall eat u. bread, and so until 12.18
dwellings you shall eat u. bread." 12.20
And they baked u. cakes of the 12.39
Seven days you shall eat u. bread, 13.06
U. bread shall be eaten for seven 13.07
You shall keep the feast of u. bread; 23.15
you shall eat u. bread for seven 23.15
and u. bread, u. cakes mixed with oil, 29.02
and u. wafers spread with oil. 29.02
the basket of u. bread that is 29.23
"The feast of u. bread you shall 34.18
seven days you shall eat u. bread, 34.18
it shall be u. cakes of fine flour Lev 2.04
or u. wafers spread with oil. 2.04
it shall be of fine flour u., 2.05
shall be eaten u. in a holy place; 6.16
thank offering u. cakes mixed with 7.12
u. wafers spread with oil, and cakes 7.12
rams, and the basket of u. bread; 8.02
the basket of u. bread which was 8.26
the LORD he took one u. cake, 8.26
and eat it u. beside the altar, for 10.12
is the feast of u. bread to the 23.06
seven days you shall eat u. bread. 23.06
and a basket of u. bread, Num 6.15
and u. wafers spread with oil, and 6.15
LORD, with the basket of u. bread; 6.17
and one u. cake out of the basket, 6.19
and one u. wafer, and shall put them 6.19
eat it with u. bread and bitter 9.11
seven days shall u. bread be eaten. 28.17
you shall eat it with u. bread, Deu 16.03
For six days you shall eat u. bread; 16.08
choose: at the feast of u. bread, 16.16
u. cakes and parched grain. Jos 5.11
and u. cakes from an ephah of flour; Ju 6.19
"Take the meat and the u. cakes, 6.20
touched the meat and the u. cakes; 6.21
consumed the flesh and the u. cakes; 6.21
it and baked u. bread of it, 1Sa 28.24
but they ate u. bread among their 2Ki 23.09
the wafers of u. bread, the baked 1Ch 23.29
the feast of u. bread, the feast of 2Ch 8.13
the feast of u. bread in the 30.13
the feast of u. bread seven days 30.21
the feast of u. bread seven days. 35.17
the feast of u. bread seven days Ez 6.22
for seven days u. bread shall be Eze 45.21
first day of U. Bread the disciples Mt 26.17
Passover and the feast of U. Bread. Mk 14.01
And on the first day of U. Bread, 14.12
Now the feast of U. Bread drew near, Lk 22.01
Then came the day of U. Bread, 22.07
was during the days of U. Bread. Ac 12.03
Philippi after the days of U. Bread, 20.06
fresh dough, as you really are u. 1Co 5.07
but with the u. bread of sincerity 5.08

UNLESS
not let you go, u. you bless me." Gen 32.26
from this place u. your youngest 42.15
my face, u. your brother is with you.' 43.03
my face, u. your brother is with you.'" 43.05
'U. your youngest brother comes 44.23
the man's face u. our youngest 44.26
not let you go u. compelled by a Ex 3.19
the holy things u. he has bathed Lev 22.06
u. their Rock had sold them, and the Deu 32.30
u. you destroy the devoted things Jos 7.12
u. you had made haste and come to 1Sa 25.34
u. you first bring Michal, Saul's 2Sa 3.13
the pace for me u. I tell you." 2Ki 4.24
u. the king delighted in her and Est 2.14
U. the LORD builds the house, those Ps 127.01
U. the LORD watches over the city, 127.01
cannot sleep u. they have done Pro 4.16
robbed of sleep u. they have made 4.16
u. the Lord has ordained it? Lam 3.37
this Daniel u. we find it in Dan 6.05
u. they have made an appointment? Amo 3.03
befall a city, u. the LORD has done it? 3.06
u. your righteousness exceeds that Mt 5.20
u. he first binds the strong man? 12.29
u. you turn and become like children, 18.03
if this cannot pass u. I drink it, 26.42
u. he first binds the strong man; Mk 3.27
do not eat u., they wash their hands, 7.03
they do not eat u. they purify 7.04
u. we are to go and buy food for Lk 9.13
but u. you repent you will all 13.03
but u. you repent you will all 13.05
that you do, u. God is with him." Jn 3.02
u. one is born anew, he cannot see 3.03
u. one is born of water and the 3.05
"U. you see signs and wonders you 4.48
can come to me u. the Father who 6.44
u. you eat the flesh of the Son of 6.53
can come to me u. it is granted 6.65
in your sins u. you believe that I 8.24
u. a grain of wheat falls into the 12.24
u. it abides in the vine, neither 15.04
can you, u. you abide in me. 15.04
power over me u. it had been given 19.11
"U. I see in his hands the print of 20.25
u. some one guides me?" And he invited Ac 8.31
"U. you are circumcised according 15.01
"U. these men stay in the ship, you 27.31
can men preach u. they are sent? Rom 10.15
u. some one interprets, so that the 1Co 14.05
I benefit you u. I bring you some 14.06
it fast—u. you believed in vain. 15.02
does not come to life u. it dies. 15.36
u. indeed you fail to meet the 2Co 13.05
u. the rebellion comes first, and 2Th 2.03
is not crowned u. he competes 2Ti 2.05
from its place, u. you repent. Rev 2.05
u. they repent of her doings; 2.22
can buy or sell u. he has the mark, 13.17

UNLIFTED
covenant, that same veil remains u., 2Co 3.14

UNLOAD
there the ship was to u. its cargo. Ac 21.03

UNLOVED
an u. woman when she gets a husband, Pro 30.23

UNMARRIED
for brother or u. sister they may Eze 44.25
And he had four u. daughters, Ac 21.09
To the u. and the widows I say that 1Co 7.08
Now concerning the u., I have no 7.25
The u. man is anxious about the 7.32
And the u. woman or girl is anxious 7.34

UNMINDFUL
You were u. of the Rock that begot Deu 32.18

UNMIXED
poured u. into the cup of his anger, Rev 14.10

UNMOVED
yet his bow remained u., his arms were Gen 49.24

UNNATURAL
exchanged natural relations for u., Rom 1.26
immorally and indulged in u. lust, Jud 1.07

UNNI
U., Eliab, Benaiah, Maaseiah, Mattithiah, 1Ch 15.18
U., Eliab, Maaseiah, and Benaiah were 15.20

UNNO
And Bakbukiah and U. their brethren Neh 12.09

UNPLEASANT
do not delay when the matter is u., Ecc 8.03

UNPRESENTABLE
and our u. parts are treated with 1Co 12.23

UNPROFITABLE
Should he argue in u. talk, Job 15.03
law, for they are u. and futile. Tit 3.09

UNPUNISHED
none who touches her will go u. Pro 6.29
assured, an evil man will not go u., 11.21
be assured, he will not go u. 16.05
is glad at calamity will not go u. 17.05
A false witness will not go u., 19.05
A false witness will not go u., 19.09
hastens to be rich will not go u. 28.20
by my name, and shall you go u.? Jer 25.29
You shall not go u., for I am 25.29
I will by no means leave you u. 30.11
I will by no means leave you u." 46.28
cup must drink it, will you go u.? 49.12
You shall not go u., but you must 49.12
Those who buy them slay them and go u.; Zec 11.05

UNQUENCHABLE
chaff he will burn with u. fire." Mt 3.12
to go to hell, to the u. fire. Mk 9.43
chaff he will burn with the u. fire." Lk 3.17

UNREASONABLE
For it seems to me u., in sending a Ac 25.27

UNRELENTING
the nations in anger with u. persecution. Is 14.06

UNREST
but u. to the inhabitants of Babylon. Jer 50.34

UNRIGHTEOUS
rises up against me be as the u. Job 27.07
I broke the fangs of the u., 29.17
Does not calamity befall the u., 31.03
and the u. man his thoughts; Is 55.07
yourselves by means of u. mammon, Lk 16.09
not been faithful in the u. mammon, 16.11
said, "Hear what the u. judge says, 18.06
law before the u. instead of the 1Co 6.01
know that the u. will not inherit 6.09
tongue is an u. world among our Jas 3.06
for all, the righteous for the u., 1Pe 3.18
and to keep the u. under punishment 2Pe 2.09

UNRIGHTEOUSNESS
if you remove u. far from your Job 22.23
my rock, and there is no u. in him. Ps 92.15
"Woe to him who builds his house by u., Jer 22.13
in the u. of your trade you profaned Eze 28.18

UNRIGHTEOUSNESS (cont.)
the truth but had pleasure in u. 2Th 2.12
sins and cleanse us from all u. 1Jn 1.09

UNRIPE
He will shake off his u. grape, like the vine, Job 15.33

UNSATISFIED
leave the craving of the hungry u., Is 32.06

UNSAVOURY
of Samaria I saw an u. thing: they prophesied Jer 23.13

UNSEARCHABLE
who does great things and u., Job 5.09
the number of his years is u. 36.26
praised, and his greatness is u. Ps 145.03
depth, so the mind of kings is u. Pro 25.03
weary, his understanding is u. Is 40.28
How u. are his judgments and how Rom 11.33
Gentiles the u. riches of Christ, Eph 3.08

UNSEEN
yet thy footprints were u. Ps 77.19
seen but to the things that are u.; 2Co 4.18
the things that are u. are eternal. 4.18
by God concerning events as yet u., Heb 11.07

UNSETTLE
I wish those who u. you would mutilate Gal 5.12

UNSETTLING
u. your minds, although we gave them Ac 15.24

UNSHAKEN
Our hope for you is u.; for we know 2Co 1.07

UNSHEATHE
and I will u. the sword after you; Lev 26.33
and I will u. the sword after them. Eze 5.02
winds and will u. the sword after 5.12
and I will u. the sword after them. 12.14

UNSHOD
feet from going u. and your throat Jer 2.25

UNSHRUNK
puts a piece of u. cloth on an old Mt 9.16
sews a piece of u. cloth on an old Mk 2.21

UNSKILLED
Even if I am u. in speaking, I am 2Co 11.06
on milk is u. in the word of Heb 5.13

UNSOLD
While it remained u., did it not Ac 5.04

UNSOWN
u., and growing nothing, where no Deu 29.23

UNSPARING
I would even exult in pain u.; for I have Job 6.10

UNSPIRITUAL
The u. man does not receive the 1Co 2.14
but is earthly, u., devilish. Jas 3.15

UNSTABLE
U. as water, you shall not have pre-eminence Gen 49.04
u. in all his ways, will receive Jas 1.07
ignorant and u. twist to their own 2Pe 3.16

UNSTAINED
the commandment u. and free from 1Ti 6.14
u., separated from sinners, exalted Heb 7.26
to keep oneself u. from the world. Jas 1.27

UNSTEADY
insatiable for sin. They entice u. souls. 2Pe 2.14

UNSTOPPED
be opened, and the ears of the deaf u.; Is 35.05

UNSUSPECTING
quiet and u., lacking nothing that is in the Ju 18.07
go, you will come to an u. people. 18.10
to Laish, to a people quiet and u., 18.27
me to terrify the u. Ethiopians; Eze 30.09

UNTIE
u. them and bring them to me. Mt 21.02
am not worthy to stoop down and u. Mk 1.07
has ever sat; u. it and bring it. 11.02
sandals I am not worthy to u.; Lk 3.16
on the sabbath u. his ox or his 13.15
has ever sat; u. it and bring it here. 19.30
whose sandal I am not worthy to u." Jn 1.27
whose feet I am not worthy to u.' Ac 13.25

UNTIED
in the open street; and they u. it. Mk 11.04

UNTIL
to abate u. the tenth month; Gen 8.05
went to and fro u. the waters were 8.07
I have not heard of it u. today." 21.26
u. they have done drinking." 24.19
"I will not eat u. I have told my 24.33
more and more u. he became very 26.13
u. your brother's fury turns away; 27.44
u. your brother's anger turns away, 27.45
not leave you u. I have done that 28.15
"We cannot u. all the flocks are 29.08
with Laban, and stayed u. now; 32.04
with him u. the breaking of the 32.24
seven times, u. he came near his brother. 33.03
children, u. I come to my lord in Seir." 33.14
Jacob held his peace u. they came. 34.05
garment by her u. his master came 39.16
u. he ceased to measure it, for it 41.49
cattle from our youth even u. now, 46.34
u. he comes to whom it belongs; 49.10
from the day it was founded u. now. Ex 9.18
serve the LORD u. we arrive there." 10.26
shall keep it u. the fourteenth 12.06
none of it remain u. the morning, 12.10
that remains u. the morning you 12.10
the first day u. the seventh day, 12.15
and so u. the twenty-first day of 12.18
door of his house u. the morning. 12.22
were steady u. the going down of 17.12
of my feast remain u. the morning. 23.18
u. you are increased and possess 23.30
u. we come to you again; and, behold, 24.14
remain u. the morning, then you 29.34
u. he had gone into the tent. 33.08
with my hand u. I have passed by; 33.22
passover be left u. the morning. 34.25
took the veil off, u. he came out; 34.34
u. he went in to speak with him. 34.35
the altar all night u. the morning, Lev 6.09
not leave any of it u. the morning. 7.15
u. the days of your ordination are 8.33
shall be unclean u. the evening, 11.24
and be unclean u. the evening. 11.25
shall be unclean u. the evening, 11.27
and be unclean u. the evening; 11.28
shall be unclean u. the evening. 11.31
it shall be unclean u. the evening; 11.32
shall be unclean u. the evening, 11.39
and be unclean u. the evening; 11.40
u. the days of her purifying are 12.04
up shall be unclean u. the evening; 14.46
and be unclean u. the evening. 15.05
and be unclean u. the evening. 15.06
and be unclean u. the evening. 15.07
and be unclean u. the evening. 15.08
shall be unclean u. the evening; 15.10

UNTIL (cont.)
and be unclean u. the evening. Lev 15.11
and be unclean u. the evening. 15.16
and be unclean u. the evening. 15.17
and be unclean u. the evening. 15.18
shall be unclean u. the evening. 15.19
and be unclean u. the evening. 15.21
and be unclean u. the evening; 15.22
he shall be unclean u. the evening. 15.23
and be unclean u. the evening. 15.27
the holy place u. he comes out and 16.17
and be unclean u. the evening; 17.15
left over u. the third day shall 19.06
with you all night u. the morning. 19.13
of the holy things u. he is clean. 22.04
be unclean u. the evening and 22.06
shall leave none of it u. morning: 22.30
parched or fresh u. this same day, 23.14
u. you have brought the offering of 23.14
u. the ninth year, when its produce 25.22
who bought it u. the year of 25.28
serve with you u. the year of the 25.40
himself to him u. the year of 25.50
but a few years u. the year of 25.52
that remain u. the year of jubilee, 27.18
u. the time is completed for which Num 6.05
leave none of it u. the morning, 9.12
the appearance of fire u. morning. 9.15
remained from evening u. morning; 9.21
u. it comes out at your nostrils 11.20
people, from Egypt even u. now." 14.19
u. the last of your dead bodies 14.33
priest shall be unclean u. evening. 19.07
and shall be unclean u. evening. 19.08
clothes, and be unclean u. evening. 19.10
impurity shall be unclean u. evening. 19.21
it shall be unclean u. evening. 19.22
u. we have passed through your 20.17
u. we have passed through your 21.22
we laid waste u. fire spread to 21.30
u. there was not one survivor left 21.35
u. all the generation that had done 32.13
u. we have brought them to their 32.17
to our homes u. the people of 32.18
u. he has driven out his enemies 32.21
may not die u. he stands before 35.12
live in it u. the death of the 35.25
city of refuge u. the death of the 35.28
that you went u. you came to this Deu 1.31
Kadeshbarnea u. we crossed the 2.14
u. the entire generation, that is, 2.14
from the camp, u. they had perished. 2.15
u. I go over the Jordan into the 2.29
we smote him u. no survivor was 3.03
u. the LORD gives rest to your 3.20
u. those who are left and hide 7.20
great confusion, u. they are destroyed. 7.23
against you, u. you have destroyed them. 7.24
u. you came to this place, you have 9.07
u. it was as fine as dust; and I threw 9.21
wilderness, u. you came to this place; 11.05
day remain all night u. morning. 16.04
makes war with you, u. it falls. 20.20
be with you u. your brother seeks 22.02
u. you are destroyed and perish 28.20
cleave to you u. he has consumed 28.21
shall pursue you u. you perish. 28.22
down upon you u. you are destroyed. 28.24
your neck, u. he has destroyed you. 28.48
u. you are destroyed; who also 28.51
u. they have caused you to perish. 28.51
u. your high and fortified walls, in 28.52
upon you, u. you are destroyed. 28.61
of this song u. they were finished, 31.30
u. the pursuers returned; for the pursuers 2.22
u. the LORD gives rest to your Jos 1.15
u. the pursuers have returned; 2.16

u. all the nation finished passing 3.17
u. everything was finished that the 4.10
Jordan for you u. you passed over, 4.23
dried up for us u. we passed over, 4.23
of Israel u. they had crossed over, 5.01
u. the day I bid you shout; then you shall 6.10
the ark of the LORD u. the evening, 7.06
u. you take away the devoted things 7.13
u. there was left none that survived 8.22
u. he had utterly destroyed all the 8.26
king of Ai on a tree u. evening; 8.29
u. the nation took vengeance on 10.13
u. they were wiped out, and when the 10.20
hung upon the trees u. evening; 10.26
his people, u. he left none remaining. 10.33
smote them, u. they left none remaining. 11.08
u. they had destroyed them, and they 11.14
in that city u. he has stood before the 20.06
u. the death of him who is high 20.06
u. he have destroyed you from off 23.15
u. they destroyed Jabin king of Ju 4.24
they ceased u. you arose, Deborah, 5.07
u. I come to thee, and bring out my 6.18
"U. now you have mocked me, and told 16.13
for u. then no inheritance among 18.01
of the Danites u. the day of the 18.30
and tarry u. the day declines." 19.08
her all night u. the morning. 19.25
of the land of Egypt u. this day; 19.30
before the LORD u. the evening; 20.23
and fasted that day u. evening, 20.26
of them went on u. they came to Ru 1.19
continued from early morning u. now, 2.07
and she ate u. she was satisfied, 2.14
gleaned in the field u. evening; 2.17
gleaning u. the end of the barley 2.23
to the man u. he has finished 3.03
kin for you. Lie down u. the morning." 3.13
she lay at his feet u. the morning, 3.14
u. you learn how the matter turns 3.18
wait u. you have weaned him; 1Sa 1.23
nursed her son, u. she weaned him. 1.23
Samuel lay u. morning; then he opened 3.15
kept for you u. the hour appointed, 9.24
u. I come to you and show you what 10.08
the Ammonites u. the heat of the 11.11
you from my youth u. this day. 12.02
'Wait u. we come to you,' then we 14.09
who eats food u. it is evening and 14.24
despoil them u. the morning light; 14.36
against them u. they are consumed." 15.18
see Saul again u. the day of his 15.35
u. he came to Naioth in Ramah. 19.23
one another, u. David recovered himself. 20.41
nothing at all u. the morning 25.36
day I entered your service u. now, 29.08
u. they had no more strength to 30.04
from twilight u. the evening of 30.17
wept and fasted u. evening for 2Sa 1.12
at Jericho u. your beards have 10.05
pressed him u. he let Amnon and 13.27
u. the people had all passed out of 15.24
u. word comes from you to inform me." 15.28
u. not even a pebble is to be found 17.13
upon you from your youth u. now." 19.07
king departed u. the day he came 19.24
were shut up u. the day of their 20.03
of harvest u. rain fell upon them 21.10
not turn back u. they were consumed. 22.38
the Philistines u. his hand was 23.10
the morning u. the appointed time; 24.15
u. he had finished building his own 1Ki 3.01
u. the LORD put them under the 5.03
u. all the house was finished. 6.22
the reports u. I came and my own 10.07
u. he had cut off every male in 11.16
was in Egypt u. the death of 11.40

UNTIL (cont.)
burns up dung u. it is all gone. 1Ki 14.10
u. he had destroyed it, according to 15.29
u. the day that the LORD sends rain 17.14
name of Baal from morning u. noon, 18.26
u. the blood gushed out upon them. 18.28
they raved on u. the time of the 18.29
the Syrians u. they are destroyed.'" 22.11
and water, u. I come in peace."'" 22.27
u. at evening he died; and the blood 22.35
threw a stone, u. it was covered; 2Ki 3.25
u. an ass's head was sold for 6.25
silent and wait u. the morning 7.09
day that she left the land u. now." 8.06
stared at him, u. he was ashamed. 8.11
entrance of the gate u. the morning." 10.08
u. he left him none remaining. 10.11
in Aphek u. you have made an end 13.17
down Syria u. you had made an end 13.19
cast them from his presence u. now. 13.23
u. he had cast them out of his 17.20
u. the LORD removed Israel out of 17.23
own land to Assyria u. this day. 17.23
for u. those days the people of 18.04
u. I come and take you away to a 18.32
were their cities u. David reigned. 1Ch 4.31
dwelt in their place u. the exile. 5.22
u. Solomon had built the house of 6.32
u. there was a great army, like an 12.22
at Jericho u. your beards have 19.05
u. all the work for the service of 28.20
LORD was laid u. it was finished. 2Ch 8.16
the reports u. I came and my own 9.06
Ethiopians fell u. none remained 14.13
was no more war u. the thirty-fifth 15.19
the Syrians u. they are destroyed.'" 18.10
and water, u. I return in peace.'" 18.26
facing the Syrians u. evening; 18.34
for themselves u. they could carry 20.25
u. your bowels come out because of 21.15
into the chest u. they had finished 24.10
this continued u. the burnt offering 29.28
so u. other priests had sanctified 29.34
u. the work was finished—for the 29.34
u. they had destroyed them all. 31.01
offerings and the fat parts u. night; 35.14
and to his sons u. the establishment 36.20
u. the land had enjoyed its sabbaths. 36.21
u. there should be a priest to Ez 2.63
even u. the reign of Darius king of 4.05
not rebuilt, u. a decree is made by me. 4.21
and it ceased u. the second year 4.24
from that time u. now it has been 5.16
and keep them u. you weigh them 8.29
I sat appalled u. the evening 9.04
me pass through u. I come to Judah; Neh 2.07
be opened u. the sun is hot; 7.03
u. a priest with Urim and Thummim 7.65
Gate from early morning u. midday, 8.03
the kings of Assyria u. this day. 9.32
the priests u. the reign of Darius 12.22
the Chronicles u. the days of 12.23
not be opened u. after the sabbath. 13.19
conceal me u. thy wrath be past, Job 14.13
u. I went into the sanctuary of God; Ps 73.17
u. a pit is dug for the wicked. 94.13
and to his labor u. the evening. 104.23
u. what he had said came to pass 105.19
u. he sees his desire on his adversaries. 112.08
u. I find a place for the LORD, a 132.05
brighter and brighter u. full day. Pro 4.18
u. the other comes and examines him. 18.17
let him be a fugitive u. death; let no one 28.17
up nor awaken love u. it please. Sol 2.07
U. the day breathes and the shadows 2.17
not let him go u. I had brought 3.04
up nor awaken love u. it please. 3.05
U. the day breathes and the shadows 4.06
up nor awaken love u. it please. 8.04
u. there is no more room, and you Is 5.08
"U. cities lie waste without inhabitant, 6.11
a little while u. the wrath is 26.20
little while u. Lebanon shall be 29.17
u. the Spirit is poured upon us 32.15
u. I come and take you away to a 36.17
I cry for help u. morning; like a lion 38.13
u. her vindication goes forth as 62.01
him no rest u. he establishes 62.07
and u. the end of the eleventh year Jer 1.03
u. the captivity of Jerusalem in 1.03
after them, u. I have consumed them." 9.16
not turn back u. he has executed 23.20
u. they shall be utterly destroyed 24.10
u. the time of his own land comes; 27.07
u. I have consumed it by his hand. 27.08
remain there u. the day when I 27.22
not turn back u. he has executed 30.24
he shall remain u. I visit him, 32.05
from the days of Josiah u. today. 36.02
u. the entire scroll was consumed 36.23
u. all the bread of the city was 37.21
of the guard u. the day that 38.28
u. there is an end of them. 44.27
after them, u. I have consumed them; 49.37
u. the day of his death as long as 52.34
u. the LORD from heaven looks down Lam 3.50
a trace of it u. he comes whose Eze 21.27
gate shall not be shut u. evening. 46.02
continued u. the first year of Dan 1.21
u. you have learned that the Most 4.32
u. he knew that the Most High God 5.21
u. the Ancient of Days came, and 7.22
u. the decreed end is poured out on 9.27
u. the time of the end, for it is 11.35
u. the time of the end. Many shall 12.04
up and sealed u. the time of the 12.09
u. they acknowledge their guilt and Hos 5.15
of the dough u. it is leavened. 7.04
the capitals u. the thresholds Amo 9.01
give them up u. the time when she Mic 5.03
u. he pleads my cause and executes 7.09
but knew her not u. she had borne a Mt 1.25
and remained there u. the death of 2.15
from the law u. all is accomplished 5.18
and stay with him u. you depart. 10.11
the Baptist u. now the kingdom of 11.12
and the law prophesied u. John; 11.13
it would have remained u. this day. 11.23
Let both grow together u. the harvest; 13.30
u. the Son of man is raised from 17.09
u. you say, 'Blessed be he who comes 23.39
the beginning of the world u. now, 24.21
u. the day when Noah entered the 24.38
did not know u. the flood came and 24.39
of the vine u. that day when I 26.29
all the land u. the ninth hour. 27.45
to be made secure u. the third day, 27.64
stay there u. you leave the place. Mk 6.10
u. the Son of man should have risen 9.09
creation which God created u. now, 13.19
of the vine u. that day when I 14.25
the whole land u. the ninth hour. 15.33
unable to speak u. the day that Lk 1.20
from him u. an opportune time. 4.13
am constrained u. it is accomplished! 12.50
you will not see me u. you say, 13.35
one which is lost, u. he finds it? 15.04
seek diligently u. she finds it? 15.08
"The law and the prophets were u. John; 16.16
u. the day when Noah entered the 17.27
u. the times of the Gentiles are 21.24
not eat it u. it is fulfilled in 22.16
of the vine u. the kingdom of God 22.18
u. you three times deny that you 22.34

UNTIL (cont.)
the whole land u. the ninth hour, Lk 23.44
u. you are clothed with power from 24.49
you have kept the good wine u. now." Jn 2.10
u. they called the parents of the 9.18
my will that he remain u. I come, 21.22
my will that he remain u. I come, 21.23
u. the day when he was taken up, Ac 1.02
baptism of John u. the day when he 1.22
must receive u. the time for establishing 3.21
put them in custody u. the morrow, 4.03
So it was u. the days of David, 7.45
them judges u. Samuel the prophet. 13.20
prolonged his speech u. midnight. 20.07
long while, u. daybreak, and so departed. 20.11
him to be held u. I could send him 25.21
groaning in travail together u. now; Rom 8.22
u. the full number of the Gentiles 11.25
the Lord's death u. he comes. 1Co 11.26
For he must reign u. he has put all 15.25
will stay in Ephesus u. Pentecost, 16.08
under restraint u. faith should be Gal 3.23
was our custodian u. Christ came, 3.24
and trustees u. the date set by 4.02
in travail u. Christ be formed in 4.19
our inheritance u. we acquire Eph 1.14
u. we all attain to the unity of 4.13
gospel from the first day u. now. Php 1.05
who are left u. the coming of the 1Th 4.15
it will do so u. he is out of the 2Th 2.07
from reproach u. the appearing of 1Ti 6.14
able to guard u. that Day what has 2Ti 1.12
full assurance of hope u. the end, Heb 6.11
body imposed u. the time of reformation. 9.10
then to wait u. his enemies should 10.13
u. the coming of the Lord. Behold, Jas 5.07
patient over it u. it receives the 5.07
u. the day dawns and the morning 2Pe 1.19
gloom to be kept u. the judgment; 2.04
punishment u. the day of judgment, 2.09
being kept u. the day of judgment 3.07
nether gloom u. the judgment of Jud 1.06
hold fast what you have, u. I come. Rev 2.25
and who keeps my works u. the end, 2.26
u. the number of their fellow servants 6.11
the temple u. the seven plagues of 15.08
u. the words of God shall be 17.17
to life again u. the thousand 20.05

UNTIMELY
why was I not as a hidden u. birth, Job 3.16
like the u. birth that never sees Ps 58.08
I say that an u. birth is better Ecc 6.03
sepulchre, like a loathed u. birth, Is 14.19
as to one u. born, he appeared also 1Co 15.08

UNTRAINED
I was chastened, like an u. calf; bring me Jer 31.18

UNTRUE
would have been u. to the generation Ps 73.15

UNTYING
to them, "What are you doing, u. the colt?" Mk 11.05
one asks you, 'Why are you u. it?' you shall Lk 19.31
And as they were u. the colt, its owners 19.33
to them, "Why are you u. the colt?" 19.33

UNUSUAL
And the natives showed us u. kindness, for Ac 28.02

UNUTTERABLE
him and rejoice with u. and exalted joy. 1Pe 1.08

UNVEILED
with her head u. dishonors her 1Co 11.05
with u. face, beholding the glory of 2Co 3.18

UNWALLED
besides very many u. villages. Deu 3.05
fortified cities and u. villages. 1Sa 6.18
up against the land of u. villages; Eze 38.11

UNWASHED
but to eat with u. hands does not Mt 15.20
with hands defiled, that is, u. Mk 7.02

UNWEIGHED
And Solomon left all the vessels u., because 1Ki 7.47

UNWILLING
the LORD was u. to destroy you. Deu 10.10
And if you be u. to serve the LORD, Jos 24.15
and he was u. to take one of his 2Sa 12.04
a just man and u. to put her to Mt 1.19
and I am u. to send them away hungry, 15.32

UNWISE
come for him, but he is an u. son; Hos 13.13
not as u. men but as wise, Eph 5.15

UNWITTINGLY
If any one sins u. in any of the Lev 4.02
commits a sin u. and the thing is 4.13
doing u. any one of all the things 4.22
people sins u. in doing any one of 4.27
faith and sins u. in any of the 5.15
the error which he committed u., 5.18
And if a man eats of a holy thing u., 22.14
then if it was done u. without the Num 15.24
"If one person sins u., he shall 15.27
when he sins u., to make atonement 15.28
law for him who does anything u., 15.29
intent or u. may flee there; they shall Jos 20.03
because he killed his neighbor u., 20.05

UNWORTHY
you, say, 'We are u. servants; Lk 17.10
yourselves u. of eternal life, Ac 13.46
the Lord in an u. manner will be 1Co 11.27

UPBRAID
Then he began to u. the cities where most Mt 11.20

UPBRAIDED
Then Jacob became angry, and u. Laban; Gen 31.36
with Midian?" And they u. him violently. Ju 8.01
and he u. them for their unbelief and * Mk 16.14

UPBUILDING
makes for peace and for mutual u. Rom 14.19
men for their u. and encouragement 1Co 14.03
and all for your u., beloved. 2Co 12.19

UPBUILDS
makes bodily growth and u. itself in love. Eph 4.16

UPHAZ
from Tarshish, and gold from U. Jer 10.09
loins were girded with gold of U. Dan 10.05

UPHELD
Your words have u. him who was Job 4.04
But thou hast u. me because of my Ps 41.12
his throne is u. by righteousness. Pro 20.28
and his righteousness u. him. Is 59.16
me victory, and my wrath u. me. 63.05
And he will be u., for the Master Rom 14.04

UPHOLD
and u. me with a willing spirit. Ps 51.12
U. me according to thy promise, that 119.116
and to u. it with justice and with Is 9.07
I will u. you with my victorious 41.10
whom I u., my chosen, in whom my 42.01
appalled, but there was no one to u.; 63.05
There is none to u. your cause, Jer 30.13
On the contrary, we u. the law. Rom 3.31

UPHOLDER
my helper; the Lord is the u. of my life. Ps 54.04

UPHOLDING
u. the universe by his word of power. Heb 1.03

UPHOLDS
but the LORD u. the righteous. Ps 37.17
clings to thee; thy right hand u. me. 63.08
The LORD u. all who are falling, and 145.14
he u. the widow and the fatherless; 146.09

UPLIFTED
withheld, and their u. arm is broken. Job 38.15
and with u. arm he led them out of Ac 13.17

UPPER
he shall cover his u. lip and cry, Lev 13.45
a mill or an u. millstone in Deu 24.06
gave her the u. springs and the Jos 15.19
Atarothaddar as far as u. Bethhoron, 16.05
gave her the u. springs and the Ju 1.15
woman threw an u. millstone upon 9.53
the leg and the u. portion and set 1Sa 9.24
a woman cast an u. millstone upon 2Sa 11.21
carried him up into the u. chamber, 1Ki 17.19
down from the u. chamber into the 17.23
lattice in his u. chamber in 2Ki 1.02
He built the u. gate of the house 15.35
by the conduit of the u. pool, 18.17
the roof of the u. chamber of Ahaz, 23.12
built both lower and u. Bethhoron, 1Ch 7.24
its u. rooms, and its inner chambers, 28.11
he overlaid the u. chambers with 2Ch 3.09
He also built U. Bethhoron and 8.05
through the u. gate to the king's 23.20
He built the u. gate of the house 27.03
closed the u. outlet of the waters 32.30
from the u. house of the king at Neh 3.25
and to the u. chamber of the corner 3.31
And between the u. chamber of the 3.32
At the u. entrance they hacked the Ps 74.05
conduit of the u. pool on the Is 7.03
conduit of the u. pool on the 36.02
were in the u. Benjamin Gate of Jer 20.02
and his u. rooms by injustice; 22.13
great house with spacious u. rooms, 22.14
secretary, which was in the u. court, 36.10
from the direction of the u. gate, Eze 9.02
Now the u. chambers were narrower, 42.05
hence the u. chambers were set back 42.06
windows in his u. chamber open Dan 6.10
who builds his u. chambers in the Amo 9.06
you a large u. room furnished and Mk 14.15
show you a large u. room furnished; Lk 22.12
they went up to the u. room, Ac 1.13
her, they laid her in an u. room. 9.37
come, they took him to the u. room. 9.39
through the u. country and came to 19.01
lights in the u. chamber where we 20.08

UPPERMOST
and in the u. basket there were all Gen 40.17

UPRIGHT
lo, my sheaf arose and stood u.; Gen 37.07
"And you shall make u. frames for Ex 26.15
Then he made the u. frames for the 36.20
and may the LORD be with the u.!" 2Ch 19.11
were more u. in heart than the 29.34
and that man was blameless and u., Job 1.01
the earth, a blameless and u. man, 1.08
the earth, a blameless and u. man, 2.03
Or where were the u. cut off? 4.07
if you are pure and u., surely then 8.06
U. men are appalled at this, and the 17.08
There an u. man could reason with 23.07
God, who saves the u. in heart. Ps 7.10
in the dark at the u. in heart; 11.02
the u. shall behold his face. 11.07
but we shall rise and stand u. 20.08
Good and u. is the LORD; therefore 25.08
shout for joy, all you u. in heart! 32.11
righteous! Praise befits the u. 33.01
For the word of the LORD is u.; 33.04
thy salvation to the u. of heart! 36.10
blameless man, and behold the u., 37.37
Let all the u. in heart glory! 64.10
Truly God is good to the u., 73.01
With u. heart he tended them, and 78.72
to show that the LORD is u.; 92.15
and all the u. in heart will follow 94.15
and joy for the u. in heart. 97.11
The u. see it and are glad; 107.42
heart, in the company of the u., 111.01
generation of the u. will be 112.02
Light rises in the darkness for the u.; 112.04
I will praise thee with an u. heart, 119.07
those who are u. in their hearts! 125.04
the u. shall dwell in thy presence. 140.13
he stores up sound wisdom for the u.; Pro 2.07
For the u. will inhabit the land, 2.21
but the u. are in his confidence. 3.32
stronghold to him whose way is u., 10.29
The integrity of the u. guides them, 11.03
righteousness of the u. delivers them, 11.06
blessing of the u. a city is 11.11
the mouth of the u. delivers men. 12.06
Righteousness guards him whose way is u., 13.06
but the u. enjoy his favor. 14.09
the tent of the u. will flourish. 14.11
prayer of the u. is his delight. 15.08
the path of the u. is a level 15.19
The highway of the u. turns aside 16.17
and the faithless for the u. 21.18
but an u. man considers his ways. 21.29
misleads the u. into an evil way 28.10
I found, that God made man u., Ecc 7.29
and stand u., for now I have been Dan 10.11
and the u. walk in them, but transgressors Hos 14.09
and there is none u. among men; Mic 7.02
the most u. of them a thorn hedge. 7.04
soul is not u. in him shall fail, Hab 2.04
an u. and God-fearing man, who is Ac 10.22
loud voice, "Stand u. on your feet." 14.10
u., holy, and self-controlled; Tit 1.08
u., and godly lives in this world, 2.12

UPRIGHTLY
needy, to slay those who walk u.; Ps 37.14
Do you judge the sons of men u.? 58.01
withhold from those who walk u. 84.11
and u. he wrote words of truth. Ecc 12.10
walks righteously and speaks u.; Is 33.15
words do good to him who walks u.? Mic 2.07

UPRIGHTNESS
righteousness or the u. of your Deu 9.05
and in u. of heart toward thee; 1Ki 3.06
with integrity of heart and u., 9.04
the heart, and hast pleasure in u.; 1Ch 29.17
in the u. of my heart I have 29.17
My words declare the u. of my heart, Job 33.03
May integrity and u. preserve me, Ps 25.21
performed with faithfulness and u. 111.08
the paths of u. to walk in the Pro 2.13
I have led you in the paths of u. 4.11
He who walks in u. fears the LORD, 14.02
in the land of u. he deals perversely Is 26.10
in their beds who walk in their u. 57.02
squares, and u. cannot enter. 59.14
and in u., then nations shall bless Jer 4.02
he walked with me in peace and u., Mal 2.06

UPROAR
outcry, he said, "What is this u.?" 1Sa 4.14
"What does this u. in the city mean?" 1Ki 1.41
so that the city is in an u. 1.45
the u. of thy adversaries which Ps 74.23
Hark, an u. of kingdoms, of nations Is 13.04
"Hark, an u. from the city! A voice 66.06
Kerioth, and Moab shall die amid u., Amo 2.02
a crowd, set the city in an u., Ac 17.05
After the u. ceased, Paul sent for 20.01
learn the facts because of the u., 21.34

UPROOT
he will u. you from the land of the Ps 52.05
I will plant them, and not u. them. Jer 24.06

UPROOTED
and the LORD u. them from their Deu 29.28
It shall not be u. or overthrown Jer 31.40
out at noon, and Ekron shall be u. Zep 2.04
in late autumn, twice dead, u.; Jud 1.12

UPSETTING
They are u. the faith of some. 2Ti 2.18
since they are u. whole families Tit 1.11

UPSIDE
and turned it u. down, so that the Ju 7.13
wiping it and turning it u. down. 2Ki 21.13
You turn things u. down! Shall the Is 29.16
the world u. down have come here Ac 17.06

UPSURGING
rain upon you, nor u. of the deep! 2Sa 1.21

UPWARD
from twenty years old and u., Ex 30.14
from twenty years old and u., 38.26
person is sixty years old and u., Lev 27.07
from twenty years old and u., Num 1.03
years old and u., head by head, 1.18
male from twenty years old and u., 1.20
male from twenty years old and u., 1.22
from twenty years old and u., 1.24
from twenty years old and u., 1.26
from twenty years old and u., 1.28
from twenty years old and u., 1.30
from twenty years old and u., 1.32
from twenty years old and u., 1.34
from twenty years old and u., 1.36
from twenty years old and u., 1.38
from twenty years old and u., 1.40
from twenty years old and u., 1.42
from twenty years old and u., 1.45
a month old and u. you shall 3.15
a month old and u. was seven 3.22
the males, from a month old and u., 3.28
a month old and u. was six thousand 3.34
the males from a month old and u., 3.39
of Israel, from a month old and u., 3.40
a month old and u. as numbered 3.43
years old and u. they shall go in 8.24
from twenty years old and u., 14.29
from twenty years old and u., 26.02
from twenty years old and u., 26.04
every male from a month old and u.; 26.62
from twenty years old and u., 32.11
and you shall tend u. only, Deu 28.13
of Akrabbim, from Sela and u. Ju 1.36
his shoulders u. he was taller 1Sa 9.02
the people from his shoulders u. 10.23
crown which projected u. one cubit; 1Ki 7.31
root downward, and bear fruit u.; 2Ki 19.30
The Levites, thirty years old and u., 1Ch 23.03
years old and u. who were to do 23.24
from twenty years old and u.— 23.27
those twenty years old and u., 2Ch 25.05
males from three years old and u., 31.16
years old and u. was according to 31.17
from twenty years old and u., Ez 3.08
to trouble as the sparks fly u. Job 5.07
The wise man's path leads u. to life, Pro 15.24
of man goes u. and the spirit of Ecc 3.21
their God, and turn their faces u.; Is 8.21
and they roll u. in a column of 9.18
root downward, and bear fruit u.; 37.31
my eyes are weary with looking u. 38.14
And u. from what had the appearance Eze 1.27
of the temple a stairway led u., 41.07
the altar hearth projecting u., 43.15
prize of the u. call of God in Php 3.14

UR
his birth, in U. of the Chaldeans. Gen 11.28
together from U. of the Chaldeans 11.31
you from U. of the Chaldeans, to 15.07
Hararite, Eliphal the son of U., 1Ch 11.35
forth out of U. of the Chaldees Neh 9.07

URBANUS
Greet U., our fellow worker in Rom 16.09

URGE
to her servant, "U. the beast on; 2Ki 4.24
Therefore I u. you to take some Ac 27.34
I u. you, then, be imitators of me. 1Co 4.16
I u. you to be subject to such men 16.16
it necessary to u. the brethren to 2Co 9.05
I u. that supplications, prayers, 1Ti 2.01
Teach and u. these duties. 6.02
Likewise u. the younger men to Tit 2.06
I u. you the more earnestly to do Heb 13.19

URGED
But he u. them strongly; so they turned Gen 19.03
the angels u. Lot, saying, "Arise, 19.15
Thus he u. him, and he took it. 33.11
she u. him to ask her father for a Jos 15.18
she u. him to ask her father for a Ju 1.14
and u. him, his soul was vexed to 16.16
up to go, his father-in-law u. him, 19.07
together with the woman, u. him; 1Sa 28.23
But when they u. him till he was 2Ki 2.17
who u. him to eat some food. 4.08
And he u. him to take it, but he refused. 5.16
And he u. him, and tied up two 5.23
u. by the king's command; and the decree Est 8.14
and Gemariah u. the king not to Jer 36.25
to them and u. them to continue in Ac 13.43
against Paul; and they u. him, 25.02
Paul u. them all to take some food, 27.33
I strongly u. him to visit you with 1Co 16.12
Accordingly we have u. Titus that 2Co 8.06
I u. Titus to go, and sent the 12.18
As I u. you when I was going to 1Ti 1.03

URGENT
The taskmasters were u., saying, "Complete Ex 5.13
Egyptians were u. with the people, 12.33
But they were u., saying, "He stirs Lk 23.05
But they were u.. demanding with 23.23
be u. in season and out of season, 2Ti 4.02
so as to help cases of u. need, Tit 3.14

URGENTLY
the prophets whom I send to you u., Jer 26.05

URGES
works for him; his mouth u. him on. Pro 16.26

URI
by name Bezalel the son of U., Ex 31.02
by name Bezalel the son of U., 35.30
Bezalel the son of U., 38.22
Geber the son of U., in the land 1Ki 4.19
Hur was the father of U., and U. was 1Ch 2.20

URI (cont.)
altar that Bezalel the son of U., 2Ch 1.05
gatekeepers: Shallum, Telem, and U. Ez 10.24

URIAH
Eliam, the wife of U. the Hittite?" 2Sa 11.03
to Joab, "Send me U. the Hittite." 11.06
And Joab sent U. to David. 11.06
When U. came to him, David asked how 11.07
Then David said to U., "Go down 11.08
And U. went out of the king's house, 11.08
But U. slept at the door of the 11.09
"U. did not go down to his house," 11.10
David said to U., "Have you not 11.10
U. said to David, "The ark and 11.11
Then David said to U., "Remain here 11.12
So U. remained in Jerusalem that 11.12
and sent it by the hand of U. 11.14
"Set U. in the forefront of the 11.15
he assigned U. to the place where 11.16
U. the Hittite was slain also. 11.17
'Your servant U. the Hittite is 11.21
your servant U. the Hittite is 11.24
When the wife of U. heard that 11.26
heard that U. her husband was dead, 11.26
have smitten U. the Hittite with 12.09
the wife of U. the Hittite to be 12.10
U. the Hittite: thirty-seven in all. 23.39
in the matter of U. the Hittite. 1Ki 15.05
U. the Hittite, Zabad the son of 1Ch 11.41
son of U., and with him was Eleazar Ez 8.33
to them Meremoth the son of U., Neh 3.04
After him Meremoth the son of U., 3.21
U., Hilkiah, and Maaseiah on his 8.04
U. the priest and Zechariah the son Is 8.02
U. the son of Shemaiah from Kiriathjearim. Jer 26.20
but when U. heard of it, he was 26.21
and they fetched U. from Egypt and 26.23
of Solomon by the wife of U., Mt 1.06

URIAH'S
the child that U. wife bore to 2Sa 12.15

URIEL
U. his son, Uzziah his son, and Shaul 1Ch 6.24
U. the chief, with a hundred and 15.05
and Abiathar, and the Levites U., 15.11
the daughter of U. of Gibeah. 2Ch 13.02

URIJAH
Ahaz sent to U. the priest a model 2Ki 16.10
And U. the priest built the altar; 16.11
so U. the priest made it, before 16.11
And King Ahaz commanded U. the priest, 2Ki 16.15
U. the priest did all this, as King 16.16

URIM
shall put the U. and the Thummim, Ex 28.30
he put the U. and the Thummim. Lev 8.08
judgment of the U. before the LORD; Num 27.21
and thy U. to thy godly one, whom Deu 33.08
O LORD, God of Israel, give U.; 1Sa 14.41
by dreams, or by U., or by prophets. 28.06
a priest to consult U. and Thummim. Ez 2.63
a priest with U. and Thummim Neh 7.65

URINE
own dung and to drink their own u.?" 2Ki 18.27
own dung and drink their own u.?" Is 36.12

URN
a golden u. holding the manna, and Heb 9.04

USE
of what u. is a birthright to me?" Gen 25.32
of the tabernacle for every u., Ex 27.19
any like it to u. as perfume shall 30.38
acacia wood of any u. in the work, 35.24
beasts, may be put to any other u., Lev 7.24
whatever be the u. of the skin, 13.51
and you shall u. them for summoning Num 10.02
you shall not u. the fruit of it. Deu 28.30
according to the u. of each lampstand 1Ch 28.15
any person or u. flattery toward Job 32.21
war were unable to u. their hands. Ps 76.05
who deride me u. my name for a 102.08
The poor u. entreaties, but the rich Pro 18.23
and of pleasure, "What u. is it?" Ecc 2.02
yourself with lye and u. much soap, Jer 2.22
who u. their tongues and say, 'Says 23.31
more they shall u. these words in 31.23
u. it as a barber's razor and pass Eze 5.01
shall no more u. it as a proverb 12.23
proverbs will u. this proverb 16.44
of the two ways, to u. divination; 21.21
be for ordinary u. for the city, 48.15
of what parable shall we u. for it? Mk 4.30
why should it u. up the ground?' Lk 13.07
sitting, who could not u. his feet; Ac 14.08
they u. their tongues to deceive. Rom 3.13
beauty and another for menial u.? 9.21
let us u. them: if prophecy, in 12.06
we have not made u. of this right, 1Co 9.12
But I have made no u. of any of 9.15
not making full u. of my right in 9.18
be severe in my u. of the authority 2Co 13.10
only do not u. your freedom as an Gal 5.13
but u. a little wine for the sake 1Ti 5.23
earthenware, and some for noble u., 2Ti 2.20
he will be a vessel for noble u., 2.21
would rather not u. paper and ink, 2Jn 1.12

USED
Now Moses u. to take the tent and Ex 33.07
Thus the LORD u. to speak to Moses 33.11
offering to be u. for the tent of 35.21
All the gold that was u. for the work, 38.24
vessel that is u. for any purpose; Lev 11.32
which are u. in the sanctuary, and Num 4.12
which are u. for the service there, 4.14
they may be u. in doing the 7.05
or u. a stone, by which a man may 35.23
toes cut off u. to pick up scraps Ju 1.07
She u. to sit under the palm of 4.05
for so the young men u. to do. 14.10
new ropes that have not been u., 16.11
Now this man u. to go up year by 1Sa 1.03
And her rival u. to provoke her 1.06
of the LORD, she u. to provoke her. 1.07
And his mother u. to make for him a 2.19
"Your servant u. to keep sheep for 17.34
to go, for he was not u. to them. 17.39
with these; for I am not u. to them." 17.39
it u. to eat of his morsel, and 2Sa 12.03
end of every year he u. to cut it; 14.26
And Absalom u. to rise early and 15.02
a maidservant u. to go and tell 17.17
Solomon u. to offer a thousand 1Ki 3.04
a year Solomon u. to offer up 9.25
of Tarshish u. to come bringing 10.22
Thus he u. to warn him, so that he 2Ki 6.10
of Moabites u. to invade the land 13.20
and u. divination and sorcery, and 17.17
of bronze u. in the temple service, 25.14
off what was u. for the burnt 2Ch 4.06
of Tarshish u. to come bringing 9.21
and had also u. all the dedicated 24.07
that were u. in the king's service, Est 8.10
that were u. in the king's service, 8.14
His sons u. to go and hold a feast Job 1.04
no survivor where he u. to live. 18.19
We u. to hold sweet converse Ps 55.14
I toiled and u. my wisdom under Ecc 2.19
they u. to go in and out of the 8.10
where there u. to be a thousand Is 7.23

USED (cont.)
the hills which u. to be hoed with Is 7.25
a wild ass u. to the wilderness, in Jer 2.24
curse shall be u. by all the 29.22
shall stand where it u. to be. 30.18
In vain you have u. many medicines; 46.11
of bronze u. in the temple service; 52.18
ornament they u. for vainglory, Eze 7.20
was whole, it was u. for nothing; 15.05
can it ever be u. for anything! 15.05
no more be u. by you in Israel. 18.03
and gold which they u. for Baal. Hos 2.08
Now at the feast he u. to release Mk 15.06
this the man who u. to sit and beg?" Jn 9.08
This figure Jesus u. with them, 10.06
money box he u. to take what was 12.06
which all perish as they are u.), Col 2.22
For we never u. either words of 1Th 2.05
and all the vessels u. in worship. Heb 9.21
hoped in God u. to adorn themselves 1Pe 3.05

USEFUL
is charred, is it u. for anything? Eze 15.04
consecrated and u. to the master 2Ti 2.21
for he is very u. in serving me. 4.11
he is indeed u. to you and to me. Phm 1.11
vegetation u. to those for whose Heb 6.07

USELESS
which hang u., is a proverb in the Pro 26.07
among the nations as a u. vessel. Hos 8.08
(Formerly he was u. to you, Phm 1.11

USELESSNESS
set aside because of its weakness and u. Heb 7.18

USES
every one who u. proverbs will use Eze 16.44
good, if any one u. it lawfully, 1Ti 1.08

USING
and he has been u. up the money Gen 31.15
yet without u. your freedom as a 1Pe 2.16

UTENSILS
it be made, with all these u. Ex 25.39
all its u. you shall make of bronze. 27.03
All the u. of the tabernacle for 27.19
and the table and all its u., 30.27
and the lampstand and its u., 30.27
with all its u. and the laver and 30.28
the table and its u., and 31.08
the pure lampstand with all its u., 31.08
of burnt offering with all its u., 31.09
with its poles and all its u., 35.13
with its u. and its lamps, and the 35.14
and all its u., the laver and its 35.16
it and all its u. of a talent of 37.24
And he made all the u. of the altar, 38.03
all its u. he made of bronze. 38.03
it and all the u. of the altar, 38.30
to Moses, the tent and all its u., 39.33
the table with all its u., and the 39.36
with the lamps set and all its u., 39.37
bronze, its poles, and all its u.; 39.39
and all the u. for the service of 39.40
of burnt offering and all its u., 40.10
anointed the altar and all its u., Lev 8.11
it with all its u. in a covering Num 4.10
put on it all the u. of the altar, 4.14
basins, all the u. of the altar; 4.14
consecrated the altar with all its u., 7.01
had charge of the u. of service, 1Ch 9.28
furniture, and over all the holy u., 9.29
it were made u. for the house of 2Ch 24.14
of burnt offering and all its u., 29.18
for the showbread and all its u. 29.18
All the u. which King Ahaz discarded 29.19

UTHAI
U. the son of Ammihud, son of Omri, 1Ch 9.04
U. and Zakkur, and with them seventy Ez 8.14

UTTER
"You shall not u. a false report. Ex 23.01
Awake, awake, u. a song! Arise, Barak, Ju 5.12
and to u. shame, as at this day. Ez 9.07
and u. words out of their understanding? Job 8.10
U. darkness is laid up for his 20.26
and my tongue will not u. deceit. 27.04
and at noon I u. my complaint and Ps 55.17
cursing and lies which they u., 59.12
the heavens thou didst u. judgment; 76.08
I will u. dark sayings from of old, 78.02
Who can u. the mighty doings of the 106.02
at the point of u. ruin in the Pro 5.14
for my mouth will u. truth; 8.07
will be put out in u. darkness. 20.20
and your mind u. perverse things. 23.33
a man cannot u. it; the eye is not Ecc 1.08
be hasty to u. a word before God, 5.02
to u. error concerning the LORD, to Is 32.06
Jacob to u. destruction and Israel 43.28
And I will u. my judgments against Jer 1.16
If you u. what is precious, and not 15.19
his holy habitation u. his voice; 25.30
far as Jahaz they u. their voice, 48.34
but shall be an u. desolation; 50.13
And u. an allegory to the rebellious Eze 24.03
of Egypt an u. waste and desolation, 29.10
wholehearted joy and u. contempt, 36.05
They u. mere words; with empty oaths Hos 10.04
go about and u. wind and lies, Mic 2.11
shall do no wrong and u. no lies, Zep 3.13
For the teraphim u. nonsense, Zec 10.02
persecute you and u. all kinds of Mt 5.11
you in the dark, u. in the light; 10.27
for every careless word they u.; 12.36
I will u. what has been hidden 13.35
and whatever blasphemies they u.; Mk 3.28
him, "You were born in u. sin, Jn 9.34
you in a tongue u. speech that is 1Co 14.09
That is why we u. the Amen through 2Co 1.20
be told, which man may not u. 12.04
its mouth to u. blasphemies Rev 13.06

UTTERANCE
any thoughtless u. of her lips by Num 30.06
and the thoughtless u. of her lips, 30.08
will give free u. to my complaint; Job 10.01
are snared in the u. of your lips, Pro 6.02
tongues, as the Spirit gave them u. Ac 2.04
the Spirit the u. of wisdom, 1Co 12.08
to another the u. of knowledge 12.08
in u., in knowledge, in all earnestness, 2Co 8.07
that u. may be given me in opening Eph 6.19
by prophetic u. when the elders 1Ti 4.14

UTTERANCES
understand the u. of the prophets Ac 13.27
the prophetic u. which pointed to 1Ti 1.18

UTTERED
you, about which you u. a curse, Ju 17.02
and the Most High u. his voice. 2Sa 22.14
He also u. three thousand proverbs; 1Ki 4.32
which he u. by Moses his servant. 8.56
how the LORD u. this oracle against 2Ki 9.25
he wrought, the judgments he u., 1Ch 16.12
Jeremiah also u. a lament for 2Ch 35.25
With whose help have you u. words, Job 26.04
Therefore I have u. what I did not 42.03
and the Most High u. his voice, Ps 18.13
that which my lips u. and my mouth 66.14
miracles, and the judgments he u., 105.05
words which I have u. against it, Jer 25.13
you have u. rebellion against the 28.16

UTTERED (cont.)
and u. a lying divination, whenever Eze 13.07
you have u. delusions and seen 13.08
which you u. against the mountains 35.12
and said, "He has u. blasphemy. Mt 26.65
And Jesus u. a loud cry, and breathed Mk 15.37

UTTERING
u. slanders against me, my adversaries Ps 27.02
conceiving and u. from the heart Is 59.13
For, u. loud boasts of folly, they 2Pe 2.18
given a mouth u. haughty and Rev 13.05

UTTERLY
that I will u. blot out the remembrance Ex 17.14
If her father u. refuses to give 22.17
LORD only, shall be u. destroyed. 22.20
but you shall u. overthrow them and 23.24
to destroy them u. and break my Lev 26.44
who is to be u. destroyed from 27.29
that person shall be u. cut off; Num 15.31
then I will u. destroy their cities." 21.02
and they u. destroyed them and 21.03
that time and u. destroyed every Deu 2.34
And we u. destroyed them, as we did 3.06
you will soon u. perish from the 4.26
upon it, but will be u. destroyed. 4.26
then you must u. destroy them; 7.02
you shall u. detest and abhor it; 7.26
destroying it u., all who are in it 13.15
but you shall u. destroy them, the 20.17
and Og, whom you u. destroyed. Jos 2.10
Then they u. destroyed all in the 6.21
until he had u. destroyed all the 8.26
and had u. destroyed it, doing to Ai 10.01
he u. destroyed every person in it, 10.28
person in it he u. destroyed that 10.35
and u. destroyed it with every 10.37
and u. destroyed every person in it 10.39
but u. destroyed all that breathed, 10.40
u. destroying them; there was none 11.11
u. destroying them, as Moses the 11.12
that they should be u. destroyed, 11.20
Joshua u. destroyed them with their 11.21
and did not u. drive them out. 17.13
Zephath, and u. destroyed it. Ju 1.17
but did not u. drive them out. 1.28
waited till they were u. a at a loss; 3.25
thought that you u. hated her; 15.02
with a male you shall u. destroy. 21.11
and u. destroy all that they have; 1Sa 15.03
and u. destroyed all the people 15.08
and would not u. destroy them; 15.09
and worthless they u. destroyed. 15.09
and the rest we have u. destroyed." 15.15
u. destroy the sinners, the Amalekites, 15.18
and I have u. destroyed the Amalekites 15.20
made himself u. abhorred by his 27.12
deed you hve u. scorned the LORD, 2Sa 12.14
of a lion, will u. melt with fear; 17.10
and they are u. consumed with fire. 23.07
Israel were unable to destroy u.— 1Ki 9.21
and will u. consume the house of 14.10
behold, I will u. sweep away Baasha 16.03
I will u. sweep you away, and will 21.21
to all lands, destroying them u. 2Ki 19.11
of Mount Seir, destroying them u., 2Ch 20.23
my fathers u. destroyed was able 32.14
I am u. bowed down and prostrate; Ps 38.06
I am u. spent and crushed; I groan 38.08
a moment, swept away u. by terrors! 73.19
themselves, "We will u. subdue them"; 74.08
of wrath, and he u. rejected Israel. 78.59
thy statutes: O forsake me not u.! 119.08
word of truth u. out of my mouth, 119.43
Godless men u. deride me, but I do 119.51
his house, it would be u. scorned. Sol 8.07
of Israel, they are u. estranged. Is 1.04
And the idols shall u. pass away. 2.18
men, and the land is u. desolate, 6.11
And the LORD will u. destroy the 11.15
Mourn, u. stricken, for the raisin-cakes 16.07
The princes of Zoan are u. foolish; 19.11
The earth shall be u. laid waste 24.03
and u. despoiled; for the LORD 24.03
The earth is u. broken, the earth is 24.19
And the forest will u. go down, 32.19
and the city will be u. laid low. 32.19
to all lands, destroying them u. 37.11
be turned back and u. put to shame, 42.17
nations shall be u. laid waste. 60.12
be u. desolate, says the LORD, Jer 2.12
thou hast u. deceived this people 4.10
Judah have been u. faithless to me, 5.11
We are u. shamed, because we have 9.19
then I will u. pluck it up and 12.17
Hast thou u. rejected Judah? 14.19
they shall be u. destroyed from 24.10
I will u. destroy them, and make 25.09
your mother shall be u. shamed, 50.12
Slay, and u. destroy after them, says 50.21
heaps of grain, and destroy her u.; 50.26
young men; u. destroy all her host. 51.03
Or hast thou u. rejected us? Lam 5.22
Will it not u. wither when the east Eze 17.10
Armies shall be u. swept away Dan 11.22
to exterminate and u. destroy many. 11.44
king of Israel shall be u. cut off. Hos 10.15
that I will not u. destroy the Amo 9.08
nations, you shall be u. despised. Ob 1.02
lamentation, and say, "We are u. ruined; Mic 2.04
come against you, he is u. cut off. Nah 1.15
"I will u. sweep away everything Zep 1.02
withered, his right eye u. blinded!" Zec 11.27
wind ceased. And they were u. astounded, Mk 6.51
for we were so u., unbearably crushed 2Co 1.08

UTTERMOST
are in the u. parts of heaven, from Deu 30.04
dwell in the u. parts of the sea, Ps 139.09
are set in the u. parts of the Pit, Eze 32.23
from the u. parts of the north 38.06
out of the u. parts of the north, 38.15
you up from the u. parts of the 39.02
salvation to the u. parts of the Ac 13.47

UTTERS
Or if any one u. with his lips a Lev 5.04
Every one u. lies to his neighbor; Ps 12.02
The mouth of the righteous u. wisdom, 37.30
he u. empty words, while his heart 41.06
he u. his voice, the earth melts. 46.06
no man who u. lies shall continue 101.07
and he who u. slander is a fool. Pro 10.18
but a false witness u. deceit. 12.17
but one who u. lies is a betrayer. 14.25
and he who u. lies will not escape. 19.05
and he who u. lies will perish. 19.09
When he u. his voice there is a Jer 10.13
When he u. his voice there is a 51.16
The LORD u. his voice before his Joe 2.11
and u. his voice from Jerusalem, and 3.16
and u. his voice from Jerusalem; Amo 1.02
the great man u. the evil desire Mic 7.03
God has sent u. the words of God, Jn 3.34
but he u. mysteries in the Spirit. 1Co 14.02
as one who u. oracles of God; 1Pe 4.11

UZ
sons of Aram: U., Hul, Gether, and Mash. Gen 10.23
U. the first-born, Buz his brother, 22.21
the sons of Dishan: U. and Aran. 36.28
U., Hul, Gether, and Meshech. 1Ch 1.17
The sons of Dishan: U. and Aran. 1.42

UZ (cont.)
There was a man in the land of U., Job 1.01
of the land of U. and all the Jer 25.20
of Edom, dweller in the land of U.; Lam 4.21

UZAI
the son of U. repaired opposite the Angle Neh 3.25

UZAL
Hadoram, U., Diklah, Gen 10.27
Hadoram, U., Diklah, 1Ch 1.21
and wine from U. they exchanged for Eze 27.19

UZZA
of his house, in the garden of U.; 2Ki 21.18
in his tomb in the garden of U.; 21.26
was the father of U. and Ahihud. 1Ch 8.07
the sons of U., the sons of Paseah, Ez 2.49
the sons of U., the sons of Paseah, Neh 7.51

UZZAH
and U. and Ahio, the sons of Abinadab, 2Sa 6.03
U. put out his hand to the ark of 6.06
of the LORD was kindled against U.; 6.07
the LORD had broken forth upon U.; 6.08
son, Shimei his son, U. his son, 1Ch 6.29
and U. and Ahio were driving the 13.07
U. put out his hand to hold the ark, 13.09
of the LORD was kindled against U.; 13.10
the LORD had broken forth upon U.; 13.11

UZZENSHEERAH
built both lower and upper Bethhoron, and U. 1Ch 7.24

UZZI
Abishua of Bukki, Bukki of U., 1Ch 6.05
U. of Zerahiah, Zerahiah of Meraioth, 6.06
Bukki his son, U. his son, Zerahiah 6.51
U., Rephaiah, Jeriel, Jahmai, Ibsam, 7.02
The sons of U.: Izrahiah. And the sons 7.03
U., Uzziel, Jerimoth, and Iri, five, 7.07
son of Jeroham, Elah the son of U., 9.08
Zerahiah, son of U., son of Bukki, Ez 7.04
Jerusalem was U. the son of Bani, Neh 11.22
Mattenai; of Jedaiah, U.; 12.19
U., Jehohanan, Malchijah, Elam, and 12.42

UZZIA
U. the Ashterathite, Shama and Jeiel the sons 1Ch 11.44

UZZIAH
thirty-ninth year of U. king of Judah, 2Ki 15.13
year of Jotham the son of U. 15.30
of Israel, Jotham the son of U., 15.32
to all that his father U. had done. 15.34
U. his son, and Shaul his son. 1Ch 6.24
towers, was Jonathan the son of U.; 27.25
And all the people of Judah took U., 2Ch 26.01
U. was sixteen years old when he 26.03
The Ammonites paid tribute to U., 26.08
Moreover U. built towers in Jerusalem 26.09
Moreover U. had an army of soldiers, 26.11
And U. prepared for all the army 26.14
and they withstood King U., 26.18
U., to burn incense to the LORD, but 26.18
Then U. was angry. Now he had a 26.19
And King U. was a leper to the day 26.21
Now the rest of the acts of U., 26.22
And U. slept with his fathers, and 26.23
all that his father U. had done— 27.02
Elijah, Shemaiah, Jehiel, and U. Ez 10.21
of Judah: Athaiah the son of U., Neh 11.04
and Jerusalem in the days of U., Is 1.01
year that King U. died I saw the 6.01
son of U., king of Judah, Rezin the 7.01
son of Beeri, in the days of U., Hos 1.01
in the days of U. king of Judah Amo 1.01
in the days of U. king of Judah. Zec 14.05
Joram, and Joram the father of U., Mt 1.08
and U. the father of Jotham, and 1.09

UZZIEL
Hebron and U., the years of the Ex 6.18
And the sons of U.: Mishael, Elzaphan, 6.22
the sons of U. the uncle of Aaron, Lev 10.04
Amram, Izhar, Hebron, and U. Num 3.19
the son of U. as head of the fathers' 3.30
Rephaiah, and U., the sons of Ishi; 1Ch 4.42
Amram, Izhar, Hebron, and U. 6.02
Amram, Izhar, Hebron, and U. 6.18
U., Jerimoth, and Iri, five, heads of 7.07
of the sons of U., Amminadab the 15.10
Amram, Izhar, Hebron, and U., four. 23.12
The sons of U.: Micah the chief and 23.20
The sons of U., Micah; of the sons 24.24
U., Shebuel, and Jerimoth, Hananiah, 25.04
sons of Jeduthun, Shemaiah and U. 2Ch 29.14
Next to them U. the son of Harhaiah, Neh 3.08

UZZIELITES
Hebronites, and the family of the U.; Num 3.27
the Hebronites, and the U.— 1Ch 26.23

V

VACILLATING
Was I v. when I wanted to do this? 2Co 1.17

VAGABOND
poverty will come upon you like a v., Pro 6.11

VAIN
name of the LORD your God in v.; Ex 20.07
guiltless who takes his name in v. 20.07
and you shall sow your seed in v., Lev 26.16
your strength shall be spent in v., 26.20
name of the LORD your God in v.: Deu 5.11
guiltless who takes his name in v. 5.11
aside after v. things which cannot 1Sa 12.21
profit or save, for they are v. 12.21
armor, and he tried in v. to go, 17.39
"Surely in v. have I guarded all 25.21
condemned; why then do I labor in v.? Job 9.29
then have you become altogether v.? 27.12
though her labor be in v., yet she has 39.16
conspire, and the peoples plot in v.? Ps 2.01
How long will you love v. words, 4.02
those who pay regard to v. idols; 31.06
The war horse is a v. hope for 33.17
against the foe, for v. is the help of man! 60.11
set no v. hopes on robbery; if riches 62.10
All in v. have I kept my heart clean 73.13
from the foe, for v. is the help of man! 108.12
consternation, "Men are all a v. hope." 116.11
yea, their cunning is in v. 119.118
those who build it labor in v. 127.01
the watchman stays awake in v. 127.01
It is in v. that you rise up early, 127.02
For in v. is a net spread in the Pro 1.17
A scoffer seeks wisdom in v., 14.06
and beauty is v., but a woman who 31.30
lives the few days of his v. life, Ecc 6.12
In my v. life I have seen everything; 7.15
days of your v. life which he has 9.09
Bring no more v. offerings; incense is Is 1.13
But I said, "I have labored in v., 49.04
They shall not labor in v., or bear 65.23
In v. have I smitten your children, Jer 2.30
In v. you beautify yourself. 4.30

VAIN (cont.)
in v. the refining goes on, for the Jer 6.29
"But they say, 'That is in v.! 18.12
to you, filling you with v. hopes; 23.16
In v. you have used many medicines; 46.11
not said in v. that I would do Eze 6.10
In v. I have wearied myself; 24.12
pay regard to v. idols forsake Jon 2.08
kindle fire upon my altar in v.! Mal 1.10
You have said, 'It is v. to serve God. 3.14
in v. do they worship me, teaching Mt 15.09
in v. do they worship me, teaching Mk 7.07
and the peoples imagine v. things? Ac 4.25
turn from these v. things to a 14.15
he does not bear the sword in v.; Rom 13.04
it fast—unless you believed in v. 1Co 15.02
his grace toward me was not in v. 15.10
preaching is in v. and your faith is in v. 15.14
the Lord your labor is not in v. 15.58
to accept the grace of God in v. 2Co 6.01
you may not prove v. in this case, 9.03
should be running or had run in v. Gal 2.02
many things in v.?—if it is in v. 3.04
I have labored over you in v. 4.11
did not run in v. or labor in v. Php 2.16
our visit to you was not in v.; 1Th 2.01
and that our labor would be in v. 3.05
wandered away into v. discussion, 1Ti 1.06
heart, this man's religion is v. Jas 1.26
it is in v. that the scripture 4.05

VAINGLORY
beautiful ornament they used for v., Eze 7.20

VAINLY
failed, ever watching v. for help; Lam 4.17

VAIZATHA
and Parmashta and Arisai and Aridai and V., Est 9.09

VALE
and portion out the V. of Succoth. Ps 60.06
and portion out the V. of Succoth. 108.07

VALIANT
or any v. man, he attached him to 1Sa 14.52
only be v. for me and fight the 18.17
all the v. men arose, and went all 31.12
your hands be strong, and be v.; 2Sa 2.07
where he knew there were v. men. 11.16
commanded you? Be courageous and be v." 13.28
Then even the v. man, whose heart is 17.10
those who are with him are v. men. 17.10
Jehoiada was a v. man of Kabzeel, 23.20
thousand v. men who drew the sword, 24.09
half-tribe of Manasseh had v. men, 1Ch 5.18
all the v. men arose, and took away 10.12
Jehoiada was a v. man of Kabzeel, 11.22
having an army of v. men of war, 2Ch 13.03
hundred and sixty-eight v. men. Neh 11.06
and v. men in mixing strong drink, Is 5.22
Behold the v. ones cry without; 33.07

VALIANTLY
dispossessed, while Israel does v. Num 24.18
And he did v., and smote the 1Sa 14.48
With God we shall do v.; it is he who Ps 60.12
With God we shall do v.; it is he who 108.13
right hand of the LORD does v., 118.15
the right hand of the LORD does v.! 118.16

VALID
by angels was v. and every transgression Heb 2.02

VALLEY
that the Jordan v. was well Gen 13.10
for himself all the Jordan v., 13.11
cities of the v. and moved his 13.12
forces in the V. of Siddim (that 14.03
joined battle in the V. of Siddim 14.08
Now the V. of Siddim was full of 14.10
the V. of Shaveh (that is, the King's V.). 14.17
back or stop anywhere in the v.; 19.17
and all the v., and all the inhabitants 19.25
and toward all the land of the v., 19.28
God destroyed the cities of the v., 19.29
encamped in the v. of Gerar and 26.17
dug in the v. and found there a 26.19
he sent him from the v. of Hebron, 37.14
And they came to the V. of Eshcol, Num 13.23
That place was called the V. of Eshcol, 13.24
and encamped in the V. of Zered. 21.12
Bamoth to the v. lying in the 21.20
they went up to the V. of Eshcol, 32.09
and came to the V. of Eshcol and Deu 1.24
and go over the v. of the Arnon; 2.24
on the edge of the v. of the Arnon, 2.36
from the city that is in the v., 2.36
from the v. of the Arnon to Mount 3.08
on the edge of the v. of the Arnon, 3.12
as far as the v. of the Arnon, 3.16
the middle of the v. as a boundary, 3.16
remained in the v. opposite Bethpeor. 3.29
Jordan in the v. opposite Bethpeor, 4.46
on the edge of the v. of the Arnon, 4.48
down to a v. with running water, 21.04
the heifer's neck there in the v. 21.04
whose neck was broken in the v.; 21.06
the v. of Jericho the city of palm 34.03
him in the v. in the land of Moab, 34.06
brought them up to the V. of Achor. Jos 7.24
place is called the V. of Achor. 7.26
Joshua spent that night in the v. 8.13
and thou Moon in the v. of Aijalon." 10.12
eastward as far as the v. of Mizpeh; 11.08
Baalgad in the v. of Lebanon below 11.17
from the v. of the Arnon to Mount 12.01
on the edge of the v. of the Arnon, 12.02
middle of the v. as far as the 12.02
Baalgad in the v. of Lebanon to 12.07
on the edge of the v. of the Arnon, 13.09
that is in the middle of the v., 13.09
on the edge of the v. of the Arnon, 13.16
that is in the middle of the v., 13.16
Zerethshahar on the hill of the v., 13.19
and in the v. Tram, Bethnimrah, 13.27
up to Debir from the V. of Achor, 15.07
is on the south side of the v.; 15.07
goes up by the v. of the son of 15.08
lies over against the v. of Hinnom, 15.08
northern end of the v. of Rephaim; 15.08
and those in the V. of Jezreel. 17.16
overlooks the v. of the son of 18.16
the north end of the v. of Rephaim; 18.16
it then goes down the v. of Hinnom, 18.16
and it ends at the v. of Iphtahel; 19.14
Zebulun and the v. of Iphtahel 19.27
they set out thither into the v., Ju 5.14
into the v. they rushed forth at 5.15
they encamped in the V. of Jezreel. 6.33
by the hill of Moreh, in the v. 7.01
of Midian was below him in the v. 7.08
lay along the v. like locusts for 7.12
loved a woman in the v. of Sorek, 16.04
It was in the v. which belongs to 18.28
their wheat harvest in the v.; 1Sa 6.13
down upon the v. of Zeboim toward 13.18
Amalek, and lay in wait in the v. 15.05
and encamped in the v. of Elah, 17.02
other side, with a v. between them. 17.03
were in the v. of Elah, fighting 17.19
whom you killed in the v. of Elah, 21.09
side of the v. and those beyond 31.07
spread out in the v. of Rephaim. 2Sa 5.18
spread out in the v. of Rephaim. 5.22

VALLEY (cont.)

thousand Edomites in the V. of Salt. 2Sa 8.13
and we shall drag it into the v., 17.13
pillar which is in the King's V., 18.18
was encamped in the v. of Rephaim. 23.13
that is in the middle of the v., 24.05
upon some mountain or into some v." 2Ki 2.16
which is by the v. of the Arnon, 10.33
Edomites in the V. of Salt and 14.07
which is in the v. of the sons of 23.10
Gedor, to the east side of the v., 1Ch 4.39
who were in the v. saw that the 10.07
was encamped in the v. of Rephaim. 11.15
made a raid in the v. of Rephaim. 14.09
yet again made a raid in the v. 14.13
thousand Edomites in the V. of Salt. 18.12
battle in the v. of Zephathah at 2Ch 14.10
find them at the end of the v., 20.16
assembled in the V. of Beracah, 20.26
been called the V. of Beracah to 20.26
and went to the V. of Salt and 25.11
Gate and at the V. Gate and at the 26.09
incense in the v. of the son of 28.03
away and threw into the Kidron v. 30.14
offering in the v. of the son of 33.06
in the v., to the entrance by the 33.14
by night by the V. Gate to the Neh 2.13
night by the v. and inspected the 2.15
back and entered by the V. Gate, 2.15
of Zanoah repaired the V. Gate; 3.13
from Beersheba to the v. of Hinnom. 11.30
Lod, and Ono, the v. of craftsmen. 11.35
The clods of the v. are sweet to Job 21.33
shafts in a v. away from where men 28.04
He paws in the v., and exults in 39.21
through the v. of the shadow of Ps 23.04
go through the v. of Baca they 84.06
ravens of the v. and eaten by the Pro 30.17
to look at the blossoms of the v., Sol 6.11
ears of grain in the V. of Rephaim. Is 17.05
oracle concerning the v. of vision. 22.01
and confusion in the v. of vision, 22.05
of the rich v. of those overcome 28.01
is on the head of the rich v., 28.04
be wroth as in the v. of Gibeon; 28.21
Every v. shall be lifted up, and 40.04
stones of the v. is your portion; 57.06
Like cattle that go down into the v., 63.14
and the V. of Achor a place for 65.10
Look at your way in the v.; Jer 2.23
which is in the v. of the son of 7.31
or the v. of the son of Hinnom, but 7.32
but the v. of Slaughter: for they 7.32
and go out to the V. of Benhinnom 19.02
or the V. of Benhinnom, but the 19.06
Benhinnom, but the V. of Slaughter. 19.06
you, O inhabitant of the v., 21.13
The whole v. of the dead bodies and 31.40
of Baal in the v. of the son of 32.35
the v. shall perish, and the plain 48.08
set me down in the midst of the v.; Eze 37.01
there were very many upon the v.; 37.02
the V. of the Travelers east of the 39.11
will be called the V. of Hamongog. 39.11
buried it in the V. of Hamongog. 39.15
bow of Israel in the v. of Jezreel. Hos 1.05
and make the V. of Achor a door of 2.15
them down to the v. of Jehoshaphat, Joe 3.02
come up to the v. of Jehoshaphat; 3.12
Multitudes, multitudes, in the v. of decision! 3.14
Lord is near in the v. of decision. 3.14
Lord and water the v. of Shittim. 3.18
inhabitants from the V. of Aven, Amo 1.05
pour down her stones into the v., Mic 1.06
east to west by a very wide v.; Zec 14.04
And the v. of my mountains shall be 14.05
for the v. of the mountains shall 14.05
Every v. shall be filled, and every Lk 3.05
his disciples across the Kidron v., Jn 18.01

VALLEYS

and the Canaanites dwell in the v., Num 14.25
Suphah, and the v. of the Arnon, 21.14
slope of the v. that extends to 21.15
Like v. that stretch afar, like 24.06
flowing forth in v. and hills, Deu 8.07
possess is a land of hills and v., 11.11
springs of water and to all the v.; 1Ki 18.05
but he is not a god of the v., 20.28
put to flight all those in the v., 1Ch 12.15
herds in the v. was Shaphat the 27.29
or will he harrow the v. after you Job 39.10
the v. deck themselves with grain, Ps 65.13
the v. sank down to the place which 104.08
springs gush forth in the v.; 104.10
a rose of Sharon, a lily of the v. Sol 2.01
Your choicest v. were full of Is 22.07
fountains in the midst of the v.; 41.18
who slay your children in the v., 57.05
Why do you boast of your v., Jer 49.04
hills, to the ravines and the v.: Eze 6.03
mountains, like doves of the v., 7.16
and in all the v. its branches 31.12
and fill the v. with your carcass. 32.05
and in your v. and in all your 35.08
the hills, the ravines and the v., 36.04
and hills, to the ravines and v., 36.06
under him and the v. will be cleft, Mic 1.04

VALOR

all your men of v. shall pass over Deu 3.18
all the men of v. among you shall Jos 1.14
with its king and mighty men of v. 6.02
thirty thousand mighty men of v., 8.03
him, and all the mighty men of v. 10.07
is with you, you mighty man of v." Ju 6.12
fell, all of them men of v. 20.44
the sword, all of them men of v. 20.46
him went men of v. whose hearts 1Sa 10.26
a man of v., a man of war, prudent 16.18
He was a mighty man of v., 2Ki 5.01
and all the mighty men of v., 24.14
to Babylon all the men of v., 24.16
for they were all mighty men of v., 1Ch 12.21
mighty men of v. for war, seven 12.25
Zadok, a young man mighty in v., 12.28
mighty men of v., famous men in 12.30
all these were mighty men of v. 2Ch 14.08
mighty men of v., in Jerusalem. 17.13
hundred thousand mighty men of v., 17.14
hundred thousand mighty men of v. 17.16
Benjamin: Eliada, a mighty man of v., 17.17
mighty men of v. from Israel for a 25.06
mighty men of v. was two thousand 26.12
of the Lord who were men of v.; 26.17
in one day, all of them men of v., 28.06
mighty men of v., a hundred and Neh 11.14

VALUABLE

and v. possessions, together with fortified 2Ch 21.03

VALUATION

of persons to the Lord at your v., Lev 27.02
then your v. of a male from twenty 27.03
your v. shall be thirty shekels. 27.04
your v. shall be for a male twenty 27.05
your v. shall be for a male five 27.06
a female your v. shall be three 27.06
then your v. for a male shall be 27.07
a man is too poor to pay your v., 27.08
it, he shall add a fifth to the v. 27.13
a fifth of the v. in money to it, 27.15
then your v. shall be according to 27.16
it shall stand at your full v.; 27.17
deduction shall be made from your v. 27.18

VALUATION (cont.)
a fifth of the v. in money to it, Lev 27.19
compute the v. for it up to the 27.23
amount of the v. on that day as a 27.23
Every v. shall be according to the 27.25
he shall buy it back at your v., 27.27
redeemed, it shall be sold at its v. 27.27

VALUE
add the fifth of its v. to it, Lev 22.14
and the priest shall v. him; 27.08
who vowed the priest shall v. him. 27.08
priest shall v. it as either good 27.12
the priest, v. it, so it shall be. 27.12
priest shall v. it as either good 27.14
I will give you its v. in money." 1Ki 21.02
Are you not of more v. than they Mt 6.26
you are of more v. than many 10.31
Of how much more v. is a man than a 12.12
who, on finding one pearl of great v., 13.46
you are of more v. than many Lk 12.07
how much more v. are you than the 12.24
counted the v. of them and found Ac 19.19
my life of any v. nor as precious 20.24
Circumcision indeed is of v. if you Rom 2.25
Or what is the v. of circumcision? 3.01
they are of no v. in checking the Col 2.23
bodily training is of some v., 1Ti 4.08
godliness is of v. in every way, 4.08

VALUED
v. by you in shekels of silver, Lev 5.15
v. by you at the price for a guilt 5.18
v. by you at the price for a guilt 6.06
barley shall be v. at fifty 27.16
It cannot be v. in the gold of Job 28.16
it, nor can it be v. in pure gold. 28.19

VALUES
or bad; as the priest v. it, so it shall Lev 27.14

VANIAH
V., Meremoth, Eliashib, Ez 10.36

VANISH
it is hot, they v. from their place. Job 6.17
they v.—like smoke they v. away. Ps 37.20
Let them v. like water that runs 58.07
made their days v. like a breath, 78.33
for the heavens will v. like smoke, Is 51.06
growing old is ready to v. away. Heb 8.13

VANISHED
of the LORD v. from his sight. Ju 6.21
The enemy have v. in everlasting Ps 9.06
faithful have v. from among the 12.01
under foot has v. from the land, Is 16.04
the prudent? Has their wisdom v.? Jer 49.07
'How you have v. from the seas, O Eze 26.17
and he v. out of their sight. Lk 24.31
the sky v. like a scroll that is Rev 6.14

VANISHES
As the cloud fades and v., Job 7.09
for a little time and then v. Jas 4.14

VANITIES
Turn my eyes from looking at v.; Ps 119.37
Vanity of v., says the Preacher, Ecc 1.02
Vanity of v.! All is vanity. 1.02
Vanity of v., says the Preacher; 12.08

VANITY
for what v. thou hast created all Ps 89.47
V. of vanities, says the Preacher, Ecc 1.02
v. of vanities! All is v. 1.02
all is v. and a striving after wind. 1.14
But behold, this also was v. 2.01
all was v. and striving after 2.11
to myself that this also is v. 2.15
for all is v. and a striving after 2.17
under the sun. This also is v. 2.19
This also is v. and a great evil. 2.21
does not rest. This also is v. 2.23
This also is v. and a striving 2.26
over the beasts; for all is v. 3.19
This also is v. and a striving 4.04
Again, I saw v. under the sun: 4.07
This also is v. and an unhappy 4.08
this also is v. and a striving 4.16
wealth, with gain: this also is v. 5.10
this is v.; it is a sore 6.02
For it comes into v. and goes into 6.04
this also is v. and a striving 6.09
the more v., and what is man the 6.11
of the fools; this also is v. 7.06
such things. This also is v. 8.10
there is a v. which takes place on 8.14
I said that this also is v. 8.14
Everything before them is v., 9.01
will be many. All that comes is v. 11.08
youth and the dawn of life are v. 11.10
V. of vanities, says the Preacher; all is v. 12.08
my strength for nothing and v.; Is 49.04
he was determined to go after v. Hos 5.11

VANQUISH
found wisdom; God may v. him, not man. Job 32.13

VAPOR
is a fleeting v. and a snare of Pro 21.06
blood, and fire, and v. of smoke; Ac 2.19

VARIATION
there is no v. or shadow due to change. Jas 1.17

VARIED
another, as good stewards of God's v. grace: 1Pe 4.10

VARIETIES
Now there are v. of gifts, but the 1Co 12.04
and there are v. of service, but the 12.05
and there are v. of working, but it 12.06

VARIOUS
filled with v. kinds of spices 2Ch 16.14
afflicted with v. diseases and Mt 4.24
and earthquakes in v. places: 24.07
who were sick with v. diseases, Mk 1.34
will be earthquakes in v. places, 13.08
were sick with v. diseases brought Lk 4.40
and in v. places famines and 21.11
to another v. kinds of tongues, to 1Co 12.10
speakers in v. kinds of tongues. 12.28
sins and swayed by v. impulses, 2Ti 3.06
slaves to v. passion and pleasures, Tit 3.03
In many and v. ways God spoke of Heb 1.01
and wonders and v. miracles and by 2.04
food and drink and v. ablutions, 9.10
brethren, when you meet v. trials, Jas 1.02
you may have to suffer v. trials, 1Pe 1.06

VASHTI
Queen V. also gave a banquet for Est 1.09
to bring Queen V. before the king 1.11
But Queen V. refused to come at the 1.12
what is to be done to Queen V., 1.15
the king has Queen V. done wrong, 1.16
commanded Queen V. to be brought 1.17
that V. is to come no more before 1.19
he remembered V. and what she had 2.01
pleases the king be queen instead of V." 2.04
and made her queen instead of V. 2.17

VASSAL
and Hoshea became his v., and paid 2Ki 17.03
among the cities has become a v. Lam 1.01

VAST
v. as it is, all women will give Est 1.20
thoughts, O God! How v. is the sum of them! Ps 139.17
For v. as the sea is your ruin; Lam 2.13

VAT
it, and hewed out a wine v. in it; Is 5.02

VATS
and your v. will be bursting with Pro 3.10
the v. shall overflow with wine and Joe 2.24
The v. overflow, for their wickedness 3.13

VAULT
and he walks on the v. of heaven.' Job 22.14
and founds his v. upon the earth; Amo 9.06

VAULTED
you built yourself a v. chamber, Eze 16.24
building your v. chamber at the 16.31
throw down your v. chamber and 16.39

VAUNT
lest Israel v. themselves against Ju 7.02
Shall the axe v. itself over him Is 10.15

VEGETABLE
that I may have it for a v. garden, 1Ki 21.02

VEGETABLES
your feet, like a garden of v.; Deu 11.10
let us be given v. to eat and water Dan 1.12
were to drink, and gave them v. 1.16
while the weak man eats only v. Rom 14.02

VEGETATION
said, "Let the earth put forth v., Gen 1.11
The earth brought forth v., 1.12
which devoured all the v. in their land, Ps 105.35
to every one the v. in the field. Zec 10.01
brings forth v. useful to those Heb 6.07

VEHEMENT
flashes are flashes of fire, a most v. flame. Sol 8.06

VEHEMENTLY
But he said v., "If I must die with Mk 14.31
scribes stood by, v. accusing him. Lk 23.10

VEIL
So she took her v. and covered Gen 24.65
and put on a v., wrapping herself 38.14
taking off her v. she put on the 38.19
shall make a v. of blue and purple Ex 26.31
shall hang the v. from the clasps, 26.33
testimony in thither within the v.; 26.33
and the v. shall separate for you 26.33
shall set the table outside the v., 26.35
outside the v. which is before the 27.21
it before the v. that is by the 30.06
with them, he put a v. on his face; 34.33
he took the v. off, until he came 34.34
would put the v. upon his face 34.35
seat, and the v. of the screen; 35.12
And he made the v. of blue and 36.35
sanctuary, and the bases of the v.; 38.27
goatskins, and the v. of the screen; 39.34
shall screen the ark with the v. 40.03
and set up the v. of the screen, 40.21
of the tabernacle, outside the v., 40.22
the tent of meeting before the v., 40.26
in front of the v. of the sanctuary. Lev 4.06
before the LORD in front of the v. 4.17
into the holy place within the v., 16.02
he shall bring it within the v. 16.12
and bring its blood within the v., 16.15
come near the v. or approach the 21.23
Outside the v. of the testimony, in 24.03
and take down the v. of the screen, Num 4.05
altar and that is within the v.; 18.07
And he made the v. of blue and 2Ch 3.14
Your eyes are doves behind your v. Sol 4.01
of a pomegranate behind your v. 4.03
of a pomegranate behind your v. 6.07
the v. that is spread over all Is 25.07
put off your v., strip off your 47.02
For if a woman will not v. herself, 1Co 11.06
shorn or shaven, let her wear a v. 11.06
ought to have a v. on her head, 11.10
who put a v. over his face so that 2Co 3.13
that same v. remains unlifted, 3.14
Moses is read a v. lies over their 3.15
to the Lord the v. is removed. 3.16

VEILED
and there he v. his power. Hab 3.04
And even if our gospel is v., 2Co 4.03
it is v. only to those who are 4.03

VEILS
garments, the turbans, and the v. Is 3.23
and make v. for the heads of Eze 13.18
Your v. also I will tear off, and 13.21

VENGEANCE
v. shall be taken on him sevenfold." Gen 4.15
You shall not take v. or bear any Lev 19.18
shall execute v. for the covenant; 26.25
to execute the LORD's v. on Midian. Num 31.03
V. is mine, and recompense, for the Deu 32.35
I will take v. on my adversaries, 32.41
and takes v. on his adversaries, and 32.43
the nation took v. on their Jos 10.13
it, may the LORD himself take v. 22.23
the LORD take v. on David's enemies." 1Sa 20.16
and from taking v. with your own 25.26
or for my lord taking v. himself. 25.31
the God who gave me v. and brought 2Sa 22.48
the God who gave me v. and subdued Ps 18.47
will rejoice when he sees the v.; 58.10
God of v., thou God of v., shine forth! 94.01
to wreak v. on the nations and 149.07
For the LORD has a day of v., Is 34.08
Behold, your God will come with v., 35.04
I will take v., and I will spare no 47.03
put on garments of v. for clothing, 59.17
and the day of v. of our God, 61.02
For the day of v. was in my heart, 63.04
mind, let me see thy v. upon them, Jer 11.20
and take v. for me on my persecutors. 15.15
mind, let me see thy v. upon them, 20.12
a day of v., to avenge himself on 46.10
For this is the v. of the LORD: 50.15
take v. on her, do to her as she has 50.15
in Zion the v. of the LORD our God, 50.28
LORD our God, v. for his temple. 50.28
this is the time of the LORD's v., 51.06
v. of the LORD, the v. for his temple. 51.11
your cause and take v. for you. 51.36
Thou hast seen all their v., Lam 3.60
to take v., I have set on the bare Eze 24.08
offended in taking v. upon them, 25.12
And I will lay my v. upon Edom by 25.14
and they shall know my v., 25.14
and took v. with malice of heart 25.15
execute great v. upon them with 25.17
LORD, when I lay my v. upon them." 25.17
I will execute v. upon the nations Mic 5.15
the LORD takes v. on his adversaries Nah 1.02
will not take v. twice on his foes. 1.09
for these are days of v., Lk 21.22
"V. is mine, I will repay, says the Rom 12.19
inflicting v. upon those who do not 2Th 1.08
"V. is mine, I will repay." Heb 10.30

VENOM
with v. of crawling things of the Deu 32.24
serpents, and the cruel v. of asps. 32.33
have v. like the v. of a serpent, Ps 58.04
"The v. of asps is under their Rom 3.13

VENT
heart is like wine that has no v.; Job 32.19
A fool gives full v. to his anger, Pro 29.11
I will v. my wrath on my enemies, Is 1.24
The LORD gave full v. to his wrath, Lam 4.11
and I will v. my fury upon them and Eze 5.13

VENTED
to the sword, and v. his wrath on his heritage. Ps 78.62

VENTURE
who would not v. to set the sole of Deu 28.56
a certain man drew his bow at a v., 1Ki 22.34
a certain man drew his bow at a v., 2Ch 18.33
those riches were lost in a bad v.; Ecc 5.14
him not to v. into the theater. Ac 19.31
For I will not v. to speak of Rom 15.18
Not that we v. to class or compare 2Co 10.12

VENTURES
"If one v. a word with you, will you Job 4.02

VERDICT
aside from the v. which they declare to you, Deu 17.11

VERDURE
the new growth fails, the v. is no more. Is 15.06

VERIFIED
words will be v., and you shall not die." Gen 42.20

VERMILION
cedar, and painting it with v. Jer 22.14
of the Chaldeans portrayed in v., Eze 23.14

VERMIN
a shepherd cleans his cloak of v.; Jer 43.12

VERSED
all who were v. in law and judgment, Est 1.13
eloquent man, well v. in the scriptures. Ac 18.24

VERSES
I address my v. to the king; my tongue is like Ps 45.01

VESSEL
And the earthen v. in which it is Lev 6.28
but if it is boiled in a bronze v., 6.28
any v. that is used for any purpose; 11.32
of them falls into any earthen v., 11.33
from every such v. shall be unclean. 11.34
the birds in an earthen v. over running 14.05
the birds in an earthen v. over running 14.50
And the earthen v. which he who has 15.12
and every v. of wood shall be 15.12
take holy water in an earthen v., Num 5.17
And every open v., which has no 19.15
water shall be added in a v.; 19.17
you shall not put any in your v. Deu 23.24
"Bring me a little water in a v., 1Ki 17.10
to her son, "Bring me another v." 2Ki 4.06
them in pieces like a potter's v. Ps 2.09
I have become like a broken v. 31.12
the smith has material for a v.; Pro 25.04
an earthen v. are smooth lips with 26.23
every small v., from the cups to Is 22.24
of a potter's v. which is smashed 30.14
an earthen v. with the potter! 45.09
in a clean v. to the house of the 66.20
And the v. he was making of clay Jer 18.04
and he reworked it into another v., 18.04
city, as one breaks a potter's v., 19.11
broken pot, a v. no one cares for? 22.28
and put them in an earthenware v., 32.14
not been emptied from v. to v., 48.11
Moab like a v. for which no one 48.38
he has made me an empty v., 51.34
and put them into a single v., Eze 4.09
a peg from it to hang any v. on? 15.03
among the nations as a useless v. Hos 8.08
lighting a lamp covers it with a v., Lk 8.16
a shoal they ran the v. aground; Ac 27.41
same lump one v. for beauty and Rom 9.21
then he will be a v. for noble use, 2Ti 2.21

VESSELS
in v. of wood and in v. of stone.'" Ex 7.19
And he made the v. of pure gold 37.16
the v. of the sanctuary with which Num 3.31
and all the v. for oil with which 4.09
take all the v. of the service 4.12
in it, of the sanctuary and its v." 4.16
silver of the v. two thousand four 7.85
near to the v. of the sanctuary or 18.03
with the v. of the sanctuary and 31.06
and v. of bronze and iron, are Jos 6.19
and the v. of bronze and of iron, 6.24
go to the v. and drink what the Ru 2.09
the v. of the young men are holy, 1Sa 21.05
more today will their v. be holy?" 21.05
and earthen v., wheat, barley, meal, 2Sa 17.28
all these v. in the house of the 1Ki 7.45
And Solomon left all the v. unweighed, 7.47
made all the v. that were in the 7.48
and the v., and stored them in the 7.51
all the holy v. that were in the 8.04
Solomon's drinking v. were of gold, 10.21
and all the v. of the House of the 10.21
silver, and gold, and v. 15.15
borrow v. of all your neighbors, 2Ki 4.03
empty v. and not too few. 4.03
sons, and pour into all these v.; 4.04
poured they brought the v. to her. 4.05
When the v. were full, she said to 4.06
of any v. of gold, or of silver, from 12.13
and all the v. that were found in 14.14
the LORD all the v. made for Baal, 23.04
pieces all the v. of gold in the 24.13
and all the v. of bronze used in 25.14
of all these v. was beyond weight. 25.16
the pillars and the v. of bronze. 1Ch 18.08
and the holy v. of God may be 22.19
for all the v. for the service in 28.13
for all golden v. for each service, 28.14
of silver v. for each service, 28.14
and all the v. in the treasuries of 2Ch 5.01
all the holy v. that were in the 5.05
Solomon's drinking v. were of gold, 9.20
and all the v. of the House of the 9.20
gifts, silver, and gold, and v. 15.18
and v. of gold and silver. 24.14
and all the v. that were found in 25.24
together the v. of the house of 28.24
in pieces the v. of the house of 28.24
and for all kinds of costly v.; 32.27
part of the v. of the house of the 36.07
the precious v. of the house of 36.10
And all the v. of the house of God, 36.18
and destroyed all its precious v. 36.19
them aided them with v. of silver, Ez 1.06
brought out the v. of the house of 1.07
of silver, and a thousand other v.; 1.10
all the v. of gold and of silver 1.11
gold and silver v. of the house of 5.14
"Take these v., go and put them in 5.15
gold and silver v. of the house of 6.05
The v. that have been give you for 7.19
the silver and the gold and the v., 8.25
and silver v. worth a hundred 8.26

VESSELS (cont.)

and two v. of fine bright bronze as Ez 8.27
to the LORD, and the v. are holy; 8.28
the silver and the gold and the v., 8.30
gold and the v. were weighed into 8.33
where are the v. of the sanctuary, Neh 10.39
the v., and the tithes of grain, 13.05
thither the v. of the house of God, 13.09
in v. of papyrus upon the waters! Is 18.02
you who bear the v. of the LORD. 52.11
abominable things is in their v.; 65.04
they return with their v. empty; Jer 14.03
the v. of the LORD's house will now 27.16
that the v. which are left in the 27.18
the rest of the v. which are left 27.19
concerning the v. which are left 27.21
place all the v. of the LORD's 28.03
Babylon the v. of the house of the 28.06
and oil, and store them in your v., 40.10
and empty his v., and break his 48.12
and all the v. of bronze used in 52.18
of men and v. of bronze for your Eze 27.13
some of the v. of the house of God; Dan 1.02
and placed the v. in the treasury 1.02
that the v. of gold and of silver 5.02
and silver v. which had been taken 5.03
and the v. of his house have been 5.23
their precious v. of silver and of 11.08
the good into v. but threw away Mt 13.48
of cups and pots and v. of bronze.) Mk 7.04
patience the v. of wrath made for Rom 9.22
of his glory for the v. of mercy, 9.23
have this treasure in earthen v., 2Co 4.07
are not only v. of gold and silver 2Ti 2.20
and all the v. used in worship. Heb 9.21

VESTIBULE

Then Ehud went out into the v., Ju 3.23
The v. in front of the nave of the 1Ki 6.03
the LORD, and the v. of the house. 7.12
pillars in the v. were of lily-work, 7.19
pillars at the v. of the temple; 7.21
the plan of the v. of the temple, 1Ch 28.11
The v. in front of the nave of the 2Ch 3.04
which he had built before the v., 8.12
in front of the v. of the house of 15.08
doors of the v. and put out the 29.07
they came to the v. of the LORD; 29.17
the gate by the v. of the gate at Eze 40.07
Then he measured the v. of the gateway, 40.08
and the v. of the gate was at the 40.09
measured also the v., twenty cubits; 40.14
round about the v. of the gateway 40.14
of the inner v. of the gate was 40.15
likewise the v. had windows round 40.16
jambs and its v. were of the same 40.21
its v., and its palm trees were of 40.22
and its v. was on the inside. 40.22
he measured its jambs and its v.; 40.24
round about in it and in its v., 40.25
and its v. was on the inside; 40.26
and its v. were of the same size as 40.29
round about in it and in its v.; 40.29
Its v. faced the outer court, and 40.31
and its v. were of the same size as 40.33
round about in it and in its v.; 40.33
Its v. faced the outer court, and it 40.34
and its v. were of the same size as 40.36
Its v. faced the outer court, and it 40.37
its door in the v. of the gate, 40.38
And in the v. of the gate were two 40.39
outside of the v. at the entrance 40.40
side of the v. of the gate were 40.40
me to the v. of the temple and 40.48
and measured the jambs of the v., 40.48
The length of the v. was twenty 40.49
inner room and the outer v. 41.15
of wood in front of the v. outside. 41.25
side, on the sidewalls of the v. 41.26
enter by way of the v. of the gate, 44.03
enter by the v. of the gate from 46.02
shall go in by the v. of the gate, 46.08
Between the v. and the altar let Joe 2.17

VESTIBULES

And there were v. round about, twenty-five Eze 40.30

VESTMENTS

"Bring out the v. for all the 2Ki 10.22
So he brought out the v. for them. 10.22
in their v. came forward with Ez 3.10

VESTURE

in wine and his v. in the blood of grapes; Gen 49.11

VEXATION

out of my great anxiety and v." 1Sa 1.16
Surely v. kills the fool, and Job 5.02
"O that my v. were weighed, and all 6.02
me, and increase thy v. toward me; 10.17
yea, thou dost note trouble and v., Ps. 10.14
The v. of a fool is known at once, Pro 12.16
For in much wisdom is much v., Ec 1.18
full of pain, and his work is a v.; 2.23
in much v. and sickness and resentment? 5.17
Remove v. from your mind, and put 11.10

VEXED

him, his soul was v. to death. Ju 16.16
into his house v. and sullen because 1Ki 21.04
your spirit so v. that you eat no 21.05
he was v. in his righteous soul day 2Pe 2.08

VIAL

Then Samuel took a v. of oil and poured it 1Sa 10.01

VICINITY

lived in Jerusalem and its v.; and the singers, Ez 2.70

VICIOUS

a matter of wrongdoing or v. crime, I should Ac 18.14

VICTIM

for many a v. has she laid low; yea, all her Pro 7.26

VICTIMS

while the Levites flayed the v. 2Ch 35.11
A lying tongue hates its v., Pro 26.28
v. of famine and sword, with none to Jer 14.16
Happier were the v. of the sword Lam 4.09
than the v. of hunger, who pined away, 4.09

VICTORIES

with mighty v. by his right hand. Ps 20.06
my God, who ordainest v. for Jacob. 44.04

VICTORIOUS

when I return v. from the Ammonites, Ju 11.31
uphold you with my v. right hand. Is 41.10
triumphant and v. is he, humble and Zec 9.09

VICTORIOUSLY

ride forth v. for the cause of truth Ps 45.04

VICTORY

not the sound of shouting for v., Ex 32.18
your enemies, to give you the v.' Deu 20.04
wrought this great v. in Israel? 1Sa 14.45
wrought a great v. for all Israel. 19.05
the LORD gave v. to David wherever 2Sa 8.06
the LORD gave v. to David wherever 8.14
So the v. that day was turned into 19.02
LORD wrought a great v. that day; 23.10
and the LORD wrought a great v. 23.12
him the LORD had given v. to Syria. 2Ki 5.01
arrow of v., the arrow of v. over Syria! 13.17

VICTORY (cont.)
the LORD saved them by a great v. 1Ch 11.14
the LORD gave v. to David wherever 18.06
the LORD gave v. to David wherever 18.13
and the v., and the majesty; for all that 29.11
and see the v. of the LORD on your 2Ch 20.17
own right hand can give you v. Job 40.14
May we shout for joy over your v., Ps 20.05
Give v. to the king, O LORD; 20.09
The war horse is a vain hope for v., 33.17
nor did their own arm give them v.; 44.03
Thy right hand is filled with v.; 48.10
give v. by thy right hand and answer 60.05
his holy arm have gotten him v. 98.01
The LORD has made known his v., 98.02
earth have seen the v. of our God. 98.03
glad songs of v. in the tents of 118.15
who givest v. to kings, who rescuest 144.10
he adorns the humble with v. 149.04
but the v. belongs to the LORD. Pro 21.31
abundance of counselors there is v. 24.06
the east whom v. meets at every Is 41.02
then his own arm brought him v., 59.16
so my own arm brought me v., 63.05
raise the shout of v. over you. Jer 51.14
thy horses, upon thy chariot of v.? Hab 3.08
your midst, a warrior who gives v.; Zep 3.17
LORD will give v. to the tents of Zec 12.07
wick, till he brings justice to v.; Mt 12.20
"Death is swallowed up in v." 1Co 15.54
"O death, where is thy v.? 15.55
gives us the v. through our Lord 15.57
and this the v. that overcomes 1Jn 5.04

VICTUALS
interest on v., interest on anything that is Deu 23.19

VIEW
and v. the land of Canaan, which I Deu 32.49
v. the land, especially Jericho." Jos 2.01
of it with a v. to their inheritances, 18.04
I think that in v. of the impending 1Co 7.26
no one from a human point of v., 2Co 5.16
Christ from a human point of v., 5.16
will take no other v. than mine; Gal 5.10

VIEWED
from Damascus, the king v. the altar. 2Ki 16.12

VIEWS
to hear from you what your v. are; for with Ac 28.22

VIGILANCE
Keep your heart with all v.; for from it Pro 4.23

VIGOR
His bones are full of youthful v., Job 20.11
their hands, men whose v. is gone? 30.02
to the days of his youthful v. 33.25
those in full v. we are like dead Is 59.10
the earth with v. and dispatch. Rom 9.28

VIGOROUS
for they are v. and are delivered before the Ex 1.19

VILE
my house, do not do this v. thing. Ju 19.23
this man do not do so v. a thing." 19.24
the land with your v. harlotry. Jer 3.02
house, when she has done v. deeds? 11.15
make them like v. figs which are 29.17
and see the v. abominations that Eze 8.09
make your grave, for you are v." Nah 1.14
be disorder and every v. practice. Jas 3.16

VILENESS
as v. is exalted among the sons of men. Ps 12.08

VILLAGE
And whatever town or v. you enter, Mt 10.11
"Go into the v. opposite you, and 21.02
hand, and led him out of the v.; Mk 8.23
saying, 'Do not even enter the v." 8.26
"Go into the v. opposite you, and 11.02
come from every v. of Galilee and Lk 5.17
and entered a v. of the Samaritans, 9.52
And they went on to another v. 9.56
went on their way, he entered a v.; 10.38
And as he entered a v., he was met 17.12
"Go into the v. opposite, where on 19.30
were going to a v. named Emmaus, 24.13
near to the v. to which they were 24.28
Bethlehem, the v. where David was?" Jn 7.42
the v. of Mary and her sister 11.01
Now Jesus had not yet come to the v., 11.30

VILLAGES
by their v. and by their encampments, Gen 25.16
houses of the v. which have no Lev 25.31
in Heshbon, and in all its v. Num 21.25
and they took its v., and dispossessed 21.32
of Manasseh went and took their v., 32.41
went and took Kenath and its v., 32.42
who lived in v. as far as Gaza, the Deu 2.23
besides very many unwalled v. 3.05
and called the v. after his own 3.14
families with their cities and v. Jos 13.23
families, with their cities and v. 13.28
twenty-nine cites, with their v. 15.32
fourteen cities with their v. 15.36
sixteen cities with their v. 15.41
Mareshah: nine cities with their v. 15.44
Ekron, with its towns and its v.; 15.45
the side of Ashdod, with their v. 15.46
Ashdod, its towns and its v.; 15.47
Gaza, its towns and its v.; 15.47
Giloh: eleven cities with their v. 15.51
Zior: nine cities with their v. 15.54
Timnah: ten cities with their v. 15.57
Eltekon: six cities with their v. 15.59
Rabbah: two cities with their v. 15.60
Engedi: six cities with their v. 15.62
all those towns with their v. 16.09
Manasseh ahd Bethshean and its v., 17.11
villages, and Ibleam and its v., 17.11
the inhabitants of Dor and its v., 17.11
inhabitants of Endor and its v., 17.11
inhabitants of Taanach and its v., 17.11
inhabitants of Megiddo and its v.; 17.11
Bethshan and its v. and those in 17.16
Geba—twelve cities with their v.: 18.24
fourteen cities with their v. This is 18.28
thirteen cities with their v.; 19.06
and Ashan—four cities with their v.; 19.07
together with all the v. round 19.08
twelve cities with their v. 19.15
families—these cities with their v. 19.16
Jordan—sixteen cities with their v. 19.22
families—the cities with their v. 19.23
twenty-two cities with their v. 19.30
families—these cities with their v. 19.31
nineteen cities with their v. 19.38
families—the cities with their v. 19.39
families—these cities with their v. 19.48
city and its v. had been given to 21.12
inhabitants of Bethshean and its v., Ju 1.27
villages, or Taanach and its v., 1.27
the inhabitants of Dor and its v., 1.27
inhabitants of Ibleam and its v., 1.27
inhabitants of Megiddo and its v.; 1.27
Israel dwelt in Heshbon and its v., 11.26
villages, and in Aroer and its v., 11.26
fortified cities and unwalled v. 1Sa 6.18
(he had the v. of Jair the son of 1Ki 4.13
Kenath and its v., sixty towns. 1Ch 2.23
And their v. were Tam, Ain, Rimmon, 4.32

VILLAGES (cont.)

along with all their v. which were	1Ch 4.33
city and its v. they gave to Caleb	6.56
dwelt in the v. of the Netophathites.	9.16
enrolled by genealogies in their v.	9.22
were in their v. were obliged to	9.25
Gath and its v. out of the hand of	18.01
in the v. and in the towers, was	27.25
Bethel with its v. and Jeshanah	2Ch 13.19
with its v. and Ephron with its v.	13.19
Soco with its v., Timnah with its v.,	28.18
and Gimzo with its v.; and they	28.18
in one of the v. in the plain of	Neh 6.02
And as for the v., with their	11.25
lived in Kiriatharba and its v.,	11.25
and in Dibon and its v., and in	11.25
and in Jekabzeel and its v.,	11.25
Hazarshual, in Beersheba and its v.,	11.27
in Ziklag, in Meconah and its v.,	11.28
Zanoah, Adullam, and their v.,	11.30
its fields, and Azekah and its v.	11.30
Michmash, Aija, Bethel and its v.,	11.31
and from the v. of the Netophathites;	12.28
for themselves v. around Jerusalem.	12.29
Therefore the Jews of the v.,	Est 9.19
He sits in ambush in the v.;	Ps 10.08
the fields, and lodge in the v.;	Sol 7.11
the v. that Kedar inhabits;	Is 42.11
and its v. shall be burned with	Jer 49.02
up against the land of unwalled v.;	Eze 38.11
and all its v. will say to you,	38.13
be inhabited as v. without walls,	Zec 2.04
went about all the cities and v.,	Mt 9.35
to go into the v. and buy food for	14.15
went about among the v. teaching.	Mk 6.06
the country and v. round about and	6.36
in v., cities, or country, they laid	6.56
to the v. of Caesarea Philippi;	8.27
he went on through cities and v.,	Lk 8.01
departed and went through the v.,	9.06
to go into the v. and country	9.12
on his way through towns and v.,	13.22
gospel to many v. of the Samaritans.	Ac 8.25

VILLAINY

to Shechem, yea, they commit v.	Hos 6.09
against the LORD, and counseled v.?	Nah 1.11
righteousness, full of all deceit and v.,	Ac 13.10

VINDICATE

For the LORD will v. his people and	Deu 32.36
V. me, O LORD, for I have walked in	Ps 26.01
V. me, O LORD, my God, according to	35.24
V. me, O God, and defend my cause	43.01
by thy name, and v. me by thy might.	54.01
For the LORD will v. his people,	135.14
And I will v. the holiness of my	Eze 36.23
through you I v. my holiness	36.23
I v. my holiness before their eyes.	38.16
'V. me against my adversary.'	Lk 18.03
I will v. her, or she will wear me	18.05
And will not God v. his elect,	18.07
tell you, he will v. them speedily.	18.08

VINDICATED

and a man full of talk be v.?	Job 11.02
I know that I shall be v.	13.18
them have v. my holiness in the	Eze 39.27
v. in the Spirit, seen by angels,	1Ti 3.16

VINDICATES

he who v. me is near, Who will contend	Is 50.08

VINDICATING

and v. the righteous by rewarding	1Ki 8.32
and v. the righteous by rewarding	2Ch 6.23

VINDICATION

it is your v. in the eyes of all	Gen 20.16
Turn now, my v. is at stake.	Job 6.29
Form thee let my v. come! Let thy eyes	Ps 17.02
and v. from the God of his salvation.	24.05
who desire my v. shout for joy and	35.27
bring forth your v. as the light,	37.06
revealed his v. in the sight of	98.02
The LORD works v. and justice for	103.06
of the LORD and their v. from me,	Is 54.17
until her v. goes forth as brightness,	62.01
The nations shall see your v.,	62.02
announcing v., mighty to save."	63.01
The LORD has brought forth our v.;	Jer 51.10
given the early rain for your v.,	Joe 2.23

VINE

my dream there was a v. before me,	Gen 40.09
and on the v. there were three	40.10
Binding his foal to the v. and his	49.11
his ass's colt to the choice v.,	49.11
your undressed v. you shall not	Lev 25.05
their v. comes from the v. of Sodom,	Deu 32.23
And the trees said to the v.,	Ju 9.12
But the v. said to them, 'Shall I	9.13
of anything that comes from the v.,	13.14
man under his v. and under his fig	1Ki 4.25
found a wild v. and gathered from	2Ki 4.39
one of you will eat of his own v.,	18.31
like the v., and cast off his	Job 15.33
Thou didst bring a v. out of Egypt;	Ps 80.08
and see; have regard for this v.,	80.14
like a fruitful v. within your	128.03
breasts be like clusters of the v.,	Sol 7.08
languish, and the v. of Sibmah;	Is 16.08
of Jazer for the v. of Sibmah;	16.09
the v. languishes, all the merry-hearted	24.07
pleasant fields, for the fruitful v.,	32.12
fall, as leaves fall from the v.,	34.04
one of you will eat of his own v.,	36.16
Yet I planted you a choice v.,	Jer 2.21
degenerate and become a wild v.?	2.21
thoroughly as a v. the remnant of	6.09
there are no grapes on the v.,	8.13
I weep for you, O v. of Sibmah!	48.32
the wood of the v. surpass any	Eze 15.02
the v. branch which is among the	15.02
the wood of the v. among the trees	15.06
and became a low spreading v.,	17.06
So it became a v., and brought forth	17.06
this v. bent its roots toward him,	17.07
bear fruit, and become a noble v.	17.08
was like a v. in a vineyard	19.10
But the v. was plucked up in fury,	19.12
Israel is a luxuriant v. that	Hos 10.01
they shall blossom as the v.,	14.07
The v. withers, the fig tree languishes.	Joe 1.12
fig tree and v. give their full	2.22
man under his v. and under his fig	Mic 4.04
Do the v., the fig tree, the pomegranate,	Hag 2.19
under his v. and under his fig	Zec 3.10
the v. shall yield its fruit, and	8.12
and your v. in the field shall not	Mal 3.11
fruit of the v. until that day	Mt 26.29
fruit of the v. until that day	Mk 14.25
fruit of the v. until the kingdom	Lk 22.18
"I am the true v., and my Father is	Jn 15.01
itself, unless it abides in the v.,	15.04
I am the v., you are the branches.	15.05
clusters of the v. of the earth,	Rev 14.18

VINEDRESSER

And he said to the v., 'Lo, these three years	Lk 13.07
true vine, and my Father is the v.	Jn 15.01

VINEDRESSERS
of the land to be v. and plowmen. 2Ki 25.12
had farmers and v. in the hills 2Ch 26.10
foreigners shall be your plowmen and v.; Is 61.05
of the land to be v. and plowmen. Jer 52.16
O v., for the wheat and the barley; Joe 1.11

VINEGAR
shall drink no v. made from wine Num 6.03
my thirst they gave me v. to drink. Ps 69.21
Like v. to the teeth, and smoke to Pro 10.26
a cold day, and like v. on a wound. 25.20
took a sponge, filled it with v., Mt 27.48
and, filling a sponge full of v., Mk 15.36
coming up and offering him v., Lk 23.36
A bowl full of v. stood there; Jn 19.29
full of the v. on hyssop and held 19.29
When Jesus had received the v., 19.30

VINE-ROWS
"Go up through her v. and destroy, Jer 5.10

VINES
the grapes from the undressed v. Lev 25.11
or v., or pomegranates; and there is Num 20.05
of v. and fig trees and pomegranates, Deu 8.08
He destroyed their v. with hail, Ps 78.47
He smote their v. and fig trees, and 105.33
figs, and the v. are in blossom; Sol 2.13
to see whether the v. had budded, 6.11
and see whether the v. have budded, 7.12
and planted it with choice v.; Is 5.02
there used to be a thousand v., 7.23
eat up your v. and your fig trees; Jer 5.17
lay waste her v. and her fig trees, Hos 2.12
It has laid waste my v., and splintered Joe 1.07
blossom, nor fruit be on the v., Hab 3.17

VINEYARD
of the soil. He planted a v.; Gen 9.20
a field or v. to be grazed over, or Ex 22.05
in his own field and in his own v. 22.05
You shall do likewise with your v., 23.11
And you shall not strip your v. bare, Lev 19.10
the fallen grapes of your v.; 19.10
six years you shall prune your v., 25.03
sow your field or prune your v. 25.04
will not pass through field or v., Num 20.17
not turn aside into field or v.; 21.22
has planted a v. and has not Deu 20.06
not sow your v. with two kinds of 22.09
have sown and the yield of the v. 22.09
"When you go into your neighbor's v., 23.24
When you gather the grapes of your v., 24.21
you shall plant a v., and you shall 28.30
the Jezreelite had a v. in Jezreel, 1Ki 21.01
"Give me your v., that I may have 21.02
I will give you a better v. for it; 21.02
to him, 'Give me your v. for money; 21.06
I will give you another v. for it'; 21.06
answered, 'I will not give you my v.'" 21.06
give you the v. of Naboth the 21.07
possession of the v. of Naboth the 21.15
go down to the v. of Naboth the 21.16
he is in the v. of Naboth, where he 21.18
they glean the v. of the wicked Job 24.06
by the v. of a man without sense; Pro 24.30
fruit of her hands she plants a v. 31.16
but, my own v. I have not kept! Sol 1.06
Solomon had a v. at Baalhamon; 8.11
he let out the v. to keepers; 8.11
My v., my very own, is for myself; 8.12
Zion is left like a booth in a v., Is 1.08
"It is you who have devoured the v., 3.14
a love song concerning his v.: 5.01
beloved had a v. on a very fertile 5.01
I pray you, between me and my v. 5.03
What more was there to do for my v., 5.04
tell you what I will do to my v. 5.05
For the v. of the LORD of hosts is 5.07
For ten acres of v. shall yield but 5.10
day: "A pleasant v., sing of it! 27.02
Many shepherds have destroyed my v., Jer 12.10
you shall not plant or have a v.; 35.07
We have no v. or field or seed; 35.09
a vine in a v. transplanted by the Eze 19.10
to hire laborers for his v. Mt 20.01
a day, he sent them into his v. 20.02
he said, 'You go into the v. too, 20.04
to them, 'You go into the v. too.' 20.07
owner of the v. said to his steward, 20.08
'Son, go and work in the v. today.' 21.28
was a householder who planted a v., 21.33
him and cast him out of the v., 21.39
therefore the owner of the v. comes, 21.40
and let out the v. to other 21.41
"A man planted a v., and set a Mk 12.01
them some of the fruit of the v. 12.02
him, and cast him out of the v. 12.08
What will the owner of the v. do? 12.09
tenants, and give the v. to others. 12.09
had a fig tree planted in his v.; Lk 13.06
this parable: "A man planted a v., 20.09
him some of the fruit of the v.; 20.10
Then the owner of the v. said, 20.13
him out of the v. and killed him. 20.15
the owner of the v. do to them? 20.15
tenants, and give the v. to others." 20.16
Who plants a v. without eating any 1Co 9.07

VINEYARDS
us inheritance of fields and v. Num 16.14
in a narrow path between the v., 22.24
and v. and olive trees, which you Deu 6.11
You shall plant v. and dress them, 28.39
the fruit of v. and oliveyards Jos 24.13
grapes from their v. and trod them, Ju 9.27
and he came to the v. of Timnah. 14.05
"Go and lie in wait in the v., 21.20
come out of the v. and seize each 21.21
your fields and v. and olive 1Sa 8.14
and of your v. and give it to his 8.15
every one of you fields and v., 22.07
garments, olive orchards and v., 2Ki 5.26
and wine, a land of bread and v., 18.32
and plant v., and eat their fruit. 19.29
and over the v. was Shimei the 1Ch 27.27
produce of the v. for the wine 27.27
our v., and our houses to get grain Neh 5.03
tax upon our fields and our v. 5.04
men have our fields and our v." 5.05
their v., their olive orchards, and 5.11
v., olive orchards and fruit trees 9.25
no treader turns toward their v. Job 24.18
and plant v., and get a fruitful Ps 107.37
houses and planted v. for myself; Ecc 2.04
me, they made me keeper of the v.; Sol 1.06
henna blossoms in the v. of Engedi. 1.14
little foxes, that spoil the v., 2.15
for our v. are in blossom. 2.15
let us go out early to the v., 7.12
and in the v. no songs are sung, no Is 16.10
and wine, a land of bread and v. 36.17
and plant v., and eat their fruit. 37.30
shall plant v. and eat their fruit. 65.21
Again you shall plant v. upon the Jer 31.05
and fields and v. shall again be 32.15
and gave them v. and fields at the 39.10
shall build houses and plant v. Eze 28.26
And there I will give her her v., Hos 2.15
waste your gardens and your v.; Amo 4.09
you have planted pleasant v., 5.11
and in all v. there shall be 5.17
shall plant v. and drink their 9.14
country, a place for planting v.; Mic 1.06
though they plant v., they shall not Zep 1.13

VINTAGE
shall last to the time of v., Lev 26.05
and the v. shall last to the time 26.05
better than the v. of Abiezer? Ju 8.02
in the presses; the v. shout is hushed. Is 16.10
the gleaning when the v. is done. 24.13
for the v. will fail, the fruit 32.10
fruits and your v. the destroyer Jer 48.32
as when the v. has been gleaned: Mic 7.01
and gathered the v. of the earth, Rev 14.19

VIOLATE
righteousness he will not v. Job 37.23
if they v. my statutes and do not Ps 89.31
I will not v. my covenant, or alter 89.34
flattery those who v. the covenant; Dan 11.32

VIOLATED
man because he v. his neighbor's Deu 22.24
be his wife, because he has v. her; 22.29
his friends, he v. his covenant. Ps 55.20
v. the statutes, broken the everlasting Is 24.05
for having v. their first pledge. 1Ti 5.12
A man who has v. the law of Moses Heb 10.28

VIOLENCE
and the earth was filled with v. Gen 6.11
is filled with v. through them; 6.13
weapons of v. are their swords. 49.05
that the v. done to the seventy Ju 9.24
my savior; thou savest me from v. 2Sa 22.03
didst deliver me from men of v. 22.49
although there is no v. in my hands, Job 16.17
'V.!' but am not answered; 19.07
With v. it seizes my garment; 30.18
on his own pate his v. descends. Ps 7.16
his soul hates him that loves v. 11.05
didst deliver me from men of v. 18.48
have risen against me, and they breathe out v. 27.12
for I see v. and strife in the city 55.09
your hands deal out v. on earth. 58.02
From oppression and v. he redeems 72.14
v. covers them as a garment. 73.06
are full of the habitations of v. 74.20
the ways of all who get gain by v.; Pro 1.19
envy a man of v. and do not choose 3.31
wickedness and drink the wine of v. 4.17
mouth of the wicked conceals v. 10.06
mouth of the wicked conceals v. 10.11
of the treacherous is for v. 13.02
A man of v. entices his neighbor 16.29
He who does v. to his father and 19.26
The v. of the wicked will sweep 21.07
for their minds devise v., 24.02
of the righteous; do not v. to his home; 24.15
off his own feet and drinks v. 26.06
cast down to the earth with v. Is 28.02
death, although he had done no v., 53.09
and deeds of v. are in their hands. 59.06
V. shall no more be heard in your 60.18
v. and destruction are heard within Jer 6.07
are lifted up, and you suffer v. 13.22
"V. and destruction!" For the word of the 20.08
And do no wrong or v. to the alien, 22.03
for practicing oppression and v. 22.17
The v. done to me and to my kinsmen 51.35
and v. is in the land, and ruler is 51.46
V. has grown up into a rod of Eze 7.11
crimes and the city is full of v., 7.23
they should fill the land with v., 8.17
account of the v. of all those who 12.19
have done v. to my law and have 22.26
your trade you were filled with v., 28.16
Put away v. and oppression, and 45.09
and the men of v. among your own Dan 11.14
they multiply falsehood and v.; Hos 12.01
for the v. done to the people of Joe 3.19
who store up v. and robbery in Amo 3.10
day, and bring near the seat of v.? 6.03
For the v. done to your brother Ob 1.10
and from the v. which is in his Jon 3.08
Your rich men are full of v.; Mic 6.12
Or cry to thee "V.!" and thou wilt not Hab 1.02
Destruction and v. are before me; 1.03
They all come for v.; terror of them goes 1.09
blood of men and v. to the earth, 2.08
The v. done to Lebanon will overwhelm 2.17
blood of men and v. to the earth, 2.17
master's house with v. and fraud. Zep 1.09
is sacred, they do v. to the law. 3.04
been taken by v. or is lame or Mal 1.13
and covering one's garment with v., 2.16
kingdom of heaven has suffered v., Mt 11.12
and men of v. take it by force. 11.12
"Rob no one by v. or false Lk 3.14
but without v., for they were Ac 5.26
because of the v. of the crowd; 21.35
Lysias came and with great v. took *24.07
great city be thrown down with v., Rev 18.21

VIOLENT
and v. men shall afflict them no 2Sa 7.10
and v. men shall waste them no 1Ch 17.09
I have avoided the ways of the v. Ps 17.04
and with what v. hatred they hate 25.19
from evil men; preserve me from v. men, 140.01
preserve me from v. men, who have planned 140.04
evil hunt down the v. man speedily! 140.11
gets honor, and v. men get riches. Pro 11.16
the king laid v. hands upon some Ac 12.01
And when the dissension became 23.10
not v. but gentle, not quarrelsome, 1Ti 3.03
a drunkard or v. or greedy for Tit 1.07

VIOLENTLY
Then Isaac trembled v., and said, Gen 27.33
ass shall be v. taken away before Deu 28.31
with Midian?" And they upbraided him v. Ju 8.01
justice and right v. taken away, Ecc 5.08
Behold, the LORD will hurl you away v., Is 22.17
asunder, the earth is v. shaken. 24.19
preached, and every one enters it v. Lk 16.16
As we were v. storm-tossed, they Ac 27.18
church of God v. and tried to Gal 1.13

VIOLET
their clothing is v. and purple; they are all Jer 10.09

VIPER
a v. by the path, that bites the Gen 49.17
the tongue of a v. will kill him. Job 20.16
the v. and the flying serpent, they Is 30.06
which is crushed a v. is hatched. 59.05
when a v. came out because of the Ac 28.03

VIPERS
their lips is the poison of v. Ps 140.03
he said to them, "You brood of v.! Mt 3.07
You brood of v.! how can you speak 12.34
you brood of v., how are you to 23.33
baptized by him, "You brood of v.! Lk 3.07

VIRGIN
a v., whom no man had known. Gen 24.16
"If a man seduces a v. who is not Ex 22.16
or his v. sister (who is near to Lev 21.03
take to wife a v. of his own 21.14
an evil name upon a v. of Israel; Deu 22.19
"If there is a betrothed v., 22.23
"If a man meets a v. who is not 22.28
destroying both young man and v., 32.25
here are my v. daughter and his Ju 19.24
for she was a v., and it seemed 2Sa 13.02
thus were the v. daughters of the 13.18
the v. daughter of Zion; she wags her 2Ki 19.21
no compassion on young man or v., 2Ch 36.17

VIRGIN (cont.)

how then could I look upon a v.? Job 31.01
with her v. companions, her escort, Ps 45.14
O oppressed v. daughter of Sidon; Is 23.12
the v. daughter of Zion; she wags her 37.22
O v. daughter of Babylon; sit on the 47.01
For as a young man married a v., 62.05
for the v. daughter of my people is Jer 14.17
The v. Israel has done a very 18.13
you shall be built, O v. Israel! 31.04
Return, O v. Israel, return to these 31.21
O v. daughter of Egypt! In vain you 46.11
wine press the v. daughter of Lam 1.15
O v. daughter of Zion? For vast as 2.13
and their v. bosoms handled. Eze 23.03
and handled her v. bosom and 23.08
but only a v. of the stock of the 44.22
Lament like a v. girded with Joe 1.08
'Fallen, no more to rise, is the v. Israel; Amo 5.02
"Behold, a v. shall conceive and Mt 1.23
to a v. betrothed to a man whose Lk 1.27

VIRGINITY

And he shall take a wife in her v. Lev 21.13
not find in her the tokens of v.,' Deu 22.14
tokens of her v. to the elders of 22.15
in your daughter the tokens of v." 22.17
are the tokens of my daughter's v.' 22.17
the tokens of v. were not found in 22.20
and bewail my v., I and my companions, Ju 11.37
bewailed her v. upon the mountains. 11.38
husband seven years from her v., Lk 2.36

VIRGIN'S

house of David; and the v. name was Mary. Lk 1.27

VIRGINS

to the marriage present for v. Ex 22.17
hundred young v. who had not known Ju 21.12
beautiful young v. be sought out Est 2.02
beautiful young v. to the harem in 2.03
in his sight more than all the v., 2.17
When the v. were gathered together 2.19
reared young men nor brought up v." Is 23.04
in Zion, v. in the towns of Judah. Lam 5.11
day the fair v. and the young men Amo 8.13

VIRTUE

not in v. of our works but in 2Ti 1.09
works but in v. of his own purpose 1.09
but in v. of his own mercy, by the Tit 3.05
faith with v., and v. with knowledge, 2Pe 1.05

VISAGE

Now their v. is blacker than soot, Lam 4.08

VISIBLE

and it was v. to the end of the Dan 4.11
and it was v. to the end of the 4.20
exposed by the light it becomes v., Eph 5.13
anything that becomes v. is light. 5.13
v. and invisible, whether thrones or Col 1.16

VISION

of the LORD came to Abram in a v., Gen 15.01
make myself known to him in a v., Num 12.06
who sees the v. of the Almighty, 24.04
who sees the v. of the Almighty, 24.16
in those days; there was no frequent v. 1Sa 3.01
was afraid to tell the v. to Eli. 3.15
and in accordance with all this v., 2Sa 7.17
and in accordance with all this v., 1Ch 17.15
written in the v. of Isaiah the 2Ch 32.32
chased away like a v. of the night. Job 20.08
in a v. of the night, when deep 33.15
speak in a v. to thy faithful one, Ps 89.19
The v. of Isaiah the son of Amoz, Is 1.01
A stern v. is told to me; 21.02
oracle concerning the valley of v. 22.01
and confusion in the valley of v., 22.05
they err in v., they stumble in 28.07
be like a dream, a v. of the night. 29.07
And the v. of all this has become 29.11
are prophesying to you a lying v., Jer 14.14
Babylon, the LORD showed me this v.: 24.01
this is the v. which the LORD has 38.21
prophets obtain no v. from the LORD. Lam 2.09
they seek a v. from the prophet, but Eze 7.26
like the v. that I saw in the plain 8.04
me in the v. by the Spirit of God 11.24
Then the v. that I had seen went up 11.24
and every v. comes to naught'? 12.22
and the fulfilment of every v. 12.23
more any false v. or flattering 12.24
'The v. that he sees is for many 12.27
Have you not seen a delusive v., 13.07
And the v. I saw was like the v. which 43.03
and like the v. which I had seen by 43.03
to Daniel in a v. of the night. Dan 2.19
"I saw in my v. by night, and behold, 7.02
Belshazzar a v. appeared to me, 8.01
And I saw in the v.; and when I 8.02
how long is the v. concerning the 8.13
had seen the v., I sought to 8.15
make this man understand the v." 8.16
that the v. is for the time of the 8.17
The v. of the evenings and the 8.26
but seal up the v., for it pertains 8.26
appalled by the v. and did not 8.27
I had seen in the v. at the first, 9.21
the word and understand the v. 9.23
to seal both v. and prophet, and to 9.24
and had understanding of the v. 10.01
alone saw the v., for the men who 10.07
were with me did not see the v., 10.07
left alone and saw this great v., 10.08
For the v. is for days yet to come." 10.14
reason of the v. pains have come 10.16
up in order to fulfil the v.; 11.14
The v. of Obadiah. Thus says the Ob 1.01
without v., and darkness to you, Mic 3.06
The book of the v. of Nahum of Nah 1.01
the LORD answered me: "Write the v.; Hab 2.02
For still the v. awaits its time; 2.03
ashamed of his v. when he prophesies; Zec 13.04
commanded them, "Tell no one the v., Mt 17.09
he had seen a v. in the temple; Lk 1.22
they had even seen a v. of angels, 24.23
Lord said to him in a v., "Ananias." Ac 9.10
clearly in a v. an angel of God 10.03
as to what the v. which he had 10.17
And while Peter was pondering the v., 10.19
and in a trance I saw a v., 11.05
but thought he was seeing a v. 12.09
And a v. appeared to Paul in the 16.09
And when he had seen the v., 16.10
said to Paul one night in a v., 18.09
disobedient to the heavenly v., 26.19
was how I saw the horses in my v.: Rev 9.17

VISIONS

spoke to Israel in v. of the night, Gen 46.02
and in the v. of Iddo the seer 2Ch 9.29
Amid thoughts from v. of night, Job 4.13
dreams and terrify me with v., 7.14
they speak v. of their own minds, Jer 23.16
for you false and deceptive v.; Lam 2.14
were opened, and I saw v. of God. Eze 1.01
brought me in v. of God to Jerusalem, 8.03
see delusive v. and who give lying 13.09
Jerusalem and saw v. of peace for 13.16
see delusive v. nor practice 13.23
while they see for you false v., 21.29
seeing false v. and divining lies 22.28
me in the v. of God into the land 40.02
understanding in all v. and dreams. Dan 1.17
dream and the v. of your head as 2.28

VISIONS (cont.)
fancies and the v. of my head Dan 4.05
The v. of my head as I lay in bed 4.10
"I saw in the v. of my head as I 4.13
had a dream and v. of his head as 7.01
After this I saw in the night v., 7.07
I saw in the night v., and behold, 7.13
anxious and the v. of my head 7.15
it was I who multiplied v., Hos 12.10
and your young men shall see v. Joe 2.28
and your young men shall see v., Ac 2.17
I will go on to v. and revelations 2Co 12.01
of angels, taking his stand on v., Col 2.18

VISIT
went out to v. the women of the Gen 34.01
but God will v. you, and bring you 50.24
"God will v. you, and you shall 50.25
of Israel, saying, "God will v. you; Ex 13.19
Nevertheless, in the day when I v., 32.34
I will v. their sin upon them." 32.34
Samson went to v. his wife with a Ju 15.01
of Judah had come down to v. Joram. 2Ki 9.16
we came down to v. the royal 10.13
through his going to v. Joram. 2Ch 22.07
dost v. him every morning, and test Job 7.18
the LORD will v. Tyre, and she will Is 23.17
remember me and v. me, and take Jer 15.15
I will v. you, and I will fulfil to 29.10
he shall remain until I v. him, 32.05
thee sick or in prison and v. thee?' Mt 25.39
in prison and you did not v. me.' 25.43
And at the second v. Joseph made Ac 7.13
into his heart to v. his brethren, 7.23
with or to v. any one of another 10.28
us return and v. the brethren in 15.36
I will v. you after passing through 1Co 16.05
urged him to v. you with the other 16.12
I wanted to v. you on my way to 2Co 1.16
not to make you another painful v. 2.01
I did when present on my second v., 13.02
went up to Jerusalem to v. Cephas, Gal 1.18
that our v. to you was not in vain; 1Th 2.01
to v. orphans and widows in their Jas 1.27

VISITATION
did not know the time of your v." Lk 19.44
and glorify God on the day of v. 1Pe 2.12

VISITED
The LORD v. Sarah as he had said, Gen 21.01
the LORD had v. the people of Ex 4.31
or if they are v. by the fate of Num 16.29
the LORD had v. his people and Ru 1.06
And the LORD v. Hannah, and she 1Sa 2.21
he will not be v. by harm. Pro 19.23
end thou hast v. them with destruction Is 26.14
you will be v. by the LORD of hosts 29.06
me, I was sick and you v. me, Mt 25.36
for he has v. and redeemed his Lk 1.68
and "God has v. his people!" 7.16
how God first v. the Gentiles, Ac 15.14
out of the prison, and v. Lydia; 16.40
and Paul v. him and prayed, and 28.08

VISITEST
if thou v. me by night, if thou Ps 17.03
Thou v. the earth and waterest it, 65.09

VISITING
v. the iniquity of the fathers upon Ex 20.05
v. the iniquity of the fathers upon 34.07
v. the iniquity of fathers upon Num 14.18
v. the iniquity of the fathers upon Deu 5.09

VISITOR
only v. to Jerusalem who does not know Lk 24.18

VISITORS
and v. from Rome, both Jews and Ac 2.10

VOICE
listened to the v. of your wife, Gen 3.17
The v. of your brother's blood is 4.10
wives: "Adah and Zillah, hear my v.; 4.23
Abram hearkened to the v. of Sarai. 16.02
child lifted up his v. and wept. 21.16
And God heard the v. of the lad; 21.17
has heard the v. of the lad where 21.17
because you have obeyed my v." 22.18
obeyed my v. and kept my charge, my 26.05
"The v. is Jacob's v., but the 27.22
And Esau lifted up his v. and wept. 27.38
Now therefore, my son, obey my v.; 27.43
also heard my v. and given me a 30.06
me, and I cried out with a loud v.; 39.14
that I lifted up my v. and cried, 39.15
as I lifted up my v. and cried, 39.18
And they will hearken to your v.; Ex 3.18
not believe me or listen to my v., 4.01
these two signs or heed your v., 4.09
should heed his v. and let Israel 5.02
hearken to the v. of the LORD your 15.26
Listen now to my v.; I will give you 18.19
heed to the v. of his father-in-law 18.24
will obey my v. and keep my 19.05
Give heed to him and hearken to his v., 23.21
attentively to his v. and do all 23.22
the people answered with one v., 24.03
he heard the v. speaking to him Num 7.89
and have not hearkened to my v., 14.22
he heard our v., and sent an angel 20.16
LORD hearkened to the v. of Israel, 21.03
hearken to your v. or give ear to Deu 1.45
saw no form; there was only a v. 4.12
the LORD your God and obey his v., 4.30
ever hear the v. of a god speaking 4.33
Out of heaven he let you hear his v., 4.36
and the deep gloom, with a loud v.; 5.22
you heard the v. out of the midst 5.23
have heard his v. out of the midst 5.24
if we hear the v. of the LORD our 5.25
has heard the v. of the living God 5.26
not obey the v. of the LORD your 8.20
did not believe him or obey his v., 9.23
his commandments and obey his v., 13.04
if you obey the v. of the LORD your 15.05
hear again the v. of the LORD my 18.16
not obey the v. of his father or 21.18
his father or the v. of his mother, 21.18
rebellious, he will not obey our v.; 21.20
fathers, and the LORD heard our v., 26.07
have obeyed the v. of the LORD my 26.14
ordinances, and will obey his v.; 26.17
obey the v. of the LORD your God, 27.10
the men of Israel with a loud v.: 27.14
"And if you obey the v. of the LORD 28.01
if you obey the v. of the LORD 28.02
not obey the v. of the LORD your 28.15
not obey the v. of the LORD your 28.45
not obey the v. of the LORD your 28.62
and obey his v. in all that I 30.02
again obey the v. of the LORD, 30.08
if you obey the v. of the LORD your 30.10
obeying his v., and cleaving to him; 30.20
the v. of Judah, and bring him in to 33.07
not hearken to the v. of the LORD; Jos 5.06
not shout or let your v. be heard, 6.10
LORD hearkened to the v. of a man; 10.14
have obeyed my v. in all that I 22.02
serve, and his v. we will obey." 24.24
fathers, and have not obeyed my v., Ju 2.20
you have not given heed to my v." 6.10
And God listened to the v. of Manoah, 13.09
recognized the v. of the young 18.03

VOICE (cont.)

"Do not let your v. be heard among Ju 18.25
listen to the v. of their brethren, 20.13
moved, and her v. was not heard; 1Sa 1.13
listen to the v. of their father; 2.25
with a mighty v. that day against 7.10
"Hearken to the v. of the people in 8.07
Now then, hearken to their v.; 8.09
to listen to the v. of Samuel; 8.19
to Samuel, "Hearken to their v., 8.22
hearkened to your v. in all that 12.01
hearken to his v. and not rebel 12.14
not hearken to the v. of the LORD, 12.15
you not obey the v. of the LORD? 15.19
"I have obeyed the v. of the LORD, 15.20
as in obeying the v. of the LORD? 15.22
the people and obeyed their v. 15.24
hearkened to the v. of Jonathan; 19.06
"Is this your v., my son David?" 24.16
And Saul lifted up his v. and wept. 24.16
see, I have hearkened to your v., 25.35
Saul recognized David's v., 26.17
"Is this your v., my son David?" 26.17
"It is my v., my lord, O king." 26.17
she cried out with a loud v.; 28.12
did not obey the v. of the LORD, 28.18
lifted up his v. and wept at the 2Sa 3.32
and lifted up their v. and wept; 13.36
and the king cried with a loud v., 19.04
listen to the v. of singing men 19.35
From his temple he heard my v., 22.07
and the Most High uttered his v. 22.14
of Israel with a loud v., saying, 1Ki 8.55
LORD hearkened to the v. of Elijah; 17.22
But there was no v., and no one 18.26
the oblation, but there was no v.; 18.29
after the fire a still small v. 19.12
there came a v. to him, and said, 19.13
hearkened to their v., and did so. 20.25
have not obeyed the v. of the LORD, 20.36
not obey the v. of the LORD their 2Ki 18.12
out in a loud v. in the language 18.28
you raised your v. and haughtily 19.22
oath to the LORD with a loud v., 2Ch 15.14
God of Israel, with a very loud v. 20.19
and their v. was heard, and their 30.27
it with a loud v. in the language 32.18
with a loud v. when they saw the Ez 3.12
answered with a loud v., "It is so; we 10.12
with a loud v. to the LORD their Neh 9.04
hear not the v. of the taskmaster. Job 3.18
the v. of the fierce lion, the teeth 4.10
was silence, then I heard a v.: 4.16
that he was listening to my v. 9.16
the v. of the nobles was hushed, and 29.10
my pipe to the v. of those who 30.31
thunder of his v. and the rumbling 37.02
After it his v. roars; he thunders 37.04
his majestic v. and he does not 37.04
lightnings when his v. is heard. 37.04
God thunders wondrously with his v.; 37.05
"Can you lift up your v. to the clouds, 38.34
can you thunder with a v. like his? 40.09
the morning thou dost hear my v.; Ps 5.03
From his temple he heard my v., 18.06
and the Most High uttered his v., 18.13
are their words; their v. is not heard; 19.03
yet their v. goes out through all 19.04
Hear the v. of my supplication, as I 28.02
has heard the v. of my supplications. 28.06
The v. of the LORD is upon the 29.03
The v. of the LORD is powerful, the 29.04
the v. of the LORD is full of 29.04
The v. of the LORD breaks the 29.05
The v. of the LORD flashes forth 29.07
The v. of the LORD shakes the 29.08
The v. of the LORD makes the oaks 29.09
he utters his v., the earth melts. 46.06
and moan, and he will hear my v. 55.17
not hear the v. of charmers or of 58.05
Hear my v., O God, in my complaint; 64.01
given heed to the v. of my prayer. 66.19
lo, he sends forth his v., 68.33
forth his voice, his mighty v. 68.33
I hear a v. I had not known: 81.05
"But my people did not listen to my v.; 81.11
the floods have lifted up their v., 93.03
today you would hearken to his v.! 95.07
hearkening to the v. of his word! 103.20
did not obey the v. of the LORD. 106.25
he has heard my v. and my supplications. 116.01
Hear my v. in thy steadfast love; 119.149
Lord, hear my v.! let thy ears 130.02
attentive to the v. of my supplications! 130.02
give ear to the v. of my supplications, 140.06
Give ear to my v., when I call 141.01
I cry with my v. to the LORD, with 142.01
with my v. I make supplication to 142.01
in the markets she raises her v.; Pro 1.20
and raise your v. for understanding, 2.03
listen to the v. of my teachers or 5.13
not understanding raise her v.? 8.01
his neighbor with a loud v., 27.14
and a fool's v. with many words. Ecc 5.03
why should God be angry at your v., 5.06
bird of the air will carry your v., 10.20
one rises up at the v. of a bird, 12.04
The v. of my beloved! Behold, he comes, Sol 2.08
and the v. of the turtledove is 2.12
see your face, let me hear your v., 2.14
for your v. is sweet, and your face 2.14
companions are listening for your v.; 8.13
shook at the v. of him who called, Is 6.04
And I heard the v. of the Lord 6.08
their v. is heard as far as Jahaz; 15.04
Give ear, and hear my v.; 28.23
your v. shall come from the ground 29.04
the ground like the v. of a ghost, 29.04
his majestic v. to be heard and 30.30
terror-stricken at the v. of the LORD, 30.31
women who are at ease, hear my v.; 32.09
out in a loud v. in the language 36.13
you raised your v. and haughtily 37.23
A v. cries: "In the wilderness 40.03
A v. says, "Cry!" And I said, 40.06
lift up your v. with strength, O 40.09
He will not cry or lift up his v., 42.02
and its cities lift up their v., 42.11
and obeys the v. of his servant, 50.10
thanksgiving and the v. of song. 51.03
Hark, your watchmen lift up their v., 52.08
lift up your v. like a trumpet; 58.01
not make your v. to be heard on 58.04
from the city! A v. from the temple! 66.06
The v. of the LORD, rendering 66.06
not obeyed my v., says the LORD. Jer 3.13
A v. on the bare heights is heard, 3.21
not obeyed the v. of the LORD our 3.25
For a v. declares from Dan and 4.15
'Obey my v., and I will be your God, 7.23
not obey the v. of the LORD their 7.28
the v. of mirth and the v. of gladness, 7.34
the v. of the bridegroom and the v. of 7.34
them, and have not obeyed my v., 9.13
When he utters his v. there is a 10.13
Listen to my v., and do all that I 11.04
to this day, saying, Obey my v. 11.07
has lifted up her v. against me; 12.08
the v. of mirth and the v. of gladness, 16.09
the v. of the bridegroom and the v. of 16.09
my sight, not listening to my v., 18.10
out, and lift up your v. in Bashan; 22.20
that you have not obeyed my v. 22.21
the v. of mirth and the v. of gladness, 25.10
v. of the bridegroom and the v. of the 25.10

VOICE (cont.)

his holy habitation utter his v.; Jer 25.30
and obey the v. of the LORD your 26.13
"A v. is heard in Ramah, lamentation 31.15
"Keep your v. from weeping, and your 31.16
not obey thy v. or walk in thy law; 32.23
the v. of mirth and the v. of gladness, 33.11
the v. of the bridegroom and the v. of 33.11
We have obeyed the v. of Jonadab 35.08
Obey now the v. of the LORD in what 38.20
the LORD, and did not obey his v., 40.03
will obey the v. of the LORD our 42.06
we obey the v. of the LORD our God." 42.06
disobeying the v. of the LORD your 42.13
not obeyed the v. of the LORD your 42.21
did not obey the v. of the LORD, 43.04
did not obey the v. of the LORD. 43.07
not obey the v. of the LORD or 44.23
far as Jahaz they utter their v., 48.34
When he utters his v. there is a 51.16
waste, and stilling her mighty v. 51.55
the noise of their v. is raised; 51.55
And there came a v. from above the Eze 1.25
and I heard the v. of one speaking. 1.28
they cry in my ears with a loud v., 8.18
he cried in my ears with a loud v., 9.01
like the v. of God Almighty when he 10.05
my face, and cried with a loud v., 11.13
that his v. should no more be heard 19.09
to lift up the v. with shouting, 21.22
a beautiful v. and plays well on 33.32
there fell a v. from heaven, "O King Dan 4.31
And I heard a man's v. between the 8.16
not obeyed the v. of the LORD our 9.10
aside, refusing to obey thy v. 9.11
and we have not obeyed his v. 9.14
The LORD utters his v. before his Joe 2.11
and utters his v. from Jerusalem, 3.16
and utters his v. from Jerusalem; Amo 1.02
I cried, and thou didst hear my v. Jon 2.02
But I with the v. of thanksgiving 2.09
and let the hills hear your v. Mic 6.01
The v. of the LORD cries to the 6.09
and the v. of your messengers shall Nah 2.13
the deep gave forth its v., Hab 3.10
She listens to no v., she accepts no Zep 3.02
obeyed the v. of the LORD their God, Hab 1.12
obey the v. of the LORD your God." Zec 6.15
"A v. was heard in Ramah, wailing Mt 2.18
"The v. of one crying in the 3.03
and lo, a v. from heaven, saying, 3.17
any one hear his v. in the streets; 12.19
and a v. from the cloud said, "This 17.05
hour Jesus cried with a loud v., 27.46
with a loud v. and yielded up his 27.50
the v. of one crying in the wilderness: Mk 1.03
and a v. came from heaven, "Thou art 1.11
him and crying with a loud v., 1.26
and crying out with a loud v., 5.07
and a v. came out of the cloud, 9.07
hour Jesus cried with a loud v., 15.34
when the v. of your greeting came Lk 1.44
"The v. of one crying in the 3.04
and a v. came from heaven, "Thou art 3.22
and he cried out with a loud v., 4.33
him, and said with a loud v., 8.28
And a v. came out of the cloud, 9.35
And when the v. had spoken, Jesus 9.36
raised her v. and said to him, 11.27
back, praising God with a loud v.; 17.15
God with a loud v. for all the 19.37
Then Jesus, crying with a loud v., 23.46
"I am the v. of one crying in the Jn 1.23
greatly at the bridegroom's v.; 3.29
will hear the v. of the Son of God, 5.25
in the tombs will hear his v. 5.28
His v. you have never heard, his 5.37
the sheep hear his v., 10.03
follow him, for they know his v. 10.04
do not know the v. of strangers." 10.05
also, and they will heed my v. 10.16
My sheep hear my v., 10.27
said this, he cried with a loud v., 11.43
Then a v. came from heaven, "I 12.28
"This v. has come for your sake, not 12.30
who is of the truth hears my v." 18.37
lifted up his v. and addressed them, Ac 2.14
near to look, the v. of the Lord came, 7.31
out with a loud v. and stopped 7.57
down and cried with a loud v., 7.60
possessed, crying with a loud v.; 8.07
and heard a v. saying to him, 9.04
hearing the v. but seeing no one. 9.07
And there came a v. to him, 10.13
And the v. came to him again a 10.15
And I heard a v. saying to me, 'Rise, 11.07
But the v. answered a second time 11.09
Recognizing Peter's v., in her joy 12.14
"The v. of a god, and not of man!" 12.22
said in a loud v., "Stand upright 14.10
But Paul cried with a loud v., 16.28
they all with one v. cried out, 19.34
ground and heard a v. saying to me, 22.07
not hear the v. of the one who was 22.09
and to hear a v. from his mouth; 22.14
I heard a v. saying to me in the 26.14
defense, Festus said with a loud v., 26.24
for "Their v. has gone out to all Rom 10.18
may with one v. glorify the God 15.06
says, "Today, when you hear his v., Heb 3.07
you hear his v. do not harden your 3.15
"Today, when you hear his v., 4.07
and a v. whose words made the 12.19
His v. then shook the earth; 12.26
Father and the v. was borne to him 2Pe 1.17
we heard this v. borne from heaven, 1.18
with human v. and restrained the 2.16
behind me a long v. like a trumpet Rev 1.10
to see the v. that was speaking to 1.12
and his v. was like the sound of 1.15
one hears my v. and opens the door, 3.20
And the first v., which I had heard 4.01
angel proclaiming with a loud v., 5.02
the elders the v. of many angels, 5.11
saying with a loud v., "Worthy is the 5.12
as with a v. of thunder, "Come!" 6.01
seemed to be a v. in the midst of 6.06
I heard the v. of the fourth living 6.07
they cried out with a loud v., 6.10
with a loud v. to the four angels 7.02
and crying out with a loud v., 7.10
an eagle crying with a loud v., 8.13
and I heard a v. from the four 9.13
and called out with a loud v., 10.03
but I heard a v. from heaven saying, 10.04
Then the v. which I had heard from 10.08
heard a loud v. from heaven saying 11.12
And I heard a loud v. in heaven, 12.10
And I heard a v. from heaven like 14.02
the v. I heard was like the sound 14.02
and he said with a loud v., 14.07
followed, saying with a loud v., 14.09
And I heard a v. from heaven saying, 14.13
with a loud v. to him who sat upon 14.15
with a loud v. to him who had the 14.18
Then I heard a loud v. from the 16.01
and a great v. came out of the 16.17
And he called out with a mighty v., 18.02
Then I heard another v. from heaven 18.04
and the v. of bridegroom and bride 18.23
be the mighty v. of a great 19.01
And from the throne came a v. crying, 19.05
to be the v. of a great multitude, 19.06
and with a loud v. he called to 19.17
and I heard a great v. from the 21.03

VOICES
people lifted up their v. and wept. Ju 2.04
lifted up their v. and wept 21.02
they lifted up their v. and wept. Ru 1.09
lifted up their v. and wept again; 1.14
with him raised their v. and wept, 1Sa 30.04
and they raised their v. and wept; Job 2.12
They lift up their v., they sing for Is 24.14
and the v. of those who make merry. Jer 30.19
the v. of those who sing, as they 33.11
and lifted up their v. and said, Lk 17.13
be crucified. And their v. prevailed. 23.23
lifted their v. together to God Ac 4.24
had done, they lifted up their v., 14.11
they lifted up their v. and said, 22.22
and v. and peals of thunder, and Rev 4.05
and there were loud v. in heaven, 11.15

VOID
The earth was without form and v., Gen 1.02
but the former time shall be v., Num 6.12
he shall make v. her vow which was 30.08
them null and v. on the day that 30.12
her husband has made them v., 30.12
establish, or her husband may make v. 30.13
them null and v. after he has 30.15
"For they are a nation v. of counsel, Deu 32.28
stretches out the north over the v., Job 26.07
earth, and lo, it was waste and v.; Jer 4.23
I will make v. the plans of Judah 19.07
you have made v. the word of God. Mt 15.06
thus making v. the word of God Mk 7.13
one dot of the law to become v. Lk 16.17
is null and the promise is v. Rom 4.14
God, so as to make the promise v. Gal 3.17

VOLUNTARILY
you have v. vowed to the LORD your God Deu 23.23

VOLUNTEER
a v. for the service of the LORD, 2Ch 17.16

VOMIT
lest the land v. you out, when you Lev 18.28
you to dwell may not v. you out. 20.22
you will v. up the morsels which Pro 23.08
you be sated with it and v. it. 25.16
returns to his v. is a fool that 26.11
a drunken man staggers in his v. Is 19.14
For all tables are full of v., 28.08
be drunk and v., fall and rise no Jer 25.27
that Moab shall wallow in his v., 48.26
The dog turns back to his own v., 2Pe 2.22

VOMITED
and the land v. out its inhabitants. Lev 18.25
as it v. out the nation that was 18.28
and it v. out Jonah upon the dry Jon 2.10

VOMITS
down riches and v. them up again; Job 20.15

VOPHSI
of Naphtali, Nahbi the son of V.; Num 13.14

VOTE
to death I cast my v. against them. Ac 26.10

VOTIVE
offering is a v. offering or a Lev 7.16
but for a v. offering it cannot be 22.23
and besides all your v. offerings, 23.38
addition to your v. offerings and Num 29.39
your v. offerings, your freewill Deu 12.06
and all your v. offerings which you 12.11
or any of your v. offerings which 12.17
and your v. offerings, you shall 12.26
of the LORD the v. gifts of his 1Ki 15.15
of his father and his own v. gifts, 15.15
took all the v. gifts that Jehoshaphat 2Ki 12.18
and his own v. gifts, and all the 12.18
of God the v. gifts of his father 2Ch 15.18
and his own v. gifts, silver, and 15.18

VOUCHES
and he that v. for me is on high. Job 16.19

VOW
Then Jacob made a v., saying, "If God Gen 28.20
a pillar and made a v. to me. 31.13
in payment of a v. or as a freewill Lev 22.18
to fulfil a v. or as a freewill 22.21
makes a special v. of persons to 27.02
man or a woman makes a special v., Num 6.02
the v. of a Nazirite, to separate 6.02
"All the days of his v. of separation 6.05
for the Nazirite who takes a v. 6.21
according to his v. as a Nazirite, 6.21
accordance with the v. which he takes, 6.21
to fulfil a v. or as a freewill 15.03
to fulfil a v., or for peace 15.08
And Israel vowed a v. to the LORD, 21.02
When a man vows a v. to the LORD, 30.02
when a woman vows a v. to the LORD, 30.03
hears of her v. and of her pledge 30.04
no v. of hers, no pledge by which 30.05
make void her v. which was on her, 30.08
But any v. of a widow or of a 30.09
Any v. and any binding oath to 30.13
offerings which you v. to the LORD. Deu 12.11
your votive offerings which you v., 12.17
your God in payment for any v.; 23.18
"When you make a v. to the LORD 23.21
And Jephthah made a v. to the LORD, Ju 11.30
and I cannot take back my v." 11.35
according to his v. which he had 11.39
And she vowed a v. and said, 1Sa 1.11
sacrifice, and to pay his v. 1.21
king, "Pray let me go and pay my v., 2Sa 15.07
servant vowed a v. while I dwelt 15.08
When you v. a v. to God, do not Ecc 5.04
pleasure in fools. Pay what you v. 5.04
you should not v. than that you 5.05
that you should v. and not pay. 5.05
he cut his hair, for he had a v. Ac 18.18
have four men who are under a v.; 21.23

VOWED
of him who v. the priest shall Lev 27.08
And Israel v. a vow to the LORD, and Num 21.02
And if she v. in her husband's house, 30.10
voluntarily v. to the LORD your Deu 23.23
And she v. a vow and said, "O LORD 1Sa 1.11
which I have v. to the LORD, in 2Sa 15.07
For your servant v. a vow while I 15.08
v. willingly for the house of their Ez 7.16
to the LORD and v. to the Mighty Ps 132.02
will do everything that we have v., Jer 44.17
what I have v. I will pay. Jon 2.09
And he v. to her, "Whatever you ask Mk 6.23

VOWING
But if you refrain from v., it shall be no Deu 23.22

VOWS
When a man v. a vow to the LORD, or Num 30.02
Or when a woman v. a vow to the 30.03
then all her v. shall stand, and 30.04
while under her v. or any thoughtless 30.06
then her v. shall stand, and her 30.07
then all her v. shall stand, and 30.11
out of her lips concerning her v., 30.12
then he establishes all her v., 30.14
and you will pay your v. Job 22.27
my v. I will pay before those who Ps 22.25
and pay your v. to the Most High; 50.14

VOWS (cont.)
My v. to thee I must perform, O God; Ps 56.12
hast heard my v., thou hast given 61.05
name, as I pay my v. day after day. 61.08
and to thee shall v. be performed, 65.01
burnt offerings; I will pay thee v., 66.13
Make your v. to the LORD your God, 76.11
I will pay my v. to the LORD in the 116.14
I will pay my v. to the LORD in the 116.18
and today I have paid my v.; Pro 7.14
reflect only after making his v. 20.25
son of my womb? What, son of my v.? 31.02
they will make v. to the LORD and Is 19.21
Can v. and sacrificial flesh avert Jer 11.15
perform our v. that we have made, 44.25
confirm your v. and perform your v.! 44.25
sacrifice to the LORD and made v. Jon 1.16
fulfil your v., for never again Nah 1.15
and v. it, and yet sacrifices to the Mal 1.14

VOYAGE
we made a direct v. to Samothrace, Ac 16.11
When we had finished the v. from Tyre, 21.07
and the v. was already dangerous 27.09
that the v. will be with injury 27.10

VULGAR
as one of the v. fellows shamelessly 2Sa 6.20

VULTURE
the water hen, the pelican, the v., Lev 11.18
the eagle, the v., the osprey, Deu 14.12
the carrion v. and the cormorant, 14.17
I am like a v. of the wilderness, Ps 102.06
for a v. is over the house of the Hos 8.01
the v. and the hedgehog shall lodge Zep 2.14

VULTURES
of the valley and eaten by the v. Pro 30.17
swifter than the v. in the heavens; Lam 4.19

W

WAFER
and one w., out of the basket of Ex 29.23
and one w., and placed them on the Lev 8.26
the basket, and one unleavened w., Num 6.19

WAFERS
of it was like w. made with honey. Ex 16.31
and unleavened w. spread with oil. 29.02
or unleavened w. spread with oil. Lev 2.04
unleavened w. spread with oil, and 7.12
and unleavened w. spread with oil, Num 6.15
the w. of unleavened bread, the 1Ch 23.29

WAFTED
let its fragrance be w. abroad. Sol 4.16

WAG
mouths at me, they w. their heads; Ps 22.07
who see them will w. their heads. 64.08
they see me, they w. their heads. 109.25
they hiss and w. their heads at the Lam 2.15

WAGE
came up to w. war on Jerusalem, and 2Ki 16.05
safety from the battle that I w., Ps 55.18
The w. of the righteous leads to Pro 10.16
by Counsel; by wise guidance w. war. 20.18
wise guidance you can w. your war, 24.06
to Jerusalem to w. war against it, Is 7.01
"His sons shall w. war and assemble Dan 11.10
the south shall w. war with an 11.25
there was no w. for man or any w. for Zec 8.10
peoples that w. war against 14.12
by them you may w. the good 1Ti 1.18
so you fight and w. war. Jas 4.02
the flesh that w. war against your 1Pe 2.11

WAGED
much blood and have w. great wars; 1Ch 22.08

WAGER
make a w. with my master the king 2Ki 18.23
make a w. with my master the king Is 36.08

WAGES
Tell me, what shall your w. be?" Gen 29.15
name your w., and I will give it." 30.28
among the goats; and such shall be my w. 30.32
come to look into my w. with you. 30.33
me and changed my w. ten times, 31.07
'The spotted shall be your w., 31.08
'The striped shall be your w., 31.08
you have changed my w. ten times. 31.41
me, and I will give you your w." Ex 2.09
The w. of a hired servant shall not Lev 19.13
or the w. of a dog, into the house Deu 23.18
your servants such w. as you set; 1Ki 5.06
a hireling who looks for his w., Job 7.02
A wicked man earns deceptive w., Pro 11.18
and does not give him his w.; Jer 22.13
it shall be the w. for his army. Eze 29.19
he who earns w. earns w. to put Hag 1.06
seems right to you, give me my w.; Zec 11.12
out as my w. thirty shekels of 11.12
who oppress the hireling in his w., Mal 3.05
the laborers and pay them their w., Mt 20.08
and be content with your w." Lk 3.14
for the laborer deserves his w.; 10.07
He who reaps receives w., and gathers Jn 4.36
his w. are not reckoned as a gift Rom 4.04
For the w. of sin is death, but the 6.23
receive his w. according to his 1Co 3.08
and, "The laborer deserves his w." 1Ti 5.18
Behold, the w. of the laborers who Jas 5.04

WAGGED
you spoke of him you w. your head? Jer 48.27

WAGGING
by derided him, w. their heads Mt 27.39
w. their heads, and saying, "Aha! Mk 15.29

WAGON
a w. for every two of the leaders, Num 7.03

WAGONS
take w. from the land of Egypt for Gen 45.19
and Joseph gave them w., 45.21
when he saw the w. which Joseph 45.27
in the w. which Pharaoh had sent to 46.05
six covered w. and twelve oxen, a Num 7.03
So Moses took the w. and the oxen, 7.06
Two w. and four oxen he gave to the 7.07
and four w. and eight oxen he gave 7.08
chariots and w. and host of Eze 23.24
the horsemen and w. and chariots, 26.10

WAGS
she w. her head behind you—the 2Ki 19.21
she w. her head behind you—the Is 37.22

WAHEB
"W. in Suphah, and the valleys of Num 21.14

WAIL
W., for the day of the LORD is near; Is 13.06
W., O gate; cry, O city, 14.31

WAIL (cont.)
Therefore let Moab w., Is 16.07
let every one w. for Moab. 16.07
W., O ships of Tarshish, for Tyre is 23.01
w., O inhabitants of the coast! 23.06
W., O ships of Tarshish, for your 23.14
Their rulers w., says the LORD, and 52.05
and shall w. for anguish of spirit. 65.14
you with sackcloth, lament and w.; Jer 4.08
you shepherds, and cry, and roll 25.34
and the w. of the lords of the 25.36
inhabitant of the land shall w. 47.02
w. and cry! Tell it by the Arnon, 48.20
Therefore I w. for Moab; 48.31
How they w.! How Moab has 48.39
"W., O Heshbon, for Ai is laid waste! 49.03
w. for her! Take balm for her 51.08
Cry and w., son of man, for it is Eze 21.12
and w. aloud over you, and cry 27.30
Lord GOD: "W., 'Alas for the day!' 30.02
"Son of man, w. over the multitude 32.18
but they w. upon their beds; Hos 7.14
idolatrous priests shall w. over it, 10.05
and w., all you drinkers of wine, Joe 1.05
w., O vinedressers, for the wheat 1.11
w., O ministers of the altar. 1.13
For this I will lament and w.; Mic 1.08
and w. with bitter lamentation, and 2.04
a w. from the Second Quarter, a loud Zep 1.10
W., O inhabitants of the Mortar! 1.11
W., O cypress, for the cedar has Zec 11.02
W., oaks of Bashan, for the thick 11.02
Hark, the w. of the shepherds, for 11.03
the earth will w. on account of Rev 1.07
will weep and w. over her when they 18.09

WAILED
we w., and you did not mourn.' Mt 11.17
we w., and you did not weep.' Lk 7.32

WAILING
w. with a loud and bitter cry; Est 4.01
the w. reaches to Eglaim, the Is 15.08
the w. reaches to Beerelim. 15.08
"Take up weeping and w. for the Jer 9.10
make haste and raise a w. over us, 9.18
For a sound of w. is heard from 9.19
In their w. they raise a lamentation Eze 27.32
all the squares there shall be w.; Amo 5.16
mourning and to w. those who are 5.16
in all vineyards there shall be w., 5.17
the w. of Bethezel shall take away Mic 1.11
w. and loud lamentation, Rachel Mt 2.18
and people weeping and w. loudly. Mk 5.38

WAILINGS
temple shall become w. in that day, Amo 8.03

WAILS
over Nebo and over Medeba Moab w. Is 15.02
every one w. and melts in tears. 15.03

WAIST
Righteousness shall be the girdle of his w., Is 11.05
and a leather girdle around his w.; Mt 3.04
had a leather girdle around his w., Mk 1.06

WAISTCLOTH
and binds a w. on their lons. Job 12.18
not a w. is loose, not a sandal-thong Is 5.27
LORD to me, "Go and buy a linen w., Jer 13.01
So I bought a w. according to the 13.02
"Take the w. which you have bought, 13.04
from there the w. which I commanded 13.06
and I took the w. from the place 13.07
And behold, the w. was spoiled; 13.07
them, shall be like this w., 13.10
For as the w. clings to the loins 13.11

WAIT
I w. for thy salvation, O LORD. Gen 49.18
w. for him by the river's brink, and Ex 7.15
in the morning and w. for Pharaoh, 8.20
But if he did not lie in w. for him, 21.13
me on the mountain, and w. there; 24.12
"W., that I may hear what the LORD Num 9.08
lying in w., so that he died, 35.20
on him without lying in w., 35.22
and lies in w. for him, and attacks Deu 19.11
you, and lie in w. in the fields. Ju 9.32
and laid w. against Shechem in four 9.34
companies, and laid w. in the fields; 9.43
and lay in w. for him all night at 16.02
"Let us w. till the light of the 16.02
men lying in w. in an inner 16.09
men lying in w. were in an inner 16.12
"Go and lie in w. in the vineyards, 21.20
would you therefore w. till they Ru 1.13
She replied, "W., my daughter, until 3.18
w. until you have weaned him; 1Sa 1.23
Seven days you shall w., 10.08
'W. until we come to you,' then we 14.09
and lay in w. in the valley. 15.05
to lie in w., as at this day." 22.08
to lie in w., as at this day?" 22.13
See, I will w. at the fords of the 2Sa 15.28
and let her w. upon the king, and be 1Ki 1.02
Why should I w. for the LORD any 2Ki 6.33
are silent and w. until the 7.09
What is my strength, that I should w.? Job 6.11
the days of my service I would w., 14.14
I have lain in w. at my neighbor's 31.09
And shall I w., because they do not 32.16
or lie in w. in their covert? 38.40
let none that w. for thee be put to Ps 25.03
for thee I w. all the day long. 25.05
preserve me, for I w. for thee. 25.21
W. for the LORD; be strong, and let 27.14
courage; yea, w. for the LORD! 27.14
all you who w. for the LORD! 31.24
and w. patiently for him; fret not yourself 37.07
but those who w. for the LORD shall 37.09
W. for the LORD, and keep to his way, 37.34
But for thee, O LORD, do I w.; 38.15
"And now, Lord, for what do I w.? 39.07
For, lo, they lie in w. for my life; 59.03
they did not w. for his counsel. 106.13
The wicked lie in w. to destroy me; 119.95
I w. for the LORD, my soul waits, and 130.05
let us lie in w. for blood, let us Pro 1.11
men lie in w. for their own blood, 1.18
and at every corner she lies in w. 7.12
of the wicked lie in w. for blood, 12.06
w. for the LORD, and he will help 20.22
She lies in w. like a robber and 23.28
Lie not in w. as a wicked man 24.15
I will w. for the LORD, who is Is 8.17
judgments, O LORD, we w. for thee; 26.08
are all those who w. for him. 30.18
we w. for thee. Be our arm 33.02
but they who w. for the LORD shall 40.31
and the coastlands w. for his law. 42.04
those who w. for me shall not be 49.23
the coastlands w. for me, and for my arm 51.05
For the coastlands shall w. for me, 60.09
who works for those who w. for him. 64.04
they lurk like fowlers lying in w. Jer 5.26
He is to me like a bear lying in w., Lam 3.10
is good to those who w. for him, 3.25
that one should w. quietly for the 3.26
they lay in w. for us in the 4.19
As robbers lie in w. for a man, Hos 6.09
and w. continually for your God." 12.06
of Maroth w. anxiously for good, Mic 1.12
not for men nor w. for the sons of 5.07

WAIT (cont.)
they all lie in w. for blood, Mic 7.02
I will w. for the God of my salvation; 7.07
If it seem slow, w. for it; Hab 2.03
I will quietly w. for the day of 3.16
"Therefore w. for me," says the LORD, Zep 3.08
"W., let us see whether Elijah will Mt 27.49
"W., let us see whether Elijah will Mk 15.36
lying in w. for him, to catch at Lk 11.54
but to w. for the promise of the Ac 1.04
And now why do you w.? Rise and be 22.16
inwardly as we w. for adoption as Rom 8.23
we w. for it with patience. 8.25
as you w. for the revealing of our 1Co 1.07
together to eat, w. for one another— 11.33
we w. for the hope of righteousness. Gal 5.05
and to w. for his Son from heaven, 1Th 1.10
then to w. until his enemies should Heb 10.13
his promise we w. for new heavens 2Pe 3.13
since you w. for these, be zealous 3.14
w. for the mercy of our Lord Jesus Jud 1.21

WAITED
He w. another seven days, and again Gen 8.10
Then he w. another seven days, and 8.12
with them, and he w. on them; 40.04
And they w. till they were utterly Ju 3.25
He w. seven days, the time appointed 1Sa 13.08
name of David; and then they w. 25.09
and w. for the king by the way, 1Ki 20.38
and she w. on Naaman's wife. 2Ki 5.02
and w., and kept silence for my Job 29.21
They w. for me as for the rain; 29.23
and when I w. for light, darkness 30.26
Now Elihu had w. to speak to Job 32.04
"Behold, I w. for your words, I 32.11
I w. patiently for the LORD; Ps 40.01
As they have w. for my life, 56.06
we have w. for him, that he might Is 25.09
we have w. for him; let us be 25.09
from among those that w. on him, Ax 10.07
They w., expecting him to swell up 28.06
when they had w. a long time and 28.06
God's patience w. in the days of 1Pe 3.20

WAITING
who were w. for them, as they came Ex 5.20
and Ahimaaz were w. at Enrogel; 2Sa 17.17
before him, and you are w. for him! Job 35.14
eyes grow dim with w. for my God. Ps 69.03
at my gates, w. beside my doors. Pro 8.34
And the people were w. for Zechariah, Lk 1.21
him, for they were all w. for him. 8.40
men who are w. for their master to 12.36
w. for the moving of the water *Jn 5.03
Now while Paul was w. for them at Ac 17.16
on and were w. for us at Troas, 20.05
w. for the promise from you." 23.21
those who are eagerly w. for him. Heb 9.28
w. for and hastening the coming of 2Pe 3.12

WAITS
adulterer also w. for the twilight, Job 24.15
Our soul w. for the LORD; Ps 33.20
For God alone my soul w. in silence; 62.01
For God alone my soul w. in silence, 62.05
my soul w., and in his word I hope; 130.05
my soul w. for the LORD more than 130.06
Therefore the LORD w. to be gracious Is 30.18
Blessed is he who w. and comes to Dan 12.12
For the creation w. with eager Rom 8.19
the farmer w. for the precious Jas 5.07

WAKE
Behind him he leaves a shining w.; Job 41.32
I w. again, for the LORD sustains me Ps 3.05
sleep and not w., says the LORD. Jer 51.39
sleep a perpetual sleep and not w., 51.57
time now for you to w. from sleep. Rom 13.11
that whether we w. or sleep we 1Th 5.10

WAKED
came again and w. me, like a man that is Zec 4.01

WAKENED
a man that is w. out of his sleep. Zec 4.01

WAKENS
Morning by morning he w., Is 50.04
he w. my ear to hear as those who 50.04

WALK
Arise w. through the length and the Gen 13.17
w. before me, and be blameless. 17.01
before whom I w., will send his 24.40
they will w. in my law or not. Ex 16.04
which they must w. and what they 18.20
You shall not w. in their statutes. Lev 18.03
keep my statutes and w. in them. 18.04
And you shall not w. in the customs 20.23
"If you w. in my statutes and 26.03
And I will w. among you, and will be 26.12
of your yoke and made you w. erect. 26.13
"Then if you w. contrary to me, and 26.21
turned to me, but w. contrary to me, 26.23
then I also will w. contrary to you, 26.24
hearken to me, but w. contrary to me, 26.27
then I will w. contrary to you, 26.24
hearken to me, but w. contrary to me, 26.27
then I will w. contrary to you in 26.28
You shall w. in all the way which Deu 5.33
and when you w. by the way, and when 6.07
to w. in all his ways, to love him, 10.12
You shall w. after the LORD your 13.04
LORD your God commanded you to w. 13.05
and that you will w. in his ways, 26.17
LORD your God, and w. in his ways. 28.09
though I w. in the stubbornness of 29.19
and to w. in all his ways, and to Jos 22.05
take care to w. in the way of the Ju 2.22
carpets and you who w. by the way. 5.10
Yet his sons did not w. in his ways, 1Sa 8.03
your sons do not w. in your ways; 8.05
to w. before me in faithfulness 1Ki 2.04
And if you will w. in my ways, 3.14
if you will w. in my statutes and 6.12
all my commandments and w. in them, 6.12
servants who w. before thee with 8.23
to w. before me as you have walked 8.25
good way in which they should w.; 8.36
to w. in all his ways, and to keep 8.58
if you will w. before me, as David 9.04
and will w. in my ways, and do what 11.38
for him to w. in the sins of 16.31
not careful to w. in the law of 2Ki 10.31
and did not w. in the way of the 21.22
to w. after the LORD and to keep 23.03
servants who w. before thee with 2Ch 6.14
to w. in my law as you have walked 6.16
good way in which they should w.; 6.27
fear thee and w. in thy ways all 6.31
if you w. before me, as David your 7.17
to w. after the LORD and to keep 34.31
you not to w. in the fear of our Neh 5.09
and an oath to w. in God's law 10.29
Even though I w. through the valley Ps 23.04
and I w. in faithfulness to thee. 26.03
I w. in my integrity; redeem me, 26.11
to slay those who w. uprightly; 37.14
W. about Zion, go round about her, 48.12
that I may w. before God in the 56.13
but refused to w. according to his 78.10
that Israel would w. in my ways! 81.13
they w. about in darkness; 82.05
from those who w. uprightly. 84.11
O LORD, that I may w. in thy truth; 86.11

WALK (cont.)

who w., O LORD, in the light of thy Ps 89.15
law and do not w. according to my 89.30
I will w. with integrity of heart 101.02
feet, but do not w.; and they do not 115.07
I w. before the LORD in the land of 116.09
who w. in the law of the LORD! 119.01
do no wrong, but w. in his ways! 119.03
and I shall w. at liberty, for I 119.45
Though I w. in the midst of trouble, 138.07
path where I w. they have hidden a 142.03
my son, do not w. in the way with Pro 1.15
to those who w. in integrity, 2.07
uprightness to w. in the ways of 2.13
So you will w. in the way of good 2.20
Then you will w. on your way 3.23
When you w., your step will not be 4.12
and do not w. in the way of evil 4.14
When you w., they will lead you; 6.22
Or can one w. upon hot coals and 6.28
I w. in the way of righteousness, in 8.20
and w. in the way of insight. 9.06
w. in the ways of your heart and Ecc 11.09
and that we may w. in his paths." Is 2.03
let us w. in the light of the LORD. 2.05
are haughty and w. with outstretched 3.16
me not to w. in the way of this 8.11
w. in it," when you turn to the 30.21
but the redeemed shall w. there. 35.09
weary, they shall w. and not faint. 40.31
and spirit to those who w. in it: 42.05
in whose ways they would not w., 42.24
when you w. through fire you shall 43.02
W. by the light of your fire, and by 50.11
their beds who w. in their uprightness. 57.02
for brightness, but we w. in gloom. 59.09
who w. in a way that is not good, 65.02
and w. in it, and find rest for your Jer 6.16
they said, 'We will not w. in it.' 6.16
into the field, nor w. on the road; 6.25
and w. in all the way that I 7.23
to be carried, for they cannot w. 10.05
commit adultery and w. in lies; 23.14
to w. in my law which I have set 26.04
will make them w. by brooks of 31.09
obey thy voice or w. in thy law; 32.23
of the LORD or w. in his law and 44.23
we could not w. in our streets; Lam 4.18
that they may w. in my statutes and Eze 11.20
not content to w. in their ways, 16.47
they did not w. in my statutes but 20.13
and did not w. in my statutes, 20.16
Do not w. in the statutes of your 20.18
w. in my statutes, and be careful to 20.19
they did not w. in my statutes, and 20.21
Yea, I will let men w. upon you, 36.12
cause you to w. in my statutes and 36.27
and those who w. in pride he is Dan 4.37
Yet it was I who taught Ephraim to w., Hos 11.03
right, and the upright w. in them, 14.09
"Do two w. together, unless they Amo 3.03
and you shall not w. haughtily, Mic 2.03
ways and we may w. in his paths." 4.02
For all the peoples w. each in the 4.05
but we will w. in the name of the 4.05
and to w. humbly with your God? 6.08
that they shall w. like the blind, Zep 1.17
If you will w. in my ways and keep Zec 3.07
forgiven,' or to say, 'Rise and w.'? Mt 9.05
their sight and the lame w., 11.05
'Rise, take up your pallet and w.'? Mk 2.09
you,' or to say, 'Rise and w.'? Lk 5.23
the lame w., lepers are cleansed, 7.22
and men w. over them without 11.44
holding with each other as you w.?" 24.17
"Rise, take up your pallet, and w." Jn 5.08
me, 'Take up your pallet, and w.'" 5.11
you, 'Take up your pallet, and w.'?" 5.12
follows me will not w. in darkness, 8.12
W. while you have the light, lest 12.35
of Jesus Christ of Nazareth, w." Ac 3.06
power or piety we had made him w.? 3.12
the nations to w. in their own 14.16
we too might w. in newness of life. Rom 6.04
who w. not according to the flesh 8.04
for we w. by faith, not by sight. 2Co 5.07
But I say, w. by the Spirit, and do Gal 5.16
let us also w. by the Spirit. 5.25
be upon all who w. by this rule, 6.16
beforehand, that we should w. in them. Eph 2.10
And w. in love, as Christ loved us 5.02
in the Lord; w. as children of light 5.08
look carefully then how you w., 5.15
with him while we w. in darkness, 1Jn 1.06
but if we w. in the light, as he is 1.07
in him ought to w. in the same way 2.06
For they w. in the way of Cain, and Jud 1.11
and they shall w. with me in white, Rev 3.04
cannot either see or hear or w.; 9.20
By its light shall the nations w.; 21.24

WALKED

Enoch w. with God after the birth Gen 5.22
Enoch w. with God; and he was not 5.24
in his generation; Noah w. with God. 6.09
and w. backward and covered the 9.23
my fathers Abraham and Isaac w., 48.15
and her maidens w. beside the Ex 2.05
of Israel w. on dry ground through 14.29
of Israel w. on dry ground in the 15.19
so that I w. contrary to them and Lev 26.41
of Israel w. forty years in the Jos 5.06
while Israel w. in the wilderness; 14.10
way in which their fathers had w., Ju 2.17
and I have w. before you from my 1Sa 12.02
because he w. before thee in 1Ki 3.06
commandments, as your father David w., 3.14
before me as you have w. before me.' 8.25
before me, as David your father w., 9.04
and has not w. in my ways, doing 11.33
And he w. in all the sins which his 15.03
and w. in the way of his father and 15.26
and w. in the way of Jeroboam and 15.34
and you have w. in the way of 16.02
For he w. in all the way of Jeroboam 16.26
He w. in all the way of Asa his 22.43
and w. in the way of his father, and 22.52
and w. once to and fro in the house, 2Ki 4.35
And he w. in the way of the kings 8.18
He also w. in the way of the house 8.27
made Israel to sin, but w. in them; 13.06
Israel to sin, but he w. in them. 13.11
but he w. in the way of the kings 16.03
and w. in the customs of the 17.08
but w. in the customs which Israel 17.19
of Israel w. in all the sins which 17.22
how I have w. before thee in 20.03
He w. in all the way in which his 21.21
all the way in which his father w., 21.21
and w. in all the way of David his 22.02
in my law as you have w. before me.' 2Ch 6.16
before me, as David your father w., 7.17
for they w. for three years in the 11.17
Because he w. in the earlier ways 17.03
his father and w. in his commandments, 17.04
He w. in the way of Asa his father 20.32
And he w. in the way of the kings 21.06
you have not w. in the ways of 21.12
but have w. in the way of the kings 21.13
He also w. in the ways of the house 22.03
but w. in the ways of the kings of 28.02
and w. in the ways of David his 34.02
day Mordecai w. in front of the Est 2.11
by his light I w. through darkness; Job 29.03
"If I have w. with falsehood, and my 31.05

WALKED (cont.)
or w. in the recesses of the deep? Job 38.16
for I have w. in my integrity, and I Ps 26.01
God's house we w. in fellowship. 55.14
The people who w. in darkness have Is 9.02
Isaiah has w. naked and barefoot 20.03
how I have w. before thee in 38.03
but w. in their own counsels and Jer 7.24
or w. in accord with it, 9.13
but every one w. in the stubbornness 11.08
nor w. in my law and my statutes 44.10
and have not w. in my statutes or Eze 5.07
for you have not w. in my statutes, 11.12
midst of the stones of fire you w. 28.14
after which their fathers w. Amo 2.04
and you have w. in their counsels; Mic 6.16
He w. with me in peace and uprightness, Mal 2.06
As he w. by the Sea of Galilee, he Mt 4.18
of the boat and w. on the water 14.29
immediately the girl got up and w.; Mk 5.42
and he looked at Jesus as he w., Jn 1.36
and he took up his pallet and w. 5.09
yourself and w. where you would; 21.18
up he stood and w. and entered the Ac 3.08
from birth, who had never w. 14.08
And he sprang up and w. 14.10
in which you once w., Eph 2.02
In these you once w., Col 3.07
in the same way in which he w. 1Jn 2.06

WALKING
of the LORD God w. in the garden Gen 3.08
w. in the field to meet us?" 24.65
and also in w. contrary to me, Lev 26.40
by w. in his ways and by fearing Deu 8.06
and when you are w. by the way, 11.19
w. in all his ways, and cleaving to 11.22
your God and by w. ever in his 19.09
by w. in his ways, and by keeping 30.16
couch and was w. upon the roof of 2Sa 11.02
w. in his ways and keeping his 1Ki 2.03
w. in the statutes of David his 3.03
w. in his statutes and keeping his 8.61
w. in the way of Jeroboam, and for 16.19
and from w. up and down on it." Job 1.07
and from w. up and down on it." 2.02
and princes w. on foot like slaves. Ecc 10.07
had done so, w. naked and barefoot— Is 20.02
ordinances and not w. in my statutes. Eze 5.06
w. in the midst of the fire, and Dan 3.25
months he was w. on the roof of 4.29
charge or of w. as in mourning Mal 3.14
he came to them, w. on the sea. Mt 14.25
disciples saw him w. on the sea, 14.26
the lame w., and the blind seeing; 15.31
he came to them, w. on the sea. Mk 6.48
they saw him w. on the sea they 6.49
but they look like trees, w." 8.24
and Jesus was w. ahead of them; 10.32
And as he was w. in the temple, the 11.27
as they were w. into the country. * 16.12
w. in all the commandments and Lk 1.06
they saw Jesus w. on the sea and Jn 6.19
and Jesus was w. in the temple, in 10.23
w. and leaping and praising God. Ac 3.08
people saw him w. and praising God, 3.09
and w. in the fear of the Lord and 9.31
eat, you are no longer w. in love. Rom 14.15

WALKS
rises again and w. abroad with his Ex 21.19
LORD your God w. in the midst of Deu 23.14
behold, the king w. before you; 1Sa 12.02
own feet, and he w. on a pitfall. Job 18.08
and he w. on the vault of heaven. 22.14
evildoers and w. with wicked men? 34.08
Blessed is the man who w. not in Ps 1.01
He who w. blamelessly, and does what 15.02
of him who w. in his guilty ways. 68.21
he who w. in the way that is 101.06
fears the LORD, who w. in his ways! 128.01
He who w. in integrity w. securely, Pro 10.09
He who w. with wise men becomes 13.20
He who w. in uprightness fears the 14.02
a man of understanding w. aright. 15.21
a poor man who w. in his integrity 19.01
righteous man who w. in his integrity— 20.07
a poor man who w. in his integrity 28.06
He who w. in integrity will be 28.18
but he who w. in wisdom will be 28.26
head, but the fool w. in darkness; Ecc 2.14
Even when the fool w. on the road, 10.03
He who w. righteously and speaks Is 33.15
who w. in darkness and has no light, 50.10
not in man who w. to direct his Jer 10.23
w. in my statutes, and is careful to Eze 18.09
ordinances, and w. in my statutes; 18.17
and w. in the statutes of life, 33.15
do good to him who w. uprightly? Mic 2.07
streets so that none w. in them; Zep 3.06
If any one w. in the day, he does Jn 11.09
But if any one w. in the night, he 11.10
he who w. in the darkness does not 12.35
darkness and w. in the darkness, 1Jn 2.11
who w. among the seven golden Rev 2.01

WALL
his branches run over the w. Gen 49.22
waters being a w. to them on their Ex 14.22
waters being a w. to them on their 14.29
which have no w. around them shall Lev 25.31
vineyards, with a w. on either side. Num 22.24
LORD, she pushed against the w., 22.25
Balaam's foot against the w.; 22.25
reach from the w. of the city 35.04
house was built into the city w., Jos 2.15
so that she dwelt in the w. 2.15
and the w. of the city will fall 6.05
and the w. fell down flat, so that 6.20
thought, "I will pin David to the w." 1Sa 18.11
pin David to the w. with the spear; 19.10
he struck the spear into the w. 19.10
times, upon the seat by the w.; 20.25
they were a w. to us both by night 25.16
his body to the w. of Bethshan. 31.10
his sons from the w. of Bethshan; 31.12
that they would shoot from the w.? 2Sa 11.20
millstone upon him from the w., 11.21
Why did you go so near the w.?' 11.21
shot at your servants from the w.; 11.24
to the roof of the gate by the w., 18.24
and they were battering the w., 20.15
shall be thrown to you over the w." 20.21
and by my God I can leap over a w. 22.30
LORD and the w. around Jerusalem. 1Ki 3.01
hyssop that grows out of the w.; 4.33
against the w. of the house, 6.05
offsets on the w. in order that 6.06
a wing of one touched the one w., 6.27
other cherub touched the other w.; 6.27
Millo and the w. of Jerusalem and 9.15
and the w. fell upon twenty-seven 20.30
for a burnt offering upon the w., 2Ki 3.27
Israel was passing by upon the w., 6.26
now he was passing by upon the w.— 6.30
spattered on the w. and on the 9.33
broke down the w. of Jerusalem for 14.13
of the people who are on the w." 18.26
not to the men sitting on the w., 18.27
Hezekiah turned his face to the w., 20.02
touched the w. of the house, and its 2Ch 3.11
touched the w. of the house, and the 3.12
broke down the w. of Jerusalem for 25.23

WALL (cont.)
broke down the w. of Gath and the 2Ch 26.06
of Gath and the w. of Jabneh and 26.06
of Jabneh and the w. of Ashdod; 26.06
much building on the w. of Ophel. 27.03
up all the w. that was broken down, 32.05
and outside it he built another w.; 32.05
of Jerusalem who were upon the w., 32.18
built an outer w. to the city of 33.14
and broke down the w. of Jerusalem, 36.19
the w. of Jerusalem is broken down, Neh 1.03
and for the w. of the city, and for 2.08
by the valley and inspected the w.; 2.15
let us build the w. of Jerusalem, 2.17
Jerusalem as far as the Broad W. 3.08
a thousand cubits of the w., 3.13
he built the w. of the Pool of 3.15
tower as far as the w. of Ophel. 3.27
heard that we were building the w., 4.01
he will break down their stone w.!" 4.03
So we built the w.; and all the w. was 4.06
we are not able to work on the w." 4.10
parts of the space behind the w., 4.13
plan, we all returned to the w., 4.15
who were building on the w. 4.17
and we are separated on the w., 4.19
I also held to the work on this w., 5.16
I had built the w. and that there 6.01
is why you are building the w.; 6.06
So the w. was finished on the 6.15
Now when the w. had been built and 7.01
dedication of the w. of Jerusalem 12.27
people and the gates and the w. 12.30
the princes of Judah upon the w., 12.31
right upon the w. to the Dung Gate; 12.31
of David, at the ascent of the w., 12.37
upon the w., above the Tower of the 12.38
of the Furnaces, to the Broad W., 12.38
"Why do you lodge before the w.? 13.21
and by my God I can leap over a w. Ps 18.29
him, all of you, like a leaning w., 62.03
and like a high w. protecting him. Pro 18.11
and its stone w. was broken down. 24.31
bite him who breaks through a w. Ecc 10.08
there he stands behind our w., Sol 2.09
If she is a w., we will build upon 8.09
I was a w., and my breasts were 8.10
and against every fortified w.; Is 2.15
I will break down its w., 5.05
down the houses to fortify the w. 22.10
is like a storm against a w., 25.04
to you like a break in a high w., 30.13
of the people who are on the w." 36.11
not to the men sitting on the w., 36.12
Hezekiah turned his face to the w., 38.02
and all your w. of precious stones. 54.12
We grope for the w. like the blind, 59.10
people a fortified w. of bronze; Jer 15.20
a fire in the w. of Damascus, 49.27
the w. of Babylon has fallen. 51.44
The broad w. of Babylon shall be 51.58
in ruins the w. of the daughter of Lam 2.08
he caused rampart and w. to lament, 2.08
and build a siege w. against it, Eze 4.02
it as an iron w. between you and 4.03
behold, there was a hole in the w. 8.07
to me, "Son of man, dig in the w."; 8.08
and when I dug in the w., 8.08
portrayed upon the w. round about, 8.10
Dig through the w. in their sight, 12.05
dug through the w. with my own 12.07
dig through the w. and go out 12.12
or built up a w. for the house of 13.05
because, when the people build a w., 13.10
and when the w. falls, will it not 13.12
break down the w. that you have 13.14
Thus will I spend my wrath upon the w., 13.15
The w. is no more, nor those who 13.15
build up the w. and stand in the 22.30
he saw men portrayed upon the w., 23.14
will set up a siege w. against you, 26.08
and every w. shall tumble to the 38.20
there was a w. all around the 40.05
the thickness of the w., one reed; 40.05
Then he measured the w. of the temple, 41.05
all around the w. of the temple to 41.06
supported by the w. of the temple. 41.06
of the outer w. of the side 41.09
and the w. of the building was five 41.12
palm trees were carved on the w. 41.20
And there was a w. outside parallel 42.07
where the outside w. begins. 42.10
opposite there was a dividing w. 42.12
It had a w. around it, five hundred 42.20
with only a w. between me and them. 43.08
plaster of the w. of the king's Dan 5.05
and I will build a w. against her, Hos 2.06
like soldiers they scale the w. Joe 2.07
send a fire upon the w. of Gaza, Amo 1.07
send a fire upon the w. of Tyre, 1.10
kindle a fire in the w. of Rabbah, 1.14
with his hand against the w., 5.19
beside a w. built with a plumb 7.07
Now you are walled about with a w.; Mic 5.01
as they go, they hasten to the w., Nah 2.05
rampart a sea, and water her w.? 3.08
the stone will cry out from the w., Hab 2.11
be to her a w. of fire round about, Zec 2.05
night and let him down over the w., Ac 9.25
strike you, you whitewashed w.! 23.03
basket through a window in the w., 2Co 11.33
down the dividing w. of hostility, Eph 2.14
high w., with twelve gates, and at Rev 21.12
And the w. of the city had twelve 21.14
He also measured its w., a hundred and 21.17
The w. was built of jasper, while 21.18
foundations of the w. of the city 21.19

WALLED
a dwelling house in a w. city, Lev 25.29
that is in the w. city shall be 25.30
He has w. up my way, so that I Job 19.08
He has w. me about so that I cannot Lam 3.07
Now you are w. about with a wall; Mic 5.01

WALLET
in his shepherd's bag, in his w.; 1Sa 17.40

WALLOW
so that Moab shall w. in his vomit, Jer 48.26
on their heads and w. in ashes; Eze 27.30
is washed only to w. in the mire. 2Pe 2.22

WALLOWING
And Amasa lay w. in his blood in 2Sa 20.12

WALLS
is in the w. of the house with Lev 14.37
has spread in the w. of the house, 14.39
were cities fortified with high w., Deu 3.05
until your high and fortified w., 28.52
cities with w. and bronze bars; 1Ki 4.13
running round the w. of the house, 6.05
inserted into the w. of the house. 6.06
He lined the w. of the house on the 6.15
He carved all the w. of the house 6.29
make a small roof chamber with w., 2Ki 4.10
way of the gate between the two w., 25.04
broke down the w. around Jerusalem. 25.10
overlaying the w. of the house, 1Ch 29.04
thresholds, its w., and its doors; 2Ch 3.07
and he carved cherubim on the w. 3.07
Bethhoron, fortified cities with w., 8.05
surround them with w. and towers, 14.07
finishing the w. and repairing the Ez 4.12

WALLS (cont.)

is rebuilt and the w. finished, Ez 4.13
is rebuilt and its w. finished, 4.16
and timber is laid in the w.; 5.08
I inspected the w. of Jerusalem Neh 2.13
repairing of the w. of Jerusalem 4.07
rebuild the w. of Jerusalem, Ps 51.18
night they go around it on its w.; 55.10
Why then hast thou broken down its w., 80.12
Thou hast breached all his w.; 89.40
Peace be within your w., and security 122.07
on the top of the w. she cries out; Pro 1.21
broken into and left without w. 25.28
mantle, those watchmen of the w. Sol 5.07
battering down of w. and a shouting Is 22.05
between the two w. for the water 22.11
fortifications of his w. he will 25.12
up salvation as w. and bulwarks. 26.01
your w. are continually before me. 49.16
and within by w. a monument and a 56.05
Foreigners shall build up your w., 60.10
you shall call your w. Salvation, 60.18
Upon your w., O Jerusalem, I have 62.06
against all its w. round about, Jer 1.15
and bronze w., against the whole 1.18
Oh, the w. of my heart! My heart is beating 4.19
are besieging you outside the w.; 21.04
the gate between the two w.; 39.04
and broke down the w. of Jerusalem. 39.08
her w. are thrown down. For this is 50.15
standard against the w. of Babylon; 51.12
way of a gate between the two w., 52.07
down all the w. round about 52.14
of the enemy the w. of her palaces; Lam 2.07
up and siege w. built to cut off Eze 17.17
They shall destroy the w. of Tyre, 26.04
his battering rams against your w., 26.09
your w. will shake at the noise of 26.10
break down your w. and destroy 26.12
were upon your w. round about, 27.11
shields upon your w. round about; 27.11
breached, and its w. broken down. 30.16
you by the w. and at the doors of 33.30
all of them dwelling without w., 38.11
yard and the building with its w., 41.13
the west and its w. on either side, 41.15
And on all the w. round about in 41.17
its base, and its w. were of wood. 41.22
such as were carved on the w.; 41.25
the city, they run upon the w.; Joe 2.09
A day for the building of your w.! Mic 7.11
inhabited as villages without w., Zec 2.04
By faith the w. of Jericho fell Heb 11.30
the city and its gates and w. Rev 21.15

WANDER

caused me to w. from my father's Gen 20.13
he made them w. in the wilderness Num 32.13
I may go and w. on the mountains, Ju 11.37
I today make you w. about with us, 2Sa 15.20
of Israel to w. any more out of 2Ki 21.08
and makes them w. in a pathless Job 12.24
and w. about for lack of food? 38.41
yea, I would w. afar, I would lodge Ps 55.07
and makes them w. in trackless 107.40
May his children w. about and beg; 109.10
let me not w. from thy commandments! 119.10
who w. from thy commandments; 119.21
her ways w., and she does not know Pro 5.06
they w. about each in his Is 47.15
people: "They have loved to w. thus, Jer 14.10
and those who w. with their flocks. 31.24
Flee, w. far away, dwell in the 49.30
They shall w. from sea to sea, and Amo 8.12
Therefore the people w. like sheep; Zec 10.02
to the truth and w. into myths. 2Ti 4.04

WANDERED

and w. in the wilderness of Beersheba. Gen 21.14
Some w. in desert wastes, finding no Ps 107.04
They w., blind, through the streets, Lam 4.14
they w. over all the mountains and Eze 34.06
or three cities w. to one city to Amo 4.08
from these have w. away into vain 1Ti 1.06
that some have w. away from the 6.10

WANDERER

a fugitive and a w. on the earth. Gen 4.12
a fugitive and a w. on the earth, 4.14

WANDERERS

So they became fugitives and w.; Lam 4.15
they shall be w. among the nations. Hos 9.17

WANDERING

And a man found him w. in the fields; Gen 37.15
'A w. Aramean was my father; Deu 26.05
w. from nation to nation, from one 1Ch 16.20
w. from nation to nation, from one Ps 105.13
of the eyes than the w. of desire; Ecc 6.09
up to Assyria, a wild ass w. alone; Hos 8.09
or seek the w., or heal the maimed, Zec 11.16
w. over deserts and mountains, and Heb 11.38
w. stars for whom the nether gloom Jud 1.13

WANDERS

He w. abroad for bread, saying, Job 15.23
A man who w. from the way of Pro 21.16
be like one who w. beside the Sol 1.07
one among you w. from the truth Jas 5.19

WANED

now the day has w. toward evening; Ju 19.09

WANT

nakedness, and in w. of all things; Deu 28.48
for w. of all things, in the siege 28.57
to the rock for w. of shelter. Job 24.08
Through w. and hard hunger they 30.03
is my shepherd, I shall not w.; Ps 23.01
for those who fear him have no w.! 34.09
The young lions suffer w. and hunger; 34.10
like a vagabond, and w. like an armed man. Pro 6.11
should give, and only suffers w. 11.24
the belly of the wicked suffers w. 13.25
but mere talk tends only to w. 14.23
one who is hasty comes only to w. 21.05
to the rich, will only come to w. 22.16
and w. like an armed man. 24.34
not know that w. will come upon 28.22
He who gives to the poor will not w., 28.27
go into exile for w. of knowledge; Is 5.13
stricken by w. of the fruits of the Lam 4.09
are afflicted for w. of a shepherd. Zec 10.02
'Then do you w. us to go and gather Mt 13.28
And he said to her, "What do you w.?" 20.21
"What do you w. me to do for you?" 20.32
"Whom do you w. me to release for 27.17
the two do you w. me to release 27.21
"I w. you to give me at once the Mk 6.25
he did not w. to break his word to 6.26
we w. you to do for us whatever we 10.35
"What do you w. me to do for you?" 10.36
"What do you w. me to do for you?" 10.51
"Do you w. me to release for you 15.09
do you w. us to bid fire come down Lk 9.54
country, and he began to be in w. 15.14
"What do you w. me to do for you?" 18.41
'We do not w. this man to reign 19.14
who did not w. me to reign over 19.27
to him, "Do you w. to be healed?" Jn 5.06
Why do you w. to hear it again? 9.27
Do you too w. to become his disciples?" 9.27
Do you w. to kill me as you killed Ax 7.28
I w. you to know, brethren, that I Rom 1.13

WANT (cont.)
For I do not do what I w., Rom 7.15
Now if I do what I do not w., 7.16
For I do not do the good I w., 7.19
the evil I do not w. is what I do. 7.19
Now if I do what I do not w., 7.20
a law that when I w. to do right, 7.21
I w. you to understand this mystery, 11.25
I w. you to be free from anxieties. 1Co 7.32
I w. you to know, brethren, that our 10.01
I do not w. you to be partners with 10.20
But I w. you to understand that the 11.03
I do not w. you to be uninformed. 12.01
Therefore I w. you to understand 12.03
Now I w. you all to speak in 14.05
For I do not w. to see you now just 16.07
For we do not w. you to be ignorant, 2Co 1.08
We w. you to know, brethren, about 8.01
time should supply their w., 8.14
their abundance may supply your w., 8.14
And when I was with you and was in w., 11.09
trouble you and w. to pervert the Gal 1.07
slaves you w. to be once more? 4.09
they w. to shut you out, that you 4.17
It is those who w. to make a good 6.12
I w. you to know, brethren, that what Php 1.12
Not that I complain of w.; 4.11
and hunger, abundance and w. 4.12
For I w. you to know now greatly I Col 2.01
I w. some benefit from you in the Phm 1.20
Do you w. to be shown, you foolish Jas 2.20
stops those who w. to welcome them 3Jn 1.10

WANTED
For they all w. to frighten us, Neh 6.09
prophets who w. to make me afraid. 6.14
And though he w. to put him to Mt 14.05
any one prisoner whom they w. 27.15
against him, and w. to kill him. Mk 6.19
also the fish, as much as they w. Jn 6.11
Some of them w. to arrest him, but 7.44
Jesus knew that they w. to ask him; 16.19
were enraged and w. to kill them. Ac 5.33
the gates and w. to offer sacrifice 14.13
And Barnabas w. to take with them 15.37
Paul w. Timothy to accompany him; 16.03
I w. to come to you first, so that 2Co 1.15
I w. to visit you on my way to 1.16
I vacillating when I w. to do this? 1.17
because we w. to come to you—I, 1Th 2.18

WANTING
in the balances and found w.; Dan 5.27

WANTON
for all the w. crime which they Ju 20.10
done in Israel; do not do this w. folly. 2Sa 13.12
as one of the w. fools in Israel. 13.13
But they had a w. craving in the Ps 106.14
she is w. and knows no shame. Pro 9.13
though you are w. as a heifer at Jer 50.11
broken their w. heart which has Eze 6.09
Her prophets are w., faithless men; Zep 3.04
when they grow w. against Christ 1Ti 5.11
glorified herself and played the w., Rev 18.07
fornication and were w. with her, 18.09

WANTONLY
you are inclined to go after w. Num 15.39
he had dealt w. in Judah and had 2Ch 28.19
be ashamed who are w. treacherous. Ps 25.03
let us w. ambush the innocent; Pro 1.11
glancing w. with their eyes, mincing Is 3.16
eyes which turn w. after their Eze 6.09

WANTONNESS
and in their w. they hamstring oxen. Gen 49.06

abomination and w. in Israel. Ju 20.06
rich with the wealth of her w. Rev 18.03

WANTS
I will care for all your w.; Ju 19.20
here, for Herod w. to kill you." Lk 13.31
supplies the w. of the saints but 2Co 9.12

WAR
these kings made w. with Bera king Gen 14.02
if w. befall us, they join our Ex 1.10
the people repent when they see w., 13.17
The LORD is a man of w.; 15.03
LORD will have w. with Amalek from 17.16
"There is a noise of w. in the camp." 32.17
who are able to go forth to w., Num 1.03
who were able to go forth to w.: 1.20
who were able to go forth to w.: 1.22
who were able to go forth to w.: 1.24
every man able to go forth to w.: 1.26
every man able to go forth to w.: 1.28
every man able to go forth to w.: 1.30
every man able to go forth to w.: 1.32
every man able to go forth to w.: 1.34
every man able to go forth to w.: 1.36
every man able to go forth to w.: 1.38
every man able to go forth to w.: 1.40
every man able to go forth to w.: 1.42
able to go forth to w. in Israel— 1.45
And when you go to w. in your land 10.09
who are able to go forth to w." 26.02
"Arm men from among you for the w., 31.03
of the tribes of Israel to the w." 31.04
from each tribe twelve thousand armed for w. 31.05
And Moses sent them to the w., 31.06
had come from service in the w. 31.14
to the men of w. who had gone to 31.21
from the men of w. who went out to 31.28
spoil that the men of w. took was: 31.32
of those who had gone out to w., 31.36
of the men who had gone to w.— 31.42
the men of w. who are under our 31.49
(The men of w. had taken booty, 31.53
go to the w. while you sit here? 32.06
to go before the LORD for the w., 32.20
every man who is armed for w., 32.27
of you girded on his weapons of w., Deu 1.41
the men or w., had perished from 2.14
all the men of w. had perished and 2.16
and by w., by a mighty hand and an 4.34
"When you go forth to w. against 20.01
but makes w. against you, then you 20.12
making w. against it in order to 20.19
the city that makes w. with you, 20.20
"When you go forth to w. against 21.10
ready armed for w. passed over Jos 4.13
out of Egypt, all the men of w., 5.04
the men of w. that came forth out 5.06
all the men of w. going around the 6.03
Gibeon, and made w. against it. 10.05
and all the people of w. with him, 10.07
of the men of w. who had gone with 10.24
them with all his people of w., 11.07
Joshua made w. a long time with all 11.18
And the land had rest from w. 11.23
for w., and for going and coming. 14.11
And the land had rest from w. 14.15
Bashan, because he was a man of w. 17.01
at Shiloh, to make w. against them. 22.12
no more of making w. against them, 22.33
no experience of any w. in Canaan; Ju 3.01
the people of Israel might know w., 3.02
he might teach w. to such at least 3.02
he went out to w., and the LORD 3.10
then w. was in the gates. Was shield 5.08
Ammonites made w. against Israel. 11.04
Ammonites made w. against Israel, 11.05
or did he ever go to w. with them? 11.25

WAR (cont.)

you do me wrong by making w. on me; Ju 11.27
of Dan, armed with weapons of w., 18.11
armed with their weapons of w., 18.16
men armed with weapons of w. 18.17
that drew sword; all these were men of w. 20.17
implements of w. and the equipment 1Sa 8.12
a man of w., prudent in speech, and 16.18
battle line, shouting the w. cry. 17.20
been a man of w. from his youth." 17.33
Saul set him over the men of w. 18.05
And there was w. again; and David went 19.08
Saul summoned all the people to w., 23.08
gathered their forces for w., 28.01
and the weapons of w. perished! 2Sa 1.27
There was a long w. between the 3.01
While there was w. between the 3.06
had often been at w. with Tou. 8.10
fared, and how the w. prospered. 11.07
your father is expert in w.; 17.08
The Philistines had w. again with 21.15
there was again w. with the 21.18
And there was again w. with the 21.19
And there was again w. at Gath, 21.20
He trains my hands for w., 22.35
blood which had been shed in w., 1Ki 2.05
And there was w. between Rehoboam 14.30
Now there was w. between Rehoboam 15.06
And there was w. between Abijam and 15.07
And there was w. between Asa and 15.16
And there was w. between Asa and 15.32
or if they have come out for w., 20.18
and Israel continued without w. 22.01
of Ahab to make w. against Hazael 2Ki 8.28
from Jehoahaz his father in w. 13.25
came up to wage w. on Jerusalem, 16.05
are counsel and strength for w.! 18.20
all of them strong and fit for w. 24.16
all the men of w. fled by night by 25.04
been in command of the men of w., 25.19
Saul they made w. on the Hagrites, 1Ch 5.10
expert in w., forty-four thousand 5.18
They made w. upon the Hagrites, 5.19
slain, because the w. was of God. 5.22
were units of the army for w., 7.04
hundred, ready for service in w. 7.11
by genealogies, for service in w., 7.40
mighty men who helped him in w. 12.01
Simeonites, mighty men of valor for w., 12.25
battle with all the weapons of w., 12.33
armed with all the weapons of w. 12.37
men of w., arrayed in battle order, 12.38
had often been at w. with Tou. 18.10
there arose w. with the Philistines 20.04
And there was again w. with the 20.05
And there was again w. at Gath, 20.06
Now there was w. between Abijah and 2Ch 13.02
an army of valiant men of w., 13.03
He had no w. in those years, for the 14.06
was no more w. until the thirty-fifth 15.19
they made no w. against Jehoshaphat 17.10
and eighty thousand armed for w. 17.18
We will be with you in the w. 18.03
Israel to make w. against Hazael 22.05
fit for w., able to handle spear 25.05
this way you will be strong for w., 25.08
out and made w. against the 26.06
fit for w., in divisions according 26.11
who could make w. with mighty 26.13
those who were coming from the w., 28.12
the house with which I am at w.; 35.21
and in w. from the power of the Job 5.20
for the day of battle and w.? 38.23
He trains my hands for w., Ps 18.34
though w. arise against me, yet I 27.03
The w. horse is a vain hope for 33.17
yet w. was in his heart; his words were 55.21
the peoples who delight in w. 68.30
the sword, and the weapons of w. 76.03
all the men of w. were unable to 76.05
but when I speak, they are for w.! 120.07
rock, who trains my hands for w., 144.01
by counsel; by wise guidance wage w. Pro 20.18
wise guidance you can wage your w., 24.06
his neighbor is like a w. club, 25.18
a time for w., and a time for peace. Ecc 3.08
there is no discharge from w., 8.08
Wisdom is better than weapons of w., 9.18
all girt with swords and expert in w., Sol 3.08
shall they learn w. any more. Is 2.04
to Jerusalem to wage w. against it, 7.01
are strategy and power for w.? 36.05
those who w. against you shall be 41.12
like a man of w. he stirs up his 42.13
of the trumpet, the alarm of w. Jer 4.19
"Prepare w. against her; up, and let us 6.04
of Babylon is making w. against us; 21.02
the weapons of w. which are in 21.04
have his life as a prize of w. 21.09
from ancient times prophesied w., 28.08
life as a prize of w., and live. 38.02
have your life as a prize of w., 39.18
Egypt, where we shall not see w., 42.14
as a prize of w. in all places to 45.05
are heroes and mighty men of w.'? 48.14
"You are my hammer and weapon w.: 51.20
the nations for w. against her, 51.27
Prepare the nations for w. against her, 51.28
all the men of w. fled and went 52.07
been in command of the men of w., 52.25
company will not help him in w., Eze 17.17
in your army as your men of w.; 27.10
for your wares w. horses, and mules. 27.14
all your men of w. who are in you, 27.27
to Sheol with their weapons of w., 32.27
the land that is restored from w., 38.08
this horn made w. with the saints, Dan 7.21
and to the end there shall be w.; 9.26
"His sons shall wage w. and assemble 11.10
shall carry the w. as far as his 11.10
shall wage w. with an exceedingly 11.25
nor by w., nor by horses, nor by Hos 1.07
the sword, and w. from the land; 2.18
Shall not w. overtake them in 10.09
therefore the tumult of w. shall 10.14
and like w. horses they run. Joe 2.04
Prepare w., stir up the mighty men. 3.09
Let all the men of w. draw near, 3.09
trustingly with no thought of w. Mic 2.08
but declare w. against him who puts 3.05
shall they learn w. any more; 4.03
Ephraim and the w. horse from Zec 9.10
that wage w. against Jerusalem: 14.12
to encounter another king in w., Lk 14.31
another law at w. with the law of Rom 7.23
are not carrying on a worldly w., 2Co 10.03
of weakness, became mighty in w., Heb 11.34
that are at w. in your members? Jas 4.01
so you fight and wage w. 4.02
flesh that wage w. against your 1Pe 2.11
to you soon and w. against them Rev 2.16
pit will make w. upon them and 11.07
Now w. arose in heaven, Michael and 12.07
off to make w. on the rest of her 12.17
allowed to make w. on the saints 13.07
they will make w. on the Lamb, and 17.14
righteousness he judges and makes w. 19.11
gathered to make w. against him who 19.19

WARD

and the lame will w. you off"— 2Sa 5.06

WARDROBE

to him who was in charge of the w., 2Ki 10.22
keeper of the w. (now she dwelt in 22.14

WARDROBE (cont.)
keeper of the w. (now she dwelt in 2Ch 34.22
to a w. of the storehouse, and took Jer 38.11

WARES
with beasts, and with costly w., Ez 1.06
land bring in w. or any grain on Neh 10.31
all kinds of w. and sold them on 13.16
of all kinds of w. lodged outside 13.20
were in you, to barter for your w. Eze 27.09
lead they exchanged for your w. 27.12
Bethtogarmah exchanged for your w. horses, 27.14
exchanged for your w. emeralds, 27.16
Uzal they exchanged for your w.; 27.19
for your w. the best of all kinds 27.22
your w., your merchandise, your 27.27
When your w. came from the seas, you 27.33
they threw the w. that were in the Jon 1.05
The merchants of these w., Rev 18.15

WARFARE
because of the w. with which his 1Ki 5.03
cry to her that her w. is ended, Is 40.02
weapons of our w. are not worldly 2Co 10.04
by them you may wage the good w., 1Ti 1.18

WARM
it was still w. when we took it Jos 9.12
with clothes, he could not get w. 1Ki 1.01
that my lord the king may be w." 1.02
the flesh of the child became w. 2Ki 4.34
and to w. themselves the roots of Job 30.04
Again, if two lie together, they are w.; Ecc 4.11
but how can one be w. alone? 4.11
I am w., I have seen the fire! Is 44.16
my compassions grows w. and tender, Hos 11.08
yourselves, but no one is w.; Hag 1.06

WARMED
if he was not w. with the fleece Job 31.20
and lets them be w. on the ground, 39.14
be w. and filled," without giving Jas 2.16

WARMING
No coal for w. oneself is this, no Is 47.14
and w. himself at the fire. Mk 14.54
and seeing Peter w. himself, 14.67
were standing and w. themselves; Jn 18.18
with them, standing and w. himself. 18.18
Peter was standing and w. himself. 18.25

WARMS
takes a part of it and w. himself, Is 44.15
also he w. himself and says, "Aha, I 44.16

WARN
"Go down and w. the people, lest Ex 19.21
I solemnly w. you this day that you Deu 8.19
only, you shall solemnly w. them, 1Sa 8.09
Thus he used to w. him, so that he 2Ki 6.10
And thou didst w. them in order to Neh 9.29
and didst w. them by thy Spirit 9.30
W. the nations that he is coming; Jer 4.16
nor speak to w. the wicked from his Eze 3.18
But if you w. the wicked, and he 3.19
Nevertheless if you w. the righteous 3.21
do not speak to w. the wicked to 33.08
But if you w. the wicked to turn 33.09
But I will w. you whom to fear: fear Lk 2.05
brothers, so that he may w. them, 16.28
let us w. them to speak no more to Ac 4.17
and I w. them now while absent, as I 2Co 13.02
I w. you, as I warned you before, Gal 5.21
as an enemy, but w. him as a brother. 2Th 3.15
I w. every one who hears the words Rev 22.18

WARNED
So Abimelech w. all the people, Gen 26.11
to him, "The man solemnly w. us, 43.03
owner has been w. but has not kept Ex 21.29
them for evil, as the LORD had w., Ju 2.15
Yet the LORD w. Israel and Judah by 2Ki 17.13
who had w. them in order to turn Neh 9.26
and I w. them on the day when they 13.15
But I w. them and said to them, "Why 13.21
be w., O rulers of the earth. Ps 2.10
Moreover by them is thy servant w.; 19.11
and w. me not to walk in the way of Is 8.11
Be w., O Jerusalem, lest I be Jer 6.08
For I solemnly w. your fathers when 11.07
that I have w. you this day 42.19
because you have not w. him, Eze 3.20
so that the people are not w., 33.06
And being w. in a dream not to Mt 2.12
and being w. in a dream he withdrew 2.22
Who w. you to flee from the wrath 3.07
Who w. you to flee from the wrath Lk 3.07
I w. those who sinned before and 2Co 13.02
as I w. you before, that those who Gal 5.21
being w. by God concerning events Heb 11.07
refused him who w. them on earth, 12.25

WARNING
and fifty men, and they became a w. Num 26.10
To whom shall I speak and give w., Jer 6.10
w. them persistently, even to this 11.07
you shall give them w. from me. Eze 3.17
die,' and you give him no w., 3.18
surely live, because he took w.; 3.21
a w. and a horror, to the nations 5.15
women may take w. and not commit 23.48
of the trumpet does not take w., 33.04
the trumpet, and did not take w.; 33.05
But if he had taken w., 33.05
you shall give them w. from me. 33.07
Without w. he shall destroy many; Dan 8.25
come in without w. and obtain the 11.21
with a small people. Without w. 11.23
things happened to them as a w., 1Co 10.11
w. every man and teaching every man Col 1.28

WARNINGS
and the w. which he gave them. 2Ki 17.15
commandments and thy w. which thou Neh 9.34
men, and terrifies them with w., Job 33.16
Now these things are w. for us, 1Co 10.06

WARNS
the trumpet and w. the people; Eze 33.03
we reject him who w. from heaven. Heb 12.25

WARP
in w. or woof of linen or wool, or Lev 13.48
whether in w. or woof or in skin or 13.49
in w. or woof, or in the skin, 13.51
whether diseased in w. or woof, 13.52
the garment in w. or woof or in 13.53
or the skin or the w. or woof; 13.56
in w. or woof, or in anything of 13.57
w. or woof, or anything of skin from 13.58
either in w. or woof, or in anything 13.59

WARRED
They w. against Midian, as the LORD Num 31.07
how he w. and how he reigned, behold, 1Ki 14.19
and how he w., are they not written 22.45

WARRING
the Philistines are w. against me, 1Sa 28.15
of Syria was w. against Israel, 2Ki 6.08

WARRIOR
the Gileadite was a mighty w., Ju 11.01
for you are a w. and have shed 1Ch 28.03
he runs upon me like a w. Job 16.14
a w. is not delivered by his great Ps 33.16
the hand of a w. are the sons of 127.04

WARRIOR (cont.)
of the tramping w. in battle Is 9.05
chariot and horse, army and w.; 43.17
But the LORD is with me as a dread w.; Jer 20.11
flee away, nor the w. escape; 46.06
for w. has stumbled against w.; 46.12
like a skilled w. who does not 50.09
let the weak say, "I am a w." Joe 3.10
a w. who gives victory; he will rejoice Zep 3.17
shall become like a mighty w., Zec 10.07

WARRIOR'S
A w. sharp arrows, with glowing Ps 120.04
and wield you like a w. sword. Zec 9.13

WARRIORS
between the w. who went out to Num 31.27
and eighty thousand chosen w., 1Ki 12.21
mighty w., famous men, heads of 1Ch 5.24
mighty w. of their generations, 7.02
eighty-seven thousand mighty w., 7.05
of fathers' houses, mighty w.; 7.07
mighty w., was twenty thousand two 7.09
mighty w., seventeen thousand and 7.11
mighty w., chief of the princes. 7.40
Ulam were men who were mighty w., 8.40
wilderness mighty and experienced w., 12.08
men, and all the seasoned w. 28.01
and eighty thousand chosen w., 2Ch 11.01
hundred thousand picked mighty w. 13.03
all the mighty w. and commanders 32.21
bucklers, all of them shields of w. Sol 4.04
sickness among his stout w., Is 10.16
with all his w. and all the princes, Jer 26.21
Their w. are beaten down, and have 46.05
Let the w. go forth: men of Ethiopia 46.09
heart of the w. of Moab shall be 48.41
heart of the w. of Edom shall be 49.22
A sword upon her w., that they may be 50.36
The w. of Babylon have ceased 51.30
her w. are taken, their bows are 51.56
governors, her commanders, and her w.; 51.57
w. clothed in purple, governors and Eze 23.06
w. clothed in full armor, horsemen 23.12
officers and w., all of them riding 23.23
mighty men and all kinds of w., 39.20
and in the multitude of your w., Hos 10.13
Like w. they charge, like soldiers Joe 2.07
Bring down thy w., O LORD. 3.11
with thy shafts the head of his w., Hab 3.14

WARS
in the Book of the W. of the LORD, Num 21.14
much blood and have waged great w.; 1Ch 22.08
were continual w. between Rehoboam 2Ch 12.15
for from now on you will have w." 16.09
and all his w., and his ways, behold, 27.07
He makes w. cease to the end of the Ps 46.09
heart, and stir up w. continually. 140.02
will hear of w. and rumors of w.; Mt 24.06
you hear of w. and rumors of w., Mk 13.07
And when you hear of w. and tumults, Lk 21.09
What causes w., and what causes Jas 4.01

WASH
and w. your feet, and rest yourselves Gen 18.04
spend the night, and w. your feet; 19.02
and water to w. his feet and the 24.32
and let them w. their garments, Ex 19.10
of meeting, and w. them with water. 29.04
and w. its entrails and its legs, 29.17
his sons shall w. their hands and 30.19
they shall w. with water, lest they 30.20
They shall w. their hands and their 30.21
of meeting, and shall w. them with water, 40.12
its legs he shall w. with water. Lev 1.09
the legs he shall w. with water. 1.13
you shall w. that on which it was 6.27
carcass shall w. his clothes and 11.25
carcass shall w. his clothes and 11.28
carcass shall w. his clothes and 11.40
and he shall w. his clothes, and be 13.06
and he shall w. his clothes, and be 13.34
that they w. the thing in which is 13.54
be cleansed shall w. his clothes, 14.08
Then he shall w. his clothes, and 14.09
in the house shall w. his clothes; 14.47
in the house shall w. his clothes. 14.47
his bed shall w. his clothes, 15.05
has sat shall w. his clothes, 15.06
the discharge shall w. his clothes, 15.07
then he shall w. his clothes, and 15.08
such a thing shall w. his clothes, 15.10
in water shall w. his clothes, 15.11
his cleansing, and w. his clothes; 15.13
her bed shall w. his clothes, 15.21
she sits shall w. his clothes, 15.22
and shall w. his clothes, and bathe 15.27
to Azazel shall w. his clothes and 16.26
them shall w. his clothes and 16.28
shall w. his clothes, and bathe 17.15
But if he does not w. them or bathe 17.16
and w. them off into the water of Num 5.23
and w. their clothes and cleanse 8.07
priest shall w. his clothes and 19.07
heifer shall w. his clothes in 19.08
of the heifer shall w. his clothes, 19.10
and he shall w. his clothes and 19.19
for impurity shall w. his clothes; 19.21
You must w. your clothes on the 31.24
slain man shall w. their hands Deu 21.06
W. therefore and anoint yourself, Ru 3.03
is a servant to w. the feet of the 1Sa 25.41
to your house, and w. your feet." 2Sa 11.08
"Go and w. in the Jordan seven 2Ki 5.10
Could I not w. in them, and be clean?" 5.12
he says to you, 'W., and be clean?'" 5.13
made ten lavers in which to w., 2Ch 4.06
sea was for the priest to w. in. 4.06
If I w. myself with snow, and Job 9.30
the torrents w. away the soil of 14.19
I w. my hands in innocence, and go Ps 26.06
W. me thoroughly from my iniquity, 51.02
w. me, and I shall be whiter than 51.07
W. yourselves; make yourselves clean; Is 1.16
Though you w. yourself with lye and Jer 2.22
O Jerusalem, w. your heart from 4.14
anoint your head and w. your face, Mt 6.17
For they do not w. their hands when 15.02
not eat unless they w. their hands, Mk 7.03
he did not first w. before dinner. Lk 11.38
w. in the pool of Siloam" (which Jn 9.07
said to me, 'Go to Siloam and w.'; 9.11
and began to w. the disciples' feet, 13.05
to him, "Lord, do you w. my feet?" 13.06
to him, "You shall never w. my feet." 13.08
"If I do not w. you, you have no 13.08
who has bathed does not need to w., 13.10
also ought to w. one another's feet. 13.14
and w. away your sins, calling on Ac 22.16
Blessed are those who w. their robes, Rev 22.14

WASHBASIN
Moab is my w.; upon Edom I cast Ps 60.08
Moab is my w.; upon Edom I cast 108.09

WASHED
and they had w. their feet, and when Gen 43.24
Then he w. his face and came out; 43.31
and they w. their garments. Ex 19.14
and his sons w. their hands and 40.31
they approached the altar, they w.; 40.32
and w. them with water. Lev 8.06

WASHED (cont.)
and the legs were w. with water, Lev 8.21
And he w. the entrails and the legs, 9.14
diseased thing after it has been w. 13.55
the disease is dim after it is w., 13.56
departs when you have w. it, 13.58
shall then be w. a second time, and 13.58
semen comes shall be w. with water, 15.17
from sin, and w. their clothes; Num 8.21
and they w. their feet, and ate and Ju 19.21
and w., and anointed himself, and 2Sa 12.20
nor w. his clothes, from the day the 19.24
And they w. the chariot by the pool 1Ki 22.38
and the harlots w. themselves in 22.38
their foundation was w. away. Job 22.16
when my steps were w. with milk, 29.06
heart clean and w. my hands in Ps 73.13
Lord shall have w. away the filth Is 4.04
nor were you w. with water to Eze 16.04
with water and w. off your blood 16.09
the burnt offering was to be w. 40.38
took water and w. his hands before Mt 27.24
So he went and w. and came back Jn 9.07
so I went and w. and received my 9.11
on my eyes, and I w., and I see. 9.15
When he had w. their feet, and taken 13.12
have w. your feet, you also ought to 13.14
and when they had w. her, they laid her Ac 9.37
and w. their wounds, and he was 16.33
But you were w., you were sanctified, 1Co 6.11
w. the feet of the saints, relieved 1Ti 5.10
and our bodies w. with pure water. Heb 10.22
and the sow is w. only to wallow 2Pe 2.22
they have w. their robes and made Rev 7.14

WASHES
he w. his garments in wine and his Gen 49.11

WASHING
with its base of bronze, for w. Ex 30.18
altar, and put water in it for w., 40.30
ewes that have come up from the w., Sol 4.02
that have come up from the w., 6.06
the w. of cups and pots and vessels Mk 7.04
out of them and were w. their nets. Lk 5.02
her by the w. of water with the Eph 5.26
by the w. of regeneration and Tit 3.05

WASTE
and fever that w. the eyes and Lev 26.16
And I will lay your cities w., 26.31
and your cities shall be a w. 26.33
and we laid w. until fire spread to Num 21.30
and salt, and a burnt-out w., Deu 29.23
in the howling w. of the wilderness; 32.10
"I will not w. time like this with 2Sa 18.14
have laid w. the nations and their 2Ki 19.17
violent men shall w. them no more, 1Ch 17.09
That was why this city was laid w. Ez 4.15
lies w., and its gates have been Neh 2.03
they go up into the w., and perish. Job 6.18
makes them wander in a pathless w. 12.24
to satisfy the w. and desolate land, 38.27
of my misery, and my bones w. away. Ps 31.10
and their form shall w. away; 49.14
Jacob, and laid w. his habitation. 79.07
like an owl of the w. places; 102.06
a fruitful land into a salty w., 107.34
and w. your pleasant words. Pro 23.08
I will make it a w.; it shall not be Is 5.06
cities lie w. without inhabitant, 6.11
Ar is laid w. in a night Moab is 15.01
Kir is laid w. in a night Moab is 15.01
of Tarshish, for Tyre is laid w., 23.01
for your stronghold is laid w. 23.14
LORD will lay w. the earth and 24.01
be utterly laid w. and utterly 24.03
The highways lie w., the wayfaring 33.08
to generation it shall lie w.; 34.10
have laid w. all the nations and 37.18
I will lay w. mountains and hills, 42.15
who laid you w. go forth from you. 49.17
"Surely your w. and your desolate 49.19
he will comfort all her w. places, 51.03
you w. places of Jerusalem; 52.09
nations shall be utterly laid w. 60.12
They have made his land a w.; Jer 2.15
his place to make your land a w.; 4.07
disaster, the whole land is laid w. 4.20
earth, and lo, it was w. and void; 4.23
for the land shall become a w. 7.34
they are laid w. so that no one 9.10
ruined and laid w. like a wilderness, 9.12
and have laid w. his habitation. 10.25
land shall become a ruin and a w., 25.11
making the land an everlasting w. 25.12
to make them a desolation and a w., 25.18
has become a w. because of the 25.38
'It is a w. without man or beast,' 33.10
hosts: In this place which is w., 33.12
they became a w. and a desolation, 44.06
a desolation and a w. and a curse, 44.22
For Memphis shall become a w., 46.19
"Woe to Nebo, for it is laid w.! 48.01
by the Arnon, that Moab is laid w. 48.20
"Wail, O Heshbon, for Ai is laid w.! 49.03
horror, a taunt, a w., and a curse; 49.13
of jackals, an everlasting w.; 49.33
be a perpetual w., says the LORD. 51.26
For the LORD is laying Babylon w., 51.55
made my flesh and my skin w. away, Lam 3.04
and w. away under their punishment. Eze 4.17
cities shall be w. and your high 6.06
your altars will be w. and ruined, 6.06
and make the land desolate and w., 6.14
inhabited cities shall be laid w., 12.20
strongholds, and laid w. their cities; 19.07
replenished, now that she is laid w.,' 26.02
When I make you a city laid w., 26.19
shall be a desolation and a w. 29.09
Egypt an utter w. and desolation, 29.10
among cities that are laid w. 29.12
midst of cities that are laid w. 30.07
and we w. away because of them; 33.10
of these w. places in the land of 33.24
who are in the w. places shall 33.27
the land a desolation and a w.; 33.28
desolation and a w. because of all 33.29
make you a desolation and a w. 35.03
I will lay your cities w., 35.04
Mount Seir a w. and a desolation; 35.07
inhabited and the w. places rebuilt; 36.10
and the w. places shall be rebuilt. 36.33
and the w. and desolate and ruined 36.35
so shall the w. cities be filled 36.38
which had been a continual w.; 38.08
to assail the w. places which are 38.12
And I will lay w. her vines and her Hos 2.12
It has laid w. my vines, and splintered Joe 1.07
The fields are laid w., the ground 1.10
I laid w. your gardens and your Amo 4.09
sanctuaries of Israel shall be laid w., 7.09
and all her idols I will lay w.; Mic 1.07
the earth is laid w. before him, Nah 1.05
plundered, and their houses laid w. Zep 1.13
and salt pits, and a w. for ever. 2.09
a dry w. like the desert. 2.13
I have laid w. their streets so 3.06
jungle of the Jordan is laid w.! Zec 11.03
I have laid w. his hill country and Mal 1.03
divided against itself is laid w., Mt 12.25
indignant, saying, "Why this w.? 26.08
divided against itself is laid w., Lk 11.17

WASTE (cont.)

But Saul laid w. the church, and	Ac 8.03
all this wealth has been laid w.	Rev 18.17
In one hour she has been laid w.	18.19

WASTED

nevertheless Kain shall be w.	Num 24.22
they shall be w. with hunger, and	Deu 32.24
so that they w. the land as they	Ju 6.05
His flesh is so w. away that it	Job 33.21
my eye is w. from grief, my soul and	Ps 31.09
my body w. away through my groaning	32.03
from you and say, W. is Nineveh;	Nah 3.07
"Why was the ointment thus w.?	Mk 14.04

WASTES

Man w. away like a rotten thing,	Job 13.08
and a river w. away and dries up,	14.11
My eye w. away because of grief, it	Ps 6.07
the destruction that w. at noonday.	91.06
Some wandered in desert w.,	107.04
makes them wander in trackless w.;	107.40
will be as when a sick man w. away.	Is 10.18
her cities shall be perpetual w."	Jer 49.13
the desolate w. and the deserted	Eze 36.04

WASTING

but sent a w. disease among them.	Ps 106.15
will send w. sickness among his	Is 10.16
him that this man was w. his goods.	Lk 16.01
Though our outer nature is w. away,	2Co 4.16

WATCH

"The LORD w. between you and me,	Gen 31.49
And in the morning w. the LORD in	Ex 14.24
at the beginning of the middle w.,	Ju 7.19
when they had just set the w.;	7.19
and w.; if the daughters	21.21
And w.; if it goes up	1Sa 6.09
of the camp in the morning w.,	11.11
messengers to David's house to w. him,	19.11
you not kept w. over your lord the	26.15
have not kept w. over your lord,	26.16
who kept the w. lifted up his eyes,	2Sa 13.34
from w. tower to fortified city;	2Ki 17.09
W. corresponded to w.	1Ch 26.16
who kept w. at the gates, were a	Neh 11.19
of God, w. corresponding to w.	12.24
wouldest not keep w. over my sin;	Job 14.16
w. is kept over his tomb.	21.32
a sacrifice for thee, and w.	Ps 5.03
eyes stealthily w. for the hapless,	10.08
they lurk, they w. my steps.	56.06
love and faithfulness w. over him!	61.07
whose eyes keep w. on the nations—	66.07
those who w. for my life consult	71.10
is past, or as a w. in the night.	90.04
keep w. over the door of my lips!	141.03
I look to the right and w.,	142.04
discretion will w. over you;	Pro 2.11
lie down, they will w. over you;	6.22
keeping w. on the evil and the good.	15.03
of the LORD w. over knowledge,	22.12
he who keeps w. over your soul	24.12
and all who w. to do evil shall be	Is 29.20
so I will w. over them to build and	Jer 31.28
Stand by the way and w.,	48.19
make the w. strong; set up watchmen;	51.12
fat and the strong I will w. over;	Eze 34.16
w. the road; gird your loins;	Nah 2.01
I will take my stand to w.,	Hab 2.01
And in the fourth w. of the night	Mt 14.25
W. therefore, for you do not know on	24.42
W. therefore, for you know neither	25.13
remain here, and w. with me."	26.38
could you not w. with me one hour?	26.40
W. and pray that you may not enter	26.41
down and kept w. over him there.	27.36
keeping w. over Jesus, saw the	27.54
the fourth w. of the night he came	Mk 6.48
Take heed, w.; for you do not	31.33
the doorkeeper to be on the w.	13.34
W. therefore—for you do not know	13.35
what I say to you I say to all: W."	13.37
to death; remain here, and w."	14.34
Could you not w. one hour?	14.37
W. and pray that you may not enter	14.38
keeping w. over their flock by	Lk 2.08
If he comes in the second w.,	12.38
But w. at all times, praying that	21.36
are keeping w. over your souls, as	Heb 13.17

WATCHED

as in the days when God w. over me;	Job 29.02
high official is w. by a higher,	Ecc 5.08
that as I have w. over them to	Jer 31.28
our watching we w. for a nation	Lam 4.17
he would have w. and would not have	Mt 24.43
And they w. him, to see whether he	Mk 3.02
and w. the multitude putting money	12.41
scribes and the Pharisees w. him,	Lk 6.07
So they w. him, and sent spies, who	20.20

WATCHER

do I do to thee, thou w. of men?	Job 7.20
a w., a holy one, came down from	Dan 4.13
And whereas the king saw a w.,	4.23

WATCHERS

sentence is by the decree of the w.,	Dan 4.17

WATCHES

in the stocks, and w. all my paths.	Job 33.11
The wicked w. the righteous, and	Ps 37.32
on thee in the w. of the night;	63.06
awake before the w. of the night,	119.148
Unless the LORD w. over the city,	127.01
The LORD w. over the sojourners, he	146.09
the LORD, and he w. all his paths.	Pro 5.21
night, at the beginning of the w.!	Lam 2.19

WATCHEST

in the stocks, and w. all my paths;	Job 13.27

WATCHFUL

Be w., stand firm in your faith, be	1Co 16.13
being w. in it with thanksgiving;	Col 4.02
Be sober, be w.	1Pe 5.08

WATCHING

It was a night of w. by the LORD,	Ex 12.42
is a night of w. kept to the LORD	12.42
upon his seat by the road w.,	1Sa 4.13
Now the men were w. for an omen,	1Ki 20.33
for upon them lay the duty of w.,	1Ch 9.27
My eyes fail with w. for thy	Ps 119.82
My eyes fail with w. for thy	119.123
w. daily at my gates, waiting beside	Pro 8.34
for I am w. over my word to perform	Jer 1.12
A leopard is w. against their	5.06
familiar friends, w. for my fall.	20.10
Behold, I am w. over them for evil	44.27
ever w. vainly for help;	Lam 4.17
in our w. we watched for a nation	4.17
who were w. me, knew that it was the	Zec 11.11
to the Pharisees, they were w. him.	Lk 14.01
And the people stood by, w.;	23.35
They were w. the gates day and	Ac 9.24
tumults, labors, w., hunger;	2Co 6.05

WATCHMAN
and the w. went up to the roof of 2Sa 18.24
And the w. called out and told the 18.25
And the w. saw another man running; 18.26
and the w. called to the gate and 18.26
And the w. said, "I think the 18.27
Now the w. was standing on the 2Ki 9.17
And the w. reported, saying, "The 9.18
Again the w. reported, "He reached 9.20
web, like a booth which a w. makes. Job 27.18
the w. stays awake in vain. Ps 127.01
set a w., let him announce what he Is 21.06
"W., what of the night? W., what of 21.11
The w. says: "Morning comes, and also 21.12
have made you a w. for the house Eze 3.17
among them, and make him their w.; 33.02
But if the w. sees the sword coming 33.06
I have made a w. for the house of 33.07
The prophet is the w. of Ephraim, Hos 9.08

WATCHMAN'S
I will require at the w. hand. Eze 33.06

WATCHMEN
And the w. of Saul in Gibeah of 1Sa 14.16
priest posted w. over the house of 2Ki 11.18
And Jehoiada posted w. for the 2Ch 23.18
LORD more than w. for the morning, Ps 130.06
more than w. for the morning. 130.06
The w. found me, as they went about Sol 3.03
The w. found me, as they went about 5.07
my mantle, those w. of the walls. 5.07
Hark, your w. lift up their voice, Is 52.08
His w. are blind, they are all 56.10
walls, O Jerusalem, I have set w.; 62.06
I set w. over you, saying, 'Give heed Jer 6.17
be a day when w. will call in the 31.06
set up w.; prepare the ambushes; 51.12
The day of their w., of their Mic 7.04

WATCHTOWER
from w. to fortified city. 2Ki 18.08
came to the w. of the wilderness, 2Ch 20.24
he built a w. in the midst of it, Is 5.02
"Upon a w. I stand, O Lord, continually 21.08
hill and the w. will become dens 32.14

WATER
out of Eden to w. the garden, Gen 2.10
by a spring of w. in the wilderness, 16.07
Let a little w. be brought, and wash 18.04
and took bread and a skin of w., 21.14
When the w. in the skin was gone, 21.15
her eyes, and she saw a well of w.; 21.19
went, and filled the skin with w., 21.19
about a well of w. which Abimelech's 21.25
by the well of w. at the time of 24.11
time when women go out to draw w. 24.11
Behold, I am standing by the spring of w., 24.13
the city are coming out to draw w. 24.13
and I will w. your camels'—let her 24.14
out with her w. jar upon her 24.15
me a little w. to drink from your 24.17
and w. to wash his feet and the 24.32
behold, I am standing by the spring of w.; 24.43
me a little w. from your jar to 24.43
out with her w. jar on her shoulder; 24.45
the wells of w. which had been dug 26.18
there a well of springing w., 26.19
herdsmen, saying, "The w. is ours." 26.20
and said to him, "We have found w." 26.32
and w. the sheep, and put the stone 29.03
w. the sheep, and go, pasture them." 29.07
of the well; then we w. the sheep." 29.08
was empty, there was no w. in it. 37.24
Joseph's house, and given them w., 43.24
Unstable as w., you shall not have 49.04
"Because I drew him out of the w." Ex 2.10
and they came and drew w., 2.16
the troughs to w. their father's 2.16
and even drew w. for us and watered 2.19
shall take some w. from the Nile 4.09
and the w. which you shall take 4.09
as he is going out to the w.; 7.15
will strike the w. that is in the 7.17
loathe to drink w. from the Nile." 7.18
ponds, and all their pools of w., 7.19
and struck the w. that was in the 7.20
and all the w. that was in the Nile 7.20
could not drink w. from the Nile; 7.21
about the Nile for w. to drink, 7.24
could not drink the w. of the Nile. 7.24
Pharaoh, as he goes out to the w., 8.20
any of it raw or boiled with w., 12.09
that the w. may come back upon the 14.26
in the wilderness and found no w. 15.22
not drink the w. of Marah because 15.23
tree, and he threw it into the w., 15.25
and the w. became sweet. 15.25
springs of w. and seventy palm 15.27
and they encamped there by the w. 15.27
there was no w. for the people to 17.01
and said, "Give us w. to drink." 17.02
But the people thirsted there for w., 17.03
and w. shall come out of it, that 17.06
that is in the w. under the earth; 20.04
will bless your bread and your w.; 23.25
of meeting, and wash them with w. 29.04
altar, and you shall put w. in it, 30.18
shall wash with w., lest they die. 30.20
and scattered it upon the w., 32.20
he neither ate bread nor drank w. 34.28
and the altar, and put w. in it. 40.07
and shall wash them with w., 40.12
and put w. in it for washing, 40.30
and its legs he shall wash with w. Lev 1.09
and the legs he shall wash with w. 1.13
shall be scoured, and rinsed in w. 6.28
his sons, and washed them with w. 8.06
and the legs were washed with w., 8.21
the w. hen, the pelican, the vulture, 11.18
it must be put into w., and it shall be 11.32
upon which w. may come, shall be 11.34
cistern holding w. shall be clean; 11.36
but if w. is put on the seed and 11.38
an earthen vessel over running w. 14.05
was killed over the running w.; 14.06
his hair, and bathe himself in w., 14.08
clothes, and bathe his body in w., 14.09
an earthen vessel over running w., 14.50
was killed and in the running w., 14.51
the bird, and with the running w., 14.52
clothes, and bathe himself in w., 15.05
clothes, and bathe himself in w., 15.06
clothes, and bathe himself in w., 15.07
clothes, and bathe himself in w., 15.08
clothes and bathe himself in w., 15.10
his hands in w. shall wash his 15.11
clothes, and bathe himself in w., 15.11
of wood shall be rinsed in w. 15.12
shall bathe his body in running w., 15.13
shall bathe his whole body in w., 15.16
comes shall be washed with w., 15.17
them shall bathe themselves in w., 15.18
clothes, and bathe himself in w., 15.21
clothes, and bathe himself in w., 15.22
clothes, and bathe himself in w., 15.27
He shall bathe his body in w., 16.04
his body in w. in a holy place, and 16.24
clothes and bathe his body in w., 16.26
clothes and bathe his body in w., 16.28
clothes, and bathe himself in w., 17.15
he has bathed his body in w. 22.06

WATER (cont.)
shall take holy w. in an earthen Num 5.17
tabernacle and put it into the w. 5.17
shall have the w. of bitterness 5.18
free from this w. of bitterness 5.19
may this w. that brings the curse 5.22
them off into the w. of bitterness; 5.23
woman drink the w. of bitterness 5.24
and the w. that brings the curse 5.24
shall make the woman drink the w. 5.26
And when he has made her drink the w., 5.27
the w. that brings the curse shall 5.27
sprinkle the w. of expiation upon 8.07
clothes and bathe his body in w., 19.07
his clothes in w. and bathe his 19.08
in water and bathe his body in w., 19.08
of Israel for the w. for impurity, 19.09
with the w. on the third day and 19.12
because the w. for impurity was not 19.13
and running w. shall be added in a 19.17
take hyssop, and dip it in the w., 19.18
clothes and bathe himself in w., 19.19
because the w. for impurity has not 19.20
sprinkles the w. for impurity 19.21
who touches the w. for impurity 19.21
Now there was no w. for the congregation; 20.02
and there is no w. to drink." 20.05
before their eyes to yield its w.; 20.08
you shall bring w. out of the rock 20.08
we bring forth w. for you out of 20.10
and w. came forth abundantly, and 20.11
will we drink w. from a well; 20.17
and if we drink of your w., 20.19
For there is no food and no w., 21.05
together, and I will give them w." 21.16
we will not drink the w. of a well; 21.22
W. shall flow from his buckets, and 24.07
purified with the w. of impurity; 31.23
you shall pass through the w. 31.23
springs of w. and seventy palm 33.09
there was no w. for the people to 33.14
shall also buy w. of them for Deu 2.06
and give me w. for money, that I may 2.28
that is in the w. under the earth. 4.18
that is in the w. under the earth; 5.08
good land, a land of brooks of w., 8.07
ground where there was no w., 8.15
who brought you w. out of the 8.15
I neither ate bread nor drank w. 9.09
I neither ate bread nor drank w., 9.18
Jotbathah, a land with brooks of w. 10.07
how he made the w. of the Red Sea 11.04
which drinks w. by the rain from 11.11
pour it out upon the earth like w. 12.16
pour it out upon the earth like w. 12.24
owl and the great owl, the w. hen 14.16
pour it out on the ground like w. 15.23
down to a valley with running w., 21.04
with bread and with w. on the way, 23.04
on, he shall bathe himself in w., 23.11
wood and he who draws your w., 29.11
dried up the w. of the Red Sea Jos 2.10
brink of the w. (the Jordan 3.15
people melted, and became as w. 7.05
and drawers of w. for all the 9.21
and drawers of w. for the house of 9.23
and drawers of w. for the congregation 9.27
Negeb, give me also springs of w." 15.19
Negeb, give me also springs of w." Ju 1.15
"Pray, give me a little w. to drink; 4.19
dropped, yea, the clouds dropped w. 5.04
He asked w. and she gave him milk, 5.25
the fleece to fill a bowl with w. 6.38
down to the w. and I will test 7.04
brought the people down to the w.; 7.05
that laps the w. with his tongue, 7.05
the people knelt down to drink w. 7.06
at Lehi, and there came w. from it; 15.19
and drew w. and poured it out 1Sa 7.06
maidens coming out to draw w., 9.11
my bread and my w. and my meat 25.11
and the jar of w., and let us go." 26.11
and the jar of w. from Saul's head; 26.12
and the jar of w. that was at his 26.16
he ate, they gave him w. to drink, 30.11
bread or drunk w. for three days 30.12
him get up the w. shaft to attack 2Sa 5.08
we are like w. spilt on the ground, 14.14
have gone over the brook of w." 17.20
"Arise, and go quickly over the w.; 17.21
thick clouds, a gathering of w. 22.12
would give me w. to drink from the 23.15
and drew w. out of the well of 23.16
bread or drink w. in this place; 1Ki 13.08
nor drink w., nor return by the way 13.09
bread nor drink w. with you in 13.16
eat bread nor drink w. there, 13.17
that he may eat bread and drink w.' " 13.18
bread in his house, and drank w. 13.19
bread and drunk w. in the place of 13.22
"Eat no bread, and drink no w."; 13.22
as a reed is shaken in the w., 14.15
"Bring me a little w. in a vessel, 17.10
and fed them with bread and w.) 18.04
the springs of w. and to all the 18.05
and fed them with bread and w.? 18.13
he said, "Fill four jars with w., 18.33
And the w. ran round about the 18.35
and filled the trench also with w. 18.35
licked up the w. that was in the 18.38
on hot stones and a jar of w. 19.06
with scant fare of bread and w., 22.27
rolled it up, and struck the w., 2Ki 2.08
and the w. was parted to the one 2.08
fallen from him, and struck the w., 2.14
And when he had struck the w., 2.14
the w. was parted to the one side 2.14
but the w. is bad, and the land is 2.19
the spring of w. and threw salt in 2.21
I have made this w. wholesome; 2.21
So the w. has been wholesome to 2.22
there was no w. for the army or for 3.09
who poured w. on the hands of 3.11
stream-bed shall be filled with w., 3.17
and stop up all springs of w., 3.19
w. came from the direction of Edom, 3.20
the country was filled with w. 3.20
and the sun shone upon the w., 3.22
Moabites saw the w. opposite them 3.22
they stopped every spring of w. 3.25
log, his axe head fell into the w.; 6.05
Set bread and w. before them, that 6.22
dipped it in w. and spread it over 8.15
will drink the w. of his own 18.31
and brought w. into the city, 20.20
would give me w. to drink from the 1Ch 11.17
and drew w. out of the well of 11.18
with scant fare of bread and w., 2Ch 18.26
men to stop the w. of the springs 32.03
of Assyria come and find much w.?" 32.04
eating bread nor drinking w.; Ez 10.06
opposite the W. Gate on the east Neh 3.26
into the square before the W. Gate; 8.01
before the W. Gate from early 8.03
square at the W. Gate and in the 8.16
and bring forth w. for them from 9.15
and gavest them w. for their 9.20
house of David, to the W. Gate on the east. 12.37
of Israel with bread and w., 13.02
groanings are poured out like w. Job 3.24
flourish where there is no w.? 8.11
yet at the scent of w. it will bud 14.09
a man who drinks iniquity like w.! 15.16
You have given no w. to the weary 22.07

WATER (cont.)
see, and a flood of w. covers you. Job 22.11
who drinks up scoffing like w., 34.07
For he draws up the drops of w., 36.27
a tree planted by streams of w., Ps 1.03
canopy thick clouds dark with w. 18.11
I am poured out like w., and all my 22.14
them vanish like w. that runs away; 58 07
dry and weary land where no w. is. 63.01
the river of God is full of w.; 65.09
went through fire and through w.; 66.12
like showers that w. the earth! 72.06
The clouds poured out w.; the skies gave 77.17
rock so that w. gushed out and 78.20
blood like w. round about Jerusalem, 79.03
the rock, and w. gushed forth; 105.41
springs of w. into thirsty ground, 107.33
He turns a desert into pools of w., 107.35
a parched land into springs of w. 107.35
may it soak into his body like w., 109.18
who turns the rock into a pool of w., 114.08
the flint into a spring of w. 114.08
Drink w. from your own cistern, Pro 5.15
flowing w. from your own well. 5.15
streams of w. in the streets? 5.16
were no springs abounding with w. 8.24
"Stolen w. is sweet, and bread eaten 9.17
of strife is like letting out w.; 17.14
in a man's mind is like deep w.; 20.05
is a stream of w. in the hand of 21.01
is thirsty, give him w. to drink; 25.21
Like cold w. to a thirsty soul, so 25.25
As in w. face answers to face, so 27.19
the earth never thirsty for w., 30.16
from which to w. the forest of Ecc 2.06
fountain, a well of living w., Sol 4.15
like doves beside springs of w., 5.12
dross, your wine mixed with w. Is 1.22
and like a garden without w. 1.30
of bread, and the whole stay of w.; 3.01
you will draw w. from the wells of 12.03
and pools of w., and I will sweep 14.23
who spread nets upon the w. 19.08
To the thirsty bring w., 21.14
walls for the w. of the old pool. 22.11
every moment I w. it. 27.03
or to dip up w. out of the cistern." 30.14
adversity and the w. of affliction, 30.20
will be brooks running with w., 30.25
like streams of w. in a dry place, 32.02
be given him, his w. will be sure. 33.16
the thirsty ground springs of w.; 35.07
will drink the w. of his own 36.16
When the poor and needy seek w., 41.17
make the wilderness a pool of w., 41.18
and the dry land springs of w. 41.18
for I give w. in the wilderness, 43.20
For I will pour w. on the thirsty 44.03
he drinks no w. and is faint. 44.12
he made w. flow for them from the 48.21
the rock and the w. gushed out. 48.21
by springs of w. will guide them. 49.10
their fish stink for lack of w., 50.02
not thither but w. the earth, 55.10
garden, like a spring of w., 58.11
and the fire causes w. to boil— 64.02
cisterns, that can hold no w. Jer 2.13
As a well keeps its w. fresh, 6.07
has given us poisoned w. to drink, 8.14
give them poisonous w. to drink. 9.15
and our eyelids gush with w. 9.18
loins, and do not dip it in w." 13.01
Her nobles send their servants for w.; 14.03
they find no w., they return with 14.03
He is like a tree planted by w., 17.08
LORD, the fountain of living w. 17.13
and give them poisoned w. to drink; 23.15
make them walk by brooks of w., 31.09
And there was no w. in the cistern, 38.06
your heart like w. before the Lam 2.19
w. closed over my head; I said, 'I am lost.' 3.54
We must pay for the w. we drink, 5.04
And w. you shall drink by measure, Eze 4.11
shall drink w. by measure and in 4.16
that they may lack bread and w., 4.17
feeble, and all knees weak as w. 7.17
and drink w. with trembling and 12.18
and drink w. in dismay, because 12.19
you washed with w. to cleanse you, 16.04
bathed you with w. and washed off 16.09
toward him that he might w. it. 17.07
a vineyard transplanted by the w., 19.10
branches by reason of abundant w. 19.10
and all knees will be weak as w. 21.07
pot, set it on, pour in w. also; 24.03
from abundant w. in its shoots. 31.05
that drink w. in its shoots. 31.05
that drink w. may reach up to them 31.14
best of Lebanon, all that drink w., 31.16
and to drink of clear w., that you must 34.18
I will sprinkle clean w. upon you, 36.25
and behold, w. was issuing from 47.01
and the w. was flowing down from 47.01
and the w. was coming out on the 47.02
and then led me through the w.; 47.03
thousand, and led me through the w.; 47.04
through the w.; and it was up to the 47.04
pass through, for the w. had risen; 47.05
"This w. flows toward the eastern 47.08
of the sea, the w. will become fresh. 47.08
for this w. goes there, that the 47.09
because the w. for them flows from 47.12
vegetables to eat and w. to drink. Dan 1.12
who give me my bread and my w., Hos 2.05
I will pour out my wrath like w. 5.10
the spring rains that w. the earth." 6.03
because the w. brooks are dried up, Joe 1.20
beds of Judah shall flow with w.; 3.18
of the LORD and w. the valley of 3.18
wandered to one city to drink w., Amo 4.08
of bread, nor a thirst for w., 8.11
let them not feed, or drink w., Jon 3.07
with w. around her, her rampart a Nah 3.08
her rampart a sea, and w. her wall? 3.08
Draw w. or the siege, strengthen 3.14
baptize you with w. for repentance, Mt 3.11
he went up immediately from the w., 3.16
a cup of cold w. because he is a 10.42
you, bid me come to you on the w." 14.28
walked on the w. and came to Jesus; 14.29
the fire, and often into the w. 17.15
he took w. and washed his hands 27.24
pierced his side, and out came w. * 27.49
I have baptized you with w.; Mk 1.08
And when he came up out of the w., 1.10
him into the fire and into the w., 9.22
you a cup of w. to drink because 9.41
carrying a jar of w. will meet you; 14.13
them all, "I baptize you with w.; Lk 3.16
you gave me no w. for my feet, 7.44
and they were filling with w., 8.23
that he commands even wind and w., 8.25
manger, and lead it away to w. it? 13.15
his finger in w. and cool my 16.24
carrying a jar of w. will meet you; 22.10
John answered them, "I baptize with w.; Jn 1.26
for this I came baptizing with w., 1.31
me to baptize with w. said to me, 1.33
to them, "Fill the jars with w." 2.07
tasted the w. now become wine, and 2.09
servants who had drawn the w. knew), 2.09
one is born of w. and the Spirit, 3.05
because there was much w. there; 3.23
came a woman of Samaria to draw w. 4.07

WATER (cont.)
he would have given you living w." Jn 4.10
where do you get that living w.? 4.11
drinks of this w. will thirst 4.13
drinks of the w. that I shall give 4.14
the w. that I shall give him will 4.14
him a spring of w. welling up to 4.14
give me this w., that I may not 4.15
So the woman left her w. jar, 4.28
where he had made the w. wine. 4.46
waiting for the moving of the w. * 5.03
into the pool, and troubled the w. * 5.04
after the troubling of the w. was * 5.04
the pool when the w. is troubled, 5.07
shall flow rivers of living w." 7.38
Then he poured w. into a basin, and 13.05
once there came out blood and w. 19.34
for John baptized with w., but before Ac 1.05
the road they came to some w., 8.36
the eunuch said, "See, here is w.! 8.36
they both went down into the w., 8.38
And when they came up out of the w., 8.39
"Can any one forbid w. for baptizing 10.47
he said, 'John baptized with w., 11.16
the washing of w. with the word, Eph 5.26
No longer drink only w., 1Ti 5.23
with w. and scarlet wool and hyssop, Heb 9.19
and our bodies washed with pure w. 10.22
same opening fresh w. and brackish? Jas 3.11
No more can salt w. yield fresh. 3.12
persons, were saved through w. 1Pe 3.20
formed out of w. and by means of 2Pe 3.05
out of water and by means of w., 3.05
was deluged with w. and perished. 3.06
This is he who came by w. and blood, 1Jn 5.06
not with the w. only but with the 5.06
only but with the w. and the blood. 5.06
the Spirit, the w., and the blood; 5.08
guide them to springs of living w.; Rev 7.17
rivers and on the fountains of w. 8.10
and many men died of the w., 8.11
The serpent poured w. like a river 12.15
the sea and the fountains of w. 14.07
the rivers and the fountains of w., 16.04
And I heard the angel of w. say, 16.05
and its w. was dried up, to prepare 16.12
I will give w. without price from 21.06
the fountain of the w. of life. 21.06
me the river of the w. of life, 22.01
take the w. of life without price. 22.17

WATERCOURSES
O LORD, like the w. in the Negeb! Ps 126.04
broken in all the w. of the land; Eze 31.12
and the w. will be full of you. 32.06

WATERED
the earth and w. the whole face of Gen 2.06
valley was well w. everywhere like 13.10
of that well the flocks were w. 29.02
and w. the flock of Laban his 29.10
helped them, and w. their flock. Ex 2.17
drew water for us and w. the flock." 2.19
your seed and w. it with your feet, Deu 11.10
of the LORD are w. abundantly, Ps 104.16
one who waters will himself be w. Pro 11.25
and you shall be like a w. garden, Is 58.11
life shall be like a w. garden, Jer 31.12
Apollos w., but God gave the growth. 1Co 3.06

WATEREST
Thou visitest the earth and w. it, Ps 65.09
Thou w. its furrows abundantly, 65.10
lofty abode thou w. the mountains; 104.13

WATERING
the w. troughs, where the flocks Gen 30.38
of musicians at the w. places, Ju 5.11

WATERLESS
your captives free from the w. pit. Zec 9.11
pass through w. places seeking Mt 12.43
passes through w. places seeking Lk 11.24
These are w. springs and mists 2Pe 2.17
w. clouds, carried along by winds; Jud 1.12

WATERS
was moving over the face of the w. Gen 1.02
a firmament in the midst of the w., 1.06
it separate the w. from the w." 1.06
separated the w. which were under 1.07
from the w. which were above the 1.07
"Let the w. under the heavens be 1.09
and the w. that were gathered 1.10
"Let the w. bring forth swarms of 1.20
moves, with which the w. swarm, 1.21
and fill the w. in the seas, 1.22
bring a flood of w. upon the earth, 6.17
the flood of w. came upon the 7.06
ark, to escape the w. of the flood. 7.07
seven days the w. of the flood 7.10
and the w. increased, and bore up 7.17
The w. prevailed and increased 7.18
ark floated on the face of the w. 7.18
And the w. prevailed so mightily 7.19
the w. prevailed above the mountains, 7.20
And the w. prevailed upon the earth 7.24
the earth, and the w. subsided; 8.01
and the w. receded from the earth 8.03
and fifty days the w. had abated; 8.03
And the w. continued to abate until 8.05
fro until the w. were dried up 8.07
to see if the w. had subsided from 8.08
for the w. were still on the face 8.09
knew that the w. had subsided from 8.11
the w. were dried from off the 8.13
be cut off by the w. of a flood, 9.11
and the w. shall never again become 9.15
out your hand over the w. of Egypt, Ex 7.19
out his hand over the w. of Egypt; 8.06
dry land, and the w. were divided. 14.21
the w. being a wall to them on 14.22
The w. returned and covered the 14.28
the w. being a wall to them on 14.29
of thy nostrils the w. piled up, 15.08
they sank as lead in the mighty w. 15.10
back the w. of the sea upon them; 15.19
may eat, of all that are in the w. Lev 11.09
Everything in the w. that has fins 11.09
creatures in the w. of the 11.10
creatures that are in the w., 11.10
Everything in the w. that had not 11.12
through the w. and every creature 11.46
These are the w. of Meribah, where Num 20.13
my command at the w. of Meribah 20.24
like cedar trees beside the w. 24.06
and his seed shall be in many w., 24.07
me at the w. before their eyes." 27.14
(These are the w. of Meribah of 27.14
that are in the w. you may eat Deu 14.09
Israel at the w. of Meribathkadesh, 32.51
didst strive at the w. of Meribah; 33.08
the brink of the w. of the Jordan, Jos 3.08
shall rest in the w. of the Jordan, 3.13
the w. of the Jordan shall be 3.13
and the w. coming down from above 3.13
the w. coming down from above stood 3.16
them that the w. of the Jordan 4.07
the w. of the Jordan were cut off. 4.07
the w. of the Jordan returned to 4.18
dried up the w. of the Jordan for 4.23
dried up the w. of the Jordan for 5.01
together at the w. of Merom, 11.05
by the w. of Merom, and fell upon 11.07
along to the w. of Enshemesh, 15.07
the spring of the W. of Nephtoah, 15.09

WATERS (cont.)

east of the w. of Jericho, into the Jos 16.01
the spring of the W. of Nephtoah; 18.15
at Taanach, by the w. of Megiddo; Ju 5.19
and seize the w. against them, 7.24
they seized the w. as far as 7.24
I have taken the city of w. 2Sa 12.27
took me, he drew me out of many w. 22.17
better than all the w. of Israel? 2Ki 5.12
I dug wells and drank foreign w., 19.24
outlet of the w. of Gihon and 2Ch 32.30
depths, as a stone into mighty w. Neh 9.11
earth and sends w. upon the fields Job 5.10
remember it as w. that have passed 11.16
If he withholds the w., they dry up; 12.15
As w. fail from a lake, and a river 14.11
the w. wear away the stones; 14.19
away upon the face of the w.; 24.18
Drought and heat snatch away the snow w.; 24.19
the w. and their inhabitants. 26.05
He binds up the w. in his thick 26.08
the face of the w. at the boundary 26.10
and meted out the w. by measure; 28.25
my roots spread out to the w., 29.19
and the broad w. are frozen fast. 37.10
The w. become hard like stone, and 38.30
that a flood of w. may cover you 38.34
took me, he drew me out of many w. Ps 18.16
He leads me beside still w.; 23.02
The voice of the Lord is upon the w.; 29.03
thunders, the Lord, upon many w. 29.03
distress, in the rush of great w., 32.06
He gathered the w. of the sea as in 33.07
though its w. roar and foam, though 46.03
For the w. have come up to my neck. 69.01
I have come into deep w., 69.02
my enemies and from the deep w. 69.14
the heads of the dragons on the w. 74.13
When the w. saw thee, O God, when the 77.16
when the w. saw thee, they were 77.16
sea, thy path through the great w.; 77.19
and made the w. stand like a heap. 78.13
and caused w. to flow down like 78.16
I tested you at the w. of Meribah. 81.07
Mightier than the thunders of many w., 93.04
beams of thy chambers on the w., 104.03
the w. stood above the mountains. 104.06
He turned their w. into blood, 105.29
And the w. covered their adversaries; 106.11
They angered him at the w. of Meribah, 106.32
doing business on the great w.; 107.23
us would have gone the raging w. 124.05
spread out the earth upon the w., 136.06
By the w. of Babylon, there we sat 137.01
me and deliver me from the many w., 144.07
his wind blow, and the w. flow. 147.18
and you w. above the heavens! 148.04
so that the w. might not transgress Pro 8.29
and one who w. will himself be 11.25
words of a man's mouth are deep w.; 18.04
has wrapped up the w. in a garment? 30.04
Cast your bread upon the w., Ecc 11.01
Many w. cannot quench love, neither Sol 8.07
refused the w. of Shiloah that Is 8.06
against them the w. of the River, 8.07
the Lord as the w. cover the sea. 11.09
the w. of Nimrim are a desolation; 15.06
For the w. of Dibon are full of 15.09
roar like the roaring of mighty w.! 17 12
roar like the roaring of many w., 17.13
in vessels of papyrus upon the w.! 18.02
And the w. of the Nile will be 19.05
collected the w. of the lower pool, 22.09
over the sea and were on many w.; 23.02
overflowing w., he will cast down 28.02
and w. will overwhelm the shelter. 28.17
Happy are you who sow beside all w., 32.20
For w. shall break forth in the 35.06
I dug wells and drank w., 37.25
measured the w. in the hollow of 40.12
through the w. I will be with you; 43.02
the sea, a path in the mighty w., 43.16
shall spring up like grass amid w., 44.04
the w. of the great deep; 51.10
swore that the w. of Noah should 54.09
one who thirsts, come to the w.; 55.01
and its w. toss up mire and dirt. 57.20
spring of water, whose w. fail not. 58.11
who divided the w. before them to 63.12
me, the fountain of living w., Jer 2.13
Egypt, to drink the w. of the Nile? 2.18
to drink the w. of the Euphrates? 2.18
O that my head were w., 9.01
is a tumult of w. in the heavens, 10.13
deceitful brook, like w. that fail? 15.18
Do the mountain w. run dry, 18.14
Nile, like rivers whose w. surge? 46.07
Nile, like rivers whose w. surge. 46.08
w. are rising out of the north, and 47.02
For the w. of Nimrim also have 48.34
A drought upon her w., that they may 50.38
O you who dwell by many w., 51.13
is a tumult of w. in the heavens, 51.16
Their waves roar like many w., 51.55
wings like the sound of many w., Eze 1.24
he placed it beside abundant w. 17.05
it to good soil by abundant w., 17.08
will cast into the midst of the w. 26.12
you, and the great w. cover you, 26.19
the seas, in the depths of the w.; 27.34
The w. nourished it, the deep made 31.04
its roots went down to abundant w. 31.07
no trees by the w. may grow to 31.14
and many w. shall be stopped; 31.15
trouble the w. with your feet, and 32.02
all its beasts from beside many w.; 32.13
Then I will make their w. clear, 32.14
was like the sound of many w.; 43.02
enters the stagnant w. of the sea, 47.08
that the w. of the sea may become 47.09
as far as the w. of Meribathkadesh, 47.19
Tamar to the w. of Meribathkadesh, 48.28
who was above the w. of the stream, Dan 12.06
who was above the w. of the stream, 12.07
like a chip on the face of the w. Hos 10.07
who calls for the w. of the sea, Amo 5.08
But let justice roll down like w., 5.24
who calls for the w. of the sea, 9.06
The w. closed in over me, the deep Jon 2.05
like w. poured down a steep place. Mic 1.04
Nineveh is like a pool whose w. run away. Nah 2.08
the Lord, as the w. cover the sea. Hab 2.14
the raging w. swept on; 3.10
horses, the surging of mighty w. 3.15
On that day living w. shall flow Zec 14.08
the sea, and perished in the w. Mt 8.32
plants nor he who w. is anything, 1Co 3.07
who plants and he who w. are equal, 3.08
was like the sound of many w.; Rev 1.15
A third of the w. became wormwood, 8.11
power over the w. to turn them 11.06
sound of many w. and like the 14.02
harlot who is seated upon many w., 17.01
"The w. that you saw, where the 17.15
sound of many w. and like the 19.06

WATERSKINS

who can tilt the w. of the heavens, Job 38.37

WAVE

and w. them for a w. offering before Ex 29.24
ordination and w. it for a w. offering 29.26
the breast of the w. offering, 29.27

WAVE (cont.)

be waved as a w. offering before Lev 7.30
waved them as a w. offering before 8.27
waved it for a w. offering before 8.29
waved for a w. offering before the 9.21
to w. for a w. offering before 10.15
and w. them for a w. offering 14.12
priest shall w. them for a w. offering 14.14
and he shall w. the sheaf before 23.11
the sabbath the priest shall w. it. 23.11
And on the day when you w. the sheaf, 23.12
the sheaf of the w. offering; 23.15
priest shall w. them with the 23.20
fruits as a w. offering before the 23.20
and shall w. the cereal offering Num 5.25
priest shall w. them for a w. offering 6.20
the LORD as a w. offering from the 8.11
offer them as a w. offering to the 8.13
and offered them as a w. offering. 8.15
them as a w. offering before the 8.21
all the w. offerings of the people 18.11
and w. his hand over the place, and 2Ki 5.11
"The wings of the ostrich w. proudly; Job 39.13
tops of the mountains may it w.; Ps 72.16
and will w. his hand over the River Is 11.15
w. the hand for them to enter the 13.02
is like a w. of the sea that is Jas 1.06

WAVED

which is w., and which is offered Ex 29.27
breast may be w. as a wave offering Lev 7.30
breast that is w. and the thigh 7.34
and w. them as a wave offering 8.27
and w. it for a wave offering 8.29
thigh Aaron w. for a wave offering 9.21
breast that is w. and the thigh 10.14
breast that is w. they shall bring 10.15
lamb for a guilt offering to be w., 14.21
two loaves of bread to be w., 23.17
breast that is w. and the thigh Num 6.20
breast that is w. and as the right 18.18
cried out and w. their garments Ac 22.23

WAVER

from my presence, and do not w., Jer 4.01
How long will you w., O faithless 31.22
made him w. concerning the promise Rom 4.20

WAVERING

trusted in the LORD without w. Ps 26.01
confession of our hope without w., Heb 10.23

WAVES

"For the w. of death encompass me, 2Sa 22.05
and trampled the w. of the sea; Job 9.08
shall your proud w. be stayed"? 38.11
all thy w. and thy billows have Ps 42.07
the seas, the roaring of their w., 65.07
dost overwhelm me with all thy w. 88.07
when its w. rise, thou stillest them 89.09
mightier than the w. of the sea, 93.04
which lifted up the w. of the sea. 107.25
and the w. of the sea were hushed. 107.29
righteousness like the w. of the sea; Is 48.18
up the sea so that its w. roar— 51.15
though the w. toss, they cannot Jer 5.22
up the sea so that its w. roar— 31.35
is covered with its tumultuous w. 51.42
Their w. roar like many waters, the 51.55
you, as the sea brings up its w. Eze 26.03
all thy w. and thy billows passed Jon 2.03
and the w. of the sea shall be Zec 10.11
boat was being swamped by the w.; Mt 8.24
from the land, beaten by the w.; 14.24
and the w. beat into the boat, so Mk 4.37
rebuked the wind and the raging w.; Lk 8.24
the roaring of the sea and the w., 21.25
wild w. of the sea, casting up the Jud 1.13

WAVY

his locks are w., black as a raven. Sol 5.11

WAX

my heart is like w., it is melted Ps 22.14
as w. melts before fire, let the 68.02
melt like w. before the LORD, 97.05
like w. before the fire, like waters Mic 1.04

WAXED

"But Jeshurun w. fat, and kicked; Deu 32.15
you w. fat, you grew thick, you 32.15

WAY

sword which turned every w., Gen 3.24
to guard the w. to the tree of life. 3.24
corrupted their w. upon the earth. 6.12
and they set him on the w., 12.20
provisions, and went their w.; 14.11
the spring on the w. to Shur. 16.07
with them to set them on their w. 18.16
him to keep the w. of the LORD by 18.19
And the LORD went his w., 18.33
rise up early and go on your w." 19.02
over against him a good w. off, 21.16
led me in the w. to the house of 24.27
angel with you and prosper your w.; 24.40
wilt prosper the w. which I go, 24.42
me by the right w. to take the 24.48
since the LORD has prospered my w.; 24.56
took Rebekah, and went his w. 24.61
drank, and rose and went his w. 25.34
and Isaac set them on their w., 26.31
will keep me in this w. that I go, 28.20
for the w. of women is upon me." 31.35
Jacob went on his w. and the angels 32.01
said, "Let us journey on our w., 33.12
returned that day on his w. to Seir. 33.16
on his w. from Paddan-aram; 33.18
buried on the w. to Ephrath (that 35.19
on their w. to carry it down to 37.25
"This is the w. your servant 39.19
of your households, and go your w. 42.33
could we in any w. know that he 43.07
to them, "Do not quarrel on the w." 45.24
in the land of Canaan on the w., 48.07
there on the w. to Ephrath (that 48.07
Dan shall be a serpent in the w., 49.17
He looked this w. and that, and Ex 2.12
place on the w. the LORD met him 4.24
lead them by w. of the land of the 13.17
round by the w. of the wilderness 13.18
of cloud to lead them along the w., 13.21
that had come upon them in the w., 18.08
them know the w. in which they 18.20
and he went his w. to his own 18.27
you on the w. and to bring you to 23.20
out of the w. which I commanded 32.08
you, lest I consume you in the w., 33.03
out the old to make w. for the new. Lev 26.10
wilderness by the w. to the Red Sea." Num 14.25
shall do these things in this w., 15.13
was coming by the w. of Atharim, 21.01
set out by the w. to the Red Sea, 21.04
people became impatient on the w. 21.04
and went up by the w. to Bashan; 21.33
stand in the w. as his adversary. 22.22
there was no w. to turn either to 22.26
of the LORD standing in the w. 22.31
because your w. is perverse before 22.32
and Balak also went his w. 24.25
In the same w. you shall offer 28.24
Horeb by the w. of Mount Seir to Deu 1.02
on the w. to the hill country of 1.19
again of the w. by which we must 1.22
in all the w. that you went until 1.31
you in the w. to seek you out a 1.33

WAY (cont.)
show you by what w. you should go, Deu 1.33
and went up the w. to Bashan; 3.01
walk in all the w. which the LORD 5.33
house, and when you walk by the w., 6.07
remember all the w. which the LORD 8.02
out of the w. which I commanded 9.12
from the w. which the LORD had 9.16
and when you are walking by the w., 11.19
aside from the w. which I command 11.28
you leave the w. in which the LORD 13.05
And if the w. is too long for you, 14.24
shall never return that w. again.' 17.16
because the w. is long, and wound 19.06
or his ox fallen down by the w., 22.04
bread and with water on the w., 23.04
Miriam on the w. as you came forth 24.09
to you on the w. as you came out 25.17
how he attacked you on the w., 25.18
shall come out against you one w., 28.07
shall go out one w. against them, 28.25
aside from the w. which I have 31.29
you shall make your w. prosperous, Jos 1.08
them on the w. to the Jordan as 2.07
then afterward you may go your w." 2.16
all along the w. and found nothing. 2.22
that you may know the w. you shall go, 3.04
you have not passed this w. before. 3.04
had died on the w. in the wilderness 5.04
born on the w. in the wilderness 5.05
had not been circumcised on the w. 5.07
no power to flee this w. or that, 8.20
them by the w. of the ascent of 10.10
So the men started on their w.; 18.08
about to go the w. of all the 23.14
us in all the w. that we went, 24.17
show us the w. into the city, and we Ju 1.24
showed them the w. into the city; 1.25
aside from the w. in which their 2.17
to walk in the w. of the LORD as 2.22
carpets and you who walk by the w. 5.10
and spoke to them in the same w.; 8.08
who passed by them along that w.; 9.25
were a good w. from the home of 18.22
Then the Danites went their w.; 18.26
So they passed on and went their w.; 19.14
house and went out to go on his w., 19.27
went on the w. to return to the Ru 1.07
go your w., for I am too old to 1.12
Then the woman went her w. and ate, 1Sa 1.18
send it off, and let it go its w. 6.08
goes up on the w. to its own land, 6.09
the man of God, to tell us our w." 9.08
them on his w. up to the high 9.14
have you spoken to me in this w.?" 9.21
"Up, that I may send you on your w." 9.26
you in the good and the right w. 12.23
Israel in opposing them on the w., 15.02
people answered him in the same w., 17.27
another, and spoke in the same w.; 17.30
fell on the w. from Shaaraim as 17.52
came to the sheepfolds by the w., 24.03
the cave, and went upon his w. 24.07
So David went his w., and Saul returned 26.25
strength when you go on your w." 28.22
them off, and went their w. 30.02
Giah on the w. to the wilderness 2Sa 2.24
after her all the w. to Bahurim. 3.16
and went by the w. of the Arabah 4.07
While they were on the w., 13.30
stand beside the w. of the gate; 15.02
Ahimaaz ran by the w. of the plain, 18.23
go a little w. over the Jordan 19.36
Israel, brought the king on his w. 19.40
This God—his w. is perfect; 22.31
refuge, and has made my w. safe. 22.33
and rose, and each went his own w. 1Ki 1.49
about to go the w. of all the 2.02
If your sons take heed to their w., 2.04
your sons take heed to their w., 8.25
them the good w. in which they 8.36
by whatever w. thou shalt send them, 8.44
nor return by the w. that you came." 13.09
So he went another w., 13.10
return by the w. that he came to 13.10
said to them, "Which w. did he go?" 13.12
showed him the w. which the man of 13.12
nor return by the w. that you came." 13.17
him back from the w. heard of it, 13.26
did not turn from his evil w., 13.33
walked in the w. of his father and 15.26
walked in the w. of Jeroboam and 15.34
have walked in the w. of Jeroboam, 16.02
walking in the w. of Jeroboam, 16.19
in all the w. of Jeroboam the son 16.26
And as Obadiah was on the w., 18.07
return on your w. to the wilderness 19.15
and waited for the king by the w., 20.38
in all the w. of Asa his father; 22.43
and walked in the w. of his father, 22.52
and in the w. of his mother, and in 22.52
and in the w. of Jeroboam the son 22.52
anger in every w. that his father 22.53
were on their w. from Gilgal. 2Ki 2.01
while he was going up on the w., 2.23
said, "By which w. shall we march?" 3.08
"By the w. of the wilderness of 3.08
So whenever he passed that w., 4.08
who is continually passing our w. 4.09
said to them, "This is not the w., 6.19
all the w. was littered with 7.15
walked in the w. of the kings of 8.18
walked in the w. of the house of 8.27
On the w., when he was at Betheked 10.12
on the w. that goes down to Silla. 12.20
walked in the w. of the kings of 16.03
And the covered w. for the sabbath 16.28
you back on the w. by which you 19.28
By the w. that he came, by the same 19.33
in all the w. in which his father 21.21
did not walk in the w. of the LORD. 21.22
in all the w. of David his father, 22.02
by night by the w. of the gate 25.04
for it in the w. that is ordained. 1Ch 15.13
your sons take heed to their w., 2Ch 6.16
them the good w. in which they 6.27
by whatever w. thou shalt send them, 6.34
years in the w. of David and 11.17
"Which w. did the Spirit of the 18.23
He walked in the w. of Asa his 20.32
walked in the w. of the kings of 21.06
walked in the w. of the kings of 21.13
enter who was in any w. unclean. 23.19
that in this w. you will be strong 25.08
him a straight w. for ourselves, Ez 8.21
us against the enemy on our w.; 8.22
enemy and from ambushes by the w. 8.31
laden in such a w. that each with Neh 4.17
times in this w. and I answered 6.04
In the same w. Sanballat for the 6.05
afraid and act in this w. and sin, 6.13
"Go your w., eat the fat and drink 8.10
went their w. to eat and drink and 8.12
for them the w. in which they 9.12
led them in the w. did not depart 9.19
for them the w. by which they 9.19
Did not your fathers act in this w., 13.18
king in this w. she was given Est 2.13
given to a man whose w. is hid, Job 3.23
Behold, this is the joy of his w.; 8.19
all w. of escape will be lost to 11.20
I shall go the w. whence I shall 16.22
Yet the righteous holds to his w., 17.09
He has walled up my w., 19.08

WAY (cont.)

Who declares his w. to his face, Job 21.31
keep to the old w. which wicked 22.15
But he knows the w. that I take; 23.10
I have kept his w. and have not 23.11
Man does not know the w. to it, 28.13
"God understands the w. to it, 28.23
and a w. for the lightning of the 28.26
I chose their w., and sat as chief, 29.25
step has turned aside from the w., 31.07
For God speaks in one w., 33.14
Who has prescribed for him his w., 36.23
"Where is the w. to the dwelling of 38.19
What is the w. to the place where 38.24
and a w. for the thunderbolt, 38.25
nor stands in the w. of sinners, Ps 1.01
LORD knows the w. of the righteous, 1.06
but the w. of the wicked will 1.06
be angry, and you perish in the w.; 2.12
make thy w. straight before me. 5.08
This God—his w. is perfect; 18.30
with strength, and made my w. safe. 18.32
he instructs sinners in the w. 25.08
and teaches the humble his w. 25.09
instruct in the w. that he should 25.12
Teach me thy w., O LORD; and lead me 27.11
and teach you the w. you should go; 32.08
Let their w. be dark and slippery, 35.06
himself in a w. that is not good; 36.04
Commit your w. to the LORD; 37.05
over him who prospers in his w., 37.07
him in whose w. he delights; 37.23
Wait for the LORD, and keep to his w., 37.34
our steps departed from thy w., 44.18
who orders his w. aright I will 50.23
They dug a pit in my w., 57.06
that thy w. may be known upon earth, 67.02
Thy w.. O God, is holy. 77.13
Thy w. was through the sea, thy path 77.19
pass along the w. pluck its fruit? 80.12
him, and make his footsteps a w. 85.13
Teach me thy w., O LORD, that I may 86.11
heed to the w. that is blameless. 101.02
walks in the w. that is blameless 101.06
finding no w. to a city to dwell in 107.04
he led them by a straight w., 107.07
drink from the brook by the w.; 110.07
Blessed are those whose w. is blameless, 119.01
How can a young man keep his w. pure? 119.09
In the w. of thy testimonies I 119.14
understand the w. of thy precepts, 119.27
I have chosen the w. of faithfulness, 119.30
I will run in the w. of thy commandments 119.32
the w. of thy statutes; and I will keep 119.33
back my feet from every evil w., 119.101
therefore I hate every false w. 119.104
I hate every false w. 119.128
if there be any wicked w. in me, 139.24
and lead me in the w. everlasting! 139.24
is faint, thou knowest my w.! 142.03
Teach me the w. I should go, for to 143.08
but the w. of the wicked he brings 146.09
do not walk in the w. with them, Pro 1.15
fruit of their w. and be sated 1.31
preserving the w. of his saints. 2.08
delivering you from the w. of evil, 2.12
walk in the w. of good men and 2.20
walk on your w. securely and your 3.23
I have taught you the w. of wisdom; 4.11
do not walk in the w. of evil men. 4.14
The w. of the wicked is like deep 4.19
Keep your w. far from her, and do 5.08
of discipline are the w. of life, 6.23
Her house is the w. to Sheol, 7.27
On the heights beside the w., 8.02
arrogance and the w. of evil and 8.13
I walk in the w. of righteousness, 8.20
and walk in the w. of insight." 9.06
are going straight on their w., 9.15
stronghold to him whose w. is upright, 10.29
blameless keeps his w. straight, 11.05
The w. of a fool is right in his 12.15
but the w. of the wicked leads them 12.26
but the w. of error leads to death. 12.28
Righteousness guards him whose w. is upright, 13.06
but the w. of the faithless is 13.15
a prudent man is to discern his w., 14.08
There is a w. which seems right to 14.12
but its end is the w. to death. 14.12
The w. of the wicked is an abomination 15.09
for him who forsakes the w.; 15.10
The w. of a sluggard is overgrown 15.19
A man's mind plans his w., 16.09
who guards his w. preserves his 16.17
there is a w. which seems right to 16.25
but its end is the w. to death. 16.25
leads him in a w. that is not good 16.29
haste with his feet misses his w. 19.02
man's folly brings his w. to ruin, 19.03
how then can man understand his w.? 20.24
Every w. of a man is right in his 21.02
The w. of the guilty is crooked, but 21.08
from the w. of understanding will 21.16
are in the w. of the perverse; 22.05
Train up a child in the w. he should go, 22.06
and direct your mind in the w. 23.19
man who gives w. before the wicked 25.26
into an evil w. will fall into his 28.10
but he whose w. is straight is an 29.27
the w. of an eagle in the sky, the 30.19
the w. of a serpent on a rock, the 30.19
the w. of a ship on the high seas, 30.19
and the w. of a man with a maiden. 30.19
This is the w. of an adulteress: she 30.20
wise man will know the time and w. Ecc 8.05
For every matter has its time and w., 8.06
does not know the w. to the city. 10.15
is high, and terrors are in the w.; 12.05
to walk in the w. of this people, Is 8.11
make glorious the w. of the sea, 9.01
by w. of the desert, to the mount of 16.01
in a sure place will give w.; 22.25
The w. of the righteous is level; 26.07
leave the w., turn aside from the 30.11
"This is the w., walk in it," when 30.21
and it shall be called the Holy W.; 35.08
you back on the w. by which you 37.29
By the w. that he came, by the same 37.34
wilderness prepare the w. of the LORD, 40.03
showed him the w. of understanding? 40.14
"My w. is hid from the LORD, and my 40.27
the blind in a w. that they know 42.16
who makes a w. in the sea, a path in 43.16
I will make a w. in the wilderness 43.19
him, and he will prosper in his w. 48.15
leads you in the w. you should go. 48.17
And I will make all my mountains a w., 49.11
of the sea a w. for the redeemed 51.10
turned every one to his own w.; 53.06
let the wicked forsake his w., 55.07
have all turned to their own w., 56.11
wearied with the length of your w., 57.10
prepare the w., remove every 57.14
obstruction from my people's w." 57.14
backsliding in the w. of his own 57.17
The w. of peace they know not, and 59.08
prepare the w. for the people; 62.10
who walk in a w. that is not good, 65.02
God, when he led you in the w.? Jer 2.17
Look at your w. in the valley; 2.23
you gad about, changing your w.! 2.36
they have perverted their w., 3.21
do not know the w. of the LORD, 5.04
for they know the w. of the LORD, 5.05

WAY (cont.)
paths, where the good w. is; Jer 6.16
walk in all the w. that I command 7.23
"Learn not the w. of the nations, 10.02
that the w. of man is not in 10.23
Why does the w. of the wicked 12.01
Return, every one from his evil w., 18.11
before you the w. of life and the w. of death. 21.08
has been your w. from your youth, 22.21
Therefore their w. shall be to them 23.12
turned them from their evil w., 23.22
from his evil w. and wrong doings, 25.05
every one turn from his evil w., 26.03
Jeremiah the prophet went his w. 28.11
give them one heart and one w., 32.39
every one of you from his evil w., 35.15
one may turn from his evil w., 36.03
one will turn from his evil w., 36.07
at night by w. of the king's garden 39.04
may show us the w. we should go, 42.03
Stand by the w. and watch, O inhabitant 48.19
They shall ask the w. to Zion, 50.05
by night by the w. of a gate 52.07
pass along the w. clap their hands Lam 2.15
he led me off my w. and tore me to 3.11
warn the wicked from his wicked w., Eze 3.18
wickedness, or from his wicked w., 3.19
to their w. I will do to them, and 7.27
from his wicked w. to save his 13.22
should turn from his w. and live? 18.23
'The w. of the LORD is not just.' 18.25
house of Israel: Is my w. not just? 18.25
'The w. of the LORD is not just.' 18.29
it at the head of the w. to a city; 21.19
mark a w. for the sword to come to 21.20
stands at the parting of the w., 21.21
their w. have I requited upon their 22.31
they both took the same w. 23.13
You have gone the w. of your sister; 23.31
the wicked to turn from his w., 33.08
the wicked to turn from his w., 33.09
and he does not turn from his w.; 33.09
wicked turn from his w. and live; 33.11
'The w. of the LORD is not just'; 33.17
it is their own w. that is not 33.17
'The w. of the LORD is not just.' 33.20
shall enter by w. of the vestibule 44.03
and shall go out by the same w." 44.03
brought me by w. of the north gate 44.04
and he shall go out by the same w. 46.08
shall return by w. of the gate by 46.09
me out by w. of the north gate, and 47.02
Great Sea by w. of Hethlon to the 47.15
from the sea by w. of Hethlon to 48.01
who is able to deliver in this w." Dan 3.29
his limbs gave w., and his knees 5.06
"Go your w., Daniel, for the words 12.09
But go your w. till the end; 12.13
I will hedge up her w. with thorns; Hos 2.06
they murder on the w. to Shechem, 6.09
leopard I will lurk beside the w. 13.07
They march each on his w., Joe 2.07
turn aside the w. of the afflicted Amo 2.07
'As the w. of Beersheba lives,' they 8.14
from his evil w. and from the Jon 3.08
how they turned from their evil w., 3.10
Pass on your w., inhabitants of Mic 1.11
His w. is in whirlwind and storm, Nah 1.03
But you have turned aside from the w.; Mal 2.08
to prepare the w. before me, 3.01
Jesus Christ took place in this w. Mt 1.18
heard the king they went their w.; 2.09
to their own country by another w. 2.12
Prepare the w. of the LORD, make his 3.03
gate is wide and the w. is easy, 7.13
gate is narrow and the w. is hard, 7.14
that no one could pass that w. 8.28
shall prepare thy w. before thee.' 11.10
hungry, lest they faint on the w." 15.32
and on the w. he said to them, 20.17
to you in the w. of righteousness, 21.32
and teach the w. of God truthfully, 22.16
also reviled him in the same w. 27.44
thy face, who shall prepare thy w.; Mk 1.02
Prepare the w. of the LORD, make his 1.03
they made their w. his disciples 2.23
"You have a fine w. of rejecting 7.09
"For this saying you may go your w.; 7.29
homes, they will faint on the w.; 8.03
some of them have come a long w." 8.03
and on the w. he asked his disciples, 8.27
"What were you discussing on the w.?" 9.33
for on the w. they had discussed 9.34
And Jesus said to him, "Go your w.; 10.52
sight and followed him on the w. 10.52
it and sought a w. to destroy him; 11.18
men, but truly teach the w. of God. 12.14
our feet into the w. of peace." Lk 1.79
Prepare the w. of the LORD, make his 3.04
but finding no w. to bring him in, 5.19
shall prepare thy w. before thee.' 7.27
go on their w. they are choked by 8.14
Go your w.; behold, I send you out 10.03
Now as they went on their w., 10.38
to settle with him on the w., 12.58
He went on his w. through towns and 13.22
Nevertheless I must go on my w. 13.33
the other is yet a great w. off, 14.32
On the w. to Jerusalem he was 17.11
said to him, "Rise and go your w.; 17.19
him, for he was to pass that w. 19.04
but truly teach the w. of God. 20.21
'Make straight the w. of the LORD, Jn 1.23
Jesus spoke to him and went his w. 4.50
door but climbs in by another w., 10.01
And you know the w. where I am 14.04
how can we know the w.?" 14.05
"I am the w., and the truth, and the 14.06
and he revealed himself in this w. 21.01
in the same w. as you saw him go Ac 1.11
finding no w. to punish them, 4.21
more, and went on his w. rejoicing. 8.39
he found any belonging to the W., 9.02
to corruption, he spoke in this w., 13.34
sent on their w. by the church, 15.03
went on their w. through the 16.04
proclaim to you the w. of salvation." 16.17
sent Paul off on his w. to the sea, 17.14
that in every w. you are very 17.22
instructed in the w. of the LORD; 18.25
to him the w. of God more accurately 18.26
evil of the W. before the congregation, 19.09
no little stir concerning the W. 19.23
us on our w. till we were outside 21.05
I persecuted this W. to the death, 22.04
in every w. and everywhere we 24.03
to you, that according to the W., 24.14
accurate knowledge of the W., 24.22
an ambush to kill him on the w. 25.03
I saw on the w. a light from heaven, 26.13
we gave w. to it and were driven. 27.15
Much in every w. To begin with, Rom 3.02
on us? (I speak in a human w.) 3.05
and the w. of peace they do not 3.17
hindrance in the w. of a brother. 14.13
you very boldly by w. of reminder, 15.15
shall go on by w. of you to Spain; 15.28
that in every w. you were enriched 1Co 1.05
I say this by w. of concession, not 7.06
obstacle in the w. of the gospel 9.12
In the same w., the LORD commanded 9.14
will also provide the w. of escape, 10.13
In the same w. also the cup, after 11.25
show you a still more excellent w. 12.31

WAY (cont.)
Love does not insist on its own w.; 1Co 13.05
Speed him on his w. in peace, 16.11
to visit you on my w. to Macedonia, 2Co 1.16
have you send me on my w. to Judea. 1.16
We are afflicted in every w., 4.08
We put no obstacle in any one's w., 6.03
we commend ourselves in every w.: 6.04
in every w. for great generosity, 9.11
to come all the w. to you with the 10.14
in every w. we have made this plain 11.06
from burdening you in any w. 11.09
up in every w. into him who is the Eph 4.15
not in the w. of eye-service, as 6.06
Only that in every w., whether in Php 1.18
LORD Jesus, direct our w. to you; 1Th 3.11
Let no one deceive you in any w.; 2Th 2.03
do so until he is out of the w. 2.07
letter of mine, it is the w. I write. 3.17
godly and respectful in every w. 1Ti 2.02
submissive and respectful in every w.; 3.04
godliness is of value in every w., 4.08
herself to doing good in every w. 5.10
talk will eat its w. like gangrene. 2Ti 2.17
who make their w. into households 3.06
the lawyer and Apollos on their w.; Tit 3.13
of the seventh day in this w., Heb 4.04
that the w. into the sanctuary is 9.08
And in the same w. he sprinkled 9.21
new and living w. which he opened 10.20
And in the same w. was not also Jas 2.25
and sent them out another w.? 2.25
error of his w. will save his soul 5.20
to arouse you by w. of reminder, 2Pe 1.13
of them the w. of truth will be 2.02
Forsaking the right w. they have 2.15
have followed the w. of Balaam, 2.15
have known the w. of righteousness 2.21
sincere mind by w. of reminder; 3.01
in the same w. in which he walked. 1Jn 2.06
For they walk in the w. of Cain, Jud 1.11
committed in such an ungodly w., 1.15
to prepare the w. for the kings Rev 16.12

WAYFARER
and saw the w. in the open square Ju 19.17
prepare for the w. who had come to 2Sa 12.04
I have opened my doors to the w.); Job 31.32
like a w. who turns aside to tarry Jer 14.08

WAYFARERS'
in the desert a w. lodging place, Jer 9.02

WAYFARING
lie waste, the w. man ceases. Is 33.08

WAYMARKS
"Set up w. for yourself, make Jer 31.21

WAYS
in thy sight, show me now thy w., Ex 33.13
so that your w. shall become Lev 26.22
walking in his w. and by fearing Deu 8.06
your God to walk in all his w., 10.12
your God, walking in all his w., 11.22
God and by walking ever in his w.— 19.09
and that you will walk in his w., 26.17
way, and flee before you seven w. 28.07
LORD your God, and walk in his w. 28.09
and flee seven w. before them; 28.25
you shall not prosper in your w.; 28.29
your God, by walking in his w., 30.16
for all his w. are justice.' 32.04
God, and to walk in all his w., Jos 22.05
practices or their stubborn w. Ju 2.19
Yet his sons did not walk in his w., 1Sa 8.03
your sons do not walk in your w.; 8.05
show them the w. of the king who 8.09
will be the w. of the king who 8.11
For I have kept the w. of the LORD, 2Sa 22.22
walking in his w. and keeping his 1Ki 2.03
And if you will walk in my w., 3.14
according to all his w. (for thou, 8.39
to him, to walk in all his w., 8.58
and has not walked in my w., 11.33
you, and will walk in my w., 11.38
from your evil w. and keep my 2Ki 17.13
according to all his w. (for thou, 2Ch 6.30
and walk in thy w. all the days 6.31
and turn from their wicked w., 7.14
his w. and his sayings, are written 13.22
in the earlier w. of his father; 17.03
not according to the w. of Israel. 17.04
courageous in the w. of the LORD; 17.06
walked in the w. of Jehoshaphat 21.12
or in the w. of Asa king of Judah, 21.12
walked in the w. of the house of 22.03
he ordered his w. before the LORD 27.06
and his w., behold, they are written 27.07
but walked in the w. of the kings 28.02
rest of his acts and all his w., 28.26
walked in the w. of David his 34.02
the integrity of your w. your hope? Job 4.06
I will defend my w. to his face. 13.15
not desire the knowledge of thy w. 21.14
him if you make your w. blameless? 22.03
and light will shine on your w. 22.28
who are not acquainted with its w., 24.13
and his eyes are upon their w. 24.23
are but the outskirts of his w.; 26.14
against me their w. of destruction. 30.12
Does not he see my w., and number 31.04
according to his w. he will make it 34.11
"For his eyes are upon the w. of a man, 34.21
had no regard for any of his w., 34.27
His w. prosper at all times; Ps 10.05
have avoided the w. of the violent. 17.04
For I have kept the w. of the LORD, 18.21
Make me to know thy w., O LORD; 25.04
I said, "I will guard my w., 39.01
Then I will teach transgressors thy w., 51.13
of him who walks in his guilty w. 68.21
that Israel would walk in my w.! 81.13
of you to guard you in all your w. 91.11
and they do not regard my w." 95.10
He made known his w. to Moses, 103.07
Some were sick through their sinful w., 107.17
do no wrong, but walk in his w.! 119.03
O that my w. may be steadfast in 119.05
precepts, and fix my eyes on thy w. 119.15
When I told of my w., thou didst 119.26
Put false w. far from me; and graciously 119.29
vanities, and give me life in thy w. 119.37
When I think of thy w., I turn my 119.59
for all my w. are before thee. 119.168
their crooked w. the LORD will 125.05
the LORD, who walks in his w.! 128.01
shall sing of the w. of the LORD, 138.05
and art acquainted with all my w. 139.03
The LORD is just in all his w., 145.17
Such are the w. of all who get gain Pro 1.19
to walk in the w. of darkness, 2.13
and who are devious in their w. 2.15
In all your w. acknowledge him, and 3.06
Her w. are w. of pleasantness, and 3.17
and do not choose any of his w.; 3.31
then all your w. will be sure. 4.26
her w. wander, and she does not know 5.06
For a man's w. are before the eyes 5.21
consider her w., and be wise. 6.06
your heart turn aside to her w., 7.25
me: happy are those who keep my w. 8.32
perverts his w. will be found out. 10.09
of blameless w. are his delight. 11.20
is devious in his w. despises him. 14.02

WAYS (cont.)
be filled with the fruit of his w., Pro 14.14
All the w. of a man are pure in his 16.02
When a man's w. please the LORD, he 16.07
bosom to pervert the w. of justice. 17.23
an upright man considers his w. 21.29
lest you learn his w. and entangle 22.25
and let your eyes observe my w. 23.26
rich man who is perverse in his w. 28.06
perverse in his w. will fall into 28.18
your w. to those who destroy kings. 31.03
well to the w. of her household, 31.27
walk in the w. of your heart and Ecc 11.09
teach us his w. and that we may Is 2.30
in whose w. they would not walk, and 42.24
I will make straight all his w.; 45.13
They shall feed along the w., 49.09
neither are your w. my w., says the 55.08
so are my w. higher than your w. 55.09
I have seen his w., but I will heal 57.18
daily, and delight to know my w., 58.02
honor it, not going your own w., 58.13
us err from thy w. and harden our 63.17
those that remember thee in thy w. 64.05
These have chosen their own w., 66.03
women you have taught your w. Jer 2.33
Your w. and your doings have 4.18
you may know and assay their w. 6.27
Amend your w. and your doings, and I 7.03
amend your w. and your doings, if 7.05
diligently learn the w. of my people, 12.16
they did not turn from their w. 15.07
For my eyes are upon all thy w.; 16.17
to every man according to his w., 17.10
and amend your w. and your doings.' 18.11
they have stumbled in their w., 18.15
amend your w. and your doings, and 26.13
eyes are open to all the w. of men, 32.19
according to his w. and according 32.19
he has blocked my w. with hewn Lam 3.09
Let us test and examine our w., 3.40
judge you according to your w.; Eze 7.03
but I will punish you for your w., 7.04
and judge you according to your w.; 7.08
punish you according to your w., 7.09
you see their w. and their doings, 14.22
you see their w. and their doings; 14.23
not content to walk in their w., 16.47
corrupt than they in all your w. 16.47
Then you will remember your w., 16.61
Is it not your w. that are not just? 18.25
of Israel, are my w. not just 18.29
Is it not your w. that are not just? 18.29
every one according to his w., 18.30
remember your w. and all the 20.43
not according to your evil w., 20.44
mark two w. for the sword of the 21.19
the way, at the head of the two w., 21.21
according to your w. and your 24.14
blameless in your w. from the day 28.15
back, turn back from your evil w.; 33.11
each of you according to his w." 33.20
it by their w. and their doings; 36.17
Then you will remember your evil w., 36.31
ashamed and confounded for your w., 36.32
are right and his w. are just; Dan 4.37
breath, and whose are all your w., 5.23
I will punish them for their w., Hos 4.09
a fowler's snare is on all is w., 9.08
punish Jacob according to his w. 12.02
for the w. of the LORD are right, 14.09
parting of the w. to cut off his Ob 1.14
teach us his w. and we may walk in Mic 4.02
hills sank low. His w. were as of old. Hab 3.06
from your evil w. and from your Zec 1.04
deal with us for our w. and deeds, 1.06
will walk in my w. and keep my 3.07
not kept my w. but have shown Mal 2.09
before the LORD to prepare his w., Lk 1.76
and the rough w. shall be made 3.05
made known to me the w. of life; Ac 2.28
nations to walk in their own w.; 14.16
judgments and how inscrutable his w.! Rom 11.33
to remind you of my w. in Christ, 1Co 4.17
a man, I gave up childish w. 13.11
disgraceful, underhanded w.; 2Co 4.02
Mend your w., heed my appeal, agree 13.11
you peace at all times in all w. 2Th 3.16
and various w. God spoke of old to Heb 1.01
their hearts; they have not known my w.' 3.10
minded man, unstable in all his w., Jas 1.07
from the futile w. inherited from 1Pe 1.18
Just and true are thy w., O king of Rev 15.03

WAYSIDE
harlot who was at Enaim by the w.?" Gen 38.21
by the w. they have set snares for Ps 140.05
a fig tree by the w. he went to it, Mt 21.19

WAYSIDES
By the w. you have sat awaiting Jer 3.02

WAYWARD
She is loud and w., her feet do Pro 7.11
against the w. people to chastise Hos 10.10
gently with the ignorant and w., Heb 5.02

WEAK
Leah's eyes were w., but Rachel was Gen 29.17
who dwell in it are strong or w., Num 13.18
been dried, then I shall become w., Ju 16.07
been used, then I shall become w., 16.11
the pin, then I shall become w., 16.13
leave me, and I shall become w., 16.17
And I am this day w., though anointed 2Sa 3.39
between the mighty and the w. 2Ch 14.11
Do not let your hands be w., 15.07
you have strengthened the w. hands. Job 4.03
it grows w. because of all my foes. Ps 6.07
deliverest the w. from him who is 35.10
the w. and needy from him who 35.10
He has pity on the w. and the needy, 72.13
Give justice to the w. and the 82.03
Rescue the w. and the needy; 82.04
My knees are w. through fasting; 109.24
'You too have become as w. as we! Is 14.10
Strengthen the w. hands, and make 35.03
feeble, and all knees w. as water. Eze 7.17
and all knees will be w. as water. 21.07
The w. you have not strengthened, 34.04
and I will strengthen the w., 34.16
at all the w. with your horns, till 34.21
let the w. say, "I am a warrior." Joe 3.10
O Zion; let not your hands grow w. Zep 3.16
is willing, but the flesh is w." Mt 26.41
is willing, but the flesh is w." Mk 14.38
by so toiling one must help the w., Ac 20.35
As for the man who is w. in faith, Rom 14.01
while the w. man eats only vegetables. 14.02
bear with the failings of the w., 15.01
chose what is w. in the world to 1Co 1.27
We are w., but you are strong. 4.10
conscience, being w., is defiled. 8.07
become a stumbling block to the w. 8.09
encouraged, if his conscience is w., 8.10
knowledge this w. man is destroyed, 8.11
their conscience when it is w., 8.12
To the w. I became w., that I might win the w. 9.22
That is why many of you are w. and ill, 11.30
but his bodily presence is w., 2Co 10.10
must say, we were too w. for that! 11.21
Who is w., and I am not w.? 11.29
for when I am w., then I am strong. 12.10

WEAK (cont.)
He is not w. in dealing with you, 2Co 13.03
For we are w. in him, but in dealing 13.04
when we are w. and you are strong. 13.09
again to the w. and beggarly Gal 4.09
help the w., be patient with them 1Th 5.14
households and capture w. women, 2Ti 3.06
and strengthen your w. knees, Heb 12.12

WEAKEN
He did not w. in faith when he Rom 4.19

WEAKENED
w. by the flesh, could not do: Rom 8.03

WEAKENING
for he is w. the hands of the Jer 38.04

WEAKER
house of Saul became w. and w. 2Sa 3.01
seem to be w. are indispensable, 1Co 12.22
honor on the woman as the w. sex, 1Pe 3.07

WEAKEST
my clan is the w. in Manasseh, Ju 6.15

WEAKNESS
come to see the w. of the land. Gen 42.09
it is the w. of the land that you 42.12
Likewise the Spirit helps us in our w.; Rom 8.26
and the w. of God is stronger than 1Co 1.25
was with you in w. and in much 2.03
It is sown in w., it is raised in 15.43
of the things that show my w. 2Co 11.30
for my power is made perfect in w." 12.09
For he was crucified in w., 13.04
since he himself is beset with w. Heb 5.02
because of its w. and uselessness 7.18
men in their w. as high priests, 7.28
the sword, won strength out of w., 11.34

WEAKNESSES
I will not boast, except of my w. 2Co 12.05
all the more gladly boast of my w., 12.09
Christ, then, I am content with w., 12.10
unable to sympathize with our w., Heb 4.15

WEAL
I make w. and create woe, I am the Is 45.07

WEALTH
father's he has gained all this w." Gen 31.01
all their w., all their little ones 34.29
of my hand have gotten me this w.' Deu 8.17
he who gives you power to get w.; 8.18
"Go back to your homes with much w., Jos 22.08
is in the earth, and possessing w., Ju 18.07
a man of w., of the family of Ru 2.01
Aphiah, a Benjaminite, a man of w.; 1Sa 9.01
w., honor, or the life of those who 2Ch 1.11
and the thirsty pant after his w. Job 5.05
'From your w. offer a bribe for me'? 6.22
and his w. will not endure, nor will 15.29
his hands will give back his w. 20.10
opens his eyes, and his w. is gone. 27.19
rejoiced because my w. was great, 31.25
with all kinds of w. The princess is Ps 45.13
trust in their w. and boast of the 49.06
and leave their w. to others. 49.10
and sought refuge in his w.! 52.07
W. and riches are in his house; 112.03
me, enduring w. and prosperity. Pro 8.18
endowing with w. those who love me, 8.21
A rich man's w. is his strong city; 10.15
diligent man will get precious w. 12.27
to be poor, yet has great w. 13.07
The ransom of a man's life is his w., 13.08
W. hastily gotten will dwindle, but 13.11
the sinner's w. is laid up for the 13.22
A rich man's w. is his strong city, 18.11
W. brings many new friends, but a 19.04
House and w. are inherited from 19.14
the poor to increase his own w., 22.16
Do not toil to acquire w.; 23.04
augments his w. by interest and 28.08
A miserly man hastens after w., 28.22
nor he who loves w., with gain; Ecc 5.10
God has given w. and possessions 5.19
a man to whom God gives w., 6.02
for love all the w. of his house, Sol 8.07
the w. of Damascus and the spoil Is 8.04
and where will you leave your w.? 10.03
like a nest the w. of the peoples; 10.14
"The w. of Egypt and the merchandise 45.14
the w. of the nations shall come to 60.05
bring to you the w. of the nations, 60.11
shall eat the w. of the nations, 61.06
and the w. of the nations like an 66.12
"Your w. and your treasures I will Jer 15.13
Your w. and all your treasures I 17.03
I will give all the w. of the city, 20.05
nor their abundance, nor their w.; Eze 7.11
of your great w. of every kind; 27.12
of your great w. of every kind; 27.18
your abundant w. and merchandise 27.33
you have gotten w. for yourself, 28.04
trade you have increased your w., 28.05
has become proud in your w.— 28.05
carry off its w. and despoil it 29.19
and her w. is carried away, and her 30.04
will put an end to the w. of Egypt, 30.10
rich, I have gained w. for myself"; Hos 12.08
that strangers carried off his w., Ob 1.11
their w. to the Lord of the whole Mic 4.13
or w. of every precious thing. Nah 2.09
and hurl her w. into the sea, Zec 9.04
And the w. of all the nations round 14.14
from this business we have our w. Ac 19.25
overflowed in a w. of liberality 2Co 8.02
Christ greater w. than the treasures Heb 11.26
power and w. and wisdom and might Rev 5.12
rich with the w. of her wantonness." 18.03
who gained w. from her, will stand 18.15
hour all this w. has been laid 18.17
ships at sea grew rich by her w.! 18.19

WEALTHY
and more until he became very w. Gen 26.13
at Mahanaim; for he was a very w. man. 2Sa 19.32
where a w. woman lived, who urged 2Ki 4.08
from all the w. men, fifty shekels 15.20

WEANED
And the child grew, and was w.; Gen 21.08
feast on the day that Isaac was w. 21.08
husband, "As soon as the child is w., 1Sa 1.22
to you, wait until you have w. him; 1.23
nursed her son, until she w. him. 1.23
And when she had w. him, she took him 1.24
whom Tahpenes w. in Pharaoh's house; 1Ki 11.20
and the w. child shall put his hand Is 11.08
Those who are w. from the milk, 28.09
When she had w. Not pitied, she Hos 1.08

WEAPON
him down with a w. of wood in the Num 35.18
every man with his w. in his hand, 2Ch 23.10
and with the other held his w. Neh 4.17
each kept his w. in his hand. 4.23
He will flee from an iron w.; Job 20.24
and produces a w. for its purpose. Is 54.16
no w. that is fashioned against you 54.17
"You are my hammer and w. of war: Jer 51.20
with his destroying w. in his hand." Eze 9.01
man with his w. for slaughter in 9.02

WEAPONS

take your w., your quiver and your	Gen 27.03
w. of violence are their swords.	49.05
man of you girded on his w. of war,	Deu 1.41
shall have a stick with your w.;	23.13
armed with w. of war, set forth from	Ju 18.11
Danites, armed with their w. of war,	18.16
hundred men armed with w. of war.	18.17
And Jonathan gave his w. to his lad,	1Sa 20.40
neither my sword nor my w. with me,	21.08
and the w. of war perished!	2Sa 1.27
fortified cities also, and w.,	2Ki 10.02
king, each with his w. in his hand;	11.08
every man with his w. in his hand,	11.11
for battle with all the w. of war,	1Ch 12.33
men armed with all the w. of war.	12.37
king, each with his w. in his hand;	2Ch 23.07
He also made w. and shields in	32.05
he goes out to meet the w.	Job 39.21
he has prepared his deadly w.,	Ps 7.13
the sword, and the w. of war.	76.03
Wisdom is better than w. of war,	Ecc 9.18
LORD and the w. of his indignation,	Is 13.05
looked to the w. of the house of	22.08
turn back the w. of war which are	Jer 21.04
against you, each with his w.;	22.07
brought out the w. of his wrath,	50.25
down to Sheol with their w. of war,	Eze 32.27
make fires of the w. and burn them,	39.09
will make their fires of the w.;	39.10
through the w. and are not halted.	Joe 2.08
with lanterns and torches and w.	Jn 18.03
with the w. of righteousness for	2Co 6.07
for the w. of our warfare are not	10.04

WEAR

bread to eat and clothing to w.,	Gen 28.20
with you will w. yourselves out,	Ex 18.18
his place shall w. them seven days,	29.30
disease shall w. torn clothes and	Lev 13.45
and w. the linen turban; these are	16.04
consecrated to w. the garments,	21.10
Your clothing did not w. out upon you,	Deu 8.04
"A woman shall not w. anything that	22.05
You shall not w. a mingled stuff,	22.11
to w. an ephod before me; and I gave	1Sa 2.28
into battle, but you w. your robes."	1Ki 22.30
into battle, but you w. your robes."	2Ch 18.29
clothes did not w. out and their	Neh 9.21
the waters w. away the stones;	Job 14.19
it up, but the just will w. it,	27.17
they will all w. out like a garment	Ps 102.26
own bread and w. our own clothes,	Is 4.01
of them will w. out like a garment	50.09
the earth will w. out like a	51.06
they shall w. linen garments;	Eze 44.17
and shall w. out the saints of the	Dan 7.25
drink?' or 'What shall we w.?'	Mt 6.31
those who w. soft raiment are in	11.08
but to w. sandals and not put on	Mk 6.09
Now the day began to w. away;	Lk 9.12
or she will w. me out by her	18.05
shorn or shaven, let her w. a veil.	1Co 11.06
for a man to w. long hair is	11.14

WEARIED

so that they w. themselves groping	Gen 19.11
or w. you with frankincense.	Is 43.23
you have w. me with your iniquities.	43.24
You are w. with your many counsels;	47.13
You were w. with the length of your	57.10
and they have w. you, how will you	Jer 12.05
In vain I have w. myself; its thick rust	Eze 24.12
In what have I w. you? Answer me	Mic 6.03
You have w. the LORD with your	Mal 2.17
Yet you say, "How have we w. him?"	2.17
w. as he was with his journey, sat	Jn 4.06

WEARIES

The toil of a fool w. him,	Ecc 10.15
when he w. himself upon the high	Is 16.12

WEARINESS

he was lying fast asleep from w.	Ju 4.21
All things are full of w.;	Ecc 1.08
much study is a w. of the flesh.	12.12
'What a w. this is,' you say, and you	Mal 1.13

WEARING

w. the holy linen garments;	Lev 16.32
mantle you are w. and hold it out."	Ru 3.15
of the LORD in Shiloh, w. an ephod.	1Sa 14.03
Now she was w. a long robe with	2Sa 13.18
Now Joab was w. a soldier's garment,	20.08
w. the crown of thorns and the	Jn 19.05
I am suffering and w. fetters,	2Ti 2.09
decoration of gold, and w. of robes,	1Pe 3.03

WEARISOME

this, it seemed to me a w. task,	Ps 73.16

WEARS

it w. him out to bring it back to	Pro 26.15
to the one who w. the fine clothing	Jas 2.03

WEARY

"I am w. of my life because of the	Gen 27.46
But Moses' hands grew w.; so they took	Ex 17.12
way, when you were faint and w.,	Deu 25.18
with him, arrived w. at the Jordan;	2Sa 16.14
him while he is w. and discouraged,	17.02
are hungry and w. and thirsty in	17.29
the Philistines; and David grew w.	21.15
Philistines until his hand was w.,	23.10
and there the w. are at rest.	Job 3.17
given no water to the w. to drink,	22.07
I am w. with my moaning; every night	Ps 6.06
as in a dry and w. land where no	63.01
I am w. with my crying;	69.03
discipline or be w. of his reproof,	Pro 3.11
lest he become w. of you and hate	25.17
burden to me, I am w. of bearing them.	Is 1.14
None is w., none stumbles, none	5.27
Is it too little for you to w. men,	7.13
men, that you w. my God also?	7.13
give rest to the w.; and this is	28.12
shade of a great rock in a w. land.	32.02
My eyes are w. with looking upward.	38.14
He does not faint or grow w.,	40.28
Even youths shall faint and be w.,	40.30
they shall run and not be w.,	40.31
but you have been w. of me,	43.22
are loaded as burdens on w. beasts.	46.01
sustain with a word him that is w.	50.04
who seek her need w. themselves;	Jer 2.24
I am w. of holding it in. "Pour it out	6.11
iniquity and are too w. to repent.	9.05
destroyed you;—I am w. of relenting.	15.06
and I am w. with holding it in, and	20.09
For I will satisfy the w. soul,	31.25
I am w. with my groaning, and I find	45.03
and the nations w. themselves only	51.58
we are w., we are given no rest.	Lam 5.05
and nations w. themselves for	Hab 2.13
And let us not grow w. in well-doing,	Gal 6.09
Brethren, do not be w. in well-doing.	2Th 3.13
may not grow w. or fainthearted	Heb 12.03
sake, and you have not grown w.	Rev 2.03

WEARYING

hand is stretched out without w.;	Ps 77.02

WEASEL

the w., the mouse, the great lizard	Lev 11.29

WEATHER
you say, 'It will be fair w.; for the sky Mt 16.02

WEAVE
"And you shall w. the coat in Ex 28.39
"If you w. the seven locks of my Ju 16.13
they w. the spider's web; he who eats Is 59.05
of his soul; thus they w. it together. Mic 7.03

WEAVER
or by a w.—by any sort of workman Ex 35.35
like a w. I have rolled up my life; Is 38.12

WEAVER'S
of his spear was like a w. beam, 1Sa 17.07
of whose spear was like a w. beam. 2Sa 21.19
in his hand a spear like a w. beam; 1Ch 11.23
of whose spear was like a w. beam. 20.05
days are swifter than a w. shuttle, Job 7.06

WEAVERS
and the w. of white cotton. Is 19.09

WEB
head with the w. and make it tight Ju 16.13
his head and wove them into the w. 16.14
away the pin, the loom, and the w. 16.14
and his trust is a spider's w. Job 8.14
he builds is like a spider's w., 27.18
eggs, they weave the spider's w.; Is 59.05

WEBS
Their w. will not serve as clothing; Is 59.06

WEDDING
crowned him on the day of his w., Sol 3.11
"Can the w. guests mourn as long as Mt 9.15
'The w. is ready, but those invited 22.08
so the w. hall was filled with 22.10
there a man who had no w. garment; 22.11
get in here without a w. garment?" 22.12
"Can the w. guests fast while the Mk 2.19
"Can you make w. guests fast while Lk 5.34

WEDLOCK
women who break w. and shed blood Eze 16.38

WEEDS
and foul w. instead of barley. Job 31.40
like poisonous w. in the furrows Hos 10.04
w. were wrapped about my head Jon 2.05
came and sowed w. among the wheat, Mt 13.25
grain, then the w. appeared also. 13.26
your field? How then has it w.?" 13.27
gathering the w. you root up the 13.29
Gather the w. first and bind them 13.30
the parable of the w. of the field." 13.36
the w. are the sons of the evil one, 13.38
Just as the w. are gathered and 13.40

WEEK
Complete the w. of this one, and we Gen 29.27
Jacob did so, and completed her w.; 29.28
covenant with many for one w.; Dan 9.27
for half of the w. he shall cause 9.27
dawn of the first day of the w., Mt 28.01
day of the w. they went to the Mk 16.02
rose early on the first day of the w., * 16.09
I fast twice a w., I give tithes of Lk 18.12
But on the first day of the w., 24.01
day of the w. Mary Magdalene came Jn 20.01
that day, the first day of the w., 20.19
On the first day of the w., Ac 20.07
On the first day of every w., 1Co 16.02

WEEKS
And you shall observe the feast of w., Ex 34.22
then she shall be unclean two w., Lev 12.05
seven full w. shall they be, 23.15
"And you shall count seven w. of years, 25.08
of the seven w. of years shall be 25.08
to the LORD at your feast of w., Num 28.26
"You shall count seven w.; begin to count Deu 16.09
count the seven w. from the time 16.09
the feast of w. to the LORD your 16.10
unleavened bread, at the feast of w., 16.16
the feast of w., and the feast of 2Ch 8.13
for us the w. appointed for the Jer 5.24
"Seventy w. of years are decreed Dan 9.24
a prince, there shall be seven w. 9.25
for sixty-two w. it shall be built 9.25
And after the sixty-two w., 9.26
Daniel, was mourning for three w. 10.02
at all, for the full three w. 10.03
and for three w. he argued with Ac 17.02

WEEP
mourn for Sarah and to w. for her. Gen 23.02
and he sought a place to w. 43.30
For they w. before me and say, 'Give Num 11.13
said to her, "Hannah, why do you w.? 1Sa 1.08
be spared to w. out his eyes and 2.33
they had no more strength to w. 30.04
w. over Saul, who clothed you 2Sa 1.24
And Hazael said, "Why does my lord w.?" 2Ki 8.12
do not mourn or w." For all the Neh 8.09
Did not I w. for him whose day was Job 30.25
pipe to the voice of those who w. 30.31
a time to w., and a time to laugh; Ec 3.04
gone up to the high places to w.; Is 15.02
Therefore I w. with the weeping of 16.09
from me, let me w. bitter tears; 22.04
you shall w. no more. He will surely 30.19
the envoys of peace w. bitterly. 33.07
that I might w. day and night for Jer 9.01
my soul will w. in secret for your 13.17
my eyes will w. bitterly and run 13.17
W. not for him who is dead, nor 22.10
but w. bitterly for him who goes 22.10
More than for Jazer I w. for you, 48.32
"For these things I w.; my tears for Lam 1.16
not mourn or w. nor shall your Eze 24.16
you shall not mourn or w., 24.23
and they w. over you in bitterness 27.31
Awake, you drunkards, and w.; Joe 1.05
w. and say, "Spare thy people, O LORD, 2.17
Tell it not in Gath, w. not at all; Mic 1.10
and w. bitterly over him, as one Zec 12.10
there men will w. and gnash their Mt 8.12
there men will w. and gnash their 13.42
there men will w. and gnash their 13.50
there men will w. and gnash their 22.13
there men will w. and gnash their 24.51
there men will w. and gnash their 25.30
"Why do you make a tumult and w.? Mk 5.39
"Blessed are you that w. now, Lk 6.21
now, for you shall mourn and w. 6.25
on her and said to her, "Do not w." 7.13
we wailed, and you did not w.' 7.32
but he said, "Do not w.; for she is not 8.52
There you will w. and gnash your 13.28
do not w. for me, but w. for yourselves 23.28
was going to the tomb to w. there. Jn 11.31
you will w. and lament, but the 16.20
rejoice, w. with those who w. Rom 12.15
Be wretched and mourn and w. Jas 4.09
w. and howl for the miseries that 5.01
of the elders said to me, "W. not; Rev 5.05
will w. and wail over her when they 18.09
of the earth w. and mourn for her, 18.11

WEEPING
the days of w. for him were past, Gen 50.04
the people w. throughout their Num 11.10
while they were w. at the door of 25.06

WEEPING (cont.)
the days of w. and mourning for Deu 34.08
ails the people, that they are w.?" 1Sa 11.05
w. after her all the way to Bahurim. 2Sa 3.16
w. as he went, barefoot and with his 15.30
and they went up, w. as they went. 15.30
the king is w. and mourning for 19.01
from the sound of the people's w., Ez 3.13
w. and casting himself down before 10.01
with fasting and w. and lamenting, Est 4.03
My face is red with w., and on my Job 16.16
I drench my couch with my w. Ps 6.06
LORD has heard the sound of my w. 6.08
W. may tarry for the night, but joy 30.05
He that goes forth w., bearing the 126.06
the ascent of Luhith they go up w.; Is 15.05
Therefore I weep with the w. of 16.09
called to w. and mourning, to 22.12
it the sound of w. and the cry of 65.19
the w. and pleading of Israel's sons, Jer 3.21
"Take up w. and wailing for the 9.10
With w. they shall come, and with 31.09
Ramah, lamentation and bitter w. 31.15
Rachel is w. for her children; 31.15
the LORD: "Keep your voice from w., 31.16
Mizpah to meet them, w. as he came. 41.06
the ascent of Luhith they go up w.; 48.05
come together, w. as they come; 50.04
My eyes are spent with w.; my soul is Lam 2.11
there sat women w. for Tammuz. Eze 8.14
with w., and with mourning; Joe 2.12
with w. and groaning because he no Mal 2.13
Rachel w. for her children; she refused Mt 2.18
and people w. and wailing loudly. Mk 5.38
w., she began to wet his feet with Lk 7.38
And all were w. and bewailing her; 8.52
When Jesus saw her w., and the Jn 11.33
the Jews who came with her also w., 11.33
But Mary stood w. outside the tomb, 20.11
said to her, "Woman why are you w.?" 20.13
said to her, "Woman, why are you w.? 20.15
All the widows stood beside him w., Ac 9.39
w. and breaking my heart? For I am 21.13
her torment, w. and mourning aloud, Rev 18.15

WEEPS
She w. bitterly in the night, tears Lam 1.02
as one w. over a first-born. Zec 12.10

WEIGH
them until you w. them before the Ez 8.29
they w. like a burden too heavy for Ps 38.04
and w. out silver in the scales, Is 46.06
all who w. out silver are cut off. Zep 1.11
and let the others w. what is said. 1Co 14.29

WEIGHED
and Abraham w. out for Ephron the Gen 23.16
knowledge, and by him actions are w. 1Sa 2.03
spear's head w. six hundred shekels 17.07
he w. the hair of his head, two 2Sa 14.26
whose spear w. three hundred shekels 21.16
money that was w. out into the 2Ki 12.11
found that it w. a talent of gold, 1Ch 20.02
And I w. out to them the silver and Ez 8.25
I w. out into their hand six 8.26
vessels were w. into the hands of 8.33
The whole was counted and w., 8.34
"O that my vexation were w., Job 6.02
silver cannot be w. as its price. 28.15
(Let me be w. in a just balance, and 31.06
where is he who w. the tribute? Is 33.18
a measure and w. the mountains in 40.12
and w. out the money to him, seventeen Jer 32.09
and w. the money on scales. 32.10
you have been w. in the balances Dan 5.27
"And they w. out as my wages Zec 11.12

your hearts be w. down with dissipation Lk 21.34
they w. anchor and sailed along Ac 27.13

WEIGHING
took a gold ring w. a half shekel, Gen 24.22
for her arms w. ten gold shekels, 24.22
each silver plate w. a hundred and Num 7.85
w. ten shekels apiece according to 7.86
and a bar of gold w. fifty shekels, Jos 7.21
as bronze in quantities beyond w., 1Ch 22.03
and bronze and iron beyond w., 22.14
w. and studying and arranging Ecc 12.09
then take balances for w., and divide Eze 5.01

WEIGHS
Anxiety in a man's heart w. him down, Pro 12.25
eyes, but the LORD w. the spirit. 16.02
eyes, but the LORD w. the heart. 21.02
does not he who w. the heart perceive it? 24.12

WEIGHT
of his sack, our money in full w.; Gen 43.21
of length or w. or quantity. Lev 19.35
deliver your bread again by w.; 26.26
plate whose w. was a hundred and Num 7.13
whose w. was a hundred and thirty 7.19
whose w. was a hundred and thirty 7.25
plate whose w. was a hundred and 7.31
whose w. was a hundred and thirty 7.37
whose w. was a hundred and thirty 7.43
whose w. was a hundred and thirty 7.49
whose w. was a hundred and thirty 7.55
whose w. was a hundred and thirty 7.61
whose w. was a hundred and thirty 7.67
whose w. was a hundred and thirty 7.73
whose w. was a hundred and thirty 7.79
bear alone the w. and burden of Deu 1.12
A full and just w. you shall have, 25.15
And the w. of the golden earrings Ju 8.26
and he leaned his w. upon them, 16.29
and the w. of the coat was five 1Sa 17.05
the w. of it was a talent of gold, 2Sa 12.30
hundred shekels by the king's w. 14.26
in my hand the w. of a thousand 18.12
the w. of the bronze was not found 1Ki 7.47
Now the w. of gold that came to 10.14
of all these vessels was beyond w. 2Ki 25.16
shekels of gold by w. for the site. 1Ch 21.25
the w. of gold for all golden 28.14
the w. of silver vessels for each 28.14
the w. of the golden lampstands and 28.15
the w. of gold for each lampstand 28.15
the w. of silver for a lampstand 28.15
the w. of gold for each table for 28.16
golden bowls and the w. of each; 28.17
silver bowls and the w. of each; 28.17
made of refined gold, and its w.; 28.18
The w. of the nails was one shekel 2Ch 3.09
so that the w. of the bronze was 4.18
Now the w. of gold that came to 9.13
took over the w. of the silver and Ez 8.30
and the w. of everything was 8.34
When he gave to the wind its w., Job 28.25
LORD, but a just w. is his delight. Pro 11.01
him the whole w. of his father's Is 22.24
of all these things was beyond w. Jer 52.20
worth their w. in fine gold, how Lam 4.02
food which you eat shall be by w., Eze 4.10
eat bread by w. and with fearfulness 4.16
down the leaden w. upon its mouth. Zec 5.08
aloes, about a hundred pounds' w. Jn 19.39
us an eternal w. of glory beyond 2Co 4.17
let us also lay aside every w., Heb 12.01

WEIGHTIER
neglected the w. matters of the Mt 23.23

WEIGHTS
according to the w. current among Gen 23.16
just w., a just ephah, and a just Lev 19.36
have in your bag two kinds of w., Deu 25.13
all the w. in the bag are his work. Pro 16.11
Diverse w. and diverse measures are 20.10
Diverse w. are an abomination to 20.23
and with a bag of deceitful w.? Mic 6.11

WEIGHTY
and sand is w., but a fool's provocation Pro 27.03
say, "His letters are w. and strong, 2Co 10.10

WELCOME
we see thee a stranger and w. thee, Mt 25.38
a stranger and you did not w. me, 25.43
arrived at Caesarea to w. Festus. Ac 25.13
w. him, but not for disputes over Rom 14.01
W. one another, therefore, as Christ 15.07
nothing unclean, then I will w. you, 2Co 6.17
us what a w. we had among you, and 1Th 1.09
had given friendly w. to the spies. Heb 11.31
refuses himself to w. the brethren, 3Jn 1.10
who want to w. them and puts them 1.10

WELCOMED
And Hezekiah w. them, and he showed 2Ki 20.13
And Hezekiah w. them; and he showed Is 39.02
I was a stranger and you w. me, Mt 25.35
the crowd w. him, for they were all Lk 8.40
and he w. them and spoke to them of 9.11
the Galileans w. him, having seen Jn 4.45
they were w. by the church and the Ac 15.04
they kindled a fire and w. us all, 28.02
and w. all who came to him, 28.30
him who eats; for God has w. him. Rom 14.03
as Christ has w. you, for the glory 15.07

WELFARE
And he inquired about their w., Gen 43.27
they asked each other of their w., Ex 18.07
of Micah, and asked him of his w. Ju 18.15
to seek the w. of the children of Neh 2.10
he sought the w. of his people and Est 10.03
delights in the w. of his servant! Ps 35.27
and abundant w. will they give you Pro 3.02
it was for my w. that I had great Is 38.17
not pray for the w. of this people. Jer 14.11
turn aside to ask about your w.? 15.05
But seek the w. of the city where I 29.07
for in its w. you will find your w. 29.07
plants for w. and not for evil, to 29.11
not seeking the w. of this people, 38.04
be genuinely anxious for your w. Php 2.20

WELL
If you do w., will you not be Gen 4.07
And if you do not do w., sin is couching 4.07
that it may go w. with me because 12.13
her sake he dealt w. with Abram; 12.16
valley was w. watered everywhere 13.10
Therefore the w. was called Beerlahairoi; 16.14
eyes, and she saw a w. of water; 21.19
Abimelech about a w. of water which 21.25
witness for me that I dug this w." 21.30
w. advanced in years; and the LORD 24.01
the city by the w. of water at the 24.11
and ran again to the w. to draw, 24.20
found there a w. of springing 26.19
he called the name of the w. Esek, 26.20
Then they dug another w., 26.21
from there and dug another w., 26.22
there Isaac's servants dug a w. 26.25
him about the w. which they had 26.32
he saw a w. in the field, and lo, 29.02
for out of that w. the flocks were 29.02
the stone from the mouth of the w., 29.03
its place upon the mouth of the w. 29.03
He said to them, "Is it w. with him?" 29.06
They said, "It is w.; and see Rachel 29.06
is rolled from the mouth of the w.; 29.08
see if it is w. with your brothers, 37.14
when it is w. with you, and do me 40.14
and said, "Is your father w., 43.27
"Your servant our father is w., 43.28
Pharaoh and his servants w. 45.16
as w. as all the household of 50.08
So God dealt w. with the midwives; Ex 1.20
and he sat down by a w. 2.15
I know that he can speak w.; and behold, he 4.14
you shall bring it w. mixed, Lev 6.21
of Aaron, one as w. as another. 7.10
of fine flour w. mixed with oil. 7.12
he sojourner as w. as the native, 24.16
For it was w. with us in Egypt." Num 11.18
for we are w. able to overcome it." 13.30
will we drink water from a w.; 20.17
that is the w. of which the LORD 21.16
sang this song: "Spring up, O w.! 21.17
the w. which the princes dug, which 21.18
will not drink the water of a w.; 21.22
day, that it may go w. with you, Deu 4.40
maidservant may rest as w. as you, 5.14
and that it may go w. with you, 5.16
it might go w. with them and with 5.29
and that it may go w. with you, 5.33
that it may go w. with you, 6.03
LORD that it may go w. with you, 6.18
that all may go w. with you and 12.25
that it may go w. with you and 12.28
since he fares w. with you, 15.16
so that it may be w. with you. 19.13
that it may go w. with you, 22.07
us this day as w. as with him who 29.15
to your brethren as w. as to you, Jos 1.15
sojourner as w. as homeborn, with 8.33
Manassites spoke, it pleased them w. 22.30
was old and w. advanced in years, 23.01
am now old and w. advanced in 23.02
"W. then, when the LORD has given Ju 8.07
you have dealt w. with Jerubbaal 9.16
for me; for she pleases me w." 14.03
the woman; and she pleased Samson w. 14.07
as w. as the olive orchards. 15.05
"It is w., my daughter, that you go Ru 2.22
you, that it may be w. with you? 3.01
of the next of kin for you, w.; 3.13
And Saul said to his servant, "W. said; 1Sa 9.10
the LORD your God, it will be w.; 12.14
will play it, and you will be w." 16.16
for me a man who can play w., 16.17
and was w., and the evil spirit 16.23
pleased David w. to be the king's 18.26
And Jonathan spoke w. of David to 19.04
to the great w. that is in Secu; 19.22
father knows w. that I have found 20.03
it will be w. with your servant; 20.07
if he is w. disposed toward David, 20.12
day how you have dealt w. with me, 24.18
the LORD has dealt w. with my lord, 25.31
"Very w., you shall know what your 28.02
"Very w., I will make you my 28.02
who had a w. in his courtyard; 2Sa 17.18
the men came up out of the w., 17.21
cried out to the king, "All is w." 18.28
"Is it w. with the young man 18.29
"Is it w. with the young man 18.32
"Is it w. with you, my brother?" 20.09
drink from the w. of Bethlehem 23.15
out of the w. of Bethlehem which 23.16
Bathsheba said, "Very w.; 1Ki 2.18
you did w. that it was in your 8.18
people answered, "It is w. spoken." 18.24
and consider w. what you have to do; 20.22
"W., she has no son, and her husband 2Ki 4.14

WELL (cont.)
She said, "It will be w." 2Ki 4.23
and say to her, Is it w. with you? 4.26
Is it w. with your husband? 4.26
Is it w. with the child?" 4.26
And she answered, "It is w." 4.26
to meet him, and said, "Is all w.?" 5.21
And he said, "All is w. 5.22
they said to him, "Is all w.? 9.11
you have done w. in carrying out 10.30
as w. as to buy timber and quarried 12.12
as w. as for buying timber and 22.06
and it shall be w. with you. 25.24
drink from the w. of Bethlehem 1Ch 11.17
out of the w. of Bethlehem which 11.18
as w. as bronze in quantities 22.03
as w. as two and two at the storehouse; 26.17
you did w. that it was in your 2Ch 6.08
to the Jackal's w. and to the Dung Neh 2.13
But I have understanding as w. as you; Job 12.03
Will it be w. with you when he 13.09
though you look w. at his place, Ps 37.10
consider w. her ramparts, go through 48.13
when he does w. for himself, 49.18
my steps had w. nigh slipped. 73.02
a cup, with foaming wine, w. mixed; 75.08
And they ate and were w. filled, 78.29
It is w. with the man who deals 112.05
Thou hast dealt w. with thy servant, 119.65
Thy promise is w. tried, and they 119.140
happy, and it shall be w. with you. 128.02
Thou knowest me right w.; 139.14
flowing water from your own w. Pro 5.15
When it goes w. with the righteous, 11.10
an adventuress is a narrow w. 23.27
Know w. the condition of your 27.23
She looks w. to the ways of her 31.27
as w. as that youth, who was to Ecc 4.15
made the one as w. as the other, 7.14
that it will be w. with those who 8.12
but it will not be w. with the 8.13
a w. of living water, and flowing Sol 4.15
new as w. as old, which I have laid 7.13
that it shall be w. with them, Is 3.10
of wine on the lees w. refined. 25.06
LORD said to me, "You have seen w., Jer 1.12
"How w. you direct your course to 2.33
saying, 'It shall be w. with you'; 4.10
As a w. keeps its water fresh, so 6.07
you, that it may be w. with you.' 7.23
righteousness? Then it was w. with him. 22.15
then it was w. Is not this to 22.16
LORD, 'It shall be w. with you'; 23.17
consider w. the highway, the road by 31.21
you, and it shall be w. with you, 38.20
look after him w. and do him no 39.12
come, and I will look after you w.; 40.04
and it shall be w. with you. 40.09
that it may be w. with us when we 42.06
the father as w. as the soul of Eze 18.04
boil w. the flesh, and empty out the 24.10
voice and plays w. on an instrument, 33.32
mark w., see with your eyes, and 44.05
and mark w. those who may be 44.05
which I have made, w. and good; Dan 3.15
said, "Do you do w. to be angry?" Jon 4.04
"Do you do w. to be angry for the 4.09
"I do w. to be angry, angry enough 4.09
Son, with whom I am w. pleased." Mt 3.17
let him have your cloak as w.; 5.40
these things shall be yours as w. 6.33
"Those who are w. have no need of a 9.12
his garment, I shall be made w." 9.21
your faith has made you w." 9.22
instantly the woman was made w. 9.22
with whom my soul is w. pleased. 12.18
as many as touched it were made w. 14.36
W. did Isaiah prophesy of you, when 15.07
it is w. that we are here; if you wish 17.04
Son, with whom I am w. pleased; 17.05
'W. done, good and faithful servant; 25.21
'W. done, good and faithful servant; 25.23
with thee I am w. pleased." Mk 1.11
"Those who are w. have no need of a 2.17
that she may be made w., and live." 5.23
his garments, I shall be made w." 5.28
"Daughter, your faith has made you w.; 5.34
as many as touched it were made w. 6.56
"W. did Isaiah prophesy of you 7.06
saying, "He has done all things w.; 7.37
it is w. that we are here; let us make 9.05
your way; your faith has made you w." 10.52
seeing that he answered them w., 12.28
with thee I am w. pleased." Lk 3.22
And all spoke w. of him, and wondered 4.22
"Those who are w. have no need of a 5.31
you, when all men speak w. of you, 6.26
do not withhold your coat as w. 6.29
it, because it had been w. built. 6.48
the house, they found the slave w. 7.10
"Daughter, your faith has made you w.; 8.48
only believe, and she shall be w." 8.50
it is w. that we are here; 9.33
these things shall be yours as w. 12.31
bears fruit next year, w. and good; 13.09
or an ox that has fallen into a w., 14.05
your faith has made you w." 17.19
your faith has made you w." 18.42
'W. done, good servant! Because you 19.17
"Teacher, you have spoken w." 20.39
Jacob's w. was there, and so Jesus, Jn 4.06
journey, sat down beside the w. 4.06
to draw with, and the w. is deep; 4.11
father Jacob, who gave us the w., 4.12
and said to him, "See, you are w.! 5.14
I made a man's whole body w.? 7.23
this man is standing before you w. Ac 4.10
who is w. spoken of by the whole 10.22
that he had faith to be made w., 14.09
yourselves from these, you will do w. 15.29
He was w. spoken of by the brethren 16.02
of high standing as w. as men. 17.12
w. versed in the scriptures. 18.24
w. spoken of by all the Jews who 22.12
done no wrong, as you know very w. 25.10
among you as w. as among the rest Rom 1.13
helper of many and of myself as w. 16.02
It is w. for a man not to touch a 1Co 7.01
say that it is w. for them to 7.08
distress it is w. for a person to 7.26
as his betrothed, he will do w. 7.37
who marries his betrothed does w.; 7.38
W., I do not run aimlessly, I do not 9.26
For you may give thanks w. enough, 14.17
refreshed my spirit as w. as yours. 16.18
as unknown, and yet w. known; as dying 2Co 6.09
You were running w.; who hindered Gal 5.07
"that it may be w. with you and Eph 6.03
yourselves know w. that the day of 1Th 5.02
He must manage his own household w., 1Ti 3.04
moreover he must be w. thought of 3.07
children and their households w.; 3.12
for those who serve w. as deacons 3.13
and she must be w. attested for her 5.10
elders who rule w. be considered 5.17
and you w. know all the service he 2Ti 1.18
his own sins as w. as for those of Heb 5.03
necessarily a change in the law as w. 7.12
though w. attested by their faith, 11.39
for it is w. that the heart be 13.09
neighbor as yourself," you do w. Jas 2.08
you do w. Even the demons 2.19
of Christ as w. as a partaker in 1Pe 5.01
Son, with whom I am w. pleased," 2Pe 1.17

WELL (cont.)
You will do w. to pay attention to 2Pe 1.19
that all may go w. with you and 3Jn 1.02
know that it is w. with your soul. 1.02
You will do w. to send them on 1.06

WELL-DOING
by patience in w. seek for glory Rom 2.07
And let us not grow weary in w., Gal 6.09
Brethren, do not be weary in w. 2Th 3.13

WELL-FED
They were w. lusty stallions, each Jer 5.08

WELL-FORTIFIED
up siegeworks, and take a w. city. Dan 11.15

WELLING
spring of water w. up to eternal Jn 4.14

WELL-KNOWN
chosen from the assembly, w. men; Num 16.02

WELL-SET
and instead of w. hair, baldness; Is 3.24

WELL'S
stone on the w. mouth was large, Gen 29.02
rolled the stone from the w. mouth, 29.10
a covering over the w. mouth, 2Sa 17.19

WELLS
earth all the w. which his father's Gen 26.15
dug again the w. of water which 26.18
I dug w. and drank foreign waters, 2Ki 19.24
water from the w. of salvation. Is 12.03
I dug w. and drank waters, and I 37.25

WELTERING
and saw you w. in your blood, I said Eze 16.06
naked and bare, w. in your blood. 16.22

WEPT
child lifted up his voice and w. Gen 21.16
Esau lifted up his voice and w. 27.38
Then Jacob kissed Rachel, and w. aloud. 29.11
neck and kissed him, and they w. 33.04
Thus his father w. for him. 37.35
Then he turned away from them and w.; 42.24
entered his chamber and w. there. 43.30
And he w. aloud, so that the Egyptians 45.02
his brother Benjamin's neck and w.; 45.14
and Benjamin w. upon his neck. 45.14
all his brothers and w. upon them; 45.15
and w. on his neck a good while. 46.29
and w. over him, and kissed him. 50.01
the Egyptians w. for him seventy 50.03
Joseph w. when they spoke to him. 50.17
the people of Israel also w. again, Num 11.04
for you have w. in the hearing of 11.18
and have w. before him, saying, "Why 11.20
and the people w. that night. 14.01
house of Israel w. for Aaron 20.29
returned and w. before the LORD; Deu 1.45
of Israel w. for Moses in the 34.08
lifted up their voices and w. Ju 2.04
And Samson's wife w. before him, 14.16
She w. before him the seven days 14.17
went up and w. before the LORD 20.23
went up and came to Bethel and w.; 20.26
up their voices and w. bitterly. 21.02
they lifted up their voices and w. Ru 1.09
up their voices and w. again; 1.14
Therefore Hannah w. and would not 1Sa 1.07
to the LORD, and w. bitterly. 1.10
and all the people w. aloud. 11.04
and w. with one another, until David 20.41
Saul lifted up his voice and w. 24.16
him raised their voices and w., 30.04
mourned and w. and fasted until 2Sa 1.12
his voice and w. at the grave of 3.32
and all the people w. 3.32
all the people w. again over him. 3.34
You fasted and w. for the child 12.21
was still alive, I fasted and w.; 12.22
and lifted up their voice and w.; 13.36
all his servants w. very bitterly. 13.36
And all the country w. aloud as all 15.23
the chamber over the gate, and w.; 18.33
was ashamed. And the man of God w. 2Ki 8.11
and w. before him, crying, "My father, 13.14
good in thy sight." And Hezekiah w. bitterly. 20.03
rent your clothes and w. before me, 22.19
rent your clothes and w. before me, 2Ch 34.27
w. with a loud voice when they saw Ez 3.12
for the people w. bitterly. 10.01
these words I sat down and w., Neh 1.04
all the people w. when they heard 8.09
they raised their voices and w.; Job 2.12
and its furrows have w. together; 31.38
Babylon, there we sat down and w., Ps 137.01
good in thy sight." And Hezekiah w. bitterly. Is 38.03
he w. and sought his favor. He met Hos 12.04
And he went out and w. bitterly. Mt 26.75
three times." And he broke down and w. Mk 14.72
him, as they mourned and w. *16.10
and saw the city he w. over it, Lk 19.41
And he went out and w. bitterly. 22.62
Jesus w. Jn 11.35
and as she w. she stooped to look 20.11
And they all w. and embraced Paul Ac 20.37
and I w. much that no one was found Rev 5.04
as they w. and mourned, crying out, 18.19

WEST
Bethel on the w. and Ai on the Gen 12.08
abroad to the w. and to the east 28.14
flock to the w. side of the Ex 3.01
LORD turned a very strong w. wind, 10.19
court on the w. side there shall 27.12
And for the w. side were hangings 38.12
"On the w. side shall be the Num 2.18
behind the tabernacle on the w., 3.23
and for the w. side two thousand 35.05
w. of the road, toward the going Deu 11.30
were beyond the Jordan to the w., Jos 5.01
Bethel and Ai, to the w. of Ai; 8.09
and Ai, to the w. of the city. 8.12
and its rear guard w. of the city. 8.13
and in Naphothdor on the w., 11.02
Canaanites in the east and the w., 11.03
defeated on the w. side of the 12.07
on the w., at the northern end of 15.08
boundary circles w. of Baalah to 15.10
And the w. boundary was the Great 15.12
on the w. it touches Carmel and 19.26
at the south, and Asher on the w., 19.34
in the land w. of the Jordan. 22.07
Jordan to the Great Sea in the w. 23.04
behold, it is w. of Kiriathjearim. Ju 18.12
out of their place w. of Geba. 20.33
all the region w. of the Euphrates 1Ki 4.24
all the kings w. of the Euphrates; 4.24
three facing w., three facing south, 7.25
four sides East w., north, and south; 1Ch 9.24
valleys, to the east and to the w. 12.15
and Hosah it came out for the w., 26.16
parbar on the w. there were four 26.18
three facing w., three facing south, 2Ch 4.04
down to the w. side of the city of 32.30
to the city of David w. of Gihon, 33.14
They of the w. are appalled at his Job 18.20
or from the w. and not from the Ps 75.06
as far as the east is from the w., 103.12

WEST (cont.)
from the east and from the w., Ps 107.03
Philistines on the w. devour Israel Is 9.12
of the Philistines in the w., 11.14
of the LORD they shout from the w. 24.14
and from the w. I will gather you; 43.05
rising of the sun and from the w., 45.06
from the north and from the w., 49.12
the name of the LORD from the w., 59.19
yard on the w. side was seventy Eze 41.12
was at the w. and its walls on 41.15
turned to the w. side and measured, 42.19
on the w. and on the east, corresponding 45.07
"On the w. side, the Great Sea shall 47.20
This shall be the w. side. 47.20
from the east side to the w., 48.01
Dan, from the east side to the w., 48.02
from the east side to the w., 48.03
from the east side to the w., 48.04
from the east side to the w., 48.05
from the east side to the w., 48.06
from the east side to the w., 48.07
from the east side to the w., 48.08
from the east side to the w., 48.08
and the w. side four thousand five 48.16
and on the w. two hundred and fifty 48.17
east, and ten thousand to the w., 48.18
thousand cubits to the w. border, 48.21
from the east side to the w., 48.23
from the east side to the w., 48.24
from the east side to the w., 48.25
from the east side to the w., 48.26
from the east side to the w., 48.27
On the w. side, which is to be four 48.34
came from the w. across the face Dan 8.05
shall come trembling from the w.; Hos 11.10
ones go toward the w. country, Zec 6.06
country and from the w. country; 8.07
from east to w. by a very wide 14.04
from east and w. and sit at table Mt 8.11
out by means of them, from east to w., * 16.08
east and shines as far as the w., 24.27
you see a cloud rising in the w., Lk 12.54
And men will come from east and w., 13.29
gates, and on the w. three gates. Rev 21.13

WESTERN
"For the w. boundary, you shall have Num 34.06
this shall be your w. boundary. 34.06
the river Euphrates, to the w. sea. Deu 11.24
of Judah as far as the W. Sea, 34.02
turning on the w. side southward Jos 18.14
This forms the w. side. 18.14
from the w. to the eastern boundary Eze 45.07
at the extreme w. end of them. 46.19
cubits in breadth on the w. side, 48.10
sea, and his rear into the w. sea; Joe 2.20
sea and half of them to the w. sea; Zec 14.08

WESTWARD
and southward and eastward and w.; Gen 13.14
the tabernacle w. you shall make Ex 26.22
of the tabernacle at the rear w. 26.27
the tabernacle w. he made six 36.27
of the tabernacle at the rear w. 36.32
up your eyes w. and northward and Deu 3.27
then it goes down w. to the territory Jos 16.03
boundary goes w. to the brook 16.08
up through the hill country w.; 18.12
then its boundary goes up w., 19.11
boundary turns w. to Aznothtabor, 19.34
and w. Gezer and its towns, Shechem 1Ch 7.28
of Israel w. of the Jordan for all 26.30
and w. from the twenty-five thousand Eze 48.21
ram charging w. and northward and Dan 8.04

WET
They are w. with the rain of the Job 24.08
for my head is w. with dew, Sol 5.02
Let him be w. with the dew of Dan 4.15
and let him be w. with the dew of 4.23
you shall be w. with the dew of 4.25
his body was w. with the dew of 4.33
his body was w. with the dew of 5.21
she began to w. his feet with her Lk 7.38
but she has w. my feet with her 7.44

WHALE
nights in the belly of the w., Mt 12.40

WHATEVER
and w. the man called every living Gen 2.19
w. Sarah says to you, do as she 21.12
now then, w. God has said to you, do." 31.16
and w. you say to me I will give. 34.11
and w. was in the city and in the 34.28
and w. was done there, he was the 39.22
and w. he did, the LORD made it 39.23
w. is the first to open the womb Ex 13.02
of his life w. is laid upon him. 21.30
w. touches the altar shall become 29.37
w. touches them will become holy. 30.29
of w. sort the uncleanness may be Lev 5.03
W. touches its flesh shall be holy; 6.27
Moreover you shall eat no blood w., 7.26
W. parts the hoof and is cloven-footed 11.03
but w. touches their carcass shall 11.36
W. goes on its belly, and whatever 11.42
and w. goes on all fours, or whatever 11.42
or w. has many feet, all the swarming 11.42
w. be the use of the skin, the 13.51
uncleanness, w. his uncleanness may be— 22.05
w. had to be done for the people of Num 3.38
w. any man gives to the priest 5.10
w. good the LORD will do to us, the 10.32
have given you w. is kept of the 18.08
And w. the unclean person touches 19.22
and w. you say to me I will do; 22.17
and w. he shows me I will tell you." 23.03
then w. proceeds out of her lips 30.12
and w. cannot stand the fire, you 31.23
every man doing w. is right in his Deu 12.08
w. has fins and scales you may eat. 14.09
And w. does not have fins and 14.10
and spend the money for w. you desire, 14.26
w. your appetite craves; and you shall 14.26
but w. of yours is with your 15.03
sufficient for his need, w. it may be. 15.08
or has any serious blemish w., 15.21
which is a blemish, any defect w.; 17.01
w. you command him, shall be put to Jos 1.18
do to us w. seems good to thee; Ju 10.15
do w. your hand finds to do, for God 1Sa 10.07
may do to us w. seems good to you." 11.10
"Do w. seems good to you." But the 14.36
"W. you say, I will do for you." 20.04
loaves of bread, or w. is here." 21.03
Pray, give w. you have at hand to 25.08
are ready to do w. my lord the 2Sa 15.15
So w. you hear from the king's house, 15.35
"W. seems best to you I will do." 18.04
and do for him w. seems good to you." 19.37
will do for him w. seems good to 19.38
forth from there to any place w. 1Ki 2.36
go forth and go to any place w., 2.42
w. plague, w. sickness there is; 8.37
w. prayer, w. supplication is made 8.38
by w. way thou shalt send them, and 8.44
and w. Solomon desired to build in 9.19
w. she asked besides what was given 10.13
and lay hands on w. pleases them, 20.06
do w. is good in your eyes." 2Ki 10.05
w. you impose on me I will bear." 18.14
Hebronites of w. genealogy or 1Ch 26.31
and we will cut w. timber you need 2Ch 2.16
w. plague, w. sickness there is; 6.28

WHATEVER (cont.)

w. prayer, w. supplication is made 2Ch 6.29
by w. way thou shalt send them, and 6.34
and w. Solomon desired to build in 8.06
w. she asked besides what she had 9.12
in w. place he sojourns, be assisted Ez 1.04
And w. is needed—young bulls, rams, 6.09
W. seems good to you and your 7.18
And w. else is required for the 7.20
W. Ezra the priest, the scribe of 7.21
W. is commanded by the God of 7.23
she was given w. she desired to Est 2.13
W. is under the whole heaven is Job 41.11
w. passes along the paths of the Ps 8.08
the heavens; he does w. he pleases. 115.03
W. the LORD pleases he does, in 135.06
and w. you get, get insight. Pro 4.07
And w. my eyes desired I did not Ecc 2.10
I know that w. God does endures for 3.14
W. has come to be has already been 6.10
unpleasant, for he does w. he pleases. 8.03
W. your hands find to do, do it with 9.10
and w. I command you you shall Jer 1.07
and w. the LORD answers you I will 42.04
and w. the LORD our God says 42.20
but in w. direction the front wheel Eze 10.11
In w. tribe the alien resides, there 47.23
and w. beasts may be in those camps Zec 14.15
So w. you wish that men would do to Mt 7.12
And w. town or village you enter, 10.11
oath to give her w. she might ask. 14.07
not see that w. goes into the 15.17
and w. you bind on earth shall be 16.19
and w. you loose on earth shall be 16.19
but did to him w. they pleased. 17.12
w. you bind on earth shall be bound 18.18
and w. you loose on earth shall be 18.18
and w. is right I will give you.' 20.04
And w. you ask in prayer, you will 21.22
and observe w. they tell you, 23.03
and w. blasphemies they utter; Mk 3.28
"Ask me for w. you wish, and I will 6.22
"W. you ask me, I will give you, even 6.23
not see that w. goes into a man 7.18
they did to him w. they pleased, 9.13
you to do for us w. we ask of you." 10.35
w. you ask in prayer, believe that 11.24
but say w. is given you in that 13.11
And w. house you enter, stay there, Lk 9.04
W. house you enter, first say, 'Peace 10.05
and w. more you spend, I will repay 10.35
will rise and give him w. he needs. 11.08
W. you have said in the dark shall 12.03
the servants, "Do w. he tells you." Jn 2.05
was healed of w. disease he had. *5.04
for w. he does, that the Son does 5.19
now I know that w. you ask from 11.22
W. you ask in my name, I will do it, 14.13
ask w. you will, and it shall be 15.07
so that w. you ask the Father in my 15.16
but w. he hears he will speak, and 16.13
listen to him in w. he tells you. Ac 3.22
to do w. thy hand and thy plan had 4.28
they put on board w. we needed. 28.10
Now we know that w. the law says it Rom 3.19
for w. does not proceed from faith 14.23
For w. was written in former days 15.04
and help her in w. she may require 16.02
in w. state each was called, there 1Co 7.24
Eat w. is sold in the meat market 10.25
eat w. is set before you without 10.27
or w. you do, do all to the glory of 10.31
But w. any one dares to boast of—I 2Co 11.21
for w. a man sows, that he will also Gal 6.07
knowing that w. good any one does, Eph 6.08
But w. gain I had, I counted as loss Php 3.07
w. is true, w. is honorable, w. is just, 4.08
w. is pure, w. is lovely, 4.08
w. is gracious, if there is any 4.08
in w. state I am, to be content. 4.11
And w. you do, in word or deed, do Col 3.17
W. your task, work heartily, as 3.23
and w. else is contrary to sound 1Ti 1.10
for w. overcomes a man, to that he 2Pe 2.19
and we received from him w. we ask, 1Jn 3.22
For w. is born of God overcomes the 5.04
know that he hears us in w. we ask, 5.15
men revile w. they do not understand, Jud 1.10

WHEAT

In the days of w. harvest Reuben Gen 30.14
But the w. and the spelt were not Ex 9.32
shall make them of fine w. flour. 29.02
the first fruits of w. harvest, 34.22
a land of w. and barley, of vines Deu 8.08
goats, with the finest of the w.— 32.14
was beating out w. in the wine Ju 6.11
a while, at the time of w. harvest, 15.01
end of the barley and w. harvests; Ru 2.33
reaping their w. harvest in the 1Sa 6.13
Is it not w. harvest today? 12.17
of the house had been cleaning w., 2Sa 4.06
w., barley, meal, parched grain, beans 17.28
thousand cors of w. as food for his 1Ki 5.11
Now Ornan was threshing w.; 1Ch 21.20
and the w. for a cereal offering. 21.23
twenty thousand cors of crushed w., 2Ch 2.10
Now therefore the w. and barley, 2.15
thousand cors of w. and ten thousand 27.05
w., salt, wine, or oil, as the priests Ez 6.09
silver, a hundred measures of w., 7.22
let thorns grow instead of w., Job 31.40
feed you with the finest of the w., Ps 81.16
you with the finest of the w. 147.14
Your belly is a heap of w., Sol 7.02
and put in w. in rows and barley in Is 28.25
They have sown w. and have reaped Jer 12.13
What has straw in common with w.? 23.28
kill us, for we have stores of w., 41.08
"And you, take w. and barley, beans Eze 4.09
exchanged for your merchandise w., 27.17
of an ephah from each homer of w., 45.13
vinedressers, for the w. and the barley; Joe 1.11
and take from him exactions of w., Amo 5.11
that we may offer w. for sale, 8.05
and sell the refuse of the w.? 8.06
and gather his w. into the granary, Mt 3.12
weeds among the w., and went away. 13.25
you root up the w. along with them 13.29
but gather the w. into my barn.'" 13.30
to gather the w. into his granary, Lk 3.17
He said, 'A hundred measures of w.' 16.07
that he might sift you like w., 22.31
a grain of w. falls into the earth Jn 12.24
throwing out the w. into the sea. Ac 27.38
perhaps of w. or of some other 1Co 15.37
"A quart of w. for a denarius, and Rev 6.06
wine, oil, fine flour and w., 18.13

WHEEL

the height of a w. was a cubit and 1Ki 7.32
wheels were made like a chariot w.; 7.33
and drives the w. over them. Pro 20.26
or the w. broken at the cistern, Ecc 12.06
nor is a cart w. rolled over cummin; Is 28.27
drives his cart w. over it with 28.28
and there he was working at his w. Jer 18.03
I saw a w. upon the earth beside Eze 1.15
as it were a w. within a w. 1.16
he went in and stood beside a w. 10.06
likeness, as if a w. were within a w. 10.10
the front w. faced the others 10.11
and rumble of w., galloping horse Nah 3.02

WHEELS

clogging their chariot w. so that Ex 14.25
had four bronze w. and axles of 1Ki 7.30
And the four w. were underneath the 7.32
axles of the w. were of one piece 7.32
The w. were made like a chariot 7.33
and their w. like the whirlwind. Is 5.28
at the rumbling of their w., Jer 47.03
appearance of the w. and their Eze 1.16
The four w. had rims and they had 1.18
the w. went beside them; 1.19
rose from the earth, the w. rose. 1.19
and the w. rose along with them; 1.20
the living creatures was in the w. 1.20
the w. rose along with them; 1.21
the living creatures was in the w. 1.21
the sound of the w. beside them, 3.13
the whirling w. underneath the 10.02
fire from between the whirling w., 10.06
there were four w. beside the 10.09
appearance of the w. was like 10.09
and the w. were full of eyes round 10.12
the w. that the four of them had. 10.12
As for the w., they were called in 10.13
in my hearing the whirling w. 10.13
the w. went beside them; 10.16
the w. did not turn from beside 10.16
forth, with the w. beside them; 10.19
wings, with the w. beside them; 11.22
its w. were burning fire. Dan 7.09

WHELP

Judah is a lion's w.; from the prey, Gen 49.09
of Dan he said, "Dan is a lion's w., Deu 33.22

WHELPS

and the w. of the lioness are scattered. Job 4.11
they shall growl like lions' w. Jer 51.38
of young lions, rearing her w. Eze 19.02
And she brought up one of her w.; 19.03
another of her w. and made him a 19.05
enough for his w. and strangled Nah 2.12

WHENCE

Casluhim (w. came the Philistines), Gen 10.14
I did not ask him w. he was, Ju 13.06
are you going? and w. do you come?" 19.17
w. shall I help you? from the threshing 2Ki 6.27
And w. did they come to you?" 20.14
Casluhim (w. come the Philistines), 1Ch 1.12
said to Satan, "W. have you come?" Job 1.07
said to Satan, "W. have you come?" 2.02
before I go w. I shall not return, 10.21
go the way w. I shall not return. 16.22
"W. then comes wisdom? And where is 28.20
to the hills. From w. does my help come? Ps 121.01
And w. did they come to you?" Is 39.03
w. then have these come?' " 49.21
And w. do you come? What is your Jon 1.08
w. shall I seek comforters for her? Nah 3.07
The baptism of John, w. was it? Mt 21.25
that they did not know w. it was. Lk 20.07
you do not know w. it comes or Jn 3.08
for I know w. I have come and 8.14
you do not know w. I come or 8.14
white robes, and w. have they come? Rev 7.13

WHENEVER

W. the stronger of the flock were Gen 30.41
W. Moses held up his hand, Israel Ex 17.11
and w. he lowered his hand, Amalek 17.11
W. Moses went out to the tent, all 33.08
but w. Moses went in before the 34.34
w. the cloud was taken up from over 40.36
And w. the cloud was taken up from Num 9.17
is to be blown w. they are to set 10.06
w. they set out from the camp. 10.34
And w. the ark set out, Moses said, 10.35
is to us, w. we call upon him? Deu 4.07
W. they marched out, the hand of the Ju 2.15
W. the LORD raised up judges for 2.18
But w. the judge died, they turned 2.19
For w. the Israelites put in seed 6.03
And w. the evil spirit from God was 1Sa 16.23
And w. a man came near to do 2Sa 15.05
ear to them w. they call to thee. 1Ki 8.52
So w. he passed that way, he would 2Ki 4.08
so that w. he comes to us, he can go 4.10
And w. they saw that there was much 12.10
and w. burnt offerings are offered 1Ch 23.31
w. David offered praises by their 2Ch 7.06
w. a case comes to you from your 19.10
And w. the chest was brought to the 24.11
For w. I speak, I cry out, I shout, Jer 20.08
that w. you spoke of him you wagged 48.27
w. you hear a word from my mouth, Eze 3.17
w. you have said, 'Says the LORD,' 13.07
w. you hear a word from my mouth, 33.07
And w. the unclean spirits beheld Mk 3.11
And w. you stand praying, forgive, if 11.25
and w. you will, you can do good to 14.07
W. you enter a town and they Lk 10.08
But w. enter a town and they do 10.10
to this day w. Moses is read a veil 2Co 3.15
w. our hearts condemn us; 1Jn 3.20
And w. the living creatures give Rev 4.09

WHERE

land of Havilah, w. there is gold; Gen 2.11
man, and said to him, "W. are you?" 3.09
"W. is Abel your brother?" 4.09
to the place w. his tent had been 13.03
to the place w. he had made an 13.04
and look from the place w. you are, 13.14
"Hagar, maid of Sarai, w. have you come 16.08
you come from and w. are you going?" 16.08
"W. is Sarah your wife?" And he said, 18.09
"W. are the men who came to you 19.05
to the place w. he had stood 19.27
dwell w. it pleases you." 20.15
the voice of the lad w. he is. 21.17
with the land w. you have sojourned." 21.23
but w. is the lamb for a burnt 22.07
w. do you come from?" They said, 29.04
w. the flocks came to drink. 30.38
into the field w. his flock was, 31.04
w. you anointed a pillar and made a 31.13
W. are you going? And whose are 32.17
in the place w. he had spoken with 35.13
in the place w. he had spoken with 35.14
of the place w. God had spoken 35.15
w. Abraham and Isaac had sojourned. 35.27
w. they are pasturing the flock." 37.16
is gone; and I, w. shall I go?" 37.30
"W. is the harlot who was at Enaim 38.21
the place w. the king's prisoners 39.20
in the prison w. Joseph was confined. 40.03
"W. do you come from?" he said. 42.07
to his daughters, "And w. is he? Ex 2.20
w. my people dwell, so that no 8.22
w. the people of Israel were, there 9.26
of Israel had light w. they dwelt. 10.23
you, upon the houses w. you are; 12.13
was not a house w. one was not 12.30
w. there were twelve springs of 15.27
the wilderness w. he was encamped 18.05
near to the thick cloud w. God was. 20.21
in every place w. I cause my name 20.24
w. I will meet with you, to speak 29.42
w. I will meet with you. 30.06
tent of meeting w. I shall meet 30.36
a place by me w. you shall stand 33.21
w. the ashes are poured out, and Lev 4.12
w. the ashes are poured out it 4.12

WHERE (cont.)
it in the place w. they kill the Lev 4.24
in the place w. they kill the 4.33
In the place w. the burnt offering 6.25
in the place w. they kill the burnt 7.02
in the place w. they kill the sin 14.13
in the place w. the blood of the 14.28
w. you dwelt, and you shall not do 18.03
that the land w. I am bringing you 20.22
in the place w. the cloud settled Num 9.17
W. am I to get meat to give to all 11.13
into the land w. I swore that I 14.30
testimony, w. I meet with you. 17.04
w. the people of Israel contended 20.13
w. there was no way to turn either 22.26
cities in the places w. they dwelt, 31.10
w. there was no water for the 33.14
you in the land w. you dwell. 33.55
w. you shall permit the manslayer 35.06
w. you have seen how the LORD your Deu 1.31
the nations w. the LORD will drive 4.27
thirsty ground w. there was no 8.15
w. you sowed your seed and watered 11.10
all the places w. the nations whom 12.02
w. he lives—and he may come when 18.06
you shall let her go w. she will; 21.14
the gate of the place w. he lives, 21.19
w. it pleases him best; you shall not 23.16
all the peoples w. the LORD will 28.37
w. no grass can sprout, an overthrow 29.23
all the nations w. the LORD your 30.01
all the peoples w. the LORD your 30.03
w. they go to be among them, and 31.16
'W. are their gods, the rock in 32.37
I did not know w. they came from; Jos 2.04
w. the men went I do not know; 2.05
the very place w. the priests' 4.03
in the place w. you lodge tonight." 4.03
them to the place w. they lodged, 4.08
in the place w. the feet of the 4.09
for the place w. you stand is holy." 5.15
open wilderness w. they pursued 8.24
And w. do you come from?" 9.08
into the cave w. they had hidden 10.27
in the land w. your possession 22.04
the LORD's land w. the LORD's 22.19
the land w. the Reubenites and the 22.33
w. he sank, there he fell dead. Ju 5.27
And w. are all his wonderful deeds 6.13
"W. are the men whom you slew at 8.18
"W. is your mouth now, you who said, 9.38
to live w. he could find a place; 17.08
said to him, "From w. do you come?" 17.09
to sojourn w. I may find a place." 17.09
a place w. there is no lack of 18.10
the old man said, "W. are you going? 19.17
the man's house w. her master was, 19.26
the same place w. they had formed 20.22
set out from the place w. she was, Ru 1.07
for w. you go I will go, and 1.16
and w. you lodge I will lodge; 1.16
w. you die I will die, and there 1.17
"W. did you glean today? And w. have 2.19
down, observe the place w. he lies; 3.04
w. the two sons of Eli, Hophni and 1Sa 1.03
of the LORD, w. the ark of God was. 3.03
to the city w. the man of God was. 9.10
"Tell me w. is the house of the 9.18
w. there is a garrison of the 10.05
and to his servant, "W. did you go?" 10.14
of the holes w. they have hid 14.11
my father in the field w. you are, 19.03
"W. are Samuel and David?" 19.22
go to the place w. you hid yourself 20.19
and see the place w. his haunt is, 23.22
all the lurking places w. he hides, 23.23
w. there was a cave; and Saul 24.03
men who come from I do not know w.?" 25.11
to the place w. Saul had encamped; 26.05
David saw the place w. Saul lay, 26.05
And now see w. the king's spear is, 26.16
w. those stayed who were left 30.09
And w. are you from?" He said, 30.13
all the places w. David and his 30.31
"W. do you come from?" And he said, 2Sa 1.03
"W. do you come from?" And he answered, 1.13
he fell there, and died w. he was. 2.23
to the place w. Asahel had fallen 2.23
In all places w. I have moved with 7.07
The king said to him, "W. is he?" 9.04
to the place w. he knew there were 11.16
w. he was lying down. And she took 13.08
As for me, w. could I carry my shame? 13.13
with us, seeing I go I know not w.? 15.20
w. God was worshiped, behold, Hushai 15.32
"And w. is your master's son 16.03
in some place w. he is to be found, 17.12
"W. are Ahimaaz and Jonathan 17.20
w. the Philistines had hanged them, 21.12
w. there was a man of great stature, 21.20
w. there was a plot of ground full 23.11
to the place w. it was required, 1Ki 4.28
of the Throne w. he was to pronounce 7.07
His own house w. he was to dwell, in 7.08
w. the LORD made a covenant with 8.09
w. he had knelt with hands outstretched 8.54
the city w. I have chosen to put my 11.36
it in the city w. the old prophet 13.25
w. he lodged, and laid him upon his 17.19
w. he has gone to take possession. 21.18
"In the place w. dogs licked up the 21.19
"W. is the LORD, the God of Elijah?" 2Ki 2.14
w. a wealthy woman lived, who urged 4.08
"W. have you been, Gehazi?" 5.25
the place w. we dwell under your 6.01
man of God said, "W. did it fall?" When he 6.06
"Go and see w. he is, that I may 6.13
w. the Syrians wounded Joram. 8.28
w. the LORD commanded, "The fathers 14.06
w. they dwell to this day. 16.06
W. are the gods of Hamath and Arpad? 18.34
W. are the gods of Sepharvaim, Hena, 18.34
W. is the king of Hamath, the king 19.13
w. the women wove hangings for the 23.07
the high places w. the priests had 23.08
w. he reigned for seven years and 1Ch 3.04
w. they found rich, good pasture, and 4.40
w. the Jebusites were, the inhabitants 11.04
In all places w. I have moved with 17.06
w. there was a man of great stature, 20.06
w. the LORD had appeared to David 2Ch 3.01
w. the LORD made a covenant with 5.10
the place w. thou hast promised to 6.20
him from all places w. they lived. 11.13
w. the LORD commanded, "The fathers 25.04
of the archives w. the documents Ez 6.01
the place w. sacrifices are offered 6.03
w. he spent the night, neither 10.06
did not know w. I had gone or what Neh 2.16
in a land w. they are captives. 4.04
all the places w. they live they 4.12
In the place w. you hear the sound 4.20
w. are the vessels of the sanctuary, 10.39
a large chamber w. they had 13.05
and w. is he, that would presume to Est 7.05
to the place w. they were drinking 7.08
falling on the couch w. Esther was; 7.08
Or w. were the upright cut off? Job 4.07
and w. the snow hides itself. 6.16
"Can papyrus grow w. there is no 8.11
reeds flourish w. there is no 8.11
and chaos, w. light is as darkness." 10.22
breathes his last, and w. is he? 14.10
for bread, saying, 'W. is it?' 15.23

WHERE (cont.)

w. then is my hope? Who will see Job 17.15
and no survivor w. he used to live. 18.19
have seen him will say, 'W. is he?' 20.07
For you say, 'W. is the house of the 21.28
W. is the tent in which the wicked 21.28
that I knew w. I might find him, 23.03
in a valley away from w. men live; 28.04
"But w. shall wisdom be found? 28.12
And w. is the place of understanding? 28.12
And w. is the place of understanding? 28.20
deep darkness w. evildoers may 34.22
'W. is God my Maker, who gives songs 35.10
a broad place w. there was no 36.16
"W. were you when I laid the 38.04
"W. is the way to the dwelling of 38.19
and w. is the place of darkness, 38.19
to the place w. the light is 38.24
or w. the east wind is scattered 38.24
to bring rain on a land w. no man is, 38.26
and w. the slain are, there is he." 39.30
down the wicked w. they stand. 40.12
food for him w. all the wild 40.20
and the place w. thy glory dwells. Ps 26.08
from w. he sits enthroned he looks 33.14
not rise again from w. he lies." 41.08
to me continually, "W. is your God?" 42.03
to me continually, "W. is your God?" 42.10
dry and weary land w. no water is. 63.01
w. the LORD will dwell for ever? 68.16
w. there is no foothold; I have come 69.02
Mount Zion, w. thou hast dwelt. 74.02
the tent w. he dwelt among men, 78.60
the nations say, "W. is their God?" 79.10
w. she may lay her young, at thy 84.03
Lord, w. is thy steadfast love of 89.49
the nations say, "W. is their God?" 115.02
In the path w. I walk they have 142.03
W. there is no guidance, a people Pro 11.14
W. there are no oxen, there is no 14.04
the prudent looks w. he is going. 14.15
dinner of herbs w. love is than a 15.17
and w. there is no whisperer, 26.20
W. there is no prophecy the people 29.18
hastens to the place w. it rises. Ecc 1.05
to the place w. the streams flow, 1.07
in the city w. they had done such 8.10
in the place w. the tree falls, 11.03
w. you pasture your flock, w. you Sol 1.07
day every place w. there used to Is 7.23
become a place w. cattle are let 7.25
are let loose and w. sheep tread. 7.25
and w. will you leave your wealth? 10.03
W. then are your wise men? 19.12
Ariel, the city w. David encamped! 29.01
from w. come the lioness and the 30.06
"W. is he who counted, w. is he who 33.18
w. is he who counted the towers?" 33.18
w. no galley with oars can go, nor 33.21
W. are the gods of Hamath and Arpad? 36.19
W. are the gods of Sepharviam? 36.19
W. are the king of Hamath, the king 37.13
"W. is your mother's bill of divorce, 50.01
And w. is the fury of the oppressor? 51.13
W. is he who brought up out of the 63.11
W. is he who put in the midst of 63.11
W. are thy zeal and thy might? 63.15
w. our fathers praised thee, has 64.11
'W. is the LORD who brought us up Jer 2.06
passes through, w. no man dwells?' 2.06
did not say, 'W. is the LORD?' 2.08
But w. are your gods that you made 2.28
W. have you not been lain with? 3.02
w. the good way is; and walk in it, 6.16
w. I made my name dwell at first, 7.12
all the places w. I have driven 8.03
from the place w. I had hidden it. 13.07
W. is the flock that was given you, 13.20
when they ask you, 'W. shall we go?' 15.02
the countries w. he had driven 16.15
"W. is the word of the LORD? 17.15
w. the LORD had sent him to prophesy, 19.14
but in the place w. they have 22.12
w. you were not born, and there you 22.26
the countries w. I have driven 23.03
the countries w. he had driven 23.08
all the places w. I shall drive 24.09
of the city w. I have sent you 29.07
all the places w. I have driven 29.14
all the nations w. I have driven 29.18
shall stand w. it used to be. 30.18
days in the land w. you sojourn.' 35.07
and let no one know w. you are." 36.19
W. are your prophets who prophesied 37.19
w. we shall not see war, or hear the 42.14
in the place w. you desire to go 42.22
land of Egypt w. you have come to 44.08
"W. is bread and wine?" Lam 2.12
the nations w. they are carried Eze 6.09
w. was the seat of the image of 8.03
in the countries w. they have gone.' 11.16
the countries w. you have been 11.17
among the nations w. they go, 12.16
'W. is the daubing with which you 13.12
and its roots remained w. it stood. 17.06
From the bed w. it was planted 17.07
wither away on the bed w. it grew?" 17.10
in the place w. the king dwells 17.16
the countries w. you are scattered, 20.34
out of the land w. they sojourn, 20.38
the countries w. you have been 20.41
right and left w. your edge is 21.16
In the place w. you were created, in 21.30
from all places w. they have been 34.12
in the land w. your fathers dwelt 37.25
the land w. people were gathered 38.08
w. the burnt offering was to be 40.38
w. the outside wall begins. 42.10
w. one enters the passage, and 42.12
w. the priests who approach the 42.13
w. I will dwell in the midst of the 43.07
is the place w. the priests shall 46.20
and w. they shall bake the cereal 46.20
the kitchens w. those who minister 46.24
will live w. the river goes. 47.09
to his house w. he had windows in Dan 6.10
came near to the den w. Daniel was, 6.20
So he came near w. I stood; 8.17
in the place w. it was said to Hos 1.10
W. now is your king, to save you; 13.10
w. are all your princes, to defend 13.10
O Death, w. are your plagues? 13.14
O Sheol, w. is your destruction? 13.14
the peoples, 'W. is their God?'" Joe 2.17
"W. is the LORD your God?" Mic 7.10
W. is the lions' den, the cave of Nah 2.11
w. the lion brought his prey, w. his cubs 2.11
no one knows w. they are. 3.17
Your fathers, w. are they? Zec 1.05
Then I said, "W. are you going?" 2.02
"W. are they taking the ephah?" 5.10
then I am a father, w. is my honor? Mal 1.06
if I am a master, w. is my fear? 1.06
"W. is the God of justice?" 2.17
"W. is he who has been born king of Mt 2.02
inquired of them w. the Christ was 2.04
over the place w. the child was. 2.09
on earth, w. moth and rust consume 6.19
and w. thieves break in and steal, 6.19
w. neither moth nor rust consumes 6.20
and w. thieves do not break in and 6.20
For w. your treasure is, there will 6.21
the cities w. most of his mighty 11.20

WHERE (cont.)

w. they had not much soil, and Mt 13.05
"W. did this man get this wisdom 13.54
W. then did this man get all this? 13.56
"W. are we to get bread enough in 15.33
For w. two or three are gathered in 18.20
reaping w. you did not sow, and 25.24
and gathering w. you did not winnow; 25.24
that I reap w. I have not sowed, 25.26
and gather w. I have not winnowed? 25.26
"W. will you have us prepare for 26.17
w. the scribes and the elders had 26.57
Come, see the place w. he lay. 28.06
w. it had not much soil, and immediately Mk 4.05
w. the word is sown; when they hear 4.15
him, and went in w. the child was. 5.40
"W. did this man get all this? 6.02
"W. you enter a house, stay there 6.10
to any place w. they heard he was. 6.55
w. their worm does not die, and the 9.48
sacrilege set up w. it ought not to 13.14
"W. will you have us go and prepare 14.12
W. is my guest room, w. I am to eat 14.14
mother of Joses saw w. he was laid. 15.47
see the place w. they laid him. 16.06
w. he had been brought up; Lk 4.16
found the place w. it was written, 4.17
He said to them, "W. is your faith?" 8.25
town and place w. he himself was 10.01
as he journeyed, came to w. he was; 10.33
w. no thief approaches and no moth 12.33
For w. your treasure is, there will 12.34
'I do not know w. you come from.' 13.25
I do not know w. you come from; 13.27
ten cleaned? W. are the nine? 17.17
And they said to him, "W., Lord?" 17.37
"W. the body is, there the eagles 17.37
w. on entering you will find a colt 19.30
w. he calls the Lord the God of 20.37
"W. will you have us prepare it?" 22.09
W. is the guest room, w. I am to eat 22.11
w. no one had ever yet been laid. 23.53
beyond the Jordan w. John was baptizing. Jn 1.28
teacher), w. are you staying?" 1.38
came and saw w. he was staying; 1.39
did not know w. it came from 2.09
The wind blows w. it wills, and you 3.08
w. do you get that living water? 4.11
is the place w. men ought to 4.20
w. he had made the water wine. 4.46
near the place w. they are the 6.23
of man ascending w. he was before? 6.62
at the feast, and saying, "W. is he?" 7.11
Yet we know w. this man comes from; 7.27
no one will know w. he comes from." 7.27
me, and you know w. I come from? 7.28
w. I am you cannot come." 7.34
"W. does this man intend to go that 7.35
'W. I am you cannot come'?" 7.36
Bethlehem, the village w. David was?" 7.42
"Woman, w. are they? Has no one * 8.10
him therefore, "W. is your Father?" 8.19
w. I am going, you cannot come." 8.21
'W. I am going, you cannot come'?" 8.22
They said to him, "W. is he?" 9.12
we do not know w. he comes from." 9.29
You do not know w. he comes from, 9.30
to the place w. John at first 10.40
days longer in the place w. he was. 11.06
in the place w. Martha had met him. 11.30
when she came w. Jesus was and saw 11.32
and he said, "W. have you laid him?" 11.34
that if any one knew w. he was, 11.57
w. Lazarus was, whom Jesus had 12.01
and w. I am, there shall my servant 12.26
darkness does not know w. he goes. 12.35
'W. I am going you cannot come.' 13.33
to him, "Lord, w. are you going?" 13.36
"W. I am going you cannot follow me 13.36
that w. I am you may be also. 14.03
And you know the way w. I am going." 14.04
we do not know w. you are going; 14.05
of you asks me, 'W. are we going?' 16.05
given me, may be with me w. I am, 17.24
w. there was a garden, which he and 18.01
w. all Jews come together; 18.20
and said to Jesus, "W. are you from?" 19.09
for the place w. Jesus was crucified 19.20
Now in the place w. he was crucified 19.41
a new tomb w. no one had ever been 19.41
we do not know w. they have laid 20.02
sitting w. the body of Jesus had 20.12
I do not know w. they have laid 20.13
tell me w. you have laid him, and I 20.15
being shut w. the disciples were, 20.19
yourself and walked w. you would; 21.18
and carry you w. you do not wish 21.18
w. they were staying, Peter and John Ac 1.13
all the house w. they were sitting. 2.02
w. he became the father of two sons. 7.29
for the place w. you are standing 7.33
w. many were gathered together and 12.12
w. they had been commended to the 14.26
in every city w. we proclaimed the 15.36
w. we supposed there was a place of 16.13
w. there was a synagogue of the 17.01
w. we stayed for seven days. 20.06
upper chamber w. we were gathered. 20.08
w. I ought to be tried; to the Jews 25.10
but w. there is no law there is no Rom 4.15
is not counted w. there is no law. 5.13
but w. sin increased, grace abounded 5.20
the very place w. it was said to 9.26
not w. Christ has already been 15.20
W. is the wise man? W. is the scribe? 1Co 1.20
W. is the debater of this age? 1.20
w. would be the hearing? If the whole 12.17
w. would be the sense of smell? 12.17
single organ, w. would the body be? 12.19
"O death, w. is thy victory? 15.55
O death, w. is thy sting?" 15.55
and w. the Spirit of the Lord is, 2Co 3.17
w. Christ is, seated at the right Col 3.01
w. your fathers put me to the test Heb 3.09
w. Jesus has gone as a forerunner 6.20
For w. a will is involved, the death 9.16
W. there is forgiveness of these, 10.18
out, not knowing w. he was to go. 11.08
For w. jealousy and selfish ambition Jas 3.16
w. will the impious and sinner 1Pe 4.18
and saying, "W. is the promise of 2Pe 3.04
and does not know w. he is going, 1Jn 2.11
"I know w. you dwell, w. Satan's throne Rev 2.13
killed among you, w. Satan dwells. 2.13
w. their Lord was crucified. 11.08
w. she has a place prepared by God, 12.06
to the place w. she is to be 12.14
w. the harlot is seated, are peoples 17.15
the great city w. all who had 18.19
and brimstone w. the beast and the 20.10

WHEREAS

w. it is because of the wickedness Deu 9.04
W. you were as the stars of heaven 28.62
w. I have repaid you evil. 1Sa 24.17
'W. it was in your heart to build a 1Ki 8.18
And now, w. my father laid upon you 12.11
'W. it was in your heart to build a 2Ch 6.08
And now, w. my father laid upon you 10.11
W. you have been forsaken and hated, Is 60.15
w. the sword has reached their very Jer 4.10
And w. the king saw a watcher, a Dan 4.23

WHEREAS (cont.)
w. the aim of our charge is love 1Ti 1.05
w. she who is self-indulgent is 5.06
w. you do not know about tomorrow. Jas 4.14
w. angels, though greater in might 2Pe 2.11

WHEREFORE
W. the people of Israel shall keep Ex 31.16
W. it is said in the Book of the Num 21.14
W., as I live, says the Lord God, Eze 5.11
"W. thus says the Lord God: Behold, 13.20
"W., O harlot, hear the word of the 16.35
W. say to the house of Israel, Thus 20.30
"W., O King Agrippa, I was not Ac 26.19

WHEREIN
and see w. his great strength lies, Ju 16.05
"Please tell me w. your great 16.06
not told me w. your great strength 16.15
And he said, "W. have I sinned, that 1Ki 18.09
"Let the day perish w. I was born, Job 3.03

WHEREON
w. hang a thousand bucklers, all of Sol 4.04

WHEREVER
you and will keep you w. you go, Gen 28.15
Lord has blessed you w. I turned. 30.30
has been with me w. I have gone." 35.03
get your straw w. you can find it; Ex 5.11
w. the lot falls to any man, that Num 33.54
and w. the Lord our God forbade us. Deu 2.37
may have good success w. you go. Jos 1.07
your God is with you w. you go." 1.09
and w. you send us we will go. 1.16
w. he turned he put them to the 1Sa 14.47
was successful w. Saul sent him; 18.05
and they went w. they could go. 23.13
and I have been with you w. you went, 2Sa 7.09
gave victory to David w. he went. 8.06
gave victory to David w. he went. 8.14
w. my lord the king shall be, 15.21
in all that you do and w. you turn; 1Ki 2.03
household, and sojourn w. you can; 2Ki 8.01
the house w. any need of repairs 12.05
w. he went forth, he prospered. 18.07
and I have been with you w. you went, 1Ch 17.08
gave victory to David w. he went. 18.06
gave victory to David w. he went. 18.13
w. the king's command and his decree Est 4.03
w. the king's command and his edict 8.17
gives it, w. he turns he prospers. Pro 17.08
of the Lord; he turns it w. he will. 21.01
go w. you think it good and right Jer 40.04
or go w. you think it right to go." 40.05
w. the spirit would go, they went, Eze 1.12
W. the spirit would go, they went, 1.20
W. you dwell your cities shall be 6.06
w. they offered pleasing odor to 6.13
then w. they saw any high hill or 20.28
w. they came, they profaned my holy 36.20
And w. the river goes every living 47.09
w. they dwell, the sons of men, the Dan 2.38
I will follow you w. you go." Mt 8.19
W. the body is, there the eagles 24.28
w. this gospel is preached in the 26.13
And w. he came, in villages, cities, Mk 6.56
and w. it seizes him, it dashes him 9.18
w. the gospel is preached in the 14.09
and w. he enters, say to the householder, 14.14
And w. they do not receive you, when Lk 9.05
him, "I will follow you w. you go." 9.57
speed me on my journey, w. I go. 1Co 16.06
small rudder w. the will of the Jas 3.04
who follow the Lamb w. he goes; Rev 14.04

WHEREWITH
w. I have made supplication before 1Ki 8.59

WHET
if I w. my glittering sword, and my Deu 32.41
not repent, God will w. his sword; Ps 7.12
who w. their tongues like swords, 64.03
and one does not w. the edge, Ecc 10.10

WHETHER
w. born in his house, or bought Gen 17.12
go down to see w. they have done 18.21
to learn w. the Lord had prospered 24.21
to know w. you are really my son 27.21
w. stolen by day or stolen by night. 31.39
see now w. it is your son's robe or 37.32
w. there is truth in you; 42.16
Egypt and see w. they are still Ex 4.18
w. he is a sojourner or a native of 12.19
w. they will walk in my law or not. 16.04
w. beast or man, he shall not live.' 19.13
w. he sells him or is found in 21.16
w. it is an ox or an ass or a sheep, 22.04
to show w. or not he has put his 22.08
w. it is for ox, for ass, for sheep, 22.09
both to see w. he has not put his 22.11
w. he has seen or come to know the Lev 5.01
w. the carcass of an unclean beast 5.02
w. the uncleanness of man or an 7.21
w. of fowl or animal, in any of 7.26
w. in the seas or in the rivers, you 11.09
w. it is an article of wood or a 11.32
w. oven or stove, it shall be broken 11.35
w. for a son or for a daughter, she 12.06
w. a woolen or a linen garment, 13.47
w. in warp or woof or in skin or in 13.49
w. diseased in warp or woof, woolen 13.52
w. the leprous spot is on the back 13.55
to decide w. it is clean or unclean. 13.59
w. his body runs with his discharge, 15.03
w. it is the bed or anything upon 15.23
w. he is a native or a sojourner, 17.15
w. born at home or born abroad. 18.09
w. in payment of a vow or as a 22.18
And w. the mother is a cow or an ewe, 22.28
w. ox or sheep, it is the Lord's. 27.26
w. of man or beast, or of his 27.28
w. of the seed of the land or of 27.30
not inquire w. it is good or bad, 27.33
W. it was two days, or a month, or a Num 9.22
you shall see w. my word will come 11.23
and w. the people who dwell in it 13.18
w. they are few or many, 13.18
and w. the land that they dwell in 13.19
and w. the cities that they dwell 13.19
and w. the land is rich or poor, and 13.20
and w. there is wood in it or not. 13.20
w. he is native or a sojourner, 15.30
w. man or beast, which they offer to 18.15
w. such a great thing as this has Deu 4.32
w. you would keep his commandments, 8.02
to know w. you love the Lord your 13.03
w. near you or far off from you, 13.07
w. it be ox or sheep: they shall 18.03
w. he is one of your brethren or 24.14
w. the daughter of is father or 27.22
w. the gods your fathers served in Jos 24.15
w. they will take care to walk in Ju 2.22
to know w. Israel would obey the 3.04
we may know w. the journey on 18.05
after young men, w. poor or rich. Ru 3.10
w. small or great, sons or daughters, 1Sa 30.19
'Who knows w. the Lord will be 2Sa 12.22
w. for death or for life, there also 15.21
w. I shall recover from this 2Ki 1.02
w. young or old, man or woman. 2Ch 15.13
w. they belonged to Israel: Ez 2.59
to see w. a decree was issued by 5.17
w. for death or for banishment or 7.26
w. they belonged to Israel: Neh 7.61

WHETHER (cont.)
in order to see w. Mordecai's words Est 3.04
And who knows w. you have not come 4.14
w. it be a nation or a man?— Job 34.29
W. for correction, or for his land, 37.13
w. green or ablaze, may he sweep Ps 58.09
w. what he does is pure and right. Pro 20.11
and who knows w. he will be a wise Ecc 2.19
Who knows w. the spirit of man goes 3.21
w. he eats little or much; 5.12
w. it is love or hate man does not 9.01
or w. both alike will be good. 11.06
secret thing, w. good or evil. 12.14
to see w. the vines had budded, Sol 6.11
w. the pomegranates were in bloom. 6.11
and see w. the vines have budded, 7.12
w. the grape blossoms have opened 7.12
W. it is good or evil, we will obey Jer 42.06
And w. they hear or refuse to hear Eze 2.05
w. they hear or refuse to hear; 2.07
w. they hear or refuse to hear." 3.11
w. bird or beast, that has died of 44.31
Who knows w. he will not turn and Joe 2.14
let us see w. Elijah will come to Mt 27.49
to see w. he would heal him on the Mk 3.02
let us see w. Elijah will come to 15.36
he asked him w. he was already dead. 15.44
w. perhaps he were the Christ, Lk 3.15
to see w. he would heal on the 6.07
w. he has enough to complete it? 14.28
take counsel w. he is able with 14.31
he asked w. the man was a Galilean. 23.06
he shall know w. the teaching is Jn 7.17
is from God or w. I am speaking on 7.17
He answered, "W. he is a sinner, I do 9.25
"W. it is right in the sight of God Ac 4.19
"Tell me w. you sold the land for 5.08
out to ask w. Simon who was called 10.18
I asked w. he wished to go to 25.20
"W. short or long, I would to God 26.29
so then, w. we live or w. we die, Rom 14.08
I do not know w. I baptized any one 1Co 1.16
w. Paul or Apollos or Cephas or the 3.22
Wife, how do you know w. you will 7.16
how do you know w. you will save 7.16
So, w. you eat or drink, or whatever 10.31
W. then it was I or they, so we 15.11
you and know w. you are obedient 2Co 2.09
So w. we are at home or away, we 5.09
w. in the body or out of the body I 12.02
w. in the body or out of the body I 12.03
to see w. you are holding to your 13.05
w. he is a slave or free. Eph 6.08
w. in the pretense or in truth, Christ Php 1.18
in my body, w. by life or by death. 1.20
so that w. I come and see you or am 1.27
w. thrones or dominions or principalities Col 1.16
w. on earth or in heaven, making 1.20
w. from you or from others, though 1Th 2.06
for us so that w. we wake or sleep 5.10
w. it be to the emperor as supreme, 1Pe 2.13
spirits to see w. they are of God; 1Jn 4.01

WHILE
and w. he slept took one of his Gen 2.21
W. the earth remains, seedtime and 8.22
w. Lot dwelt among the cities of 13.12
w. I fetch a morsel of bread, that 18.05
by them under the tree w. they ate. 18.08
"Let the maiden remain with us a w., 24.55
and w. he was still living he sent 25.06
w. Jacob was a quiet man, dwelling 25.27
and stay with him a w., 27.44
W. he was still speaking with them, 29.09
W. Israel dwelt in that land Reuben 35.22
w. you remain in prison, that your 42.16
and wept on his neck a good w. 46.29
w. Moses drew near to the thick Ex 20.21
and w. my glory passes by I will 33.22
w. the rest of the blood shall be Lev 5.09
peace offerings w. an uncleanness 7.20
the house w. it is shut up shall 14.46
her nakedness w. her sister is yet 18.18
her nakedness w. she is in her 18.19
w. he has an uncleanness, that 22.03
w. you are in your enemies' land; 26.34
its sabbaths w. it lies desolate 26.43
w. you were under your husband's Num 5.19
W. the meat was yet between their 11.33
W. the people of Israel were in the 15.32
minister to you w. you and your 18.02
offering, w. I meet the LORD yonder." 23.15
dispossessed w. Israel does valiantly. 24.18
W. Israel dwelt in Shittim the 25.01
w. they were weeping at the door of 25.06
w. within her father's house, in her 30.03
w. under her vows or any thoughtless 30.06
w. in her youth, within her father's 30.16
go to the war w. you sit here? 32.06
w. the Egyptians were burying all 33.04
w. the Amorites call it Senir), Deu 3.09
w. the mountain burned with fire to 4.11
w. I stood between the LORD and you 5.05
w. the mountain was burning with 5.23
of the tithe w. I was mourning, 26.14
removed any of it w. I was unclean, 26.14
w. your eyes look on and fail with 28.32
behold, w. I am yet alive with you, 31.27
And w. all Israel were passing over Jos 3.17
W. the people of Israel were 5.10
w. the trumpets blew continually. 6.09
w. the trumpets blew continually. 6.13
w. they were going down the ascent 10.11
w. Israel walked in the wilderness; 14.10
Ehud escaped w. they delayed, and Ju 3.26
w. the two companies rushed upon 9.44
W. Israel dwelt in Heshbon and its 11.26
of the altar w. Manoah and his 13.20
And after a w. he returned to take 14.08
After a w., at the time of wheat 15.01
So w. he slept, Delilah took the 16.14
who looked on w. Samson made sport. 16.27
w. the priest stood by the entrance 18.17
w. the meat was boiling, with a 1Sa 2.13
on stop here yourself for a w., 9.27
And w. Saul was talking to the 14.19
w. David was playing the lyre, as he 18.10
w. two hundred remained with the 25.13
all the w. we were with them 25.16
w. the army was encamped around him. 26.05
custom all the w. he dwelt in the 27.11
w. the house of Saul became weaker 2Sa 3.01
W. there was war between the house 3.06
to eat bread w. it was yet day; 3.35
house for a great w. to come, 7.19
w. the child was yet alive, we spoke 12.18
wept for the child w. it was alive; 12.21
He said, "W. the child was still 12.22
W. they were on the way, tidings 13.30
vowed a vow w. I dwelt at Geshur 15.08
And w. Absalom was offering the 15.12
w. Shimei went along on the hillside 16.13
come upon him w. he is weary and 17.02
w. all the army marched out by 18.04
w. the mule that was under him went 18.09
w. he was still alive in the oak. 18.14
king with food w. he stayed at 19.32
w. the eyes of my lord the king 24.03
your foes w. they pursue you 24.13
Then w. you are still speaking with 1Ki 1.14
W. she was still speaking with the 1.22
W. he was still speaking, behold, 1.42
to a child w. she was in the house. 3.17

WHILE (cont.)

w. your maidservant slept, and laid 1Ki 3.20
w. Solomon gave Hiram twenty 5.11
the temple, w. it was being built. 6.07
w. all the assembly of Israel stood 8.14
w. twelve lions stood there, one on 10.20
his father w. he was yet alive, 12.06
And after a w. the brook dried up, 17.07
And in a little w. heavens grew 18.45
w. Benhadad was drinking himself 20.16
w. he tarried at Jericho, and he 2Ki 2.18
and w. he was going up on the way, 2.23
But w. they were eating of the 4.40
And w. he was still speaking with 6.33
And w. he was telling the king how 8.05
w. Athaliah reigned over the land. 11.03
w. their inhabitants, shorn of 19.26
w. his servants were besieging it; 24.11
w. he could not move about freely 1Ch 12.01
w. Obededom, the son of Jeduthun, 16.38
house for a great w. to come, 17.17
w. the sword of your enemies 21.12
w. all the assembly of Israel stood 2Ch 6.03
w. twelve lions stood there, one on 9.19
his father w. he was yet alive, 10.06
w. you are with him. If you seek 15.02
he was captured w. hiding in 22.09
w. Athaliah reigned over the land. 22.12
w. Jehiel, Azaziah, Nahath, Asahel, 31.13
w. he was yet a boy, he began to 34.03
W. they were bringing out the money 34.14
from them w. the Levites flayed 35.11
round me w. I sat appalled until Ez 9.04
W. Ezra prayed and made confession, 10.01
girded at his side w. he built. Neh 4.18
the work stop w. I leave it and 6.03
and w. they are still standing 7.03
w. the people remained in their 8.07
w. nine tenths remained in the 11.01
W. this was taking place I was not 13.06
w. he showed the riches of his Est 1.04
W. they were yet talking with him, 6.14
w. the city of Susa shouted and 8.15
W. he was yet speaking, there came Job 1.16
W. he was yet speaking, there came 1.17
W. he was yet speaking, there came 1.18
w. thy eyes are upon me, I shall be 7.08
W. yet in flower and not cut down, 8.12
They are exalted a little w., 24.24
w. you searched out what to say. 32.11
w. they slumber on their beds, 33.15
w. mischief is in their hearts. Ps 28.03
He plots mischief w. on his bed; 36.04
Yet a little w., and the wicked 37.10
w. his heart gathers mischief; 41.06
w. men say to me continually, "Where 42.03
w. they say to me continually, 42.10
Though, w. he lives, he counts 49.18
May he live w. the sun endures, and 72.05
w. the food was still in their 78.30
Hear, O my people, w. I admonish you! 81.08
stand firm w. the skies endure. 89.37
praise to my God w. I have being. 104.33
w. those who pass by do not say, 129.08
into their own nets, w. I escape. 141.10
praises to my God w. I have being. 146.02
w. the slothful will be put to Pro 12.24
w. the soul of the diligent is 13.04
Discipline your son w. there is hope; 19.18
She rises w. it is yet night and 31.15
is good for man w. he lives the Ecc 6.12
All this I observed w. applying my 8.09
w. man lords it over man to his 8.09
is in their hearts w. they live, 9.03
W. the king was on his couch, my Sol 1.12
a very little w. my indignation Is 10.25
for a little w. until the wrath is 26.20
w. their hearts are far from me, and 29.13
a very little w. until Lebanon 29.17
w. their inhabitants, shorn of 37.27
"Seek the Lord w. he may be found, 55.06
found, call upon him w. he is near; 55.06
w. no one understands. For the righteous 57.01
possessed thy sanctuary a little w.; 63.18
w. they are yet speaking I will 65.24
and w. you look for light he turns Jer 13.16
sun went down w. it was yet day; 15.09
w. their children remember their 17.02
of their enemies w. you look on. 20.04
w. he was still shut up in the 33.01
w. I wrote them with ink on the 36.18
to Jeremiah w. he was shut up in 39.15
yet a little w. and the time of her 51.33
W. they are inflamed I will prepare 51.39
w. the Chaldeans were round about 52.07
w. they sought food to revive their Lam 1.19
w. two covered their bodies. Eze 1.11
w. your abominations are in your 7.04
w. your abominations are in your 7.09
to what he has sold, w. they live. 7.13
And w. they were smiting, and I was 9.08
w. I was prophesying, that Pelatiah 11.13
to them for a w. in the countries 11.16
w. no hire was given to you; 16.34
w. they see for you false visions, 21.29
w. they divine lies for you—to be 21.29
"Oholah played the harlot w. she was mine; 23.05
w. those opposite the temple were a 42.08
W. the man was standing beside me, I 43.06
w. they minister at the gates of 44.17
W. the words were still in the Dan 4.31
W. I was speaking and praying, 9.20
w. I was speaking in prayer, the man 9.21
"W. he was speaking this word to 10.11
for yet a little w., and I will Hos 1.04
for a little w. from anointing 8.10
w. this house lies in ruins? Hag 1.04
w. you busy yourselves each with 1.09
in a little w., I will shake the 2.06
for w. I was angry but a little Zec 1.15
w. Jerusalem shall still be inhabited 12.06
flesh shall rot w. they are still 14.12
w. you are going with him to court, Mt 5.25
w. the sons of the kingdom will be 8.12
W. he was thus speaking to them, 9.18
W. he was still speaking to the 12.46
in himself, but endures for a w., 13.21
but w. men were sleeping, his enemy 13.25
w. he dismissed the crowds. 14.22
w. the rest seized his servants, 22.06
Now w. the Pharisees were gathered 22.41
And w. they went to buy, the bridegroom 25.10
w. I go yonder and pray." 26.36
W. he was still speaking, Judas came, 26.47
After a little w. the bystanders 26.73
Besides, w. he was sitting on the 27.19
w. he was still alive, 'After three 27.63
W. they were going, behold, some of 28.11
stole him away w. we were asleep.' 28.13
a great w. before day, he rose and Mk 1.35
guests fast w. the bridegroom is 2.19
in themselves, but endure for a w.; 4.17
W. he was still speaking, there came 5.35
to a lonely place, and rest a w." 6.31
w. he dismissed the crowd. 6.45
And w. he was at Bethany in the 14.03
his disciples, "Sit here, w. I pray." 14.32
w. he was still speaking, Judas came, 14.43
after a little w. again the bystanders 14.70
Now w. he was serving as priest Lk 1.08
And w. they were there, the time 2.06
W. the people pressed upon him to 5.01
W. he was in one of the cities, 5.12
guests fast w. the bridegroom is 5.34

WHILE (cont.)

On a sabbath, w. he was going Lk 6.01
believe for a w. and in time of 8.13
W. he was still speaking, a man from 8.49
W. he was coming, the demon tore him 9.42
But w. they were all marveling at 9.43
w. others, to test him, sought from 11.16
W. he was speaking, a Pharisee asked 11.37
And if not, w. the other is yet a 14.32
But w. he was yet at a distance, his 15.20
For a w. he refused; but afterward 18.04
into another country for a long w. 20.09
W. he was still speaking, there came 22.47
w. he was still speaking, the cock 22.60
w. the sun's light failed; 23.45
W. they were perplexed about this, 24.04
w. he was still in Galilee, 24.06
W. they were talking and discussing 24.15
burn within us w. he talked to us 24.32
w. he opened to us the scriptures?" 24.32
And w. they still disbelieved for 24.41
w. I was still with you, that 24.44
W. he blessed them, he parted from 24.51
and w. I am going another steps Jn 5.07
to rejoice for a w. in his light. 5.35
W. some said, "He is a good man," 7.12
of him who sent me, w. it is day; 9.04
w. Mary sat in the house. 11.20
Walk w. you have the light, lest the 12.35
W. you have the light, believe in 12.36
yet a little w. I am with you. 13.33
Yet a little w., and the word will 14.19
spoken to you, w. I am still with you. 14.25
"A little w., and you will see me 16.16
again a little w., again a little, 16.16
'A little w., and you will not see 16.17
not see me, and again a little w., 16.17
"What does he mean by 'a little w.'? 16.18
'A little w., and you will not see 16.19
not see me, and again a little w., 16.19
W. I was with them, I kept them in 17.12
w. Peter stood outside at the door. 18.16
w. it was still dark, and saw that 20.01
And w. staying with them he charged Ac 1.04
And w. they were gazing into heaven 1.10
W. he clung to Peter and John, all 3.11
w. thou stretchest out thy hand to 4.30
W. it remained unsold, did it not 5.04
the men to be put outside for a w. 5.34
Dorcas made w. she was with them. 9.39
but w. they were preparing it, he 10.10
Now w. Peter was inwardly perplexed 10.17
And w. Peter was pondering the 10.19
W. Peter was still saying this, the 10.44
W. they were worshiping the Lord 13.02
Now w. Paul was waiting for them at 17.16
W. Apollos was at Corinth, Paul 19.01
he himself stayed in Asia for a w. 19.22
he conversed with them a long w., 20.11
W. we were staying for some days, a 21.10
I cried out w. standing among them, 24.21
he said, w. others disbelieved. 28.24
w. their conscience also bears Rom 2.15
W. you preach against stealing, do 2.21
he had by faith w. he was still 4.11
W. we were yet helpless, at the 5.06
for us in that w. we were yet 5.08
For if w. we were enemies we were 5.10
another man w. her husband is 7.03
W. we were living in the flesh, our 7.05
w. the weak man eats only vegetables 14.02
w. the weak man eats only vegetables. 14.02
w. he who abstains, abstains in 14.06
For w. your obedience is known to 16.19
For w. there is jealousy and strife 1Co 3.03
w. prophecy is not for unbelievers 14.22
For w. we live we are always being 2Co 4.11
For w. we are still in this tent, we 5.04
we know that w. we are at home in 5.06
grieved you, though only for a w. 7.08
w. they long for you and pray for 9.14
and I warn them now w. absent, 13.02
I write this w. I am away from you, 13.10
w. we preached to you the gospel of 1Th 2.09
for w. bodily training is of some 1Ti 4.08
self-indulgent is dead even w. she lives. 5.06
w. evil men and impostors will go 2Ti 3.13
he was parted from you for a w., Phm 1.15
w. God also bore witness by signs Heb 2.04
for a little w. lower than the 2.07
for a little w. was made lower 2.09
w. it is said, "Today, when you hear 3.15
Therefore, w. the promise of entering 4.01
"For yet a little w., and the coming 10.37
w. you say to the poor man, "Stand Jas 2.03
for a little w. you may have to 1Pe 1.06
he endures pain w. suffering 2.19
you have suffered a little w., 5.10
with him w. we walk in darkness, we 1Jn 1.06
he must remain only a little w. Rev 17.10
he must be loosed for a little w. 20.03
w. the city was pure gold, clear as 21.18

WHIP

city shall take the man and w. him; Deu 22.18
A w. for the horse, a bridle for the Pro 26.03
The crack of w., and rumble of Nah 3.02
And making a w. of cords, he drove Jn 2.15

WHIPPED

they have been w. out of the land. Job 30.08

WHIPS

My father chastised you with w., 1Ki 12.11
my father chastised you with w., 12.14
My father chastised you with w., 2Ch 10.11
my father chastised you with w., 10.14

WHIRL

of the LORD makes the oaks to w., Ps 29.09
and w. you round and round, and Is 22.18

WHIRLING

O my God, make them like w. dust, Ps 83.13
the wind and w. dust before the Is 17.13
Wrath has gone forth, a w. tempest; Jer 23.19
Wrath has gone forth, a w. tempest; 30.23
"Go in among the w. wheels underneath Eze 10.02
fire from between the w. wheels, 10.06
called in my hearing the w. wheels. 10.13

WHIRLWIND

take Elijah up to heaven by a w., 2Ki 2.01
Elijah went up by a w. into heaven. 2.11
in the night a w. carries him off. Job 27.20
From its chamber comes the w., 37.09
LORD answered Job out of the w.: 38.01
LORD answered Job out of the w.: 40.06
crash of thy thunder was in the w.; Ps 77.18
and your calamity comes like a w., Pro 1.27
and their wheels like the w. Is 5.28
with w. and tempest, and the flame 29.06
clouds, his chariots like the w.; Jer 4.13
shall rush upon him like a w.; Dan 11.40
wind, and they shall reap the w. Hos 8.07
a tempest in the day of the w.; Amo 1.14
His way is in w. and storm, and the Nah 1.03
who came like a w. to scatter me, Hab 3.14
them with a w. among all the Zec 7.14

WHIRLWINDS

As w. in the Negeb sweep on, it Is 21.01
march forth in the w. of the south. Zec 9.14

WHIRRING

Ah, land of w. wings which is beyond Is 18.01

WHISPER
my ear received the w. of it. Job 4.12
and how small a w. do we hear of 26.14
All who hate me w. together about Ps 41.07
speech shall w. out of the dust. Is 29.04

WHISPERED
and what you hear w., proclaim Mt 10.27
what you have w. in private rooms Lk 12.03

WHISPERER
and a w. separates close friends. Pro 16.28
The words of a w. are like delicious 18.08
and where there is no w., 26.20
The words of a w. are like delicious 26.22

WHISPERING
that his servants were w. together, 2Sa 12.19
I hear the w. of many—terror on Ps 31.13
For I hear many w. Terror is on Jer 20.10

WHISTLE
and w. for it from the ends of the Is 5.26
the LORD will w. for the fly which 7.18

WHITE
every one that had w. on it, Gen 30.35
and peeled w. streaks in them, 30.37
them, exposing the w. of the rods. 30.37
wine, and his teeth w. with milk. 49.12
hand was leprous, as w. as snow. Ex 4.06
w., and the taste of it was like 16.31
spot has turned w. and the disease Lev 13.03
the spot is w. in the skin 13.04
the hair in it has not turned w., 13.04
if there is a w. swelling in the 13.10
skin, which has turned the hair w., 13.10
it has all turned w., and he is 13.13
turns again and is changed to w., 13.16
and if the disease has turned w., 13.17
there comes a w. swelling or a 13.19
skin and its hair has turned w., 13.20
on it is not w. and it is not 13.21
a spot, reddish-white or w., 13.24
spot has turned w. and it appears 13.25
the spot is not w. and it is no 13.26
on the skin of the body, w. spots, 13.38
skin of the body are of a dull w., 13.39
Miriam was leprous, as w. as snow. Num 12.10
presence a leper, as w. as snow. 2Ki 5.27
There were w. cotton curtains and Est 1.06
king in royal robes of blue and w., 8.15
Let your garments be always w.; Ecc 9.08
they shall be as w. as snow; Is 1.18
and the weavers of w. cotton. 19.09
wine of Helbon, and w. wool, Eze 27.18
his raiment was w. as snow, Dan 7.09
cleanse them and to make them w., 11.35
themselves, and make themselves w. 12.10
their branches are made w. Joe 1.07
were red, sorrel, and w. horses. Zec 1.08
the third w. horses, and the fourth 6.03
the w. ones go toward the west 6.06
cannot make one hair w. or black. Mt 5.36
his garments became w. as light. 17.02
lightning, and his raiment w. as snow. 28.03
intensely w., as no fuller on earth Mk 9.03
right side, dressed in a w. robe; 16.05
and his raiment became dazzling w. Lk 9.29
fields are already w. for harvest. Jn 4.35
and she saw two angels in w., 20.12
two men stood by them in w. robes, Ac 1.10
and his hair were w. as w. wool, w. as snow; Rev 1.14
and I will give him a w. stone, 2.17
and they shall walk with me in w., 3.04
shall be clad thus in w. garments, 3.05
and w. garments to clothe you and 3.18
clad in w. garments, with golden 4.04
a w. horse, and its rider had a bow; 6.02
each given a w. robe and told to 6.11
clothed in w. robes, with palm 7.09
clothed in w. robes, and whence have 7.13
and made them w. in the blood of 7.14
a w. cloud, and seated on the cloud 14.14
opened, and behold, a w. horse! 19.11
w. and pure, followed him on w. horses. 19.14
Then I saw a great w. throne and 20.11

WHITER
me, and I shall be w. than snow. Ps 51.07
were purer than snow, w. than milk; Lam 4.07

WHITEWASH
As for you, you w. with lies; Job 13.04
these prophets daub it with w.; Eze 13.10
daub it with w. that it shall fall 13.11
wall that you have daubed with w., 13.14
those who have daubed it with w.; 13.15
have daubed for them with w., 22.28

WHITEWASHED
for you are like w. tombs, which Mt 23.27
"God shall strike you, you w. wall! Ac 23.03

WHITHER
inhabitants of the land w. you go, Ex 34.12
W. are we going up? Our brethren Deu 1.28
w. he had fled from King Solomon), 1Ki 12.02
or kingdom w. my lord has not sent 18.10
LORD will carry you w. I know not; 18.12
w. he had fled from King Solomon), 2Ch 10.02
W. shall I go from thy Spirit? Ps 139.07
Or w. shall I flee from thy presence? 139.07
W. has your beloved gone, O fairest Sol 6.01
W. has your beloved turned, that we 6.01
the nations w. I will drive them." Eze 4.13
know whence it comes or w. it goes; Jn 3.08
I have come and w. I am going, 8.14
whence I come or w. I am going. 8.14

WHOEVER
and w. finds me will slay me." Gen 4.14
W. sheds the blood of man, by man 9.06
"W. touches this man or his wife 26.11
w. touches the mountain shall be Ex 19.12
"W. strikes a man so that he dies 21.12
"W. strikes his father or his 21.15
"W. steals a man, whether he sells 21.16
"W. curses his father or his mother 21.17
"W. lies with a beast shall be put 22.19
"W. sacrifices to any god, save to 22.20
w. has a cause, let him go to them." 24.14
W. compounds any like it or w. puts 30.33
W. makes any like it to use as 30.38
w. does any work on it, that soul 31.14
w. does any work on the sabbath day 31.15
"W. has sinned against me, him will 32.33
w. does any work on it shall be put 35.02
w. is of a generous heart, let him 35.05
w. touches them shall become holy." Lev 6.18
W. eats any blood, that person shall 7.27
w. touches their carcass shall be 11.24
and w. carries any part of their 11.25
w. touches their carcass shall be 11.27
w. touches them when they are dead 11.31
And w. sits on anything on which he 15.06
And w. touches the body of him who 15.07
And w. touches anything that was 15.10
and w. touches her shall be unclean 15.19
And w. touches her bed shall wash 15.21
And w. touches anything upon which 15.22
And w. touches these things shall 15.27
w. eats it shall be cut off. 17.14
For w. shall do any of these 18.29
W. touches anything that is unclean 22.04

WHOEVER (cont.)
and w. touches a creeping thing by Lev 22.05
For w. is not afflicted on this 23.29
And w. does any work on this same 23.30
W. curses his God shall bear his 24.15
W. touches a dead person, the body Num 19.13
W. in the open field touches one 19.16
w. of you has killed any person, and 31.19
and w. has touched any slain, purify 31.19
For w. does these things is an Deu 18.12
And w. will not give heed to my 18.19
for w. does these things is an 22.05
W. rebels against your commandment Jos 1.18
"W. smites Kiriathsepher, and takes 15.16
W. contends for him shall be put to Ju 6.31
'W. is fearful and trembling, let 7.03
then w. comes forth from the doors 11.31
"W. does not come out after Saul 1Sa 11.07
"W. would smite the Jebusites, let 2Sa 5.08
w. hears it will say, 'There has 17.09
"W. favors Joab, and w. is for David, 20.11
w. is missing shall not live." 2Ki 10.19
and w. approaches the ranks is to 11.08
David said, "We shall smite the 1Ch 11.06
And w. had precious stones gave 29.08
W. comes to consecrate himself with 2Ch 13.09
and that w. would not seek the LORD, 15.13
and w. enters the house shall be 23.07
W. is among you of all his people, 36.23
W. is among you of all his people, Ez 1.03
W. will not obey the law of your 7.26
W. is wise, let him give heed to Ps 107.43
"W. is simple, let him turn in here!" Pro 9.04
"W. is simple, let him turn in here!" 9.16
W. loves discipline loves knowledge, 12.01
and w. is led astray by it is not 20.01
W. is found will be thrust through, Is 13.15
and w. is caught will fall by the 13.15
w. stirs up strife with you shall 54.15
and w. does not fall down and Dan 3.06
and w. does not fall down and 3.11
"W. reads this writing, and shows me 5.07
that w. makes petition to any god 6.07
W. is wise, let him understand these Hos 14.09
w. is discerning, let him know them; 14.09
For w. has despised the day of Zec 4.10
W. then relaxes one of the least of Mt 5.19
and w. kills shall be liable to 5.21
w. insults his brother shall be 5.22
and w. says, 'You fool!' shall be 5.22
'W. divorces his wife, let him give 5.31
and w. marries a divorced woman 5.32
but w. denies me before men, I also 10.33
And w. gives to one of these little 10.42
And w. says a word against the Son 12.32
but w. speaks against the Holy 12.32
For w. does the will of my Father 12.50
For w. would save his life will 16.25
and w. loses his life for my sake 16.25
W. humbles himself like this child, 18.04
"W. receives one such child in my 18.05
but w. causes one of these little 18.06
w. divorces his wife, except for 19.09
but w. would be great among you 20.26
and w. would be first among you 20.27
w. exalts himself will be humbled, 23.12
and w. humbles himself will be 23.12
but w. blasphemes against the Holy Mk 3.29
W. does the will of God is my 3.35
For w. would save his life will 8.35
and w. loses his life for my sake 8.35
For w. is ashamed of me and of my 8.38
"W. receives one such child in my 9.37
and w. receives me, receives not me 9.37
w. gives you a cup of water to 9.41
"W. causes one of these little ones 9.42
"W. divorces his wife and marries 10.11
w. does not receive the kingdom of 10.15
but w. would be great among you 10.43
and w. would be first among you 10.44
w. says to this mountain, 'Be taken 11.23
For w. would save his life will Lk 9.24
and w. loses his life for my sake, 9.24
For w. is ashamed of me and of my 9.26
"W. receives this child in my name 9.48
and w. receives me receives him who 9.48
W. does not bear his own cross and 14.27
So therefore, w. of you does not 14.33
W. seeks to gain his life will lose 17.33
but w. loses his life will preserve 17.33
w. does not receive the kingdom of 18.17
that w. believes in him may have Jn 3.15
that w. believes in him should not 3.16
but w. drinks of the water that I 4.14
w. stepped in first after the * 5.04
and w. lives and believes in me 11.26
that w. believes in me may not 12.46
is coming when w. kills you will 16.02
shall be that w. calls on the name Ac 2.21
w. you are, when you judge another; Rom 2.01
But w. is firmly established in his 1Co 7.37
W., therefore, eats the bread or 11.27
will bear his judgment, w. he is. Gal 5.10
Therefore w. disregards this, 1Th 4.08
for w. enters God's rest also ceases Heb 4.10
For w. would draw near to God must 11.06
For w. keeps the whole law but Jas 2.10
Therefore w. wishes to be a friend 4.04
W. knows what is right to do and 4.17
let him know that w. brings back a 5.20
for w. has suffered in the flesh 1Pe 4.01
w. speaks, as one who utters oracles 4.11
w. renders service, as one who 4.11
For w. lacks these things is blind 2Pe 1.09
but w. keeps his word, in him truly 1Jn 2.05
w. does not do right is not of God, 3.10
W. knows God listens to us, and he 4.06
W. confesses that Jesus is the Son 4.15
and w. receives the mark of its Rev 14.11

WHOLE
and watered the w. face of the Gen 2.06
around the w. land of Havilah, 2.11
flows around the w. land of Cush. 2.13
under the w. heaven were covered; 7.19
still on the face of the w. earth. 8.09
from these the w. earth was 9.19
Now the w. earth had one language 11.01
upon the face of the w. earth." 11.04
Is not the w. land before you? 13.09
will spare the w. place for their 18.26
destroy the w. city for lack of 18.28
the field, throughout its w. area, 23.17
After two w. years, Pharaoh dreamed 41.01
settled on the w. country of Egypt, Ex 10.14
covered the face of the w. land, 10.15
when the w. assembly of the congregation 12.06
And the w. congregation of the 16.02
to kill this w. assembly with hunger." 16.03
"Say to the w. congregation of the 16.09
spoke to the w. congregation of 16.10
and the w. mountain quaked greatly. 19.18
the w. of it one piece of hammered 25.36
that the tabernacle may be one w. 26.06
together that it may be one w. 26.11
and burn the w. ram upon the altar; 29.18
so the tabernacle was one w. 36.13
together that it might be one w. 36.18
the w. of it was one piece of 37.22
shall burn the w. on the altar, Lev 1.09
and the priest shall offer the w., 1.13
the w. bull he shall carry forth 4.12
"If the w. congregation of Israel 4.13
the w. of it shall be burned. 6.22

WHOLE (cont.)
burned the w. ram on the altar, as Lev 8.21
the w. house of Israel, may bewail 10.06
shall bathe his w. body in water, 15.16
it within a w. year after its sale 25.29
assembled the w. congregation together, Num 1.18
So the w. number of the people of 1.45
their w. number was six hundred and 1.46
The w. number of the camp of Judah, 2.09
The w. number of the camp of Reuben, 2.16
The w. number of the camp of Ephraim, 2.24
The w. number of the camp of Dan is 2.31
him and for the w. congregation 3.07
as the w. of their service in the 4.31
the w. of their service in the tent 4.33
assemble the w. congregation of 8.09
but a w. month, until it comes out 11.20
meat, that they may eat a w. month!' 11.21
the w. congregation said to them, 14.02
because the w. population was involved 15.26
the w. congregation, came into the 20.01
the w. congregation, came to Mount 20.22
sight of the w. congregation of 25.06
Israel with him, the w. congregation." 27.21
priest and the w. congregation, 27.22
that are under the w. heaven, Deu 2.25
the w. region of Argob, the kingdom 3.04
(The w. of that Bashan is called 3.13
the peoples under the w. heaven. 4.19
as a w. burnt offering to the LORD 13.16
lest the w. yield be forfeited to 22.09
the w. land brimstone and salt, and 29.23
and w. burnt offering upon thy 33.10
do not make the w. people toil up Jos 7.03
to go down for about a w. day. 10.13
So Joshua defeated the w. land, 10.40
So Joshua took the w. land, 11.23
the w. kingdom of Og king of Bashan, 13.30
Then the w. congregation of the 18.01
the w. assembly of the people of 22.12
"Thus says the w. congregation of 22.16
angry with the w. congregation of 22.18
them and to the w. clan of his Ju 9.01
men from the w. number of their 18.02
the w. army, went up and came to 20.26
the w. of the city went up in smoke 20.40
Then the w. congregation sent word 21.13
the w. town was stirred because of Ru 1.19
panic throughout the w. city. 1Sa 5.11
offered it as a w. burnt offering 7.09
marching the w. forenoon they came 2Sa 2.29
Israel and the w. house of Benjamin 3.19
the w. multitude of Israel, both men 6.19
defeated the w. army of Hadadezer, 8.09
And now the w. family has risen 14.07
the structure against the w. house, 1Ki 6.10
And he overlaid the w. house with 6.22
Also the w. altar that belonged to 6.22
And the w. earth sought the presence 10.24
not take the w. kingdom out of his 11.34
fare like the w. multitude of 2Ki 7.13
For the w. house of Ahab shall 9.08
faithfulness and with a w. heart, 20.03
defeated the w. army of Hadadezer, 1Ch 18.09
him with a w. heart and with a 28.09
for with a w. heart they had 29.09
son that with a w. heart he may 29.19
sought him with their w. desire, 2Ch 15.15
to and fro throughout the w. earth, 16.09
faithfulness, and with your w. heart: 19.09
The w. number of the heads of 26.12
The w. assembly worshiped, and the 29.28
Then the w. assembly agreed together 30.23
The w. assembly of Judah, and the 30.25
and the w. assembly that came out 30.25
their daughters, the w. multitude; 31.18
The w. assembly together was forty-two Ez 2.64
ruled over the w. province Beyond 4.20
find in the w. province of Babylonia, 7.16
The w. was counted and weighed, and 8.34
officials stand for the w. assembly; 10.14
The w. assembly together was forty-two Neh 7.66
throughout the w. kingdom of Ahasuerus. Est 3.06
and who laid on him the w. world? Job 34.13
Under the w. heaven he lets it go, 37.03
is under the w. heaven is mine. 41.11
to the LORD with my w. heart; Ps 9.01
offerings and w. burnt offerings; 51.19
may his glory fill the w. earth! 72.19
with my w. heart, and I will glorify 86.12
to the LORD with my w. heart, 111.01
who seek him with their w. heart, 119.02
With my w. heart I seek thee; 119.10
and observe it with my w. heart. 119.34
but with my w. heart I keep thy 119.69
With my w. heart I cry; answer 119.145
thanks, O LORD, with my w. heart; 138.01
let us swallow them alive and w., Pro 1.12
for this is the w. duty of man. Ecc 12.13
The w. head is sick, and the w. heart Is 1.05
the w. stay of bread, and the w. stay 3.01
create over the w. site of Mount 4.05
the w. earth is full of his glory." 6.03
indignation, to destroy the w. earth. 13.05
The w. earth is at rest and quiet; 14.07
purposed concerning the w. earth; 14.26
my post I am stationed w. nights. 21.08
hang on him the w. weight of his 22.24
and fill the w. world with fruit. 27.06
Lord GOD of hosts upon the w. land. 28.22
faithfulness and with a w. heart, 38.03
his w. armory, all that was found in 39.02
the chastisement that made us w., 53.05
the God of the w. earth he is 54.05
against the w. land, against the Jer 1.18
not return to me with her w. heart, 3.10
the w. land is laid waste. Suddenly 4.20
"The w. land shall be a desolation; 4.27
their stallions the w. land quakes. 8.16
The w. land is made desolate, but no 12.11
so I made the w. house of Israel 13.11
Israel and the w. house of Judah 13.11
and contention to the w. land! 15.10
return to me with their w. heart. 24.07
This w. land shall become a ruin 25.11
The w. valley of the dead bodies 31.40
and the w. house of the Rechabites. 35.03
defeat the w. army of Chaldeans 37.10
See, the w. land is before you; 40.04
am plucking up—that is, the w. land. 45.04
hammer of the w. earth is cut down 50.23
LORD, which destroys the w. earth; 51.25
the praise of the w. earth seized! 51.41
her w. land shall be put to shame, 51.47
again and again the w. day long. Lam 3.03
the w. house of Israel, all of them, Eze 11.15
when it was w., it was used for 15.05
beasts of the w. earth with you. 32.04
rejoicing of the w. earth I will 35.14
the w. house of Israel, all of it; 36.10
bones are the w. house of Israel. 37.11
mercy upon the w. house of Israel; 39.25
carved on the w. temple round 41.19
and its entrances, and its w. form; 43.11
the w. territory round about upon 43.12
be holy throughout its w. extent. 45.01
belong to the w. house of Israel. 45.06
The w. length shall be twenty-five 48.13
The w. portion which you shall set 48.20
mountain and filled the w. earth. Dan 2.35
ruler over the w. province of 2.48
visible to the end of the w. earth. 4.11
visible to the end of the w. earth; 4.20
to be throughout the w. kingdom; 6.01

WHOLE (cont.)

to set him over the w. kingdom. Dan 6.03
and it shall devour the w. earth, 7.23
under the w. heaven shall be given 7.27
across the face of the w. earth, 8.05
for under the w. heaven there has 9.12
the strength of his w. kingdom, 11.17
into exile a w. people to deliver Amo 1.06
delivered up a w. people to Edom, 1.09
against the w. family which I 3.01
wealth to the Lord of the w. earth. Mic 4.13
which range through the w. earth. Zec 4.10
stand by the LORD of the w. earth. 4.14
out over the face of the w. land; 5.03
In the w. land, says the LORD, two 13.08
The w. land shall be turned into a 14.10
robbing me; the w. nation of you. Mal 3.09
than that your w. body be thrown Mt 5.29
than that your w. body go into 5.30
your w. body will be full of light; 6.22
your w. body will be full of 6.23
the w. herd rushed down the steep 8.32
it was restored, w. like the other. 12.13
and the w. crowd stood on the beach. 13.02
the maimed w., the lame walking, and 15.31
if he gains the w. world and 16.26
preached throughout the w. world, 24.14
gospel is preached in the w. world, 26.13
priests and the w. council sought 26.59
gathered the w. battalion before 27.27
And the w. city was gathered Mk 1.33
and the w. crowd was beside the sea. 4.01
him, and told him the w. truth. 5.33
and ran about the w. neighborhood 6.55
to gain the w. world and forfeit 8.36
more than all w. burnt offerings 12.33
everything she had, her w. living." 12.44
gospel is preached in the w. world, 14.09
priests and the w. council sought 14.55
and the w. council held a consultation; 15.01
called together the w. battalion. 15.16
over the w. land until the ninth 15.33
the gospel to the w. creation. * 16.15
And the w. multitude of the people Lk 1.10
through the w. of Judea and all 7.17
throughout the w. city how much 8.39
if he gains the w. world and loses 9.25
your w. body is full of light; 11.34
If then your w. body is full of 11.36
the w. multitude of the disciples 19.37
upon the face of the w. earth. 21.35
Then the w. company of them arose, 23.01
over the w. land until the ninth 23.44
I made a man's w. body well? Jn 7.23
and that the w. nation should not 11.50
great fear came upon the w. church, Ac 5.11
they said pleased the w. multitude, 6.05
spoken of by the w. Jewish nation, 10.22
For a w. year they met with the 11.26
through the w. island as far as 13.06
almost the w. city gathered 13.44
with the w. church, to choose men 15.22
to you the w. counsel of God. 20.27
priest and the w. council of 22.05
about whom the w. Jewish people 25.24
lived there two w. years at his 28.30
and the w. world may be held Rom 3.19
We know that the w. creation has 8.22
fruits is holy, so is the w. lump; 11.16
is host to me and to the w. church, 16.23
ferments the w. lump of dough? 1Co 5.06
If the w. body were an eye, where 12.17
If the w. body were an ear, where 12.17
the w. church assembles and all 14.23
who are in the w. of Achaia: 2Co 1.01
he is bound to keep the w. law. Gal 5.03
A little yeast leavens the w. lump. 5.09
For the w. law is fulfilled in one 5.14
in whom the w. structure is joined Eph 2.21
from whom the w. body, joined and 4.16
Put on the w. armor of God, that you 6.11
Therefore take the w. armor of God, 6.13
throughout the w. praetorian guard Php 1.13
indeed in the w. world it is Col 1.06
For in him the w. fulness of deity 2.09
from whom the w. body, nourished and 2.19
are upsetting w. families by Tit 1.11
keeps the w. law but fails in one Jas 2.10
able to bridle the w. body also. 3.02
obey us, we guide their w. bodies. 3.03
staining the w. body, setting on 3.06
also for the sins of the w. world. 1Jn 2.02
and the w. world is in the power of 5.19
which is coming on the w. world, Rev 3.10
the deceiver of the w. world— 12.09
and w. earth followed the beast 13.03
to the kings of the w. world, 16.14

WHOLEHEARTED

possession with w. joy and utter Eze 36.05

WHOLESOME

LORD, I have made this water w.; 2Ki 2.21
So the water has been w. to this day, 2.22
He whose ear heeds w. admonition Pro 15.31

WHOLLY

of a priest shall be w. burned; Lev 6.23
they are w. given to him from among Num 3.09
For they are w. given to me from 8.16
they have not w. followed me; 32.11
for they have w. followed the LORD. 32.12
because he has w. followed the Deu 1.36
the Salt Sea, were w. cut off; Jos 3.16
yet I w. followed the LORD my God. 14.08
you have w. followed the LORD my 14.09
because he w. followed the LORD, the 14.14
therefore be w. true to the LORD 1Ki 8.61
heart was not w. true to the LORD 11.04
and did not w. follow the LORD, as 11.06
heart was not w. true to the LORD 15.03
of Asa was w. true to the LORD all 15.14
people will be w. at your command." 1Ch 28.21
acquaintances are w. estranged from Job 19.13
being w. at ease and secure, 21.23
the decision is w. from the LORD. Pro 16.33
you a choice vine, w. of pure seed. Jer 2.21
into exile, w. taken into exile. 13.19
Let his arm be w. withered, Zec 11.17
it will be w. bright, as when a lamp Lk 11.36
of peace himself sanctify you w.; 1Th 5.23

WHOMEVER

With w. of your servants it be Gen 44.09
bring up for me w. I shall name to 1Sa 28.08
I give it to w. it seems right to Jer 27.05
will appoint over her w. I choose. 49.19
will appoint over her w. I choose. 50.44
then he has mercy upon w. he wills, Rom 9.18
hardens the heart of w. he wills. 9.18

WICK

a dimly burning w. he will not Is 42.03
extinguished, quenched like a w.: 43.17
reed or quench a smoldering w., Mt 12.20

WICKED

Now the men of Sodom were w., Gen 13.13
destroy the righteous with the w.? 18.23
to slay the righteous with the w., 18.25
that the righteous fare as the w.! 18.25
was w. in the sight of the LORD; 38.07
shall not join hands with a w. man, Ex 23.01
for I will not acquit the w. 23.07
"How long shall this w. congregation Num 14.27

WICKED (cont.)

do to all this w. congregation	Num 14.35
from the tents of these w. men,	16.26
but the w. shall be cut off in	1Sa 2.09
'Out of the w. comes forth wickedness';	24.13
Then all the w. and base fellows	30.22
before the w. you have fallen."	2Sa 3.34
when w. men have slain a righteous	4.11
And they did w. things, provoking	2Ki 17.11
things more w. than all that the	21.11
was w. in the sight of the LORD, and	1Ch 2.03
face, and turn from their w. ways,	2Ch 7.14
you help the w. and love those who	19.02
that w. woman, had broken into the	24.07
that rebellious and w. city;	Ez 4.12
did not turn from their w. works.	Neh 9.35
This w. Haman!" Then Haman	Est 7.06
that his w. plot which he had	9.25
There the w. cease from troubling,	Job 3.17
the tent of the w. will be no more."	8.22
both the blameless and the w.	9.22
is given into the hand of the w.;	9.24
and favor the designs of the w.?	10.03
If I am w., woe to me! If I am	10.15
But the eyes of the w. will fail;	11.20
The w. man writhes in pain all his	15.20
casts me into the hands of the w.	16.11
"Yea, the light of the w. is put out,	18.05
that the exulting of the w. is short,	20.05
This is the w. man's portion from	20.29
Why do the w. live, reach old age,	21.07
counsel of the w. is far from me.	21.16
that the lamp of the w. is put out?	21.17
is the tent in which the w. dwelt?'	21.28
that the w. man is spared in the	21.30
the old way which w. men have trod?	22.15
counsel of the w. is far from me.	22.18
clean the vineyard of the w. man.	24.06
olive rows of the w. they make oil;	24.11
"Let my enemy be as the w., and let him	27.07
the portion of a w. man with God,	27.13
evildoers and walks with w. men?	34.08
one,' and to nobles, 'W. man';	34.18
because he answers like w. men.	34.36
He does not keep the w. alive,	36.06
are full of the judgment on the w.;	36.17
and the w. be shaken out of it?	38.13
from the w. their light is withheld,	38.15
tread down the w. where they stand.	40.12
walks not in the counsel of the w.,	Ps 1.01
The w. are not so, but are like	1.04
Therefore the w. will not stand in	1.05
but the way of the w. will perish.	1.06
dost break the teeth of the w.	3.07
the evil of the w. come to an end,	7.09
behold, the w. man conceives evil,	7.14
nations, thou hast destroyed the w.;	9.05
the w. are snared in the work of	9.16
The w. shall depart to Sheol, all	9.17
In arrogance the w. hotly pursue	10.02
For the w. boasts of the desires of	10.03
countenance the w. does not seek	10.04
Why does the w. renounce God, and	10.13
the arm of the w. and evildoer;	10.15
for lo, the w. bend the bow, they	11.02
tests the righteous and the w.,	11.05
On the w. he will rain coals of	11.06
On every side the w. prowl,	12.08
from the w. who despoil me, my	17.09
my life from the w. by thy sword,	17.13
and I will not sit with the w.	26.05
Take me not off with the w.,	28.03
let the w. be put to shame, let them	31.17
Many are the pangs of the w.;	32.10
Evil shall slay the w.;	34.21
Transgression speaks to the w. deep	36.01
the hand of the w. drive me away.	36.11

Fret not yourself because of the w.,	37.01
For the w. shall be cut off;	37.09
and the w. will be no more;	37.10
The w. plots against the righteous,	37.12
but the LORD laughs at the w.,	37.13
The w. draw the sword and bend	37.14
has than the abundance of many w.	37.16
For the arms of the w. shall be	37.17
But the w. perish; the enemies of	37.20
The w. borrows, and cannot pay back,	37.21
children of the w. shall be cut	37.28
The w. watches the righteous, and	37.32
look on the destruction of the w.	37.34
I have seen a w. man overbearing,	37.35
posterity of the w. shall be cut	37.38
he delivers them from the w.,	37.40
so long as the w. are in my	39.01
But to the w. God says: "What right	50.16
of the oppression of the w.	55.03
The w. go astray from the womb, they	58.03
his feet in the blood of the w.	58.10
me from the secret plots of the w.,	64.02
let the w. perish before God!	68.02
O my God, from the hand of the w.,	71.04
I saw the prosperity of the w.	73.03
Behold, these are the w.;	73.12
and to the w., "Do not lift up	75.04
and all the w. of the earth shall	75.08
horns of the w. he will cut off,	75.10
and show partiality to the w.?	82.02
them from the hand of the w.	82.04
outwit him the w. shall not humble him.	89.22
and see the recompense of the w.	91.08
though the w. sprout like grass and	92.07
O LORD, how long shall the w.,	94.03
how long shall the w. exult?	94.03
until a pit is dug for the w.	94.13
Who rises up for me against the w.?	94.16
Can w. rulers be allied with thee,	94.20
them from the hand of the w.	97.10
destroy all the w. in the land,	101.08
earth, and let the w. be no more!	104.35
the flame burned up the w.	106.18
For w. and deceitful mouths are	109.02
Appoint a w. man against him;	109.06
The w. man sees it and is angry;	112.10
desire of the w. man comes to	112.10
seizes me because of the w.,	119.53
Though the cords of the w. ensnare me,	119.61
The w. lie in wait to destroy me;	119.95
The w. have laid a snare for me, but	119.110
All the w. of the earth thou dost	119.119
Salvation is far from the w.,	119.155
he has cut the cords of the w.	129.04
O that hou wouldst slay the w.,	139.19
And see if there be any w. way in me,	139.24
O LORD, from the hands of the w.;	140.04
not, O LORD the desires of the w.;	140.08
myself with w. deeds in company	141.04
the oil of the w. never anoint my	141.05
continually against their w. deeds.	141.05
Let the w. together fall into their	141.10
but all the w. he will destroy.	145.20
the way of the w. he brings to	146.09
he casts the w. to the ground.	147.06
but the w. will be cut off from the	Pro 2.22
the ruin of the w., when it comes;	3.25
curse is on the house of the w.,	3.33
Do not enter the path of the w.,	4.14
The way of the w. is like deep	4.19
The iniquities of the w. ensnare him,	5.22
a w. man, goes about with crooked	6.12
a heart that devises w. plans,	6.18
who reproves a w. man incurs	9.07
he thwarts the craving of the w.	10.03
mouth of the w. conceals violence.	10.06
but the name of the w. will rot.	10.07

WICKED (cont.)
mouth of the w. conceals violence. Pro 10.11
to life, the gain of the w. to sin. 10.16
the mind of the w. is of little 10.20
What the w. dreads will come upon 10.24
the w. is no more, but the righteous 10.25
the years of the w. will be short. 10.27
expectation of the w. comes to 10.28
but the w. will not dwell in the 10.30
acceptable, but the mouth of the w., 10.32
but the w. falls by his own wickedness. 11.05
When the w. dies, his hope perishes, 11.07
and the w. gets into it instead. 11.08
and when the w. perish there are 11.10
overthrown by the mouth of the w. 11.11
A w. man earns deceptive wages, but 11.18
the expectation of the w. in wrath. 11.23
much more the w. and the sinner! 11.31
counsels of the w. are treacherous. 12.05
The words of the w. lie in wait for 12.06
The w. are overthrown and are no 12.07
but the mercy of the w. is cruel. 12.10
tower of the w. comes to ruin, 12.12
but the w. are filled with trouble. 12.21
the way of the w. leads them 12.26
but a w. man acts shamefully and 13.05
upright, but sin overthrows the w. 13.06
the lamp of the w. will be put out 13.09
the belly of the w. suffers want. 13.25
God scorns the w., but the upright 14.09
The house of the w. will be destroyed, 14.11
the w. at the gates of the righteous. 14.19
The w. is overthrown through his 14.32
befalls the income of the w. 15.06
sacrifice of the w. is an abomination 15.08
The way of the w. is an abomination 15.09
The thoughts of the w. are an 15.26
mouth of the w. pours out evil 15.28
The LORD is far from the w., 15.29
even the w. for the day of trouble. 16.04
An evildoer listens to w. lips; 17.04
justifies the w. and he who 17.15
A w. man accepts a bribe from the 17.23
not good to be partial to a w. man, 18.05
mouth of the w. devours iniquity. 19.28
A wise king winnows the w., 20.26
heart, the lamp of the w., are sin. 21.04
The violence of the w. will sweep 21.07
The soul of the w. desires evil; 21.10
observes the house of the w.; 21.12
the w. are cast down to ruin. 21.12
The w. is a ransom for the righteous, 21.18
All day long the w. covets, but the 21.26
sacrifice of the w. is an abomination; 21.27
A w. man puts on a bold face, but an 21.29
in wait as a w. man against the dwelling 24.15
but the w. are overthrown by calamity. 24.16
of evildoers, and be not envious of the w.; 24.19
the lamp of the w. will be put out. 24.20
He who says to the w., "You are 24.24
who rebuke the w. will have delight, 24.25
take away the w. from the presence 25.05
man who gives way before the w. 25.26
The w. flee when no one pursues, but 28.01
Those who forsake the law praise the w., 28.04
but when the w. rise, men hide themselves. 28.12
bear is a w. ruler over a poor 28.15
When the w. rise, men hide themselves, 28.28
but when the w. rule, the people 29.02
a w. man does not understand such 29.07
blameless, and the w. seek his life. 29.10
falsehood all his officials will be w. 29.12
When the w. are in authority, transgression 29.16
straight is an abomination to the w. 29.27
judge the righteous and the w., Ecc 3.17
and there is a w. man who prolongs 7.15
Be not w. overmuch, neither be a 7.17
Then I saw the w. buried; they used 8.10
but it will not be well with the w., 8.13
accordng to the deeds of the w., 8.14
and there are w. men to whom it 8.14
all, to the righteous and the w., 9.02
the end of his talk is w. madness. 10.13
Woe to the w.! It shall be Is 3.11
of his lips he shall slay the w. 11.04
and the w. for their iniquity; 13.11
has broken the staff of the w., 14.05
If favor is shown to the w., 26.10
he devises w. devices to ruin the 32.07
peace," says the LORD, "for the w." 48.22
grave with the w. and with a rich 53.09
let the w. forsake his way, and the 55.07
But the w. are like the tossing sea 57.20
no peace, says my God, for the w." 57.21
to fight and to hit with w. fist. 58.04
So that even to w. women you have Jer 2.33
For w. men are found among my 5.26
goes on, for the w. are not removed. 6.29
Why does the way of the w. prosper? 12.01
you out of the hand of the w., 15.21
will burst upon the head of the w. 23.19
and the w. he will put to the sword, 25.31
will burst upon the head of the w. 30.23
If I say to the w., 'You shall Eze 3.18
to warn the w. from his w. way, 3.18
that w. man shall die in his 3.18
But if you warn the w., and he does 3.19
or from his w. way, he shall die in 3.19
and to the w. of the earth for a 7.21
and who give w. counsel in this 11.02
and you have encouraged the w., 13.22
turn from his w. way to save his 13.22
wickedness of the w. shall be upon 18.20
"But if a w. man turns away from 18.21
pleasure in the death of the w., 18.23
things that the w. man does, 18.24
Again, when a w. man turns away from 18.27
off from you both righteous and w. 21.03
off from you both righteous and w., 21.04
O unhallowed w. one, prince of 21.25
on the necks of the unhallowed w., 21.29
If I say to the w., O w. man, 33.08
to warn the w. to turn from his 33.08
that w. man shall die in his 33.08
But if you warn the w. to turn from 33.09
no pleasure in the death of the w., 33.11
but that the w. turn from his way 33.11
as for the wickedness of the w., he shall 33.12
Again, though I say to the w., 33.14
if the w. restores the pledge, gives 33.15
And when the w. turns from his 33.19
but the w. shall do wickedly; Dan 12.10
and none of the w. shall understand; 12.10
and the w. deeds of Samaria; Hos 7.01
chastise them for their w. deeds. 7.12
wickedness in the house of the w., Mic 6.10
the man with w. scales and with a 6.11
again shall the w. come against Nah 1.15
For the w. surround the righteous, Hab 1.04
silent when the w. swallows up the 1.13
didst crush the head of the w., 3.13
I will overthrow the w.; I will cut Zep 1.03
they are called the w. country, Mal 1.04
between the righteous and the w., 3.18
And you shall tread down the w., 4.03
and said to him, 'You w. servant! Mt 18.32
But if that w. servant says to 24.48
'You w. and slothful servant! 25.26
of your own mouth, you w. servant! Lk 19.22
and taking some w. fellows of the Ac 17.05
Drive out the w. person from among 1Co 5.13
and with all w. deception for those 2Th 2.10
be delivered from w. and evil men; 3.02

WICKED (cont.)
the licentiousness of the w. 2Pe 2.07
who greets him shares his w. work. 2Jn 1.11

WICKEDLY
you, my brothers, do not act so w. Gen 19.07
"No, my brethren, do not act so w.; Ju 19.23
But if you still do w., you shall be 1Sa 12.25
and have not w. departed from my 2Sa 22.22
I have sinned, and I have done w.; 24.17
and have acted perversely and w.'; 1Ki 8.47
I who have sinned and done very w. 1Ch 21.17
and have acted perversely and w.'; 2Ch 6.37
Ahaziah king of Israel, who did w. 20.35
was his counselor in doing w. 22.03
faithfully and we have acted w.; Neh 9.33
Of a truth, God will not do w., Job 34.12
and have not w. departed from my Ps 18.21
committed iniquity, we have done w. 106.06
And she has w. rebelled against my Eze 5.06
wrong and acted w. and rebelled, Dan 9.05
we have sinned, we have done w. 9.15
but the wicked shall do w.; 12.10

WICKEDNESS
saw that the w. of man was great Gen 6.05
how then can I do this great w., 39.09
near kinswomen, it is w. Lev 18.17
and the land become full of w. 19.29
wife and her mother also, it is w.; 20.14
that there may be no w. among you. 20.14
because of the w. of these nations Deu 9.04
because of the w. of these nations 9.05
people, or their w., or their sin, 9.27
do any such w. as this among you. 13.11
made all the w. of the men of Ju 9.57
how was this w. brought to pass?" 20.03
"What w. is this that has taken 20.12
know and see that your w. is great, 1Sa 12.17
'Out of the wicked comes forth w.'; 24.13
the evildoer according to his w.!" 2Sa 3.39
but if w. is found in him, he shall 1Ki 1.52
and let not w. dwell in your tents. Job 11.14
"Though w. is sweet in his mouth, 20.12
Is not your w. great? There is no 22.05
so w. is broken like a tree. 24.20
it from God that he should do w., 34.10
them for their w. in the sight of 34.26
Your w. concerns a man like yourself, 35.08
art not a God who delights in w.; Ps 5.04
seek out his w. till thou find none 10.15
me, thou wilt find no w. in me; 17.03
you love righteousness and hate w. 45.07
God than dwell in the tents of w. 84.10
and wipe them out for their w.; 94.23
because of the w. of its inhabitants. 107.34
and all w. stops its mouth. 107.42
For the scepter of w. shall not 125.03
the bread of w. and drink the wine Pro 4.17
w. is an abomination to my lips. 8.07
Treasures gained by w. do not profit, 10.02
but the wicked falls by his own w. 11.05
A man is not established by w., 12.03
When w. comes, contempt comes also; 18.03
his w. will be exposed in the 26.26
of justice, even there was w., Ecc 3.16
righteousness, even there was w. 3.16
and to know the w. of folly and 7.25
nor will w. deliver those who are 8.08
For w. burns like a fire, it consumes Is 9.18
You felt secure in your w., 47.10
I choose: to loose the bonds of w., 58.06
of the finger, and speaking w., 58.09
lies, your tongue mutters w. 59.03
for all their w. in forsaking me; Jer 1.16
Your w. will chasten you, and your 2.19
Jerusalem, wash your heart from w., 4.14
They know no bounds in deeds of w.; 5.28
fresh, so she keeps fresh her w.; 6.07
to it for the w. of my people 7.12
no man repents of his w., saying, 8.06
For the w. of those who dwell in it 12.04
I will pour out their w. upon them. 14.16
We acknowledge out w., O LORD, 14.20
confounded because of all your w. 22.22
have found their w., says the LORD. 23.11
so that no one turns from his w.; 23.14
this city because of all their w. 33.05
because of the w. which they 44.03
turn from their w. and burn no 44.05
forgotten the w. of your fathers, 44.09
the w. of the kings of Judah, the 44.09
the w. of their wives, your own w., 44.09
and the w. of your wives, which they 44.09
and he does not turn from his w., Eze 3.19
Violence has grown up into a rod of w.; 7.11
"And after all your w. (woe, woe to you! 16.23
before your w. was uncovered? Now you 16.57
and the w. of the wicked shall be 18.20
away from the w. he has committed 18.27
deal with it as its w. deserves. 31.11
and as for the w. of the wicked, 33.12
by it when he turns from his w.; 33.12
And when the wicked turns from his w., 33.19
By their w. they make the king glad, Hos 7.03
Because of the w. of their deeds I 9.15
Israel, because of your great w. 10.15
overflow, for their w. is great. Joe 3.13
for their w. has come up before me. Jon 1.02
who devise w. and work evil upon Mic 2.01
treasures of w. in the house of 6.10
And he said, "This is W." And he Zec 5.08
And because w. is multiplied, most Mt 24.12
coveting, w., deceit, licentiousness, Mk 7.22
you are full of extortion and w. Lk 11.39
a field with the reward of his w.; Ac 1.18
every one of you from your w." 3.26
Repent therefore of this w. of yours, 8.22
ungodliness and w. of men who by Rom 1.18
who by their w. suppress the truth. 1.18
They were filled with all manner of w., 1.29
but obey w., there will be wrath 2.08
But if our w. serves to show the 3.05
to sin as instruments of w., 6.13
hosts of w. in the heavenly places. Eph 6.12
rank growth of w. and receive with Jas 1.21

WIDE
around it a frame a handbreadth w., Ex 25.25
around it a frame a handbreadth w., 37.12
then scatter the fire far and w. Num 16.37
You shall open w. your hand to Deu 15.11
Thou didst give a w. place for my 2Sa 22.37
twenty cubits w., and thirty cubits 1Ki 6.02
twenty cubits w., and twenty cubits 6.20
four cubits w., and three cubits 7.27
cubits long, and twenty cubits w., 2Ch 4.01
five cubits w., and three cubits 6.13
The city was w. and large, but the Neh 7.04
As through a w. breach they come; Job 30.14
Thou didst give a w. place for my Ps 18.36
they open w. their mouths at me, 22.13
They open w. their mouths against 35.21
Open your mouth w., and I will 81.10
great and w., which teems with 104.25
shatter chiefs over the w. earth. 110.06
he who opens w. his lips comes to Pro 13.03
you like a ball into a w. land; Is 22.18
ready, its pyre made deep and w., 30.33
open your mouth w. and put out 57.04
gone up to it, you have made it w.; 57.08
ten cubits w. and a hundred cubits Eze 42.04
your land are w. open to your foes; Nah 3.13
His greed is as w. as Sheol; Hab 2.05

WIDE (cont.)
east to west by a very w. valley; Zec 14.04
for the gate is w. and the way is Mt 7.13
for a w. door for effective work 1Co 16.09
Corinthians; our heart is w. 2Co 6.11

WIDELY
"The work is great and w. spread, Neh 4.19

WIDEN
as to children—w. your hearts also. 2Co 6.13

WIDOW
"Remain a w. in your father's house, Gen 38.11
shall not afflict any w. or orphan. Ex 22.22
A w., or one divorced, or a woman Lev 21.14
daughter is a w. or divorced, 22.13
But any vow of a w. or of a divorced Num 30.09
for the fatherless and the w., Deu 10.18
and the w., who are within your 14.29
and the w. who are among you, at the 16.11
and the w. who are within your 16.14
sojourner, the fatherless, and the w.; 24.19
sojourner, the fatherless, and the w. 24.20
sojourner, the fatherless, and the w. 24.21
and the w., that they may eat 26.12
and the w., according to all thy 26.13
sojourner, the fatherless, and the w. 27.19
the w. of the dead, in order to Ru 4.05
the w. of Mahlon, I have bought to 4.10
and Abigail of Carmel, Nabal's w. 1Sa 27.03
and Abigail the w. of Nabal of 30.05
and Abigail the w. of Nabal of 2Sa 2.02
of Abigail the w. of Nabal of 3.03
She answered, "Alas, I am a w.; 14.05
the son of a w. of the tribe of 1Ki 7.14
a w., also lifted up his hand 11.26
commanded a w. there to feed you." 17.09
a w. was there gathering sticks; 17.10
even upon the w. with whom I 17.20
woman, and do no good to the w. Job 24.21
caused the eyes of the w. to fail, 31.16
They slay the w. and the sojourner, Ps 94.06
be fatherless, and his wife a w.! 109.09
he upholds the w. and the fatherless; 146.09
the fatherless, plead for the w. Is 1.17
not sit as a w. or know the loss 47.08
alien, the fatherless or the w., Jer 7.06
and the w., nor shed innocent blood 22.03
How like a w. has she become, she Lam 1.01
fatherless and the w. are wronged Eze 22.07
They shall not marry a w., 44.22
or a w. who is the w. of a priest. 44.22
do not oppress the w., the fatherless, Zec 7.10
the w. and the orphan, against those Mal 3.05
his brother must marry the w., Mt 22.24
And a poor w. came, and put in two Mk 12.42
this poor w. has put in more than 12.43
and as a w. till she was eighty-four. Lk 2.37
of Sidon, to a woman who was a w. 4.26
of his mother, and she was a w.; 7.12
and there was a w. in that city who 18.03
yet because this w. bothers me, 18.05
and he saw a poor w. put in two 21.02
this poor w. has put in more than 21.03
If a w. has children or grandchildren, 1Ti 5.04
She who is a real w., and is left 5.05
enrolled as a w. who is under 5.09
I am no w., mourning I shall never Rev 18.07

WIDOWED
wives become childless and w. Jer 18.21

WIDOWHOOD
she put on the garments of her w. Gen 38.19
of their death, living as if in w. 2Sa 20.03
of children and w. shall come upon Is 47.09
reproach of your w. you will 54.04

WIDOW'S
she put off her w. garments, Gen 38.14
or take a w. garment in pledge; Deu 24.17
they take the w. ox for a pledge. Job 24.03
I caused the w. heart to sing for 29.13
but maintains the w. boundaries. Pro 15.25
and the w. cause does not come to Is 1.23

WIDOWS
shall become w. and your children Ex 22.24
You have sent w. away empty, and the Job 22.09
and their w. make no lamentation. 27.15
protector of w. is God in his holy Ps 68.05
and their w. made no lamentation. 78.64
compassion on their fatherless and w.; Is 9.17
that w. may be their spoil, and that 10.02
I have made their w. more in number Jer 15.08
and let your w. trust in me." 49.11
fatherless; our mothers are like w. Lam 5.03
have made many w. in the midst of Eze 22.25
there were many w. in Israel in Lk 4.25
because their w. were neglected in Ac 6.01
All the w. stood beside him weeping, 9.39
the saints and w. he presented her 9.41
unmarried and the w. I say that it 1Co 7.08
Honor w. who are real w. 1Ti 5.03
But refuse to enrol younger w.; 5.11
So I would have younger w. marry, 5.14
woman has relatives who are w., 5.16
may assist those who are real w. 5.16
orphans and w. in their affliction, Jas 1.27

WIDOWS'
for you devour w. houses and for a *Mt 23.14
who devour w. houses and for a Mk 12.40
who devour w. houses and for a Lk 20.47

WIDTH
equal to the w. of the house, and 1Ki 6.03
long, equal to the w. of the house; 2Ch 3.04

WIELD
for if you w. your tool upon it you Ex 20.25
if a rod should w. him who lifts Is 10.15
of hosts will w. against them a 10.26
may become strong to w. the sword. Eze 30.21
and w. you like a warrior's sword. Zec 9.13

WIELDED
he w. his spear against eight 2Sa 23.08
And he w. his spear against three 23.18
he w. his spear against three 1Ch 11.11
And he w. his spear against three 11.20

WIELDING
its trees by w. an axe against Deu 20.19
with buckler and shield, w. swords; Eze 38.04

WIELDS
itself against him who w. it? Is 10.15

WIFE
his mother and cleaves to his w., Gen 2.24
And the man and his w. were both 2.25
the man and his w. hid themselves 3.08
listened to the voice of your w., 3.17
and for his w. garments of skins, 3.21
Now Adam knew Eve his w., and she 4.01
Cain knew his w., and she conceived 4.17
And Adam knew his w. again, 4.25
they took to w. such of them as 6.02
your w., and your sons' wives with 6.18
sons and his w. and his sons' 7.07
And Noah's w. and the three wives of 7.13

WIFE (cont.)

you and your w., and your sons and	Gen 8.16
sons and his w. and his sons'	8.18
the name of Abram's w. was Sarai,	11.29
Sarai, and the name of Nahor's w.,	11.29
daughter-in-law, his son Abram's w.,	11.31
And Abram took Sarai his w.,	12.05
Egypt, he said to Sarai his w.,	12.11
they will say, 'This is his w.';	12.12
because of Sarai, Abram's w.	12.17
not tell me that she was your w.?	12.18
so that I took her for my w.?	12.19
here is your w., take her, and be	12.19
with his w. and all that he had.	12.20
he and his w., and all that he had,	13.01
Abram's w., bore him no children.	16.01
Abram's w., took Hagar the Egyptian	16.03
her to Abram her husband as a w.	16.03
to Abraham, "As for Sarai your w.,	17.15
but Sarah your w. shall bear you a	17.19
to him, "Where is Sarah your w.?"	18.09
and Sarah your w. shall have a son."	18.10
take your w. and your two daughters	19.15
him and his w. and his two daughters	19.16
But Lot's w. behind him looked back,	19.26
And Abraham said of Sarah his w.,	20.02
have taken; for she is a man's w."	20.03
Now then restore the man's w.;	20.07
they will kill me because of my w.	20.11
my mother; and she became my w.	20.12
and restored Sarah his w. to him.	20.14
also healed his w. and female	20.17
because of Sarah, Abraham's w.	20.18
mother took a w. for him from the	21.21
Sarah his w. in the cave of the	23.19
will not take a w. for my son from	24.03
and take a w. for my son Isaac."	24.04
shall take a w. for my son from	24.07
the w. of Nahor, Abraham's brother,	24.15
my master's w. bore a son to my	24.36
not take a w. for my son from the	24.37
kindred, and take a w. for my son.'	24.38
shall take a w. for my son from my	24.40
let her be the w. of your master's	24.51
Rebekah, and she became his w.;	24.67
Abraham took another w., whose name	25.01
was buried, with Sarah his w.	25.10
old when he took to w. Rebekah,	25.20
prayed to the LORD for his w.,	25.21
and Rebekah his w. conceived.	25.21
the place asked him about his w.,	26.07
"My w.," thinking, "lest the men of	26.07
saw Isaac fondling Rebekah his w.	26.08
and said, "Behold, she is your w.;	26.09
easily have lain with your w.,	26.10
this man or his w. shall be put to	26.11
he took to w. Judith the daughter	26.34
and take as w. from there one of	28.02
Paddan-aram to take a w. from there,	28.06
Esau went to Ishmael and took to w.,	28.09
"Give me my w. that I may go in to	29.21
gave him his daughter Rachel to w.	29.28
gave him her maid Bilhah as a w.;	30.04
and gave her to Jacob as a w.	30.09
"Get me this maiden for my w."	34.04
give me the maiden to be my w."	34.12
the son of Adah the w. of Esau,	36.10
the son of Basemath the w. of Esau.	36.10
are the sons of Adah, Esau's w.	36.12
the sons of Basemath, Esau's w.	36.13
Esau's w.: she bore to Esau Jeush,	36.14
the sons of Basemath, Esau's w.	36.17
Esau's w.: the chiefs Jeush, Jalam, and	36.18
the daughter of Anah, Esau's w.	36.18
And Judah took a w. for Er his	38.06
Onan, "Go in to your brother's w.,	38.08
his brother's w. he spilled the	38.09

In course of time the w. of Judah,	38.12
his master's w. cast her eyes upon	39.07
and said to his master's w.,	39.08
yourself, because you are his w.;	39.09
words which his w. spoke to him,	39.19
know that my w. bore me two sons;	44.27
Jacob's w.: Joseph and Benjamin.	46.19
buried Abraham and Sarah his w.;	49.31
buried Isaac and Rebekah his w.;	49.31
and took to w. a daughter of Levi.	Ex 2.01
So Moses took his w. and his sons	4.20
Amram took to w. Jochebed his	6.20
Aaron took to w. Elisheba, the	6.23
took to w. one of the daughters of	6.25
Moses' w., after he had sent her	18.02
sons and his w. to Moses in the	18.05
you with your w. and her two sons	18.06
shall not covet your neighbor's w.,	20.17
then his w. shall go out with him.	21.03
gives him a w. and she bears him	21.04
the w. and her children shall be	21.04
my w., and my children; I will not	21.05
If he takes another w. to himself,	21.10
for her, and make her his w.	22.16
the nakedness of your father's w.;	Lev 18.08
is, you shall not approach his w.;	18.14
she is your son's w., you shall not	18.15
the nakedness of your brother's w.;	18.16
woman as a rival w. to her sister,	18.18
carnally with your neighbor's w.,	18.20
with the w. of his neighbor, both	20.10
his father's w. has uncovered his	20.11
If a man takes a w. and her mother	20.14
If a man lies with his uncle's w.,	20.20
If a man takes his brother's w.,	20.21
And he shall take a w. in her	21.13
shall take to w. a virgin of his	21.14
If any man's w. goes astray and acts	Num 5.12
jealous of his w. who has defiled	5.14
him, and he is jealous of his w.,	5.14
shall bring his w. to the priest,	5.15
when a w., though under her husband's	5.29
a man and he is jealous of his w.;	5.30
The name of Amram's w. was Jochebed	26.59
Moses, as between a man and his w.,	30.16
shall be w. to one of the family of	36.08
shall you covet your neighbor's w.;	Deu 5.21
or the w. of your bosom, or your	13.06
has betrothed a w. and has not	20.07
would take her for yourself as w.,	21.11
husband, and she shall be your w.	21.13
"If any man takes a w., and goes	22.13
gave my daughter to this man to w.,	22.16
and she shall be his w.; he may	22.19
lying with the w. of another man,	22.22
he violated his neighbor's w.;	22.24
of silver, and she shall be his w.,	22.29
man shall not take his father's w.,	22.30
"When a man takes a w. and marries	24.01
goes and becomes another man's w.,	24.02
dies, who took her to be his w.,	24.03
not take her again to be his w.,	24.04
happy with his w. whom he has	24.05
the w. of the dead shall not be	25.05
in to her, and take her as his w.,	25.05
not wish to take his brother's w.,	25.07
his brother's w. shall go up to	25.07
then his brother's w. shall go up to	25.09
and the w. of the one draws near to	25.11
he who lies with his father's w.,	27.20
You shall betroth a w., and another	28.30
to the w. of his bosom, and to the	28.54
I give Achsah my daughter as w.	Jos 15.16
gave him Achsah his daughter as w.	15.17
give him Achsah my daughter as w."	Ju 1.12
gave him Achsah his daughter as w.	1.13
the w. of Lappidoth, was judging	4.04

WIFE (cont.)
the w. of Heber the Kenite; for there Ju 4.17
But Jael the w. of Heber took a 4.21
the w. of Heber the Kenite, of 5.24
And Gilead's w. also bore him sons; 11.02
and his w. was barren and had no 13.02
Manoah arose and went after his w., 13.11
while Manoah and his w. looked on; 13.20
no more to Manoah and to his w. 13.21
And Manoah said to his w., 13.22
But his w. said to him, "If the LORD 13.23
now get her for me as my w." 14.02
go to take a w. from the uncircumcised 14.03
day they said to Samson's w., 14.15
And Samson's w. wept before him, and 14.16
And Samson's w. was given to his 14.20
went to visit his w. with a kid; 15.01
will go in to my w. in the chamber." 15.01
has taken his w. and given her to 15.06
be he who gives a w. to Benjamin." 21.18
each man his w. from the daughters 21.21
each man of them his w. in battle, 21.22
he and his w. and his two sons. Ru 1.01
and the name of his w. Naomi, 1.02
Mahlon, I have bought to be my w., 4.10
took Ruth and she became his w.; 4.13
to Peninnah his w. and to all her 1Sa 1.04
And Elkanah knew Hannah his w., 1.19
Eli would bless Elkanah and his w., 2.20
the w. of Phinehas, was with child, 4.19
name of Saul's w. was Ahinoam the 14.50
I will give her to you for a w.; 18.17
to Adriel the Meholathite for a w. 18.19
him his daughter Michal for a w. 18.27
David's w., told him, "If you do not 19.11
and the name of his w. Abigail. 25.03
Nabal's w., "Behold, David sent 25.14
his w. told him these things, and 25.37
wooed Abigail, to make her his w. 25.39
you to take you to him as his w." 25.40
of David, and became his w. 25.42
David's w., to Palti the son of 25.44
may lead away his w. and children, 30.22
Ithream of Eglah, David's w. 2Sa 3.05
"Give me my w. Michal, whom I 3.14
the w. of Uriah the Hittite?" 11.03
to drink, and to lie with my w.? 11.11
When the w. of Uriah heard that 11.26
his house, and she became his w., 11.27
have taken his w. to be your w., 12.09
the w. of Uriah the Hittite to be your w.' 12.10
that Uriah's w. bore to David, 12.15
Then David comforted his w., 12.24
me Abishag the Shunammite as my w." 1Ki 2.17
to Adonijah your brother as his w." 2.21
the daughter of Solomon as his w.); 4.11
the daughter of Solomon as his w.); 4.15
to his daughter, Solomon's w.; 9.16
marriage the sister of his own w., 11.19
And Jeroboam said to his w., 14.02
that you are the w. of Jeroboam, 14.02
Jeroboam's w. did so; she arose 14.04
the w. of Jeroboam is coming to 14.05
he said, "Come in, w. of Jeroboam; 14.06
Then Jeroboam's w. arose, and departed, 14.17
he took for w. Jezebel the daughter 16.31
But Jezebel his w. came to him, 21.05
And Jezebel his w. said to him, 21.07
Ahab, whom Jezebel his w. incited. 21.25
Now the w. of one of the sons of 2Ki 4.01
and she waited on Naaman's w. 5.02
the daughter of Ahab was his w. 8.18
your daughter to my son for a w.'; 14.09
the w. of Shallum the son of Tikvah, 22.14
had children by his w. Azubah, 1Ch 2.18
the w. of Hezron his father, and she 2.24
Jerahmeel also had another w., 2.26
The name of Abishur's w. was Abihail, 2.29
the sixth Ithream, by his w. Eglah; 3.03
And his Jewish w. bore Jered the 4.18
The sons of the w. of Hodiah, 4.19
And Machir took a w. for Huppim and 7.15
And Maacah the w. of Machir bore a 7.16
And Ephraim went in to his w., 7.23
He had sons by Hodesh his w.: 8.09
and the name of his w. was Maacah, 8.29
and the name of his w. was Maacah, 9.35
"My w. shall not live in the house 2Ch 8.11
Rehoboam took as w. Mahalath the 11.18
the daughter of Ahab was his w. 21.06
Jehoram and w. of Jehoiada the 22.11
your daughter to my son for a w.'; 25.18
the w. of Shallum the son of 34.22
(who had taken a w. from the Ez 2.61
the son of Berechiah as his w. Neh 6.18
(who had taken a w. of the daughters 7.63
his friends and his w. Zeresh. Est 5.10
Then his w. Zeresh and all his 5.14
And Haman told his w. Zeresh and 6.13
men and his w. Zeresh said to him, 6.13
Then his w. said to him, "Do you Job 2.09
I am repulsive to my w., loathsome 19.17
then let my w. grind for another, 31.10
be fatherless, and his w. a widow! Ps 109.09
Your w. will be like a fruitful 128.03
rejoice in the w. of your youth, Pro 5.18
who goes in to his neighbor's w.; 6.29
A good w. is the crown of her 12.04
He who finds a w. finds a good 18.22
but a prudent w. is from the LORD. 19.14
A good w. who can find? 31.10
Enjoy life with the w. whom you love, Ecc 9.09
you like a w. forsaken and grieved Is 54.06
like a w. of youth when she is cast 54.06
divorces his w. and she goes from Jer.3.01
him and becomes another man's w., 3.01
Surely, as a faithless w. leaves her 3.20
neighing for his neighbor's w. 5.08
both husband and w. shall be taken, 6.11
"You shall not take a w., nor shall 16.02
Adulterous w., who receives strangers Eze 16.32
his neighbor's w. or approach a 18.06
mountains, defiles his neighbor's w., 18.11
does not defile his neighbor's w., 18.15
abomination with his neighbor's w.; 22.11
morning, and at evening my w. died. 24.18
of you defiles his neighbor's w.; 33.26
to yourself a w. of harlotry and Hos 1.02
mother, plead—for she is not my w., 2.02
there Israel did service for a w., 12.12
and for a w. he herded sheep. 12.12
'Your w. shall be a harlot in the Amo 7.17
you and the w. of your youth, Mal 2.14
companion and your w. by covenant. 2.14
faithless to the w. of his youth. 2.15
of Solomon by the w. of Uriah, Mt 1.06
do not fear to take Mary your w., 1.20
commanded him; he took his w., 1.24
said, 'Whoever divorces his w., 5.31
that every one who divorces his w., 5.32
Herodias, his brother Philip's w.; 14.03
with his w. and children and all 18.25
to divorce one's w. for any cause?" 19.03
and mother and be joined to his w., 19.05
to you: whoever divorces his w., 19.09
is the case of a man with his w., 19.10
children left his w. to his brother. 22.25
which of the seven will she be w.? 22.28
his w. sent word to him, "Have 27.19
Herodias, his brother Philip's w.; Mk 6.17
for you to have your brother's w." 6.18
lawful for a man to divorce his w.?" 10.02
mother and be joined to his w., 10.07

WIFE (cont.)

divorces his w. and marries Mk 10.11
man's brother dies and leaves a w., 12.19
no child, the man must take the w., 12.19
the first took a w., and when he 12.20
resurrection whose w. will she be? 12.23
For the seven had her as w." 12.23
and he had a w. of the daughters of Lk 1.05
and your w. Elizabeth will bear you 1.13
and my w. is advanced in years." 1.18
After these days his w. Elizabeth 1.24
his brother's w., and for all the 3.19
the w. of Chuza, Herod's steward, and 8.03
another said, 'I have married a w., 14.20
and mother and w. and children and 14.26
divorces his w. and marries 16.18
not turn back. Remember Lot's w. 17.32
left house or w. or brothers or 18.29
having a w. but no children, the man 20.28
must take the w. and raise up 20.28
the first took a w., and died 20.29
whose w. will the woman be? 20.33
For the seven had her as w." 20.33
Mary the w. of Clopas, and Mary Jn 19.25
with his w. Sapphira sold a piece Ac 5.01
about three hours his w. came in, 5.07
from Italy with his w. Priscilla, 18.02
Felix came with his w. Drusilla, 24.24
man is living with his father's w. 1Co 5.01
have his own w. and each woman her 7.02
give to his w. her conjugal rights, 7.03
and likewise the w. to her husband. 7.03
For the w. does not rule over her 7.04
over his own body, but the w. does. 7.04
that the w. should not separate 7.10
husband should not divorce his w. 7.11
brother has a w. who is an unbeliever, 7.12
is consecrated through his w., 7.14
the unbelieving w. is consecrated 7.14
W., how do you know whether you 7.16
know whether you will save your w.? 7.16
Are you bound to a w.? Do not seek 7.27
Are you free from a w.? Do not seek 7.27
affairs, how to please his w., 7.33
A w. is bound to her husband as 7.39
right to be accompanied by a w., 9.05
the head of the w. as Christ is Eph 5.23
he who loves his w. loves himself. 5.28
and mother and be joined to his w., 5.31
one of you love his w. as himself, 5.33
and let the w. see that she respects 5.33
how to take a w. for himself in 1Th 4.04
you the Bride, the w. of the Lamb." Rev 21.09

WIFE'S

The man called his w. name Eve, Gen 3.20
his w. name was Mehetabel, the 36.39
of your father's w. daughter, Lev 18.11
and when his w. sons grew up, they Ju 11.02
and his w. name Mehetabel the 1Ch 1.50
and a w. quarreling is a continual Pro 19.13
and with his w. knowledge he kept Ac 5.02

WILD

than any other w. creature that Gen 3.01
cattle, and above all w. animals; 3.14
He shall be a w. ass of a man, his 16.12
was torn by w. beasts I did not 31.39
say that a w. beast has devoured 37.20
a w. beast has devoured him; 37.33
they leave the w. beasts may eat. Ex 23.11
desolate and the w. beasts multiply 23.29
let loose the w. beasts among you, Lev 26.22
as it were the horns of the w. ox. Num 23.22
as it were the horns of the w. ox, 24.08
lest the w. beasts grow too numerous Deu 7.22
the w. goat, the ibex, the antelope, 14.05
his horns are the horns of a w. ox; 33.17
air and to the w. beasts of the 1Sa 17.46
as swift of foot as a w. gazelle; 2Sa 2.18
and found a w. vine and gathered 2Ki 4.39
from it his lap full of w. gourds, 4.39
and a w. beast of Lebanon passed 14.09
and a w. beast of Lebanon passed 2Ch 25.18
w. olive, myrtle, palm, and other Neh 8.15
Does the w. ass bray when he has Job 6.05
when a w. ass's colt is born a man. 11.12
Behold, like w. asses in the desert 24.05
"Who has let the w. ass go free? 39.05
"Is the w. ox willing to serve you? 39.09
and that the w. beast may trample 39.15
him where all the w. beasts play. 40.20
soul from the horns of the w. oxen! Ps 22.21
and Sirion like a young w. ox 29.06
soul of thy dove to the w. beasts; 74.19
my horn like that of the w. ox; 92.10
the w. asses quench their thirst. 104.11
mountains are for the w. goats; 104.18
grapes, but it yielded w. grapes. Is 5.02
grapes, why did it yield w. grapes? 5.04
But w. beasts will lie down there, 13.21
They destined Tyre for w. beasts. 23.13
a joy of w. asses, a pasture of 32.14
W. oxen shall fall with them, and 34.07
And w. beasts shall meet with 34.14
The w. beasts will honor me, the 43.20
degenerate and become a w. vine? Jer 2.21
a w. ass used to the wilderness, in 2.24
Go, assemble all the w. beasts; 12.09
The w. asses stand on the bare 14.06
Be like a w. ass in the desert! 48.06
"Therefore w. beasts and jackals 50.39
send famine and w. beasts against Eze 5.17
If I cause w. beasts to pass 14.15
became food for all the w. beasts. 34.05
became food for all the w. beasts, 34.08
and banish w. beasts from the land, 34.25
sort and to the w. beasts to be 39.04
his dwelling was with the w. asses; Dan 5.21
a w. ass wandering alone; Ephraim has Hos 8.09
as a w. beast would rend them. 13.08
Even the w. beasts cry to thee Joe 1.20
has become, a lair for w. beasts! Zep 2.15
his food was locusts and w. honey. Mt 3.04
and ate locusts and w. honey. Mk 1.06
and he was with the w. beasts; 1.13
a w. olive shoot, were grafted in Rom 11.17
what is by nature a w. olive tree, 11.24
them in the same w. profligacy, 1Pe 4.04
w. waves of the sea, casting up the Jud 1.13
pestilence and by w. beasts of the Rev 6.08

WILDERNESS

as Elparan on the border of the w.; Gen 14.06
her by a spring of water in the w., 16.07
wandered in the w. of Beersheba. 21.14
he lived in the w. and became an 21.20
He lived in the w. of Paran; 21.21
found the hot springs in the w., 36.24
him into this pit here in the w., 37.22
flock to the west side of the w., Ex 3.01
a three days' journey into the w., 3.18
"Go into the w. to meet Moses." 4.27
may hold a feast to me in the w.' " 5.01
a three days' journey into the w., 5.03
that they may serve me in the w.; 7.16
into the w. and sacrifice to the 8.27
to the LORD your God in the w.; 8.28
the way of the w. toward the Red 13.18
at Etham, on the edge of the w. 13.20
in the land; the w. has shut them in.' 14.03
taken us away to die in the w.? 14.11
Egyptians than to die in the w." 14.12
and they went into the w. of Shur; 15.22

WILDERNESS (cont.)

days in the w. and found no water. Ex 15.22
of Israel came to the w. of Sin, 16.01
against Moses and Aaron in the w., 16.02
out into this w. to kill this 16.03
Israel, they looked toward the w., 16.10
was on the face of the w. a fine, 16.14
with which I fed you in the w., 16.32
on from the w. of Sin by stages, 17.01
to Moses in the w. where he was 18.05
day they came into the w. of Sinai. 19.01
and came into the w. of Sinai, 19.02
of Sinai, they encamped in the w.; 19.02
and from the w. to the Euphrates; 23.31
to the LORD, in the w. of Sinai. Lev 7.38
be sent away into the w. to Azazel. 16.10
away into the w. by the hand of a 16.21
he shall let the goat go in the w. 16.22
spoke to Moses in the w. of Sinai, Num 1.01
numbered them in the w. of Sinai. 1.19
before the LORD in the w. of Sinai; 3.04
said to Moses in the w. of Sinai, 3.14
spoke to Moses in the w. of Sinai, 9.01
in the evening, in the w. of Sinai; 9.05
out by stages from the w. of Sinai; 10.12
settled down in the w. of Paran. 10.12
how we are to encamp in the w., 10.31
and encamped in the w. of Paran. 12.16
sent them from the w. of Paran, 13.03
land from the w. of Zin to Rehob, 13.21
of Israel in the w. of Paran, 13.26
would that we had died in this w.! 14.02
he has slain them in the w.' 14.16
I wrought in Egypt and in the w., 14.22
set out for the w. by the way to 14.25
your dead bodies shall fall in this w.; 14.29
dead bodies shall fall in this w. 14.32
be shepherds in the w. forty years, 14.33
of your dead bodies lies in the w. 14.33
in this w. they shall come to a 14.35
people of Israel were in the w., 15.32
and honey, to kill us in the w., 16.13
came into the w. of Zin in the 20.01
assembly of the LORD into this w., 20.04
up out of Egypt to die in the w.? 21.05
in the w. which is opposite Moab, 21.11
of the Arnon, which is in the w., 21.13
And from the w. they went on to 21.18
went out against Israel to the w., 21.23
but set his face toward the w. 24.01
of Israel in the w. of Sinai. 26.64
of them, "They shall die in the w." 26.65
"Our father died in the w.; 27.03
my word in the w. of Zin during 27.14
Meribah of Kadesh in the w. of Zin. 27.14
them wander in the w. forty years, 32.13
will again abandon them in the w.; 32.15
which is on the edge of the w. 33.06
the midst of the sea into the w., 33.08
days' journey in the w. of Etham, 33.08
Sea, and encamped in the w. of Sin. 33.11
And they set out from the w. of Sin, 33.12
and encamped in the w. of Sinai. 33.15
And they set out from the w. of Sinai, 33.16
encamped in the w. of Zin (that is, 33.36
be from the w. of Zin along the 34.03
Israel beyond the Jordan in the w., Deu 1.01
and terrible w. which you saw, 1.19
and in the w., where you have seen 1.31
into the w. in the direction of 1.40
into the w. in the direction of 2.01
your going through this great w.; 2.07
in the direction of the w. of Moab. 2.08
from the w. of Kedemoth to Sihon 2.26
Bezer in the w. on the tableland 4.43
you these forty years in the w., 8.02
through the great and terrible w., 8.15
who fed you in the w. with manna 8.16
LORD your God to wrath in the w.; 9.07
them out to slay them in the w." 9.28
and what he did to you in the w., 11.05
be from the w. to Lebanon and from 11.24
have led you forty years in the w.; 29.05
and in the howling waste of the w.; 32.10
Meribathkadesh, in the w. of Zin; 32.51
From the w. and this Lebanon as far Jos 1.04
the way in the w. after they had 5.04
the way in the w. after they had 5.05
walked forty years in the w., 5.06
fled in the direction of the w. 8.15
fled to the w. turned back upon 8.20
Ai in the open w. where they 8.24
in the w., and in the Negeb, the 12.08
while Israel walked in the w.; 14.10
to the w. of Zin at the farthest 15.01
In the w., Betharabah, Middin, 15.61
into the w., going up from Jericho 16.01
and it ends at the w. of Bethaven. 18.12
Bezer in the w. on the tableland, 20.08
you lived in the w. a long time. 24.07
city of palms into the w. of Judah, Ju 1.16
thorns of the w. and with briers. 8.07
thorns of the w. and briers and 8.16
through the w. to the Red Sea and 11.16
Then they journeyed through the w., 11.18
and from the w. to the Jordan. 11.22
Israel in the direction of the w.; 20.42
fled toward the w. to the rock of 20.45
fled toward the w. to the rock of 20.47
every sort of plague in the w. 1Sa 4.08
the valley of Zeboim toward the w. 13.18
you left those few sheep in the w.? 17.28
in the strongholds in the w., 23.14
the hill country of the W. of Ziph. 23.14
was in the W. of Ziph at Horesh. 23.15
and his men were in the w. of Maon, 23.24
rock which is in the w. of Maon. 23.25
after David in the w. of Maon. 23.25
David is in the w. of Engedi. 24.01
and went down to the w. of Paran. 25.01
David heard in the w. that Nabal 25.04
out of the w. to salute our master 25.14
all that this fellow has in the w., 25.21
and went down to the w. of Ziph, 26.02
to seek David in the w. of Ziph. 26.02
But David remained in the w.; 26.03
Saul came after him into the w., 26.03
on the way to the w. of Gibeon. 2Sa 2.24
the people passed on toward the w. 15.23
I will wait at the fords of the w., 15.28
those who faint in the w. to drink." 16.02
tonight at the fords of the w., 17.16
and weary and thirsty in the w." 17.29
buried in his own house in the w. 1Ki 2.34
and Baalath and Tamir in the w., 9.18
went a day's journey into the w., 19.04
on your way to the w. of Damascus; 19.15
"By the way of the w. of Edom." 2Ki 3.08
stronghold in the w. mighty and 1Ch 12.08
which Moses had made in the w., 21.29
LORD had made in the w., was there. 2Ch 1.03
Tadmor in the w. and all the store 8.04
valley, east of the w. of Jeruel. 20.16
and went out into the w. of Tekoa; 20.20
came to the watchtower of the w., 20.24
of God laid upon Israel in the w. 24.09
And he built towers in the w., 26.10
didst not forsake them in the w.; Neh 9.19
didst thou sustain them in the w., 9.21
a great wind came across the w., Job 1.19
prey in the w. as food for their 24.05
The voice of the LORD shakes the w., Ps 29.08
the LORD shakes the w. of Kadesh. 29.08
afar, I would lodge in the w., 55.07

WILDERNESS (cont.)
The pastures of the w. drip, Ps 65.12
thou didst march through the w., 68.07
food for the creatures of the w. 74.14
not from the w. comes lifting up; 75.06
He cleft rocks in the w., and gave them 78.15
"Can God spread a table in the w.? 78.19
him in the w. and grieved him in 78.40
guided them in the w. like a flock. 78.52
as on the day at Massah in the w., 95.08
I am like a vulture of the w., 102.06
had a wanton craving in the w., 106.14
he would make them fall in the w., 106.26
who led his people through the w., 136.16
What is that coming up from the w., Sol 3.06
Who is that coming up from the w., 8.05
concerning the w. of the sea. Is 21.01
deserted and forsaken, like the w.; 27.10
and the w. becomes a fruitful field, 32.15
Then justice will dwell in the w., 32.16
The w. and the dry land shall be 35.01
waters shall break forth in the w., 35.06
"In the w. prepare the way of the 40.03
I will make the w. a pool of water, 41.18
I will put in the w. the cedar, 41.19
a way in the w. and rivers in the 43.19
for I give water in the w., rivers in 43.20
and will make her w. like Eden, 51.03
Thy holy cities have become a w., 64.10
a wilderness, Zion has become a w., 64.10
how you followed me in the w., Jer 2.02
of Egypt, who led us in the w., 2.06
a wild ass used to the w., 2.24
Have I been a w. to Israel, or a 2.31
lovers like an Arab in the w. 3.02
lamentation for the pastures of the w., 9.10
ruined and laid waste like a w., 9.12
my pleasant portion a desolate w. 12.10
in the parched places of the w., 17.06
pastures of the w. are dried up. 23.10
the sword found grace in the w.; 31.02
the nations, a w. dry and desert. 50.12
like the ostriches in the w. Lam 4.03
they lay in wait for us in the w. 4.19
because of the sword in the w. 5.09
habitations, from the w. to Riblah. Eze 6.14
Now it is transplanted in the w., 19.13
Egypt and brought them into the w. 20.10
rebelled against me in the w.; 20.13
out my wrath upon them in the w., 20.13
to them in the w. that I would not 20.15
make a full end of them in the w. 20.17
I said to their children in the w., 20.18
my anger against them in the w. 20.21
to them in the w. that I would 20.23
you into the w. of the peoples, 20.35
fathers in the w. of the land of 20.36
drunkards were brought from the w.; 23.42
And I will cast you forth into the w., 29.05
securely in the w. and sleep in 34.25
was born, and make her like a w., Hos 2.03
her, and bring her into the w., 2.14
Like grapes in the w., I found 9.10
It was I who knew you in the w., 13.05
shall come, rising from the w.; 13.15
devoured the pastures of the w., Joe 1.19
devoured the pastures of the w. 1.20
them, but after them a desolate w., 2.03
the pastures of the w. are green; 2.22
desolation and Edom a desolate w., 3.19
and led you forty years in the w., Amo 2.10
offerings the forty years in the w., 5.25
preaching in the w. of Judea, Mt 3.01
"The voice of one crying in the w.: 3.03
Spirit into the w. to be tempted 4.01
you go out into the w. to behold? 11.07
he is in the w.,' do not go out; 24.26
the voice of one crying in the w.: Mk 1.03
John the baptizer appeared in the w., 1.04
immediately drove him out into the w. 1.12
And he was in the w. forty days, 1.13
he was in the w. till the day of Lk 1.80
the son of Zechariah in the w.; 3.02
"The voice of one crying in the w.: 3.04
for forty days in the w., tempted by 4.02
But he withdrew to the w. and prayed. 5.16
you go out into the w. to behold? 7.24
leave the ninety-nine in the w., 15.04
the voice of one crying in the w., Jn 1.23
lifted up the serpent in the w., 3.14
Our fathers ate the manna in the w.; 6.31
the manna in the w., and they died. 6.49
there to the country near the w., 11.54
to him in the w. of Mount Sinai, Ac 7.30
and in the w. for forty years. 7.36
congregation in the w. with the 7.38
sacrifices, forty years in the w., 7.42
had the tent of witness in the w., 7.44
years he bore with them in the w. 13.18
of the Assassins out into the w.? 21.38
for they were overthrown in the w. 1Co10.05
danger in the w., danger at sea, 2Co 11.26
on the day of testing in the w., Heb 3.08
whose bodies fell in the w.? 3.17
and the woman fled into the w., Rev 12.06
fly from the serpent into the w., 12.14
me away in the Spirit into a w., 17.03

WILDGOATS'
his men in front of the W. Rocks. 1Sa 24.02

WILDLY
My heart is beating w.; I cannot Jer 4.19

WILES
have harassed you with their w., Num 25.18
their craftiness in deceitful w. Eph 4.14
stand against the w. of the devil. 6.11

WILFUL
Bold and w., they are not afraid to 2Pe 2.10

WILFULLY
But if a man w. attacks another to Ex 21.14

WILL
he w. not perform the duty of a Deu 25.07
if he w. do the part of the next of Ru 3.13
I w. do the part of the next of kin 3.13
according to the w. of your God. Ez 7.18
not up to the w. of my adversaries; Ps 27.12
I delight to do thy w., O my God; 40.08
him up to the w. of his enemies. 41.02
Teach me to do thy w., for thou art 143.10
he turns it wherever he w. Pro 21.01
who w. no longer take advice, Ecc 4.13
here w. be dedicated to the LORD; Is 23.18
it w. not be stored or hoarded, 23.18
but her merchandise w. supply 23.18
sons who w. not hear the instruction 30.09
house of Israel w. not listen to Eze 3.07
of men, and gives it to whom he w., Dan 4.17
of men, and gives it to whom he w. 4.25
according to his w. in the host of 4.35
men, and sets over it whom he w. 5.21
dominion and do according to his w. 11.03
shall do according to his own w., 11.16
king shall do according to his w.; 11.36
Thy w. be done, On earth as it is in Mt 6.10
he who does the w. of my Father 7.21
hand and touched him, saying, "I w.; 8.03
does the w. of my Father in heaven 12.50
So it is not the w. of my Father 18.14
And he answered, 'I w. not'; 21.29
the two did the w. of his father?" 21.31

WILL (cont.)

they themselves w. not move them Mt 23.04
"What w. you give me if I deliver 26.15
not as I w., but as thou wilt." 26.39
unless I drink it, thy w. be done." 26.42
touched him, and said to him, "I w.; Mk 1.41
Whoever does the w. of God is my 3.35
poor with you, and whenever you w., 14.07
but you w. not always have me. 14.07
yet not what I w., but what thou 14.36
"To you I w. give all this authority Lk 4.06
to me, and I give it to whom I w. 4.06
and touched him, saying, "I w.; 5.13
servant who knew his master's w., 12.47
ready or act according to his w., 12.47
nevertheless not my w., but thine 22.42
Jesus he delivered up to their w. 23.25
nor of the w. of the flesh nor of Jn 1.13
of the flesh nor of the w. of man, 1.13
is to do the w. of him who sent me, 4.34
the Son gives life to whom he w. 5.21
not my own w. but the w. of him who 5.30
from heaven, not to do my own w., 6.38
but the w. of him who sent me; 6.38
and this is the w. of him who sent 6.39
For this is the w. of my Father, 6.40
and I w. raise him up at the last 6.40
the twelve, "W. you also go away?" 6.67
if any man's w. is to do his w., he 7.17
and your w. is to do your father's 8.44
a worshiper of God and does his w., 9.31
abide in you, ask whatever you w., 15.07
w. you have me release for you the 18.39
"If it is my w. that he remain 21.22
"If it is my w. that he remain 21.23
my heart, who w. do all my w.' Ac 13.22
day on which he w. judge the world 17.31
"The w. of the Lord be done." 21.14
appointed you to know his w., 22.14
by God's w. I may now at last Rom 1.10
and know his w. and approve what is 2.18
I can w. what is right, but I cannot 7.18
You w. say to me then, "Why does he 9.19
For who can resist his w.?" 9.19
may prove what is the w. of God, 12.02
so that by God's w. I may come to 15.32
called by the w. of God to be an 1Co 1.01
For if I do this of my own w., 9.17
but if not of my own w., 9.17
at all God's w. for him to go now. 16.12
He w. come when he has opportunity. 16.12
of Christ Jesus by the w. of God, 2Co 1.01
Lord and to us by the w. of God. 8.05
according to the w. of our God and Gal 1.04
of Christ Jesus by the w. of God, Eph 1.01
according to the purpose of his w., 1.05
and insight the mystery of his w., 1.09
according to the counsel of his w. 1.11
understand what the w. of the Lord is. 5.17
doing the w. of God from the heart, 6.06
with a good w. as to the Lord and 6.07
rivalry, but others from good w. Php 1.15
both to w. and to work for his good 2.13
of Christ Jesus by the w. of God, Col 1.01
knowledge of his w. in all spiritual 1.09
fully assured in all the w. of God. 4.12
For this is the w. of God, your 1Th 4.03
for this is the w. of God in Christ 5.18
Jesus by the w. of God according 2Ti 1.01
being captured by him to do his w. 2.26
distributed according to his own w. Heb 2.04
'Lo, I have come to do thy w., 10.07
"Lo, I have come to do thy w." 10.09
And by that w. we have been sanctified 10.10
you may do the w. of God and 10.36
good that you may do his w., 13.21
Of his own w. he brought us forth Jas 1.18
For it is God's w. that by doing 1Pe 2.15
right, if that should be God's w., 3.17
passions but by the w. of God. 4.02
to God's w. do right and entrust 4.19
he who does the w. of God abides 1Jn 2.17
according to his w. he hears us. 5.14
I w. spew you out of my mouth. Rev 3.16

WILLING

"If you are w. that I should bury Gen 23.08
may not be w. to follow me to this 24.05
the woman is not w. to follow you, 24.08
heart makes him w. you shall Ex 25.02
who were of a w. heart brought 35.22
if he is not w. to do the part of Ru 3.13
So David was not w. to take the ark 2Sa 6.10
ships," but Jehoshaphat was not w. 1Ki 22.49
were not w. to help the Ammonites 1Ch 19.19
a whole heart and with a w. mind; 28.09
will be every w. man who has skill 28.21
who were of a w. heart brought 2Ch 29.31
"Is the wild ox w. to serve you? Job 39.09
and uphold me with a w. spirit. Ps 51.12
and flax, and works with w. hands. Pro 31.13
If you are w. and obedient, you Is 1.19
they are not w. to listen to me; Eze 3.07
and if you are w. to accept it, he Mt 11.14
the spirit indeed is w., but the flesh 26.41
the spirit indeed is w., but the flesh Mk 14.38
if thou art w., remove this cup Lk 22.42
and you were w. to rejoice for a Jn 5.35
if they are w. to testify, that Ac 26.05
as an exaction but as a w. gift. 2Co 9.05
we were w. to be left behind at 1Th 3.01

WILLINGLY

the people offered themselves w., Ju 5.02
themselves w. among the people. 5.09
answered, "We will w. give them." 8.25
Who then will offer w., consecrating 1Ch 29.05
rejoiced because these had given w., 29.09
we should be able thus to offer w.? 29.14
contributed w. to the people, 2Ch 35.08
vowed w. for the house of their God Ez 7.16
all the men who w. offered to live Neh 11.02
for he does not w. afflict or Lam 3.33
charge, not by constraint but w., 1Pe 5.02

WILLOW

abundant waters. He set it like a w. twig, Eze 17.05

WILLOWS

leafy trees, and w. of the brook; Lev 23.40
the w. of the brook surround him. Job 40.22
On the w. there we hung up our Ps 137.02
carry away over the Brook of the W. Is 15.07
amid waters, like w. by flowing streams. 44.04

WILLS

The wind blows where it w., Jn 3.08
"I will return to you if God w., Ac 18.21
he has mercy upon whomever he w., Rom 9.18
the heart of whomever he w. 9.18
if the Lord w., and I will find out 1Co 4.19
to each one individually as he w. 12.11
"If the Lord w., we shall live and Jas 4.15

WILT

what w. thou give me, for I continue Gen 15.02
"W. thou indeed destroy the righteous 18.23
w. thou then destroy the place and 18.24
W. thou destroy the whole city for 18.28
w. thou slay an innocent people? 20.04
if now thou w. prosper the way 24.42
Thou w. bring them in, and plant Ex 15.17
if thou w. forgive their sin—and 32.32
me know whom thou w. send with me. 33.12
If thou w. deal thus with me, kill Num 11.15

WILT (cont.)
and w. thou be angry with all the Num 16.22
"If thou w. indeed give this poeple 21.02
and what w. thou do for thy great Jos 7.09
"If thou w. deliver Israel by my Ju 6.36
know that thou w. deliver Israel 6.37
"If thou w. give the Ammonites into 11.30
if thou w. indeed look on the 1Sa 1.11
but w. give to thy maidservant a 1.11
W. thou give them into the hand of 14.37
W. thou give them into my hand?" 2Sa 5.19
W. thou give them into my hand?" 1Ch 14.10
that thou w. build a house for him; 17.25
affliction, and thou w. hear and save. 2Ch 20.09
O our God, w. thou not execute 20.12
How long w. thou not look away from Job 7.19
thou w. seek me, but I shall not be." 7.21
for I know thou w. not hold me 9.28
yet thou w. plunge me into a pit, 9.31
and w. thou turn me to dust again? 10.09
W. thou frighten a driven leaf and 13.25
therefore thou w. not let them 17.04
know that thou w. bring me to 30.23
"Thou w. not call to account"? Ps 10.13
O LORD, thou w. hear the desire of 10.17
thou w. strengthen their heart, thou 10.17
their heart, thou w. incline thy ear 10.17
W. thou forget me for ever? 13.01
How long w. thou hide thy face from 13.01
thou w. find no wickedness in me; 17.03
for thou w. answer me, O God; 17.06
How long, O LORD, w. thou look on? 35.17
thou, O LORD my God, who w. answer. 38.15
heart, O God, thou w. not despise. 51.17
then w. thou delight in right 51.19
w. cast them down into the lowest 55.23
sore troubles w. revive me again; 71.20
the earth thou w. bring me up again. 71.20
Thou w. increase my honor, and 71.21
afterward thou w. receive me to 73.24
of wrath thou w. gird upon thee. 76.10
W. thou be angry for ever? Will thy 79.05
how long w. thou be angry with thy 80.04
W. thou be angry with us for ever? 85.05
W. thou prolong thy anger to all 85.05
W. thou not revive us again, that 85.06
W. thou hide thyself for ever? 89.46
Oh when w. thou come to me? 101.02
Thou w. arise and have pity on Zion; 102.13
I ask, "When w. thou comfort me?" 119.82
When w. thou judge those who 119.84
for thou w. deal bountifully with 142.07
O LORD, thou w. ordain peace for us, Is 26.12
of the shades thou w. let it fall. 26.19
W. thou restrain thyself at these 64.12
W. thou keep silent, and afflict us 64.12
W. thou be to me like a deceitful Jer 15.18
this place that thou w. cut it off, 51.62
"Thou w. requite them, O LORD, Lam 3.64
Thou w. give them dullness of heart; 3.65
Thou w. pursue them in anger and 3.66
w. thou destroy all that remains of Eze 9.08
w. thou make a full end of the 11.13
Give them, O LORD— what w. thou give? Hos 9.14
Thou w. cast all our sins into the Mic 7.19
Thou w. show faithfulness to Jacob 7.20
cry for help, and thou w. not hear? Hab 1.02
"Violence!" and thou w. not save? 1.02
how long w. thou have no mercy on Zec 1.12
not as I will, but as thou w." Mt 26.39
not what I will, but what thou w." Mk 14.36
For thou w. not abandon my soul to Ac 2.27
thou w. make me full of gladness 2.28
'Thou w. not let thy Holy One see 13.35
like a mantle thou w. roll them up, Heb 1.12
before thou w. judge and avenge Rev 6.10

WILY
schemes of the w. are brought to a Job 5.13
dressed as a harlot, w. of heart. Pro 7.10

WIN
thinking to w. them for himself. 2Ch 32.01
own sword did they w. the land, Ps 44.03
of a wise man's mouth w. him favor, Ecc 10.12
through me to w. obedience from Rom15.18
to all, that I might w. the more. 1Co 9.19
as a Jew, in order to w. Jews; 9.20
that I might w. those under the law. 9.20
that I might w. those outside the 9.21
weak, that I might w. the weak. 9.22
for, but may w. a full reward. 2Jn 1.08

WIND
And God made a w. blow over the Gen 8.01
thin and blighted by the east w. 41.06
thin, and blighted by the east w., 41.23
by the east w. are also seven 41.27
brought an east w. upon the land Ex 10.13
the east w. had brought the 10.13
LORD turned a very strong west w., 10.19
back by a strong east w. all night, 14.21
Thou didst blow with thy w., 15.10
went forth a w. from the LORD, Num 11.31
was seen upon the wings of the w. 2Sa 22.11
grew black with clouds and w., 1Ki 18.45
and strong w. rent the mountains, 19.11
but the LORD was not in the w.; 19.11
and after the w. an earthquake, but 19.11
'You shall not see w. or rain, 2Ki 3.17
a great w. came across the wilderness, Job 1.19
speech of a despairing man is w.? 6.26
words of your mouth be a great w.? 8.02
and fill himself with the east w.? 15.02
will be swept away by the w. 15.30
That they are like straw before the w., 21.18
By his w. the heavens were made 26.13
The east w. lifts him up and he is 27.21
When he gave to the w. its weight, 28.25
my honor is pursued as by the w., 30.15
thou liftest me up on the w., 30.22
is still because of the south w.? 37.17
when the w. has passed and cleared 37.21
where the east w. is scattered 38.24
chaff which the w. drives away. Ps 1.04
a scorching w. shall be the portion 11.06
swiftly upon the wings of the w. 18.10
them fine as dust before the w.; 18.42
Let them be like chaff before the w., 35.05
By the east w. thou didst shatter 48.07
from the raging w. and tempest." 55.08
He caused the east w. to blow in 78.26
his power he led out the south w.; 78.26
a w. that passes and comes not 78.39
dust, like chaff before the w. 83.13
for the w. passes over it, and it is 103.16
who ridest on the wings of the w., 104.03
commanded, and raised the stormy w., 107.25
forth the w. from his storehouses. 135.07
he makes his w. blow, and the waters 147.18
stormy w. fulfilling his command! 148.08
his household will inherit w., Pro11.29
Like clouds and w. without rain is 25.14
The north w. brings forth rain; 25.23
to restrain the w. or to grasp oil 27.16
has gathered the w. in his fists? 30.04
The w. blows to the south, and goes Ecc 1.06
round and round goes the w., 1.06
and on its circuits the w. returns. 1.06
is vanity and a striving after w. 1.14
also is but a striving after w. 1.17
was vanity and a striving after w., 2.11
is vanity and a striving after w. 2.17
is vanity and a striving after w. 2.26
is vanity and a striving after w. 4.04

WIND (cont.)
of toil and a striving after w. Ecc 4.06
is vanity and a striving after w. 4.16
has he that he toiled for the w., 5.16
is vanity and a striving after w. 6.09
He who observes the w. will not sow; 11.04
Awake, O north w., and come, O south w.! Sol 4.16
of the forest shake before the w. Is 7.02
the River with his scorching w., 11.15
before the w. and whirling dust 17.13
have as it were brought forth w. 26.18
blast in the day of the east w. 27.08
be like a hiding place from the w., 32.02
them and the w. shall carry them 41.16
their molten images are empty w. 41.29
scorching w. nor sun shall smite 49.10
The w. will carry them off, a breath 57.13
which the w. of the LORD drives. 59.19
iniquities, like the w., take us away. 64.06
in her heat sniffing the w.! Jer 2.24
"A hot w. from the bare heights in 4.11
a w. too full for this comes for me. 4.12
The prophets will become w.; 5.13
forth the w. from his storehouses. 10.13
driven by the w. from the desert. 13.24
Like the east w. I will scatter 18.17
The w. shall shepherd all your 22.22
to every w. those who cut the 49.32
forth the w. from his storehouses. 51.16
a stormy w. came out of the north, Eze 1.04
part you shall scatter to the w., 5.02
toward every w. all who are round 12.14
fall, and a stormy w. break out; 13.11
make a stormy w. break out in my 13.13
when the east w. strikes it—wither 17.10
shall be scattered to every w.; 17.21
the east w. dried it up; its fruit was 19.12
The east w. has wrecked you in the 27.26
and the w. carried them away, so Dan 2.35
A w. has wrapped them in its wings, Hos 4.19
For they sow the w., and they shall 8.07
Ephraim herds the w., and 12.01
pursues the east w. all day long; 12.01
the east w., the w. of the Lord, shall come, 13.15
the mountains, and creates the w., Amo 4.13
hurled a great w. upon the sea, Jon 1.04
God appointed a sultry east w., 4.08
go about and utter w. and lies, Mic 2.11
sweep by like the w. and go on, Hab 1.11
The w. was in their wings; Zec 5.09
A reed shaken by the w.? Mt 11.07
for the w. was against them. 14.24
but when he saw the w., 14.30
got into the boat, the w. ceased. 14.32
And a great storm of w. arose, Mk 4.37
And he awoke and rebuked the w., 4.39
"And the w. ceased, and there was a 4.39
that even w. and sea obey him?" 4.41
for the w. was against them. 6.48
boat with them and the w. ceased. 6.51
A reed shaken by the w.? Lk 7.24
And a storm of w. came down on the 8.23
and rebuked the w. and the raging 8.24
that he commands even w. and water, 8.25
And when you see the south w. blowing, 12.55
The w. blows where it wills, and you Jn 3.08
because a strong w. was blowing. 6.18
like the rush of a mighty w., Ac 2.02
and as the w. did not allow us to 27.07
And when the south w. blew gently, 27.13
But soon a tempestuous w., 27.14
caught and could not face the w., 27.15
foresail to the w. they made for 27.40
after one day a south w. sprang up, 28.13
about with every w. of doctrine, Eph 4.14
is driven and tossed by the w. Jas 1.06
that no w. might blow on earth or Rev 7.01

WINDOW
Noah opened the w. of the ark Gen 8.06
looked out of a w. and saw Isaac 26.08
them down by a rope through the w., Jos 2.15
cord in the w. through which you 2.18
bound the scarlet cord in the w. 2.21
"Out of the w. she peered, the Ju 5.28
let David down through the w.; 1Sa 19.12
of Saul looked out of the w., 2Sa 6.16
There were w. frames in three rows, 1Ki 7.04
and w. opposite w. in three tiers. 7.04
and w. was opposite w. in three tiers. 7.05
her head, and looked out of the w. 2Ki 9.30
And he lifted up his face to the w., 9.32
And he said, "Open the w. eastward"; 13.17
of Saul looked out of the w., 1Ch 15.29
For at the w. of my house I have Pro 7.06
floor or like smoke from a w. Hos 13.03
the owl shall hoot in the w., Zep 2.14
Eutychus was sitting in the w. Ac 20.09
a basket through a w. in the wall, 2Co 11.33

WINDOWS
and the w. of the heavens were Gen 7.11
deep and the w. of the heavens 8.02
for the house w. with recessed 1Ki 6.04
doorways and w. had square frames, 7.05
himself should make w. in heaven, 2Ki 7.02
himself should make w. in heaven, 7.19
look through the w. are dimmed, Ecc 12.03
our wall, gazing in at the w., Sol 2.09
For the w. of heaven are opened, and Is 24.18
cloud, and like doves to their w.? 60.08
For death has come up into our w., Jer 9.21
and cuts out w. for it, paneling 22.14
And the gateway had w. round about, Eze 40.16
vestibule had w. round about 40.16
And its w., its vestibule, and its 40.22
And there were w. round about in it 40.25
vestibule, like the w. of the others; 40.25
and there were w. round about in it 40.29
and there were w. round about in it 40.33
and it had w. round about; 40.36
all three had w. with recessed frames. 41.16
floor up to the w. (now the w. were covered), 41.16
were recessed w. and palm trees on 41.26
where he had w. in his upper chamber Dan 6.10
enter through the w. like a thief. Joe 2.09
not open the w. of heaven for you Mal 3.10

WINDS
and cold from the scattering w. Job 37.09
who makest the w. thy messengers, Ps 104.04
Elam the four w. from the four Jer 49.36
will scatter them to all those w., 49.36
I will scatter to all the w. Eze 5.10
to all the w. and will unsheathe 5.12
Lord GOD: Come from the four w., 37.09
the four w. of heaven were stirring Dan 7.02
horns toward the four w. of heaven. 8.08
toward the four w. of heaven, 11.04
as the four w. of the heavens, Zec 2.06
forth to the four w. of heaven, 6.05
and the w. blew and beat upon that Mt 7.25
and the w. blew and beat against 7.27
and rebuked the w. and the sea; 8.26
that even w. and sea obey him?" 8.27
gather his elect from the four w., 24.31
gather his elect from the four w., Mk 13.27
because the w. were against us. Ac 27.04
he says, "Who makes his angels w., Heb 1.07
great and are driven by strong w., Jas 3.04
clouds, carried along by w.; Jud 1.12
back the four w. of the earth, Rev 7.01

WINDY

wise man answer with w. knowledge, Job 15.02
Shall w. words have an end? 16.03

WINE

and he drank of the w., and became Gen 9.21
awoke from his w. and knew what 9.24
of Salem brought out bread and w.; 14.18
Come, let us make our father drink w., 19.32
their father drink w. that night; 19.33
us make him drink w. tonight also; 19.34
father drink w. that night also; 19.35
he brought him w., and he drank. 27.25
earth, and plenty of grain and w. 27.28
with grain and w. I have sustained 27.37
his garments in w. and his vesture 49.11
his eyes shall be red with w., 49.12
of a hin of w. for a libation. Ex 29.40
"Drink no w. nor strong drink, you Lev 10.09
offering with it shall be of w., 23.13
himself from w. and strong drink; Num 6.03
made from w. or strong drink, and 6.03
that the Nazirite may drink w. 6.20
and w. for the drink offering, a 15.05
shall offer a third of a hin of w., 15.07
drink offering half a hin of w., 15.10
the best of the w. and of the 18.12
and as the fulness of the w. press. 18.27
and as produce of the w. press; 18.30
be half a hin of w. for a bull, 28.14
grain and your w. and your oil, Deu 7.13
grain and your w. and your oil. 11.14
grain or of your w. or of your oil, 12.17
of your w., and of your oil, and the 14.23
or w. or strong drink, whatever your 14.26
floor, and out of your w. press; 15.14
threshing floor and your w. press; 16.13
of your w. and of your oil, and the 18.04
drink of the w. not gather the 28.39
w., or oil, the increase of your 28.51
have not drunk w. or strong drink; 29.06
blood of the grape you drank w. 32.14
their w. is the poison of serpents, 32.33
and drank the w. of their drink 32.38
alone, in a land of grain and w.; 33.28
beating out wheat in the w. press, Ju 6.11
killed at the w. press of Zeeb, 7.25
I leave my w. which cheers gods 9.13
and drink no w. or strong drink, and 13.04
then drink no w. or strong drink, 13.07
let her drink w. or strong drink, 13.14
with bread and w. for me and your 19.19
and dip your morsel in the w. Ru 2.14
Put away your w. from you." 1Sa 1.14
drunk neither w. nor strong drink, 1.15
ephah of flour, and a skin of w.; 1.24
and another carrying a skin of w. 10.03
and a skin of w. and a kid, and sent 16.20
loaves, and two skins of w., 25.18
when the w. had gone out of Nabal, 25.37
Amnon's heart is merry with w., 2Sa 13.28
of summer fruits, and a skin of w. 16.01
and the w. for those who faint in 16.02
floor, or from the w. press? 2Ki 6.27
own land, a land of grain and w., 18.32
the w., the oil, the incense, and the 1Ch 9.29
and w. and oil, oxen and sheep, for 12.40
vineyards for the w. cellars was 27.27
twenty thousand baths of w., 2Ch 2.10
oil and w., of which my lord has 2.15
and stores of food, oil, and w. 11.11
w., oil, honey, and of all the 31.05
the yield of grain, w., and oil; 32.28
w., or oil, as the priests at Ez 6.09
of wheat, a hundred baths of w., 7.22
when w. was before him, I took up Neh 2.01
I took up the w. and gave it to the 2.01
w., and oil which you have been 5.11
and took from them food and w., 5.15
ten days skins of w. in abundance; 5.18
and drink sweet w. and send 8.10
the w. and the oil, to the priests, 10.37
w., and oil to the chambers, where 10.39
w., and oil, which were given by 13.05
w., and oil into the storehouses. 13.12
men trading w. presses on the 13.15
and also w., grapes, figs, and all 13.15
and the royal w. was lavished Est 1.07
of the king was merry with w., 1.10
And as they were drinking w., 5.06
day, as they were drinking w., 7.02
place where they were drinking w., 7.08
and drinking w. in their eldest Job 1.13
and drinking w. in their eldest 1.18
they tread the w. presses, 24.11
heart is like w. that has no vent; 32.19
when their grain and w. abound. Ps 4.07
hast given us w. to drink that 60.03
a cup, with foaming w., well mixed; 75.08
strong man shouting because of w. 78.65
and w. to gladden the heart of man, 104.15
your vats will be bursting with w. Pro 3.10
and drink the w. of violence. 4.17
her beasts, she has mixed her w., 9.02
and drink of the w. I have mixed. 9.05
W. is a mocker, strong drink a 20.01
he who loves w. and oil will not be 21.17
Those who tarry long over w., 23.30
those who go to try mixed w. 23.30
Do not look at w. when it is red, 23.31
it is not for kings to drink w., 31.04
and w. to those in bitter distress; 31.06
mind how to cheer my body with w.— Ecc 2.03
and drink your w. with a merry 9.07
and w. gladdens life, and money 10.19
For your love is better than w., Sol 1.02
will extol your love more than w.; 1.04
much better is your love than w., 4.10
honey, I drink my w. with my milk. 5.01
bowl that never lacks mixed w. 7.02
like the best w. that goes down 7.09
would give you spiced w. to drink, 8.02
become dross, your w. mixed with water. Is 1.22
it, and hewed out a w. vat in it; 5.02
the evening till w. inflames them! 5.11
and flute and w. at their feasts; 5.12
who are heroes at drinking w., 5.22
treads out w. in the presses; 16.10
eating flesh and drinking w. 22.13
The w. mourns, the vine languishes, 24.07
more do they drink w. with singing; 24.09
in the streets for lack of w.; 24.11
a feast of w. on the lees, of fat 25.06
of w. on the lees well refined. 25.06
valley of those overcome with w.! 28.01
These also reel with w. and stagger 28.07
drink, they are confused with w., 28.07
Be drunk, but not with w.; 29.09
own land, a land of grain and w., 36.17
with their own blood as with w. 49.26
who are drunk, but not with w.: 51.21
Come, buy w. and milk without money 55.01
"let us get w., let us fill ourselves 56.12
not drink your w. for which you 62.08
his that treads in the w. press? 63.02
"I have trodden the w. press alone, 63.03
"As the w. is found in the cluster, 65.08
fill cups of mixed w. for Destiny; 65.11
"Every jar shall be filled with w." Jer 13.12
every jar will be filled with w.?' 13.12
man, like a man overcome by w., 23.09
hand this cup of the w. of wrath, 25.15
the w., and the oil, and over the 31.12
then offer them w. to drink." 35.02

WINE (cont.)

pitchers full of w., and cups; Jer 35.05
and I said to them, "Drink w." 35.05
they answered, "We will drink no w., 35.06
us, 'You shall not drink w., 35.06
to drink no w. all our days, ourselves, 35.08
to drink no w., has been kept; 35.14
gather w. and summer fruits and oil, 40.10
they gathered w. and summer fruits 40.12
I have made the w. cease from the 48.33
the wine cease from the w. presses; 48.33
the nations drank of her w., 51.07
trodden as in a w. press the Lam 1.15
mothers, "Where is bread and w.?" 2.12
w. of Helbon, and white wool, Eze 27.18
and w. from Uzal they exchanged for 27.19
No priest shall drink w., 44.21
ate, and of the w. which he drank. Dan 1.05
or with the w. which he drank; 1.08
food and the w. they were to drink, 1.16
and drank w. in front of the 5.01
Belshazzar, when he tasted the w., 5.02
They drank w., and praised the gods 5.04
concubines have drunk w. from them; 5.23
no meat or w. entered my mouth, nor 10.03
the w., and the oil, and who lavished Hos 2.08
its time, and my w. in its season: 2.09
the w., and the oil, and they shall 2.22
W. and new w. take away the 4.11
became sick with the heat of w.; 7.05
for grain and w. they gash themselves, 7.14
and the new w. shall fail them. 9.02
pour libations of w. to the LORD; 9.04
shall be like the w. of Lebanon. 14.07
and wail, all you drinkers of w., Joe 1.05
because of the sweet w., for it is 1.05
the w. fails, the oil languishes. 1.10
w., and oil, and you will be satisfied; 2.19
shall overflow with w. and oil. 2.24
and have sold a girl for w., 3.03
tread, for the w. press is full. 3.13
the mountains shall drip sweet w., 3.18
they drink the w. of those who Amo 2.08
"But you made the Nazarites drink w., 2.12
but you shall not drink their w. 5.11
who drink w. in bowls, and anoint 6.06
the mountains shall drip sweet w., 9.13
plant vineyards and drink their w., 9.14
to you of w. and strong drink," he Mic 2.11
tread grapes, but not drink w. 6.15
Moreover, w. is treacherous; Hab 2.05
they shall not drink w. from them." Zep 1.13
the new w., the oil, upon what the Hag 1.11
or w., or oil, or any kind of food, 2.12
shall drink their blood like w., Zec 9.15
flourish, and new w. the maidens. 9.17
hearts shall be glad as with w. 10.07
Hananel to the king's w. presses. 14.10
Neither is new w. put into old Mt 9.17
and the w. is spilled, and the skins 9.17
but new w. is put into fresh 9.17
and dug a w. press in it, and built 21.33
they offered him w. to drink, 27.34
And no one puts new w. into old Mk 2.22
the w. will burst the skins, and the 2.22
and the w. is lost, and so are the 2.22
but new w. is for fresh skins. 2.22
it, and dug a pit for the w. press, 12.01
offered him w. mingled with myrrh; 15.23
shall drink no w. nor strong drink, Lk 1.15
And no one puts new w. into old 5.37
the new w. will burst the skins and 5.37
But new w. must be put into fresh 5.38
after drinking old w. desires new; 5.39
eating no bread and drinking no w.; 7.33
his wounds, pouring on oil and w.; 10.34
When the w. failed, the mother of Jn 2.03
Jesus said to him, "They have no w." 2.03
tasted the water now become w., 2.09
"Every man serves the good w. first; 2.10
drunk freely, then the poor w.; 2.10
have kept the good w. until now." 2.10
where he had made the water w. 4.46
said, "They are filled with new w." Ac 2.13
meat or drink w. or do anything Rom 14.21
And do not get drunk with w., Eph 5.18
double-tongued, not addicted to much w., 1Ti 3.08
use a little w. for the sake of 5.23
but do not harm oil and w.! Rev 6.06
drink the w. of her impure passion." 14.08
shall drink the w. of God's wrath, 14.10
into the great w. press of the 14.19
and the w. press was trodden 14.20
and blood flowed from the w. press, 14.20
and with the w. of whose fornication 17.02
have drunk the w. of her impure 18.03
w., oil, fine flour and wheat, cattle 18.13
will tread the w. press of the 19.15

WINEBIBBERS

Be not among w., or among gluttonous Pro 23.20

WINESKIN

have become like a w. in the smoke, Ps 119.83

WINESKINS

and w., worn-out and torn and Jos 9.04
these w. were new when we filled 9.13
like new w., it is ready to burst. Job 32.19
Neither is new wine put into old w.; Mt 9.17
but new wine is put into fresh w., 9.17
And no one puts new wine into old w.; Mk 2.22
And no one puts new wine into old w.; Lk 5.37
new wine must be put into fresh w. 5.38

WINEVAT

Threshing floor and w. shall not Hos 9.02
one came to the w. to draw fifty Hag 2.16

WING

the length of one w. of the cherub, 1Ki 6.24
of the other w. of the cherub; 6.24
the tip of one w. to the tip of 6.24
out so that a w. of one touched 6.27
and a w. of the other cherub 6.27
one w. of the one, of five cubits, 2Ch 3.11
and its other w., of five cubits, 3.11
touched the w. of the other cherub; 3.11
one w., of five cubits, touched the 3.12
and the other w., also of five 3.12
joined to the w. of the first 3.12
and there was none that moved a w., Is 10.14
of which touched the w. of another, Eze 1.11
and upon the w. of abominations Dan 9.27

WINGED

and every w. bird according to its Gen 1.21
"All w. insects that go upon all Lev 11.20
Yet among the w. insects that go on 11.21
But all other w. insects which have 11.23
likeness of any w. bird that flies Deu 4.17
And all w. insects are unclean for 14.19
All clean w. things you may eat. 14.20
w. birds like the sand of the seas; Ps 78.27
or some w. creature tell the matter Ecc 10.20

WINGS

you on eagles' w. and brought you Ex 19.04
shall spread out their w. above, 25.20
the mercy seat with their w., 25.20
cherubim spread out their w. above, 37.09
the mercy seat with their w., 37.09
he shall tear it by its w., Lev 1.17
its young, spreading out its w., Deu 32.11
under whose w. you have come to Ru 2.12

WINGS (cont.)

was seen upon the w. of the wind. 2Sa 22.11
and the w. of the cherubim were 1Ki 6.27
their other w. touched each other 6.27
underneath the w. of the cherubim. 8.06
out their w. over the place of the 8.07
spread their w. and covered the 1Ch 28.18
The w. of the cherubim together 2Ch 3.11
The w. of these cherubim extended 3.13
underneath the w. of the cherubim. 5.07
out their w. over the place of the 5.08
"The w. of the ostrich wave proudly Job 39.13
and spreads his w. toward the 39.26
hide me in the shadow of thy w., Ps 17.08
swiftly upon the w. of the wind. 18.10
refuge in the shadow of thy w. 36.07
I say, "O that I had w. like a dove! 55.06
shadow of thy w. I will take 57.01
safe under the shelter of thy w.! 61.04
shadow of thy w. I sing for joy. 63.07
the w. of a dove covered with 68.13
and under his w. you will find 91.04
who ridest on the w. of the wind, 104.03
If I take the w. of the morning and 139.09
for suddenly it takes to itself w., Pro 23.05
each had six w.: with two he covered Is 6.02
its outspread w. will fill the 8.08
of whirring w. which is beyond the 18.01
shall mount up with w. like eagles, 40.31
"Give w. to Moab, for she would fly Jer 48.09
and spread his w. against Moab; 48.40
and spread his w. against Bozrah, 49.22
and each of them had four w. Eze 1.06
Under their w. on their four sides 1.08
had their faces and their w. thus: 1.08
their w. touched one another; 1.09
And their w. were spread out above; 1.11
each creature had two w., 1.11
firmament their w. were stretched 1.23
creature had two w. covering its 1.23
sound of their w. like the sound 1.24
still, they let down their w. 1.24
still, they let down their w. 1.25
sound of the w. of the living 3.13
sound of the w. of the cherubim 10.05
of a human hand under their w. 10.08
lifted up their w. to mount up 10.16
lifted up their w. and mounted up 10.19
and each four w., and underneath 10.21
underneath their w. the semblance 10.21
Then the cherubim lifted up their w., 11.22
with great w. and long pinions, 17.03
with great w. and much plumage; 17.07
was like a lion and had eagles' w. Dan 7.04
as I looked its w. were plucked 7.04
with four w. of a bird on its back; 7.06
A wind has wrapped them in its w., Hos 4.19
spreads its w. and flies away. Nah 3.16
The wind was in their w.; Zec 5.09
they had w. like the w. of a stork, 5.09
shall rise, with healing in its w. Mal 4.02
hen gathers her brood under her w., Mt 23.37
hen gathers her brood under her w., Lk 13.34
creatures, each of them with six w., Rev 4.08
noise of their w. was like the 9.09
given the two w. of the great 12.14

WINK

let not those w. the eye who hate Ps 35.19

WINKS

w. with his eyes, scrapes with his Pro 6.13
He who w. the eye causes trouble, 10.10
He who w. his eyes plans perverse 16.30

WINNOW

You shall w. them and the wind Is 41.16
my people, not to w. or cleanse, Jer 4.11
winnowers, and they shall w. her, 51.02
and gathering where you did not w.; Mt 25.24

WINNOWED

O my threshed and w. one, what I have Is 21.10
which has been w. with shovel and 30.24
I have w. them with a winnowing Jer 15.07
and gather where I have not w.? Mt 25.26

WINNOWERS

and I will send to Babylon w., Jer 51.02

WINNOWING

See, he is w. barley tonight at the Ru 3.02
them with a w. fork in the gates Jer 15.07
His w. fork is in his hand, and he Mt 3.12
His w. fork is in his hand, to clear Lk 3.17

WINNOWS

of judgment w. all evil with his Pro 20.08
A wise king w. the wicked, and 20.26

WINS

Good sense w. favor, but the way of Pro 13.15

WINTER

summer and w., day and night, shall Gen 8.22
thou hast made summer and w. Ps 74.17
for lo, the w. is past, the rain is Sol 2.11
of the earth will w. upon them. Is 18.06
sitting in the w. house and there Jer 36.22
I will smite the w. house with the Amo 3.15
shall continue in summer as in w. Zec 14.08
may not be in w. or on a sabbath. Mt 24.20
Pray that it may not happen in w. Mk 13.18
it was w., and Jesus was walking in Jn 10.23
harbor was not suitable to w. in, Ac 27.12
and southeast, and w. there. 27.12
stay with you or even spend the w., 1Co 16.06
Do your best to come before w. 2Ti 4.21
have decided to spend the w. there. Tit 3.12
tree sheds its w. fruit when Rev 6.13

WINTERED

a ship which had w. in the island, Ac 28.11

WIPE

and I will w. Jerusalem as one 2Ki 21.13
and w. not out my good deeds that I Neh 13.14
let us w. them out as a nation; Ps 83.04
iniquity and w. them out for their 94.23
the LORD our God will w. them out. 94.23
Lord GOD will w. away tears from Is 25.08
we w. off against you; nevertheless Lk 10.11
and to w. them with the towel with Jn 13.05
and God will w. away every tear Rev 7.17
he will w. away every tear from 21.04

WIPED

slaughter, until they were w. out, Jos 10.20
and w. out the Anakim from the hill 11.21
till he had w. them out, according 2Ki 10.17
Thus Jehu w. out Baal from Israel. 10.28
his disgrace will not be w. away. Pro 6.33
destruction and w. out all remembrance Is 26.14
cut down, and your works w. out. Eze 6.06
and w. them with the hair of her Lk 7.38
her tears and w. them with her 7.44
ointment and w. his feet with her Jn 11.02
of Jesus and w. his feet with her 12.03

WIPES

wipe Jerusalem as one w. a dish, 2Ki 21.13
and w. her mouth, and says "I have Pro 30.20

WIPING

w. it and turning it upside down. 2Ki 21.13

WISDOM

will be your w. and your understanding Deu 4.06
Nun was full of the spirit of w., 34.09
But my lord has w. like the wisdom 2Sa 14.20
wisdom like the w. of the angel of 14.20
went to all the people in her w. 20.22
Act therefore according to your w., 1Ki 2.06
that the w. of God was in him, to 3.28
gave Solomon w. and understanding 4.29
so that Solomon's w. surpassed the 4.30
surpassed the w. of all the people 4.30
the east, and all the w. of Egypt. 4.30
peoples to hear the w. of Solomon, 4.34
the earth, who had heard of his w. 4.34
And the LORD gave Solomon w., 5.12
and he was full of w., understanding, 7.14
had seen all the w. of Solomon, 10.04
of your affairs and of your w., 10.06
your w. and prosperity surpass the 10.07
stand before you and hear your w.! 10.08
of the earth in riches and in w. 10.23
presence of Solomon to hear his w., 10.24
and his w., are they not written in 11.41
Give me now w. and knowledge to go 2Ch 1.10
but have asked w. and knowledge 1.11
w. and knowledge are granted to you 1.12
Sheba had seen the w. of Solomon, 9.03
of your affairs and of your w., 9.05
greatness of your w. was not told 9.06
stand before you and hear your w.! 9.07
of the earth in riches and in w. 9.22
presence of Solomon to hear his w., 9.23
according to the w. of your God Ez 7.25
they not die, and that without w.?' Job 4.21
would tell you the secrets of w.! 11.06
are the people and w. will die with you. 12.02
W. is with the aged, and understanding 12.12
"With God are w. and might; he has 12.13
With him are strength and w.; 12.16
silent, and it would be your w.! 13.05
And do you limit w. to yourself? 15.08
have counseled him who has no w., 26.03
"But where shall w. be found? and where 28.12
the price of w. is above pearls. 28.18
"Whence then comes w.? and where 28.20
the fear of the Lord, that is w.; 28.28
speak, and many years teach w. 32.07
Beware lest you say, 'We have found w.; 32.13
be silent, and I will teach you w. 33.33
Who has put w. in the clouds, or 38.36
Who can number the clouds by w.? 38.37
because God has made her forget w., 39.17
"Is it by your w. that the hawk 39.26
The mouth of the righteous utters w., Ps 37.30
My mouth shall speak w.; 49.03
teach me w. in my secret heart. 51.06
days that we may get a heart of w. 90.12
In w. hast thou made them all; 104.24
pleasure, and to teach his elders w. 105.22
of the LORD is the beginning of w.; 111.10
That men may know w. and instruction, Pro 1.02
fools despise w. and instruction. 1.07
W. cries aloud in the street; 1.20
attentive to w. and inclining your 2.02
For the LORD gives w.; from his 2.06
he stores up sound w. for the 2.07
for w. will come into your heart, 2.10
Happy is the man who finds w., 3.13
The LORD by w. founded the earth; 3.19
My son, keep sound w. and discretion; 3.21
my mouth. Get w.; get insight. 4.05
The beginning of w. is this: 4.07
Get w., and whatever you get, get 4.07
I have taught you the way of w.; 4.11
My son, be attentive to my w., 5.01
Say to w., "You are my sister," and 7.04
Does not w. call, does not understanding 8.01
for w. is better than jewels, and 8.11
I, w. dwell in prudence, and I find 8.12
I have counsel and sound w., 8.14
W. has built her house, she has set 9.01
of the LORD is the beginning of w., 9.10
who has understanding w. is found, 10.13
of the righteous brings forth w., 10.31
but with the humble is w. 11.02
with those who take advice is w. 13.10
W. builds her house, but folly with 14.01
A scoffer seeks w. in vain, 14.06
The w. of a prudent man is to 14.08
The crown of the wise is their w., 14.24
W. abides in the mind of a man of 14.33
of the LORD is instruction in w., 15.33
To get w. is better than gold; 16.16
W. is a fountain of life to him who 16.22
have a price in his hand to buy w., 17.16
understanding sets his face toward w., 17.24
the fountain of w. is a gushing 18.04
He who gets w. loves himself; 19.08
you may gain w. for the future. 19.20
No w., no understanding, no counsel, 21.30
will despise the w. of your words. 23.09
buy w., instruction, and understanding. 23.23
By w. a house is built, and by 24.03
W. is too high for a fool; in the gate 24.07
Know that w. is such to your soul; 24.14
he who walks in w. will be delivered 28.26
He who loves w. makes his father 29.03
The rod and reproof give w., 29.15
I have not learned w., nor have I 30.03
She opens her mouth with w., 31.26
search out by w. all that is done Ecc 1.13
myself, "I have acquired great w., 1.16
experience of w. and knowledge. 1.16
my mind to know w. and to know 1.17
For in much w. is much vexation, and 1.18
my mind still guiding me with w.— 2.03
also my w. remained with me. 2.09
to consider w. and madness and 2.12
Then I saw that w. excels folly as 2.13
and used my w. under the sun. 2.19
has toiled with w. and knowledge 2.21
him God gives w. and knowledge and 2.26
it is not from w. that you ask 7.10
W. is good with an inheritance, an 7.11
protection of w. is like the 7.12
knowledge is that w. preserves the 7.12
W. gives strength to the wise man 7.19
All this I have tested by w.; 7.23
out and to seek w. and the sum of 7.25
A man's w. makes his face shine, and 8.01
When I applied my mind to know w., 8.16
or knowledge or w. in Sheol, 9.10
this example of w. under the sun, 9.13
and he by his w. delivered the city 9.15
But I say that w. is better than 9.16
the poor man's w. is despised, 9.16
W. is better than weapons of war, 9.18
folly outweighs w. and honor. 10.01
but w. helps one to succeed. 10.10
and by my w., for I have understanding Is 10.13
the spirit of w. and understanding, 11.02
in counsel, and excellent in w. 28.29
and the w. of their wise men shall 29.14
of salvation, w., and knowledge; 33.06
your w. and your knowledge led you 47.10
the LORD, and what w. is in them? Jer 8.09
not the wise man glory in his w., 9.23
established the world by his w., 10.12
"Is w. no more in Teman? Has counsel 49.07
prudent? Has their w. vanished? 49.07
established the world by his w., 51.15
by your w. and your understanding Eze 28.04
by your great w. in trade you have 28.05
beauty of your w. and defile your 28.07

WISDOM (cont.)
full of w. and perfect in beauty. Eze 28.12
corrupted your w. for the sake of 28.17
handsome and skilful in all w., Dan 1.04
and skill in all letters and w.; 1.17
every matter of w. and understanding 1.20
ever, to whom belong w. and might. 2.20
he gives w. to the wise and knowledge 2.21
thou hast given me w. and strength, 2.23
because of any w. that I have more 2.30
light and understanding and w., 5.11
like the w. of the gods, were found 5.11
and excellent w. are found in you. 5.14
out to give you w. and understanding. 9.22
and it is sound w. to fear thy Mic 6.09
Yet w. is justified by her deeds. Mt 11.19
earth to hear the w. of Solomon, 12.42
man get this w. and these mighty 13.54
What is the w. given to him? Mk 6.02
disobedient to the w. of the just, Lk 1.17
and became strong, filled with w.; 2.40
increased in w. and in stature, 2.52
Yet w. is justified by all her 7.35
earth to hear the w. of Solomon, 11.31
Therefore also the W. of God said, 11.49
for I will give you a mouth and w., 21.15
full of the Spirit and of w., Ac 6.03
withstand the w. and the Spirit 6.10
him favor and w. before Pharaoh, 7.10
in all the w. of the Egyptians, and 7.22
the riches and w. and knowledge of Rom 11.33
gospel, and not with eloquent w., 1Co 1.17
"I will destroy the w. of the wise, 1.19
made foolish the w. of the world? 1.20
in the w. of God, the world did not 1.21
world did not know God through w., 1.21
demand signs and Greeks seek w., 1.22
the power of God and the w. of God. 1.24
Christ Jesus, whom God made our w., 1.30
of God in lofty words or w. 2.01
were not in plausible words of w., 2.04
not rest in the w. of men but in 2.05
Yet among the mature we do impart w., 2.06
it is not a w. of this age or of 2.06
a secret and hidden w. of God, 2.07
taught by human w. but taught by 2.13
For the w. of this world is folly 3.19
the Spirit the utterance of w., 12.08
not by earthly w. but by the grace 2Co 1.12
to us in all w. and insight the Eph 1.09
you a spirit of w. and of revelation 1.17
the manifold w. of God might now 3.10
all spiritual w. and understanding, Col 1.09
and teaching every man in all w., 1.28
the treasures of w. and knowledge. 2.03
appearance of w. in promoting 2.23
and admonish one another in all w., 3.16
If any of you lacks w., let him ask Jas 1.05
his works in the meekness of w. 3.13
This w. is not such as comes down 3.15
But the w. from above is first pure, 3.17
you according to the w. given him, 2Pe 3.15
and wealth and w. and might and Rev 5.12
and glory and w. and thanksgiving 7.12
This calls for w. let him who has 13.18
This calls for a mind with w.: 17.09

WISE
was to be desired to make one w., Gen 3.06
of Egypt and all its w. men; 41.08
select a man discreet and w., 41.33
none so discreet and w. as you are; 41.39
summoned the w. men and the Ex 7.11
Choose w., understanding, and Deu 1.13
w. and experienced men, and set them 1.15
nation is a w. and understanding 4.06
the eyes of the w. and subverts 16.19
If they were w., they would understand 32.29
and fetched from there a w. woman, 2Sa 14.02
Then a w. woman called from the 20.16
guiltless, for you are a w. man; 1Ki 2.09
I give you a w. and discerning mind, 3.12
to David a w. son to be over this 5.07
who has given King David a w. son, 2Ch 2.12
said to the w. men who knew the Est 1.13
Then his w. men and his wife Zeresh 6.13
He takes the w. in their own Job 5.13
He is w. in heart, and mighty in 9.04
"Should a w. man answer with windy 15.02
(what w. men have told, and their 15.18
shall not find a w. man among you. 17.10
he who is w. is profitable to 22.02
It is not the old that are w., 32.09
I listened for your w. sayings, 32.11
you w. men, and give ear to me, you 34.02
and the w. man who hears me will 34.34
any who are w. in their own 37.24
Now therefore, O kings, be w.; Ps 2.10
LORD is sure, making w. the simple; 19.07
Yea, he shall see that even the w. die, 49.10
see if there are any that are w., 53.02
Fools, when will you be w.? 94.08
Whoever is w., let him give heed to 107.43
receive instruction in w. dealing, Pro 1.03
the w. man also may hear and 1.05
words of the w. and their riddles. 1.06
Be not w. in your own eyes; 3.07
The w. will inherit honor, but fools 3.35
consider her ways, and be w. 6.06
Hear instruction and be w., 8.33
reprove a w. man, and he will love 9.08
Give instruction to a w. man, 9.09
If you are w., you are w. for yourself; 9.12
A w. son makes a glad father, but a 10.01
The w. of heart will heed commandments, 10.08
W. men lay up knowledge, but the 10.14
but w. conduct is pleasure to a man 10.23
the fool will be servant to the w. 11.29
but a w. man listens to advice. 12.15
tongue of the w. brings healing. 12.18
A w. son hears his father's instruction, 13.01
The teaching of the w. is a fountain 13.14
He who walks with w. men becomes w., 13.20
the lips of the w. will preserve 14.03
A w. man is cautious and turns away 14.16
The crown of the w. is their wisdom, 14.24
The tongue of the w. dispenses 15.02
The lips of the w. spread knowledge 15.07
reproved; he will not go to the w. 15.12
A w. son makes a glad father, but a 15.20
The w. man's path leads upward to 15.24
admonition will abide among the w. 15.31
and a w. man will appease it. 16.14
The w. of heart is called a man of 16.21
The mind of the w. makes his speech 16.23
who keeps silent is considered w.; 17.28
the ear of the w. seeks knowledge. 18.15
is led astray by it is not w. 20.01
by counsel; by w. guidance wage war. 20.18
A w. king winnows the wicked, and 20.26
is punished, the simple becomes w.; 21.11
when a w. man is instructed, he 21.11
remains in a w. man's dwelling, 21.20
A w. man scales the city of the 21.22
ear, and hear the words of the w., 22.17
wealth; be w. enough to desist. 23.04
My son, if your heart is w., 23.15
and be w., and direct your mind in 23.19
he who begets a w. son will be glad 23.24
A w. man is mightier than a strong 24.05
for by w. guidance you can wage 24.06
These also are sayings of the w. 24.23
of gold is a w. reprover to a 25.12
lest he be w. in his own eyes. 26.05

WISE (cont.)

a man who is w. in his own eyes? Pro 26.12
Be w., my son, and make my heart 27.11
He who keeps the law is a w. son, 28.07
A rich man is w. in his own eyes, 28.11
but w. men turn away wrath. 29.08
If a w. man has an argument with a 29.09
but a w. man quietly holds it back. 29.11
are small, but they are exceedingly w.: 30.24
The w. man has his eyes in his head, Ecc 2.14
why then have I been so very w.? 2.15
For of the w. man as of the fool 2.16
How the w. man dies just like the 2.16
he will be a w. man or a fool? 2.19
Better is a poor and w. youth than 4.13
advantage has the w. man over the 6.08
The heart of the w. is in the house 7.04
rebuke of the w. than to hear the 7.05
oppression makes the w. man foolish, 7.07
strength to the w. man more than 7.19
I said, "I will be w."; but it was 7.23
Who is like the w. man? And who knows 8.01
the mind of a w. man will know the 8.05
even though a w. man claims to know, 8.17
righteous and the w. and their 9.01
to the strong, nor bread to the w., 9.11
was found in it a poor w. man, 9.15
The words of the w. heard in quiet 9.17
A w. man's heart inclines him toward 10.02
The words of a w. man's mouth win 10.12
Besides being w., the Preacher also 12.09
The sayings of the w. are like goads, 12.11
those who are w. in their own eyes, Is 5.21
the w. counselors of Pharaoh give 19.11
to Pharaoh, "I am a son of the w., a son of 19.11
Where then are your w. men? Let them tell 19.12
wisdom of their w. men shall perish 29.14
And yet he is w. and brings disaster, 31.02
who turns w. men back, and makes 44.25
'We are w., and the law of the LORD Jer 8.08
The w. men shall be put to shame, 8.09
Who is the man so w. that he can 9.12
"Let not the w. man glory in his 9.23
among all the w. ones of the nations 10.07
priest, nor counsel from the w., 18.18
upon her princes and her w. men! 50.35
drunk her princes and her w. men, 51.57
consider yourself as w. as a god— Eze 28.02
consider yourself as w. as a god, 28.06
that all the w. men of Babylon be Dan 2.12
forth that the w. men were to be 2.13
out to slay the w. men of Babylon; 2.14
the rest of the w. men of Babylon. 2.18
wisdom to the w. and knowledge to 2.21
to destroy the w. men of Babylon; 2.24
not destroy the w. men of Babylon; 2.24
"No w. men, enchanters, magicians, or 2.27
chief prefect over all the w. men of Babylon. 2.48
that all the w. men of Babylon should be 4.06
because all the w. men of my kingdom 4.18
king said to the w. men of Babylon, 5.07
Then all the king's w. men came in, 5.08
Now the w. men, the enchanters, have 5.15
people who are w. shall make many 11.33
of those who are w. shall fall, 11.35
And those who are w. shall shine 12.03
those who are w. shall understand. 12.10
Whoever is w., let him understand Hos 14.09
destroy the w. men out of Edom, and Ob 1.08
and Sidon, though they are very w. Zec 9.02
w. men from the East came to Mt 2.01
summoned the w. men secretly and 2.07
he had been tricked by the w. men, 2.16
he had ascertained from the w. men. 2.16
will be like a w. man who built 7.24
so be w. as serpents and innocent 10.16
things from the w. and understanding 11.25
prophets and w. men and scribes, 23.34
is the faithful and w. servant, 24.45
were foolish, and five were w. 25.02
but the w. took flasks of oil with 25.04
And the foolish said to the w., 25.08
But the w. replied, 'Perhaps there 25.09
things from the w. and understanding Lk 10.21
is the faithful and w. steward, 12.42
both to the w. and to the foolish: Rom 1.14
Claiming to be w., they became 1.22
Lest you be w. in your own conceits, 11.25
would have you w. as to what is 16.19
to the only w. God be glory for 16.27
will destroy the wisdom of the w., 1Co 1.19
Where is the w. man? Where is the 1.20
of you were w. according to worldly standards, 1.26
in the world to shame the w., 1.27
thinks that he is w. in this age, 3.18
a fool that he may become w. 3.18
"He catches the w. in their craftiness," 3.19
the thoughts of the w. are futile. 3.20
sake, but you are w. in Christ. 4.10
man among you w. enough to decide 6.05
with fools, being w. yourselves! 2Co 11.19
walk, not as unwise men but as w., Eph 5.15
Who is w. and understanding among Jas 3.13

WISELY

And he dealt w., and distributed 2Ch 11.23
see if there are any that act w., Ps 14.02
has ceased to act w. and do good. 36.03
who deals w. has the king's favor, Pro 14.35
A slave who deals w. will rule over 17.02
he shall reign as king and deal w., Jer 23.05
when Jesus saw that he answered w., Mk 12.34
Conduct yourselves w. toward Col 4.05

WISER

For he was w. than all other men, 1Ki 4.31
w. than Ethan the Ezrahite, and 4.31
and makes us w. than the birds of Job 35.11
makes me w. than my enemies, for it Ps 119.98
wise man, and he will be still w.; Pro 9.09
The sluggard is w. in his own eyes 26.16
you are indeed w. than Daniel; Eze 28.03
this world are w. in their own Lk 16.08
foolishness of God is w. than men, 1Co 1.25

WISEST

Her w. ladies make answer, nay, she Ju 5.29

WISH

But if he does not w. to redeem the Lev 27.20
I w. I had a sword in my hand, for Num 22.29
fill of grapes, as many as you w., Deu 23.24
man does not w. to take his 25.07
saying, 'I do not w. to take her,' 25.08
Caleb said to her, "What do you w.?" Jos 15.18
Caleb said to her, "What do you w.?" Ju 1.14
and then take as much as you w., 1Sa 2.16
and you w. to become their king, Neh 6.06
Did a man ever w. that he would be Job 37.20
So whatever you w. that men would Mt 7.12
we w. to see a sign from you." 12.38
if you w., I will make three booths 17.04
girl, "Ask me for whatever you w., Mk 6.22
And as you w. that men would do to Lk 6.31
but none said, "What do you w.?" Jn 4.27
to him, "Sir, we w. to see Jesus." 12.21
you where you do not w. to go." 21.18
we w. to know therefore what these Ac 17.20
"Do you w. to go up to Jerusalem, 25.09
For I could w. that I myself were Rom 9.03
What do you w.? Shall I come 1Co 4.21
I w. that all were as I myself am. 7.07
I w. you would bear with me in a 2Co 11.01
Though if I w. to boast, I shall not 12.06
come and find you not what I w., 12.20

WISH (cont.)

you may find me not what you w.; 2Co 12.20
I could w. to be present with you Gal 4.20
I w. those who unsettle you would 5.12

WISHED

If one w. to contend with him, one Job 9.03
to a king who w. to settle accounts Mt 18.23
And when he w. to cross to Achaia, Ac 18.27
Paul w. to go in among the crowd, 19.30
whether he w. to go to Jerusalem 25.20
they w. to set me at liberty, 28.18

WISHES

But if he w. to redeem it, he shall Lev 27.13
dedicates it w. to redeem his 27.15
dedicates the field w. to redeem it, 27.19
If a man w. to redeem any of his 27.31
and he w. to offer an offering by Num 15.14
shall meet my w. by providing food 1Ki 5.09
it has to be, let him do as he w.: 1Co 7.36
free to be married to whom she w., 7.39
Therefore whoever w. to be a friend Jas 4.04

WISHING

So Pilate, w. to satisfy the crowd, Mk 15.15
w. to make a defense to the people. Ac 19.33
But Festus, w. t do the Jews a 25.09
w. to save Paul, kept them from 27.43
not w. that any should perish, but 2Pe 3.09

WITCHCRAFT

blood in it, shall not practice augury or w. Lev 19.26

WITHDRAW

they shall w. from the work of the Num 8.25
said to the priest, "W. your hand." 1Sa 14.19
alone, and I will w. from the city." 2Sa 20.21
of Israel, that he may w. from me." 1Ki 15.19
w. from me; whatever you impose 2Ki 18.14
of Israel, that he may w. from me." 2Ch 16.03
w. thy hand far from me, and let not Job 13.21
He does not w. his eyes from the 36.07
Thou didst w. all thy wrath; Ps 85.03
go down, nor your moon w. itself; Is 60.20
and will make him w. from us. Jer 21.02
him, and he shall be afraid and w., Dan 11.30
and the stars w. their shining. Joe 2.10
and the stars w. their shining. 3.15
of the Mount shall w. northward, Zec 14.04

WITHDRAWN

of Babylon which has w. from you. Jer 34.21
army had w. from Jerusalem at the 37.11
he has w. from them his right hand Lam 2.03
not find him; he has w. from them. Hos 5.06
for Jesus had w., as there was a Jn 5.13
one who had w. from them in Ac 15.38
and when they had w., they said to 26.31

WITHDRAWS

If he w. into a city, then all 2Sa 17.13

WITHDREW

the men of Israel w. from David, 2Sa 20.02
battle, and the men of Israel w. 23.09
and they w. from him and returned 2Ki 3.27
Then Ezra w. from before the house Ez 10.06
the young men saw me and w., Job 29.08
of them, they w. from Jerusalem. Jer 37.05
in a dream he w. to the district Mt 2.22
been arrested, he w. into Galilee; 4.12
Jesus, aware of this, w. from there. 12.15
he w. from there in a boat to a 14.13
from there and w. to the district 15.21
Jesus w. with his disciples to the Mk 3.07
But he w. to the wilderness and Lk 5.16
took them and w. apart to a city 9.10
And he w. from them about a stone's 22.41
Jesus w. again to the hills by Jn 6.15
he w. from them, taking the disciples Ac 19.09
to examine him w. from him instantly 22.29

WITHER

they w. before any other plant. Job 8.12
beneath, and his branches w. above. 18.16
they w. and fade like the mallow; 24.24
season, and its leaf does not w. Ps 1.03
the grass, and w. like the green herb. 37.02
let them be trodden down and w. 58.07
evening shadow; I w. away like grass. 102.11
O Jerusalem, let my right hand w.! 137.05
He who trusts in his riches will w., Pro 11.28
and they w., and the tempest carries Is 40.24
and the grass of every field w.? Jer 12.04
all its fresh sprouting leaves w.? Eze 17.09
it not utterly w. when the east 17.10
w. away on the bed where it grew?" 17.10
leaves will not w. nor their fruit 47.12
Bashan and Carmel w., the bloom of Nah 1.04
"How did the fig tree w. at once?" Mt 21.20

WITHERED

w., thin, and blighted by the east Gen 41.23
is smitten like grass, and w.; Ps 102.04
the grass is w., the new growth Is 15.06
even the leaves are w., and what I Jer 8.13
off, its strong stem was w.; Eze 19.12
all the trees of the field are w.; Joe 1.12
field on which it did not rain w.; Amo 4.07
attacked the plant, so that it w. Jon 4.07
Let his arm be wholly w., his right eye Zec 11.17
there was a man with a w. hand. Mt 12.10
they had no root they w. away. 13.06
And the fig tree w. at once. 21.19
a man was there who had a w. hand. Mk 3.01
to the man who had the w. hand, 3.03
since it had no root it w. away. 4.06
the fig tree w. away to its roots. 11.20
fig tree which you cursed has w." 11.21
was there whose right hand was w. Lk 6.06
to the man who had the w. hand, 6.08
it w. away, because it had no 8.06

WITHERS

He comes forth like a flower, and w.; Job 14.02
in the evening it fades and w. Ps 90.06
which w. before it grows up, 129.06
shall be like an oak whose leaf w., Is 1.30
The earth mourns and w., 24.04
the world languishes and w.; 24.04
Lebanon is confounded and w. away; 33.09
The grass w., the flower fades, when 40.07
The grass w., the flower fades; 40.08
The vine w., the fig tree languishes Joe 1.12
mourn, and the top of Carmel w. Amo 1.02
is cast forth as a branch and w.; Jn 15.06
scorching heat and w. the grass; Jas 1.11
The grass w., and the flower falls, 1Pe 1.24

WITHHELD

seeing you have not w. your son, Gen 22.12
and have not w. your son, your only 22.16
who has w. from you the fruit of 30.02
and you have w. bread from the Job 22.07
"If I have w. anything that the 31.16
From the wicked their light is w., 38.15
and hast not w. the request of his Ps 21.02
and thy compassion are w. from me. Is 63.15
Therefore the showers have been w., Jer 3.03
But I w. my hand, and acted for the Eze 20.22
offering are w. from the house of Joe 1.13
"And I also w. the rain from you Amo 4.07
heavens above you have w. the dew, Hag 1.10
and the earth has w. its produce. 1.10

WITHHOLD
none of us will w. from you his Gen 23.06
and w. your help from them; Deu 22.01
you find; you may not w. your help. 22.03
and w. your help from them; 22.04
for he will not w. me from you. 2Sa 13.13
and didst not w. thy manna from Neh 9.20
w. thy mercy from me, let thy Ps 40.11
does the LORD w. from those who 84.11
Do not w. good from those to whom Pro 3.27
Do not w. discipline from a child; 23.13
and from that w. not your hand; Ecc 7.18
and at evening w. not your hand; 11.06
up, and to the south, Do not w.; Is 43.06
cloak do not w. your coat as well. Lk 6.29

WITHHOLDS
"He who w. kindness from a friend Job 6.14
If he w. the waters, they dry up; 12.15
another w. what he should give, and Pro 11.24
w. his hand from iniquity, executes Eze 18.08
w. his hand from iniquity, takes no 18.17

WITHOUT
The earth was w. form and void, and Gen 1.02
Joseph is w. doubt torn to pieces." 37.33
and w. your consent no man shall 41.44
Your lamb shall be w. blemish, Ex 12.05
night passed w. one coming near 14.20
for nothing, w. payment of money. 21.11
driven away, w. any one seeing it, 22.10
within and w. shall you overlay it, 25.11
bull and two rams w. blemish, 29.01
it with pure gold within and w., 37.02
he shall offer a male w. blemish; Lev 1.03
he shall offer a male w. blemish; 1.10
shall offer it w. blemish before 3.01
he shall offer it w. blemish. 3.06
a young bull w. blemish to the 4.03
offering a goat, a male w. blemish, 4.23
a female w. blemish, for his sin 4.28
shall bring a female w. blemish, 4.32
a ram w. blemish out of the flock, 5.15
priest a ram w. blemish out of the 5.18
a ram w. blemish out of the flock, 6.06
both w. blemish, and offer them 9.02
a lamb, both a year old w. blemish, 9.03
take two male lambs w. blemish, 14.10
one ewe lamb a year old w. blemish, 14.10
discharge touches w. having rinsed 15.11
you shall offer a male w. blemish, 22.19
lamb a year old w. blemish as a 23.12
seven lambs a year old w. blemish, 23.18
while it lies desolate w. them; 26.43
lamb a year old w. blemish for a Num 6.14
lamb a year old w. blemish as a 6.14
and one ram w. blemish as a peace 6.14
unwittingly w. the knowledge of 15.24
bring you a red heifer w. defect, 19.02
male lambs a year old w. blemish, 28.03
male lambs a year old w. blemish, 28.09
male lambs a year old w. blemish; 28.11
see that they are w. blemish; 28.19
See that they are w. blemish. 28.31
male lambs a year old w. blemish; 29.02
they shall be to you w. blemish; 29.08
they shall be w. blemish; 29.13
male lambs a year old w. blemish, 29.17
male lambs a year old w. blemish, 29.20
male lambs a year old w. blemish, 29.23
male lambs a year old w. blemish, 29.26
male lambs a year old w. blemish, 29.29
male lambs a year old w. blemish, 29.32
male lambs a year old w. blemish, 29.36
any person w. intent may flee 35.11
any person w. intent may flee 35.15
he stabbed him suddenly w. enmity, 35.22
anything on him w. lying in wait, 35.22
and w. seeing him cast it upon him, 35.23
w. being at enmity with him in time Deu 4.42
you will eat bread w. scarcity, 8.09
unintentionally w. having been at 19.04
of faithfulness and w. iniquity, 32.04
that he will w. fail drive out Jos 3.10
within and from w. because of the 6.01
any person w. intent or unwittingly 20.03
killed a person w. intent could 20.09
and their camels were w. number, Ju 7.12
w. resting even for a moment." Ru 2.07
left you this day w. next of kin; 4.14
blood by killing David w. cause? 1Sa 19.05
great or small w. disclosing it to 20.02
shed blood w. cause or for my lord 25.31
Joab never be w. one who has a 2Sa 3.29
w. coming into the king's presence. 14.28
w. striking a second blow; 20.10
the blood which Joab shed w. cause. 1Ki 2.31
w. the knowledge of my father David, 2.32
Syria and Israel continued w. war. 22.01
is it w. the LORD that I have come 2Ki 18.25
and cedar timbers w. number; 1Ch 22.04
all kinds of craftsmen w. number, 22.15
w. regard to their divisions; 2Ch 5.11
the people were w. number who came 12.03
time Israel was w. the true God, 15.03
and w. a teaching priest, and w. law; 15.03
w. letting go with him to battle, 25.13
men in full and w. delay from the Ez 6.08
given to them day by day w. fail, 6.09
and salt w. prescribing how much. 7.22
the inner court w. being called, Est 4.11
that w. fail they would keep these 9.27
him, to destroy him w. cause." Job 2.03
perish for ever w. any regarding 4.20
they not die, and that w. wisdom? 4.21
marvelous things w. number: 5.09
it tasteless be eaten w. salt, 6.06
and come to their end w. hope. 7.06
and marvelous things w. number. 9.10
and multiplies my wounds w. cause; 9.17
Then I would speak w. fear of him, 9.35
will lift up your face w. blemish; 11.15
They grope in the dark w. light; 12.25
then w. my flesh I shall see God, 19.26
Their bull breeds w. fail; their cow calves 21.10
w. clothing, and have no covering in 24.07
They go about naked, w. clothing; 24.10
It hurls at him w. pity; he flees from 27.22
clothing, or a poor man w. covering; 31.19
if I have eaten its yield w. payment, 31.39
say, 'I am clean, w. transgression; 33.09
incurable, though I am w. transgression.' 34.06
the mighty w. investigation, and sets 34.24
'Job speaks w. knowledge, his words 34.35
knowledge, his words are w. insight.' 34.35
he multiplies words w. knowledge." 35.16
by the sword, and die w. knowledge. 36.12
counsel by words w. knowledge? 38.02
not his like, a creature w. fear. 41.33
that hides counsel w. knowledge?' 42.03
or plundered my enemy w. cause, Ps 7.04
trusted in the LORD w. wavering. 26.01
w. understanding, which must be 32.09
For w. cause they hid their net for 35.07
w. cause they dug a pit for my life 35.07
I knew not slandered me w. ceasing; 35.15
wink the eye who hate me w. cause. 35.19
Those who are my foes w. cause are 38.19
have encompassed me w. number; 40.12
I praise, in God I trust w. a fear. 56.04
in God I trust w. a fear. What can man 56.11
shooting at him suddenly and w. fear. 64.04
are those who hate me w. cause; 69.04
hand is stretched out w. wearying; 77.02

WITHOUT (cont.)

came, and young locusts w. number; Ps 105.34
of hate, and attack me w. cause. 109.03
Princes persecute me w. cause, 119.161
will be at ease, w. dread of evil." Pro 1.33
W. having any chief, officer or 6.07
the youths, a young man w. sense, 7.07
To him who is w. sense she says, 9.04
to him who is w. sense she says, 9.16
is a beautiful woman w. discretion. 11.22
but w. people a prince is ruined. 14.28
W. counsel plans go wrong, but with 15.22
A man w. sense gives a pledge, and 17.18
good for a man to be w. knowledge, 19.02
Who has wounds w. cause? Who has redness 23.29
against your neighbor w. cause, 24.28
by the vineyard of a man w. sense; 24.30
Like clouds and wind w. rain is a 25.14
A man w. self-control is like a 25.28
city broken into and left w. walls. 25.28
concubines, and maidens w. number. Sol 6.08
withers, and like a garden w. water. Is 1.30
beautiful houses, w. inhabitant. 5.09
cities lie waste w. inhabitant, 6.11
and houses w. men, and the land is 6.11
w. the bow they were captured. 22.03
is laid waste, w. house or haven! 23.01
this is a people w. discernment; 27.11
vomit, no place is w. filthiness. 28.08
w. asking for my counsel, to take 30.02
Behold the valiant ones cry w.; 33.07
none shall be w. her mate. 34.16
is it w. the LORD that I have come 36.10
sit on the ground w. a throne, 47.01
and you shall be redeemed w. money. 52.03
wine and milk w. money and w. price. 55.01
blind, they are all w. knowledge; 56.10
cities are in ruins, w. inhabitant. Jer 2.15
have forgotten me days w. number. 2.32
cities will be ruins w. inhabitant. 4.07
Judah a desolation, w. inhabitant. 9.11
Every man is stupid and w. knowledge; 10.14
w. price, for all your sins, throughout 15.13
which the LORD overthrew w. pity; 20.16
shall be desolate, w. inhabitant'? 26.09
is a desolation, w. man or beast; 32.43
'It is a waste w. man or beast,' 33.10
w. man or inhabitant or beast, 33.10
w. man or beast, and in all of its 33.12
Judah a desolation w. inhabitant." 34.22
was it w. our husbands' approval 44.19
w. inhabitant, as it is this day. 44.22
a waste, a ruin, w. inhabitant. 46.19
than locusts; they are w. number. 46.23
Heshbon fugitives stop w. strength; 48.45
Every man is stupid and w. knowledge; 51.17
a desolation, w. inhabitant. 51.29
and a hissing, w. inhabitant. 51.37
they fled w. strength before the Lam 1.06
has destroyed w. mercy all the 2.02
ago, he has demolished w. pity; 2.17
slain them, slaughtering w. mercy. 2.21
me into darkness w. any light; 3.02
and pursued us, slaying w. pity; 3.43
"My eyes will flow w. ceasing, w. respite, 3.49
those who were my enemies w. cause; 3.52
forward, w. turning as they went. Eze 1.09
they went, w. turning as they went. 1.12
four directions w. turning as they 1.17
The sword is w., pestilence and 7.15
four directions w. turning as they 10.11
others followed w. turning as they 10.11
I have not done w. cause all that 14.23
from the sojourner w. redress. 22.29
after piece, w. making any choice. 24.06
all of them dwelling w. walls, 38.11
brought me from w. into the inner 40.44
the outer court w. laying there 42.14
offer a he-goat w. blemish for a 43.22
offer a bull w. blemish and a ram 43.23
a ram from the flock w. blemish. 43.23
w. blemish, shall be provided. 43.25
shall take a young bull w. blemish, 45.18
bulls and seven rams w. blemish, 45.23
the vestibule of the gate from w., 46.02
six lambs w. blemish and a ram w. blemish; 46.04
offer a young bull w. blemish, 46.06
a ram, which shall be w. blemish; 46.06
lamb a year old w. blemish for a 46.13
youths w. blemish, handsome and Dan 1.04
w. touching the ground; and the goat 8.05
W. warning he shall destroy many; 8.25
shall come in w. warning and 11.21
a small people. W. warning 11.23
dwell many days w. king or prince, Hos 3.04
w. sacrifice or pillar, w. ephod or 3.04
and a people w. understanding shall 4.14
breaks in, and the bandits raid w. 7.01
silly and w. sense, calling to Egypt, 7.11
up princes, but w. my knowledge. 8.04
my land, powerful and w. number; Joe 1.06
w. revealing his secret to his Amo 3.07
w. vision, and darkness to you, Mic 3.06
and darkness to you, w. divination. 3.06
dead bodies w. end—they stumble Nah 3.03
Egypt too, and that w. limit; 3.09
w. a man, w. an inhabitant. Zep 3.06
be inhabited as villages w. walls, Zec 2.04
helpless, like sheep w. a shepherd. Mt 9.36
You received w. pay, give w. pay. 10.08
to the ground w. your Father's will 10.29
said nothing to them w. a parable. 13.34
prophet is not w. honor except in 13.57
you also still w. understanding? 15.16
you get in here w. a wedding 22.12
w. neglecting the others. 23.23
did not speak to them w. a parable, Mk 4.34
to them, "A prophet is not w. honor, 6.04
they were like sheep w. a shepherd; 6.34
"Then are you also w. understanding? 7.18
enemies, might serve him w. fear, Lk 1.74
on the ground w. a foundation; 6.49
have done, w. neglecting the others. 11.42
men walk over them w. knowing it." 11.44
took a wife, and died w. children; 20.29
and w. him was not anything made Jn 1.03
law judge a man w. first giving 7.51
"Let him who is w. sin among you * 8.07
law, 'They hated me w. a cause.' 15.25
But his tunic was w. seam, 19.23
but w. violence, for they were Ac 5.26
And for three days he was w. sight, 9.09
him, "Please come to us w. delay." 9.38
and accompany them w. hesitation. 10.20
was sent for, I came w. objection. 10.29
me to go with them w. hesitation. 11.12
did not leave himself w. witness, 14.17
w. any crowd or tumult. But some 24.18
As they had been long w. food, 27.21
continued in suspense and w. food, 27.33
that w. ceasing I mention you Rom 1.09
been made. So they are w. excuse; 1.20
All who have sinned w. the law will 2.12
law will also perish w. the law, 2.12
all who believe w. being circumcised 4.11
how are they to hear w. a preacher 10.14
W. us you have become kings! And would 1Co 4.08
a vineyard w. eating any of its 9.07
tends a flock w. getting some of 9.07
not being w. law toward God but 9.21
the meat market w. raising any 10.25
set before you w. raising any 10.27
eats and drinks w. discerning the 11.29
the world, and none is w. meaning; 14.10

WITHOUT (cont.)

fighting w. and fear within. 2Co 7.05
another, they are w. understanding. 10.12
w. boasting of work already done in 10.16
God's gospel w. cost to you? 11.07
often w. food, in cold and exposure. 11.27
no hope and w. God in the world. Eph 2.12
w. spot or wrinkle or any such 5.27
she might be holy and w. blemish. 5.27
to speak the word of God w. fear. Php 1.14
Do all things w. grumbling or 2.14
children of God w. blemish in the 2.15
with a circumcision made w. hands, Col 2.11
puffed up w. reason by his sensuous 2.18
not eat any one's bread w. paying, 2Th 3.08
w. understanding either what they 1Ti 1.07
holy hands w. anger or quarreling; 2.08
so that they may be w. reproach. 5.07
you to keep these rules w. favor, 5.21
to do nothing w. your consent in Phm 1.14
tempted as we are, yet w. sinning. Heb 4.15
He is w. father or mother or 7.03
And it was not w. an oath. 7.20
took their office w. an oath, 7.21
and not w. taking blood which he 9.07
offered himself w. blemish to God, 9.14
covenant was not ratified w. blood. 9.18
and w. the shedding of blood there 9.22
confession of our hope w. wavering, 10.23
of Moses dies w. mercy at the 10.28
And w. faith it is impossible to 11.06
If you are left w discipline, 12.08
the holiness w. which no one will 12.14
men generously and w. reproaching, Jas 1.05
For judgment is w. mercy to one who 2.13
w. giving them the things needed 2.16
w. uncertainty or insincerity. 3.17
W. having seen him you love him; 1Pe 1.08
that of a lamb w. blemish or spot. 1.19
yet w. using your freedom as a 2.16
may be won w. a word by the behavior 3.01
be found by him w. spot or blemish, 2Pe 3.14
to present you w. blemish before Jud 1.24
will give water w. price from the Rev 21.06
take the water of life w. price. 22.17

WITHSTAND

I have come forth to w. you, Num 22.32
been able to w. you to this day. Jos 23.09
could no longer w. their enemies. Ju 2.14
irresolute and could not w. them. 2Ch 13.07
you think to w. the kingdom of the 13.08
so that none is able to w. thee. 20.06
one who is alone, two will w. him. Ecc 4.12
hands of those whom I cannot w. Lam 1.14
will be able to w. or contradict. Lk 21.15
But they could not w. the wisdom Ac 6.10
who was I that I could w. God? 11.17
may be able to w. in the evil day, Eph 6.13

WITHSTOOD

of all their enemies had w. them, Jos 21.44
and they w. King Uzziah, and said to 2Ch 26.18
of Persia w. me twenty-one days; Dan 10.13
the meaning of his name) w. them, Ac 13.08

WITNESS

you may be a w. for me that I dug Gen 21.30
and let it be a w. between you and 31.44
"This heap is a w. between you and 31.48
God is w. between you and me." 31.50
This heap is a w., and the pillar is a w., 31.52
not bear false w. against your Ex 20.16
a wicked man, to be a malicious w. 23.01
nor shall you bear w. in a suit, 23.02
to testify and though he is a w., Lev 5.01
and there is no w. against her, Num 5.13
death on the testimony of one w. 35.30
and earth to w. against you this Deu 4.26
you bear false w. against your 5.20
to death on the evidence of one w. 17.06
"A single w. shall not prevail 19.15
If a malicious w. rises against any 19.16
and if the w. is a false witness 19.18
is a false w. and has accused his 19.18
and earth to w. against you this 30.19
song may be a w. for me against 31.19
them as a w. (for it will live 31.21
may be there for a w. against you. 31.26
and earth to w. against them. 31.28
but to be a w. between us and you, Jos 22.27
but to be a w. between us and you.' 22.28
the Gadites called the altar w.; 22.34
"it is a w. between us that the 22.34
stone shall be a w. against us; 24.27
it shall be a w. against you, 24.27
"The Lord will be w. between us; Ju 11.10
is a w. to this day in the field of 1Sa 6.18
"The Lord is w. against you, and his 12.05
and his anointed is w. this day, 12.05
And they said, "He is w." 12.05
"The Lord is w., who appointed 12.06
"The Lord, the God of Israel, be w.! 20.12
for us to w. the king's dishonor, Ez 4.14
me up, which is a w. against me; Job 16.08
my w. is in heaven, and he that 16.19
a false w. who breathes out lies, Pro 6.19
but a false w. utters deceit. 12.17
A faithful w. does not lie, but a 14.05
but a false w. breathes out lies. 14.05
A truthful w. saves lives, but one 14.25
A false w. will not go unpunished, 19.05
A false w. will not go unpunished, 19.09
A worthless w. mocks at justice, and 19.28
A false w. will perish, but the word 21.28
Be not a w. against your neighbor 24.28
who bears false w. against his 25.18
be a sign and a w. to the Lord of Is 19.20
the time to come as a w. for ever. 30.08
I made him a w. to the peoples, a 55.04
knows, and I am w., says the Lord.'" Jer 29.23
and faithful w. against us if we 42.05
the Lord God be a w. against you, Mic 1.02
"for the day when I arise as a w. Zep 3.08
any to w. or answer, or to bring an Mal 2.12
the Lord was w. to the covenant 2.14
will be a swift w. against the 3.05
fornication, theft, false w., slander. Mt 15.19
You shall not bear false w., 19.18
Thus you w. against yourselves, that 23.31
Do not steal, Do not bear false w., Mk 10.19
For many bore false w. against him, 14.56
him, and their w. did not agree. 14.56
up and bore false w. against him, 14.57
Do not steal, Do not bear false w., Lk 18.20
to bear w. to the light, that all Jn 1.07
but came to bear w. to the light. 1.08
(John bore w. to him, and cried, 1.15
And John bore w., "I saw the Spirit 1.32
and have borne w. that this is the 1.34
needed no one to bear w. of man; 2.25
and bear w. to what we have seen; 3.11
the Jordan, to whom you bore w., 3.26
You yourselves bear me w., 3.28
He bears w. to what he has seen and 3.32
If I bear w. to myself, my testimony 5.31
there is another who bears w. to me, 5.32
and he has borne w. to the truth. 5.33
bear me w. that the Father has sent 5.36
sent me has himself borne w. to me. 5.37
and it is they that bear w. to me; 5.39
"You are bearing w. to yourself; 8.13
"Even if I do bear w. to myself, 8.14
I bear w. to myself, and the Father 8.18

WITNESS (cont.)
Father who sent me bears w. to me. Jn 8.18
Father's name, they bear w. to me; 10.25
rasied him from the dead bore w. 12.17
the Father, he will bear w. to me; 15.26
wrongly, bear w. to the wrong; 18.23
the world, to bear w. to the truth. 18.37
He who saw it has borne w.— 19.35
who is bearing w. to these things, 21.24
with us a w. to his resurrection. Ac 1.22
had the tent of w. in the wilderness, 7.44
prophets bear w. that every one 10.43
who bore w. to the word of his 14.03
did not leave himself without w., 14.17
knows the heart bore w. to them, 15.08
whole council of elders bear me w. 22.05
for you will be a w. for him to all 22.15
blood of Stephen thy w. was shed, 22.20
so you must bear w. also at Rome." 23.11
serve and bear w. to the things in 26.16
For God is my w., whom I serve with Rom 1.09
also bears w. and their conflicting 2.15
and the prophets bear w. to it, 3.21
himself bearing w. with our spirit 8.16
bears me w. in the Holy Spirit, 9.01
I bear them w. that they have a 10.02
But I call God to w. against me— 2Co 1.23
For I bear you w. that, if possible, Gal 4.15
For God is my w., how I yearn for Php 1.08
For I bear him w. that he has Col 4.13
or a cloak for greed, as God is w.; 1Th 2.05
while God also bore w. by signs and Heb 2.04
Holy Spirit also bears w. to us; 10.15
God bearing w. by accepting his 11.04
elder and a w. of the sufferings 1Pe 5.01
And the Spirit is the w., 1Jn 5.07
that he has borne w. to his Son. 5.09
who bore w. to the word of God and Rev 1.02
and from Jesus Christ the faithful w. 1.05
even in the days of Antipas my w., 2.13
the Amen, the faihtful and true w., 3.14
God and for the w. they had borne; 6.09
of the tent of the w. in heaven was 15.05

WITNESSED
shall be signed and sealed and w., Jer 32.44
For it is w. of him, "Thou art a Heb 7.17

WITNESSES
put to death on the evidence of w.; Num 35.30
evidence of two w. or of three Deu 17.06
or of three w. he that is to die 17.06
The hand of the w. shall be first 17.07
only on the evidence of two w., 19.15
or of three w., shall a charge be 19.15
"You are w. against yourselves that Jos 24.22
And they said, "We are w." 24.22
"You are w. this day that I have Ru 4.09
native place; you are w. this day." 4.10
and the elders, said, "We are w. 4.11
thou dost renew thy w. against me, Job 10.17
for false w. have risen against me, Ps 27.12
Malicious w. rise up; they ask me 35.11
Their partiality w. against them; Is 3.09
And I got reliable w., Uriah, the priest 8.02
w. are despised, there is no regard 33.08
bring their w. to justify them, and 43.09
"You are my w.," says the LORD, "and 43.10
and you are my w.," says the LORD. 43.12
declared it? And you are my w.! 44.08
their w. neither see nor know, that 44.09
got w., and weighed the money on Jer 32.10
presence of the w. who signed the 32.12
the field for money and get w."— 32.25
the pride of Israel w. against him; Hos 7.10
by the evidence of two or three w. Mt 18.16
though many false w. came forward, 26.60
Why do we still need w.? You have now 26.65
and said, 'Why do we still need w.? Mk 14.63
So you are w. and consent to the Lk 11.48
You are w. of these things, 24.48
and you also are w., because you Jn 15.27
you shall be my w. in Jerusalem Ac 1.08
up, and of that we all are w. 2.32
from the dead. To this we are w. 3.15
And we are w. to these things, and 5.32
and set up false w. who said, 6.13
and the w. laid down their garments 7.58
And we are w. to all that he did 10.39
to us who were chosen by God as w., 10.41
who are now his w. to the people. 13.31
by the evidence of two or three w. 2Co 13.01
You are w., and God also, how holy 1Th 2.10
on the evidence of two or three w. 1Ti 5.19
confession in the presence of many w. 6.12
me before many w. entrust to 2Ti 2.02
the testimony of two or three w. Heb 10.28
surrounded by so great a cloud of w., 12.01
There are three w., the Spirit, 1Jn 5.08
grant my two w. power of prophesy Rev 11.03

WITS'
drunken men, and were at their w. end. Ps 107.27

WIVES
And Lamech took two w.; the name Gen 4.19
Lamech said to his w.: "Adah and Zillah, 4.23
you w. of Lamech, hearken to what I 4.23
wife, and your sons' w. with you. 6.18
and his sons' w. with him went 7.07
and the three w. of his sons with 7.13
sons and your son's w. with you. 8.16
his wife and his sons' w. with him. 8.18
And Abram and Nahor took w.; 11.29
besides the w. he had, Mahalath the 28.09
Give me my w. and my children for 30.26
set his sons and his w. on camels; 31.17
or if you take w. besides my 31.50
night he arose and took his two w.. 32.22
all their little ones and their w., 34.29
Esau took his w. from the Canaanites: 36.02
Then Esau took his w., his sons, 36.06
Bilhah and Zilpah, his father's w.; 37.02
your little ones and for your w., 45.19
and their w., in the wagons which 46.05
not including Jacob's sons' w., 46.26
and your w. shall become widows and Ex 22.24
which are in the ears of your w., 32.02
Our w. and our little ones will Num 14.03
tents, together with their w., 16.27
our w., our flocks, and all our 32.26
But your w., your little ones, and Deu 3.19
shall not multiply w. for himself, 17.17
"If a man has two w., the one loved 21.15
your w., and the sojourner who is 29.11
Your w., your little ones, and your Jos 1.14
daughters to themselves for w., Ju 3.06
own offspring, for he had many w. 8.30
What shall we do for w. for those 21.07
them any of our daughters for w.?" 21.07
shall we do for w. for those who 21.16
give them w. of our daughters. 21.18
Benjaminites did so, and took their w., 21.23
These took Moabite w.; Ru 1.04
He had two w.; the name of the 1Sa 1.02
and both of them became his w. 25.43
household, and David with his two w., 27.03
and their w. and sons and daughters 30.03
David's two w. also had been taken 30.05
and David rescued his two w. 30.18
and his two w. also, Ahinoam of 2Sa 2.02
concubines and w. from Jerusalem, 5.13
your master's w. into your bosom, 12.08
will take your w. before your eyes, 12.11
lie with your w. in the sight of 12.11

WIVES (cont.)

lives of your w. and your concubines, 2Sa 19.05
Happy are your w.! Happy are these 1Ki 10.08
He had seven hundred w., princesses, 11.03
and his w. turned away his heart. 11.03
was old his w. turned away his 11.04
And so he did for all his foreign w., 11.08
your fairest w. and children also 20.03
your w. and your children"; 20.05
to me for my w. and my children, 20.07
the king's w., his officials, and the 2Ki 24.15
had two w., Helah and Naarah; 1Ch 4.05
for they had many w. and sons. 7.04
sent away Hushim and Baara his w. 8.08
And David took more w. in Jerusalem, 14.03
Happy are your w.! Happy are these 2Ch 9.07
above all his w. and concubines 11.21
took eighteen w. and sixty concubines, 11.21
provisions, and procured w. for them. 11.23
And he took fourteen w., and had 13.21
little ones, their w., and their children. 20.13
your w., and all your possessions, 21.14
and also his sons and his w., 21.17
Jehoiada got for him two w., 24.03
daughters and our w. are in captivity 29.09
their w., their sons, and their 31.18
daughters to be w. for themselves Ez 9.02
away all these w. and their 10.03
the land and from the foreign w. 10.11
taken foreign w. come at appointed 10.14
themselves to put away their w., 10.19
your daughters, your w., and your homes." Neh 4.14
and of their w. against their 5.01
their w., their sons, their daughters, 10.28
be plundered and their w. ravished. Is 13.16
their fields and w. together; Jer 6.12
will give their w. to others and 8.10
their w., their sons, and their 14.16
let their w. become childless and 18.21
Take w. and have sons and daughters; 29.06
take w. for your sons, and give your 29.06
adultery with their neighbors' w., 29.23
our w., our sons, or our daughters, 35.08
All your w. and your sons shall be 38.23
Judah, the wickedness of their w., 44.09
and the wickedness of your w., 44.09
knew that their w. had offered 44.15
You and your w. have declared with 44.25
his w., and his concubines might Dan 5.02
his w., and his concubines drank 5.03
your w., and your concubines have 5.23
they, their children, and their w.; 6.24
of David by itself, and their w. by themselves; Zec 12.12
of Nathan by itself, and their w. by themselves; 12.12
of Levi by itself, and their w. by themselves; 12.13
Shimeites by itself, and their w. by 12.13
itself, and their w. by themselves. 12.14
allowed you to divorce your w., Mt 19.08
with w. and children, brought us on Ac 21.05
those who have w. live as though 1Co 7.29
W., be subject to your husbands, as Eph 5.22
so let w. also be subject in 5.24
love your w., as Christ loved the 5.25
love their w. as their own bodies. 5.28
W., be subject to your husbands, as Col 3.18
love your w., and do not be harsh 3.19
Likewise you w., be submissive to 1Pe 3.01
word by the behavior of thier w., 3.01
live considerately with your w., 3.07

WIZARD

a medium or a w. shall be put to Lev 20.27
or a medium, or a w., or a necromancer. Dec 18.11

WIZARDS

"Do not turn to mediums or w.; Lev 19.31
"If a person turns to mediums and w., 20.06
mediums and the w. out of the land 1Sa 28.03
mediums and the w. from the land. 28.09
and dealt with mediums and with w. 2Ki 21.06
mediums and the w. and the teraphim 23.24
and dealt with mediums and with w. 2Ch 33.06
mediums and the w. who chirp and Is 8.19
sorcerers, and the mediums and the w.; 19.03

WOE

W. to you, O Moab! You are undone Num 21.29
And they said, "W. to us! For nothing 1Sa 4.07
W. to us! Who can deliver 4.08
If I am wicked, w. to me! If I am Job 10.15
W. is me, that I sojourn in Meshech, Ps 120.05
Who has w.? Who has sorrow? Pro 23.29
but w. to him who is alone when he Ecc 4.10
W. to you, O land, when your king is 10.16
W. to them! For they have Is 3.09
W. to the wicked! It shall be 3.11
W. to those who join house to house, 5.08
W. to those who rise early in the 5.11
W. to those who draw iniquity with 5.18
W. to those who call evil good and 5.20
W. to those who are wise in their 5.21
W. to those who are heroes at 5.22
And I said: "W. is me! For I am lost; 6.05
W. to those who decree iniquitous 10.01
W. is me! For the treacherous 24.16
W. to the proud crown of the 28.01
W. to those who hide deep from the 29.15
"W. to the rebellious children," 30.01
W. to those who go down to Egypt 31.01
W. to you, destroyer, who yourself 33.01
darkness, I make weal and create w., 45.07
"W. to him who strives with his 45.09
W. to him who says to a father, 45.10
w. to us, for we are ruined! Jer 4.13
stretching out her hands, "W. is me! 4.31
"W. to us, for the day declines, 6.04
W. is me because of my hurt! 10.19
W. to you, O Jerusalem! How long 13.27
W. is me, my mother, that you bore me, 15.10
"W. to him who builds his house by 22.13
"W. to the shepherds who destroy 23.01
You said, 'W. is me! for the LORD 45.03
"W. to Nebo, for it is laid waste! 48.01
W. to you, O Moab! The people of 48.46
W. to them, for their day has come, 50.27
w. to us, for we have sinned! Lam 5.16
of lamentation and mourning and w. Eze 2.10
W. to the foolish prophets who 13.03
W. to the women who sew magic bands 13.18
all your wickedness (w., w. to you! 16.23
W. to the bloody city, to the pot 24.06
W. to the bloody city! I also will 24.09
W. to them, for they have strayed Hos 7.13
W. to them when I depart from them! 9.12
W. to you who desire the day of the Amo 5.18
"W. to those who are at ease in 6.01
W. to those who lie upon beds of 6.04
W. to those who devise wickedness Mic 2.01
W. is me! For I have Mic 7.01
W. to the bloody city, all full of Nah 3.01
"W. to him who heaps up what is not Hab 2.06
W. to him who gets evil gain for 2.09
W. to him who builds a town with 2.12
W. to him who makes his neighbors 2.15
W. to him who says to a wooden 2.19
W. to you inhabitants of the Zep 2.05
W. to her that is rebellious and 3.01
W. to my worthless shepherd, who Zec 11.17
"W. to you, Chorazin! W. to you, Mt 11.21
"W. to the world for temptations to 18.07
but w. to the man by whom the 18.07
"But w. to you, scribes an Pharisees, 23.13
W. to you, scribes and Pharisees, * 23.14

WOE (cont.)

W. to you, scribes and Pharisees, Mt 23.15
"W. to you, blind guides, who say, 'If 23.16
"W. to you, scribes and Pharisees, 23.23
"W. to you, scribes and Pharisees, 23.25
"W. to you, scribes and Pharisees, 23.27
"W. to you, scribes and Pharisees, 23.29
but w. to that man by whom the Son 26.24
but w. to that man by whom the Son Mk 14.21
"But w. to you that are rich, for Lk 6.24
"W. to you that are full now, for 6.25
"W. to you that laugh now, for you 6.25
"W. to you, when all men speak well 6.26
"W. to you, Chorazin! 10.13
w. to you, Bethsaida! for if the mighty 10.13
"But w. to you Pharisees! for you tithe 11.42
W. to you Pharisees! for you love 11.43
W. to you! for you are like 11.44
And he said, "W. to you lawyers also 11.46
W. to you! for your build 11.47
W. to you lawyers! for you have taken away 11.52
but w. to him by whom they come! 17.01
but w. to that man by whom he is 22.22
W. to me if I do not preach the 1Co 9.16
W. to them! For they walk Jud 1.11
"W., w., w. to those who dwell on Rev 8.13
The first w. has passed; behold, two 9.12
The second w. has passed; behold, the 11.14
the third w. is soon to come. 11.14
But w. to you, O earth and sea, for 12.12

WOES

behold, two w. are still to come. Rev 9.12

WOKE

When Joseph w. from sleep, he did as Mt 1.24
And they went and w. him, saying, 8.25
and they w. him and said to him, Mk 4.38
And they went and w. him, saying, Lk 8.24
Peter on the side and w. him, Ac 12.07
When the jailer w. and saw that the 16.27

WOLF

Benjamin is a ravenous w., in the morning Gen 49.27
The w. shall dwell with the lamb, Is 11.06
The w. and the lamb shall feed 65.25
a w. from the desert shall destroy Jer 5.06
sees the w. coming and leaves the Jn 10.12
and the w. snatches them and 10.12

WOLVES

of her are like w. tearing the Eze 22.27
more fierce than the evening w.; Hab 1.08
are evening w. that leave nothing Zep 3.03
but inwardly are ravenous w. Mt 7.15
out as sheep in the midst of w.; 10.16
out as lambs in the midst of w. Lk 10.03
departure fierce w. will come in Ac 20.29

WOMAN

he made into a w. and brought her Gen 2.22
she shall be called W., because she 2.23
He said to the w., "Did God say, 3.01
And the w. said to the serpent, "We 3.02
But the serpent said to the w., 3.04
So when the w. saw that the tree 3.06
"The w. whom thou gavest to be with 3.12
Then the LORD God said to the w., 3.13
The w. said. "The serpent beguiled 3.13
put enmity between you and the w. 3.15
To the w. he said, "I will greatly 3.16
that you are a w. beautiful to 12.11
saw that the w. was very beautiful. 12.14
And the w. was taken into Pharaoh's 12.15
because of the w. whom you have 20.03
out this slave w. with her son; 21.10
of this slave w. shall not be heir 21.10
lad and because of your slave w.; 21.12
of the son of the slave w. also, 21.13
"Perhaps the w. may not be willing 24.05
But if the w. is not willing to 24.08
'Perhaps the w. will not follow me.' 24.39
let the young w. who comes out to 24.43
let her be the w. whom the LORD 24.44
Shaul, the son of Canaanitish w. 46.10
The w. conceived and bore a son; Ex 2.02
So the w. took the child and nursed 2.09
but each w. shall ask of her 3.22
Shaul, the son of a Canaanite w.; 6.15
and every w. of her neighbor, 11.02
the third day; do not go near a w." 19.15
and hurt a w. with child, so that 21.22
an ox gores a man or a w. to death, 21.28
it in, and it kills a man or a w., 21.29
neither man nor w. do anything 36.06
If a w. conceives, and bears a male Lev 12.02
"When a man or w. has a disease on 13.29
"When a man or a w. has spots on 13.38
man lies with a w. and has an 15.18
"When a w. has a discharge of blood 15.19
"If a w. has a discharge of blood 15.25
who lies with a w. who is unclean. 15.33
nakedness of a w. and of her 18.17
not take a w. as a rival wife to 18.18
not approach a w. to uncover her 18.19
not lie with a male as with a w.; 18.22
shall any w. give herself to a 18.23
carnally with a w. who is a slave, 19.20
man lies with a male as with a w., 20.13
If w. approaches any beast and 20.16
shall kill the w. and the beast; 20.16
man lies with a w. having her 20.18
"A man or a w. who is a medium or a 20.27
a harlot or a w. who has been 21.07
they marry a w. divorced from her 21.07
or a w. who has been defiled, or a 21.14
When a man or w. commits any of the Num 5.06
shall set the w. before the LORD, 5.18
priest make the w. take the oath 5.21
and say to the w.) 'the LORD make 5.21
And the w. shall say, 'Amen, Amen.' 5.22
shall make the w. drink the water 5.24
shall make the w. drink the water. 5.26
and the w. shall become an execration 5.27
But if the w. has not defiled 5.28
shall set the w. before the LORD, 5.30
but the w. shall bear her iniquity. 5.31
a man or a w. makes a special vow, 6.02
of the Cushite w. whom he had 12.01
for he had married a Cushite w.; 12.01
a Midianite w. to his family, 25.06
them, the man of Israel and the w., 25.08
was slain with the Midianite w., 25.14
the Midianite w. who was slain was 25.15
Or when a w. vows a vow to the LORD, 30.03
vow of a widow or of a divorced w., 30.09
and kill every w. who has known 31.17
or a Hebrew w., is sold to you, he Deu 15.12
a man or w. who does what is evil 17.02
that man or w. who has done this 17.05
that man or w. to death with 17.05
among the captives a beautiful w., 21.11
"A. w. shall not wear anything that 22.05
'I took this w., and when I came 22.14
of the young w. and her mother 22.15
of the young w. shall say to the 22.16
them to the father of the young w., 22.19
were not found in the young w., 22.20
out the young w. to the door of 22.21
who lay with the w., and the w.; 22.22
the young w. because she did not 22.24
meets a young w. who is betrothed, 22.25
But to the young w. you shall do 22.26
in the young w. there is no offence 22.26
betrothed young w. cried for help 22.27

WOMAN (cont.)

of the young w. fifty shekels of Deu 22.29
and delicately bred w. among you, 28.56
you a man or w. or family or tribe, 29.18
But the w. had taken the two men Jos 2.04
and bring out from it the w., 6.22
sell Sisera into the hand of a w. Ju 4.09
And a certain w. threw an upper 9.53
men say to me, 'A w. killed him.'" 9.54
or you are the son of another w. 11.02
appeared to the w. and said to her, 13.03
Then the w. came and told her 13.06
again to the w. as she sat in the 13.09
And the w. ran in haste and told 13.10
you the man who spoke to this w.?" 13.11
I said to the w. let her beware. 13.13
And the w. bore a son, and called 13.24
"Is there not a w. among the 14.03
went down and talked with the w.; 14.07
And his father went down to the w., 14.10
After this he loved a w. in the 16.04
the w. came and fell down at the 19.26
husband of the w. who was murdered, 20.04
male and every w. that has lain 21.11
so that the w. was bereft of her Ru 1.05
and behold, a w. lay at his feet! 3.08
know that you are a w. of worth. 3.11
known that the w. came to the 3.14
May the Lord make the w., 4.11
will give you by this young w." 4.12
Eli took her to be a drunken w. 1Sa 1.13
I am a w. sorely troubled; 1.15
your maidservant as a base w., 1.16
Then the w. went her way and ate, 1.18
So the w. remained and nursed her 1.23
I am the w. who was standing here 1.26
children by this w. for the loan 2.20
them, but kill both man and w., 15.03
rebellious w., do I not know that 20.30
The w. was of good understanding 25.03
and left neither man nor w. alive, 27.09
saved neither man nor w. alive, 27.11
out for me a w. who is a medium, 28.07
and they came to the w. by night. 28.08
The w. said to him, "Surely you know 28.09
Then the w. said, "Whom shall I 28.11
When the w. saw Samuel, she cried 28.12
and the w. said to Saul, "Why have 28.12
And the w. said to Saul, "I see a 28.13
And the w. came to Saul and when 28.21
together with the w., urged him; 28.23
Now the w. had a fatted calf in the 28.24
today with a fault concerning a w. 2Sa 3.08
he saw from the roof a w. bathing; 11.02
and the w. was very beautiful. 11.02
sent and inquired about the w. 11.03
And the w. conceived; and she sent 11.05
Did not a w. cast an upper millstone 11.21
"Put this w. out of my presence, and 13.17
a desolate w., in her brother 13.20
and fetched from there a wise w., 14.02
behave like a w. who has been 14.02
When the w. of Tekoa came to the 14.04
Then the king said to the w., 14.08
And the w. of Tekoa said to the 14.09
Then the w. said, "Pray let your 14.12
And the w. said, "Why then have you 14.13
Then the king answered the w., 14.18
And the w. said, "Let my lord the 14.18
The w. answered and said, "As surely 14.19
was Tamar; she was a beautiful w. 14.27
And the w. took and spread a 17.19
came to the w. at the house, 17.20
And the w. said to them, "They have 17.20
Then a wise w. called from the city, 20.16
and the w. said, "Are you Joab 20.17
And the w. said to Joab, "Behold, his 20.21
Then the w. went to all the people 20.22
The one w. said, "Oh, my lord, this 1Ki 3.17
this w. and I dwell in the same 3.17
this w. also gave birth; and we were 3.18
But the other w. said, "No, the 3.22
Then the w. whose son was alive 3.26
the living child to the first w., 3.27
she pretended to be another w. 14.05
After this the son of the w., 17.17
And the w. said to Elijah, "Now I 17.24
Shunem, where a wealthy w. lived, 2Ki 4.08
But the w. conceived, and she bore a 4.17
a w. cried out to him, saying, "Help, 6.26
This w. said to me, 'Give your son, 6.28
words of the w. he rent his 6.30
had said to the w. whose son he 8.01
So the w. arose, and did according 8.02
when the w. returned from the land 8.03
the w. whose son he had restored to 8.05
here is the w., and here is her son 8.05
king asked the w., she told him. 8.06
to this cursed w., and bury her; 9.34
the son of a w. of the daughters of 2Ch 2.14
whether young or old, man or w. 15.13
that wicked w., had broken into the 24.07
if any man or w. goes to the king Est 4.11
is born of a w. is of few days, Job 14.01
Or he that is born of a w. 15.14
"They feed on the barren childless w., 24.21
can he who is born of w. be clean? 25.04
"If my heart has been enticed to a w., 31.09
anguish as of a w. in travail. Ps 48.06
He gives the barren w. a home, 113.09
You will be saved from the loose w., Pro 2.16
For the lips of a loose w. drip honey, 5.03
with a loose w. and embrace the 5.20
to preserve you from he evil w., 6.24
to preserve you from the loose w., 7.05
And lo, a w. meets him, dressed as a 7.10
A foolish w. is noisy; she is wanton 9.13
A gracious w. gets honor, and 11.16
is a beautiful w. without discretion 11.22
house shared with a contentious w. 21.09
with a contentious and fretful w. 21.19
The mouth of a loose w. is a deep pit; 22.14
house shared with a contentious w. 25.24
day and a contentious w. are alike; 27.15
an unloved w. when she gets a 30.23
but a w. who fears the Lord is to 31.30
than death the w. whose heart is Ecc 7.26
but a w. among all these I have not 7.28
in the womb of a w. with child, 11.05
a young w. shall conceive and bear Is 7.14
be in anguish like a w. in travail. 13.08
like the pangs of a w. in travail; 21.03
Like a w. with child, who writhes 26.17
will cry out like a w. in travail, 42.14
or to a w., 'With what are you in 45.10
"Can a w. forget her sucking child, 49.15
heard a cry as of a w. in travail, Jer 4.31
of us, pain as of a w. in travail. 6.24
you, like those of a w. in travail? 13.21
you, pain as of a w. in travail! 22.23
on his loins like a w. in labor? 30.06
the w. with child and her who is in 31.08
on the earth: a w. protects a man." 31.22
to cut off from you man and w., 44.07
the heart of a w. in her pangs; 48.41
the heart of a w. in her pangs. 49.22
hold of her, as of a w. in travail. 49.24
him, pain as of a w. in travail. 50.43
with you I break in pieces man and w.; 51.22
or approach a w. in her time of Eze 18.06
uncleanness of a w. in her impurity 36.17
or a divorced w., but only a virgin 44.22
love a w. who is beloved of a Hos 3.01
seized you like a w. in travail? Mic 4.09

WOMAN (cont.)
of Zion, like a w. in travail; Mic 4.10
and there was a w. sitting in the Zec 5.07
who looks at a w. lustfully has Mt 5.28
a divorced w. commits adultery. 5.32
And behold, a w. who had suffered 9.20
And instantly the w. was made well. 9.22
leaven which a w. took and hid in 13.33
a Canaanite w. from that region 15.22
"O w., great is your faith! 15.28
a divorced w. commits adultery. * 19.09
After them all, the w. died. 22.27
a w. came up to him with an alabaster 26.07
to them, "Why do you trouble the w.? 26.10
And there was a w. who had had a Mk 5.25
But the w., knowing what had been 5.33
But immediately a w., whose little daughter 7.25
Now the w. was a Greek, a Syrophoenician 7.26
no children. Last of all the w. also died. 12.22
a w. came with an alabaster jar of 14.03
land of Sidon, to a w. who was a widow. Lk 4.26
And behold, a w. of the city, who was 7.37
what sort of w. this is who is 7.39
toward the w. he said to Simon, "Do 7.44
said to Simon, "Do you see this w.? 7.44
And he said to the w., "Your faith 7.50
And a w. who had had a flow of 8.43
And when the w. saw that she was 8.47
and a w. named Martha received him 10.38
a w. in the crowd raised her voice 11.27
And there was a w. who had had a 13.11
"W., you are freed from your 13.12
And ought not this w., a daughter of 13.16
leaven which a w. took and hid in 13.21
"Or what w., having ten silver 15.08
who marries a w. divorced from her 16.18
Afterward the w. also died. 20.32
therefore, whose wife will the w. be? 20.33
"W., I do not know him." 22.57
"O w., what have you to do with me? Jn 2.04
There came a w. of Samaria to draw 4.07
The Samaritan w. said to him, "How 4.09
ask a drink of me, a w. of Samaria?" 4.09
The w. said to him, "Sir, you have 4.11
The w. said to him, "Sir, give me 4.15
The w. answered him, "I have no 4.17
The w. said to him, "Sir, I perceive 4.19
"W., believe me, the hour is coming 4.21
The w. said to him, "I know that 4.25
that he was talking with a w., 4.27
So the w. left her water jar, and 4.28
Then said to the w., "It is no longer 4.42
w. who had been caught in adultery, * 8.03
this w. has been caught in the act * 8.04
Jesus was left alone with the w. * 8.09
"W., where are they? Has no one * 8.10
When a w. is in travail she has 16.21
mother, "W., behold your son!" 19.26
"W., why are you weeping?" She said to them, 20.13
"W., why are you weeping? Whom do 20.15
son of a Jewish w. who was a Ac 16.01
One who heard us was a w. named Lydia, 16.14
Areopagite and a w. named Damaris 17.34
Thus a married w. is bound by law Rom 7.02
well for a man not to touch a w. 1Co 7.01
wife and each w. her own husband. 7.02
If any w. has a husband who is an 7.13
the unmarried w. or girl is 7.34
but the married w. is anxious about 7.34
the head of a w. is her husband, and 11.03
but any w. who prays or prophesies 11.05
For if a w. will not veil herself, 11.06
disgraceful for a w. to be shorn or 11.06
but w. is the glory of man. 11.07
(For man was not made from w., but w. from 11.08
Neither was man created for w., but w. for man. 11.09
That is why a w. ought to have a 11.10
in the Lord w. is not independent 11.11
independent of man nor man of w.; 11.11
for as w. was made from man, so man 11.12
from man, so man is now born of w. 11.12
it proper for a w. to pray to God 11.13
but if a w. has long hair, it is her 11.15
shameful for a w. to speak in 14.35
born of w., born under the law, Gal 4.04
by a slave and one by a free w. 4.22
son of the free w. through promise 4.23
with the son of the free w. 4.30
of the slave but of the free w. 4.31
travail comes upon a w. with child, 1Th 5.03
Let a w. learn in silence with all 1Ti 2.11
I permit no w. to teach or to have 2.12
but the w. was deceived and became 2.14
Yet w. will be saved through bearing 2.15
If any believing w. has relatives 5.16
honor on the w. as the weaker sex, 1Pe 3.07
that you tolerate the w. Jezebel, Rev 2.20
a w. clothed with the sun, with the 12.01
before the w. who was about to 12.04
and the w. fled into the wilderness, 12.06
he pursued the w. who had borne 12.13
But the w. was given the two wings 12.14
out of his mouth after the w., 12.15
earth came to the help of the w., 12.16
Then the dragon was angry with the w., 12.17
and I saw a w. sitting on a scarlet 17.03
The w. was arrayed in purple and 17.04
And I saw the w., drunk with the 17.06
tell you the mystery of the w., 17.07
hills on which the w. is seated; 17.09
And the w. that you saw is the 17.18

WOMAN'S
the pledge from the w. hand, Gen 38.20
according as the w. husband shall Ex 21.22
Now an Israelite w. son whose Lev 24.10
and the Israelite w. son blasphemed 24.11
and unbind the hair of the w. head, Num 5.18
of jealousy out of the w. hand, 5.25
shall a man put on a w. garment; Deu 22.05
And this w. son died in the night, 1Ki 3.19
in him because of the w. testimony, Jn 4.39

WOMB
to her, "Two nations are in your w., Gen 25.23
behold, there were twins in her w. 25.24
Leah was hated, he opened her w.; 29.31
from you the fruit of the w.?" 30.02
hearkened to her and opened her w. 30.22
came, there were twins in her w. 38.27
of the breasts and of the w. 49.25
to open the w. among the people of Ex 13.02
LORD all that first opens the w. 13.12
the males that first open the w.; 13.15
All that opens the w. is mine, 34.19
that opens the w. among the people Num 3.12
instead of all that open the w., 8.16
he comes out of his mother's w. 12.12
Everything that opens the w. of all flesh, 18.15
Nazirite to God from my mother's w. Ju 16.17
yet sons in my w. that they may Ru 1.11
because the LORD had closed her w. 1Sa 1.05
because the LORD had closed her w. 1.06
"Naked I came from my mother's w., Job 1.21
shut the doors of my mother's w., 3.10
come forth from the w. and expire? 3.11
thou bring me forth from the w.? 10.18
carried from the w. to the grave. 10.19
he who made me in the w. make him? 31.15
did not one fashion us in the w.? 31.15
from his mother's w. I guided him); 31.18
when it burst forth from the w.; 38.08
From whose w. did the ice come 38.29
art he who took me from the w.; Ps 22.09

WOMB (cont.)

The wicked go astray from the w., Ps 58.03
he who took me from my mother's w. 71.06
From the w. of the morning like dew 110.03
LORD, the fruit of the w. a reward. 127.03
knit me together in my mother's w. 139.13
the barren w., the earth ever Pro 30.16
What, son of my w.? What son of my sons? 31.02
his mother's w. he shall go again, Ecc 5.15
bones in the w. of a woman with 11.05
no mercy on the fruit of the w.; Is 13.18
you from the w. and will help you: 44.02
Redeemer, who formed you from the w.: 44.24
your birth, carried from the w.; 46.03
The LORD called me from the w., 49.01
me from the w. to be his servant, 49.05
no compassion on the son of her w.? 49.15
cause to bring forth, shut the w.? 66.09
"Before I formed you in the w. I knew you, Jer 1.05
because he did not kill me in the w.; 20.17
grave, and her w. for ever great. 20.17
forth from the w. to see toil and 20.18
a miscarrying w. and dry breasts. Hos 9.14
In the w. he took his brother by 12.03
himself at the mouth of the w. 13.13
Spirit, even from his mother's w. Lk 1.15
conceive in your w. and bear a son, 1.31
of Mary, the babe leaped in her w.; 1.41
blessed is the fruit of your w.! 1.42
the babe in my w. leaped for joy. 1.44
before he was conceived in the w. 2.21
that opens the w. shall be called 2.23
"Blessed is the w. that bore you, 11.27
into his mother's w. and be born? Jn 3.04
the barrenness of Sarah's w. Rom 4.19

WOMBS

closed all the w. of the house of Gen 20.18
and the w. that never bore, and the Lk 23.29

WOMEN

goods, and the w. and the people. Gen 14.16
with Sarah after the manner of w. 18.11
the time when w. go out to draw 24.11
my life because of the Hittite w. 27.46
of the Hittite w. such as these, 27.46
one of the w. of the land, what good 27.46
not marry one of the Canaanite w. 28.01
marry one of the Canaanite w.," 28.06
the Canaanite w. did not please 28.08
For the w. will call me happy"; so 30.13
you, for the way of w. is upon me. 31.35
eyes and saw the w. and children, 33.05
out to visit the w. of the land; 34.01
serve as midwife to the Hebrew w., Ex 1.16
Hebrew w. are not like the Egyptian w.; 1.19
from the Hebrew w. to nurse the 2.07
on foot, besides w. and children. 12.37
and all the w. went out after her 15.20
So they came, both men and w.; 35.22
And all w. who had ability spun 35.25
all the w. whose hearts were moved 35.26
All the men and w., the people 35.29
the ministering w. who ministered 38.08
ten w. shall bake your bread in one Lev 26.26
captive the w. of Midian and their Num 31.09
them, 'Have you let all the w. live? 31.15
w. who had not known man by lying 31.35
every city, men, w., and children; Deu 2.34
every city, men, w., and children. 3.06
but the w. and the little ones, the 20.14
w., and little ones, and the sojourner 31.12
both men and w., young and old, oxen, Jos 6.21
both men and w., were twelve 8.25
and the w., and the little ones, and 8.35
you marry their w. and they yours, 23.12
"Most blessed of w. be Jael, Ju 5.24
of tent-dwelling w. most blessed. 5.24
died, about a thousand men and w. 9.49
fled to it, all the men and w., 9.51
Now the house was full of men and w.; 16.27
about three thousand men and w., 16.27
also the w. and the little ones. 21.10
gave them the w. whom they had 21.14
alive of the w. of Jabeshgilead; 21.14
since the w. are destroyed out of 21.16
and the w. said, "Is this Naomi?" Ru 1.19
Then the w. said to Naomi, "Blessed 4.14
And the w. of the neighborhood gave 4.17
lay with the w. who served at the 1Sa 2.22
her death the w. attending her 4.20
your sword has made w. childless, 15.33
your mother be childless among w. 15.33
the w. came out of all the cities 18.06
And the w. sang to one another as 18.07
men have kept themselves from w. 21.04
"Of a truth w. have been kept from 21.05
both men and w., children and 22.19
captive the w. and all who were in 30.02
wonderful, passing the love of w. 2Sa 1.26
both men and w., to each a cake of 6.19
of singing men and singing w.? 19.35
King Solomon loved many foreign w.: 1Ki 11.01
Edomite, Sidonian, and Hittite w., 11.01
and rip up their w. with child." 2Ki 8.12
up all the w. in it who were with 15.16
where the w. wove hangings for the 23.07
both men and w., to each a loaf of 1Ch 16.03
w., sons, and daughters; they also took 2Ch 28.08
men and singing w. have spoken of 35.25
w., and children, gathered to him Ez 10.01
married foreign w. from the 10.02
trespassed and married foreign w., 10.10
the men who had married foreign w. 10.17
married foreign w. were found 10.18
All these had married foreign w. 10.44
both men and w. and all who could Neh 8.02
the men and the w. and those who 8.03
the w. and children also rejoiced. 12.43
Jews who had married w. of Ashdod, 13.23
Israel sin on account of such w. 13.26
nevertheless foreign w. made even 13.26
our God by marrying foreign w.? 13.27
banquet for the w. in the palace Est 1.09
queen will be made known to all w., 1.17
all w. will give honor to their 1.20
eunuch who is in charge of the w.; 2.03
of Hegai who had charge of the w. 2.08
under the regulations for the w., 2.12
with spices and ointments for w.— 2.12
who had charge of the w., advised. 2.15
loved Esther more than all the w., 2.17
w. and children, in one day, the 3.13
men and w., I would have held my 7.04
them, with their children and w., 8.11
one of the foolish w. would speak. Job 2.10
there were no w. so fair as Job's 42.15
"The w. at home divide the spoil, Ps 68.12
Give not your strength to w., Pro 31.03
Many w. have done excellently, but 31.29
both men and w., and many concubines, Ecc 2.08
do not know, O fairest among w., Sol 1.08
beloved, O fairest among w.? 5.09
beloved gone, O fairest among w.? 6.01
oppressors, and w. rule over them. Is 3.12
And seven w. shall take hold of one 4.01
day the Egyptians will be like w., 19.16
w. come and make a fire of them. 27.11
Rise up, you w. who are at ease, hear 32.09
will shudder, you complacent w.; 32.10
Tremble, you w. who are at ease, 32.11
even to wicked w. you have taught Jer 2.33
and the w. knead dough, to make 7.18
call for the mourning w. to come; 9.17
send for the skilful w. to come; 9.17

WOMEN (cont.)
Hear, O w., the word of the LORD, and Jer 9.20
all the w. left in the house of the 38.22
w., and children, those of the 40.07
w., children, and eunuchs, whom 41.16
the men, the w., the children, the 43.06
and all the w. who stood by, a great 44.15
And the w. said, "When we burned 44.19
men and w., all the people who had 44.20
to all the people and all the w., 44.24
her midst, that they may become w.! 50.37
has failed, they have become w.; 51.30
Should w. eat their offspring, the Lam 2.20
compassionate w. have boiled their 4.10
W. are ravished in Zion, virgins in 5.11
there sat w. weeping for Tammuz. Eze 8.14
maidens, little children and w., 9.06
Woe to the w. who sew magic bands 13.18
from other w. in your harlotries: 16.34
judge you as w. who break wedlock 16.38
upon you in the sight of many w.; 16.41
you they humble w. who are unclean 22.10
"Son of man, there were two w., 23.02
and she became a byword among w., 23.10
bracelets upon the hands of the w., 23.42
the sentence of w. that shed blood 23.45
that all w. may take warning and 23.48
and the w. shall go into captivity. 30.17
the daughter of w. to destroy the Dan 11.17
or to the one beloved by w.; 11.37
and their pregnant w. ripped open. Hos 13.16
have ripped up w. with child in Amo 1.13
The w. of my people you drive out Mic 2.09
Behold your troops are w. in your midst. Nah 3.13
and behold, two w. coming forward! Zec 5.09
Old men and old w. shall again sit 8.04
plundered and the w. ravished; 14.02
those born of w. there has risen Mt 11.11
men, besides w. and children. 14.21
men, besides w. and children. 15.38
Two w. will be grinding at the mill 24.41
There were also many w. there, 27.55
But the angel said to the w., 28.05
There were also w. looking on from Mk 15.40
also many other w. who came up 15.41
loud cry, "Blessed are you among w., Lk 1.42
those born of w. none is greater 7.28
and also some w. who had been 8.02
There will be two w. grinding 17.35
and of w. who bewailed and lamented 23.27
acquaintances and the w. who had 23.49
The w. who had come with him from 23.55
and the other w. with them who 24.10
Moreover, some w. of our company 24.22
found it just as the w. had said; 24.24
with the w. and Mary the mother of Ac 1.14
multitudes both of men and w., 5.14
off men and w. and committed them 8.03
were baptized, both men and w. 8.12
men or w., he might bring them 9.02
the devout w. of high standing and 13.50
spoke to the w. who had come 16.13
and not a few of the leading w. 17.04
not a few Greek w. of high standing 17.12
delivering to prison both men and w., 22.04
Their w. exchanged natural relations Rom 1.26
relations with w. and were consumed 1.27
the w. should keep silence in the 1Co 14.34
these w. are two covenants. One is from Gal 4.24
help these w., for they have labored Php 4.03
also that w. should adorn themselves 1Ti 2.09
as befits w. who profess religion. 2.10
The w. likewise must be serious, no 3.11
older w. like mothers, younger women 5.02
younger w. like sisters, in all 5.02
households and capture weak w., 2Ti 3.06
Bid the older w. likewise to be Tit 2.03
train the young w. to love their 2.04
W. received their dead by resurrection Heb 11.35
So once the holy w. who hoped in 1Pe 3.05
not defiled themselves with w., Rev 14.04

WOMEN'S
their hair like w. hair, and their teeth Rev 9.08

WON
And David w. a name for himself. 2Sa 8.13
and w. a name beside the three. 23.18
and w. a name beside the three 23.22
and w. a name beside the three. 1Ch 11.20
and w. a name beside the three 11.24
From spoil w. in battles they 26.27
pleased him and w. his favor; Est 2.09
which his right hand had w. Ps 78.54
w. strength out of weakness, became Heb 11.34
may be w. without a word by the 1Pe 3.01

WONDER
and gives you a sign or a w., Deu 13.01
and the sign or w. which he tells 13.02
be upon you as a sign and a w., 28.46
w. and be astounded. For I am doing Hab 1.05
filled with w. and amazement at Ac 3.10
why do you w. at this, or why do you 3.12
'Behold, you scoffers, and w., and perish; 13.41
And no w., for even Satan disguises 2Co 11.14
Do not w., brethren, that the world 1Jn 3.13
earth followed the beast with w. Rev 13.03

WONDERED
and w. that there was no one to Is 59.16
so that the throng w., when they saw Mt 15.31
so that the governor w. greatly. 27.14
further answer, so that Pilate w. Mk 15.05
And Pilate w. if he were already 15.44
and they w. at his delay in the Lk 1.21
who heard it w. at what the 2.18
and w. at the gracious words which 4.22
and w., he said to them, "Have you 24.41
And they were amazed and w., Ac 2.07
uneducated, common men, they w.; 4.13
When Moses saw it he w. at the sight; 7.31

WONDERFUL
are all his w. deeds which our Ju 6.13
you ask my name, seeing it is w.?" 13.18
your love to me was w., passing the 2Sa 1.26
to him, tell of all his w. works! 1Ch 16.09
Remember the w. works that he has 16.12
I am to build will be great and w. 2Ch 2.09
things too w. for me, which I did Job 42.03
I will tell of all thy w. deeds. Ps 9.01
to him, tell of all his w. works! 105.02
Remember the w. works that he has 105.05
did not consider thy w. works; 106.07
for his w. works to the sons of men 107.08
for his w. works to the sons of men 107.15
for his w. works to the sons of men 107.21
for his w. works to the sons of men 107.31
He has caused his w. works to be 111.04
Thy testimonies are w.; therefore my soul 119.129
Such knowledge is too w. for me; 139.06
thee, for thou art fearful and w. 139.14
W. are thy works! Thou knowest 139.14
Three things are too w. for me; Pro 30.18
name will be called "W. Counselor, Is 9.06
for thou hast done w. things, 25.01
he is w. in counsel, and excellent 28.29
with this people, w. and marvelous; 29.14
us according to all his w. deeds, Jer 21.02
scribes saw the w. things that he Mt 21.15
what w. stones and what w. buildings! Mk 13.01
may declare the w. deeds of him 1Pe 2.09
great and w., seven angels with Rev 15.01
"Great and w. are thy deeds, O Lord 15.03

WONDERING

went home w. at what had happened. *Lk 24.12
w. what this would come to. Ac 5.24

WONDERS

with all the w. which I will do in Ex 3.20
my signs and w. in the land of 7.03
that my w. may be multiplied in the 11.09
did all these w. before Pharaoh; 11.10
in glorious deeds, doing w.? 15.11
by w., and by war, by a mighty hand Deu 4.34
and the LORD showed signs and w., 6.22
the w., the mighty hand, and the 7.19
great terror, with signs and w.; 26.08
saw, the signs, and those great w.; 29.03
signs and the w. which the LORD 34.11
the LORD will do w. among you. Jos 3.05
to the LORD, to him who works w. Ju 13.19
the w. he wrought, the judgments he 1Ch 16.12
signs and w. against Pharaoh and Neh 9.10
mindful of the w. which thou didst 9.17
lion, and again work w. gainst me; Job 10.16
yea, I will remember thy w. of old. Ps 77.11
Thou art the God who workest w., 77.14
and the w. which he has wrought. 78.04
despite his w. they did not believe 78.32
Dost thou work w. for the dead? 88.10
Are thy w. known in the darkness, or 88.12
Let the heavens praise thy w., 89.05
sent signs and w. against Pharaoh 135.09
to him who alone does great w., 136.04
shown signs and w. in the land of Jer 32.20
land of Egypt with signs and w., 32.21
the signs and w. that the Most Dan 4.02
are his signs, how mighty his w.! 4.03
works signs and w. in heaven and 6.27
it be till the end of these w.?" 12.06
arise and show great signs and w., Mt 24.24
will arise and show signs and w., Mk 13.22
see signs and w. you will not Jn 4.48
And I will show w. in the heaven Ac 2.19
works and w. and signs which God 2.22
and many w. and signs were done 2.43
and signs and w. are performed 4.30
Now many signs and w. were done 5.12
did great w. and signs among the 6.08
performed w. and signs in Egypt 7.36
signs and w. to be done by their 14.03
what signs and w. God had done 15.12
by the power of signs and w., Rom 15.19
with signs and w. and mighty works 2Co 12.12
and with pretended signs and w., 2Th 2.09
by signs and w. and various Heb 2.04

WONDROUS

and consider the w. works of God. Job 37.14
the w. works of him who is perfect 37.16
and telling all thy w. deeds. Ps 26.07
thy w. deeds and thy thoughts 40.05
and I still proclaim thy w. deeds. 71.17
Israel, who alone does w. things. 72.18
thy name and recount thy w. deeds. 75.01
thou art great and doest w. things, 86.10
w. works in the land of Ham, and 106.22
of the LORD, his works in the deep. 107.24
I may behold w. things out of thy 119.18
I will meditate on thy w. works. 119.27
and of thy w. works, I will meditate 145.05

WONDROUSLY

God thunders w. with his voice; Job 37.05
W. show thy steadfast love, O savior Ps 17.07
for he has w. shown his steadfast 31.21
God, who has dealt w. with you. Joe 2.26

WONT

"They were w. to say in old time, 2Sa 20.18
as is thy w. toward those who love Ps 119.132
more than it was w. to be heated. Dan 3.19
to do as he was w. to do for them. Mk 15.08

WONTED

returned to its w. flow when the Ex 14.27

WOOD

Make yourself an ark of gopher w.; Gen 6.14
and he cut the w. for the burnt 22.03
took the w. of the burnt offering, 22.06
said, "Behold, the fire and the w.; 22.07
and laid the w. in order, and bound 22.09
laid him on the altar, upon the w. 22.09
in vessels of w. and in vessels of Ex 7.19
rams' skins, goatskins, acacia w., 25.05
"They shall make an ark of acacia w.; 25.10
You shall make poles of acacia w., 25.13
shall make a table of acacia w.; 25.23
You shall make the poles of acacia w., 25.28
for the tabernacle of acacia w. 26.15
"And you shll make bars of acacia w., 26.26
"You shall make the altar of acacia w., 27.01
for the altar, poles of acacia w., 27.06
of acacia w. shall you make it. 30.01
You shall make the poles of acacia w., 30.05
for setting, and in carving w., 31.05
skins and goat skins, acacia w., 35.07
found acacia w. of any use in the 35.24
for setting, and in carving w., 35.33
for the tabernacle of acacia w. 36.20
And he made bars of acacia w., 36.31
Bezalel made the ark of acacia w.; 37.01
And he made poles of acacia w., 37.04
He also made the table of acacia w.; 37.10
poles of acacia w. to carry the 37.15
the altar of incense of acacia w.; 37.25
And he made the poles of acacia w., 37.28
burnt offering also of acacia w.; 38.01
he made the poles of acacia w., 38.06
and lay w. in order upon the fire; Lev 1.07
order upon the w. that is on the 1.08
order upon the w. that is on the 1.12
upon the w. that is on the fire; 1.17
which is upon the w. on the fire; 3.05
and shall burn it on a fire of w.; 4.12
shall burn w. on it every morning, 6.12
an article of w. or a garment or a 11.32
every vessel of w. shall be rinsed 15.12
whether there is w. in it or not. Num 13.20
hair, and every article of w. 31.20
with a weapon of w. in the hand, 35.18
will serve gods of w. and stone, Deu 4.28
mountain, and make an ark of w. 10.01
So I made an ark of acacia w., 10.03
forest with his neighbor to cut w., 19.05
serve other gods, of w. and stone. 28.36
of w. and stone, which neither you 28.64
who hews your w. and he who draws 29.11
their idols of w. and stone, 29.17
hewers of w. and drawers of water Jos 9.21
hewers of w. and drawers of water 9.23
day hewers of w. and drawers of 9.27
with the w. of the Asherah which Ju 6.26
split up the w. of the cart and 1Sa 6.14
the yokes of the oxen for the w. 2Sa 24.22
covered them on the inside with w.; 1Ki 6.15
and two doors of cypress w.; 6.34
amount of almug w. and precious 10.11
of the almug w. supports for the 10.12
no such almug w. has come or been 10.12
it in pieces and lay it on the w., 18.23
other bull and lay it on the w., 18.23
And he put the w. in order, and cut 18.33
in pieces and laid it on the w. 18.33
the burnt offering, and on the w. 18.33
and the w., and the stones, and the 18.38
work of men's hands, w. and stone; 2Ki 19.18
trees of the w. sing for joy 1Ch 16.33

WOOD (cont.)
the threshing sledges for the w., 1Ch 21.23
and w. for the things of wood, 29.02
and wood for the things of w., 29.02
and w., and in purple, blue, and 2Ch 2.14
two cherubim of w. and overlaid 3.10
brought algum w. and precious 9.10
of the algum w. steps for the 9.11
for the w. offering, to bring it Neh 10.34
and I provided for the w. offering, 13.31
as straw, and bronze as rotten w. Job 41.27
all its carved w. they broke down Ps 74.06
the trees of the w. sing for joy 96.12
For lack of w. the fire goes out; Pro 26.20
to hot embers and w. to fire, 26.21
tree among the trees of the w., Sol 2.03
a palanquin from the w. of Lebanon. 3.09
should lift him who is not w.! Is 10.15
with fire and w. in abundance; 30.33
work of men's hands, w. and stone; 37.19
for an offering w. that will not 40.20
I fall down before a block of w.? 44.19
instead of w., bronze, instead of 60.17
mouth a fire, and this people w., Jer 5.14
The children gather w., the fathers 7.18
the instruction of idols is but w.! 10.08
bones, it has become as dry as w. Lam 4.08
the w. we get must be bought. 5.04
and boys stagger under loads of w. 5.13
does the w. of the vine surpass any w. Eze 15.02
Is w. taken from it to make anything? 15.03
Like the w. of the vine among the 15.06
countries, and worship w. and stone.' 20.32
rod, my son, with everything of w. 21.10
need to take w. out of the field 39.10
was paneled with w. round about, 41.16
an altar of w., three cubits high, 41.22
its base, and its walls were of w. 41.22
was a canopy of w. in front of the 41.25
bronze, iron, w., and stone. Dan 5.04
w., and stone, which do not see or 5.23
My people inquire of a thing of w., Hos 4.12
hills and bring w. and build the Hag 1.08
a blazing pot in the midst of w., Zec 12.06
they do this when the w. is green, Lk 23.31
silver precious stones, w., hay, stubble— 1Co 3.12
but also of w. and earthenware, and 2Ti 2.20
silver and bronze and stone and w., Rev 9.20
scarlet, all kinds of scented w., 18.12
ivory, all articles of costly w., 18.12

WOODED
forts and towers on the w. hills. 2Ch 27.04
mountain of the house a w. height. Jer 26.18
mountain of the house a w. height. Mic 3.12

WOODEN
stood on a w. pulpit which they Neh 8.04
they hacked the w. trellis with Ps 74.05
who carry about their w. idols, Is 45.20
the LORD: You have broken w. bars, Jer 28.13
him who says to a w. thing, Awake; Hab 2.19

WOODS
came out of the w. and tore 2Ki 2.24
the wilderness and sleep in the w. Eze 34.25

WOODWORK
and the beam from the w. respond. Hab 2.11

WOOED
Then David sent and w. Abigail, 1Sa 25.39

WOOF
in warp or w. of linen or wool, or Lev 13.48
in warp or w. or in skin or in 13.49
in warp or w., or in the skin, 13.51
whether diseased in warp or w., 13.52
in warp or w. or in anything of skin 13.53
or the skin or the warp or w.; 13.56
in warp or w., or in anything of 13.57
warp or w., or anything of skin 13.58
or linen, either in warp or w., 13.59

WOOL
in warp or woof of linen or w., Lev 13.48
in a garment of w. or linen, 13.59
mingled stuff, w. and linen together. Deu 22.11
a fleece of w. on the threshing Ju 6.37
and the w. of a hundred thousand 2Ki 3.04
He gives snow like w.; the scatters Ps 147.16
She seeks w. and flax, and works Pro 31.13
crimson, they shall become like w. Is 1.18
and the worm will eat them like w.; 51.08
wine of Helbon, and white w., Eze 27.18
you clothe yourselves with the w., 34.03
shall have nothing of w. on them, 44.17
the hair of his head like pure w.; Dan 7.09
my w. and my flax, my oil and my Hos 2.05
I will take away my w. and my flax, 2.09
water and scarlet w. and hyssop, Heb 9.19
white as white w., white as snow; Rev 1.14

WOOLEN
whether a w. or a linen garment, Lev 13.47
w. or linen, or anything of skin, for 13.52

WORD
things the w. of the LORD came to Gen 15.01
the w. of the LORD came to him, 15.04
obey my w. as I command you. 27.08
only obey my w., and go, fetch them 27.13
that you say not a w. to Jacob, 31.24
and bring me w. again. So he sent him 37.14
she sent w. to her father-in-law, 38.25
speak a w. in my lord's ears, and let 44.18
did according to the w. of Moses; Ex 8.13
who feared the w. of the LORD 9.20
not regard the w. of the LORD left 9.21
did according to the w. of Moses; 32.28
and w. was proclaimed throughout 36.06
did according to the w. of Moses. Lev 10.07
according to the w. of the LORD, Num 3.16
according to the w. of the LORD, 3.51
see whether my w. will come true 11.23
brought back w. to them and to all 13.26
pardoned, according to your w.; 14.20
he has despised the w. of the LORD, 15.31
and I will bring back w. to you, 22.08
but only the w. which I bid you, 22.35
The w. that God puts in my mouth, 22.38
And the LORD put a w. in Balaam's 23.05
and put a w. in his mouth, and said, 23.16
to go beyond the w. of the LORD, 24.13
against my w. in the wilderness of 27.14
at his w. they shall go out, and at 27.21
and at his w. they shall come in, 27.21
pledge, he shall not break his w.; 30.02
according to the w. of the LORD, 36.05
and bring us w. again of the way by Deu 1.22
to us, and brought us w. again, 1.25
spite of this w. you did not 1.32
not add to the w. which I command 4.02
declare to you the w. of the LORD; 5.05
may confirm the w. which the LORD 9.05
to speak a w. in my name which I 18.20
may we know the w. which the LORD 18.21
if the w. does not come to pass or 18.22
that is a w. which the LORD has not 18.22
and by their w. every dispute and 21.05
But the w. is very near you 30.14
For they observed thy w., 33.09
according to the w. of the LORD, 34.05
'Remember the w. which Moses the Jos 1.13
shall any w. go out of your mouth, 6.10
according to the w. of the LORD 8.27

WORD (cont.)

There was not a w. of all that	Jos 8.35
I brought him w. again as it was	14.07
the LORD spoke this w. to Moses,	14.10
and brought back w. to them.	22.32
congregation sent w. to the Benjaminites	Ju 21.13
may the LORD establish his w.	1Sa 1.23
And the w. of the LORD was rare in	3.01
and the w. of the LORD had not yet	3.07
at Shiloh by the w. of the LORD.	3.21
And the w. of Samuel came to all	4.01
make known to you the w. of God.	9.27
The w. of the LORD came to Samuel:	15.10
have rejected the w. of the LORD,	15.23
have rejected the w. of the LORD,	15.26
have I done now? Was it not but a w.?"	17.29
could not answer Abner another w.,	2Sa 3.11
same night the w. of the LORD came	7.04
did I speak a w. with any of the	7.07
for ever the w. which thou hast	7.25
So David sent w. to Joab, "Send me	11.06
you despised the w. of the LORD,	12.09
handmaid speak a w. to my lord the	14.12
'The w. of my lord the king will	14.17
I sent w. to you, 'Come here, that I	14.32
until w. comes from you to inform	15.28
when the w. of all Israel has come	19.11
so that they sent w. to the king,	19.14
his w. is upon my tongue.	23.02
But the king's w. prevailed against	24.04
the w. of the LORD came to the	24.11
So David went up at Gad's w.,	24.19
establish his w. which he spoke	1Ki 2.04
also if this w. does not cost	2.23
fulfilling the w. of the LORD	2.27
Benaiah brought the king w. again,	2.30
behold, I now do according to your w.	3.12
And Solomon sent w. to Hiram,	5.02
Now the w. of the LORD came to	6.11
I will establish my w. with you,	6.12
let thy w. be confirmed, which thou	8.26
not one w. has failed of all his	8.56
LORD that he might fulfil his w.,	12.15
But the w. of God came to Shemaiah	12.22
hearkened to the w. of the LORD,	12.24
according to the w. of the LORD.	12.24
of Judah by the w. of the LORD to	13.01
the altar by the w. of the LORD,	13.02
had given by the w. of the LORD.	13.05
commanded me by the w. of the LORD,	13.09
said to me by the w. of the LORD,	13.17
spoke to me by the w. of the LORD,	13.18
the w. of the LORD came to the	13.20
have disobeyed the w. of the LORD,	13.21
who disobeyed the w. of the LORD;	13.26
according to the w. which the LORD	13.26
he cried by the w. of the LORD	13.32
according to the w. of the LORD,	14.18
according to the w. of the LORD	15.29
And the w. of the LORD came to Jehu	16.01
Moreover the w. of the LORD came by	16.07
according to the w. of the LORD,	16.12
according to the w. of the LORD,	16.34
rain these years, except by my w."	17.01
And the w. of the LORD came to him,	17.02
according to the w. of the LORD;	17.05
Then the w. of the LORD came to him,	17.08
according to the w. of the LORD	17.16
and that the w. of the LORD in your	17.24
After many days the w. of the LORD	18.01
the people did not answer him a w.	18.21
to whom the w. of the LORD came,	18.31
done all these things at thy w.	18.36
the w. of the LORD came to him, and	19.09
departed and brought him w. again.	20.09
did as Jezebel had sent w. to them.	21.11
Then the w. of the LORD came to	21.17
And the w. of the LORD came to	21.28
first for the w. of the LORD.	22.05
let your w. be like the word of one	22.13
word be like the w. of one of them,	22.13
"Therefore hear the w. of the LORD:	22.19
according to the w. of the LORD	22.38
God in Israel to inquire of his w.?	2Ki 1.16
according to the w. of the LORD	1.17
according to the w. which Elisha	2.22
went and sent w. to Jehoshaphat	3.07
"The w. of the LORD is with him."	3.12
you have a w. spoken on your	4.13
according to the w. of the LORD.	4.44
this man sends w. to me to cure a	5.07
according to the w. of the man of	5.14
man of God sent w. to the king of	6.09
"Hear the w. of the LORD: thus says	7.01
according to the w. of the LORD.	7.16
according to the w. of the man of	8.02
accordance with the w. of the LORD.	9.26
"This is the w. of the LORD, which	9.36
nothing of the w. of the LORD,	10.10
according to the w. of the LORD	10.17
of Israel sent w. to Amaziah king	14.09
according to the w. of the LORD,	14.25
"Hear the w. of the great king, the	18.28
silent and answered him not a w.,	18.36
This is the w. that the LORD has	19.21
the w. of the LORD came to him:	20.04
Hezekiah, "Hear the w. of the LORD:	20.16
'The w. of the LORD which you have	20.19
they brought back w. to the king.	22.20
according to the w. of the LORD	23.16
according to the w. of the LORD	24.02
according to the w. of the LORD by	1Ch 11.03
according to the w. of the LORD	11.10
according to the w. of the LORD.	12.23
according to the w. of the LORD.	15.15
of the w. that he commanded, for a	16.15
same night the w. of the LORD came	17.03
did I speak a w. with any of the	17.06
let the w. which thou hast spoken	17.23
But the king's w. prevailed against	21.04
So David went up at Gad's w.,	21.19
But the w. of the LORD came to me,	22.08
And Solomon sent w. to Huram the	2Ch 2.03
let thy w. be confirmed, which thou	6.17
that the LORD might fulfil his w.,	10.15
But the w. of the LORD came to	11.02
hearkened to the w. of the LORD,	11.04
the w. of the LORD came to Shemaiah:	12.07
first for the w. of the LORD.	18.04
your w. be like the word of one of them,	18.12
Therefore hear the w. of the LORD:	18.18
of Israel sent w. to Amaziah king	25.18
commanded by the w. of the LORD.	30.12
have not kept the w. of the LORD,	34.21
they brought back w. to the king.	34.28
according to the w. of the LORD by	35.06
to fulfil the w. of the LORD by the	36.21
that the w. of the LORD by the	36.22
that the w. of the LORD by the	Ez 1.01
according to the w. sent by Darius	6.13
Remember the w. which thou didst	Neh 1.08
and could not find a w. to say.	5.08
whose w. saved the king, is standing	Est 7.09
and no one spoke a w. to him,	Job 2.13
"If one ventures a w. with you,	4.02
"Now a w. was brought to me stealthily,	4.12
or the w. that deals gently with	15.11
and my w. dropped upon them.	29.22
they have not a w. to say.	32.15
by the w. of thy lips I have	Ps 17.04
For the w. of the LORD is upright;	33.04
By the w. of the LORD the heavens	33.06
In God, whose w. I praise, in God I	56.04
In God, whose w. I praise, in the	56.10
in the LORD, whose w. I praise,	56.10
or alter the w. that went forth	89.34

WORD (cont.)

you mighty ones who do his w., Ps 103.20
hearkening to the voice of his w.! 103.20
of the w. that he commanded, for a 105.08
to pass the w. of the LORD tested 105.19
he sent forth his w., and healed 107.20
By guarding it according to thy w. 119.09
I have laid up thy w. in my heart, 119.11
I will not forget thy w. 119.16
that I may live and observe thy w. 119.17
revive me according to thy w.! 119.25
strengthen me according to thy w.! 119.28
taunt me, for I trust in thy w. 119.42
And take not the w. of truth 119.43
Remember thy w. to thy servant, in 119.49
O LORD, according to thy w. 119.65
went astray; but now I keep thy w. 119.67
because I have hoped in thy w. 119.74
thy salvation; I hope in thy w. 119.81
thy w. is firmly fixed in the 119.89
evil way, in order to keep thy w. 119.101
Thy w. is a lamp to my feet and a 119.105
life, O LORD, according to thy w.! 119.107
my shield; I hope in thy w. 119.114
The sum of thy w. is truth; 119.160
I rejoice at thy w. like one who 119.162
understanding according to thy w.! 119.169
deliver me according to thy w. 119.170
My tongue will sing of thy w., 119.172
soul waits, and in his w. I hope; 130.05
everything thy name and thy w. 138.02
Even before a w. is on my tongue, lo, 139.04
learn that the w. of the LORD is 141.06
to the earth; his w. runs swiftly. 147.15
He sends forth his w., and melts them; 147.18
He declares his w. to Jacob, 147.19
down, but a good w. makes him glad. Pro 12.25
despises the w. brings destruction 13.13
but a harsh w. stirs up anger. 15.01
and a w. in season, how good it is! 15.23
gives heed to the w. will prosper, 16.20
he who despises the w. will die. 19.16
but the w. of a man who hears will 21.28
A w. fitly spoken is like apples of 25.11
Every w. of God proves true; 30.05
be hasty to utter a w. before God, Ecc 5.02
For the w. of the king is supreme, 8.04
Hear the w. of the LORD, you rulers Is 1.10
The w. which Isaiah the son of Amoz 2.01
and the w. of the LORD form Jerusalem 2.03
despised the w. of the Holy One of 5.24
speak a w., but it will not stand, 8.10
Surely for this w. which they speak 8.20
he Lord has sent a w. against Jacob, 9.08
This is the w. which the LORD spoke 16.13
for the LORD has spoken this w. 24.03
Therefore the w. of the LORD will 28.13
Therefore hear the w. of the LORD 28.14
who by a w. make a man out to be an 29.21
"Because you despise this w., 30.12
ears shall hear a w. behind you, 30.21
silent and answered him not a w., 36.21
this is the w. that the LORD has 37.22
Then the w. of the LORD came to 38.04
"Hear the w. of the LORD of hosts: 39.05
"The w. of the LORD which you have 39.08
but the w. of our God will stand 40.08
who confirms the w. of his servant, 44.26
righteousness a w. that shall not 45.23
sustain with a w. him that is 50.04
so shall my w. be that goes forth 55.11
in spirit, and trembles at my w. 66.02
Hear the w. of the LORD, you who 66.05
LORD, you who tremble at his w.: 66.05
to whom the w. of the LORD came in Jer 1.02
Now the w. of the LORD came to me 1.04
And the w. of the LORD came to me, 1.11
watching over my w. to perform it." 1.12

The w. of the LORD came to me a 1.13
The w. of the LORD came to me, 2.01
Hear the w. of the LORD, O house of 2.04
generation, heed the w. of the LORD. 2.31
the w. is not in them. Thus shall it 5.13
"Because they have spoken this w., 5.14
behold, the w. of the LORD is to 6.10
The w. that came to Jeremiah from 7.01
house, and proclaim there this w., 7.02
Hear the w. of the LORD, all you men 7.02
have rejected the w. of the LORD, 8.09
the w. of the LORD, and let your ear 9.20
ear receive the w. of his mouth; 9.20
Hear the w. which the LORD speaks 10.01
The w. that came to Jeremiah from 11.01
according to the w. of the LORD, 13.02
And the w. of the LORD came to me a 13.03
Then the w. of the LORD came to me: 13.08
"You shall speak to them this w.: 13.12
The w. of the LORD which came to 14.01
"You shall say to them this w.: 14.17
The w. of the LORD came to me: 16.01
to me, 'Where is the w. of the LORD? 17.15
'Hear the w. of the LORD, you kings 17.20
The w. that came to Jeremiah from 18.01
Then the w. of the LORD came to me: 18.05
nor the w. from the prophet. 18.18
'Hear the w. of the LORD, O kings of 19.03
For the w. of the LORD has become 20.08
This is the w. which came to 21.01
say, 'Hear the w. of the LORD, 21.11
of Judah, and speak there this w., 22.01
'Hear the w. of the LORD, O King of 22.02
For if you will indeed obey this w., 22.04
land, hear the w. of the LORD! 22.29
who despise the w. of the LORD, 23.17
to perceive and to hear his w., 23.18
given heed to his w. and listened? 23.18
him who has my w. speak my word 23.28
has my word speak my w. faithfully. 23.28
Is not my w. like fire, says the 23.29
the burden is every man's own w., 23.36
Then the w. of the LORD came to me: 24.04
The w. that came to Jeremiah 25.01
the w. of the LORD has come to me, 25.03
this w. came from the LORD, 26.01
speak to them; do not hold back a w. 26.02
this w. came to Jeremiah from the 27.01
Send w. to the king of Edom, the 27.03
and if the w. of the LORD is with 27.18
Yet hear now this w. which I speak 28.07
when the w. of that prophet comes 28.09
the w. of the LORD came to Jeremiah: 28.12
Hear the w. of the LORD, all you 29.20
Then the w. of the LORD came to 29.30
The w. that came to Jeremiah from 30.01
"Hear the w. of the LORD, O nations, 31.10
The w. that came to Jeremiah from 32.01
'The w. of the LORD came to me: 32.06
accordance with the w. of the LORD, 32.08
that this was the w. of the LORD.' 32.08
The w. of the LORD came to Jeremiah: 32.26
The w. of the LORD came to Jeremiah 33.01
The w. of the LORD came to Jeremiah: 33.19
The w. of the LORD came to Jeremiah: 33.23
The w. which came to Jeremiah from 34.01
Yet hear the w. of the LORD, O 34.04
have spoken the w., says the LORD. 34.05
The w. which came to Jeremiah from 34.08
The w. of the LORD came to Jeremiah 34.12
The w. which came to Jeremiah from 35.01
Then the w. of the LORD came to 35.12
this w. came to Jeremiah from the 36.01
the w. of the LORD came to Jeremiah: 36.27
Then the w. of the LORD came to 37.06
"Is there any w. from the LORD?" 37.17
The w. of the LORD came to Jeremiah 39.15
The w. that came to Jeremiah from 40.01

WORD (cont.)

to all the w. with which the LORD Jer 42.05
of ten days the w. of the LORD 42.07
then hear the w. of the LORD, O 42.15
Then the w. of the LORD came to 43.08
The w. that came to Jeremiah 44.01
"As for the w. which you have 44.16
"Hear the w. of the LORD, all you of 44.24
Therefore hear the w. of the LORD, 44.26
shall know whose w. will stand, 44.28
The w. that Jeremiah the prophet 45.01
The w. of the LORD which came to 46.01
The w. which the LORD spoke to 46.13
The w. of the LORD that came to 47.01
The w. of the LORD that came to 49.34
The w. which the LORD spoke concerning 50.01
The w. which Jeremiah the prophet 51.59
for I have rebelled against his w.; Lam 1.18
the w. of the LORD came to Ezekiel Eze 1.03
the w. of the LORD came to me: 3.16
you hear a w. from my mouth, 3.17
The w. of the LORD came to me: 6.01
hear the w. of the LORD GOD 6.03
The w. of the LORD came to me: 7.01
brought back w., saying, "I have 9.11
And the w. of the LORD came to me: 11.14
The w. of the LORD came to me: 12.01
In the morning the w. of the LORD 12.08
Moreover the w. of the LORD came to 12.17
And the w. of the LORD came to me: 12.21
will speak the w. which I will 12.25
I will speak the w. and perform it, 12.25
Again the w. of the LORD came to me: 12.26
but the w. which I speak will be 12.28
The w. of the LORD came to me: 13.01
minds: 'Hear the w. of the LORD!' 13.02
they expect him to fulfil their w. 13.06
And the w. of the LORD came to me: 14.02
prophet be deceived and speak a w., 14.09
And the w. of the LORD came to me: 14.12
And the w. of the LORD came to me: 15.01
Again the w. of the LORD came to me: 16.01
O harlot, hear the w. of the LORD: 16.35
The w. of the LORD came to me: 17.01
Then the w. of the LORD came to me: 17.11
The w. of the LORD came to me again: 18.01
And the w. of the LORD came to me: 20.02
And the w. of the LORD came to me: 20.45
Hear the w. of the LORD: Thus says 20.47
The w. of the LORD came to me: 21.01
And the w. of the LORD came to me; 21.08
The w. of the LORD came to me again: 21.18
Moreover the w. of the LORD came to 22.01
And the w. of the LORD came to me: 22.17
And the w. of the LORD came to me: 22.23
The w. of the LORD came to me: 23.01
the w. of the LORD came to me: 24.01
Also the w. of the LORD came to me: 24.15
"The w. of the LORD came to me: 24.20
The w. of the LORD came to me: 25.01
Hear the w. of the Lord GOD: Thus 25.03
the w. of the LORD came to me: 26.01
The w. of the LORD came to me: 27.01
The w. of the LORD came to me: 28.01
Moreover the w. of the LORD came to 28.11
The w. of the LORD came to me: 28.20
the w. of the LORD came to me: 29.01
the w. of the LORD came to me: 29.17
The w. of the LORD came to me: 30.01
the w. of the LORD came to me: 30.20
the w. of the LORD came to me: 31.01
the w. of the LORD came to me: 32.01
the w. of the LORD came to me: 32.17
The w. of the LORD came to me: 33.01
you hear a w. from my mouth, 33.07
The w. of the LORD came to me: 33.23
hear what the w. is that comes 33.30
The w. of the LORD came to me: 34.01
shepherds, hear the w. of the LORD: 34.07
shepherds, hear the w. of the LORD: 34.09
The w. of the LORD came to me: 35.01
of Israel, hear the w. of the LORD. 36.01
hear the w. of the Lord GOD: Thus 36.04
The w. of the LORD came to me: 36.16
dry bones, hear the w. of the LORD. 37.04
The w. of the LORD came to me: 37.15
The w. of the LORD came to me: 38.01
"The w. from me is sure: if you do Dan 2.05
see that the w. from me is sure 2.08
decision by the w. of the holy 4.17
Immediately the w. was fulfilled 4.33
according to the w. of the LORD to 9.02
your supplications a w. went forth, 9.23
consider the w. and understand the 9.23
forth of the w. to restore and 9.25
of Persia a w. was revealed to 10.01
And the w. was true, and it was a 10.01
understood the w. and had understanding 10.01
he was speaking this w. to me, 10.11
The w. of the LORD that came to Hos 1.01
Hear the w. of the LORD, O people of 4.01
The w. of the LORD that came to Joe 1.01
that executes his w. is powerful. 2.11
Hear this w. that the LORD has Amo 3.01
"Hear this w., you cows of Bashan, 4.01
Hear this w. which I take up over 5.01
"Now therefore hear the w. of the LORD. 7.16
to seek the w. of the LORD, but they 8.12
Now the w. of the LORD came to Jon 1.01
Then the w. of the LORD came to 3.01
according to the w. of the LORD. 3.03
The w. of the LORD that came to Mic 1.01
and the w. of the LORD from Jerusalem 4.02
The w. of the LORD which came to Zep 1.01
The w. of the LORD is against you, O 2.05
the w. of the LORD came by Haggai Hag 1.01
Then the w. of the LORD came by 1.03
the w. of the LORD came by Haggai 2.01
the w. of the LORD came by Haggai 2.10
The w. of the LORD came a second 2.20
the w. of the LORD came to Zechariah Zec 1.01
the w. of the LORD came to Zechariah 1.07
"This is the w. of the LORD to 4.06
Moreover the w. of the LORD came to 4.08
And the w. of the LORD came to me: 6.09
the w. of the LORD came to Zechariah 7.01
Then the w. of the LORD of hosts 7.04
And the w. of the LORD came to 7.08
And the w. of the LORD of hosts 8.01
And the w. of the LORD of hosts 8.18
The w. of the LORD is against the 9.01
that it was the w. of the LORD. 11.11
The w. of the LORD concerning 12.01
The oracle of the w. of the LORD to Mal 1.01
you have found him bring me w., Mt 2.08
but by every w. that proceeds from 4.04
but only say the w., and my servant 8.08
he cast out the spirits with a w., 8.16
he sent w. by his disciples 11.02
And whoever says a w. against the 12.32
for every careless w. they utter; 12.36
one hears the w. of the kingdom 13.19
who hears the w. and immediately 13.20
arises on account of the w., 13.21
this is he who hears the w., 13.22
the delight in riches choke the w., 13.22
who hears the w. and understands 13.23
you have made void the w. of God. 15.06
But he did not answer her a w. 15.23
that every w. may be confirmed by 18.16
no one was able to answer him a w, 22.46
his wife sent w. to him, "Have 27.19
he was preaching the w. to them. Mk 2.02
the parables? The sower sows the w. 4.14
the path, where the w. is sown; 4.15
takes away the w. which is sown in 4.15

WORD (cont.)

ground, who, when they hear the w., Mk 4.16
arises on account of the w., 4.17
they are those who hear the w., 4.18
things, enter in and choke the w., 4.19
who hear the w. and accept it and 4.20
parables he spoke the w. to them, 4.33
not want to break his w. to her. 6.26
thus making void the w. of God 7.13
eyewitnesses and ministers of the w., Lk 1.02
it be to me according to your w." 1.38
in peace, according to thy w.; 2.29
the w. of God came to John the son 3.02
for his w. was with authority. 4.32
to one another, "What is this w.? 4.36
upon him to hear the w. of God, 5.01
But at your w. I will let down the 5.05
But say the w., and let my servant 7.07
is this: The seed is the w. of God. 8.11
takes away the w. from their 8.12
those who, when they hear the w., 8.13
hearing the w., hold it fast in an 8.15
who hear the w. of God and do it. 8.21
who hear the w. of God and keep it 11.28
who speaks a w. against the Son of 12.10
remembered the w. of the Lord, 22.61
in deed and w. before God and all 24.19
In the beginning was the W., Jn 1.01
and the W. was with God, and the 1.01
was with God, and the W. was God. 1.01
And the W. became flesh and dwelt 1.14
scripture and the w. which Jesus 2.22
more believed because of his w. 4.41
believed the w. that Jesus spoke 4.50
he who hears my w. and believes 5.24
do not have his w. abiding in you, 5.38
in him, "If you continue in my w., 8.31
because my w. finds no place in you 8.37
you cannot bear to hear my w. 8.43
say to you, if any one keeps my w., 8.51
you say, 'If any one keeps my w., 8.52
I do know him and I keep his w. 8.55
to whom the w. of God came and 10.35
it was that the w. spoken by the 12.38
the w. that I have spoken will be 12.48
a man loves me, he will keep my w., 14.23
and the w. which you hear is not 14.24
clean by the w. which I have 15.03
Remember the w. that I said to you, 15.20
if they kept my w., they will keep 15.20
to fulfil the w. that is written 15.25
to me, and they have kept thy w. 17.06
I have given them thy w.; 17.14
in the truth, thy w. is truth. 17.17
to believe in me through their w., 17.20
to fulfil the w. which he had 18.09
to fulfil the w. which Jesus had 18.32
who received his w. were baptized, Ac 2.41
of those who heard the w. believed; 4.04
to speak thy w. with all boldness, 4.29
and spoke the w. of God with 4.31
preaching the w. of God to serve 6.02
and to the ministry of the w. 6.04
And the w. of God increased; 6.07
went about preaching the w. 8.04
Samaria had received the w. of God, 8.14
and spoken the w. of the Lord, 8.25
You know the w. which he sent to 10.36
the w. which was proclaimed throughout 10.37
fell on all who heard the w. 10.44
also had received the w. of God. 11.01
And I remembered the w. of the Lord, 11.16
speaking the w. to none except Jews 11.19
But the w. of God grew and multiplied 12.24
proclaimed the w. of God in the 13.05
and sought to hear the w. of God. 13.07
if you have any w. of exhortation 13.15
together to hear the w. of God. 13.44
that the w. of God should be 13.46
glad and glorified the w. of God; 13.48
And the w. of the Lord spread 13.49
witness to the w. of his grace, 14.03
they had spoken the w. in Perga, 14.25
should hear the w. of the gospel 15.07
you the same things by w. of mouth. 15.27
and preaching the w. of the Lord, 15.35
we proclaimed the w. of the Lord, 15.36
Spirit to speak the w. in Asia. 16.06
And they spoke the w. of the Lord 16.32
received the w. with all eagerness, 17.11
that the w. of God was proclaimed 17.13
teaching the w. of God among them. 18.11
of Asia heard the w. of the Lord, 19.10
So the w. of the Lord grew and 19.20
to God and to the w. of his grace, 20.32
because of the w. he had spoken, 20.38
w. came to the tribune of the 21.31
Up to this w. they listened to him; 22.22
as though the w. of God had failed Rom 9.06
The w. is near you, on your lips and 10.08
the w. of faith which we preach); 10.08
from the Gentiles, by w. and deed, 15.18
For the w. of the cross is folly to 1Co 1.18
Did the w. of God originate with 14.36
our w. to you has not been Yes and 2Co 1.18
like so many, peddlers of God's w.; 2.17
cunning or to tamper with God's w., 4.02
whole law is fulfilled in one w., Gal 5.14
is taught the w. share all good 6.06
who have heard the w. of truth, Eph 1.13
the washing of water with the w., 5.26
the Spirit, which is the w. of God. 6.17
to speak the w. of God without Php 1.14
holding fast the w. of life, 2.16
before in the w. of the truth, Col 1.05
to make the w. of God fully known, 1.25
Let the w. of Christ dwell in you 3.16
in w. or deed, do everything in the 3.17
may open to us a door for the w., 4.03
gospel came to you not only in w., 1Th 1.05
received the w. in much affliction, 1.06
only has the w. of the Lord sounded 1.08
received the w. of God which you 2.13
it not as the w. of men but as 2.13
the w. of God, which is at work in 2.13
to you by the w. of the Lord, 4.15
excited, either by spirit or by w., 2Th 2.02
either by w. of mouth or by letter. 2.15
them in every good work and w. 2.17
that the w. of the Lord may speed 3.01
consecrated by the w. of God and 1Ti 4.05
But the w. of God is not fettered. 2Ti 2.09
rightly handling the w. of truth. 2.15
preach the w., be urgent in season 4.02
strength to proclaim the w. fully, 4.17
manifested in his w. through the Tit 1.03
hold firm to the sure w. as taught, 1.09
that the w. of God may not be 2.05
the universe by his w. of power. Heb 1.03
For the w. of God is living and 4.12
the first principles of God's w. 5.12
unskilled in the w. of righteousness, 5.13
goodness of the w. of God and the 6.05
but the w. of the oath, which came 7.28
world was created by the w. of God, 11.03
who spoke to you the w. of God; 13.07
bear with my w. of exhortation, for 13.22
us forth by the w. of truth that Jas 1.18
with meekness the implanted w., 1.21
But be doers of the w., and not hearers 1.22
a hearer of the w. and not a doer, 1.23
the living and abiding w. of God; 1Pe 1.23
but the w. of the Lord abides for ever." 1.25
That w. is the good news which 1.25
because they disobey the w., 2.08
though they do not obey the w., 3.01

WORD (cont.)
won without a w. by the behavior 1Pe 3.01
the prophetic w. made more sure. 2Pe 1.19
that by the w. of God heavens 3.05
But by the same w. the heavens and 3.07
hands, concerning the w. of life— 1Jn 1.01
a liar, and his w. is not in us. 1.10
but whoever keeps his w., 2.05
commandment is the w. which you 2.07
and the w. of God abides in you, and 2.14
us not love in w. or speech but in 3.18
witness to the w. of God and to Rev 1.02
account of the w. of God and the 1.09
have kept my w. and have not 3.08
have kept my w. of patient endurance, 3.10
slain for the w. of God and for 6.09
Lamb and by the w. of their 12.11
he is called is The W. of God. 19.13
to Jesus and for the w. of God, 20.04

WORDS
earth had one language and few w. Gen 11.01
he heard the w. of Rebekah his 24.30
When Abraham's servant heard their w., 24.52
When Esau heard the w. of his father, 27.34
But the w. of Esau her older son 27.42
Their w. pleased Hamor and Hamor's 34.18
more for his dreams and for his w. 37.08
heard the w. which his wife spoke 39.19
that your w. may be tested, whether 42.16
so your w. will be verified, and you 42.20
them, he spoke to them these w. 44.06
my lord speak such w. as these? 44.07
we told him the w. of my lord. 44.24
they told him all the w. of Joseph, 45.27
to him and put the w. in his mouth; Ex 4.15
Aaron all the w. of the LORD with 4.28
spoke all the w. which the LORD 4.30
it and pay no regard to lying w. 5.09
These are the w. which you shall 19.06
them all these w. which the LORD 19.07
reported the w. of the people to 19.08
Moses told the w. of the people to 19.09
And God spoke all these w., saying, 20.01
people all the w. of the LORD and 24.03
"All the w. which the LORD has 24.03
Moses wrote all the w. of the LORD. 24.04
in accordance with all these w. 24.08
the tables the w. that were on the 34.01
LORD said to Moses, "Write these w.; 34.27
with these w. I have made a 34.27
the tables the w. of the covenant, 34.28
told the people the w. of the LORD; Num 11.24
"Hear my w.: If there is a prophet 12.06
told these w. to all the people of 14.39
he finished speaking all these w., 16.31
of him who hears the w. of God, 24.04
of him who hears the w. of God, 24.16
These are the w. that Moses spoke Deu 1.01
"And the LORD heard your w., 1.34
with w. of peace, saying, 2.26
me, that I may let them hear my w., 4.10
you heard the sound of w., 4.12
you heard his w. out of the midst 4.36
"These w. the LORD spoke to all 5.22
"And the LORD heard your w., 5.28
I have heard the w. of this people, 5.28
And these w. which I command you 6.06
were all the w. which the LORD had 9.10
the tables the w. that were on the 10.02
lay up these w. of mine in your 11.18
heed all these w. which I command 12.28
listen to the w. of that prophet 13.03
keeping all the w. of this law and 17.19
and I will put my w. in his mouth, 18.18
give heed to my w. which he shall 18.19
upon them all the w. of this law, 27.03
stones all the w. of this law very 27.08
not confirm the w. of this law by 27.26
from any of the w. which I command 28.14
to do all the w. of this law which 28.58
These are the w. of the covenant 29.01
to do the w. of this covenant, that 29.09
he hears the w. of this sworn 29.19
we may do all the w. of this law. 29.29
to speak these w. to all Israel. 31.01
to do all the w. of this law, 31.12
writing the w. of this law in a 31.24
may speak these w. in their ears 31.28
Then Moses spoke the w. of this 31.30
the earth hear the w. of my mouth. 32.01
recited all the w. of this song in 32.44
all these w. to all Israel, 32.45
heart all the w. which I enjoin 32.46
to do all the w. of this law. 32.46
commandment and disobeys your w., Jos 1.18
"According to your w., so be it." 2.21
and hear the w. of the LORD your 3.09
he read all the w. of the law, 8.34
heard the w. that the Reubenites 22.30
wrote these w. in the book of the 24.26
heard all the w. of the LORD which 24.27
spoke these w. to all the people Ju 2.04
spoke all these w. on his behalf 9.03
city heard the w. of Gaal the son 9.30
spoke all his w. before the LORD 11.11
said, "Now when your w. come true, 13.12
when your w. come true, we may honor 13.17
him hard with her w. day after day, 16.16
let none of his w. fall to the 1Sa 3.19
told all the w. of the LORD to the 8.10
had heard all the w. of the people, 8.21
upon Saul when he heard these w., 11.06
hearken to the w. of the LORD. 15.01
commandment of the LORD and your w., 15.24
heard these w. of the Philistine, 17.11
and spoke the same w. as before. 17.23
When the w. which David spoke were 17.31
spoke those w. in the ears of 18.23
his servants told David these w., 18.26
And David took these w. to heart, 21.12
persuaded his men with these w., 24.07
listen to the w. of men who say, 24.09
finished speaking these w. to Saul, 24.16
and hear the w. of your handmaid. 25.24
king hear the w. of his servant. 26.19
fear because of the w. of Samuel; 28.20
and he hearkened to their w. 28.23
angry over the w. of Ishbosheth, 2Sa 3.08
In accordance with all these w., 7.17
and thy w. are true, and thou hast 7.28
So Joab put the w. in her mouth. 14.03
put all these w. in the mouth of 14.19
But the w. of the men of Judah were 19.43
than the w. of the men of Israel. 19.43
"Listen to the w. of your maidservant 20.17
to the LORD the w. of this song on 22.01
Now these are the last w. of David: 23.01
in after you and confirm your w. 1Ki 1.14
When Hiram heard the w. of Solomon, 5.07
Let these w. of mine, wherewith I 8.59
and speak good w. to them when you 12.07
the w. also which he had spoken to 13.11
And when Ahab heard those w., 21.27
the w. of the prophets with one 22.13
of Israel the w. that you speak in 2Ki 6.12
king heard the w. of the woman he 6.30
You think that mere w. are counsel 18.20
to speak these w. to your master 18.27
told him the w. of the Rabshakeh. 18.37
heard all the w. of the Rabshakeh, 19.04
will rebuke the w. which the LORD 19.04
because of the w. that you have 19.06
and hear the w. of Sennacherib, 19.16
king heard the w. of the book of 22.11
concerning the w. of this book 22.13

WORDS (cont.)

not obeyed the w. of this book, 2Ki 22.13
all the w. of the book which the 22.16
Regarding the w. which you have 22.18
hearing all the w. of the book of 23.02
to perform the w. of this covenant 23.03
establish the w. of the law which 23.24
In accordance with all these w., 1Ch 17.15
for by the last w. of David these 23.27
them, and speak good w. to them, 2Ch 10.07
When Asa heard these w., the prophecy 15.08
the w. of the prophets with one 18.12
by the w. of the LORD, to cleanse 29.15
LORD with the w. of David and of 29.30
from the w. of Hezekiah king of 32.08
and the w. of the seers who spoke 33.18
king heard the w. of the law he 34.19
concerning the w. of the book that 34.21
Regarding the w. which you have 34.26
you heard his w. against this 34.27
hearing all the w. of the book of 34.30
to perform the w. of the covenant 34.31
listen to the w. of Neco from the 35.22
despising his w., and scoffing at 36.16
trembled at the w. of the God of Ez 9.04
The w. of Nehemiah the son of Neh 1.01
When I heard these w. I sat down 1.04
and also of the w. which the king 2.18
I heard their outcry and these w. 5.06
to the king according to these w. 6.07
presence, and reported my w. to him. 6.19
when they heard the w. of the law. 8.09
understood the w. that were 8.12
order to study the w. of the law. 8.13
whether Mordecai's w. would avail; Est 3.04
As the w. left the mouth of the 7.08
in w. of peace and truth, 9.30
Your w. have upheld him who was Job 4.04
therefore my w. have been rash. 6.03
not denied the w. of the Holy One. 6.10
How forceful are honest w.! 6.25
Do you think that you can reprove w., 6.26
and the w. of your mouth be a great 8.02
and utter w. out of their understanding 8.10
him, choosing my w. with him? 9.14
"Should a multitude of w. go unanswered, 11.02
Does not the ear try w. as the 12.11
Listen carefully to my w., 13.17
or in w. with which he can do no 15.03
and let such w. go out of your 15.13
Shall windy w. have an end? 16.03
I could join w. together against 16.04
"How long will you hunt for w.? 18.02
me, and break me in pieces with w.? 19.02
"Oh that my w. were written! 19.23
"Listen carefully to my w., 21.02
and lay up his w. in your heart. 22.22
in my bosom the w. of his mouth. 23.12
With whose help have you uttered w., 26.04
The w. of Job are ended. 31.40
"Behold, I waited for your w., 32.11
or that answered his w., among you. 32.12
has not directed his w. against me, 32.14
For I am full of w., the spirit within 32.18
O Job, and listen to all my w. 33.01
My w. declare the uprightness of my 33.03
set your w. in order before me; 33.05
I have heard the sound of your w. 33.08
'He will answer none of my w.'? 33.13
"Hear my w., you wise men, and give 34.02
for the ear tests w. as the palate 34.03
his w. are without insight.' 34.35
and multiplies his w. against God." 34.37
he multiplies w. without knowledge." 35.16
For truly my w. are not false; 36.04
counsel by w. without knowledge? 38.02
Will he speak to you soft w.? 41.03
LORD had spoken these w. to Job, 42.07

How long will you love vain w., Ps 4.02
Give ear to my w., O LORD; 5.01
incline thy ear to me, hear my w. 17.06
There is no speech, nor are there w.; 19.03
and their w. to the end of the 19.04
Let the w. of my mouth and the 19.14
me, from the w. of my groaning? 22.01
land they conceive w. of deceit. 35.20
The w. of his mouth are mischief 36.03
to see me, he utters empty w., 41.06
at the w. of the taunters and 44.16
and you cast my w. behind you. 50.17
You love all w. that devour, O 52.04
give ear to the w. of my mouth. 54.02
his w. were softer than oil, yet 55.21
the w. of their lips, let them be 59.12
who aim bitter w. like arrows, 64.03
your ears to the w. of my mouth! 78.01
They pour out their arrogant w., 94.04
they rebelled against his w. 105.28
Then they believed his w.; 106.12
and he spoke w. that were rash. 106.33
had rebelled against the w. of God, 107.11
They beset me with w. of hate, 109.03
my portion; I promise to keep thy w. 119.57
How sweet are thy w. to my taste, 119.103
The unfolding of thy w. gives light; 119.130
me, because my foes forget thy w. 119.139
cry for help; I hope in thy w. 119.147
my heart stands in awe of thy w. 119.161
have heard the w. of thy mouth; 138.04
The LORD is faithful in all his w., 145.13
instruction, understand w. of insight, Pro 1.02
the w. of the wise and their 1.06
I will make my w. known to you. 1.23
you receive my w. and treasure up 2.01
adventuress with her smooth w., 2.16
me, "Let your heart hold fast my w.; 4.04
turn away from the w. of my mouth. 4.05
and accept my w., that the years of 4.10
My son, be attentive to my w.; 4.20
not depart from the w. of my mouth. 5.07
caught in the w. of your mouth; 6.02
keep my w. and treasure up my 7.01
the adventuress with her smooth w. 7.05
be attentive to the w. of my mouth. 7.24
All the w. of my mouth are righteous 8.08
When w. are many, transgression is 10.19
The w. of the wicked lie in wait 12.06
fruit of his w. a man is satisfied 12.14
one whose rash w. are like sword 12.18
you do not meet w. of knowledge. 14.07
the w. of the pure are pleasing to 15.26
Pleasant w. are like a honeycomb, 16.24
who restrains his w. has knowledge, 17.27
The w. of a man's mouth are deep 18.04
The w. of a whisperer are like 18.08
He pursues them with w., 19.07
to stray from the w. of knowledge. 19.27
overthrows the w. of the faithless 22.12
and hear the w. of the wise, and 22.17
eaten, and waste your pleasant w. 23.08
will despise the wisdom of your w. 23.09
and your ear to w. of knowledge. 23.12
so be sparing of complimentary w. 25.27
The w. of a whisperer are like 26.22
By mere w. a servant is not diciplined, 29.19
see a man who is hasty in his w.? 29.20
The w. of Agur son of Jakeh of 30.01
Do not add to his w., lest he rebuke 30.06
The w. of Lemuel, king of Massa, 31.01
The w. of the Preacher, the son of Ecc 1.01
therefore let your w. be few. 5.02
and a fool's voice with many w. 5.03
empty w. grow many: but do you fear 5.07
The more w., the more vanity, and 6.11
despised, and his w. are not heeded. 9.16
The w. of the wise heard in quiet 9.17

WORDS (cont.)

The w. of a wise man's mouth win him Ecc 10.12
beginning of the w. of his mouth is 10.13
A fool multiplies w., though no man 10.14
Preacher sought to find pleasing w., 12.10
and uprightly he wrote w. of truth. 12.10
low in the dust your w. shall come; Is 29.04
to you like the w. of a book that 29.11
deaf shall hear the w. of a book, 29.18
he does not call back his w., 31.02
to ruin the poor with lying w., 32.07
think that mere w. are strategy 36.05
to speak these w. to your master 36.12
"Hear the w. of the great king, the 36.13
told him the w. of the Rabshakeh. 36.22
God heard the w. of the Rabshakeh, 37.04
will rebuke the w. which the LORD 37.04
because of the w. that you have 37.06
and hear all the w. of Sennacherib, 37.17
proclaimed, none who heard your w. 41.26
And I have put my w. in your mouth, 51.16
uttering from the heart lying w. 59.13
and my w. which I have put in your 59.21
The w. of Jeremiah, the son of Jer 1.01
I have put my w. in your mouth. 1.09
proclaim these w. toward the north, 3.12
I am making my w. in your mouth a 5.14
they have not given heed to my w.; 6.19
Do not trust in these deceptive w.: 7.04
trust in deceptive w. to no avail. 7.08
shall speak all these w. to them, 7.27
"Hear the w. of this covenant, and 11.02
not heed the w. of this covenant 11.03
all these w. in the cities of 11.06
Hear the w. of this covenant and do 11.06
them all the w. of this covenant, 11.08
forefathers, who refused to hear my w.; 11.10
though they speak fair w. to you. 12.06
people, who refuse to hear my w., 13.10
Thy w. were found, and I ate them, 15.16
and thy w. became to me a joy and 15.16
you tell this people all these w., 16.10
there I will let you hear my w." 18.02
and let us not heed any of his w." 18.18
there the w. that I tell you. 19.02
their neck, refusing to hear my w." 19.15
But if you will not heed these w., 22.05
LORD and because of his holy w. 23.09
listen to the w. of the prophets 23.16
have proclaimed my w. to my people, 23.22
who steal my w. from one another. 23.30
you pervert the w. of the living 23.36
'Because you have said these w., 23.38
Because you have not obeyed my w., 25.08
land all the w. which I have 25.13
prophesy against them all these w., 25.30
LORD all the w. that I command you 26.02
and to heed the w. of my servants 26.05
speaking these w. in the house of 26.07
city all the w. you have heard. 26.12
to speak all these w. in your ears. 26.15
this land in w. like those of 26.20
heard his w., the king sought to 26.21
listen to the w. of the prophets 27.14
listen to the w. of your prophets 27.16
LORD make the w. which you have 28.06
These are the w. of the letter 29.01
because they did not heed my w., 29.19
my name lying w. which I did not 29.23
a book all the w. that I have 30.02
These are the w. which the LORD 30.04
shall use these w. in the land of 31.23
spoke all these w. to Zedekiah 34.06
instruction and listen to my w.? 35.13
on it all the w. that I have 36.02
Jeremiah all the w. of the LORD 36.04
shall read the w. of the LORD from 36.06
the scroll the w. of the LORD in 36.08
Baruch read the w. of Jeremiah 36.10
heard all the w. of the LORD from 36.11
them all the w. that he had heard, 36.13
When they heard all the w., 36.16
report all these w. to the king. 36.16
us, how did you write all these w.? 36.17
"He dictated all these w. to me, 36.18
reported all the w. to the king. 36.20
servants who heard all these w., 36.24
scroll with the w. which Baruch 36.27
all the former w. that were in the 36.28
Jeremiah all the w. of the scroll 36.32
many similar w. were added to them 36.32
listened to the w. of the LORD 37.02
heard the w. that Jeremiah was 38.01
by speaking such w. to them. 38.04
know of these w. and you shall not 38.24
will fulfil my w. against this 39.16
all these w. of the LORD their God, 43.01
know that my w. will surely stand 44.29
he wrote these w. in a book at the 45.01
all these w. that are written 51.60
see that you are read all these w., 51.61
thus far are the w. of Jeremiah. 51.64
of them, nor be afraid of their w., Eze 2.06
be not afraid of their w., 2.06
And you shall speak my w. to them, 2.07
written on it w. of lamentation 2.10
and speak with my w. to them. 3.04
whose w. you cannot understand. 3.06
all my w. that I shall speak to you 3.10
None of my w. will be delayed any 12.28
and multiplied your w. against me; 35.13
and corrupt w. before me till the Dan 2.09
While the w. were still in the 4.31
because of the w. of the king and 5.10
Then the king, when he heard these w., 6.14
of the great w. which the horn was 7.11
He shall speak w. against the Most 7.25
He has confirmed his w., which he spoke 9.12
sound of his w. like the noise of 10.06
Then I heard the sound of his w.; 10.09
when I heard the sound of his w. 10.09
heed to the w. that I speak to you, 10.11
your w. have been heard, and I have 10.12
and I have come because of your w. 10.12
spoken to me according to these w., 10.15
shut up the w., and seal the book, 12.04
for the w. are shut up and sealed 12.09
slain them by the w. of my mouth, Hos 6.05
They utter mere w.; with empty oaths 10.04
Take with you w. and return to the 14.02
The w. of Amos, who was among the Amo 1.01
is not able to bear all his w. 7.10
but of hearing the w. of the LORD. 8.11
Do not my w. do good to him who Mic 2.07
and the w. of Haggai the prophet, as Hag 1.12
But my w. and my statutes, which I Zec 1.06
and comforting w. to the angel who 1.13
not these the w. which the LORD 7.07
the law and the w. which the LORD 7.12
hearing these w. from the mouth of 8.09
have wearied the LORD with your w. Mal 2.17
"Your w. have been stout against me, 3.13
will be heard for their many w. Mt 6.07
who hears these w. of mine and 7.24
who hears these w. of mine and 7.26
receive you or listen to your w., 10.14
for by your w. you will be justified, 12.37
and by your w. you will be condemned 12.37
but my w. will not pass away. 24.35
the third time, saying the same w. 26.44
of me and of my w. in this adulterous Mk 8.38
disciples were amazed at his w. 10.24
but my w. will not pass away. 13.31
and prayed, saying the same w. 14.39
because you did not believe my w., Lk 1.20
the book of the w. of Isaiah the 3.04

WORDS (cont.)
at the gracious w. which proceeded Lk 4.22
me and hears my w. and does them, 6.47
is ashamed of me and of my w., 9.26
"Let these w. sink into your ears; 9.44
all the people hung upon his w. 19.48
but my w. will not pass away. 21.33
spoke many other w. against him, 22.65
And they remembered his w., 24.08
but these w. seemed to them an idle 24.11
"These are my w. which I spoke to 24.44
God has sent utters the w. of God, Jn 3.34
because of your w. that we believe, 4.42
writings, how will you believe my w.? 5.47
the w. that I have spoken to you 6.63
You have the w. of eternal life; 6.68
When they heard these w., some of the 7.40
These w. he spoke in the treasury, 8.20
He who is of God hears the w. of God; 8.47
among the Jews because of these w. 10.19
The w. that I say to you I do not 14.10
not love me does not keep my w.; 14.24
and my w. abide in you, ask whatever 15.07
When Jesus had spoken these w., 17.01
given them the w. which thou 17.08
When Jesus had spoken these w., 18.01
When Pilate heard these w., 19.08
When Pilate heard these w., 19.13
to you, and give ear to my w. Ac 2.14
hear these w.: Jesus of Nazareth, a 2.22
with many other w. and exhorted 2.40
when Ananias heard these w., 5.05
the people all the w. of this Life." 5.20
the chief priests heard these w., 5.24
blasphemous w. against Moses and 6.11
ceases to speak w. against this 6.13
he was mighty in his w. and deeds. 7.22
With these w. they scarcely restrained 14.18
And with this the w. of the prophets 15.15
from us have troubled you with w., 15.24
with many w. and strengthened them 15.32
the jailer reported the w. to Paul, 16.36
reported these w. to the magistrates, 16.38
questions about w. and names and 18.15
remembering the w. of the Lord 20.35
And when he had said these w., * 28.29
thou mayest be justified in thy w., Rom 3.04
But the w., "it was reckoned to him," 4.23
for us with sighs too deep for w. 8.26
and their w. to the ends of the 10.18
and flattering w. they deceive the 16.18
of God in lofty w. or wisdom. 1Co 2.01
were not in plausible w. of wisdom, 2.04
impart this in w. not taught by 2.13
rather speak five w. with my mind, 14.19
than ten thousand w. in a tongue. 14.19
Let no one deceive you with empty w., Eph 5.06
never used either w. of flattery, 1Th 2.05
Therefore comfort one another with these w. 4.18
nourished on the w. of the faith 1Ti 4.06
with the sound w. of our Lord 6.03
controversy and for disputes about w., 6.04
of the sound w. which you have 2Ti 1.13
Lord to avoid disputing about w., 2.14
in the w. already quoted, "Today, Heb 4.07
a voice whose w. made the hearers 12.19
will exploit you with false w.; 2Pe 2.03
prating against me with evil w. 3Jn 1.10
reads aloud the w. of the prophecy, Rev 1.03
'The w. of him who holds the seven 2.01
'The w. of the first and the last, 2.08
'The w. of him who has the sharp 2.12
'The w. of the Son of God, who has 2.18
'The w. of him who has the seven 3.01
'The w. of the holy one, the true 3.07
'The w. of the Amen, the faithful 3.14
uttering haughty and blasphemous w., 13.05
until the w. of God shall be 17.17
to me, "These are true w. of God." 19.09
for these w. are trustworthy and 21.05
"These w. are trustworthy and true. 22.06
who keeps the w. of the prophecy 22.07
those who keep the w. of this book. 22.09
not seal up the w. of the prophecy 22.10
who hears the w. of the prophecy 22.18
away from the w. of the book of 22.19

WORE
long robe with sleeves that he w.; Gen 37.23
persons who w. the linen ephod. 1Sa 22.18
the long-sleeved robe which she w.; 2Sa 13.19
"He w. a garment of haircloth, with 2Ki 1.08
of the singers; and David w. a linen ephod. 1Ch 15.27
I w. sackcloth, I afflicted myself Ps 35.13
Now John w. a garment of camel's Mt 3.04
the riders w. breastplates the Rev 9.17

WORK
finished his w. which he had done, Gen 2.02
from all his w. which he had done. 2.02
from all his w. which he had done 2.03
relief from our w. and from the 5.29
house to do his w. and none of the 39.11
in all kinds of w. in the field; Ex 1.14
in all their w. they made them 1.14
take the people away from their w.? 5.04
Let heavier w. be laid upon the men 5.09
but your w. will not be lessened in 5.11
urgent, saying, "Complete your w., 5.13
Go now, and w.; for no straw 5.18
no w. shall be done on those days; 12.16
which he will w. for you today; 14.13
saw the great w. which the LORD 14.31
shall labor, and do all your w.; 20.09
in it you shall not do any w., 20.10
"Six days you shall do your w., 23.12
of hammered w. shall you make them, 25.18
shall be made of hammered w.; 25.31
piece of hammered w. of pure gold. 25.36
in skilled w. shall it be made, with 26.31
a robe, a coat of checker w., 28.04
breastpiece of judgment, in skilled w.; 28.15
like the w. of the ephod you shall 28.15
coat in checker w. of linen, 28.39
to w. in gold, silver, and bronze, 31.04
wood, for w. in every craft. 31.05
whoever does any w. on it, 31.14
Six days shall w. be done, but the 31.15
does any w. on the sabbath day 31.15
And the tables were the w. of God, 32.16
are shall see the w. of the LORD; 34.10
"Six days you shall w., but on the 34.21
Six days shall w. be done, but on 35.02
does any w. on it shall be put to 35.02
of any use in the w., brought it. 35.24
anything for the w. which the LORD 35.29
to w. in gold and silver and bronze, 35.32
for w. in every skilled craft. 35.33
every sort of w. done by a craftsman 35.35
sanctuary shall w. in accordance 36.01
him up to come to do the w.; 36.02
for doing the w. on the sanctuary. 36.03
for doing the w. which the LORD 36.05
sufficient to do all the w., and more. 36.07
lampstand were made of hammered w.; 37.17
piece of hammered w. of pure gold. 37.22
for the w. of the Levites under the 38.21
All the gold that was used for the w., 38.24
into threads to w. into the blue 39.03
in skilled w., like the work of the 39.08
like the w. of the ephod, of gold, 39.08
Thus all the w. of the tabernacle 39.32
of Israel had done all the w. 39.42
And Moses saw all the w., and behold, 39.43
of the court. So Moses finished the w. 40.33
yourselves, and shall do no w., Lev 16.29

WORK (cont.)

Six days shall w. be done; but in the seventh Lev 23.03
you shall do no w.; it is a sabbath 23.03
you shall do no laborious w. 23.07
you shall do no laborious w. 23.08
you shall do no laborious w.: 23.21
You shall do no laborious w.; 23.25
And you shall do no w. on this same 23.28
does any w. on this same day, that 23.30
You shall do no w.: it is a statute 23.31
you shall do no laborious w. 23.35
you shall do no laborious w. 23.36
to do the w. in the tent of meeting Num 4.03
to do the w. in the tent of meeting 4.23
and their w. is to be under the 4.28
to do the w. of the tent of meeting 4.30
for w. in the tent of meeting; 4.35
the service for w. in the tent of 4.39
for w. in the tent of meeting— 4.43
enter to do the w. of service and 4.47
service and the w. of bearing 4.47
the lampstand, hammered w. of gold; 8.04
to its flowers, it was hammered w.; 8.04
to perform the w. in the service 8.24
from the w. of the service and 8.25
of hammered w. you shall make them; 10.02
you shall do no laborious w., 28.18
you shall do no laborious w. 28.25
you shall do no laborious w. 28.26
you shall do no laborious w. 29.01
afflict yourselves; you shall do no w., 29.07
you shall do no laborious w., 29.12
you shall do no laborious w., 29.35
all w. of goats' hair, and every 31.20
you in all the w. of your hands; Deu 2.07
the w. of men's hands, that neither 4.28
shall labor, and do all your w.; 5.13
in it you shall not do any w., 5.14
all the great w. of the LORD which 11.07
you in all the w. of your hands 14.29
you in all your w. and in all that 15.10
you shall do no w. with the firstling 15.19
your God; you shall do no w. on it. 16.08
and in all the w. of your hands, 16.15
you in all the w. of your hands. 24.19
to bless all the w. of your hands; 28.12
prosperous in all the w. of your hand, 30.09
anger through the w. of your hands. 31.29
"The Rock, his w. is perfect; 32.04
and accept the w. of his hands; 33.11
known all the w. which the LORD Jos 24.31
all the great w. which the LORD Ju 2.07
the LORD or the w. which he had 2.10
pieces of dyed w. embroidered for 5.30
coming from his w. in the field at 19.16
your asses, and put them to his w. 1Sa 8.16
be that the LORD will w. for us; 14.06
officers who were over the w., 1Ki 5.16
the people who carried on the w. 5.16
evenly applied upon the carved w. 6.35
skill, for making any w. in bronze. 7.14
King Solomon, and did all his w. 7.14
nets of checker w. with wreaths of 7.17
of chain w. for the capitals upon 7.17
Thus the w. of the pillars was 7.22
there were wreaths of beveled w. 7.29
finished all the w. that he did for 7.40
Thus all the w. that King Solomon 7.51
officers who were over Solomon's w.: 9.23
the people who carried on the w. 9.23
to anger with the w. of his hands, 16.07
but the w. of men's hands, wood and 2Ki 19.18
with all the w. of their hands, 22.17
there with the king for his w. 1Ch 4.23
for all the w. of the most holy 6.49
men for the w. of the service of 9.13
in charge of the w. of the service, 9.19
charge of the w. in the house of 23.04
were to do the w. for the service 23.24
and any w. for the service of the 23.28
who did the w. and of their duties 25.01
for all the w. of the LORD and for 26.30
who did the w. of the field for 27.26
and all the w. of the service in 28.13
all the w. to be done according to 28.19
until all the w. for the service of 28.20
you in all the w. will be every 28.21
inexperienced, and the w. is great; 29.01
and for all the w. to be done by 29.05
the officers over the king's w. 29.06
me a man skilled to w. in gold, 2Ch 2.07
He is trained to w. in gold, 2.14
as overseers to make the people w. 2.18
finished the w. that he did for 4.11
Thus all the w. that Solomon did 5.01
Solomon made no slaves for his w.; 8.09
accomplished all the w. of Solomon 8.16
for your w. shall be rewarded." 15.07
Ramah, and let his w. cease. 16.05
charge of the w. of the house of 24.12
who were engaged in the w. labored, 24.13
until the w. was finished—for the 29.34
They set to w. and removed the 30.14
And every w. that he undertook in 31.21
He set to w. resolutely and built 32.05
which are the w. of men's hands. 32.19
And the men did the w. faithfully. 34.12
all who did w. in every kind of 34.13
treasury of the w. sixty-one thousand Ez 2.69
oversight of the w. of the house of 3.08
Then the w. on the house of God 4.24
this w. goes on diligently and 5.08
let the w. on this house of God 6.07
them in the w. of the house of God, 6.22
Nor is this a w. for one day or for 10.13
the rest that were to do the w. Neh 2.16
strengthened their hands for he good w. 2.18
necks to the w. of their Lord. 3.05
For the people had a mind to w. 4.06
we are not able to w. on the wall." 4.10
them and kill them and stop the w. 4.11
returned to the wall, each to his w. 4.15
labored on the w. and with the 4.17
"The w. is great and widely spread, 4.19
So we labored at the w., and half 4.21
I also held to the w. on this wall, 5.16
were gathered there for the w. 5.16
doing a great w. and I cannot come 6.03
Why should the w. stop while I 6.03
"Their hands will drop from the w., 6.09
that this w. had been accomplished 6.16
of fathers' houses gave to the w. 7.70
treasury of the w. twenty thousand 7.71
and for all the w. of the house of 10.33
who did the w. of the house, eight hundred 11.12
the outside w. of the house of God 11.16
over the w. of the house of God. 11.22
who did the w., had fled each to 13.10
and Levites, each in his w.; 13.30
hast blessed the w. of his hands, Job 1.10
to despise the w. of thy hands and 10.03
and again w. wonders against me; 10.16
long for the w. of thy hands. 14.15
according to the w. of a man he 34.11
they are all the w. of his hands? 34.19
to them their w. and their transgressions, 36.09
"Remember to extol his w., 36.24
man, that all men may know his w. 37.07
the w. of thy fingers, the moon and Ps 8.03
snared in the w. of their own 9.16
Requite them according to their w., 28.04
according to the w. of their hands; 28.04
or the w. of his hands, he will 28.05
and all his w. is done in faithfulness 33.04
Have those who w. evil no understanding, 53.04
deliver me from those who w. evil, 59.02

WORK (cont.)

requite a man according to his w.	Ps 62.12
I will meditate on all thy w.,	77.12
Dost thou w. wonders for the dead?	88.10
Let thy w. be manifest to thy	90.16
thou the w. of our hands upon us,	90.17
he w. of our hands establish thou	90.17
LORD, hast made me glad by thy w.;	92.04
proof, though they had seen my w.	95.09
I hate the w. of those who fall	101.03
heavens are the w. of thy hands.	102.25
satisfied with the fruit of thy w.	104.13
forth to his w. and to his labor	104.23
Full of honor and majesty is his w.,	111.03
and gold, the w. of men's hands.	115.04
and gold, the w. of men's hands.	135.15
Do not forsake the w. of thy hands.	138.08
company with men who w. iniquity;	141.04
me at the beginning of his w.,	Pro 8.22
and the w. of a man's hand comes	12.14
Commit your w. to the LORD, and your	16.03
the weights in the bag are his w.	16.11
is slack in his w. is a brother to	18.09
Do you see a man skilful in his w.?	22.29
requite man according to his w.?	24.12
Prepare your w. outside, get everything	24.27
of pain, and his w. is a vexation;	Ecc 2.23
he gives the w. of gathering and	2.26
for every matter, and for every w.	3.17
that a man should enjoy his w.,	3.22
all skill in w. come from a man's	4.04
and destroy the w. of your hands?	5.06
Consider the w. of God; who can make	7.13
then I saw all the w. of God,	8.17
find out the w. that is done under	8.17
for there is no w. or thought or	9.10
do not know the w. of God who	11.05
His body is ivory w., encrusted with	Sol 5.14
like jewels, the w. of a master hand.	7.01
and his w. a spark, and both of them	Is 1.31
bow down to the w. of their hands,	2.08
LORD, or see the w. of his hands.	5.12
him speed his w. that we may see	5.19
finished all his w. on Mount Zion	10.12
the w. of their hands, and they will	17.08
and all who w. for hire will be	19.10
and Assyria the w. of my hands,	19.25
and to w. his w.—alien is his w.!	28.21
the w. of my hands, in his midst,	29.23
helpers of those who w. iniquity.	31.02
but the w. of men's hands, wood and	37.19
are nothing, and your w. is nought;	41.24
from my hand; I w. and who can hinder it?"	43.13
making'? or 'Your w. has no handles'?	45.09
me concerning the w. of my hands?	45.11
the w. of my hands, that I might be	60.21
we are all the w. of thy hand.	64.08
long enjoy the w. of their hands.	65.22
They are the w. of the craftsman	Jer 10.09
they are all the w. of skilled men.	10.09
They are worthless, a w. of delusion;	10.15
houses on the sabbath or do any w.,	17.22
day holy and do no w. on it,	17.24
to anger with the w. of your hands.	25.06
anger with the w. of your hands to	25.07
deeds and the w. of their hands.	25.14
I begin to w. evil at the city	25.29
for your w. shall be rewarded, says	31.16
to anger by the w. of their hands,	32.30
he who does the w. of the LORD	48.10
of hosts has a w. to do in the	50.25
in Zion the w. of the LORD our God	51.10
They are worthless, a w. of delusion;	51.18
according to the w. of their hands.	Lam 3.64
earthen pots, the w. of a potter's hands!	4.02
embroidered w., fine linen, coral,	Eze 27.16
clothes of blue and embroidered w.,	27.24
And he shall w. his will, and return	Dan 11.28
all of them the w. of craftsmen.	Hos 13.02
'Our God,' to the w. of our hands.	14.03
wickedness and w. evil upon their	Mic 2.01
no more to the w. of your hands;	5.13
I am doing a w. in your days that	Hab 1.05
and thy w., O LORD, do I fear.	3.02
for her cedar w. will be laid bare.	Zep 2.14
w., for I am with you, says the LORD	Hag 2.04
so with every w. of their hands;	2.14
why these powers are at w. in him.	Mt 14.02
go and w. in the vineyard today.'	21.28
And he could do no mighty w. there,	Mk 6.05
why these powers are at w. in him.	6.14
does a mighty w. in my name will	9.39
each with his w., and commands the	Mk 13.34
days on which w. ought to be done;	Lk 13.14
sent me, and to accomplish his w.	Jn 4.34
we do, to be doing the w. of God?	6.28
"This is the w. of God, that you	6.29
and believe you? What w. do you perform	6.30
We must w. the works of him who	9.04
night comes, when no one can w.	9.04
you for no good w. but for blasphemy	10.33
accomplished the w. which thou	17.04
clothes, for he was stripped for w.,	21.07
Saul for the w. to which I have	Ac 13.02
of God for the w. which they had	14.26
had not gone with them to the w.	15.38
who does not w. but trusts him who	Rom 4.05
were a w. in our members to bear	7.05
of food, destroy the w. of God.	14.20
to be proud of my w. for God.	15.17
any room for w. in these regions,	15.23
each man's w. will become manifest;	1Co 3.13
what sort of w. each one has done.	3.13
If the w. which any man has built	3.14
If any man's w. is burned up, he will	3.15
Are all teachers? Do all w. miracles?	12.29
abounding in the w. of the Lord,	15.58
for effective w. has opened to me,	16.09
for he is doing the w. of the Lord,	16.10
we w. with you for your joy, for you	2Co 1.24
So death is at w. in us, but life in	4.12
complete among you this gracious w.	8.06
you excel in this gracious w. also.	8.07
this gracious w. which we are	8.19
in abundance for every good w.	9.08
boasting of w. already done in	10.16
mission they w. on the same terms	11.12
But let each one test his own w.,	Gal 6.04
that is now at w. in the sons of	Eph 2.02
by the power at w. within us is	3.20
for the w. of ministry, for building	4.12
doing honest w. with his hands, so	4.28
began a good w. in you will bring	Php 1.06
w. out your own salvation with fear	2.12
for God is at w. in you, both to	2.13
to will and to w. for his good	2.13
nearly died for the w. of Christ,	2.30
in every good w. and increasing in	Col 1.10
w. heartily, as serving the Lord and	3.23
and Father your w. of faith and	1Th 1.03
which is at w. in you believers.	2.13
and to w. with your hands, as we	4.11
highly in love because of their w.	5.13
resolve and w. of faith by his	2Th 1.11
of lawlessness is already at w.;	2.07
them in every good w. and word.	2.17
command: If any one will not w.,	3.10
mere busybodies, not doing any w.	3.11
to do their w. in quietness and to	3.12
the house, ready for any good w.	2Ti 2.21
complete, equipped for every good w.	3.17
do the w. of an evangelist, fulfil	4.05
to be ready for any honest w.,	Tit 3.01
heavens are the w. of thy hands;	Heb 1.10
overlook your w. and the love	6.10
of man does not w. the righteousness	Jas 1.20

WORK (cont.)
greets him shares his wicked w. 2Jn 1.11
is allowed to w. in the presence Rev 13.14

WORKED
skilfully w. shall you make them. Ex 26.01
of fine twined linen, skilfully w. 28.06
and the finely w. garments, the holy 31.10
stuff, with cherubim skilfully w. 36.08
cherubim skilfully w. he made it. 36.35
the finely w. garments for ministering 39.41
has never been w. and which has Deu 21.03
And where have you w.? Blessed be the Ru 2.19
mother-in-law with whom she had w., 2.19
name with whom I w. today is Boaz. 2.19
builders who w. upon the house of 2Ki 12.11
fine linen, and w. cherubim on it. 2Ch 3.14
of my servants w. on construction, Neh 4.16
and w. with an axe by the hands of Jer 10.03
because they w. for me, says the Eze 29.20
they came and w. on the house of Hag 1.14
'These last w. only one hour, and Mt 20.12
while the Lord w. with them * Mk 16.20
and they w., for by trade they were Ac 18.03
Greet Mary, who has w. hard among you. Rom 16.06
Persis, who has w. hard in the Lord. 16.12
I w. harder than any of them, though 1Co 15.10
(for he who w. through Peter for Gal 2.08
the circumcised w. through me also 2.08
that he has w. hard for you and Col 4.13
we w. night and day, that we might 1Th 2.09
toil and labor we w. night and day, 2Th 3.08
may not lose what you have w. for, 2Jn 1.08
presence had w. the signs by which Rev 19.20

WORKER
was a man of Tyre, a w. in bronze; 1Ki 7.14
a sharp razor, you w. of treachery. Ps 52.02
What gain has the w. from his toil? Ecc 3.09
our fellow w. in Christ, and my Rom 16.09
Timothy, my fellow w., greets you; 16.21
and to every fellow w. and laborer. 1Co 16.16
and fellow w. in your service; 2Co 8.23
and fellow w. and fellow soldier, Php 2.25
To Philemon our beloved fellow w. Phm 1.01

WORKER'S
A w. appetite works for him; his mouth Pro 16.26

WORKERS
house of linen w. at Bethashbea; 1Ch 4.21
the skilled w. who are with me in 2Ch 2.07
and also w. in iron and bronze to 24.12
and disaster the w. of iniquity? Job 31.03
Depart from me, all you w. of evil; Ps 6.08
with those who are w. of evil, 28.03
The w. in combed flaz will be in Is 19.09
pleasure, and oppress all your w. 58.03
be food for the w. of the city. Eze 48.18
And the w. of the city, from all the 48.19
from me, all you w. of iniquity! Lk 13.27
my fellow w. in Christ Jesus, Rom 16.03
Greet those w. in the Lord, Tryphaena 16.12
then w. of miracles, then healers, 1Co 12.28
and the rest of my fellow w., Php 4.03
among my fellow w. for the kingdom Col 4.11
Demas, and Luke, my fellow w. Phm 1.24
we may be fellow w. in the truth. 3Jn 1.08

WORKEST
Thou art the God who w. wonders, who has Ps 77.14

WORKING
'Prove yourselves by w. a miracle,' Ex 7.09
angel who has w. destruction among 2Sa 24.16
craftsmen without number, skilled in w. 1Ch 22.15
who were w. in the house of the 2Ch 34.10
w. salvation in the midst of the Ps 74.12
and there he was w. at his wheel. Jer 18.03
shall be shut on the six w. days; Eze 46.01
"My Father is w. still, and I am w." Jn 5.17
it was sin, w. death in me through Rom 7.13
and we labor, w. with our own hands. 1Co 4.12
to refrain from w. for a living? 9.06
and there are varieties of w., 12.06
to another the w. of miracles, to 12.10
W. together with him, then, we 2Co 6.01
avail, but faith w. through love. Col 5.06
according to the w. of his great Eph 1.19
given me by the w. of his power. 3.07
when each part is w. properly, 4.16
him through faith in the w. of God, Col 2.12
w. in you that which is pleasing in Heb 13.21

WORKMAN
by any sort of w. or skilled Ex 35.35
I was beside him, like a master w.; Pro 8.30
a w. casts it, and a goldsmith Is 40.19
A w. made it; it is not God. Hos 8.06
For the w. trusts in his own Hab 2.18
a w. who has no need to be ashamed, 2Ti 2.15

WORKMANSHIP
be of the same w. and materials, Ex 28.08
was of the same materials and w., 39.05
And this was the w. of the lampstand, Num 8.04
back of the hall, was of like w. 1Ki 7.08
Are not you my w. in the Lord? 1Co 9.01
For we are his w., created in Eph 2.10

WORKMEN
men among the w. made the tabernacle Ex 36.08
hands of the w. who had the 2Ki 12.11
given to the w. who were repairing 12.14
the money to pay out to the w., 12.15
the hand of the w. who have the 22.05
give it to the w. who are at the 22.05
the hand of the w. who have the 22.09
You have an abundance of w.: 1Ch 22.15
it to the w. who had the oversight 2Ch 34.10
and the w. who were working in 34.10
hand of the overseers and the w. 34.17
oversight of the w. in the house of Ez 3.09
with the w. of like occupation, and Ac 19.25
For we are fellow w. for God; 1Co 3.09
deceitful w., disguising themselves 2Co 11.13

WORKMEN'S
her right hand to the w. mallet; Ju 5.26

WORKS
them, nor do according to their w., Ex 23.24
has sent me to do all these w., Num 16.28
who can do such w. and mighty acts Deu 3.24
to the LORD, to him who w. wonders. Ju 13.19
him, tell of all his wonderful w.! 1Ch 16.09
Remember the wonderful w. that he 16.12
his marvelous w. among all the 16.24
Hezekiah prospered in all his w. 2Ch 32.30
with all the w. of their hands, 34.25
did not turn from their wicked w. Neh 9.35
knowing their w., he overturns them Job 34.25
consider the wondrous w. of God. 37.14
the wondrous w. of him who is 37.16
"He is the first of the w. of God; 40.19
dominion over the w. of thy hands; Ps 8.06
With regard to the w. of men, 17.04
do not regard the w. of the LORD, 28.05
behold the w. of the LORD, how he 46.08
that I may tell of all thy w. 73.28
God, and not forget the w. of God, 78.07
nor are there any w. like thine. 86.08
at the w. of thy hands I sing for 92.04
How great are thy w., O LORD! 92.05
his marvelous w. among all the 96.03

WORKS (cont.)

The LORD w. vindication and justice Ps 103.06
all his w., in all places of his 103.22
O LORD, how manifold are thy w.! 104.24
may the LORD rejoice in his w., 104.31
him, tell of all his wonderful w.! 105.02
Remember the wonderful w. that he 105.05
did not consider thy wonderful w.; 106.07
But they soon forgot his w.; they did not 106.13
wondrous w. in the land of Ham, and 106.22
his wonderful w. to the sons of 107.08
his wonderful w. to the sons of 107.15
his wonderful w. to the sons of 107.21
LORD, his wondrous w. in the deep. 107.24
his wonderful w. to the sons of 107.31
Great are the w. of the LORD, 111.02
his wonderful w. to be remembered; 111.04
his people the power of his w., 111.06
The w. of his hands are faithful 111.07
I will meditate on thy wondrous w. 119.27
Wonderful are thy w.! Thou knowest 139.14
shall laud thy w. to another, 145.04
majesty, and of thy wondrous w., 145.05
All thy w. shall give thanks to 145.10
standing who w. for himself than Pro 12.09
A worker's appetite w. for him; 16.26
and a flattering mouth w. ruin. 26.28
and w. with willing hands. 31.13
and let her w. praise her in the 31.31
I made great w.; I built houses Ecc 2.04
hast wrought for us all our w. Is 26.12
their w. are nothing; their molten 41.29
fashions it and w. it over the 44.12
Their w. are w. of iniquity, and 59.06
who w. for those who wait for him. 64.04
him that joyfully w. righteousness, 64.05
"For I know their w. and their 66.18
worshiped the w. of their own Jer 1.16
to anger with the w. of your hands, 44.08
cut down, and your w. wiped out. Eze 6.06
for all his w. are right and his Dan 4.37
he w. signs and wonders in heaven 6.27
in all the w. which he has done, 9.14
that I remember all their evil w. Hos 7.02
and all the w. of the house of Ahab Mic 6.16
see your good w. and give glory to Mt 5.16
and do many mighty w. in your name? 7.22
of his mighty w. had been done, 11.20
if the mighty w. done in you had 11.21
if the mighty w. done in you had 11.23
this wisdom and these mighty w.? 13.54
he did not do many mighty w. there, 13.58
What mighty w. are wrought by his Mk 6.02
if the mighty w. done in you had Lk 10.13
all the mighty w. that they had 19.37
and greater w. than these will he Jn 5.20
for the w. which the Father has 5.36
these very w. which I am doing, bear 5.36
may see the w. you are doing. 7.03
For no man w. in secret if he seeks 7.04
testify of it that its w. are evil. 7.07
but that the w. of God might be 9.03
We must work the w. of him who sent 9.04
The w. that I do in my Father's name, 10.25
you many good w. from the Father; 10.32
I am not doing the w. of my Father, 10.37
believe the w., that you may know 10.38
who dwells in me does his w. 14.10
for the sake of the w. themselves. 14.11
me will also do the w. that I do; 14.12
and greater w. than these will he 14.12
among them the w. which no one 15.24
own tongues the mighty w. of God. Ac 2.11
God with mighty w. and wonders and 2.22
rejoiced in the w. of their hands. 7.41
full of good w. and acts of 9.36
to every man according to his w.: Rom 2.06
in his sight by w. of the law 3.20
On the principle of w.? No, but on the 3.27
by faith apart from w. of law. 3.28
For if Abraham was justified by w., 4.02
Now to one who w., his wages are 4.04
righteousness apart from w.: 4.06
everything God w. for good with 8.28
not because of w. but because of 9.11
but as if it were based on w. 9.32
it is no longer on the basis of w.; 11.06
cast off the w. of darkness and 13.12
signs and wonders and mighty w. 2Co 12.12
justified by w. of the law but Gal 2.16
and not by w. of the law, because by 2.16
because by w. of the law shall no 2.16
the Spirit by w. of the law, 3.02
to you and w. miracles among you 3.05
among you do so by w. of the law, 3.05
For all who rely on w. of the law 3.10
Now the w. of the flesh are plain: 5.19
not because of w., lest any man Eph 2.09
in Christ Jesus for good w., 2.10
in the unfruitful w. of darkness, 5.11
virtue of our w. but in virtue of 2Ti 1.09
test and saw my w. for forty years Heb 3.09
although his w. were finished from 4.03
on the seventh day from all his w. 4.04
from dead w. and of faith toward 6.01
from dead w. to serve the living 9.14
one another to love and good w., 10.24
says he has faith but has not w.? Jas 2.14
itself, if it has no w., is dead. 2.17
say, "You have faith and I have w. 2.18
me your faith apart from your w., 2.18
and I by my w. will show you my 2.18
that faith apart from w. is barren? 2.20
Abraham our father justified by w., 2.21
faith was active along with his w., 2.22
and faith was completed by w., 2.22
is justified by w. and not by 2.24
justified by w. when she received 2.25
so faith apart from w. is dead. 2.26
him show his w. in the meekness of 3.13
earth and the w. that are upon it 2Pe 3.10
was to destroy the w. of the devil. 1Jn 3.08
" 'I know your w., your toil and Rev 2.02
and do the w. you did at first. 2.05
you hate the w. of the Nicolaitans, 2.06
" 'I know your w., your love and 2.19
your latter w. exceed the first. 2.19
to each of you as your w. deserve. 2.23
and who keeps my w. until the end, 2.26
" 'I know your w.; you have the 3.01
not found your w. perfect in the 3.02
" 'I know your w. Behold, I have 3.08
" 'I know your w.: you are neither 3.15
repent of the w. of their hands 9.20
It w. great signs, even making fire 13.13

WORLD

and on them he has set the w. 1Sa 2.08
foundations of the w. were laid bare, 2Sa 22.16
yea, the w. stands firm, never to 1Ch 16.30
darkness, and driven out of the w. Job 18.18
and who laid on him the whole w.? 34.13
on the face of the habitable w. 37.12
bind their faces in the w. below. 40.13
and he judges the w. with righteousness, Ps 9.08
whose portion in life is of the w. 17.14
foundations of the w. were laid bare, 18.15
their words to the end of the w. 19.04
the w. and those who dwell therein; 24.01
inhabitants of the w. stand in awe 33.08
ear, all inhabitants of the w., 49.01
for the w. and all that is in it is 50.12
thy lightining lighted up the w.; 77.18
the w. and all that is in it, thou 89.11
hadst formed the earth and the w., 90.02

WORLD (cont.)

Yea, the w. is established; Ps 93.01
Yea, the w. is established, it shall 96.10
will judge the w. with righteousness, 96.13
His lightnings lighten the w.; 97.04
the w. and those who dwell in it! 98.07
will judge the w. with righteousness, 98.09
or the first of the dust of the w. Pro 8.26
his inhabited w. and delighting in 8.31
I will punish the w. for its evil, Is 13.11
who made the w. like a desert and 14.17
the face of the w. with cities. 14.21
All you inhabitants of the w., 18.03
kingdoms of the w. upon the face 23.17
the w. languishes and withers; 24.04
inhabitants of the w. learn righteousness 26.09
inhabitants of the w. have not 26.18
and fill the whole w. with fruit. 27.06
the w., and all that comes from it. 34.01
among the inhabitants of the w. 38.11
established the w. by his wisdom, Jer 10.12
kingdoms of the w. which are on 25.26
established the w. by his wisdom, 51.15
any of the inhabitants of the w., Lam 4.12
make you to dwell in the nether w., Eze 26.20
to the nether w. among mortal men, 31.14
will be comforted in the nether w. 31.16
the trees of Eden to the nether w.; 31.18
to the nether w., to those who have 32.18
uncircumcised into the nether w., 32.24
the w. and all that dwell therein. Nah 1.05
kingdoms of the w. and the glory Mt 4.08
"You are the light of the w. 5.14
cares of the w. and the delight in 13.22
since the foundation of the w. 13.35
the field is the w., and the good 13.38
gains the whole w. and forfeits 16.26
"Woe to the w. for temptations to 18.07
in the new w., when the Son of man 19.28
preached throughout the whole w., 24.14
the beginning of the w. until now, 24.21
you from the foundation of the w.; 25.34
gospel is preached in the whole w., 26.13
but the cares of the w., and the delight Mk 4.19
gain the whole w. and forfeit his 8.36
gospel is preached in the whole w., 14.09
"Go into all the w. and preach the gospel * 16.15
that all the w. should be enrolled Lk 2.01
kingdoms of the w. in a moment of 4.05
gains the whole w. and loses or 9.25
shed from the foundation of the w., 11.50
nations of the w. seek these 12.30
sons of this w. are wiser in their 16.08
of what is coming on the w.; 21.26
every man was coming into the w. Jn 1.09
in the w., and the w. was made through him, 1.10
him, yet the w. knew him not. 1.10
who takes away the sin of the w.! 1.29
so loved the w. that he gave his 3.16
For God sent the Son into the w., 3.17
not to condemn the w., but that the w. 3.17
the light has come into the w., 3.19
is indeed the Savior of the w. 4.42
prophet who is to come into the w.! 6.14
heaven, and gives life to the w. 6.33
for the life of the w. is my flesh. 6.51
things, show yourself to the w. 7.04
The w. cannot hate you, but it hates 7.07
saying, "I am the light of the w.; 8.12
you are of this w., I am not of this w., 8.23
declare to the w. what I have 8.26
As long as I am in the w., 9.05
world, I am the light of the w. 9.05
Never since the w. began has it 9.32
"For judgment I came into this w., 9.39
consecrated and sent into the w., 10.36
he sees the light of this w. 11.09
God, he who is coming into the w. 11.27
look, the w. has gone after him." 12.19
life in this w. will keep it for 12.25
Now is the judgment of this w., 12.31
the ruler of this w. be cast out; 12.31
I have come as light into the w., 12.46
to judge the w. but to save the w. 12.47
out of this w. to the Father, 13.01
loved his own who were in the w., 13.01
whom the w. cannot receive, because 14.17
and the w. will see me no more, but 14.19
yourself to us, and not to the w.? 14.22
not as the w. gives do I give to 14.27
for the ruler of this w. is coming. 14.30
so that the w. may know that I love 14.31
"If the w. hates you, know that it 15.18
If you were of the w., 15.19
the w. would love its own; 15.19
But because you are not of the w., 15.19
but I chose you out of the w., 15.19
therefore the w. hates you. 15.19
convince the w. of sin and of 16.08
the ruler of this w. is judged. 16.11
lament, but the w. will rejoice; 16.20
that a child is born into the w. 16.21
Father and have come into the w.; 16.28
am leaving the w. and going to the 16.28
In the w. you have tribulation; 16.33
good cheer, I have overcome the w. 16.33
with thee before the w. was made. 17.05
whom thou gavest me out of the w.; 17.06
praying for the w. but for those 17.09
And now I am no more in the w., 17.11
the w., but they are in the w., 17.11
and these things I speak in the w., 17.13
and the w. has hated them because 17.14
because they are not of the w., 17.14
world, even as I am not of the w. 17.14
shouldst take them out of the w., 17.15
They are not of the w., 17.16
even as I am not of the w. 17.16
As thou didst send me into the w., 17.18
so I have sent them into the w. 17.18
so that the w. may believe that 17.21
so that the w. may know that thou 17.23
me before the foundation of the w. 17.24
the w. has not known thee, but I 17.25
"I have spoken openly to the w.; 18.20
"My kingship is not of this w.; 18.36
if my kingship were of this w., 18.36
but my kingship is not from the w. 18.36
for this I have come into the w., 18.37
that the w. itself could not 21.25
be a great famine over all the w.; Ac 11.28
have turned the w. upside down 17.06
who made the w. and everything in 17.24
judge the w. in righteousness 17.31
whom all Asia and the w. worship. 19.27
all the Jews throughout the w., 24.05
faith is proclaimed in all the w. Rom 1.08
creation of the w. his invisible 1.20
then how could God judge the w.? 3.06
and the whole w. may be held 3.19
that they should inherit the w., 4.13
came into the w. through one man 5.12
was in the w. before the law was 5.13
their words to the ends of the w. 10.18
trespass means riches for the w., 11.12
means the reconciliation of the w., 11.15
conformed to this w. but be transformed 12.02
made foolish the wisdom of the w.? 1Co 1.20
the w. did not know God through 1.21
foolish in the w. to shame the 1.27
is weak in the w. to shame the 1.27
what is low and despised in the w., 1.28
received not the spirit of the w., 2.12
wisdom of this w. is folly with 3.19

WORLD (cont.)

Cephas or the w. or life or death 1Co 3.22
have become a spectacle to the w., 4.09
are now, as the refuse of the w., 4.13
all meaning the immoral of this w., 5.10
you would need to go out of the w. 5.10
that the saints will judge the w.? 6.02
And if the w. is to be judged by 6.02
deal with the w. as though they 7.31
form of this w. is passing away. 7.31
not be condemned along with the w. 11.32
many different languages in the w., 14.10
that we have behaved in the w., 2Co 1.12
the god of this w. has blinded the 4.04
reconciling the w. to himself, 5.19
we live in the w. we are not 10.03
by which the w. has been crucified Gal 6.14
crucified to me, and I to the w. 6.14
before the foundation of the w., Eph 1.04
following the course of this w., 2.02
no hope and without God in the w. 2.12
against the w. rulers of this 6.12
you shine as lights in the w., Php 2.15
in the whole w. it is bearing Col 1.06
as if you still belonged to the w.? 2.20
came into the w. to save sinners. 1Ti 1.15
the nations, believed on in the w., 3.16
for we brought nothing into the w., 6.07
cannot take anything out of the w.; 6.07
As for the rich in this w., charge them 6.17
in love with this present w., 2Ti 4.10
and godly lives in this w., Tit 2.12
whom also he created the w. Heb 1.02
brings the first-born into the w., 1.06
that God subjected the w. to come, 2.05
from the foundation of the w. 4.03
since the foundation of the w. 9.26
Consequently, when Christ came into the w., 10.05
that the w. was created by the 11.03
condemned the w. and became an 11.07
of whom the w. was not worthy— 11.38
keep oneself unstained from the w. Jas 1.27
are poor in the w. to be rich in 2.05
an unrighteous w. among our 3.06
with the w. is enmity with God? 4.04
a friend of the w. makes himself 4.04
foundation of the w. but was made 1Pe 1.20
your brotherhood throughout the w. 5.09
that is in the w. because of 2Pe 1.04
if he did not spare the ancient w., 2.05
a flood upon the w. of the ungodly; 2.05
defilements of the w. through the 2.20
through which the w. that then 3.06
also for the sins of the whole w. 1Jn 2.02
Do not love the w. of the things in 2.15
the world or the things in the w. 2.15
If any one loves the w., 2.15
For all that is in the w., 2.16
not of the Father but is of the w. 2.16
And the w. passes away, and the lust 2.17
reason why the w. does not know us 3.01
brethren, that the w. hates you. 3.13
prophets have gone out into the w. 4.01
and now it is in the w. already. 4.03
greater than he who is in the w. 4.04
They are of the w., 4.05
therefore what they say is of the w., 4.05
and the w. listens to them. 4.05
God sent his only Son into the w., 4.09
his Son as the Savior of the w. 4.14
as he is so are we in this w. 4.17
is born of God overcomes the w.; 5.04
that overcomes the w., our faith. 5.04
overcomes the w. but he who 5.05
and the whole w. is in the power of 5.19
deceivers have gone out into the w., 2Jn 1.07
which is coming on the whole w., Rev 3.10
kingdom of the w. has become the 11.15
the deceiver of the whole w.— 12.09
foundation of the w. in the book of 13.08
to the kings of the whole w., 16.14
life from the foundation of the w., 17.08

WORLDLY

wise according to w. standards, 1Co 1.26
who marry will have w. troubles, 7.28
man is anxious about w. affairs, 7.33
woman is anxious about w. affairs, 7.34
Do I make my plans like a w. man, 2Co 1.17
but w. grief produces death. 7.10
suspect us of acting in w. fashion. 10.02
we are not carrying on a w. war, 10.03
warfare are not w. but have divine 10.04
since many boast of w. things, 11.18
renounce irreligion and w. passions, Tit 2.12
w. people, devoid of the Spirit. Jud 1.19

WORLD'S

anyone has the w. goods and sees his brother 1Jn 3.17

WORM

for the w. shall eat them. Deu28.39
'and to the w., 'My mother,' or 'My Job 17.14
and the son of man, who is a w.! 25.06
But I am a w., and no man; Ps 22.06
Fear not, you w. Jacob, you men of Is 41.14
and the w. will eat them like wool; 51.08
for their w. shall not die, their 66.24
God appointed a w. which attacked Jon 4.07
where their w. does not die and *Mk 9.44
where their w. does not die and * 9.46
where their w. does not die, and the 9.48

WORMS

and it bred w. and became foul; Ex 16.20
foul, and there were no w. in it. 16.24
My flesh is clothed with w. and dirt; Job 7.05
in the dust, and the w. cover them. 21.26
and w. are your covering. Is 14.11
and he was eaten by w. and died. Ac 12.23

WORMWOOD

but in the end she is bitter as w., Pro 5.04
I will feed this people with w., Jer 9.15
"Behold, I will feed them with w., 23.15
bitterness, he has sated me with w. Lam 3.15
my bitterness, the w. and the gall! 3.19
O you who turn justice to w., Amo 5.07
fruit of righteousness into w.— 6.12
The name of the star is W. Rev 8.11
A third of the waters became w., 8.11

WORN

clothes have not w. out upon you, Deu 29.05
sandals have not w. off your feet; 29.05
of ours are w. out from the very Jos 9.13
purple garments w. by the kings of Ju 8.26
be brought, which the king has w., Est 6.08
Surely now God has w. me out; Job 16.07
a long time he had w. no clothes, Lk 82.7

WORN-OUT

and took w. sacks upon their asses, Jos 9.04
wineskins, w. and torn and mended, 9.04
with w., patched sandals on their 9.05
on their feet, and w. clothes; 9.05
from there old rags and w. clothes, Jer 38.11

WORSE

we will deal w. with you than with Gen 19.09
and behaved w. than their fathers, Ju 2.19
he turned he put them to the w. 1Sa 14.47
this will be w. for you than all 2Sa 19.07
to no avail; my distress grew w., Ps 39.02
They did w. than their fathers. Jer 7.26

WORSE (cont.)
you have done w. than your fathers, Jer 16.12
which was w. than that of her Eze 23.11
the garment, and a w. tear is made. Mt 9.16
that man becomes w. than the first. 12.45
fraud will be w. than the first. 27.64
the old, and a w. tear is made. Mk 2.21
was no better but rather grew w. 5.26
that man becomes w. than the first." Lk 11.26
Galileans were w. sinners than all 13.02
that they were w. offenders than 13.04
more, that nothing w. befall you." Jn 5.14
We are no w. off if we do not eat, 1Co 8.08
not for the better but for the w. 11.17
faith and is w. than an unbeliever 1Ti 5.08
impostors will go on from bad to w., 2Ti 3.13
How much w. punishment do you think Heb 10.29
has become w. for them than the 2Pe 2.20

WORSHIP
and the lad will go yonder and w., Gen 22.05
elders of Israel, and w. afar off. Ex 24.01
the people would rise up and w., 33.10
(for you shall w. no other god, for 34.14
drawn away and w. them and serve Deu 4.19
gods and serve them and w. them, 8.19
and serve other gods and w. them, 11.16
and w. before the LORD your God; 26.10
drawn away to w. other gods and 30.17
our children cease to w. the LORD. Jos 22.25
his city to w. and to sacrifice to 1Sa 1.03
with me, that I may w. the LORD." 15.25
that I may w. the LORD your God." 15.30
then I will offer w. to the LORD.'" 2Sa 15.08
and serve other gods and w. them, 1Ki 9.06
the house of Rimmon to w. there, 2Ki 5.18
"You shall w. before this altar in 18.22
before him! W. the LORD in holy array; 1Ch 16.29
and serve other gods and w. them, 2Ch 7.19
"Before one altar you shall w., 32.12
for we w. your God as you do, and Ez 4.02
peoples of the land to w. the LORD, 6.21
I will w. toward thy holy temple in Ps 5.07
of the nations shall w. before him. 22.27
of his name; w. the LORD in holy array. 29.02
O come, let us w. and bow down, let 95.06
W. the LORD in holy array; tremble 96.09
w. at his footstool! Holy is he! 99.05
and w. at his holy mountain; 99.09
and kingdoms, to w. the LORD. 102.22
let us w. at his footstool! 132.07
they made for themselves to w., Is 2.20
in that day and w. with sacrifice 19.21
Egyptians will w. with the Assyrians 19.23
will come and w. the LORD on the 27.13
"You shall w. before this altar"? 36.07
into a god; then they fall down and w.! 46.06
flesh shall come to w. before me, 66.23
enter these gates to w. the LORD. Jer 7.02
gods to serve them and w. them, 13.10
other gods to serve and w. them, 25.06
which come to w. in the house of 26.02
countries, and w. wood and stone. Eze 20.32
and he shall w. at the threshold of 46.02
the land shall w. at the entrance 46.03
north gate to w. shall go out by 46.09
fall down and w. the golden image Dan 3.05
fall down and w. shall immediately 3.06
fall down and w. the golden image; 3.10
fall down and w. shall be cast 3.11
your gods or w. the golden image 3.12
my gods or w. the golden image 3.14
fall down and w. the image which I 3.15
but if you do not w., you shall 3.15
your gods or w. the golden image 3.18
than serve and w. any god except 3.28
up year after year to w. the King, Zec 14.16
go up to Jerusalem to w. the King, 14.17
the East, and have come to w. him. Mt 2.02
that I too may come and w. him. 2.08
if you will fall down and w. me. 4.09
'You shall w. the Lord your God and 4.10
in vain do they w. me, teaching as 15.09
in vain do they w. me, teaching as Mk 7.07
will w. me, it shall all be yours. Lk 4.07
'You shall w. the Lord your God, and 4.08
is the place where men ought to w. Jn 4.20
Jerusalem will you w. the Father. 4.21
You w. what you do not know; 4.22
we w. what we know, for salvation is 4.22
worshipers will w. the Father in 4.23
such the Father seeks to w. him. 4.23
and those who w. him must worship 4.24
him must w. in spirit and truth. 4.24
who went up to w. at the feast 12.20
come out and w. me in this place. Ac 7.07
them over to w. the host of heaven, 7.42
the figures which you made to w.; 7.43
had come to Jerusalem to w. 8.27
observed the objects of your w., 17.23
what therefore you w. as unknown, 17.23
persuading men to w. God contrary 18.13
she whom all Asia and the world w. 19.27
since I went up to w. at Jerusalem; 24.11
I w. the God of our fathers, believing 24.14
as they earnestly w. night and day. 26.07
to whom I belong and whom I w., 27.23
of the law, the w., and the promises; Rom 9.04
to God, which is your spiritual w. 12.01
Therefore, my beloved, shun the w. of idols. 1Co 10.14
he will w. God and declare that God 14.25
who w. God in spirit, and glory in Php 3.03
on self-abasement and w. of angels, Col 2.18
so-called god or object of w., 2Th 2.04
says, "Let all God's angels w. him." Heb 1.06
regulations for w. and an earthly 9.01
and all the vessels used in w. 9.21
bowing in w. over the head of his 11.21
let us offer to God acceptable w., 12.28
the throne and w. him who lives Rev 4.10
the altar and those who w. there, 11.01
and all who dwell on earth will w. it, 13.08
its inhabitants w. the first beast, 13.12
who will not w. the image of the 13.15
and w. him who made heaven and 14.07
All nations shall come and w. thee, 15.04
Then I fell down at his feet to w. him, 19.10
W. God. For the testimony of 19.10
it, and his servants shall w. him; 22.03
I fell down to w. at the feet of 22.08
of this book, W. God. 22.09

WORSHIPED
bowed his head and w. the LORD, Gen 24.26
Then I bowed my head and w. the LORD, 24.48
they bowed their heads and w. Ex 4.31
people bowed their heads and w. 12.27
and have w. it and sacrificed to it, 32.08
his head toward the earth, and w. 34.08
and served other gods and w. them, Deu 17.03
and served other gods and w. them, 29.26
and w., and said to him, "What does Jos 5.14
and its interpretation, he w.; Ju 7.15
the morning and w. before the LORD 1Sa 1.19
And they w. the LORD there. 1.28
after Saul; and Saul w. the LORD. 15.31
into the house of the LORD, and w.; 2Sa 12.20
where God was w., behold, Hushai the 15.32
and w. them and served them; 1Ki 9.09
and w. Ashtoreth the goddess of the 11.33
went and served Baal, and w. him. 16.31
He served Baal and w. him, 22.53
and w. all the host of heaven, and 2Ki 17.16
and w. all the host of heaven, and 21.03

WORSHIPED (cont.)
his father served, and w. them; 2Ki 21.21
and w. the LORD, and did obeisance 1Ch 29.20
and w. and gave thanks to the LORD, 2Ch 7.03
and w. them and served them; 7.22
and w. them, making offerings to 25.14
The whole assembly w., and the singers 29.28
with him bowed themselves and w. 29.29
gladness, and they bowed down and w. 29.30
and w. all the host of heaven, and 33.03
their heads and w. the LORD with Neh 8.06
confession and w. the LORD their 9.03
and fell upon the ground, and w. Job 1.20
in Horeb and w. a molten image. Ps 106.19
and w. the works of their own hands Jer 1.16
and which they have sought and w.; 8.02
gods and have served and w. them, 16.11
and w. other gods and served them. 22.09
fell down and w. the golden image Dan 3.07
and they fell down and w. him. Mt 2.11
And those in the boat w. him, 14.33
took hold of his feet and w. him. 28.09
And when they saw him they w. him; 28.17
Jesus from afar, he ran and w. him Mk 5.06
Our fathers w. on this mountain; Jn 4.20
I believe"; and he w. him. 9.38
fell down at his feet and w. him. Ac 10.25
for a lie and w. and served the Rom 1.25
and the elders fell down and w. Rev 5.14
before the throne and w. God, 7.11
fell on their faces and w. God, 11.16
Men w. the dragon, for he had given 13.04
and they w. the beast, saying, "Who 13.04
mark of the beast and w. its image. 16.02
fell down and w. God who is seated 19.04
beast and those who w. its image. 19.20
and who had not w. the beast or 20.04

WORSHIPER
if any one is a w. of God and does Jn 9.31
purple goods, who was a w. of God. Ac 16.14
named Titius Justus, a w. of God; 18.07
perfect the conscience of the w., Heb 9.09

WORSHIPERS
all his w. and all his priests; 2Ki 10.19
in order to destroy the w. of Baal. 10.19
and all the w. of Baal came, so that 10.21
vestments for all the w. of Baal. 10.22
and he said to the w. of Baal, 10.23
among you, but only the w. of Baal." 10.23
All w. of images are put to shame, Ps 97.07
when the true w. will worship the Jn 4.23
If the w. had once been cleansed, Heb 10.02
these w. of the beast and its image, Rev 14.11

WORSHIPING
And as he was w. in the house of 2Ki 19.37
down before the LORD, w. the LORD. 2Ch 20.18
And as he was w. in the house of Is 37.38
w. the sun toward the east. Eze 8.16
w. with fasting and prayer night Lk 2.37
While they were w. the Lord and Ac 13.02
nor give up w. demons and idols of Rev 9.20

WORSHIPS
and the host of heaven w. thee. Neh 9.06
All the earth w. thee; they sing praises Ps 66.04
also he makes a god and w. it, Is 44.15
and falls down to it and w. it; 44.17
"If any one w. the beast and its Rev 14.09

WORST
about me; they imagine the w. for me. Ps 41.07
I will bring the w. of the nations Eze 7.24

WORTH
a piece of land w. four hundred Gen 23.15
know that you are a woman of w. Ru 3.11
But you are w. ten thousand of us; 2Sa 18.03
silver vessels w. a hundred talents, Ez 8.26
twenty bowls of gold w. a thousand 8.27
mind of the wicked is of little w. Pro 10.20
w. a thousand shekels of silver, Is 7.23
w. their weight in fine gold, how Lam 4.02
two hundred denarii w. of bread, Mk 6.37
time are not w. comparing with the Rom 8.18
But Timothy's w. you know, how as a Php 2.22
the surpassing w. of knowing 3.08

WORTHLESS
water, and we loathe this w. food." Num 21.05
Abimelech hired w. and reckless Ju 9.04
and w. fellows collected round 11.03
Now the sons of Eli were w. men; 1Sa 2.12
But some w. fellows said, "How can 10.27
despised and w. they utterly 15.09
you man of blood, you w. fellow! 2Sa 16.07
happened to be there a w. fellow, 20.01
and certain w. scoundrels gathered 2Ch 13.07
For he knows w. men; when he sees Job 11.11
w. physicians are you all. 13.04
'W. one,' and to nobles, 'Wicked man'; 34.18
who make their boast in w. idols; Ps 97.07
A w. person, a wicked man, goes about Pro 6.12
he who follows w. pursuits has no 12.11
A w. man plots evil, and his speech 16.27
A w. witness mocks at justice, and 19.28
he who follows w. pursuits will 28.19
For Egypt's help is w. and empty, Is 30.07
after worthlessness, and became w.? Jer 2.05
They are w., a work of delusion; 10.15
w. divination, and the deceit of 14.14
is precious, and not what is w., 15.19
w. things in which there is no 16.19
They are w., a work of delusion; 51.18
the implements of a w. shepherd. Zec 11.15
Woe to my w. shepherd, who deserts 11.17
And cast the w. servant into the Mt 25.30
it is w. and near to being cursed; Heb 6.08

WORTHLESSNESS
far from me, and went after w., Jer 2.05

WORTHY
I am not w. of the least of all the Gen 32.10
who is w. to be praised, and I am 2Sa 22.04
for you are a w. man and bring good 1Ki 1.42
said, "If he prove to be a w. man, 1.52
who is w. to be praised, and I am Ps 18.03
whose sandals I am not w. to carry; Mt 3.11
I am not w. to have you come under 8.08
enter, find out who is w. in it, 10.11
And if the house is w., let your peace 10.13
but if it is not w., let your peace 10.13
mother more than me is not w. of me; 10.37
daughter more than me is not w. 10.37
and follow me is not w. of me. 10.38
but those invited were not w. 22.08
I am not w. to stoop down and Mk 1.07
whose sandals I am not w. to untie; Lk 3.16
"He is w. to have you do this for 7.04
for I am not w. to have you come 7.06
I am no longer w. to be called your 15.19
I am no longer w. to be called your 15.21
are accounted w. to attain to that 20.35
whose sandal I am not w. to untie. Jn 1.27
were counted w. to suffer dishonor Ac 5.41
of whose feet I am not w. to untie. 13.25
perform deeds w. of their repentance 26.20
to lead a life w. of the calling Eph 4.01
of life be w. of the gospel of Php 1.27
if there is anything w. of praise, 4.08
to lead a life w. of the Lord, fully Col 1.10
to lead a life w. of God, who calls 1Th 2.12
you may be made w. of the kingdom 2Th 1.05
God may make you w. of his call, 1.11

WORTHY (cont.)

is sure and w. of full acceptance, 1Ti 1.15
is sure and w. of full acceptance. 4.09
be considered w. of double honor, 5.17
their masters as w. of all honor, 6.01
been counted w. of as much more Heb 3.03
of whom the world was not w.— 11.38
with me in white, for they are w. Rev 3.04
"W. art thou, our Lord and God, to 4.11
"Who is w. to open the scroll and 5.02
one was found w. to open the 5.04
"W. art thou to take the scroll and 5.09
'W. is the Lamb who was slain, to 5.12

WOUND

burn for burn, w. for w., stripe for stripe. Ex 21.25
and w. him mortally, though the man Deu 19.06
I w. and I heal; and there is none 32.39
blood of the w. flowed into the 1Ki 22.35
my w. is incurable, though I am Job 34.06
As with a deadly w. in my body, Ps 42.10
Blows that w. cleanse away evil; Pro 20.30
cold day, and like vinegar on a w. 25.20
They have healed the w. of my Jer 6.14
They have healed the w. of my 8.11
For the w. of the daughter of my 8.21
My w. is grievous. But I said, 10.19
people is smitten with a great w., 14.17
my w. incurable, refusing to be 15.18
incurable, and your w. is grievous. 30.12
cause, no medicine for your w., 30.13
in the hands of those who w. you? Eze 28.09
and Judah his w., then Ephraim went Hos 5.13
able to cure you or heal your w. 5.13
For her w. is incurable; and it has Mic 1.09
your hurt, your w. is grievous. Nah 3.19
and by means of them they w. Rev 9.19
heads seemed to have a mortal w., 13.03
but its mortal w. was healed. 13.03
beast, whose mortal w. was healed. 13.12

WOUNDED

and many fell w., up to the entrance Ju 9.40
so that the w. Philistines fell on 1Sa 17.52
and he was badly w. by the archers. 31.03
and w. Shobach the commander of 2Sa 10.18
me out of the battle, for I am w." 1Ki 22.34
Ramothgilead, where the Syrians w. Joram. 2Ki 8.28
and he was w. by the archers. 1Ch 10.03
me out of the battle, for I am w." 2Ch 18.33
And the Syrians w. Joram, 22.05
from him, leaving him severely w., 24.25
"Take me away, for I am badly w." 35.23
the soul of the w. cries for help; Job 24.12
arrow at them; they will be w. suddenly. Ps 64.07
smitten, and him whom thou hast w., 69.26
they w. me, they took away my mantle, Sol 5.07
But he was w. for our transgressions, Is 53.05
of my people is my heart w., I mourn, Jer 8.21
there remained of them only w. men, 37.10
Chaldeans, and w. in her streets. 51.04
all her land the w. shall groan. 51.52
they faint like w. men in the Lam 2.12
when the w. groan, when slaughter is Eze 26.15
before him like a man mortally w. 30.24
and they w. him in the head, and Mk 12.04
this one they w. and cast out. Lk 20.12
out of that house naked and w. Ac 19.16
beast which was w. by the sword Rev 13.14

WOUNDING

say: I have slain a man for w. me, Gen 4.23
man struck him, smiting and w. him. 1Ki 20.37
brethren and w. their conscience 1Co 8.12

WOUNDS

and w. him mortally so that he dies, Deu 19.11
Jezreel of the w. which the 2Ki 8.29
Jezreel of the w. which the 9.15
Jezreel of the w. which he had 2Ch 22.06
For he w., but he binds up; Job 5.18
and multiplies my w. without cause; 9.17
My w. grow foul and fester because Ps 38.05
brokenhearted, and binds up their w. 147.03
W. and dishonor will he get, and his Pro 6.33
Who has w. without cause? Who has 23.29
Like an archer who w. everybody is 26.10
Faithful are the w. of a friend; 27.06
bruises and sores and bleeding w.; Is 1.06
and heals the w. inflicted by his 30.26
sickness and w. are ever before me. Jer 6.07
and your w. I will heal, says the 30.17
and hiss because of all her w. 50.13
'What are these w. on your back?' Zec 13.06
'The w. I received in the house of 13.06
and went to him and bound up his w., Lk 10.34
of the night, and washed their w., Ac 16.33
By his w. you have been healed. 1Pe 2.24

WOVE

of his head and w. them into the Ju 16.14
where the women w. hangings for 2Ki 23.07

WOVEN

And the skilfully w. band upon it, Ex 28.08
the skilfully w. band of the ephod 28.27
the skilfully w. band of the ephod, 28.28
with a w. binding around the 28.32
the skilfully w. band of the ephod 29.05
And the skilfully w. band upon it, 39.05
the skilfully w. band of the ephod 39.20
the skilfully w. band of the ephod, 39.21
robe of the ephod w. all of blue; 39.22
w. of fine linen, for Aaron and his 39.27
the skilfully w. band of the ephod, Lev 8.07
without seam, w. from top to bottom; Jn 19.23

WRANGLE

He will not w. or cry aloud, nor Mt 12.19

WRANGLING

and w. among men who are depraved 1Ti 6.05

WRAP

too narrow to w. oneself in it. Is 28.20
"W. your mantle around you and Ac 12.08

WRAPPED

And Mount Sinai was w. in smoke, Ex 19.18
w. in darkness, cloud, and gloom. Deu 4.11
it is here w. in a cloth behind the 1Sa 21.09
and he is w. in a robe." And Saul knew 28.14
he w. his face in his mantle and 1Ki 19.13
may they be w. in their own shame Ps 109.29
Who has w. up the waters in a garment? Pro 30.04
and w. himself in fury as a mantle. Is 59.17
"Thou hast w. thyself with anger Lam 3.43
thou hast w. thyself with a cloud 3.44
the prince is w. in despair, and the Eze 7.27
A wind has w. them in its wings, and Hos 4.19
about me, weeds were w. about my head Jon 2.05
and w. it in a clean linen shroud, Mt 27.59
w. him in the linen shroud, and laid Mk 15.46
first-born son and w. him in Lk 2.07
find a babe w. in swaddling cloths 2.12
it down and w. it in a linen 23.53
and his face w. with a cloth. Jn 11.44
men rose and w. him up and carried Ac 5.06
w. in a cloud, with a rainbow over Rev 10.01

WRAPPING

w. herself up, and sat at the Gen 38.14

WRAPS

a garment which he w. round him, Ps 109.19

WRATH

and their w., for it is cruel! Gen 49.07
and my w. will burn, and I will kill Ex 22.24
that my w. may burn hot against 32.10
why does thy w. burn hot against 32.11
Turn from thy fierce w., 32.12
and lest w. come upon all the Lev 10.06
there may be no w. upon the Num 1.53
for w. has gone forth from the LORD, 16.46
that there be w. no more upon the 18.05
turned back my w. from the people 25.11
your God to w. in the wilderness; Deu 9.07
Horeb you provoked the LORD to w., 9.08
you provoked the LORD to w. 9.22
overthrew in his anger and w.— 29.23
in anger and fury and great w., 29.28
lest w. be upon us, because of the Jos 9.20
and w. fell upon all the congregation 22.20
out his fierce w. against Amalek, 1Sa 28.18
there came great w. upon Israel; 2Ki 3.27
great is the w. of the LORD that 22.13
therefore my w. will be kindled 22.17
the fierceness of his great w., 23.26
yet w. came upon Israel for this, 1Ch 27.24
and my w. shall not be poured out 2Ch 12.07
himself the w. of the LORD turned 12.12
w. has gone out against you from 19.02
the LORD and w. may not come upon 19.10
And w. came upon Judah and Jerusalem 24.18
for the fierce w. of the LORD is 28.11
there is fierce w. against Israel." 28.13
Therefore the w. of the LORD came 29.08
Therefore w. came upon him and 32.25
so that the w. of the LORD did not 32.26
great is the w. of the LORD that 34.21
therefore my w. will be poured out 34.25
till the w. of the LORD rose 36.16
lest his w. be against the realm of Ez 7.23
power of his w. is against all 8.22
till the fierce w. of our God over 10.14
you bring more w. upon Israel by Neh 13.18
will be contempt and w. in plenty. Est 1.18
was filled with w. against Mordecai 5.09
the feast in w. and went into the 7.07
conceal me until thy w. be past, Job 14.13
torn me in his w., and hated me; 16.09
He has kindled his w. against me, 19.11
for w. brings the punishment of the 19.29
dragged off in the day of God's w. 20.28
drink of the w. of the Almighty. 21.20
he is rescued in the day of w.? 21.30
Beware lest w. entice you into 36.18
"My w. is kindled against you and 42.07
Then he will speak to them in his w., Ps 2.05
for his w. is quickly kindled. 2.12
anger, nor chasten me in thy w. 6.01
will swallow them up in his w.; 21.09
Refrain from anger, and forsake w.! 37.08
anger, nor chasten me in thy w.! 38.01
in w. cast down the peoples, O God! 56.07
consume them in w., consume them 59.13
Surely the w. of men shall praise 76.10
the residue of w. thou wilt gird 76.10
the LORD heard, he was full of w.; 78.21
and did not stir up all his w. 78.38
w., indignation, and distress, a 78.49
When God heard, he was full of w., 78.59
and vented his w. on his heritage. 78.62
Will thy jealous w. burn like fire? 79.05
Thou didst withdraw all thy w.; 85.03
Thy w. lies heavy upon me, and thou 88.07
Thy w. has swept over me; thy dread 88.16
art full of w. against thy anointed 89.38
long will thy w. burn like fire? 89.46
by thy w. we are overwhelmed. 90.07
our days pass away under thy w., 90.09
and thy w. acording to the fear of 90.11
turn away his w. from destroying 106.23
shatter kings on the day of his w. 110.05
hand against the w. of my enemies, 138.07
Riches do not profit in the day of w., Pro 11.04
expectation of the wicked in w. 11.23
but his w. falls on one who acts 14.35
A soft answer turns away w., 15.01
A king's w. is a messenger of death, 16.14
A king's w. is like the growling of 19.12
A man of great w. will pay the 19.19
The dread w. of a king is like the 20.02
a bribe in the bosom, strong w. 21.14
W. is cruel, anger is overwhelming; 27.04
aflame, but wise men turn away w. 29.08
A man of w. stirs up strife, and a 29.22
I will vent my w. on my enemies, Is 1.24
Through the w. of the LORD of hosts 9.19
the people of my w. I command him, 10.06
with w. and fierce anger, to make 13.09
at the w. of the LORD of hosts in 13.13
the peoples in w. with unceasing 14.06
little while until the w. is past. 26.20
I have no w. Would that I had 27.04
hand of the LORD the cup of his w., 51.17
are full of the w. of the LORD, 51.20
the bowl of my w. you shall drink 51.22
In overflowing w. for a moment I 54.08
w. to his adversaries, requital to 59.18
for in my w. I smote you, but in my 60.10
anger and trampled them in my w.; 63.03
me victory, and my w. upheld me. 63.05
anger, I made them drunk in my w., 63.06
lest my w. go forth like fire, and Jer 4.04
Therefore I am full of the w. of the LORD; 6.11
my anger and my w. will be poured 7.20
forsaken the generation of his w. 7.29
At his w. the earth quakes, and the 10.10
Pour out thy w. upon the nations 10.25
to turn away thy w. from them. 18.20
and in fury, and in great w. 21.05
lest my w. go forth like fire, and 21.12
W. has gone forth, a whirling 23.19
my hand this cup of the wine of w., 25.15
W. has gone forth, a whirling 30.23
This city has aroused my anger and w., 32.31
my anger and my w. and in great 32.37
shall smite in my anger and my w., 33.05
the anger and w. that the LORD has 36.07
my anger and my w. were poured out 42.18
so my w. will be poured out on you 42.18
Therefore my w. and my anger were 44.06
Because of the w. of the LORD she 50.13
brought out the weapons of his w., 50.25
in his w. he has broken down the Lam 2.02
affliction under the rod of his w.; 3.01
The LORD gave full vent to his w., 4.11
will soon pour out my w. upon you, Eze 7.08
for w. is upon all their multitude. 7.12
For w. is upon all their multitude; 7.13
for my w. is upon all their multitude 7.14
in the day of the w. of the LORD; 7.19
Therefore I will deal in w.; 8.18
outpouring of thy w. upon Jerusalem? 9.08
a stormy wind break out in my w.; 13.13
hailstones in w. to destroy it. 13.13
Thus will I spend my w. upon the wall, 13.15
and pour out my w. upon it with 14.19
you the blood of w. and jealousy. 16.38
pour out my w. upon them and spend 20.08
pour out my w. upon them in the 20.13
pour out my w. upon them and spend 20.21
and with w. poured out, I will be 20.33
arm, and with w. poured out; 20.34
upon you with the fire of my w.; 21.31

WRATH (cont.)
you in my anger and in my w., Eze 22.20
upon you with the fire of my w., 22.21
have poured out my w. upon you." 22.22
them with the fire of my w.; 22.31
To rouse my w., to take vengeance, I 24.08
to my anger and according to my w.; 25.14
And I will pour my w. upon Pelusium, 30.15
Behold, I speak in my jealous w., 36.06
So I poured out my w. upon them for 36.18
the Lord GOD, my w. will be roused. 38.18
and in my blazing w. I delcare, 38.19
and he ran at him in his mighty w. Dan 8.06
anger and thy w. turn away from 9.16
I will pour out my w. like water. Hos 5.10
I have taken them away in my w. 13.11
and he kept his w. for ever. Amo 1.11
And in anger and w. I will execute Mic 5.15
and keeps w. for his enemies. Nah 1.02
His w. is poured out like fire, and 1.06
neighbors drink of the cup of his w., Hab 2.15
Make it known; in w. remember mercy. 3.02
Was thy w. against the rivers, O 3.08
A day of w. is that day, a day of Zep 1.15
on the day of the w. of the LORD. 1.18
In the fire of his jealous w., 1.18
you the day of the w. of the LORD. 2.02
on the day of the w. of the LORD. 2.03
of my jealous w. all the earth 3.08
Therefore great w. came from the Zec 7.12
I am jealous for her with great w. 8.02
your fathers provoked me to w., 8.14
you to flee from the w. to come? Mt 3.07
you to flee from the w. to come? Lk 3.07
the synagogue were filled with w. 4.28
the earth and w. upon this people; 21.23
but the w. of God rests upon him. Jn 3.36
For the w. of God is revealed from Rom 1.18
are storing up w. for yourself on 2.05
on the day of w. when God's righteous 2.05
wickedness, there will be w. and fury. 2.08
God is unjust to inflict w. on us? 3.05
For the law brings w., but where there is 4.15
be saved by him from the w. of God. 5.09
to show his w. and to make known 9.22
the vessels of w. made for destruction, 9.22
but leave it to the w. of God; 12.19
to execute his w. on the wrongdoer. 13.04
to avoid God's w. but also for the 13.05
we were by nature children of w., Eph 2.03
bitterness and w. and anger and 4.31
things that the w. of God comes 5.06
of these the w. of God is coming. Col 3.06
w., malice, slander, and foul talk 3.08
delivers us from the w. to come. 1Th 1.10
But God's w. has come upon them at 2.16
For God has not destined us for w., 5.09
As I swore in my w., They shall never Heb 3.11
he has said, "As I swore in my w., 4.03
and from the w. of the Lamb; Rev 6.16
the great day of their w. has come, 6.17
but thy w. came, and the time for 11.18
has come down to you in great w., 12.12
shall drink the wine of God's w., 14.10
great wine press of the w. of God; 14.19
with them the w. of God is ended. 15.01
full of the w. of God who lives 15.07
the seven bowls of the w. of God. 16.01
the cup of the fury of his w. 16.19
the fury of the w. of God the 19.15

WRATHFUL
to anger, nor go with a w. man, Pro 22.24
upon them with w. chastisements. Eze 25.17
the LORD is avenging and w.; Nah 1.02

WREAK
to w. vengeance on the nations and Ps 149.07

WREATH
do it to receive a perishable w., 1Co 9.25

WREATHS
work with w. of chain work for the 1Ki 7.17
there were w. of beveled work. 7.29
with w. at the side of each. 7.30
space of each, with w. round about. 7.36

WRECKED
the ships were w. at Eziongeber. 1Ki 22.48
the ships were w. and were not 2Ch 20.37
east wind has w. you in the heart Eze 27.26
Now you are w. by the seas, in the 27.34

WRENCHED
chains, but the chains he w. apart, Mk 5.04

WRESTLED
wrestlings I have w. with my sister, Gen 30.08
and a man w. with him until the 32.24
put out of joint as he w. with him. 32.25

WRESTLINGS
"With mighty w. I have wrestled Gen 30.08

WRETCHED
W. man that I am! Who will deliver Rom 7.24
Be w. and mourn and weep. Jas 4.09
not knowing that you are w., Rev 3.17

WRETCHEDNESS
sight, that I may not see my w. Num 11.15

WRETCHES
will put those w. to a miserable death, Mt 21.41

WRING
to the altar and w. off its head, Lev 1.15
he shall w. its head from its neck, 5.08

WRINKLE
without spot or w. or any such Eph 5.27

WRISTS
who sew magic bands upon all w., Eze 13.18

WRITE
"W. this as a memorial in a book Ex 17.14
and I will w. upon the tables the 34.01
LORD said to Moses, "W. these words; 34.27
priest shall w. these curses in a Num 5.23
W. each man's name upon his rod, 17.02
and w. Aaron's name upon the rod of 17.03
And you shall w. them on the Deu 6.09
And I will w. on the tables the 10.02
And you shall w. them upon the 11.20
he shall w. for himself in a book a 17.18
and you shall w. upon them all the 27.03
And you shall w. upon the stones 27.08
Now therefore w. this song, and 31.19
who went to w. the description of Jos 18.08
up and down and w. a description 18.08
that we might w. down the names of Ez 5.10
we make a firm covenant and w. it, Neh 9.38
And you may w. as you please with Est 8.08
w. them on the tablet of your heart. Pro 3.03
w. them on the tablet of your heart. 7.03
tablet and w. upon it in common Is 8.01
few that a child can w. them down. 10.19
And now, go, w. it before them on a 30.08
and another will w. on his hand, 44.05
"W. this man down as childless, a Jer 22.30
W. in a book all the words that I 30.02
and I will w. it upon their hearts; 31.33

WRITE (cont.)
"Take a scroll and w. on it all the Jer 36.02
how did you w. all these words? 36.17
scroll and w. on it all the former 36.28
"Son of man, w. down the name of Eze 24.02
"Son of man, take a stick and w. on it, 37.16
take another stick and w. upon it, 37.16
on which you w. are in your hand 37.20
and w. it down in their sight, so 43.11
Were I to w. for him my laws by ten Hos 8.12
LORD answered me: "W. the vision; Hab 2.02
a man to w. a certificate of Mk 10.04
to w. an orderly account for you, Lk 1.03
and sit down quickly and w. fifty.' 16.06
'Take your bill, and w. eighty.' 16.07
"Do not w., 'The King of the Jews,' Jn 19.21
but should w. to them to abstain Ac 15.20
definite to w. to my lord about 25.26
him, I may have something to w. 25.26
I do not w. this to make you 1Co 4.14
I, Paul, w. this greeting with my own 16.21
For we w. you nothing but what you 2Co 1.13
for me to w. to you about the 9.01
I w. this while I am away from you, 13.10
To w. the same things to you is not Php 3.01
I, Paul, w. this greeting with my own Col 4.18
no need to have any one w. to you, 1Th 4.09
I, Paul, w. this greeting with my own 2Th 3.17
letter of mine, it is the way I w. 3.17
I, Paul, w. this with my own hand, I Phm 1.19
I w. to you, knowing that you will 1.21
and w. them on their hearts, and I Heb 8.10
and w. them on their minds," 10.16
I w. to you, children, because you 1Jn 2.13
I w. to you, fathers, because you 2.14
I w. to you, young men, because you 2.14
I w. to you, not because you do not 2.21
I w. this to you about those who 2.26
I w. this to you who believe in the 5.13
Though I have much to w. to you, 2Jn 1.12
I had much to w. to you, but I would 3Jn 1.13
rather not w. with pen and ink; 1.13
very eager to w. to you of our Jud 1.03
it necessary to w. appealing to 1.03
saying, "W. what you see in a book Rev 1.11
Now w. what you see, what is and 1.19
angel of the church in Ephesus w.: 2.01
angel of the church in Smyrna w.: 2.08
angel of the church in Pergamum w.: 2.12
angel of the church in Thyatira w.: 2.18
angel of the church in Sardis w.: 3.01
of the church in Philadelphia w.: 3.07
and I will w. on him the name of my 3.12
angel of the church in Laodicea w.: 3.14
had sounded, I was about to w., 10.04
have said, and do not w. it down." 10.04
"W. this: Blessed are the dead who 14.13
"W. this: Blessed are those who are 19.09
"W. this, for these words are 21.05

WRITER
I tertius, the w. of this letter, Rom 16.22

WRITERS
and the w. who keep writing oppression, Is 10.01

WRITES
and he w. her a bill of divorce and Deu 24.01
dislikes her and w. her a bill of 24.03
Moses w. that the man who practices Rom 10.05

WRITEST
For thou w. bitter things against Job 13.26

WRITHE
I w. in pain! Oh, the walls of my Jer 4.19
W. and groan, O daughter of Zion, Mic 4.10
Gaza too, and shall w. in anguish; Zec 9.05

WRITHED
we w., we have as it were brought Is 26.18
The mountains saw thee, and w.; Hab 3.10

WRITHES
The wicked man w. in pain all his Job 15.20
who w. and cries out in her pangs, Is 26.17
The land trembles and w. in pain, Jer 51.29

WRITING
and the w. was the w. of God, Ex 32.16
on the tables, as at the first w., Deu 10.04
had finished w. the words of this 31.24
w. a description of it with a view Jos 18.04
clear by the w. from the hand of 1Ch 28.19
his kingdom and also put it in w.: 2Ch 36.22
his kingdom and also put it in w.: Ez 1.01
The w. was in the name of King Est 8.10
gave orders in w. that his wicked 9.25
Purim, and it was recorded in w. 9.32
writers who keep w. oppression, Is 10.01
A w. of Hezekiah king of Judah, 38.09
and it had w. on the front and on Eze 2.10
with a w. case at his side. 9.02
who had the w. case at his side. 9.03
with the w. case at his side, 9.11
of Babylon, "Whoever reads this w., Dan 5.07
not read the w. or make known to 5.08
me to read this w. and make known 5.15
can read the w. and make known to 5.16
I will read the w. to the king and 5.17
sent, and this w. was inscribed. 5.24
And this is the w. that was inscribed: 5.25
And he asked for a w. tablet, Lk 1.63
nor am I w. this to secure any such 1Co 9.15
that what I am w. to you is a 14.37
(In what I am w. to you, before God, Gal 1.20
letters I am w. to you with my own 6.11
but I am w. these instructions to 1Ti 3.14
And we are w. this that our joy may 1Jn 1.04
I am w. this to you so that you may 2.01
Beloved, I am w. you no new commandment, 2.07
Yet I am w. you a new commandment, 2.08
I am w. to you, little children, 2.12
I am w. to you, fathers, because you 2.13
I am w. to you, young men, because 2.13
though I were w. you a new commandment, 2Jn 1.05

WRITINGS
But if you do not believe his w., Jn 5.47
the prophetic w. is made known to Rom 16.26
with the sacred w. which are able 2Ti 3.15

WRITTEN
which I have w. for their instruction Ex 24.12
w. with the finger of God. 31.18
tables that were w. on both sides; 32.15
side and on the other were they w. 32.15
out of thy book which thou hast w. 32.32
tables of stone w. with the finger Deu 9.10
this law which are w. in this book, 28.58
and the curses w. in this book 29.20
of the covenant w. in this book of 29.21
it all the curses w. in this book; 29.27
which are w. in this book of the 30.10
according to all that is w. in it; Jos 1.08
as it is w. in the book of the law 8.31
the law of Moses, which he had w. 8.32
to all that is w. in the book of 8.34
Is this not w. in the Book of 10.13
do all that is w. in the book of 23.06
behold, it is w. in the Book of 2Sa 1.18
as it is w. in the law of Moses, 1Ki 2.03
are they not w. in the book of the 11.41
they are w. in the Book of the 14.19

WRITTEN (cont.)

are they not w. in the Book of the 1Ki 14.29
are they not w. in the Book of the 15.07
are they not w. in the Book of the 15.23
are they not w. in the Book of the 15.31
are they not w. in the Book of the 16.05
are they not w. in the Book of the 16.14
are they not w. in the Book of the 16.20
are they not w. in the Book of the 16.27
As it was w. in the letters which 21.11
are they not w. in the Book of the 22.39
are they not w. in the Book of the 22.45
are they not w. in the Book of the 2Ki 1.18
are they not w. in the Book of the 8.23
are they not w. in the Book of the 10.34
are they not w. in the Book of the 12.19
are they not w. in the Book of the 13.08
are they not w. in the Book of the 13.12
to what is w. in the book of the 14.06
are they not w. in the Book of the 14.15
are they not w. in the Book of the 14.18
are they not w. in the Book of the 14.28
are they not w. in the Book of the 15.06
they are w. in the Book of the 15.11
they are w. in the Book of the 15.15
are they not w. in the Book of the 15.21
they are w. in the Book of the 15.26
they are w. in the Book of the 15.31
are they not w. in the Book of the 15.36
are they not w. in the Book of the 16.19
are they not w. in the Book of the 20.20
are they not w. in the Book of the 21.17
are they not w. in the Book of the 21.25
to all that is w. concerning us. 22.13
covenant that were w. in this book; 23.03
as it is w. in this book of the 23.21
law which were w. in the book that 23.24
are they not w. in the Book of the 23.28
are they not w. in the Book of the 24.05
and these are w. in the Book of 1Ch 9.01
to all that is w. in the law of 16.40
are w. in the Chronicles of Samuel 29.29
are they not w. in the history of 2Ch 9.29
are they not w. in the chronicles 12.15
are w. in the story of he prophet 13.22
are w. in the Book of the Kings of 16.11
are w. in the chronicles of Jehu 20.34
as it is w. in the law of Moses, 23.18
of God are w. in the Commentary on 24.27
according to what is w. in the law, 25.04
are thy not w. in the Book of the 25.26
they are w. in the Book of the 27.07
they are w. in the Book of the 28.26
as it is w. in the law of the LORD. 31.03
they are w. in the vision of Isaiah 32.32
they are w. in the Chronicles of 33.19
to all that is w. in this book. 34.21
curses that are w. in the book 34.24
covenant that were w. in this book. 34.31
as it is w. in the book of Moses. 35.12
behold, they are w. in the Laments. 35.25
to what is w. in the law of the 35.26
they are w. in the Book of the 35.27
they are w. in the Book of the 36.08
as it is w. in the law of Moses the Ez 3.02
as it is w., and offered the daily 3.04
the letter was w. in Aramaic and 4.07
in which was w. as follows: "To 5.07
on which this was w.: "A record. 6.02
as it is w. in the book of Moses. 6.18
In it was w., "It is reported among Neh 6.06
the first, and I found w. in it: 7.05
And they found it w. in the law 8.14
trees to make booths, as it is w. 8.15
our God, as it is w. in the law. 10.34
as it is w. in the law, and the 10.36
were w. in the Book of the Chronicles 12.23

in it was found w. that no Ammonite 13.01
and let it be w. among the laws of Est 1.19
was w. to the king's satraps and to 3.12
it was w. in the name of King 3.12
a copy of the w. decree issued in 4.08
And it was found w. how Mordecai 6.02
let an order be w. to revoke the 8.05
for an edict w. in the name of the 8.08
an edict was w. according to all 8.09
of what was w. was to be issued as 8.13
and as Mordecai had w. to them. 9.23
of all that was w. in this letter, 9.26
to what was w. and at the time 9.27
the Jew gave full w. authority, 9.29
are they not w. in the Book of the 10.02
"Oh that my words were w.! Job 19.23
the indictment w. by my adversary! 31.35
roll of the book it is w. of me; Ps 40.07
in thy book were w., everyone of 139.16
to execute on them the judgment w.! 149.09
Have I not w. for you thrity Pro 22.20
Behold, it is w. before me: "I will Is 65.06
"The sin of Judah is w. with a pen Jer 17.01
from thee shall be w. in the earth, 17.13
everything w. in this book, which 25.13
which you have w. at my dictation. 36.06
"Why have you w. in it that the 36.29
words that are w. concerning 51.60
to me, and lo, a w. scroll was in it; Eze 2.09
and there were w. on it words of 2.10
oath which are w. in the law of Dan 9.11
As it is w. in the law of Moses, all 9.13
name shall be found w. in the book. 12.01
remembrance was w. before him of Mal 3.16
for so it is w. by the prophet: Mt 2.05
"It is w., 'Man shall not live by 4.04
for it is w., 'He will give his 4.06
"Again it is w., 'You shall not 4.07
for it is w., 'You shall worship 4.10
This is he of whom it is w., 11.10
"It is w., 'My house shall be 21.13
Son of man goes as it is w. of him, 26.24
for it is., 'I will strike the 26.31
As it is w. in Isaiah the prophet, Mk 1.02
as it is w., 'This people honors me 7.06
and how is it w. of the Son of man, 9.12
they pleased, as it is w. of him." 9.13
"Is it not w., 'My house shall be 11.17
Son of man goes as it is w. of him, 14.21
for it is w., 'I will strike the 14.27
(as it is w. in the law of the Lord, Lk 2.23
As it is w. in the book of the 3.04
"It is w., 'Man shall not live by 4.04
"It is w., 'You shall worship the 4.08
for it is w., 'He will give his 4.10
found the place where it was w., 4.17
This is he of whom it is w., 7.27
that your names are w. in heaven." 10.20
said to him, 'What is w. in the law? 10.26
everything that is w. of the Son of 18.31
"It is w., 'My house shall be a 19.46
said, "What then is this that is w.: 20.17
vengeance, to fulfil all that is w. 21.22
for what is w. about me has its 22.37
that everything w. about me in the 24.44
"Thus it is w., that he Christ 24.46
disciples remembered that it was w., Jn 2.17
as it is w., 'He gave them bread 6.31
It is w. in the prophets, 'And they 6.45
In your law it is w. that the 8.17
"Is it not w. in your law, 'I said, 10.34
sat upon it; as it is w., 12.14
this had been w. of him and had 12.16
the word that is w. in their law, 15.25
and it was w. in Hebrew, in Latin, 19.20
"What I have w. I have w." 19.22
which are not w. in this book; 20.30

WRITTEN (cont.)
but these are w. that you may Jn 20.31
and who has w. these things; 21.24
were every one of them to be w., 21.25
contain the books that would be w. 21.25
For it is w. in the Book of Psalms, Ac 1.20
as it is w. in the book of the 7.42
fulfilled all that was w. of him, 13.29
as also it is w. in the second 13.33
the prophets agree, as it is w., 15.15
for it is w., 'You shall not speak 23.05
by the law or w. in the prophets, 24.14
as it is w., "He who through faith Rom 1.17
law requires is w. on their hearts, 2.15
For, as it is w., "The name of God 2.24
who have the w. code and circumcision 2.27
as it is w., "That thou mayest be 3.04
as it is w.: "None is righteous, no, 3.10
as it is w., "I have made you the 4.17
were w. not for his sake alone, 4.23
under the old w. code but in the 7.06
As it is w., "For thy sake we are 8.36
As it is w., "Jacob I loved, but 9.13
as it is w., "Behold I am laying in 9.33
As it is w., "How beautiful are the 10.15
as it is w., "God gave them a 11.08
as it is w., "The Deliverer will 11.26
for it is w., "Vengenace is mine, I 12.19
for it is w., "As I live, says the 14.11
but, as it is w., "The reproaches of 15.03
For whatever was w. in former days 15.04
former days was w. for our instruction, 15.04
As it is w., "Therefore I will 15.09
points I have w. to you very 15.15
but as it is w., "They shall see 15.21
For it is w., "I will destroy the 1Co 1.19
as it is w., "Let him who boasts, 1.31
But, as it is w., "What no eye has 2.09
For it is w., "He catches the wise 3.19
For, as it is w., "The two shall 6.16
For it is w. in the law of Moses, 9.09
It was w. for our sake, because the 9.10
as it is w., "The people sat down 10.07
but they were w. down for our 10.11
In the law it is w., "By men of 14.21
Thus it is w., "The first man Adam 15.45
come to pass the saying that is w.: 15.54
w. on your hearts, to be known and 2Co 3.02
w. not with ink but with the Spirit 3.03
not in a w. code but in the Spirit; 3.06
for the w. code kills, but the 3.06
As it is w., "He who gathered much 8.15
As it is w., "He scatters abroad, he 9.09
for it is w., "Cursed be every one Gal 3.10
by all things w. in the book of 3.10
for it is w., "Cursed be every one 3.13
For it is w. that Abraham had two 4.22
For it is w., "Rejoice, O barren one 4.27
revelations, as I have w. briefly. Eph 3.03
no need to have anything w. to you. 1Th 5.01
as it is w. of me in the roll of Heb 10.07
for I have w. to you briefly. 13.22
since it is w., "You shall be holy, 1Pe 1.16
I have w. briefly to you, exhorting 5.12
letter that I have w. to you, 2Pe 3.01
I have w. something to the church; 3Jn 1.09
and who keep what is w. therein; Rev 1.03
with a new name w. on the stone 2.17
throne a scroll w. within and on 5.01
has not been w. before the foundation 13.08
Father's name w. on their foreheads 14.01
forehead was w. a name of mystery: 17.05
have not been w. in the book of 17.08
judged by what was w. in the books, 20.12
was not found w. in the book of 20.15
those who are w. in the Lamb's book 21.27

WRONG
"May the w. done to me be on you! Gen 16.05
You have done w. in so doing.'" 44.05
he said to the man that did the w., Ex 2.13
and I and my people are in the w., 9.27
"You shall not w. a stranger or 22.21
your land, you shall not do him w. Lev 19.33
"You shall do no w. in judgment, 19.35
you shall not w. one another. 25.14
You shall not w. one another, but 25.17
make full restitution for his w., Num 5.07
it to him to whom he did the w. 5.07
restitution may be made for the w., 5.08
restitution for w. shall go to the 5.08
or for any w. in connection with Deu 19.15
and you do me w. by making war on Ju 11.27
there is no w. or treason in my 1Sa 24.11
Then Saul said, "I have done w.; 26.21
found nothing w. in you from the 29.06
for this w. in sending me away is 2Sa 13.16
servant did w. on the day my lord 19.19
at Lachish, saying, "I have done w.; 2Ki 18.14
although there is no w. in my hands, 1Ch 12.17
for you have done w., and it will 2Ch 26.18
the king has Queen Vashti done w., Est 1.16
did not sin or charge God with w. Job 1.22
Turn, I pray, let no w. be done. 6.29
Is there any w. on my tongue? 6.30
are you not ashamed to w. me? 19.03
then that God has put me in the w., 19.06
thoughts, and your schemes to w. me. 21.27
had declared Job to be in the w. 32.03
the Almighty that he should do w. 34.10
who can say, 'Thou hast done w.'? 36.23
Will you even put me in the w.? 40.08
this, if there is w. in my hands, Ps 7.03
who also do no w., but walk in his 119.03
put forth their hands to do w. 125.03
sleep unless they have done w.; Pro 4.16
It is like sport to a fool to do w., 10.23
Without counsel plans go w., 15.22
to flog noble men is w. 17.26
a piece of bread a man will do w. 28.21
mouth, and says "I have done no w." 30.20
justice, I hate robbery and w.; Is 61.08
"What w. did your fathers find in Jer 2.05
And do no w. or violence to the 22.03
from his evil way and w. doings, 25.05
"What w. have I done to you or your 37.18
but if it seems w. to you to come 40.04
Thou hast seen the w. done to me, Lam 3.59
does not w. any one, exacts no Eze 18.16
you, O king, I have done no w." Dan 6.22
sinned and done w. and acted 9.05
with blood and Jerusalem with w. Mic 3.10
evil and canst not look on w., Hab 1.13
her is righteous, he does no w.; Zep 3.05
shall do no w. and utter no lies, 3.13
and no w. was found on his lips. Mal 2.06
'Friend, I am doing you no w.; Mt 20.13
"You are w., because you know 22.29
them, "Is not this why you are w., Mk 12.24
of the living; you are quite w." 12.27
but this man has done nothing w." Lk 23.41
wrongly, bear witness to the w.; Jn 18.23
brethren, why do you w. each other?' Ac 7.26
"We find nothing w. in this man. 23.09
there is anything w. about the man, 25.05
to the Jews I have done no w., 25.10
aside, together they have gone w.; Rom 3.12
But if you do w., be afraid, for he 13.04
Love does no w. to a neighbor; 13.10
but it is w. for any one to make 14.20
Why not rather suffer w.? 1Co 6.07
But you yourselves w. and defraud, 6.08
it does not rejoice at w., 13.06
account of the one who did the w., 2Co 7.12

WRONG (cont.)

of the one who suffered the w., 2Co 7.12
not burden you? Forgive me this w.! 12.13
pray God that you may not do w.— 13.07
as you are. You did me no w.; Gal 4.12
paid back for the w. he has done, Col 3.25
and w. his brother in this matter, 1Th 4.06
those who do w. and to praise 1Pe 2.14
if when you do w. and are beaten 2.20
be God's will, than for doing w. 3.17
suffering w. for their wrongdoing. 2Pe 2.13

WRONGDOER

If then I am a w., and have committed Ac 25.11
God to execute his wrath on the w. Rom 13.04
For the w. will be paid back for Col 3.25
or a w., or a mischief-maker; 1Pe 4.15

WRONGDOERS

the wicked, be not envious of w.! Ps 37.01
case they speak against you as w., 1Pe 2.12

WRONGDOING

any man to accuse him of w., Deu 19.16
a matter of w. or vicious crime, I Ac 18.14
say what w. they found when I 24.20
suffering wrong for their w. 2Pe 2.13
of Beor, who loved gain from w., 2.15
All w. is sin, but there is sin 1Jn 5.17

WRONGDOINGS

them, but an avenger of their w. Ps 99.08

WRONGED

and the widow are w. in you. Eze 22.07
And seeing one of them being w., Ac 7.24
we have w. no one, we have corrupted 2Co 7.02
If he has w. you at all, or owes you Phm 1.18

WRONGFULLY

rejoice over me who are w. my foes, Ps 35.19
and many are those who hate me w. 38.19

WRONGING

But the man who was w. his neighbor Ac 7.27

WRONGLY

Jesus answered him, "If I have spoken w., Jn 18.23
do not receive, because you ask w., Jas 4.03

WRONGS

Nay, in your hearts you devise w.; Ps 58.02
the w. I have done are not hidden 69.05
make me see w. and look upon Hab 1.03

WROTE

And Moses w. all the words of the Ex 24.04
And he w. upon the tables the words 34.28
and w. upon it an inscription, like 39.30
Moses w. down their starting places, Num 33.02
and he w. them upon two tables of Deu 4.13
And he w. them upon two tables of 5.22
And he w. on the tables, as at the 10.04
And Moses w. this law, and gave it 31.09
So Moses w. this song the same day, 31.22
he w. upon the stones a copy of the Jos 8.32
And Joshua w. these words in the 24.26
and he w. down for him the officials Ju 8.14
and he w. them in a book and laid 1Sa 10.25
morning David w. a letter to Joab, 2Sa 11.14
In the letter he w., "Set Uriah in 11.15
So she w. letters in Ahab's name and 1Ki 21.08
And she w. in the letters, "Proclaim 21.09
So Jehu w. letters, and sent them to 2Ki 10.01
Then he w. to them a second letter, 10.06
commandment which he w. for you, 17.37
the prophet the son of Amoz w. 2Ch 26.22
and w. letters also to Ephraim and 30.01
And he w. letters to cast contempt 32.17
they w. an accusation against the Ez 4.06
associates w. to Artaxerxes king 4.07
the scribe w. a letter against 4.08
then w. Rehum he commander, Shimshai 4.09
which he w. to destroy the Jews who Est 8.05
and uprightly he w. words of truth. Ecc 12.10
and Baruch w. upon a scroll at the Jer 36.04
while I w. them with ink on the 36.18
which Baruch w. at Jeremiah's 36.27
who w. on it at the dictation of 36.32
when he w. these words in a book at 45.01
Jeremiah w. in a book all the evil 51.60
appeared and w. on the plaster of Dan 5.05
and the king saw the hand as it w. 5.05
Then King Darius w. to all the 6.25
Then the w. down the dream, and told 7.01
of heart he w. you this commandment Mk 10.05
Moses w. for us that if a man's 12.19
and w., "His name is John." Lk 1.63
Moses w. for us that if a man's 20.28
the law and also the prophets w., Jn 1.45
would believe me, for he w. of me. 5.46
Jesus bent down and w. with his * 8.06
he bent down and w. with his finger * 8.08
Pilate also w. a title and put it 19.19
and w. to the disciples to receive Ac 18.27
And he w. a letter to this effect: 23.25
I w. to you in my letter not to 1Co 5.09
But rather I w. to you not to 5.11
the matters about which you w. 7.01
And I w. as I did, so that when I 2Co 2.03
For I w. you out of much affliction 2.04
For this is why I w., that I might 2.09
spirit of faith as he had who w., 4.13
So although I w. to you, it was not 7.12
brother Paul w. to you according 2Pe 3.15

WROTH

he will be w. as in the valley of Is 28.21

WROUGHT

because he had w. folly in Israel Gen 34.07
have not been w. in all the earth Ex 34.10
the finely w. garments for ministering 35.19
stuff they made finely w. garments, 39.01
signs which I have w. among them? Num 14.11
signs which I w. in Egypt and in 14.22
Jacob and Israel, 'What has God w.!' 23.23
them the gold, all w. articles. 31.51
because she has w. folly in Israel Deu 22.21
the LORD has not w. all this." 32.27
which Moses w. in the sight of all 34.12
the LORD has w. deliverance in 1Sa 11.13
who has w. this great victory in 14.45
for he has w. with God this day." 14.45
and the LORD w. a great victory for 19.05
thou hast w. all this greatness, to 2Sa 7.21
and the LORD w. a great victory 23.10
and the LORD w. a great victory. 23.12
he has done, the wonders he w., 1Ch 16.12
thou hast w. all this greatness, in 17.19
yet unborn, that he has w. it. Ps 22.31
and w. for those who take refuge in 31.19
how he has w. desolations in the 46.08
they will tell what God has w., 64.09
O God, thou who hast w. for us. 68.28
and the wonders which he has w. 78.04
fathers he w. marvels in the land 78.12
when he w. his signs in Egypt, and 78.43
They w. his signs among them, and 105.27
intricately w. in the depths of the 139.15
I muse on what thy hands have w. 143.05
it was lovingly w. within by the Sol 3.10
thou hast w. for us all our works. Is 26.12
We have w. no deliverance in the 26.18

WROUGHT (cont.)
w. iron, cassia, and calamus were Eze 27.19
and w. in gold were your settings 28.13
the Most High God has w. toward me. Dan 4.02
mighty works are w. by his hands! Mk 6.02
that his deeds have been w. in God. Jn 3.21
w. in me all kinds of covetousness. Rom 7.08
what Christ has w. through me to 15.18

WRUNG
he w. enough dew from the fleece to Ju 6.38
my heart is w. within me, because I Lam 1.20

Y

YARD
the temple y. on the west side was Eze 41.12
and the y. and the building with 41.13
front of the temple and the y., 41.14
facing the y. which was at the 41.15
the temple y. and opposite the 42.01
opposite the y. and opposite the 42.10
opposite the y. are the holy 42.13

YARDS
land, but about a hundred y. off. Jn 21.08

YEA
y., with a strong hand he will Ex 6.01
y., all the nations would say, 'Why Deu 29.24
Y., he loved his people; all those 33.03
y., his heavens drop down dew. 33.28
y., the clouds dropped water. Ju 5.04
y., God has given it into your 18.10
Y., thou art my lamp, O LORD, and my 2Sa 22.29
Y., by thee I can crush a troop, and 22.30
Y., does not my house stand so with God? 23.05
Y., thou didst speak with thy mouth, 1Ki 8.24
y., hear thou in heaven thy dwelling 8.30
y., the world stands firm, never 1Ch 16.30
y., thou didst speak with thy 2Ch 6.15
y., hear thou from heaven thy 6.21
Y., I and my father's house have Neh 1.06
Y., let that night be barren; Job 3.07
"Y., the light of the wicked is put 18.05
Y., I know that thou wilt bring me 30.23
y., thou dost note trouble and Ps 10.14
y., I have a goodly heritage. 16.06
Y., thou dost light my lamp; 18.28
Y., by thee I can crush a troop; 18.29
y., thou didst exalt me above my 18.48
Y., thou dost make him most blessed 21.06
Y., dogs are round about me; 22.16
Y., to him shall all the proud of 22.29
Y., let none that wait for thee be 25.03
take courage; y., wait for the LORD! 27.14
Y., thou art my rock and my fortress; 31.03
Y., I hear the whispering of many— 31.13
Y., our heart is glad in him, 33.21
Y., I am like a man who does not 38.14
Y., he shall see that even the wise 49.10
y., I would wander afar, I would 55.07
y., my feet from falling, that I may 56.13
y., where the LORD will dwell for 68.16
y., I will remember thy wonders of 77.11
were afraid, y., the deep trembled. 77.16
Y., they conspire with one accord; 83.05
My soul longs, y., faints for the 84.02
Y., the LORD will give what is good, 85.12
Y., thou hast turned back the edge 89.43
y., the work of our hands establish 90.17
Y., the world is established; 93.01
Y., the world is established, it 96.10
y., they are the joy of my heart. 119.111
y., their cunning is in vain. 119.118
y., every one who trusts in them! 135.18
y., all her slain are a mighty host. Pro 7.26
Y., O people in Zion who dwell at Is 30.19
y., for the king it is made ready, 30.33
y., for all the joyous houses in 32.13
y., there shall the night hag alight, 34.14
y., there shall the kites be 34.15
y., I will repay into their bosom 65.06
Y., upon every high hill and Jer 2.20
y., they have turned and fled 46.21
y., she herself groans, and turns Lam 1.08
y., she has seen the nations invade 1.10
Because, y., because they have Eze 13.10
y., I plighted my troth to you and 16.08
y., you played the harlot with them, 16.28
"Y., thus says the Lord GOD: I will 16.59
y. thrice, the sword for those to be 21.14
y., the isles that are in the sea 26.18
y., those who dwelt under its 31.17
y., because they made you desolate, 36.03
Y., I will let men walk upon you, 36.12
to Shechem, y., they commit villainy. Hos 6.09
Y., the thing itself shall be 10.06
y., he will roar, and his sons shall 11.10
y., let every one turn from his Jon 3.08
Y., their horsemen come from afar; Hab 1.08
for a full, y., sudden end he will Zep 1.18
y., he will famish all the gods of 2.11
"Y., at that time I will change the 3.09
y., I will make you renowned and 3.20
Y., how good and how fair it shall Zec 9.17
y., Father, for such was thy gracious Mt 11.26
y., Father, for such was thy gracious Lk 10.21
y., and on my menservants and my Ac 2.18
"Y., Lord God the Almighty, true and Rev 16.07

YEAR
six hundredth y. of Noah's life, Gen 7.11
In the six hundred and first y., 8.13
in the thirteenth y. they rebelled. 14.04
In the fourteenth y. Chedorlaomer 14.05
bear to you at this season next y." 17.21
in the same y. a hundredfold. 26.12
Before the y. of famine came, Joseph 41.50
for all their cattle that y. 47.17
And when that y. was ended, they 47.18
they came to him the following y., 47.18
the first month of the y. for you. Ex 12.02
without blemish, a male a y. old; 12.05
its appointed time from y. to y. 13.10
but the seventh y. you shall let it 23.11
"Three times in the y. you shall 23.14
ingathering at the end of the y., 23.16
Three times in the y. shall all 23.17
them out from before you in one y., 23.29
two lambs a y. old day by day 29.38
atonement upon its horns once a y.; 30.10
it once in the y. throughout your 30.10
Three times in the y. shall all 34.23
your God three times in the y. 34.24
the first month in the second y., 40.17
both a y. old without blemish, for a Lev 9.03
a lamb a y. old for a burnt 12.06
one ewe lamb a y. old without 14.10
once in the y. because of all 16.34
And in the fourth y. all their 19.24
But in the fifth y. you may eat of 19.25
a male lamb a y. old without 23.12
seven lambs a y. old without 23.18
male lambs a y. old as a sacrifice 23.19

YEAR (cont.)
to the LORD seven days in the y.; Lev 23.41
but in the seventh y. there shall 25.04
it shall be a y. of solemn rest for 25.05
And you shall hallow the fiftieth y., 25.10
shall that fiftieth y. be to you; 25.11
"In this y. of jubilee each of you 25.13
shall we eat in the seventh y., 25.20
blessing upon you in the sixth y., 25.21
When you sow in the eighth y., 25.22
until the ninth y., when its produce 25.22
bought it until the y. of jubilee; 25.28
within a whole y. after its sale; 25.29
for a full y. he shall have the 25.29
is not redeemed within a full y., 25.30
you until the y. of the jubilee; 25.40
him from the y. when he sold 25.50
to him until the y. of jubilee, 25.50
few years until the y. of jubilee, 25.52
As a servant hired y. by y. shall 25.53
be released in the y. of jubilee, 25.54
his field from the y. of jubilee, 27.17
remain until the y. of jubilee, 27.18
for it up to the y. of jubilee, 27.23
In the y. of jubilee the field 27.24
in the second y. after they had Num 1.01
a male lamb a y. old for a guilt 6.12
one male lamb a y. old without 6.14
one ewe lamb a y. old without 6.14
one ram, one male lamb a y. old, 7.15
and five male lambs a y. old. 7.17
one ram, one male lamb a y. old, 7.21
and five male lambs a y. old. 7.23
one ram, one male lamb a y. old, 7.27
and five male lambs a y. old. 7.29
one ram, one male lamb a y. old, 7.33
and five male lambs a y. old. 7.35
one ram, one male lamb a y. old, 7.39
and five male lambs a y. old. 7.41
one ram, one male lamb a y. old, 7.45
and five male lambs a y. old. 7.47
one ram, one male lamb a y. old, 7.51
and five male lambs a y. old. 7.53
one ram, one male lamb a y. old, 7.57
and five male lambs a y. old. 7.59
one ram, one male lamb a y. old, 7.63
and five male lambs a y. old. 7.65
one ram, one male lamb a y. old, 7.69
and five male lambs a y. old. 7.71
one ram, one male lamb a y. old, 7.75
and five male lambs a y. old. 7.77
one ram, one male lamb a y. old, 7.81
and five male lambs a y. old. 7.83
rams, twelve male lambs a y. old, 7.87
the male lambs a y. old sixty. 7.88
of the second y. after they had 9.01
In the second y., in the second month, 10.11
forty days, for every day a y., 14.34
a female goat a y. old for a sin 15.27
male lambs a y. old without 28.03
male lambs a y. old without 28.09
male lambs a y. old without 28.11
throughout the months of the y. 28.14
ram, and seven male lambs a y. old; 28.19
one ram, seven male lambs a y. old; 28.27
male lambs a y. old without 29.02
one ram, seven male lambs a y. old; 29.08
rams, fourteen male lambs a y. old; 29.13
male lambs a y. old without 29.17
male lambs a y. old without 29.20
male lambs a y. old without 29.23
male lambs a y. old without 29.26
male lambs a y. old without 29.29
male lambs a y. old without 29.32
male lambs a y. old without 29.36
in the fortieth y. after the 33.38
And in the fortieth y., Deu 1.03
beginning of the y. to the end of the y. 11.12
forth from the field y. by y. 14.22
of your produce in the same y., 14.28
'The seventh y., the y. of release 15.09
in the seventh y. you shall let 15.12
LORD your God y. by y. at the place 15.20
"Three times a y. all your males 16.16
he shall be free at home one y., 24.05
of your produce in the third y., 26.12
which is the y. of tithing, giving 26.12
the set time of the y. of release, 31.10
of the land of Canaan that y. Jos 5.12
the children of Israel that y. Ju 10.08
of Israel went y. by y. to lament 11.40
the Gileadite four days in the y. 11.40
give you ten pieces of silver a y., 17.10
used to go up y. by y. from his city to 1Sa 1.03
So it went on y. by y.; 1.07
robe and take it to him each y., 2.19
on a circuit y. by y. to Bethel, 7.16
Philistines was a y. and four 27.07
In the spring of the y., 2Sa 11.01
end of every y. he used to cut it; 14.26
for three years, y. after y.; 21.01
provision for one month in the y. 1Ki 4.07
gave this to Hiram y. by y. 5.11
and eightieth y. after the people 6.01
in the fourth y. of Solomon's reign 6.01
In the fourth y. the foundation of 6.37
And in the eleventh y., in the month 6.38
Three times a y. Solomon used to 9.25
Solomon in one y. was six hundred 10.14
and mules, so much y. by y. 10.25
In the fifth y. of King Rehoboam, 14.25
the eighteenth y. of King Jeroboam 15.01
In the twentieth y. of Jeroboam 15.09
in the second y. of Asa king of 15.25
in the third y. of Asa king of 15.28
In the third y. of Asa king of 15.33
twenty-sixth y. of Asa king of 16.08
twenty-seventh y. of Asa king of 16.10
twenty-seventh y. of Asa king of 16.15
thirty-first y. of Asa king of 16.23
thirty-eighth y. of Asa king of 16.29
in the third y., saying, "Go, show 18.01
But in the third y. Jehoshaphat the 22.02
in the fourth y. of Ahab king of 22.41
the seventeenth y. of Jehoshaphat 22.51
in the second y. of Jehoram the 2Ki 1.17
In the eighteenth y. of Jehoshaphat 3.01
In the fifth y. of Joram the son of 8.16
In the twelfth y. of Joram the son 8.25
and he reigned on y. in Jerusalem. 8.26
In the eleventh y. of Joram the son 9.29
But in the seventh y. of Jehoiada sent 11.04
In the seventh y. of Jehu Jehoash 12.01
twenty-third y. of King Jehoash 12.06
twenty-third y. of Joash the son 13.01
thirty-seventh y. of Joash king of 13.10
the land in the spring of the y. 13.20
In the second y. of Joash the son 14.01
In the fifteenth y. of Amaziah the 14.23
twenty-seventh y. of Jeroboam king 15.01
thirty-eighth y. of Azariah king 15.08
thirty-ninth y. of Uzziah king of 15.13
thirty-ninth y. of Azariah king of 15.17
In the fiftieth y. of Azariah king 15.23
fifty-second y. of Azariah king of 15.27
the twentieth y. of Jotham the son 15.30
In the second y. of Pekah the son 15.32
In the seveneenth y. of Pekah the 16.01
In the twelfth y. of Ahaz king of 17.01
Assyria, as he had done y. by y.; 17.04
In the ninth y. of Hoshea the king 17.06
In the third y. of Hoshea son of 18.01
In the fourth y. of King Hezekiah, 18.09
was the seventh y. of Hoshea son 18.09

YEAR (cont.)
In the sixth y. of Hezekiah, which 2Ki 18.10
was the ninth y. of Hoshea king of 18.10
In the fourteenth y. of King 18.13
this y. you shall eat what grows of 19.29
in the second y. what springs of 19.29
then in the third y. sow, and reap. 19.29
In the eighteenth y. of King Josiah, 22.03
the eighteenth y. of King Josiah 23.23
in the eighth y. of his reign, 24.12
And in the ninth y. of his reign, 25.01
the eleventh y. of King Zedekiah. 25.02
the nineteenth y. of King Nebuchadnezzar, 25.08
thirty-seventh y. of the exile of 25.27
in the y. that he began to reign, 25.27
In the spring of the y., the time when 1Ch 20.01
(In the fortieth y. of David's reign 26.31
after month throughout the y., 27.01
of the fourth y. of his reign. 2Ch 3.02
Solomon in one y. was six hundred 9.13
and mules, so much y. by y. 9.24
In the fifth y. of King Rehoboam, 12.02
In the eighteenth y. of King 13.01
the fifteenth y. of the reign of 15.10
thirty-fifth y. of the reign of 15.19
thirty-sixth y. of the reign of 16.01
thirty-ninth y. of his reign Asa 16.12
in the forty-first y. of his reign. 16.13
In the third y. of his reign he 17.07
and he reigned one y. in Jerusalem. 22.02
But in the seventh y. Jehoiada took 23.01
house of your God from y. to y.; 24.05
At the end of the y. the army of 24.23
gave him that y. a hundred talents 27.05
In the first y. of his reign, in the 29.03
For in the eighth y. of his reign, 34.03
in the twelfth y. he began to 34.03
Now in the eighteenth y. of his reign, 34.08
In the eighteenth y. of the reign 35.19
spring of the y. King Nebuchadnezzar 36.10
Now in the first y. of Cyrus king 36.22
In the first y. of Cyrus king of Ez 1.01
Now in the second y. of their 3.08
the second y. of the reign of 4.24
However in the first y. of Cyrus 5.13
In the first y. of Cyrus the king, 6.03
in the sixth y. of the reign of 6.15
in the seventh y. of Artaxerxes 7.07
was in the seventh y. of the king; 7.08
of Chislev, in the twentieth y., Neh 1.01
the twentieth y. of King Artaxerxes, 2.01
the twentieth y. to the thirty-seconc 5.14
thirty-second y. of Artaxerxes the 5.14
of the seventh y. and the exaction 10.31
y. by y., to burn upon the altar 10.34
y. by y., to the house of the LORD; 10.35
thirty-second y. of Artaxerxes 13.06
in the third y. of his reign he Est 1.03
in the seventh y. of his reign, 2.16
in the twelfth y. of King Ahasuerus, 3.07
day of the same, y. by y., 9.21
at the time appointed every y., 9.27
rejoice among the days of the y., Job 3.06
Thou crownest the y. with thy Ps 65.11
In the y. that King Uzziah died I Is 6.01
In the y. that King Ahaz died came 14.28
In the y. that the commander in 20.01
"Within a y., according to the 21.16
Add y. to y.; let the feasts 29.01
more than a y. you will shudder, 32.10
a y. of recompense for the cause of 34.08
In the fourteenth y. of King 36.01
this y. eat what grows of itself, 37.30
in the second y. what springs of 37.30
then in the third y. sow and reap, 37.30
to proclaim the y. of the LORD's 61.02
and my y. of redemption has come. 63.04
in the thirteenth y. of his reign. Jer 1.02
end of the eleventh y. of Zedekiah, 1.03
the y. of their punishment. 11.23
not anxious in the y. of drought, 17.08
them in the y. of their punishment, 23.12
in the fourth y. of Jehoiakim the 25.01
was the first y. of Nebuchadrezzar 25.01
the thirteenth y. of Josiah the 25.03
In that same y., at the beginning 28.01
the fifth month of the fourth y., 28.01
This very y. you shall die, because 28.16
In that same y., in the seventh 28.17
in the tenth y. of Zedekiah king 32.01
the eighteenth y. of Nebuchadrezzar. 32.01
In the fourth y. of Jehoiakim the 36.01
In the fifth y. of Jehoiakim the 36.09
In the ninth y. of Zedekiah king of 39.01
in the eleventh y. of Zedekiah, 39.02
in the fourth y. of Jehoiakim the 45.01
in the fourth y. of Jehoiakim the 46.02
Moab in the y. of their punishment, 48.44
one y. and afterward a report in another y., 51.46
in the fourth y. of his reign. 51.59
And in the ninth y. of his reign, 52.04
the eleventh y. of King Zedekiah. 52.05
the nineteenth y. of King Nebuchadrezzar, 52.12
away captive: in the seventy y., 52.28
in the eighteenth y. of Nebuchadrezzar 52.29
twenty-third y. of Nebuchadrezzar, 52.30
thirty-seventh y. of the captivity 52.31
in the y. that he became king, 52.31
In the thirtieth y., in the fourth Eze 1.01
was the fifth y. of the exile of 1.02
I assign you, a day for each y. 4.06
In the sixth y., in the sixth month, 8.01
In the seventh y., in the fifth 20.01
In the ninth y., in the tenth month, 24.01
In the eleventh y., on the first 26.01
In the tenth y., in the tenth month, 29.01
In the twenty-seventh y., in the first month, 29.17
In the eleventh y., in the first 30.20
In the eleventh y., in the third 31.01
In the twelfth y., in the twelfth 32.01
In the twelfth y., in the first 32.17
In the twelfth y. of our exile, in 33.21
In the twenty-fifth y. of our exile, 40.01
at the beginning of the y., on the tenth 40.01
the fourteenth y. after the city 40.01
a lamb a y. old without blemish 46.13
shall be his to the y. of liberty; 46.17
In the third y. of the reign of Dan 1.01
until the first y. of King Cyrus. 1.21
In the second y. of the reign of 2.01
In the first y. of Belshazzar king 7.01
In the third y. of the reign of 8.01
In the first y. of Darius the son 9.01
in the first y. of his reign, I, 9.02
In the third y. of Cyrus king of 10.01
in the first y. of Darius the Mede, 11.01
offerings, with calves a y. old? Mic 6.06
In the second y. of Darius the king, Hag 1.01
In the second y. of Darius the king, 2.01
in the second y. of Darius, the word 2.10
in the second y. of Darius, the word Zec 1.01
in the second y. of Darius, the word 1.07
In the fourth y. of King Darius, the 7.01
shall go up y. after y. to worship 14.16
Jerusalem every y. at the feast of Lk 2.41
In the fifteenth y. of the reign of 3.01
the acceptable y. of the Lord. 4.19
this y. also, till I dig about it 13.08
bears fruit next y., well and good; 13.09
who was high priest that y., Jn 11.49
priest that y. he prophesied that 11.51
who was high priest that y. 18.13
For a whole y. they met with the Ac 11.26
And he stayed a y. and six months, 18.11

YEAR (cont.)
complete what a y. ago you began 2Co 8.10
has been ready since last y.; 9.02
priest goes, and he but once a y., Heb 9.07
continually offered y. after y., 10.01
is a reminder of sin y. after y. 10.03
and spend a y. there and trade and Jas 4.13
and the y., to kill a third of Rev 9.15

YEARLY
there is the y. feast of the LORD Ju 21.19
offer to the LORD the y. sacrifice, 1Sa 1.21
husband to offer the y. sacrifice. 2.19
for there is a y. sacrifice there 20.06
ourselves y. with the third part Neh 10.32
the Holy Place y. with blood not Heb 9.25

YEARN
how I y. for you all with the Php 1.08

YEARNED
for his heart y. for his brother, Gen 43.30
because her heart y. for her son, 1Ki 3.26

YEARNING
The y. of thy heart and thy compassion Is 63.15

YEARNS
My soul y. for thee in the night, my Is 26.09
Therefore my heart y. for him; Jer 31.20
"He y. jealously over the spirit Jas 4.05

YEAR'S
feast of ingathering at the y. end. Ex 34.22

YEARS
for seasons and for days and y., Gen 1.14
had lived a hundred and thirty y., 5.03
of Seth were eight hundred y.; 5.04
were nine hundred and thirty y.; 5.05
had lived a hundred and five y., 5.06
Enosh eight hundred and seven y., 5.07
were nine hundred and twelve y.; 5.08
When Enosh had lived ninety y., 5.09
Kenan eight hundred and fifteen y., 5.10
were nine hundred and five y.; 5.11
When Kenan had lived seventy y., 5.12
Mahalalel eight hundred and forty y., 5.13
Kenan were nine hundred and ten y.; 5.14
When Mahalalel had lived sixty-five y., 5.15
Jared eight hundred and thirty y., 5.16
eight hundred and ninety-five y.; 5.17
and sixty-two y. he became the 5.18
birth of Enoch eight hundred y., 5.19
were nine hundred and sixty-two y.; 5.20
When Enoch had lived sixty-five y., 5.21
of Methuselah three hundred y., 5.22
three hundred and sixty-five y. 5.23
a hundred and eighty-seven y., 5.25
seven hundred and eighty-two y., 5.26
nine hundred and sixty-nine y.; 5.27
lived a hundred and eighty-two y., 5.28
five hundred and ninety-five y., 5.30
seven hundred and seventy-seven y.; 5.31
After Noah was five hundred y. old, 5.32
shall be a hundred and twenty y. 6.03
Noah was six hundred y. old when 7.06
lived three hundred and fifty y. 9.28
were nine hundred and fifty y.; 9.29
When Shem was a hundred y. old, 11.10
Arpachshad two y. after the flood; 11.10
of Arpachshad five hundred y., 11.11
thirty-five y. he became the 11.12
Shelah four hundred and three y., 11.13
When Shelah had lived thirty y., 11.14
of Eber four hundred and three y., 11.15
When Eber had lived thirty-four y., 11.16
Peleg four hundred and thirty y., 11.17
When Peleg had lived thirty y., 11.18
of Reu two hundred and nine y., 11.19
When Reu had lived thirty-two y., 11.20
of Serug two hundred and seven y., 11.21
When Serug had lived thirty y., 11.22
the birth of Nahor two hundred y., 11.23
When Nahor had lived twenty-nine y., 11.24
of Terah a hundred and nineteen y., 11.25
When Terah had lived seventy y., 11.26
Terah were two hundred and five y.; 11.32
seventy-five y. old when he 12.04
Twelve y. they had served Chedorlaomer, 14.04
"Bring me a heifer three y. old, 15.09
years old, a she-goat three y. old, 15.09
a ram three y. old, a turtledove, and 15.09
be oppressed for four hundred y.; 15.13
had dwelt ten y. in the land of 16.03
Abram was eighty-six y. old when 16.16
was ninety-nine y. old the LORD 17.01
who is ninety y. old, bear a child?" 17.17
Abraham was ninety-nine y. old when 17.24
was thirteen y. old when he was 17.25
Abraham was a hundred y. old when 21.05
a hundred and twenty-seven y.; 23.01
these were the y. of the life of 23.01
was old, well advanced in y.; 24.01
the days of the y. of Abraham's 25.07
a hundred and seventy-five y. 25.07
old age, an old man and full of y., 25.08
(These are the y. of the life of 25.17
a hundred and thirty-seven y.; 25.17
and Isaac was forty y. old when he 25.20
Isaac was sixty y. old when she 25.26
When Esau was forty y. old, 26.34
serve you seven y. for your 29.18
So Jacob served seven y. for Rachel, 29.20
for serving me another seven y." 29.27
served Laban for another seven y. 29.30
These twenty y. I have been with 31.38
These twenty y. I have been in your 31.41
you fourteen y. for your two 31.41
and six y. for your flock, and you 31.41
Isaac were a hundred and eighty y. 35.28
Joseph, being seventeen y. old, 37.02
After two whole y., Pharaoh dreamed 41.01
The seven good cows are seven y., 41.26
the seven good ears are seven y.; 41.26
came up after them are seven y., 41.27
wind are also seven y. of famine. 41.27
There will come seven y. of great 41.29
will arise seven y. of famine, 41.30
during the seven plenteous y. 41.34
of these good y. that are coming, 41.35
the seven y. of famine which are 41.36
Joseph was thirty y. old when he 41.46
seven plenteous y. the earth 41.47
of the seven y. when there was 41.48
The seven y. of plenty that prevailed 41.53
and the seven y. of famine began to 41.54
has been in the land these two y.; 45.06
are yet five y. in which there 45.06
are yet five y. of famine to come; 45.11
the days of the y. of your life?" 47.08
"The days of the y. of my sojourning 47.09
are a hundred and thirty y.; 47.09
been the days of the y. of my life, 47.09
the days of the y. of the life of 47.09
in the land of Egypt seventeen y.; 47.28
the y. of his life, were a hundred 47.28
were a hundred and forty-seven y. 47.28
Joseph lived a hundred and ten y. 50.22
being a hundred and ten y. old; 50.26
the y. of the life of Levi being a Ex 6.16
a hundred and thirty-seven y. 6.16
the y. of the life of Kohath being 6.18
a hundred and thirty-three y. 6.18

YEARS (cont.)

the y. of the life of Amram being Ex 6.20
one hundred and thirty-seven y. 6.20
Now Moses was eighty y. old, 7.07
old, and Aaron eighty-three y. old, 7.07
was four hundred and thirty y. 12.40
end of four hundred and thirty y. 12.41
of Israel ate the manna forty y., 16.35
slave, he shall serve six y., 21.02
"For six y. you shall sow your land 23.10
from twenty y. old and upward, shall 30.14
from twenty y. old and upward, for 38.26
three y. it shall be forbidden to Lev 19.23
Six y. you shall sow your field, and 25.03
and six y. you shall prune your 25.03
"And you shall count seven weeks of y., 25.08
seven times seven y., 25.08
weeks of y. shall be to you forty-nine y. 25.08
the number of y. after the jubilee, 25.15
the number of y. for crops he 25.15
If the y. are many you shall 25.16
and if the y. are few you shall 25.16
bring forth fruit for three y. 25.21
let him reckon the y. since he sold 25.27
be according to the number of y.; 25.50
If there are still many y., 25.51
but a few y. until the year of 25.52
according to the y. of service due 25.52
from twenty y. old up to sixty y. old 27.03
is from five y. old up to twenty y. old, 27.05
from a month old up to five y. old, 27.06
person is sixty y. old and upward, 27.07
according to the y. that remain 27.18
from twenty y. old and upward, all Num 1.03
from twenty y. old and upward, 1.18
male from twenty y. old and upward, 1.20
male from twenty y. old and upward, 1.22
from twenty y. old and upward, all 1.24
from twenty y. old and upward, every 1.26
from twenty y. old and upward, every 1.28
from twenty y. old and upward, every 1.30
from twenty y. old and upward, every 1.32
from twenty y. old and upward, every 1.34
from twenty y. old and upward, every 1.36
from twenty y. old and upward, every 1.38
from twenty y. old and upward, every 1.40
from twenty y. old and upward, every 1.42
from twenty y. old and upward, every 1.45
from thirty y. old up to fifty y. old, 4.03
from thirty y. old up to fifty y. old, 4.23
from thirty y. old up to fifty y. old, 4.30
from thirty y. old up to fifty y. old, 4.35
from thirty y. old up to fifty y. old, 4.39
from thirty y. old up to fifty y. old, 4.43
from thirty y. old up to fifty y. old, 4.47
twenty-five y. old and upward they 8.24
age of fifty y. they shall withdraw 8.25
was built seven y. before Zoan in 13.22
from twenty y. old and upward, 14.29
shepherds in the wilderness forty y., 14.33
forty y., and you shall know my 14.34
from twenty y. old and upward, by 26.02
from twenty y. old and upward," as 26.04
from twenty y. old and upward, shall 32.11
wander in the wilderness forty y., 32.13
twenty-three y. old when he died 33.39
these forty y. the LORD your God Deu 2.07
brook Zered was thirty-eight y., 2.14
you these forty y. in the wilderness, 8.02
foot did not swell, these forty y. 8.04
of every three y. you shall bring 14.28
of every seven y. you shall grant 15.01
to you, he shall serve you six y., 15.12
servant he has served you six y. 15.18
led you forty y. in the wilderness; 29.05
hundred and twenty y. old this day; 31.02
them, "At the end of every seven y., 31.10
consider the y. of many generations; 32.07
and twenty y. old when he died; 34.07
walked forty y. in the wilderness, Jos 5.06
Now Joshua was old and advanced in y.; 13.01
"You are old and advanced in y., 13.01
I was forty y. old when Moses the 14.07
forty-five y. since the time that 14.10
I am this day eighty-five y. old. 14.10
was old and well advanced in y., 23.01
am now old and well advanced in y.; 23.02
being a hundred and ten y. old. 24.29
the age of one hundred and ten y. Ju 2.08
served Cushanrishathaim eight y. 3.08
So the land had rest forty y. 3.11
Eglon the king of Moab eighteen y. 3.14
the land had rest for eighty y. 3.30
of Israel cruelly for twenty y. 4.03
And the land had rest for forty y. 5.31
into the hand of Midian seven y. 6.01
bull, the second bull seven y. old, 6.25
had rest forty y. in the days of 8.28
Abimelech ruled over Israel three y. 9.22
And he judged Israel twenty-three y. 10.02
who judged Israel twenty-two y. 10.03
For eighteen y. they oppressed all 10.08
three hundred y., why did you not 11.26
Jephthah judged Israel six y. 12.07
And he judged Israel seven y. 12.09
and he judged Israel ten y. 12.11
and he judged Israel eight y. 12.14
of the Philistines for forty y. 13.01
days of the Philistines twenty y. 15.20
He had judged Israel twenty y. 16.31
They lived there about ten y.; Ru 1.04
ninety-eight y. old and his eyes 1Sa 4.15
He had judged Israel forty y. 4.18
some twenty y., and all the house 7.02
y. old when he began to reign; 13.01
and two y. over Israel. 13.01
was already old and advanced in y. 17.12
been with me now for days and y., 29.03
was forty y. old when he began to 2Sa 2.10
over Israel, and he reigned two y. 2.10
Judah was seven y. and six months. 2.11
He was five y. old when the news 4.04
David was thirty y. old when he 5.04
to reign, and he reigned forty y. 5.04
over Judah seven y. and six months; 5.05
Israel and Judah thirty-three y. 5.05
After two full y. Absalom had 13.23
to Geshur, and was there three y. 13.38
dwelt two full y. in Jerusalem, 14.28
the end of four y. Absalom said to 15.07
was a very aged man, eighty y. old; 19.32
"How many y. have I still to live, 19.34
I am this day eighty y. old; 19.35
in the days of David for three y., 21.01
"Shall three y. of famine come to 24.13
David was old and advanced in y.; 1Ki 1.01
reigned over Israel was forty y.; 2.11
he reigned seven y. in Hebron, 2.11
and thirty-three y. in Jerusalem. 2.11
end of three y. that two of 2.39
He was seven y. in building it. 6.38
building his own house thirteen y., 7.01
At the end of twenty y., in which 9.10
every three y. the fleet of ships 10.22
over all Israel was forty y. 11.42
Jeroboam reigned was twenty-two y.; 14.20
was forty-one y. old when he began 14.21
reigned seventeen y. in Jerusalem, 14.21
He reigned for three y. in Jerusalem. 15.02
reigned forty-one y. in Jerusalem. 15.10
and he reigned over Israel two y. 15.25
Tirzah, and reigned twenty-four y. 15.33
in Tirzah, and reigned two y. 16.08
Israel, and reigned for twelve y.; 16.23

YEARS (cont.)
six y. he reigned in Tirzah. 1Ki 16.23
Israel in Samaria twenty-two y. 16.29
be neither dew nor rain these y., 17.01
For three y. Syria and Israel 22.01
Jehoshaphat was thirty-five y. old 22.42
twenty-five y. in Jerusalem. 22.42
and he reigned two y. over Israel. 22.51
Samaria, and he reigned twelve y. 2Ki 3.01
come upon the land for seven y." 8.01
land of the Philistines seven y. 8.02
And at the end of the seven y., 8.03
He was thirty-two y. old when he 8.17
he reigned eight y. in Jerusalem. 8.17
Ahaziah was twenty-two y. old when 8.26
in Samaria was twenty-eight y. 10.36
and he remained with her six y., 11.03
Jehoash was seven y. old when he 11.21
he reigned forty y. in Jerusalem. 12.01
and he reigned seventeen y. 13.01
Samaria, and he reigned sixteen y. 13.10
He was twenty-five y. old when he 14.02
twenty-nine y. in Jerusalem. 14.02
lived fifteen y. after the death of 14.17
Azariah, who was sixteen y. old, 14.21
and he reigned forty-one y. 14.23
He was sixteen y. old when he began 15.02
reigned fifty-two y. in Jerusalem. 15.02
and he reigned ten y. in Samaria. 15.17
in Samaria, and he reigned two y. 15.23
in Samaria, and reigned twenty y. 15.27
He was twenty-five y. old when he 15.33
he reigned sixteen y. in Jerusalem. 15.33
Ahaz was twenty y. old when he 16.02
he reigned sixteen y. in Jerusalem. 16.02
Israel, and he reigned nine y. 17.01
and for three y. he besieged it. 17.05
He was twenty-five y. old when he 18.02
twenty-nine y. in Jerusalem. 18.02
and at the end of three y. he took it. 18.10
I will add fifteen y. to your life. 20.06
Manasseh was twelve y. old when he 21.01
reigned fifty-five y. in Jerusalem. 21.01
Amon was twenty-two y. old when he 21.19
and he reigned two y. in Jerusalem. 21.19
Josiah was eight y. old when he 22.01
reigned thirty-one y. in Jerusalem. 22.01
twenty-three y. old when he began 23.31
Jehoiakim was twenty-five y. old 23.36
he reigned eleven y. in Jerusalem. 23.36
became his servant three y.; 24.01
Jehoiachin was eighteen y. old when 24.08
Zedekiah was twenty-one y. old when 24.18
he reigned eleven y. in Jerusalem. 24.18
married when he was sixty y. old; 1Ch 2.21
for seven y. and six months. 3.04
he reigned thirty three y. in Jerusalem. 3.04
either three y. of famine; or three months 21.12
thirty y. old and upward, were numbered, 23.03
from twenty y. old and upward who 23.24
from twenty y. old and upward— 23.27
those below twenty y. of age, 27.23
reigned over Israel was forty y.; 29.27
he reigned seven y. in Hebron, 29.27
and thirty-three y. in Jerusalem. 29.27
At the end of twenty y., in which 2Ch 8.01
every three y. the ships of Tarshish 9.21
Jerusalem over all Israel forty y. 9.30
and for three y. they made Rehoboam 11.17
for three y. in the way of David 11.17
was forty-one y. old when he began 12.13
reigned seventeen y. in Jerusalem, 12.13
He reigned for three y. in Jerusalem. 13.02
days the land had rest for ten y. 14.01
He had no war in those y., for the LORD 14.06
After some y. he went down to Ahab 18.02
was thirty-five y. old when he 20.31
twenty-five y. in Jerusalem. 20.31
Jehoram was thirty-two y. old when 21.05
he reigned eight y. in Jerusalem. 21.05
of time, at the end of two y., 21.19
He was thirty-two y. old when he 21.20
he reigned eight y. in Jerusalem; 21.20
Ahaziah was forty-two y. old when 22.02
and he remained with them six y., 22.12
Joash was seven y. old when he 24.01
he reigned forty y. in Jerusalem; 24.01
and thirty y. old at his death. 24.15
Amaziah was twenty-five y. old when 25.01
twenty-nine y. in Jerusalem. 25.01
those twenty y. old and upward, 25.05
lived fifteen y. after the death 25.25
Uzziah, who was sixteen y. old, 26.01
Uzziah was sixteen y. old when he 26.03
reigned fifty-two y. in Jerusalem. 26.03
Jotham was twenty-five y. old when 27.01
he reigned sixteen y. in Jerusalem. 27.01
in the second and the third y. 27.05
He was twenty-five y. old when he 27.08
he reigned sixteen y. in Jerusalem. 27.08
Ahaz was twenty y. old when he 28.01
he reigned sixteen y. in Jerusalem. 28.01
when he was twenty-five y. old, 29.01
twenty-nine y. in Jerusalem. 29.01
from three y. old and upwards, all 31.16
from twenty y. old and upwards was 31.17
Manasseh was twelve y. old when he 33.01
reigned fifty-five y. in Jerusalem. 33.01
Amon was twenty-two y. old when he 33.21
and he reigned two y. in Jerusalem. 33.21
Josiah was eight y. old when he 34.01
reigned thirty-one y. in Jerusalem. 34.01
twenty-three y. old when he began 36.02
Jehoiakim was twenty-five y. old 36.05
he reigned eleven y. in Jerusalem. 36.05
Jehoiachin was eight y. old when he 36.09
Zedekiah was twenty-one y. old when 36.11
he reigned eleven y. in Jerusalem. 36.11
sabbath, to fulfill seventy y. 36.21
from twenty y. old and upward, to Ez 3.08
house that was built many y. ago, 5.11
twelve y., neither I nor my brethren Neh 5.14
Forty y. didst thou sustain them in 9.21
Many y. thou didst bear with them, 9.30
or thy y. as man's years, Job 10.05
of man, or thy years as man's y., 10.05
through all the y. that are laid 15.20
For when a few y. have come I shall 16.22
Buzite answered: "I am young in y., 32.06
speak, and many y. teach wisdom.' 32.07
and their y. in pleasantness. 36.11
number of his y. is unsearchable. 36.26
Job lived a hundred and forty y., 42.16
sorrow, and my y. with sighing; Ps 31.10
may his y. endure to all generations! 61.06
of old, I remember the y. long ago. 77.05
a breath, and their y. in terror. 78.33
For a thousand y. in thy sight are 90.04
our y. come to an end like a sigh. 90.09
The y. of our life are threescore 90.10
and as many y. as we have seen evil. 90.15
For forty y. I loathed that generation 95.10
thou whose y. endure throughout all 102.24
the same, and thy y. have no end. 102.27
of days and y. of life and abundant Pro 3.02
that the y. of your life may be 4.10
others and your y. to the merciless 5.09
and y. will be added to your life. 9.11
but the y. of the wicked will be 10.27
children, and lives many y., Ecc 6.03
that the days of his y. are many, 6.03
live a thousand y. twice told, 6.06
For if a man lives many y., 11.08
and the y. draw nigh, when you will 12.01

YEARS (cont.)

sixty-five y. Ephraim will be	Is 7.08
"In three y., like the y. of a hireling,	16.14
for three y. as a sign and a	20.03
according to the y. of a hireling,	21.16
will be forgotten for seventy y.,	23.15
At the end of seventy y., it will happen	23.15
At the end of seventy y., the LORD	23.17
I will add fifteen y. to your life.	38.05
of Sheol for the rest of my y.	38.10
child shall die a hundred y. old,	65.20
a hundred y. old shall be accursed.	65.20
"For twenty-three y., from the	Jer 25.03
the king of Babylon seventy y.	25.11
Then after seventy y. are completed,	25.12
Within two y. I will bring back to	28.03
of all the nations within two y."	28.11
When seventy y. are completed for	29.10
'At the end of six y. each of you	34.14
to you and has served you six y.;	34.14
Zedekiah was twenty-one y. old when	52.01
he reigned eleven y. in Jerusalem.	52.01
number of the y. of their punishment;	Eze 4.05
appointed time of your y. has come.	22.04
it shall be uninhabited forty y.	29.11
desolation forty y. among cities	29.12
end of forty y. I will gather the	29.13
in the latter y. you will go against the	38.08
prophesied for y. that I would	38.17
make fires of them for seven y.;	39.09
were to be educated for three y.,	Dan 1.05
being about sixty-two y. old.	5.31
the books the number of y. which,	9.02
of Jerusalem, namely, seventy y.	9.02
"Seventy weeks of y. are decreed	9.24
After some y. they shall make an	11.06
and for some y. he shall refrain	11.08
and after some y. he shall come on	11.13
through the y. of all generations.	Joe 2.02
to you the y. which the swarming	2.25
two y. before the earthquake.	Amo 1.01
led you forty y. in the wilderness,	2.10
the forty y. in the wilderness, O	5.25
In the midst of the y. renew it;	Hab 3.02
the midst of the y. make it known;	3.02
had indignation these seventy y.?'	Zec 1.12
as I have done for so many y.?"	7.03
the seventh, for these seventy y.,	7.05
days of old and as in former y.	Mal 3.04
who were two y. old or under,	Mt 2.16
for twelve y. came up behind him	9.20
had a flow of blood for twelve y.,	Mk 5.25
for she was twelve y. old, and immediately	5.42
and both were advanced in y.	Lk 1.07
man, and my wife is advanced in y."	1.18
husband seven y. from her virginity,	2.36
And when he was twelve y. old,	2.42
ministry, was about thirty y. of age,	3.23
shut up three y. and six months,	4.25
about twelve y. of age, and she was	8.42
for twelve y. and could not be	8.43
ample goods laid up for many y.;	12.19
these three y. I have come seeking	13.07
of infirmity for eighteen y.;	13.11
whom Satan bound for eighteen y.,	13.16
these many y. I have served you, and	15.29
taken forty-six y. to build this	Jn 2.20
had been ill for thirty-eight y.	5.05
him, "You are not yet fifty y. old,	8.57
performed was more than forty y. old.	Ac 4.22
and ill-treat them four hundred y.	7.06
"When he was forty y. old, it came	7.23
"Now when forty y. had passed,	7.30
and in the wilderness for forty y.	7.36
forty y. in the wilderness, O house	7.42
for eight y. and was paralyzed.	9.33
And for about forty y. he bore with	13.18
about four hundred and fifty y.	13.19
tribe of Benjamin, for forty y.	13.21
This continued for two y., so that all	19.10
that for three y. I did not cease	20.31
that for many y. you have been	24.10
Now after some y. I came to bring	24.17
But when two y. had elapsed, Felix	24.27
there two whole y. at his own	28.30
he was about a hundred y. old,	Rom 4.19
longed for many y. to come to you,	15.23
who fourteen y. ago was caught up	2Co 12.02
Then after three y. I went up to	Gal 1.18
Then after fourteen y. I went up	2.01
hundred and thirty y. afterward,	3.17
and months, and seasons, and y.!	4.10
widow who is under sixty y. of age,	1Ti 5.09
same, and thy y. will never end."	Heb 1.12
test and saw my works for forty y.	3.09
with whom was he provoked forty y.?	3.17
and for three y. and six months it	Jas 5.17
Lord one day is as a thousand y.,	1Pe 3.08
and a thousand y. as one day.	3.08
and bound him for a thousand y.,	Rev 20.02
till the thousand y. were ended.	20.03
reigned with Christ a thousand y.	20.04
until the thousand y. were ended.	20.05
shall reign with him a thousand y.	20.06
And when the thousand y. are ended,	20.07

YEAST

A little y. leavens the whole lump.	Gal 5.09

YELLOW

and the hair in it is y. and thin,	Lev 13.30
and there is in it no y. hair,	13.32
need not seek for the y. hair;	13.36

YES

"Y., I know that you have done this	Gen 20.06
y. and he shall be blessed."	27.33
"Y., your brother Benhadad." Then he said	1Ki 20.33
And he said, "Y., I know it; hold your	2Ki 2.03
And he answered, "Y., I know it;	2.05
"Y., what they are building—if a	Neh 4.03
y., if you cry out for insight and	Pro 2.03
What you say be simply "Y." or "No";	Mt 5.37
They said to him, "Y., Lord."	9.28
Y., I tell you, and more than a	11.09
They said to him, "Y."	13.51
She said, "Y., Lord, yet even the	15.27
He said, "Y."	17.25
And Jesus said to them, "Y.;	21.16
But she answered him, "Y., Lord;	Mk 7.28
Y., I tell you, and more than a	Lk 7.26
Y., I tell you, it shall be required	11.51
y., I tell you, fear him!	12.05
y., and even his own life, he cannot	14.26
Y., and besides all this, it is now	24.21
She said to him, "Y., Lord;	Jn 11.27
He said to him, "Y., Lord;	21.15
He said to him, "Y., Lord;	21.16
And she said, "Y., for so much."	Ac 5.08
And he said, "Y."	22.27
Gentiles also? Y., of Gentiles also,	Rom 3.29
y., who was raised from the dead,	8.34
ready to say Y. and No at once?	2Co 1.17
word to you has not been Y. and No.	1.18
Timothy and I, was not Y. and No;	1.19
but in him it is always Y.	1.19
of God find their Y. in him.	1.20
Y., to this day whenever Moses is	3.15
Y., and I shall rejoice.	Php 1.19
Y., brother, I want some benefit	Phm 1.20
but let your y. be y. and your no	Jas 5.12

YESTERDAY

to the meal, either y. or today?"	1Sa 20.27
You came only y., and shall I today	2Sa 15.20

YESTERDAY (cont.)

'As surely as I saw y. the blood of 2Ki 9.26
for we are but of y., and know Job 8.09
are but as y. when it is past, or Ps 90.04
"Y. at the seventh hour the fever Jn 4.52
me as you killed the Egyptian y.?' Ac 7.28
is the same y. and today and for Heb 13.08

YET

the field was y. in the earth and Gen 2.05
of the field had y. sprung up— 2.05
y. your desire shall be for your 3.16
of the Amorites is not y. complete." 15.16
Y. I have borne him a son in his 21.07
y. your father has cheated me and 31.07
and y. my life is preserved." 32.30
they hated him y. more for his 37.08
Y. again she bore a son, and she 38.05
Y. the chief butler did not remember 40.23
and there are y. five years in 45.06
for there are y. five years of 45.11
y. his bow remained unmoved, his 49.24
was burning, y. it was not consumed. Ex 3.02
y. they say to us, 'Make bricks!' 5.16
y. you shall deliver the same 5.18
and behold, you have not y. obeyed." 7.16
that you do not y. fear the LORD 9.30
he sinned y. again, and hardened his 9.34
do you not y. understand that Egypt 10.07
"Y. one plague more I will bring 11.01
and y. no harm follows, the one who 21.22
Y. thou hast said, 'I know you by 33.12
y. does not speak, he shall bear his Lev 5.01
y. he is guilty and shall bear his 5.17
and y. such things as these have 10.19
Y. among the winged insects that go 11.21
while her sister is y. alive. 18.18
man and not y. ransomed or given 19.20
y. no outsider shall eat of it. 22.13
Y. for all that, when they are in 26.44
y. refrains from keeping the Num 9.13
While the meat was y. between their 11.33
Y. the people who dwell in the land 13.28
and y. have put me to the proof 14.22
"Y. you would not go up, but rebelled Deu 1.26
Y. in spite of this word you did 1.32
y. the LORD set his heart in love 10.15
for you have not as y. come to the 12.09
Y. of those that chew the cud or 14.07
And y. these are the tokens of my 22.17
while I am y. alive with you, today 31.27
Y. there shall be a space between Jos 3.04
y. all the people that were born on 5.05
there remains y. very much land to 13.01
This is the land that y. remains: 13.02
Y. the people of Israel did not 13.13
y. I wholly followed the LORD my 14.08
Y. the sons of Manasseh could not 17.12
y. all the Canaanites who dwell in 17.16
inheritance had not y. been apportioned. 18.02
from which even y. we have not 22.17
And y. they did not listen to their Ju 2.17
were with him, faint y. pursuing. 8.04
Y. you have forsaken me and served 10.13
"Shall we y. again go out to battle 20.28
Y. we cannot give them wives of our 21.18
Have I y. sons in my womb that they Ru 1.11
y. there is a kinsman nearer than I. 3.12
the lamp of God had not y. gone out, 1Sa 3.03
Now Samuel did not y. know the LORD, 3.07
LORD had not y. been revealed to 3.07
Y. his sons did not walk in his 8.03
y. do not turn aside from following 12.20
y. honor me now before the elders 15.30
"There remains y. the youngest, 16.11
Y. Saul did not say anything that 20.26
Go, make y. more sure; know and see 23.22
Y. the men were very good to us, and 25.15
and y. my life still lingers.' 2Sa 1.09
and y. you charge me today with a 3.08
to eat bread while it was y. day; 3.35
And the Philistines came up y. again, 5.22
make myself y. more contemptible 6.22
And y. this was a small thing in 7.19
while the child was y. alive, 12.18
no house had y. been built for the 1Ki 3.02
Y. have regard to the prayer of thy 8.28
y. if they lay it to heart in the 8.47
y. for the sake of David your 11.12
Hadad being y. a little child. 11.17
Y. to his son I will give one tribe, 11.36
his father while he was y. alive, 12.06
and y. you have not been like my 14.08
Y. I will leave seven thousand in 19.18
"There is y. one man by whom we may 22.08
y. the high places were not taken 22.43
y., if you see me as I am being 2Ki 2.10
Y. the LORD would not destroy Judah, 8.19
y. not like David his father; 14.03
y. not as the kings of Israel who 17.02
Y. the LORD warned Israel and Judah 17.13
y. the birthright belonged to 1Ch 5.02
(Y. he did not help them, for the 12.19
And the Philistines y. again made a 14.13
y. wrath came upon Israel for 27.24
Y. the LORD God of Israel chose me 28.04
Y. have regard to the prayer of thy 2Ch 6.19
y. if they lay it to heart in the 6.37
his father while he was y. alive, 10.06
Y. Jeroboam the son of Nebat, a 13.06
Y. because you relied on the LORD, 16.08
y. even in his disease he did not 16.12
"There is y. one man by whom we may 18.07
people had not y. set their hearts 20.33
Y. the LORD would not destroy the 21.07
y. he sent prophets among them to 24.19
y. not with a blameless heart. 25.02
he became y. more faithless to the 28.22
y. they ate the passover otherwise 30.18
while he was y. a boy, he began to 34.03
temple of the LORD was not y. laid. Ez 3.06
building, and it is not y. finished.' 5.16
y. our God has not forsaken us in 9.09
and I had not y. told the Jews, the Neh 2.16
y. we are forcing our sons and our 5.05
y. with all this I did not demand 5.18
y. when they turned and cried to 9.28
y. they acted presumptuously and 9.29
y. they would not give ear. 9.30
y. thou hast been just in all that 9.33
y. our God turned the curse into a 13.02
Y. you bring more wrath upon Israel 13.18
Y. all this does me no good, so long Est 5.13
While they were y. talking with him, 6.14
While he was y. speaking, there came Job 1.16
While he was y. speaking, there came 1.17
While he was y. speaking, there came 1.18
Y. who can keep from speaking? 4.02
While y. in flower and not cut down, 8.12
He will y. fill your mouth with 8.21
y. thou wilt plunge me into a pit, 9.31
Y. these things thou didst hide in 10.13
y. I will defend my ways to his 13.15
y. at the scent of water it will 14.09
Y. the righteous holds to his way, 17.09
y. his food is turned in his 20.14
Y. he filled their houses with good 22.18
y. God pays no attention to their 24.12
Y. God prolongs the life of the 24.22
when the Almighty was y. with me, 29.05
"Y. does not one in a heap of ruins 30.24
for I have y. something to say on 36.02
y. she has no fear; 39.16

YET (cont.)
Y. thou hast made him little less Ps 8.05
y. their voice goes out through all 19.04
Y. thou art holy, enthroned on the 22.03
Y. thou art he who took me from the 22.09
deliverance to a people y. unborn, 22.31
against me, y. I will be confident. 27.03
Y. a little while, and the wicked 37.10
y. I have not seen the righteous 37.25
Y. thou hast cast us off and abased 44.09
y. war was in his heart; his words 55.21
y. they were drawn swords. 55.21
y. thou hast brought us forth to a 66.12
will praise thee y. more and more. 71.14
Y. God my King is from of old, 74.12
y. thy footprints were unseen. 77.19
the children y. unborn, and arise 78.06
Y. they sinned still more against 78.17
Y. he commanded the skies above, and 78.23
Y. he, being compassionate, forgave 78.38
Y. they tested and rebelled against 78.56
y. their span is but toil and 90.10
that a people y. unborn may praise 102.18
Y. he saved them for his name's sake, 106.08
y. I have not forgotten thy statutes. 119.83
y. I do not forget thy precepts. 119.141
y. they have not prevailed against 129.02
when as y. there was none of them. 139.16
y. grows all the richer; Pro 11.24
pretends to be rich, y. has nothing; 13.07
to be poor, y. has great wealth. 13.07
y. his folly will not depart from 27.22
y. stiffens his neck will suddenly 29.01
y. they provide their food in the 30.25
y. they make their homes in the 30.26
y. all of them march in rank; 30.27
y. it is in kings' palaces. 30.28
while it is y. night and provides 31.15
of later things y. to happen among Ecc 1.11
and y. I perceived that one fate 2.14
Y. he will be master of all for 2.19
y. so that he cannot find out what 3.11
both is he who has not y. been, 4.03
y. there is no end to all his toil, 4.08
Y. those who come later will not 4.16
and there are y. higher ones over 5.08
y. God does not give him power to 6.02
y. it finds rest rather than he. 6.05
y. enjoy no good—do not all go to 6.06
y. his appetite is not satisfied. 6.07
y. know that it will be well with 8.12
Y. no one remembered that poor man. 9.15
extend his hand y. a second time Is 11.11
y. I will bring upon Dibon even 15.09
y. the harvest will flee away in a 17.11
is repose"; y. they would not hear. 28.12
Y. I will distress Ariel, and there 29.02
Is it not y. a very little while 29.17
y. your Teacher will not hide 30.20
And y. he is wise and brings 31.02
y. have eyes, who are deaf, y. have ears! 43.08
"Y. you did not call upon me, O 43.22
let them tell us what is y. to be. 44.07
ancient times things not y. done, 46.10
y. surely my right is with the LORD, 49.04
may forget, y. I will not forget you. 49.15
bereavement will y. say in your 49.20
y. trusts in the name of the LORD 50.10
y. we esteemed him stricken, smitten 53.04
y. he opened not his mouth; 53.07
Y. it was the will of the LORD to 53.10
y. he bore the sin of many, and made 53.12
I will gather y. others to him 56.08
Y. they seek me daily, and delight 58.02
Y., O LORD, thou art our Father; 64.08
while they are y. speaking I will 65.24
Y. I planted you a choice vine, Jer 2.21
Y. my people have forgotten me days 2.32
Y. in spite of all these things 2.34
y. you have a harlot's brow, you 3.03
y. her false sister Judah did not 3.08
Y. for all this her false sister 3.10
y. I will not make a full end. 4.27
LORD lives," y. they swear falsely. 5.02
y. they did not listen to me, or 7.26
circumcised but y. uncircumcised— 9.25
Y. they did not obey or incline 11.08
y. I would plead my case before 12.01
Y. thou, O LORD, art in the midst of 14.09
y. my heart would not turn toward 15.01
sun went down while it was y. day; 15.09
y. all of them curse me. 15.10
Y. they did not listen or incline 17.23
Y. they have dug a pit for my life. 18.20
Y., thou, O LORD, knowest all their 18.23
y. surely I will make you a desert, 22.06
right hand, y. I would tear you off 22.24
not send the prophets, y. they ran; 23.21
speak to them, y. they prophesied. 23.21
Y. you have not listened to me, says 25.07
Y. hear now this word which I speak 28.07
y. he shall be saved out of it. 30.07
Y. thou, O Lord GOD, hast said to me, 32.25
Y. hear the word of the LORD, O 34.04
Y. neither the king, nor any of his 36.24
for he had not y. been put in 37.04
Y. I persistently sent to you all 44.04
Y. I will restore the fortunes of 48.47
y. a little while and the time of 51.33
y. destroyers would come from me 51.53
in the dust—there may y. be hope; Lam 3.29
with you what I have never y. done, Eze 5.09
"Y. I will leave some of you alive. 6.08
y. I have been a sanctuary to them 11.16
y. he shall not see it; and he shall 12.13
and y. they expect him to fulfil 13.06
and y. comes to the prophet, I the LORD 14.04
and y. comes to a prophet to inquire 14.07
Y., if there should be left in it 14.22
the fire shall y. consume them; 15.07
y. you were naked and bare. 16.07
Y. you were not like a harlot, 16.31
Y. you were not content to walk in 16.47
y. I will remember my covenant with 16.60
break the covenant and y. escape? 17.15
his hand y. did all these 17.18
"Y. you say, 'Why should not the son 18.19
"Y. you say, 'The way of the Lord is 18.25
Y. the house of Israel says, 'The 18.29
y. she was more corrupt than she in 23.11
Y. she increased her harlotry, 23.19
y. you shall not mourn or weep nor 24.16
y. you are but a man, and no god, 28.02
y. neither he nor his army got 29.18
y. if he trusts in his righteousness 33.13
y. if he turns from his sin and 33.14
"Y. your people say, 'The way of the 33.17
Y. you say, 'The way of the Lord is 33.20
y. he got possession of the land; 33.24
and y. they had to go out of his 36.20
Y. I will appoint them to keep 44.14
and y. a third kingdom of bronze, Dan 2.39
y. we have not entreated the favor 9.13
the vision is for days y. to come." 10.14
for the end is y. to be at the time 11.27
for it is y. for the time appointed. 11.35
y. he shall come to his end, with 11.45
for y. a little while, and I will Hos 1.04
Y. the number of the people of 1.10
Y. let no one contend, and let none 4.04
y. they do not return to the LORD 7.10
y. they devise evil against me. 7.15
y. a fowler's snare is on all his 9.08
Y. it was I who taught Ephraim to 11.03

YET (cont.)

"Y. even now," says the LORD, "return Joe 2.12
"Y. I destroyed the Amorite before Amo 2.09
y. you did not return to me," says 4.06
when there were y. three months to 4.07
y. you did not return to me," says 4.08
y. you did not return to me," says 4.09
y. you did not return to me," says 4.10
y. you did not return to me," says 4.11
y. thou didst bring up my life from Jon 2.06
"Y. forty days, and Nineveh shall be 3.04
God may y. repent and turn from his 3.09
I said when I was y. in my country? 4.02
y. they lean upon the LORD and say, Mic 3.11
Y. she was carried away, she went Nah 3.10
y. I will rejoice in the LORD, I Hab 3.18
to the LORD and y. swear by Milcom; Zep 1.05
time has not y. come to rebuild Hag 1.02
Y. now take courage, O Zerubbabel, 2.04
y. you did not return to me, says 2.17
Is the seed y. in the barn? 2.19
Peoples shall y. come, even the Zec 8.20
y. in far countries they shall 10.09
says the LORD, "Y. I have loved Jacob Mal 1.02
and y. sacrifices to the Lord what 1.14
Y. you say, "How have we wearied him?" 2.17
Y. you are robbing me. But you say, 3.08
Y. you say, 'How have we spoken 3.13
and y. your heavenly Father feeds Mt 6.26
y. I tell you, even Solomon in all 6.29
y. he who is least in the kingdom 11.11
Y. wisdom is justified by her 11.19
y. he has no root in himself, but 13.21
y. even the dogs eat the crumbs 15.27
Do you not y. perceive? Do you not 16.09
take place, but the end is not y. 24.06
y. when it is sown it grows up and Mk 4.32
and y. you say, 'Who touched me?' 5.31
and y. he heard him gladly. 6.20
know it; y. he could not be hid. 7.24
y. even the dogs under the table 7.28
Do you not y. perceive or understand? 8.17
to them, "Do you not y. understand?" 8.21
take place, but the end is not y. 13.07
y. not what I will, but what thou 14.36
Y. not even so did their testimony 14.59
y. he who is least in the kingdom Lk 7.28
Y. wisdom is justified by all her 7.35
y. because of his importunity he 11.08
nor barn, and y. God feeds them. 12.24
y. I tell you, even Solomon in all 12.27
the other is y. a great way off, he 14.32
but while he was y. at a distance, 15.20
y. you never gave me a kid, that I 15.29
y. because this widow bothers me, I 18.05
on which no one has ever y. sat; 19.30
And he sent y. a third; 20.12
where no one had ever y. been laid. 23.53
y. the world knew him not. Jn 1.10
My hour has not y. come." 2.04
and y. you do not understand this? 3.10
For John had not y. been put in 3.24
y. no one receives his testimony; 3.32
'There are y. four months, then 4.35
y. you refuse to come to me that 5.40
and Jesus had not y. come to them. 6.17
have seen me and y. do not believe. 6.36
to them, "My time has not y. come, 7.06
for my time has not y. fully come." 7.08
Y. for fear of the Jews no one 7.13
Y. none of you keeps the law. 7.19
Y. we know where this man comes 7.27
because his hour had not y. come. 7.30
Y. many of the people believed in 7.31
for as y. the Spirit had not been 7.39
because Jesus was not y. glorified. 7.39
Y. even if I do judge, my judgment 8.16
because his hour had not y. come. 8.20
y. you seek to kill me, because my 8.37
Y. I do not seek my own glory; 8.50
"You are not y. fifty years old, and 8.57
comes from, and y. he opened my eyes. 9.30
though he die, y. shall he live, 11.25
Now Jesus had not y. come to the 11.30
y. they did not believe in him; 12.37
y. a little while I am with you. 13.33
and y. you do not know me, Philip? 14.09
Y. a little while, and the world 14.19
y. none of you asks me, 'Where are 16.05
"I have y. many things to say to 16.12
y. I am not alone, for the Father is 16.32
for as y. they did not know the 20.09
for I have not y. ascended to the 20.17
who have not seen and y. believe." 20.29
y. the disciples did not know that 21.04
y. Jesus did not say to him that he 21.23
y. here you have filled Jerusalem Ac 5.28
y. he gave him no inheritance in it, 7.05
Y. the Most High does not dwell in 7.48
for it had not y. fallen on any of 8.16
y. they asked Pilate to have him 13.28
y. he did not leave himself without 14.17
Y. he is not far from each one of 17.27
and y. contrary to the law you 23.03
y. I was delivered prisoner from 28.17
such things and y. do them yourself, Rom 2.03
While we were y. helpless, at the 5.06
while we were y. sinners Christ 5.08
Y. death reigned from Adam to Moses, 5.14
Y., if it had not been for the law, 7.07
though they were not y. born and 9.11
Y. among the mature we do impart 1Co 2.06
and even y. you are not ready, 3.02
Y. those who marry will have 7.28
he does not y. know as he ought to 8.02
y. for us there is one God, the 8.06
there are many parts, y. one body. 12.20
as impostors, and y. are true; 2Co 6.08
as unknown, and y. well known; 6.09
as punished, and y. not killed; 6.09
as sorrowful, y. always rejoicing; 6.10
as poor, y. making many rich; 6.10
and y. possessing everything. 6.10
y. for your sake he became poor, so 8.09
y. who know that a man is not Gal 2.16
Y. which I shall choose I cannot Php 1.22
Y. it was kind of you to share my 4.14
y. I am with you in spirit, rejoicing Col 2.05
Y. woman will be saved through 1Ti 2.15
y. from them all the Lord rescued 2Ti 3.11
y. for love's sake I prefer to Phm 1.09
we do not y. see everything in Heb 2.08
Y. Jesus has been counted worthy of 3.03
that heard and y. were rebellious? 3.16
as we are, y. without sinning. 4.15
y. in your case, beloved, we feel 6.09
sanctuary is not y. opened as long 9.08
"For y. a little while, and the 10.37
God concerning events as y. unseen, 11.07
you have not y. resisted to the 12.04
"Y. once more I will shake not only 12.26
This phrase, "Y. once more," indicates 12.27
y. mercy triumphs over judgment. Jas 2.13
y. without using your freedom as a 1Pe 2.16
y. do it with gentleness and 3.15
y. if one suffers as a Christian, 4.16
Y. I am writing you a new commandment, 1Jn 2.08
it does not y. appear what we shall 3.02
y. closes his heart against him, how 3.17
Y. in like manner these men in Jud 1.08
Y. this you have, you hate the works Rev 2.06
Y. you have still a few names in 3.04
and y. you have kept my word and 3.08
wounded by the sword and y. lived; 13.14

YET (cont.)
one is, the other has not y. come, Rev 17.10
who have not y. received royal 17.12

YIELD
shall no longer y. to you its Gen 4.12
and he shall y. royal dainties. 49.20
sow your land and gather in its y.; Ex 23.10
that they may y. more richly for Lev 19.25
land all its y. shall be for food. 25.07
The land will y. its fruit, and you 25.19
and the land shall y. its increase, 26.04
of the field shall y. their fruit. 26.04
land shall not y. its increase, 26.20
the land shall not y. their fruit. 26.20
before their eyes to y. its water; Num 20.08
and the land y. no fruit, and you Deu 11.17
you shall not y. to him or listen 13.08
tithe all the y. of your seed, 14.22
lest the whole y. be forfeited to 22.09
sown and the y. of the vineyard. 22.09
and the rich y. of the months, 33.14
but y. yourselves to the LORD, and 2Ch 30.08
storehouses also for the y. of grain, 32.28
And its rich y. goes to the kings Neh 9.37
have eaten its y. without payment, Job 31.39
For the mountains y. food for him 40.20
and our land will y. its increase. Ps 85.12
vineyards, and get a fruitful y. 107.37
and my y. than choice silver. Pro 8.19
is satisfied by the y. of his lips. 18.20
and he looked for it to y. grapes, Is 5.02
when I looked for it to y. grapes, 5.04
grapes, why did it y. wild grapes? 5.04
of vineyard shall y. but one bath, 5.10
of seed shall y. but an ephah. 5.10
of the field shall y. their fruit, Eze 34.27
the earth shall y. its increase, 34.27
and y. your fruit to my people 36.08
has no heads, it shall y. no meal; Hos 8.07
if it were to y., aliens would 8.07
tree and vine give their full y. Joe 2.22
fail and the fields y. no good, Hab 3.17
the olive tree still y. nothing? Hag 2.19
the vine shall y. its fruit, Zec 8.12
But do not y. to them; Ac 23.21
Do not y. your members to sin as Rom 6.13
but y. yourselves to God as men who 6.13
that if you y. yourselves to any 6.16
so now y. your members to righteousness 6.19
to them we did not y. submission Gal 2.05
y. olives, or a grapevine figs? Jas 3.12
No more can salt water y. fresh. 3.12

YIELDED
The earth has y. its increase; Ps 67.06
grapes, but it y. wild grapes. Is 5.02
and y. up their bodies rather than Dan 3.28
a loud voice and y. up his spirit. Mt 27.50
and choked it, and it y. no grain. Mk 4.07
and grew, and y. a hundredfold. Lk 8.08
as you once y. your members to Rom 6.19

YIELDING
plants y. seed, and fruit trees Gen 1.11
plants y. seed according to their 1.12
you every plant y. seed which is 1.29
like beds of spices, y. fragrance. Sol 5.13
increasing and y. thirtyfold and Mk 4.08
y. its fruit each month; and the leaves Rev 22.02

YIELDS
eat what it y. out of the field. Lev 25.12
that y. its fruit in its season, and Ps 1.03
a luxuriant vine that y. its fruit. Hos 10.01
and y., in one case a hundredfold, Mt 13.23
later it y. the peaceful fruit of Heb 12.11

YIRON
Y., Migdalel, Horem, Bethanath, and Jos 19.38

YOKE
shall break his y. from your neck." Gen 27.40
bars of your y. and made you walk Lev 26.13
and upon which a y. has never come. Num 19.02
and which has not pulled in the y. Deu 21.03
he will put a y. of iron upon your 28.48
which there has never come a y., 1Sa 6.07
and y. the cows to the cart, but 6.07
He took a y. of oxen, and cut them 11.07
"Your father made our y. heavy. 1Ki 12.04
father and his heavy y. upon us, 12.04
'Lighten the y. that your father 12.09
'Your father made our y. heavy, 12.10
my father laid upon you a heavy y., 12.11
I will add to your y. My father 12.11
"My father made your y. heavy, 12.14
heavy, but I will add to your y.; 12.14
with twelve y. of oxen before him, 19.19
and took the y. of oxen, and slew 19.21
"Your father made our y. heavy. 2Ch 10.04
father and his heavy y. upon us, 10.04
'Lighten the y. that your father 10.09
'Your father made our y. heavy, 10.10
my father laid upon you a heavy y., 10.11
I will add to your y. My father 10.11
"My father made your y. heavy, 10.14
five hundred y. of oxen, and five Job 1.03
a thousand y. of oxen, and a thousand 42.12
For the y. of his burden, and the Is 9.04
and his y. will be destroyed from 10.27
and his y. shall depart from them, 14.25
you made your y. exceedingly heavy. 47.06
to undo the thongs of the y., 58.06
go free, and to break every y.? 58.06
away from the midst of you the y., 58.09
you broke your y. and burst your Jer 2.20
they all alike had broken the y., 5.05
neck under the y. of the king of 27.08
neck under the y. of the king of 27.11
necks under the y. of the king of 27.12
have broken the y. of the king of 28.02
will break the y. of the king of 28.04
I break the y. of Nebuchadnezzar 28.11
nations an iron y. of servitude to 28.14
will break the y. from off their 30.08
transgressions were bound into a y.; Lam 1.14
that he bear the y. in his youth. 3.27
With a y. on our necks we are hard 5.05
when I break the bars of their y., Eze 34.27
but I will put Ephraim to the y., Hos 10.11
one who eases the y. on their jaws, 11.04
so they are appointed to the y., 11.07
will break his y. from off you and Nah 1.13
Take my y. upon you, and learn from Mt 11.29
For my y. is easy, and my burden is 11.30
'I have bought five y. of oxen, Lk 14.19
by putting a y. upon the neck of Ac 15.10
submit again to a y. of slavery. Gal 5.01
are under the y. of slavery regard 1Ti 6.01

YOKE-BARS
to me: "Make yourself thongs and y., Jer 27.02
took the y. from the neck of Jeremiah 28.10
had broken the y. from off the 28.12

YOKED
So Israel y. himself to Baal of Num 25.03
men who have y. themselves to Baal 25.05
milch cows and y. them to the cart, 1Sa 6.10

YOKEFELLOW
true y., help these women, for they have Php 4.03

YOKES
sledges and the y. of the oxen for 2Sa 24.22
flesh with the y. of the oxen, 1Ki 19.21

YON
y. Sinai before the LORD, the God of Ju 5.05
y. Sinai quaked at the presence of Ps 68.08

YONDER
Behold, y. city is near enough to Gen 19.20
and the lad will go y. and worship, 22.05
to the servant, "Who is the man y., 24.65
to them, "Go up into the Negeb y., Num 13.17
offering, while I meet the LORD y." 23.15
the Philistine garrison on y. side." 1Sa 14.01
and remain beside y. stone heap. 20.19
servant, "Look, y. is the Shunammite; 2Ki 4.25
"What is y. monument that I see?" 23.17
Y. is the sea, great and wide, which Ps 104.25
mountain, 'Move hence to y. place,' Mt 17.20
"Sit here, while I go y. and pray." 26.36

YOUNG
wounding me, a y. man for striking me. Gen 4.23
but what the y. men have eaten, 14.24
old, a turtledove, and a y. pigeon. 15.09
both y. and old, all the people to 19.04
took two of his y. men with him, 22.03
Then Abraham said to his y. men, 22.05
So Abraham returned to his y. men, 22.19
let the y. woman who comes out to 24.43
And the y. man did not delay to do 34.19
A y. Hebrew was there with us, a 41.12
and a y. brother, the child of his 44.20
"We will go with our y. and our old; Ex 10.09
None shall cast her y. or be barren 23.26
And he sent y. men of the people of 24.05
Take one y. bull and two rams 29.01
a y. man, did not depart from the 33.11
of turtledoves or of y. pigeons. Lev 1.14
has committed a y. bull without 4.03
shall offer a y. bull for a sin 4.14
two turtledoves or two y. pigeons, 5.07
two turtledoves or two y. pigeons, 5.11
and a y. pigeon or a turtledove for 12.06
two turtledoves or two y. pigeons, 12.08
also two turtledoves or two y. pigeons, 14.22
turtledoves or y. pigeons such as 14.30
two turtledoves or two y. pigeons, 15.14
two turtledoves or two y. pigeons, 15.29
with a y. bull for a sin offering 16.03
both her and her y. in one day. 22.28
and one y. bull, and two rams; 23.18
turtledoves or two y. pigeons to Num 6.10
one y. bull, one ram, one male lamb a 7.15
one y. bull, one ram, one male lamb a 7.21
one y. bull, one ram, one male lamb a 7.27
one y. bull, one ram, one male lamb a 7.33
one y. bull, one ram, one male lamb a 7.39
one y. bull, one ram, one male lamb a 7.45
one y. bull, one ram, one male lamb a 7.51
one y. bull, one ram, one male lamb a 7.57
one y. bull, one ram, one male lamb a 7.63
one y. bull, one ram, one male lamb a 7.69
one y. bull, one ram, one male lamb a 7.75
one y. bull, one ram, one male lamb a 7.81
Then let them take a y. bull and 8.08
take another y. bull for a sin 8.08
And a y. man ran and told Moses, 11.27
shall offer one y. bull for a 15.24
two y. bulls, one ram, seven male 28.11
two y. bulls, one ram, and seven male 28.19
two y. bulls, one ram, seven male 28.27
one y. bull, one ram, seven male 29.02
one y. bull, one ram, seven male 29.08
thirteen y. bulls, two rams, fourteen 29.13
"On the second day twelve y. bulls, 29.17
But all the y. girls who have not 31.18
cattle and the y. of your flock, Deu 7.13
with y. ones or eggs and the mother 22.06
upon the y. or upon the eggs, you 22.06
not take the mother with the y.; 22.06
but the y. you may take to yourself; 22.07
father of the y. woman and her 22.15
father of the y. woman shall say 22.16
them to the father of the y. woman, 22.19
were not found in the y. woman, 22.20
bring out the y. woman to the door 22.21
the y. woman because she did not 22.24
a man meets a y. woman who is 22.25
But to the y. woman you shall do 22.26
in the y. woman there is no offense 22.26
the betrothed y. woman cried for 22.27
father of the y. woman fifty shekels 22.29
cattle, and the y. of your flock. 28.04
cattle, and the y. of your flock. 28.18
the old or show favor to the y., 28.50
cattle or the y. of your flock, 28.51
nest, that flutters over its y., 32.11
destroying both y. man and virgin, 32.25
y. and old, oxen, sheep, and asses, Jos 6.21
So the y. men who had been spies 6.23
And he caught a y. man of Succoth, Ju 8.14
hastily to the y. man his armor-bearer, 9.54
And his y. man thrust him through, 9.54
And behold, a y. lion roared against 14.05
for so the y. men used to do. 14.10
Now there was a y. man of Bethlehem 17.07
and the y. man became to him like 17.11
and the y. man became his priest, 17.12
recognized the voice of the y. Levite; 18.03
came to the house of the y. Levite, 18.15
maidservant and the y. man with 19.19
four hundred y. virgins who had 21.12
not charged the y. men not to molest Ru 2.09
drink what the y. men have drawn." 2.09
glean, Boaz instructed his y. men, 2.15
you have not gone after y. men, 3.10
will give you by this y. woman, 4.12
at Shiloh; and the child was y. 1Sa 1.24
Thus the sin of the y. men was very 2.17
both y. and old, so that tumors 5.09
name was Saul, a handsome y. man. 9.02
they met y. maidens coming out to 9.11
said to the y. man who bore his 14.01
said to the y. man who bore his 14.06
One of the y. men answered, "Behold, 16.18
to him, "Whose son are you, y. man?" 17.58
with the y. men for such and such 21.02
if only the y. men have kept 21.04
the vessels of the y. men are holy, 21.05
ten y. men; and David said to the y. men, 25.05
Ask your y. men, and they will tell 25.08
Therefore let my y. men find favor 25.08
When David's y. men came, they said 25.09
So David's y. men turned away, and 25.12
But one of the y. men told Abigail, 25.14
And she said to her y. men, "Go on before 25.19
did not see the y. men of my lord, 25.25
be given to the y. men who follow 25.27
Let one of the y. men come over and 26.22
"I am a y. man of Egypt, servant to 30.13
escaped, except four hundred y. men, 30.17
said to the y. man who told him, 2Sa 1.05
And the y. man who told him said, 1.06
said to the y. man who told him, 1.13
called one of the y. men and said, 1.15
"Let the y. men arise and play 2.14
left, and seize one of the y. men, 2.21
And David commanded his y. men, 4.12
And Mephibosheth had a y. son, 9.12
He called the y. man who served him 13.17
killed all the y. men the king's 13.32
And the y. man who kept the watch 13.34

YOUNG (cont.)

go, bring back the y. man Absalom." 2Sa 14.21
summer fruit for the y. men to eat, 16.02
my sake with the y. man Absalom." 18.05
my sake protect the y. man Absalom.' 18.12
And ten y. men, Joab's armor-bearers, 18.15
"Is it well with the y. man Absalom?" 18.29
"Is it well with the y. man Absalom?" 18.32
you for evil, be like that y. man." 18.32
"Let a y. maiden be sought for my 1Ki 1.02
saw that the y. man was industrious 11.28
with the y. men who had grown up 12.08
And the y. men who had grown up 12.10
to the counsel of the y. men, 12.14
of Ephraim two y. men of the sons 2Ki 5.22
LORD opened the eyes of the y. man, 6.17
will slay their y. men with the 8.12
So the y. man, the prophet, went to 9.04
and the y. man poured the oil on 9.06
Zadok, a y. man mighty in valor, and 1Ch 12.28
my son is y. and inexperienced, and 22.05
is y. and inexperienced, and the 29.01
with the y. men who had grown up 2Ch 10.08
And the y. men who had grown up 10.10
to the counsel of the y. men, 10.14
Rehoboam was y. and irresolute and 13.07
himself with a y. bull or seven 13.09
whether y. or old, man or woman. 15.13
old and y. alike, by divisions, 31.15
who slew their y. men with the 36.17
no compassion on y. man or virgin, 36.17
y. bulls, rams, or sheep for burnt Ez 6.09
"Let beautiful y. virgins be sought Est 2.02
the beautiful y. virgins to the 2.03
y. and old, women and children, in 3.13
and it fell upon the y. people, Job 1.19
lion, the teeth of the y. lions, 4.10
put forth branches like a y. plant. 14.09
Even y. children despise me; 19.18
the y. men saw me and withdrew, and 29.08
"I am y. in years, and you are aged; 32.06
the appetite of the y. lions, 38.39
when its y. ones cry to God, and 38.41
and are delivered of their y.? 39.03
Their y. ones become strong, they 39.04
She deals cruelly with her y., 39.16
His y. ones suck up blood; 39.30
as a y. lion lurking in ambush. Ps 17.12
calf, and Sirion like a y. wild ox. 29.06
The y. lions suffer want and hunger; 34.10
I have been y., and now am old; 37.25
the fangs of the y. lions, O LORD! 58.06
Fire devoured their y. men, 78.63
ewes that had y. he brought him to 78.71
herself, where she may lay her y., 84.03
the y. lion and the serpent you 91.13
The y. lions roar for their prey, 104.21
and y. locusts without number; 105.34
How can a y. man keep his way pure? 119.09
may our cattle be heavy with y., 144.14
and to the y. ravens which cry. 147.09
Y. men and maidens together, old men 148.12
among the youths, a y. man without sense, Pro 7.07
The glory of y. men is their 20.29
Rejoice, O y. man, in your youth, and Ecc 11.09
so is my beloved among y. men. Sol 2.03
is like a gazelle, or a y. stag. 2.09
or a y. stag upon rugged mountains. 2.17
a gazelle or a y. stag upon the 8.14
like y. lions they roar; they growl Is 5.29
Behold, a y. woman shall conceive 7.14
keep alive a y. cow and two sheep; 7.21
does not rejoice over their y. men, 9.17
their y. shall lie down together; 11.07
Their bows will slaughter the y. men; 13.18
both the y. and the old, naked and 20.04
neither reared y. men nor brought 23.04
As a lion or a y. lion growls over 31.04
and his y. men shall be put to 31.08
and y. steers with the mighty bulls 34.07
and gather her y. in her shadow; 34.15
gently lead those that are with y. 40.11
and y. men shall fall exhausted; 40.30
grew up before him like a y. plant, 53.02
the y. camels of Midian and Ephah; 60.06
For as a y. man marries a virgin, so 62.05
a restive y. camel interlacing her Jer 2.23
the gatherings of y. men, also; 6.11
streets and the y. men from the 9.21
the y. men shall die by the sword; 11.22
the mothers of y. men a destroyer 15.08
and over the y. of the flock and 31.12
and the y. men and the old shall be 31.13
choicest of his y. men have gone 48.15
Therefore her y. men shall fall in 49.26
Therefore her y. men shall fall in 50.30
Spare not her y. men; utterly destroy 51.03
in pieces the y. man and the 51.22
against me to crush my y. men; Lam 1.15
maidens and my y. men have gone 1.18
the streets lie the y. and the old; 2.21
maidens and my y. men have fallen 2.21
the breast and suckle their y., 4.03
Y. men are compelled to grind at 5.13
the city gate, the y. men their music. 5.14
y. men and maidens, little children Eze 9.06
topmost of its y. twigs and 17.04
topmost of its y. twigs a tender 17.22
couched in the midst of y. lions, 19.02
he became a y. lion, and he learned 19.03
her whelps and made him a y. lion. 19.05
he became a y. lion, and he learned 19.06
all of them desirable y. men, 23.06
all of them desirable y. men. 23.12
bosom and pressed your y. breasts." 23.21
desirable y. men, governors and 23.23
The y. men of On and of Pibeseth 30.17
the field brought forth their y.; 31.06
the face of a y. lion toward the 41.19
shall take a y. bull without blemish, 45.18
of the land a y. bull for a sin 45.22
the LORD seven y. bulls and seven 45.23
shall offer a y. bull without 46.06
offering with a y. bull shall be 46.11
and like a y. lion to the house of Hos 5.14
and your y. men shall see visions. Joe 2.28
some of your y. men for Nazirites. Amo 2.11
Does a y. lion cry out from his den, 3.04
I slew your y. men with the sword; 4.10
virgins and the y. men shall faint 8.13
from their y. children you take Mic 2.09
like a y. lion among the flocks of 5.08
den, the cave of the y. lions, Nah 2.11
sword shall devour your y. lions; 2.13
say to that y. man, 'Jerusalem shall Zec 2.04
shall make the y. men flourish, 9.17
The y. man said to him, "All these I Mt 19.20
When the y. man heard this he went 19.22
And a y. man followed him, with Mk 14.51
they saw a y. man sitting on the 16.05
of turtledoves, or two y. pigeons." Lk 2.24
And he said, "Y. man, I say to you, 7.14
And Jesus found a y. ass and sat Jn 12.14
when you were y. you girded 21.18
and your y. men shall see visions, Ac 2.17
The y. men rose and wrapped him up 5.06
When the y. men came in they found 5.10
at the feet of a y. man named Saul. 7.58
And a y. man named Eutychus was 20.09
"Bring this y. man to the tribune; 23.17
me to bring this y. man to you, 23.18
So the tribune dismissed the y. man, 23.22
and so train the y. women to love Tit 2.04

YOUNG (cont.)
y. men, because you have overcome 1Jn 2.13
y. men, because you are strong, and 2.14

YOUNGER
And the first-born said to the y., Gen 19.31
day, the first-born said to the y., 19.34
and the y. arose, and lay with him; 19.35
The y. also bore a son, and called 19.38
the elder shall serve the y." 25.23
and put them on Jacob her y. son; 27.15
sent and called Jacob her y. son, 27.42
and the name of the y. was Rachel. 29.16
years for your y. daughter Rachel." 29.18
to give the y. before the first-born. 29.26
who was the y., and his left hand 48.14
nevertheless his y. brother shall 48.19
Caleb's y. brother, took it; and he gave Ju 1.13
son of Kenaz, Caleb's y. brother. 3.09
Is not her y. sister fairer than 15.02
and the name of the y. Michal; 1Sa 14.49
house and his y. brother alike, 1Ch 24.31
men who are y. than I, whose fathers Job 30.01
and your y. sister, who lived to the Eze 16.46
both your elder and your y., and give 16.61
of James the y. and of Joses, Mk 15.40
and the y. of them said to his Lk 15.12
the y. son gathered all he had and 15.13
told, "The elder will serve the y." Rom 9.12
a father; treat y. men like brothers, 1Ti 5.01
y. women like sisters, in all purity. 5.02
But refuse to enrol y. widows; 5.11
So I would have y. widows marry, 5.14
Likewise urge the y. men to control Tit 2.06
Likewise you that are y. be subject 1 Pe 5.05

YOUNGEST
knew what his y. son had done to Gen 9.24
the y. is this day with our father, 42.13
unless your y. brother comes here. 42.15
and bring your y. brother to me; 42.20
and the y. is this day with our 42.32
Bring your y. brother to me; then I shall 42.34
"Is this your y. brother, of whom 43.29
birthright and the y. according to 43.33
in the mouth of the sack of the y., 44.02
the eldest and ending with the y.; 44.12
'Unless your y. brother comes down 44.23
If our y. brother goes with us, then 44.26
face unless our y. brother is with 44.26
the cost of his y. son shall he Jos 6.26
but Jotham the y. son of Jerubbaal Ju 9.05
he said, "There remains yet the y., 1Sa 16.11
David was the y.; the three eldest 17.14
at the cost of his y. son Segub, 1Ki 16.34
from the y. to the oldest, were 2Ki 3.21
to him except Jehoahaz, his y. son. 2Ch 21.17
Ahaziah his y. son king in his 22.01
greatest among you become as the y., Lk 22.26

YOURSELF
Make y. an ark of gopher wood; Gen 6.14
Separate y. from me. If you take 13.09
persons, but take the goods for y." 14.21
As for y., you shall go to your 15.15
"You y. know how I have served you, 30.29
my brother, keep what you have for y." 33.09
"What a breach you have made for y.!" 38.29
back anything from me except y., 39.09
still exalting y. against my Ex 9.17
you refuse to humble y. before me? 10.03
take heed to y.; never see my 10.28
"You shall not make y. a graven image, 20.04
and present y. there to me on the 34.02
Take heed to y., lest you make a 34.12
"You shall make for y. no molten gods. 34.17
atonement for y. and for the Lev 9.07
wife, and defile y. with her. 18.20
any beast and defile y. with it, 18.23
your neighbor as y.: I am the LORD. 19.18
you, and you shall love him as y.; 19.34
for y. and for your male and female 25.06
authority, and if you have defiled y., Num 5.20
that you may not bear it y. alone. 11.17
must also make y. a prince over us 16.13
not make for y. a graven image, Deu 5.08
and would take her for y. as wife, 21.11
but the young you may take to y.; 22.07
"You shall make y. tassels on the 22.12
your cloak with which you cover y. 22.12
you shall keep y. from every evil 23.09
shall not anoint y. with the oil; 28.40
"Rise y., and fall upon us; Ju 8.21
Wash therefore and anoint y., Ru 3.03
but do not make y. known to the man 3.03
Take my right of redemption y., 4.06
"Buy it for y.," he drew off his 4.08
passed on stop here y. for a while, 1Sa 9.27
take heed to y. in the morning, 19.02
stay in a secret place and hide y.; 19.02
there is guilt in me, slay me y.; 20.08
where you hid y. when the matter 20.19
the balsam trees, then bestir y.; 2Sa 5.24
do not anoint y. with oil, but 14.02
you have made y. odious to your 16.21
then you y. would have stood aloof." 18.13
within three days, and be here y." 20.04
Be strong, and show y. a man, 1Ki 2.02
"Build y. a house in Jerusalem, and 2.36
not asked for y. long life or 3.11
have asked for y. understanding to 3.11
Jeroboam, "Take for y. ten pieces; 11.31
and refresh y., and I will give you 13.07
and disguise y., that it be not 14.02
gone and made for y. other gods, 14.09
and hide y. by the brook Cherith, 17.03
afterward make for y. and your son. 17.13
year, saying, "Go, show y. to Ahab; 18.01
strengthen y., and consider well 20.22
establish bazaars for y. in Damascus, 20.34
judgment be: you y. have decided it." 20.40
you have sold y. to do what is 21.20
into an inner chamber to hide y." 22.25
and as you y. live, I will not leave 2Ki 2.02
and as you y. live, I will not leave 2.04
and as you y. live, I will not leave 2.06
the door upon y. and your sons, 4.04
and as you y. live, I will not leave 4.30
and you humbled y. before the LORD, 22.19
knowledge for y. that you may rule 2Ch 1.11
into an inner chamber to hide y." 18.24
house, who were better than y.; 21.13
and you y. will have a severe 21.15
and you humbled y. before God when 34.27
and you have humbled y. before me, 34.27
And do you limit wisdom to y.? Job 15.08
You who tear y. in your anger, shall 18.04
to the Almighty and humble y., 22.23
will delight y. in the Almighty, 22.26
Your wickedness concerns a man like y., 35.08
"Deck y. with majesty and dignity; 40.10
clothe y. with glory and splendor. 40.10
Fret not y. because of the wicked, Ps 37.01
fret not y. over him who prospers 37.07
Fret not y.; it tends only to 37.08
you thought that I was one like y. 50.21
Let them be for y. alone, and not for Pro 5.17
and save y., for you have come into 6.03
save y. like a gazelle from the 6.05
If you are wise, you are wise for y.; 9.12
ways and entangle y. in a snare. 22.25
Fret not y. because of evildoers, 24.19
Do not put y. forward in the king's 25.04
his folly, lest you be like him y. 26.04

YOURSELF (cont.)

exalting y., or if you have been Pro 30.32
enjoy y." But behold, this Ecc 2.01
and do not make y. overwise; 7.16
why should you destroy y.? 7.16
times you have y. cursed others. 7.22
you have hewn here a tomb for y., Is 22.16
a habitation for y. in the rock? 22.16
who y. have not been destroyed; 33.01
Rouse y., rouse y., stand up, O 51.17
Shake y. from the dust, arise; 52.02
made a bargain for y. with them, 57.08
and not to hide y. from your own 58.07
if you pour y. out for the hungry 58.10
"Keep to y., do not come near me, 65.05
this upon y. by forsaking the LORD Jer 2.17
Though you wash y. with lye and use 2.22
are your gods that you made for y.? 2.28
that you deck y. with ornaments of 4.30
In vain you beautify y. Your lovers 4.30
those whom you y. have taught to 13.21
you a terror to y. and to all your 20.04
"Make y. thongs and yoke-bars, and 27.02
you shall adorn y. with timbrels, 31.04
"Set up waymarks for y., 31.21
make y. guideposts; consider well 31.21
buy it for y. Then I knew 32.08
and you y. shall not escape from 38.23
And do you seek great things for y.? 45.05
Put y. into your scabbard, rest and 47.06
Give y. no rest, your eyes no Lam 2.18
become drunk and strip y. bare. 4.21
"Go, shut y. within your house. Eze 3.24
prepare for y. an exile's baggage, 12.03
shall go forth y. at evening in 12.04
and made for y. gaily decked 16.16
and made for y. images of men, and 16.17
you built y. a vaulted chamber, and 16.24
and made y. a lofty place in every 16.24
offering y. to any passer-by, and 16.25
and polluted y. with their idols. 23.30
For them you bathed y., painted your 23.40
eyes, and decked y. with ornaments; 23.40
you consider y. as wise as a god— 28.02
you have gotten wealth for y., 28.04
you consider y. as wise as a god, 28.06
"You consider y. a lion among the 32.02
securely, you will bestir y. 38.14
the king, "Let your gifts be for y., Dan 5.17
have lifted up y. against the Lord 5.23
and humbled y. before your God, 10.12
take to y. a wife of harlotry and Hos 1.02
you y. shall die in an unclean land, Amo 7.17
Drink y., and stagger! The cup in the Hab 2.16
are the Son of God, throw y. down; Mt 4.06
but go, show y. to the priest, and 8.04
give it to them for me and for y." 17.27
You shall love your neighbor as y." 19.19
You shall love your neighbor as y. 22.39
that to us? See to it y." 27.04
build it in three days, save y.! 27.40
but go, show y. to the priest, and Mk 1.44
You shall love your neighbor as y.' 12.31
save y., and come down from the 15.30
of God, throw y. down from here; Lk 4.09
this proverb, 'Physician, heal y.; 4.23
but "go and show y. to the priest, 5.14
when you y. do not see the log 6.42
to him, "Lord, do not trouble y., 7.06
your mind; and your neighbor as y." 10.27
and gird y. and serve me, till I eat 17.08
are the King of the Jews, save y.!" 23.37
not the Christ? Save y. and us!" 23.39
What do you say about y.?" Jn 1.22
these things, show y. to the world." 7.04
him, "You are bearing witness to y.; 8.13
you, being a man, make y. God." 10.33
it that you will manifest y. to us, 14.22
you girded y. and walked where you 21.18
"Dress y. and put on your sandals." Ac 12.08
"Do not harm y., for we are all 16.28
men and purify y. along with them 21.24
but that you y. live in observance 21.24
By examining him y. you will be 24.08
have permission to speak for y." 26.01
judgment upon him you condemn y., Rom 2.01
do such things and yet do them y., 2.03
up wrath for y. on the day of 2.05
But if you call y. a Jew and rely 2.17
others, will you not teach y.? 2.21
"You shall love your neighbor as y." 13.09
you have, keep between y. and God; 14.22
avail y. of the opportunity. 1Co 7.21
"You shall love your neighbor as y." Gal 5.14
Look to y., lest you too be tempted. 6.01
Train y. in godliness; 1Ti 4.07
devote y. to them, so that all may 4.15
Take heed to y. and to your teaching; 4.16
will save both y. and your hearers. 4.16
another man's sins; keep y. pure. 5.22
best to present y. to God as one 2Ti 2.15
Beware of him y., for he strongly 4.15
Show y. in all respects a model of Tit 2.07
your neighbor as y.," you do well. Jas 2.08

YOURSELVES

and rest y. under the tree, Gen 18.04
of bread, that you may refresh y., 18.05
us, and take our daughters for y. 34.09
and purify y., and change your 35.02
or angry with y., because you sold 45.05
and as food for y. and your 47.24
"Gather y. together, that I may tell 49.01
Go y., get your straw wherever you Ex 5.11
'Prove y. by working a miracle,' 7.09
lambs for y. according to your 12.21
people with you will wear y. out, 18.18
have seen for y. that I have 20.22
shall you make for y. gods of gold. 20.23
offering to make atonement for y. 30.15
so as to make atonement for y." 30.16
compositon, you shall not make for y.; 30.37
have ordained y. for the service 32.29
You shall not make y. abominable Lev 11.43
you shall not defile y. with them, 11.43
consecrate y. therefore, and be holy, 11.44
not defile y. with any swarming 11.44
of the month, you shall afflict y., 16.29
to you, and you shall afflict y.; 16.31
"Do not defile y. by any of these 18.24
and never to defile y. by them: 18.30
idols or make for y. molten gods: 19.04
Consecrate y. therefore, and be holy; 20.07
shall not make y. abominable by 20.25
shall afflict y. and present an 23.27
rest, and you shall afflict y.; 23.32
"You shall make for y. no idols and 26.01
'Consecrate y. for tomorrow, and you Num 11.18
do you exalt y. above the assembly 16.03
"Separate y. from among this 16.21
a holy convocation, and afflict y.; 29.07
lying with him, keep alive for y. 31.18
purify y. and your captives on the 31.19
"Therefore take good heed to y. Deu 4.15
by making a graven image for y., 4.16
Take heed to y., lest you forget 4.23
greater and mightier than y., 4.38
greater and mightier than y., 7.01
that is on them, or take it for y., 7.25
greater and mightier than y., 9.01
you had made y. a molten calf; 9.16
greater and mightier than y. 11.23
shall not cut y. or make any 14.01
you shall take as booty for y.; 20.14

YOURSELVES (cont.)
you shall offer y. for sale to Deu 28.68
and present y. in the tent of 31.14
and hide y. there three days, until Jos 2.16
said to the people, "Sanctify y.; 3.05
But you, keep y. from the things 6.18
and say, 'Sanctify y. for tomorrow; 7.13
you shall take as booty for y.; 8.02
but hold y. all in readiness; 8.04
but do not stay there y., 10.19
ground for y. in the land of the 17.15
by building y. an altar this day in 22.16
and take for y. a possession among 22.19
by building y. an altar other than 22.19
them, or bow down y. to them, 23.07
Take good heed to y., 23.11
witnesses against y. that you have 24.22
that you will not fall upon me y. Ju 15.12
me by fattening y. upon the 1Sa 2.29
and acquit y. like men, O Philistines, 4.09
acquit y. like men and fight." 4.09
king, whom you have chosen for y.; 8.18
therefore present y. before the 10.19
the LORD, in asking for y. a king." 12.17
"disperse y. among the people, and 14.34
consecrate y., and come with me to 16.05
Choose a man for y., and let him 17.08
"Choose for y. one bull and prepare 1Ki 18.25
gods or bow y. to them or serve 2Ki 17.35
you shall bow y. to him, and to 17.36
sanctify y., you and your brethren, 1Ch 15.12
priests for y. like the peoples of 2Ch 13.09
Now sanctify y., and sanctify the 29.05
now consecrated y. to the LORD; 29.31
but yield y. to the LORD, and come 30.08
Prepare y. according to your 35.04
and sanctify y., and prepare for 35.06
separate y. from the peoples of the Ez 10.11
daughters for your sons or for y. Neh 13.25
If indeed you magnify y. against me, Job 19.05
Behold, all of you have seen it y.; 27.12
offer up for y. a burnt offering; 42.08
Wash y.; make y. clean; Is 1.16
countries; gird y. and be dismayed; 8.09
hide y. for a little while until 26.20
Stupefy y. and be in a stupor, blind 29.09
in a stupor, blind y. and be blind! 29.09
and make y. bare, and gird sackcloth 32.11
"Assembly y. and come, draw near 45.20
purify y., you who bear the vessels 52.11
is good, and delight y. in fatness. 55.02
Circumcise y. to the LORD, remove Jer 4.04
blood upon y. and upon this city 26.15
Thus says the LORD, Do not deceive y., 37.09
commit this great evil against y., 44.07
Prepare y. baggage for exile, O 46.19
Anakim, how long will you gash y.? 47.05
Save y.! be like a wild 48.06
Gird y. with sackcloth, lament, and 49.03
"Gather y. together and come 49.14
Set y. in array against Babylon 50.14
and get y. a new heart and a new Eze 18.31
do not defile y. with the idols of 20.07
nor defile y. with their idols. 20.18
Will you defile y. after the 20.30
you defile y. with all your idols 20.31
with which you have polluted y.; 20.43
shall loathe y. for all the evils 20.43
of Israel who have been feeding y.! 34.02
you clothe y. with the wool, you 34.03
And you magnified y. against me 35.13
you will loathe y. for your 36.31
inheritance for y. and for the 47.22
Sow for y. righteousness, reap the Hos 10.12
round about, gather y. there. Joe 3.11
"Assemble y. upon the mountains of Amo 3.09
your images, which you made for y.; 5.26
Bethleaphrah roll y. in the dust. Mic 1.10
Make y. bald and cut off your hair, 1.16
make y. as bald as the eagle, for 1.16
olives, but not anoint y. with oil; 6.15
Multiply y. like the locust, multiply Nah 3.15
a time for you y. to dwell in your Hag 1.04
you clothe y., but no one is warm; 1.06
while you busy y. each with his 1.09
you not eat for y. and drink for y.? Zec 7.06
So take heed to y., and let none Mal 2.15
So take heed to y. and do not be 2.16
and do not presume to say to y., Mt 3.09
"Do not lay up for y. treasures on 6.19
but lay up for y. treasures in 6.20
discuss among y. the fact that you 16.08
for you neither enter y., nor allow 23.13
as much a child of hell as y. 23.15
Thus you witness against y., that you are 23.31
to the dealers and buy for y. 25.09
this man's blood; see to it y." 27.24
"Come away by y. to a lonely place, Mk 6.31
Have salt in y., and be at peace 9.50
"But take heed to y.; for they will 13.09
and do not begin to say to y., Lk 3.08
and you y. do not touch the burdens 11.46
you did not enter y., and you hindered 11.52
provide y. with purses that do not 12.33
you not judge for y. what is right? 12.57
of God and you y. thrust out. 13.28
friends for y. by means of unrighteous 16.09
those who justify y. before men, 16.15
Take heed to y.; if your brother 17.03
"Go and show y. to the priests." 17.14
you see for y. and know that the 21.30
"But take heed to y. lest your 21.34
"Take this, and divide it among y.; 22.17
but weep for y. and for your 23.28
You y. bear me witness, that I said, Jn 3.28
them, "Do not murmur among y. 6.43
Go to the feast y.; I am not 7.08
"Is this what you are asking y., 16.19
"Take him y. and judge him by your 18.31
"Take him y. and crucify him, for I 19.06
in your midst, as you y. know— Ac 2.22
"Save y. from this crooked generation." 2.40
"You y. know how unlawful it is for 10.28
and judge y. unworthy of eternal 13.46
If you keep y. from these, you will 15.29
and your own law, see to it y.; 18.15
"You y. know how I lived among you 20.18
Take heed to y. and to all the 20.28
You y. know that these hands 20.34
including y. who are called to Rom 1.06
must consider y. dead to sin and 6.11
but yield y. to God as men who have 6.13
if you yield y. to any one as 6.16
never avenge y., but leave it to 12.19
that you y. are full of goodness, 15.14
But you y. wrong and defraud, and 1Co 6.08
that you may devote y. to prayer; 7.05
judge for y. what I say. 10.15
Judge for y.; is it proper 11.13
So with y.; if you in a 14.09
So with y.; since you are 14.12
You y. are our letter of recommendation, 2Co 3.02
in you, what eagerness to clear y., 7.11
you have proved y. guiltless in 7.11
bear with fools, being wise y.! 11.19
Examine y., to see whether you are 13.05
Test y. Do you not realize 13.05
count others better than y. Php 2.03
Have this mind among y., which you have 2.05
And you Philippians y. know that in 4.15
so among y., from the day you heard Col 1.06
Conduct y. wisely toward outsiders, 4.05
beloved brother, who is one of y. 4.09

YOURSELVES (cont.)
who is one of y., a servant of Col 4.12
For you y. know, brethren, that our 1Th 2.01
You y. know that this is to be our 3.03
for you y. have been taught by God 4.09
For you y. know well that the day 5.02
of their work. Be at peace among y. 5.13
For you y. know how you ought to 2Th 3.07
knew that you y. had a better Heb 10.34
and not hearers only, deceiving y. Jas 1.22
you not made distinctions among y., 2.04
Submit y. therefore to God. Resist 4.07
Humble y. before the Lord and he 4.10
be holy y. in all your conduct; 1Pe 1.15
conduct y. with fear throughout the 1.17
stones be y. built into a spiritual 2.05
arm y. with the same thought, for 4.01
Clothe y., all of you, with humility 5.05
Humble y. therefore under the 5.06
Little children, keep y. from idols. 1Jn 5.21
Look to y., that you may not lose 2Jn 1.08
build y. up on your most holy faith Jud 1.20
keep y. in the love of God; 1.21

YOUTH
of man's heart is evil from his y.; Gen 8.21
the youngest according to his y.; 43.33
cattle from our y. even until now, 46.34
as in her y., she may eat of her Lev 22.13
her father's house, in her y., Num 30.03
while in her y., within her father's 30.16
But the y. did not draw his sword; Ju 8.20
afraid, because he was still a y. 8.20
you from my y. until this day. 1Sa 12.02
for you are but a y., and he has been 17.33
has been a man of war from his y." 17.33
for he was but a y., ruddy and comely 17.42
army, "Abner, whose son is this y.?" 17.55
But if I say to the y., 'Look, the arrows 20.22
upon you from your y. until now." 2Sa 19.07
have revered the LORD from my y. 1Ki 18.12
me inherit the iniquities of my y. Job 13.26
(for from his y. I reared him as a 31.18
let his flesh become fresh with y.; 33.25
They die in y., and their life ends 36.14
Remember not the sins of my y., Ps 25.07
hope, my trust, O LORD, from my y. 71.05
O God, from my y. thou hast taught 71.17
Afflicted and close to death from my y. up, 88.15
Thou hast cut short the days of his y.; 89.45
so that your y. is renewed like 103.05
like dew your y. will come to you. 110.03
a warrior are the sons of one's y. 127.04
"Sorely have they afflicted me from my y.," 129.01
"Sorely have they afflicted me from my y., 129.02
sons in their y. be like plants 144.12
knowledge and discretion to the y.— Pro 1.04
companion of her y. and forgets the 2.17
rejoice in the wife of your y., 5.18
a poor and wise y. than an old and Ecc 4.13
under the sun, as well as that y., 4.15
in your y., and let your heart 11.09
cheer you in the days of your y.; 11.09
for y. and the dawn of life are 11.10
Creator in the days of your y., 12.01
the y. will be insolent to the Is 3.05
you have labored from your y.; 47.12
trafficked with you from your y.; 47.15
will forget the shame of your y., 54.04
like a wife of y. when she is cast 54.06
how to speak, for I am only a y." Jer 1.06
me, "Do not say, 'I am only a y.'; 1.07
I remember the devotion of your y., 2.02
thou art the friend of my y.— 3.04
"But from our y. the shameful thing 3.24
from our y. even to this day; 3.25
has been your way from your y., 22.21
I bore the disgrace of my y.' 31.19
but evil in my sight from their y.; 32.30
ease from his y. and has settled 48.11
in pieces the old man and the y.; 51.22
that he bear the yoke in his y. Lam 3.27
from my y. up till now I have never Eze 4.14
not remember the days of your y., 16.22
not remembered the days of your y., 16.43
with you in the days of your y., 16.60
they played the harlot in their y.; 23.03
for in her y. men had lain with her 23.08
remembering the days of her y., 23.19
longed for the lewdness of your y., 23.21
answer as in the days of her y., Hos 2.15
for the bridegroom of her y. Joe 1.08
has been my possession since my y.' Zec 13.05
you and the wife of your y., Mal 2.14
be faithless to the wife of his y. 2.15
these I have observed from my y." Mk 10.20
these I have observed from my y." Lk 18.21
"My manner of life from my y., Ac 26.04
Let no one despise your y., 1Ti 4.12

YOUTHFUL
His bones are full of y. vigor, Job 20.11
return to the days of his y. vigor. 33.25
So shun y. passions and aim at 2Ti 2.22

YOUTHS
I have perceived among the y., Pro 7.07
Even y. shall faint and be weary, Is 40.30
their y. be slain by the sword in Jer 18.21
y. without blemish, handsome and Dan 1.04
than the y. who are of your own 1.10
appearance of the y. who eat the 1.13
than all the y. who ate the king's 1.15
As for these four y., 1.17

Z

ZAANAN
inhabitants of Z. do not come Mic 1.11

ZAANANNIM
from Heleph, from the oak in Z., Jos 19.33
tent as far away as the oak in Z., Ju 4.11

ZAAVAN
sons of Ezer: Bilhan, Z., and Akan. Gen 36.27
of Ezer: Bilhan, Z., and Jaakan. 1Ch 1.42

ZABAD
father of Nathan and Nathan of Z. 1Ch 2.36
Z. was the father of Ephlal, and 2.37
Z. his son, Shuthelah his son, and 7.21
the Hittite, Z. the son of Ahlai, 11.41
him were Z. the son of Shimeath 2Ch 24.26
Mattaniah, Jeremoth, Z., and Aziza. Ez 10.27
Z., Eliphelet, Jeremai, Manasseh, and 10.33
Z., Zebina, Jaddai, Joel, and Benaiah. 10.43

ZABBAI
Jehohanan, Hananiah, Z., and Athlai. Ez. 10.28
the son of Z. repaired another Neh 3.20

ZABDI
son of Z., son of Zerah, of the Jos 7.01
man by man, and Z. was taken; 7.17
son of Z., son of Zerah, of the 7.18
Jakim, Zichri, Z., 1Ch 8.19
wine cellars was Z. the Shiphmite. 27.27
son of Z., son of Asaph, who was the Neh 11.17

ZABDIEL
Jashobeam the son of Z. was in 1Ch 27.02
overseer was Z. the son of Haggedolim. Neh 11.14

ZABOIIM
Admahh and Z., which the LORD Deu 29.23

ZABUD
Z. the son of Nathan was priest and 1Ki 4.05

ZACCAI
The sons of Z., seven hundred and Ez 2.09
The sons of Z., seven hundred and Neh 7.14

ZACCHEAUS
And there was a man named Z.; Lk 19.02
"Z., make haste and come down; 19.05
And Z. stood and said to the Lord, 19.08

ZACCUR
of Reuben, Shammua the son of Z.; Num 13.04
Z. his son, Shimei his son. 1Ch 4.26
Jaaziah, Beno, Shoham, Z., and Ibri. 24.27
Z., Joseph, Nethaniah, and Asharelah, 25.02
the third to Z., his sons and his 25.10
next to them Z. the son of Imri Neh 3.02
Z., Sherebiah, Shebaniah, 10.12
Micaiah, son of Z., son of Asaph; 12.35
assistant Hanan the son of Z., 13.13

ZADOK
and Z. the son of Ahitub and 2Sa 8.17
Z. came also, with all the Levites, 15.24
Then the king said to Z., "Carry the ark 15.25
The king also said to Z. the priest, 15.27
So Z. and Abiathar carried the ark 15.29
Are not Z. and Abiathar the priests 15.35
tell it to Z. and Abiathar the 15.35
Then Hushai said to Z. and Abiathar 17.15
Then said Ahimaaz the son of Z., 18.19
the son of Z. said again to Joab, 18.22
running of Ahimaaz the son of Z. 18.27
this message to Z. and Abiathar 19.11
and Z. and Abiathar were priests; 20.25
But Z. the priest, and Benaiah the 1Ki 1.08
and Z. the priest, and Benaiah the 1.26
"Call to me Z. the priest, Nathan 1.32
and let Z. the priest and Nathan 1.34
So Z. the priest, Nathan the prophet, 1.38
There Z. the priest took the horn 1.39
has sent with him Z. the priest, 1.44
and Z. the priest and Nathan the 1.45
the king put Z. the priest in the 2.35
the son of Z. was the priest; 4.02
Z. and Abiathar were priests; 4.04
was Jerusha the daughter of Z. 2Ki 15.33
Ahitub of Z., Z. of Ahimaaz, 1Ch 6.08
Ahitub of Z., Z. of Shallum, 6.12
Z. his son, Ahimaaz his son. 6.53
son of Z., son of Meraioth, son of 9.11
Z., a young man mighty in valor, and 12.28
the priests Z. and Abiathar, 15.11
And he left Z. the priest and his 16.39
and Z. the son of Ahitub and 18.16
With the help of Z. of the sons of 24.03
and Z. the priest, and Ahimelech the 24.06
Z., Ahimelech, and the heads of 24.31
son of Kemuel; for Aaron, Z.; 27.17
for the LORD, and Z. as priest. 29.22
was Jerushah the daughter of Z. 2Ch 27.01
priest, who was of the house of Z., 31.10
of Shallum, son of Z., son of Ahitub, Ez 7.02
next to them Z. the son of Baana Neh 3.04
After them Z. the son of Immer 3.29
Meshezabel, Z., Jaddua, 10.21
son of Z., son of Meraioth, son of 11.11
Z. the scribe, and Pedaiah of the 13.13
these are the sons of Z., who alone among Eze 40.46
priests of the family of Z., who drew 43.19
the sons of Z., who kept the charge 44.15
the sons of Z., who kept my charge, 48.11
and Azor the father of Z., Mt 1.14
and Z. the father of Achim, and 1.14

ZADOK'S
Z. son, and Jonathan, Abiathar's son; 2Sa 15.36

ZAHAM
him sons, Jeush, Shemariah, and Z. 2Ch 11.19

ZAIR
passed over to Z. with all his chariots, 2Ki 8.21

ZAKKUR
Uthai and Z., and with them seventy Ez 8.14

ZALAPH
sixth son of Z. repaired another Neh 3.30

ZALMON
And Abimelech went up to Mount Z., Ju 9.48
Z. the Ahohite, Maharai of Netophah, 2Sa 23.28
kings there, snow fell on Z. Ps 68.14

ZALMONAH
from Mount Hor, and encamped at Z. Num 33.41
And they set out from Z., and encamped 33.42

ZALMUNNA
I am pursuing after Zebah and Z., Ju 8.05
"Are Zebah and Z. already in your 8.06
given Zebah and Z. into my hand, 8.07
Now Zebah and Z. were in Karkor 8.10
And Zebah and Z. fled; and he pursued 8.12
Zebah and Z., and he threw all the 8.12
and said, "Behold Zebah and Z., about 8.15
'Are Zebah and Z. already in your 8.15
Then he said to Zebah and Z., 8.18
Then Zebah and Z. said, "Rise 8.21
Gideon arose and slew Zebah and Z.; 8.21
their princes like Zebah and Z., Ps 83.11

ZAMZUMMIM
but the Ammonites call them Z., Deu 2.20

ZANOAH
Z., Engannim, Tappuah, Enam, Jos 15.34
Jezreel, Jokdeam, Z., 15.56
and Jekuthiel the father of Z. 1Ch 4.18
inhabitants of Z. repaired the Neh 3.13
Z., Adullam, and their villages, 11.30

ZAPHENATHPANEAH
And Pharaoh called Joseph's name Z.; Gen 41.45

ZAPHON
and Z., the rest of the kingdom of Jos 13.27
they crossed to Z. and said to Jephthah, Ju 12.01

ZAREPHATH
"Arise, go to Z., which belongs to 1Ki 17.09
So he arose and went to Z.; 17.10
possess Phoenicia as far as Z.; Ob 1.20
to none of them but only to Z., Lk 4.26

ZARETHAN
Adam, the city that is beside Z., Jos 3.16
which is beside Z. below Jezreel, 1Ki 4.12
clay ground between Succoth and Z. 7.46

ZATTU
The sons of Z., nine hundred and Ez 2.08
Of the sons of Z., Shecaniah the 8.05

ZATTU (cont.)
Of the sons of Z.: Elioenai, Eliashib, Ez 10.27
The sons of Z., eight hundred and Neh 7.13
Pahathmoab, Elam, Z., Bani, 10.14

ZAZA
The sons of Jonathan: Peleth and Z. 1Ch 2.33

ZEAL
them in his z. for the people of 2Sa 21.02
me, and see my z. for the LORD. 2K8 10.16
The z. of the LORD will do this. 19.31
For z. for thy house has consumed Ps 69.09
My z. consumes me, because my foes 119.139
The z. of the LORD of hosts will do Is 9.07
Let them see thy z. for thy people, 26.11
The z. of the LORD of hosts will 37.32
Where are thy z. and thy might? 63.15
"Z. for thy house will consume me." Jn 2.17
that they have a z. for God, Rom 10.02
he who gives aid, with z.; he who does 12.08
Never flag in z., be aglow with the 12.11
your z. for me, so that I rejoiced 2Co 7.07
what z., what punishment! At every point 7.11
order that your z. for us might be 7.12
and your z. has stirred up most of 9.02
as to z. a persecutor of the church, Php 3.06

ZEALOT
and Simon who was called the Z., Lk 6.15
and Simon the Z. and Judas the son Ac 1.13

ZEALOUS
they are all z. for the law, Ac 21.20
being z. for God as you all are 22.03
so extremely z. was I for the Gal 1.14
his own who are z. for good deeds. Tit 2.14
you if you are z. for what is 1Pe 3.13
be the more z. to confirm your call 2Pe 1.10
be z. to be found by him without 3.14
and chasten; so be z. and repent. Rev 3.19

ZEALOUSLY
charged them, the more z. they proclaimed it. Mk 7.36

ZEBADIAH
Z., Arad, Eder, 1Ch 8.15
Z., Meshullam, Hizki, Heber, 8.17
and Joelah and Z., the sons of 12.07
Z. the third, Jathniel the fourth, 26.02
month, and his son Z. after him; 27.07
Z., Asahel, Shemiramoth, Jehonathan, 2Ch 17.08
and Z. the son of Ishmael, the 19.11
Z. the son of Michael, and with him Ez 8.08
Of the sons of Immer: Hanani and Z. 10.20

ZEBAH
am pursuing after Z. and Zalmunna, Ju 8.05
"Are Z. and Zalmunna already in 8.06
LORD has given Z. and Zalmunna 8.07
Now Z. and Zalmunna were in Karkor 8.10
And Z. and Zalmunna fled; 8.12
Z. and Zalmunna, and he threw all 8.12
"Behold Z. and Zalmunna, about whom 8.15
'Are Z. and Zalmunna already in 8.15
Then he said to Z. and Zalmunna, 8.18
Then Z. and Zalmunna said, "Rise 8.21
arose and slew Z. and Zalmunna; 8.21
princes like Z. and Zalmunna, Ps 83.11

ZEBEDEE
the son of Z. and John his brother, Mt 4.21
in the boat with Z. their father, 4.21
James the son of Z., and John his 10.02
of the sons of Z. came up to him, 20.20
him Peter and the two sons of Z., 26.37
and the mother of the sons of Z. 27.56
the son of Z. and John his brother, Mk 1.19
their father Z. in the boat with 1.20
James the son of Z. and John the 3.17
the sons of Z., came forward to him, 10.35
sons of Z., who were partners with Lk 5.10
the sons of Z., and two others of Jn 21.02

ZEBIDAH
name was Z. the daughter of 2Ki 23.36

ZEBINA
Z., Jaddai, Joel, and Benaiah. Ez 10.43

ZEBOIIM
and Z., as far as Lasha. Gen 10.19
king of Admah, Shemeber king of Z., 14.02
the king of Z., and the king of 14.08
How can I treat you like Z.! Hos 11.08

ZEBOIM
the valley of Z. toward the 1Sa 13.18
Hadid, Z., Neballat, Neh 11.34

ZEBUL
Jerubbaal and Z. his officer serve Ju 9.28
when Z. the ruler of the city heard 9.30
he said to Z., "Look, men are coming 9.36
And Z. said to him, "You see the 9.36
Then Z. said to him, "Where is your 9.38
and Z. drove out Gaal and his 9.41

ZEBULUN
so she called his name Z. Gen 30.20
Levi, Judah, Issachar, and Z. 35.23
The sons of Z.: Sered, Elon, and 46.14
Z. shall dwell at the shore of the 49.13
Issachar, Z., and Benjamin, Ex 1.03
from Z., Eliab the son of Helon; Num 1.09
Of the people of Z., their generations, 1.30
of the tribe of Z. was fifty-seven 1.31
Then the tribe of Z., 2.07
the people of Z. being Eliab the 2.07
the leader of the men of Z.: 7.24
of the men of Z. was Eliab the son 10.16
from the tribe of Z., Gaddiel 13.10
The sons of Z., according to their 26.26
tribe of the sons of Z. a leader, 34.25
Gad, Asher, Z., Dan, and Naphtali. Deu 27.13
And of Z. he said, "Rejoice, Z., in your 33.18
Lot came up for the tribe of Z., Jos 19.10
the inheritance of the tribe of Z., 19.16
and touches Z. and the valley of 19.27
touching Z. at the south, and Asher 19.34
and the tribe of Z., twelve cities. 21.07
were given out of the tribe of Z., 21.34
Z. did not drive out the inhabitants Ju 1.30
of Naphtali and the tribe of Z.? 4.06
And Barak summoned Z. and Naphtali 4.10
and from Z. those who bear the 5.14
Z. is a people that jeoparded their 5.18
messengers to Asher, Z., and Naphtali; 6.35
at Aijalon in the land of Z. 12.12
Simeon, Levi, Judah, Issachar, Z., 1Ch 2.01
the tribes of Reuben, Gad, and Z. 6.63
allotted out of the tribe of Z.: 6.77
Of Z. fifty thousand seasoned 12.33
as Issachar and Z. and Naphtali, 12.40
for Z., Ishmaiah the son of Obadiah 27.19
and Manasseh, and as far as Z.; 2Ch 30.10
and of Z. humbled themselves and 30.11
and Z., had not cleansed themselves, 30.18
in their throng, the princes of Z., Ps 68.27
the land of Z. and the land of Is 9.01
side to the west, Z., one portion. Eze 48.26
Adjoining the territory of Z., 48.27
of Issachar, and the gate of Z. 48.33
the territory of Z. and Naphtali, Mt 4.13
"The land of Z. and the land of 4.15
twelve thousand of the tribe of Z., Rev 7.08

ZEBULUNITE
After him Elon the Z. judged Israel; Ju 12.11
Then Elon the Z. died, and was 12.12

ZEBULUNITES
families of the Z. according to Num 26.27

ZECHARIAH
and Z. his son reigned in his stead. 2Ki 14.29
king of Judah Z. the son of 15.08
Now the rest of the deeds of Z., 15.11
name was Abi the daughter of Z. 18.02
reckoned: the chief, Jeiel, and Z., 1Ch 5.07
Z. the son of Meshelemiah was gatekeeper 9.21
Gedor, Ahio, Z., and Mikloth; 9.37
Z., Jaaziel, Shemiramoth, Jehiel, Unni, 15.18
Z., Aziel, Shemiramoth, Jehiel, Unni, 15.20
Z., Benaiah, and Eliezer, the priests, 15.24
chief, and second to him were Z., 16.05
of the sons of Isshiah, Z. 24.25
Z. the first-born, Jediael the 26.02
Z. the fourth: all the sons and 26.11
They cast lots also for his son Z., 26.14
in Gilead, Iddo the son of Z.; 27.21
Z., Nethanel, and Micaiah, to teach 2Ch 17.07
came upon Jahaziel the son of Z., 20.14
Z., Azariah, Michael, and Shephatiah; 21.02
possession of Z. the son of 24.20
to seek God in the days of Z., 26.05
name was Abijah the daughter of Z. 29.01
sons of Asaph, Z. and Mattaniah; 29.13
and Z. and Meshullam, of the sons of 34.12
Hilkiah, Z., and Jehiel, the chief 35.08
Haggai and Z. the son of Iddo, Ez 5.01
the prophet and Z. the son of Iddo. 6.14
Z., with whom were registered one 8.03
Z., the son of Bebai, and with him 8.11
Z., and Meshullam, leading men, and 8.16
Z., Jehiel, Abdi, Jeremoth, and Elijah 10.26
Z., and Meshullam on his left hand. Neh 8.04
son of Z., son of Amariah, son of 11.04
son of Z., son of the Shilonite. 11.05
son of Z., son of Pashhur, son of 11.12
of Iddo, Z.; of Ginnethon, Meshullam; 12.16
Z. the son of Jonathan, son of 12.35
Z., and Hananiah, with trumpets; 12.41
the priest and Z. the son of Is 8.02
LORD came to Z. the son of Berechiah, Zec 1.01
LORD came to Z. the son of Berechiah, 1.07
son of Iddo, the prophet; and Z. said, 1.07
LORD came to Z. in the fourth day 7.01
of the LORD came to Z., saying, 7.08
to the blood of Z. the son of Mt 23.35
Judea, there was a priest named Z., Lk 1.05
And Z. was troubled when he saw him, 1.12
Z., for your prayer is heard, and 1.13
And Z. said to the angel, "How shall 1.18
And the people were waiting for Z., 1.21
the house of Z. and greeted 1.40
have named him Z. after his father, 1.59
And his father Z. was filled with 1.67
John the son of Z. in the wilderness; 3.02
blood of Abel to the blood of Z., 11.51

ZECHARIAH'S
Z. father, had shown him, but killed 2Ch 24.22

ZECHER
Gedor, Ahio, Z., 1Ch 8.31

ZEDAD
end of the boundary shall be at Z.; Num 34.08
entrance of Hamath, and on to Z., Eze 47.15

ZEDEKIAH
And Z. the son of Chenaanah made 1Ki 22.11
Then Z. the son of Chenaanah came 22.24
stead, and changed his name to Z. 2Ki 24.17
Z. was twenty-one years old when he 24.18
And Z. rebelled against the king of 24.20
till the eleventh year of King Z. 25.02
the sons of Z. before his eyes, and 25.07
eyes, and put out the eyes of Z., 25.07
the third Z., the fourth Shallum. 1Ch 3.15
Jeconiah his son, Z. his son; 3.16
And Z. the son of Chenaanah made 2Ch 18.10
Then Z. the son of Chenaanah came 18.23
his brother Z. king over Judah and 36.10
Z. was twenty-one years old when he 36.11
governor, the son of Hacaliah, Z., Neh 10.01
the end of the eleventh year of Z., Jer 1.03
when King Z. sent to him Pashhur 21.01
"Thus you shall say to Z., 'Thus says the 21.04
I will deliver Z. king of Judah, 21.07
so will I treat Z. the king of 24.08
of the reign of Z. the son of 27.01
to Jerusalem to Z. king of Judah. 27.03
To Z. king of Judah I spoke in like 27.12
of the reign of Z. king of Judah, 28.01
whom Z. king of Judah sent to 29.03
of Kolaiah and Z. the son of 29.21
"The LORD make you like Z. and Ahab, 29.22
the tenth year of Z. king of Judah, 32.01
For Z. king of Judah had imprisoned 32.03
Z. king of Judah shall not escape 32.04
and he shall take Z. to Babylon, 32.05
Go and speak to Z. king of Judah 34.02
of the LORD, O Z. king of Judah! 34.04
these words to Z. king of Judah, 34.06
after King Z. had made a covenant 34.08
And Z. king of Judah, and his 34.21
Z. the son of Hahaniah, and all the 36.12
Z. the son of Josiah, whom Nebuchadrezzar 37.01
King Z. sent Jehucal the son of 37.03
King Z. sent for him, and received 37.17
Jeremiah also said to King Z., 37.18
So King Z. gave orders, and they 37.21
King Z. said, "Behold, he is in your 38.05
King Z. sent for Jeremiah the 38.14
Jeremiah said to Z., "If I tell you, 38.15
Then King Z. swore secretly to 38.16
Then Jeremiah said to Z., "Thus says 38.17
King Z. said to Jeremiah, "I am 38.19
Then Z. said to Jeremiah, "Let no 38.24
the ninth year of Z. king of Judah, 39.01
in the eleventh year of Z., 39.02
When Z. king of Judah and all the 39.04
and overtook Z. in the plains of 39.05
the sons of Z. at Riblah before 39.06
He put out the eyes of Z., 39.07
as I gave Z. king of Judah into the 44.30
of the reign of Z. king of Judah. 49.34
he went with Z. king of Judah to 51.59
Z. was twenty-one years old when he 52.01
And Z. rebelled against the king of 52.03
till the eleventh year of King Z. 52.05
and overtook Z. in the plains of 52.08
the sons of Z. before his eyes, and 52.10
He put out the eyes of Z., 52.11

ZEEB
two princes of Midian, Oreb and Z.; Ju 7.25
and Z. they killed at the wine press of Z., 7.25
of Oreb and Z. to Gideon beyond 7.25
the princes of Midian, Oreb and Z.; 8.03
Make their nobles like Oreb and Z., Ps 83.11

ZELA
Z., Haeleph, Jebus (that is, Jerusalem), Jos 18.28
in the land of Benjamin in Z., 2Sa 21.14

ZELEK
Z. the Ammonite, Naharai of Beeroth, 2Sa 23.37
Z. the Ammonite, Naharai of Beeroth, 1Ch 11.39

ZELOPHEHAD
Now Z. the son of Hepher had no Num 26.33
of the daughters of Z. were Mahlah, 26.33
daughters of Z. the son of Hepher, 27.01
"The daughters of Z. are right; 27.07
inheritance of Z. our brother to 36.02
concerning the daughters of Z., 36.06
The daughters of Z. did as the LORD 36.10
and Noah, the daughters of Z., 36.11
Now Z. the son of Hepher, son of Jos 17.03
and the name of the second was Z.; 1Ch 7.15
and Z. had daughters. 7.15

ZELZAH
in the territory of Benjamin at Z., 1Sa 10.02

ZEMARAIM
Betharabah, Z., Bethel, Jos 18.22
up on Mount Z. which is in the 2Ch 13.04

ZEMARITES
the Z. and the Hamathites. Gen 10.18
the Z., and the Hamathites. 1Ch 1.16

ZEMER
skilled men of Z. were in you, Eze 27.08

ZEMIRAH
Z., Joash, Eliezer, Elioenai, Omri, 1Ch 7.08

ZENAN
Z., Hadashah, Migdalgad, Jos 15.37

ZENAS
best to speed Z. the lawyer and Tit 3.13

ZEPHANIAH
and Z. the second priest, and the 2Ki 25.18
Joel, son of Azariah, son of Z., 1Ch 6.36
son of Malchiah and Z. the priest, Jer 21.01
and to Z. the son of Maaseiah the 29.25
Z. the priest read this letter in 29.29
and Z. the priest, the son of 37.03
and Z. the second priest, and the 52.24
which came to Z. the son of Cushi, Zep 1.01
the house of Josiah, the son of Z. Zec 6.10
Jedaiah, and Josiah the son of Z. 6.14

ZEPHATH
the Canaanites who inhabited Z., and utterly Ju 1.17

ZEPHATHAH
in the valley of Z. at Mareshah. 2Ch 14.10

ZEPHI
Z., Gatam, Kenaz, Timna, and Amalek. 1Ch 1.36

ZEPHO
Teman, Omar, Z., Gatam, and Kenaz. Gen 36.11
the chiefs Teman, Omar, Z., Kenaz, 36.15

ZEPHON
of Z., the family of the Zephonites Num 26.15

ZEPHONITES
of Zephon, the family of the Z.; Num 26.15

ZER
Z., Hammath, Rakkath, Chinnereth, Jos 19.35

ZERAH
Nahath, Z., Shammah, and Mizzah. Gen 36.13
chiefs Nahath, Z., Shammah, and Mizzah; 36.17
the son of Z. of Bozrah reigned in 36.33
his hand; and his name was called Z. 38.30
and Z. (but Er and Onan died in the 46.12
of Z., the family of the Zerahites; Num 26.13
of Z., the family of the Zerahites. 26.20
son of Z., of the tribe of Judah, Jos 7.01
son of Z., of the tribe of Judah, 7.18
with him took Achan the son of Z., 7.24
the son of Z. break faith in the 22.20
Nahath, Z., Shammah, and Mizzah. 1Ch 1.37
the son of Z. of Bozrah reigned in 1.44
Tamar also bore him Perez and Z. 2.04
The sons of Z.: Zimri, Ethan, Heman, 2.06
Nemuel, Jamin, Jarib, Z., Shaul; 4.24
Z. his son, Jeatherai his son. 6.21
son of Z., son of Adaiah, 6.41
Of the sons of Z.: Jeuel and their 9.06
Z. the Ethiopian came out against 2Ch 14.09
of the sons of Z. the son of Judah, Neh 11.24
father of Perez and Z. by Tamar, Mt 1.03

ZERAHIAH
Uzzi of Z., Z. of Meraioth, 1Ch 6.06
his son, Uzzi his son, Z. his son, 6.51
son of Z., son of Uzzi, son of Bukki, Ez 7.04
Pahathmoab, Eliehoenai the son of Z., 8.04

ZERAHITES
of Zerah, the family of the Z.; Num 26.13
of Zerah, the family of the Z. 26.20
and the family of the Z. was taken; Jos 7.17
the family of the Z. man by man, 7.17
Sibbecai the Hushathite, of the Z.; 1Ch 27.11
was Maharai of Netophah, of the Z.; 27.13

ZERED
and encamped in the Valley of Z. Num 21.12
'Now rise up, and go over the brook Z.' Deu 2.13
So we went over the brook Z. 2.13
the brook Z. was thirty-eight years, 2.14

ZEREDAH
son of Nebat, an Ephraimite of Z., 1Ki 11.26
clay ground between Succoth and Z. 2Ch 4.17

ZERERAH
as far as Bethshittah toward Z., Ju 7.22

ZERESH
his friends and his wife Z. Est 5.10
Then his wife Z. and all his 5.14
told his wife Z. and all his 6.13
men and his wife Z. said to him, 6.13

ZERETH
sons of Helah: Z., Izhar, and Ethnan. 1Ch 4.07

ZERETHSHAHAR
and Sibmah, and Z. on the hill of the Jos 13.19

ZERI
Z., Jeshaiah, Shimei, Hashabiah, and 1Ch 25.03

ZEROR
son of Z., son of Becorath, son of 1Sa 9.01

ZERUAH
Solomon, whose mother's name was Z., 1Ki 11.26

ZERUBBABEL
the sons of Pedaiah: Z. and Shimei; 1Ch 3.19
and the sons of Z.: Meshullam 3.19
They came with Z., Jeshua, Nehemiah, Ez 2.02
and Z. the son of Shealtiel with 3.02
Z. the son of Shealtiel and Jeshua 3.08
they approached Z. and the heads of 4.02
But Z., Jeshua, and the rest of the 4.03
Then Z. the son of Shealtiel and 5.02
They came with Z., Jeshua, Nehemiah Neh 7.07
came up with Z. the son of Shealtiel, 12.01
in the days of Z. and in the days 12.47
came up with Z. the son of Shealitel, 12.01
in the days of Z. and in the days 12.47
the prophet to Z. the son of Hag 1.01
Then Z. the son of Shealtiel, and 1.12

ZERUBBABEL (cont.)
the spirit of Z. the son of Hag 1.14
"Speak now to Z. the son of Shealtiel, 2.02
take courage, O Z., says the LORD; 2.04
"Speak to Z., governor of Judah, 2.21
O Z. my servant, the son of Shealtiel, 2.23
"This is the word of the LORD to Z.: Zec 4.06
Before Z. you shall become a plain; 4.07
"The hands of Z. have laid the 4.09
see the plummet in the hand of Z. 4.10
and Shealtiel the father of Z., Mt 1.12
and Z. the father of Abiud, and 1.13
the son of Z., the son Shealtiel, Lk 3.27

ZERUIAH
brother Abishai the son of Z., 1Sa 26.06
And Joab the son of Z., and the 2Sa 2.13
And the three sons of Z. were there, 2.18
men the sons of Z. are too hard 3.39
And Joab the son of Z. was over the 8.16
Now Joab the son of Z. perceived 14.01
the son of Z. said to the king, 16.09
I to do with you, you sons of Z.? 16.10
sister of Z., Joab's mother. 17.25
command of Abishai the son of Z., 18.02
Abishai the son of Z. answered, 19.21
you sons of Z., that you should 19.22
the son of Z. came to his aid, and 21.17
the son of Z., was chief of the 23.18
armor-bearer of Joab the son of Z., 23.37
Joab the son of Z. and with 1Ki 1.07
what Joab the son of Z. did to me, 2.05
the priest and Joab the son of Z. 2.22
and their sisters were Z. and Abigail. 1Ch 2.16
The sons of Z.: Abishai, Joab, and 2.16
Joab the son of Z. went up first, 11.06
armor-bearer of Joab the son of Z., 11.39
the son of Z., slew eighteen 18.12
And Joab the son of Z. was over the 18.15
Joab the son of Z. had dedicated— 26.28
Joab the son of Z. began to number, 27.24

ZETHAM
Jehiel the chief, and Z., and Joel, three. 1Ch 23.08
Z. and Joel his brother, were in 26.22

ZETHAN
Z., Tarshish, and Ahishahar. 1Ch 7.10

ZETHAR
Z. and Carkas, the seven eunuchs who Est 1.10

ZEUS
Barnabas they called Z., and Paul, because Ac 14.12
And the priest of Z., whose temple 14.13

ZIA
Jorai, Jacan, Z., and Eber, seven. 1Ch 5.13

ZIBA
house of Saul whose name was Z., 2Sa 9.02
the king said to him, "Are you Z.?" 9.02
Z. said to the king, "There is still 9.03
And Z. said to the king, "He is in 9.04
Then the king called Z., 9.09
Now Z. had fifteen sons and twenty 9.10
Then Z. said to the king, "According 9.11
Z. the servant of Mephibosheth met 16.01
And the king said to Z., 16.02
Z. answered, "The asses are for the 16.02
Z. said to the king, "Behold, he 16.03
Then the king said to Z., 16.04
And Z. said, "I do obeisance; 16.04
And Z. the servant of the house of 19.17
you and Z. shall divide the land." 19.29

ZIBA'S
who dwelt in Z. house became 2Sa 9.12

ZIBEON
of Anah the son of Z. the Hivite, Gen 36.02
the daughter of Anah the son of Z., 36.14
the land: Lotan, Shobal, Z., Anah, 36.20
These are the sons of Z.: Aiah and Anah; 36.24
pastured the asses of Z. his father. 36.24
chiefs Lotan, Shobal, Z., Anah, 36.29
Z., Anah, Dishon, Ezer, and Dishan. 1Ch 1.38
The sons of Z.: Aiah and Anah. 1.40

ZIBIA
wife: Jobab, Z., Mesha, Malcam, 1Ch 8.09

ZIBIAH
mother's name was Z. of Beersheba. 2Ki 12.01
mother's name was Z. of Beersheba. 2Ch 24.01

ZICHRI
of Izhar: Korah, Nepheg, and Z. Ex 6.21
Jakim, Z., Zabdi, 1Ch 8.19
Abdon, Z., Hanan, 8.23
and Z. were the sons of Jeroham. 8.27
of Mica, son of Z., son of Asaph; 9.15
and his son Z., and his son Shelomoth 26.25
the son of Z. was chief officer; 27.16
and next to him Amasiah the son of Z., 2Ch 17.16
and Elishaphat the son of Z. 23.01
And Z., a mighty man of Ephraim, 28.07
Joel the son of Z. was their Neh 11.09
of Abijah, Z.; of Miniamin, 12.17

ZIDDIM
The fortified cities are Z., Jos 19.35

ZIHA
the sons of Z., the sons of Hasupha, Ez 2.43
the sons of Z., the sons of Hasupha, Neh 7.46
and Z. and Gishpa were over the 11.21

ZIKLAG
Z., Madmannah, Sansannah, Jos 15.31
Z., Bethmarcaboth, Hazarsusah, 19.05
So that day Achish gave him Z.; 1Sa 27.06
therefore Z. has belonged to the 27.06
his men came to Z. on the third 30.01
a raid upon the Negeb and upon Z. 30.01
They had overcome Z., and burned 30.01
and we burned Z. with fire." 30.14
When David came to Z., 30.26
David remained two days in Z.; 2Sa 1.01
I seized him and slew him at Z., 4.10
Bethuel, Hormah, Z., 1Ch 4.30
the men who came to David at Z., 12.01
As he went to Z. these men of 12.20
in Z., in Meconah and its villages, Neh 11.28

ZILLAH
Adah, and the name of the other Z. Gen 4.19
Z. bore Tubalcain; 4.22
wives: "Adah and Z., hear my voice; 4.23

ZILLETHAI
Elienai Z., Eliel, 1Ch 8.20
and Z., chiefs of thousands in 12.20

ZILPAH
(Laban gave his maid Z. to his daughter Gen 29.24
took her maid Z. and gave her to 30.09
Then Leah's maid Z. bore Jacob a son. 30.10
Leah's maid Z. bore Jacob a second 30.12
The sons of Z., Leah's maid: Gad and 35.26
lad with the sons of Bilhah and Z., 37.02
(these are the sons of Z., 46.18

ZIMMAH
son, Jahath his son, Z. his son, 1Ch 6.20
son of Ethan, son of Z., son of Shimei, 6.42
Gershonites, Joah the son of Z., 2Ch 29.12

ZIMRAN

She bore him Z., Jokshan, Medan,	Gen 25.02
she bore Z., Jokshan, Medan, Midian,	1Ch 1.32

ZIMRI

was Z. the son of Salu, head of a	Num 25.14
But his servant Z., commander of	1Ki 16.09
Z. came in and struck him down and	16.10
Thus Z. destroyed all the house of	16.12
king of Judah Z. reigned seven	16.15
"Z. has conspired, and he has killed	16.16
And when Z. saw that the city was	16.18
Now the rest of the acts of Z.,	16.20
you Z., murderer of your master?"	2Ki 9.31
Z., Ethan, Heman, Calcol, and Dara,	1Ch 2.06
of Alemeth, Azmaveth, and Z.;	8.36
Z. was the father of Moza.	8.36
Jarah of Alemeth, Azmaveth, and Z.;	9.42
and Z. was the father of Moza.	9.42
all the kings of Z., all the kings of	Jer 25.25

ZIN

from the wilderness of Z. to Rehob,	Num 13.21
wilderness of Z. in the first	20.01
wilderness of X. during the strife	27.14
of Kadesh in the wilderness of Z.	27.14
in the wilderness of Z. that is,	33.36
wilderness of Z. along the side of	34.03
and cross to Z., and its end shall	34.04
Meribathkadesh, in the wilderness of Z.;	Deu 32.51
wilderness of Z. at the farthest	Jos 15.01
of Akrabbim, passes along to Z.,	15.03

ZINA

Z., and Jeush, and Beriah. These four were	1Ch 23.10

ZION

Nevertheless David took the stronghold of Z.,	2Sa 5.07
of the city of David, which is Z.	1Ki 8.01
you—the virgin daugher of Z.;	2Ki 19.21
out of Mount Z. a band of survivors	19.31
David took the stronghold of Z.,	1Ch 11.05
of the city of David, which is Z.	2Ch 5.02
set my king on Z., my holy hill.	Ps 2.06
to the LORD, who dwells in Z.!	9.11
the daughter of Z. I may rejoice	9.14
for Israel would come out of Z.!	14.07
and give you support from Z.!	20.02
Mount Z., in the far north, the city	48.02
let Mount Z. be glad! Let the daughters	48.11
Walk about Z., go round about her,	48.12
Out of Z., the perfection of beauty,	50.02
Do good to Z. in thy good pleasure;	51.18
for Israel would come from Z.!	53.06
Praise is due to thee, O God, in Z.;	65.01
For God will save Z. and rebuild	69.35
Remember Mount Z., where thou hast	74.02
in Salem, his dwelling place in Z.	76.02
of Judah, Mount Z., which he loves.	78.68
whose heart are the highways to Z.	84.05
the God of gods will be seen in Z.	84.07
the gates of Z. more than all the	87.02
And of Z. it shall be said, "This	87.05
Z. hears and is glad, and the	97.08
The LORD is great in Z.; he is exalted	99.02
Thou wilt arise and have pity on Z.;	102.13
For the LORD will build up Z.,	102.16
may delcare in Z. the name of the	102.21
forth from Z. your mighty scepter.	110.02
in the LORD are like Mount Z.,	125.01
LORD restored the fortunes of Z.,	126.01
The LORD bless you from Z.!	128.05
May all who hate Z. be put to shame	129.05
For the LORD has chosen Z.;	132.13
which falls on the mountains of Z.!	133.03
May the LORD bless you from Z.,	134.03
Blessed be the LORD from Z.,	135.21
and wept, when we remembered Z.	137.01
"Sing us one of the songs of Z.!"	137.03
O Z., to all generations. Praise the LORD!	146.10
O Jerusalem! Praise your God, O Z.!	147.12
let the sons of Z. rejoice in	149.02
Go forth, O daughters of Z.,	Sol 3.11
and the daughter of Z. is left like	Is 1.08
Z. shall be redeemed by justice, and	1.27
"For out of Z. shall go forth the	2.03
daughters of Z. are haughty and	3.16
the heads of the daughters of Z.,	3.17
who is left in Z. and remains in	4.03
daughters of Z. and cleansed the	4.04
site of Mount Z. and over her	4.05
of hosts, who dwells on Mount Z.	8.18
work on Mount Z. and on Jerusalem	10.12
who dwell in Z., be not afraid of	10.24
at the mount of the daughter of Z.,	10.32
sing for joy, O inhabitant of Z.,	12.06
"The LORD has founded Z.,	14.32
to the mount of the daughter of Z.	16.01
to Mount Z., the place of the name	18.07
reign on Mount Z. and in Jerusalem	24.23
I am laying in Z. for a foundation	28.16
be that fight against Mount Z.	29.08
O people in Z. who dwell at Jerusalem;	30.19
upon Mount Z. and upon its hill.	31.04
says the LORD, whose fire is in Z.,	31.09
he will fill Z. with justice and	33.05
The sinners in Z. are afraid;	33.14
Look upon Z., the city of our	33.20
of recompense for the cause of Z.	34.08
and come to Z. with singing, with	35.10
you—the virgin daughter of Z.;	37.22
out of Mount Z. a band of survivors	37.32
O Z., herald of good tidings;	40.09
I first have declared it to Z.,	41.27
I will put salvation in Z.,	46.13
But Z. said, "The LORD has forsaken	49.14
For the LORD will comfort Z.;	51.03
and come with singing to Z.;	51.11
and saying to Z., 'You are my	51.16
Awake, awake, put on your strength, O Z.;	52.01
neck, O captive daughter of Z.	52.02
who says to Z., "Your God reigns."	52.07
see the return of the LORD to Z.	52.08
"And he will come to Z. as Redeemer,	59.20
the Z. of the Holy One of Israel.	60.14
to grant to those who mourn in Z.—	61.03
earth: Say to the daughter of Z.,	62.11
Z. has become a wilderness, Jerusalem	64.10
For as soon as Z. was in labor she	66.08
family, and I will bring you to Z.	Jer 3.14
Raise a standard toward Z.,	4.06
the daughter of Z. gasping for	4.31
I will destroy, the daughter of Z.	6.02
against you, O daughter of Z.!	6.23
of the land: "Is the LORD not in Z.?	8.19
sound of wailing is heard from Z.:	9.19
Does thy soul loathe Z.?	14.19
Z. shall be plowed as a field;	26.18
'It is Z., for whom no one cares!'	30.17
'Arise, and let us go up to Z.,	31.06
and sing aloud on the height of Z.,	31.12
They shall ask the way to Z.,	50.05
to declare in Z. the vengeance of	50.28
us declare in Z. the work of the	51.10
have done in Z., says the LORD.	51.24
let the inhabitant of Z. say.	51.35
The roads to Z. mourn, for none come	Lam 1.04
From the daughter of Z. has departed	1.06
Z. stretches out her hands, but	1.17
the daughter of Z. under a cloud!	2.01
in the tent of the daughter of Z.;	2.04
to an end in Z. appointed feast	2.06
the wall of the daughter of Z.;	2.08
the daughter of Z. sit on the	2.10
you, O virgin daughter of Z.?	2.13

ZION (cont.)

O daughter of Z.! Let tears stream Lam 2.18
The precious sons of Z., worth 4.02
and he kindled a fire in Z., 4.11
O daughter of Z., is accomplished, 4.22
Women are ravished in Z., virgins in the 5.11
for Mount Z. which lies desolate; 5.18
Blow the trumpet in Z.; sound the alarm Joe 2.01
Blow the trumpet in Z.; sanctify a fast; 2.15
O sons of Z., and rejoice in the 2.23
for in Mount Z. and in Jerusalem 2.32
And the LORD roars from Z., and utters 3.16
who dwell in Z., my holy mountain. 3.17
guilty, for the LORD dwells in Z. 3.21
And he said: "The LORD roars from Z., Amo 1.02
"Woe to those who are at ease in Z., 6.01
But in Mount Z. there shall be Ob 1.17
go up to Mount Z. to rule Mount 1.21
of sin to the daughter of Z.,, Mic 1.13
who build Z. with blood and Jerusalem 3.10
Therefore because of you Z. shall 3.12
For out of Z. shall go forth the 4.02
them in Mount Z. from this time 4.07
flock, hill of the daughter of Z., 4.08
O daughter of Z., like a woman in 4.10
and let our eyes gaze upon Z. 4.11
O daughter of Z., for I will make 4.13
Sing aloud, O daughter of Z.; Zep 3.14
to Jerusalem: "Do not fear, O Z.; 3.16
jealous for Jerusalem and for Z. Zec 1.14
again comfort Z. and again choose 1.17
Escape to Z., you who dwell with 2.07
Sing and rejoice, O daughter of Z.; 2.10
am jealous for Z. with great 8.02
says the LORD: I will return to Z., 8.03
Rejoice greatly, O daughter of Z.! 9.09
O Z., over your sons, O Greece, and 9.13
"Tell the daughter of Z., Behold, your Mt 21.05
"Fear not, daughter of Z.; behold, your Jn 12.15
I am laying in Z. a stone that Rom 9.33
"The Deliverer will come from Z., 11.26
come to Mount Z. and to the city Heb 12.22
"Behold, I am laying in Z. a stone, 1Pe 2.06
on Mount Z. stood the Lamb, and with Rev 14.01

ZION'S

For Z. sake I will not keep silent, Is 62.01

ZIOR

and Z.: nine cities with their Jos 15.54

ZIPH

Z., Telem, Bealoth, Jos 15.24
Maon, Carmel, Z., Juttah, 15.55
country of the Wilderness of Z. 1Sa 23.14
in the Wilderness of Z. at Horesh. 23.15
and went to Z. ahead of Saul. 23.24
went down to the wilderness of Z., 26.02
seek David in the wilderness of Z. 26.02
first-born, who was the father of Z. 1Ch 2.42
of Jehallelel, Z., Ziphah, Tiria, and Asarel. 4.16
Gath, Mareshah, Z., 2Ch 11.08

ZIPHAH

of Jehallelel: Ziph, Z., Tiria, and Asarel. 1Ch 4.16

ZIPHION

Z., Haggi, Shuni, Ezbon, Eri, Arodi, and Gen 46.16

ZIPHITES

Then the Z. went up to Saul at 1Sa 23.19
Then the Z. came to Saul at Gibeah, 26.01

ZIPHRON

then the boundary shall extend to Z., Num 34.09

ZIPPOR

the son of Z. saw all that Israel Num 22.02
So Balak the son of Z., who was king 22.04
said to God, "Balak the son of Z., 22.10
him, "Thus says Balak the son of Z.: 22.16
hearken to me, O son of Z.: 23.18
Then Balak the son of Z., Jos 24.09
Balak the son of Z., king of Moab? Ju 11.25

ZIPPORAH

and he gave Moses his daughter Z. Ex 2.21
Then Z. took a flint and cut off 4.25
had taken Z., Moses' wife, after he 18.02

ZIV

over Israel, in the month of Z., 1Ki 6.01
LORD was laid, in the month of Z. 6.37

ZIZ

will come up by the ascent of Z.; 2Ch 20.16

ZIZA

Z. the son of Shiphi, son of Allon, 1Ch 4.37
Abijah, Attai, Z., and Shelomith. 2Ch 11.20

ZIZAH

Jahath was the chief, and Z. the second; 1Ch 23.11

ZOAN

seven years before Z. in Egypt. Num 13.22
land of Egypt, in the fields of Z. Ps 78.12
his miracles in the fields of Z. 78.43
The princes of Z. are utterly Is 19.11
The princes of Z. have become fools, 19.13
officials are at Z. and his envoys 30.04
desolation, and will set fire to Z., Eze 30.14

ZOAR

of Egypt in the direction of Z.; Gen 13.10
and the king of Bela (that is, Z.). 14.02
Z.) went out, and they joined battle 14.08
the name of the city was called Z. 19.22
on the earth when Lot came to Z. 19.23
Now Lot went up out of Z., 19.30
for he was afraid to dwell in Z.; 19.30
city of palm trees, as far as Z. Deu 34.03
his fugitives flee to Z., Is 15.05
a cry is heard as far as Z. Jer 48.04
from Z. to Horonaim and 48.34

ZOBAH

Edom, against the kings of Z., 1Sa 14.47
king of Z., as he went to restore 2Sa 8.03
came to help Hadadezer king of Z., 8.05
the son of Rehob, king of Z. 8.12
Bethrehob, and the Syrians of Z., 10.06
and the Syrians of Z. and of Rehob, 10.08
Igal the son of Nathan of Z., 23.36
his master Hadadezer king of Z. 1Ki 11.23
also defeated Hadadezar king of Z., 1Ch 18.03
came to help Hadadezer king of Z., 18.05
army of Hadadezer, king of Z., 18.09
from Arammaacah, and from Z. 19.06

ZOBEBAH

Z., and the families of Aharhel the 1Ch 4.08

ZOHAR

for me Ephron the son of Z., Gen 23.08
Ephron the son of Z. the Hittite, 25.09
Z., and Shaul, the son of a Canaanitish 46.10
Z., and Shaul, the son of a Canaanite Ex 6.15

ZOHETH

The sons of Ishi: Z. and Benzoheth. 1Ch 4.20

ZOPHAH

Z., Imna, Shelesh, and Amal. 1Ch 7.35
The sons of Z.: Suah, Harnepher, Shual, 7.36

ZOPHAI

his son, Z. his son, Nahath his son, 1Ch 6.26

ZOPHAR

the Shuhite, and Z. the Naamathite. Job 2.11
Then Z. the Naamathite answered: 11.01
Then Z. the Naamathite answered: 20.01
the Shuhite and Z. the Naamathite 42.09

ZOPHIM

And he took him to the field of Z., Num 23.14

ZORAH

the lowland, Eshtaol, Z., Ashnah, Jos 15.33
of its inheritance included Z., 19.41
And there was a certain man of Z., Ju 13.02
Mahanehdan, between Z. and Eshtaol. 13.25
him between Z. and Eshtaol in the 16.31
from Z. and from Eshtaol, to spy out 18.02
their brethern at Z. and Eshtaol, 18.08
set forth from Z. and Eshtaol, 18.11
Z., Aijalon, and Hebron, fortified 2Ch 11.10
in Enrimmon, in Z., in Jarmuth, Neh 11.29

ZORATHITES

these came the Z. and the Eshtaolites 1Ch 2.53
these were the families of the Z. 4.02

ZORITES

half of the Manahathites, the Z. 1Ch 2.54

ZUAR

from Issachar, Nethanel the son of Z.; Num 1.08
being Nethanel the son of Z., 2.05
second day Nethanel the son of Z., 7.18
offering of Nethanel the son of Z. 7.23
Issachar was Nethanel the son of Z. 10.15

ZUPH

of Tohu, son of Z., and Ephraimite. 1Sa 1.01
When they came to the land of Z., 9.05
son of Z., son of Elkanah, son of 1Ch 6.35

ZUR

slain was Cozbi the daughter of Z., Num 25.15
Z., Hur, and Reba, the five kings of 31.08
and Rekem and Z. and Hur and Reba, Jos 13.21
then Z., Kish, Baal, Nadab, 1Ch 8.30
then Z., Kish, Baal, Ner, Nadab, 9.36

ZURIEL

of Merari was Z. the son of Abihail; Num 3.35

ZURISHADDAI

from Simeon, Shelumiel the son of Z.; Num 1.06
being Shelumiel the son of Z., 2.12
fifth day Shelumiel the son of Z., 7.36
offering of Shelumiel the son of Z. 7.41
Simeon was Shelumiel the son of Z. 10.19

ZUZIM

the Z. in Ham, the Emim in Gen 14.05